~~Property of Donald M. Silversthorn~~

To my friend

Chris A. McLemore

Hang in There old Pard

JMS

A Concordance to *Alcoholics Anonymous*

A Concordance to *Alcoholics Anonymous*

Compiled by Stephen E. Poe *and* Frances E. Poe

For
Mark Emory Poe
...wherever you are....

First Printing August 1990
Second Printing February 1999

Published by:
purple salamander press®
1625 Heitman Court
Reno, NV 89509 USA
Tel: 775-322-1201 • Fax: 775-348-8832
www.aaconcordance.com
email: PSP@aaconcordance.com

Database Manager & Computer Expert Extraordinaire:
James D. Whitfield, IBM (ret.)

Webmaster: Douglas S. Barrie
email: Douglas@aahistory.com

ISBN 0-9627480-0-5

Printed in the United States of America

Contents

Forward • vii

Preface • ix

A Concordance Is Not • ix

A Concordance Is • x

A Concordance for A.A.'s • xi

Selection of Third Edition Printing • xii

Concordance by Computer • xiii

Omitted Words • xiv

Footnotes • xv

Other Omissions • xv

Special Problems • xv

Acknowledgements • xvii

The Concordance • 1

Appendices • 889

Appendix I - Table of Footnotes • 891

Appendix II - Tables of Dates • 892

Table 1: Dates by Year • 892

Table 2: Dates by Month • 897

Table 3: Miscellaneous Dates • 899

Appendix III - Tables of Numbers • 900
Table 1: Numbers of Quantity • 900
Table 2: Numbers of Enumeration • 902
Table 3: Numbers As Percentages • 904
Table 4: Numbers Expressing Geographical Locations • 905
Table 5: Numbers As Denominations of Money • 906
Table 6: Miscellaneous Numbers • 907
Appendix IV - Frequency of Words: Alpha Sort • 908
Appendix V - Frequency of Words: Numerical Sort • 932

Forward

The work involved in compiling a concordance is so detailed and at the same time so massive a project that I suppose one has to be a bit crazy to tackle it. Or at least more than mildly interested in the book upon which the concordance is based. I guess I qualify on both counts. (Certain friends of mine are convinced it's more of the former, than the latter.)

What also seems to be true is that producing a concordance is not a task that appeals to everyone. I mean, it isn't exactly a mainstream activity. Most people don't even know what a concordance is. How's that for obscurity?

That's because concordances are usually compiled by people like monks -- people with 40 years or so available to devote to the task, and no worries about bills to pay. Or university professors whose scholarly occupations allow for plenty of time to devote to the undertaking without the concurrent concern over the loss of their jobs.

Neither Fran nor I fall into either category.

No matter. This book has truly been a labor of love.

For me, compiling a concordance on Alcoholics Anonymous has been a personal dream for more than ten years. Realizing that dream at last is sweet, indeed. I have a great personal affection for the Big Book. I make my living as a writer, and have for most of my adult life. Again and again I have read the Big Book text with a writer's eye for structure, nuance, flow, style, and other tell-tale signs of the professionalism with which the author approached the task.

Always I am struck by the quaintness of style, often cumbersome sentence structure, and use of outmoded phraseology.

And yet...I don't know...there is something more. A power...a kind of majesty in the words. A deeper meaning that transcends time and quaintness. Even as the words seem to change. Timeless, but somehow always changing. How often have I read a passage and felt I understood its meaning...only to re-read the same passage on some later date when my life was in emotional turmoil...and come away with a different meaning? And have both meanings be exactly what I needed on each occasion!

I don't even pretend to understand it. I do believe, however, that this particular text was inspired by a Higher Source.

And while I thought I knew the Big Book fairly well, the actual process of compiling this concordance has taught me more about A.A.'s basic text than I ever could have guessed. The more Fran and I worked on the sentences, the more I "discovered" new thoughts, new ideas, new concepts.

Are these discoveries really "new?" No, of course not. They've been there all along. It's just that now I can see them -- and others -- in a different light, a different perspective, and a different context.

Does that mean they add more meaning to my life? You bet they do.

And so the more astonished I have become at the very special nature of this book. My admiration for it has grown daily.

One thing is certain.

Anyone who uses this concordance to study the Big Book will find their appreciation for, and understanding of, A.A.'s basic text irrevocably enhanced. Over time, they will gain a new dimension of delight, wonder, and perhaps even a sense of awe over the power within the pages of Alcoholics Anonymous. They will experience, as have I, a profound change.

And they will never again be the same.

Stephen E. Poe
Minden, Nevada
June 26, 1990

Preface

A Concordance Is Not

A concordance is not a dictionary.

A dictionary defines words. A concordance defines nothing. To be sure, a dictionary is quite useful, since it gives the reader a generally accepted definition for what a word means. That's important, if what you are looking for is society's collective opinion on the meaning of a particular word. And if that's what you want, well, a concordance is not for you. You need a dictionary.

A concordance is not someone's "interpretation."

A concordance interprets nothing. If what you are looking for is someone's interpretation of what a particular book means, then you need an annotated edition of that particular book.

In annotated editions, you will find lots of remarks, clarifications, interpretations, comments, and other such stuff clearly spelled out in a wide margin on every page throughout the book. Annotated editions are very useful for anyone studying the writings of a particular author, such as Hemingway, Thoreau, Tolstoy, J.D. Salinger, Dante, etc. So, if what you are looking for is someone else's interpretation of what has been written in a particular book, please do not turn to a concordance. You will be sadly disappointed. A concordance interprets nothing.

A concordance is not an "updated" edition of a particular book.

A concordance updates nothing, changes nothing, shortens nothing, lengthens nothing. If what you are looking for is something new or updated or shortened regarding a particular book, then what you need is an abridged version of the book.

An abridged version of a book can be quite useful under certain circumstances. *Reader's Digest* editions of any previously published work have become the classic example of abridged stories and books. They're useful if you're in a hurry, like to skip over a lot of material that some editor somewhere thinks isn't very important for you to read anyway and so you don't have to waste time with it. Abridged versions of books are always useful for busy people, those who would rather rely on someone else's opinion, or those who generally would prefer to have someone else decide for them in advance what is meaningful and what is not.

Therefore if what you are looking for is someone else's opinion of what is or is not important for you to read in a particular book, then you don't need a concordance. You need an abridged version of that book. A concordance accurately reproduces every sentence, word, comma -- everything in the original book, exactly as it appears in the original book. The interpretation or opinion, if any, is left to you.

A concordance is not a review or an opinion of what a particular book says or is about.

A concordance reviews nothing, editorializes nothing, gives no opinions on anything. If you are looking for book reviews or editorialized opinions of a book, you need to read the book review section of newspapers and magazines. These reviews are sometimes helpful, in the same way that eating someone else's pre-digested food is helpful. For people who like to make up their own minds about something, such reviews are a dubious benefit at best.

And finally, if what you are looking for is someone else's opinion of what is in the Big Book and what the Big Book "says," you most certainly do not need a concordance. Simply go to any meeting, at any time, and listen. You won't even have to ask. You will hear people gladly volunteer what they think the Big Book says about anything. Including things that aren't even in the Big Book.

In short, a concordance does not define, interpret, editorialize, give opinion, update, shorten, lengthen, or change the work upon which it is based in any manner whatever.

A Concordance Is

A concordance is one of the most widely-used standard reference works in the realm of the written word. It's purpose is to enable the student of a particular book or author to study, sentence by sentence, precisely what was written in that book. The first principal advantage of a concordance is that it allows the reader to see the contextual usage of each word.

For example, if you want to know what Bill Wilson meant when he used the word "suggested" in the Big Book, and you happen to have a concordance on the Big Book, then you simply look up the word "suggested." Under that word you will find every sentence in the Big Book in which the word "suggested" is used, from beginning to end, including all the stories.

No interpretations. No definitions. No opinions. No changes. Just pure, precise, Big Book text.

In this example, the advantage is that by reading all the sentences in which the word "suggested" is used, the contextual meaning of the word becomes quite clear. And you won't need a (usually) self-appointed Big Book Expert interpreting for you, either.

Probably the most common example of a concordance is one prepared for use in studying the *Bible*. There are any number of concordances available today for use in studying the *Bible*, and concordances like these have been around for more than a hundred years. As you might imagine, each must be complete and accurate, else it would be of no value at all to anyone studying the *Bible*.

So it is, with any true concordance.

The second principal advantage of a concordance is that it allows you the reader to make up your own mind as to what a word means, what a sentence means, or indeed what a book "says" about anything at all, based not on what someone else thinks, but on what you yourself have read and studied in the text. You then get to make up your own mind. Each of us gets to read for ourselves, see for ourselves, and make up our own minds.

Somehow, that sounds just right.

A Concordance for A.A.'s

The text of *Alcoholics Anonymous*, affectionately known as the "Big Book" to millions of sober alcoholics the world over, is -- at the very least -- an astonishing work of literature. To date, more than 7 million English-language copies have been printed, not counting the 15 foreign-language editions available throughout the world. This one book is studied by more people, every day, than any other book outside of organized religion.

By any standard of comparison, the Big Book is a giant in the annals of literature.

Yet, until now, it has lacked a concordance.

Survey any of the classics of literature at the nearest library, and you will find that someone has prepared a concordance on most of them. Shakespeare, Melville, Joyce, the list seems endless. And each to serve but one purpose: to enable serious students of those works to better study, and understand, what the authors meant when they wrote their famous lines.

Alcoholics Anonymous, too, has it's famous lines.

Listen to what is shared at any meeting, and you'll hear them. "Easy does it." "Rarely have we seen a person fail..." "...a Fellowship of men and women who share..." "Resentments are the number one offender." "Lack of power was our dilemma." "Trust God and clean house."

Among the members of Alcoholics Anonymous are many who seriously study the Big Book. Indeed, one of the more popular meeting formats is a Big Book Study Meeting. The need for a concordance as a tool in studying the Big Book therefore seems obvious.

Now, in keeping with the study of other great works of literature, A.A.'s need no longer be denied access to a truly invaluable reference guide.

Selection of Third Edition Printing

As of June 1990, there were no less than 66 different "texts" of *Alcoholics Anonymous* in circulation. The First Edition produced 16 separate printings from 1939 to 1955. The Second Edition also produced, coincidentally, 16 printings from 1955 to 1976. The Third Edition, which is the current one still being printed, has to date produced 34 printings.

With so many printings floating around out there, selection of the appropriate text upon which to base a concordance seemed to be of particular importance. But which one to use?

Surprisingly, the choice wasn't that easy.

First of all, most of the 66 printings are different from each other.

This probably comes as just as much of a shock to the reader as it did to us when we made this discovery. As nearly as we can determine, most of the differences between printings are not substantial. Within each Edition certain additions, deletions, or changes were periodically made to most printings -- usually in the form of footnotes or other forms of reference data.

However, certain printings (true within First Edition texts, but especially so in the Second and Third Editions) also contain other differences, such as occurs in the wording of the original Forward to the First Edition. Then too, from Edition to Edition there have been larger changes, although these tend to be primarily in the stories which make up the latter two-thirds of the book.

With no clear majority of printings absolutely identical to each other, the question remained: which to choose for the concordance.

The selection is important, for very practical reasons.

The format for this *Concordance* calls for a display of the complete sentence in which the word is used, followed by a page number reference indicating the page on which that word and sentence appears. And therein lies the problem.

If printings are different from each other, then the page numbers will be different as well. Which means some of the page numbers referenced in the *Concordance* will be different from the actual pages in some printings in the hands of many members.

The problem began to look like the proverbial Gordian Knot.

In the end, our solution lay partially in a process of elimination.

First Edition printings were automatically eliminated, on the grounds that most people in A.A. don't have them. Second Edition printings were pretty much eliminated for the same reason. We felt that while many A.A.'s may well own a copy of a Second Edition printing, the majority of A.A.'s probably use a Third Edition printing in their everyday lives.

But again, which one?

We didn't know, so we "split the difference." This *Concordance to Alcoholics Anonymous* is based on the Third Edition, 21st printing, 1985. We believe this printing fairly represents the majority of "Big Book" texts now in use by A.A.'s, and will therefore provide the greatest benefit to the largest number.

No changes have been made to the text.

We wish to emphasize this very important point:

All text on every page of the Concordance is pure Third Edition Big Book text. There are no changes, interpretations, or modifications whatever.

Concordance By Computer

Contrary to popular belief, computers are very stupid machines. Quick, yes. Intelligent, no way. At least not ours.

So, while computers were used extensively in creating this reference book, human intervention was constantly required in order to help these marvelous little machines figure out what they were supposed to do. Despite the problems, computer-assisted concordances are preferred over the life style of a monk-assisted concordance.

For those technically-minded folks, the following data is provided: this *Concordance* was produced by the joint efforts of four MS-DOS AT's, each running at a clock speed of almost 22MHz. Original inputting was by human digital interface-with-keyboard. File-building was by means of a special concordance software program (see Acknowledgements) written in Turbo Pascal and utilizing more than 3,000 lines of code.

Typesetting and page formatting was accomplished via Ventura 2.0 with Professional Extension. Camera-ready-art was prepared with an NEC LCD 890 LED-array Postscript printer. Results were left in the hands of our Higher Power.

Omitted Words

The computer may not be very smart, but it certainly is tireless and faithful. To a fault. Without the imposition of certain restraints, our "trusted servant" would crunch on indiscriminately and, ultimately, produce enough sentences to fill a book 3,000 pages in length.

Not a good idea. Can you imagine wading through 47 pages of sentences simply because they contain the word "the"? Neither can we.

We decided to impose a few restraints.

Accordingly, certain words -- although appearing frequently throughout the Big Book -- have not been included in the lists of sentences in the *Concordance*. These words do appear, however, in both *Appendix IV, "Frequency of Words - Alpha Sort;"* and *Appendix V, "Frequency of Words - Numerical Sort."*

In keeping with accepted scholarly practices for the preparation of concordances, following is a list of words which have been excluded from the lists of sentences:

a	*could*	*her*	*in*	*or*	*the*	*those're*	*went*
an	*did*	*hers*	*is*	*other*	*them*	*to*	*were*
and	*do*	*herself*	*it*	*out*	*then*	*too*	*what*
any	*for*	*him*	*it'll*	*said*	*there*	*up*	*what's*
are	*from*	*himself*	*it's*	*she*	*there's*	*very*	*when*
as	*had*	*his*	*its*	*she'd*	*these*	*was*	*which*
at	*has*	*I*	*me*	*she's*	*they*	*wasn't*	*who*
be	*have*	*I'd*	*my*	*so*	*they'd*	*we*	*with*
been	*he*	*I'll*	*no*	*some*	*they're*	*we'd*	*would*
but	*he'd*	*I'm*	*not*	*than*	*they've*	*we'll*	*you*
by	*he'll*	*I've*	*of*	*that*	*this*	*we're*	
can	*he's*	*if*	*on*	*that's*	*those*	*we've*	

Footnotes

An increasing number of Big Book printings incorporate footnotes. With later printings, these footnotes get updated. Which means they change. Additionally, new footnotes are added to pages where, previously, none existed. Referencing the words and sentences in these footnotes would be meaningless for those printings not containing them.

We therefore extracted all footnotes from the main body of the text, and have listed them all in *Appendix I,* in the page number order in which they appear in the text.

Other Omissions

Certain textual omissions were intentionally made during production. Chief among these was the *Table of Contents.* None of the words appearing in the *Table of Contents* were included in the sentence listings within the body of the *Concordance.* Nor were these words included in the word count, for word frequency purposes.

Unlike the individual words in the Big Book, numbers -- such as addresses, dates and so forth -- have not been included with the word list. Thus you will not find a list of sentences under a number entry such as "1939," or "50,000" (but sentences containing these numbers will be found in connection with listings for the words which also appear in those sentences).

Instead, all numerical expressions of numbers have been listed in two different appendices. *Appendix II* lists all numbers expressed as dates. *Appendix III* lists all other numbers. Both appendices give specific page number references for each listing.

Special Problems

A number of special problems were encountered in the preparation of this reference work. While most have already been cited elsewhere in the *Preface,* there were some which deserve special mention. One of these involved sentences which begin on one page and end on the following page.

For example, at the bottom of page 156 in the Big Book, you will find a sentence which begins, "The use of spiritual principles in" -- and that's it. This particular sentence is then completed at the top of page 157 as, "such cases was not so well understood as it is now." This produces a situation in which the words of the sentence span two different pages, and thus present a problem for the computer in assigning a single page number reference.

Take the word "understood," for instance. It appears on page 157. But the sentence in which it is found begins on page 156. Which page number do we reference?

The ideal solution would be to simply reference the page number of the page upon which the word in question actually appears. Ah, but we live in an imperfect world. Suffice it to say that operating under certain constraints and realities as we indeed were, we decided to keep it simple. Therefore in all cases of this type, the page number referenced is the one on which the sentence itself actually begins.

Another problem which caused particular trauma was the sheer length of many of the sentences in the Big Book. Computer program after computer program simply choked up and died, while attempting to "swallow" these extraordinarily lengthy sentences.

Persistence, faith, and the timely aid of a Master Programmer saved the day. But we don't mind admitting it was tough going for a while.

Acknowledgements

(Revised for the 2nd Printing)

In the First Printing of the *Concordance* we acknowledged the contributions of those who, in one way or another, made this whole project possible. We would here like to do the same with respect to the Second Printing.

The Second Printing very nearly did not happen.

In 1993, three years after the *Concordance* was first published, I was diagnosed with Chronic Myelogenous Leukemia, a form of cancer for which there is no cure. Statistically, I had a year to live, 18 months at the outside. Understandably, my wife and I readjusted our priorities. A Second Printing was not on the list. Over the next 18 months my body was assaulted by a variety of daily chemo therapies, 11 sessions of total body irradiation (it's a wonder I'm not a walking nuclear reactor), and – in March of 1995 -- a stem cell transplant.

Eleven months later, in February of 1996, the doctors at Stanford told me I was no longer in remission. Nevertheless, I am grateful to Dr. Rob Negren and the staff at Stanford Medical Center's Bone Marrow Transplant Unit. They saved my life, no question about it. I am also especially indebted to Dr. John Shields, Dr. John Diamond, and Yat Ki Lai, my Chinese herbalist. Without them, this Second Printing probably would not even be a topic of conversation.

We eventually sold our last copies of the First Printing in 1996. But as time passed, we kept getting phone calls and letters from people desperate to obtain a copy. We had none available. All we could do was take names and addresses for possible future reference. During this time I periodically received encouragement from Ray and Ginny Grumney of Akron, Ohio (and somewhere in Florida), who have been stalwart supporters throughout this process. They, like many others, urged me to do a Second Printing.

While I repeatedly made it clear to everyone that we intended to maintain our copyright in force and effect indefinitely, still, I was not convinced my wife and I could take on this burden again all by ourselves. My health was holding, but my future was, and still is, rather uncertain. The pressure from all sides during the latter half of 1998 seemed to increase dramatically. Somehow, the push for a Second Printing would not go away.

The die was finally cast by two separate, but related events. First was Ray and Ginney's offer of material assistance. Both Fran and I are grateful for their support of this project. The second was when Douglas Barrie of Riverside, California stepped in and, unasked, designed a fully functioning web site for us. At that point I finally knew the Great Spirit who has been guiding my Cherokee ancestors since the beginning of time was trying to tell me something. We decided to go ahead.

There was considerable work to do however, in gearing up, not the least of which was the need for database management and computer support. We needed a customized method of keeping track of everyone, while handling each order accurately and efficiently. This support has been provided by my brother James Whitfield in Vail, Arizona...the same man whose wizardry created the incredible software program with which we were able to compile the *Concordance* in the first place. He was then, and remains to this day, unquestionably a Master Programmer and World Class Bug Shooter. This book literally would not exist, had it not been for his work.

I would also like to thank Roger Baron of Vermillion, South Dakota for having the courage to follow his instincts. He maintains a web site that gives folks in AA a daily Just For Today message. Against all precedent, he sent a message to everyone on his list, letting them know about our *Concordance*. That act of courage and unselfishness gave the Second Printing the push that it needed. Roger can be emailed at: Baron@jurist.law.usd.edu.

And last but by no means least, I would like to thank Sanford Chernin, my good friend from Las Vegas, Nevada, for his continuing assistance. He is such a wonderful human being, and through thick and thin has always been there for us. No man could ever ask for a truer, more loyal friendship. My wife and I both are definitely blessed to have him in our lives.

So, here is the Second Printing of *A Concordance to Alcoholics Anonymous*, back by popular demand.

Stephen E. Poe
Reno, Nevada
February 6, 1999

A Concordance to *Alcoholics Anonymous*

Aa

A.A.

• Therefore, the first portion of this volume, describing the *A.A.* recovery program, has been left untouched in the course of revisions made for both the second and the third editions.(p.xi)
• The second edition added the appendices, the Twelve Traditions, and the directions for getting in touch with *A.A.*(p.xi)
• In this third edition, Part I ("Pioneers of *A.A.*") stands unchanged.(p.xii)
• All changes made over the years in the Big Book (*A.A.* members' fond nickname for this volume) have had the same purpose: to represent the current membership of Alcoholics Anonymous more accurately, and thereby to reach more alcoholics.(p.xii)
• *A.A.* has flourishing communities in the British Isles, the Scandinavian countries, South Africa, South America, Mexico, Alaska, Australia and Hawaii.(p.xv)
• The spark that was to flare into the first *A.A.* group was struck at Akron, Ohio, in June 1935, during a talk between a New York stockbroker and an Akron physician.(p.xv)
• He had also been greatly helped by the late Dr. William D. Silkworth, a New York specialist in alcoholism who is now accounted no less than a medical saint by *A.A.* members, and whose story of the early days of our Society appears in the next pages.(p.xvi)
• Their very first case, a desperate one, recovered immediately and became *A.A.* number three.(p.xvii)
• When the broker returned to New York in the fall of 1935, the first *A.A.* group had actually been formed, though no one realized it at the time.(p.xvii)
• And besides, there were scattered alcoholics who had picked up the basic ideas in Akron or New York and were trying to form *A.A.* groups in other cities.(p.xvii)
• The flying-blind period ended and *A.A.* entered a new phase of its pioneering time.(p.xvii)
• In the spring of 1940, John D. Rockefeller, Jr. gave a dinner for many of his friends to which he invited *A.A.* members to tell their stories.(p.xviii)
• Then Jack Alexander wrote a feature article in the Saturday Evening Post and placed such a compelling picture of *A.A.* before the general public that alcoholics in need of help really deluged us.(p.xviii)
• By the close of 1941, *A.A.* numbered 8,000 members.(p.xviii)
• *A.A.* had become a national institution.(p.xviii)
• Would there be schisms which would split *A.A.* apart?(p.xix)
• Soon *A.A.* was beset by these very problems on every side and in every group.(p.xix)
• As we discovered the principles by which the individual alcoholic could live, so we had to evolve principles by which the *A.A.* groups and *A.A.* as a whole could survive and function effectively.(p.xix)
• Today the remarkable unity of *A.A.* is one of the greatest assets that our Society has.(p.xix)
• While the internal difficulties of our adolescent period were being ironed out, public acceptance of *A.A.* grew by leaps and bounds.(p.xix)
• Of alcoholics who came to *A.A.* and really tried, 50% got sober at once and remained that way; 25% sobered up after some relapses, and among the remainder, those who stayed on with *A.A.* showed improvement.(p.xx)
• Other thousands came to a few *A.A.* meetings and at first decided they didn't want the program.(p.xx)
• Another reason for the wide acceptance of *A.A.* was the ministration of friends -- friends in medicine, religion, and the press, together with innumerable others who became our able and persistent advocates.(p.xx)
• Without such support, *A.A.* could have made only the slowest progress.(p.xx)
• Neither does *A.A.* take any particular medical point of view, though we cooperate widely with the men of medicine as well as with the men of religion.(p.xx)
• Surveys of groups in the United States and Canada indicate that *A.A.* is reaching out, not only to more and more people, but to a wider and wider range.(p.xxii)
• The basic principles of the *A.A.* program, it appears, hold good for individuals with many different lifestyles, just as the program has brought recovery to those of many different nationalities.(p.xxii)
• Bill W., co-founder of *A.A.*, died January 24, 1971.(p.16)
• Since this book was first published, *A.A.* has released thousands of alcoholics from asylums and hospitals of every kind.(p.114)
• Though it is entirely separate from Alcoholics Anonymous, it uses the general principles of the *A.A.* program as a guide for husbands, wives, relatives, friends, and others close to alcoholics.(p.121)
• We know of an *A.A.* member who was living in a large community.(p.163)
• Beginning with the story of "Dr. Bob," a co-founder of *A.A.*, there are here presented three groups of personal histories.(p.165)
• PIONEERS OF *A.A.*(p.167)
• This group of thirteen stories shows that sobriety in *A.A.* can be lasting.(p.167)
• Seventeen stories may help you decide whether you are alcoholic; also, whether *A.A.* is for you.(p.167)
• PIONEERS OF *A.A.*(p.169)
• Today, hundreds of additional *A.A.* members can be found who have had no relapse for more than thirty years.(p.169)
• All of these, then, are the pioneers of *A.A.*(p.169)
• To 1950, the year of his death, he carried the *A.A.* message to more than 5,000 alcoholic men and women, and to all these he gave his medical services without thought of charge.(p.171)
• Pioneer member of Akron's Group No. 1, the first *A.A.* group in the world.(p.182)
• It would be hard to estimate how much *A.A.* has done for me.(p.191)
• That sentence, "The Lord has been so wonderful to me, curing me of this terrible disease, that I just want to keep telling people about it," has been sort of a golden text for the *A.A.* program and for me.(p.191)
• I'm so grateful for both the program and the people in it that I still want to go, and then probably the most wonderful thing that I learned from the program -- I've seen this in the '*A.A.* Grapevine' a lot of times, and I've had people say it to me personally, and I've heard people get up in meetings and make the same statement: The statement is, "I came into *A.A.* solely for the purpose of sobriety, but it has been through *A.A.* that I have found God."(p.192)
• When I had been in the hospital ten days, Sister Ignatia, who has played such a part in the development of *A.A.* in this area, stuck her head in the door one morning and announced, looking at me quizzically, that they might be able to make something human out of my face after all.(p.205)
• The man turned out to be Bill D., a very early member of *A.A.*, and I couldn't tell you a word of what he said.(p.208)
• I could not see why I couldn't drink like a gentleman, and that was my primary ambition -- until I landed in *A.A.*(p.214)
• Had anyone undertaken to explain to me what the *A.A.* movement was, what its real function was, I probably would have been set back several years and I doubt if I would have survived at all.(p.216)
• So the story of my introduction into *A.A.* begins with the activities of my wife.(p.216)
• I do not recollect the specific conversation that went on but I believe I did challenge Bill to tell me something about *A.A.* and I do recall one other thing: I wanted to know what this was that worked so many wonders, and hanging over the mantel was a picture of Gethsemane and Bill pointed to it and said, "There it is," which didn't make much sense to me.(p.216)
• That was an experience that I have never forgotten, and many times in my own work with *A.A.* newcomers I feel kind of guilty because I haven't done the same thing.(p.219)
• I believe though that it helped my family tremendously to have the *A.A.* meetings every week in my own home.(p.220)
• In summing up, I can say that *A.A.* had made me, I hope, a real Catholic.(p.221)
• An active member of *A.A.* since 1939, I feel myself a useful member of the human race at last.(p.229)
• How it finally broke a Southerner's obstinacy and destined this salesman to start *A.A.* at Philadelphia.(p.238)
• All of us in *A.A.* know the tremendous happiness that is in our sobriety, but there are also tragedies.(p.239)
• The age-old question in *A.A.* is which came first, the neurosis or the alcoholism.(p.240)
• Oddly enough, the big shot who fired me from this company was one of the first men I met when I later joined the New York *A.A.* Group.(p.242)
• In the eight years before *A.A.* found me, I had over forty jobs -- selling and travelling -- one thing after another, and the same old routine.(p.244)
• Around this time our big *A.A.* book was being written and it all became much simpler; we had a definite formula which some sixty of us agreed was the middle course for all alcoholics who wanted sobriety, and that formula has not been changed one iota down through the years.(p.248)
• After the book appeared we all became very busy in our efforts to save all and sundry, but I was still actually on the fringes of *A.A.*(p.248)
• We can share in the laughter and tears of our many friends, and most important, we can share our *A.A.* way of life and are given a daily opportunity to help others.(p.249)
• Very rarely do I miss the meetings of my neighborhood *A.A.* group, and my average has never been less than two meetings a week.(p.249)
• We now live in the West and are very fortunate in our area *A.A.*; it is good, simple and friendly, and our one desire is to stay in *A.A.* and not on it.(p.250)
• She tells how *A.A.* works when the going is rough.(p.261)
• I think his entry into *A.A.* was through spending some hours with Dr. Bob at his office.(p.267)
• He brought many people into *A.A.* through his barroom.)(p.267)
• Men from *A.A.* started coming out to the house the next day.(p.268)
• "Well," I said to dad, when the *A.A.* people kept coming with these lovely cars and looked so nice, "I suppose the neighbors say, 'Now those old fools must have up and died, but where's the hearse?'"(p.269)
• He talked about his wife taking his little boy away from him because of his drinking, and how he got back together with them through *A.A.*, and we began feeling grateful right then that all these things hadn't been taken from us.(p.270)
• We were in *A.A.* three and a half years when he was taken from me.(p.270)
• I always feel that our God Consciousness was a steady growth after we became associated with *A.A.*(p.270)
• We had big picnics out at the house with *A.A.*(p.270)
• In the spiritual strength I had found, because of *A.A.*, I felt that I had made a complete surrender, that I had really turned my life over that summer.(p.271)
• I can't express what *A.A.* meant to us during that year.(p.272)
• I feel that one of the things that I still have to guard against is that I used to be set in my way about what I considered the old-time *A.A.*(p.272)
• I have to tell myself, "Other things are progressing and *A.A.* must too."(p.272)
• We old-timers who get scattered and separated and then witness the construction of services to get in more people and to make this thing function, we think that *A.A.* has changed, but the root of it hasn't.(p.272)
• We are older in *A.A.*, and we're older in years.(p.273)
• And, anyhow, if I went on for ten or a hundred times as long I couldn't even begin to tell you all that *A.A.* has meant to me.(p.274)
• So he started *A.A.* in Detroit.(p.275)
• It was simple, they said, and went on to explain to me in their own language the program of recovery and daily living which we know today as the Twelve Steps of *A.A.*(p.279)
• After six months of sobriety I saw the picture in a different light: Detroit was the place I had to return to, not only because I must face the mess I had made there, but because it was there that I could be of the most service to *A.A.*(p.281)
• The rest of my time was devoted to *A.A.* spadework.(p.281)
• I also talked *A.A.* to every friend who would listen, at lunch, at dinner, on street corners.(p.282)
• But it took six more months of work and disappointments before a group of three men got together in my rooming house bedroom for their first *A.A.* meeting.(p.282)
• This gave me the freedom to do *A.A.* work, and to rest for periods of two or three days when I became too exhausted to carry on.(p.283)
• I, carried away with the desire to serve *A.A.*, gave what was probably one of the first radio broadcasts about *A.A.*, living through a case of mike fright and

feeling like a million dollars when it was all over.(p.283)
• Within a year of my return to Detroit, A.A. was a definitely established little group of about a dozen members and I too was established in a modest but steady job handling an independent dry-cleaning route of my own.(p.283)
• It took five years of A.A. living, and a substantial improvement in my health, before I could take a full-time office job where someone else was boss.(p.283)
• Seven years of work in this field brought an opportunity to affiliate myself actively with one of my clients, a fellow A.A.(p.284)
• The A.A. program showed me the way to come down to earth, start from the bottom and work up.(p.284)
• I had been in A.A. a year, and the last thing in my mind was a drink.(p.285)
• I learned early in my A.A. life that I could not afford to fondle such thoughts, as you might fondle a pet, because this particular pet could grow into a monster.(p.285)
• It was therefore not extraordinary that I should shy away from any serious thought of marriage for a great many years after joining A.A.(p.286)
• My wife, a sister member in A.A., had been a widow nine years and I had been single eighteen years.(p.286)
• We are both depending upon God and our use of the A.A. program to help us make a success of this joint undertaking.(p.286)
• Thus, A.A. was born in Chicago.(p.287)
• The big A.A. book had not been written and there was no literature except various religious pamphlets.(p.291)
• It was very impressive and I wish that every A.A. could have the benefit of this type of sponsorship today.(p.292)
• So I suggested that he take a trip to Akron for a couple of weeks, which he did, living with one of the A.A. families there.(p.294)
• I suggested to her that she should see the son's minister or doctor, and that perhaps he would recommend the A.A. program.(p.294)
• And over my A.A. years I have made many real, honest, sincere friendships that I shall always cherish.(p.296)
• This worldly lady helped to develop A.A. in Chicago and thus passed her keys to many.(p.304)
• Shortly after I returned to Chicago, my doctor, encouraged by the results of my contact with A.A., sent us two more of his alcoholic patients.(p.310)
• A.A. is not a plan for recovery that can be finished and done with.(p.311)
• Instead of wanting to escape some perplexing problem, we experience a thrill of challenge in the opportunity it affords for another application of A.A. techniques, and we find ourselves tackling it with surprising vigor.(p.311)
• I have had my share of problems, heartaches and disappointments, because that is life, but also I have known a great deal of joy, and a peace that is the handmaiden of an inner freedom, I have a wealth of friends and, with my A.A. friends, an unusual quality of fellowship.(p.312)
• Among today's incoming A.A. members, many have never reached the advanced stages of alcoholism, though, given time, all might have.(p.315)
• Why do men and women like these join A.A.?(p.315)
• Seeing this danger, they came to A.A.(p.315)
• I talked to the first sergeant and the battalion commander, and they got me in contact with an A.A. member.(p.319)
• I was sure I wouldn't belong in an A.A. group -- they were all old men, I thought, and all skid-row bums.(p.319)
• But I was in such deep trouble that I decided to try A.A. anyhow.(p.319)
• I went to A.A. meetings twice a week.(p.320)
• I found out that the people in all A.A. groups were as nice as the people in the first one.(p.320)
• I started to take A.A. seriously, and A.A. gave me a new way of life.(p.320)
• And when my husband found A.A., I came to the second meeting with him.(p.321)
• This girl and her husband are both in A.A., and she said to me, "Oh, but you're not the alcoholic; it's your husband."(p.322)
• We have only been in A.A. a few years, but now we're trying to make up for lost time.(p.325)
• A.A. has given us that.(p.325)
• But A.A. has shown me that I can help other alcoholics.(p.326)
• Two years later, a month beyond age seventy, I was crying for help from A.A.(p.327)
• He's now in A.A. and works as a volunteer for the local alcoholism council.(p.330)
• I knew about A.A.(p.332)
• I had forgotten "If I ever I get that bad, I'll try A.A."(p.333)
• I told her I had to go to A.A.(p.334)
• I did go to A.A., two days later, walking in alone.(p.334)
• I had worked so long in a profession where fakery, deceit, and untruths are tools of trade that I instantly recognized honesty when I heard it, from the mouths of A.A. members.(p.334)
• A.A. has not let me down there.(p.334)
• He did not know it was A.A., and it was useless to tell him, for he doesn't have our disease.(p.334)
• In A.A., she discovered she had lost nothing and had found everything.(p.335)
• But in the light of the new understanding that I have found in A.A., I have been able to interpret that defeat, and that failure, and that shame, as seeds of victory.(p.335)
• I had to hide, as a great many people in A.A. have had to do.(p.336)
• The fellowship I found in A.A. enabled me to face my problem honestly and squarely.(p.340)
• But when we come into A.A., we can face our problem honestly and openly.(p.340)
• And I took everything that A.A. had to give me.(p.340)
• I heard one very ill woman say that she didn't believe in the surrender part of the A.A. program.(p.340)
• Since I gave my will over to A.A., whatever A.A. has wanted of me I've tried to do to the best of my ability.(p.340)
• I'm not going; A.A. is leading me there.(p.340)
• A.A. gives us alcoholics direction into a way of life without the need for alcohol.(p.340)
• I had been brought up to believe in God, but I know that until I found this A.A. program, I had never found or known faith in the reality of God, the reality of His power that is now with me in everything I do.(p.341)
• The encouragement received in the early days, especially from the A.A. General Service Office, made a tremendous difference to my sobriety.(p.342)
• I have never attended an A.A. meeting, so it is essentially the literature that has kept me on the A.A. program.(p.342)
• Then I saw an A.A. advertisement in a newspaper, and I wrote to the address it gave.(p.343)
• I have read systematically since then, and A.A. literature has kept me sober.(p.343)
• Last year, I decided on an A.A. vacation in Naini Tal.(p.343)
• I read, studied, and meditated on every bit of A.A. literature in my possession.(p.344)
• I owe everything to A.A.(p.344)
• First, we all hear at A.A. meetings about those who have lost everything, those who have been in jail, those who have been in prison, those who have lost their families, those who have lost their income.(p.345)
• As someone in A.A. said to me once upon a time, there is nothing worse than a confused psychiatrist.(p.347)
• And the first thing you know I was lifted right out of the A.A. group, and I floated higher, and higher, and even higher, until I was way up on a pink cloud which is known as Pink Seven, and I felt miserable again.(p.348)
• What is this power that A.A. possesses?(p.352)
• Thank God I knew of A.A., so I called.(p.355)
• When I walked into the friendly atmosphere of my first A.A. meeting, I knew I was where I belonged.(p.355)
• A.A. has become a way of life and living for me.(p.355)
• This man faced the last ditch when his wife's voice from 1,300 miles away sent him to A.A.(p.356)
• Many times have I heard the above expressions since I have been in A.A., and many times I have had to reply "Definitely I am an alcoholic, and while it may be hard for you to believe, it is not hard for me, for I have learned many things about alcohol and myself that would, perhaps, be difficult for you to understand."(p.356)
• As these words are written at fifty-three years of age, with over nine years of A.A. behind me, with all its wonderful teachings, I haven't the slightest doubt about being an alcoholic.(p.356)
• I had read and heard a little about A.A. and so, groping for the phone book, I found the A.A. number and with hope in my heart eagerly telephoned.(p.363)
• That night she too had new hope because I had made sure she would know what I was doing about my drinking by packing every bit of A.A. literature I could put my hands on right on top so she couldn't help but see it when she opened my bag.(p.364)
• His enthusiasm and keen interest in A.A. fired my spirits again.(p.365)
• One night at the dinner table my wife said that tonight was my first birthday in A.A., and that the group would have the usual ice cream and cake for the "one year man."(p.365)
• When I was called upon for a few words I had to tell my friends that I wasn't one year old in A.A. that evening but only a "nine month baby."(p.366)
• My first spiritual experience in A.A. came quite early to me.(p.366)
• You will recall that I said the time that I got the idea out of a clear sky to call A.A. on a certain night was at about ten.(p.366)
• While I was in Florida trying to convince my wife with all the A.A. literature that she should come back to me, she went over to her desk and picked up a clipping she had taken from the St. Petersburg Times about A.A.(p.366)
• She said she cut this clipping from the paper at about ten on the same night, and at the same time as I called A.A. in Pittsburgh – some 1300 miles away.(p.367)
• I have had many more reasons to drink since I have been in A.A. than I had in all the years of my drinking.(p.367)
• I've had more problems but, thank God, I have had the teachings of A.A. with which to face them.(p.367)
• And, believe me, I thank God that I found out about A.A. before I had to beat my brains out – before I had been hospitalized, jailed or lost a job.(p.367)
• In meeting me casually, I don't think my strong belief in "The Man Upstairs" shows, but I have no other explanation for the many good things that have happened to me since I have been in A.A. – they came to me from a Greater Power.(p.367)
• I repeat, I am one of the fortunate members of A.A. – a lucky guy who is very grateful.(p.368)
• I'm very active in A.A. work and active at home, too, with my family.(p.372)
• During three years in A.A., I haven't lost so much as one shirt.(p.372)
• Two years before I joined A.A. my wife took a long trip during which she wrote me she just couldn't return unless I did something about my drinking.(p.377)
• Within thirty minutes I knew A.A. was the answer for me.(p.378)
• The answer came to me very simply in the first step of the Twelve Steps of A.A.(p.379)
• There may be many reasons which bring one to A.A. for the first time, but the lasting one must be to want sobriety and the A.A. way of living for oneself.(p.379)
• From the start I liked everything about the A.A. program.(p.380)
• It took me some time to realize that the Twelve Steps of A.A. were designed to help correct these defects of character and so help remove the obsession to drink.(p.380)
• Study the A.A. book – don't just read it.(p.381)
• A "spiritual experience" to me meant attending meetings, seeing a group of people, all there for the purpose of helping each other; hearing the Twelve Steps and the Twelve Traditions read at a meeting, and hearing the Lord's Prayer, which in an A.A. meeting has such great meaning – "Thy will be done, not mine."(p.381)
• I was desperately in earnest to follow through and understand what was expected of me as a member of A.A. and to take each Step of the Twelve as rapidly as possible.(p.382)
• To me this meant telling my associates that I had joined Alcoholics Anonymous; that I didn't know what was expected of me by A.A., but that whatever it was, it was the most important thing in life for me; that sobriety meant more to me than anything in this world.(p.382)
• There are many short phrases and expressions in A.A. which make sound sense.(p.382)
• The A.A. way of life is the way we always should have tried to live.(p.382)
• The fact that A.A. is a spiritual program didn't scare me or raise any prejudice in my mind.(p.383)
• When I joined A.A. I did so for the sole purpose of getting sober and staying sober.(p.383)
• Above all, I am grateful to A.A. for my sobriety, which means so much to my family, friends and business associates, because God and A.A. were able to do for me something I was unable to do for myself.(p.383)
• She still had her husband, her home, and a chance

to help start *A.A.* in Texas.(p.384)
• I didn't know that when I came into *A.A.*(p.384)
• I knew that I wanted to try *A.A.* and if that didn't work, I didn't think anything would.(p.384)
• I wish I could tell you how and why *A.A.* works, but I don't know.(p.384)
• I think that no one comes to *A.A.* until he's tried everything else.(p.384)
• As I grow in *A.A.*, I realize that a person with as much self-will as I had, as hard a head and as diseased an ego, had to try everything that I could think of, butting my head against every stone wall before I was ready to come in.(p.384)
• Anyhow, after Christmas my husband gave me a cocker spaniel who is, I think, just as notorious in *A.A.* as I am.(p.388)
• I think I actually read more contempt than was really there because just a week before someone had sent him the Saturday Evening Post article on *A.A.*, and there was some glimmer of hope in it for him.(p.391)
• There was something else that I could try -- *A.A.*(p.391)
• So, as I have said, I don't know how or why *A.A.* works.(p.392)
• It was the *A.A.* General Service Office in New York that I wrote to, and that office has always meant a lot to me.(p.392)
• So I wrote this letter in very shaky handwriting, and in just one week came back a letter with *A.A.* literature from New York.(p.392)
• (That was the man the *A.A.* office had referred me to.)(p.393)
• I wanted to try *A.A.* with my whole heart and soul.(p.393)
• The letter from *A.A.* had said this man would see me -- there weren't any women.(p.393)
• I stayed drunk from Monday until Friday, and I call that my spill into *A.A.*(p.393)
• There are so many to whom I feel deeply grateful; to my husband (and best critic), whose generous love, compassion and understanding have helped me along the way; to those before me in *A.A.* who inspired the first article I read, and the friend who sent that article to Frank; to Ruth for her personal note, and the first *A.A.* to talk to me; to my Bishop, whose loving and believing spirit inspired me; and to all the members of the Houston Group who were so patient, kind and helpful -- and to countless others.(p.393)
• In my second year in *A.A.* we were transferred to Dallas.(p.394)
• I wish I could tell you all that *A.A.* has done for me, all that I think and feel about *A.A.*, but it's something that I have experienced and have never been able to put into words.(p.394)
• To me, *A.A.* is within the reach of every alcoholic, because it can be achieved in any walk of life and because the achievement is not ours but God's.(p.395)
• A retired Navy man looks back over twenty years of drinking, to add up his *A.A.* "initiation fee."(p.396)
• A few times at meetings, I have heard this statement: "Members of *A.A.* have paid the highest initiation fee of any club members in the world."(p.396)
• Alcoholics being the argumentative lot that we are, the *A.A.* membership will undoubtedly come up with a few who will dispute these figures.(p.399)
• Incalculable are the intangible initiation fees that *A.A.* members have paid: the sick, sick hangovers, the remorse, guilt, broken homes, jails, and institutions, and the mental anguish in general that has been generated over the years.(p.399)
• Until I reached *A.A.* my life was a shambles; I was a mess, and I made everybody near and dear to me miserable.(p.400)
• It took me three psychoanalysts and several years in *A.A.* to really get this through my head.(p.401)
• With ten years of *A.A.* behind me, I was able to tell him that I'd have been alcoholic, no matter what; that I had been a sick person, unfit for marriage.(p.403)
• But I got drunk that night and stayed drunk, getting increasingly worse until I found *A.A.* ten years later.(p.404)
• An alcoholic cannot accept the news that he's an alcoholic unless there is a meaningful explanation given, and an offer of help, such as you get in *A.A.*(p.406)
• *A.A.* had to stop my drinking first.(p.409)
• In those days, psychiatry and *A.A.* had not gotten together as they have since.(p.412)
• My analyst was one of the first to learn of *A.A.* and to make subsequent use of it in her work.(p.412)
• In those days the *A.A.* Foundation was down in the Wall Street district of New York.(p.413)
• I did not reflect that half the office was composed of *A.A.* members, and that I was as unexciting as any client in any office.(p.413)
• A friend of Marty's, another *A.A.* let me in.(p.413)
• The strange *A.A.* put me at ease.(p.413)
• I had been on the wagon when I came to *A.A.* and this sobriety-tension eventually popped.(p.414)
• A fellow *A.A.*, called Anne, who had helped me, went on a terrible bender.(p.414)
• Priscilla, an *A.A.* who, like Marty, has become one of my greatest friends, decided that I was a stubborn case.(p.414)
• We were to go up to our *A.A.* farm in Kent, and I spent the evening before riding herd on Anne.(p.415)
• In the first year there were episodes such as kicking Priscilla in the shins, getting the lock changed on the desk in the *A.A.* Club, because I, as secretary, didn't want the Intergroup secretary "interfering," and taking an older woman member out to lunch for the express purpose of informing her that she was "a phony."(p.416)
• *A.A.* taught me how not to drink.(p.416)
• Through going to meetings and listening, and occasionally speaking, through doing Twelve Step work, whereby in helping others you are both the teacher and the student, by making many wonderful *A.A.* friends, I have been taught all the things in life that are worth having.(p.416)
• I have my *A.A.* friends, and I have become reacquainted with my old friends on a new basis.(p.416)
• My spiritual awakening in *A.A.* finally resulted in my joining a church some years ago.(p.417)
• I am a part of *A.A.* which is a way of life.(p.417)
• If I had not become an active alcoholic and joined *A.A.*, I might never have found my own identity or become a part of anything.(p.417)
• I tried the church and psychiatry and finally came to *A.A.*(p.418)
• I am one of the growing number of *A.A.* members who are second-generation.(p.419)
• In fact, I was taken to *A.A.* by a woman whom my father had taken to *A.A.* thirteen years earlier.(p.419)
• Oddly enough, the dentist who started *A.A.* in Amarillo, Tex., benevolently arranged my admission to dental college.(p.419)
• I came to *A.A.* simply because there were no other doors of help open to me in my hometown.(p.420)
• In *A.A.*, I have had to be torn down and then put back together differently.(p.420)
• *A.A.* made it possible for me to face the consequences of my past actions.(p.420)
• After I came to *A.A.*, I was divorced by my wife; I lost my practice; I was legally restrained from seeing my children; I went broke; and the dental society threatened me with the loss of my license.(p.420)
• Only *A.A.* kept me from running away.(p.420)
• My experience has been active: three meetings a week, many tapes, many *A.A.* conferences, much work on the Twelve Steps, and much work with other alcoholics and their families.(p.420)
• *A.A.* has given me a new wife, a beautiful stepdaughter, a new practice, a new home, and a new relationship with my four children.(p.420)
• Most important, *A.A.* has enabled me to go back and start growing up all over again in all areas of my life.(p.420)
• My gratitude to *A.A.* grows deeper each day I am sober.(p.420)
• My second wife is a young *A.A.* member, too, and what a terrific adventure this is for us!(p.420)
• Because *A.A.* really works for me!(p.421)
• A young veteran tells how a few rough experiences pushed him into *A.A.* -- and how he was therefore spared years of suffering.(p.422)
• About this time my folks found *A.A.*(p.427)
• Or maybe I'd come home wild drunk, singing and raving about what a fine place home was and what grand parents I had since they joined *A.A.*(p.428)
• I'd heard a lot about *A.A.* and met a great many A.A.'s during that year at home, but I hadn't thought of it for myself.(p.429)
• And the folks said *A.A.* was for people who wanted to quit, otherwise it wouldn't work.(p.429)
• I'll join *A.A.* if it kills me.(p.430)
• That is how I came into *A.A.*(p.430)
• A week after my decision to join *A.A.*, she called it quits.(p.430)
• I thought, "If this is *A.A.* why not go back to drinking, kill myself with booze in the next three years the doctor had given me, and call it a bad job?"(p.430)
• I joined *A.A.* at twenty-two.(p.430)
• Were I to revert to drinking, even now, I wouldn't give anything for these four years in *A.A.*(p.430)
• I have been helped morally, spiritually, mentally and materially through *A.A.*(p.430)
• Now I know I can't live without *A.A.*(p.430)
• I owe no one -- except *A.A.*(p.431)
• I looked up an *A.A.* meeting and went there -- alone.(p.436)
• That was seven years ago -- and many *A.A.* meetings ago -- and I haven't had a drink during those seven years.(p.437)
• With my *A.A.* friends, all I can say is that it's a power greater than myself.(p.437)
• The most terrible blow of my life befell me after I'd found sobriety through *A.A.*(p.437)
• If there ever was anyone who came to *A.A.* by mistake, it was I.(p.439)
• Never once had my mother even hinted at the idea that, when I grew up, I might like to be president of *A.A.*(p.439)
• Max and I had been married for twenty-eight years when I ended up in *A.A.*(p.439)
• (That dog hasn't wet my pants once since I joined *A.A.*, and neither have I!)(p.440)
• Today, I find I can't work my *A.A.* program while taking pills, nor may I even have them around for dire emergencies only.(p.443)
• (I am pleased to state, however, that I had gone to only a very few *A.A.* meetings before I was able to make a really beautiful pair of moccasins -- and half a wallet.(p.445)
• For my seventh *A.A.* birthday, my program-oriented, Al-Anon wife had my moccasins bronzed.(p.445)
• One day as I sat there in the hospital, my psychiatrist walked up behind me and asked, "How'd you like to talk to the man from *A.A.*?"(p.446)
• My reaction was that I'd already helped all the patients on the ward, and I still had plenty of problems of my own without trying to help some drunk from *A.A.*(p.446)
• The psychiatrist, who had generally been ignoring me, now became quite interested; every day, he would ask me all kinds of questions about the *A.A.* meetings.(p.446)
• At first, I wondered whether he was alcoholic himself, and was sending me to find out about *A.A.*(p.446)
• It was precisely a year before I spoke at an *A.A.* meeting.(p.447)
• I had already given up all the narcotics, most of the pills, and some of the alcohol when I first came to *A.A.*(p.448)
• The people of *A.A.* had something that looked much better than what I had, but I was afraid to let go of what I had in order to try something new; there was a certain sense of security in the familiar.(p.448)
• After I had been around *A.A.* for seven months, tapering off alcohol and pills, not finding the program working very well, I was finally able to say, "Okay, God.(p.448)
• *A.A.* and acceptance have taught me that there is a bit of good in the worst of us and a bit of bad in the best of us; that we are all children of God and we each have a right to be here.(p.449)
• Before *A.A.*, I judged myself by my intentions, while the world was judging me by my actions.(p.450)
• It's as though *A.A.* had given me a new pair of glasses.(p.450)
• Then, one day in *A.A.*, I was told that I had the lenses in my glasses backwards; "the courage to change" in the Serenity Prayer meant, not that I should change my marriage, but rather that I should change myself and learn to accept my spouse as she was.(p.451)
• *A.A.* has given me a new pair of glasses.(p.451)
• I can do the same thing with an *A.A.* meeting.(p.451)
• It seems I should have learned to love my wife and family first; the newcomer to *A.A.*, last.(p.451)
• Eventually, I had to redo each of the Twelve Steps specifically with Max in mind, from the First, saying, "I am powerless over alcohol, and my homelife is unmanageable by me," to the Twelfth, in which I tried to think of her as a sick Al-Anon and treat her with the love I would give a sick *A.A.* newcomer.(p.452)
• Thank God for *A.A.*!(p.452)
• Had it not been for *A.A.* in prison. . . I'll never know, but my educated guess is that I would not be alive today.(p.457)
• However, one thing I am certain of: Inmates in prison who attend *A.A.* have their chances of remaining free greatly enhanced -- this is a proved fact.(p.458)
• Of course, an inmate must begin living the *A.A.* way "inside," if he is to stand a chance "outside."(p.458)
• Yet prisoners often can't identify with many *A.A.*

members' drinking stories.(p.458)
• Most of us did not stay out of prison long enough to run the alcoholic gamut -- to develop the ongoing kind of alcoholism or alcoholic drinking you hear about in *A.A.* talks.(p.458)
• Through *A.A.*, many receive the needed change and awakening just by trying to live by *A.A.* principles and associating with *A.A.* people.(p.459)
• We do this by going to many *A.A.* meetings with an open mind and a desire to live the good-feeling life without chemicals -- liquid or otherwise.(p.459)
• Through *A.A.*, we can experience freedom from self.(p.459)
• All Twelve Steps of *A.A.* are designed to kill the old self (deflate the old ego) and build a new, free self.(p.459)
• I would rather talk about the good things *A.A.* has taught me; I feel that hitting on just a few sordid points should be sufficient to let those of you in institutions know where I came from.(p.459)
• The first time I remember seeing or hearing of *A.A.* was twenty years ago.(p.460)
• They were having a large *A.A.* meeting in the prison auditorium.(p.460)
• In those days, I trusted no church-goer, and thought *A.A.* was for weaklings.(p.460)
• Four years later, I was taken to my first *A.A.* meeting out of prison, in Los Angeles.(p.460)
• For the next five years, I was in and out of *A.A.* in Los Angeles, Phoenix, and San Francisco.(p.460)
• Finally, I threw away all my books and decided never to return to *A.A.*(p.460)
• However, I still would not attend *A.A.* in prison.(p.461)
• I suddenly remembered one of my first *A.A.* meetings, where I heard, "If you are an alcoholic and if you continue to drink, the end is death or insanity."(p.461)
• Yes, I knew what the Serenity Prayer was -- *A.A.* had taught me.(p.461)
• (I am looking at it now in my bedroom -- a copy that was presented to me a couple of years ago by the *A.A.* group in that same prison.)(p.461)
• I started going to *A.A.* in prison at the group's next meeting.(p.461)
• It is painful to grow, and without the help of my "civilian" *A.A.* companion, big Gene, I might not have survived that critical year of adjustment.(p.462)
• This *A.A.* friend took me into his home when he had me out on pass.(p.462)
• I go back to my old alma mater occasionally to give *A.A.* talks, and -- just think! -- the warden is my friend.(p.462)
• I count my sobriety date from the day I began going to *A.A.* in prison, not from the date of my last drink.(p.462)
• I owe everything to *A.A.* and God.(p.463)
• Guess I'll never be a saint, but whatever I am, I want to be sober and in *A.A.*(p.463)
• God bless all you people in *A.A.* and especially you fellows in prison.(p.463)
• You may wonder why, since I was having all this trouble, and was having to seek the assistance of others, *A.A.* hadn't come into the picture.(p.469)
• My husband said, "What is *A.A.*?"(p.469)
• And so, in those following years, whenever *A.A.* was mentioned I would have no part of it.(p.469)
• In my screwed up mind I kept thinking I could have gone to *A.A.* way back there in 1940, and perhaps saved my marriage and home.(p.469)
• Finally, however, in November of 1944, at long last I went to *A.A.*(p.470)
• And *A.A.* took this wreck of a woman and brought her back to life.(p.470)
• Was it because they told me in *A.A.* that I was an alcoholic?(p.470)
• *A.A.* didn't teach me I was an alcoholic; rather it taught me that because I was an alcoholic my life had become unmanageable.(p.470)
• But to another woman, the first woman I met in *A.A.*, I could talk.(p.471)
• (I've met some of these same women since in *A.A.*)(p.471)
• But the older members in *A.A.* told me, "easy does it."(p.471)
• When I first came into *A.A.*, the woman who was my sponsor was the first woman I had ever met who admitted that she was an alcoholic.(p.472)
• And so for three months this one woman was my *A.A.*(p.472)
• And when she broke a luncheon date with me one Saturday, after I had been in *A.A.* for about three months, I said, "I'll show her!(p.472)
• That was over seven years ago, and thank God and *A.A.*, I haven't had a drink since.(p.473)
• From a Canadian reservation to overseas bars to New England lockups, an Indian traveled a long trail that finally led him home to *A.A.*(p.474)
• I proud to be son of Tall Man, American Indian, and member of *A.A.* for many moons.(p.474)
• We all one as Great Spirit walks through *A.A.* like sun walks through day.(p.474)
• I hear about *A.A.*, but think it religion.(p.475)
• He say he take me to *A.A.* meeting.(p.476)
• Two weeks later, he come to *A.A.* meeting.(p.476)
• Find same *A.A.*, same Spirit.(p.476)
• Miracle happen all time in *A.A.*(p.476)
• Two years later, my brother take Tall Man to first *A.A.* meeting.(p.476)
• He was old, but now he grow young with new life in *A.A.* and travel all time.(p.476)
• At every place, I find *A.A.* group first.(p.476)
• I feel Great Spirit at all meetings and when talk to *A.A.* friends.(p.477)
• Go to *A.A.* meetings.(p.477)
• Call friend in *A.A.* when bad thoughts come.(p.477)
• Walk with me up Twelve Steps of *A.A.* to peace."(p.477)
• To Indians, I say: "Don't be afraid to join *A.A.*(p.477)
• If so, *A.A.* full of Indians.(p.477)
• Then *A.A.* showed her the beauty of normal living, in a whole family reborn.(p.478)
• When I came into *A.A.*, I had no intention of quitting drinking -- I figured I was doing all right.(p.478)
• You see how much work some of us have to do on ourselves when we finally come into *A.A.*!(p.480)
• We survivors are all in *A.A.* now, and my mother is in Al-Anon.(p.480)
• There is no cure for alcoholism, but it can be arrested in the program of *A.A.*(p.480)
• I met and married a man in *A.A.*, and I am the happiest I have ever been in my life.(p.481)
• I know the biggest word for me in *A.A.* is "honesty."(p.482)
• She didn't say anything about *A.A.* or getting me a sponsor at that time, but she did ask about Vi, and I told her Vi was working and how she could locate her.(p.494)
• That was the next meeting, and the first meeting of a colored group in *A.A.*, so far as I know.(p.495)
• That's my story of what *A.A.* has done for me.(p.496)
• Pioneer *A.A.*, minister's son, and southern farmer, he asked, "Who am I to say there is no God?"(p.497)
• After twenty years in prison for murder, he knew *A.A.* was the spot for him . . . if he wanted to stay on the outside.(p.508)
• I spent my last seventeen months in Wallkill, and it was there that I first got my introduction to *A.A.*(p.509)
• That was my attitude toward *A.A.* at that time.(p.510)
• I had an advantage in having an idea of what *A.A.* was about before coming out on the street.(p.510)
• So instead of going near *A.A.*, I just browsed around for that first month.(p.510)
• Each time I would make a report to the parole officer he would ask me, "Have you been to an *A.A.* meeting yet?"(p.510)
• So I went to an *A.A.* meeting the first chance I got, and I listened.(p.511)
• I started prowling around with a couple of these *A.A.* boys, which kept me pretty busy and kept my mind off of down town.(p.511)
• Then instead of going out with *A.A.* again I went out with some of the other crowd, and off again I went.(p.511)
• I've stuck pretty close to *A.A.* ever since then, taken it day by day, not biting off more than I can chew.(p.511)
• It's no bed of roses, but somehow or other I've been able to make it, through the kindness of people in *A.A.*(p.511)
• I think I am very lucky that there are people like A.A.'s and an *A.A.* program to hang on to and carry me through.(p.511)
• I'm fortunate because I live in an era when *A.A.* is available, and I'm able to take advantage of it.(p.512)
• I'm grateful because that Higher Power led me to *A.A.* a little over three years ago, when I needed it very badly.(p.512)
• My drinking pattern isn't very different from the average you find in *A.A.*(p.512)
• When we first come into *A.A.*, many of us are confused because as a general rule we're at the end of our respective ropes, and we don't know what to do.(p.512)
• It's like the fellow who came in *A.A.*, and his sponsor said to him, "Listen, buddy, do you believe in a Higher Power?"(p.512)
• We talked for a while, and then he sent me down to the Alanon House over on the west side, and there I had my introduction to *A.A.*(p.515)
• For me, *A.A.* has become a way of life.(p.516)
• He survived to become a mainstay of *A.A.* in Eire.(p.517)
• I am an Irishman and I was forty-nine when I joined *A.A.*(p.517)
• Just as I was wondering what on earth I could do -- I was too drunk even to pack a handkerchief -- the memory of an *A.A.* write-up that I had seen in the Evening Mail flashed across my mind -- and I thought to myself, this is something I haven't tried yet.(p.523)
• So I did manage to get myself down to an *A.A.* meeting that night.(p.523)
• Providentially, this was a Monday might when the Dublin Group met in those days, and my family agreed that if *A.A.* could do anything for me at all, that I'd be allowed to stay on at home on probation.(p.523)
• I was taking Benzedrine and paraldehyde quite impartially during the day then, and by the time I arrived at my first *A.A.* meeting, I was pretty drunk and certainly doped up to the eyes and completely jittery.(p.523)
• Since I joined on that April night, *A.A.* has done more for me than just stop me from drinking; it has brought me back to life again.(p.524)
• My mother lived on for five years after I joined *A.A.*, the last two in complete blindness.(p.525)
• Not least of my debts to *A.A.* is the knowledge that in that time when she wanted me most, I was there -- and that I wasn't drunk.(p.525)
• On one of these trips, the judge must have thought I was worth saving, for instead of sending me to jail, he sent me to *A.A.* for one month.(p.526)
• I went to *A.A.*(p.526)
• It was there that I really found out what *A.A.* was.(p.528)
• I had rejected *A.A.* on the outside, but now it came to me in prison.(p.528)
• Today, I thank my Higher Power for giving me another chance at life and *A.A.* and being able to try and help some other alcoholic.(p.529)
• Since I have been in *A.A.*, I have more friends than I ever had in my life -- friends who care about me and my welfare, friends who don't care that I am black and that I have been in prison.(p.529)
• The only thing that bothers me is that there are only about five Negroes in *A.A.* in my city.(p.529)
• Even those don't take part in *A.A.* functions as I would like to see them do.(p.529)
• I don't know if it's force of habit or something else that keeps them in one place, but I do know that in *A.A.* there is much work to do, and none of us can do it standing still.(p.529)
• I just want to say that you don't have to be afraid, because no one at any *A.A.* meeting will bite you.(p.529)
• There are no color bars in *A.A.*(p.529)
• I am talking about *A.A.* people, who have gone through some of the same things that you might be going through now.(p.529)
• I'm writing this during an *A.A.* convention, where I have spent the weekend with nothing but white people.(p.529)
• Sometimes we are told in *A.A.* not to try and learn the reasons for our drinking.(p.533)
• After nearly eight years of sobriety in *A.A.*, I still can set down such thoughts, "against my instinct and training," showing that I still consider myself a "special" person, entitled to special privileges.(p.536)
• For by now I had been exposed once to *A.A.*, but I had treated it as a vaudeville and had taken friends to meetings so that they too could enjoy the fascination of the naked revelation of suffering and recovery.(p.539)
• *A.A.* had not worked for me.(p.539)
• The reason, as I learned later, was that I had not worked for *A.A.*(p.539)
• But for the next years, I worked hard and exultantly in *A.A.*(p.541)
• In the nearby little town there was a plumber who once had tried to get an *A.A.* group going.(p.541)
• It is going strong still, these eight years later, and some of its members have been of great influence for good in state-wide *A.A.* work.(p.541)
• I wish we did not have to have jails; I wish everyone could be in *A.A.*, and if everyone were there would be no need for jails, in my opinion.(p.542)
• For me, *A.A.* is a synthesis of all the philosophy I've ever read, all of the positive, good philosophy, all of it based on love.(p.542)

• In *A.A.* we can begin again no matter how late it may be.(p.543)
• Young when she joined, this *A.A.* believes her serious drinking was the result of even deeper defects.(p.544)
• And I am sure they would be right as far as they go, but *A.A.* has taught me I am the result of the way I reacted to what happened to me as a child.(p.544)
• What is much more important to me, *A.A.* has taught me that through this simple program I may experience a change in this reaction pattern that will indeed allow me to "match calamity with serenity."(p.544)
• The only importance in all of this lies in the fact that at twenty-three I was just as sick as I was at thirty three, when I came into *A.A.*, but at that time I apparently had no place to go because I had no drinking problem.(p.546)
• Had I been able to explain to a psychiatrist the feeling of futility, loneliness and lack of purpose that had come with my deep sense of personal failure at this second divorce, I seriously doubt that the good doctor could have convinced me that my basic problem was a spiritual hunger, but *A.A.* has shown me this was the truth.(p.546)
• And if I had been able to turn to the church at that time I'm sure they could not have convinced me my sickness was within myself, nor could they have shown me the need for self-analysis that *A.A.* has shown me is vital if I am to survive.(p.546)
• This caused the rather cryptic comment from one of my *A.A.* friends, when I told my story after coming into the program, that I had always been a cinch for the program, for I had always been interested in mankind, but that I was just taking them one man at a time.(p.548)
• I've heard it said many times in *A.A.*, "There is just one good drunk in every alcoholic's life, and that's the one that brings us into *A.A.*," and I believe it.(p.549)
• Finally, in desperation, my family appealed to a doctor for advice and he suggested *A.A.*(p.549)
• I attended my first *A.A.* meeting eight years ago, and it is with deep gratitude that I'm able to say I've not had a drink since that time, and that I take no sedation or narcotics, for this program is to me one of complete sobriety and I no longer need to escape reality.(p.549)
• One of the truly great things *A.A.* has taught me is that reality too has two sides; I had only known the grim side before the program, but now I had a chance to learn about the pleasant side as well.(p.550)
• The *A.A.* members who sponsored me told me in the beginning that I would not only find a way to live without having a drink, but that I would find a way to live without wanting to drink, if I would do these simple things.(p.550)
• They suggested that I study the *A.A.* book and try to take the Twelve Steps according to the explanation in the Book, for it was their opinion that the application of these principles in our daily lives will get us sober and keep us sober.(p.550)
• *A.A.* taught me that willingness to believe was enough for a beginning.(p.550)
• It's been true in my case, nor could I quarrel with "restore us to sanity," for my actions drunk or sober, before *A.A.*, were not those of a sane person.(p.550)
• *A.A.* has given me serenity of purpose, the opportunity to be of service to God and to the people about me, and I am serene in the infallibility of these principles that provide the fulfillment of my purpose.(p.551)
• *A.A.* has taught me that I will have peace of mind in exact proportion to the peace of mind I bring into the lives of other people, and it has taught me the true meaning of the admonition "happy are ye who know these things and do them."(p.551)
• *A.A.* TAUGHT HIM TO HANDLE SOBRIETY(p.554)
• When I had been in *A.A.* only a short while, an oldtimer told me something that has affected my life ever since.(p.554)
• "*A.A.* does not teach us how to handle our drinking," he said.(p.554)
• To do that, I had come to *A.A.* to learn how to handle sobriety -- which is what I could not handle in the first place.(p.554)
• It was the late Dr. Tiebout, then, who persuaded me to seek help through *A.A.*(p.559)
• While there, I read the Big Book and the Grapevine and began the slow road back to health and sanity through the recovery program of *A.A.*(p.559)
• All these things and many, many more, *A.A.* gave me.(p.559)
• I have learned how to relate to people; before *A.A.*, I could never do that comfortably without alcohol.(p.559)
• God willing, we members of *A.A.* may never again have to deal with drinking, but we have to deal with sobriety every day.(p.560)
• For example, we are told in *A.A.* that we cannot afford resentments and self-pity, so we learn to avoid these festering mental attitudes.(p.560)
• *A.A.* led me gently from this fantasizing to embrace reality with open arms.(p.561)
• I. The *A.A.* Tradition(p.563)
• III. The Medical View on *A.A.*(p.563)
• V. The Religious View on *A.A.*(p.563)
• VI. How to Get in Touch With *A.A.*(p.563)
• THE *A.A.* TRADITION(p.563)
• *A.A.* can, of course, mean just as much to uncounted alcoholics not yet reached.(p.563)
• The "12 Traditions" of Alcoholics Anonymous are, we A.A.'s believe, the best answers that our experience has yet given to those ever urgent questions, "How can *A.A.* best function?" and, "How can *A.A.* best stay whole and so survive?"(p.563)
• This is a condensed version of the original "long form" *A.A.* Traditions as first printed in 1946.(p.563)
• One -- Our common welfare should come first; personal recovery depends upon *A.A.* unity.(p.564)
• Three -- The only requirement for *A.A.* membership is a desire to stop drinking.(p.564)
• Four -- Each group should be autonomous except in matters affecting other groups or *A.A.* as a whole.(p.564)
• Six -- An *A.A.* group ought never endorse, finance or lend the *A.A.* name to any related facility or outside enterprise, lest problems of money, property and prestige divert us from our primary purpose.(p.564)
• Seven -- Every *A.A.* group ought to be fully self-supporting, declining outside contributions.(p.564)
• Nine -- *A.A.*, as such, ought never be organized; but we may create service boards or committees directly responsible to those they serve.(p.564)
• Ten -- Alcoholics Anonymous has no opinion on outside issues; hence the *A.A.* name ought never be drawn into public controversy.(p.564)
• Our *A.A.* experience has taught us that:(p.565)
• *A.A.* must continue to live or most of us will surely die.(p.565)
• Nor ought *A.A.* membership ever depend upon money or conformity.(p.565)
• Any two or three alcoholics gathered together for sobriety may call themselves an *A.A.* group, provided that, as a group, they have no other affiliation.(p.565)
• And no group, regional committee, or individual should ever take any action that might greatly affect *A.A.* as a whole without conferring with the trustees of the General Service Board.(p.565)
• We think, therefore, that any considerable property of genuine use to *A.A.* should be separately incorporated and managed, thus dividing the material from the spiritual.(p.565)
• An *A.A.* group, as such, should never go into business.(p.566)
• Secondary aids to *A.A.*, such as clubs or hospitals which require much property or administration, ought to be incorporated and so set apart that, if necessary, they can be freely discarded by the groups.(p.566)
• Hence such facilities ought not to use the *A.A.* name.(p.566)
• For clubs, *A.A.* managers are usually preferred.(p.566)
• But hospitals, as well as other places of recuperation, ought to be well outside *A.A.* -- and medically supervised.(p.566)
• While an *A.A.* group may cooperate with anyone, such cooperation ought never go so far as affiliation or endorsement, actual or implied.(p.566)
• An *A.A.* group can bind itself to no one.(p.566)
• 7. -- The *A.A.* groups themselves ought to be fully supported by the voluntary contributions of their own members.(p.566)
• Then too, we view with much concern those *A.A.* treasuries which continue, beyond prudent reserves, to accumulate funds for no stated *A.A.* purpose.(p.566)
• But our usual *A.A.* "12th Step" work is never to be paid for.(p.567)
• 9. -- Each *A.A.* group needs the least possible organization.(p.567)
• The trustees of the General Service Board are, in effect, our *A.A.* General Service Committee.(p.567)
• They are the custodians of our *A.A.* Tradition and the receivers of voluntary *A.A.* contributions by which we maintain our *A.A.* General Service Office at New York.(p.567)
• They are authorized by the groups to handle our over-all public relations and they guarantee the integrity of our principal newspaper, the *A.A.* Grapevine.(p.567)
• All such representatives are to be guided in the spirit of service, for true leaders in *A.A.* are but trusted and experienced servants of the whole.(p.567)
• 10. -- No *A.A.* group or member should ever, in such a way as to implicate *A.A.*, express any opinion on outside controversial issues -- particularly those of politics, alcohol reform, or sectarian religion.(p.567)
• We think *A.A.* ought to avoid sensational advertising.(p.567)
• Our names and pictures as *A.A.* members ought not be broadcast, filmed, or publicly printed.(p.567)
• THE MEDICAL VIEW ON *A.A.*(p.571)
• Following are excerpts from the comments of doctors present at the annual meeting of the Medical Society of the State of New York where a paper on *A.A.* was read:(p.571)
• Dr. G. Kirby Collier, psychiatrist: "I have felt that *A.A.* is a group unto themselves and their best results can be had under their own guidance, as a result of their philosophy.(p.571)
• Dr. Harry M. Tiebout, psychiatrist: "As a psychiatrist, I have thought a great deal about the relationship of my specialty to *A.A.* and I have come to the conclusion that our particular function can very often lie in preparing the way for the patient to accept any sort of treatment or outside help.(p.571)
• I now conceive the psychiatrist's job to be the task of breaking down the patient's inner resistance so that which is inside him will flower, as under the activity of the *A.A.* program."(p.571)
• Dr. John F. Stouffer, Chief Psychiatrist, Philadelphia General Hospital, citing his experience with *A.A.*, said: "The alcoholics we get here at Philadelphia General are mostly those who cannot afford private treatment, and *A.A.* is by far the greatest thing we have been able to offer them.(p.572)
• (This address is now available in pamphlet form at nominal cost through most *A.A.* groups or from Box 459, Grand Central Station, New York, NY 10163, under the title "Three Talks to Medical Societies by Bill W." -- formerly called "Bill on Alcoholism" and earlier "Alcoholism the Illness.")(p.572)
• THE RELIGIOUS VIEW ON *A.A.*(p.574)
• Clergymen of practically every denomination have given *A.A.* their blessing.(p.574)
• There is something spiritual about *A.A.* too, and Catholic participation in it almost invariably results in poor Catholics becoming better Catholics."(p.574)
• The *A.A.* plan is described by the members themselves as 'self-insurance.'(p.574)
• HOW TO GET IN TOUCH WITH *A.A.*(p.575)
• In the United States and Canada, most towns and cities have *A.A.* groups.(p.575)
• In such places, *A.A.* can be located through the local telephone directory, newspaper office, or police station, or by contacting local priests or ministers.(p.575)
• These so-called intergroup associations are found under the listing "*A.A.*" or "Alcoholics Anonymous" in telephone directories.(p.575)
• The General Service Board of *A.A.* (the trustees) administers A.A.'s General Service Office, *A.A.* World Services, Inc., and our monthly magazine, the *A.A.* Grapevine.(p.575)
• If you cannot find *A.A.* in your locality, a letter addressed to Alcoholics Anonymous, Box 459, Grand Central Station, New York, NY 10163, U.S.A., will receive a prompt reply from this world center, referring you to the nearest *A.A.* group.(p.575)
• Should you be the relative or friend of an alcoholic who shows no immediate interest in *A.A.*, it is suggested that you write the Al-Anon Family Groups, Inc., Box 182, Madison Square Station, New York, NY 10159, U.S.A.(p.575)
• This is a world clearing house for the Al-Anon Family Groups, composed largely of the wives, husbands and friends of *A.A.* members.(p.575)

A.A.'s

• New groups started up and it was found, to the astonishment of everyone, that *A.A.'s* message could be transmitted in the mail as well as by word of mouth.(p.xviii)
• But out of this frightening and at first disrupting experience the conviction grew that *A.A.'s* had to hang together or die separately.(p.xix)
• This was the substance of *A.A.'s* Twelve Traditions, which are stated in full on page 564 of this book.(p.xix)
• Some of the recommendations of *A.A.'s* early medical and religious friends will be found further on in this book.(p.xx)
• Seven percent of the *A.A.'s* surveyed are less than 30 years of age -- among them, many in their teens.(p.xxii)

• Dr. Bob and the twelve men and women who here tell their stories were among the early members of ***A.A.'s*** first groups.(p.169)
• The periods of sobriety attained by these thirteen ***A.A.'s*** range from fifteen to forty-six years.(p.169)
• ***A.A.'s*** Number One Group dates from that very day.(p.189)
• A pioneer woman member of ***A.A.'s*** first Group.(p.261)
• Therefore, these seventeen ***A.A.'s***, and hundreds of thousands like them, have been saved years of infinite suffering.(p.315)
• ***A.A.'s*** Twelve Steps showed me the way to sobriety if I wanted it.(p.320)
• Once I did have a slip – tried drinking again – but the ***A.A.'s*** tell me not to worry about yesterday, because nobody can change it, and not to worry about tomorrow, because it hasn't come yet.(p.320)
• Today, because of ***A.A.'s*** growth during the intervening years, it is of course much bigger than it was then.(p.392)
• However, I had phoned New York from the farm, appealing for help, and there in the station to meet us were two ***A.A.'s***, John and Bud.(p.415)
• Many good ***A.A.'s*** never join a church, and do not need to.(p.417)
• I'd heard a lot about A.A. and met a great many ***A.A.'s*** during that year at home, but I hadn't thought of it for myself.(p.429)
• It seemed to me that those ***A.A.'s*** to whom I talked knew all about me.(p.470)
• But the difference lay in the fact that the ***A.A.'s*** knew from their own bitter experience.(p.471)
• But by listening and talking to these ***A.A.'s*** -- talking to them as I had never talked to anyone in my whole life, I saw that it was my life that was unmanageable -- not just my drinking.(p.471)
• This physician, the originator of ***A.A.'s*** first black group, but badly caught in the toils, tells of his release and of how freedom came as he worked among his own people.(p.483)
• I think I am very lucky that there are people like ***A.A.'s*** and an A.A. program to hang on to and carry me through.(p.511)
• ***A.A.'s*** Twelve Steps may confuse you when you read them over.(p.516)
• The "12 Traditions" of Alcoholics Anonymous are, we ***A.A.'s*** believe, the best answers that our experience has yet given to those ever urgent questions, "How can A.A. best function?" and, "How can A.A. best stay whole and so survive?"(p.563)
• On the next page, ***A.A.'s*** "12 Traditions" are seen in their so-called "short form," the form in general use today.(p.563)
• The General Service Board of A.A. (the trustees) administers ***A.A.'s*** General Service Office, A.A. World Services, Inc., and our monthly magazine, the A.A. Grapevine.(p.575)

abandon
• We asked His protection and care with complete ***abandon***.(p.59)
• We thought well before taking this step making sure we were ready; that we could at last ***abandon*** ourselves utterly to Him.(p.63)
• ***Abandon*** yourself to God as you understand God.(p.164)
• And the last sentence was "We asked His protection and care with complete ***abandon***."(p.349)
• "Complete ***abandon***"; "Half measures availed us nothing"; "Thoroughly follow our path"; "Completely give oneself to this simple program" – rang in my swelled head.(p.349)

abandoned
• My wife and I ***abandoned*** ourselves with enthusiasm to the idea of helping other alcoholics to a solution of their problems.(p.15)
• With that rejection we imagined we had ***abandoned*** the God idea entirely.(p.45)
• This sort of thinking had to be ***abandoned***.(p.48)

aberrations
• Normal drinkers are not so affected, nor can they understand the ***aberrations*** of the alcoholic.(p.140)

abetted
• With the bravery born of desperation, and ***abetted*** by alcohol, I married a young and lovely girl.(p.277)
• In this I was greatly aided and ***abetted*** by one John Barleycorn.(p.358)

abide
• When the man is presented with this volume it is best that no one tell him he must ***abide*** by its suggestions.(p.144)

abilities
• I, who had thought so well of myself and my ***abilities***, of my capacity to surmount obstacles, was cornered at last.(p.8)
• He often possesses special ***abilities***, skills, and aptitudes, and has a promising career ahead of him.(p.21)
• You might say you appreciated his ***abilities***, would like to keep him, but cannot if he continues to drink.(p.141)
• I thought of what liquor had done to me, the opportunities that I had discarded, the ***abilities*** that had been given me and how I had wasted them, and I finally came to the conclusion, that if I didn't want to quit, I certainly ought to want to, and that I was willing to do anything in the world to stop drinking.(p.186)
• But I have a fortune in friendships, courage, self assurance and honest appraisal of my own ***abilities***.(p.296)
• He further explained that alcohol was no respecter of sex or background, but that most of the alcoholics he had encountered had better than average minds and ***abilities***.(p.308)
• And we wonder how much further this man could go if his alcoholic problem could be removed and he could throw one hundred per cent of his ***abilities*** into action.(p.308)
• Making amends is sometimes doing what we are capable of doing but failed to do because of alcohol; carrying out community responsibilities such as Community Funds, Red Cross, educational and religious activities in proportion to our ***abilities*** and energy.(p.381)

ability
• I was to right all such matters to the utmost of my ***ability***.(p.13)
• A certain American business man had ***ability***, good sense, and high character.(p.26)
• We alcoholics are men and women who have lost the ***ability*** to control our drinking.(p.30)
• How can such a lack of proportion, of the ***ability*** to think straight, be called anything else?(p.37)
• "As soon as I regained my ***ability*** to think, I went carefully over that evening in Washington.(p.41)
• Did we not have confidence in our ***ability*** to think?(p.54)
• Because of the employee's special ***ability***, or of his own strong personal attachment to him, the employer has sometimes kept such a man at work long beyond a reasonable period.(p.137)
• Can you have every confidence in his ***ability*** to recover?(p.143)
• My father was a professional man of recognized ***ability*** and both my father and mother were most active in church affairs.(p.171)
• The very simple program they advised me to follow was that I should ask to know God's will for me for that one day, and then, to the best of my ***ability***, to follow that, and at night to express my gratefulness to God for the things that had happened to me during the day.(p.208)
• I had some financial success through no ***ability*** of my own and, when jobless and almost wiped out in 1930, I began to trade and sell my collection; much of the proceeds went to keep my apartment stocked with liquor and almost every night saw me helpless to bed.(p.255)
• Now I feel so very grateful not only for my sobriety, which I try to maintain day by day, but I'm grateful also for the ***ability*** to help other people.(p.326)
• Surrender to me has meant the ***ability*** to run my home, to face my responsibilities as they should be faced, to take life as it comes to me day by day, and work my problems out.(p.340)
• Since I gave my will over to A.A., whatever A.A. has wanted of me I've tried to do to the best of my ***ability***.(p.340)
• Today I think of life in terms of happiness, contentment, freedom from fear and despair, sane thinking, ***ability*** to face problems as they occur, the opportunity to help other alcoholics and to be decent.(p.430)
• We are told to practice the Twelve Steps and Twelve Traditions to the best of our ***ability*** every day, one day at a time.(p.481)
• I believe this, and I believe too that it is equally impossible to practice these principles to the best of our ***ability***, a day at a time, and still drink, for I don't think the two things are compatible.(p.550)
• And yet my ***ability*** to lie outwardly and to kid myself inwardly grew with every drink I took.(p.556)

abjectly
• Yes, we had been faithful, ***abjectly*** faithful to the God of Reason.(p.54)

ablaze
• My Quaker mother-in-law, bless her heart, used to set the Christmas pudding ***ablaze*** with lumps of sugar dipped in rubbing alcohol.(p.402)

able
• But when the broker gave him Dr. Silkworth's description of alcoholism and its hopelessness, the physician began to pursue the spiritual remedy for his malady with a willingness he had never before been ***able*** to muster.(p.xvi)
• Another reason for the wide acceptance of A.A. was the ministration of friends -- friends in medicine, religion, and the press, together with innumerable others who became our ***able*** and persistent advocates.(p.xx)
• In all probability, we shall never be ***able*** to touch more than a fair fraction of the alcohol problem in all its ramifications.(p.xxi)
• On the other hand – and strange as this may seem to those who do not understand -- once a psychic change has occurred, the very same person who seemed doomed, who had so many problems he despaired of ever solving them, suddenly finds himself easily ***able*** to control his desire for alcohol, the only effort necessary being that required to follow a few simple rules.(p.xxvii)
• They are often ***able***, intelligent, friendly people.(p.xxviii)
• I talked with him for some time, but was not ***able*** to bring myself to feel that I had known him before.(p.xxix)
• We have heard of few instances where people, who showed definite signs of alcoholism, were ***able*** to stop for a long period because of an overpowering desire to do so.(p.32)
• Though you may be ***able*** to stop for a considerable period, you may yet be a potential alcoholic.(p.34)
• That may be true of certain nonalcoholic people who, though drinking foolishly and heavily at the present time, are ***able*** to stop or moderate, because their brains and bodies have not been damaged as ours were.(p.39)
• I had never been ***able*** to understand people who said that a problem had them hopelessly defeated.(p.42)
• Had you offered yourselves as patients at this hospital, I would not have taken you, if I had been ***able*** to avoid it.(p.43)
• We found that as soon as we were ***able*** to lay aside prejudice and express even a willingness to believe in a Power greater than ourselves, we commenced to get results, even though it was impossible for any of us to fully define or comprehend that Power, which is God.(p.46)
• When many hundreds of people are ***able*** to say that the consciousness of the Presence of God is today the most important fact of their lives, they present a powerful reason why one should have faith.(p.51)
• No one among us has been ***able*** to maintain anything like perfect adherence to these principles.(p.60)
• It is important that he be ***able*** to keep a confidence; that he fully understand and approve what we are driving at; that he will not try to change our plan.(p.74)
• We may not be ***able*** to determine which course to take.(p.86)
• For the type of alcoholic who is ***able*** and willing to get well, little charity, in the ordinary sense of the word, is needed or wanted.(p.97)
• They should be thankful he is sober and ***able*** to be of this world once more.(p.127)
• I know, in my own particular case, that nothing my company could have done would have stopped me for, so long as I was ***able*** to hold my position, I could not possibly realize how serious my situation was.(p.141)
• If he says yes, does he really mean it, or down inside does he think he is fooling you, and that after rest and treatment he will be ***able*** to get away with a few drinks now and then?(p.142)
• If the book is read the moment the patient is ***able***, while acutely depressed, realization of his condition may come to him.(p.144)
• After your man has gone along without drinking for a few months, you may be ***able*** to make use of his services with other employees who are giving you the alcoholic run-around -- provided, of course, they are willing to have a third party in the picture.(p.146)
• He will be ***able*** to take a position with such a man which is eminently fair and square.(p.148)
• His call to the clergyman led him presently to a certain resident of the town, who, though formerly ***able*** and respected, was then nearing the nadir of alcoholic despair.(p.155)
• "God ought to be ***able*** to do anything."(p.158)
• Understanding our work, he can do this with an eye to selecting those who are willing and ***able*** to recover on a spiritual basis.(p.162)
• The doctor proved to be ***able*** and exceedingly anxious to adopt any workable method of handling the situation.(p.163)

• I seemed to be ***able*** to snap back the next morning better than most of my fellow drinkers, who were cursed (or perhaps blessed) with a great deal of morning-after nausea.(p.172)

• I conducted myself so creditably that I was ***able*** to secure a much coveted internship in a western city, where I spent two years.(p.174)

• I wasn't afraid that the program wouldn't work, but I still was doubtful whether I would be ***able*** to hang on to the program, but I did come to the conclusion that I was willing to put everything I had into it, with God's power, and that I wanted to do just that.(p.189)

• I was always ***able*** to skate along the fringe of big money.(p.197)

• I was ***able*** to rationalize it anyway.(p.198)

• When I had been in the hospital ten days, Sister Ignatia, who has played such a part in the development of A.A. in this area, stuck her head in the door one morning and announced, looking at me quizzically, that they might be ***able*** to make something human out of my face after all.(p.205)

• The successful demonstration I had made of my life problems in other respects convinced me that some day I was going to be ***able*** to drink like a gentleman.(p.214)

• After two or three years of effort along this line, I reached the point of actual despair that I ever would be ***able*** to drink only a harmless amount each day.(p.215)

• For me, work was only a different means to the same end, to be ***able*** to do exactly what I wanted to do.(p.225)

• I had to persist in my attempts to get straightened out enough to be ***able*** to use the drinks I needed, without their turning on me.(p.227)

• In a few sentences he made God seem personal to me, explained Him as a being who was interested in me, the alcoholic, and that all I needed to do was to be willing to follow His way; that as long as I followed it I would be ***able*** to overcome my desire for liquor.(p.236)

• As I go along I seem to get strength daily to be ***able*** to resist more easily.(p.237)

• One evening, the book, after checking up, was very definitely in the red for plenty through a piece of studied carelessness on my part, and my boss, very shrewd and ***able***, fired me with a parting statement to the effect that once was enough.(p.251)

• Young and ***able*** to travel with the best of them, I managed to hold my job and keep my end up in the barrooms.(p.252)

• I had never, since the believing days of childhood, been ***able*** to conceive an authority directing the universe.(p.259)

• I remember starting to city school, coming from a country school, and wanting so very, very much to be like the other girls and trying flour on my face for powder because I wasn't ***able*** to have any real powder.(p.261)

• Time went on and the drinking got worse and worse, and I was in another barroom, down the road the other way, a small one, and I took my glass – that morning I'd been ***able*** to lift it from the bar – and I said to the woman behind the bar, "I wish I might never take another drop of that stuff.(p.266)

• Before the end finally came, I had, I guess made the surrender because I finally had been ***able*** to say that I would not mind too much.(p.272)

• Probably only a few readers of this story will be ***able***, from personal experiences of their own, to understand the exhilaration and sense of accomplishment which I felt after finishing this seemingly simple assignment.(p.276)

• A year later I was ***able*** to buy a Model T roadster and take a better job with a downtown printer.(p.276)

• When the day of their return was almost upon me, and suicide was the only answer I had been ***able*** to think of, I went into Ralph's room one evening and told him the truth.(p.278)

• With this specialized training, and a liberal business education in the school of hard knocks, I was ***able*** to set up shop some two years later as an independent accountant.(p.284)

• With God's help I am ***able***, for one day at a time, to carry business responsibilities which, not many years ago, I would not have dreamed of assuming.(p.284)

• It would be wonderful were I ***able*** to tell you that my confidence in God and my application of the Twelve Steps to my daily living have utterly banished fear.(p.284)

• Above all, I have gained the greatest thing accorded to any man, the love and understanding of a gracious God, who has lifted me from the alcoholic scrap-heap to a position of trust where I have been ***able*** to reap the rich rewards that come from showing a little love for others and from serving them as I can.(p.296)

• How I was ***able*** to discharge my duties at the office during those horrible mornings, I will never be ***able*** to explain.(p.299)

• "We watch the alcoholic performing in a position of responsibility and we know that because he is drinking heavily and daily he has cut his capacities by fifty per cent, and still he seems ***able*** to do a satisfactory job.(p.308)

• Perhaps I could find freedom and peace and be ***able*** once again to call my soul my own.(p.309)

• And I was ***able*** to go on the wagon for long periods of time – once for four years, to cure an ulcer.(p.328)

• But in the light of the new understanding that I have found in A.A., I have been ***able*** to interpret that defeat, and that failure, and that shame, as seeds of victory.(p.335)

• Because it was only through feeling defeat and feeling failure, the inability to cope with my life and with alcohol, that I was ***able*** to surrender and accept the fact that I had this disease, and that I had to learn to live again without alcohol.(p.335)

• However, I am an alcoholic, so I always looked forward to the day when I would be ***able*** to drink again.(p.343)

• I tried every gimmick that there was to get some peace of mind, but it was not until I was brought to my alcoholic knees, when I was brought to a group in my own community with the butcher, the baker, the carpenter and the mechanic, who were ***able*** to give me the Twelve Steps, that I was finally given some semblance of an answer to the last half of the First Step.(p.349)

• They have contributed fantastic amounts of time and work to our problem, but they aren't ***able***, it seems, to arrest either your alcoholism or mine.(p.352)

• With these new and enlightening doors opening up to me, I was ***able*** to make the eventual decision to stop drinking, a day at a time -- because I, too, was an alcoholic.(p.355)

• Above all, I am grateful to A.A. for my sobriety, which means so much to my family, friends and business associates, because God and A.A. were ***able*** to do for me something I was unable to do for myself.(p.383)

• I wish I could tell you all that A.A. has done for me, all that I think and feel about A.A., but it's something that I have experienced and have never been ***able*** to put into words.(p.394)

• It is also stated that we will never be ***able*** to figure out how much we have spent on alcohol.(p.396)

• With ten years of A.A. behind me, I was ***able*** to tell him that I'd have been alcoholic, no matter what; that I had been a sick person, unfit for marriage.(p.403)

• But I was not ***able*** to make use of this knowledge until after I became sober.(p.409)

• Then I was ***able*** to do something about me.(p.409)

• To this day I haven't been ***able*** to decipher what I wrote to them.(p.427)

• After going to school all day, working in the family drugstore all evening, and then studying until one or two in the morning, I would not be ***able*** to sleep soundly, with everything I had been studying going round in my head.(p.440)

• In the garage, I would put the needle in my vein and then try to figure out exactly how much medication to inject to overcome the pep pills while adding to the sleeping pills while ignoring the tranquilizers, in order to get just enough to be ***able*** to pull out the needle, jerk the tourniquet, throw it in the car, slam the car door shut, run down the hall, and fall in bed before I fell asleep.(p.442)

• I wasn't ***able*** to quit chemicals as long as they were in the house.(p.443)

• (I am pleased to state, however, that I had gone to only a very few A.A. meetings before I was ***able*** to make a really beautiful pair of moccasins – and half a wallet.(p.445)

• After I had been around A.A. for seven months, tapering off alcohol and pills, not finding the program working very well, I was finally ***able*** to say, "Okay, God.(p.448)

• I was always ***able*** to see the flaw in every person, every situation.(p.449)

• Prior to our marriage, when she was a shy, scrawny adolescent, I was ***able*** to see things in her that others couldn't necessarily see – things like beauty, charm, gaiety, a gift for being easy to talk to, a sense of humor, and many other fine qualities.(p.450)

• He has also taught me that I must help myself first; only then may I be ***able*** to help others.(p.481)

• It is so beautiful to get up in the morning not being hung-over and being ***able*** to remember where we were the night before.(p.481)

• On the other hand, I believe that I've always been medically inclined, though I have never been ***able*** to see medicine quite as the average person sees it.(p.485)

• I was ***able*** to get my work out.(p.486)

• I wasn't ***able*** to comprehend it.(p.489)

• I don't seem to be ***able*** to keep my mind on what I am doing.(p.499)

• It's no bed of roses, but somehow or other I've been ***able*** to make it, through the kindness of people in A.A.(p.511)

• I'm fortunate because I live in an era when A.A. is available, and I'm ***able*** to take advantage of it.(p.512)

• I was intensely unhappy the whole time, but I didn't seem to be ***able*** to do anything about it, and the worst part to me was the realization that all this was going to happen again and again until I died.(p.522)

• My mind was too screwy to be ***able*** to understand much of what was being said.(p.524)

• I was not ***able*** to hold a job – no one wants a drunk around.(p.526)

• I was always ***able*** to get a boyfriend who had a drinking joint or sold whiskey, but it didn't last long.(p.526)

• Today, I thank my Higher Power for giving me another chance at life and A.A. and being ***able*** to try and help some other alcoholic.(p.529)

• Since I've been home, I have been ***able*** to gain the respect of my two sons again.(p.529)

• We all have the same sickness, and in helping one another, we are ***able*** to stay sober.(p.530)

• There was the love affair which was ridiculous -- "imagine that midget being ***able*** to fall in love!" – and my head knew it while my heart pumped real, genuine anguish, for it hurt like hell, and since it was first love, things have never been quite the same.(p.534)

• I went back home, to a job of manual labor where for a little while I was ***able*** to keep away from alcohol.(p.539)

• I hope I have been ***able*** to impart to you, the reader, at least a bit of what I know; the joy of living, the irresistible power of divine love and its healing strength, and the fact that we, as sentient beings, have the knowledge to choose between good and evil, and, choosing good, are made happy.(p.543)

• Had I been ***able*** to explain to a psychiatrist the feeling of futility, loneliness and lack of purpose that had come with my deep sense of personal failure at this second divorce, I seriously doubt that the good doctor could have convinced me that my basic problem was a spiritual hunger, but A.A. has shown me this was the truth.(p.546)

• And if I had been ***able*** to turn to the church at that time I'm sure they could not have convinced me my sickness was within myself, nor could they have shown me the need for self-analysis that A.A. has shown me is vital if I am to survive.(p.546)

• Maybe I wouldn't be ***able*** to hold any job, or maybe (and this was my greatest fear) I wouldn't care whether I had a job or not.(p.548)

• The only reality I was ***able*** to face had been forced upon me by its very repetition – I had to drink; and I didn't know there was anything in the world that could be done about it.(p.548)

• I attended my first A.A. meeting eight years ago, and it is with deep gratitude that I'm ***able*** to say I've not had a drink since that time, and that I take no sedation or narcotics, for this program is to me one of complete sobriety and I no longer need to escape reality.(p.549)

• As our children grew up, I was ***able*** to be a father to them when they most needed one.(p.559)

• Dr. John F. Stouffer, Chief Psychiatrist, Philadelphia General Hospital, citing his experience with A.A., said: "The alcoholics we get here at Philadelphia General are mostly those who cannot afford private treatment, and A.A. is by far the greatest thing we have been ***able*** to offer them.(p.572)

abnormal

• In this statement he confirms what we who have suffered alcoholic torture must believe – that the body of the alcoholic is quite as ***abnormal*** as his mind.(p.xxiv)

• In a vague way their families and friends sense that these drinkers are ***abnormal***, but everybody hopefully awaits the day when the sufferer will rouse himself from his lethargy and assert his power of will.(p.23)

• The idea that somehow, someday he will control and enjoy his drinking is the great obsession of every ***abnormal*** drinker.(p.30)

• If he is already committed to an institution, but can convince you and your doctor that he means business, give him a chance to try our method, unless the doctor thinks his mental condition too ***abnormal*** or dangerous.(p.114)

• Cessation of drinking is but the first step away from a highly strained, ***abnormal*** condition.(p.122)

- But these scrapes can generally be charged, no matter how bad, to the ***abnormal*** action of alcohol on his mind.(p.140)
- Painfully aware of being somehow ***abnormal***, the man did not fully realize what it meant to be alcoholic.(p.155)
- To the best of my recollection I was completely free from any ***abnormal*** fears.(p.275)
- I hadn't been drinking much about that time, for I had begun to realize that there was something ***abnormal*** about my drinking, although as yet, I didn't realize that it was so out of control.(p.465)

aboard

- A friend who knew I would soon be broke mounted guard over me when I left my job of writing the histories of Texas cities and put me ***aboard*** a bus for the town I had left almost five years before.(p.256)
- The short tours could be taken care of by sneaking enough whiskey ***aboard*** ship so that it could be rationed out until another supply could be laid in.(p.398)

about

- When writing or speaking publicly ***about*** alcoholism, we urge each of our Fellowship to omit his personal name, designating himself instead as "a member of Alcoholics Anonymous."(p.xiii)
- The membership had then reached ***about*** 100 men and women.(p.xvii)
- But great numbers of these – ***about*** two out of three – began to return as time passed.(p.xx)
- At present, our membership is increasing at the rate of ***about*** seven per cent a year.(p.xx)
- You may rely absolutely on anything they say ***about*** themselves.(p.xxiv)
- There is the manic-depressive type, who is, perhaps, the least understood by his friends, and ***about*** whom a whole chapter could be written.(p.xxviii)
- ***About*** one year prior to this experience a man was brought in to be treated for chronic alcoholism.(p.xxix)
- My work took me ***about*** Wall street and little by little I became interested in the market.(p.2)
- With a certain satisfaction I reflected there was enough gin concealed ***about*** the house to carry me through that night and the next day.(p.8)
- There was something ***about*** his eyes.(p.9)
- "Come, what's all this ***about***?" I queried.(p.9)
- So that was it -- last summer an alcoholic crackpot; now, I suspected, a little cracked ***about*** religion.(p.9)
- Society was ***about*** to lock him up.(p.11)
- My ideas ***about*** miracles were drastically revised right then.(p.11)
- There is, however, a vast amount of fun ***about*** it all.(p.16)
- An illness of this sort – and we have come to believe it an illness --involves those ***about*** us in a way no other human sickness can.(p.18)
- But the ex-problem drinker who has found this solution, who is properly armed with facts ***about*** himself, can generally win the entire confidence of another alcoholic in a few hours.(p.18)
- That the man who is making the approach has had the same difficulty, that he obviously knows what he is talking ***about***, that his whole deportment shouts at the new prospect that he is a man with a real answer, that he has no attitude of Holier Than Thou, nothing whatever except the sincere desire to be helpful; that there are no fees to pay, no axes to grind, no people to please, no lectures to be endured -- these are the conditions we have found most effective.(p.18)
- But what ***about*** the real alcoholic?(p.21)
- MORE *ABOUT* ALCOHOLISM(p.30)
- It will not take long for you to decide if you are honest with yourself ***about*** it.(p.32)
- He had much knowledge ***about*** himself as an alcoholic.(p.36)
- We first saw Fred ***about*** a year ago in a hospital where he had gone to recover from a bad case of jitters.(p.39)
- For a few days he was depressed ***about*** his condition.(p.39)
- We told him what we knew ***about*** alcoholism.(p.39)
- He was interested and conceded that he had some of the symptoms, but he was a long way from admitting that he could do nothing ***about*** it himself.(p.40)
- Let him tell you ***about*** it:"I was much impressed with what you fellows said ***about*** alcoholism, and I frankly did not believe it would be possible for me to drink again.(p.40)
- I rather appreciated your ideas ***about*** the subtle insanity which precedes the first drink, but I was confident it could not happen to me after what I had learned.(p.40)
- "In this frame of mind, I went ***about*** my business and for a time all was well.(p.40)
- I had been out of town before during this particular dry spell, so there was nothing new ***about*** that.(p.41)
- The driver escorted me ***about*** for several days.(p.41)
- One of these men, staff member of a world-renowned hospital, recently made this statement to some of us: "What you say ***about*** the general hopelessness of the average alcoholic's plight is, in my opinion, correct.(p.43)
- ***About*** half our original fellowship were of exactly that type.(p.44)
- Well, that's exactly what this book is ***about***.(p.45)
- And it means, of course, that we are going to talk ***about*** God.(p.45)
- We have numerous theories, for example, ***about*** electricity.(p.48)
- People of faith have a logical idea of what life is all ***about***.(p.49)
- Experience has taught us that these are matters ***about*** which, for our purpose, we need not be worried.(p.50)
- We asked ourselves this: Are not some of us just as biased and unreasonable ***about*** the realm of the material?(p.51)
- What ***about*** people who proved that man could never fly?(p.55)
- It is an effort to discover the truth ***about*** the stock-in-trade.(p.64)
- If the owner of the business is to be successful, he cannot fool himself ***about*** values.(p.64)
- This short word somehow touches ***about*** every aspect of our lives.(p.67)
- Now ***about*** sex.(p.68)
- What can we do ***about*** them?(p.69)
- We must be willing to make amends where we have done harm, provided that we do not bring ***about*** still more harm in so doing.(p.69)
- In meditation, we ask God what we should do ***about*** each specific matter.(p.69)
- We realize that some people are as fanatical ***about*** sex as others are loose.(p.70)
- To sum up ***about*** sex: We earnestly pray for the right ideal, for guidance in each questionable situation, for sanity, and for the strength to do the right thing.(p.70)
- If we have been thorough ***about*** our personal inventory, we have written down a lot.(p.70)
- That being so you have swallowed and digested some big chunks of truth ***about*** yourself.(p.71)
- Having made our personal inventory, what shall we do ***about*** it?(p.72)
- Now these are ***about*** to be cast out.(p.72)
- There is doubt ***about*** that.(p.72)
- Time after time newcomers have tried to keep to themselves certain facts ***about*** their lives.(p.72)
- We explain to our partner what we are ***about*** to do and why we have to do it.(p.75)
- As we look over the list of business acquaintances and friends we have hurt, we may feel diffident ***about*** going to some of them on a spiritual basis.(p.76)
- Our real purpose is to fit ourselves to be of maximum service to God and the people ***about*** us.(p.77)
- It may be he has done us more harm than we have done him and, though we may have acquired a better attitude toward him, we are still not too keen ***about*** admitting our faults.(p.77)
- Telling them what we are trying to do, we make no bones ***about*** our drinking; they usually know it anyway, whether we think so or not.(p.78)
- She is indignant ***about*** it, and has a warrant out for our arrest.(p.79)
- This brings to mind a story ***about*** one of our friends.(p.80)
- In fairness we must say that she may understand, but what are we going to do ***about*** a thing like that?(p.81)
- Whatever the situation, we usually have to do something ***about*** it.(p.81)
- Each might pray ***about*** it, having the other one's happiness uppermost in mind.(p.82)
- We should not talk incessantly to them ***about*** spiritual matters.(p.83)
- We don't worry ***about*** them if we can honestly say to ourselves that we would right them if we could.(p.83)
- If we are painstaking ***about*** this phase of our development, we will be amazed before we are half way through.(p.83)
- Much has already been said ***about*** receiving strength, inspiration, and direction from Him who has all knowledge and power.(p.85)
- It would be easy to be vague ***about*** this matter.(p.86)
- On awakening let us think ***about*** the twenty-four hours ahead.(p.86)
- In thinking ***about*** our day we may face indecision.(p.86)
- Suggestions ***about*** these may be obtained from one's priest, minister, or rabbi.(p.87)
- To watch people recover, to see them help others, to watch loneliness vanish, to see a fellowship grow up ***about*** you, to have a host of friends – this is an experience you must not miss.(p.89)
- When you discover a prospect for Alcoholics Anonymous, find out all you can ***about*** him.(p.90)
- Neither should the family hysterically plead with him to do anything, nor should they tell him much ***about*** you.(p.90)
- Tell him enough ***about*** your drinking habits, symptoms, and experiences to encourage him to speak of himself.(p.91)
- When he sees you know all ***about*** the drinking game, commence to describe yourself as an alcoholic.(p.91)
- Talk ***about*** the conditions of body and mind which accompany it.(p.92)
- But you may talk to him ***about*** the hopelessness of alcoholism because you offer a solution.(p.92)
- There is no use arousing any prejudice he may have against certain theological terms and conceptions ***about*** which he may already be confused.(p.93)
- Admit that he probably knows more ***about*** it than you do, but call to his attention the fact that however deep his faith and knowledge, he could not have applied it or he would not drink.(p.93)
- Maybe you have disturbed him ***about*** the question of alcoholism.(p.94)
- On your first visit tell him ***about*** the Fellowship of Alcoholics Anonymous.(p.94)
- Unless your friend wants to talk further ***about*** himself, do not wear out your welcome.(p.95)
- If he is, you might try to help him ***about*** getting a job, or give him a little financial assistance.(p.96)
- Though his family be at fault in many respects, he should not be concerned ***about*** that.(p.98)
- People have said we must not go where liquor is served; we must not have it in our homes; we must shun friends who drink; we must avoid moving pictures which show drinking scenes; we must not go into bars; our friends must hide their bottles if we go to their houses; we mustn't think or be reminded ***about*** alcohol at all.(p.100)
- Why sit with a long face in places where there is drinking, sighing ***about*** the good old days.(p.102)
- We would not even do the cause of temperate drinking any good, for not one drinker in a thousand likes to be told anything ***about*** alcohol by one who hates it.(p.103)
- We have traveled a rocky road, there is no mistake ***about*** that.(p.104)
- And even if they did not love their families, how could they be so blind ***about*** themselves?(p.107)
- We know all ***about*** liquor as a social lubricant.(p.110)
- Our next thought is that you should never tell him what he must do ***about*** his drinking.(p.111)
- This may lay the groundwork for a friendly talk ***about*** his alcoholic problem.(p.111)
- Show him your copy of this book and tell him what you have found out ***about*** alcoholism.(p.112)
- Talk ***about*** his condition or this book only when he raises the issue.(p.113)
- You draw more and more into yourself and you think everyone is talking ***about*** conditions at your home.(p.114)
- But be careful not to be resentful ***about*** the last time he did so.(p.116)
- Let's talk ***about*** it later."(p.118)
- He gets stirred up ***about*** their troubles, but not at all ***about*** yours.(p.119)
- The fellowship of Al-Anon Family Groups was formed ***about*** thirteen years after this chapter was written.(p.121)
- The alcoholic, his wife, his children, his "in-laws," each one is likely to have fixed ideas ***about*** the family's attitude toward himself or herself.(p.122)
- Then, under one provocation or another, the aggrieved one would unearth the old affair and angrily cast its ashes ***about***.(p.124)
- Everyone knows ***about*** the others' alcoholic troubles.(p.125)
- We do talk ***about*** each other a great deal, but we almost invariably temper such talk by a spirit of love and tolerance.(p.125)
- The family will be affected also, pleasantly at first, as they feel their money troubles are ***about*** to be solved, then not so pleasantly as they find themselves neglected.(p.126)

• There is talk ***about*** spiritual matters morning, noon and night.(p.128)
• He may tell mother, who has been religious all her life, that she doesn't know what it's all ***about***, and that she had better get his brand of spirituality while there is yet time.(p.128)
• What ***about*** his talk that God will take care of them?(p.128)
• This means trouble, unless the family watches for these tendencies in each other and comes to a friendly agreement ***about*** them.(p.131)
• If he does not argue ***about*** religion, he will make new friends and is sure to find new avenues of usefulness and pleasure.(p.132)
• So far as we are concerned, there is nothing obligatory ***about*** it.(p.132)
• Now ***about*** health: A body badly burned by alcohol does not often recover overnight nor do twisted thinking and depression vanish in a twinkling.(p.133)
• A word ***about*** sex relations.(p.134)
• Seeing this, and meaning to be helpful, his wife commenced to admonish him ***about*** it.(p.135)
• His wife is one of those persons who really feels there is something rather sinful ***about*** these commodities, so she nagged, and her intolerance finally threw him into a fit of anger.(p.135)
• One day he told me ***about*** an executive of the same bank who, from his description, was undoubtedly alcoholic.(p.138)
• This seemed to me like an opportunity to be helpful, so I spent two hours talking ***about*** alcoholism, the malady, and described the symptoms and results as well as I could.(p.138)
• You now know more ***about*** alcoholism.(p.141)
• State that you know ***about*** his drinking, and that it must stop.(p.141)
• While on the subject of confidence, can you adopt the attitude that so far as you are concerned this will be a strictly personal matter, that his alcoholic derelictions, the treatment ***about*** to be undertaken, will never be discussed without his consent?(p.143)
• Whether your employee likes it or not, he will learn the grim truth ***about*** alcoholism.(p.144)
• We hope the doctor will tell the patient the truth ***about*** his condition, whatever that happens to be.(p.144)
• One instance comes to mind in which a malicious individual was always making friendly little jokes ***about*** an alcoholic's drinking exploits.(p.145)
• If he is, and is still trying to recover, he will tell you ***about*** it even if it means the loss of his job.(p.146)
• He will appreciate knowing you are not bothering your head ***about*** him, that you are not suspicious nor are you trying to run his life so he will be shielded from temptation to drink.(p.146)
• I have been learning something ***about*** alcoholism.(p.147)
• He will presently try the old game again, for he isn't happy ***about*** his sobriety.(p.152)
• "How is that to come ***about***?" you ask.(p.152)
• But what ***about*** his responsibilities – his family and the men who would die because they would not know how to get well, ah -- yes, those other alcoholics?(p.154)
• He told how he lived in constant worry ***about*** those who might find out ***about*** his alcoholism.(p.155)
• He trembled as he went ***about***, for this might mean ruin, particularly to a person in his line of business.(p.156)
• For an hour, the two friends told him ***about*** their drinking experiences.(p.157)
• There was much talk ***about*** the mental state preceding the first drink.(p.157)
• Said the future Fellow Anonymous: "Damn little to laugh ***about*** that I can see."(p.157)
• The two friends spoke of their spiritual experience and told him ***about*** the course of action they carried out.(p.157)
• His wife came, scarcely daring to be hopeful, though she thought she saw something different ***about*** her husband already.(p.158)
• Some of us are salesmen and go ***about***.(p.162)
• This practice enables us to lend a hand, at the same time avoiding certain alluring distractions of the road, ***about*** which any traveling man can inform you.(p.162)
• I was born in a small New England village of ***about*** seven thousand souls.(p.171)
• After three years of this, I wound up in the local hospital where they attempted to help me, but I would get my friends to smuggle me a quart, or I would steal the alcohol ***about*** the building, so that I got rapidly worse.(p.175)
• Finally my father had to send a doctor out from my home town who managed to get me back there in some way, and I was in bed ***about*** two months before I could venture out of the house.(p.175)
• I stayed ***about*** town a couple of months more and then returned to resume my practice.(p.175)
• I put on thirty pounds of weight in ***about*** two months, looked like a pig, and was uncomfortable from shortness of breath.(p.177)
• ***About*** the time of the beer experiment I was thrown in with a crowd of people who attracted me because of their seeming poise, health, and happiness.(p.178)
• I read everything I could find, and talked to everyone who I thought knew anything ***about*** it.(p.178)
• ***About*** this time a lady called up my wife one Saturday afternoon, saying she wanted me to come over that evening to meet a friend of hers who might help me.(p.179)
• This dry spell lasted for ***about*** three weeks; then I went to Atlantic City to attend several days' meeting of a national society of which I was a member.(p.179)
• It must be remembered that I had read a great deal and talked to everyone who knew, or thought they knew anything ***about*** the subject of alcoholism.(p.180)
• He gave me information ***about*** the subject of alcoholism which was undoubtedly helpful.(p.180)
• Of far more importance was the fact that he was the first living human with whom I had ever talked, who knew what he was talking ***about*** in regard to alcoholism from actual experience.(p.180)
• So it doesn't behoove me to squawk ***about*** it for, after all, nobody ever had to throw me down and pour liquor down my throat.(p.181)
• It never fails, if you go ***about*** it with one half the zeal you have been in the habit of showing when you were getting another drink.(p.181)
• So, at the time Dr. Bob and Bill came along I had ***about*** run out my strength.(p.182)
• I remember that my father kept whiskey around the house for medical purposes and entertainment, and I would drink from this when no one was ***about*** and then water it to keep my parents from knowing I was drinking.(p.183)
• She told me that she had been talking to a couple of fellows ***about*** drinking.(p.184)
• Before very long we began to relate some incidents of our drinking and, naturally, pretty soon, I realized both of them knew what they were talking ***about*** because you can see things and smell things when you're drunk, that you can't other times, and, if I had thought they didn't know what they were talking ***about***, I wouldn't have been willing to talk to them at all.(p.185)
• It's none of our business ***about*** your drinking.(p.186)
• They said, "That's what we're talking ***about***.(p.188)
• Every time I'd start thinking ***about*** drinking, I would think of the long, dry years ahead without having a drink; but this idea of twenty-four hours, that it was up to me from then on, was a lot of help.(p.188)
• You certainly know what you are talking ***about***."(p.189)
• Eagerly he pointed to us saying, "These are the fellows I told you ***about***; they are the ones who understand."(p.189)
• They said, "Let's forget ***about*** those other things, that is, trying to eliminate them all at once, and concentrate on the drink."(p.190)
• Of course, we had talked over quite a number of the failings that I had and made a sort of an inventory, which wasn't too difficult, because I had an awful lot of things wrong that were very apparent to me, because I knew all ***about*** them.(p.190)
• Bill looked across at my wife, and said to her, "Henrietta, the Lord has been so wonderful to me, curing me of this terrible disease, that I just want to keep talking ***about*** it and telling people."(p.191)
• Bill was very, very grateful that he had been released from this terrible thing and he had given God the credit for having done it, and he's so grateful ***about*** it he wants to tell other people ***about*** it.(p.191)
• That sentence, "The Lord has been so wonderful to me, curing me of this terrible disease, that I just want to keep telling people ***about*** it," has been sort of a golden text for the A.A. program and for me.(p.191)
• I feel that is ***about*** the most wonderful thing that a person can do.(p.192)
• I always built up in my own mind the great things that I was going to do, and in fact I accomplished ***about*** fifty percent of them and then lost interest.(p.193)
• There was nothing ***about*** that drink that I liked.(p.195)
• ***About*** that period, too, came increasing procrastination and the avoidance of responsibilities.(p.197)
• But I didn't do a thing ***about*** giving them any part of the seven bucks I had in my pocket.(p.197)
• The rubber prosperity went on for ***about*** six years -- 1916 to 1922.(p.197)
• We had two children, a boy and a girl, and when the boy was ***about*** twelve, we broke up the marriage.(p.199)
• I think this was ***about*** 1927.(p.199)
• He had known something of my drinking pattern, and he asked me what I was doing ***about*** it.(p.200)
• At the end of ***about*** four months, I not only had good looking clothes —and I might say that at the time I first talked to Max I didn't have a suit of clothes I could bend over in real sudden; now I had six suits of clothes.(p.200)
• I attended their meetings every Sunday and Wednesday for ***about*** nine months.(p.202)
• After drinking one glass of beer at the end of my work period for ***about*** five days, I thought I'd better find out whether I really had the stuff licked.(p.203)
• So I had one double-header every night for ***about*** two or three weeks.(p.203)
• One morning, after I had been on a binge for a couple of days, I awoke to find my brother and Doctor Bob in my room talking to me ***about*** not drinking.(p.206)
• I then began asking a lot of questions of both my brother and Dr. Bob ***about*** how this thing worked, and I suppose I was becoming more glassy-eyed all the while, for eventually I said to Bob, "You're all dried up.(p.206)
• And I said, "Well, what ***about*** Paul, have you got him all dried up?"(p.207)
• Then he started to talk to me ***about*** his drinking experiences, what his drinking had cost him, how much he had drunk and where, things like that, and I remember I was quite bored because I had never seen the guy before and had no interest at all in what, where and when he drank.(p.208)
• I was then ***about*** sixteen years old.(p.211)
• I was always interested in mechanics and after having ***about*** twenty miscellaneous jobs, lasting from one day to two weeks, I obtained a job as a toolmaker apprentice.(p.211)
• After I was on the drafting board ***about*** two years I decided I wanted a technical education.(p.211)
• I was then ***about*** eighteen.(p.211)
• This work consumed a period of ***about*** two-thirds of a year, and worked out successfully so I decided to follow patent law.(p.212)
• My drinking career began ***about*** four years after I had moved up into partnership and had joined certain clubs, societies and so fourth, and during which period we had Prohibition.(p.213)
• I was then ***about*** thirty-seven or thirty-eight.(p.213)
• When I was ***about*** forty-seven, after indulging in all kinds of self-deception to control my drinking, I arrived at a period when I felt convinced I had to have so much alcohol every day and that the real problem was to control how much.(p.214)
• By that time, I had one boy in college, another a senior in high school, and a daughter ***about*** twelve years old.(p.215)
• I was forty-nine and a half years old when I was first approached ***about*** the Akron Group.(p.215)
• It was not known to me as a group, but I later learned that my wife had known ***about*** it for nine months and had prayed constantly that I would stumble into Akron some way or another.(p.215)
• She knew that at that time any suggestion she made ***about*** my drinking would only build up a barrier, a consideration for which I am ever grateful.(p.216)
• She had a hairdresser who used to tell her ***about*** a brother-in-law who had been quite a drinker and ***about*** some doctor in Akron who had straightened him out.(p.216)
• I was kind of shocked ***about*** anybody talking ***about*** themselves the way he did, and my impression was that the guy was a little "touched."(p.216)
• I do not recollect the specific conversation that went on but I believe I did challenge Bill to tell me something ***about*** A.A. and I do recall one other thing: I wanted to know what this was that worked so many wonders, and hanging over the mantel was a picture of Gethsemane and Bill pointed to it and said, "There it is," which didn't make much sense to me.(p.216)
• There was also some conversation ***about*** Dr. Bob and I must have said that I would go down to Akron with Bill in the morning.(p.217)
• That's ***about*** the spirit in which I went to Akron.(p.217)
• The interne came along with a glassful of bleached lightning that put me away for ***about*** fifteen hours.(p.217)
• In fact, the last three years of my drinking was a routine of barbiturates in the morning, so that I could

stop shaking enough to shave, and then alcohol beginning ***about*** four-thirty or five o'clock, with a struggle not to take a drink at noon or during the day, because I had the idea that if I took one drink, I would smell as though I had had a pint.(p.217)

• We went to Akron for ***about*** six weeks and we did a lot of visiting among the people in Akron.(p.219)

• I found in the fall of 1939, that I was not mentally impaired, so far as trial work was concerned, and thereafter took up where I had left off when I was ***about*** forty-five years old.(p.220)

• In fact, after six months of living on food instead of on whiskey, I gained ***about*** thirty pounds.(p.220)

• I'd been sitting comfortably in a restaurant with Rita, drinking my sixth martini and hoping the waiter would forget ***about*** the lunch order – at least long enough for me to have a couple more.(p.223)

• I remembered my loud resolution to find him and ask him to help me get into that "Asylum" he had written ***about***.(p.224)

• I remembered asserting that I was going to do something ***about*** this, that I couldn't go on . . .(p.224)

• And so on and on, for several weeks, while I grudgingly plowed through some more of the offending book, and felt more and more hopeless ***about*** myself.(p.227)

• And, accepting, I felt a new inner comfort, and the willingness and strength to do something ***about*** the traits I couldn't live with.(p.229)

• They knew what to do ***about*** those black abysses that yawned ready to swallow me when I felt depressed, or nervous.(p.229)

• My parents had some vague idea of making a priest out of me and for some years I attended the Franciscan school at Basle, Switzerland, just across the border, ***about*** six miles from my home.(p.230)

• My daily consumption of wine was ***about*** a quart, but that was common where I lived.(p.230)

• At that time I could go into any saloon, have one or two beers, walk out and forget ***about*** it.(p.231)

• I came of good stock, of men and women who drank wine all their lives as a beverage, and while they occasionally got drunk at special celebrations, they were up and ***about*** their business the next day.(p.231)

• Unfortunately, I had no desire to consult my priest ***about*** my drinking.(p.234)

• In fact I was scared to talk to him ***about*** it, for I feared the kind of talk he would give me.(p.234)

• He had no desire to know anything, except whether I was definite ***about*** my desire to quit drinking.(p.235)

• Even then he went into no great detail ***about*** how he and a crowd of alcoholics, with whom he associated, had mastered their difficulty.(p.235)

• And he further said that God could not accept me as a sincere follower of His Divine Law unless I was ready to be thoroughly honest ***about*** it.(p.236)

• We talked, too, ***about*** personal morals.(p.236)

• But I have never thought of that as something to do and then forget ***about***.(p.237)

• Jackie arrived ***about*** seven in the evening and talked until three a.m.(p.239)

• Jackie told me ***about*** a group of fellows in New York, of whom my old friend Fitz was one, who had the same problem I had, and who by working together to help each other were not now drinking and were happy like himself.(p.239)

• He said something ***about*** God or a Higher Power, but I brushed that off – that was for the birds, not for me.(p.239)

• My thoughts went round and round with "What's it all ***about*** anyhow?(p.244)

• At that time the group in New York was composed of ***about*** twelve men who were working on the principle of every drunk for himself; we had no real formula and no name.(p.246)

• There was one meeting a week at Bill's home in Brooklyn, and we all took turns there spouting off ***about*** how we had changed our lives overnight, how many drunks we had saved and straightened out, and last, but not least, how God had touched each of us personally on the shoulder.(p.246)

• When I started to tell the boys how we did it in New York and all ***about*** the spiritual part of the program, I found they would not believe me unless I was practicing what I preached.(p.249)

• Curious ***about*** it, feeling I was missing something, absolutely without any illusions ***about*** the aftermath, with no pronounced feeling of patriotism, I joined up with a Canadian regiment, serving a little over two years.(p.253)

• Now on a new job I was always thinking ***about*** payday and how much liquor I could buy and the pleasure I could have.(p.255)

• He introduced himself and began to tell me ***about*** a bunch of some sixty former drinkers and drunkards who met once a week, and he invited me to go with him to the next meeting.(p.257)

• I don't feel bothered ***about*** liquor."(p.257)

• As I look back on the events of two months, I can clearly see that I had been circling around, half-afraid of encountering the remedy for my situation, half wanting it, deferring fulfillment of my promise to get in touch with the doctor I had heard ***about***.(p.258)

• An accident while drunk laid me low for ***about*** three weeks.(p.258)

• I had been drinking heavily from one state of semi-coma to another and it was several days before I got "defogged," but subconsciously I was in earnest ***about*** wanting to quit liquor forever.(p.258)

• I was ***about*** twenty-five then, and I had never touched a drop.(p.262)

• I had gone to an attorney to see ***about*** getting a divorce during that year.(p.263)

• I didn't realize how I still felt ***about*** him.(p.263)

• As I look back, I was very broken up ***about*** it.(p.263)

• It was just ***about*** this time, in 1940, that we met up with A.A.(p.265)

• "Oh, some darn thing they've got here in the paper ***about*** it."(p.266)

• We talked ***about*** it afterwards, and we felt that there might be some time we'd need it.(p.266)

• There was a man watching, and I turned to him and said with a defiant air I carried with me all the time, "If I don't quit this I'm going to have to join that alcoholic business they're talking ***about***."(p.266)

• But right then the hope died that had been in my heart when we read ***about*** John D.(p.266)

• Right away, I saw it was the same outfit this other guy told me ***about***, and then again hope died.(p.267)

• He gave my husband one and me one ***about*** ten-thirty on the eighth day of May in 1941.(p.267)

• Jack said, "Now you start and go to these meetings, and then you'll find out all ***about*** it."(p.268)

• I don't think that there was anything said ***about*** religion.(p.268)

• I didn't know anything ***about*** the Sermon on the Mount.(p.268)

• And we went down through the valley, and I remembered reading ***about*** the Ku Klux Klan and how they burnt crosses, and I thought, "God alone knows what we are getting into this time!"(p.269)

• He talked ***about*** his wife taking his little boy away from him because of his drinking, and how he got back together with them through A.A., and we began feeling grateful right then that all these things hadn't been taken from us.(p.270)

• Jack had been sober ***about*** a year and a half.(p.271)

• I feel that one of the things that I still have to guard against is that I used to be set in my way ***about*** what I considered the old-time A.A.(p.272)

• I don't ever remember that I was bored myself when we first came in, and they came out to the house and talked to us ***about*** these things.(p.273)

• Before I stop -- I always was a great talker -- I want to say that nobody will ever know how I miss Annie's advice ***about*** things.(p.273)

• I would get in the biggest dither ***about*** something.(p.273)

• Well, I wasn't sure I did, and it was awful foggy, and I wept and asked her what she thought I ought to do ***about*** it.(p.273)

• She talked to me and laughed ***about*** it and got me all over it.(p.273)

• If it isn't anything that's going to help you or anybody else, why should you become involved in it, and get all disturbed ***about*** it?"(p.273)

• I had been brought up to believe this, and I had shown during my 'teens considerable enterprise and imagination ***about*** earning money.(p.275)

• I told our family doctor, an understanding man who gave hours of his time trying to help me, ***about*** this experience.(p.276)

• My thinking ***about*** drinking had undergone a great change.(p.277)

• Here, while in a hospital bed, men with clear eyes, happy faces, and a look of assurance and purposefulness ***about*** them, came to see me and told me their stories.(p.279)

• Here was a tall, rugged, highly educated Yankee talking in a matter of course way ***about*** God and prayer.(p.279)

• It ran something like this: If I go around shouting from the rooftops ***about*** my alcoholism, it might very possibly prevent me from getting a good job.(p.282)

• I, who had never made a speech in my life and who would have been frightened sick at the prospect, stood up in front of Rotary groups in different parts of the city and talked ***about*** Alcoholics Anonymous.(p.283)

• I, carried away with the desire to serve A.A., gave what was probably one of the first radio broadcasts ***about*** A.A., living through a case of mike fright and feeling like a million dollars when it was all over.(p.283)

• Within a year of my return to Detroit, A.A. was a definitely established little group of ***about*** a dozen members and I too was established in a modest but steady job handling an independent dry-cleaning route of my own.(p.283)

• This time I did something ***about*** it.(p.284)

• But what ***about*** my social life?(p.284)

• What ***about*** those fears which once paralyzed me to the point of my becoming a semi-hermit?(p.284)

• What ***about*** my fear of travel?(p.284)

• There have also been numerous times when I have thought ***about*** taking a drink.(p.285)

• She asked him to do something ***about*** me because she couldn't.(p.288)

• He waited until I was completely sober and the day before I was to head back for Chicago, he told me of a small group of men in Akron who apparently had the same problem that I had but were doing something ***about*** it.(p.289)

• I can still remember very distinctly getting into Akron at eleven p.m. and routing this same Howard out of bed to do something ***about*** me.(p.290)

• Here was a man with essentially the same outlook on life, except that he had done something ***about*** it.(p.290)

• On my trips back to Akron to get my spirits recharged and to work with other alcoholics, I would ask Dr. Bob ***about*** this delay and wonder just what was wrong with me.(p.293)

• In the summer of 1938, almost a year from the time I made my original contact with Akron, the man for whom I was working and who knew ***about*** the program, approached me and asked if I could do anything ***about*** one of his salesmen who was drinking very heavily.(p.294)

• He had been wanting to do something ***about*** his drinking for a long time, but did not know how.(p.294)

• In the meantime, another doctor in Evanston became convinced that the program had possibilities, and turned over a woman to us to do something ***about***.(p.295)

• Upon leaving the office in the evening, my first stop would be a saloon ***about*** a block away.(p.298)

• One is that I don't remember too many of them, as I was one of those drunks who could be on his feet and attend a meeting or a party, engage in a conversation with people and do things that any nearly normal person would do, and the next day not remember a thing ***about*** where I was, what I did, whom I saw, or how I got home.(p.301)

• He talked ***about*** himself, but I was sure it was ***about*** me.(p.302)

• I definitely liked it, everything ***about*** it, the taste, the effects; and I realize now that a drink did something for me or to me that was different from the way it affected others.(p.305)

• For ***about*** one year, prior to this time, there was one doctor who had continued to struggle with me.(p.306)

• But somehow my good doctor heard of this book and also he learned a little ***about*** the people responsible for its publication.(p.307)

• It explained so much I had not understood ***about*** myself and, best of all, it promised recovery if I would do a few simple things and be willing to have the desire to drink removed.(p.309)

• I started drinking ***about*** age thirteen.(p.317)

• Somehow, I made it through basic and then laid off the booze for ***about*** three months, because I was in school at night.(p.317)

• If I could lay off it, that meant I didn't have to worry ***about*** a drinking problem, I thought.(p.317)

• We got along fine for ***about*** two weeks, until she told me where to go and to take my damn bottle with me.(p.318)

• After ***about*** three months, no more weekends.(p.318)

• The doctor asked ***about*** my drinking, but I wouldn't talk to him.(p.319)

• Once I did have a slip – tried drinking again – but the A.A.'s tell me not to worry ***about*** yesterday, because nobody can change it, and not to worry ***about*** tomorrow, because it hasn't come yet.(p.320)

• I didn't think my children knew ***about*** it, but I found out they did.(p.324)

• It has changed my thinking entirely, ***about*** everything I do.(p.325)

• I just didn't give a whoop ***about*** myself or anyone else.(p.325)

- I knew ***about*** A.A.(p.332)
- No matter how often I had gone into and come out of alcoholic lows during the day, the pattern bounced me out of bed each night ***about*** 2:00 a.m., shaking and hurting in the agitation that always follows a drug's sedation.(p.332)
- But during a period of particular stress and strain ***about*** thirteen years ago, I resorted to alcohol in my home, alone, as a means of temporary release, as a means of getting a little extra sleep.(p.335)
- I cared nothing ***about*** my personal appearance.(p.337)
- I went on, realizing what I was becoming, hating myself for it, bitter, blaming life, blaming everything else but the fact that I should turn ***about*** and do something ***about*** my drinking.(p.337)
- I knew nothing ***about*** alcoholism or the D.T.'s, but when I woke up on this last morning of my son's illness, I taped the keyhole on my door because "everyone was out there."(p.338)
- On the second, I knew – as I know now – that if I remained away from the first drink, then I had not to worry ***about*** the hundredth one.(p.344)
- First, we all hear at A.A. meetings ***about*** those who have lost everything, those who have been in jail, those who have been in prison, those who have lost their families, those who have lost their income.(p.345)
- She's a good-natured soul and said, "I wouldn't worry ***about*** it; probably something will happen."(p.346)
- ***About*** two days later I was called by a friend of mine from Nevada City – he's a brother of my wife's closest friend.(p.347)
- I don't mean that in any sense as a derogatory statement ***about*** psychotherapy; it's a great tool, not too potent, but a great tool.(p.349)
- So I went to my wife and asked her, wasn't there something that she and I could do to somehow get together, and she turned on her heel and looked me squarely in the eye, and said, "You don't care anything ***about*** my problem," and I could have smacked her, but I said to myself, "Grab on to your serenity!"(p.351)
- We did, and spent a month boozing it up, popping pills, and smoking marijuana; taking shelter where we could, which included a veterinary hospital one night; accepting meals from anyone; actually begging; stealing anything we were in need of, which was ***about*** everything.(p.354)
- It has brought ***about*** a revelation of self, the discovery of an inner being, an awareness of God.(p.355)
- Many times have I heard the above expressions since I have been in A.A., and many times I have had to reply "Definitely I am an alcoholic, and while it may be hard for you to believe, it is not hard for me, for I have learned many things ***about*** alcohol and myself that would, perhaps, be difficult for you to understand."(p.356)
- As these words are written at fifty-three years of age, with over nine years of A.A. behind me, with all its wonderful teachings, I haven't the slightest doubt ***about*** being an alcoholic.(p.356)
- All I can remember ***about*** the Roaring Twenties is that I drank a great deal, thought I was having a grand time, managed to get to Europe for a few weeks, was very proud of the dozens of speak-easy cards entitling me to an entree in the better joints between Cleveland and New York, took on a wife, and built a home in a fashionable suburb of Cleveland.(p.358)
- In January 1938, I had the opportunity to go to northern Vermont to manage a small daytime radio station that was up against it financially, and was ***about*** to fold its antenna.(p.359)
- This was ***about*** ten p.m., and the time here is important.(p.363)
- It had happened to me and I had to do something ***about*** it.(p.363)
- I had read and heard a little ***about*** A.A. and so, groping for the phone book, I found the A.A. number and with hope in my heart eagerly telephoned.(p.363)
- Sure enough in a couple of hours two men were at my door and for the first time I heard some facts ***about*** liquor and my problem that sounded sensible to me.(p.363)
- After a few meetings I decided to drive to Florida unannounced to see my wife and tell her ***about*** my new found friends and association.(p.364)
- That night she too had new hope because I had made sure she would know what I was doing ***about*** my drinking by packing every bit of A.A. literature I could put my hands on right on top so she couldn't help but see it when she opened my bag.(p.364)
- I didn't say a word to anyone ***about*** my lapse.(p.364)
- It was worrying my wife a little, but she had the good sense not to take me to task ***about*** it or goad me into going.(p.364)
- I had never told a soul ***about*** my lapse in New York.(p.366)
- You'll read and hear a great deal ***about*** the spiritual part of our program.(p.366)
- I haven't written anything ***about*** that part of my story, but I believe in a Greater Power which I call God and I ask for His wisdom and guidance daily.(p.366)
- You will recall that I said the time that I got the idea out of a clear sky to call A.A. on a certain night was at ***about*** ten.(p.366)
- While I was in Florida trying to convince my wife with all the A.A. literature that she should come back to me, she went over to her desk and picked up a clipping she had taken from the St. Petersburg Times ***about*** A.A.(p.366)
- It was the first she had heard or read ***about*** it and she said she had considered sending it to me or trying to have someone in Pittsburgh send it to me so I wouldn't know where it came from.(p.366)
- She said she cut this clipping from the paper at ***about*** ten on the same night, and at the same time as I called A.A. in Pittsburgh -- some 1300 miles away.(p.367)
- And, believe me, I thank God that I found out ***about*** A.A. before I had to beat my brains out – before I had been hospitalized, jailed or lost a job.(p.367)
- My sister-in-law took me to a place she had heard ***about*** that helps women like me.(p.371)
- Two years before I joined A.A. my wife took a long trip during which she wrote me she just couldn't return unless I did something ***about*** my drinking.(p.377)
- Again I promised to do something ***about*** it.(p.377)
- Some crisis brings you to a point of making a decision to do something ***about*** your drinking problem.(p.377)
- I don't know what I expected, but I most certainly didn't visualize a group of people talking ***about*** their drinking problems, making light of their personal tragedies and at the same time enjoying themselves.(p.378)
- From the start I liked everything ***about*** the A.A. program.(p.380)
- The allergy we could do nothing ***about***.(p.380)
- If we do a good job of living today, and if tomorrow comes for us, then the chances are we will do a good job when it arrives -- so why worry ***about*** it?(p.382)
- So I was used to it, but I didn't know what the effect of alcohol was because I always had wine, usually with dinner, but always with a lot of ice and ***about*** two tablespoons of sugar in it.(p.385)
- By the time all this was over, I was really in a terrific state, and my father taking in things said, "Miss Esther is ***about*** to faint.(p.385)
- For some reason I can't remember, it finally dawned on me that I had a problem, and yet nobody was very critical ***about*** it except my family, and that was only because I decided, after seven years of marriage, that I would divorce my husband.(p.386)
- They would talk ***about*** it.(p.386)
- That went on for ***about*** three years, and then we moved back to Texas again.(p.386)
- I had been reading a lot ***about*** psychiatry and I thought, "Maybe if I talk to a psychiatrist he can find out what is happening, and then I can drink like a lady."(p.387)
- I was crazy ***about*** my doctor.(p.387)
- I know now that I asked questions and told him what I wanted to learn, but I told him only what I wanted to believe ***about*** myself.(p.388)
- ***About*** this time, at Christmas, after being under this doctor's care, we decided that there wasn't anything more to do.(p.388)
- My husband couldn't tell whether I wanted to do something ***about*** my drinking.(p.391)
- It was such a feeling of relief that I wanted to know more ***about*** it and with that, I think for the first time, came the realization that there was something horribly, horribly wrong with me.(p.392)
- I had learned an awful lot ***about*** myself in that one little article.(p.393)
- I wish I could tell you all that A.A. has done for me, all that I think and feel ***about*** A.A., but it's something that I have experienced and have never been able to put into words.(p.394)
- Dr. Bob tells ***about*** keeping it simple and not to louse it up.(p.395)
- I displayed alcoholic tendencies actually from the age of fourteen, when I started to steal wine from the family jug, siphoning it off one drink at a time so it wouldn't be missed, not drinking it immediately, but saving it until ***about*** a pint was accumulated, so that I could get drunk.(p.397)
- Even when I was old enough to know better, I dreamed ***about*** being as beautiful as Venus, as pure as the Madonna and as brilliant as the President of the United States is supposed to be.(p.400)
- I resented this, but I did nothing constructive ***about*** it.(p.402)
- It was all ***about*** Scott Fitzgerald's little lost debutante, abused, misunderstood and running wild.(p.402)
- I also wrote another novel, all ***about*** Scott Fitzgerald's poor, misbegotten, unloved, tipsy little debutante.(p.405)
- Even the critics kidded me ***about*** this one.(p.405)
- Then I was able to do something ***about*** me.(p.409)
- I saw that my Village friends, all of whom had small jobs, were living happily on ***about*** a tenth of my sinecure.(p.409)
- They were awfully good ***about*** not cutting me off.(p.409)
- I felt like a gangster's moll ***about*** to be interviewed by the Salvation Army.(p.413)
- I thought it was my duty to keep her from drinking, not knowing that if the other fellow is really determined to drink there is nothing you can do ***about*** it.(p.415)
- All the people involved in these flare-ups took it with remarkable grace, have teased me ***about*** it since, and have become good friends of mine.(p.416)
- In ending my story I like to think ***about*** this.(p.417)
- I looked ***about*** the room.(p.422)
- I moved ***about*** a little.(p.423)
- I didn't give a whoop ***about*** anything scholastic.(p.423)
- I was skipping classes ***about*** two days a week and doing no book work whatever.(p.423)
- They were kind when they thought ***about*** it, but that wasn't often.(p.424)
- ***About*** this time I got my first crush on a girl.(p.425)
- I teamed up with a cute little blonde with whom I was working at the office, and for ***about*** a year we were inseparable.(p.425)
- There wasn't much I could do ***about*** it, and I didn't want to do anything anyway.(p.427)
- ***About*** this time my folks found A.A.(p.427)
- They wrote me many long letters ***about*** it.(p.427)
- Meanwhile the letters from home were telling ***about*** how much my folks wanted to make up to me for some of the things I'd missed.(p.427)
- I hadn't told them ***about*** my drinking, but I guess they knew.(p.427)
- I took it easy, because they didn't know ***about*** me.(p.428)
- I would drink all night in bars, come home ***about*** five a.m., down a good big glass of whiskey straight, and tumble into bed.(p.428)
- Or maybe I'd come home wild drunk, singing and raving ***about*** what a fine place home was and what grand parents I had since they joined A.A.(p.428)
- I'd heard a lot ***about*** A.A. and met a great many A.A.'s during that year at home, but I hadn't thought of it for myself.(p.429)
- My growing inward unhappiness was a very real thing, however, and I knew that something would have to be done ***about*** it.(p.434)
- How exciting to learn the inward mysteries that govern the behavior of people, how wonderful to know, at last, all ***about*** myself!(p.434)
- My daily alcoholic consumption remained ***about*** the same through all this, with perhaps a slight increase, and my binges remained one-nighters.(p.434)
- The next day, Max called the neurologist and told him ***about*** the Mayo psychiatrist's opinion.(p.445)
- I really felt sorry for him; the only thing in life he had to brag ***about*** was the fact that he was an alcoholic.(p.446)
- The psychiatrist, who had generally been ignoring me, now became quite interested; every day, he would ask me all kinds of questions ***about*** the A.A. meetings.(p.446)
- At first, I wondered whether he was alcoholic himself, and was sending me to find out ***about*** A.A.(p.446)
- When a big, healthy-looking young fellow stood up there and said, "I'm a success today if I don't drink today," I thought, "Man, I've got a thousand things to do today before I can brag ***about*** not taking a drink, for God's sake!"(p.447)
- It seemed that all they talked ***about*** at meetings was drinking, drinking, drinking.(p.447)
- I wanted to talk ***about*** my many big problems; drinking seemed a small one.(p.447)
- Now, what am I going to do ***about*** it?"(p.449)

• When I complain ***about*** me or ***about*** you, I am complaining ***about*** God's handiwork.(p.449)
• Over the years, as I thought ***about*** Max, her good qualities grew and grew, and we married, and all these qualities became more and more apparent to me, and we were happier and happier.(p.450)
• But then, as I drank more and more, the alcohol seemed to affect my vision: Instead of continuing to see what was good ***about*** my wife, I began to see her defects.(p.450)
• But when I try to see what I can add to the meeting, rather than what I can get out of it, and when I focus my mind on what's good ***about*** it, rather than what's wrong with it, the meeting keeps getting better and better.(p.451)
• We used to argue ***about*** our differing ideas, but we can't argue ***about*** our feelings.(p.451)
• Most of us did not stay out of prison long enough to run the alcoholic gamut -- to develop the ongoing kind of alcoholism or alcoholic drinking you hear ***about*** in A.A. talks.(p.458)
• I would rather talk ***about*** the good things A.A. has taught me; I feel that hitting on just a few sordid points should be sufficient to let those of you in institutions know where I came from.(p.459)
• In a prison in my native state, I spent eleven months in solitary confinement, bouncing in and out of the "hole" (a bare concrete-and-steel cubicle) ***about*** five times during those eleven months.(p.459)
• I'm talking ***about*** the good things that have happened.(p.463)
• Forgive me -- I cannot write further ***about*** this latest turn of events, anticipating seeing the family I deserted so long ago.(p.463)
• I started drinking socially and at parties and proms when I was ***about*** twenty years old.(p.464)
• And there didn't seem to be anything to do ***about*** it.)(p.465)
• I hadn't been drinking much ***about*** that time, for I had begun to realize that there was something abnormal ***about*** my drinking, although as yet, I didn't realize that it was so out of control.(p.465)
• I was frightened – terribly frightened, and in ***about*** three days I was sober.(p.467)
• And then I went back home to live with my parents, and the merry-go-round started again – only this time I didn't have to worry ***about*** waking up behind bars in a psychiatric ward.(p.468)
• I won't go into detail ***about*** that, but I can assure you it's no fun.(p.469)
• So the doctor said, "I really don't know too much ***about*** it, but they tell me it is a bunch of drunks who get together . . ."(p.469)
• It seemed to me that those A.A.'s to whom I talked knew all ***about*** me.(p.470)
• In other words, the kindest doctor in the whole world, and I had one such, couldn't help me because I always felt, "You can't know ***about*** me -- you can't possibly know – you don't even drink!"(p.471)
• It came ***about*** in this way.(p.472)
• And when she broke a luncheon date with me one Saturday, after I had been in A.A. for ***about*** three months, I said, "I'll show her!(p.472)
• My aunt had sharp words for me ***about*** drinking.(p.474)
• Think ***about*** kill myself.(p.475)
• By grace of God I stop, think two things: This would kill good mother and father; then remember boys talk ***about*** Indian fellow who been sober three years.(p.475)
• I hear ***about*** A.A., but think it religion.(p.475)
• When I got out of there, I lasted ***about*** fifteen minutes at home, before I headed for the drugstore and more pills, and then the bar.(p.479)
• Some of us always remember our big mouths when it comes to a drink, but somewhere along the line, we seem to have forgotten ***about*** taking care of our teeth.(p.479)
• I wasted twenty years of my life, and there is nothing I can do ***about*** that, but there is something I can do ***about*** now.(p.480)
• If someone had told me last year that I would be excited ***about*** gardening this year, I would have said he was off his rocker.(p.481)
• I don't believe this program would work for me if I didn't get honest with myself ***about*** everything.(p.482)
• I was ***about*** six then.(p.483)
• ***About*** this time an incident took place in grade school that I have never forgotten because it made me realize that I was actually a physical coward.(p.484)
• ***About*** then too, I realized that my point of view on the opposite sex wasn't entirely like that of most of the boys I knew.(p.484)
• I had quite a heartache ***about*** her then because she wasn't the type of girl that my mother wanted me to marry.(p.485)
• He could do nothing ***about*** it.(p.486)
• This was around 1935, and it was ***about*** this time that I actually started drinking.(p.486)
• A very good friend of mine who owned a drug store across the street from us, came by only ***about*** two hours later and said that he had seen Vi down town.(p.487)
• I said that she told me she was going to the movies, and I became foolishly disturbed ***about*** it and, as things snowballed, I decided to go out and get drunk.(p.487)
• The fear of the loss of Vi and the feeling that, though she had the right to do as she pleased, she should have told me the truth ***about*** it, upset me.(p.487)
• ***About*** that time I had lost practically all my property except the place we were living in.(p.487)
• There came a time when she spoke to me ***about*** it, and I would say that I had a bad cold or that I wasn't feeling well.(p.487)
• That went on for maybe two months, and then she got after me again ***about*** drinking.(p.488)
• Ask him ***about*** it.(p.488)
• I don't know anything ***about*** the bottles."(p.488)
• Fear gripped me then, because I could remember nothing ***about*** it.(p.489)
• I had a long talk with a psychiatrist, but nothing came of that, and I had also, just ***about*** that time, talked with a minister for whom I had a great deal of respect.(p.489)
• I rebelled against this, because just ***about*** the time that I was getting ready to leave high school, a revelation came to me ***about*** God and it made things very complicated for me.(p.489)
• I had a very good friend who was in the Government service, and I went to him ***about*** a job.(p.489)
• I worked for the Government ***about*** a year and still maintained my evening office practice when the Government agencies were decentralized.(p.489)
• Nevertheless, I stayed sober there ***about*** six months, because I knew that Vi was to come later and bring the children.(p.490)
• I was out of work for ***about*** four days.(p.490)
• Within ***about*** ten days I got locked up for being drunk and this same policeman was in the station house as I was being booked.(p.491)
• I was just ***about*** broke.(p.491)
• I was there ***about*** three weeks, and then I got restless and started to tramp across the country, here and there, until I finally wound up in Pennsylvania, in a steel mill.(p.492)
• I'd been home ***about*** a week or ten days when one of my friends asked if I could repair one of his electrical outlets.(p.493)
• She didn't say anything ***about*** A.A. or getting me a sponsor at that time, but she did ask ***about*** Vi, and I told her Vi was working and how she could locate her.(p.494)
• She never mentioned anything ***about*** my whiskey drinking because if she had I would have told her, "No" right then.(p.494)
• ***About*** seven that evening my sponsor walked in, Charlie G.(p.494)
• Anyhow, he started talking ***about*** himself.(p.494)
• When he left I walked with him to the streetcar line, which was just ***about*** a half a block, but there were two liquor stores, one on each corner from my home.(p.495)
• I put Charlie on the car and when I left him I passed both of those liquor stores without even thinking ***about*** them.(p.495)
• They taught us a great deal ***about*** Twelve Step work too.(p.496)
• Father had never directly spoken to me ***about*** drinking but he never drank any, so far as I knew.(p.498)
• I see her ***about*** to go.(p.501)
• Am I willing to be honest with myself ***about*** myself and tell someone ***about*** myself, and am I willing to think of other people, of their needs instead of myself, in order to get rid of the drink problem?(p.503)
• Can all the worth while people I have known be wrong ***about*** God?(p.503)
• Then I find myself thinking ***about*** myself, and a few things that I had wanted to forget.(p.503)
• I've made a mess of things and can't do anything ***about*** it.(p.504)
• I have forgotten ***about*** a drink.(p.505)
• I didn't have to worry ***about*** him any longer.(p.508)
• The trial lasted ***about*** a week, and whether or not I was going to the death house was anybody's guess.(p.508)
• I spent ***about*** six or seven weeks in Sing Sing, and was finally sent off to Dannemora in the Adirondacks.(p.509)
• I remained there for ***about*** ten months, and then I was sent to a place called Wallkill, a so-called rehabilitation center.(p.509)
• When I had heard ***about*** it, it meant nothing but just two letters to me, but some friends of mine in the institution were very active in the program and really believed in it.(p.509)
• I had an advantage in having an idea of what A.A. was ***about*** before coming out on the street.(p.510)
• I had a rough lot, but I don't worry ***about*** that, after hearing the stories of many others.(p.511)
• It was a thorn in my side, because I knew it was the truth, and I hated to hear the truth, especially ***about*** myself.(p.513)
• For me, it was a little different because I couldn't help thinking ***about*** the past, and I saw the future more or less mirrored in the past.(p.513)
• She certainly wasn't in the dark ***about*** my drinking.(p.513)
• I had a habit of getting up just prior to the closing time of the saloons, ***about*** two or three o'clock in the morning.(p.514)
• You hit the street ***about*** ten minutes to eight, and you walk around the block, God knows how many times, waiting for that joint to open.(p.514)
• I wasn't a happy man that morning, but I'm happy now that it came ***about***.(p.515)
• Oh yes, I get the dry jitters once in a while, but that isn't anything to worry ***about***.(p.516)
• The war was on and it was a fairly short course, ***about*** eight months.(p.518)
• When the war was over, we had ***about*** a year in Germany, occupying the place.(p.518)
• Lots of the older people had taken to drinking quite a good deal more during the war, but the younger generation was, I think, ***about*** the same.(p.518)
• This was ***about*** 1926.(p.519)
• However, I kept that job in Egypt and Palestine for ***about*** two years, and then I changed over to the other battalion in my regiment.(p.520)
• They weren't quite so up-to-date on my history and I got away with ***about*** four years with them.(p.520)
• Then I had ***about*** six months on a small island in command of the troops there.(p.520)
• I buttonholed him after dinner and gave him a few tips on how to run his colony better and the result of that was ***about*** a fortnight or so later I was shipped back to my regiment.(p.520)
• ***About*** three months after that, my record reached home and I got a letter telling me I was retired from the Army, they put it very kindly, on medical grounds.(p.521)
• I had two or three feelings ***about*** that.(p.521)
• I thought, well, now that I've been put out for drinking, I'll just show them that they were completely wrong, so I went off on the biggest bout I had been on up to then, involving ***about*** a fortnight's blackout.(p.521)
• I was in a world that I knew nothing at all ***about***, and I felt intensely afraid.(p.521)
• In any case, I made myself believe that, so I just drifted ***about***, existing on my retired pay, drinking, and living at home.(p.522)
• That went on for ***about*** six years.(p.522)
• That put a scare in me for ***about*** a fortnight.(p.522)
• I was intensely unhappy the whole time, but I didn't seem to be able to do anything ***about*** it, and the worst part to me was the realization that all this was going to happen again and again until I died.(p.522)
• As I say, this specialist put a scare in me for ***about*** a fortnight or three weeks, then I started my last bout which went on and off for ***about*** three months.(p.523)
• When I arrived at The Country Shop, which was a restaurant where they met in Dublin, I found ***about*** thirty-five or forty people in the room.(p.524)
• Since I have been in A.A., I have more friends than I ever had in my life -- friends who care ***about*** me and my welfare, friends who don't care that I am black and that I have been in prison.(p.529)
• All they care ***about*** is that I am a human being and that I want to stay sober.(p.529)
• The only thing that bothers me is that there are only ***about*** five Negroes in A.A. in my city.(p.529)
• I am talking ***about*** A.A. people, who have gone through some of the same things that you might be going through now.(p.529)
• I remember the day when I decided to drink myself to death quietly, without bothering anyone, because I was tired of having been a dependable, trustworthy person for ***about*** thirty-nine years without having received what I thought was a proper reward for my virtue.(p.531)

• (There was a time, for ***about*** three months, when I bought a ten-dollar wrist watch every pay day – that is every two weeks.(p.532)
• But such is my nature that I must know the reason for things and I didn't stop until I had satisfied myself ***about*** the reasons for my drinking.(p.533)
• My serious drinking covered ***about*** seven years.(p.536)
• Simply, yes it did end; for I had changed my mind ***about*** alcohol, and it stayed changed.(p.541)
• I don't care too much ***about*** personal fame or glory, and I want only enough money to enable me to do the work I feel I can perhaps do best.(p.542)
• The only kind of security I knew anything ***about*** at that time was material security and I decided that all these intruders would vanish immediately if I only had a lot of money.(p.545)
• With cold calculation I set ***about*** to marry a fortune, and I did.(p.545)
• I wasn't afraid of anything or anybody after I learned ***about*** drinking, for it seemed right from the beginning that with liquor I could always retire to my little private world where nobody could get at me to hurt me.(p.547)
• The only reality I was able to face had been forced upon me by its very repetition – I had to drink; and I didn't know there was anything in the world that could be done ***about*** it.(p.548)
• ***About*** this time, I met a man who had three motherless children and it seemed that might be a solution to my problem.(p.548)
• The people who came knew immediately I was in no condition to absorb anything of the program, and I was put in a sanitarium to be defogged so that I could make a sober decision ***about*** this for myself.(p.549)
• One of the truly great things A.A. has taught me is that reality too has two sides; I had only known the grim side before the program, but now I had a chance to learn ***about*** the pleasant side as well.(p.550)
• A.A. has given me serenity of purpose, the opportunity to be of service to God and to the people ***about*** me, and I am serene in the infallibility of these principles that provide the fulfillment of my purpose.(p.551)
• What my doctor had warned me ***about*** finally happened.(p.558)
• He happened to be, by the grace of God, Dr. Harry Tiebout, the psychiatrist who probably knew more ***about*** alcoholism than any other in the world.(p.559)
• The terms "spiritual experience" and "spiritual awakening" are used many times in this book which, upon careful reading, shows that the personality change sufficient to bring ***about*** recovery from alcoholism has manifested itself among us in many different forms.(p.569)
• He finally realizes that he has undergone a profound alteration in his reaction to life; that such a change could hardly have been brought ***about*** by himself alone.(p.569)
• Dr. Harry M. Tiebout, psychiatrist: "As a psychiatrist, I have thought a great deal ***about*** the relationship of my specialty to A.A. and I have come to the conclusion that our particular function can very often lie in preparing the way for the patient to accept any sort of treatment or outside help.(p.571)
• There is something spiritual ***about*** an art museum or a symphony, and the Catholic Church approves of our use of them.(p.574)
• There is something spiritual ***about*** A.A. too, and Catholic participation in it almost invariably results in poor Catholics becoming better Catholics."(p.574)
• This headquarters will give the location of the nearest family group and will if you wish, correspond with you ***about*** your special problems.(p.575)

above

• In that brief space, Alcoholics Anonymous has mushroomed into nearly 6,000 groups whose membership is far ***above*** 150,000 recovered alcoholics.(p.xv)
• ***Above*** all, he believed he had acquired such a profound knowledge of the inner workings of his mind and its hidden springs that relapse was unthinkable.(p.26)
• He wished ***above*** all things to regain self-control.(p.26)
• Yet we had been seeing another kind of flight, a spiritual liberation from this world, people who rose ***above*** their problems.(p.55)
• ***Above*** everything, we alcoholics must be rid of this selfishness.(p.62)
• But ***above*** all, we tried to be sensible on this question.(p.68)
• He had commenced our way of life, had secured a position, and was getting his head ***above*** water.(p.79)
• We wives found that, like everybody else, we were afflicted with pride, self-pity, vanity and all the things which go to make up the self-centered person; and we were not ***above*** selfishness or dishonesty.(p.116)
• He may demand that the family find God in a hurry, or exhibit amazing indifference to them and say he is ***above*** worldly considerations.(p.128)
• We all had to place recovery ***above*** everything, for without recovery we would have lost both home and business.(p.143)
• Should you wish them ***above*** all else, and be willing to make use of our experience, we are sure they will come.(p.153)
• The general moral standard was, as I recall it, far ***above*** the average.(p.171)
• Both father and mother were considerably ***above*** the average in intelligence.(p.172)
• Then I remember when the boys came back, that I told them, "I have gone to this Higher Power and I have told Him that I am willing to put His world first, ***above*** everything.(p.190)
• One of them was that I would try to get a group started in Chicago; the second was that I would have to return to Akron to attend meetings at least every two months until I did get a group started in Chicago; third, I decided I must place this program ***above*** everything else, even my family, because if I did not maintain my sobriety I would lose my family anyway.(p.292)
• ***Above*** all, I have gained the greatest thing accorded to any man, the love and understanding of a gracious God, who has lifted me from the alcoholic scrap-heap to a position of trust where I have been able to reap the rich rewards that come from showing a little love for others and from serving them as I can.(p.296)
• Many times have I heard the ***above*** expressions since I have been in A.A., and many times I have had to reply "Definitely I am an alcoholic, and while it may be hard for you to believe, it is not hard for me, for I have learned many things about alcohol and myself that would, perhaps, be difficult for you to understand."(p.356)
• I can't bear to be here when you lose the respect of others, and ***above*** all -- when you lose your own self respect."(p.362)
• I was going to prove to her that liquor wasn't necessary in my life, and ***above*** all that I still loved her more than anything else in the world and that I wanted her back.(p.362)
• I can't bear to be here when you lose the respect of others, and ***above*** all when you lose your own self respect."(p.363)
• They meant patience, tolerance and humility, and ***above*** all the belief that a Power greater than myself could help.(p.381)
• ***Above*** all, I am grateful to A.A. for my sobriety, which means so much to my family, friends and business associates, because God and A.A. were able to do for me something I was unable to do for myself.(p.383)
• ***Above*** all, he noticed that I drank a good deal, often got tight in his company and told him naughty stories.(p.403)
• I think the thing that galled me was that just after Easter I had drawn my salary for two weeks' work and had decided that I was going to send some money to Vi; and ***above*** all else I was going to send my baby daughter an Easter outfit.(p.493)
• For always, over and ***above*** everything else, was the awfulness of the lack of meaning in life.(p.535)
• ***Above*** all, I was suffering inner pain because my performance and my accomplishments in life failed to live up to my own expectations of myself.(p.557)
• But ***above*** all, it taught me how to handle sobriety.(p.559)
• ***Above*** all, we reject fantasizing and accept reality.(p.560)

above-board

• You may be at a loss to understand how such a seemingly ***above-board*** chap could be so involved.(p.140)

abroad

• For greater freedom and excitement I went ***abroad*** to live.(p.225)

abruptly

• ***Abruptly*** in October 1929 hell broke loose on the New York stock exchange.(p.4)
• Try to drink and stop ***abruptly***.(p.31)
• I had a couple of shorter talks with this man afterward, and stopped drinking ***abruptly***.(p.179)
• ***Abruptly*** I stopped speaking.(p.222)
• I am an only child, and when I was seven years old my parents separated very ***abruptly***.(p.544)

absence

• The unselfishness of these men as we have come to know them, the entire ***absence*** of profit motive, and their community spirit, is indeed inspiring to one who has labored long and wearily in this alcoholic field.(p.xxv)
• He has just returned from a three-months leave of ***absence***, has taken a cure, looks fine, and to clinch the matter, the board of directors told him this was his last chance."(p.138)
• The very practical approach to his problems, the ***absence*** of intolerance of any kind, the informality, the genuine democracy, the uncanny understanding which these people had were irresistible.(p.160)

absent

• He has helped other men recover, and is a power in the church from which he was long ***absent***.(p.158)
• This resolution I kept steadfastly for the next forty years, except when circumstances made it seem unwise to ***absent*** myself.(p.172)
• I had never doubted the existence of the Supreme Being, but now I began to ***absent*** myself from my church where I had formerly been a member of the choir.(p.234)

absolute

• My friend had emphasized the ***absolute*** necessity of demonstrating these principles in all my affairs.(p.14)
• The central fact of our lives today is the ***absolute*** certainty that our Creator has entered into our hearts and lives in a way which is indeed miraculous.(p.25)
• For myself, I have an ***absolute*** proof of the existence of God.(p.350)
• I'd had ***absolute*** faith in science, and only in science.(p.435)

absolutely

• You may rely ***absolutely*** on anything they say about themselves.(p.xxiv)
• We have a way out on which we can ***absolutely*** agree, and upon which we can join in brotherly and harmonious action.(p.17)
• At a certain point in the drinking of every alcoholic, he passes into a state where the most powerful desire to stop drinking is of ***absolutely*** no avail.(p.24)
• But the actual or potential alcoholic, with hardly an exception, will be ***absolutely*** unable to stop drinking on the basis of self-knowledge.(p.39)
• The story he told is most instructive, for here was a chap ***absolutely*** convinced he had to stop drinking, who had no excuse for drinking, who exhibited splendid judgment and determination in all his other concerns, yet was flat on his back nevertheless.(p.40)
• Some of us have tried to hold on to our old ideas and the result was nil until we let go ***absolutely***.(p.58)
• Make him feel ***absolutely*** free to come and go as he likes.(p.120)
• We ***absolutely*** insist on enjoying life.(p.132)
• A spiritual experience, he conceded, was ***absolutely*** necessary, but the price seemed high upon the basis suggested.(p.155)
• I passed in at least three ***absolutely*** blank books.(p.174)
• I was, of course, soon on the carpet and the upshot was that I had to go back for two more quarters and remain ***absolutely*** dry, if I wished to graduate.(p.174)
• Their talk and action had instilled me with a certain amount of confidence, although I was not too ***absolutely*** certain.(p.189)
• Curious about it, feeling I was missing something, ***absolutely*** without any illusions about the aftermath, with no pronounced feeling of patriotism, I joined up with a Canadian regiment, serving a little over two years.(p.253)
• Eventually I would arrive home for a late supper for which, of course, I had ***absolutely*** no relish.(p.299)
• My son had ***absolutely*** no use for me.(p.301)
• On two occasions, over weekends, I decided I would take ***absolutely*** nothing.(p.443)
• (Today, there is ***absolutely*** nothing in the world more important to me than my keeping this alcoholic sober; not taking a drink is by far the most important thing I do each day.)(p.447)
• Nothing, ***absolutely*** nothing happens in God's world by mistake.(p.449)
• Mind you, I had ***absolutely*** nothing to show for that eighteen years, except a beat-up car that I hadn't even paid for, but I was doing all right.(p.478)
• I couldn't see that there was any way out of it, and I got ***absolutely*** despairing.(p.522)

absorb

• I stayed in Akron two or three weeks on my initial trip trying to ***absorb*** as much of the program and philosophy as possible.(p.291)
• Somehow our bodies had reached the point where we could no longer ***absorb*** alcohol in our systems.(p.380)

• The atmosphere of "eat, drink, and be merry" prevails and I ***absorb*** it.(p.499)
• The people who came knew immediately I was in no condition to ***absorb*** anything of the program, and I was put in a sanitarium to be defogged so that I could make a sober decision about this for myself.(p.549)
• Learning to depend upon a higher power and ***absorb*** himself in his work with other alcoholics, he remains sober day by day.(p.572)

abstainer
• Those who drink moderately may be more annoyed with an alcoholic than a total ***abstainer*** would be.(p.139)

abstemious
• In foreign parts many a soldier who has been ***abstemious*** at home learns to use new and potent drinks.(p.230)
• Remarkably enough, I was a very ***abstemious*** soldier.(p.253)

abstinence
• The only relief we have to suggest is entire ***abstinence***.(p.xxviii)
• Unlike most of our crowd, I did not get over my craving for liquor much during the first two and one-half years of ***abstinence***.(p.181)
• My four years of ***abstinence*** had something to do with it, but soldiering is a tough enough game for a sober man, and I had no yen for full-pack slogging through mud with a cognac or vin rouge hang-over.(p.253)
• After such often-painful vigilance (and numerous phony stints of ***abstinence***), retirement naturally created an impulse to live without restraints.(p.328)
• I told her that I was an alcoholic, victim of a disease, that there was no cure, only arrestment through total ***abstinence***.(p.333)

absurd
• He does ***absurd***, incredible, tragic things while drinking.(p.21)
• Our behavior is as ***absurd*** and incomprehensible with respect to the first drink as that of an individual with a passion, say, for jay-walking.(p.37)
• Here we find human opinions running to extremes -- ***absurd*** extremes, perhaps.(p.68)
• We might pay for this presumption in all sorts of ***absurd*** actions and ideas.(p.87)
• When I am through speaking, the whole idea has become ***absurd***.(p.507)

absurdities
• Can his past ***absurdities*** be forgotten?(p.140)

abundantly
• The experience of any alcoholic will ***abundantly*** confirm this.(p.23)
• God has ***abundantly*** supplied this world with fine doctors, psychologists, and practitioners of various kinds.(p.133)

abuse
• Especially when he has before him a way to stop his drinking and ***abuse*** if he really wants to pay the price.(p.108)
• My practice had advanced to the point where it could stand a lot of ***abuse*** and it got it.(p.214)

abused
• I used to get terribly upset when I saw my friends drink and knew I could not, but I schooled myself to believe that though I once had the same privilege, I had ***abused*** it so frightfully that it was withdrawn.(p.181)
• I tried the wagon on numerous occasions but I always felt unhappy and ***abused***.(p.375)
• I will never know all the people I hurt, all the friends I ***abused***, the humiliation of my family, the worry of my business associates, or how far reaching it was.(p.376)
• It was all about Scott Fitzgerald's little lost debutante, ***abused***, misunderstood and running wild.(p.402)

abusive
• But my attempts at community service ended in a drunken and ***abusive*** row with a fellow volunteer.(p.410)

abysmal
• In any case I must get out of here before I let slip my ***abysmal*** ignorance of how I came to be here, and she realized that I was stark, staring mad.(p.223)

abyss
• Nothing could pull me out of the ***abyss*** but more alcohol.(p.457)

abysses
• They knew what to do about those black ***abysses*** that yawned ready to swallow me when I felt depressed, or nervous.(p.229)

Abyssinian
• The ***Abyssinian*** war broke out just as things were going very badly for me, and I went off to Egypt on a job there.(p.519)

academic
• These observations would be ***academic*** and pointless if our friend never took the first drink, thereby setting the terrible cycle in motion.(p.23)

academies
• I don't remember much of what he said, but I did realize that there was another guy exactly like me; he had been in the same laughing ***academies*** and the same jails, known the same loss of jobs, same frustrations, same boredom and the same loneliness.(p.239)

academy
• I'd been on the board of governors of the ***Academy*** of Motion Picture Arts and Sciences for six years.(p.328)

accept
• Though he could not ***accept*** all the tenets of the Oxford Groups, he was convinced of the need for moral inventory, confession of personality defects, restitution to those harmed, helpfulness to others, and the necessity of belief in and dependence upon God.(p.xvi)
• We were in a position where life was becoming impossible, and if we had passed into the region from which there is no return through human aid we had but two alternatives: One was to go on to the bitter end, blotting out the consciousness of our intolerable situation as best we could; and the other, to ***accept*** spiritual help.(p.25)
• Fred would not believe himself an alcoholic, much less ***accept*** a spiritual remedy for his problem.(p.39)
• But I cannot ***accept*** as surely true the many articles of faith which are so plain to him."(p.47)
• Besides a seeming inability to ***accept*** much on faith, we often found ourselves handicapped by obstinacy, sensitiveness, and unreasoning prejudice.(p.47)
• You are sure to find someone desperate enough to ***accept*** with eagerness what you offer.(p.96)
• Should they ***accept*** and practice spiritual principles, there is a much better chance that the head of the family will recover.(p.97)
• My inability to ***accept*** the harsh realities of life had resulted in a disillusioned cynic, clothed in protective armor against the world's misunderstanding.(p.226)
• Suddenly I could ***accept*** myself, faults and all, as I was -- for weren't we all like that?(p.229)
• And he further said that God could not ***accept*** me as a sincere follower of His Divine Law unless I was ready to be thoroughly honest about it.(p.236)
• I don't think the boys were completely convinced of my personality change, for they fought shy of including my story in the book, so my only contribution to their literary efforts was my firm conviction, being still a theological rebel, that the word God should be qualified with the phrase "as we understand him" -- for that was the only way I could ***accept*** spirituality.(p.248)
• Where once I had casual acquaintances, all of whom were fair weather friends, I now have a host of friends who ***accept*** me for what I am.(p.296)
• Because it was only through feeling defeat and feeling failure, the inability to cope with my life and with alcohol, that I was able to surrender and ***accept*** the fact that I had this disease, and that I had to learn to live again without alcohol.(p.335)
• The Twelve Steps, which to me are a spiritual way of living, soon meant honest thinking, not wishful thinking, open mindedness, a willingness to try and a faith to ***accept***.(p.381)
• "Grant us the serenity to ***accept*** the things we cannot change, courage to change the things we can, and the wisdom to know the difference."(p.382)
• So please ***accept*** these humble calculations as, if anything, an underestimation.(p.396)
• An alcoholic cannot ***accept*** the news that he's an alcoholic unless there is a meaningful explanation given, and an offer of help, such as you get in A.A.(p.406)
• When I am disturbed, it is because I find some person, place, thing, or situation -- some fact of my life -- unacceptable to me, and I can find no serenity until I ***accept*** that person, place, thing, or situation as being exactly the way it is supposed to be at this moment.(p.449)
• Until I could ***accept*** my alcoholism, I could not stay sober; unless I ***accept*** life completely on life's terms, I cannot be happy.(p.449)
• So I'm better off if I don't give advice, don't figure I know what's best, and just ***accept*** life on life's terms, as it is today -- especially my own life, as it actually is.(p.450)
• Then, one day in A.A., I was told that I had the lenses in my glasses backwards; "the courage to change" in the Serenity Prayer meant, not that I should change my marriage, but rather that I should change myself and learn to ***accept*** my spouse as she was.(p.451)
• I began to sleep, to relax, to ***accept*** my plight.(p.461)
• And having sung that phrase, I'd chuckle with amusement, turning into irony turning into self-contempt turning into self-pity, at the sad fate of Bob, that wonderful, poor little motherless boy who was so smart in school and who grew up to ***accept*** responsibility so early and so fast and who staggered under his burdens without a whimper until the time came when he thought he was too good for this world and so he ought to be out of it.(p.532)
• We are granted "the serenity to ***accept*** the things we cannot change" -- and thus lose our quickness to anger and our sensitivity to criticism.(p.560)
• Above all, we reject fantasizing and ***accept*** reality.(p.560)
• Dr. Harry M. Tiebout, psychiatrist: "As a psychiatrist, I have thought a great deal about the relationship of my specialty to A.A. and I have come to the conclusion that our particular function can very often lie in preparing the way for the patient to ***accept*** any sort of treatment or outside help.(p.571)

acceptable
• I came from a family where alcohol was socially ***acceptable***.(p.384)
• But as long as you did your work and didn't disgrace yourself, you were socially ***acceptable*** and nobody really intruded on your private life very much.(p.518)
• I've been benefited from a dictionary definition I found that reads: "rationalization is giving a socially ***acceptable*** reason for socially unacceptable behavior, and socially unacceptable behavior is a form of insanity."(p.551)

acceptance
• While the internal difficulties of our adolescent period were being ironed out, public ***acceptance*** of A.A. grew by leaps and bounds.(p.xix)
• Another reason for the wide ***acceptance*** of A.A. was the ministration of friends -- friends in medicine, religion, and the press, together with innumerable others who became our able and persistent advocates.(p.xx)
• Why this ready ***acceptance***?(p.48)
• ***Acceptance*** of things as they are has replaced the old impatient champing at the bit to conquer the world.(p.295)
• ***Acceptance*** was his key to liberation.(p.439)
• At last, ***acceptance*** proved to be the key to my drinking problem.(p.448)
• And ***acceptance*** is the answer to all my problems today.(p.449)
• A.A. and ***acceptance*** have taught me that there is a bit of good in the worst of us and a bit of bad in the best of us; that we are all children of God and we each have a right to be here.(p.449)
• ***Acceptance*** has been the answer to my marital problems.(p.450)
• ***Acceptance*** is the key to my relationship with God today.(p.452)
• I must keep my magic magnifying mind on my ***acceptance*** and off my expectations, for my serenity is directly proportional to my level of ***acceptance***.(p.452)
• We think that each group should soon achieve this ideal; that any public solicitation of funds using the name of Alcoholics Anonymous is highly dangerous, whether by groups, clubs, hospitals, or other outside agencies; that ***acceptance*** of large gifts from any source, or of contributions carrying any obligation whatever, is unwise.(p.566)

accepted
• Though none of these principles had the force of rules or laws, they had become so widely ***accepted*** by 1950 that they were confirmed by our first International Conference held at Cleveland.(p.xix)
• If any feel that as psychiatrists directing a hospital for alcoholics we appear somewhat sentimental, let them stand with us a while on the firing line, see the tragedies, the despairing wives, the little children; let the solving of these problems become a part of their daily work, and even of their sleeping moments, and the most cynical will not wonder that we have ***accepted*** and encouraged this movement.(p.xxvi)
• He ***accepted*** the plan outlined in this book.(p.xxix)
• These were revolutionary and drastic proposals, but the moment I fully ***accepted*** them, the effect was electric.(p.14)
• That was great news to us, for we had assumed we could not make use of spiritual principles unless we ***accepted*** many things on faith which seemed difficult to believe.(p.47)

• While drinking, he *accepted* a sum of money from a bitterly-hated business rival, giving him no receipt for it.(p.80)
• This may hang on for months, long after their mother has *accepted* dad's new way of living and thinking.(p.134)
• Without much ado, he *accepted* the principles and procedure that had helped us.(p.139)
• In fact, he may say almost anything if he has *accepted* our solution which, as you know, demands rigorous honesty.(p.145)
• I *accepted* their help, and it was helpful.(p.202)
• One of the things that came up repeatedly in the stories they told me was that once they had *accepted* the program, they never had a desire to take a drink.(p.219)
• I had *accepted* Catholicism somewhat as an inheritance.(p.220)
• At the age of sixteen, I was invited to spend the summer with an aunt and I, very delightedly, *accepted* the invitation.(p.261)
• We drank with exactly the same accord that we finally *accepted* A.A.(p.265)
• Help which you once continually rejected, suggestions once turned aside are finally *accepted* in desperation.(p.377)
• His were good, simple Quaker folk who *accepted* me with love.(p.402)
• I *accepted* a big tax-free income from the family, but I didn't like it when they told me how to live.(p.405)
• Only through being beaten down by my own misery would I ever have *accepted* the term "alcoholic" as applied to myself.(p.436)
• Now, however, I *accepted* it fully.(p.436)
• Max *accepted* responsibility for me after I had promised never to drink again, never to take another pill, never to swear again, and never to talk to girls again.(p.444)
• He and his wife more than *accepted* me; he listened to all my woes; both of them treated me as a human being.(p.462)
• For to have *accepted* the reasons and to have acted on them would have been too great a blow to my ego, which was as great, in reverse, as my body was small.(p.534)
• As soon as I had made a few friends and had begun to feel *accepted*, we moved again.(p.555)

accepting

• More often than not, it is imperative that a man's brain be cleared before he is approached, as he has then a better chance of understanding and *accepting* what we have to offer.(p.xxiv)
• Here are some of the methods we have tried: Drinking beer only, limiting the number of drinks, never drinking alone, never drinking in the morning, drinking only at home, never having it in the house, never drinking during business hours, drinking only at parties, switching from scotch to brandy, drinking only natural wines, agreeing to resign if ever drunk on the job, taking a trip, not taking a trip, swearing off forever (with and without a solemn oath), taking more physical exercise, reading inspirational books, going to health farms and sanitariums, *accepting* voluntary commitment to asylums -- we could increase the list ad infinitum.(p.31)
• Afterward, we found ourselves *accepting* many things which then seemed entirely out of reach.(p.47)
• If you think you are an atheist, an agnostic, a skeptic, or have any other form of intellectual pride which keeps you from *accepting* what is in this book, I feel sorry for you.(p.181)
• Sitting in a Second Avenue bar, *accepting* drinks from anyone who offered, after my small stake was gone; or sitting at home alone, with the inevitable glass in my hand, I would remember, and remembering, I would drink faster, seeking speedy oblivion.(p.225)
• And, *accepting*, I felt a new inner comfort, and the willingness and strength to do something about the traits I couldn't live with.(p.229)
• I felt that his family were *accepting* me because it was good sense.(p.262)
• Where we used to run from responsibility, we find ourselves *accepting* it with gratitude that we can successfully shoulder it.(p.311)
• We did, and spent a month boozing it up, popping pills, and smoking marijuana; taking shelter where we could, which included a veterinary hospital one night; *accepting* meals from anyone; actually begging; stealing anything we were in need of, which was about everything.(p.354)
• I was *accepting* help with one hand and pushing it away with the other.(p.407)

accepts

• Nevertheless, the twentieth century readily *accepts* theories of all kinds, provided they are firmly grounded in fact.(p.48)
• If your man *accepts* your offer, it should be pointed out that physical treatment is but a small part of the picture.(p.143)

access

• Every one of them has gained *access* to, and believes in, a Power greater than himself.(p.50)

accident

• An *accident* while drunk laid me low for about three weeks.(p.258)

accidentally

• During recess we were playing basketball and I had *accidentally* tripped a fellow just a little larger than I was.(p.484)

accommodate

• Now, this house will hardly *accommodate* its weekly visitors, for they number sixty or eighty as a rule.(p.161)

accompanied

• On through the years this conduct continues, *accompanied* by his continual promises to be careful or to keep off the streets altogether.(p.38)
• To be vital, faith must be *accompanied* by self sacrifice and unselfish, constructive action.(p.93)
• This dream world has been replaced by a great sense of purpose, *accompanied* by a growing consciousness of the power of God in our lives.(p.130)
• My wife *accompanied* me on my visit and the doctor really told me some things that in my state of jitters nearly knocked me out of the chair.(p.302)
• The next recollection I have is of my husband coming into my room (later found out it was on New Year's Eve) *accompanied* by two policemen.(p.468)

accompany

• Talk about the conditions of body and mind which *accompany* it.(p.92)
• I jumped at the suggestion that I *accompany* him.(p.281)

accomplish

• He has commenced to *accomplish* those things for us which we could never do by ourselves.(p.25)
• Science may one day *accomplish* this, but it hasn't done so yet.(p.31)
• We think this method of approach will *accomplish* several things.(p.148)
• I have stopped tilting at windmills, and instead have tried to *accomplish* the little daily tasks, unimportant in themselves, but tasks that are an integral part of living fully.(p.295)
• In all honesty though, I was skeptical, but I wanted so definitely to quit drinking that I would have welcomed any sort of physical torture or pain to *accomplish* the result.(p.302)

accomplished

• Until such an understanding is reached, little or nothing can be *accomplished*.(p.18)
• This Power has in each case *accomplished* the miraculous, the humanly impossible.(p.50)
• We are there to sweep off our side of the street realizing that nothing worth while can be *accomplished* until we do so, never trying to tell him what he should do.(p.77)
• But say nothing, for the moment, of how that was *accomplished*.(p.91)
• If you have been successful in solving your own domestic problems, tell the newcomer's family how that was *accomplished*.(p.100)
• We do not like the thought that the contents of a book or the work of another alcoholic has *accomplished* in a few weeks that for which we struggled for years.(p.118)
• While grateful that he drinks no more, they may not like the idea that God has *accomplished* the miracle where they failed.(p.128)
• Meanwhile, we are sure a great deal can be *accomplished* by the use of the book alone.(p.144)
• To duplicate, with such backing, what we have *accomplished* is only a matter of willingness, patience and labor.(p.163)
• I always built up in my own mind the great things that I was going to do, and in fact I *accomplished* about fifty percent of them and then lost interest.(p.193)
• This last real merry-go-round had started the day before Christmas and I had really *accomplished* a lot in those fourteen days.(p.238)
• Haven't I been successful, haven't I *accomplished* extraordinary things in business?(p.245)
• There was the same reward -- exhilaration at a mission *accomplished*.(p.283)
• This latest part of my life has had a purpose, not in great things *accomplished* but in daily living.(p.295)
• I could never have *accomplished* this alone.(p.311)
• I had *accomplished* all the right things that our society expected, and I had no real peace of mind nor gratitude.(p.418)
• What often takes place in a few months could seldom have been *accomplished* by years of self discipline.(p.569)

accomplishing

• If he gets the idea that you are a nag or a killjoy, your chance of *accomplishing* anything useful may be zero.(p.111)

accomplishment

• The Wright brothers' almost childish faith that they could build a machine which would fly was the mainspring of their *accomplishment*.(p.52)
• I get my greatest thrill of *accomplishment* from the knowledge that I have played a part in the new happiness achieved by countless others like myself.(p.229)
• Probably only a few readers of this story will be able, from personal experiences of their own, to understand the exhilaration and sense of *accomplishment* which I felt after finishing this seemingly simple assignment.(p.276)

accomplishments

• Above all, I was suffering inner pain because my performance and my *accomplishments* in life failed to live up to my own expectations of myself.(p.557)

accord

• The next thing they wanted to know was if I thought I could quit of my own *accord*, without any help, if I could just walk out of the hospital and never take another drink.(p.186)
• We drank with exactly the same *accord* that we finally accepted A.A.(p.265)

accorded

• Occasionally, it is *accorded* to a few of us to watch something fine grow from a tiny kernel into something of gigantic goodness.(p.295)
• Above all, I have gained the greatest thing *accorded* to any man, the love and understanding of a gracious God, who has lifted me from the alcoholic scrap-heap to a position of trust where I have been able to reap the rich rewards that come from showing a little love for others and from serving them as I can.(p.296)

according

• So far, so good -- all *according* to plan, like thousands of others.(p.225)
• Also, I was insane at times – *according* to society's yardstick.(p.458)
• They suggested that I study the A.A. book and try to take the Twelve Steps *according* to the explanation in the Book, for it was their opinion that the application of these principles in our daily lives will get us sober and keep us sober.(p.550)

accordingly

• But urge upon a man's family that he has been a very sick person and should be treated *accordingly*.(p.100)

account

• We think this *account* of our experiences will help everyone to better understand the alcoholic.(p.xiii)
• It explains many things for which we cannot otherwise *account*.(p.xxiv)
• At the end of it, my reports to Wall street procured me a position there and the use of a large expense *account*.(p.3)
• Even in the present century, American newspapers were afraid to print an *account* of the Wright brothers' first successful flight at Kitty Hawk.(p.51)
• Threatens to fire me for drinking and padding my expense *account*.(p.65)
• Maybe it's only a petty offense such as padding the expense *account*.(p.78)
• Give him an *account* of the struggles you made to stop.(p.92)
• Let your friends know they are not to change their habits on your *account*.(p.102)
• The checking *account* melted like snow in June.(p.106)
• God, they believe, almost owes this recompense on a long overdue *account*.(p.123)
• That is true only if one is willing to turn the past to good *account*.(p.124)
• He can scarcely square the *account* in his lifetime.(p.127)
• He may, for example, reveal that he has padded his expense *account* or that he has planned to take your best customers away from you.(p.145)
• Can you charge this off as you would a bad *account* and start fresh with him?(p.145)
• Here is a brief *account*:(p.153)

• On *account* of my enormous capacity for beer, I was elected to membership in one of the drinking societies, and soon became one of the leading spirits.(p.173)
• There were no childhood episodes of unhappiness to *account* for my alcoholism.(p.182)
• (At this point, the Editors intrude just long enough to supplement Bill D.'s *account*, that of the man on the bed, with that of Bill W., the man who sat by the side of the bed.)(p.188)
• My fright was real enough, but it didn't *account* for these violent reactions.(p.222)
• Then I started traveling, with the United States and Canada as my territory, and with so much freedom and with an unlimited expense *account*, I was soon drinking every night and kidding myself that it was all part of the job.(p.287)
• For three generations, my family had had a charge *account* in one of the big New York hotels.(p.410)
• The doctor bills are heavy and the bank *account* is low.(p.501)
• I'd gladly do it anonymously, as I have done this brief *account* of my struggle with alcohol – merely to present certain ideas for the consideration of the reader.(p.542)
• The only thing this changed, however, was my surroundings, and it was soon apparent that I could have the same uncomfortable emotions with an unlimited checking *account* that I could on a working girl's salary.(p.545)

accountable
• I early discovered that if I drank anything, I was not *accountable* for what happened.(p.196)

accountant
• With this specialized training, and a liberal business education in the school of hard knocks, I was able to set up shop some two years later as an independent *accountant*.(p.284)

accounted
• He had also been greatly helped by the late Dr. William D. Silkworth, a New York specialist in alcoholism who is now *accounted* no less than a medical saint by A.A. members, and whose story of the early days of our Society appears in the next pages.(p.xvi)

accounting
• Fred is partner in a well known *accounting* firm.(p.39)
• One day I went to Washington to present some *accounting* evidence to a government bureau.(p.40)
• I enrolled in a correspondence school which taught nothing but *accounting*.(p.284)
• I have had experience in selling, collecting, and *accounting*, and am on my way up the ladder.(p.500)

accounts
• We hope no one will consider these self-revealing *accounts* in bad taste.(p.29)
• We may be short in our *accounts* and unable to make good.(p.78)
• Returning to the town I had left three months before, I became editor of a monthly magazine, soon had additional publicity and advertising *accounts* and the money rolled in.(p.254)

accumulate
• Then too, we view with much concern those A.A. treasuries which continue, beyond prudent reserves, to *accumulate* funds for no stated A.A. purpose.(p.566)

accumulated
• We attempt to sweep away the debris which has *accumulated* out of our effort to live on self-will and run the show ourselves.(p.76)
• I displayed alcoholic tendencies actually from the age of fourteen, when I started to steal wine from the family jug, siphoning it off one drink at a time so it wouldn't be missed, not drinking it immediately, but saving it until about a pint was *accumulated*, so that I could get drunk.(p.397)

accumulating
• I began making the rounds of the doctors in the hope that one of them might find some cure for my *accumulating* ailments, preferably something that could be removed surgically.(p.305)

accumulation
• At that time the repeal whiskies were back, and I'd go to the store and buy my whiskey and take it to my office and put it under the desk, first in one place and then in another, and there soon was an *accumulation* of empty bottles.(p.488)

accurate
• Alcohol being no respecter of persons, we are an *accurate* cross section of America, and in distant lands, the same democratic evening-up process is now going on.(p.xx)
• The most *accurate* answer I can give you is this: Fear has never again ruled my life since that day in September, 1938, when I found that a Power greater than myself could not only restore me to sanity but could keep me both sober and sane.(p.285)

accurately
• All changes made over the years in the Big Book (A.A. members' fond nickname for this volume) have had the same purpose: to represent the current membership of Alcoholics Anonymous more *accurately*, and thereby to reach more alcoholics.(p.xii)

accused
• I was *accused* of it many times when I went to play bridge in the afternoon, but I really never did take a morning drink.(p.323)
• For you learned that he had been guilty of the thing he had *accused* you of, and his guilt had brought suffering to his entire family; and he thought he saw his young son beginning his own tragic pattern.(p.533)

accustomed
• By the following spring we were living in our *accustomed* style.(p.4)
• Thus mother, through no fault of her own, became *accustomed* to wearing the family trousers.(p.131)
• Having regard for the law of the land, I resigned myself to the will of the national legislators and quit drinking altogether, not because I had found it harmful, but because I couldn't get what I was *accustomed* to drink.(p.232)
• It meant that I had to give up a lot of the things that I had been *accustomed* to and that wasn't the easiest thing in the world for me.(p.487)

ace
• "*Ace* crime photographer," that's me.(p.425)

ache
• They sound like the philosophy of the man who, having a headache, beats himself on the head with a hammer so that he can't feel the *ache*.(p.23)
• There is no more "aloneness," with that awful *ache*, so deep in the heart of every alcoholic that nothing, before, could ever reach it.(p.312)
• That *ache* is gone and never need return again.(p.312)

ached
• When we went to bed my sides *ached*, and I said to my husband, "I thought I would never laugh again, but I have laughed."(p.269)

achieve
• We shall do our utmost to *achieve* that ideal.(p.19)
• We think that each group should soon *achieve* this ideal; that any public solicitation of funds using the name of Alcoholics Anonymous is highly dangerous, whether by groups, clubs, hospitals, or other outside agencies; that acceptance of large gifts from any source, or of contributions carrying any obligation whatever, is unwise.(p.566)

achieved
• Before my drinking had cut me down completely, I *achieved* a considerable measure of success, having been a City Councilman for five years and a financial director of Kenmore, a suburb later taken into the city itself.(p.182)
• I get my greatest thrill of accomplishment from the knowledge that I have played a part in the new happiness *achieved* by countless others like myself.(p.229)
• I *achieved* recognized and national standing in my profession, as well as becoming a director in many important institutions having to do with the civic life of a large city.(p.374)
• To me, A.A. is within the reach of every alcoholic, because it can be *achieved* in any walk of life and because the achievement is not ours but God's.(p.395)
• I have *achieved* the inner confidence to write quite unlike Shakespeare, and I have sold a good deal of what I've written.(p.416)

achievement
• To me, A.A. is within the reach of every alcoholic, because it can be achieved in any walk of life and because the *achievement* is not ours but God's.(p.395)
• I was listed in "Who's Who in America" as an American who, by distinguished *achievement*, had arrived.(p.432)
• There would be times when the life of respectability and *achievement* seemed insufferably dull – I had to break out.(p.432)

achievements
• At thirteen I was packed off to a very fine Protestant boarding school in Virginia where I stayed four years, graduating without any special *achievements*.(p.240)

achieving
• A "good boy" reached adulthood and success without *achieving* maturity or fulfillment.(p.418)

acknowledge
• On that day of decision, I didn't *acknowledge* that I was an alcoholic.(p.532)

acquaintance
• If we cannot or would rather not do this, we search our *acquaintance* for a close-mouthed, understanding friend.(p.74)
• Unless he took some drinks, he might not have the courage to scrape an *acquaintance* and would have a lonely week-end.(p.154)
• He came through an *acquaintance* who had heard the good news.(p.158)
• He now returned home, leaving behind his first *acquaintance*, the lawyer and the devil-may-care chap.(p.159)
• He and his wife would leave elated by the thought of what they could now do for some stricken *acquaintance* and his family.(p.160)
• During my visit there, renewing *acquaintance* with former friends, I soon spent most of my money.(p.252)
• I really worked for several weeks, and having had a fairly wide *acquaintance* with the dealer trade, it was not difficult for me to line up enough of them to give me a very substantial volume of business with a minimum of effort.(p.300)
• Finally, an old business *acquaintance* of mine, whom I hadn't seen for several years offered me a job.(p.301)
• Most of these fortunate ones have had little or no *acquaintance* with delirium, with hospitals, asylums, and jails.(p.315)
• After several months of *acquaintance* I asked her to marry me, but was politely refused.(p.359)

acquaintances
• As we look over the list of business *acquaintances* and friends we have hurt, we may feel diffident about going to some of them on a spiritual basis.(p.76)
• He probably has several alcoholics among his own *acquaintances*.(p.112)
• New *acquaintances* who know nothing of alcoholism might be made and thoughtful consideration given their needs.(p.131)
• In sports I made the track and tennis teams; I got along well with the other boys and had a fairly large circle of *acquaintances* but no intimate friends.(p.240)
• Where once I had casual *acquaintances*, all of whom were fair weather friends, I now have a host of friends who accept me for what I am.(p.296)
• I continued to work and continued to go to lunch with Vi, and none of our *acquaintances* on the job knew that we had separated.(p.491)

acquainted
• My schoolmate visited me, and I fully *acquainted* him with my problems and deficiencies.(p.13)
• Perhaps you are not *acquainted* with any drinkers who want to recover.(p.89)
• Strangely enough, I became *acquainted* with the "hilarious life" just at the time in my own life when I was beginning really to settle down to a common-sense, sane domesticity.(p.297)

acquire
• I didn't dare hope I might find for myself all that these people had found, but if I could *acquire* some small part of their intriguing quality of living -- and sobriety – that would be enough.(p.310)
• In learning to practice these steps in my daily living I began to *acquire* faith and a philosophy to live by.(p.311)
• And, as the years go by, working together, sharing our experiences with one another, and also sharing a mutual trust, understanding and love – without strings, without obligation – we *acquire* relationships that are unique and priceless.(p.312)
• During these years, I did *acquire* some good friends.(p.404)
• Though it was not our intention to create such an impression, many alcoholics have nevertheless concluded that in order to recover they must *acquire* an immediate and overwhelming "God-consciousness" followed at once by a vast change in feeling and outlook.(p.569)

acquired
• In the course of his third treatment he *acquired* certain ideas concerning a possible means of recovery.(p.xxiii)
• Many years ago one of the leading contributors to this book came under our care in this hospital and while here he *acquired* some ideas which he put into practical application at once.(p.xxv)
• I *acquired* the impeccable coat of tan one sees upon the well-to-do.(p.4)
• Above all, he believed he had *acquired* such a profound knowledge of the inner workings of his mind

and its hidden springs that relapse was unthinkable.(p.26)
• We have no desire to convince anyone that there is only one way by which faith can be ***acquired.***(p.28)
• We doubt if many of them can do it, because none will really want to stop, and hardly one of them, because of the peculiar mental twist already ***acquired,*** will find he can win out.(p.33)
• He was positive that his humiliating experience, plus the knowledge he had ***acquired,*** would keep him sober the rest of his life.(p.40)
• It may be he has done us more harm than we have done him and, though we may have ***acquired*** a better attitude toward him, we are still not too keen about admitting our faults.(p.77)
• In 1924, I had ***acquired*** enough clients of my own so that the firm made me a junior partner.(p.213)
• Very early I became apprenticed to harness-making and ***acquired*** considerable knowledge of upholstering.(p.230)
• I cannot say, however, that I ***acquired*** any craving for hard liquor as a result.(p.231)
• So six months ago I ***acquired*** a ready made family consisting of one charming wife, four grown children to whom I am devoted, and three grandchildren.(p.286)
• They inherited wealth and ***acquired*** more.(p.401)
• I'd ***acquired*** a new girl, a lovely girl who knew of my problem and had tried to help me.(p.430)
• Dad, due to having spent most of his time in a small Virginia town, didn't have any too much money, and the money he had saved and the property he had ***acquired*** were in Washington.(p.486)
• He didn't have to lie in wait very long, but fortunately by that time, I had ***acquired*** friends upstairs and they covered me for quite a time.(p.519)
• Apparently I'd grown physically at the customary rate of speed, and I had ***acquired*** an average amount of intellectual training in the intervening years, but there had been no emotional maturity at all.(p.547)
• I ***acquired*** a sponsor and began attending meetings, but continued to drink.(p.559)

across

• I pushed a drink ***across*** the table.(p.9)
• Never mind the musty past; here sat a miracle directly ***across*** the kitchen table.(p.11)
• Bill looked ***across*** at my wife, and said to her, "Henrietta, the Lord has been so wonderful to me, curing me of this terrible disease, that I just want to keep talking about it and telling people."(p.191)
• He wouldn't give me any money for the groceries, but he did take me ***across*** the street and buy me a bag of candy, which I later took back and traded for a loaf of bread.(p.193)
• My parents had some vague idea of making a priest out of me and for some years I attended the Franciscan school at Basle, Switzerland, just ***across*** the border, about six miles from my home.(p.230)
• As we left, and they were escorting us ***across*** the bridge into Wheeling, I, with great dignity and sarcasm, told them if their wives were ever visiting in Akron, and they, too, were looking for their route sign as I was, that I hoped I could extend to them the hospitality that had been shown to me in Bellaire.(p.264)
• I lay ***across*** the bed on my stomach with nothing but pain and sickness.(p.267)
• And then one ill-defined day, one day that I can't recall, I stepped ***across*** the line that alcoholics know so well, and from that day on drinking was miserable.(p.346)
• So I went down to him quite a few times a month and had him shoot me full of the stuff; and then I went ***across*** the street to a little drug store to take a glass of beer or two beers, and then stopped at the liquor store to get myself a pint and go home.(p.389)
• I opened my eyes again and a shadow fell ***across*** the bed.(p.422)
• I was transferred to Kaneohe Bay, ***across*** the hump to the windward side of Oahu, to the aviation base.(p.426)
• A very good friend of mine who owned a drug store ***across*** the street from us, came by only about two hours later and said that he had seen Vi down town.(p.487)
• I was there about three weeks, and then I got restless and started to tramp ***across*** the country, here and there, until I finally wound up in Pennsylvania, in a steel mill.(p.492)
• Just as I was wondering what on earth I could do -- I was too drunk even to pack a handkerchief – the memory of an A.A. write-up that I had seen in the Evening Mail flashed ***across*** my mind – and I thought to myself, this is something I haven't tried yet.(p.523)
• During the day a friend of mine brought me some magazines to take to a hospital group I was interested in, and I looked through them and a "banner" ***across*** the front of one featured an article by a prominent clergyman in which I caught the word "resentment."(p.552)

act

• If he is not interested in your solution, if he expects you to ***act*** only as a banker for his financial difficulties or a nurse for his sprees, you may have to drop him until he changes his mind.(p.95)
• A kindly ***act*** once in a while isn't enough.(p.97)
• You have to ***act*** the Good Samaritan every day, if need be.(p.97)
• If you ***act*** upon these principles, your husband may stop or moderate.(p.112)
• Wait until repeated stumbling convinces him he must ***act,*** for the more you hurry him the longer his recovery may be delayed.(p.113)
• You ***act*** like one.(p.147)
• It took me a year, or a year and a half to get to feeling physically well, and it was rather tough, but I soon found folks whose friendship I had once had, and I found, after I had been sober for quite some little time, that these people began to ***act*** like they had in previous years, before I had gotten so bad, so that I didn't pay too awful much attention to financial gains.(p.190)
• My life was always ***act*** and react.(p.325)
• Or: If I'm really a genius, I must produce a great work, to show why I ***act*** like a genius.(p.408)
• If it was one minute after, I'd stay up and ***act*** like a martyr all day.(p.441)
• What else can I do except what I have always done in the past? – ***act*** as my old self and return to prison.(p.458)
• It was the one redeeming ***act*** of that Christmas.(p.467)
• I learn that when we ***act*** upon the highest conception of honesty which is given us, our sense of honesty becomes more acute.(p.507)

acted

• They ***acted*** on me like the beating of a club.(p.195)
• I realized that there were other people in this world who behaved and ***acted*** as I did, and that I was a sick person, that I was suffering from an actual disease.(p.392)
• This was how I had looked and ***acted*** a few short weeks ago.(p.415)
• For to have accepted the reasons and to have ***acted*** on them would have been too great a blow to my ego, which was as great, in reverse, as my body was small.(p.534)

action

• We believe, and so suggested a few years ago, that the ***action*** of alcohol on these chronic alcoholics is a manifestation of an allergy; that the phenomenon of craving is limited to this class and never occurs in the average temperate drinker.(p.xxvi)
• They had told of a simple religious idea and a practical program of ***action.***(p.9)
• We have a way out on which we can absolutely agree, and upon which we can join in brotherly and harmonious ***action.***(p.17)
• "Then they outlined the spiritual answer and program of ***action*** which a hundred of them had followed successfully.(p.42)
• But the program of ***action,*** though entirely sensible, was pretty drastic.(p.42)
• Next we launched out on a course of vigorous ***action,*** the first step of which is a personal housecleaning, which many of us had never attempted.(p.63)
• INTO ***ACTION***(p.72)
• This requires ***action*** on our part, which, when completed, will mean that we have admitted to God, to ourselves, and to another human being the exact nature of our defects.(p.72)
• Now we need more ***action,*** without which we find that "Faith without works is dead."(p.76)
• Before taking drastic ***action*** which might implicate other people we secure their consent.(p.80)
• His ***action*** met widespread approval, and today his is one of the most trusted citizens of his town.(p.80)
• It is easy to let up on the spiritual program of ***action*** and rest on our laurels.(p.85)
• But we must go further and that means more ***action.***(p.85)
• As we go through the day we pause, when agitated or doubtful, and ask for the right thought or ***action.***(p.87)
• There is ***action*** and more ***action.***(p.88)
• To be vital, faith must be accompanied by self sacrifice and unselfish, constructive ***action.***(p.93)
• Outline the program of ***action,*** explaining how you made a self-appraisal, how you straightened out your past and why you are now endeavoring to be helpful to him.(p.94)
• Tell him you once felt as he does, but you doubt whether you would have made much progress had you not taken ***action.***(p.94)
• Yet we do go to great extremes to provide each other with these very things, when such ***action*** is warranted.(p.98)
• When your prospect has made such reparation as he can to his family, and has thoroughly explained to them the new principles by which he is living, he should proceed to put those principles into ***action*** at home.(p.98)
• They can urge ***action*** without arousing hostility.(p.113)
• Can it be appreciated that he has been a victim of crooked thinking, directly caused by the ***action*** of alcohol on his brain?(p.140)
• But these scrapes can generally be charged, no matter how bad, to the abnormal ***action*** of alcohol on his mind.(p.140)
• After satisfying yourself that your man wants to recover and that he will go to any extreme to do so, you may suggest a definite course of ***action.***(p.142)
• The two friends spoke of their spiritual experience and told him about the course of ***action*** they carried out.(p.157)
• Their talk and ***action*** had instilled me with a certain amount of confidence, although I was not too absolutely certain.(p.189)
• The three of us did not feel up to the job, and after a few meetings we convinced the prospects that they too should go to Akron where they could see an older group in ***action.***(p.295)
• And we wonder how much further this man could go if his alcoholic problem could be removed and he could throw one hundred per cent of his abilities into ***action.***(p.308)
• I went into ***action.***(p.333)
• There was the economic fear which made me too timid to take any ***action*** which might improve my circumstances.(p.534)
• And no group, regional committee, or individual should ever take any ***action*** that might greatly affect A.A. as a whole without conferring with the trustees of the General Service Board.(p.565)
• Historians may one day recognize Alcoholics Anonymous to have been a great venture in social pioneering which forged a new instrument for social ***action;*** a new therapy based on the kinship of common suffering; one having a vast potential for the myriad other ills of mankind."(p.573)

actions

• And do not his ***actions*** make each of them wish to retaliate, snatching all they can get out of the show?(p.61)
• Their defects may be glaring, but the chances are that our own ***actions*** are partly responsible.(p.83)
• We might pay for this presumption in all sorts of absurd ***actions*** and ideas.(p.87)
• I had been too self-sufficient to write a moral inventory, but I discovered in pointing out to the new man his wrong attitudes and ***actions*** that I was really taking my own inventory, and that if I expected him to change I would have to work on myself too.(p.249)
• It was hard for her to believe in my love by my ***actions.***(p.362)
• Just being sober will be making amends to many we have hurt by our drunken ***actions.***(p.381)
• A.A. made it possible for me to face the consequences of my past ***actions.***(p.420)
• Before A.A., I judged myself by my intentions, while the world was judging me by my ***actions.***(p.450)
• It's been true in my case, nor could I quarrel with "restore us to sanity," for my ***actions*** drunk or sober, before A.A., were not those of a sane person.(p.550)

active

• Both saw that they must keep spiritually ***active.***(p.156)
• My father was a professional man of recognized ability and both my father and mother were most ***active*** in church affairs.(p.171)
• An ***active*** member of A.A. since 1939, I feel myself a useful member of the human race at last.(p.229)
• While I went along with all that was done and attended the meetings, I never took an ***active*** job of leadership until February 1940.(p.249)
• From that point on, I secured crocks of ten gallon capacity and really took quite an ***active*** interest in the manufacture of home brew.(p.297)
• I became one of the most ***active*** women in the community, what with P.T.A., other community organiza-

tions and drives.(p.339)
• I was ***active*** and did well, however, in school publications, dramatics (which came in handy during my drinking career), and Greek letter societies.(p.357)
• I'm very ***active*** in A.A. work and ***active*** at home, too, with my family.(p.372)
• They said "Get ***active***," so I helped whenever I could, and I still do.(p.381)
• After all, upon coming out of a week-long or ten-day drunk, it was hard enough to figure up just how much that one drunk cost, let alone trying to calculate the cost of approximately twenty-five years of ***active*** alcoholism.(p.396)
• If I had not become an ***active*** alcoholic and joined A.A., I might never have found my own identity or become a part of anything.(p.417)
• My experience has been ***active***: three meetings a week, many tapes, many A.A. conferences, much work on the Twelve Steps, and much work with other alcoholics and their families.(p.420)
• Had I tried honestly and sincerely to practice the Twelve Steps I would have seen from my continuous moral inventory that I was getting off the beam -- I would have found that there were some ***active*** resentments in my life, a terrific amount of self-pity.(p.471)
• When I had heard about it, it meant nothing but just two letters to me, but some friends of mine in the institution were very ***active*** in the program and really believed in it.(p.509)
• That was the day, that was the decision, I know now, when I crossed over the line and became an ***active*** alcoholic.(p.531)

actively

• Seven years of work in this field brought an opportunity to affiliate myself ***actively*** with one of my clients, a fellow A.A.(p.284)
• I had a family to be proud of, ***actively*** sharing in the responsibilities of good citizenship.(p.374)

activities

• Every day is a day when we must carry the vision of God's will into all of our ***activities***.(p.85)
• It works when other ***activities*** fail.(p.89)
• Our ***activities*** in behalf of women who drink are on the increase.(p.104)
• Your husband will see at once that he must redouble his spiritual ***activities*** if he expects to survive.(p.120)
• Though the family does not fully agree with dad's spiritual ***activities***, they should let him have his head.(p.129)
• Father may have laid aside for years all normal ***activities*** -- clubs, civic duties, sports.(p.131)
• The town was well supplied with churches and schools in which I pursued my early educational ***activities***.(p.171)
• So the story of my introduction into A.A. begins with the ***activities*** of my wife.(p.216)
• This widened the scope of my ***activities***.(p.276)
• During the first three months I carried on all these ***activities*** without a car, depending entirely on buses and streetcars -- I, who had always to have a car at my immediate command.(p.283)
• Too many outside ***activities*** to do much studying.(p.357)
• But success brought increased social ***activities*** and I realized that many of my friends enjoyed a social drink with no apparent harm to themselves or others.(p.374)
• Never having enough, always craving more, the obsession for alcohol gradually dominated all my ***activities***, particularly while travelling.(p.375)
• Making amends is sometimes doing what we are capable of doing but failed to do because of alcohol; carrying out community responsibilities such as Community Funds, Red Cross, educational and religious ***activities*** in proportion to our abilities and energy.(p.381)
• My job was to make out the guard schedules and thus I was exempt from ordinary recruit training ***activities***.(p.425)

activity

• Instead of developing new channels of ***activity*** for themselves, mother and children demand that he stay home and make up the deficiency.(p.131)
• Father will necessarily spend much time with other alcoholics, but this ***activity*** should be balanced.(p.131)
• After high school came four years in one of the best colleges in the country where drinking seemed to be a major extra-curricular ***activity***.(p.172)
• I did not know there was such a thing as group ***activity*** until I left the hospital.(p.218)
• He was close to tears in describing his boredom without an ***activity***.(p.334)
• I tried volunteer ***activity***.(p.410)
• My personal definition, which I submit as applying only to myself (although everyone is welcome to it who wants it), includes every waking ***activity*** of the human being; to have a creative attitude towards things is a more exact meaning, to live and to deal with other human beings creatively, which to me means seeing the God in them, and respecting and worshipping this God.(p.535)
• I now conceive the psychiatrist's job to be the task of breaking down the patient's inner resistance so that which is inside him will flower, as under the ***activity*** of the A.A. program."(p.571)

actor

• Each person is like an ***actor*** who wants to run the whole show; is forever trying to arrange the lights, the ballet, the scenery and the rest of the players in his own way.(p.60)
• In trying to make these arrangements our ***actor*** may sometimes be quite virtuous.(p.61)
• Our ***actor*** is self-centered -- ego-centric, as people like to call it nowadays.(p.61)
• He is very much the ***actor***.(p.73)

acts

• But I have not seen yet that I should do some constructive ***acts*** of love without expecting any return.(p.505)

actual

• So far, upon the total problem of several million ***actual*** and potential alcoholics in the world, we have made only a scratch.(p.xx)
• But the ***actual*** or potential alcoholic, with hardly an exception, will be absolutely unable to stop drinking on the basis of self-knowledge.(p.39)
• In ***actual*** practice, we usually find a solitary self-appraisal insufficient.(p.72)
• That company may harbor many ***actual*** or potential alcoholics.(p.149)
• Of far more importance was the fact that he was the first living human with whom I had ever talked, who knew what he was talking about in regard to alcoholism from ***actual*** experience.(p.180)
• After two or three years of effort along this line, I reached the point of ***actual*** despair that I ever would be able to drink only a harmless amount each day.(p.215)
• I was suffering from an ***actual*** disease that had a name and symptoms like diabetes or cancer or TB -- and a disease was respectable, not a moral stigma!(p.227)
• They saw that they had become ***actual*** or potential alcoholics, even though no serious harm had yet been done.(p.315)
• I realized that there were other people in this world who behaved and acted as I did, and that I was a sick person, that I was suffering from an ***actual*** disease.(p.392)
• While an A.A. group may cooperate with anyone, such cooperation ought never go so far as affiliation or endorsement, ***actual*** or implied.(p.566)

actually

• When the broker returned to New York in the fall of 1935, the first A.A. group had ***actually*** been formed, though no one realized it at the time.(p.xvii)
• These give a fair cross section of our membership and a clear-cut idea of what has ***actually*** happened in their lives.(p.29)
• ***Actually***, we used to have no reasonable conception whatever.(p.49)
• ***Actually*** we were fooling ourselves, for deep down in every man, woman, and child, is the fundamental idea of God.(p.55)
• In that state, the wrong-doing of others, fancied or real, had power to ***actually*** kill.(p.66)
• ***Actually***, he may be helping you more than you are helping him.(p.94)
• Unless they ***actually*** need protection from their father, it is best not to take sides in any argument he has with them while drinking.(p.115)
• I well remember the shock I received when a prominent doctor in Chicago told me of cases where pressure of the spinal fluid ***actually*** ruptured the brain.(p.140)
• I had no trouble there because I had never ***actually*** ceased to believe in God, and had tried lots of times to get help but hadn't succeeded.(p.186)
• I didn't like having to come home at a certain time; I didn't like this, I didn't like that, and I think the poor girl ***actually*** divorced me to help me stop drinking!(p.199)
• After the book appeared we all became very busy in our efforts to save all and sundry, but I was still ***actually*** on the fringes of A.A.(p.248)
• I can ***actually*** take my problems to Him and He gives me comfort, peace, and happiness.(p.303)
• ***Actually***, the bottom came up and hit us.(p.315)
• We did, and spent a month boozing it up, popping pills, and smoking marijuana; taking shelter where we could, which included a veterinary hospital one night; accepting meals from anyone; ***actually*** begging; stealing anything we were in need of, which was about everything.(p.354)
• When I did make it home in 1920, I re-entered school and caught up with my class in a few short months -- I ***actually*** did a year's work in three months, proving much to the disgust of my dad that I could do it when I wanted to.(p.358)
• I think I ***actually*** read more contempt than was really there because just a week before someone had sent him the Saturday Evening Post article on A.A., and there was some glimmer of hope in it for him.(p.391)
• I displayed alcoholic tendencies ***actually*** from the age of fourteen, when I started to steal wine from the family jug, siphoning it off one drink at a time so it wouldn't be missed, not drinking it immediately, but saving it until about a pint was accumulated, so that I could get drunk.(p.397)
• So I'm better off if I don't give advice, don't figure I know what's best, and just accept life on life's terms, as it is today -- especially my own life, as it ***actually*** is.(p.450)
• ***Actually*** it had, way back in 1940.(p.469)
• (***Actually***, he does it solely to get rid of us.)(p.480)
• I planted my first flower garden this year and am ***actually*** excited to see the results.(p.481)
• My mother had been recently converted and, ***actually***, had become a religious fanatic.(p.483)
• About this time an incident took place in grade school that I have never forgotten because it made me realize that I was ***actually*** a physical coward.(p.484)
• A man wasn't ***actually*** mistreated, though if he was he could only resent it.(p.485)
• This was around 1935, and it was about this time that I ***actually*** started drinking.(p.486)
• I don't think I ***actually*** started to drink pathologically until approximately 1935.(p.487)
• I ***actually*** wanted a drink, besides feeling that I had to have a drink.(p.488)
• What ***actually*** happened was that I had taken a penknife and stabbed Vi three times with it.(p.492)
• I was terribly afraid that I was ***actually*** going mad, if I hadn't gone mad already.(p.522)
• Since, perhaps, suicide was a bit too drastic (***actually***, I was afraid), dry martinis were chosen as the slow, pleasant, private, gradual instrument of self-destruction.(p.531)
• ***Actually***, of course, I wanted someone to listen to me, because when I had a few martinis inside, I became the great author I longed to be; and the right listener was in for some pretty highflown theories of literature and of genius.(p.536)
• It reminds us that we are to place principles before personalities; that we are ***actually*** to practice a genuine humility.(p.568)

acute

• The man in the bed was told of the ***acute*** poisoning from which he suffered, how it deteriorates the body of an alcoholic and warps his mind.(p.157)
• Formerly, in the ***acute*** mental and physical pain during the remorseful periods succeeding each drunk, I found my recollection of the misery I had gone through a bolsterer of resolution and afterward, perhaps, a deterrent for a time.(p.260)
• Either they die of ***acute*** alcoholism or they develop wet brains and have to be put away permanently."(p.308)
• I couldn't focus enough to make out the chart, but the card contained two words -- "***ACUTE*** ALCOHOLISM."(p.422)
• I learn that when we act upon the highest conception of honesty which is given us, our sense of honesty becomes more ***acute***.(p.507)
• The relationship between my wife and me was restored to a love and happiness that we had not known even before my alcoholism became ***acute***.(p.559)

acutely

• If the book is read the moment the patient is able, while ***acutely*** depressed, realization of his condition may come to him.(p.144)
• I had always been oversensitive to criticism and was ***acutely*** so now.(p.556)

acuteness

• He said the alcoholic seemed to possess a native ***acuteness*** and usually excelled in his field, regardless of environmental or educational advantages.(p.308)

ad infinitum

• Here are some of the methods we have tried: Drinking beer only, limiting the number of drinks, never drinking alone, never drinking in the morning, drinking only at home, never having it in the house, never drinking during business hours, drinking only at parties, switching from scotch to brandy, drinking only natural wines, agreeing to resign if ever drunk on the job, taking a trip, not taking a trip, swearing off forever (with and without a solemn oath), taking more physical exercise, reading inspirational books, going to health farms and sanitariums, accepting voluntary commitment to asylums -- we could increase the list ***ad infinitum***.(p.31)

ad nauseam

• It was really a horrible nightmare, this earning money, getting liquor, smuggling it home, getting drunk, morning jitters, taking large doses of sedatives to make it possible for me to earn more money, and so on, ***ad nauseam***.(p.177)

adapt

• I had to ***adapt*** to new associations and associates, and it seemed to be the smart thing to drink and smoke.(p.287)

add

• In that case he is going to wonder how you can ***add*** anything to what he already knows.(p.93)

• I could end my story here, but for the new man I would like to ***add*** a few words.(p.366)

• A retired Navy man looks back over twenty years of drinking, to ***add*** up his A.A. "initiation fee."(p.396)

• But when I try to see what I can ***add*** to the meeting, rather than what I can get out of it, and when I focus my mind on what's good about it, rather than what's wrong with it, the meeting keeps getting better and better.(p.451)

• Need I ***add*** that such was the case because I had no money to provide a roof over my head?(p.538)

• The days ***add*** up into weeks, the weeks into months and years."(p.572)

added

• The second edition ***added*** the appendices, the Twelve Traditions, and the directions for getting in touch with A.A.(p.xi)

• "Bill's Story," "Doctor Bob's Nightmare," and one other personal history from the first edition were retained intact; three were edited and one of these was retitled; new versions of two stories were written with new titles; thirty completely new stories were ***added***; and the story section was divided into three parts, under the same headings that are used now.(p.xi)

• Nine of the stories in Part II ("They Stopped in Time") are carried over from the second edition; eight new stories have been ***added***.(p.xii)

• He ***added*** that occasionally in the night a vague craving arose which would be satisfied by candy.(p.134)

• Then he ***added***, "He sure didn't do much for me when I was trying to fight this booze racket alone."(p.158)

• So one more was ***added*** to the Fellowship.(p.159)

• Paul measured the medicine out, but he figured that with my track record that little bit wouldn't be enough, so he doubled it and ***added*** a few drops more and then gave it to me.(p.207)

• All sorts were represented and their relation of experiences and how they had found the only remedy, ***added*** to their human existence as sober men, laid the foundation of a very necessary faith.(p.258)

• I look back and remember these things because they made me very unhappy, and ***added*** to my feeling of inferiority at never being the same as other people.(p.261)

• It made me feel quite grown-up and mature, and I think another ***added*** attraction was the fact that so far as my family was concerned, it was forbidden, and it had a special attraction for that reason.(p.464)

• It wasn't strong enough, so I ***added*** a shot of vodka -- and was right back to worse trouble than before.(p.556)

addict

• No one could have told me then that I had not earned all my success, nor could anyone have told me that I was an alcoholic and a drug ***addict***.(p.418)

addicted

• Although, during this period I was not ***addicted*** to any pattern of alcohol consumption, when I did drink the drinking was pretty wild.(p.212)

• For two years, I was also ***addicted*** to heroin.(p.480)

addiction

• A well-known doctor, chief physician at a nationally prominent hospital specializing in alcoholic and drug ***addiction***, gave Alcoholics Anonymous this letter:(p.xxiii)

• The subject presented in this book seems to me to be of paramount importance to those afflicted with alcoholic ***addiction***.(p.xxv)

• I say this after many years' experience as Medical Director of one of the oldest hospitals in the country treating alcoholic and drug ***addiction***.(p.xxv)

• In one of these there is a well-known hospital for the treatment of alcoholic and drug ***addiction***.(p.161)

• (My ***addiction*** bloomed within a small apartment I shared with my wife, a heart patient.)(p.329)

• When I went back to my hometown to go into private practice, I experienced another brief lull in my ***addiction*** to alcohol and drugs.(p.420)

adding

• In the garage, I would put the needle in my vein and then try to figure out exactly how much medication to inject to overcome the pep pills while ***adding*** to the sleeping pills while ignoring the tranquilizers, in order to get just enough to be able to pull out the needle, jerk the tourniquet, throw it in the car, slam the car door shut, run down the hall, and fall in bed before I fell asleep.(p.442)

addition

• In ***addition*** to these casual get-togethers, it became customary to set apart one night a week for a meeting to be attended by anyone or everyone interested in a spiritual way of life.(p.159)

additional

• His case presents ***additional*** questions which we shall try to answer for you.(p.110)

• Today, hundreds of ***additional*** A.A. members can be found who have had no relapse for more than thirty years.(p.169)

• Returning to the town I had left three months before, I became editor of a monthly magazine, soon had ***additional*** publicity and advertising accounts and the money rolled in.(p.254)

• I received an ***additional*** fifteen years for that, making a minimum of thirty-five years and a maximum of natural life.(p.509)

address

• We want the wives of Alcoholics Anonymous to ***address*** the wives of men who drink too much.(p.104)

• I lived through a week of the fidgets because I had agreed to ***address*** a group of alcoholic inmates in one of our state mental hospitals.(p.283)

• Then I saw an A.A. advertisement in a newspaper, and I wrote to the ***address*** it gave.(p.343)

• There at the top of the folder was my name, age and ***address***, and underneath were the words, "Periodic Drinker."(p.470)

• (This ***address*** is now available in pamphlet form at nominal cost through most A.A. groups or from Box 459, Grand Central Station, New York, NY 10163, under the title "Three Talks to Medical Societies by Bill W." -- formerly called "Bill on Alcoholism" and earlier "Alcoholism the Illness.")(p.572)

addressed

• In the following chapter, there appears an explanation of alcoholism, as we understand it, then a chapter ***addressed*** to the agnostic.(p.28)

• The foregoing pages (though ***addressed*** only to wives) indicate the problems such people may face.(p.121)

• My opinions were quoted in Time and Newsweek with pictures, and I ***addressed*** the public by radio and television.(p.435)

• If you cannot find A.A. in your locality, a letter ***addressed*** to Alcoholics Anonymous, Box 459, Grand Central Station, New York, NY 10163, U.S.A., will receive a prompt reply from this world center, referring you to the nearest A.A. group.(p.575)

adds

• If our hair is half-bleached (with dark roots), poker-straight, and not combed, this ***adds*** to our beauty.(p.479)

Adeline

• The grand fellow who at my call made me a hail-fellow-well-met, who gave me such a fine voice, as we sang "Hail, hail, the gang's all here," and "Sweet ***Adeline***," who gave me freedom from fear and feelings of inferiority.(p.498)

adepts

• Within a month, the police, the hospital authorities, several kind strangers, most of my friends, all of my close relatives, and a few ***adepts*** at rolling a drunk and removing his wrist watch and wallet had been involved.(p.532)

adequate

• I spent several days with him, but I did not feel ***adequate*** to pass the program on to him alone.(p.294)

• I was never drunk on the job, never missed a day's work, was seldom rendered totally ineffective by a hangover and kept my liquor expenses well within my ***adequate*** budget.(p.433)

adherence

• No one among us has been able to maintain anything like perfect ***adherence*** to these principles.(p.60)

adherents

• I was an honest agnostic, but definitely not a hater of the church or its ***adherents***.(p.256)

Adirondacks

• I spent about six or seven weeks in Sing Sing, and was finally sent off to Dannemora in the ***Adirondacks***.(p.509)

adjacent

• I managed to maintain myself with odd jobs, did ten weeks in a social rescue institution, and at length wound up in a second-hand bookstore in an ***adjacent*** town as manager.(p.257)

adjusted

• Of course she did not, and the whole situation has long since been ***adjusted***.(p.79)

• Just an unstable woman, undisciplined, poorly ***adjusted*** and filled with nameless fears.(p.305)

adjustment

• It is painful to grow, and without the help of my "civilian" A.A. companion, big Gene, I might not have survived that critical year of ***adjustment***.(p.462)

• I realize now that this phase of my development had been arrested by my obsession with self, and my egocentricity had reached such proportions that ***adjustment*** to anything outside my personal control was impossible for me.(p.547)

adjustments

• The ***adjustments*** in such a case are difficult and take time, but we both feel that they are certainly worth it.(p.286)

administer

• Sometimes you will have to call a doctor and ***administer*** sedatives under his direction.(p.97)

administers

• The General Service Board of A.A. (the trustees) ***administers*** A.A.'s General Service Office, A.A. World Services, Inc., and our monthly magazine, the A.A. Grapevine.(p.575)

administration

• Secondary aids to A.A., such as clubs or hospitals which require much property or ***administration***, ought to be incorporated and so set apart that, if necessary, they can be freely discarded by the groups.(p.566)

administrative

• Federal Theatre in Texas gave me an ***administrative*** job which I held for a year, only because I worked hard and productively when I worked, and because my very tolerant chief ascribed my frequent lapses to a bohemian temperament.(p.256)

admirals

• Then I joined the Navy and was commissioned as an ensign to write speeches for ***admirals***.(p.555)

admire

• But the wise family will ***admire*** him for what he is trying to be, rather than for what he is trying to get.(p.123)

admired

• So he returned to this doctor, whom he ***admired***, and asked him point-blank why he could not recover.(p.26)

• My associates, and all the wits and literary lights I so much ***admired***, also drank.(p.433)

admission

• At one time, the ***admission*** that I was and am an alcoholic meant shame, defeat, and failure to me.(p.335)

• But I made my ***admission*** just the same.(p.350)

• Oddly enough, the dentist who started A.A. in Amarillo, Tex., benevolently arranged my ***admission*** to dental college.(p.419)

admit

• The sensation is so elusive that, while they ***admit*** it is injurious, they cannot after a time differentiate the true from the false.(p.xxvi)

• Though the aggregate of recoveries resulting from psychiatric effort is considerable, we physicians must ***admit*** we have made little impression upon the problem as a whole.(p.xxvii)

• There is the type of man who is unwilling to ***admit*** that he cannot take a drink.(p.xxviii)

• Most of us have been unwilling to ***admit*** we were real alcoholics.(p.30)

• But even in this type of beginning we are obliged to ***admit*** that our justification for a spree was insanely insufficient in the light of what always happened.(p.37)

• We, who have been through the wringer, have to

admit if we substituted alcoholism for jay-walking, the illustration would fit us exactly.(p.38)
• We ***admit*** we have some of these symptoms, but we have not gone to the extremes you fellows did, nor are we likely to, for we understand ourselves so well after what you have told us that such things cannot happen again.(p.38)
• Undoubtedly we should ***admit*** our fault.(p.81)
• ***Admit*** that he probably knows more about it than you do, but call to his attention the fact that however deep his faith and knowledge, he could not have applied it or he would not drink.(p.93)
• Little by little the family may see their own defects and ***admit*** them.(p.99)
• He had to painfully ***admit*** that and mend his spiritual fences.(p.135)
• ***Admit*** your faults to Him and to your fellows.(p.164)
• I was willing to ***admit*** to myself that I had hit bottom, that I had gotten hold of something that I didn't know how to handle by myself.(p.187)
• I realized that I had a problem, although my realization was not very deep because my own conceit wouldn't ***admit*** that I had any personality problems.(p.214)
• I never left the church, but I was a fringe member, and the thought simply never occurred to me that through the exercise of what I had I might find the answer to my problem, simply because I wouldn't ***admit*** that I had a problem.(p.214)
• I couldn't ***admit*** that I was.(p.319)
• The unwillingness to ***admit*** failure requires even further friendly intake.(p.331)
• No one likes to ***admit*** that they're a drunk, that they can't control this thing.(p.340)
• I had to ***admit*** to myself that he was right.(p.436)
• Many times in the intervening years I have thanked God for that man, a man who had the courage to ***admit*** failure, a man who had the humility to confess that all the hard-won learning of his profession could not turn up the answer.(p.436)
• Why don't you ***admit*** it?"(p.439)
• Why don't you ***admit*** it?"(p.439)
• Why don't you ***admit*** you hate me?"(p.439)
• I would never ***admit*** that I was drinking too much, or spending money that I should have used to buy food for my two little boys.(p.526)
• Rather, I embraced it – I must in honesty ***admit*** it -- with a great sense of relief.(p.531)

admits
• Sometimes the man we are calling upon ***admits*** his own fault, so feuds of years' standing melt away in an hour.(p.78)
• He ***admits*** this is true, but is positive that he will do better.(p.109)
• He ***admits*** he cannot drink like other people, but does not see why.(p.110)
• As each member of a resentful family begins to see his short comings and ***admits*** them to the others, he lays a basis for helpful discussion.(p.127)

admitted
• He frankly ***admitted*** and believed that for him there was no hope.(p.xxix)
• Like myself, he had ***admitted*** complete defeat.(p.11)
• I ***admitted*** for the first time that of myself I was nothing; that without Him I was lost.(p.13)
• As soon as we ***admitted*** the possible existence of a Creative Intelligence, a Spirit of the Universe underlying the totality of things, we began to be possessed of a new sense of power and direction, provided we took other simple steps.(p.46)
• 1.We ***admitted*** we were powerless over alcohol -- that our lives had become unmanageable.(p.59)
• 10.Continued to take personal inventory and when we were wrong promptly ***admitted*** it.(p.59)
• We ***admitted*** our wrongs honestly and were willing to set these matters straight.(p.67)
• We have ***admitted*** certain defects; we have ascertained in a rough way what the trouble is; we have put our finger on the weak items in our personal inventory.(p.72)
• This requires action on our part, which, when completed, will mean that we have ***admitted*** to God, to ourselves, and to another human being the exact nature of our defects.(p.72)
• Are we now ready to let God remove from us all the things which we have ***admitted*** are objectionable?(p.76)
• We have already ***admitted*** this in confidence to another person, but we are sure we would be imprisoned or lose our job if it were known.(p.78)
• Even though your protege may not have entirely ***admitted*** his condition, he has become very curious to know how you got well.(p.92)
• He ***admitted*** he was overdoing these things, but frankly said that he was not ready to stop.(p.135)
• So, after reviewing these things and realizing what liquor had cost me, I went to this Higher Power which, to me was God, without any reservation, and ***admitted*** that I was completely powerless over alcohol, and that I was willing to do anything in the world to get rid of the problem.(p.187)
• In fact, I ***admitted*** that from now on I was willing to let God take over, instead of me.(p.187)
• As a matter of fact, I had two children at the time I was ***admitted*** to the bar.(p.212)
• That night for the first time in my life I really let down my hair and ***admitted*** my general loneliness.(p.239)
• But after hearing their stories, I knew that I was, and I ***admitted*** it.(p.320)
• Within a few months, I was ***admitted*** to a state hospital for the mentally ill.(p.370)
• "We ***admitted*** we were powerless over alcohol -- that our lives had become unmanageable."(p.379)
• It did say, "***admitted*** I was powerless over alcohol; that my life had become unmanageable."(p.379)
• So I ***admitted*** it.(p.439)
• When I first came into A.A., the woman who was my sponsor was the first woman I had ever met who ***admitted*** that she was an alcoholic.(p.472)

admitting
• I expressed my entire willingness to approach these individuals, ***admitting*** my wrong.(p.13)
• Far from ***admitting*** he was an alcoholic, he told himself he came to the hospital to rest his nerves.(p.39)
• He was interested and conceded that he had some of the symptoms, but he was a long way from ***admitting*** that he could do nothing about it himself.(p.40)
• ***Admitting*** he may be somewhat at fault, he is sure that other people are more to blame.(p.61)
• We think we have done well enough in ***admitting*** these things to ourselves.(p.72)
• It may be he has done us more harm than we have done him and, though we may have acquired a better attitude toward him, we are still not too keen about ***admitting*** our faults.(p.77)
• We suggested he write his first wife ***admitting*** his faults and asking forgiveness.(p.79)
• You will soon have your friend ***admitting*** he has many, if not all, of the traits of the alcoholic.(p.92)
• Why, he argued, should he lose the remainder of his business, only to bring still more suffering to his family by foolishly ***admitting*** his plight to people from whom he made his livelihood?(p.155)
• So, after taking the first half of the First Step, and very gingerly ***admitting*** myself to Alcoholics Anonymous, something happened.(p.349)
• And then I thought to myself: "Imagine an alcoholic ***admitting*** anything!"(p.349)
• ***Admitting*** that I am wrong or that I do not know is difficult for me.(p.420)
• I had no problem ***admitting*** I was powerless over alcohol, and I certainly agreed that my life had become unmanageable.(p.550)

admonish
• Seeing this, and meaning to be helpful, his wife commenced to ***admonish*** him about it.(p.135)

admonition
• A.A. has taught me that I will have peace of mind in exact proportion to the peace of mind I bring into the lives of other people, and it has taught me the true meaning of the ***admonition*** "happy are ye who know these things and do them."(p.551)

ado
• Without much ***ado***, he accepted the principles and procedure that had helped us.(p.139)

adolescent
• Our Society then entered a fearsome and exciting ***adolescent*** period.(p.xviii)
• While the internal difficulties of our ***adolescent*** period were being ironed out, public acceptance of A.A. grew by leaps and bounds.(p.xix)
• Prior to our marriage, when she was a shy, scrawny ***adolescent***, I was able to see things in her that others couldn't necessarily see – things like beauty, charm, gaiety, a gift for being easy to talk to, a sense of humor, and many other fine qualities.(p.450)

adopt
• If such women ***adopt*** a spiritual way of life their road will be smoother.(p.114)
• While on the subject of confidence, can you ***adopt*** the attitude that so far as you are concerned this will be a strictly personal matter, that his alcoholic derelictions, the treatment about to be undertaken, will never be discussed without his consent?(p.143)
• The doctor proved to be able and exceedingly anxious to ***adopt*** any workable method of handling the situation.(p.163)

adopted
• For myself, I had ***adopted*** those parts which seemed convenient and not too difficult; the rest I disregarded.(p.11)
• Suppose now that through you several families have ***adopted*** this way of life.(p.153)
• My youngster has ***adopted*** me.(p.303)

adopts
• Nothing will help the man who is off on a spiritual tangent so much as the wife who ***adopts*** a sane spiritual program, making a better practical use of it.(p.130)

adored
• I loved my father dearly and I ***adored*** my dog, and I'd gotten this new house and Frank had just given me a new fur coat and I was thrilled to death.(p.389)

adult
• I felt having gotten married, I was an ***adult*** and one of the first things I did was to buy two cases of whiskey with no idea of drinking it.(p.196)
• The differences between my father and my sisters, who were school teachers, made an excellent environment for the type of child I was – that is, slick and cute enough to take advantage of any ***adult*** quarrel.(p.210)
• This office job brought me face to face with a problem which I had sidestepped all my ***adult*** life, lack of training.(p.284)
• To be sure, this had been a dizzy and confused interval, but most everyone else I knew had emerged from it with both feet on the ground and a fair amount of ***adult*** maturity.(p.304)
• I came to understand the intricate processes of projection, by which we cast into our ***adult*** world the images of the horrors of our childhood.(p.434)

adultery
• My life there was a nightmare of periodic binges on alcohol and pills, ***adultery***, unhappy hours at the dental office, seeing my wife give birth to our second child and have several miscarriages, living in a turbulent household, and making continual attempts to be the respectable dentist, husband, father, and community leader.(p.419)

adulthood
• Slowly, my life seemed to unfold before me, shedding insights on childhood resentments, jealousies, and fears that had mushroomed in ***adulthood***, and also on the self-pity that I had wallowed in at every opportunity.(p.371)
• A "good boy" reached ***adulthood*** and success without achieving maturity or fulfillment.(p.418)

advance
• If you propose such a procedure to him, it may be necessary to ***advance*** the cost of treatment, but we believe it should be made plain that any expense will later be deducted from his pay.(p.143)
• I continued to ***advance*** in my chosen field.(p.433)

advanced
• If he is a real alcoholic and very far ***advanced***, there is scant chance of success.(p.34)
• I reasoned I was not so far ***advanced*** as most of you fellows, that I had been usually successful in licking my other personal problems, and that I would therefore be successful where you men failed.(p.40)
• I proceeded to take up the drawing and ***advanced*** rapidly in it.(p.211)
• Forty came and went and then the resolution was ***advanced*** to forty-one, forty-two, and so on in the usual pattern.(p.214)
• My practice had ***advanced*** to the point where it could stand a lot of abuse and it got it.(p.214)
• It was with grim foreboding and ***advanced*** jitters that I checked in at the hospital.(p.302)
• Among today's incoming A.A. members, many have never reached the ***advanced*** stages of alcoholism, though, given time, all might have.(p.315)
• My company ***advanced*** me rapidly, once my reliability was established again.(p.559)

advancement
• I still have my job, and just prior to the writing of this narrative, I received an ***advancement***.(p.303)

advancing
• Instead of regarding ourselves as intelligent agents, spearheads of God's ever ***advancing*** Creation, we agnostics and atheists chose to believe that our human intelligence was the last word, the alpha and the omega, the beginning and end of all.(p.49)
• I swung, I swore, I started throwing beer cans at the ***advancing*** hordes of pineapple faces.(p.427)

advantage
• This is a condition which, in ordinary life, would produce untold grief; there might be scandalous gossip, laughter at the expense of other people, and a tendency to take ***advantage*** of intimate information.(p.125)
• Seeing your attempt to understand and help, some men will try to take ***advantage*** of your kindness.(p.141)
• Being on a radically different basis of life, he will never take ***advantage*** of the situation.(p.146)
• The differences between my father and my sisters, who were school teachers, made an excellent environment for the type of child I was – that is, slick and cute enough to take ***advantage*** of any adult quarrel.(p.210)
• I was given every ***advantage*** in a well ordered home.(p.304)
• I had every ***advantage*** a child could have, private schools (several of them), dancing schools, two colleges, coon skin coats, automobiles, a listing in the social register and all the rest.(p.357)
• I begin to see I am not the person I had thought myself, that I had judged myself by comparing myself to others, and always to my own ***advantage.***(p.504)
• I had an ***advantage*** in having an idea of what A.A. was about before coming out on the street.(p.510)
• I'm fortunate because I live in an era when A.A. is available, and I'm able to take ***advantage*** of it.(p.512)
• Speaking at a dinner given by John D. Rockefeller Jr. to introduce Alcoholics Anonymous to some of his friends, Dr. Harry Emerson Fosdick remarked: "I think that psychologically speaking there is a point of ***advantage*** in the approach that is being made in this movement that cannot be duplicated.(p.574)

advantages
• And besides, we are sure that our way of living has its ***advantages*** for all.(p.xiii)
• Some, but not all of us, think it has its ***advantages*** when reasonably used.(p.110)
• He said the alcoholic seemed to possess a native acuteness and usually excelled in his field, regardless of environmental or educational ***advantages.***(p.308)

advent
• At age twenty-one, I enlisted in the Navy for two reasons: (1) to avoid being drafted into the Army, and (2) out of a burst of patriotic fervor inspired by the ***advent*** of World War II and as the result of an all-night drinking binge which found me sitting on the doorstep of the Navy recruiting office when the chief petty officer arrived to open for business at nine o'clock Monday morning.(p.398)

adventure
• Living just for today is a pleasant ***adventure.***(p.383)
• My second wife is a young A.A. member, too, and what a terrific ***adventure*** this is for us!(p.420)
• It would be a sure cure and also an ***adventure.***(p.434)
• To cut a long story short, I spent seven years and ten thousand dollars on my psychiatric ***adventure,*** and emerged in worse condition than ever.(p.434)

adventures
• Our description of the alcoholic, the chapter to the agnostic, and our personal ***adventures*** before and after make clear three pertinent ideas:(p.60)
• I was there for another couple of months and then, after a few more ***adventures*** in the East, I was shipped home.(p.521)

adverse
• And I still felt it was a weakness – plus, in her case, ***adverse*** circumstances.(p.370)

adversity
• A normal person, hit with ***adversity,*** can go on a drinking spree and then snap out of it.(p.404)

advertised
• Perhaps we are mixed up with women in a fashion we wouldn't care to have ***advertised.***(p.80)
• My wife wrote away for ***advertised*** cures for the liquor habit and gave them to me in coffee.(p.235)

advertisement
• Then I saw an A.A. ***advertisement*** in a newspaper, and I wrote to the address it gave.(p.343)
• But I pointed out to him that as I was the first British boy who had been to the school, it wouldn't be a very good ***advertisement*** for him, so I got over that all right.(p.518)

advertising
• Returning to the town I had left three months before, I became editor of a monthly magazine, soon had additional publicity and ***advertising*** accounts and the money rolled in.(p.254)
• Offered the job of ***advertising*** manager for an eastern automotive company, I moved to Philadelphia to begin life anew.(p.254)
• I did six years of newspaper ***advertising,*** and trade journal work with many, many drunks of drab and dreary hue woven into the pattern of my life.(p.254)
• It was my job to sell time on these stations to ***advertising*** agencies in New York.(p.359)
• We think A.A. ought to avoid sensational ***advertising.***(p.567)

advice
• We avoid hysterical thinking or ***advice.***(p.70)
• We have seldom told them the whole truth nor have we followed their ***advice.***(p.73)
• This ***advice*** is given for his family also.(p.90)
• Having had the experience yourself, you can give him much practical ***advice.***(p.96)
• We began to ask medical ***advice*** as the sprees got closer together.(p.106)
• We realize that we have been giving you much direction and ***advice.***(p.121)
• One of the many doctors who had the opportunity of reading this book in manuscript form told us that the use of sweets was often helpful, of course depending upon a doctor's ***advice.***(p.133)
• Before I stop – I always was a great talker – I want to say that nobody will ever know how I miss Annie's ***advice*** about things.(p.273)
• My wife became pregnant and the doctor recommended the use of port or ale . . . so . . . I bought a six gallon crock and a few bottles, listened to ***advice*** from amateur brewmeisters, and was off on my beer manufacturing career on a small scale (for the time being).(p.297)
• In my cups I used to tell them off, giving them lengthy ***advice*** on how to lead the right life.(p.410)
• So I raised enough fuss that they finally agreed to let me sign out, against medical ***advice.***(p.444)
• So I'm better off if I don't give ***advice,*** don't figure I know what's best, and just accept life on life's terms, as it is today -- especially my own life, as it actually is.(p.450)
• In the light of subsequent events it became evident that I took their ***advice*** far too literally, for, after some months of happy sobriety I drank again.(p.471)
• I took the ***advice*** of people I had heard at meetings, the people in the group.(p.516)
• Finally, in desperation, my family appealed to a doctor for ***advice*** and he suggested A.A.(p.549)

advise
• I earnestly ***advise*** every alcoholic to read this book through, and though perhaps he came to scoff, he may remain to pray.(p.xxx)
• Doctors may shake their heads and ***advise*** you to have him committed.(p.110)

advised
• Many a distracted wife has visited this house to find loving and understanding companionship among women who knew her problem, to hear from the lips of their husbands what had happened to them, to be ***advised*** how her own wayward mate might be hospitalized and approached when next he stumbled.(p.160)
• In 1932, some friends of mine ***advised*** me that I might try Christian Science, which had done a lot for some of their friends.(p.202)
• The very simple program they ***advised*** me to follow was that I should ask to know God's will for me for that one day, and then, to the best of my ability, to follow that, and at night to express my gratefulness to God for the things that had happened to me during the day.(p.208)
• He ***advised*** me to enter the particular hospital with which he was connected and I readily agreed.(p.302)
• Most of them prescribed sedatives and ***advised*** rest and moderation.(p.305)
• Doctors were ***advised*** to attend patients who could be benefited by medicine.(p.307)
• So oldsters are ***advised*** to develop interest, find hobbies.(p.330)

adviser
• We found it very desirable to take this spiritual step with an understanding person, such as our wife, best friend or spiritual ***adviser.***(p.63)

advocates
• Another reason for the wide acceptance of A.A. was the ministration of friends -- friends in medicine, religion, and the press, together with innumerable others who became our able and persistent ***advocates.***(p.xx)

aerial
• I don't know why I didn't fall out of the open cockpit of some of those planes I flew in while taking ***aerial*** pictures.(p.426)

affair
• This should be an entirely personal ***affair*** which each one decides for himself in the light of past associations, or his present choice.(p.28)
• If he opened that old ***affair,*** he was afraid it would destroy the reputation of his partner, disgrace his family and take away his means of livelihood.(p.80)
• Perhaps he is having a secret and exciting ***affair*** with "the girl who understands."(p.81)
• Then, under one provocation or another, the aggrieved one would unearth the old ***affair*** and angrily cast its ashes about.(p.124)
• If you still think you are strong enough to beat the game alone, that is your ***affair.***(p.181)
• Slowly I realized I was in bed and that the objects were my feet, encased in a harness ***affair.***(p.422)
• My wife received me graciously, although she was living in a one room with kitchen ***affair.***(p.490)
• There was the love ***affair*** which was ridiculous -- "imagine that midget being able to fall in love!" -- and my head knew it while my heart pumped real, genuine anguish, for it hurt like hell, and since it was first love, things have never been quite the same.(p.534)

affairs
• Judging from what I had seen in Europe and since, the power of God in human ***affairs*** was negligible, the Brotherhood of Man a grim jest.(p.11)
• My friend had emphasized the absolute necessity of demonstrating these principles in all my ***affairs.***(p.14)
• A much more important demonstration of our principles lies before us in our respective homes, occupations and ***affairs.***(p.19)
• 12.Having had a spiritual awakening as the result of these steps, we tried to carry this message to alcoholics, and to practice these principles in all our ***affairs.***(p.60)
• We have had retaliatory love ***affairs*** with other men.(p.105)
• The slightest disposition on your part to guide his appointments or his ***affairs*** so he will not be tempted will be noticed.(p.120)
• For example, we know of situations in which the alcoholic or his wife have had love ***affairs.***(p.124)
• My father was a professional man of recognized ability and both my father and mother were most active in church ***affairs.***(p.171)
• 4. -- With respect to its own ***affairs,*** each A.A group should be responsible to no other authority than its own conscience.(p.565)

affect
• This seemed to prove that one alcoholic could ***affect*** another as no nonalcoholic could.(p.xvi)
• A man may criticize or laugh at himself and it will ***affect*** others favorably, but criticism or ridicule coming from another often produces the contrary effect.(p.125)
• But then, as I drank more and more, the alcohol seemed to ***affect*** my vision: Instead of continuing to see what was good about my wife, I began to see her defects.(p.450)
• And no group, regional committee, or individual should ever take any action that might greatly ***affect*** A.A. as a whole without conferring with the trustees of the General Service Board.(p.565)

affected
• We hope this volume will inform and comfort those who are, or who may be ***affected.***(p.18)
• To be gravely ***affected,*** one does not necessarily have to drink a long time nor take the quantities some of us have.(p.33)
• The family will be ***affected*** also, pleasantly at first, as they feel their money troubles are about to be solved, then not so pleasantly as they find themselves neglected.(p.126)
• Normal drinkers are not so ***affected,*** nor can they understand the aberrations of the alcoholic.(p.140)
• Because it ***affected*** me so strenuously, they felt that hospitalization was indicated and I awoke in a hospital.(p.207)
• I myself could see deterioration in my work from being physically and mentally ***affected*** by liquor, although I had not yet reached the point where all I wanted was more to drink.(p.254)
• I definitely liked it, everything about it, the taste, the effects; and I realize now that a drink did something for me or to me that was different from the way it ***affected*** others.(p.305)
• The pep pills ***affected*** my hearing at times: I couldn't listen fast enough to hear what I was saying.(p.442)
• When I had been in A.A. only a short while, an oldtimer told me something that has ***affected*** my life ever since.(p.554)

affecting
• Four – Each group should be autonomous except in matters *affecting* other groups or A.A. as a whole.(p.564)

affection
• Moreover, he would lose his family for whom he had a deep *affection*.(p.35)
• For a while they would be their old sweet selves, only to dash the new structure of *affection* to pieces once more.(p.107)
• I wanted love and *affection* but I didn't get it.(p.424)
• Perhaps the single flicker of decency that shone through the fog of my drinking days was a clumsy *affection* for my two children, a boy and a girl.(p.437)

affectionate
• If not irritable, he may seem dull and boring, not gay and *affectionate* as the family would like him to be.(p.126)

affections
• *Affections* have been uprooted.(p.82)
• What they say will apply to nearly everyone bound by ties of blood or *affections* to an alcoholic.(p.104)
• They may be jealous of a God who has stolen dad's *affections*.(p.128)

affects
• *Affects* my:(p.65)

affiliate
• Seven years of work in this field brought an opportunity to *affiliate* myself actively with one of my clients, a fellow A.A.(p.284)

affiliation
• By personal religious *affiliation*, we include Catholics, Protestants, Jews, Hindus, and a sprinkling of Moslems and Buddhists.(p.xx)
• Any two or three alcoholics gathered together for sobriety may call themselves an A.A. group, provided that, as a group, they have no other *affiliation*.(p.565)
• While an A.A. group may cooperate with anyone, such cooperation ought never go so far as *affiliation* or endorsement, actual or implied.(p.566)

affiliations
• Those having religious *affiliations* will find here nothing disturbing to their beliefs or ceremonies.(p.28)

affinity
• I had, seemingly, just a natural *affinity* for grog.(p.182)

affirmation
• This great experience that released me from the bondage of hatred and replaced it with love is really just another *affirmation* of the truth I know: I get everything I need in Alcoholics Anonymous – everything I need I get – and when I get what I need I invariably find that it was just what I wanted all the time.(p.553)

affixed
• Shackles were permanently *affixed* to my ankles.(p.460)

afflicted
• We simply wish to be helpful to those who are *afflicted*.(p.xiv)
• The subject presented in this book seems to me to be of paramount importance to those *afflicted* with alcoholic addiction.(p.xxv)
• But insist that if he is severely *afflicted*, there may be little chance he can recover by himself.(p.92)
• We wives found that, like everybody else, we were *afflicted* with pride, self-pity, vanity and all the things which go to make up the self-centered person; and we were not above selfishness or dishonesty.(p.116)
• It is a most wonderful blessing to be relieved of the terrible curse with which I was *afflicted*.(p.180)

affliction
• When I hear the more rugged stories of alcoholics who became sicker than I did with this *affliction*, I humbly thank God for showing me "the handwriting on the wall."(p.367)
• Aside from being a common drunk, I had a very serious pill *affliction* and all the garbage that goes with it -- lying, stealing, cheating anybody and everybody, conning the people I could, and staying clear of the ones I couldn't.(p.478)

affluence
• But for him, financial security or even *affluence* can be a tragedy.(p.330)

afford
• If he can *afford* it, he may have liquor concealed all over his house to be certain no one gets his entire supply away from him to throw down the waterpipe.(p.22)
• Why not at least *afford* him an opportunity to hear my story?(p.138)
• I couldn't *afford* to be found with those people, but I said I would certainly pay his dues if it would keep him from drinking.(p.205)
• When my doctor told me I should never touch a drink again, I couldn't *afford* to believe him.(p.226)
• I learned early in my A.A. life that I could not *afford* to fondle such thoughts, as you might fondle a pet, because this particular pet could grow into a monster.(p.285)
• I can't *afford* resentments against anyone, because they are the build-up of another drunk.(p.325)
• I couldn't *afford* the luxury of prejudice.(p.383)
• Then the time came when I couldn't *afford* whiskey, so I turned to wine.(p.527)
• For example, we are told in A.A. that we cannot *afford* resentments and self-pity, so we learn to avoid these festering mental attitudes.(p.560)
• Dr. John F. Stouffer, Chief Psychiatrist, Philadelphia General Hospital, citing his experience with A.A., said: "The alcoholics we get here at Philadelphia General are mostly those who cannot *afford* private treatment, and A.A. is by far the greatest thing we have been able to offer them.(p.572)

afforded
• If he wants to stop, he should be *afforded* a real chance.(p.148)
• In describing his suffering, his fears, his many years of groping for some answer to that which always seemed to remain unanswerable, he could have been describing me, and nothing short of experience and knowledge could have *afforded* him that much insight!(p.309)

affords
• Instead of wanting to escape some perplexing problem, we experience a thrill of challenge in the opportunity it *affords* for another application of A.A. techniques, and we find ourselves tackling it with surprising vigor.(p.311)

afraid
• Even in the present century, American newspapers were *afraid* to print an account of the Wright brothers' first successful flight at Kitty Hawk.(p.51)
• Nor are we *afraid* of disclosing our alcoholism on the theory it may cause financial harm.(p.78)
• We must lose our fear of creditors no matter how far we have to go, for we are liable to drink if we are *afraid* to face them.(p.78)
• If he opened that old affair, he was *afraid* it would destroy the reputation of his partner, disgrace his family and take away his means of livelihood.(p.80)
• We are neither cocky nor are we *afraid*.(p.85)
• Were we resentful, selfish, dishonest or *afraid*?(p.86)
• You may be *afraid* your husband will lose his position; you are thinking of the disgrace and hard times which will befall you and the children.(p.116)
• I'm *afraid* to go out the door.(p.157)
• I wasn't *afraid* that the program wouldn't work, but I still was doubtful whether I would be able to hang on to the program, but I did come to the conclusion that I was willing to put everything I had into it, with God's power, and that I wanted to do just that.(p.189)
• I'd waked up in strange rooms before, fully dressed on a bed or a couch; I'd waked up in my own room, in or on my own bed, not knowing what hour or day it was, *afraid* to ask . . . but this was different.(p.222)
• I'm pretty near *afraid* of Labor Day yet.(p.264)
• Never in sixteen years have I dodged anything because I was *afraid* of it.(p.285)
• I was *afraid*, and I had made my mind up that I would never get drunk, so I was watchful and careful.(p.322)
• I needed a drink, but I was *afraid* to take a morning drink, because I didn't want to be a drunk.(p.323)
• I was *afraid* to set even one day.(p.326)
• I was keenly aware that my all-important security, which I had been constantly *afraid* of losing for four decades, no longer was endangered.(p.329)
• In fact I was *afraid* to try it for fear that I would wind up like many examples I had seen of excessive drinking in the Army.(p.374)
• There comes a time when you don't want to live and are *afraid* to die.(p.377)
• Scared that my dress wasn't going to fit right, that the church wasn't going to be filled, that I'd fall flat on my face walking up the aisle; in fact, I was *afraid* I wasn't going to be a prima donna in the place where I should be.(p.385)
• But I was *afraid*.(p.401)
• I was *afraid* to think why.(p.406)
• Bill was tall, grey haired, with the kind of asymmetrical good looks and pleasant easy manner that inspire confidence in the shaken and *afraid*.(p.413)
• The people of A.A. had something that looked much better than what I had, but I was *afraid* to let go of what I had in order to try something new; there was a certain sense of security in the familiar.(p.448)
• To Indians, I say: "Don't be *afraid* to join A.A.(p.477)
• I was *afraid* that sometime I would get half drunk and go through with it.(p.515)
• I was in a world that I knew nothing at all about, and I felt intensely *afraid*.(p.521)
• I was terribly *afraid* that I was actually going mad, if I hadn't gone mad already.(p.522)
• I was *afraid* to drink before the meeting.(p.526)
• Things got so bad, I was *afraid* to go on the street, so I turned to Mothers' Aid.(p.527)
• My father was and still is a minister, and I was *afraid* that I might run into him, or that someone might tell him where I was, and I could still remember what he had done to me when I got drunk one Christmas when I was very young.(p.527)
• I do think that some of the Negroes here – and other places, too – are *afraid* to go to other meetings.(p.529)
• I just want to say that you don't have to be *afraid*, because no one at any A.A. meeting will bite you.(p.529)
• Since, perhaps, suicide was a bit too drastic (actually, I was *afraid*), dry martinis were chosen as the slow, pleasant, private, gradual instrument of self-destruction.(p.531)
• I wasn't *afraid* of anything or anybody after I learned about drinking, for it seemed right from the beginning that with liquor I could always retire to my little private world where nobody could get at me to hurt me.(p.547)

afresh
• Somewhat faded, she nevertheless bloomed *afresh*.(p.384)

African
• By this time, with the doctor's explanation, the revelations contained in the book, and the hope-inspiring interview with Mr. T., I was ready and willing to go into the interior of the *African* jungles, if that was what it took, for me to find what these people had.(p.309)

Afro-American
• I am an *Afro-American* alcoholic.(p.526)

after
• Of alcoholics who came to A.A. and really tried, 50% got sober at once and remained that way; 25% sobered up *after* some relapses, and among the remainder, those who stayed on with A.A. showed improvement.(p.xx)
• I say this *after* many years' experience as Medical Director of one of the oldest hospitals in the country treating alcoholic and drug addiction.(p.xxv)
• We feel, *after* many years of experience, that we have found nothing which has contributed more to the rehabilitation of these men than the altruistic movement now growing up among them.(p.xxvi)
• The sensation is so elusive that, while they admit it is injurious, they cannot *after* a time differentiate the true from the false.(p.xxvi)
• *After* they have succumbed to the desire again, as so many do, and the phenomenon of craving develops, they pass through the well-known stages of a spree, emerging remorseful, with a firm resolution not to drink again.(p.xxvii)
• There is the type who always believes that *after* being entirely free from alcohol for a period of time he can take a drink without danger.(p.xxviii)
• *After* one of those days of inferno, I wobbled from a hotel bar to a brokerage office.(p.4)
• It was eight o'clock -- five hours *after* the market closed.(p.4)
• *After* a time I returned to the hospital.(p.7)
• There had been much happiness *after* all.(p.8)
• It began to look as though religious people were right *after* all.(p.11)
• We are like the passengers of a great liner the moment *after* rescue from shipwreck when camaraderie, joyousness and democracy pervade the vessel from steerage to Captain's table.(p.17)
• *After* such an approach many take up their beds and walk again.(p.19)
• How often have some of us begun to drink in this nonchalant way, and *after* the third or fourth, pounded on the bar and said to ourselves, "For God's sake, how did I ever get started again?"(p.24)
• Upon hearing this, our friend was somewhat relieved, for he reflected that *after* all, he was a good church member.(p.27)
• He was very nervous in the morning *after* these bouts and quieted himself with more liquor.(p.32)

• An exceptional man, he remained bone dry for twenty-five years and retired at the age of fifty-five, ***after*** a successful and happy business career.(p.32)
• Commencing to drink ***after*** a period of sobriety, we are in a short time as bad as ever.(p.33)
• Some will be drunk the day ***after*** making their resolutions; most of them within a few weeks.(p.34)
• What sort of thinking dominates an alcoholic who repeats time ***after*** time the desperate experiment of the first drink?(p.35)
• Friends who have reasoned with him ***after*** a spree which has brought him to the point of divorce or bankruptcy are mystified when he walks directly into a saloon.(p.35)
• Within a week ***after*** leaving the hospital a fast-moving trolley car breaks his arm.(p.38)
• We admit we have some of these symptoms, but we have not gone to the extremes you fellows did, nor are we likely to, for we understand ourselves so well ***after*** what you have told us that such things cannot happen again.(p.38)
• I rather appreciated your ideas about the subtle insanity which precedes the first drink, but I was confident it could not happen to me ***after*** what I had learned.(p.40)
• ***After*** dinner I decided to take a walk.(p.41)
• But ***after*** a while we had to face the fact that we must find a spiritual basis of life -- or else.(p.44)
• This happened soon ***after*** they wholeheartedly met a few simple requirements.(p.50)
• Did not these feelings, ***after*** all, determine the course of our existence?(p.54)
• Our description of the alcoholic, the chapter to the agnostic, and our personal adventures before and ***after*** make clear three pertinent ideas:(p.60)
• Time ***after*** time newcomers have tried to keep to themselves certain facts about their lives.(p.72)
• ***After*** consulting with his wife and partner he came to the conclusion that it was better to take those risks than to stand before his Creator guilty of such ruinous slander.(p.80)
• ***After*** the sermon, he quietly got up and made an explanation.(p.80)
• ***After*** a few years with an alcoholic, a wife gets worn out, resentful and uncommunicative.(p.81)
• ***After*** making our review we ask God's forgiveness and inquire what corrective measures should be taken.(p.86)
• Under these conditions we can employ our mental faculties with assurance, for ***after*** all God gave us brains to use.(p.86)
• We are often surprised how the right answers come ***after*** we have tried this for a while.(p.86)
• ***After*** a while, turn the talk to some phase of drinking.(p.91)
• This he may do ***after*** he gets hurt some more.(p.95)
• ***After*** doing that, he must decide for himself whether he wants to go on.(p.95)
• ***After*** they have seen tangible results, the family will perhaps want to go along.(p.99)
• ***After*** all, our problems were of our own making.(p.103)
• As animals on a treadmill, we have patiently and wearily climbed, falling back in exhaustion ***after*** each futile effort to reach solid ground.(p.107)
• Of those who keep on, a good number will become true alcoholics ***after*** a while.(p.109)
• He is remorseful ***after*** serious drinking bouts and tells you he wants to stop.(p.109)
• He has been placed in one institution ***after*** another.(p.110)
• If this kind of approach does not catch your husband's interest, it may be best to drop the subject, but ***after*** a friendly talk your husband will usually revive the topic himself.(p.112)
• But ***after*** his next binge, ask him if he would really like to get over drinking for good.(p.112)
• But don't remind him of this ***after*** he has been drinking, for he may be angry.(p.113)
• Time ***after*** time, this apparent calamity has been a boon to us, for it opened up a path which led to the discovery of God.(p.116)
• ***After*** all, your family is reunited, alcohol is no longer a problem and you and your husband are working together toward an undreamed-of future.(p.119)
• The fellowship of Al-Anon Family Groups was formed about thirteen years ***after*** this chapter was written.(p.121)
• Dad is not so spiritual ***after*** all, they say.(p.128)
• He will perceive that his spiritual growth is lopsided, that for an average man like himself, a spiritual life which does not include his family obligations may not be so perfect ***after*** all.(p.129)
• This may hang on for months, long ***after*** their mother has accepted dad's new way of living and thinking.(p.134)
• ***After*** two weeks of drinking, he had placed his toe on the trigger of a loaded shotgun -- the barrel in his mouth.(p.137)
• If he says yes, does he really mean it, or down inside does he think he is fooling you, and that ***after*** rest and treatment he will be able to get away with a few drinks now and then?(p.142)
• If he temporizes and still thinks he can ever drink again, even beer, he might as well be discharged ***after*** the next bender which, if an alcoholic, he is almost certain to have.(p.142)
• ***After*** satisfying yourself that your man wants to recover and that he will go to any extreme to do so, you may suggest a definite course of action.(p.142)
• ***After*** all, are you not looking for results rather than methods?(p.144)
• ***After*** your man has gone along without drinking for a few months, you may be able to make use of his services with other employees who are giving you the alcoholic run-around -- provided, of course, they are willing to have a third party in the picture.(p.146)
• ***After*** reading this book, a junior executive can go to such a man and say approximately this, "Look here, Ed.(p.147)
• ***After*** all, had he not been sober six months now?(p.154)
• ***After*** several failures to find others, a fourth turned up.(p.158)
• ***After*** a bit, he said, "The way you fellows put this spiritual stuff makes sense.(p.159)
• I guess the old folks were right ***after*** all."(p.159)
• ***After*** high school came four years in one of the best colleges in the country where drinking seemed to be a major extra-curricular activity.(p.172)
• This went from bad to worse until Sophomore spring when, ***after*** a prolonged period of drinking, I made up my mind that I could not complete my course, so I packed my grip and went South to spend a month on a large farm owned by a friend of mine.(p.173)
• ***After*** much argument they allowed me to return and take my exams, all of which I passed creditably.(p.173)
• ***After*** many painful discussions, they finally gave me my credits and I migrated to another of the leading universities of the country and entered as a Junior that fall.(p.173)
• ***After*** three years of this, I wound up in the local hospital where they attempted to help me, but I would get my friends to smuggle me a quart, or I would steal the alcohol about the building, so that I got rapidly worse.(p.175)
• This worked nicely until my wife and I went to see Wallace Beery in "Tugboat Annie," ***after*** which the pant-leg and stocking racket were out!(p.177)
• It then occurred to me that ***after*** one was all smelled up with beer nobody could tell what had been drunk, so I began to fortify my beer with straight alcohol.(p.178)
• I got tight that night, stayed sober Monday till ***after*** the dinner and then proceeded to get tight again.(p.179)
• So it doesn't behoove me to squawk about it for, ***after*** all, nobody ever had to throw me down and pour liquor down my throat.(p.181)
• On the return trip, ***after*** two or three loads, I passed out and had to be carried to the house.(p.183)
• Morning ***after*** morning I would awake sick and with terrible jitters, but there was always a flask of liquor sitting on the table beside my bed.(p.183)
• Then Prohibition came into effect, and the facts that the stuff obtainable was so horrible and sometimes deadly, and that I had married and had a job which I had to look ***after***, helped me for a period of some three or four years, although I would get drunk every time I could get hold of enough to drink to get started.(p.183)
• However, ***after*** two or three trials, I found this was not satisfactory because they did not serve enough to satisfy me.(p.184)
• ***After*** a while, Bill said, "Well, now, you've been talking a good long time, let me talk a minute or two."(p.185)
• So, ***after*** hearing some more of my story, he turned around and said to Doc -- I don't think he knew I heard him, but I did -- he said, "Well, I believe he's worth saving and working on."(p.185)
• So, ***after*** reviewing these things and realizing what liquor had cost me, I went to this Higher Power which, to me was God, without any reservation, and admitted that I was completely powerless over alcohol, and that I was willing to do anything in the world to get rid of the problem.(p.187)
• And they said, "No, you have a disease, and it doesn't make any difference how long you do without it, ***after*** a drink or two you'll end up just like you are now."(p.187)
• ***After*** prescribing medicines, Dr. Bob ordered, "Put him in a private room.(p.188)
• It was in the next two or three days ***after*** I had first met Doc and Bill, that I finally came to a decision to turn my will over to God and to go along with this program the best that I could.(p.189)
• It took me a year, or a year and a half to get to feeling physically well, and it was rather tough, but I soon found folks whose friendship I had once had, and I found, ***after*** I had been sober for quite some little time, that these people began to act like they had in previous years, before I had gotten so bad, so that I didn't pay too awful much attention to financial gains.(p.190)
• I know there was even more, something that I hadn't got, and I remember one day, a week or two ***after*** I had come out of the hospital, Bill was over to my house talking to my wife and me.(p.191)
• This was six or eight months ***after*** the last drinking episode.(p.196)
• I can remember telling the poor little soul that I could probably quit drinking if I wasn't married to her, and told her that, ***after*** all, I didn't like restraint!(p.199)
• ***After*** drinking one glass of beer at the end of my work period for about five days, I thought I'd better find out whether I really had the stuff licked.(p.203)
• When I had been in the hospital ten days, Sister Ignatia, who has played such a part in the development of A.A. in this area, stuck her head in the door one morning and announced, looking at me quizzically, that they might be able to make something human out of my face ***after*** all.(p.205)
• Shortly ***after*** that, my brother, who had then become associated with a group of people and had stopped drinking, urged me to attend meetings with him.(p.205)
• One morning, ***after*** I had been on a binge for a couple of days, I awoke to find my brother and Doctor Bob in my room talking to me about not drinking.(p.206)
• I was always interested in mechanics and ***after*** having about twenty miscellaneous jobs, lasting from one day to two weeks, I obtained a job as a toolmaker apprentice.(p.211)
• ***After*** I was on the drafting board about two years I decided I wanted a technical education.(p.211)
• A year later, ***after*** I completed the course in contracts, I quit the law school, and undertook some engineering work for a patent law firm on behalf of clients who were in difficulties and who desired to keep their troubles from their own engineering department.(p.212)
• I married when I was twenty-eight years old, and started in law school ***after*** I was married.(p.212)
• My drinking career began about four years ***after*** I had moved up into partnership and had joined certain clubs, societies and so fourth, and during which period we had Prohibition.(p.213)
• When I was about forty-seven, ***after*** indulging in all kinds of self-deception to control my drinking, I arrived at a period when I felt convinced I had to have so much alcohol every day and that the real problem was to control how much.(p.214)
• ***After*** two or three years of effort along this line, I reached the point of actual despair that I ever would be able to drink only a harmless amount each day.(p.215)
• My children had lost respect for me and, in fact, it was only ***after*** three or four years of sobriety that any of them ever said anything to me to indicate that I had recouped even a little of their respect.(p.215)
• One evening I had gone out ***after*** dinner to take on a couple of double-headers and stayed a little later than usual, and when I came home Clarence was sitting on the davenport with Bill W.(p.216)
• That was skeptically received by me when I first heard it, but ***after*** some twenty-eight or thirty fellows had come to see me, and pretty nearly all of them had said the same thing, I began to believe it.(p.219)
• Professionally, ***after*** I was sober for a month or so I realized that I should school myself to dissolve the partnership I was in because I felt that I would never regain the respect of my partners no matter how long I was sober, and that I would be at a disadvantage.(p.220)
• Shortly ***after*** I came to this conclusion, I was importuned by another well-known patent law firm to help them out on some trial work because their trial man had had a heart attack and had been forbidden to go into the courtroom.(p.220)
• In fact, ***after*** six months of living on food instead of on whiskey, I gained about thirty pounds.(p.220)

• Sitting in a Second Avenue bar, accepting drinks from anyone who offered, ***after*** my small stake was gone; or sitting at home alone, with the inevitable glass in my hand, I would remember, and remembering, I would drink faster, seeking speedy oblivion.(p.225)
• The year ***after*** coming out, I married.(p.225)
• I was born in Europe, in Alsace to be exact, shortly ***after*** it had become German, and practically grew up with the "good Rhine wine" of song and story.(p.230)
• For weeks ***after*** my arrival I was feted and entertained in the already large colony of Alsatians in the city, and among the Germans in their saloons and clubs.(p.231)
• You can all remember that in the first few months ***after*** the change, a great many men, who had formerly been used to a few beers every day or an occasional drink of whiskey, simply quit all alcoholic drinks.(p.232)
• More and more I formed the habit of doing some of my business in the speakeasy, and ***after*** a time I did not need that as an excuse.(p.233)
• Sometimes, ***after*** sobering up ***after*** a bout of several weeks, I would righteously resolve to quit.(p.233)
• ***After*** a couple of days in dollar hotels and one night in the pokey, I finally landed on my mother's doorstep -- shaking apart, with several days' beard and, of course, broke as usual.(p.238)
• But each drink ***after*** the "first" seemed to become less effective and ***after*** three or four they all seemed like water.(p.241)
• ***After*** the oil job blew up, I went back to Baltimore and mother, my first wife having said a permanent "Goodbye."(p.243)
• ***After*** the tire job came the thirties, the Depression and the down hill road.(p.244)
• In the eight years before A.A. found me, I had over forty jobs – selling and travelling – one thing ***after*** another, and the same old routine.(p.244)
• ***After*** being dry two weeks and sticking close to Jackie, all of a sudden I found I had become the sponsor of my sponsor, for he was suddenly taken drunk.(p.245)
• ***After*** a very good week, two of my customers took me to lunch on Saturday.(p.247)
• ***After*** a bit, the other man said "Three beers."(p.247)
• So I drank all three beers, one ***after*** the other, said "I'll be seeing you, boys," and went around the corner for a bottle.(p.247)
• ***After*** the book appeared we all became very busy in our efforts to save all and sundry, but I was still actually on the fringes of A.A.(p.248)
• With nothing but a liberal arts education, very definitely estranged from my family and already married, soon ***after*** graduation from college I became a bookmaker's clerk on the British racing circuits, far better off financially than the average professional man.(p.251)
• One evening, the book, ***after*** checking up, was very definitely in the red for plenty through a piece of studied carelessness on my part, and my boss, very shrewd and able, fired me with a parting statement to the effect that once was enough.(p.251)
• Some days later, ***after*** he had been discharged, a stranger came into my shop in the nearby town.(p.257)
• That was seven or eight years ***after*** we were married.(p.262)
• One morning ***after*** a terrific drinking bout, I was in a little bar near our house, and I shook so that I was very much ashamed, because I was getting the shakes worse and worse.(p.266)
• This was ***after*** his illness.(p.270)
• I always feel that our God Consciousness was a steady growth ***after*** we became associated with A.A.(p.270)
• I remember sometime, it was possibly six months ***after*** we had been going steadily to King School, that we were coming home from a meeting and saw a car along the way, and a fellow in back drinking a bottle of beer.(p.271)
• And that woman told me long ***after*** that was the surest proof to her that this program could work.(p.272)
• Probably only a few readers of this story will be able, from personal experiences of their own, to understand the exhilaration and sense of accomplishment which I felt ***after*** finishing this seemingly simple assignment.(p.276)
• But – I also stayed up week nights ***after*** they had retired and drank myself into bed.(p.277)
• It is, however, only the first of a series of miracles which have followed one ***after*** another as a result of my trying to apply to my daily life the principles embodies in our Twelve Steps.(p.280)
• ***After*** six months of sobriety I saw the picture in a different light: Detroit was the place I had to return to, not only because I must face the mess I had made there, but because it was there that I could be of the most service to A.A.(p.281)
• I well remember a session I had with myself soon ***after*** I returned.(p.282)
• It was therefore not extraordinary that I should shy away from any serious thought of marriage for a great many years ***after*** joining A.A.(p.286)
• ***After*** I left school, I went to work in Akron, living at home with my parents.(p.287)
• Once dad came all the way to Florida to sober me up, ***after*** a hotel manager called him and said that if he wanted to see me alive he better get there fast.(p.288)
• ***After*** finding every bottle that I had hidden around the apartment, she took away my pants, my shoes, my money and my keys, threw them under the bed in the back bedroom and slip-locked our door.(p.288)
• ***After*** a particularly bad Christmas and New Year's holiday, dad picked me up again early in January, 1937, to go through the usual sobering up routine.(p.289)
• So I told dad that I would lick it on my own, that I would drink nothing for a month and ***after*** that only beer.(p.289)
• Then and then only, ***after*** a thorough indoctrination by eight or nine individuals, was I allowed to attend my first meeting.(p.291)
• ***After*** it was closed we all retired to the kitchen and had coffee and doughnuts and more discussion until the small hours of the morning.(p.291)
• A few months ***after*** I made my original trip to Akron I was feeling pretty cocky, and I didn't think my wife was treating me with proper respect, now that I was an outstanding citizen.(p.293)
• The three of us did not feel up to the job, and ***after*** a few meetings we convinced the prospects that they too should go to Akron where they could see an older group in action.(p.295)
• Three years ***after*** I started on my drinking career, I lost my first job.(p.298)
• ***After*** being fired, I lined up with a new finance company that was just starting in business, and took the position of business promotion man, contacting automobile dealers.(p.300)
• ***After*** holding good positions, making better than an average income for over ten years, I was in debt, had no clothes to speak of, no money, no friends, and no one any longer tolerating me but my wife.(p.301)
• ***After*** being in the hospital for several days, a plan of living was outlined to me.(p.302)
• I am anxious to get home ***after*** dark.(p.303)
• He sent to New York for a copy, and ***after*** reading it he tucked it under his arm and called on me.(p.307)
• Shortly ***after*** I returned to Chicago, my doctor, encouraged by the results of my contact with A.A., sent us two more of his alcoholic patients.(p.310)
• But who wasn't ***after*** drinking that much?(p.317)
• ***After*** about three months, no more weekends.(p.318)
• The third time, ***after*** almost five years as an S.P. 4, I finally made sergeant.(p.318)
• ***After*** having a few drinks, I went to a meeting -- and the people there were not all old men and definitely not skid-row types!(p.319)
• But ***after*** hearing their stories, I knew that I was, and I admitted it.(p.320)
• ***After*** a time, my mind began to clear of the fog that had covered it.(p.320)
• That was on a hot summer evening, down in the Greenwich Village Group, and there was a little porch out there in the old meeting place on Sullivan Street, and ***after*** the meeting I went out on the steps for some air.(p.321)
• I started my drinking nearly thirty years ago – right ***after*** I was married.(p.322)
• Until I took Social Security and a pension at the age of sixty-eight, ***after*** forty years in motion-picture-studio public relations, I had successfully hidden even any hints of approaching alcoholism.(p.327)
• ***After*** such often-painful vigilance (and numerous phony stints of abstinence), retirement naturally created an impulse to live without restraints.(p.328)
• Even obvious intoxication is excused by younger people as something "he's earned the right to do," and they say, "***After*** all, who's he hurting?"(p.330)
• He may even read in a newspaper that one out of every seven drinkers will become alcoholic, but he rarely is told that it holds true for all ages – or that the tolerance to alcohol (and other drugs) decreases steadily, year ***after*** year, in the bodies of all persons.(p.330)
• Best that they not be found ***after*** I'd had my last drink on earth.(p.333)
• Toward five o'clock, helter-skelter, I'd get everything put away and try to get supper on the table, and ***after*** supper I'd finish the job up and knock myself out.(p.337)
• I just wanted to live to a certain age, carry through with what I felt was my job with the children, and ***after*** that – no matter.(p.337)
• And that came ***after*** a three-weeks' illness of my son.(p.338)
• ***After*** that I sat for a week, a body in a chair, a mind off in space.(p.338)
• I had always hated beer, but now I grew to love it, bottle ***after*** bottle of it, warm or cold.(p.339)
• ***After*** training, I was commissioned as a first lieutenant.(p.342)
• ***After*** my wife had read this to me, I said to her, as I had said many times in desperation, "I have got to do something."(p.346)
• So, ***after*** taking the first half of the First Step, and very gingerly admitting myself to Alcoholics Anonymous, something happened.(p.349)
• I was sitting in my office one time ***after*** I had operated on a woman.(p.350)
• Shortly ***after*** I was starting to work on the program I realized that I was not a good father; I wasn't a good husband, but, oh, I was a good provider.(p.351)
• But I remembered that every night ***after*** dinner my wife would get up and do the dishes.(p.351)
• ***After*** several months of acquaintance I asked her to marry me, but was politely refused.(p.359)
• ***After*** all -- wasn't I entitled to it?(p.360)
• Time ***after*** time I would beg forgiveness on bended knees, with tears rolling down my cheeks, and promise I would never again drink too much.(p.362)
• ***After*** another of my "never again episodes" she packed up and left for her parents' home in Florida.(p.362)
• ***After*** a few meetings I decided to drive to Florida unannounced to see my wife and tell her about my new found friends and association.(p.364)
• I said I was okay, but if it would make her feel better I would go "as tired as I was ***after*** the strenuous holidays."(p.365)
• ***After*** his death, my mother soon picked up drinking where Dad left off, and in a very short time she died of cirrhosis of the liver.(p.370)
• Very soon ***after*** I lost Mother, my five-year-old little girl was killed by a neighbor's car.(p.370)
• A few months ***after*** that, I was released and left the world of insanity, only to return to the world of alcoholic insanity.(p.370)
• One night, a few weeks ***after*** joining the Fellowship, much to my surprise and delight I saw a familiar but no longer frowning face.(p.371)
• I did work of all kinds ***after*** school and during vacations, trying to find that which would appeal most as a goal for a life work.(p.373)
• Then there was wartime service to interrupt my plans, and an education to be picked up ***after*** the war.(p.373)
• ***After*** that came marriage, getting started in business, and a family.(p.373)
• My drinking did not start until ***after*** I was thirty-five, and a fairly successful career had been established.(p.374)
• We had always encouraged our children to bring their friends home at any time, but ***after*** a few experiences with a drunken father they eliminated home as a place to entertain friends.(p.376)
• ***After*** every cocktail party or dinner party she would say she couldn't understand how I could get in such a drunken stupor on one drink.(p.377)
• She of course didn't realize how cunning an alcoholic can be and the lengths to which he will go in finding ways to satisfy the compulsion for more and more drinks ***after*** having had the first one.(p.377)
• However, ***after*** I heard a few stories of jails, sanitariums, broken homes and skid row, I wondered if I really was an alcoholic.(p.378)
• ***After*** all, I hadn't started to drink early in life, so I had some stability and maturity to guide me for a while.(p.379)
• Meetings are both relaxing and refreshing to me ***after*** a hard day.(p.381)
• We always had cordials ***after*** dinner and I know my sister and my brother and I loved creme de menthe.(p.384)
• It was really medicinal that night, that whiskey, and it was a medication ***after*** that.(p.386)
• For some reason I can't remember, it finally dawned on me that I had a problem, and yet nobody was very critical about it except my family, and that was only because I decided, ***after*** seven years of marriage, that I would divorce my husband.(p.386)
• Frank, my husband, would come home day ***after*** day and find me passed out.(p.386)

• He asked if I would cooperate with him ***after*** I went home, and if I would have a trained nurse stay with me for at least two weeks.(p.387)
• About this time, at Christmas, ***after*** being under this doctor's care, we decided that there wasn't anything more to do.(p.388)
• Anyhow, ***after*** Christmas my husband gave me a cocker spaniel who is, I think, just as notorious in A.A. as I am.(p.388)
• One afternoon, the year ***after*** moving to Houston, I got as drunk as a skunk, and while I do not walk very straight sober, you should see me when I'm drunk!(p.390)
• ***After*** all, upon coming out of a week-long or ten-day drunk, it was hard enough to figure up just how much that one drunk cost, let alone trying to calculate the cost of approximately twenty-five years of active alcoholism.(p.396)
• ***After*** a few more estimates as to income and expenditures for booze over a few sample years, taken at random, I conclude that this twenty per cent stayed fairly constant.(p.398)
• For an estimate of salary from the twenty-one a month to start with, to over $400 per month upon my retirement ***after*** twenty years in the Navy, I believe that an average income of $2,000 a year over this period is low, but as I stated earlier, an underestimate is best.(p.399)
• ***After*** eight months, the family found me.(p.401)
• I saw him recently and he told me that he had always felt guilty, because, ***after*** our separation, I had become a serious alcoholic.(p.403)
• Couldn't I stop, ***after*** a few?(p.404)
• I returned from Europe a while ***after*** that encounter, and I never went back.(p.406)
• Other girls whom I had known all my life asked for one weak scotch ***after*** dinner.(p.406)
• For, ***after*** those daily self-punishing sessions with myself, ***after*** the vows to stop, I would change entirely as evening came on.(p.408)
• But I was not able to make use of this knowledge until ***after*** I became sober.(p.409)
• And again these were things that I really profited by ***after*** I sobered up.(p.409)
• It was I who had to tell the bank, ***after*** a certain time, to refuse all further deposits.(p.409)
• I think now that a God, in whom I did not believe, was looking ***after*** me.(p.412)
• Something in the book had reached me ***after*** all.(p.412)
• Since they could do nothing with Anne either, Priscilla suggested that I go and look ***after*** Anne.(p.414)
• ***After*** I came to A.A., I was divorced by my wife; I lost my practice; I was legally restrained from seeing my children; I went broke; and the dental society threatened me with the loss of my license.(p.420)
• The other kids would light out for the hamburger huts or ice cream parlors, the pizza joints or bowling alleys, ***after*** football games and dances.(p.423)
• I got a job ***after*** school pumping gas and worked until ten or eleven at night.(p.423)
• But my dad pulled some strings and got in to see me ***after*** three weeks.(p.425)
• I spent eighteen hundred dollars fixing up that car in the first year I was home, ***after*** four bad smash-ups.(p.429)
• A week ***after*** my decision to join A.A., she called it quits.(p.430)
• ***After*** a day or two of grovelling remorse I'd come up with an explanation.(p.433)
• ***After*** a month it seemed unlikely that it ever really happened.(p.433)
• ***After*** three months it was forgotten.(p.434)
• ***After*** a particularly ugly one-nighter, my wife suggested I try it, and I agreed.(p.434)
• ***After*** my last binge I came home and smashed my dining room furniture to splinters, kicked out six windows and two balustrades.(p.435)
• ***After*** talking with him for a time I heard myself saying, "Doc, I think I'm an alcoholic."(p.436)
• The most terrible blow of my life befell me ***after*** I'd found sobriety through A.A.(p.437)
• ***After*** going to school all day, working in the family drugstore all evening, and then studying until one or two in the morning, I would not be able to sleep soundly, with everything I had been studying going round in my head.(p.440)
• My drinking took place ***after*** work hours.(p.441)
• If it was one minute ***after***, I'd stay up and act like a martyr all day.(p.441)
• ***After*** nine days of tests at Mayo, I was put in the locked ward -- of all places!(p.444)
• Max accepted responsibility for me ***after*** I had promised never to drink again, never to take another pill, never to swear again, and never to talk to girls again.(p.444)
• But it quickly became obvious that he had this childish notion instead: If he could get me to go to enough meetings while in the hospital, I would continue to go ***after*** he let me out.(p.447)
• Finally ***after*** seven months, I decided to try it.(p.448)
• ***After*** I had been around A.A. for seven months, tapering off alcohol and pills, not finding the program working very well, I was finally able to say, "Okay, God.(p.448)
• ***After*** all, it was self (you, me) that stood in our own way, that ran the show and ran ourselves into bankruptcy, that hurt the ones we loved.(p.459)
• Three weeks ***after*** an armed robbery in which one person received a superficial flesh wound (I could have killed someone!), I was apprehended.(p.460)
• During the twenty-four hours ***after*** running into the Serenity Prayer, I think I took the first three Steps for the first time.(p.461)
• ***After*** nine months of training, all the rest of my class was paroled and I went to work in the Department of Corrections.(p.462)
• ***After*** a few months there, I went to County Mental Health as an alcoholism worker.(p.462)
• ***After*** a while I really did enjoy drinking and what it did to me, and I became dependent upon it for every occasion.(p.464)
• On the day set for the extractions, on my way to the dentist's I felt a little nervous, so I had a couple of drinks, and ***after*** the teeth were out I was very nervous, so I had a few more.(p.466)
• Instead, I started going to a nice private sanitarium which, ***after*** the first visit, turned out to be more like a country club than anything else.(p.468)
• ***After*** the first two or three days you were allowed the run of the place and it was a lot of fun.(p.468)
• Also, ***after*** that first visit I learned I could refuse to sign myself in unless they gave me a glass of whiskey in one hand and a glass of paraldehyde in the other.(p.468)
• In the light of subsequent events it became evident that I took their advice far too literally, for, ***after*** some months of happy sobriety I drank again.(p.471)
• And when she broke a luncheon date with me one Saturday, ***after*** I had been in A.A. for about three months, I said, "I'll show her!(p.472)
• ***After*** six months, we move to Bridgeport, Conn.(p.476)
• ***After*** all, I had been working for eighteen years, slinging hash, and I was managing.(p.478)
• That was enough provocation to fight but I didn't fight, and I realized ***after*** recess why I didn't.(p.484)
• My mother resented it so that the first Christmas ***after*** our marriage, she didn't even invite us to dinner.(p.485)
• ***After*** our first child came my parents both became allies, but in later days, ***after*** I became an alcoholic, they both turned against me.(p.485)
• That went on for maybe two months, and then she got ***after*** me again about drinking.(p.488)
• ***After*** this incident in 1940, I sought some other means of livelihood.(p.489)
• But I found that ***after*** I got to North Carolina it wasn't any different.(p.490)
• The November following, I took a few days off ***after*** pay day to celebrate my birthday on the 25th of the month.(p.491)
• Anyhow, on the 24th, ***after*** drinking all day on the 23rd, I must have decided I wanted to see my wife and have some kind of reconciliation or at least talk with her.(p.491)
• I remember talking to her, but what happened ***after*** that I don't know.(p.492)
• ***After*** the trial, I got big-hearted again and felt that I should do something in payment for Vi's kindness to me; so I left Washington and went to Seattle to work.(p.492)
• I think the thing that galled me was that just ***after*** Easter I had drawn my salary for two weeks' work and had decided that I was going to send some money to Vi; and above all else I was going to send my baby daughter an Easter outfit.(p.493)
• ***After*** he'd talked half an hour, I still wanted him to hurry up and get out so I could go and get some whiskey before the liquor store closed.(p.494)
• ***After*** Charlie had talked a while, I knew that this man had something.(p.495)
• This wasn't so bad ***after*** all.(p.498)
• I'd drink like a gentleman ***after*** this.(p.498)
• She had looked for me last evening ***after*** I left the car and wandered off into the night.(p.502)
• I shall learn this ***after*** some more explosions.(p.506)
• ***After*** twenty years in prison for murder, he knew A.A. was the spot for him . . . if he wanted to stay on the outside.(p.508)
• I began drinking as a kid, shortly ***after*** I reached my fourteenth birthday.(p.508)
• ***After*** hearing the first speaker I could tell myself that my own lot was rather mild.(p.509)
• ***After*** the meeting was over and we had returned to the cell block again, I was asked how I was impressed.(p.510)
• I clung to the outfit for the balance of my time, and finally I was released, ***after*** having spent twenty years and nine months behind bars.(p.510)
• But ***after*** I passed through the gates I took a change of heart and mind.(p.510)
• ***After*** I had made my third report, I stepped down town, met some of the old crowd, and of course you know the answer.(p.510)
• I had a rough lot, but I don't worry about that, ***after*** hearing the stories of many others.(p.511)
• ***After*** I came in I found I wasn't an exceptional drunk.(p.512)
• One morning I didn't wake up until ***after*** four o'clock.(p.515)
• I buttonholed him ***after*** dinner and gave him a few tips on how to run his colony better and the result of that was about a fortnight or so later I was shipped back to my regiment.(p.520)
• I was there for another couple of months and then, ***after*** a few more adventures in the East, I was shipped home.(p.521)
• About three months ***after*** that, my record reached home and I got a letter telling me I was retired from the Army, they put it very kindly, on medical grounds.(p.521)
• My mother lived on for five years ***after*** I joined A.A., the last two in complete blindness.(p.525)
• ***After*** a while, I found that the psycho ward was a good place to hide when I had taken something stolen to the pawnshop.(p.528)
• I know there are some alcoholics who seem terribly, terribly grown-up, but I think that they are trying to make themselves think they are grown-up, and the strain of their effort is what is causing them to drink -- a sense of inadequacy, a childish vanity to be the most popular, the most sought ***after***, the mostest of the most.(p.535)
• ***After*** nearly eight years of sobriety in A.A., I still can set down such thoughts, "against my instinct and training," showing that I still consider myself a "special" person, entitled to special privileges.(p.536)
• I'd visit one bar ***after*** another, having one martini in each, and in each hoping to find someone interesting to talk to.(p.536)
• Still another friend and temporary host received me at four in the morning from the charge of a policeman who had found me "going to bed" in a garage far from the last place I could remember having been, a fashionable bar and restaurant in the theatrical district of New York, to which I had repaired ***after*** my date for that evening, a charming lady of the theatre who had refused my company for obvious reasons.(p.538)
• I fled, finally, ***after*** having been fired from my job by a boss who wept a little (since I had worked hard) as he gave notice for me to clear out.(p.539)
• I left this home town, then, ***after*** I had made a public spectacle of myself in the presence of a revered teacher whose favorite pupil I had been.(p.539)
• I thought that life was a pretty simple thing; you simply made a plan for your life, based upon what you wanted, and then you needed only the courage to go ***after*** it.(p.545)
• I wasn't afraid of anything or anybody ***after*** I learned about drinking, for it seemed right from the beginning that with liquor I could always retire to my little private world where nobody could get at me to hurt me.(p.547)
• This caused the rather cryptic comment from one of my A.A. friends, when I told my story ***after*** coming into the program, that I had always been a cinch for the program, for I had always been interested in mankind, but that I was just taking them one man at a time.(p.548)
• ***After*** my very first drink -- a tiny glass of sherry my father gave me to celebrate the New Year when I was thirteen -- I went up to bed, dizzy with exhilaration and excitement, and I prayed I wouldn't drink any more!(p.554)
• I also began visiting bars ***after*** work, with my older associates.(p.555)
• So, when my liver had recovered ***after*** ten months, I resumed drinking.(p.557)

aftermath

• Curious about it, feeling I was missing something, absolutely without any illusions about the ***aftermath***,

with no pronounced feeling of patriotism, I joined up with a Canadian regiment, serving a little over two years.(p.253)
• During the years 1930 to 1935, due to the Depression and its ***aftermath***, business went from bad to worse.(p.486)

afternoon

• One dismal ***afternoon*** he paced a hotel lobby wondering how his bill was to be paid.(p.154)
• That ***afternoon*** he put on his clothes and walked from the hospital a free man.(p.158)
• If my wife was planning to go out in the ***afternoon***, I would get a large supply of liquor and smuggle it home and hide it in the coal bin, the clothes chute, over door jambs, over beams in the cellar and in cracks in the cellar tile.(p.176)
• About this time a lady called up my wife one Saturday ***afternoon***, saying she wanted me to come over that evening to meet a friend of hers who might help me.(p.179)
• That was at three-thirty in the ***afternoon***.(p.201)
• My wife didn't tell me this, but one Sunday ***afternoon*** when Mary was trying to get the cobwebs out of my mind, Clarence and his sister-in-law, the hairdresser, called at the house.(p.216)
• I left on a Wednesday ***afternoon***, had dinner in Akron and then went to a house where I encountered my first meeting.(p.218)
• The ***afternoon*** that I was to leave the hospital, he came in to see me and asked me if I were willing to attempt to follow the program.(p.218)
• I had no desire whatever to sit down at a table and stay a whole morning or ***afternoon*** drinking.(p.231)
• I had repaired to one of these one morning with my jug and when I left late in the ***afternoon***, I picked up a newspaper on the way home.(p.244)
• One Sunday ***afternoon***, the only time I ever got picked up for drunken driving, I got picked up in Bellaire.(p.264)
• (Russ was buried on Friday, and on Sunday ***afternoon*** Hilda S. had invited me there to dinner Sunday night, and I didn't think I could do it.(p.272)
• Almost simultaneously, I discovered that cocktails in the late ***afternoon*** and highballs in the evening relieved the many tensions of the day.(p.277)
• The next ***afternoon*** and evening, two other men visited me and each told me his story and the things that they were doing to try to recover from this tragic illness.(p.290)
• The day before I was due to go back to Chicago, a Wednesday and Dr. Bob's ***afternoon*** off, he had me down to the office and we spent three or four hours formally going through the Six-Step program as it was at that time.(p.291)
• I was accused of it many times when I went to play bridge in the ***afternoon***, but I really never did take a morning drink.(p.323)
• But from one or two drinks of an ***afternoon*** or evening, my intake mounted, and mounted fast.(p.336)
• One ***afternoon***, the year after moving to Houston, I got as drunk as a skunk, and while I do not walk very straight sober, you should see me when I'm drunk!(p.390)
• I was just as drunk as I could be, getting ready to take an ***afternoon*** walk.(p.390)
• By two-thirty in the ***afternoon*** I was always tight.(p.404)
• All ***afternoon*** I sat there and drank and played Bing Crosby's recording of "Silent Night" over and over again on the juke box.(p.467)

afternoons

• I had a crew of men working there and I wanted them to work Sunday ***afternoons*** so that I could sell lots on Sunday.(p.195)

afterward

• Shortly ***afterward*** I came home drunk.(p.5)
• ***Afterward***, we found ourselves accepting many things which then seemed entirely out of reach.(p.47)
• THE FAMILY ***AFTERWARD***(p.122)
• Their services are often indispensable in treating a newcomer and in following his case ***afterward***.(p.133)
• Not long ***afterward*** he had called me from Hartford on two successive days, so drunk he could hardly speak.(p.136)
• ***Afterward***, his revulsion will be terrible.(p.141)
• They were willing, by day or night, to place a new man in the hospital and visit him ***afterward***.(p.159)
• I had a couple of shorter talks with this man ***afterward***, and stopped drinking abruptly.(p.179)
• Formerly, in the acute mental and physical pain during the remorseful periods succeeding each drunk, I found my recollection of the misery I had gone through a bolsterer of resolution and ***afterward***, perhaps, a deterrent for a time.(p.260)
• But individual welfare follows close ***afterward***.(p.565)

afterwards

• (I knew ***afterwards*** that the two who came in were Bill W. and Doctor Bob.)(p.185)
• That is where I had my first drink and I still remember it, for every "first" drink ***afterwards*** did exactly the same trick -- I could feel it go right through every bit of my body and down to my very toes.(p.241)
• We talked about it ***afterwards***, and we felt that there might be some time we'd need it.(p.266)
• What happened ***afterwards*** I don't know.(p.468)
• There was nothing in my school life that I can look back on which was responsible for anything that happened ***afterwards***.(p.517)

again

• The broker had gone to Akron on a business venture which had collapsed, leaving him greatly in fear that he might start drinking ***again***.(p.xvi)
• He sobered, never to drink ***again*** up to the moment of his death in 1950.(p.xvi)
• News of this got on the world wires; inquiries poured in ***again*** and many people went to the bookstores to get the book "Alcoholics Anonymous."(p.xviii)
• They are restless, irritable and discontented, unless they can ***again*** experience the sense of ease and comfort which comes at once by taking a few drinks -- drinks which they see others taking with impunity.(p.xxvi)
• After they have succumbed to the desire ***again***, as so many do, and the phenomenon of craving develops, they pass through the well-known stages of a spree, emerging remorseful, with a firm resolution not to drink ***again***.(p.xxvii)
• I was very lonely and ***again*** turned to alcohol.(p.1)
• But drinking caught up with me ***again*** and my generous friend had to let me go.(p.4)
• Renewing my resolve, I tried ***again***.(p.5)
• A morning paper told me the market had gone to hell ***again***.(p.6)
• ***Again*** I swayed dizzily before an open window, or the medicine cabinet where there was poison, cursing myself for a weakling.(p.6)
• Then came the insidious insanity of that first drink, and on Armistice Day 1935, I was off ***again***.(p.8)
• That war-time day in old Winchester Cathedral came back ***again***.(p.10)
• If he did not work, he would surely drink ***again***, and if he drank, he would surely die.(p.15)
• After such an approach many take up their beds and walk ***again***.(p.19)
• "The doctor told him that if he ever drank ***again*** it would kill him, but there he is all lit up ***again***."(p.20)
• Then comes the day when he simply cannot make it and gets drunk all over ***again***.(p.22)
• How often have some of us begun to drink in this nonchalant way, and after the third or fourth, pounded on the bar and said to ourselves, "For God's sake, how did I ever get started ***again***?"(p.24)
• We have seen the truth demonstrated ***again*** and ***again***: "Once an alcoholic, always an alcoholic."(p.33)
• In the early days of our drinking we occasionally remained sober for a year or more, becoming serious drinkers ***again*** later.(p.34)
• Yet he got drunk ***again***.(p.36)
• Presently he is hit ***again*** and this time has a fractured skull.(p.38)
• We admit we have some of these symptoms, but we have not gone to the extremes you fellows did, nor are we likely to, for we understand ourselves so well after what you have told us that such things cannot happen ***again***.(p.38)
• Let him tell you about it: "I was much impressed with what you fellows said about alcoholism, and I frankly did not believe it would be possible for me to drink ***again***.(p.40)
• I now remembered what my alcoholic friends had told me, how they prophesied that if I had an alcoholic mind, the time and place would come -- I would drink ***again***.(p.41)
• The insanity of alcohol returns and we drink ***again***.(p.66)
• Referring to our list ***again***.(p.67)
• In this book you read ***again*** and ***again*** that faith did for us what we could not do for ourselves.(p.70)
• He saw that he had to place the outcome in God's hands or he would soon start drinking ***again***, and all would be lost anyhow.(p.80)
• Make it clear that he is not under pressure, that he needn't see you ***again*** if he doesn't want to.(p.94)
• If he is sincerely interested and wants to see you ***again***, ask him to read this book in the interval.(p.95)
• Search out another alcoholic and try ***again***.(p.96)
• Don't start to withdraw ***again*** just because your friends drink liquor.(p.102)
• Next day they would be themselves ***again*** and we would forgive and try to forget.(p.106)
• Asked why they commenced to drink ***again***, they would reply with some silly excuse, or none.(p.107)
• Why was it, when these dangers were pointed out that they agreed, and then got drunk ***again*** immediately?(p.107)
• ***Again***, you should not crowd him.(p.113)
• Ask him what you should do if he places you in such a position ***again***.(p.116)
• Should it happen ***again***, regard it in a different light.(p.116)
• Perhaps he will never have much money ***again***.(p.123)
• He will be less likely to drink ***again***, and anything is preferable to that.(p.130)
• Father, coming suddenly to life ***again***, often begins to assert himself.(p.131)
• If he temporizes and still thinks he can ever drink ***again***, even beer, he might as well be discharged after the next bender which, if an alcoholic, he is almost certain to have.(p.142)
• He will presently try the old game ***again***, for he isn't happy about his sobriety.(p.152)
• ***Again*** it was the old, insidious insanity -- that first drink.(p.154)
• He never drank ***again***.(p.158)
• When a few men in this city have found themselves, and have discovered the joy of helping others to face life ***again***, there will be no stopping until everyone in that town has had his opportunity to recover -- if he can and will.(p.163)
• Those who believe their drinking to be hopeless may ***again*** find hope in these thirteen impressive tales.(p.167)
• This had the effect of making me resolve that when I was free from parental domination, I would never ***again*** darken the doors of a church.(p.172)
• I think I must have been thoroughly scared by what had happened, or by the doctor, or probably both, so that I did not touch a drink ***again*** until the country went dry.(p.175)
• The next day she called ***again***.(p.179)
• I got tight that night, stayed sober Monday till after the dinner and then proceeded to get tight ***again***.(p.179)
• Each of the seven times that I had left this hospital in the last six months, I had come out fully determined in my own mind that I would not get drunk ***again*** -- for at least six or eight months.(p.184)
• Wouldn't you like to see us ***again***?"(p.189)
• Bill D. walked out of that hospital a free man never to drink ***again***.(p.189)
• I have already done it, and I am willing to do it ***again*** here in the presence of you or I am willing to say it any place, anywhere in the world from now on and not be ashamed of it."(p.190)
• I kept watching the man down the bar to see what he did with a contraption like that, and he just smelled of his drink and set it down ***again***, so I did the same.(p.195)
• I can remember well thinking that I would quit drinking, really go to work hard, apply myself eight hours a day, five days a week, make a lot of money, and then I could start drinking ***again***.(p.199)
• So I was driving to Cleveland when I made this solemn promise never to drink ***again***.(p.201)
• And I continued to drink, on and off then, until every dollar I had in the world was gone ***again*** and I was right back living at my sister's, getting my cigarettes by calling her grocer and telling him to put in a couple of cartons with her order, exactly as I had before I started to work at Max's.(p.202)
• Then I started drinking ***again***, with possibly a little more restraint, periods a little bit longer than they had been before, but substantially the same pattern.(p.203)
• Bill left me at the elevator and said, "Your room is so and so," and I didn't see him ***again*** for six months.(p.217)
• And I remembered the creeping horror of the interminable night, in which I slept for short spells and woke up dripping with cold sweat and shaken with utter despair, to drink hastily from my bottle and mercifully pass out ***again***, "You're mad, you're mad, you're mad!" pounded through my brain with each returning ray of consciousness, and I drowned the refrain with drink.(p.224)
• When my doctor told me I should never touch a drink ***again***, I couldn't afford to believe him.(p.226)
• The fact that I can work ***again*** and earn my living, is important, but secondary.(p.229)
• Searching where I have been at fault, it is not hard to discover and get right ***again***, for I have proven to

myself and to many others who know me that God can keep a man sober if he will let Him.(p.237)
• Then I turned two company cars over in a short time and Bingo – fired ***again***.(p.242)
• He had also gone all the way through the wringer and had been dry two years when I saw him ***again***.(p.243)
• No one in that company saw me ***again*** – ten days later I wired my resignation.(p.243)
• As long as things were tough and the job a challenge I could always manage to hold on pretty well, but as soon as I learned the combination, got the puzzle under control and the boss to pat me on the back, I was gone ***again***.(p.243)
• Then broke ***again***, hiding out in cheap hotels all over the country, one night jail stands here and there, and always that horrible feeling "What's the use -- nothing is worth while."(p.244)
• Many alcoholics have learned they can bring their bottle to a cheap movie theater and drink, sleep, wake up and drink ***again*** in the darkness.(p.244)
• For the last two years of my drinking I prayed on every drunk that I wouldn't wake up ***again***.(p.245)
• Despite all this, I did like these new friends because, ***again***, they were like me.(p.245)
• I never saw either of them ***again***.(p.247)
• Once ***again***, there was the challenge of a tough job, but this time I was determined to follow through.(p.248)
• I wanted to roam ***again*** and through relatives got a supercargo job on an Australian packet which allowed me to visit my people in Australia where I was born.(p.252)
• In my mind's eye I saw Broadway ***again*** and Tom Sharkey's bar; the roar of the subway was in my ears.(p.252)
• ***Again*** I spent my bankroll, by no means as thick as the one I had when I first saw the skyline of Gotham.(p.252)
• I ***again*** became a reporter on a Pittsburgh daily.(p.254)
• The strain of overwork led me to the bottle ***again***.(p.254)
• As soon as I could get up and walk I started to drink ***again*** and kept it up until my friend of the hospital, who, in his first try at the new way of life had stubbed his toe in Chicago but had come back to the town to take counsel and make a new start, picked me up and got me into a hospital.(p.258)
• He told me that he would never drink ***again***.(p.263)
• Right away, I saw it was the same outfit this other guy told me about, and then ***again*** hope died.(p.267)
• He said, "Let's put the Big Book away ***again***, and when you read it ***again***, turn to the back and read some of the stories.(p.269)
• When we went to bed my sides ached, and I said to my husband, "I thought I would never laugh ***again***, but I have laughed."(p.269)
• He wants to go to the hospital, and I'm not paying for the hospital ***again***!"(p.271)
• I sat down on the side of one of their beds, and I started to weep, and I couldn't stop, and I was so startled, and I apologized ***again*** and ***again*** for it.(p.272)
• Dr. Bob dwelt at length on how prayer had given him release, time and time ***again***, from the nearly over-powering compulsion to take a drink.(p.279)
• During my first few months in Akron I was quite sure that I never wanted to see my home town ***again***.(p.281)
• The most accurate answer I can give you is this: Fear has never ***again*** ruled my life since that day in September, 1938, when I found that a Power greater than myself could not only restore me to sanity but could keep me both sober and sane.(p.285)
• Home life was ***again*** a restraining influence.(p.287)
• After a particularly bad Christmas and New Year's holiday, dad picked me up ***again*** early in January, 1937, to go through the usual sobering up routine.(p.289)
• Several months later dad was back in Chicago to pick me up ***again***, but this time my attitude was entirely different.(p.289)
• He was happy, getting a kick out of life and people, and beginning to get his medical practice back ***again***.(p.290)
• It wasn't necessary to report to the office in person every day, and when I did go in, it was just to make an appearance and bounce right out ***again***.(p.300)
• I had never seen him before, and at the time hoped I would never see him ***again***.(p.302)
• Perhaps I could find freedom and peace and be able once ***again*** to call my soul my own.(p.309)
• That ache is gone and never need return ***again***.(p.312)
• I halfway washed them, and he told me to do them ***again***, and I did, and he yelled at me to do them ***again***, and I picked up one of the cans and threw it at him and told him to do them himself.(p.317)
• When I came home ***again***, the only thing I had left to love was the bottle.(p.318)
• Once I did have a slip – tried drinking ***again*** -- but the A.A.'s tell me not to worry about yesterday, because nobody can change it, and not to worry about tomorrow, because it hasn't come yet.(p.320)
• Sometimes I would lie on the bathroom floor, deathly sick, praying I would die, and praying to God as I always had prayed to Him when I was drinking: "Dear God, get me out of this one and I'll never do it ***again***."(p.324)
• I'd get so fed up with drinking all alone and bearing the burden of guilt all by myself, that I'd egg him on to drink, to get started ***again***.(p.325)
• And the whole merry-go-round would be on ***again***.(p.325)
• I vowed that never ***again*** would any important person whom I wished to please and impress ever see me drunk.(p.328)
• "I'll Never Smile ***Again***" – how perfect.(p.332)
• They described what had happened when they went out and tried drinking ***again***, and I knew they were sincere in saying that it could happen to me.(p.334)
• Because it was only through feeling defeat and feeling failure, the inability to cope with my life and with alcohol, that I was able to surrender and accept the fact that I had this disease, and that I had to learn to live ***again*** without alcohol.(p.335)
• I had to give him a story and ask him the same question over and over ***again***, "Well, now, how many will that bottle serve?"(p.336)
• I went to my doctor ***again***.(p.339)
• However, I am an alcoholic, so I always looked forward to the day when I would be able to drink ***again***.(p.343)
• During the next three years, I tried often ***again*** to give it up, but failed miserably.(p.343)
• Studied the Big Book ***again***.(p.344)
• And the first thing you know I was lifted right out of the A.A. group, and I floated higher, and higher, and even higher, until I was way up on a pink cloud which is known as Pink Seven, and I felt miserable ***again***.(p.348)
• I would do it ***again***.(p.349)
• Once ***again*** I asked my girl to marry me and join me in this new venture.(p.359)
• Once ***again*** I was back in the big time operations, and along with them, big shot complexes.(p.361)
• Time after time I would beg forgiveness on bended knees, with tears rolling down my cheeks, and promise I would never ***again*** drink too much.(p.362)
• After another of my "never ***again*** episodes" she packed up and left for her parents' home in Florida.(p.362)
• I began hitting the bottle ***again***, and with it self-pity, resentment, loneliness and remorse set in deeply.(p.362)
• I was scared – would she leave me ***again***?(p.365)
• His enthusiasm and keen interest in A.A. fired my spirits ***again***.(p.365)
• With that utterance I ***again*** made a wonderful discovery.(p.366)
• My mother said so, ***again*** and ***again***.(p.369)
• I promised, but within two months, I began ***again***.(p.377)
• ***Again*** I promised to do something about it.(p.377)
• I wanted to do it all over ***again***.(p.386)
• That went on for about three years, and then we moved back to Texas ***again***.(p.386)
• I don't want anybody ever to look at me like that ***again***.(p.391)
• In spite of knowing that my drunkenness was a symptom of the things that were wrong with me, and that I could never drink ***again***, I thought I couldn't yet give it up, although I was going to try.(p.393)
• When I was a baby, my mother brought me to America, and I never ***again*** saw my father.(p.401)
• But ***again***, the living was easy.(p.401)
• Responsibility ***again***.(p.402)
• During this period I married ***again***.(p.405)
• I was going to get drunk ***again*** -- Drunk!(p.408)
• And ***again*** these were things that I really profited by after I sobered up.(p.409)
• GROWING UP ALL OVER ***AGAIN***(p.418)
• Most important, A.A. has enabled me to go back and start growing up all over ***again*** in all areas of my life.(p.420)
• I opened my eyes ***again*** and a shadow fell across the bed.(p.422)
• Back home ***again***!(p.424)
• It solved their problems and they started living a sane life ***again***.(p.427)
• I'd lost my car ***again***, pawned my wallet and all identification papers for a bottle, and gotten home somehow.(p.429)
• ***Again*** I went into a mild form of D.T.'s, but with no pineapples this time.(p.429)
• And I'd proved I couldn't handle it, time and ***again***.(p.429)
• Science could take my mind apart expertly, but it couldn't seem to put it together ***again***.(p.435)
• And should I have more bad times, I know that I'll never ***again*** have to go through them alone.(p.438)
• The longer the drinking continued, the shorter the time the alcohol would keep me asleep; I would have to drink myself back to sleep ***again*** and ***again*** throughout the night.(p.441)
• I'd think, "I wonder why I'm saying that ***again*** -- I've already said it three times."(p.442)
• Max accepted responsibility for me after I had promised never to drink ***again***, never to take another pill, never to swear ***again***, and never to talk to girls ***again***.(p.444)
• The girl had explained them to me four times, and I was too embarrassed to ask her ***again***.(p.445)
• I can ***again*** focus on my wife's good qualities and watch them grow and grow and grow.(p.451)
• There, I received several soda crackers and water daily, and before I could have my third-day meal (***again*** the only meal in ten days), I had to drink a glass of castor oil or mineral oil, depending on the cruelty of the person who was doing the dispensing.(p.459)
• If I failed, they would throw away the key, and I would never get out ***again***.(p.461)
• I thought I would be quite happy and never would I drink too much ***again***.(p.465)
• I remember vaguely violent quarrels with my husband, his finding my liquor supply time and time ***again*** and throwing it out.(p.466)
• He said he was finally and completely through -- that he never wanted to see me ***again***.(p.467)
• All afternoon I sat there and drank and played Bing Crosby's recording of "Silent Night" over and over ***again*** on the juke box.(p.467)
• And then I went back home to live with my parents, and the merry-go-round started ***again*** -- only this time I didn't have to worry about waking up behind bars in a psychiatric ward.(p.468)
• In the light of subsequent events it became evident that I took their advice far too literally, for, after some months of happy sobriety I drank ***again***.(p.471)
• But more important, I would have found that once ***again*** I was sitting in the driver's seat – I was running the show.(p.471)
• The Higher Power to whom I had turned, and who had sustained me, had once ***again*** been thrust into the background, while my emotions were running my life and, as always, my emotions ran me to the bottle.(p.472)
• I get arrested ***again***.(p.475)
• Then I drink ***again***, but more miserable.(p.475)
• He said he never wanted to set foot in the deep south ***again*** and he didn't.(p.486)
• That went on for maybe two months, and then she got after me ***again*** about drinking.(p.488)
• After the trial, I got big-hearted ***again*** and felt that I should do something in payment for Vi's kindness to me; so I left Washington and went to Seattle to work.(p.492)
• The indescribable torture has me ***again***.(p.501)
• I am home ***again***.(p.505)
• I am quiet ***again***.(p.505)
• I am blue ***again***.(p.506)
• After the meeting was over and we had returned to the cell block ***again***, I was asked how I was impressed.(p.510)
• However, my two friends kept coaxing and cajoling to get me back ***again***.(p.510)
• She asked me, was I going to do this to her all over ***again***?(p.510)
• Then instead of going out with A.A. ***again*** I went out with some of the other crowd, and off ***again*** I went.(p.511)
• And I was off ***again***.(p.514)
• Then I went over ***again*** to Germany for four years on an occupation job.(p.519)
• I was up to international standards in one particular game, and that ***again*** covered quite a lot of my sins.(p.519)
• I was lucky ***again***.(p.520)
• Then Hitler's war broke out, and ***again***, I was given a really important job on the Suez Canal,

dealing with military shipping.(p.520)
• At the end of that time, they shipped me back to my regiment *again*.(p.520)
• I stayed there just long enough to work up a real good resentment against the doctor in charge, who I didn't think was doing anything at all except collecting fees, and I left there fully determined that I'd never put myself in the power of medical people *again*.(p.521)
• I stopped off just to have one drink to see if it tasted the same on the way back to London, and that night I was carried back to bed *again*.(p.522)
• I was intensely unhappy the whole time, but I didn't seem to be able to do anything about it, and the worst part to me was the realization that all this was going to happen *again* and *again* until I died.(p.522)
• It was no use talking of putting myself into a home, a hospital, or of going to see a doctor *again*, or of going to see a priest or anyone else.(p.523)
• I suppose I had reached my spiritual gutter that night, but I have never had what you could call a real urge to drink *again*.(p.524)
• Since I joined on that April night, A.A. has done more for me than just stop me from drinking; it has brought me back to life *again*.(p.524)
• He said if I came back *again*, they would send me to the state hospital.(p.528)
• Since I've been home, I have been able to gain the respect of my two sons *again*.(p.529)
• The sacred word was broken and you never trusted your father *again*, and avoided him.(p.533)
• You were thirty-five before you understood your father's horrible anguish, and forgave him, and loved him *again*.(p.533)
• This question so insulted the emotions that clearly there was only one thing to do, go and get drunk *again*, and put that enquiring mind in its proper place, which was oblivion.(p.537)
• I went over and met him, and we two started the group up *again*.(p.541)
• I have had the joy of seeing many a human being, down and out, learn to stand straight *again*, and to proceed under his own power to happiness in life.(p.541)
• In A.A. we can begin *again* no matter how late it may be.(p.543)
• I have begun *again*.(p.543)
• That's what I am doing, living *again*, knowing what I know.(p.543)
• In time I concluded that the reason I was hurt was because I loved my parents, and I concluded too that if I never allowed myself to love anybody or anything I could never be hurt *again*.(p.545)
• I was married and divorced *again* before I was twenty-three years old, this time to a prominent band leader -- a man that many women wanted.(p.546)
• I thought this would give me ego-strength, make me feel wanted and secure, and alleviate my fears, but *again* nothing changed inside me.(p.546)
• So I married *again*.(p.548)
• "God willing, we . . . may never *again* have to deal with drinking, but we have to deal with sobriety every day."(p.554)
• As soon as I had made a few friends and had begun to feel accepted, we moved *again*.(p.555)
• Within two months, I was drinking *again*.(p.558)
• My company advanced me rapidly, once my reliability was established *again*.(p.559)
• God willing, we members of A.A. may never *again* have to deal with drinking, but we have to deal with sobriety every day.(p.560)
• Even among those who occasionally land back in here *again*, we observe a profound change in personality.(p.572)

against

• Because this book has become the basic text for our Society and has helped such large numbers of alcoholic men and women to recover, there exists a sentiment *against* any radical changes being made in it.(p.xi)
• When they talked of a God personal to me, who was love, superhuman strength and direction, I became irritated and my mind snapped shut *against* such a theory.(p.10)
• We are without defense *against* the first drink.(p.24)
• Not only had I been off guard, I had made no fight whatever *against* the first drink.(p.41)
• Once more: The alcoholic at certain times has no effective mental defense *against* the first drink.(p.43)
• At first some of us tried to avoid the issue, hoping *against* hope we were not true alcoholics.(p.44)
• Do not let any prejudice you may have *against* spiritual terms deter you from honestly asking yourself what they mean to you.(p.47)
• We, who have traveled this dubious path, beg you to lay aside prejudice, even *against* organized religion.(p.49)
• There is no use arousing any prejudice he may have *against* certain theological terms and conceptions about which he may already be confused.(p.93)
• You should warn *against* arousing resentment or jealousy.(p.100)
• Today's life is measured *against* that of other years and, when it falls short, the family may be unhappy.(p.123)
• 4.Because every time I do it I take out a little more insurance for myself *against* a possible slip.(p.181)
• "Who is convinced *against* his will is of the same opinion still."(p.193)
• My inability to accept the harsh realities of life had resulted in a disillusioned cynic, clothed in protective armor *against* the world's misunderstanding.(p.226)
• I had no resentments *against* individuals – the whole world was all wrong.(p.244)
• My loneliness was worse than it had ever been before, for now even my own kind had turned *against* me.(p.247)
• I feel that one of the things that I still have to guard *against* is that I used to be set in my way about what I considered the old-time A.A.(p.272)
• Everyone was *against* me -- I'd show them I didn't need them.(p.318)
• I got orders to go to Germany, and everyone in Germany was *against* me.(p.318)
• I can't afford resentments *against* anyone, because they are the build-up of another drunk.(p.325)
• Now, no longer under pressure, I could safely guard *against* loss of control.(p.327)
• The very person who stood with me through it all and has been my greatest help was the person that I turned *against*, my husband.(p.338)
• I also turned *against* my family, my mother.(p.338)
• In January 1938, I had the opportunity to go to northern Vermont to manage a small daytime radio station that was up *against* it financially, and was about to fold its antenna.(p.359)
• As I grow in A.A., I realize that a person with as much self-will as I had, as hard a head and as diseased an ego, had to try everything that I could think of, butting my head *against* every stone wall before I was ready to come in.(p.384)
• They phoned my husband that I was in jail and in such terrible shape that they didn't know what I would do to myself; and they realized that jail was no place for me, but that he was to wait a while before he got me, because at the time they called him to come over for me I was beating a tin cup *against* the wall.(p.390)
• Age and the law were still *against* me, but laws were not as strictly enforced in those days as they are now, and I discovered that as long as I had the green blood, there was always a way to get alcohol, either from a nondiscriminatory bartender or from an older friend who would be glad to purchase the joy juice for the privilege of sharing it.(p.397)
• All the statistics are *against* me.(p.420)
• So I raised enough fuss that they finally agreed to let me sign out, *against* medical advice.(p.444)
• *Against* my better judgment, I went to a meeting with him that night, and a strange thing began to happen.(p.446)
• I woke up in jail, sick, withdrawing from alcohol and speed, already a four-time loser, and now with a fifth felony charge *against* me.(p.460)
• After our first child came my parents both became allies, but in later days, after I became an alcoholic, they both turned *against* me.(p.485)
• I rebelled *against* this, because just about the time that I was getting ready to leave high school, a revelation came to me about God and it made things very complicated for me.(p.489)
• But I knew that they knew what the medical grounds were, and that they had put a big black mark *against* my name.(p.521)
• I stayed there just long enough to work up a real good resentment *against* the doctor in charge, who I didn't think was doing anything at all except collecting fees, and I left there fully determined that I'd never put myself in the power of medical people again.(p.521)
• As I write these words, it seems incredible that these things should have happened to me, for they are, truly, *against* all my instincts and training.(p.536)
• After nearly eight years of sobriety in A.A., I still can set down such thoughts, "*against* my instinct and training," showing that I still consider myself a "special" person, entitled to special privileges.(p.536)
• He had a shot of brandy *against* the cold and passed me the bottle.(p.541)
• As I said earlier, self-pity and resentment were my constant companions and my inventory began to look like a thirty-three year diary, for I seemed to have a resentment *against* everybody I had ever known.(p.551)
• It was *against* my mother and it was twenty-five years old.(p.551)
• "There is a principle which is a bar *against* all information, which is proof *against* all arguments and which cannot fail to keep a man in everlasting ignorance – that principle is contempt prior to investigation."(p.570)

age

• Seven percent of the A.A.'s surveyed are less than 30 years of *age* -- among them, many in their teens.(p.xxii)
• An exceptional man, he remained bone dry for twenty-five years and retired at the *age* of fifty-five, after a successful and happy business career.(p.32)
• His income is good, he has a fine home, is happily married and the father of promising children of college *age*.(p.39)
• Is not our *age* characterized by the ease with which we discard old ideas for new, by the complete readiness with which we throw away the theory or gadget which does not work for something new which does?(p.52)
• The *age* of miracles is still with us.(p.153)
• I immediately quit school and went to work, and from that time until I was high school *age* there was never a return to school.(p.193)
• At a comparatively early *age*, I can remember being jealous of my brother.(p.194)
• I was married at the *age* of nineteen to a grand girl and had good business prospects.(p.194)
• I went back to law school, and doubled up on the courses because I was then approaching thirty years of *age* and I wanted to get through as quickly as possible.(p.212)
• Military service was compulsory and I did my stretch with the class of my *age*, goose-stepping in German barracks and taking part in the Boxer Rebellion in China, my first time at any great distance from home.(p.230)
• I was doing very well with that and general upholstering work, and there was every indication that I would be financially independent by the time I reached middle *age*.(p.232)
• We moved in from the country at the *age* when girls want all sorts of nice things.(p.261)
• At the *age* of sixteen, I was invited to spend the summer with an aunt and I, very delightedly, accepted the invitation.(p.261)
• For eighteen years, from the *age* of twenty-one to thirty-nine, fear governed my life.(p.275)
• That *age* of the flapper and the "It" girl, speakeasies and the hip flask, the boyish bob and the drugstore cowboy, John Held Jr. and F. Scott Fitzgerald, all generously sprinkled with a patent pseudo-sophistication.(p.304)
• But he couldn't be an alcoholic at his *age*, could he?(p.317)
• I started drinking about *age* thirteen.(p.317)
• Since I didn't do well in school, I quit and joined the Army at *age* seventeen.(p.317)
• As my son, our second child, came along, and as he became school *age* and was away at school most of the time, something happened.(p.323)
• Until I took Social Security and a pension at the *age* of sixty-eight, after forty years in motion-picture-studio public relations, I had successfully hidden even any hints of approaching alcoholism.(p.327)
• Two years later, a month beyond *age* seventy, I was crying for help from A.A.(p.327)
• I just wanted to live to a certain *age*, carry through with what I felt was my job with the children, and after that – no matter.(p.337)
• As these words are written at fifty-three years of *age*, with over nine years of A.A. behind me, with all its wonderful teachings, I haven't the slightest doubt about being an alcoholic.(p.356)
• My drinking career extended from *age* eighteen to forty-three.(p.397)
• Eighteen will be used as the starting point, because my drinking before was limited by *age*, the law, and money.(p.397)
• I displayed alcoholic tendencies actually from the *age* of fourteen, when I started to steal wine from the family jug, siphoning it off one drink at a time so it wouldn't be missed, not drinking it immediately, but saving it until about a pint was accumulated, so that I could get drunk.(p.397)
• Even at that *age*, I had learned that one drink was not enough.(p.397)
• *Age* and the law were still against me, but laws were not as strictly enforced in those days as they are

now, and I discovered that as long as I had the green blood, there was always a way to get alcohol, either from a nondiscriminatory bartender or from an older friend who would be glad to purchase the joy juice for the privilege of sharing it.(p.397)
• At *age* twenty-one, I enlisted in the Navy for two reasons: (1) to avoid being drafted into the Army, and (2) out of a burst of patriotic fervor inspired by the advent of World War II and as the result of an all-night drinking binge which found me sitting on the doorstep of the Navy recruiting office when the chief petty officer arrived to open for business at nine o'clock Monday morning.(p.398)
• At the tender *age* of twenty-three, I got a divorce.(p.402)
• I could tell him a lot of reasons why I am here in an alky ward at the *age* of twenty.(p.423)
• Educated child of the scientific *age* that I was, I had complete faith in the science of the mind.(p.434)
• There at the top of the folder was my name, *age* and address, and underneath were the words, "Periodic Drinker."(p.470)
• I drank from the *age* of twelve until I was thirty-two.(p.480)
• I remember in my early youth my mother dressed me just as she did my two sisters, and I wore curls until I was six years of *age*.(p.483)
• For that reason, I believe, I married at a much younger *age* than I would have, had it not been for my home training.(p.485)
• She's still alive today at the *age* of eighty-two.(p.511)
• I started drinking rather early, at the *age* of sixteen.(p.512)
• When I came home to ordinary garrison life in England, I found that I was drinking rather more than most people of may *age*.(p.518)
• I had no work to do and I was at an *age* where it seemed too late to start anything new.(p.522)
• There was the father one lost respect for at the *age* of eleven, because the father broke his solemn word in a circumstance where you, eleven years old, had assumed guilt when you were innocent; but the father would not believe you, no matter what; and to ease his suffering you "confessed" and were "forgiven," only – months later – to have your "guilt" brought up – only he and you knew what he was talking bout -- brought up in front of the stern grandmother.(p.533)
• But I did, when I reached college *age*.(p.554)
• By *age* twenty-two, I was a daily drinker.(p.555)
• At *age* forty, I developed a large lump in my potbelly, and I feared it was a tumor.(p.557)

age-old
• If God can solve the *age-old* riddle of alcoholism, He can solve your problems too.(p.116)
• The *age-old* question in A.A. is which came first, the neurosis or the alcoholism.(p.240)
• "The American Public Health Association presents a Lasker Group Award for 1951 to Alcoholics Anonymous in recognition of its unique and highly successful approach to that *age-old* public health and social problem, alcoholism . . .(p.573)

agencies
• It was my job to sell time on these stations to advertising *agencies* in New York.(p.359)
• Why did it work for me when all other *agencies* had failed?(p.470)
• I worked for the Government about a year and still maintained my evening office practice when the Government *agencies* were decentralized.(p.489)
• We think that each group should soon achieve this ideal; that any public solicitation of funds using the name of Alcoholics Anonymous is highly dangerous, whether by groups, clubs, hospitals, or other outside *agencies*; that acceptance of large gifts from any source, or of contributions carrying any obligation whatever, is unwise.(p.566)

agency
• He inherited a lucrative automobile *agency*.(p.35)
• No beer or liquor was sold in the neighborhood, except at the State liquor *agency* where perhaps one might procure a pint if he could convince the agent that he really needed it.(p.171)
• Washington, D.C. and news-gathering *agency* work followed, along with many parties.(p.254)
• We were now both working in the same *agency*.(p.490)

agent
• No beer or liquor was sold in the neighborhood, except at the State liquor agency where perhaps one might procure a pint if he could convince the *agent* that he really needed it.(p.171)
• My wife traveled with me, but with a baby coming I decided to settle in a large city where I got a job with a commission *agent* which is a polite term for a handbook operator.(p.251)
• Out of those forty years as a movie press *agent* came one blessing that granted me a blind faith in the program.(p.334)

agents
• Instead of regarding ourselves as intelligent *agents*, spearheads of God's ever advancing Creation, we agnostics and atheists chose to believe that our human intelligence was the last word, the alpha and the omega, the beginning and end of all.(p.49)
• He is the Principal; we are His *agents*.(p.62)

ages
• The verdict of the *ages* is that faith means courage.(p.68)
• I kept myself so busy that outside of some school and group parties, I didn't go overboard on drinking very much between the *ages* of twenty-five and thirty.(p.213)
• Between the *ages* of twenty-five and thirty I tried everything.(p.305)
• He may even read in a newspaper that one out of every seven drinkers will become alcoholic, but he rarely is told that it holds true for all *ages* – or that the tolerance to alcohol (and other drugs) decreases steadily, year after year, in the bodies of all persons.(p.330)

aggregate
• Though the *aggregate* of recoveries resulting from psychiatric effort is considerable, we physicians must admit we have made little impression upon the problem as a whole.(p.xxvii)

aggrieved
• Then, under one provocation or another, the *aggrieved* one would unearth the old affair and angrily cast its ashes about.(p.124)

aghast
• I was *aghast*.(p.9)

agitated
• As we go through the day we pause, when *agitated* or doubtful, and ask for the right thought or action.(p.87)

agitation
• No matter how often I had gone into and come out of alcoholic lows during the day, the pattern bounced me out of bed each night about 2:00 a.m., shaking and hurting in the *agitation* that always follows a drug's sedation.(p.332)

agitator
• I was an *agitator*, a troublemaker, and many men as bitter as I was followed me.(p.458)

agnostic
• In the following chapter, there appears an explanation of alcoholism, as we understand it, then a chapter addressed to the *agnostic*.(p.28)
• To one who feels he is an atheist or *agnostic* such an experience seems impossible, but to continue as he is means disaster, especially if he is an alcoholic of the hopeless variety.(p.44)
• Yes, we of *agnostic* temperament have had these thoughts and experiences.(p.46)
• Our description of the alcoholic, the chapter to the *agnostic*, and our personal adventures before and after make clear three pertinent ideas:(p.60)
• If the man be *agnostic* or atheist, make it emphatic that he does not have to agree with your conception of God.(p.93)
• If you think you are an atheist, an *agnostic*, a skeptic, or have any other form of intellectual pride which keeps you from accepting what is in this book, I feel sorry for you.(p.181)
• I was an honest *agnostic*, but definitely not a hater of the church or its adherents.(p.256)
• I was an *agnostic*, so I thought.(p.408)

agnostically
• We *agnostically* inclined would not feel satisfied with a proposal which does not lend itself to reasonable approach and interpretation.(p.53)

agnosticism
• My brilliant *agnosticism* vanished, and I saw for the first time that those who really believed, or at least honestly tried to find a Power greater than themselves, were much more composed and contented than I had ever been, and they seemed to have a degree of happiness which I had never known.(p.247)

agnostics
• WE *AGNOSTICS*(p.44)
• But cheer up, something like half of us thought we were atheists or *agnostics*.(p.44)
• Here difficulty arises with *agnostics*.(p.45)
• Instead of regarding ourselves as intelligent agents, spearheads of God's ever advancing Creation, we *agnostics* and atheists chose to believe that our human intelligence was the last word, the alpha and the omega, the beginning and end of all.(p.49)
• We *agnostics* and atheists were sticking to the idea that self-sufficiency would solve our problems.(p.52)
• Some even remain *agnostics*.)(p.417)

ago
• Many years *ago* one of the leading contributors to this book came under our care in this hospital and while here he acquired some ideas which he put into practical application at once.(p.xxv)
• We believe, and so suggested a few years *ago*, that the action of alcohol on these chronic alcoholics is a manifestation of an allergy; that the phenomenon of craving is limited to this class and never occurs in the average temperate drinker.(p.xxvi)
• That was two months *ago* and the result was self-evident.(p.9)
• We are unable, at certain times, to bring into our consciousness with sufficient force the memory of the suffering and humiliation of even a week or a month *ago*.(p.24)
• We first saw Fred about a year *ago* in a hospital where he had gone to recover from a bad case of jitters.(p.39)
• If a mere code of morals or a better philosophy of life were sufficient to overcome alcoholism, many of us would have recovered long *ago*.(p.44)
• That very night, years *ago*, it disappeared.(p.56)
• This all happened years *ago*.(p.80)
• Without you he would have gone to pieces long *ago*.(p.119)
• They often jeopardize their own positions by trying to help serious drinkers who should have been fired long *ago*, or else given an opportunity to get well.(p.147)
• Years *ago*, in 1935, one of our number made a journey to a certain western city.(p.153)
• Six years *ago* one of our number was a patient there.(p.162)
• This was only a few days *ago* at this writing.(p.163)
• If she had not, I know I would have been dead a long time *ago*.(p.178)
• Nineteen years *ago* last summer, Dr. Bob and I saw him (Bill D.) for the first time.(p.188)
• I quit the factory and got a job on a small newspaper, going from that to a Pittsburgh daily, long *ago* defunct.(p.252)
• In the long *ago* past I used to start at the top as president or treasurer and end up with the sheriff breathing down my neck.(p.284)
• With God's help I am able, for one day at a time, to carry business responsibilities which, not many years *ago*, I would not have dreamed of assuming.(p.284)
• Twenty-odd years *ago* I made a mess out of my one and only marriage.(p.286)
• So six months *ago* I acquired a ready made family consisting of one charming wife, four grown children to whom I am devoted, and three grandchildren.(p.286)
• Why, even a year *ago*, I had seen Howard, an ex-doctor, mooching a dime for a drink.(p.289)
• A little more than fifteen years *ago*, through a long and calamitous series of shattering experiences, I found myself being helplessly propelled toward total destruction.(p.304)
• I couldn't remember what had been said five minutes *ago*.(p.319)
• I started my drinking nearly thirty years *ago* -- right after I was married.(p.322)
• Not long *ago*, I was lunching with another retired publicist.(p.334)
• But during a period of particular stress and strain about thirteen years *ago*, I resorted to alcohol in my home, alone, as a means of temporary release, as a means of getting a little extra sleep.(p.335)
• Eight years *ago*, my wife and I decided to spend a vacation in Naini Tal, the mountain resort.(p.343)
• He has loaned it to me and I did my job, but that ended nine days *ago*.(p.351)
• This was how I had looked and acted a few short weeks *ago*.(p.415)
• My spiritual awakening in A.A. finally resulted in my joining a church some years *ago*.(p.417)
• Four years *ago* I had nothing but a jumbled, mad existence.(p.430)
• That was seven years *ago* -- and many A.A. meetings *ago* -- and I haven't had a drink during those seven years.(p.437)
• And that was how Max and I and our two daughters spent Christmas Day, eight years *ago*.(p.444)
• The first time I remember seeing or hearing of A.A. was twenty years *ago*.(p.460)

• (I am looking at it now in my bedroom — a copy that was presented to me a couple of years ***ago*** by the A.A. group in that same prison.)(p.461)
• Three weeks ***ago***, my phone rang, and a voice I hadn't heard in over twenty-three years spoke.(p.462)
• I attempted nearly two years ***ago*** to make some amends and contact my children, but it wasn't God's time yet.(p.463)
• Forgive me — I cannot write further about this latest turn of events, anticipating seeing the family I deserted so long ***ago***.(p.463)
• The last Christmas I spent in Washington, fourteen years ***ago***, comes to mind.(p.465)
• That was over seven years ***ago***, and thank God and A.A., I haven't had a drink since.(p.473)
• Tall Man die five years ***ago***, a sober, peaceful, happy man.(p.476)
• "I went out of here nine days ***ago*** saying that I was going to be honest, and I wasn't," he answers.(p.503)
• I'm grateful because that Higher Power led me to A.A. a little over three years ***ago***, when I needed it very badly.(p.512)
• A former employer of mine said to me a little over ten years ***ago***, "Pat, you seem to be one of those unfortunate people who at least once every six months must go out and roll in the gutter."(p.513)
• I had played all that out long ***ago***.(p.523)
• The pressures had started long ***ago***.(p.533)
• All of my family and loved ones, all of my friends, are nearer and dearer to me than ever before and I have literally dozens of new friends who say they cannot believe that a short eight years ***ago*** I was ready for the scrap heap.(p.541)
• I attended my first A.A. meeting eight years ***ago***, and it is with deep gratitude that I'm able to say I've not had a drink since that time, and that I take no sedation or narcotics, for this program is to me one of complete sobriety and I no longer need to escape reality.(p.549)
• I had only to reflect on the contrast between the plans I made so many years ***ago*** for my life with what really happened to know I couldn't manage my life drunk or sober.(p.550)

agonies
• I put my poor mother and father through ***agonies*** but, finally, I couldn't stand living with them and having them watch everything I did.(p.386)

agonizedly
• I stumbled ***agonizedly*** past the theatre where in years gone by a great star had played my play.(p.540)

agonizing
• I remember looking longingly at the window as an easier solution, and shuddering at the memory of that other window, three years before, and the six ***agonizing*** months in a London hospital ward.(p.224)
• Maybe I could find my way out of this ***agonizing*** existence.(p.309)

agony
• The mind and body are marvelous mechanisms, for mine endured this ***agony*** two more years.(p.6)
• He told me that it was imperative that I walk around the entire block, cost me what it might in mental ***agony***.(p.276)
• Under the skilled guidance of an expert practitioner I wallowed in the world's individual and collective mental ***agony***.(p.434)
• Loneliness, great physical and mental ***agony*** -- these were the common lot.(p.455)
• But I remembered the years of ***agony*** preceding the binge, I remembered the years I had thrown away.(p.540)

agree
• We have a way out on which we can absolutely ***agree***, and upon which we can join in brotherly and harmonious action.(p.17)
• Physicians who are familiar with alcoholism ***agree*** there is no such thing as making a normal drinker out of an alcoholic.(p.31)
• Many doctors and psychiatrists ***agree*** with our conclusions.(p.43)
• Whether we ***agree*** with a particular approach or conception seems to make little difference.(p.50)
• Psychologists are inclined to ***agree*** with us.(p.73)
• If the man be agnostic or atheist, make it emphatic that he does not have to ***agree*** with your conception of God.(p.93)
• We do not mean that you have to ***agree*** with your husband whenever there is an honest difference of opinion.(p.117)
• Though the family does not fully ***agree*** with dad's spiritual activities, they should let him have his head.(p.129)
• Your junior executive may not ***agree*** with the contents of our book.(p.148)
• Each day I would try to find out what His will was, and try to follow that, rather than trying to get Him to always ***agree*** that the things I thought of myself were the things best for me.(p.187)

agreeably
• I don't know what sort of person I was expecting, but I was very ***agreeably*** surprised to find Mr. T. a poised, intelligent, well groomed and mannered gentleman.(p.309)

agreed
• He ***agreed*** he was a real alcoholic and in a serious condition.(p.35)
• On one proposition, however, these men and women are strikingly ***agreed***.(p.50)
• Remember it was ***agreed*** at the beginning we would go to any lengths for victory over alcohol.(p.76)
• Why was it, when these dangers were pointed out that they ***agreed***, and then got drunk again immediately?(p.107)
• When our friend related his experience, the man ***agreed*** that no amount of will power he might muster could stop his drinking for long.(p.155)
• And with such good effect that the doctor ***agreed*** to a test among his patients and certain other alcoholics from a clinic which he attends.(p.163)
• Nobody would know it, so I ***agreed*** to have the one drink.(p.202)
• I ***agreed*** with him and told him in no uncertain terms that I never broke my word in my life.(p.206)
• Around this time our big A.A. book was being written and it all became much simpler; we had a definite formula which some sixty of us ***agreed*** was the middle course for all alcoholics who wanted sobriety, and that formula has not been changed one iota down through the years.(p.248)
• I lived through a week of the fidgets because I had ***agreed*** to address a group of alcoholic inmates in one of our state mental hospitals.(p.283)
• Well . . . I had a job, and I really wanted desperately to stop drinking, but couldn't, so I readily ***agreed*** to visit the doctor she recommended.(p.301)
• He advised me to enter the particular hospital with which he was connected and I readily ***agreed***.(p.302)
• Certainly now, anyone would have ***agreed*** that only a miracle could prevent my final breakdown.(p.306)
• I ***agreed*** it was great stuff -- for those who needed it.(p.332)
• My salesmanship was still good, for in the fall of 1938 she called me from Salt Lake and finally ***agreed*** to take me on for better or for worse.(p.360)
• After a particularly ugly one-nighter, my wife suggested I try it, and I ***agreed***.(p.434)
• So I raised enough fuss that they finally ***agreed*** to let me sign out, against medical advice.(p.444)
• But, by the look on the psychiatrist's face, I could tell that it would really make him happy if I ***agreed***.(p.446)
• So, for no better reason than to make him happy, I ***agreed***.(p.446)
• Providentially, this was a Monday might when the Dublin Group met in those days, and my family ***agreed*** that if A.A. could do anything for me at all, that I'd be allowed to stay on at home on probation.(p.523)
• I had no problem admitting I was powerless over alcohol, and I certainly ***agreed*** that my life had become unmanageable.(p.550)

agreeing
• Here are some of the methods we have tried: Drinking beer only, limiting the number of drinks, never drinking alone, never drinking in the morning, drinking only at home, never having it in the house, never drinking during business hours, drinking only at parties, switching from scotch to brandy, drinking only natural wines, ***agreeing*** to resign if ever drunk on the job, taking a trip, not taking a trip, swearing off forever (with and without a solemn oath), taking more physical exercise, reading inspirational books, going to health farms and sanitariums, accepting voluntary commitment to asylums -- we could increase the list ad infinitum.(p.31)

agreement
• This means trouble, unless the family watches for these tendencies in each other and comes to a friendly ***agreement*** about them.(p.131)

ah
• But what about his responsibilities — his family and the men who would die because they would not know how to get well, ***ah*** -- yes, those other alcoholics?(p.154)
• When the policeman released me to my stupefied and exasperated friend at four in the morning, I went to my traveling bag and groped until I found — well, let the officer speak: "***Ah***," said the policeman, "he's got anuder pair, t'ank God!"(p.538)

aha
• I thought, "***Aha***, he's passing the buck.(p.413)

ahead
• Many of our friends encourage us by saying that this is but a beginning, only the augury of a much larger future ***ahead***.(p.xv)
• For if an alcoholic failed to perfect and enlarge his spiritual life through work and self-sacrifice for others, he could not survive the certain trials and low spots ***ahead***.(p.14)
• He often possesses special abilities, skills, and aptitudes, and has a promising career ***ahead*** of him.(p.21)
• Yes, there is a long period of reconstruction ***ahead***.(p.83)
• On awakening let us think about the twenty-four hours ***ahead***.(p.86)
• Suggest how important it is that he place the welfare of other people ***ahead*** of his own.(p.94)
• Some of us have taken very hard knocks to learn this truth: Job or no job -- wife or no wife -- we simply do not stop drinking so long as we place dependence upon other people ***ahead*** of dependence on God.(p.98)
• Though some of his manifestations are alarming and disagreeable, we think dad will be on a firmer foundation than the man who is placing business or professional success ***ahead*** of spiritual development.(p.129)
• The most satisfactory years of your existence lie ***ahead***.(p.152)
• Every time I'd start thinking about drinking, I would think of the long, dry years ***ahead*** without having a drink; but this idea of twenty-four hours, that it was up to me from then on, was a lot of help.(p.188)
• I could work a deal up to where all I had to do was to go ***ahead*** with it; all the planning had been done, all the financing had been done, but then I'd say "Nuts to it!" and walk away.(p.197)
• I entered the business world with every confidence that success lay ***ahead*** of me.(p.275)
• At any rate the last great step toward a well rounded life still lay ***ahead*** of me.(p.286)
• All the joys of retirement lay ***ahead*** for this movie publicist.(p.327)
• The drive to get ***ahead***, to succeed, kept me too busy for many years to have any great experience with social life.(p.374)
• It was so important that it must come ***ahead*** of anything.(p.382)
• I figured that perhaps if I went ***ahead*** with that marriage, which I was sure was right for me, that would be the answer to my drinking problem.(p.465)
• The insane asylum lies ***ahead***.(p.502)
• An ambitious playwright, he let his brains get so far ***ahead*** of his emotions that he collapsed into suicidal drinking.(p.531)
• For a while, for a long time, we can endure the intellect's being ***ahead*** of the emotions, which is the import of Millay's couplet.(p.534)
• Sobering up, the mind that was ***ahead*** of the emotions would impel the question: What have you written or done to be the great man?(p.537)
• Even when you don't really want it for them, and your prayers are only words and you don't mean it, go ***ahead*** and do it anyway.(p.552)
• Hopeless now, I felt it would be better for my wife, my children, and everyone in my life if I went ***ahead*** and died.(p.558)
• I suspect that if it is wisely handled — and it seems to be in wise and prudent hands — there are doors of opportunity ***ahead*** of this project that may surpass our capacities to imagine."(p.574)

aid
• When this sort of thinking is fully established in an individual with alcoholic tendencies, he has probably placed himself beyond human ***aid***, and unless locked up, may die or go permanently insane.(p.24)
• We were in a position where life was becoming impossible, and if we had passed into the region from which there is no return through human ***aid*** we had but two alternatives: One was to go on to the bitter end, blotting out the consciousness of our intolerable situation as best we could; and the other, to accept spiritual help.(p.25)
• And there often seems no way of entirely getting rid of self without His ***aid***.(p.62)
• They often forget father was beyond human ***aid***.(p.128)
• When we see a man sinking into the mire that is alcoholism, we give him first ***aid*** and place what we have at his disposal.(p.132)
• In the chapter "Working With Others" you gathered

an idea of how we approach and *aid* others to health.(p.153)
• I have something to contribute to humanity, since I am peculiarly qualified, as a fellow-sufferer, to give *aid* and comfort to those who have stumbled and fallen over this business of meeting life.(p.229)
• Indeed, without their *aid* we couldn't possibly have gone on.(p.496)
• Things got so bad, I was afraid to go on the street, so I turned to Mothers' *Aid*.(p.527)

aided
• Shortly thereafter, *aided* by the Depression, I found that I had a great deal of spare time and that a little drink in the morning helped.(p.287)
• In this I was greatly *aided* and abetted by one John Barleycorn.(p.358)

aiding
• You may be *aiding* in his destruction rather than his recovery.(p.97)

aids
• Secondary *aids* to A.A., such as clubs or hospitals which require much property or administration, ought to be incorporated and so set apart that, if necessary, they can be freely discarded by the groups.(p.566)

ailed
• She, more than the others, showed me what *ailed* me basically, why I was immature and insecure.(p.409)

ailing
• Should he have the same consideration as other *ailing* employees?(p.140)

ailment
• An *ailment* developed in one of my eyes, and I was transferred back to Sing Sing and operated upon.(p.509)

ailments
• She sees she was wrong to make a burning issue out of such a matter when his more serious *ailments* were being rapidly cured.(p.135)
• I began making the rounds of the doctors in the hope that one of them might find some cure for my accumulating *ailments*, preferably something that could be removed surgically.(p.305)
• The physician wasn't hooked, he thought -- he just prescribed drugs medically indicated for his many *ailments*.(p.439)

ails
• To me, this incident illustrates lack of understanding as to what really *ails* the alcoholic, and lack of knowledge as to what part employers might profitably take in salvaging their sick employees.(p.139)

aim
• To be helpful is our only *aim*.(p.89)
• Of course, it was always my *aim* to have my own way without being caught.(p.210)
• 6. -- Problems of money, property, and authority may easily divert us from our primary spiritual *aim*.(p.565)

aimlessly
• Few people really are, for that means blind faith in the strange proposition that this universe originated in a cipher and *aimlessly* rushes nowhere.(p.10)

ain't
• *Ain't* it grand the wind stopped blowin'?"(p.82)

air
• Only thirty years later the conquest of the *air* was almost an old story and airplane travel was in full swing.(p.52)
• There was a man watching, and I turned to him and said with a defiant *air* I carried with me all the time, "If I don't quit this I'm going to have to join that alcoholic business they're talking about."(p.266)
• That was on a hot summer evening, down in the Greenwich Village Group, and there was a little porch out there in the old meeting place on Sullivan Street, and after the meeting I went out on the steps for some *air*.(p.321)
• I applied for photo school at Pensacola *Air* Base and made it.(p.426)
• If I write with the *air* of one who has discovered the obvious, which is to say, the eternal truths which have been offered to us since the beginning, forgive my callowness; I had to find these things out for myself.(p.536)

aircraft
• I was club-man, athlete, artist, musician, author, editor, *aircraft* pilot and world traveller.(p.432)

airing
• I used to put eight or twelve ounce bottles of alcohol in a fur lined glove and toss it onto the back *airing* porch when winter days got dark enough.(p.176)

airplane
• There was that time we had chartered an *airplane* to complete a jag!(p.9)
• I have a shadowy recollection of being in an *airplane* bound for New York, and of finding a friendly taxicab driver at the landing field instead of my wife.(p.41)
• Only thirty years later the conquest of the air was almost an old story and *airplane* travel was in full swing.(p.52)

aisle
• Scared that my dress wasn't going to fit right, that the church wasn't going to be filled, that I'd fall flat on my face walking up the *aisle*; in fact, I was afraid I wasn't going to be a prima donna in the place where I should be.(p.385)
• You didn't carry a little orchid up the *aisle* in those days; you carried a great big bouquet, like a funeral spray, and you didn't have your picture taken until just before you went to the church.(p.385)
• As I started down the *aisle*, that bourbon went right through me.(p.385)
• I walked up that *aisle* just like Mae West in her prime.(p.385)

Akron
• The spark that was to flare into the first A.A. group was struck at *Akron*, Ohio, in June 1935, during a talk between a New York stockbroker and an *Akron* physician.(p.xv)
• Prior to his journey to *Akron*, the broker had worked hard with many alcoholics on the theory that only an alcoholic could help an alcoholic, but he had succeeded only in keeping sober himself.(p.xvi)
• The broker had gone to *Akron* on a business venture which had collapsed, leaving him greatly in fear that he might start drinking again.(p.xvi)
• That alcoholic turned out to be the *Akron* physician.(p.xvi)
• Hence the two men set to work almost frantically upon alcoholics arriving in the ward of the *Akron* City Hospital.(p.xvii)
• This work at *Akron* continued through the summer of 1935.(p.xvii)
• And besides, there were scattered alcoholics who had picked up the basic ideas in *Akron* or New York and were trying to form A.A. groups in other cities.(p.xvii)
• In his prodigy of service, he was well assisted by Sister Ignatia at St. Thomas Hospital in *Akron*, Ohio, one of the greatest friends our Fellowship will ever know.(p.171)
• My wife, a Kentucky girl, came with me to *Akron* where I completed my course in law at the *Akron* Law School.(p.182)
• When I was eighteen, at the end of high school, the high school team had a banquet at a well-known roadhouse outside of *Akron*.(p.194)
• At the end of this selling of lots, just prior to World War I, I got into the crude rubber business, and six months later there was only one broker and myself left in *Akron*.(p.197)
• I found, however, that when I would leave *Akron* to go to Chicago, I would get drunk.(p.197)
• *Akron* was really on the boom in those days, 1919-1920; expansion was terrific.(p.198)
• Everything in the world a man could possibly want, and I was driving from *Akron* to Cleveland, having just been to the bank and discovered that I had approximately $5,000.(p.200)
• If there was a lecture on the subject within a hundred miles of *Akron*, I attended.(p.202)
• I was forty-nine and a half years old when I was first approached about the *Akron* Group.(p.215)
• It was not known to me as a group, but I later learned that my wife had known about it for nine months and had prayed constantly that I would stumble into *Akron* some way or another.(p.215)
• She had a hairdresser who used to tell her about a brother-in-law who had been quite a drinker and about some doctor in *Akron* who had straightened him out.(p.216)
• There was also some conversation about Dr. Bob and I must have said that I would go down to *Akron* with Bill in the morning.(p.217)
• The next morning, my wife came into my room and wakened me and said, "That man is downstairs and he said you said you'd go to *Akron*."(p.217)
• That's about the spirit in which I went to *Akron*.(p.217)
• I believe every member of the *Akron* Group did come to see me, which impressed me terrifically, not so much because of the stories they told, but because they would take the time to come and talk to me without even knowing who I was.(p.218)
• I left on a Wednesday afternoon, had dinner in *Akron* and then went to a house where I encountered my first meeting.(p.218)
• We went to *Akron* for about six weeks and we did a lot of visiting among the people in *Akron*.(p.219)
• They had all been to *Akron*.(p.219)
• At that meeting, there were a number of *Akron* people and all the Cleveland people.(p.219)
• As we left, and they were escorting us across the bridge into Wheeling, I, with great dignity and sarcasm, told them if their wives were ever visiting in *Akron*, and they, too, were looking for their route sign as I was, that I hoped I could extend to them the hospitality that had been shown to me in Bellaire.(p.264)
• He used to drink, and then he found something that started up in *Akron* that helped him quit drinking."(p.267)
• He said, "There's a doctor here in *Akron*.(p.267)
• Jack said there was a meeting in *Akron* every Wednesday night and that it was very important that we go.(p.268)
• The next day he turned me over to a couple who, although neither was an alcoholic, knew Dr. Bob and were willing to drive me to *Akron* where they would turn me over to his care.(p.278)
• So I was driven to *Akron* the very next day by these Good Samaritans, and turned over to Dr. Bob and the then tiny *Akron* Group.(p.279)
• The example which they and Bill W., whose visits to *Akron* were fairly frequent, set me of service to their fellow men imbued me with a great desire to emulate them.(p.281)
• During my first few months in *Akron* I was quite sure that I never wanted to see my home town again.(p.281)
• In the spring of 1939, Bill stopped off in *Akron* on his way to Detroit on business.(p.281)
• I landed him and shipped him by train to *Akron*, with a pint of whiskey in his pocket to keep him from wanting to get off the train in Toledo!(p.282)
• Those three weeks left me completely exhausted and I had to return to *Akron* for three more months of rest.(p.282)
• I grew up in a small town outside *Akron*, Ohio, where the life was typical of any average small town.(p.287)
• After I left school, I went to work in *Akron*, living at home with my parents.(p.287)
• That same year, my wife became fed up with my drinking around the house and called my dad in *Akron* to come and pick me up.(p.288)
• This was the beginning of five years of bounding back and forth between my home in Chicago and *Akron* to sober up.(p.288)
• He waited until I was completely sober and the day before I was to head back for Chicago, he told me of a small group of men in *Akron* who apparently had the same problem that I had but were doing something about it.(p.289)
• I could not wait to tell him that I wanted help, that if these men in *Akron* had anything I wanted it, and would do anything to get it.(p.289)
• I can still remember very distinctly getting into *Akron* at eleven p.m. and routing this same Howard out of bed to do something about me.(p.290)
• I stayed in *Akron* two or three weeks on my initial trip trying to absorb as much of the program and philosophy as possible.(p.291)
• One of them was that I would try to get a group started in Chicago; the second was that I would have to return to *Akron* to attend meetings at least every two months until I did get a group started in Chicago; third, I decided I must place this program above everything else, even my family, because if I did not maintain my sobriety I would lose my family anyway.(p.292)
• On my trips back to *Akron* to get my spirits recharged and to work with other alcoholics, I would ask Dr. Bob about this delay and wonder just what was wrong with me.(p.293)
• A few months after I made my original trip to *Akron* I was feeling pretty cocky, and I didn't think my wife was treating me with proper respect, now that I was an outstanding citizen.(p.293)
• A week later, I had to get an old friend from *Akron* to spend two days sobering me up.(p.293)
• In the summer of 1938, almost a year from the time I made my original contact with *Akron*, the man for whom I was working and who knew about the program, approached me and asked if I could do anything about one of his salesmen who was drinking very heavily.(p.294)
• So I suggested that he take a trip to *Akron* for a couple of weeks, which he did, living with one of

the A.A. families there.(p.294)
• A few months later one of the men who had been in touch with the group in ***Akron*** came to Chicago to live, and then there were three of us who continued to have informal meetings quite regularly.(p.294)
• The three of us did not feel up to the job, and after a few meetings we convinced the prospects that they too should go to ***Akron*** where they could see an older group in action.(p.295)
• The girl was full of enthusiasm and she made the trip to ***Akron*** too.(p.295)
• From a mere handful in ***Akron*** we have spread throughout the world.(p.295)
• From a single member in the Chicago area, commuting to ***Akron***, we now exceed six thousand.(p.295)
• Then he told me there was a handful of people in ***Akron*** and New York who had worked out a technique for arresting their alcoholism.(p.308)
• He had been dry for two and a half years and had been maintaining his contact with a group of recovered alcoholics in ***Akron***.(p.309)
• He thought it would be helpful for me to visit the ***Akron*** group and meet many like himself.(p.309)
• So I went to ***Akron***, and also to Cleveland, and I met more recovered alcoholics.(p.310)

Akron's
• Pioneer member of ***Akron's*** Group No. 1, the first A.A. group in the world.(p.182)
• Straightway, Bob called ***Akron's*** City Hospital and asked for the nurse on the receiving ward.(p.188)

Al-Anon
• The fellowship of ***Al-Anon*** Family Groups was formed about thirteen years after this chapter was written.(p.121)
• Alateen, for teen-aged children of alcoholics, is a part of ***Al-Anon***.(p.121)
• If there is no ***Al-Anon*** listing in your local telephone book, you may obtain further information on ***Al-Anon*** Family Groups by writing to its World Service Office: Box 182, Madison Square Station, New York, NY 10159.(p.121)
• It started out as a good marriage, but it deteriorated over the years as she progressed through the various stages of qualifying for ***Al-Anon***.(p.439)
• For my seventh A.A. birthday, my program-oriented, ***Al-Anon*** wife had my moccasins bronzed.(p.445)
• Eventually, I had to redo each of the Twelve Steps specifically with Max in mind, from the First, saying, "I am powerless over alcohol, and my homelife is unmanageable by me," to the Twelfth, in which I tried to think of her as a sick ***Al-Anon*** and treat her with the love I would give a sick A.A. newcomer.(p.452)
• We survivors are all in A.A. now, and my mother is in ***Al-Anon***.(p.480)
• Should you be the relative or friend of an alcoholic who shows no immediate interest in A.A., it is suggested that you write the ***Al-Anon*** Family Groups, Inc., Box 182, Madison Square Station, New York, NY 10159, U.S.A.(p.575)
• This is a world clearing house for the ***Al-Anon*** Family Groups, composed largely of the wives, husbands and friends of A.A. members.(p.575)

Alan
• One night, I was struck with the memory of a line ***Alan*** Ladd used in "Shane," a movie that I'd worked on.(p.333)

Alanon
• We talked for a while, and then he sent me down to the ***Alanon*** House over on the west side, and there I had my introduction to A.A.(p.515)

alarm
• Gone are time cards to punch, ***alarm*** clocks to obey, nosey rumor-mongers and talebearers to evade.(p.329)

alarmed
• For a moment I was ***alarmed***, and called my friend, the doctor, to ask if I were still sane.(p.14)
• If you are satisfied he really wants to get over drinking, you need not be ***alarmed***.(p.120)

alarming
• The ***alarming*** physical and mental symptoms, the deepening pall of remorse, depression and inferiority that settled down on our loved ones -- these things terrified and distracted us.(p.106)
• Though some of his manifestations are ***alarming*** and disagreeable, we think dad will be on a firmer foundation than the man who is placing business or professional success ahead of spiritual development.(p.129)
• But they were occurring with ***alarming*** frequency.(p.434)

alas
• We "instant perfectionists" also are hypersensitive, ***alas***.(p.331)
• ***Alas*** for us men toward whom Shaw hurled his cry, "Must a Christ be crucified in every generation for the benefit of those who have no imagination?"(p.536)

Alaska
• A.A. has flourishing communities in the British Isles, the Scandinavian countries, South Africa, South America, Mexico, ***Alaska***, Australia and Hawaii.(p.xv)

Alateen
• ***Alateen***, for teen-aged children of alcoholics, is a part of Al-Anon.(p.121)

alcohol
• ***Alcohol*** being no respecter of persons, we are an accurate cross section of America, and in distant lands, the same democratic evening-up process is now going on.(p.xx)
• In all probability, we shall never be able to touch more than a fair fraction of the ***alcohol*** problem in all its ramifications.(p.xxi)
• The doctor's theory that we have an allergy to ***alcohol*** interests us.(p.xxiv)
• We believe, and so suggested a few years ago, that the action of ***alcohol*** on these chronic alcoholics is a manifestation of an allergy; that the phenomenon of craving is limited to this class and never occurs in the average temperate drinker.(p.xxvi)
• These allergic types can never safely use ***alcohol*** in any form at all; and once having formed the habit and found they cannot break it, once having lost their self-confidence, their reliance upon things human, their problems pile up on them and become astonishingly difficult to solve.(p.xxvi)
• Men and women drink essentially because they like the effect produced by ***alcohol***.(p.xxvi)
• On the other hand — and strange as this may seem to those who do not understand -- once a psychic change has occurred, the very same person who seemed doomed, who had so many problems he despaired of ever solving them, suddenly finds himself easily able to control his desire for ***alcohol***, the only effort necessary being that required to follow a few simple rules.(p.xxvii)
• There is the type who always believes that after being entirely free from ***alcohol*** for a period of time he can take a drink without danger.(p.xxviii)
• Then there are types entirely normal in every respect except in the effect ***alcohol*** has upon them.(p.xxviii)
• Following the elimination of ***alcohol***, there was found to be no permanent brain injury.(p.xxix)
• A long time has passed with no return to ***alcohol***.(p.xxix)
• I was very lonely and again turned to ***alcohol***.(p.1)
• ***Alcohol*** was my master.(p.8)
• At the hospital I was separated from ***alcohol*** for the last time.(p.13)
• We are equally positive that once he takes any ***alcohol*** whatever into his system, something happens, both in the bodily and mental sense, which makes it virtually impossible for him to stop.(p.22)
• Yet he had no control whatever over ***alcohol***.(p.26)
• If we are planning to stop drinking, there must be no reservation of any kind, nor any lurking notion that someday we will be immune to ***alcohol***.(p.33)
• However intelligent we may have been in other respects, where ***alcohol*** has been involved, we have been strangely insane.(p.38)
• In this respect ***alcohol*** was a great persuader.(p.48)
• Remember that we deal with ***alcohol*** -- cunning, baffling, powerful!(p.58)
• 1.We admitted we were powerless over ***alcohol*** -- that our lives had become unmanageable.(p.59)
• The insanity of ***alcohol*** returns and we drink again.(p.66)
• We could not wish them away any more than ***alcohol***.(p.66)
• Remember it was agreed at the beginning we would go to any lengths for victory over ***alcohol***.(p.76)
• And we have ceased fighting anything or anyone -- even ***alcohol***.(p.84)
• We are headed for trouble if we do, for ***alcohol*** is a subtle foe.(p.85)
• The men who cry for money and shelter before conquering ***alcohol***, are on the wrong track.(p.98)
• He clamors for this or that, claiming he cannot master ***alcohol*** until his material needs are cared for.(p.98)
• People have said we must not go where liquor is served; we must not have it in our homes; we must shun friends who drink; we must avoid moving pictures which show drinking scenes; we must not go into bars; our friends must hide their bottles if we go to their houses; we mustn't think or be reminded about ***alcohol*** at all.(p.100)
• Ask any woman who has sent her husband to distant places on the theory he would escape the ***alcohol*** problem.(p.101)
• At proper time and place explain to all your friends why ***alcohol*** disagrees with you.(p.102)
• We would not even do the cause of temperate drinking any good, for not one drinker in a thousand likes to be told anything about ***alcohol*** by one who hates it.(p.103)
• Some men have been so impaired by ***alcohol*** that they cannot stop.(p.114)
• After all, your family is reunited, ***alcohol*** is no longer a problem and you and your husband are working together toward an undreamed-of future.(p.119)
• We have been dealing with ***alcohol*** in its worst aspect.(p.132)
• Now about health: A body badly burned by ***alcohol*** does not often recover overnight nor do twisted thinking and depression vanish in a twinkling.(p.133)
• ***Alcohol*** is so sexually stimulating to some men that they have over-indulged.(p.134)
• Can it be appreciated that he has been a victim of crooked thinking, directly caused by the action of ***alcohol*** on his brain?(p.140)
• But these scrapes can generally be charged, no matter how bad, to the abnormal action of ***alcohol*** on his mind.(p.140)
• Whatever the method, its object is to thoroughly clear mind and body of the effects of ***alcohol***.(p.143)
• Being somewhat weakened, and faced with physical and mental readjustment to a life which knows no ***alcohol***, he may overdo.(p.146)
• As we became subjects of King ***Alcohol***, shivering denizens of his mad realm, the chilling vapor that is loneliness settled down.(p.151)
• He cannot picture life without ***alcohol***.(p.152)
• Some day he will be unable to imagine life either with ***alcohol*** or without it.(p.152)
• After three years of this, I wound up in the local hospital where they attempted to help me, but I would get my friends to smuggle me a quart, or I would steal the ***alcohol*** about the building, so that I got rapidly worse.(p.175)
• I used to put eight or twelve ounce bottles of ***alcohol*** in a fur lined glove and toss it onto the back airing porch when winter days got dark enough.(p.176)
• My bootlegger had hidden ***alcohol*** at the back steps where I could get it at my convenience.(p.176)
• It then occurred to me that after one was all smelled up with beer nobody could tell what had been drunk, so I began to fortify my beer with straight ***alcohol***.(p.178)
• Later, I realized that I was running from ***alcohol***.(p.183)
• So, after reviewing these things and realizing what liquor had cost me, I went to this Higher Power which, to me was God, without any reservation, and admitted that I was completely powerless over ***alcohol***, and that I was willing to do anything in the world to get rid of the problem.(p.187)
• Twenty-two years later, Doctor Bob told me that what I had done was like turning a switch and setting up a demand for more ***alcohol*** in my system.(p.195)
• I very early sampled the effects of ***alcohol***.(p.211)
• Although, during this period I was not addicted to any pattern of ***alcohol*** consumption, when I did drink the drinking was pretty wild.(p.212)
• When I was about forty-seven, after indulging in all kinds of self-deception to control my drinking, I arrived at a period when I felt convinced I had to have so much ***alcohol*** every day and that the real problem was to control how much.(p.214)
• In fact, the last three years of my drinking was a routine of barbiturates in the morning, so that I could stop shaking enough to shave, and then ***alcohol*** beginning about four-thirty or five o'clock, with a struggle not to take a drink at noon or during the day, because I had the idea that if I took one drink, I would smell as though I had had a pint.(p.217)
• Despite great opportunities, ***alcohol*** nearly ended her life.(p.222)
• ***Alcohol*** was that prop, and I didn't see how I could live without it.(p.226)
• I like to think I was fairly normal before ***alcohol*** took over.(p.240)
• I'd work like mad for three or four weeks without a single drink, save my money, pay a few bills and then "reward" myself with ***alcohol***.(p.244)
• By the time I was thirty I had found that ***alcohol*** dissolved fear.(p.275)
• In the end I had two problems instead of one: Fear and ***alcohol***.(p.275)

• This happy combination of pleasant work and ***alcohol*** lasted for five years.(p.277)
• At last I discovered ***alcohol*** as a cure-all.(p.277)
• With the bravery born of desperation, and abetted by ***alcohol***, I married a young and lovely girl.(p.277)
• I was completely licked by ***alcohol***.(p.290)
• I was caught in a cycle of ***alcohol*** and sedation that was proving inescapable and consciousness had become intolerable.(p.304)
• He further explained that ***alcohol*** was no respecter of sex or background, but that most of the alcoholics he had encountered had better than average minds and abilities.(p.308)
• It had been so many years since I had not relied on some artificial crutch, either ***alcohol*** or sedatives.(p.310)
• He may even read in a newspaper that one out of every seven drinkers will become alcoholic, but he rarely is told that it holds true for all ages -- or that the tolerance to ***alcohol*** (and other drugs) decreases steadily, year after year, in the bodies of all persons.(p.330)
• My writing career was described in the couplet "***Alcohol*** gave me wings to fly,/And then it took away the sky."(p.331)
• While I sought the comforting arms of ***alcohol***, I knew this was a sign of weakness on the part of a longtime-successful old codger with white hair, the image of dignity.(p.331)
• I'd just take a couple or three barbiturates to get back to sleep -- eating my ***alcohol***.(p.333)
• When ***alcohol*** took me over, my bar was my kitchen, my living room, my bedroom, the back bathroom, and the two hampers.(p.335)
• Because it was only through feeling defeat and feeling failure, the inability to cope with my life and with ***alcohol***, that I was able to surrender and accept the fact that I had this disease, and that I had to learn to live again without ***alcohol***.(p.335)
• But during a period of particular stress and strain about thirteen years ago, I resorted to ***alcohol*** in my home, alone, as a means of temporary release, as a means of getting a little extra sleep.(p.335)
• I should have realized that ***alcohol*** was getting hold of me when I started to become secretive in my drinking.(p.336)
• When we begin to do things like that with ***alcohol***, something's gone wrong.(p.336)
• I needed that ***alcohol***.(p.337)
• I knew that ***alcohol*** and I had to part.(p.338)
• Nevertheless, I began to try to live without ***alcohol***.(p.338)
• And believe me, an alcoholic cannot fight ***alcohol***.(p.338)
• The first time was when I knew I couldn't live with ***alcohol***.(p.340)
• A.A. gives us alcoholics direction into a way of life without the need for ***alcohol***.(p.340)
• It was here I came to know properly what ***alcohol*** was.(p.343)
• At Christmastime next year, I convinced my wife that I had ***alcohol*** under control and that I would do controlled drinking over Christmas and the New Year.(p.343)
• The second way in which, perhaps, I differ from some other alcoholics is this; many alcoholics state that they didn't particularly like the taste of ***alcohol***, but that they liked the effect.(p.345)
• I loved ***alcohol***!(p.346)
• ***Alcohol*** failed to serve the purpose.(p.346)
• On the last day I was drinking I went up to see a friend who had had a good deal of trouble with ***alcohol***, and whose wife had left him a number of times.(p.346)
• I needed ***alcohol*** from that night on, and it in turn used me, ruling my life for three years.(p.353)
• Many times have I heard the above expressions since I have been in A.A., and many times I have had to reply "Definitely I am an alcoholic, and while it may be hard for you to believe, it is not hard for me, for I have learned many things about ***alcohol*** and myself that would, perhaps, be difficult for you to understand."(p.356)
• My childhood was shrouded in the fumes of ***alcohol***.(p.369)
• ***Alcohol*** was a looming cloud in this banker's bright sky.(p.373)
• As I later found out through Alcoholics Anonymous, ***alcohol*** is no respecter of economic status, social and business standing or intelligence.(p.373)
• I would have begrudged the time or money for ***alcohol***.(p.374)
• Why did I want increasingly greater quantities of ***alcohol***?(p.374)
• Cunning, baffling, powerful -- the gradual creeping up of the frequency and quantity of ***alcohol***, and what it does to a person is apparent to everyone but the person involved.(p.375)
• Never having enough, always craving more, the obsession for ***alcohol*** gradually dominated all my activities, particularly while travelling.(p.375)
• By now it had become difficult to visualize a life without ***alcohol***.(p.378)
• "We admitted we were powerless over ***alcohol*** -- that our lives had become unmanageable."(p.379)
• It did say, "admitted I was powerless over ***alcohol***; that my life had become unmanageable."(p.379)
• Most certainly I was powerless over ***alcohol***, and for me, my life had become unmanageable.(p.379)
• It was important to me to see what ***alcohol*** had done to me and would continue to do if I didn't have help.(p.379)
• I liked the description of the alcoholic as a person who had found that ***alcohol*** is interfering with his social or business life.(p.380)
• What could be more reasonable than that some people, including myself, were allergic to ***alcohol***?(p.380)
• Somehow our bodies had reached the point where we could no longer absorb ***alcohol*** in our systems.(p.380)
• Living with fear and tension inevitably results in wanting to ease that tension, which ***alcohol*** seems to do temporarily.(p.380)
• Making amends is sometimes doing what we are capable of doing but failed to do because of ***alcohol***; carrying out community responsibilities such as Community Funds, Red Cross, educational and religious activities in proportion to our abilities and energy.(p.381)
• I came from a family where ***alcohol*** was socially acceptable.(p.384)
• So I was used to it, but I didn't know what the effect of ***alcohol*** was because I always had wine, usually with dinner, but always with a lot of ice and about two tablespoons of sugar in it.(p.385)
• I believe the first time I ever realized what ***alcohol*** would do for me was at my own wedding.(p.385)
• It is also stated that we will never be able to figure out how much we have spent on ***alcohol***.(p.396)
• Age and the law were still against me, but laws were not as strictly enforced in those days as they are now, and I discovered that as long as I had the green blood, there was always a way to get ***alcohol***, either from a nondiscriminatory bartender or from an older friend who would be glad to purchase the joy juice for the privilege of sharing it.(p.397)
• My Quaker mother-in-law, bless her heart, used to set the Christmas pudding ablaze with lumps of sugar dipped in rubbing ***alcohol***.(p.402)
• What we had in common was ***alcohol***.(p.405)
• I did not know that I had no power over ***alcohol***, that I, alone and unaided, could not stop; that I was on a downgrade, tearing along at full speed with all my brakes gone, and that the end would be a total smash-up, death or insanity.(p.408)
• Defeated by ***alcohol*** and pills, he found the way to a new life.(p.418)
• My life there was a nightmare of periodic binges on ***alcohol*** and pills, adultery, unhappy hours at the dental office, seeing my wife give birth to our second child and have several miscarriages, living in a turbulent household, and making continual attempts to be the respectable dentist, husband, father, and community leader.(p.419)
• When I went back to my hometown to go into private practice, I experienced another brief lull in my addiction to ***alcohol*** and drugs.(p.420)
• The longer the drinking continued, the shorter the time the ***alcohol*** would keep me asleep; I would have to drink myself back to sleep again and again throughout the night.(p.441)
• In the end, I had to do the same with ***alcohol*** and all pills.(p.443)
• I can't say, "I'm powerless over ***alcohol***, but solid ***alcohol*** is okay."(p.443)
• Giving up ***alcohol*** alone was not enough for me; I've had to give up all mood-and mind-affecting chemicals in order to stay sober and comfortable.(p.443)
• Both times, my reaction was that I had had nothing to drink the night before, so obviously ***alcohol*** had nothing to do with it.(p.444)
• I had already given up all the narcotics, most of the pills, and some of the ***alcohol*** when I first came to A.A.(p.448)
• By early July, I had tapered off ***alcohol*** completely, and I got off all pills in the ensuing few months.(p.448)
• When the compulsion to drink left, it was relatively easy to stay off ***alcohol***.(p.448)
• After I had been around A.A. for seven months, tapering off ***alcohol*** and pills, not finding the program working very well, I was finally able to say, "Okay, God.(p.448)
• But then, as I drank more and more, the ***alcohol*** seemed to affect my vision: Instead of continuing to see what was good about my wife, I began to see her defects.(p.450)
• Eventually, I had to redo each of the Twelve Steps specifically with Max in mind, from the First, saying, "I am powerless over ***alcohol***, and my homelife is unmanageable by me," to the Twelfth, in which I tried to think of her as a sick Al-Anon and treat her with the love I would give a sick A.A. newcomer.(p.452)
• Some went on trying to live with ***alcohol***.(p.455)
• Nothing could pull me out of the abyss but more ***alcohol***.(p.457)
• Later on, it took ***alcohol*** fortified with other drugs to pull me up.(p.457)
• Still later, even ***alcohol*** and chemicals together could not lift me.(p.457)
• ***Alcohol*** wrings the guts out of life, eats into the brain in such a way as to make the alcoholic blind to the truth.(p.457)
• I served twelve years in prison, never suspecting that without ***alcohol*** I would not have been in prison at all.(p.457)
• Intake of ***alcohol*** changes one's personality -- even the healthy personality.(p.458)
• If my personality is inadequate, antisocial, or full of kinks and I alter it with ***alcohol*** or any chemical, bingo!(p.458)
• It is estimated that two-thirds of the men in prison were under the influence of ***alcohol*** and/or drugs when they committed their offenses.(p.458)
• I didn't know I was an alcoholic and (like most men in prison today) could not relate ***alcohol*** to any of my past troubles.(p.460)
• I woke up in jail, sick, withdrawing from ***alcohol*** and speed, already a four-time loser, and now with a fifth felony charge against me.(p.460)
• The idea behind it is that, having taken the treatment, your system is so "conditioned" that the mere sight or smell or taste of ***alcohol*** produces a violent reaction, and you become ill.(p.469)
• That my own innate selfishness and stubbornness are the evils which, if left unguarded, can drive me to ***alcohol***.(p.473)
• I pour out half a tumbler of grain ***alcohol*** and fill it with ginger ale.(p.499)
• My life had become unmanageable due to the excessive use of ***alcohol***.(p.515)
• I lasted at that for four months chiefly on ***alcohol***, because I never seemed to find any time to eat.(p.520)
• Poor, black, totally ruled by ***alcohol***, she felt shut away from any life worth living.(p.526)
• Bob found ***alcohol***!"(p.532)
• But as the years go by, the stretch becomes unbearable; and the man with the grown-up brain and the childish emotions -- vanity, self-interest, false pride, jealousy, longing for social approval, to name few -- becomes a prime candidate for ***alcohol***.(p.534)
• So it was that in ***alcohol*** I found fulfillment.(p.537)
• I had nothing to put in the place of ***alcohol***, of the forgetfulness, of the oblivion, which ***alcohol*** provides.(p.539)
• Without ***alcohol***, I would be really alone.(p.539)
• I went back home, to a job of manual labor where for a little while I was able to keep away from ***alcohol***.(p.539)
• Simply, yes it did end; for I had changed my mind about ***alcohol***, and it stayed changed.(p.541)
• I'd gladly do it anonymously, as I have done this brief account of my struggle with ***alcohol*** -- merely to present certain ideas for the consideration of the reader.(p.542)
• Fear of rejection and its ensuing pain were not to be risked, and I turned away from myself once more for the answer, this time to the drinks I had always refused before, and in ***alcohol*** I found a false courage.(p.546)
• I had no problem admitting I was powerless over ***alcohol***, and I certainly agreed that my life had become unmanageable.(p.550)
• I had to anesthetize that pain with ***alcohol***.(p.557)
• I have learned how to relate to people; before A.A., I could never do that comfortably without ***alcohol***.(p.559)
• 10. -- No A.A. group or member should ever, in such a way as to implicate A.A., express any opinion on outside controversial issues -- particularly those of politics, ***alcohol*** reform, or sectarian religion.(p.567)

alcoholic

• Because this book has become the basic text for our Society and has helped such large numbers of *alcoholic* men and women to recover, there exists a sentiment against any radical changes being made in it.(p.xi)
• We think this account of our experiences will help everyone to better understand the *alcoholic*.(p.xiii)
• Many do not comprehend that the *alcoholic* is a very sick person.(p.xiii)
• We would like it understood that our *alcoholic* work is an avocation.(p.xiii)
• Our earliest printing voiced the hope "that every *alcoholic* who journeys will find the Fellowship of Alcoholics Anonymous at his destination.(p.xv)
• Six months earlier, the broker had been relieved of his drink obsession by a sudden spiritual experience, following a meeting with an *alcoholic* friend who had been in contact with the Oxford Groups of that day.(p.xv)
• Prior to his journey to Akron, the broker had worked hard with many alcoholics on the theory that only an *alcoholic* could help an *alcoholic*, but he had succeeded only in keeping sober himself.(p.xvi)
• He suddenly realized that in order to save himself he must carry his message to another *alcoholic*.(p.xvi)
• That *alcoholic* turned out to be the Akron physician.(p.xvi)
• This physician had repeatedly tried spiritual means to resolve his *alcoholic* dilemma but had failed.(p.xvi)
• This seemed to prove that one *alcoholic* could affect another as no nonalcoholic could.(p.xvi)
• It also indicated that strenuous work, one *alcoholic* with another, was vital to permanent recovery.(p.xvii)
• By late 1937, the number of members having substantial sobriety time behind them was sufficient to convince the membership that a new light had entered the dark world of the *alcoholic*.(p.xvii)
• As we discovered the principles by which the individual *alcoholic* could live, so we had to evolve principles by which the A.A. groups and A.A. as a whole could survive and function effectively.(p.xix)
• It was thought that no *alcoholic* man or woman could be excluded from our Society; that our leaders might serve but never govern; that each group was to be autonomous and there was to be no professional class of therapy.(p.xix)
• Upon therapy for the *alcoholic* himself, we surely have no monopoly.(p.xxi)
• Each day, somewhere in the world, recovery begins when one *alcoholic* talks with another *alcoholic*, sharing experience, strength, and hope.(p.xxii)
• A well-known doctor, chief physician at a nationally prominent hospital specializing in *alcoholic* and drug addiction, gave Alcoholics Anonymous this letter:(p.xxiii)
• In late 1934 I attended a patient who, though he had been a competent businessman of good earning capacity, was an *alcoholic* of a type I had come to regard as hopeless.(p.xxiii)
• In this statement he confirms what we who have suffered *alcoholic* torture must believe – that the body of the *alcoholic* is quite as abnormal as his mind.(p.xxiv)
• In our belief, any picture of the *alcoholic* which leaves out this physical factor is incomplete.(p.xxiv)
• Though we work out our solution on the spiritual as well as an altruistic plane, we favor hospitalization for the *alcoholic* who is very jittery or befogged.(p.xxiv)
• The subject presented in this book seems to me to be of paramount importance to those afflicted with *alcoholic* addiction.(p.xxv)
• I say this after many years' experience as Medical Director of one of the oldest hospitals in the country treating *alcoholic* and drug addiction.(p.xxv)
• The unselfishness of these men as we have come to know them, the entire absence of profit motive, and their community spirit, is indeed inspiring to one who has labored long and wearily in this *alcoholic* field.(p.xxv)
• Of course an *alcoholic* ought to be freed from his physical craving for liquor, and this often requires a definite hospital procedure, before psychological measures can be of maximum benefit.(p.xxv)
• The message which can interest and hold these *alcoholic* people must have depth and weight.(p.xxvi)
• To them, their *alcoholic* life seems the only normal one.(p.xxvi)
• His *alcoholic* problem was so complex, and his depression so great, that we felt his only hope would be through what we then called "moral psychology," and we doubted if even that would have any effect.(p.xxix)
• I earnestly advise every *alcoholic* to read this book through, and though perhaps he came to scoff, he may remain to pray.(p.xxx)
• Potential *alcoholic* that I was, I nearly failed my law course.(p.2)
• Rumor had it that he had been committed for *alcoholic* insanity.(p.9)
• So that was it – last summer an *alcoholic* crackpot; now, I suspected, a little cracked about religion.(p.9)
• And how appallingly true for the *alcoholic*!(p.14)
• For if an *alcoholic* failed to perfect and enlarge his spiritual life through work and self-sacrifice for others, he could not survive the certain trials and low spots ahead.(p.14)
• This sometimes nearly drove me back to drink, but I soon found that when all other measures failed, work with another *alcoholic* would save the day.(p.15)
• An *alcoholic* in his cups is an unlovely creature.(p.16)
• But not so with the *alcoholic* illness, for with it there goes annihilation of all the things worth while in life.(p.18)
• Highly competent psychiatrists who have dealt with us have found it sometimes impossible to persuade an *alcoholic* to discuss his situation without reserve.(p.18)
• But the ex-problem drinker who has found this solution, who is properly armed with facts about himself, can generally win the entire confidence of another *alcoholic* in a few hours.(p.18)
• If your are an *alcoholic* who wants to get over it, you may already be asking – "What do I have to do?"(p.20)
• But what about the real *alcoholic*?(p.21)
• This is by no means a comprehensive picture of the true *alcoholic*, as our behavior patterns vary.(p.22)
• Opinions vary considerably as to why the *alcoholic* reacts differently from normal people.(p.22)
• We know that while the *alcoholic* keeps away from drink, as he may do for months or years, he reacts much like other men.(p.22)
• The experience of any *alcoholic* will abundantly confirm this.(p.23)
• Therefore, the main problem of the *alcoholic* centers in his mind, rather than in his body.(p.23)
• If you draw this fallacious reasoning to the attention of an *alcoholic*, he will laugh it off, or become irritated and refuse to talk.(p.23)
• The tragic truth is that if the man be a real *alcoholic*, the happy day may not arrive.(p.23)
• At a certain point in the drinking of every *alcoholic*, he passes into a state where the most powerful desire to stop drinking is of absolutely no avail.(p.24)
• The *alcoholic* may say to himself in the most casual way, "It won't burn me this time, so here's how!"(p.24)
• When this sort of thinking is fully established in an individual with *alcoholic* tendencies, he has probably placed himself beyond human aid, and unless locked up, may die or go permanently insane.(p.24)
• If you are as seriously *alcoholic* as we were, we believe there is no middle-of-the-road solution.(p.25)
• Some of our *alcoholic* readers may think they can do without spiritual help.(p.27)
• The doctor said: "You have the mind of a chronic *alcoholic*.(p.27)
• With many individuals the methods which I employed are successful, but I have never been successful with an *alcoholic* of your description."(p.27)
• Our hope is that many *alcoholic* men and women, desperately in need, will see these pages, and we believe that it is only by fully disclosing ourselves and our problems that they will be persuaded to say, "Yes, I am one of them too; I must have this thing."(p.29)
• We know that no real *alcoholic* ever recovers control.(p.30)
• Physicians who are familiar with alcoholism agree there is no such thing as making a normal drinker out of an *alcoholic*.(p.31)
• We do not like to pronounce any individual as *alcoholic*, but you can quickly diagnose yourself.(p.31)
• Then he fell victim to a belief which practically every *alcoholic* has – that his long period of sobriety and self-discipline had qualified him to drink as other men.(p.32)
• We have seen the truth demonstrated again and again: "Once an *alcoholic*, always an *alcoholic*."(p.33)
• If he is a real *alcoholic* and very far advanced, there is scant chance of success.(p.34)
• Though you may be able to stop for a considerable period, you may yet be a potential *alcoholic*.(p.34)
• The experiment of quitting for a period of time will be helpful, but we think we can render an even greater service to *alcoholic* sufferers and perhaps to the medical fraternity.(p.34)
• What sort of thinking dominates an *alcoholic* who repeats time after time the desperate experiment of the first drink?(p.35)
• He agreed he was a real *alcoholic* and in a serious condition.(p.35)
• He had much knowledge about himself as an *alcoholic*.(p.36)
• But the actual or potential *alcoholic*, with hardly an exception, will be absolutely unable to stop drinking on the basis of self-knowledge.(p.39)
• This is a point we wish to emphasize and re-emphasize, to smash home upon our *alcoholic* readers as it has been revealed to us out of bitter experience.(p.39)
• Yet, he is *alcoholic*.(p.39)
• Far from admitting he was an *alcoholic*, he told himself he came to the hospital to rest his nerves.(p.39)
• Fred would not believe himself an *alcoholic*, much less accept a spiritual remedy for his problem.(p.39)
• I now remembered what my *alcoholic* friends had told me, how they prophesied that if I had an *alcoholic* mind, the time and place would come – I would drink again.(p.41)
• I knew from that moment that I had an *alcoholic* mind.(p.42)
• They grinned, which I didn't like so much, and then asked me if I thought myself *alcoholic* and if I were really licked this time.(p.42)
• They piled on me heaps of evidence to the effect that an *alcoholic* mentality, such as I had exhibited in Washington, was a hopeless condition.(p.42)
• But the moment I made up my mind to go through with the process, I had the curious feeling that my *alcoholic* condition was relieved, as in fact it proved to be.(p.42)
• Once more: The *alcoholic* at certain times has no effective mental defense against the first drink.(p.43)
• We hope we have made clear the distinction between the *alcoholic* and the non-alcoholic.(p.44)
• To one who feels he is an atheist or agnostic such an experience seems impossible, but to continue as he is means disaster, especially if he is an *alcoholic* of the hopeless variety.(p.44)
• To be doomed to an *alcoholic* death or to live on a spiritual basis are not always easy alternatives to face.(p.44)
• Many times we talk to a new man and watch his hope rise as we discuss his *alcoholic* problems and explain our fellowship.(p.45)
• Faced with *alcoholic* destruction, we soon became as open minded on spiritual matters as we tried to be on other questions.(p.48)
• His *alcoholic* problem was taken away.(p.56)
• Our description of the *alcoholic*, the chapter to the agnostic, and our personal adventures before and after make clear three pertinent ideas:(p.60)
• (a) That we were *alcoholic* and could not manage our own lives.(p.60)
• He is like the retired business man who lolls in the Florida sunshine in the winter complaining of the sad state of the nation; the minister who sighs over the sins of the twentieth century; politicians and reformers who are sure all would be Utopia if the rest of the world would only behave; the outlaw safe cracker who thinks society has wronged him; and the *alcoholic* who has lost all and is locked up.(p.61)
• They arise out of ourselves, and the *alcoholic* is an extreme example of self-will run riot, though he usually doesn't think so.(p.62)
• But with the *alcoholic*, whose hope is the maintenance and growth of a spiritual experience, this business of resentment is infinitely grave.(p.66)
• More than most people, the *alcoholic* leads a double life.(p.73)
• Therefore, we are not to be the hasty and foolish martyr who would needlessly sacrifice others to save himself from the *alcoholic* pit.(p.79)
• After a few years with an *alcoholic*, a wife gets worn out, resentful and uncommunicative.(p.81)
• Sometimes we hear an *alcoholic* say that the only thing he needs to do is to keep sober.(p.82)
• The *alcoholic* is like a tornado roaring his way through the lives of others.(p.82)
• When he sees you know all about the drinking game, commence to describe yourself as an *alcoholic*.(p.91)
• If he is *alcoholic*, he will understand you at once.(p.92)
• If you are satisfied that he is a real *alcoholic*, begin to dwell on the hopeless feature of the malady.(p.92)
• And be careful not to brand him as an *alcoholic*.(p.92)
• If he sticks to the ideas that he can still control his drinking, tell him that possibly he can – if he is not too *alcoholic*.(p.92)
• Doctors are rightly loath to tell *alcoholic* patients the whole story unless it will serve some good purpose.(p.92)
• You will soon have your friend admitting he has

many, if not all, of the traits of the ***alcoholic***.(p.92)
• If his own doctor is willing to tell him that he is ***alcoholic***, so much the better.(p.92)
• Never talk down to an ***alcoholic*** from any moral or spiritual hilltop; simply lay out the kit of spiritual tools for his inspection.(p.95)
• Search out another ***alcoholic*** and try again.(p.96)
• To spend too much time on any one situation is to deny some other ***alcoholic*** an opportunity to live and be happy.(p.96)
• We seldom allow an ***alcoholic*** to live in our homes for long at a time.(p.97)
• Though an ***alcoholic*** does not respond, there is no reason why you should neglect his family.(p.97)
• For the type of ***alcoholic*** who is able and willing to get well, little charity, in the ordinary sense of the word, is needed or wanted.(p.97)
• The minute we put our work on a service plane, the ***alcoholic*** commences to rely upon our assistance rather than upon God.(p.98)
• These things will come to pass naturally and in good time provided, however, the ***alcoholic*** continues to demonstrate that he can be sober, considerate, and helpful, regardless of what anyone says or does.(p.99)
• Let the ***alcoholic*** continue his program day by day.(p.99)
• Let no ***alcoholic*** say he cannot recover unless he has his family back.(p.99)
• An ***alcoholic*** who cannot meet them, still has an ***alcoholic*** mind; there is something the matter with his spiritual status.(p.101)
• If the ***alcoholic*** tries to shield himself he may succeed for a time, but he usually winds up with a bigger explosion than ever.(p.101)
• To a person who has had experience with an ***alcoholic***, this may seem like tempting Providence, but it isn't.(p.101)
• But if you are shaky, you had better work with another ***alcoholic*** instead!(p.102)
• Some of us still serve it to our friends provided they are not ***alcoholic***.(p.102)
• Every new ***alcoholic*** looks for this spirit among us and is immensely relieved when he finds we are not witch-burners.(p.103)
• Some day we hope that Alcoholics Anonymous will help the public to a better realization of the gravity of the ***alcoholic*** problem, but we shall be of little use if our attitude is one of bitterness or hostility.(p.103)
• What they say will apply to nearly everyone bound by ties of blood or affections to an ***alcoholic***.(p.104)
• Had we fully understood the nature of the ***alcoholic*** illness, we might have behaved differently.(p.107)
• These are some of the questions which race through the mind of every woman who has an ***alcoholic*** husband.(p.108)
• Of course, there is such a thing as incompatibility, but in nearly every instance the ***alcoholic*** only seems to be unloving and inconsiderate; it is usually because he is warped and sickened that he says and does these appalling things.(p.108)
• Try not to condemn your ***alcoholic*** husband no matter what he says or does.(p.108)
• An ***alcoholic*** of this temperament may be quick to use this chapter as a club over your head.(p.108)
• He would probably be insulted if he were called an ***alcoholic***.(p.109)
• These are the earmarks of a real ***alcoholic***.(p.109)
• This may lay the groundwork for a friendly talk about his ***alcoholic*** problem.(p.111)
• If he is lukewarm or thinks he is not an ***alcoholic***, we suggest you leave him alone.(p.113)
• Never forget that resentment is a deadly hazard to an ***alcoholic***.(p.117)
• We do not like the thought that the contents of a book or the work of another ***alcoholic*** has accomplished in a few weeks that for which we struggled for years.(p.118)
• We find it a real mistake to dampen his enthusiasm for ***alcoholic*** work.(p.119)
• We suggest that you direct some of your thought to the wives of his new ***alcoholic*** friends.(p.119)
• It is probably true that you and your husband have been living too much alone, for drinking many times isolates the wife of an ***alcoholic***.(p.119)
• The ***alcoholic***, his wife, his children, his "in-laws," each one is likely to have fixed ideas about the family's attitude toward himself or herself.(p.122)
• A doctor said to us, "Years of living with an ***alcoholic*** is almost sure to make any wife or child neurotic.(p.122)
• The family of an ***alcoholic*** longs for the return of happiness and security.(p.123)
• Now and then the family will be plagued by spectres from the past, for the drinking career of almost every ***alcoholic*** has been marked by escapades, funny, humiliating, shameful or tragic.(p.123)
• For example, we know of situations in which the ***alcoholic*** or his wife have had love affairs.(p.124)
• In most cases, the ***alcoholic*** survived this ordeal without relapse, but not always.(p.125)
• Everyone knows about the others' ***alcoholic*** troubles.(p.125)
• One more suggestion: Whether the family has spiritual convictions or not, they may do well to examine the principles by which the ***alcoholic*** member is trying to live.(p.130)
• Being possessed of a spiritual experience, the ***alcoholic*** will find he has much in common with these people, though he may differ with them on many matters.(p.131)
• The ***alcoholic*** may find it hard to re-establish friendly relations with his children.(p.134)
• Whether the family goes on a spiritual basis or not, the ***alcoholic*** member has to if he would recover.(p.135)
• He knows the ***alcoholic*** as the employer sees him.(p.136)
• What irony -- I became an ***alcoholic*** myself!(p.137)
• That he has not always done so for the ***alcoholic*** is easily understood.(p.137)
• To him the ***alcoholic*** has often seemed a fool of the first magnitude.(p.137)
• One day he told me about an executive of the same bank who, from his description, was undoubtedly ***alcoholic***.(p.138)
• Why not bring him into contact with some of our ***alcoholic*** crowd?(p.138)
• To me, this incident illustrates lack of understanding as to what really ails the ***alcoholic***, and lack of knowledge as to what part employers might profitably take in salvaging their sick employees.(p.139)
• Those who drink moderately may be more annoyed with an ***alcoholic*** than a total abstainer would be.(p.139)
• Drinking occasionally, and understanding your own reactions, it is possible for you to become quite sure of many things which, so far as the ***alcoholic*** is concerned, are not always so.(p.139)
• When dealing with an ***alcoholic***, there may be a natural annoyance that a man could be so weak, stupid and irresponsible.(p.139)
• A look at the ***alcoholic*** in your organization is many times illuminating.(p.139)
• If this presents difficulty, re-reading chapters two and three, where the ***alcoholic*** sickness is discussed at length might be worth while.(p.140)
• No wonder an ***alcoholic*** is strangely irrational.(p.140)
• Normal drinkers are not so affected, nor can they understand the aberrations of the ***alcoholic***.(p.140)
• When drinking, or getting over a bout, an ***alcoholic***, sometimes the model of honesty when normal, will do incredible things.(p.140)
• If he temporizes and still thinks he can ever drink again, even beer, he might as well be discharged after the next bender which, if an ***alcoholic***, he is almost certain to have.(p.142)
• While on the subject of confidence, can you adopt the attitude that so far as you are concerned this will be a strictly personal matter, that his ***alcoholic*** derelictions, the treatment about to be undertaken, will never be discussed without his consent?(p.143)
• In another case, an ***alcoholic*** was sent to a hospital for treatment.(p.145)
• After your man has gone along without drinking for a few months, you may be able to make use of his services with other employees who are giving you the ***alcoholic*** run-around -- provided, of course, they are willing to have a third party in the picture.(p.146)
• An ***alcoholic*** who has recovered, but holds a relatively unimportant job, can talk to a man with a better position.(p.146)
• Long experience with ***alcoholic*** excuses naturally arouses suspicion.(p.146)
• If you are an ***alcoholic***, you are a mighty sick man.(p.147)
• He need not, and often should not show it to his ***alcoholic*** prospect.(p.148)
• He will have no further reason for covering up an ***alcoholic*** employee.(p.148)
• It boils right down to this: No man should be fired just because he is ***alcoholic***.(p.148)
• I don't see how you can be of any help to us for, as you see, we don't have any ***alcoholic*** problem."(p.148)
• We, who have collectively seen a great deal of business life, at least from the ***alcoholic*** angle, had to smile at this gentleman's sincere opinion.(p.149)
• Even if you feel your organization has no ***alcoholic*** problem, it might pay to take another look down the line.(p.149)
• As to them, his policy is undoubtedly sound, but he did not distinguish between such people and the ***alcoholic***.(p.149)
• It is not to be expected that an ***alcoholic*** employee will receive a disproportionate amount of time and attention.(p.149)
• There are two ***alcoholic*** employees, who produce as much as five normal salesmen.(p.149)
• His call to the clergyman led him presently to a certain resident of the town, who, though formerly able and respected, was then nearing the nadir of ***alcoholic*** despair.(p.155)
• Painfully aware of being somehow abnormal, the man did not fully realize what it meant to be ***alcoholic***.(p.155)
• He had, of course, the familiar ***alcoholic*** obsession that few knew of his drinking.(p.155)
• They explained their need and inquired if she had a first class ***alcoholic*** prospect.(p.156)
• The man in the bed was told of the acute poisoning from which he suffered, how it deteriorates the body of an ***alcoholic*** and warps his mind.(p.157)
• Many an ***alcoholic*** who entered there came away with an answer.(p.160)
• In one of these there is a well-known hospital for the treatment of ***alcoholic*** and drug addiction.(p.161)
• Some day we hope that every ***alcoholic*** who journeys will find a Fellowship of Alcoholics Anonymous at his destination.(p.162)
• Seventeen stories may help you decide whether you are ***alcoholic***; also, whether A.A. is for you.(p.167)
• To 1950, the year of his death, he carried the A.A. message to more than 5,000 ***alcoholic*** men and women, and to all these he gave his medical services without thought of charge.(p.171)
• Never once in my life have I had a headache, which fact leads me to believe that I was an ***alcoholic*** almost from the start.(p.172)
• ***ALCOHOLIC*** ANONYMOUS NUMBER THREE(p.182)
• You are an ***alcoholic***."(p.187)
• Did she have an ***alcoholic*** customer on whom it could be tried?(p.188)
• I was the oldest of three children, and my father was an ***alcoholic***.(p.193)
• My mother was eighty-nine years old when she died, and I was a full-blown ***alcoholic*** at the time of her death.(p.210)
• All during Prohibition, every ***alcoholic*** felt that he made the best hooch, regardless of how bad it was.(p.213)
• The first definite indications of an ***alcoholic*** pattern began to arise when I would go to New York on business and disappear, and wind up in Philadelphia or Boston for two or three day periods.(p.213)
• I resented it of course, and I offered Clarence his commission, whatever it might be, if he would please not bother me because I had arrived at the conclusion that he was a solicitor for some ***alcoholic*** institute.(p.216)
• He startled me by informing me that he was an ***alcoholic***, that he had found a way which so far enabled him to live without taking a drink, and that the main idea was to find a way how not to take that first drink.(p.218)
• That is, it was sort of a mixed bunch of Oxford Groupers, who were interested in the ***alcoholic*** problem, and of alcoholics themselves.(p.218)
• My husband was an ***alcoholic*** -- I had only contempt for those without my own amazing capacity -- the outcome was inevitable.(p.225)
• You can all remember that in the first few months after the change, a great many men, who had formerly been used to a few beers every day or an occasional drink of whiskey, simply quit all ***alcoholic*** drinks.(p.232)
• I had all the usual experiences of the ***alcoholic***, for I was certainly one by this time.(p.233)
• An ***alcoholic*** who was a doctor came to see me.(p.235)
• In a few sentences he made God seem personal to me, explained Him as a being who was interested in me, the ***alcoholic***, and that all I needed to do was to be willing to follow His way; that as long as I followed it I would be able to overcome my desire for liquor.(p.236)
• It wasn't very long until my doctor friend sent me to tell another ***alcoholic*** what my experience had been.(p.237)
• My family lived in very prosperous circumstances, and while both my parents drank, sometimes too much, neither was an ***alcoholic***.(p.240)

• There were four of us children, and although both of my brothers later became *alcoholic* -- one died of alcoholism -- my sister has never taken a drink in her life.(p.240)
• Even that first night I blacked out, which leads me to believe that I was an *alcoholic* from my very first drink.(p.241)
• In the Army, I became a periodic *alcoholic* -- the periods always coming whenever I could make the opportunity.(p.241)
• Back at camp, all was forgiven because it was the End, but in the light of what I have since learned I know I was a confirmed *alcoholic* at nineteen.(p.242)
• The mental state of the sick *alcoholic* is beyond description.(p.244)
• In June, 1945, with another member, I made my first -- and only -- Twelfth Step call on a female *alcoholic* and a year later I married her.(p.249)
• Enduring all the hangover hells that every *alcoholic* experiences, I made the usual resolutions.(p.256)
• That night I was taken home by a former *alcoholic* and his wife.(p.259)
• I was the oldest in a family of seven, and my father was an *alcoholic*.(p.261)
• Dr. Bob often said that it was a record for what he felt was a typical *alcoholic*.(p.263)
• There was a man watching, and I turned to him and said with a defiant air I carried with me all the time, "If I don't quit this I'm going to have to join that *alcoholic* business they're talking about."(p.266)
• That was our last drink of anything *alcoholic*.(p.267)
• The next day he turned me over to a couple who, although neither was an *alcoholic*, knew Dr. Bob and were willing to drive me to Akron where they would turn me over to his care.(p.278)
• So I spent much of my time calling on the people who I felt would logically come in contact with *alcoholic* cases, doctors, ministers, lawyers and the personnel men in industry.(p.281)
• I lived through a week of the fidgets because I had agreed to address a group of *alcoholic* inmates in one of our state mental hospitals.(p.283)
• Being an *alcoholic*, I couldn't dream of doing anything by halves!(p.286)
• When I told them six weeks, they were polite and said that they would contact me in case they had anyone with an *alcoholic* problem.(p.293)
• That was my lesson, that one could not take the moral inventory and then file it away; that the *alcoholic* has to continue to take inventory every day if he expects to get well and stay well.(p.293)
• Above all, I have gained the greatest thing accorded to any man, the love and understanding of a gracious God, who has lifted me from the *alcoholic* scrap-heap to a position of trust where I have been able to reap the rich rewards that come from showing a little love for others and from serving them as I can.(p.296)
• At twenty-five I had developed an *alcoholic* problem.(p.305)
• Why he bothered with me as long as he did I shall never know, for he knew there was no answer for me in medicine and he, like all doctors of his day, had been taught that the *alcoholic* was incurable and should be ignored.(p.307)
• With the *alcoholic*, they could only give temporary relief and in the last stages not even that.(p.307)
• Nevertheless, there were a few doctors who saw alcoholism as a disease and felt that the *alcoholic* was a victim of something over which he had no control.(p.307)
• Until now, I had never been told that I was an *alcoholic*.(p.307)
• Every doctor gets his quota of *alcoholic* patients.(p.308)
• He said the *alcoholic* seemed to possess a native acuteness and usually excelled in his field, regardless of environmental or educational advantages.(p.308)
• "We watch the *alcoholic* performing in a position of responsibility and we know that because he is drinking heavily and daily he has cut his capacities by fifty per cent, and still he seems able to do a satisfactory job.(p.308)
• And we wonder how much further this man could go if his *alcoholic* problem could be removed and he could throw one hundred per cent of his abilities into action.(p.308)
• But, of course," he continued, "eventually the *alcoholic* loses all of his capacities as his disease gets progressively worse, and this is a tragedy that is painful to watch; the disintegration of a sound mind and body."(p.308)
• The next day I received a visit from Mr. T., a recovered *alcoholic*.(p.309)
• Nothing in their lives took precedence over their response to a call for help from some *alcoholic* in need.(p.310)
• Shortly after I returned to Chicago, my doctor, encouraged by the results of my contact with A.A., sent us two more of his *alcoholic* patients.(p.310)
• There is no more "aloneness," with that awful ache, so deep in the heart of every *alcoholic* that nothing, before, could ever reach it.(p.312)
• But he couldn't be an *alcoholic* at his age, could he?(p.317)
• I am a twenty-four-year-old *alcoholic*.(p.317)
• An *alcoholic* can't lay off the booze -- right?(p.317)
• "I'm not crazy," I thought, "and I can't be an *alcoholic* -- I'm too young."(p.319)
• I sat and listened and heard the first speaker say, "I'm an *alcoholic*."(p.319)
• Like I said, I'm a twenty-four-year-old *alcoholic* -- and I'm happy.(p.320)
• I didn't think I was an *alcoholic*.(p.321)
• This girl and her husband are both in A.A., and she said to me, "Oh, but you're not the *alcoholic*; it's your husband."(p.322)
• She said, "Twenty-seven years to an *alcoholic*!(p.322)
• I should have lost my husband, and I think that only the fact that he was an *alcoholic* too kept us together.(p.323)
• Retirement rids the potential *alcoholic* of many shackles.(p.329)
• He may even read in a newspaper that one out of every seven drinkers will become *alcoholic*, but he rarely is told that it holds true for all ages -- or that the tolerance to alcohol (and other drugs) decreases steadily, year after year, in the bodies of all persons.(p.330)
• What *alcoholic* can live with rejection?(p.331)
• I could hide my *alcoholic* stupor behind pretense.(p.332)
• No matter how often I had gone into and come out of *alcoholic* lows during the day, the pattern bounced me out of bed each night about 2:00 a.m., shaking and hurting in the agitation that always follows a drug's sedation.(p.332)
• I told her that I was an *alcoholic*, victim of a disease, that there was no cure, only arrestment through total abstinence.(p.333)
• You're not an *alcoholic*.(p.334)
• At one time, the admission that I was and am an *alcoholic* meant shame, defeat, and failure to me.(p.335)
• And believe me, an *alcoholic* cannot fight alcohol.(p.338)
• Mere cessation from drinking is not enough for an *alcoholic* while the need for that drink goes on.(p.339)
• However, I am an *alcoholic*, so I always looked forward to the day when I would be able to drink again.(p.343)
• And I knew this: Once an *alcoholic*, always an *alcoholic*.(p.344)
• I am also an *alcoholic*.(p.345)
• He said, "I'm an *alcoholic*, what do I do?"(p.347)
• I tried every gimmick that there was to get some peace of mind, but it was not until I was brought to my *alcoholic* knees, when I was brought to a group in my own community with the butcher, the baker, the carpenter and the mechanic, who were able to give me the Twelve Steps, that I was finally given some semblance of an answer to the last half of the First Step.(p.349)
• And then I thought to myself: "Imagine an *alcoholic* admitting anything!"(p.349)
• And this chokes the *alcoholic*.(p.350)
• It fills the *alcoholic* with rage.(p.350)
• I had my first drink when I was fifteen and my *alcoholic* potential had ripened me to the point of necessary escapism.(p.353)
• With these new and enlightening doors opening up to me, I was able to make the eventual decision to stop drinking, a day at a time -- because I, too, was an *alcoholic*.(p.355)
• "You an *alcoholic*!(p.356)
• "Sure, I've seen you tight several times, but you're no *alcoholic*!"(p.356)
• "You kidding -- you an *alcoholic*?"(p.356)
• Many times have I heard the above expressions since I have been in A.A., and many times I have had to reply "Definitely I am an *alcoholic*, and while it may be hard for you to believe, it is not hard for me, for I have learned many things about alcohol and myself that would, perhaps, be difficult for you to understand."(p.356)
• As these words are written at fifty-three years of age, with over nine years of A.A. behind me, with all its wonderful teachings, I haven't the slightest doubt about being an *alcoholic*.(p.356)
• Before long I was at the luncheon meeting an hour before the others, that old and familiar trademark of every *alcoholic*.(p.360)
• It wasn't long before I became a five o'clock *alcoholic*.(p.360)
• I graduated there from a five o'clock *alcoholic* to a noon-day one.(p.361)
• I did everything to make her an *alcoholic* too.(p.361)
• In my drinking days, I found the ideal spot for the *alcoholic* housewife: the neighborhood Laundromat.(p.369)
• A few months after that, I was released and left the world of insanity, only to return to the world of *alcoholic* insanity.(p.370)
• How can a person with a fine family, an attractive home, an excellent position and high standing in an important city become an *alcoholic*?(p.373)
• What *alcoholic* can be satisfied with one drink?(p.377)
• She of course didn't realize how cunning an *alcoholic* can be and the lengths to which he will go in finding ways to satisfy the compulsion for more and more drinks after having had the first one.(p.377)
• However, after I heard a few stories of jails, sanitariums, broken homes and skid row, I wondered if I really was an *alcoholic*.(p.378)
• Could I be an *alcoholic* without some of the hair-raising experiences I had heard of in meetings?(p.379)
• At first it was a shock to realize I was an *alcoholic*, but the realization that there was hope made it easier.(p.379)
• I liked the description of the *alcoholic* as a person who had found that alcohol is interfering with his social or business life.(p.380)
• The *alcoholic* has them to an exaggerated degree.(p.380)
• Frank found the doctor, but the doctor didn't want to take an *alcoholic*.(p.387)
• Dr. Bob said, "Love and service keep us dry," and Bill said, "Always we must remember that our first duty is face-to-face help for the *alcoholic* who still suffers."(p.395)
• To me, A.A. is within the reach of every *alcoholic*, because it can be achieved in any walk of life and because the achievement is not ours but God's.(p.395)
• I displayed *alcoholic* tendencies actually from the age of fourteen, when I started to steal wine from the family jug, siphoning it off one drink at a time so it wouldn't be missed, not drinking it immediately, but saving it until about a pint was accumulated, so that I could get drunk.(p.397)
• But I was a careful and cunning *alcoholic*, and this didn't happen very often.(p.399)
• My *alcoholic* problem began long before I drank.(p.400)
• My personality, from the time I can remember anything, was the perfect set-up for an *alcoholic* career.(p.400)
• I saw him recently and he told me that he had always felt guilty, because, after our separation, I had become a serious *alcoholic*.(p.403)
• With ten years of A.A. behind me, I was able to tell him that I'd have been *alcoholic*, no matter what; that I had been a sick person, unfit for marriage.(p.403)
• He also said, "You are an *alcoholic* and there's nothing I can do for you."(p.406)
• An *alcoholic* cannot accept the news that he's an *alcoholic* unless there is a meaningful explanation given, and an offer of help, such as you get in A.A.(p.406)
• My first analyst said, "You are becoming more and more of an *alcoholic*," and sent me to another analyst.(p.407)
• I was an *alcoholic*, with a recognizable behavior pattern.(p.414)
• If I had not become an active *alcoholic* and joined A.A., I might never have found my own identity or become a part of anything.(p.417)
• No one could have told me then that I had not earned all my success, nor could anyone have told me that I was an *alcoholic* and a drug addict.(p.418)
• I am a young *alcoholic* with a drug problem, a doctor, the husband of an *alcoholic*, the son of an *alcoholic*, and a man once diagnosed as a violent manic-depressive.(p.421)
• I'm an *alcoholic*.(p.423)
• ME AN *ALCOHOLIC*?(p.432)
• How could such a man possibly be called an *alcoholic*?(p.433)
• My daily *alcoholic* consumption remained about the same through all this, with perhaps a slight increase, and my binges remained one-nighters.(p.434)
• After talking with him for a time I heard myself saying, "Doc, I think I'm an *alcoholic*."(p.436)
• The line between a heavy drinker and an *alcoholic*

is not always clear.(p.436)
• Only through being beaten down by my own misery would I ever have accepted the term "*alcoholic*" as applied to myself.(p.436)
• My *alcoholic* associates fired me, took control, and ran the enterprise into bankruptcy.(p.437)
• My *alcoholic* wife took up someone else, divorced me, and took with her all my remaining property.(p.437)
• DOCTOR, *ALCOHOLIC*, ADDICT(p.439)
• Never in my wildest moments had it occurred to me that I might like to be an *alcoholic*.(p.439)
• Not only did I not think that being an *alcoholic* was a good idea, I didn't even feel that I had all that much of a drinking problem!(p.439)
• Very shortly, I realized that had been a mistake -- when this big clown came bounding into the room, almost shouting, "My name is Frank, and I'm an *alcoholic*, ha-ha-ha!"(p.446)
• I really felt sorry for him; the only thing in life he had to brag about was the fact that he was an *alcoholic*.(p.446)
• At first, I wondered whether he was *alcoholic* himself, and was sending me to find out about A.A.(p.446)
• (Today, there is absolutely nothing in the world more important to me than my keeping this *alcoholic* sober; not taking a drink is by far the most important thing I do each day.)(p.447)
• It is true that I -- of all people, strange as it may seem, and even though I didn't give my permission -- really, really am an *alcoholic* of sorts.(p.448)
• For years, I was sure the worst thing that could happen to a nice guy like me would be that I would turn out to be an *alcoholic*.(p.449)
• There are many things worse than dying, but is there any death worse than the progressive, self-induced, slow suicide of the practicing *alcoholic*?(p.457)
• The *alcoholic* suffers death many times over.(p.457)
• Alcohol wrings the guts out of life, eats into the brain in such a way as to make the *alcoholic* blind to the truth.(p.457)
• Most of us did not stay out of prison long enough to run the *alcoholic* gamut -- to develop the ongoing kind of alcoholism or *alcoholic* drinking you hear about in A.A. talks.(p.458)
• I didn't know I was an *alcoholic* and (like most men in prison today) could not relate alcohol to any of my past troubles.(p.460)
• I suddenly remembered one of my first A.A. meetings, where I heard, "If you are an *alcoholic* and if you continue to drink, the end is death or insanity."(p.461)
• The word "*alcoholic*" does not turn me off any more; in fact, it is music to my ears when it applies to me.(p.463)
• I wasn't always an *alcoholic*.(p.464)
• In fact it has been only within the last fifteen years that I changed from a fairly normal, controlled drinker into an *alcoholic*.(p.464)
• I don't mean that I went to bed one night a normal drinker, and awoke the next morning an *alcoholic*.(p.464)
• There was that awful *alcoholic* loneliness.(p.467)
• Was it because they told me in A.A. that I was an *alcoholic*?(p.470)
• Yes, I even knew I was a "chronic *alcoholic*."(p.470)
• Only they had been scratched out and over them was written, "Chronic *Alcoholic*."(p.470)
• I had been promoted from a periodic drinker to a chronic *alcoholic*!(p.470)
• A.A. didn't teach me I was an *alcoholic*; rather it taught me that because I was an *alcoholic* my life had become unmanageable.(p.470)
• In all the sanitariums and psycho wards I had never met a single woman who said she was an *alcoholic*.(p.471)
• When I first came into A.A., the woman who was my sponsor was the first woman I had ever met who admitted that she was an *alcoholic*.(p.472)
• Of course I had the sensitive, hurt feelings of the *alcoholic*.(p.472)
• Now think I was *alcoholic* from first drink.(p.474)
• This sober Indian say to sick, red-eyed *alcoholic* who want good medicine: "Put cork in bottle.(p.477)
• The only time that I have ever seen my mother take anything *alcoholic* was around Christmas time, when she would drink some eggnog or light wine.(p.484)
• After our first child came my parents both became allies, but in later days, after I became an *alcoholic*, they both turned against me.(p.485)
• Being an *alcoholic*, slick, and having some good sense left, I survived the investigation.(p.490)
• I just gathered up this and that *alcoholic*, because, in the back of my mind, I wanted to save all the world.(p.496)
• I am an *alcoholic*.(p.502)
• But somehow or other, with my old *alcoholic* brain, sitting there in that chair, I kept saying to myself, "I wonder if it'll work?(p.515)
• They brought me in and of course, they hadn't very much trouble in finding that I was *alcoholic*.(p.521)
• I didn't know what an *alcoholic* was.(p.521)
• I am an Afro-American *alcoholic*.(p.526)
• I don't know when I became an *alcoholic*, but I do believe I became one because I drank too much too often.(p.526)
• I wasn't an *alcoholic*!(p.527)
• That was one of the worst things that could have happened to an *alcoholic* woman.(p.527)
• I would wait for the mailman each month, like any good mother, but as soon as he handed me my check, I put on my best dress and went looking for my *alcoholic* friend.(p.527)
• Today, I thank my Higher Power for giving me another chance at life and A.A. and being able to try and help some other *alcoholic*.(p.529)
• That was the day, that was the decision, I know now, when I crossed over the line and became an active *alcoholic*.(p.531)
• On that day of decision, I didn't acknowledge that I was an *alcoholic*.(p.532)
• In those years I was in jail nine times, in an *alcoholic* ward, overnight, twice; and I was fired from three jobs, two of them very good ones.(p.536)
• What a revelation of ego and arrogance still remaining in me -- as if anyone, instinct and training apart, likes to be in jail or in an *alcoholic* ward or fired from his job.(p.536)
• I have not had a drink of anything *alcoholic* since that ten-day binge.(p.541)
• When I remark that I have been in jail nine times, and in an *alcoholic* ward twice, they think I'm kidding, or possibly dramatizing for the sake of a good yarn.(p.542)
• My mother went to a nearby city to go to work, and my father, being an *alcoholic*, simply went.(p.544)
• It seems only fitting that when I did finally fall in love it was with an *alcoholic*, and for the next ten years I progressed as rapidly as is humanly possible into what I believed to be hopeless alcoholism.(p.547)
• By this time I was such a past master at kidding myself that I had convinced myself I had sat out a war and waited for this man to come home and, as my resentment and self-pity grew, so did my *alcoholic* problem.(p.548)
• It was here that I realized for the first time that as a practicing *alcoholic* I had no rights.(p.549)
• Five -- Each group has but one primary purpose -- to carry its message to the *alcoholic* who still suffers.(p.564)
• 5. -- Each Alcoholics Anonymous group ought to be a spiritual entity having but one primary purpose -- that of carrying its message to the *alcoholic* who still suffers.(p.565)
• Most emphatically we wish to say that any *alcoholic* capable of honestly facing his problems in the light of our experience can recover, provided he does not close his mind to all spiritual concepts.(p.570)
• In this atmosphere the *alcoholic* often overcomes his excessive concentration upon himself.(p.572)
• Should you be the relative or friend of an *alcoholic* who shows no immediate interest in A.A., it is suggested that you write the Al-Anon Family Groups, Inc., Box 182, Madison Square Station, New York, NY 10159, U.S.A.(p.575)

alcoholic's

• Sometimes these excuses have a certain plausibility, but none of them really makes sense in the light of the havoc an *alcoholic's* drinking bout creates.(p.23)
• One of these men, staff member of a world-renowned hospital, recently made this statement to some of us: "What you say about the general hopelessness of the average *alcoholic's* plight is, in my opinion, correct.(p.43)
• The *alcoholic's* past thus becomes the principal asset of the family and frequently it is almost the only one!(p.124)
• One instance comes to mind in which a malicious individual was always making friendly little jokes about an *alcoholic's* drinking exploits.(p.145)
• However, a rough estimate of one *alcoholic's* initiation fee seemed possible.(p.396)
• I've heard it said many times in A.A., "There is just one good drunk in every *alcoholic's* life, and that's the one that brings us into A.A.," and I believe it.(p.549)

alcoholics

• This is the third edition of the book "*Alcoholics* Anonymous."(p.xi)
• All changes made over the years in the Big Book (A.A. members' fond nickname for this volume) have had the same purpose: to represent the current membership of *Alcoholics* Anonymous more accurately, and thereby to reach more *alcoholics*.(p.xii)
• We, of *Alcoholics* Anonymous, are more than one hundred men and women who have recovered from a seemingly hopeless state of mind and body.(p.xiii)
• To show other *alcoholics* precisely how we have recovered is the main purpose of this book.(p.xiii)
• When writing or speaking publicly about alcoholism, we urge each of our Fellowship to omit his personal name, designating himself instead as "a member of *Alcoholics* Anonymous."(p.xiii)
• We shall be interested to hear from those who are getting results from this book, particularly from those who have commenced work with other *alcoholics*.(p.xiv)
• *ALCOHOLICS* ANONYMOUS.(p.xiv)
• Our earliest printing voiced the hope "that every alcoholic who journeys will find the Fellowship of *Alcoholics* Anonymous at his destination.(p.xv)
• In that brief space, *Alcoholics* Anonymous has mushroomed into nearly 6,000 groups whose membership is far above 150,000 recovered *alcoholics*.(p.xv)
• Prior to his journey to Akron, the broker had worked hard with many *alcoholics* on the theory that only an alcoholic could help an alcoholic, but he had succeeded only in keeping sober himself.(p.xvi)
• Hence the two men set to work almost frantically upon *alcoholics* arriving in the ward of the Akron City Hospital.(p.xvii)
• And besides, there were scattered *alcoholics* who had picked up the basic ideas in Akron or New York and were trying to form A.A. groups in other cities.(p.xvii)
• The fledgling society, which had been nameless, now began to be called *Alcoholics* Anonymous, from the title of its own book.(p.xvii)
• In the fall of 1939, Fulton Oursler, then editor of Liberty, printed a piece in his magazine, called "*Alcoholics* and God."(p.xviii)
• By the end of 1939, it was estimated that 800 *alcoholics* were on their way to recovery.(p.xviii)
• News of this got on the world wires; inquiries poured in again and many people went to the bookstores to get the book "*Alcoholics* Anonymous."(p.xviii)
• Then Jack Alexander wrote a feature article in the Saturday Evening Post and placed such a compelling picture of A.A. before the general public that *alcoholics* in need of help really deluged us.(p.xviii)
• The test that it faced was this: Could these large numbers of erstwhile erratic *alcoholics* successfully meet and work together?(p.xviii)
• Of *alcoholics* who came to A.A. and really tried, 50% got sober at once and remained that way; 25% sobered up after some relapses, and among the remainder, those who stayed on with A.A. showed improvement.(p.xx)
• *Alcoholics* Anonymous is not a religious organization.(p.xx)
• So far, upon the total problem of several million actual and potential *alcoholics* in the world, we have made only a scratch.(p.xx)
• By March 1976, when this edition went to the printer, the total worldwide membership of *Alcoholics* Anonymous was conservatively estimated at more than 1,000,000, with almost 28,000 groups meeting in over 90 countries.(p.xxi)
• The Twelve Steps that summarize the program may be called los Doce Pasos in one country, los Douze Etapes in another, but they trace exactly the same path to recovery that was blazed by the earliest members of *Alcoholics* Anonymous.(p.xxii)
• We of *Alcoholics* Anonymous believe that the reader will be interested in the medical estimate of the plan of recovery described in this book.(p.xxiii)
• A well-known doctor, chief physician at a nationally prominent hospital specializing in alcoholic and drug addiction, gave *Alcoholics* Anonymous this letter:(p.xxiii)
• As part of his rehabilitation he commenced to present his conceptions to other *alcoholics*, impressing upon them that they must do likewise with still others.(p.xxiii)
• We doctors have realized for a long time that some form of moral psychology was of urgent importance to *alcoholics*, but its application presented difficulties beyond our conception.(p.xxv)
• They believe in themselves, and still more in the Power which pulls chronic *alcoholics* back from the

gates of death.(p.xxv)
• We believe, and so suggested a few years ago, that the action of alcohol on these chronic ***alcoholics*** is a manifestation of an allergy; that the phenomenon of craving is limited to this class and never occurs in the average temperate drinker.(p.xxvi)
• If any feel that as psychiatrists directing a hospital for ***alcoholics*** we appear somewhat sentimental, let them stand with us a while on the firing line, see the tragedies, the despairing wives, the little children; let the solving of these problems become a part of their daily work, and even of their sleeping moments, and the most cynical will not wonder that we have accepted and encouraged this movement.(p.xxvi)
• The classification of ***alcoholics*** seems most difficult, and in much detail is outside the scope of this book.(p.xxviii)
• Much has been written pro and con, but among physicians, the general opinion seems to be that most chronic ***alcoholics*** are doomed.(p.xxviii)
• My bother-in-law is a physician, and through his kindness and that of my mother I was placed in a nationally-known hospital for the mental and physical rehabilitation of ***alcoholics***.(p.7)
• It relieved me somewhat to learn that in ***alcoholics*** the will is amazingly weakened when it comes to combating liquor, though it often remains strong in other respects.(p.7)
• While I lay in the hospital the thought came that there were thousands of hopeless ***alcoholics*** who might be glad to have what had been so freely given me.(p.14)
• My wife and I abandoned ourselves with enthusiasm to the idea of helping other ***alcoholics*** to a solution of their problems.(p.15)
• We of *ALCOHOLICS* ANONYMOUS, know thousands of men and women who were once just as hopeless as Bill.(p.17)
• The fact is that most ***alcoholics***, for reasons yet obscure, have lost the power of choice in drink.(p.24)
• These stark and ugly facts have been confirmed by legions of ***alcoholics*** throughout history.(p.24)
• Here and there, once in a while, ***alcoholics*** have had what are called vital spiritual experiences.(p.27)
• Most of us have been unwilling to admit we were real ***alcoholics***.(p.30)
• We learned that we had to fully concede to our innermost selves that we were ***alcoholics***.(p.30)
• We ***alcoholics*** are men and women who have lost the ability to control our drinking.(p.30)
• We are convinced to a man that ***alcoholics*** of our type are in the grip of a progressive illness.(p.30)
• Neither does there appear to be any kind of treatment which will make ***alcoholics*** of our kind like other men.(p.30)
• Despite all we can say, many who are real ***alcoholics*** are not going to believe they are in that class.(p.31)
• But the difficulty is that few ***alcoholics*** have enough desire to stop while there is yet time.(p.32)
• Potential female ***alcoholics*** often turn into the real thing and are gone beyond recall in a few years.(p.33)
• Certain drinkers, who would be greatly insulted if called ***alcoholics***, are astonished at their inability to stop.(p.33)
• We, who are familiar with the symptoms, see large numbers of potential ***alcoholics*** among young people everywhere.(p.33)
• "Two of the members of *Alcoholics* Anonymous came to see me.(p.42)
• Most ***alcoholics*** have to be pretty badly mangled before they really commence to solve their problems.(p.43)
• At first some of us tried to avoid the issue, hoping against hope we were not true ***alcoholics***.(p.44)
• When we became ***alcoholics***, crushed by a self-imposed crisis we could not postpone or evade, we had to fearlessly face the proposition that either God is everything or else He is nothing.(p.53)
• 12.Having had a spiritual awakening as the result of these steps, we tried to carry this message to ***alcoholics***, and to practice these principles in all our affairs.(p.60)
• Above everything, we ***alcoholics*** must be rid of this selfishness.(p.62)
• It destroys more ***alcoholics*** than anything else.(p.64)
• They may be the dubious luxury of normal men, but for ***alcoholics*** these things are poison.(p.66)
• Small wonder many in the medical profession have a low opinion of ***alcoholics*** and their chance for recovery!(p.73)
• Of course, we sometimes encounter people who do not understand ***alcoholics***.(p.74)
• Most ***alcoholics*** owe money.(p.78)
• We doubt if, in this respect, ***alcoholics*** are fundamentally much worse than other people.(p.81)
• Passing all understanding is the patience mothers and wives have had with ***alcoholics***.(p.82)
• We ***alcoholics*** are undisciplined.(p.88)
• Practical experience shows that nothing will so much insure immunity from drinking as intensive work with other ***alcoholics***.(p.89)
• This is our twelfth suggestion: Carry this message to other ***alcoholics***!(p.89)
• Ministers and doctors are competent and you can learn much from them if you wish, but it happens that because of your own drinking experience you can be uniquely useful to other ***alcoholics***.(p.89)
• When you discover a prospect for *Alcoholics* Anonymous, find out all you can about him.(p.90)
• Make it plain he is under no obligation to you, that you hope only that he will try to help other ***alcoholics*** when he escapes his own difficulties.(p.94)
• On your first visit tell him about the Fellowship of *Alcoholics* Anonymous.(p.94)
• You will be most successful with ***alcoholics*** if you do not exhibit any passion for crusade or reform.(p.95)
• But point out that we ***alcoholics*** have much in common and that you would like, in any case, to be friendly.(p.95)
• Assuming we are spiritually fit, we can do all sorts of things ***alcoholics*** are not supposed to do.(p.100)
• A spirit of intolerance might repel ***alcoholics*** whose lives could have been saved, had it not been for such stupidity.(p.103)
• Some day we hope that *Alcoholics* Anonymous will help the public to a better realization of the gravity of the alcoholic problem, but we shall be of little use if our attitude is one of bitterness or hostility.(p.103)
• We want the wives of *Alcoholics* Anonymous to address the wives of men who drink too much.(p.104)
• As wives of *Alcoholics* Anonymous, we would like you to feel that we understand as perhaps few can.(p.104)
• Of those who keep on, a good number will become true ***alcoholics*** after a while.(p.109)
• He probably has several ***alcoholics*** among his own acquaintances.(p.112)
• Show him that as ***alcoholics***, the writers of the book understand.(p.112)
• Many of *Alcoholics* Anonymous were like that.(p.113)
• For years we have been working with ***alcoholics*** committed to institutions.(p.114)
• Since this book was first published, A.A. has released thousands of ***alcoholics*** from asylums and hospitals of every kind.(p.114)
• Still another difficulty is that you may become jealous of the attention he bestows on other people, especially ***alcoholics***.(p.119)
• Though it is entirely separate from *Alcoholics* Anonymous, it uses the general principles of the A.A. program as a guide for husbands, wives, relatives, friends, and others close to ***alcoholics***.(p.121)
• Alateen, for teen-aged children of ***alcoholics***, is a part of Al-Anon.(p.121)
• We families of *Alcoholics* Anonymous keep few skeletons in the closet.(p.125)
• We ***alcoholics*** are sensitive people.(p.125)
• Many ***alcoholics*** are enthusiasts.(p.125)
• Even if he displays a certain amount of neglect and irresponsibility towards the family, it is well to let him go as far as he likes in helping other ***alcoholics***.(p.129)
• Father will necessarily spend much time with other ***alcoholics***, but this activity should be balanced.(p.131)
• ***Alcoholics*** who have derided religious people will be helped by such contacts.(p.131)
• He thought all ***alcoholics*** should constantly have chocolate available for its quick energy value at times of fatigue.(p.133)
• Though he is now a most effective member of *Alcoholics* Anonymous, he still smokes and drinks coffee, but neither his wife or anyone else stands in judgment.(p.135)
• This is not to say that all ***alcoholics*** are honest and upright when not drinking.(p.141)
• You ask, because many ***alcoholics***, being warped and drugged, do not want to quit.(p.142)
• For most ***alcoholics*** who are drinking, or who are just getting over a spree, a certain amount of physical treatment is desirable, even imperative.(p.142)
• The greatest enemies of us ***alcoholics*** are resentment, jealousy, envy, frustration, and fear.(p.145)
• Sometimes we ***alcoholics*** have an idea that people are trying to pull us down.(p.145)
• As a class, ***alcoholics*** are energetic people.(p.146)
• He may wish to do a lot for other ***alcoholics*** and something of the sort may come up during business hours.(p.146)
• You might let them know you have no quarrel with the ***alcoholics*** of your organization.(p.147)
• That company may harbor many actual or potential ***alcoholics***.(p.149)
• Of course, this chapter refers to ***alcoholics***, sick people, deranged men.(p.149)
• It is a fellowship in *Alcoholics* Anonymous.(p.152)
• Near you, ***alcoholics*** are dying helplessly like people in a sinking ship.(p.152)
• High and low, rich and poor, these are future fellows of *Alcoholics* Anonymous.(p.152)
• They will approach still other sick ones and fellowships of *Alcoholics* Anonymous may spring up in each city and hamlet, havens for those who must find a way out.(p.153)
• But what about his responsibilities -- his family and the men who would die because they would not know how to get well, ah -- yes, those other ***alcoholics***?(p.154)
• Two days later, a future fellow of *Alcoholics* Anonymous stared glassily at the strangers beside his bed.(p.157)
• So, you see, there were three ***alcoholics*** in that town, who now felt they had to give to others what they had found, or be sunk.(p.158)
• Though they knew they must help other ***alcoholics*** if they would remain sober, that motive became secondary.(p.159)
• ***Alcoholics*** are being attracted from far and near.(p.161)
• A community thirty miles away has fifteen fellows of *Alcoholics* Anonymous.(p.161)
• But life among *Alcoholics* Anonymous is more than attending gatherings and visiting hospitals.(p.161)
• Some day we hope that every alcoholic who journeys will find a Fellowship of *Alcoholics* Anonymous at his destination.(p.162)
• He had lived there but a few weeks when he found that the place probably contained more ***alcoholics*** per square mile than any city in the country.(p.163)
• And with such good effect that the doctor agreed to a test among his patients and certain other ***alcoholics*** from a clinic which he attends.(p.163)
• Some of them may sink and perhaps never get up, but if our experience is a criterion, more than half of those approached will become fellows of *Alcoholics* Anonymous.(p.163)
• How Forty-Three *Alcoholics* Recovered From Their Malady(p.165)
• A co-founder of *Alcoholics* Anonymous.(p.171)
• For some reason, we ***alcoholics*** seem to have the gift of picking out the world's finest women.(p.178)
• They came in and began to give me instruction in the program which later became known as *Alcoholics* Anonymous.(p.185)
• I had attended several of these meetings before I discovered that all those who were there were not ***alcoholics***.(p.218)
• That is, it was sort of a mixed bunch of Oxford Groupers, who were interested in the alcoholic problem, and of ***alcoholics*** themselves.(p.218)
• That was the point at which my doctor gave me the book "*Alcoholics* Anonymous" to read.(p.227)
• They were undoubtedly the ***alcoholics*** of our village.(p.230)
• Even then he went into no great detail about how he and a crowd of ***alcoholics***, with whom he associated, had mastered their difficulty.(p.235)
• And, because as I have discovered since, it is part of the "treatment" that these men be sent to see and talk with ***alcoholics*** who want to quit, he kept them busy.(p.235)
• This duty together with my weekly meetings with my fellow ***alcoholics***, and my daily renewal of the contract I originally made with God, have kept me sober when nothing else ever did.(p.237)
• This was my introduction to this "understanding fellowship" although it was to be more than a year later before our Society was to bear the name, *Alcoholics* Anonymous.(p.239)
• Many ***alcoholics*** have learned they can bring their bottle to a cheap movie theater and drink, sleep, wake up and drink again in the darkness.(p.244)
• Around this time our big A.A. book was being written and it all became much simpler; we had a definite formula which some sixty of us agreed was the middle course for all ***alcoholics*** who wanted sobriety, and that formula has not been changed one iota down through the years.(p.248)
• Then I got a very good position in Philadelphia and quickly found I would need a few fellow ***alcoholics*** around me if I was to stay sober.(p.249)
• I stayed so sober that I used to keep a quart of medicinal whiskey in my bureau which I used to taper off the occasional newspaper ***alcoholics*** who were

sent to see me.(p.253)
• The story of *Alcoholics* Anonymous fascinated me.(p.258)
• Today I have Someone who will always hear me; I have a warm fellowship among men who understand my problems; I have tasks to do and am glad to do them, to see others who are *alcoholics* and to help them in any way I can to become sober men.(p.260)
• I had the Big Book ("*Alcoholics* Anonymous") that had been brought to me.(p.268)
• I often think how that could have turned some people away, because there were no other women *alcoholics* there then.(p.269)
• I, who had never made a speech in my life and who would have been frightened sick at the prospect, stood up in front of Rotary groups in different parts of the city and talked about *Alcoholics* Anonymous.(p.283)
• The meeting consisted of perhaps eight or nine *alcoholics* and seven or eight wives.(p.291)
• 6.Continued work with other *alcoholics*.(p.292)
• On my trips back to Akron to get my spirits recharged and to work with other *alcoholics*, I would ask Dr. Bob about this delay and wonder just what was wrong with me.(p.293)
• And then, in the spring of 1939, a very remarkable book was rolled off a New York press with the title "*Alcoholics* Anonymous."(p.307)
• He further explained that alcohol was no respecter of sex or background, but that most of the *alcoholics* he had encountered had better than average minds and abilities.(p.308)
• He asked me to read the book "*Alcoholics* Anonymous," and then he wanted me to talk with a man who was experiencing success with his own arrestment.(p.308)
• He had been dry for two and a half years and had been maintaining his contact with a group of recovered *alcoholics* in Akron.(p.309)
• So I went to Akron, and also to Cleveland, and I met more recovered *alcoholics*.(p.310)
• As arrested *alcoholics*, we must have a program for living that allows for limitless expansion.(p.311)
• They saw that they had become actual or potential *alcoholics*, even though no serious harm had yet been done.(p.315)
• That sold us on *Alcoholics* Anonymous."(p.315)
• But A.A. has shown me that I can help other *alcoholics*.(p.326)
• I was sure those who needed a bit of the hair of the dog really were *alcoholics*.(p.332)
• You can never know the pure joy of recovering within the Fellowship of *Alcoholics* Anonymous."(p.334)
• He said, "Why don't you try *Alcoholics* Anonymous?"(p.340)
• A.A. gives us *alcoholics* direction into a way of life without the need for alcohol.(p.340)
• In two ways I may be a little different from other *alcoholics*.(p.345)
• The second way in which, perhaps, I differ from some other *alcoholics* is this; many *alcoholics* state that they didn't particularly like the taste of alcohol, but that they liked the effect.(p.345)
• And then one ill-defined day, one day that I can't recall, I stepped across the line that *alcoholics* know so well, and from that day on drinking was miserable.(p.346)
• In my stupid way I went up to see him with the idea in the back of my mind that I would investigate *Alcoholics* Anonymous from a medical standpoint.(p.346)
• We have here in this community an organization which helps people, and this organization is known as *Alcoholics* Anonymous.(p.348)
• So, after taking the first half of the First Step, and very gingerly admitting myself to *Alcoholics* Anonymous, something happened.(p.349)
• Doctors have been notoriously unsuccessful in helping *alcoholics*.(p.352)
• But – *Alcoholics* Anonymous has helped.(p.352)
• As a matter of fact, when I came into *Alcoholics* Anonymous I was close to being at the peak of my career.(p.356)
• Like all *alcoholics* endeavoring to run away from themselves and their environment, I decided to go to New York.(p.358)
• When I hear the more rugged stories of *alcoholics* who became sicker than I did with this affliction, I humbly thank God for showing me "the handwriting on the wall."(p.367)
• At a women's halfway house, I became associated with *Alcoholics* Anonymous and became aware of alcoholism as a disease, not just a "weakness."(p.371)
• But what is more important is that I found a new life in *Alcoholics* Anonymous.(p.372)
• As I later found out through *Alcoholics* Anonymous, alcohol is no respecter of economic status, social and business standing or intelligence.(p.373)
• The final decision came when my daughter, following a drunk which ruined my wife's birthday, said, "It's *Alcoholics* Anonymous – or else!"(p.378)
• This suggestion had been made before on a number of occasions, but like all *alcoholics* I wanted to handle my problem my own way, which really meant I didn't want anything to interfere with my drinking.(p.378)
• The time for decision had arrived, and it was a relief to say "Yes" when my family said they would call *Alcoholics* Anonymous for me.(p.378)
• To me this meant telling my associates that I had joined *Alcoholics* Anonymous; that I didn't know what was expected of me by A.A., but that whatever it was, it was the most important thing in life for me; that sobriety meant more to me than anything in this world.(p.382)
• My work with other *alcoholics* has led me, day by day, into ever wider and richer experiences.(p.394)
• I feel that there is no situation too difficult, none too desperate, no unhappiness too great to be overcome in this great fellowship – *Alcoholics* Anonymous.(p.395)
• *Alcoholics* being the argumentative lot that we are, the A.A. membership will undoubtedly come up with a few who will dispute these figures.(p.399)
• None of them were *alcoholics*, but at this time they were drinking as much as I was.(p.407)
• So here, in this dive, this hangout for dead-end *alcoholics* and neurotics, here was I.(p.410)
• My experience has been active: three meetings a week, many tapes, many A.A. conferences, much work on the Twelve Steps, and much work with other *alcoholics* and their families.(p.420)
• Today I think of life in terms of happiness, contentment, freedom from fear and despair, sane thinking, ability to face problems as they occur, the opportunity to help other *alcoholics* and to be decent.(p.430)
• However, I've heard of an organization called *Alcoholics* Anonymous that has had some success with people like you.(p.436)
• They prove to almost anyone's satisfaction that it's never too late to try *Alcoholics* Anonymous.(p.455)
• For me, as for most *alcoholics*, it was "Eat, drink, and be merry, for tomorrow you die."(p.457)
• Then in a couple of hours, when there was still no word from my husband and no sign of him, I had the feeling we *alcoholics* all know.(p.467)
• The same doctor who had sent me to the psycho had asked my husband, "Why don't you send her to this *Alcoholics* Anonymous?"(p.469)
• The other of the Twelve Steps of *Alcoholics* Anonymous seemed insurmountable to me at first.(p.471)
• Carry this message to other *alcoholics*.(p.473)
• She begs me to go to a hospital for *alcoholics* which has been recommended.(p.502)
• I am in the hospital for *alcoholics*.(p.502)
• Four *alcoholics* play bridge in a smoke-filled room.(p.502)
• I want to get where I can find some *alcoholics* to help, and where I can have some fellowship.(p.506)
• Soon I have others who are *alcoholics* and some who have other problems.(p.506)
• It was a revelation to me to find that there were such people as those I found in *Alcoholics* Anonymous.(p.515)
• It was their open night meeting, but of course I thought they were all *alcoholics*; I couldn't imagine why anybody else would want to go there, and my first reaction was, well, I've come to something that's not for me.(p.524)
• It has shown me, through the tragic stories of so many other *alcoholics*, the utter futility of self pity.(p.525)
• I know there are some *alcoholics* who seem terribly, terribly grown-up, but I think that they are trying to make themselves think they are grown-up, and the strain of their effort is what is causing them to drink -- a sense of inadequacy, a childish vanity to be the most popular, the most sought after, the mostest of the most.(p.535)
• This great experience that released me from the bondage of hatred and replaced it with love is really just another affirmation of the truth I know: I get everything I need in *Alcoholics* Anonymous – everything I need I get – and when I get what I need I invariably find that it was just what I wanted all the time.(p.553)
• Like most other *alcoholics* I have known, I did quit drinking at various times – once for ten months on my own and during other interludes when I was hospitalized.(p.554)
• At that very time, he was a nonalcoholic trustee on the General Service Board of *Alcoholics* Anonymous!(p.559)
• *Alcoholics* can stop drinking in many places and many ways – but *Alcoholics* Anonymous offers us a way to stay sober.(p.559)
• To those now in its fold, *Alcoholics* Anonymous has made the difference between misery and sobriety, and often the difference between life and death.(p.563)
• A.A. can, of course, mean just as much to uncounted *alcoholics* not yet reached.(p.563)
• We *alcoholics* see that we must work together and hang together, else most of us will finally die alone.(p.563)
• The "12 Traditions" of *Alcoholics* Anonymous are, we A.A.'s believe, the best answers that our experience has yet given to those ever urgent questions, "How can A.A. best function?" and, "How can A.A. best stay whole and so survive?"(p.563)
• Eight – *Alcoholics* Anonymous should remain forever nonprofessional, but our service centers may employ special workers.(p.564)
• Ten – *Alcoholics* Anonymous has no opinion on outside issues; hence the A.A. name ought never be drawn into public controversy.(p.564)
• 1. -- Each member of *Alcoholics* Anonymous is but a small part of a great whole.(p.565)
• Any two or three *alcoholics* gathered together for sobriety may call themselves an A.A. group, provided that, as a group, they have no other affiliation.(p.565)
• 5. -- Each *Alcoholics* Anonymous group ought to be a spiritual entity having but one primary purpose -- that of carrying its message to the alcoholic who still suffers.(p.565)
• We think that each group should soon achieve this ideal; that any public solicitation of funds using the name of *Alcoholics* Anonymous is highly dangerous, whether by groups, clubs, hospitals, or other outside agencies; that acceptance of large gifts from any source, or of contributions carrying any obligation whatever, is unwise.(p.566)
• 8. – *Alcoholics* Anonymous should remain forever nonprofessional.(p.566)
• We define professionalism as the occupation of counseling *alcoholics* for fees or hire.(p.566)
• But we may employ *alcoholics* where they are going to perform those services for which we might otherwise have to engage nonalcoholics.(p.566)
• The *Alcoholics* Anonymous groups oppose no one.(p.567)
• 12. – And finally, we of *Alcoholics* Anonymous believe that the principle of anonymity has immense spiritual significance.(p.567)
• Though it was not our intention to create such an impression, many *alcoholics* have nevertheless concluded that in order to recover they must acquire an immediate and overwhelming "God-consciousness" followed at once by a vast change in feeling and outlook.(p.569)
• Among our rapidly growing membership of thousands of *alcoholics* such transformations, though frequent, are by no means the rule.(p.569)
• Since Dr. Silkworth's first endorsement of *Alcoholics* Anonymous, medical societies and physicians throughout the world have set their approval upon us.(p.571)
• Dr. Foster Kennedy, neurologist: "This organization of *Alcoholics* Anonymous calls on two of the greatest reservoirs of power known to man, religion and that instinct for association with one's fellows . . . the 'herd instinct.'(p.571)
• Dr. W.W. Bauer, broadcasting under the auspices of The American Medical Association in 1946, over the NBC network, said, in part: "*Alcoholics* Anonymous are no crusaders; not a temperance society.(p.572)
• Learning to depend upon a higher power and absorb himself in his work with other *alcoholics*, he remains sober day by day.(p.572)
• Dr. John F. Stouffer, Chief Psychiatrist, Philadelphia General Hospital, citing his experience with A.A., said: "The *alcoholics* we get here at Philadelphia General are mostly those who cannot afford private treatment, and A.A. is by far the greatest thing we have been able to offer them.(p.572)
• The American Psychiatric Association requested, in 1949, that a paper be prepared by one of the older members of *Alcoholics* Anonymous to be read at the Association's annual meeting of that year.(p.572)
• In 1951 the Lasker Award was given *Alcoholics* Anonymous.(p.573)
• "The American Public Health Association presents a Lasker Group Award for 1951 to *Alcoholics* Anonymous in recognition of its unique and highly successful approach to that age-old public health and social

problem, alcoholism . . .(p.573)
• Historians may one day recognize ***Alcoholics*** Anonymous to have been a great venture in social pioneering which forged a new instrument for social action; a new therapy based on the kinship of common suffering; one having a vast potential for the myriad other ills of mankind."(p.573)
• Edward Dowling, S.J., of the Queen's Work staff says, "***Alcoholics*** Anonymous is natural; it is natural at the point where nature comes closest to the supernatural, namely in humiliations and in consequent humility.(p.574)
• The Episcopal magazine, The Living Church, observes editorially: "The basis of the technique of ***Alcoholics*** Anonymous is the truly Christian principle that a man cannot help himself except by helping others.(p.574)
• Speaking at a dinner given by John D. Rockefeller Jr. to introduce ***Alcoholics*** Anonymous to some of his friends, Dr. Harry Emerson Fosdick remarked: "I think that psychologically speaking there is a point of advantage in the approach that is being made in this movement that cannot be duplicated.(p.574)
• In large cities, groups often maintain local offices where ***alcoholics*** or their families may arrange for interviews or hospitalization.(p.575)
• These so-called intergroup associations are found under the listing "A.A." or "***Alcoholics*** Anonymous" in telephone directories.(p.575)
• At New York, U.S.A., ***Alcoholics*** Anonymous maintains its international service center.(p.575)
• If you cannot find A.A. in your locality, a letter addressed to ***Alcoholics*** Anonymous, Box 459, Grand Central Station, New York, NY 10163, U.S.A., will receive a prompt reply from this world center, referring you to the nearest A.A. group.(p.575)

Alcoholics Anonymous

• This is the third edition of the book "***Alcoholics Anonymous***."(p.xi)
• All changes made over the years in the Big Book (A.A. members' fond nickname for this volume) have had the same purpose: to represent the current membership of ***Alcoholics Anonymous*** more accurately, and thereby to reach more alcoholics.(p.xii)
• We, of ***Alcoholics Anonymous***, are more than one hundred men and women who have recovered from a seemingly hopeless state of mind and body.(p.xiii)
• When writing or speaking publicly about alcoholism, we urge each of our Fellowship to omit his personal name, designating himself instead as "a member of ***Alcoholics Anonymous***."(p.xiii)
• ***ALCOHOLICS ANONYMOUS***.(p.xiv)
• Our earliest printing voiced the hope "that every alcoholic who journeys will find the Fellowship of ***Alcoholics Anonymous*** at his destination.(p.xv)
• In that brief space, ***Alcoholics Anonymous*** has mushroomed into nearly 6,000 groups whose membership is far above 150,000 recovered alcoholics.(p.xv)
• The fledgling society, which had been nameless, now began to be called ***Alcoholics Anonymous***, from the title of its own book.(p.xvii)
• News of this got on the world wires; inquiries poured in again and many people went to the bookstores to get the book "***Alcoholics Anonymous***."(p.xviii)
• ***Alcoholics Anonymous*** is not a religious organization.(p.xx)
• By March 1976, when this edition went to the printer, the total worldwide membership of ***Alcoholics Anonymous*** was conservatively estimated at more than 1,000,000, with almost 28,000 groups meeting in over 90 countries.(p.xxii)
• The Twelve Steps that summarize the program may be called los Doce Pasos in one country, los Douze Etapes in another, but they trace exactly the same path to recovery that was blazed by the earliest members of ***Alcoholics Anonymous***.(p.xxii)
• We of ***Alcoholics Anonymous*** believe that the reader will be interested in the medical estimate of the plan of recovery described in this book.(p.xxiii)
• A well-known doctor, chief physician at a nationally prominent hospital specializing in alcoholic and drug addiction, gave ***Alcoholics Anonymous*** this letter:(p.xxiii)
• We of ***ALCOHOLICS ANONYMOUS***, know thousands of men and women who were once just as hopeless as Bill.(p.17)
• "Two of the members of ***Alcoholics Anonymous*** came to see me.(p.42)
• When you discover a prospect for ***Alcoholics Anonymous***, find out all you can about him.(p.90)
• On your first visit tell him about the Fellowship of ***Alcoholics Anonymous***.(p.94)
• Some day we hope that ***Alcoholics Anonymous*** will help the public to a better realization of the gravity of the alcoholic problem, but we shall be of little use if our attitude is one of bitterness or hostility.(p.103)
• We want the wives of ***Alcoholics Anonymous*** to address the wives of men who drink too much.(p.104)
• As wives of ***Alcoholics Anonymous***, we would like you to feel that we understand as perhaps few can.(p.104)
• Many of ***Alcoholics Anonymous*** were like that.(p.113)
• Though it is entirely separate from ***Alcoholics Anonymous***, it uses the general principles of the A.A. program as a guide for husbands, wives, relatives, friends, and others close to alcoholics.(p.121)
• We families of ***Alcoholics Anonymous*** keep few skeletons in the closet.(p.125)
• Though he is now a most effective member of ***Alcoholics Anonymous***, he still smokes and drinks coffee, but neither his wife or anyone else stands in judgment.(p.135)
• It is a fellowship in ***Alcoholics Anonymous***.(p.152)
• High and low, rich and poor, these are future fellows of ***Alcoholics Anonymous***.(p.152)
• They will approach still other sick ones and fellowships of ***Alcoholics Anonymous*** may spring up in each city and hamlet, havens for those who must find a way out.(p.153)
• Two days later, a future fellow of ***Alcoholics Anonymous*** stared glassily at the strangers beside his bed.(p.157)
• A community thirty miles away has fifteen fellows of ***Alcoholics Anonymous***.(p.161)
• But life among ***Alcoholics Anonymous*** is more than attending gatherings and visiting hospitals.(p.161)
• Some day we hope that every alcoholic who journeys will find a Fellowship of ***Alcoholics Anonymous*** at his destination.(p.162)
• Some of them may sink and perhaps never get up, but if our experience is a criterion, more than half of those approached will become fellows of ***Alcoholics Anonymous***.(p.163)
• A co-founder of ***Alcoholics Anonymous***.(p.171)
• They came in and began to give me instruction in the program which later became known as ***Alcoholics Anonymous***.(p.185)
• That was the point at which my doctor gave me the book "***Alcoholics Anonymous***" to read.(p.227)
• This was my introduction to this "understanding fellowship" although it was to be more than a year later before our Society was to bear the name, ***Alcoholics Anonymous***.(p.239)
• The story of ***Alcoholics Anonymous*** fascinated me.(p.258)
• I had the Big Book ("***Alcoholics Anonymous***") that had been brought to me.(p.268)
• I, who had never made a speech in my life and who would have been frightened sick at the prospect, stood up in front of Rotary groups in different parts of the city and talked about ***Alcoholics Anonymous***.(p.283)
• And then, in the spring of 1939, a very remarkable book was rolled off a New York press with the title "***Alcoholics Anonymous***."(p.307)
• He asked me to read the book "***Alcoholics Anonymous***," and then he wanted me to talk with a man who was experiencing success with his own arrestment.(p.308)
• That sold us on ***Alcoholics Anonymous***."(p.315)
• You can never know the pure joy of recovering within the Fellowship of ***Alcoholics Anonymous***."(p.334)
• He said, "Why don't you try ***Alcoholics Anonymous***?"(p.340)
• In my stupid way I went up to see him with the idea in the back of my mind that I would investigate ***Alcoholics Anonymous*** from a medical standpoint.(p.346)
• We have here in this community an organization which helps people, and this organization is known as ***Alcoholics Anonymous***.(p.348)
• So, after taking the first half of the First Step, and very gingerly admitting myself to ***Alcoholics Anonymous***, something happened.(p.349)
• But – ***Alcoholics Anonymous*** has helped.(p.352)
• As a matter of fact, when I came into ***Alcoholics Anonymous*** I was close to being at the peak of my career.(p.356)
• At a women's halfway house, I became associated with ***Alcoholics Anonymous*** and became aware of alcoholism as a disease, not just a "weakness."(p.371)
• But what is more important is that I found a new life in ***Alcoholics Anonymous***.(p.372)
• As I later found out through ***Alcoholics Anonymous***, alcohol is no respecter of economic status, social and business standing or intelligence.(p.373)
• The final decision came when my daughter, following a drunk which ruined my wife's birthday, said, "It's ***Alcoholics Anonymous*** -- or else!"(p.378)
• The time for decision had arrived, and it was a relief to say "Yes" when my family said they would call ***Alcoholics Anonymous*** for me.(p.378)
• To me this meant telling my associates that I had joined ***Alcoholics Anonymous***; that I didn't know what was expected of me by A.A., but that whatever it was, it was the most important thing in life for me; that sobriety meant more to me than anything in this world.(p.382)
• I feel that there is no situation too difficult, none too desperate, no unhappiness too great to be overcome in this great fellowship – ***Alcoholics Anonymous***.(p.395)
• However, I've heard of an organization called ***Alcoholics Anonymous*** that has had some success with people like you.(p.436)
• They prove to almost anyone's satisfaction that it's never too late to try ***Alcoholics Anonymous***.(p.455)
• The same doctor who had sent me to the psycho had asked my husband, "Why don't you send her to this ***Alcoholics Anonymous***?"(p.469)
• The other of the Twelve Steps of ***Alcoholics Anonymous*** seemed insurmountable to me at first.(p.471)
• It was a revelation to me to find that there were such people as those I found in ***Alcoholics Anonymous***.(p.515)
• This great experience that released me from the bondage of hatred and replaced it with love is really just another affirmation of the truth I know: I get everything I need in ***Alcoholics Anonymous*** -- everything I need I get – and when I get what I need I invariably find that it was just what I wanted all the time.(p.553)
• At that very time, he was a nonalcoholic trustee on the General Service Board of ***Alcoholics Anonymous***!(p.559)
• Alcoholics can stop drinking in many places and many ways – but ***Alcoholics Anonymous*** offers us a way to stay sober.(p.559)
• To those now in its fold, ***Alcoholics Anonymous*** has made the difference between misery and sobriety, and often the difference between life and death.(p.563)
• The "12 Traditions" of ***Alcoholics Anonymous*** are, we A.A.'s believe, the best answers that our experience has yet given to those ever urgent questions, "How can A.A. best function?" and, "How can A.A. best stay whole and so survive?"(p.563)
• Eight – ***Alcoholics Anonymous*** should remain forever nonprofessional, but our service centers may employ special workers.(p.564)
• Ten – ***Alcoholics Anonymous*** has no opinion on outside issues; hence the A.A. name ought never be drawn into public controversy.(p.564)
• 1. -- Each member of ***Alcoholics Anonymous*** is but a small part of a great whole.(p.565)
• 5. -- Each ***Alcoholics Anonymous*** group ought to be a spiritual entity having but one primary purpose -- that of carrying its message to the alcoholic who still suffers.(p.565)
• We think that each group should soon achieve this ideal; that any public solicitation of funds using the name of ***Alcoholics Anonymous*** is highly dangerous, whether by groups, clubs, hospitals, or other outside agencies; that acceptance of large gifts from any source, or of contributions carrying any obligation whatever, is unwise.(p.566)
• 8. – ***Alcoholics Anonymous*** should remain forever nonprofessional.(p.566)
• The ***Alcoholics Anonymous*** groups oppose no one.(p.567)
• 12. – And finally, we of ***Alcoholics Anonymous*** believe that the principle of anonymity has immense spiritual significance.(p.567)
• Since Dr. Silkworth's first endorsement of ***Alcoholics Anonymous***, medical societies and physicians throughout the world have set their approval upon us.(p.571)
• Dr. Foster Kennedy, neurologist: "This organization of ***Alcoholics Anonymous*** calls on two of the greatest reservoirs of power known to man, religion and that instinct for association with one's fellows . . . the 'herd instinct.'(p.571)
• Dr. W.W. Bauer, broadcasting under the auspices of The American Medical Association in 1946, over the NBC network, said, in part: "***Alcoholics Anonymous*** are no crusaders; not a temperance society.(p.572)
• The American Psychiatric Association requested, in 1949, that a paper be prepared by one of the older members of ***Alcoholics Anonymous*** to be read at the Association's annual meeting of that year.(p.572)
• In 1951 the Lasker Award was given ***Alcoholics Anonymous***.(p.573)
• "The American Public Health Association presents a Lasker Group Award for 1951 to ***Alcoholics Anonymous*** in recognition of its unique and highly successful approach to that age-old public health and social

problem, alcoholism . . .(p.573)
• Historians may one day recognize ***Alcoholics Anonymous*** to have been a great venture in social pioneering which forged a new instrument for social action; a new therapy based on the kinship of common suffering; one having a vast potential for the myriad other ills of mankind."(p.573)
• Edward Dowling, S.J., of the Queen's Work staff says, "***Alcoholics Anonymous*** is natural; it is natural at the point where nature comes closest to the supernatural, namely in humiliations and in consequent humility.(p.574)
• The Episcopal magazine, The Living Church, observes editorially: "The basis of the technique of ***Alcoholics Anonymous*** is the truly Christian principle that a man cannot help himself except by helping others.(p.574)
• Speaking at a dinner given by John D. Rockefeller Jr. to introduce ***Alcoholics Anonymous*** to some of his friends, Dr. Harry Emerson Fosdick remarked: "I think that psychologically speaking there is a point of advantage in the approach that is being made in this movement that cannot be duplicated.(p.574)
• These so-called intergroup associations are found under the listing "A.A." or "***Alcoholics Anonymous***" in telephone directories.(p.575)
• At New York, U.S.A., ***Alcoholics Anonymous*** maintains its international service center.(p.575)
• If you cannot find A.A. in your locality, a letter addressed to ***Alcoholics Anonymous***, Box 459, Grand Central Station, New York, NY 10163, U.S.A., will receive a prompt reply from this world center, referring you to the nearest A.A. group.(p.575)

alcoholism

• When writing or speaking publicly about ***alcoholism***, we urge each of our Fellowship to omit his personal name, designating himself instead as "a member of Alcoholics Anonymous."(p.xiii)
• He had also been greatly helped by the late Dr. William D. Silkworth, a New York specialist in ***alcoholism*** who is now accounted no less than a medical saint by A.A. members, and whose story of the early days of our Society appears in the next pages.(p.xvi)
• From this doctor, the broker had learned the grave nature of ***alcoholism***.(p.xvi)
• But when the broker gave him Dr. Silkworth's description of ***alcoholism*** and its hopelessness, the physician began to pursue the spiritual remedy for his malady with a willingness he had never before been able to muster.(p.xvi)
• I have specialized in the treatment of ***alcoholism*** for many years.(p.xxiii)
• These facts appear to be of extreme medical importance; because of the extraordinary possibilities of rapid growth inherent in this group they may mark a new epoch in the annals of ***alcoholism***.(p.xxiii)
• I do not hold with those who believe that ***alcoholism*** is entirely a problem of mental control.(p.xxvii)
• About one year prior to this experience a man was brought in to be treated for chronic ***alcoholism***.(p.xxix)
• This is the great news this book carries to those who suffer from ***alcoholism***.(p.17)
• In the following chapter, there appears an explanation of ***alcoholism***, as we understand it, then a chapter addressed to the agnostic.(p.28)
• MORE ABOUT ***ALCOHOLISM***(p.30)
• Physicians who are familiar with ***alcoholism*** agree there is no such thing as making a normal drinker out of an alcoholic.(p.31)
• We have heard of few instances where people, who showed definite signs of ***alcoholism***, were able to stop for a long period because of an overpowering desire to do so.(p.32)
• This is the baffling feature of ***alcoholism*** as we know it -- this utter inability to leave it alone, no matter how great the necessity or the wish.(p.34)
• We told him what we knew of ***alcoholism*** and the answer we had found.(p.35)
• We, who have been through the wringer, have to admit if we substituted ***alcoholism*** for jay-walking, the illustration would fit us exactly.(p.38)
• We told him what we knew about ***alcoholism***.(p.39)
• Let him tell you about it: "I was much impressed with what you fellows said about ***alcoholism***, and I frankly did not believe it would be possible for me to drink again.(p.40)
• Well, just that did happen and more, for what I had learned of ***alcoholism*** did not occur to me at all.(p.42)
• In the preceding chapters you have learned something of ***alcoholism***.(p.44)
• If a mere code of morals or a better philosophy of life were sufficient to overcome ***alcoholism***, many of us would have recovered long ago.(p.44)
• Post-war disillusionment, ever more serious ***alcoholism***, impending mental and physical collapse, brought him to the point of self-destruction.(p.56)
• (b) That probably no human power could have relieved our ***alcoholism***.(p.60)
• Nor are we afraid of disclosing our ***alcoholism*** on the theory it may cause financial harm.(p.78)
• We are not cured of ***alcoholism***.(p.85)
• We suggest you do this as we have done it in the chapter on ***alcoholism***.(p.92)
• Continue to speak of ***alcoholism*** as an illness, a fatal malady.(p.92)
• But you may talk to him about the hopelessness of ***alcoholism*** because you offer a solution.(p.92)
• Maybe you have disturbed him about the question of ***alcoholism***.(p.94)
• In our belief any scheme of combating ***alcoholism*** which proposes to shield the sick man from temptation is doomed to failure.(p.101)
• Some of them rose out of ignorance of ***alcoholism***.(p.107)
• Perhaps your husband has been living in that strange world of ***alcoholism*** where everything is distorted and exaggerated.(p.108)
• When a discussion does arise, you might suggest he read this book or at least the chapter on ***alcoholism***.(p.111)
• Thus you may succeed in interesting him in ***alcoholism***.(p.112)
• Show him your copy of this book and tell him what you have found out about ***alcoholism***.(p.112)
• If you think he will be shy of a spiritual remedy, ask him to look at the chapter on ***alcoholism***.(p.112)
• Sometimes there are cases where ***alcoholism*** is complicated by other disorders.(p.114)
• Some men cannot or will not get over ***alcoholism***.(p.114)
• If God can solve the age-old riddle of ***alcoholism***, He can solve your problems too.(p.116)
• Another feeling we are very likely to entertain is one of resentment that love and loyalty could not cure our husbands of ***alcoholism***.(p.118)
• At such moments we forget that ***alcoholism*** is an illness over which we could not possibly have had any power.(p.118)
• We know there are difficult wives and families, but the man who is getting over ***alcoholism*** must remember he did much to make them so.(p.127)
• New acquaintances who know nothing of ***alcoholism*** might be made and thoughtful consideration given their needs.(p.131)
• When we see a man sinking into the mire that is ***alcoholism***, we give him first aid and place what we have at his disposal.(p.132)
• Here were three exceptional men lost to this world because I did not understand ***alcoholism*** as I do now.(p.137)
• This seemed to me like an opportunity to be helpful, so I spent two hours talking about ***alcoholism***, the malady, and described the symptoms and results as well as I could.(p.138)
• You now know more about ***alcoholism***.(p.141)
• At this point, it might be well to explain ***alcoholism***, the illness.(p.142)
• Whether your employee likes it or not, he will learn the grim truth about ***alcoholism***.(p.144)
• I have been learning something about ***alcoholism***.(p.147)
• ***Alcoholism*** may be causing your organization considerable damage in its waste of time, men and reputation.(p.148)
• But ***alcoholism*** -- well, they just don't believe they have it.(p.149)
• He might be shocked if he knew how much ***alcoholism*** is costing his organization a year.(p.149)
• Our hope is that when this chip of a book is launched on the world tide of ***alcoholism***, defeated drinkers will seize upon it, to follow its suggestions.(p.153)
• He told how he lived in constant worry about those who might find out about his ***alcoholism***.(p.155)
• Said one of the visitors, "We're giving you a treatment for ***alcoholism***."(p.157)
• They bear witness that release from ***alcoholism*** can really be permanent.(p.169)
• Unfortunately for me, I was the only child, which perhaps engendered the selfishness which played such an important part in bringing on my ***alcoholism***.(p.172)
• It must be remembered that I had read a great deal and talked to everyone who knew, or thought they knew anything about the subject of ***alcoholism***.(p.180)
• He gave me information about the subject of ***alcoholism*** which was undoubtedly helpful.(p.180)
• Of far more importance was the fact that he was the first living human with whom I had ever talked, who knew what he was talking about in regard to ***alcoholism*** from actual experience.(p.180)
• There were no childhood episodes of unhappiness to account for my ***alcoholism***.(p.182)
• He explained that he and a man from New York had a cure for ***alcoholism***.(p.188)
• You're never going to want another drink, are you?"; and this answer of his is very important to those of us who are victims of ***alcoholism***.(p.206)
• He was released, relieved from his ***alcoholism*** and was happy and contented because of it.(p.208)
• He brought in many of our original members, yet he himself could not make it and died of ***alcoholism***.(p.239)
• The age-old question in A.A. is which came first, the neurosis or the ***alcoholism***.(p.240)
• There were four of us children, and although both of my brothers later became alcoholic -- one died of ***alcoholism*** -- my sister has never taken a drink in her life.(p.240)
• However, here I probably took my first step towards my coming ***alcoholism*** by developing a terrific aversion to all churches and established religions.(p.240)
• I found my friend was there for ***alcoholism*** and now he was insisting that he had found the only cure.(p.257)
• As he talked I gathered vaguely, (because he was a faltering beginner then, just as I am now) that to be relieved of ***alcoholism*** I would have to be different.(p.257)
• It ran something like this: If I go around shouting from the rooftops about my ***alcoholism***, it might very possibly prevent me from getting a good job.(p.282)
• Nevertheless, there were a few doctors who saw ***alcoholism*** as a disease and felt that the alcoholic was a victim of something over which he had no control.(p.307)
• Either they die of acute ***alcoholism*** or they develop wet brains and have to be put away permanently."(p.308)
• Then he told me there was a handful of people in Akron and New York who had worked out a technique for arresting their ***alcoholism***.(p.308)
• Among today's incoming A.A. members, many have never reached the advanced stages of ***alcoholism***, though, given time, all might have.(p.315)
• This, plus mounting emotional disturbances, convinced them that compulsive ***alcoholism*** already had them; that complete ruin would be only a question of time.(p.315)
• They realized that in the end ***alcoholism*** could be a mortal as cancer; certainly no sane man would wait for a malignant growth to become fatal before seeking help.(p.315)
• Until I took Social Security and a pension at the age of sixty-eight, after forty years in motion-picture-studio public relations, I had successfully hidden even any hints of approaching ***alcoholism***.(p.327)
• Many retirees embrace ***alcoholism*** while secluded in motor trailers, rest homes, leisure-world bungalows, mountain cabins, or beach cottages, or even in penthouses, on yachts, and inside Palm Springs cabanas.(p.329)
• Boredom sets up every retiree for two chief dangers: obesity and ***alcoholism***.(p.330)
• He's now in A.A. and works as a volunteer for the local ***alcoholism*** council.(p.330)
• That fear, of course, necessitated a program of hidden ***alcoholism***.(p.331)
• Somehow, I managed to read pieces on ***alcoholism***.(p.332)
• I knew nothing about ***alcoholism*** or the D.T.'s, but when I woke up on this last morning of my son's illness, I taped the keyhole on my door because "everyone was out there."(p.338)
• They have contributed fantastic amounts of time and work to our problem, but they aren't able, it seems, to arrest either your ***alcoholism*** or mine.(p.352)
• And the psychiatrist has had thousands of couches, and has put you and me on them many, many times, but he hasn't helped us very much, though he has tried hard; and we owe the clergy and the doctor and the psychiatrist a deep debt of gratitude, but they haven't helped our ***alcoholism***, except in a rare few instances.(p.352)
• At a women's halfway house, I became associated with Alcoholics Anonymous and became aware of ***alcoholism*** as a disease, not just a "weakness."(p.371)
• It shows nothing or no one to blame for ***alcoholism***.(p.373)
• The explanation that ***alcoholism*** was a disease of a two fold nature, an allergy of the body and an obsession of the mind, cleared up a number of puzzling questions for me.(p.380)

• After all, upon coming out of a week-long or ten-day drunk, it was hard enough to figure up just how much that one drunk cost, let alone trying to calculate the cost of approximately twenty-five years of active ***alcoholism***.(p.396)
• I had to go through extreme ***alcoholism*** to find my answer.(p.400)
• I couldn't focus enough to make out the chart, but the card contained two words – "ACUTE ***ALCOHOLISM***."(p.422)
• The insidiousness of ***alcoholism*** is an appalling thing.(p.432)
• I knew from my general reading that ***alcoholism*** was irreversible and fatal.(p.436)
• It helped me a great deal to become convinced that ***alcoholism*** was a disease, not a moral issue; that I had been drinking as a result of a compulsion, even though I had not been aware of the compulsion at the time; and that sobriety was not a matter of will-power.(p.448)
• Until I could accept my ***alcoholism***, I could not stay sober; unless I accept life completely on life's terms, I cannot be happy.(p.449)
• The thirteen stories in this group tell of ***alcoholism*** at its miserable worst.(p.455)
• ***Alcoholism*** had respected nobody, neither rich nor poor, learned nor unlettered.(p.455)
• Most of us did not stay out of prison long enough to run the alcoholic gamut -- to develop the ongoing kind of ***alcoholism*** or alcoholic drinking you hear about in A.A. talks.(p.458)
• I had been in several hospitals for ***alcoholism***.(p.460)
• After a few months there, I went to County Mental Health as an ***alcoholism*** worker.(p.462)
• Now, I have been an ***alcoholism*** counselor for over a year and am off parole.(p.462)
• It was in Washington, D.C. that this transition took place, and that the really bad part of ***alcoholism*** began happening.(p.465)
• There is no cure for ***alcoholism***, but it can be arrested in the program of A.A.(p.480)
• To my way of thinking, that is a definition of ***alcoholism***; a state of being in which the emotions have failed to grow to the stature of the intellect.(p.535)
• The medical profession would probably tell me I was conditioned for ***alcoholism*** by the things that happened to me in my childhood.(p.544)
• It seems only fitting that when I did finally fall in love it was with an alcoholic, and for the next ten years I progressed as rapidly as is humanly possible into what I believed to be hopeless ***alcoholism***.(p.547)
• It had provided me with excuses for my lack of education, my marital failures, personal failures, inadequacy, and of course, my ***alcoholism*** and, though I really thought I had been willing to part with it, now I knew I was reluctant to let it go.(p.552)
• Much later, when I had progressed to full-blown ***alcoholism***, people told me I should quit.(p.554)
• He happened to be, by the grace of God, Dr. Harry Tiebout, the psychiatrist who probably knew more about ***alcoholism*** than any other in the world.(p.559)
• The relationship between my wife and me was restored to a love and happiness that we had not known even before my ***alcoholism*** became acute.(p.559)
• 3. – Our membership ought to include all who suffer from ***alcoholism***.(p.565)
• The terms "spiritual experience" and "spiritual awakening" are used many times in this book which, upon careful reading, shows that the personality change sufficient to bring about recovery from ***alcoholism*** has manifested itself among us in many different forms.(p.569)
• (This address is now available in pamphlet form at nominal cost through most A.A. groups or from Box 459, Grand Central Station, New York, NY 10163, under the title "Three Talks to Medical Societies by Bill W." – formerly called "Bill on ***Alcoholism***" and earlier "***Alcoholism*** the Illness.")(p.572)
• "The American Public Health Association presents a Lasker Group Award for 1951 to Alcoholics Anonymous in recognition of its unique and highly successful approach to that age-old public health and social problem, ***alcoholism*** . . .(p.573)
• In emphasizing ***alcoholism*** as an illness, the social stigma associated with this condition is being blotted out . . .(p.573)

alcoholism-prone

• My ***alcoholism-prone*** mind, however, reminded me that all great authors had needed a stimulus to build up inspiration and inventiveness before each day's work.(p.331)

ale

• An all night place supplied me with a dozen glasses of ***ale***.(p.6)
• I had commenced to drink as carelessly as though the cocktails were ginger ***ale***.(p.41)
• Of course he couldn't drink, but why not sit hopefully at a table, a bottle of ginger ***ale*** before him?(p.154)
• My wife became pregnant and the doctor recommended the use of port or ***ale*** . . . so . . . I bought a six gallon crock and a few bottles, listened to advice from amateur brewmeisters, and was off on my beer manufacturing career on a small scale (for the time being).(p.297)
• I pour out half a tumbler of grain alcohol and fill it with ginger ***ale***.(p.499)
• I got sick of the sweetness and turned to ***ale***.(p.556)

alert

• I had been obliged to discharge him for drinking, though he was brilliant, ***alert***, and one of the best organizers I have ever known.(p.137)
• They are far more ***alert*** and progressive than we floundering fathers were, and the future of our fellowship is in their hands.(p.250)
• Creativity at the typewriter would keep me busy and ***alert***, I said.(p.331)
• If it hadn't been for an ***alert*** hotel maid, I might have died then.(p.465)

Alexander

• Then Jack ***Alexander*** wrote a feature article in the Saturday Evening Post and placed such a compelling picture of A.A. before the general public that alcoholics in need of help really deluged us.(p.xviii)
• Even the Jack ***Alexander*** Saturday Evening Post article hadn't been written, and there was only a tiny group of people in Washington.(p.469)

Alexander's

• Jack brought the Saturday Post with Jack ***Alexander's*** story.(p.268)

alibi

• True, I have recently recovered from pneumonia and have an ***alibi***, but my friends are in the war or going, and I am not.(p.499)

alibis

• If you ask him why he started on that last bender, the chances are he will offer you any one of a hundred ***alibis***.(p.23)

Alice

• I was crying, and I said, "***Alice*** says she knows I don't have any part of the program."(p.273)

alien

• All I had left was an iron determination to live my own life in spite of the ***alien*** world – and here I was, an inwardly frightened, outwardly defiant woman, who desperately needed a prop to keep going.(p.226)

alimony

• Maybe we are divorced, and have remarried but haven't kept up the ***alimony*** to number one.(p.79)
• Because of resentment and drinking, he had not paid ***alimony*** to his first wife.(p.79)

alive

• Once dad came all the way to Florida to sober me up, after a hotel manager called him and said that if he wanted to see me ***alive*** he better get there fast.(p.288)
• Why am I ***alive***, free, a respected member of my community?(p.421)
• Had it not been for A.A. in prison. . . I'll never know, but my educated guess is that I would not be ***alive*** today.(p.457)
• My father was ***alive***, and I had to do as he wanted, so I drank under cover.(p.508)
• She's still ***alive*** today at the age of eighty-two.(p.511)

alky

• I could tell him a lot of reasons why I am here in an ***alky*** ward at the age of twenty.(p.423)

all

• In Part III ("They Lost Nearly ***All***"), eight stories have been retained; five are new.(p.xii)
• ***All*** changes made over the years in the Big Book (A.A. members' fond nickname for this volume) have had the same purpose: to represent the current membership of Alcoholics Anonymous more accurately, and thereby to reach more alcoholics.(p.xii)
• And besides, we are sure that our way of living has its advantages for ***all***.(p.xiii)
• Groups are to be found in each of the United States and ***all*** of the provinces of Canada.(p.xv)
• ***All*** told, promising beginnings have been made in some 50 foreign countries and U.S. possessions.(p.xv)
• Though he could not accept ***all*** the tenets of the Oxford Groups, he was convinced of the need for moral inventory, confession of personality defects, restitution to those harmed, helpfulness to others, and the necessity of belief in and dependence upon God.(p.xvi)
• It was decided that ***all*** members ought to be anonymous at the level of press, radio, TV and films.(p.xix)
• In ***all*** probability, we shall never be able to touch more than a fair fraction of the alcohol problem in ***all*** its ramifications.(p.xxi)
• Yet it is our great hope that ***all*** those who have as yet found no answer may begin to find one in the pages of this book and will presently join us on the highroad to a new freedom.(p.xxi)
• These allergic types can never safely use alcohol in any form at ***all***; and once having formed the habit and found they cannot break it, once having lost their self-confidence, their reliance upon things human, their problems pile up on them and become astonishingly difficult to solve.(p.xxvi)
• In nearly ***all*** cases, their ideals must be grounded in a power greater than themselves, if they are to re-create their lives.(p.xxvi)
• Although he gives ***all*** that is in him, it often is not enough.(p.xxvii)
• They took a drink a day or so prior to the date, and then the phenomenon of craving at once became paramount to ***all*** other interests so that the important appointment was not met.(p.xxvii)
• We are ***all*** familiar with this type.(p.xxviii)
• ***All*** these, and many others, have one symptom in common: they cannot start drinking without developing the phenomenon of craving.(p.xxviii)
• I knew the man by name, and partly recognized his features, but there ***all*** resemblance ended.(p.xxix)
• Out of this alloy of drink and speculation, I commenced to forge the weapon that one day would turn in its flight like a boomerang and ***all*** but cut me to ribbons.(p.2)
• My drinking assumed more serious proportions, continuing ***all*** day and almost every night.(p.3)
• An ***all*** night place supplied me with a dozen glasses of ale.(p.6)
• Then came the night when the physical and mental torture was so hellish I feared I would burst through my window, sash and ***all***.(p.6)
• Best of ***all***, I met a kind doctor who explained that though certainly selfish and foolish, I had been seriously ill, bodily and mentally.(p.7)
• My weary and despairing wife was informed that it would ***all*** end with heart failure during delirium tremens, or I would develop a wet brain, perhaps within a year.(p.7)
• There had been much happiness after ***all***.(p.8)
• Quicksand stretched around me in ***all*** directions.(p.8)
• "Come, what's ***all*** this about?" I queried.(p.9)
• Yes, the old boy was on fire ***all*** right.(p.9)
• Despite contrary indications, I had little doubt that a mighty purpose and rhythm underlay ***all***.(p.10)
• There had been no more power in him than there was in me at the minute; and this was none at ***all***.(p.11)
• It began to look as though religious people were right after ***all***.(p.11)
• I was to right ***all*** such matters to the utmost of my ability.(p.13)
• My friend promised when these things were done I would enter upon a new relationship with my Creator; that I would have the elements of a way of living which answered ***all*** my problems.(p.13)
• I must turn in ***all*** things the Father of Light who presides over us ***all***.(p.14)
• My friend had emphasized the absolute necessity of demonstrating these principles in ***all*** my affairs.(p.14)
• This sometimes nearly drove me back to drink, but I soon found that when ***all*** other measures failed, work with another alcoholic would save the day.(p.15)
• I have seen hundreds of families set their feet in the path that really goes somewhere; have seen the most impossible domestic situations righted; feuds and bitterness of ***all*** sorts wiped out.(p.15)
• There is, however, a vast amount of fun about it ***all***.(p.16)
• Nearly ***all*** have recovered.(p.17)
• ***All*** sections of this country and many of its occupations are represented, as well as many political, economic, social, and religious backgrounds.(p.17)
• If a person has cancer ***all*** are sorry for him and no one is angry or hurt.(p.18)
• But not so with the alcoholic illness, for with it there goes annihilation of ***all*** the things worth while in life.(p.18)
• It engulfs ***all*** whose lives touch the sufferer's.(p.18)
• ***All*** of us spend much of our spare time in the sort of effort which we are going to describe.(p.19)
• A few are fortunate enough to be so situated that

they can give nearly ***all*** their time to the work.(p.19)
• You may already have asked yourself why it is that ***all*** of us became so very ill from drinking.(p.20)
• "The doctor told him that if he ever drank again it would kill him, but there he is ***all*** lit up again."(p.20)
• Now these are commonplace observations on drinkers which we hear ***all*** the time.(p.20)
• He may start off as a moderate drinker; he may or may not become a continuous hard drinker; but at some stage of his drinking career he begins to lose ***all*** control of his liquor consumption, once he starts to drink.(p.21)
• If he can afford it, he may have liquor concealed ***all*** over his house to be certain no one gets his entire supply away from him to throw down the waterpipe.(p.22)
• Then comes the day when he simply cannot make it and gets drunk ***all*** over again.(p.22)
• If hundreds of experiences have shown him that one drink means another debacle with ***all*** its attendant suffering and humiliation, why is it he takes that one drink?(p.22)
• Or perhaps he doesn't think at ***all***.(p.24)
• Above ***all***, he believed he had acquired such a profound knowledge of the inner workings of his mind and its hidden springs that relapse was unthinkable.(p.26)
• He wished above ***all*** things to regain self-control.(p.26)
• Upon hearing this, our friend was somewhat relieved, for he reflected that after ***all***, he was a good church member.(p.27)
• We, in our turn, sought the same escape with ***all*** the desperation of drowning men.(p.28)
• If what we have learned and felt and seen means anything at ***all***, it means that ***all*** of us, whatever our race, creed, or color are the children of a living Creator with whom we may form a relationship upon simple and understandable terms as soon as we are willing and honest enough to try.(p.28)
• Not ***all*** of us join religious bodies, but most of us favor such memberships.(p.28)
• ***All*** of us felt at times that we were regaining control, but such intervals — usually brief — were inevitably followed by still less control, which led in time to pitiful and incomprehensible demoralization.(p.30)
• Despite ***all*** we can say, many who are real alcoholics are not going to believe they are in that class.(p.31)
• He was ambitious to succeed in business, but saw that he would get nowhere if he drank at ***all***.(p.32)
• Then, gathering ***all*** his forces, he attempted to stop altogether and found he could not.(p.32)
• ***All*** went well for a time, but he failed to enlarge his spiritual life.(p.35)
• Yet ***all*** reasons for not drinking were easily pushed aside in favor of the foolish idea that he could take whiskey if only he mixed it with milk!(p.36)
• Next day we would ask ourselves, in ***all*** earnestness and sincerity, how it could have happened.(p.37)
• To ***all*** appearance he is a stable, well balanced individual.(p.39)
• The story he told is most instructive, for here was a chap absolutely convinced he had to stop drinking, who had no excuse for drinking, who exhibited splendid judgment and determination in ***all*** his other concerns, yet was flat on his back nevertheless.(p.40)
• "In this frame of mind, I went about my business and for a time ***all*** was well.(p.40)
• That was ***all***.(p.41)
• This time I had not thought of the consequences at ***all***.(p.41)
• Well, just that did happen and more, for what I had learned of alcoholism did not occur to me at ***all***.(p.42)
• "Quite as important was the discovery that spiritual principles would solve ***all*** my problems.(p.42)
• We could wish to be moral, we could wish to be philosophically comforted, in fact, we could will these things with ***all*** our might, but the needed power wasn't there.(p.45)
• How could a Supreme Being have anything to do with it ***all***?(p.46)
• Yet, in other moments, we found ourselves thinking, when enchanted by a starlit night, "Who, then, made ***all*** this?"(p.46)
• To us, the Realm of Spirit is broad, roomy, ***all*** inclusive; never exclusive or forbidding to those who earnestly seek.(p.46)
• It is open, we believe, to ***all*** men.(p.46)
• At the start, this was ***all*** we needed to commence spiritual growth, to effect our first conscious relation with God as we understood Him.(p.47)
• When people presented us with spiritual approaches, how frequently did we ***all*** say, "I wish I had what that man has.(p.47)
• Nevertheless, the twentieth century readily accepts theories of ***all*** kinds, provided they are firmly grounded in fact.(p.48)
• It is being constantly revealed, as mankind studies the material world, that outward appearances are not inward reality at ***all***.(p.48)
• When, however, the perfectly logical assumption is suggested that underneath the material world and life as we see it, there is an ***All*** Powerful, Guiding, Creative Intelligence, right there our perverse streak comes to the surface and we laboriously set out to convince ourselves it isn't so.(p.49)
• Instead of regarding ourselves as intelligent agents, spearheads of God's ever advancing Creation, we agnostics and atheists chose to believe that our human intelligence was the last word, the alpha and the omega, the beginning and end of ***all***.(p.49)
• People of faith have a logical idea of what life is ***all*** about.(p.49)
• We used to amuse ourselves by cynically dissecting spiritual beliefs and practices when we might have observed that many spiritually-minded persons of ***all*** races, colors, and creeds were demonstrating a degree of stability, happiness and usefulness which we should have sought ourselves.(p.49)
• This world of ours has made more material progress in the last century than in ***all*** the millenniums which went before.(p.51)
• In the realm of the material, men's minds were fettered by superstition, tradition, and ***all*** sorts of fixed ideas.(p.51)
• Had not ***all*** efforts at flight failed before?(p.51)
• So, in one way or another, we discovered that faith had been involved ***all*** the time!(p.54)
• Did not these feelings, after ***all***, determine the course of our existence?(p.54)
• But later, alone in his room, he asked himself this question: "Is it possible that ***all*** the religious people I have known are wrong?"(p.56)
• It crowded out ***all*** else:(p.56)
• Even so has God restored us ***all*** to our right minds.(p.57)
• But He has come to ***all*** who have honestly sought Him.(p.57)
• With ***all*** the earnestness at our command, we beg of you to be fearless and thorough from the very start.(p.58)
• But there is One who has ***all*** power — that One is God.(p.59)
• 6.Were entirely ready to have God remove ***all*** these defects of character.(p.59)
• 8.Made a list of ***all*** persons we had harmed, and became willing to make amends to them ***all***.(p.59)
• 12.Having had a spiritual awakening as the result of these steps, we tried to carry this message to alcoholics, and to practice these principles in ***all*** our affairs.(p.60)
• Is it not evident to ***all*** the rest of the players that these are the things he wants?(p.61)
• And do not his actions make each of them wish to retaliate, snatching ***all*** they can get out of the show?(p.61)
• He is like the retired business man who lolls in the Florida sunshine in the winter complaining of the sad state of the nation; the minister who sighs over the sins of the twentieth century; politicians and reformers who are sure ***all*** would be Utopia if the rest of the world would only behave; the outlaw safe cracker who thinks society has wronged him; and the alcoholic who has lost ***all*** and is locked up.(p.61)
• First of ***all***, we had to quit playing God.(p.62)
• When we sincerely took such a position, ***all*** sorts of remarkable things followed.(p.63)
• Being ***all*** powerful, He provided what we needed, if we kept close to Him and performed His work well.(p.63)
• From it stem ***all*** forms of spiritual disease, for we have been not only mentally and physically ill, we have been spiritually sick.(p.64)
• We cannot be helpful to ***all*** people, but at least God will show us how to take a kindly and tolerant view of each and every one.(p.67)
• ***All*** men of faith have courage.(p.68)
• But above ***all***, we tried to be sensible on this question.(p.68)
• One school would allow man no flavor for his fare and the other would have us ***all*** on a straight pepper diet.(p.69)
• We ***all*** have sex problems.(p.69)
• We got this ***all*** down on paper and looked at it.(p.69)
• We have begun to learn tolerance, patience and good will toward ***all*** men, even our enemies, for we look on them as sick people.(p.70)
• They took inventory ***all*** right, but hung on to some of the worst items in stock.(p.73)
• But they had not learned enough of humility, fearlessness and honesty, in the sense we find it necessary, until they told someone else ***all*** their life story.(p.73)
• Are we now ready to let God remove from us ***all*** the things which we have admitted are objectionable?(p.76)
• Can He now take them ***all*** -- every one?(p.76)
• When ready, we say something like this: "My Creator, I am now willing that you should have ***all*** of me, good and bad.(p.76)
• We have a list of ***all*** persons we have harmed and to whom we are willing to make amends.(p.76)
• He saw that he had to place the outcome in God's hands or he would soon start drinking again, and ***all*** would be lost anyhow.(p.80)
• This ***all*** happened years ago.(p.80)
• She may insist on knowing ***all*** the particulars.(p.81)
• Passing ***all*** understanding is the patience mothers and wives have had with alcoholics.(p.82)
• A remorseful mumbling that we are sorry won't fill the bill at ***all***.(p.83)
• Every day is a day when we must carry the vision of God's will into ***all*** of our activities.(p.85)
• We can exercise our will power along this line ***all*** we wish.(p.85)
• Much has already been said about receiving strength, inspiration, and direction from Him who has ***all*** knowledge and power.(p.85)
• Were we kind and loving toward ***all***?(p.86)
• Under these conditions we can employ our mental faculties with assurance, for after ***all*** God gave us brains to use.(p.86)
• Being still inexperienced and having just made conscious contact with God, it is not probable that we are going to be inspired at ***all*** times.(p.87)
• We might pay for this presumption in ***all*** sorts of absurd actions and ideas.(p.87)
• We usually conclude the period of meditation with a prayer that we be shown ***all*** through the day what our next step is to be, that we be given whatever we need to take care of such problems.(p.87)
• But this is not ***all***.(p.88)
• When you discover a prospect for Alcoholics Anonymous, find out ***all*** you can about him.(p.90)
• When he sees you know ***all*** about the drinking game, commence to describe yourself as an alcoholic.(p.91)
• You will soon have your friend admitting he has many, if not ***all***, of the traits of the alcoholic.(p.92)
• This is ***all*** to the good.(p.94)
• Your candidate may give reasons why he need not follow ***all*** of the program.(p.94)
• Of course, we ***all*** fall much below this standard many times.(p.99)
• This means a new attitude and spirit ***all*** around.(p.99)
• Sometimes it is to the best interests of ***all*** concerned that a couple remain apart.(p.99)
• We have seen men get well whose families have not returned at ***all***.(p.100)
• Assuming we are spiritually fit, we can do ***all*** sorts of things alcoholics are not supposed to do.(p.100)
• People have said we must not go where liquor is served; we must not have it in our homes; we must shun friends who drink; we must avoid moving pictures which show drinking scenes; we must not go into bars; our friends must hide their bottles if we go to their houses; we mustn't think or be reminded about alcohol at ***all***.(p.100)
• If you are with a person who wants to eat in a bar, by ***all*** means go along.(p.102)
• At proper time and place explain to ***all*** your friends why alcohol disagrees with you.(p.102)
• After ***all***, our problems were of our own making.(p.103)
• Our loyalty and the desire that our husbands hold up their heads and be like other men have begotten ***all*** sorts of predicaments.(p.105)
• In desperation, we have even got tight ourselves -- the drunk to end ***all*** drunks.(p.106)
• We know ***all*** about liquor as a social lubricant.(p.110)
• Some, but not ***all*** of us, think it has its advantages when reasonably used.(p.110)
• Use your energies to promote a better understanding ***all*** around.(p.115)
• We wives found that, like everybody else, we were afflicted with pride, self-pity, vanity and ***all*** the things which go to make up the self-centered person; and we were not above selfishness or dishonesty.(p.116)

• But *all* problems will not be solved at once.(p.117)
• After *all*, your family is reunited, alcohol is no longer a problem and you and your husband are working together toward an undreamed-of future.(p.119)
• He gets stirred up about their troubles, but not at *all* about yours.(p.119)
• Though it is infinitely better that he have no relapse at *all*, as has been true with many of our men, it is by no means a bad thing in some cases.(p.120)
• *All* members of the family should meet upon the common ground of tolerance, understanding and love.(p.122)
• Let families realize, as they start their journey, that *all* will not be fair weather.(p.122)
• They are *all* disappointed, and often let him feel it.(p.126)
• Let them remember that his drinking wrought *all* kinds of damage that may take long to repair.(p.127)
• He may tell mother, who has been religious *all* her life, that she doesn't know what it's *all* about, and that she had better get his brand of spirituality while there is yet time.(p.128)
• Dad is not so spiritual after *all*, they say.(p.128)
• If he means to right his past wrongs, why *all* this concern for everyone in the world but his family?(p.128)
• He will perceive that his spiritual growth is lopsided, that for an average man like himself, a spiritual life which does not include his family obligations may not be so perfect after *all*.(p.129)
• If the family will appreciate that dad's current behavior is but a phase of his development, *all* will be well.(p.129)
• Mother made *all* the plans and gave the directions.(p.131)
• Father may have laid aside for years *all* normal activities – clubs, civic duties, sports.(p.131)
• He may bring new hope and new courage to many a priest, minister, or rabbi, who gives his *all* to minister to our troubled world.(p.132)
• He thought *all* alcoholics should constantly have chocolate available for its quick energy value at times of fatigue.(p.133)
• We think the business fabric is shot through with a situation which might be helped by better understanding *all* around.(p.137)
• This is not to say that *all* alcoholics are honest and upright when not drinking.(p.141)
• We *all* had to place recovery above everything, for without recovery we would have lost both home and business.(p.143)
• After *all*, are you not looking for results rather than methods?(p.144)
• Often this is not so at *all*.(p.145)
• For he knows he must be honest if he would live at *all*.(p.146)
• Now and then a serious drinker, being dry at the moment says, "I don't miss it at *all*.(p.151)
• Should you wish them above *all* else, and be willing to make use of our experience, we are sure they will come.(p.153)
• After *all*, had he not been sober six months now?(p.154)
• For him, this was the spree that ended *all* sprees.(p.155)
• Here was a prospect *all* right but, by the description, none too promising.(p.156)
• You fellows know your stuff *all* right, but I don't see what good it'll do.(p.157)
• He entered a political campaign, making speeches, frequenting men's gathering places of *all* sorts, often staying up *all* night.(p.158)
• I guess the old folks were right after *all*."(p.159)
• *All* this time our friend of the hotel lobby incident remained in that town.(p.159)
• They had visioned the Great Reality – their loving and *All* Powerful Creator.(p.161)
• We believe and hope it contains *all* you will need to begin.(p.163)
• THEY LOST NEARLY *ALL*(p.167)
• *All* have now passed away from natural causes, having maintained complete sobriety.(p.169)
• *All* of these, then, are the pioneers of A.A.(p.169)
• To 1950, the year of his death, he carried the A.A. message to more than 5,000 alcoholic men and women, and to *all* these he gave his medical services without thought of charge.(p.171)
• Without this proof the expectant purchaser would be forced to depart empty handed with none of what I later came to believe was the great panacea for *all* human ills.(p.171)
• The next three years I spent in Boston, Chicago, and Montreal in the employ of a large manufacturing concern, selling railway supplies, gas engines of *all* sorts, and many other items of heavy hardware.(p.172)
• After much argument they allowed me to return and take my exams, *all* of which I passed creditably.(p.173)
• During these two years I was kept so busy that I hardly left the hospital at *all*.(p.174)
• I had some money, *all* the time in the world, and considerable stomach trouble.(p.174)
• I soon discovered that a couple of drinks would alleviate my gastric distress, at least for a few hours at a time, so it was not at *all* difficult for me to return to my former excessive indulgence.(p.174)
• I will not take space to relate *all* my hospital or sanitarium experiences.(p.177)
• During *all* this time we became more or less ostracized by our friends.(p.177)
• I could drink *all* I wanted of that.(p.177)
• It then occurred to me that after one was *all* smelled up with beer nobody could tell what had been drunk, so I began to fortify my beer with straight alcohol.(p.178)
• They spoke with great freedom from embarrassment, which I could never do, and they seemed very much at ease on *all* occasions and appeared very healthy.(p.178)
• How my wife kept her faith and courage during *all* those years, I'll never know, but she did.(p.178)
• I drank *all* the scotch they had on the train and bought several quarts on my way to the hotel.(p.179)
• I drank *all* I dared in the bar, and then went to my room to finish the job.(p.179)
• But this was a man who had experienced many years of frightful drinking, who had had most *all* the drunkard's experiences known to man, but who had been cured by the very means I had been trying to employ, that is to say the spiritual approach.(p.180)
• He knew *all* the answers, and certainly not because he had picked them up in his reading.(p.180)
• So it doesn't behoove me to squawk about it for, after *all*, nobody ever had to throw me down and pour liquor down my throat.(p.181)
• But if you really and truly want to quit drinking liquor for good and *all*, and sincerely feel that you must have some help, we know that we have an answer for you.(p.181)
• But, of course, this *all* went up the spout with my increased drinking.(p.182)
• *All* the other people that had talked to me wanted to help me, and my pride prevented me from listening to them, and caused only resentment on my part, but I felt as if I would be a real stinker if I did not listen to a couple of fellows for a short time, if that would cure them.(p.185)
• Before very long we began to relate some incidents of our drinking and, naturally, pretty soon, I realized both of them knew what they were talking about because you can see things and smell things when you're drunk, that you can't other times, and, if I had thought they didn't know what they were talking about, I wouldn't have been willing to talk to them at *all*.(p.185)
• My case is so terrible that I'm scared to go out of this hospital at *all*.(p.188)
• Bill then related how he had lain awake nearly *all* night.(p.189)
• Don't you believe you are going to have *all* you can do to get rid of that?"(p.190)
• They said, "Let's forget about those other things, that is, trying to eliminate them *all* at once, and concentrate on the drink."(p.190)
• Of course, we had talked over quite a number of the failings that I had and made a sort of an inventory, which wasn't too difficult, because I had an awful lot of things wrong that were very apparent to me, because I knew *all* about them.(p.190)
• Of course, as time went on, and I began to get my health back and began to be so I didn't have to hide from people *all* the time, it's just been wonderful.(p.192)
• I went into the high school grades, but having missed *all* the intermediate grades, I didn't get along too well, so I developed the habit of going back to school just long enough for the football season and then quitting.(p.193)
• They looked at one another queerly and, finally, one of them allowed he'd have a beer and they *all* followed him, each of them saying he'd have a beer too.(p.194)
• I had no pleasure out of the drinking at *all*.(p.195)
• *All* of a sudden I found myself guzzling.(p.195)
• I could work a deal up to where *all* I had to do was to go ahead with it; *all* the planning had been done, *all* the financing had been done, but then I'd say "Nuts to it!" and walk away.(p.197)
• My idea was to have *all* the companies pool their funds and buy rubber when rubber was cheap and then put it in a pool.(p.198)
• I can remember telling the poor little soul that I could probably quit drinking if I wasn't married to her, and told her that, after *all*, I didn't like restraint!(p.199)
• Pretty soon, I wasn't going at *all*, and was avoiding those people who had been so kind to me.(p.203)
• I was black and blue, with my lips *all* swollen, when they roused us to go into court in the morning.(p.204)
• I looked so terrible in the court that the judge suggested that I get a continuance and let me sign *all* the papers to go to a hospital and to a doctor.(p.204)
• I said, "*All* right, call me a cab," as though I was talking to a bell boy.(p.204)
• When I had been in the hospital ten days, Sister Ignatia, who has played such a part in the development of A.A. in this area, stuck her head in the door one morning and announced, looking at me quizzically, that they might be able to make something human out of my face after *all*.(p.205)
• I then began asking a lot of questions of both my brother and Dr. Bob about how this thing worked, and I suppose I was becoming more glassy-eyed *all* the while, for eventually I said to Bob, "You're *all* dried up.(p.206)
• And I said, "Well, what about Paul, have you got him *all* dried up?"(p.207)
• Then he started to talk to me about his drinking experiences, what his drinking had cost him, how much he had drunk and where, things like that, and I remember I was quite bored because I had never seen the guy before and had no interest at *all* in what, where and when he drank.(p.208)
• There were only seven or eight people in the group before me and they *all* visited me during my period in the hospital.(p.208)
• As I look back, *all* the brothers developed personality problems.(p.210)
• I was supporting myself through *all* this education by being a toolmaker and a draftsman.(p.212)
• *All* during Prohibition, every alcoholic felt that he made the best hooch, regardless of how bad it was.(p.213)
• There had been some occasions -- there was an automobile wreck, for instance -- when I had police escort home but not to jail, *all* of which, instead of doing me a favor, did me harm because I was then full of self-esteem as to the progress I had made both professionally and financially.(p.213)
• When I was about forty-seven, after indulging in *all* kinds of self-deception to control my drinking, I arrived at a period when I felt convinced I had to have so much alcohol every day and that the real problem was to control how much.(p.214)
• Had anyone undertaken to explain to me what the A.A. movement was, what its real function was, I probably would have been set back several years and I doubt if I would have survived at *all*.(p.216)
• I had attended several of these meetings before I discovered that *all* those who were there were not alcoholics.(p.218)
• That was skeptically received by me when I first heard it, but after some twenty-eight or thirty fellows had come to see me, and pretty nearly *all* of them had said the same thing, I began to believe it.(p.219)
• They had *all* been to Akron.(p.219)
• At that meeting, there were a number of Akron people and *all* the Cleveland people.(p.219)
• I knew what they were *all* right – a drink would fix them.(p.223)
• The times in which I grew up (the Prohibition era immortalized by Scott Fitzgerald and John Held Jr.) had taught me to be gay with the gayest; my own inner urges led me to outdo them *all*.(p.225)
• So far, so good – *all* according to plan, like thousands of others.(p.225)
• My divorce coincided with my father's bankruptcy, and I went to work, casting off *all* allegiances and responsibilities to any other than myself.(p.225)
• I met *all* the people I wanted to meet; I saw *all* the places I wanted to see; I did *all* the things I wanted to do -- and I was increasingly miserable.(p.225)
• *All* I had left was an iron determination to live my own life in spite of the alien world -- and here I was, an inwardly frightened, outwardly defiant woman, who desperately needed a prop to keep going.(p.226)
• To go into a gathering of people was the sort of thing that *all* my life, from the time I left my private world of books and dreams to meet the real world of people and parties and jobs, had left me feeling an uncomfortable outsider, needing the warming stimulus of drinks to join in.(p.228)
• We *all* had hundreds of character traits, of fears and

phobias, likes and dislikes, in common.(p.229)
• Suddenly I could accept myself, faults and *all*, as I was -- for weren't we *all* like that?(p.229)
• There I sat in the evenings, enjoying with my friends our memories of the "old country," singing the old songs we *all* knew, playing simple card games for drinks and consuming great quantities of beer.(p.231)
• I came of good stock, of men and women who drank wine *all* their lives as a beverage, and while they occasionally got drunk at special celebrations, they were up and about their business the next day.(p.231)
• You can *all* remember that in the first few months after the change, a great many men, who had formerly been used to a few beers every day or an occasional drink of whiskey, simply quit *all* alcoholic drinks.(p.232)
• I had them hidden away in the house and *all* over my shop in careful concealment.(p.233)
• I had *all* the usual experiences of the alcoholic, for I was certainly one by this time.(p.233)
• In four or five days I would be hunting *all* over the place, at home and in my workshop, for the bottles I had destroyed, cursing myself for being a fool.(p.234)
• My "periodics" became more frequent until I reached the point where I wanted to devote *all* my time to drinking, working as little as possible, and then only when the necessity of my family demanded it.(p.234)
• He didn't talk like a preacher at *all*.(p.235)
• I told him with *all* the sincerity at my command that I did.(p.235)
• He had already imbued them with his own spirit until they were ready and willing at *all* times to go where sent, and as a doctor he well knew that this mission and duty would strengthen them as it later helped me.(p.235)
• In a few sentences he made God seem personal to me, explained Him as a being who was interested in me, the alcoholic, and that *all* I needed to do was to be willing to follow His way; that as long as I followed it I would be able to overcome my desire for liquor.(p.236)
• If that was *all*, then I was a little doubtful that it was the answer I was looking for.(p.236)
• Many of these same things had happened to me many times before, but this time they had *all* descended together.(p.238)
• That is the way Jackie found me, lying on a cot in my skivvies, with hot and cold sweats, pounding heart and that awful itchy scratchiness *all* over.(p.238)
• If anything, he had known *all* of them even better and more often than I.(p.239)
• *All* of us in A.A. know the tremendous happiness that is in our sobriety, but there are also tragedies.(p.239)
• However, here I probably took my first step towards my coming alcoholism by developing a terrific aversion to *all* churches and established religions.(p.240)
• But each drink after the "first" seemed to become less effective and after three or four they *all* seemed like water.(p.241)
• So it is clear that I never had any fun out of drinking – I would be the soberest-seeming one in the crowd and *all* of a sudden I would be the drunkest.(p.241)
• There I was, unshaven, clothes torn and dirty with no recollection of wandering *all* over France but, of course, a hero to the local French.(p.242)
• Back at camp, *all* was forgiven because it was the End, but in the light of what I have since learned I know I was a confirmed alcoholic at nineteen.(p.242)
• I was the fair-haired boy *all* right, but two years later I was blacklisted as an irresponsible drunk.(p.242)
• He had also gone *all* the way through the wringer and had been dry two years when I saw him again.(p.243)
• At this time I was holding what drinking I did down to weekends, but I hadn't had a drink at *all* in a month.(p.243)
• Routine jobs bored me, but I would take on the toughest one I could find, work day and night until I had it under control; then it would become tedious and I'd lose *all* interest in it.(p.243)
• Then broke again, hiding out in cheap hotels *all* over the country, one night jail stands here and there, and always that horrible feeling "What's the use -- nothing is worth while."(p.244)
• I had no resentments against individuals – the whole world was *all* wrong.(p.244)
• My thoughts went round and round with "What's it *all* about anyhow?(p.244)
• Everything's *all* wrong and the hell with it."(p.245)
• After being dry two weeks and sticking close to Jackie, *all* of a sudden I found I had become the sponsor of my sponsor, for he was suddenly taken drunk.(p.245)
• At the time, I thought them just a swell pair of screwballs, for they were not only going to save *all* the drunks in the world but also *all* the so-called normal people!(p.245)
• *All* they talked of that first week-end was God, and how they were going to straighten out Jackie's and my life.(p.245)
• Despite *all* this, I did like these new friends because, again, they were like me.(p.245)
• The same old routines seemed to be common to us *all*.(p.246)
• During that first week-end I decided to stay in New York and take *all* they gave out with, except the "God stuff."(p.246)
• I knew they needed to straighten out their thinking and habits, but I was *all* right, I just drank too much.(p.246)
• I'd been dry three weeks, had the wrinkles out and had sobered up my sponsor *all* by myself!(p.246)
• We were *all* set to put DuPont out of business.(p.246)
• There was one meeting a week at Bill's home in Brooklyn, and we *all* took turns there spouting off about how we had changed our lives overnight, how many drunks we had saved and straightened out, and last, but not least, how God had touched each of us personally on the shoulder.(p.246)
• Yet we *all* had one really sincere purpose in our hearts and that was not to drink.(p.246)
• So I drank *all* three beers, one after the other, said "I'll be seeing you, boys," and went around the corner for a bottle.(p.247)
• Around this time our big A.A. book was being written and it *all* became much simpler; we had a definite formula which some sixty of us agreed was the middle course for *all* alcoholics who wanted sobriety, and that formula has not been changed one iota down through the years.(p.248)
• After the book appeared we *all* became very busy in our efforts to save *all* and sundry, but I was still actually on the fringes of A.A.(p.248)
• While I went along with *all* that was done and attended the meetings, I never took an active job of leadership until February 1940.(p.249)
• When I started to tell the boys how we did it in New York and *all* about the spiritual part of the program, I found they would not believe me unless I was practicing what I preached.(p.249)
• In telling newcomers how to change their lives and attitudes, *all* of a sudden I found I was doing a little changing myself.(p.249)
• She has been sober *all* the way through and for me that has been good.(p.249)
• Drinking was *all* in the day's work.(p.251)
• I myself could see deterioration in my work from being physically and mentally affected by liquor, although I had not yet reached the point where *all* I wanted was more to drink.(p.254)
• Enduring *all* the hangover hells that every alcoholic experiences, I made the usual resolutions.(p.256)
• What philosophy I had was thoroughly paganistic -- *all* my life was devoted to a search for pleasure.(p.256)
• *All* sorts were represented and their relation of experiences and how they had found the only remedy, added to their human existence as sober men, laid the foundation of a very necessary faith.(p.258)
• The big thing was that these men were *all* sober and evidently had something I didn't have.(p.259)
• We moved in from the country at the age when girls want *all* sorts of nice things.(p.261)
• I remember feeling that they were *all* making fun of me.(p.261)
• But he's in *all* sorts of scrapes because he drinks too much."(p.262)
• He had taken up light work, and he had a safety valve and a pair of spurs and the clothes on his back, and that was *all*.(p.263)
• We were together *all* the time, but this night I got up and saw it was late.(p.263)
• So, sometimes we'd end up in Charleston, West Virginia, or here or there, drinking *all* along the way.(p.264)
• There was a man watching, and I turned to him and said with a defiant air I carried with me *all* the time, "If I don't quit this I'm going to have to join that alcoholic business they're talking about."(p.266)
• He said, "Sister, if you think you're a screwball now, *all* you have to do is join up with that.(p.266)
• Finally, one morning, I got up and got in the car and cried *all* the way down to the M.'s – the people who owned the bar -- and told her I was licked and wanted help.(p.267)
• Jack said, "Now you start and go to these meetings, and then you'll find out *all* about it."(p.268)
• I was reading it for *all* that was in it, and I said to Russ, "We can't do this.(p.269)
• I could never go and make up to *all* the people I've done wrong to."(p.269)
• No, I was *all* interested in this part that told you how to do it.(p.269)
• He talked about his wife taking his little boy away from him because of his drinking, and how he got back together with them through A.A., and we began feeling grateful right then that *all* these things hadn't been taken from us.(p.270)
• They opened with a little prayer, and I thought it was very fine that we stood, *all* of us together, and closed with the Lord's Prayer.(p.270)
• I'd like to say here how important it was to us then that we do *all* the little things that people said were important, because later when Russ was so sick that I had to hold him up, they had a meeting out at the house.(p.270)
• I knew Doc and Anne were going to be there, and *all* of them thought it would be good for me, but the first thing I did was to go to St. Thomas and try to talk to those women.)(p.272)
• She talked to me and laughed about it and got me *all* over it.(p.273)
• If it isn't anything that's going to help you or anybody else, why should you become involved in it, and get *all* disturbed about it?"(p.273)
• And, anyhow, if I went on for ten or a hundred times as long I couldn't even begin to tell you *all* that A.A. has meant to me.(p.274)
• Suddenly *all* this changed.(p.275)
• *All* this changed when I was thirty years old.(p.277)
• These men *all* drank on Saturday nights, and enjoyed themselves.(p.277)
• During the first three months I carried on *all* these activities without a car, depending entirely on buses and streetcars – I, who had always to have a car at my immediate command.(p.283)
• I, carried away with the desire to serve A.A., gave what was probably one of the first radio broadcasts about A.A., living through a case of mike fright and feeling like a million dollars when it was *all* over.(p.283)
• Do I have to tell you who gained the most out of *all* this?(p.283)
• This office job brought me face to face with a problem which I had sidestepped *all* my adult life, lack of training.(p.284)
• *All* of this changed when I went to college.(p.287)
• Then I started traveling, with the United States and Canada as my territory, and with so much freedom and with an unlimited expense account, I was soon drinking every night and kidding myself that it was *all* part of the job.(p.287)
• Once dad came *all* the way to Florida to sober me up, after a hotel manager called him and said that if he wanted to see me alive he better get there fast.(p.288)
• After it was closed we *all* retired to the kitchen and had coffee and doughnuts and more discussion until the small hours of the morning.(p.291)
• Dr. Bob led me through *all* of these steps.(p.292)
• Dr. Bob then led me through the restitution step, in which I made a list of *all* of the persons I had harmed, and worked out ways and means of slowly making restitution.(p.292)
• Where once I had casual acquaintances, *all* of whom were fair weather friends, I now have a host of friends who accept me for what I am.(p.296)
• Above *all*, I have gained the greatest thing accorded to any man, the love and understanding of a gracious God, who has lifted me from the alcoholic scrap-heap to a position of trust where I have been able to reap the rich rewards that come from showing a little love for others and from serving them as I can.(p.296)
• Eventually, of course, what with *all* the hilarity that could be provoked with a few gallons of beer, there seemed to be no need of bridge or poker playing for entertainment.(p.297)
• I had a mortal fear of going to bed and tossing *all* night.(p.299)
• Handling customers, dealers, insurance people, dictation, telephoning, directing new employees, answering to superiors, and *all* the rest of it.(p.299)
• During this time, I had been threatened, beaten, kissed, praised and damned alternately by relatives, family, friends and strangers, but of course it *all* went for naught.(p.300)
• Now I was getting drunk *all* the time.(p.300)
• I learned that a person just can't find a job hanging

in a dive or barroom ***all*** day and ***all*** night, as jobs don't seem to turn up in those places.(p.300)
• Indeed, I was always well on my way before I would undertake to go visiting at ***all***.(p.301)
• She offered me the alternative of going to see him or her leaving me for good and ***all***.(p.301)
• How did he know ***all*** this?(p.302)
• In ***all*** honesty though, I was skeptical, but I wanted so definitely to quit drinking that I would have welcomed any sort of physical torture or pain to accomplish the result.(p.302)
• It is impossible to put on paper ***all*** the benefits I have derived . . . physical, mental, domestic, spiritual, and monetary.(p.302)
• For ***all*** of these blessings, I thank Him.(p.303)
• That age of the flapper and the "It" girl, speakeasies and the hip flask, the boyish bob and the drugstore cowboy, John Held Jr. and F. Scott Fitzgerald, ***all*** generously sprinkled with a patent pseudo-sophistication.(p.304)
• And ***all*** the while my fear fed a growing conviction that before long it would be necessary for me to be put away in some institution.(p.306)
• Why he bothered with me as long as he did I shall never know, for he knew there was no answer for me in medicine and he, like ***all*** doctors of his day, had been taught that the alcoholic was incurable and should be ignored.(p.307)
• But, of course," he continued, "eventually the alcoholic loses ***all*** of his capacities as his disease gets progressively worse, and this is a tragedy that is painful to watch; the disintegration of a sound mind and body."(p.308)
• I stayed up ***all*** night reading that book.(p.309)
• It explained so much I had not understood about myself and, best of ***all***, it promised recovery if I would do a few simple things and be willing to have the desire to drink removed.(p.309)
• They seemed to have ***all*** the ingredients for successful living.(p.310)
• They would travel miles and stay up ***all*** night with someone they had never laid eyes on before and think nothing of it.(p.310)
• I didn't dare hope I might find for myself ***all*** that these people had found, but if I could acquire some small part of their intriguing quality of living -- and sobriety – that would be enough.(p.310)
• Among today's incoming A.A. members, many have never reached the advanced stages of alcoholism, though, given time, ***all*** might have.(p.315)
• He turned me in to the company commander, but I got off the hook, and that was ***all*** that mattered.(p.317)
• They were ***all*** picking on me.(p.319)
• I was sure I wouldn't belong in an A.A. group -- they were ***all*** old men, I thought, and ***all*** skid-row bums.(p.319)
• After having a few drinks, I went to a meeting -- and the people there were not ***all*** old men and definitely not skid-row types!(p.319)
• ***All*** of them were so nice to me that I figured I must be careful – they were bound to want something, being that nice.(p.319)
• I found out that the people in ***all*** A.A. groups were as nice as the people in the first one.(p.320)
• I also found out that ***all*** they wanted was to help me get sober and to stay sober themselves.(p.320)
• I noticed that I was avoiding ***all*** my social friends except for my bridge.(p.324)
• I had bottles hidden ***all*** over the apartment.(p.324)
• I'd get so fed up with drinking ***all*** alone and bearing the burden of guilt ***all*** by myself, that I'd egg him on to drink, to get started again.(p.325)
• I myself didn't know ***all*** the places I had them hidden.(p.325)
• And unless I had some rosy picture of what was going to happen that day, I wouldn't even feel like getting up in the morning at ***all***.(p.325)
• I am trying now, each day, to make up for ***all*** those selfish, thoughtless, foolish things I did in my drinking days.(p.326)
• ***All*** the joys of retirement lay ahead for this movie publicist.(p.327)
• I had been far too busy building, protecting, and maintaining an image of respectability and ***all*** the other business pluses.(p.327)
• Aren't we ***all***?(p.328)
• ***All*** hidden drunks aren't at home in housewives' dresses.(p.328)
• Even obvious intoxication is excused by younger people as something "he's earned the right to do," and they say, "After ***all***, who's he hurting?"(p.330)
• He may even read in a newspaper that one out of every seven drinkers will become alcoholic, but he rarely is told that it holds true for ***all*** ages – or that the tolerance to alcohol (and other drugs) decreases steadily, year after year, in the bodies of ***all*** persons.(p.330)
• My alcoholism-prone mind, however, reminded me that ***all*** great authors had needed a stimulus to build up inspiration and inventiveness before each day's work.(p.331)
• In succession came "What Made Milwaukee Famous Made a Loser Out of Me" and "I'm Drinking My Christmas Dinner ***All*** Alone."(p.332)
• Where were ***all*** those words coming from?(p.333)
• Whatever it was, it brushed ***all*** the heavy burdens off my back.(p.334)
• We ***all*** have them, and I thought a little brandy or a little wine now and then could certainly hurt no one.(p.336)
• It wasn't long before I was drinking ***all*** day.(p.336)
• But they were ***all*** mixed up together, and I was ***all*** mixed up inside.(p.337)
• Half a mother was better than no mother at ***all***.(p.337)
• Well, of course that was ***all*** I needed – to switch from wine to brandy for three weeks.(p.338)
• The very person who stood with me through it ***all*** and has been my greatest help was the person that I turned against, my husband.(p.338)
• I had ***all*** kinds of reasons for my drinking.(p.338)
• I figured I'd be ***all*** right if I could find something I liked to do.(p.339)
• And when ***all*** of life is a substitute for drink, there's no happiness, no peace.(p.339)
• It's either ***all*** work, or I drink."(p.340)
• The regular flow of ***all*** the literature, which I keep meticulously and which, of course, I study, has been wonderful.(p.342)
• I have been of a very religious outlook ***all*** my life, but that made no difference once John Barleycorn got the better of me.(p.343)
• First, we ***all*** hear at A.A. meetings about those who have lost everything, those who have been in jail, those who have been in prison, those who have lost their families, those who have lost their income.(p.345)
• I was president of ***all*** my classes in high school and in my last year I was president of that student body.(p.345)
• In an attempt to get over that feeling, there was a quick onslaught of a greater number of drinks, and then ***all*** was lost.(p.346)
• This was such a new thought that I got ***all*** sorts of books on Higher Powers, and I put a Bible by my bedside, and I put a Bible in my car.(p.348)
• And I put a Big Book by my night stand, and I put a "Twelve Steps and Twelve Tradition" in my locker at the hospital, and I got books by Emmet Fox, and I got books by God-knows-who, and I got to reading ***all*** these things.(p.348)
• You've been doing ***all*** right."(p.348)
• ***All*** I do in a very simple way, is to help Him cure my patients.(p.351)
• ***All*** my life, it seemed, was spent on the outside looking in.(p.353)
• I had been unhappy, lonely, and scared for so long that the discovery of liquor seemed to be the answer to ***all*** my problems.(p.353)
• I could hardly see at ***all***, and my memory kept eluding me.(p.353)
• I'd managed to drink my way through ***all*** my friends.(p.355)
• Here was the understanding I'd been searching for ***all*** my life.(p.355)
• As these words are written at fifty-three years of age, with over nine years of A.A. behind me, with ***all*** its wonderful teachings, I haven't the slightest doubt about being an alcoholic.(p.356)
• I had every advantage a child could have, private schools (several of them), dancing schools, two colleges, coon skin coats, automobiles, a listing in the social register and ***all*** the rest.(p.357)
• ***All*** of which could turn out but one thing – a very popular, but spoiled, brat.(p.357)
• I had no trouble at ***all*** in being elected to the two drinking societies at my college.(p.357)
• ***All*** I can remember about the Roaring Twenties is that I drank a great deal, thought I was having a grand time, managed to get to Europe for a few weeks, was very proud of the dozens of speak-easy cards entitling me to an entree in the better joints between Cleveland and New York, took on a wife, and built a home in a fashionable suburb of Cleveland.(p.358)
• Like ***all*** alcoholics endeavoring to run away from themselves and their environment, I decided to go to New York.(p.358)
• After ***all*** -- wasn't I entitled to it?(p.360)
• She was tolerant beyond ***all*** belief.(p.361)
• She tried reasoning with me, endeavored to work out various drinking schedules, in fact ***all*** the tricks were practised faithfully for a short time somewhere along my shaky road to unhappiness.(p.361)
• I can't bear to be here when you lose the respect of others, and above ***all*** -- when you lose your own self respect."(p.362)
• I was going to prove to her that liquor wasn't necessary in my life, and above ***all*** that I still loved her more than anything else in the world and that I wanted her back.(p.362)
• Sure I still loved her, but hang it ***all***, she was unreasonable!(p.362)
• I would end it ***all***, and then, by George, she'd be sorry!(p.363)
• I can't bear to be here when you lose the respect of others, and above ***all*** when you lose your own self respect."(p.363)
• I got through the holidays ***all*** right until New Year's Day.(p.365)
• Later I told her I had not taken the drink and that I was ***all*** right.(p.365)
• While I was in Florida trying to convince my wife with ***all*** the A.A. literature that she should come back to me, she went over to her desk and picked up a clipping she had taken from the St. Petersburg Times about A.A.(p.366)
• I have had many more reasons to drink since I have been in A.A. than I had in ***all*** the years of my drinking.(p.367)
• Also, I believed I was the image of ***all*** domestic virtues, secluded in my washday (any day) refuge.(p.369)
• I had no qualms, because I felt the source of a drinking problem was ***all*** in how weak one was, and I wasn't like my dad (I thought).(p.370)
• I would gather up ***all*** my soiled clothes, as much as I could cram into a grocery cart, and be off.(p.370)
• ***All*** this while, I wondered whether I could do laundry for the neighbors as a part-time job.(p.371)
• I did work of ***all*** kinds after school and during vacations, trying to find that which would appeal most as a goal for a life work.(p.373)
• Never having enough, always craving more, the obsession for alcohol gradually dominated ***all*** my activities, particularly while travelling.(p.375)
• I will never know ***all*** the people I hurt, ***all*** the friends I abused, the humiliation of my family, the worry of my business associates, or how far reaching it was.(p.376)
• We rationalize and excuse our conduct beyond ***all*** reason.(p.376)
• It seemed to me my wife was becoming more intolerant and narrow minded ***all*** the time.(p.376)
• This suggestion had been made before on a number of occasions, but like ***all*** alcoholics I wanted to handle my problem my own way, which really meant I didn't want anything to interfere with my drinking.(p.378)
• I was unhappy myself and I had brought unhappiness to ***all*** who cared for me.(p.378)
• After ***all***, I hadn't started to drink early in life, so I had some stability and maturity to guide me for a while.(p.379)
• They meant patience, tolerance and humility, and above ***all*** the belief that a Power greater than myself could help.(p.381)
• A "spiritual experience" to me meant attending meetings, seeing a group of people, ***all*** there for the purpose of helping each other; hearing the Twelve Steps and the Twelve Traditions read at a meeting, and hearing the Lord's Prayer, which in an A.A. meeting has such great meaning – "Thy will be done, not mine."(p.381)
• "First Things First": solving our immediate problems before we try to solve ***all*** the others and get muddled in our thinking and doing.(p.382)
• No one individual can carry ***all*** the burdens of the world.(p.382)
• Above ***all***, I am grateful to A.A. for my sobriety, which means so much to my family, friends and business associates, because God and A.A. were able to do for me something I was unable to do for myself.(p.383)
• I was an extremely sensitive person and so self-conscious that I hurt ***all*** over.(p.385)
• By the time ***all*** this was over, I was really in a terrific state, and my father taking in things said, "Miss Esther is about to faint.(p.385)
• I wanted to do it ***all*** over again.(p.386)
• That was when ***all*** the boys and Esther got drunk and the wives didn't.(p.386)
• So Frank went to New York and despite ***all*** these

things, I got drunk.(p.389)
• We moved once more, to Houston; my husband thought maybe a change of environment would help and I'd be *all* right.(p.389)
• The only time my dog would have anything to do with me was when I had a hangover, and when I was so sick he was the only one who would have anything to do with me at *all*.(p.390)
• So he waited another week or two and I don't think I stayed sober hardly at *all*.(p.391)
• Up to that time, I was so completely baffled by my behavior that I had never really stopped to think at *all*.(p.392)
• This was something I had to do *all* by myself.(p.392)
• Monday morning I was feeling just like a million dollars -- *all* I needed was half a pint!(p.393)
• There are so many to whom I feel deeply grateful; to my husband (and best critic), whose generous love, compassion and understanding have helped me along the way; to those before me in A.A. who inspired the first article I read, and the friend who sent that article to Frank; to Ruth for her personal note, and the first A.A. to talk to me; to my Bishop, whose loving and believing spirit inspired me; and to *all* the members of the Houston Group who were so patient, kind and helpful -- and to countless others.(p.393)
• I wish I could tell you *all* that A.A. has done for me, *all* that I think and feel about A.A., but it's something that I have experienced and have never been able to put into words.(p.394)
• In *all* these ways I've experienced, in ever growing measure and beyond *all* expectations and rewards, a joy which I had never before imagined.(p.395)
• The words of Dr. Bob and Bill are with me *all* the time.(p.395)
• After *all*, upon coming out of a week-long or ten-day drunk, it was hard enough to figure up just how much that one drunk cost, let alone trying to calculate the cost of approximately twenty-five years of active alcoholism.(p.396)
• But now, with His help and grace, this child of His has paid his initiation fee for good, as long as he remembers to stay away from that first drink (the one that does *all* the damage) one day at a time.(p.399)
• Up to my early thirties, when my drinking had become a major problem, I lived in large houses, with servants and *all* the luxuries that I could possibly ask for.(p.401)
• Showing *all* the courage and ingenuity that I had not used in a positive way, I covered my tracks and hid from my family so successfully that they did not find me for months.(p.401)
• It was *all* about Scott Fitzgerald's little lost debutante, abused, misunderstood and running wild.(p.402)
• Above *all*, he noticed that I drank a good deal, often got tight in his company and told him naughty stories.(p.403)
• Many of them carried a flask and sandwich case, strapped to their saddles so they could stay out *all* day.(p.404)
• It was nothing to my own inner distress, my self-reproach, and my self-loathing, for was I not bearing out *all* the horrible things I had always suspected of myself?(p.404)
• I also wrote another novel, *all* about Scott Fitzgerald's poor, misbegotten, unloved, tipsy little debutante.(p.405)
• During this time, you are supposed to behave yourself, but I took a little wine-tasting tour through France, *all* by my lone, with car and chauffeur.(p.405)
• Other girls whom I had known *all* my life asked for one weak scotch after dinner.(p.406)
• It combined running away from my world, and drinking *all* I wanted to.(p.407)
• They were *all* kids, most of them younger than I was.(p.407)
• *All* of them have since settled down to jobs and good marriages.(p.407)
• Ribaldry was the substance of the conversation, and I set out to be the funniest and most ribald of them *all*.(p.407)
• Underneath, I knew this was *all* wrong.(p.407)
• I used *all* those well-known phrases.(p.408)
• My new friends made fun of God and *all* the orthodox beliefs.(p.408)
• I did not know that I had no power over alcohol, that I, alone and unaided, could not stop; that I was on a downgrade, tearing along at full speed with *all* my brakes gone, and that the end would be a total smash-up, death or insanity.(p.408)
• My child was being exposed to *all* this.(p.408)
• She did *all* she could to help this situation and to protect my child.(p.409)
• I saw that my Village friends, *all* of whom had small jobs, were living happily on about a tenth of my sinecure.(p.409)
• It was I who had to tell the bank, after a certain time, to refuse *all* further deposits.(p.409)
• Yes, I, the queen of them *all*!(p.411)
• What I had secretly believed myself to be *all* along, this I had become.(p.411)
• I could not live on that tiny trust fund and still drink *all* I wanted to.(p.411)
• But *all* these things could have happened.(p.412)
• "These people *all* had your problem," she told me.(p.412)
• Something in the book had reached me after *all*.(p.412)
• They would *all* stare at me and whisper!(p.413)
• But my life, even sober, was *all* askew and so were my emotions.(p.414)
• I tried to wash a little, but Anne refused to wash at *all*.(p.415)
• *All* these things together brought me into A.A.(p.415)
• *All* the people involved in these flare-ups took it with remarkable grace, have teased me about it since, and have become good friends of mine.(p.416)
• I know I do not have to be "queen of them *all*" to salve a frightened ego.(p.416)
• Through going to meetings and listening, and occasionally speaking, through doing Twelve Step work, whereby in helping others you are both the teacher and the student, by making many wonderful A.A. friends, I have been taught *all* the things in life that are worth having.(p.416)
• GROWING UP *ALL* OVER AGAIN(p.418)
• No one could have told me then that I had not earned *all* my success, nor could anyone have told me that I was an alcoholic and a drug addict.(p.418)
• I had accomplished *all* the right things that our society expected, and I had no real peace of mind nor gratitude.(p.418)
• Most important, A.A. has enabled me to go back and start growing up *all* over again in *all* areas of my life.(p.420)
• *All* the statistics are against me.(p.420)
• We *all* had lockers.(p.423)
• My dad, who was a newspaper man and had some connections, had meantime put a stop on me, and I guess that report went *all* over the country.(p.424)
• I stayed in the barracks *all* day, "making out guard schedules," and getting mildly plastered from the jug under my desk.(p.426)
• He was interested and said he'd help me *all* he could.(p.428)
• *All* I'd wanted was one more drink.(p.428)
• I headed home for the most wonderful experience of *all* time -- meeting my "new" parents -- mom and dad looked different than I had pictured them.(p.428)
• I would drink *all* night in bars, come home about five a.m., down a good big glass of whiskey straight, and tumble into bed.(p.428)
• Sometimes I'd make it home and go to sleep at the wheel of my car, for *all* the neighbors to see next morning as they left for work.(p.429)
• I'd lost my car again, pawned my wallet and *all* identification papers for a bottle, and gotten home somehow.(p.429)
• Today I have *all* that anyone could ask.(p.431)
• In *all* the twenty-five years of my drinking there were only a few occasions when I took a morning drink.(p.432)
• My associates, and *all* the wits and literary lights I so much admired, also drank.(p.433)
• How exciting to learn the inward mysteries that govern the behavior of people, how wonderful to know, at last, *all* about myself!(p.434)
• My daily alcoholic consumption remained about the same through *all* this, with perhaps a slight increase, and my binges remained one-nighters.(p.434)
• With *all* this, it was becoming increasingly hard to maintain my front of distinction and respectability to the world.(p.435)
• "Then why in God's name haven't you told me so, during *all* these years?"(p.436)
• Many times in the intervening years I have thanked God for that man, a man who had the courage to admit failure, a man who had the humility to confess that *all* the hard-won learning of his profession could not turn up the answer.(p.436)
• With my A.A. friends, *all* I can say is that it's a power greater than myself.(p.437)
• If pressed further, *all* I can do is follow the psalmist who said it long, long before me: "Be still, and know that I am God."(p.437)
• My alcoholic wife took up someone else, divorced me, and took with her *all* my remaining property.(p.437)
• I think He's on hand to see *all* of us through whatever may come to us.(p.437)
• Not only did I not think that being an alcoholic was a good idea, I didn't even feel that I had *all* that much of a drinking problem!(p.439)
• Of course, I had problems, *all* sort of problems.(p.439)
• *All* I want to know is, why does that dog wet in my lap every time I hold him?"(p.440)
• So, when it ended up at a psycho ward, I wasn't *all* that surprised.(p.440)
• After going to school *all* day, working in the family drugstore *all* evening, and then studying until one or two in the morning, I would not be able to sleep soundly, with everything I had been studying going round in my head.(p.440)
• If it was one minute after, I'd stay up and act like a martyr *all* day.(p.441)
• But to do so, I had to get *all* the stuff out of the house and out of my possession.(p.443)
• In the end, I had to do the same with alcohol and *all* pills.(p.443)
• Giving up alcohol alone was not enough for me; I've had to give up *all* mood-and mind-affecting chemicals in order to stay sober and comfortable.(p.443)
• After nine days of tests at Mayo, I was put in the locked ward -- of *all* places!(p.444)
• They wanted me to make leather belts, of *all* things!(p.445)
• Had I gone to school *all* those years just to sit and make leather belts?(p.445)
• My reaction was that I'd already helped *all* the patients on the ward, and I still had plenty of problems of my own without trying to help some drunk from A.A.(p.446)
• The psychiatrist, who had generally been ignoring me, now became quite interested; every day, he would ask me *all* kinds of questions about the A.A. meetings.(p.446)
• It seemed that *all* they talked about at meetings was drinking, drinking, drinking.(p.447)
• I had already given up *all* the narcotics, most of the pills, and some of the alcohol when I first came to A.A.(p.448)
• By early July, I had tapered off alcohol completely, and I got off *all* pills in the ensuing few months.(p.448)
• It is true that I -- of *all* people, strange as it may seem, and even though I didn't give my permission -- really, really am an alcoholic of sorts.(p.448)
• And it's *all* right with me.(p.449)
• And acceptance is the answer to *all* my problems today.(p.449)
• Shakespeare said, "*All* the world's a stage, *all* the men and women merely players."(p.449)
• A.A. and acceptance have taught me that there is a bit of good in the worst of us and a bit of bad in the best of us; that we are *all* children of God and we each have a right to be here.(p.449)
• Over the years, as I thought about Max, her good qualities grew and grew, and we married, and *all* these qualities became more and more apparent to me, and we were happier and happier.(p.450)
• Perhaps the best thing of *all* for me is to remember that my serenity is inversely proportional to my expectations.(p.452)
• *All* found themselves headed for the same destruction, and it seemed they could to nothing whatever to stop it.(p.455)
• I served twelve years in prison, never suspecting that without alcohol I would not have been in prison at *all*.(p.457)
• After *all*, it was self (you, me) that stood in our own way, that ran the show and ran ourselves into bankruptcy, that hurt the ones we loved.(p.459)
• *All* Twelve Steps of A.A. are designed to kill the old self (deflate the old ego) and build a new, free self.(p.459)
• Finally, I threw away *all* my books and decided never to return to A.A.(p.460)
• He and his wife more than accepted me; he listened to *all* my woes; both of them treated me as a human being.(p.462)
• After nine months of training, *all* the rest of my class was paroled and I went to work in the Department of Corrections.(p.462)
• It is *all* like a dream.(p.463)
• God bless *all* you people in A.A. and especially you fellows in prison.(p.463)
• The doctor, apparently realizing that one thing that I certainly needed was sleep, left a bottle of sleeping

pills there and in my drunken state I took them *all*, instead of the one or two he had prescribed.(p.465)
• I waited *all* the rest of that day and paced the floor *all* that night.(p.467)
• Then in a couple of hours, when there was still no word from my husband and no sign of him, I had the feeling we alcoholics *all* know.(p.467)
• *All* afternoon I sat there and drank and played Bing Crosby's recording of "Silent Night" over and over again on the juke box.(p.467)
• You may wonder why, since I was having *all* this trouble, and was having to seek the assistance of others, A.A. hadn't come into the picture.(p.469)
• Why did it work for me when *all* other agencies had failed?(p.470)
• It seemed to me that those A.A.'s to whom I talked knew *all* about me.(p.470)
• In *all* the sanitariums and psycho wards I had never met a single woman who said she was an alcoholic.(p.471)
• I went to meetings, I spent a lot of time at the clubroom, but it was *all* centered in this one woman.(p.472)
• I thought, "Oh well, these people are just like *all* the people I've known *all* my life.(p.472)
• They build you up with a lot of false hopes and promises, and rush you around here and there and then, *all* of a sudden, it's gone."(p.472)
• Here was a book that said I could do something that *all* these doctors and priests and ministers and psychiatrists that I'd been going to for years couldn't do!(p.473)
• I realize that *all* I'm guaranteed in life is today.(p.473)
• We *all* one as Great Spirit walks through A.A. like sun walks through day.(p.474)
• Miracle happen *all* time in A.A.(p.476)
• Start group on reservation and carry message, help start other groups *all* over Maritimes and New England.(p.476)
• He was old, but now he grow young with new life in A.A. and travel *all* time.(p.476)
• I feel Great Spirit at *all* meetings and when talk to A.A. friends.(p.477)
• When I came into A.A., I had no intention of quitting drinking -- I figured I was doing *all* right.(p.478)
• After *all*, I had been working for eighteen years, slinging hash, and I was managing.(p.478)
• Mind you, I had absolutely nothing to show for that eighteen years, except a beat-up car that I hadn't even paid for, but I was doing *all* right.(p.478)
• No clothes, no money, no home, no real friends to speak of, mentally and physically pooped, but I was doing *all* right!(p.478)
• Aside from being a common drunk, I had a very serious pill affliction and *all* the garbage that goes with it -- lying, stealing, cheating anybody and everybody, conning the people I could, and staying clear of the ones I couldn't.(p.478)
• We survivors are *all* in A.A. now, and my mother is in Al-Anon.(p.480)
• I can't begin to tell you of *all* the benefits I have derived from this new way of living.(p.481)
• He has taught me that, in our new life, I am the most important person of *all*.(p.481)
• If anyone had told me I would be enjoying a hockey game with my husband and my brother without being *all* boozed up, I would not have believed it.(p.481)
• I went to church on Easter Sunday with my husband, and it didn't hurt at *all*.(p.482)
• Honesty is the easiest word for me to understand because it is the exact opposite of what I've been doing *all* my life.(p.482)
• *All* my troubles arose when I was thrown socially among groups of people.(p.486)
• He was in his late fifties, and *all* that he had undertaken fell upon my shoulders at his death in 1928.(p.486)
• I thought that *all* women should be perfect.(p.487)
• About that time I had lost practically *all* my property except the place we were living in.(p.487)
• I took that bottle of medicine and gave it to a very good friend of mine who was a pharmacist and had it analyzed, and the bottle was perfectly *all* right.(p.489)
• Matters got worse *all* the time until finally they got so bad that I was reinvestigated by the Government.(p.490)
• Anyhow, on the 24th, after drinking *all* day on the 23rd, I must have decided I wanted to see my wife and have some kind of reconciliation or at least talk with her.(p.491)
• I think the thing that galled me was that just after Easter I had drawn my salary for two weeks' work and had decided that I was going to send some money to Vi; and above *all* else I was going to send my baby daughter an Easter outfit.(p.493)
• He started telling me how much trouble he had, and I said to myself, "I wonder why this guy is telling me *all* his troubles.(p.494)
• I knew my wife didn't because I had been sincere in *all* my promises to her as well as to my mother and to my close friends, but the urge to take that drink was more powerful than anything else.(p.494)
• I approached several ministers and *all* of them thought it was a very good idea, but they never relinquished any space.(p.495)
• Vi was taking care of me and I was devoting *all* my time to the building of that group.(p.496)
• I just gathered up this and that alcoholic, because, in the back of my mind, I wanted to save *all* the world.(p.496)
• This wasn't so bad after *all*.(p.498)
• The grand fellow who at my call made me a hail-fellow-well-met, who gave me such a fine voice, as we sang "Hail, hail, the gang's *all* here," and "Sweet Adeline," who gave me freedom from fear and feelings of inferiority.(p.498)
• He was my pal, *all* right.(p.498)
• I'll do it *all* myself.(p.502)
• Then he asks me if I am willing to right *all* the wrongs I have ever done to anyone, no matter how wrong I thought the others were.(p.503)
• "Then *all* of your troubles are over," says the man and leaves the room.(p.503)
• Can *all* the worth while people I have known be wrong about God?(p.503)
• "The thing I do is to say 'God here I am and here are *all* my troubles.(p.504)
• You take me, and *all* my troubles, and do anything you want with me.'(p.504)
• I feel that I can fix them *all*.(p.506)
• She asked me, was I going to do this to her *all* over again?(p.510)
• Yes, we find it rather confusing, but as we get around and get to know people in the group, they lead the way and *all* we have to do is to follow.(p.512)
• You went *all* the way.(p.516)
• In here you must go *all* the way too."(p.516)
• We *all* use them differently.(p.516)
• I have to watch myself *all* the time.(p.516)
• But I pointed out to him that as I was the first British boy who had been to the school, it wouldn't be a very good advertisement for him, so I got over that *all* right.(p.518)
• Up to that time, drinking didn't really mean anything to me at *all*.(p.518)
• India lent itself to drinking then, if you were disposed to drink, because you lived in bungalows; you didn't live *all* together as you do at home in an Officer's Mess.(p.519)
• I was in a world that I knew nothing at *all* about, and I felt intensely afraid.(p.521)
• I stayed there just long enough to work up a real good resentment against the doctor in charge, who I didn't think was doing anything at *all* except collecting fees, and I left there fully determined that I'd never put myself in the power of medical people again.(p.521)
• I was intensely unhappy the whole time, but I didn't seem to be able to do anything about it, and the worst part to me was the realization that *all* this was going to happen again and again until I died.(p.522)
• I couldn't think of anything at *all* to do.(p.523)
• I had played *all* that out long ago.(p.523)
• Providentially, this was a Monday might when the Dublin Group met in those days, and my family agreed that if A.A. could do anything for me at *all*, that I'd be allowed to stay on at home on probation.(p.523)
• It was their open night meeting, but of course I thought they were *all* alcoholics; I couldn't imagine why anybody else would want to go there, and my first reaction was, well, I've come to something that's not for me.(p.524)
• What struck me most was that they *all* seemed to be quite pleased with having made a job of it and having stopped drinking.(p.524)
• I hated that judge for sending me to a place with *all* those drunks.(p.527)
• *All* they care about is that I am a human being and that I want to stay sober.(p.529)
• I hope I haven't hurt anyone's feelings, but maybe we could *all* grow and change.(p.529)
• We *all* have the same sickness, and in helping one another, we are able to stay sober.(p.530)
• Things weren't going as I thought they should, for my greater enjoyment, comfort and fame; therefore, if the universe wouldn't play my way, I wouldn't play at *all*.(p.531)
• Within a month, the police, the hospital authorities, several kind strangers, most of my friends, *all* of my close relatives, and a few adepts at rolling a drunk and removing his wrist watch and wallet had been involved.(p.532)
• These things were *all* pressures.(p.533)
• And *all* this, of course, is, in the popular modern jargon, "compensation" for immaturity.(p.535)
• But I wanted a cosmos, a universe *all* my own which I had created and where I reigned as chief top reigner and ruler over everyone else.(p.535)
• Which is only another way of saying, I had to be right *all* the time, and only God can be that.(p.535)
• As I write these words, it seems incredible that these things should have happened to me, for they are, truly, against *all* my instincts and training.(p.536)
• I wonder if ever there has been a sillier reason for getting drunk *all* the time.(p.537)
• *All* of my family and loved ones, *all* of my friends, are nearer and dearer to me than ever before and I have literally dozens of new friends who say they cannot believe that a short eight years ago I was ready for the scrap heap.(p.541)
• For me, A.A. is a synthesis of *all* the philosophy I've ever read, *all* of the positive, good philosophy, *all* of it based on love.(p.542)
• With no explanation at *all*, I was taken from my home in Florida to my grandparents' home in the middle west.(p.544)
• The only kind of security I knew anything about at that time was material security and I decided that *all* these intruders would vanish immediately if I only had a lot of money.(p.545)
• The only importance in *all* of this lies in the fact that at twenty-three I was just as sick as I was at thirty three, when I came into A.A., but at that time I apparently had no place to go because I had no drinking problem.(p.546)
• Apparently I'd grown physically at the customary rate of speed, and I had acquired an average amount of intellectual training in the intervening years, but there had been no emotional maturity at *all*.(p.547)
• I was immersed in self-pity and resentment, and the only people who would support this attitude or who I felt understood me at *all* were the people I met in bars and the ones who drank as I did.(p.547)
• *All* but one "responded to the treatment" suggested in the Steps immediately, but this one posed a problem.(p.551)
• And because it works for me, it will work for *all* of us.(p.552)
• This great experience that released me from the bondage of hatred and replaced it with love is really just another affirmation of the truth I know: I get everything I need in Alcoholics Anonymous -- everything I need I get -- and when I get what I need I invariably find that it was just what I wanted *all* the time.(p.553)
• Above *all*, I was suffering inner pain because my performance and my accomplishments in life failed to live up to my own expectations of myself.(p.557)
• Soon my drinking was as bad as ever -- *all* day long every day.(p.557)
• Angry bruises appeared mysteriously *all* over my body.(p.558)
• But now *all* choice was gone.(p.558)
• *All* these things and many, many more, A.A. gave me.(p.559)
• But above *all*, it taught me how to handle sobriety.(p.559)
• Above *all*, we reject fantasizing and accept reality.(p.560)
• Twelve -- Anonymity is the spiritual foundation of *all* our Traditions, ever reminding us to place principles before personalities.(p.564)
• 3. -- Our membership ought to include *all* who suffer from alcoholism.(p.565)
• *All* such representatives are to be guided in the spirit of service, for true leaders in A.A. are but trusted and experienced servants of the whole.(p.567)
• This to the end that our great blessings may never spoil us; that we shall forever live in thankful contemplation of Him who presides over us *all*.(p.568)
• Most emphatically we wish to say that any alcoholic capable of honestly facing his problems in the light of our experience can recover, provided he does not close his mind to *all* spiritual concepts.(p.570)
• "There is a principle which is a bar against *all* information, which is proof against *all* arguments and which cannot fail to keep a man in everlasting ignorance -- that principle is contempt prior to investigation."(p.570)

all-important
- I was keenly aware that my ***all-important*** security, which I had been constantly afraid of losing for four decades, no longer was endangered.(p.329)

all-night
- At age twenty-one, I enlisted in the Navy for two reasons: (1) to avoid being drafted into the Army, and (2) out of a burst of patriotic fervor inspired by the advent of World War II and as the result of an ***all-night*** drinking binge which found me sitting on the doorstep of the Navy recruiting office when the chief petty officer arrived to open for business at nine o'clock Monday morning.(p.398)
- So I'd sit up, watch old Wallace Beery movies on ***all-night*** TV, and drink.(p.441)

Allah
- Then he asks me if I believe in a power greater than myself, whether I call that power God, ***Allah***, Confucius, Prime Cause, Divine Mind, or any other name.(p.503)

allegiances
- My divorce coincided with my father's bankruptcy, and I went to work, casting off all ***allegiances*** and responsibilities to any other than myself.(p.225)

allergic
- These ***allergic*** types can never safely use alcohol in any form at all; and once having formed the habit and found they cannot break it, once having lost their self-confidence, their reliance upon things human, their problems pile up on them and become astonishingly difficult to solve.(p.xxvi)
- My first drinking spree was on corn liquor and I was ***allergic*** to it, believe me.(p.322)
- The allergy I could understand because I am ***allergic*** to certain pollens.(p.380)
- Some of my family are ***allergic*** to certain foods.(p.380)
- What could be more reasonable than that some people, including myself, were ***allergic*** to alcohol?(p.380)

allergy
- The doctor's theory that we have an ***allergy*** to alcohol interests us.(p.xxiv)
- We believe, and so suggested a few years ago, that the action of alcohol on these chronic alcoholics is a manifestation of an ***allergy***; that the phenomenon of craving is limited to this class and never occurs in the average temperate drinker.(p.xxvi)
- This phenomenon, as we have suggested, may be the manifestation of an ***allergy*** which differentiates these people, and sets them apart as a distinct entity.(p.xxviii)
- He said he had finally learned that drinking was a fatal illness made up of an ***allergy*** plus an obsession, and once the drinking had passed from habit to obsession, we were completely hopeless, and could look forward only to spending the balance of our lives in mental institutions or to death.(p.290)
- The ***allergy*** I could understand because I am allergic to certain pollens.(p.380)
- The explanation that alcoholism was a disease of a two fold nature, an ***allergy*** of the body and an obsession of the mind, cleared up a number of puzzling questions for me.(p.380)
- The ***allergy*** we could do nothing about.(p.380)
- I think I had the physical ***allergy*** right away.(p.402)
- He now said that we had a physical ***allergy*** combined with a mental obsession, and he explained this so that I saw for the first time how this could be.(p.413)

alleviate
- I soon discovered that a couple of drinks would ***alleviate*** my gastric distress, at least for a few hours at a time, so it was not at all difficult for me to return to my former excessive indulgence.(p.174)
- I thought this would give me ego-strength, make me feel wanted and secure, and ***alleviate*** my fears, but again nothing changed inside me.(p.546)

alley
- This phase was right down my ***alley***; I had my master's degree in the art of making "whoopee."(p.359)

alleys
- Unlike his skid-row brother, he isn't heckled for sleeping in ***alleys*** or doorways.(p.330)
- The other kids would light out for the hamburger huts or ice cream parlors, the pizza joints or bowling ***alleys***, after football games and dances.(p.423)
- If it was daylight, I would go down ***alleys*** to make sure no one saw me.(p.527)

alliances
- And in no circumstances should we give endorsements, make ***alliances***, or enter public controversies.(p.xix)

allied
- We are not ***allied*** with any particular faith, sect or denomination, nor do we oppose anyone.(p.xiv)

allies
- After our first child came my parents both became ***allies***, but in later days, after I became an alcoholic, they both turned against me.(p.485)

allotment
- On that statement and the fact that I had been sober for ninety days, he gave me a job selling lots in an ***allotment*** he had.(p.200)

allow
- One school would ***allow*** man no flavor for his fare and the other would have us all on a straight pepper diet.(p.69)
- We seldom ***allow*** an alcoholic to live in our homes for long at a time.(p.97)
- I had found friends, understanding friends who often knew what I was thinking and feeling better than I knew myself, and didn't ***allow*** me to retreat into my prison of loneliness and fear over a fancied slight or hurt.(p.228)
- What is much more important to me, A.A. has taught me that through this simple program I may experience a change in this reaction pattern that will indeed ***allow*** me to "match calamity with serenity."(p.544)

allowance
- I had saved my ***allowance***.(p.409)

allowed
- Later, he requested the privilege of being ***allowed*** to tell his story to other patients here and with some misgiving, we consented.(p.xxv)
- After much argument they ***allowed*** me to return and take my exams, all of which I passed creditably.(p.173)
- They looked at one another queerly and, finally, one of them ***allowed*** he'd have a beer and they all followed him, each of them saying he'd have a beer too.(p.194)
- I wanted to roam again and through relatives got a supercargo job on an Australian packet which ***allowed*** me to visit my people in Australia where I was born.(p.252)
- Then and then only, after a thorough indoctrination by eight or nine individuals, was I ***allowed*** to attend my first meeting.(p.291)
- This went on for thirteen weeks, the first eight of which I wasn't ***allowed*** visitors.(p.425)
- After the first two or three days you were ***allowed*** the run of the place and it was a lot of fun.(p.468)
- I even wanted to -- but I wasn't ***allowed*** to, so I won't go now.(p.470)
- I was never to be ***allowed*** back.(p.521)
- Providentially, this was a Monday might when the Dublin Group met in those days, and my family agreed that if A.A. could do anything for me at all, that I'd be ***allowed*** to stay on at home on probation.(p.523)
- I have been ***allowed*** to build an entirely new career in a field I had never worked in.(p.541)
- In time I concluded that the reason I was hurt was because I loved my parents, and I concluded too that if I never ***allowed*** myself to love anybody or anything I could never be hurt again.(p.545)

allows
- As arrested alcoholics, we must have a program for living that ***allows*** for limitless expansion.(p.311)
- I leave the room, which the honor system ***allows***.(p.499)

alloy
- Out of this ***alloy*** of drink and speculation, I commenced to forge the weapon that one day would turn in its flight like a boomerang and all but cut me to ribbons.(p.2)

alluring
- There will be ***alluring*** shortcuts and by-paths down which they may wander and lose their way.(p.123)
- This practice enables us to lend a hand, at the same time avoiding certain ***alluring*** distractions of the road, about which any traveling man can inform you.(p.162)

alma mater
- Fortunately, I received only fifteen-twenty years, and I went back to my ***alma mater*** (where I had spent so much time in the hole).(p.461)
- I go back to my old ***alma mater*** occasionally to give A.A. talks, and -- just think! -- the warden is my friend.(p.462)

Almighty
- He found that I had enough faith in the ***Almighty*** to be fairly frank.(p.219)

almost
- Hence the two men set to work ***almost*** frantically upon alcoholics arriving in the ward of the Akron City Hospital.(p.xvii)
- By March 1976, when this edition went to the printer, the total worldwide membership of Alcoholics Anonymous was conservatively estimated at more than 1,000,000, with ***almost*** 28,000 groups meeting in over 90 countries.(p.xxii)
- My drinking assumed more serious proportions, continuing all day and ***almost*** every night.(p.3)
- I knew, and ***almost*** welcomed the idea.(p.7)
- I could ***almost*** hear the sound of the preacher's voice as I sat, on still Sundays, way over there on the hillside; there was that proffered temperance pledge I never signed; my grandfather's good natured contempt of some church folk and their doings; his insistence that the spheres really had their music; but his denial of the preacher's right to tell him how he must listen; his fearlessness as he spoke of these things just before he died; these recollections welled up from the past.(p.10)
- The ***almost*** certain consequences that follow taking even a glass of beer do not crowd into the mind to deter us.(p.24)
- ***Almost*** none of us liked the self-searching, the leveling of our pride, the confession of shortcomings which the process requires for its successful consummation.(p.25)
- ***Almost*** everyone knows the reason.(p.51)
- The spirit of modern scientific inquiry, research and invention was ***almost*** unknown.(p.51)
- Only thirty years later the conquest of the air was ***almost*** an old story and airplane travel was in full swing.(p.52)
- The Wright brothers' ***almost*** childish faith that they could build a machine which would fly was the mainspring of their accomplishment.(p.52)
- On that basis we are ***almost*** always in collision with something or somebody, even though our motives are good.(p.60)
- ***Almost*** invariably they got drunk.(p.72)
- We came to live ***almost*** alone.(p.105)
- A doctor said to us, "Years of living with an alcoholic is ***almost*** sure to make any wife or child neurotic.(p.122)
- God, they believe, ***almost*** owes this recompense on a long overdue account.(p.123)
- Now and then the family will be plagued by spectres from the past, for the drinking career of ***almost*** every alcoholic has been marked by escapades, funny, humiliating, shameful or tragic.(p.123)
- The alcoholic's past thus becomes the principal asset of the family and frequently it is ***almost*** the only one!(p.124)
- We do talk about each other a great deal, but we ***almost*** invariably temper such talk by a spirit of love and tolerance.(p.125)
- For his sake, we do recount and ***almost*** relive the horrors of our past.(p.132)
- If he temporizes and still thinks he can ever drink again, even beer, he might as well be discharged after the next bender which, if an alcoholic, he is ***almost*** certain to have.(p.142)
- In fact, he may say ***almost*** anything if he has accepted our solution which, as you know, demands rigorous honesty.(p.145)
- Bitterly discouraged, he found himself in a strange place, discredited and ***almost*** broke.(p.154)
- ***Almost*** everyone seemed to do it.(p.172)
- Never once in my life have I had a headache, which fact leads me to believe that I was an alcoholic ***almost*** from the start.(p.172)
- At that time I was not aware of the ***almost*** unlimited supply the government made it possible for us doctors to obtain, neither had I any knowledge of the bootlegger who soon appeared on the horizon.(p.175)
- It was ***almost*** always with me.(p.181)
- I had some financial success through no ability of my own and, when jobless and ***almost*** wiped out in 1930, I began to trade and sell my collection; much of the proceeds went to keep my apartment stocked with liquor and ***almost*** every night saw me helpless to bed.(p.255)
- A friend who knew I would soon be broke mounted guard over me when I left my job of writing the histories of Texas cities and put me aboard a bus for the town I had left ***almost*** five years before.(p.256)
- The doctor who came to see me ***almost*** at once did not assail me with any new doctrines; he made sure that I had a need and that I wanted to have that need

filled, and little by little I learned how my need could be met.(p.258)

- When I reached a point directly back of our house, where I could have cut through a friend's garden, I was *almost* overpowered by the desire to get home, but I made the whole journey.(p.276)
- *Almost* simultaneously, I discovered that cocktails in the late afternoon and highballs in the evening relieved the many tensions of the day.(p.277)
- When the day of their return was *almost* upon me, and suicide was the only answer I had been able to think of, I went into Ralph's room one evening and told him the truth.(p.278)
- I was seized with an *almost* uncontrollable desire to reach out for it.(p.285)
- In the summer of 1938, *almost* a year from the time I made my original contact with Akron, the man for whom I was working and who knew about the program, approached me and asked if I could do anything about one of his salesmen who was drinking very heavily.(p.294)
- That discovery so intrigued me, that I stayed on that diet *almost* entirely for the balance of my extensive drinking life.(p.298)
- From a monetary standpoint . . . in the past few years, I have reduced my reckless debts to *almost* nothing, and have had money to get along on comfortably.(p.303)
- While I was in basic, I got high off booze *almost* every night.(p.317)
- The third time, after *almost* five years as an S.P. 4, I finally made sergeant.(p.318)
- I didn't realize I would find so much more, but a new and different outlook on life started opening up *almost* immediately.(p.383)
- I lived in New Orleans where, at that time, cocktail parties, dances and night spots were *almost* the order of the day -- or rather the night.(p.384)
- While I was at Pensacola my dad became dangerously ill and *almost* died of pneumonia plus a heart attack.(p.426)
- My personality was stretched *almost* to splitting in the effort; schizophrenia stared me in the face, and one night I was in a suicidal despair.(p.435)
- Very shortly, I realized that had been a mistake -- when this big clown came bounding into the room, *almost* shouting, "My name is Frank, and I'm an alcoholic, ha-ha-ha!"(p.446)
- They prove to *almost* anyone's satisfaction that it's never too late to try Alcoholics Anonymous.(p.455)
- I *almost* broke down and cried when I talked with them but I didn't.(p.467)
- During the course of that drinking, I had shot and killed one person and *almost* completed the job on a second one.(p.508)
- When my mother opened the door, I *almost* fell in on my face.(p.510)
- This was the only time in my life that I'd ever known my mother to be *almost* pitiless, but she couldn't be blamed for that.(p.523)
- They are *almost* paid; the end is in sight.(p.541)
- It became more and more necessary to escape from myself, for my remorse and shame and humiliation when I was sober were *almost* unbearable.(p.547)
- There is something spiritual about A.A. too, and Catholic participation in it *almost* invariably results in poor Catholics becoming better Catholics."(p.574)

alone

- How many times people have said to us: "I can take it or leave it *alone*.(p.20)
- They can take it or leave it *alone*.(p.20)
- Here are some of the methods we have tried: Drinking beer only, limiting the number of drinks, never drinking *alone*, never drinking in the morning, drinking only at home, never having it in the house, never drinking during business hours, drinking only at parties, switching from scotch to brandy, drinking only natural wines, agreeing to resign if ever drunk on the job, taking a trip, not taking a trip, swearing off forever (with and without a solemn oath), taking more physical exercise, reading inspirational books, going to health farms and sanitariums, accepting voluntary commitment to asylums -- we could increase the list ad infinitum.(p.31)
- If anyone questions whether he has entered this dangerous area, let him try leaving liquor *alone* for one year.(p.34)
- This is the baffling feature of alcoholism as we know it -- this utter inability to leave it *alone*, no matter how great the necessity or the wish.(p.34)
- But later, *alone* in his room, he asked himself this question: "Is it possible that all the religious people I have known are wrong?"(p.56)
- But it is better to meet God *alone* than with one who might misunderstand.(p.63)
- God *alone* can judge our sex situation.(p.69)
- We can be *alone* at perfect peace and ease.(p.75)
- See your man *alone*, if possible.(p.91)
- He may be an example of the truth that faith *alone* is insufficient.(p.93)
- If you leave such a person *alone*, he may soon become convinced that he cannot recover by himself.(p.96)
- We came to live almost *alone*.(p.105)
- If he is lukewarm or thinks he is not an alcoholic, we suggest you leave him *alone*.(p.113)
- It is probably true that you and your husband have been living too much *alone*, for drinking many times isolates the wife of an alcoholic.(p.119)
- As a moderate drinker, you can take your liquor or leave it *alone*.(p.139)
- Meanwhile, we are sure a great deal can be accomplished by the use of the book *alone*.(p.144)
- Then he added, "He sure didn't do much for me when I was trying to fight this booze racket *alone*."(p.158)
- You are saying to yourself: "I'm jittery and *alone*.(p.163)
- If you still think you are strong enough to beat the game *alone*, that is your affair.(p.181)
- Sitting in a Second Avenue bar, accepting drinks from anyone who offered, after my small stake was gone; or sitting at home *alone*, with the inevitable glass in my hand, I would remember, and remembering, I would drink faster, seeking speedy oblivion.(p.225)
- I wasn't *alone* any more.(p.228)
- Certainly, at that time I was one of those who "can take it or leave it *alone*."(p.231)
- It was also an ending, for never since June 16th, 1938, have I had to walk *alone*.(p.248)
- And we went down through the valley, and I remembered reading about the Ku Klux Klan and how they burnt crosses, and I thought, "God *alone* knows what we are getting into this time!"(p.269)
- This *alone* is a miracle.(p.280)
- By living *alone* you can pretty much eliminate grief from you life, but you also eliminate joy.(p.286)
- I know now that sixty per cent of the time I drank *alone* without benefit of customers.(p.287)
- I had thought that I was completely different from other people, that I was beginning to become a little balmy, even to the point of withdrawing more and more from society and wanting to be *alone* with my bottle.(p.290)
- I spent several days with him, but I did not feel adequate to pass the program on to him *alone*.(p.294)
- If I were *alone* I would stop at four or five of them, but only one or two in the event I had my mistrusting wife with me.(p.299)
- This was drinking in sheer desperation, *alone* and locked behind my own door.(p.306)
- *Alone* in the relative safety of my home because I knew I dare not risk the danger of blacking out in some public place or at the wheel of a car.(p.306)
- I could never have accomplished this *alone*.(p.311)
- I'd get so fed up with drinking all *alone* and bearing the burden of guilt all by myself, that I'd egg him on to drink, to get started again.(p.325)
- Although I did drink, it always was with caution -- unless I was *alone*.(p.328)
- They daily pass into oblivion, *alone* or with mates.(p.329)
- In succession came "What Made Milwaukee Famous Made a Loser Out of Me" and "I'm Drinking My Christmas Dinner All *Alone*."(p.332)
- I did go to A.A., two days later, walking in *alone*.(p.334)
- But during a period of particular stress and strain about thirteen years ago, I resorted to alcohol in my home, *alone*, as a means of temporary release, as a means of getting a little extra sleep.(p.335)
- In September of this same year I went to New York *alone*.(p.364)
- When I was nineteen, I married a fine man who had never known an insecure moment in his life, let *alone* the trials and tribulations of booze.(p.369)
- After all, upon coming out of a week-long or ten-day drunk, it was hard enough to figure up just how much that one drunk cost, let *alone* trying to calculate the cost of approximately twenty-five years of active alcoholism.(p.396)
- I drank *alone* or with someone, anyone who would stay and drink with me.(p.406)
- I passed out frequently in my home, *alone*.(p.406)
- I did not know that I had no power over alcohol, that I, *alone* and unaided, could not stop; that I was on a downgrade, tearing along at full speed with all my brakes gone, and that the end would be a total smash-up, death or insanity.(p.408)
- I went to bars *alone* to drink.(p.410)
- One night I was sitting in the lab *alone* with a fifth and a case of beer listening to dreamy Hawaiian music on the radio.(p.427)
- Well, I'm willing, if it will curb this awful desire to drink, this fear of not having a drink, this feeling of always being *alone*, scared, deserted, sick.(p.430)
- I looked up an A.A. meeting and went there -- *alone*.(p.436)
- And should I have more bad times, I know that I'll never again have to go through them *alone*.(p.438)
- Giving up alcohol *alone* was not enough for me; I've had to give up all mood-and mind-affecting chemicals in order to stay sober and comfortable.(p.443)
- I feel that I have been restored to health and sanity these past years not through my own efforts nor as a result of anything I may have done, but because I've come to believe -- to really believe -- that *alone* I can do nothing.(p.473)
- He old, sick, want to be *alone* with bottle.(p.476)
- I started drinking *alone* then.(p.487)
- I worked at that *alone* for six months.(p.496)
- The Army drinking *alone* covered a lot of territory.(p.513)
- I was *alone* by myself in that job for a long time.(p.519)
- Without alcohol, I would be really *alone*.(p.539)
- We alcoholics see that we must work together and hang together, else most of us will finally die *alone*.(p.563)
- He finally realizes that he has undergone a profound alteration in his reaction to life; that such a change could hardly have been brought about by himself *alone*.(p.569)

aloneness

- There is no more "*aloneness*," with that awful ache, so deep in the heart of every alcoholic that nothing, before, could ever reach it.(p.312)

along

- Everyone became resigned to the certainty that I would have to be shut up somewhere, or would stumble *along* to a miserable end.(p.8)
- He had come to pass his experience *along* to me -- if I cared to have it.(p.9)
- The point is, that we are willing to grow *along* spiritual lines.(p.60)
- This thought brings us to Step Ten, which suggests we continue to take personal inventory and continue to set right any new mistakes as we go *along*.(p.84)
- We can exercise our will power *along* this line all we wish.(p.85)
- After they have seen tangible results, the family will perhaps want to go *along*.(p.99)
- If you are with a person who wants to eat in a bar, by all means go *along*.(p.102)
- Go *along* with your husband if you possibly can.(p.117)
- If a repetition is to be prevented, place the problem, *along* with everything else, in God's hands.(p.120)
- After your man has gone *along* without drinking for a few months, you may be able to make use of his services with other employees who are giving you the alcoholic run-around -- provided, of course, they are willing to have a third party in the picture.(p.146)
- I know I must get *along* without liquor, but how can I?(p.152)
- But they were much disgusted and told me they would attempt to struggle *along* without my presence.(p.173)
- So, at the time Dr. Bob and Bill came *along* I had about run out my strength.(p.182)
- This problem was soon solved, however, as I began to take my bottle *along* with me and hide it in the bathroom or in the shrubbery outside.(p.184)
- It was in the next two or three days after I had first met Doc and Bill, that I finally came to a decision to turn my will over to God and to go *along* with this program the best that I could.(p.189)
- I really wanted the program and I wanted to go *along* with it.(p.191)
- I went into the high school grades, but having missed all the intermediate grades, I didn't get *along* too well, so I developed the habit of going back to school just long enough for the football season and then quitting.(p.193)
- I was always able to skate *along* the fringe of big money.(p.197)
- I worked *along* until I had really big names in rubber on a tentative contract, and then I neglected to go through with it.(p.198)
- In the meantime, the domestic situation was not getting *along* too well.(p.199)

• I was bounding *along* and not doing too badly.(p.204)
• I got two drinks, each of them a quarter of that pint, in me, and was talking *along* with these people, but I felt that sooner or later they were going to have me cornered because they were smarter than I was and the drink was beginning to take effect; but as I reached for the third drink Bob said, "Listen, Buster, you promised to take some medicine if we got you a drink.(p.206)
• In other words, I was always safe from the discipline of my father, and having developed *along* that line, I had considerable difficulty in school.(p.210)
• I could discipline myself but *along* the way there would be festivities and occasions when I got drunk.(p.211)
• After two or three years of effort *along* this line, I reached the point of actual despair that I ever would be able to drink only a harmless amount each day.(p.215)
• The interne came *along* with a glassful of bleached lightning that put me away for about fifteen hours.(p.217)
• In fact, I never lost my faith, since I had been prepared by some conversations toward the end of my sojourn in the hospital with Dr. Bob, conversations pretty much *along* spiritual lines.(p.218)
• I condoned my domestic brewing *along* with the bootleggers and their business.(p.233)
• As I go *along* I seem to get strength daily to be able to resist more easily.(p.237)
• In sports I made the track and tennis teams; I got *along* well with the other boys and had a fairly large circle of acquaintances but no intimate friends.(p.240)
• So I rocked *along* my merry independent way until June, when I went out selling auto polish in New England.(p.247)
• While I went *along* with all that was done and attended the meetings, I never took an active job of leadership until February 1940.(p.249)
• The war was getting *along*.(p.253)
• Washington, D.C. and news-gathering agency work followed, *along* with many parties.(p.254)
• Need I say that in a very short time I was walking *along* a prairie highway with arm extended and thumb pointed?(p.255)
• So, sometimes we'd end up in Charleston, West Virginia, or here or there, drinking all *along* the way.(p.264)
• I remember sometime, it was possibly six months after we had been going steadily to King School, that we were coming home from a meeting and saw a car *along* the way, and a fellow in back drinking a bottle of beer.(p.271)
• I got *along* fairly well with my party drinking for quite some time, but eventually I began to visit beer joints in between parties.(p.298)
• A night or so a week in a joint, and a party or so a week at home or with friends, *along* with a little lone drinking, soon had me preparing for the existence of a top flight drunkard.(p.298)
• From a monetary standpoint . . . in the past few years, I have reduced my reckless debts to almost nothing, and have had money to get *along* on comfortably.(p.303)
• We got *along* fine for about two weeks, until she told me where to go and to take my damn bottle with me.(p.318)
• The only way I knew to do it was to drink right *along* with him.(p.322)
• As my son, our second child, came *along*, and as he became school age and was away at school most of the time, something happened.(p.323)
• Prohibition came *along*, and with it my first taste of moonshine.(p.357)
• Once again I was back in the big time operations, and *along* with them, big shot complexes.(p.361)
• My wonderful wife did everything to play *along* with me.(p.361)
• She tried reasoning with me, endeavored to work out various drinking schedules, in fact all the tricks were practised faithfully for a short time somewhere *along* my shaky road to unhappiness.(p.361)
• I would follow certain drinking schedules or diets faithfully for a few days, and then somewhere *along* the line would over-train and upset the applecart.(p.361)
• As long as it eased situations socially, it helped just fine, but somewhere *along* the line, it backfired.(p.386)
• If you will try this thing, I'll go *along* with you.(p.391)
• They sent me the regular letter they send to everybody else, but *along* with it, Ruth Hock, the nonalcoholic secretary, wrote a longhand note because she could see from the letter that I really needed help badly.(p.392)
• There are so many to whom I feel deeply grateful; to my husband (and best critic), whose generous love, compassion and understanding have helped me *along* the way; to those before me in A.A. who inspired the first article I read, and the friend who sent that article to Frank; to Ruth for her personal note, and the first A.A. to talk to me; to my Bishop, whose loving and believing spirit inspired me; and to all the members of the Houston Group who were so patient, kind and helpful -- and to countless others.(p.393)
• Imagine my surprise when I came to, in Europe, and discovered I had brought myself *along*!(p.405)
• I did not know that I had no power over alcohol, that I, alone and unaided, could not stop; that I was on a downgrade, tearing *along* at full speed with all my brakes gone, and that the end would be a total smash-up, death or insanity.(p.408)
• What I had secretly believed myself to be all *along*, this I had become.(p.411)
• And I knew that somewhere *along* the line I'd lost the power to stop drinking.(p.436)
• When I do this, we get *along* fine.(p.452)
• No drunk hopeless if he want to follow guide *along* right trail.(p.477)
• Some of us always remember our big mouths when it comes to a drink, but somewhere *along* the line, we seem to have forgotten about taking care of our teeth.(p.479)
• I rolled *along* with the mob this way, that way and the other way, but in those years nothing really bad happened to me.(p.508)
• I went *along* pretty well for the next ten months.(p.511)
• If something does come *along* that sort of upsets me, instead of walking in and throwing a buck at the barman and asking for a drink, I walk into a telephone booth, drop a dime in the box, and call somebody who was so kind as to give me his name and telephone number to meet such an emergency.(p.511)
• I got *along* well there.(p.517)

alongside

• Notice that the word "fear" is bracketed *alongside* the difficulties with Mr. Brown, Mrs. Jones, the employer, and the wife.(p.67)

alpha

• Instead of regarding ourselves as intelligent agents, spearheads of God's ever advancing Creation, we agnostics and atheists chose to believe that our human intelligence was the last word, the *alpha* and the omega, the beginning and end of all.(p.49)

already

• *Already,*" continues the early text, "twos and threes and fives of us have sprung up in other communities."(p.xv)
• You may *already* have asked yourself why it is that all of us became so very ill from drinking.(p.20)
• If your are an alcoholic who wants to get over it, you may *already* be asking -- "What do I have to do?"(p.20)
• This tragic situation has *already* arrived in practically every case long before it is suspected.(p.24)
• Here was the terrible dilemma in which our friend found himself when he had the extraordinary experience which as we have *already* told you, made him a free man.(p.28)
• We doubt if many of them can do it, because none will really want to stop, and hardly one of them, because of the peculiar mental twist *already* acquired, will find he can win out.(p.33)
• Whether such a person can quit upon a nonspiritual basis depends upon the extent to which he has *already* lost the power to choose whether he will drink or not.(p.34)
• Some of us had *already* walked far over the Bridge of Reason toward the desired shore of faith.(p.53)
• If you have *already* made a decision, and an inventory of your grosser handicaps, you have made a good beginning.(p.71)
• We have *already* admitted this in confidence to another person, but we are sure we would be imprisoned or lose our job if it were known.(p.78)
• Much has *already* been said about receiving strength, inspiration, and direction from Him who has all knowledge and power.(p.85)
• There is no use arousing any prejudice he may have against certain theological terms and conceptions about which he may *already* be confused.(p.93)
• In that case he is going to wonder how you can add anything to what he *already* knows.(p.93)
• Maybe you have *already* been obliged to put him away.(p.110)
• If he is *already* committed to an institution, but can convince you and your doctor that he means business, give him a chance to try our method, unless the doctor thinks his mental condition too abnormal or dangerous.(p.114)
• Or you may *already* have had it several times.(p.116)
• But you should feel under no obligation to keep him on, for your obligation has been well discharged *already*.(p.147)
• His wife came, scarcely daring to be hopeful, though she thought she saw something different about her husband *already*.(p.158)
• To some extent this is *already* true.(p.162)
• Knowing Bob of old, she jokingly replied, "Well, Doctor, I suppose you've *already* tried it yourself?"(p.188)
• I have *already* done it, and I am willing to do it again here in the presence of you or I am willing to say it any place, anywhere in the world from now on and not be ashamed of it."(p.190)
• I was arrested and taken to jail where I was beaten up by two or three fellows who were *already* in there and whom I tried to boss.(p.204)
• This time I seemed to be *already* awake, sitting upright in a big easy chair, in the middle of an animated conversation with a perfectly strange young woman, who didn't appear to think it strange.(p.222)
• For weeks after my arrival I was feted and entertained in the *already* large colony of Alsatians in the city, and among the Germans in their saloons and clubs.(p.231)
• He had *already* imbued them with his own spirit until they were ready and willing at all times to go where sent, and as a doctor he well knew that this mission and duty would strengthen them as it later helped me.(p.235)
• With nothing but a liberal arts education, very definitely estranged from my family and *already* married, soon after graduation from college I became a bookmaker's clerk on the British racing circuits, far better off financially than the average professional man.(p.251)
• When I finally returned to Detroit to find work and to learn to stand on my own feet, the ball was *already* rolling, however slowly.(p.282)
• This, plus mounting emotional disturbances, convinced them that compulsive alcoholism *already* had them; that complete ruin would be only a question of time.(p.315)
• My husband was made miserable by this, but I had *already* made him and myself miserable.(p.402)
• I had *already* been to one analyst at home.(p.406)
• I had *already* feared insanity for a long time.(p.408)
• I'd think, "I wonder why I'm saying that again -- I've *already* said it three times."(p.442)
• My reaction was that I'd *already* helped all the patients on the ward, and I still had plenty of problems of my own without trying to help some drunk from A.A.(p.446)
• I had *already* given up all the narcotics, most of the pills, and some of the alcohol when I first came to A.A.(p.448)
• I woke up in jail, sick, withdrawing from alcohol and speed, *already* a four-time loser, and now with a fifth felony charge against me.(p.460)
• Once, I phoned my brother-in-law and told him I was going to take a handful of pills (in fact, I *already* had) and I would slash my wrists if he didn't come over to stop me.(p.479)
• I was terribly afraid that I was actually going mad, if I hadn't gone mad *already*.(p.522)

Alsace

• I was born in Europe, in *Alsace* to be exact, shortly after it had become German, and practically grew up with the "good Rhine wine" of song and story.(p.230)

Alsatians

• For weeks after my arrival I was feted and entertained in the already large colony of *Alsatians* in the city, and among the Germans in their saloons and clubs.(p.231)

also

• Very earnestly we ask the press *also*, to observe this request, for otherwise we shall be greatly handicapped.(p.xiii)
• He had *also* been greatly helped by the late Dr. William D. Silkworth, a New York specialist in alcoholism who is now accounted no less than a medical saint by A.A. members, and whose story of the early days of our Society appears in the next pages.(p.xvi)
• It *also* indicated that strenuous work, one alcoholic with another, was vital to permanent recovery.(p.xvii)
• If a sufficiently strong reason – ill health, falling in love, change of environment, or the warning of a doctor – becomes operative, this man can *also* stop or moderate, although he may find it difficult and trou-

blesome and may even need medical attention.(p.21)
• I ***also*** had the notion that I might find a customer for a car at this place, which was familiar for I had been going to it for years.(p.36)
• He did, and ***also*** sent a small amount of money.(p.79)
• If we belong to a religious denomination which requires a definite morning devotion, we attend to that ***also***.(p.87)
• There are many helpful books ***also***.(p.87)
• This advice is given for his family ***also***.(p.90)
• He sometimes drinks in the morning and through the day ***also***, to hold his nervousness in check.(p.109)
• If your husband is trying to live on a spiritual basis, he will ***also*** be doing everything in his power to avoid disagreement or contention.(p.118)
• The family will be affected ***also***, pleasantly at first, as they feel their money troubles are about to be solved, then not so pleasantly as they find themselves neglected.(p.126)
• Arrangements were ***also*** made with the chief psychiatrist of a large public hospital to select still others from the stream of misery which flows through that institution.(p.163)
• Seventeen stories may help you decide whether you are alcoholic; ***also***, whether A.A. is for you.(p.167)
• I ***also*** made use of old trunks and chests, the old can container, and even the ash container.(p.176)
• I used ***also*** to put it up in four ounce bottles and stick several in my stocking tops.(p.177)
• She ***also*** told me that I could not pay them even if I wanted to and had the money, which I did not.(p.185)
• I can ***also*** remember that he was a salesman and a very good one.(p.193)
• There was ***also*** some conversation about Dr. Bob and I must have said that I would go down to Akron with Bill in the morning.(p.217)
• I realized that there wasn't anything I could say to place myself in a more favorable light with my children, that it was going to be a matter of time; for I ***also*** understood the intolerance of young people towards deficiencies in their elders.(p.220)
• All of us in A.A. know the tremendous happiness that is in our sobriety, but there are ***also*** tragedies.(p.239)
• He had ***also*** gone all the way through the wringer and had been dry two years when I saw him again.(p.243)
• At the time, I thought them just a swell pair of screwballs, for they were not only going to save all the drunks in the world but ***also*** all the so-called normal people!(p.245)
• They had ***also*** been periodic big shots who had goofed out repeatedly at the wrong time, and they ***also*** knew how to split one paper match into three separate matches.(p.245)
• It was ***also*** an ending, for never since June 16th, 1938, have I had to walk alone.(p.248)
• But -- I ***also*** stayed up week nights after they had retired and drank myself into bed.(p.277)
• I ***also*** talked A.A. to every friend who would listen, at lunch, at dinner, on street corners.(p.282)
• There have ***also*** been numerous times when I have thought about taking a drink.(p.285)
• By living alone you can pretty much eliminate grief from you life, but you ***also*** eliminate joy.(p.286)
• Somehow or other, I must have misunderstood the doctor's instructions, for I not only made the beer for my wife, I ***also*** drank it for her.(p.297)
• Eventually, the noon meal was ***also*** dispensed with.(p.299)
• Finally this company ***also*** became involved and I was once more looking for a job.(p.300)
• ***Also***, I have no fear of anything.(p.303)
• But somehow my good doctor heard of this book and ***also*** he learned a little about the people responsible for its publication.(p.307)
• Some of us struggle with these people because we know that they are really very sick, but we ***also*** know that short of some miracle, we are not going to help them except temporarily, and that they will inevitably get worse and worse until one of two things happens.(p.308)
• So I went to Akron, and ***also*** to Cleveland, and I met more recovered alcoholics.(p.310)
• I have had my share of problems, heartaches and disappointments, because that is life, but ***also*** I have known a great deal of joy, and a peace that is the handmaiden of an inner freedom, I have a wealth of friends and, with my A.A. friends, an unusual quality of fellowship.(p.312)
• And, as the years go by, working together, sharing our experiences with one another, and ***also*** sharing a mutual trust, understanding and love -- without strings, without obligation -- we acquire relationships that are unique and priceless.(p.312)
• I ***also*** found out that all they wanted was to help me get sober and to stay sober themselves.(p.320)
• Now I feel so very grateful not only for my sobriety, which I try to maintain day by day, but I'm grateful ***also*** for the ability to help other people.(p.326)
• We "instant perfectionists" ***also*** are hypersensitive, alas.(p.331)
• It becomes vital, ***also***, that others not know of our defeats, nor suspect our loss of confidence.(p.331)
• I ***also*** turned against my family, my mother.(p.338)
• I am ***also*** an alcoholic.(p.345)
• This escapade ***also*** ended up in the clutches of the law, and my friend was institutionalized for eight months.(p.354)
• It was ***also*** my job to entertain the owners of these stations when they came East on business -- or the pretense of business.(p.359)
• The challenge intrigued me; ***also*** it was another opportunity to run away from myself and the "fast life of the big city."(p.359)
• It ***also*** was the beginning of another cycle in my drinking.(p.360)
• I had not only let my wife down but ***also*** a lot of other wonderful people who had helped me.(p.364)
• To the new man I would ***also*** like to say that this program is not for sissies for, in my humble opinion, it takes a man to make the grade.(p.367)
• ***Also***, I believed I was the image of all domestic virtues, secluded in my washday (any day) refuge.(p.369)
• As my father climbed the ladder of success in the oilfield business, his drinking ***also*** climbed.(p.369)
• Slowly, my life seemed to unfold before me, shedding insights on childhood resentments, jealousies, and fears that had mushroomed in adulthood, and ***also*** on the self-pity that I had wallowed in at every opportunity.(p.371)
• It is ***also*** stated that we will never be able to figure out how much we have spent on alcohol.(p.396)
• I ***also*** wanted to be the queen of society, with a glittering salon, the bride of a dream prince and the mother of a happy brood.(p.400)
• I ***also*** wrote another novel, all about Scott Fitzgerald's poor, misbegotten, unloved, tipsy little debutante.(p.405)
• He ***also*** said, "You are an alcoholic and there's nothing I can do for you."(p.406)
• Here, ***also***, I had good friends, but I became more and more separated from them.(p.406)
• I ***also*** thought that I must have power over myself.(p.408)
• She was ***also*** the victim of my scolding and incessant nagging.(p.408)
• And ***also***, on the twenty-four hour plan, it taught me how to live.(p.416)
• They ***also*** were held in some sort of strap arrangement.(p.422)
• I ***also*** kept beer.(p.423)
• My associates, and all the wits and literary lights I so much admired, ***also*** drank.(p.433)
• It would be a sure cure and ***also*** an adventure.(p.434)
• I ***also*** sent my kids to psychiatrists.(p.440)
• Following an injection I would have to keep one hand busy scratching my constantly itching nose and would ***also*** have sudden uncontrollable urges to vomit.(p.442)
• Much of my time was spent writing letters, notes, orders, and lists of things for Max, who was ***also*** my office nurse, to do to keep the world running while I was locked up.(p.445)
• ***Also***, I was insane at times -- according to society's yardstick.(p.458)
• At the wedding, I hope I will ***also*** get to see my daughter and their mother.(p.463)
• ***Also***, after that first visit I learned I could refuse to sign myself in unless they gave me a glass of whiskey in one hand and a glass of paraldehyde in the other.(p.468)
• With their help I ***also*** saw that certainly, because of some of the things I had done during the years, I was bordering on insanity, and so, facing the record, I tried to believe that a Power greater than I could and would restore me to sanity.(p.471)
• For two years, I was ***also*** addicted to heroin.(p.480)
• He ***also*** cares; he really cares.(p.481)
• He has ***also*** taught me that I must help myself first; only then may I be able to help others.(p.481)
• I had a long talk with a psychiatrist, but nothing came of that, and I had ***also***, just about that time, talked with a minister for whom I had a great deal of respect.(p.489)
• She ***also*** was in the government service.(p.490)
• I ***also*** thought I was a brilliant drunk.(p.512)
• I ***also*** began to drink at fraternity parties and beer busts.(p.555)
• I ***also*** began visiting bars after work, with my older associates.(p.555)
• I ***also*** got into my first disciplinary trouble caused by drinking, on two separate occasions.(p.555)
• Because the "long form" is more explicit and of possible historic value, it is ***also*** reproduced.(p.563)
• But when its plans concern the welfare of neighboring groups ***also***, those groups ought to be consulted.(p.565)

altar
• Was ***altar*** boy at church on reservation.(p.474)

alter
• If my personality is inadequate, antisocial, or full of kinks and I ***alter*** it with alcohol or any chemical, bingo!(p.458)

alteration
• He finally realizes that he has undergone a profound ***alteration*** in his reaction to life; that such a change could hardly have been brought about by himself alone.(p.569)

altered
• When the others saw my ***altered*** attitude they took me back in, but for me they had to make it tough; if they hadn't I don't think I ever would have stuck it out.(p.248)

altering
• I was living in a small room on West 53rd Street right off Fifth Avenue, when I met a young lady who eventually was responsible for ***altering*** my entire way of living.(p.359)

alternately
• During this time, I had been threatened, beaten, kissed, praised and damned ***alternately*** by relatives, family, friends and strangers, but of course it all went for naught.(p.300)

alternative
• She offered me the ***alternative*** of going to see him or her leaving me for good and all.(p.301)
• The principal had no ***alternative*** but to expel me.(p.424)

alternatives
• We were in a position where life was becoming impossible, and if we had passed into the region from which there is no return through human aid we had but two ***alternatives***: One was to go on to the bitter end, blotting out the consciousness of our intolerable situation as best we could; and the other, to accept spiritual help.(p.25)
• To be doomed to an alcoholic death or to live on a spiritual basis are not always easy ***alternatives*** to face.(p.44)

although
• ***Although*** he gives all that is in him, it often is not enough.(p.xxvii)
• If a sufficiently strong reason -- ill health, falling in love, change of environment, or the warning of a doctor -- becomes operative, this man can also stop or moderate, ***although*** he may find it difficult and troublesome and may even need medical attention.(p.21)
• ***Although*** these reparations take innumerable forms, there are some general principles which we find guiding.(p.79)
• ***Although*** financial recovery is on the way for many of us, we found we could not place money first.(p.127)
• We are greatly indebted to the doctor in attendance there, for he, ***although*** it might prejudice his own work, has told us of his belief in ours.(p.162)
• During these years, I drank as much as my purse permitted, still without paying too great a penalty, ***although*** I was beginning to have morning jitters at times.(p.173)
• Then Prohibition came into effect, and the facts that the stuff obtainable was so horrible and sometimes deadly, and that I had married and had a job which I had to look after, helped me for a period of some three or four years, ***although*** I would get drunk every time I could get hold of enough to drink to get started.(p.183)
• Their talk and action had instilled me with a certain amount of confidence, ***although*** I was not too absolutely certain.(p.189)
• ***Although***, during this period I was not addicted to any pattern of alcohol consumption, when I did drink the drinking was pretty wild.(p.212)
• I realized that I had a problem, ***although*** my realization was not very deep because my own conceit wouldn't admit that I had any personality problems.(p.214)
• But, ***although*** I was a good Catholic, the monastic life had little appeal for me.(p.230)

- This was my introduction to this "understanding fellowship" ***although*** it was to be more than a year later before our Society was to bear the name, Alcoholics Anonymous.(p.239)
- There were four of us children, and ***although*** both of my brothers later became alcoholic -- one died of alcoholism -- my sister has never taken a drink in her life.(p.240)
- I myself could see deterioration in my work from being physically and mentally affected by liquor, ***although*** I had not yet reached the point where all I wanted was more to drink.(p.254)
- The next day he turned me over to a couple who, ***although*** neither was an alcoholic, knew Dr. Bob and were willing to drive me to Akron where they would turn me over to his care.(p.278)
- Having no one else to turn to, I was willing to give Him a chance, ***although*** with considerable doubt.(p.280)
- I couldn't look them straight in the eyes, ***although*** I was always a self-possessed brazen sort of person.(p.323)
- ***Although*** I did drink, it always was with caution -- unless I was alone.(p.328)
- In spite of knowing that my drunkenness was a symptom of the things that were wrong with me, and that I could never drink again, I thought I couldn't yet give it up, ***although*** I was going to try.(p.393)
- ***Although*** we enjoyed the laughter in the early days, I heard a lot of things that I thought were stupid.(p.447)
- I hadn't been drinking much about that time, for I had begun to realize that there was something abnormal about my drinking, ***although*** as yet, I didn't realize that it was so out of control.(p.465)
- I've never seen him drunk in my life, ***although*** he'd take a shot in the morning and usually one in the evening, and so did I; but for the most part he kept his whiskey in his office.(p.484)
- My wife received me graciously, ***although*** she was living in a one room with kitchen affair.(p.490)
- She continued to watch me, ***although*** she didn't say anything.(p.493)
- There was the sense of being "misunderstood," when as a matter of fact by my middle twenties I was quite popular, ***although*** I hadn't grown much bigger physically.(p.534)
- My personal definition, which I submit as applying only to myself (***although*** everyone is welcome to it who wants it), includes every waking activity of the human being; to have a creative attitude towards things is a more exact meaning, to live and to deal with other human beings creatively, which to me means seeing the God in them, and respecting and worshipping this God.(p.535)
- ***Although*** my ambition still flickered, it now took the form of fantasizing.(p.556)

altogether

- Then, gathering all his forces, he attempted to stop ***altogether*** and found he could not.(p.32)
- For those who are unable to drink moderately the question is how to stop ***altogether***.(p.34)
- On through the years this conduct continues, accompanied by his continual promises to be careful or to keep off the streets ***altogether***.(p.38)
- He made up his mind to quit drinking ***altogether***.(p.39)
- Some will moderate or stop ***altogether***, and some will not.(p.109)
- Having regard for the law of the land, I resigned myself to the will of the national legislators and quit drinking ***altogether***, not because I had found it harmful, but because I couldn't get what I was accustomed to drink.(p.232)

altruistic

- Though we work out our solution on the spiritual as well as an ***altruistic*** plane, we favor hospitalization for the alcoholic who is very jittery or befogged.(p.xxiv)
- We feel, after many years of experience, that we have found nothing which has contributed more to the rehabilitation of these men than the ***altruistic*** movement now growing up among them.(p.xxvi)

always

- They are ***always*** "going on the wagon for keeps."(p.xxviii)
- There is the type who ***always*** believes that after being entirely free from alcohol for a period of time he can take a drink without danger.(p.xxviii)
- I had ***always*** believed in a Power greater than myself.(p.10)
- He is ***always*** more or less insanely drunk.(p.21)
- In some instances there has been brief recovery, followed ***always*** by a still worse relapse.(p.31)
- We have seen the truth demonstrated again and again: "Once an alcoholic, ***always*** an alcoholic."(p.33)
- Here was the threat of commitment, the loss of family and position, to say nothing of that intense mental and physical suffering which drinking ***always*** caused him.(p.36)
- But there was ***always*** the curious mental phenomenon that parallel with our sound reasoning there inevitably ran some insanely trivial excuse for taking the first drink.(p.37)
- But even in this type of beginning we are obliged to admit that our justification for a spree was insanely insufficient in the light of what ***always*** happened.(p.37)
- To be doomed to an alcoholic death or to live on a spiritual basis are not ***always*** easy alternatives to face.(p.44)
- On that basis we are almost ***always*** in collision with something or somebody, even though our motives are good.(p.60)
- May I do Thy will ***always***!"(p.63)
- We remembered ***always*** that our sex powers were God-given and therefore good, neither to be used lightly or selfishly nor to be despised and loathed.(p.69)
- The rule is we must be hard on ourself, but ***always*** considerate of others.(p.74)
- Not ***always*** we think.(p.81)
- Keep it ***always*** in sight that we are dealing with that most terrible human emotion -- jealousy.(p.82)
- They will ***always*** materialize if we work for them.(p.84)
- These attempts to do the impossible have ***always*** failed.(p.101)
- Our friends have counseled chucking the men and we have done so with finality, only to be back in a little while hoping, ***always*** hoping.(p.105)
- Positions were ***always*** in jeopardy or gone.(p.105)
- He may seek someone else to console him -- not ***always*** another man.(p.111)
- When they become too dangerous, we think the kind thing is to lock them up, but of course a good doctor should ***always*** be consulted.(p.114)
- If that is so we are sorry, for we ourselves don't ***always*** care for people who lecture us.(p.121)
- In most cases, the alcoholic survived this ordeal without relapse, but not ***always***.(p.125)
- For us, material well-being ***always*** followed spiritual progress; it never preceded.(p.127)
- That he has not ***always*** done so for the alcoholic is easily understood.(p.137)
- Drinking occasionally, and understanding your own reactions, it is possible for you to become quite sure of many things which, so far as the alcoholic is concerned, are not ***always*** so.(p.139)
- Nearly ***always***, these antics indicate nothing more than temporary conditions.(p.141)
- One instance comes to mind in which a malicious individual was ***always*** making friendly little jokes about an alcoholic's drinking exploits.(p.145)
- The employer cannot play favorites, but he can ***always*** defend a man from needless provocation and unfair criticism.(p.146)
- There was ***always*** one more attempt -- and one more failure.(p.151)
- I was ***always*** in a ward before."(p.157)
- They knew they had a host of new friends; it seemed they had known these strangers ***always***.(p.161)
- God will determine that, so you must remember that your real reliance is ***always*** upon Him.(p.164)
- It was almost ***always*** with me.(p.181)
- Morning after morning I would awake sick and with terrible jitters, but there was ***always*** a flask of liquor sitting on the table beside my bed.(p.183)
- Each day I would try to find out what His will was, and try to follow that, rather than trying to get Him to ***always*** agree that the things I thought of myself were the things best for me.(p.187)
- I ***always*** built up in my own mind the great things that I was going to do, and in fact I accomplished about fifty percent of them and then lost interest.(p.193)
- There was ***always*** a tremendous drive and ambition to become a great guy, because I think I recognized inwardly that I didn't have any special talents.(p.194)
- I was ***always*** able to skate along the fringe of big money.(p.197)
- ***Always*** at the end of these dreams was drinking.(p.199)
- I had run into a man I ***always*** drank with.(p.201)
- Whenever this man and I met -- I didn't know his name then nor do I know it now -- we would ***always*** get drunk.(p.201)
- In other words, I was ***always*** safe from the discipline of my father, and having developed along that line, I had considerable difficulty in school.(p.210)
- Of course, it was ***always*** my aim to have my own way without being caught.(p.210)
- I was ***always*** interested in mechanics and after having about twenty miscellaneous jobs, lasting from one day to two weeks, I obtained a job as a toolmaker apprentice.(p.211)
- It isn't ***always*** so sudden with everyone, but I ran into a personal crisis which filled me with a raging and righteous anger.(p.228)
- I had ***always*** been a good Catholic, possibly not so devoted as I should have been, but fairly regular in my attendance at services.(p.234)
- "You've been trying man's ways and they ***always*** fail," he told me.(p.236)
- I had ***always*** known that, in theory.(p.236)
- Somehow I had ***always*** managed to avoid D.T.'s.(p.238)
- So I ***always*** say that as long as I remember January 8th that is how long I will remain sober.(p.240)
- I was never homesick and was ***always*** pretty self-sufficient.(p.240)
- In the Army, I became a periodic alcoholic -- the periods ***always*** coming whenever I could make the opportunity.(p.241)
- As long as things were tough and the job a challenge I could ***always*** manage to hold on pretty well, but as soon as I learned the combination, got the puzzle under control and the boss to pat me on the back, I was gone again.(p.243)
- Then broke again, hiding out in cheap hotels all over the country, one night jail stands here and there, and ***always*** that horrible feeling "What's the use -- nothing is worth while."(p.244)
- Every time I blacked out, and that was every time I drank, there was ***always*** that gnawing fear, "What did I do this time?"(p.244)
- My drinking was never the spaced doses of the careful tippler; it was ***always*** gluttonous.(p.254)
- My wife made several attempts to get me to stop and I had the usual visits from persons who would ***always*** ask me "Why?" -- as if I knew!(p.254)
- ***Always***, in between, there were intervals of being broke, riding freights and hitch-hiking interminable distances from one big town to another in three states.(p.255)
- Now on a new job I was ***always*** thinking about payday and how much liquor I could buy and the pleasure I could have.(p.255)
- They seemed to be happy in their fashion, they and their little groups of supporters, but ***always*** pride of intellect stopped me from seeking what they evidently had.(p.256)
- In those days my system was ***always*** to drink up my last pay check and believe that necessity would bring the next job.(p.256)
- Today I have Someone who will ***always*** hear me; I have a warm fellowship among men who understand my problems; I have tasks to do and am glad to do them, to see others who are alcoholics and to help them in any way I can to become sober men.(p.260)
- I looked much older than I was, I was ***always*** large, and I went back to work in this job.(p.262)
- He'd ***always*** say, "Take me for a ride, Ma."(p.264)
- These vacations became quite something, and he ***always*** had two weeks vacation the first two weeks of every September.(p.264)
- We ***always*** started out on the Saturday before Labor Day.(p.264)
- We ***always*** tried to buy him a drink, and he ***always*** told us he had liquor trouble -- couldn't drink.)(p.266)
- I ***always*** feel that our God Consciousness was a steady growth after we became associated with A.A.(p.270)
- Before I stop -- I ***always*** was a great talker -- I want to say that nobody will ever know how I miss Annie's advice about things.(p.273)
- I know I've talked too long, but I ***always*** do.(p.274)
- During the first three months I carried on all these activities without a car, depending entirely on buses and streetcars -- I, who had ***always*** to have a car at my immediate command.(p.283)
- At long last I am doing the kind of work I have ***always*** wanted to do, but never had the patience and emotional stability to train myself for.(p.284)
- If I live to be a hundred, it will ***always*** stand out in my mind.(p.292)
- Dr. Bob ***always*** emphasized the religious angle very strongly, and I think it helped.(p.292)
- Their answer was ***always*** the same: If they should need it at any time they would surely get in touch with me.(p.293)
- You must ***always*** be willing and continue to

make contacts."(p.293)
• And over my A.A. years I have made many real, honest, sincere friendships that I shall *always* cherish.(p.296)
• Indeed, I was *always* well on my way before I would undertake to go visiting at all.(p.301)
• Our home is *always* full of friends and visitors.(p.303)
• I would hang on to sobriety for short intervals, but *always* there would come the tide of an overpowering necessity to drink and, as I was engulfed in it, I felt such a sense of panic that I really believed I would die if I didn't get that drink inside.(p.306)
• In describing his suffering, his fears, his many years of groping for some answer to that which *always* seemed to remain unanswerable, he could have been describing me, and nothing short of experience and knowledge could have afforded him that much insight!(p.309)
• I *always* wanted to drink too much, so I was watchful, *always* watchful, counting my drinks.(p.322)
• I couldn't look them straight in the eyes, although I was *always* a self-possessed brazen sort of person.(p.323)
• I did try, for a day or two, but something *always* would come up that would throw me.(p.324)
• Sometimes I would lie on the bathroom floor, deathly sick, praying I would die, and praying to God as I *always* had prayed to Him when I was drinking: "Dear God, get me out of this one and I'll never do it again."(p.324)
• My life was *always* act and react.(p.325)
• Although I did drink, it *always* was with caution -- unless I was alone.(p.328)
• I *always* succumbed to its seduction.(p.332)
• No matter how often I had gone into and come out of alcoholic lows during the day, the pattern bounced me out of bed each night about 2:00 a.m., shaking and hurting in the agitation that *always* follows a drug's sedation.(p.332)
• That *always* has been good enough for me.(p.334)
• But I was *always* the unexpected person who had to finish the bottle.(p.336)
• I had *always* hated beer, but now I grew to love it, bottle after bottle of it, warm or cold.(p.339)
• However, I am an alcoholic, so I *always* looked forward to the day when I would be able to drink again.(p.343)
• And I knew this: Once an alcoholic, *always* an alcoholic.(p.344)
• So I went to her and said, "There's only one thing I want in my whole life, and I don't want any commendation; I don't want any credit; I don't want anything from you or Janey for the rest of your life except one thing; and that is, the opportunity to do anything you want *always*, and I would like to start off by doing the dishes."(p.351)
• I have *always* considered myself one of the lucky members of our fraternity.(p.356)
• In the various schools I attended, it was *always* a case of just getting by.(p.357)
• By hook or crook I usually managed to sober up before I reached home, but *always* "terribly tired" from a "hard day's work," and just having to have one or two before dinner.(p.361)
• The inevitable *always* happened.(p.361)
• The only drawback was, I *always* knew how I arrived there, but somehow, between the rest room, the rinse, and the fluff-dry, I never knew when or how I got home.(p.370)
• "Keep busy; *always* have something constructive to do."(p.373)
• Hangovers and remorse were *always* with me.(p.375)
• Never having enough, *always* craving more, the obsession for alcohol gradually dominated all my activities, particularly while travelling.(p.375)
• I tried the wagon on numerous occasions but I *always* felt unhappy and abused.(p.375)
• My hours of work were flexible so that returning to the office was not *always* important.(p.376)
• We had *always* encouraged our children to bring their friends home at any time, but after a few experiences with a drunken father they eliminated home as a place to entertain friends.(p.376)
• The A.A. way of life is the way we *always* should have tried to live.(p.382)
• We *always* had cordials after dinner and I know my sister and my brother and I loved creme de menthe.(p.384)
• So I was used to it, but I didn't know what the effect of alcohol was because I *always* had wine, usually with dinner, but *always* with a lot of ice and about two tablespoons of sugar in it.(p.385)
• He *always* thought that maybe I was safer in a building where there were other people.(p.388)
• It was the A.A. General Service Office in New York that I wrote to, and that office has *always* meant a lot to me.(p.392)
• Dr. Bob said, "Love and service keep us dry," and Bill said, "*Always* we must remember that our first duty is face-to-face help for the alcoholic who still suffers."(p.395)
• Age and the law were still against me, but laws were not as strictly enforced in those days as they are now, and I discovered that as long as I had the green blood, there was *always* a way to get alcohol, either from a nondiscriminatory bartender or from an older friend who would be glad to purchase the joy juice for the privilege of sharing it.(p.397)
• I was *always* at odds with the entire world, not to say the universe.(p.400)
• My family *always* bought the best, and the embassies were flowing.(p.402)
• I saw him recently and he told me that he had *always* felt guilty, because, after our separation, I had become a serious alcoholic.(p.403)
• But whereas my horse was *always* equipped with a flask, I merely endured the fox hunting so I could start drinking at lunch time.(p.404)
• By two-thirty in the afternoon I was *always* tight.(p.404)
• It was nothing to my own inner distress, my self-reproach, and my self-loathing, for was I not bearing out all the horrible things I had *always* suspected of myself?(p.404)
• Well, I'm willing, if it will curb this awful desire to drink, this fear of not having a drink, this feeling of *always* being alone, scared, deserted, sick.(p.430)
• *Always* we'd emerge with a new formula for avoiding future trouble.(p.433)
• "Knowledge is power," I'd *always* been taught.(p.435)
• The line between a heavy drinker and an alcoholic is not *always* clear.(p.436)
• They make no guarantees and are not *always* successful.(p.436)
• I drank my way through schools and *always* got honors.(p.441)
• If they were around, I *always* found a need for them – especially the pills.(p.443)
• I *always* took it because I had the symptom that only that pill would relieve.(p.443)
• I was *always* able to see the flaw in every person, every situation.(p.449)
• And I was *always* glad to point it out, because I knew you wanted perfection, just as I did.(p.449)
• What else can I do except what I have *always* done in the past? -- act as my old self and return to prison.(p.458)
• We *always*, or nearly *always*, had good intentions when we were released from prison.(p.458)
• I wasn't *always* an alcoholic.(p.464)
• In other words, the kindest doctor in the whole world, and I had one such, couldn't help me because I *always* felt, "You can't know about me – you can't possibly know – you don't even drink!"(p.471)
• They were *always* there because of a nervous breakdown, or for a "rest cure" -- any reason except because of drinking.(p.471)
• The Higher Power to whom I had turned, and who had sustained me, had once again been thrust into the background, while my emotions were running my life and, as *always*, my emotions ran me to the bottle.(p.472)
• I felt very sorry for myself and attempted suicide on many occasions, making sure there was *always* somebody within reaching distance to see that I didn't finish the job.(p.478)
• Then, of course, there are *always* the wrinkled slacks, which have been slept in and are so dirty, they could walk away by themselves.(p.479)
• Some of us *always* remember our big mouths when it comes to a drink, but somewhere along the line, we seem to have forgotten about taking care of our teeth.(p.479)
• This means a great deal to me, because I had *always* figured that nobody cared.(p.481)
• On the other hand, I believe that I've *always* been medically inclined, though I have never been able to see medicine quite as the average person sees it.(p.485)
• I begin to see I am not the person I had thought myself, that I had judged myself by comparing myself to others, and *always* to my own advantage.(p.504)
• At first, like everybody else, I could keep control when I drank, but if I did start to drink, even in those days, I was *always* one of the last to leave the party.(p.518)
• I *always* blamed my drinking on being poor, or on anything other than the truth – that I liked what booze did for me, that when I had a drink I was as big and had as much as the next person.(p.526)
• I was *always* able to get a boyfriend who had a drinking joint or sold whiskey, but it didn't last long.(p.526)
• But I would *always* wake up in the psychiatric ward to begin another long treatment.(p.528)
• For *always*, over and above everything else, was the awfulness of the lack of meaning in life.(p.535)
• I bear a few scars on my face from these fights, which I *always* lost, because the "stick" existed only in my mind.(p.537)
• But not for long; now, for five Friday nights in a row, I went to jail, picked up sodden with beer (which I *always* disliked, but which was the only drink available); in jail five consecutive Friday nights in the town where I had grown up, where I had been an honor student in high school, where a kindly uncle, bailing me out, said, "Bob, our family just doesn't do this sort of thing."(p.539)
• Fear of rejection and its ensuing pain were not to be risked, and I turned away from myself once more for the answer, this time to the drinks I had *always* refused before, and in alcohol I found a false courage.(p.546)
• I wasn't afraid of anything or anybody after I learned about drinking, for it seemed right from the beginning that with liquor I could *always* retire to my little private world where nobody could get at me to hurt me.(p.547)
• This caused the rather cryptic comment from one of my A.A. friends, when I told my story after coming into the program, that I had *always* been a cinch for the program, for I had *always* been interested in mankind, but that I was just taking them one man at a time.(p.548)
• Sometimes I have to ask first for the willingness, but it too *always* comes.(p.552)
• I guess I *always* knew that the way to handle my drinking was to quit.(p.554)
• I had *always* been oversensitive to criticism and was acutely so now.(p.556)
• We are taught to differentiate between our wants (which are never satisfied) and our needs (which are *always* provided for).(p.560)
• Eleven -- Our public relations policy is based on attraction rather than promotion; we need *always* maintain personal anonymity at the level of press, radio and films.(p.564)

am

• Our hope is that many alcoholic men and women, desperately in need, will see these pages, and we believe that it is only by fully disclosing ourselves and our problems that they will be persuaded to say, "Yes, I *am* one of them too; I must have this thing."(p.29)
• "Do I now believe, or *am* I even willing to believe, that there is a Power greater than myself?"(p.47)
• When ready, we say something like this: "My Creator, I *am* now willing that you should have all of me, good and bad.(p.76)
• It would have been impressive heroics if he had walked up to the Judge and said, "Here I *am*."(p.79)
• Or *am* I expecting to steal a little vicarious pleasure from the atmosphere of such places?"(p.101)
• But *am* I to be consigned to a life where I shall be stupid, boring and glum, like some righteous people I see?(p.152)
• "Where *am* I to find these people?"(p.152)
• 3.Because in so doing I *am* paying my debt to the man who took time to pass it on to me.(p.181)
• Then I remember when the boys came back, that I told them, "I have gone to this Higher Power and I have told Him that I *am* willing to put His world first, above everything.(p.190)
• I have already done it, and I *am* willing to do it again here in the presence of you or I *am* willing to say it any place, anywhere in the world from now on and not be ashamed of it."(p.190)
• She knew that at that time any suggestion she made about my drinking would only build up a barrier, a consideration for which I *am* ever grateful.(p.216)
• I have something to contribute to humanity, since I *am* peculiarly qualified, as a fellow-sufferer, to give aid and comfort to those who have stumbled and fallen over this business of meeting life.(p.229)
• And when I get upset, cross-grained and out of tune with my fellow man I know that I *am* out of tune with God.(p.237)
• I *am* one of the lads who came out of the service with a lower rank than when I went in.(p.241)
• As he talked I gathered vaguely, (because he was a faltering beginner then, just as I *am* now) that to be relieved of alcoholism I would have to be different.(p.257)

• Today I have Someone who will always hear me; I have a warm fellowship among men who understand my problems; I have tasks to do and *am* glad to do them, to see others who are alcoholics and to help them in any way I can to become sober men.(p.260)
• I used to think I was cowardly because when things came out pertaining to the program that troubled me, I said to her many times, "Annie, *am* I being a coward because I lay those things away on the shelf and skip it?"(p.273)
• At long last I *am* doing the kind of work I have always wanted to do, but never had the patience and emotional stability to train myself for.(p.284)
• With God's help I *am* able, for one day at a time, to carry business responsibilities which, not many years ago, I would not have dreamed of assuming.(p.284)
• I *am* very apt to get into quite an uproar for a day or two before starting, but I do start, and once started, I have a swell time.(p.285)
• So six months ago I acquired a ready made family consisting of one charming wife, four grown children to whom I *am* devoted, and three grandchildren.(p.286)
• Where once I had casual acquaintances, all of whom were fair weather friends, I now have a host of friends who accept me for what I *am*.(p.296)
• I can think clearly and *am* helped much in my thinking and judgment by my spiritual development which grows daily.(p.303)
• I *am* anxious to get home after dark.(p.303)
• For, to these people, I *am* truly related.(p.312)
• I *am* a twenty-four-year-old alcoholic.(p.317)
• I *am* trying now, each day, to make up for all those selfish, thoughtless, foolish things I did in my drinking days.(p.326)
• At one time, the admission that I was and *am* an alcoholic meant shame, defeat, and failure to me.(p.335)
• However, I *am* an alcoholic, so I always looked forward to the day when I would be able to drink again.(p.343)
• I *am* a physician, licensed to practice in a western state.(p.345)
• I *am* also an alcoholic.(p.345)
• I *am* a surgeon.)(p.347)
• I recall, as I walked into that meeting, saying to myself, "Here I *am*, a fellow of the American College of Surgeons, a Fellow of the International College of Surgeons, a diplomate of one of the great specialty boards in these United States, a member of the American Psychiatric Society, and I have to go to the butcher, the baker and the carpenter to help make a man out of me!"(p.347)
• Here I *am* down at my office behind my desk and there she is out at the hospital.(p.350)
• I *am* not even there, and if I was there the only thing I could do would be to give her moral support, and yet he thanks me for curing his wife."(p.350)
• This to me is the proof of the existence of a Somethingness greater than I *am*.(p.351)
• And now I *am* doing the darn dishes every night!(p.352)
• Many times have I heard the above expressions since I have been in A.A., and many times I have had to reply "Definitely I *am* an alcoholic, and while it may be hard for you to believe, it is not hard for me, for I have learned many things about alcohol and myself that would, perhaps, be difficult for you to understand."(p.356)
• Her parting words were "I *am* not leaving you because I don't love you; it's because I do love you.(p.362)
• Looking directly at me was a large oil painting of my wife, and her very words seemed to shout at me -- "I *am* not leaving you because I don't love you; it's because I do love you.(p.363)
• I repeat, I *am* one of the fortunate members of A.A. -- a lucky guy who is very grateful.(p.368)
• I was told that I must want sobriety for my own sake and I *am* convinced this is true.(p.379)
• The allergy I could understand because I *am* allergic to certain pollens.(p.380)
• They told me to go to meetings, and I still do at every available opportunity, whether I *am* at home or in some other city.(p.381)
• Above all, I *am* grateful to A.A. for my sobriety, which means so much to my family, friends and business associates, because God and A.A. were able to do for me something I was unable to do for myself.(p.383)
• Anyhow, after Christmas my husband gave me a cocker spaniel who is, I think, just as notorious in A.A. as I *am*.(p.388)
• In the back of my mind, I probably thought, "They won't take me as drunk as I *am*."(p.398)
• Now, I *am* big and weak, but Anne was bigger than I and strong.(p.414)
• I *am* no longer interested in living in a palace, because palace living was not the answer for me.(p.416)
• My friendships are meaningful, loving and interesting because I *am* sober.(p.416)
• I *am* a part of A.A. which is a way of life.(p.417)
• I *am* one of the growing number of A.A. members who are second-generation.(p.419)
• Admitting that I *am* wrong or that I do not know is difficult for me.(p.420)
• My gratitude to A.A. grows deeper each day I *am* sober.(p.420)
• I *am* a young alcoholic with a drug problem, a doctor, the husband of an alcoholic, the son of an alcoholic, and a man once diagnosed as a violent manic-depressive.(p.421)
• Why *am* I alive, free, a respected member of my community?(p.421)
• I could tell him a lot of reasons why I *am* here in an alky ward at the age of twenty.(p.423)
• Moreover, I *am* deeply convinced that so long as I continue to strive, in my bumbling way, toward the principles I first encountered in the earlier chapters of this book, this remarkable power will continue to flow through me.(p.437)
• If pressed further, all I can do is follow the psalmist who said it long, long before me: "Be still, and know that I *am* God."(p.437)
• My work is on a much deeper and more significant level than it ever was before, and I *am* today a fairly creative, relatively sane human being.(p.438)
• (I *am* pleased to state, however, that I had gone to only a very few A.A. meetings before I was able to make a really beautiful pair of moccasins – and half a wallet.(p.445)
• To this day, I *am* amazed at how many of my problems -- most of which had nothing to do with drinking, I believed -- have become manageable or have simply disappeared since I quit drinking.(p.448)
• It is true that I -- of all people, strange as it may seem, and even though I didn't give my permission -- really, really *am* an alcoholic of sorts.(p.448)
• Now, what *am* I going to do about it?"(p.449)
• When I *am* disturbed, it is because I find some person, place, thing, or situation – some fact of my life -- unacceptable to me, and I can find no serenity until I accept that person, place, thing, or situation as being exactly the way it is supposed to be at this moment.(p.449)
• When I complain about me or about you, I *am* complaining about God's handiwork.(p.449)
• I *am* saying that I know better than God.(p.449)
• Eventually, I had to redo each of the Twelve Steps specifically with Max in mind, from the First, saying, "I *am* powerless over alcohol, and my homelife is unmanageable by me," to the Twelfth, in which I tried to think of her as a sick Al-Anon and treat her with the love I would give a sick A.A. newcomer.(p.452)
• You see, I *am* a five-time loser, which means five felony convictions (not including the cases beaten).(p.457)
• However, one thing I *am* certain of: Inmates in prison who attend A.A. have their chances of remaining free greatly enhanced – this is a proved fact.(p.458)
• (I *am* looking at it now in my bedroom – a copy that was presented to me a couple of years ago by the A.A. group in that same prison.)(p.461)
• Now, I have been an alcoholism counselor for over a year and *am* off parole.(p.462)
• I thank God I *am* to see him this month.(p.463)
• I will be fifty years old next month, haven't seen my son or daughter yet, nor my daughter's two children, my grandchildren; but I *am* grateful.(p.463)
• I *am* still arrogant, egocentric, self-righteous, with no humility, even phony at times, but I'm trying to be a better person and help my fellowman.(p.463)
• Guess I'll never be a saint, but whatever I *am*, I want to be sober and in A.A.(p.463)
• I met and married a man in A.A., and I *am* the happiest I have ever been in my life.(p.481)
• He is my best teacher; without him, I *am* sure I would never have made the progress I have.(p.481)
• He has taught me that, in our new life, I *am* the most important person of all.(p.481)
• I planted my first flower garden this year and *am* actually excited to see the results.(p.481)
• Pioneer A.A., minister's son, and southern farmer, he asked, "Who *am* I to say there is no God?"(p.497)
• But I *am* safe and warm.(p.497)
• I *am* in church.(p.497)
• I *am* in another fellow's room at college.(p.497)
• I don't seem to be able to keep my mind on what I *am* doing.(p.499)
• True, I have recently recovered from pneumonia and have an alibi, but my friends are in the war or going, and I *am* not.(p.499)
• I *am* examined for the draft and pass the physical test.(p.499)
• I *am* to go to camp on November 13th.(p.499)
• I *am* working hard on the books of a subsidiary company of a large corporation.(p.500)
• I have had experience in selling, collecting, and accounting, and *am* on my way up the ladder.(p.500)
• I have no assistance and *am* working nights, Saturdays and Sundays.(p.500)
• But what *am* I to do?(p.500)
• I *am* a traveling salesman.(p.500)
• Yet I *am* fairly steady when I go to bed.(p.500)
• I *am* happy in my work.(p.500)
• I *am* filled with hurt pride and self-pity.(p.501)
• I return to the hotel where I *am* staying and get gin from the bellboy.(p.501)
• I *am* at the hospital to see my wife.(p.501)
• "I *am* going to do something."(p.502)
• I *am* in the hospital for alcoholics.(p.502)
• I *am* an alcoholic.(p.502)
• I *am* too yellow to kill myself.(p.502)
• Then he asks me if I *am* willing to right all the wrongs I have ever done to anyone, no matter how wrong I thought the others were.(p.503)
• *Am* I willing to be honest with myself about myself and tell someone about myself, and *am* I willing to think of other people, of their needs instead of myself, in order to get rid of the drink problem?(p.503)
• I begin to see I *am* not the person I had thought myself, that I had judged myself by comparing myself to others, and always to my own advantage.(p.504)
• "The thing I do is to say 'God here I *am* and here are all my troubles.(p.504)
• I *am* in the bottom of hell.(p.504)
• I *am* home again.(p.505)
• I *am* blue and unhappy.(p.505)
• I *am* on a train headed for a city.(p.505)
• I *am* very unhappy.(p.505)
• I *am* learning that I cannot have my own way as I used to.(p.505)
• I return home and say I *am* sorry for my wrong.(p.505)
• I *am* quiet again.(p.505)
• I *am* blue again.(p.506)
• I do not fix anyone, but I *am* getting part of a tremendous education and I have made some new friends.(p.506)
• I *am* going to town to get some liquor and food.(p.506)
• I'll tell my wife what I *am* going to do.(p.506)
• When I *am* through speaking, the whole idea has become absurd.(p.507)
• But I *am* to learn later that it began with my desire for material success becoming greater than my interest in the welfare of my fellow man.(p.507)
• I think I *am* very lucky that there are people like A.A.'s and an A.A. program to hang on to and carry me through.(p.511)
• I *am* an Irishman and I was forty-nine when I joined A.A.(p.517)
• I *am* an Afro-American alcoholic.(p.526)
• Since I have been in A.A., I have more friends than I ever had in my life – friends who care about me and my welfare, friends who don't care that I *am* black and that I have been in prison.(p.529)
• All they care about is that I *am* a human being and that I want to stay sober.(p.529)
• I think I *am* dreaming and will soon wake up.(p.529)
• I *am* talking about A.A. people, who have gone through some of the same things that you might be going through now.(p.529)
• I have not seen a black face but mine since I've been here, and if I didn't look in the mirror, I wouldn't know that I was black, because these people treat me as one of them, which I *am*.(p.530)
• I *am* hoping that writing this may bring some poor, mixed-up soul into the program.(p.530)
• For I *am* happy.(p.542)
• That's what I *am* doing, living again, knowing what I know.(p.543)
• The mental twists that led up to my drinking began many years before I ever took a drink for I *am* one of those whose history proves conclusively that my drinking was "a symptom of a deeper trouble."(p.544)
• And I *am* sure they would be right as far as they go, but A.A. has taught me I *am* the result of the way I reacted to what happened to me as a child.(p.544)
• I *am* an only child, and when I was seven years old

my parents separated very abruptly.(p.544)
• And if I had been able to turn to the church at that time I'm sure they could not have convinced me my sickness was within myself, nor could they have shown me the need for self-analysis that A.A. has shown me is vital if I *am* to survive.(p.546)
• Society can do anything it chooses to do with me when I *am* drunk and I can't lift a finger to stop it, for I forfeit my rights through the simple expedient of becoming a menace to myself and to the people around me.(p.549)
• A.A. has given me serenity of purpose, the opportunity to be of service to God and to the people about me, and I *am* serene in the infallibility of these principles that provide the fulfillment of my purpose.(p.551)
• It worked for me then, and it has worked for me many times since, and it will work for me every time I *am* willing to work it.(p.552)

Amarillo
• Oddly enough, the dentist who started A.A. in *Amarillo*, Tex., benevolently arranged my admission to dental college.(p.419)

amateur
• My wife became pregnant and the doctor recommended the use of port or ale . . . so . . . I bought a six gallon crock and a few bottles, listened to advice from *amateur* brewmeisters, and was off on my beer manufacturing career on a small scale (for the time being).(p.297)

amazed
• I was *amazed*.(p.9)
• If we are painstaking about this phase of our development, we will be *amazed* before we are half way through.(p.83)
• I noticed a Bible on his table and it *amazed* me.(p.257)
• But then, when that steel door slammed shut, and she was the one that went home, I was *amazed*.(p.440)
• To this day, I am *amazed* at how many of my problems -- most of which had nothing to do with drinking, I believed -- have become manageable or have simply disappeared since I quit drinking.(p.448)
• Around eight or nine o'clock there came two big detectives and a policeman to arrest me for assault; and I was the most *amazed* person in the world when they said I had assaulted someone, and especially that I had assaulted my wife.(p.492)

amazing
• The cases we have followed through have been most interesting; in fact, many of them are *amazing*.(p.xxv)
• He may demand that the family find God in a hurry, or exhibit *amazing* indifference to them and say he is above worldly considerations.(p.128)
• My husband was an alcoholic -- I had only contempt for those without my own *amazing* capacity -- the outcome was inevitable.(p.225)
• But he told a story of drinking that was *amazing* to me.(p.268)

amazingly
• It relieved me somewhat to learn that in alcoholics the will is *amazingly* weakened when it comes to combating liquor, though it often remains strong in other respects.(p.7)
• On talking to a man there, I would be *amazingly* lifted up and set on my feet.(p.15)

ambition
• There was always a tremendous drive and *ambition* to become a great guy, because I think I recognized inwardly that I didn't have any special talents.(p.194)
• I could not see why I couldn't drink like a gentleman, and that was my primary *ambition* -- until I landed in A.A.(p.214)
• The *ambition* to succeed was instilled in me by my Scandinavian parents who came to this country where opportunities were so great.(p.373)
• I depended on optimism and *ambition* to live in society; when I began to tire, I had to depend on chemicals instead to keep going.(p.420)
• There was the over-weening *ambition* to be the world's greatest author, when -- at thirty-nine -- I had nothing of importance to say to the world.(p.534)
• Although my *ambition* still flickered, it now took the form of fantasizing.(p.556)

ambitions
• In most cases it was found that our self-esteem, our pocketbooks, our *ambitions*, our personal relationships (including sex) were hurt or threatened.(p.64)
• Was it our self-esteem, our security, our *ambitions*, our personal, or sex relations, which had been interfered with?(p.65)
• I have never shown any particular talents nor have I had any really frustrating *ambitions*.(p.240)
• I tried to compensate with impossible dreams and *ambitions*, which were simply early forms of escape.(p.400)
• I had writing *ambitions*, and nothing would do but that I'd write like Shakespeare.(p.400)

ambitious
• He was *ambitious* to succeed in business, but saw that he would get nowhere if he drank at all.(p.32)
• They were *ambitious*, successful, strong and famous.(p.401)
• He was brilliant and *ambitious*.(p.403)
• An *ambitious* playwright, he let his brains get so far ahead of his emotions that he collapsed into suicidal drinking.(p.531)

ambulance
• Another time you may have to send for the police or an *ambulance*.(p.97)
• Imagine my surprise when I read in a page one "box" that I had been taken from the theater unconscious around noon that day, removed by *ambulance* to a hospital and stomach-pumped and then released.(p.244)
• I was down to my shorts, unaware of wrong-doing, before the *ambulance* got there and hauled me off to a hospital from which anxious friends rescued me, later that night.(p.537)
• I found myself being lifted onto a stretcher and whisked away in an *ambulance* to a strange hospital.(p.558)

Amen
• *Amen*."(p.76)

Amendment
• With the passing of the Eighteenth *Amendment* I felt quite safe.(p.175)

amends
• What would I not give to make *amends*.(p.8)
• 8.Made a list of all persons we had harmed, and became willing to make *amends* to them all.(p.59)
• 9.Made direct *amends* to such people wherever possible, except when to do so would injure them or others.(p.59)
• We must be willing to make *amends* where we have done harm, provided that we do not bring about still more harm in so doing.(p.69)
• We have a list of all persons we have harmed and to whom we are willing to make *amends*.(p.76)
• We discuss them with someone immediately and make *amends* quickly if we have harmed anyone.(p.84)
• I remained with them for three weeks, using part of the time in making many *amends*, which I had had no earlier opportunity of making.(p.281)
• To most of us, making *amends* will take the rest of our lives, but we can start immediately.(p.381)
• Just being sober will be making *amends* to many we have hurt by our drunken actions.(p.381)
• Making *amends* is sometimes doing what we are capable of doing but failed to do because of alcohol; carrying out community responsibilities such as Community Funds, Red Cross, educational and religious activities in proportion to our abilities and energy.(p.381)
• I attempted nearly two years ago to make some *amends* and contact my children, but it wasn't God's time yet.(p.463)
• I know I will be grateful for a chance to make *amends* to everybody I have hurt in the past.(p.482)

America
• A.A. has flourishing communities in the British Isles, the Scandinavian countries, South Africa, South *America*, Mexico, Alaska, Australia and Hawaii.(p.xv)
• Alcohol being no respecter of persons, we are an accurate cross section of *America*, and in distant lands, the same democratic evening-up process is now going on.(p.xx)
• Here, for instance, is a typical example: An officer of one of the largest banking institutions in *America* knows I no longer drink.(p.138)
• No doubt I had been an exile too long -- I should go home to *America*.(p.226)
• Many friends of my family had emigrated to *America*, so at twenty-four I decided that the United States offered me the opportunity I was never likely to find in my native land.(p.231)
• I early decided that the wine of *America* was very inferior stuff and took up beer instead.(p.231)
• When I was a baby, my mother brought me to *America*, and I never again saw my father.(p.401)
• I was listed in "Who's Who in *America*" as an American who, by distinguished achievement, had arrived.(p.432)

American
• A certain *American* business man had ability, good sense, and high character.(p.26)
• He had consulted the best known *American* psychiatrists.(p.26)
• The distinguished *American* psychologist, William James, in his book "Varieties of Religious Experience," indicates a multitude of ways in which men have discovered God.(p.28)
• As a celebrated *American* statesman put it, "Let's look at the record."(p.50)
• Even in the present century, *American* newspapers were afraid to print an account of the Wright brothers' first successful flight at Kitty Hawk.(p.51)
• (I belong to the *American* Psychiatric Society, but I don't practice psychiatry as such.(p.347)
• I recall, as I walked into that meeting, saying to myself, "Here I am, a fellow of the *American* College of Surgeons, a Fellow of the International College of Surgeons, a diplomate of one of the great specialty boards in these United States, a member of the *American* Psychiatric Society, and I have to go to the butcher, the baker and the carpenter to help make a man out of me!"(p.347)
• I was raised like the majority of *American* boys, coming from a family of modest circumstances, attending public schools, having the social life of a small midwestern town, with part-time work and some athletics.(p.373)
• An *American* doctor in Paris said I had an enlarged liver.(p.406)
• I was listed in "Who's Who in America" as an *American* who, by distinguished achievement, had arrived.(p.432)
• I proud to be son of Tall Man, *American* Indian, and member of A.A. for many moons.(p.474)
• Dr. W.W. Bauer, broadcasting under the auspices of The *American* Medical Association in 1946, over the NBC network, said, in part: "Alcoholics Anonymous are no crusaders; not a temperance society.(p.572)
• The *American* Psychiatric Association requested, in 1949, that a paper be prepared by one of the older members of Alcoholics Anonymous to be read at the Association's annual meeting of that year.(p.572)
• This was done, and the paper was printed in the *American* Journal of Psychiatry for November, 1949.(p.572)
• "The *American* Public Health Association presents a Lasker Group Award for 1951 to Alcoholics Anonymous in recognition of its unique and highly successful approach to that age-old public health and social problem, alcoholism . . .(p.573)

American-sponsored
• I finished high school here in an *American-sponsored* Methodist public school, know as Philander Smith College.(p.342)

Americana
• An old avocation, the collecting of first editions, rare books and *Americana*, fascinated me between times.(p.255)

Americans
• We are average *Americans*.(p.17)

amid
• But the firm became violently ill with my drunkenness and their course of treatment was to remove their ulcer, in the form of me, from the payroll, *amid* much fanfare and very personal and slighting remarks and insinuations.(p.300)

among
• Of alcoholics who came to A.A. and really tried, 50% got sober at once and remained that way; 25% sobered up after some relapses, and *among* the remainder, those who stayed on with A.A. showed improvement.(p.xx)
• Women now make up more than one-fourth of the membership; *among* newer members, the proportion is nearly one-third.(p.xxii)
• Seven percent of the A.A.'s surveyed are less than 30 years of age — *among* them, many in their teens.(p.xxii)
• We feel, after many years of experience, that we have found nothing which has contributed more to the rehabilitation of these men than the altruistic movement now growing up *among* them.(p.xxvi)
• Much has been written pro and con, but *among* physicians, the general opinion seems to be that most chronic alcoholics are doomed.(p.xxviii)
• We commenced to make many fast friends and a fellowship has grown up *among* us of which it is a wonderful thing to feel a part.(p.15)
• There is scarcely any form of trouble and misery which has not been overcome *among* us.(p.15)
• But there exists among us a fellowship, a friendliness, and an understanding which is indescribably

wonderful.(p.17)
• There is no friction ***among*** us over such matters.(p.28)
• Many who once were in this class are now ***among*** our members.(p.28)
• We, who are familiar with the symptoms, see large numbers of potential alcoholics ***among*** young people everywhere.(p.33)
• It has been repeatedly proven ***among*** us that upon this simple cornerstone a wonderfully effective spiritual structure can be built.(p.47)
• No one ***among*** us has been able to maintain anything like perfect adherence to these principles.(p.60)
• They are being fulfilled ***among*** us – sometimes quickly, sometimes slowly.(p.84)
• Every new alcoholic looks for this spirit ***among*** us and is immensely relieved when he finds we are not witch-burners.(p.103)
• ***Among*** us are wives, relatives and friends whose problem has been solved, as well as some who have not yet found a happy solution.(p.104)
• As we say ***among*** ourselves, "He wants to want to stop."(p.109)
• He probably has several alcoholics ***among*** his own acquaintances.(p.112)
• ***Among*** us, these are rare occurrences.(p.125)
• Try to remember that though God has wrought miracles ***among*** us, we should never belittle a good doctor or psychiatrist.(p.133)
• ***Among*** many employers nowadays, we think of one member who has spent much of his life in the world of big business.(p.136)
• ***Among*** them you will make lifelong friends.(p.152)
• The practical answer is that since these things have happened ***among*** us, they can happen with you.(p.153)
• Perhaps the best way of treating you to a glimpse of your future will be to describe the growth of the fellowship ***among*** us.(p.153)
• Many a distracted wife has visited this house to find loving and understanding companionship ***among*** women who knew her problem, to hear from the lips of their husbands what had happened to them, to be advised how her own wayward mate might be hospitalized and approached when next he stumbled.(p.160)
• But life ***among*** Alcoholics Anonymous is more than attending gatherings and visiting hospitals.(p.161)
• There are the same fast friendships, there is the same helpfulness to one another as you find ***among*** our western friends.(p.162)
• And with such good effect that the doctor agreed to a test ***among*** his patients and certain other alcoholics from a clinic which he attends.(p.163)
• Dr. Bob and the twelve men and women who here tell their stories were ***among*** the early members of A.A.'s first groups.(p.169)
• We went to Akron for about six weeks and we did a lot of visiting ***among*** the people in Akron.(p.219)
• Early member, she spread the word ***among*** women in our pioneering period.(p.222)
• I wanted to live, not in a desert, but in a normal world; and my idea of a normal world was ***among*** people who drank – teetotallers were not included.(p.227)
• For weeks after my arrival I was feted and entertained in the already large colony of Alsatians in the city, and ***among*** the Germans in their saloons and clubs.(p.231)
• Successful home-brewers ***among*** my friends began to invite me to their homes.(p.232)
• I knew I was through ***among*** the English "bookies."(p.251)
• Today I have Someone who will always hear me; I have a warm fellowship ***among*** men who understand my problems; I have tasks to do and am glad to do them, to see others who are alcoholics and to help them in any way I can to become sober men.(p.260)
• The next day I went back to Chicago and started a vigorous campaign ***among*** my so-called friends or drinking companions.(p.293)
• I studied art; I desperately endeavored to create an interest in many things, in a new place ***among*** new people.(p.305)
• ***Among*** today's incoming A.A. members, many have never reached the advanced stages of alcoholism, though, given time, all might have.(p.315)
• I couldn't do it ***among*** my relatives, I couldn't do it ***among*** my friends.(p.340)
• Furthermore, I knew that I was looked upon as a city slicker from New York, and I had to be pretty cautious ***among*** small town, conservative Yankees.(p.360)
• In a sick people's place, myself ***among*** the sickest.(p.410)
• This physician, the originator of A.A.'s first black group, but badly caught in the toils, tells of his release and of how freedom came as he worked ***among*** his own people.(p.483)
• All my troubles arose when I was thrown socially ***among*** groups of people.(p.486)
• My husband was soon in uniform and ***among*** the first to go overseas.(p.547)
• The terms "spiritual experience" and "spiritual awakening" are used many times in this book which, upon careful reading, shows that the personality change sufficient to bring about recovery from alcoholism has manifested itself ***among*** us in many different forms.(p.569)
• ***Among*** our rapidly growing membership of thousands of alcoholics such transformations, though frequent, are by no means the rule.(p.569)
• Even ***among*** those who occasionally land back in here again, we observe a profound change in personality.(p.572)

amount

• There is, however, a vast ***amount*** of fun about it all.(p.16)
• He did, and also sent a small ***amount*** of money.(p.79)
• The story of how you and your wife settled your difficulties is worth any ***amount*** of criticism.(p.100)
• We realize some men are thoroughly bad-intentioned, that no ***amount*** of patience will make any difference.(p.108)
• Even if he displays a certain ***amount*** of neglect and irresponsibility towards the family, it is well to let him go as far as he likes in helping other alcoholics.(p.129)
• For most alcoholics who are drinking, or who are just getting over a spree, a certain ***amount*** of physical treatment is desirable, even imperative.(p.142)
• Wherever men are gathered together in business there will be rivalries and, arising out of these, a certain ***amount*** of office politics.(p.145)
• A reasonable ***amount*** of latitude will be helpful.(p.146)
• It is not to be expected that an alcoholic employee will receive a disproportionate ***amount*** of time and attention.(p.149)
• When our friend related his experience, the man agreed that no ***amount*** of will power he might muster could stop his drinking for long.(p.155)
• Their talk and action had instilled me with a certain ***amount*** of confidence, although I was not too absolutely certain.(p.189)
• With the big companies, and with the ***amount*** of money we could have gotten and the promises I had, it could have been done.(p.198)
• I became a constant drinker with a terrific fight to control the ***amount*** of my consumption each day.(p.214)
• After two or three years of effort along this line, I reached the point of actual despair that I ever would be able to drink only a harmless ***amount*** each day.(p.215)
• And it is true that there was no great ***amount*** of drunkenness.(p.230)
• To be sure, this had been a dizzy and confused interval, but most everyone else I knew had emerged from it with both feet on the ground and a fair ***amount*** of adult maturity.(p.304)
• I still had a wife and family, a home and a car, my driver's license, and a proper ***amount*** of insurance.(p.327)
• So I believe that twenty percent is a very conservative estimate of the ***amount*** of income I blew.(p.399)
• It was hard to judge the right ***amount***.(p.443)
• Had I tried honestly and sincerely to practice the Twelve Steps I would have seen from my continuous moral inventory that I was getting off the beam -- I would have found that there were some active resentments in my life, a terrific ***amount*** of self-pity.(p.471)
• I was going to be sent to the Indian Civil Service, which, in those days, meant that people thought you had a certain ***amount*** of brains.(p.517)
• Apparently I'd grown physically at the customary rate of speed, and I had acquired an average ***amount*** of intellectual training in the intervening years, but there had been no emotional maturity at all.(p.547)
• The ***amount*** of will power exercised to control my drinking during working hours, diverted into a constructive channel, would have made me President, and the thing that made the will power possible was the knowledge that as soon as my day was finished I could drink myself into oblivion.(p.548)

amounts

• They have contributed fantastic ***amounts*** of time and work to our problem, but they aren't able, it seems, to arrest either your alcoholism or mine.(p.352)

amuse

• We used to ***amuse*** ourselves by cynically dissecting spiritual beliefs and practices when we might have observed that many spiritually-minded persons of all races, colors, and creeds were demonstrating a degree of stability, happiness and usefulness which we should have sought ourselves.(p.49)

amused

• The local banker watched me whirl fat checks in and out of his till with ***amused*** skepticism.(p.4)

amusement

• And having sung that phrase, I'd chuckle with ***amusement***, turning into irony turning into self-contempt turning into self-pity, at the sad fate of Bob, that wonderful, poor little motherless boy who was so smart in school and who grew up to accept responsibility so early and so fast and who staggered under his burdens without a whimper until the time came when he thought he was too good for this world and so he ought to be out of it.(p.532)

amusing

• I was so ***amusing***!(p.402)
• At first they were rather ***amusing***, but a little later on they became serious.(p.513)
• Once, or even twice, such incidents might be ***amusing***.(p.538)

analyses

• One day soon, the ***analyses*** would reveal why I drank and how to stop.(p.408)

analysis

• In the last ***analysis*** it is only there that He may be found.(p.55)

analyst

• I had already been to one ***analyst*** at home.(p.406)
• My first ***analyst*** said, "You are becoming more and more of an alcoholic," and sent me to another ***analyst***.(p.407)
• When I protested, his lawyer, my lawyer, and my third and last ***analyst*** had a conference.(p.409)
• This new ***analyst*** was a woman doctor, one of the best in the country.(p.409)
• Once, when I called my ***analyst***, and told her I was contemplating death, she came over and tried to get me into a sanitarium.(p.411)
• Perhaps it was He who sent my ***analyst*** to a psychiatrist's meeting at which Bill spoke.(p.412)
• My ***analyst*** was one of the first to learn of A.A. and to make subsequent use of it in her work.(p.412)
• I returned the book to my ***analyst*** and shook my head.(p.412)
• My ***analyst*** pricked up her ears.(p.412)
• I crawled back to my ***analyst***, not so much because I had faith in him, but because I had nowhere else to turn.(p.435)

analyze

• We ought to sit down with the family and frankly ***analyze*** the past as we now see it, being very careful not to criticize them.(p.83)
• We want to ***analyze*** mistakes we have made.(p.104)
• I looked around me at people who seemed happy and tried to ***analyze*** their happiness, and it seemed to me that without exception these people had something or somebody they loved very much.(p.546)

analyzed

• We have listed and ***analyzed*** our resentments.(p.70)
• I took that bottle of medicine and gave it to a very good friend of mine who was a pharmacist and had it ***analyzed***, and the bottle was perfectly all right.(p.489)

ancient

• Students of ***ancient*** history tell us that the intellect of men in those days was equal to the best of today.(p.51)
• Yet in ***ancient*** times material progress was painfully slow.(p.51)

anesthetic

• I had to cope with the demands of everyday living without my comforter, my ***anesthetic***, my crutch.(p.557)

anesthetize

• I had to ***anesthetize*** that pain with alcohol.(p.557)

anew

• But sometimes you must start life ***anew***.(p.114)
• Offered the job of advertising manager for an eastern automotive company, I moved to Philadelphia to begin life ***anew***.(p.254)

angel

• I had no trouble making the right decision when I saw my wife open her purse at the meeting that night and deposit a cute little ***angel*** in the middle of my birthday cake.(p.366)

anger

- In some circumstances we have gone out deliberately to get drunk, feeling ourselves justified by nervousness, *anger*, worry, depression, jealousy or the like.(p.37)
- If we were to live, we had to be free of *anger*.(p.66)
- We are then in much less danger of excitement, fear, *anger*, worry, self-pity, or foolish decisions.(p.88)
- His wife is one of those persons who really feels there is something rather sinful about these commodities, so she nagged, and her intolerance finally threw him into a fit of *anger*.(p.135)
- It isn't always so sudden with everyone, but I ran into a personal crisis which filled me with a raging and righteous *anger*.(p.228)
- And as I fumed helplessly and planned to get good and drunk and show them, my eye caught a sentence in the book lying open on my bed: "We cannot live with *anger*."(p.228)
- Freedom from *anger* and fear, freedom to know happiness and love.(p.228)
- But I can remember, in my teens, that there were a few characters who caused the village heads to nod pityingly and sometimes in *anger* as they paused to say, "That sot, Henri" and "Ce pauvre Jules," who drank too much.(p.230)
- So, with mixed feelings of humiliation, *anger*, and fear, I decided to look for an answer.(p.371)
- We reverted to the old way of life we knew -- a life full of *anger*, vindictiveness, resentment, fear, dependence, denial, self-will, irresponsibility.(p.459)
- *Anger* possesses me, *anger* such as I have never felt before.(p.505)
- We are granted "the serenity to accept the things we cannot change" -- and thus lose our quickness to *anger* and our sensitivity to criticism.(p.560)

angers

- When he *angers* you, remember that he is very ill.(p.108)

angle

- We were prepared to look at it from an entirely different *angle*.(p.66)
- We, who have collectively seen a great deal of business life, at least from the alcoholic *angle*, had to smile at this gentleman's sincere opinion.(p.149)
- (My mother and father were Catholics and I had been baptized, but at the end of my instructions for Confirmation I had not gone to church, and then when my mother remarried, she married a Protestant and the whole religious *angle* was forgotten.(p.201)
- At our weekly meeting I was a menace to serenity those first few months, for I took every opportunity to lambaste the "spiritual *angle*" as we called it, or anything else that had any tinge of theology.(p.246)
- Dr. Bob always emphasized the religious *angle* very strongly, and I think it helped.(p.292)
- Finally, he brought in the *angle* of whiskey.(p.494)

angling

- He'll never read in his "sweetness and light" senior-citizen publications anything but the joys of lolling in the rocking chair, *angling* on the riverbank, or bowling on the green.(p.330)

angrily

- Then, under one provocation or another, the aggrieved one would unearth the old affair and *angrily* cast its ashes about.(p.124)

angry

- If a person has cancer all are sorry for him and no one is *angry* or hurt.(p.18)
- He becomes *angry*, indignant, self-pitying.(p.61)
- We listed people, institutions or principles with whom we were *angry*.(p.64)
- We asked ourselves why we were *angry*.(p.64)
- God save me from being *angry*.(p.67)
- The bill collectors, the sheriffs, the *angry* taxi drivers, the policemen, the bums, the pals, and even the ladies they sometimes brought home -- our husbands thought we were so inhospitable.(p.106)
- The first principle of success is that you should never be *angry*.(p.111)
- But don't remind him of this after he has been drinking, for he may be *angry*.(p.113)
- My friends were understandably hurt and *angry*.(p.406)
- Except for one short slip, during the first eight months, which was an *angry* "the world can't do this to me" reaction to a personal tragedy in my life, I have been sober for twelve years.(p.416)
- I do not feel *angry* any more.(p.505)
- *Angry* bruises appeared mysteriously all over my body.(p.558)

anguish

- Incalculable are the intangible initiation fees that A.A. members have paid: the sick, sick hangovers, the remorse, guilt, broken homes, jails, and institutions, and the mental *anguish* in general that has been generated over the years.(p.399)
- You were thirty-five before you understood your father's horrible *anguish*, and forgave him, and loved him again.(p.533)
- There was the love affair which was ridiculous -- "imagine that midget being able to fall in love!" -- and my head knew it while my heart pumped real, genuine *anguish*, for it hurt like hell, and since it was first love, things have never been quite the same.(p.534)

animals

- As *animals* on a treadmill, we have patiently and wearily climbed, falling back in exhaustion after each futile effort to reach solid ground.(p.107)

animated

- This time I seemed to be already awake, sitting upright in a big easy chair, in the middle of an *animated* conversation with a perfectly strange young woman, who didn't appear to think it strange.(p.222)

ankles

- Shackles were permanently affixed to my *ankles*.(p.460)

Annabelle

- And they introduced me to Miriam and *Annabelle*.(p.269)
- They told *Annabelle* to take me under her wing, and I shall never forget how she sort of curled up her nose and said, "They tell me you drink too."(p.269)

annals

- These facts appear to be of extreme medical importance; because of the extraordinary possibilities of rapid growth inherent in this group they may mark a new epoch in the *annals* of alcoholism.(p.xxiii)

Anne

- I give a great deal of credit to Doc and *Anne* for changing our life.(p.270)
- I knew Doc and *Anne* were going to be there, and all of them thought it would be good for me, but the first thing I did was to go to St. Thomas and try to talk to those women.)(p.272)
- I didn't think I was going to get drunk right then, but I remember how comforting it was when I called *Anne* and told her.(p.273)
- When I got out of the hospital, I was invited to stay with Dr. Bob and his dear wife, *Anne*.(p.279)
- Poor health and a complete lack of money necessitated my remaining with Dr. Bob and *Anne* for very close to a year.(p.280)
- A fellow A.A., called *Anne*, who had helped me, went on a terrible bender.(p.414)
- Since they could do nothing with *Anne* either, Priscilla suggested that I go and look after *Anne*.(p.414)
- Now, I am big and weak, but *Anne* was bigger than I and strong.(p.414)
- We were to go up to our A.A. farm in Kent, and I spent the evening before riding herd on *Anne*.(p.415)
- *Anne* and I went up in ski clothes and fur coats, and it was so cold we slept in them.(p.415)
- I tried to wash a little, but *Anne* refused to wash at all.(p.415)
- I completely forgot myself in trying vainly to help *Anne*, whose misery I understood.(p.415)
- They took *Anne* and me to dinner.(p.415)

Anne's

- On the train going back, *Anne's* one idea was to get to the nearest bar.(p.415)

Annie

- This worked nicely until my wife and I went to see Wallace Beery in "Tugboat *Annie*," after which the pant-leg and stocking racket were out!(p.177)
- I used to think I was cowardly because when things came out pertaining to the program that troubled me, I said to her many times, "*Annie*, am I being a coward because I lay those things away on the shelf and skip it?"(p.273)

Annie's

- Before I stop -- I always was a great talker -- I want to say that nobody will ever know how I miss *Annie's* advice about things.(p.273)

annihilation

- But not so with the alcoholic illness, for with it there goes *annihilation* of all the things worth while in life.(p.18)

anniversary

- For instance, the fiftieth wedding *anniversary* of my wife's parents was the occasion for a huge family reunion at our home.(p.556)

announce

- It is seldom wise to approach an individual, who still smarts from our injustice to him, and *announce* that we have gone religious.(p.77)
- When it will serve any good purpose, we are willing to *announce* our convictions with tact and common sense.(p.77)

announced

- When I had been in the hospital ten days, Sister Ignatia, who has played such a part in the development of A.A. in this area, stuck her head in the door one morning and *announced*, looking at me quizzically, that they might be able to make something human out of my face after all.(p.205)

annoy

- Members of my family *annoy* me.(p.505)
- People *annoy* me.(p.506)

annoyance

- When dealing with an alcoholic, there may be a natural *annoyance* that a man could be so weak, stupid and irresponsible.(p.139)

annoyed

- Those who drink moderately may be more *annoyed* with an alcoholic than a total abstainer would be.(p.139)

annual

- Following are excerpts from the comments of doctors present at the *annual* meeting of the Medical Society of the State of New York where a paper on A.A. was read:(p.571)
- The American Psychiatric Association requested, in 1949, that a paper be prepared by one of the older members of Alcoholics Anonymous to be read at the Association's *annual* meeting of that year.(p.572)

annually

- This company now does a volume of over three billion dollars *annually*.(p.242)

anon

- Of course, the latter ultimately killed the former, but of this, more *anon*.(p.277)

anonymity

- Eleven -- Our public relations policy is based on attraction rather than promotion; we need always maintain personal *anonymity* at the level of press, radio and films.(p.564)
- Twelve -- *Anonymity* is the spiritual foundation of all our Traditions, ever reminding us to place principles before personalities.(p.564)
- 11. -- Our relations with the general public should be characterized by personal *anonymity*.(p.567)
- 12. -- And finally, we of Alcoholics Anonymous believe that the principle of *anonymity* has immense spiritual significance.(p.567)

anonymous

- This is the third edition of the book "Alcoholics *Anonymous*."(p.xi)
- All changes made over the years in the Big Book (A.A. members' fond nickname for this volume) have had the same purpose: to represent the current membership of Alcoholics *Anonymous* more accurately, and thereby to reach more alcoholics.(p.xii)
- We, of Alcoholics *Anonymous*, are more than one hundred men and women who have recovered from a seemingly hopeless state of mind and body.(p.xiii)
- It is important that we remain *anonymous* because we are too few, at present to handle the overwhelming number of personal appeals which may result from this publication.(p.xiii)
- When writing or speaking publicly about alcoholism, we urge each of our Fellowship to omit his personal name, designating himself instead as "a member of Alcoholics *Anonymous*."(p.xiii)
- ALCOHOLICS *ANONYMOUS*.(p.xiv)
- Our earliest printing voiced the hope "that every alcoholic who journeys will find the Fellowship of Alcoholics *Anonymous* at his destination.(p.xv)
- In that brief space, Alcoholics *Anonymous* has mushroomed into nearly 6,000 groups whose membership is far above 150,000 recovered alcoholics.(p.xv)
- The fledgling society, which had been nameless, now began to be called Alcoholics *Anonymous*, from the title of its own book.(p.xvii)
- News of this got on the world wires; inquiries poured in again and many people went to the bookstores to get the book "Alcoholics *Anonymous*."(p.xviii)
- It was decided that all members ought to be *anonymous* at the level of press, radio, TV and films.(p.xix)
- Alcoholics *Anonymous* is not a religious organization.(p.xx)
- By March 1976, when this edition went to the printer, the total worldwide membership of Alcoholics *Anonymous* was conservatively estimated at more

than 1,000,000, with almost 28,000 groups meeting in over 90 countries.(p.xxii)
• The Twelve Steps that summarize the program may be called los Doce Pasos in one country, los Douze Etapes in another, but they trace exactly the same path to recovery that was blazed by the earliest members of Alcoholics ***Anonymous***.(p.xxii)
• We of Alcoholics ***Anonymous*** believe that the reader will be interested in the medical estimate of the plan of recovery described in this book.(p.xxiii)
• A well-known doctor, chief physician at a nationally prominent hospital specializing in alcoholic and drug addiction, gave Alcoholics ***Anonymous*** this letter:(p.xxiii)
• We of ALCOHOLICS ***ANONYMOUS***, know thousands of men and women who were once just as hopeless as Bill.(p.17)
• We have concluded to publish an ***anonymous*** volume setting forth the problem as we see it.(p.19)
• "Two of the members of Alcoholics ***Anonymous*** came to see me.(p.42)
• When you discover a prospect for Alcoholics ***Anonymous***, find out all you can about him.(p.90)
• On your first visit tell him about the Fellowship of Alcoholics ***Anonymous***.(p.94)
• Some day we hope that Alcoholics ***Anonymous*** will help the public to a better realization of the gravity of the alcoholic problem, but we shall be of little use if our attitude is one of bitterness or hostility.(p.103)
• We want the wives of Alcoholics ***Anonymous*** to address the wives of men who drink too much.(p.104)
• As wives of Alcoholics ***Anonymous***, we would like you to feel that we understand as perhaps few can.(p.104)
• Many of Alcoholics ***Anonymous*** were like that.(p.113)
• Though it is entirely separate from Alcoholics ***Anonymous***, it uses the general principles of the A.A. program as a guide for husbands, wives, relatives, friends, and others close to alcoholics.(p.121)
• We families of Alcoholics ***Anonymous*** keep few skeletons in the closet.(p.125)
• Though he is now a most effective member of Alcoholics ***Anonymous***, he still smokes and drinks coffee, but neither his wife or anyone else stands in judgment.(p.135)
• It is a fellowship in Alcoholics ***Anonymous***.(p.152)
• High and low, rich and poor, these are future fellows of Alcoholics ***Anonymous***.(p.152)
• They will approach still other sick ones and fellowships of Alcoholics ***Anonymous*** may spring up in each city and hamlet, havens for those who must find a way out.(p.153)
• Two days later, a future fellow of Alcoholics ***Anonymous*** stared glassily at the strangers beside his bed.(p.157)
• Said the future Fellow ***Anonymous***: "Damn little to laugh about that I can see."(p.157)
• A community thirty miles away has fifteen fellows of Alcoholics ***Anonymous***.(p.161)
• But life among Alcoholics ***Anonymous*** is more than attending gatherings and visiting hospitals.(p.161)
• Some day we hope that every alcoholic who journeys will find a Fellowship of Alcoholics ***Anonymous*** at his destination.(p.162)
• Some of them may sink and perhaps never get up, but if our experience is a criterion, more than half of those approached will become fellows of Alcoholics ***Anonymous***.(p.163)
• A co-founder of Alcoholics ***Anonymous***.(p.171)
• ALCOHOLIC ***ANONYMOUS*** NUMBER THREE(p.182)
• They came in and began to give me instruction in the program which later became known as Alcoholics ***Anonymous***.(p.185)
• That was the point at which my doctor gave me the book "Alcoholics ***Anonymous***" to read.(p.227)
• This was my introduction to this "understanding fellowship" although it was to be more than a year later before our Society was to bear the name, Alcoholics ***Anonymous***.(p.239)
• The story of Alcoholics ***Anonymous*** fascinated me.(p.258)
• I had the Big Book ("Alcoholics ***Anonymous***") that had been brought to me.(p.268)
• I, who had never made a speech in my life and who would have been frightened sick at the prospect, stood up in front of Rotary groups in different parts of the city and talked about Alcoholics ***Anonymous***.(p.283)
• And then, in the spring of 1939, a very remarkable book was rolled off a New York press with the title "Alcoholics ***Anonymous***."(p.307)
• He asked me to read the book "Alcoholics ***Anonymous***," and then he wanted me to talk with a man who was experiencing success with his own arrestment.(p.308)
• That sold us on Alcoholics ***Anonymous***."(p.315)
• You can never know the pure joy of recovering within the Fellowship of Alcoholics ***Anonymous***."(p.334)
• He said, "Why don't you try Alcoholics ***Anonymous***?"(p.340)
• In my stupid way I went up to see him with the idea in the back of my mind that I would investigate Alcoholics ***Anonymous*** from a medical standpoint.(p.346)
• We have here in this community an organization which helps people, and this organization is known as Alcoholics ***Anonymous***.(p.348)
• So, after taking the first half of the First Step, and very gingerly admitting myself to Alcoholics ***Anonymous***, something happened.(p.349)
• But -- Alcoholics ***Anonymous*** has helped.(p.352)
• As a matter of fact, when I came into Alcoholics ***Anonymous*** I was close to being at the peak of my career.(p.356)
• At a women's halfway house, I became associated with Alcoholics ***Anonymous*** and became aware of alcoholism as a disease, not just a "weakness."(p.371)
• But what is more important is that I found a new life in Alcoholics ***Anonymous***.(p.372)
• As I later found out through Alcoholics ***Anonymous***, alcohol is no respecter of economic status, social and business standing or intelligence.(p.373)
• The final decision came when my daughter, following a drunk which ruined my wife's birthday, said, "It's Alcoholics ***Anonymous*** -- or else!"(p.378)
• The time for decision had arrived, and it was a relief to say "Yes" when my family said they would call Alcoholics ***Anonymous*** for me.(p.378)
• To me this meant telling my associates that I had joined Alcoholics ***Anonymous***; that I didn't know what was expected of me by A.A., but that whatever it was, it was the most important thing in life for me; that sobriety meant more to me than anything in this world.(p.382)
• I feel that there is no situation too difficult, none too desperate, no unhappiness too great to be overcome in this great fellowship -- Alcoholics ***Anonymous***.(p.395)
• However, I've heard of an organization called Alcoholics ***Anonymous*** that has had some success with people like you.(p.436)
• They prove to almost anyone's satisfaction that it's never too late to try Alcoholics ***Anonymous***.(p.455)
• The same doctor who had sent me to the psycho had asked my husband, "Why don't you send her to this Alcoholics ***Anonymous***?"(p.469)
• The other of the Twelve Steps of Alcoholics ***Anonymous*** seemed insurmountable to me at first.(p.471)
• It was a revelation to me to find that there were such people as those I found in Alcoholics ***Anonymous***.(p.515)
• This great experience that released me from the bondage of hatred and replaced it with love is really just another affirmation of the truth I know: I get everything I need in Alcoholics ***Anonymous*** -- everything I need I get -- and when I get what I need I invariably find that it was just what I wanted all the time.(p.553)
• At that very time, he was a nonalcoholic trustee on the General Service Board of Alcoholics ***Anonymous***!(p.559)
• Alcoholics can stop drinking in many places and many ways -- but Alcoholics ***Anonymous*** offers us a way to stay sober.(p.559)
• To those now in its fold, Alcoholics ***Anonymous*** has made the difference between misery and sobriety, and often the difference between life and death.(p.563)
• The "12 Traditions" of Alcoholics ***Anonymous*** are, we A.A.'s believe, the best answers that our experience has yet given to those ever urgent questions, "How can A.A. best function?" and, "How can A.A. best stay whole and so survive?"(p.563)
• Eight -- Alcoholics ***Anonymous*** should remain forever nonprofessional, but our service centers may employ special workers.(p.564)
• Ten -- Alcoholics ***Anonymous*** has no opinion on outside issues; hence the A.A. name ought never be drawn into public controversy.(p.564)
• 1. -- Each member of Alcoholics ***Anonymous*** is but a small part of a great whole.(p.565)
• 5. -- Each Alcoholics ***Anonymous*** group ought to be a spiritual entity having but one primary purpose -- that of carrying its message to the alcoholic who still suffers.(p.565)
• We think that each group should soon achieve this ideal; that any public solicitation of funds using the name of Alcoholics ***Anonymous*** is highly dangerous, whether by groups, clubs, hospitals, or other outside agencies; that acceptance of large gifts from any source, or of contributions carrying any obligation whatever, is unwise.(p.566)
• 8. -- Alcoholics ***Anonymous*** should remain forever nonprofessional.(p.566)
• The Alcoholics ***Anonymous*** groups oppose no one.(p.567)
• 12. -- And finally, we of Alcoholics ***Anonymous*** believe that the principle of anonymity has immense spiritual significance.(p.567)
• Since Dr. Silkworth's first endorsement of Alcoholics ***Anonymous***, medical societies and physicians throughout the world have set their approval upon us.(p.571)
• Dr. Foster Kennedy, neurologist: "This organization of Alcoholics ***Anonymous*** calls on two of the greatest reservoirs of power known to man, religion and that instinct for association with one's fellows . . . the 'herd instinct.'(p.571)
• Dr. W.W. Bauer, broadcasting under the auspices of The American Medical Association in 1946, over the NBC network, said, in part: "Alcoholics ***Anonymous*** are no crusaders; not a temperance society.(p.572)
• The American Psychiatric Association requested, in 1949, that a paper be prepared by one of the older members of Alcoholics ***Anonymous*** to be read at the Association's annual meeting of that year.(p.572)
• In 1951 the Lasker Award was given Alcoholics ***Anonymous***.(p.573)
• "The American Public Health Association presents a Lasker Group Award for 1951 to Alcoholics ***Anonymous*** in recognition of its unique and highly successful approach to that age-old public health and social problem, alcoholism . . .(p.573)
• Historians may one day recognize Alcoholics ***Anonymous*** to have been a great venture in social pioneering which forged a new instrument for social action; a new therapy based on the kinship of common suffering; one having a vast potential for the myriad other ills of mankind."(p.573)
• Edward Dowling, S.J., of the Queen's Work staff says, "Alcoholics ***Anonymous*** is natural; it is natural at the point where nature comes closest to the supernatural, namely in humiliations and in consequent humility.(p.574)
• The Episcopal magazine, The Living Church, observes editorially: "The basis of the technique of Alcoholics ***Anonymous*** is the truly Christian principle that a man cannot help himself except by helping others.(p.574)
• Speaking at a dinner given by John D. Rockefeller Jr. to introduce Alcoholics ***Anonymous*** to some of his friends, Dr. Harry Emerson Fosdick remarked: "I think that psychologically speaking there is a point of advantage in the approach that is being made in this movement that cannot be duplicated.(p.574)
• These so-called intergroup associations are found under the listing "A.A." or "Alcoholics ***Anonymous***" in telephone directories.(p.575)
• At New York, U.S.A., Alcoholics ***Anonymous*** maintains its international service center.(p.575)
• If you cannot find A.A. in your locality, a letter addressed to Alcoholics ***Anonymous***, Box 459, Grand Central Station, New York, NY 10163, U.S.A., will receive a prompt reply from this world center, referring you to the nearest A.A. group.(p.575)

anonymously

• I'd gladly do it ***anonymously***, as I have done this brief account of my struggle with alcohol -- merely to present certain ideas for the consideration of the reader.(p.542)

another

• He suddenly realized that in order to save himself he must carry his message to ***another*** alcoholic.(p.xvi)
• This seemed to prove that one alcoholic could affect ***another*** as no nonalcoholic could.(p.xvi)
• It also indicated that strenuous work, one alcoholic with ***another***, was vital to permanent recovery.(p.xvii)
• He never had ***another*** drink.(p.xvii)
• ***Another*** reason for the wide acceptance of A.A. was the ministration of friends -- friends in medicine, religion, and the press, together with innumerable others who became our able and persistent advocates.(p.xx)
• The Twelve Steps that summarize the program may be called los Doce Pasos in one country, los Douze Etapes in ***another***, but they trace exactly the same path to recovery that was blazed by the earliest members of Alcoholics Anonymous.(p.xxii)
• Each day, somewhere in the world, recovery begins when one alcoholic talks with ***another*** alcoholic, sharing experience, strength, and hope.(p.xxii)
• The physician who at our request, gave us this letter, has been kind enough to enlarge upon his views in ***another*** statement which follows.(p.xxiv)

• When I need a mental uplift, I often think of ***another*** case brought in by a physician prominent in New York.(p.xxix)
• Tomorrow was ***another*** day.(p.4)
• This sometimes nearly drove me back to drink, but I soon found that when all other measures failed, work with ***another*** alcoholic would save the day.(p.15)
• But the ex-problem drinker who has found this solution, who is properly armed with facts about himself, can generally win the entire confidence of ***another*** alcoholic in a few hours.(p.18)
• If hundreds of experiences have shown him that one drink means ***another*** debacle with all its attendant suffering and humiliation, why is it he takes that one drink?(p.22)
• For years he had floundered from one sanitarium to ***another.***(p.26)
• He made up his mind that until he had been successful in business and had retired, he would not touch ***another*** drop.(p.32)
• He knew he faced ***another*** trip to the asylum if he kept on.(p.35)
• I ordered ***another*** sandwich and decided to have ***another*** glass of milk.(p.36)
• The experiment went so well that I ordered ***another*** whiskey and poured it into more milk.(p.36)
• That didn't seem to bother me so I tried ***another.***"(p.36)
• Let us take ***another*** illustration.(p.39)
• Then I ordered ***another*** cocktail.(p.41)
• So, in one way or ***another***, we discovered that faith had been involved all the time!(p.54)
• In one form or ***another*** we had been living by faith and little else.(p.54)
• Yet we had been seeing ***another*** kind of flight, a spiritual liberation from this world, people who rose above their problems.(p.55)
• 5.Admitted to God, to ourselves, and to ***another*** human being the exact nature of our wrongs.(p.59)
• This requires action on our part, which, when completed, will mean that we have admitted to God, to ourselves, and to ***another*** human being the exact nature of our defects.(p.72)
• This is perhaps difficult – especially discussing our defects with ***another*** person.(p.72)
• We will be more reconciled to discussing ourselves with ***another*** person when we see good reasons why we should do so.(p.72)
• We have no right to save our own skin at ***another*** person's expense.(p.74)
• We have already admitted this in confidence to ***another*** person, but we are sure we would be imprisoned or lose our job if it were known.(p.78)
• He thus used his own wrong-doing as a means of destroying the reputation of ***another.***(p.80)
• We feel we ought to say to her that we have no right to involve ***another*** person.(p.81)
• Have we kept something to ourselves which should be discussed with ***another*** person at once?(p.86)
• Search out ***another*** alcoholic and try again.(p.96)
• ***Another*** time you may have to send for the police or an ambulance.(p.97)
• In some cases the wife will never come back for one reason or ***another.***(p.99)
• But if you are shaky, you had better work with ***another*** alcoholic instead!(p.102)
• He is just ***another*** very sick, unreasonable person.(p.108)
• He has been placed in one institution after ***another.***(p.110)
• He may seek someone else to console him -- not always ***another*** man.(p.111)
• Meanwhile you might try to help the wife of ***another*** serious drinker.(p.112)
• There is ***another*** paralyzing fear.(p.116)
• ***Another*** feeling we are very likely to entertain is one of resentment that love and loyalty could not cure our husbands of alcoholism.(p.118)
• We do not like the thought that the contents of a book or the work of ***another*** alcoholic has accomplished in a few weeks that for which we struggled for years.(p.118)
• Still ***another*** difficulty is that you may become jealous of the attention he bestows on other people, especially alcoholics.(p.119)
• Then, under one provocation or ***another***, the aggrieved one would unearth the old affair and angrily cast its ashes about.(p.124)
• ***Another*** principle we observe carefully is that we do not relate intimate experiences of ***another*** person unless we are sure he would approve.(p.125)
• A man may criticize or laugh at himself and it will affect others favorably, but criticism or ridicule coming from ***another*** often produces the contrary effect.(p.125)
• ***Another*** time, as I opened a letter which lay on my desk, a newspaper clipping fell out.(p.136)
• Still ***another*** experience: A woman's voice came faintly over long distance from Virginia.(p.137)
• In ***another*** case, an alcoholic was sent to a hospital for treatment.(p.145)
• If, on the contrary, you are sure he is doing his utmost, you may wish to give him ***another*** chance.(p.147)
• There is ***another*** thing you might wish to do.(p.147)
• So, for one reason or ***another***, they cover these men, hoping matters will take a turn for the better.(p.147)
• Even if you feel your organization has no alcoholic problem, it might pay to take ***another*** look down the line.(p.149)
• I've prayed to God on hangover mornings and sworn that I'd never touch ***another*** drop but by nine o'clock I'd be boiled as an owl."(p.158)
• There are the same fast friendships, there is the same helpfulness to one ***another*** as you find among our western friends.(p.162)
• After many painful discussions, they finally gave me my credits and I migrated to ***another*** of the leading universities of the country and entered as a Junior that fall.(p.173)
• It never fails, if you go about it with one half the zeal you have been in the habit of showing when you were getting ***another*** drink.(p.181)
• I would reach over and get this and take a shot and in a few moments get up and take ***another***, shave and eat my breakfast, slip a half pint of liquor in my hip pocket, and go on to school.(p.183)
• I was moved into ***another*** room that morning and there was my wife.(p.184)
• That wasn't so bad, to tell it to ***another*** drunk.(p.185)
• Then she told me that these two drunks she had been talking to had a plan whereby they thought they could quit drinking, and part of that plan was that they tell it to ***another*** drunk.(p.185)
• The next thing they wanted to know was if I thought I could quit of my own accord, without any help, if I could just walk out of the hospital and never take ***another*** drink.(p.186)
• ***Another*** reason I go is that I'm still grateful for the good years that I've had.(p.192)
• At that time, as I remember, he had promised never to take ***another*** drink.(p.193)
• They looked at one ***another*** queerly and, finally, one of them allowed he'd have a beer and they all followed him, each of them saying he'd have a beer too.(p.194)
• ***Another*** blackout.(p.196)
• ***Another*** time, I had a rubber pool project.(p.198)
• ***Another*** time, I had gone around to Max R. trying to get a job driving one of his trucks.(p.200)
• So, knowing that, I had determined that so long as I lived I would never take ***another*** drink.(p.200)
• An offer of appreciation for not having had a drink for those few months and then and there, without anybody promising me anything or threatening me, I made a solemn vow that never so long as I lived would I take ***another*** drink.(p.200)
• My sobriety continued for ***another*** six months.(p.203)
• You're never going to want ***another*** drink, are you?"; and this answer of his is very important to those of us who are victims of alcoholism.(p.206)
• He said, "So long as I'm thinking as I'm thinking now, and so long as I'm doing the things I'm doing now, I don't believe I'll ever take ***another*** drink."(p.206)
• I'm not going to want ***another*** drink?"(p.207)
• The school then obtained a job for me in the drafting department of ***another*** company.(p.211)
• By that time, I had one boy in college, ***another*** a senior in high school, and a daughter about twelve years old.(p.215)
• It was not known to me as a group, but I later learned that my wife had known about it for nine months and had prayed constantly that I would stumble into Akron some way or ***another.***(p.215)
• Shortly after I came to this conclusion, I was importuned by ***another*** well-known patent law firm to help them out on some trial work because their trial man had had a heart attack and had been forbidden to go into the courtroom.(p.220)
• I wanted to learn to stand on my own feet, not to change one prop for ***another***, and an intangible and dubious one at that.(p.227)
• There is ***another*** meaning for the Hebrew word that in the King James version of the Bible is translated "salvation."(p.228)
• With a great deal of determination, I would throw out full pints – pour them out and smash the bottles -- firmly resolved never to take ***another*** drink of the stuff.(p.234)
• It wasn't very long until my doctor friend sent me to tell ***another*** alcoholic what my experience had been.(p.237)
• First, my new wife had walked out, bag, baggage and furniture; then the apartment landlord had thrown me out of the empty apartment and the finish was the loss of ***another*** job.(p.238)
• I don't remember much of what he said, but I did realize that here was ***another*** guy exactly like me; he had been in the same laughing academies and the same jails, known the same loss of jobs, same frustrations, same boredom and the same loneliness.(p.239)
• In the eight years before A.A. found me, I had over forty jobs – selling and travelling – one thing after ***another***, and the same old routine.(p.244)
• In June, 1945, with ***another*** member, I made my first – and only – Twelfth Step call on a female alcoholic and a year later I married her.(p.249)
• Always, in between, there were intervals of being broke, riding freights and hitch-hiking interminable distances from one big town to ***another*** in three states.(p.255)
• He knew too well that didn't mean a thing, just as I knew in my heart that it would be only a question of time -- a few days, a week, or even a month, it was inevitable -- till I would be off on ***another*** bender.(p.257)
• I had been drinking heavily from one state of semi-coma to ***another*** and it was several days before I got "defogged," but subconsciously I was in earnest about wanting to quit liquor forever.(p.258)
• At the end of these thirteen years I never dreamed that he'd ever take ***another*** drink.(p.263)
• And ***another*** thing, it's a wonder they didn't throw us back in because I could become very dignified and sarcastic.(p.264)
• Time went on and the drinking got worse and worse, and I was in ***another*** barroom, down the road the other way, a small one, and I took my glass – that morning I'd been able to lift it from the bar -- and I said to the woman behind the bar, "I wish I might never take ***another*** drop of that stuff.(p.266)
• Russ said, "Don't do ***another*** thing today but help him.(p.271)
• It's only natural that we don't have the capacity to change, but we ought not to criticize those who have, There's ***another*** thing I would stress.(p.273)
• ***Another*** thing that was helpful to me.(p.273)
• From this job and the next one with ***another*** printer I was courteously dismissed.(p.277)
• It is, however, only the first of a series of miracles which have followed one after ***another*** as a result of my trying to apply to my daily life the principles embodies in our Twelve Steps.(p.280)
• This represents ***another*** great change for me.(p.284)
• Instead, I quickly substituted one or ***another*** vivid scene from the nightmare of my later drinking.(p.286)
• In the meantime, ***another*** doctor in Evanston became convinced that the program had possibilities, and turned over a woman to us to do something about.(p.295)
• Just at this time my wife heard of a doctor in ***another*** city who had been very successful with drunks.(p.301)
• My broken home and broken heart fanned my smoldering self-pity into a fair-sized bonfire and this kept me well supplied with reasons for having ***another*** drink, and then ***another.***(p.305)
• Instead of wanting to escape some perplexing problem, we experience a thrill of challenge in the opportunity it affords for ***another*** application of A.A. techniques, and we find ourselves tackling it with surprising vigor.(p.311)
• And, as the years go by, working together, sharing our experiences with one ***another***, and also sharing a mutual trust, understanding and love – without strings, without obligation – we acquire relationships that are unique and priceless.(p.312)
• I had to get a drink, and then ***another*** drink, and then . . .(p.319)
• Then I went to ***another*** meeting, and I still thought it was wonderful --for him, but not for me.(p.321)
• As we walked back through the hall, I, for the first time in my life, said to ***another*** human being, "I'm having trouble with my drinking, too."(p.321)
• I can't afford resentments against anyone, because they are the build-up of ***another*** drunk.(p.325)
• I foresaw ***another*** heart attack.(p.333)
• Not long ago, I was lunching with ***another*** retired publicist.(p.334)
• I used to like to get it on my fingers so I could lick them and get ***another*** taste.(p.346)

• It only became ***another*** excuse to drink.(p.354)
• The challenge intrigued me; also it was ***another*** opportunity to run away from myself and the "fast life of the big city."(p.359)
• It also was the beginning of ***another*** cycle in my drinking.(p.360)
• In 1940 ***another*** good opportunity came up and we moved to Pittsburgh where I was to manage two radio stations under the same ownership.(p.361)
• After ***another*** of my "never again episodes" she packed up and left for her parents' home in Florida.(p.362)
• I was told that someone would call on me shortly, to sit tight and not take ***another*** drink.(p.363)
• So he waited ***another*** week or two and I don't think I stayed sober hardly at all.(p.391)
• The short tours could be taken care of by sneaking enough whiskey aboard ship so that it could be rationed out until ***another*** supply could be laid in.(p.398)
• He finally decided that he did not love me enough, and soon he told me so and said he was engaged to ***another*** girl.(p.403)
• I also wrote ***another*** novel, all about Scott Fitzgerald's poor, misbegotten, unloved, tipsy little debutante.(p.405)
• My first analyst said, "You are becoming more and more of an alcoholic," and sent me to ***another*** analyst.(p.407)
• Meanwhile I had found ***another*** escape.(p.407)
• I would get wildly excited and look forward to ***another*** night of drinking.(p.408)
• A friend of Marty's, ***another*** A.A. let me in.(p.413)
• When I went back to my hometown to go into private practice, I experienced ***another*** brief lull in my addiction to alcohol and drugs.(p.420)
• I ran away for the second time, with ***another*** lad.(p.424)
• One night I barely made my downtown club; if I'd had to go ***another*** fifty feet I'd have collapsed in the gutter.(p.435)
• On ***another*** occasion I arrived home covered with blood.(p.435)
• My new wife and I don't own any property to speak of, and the flashy successes of ***another*** day are no longer mine.(p.438)
• I cried a bit and then mixed me ***another*** drink.(p.440)
• Max accepted responsibility for me after I had promised never to drink again, never to take ***another*** pill, never to swear again, and never to talk to girls again.(p.444)
• It made me feel quite grown-up and mature, and I think ***another*** added attraction was the fact that so far as my family was concerned, it was forbidden, and it had a special attraction for that reason.(p.464)
• But to ***another*** woman, the first woman I met in A.A., I could talk.(p.471)
• He planted many seeds, and it will be many moons before ***another*** rises to walk in his shoes."(p.476)
• ***Another*** thing that mother drilled into me was a very Puritanical point of view as to sex relations and as to motherhood and womanhood.(p.483)
• I don't know whether she was a pacifist or whether she just thought that in the event of ***another*** war it would have some bearing on my joining up.(p.484)
• To get rid of me one evening, she decided to go to the movies, she and ***another*** friend.(p.487)
• At that time the repeal whiskies were back, and I'd go to the store and buy my whiskey and take it to my office and put it under the desk, first in one place and then in ***another***, and there soon was an accumulation of empty bottles.(p.488)
• The next morning I carried ***another*** prescription to this man's house and exchanged it for the bottle his wife had.(p.489)
• I am in ***another*** fellow's room at college.(p.497)
• Sure, I'd have ***another***.(p.498)
• I have a family to support and have no time to be looking for ***another*** job.(p.500)
• We have ***another*** child.(p.501)
• ***Another*** foolish idea.(p.502)
• I was there for ***another*** couple of months and then, after a few more adventures in the East, I was shipped home.(p.521)
• *ANOTHER* CHANCE(p.526)
• But I would always wake up in the psychiatric ward to begin ***another*** long treatment.(p.528)
• Today, I thank my Higher Power for giving me ***another*** chance at life and A.A. and being able to try and help some other alcoholic.(p.529)
• We all have the same sickness, and in helping one ***another***, we are able to stay sober.(p.530)
• Only, having found them, I threw them away, and ordered ***another*** extra dry martini.(p.533)
• Which is only ***another*** way of saying, I had to be right all the time, and only God can be that.(p.535)
• I'd visit one bar after ***another***, having one martini in each, and in each hoping to find someone interesting to talk to.(p.536)
• If he were still sober, chances are that very quickly I put him down as a Philistine with no appreciation of literary genius; and then I went on to ***another*** bar to find a new victim.(p.537)
• Still ***another*** friend and temporary host received me at four in the morning from the charge of a policeman who had found me "going to bed" in a garage far from the last place I could remember having been, a fashionable bar and restaurant in the theatrical district of New York, to which I had repaired after my date for that evening, a charming lady of the theatre who had refused my company for obvious reasons.(p.538)
• I wandered, craving peace, from one spot to ***another*** of youthful happy memory, and loathed the man I had become.(p.539)
• Back to the big city, for ***another*** year of precarious living, paid for largely by one or two friends I still had not milked dry or worn to exhaustion with demands on their bounty.(p.540)
• On ***another*** small borrowed sum, I went up into the country to the home of a doctor I had known since boyhood.(p.540)
• A happy man is not likely to do harm to ***another*** human being.(p.542)
• I have seen that there is only one law, the law of love, and there are only two sins; the first is to interfere with the growth of ***another*** human being, and the second is to interfere with one's own growth.(p.542)
• I grew up believing that one had to be totally self-sufficient, for one never dared to depend on ***another*** human being.(p.545)
• As ***another*** great man says, "The only real freedom a human being can ever know is doing what you ought to do because you want to do it."(p.553)
• This great experience that released me from the bondage of hatred and replaced it with love is really just ***another*** affirmation of the truth I know: I get everything I need in Alcoholics Anonymous – everything I need I get – and when I get what I need I invariably find that it was just what I wanted all the time.(p.553)
• My employer gave me one warning, then ***another***.(p.558)
• The doctors told me that if I ever took ***another*** drink, it might be my last.(p.558)

another's

• Much to our relief, we discovered we did not need to consider ***another's*** conception of God.(p.46)
• We would follow one man's ideas for a while, decide he was wrong and switch to ***another's*** method.(p.246)

answer

• Yet it is our great hope that all those who have as yet found no ***answer*** may begin to find one in the pages of this book and will presently join us on the highroad to a new freedom.(p.xxi)
• Perhaps I can best ***answer*** this by relating one of my experiences.(p.xxix)
• Surely this was the ***answer*** – self-knowledge.(p.7)
• That the man who is making the approach has had the same difficulty, that he obviously knows what he is talking about, that his whole deportment shouts at the new prospect that he is a man with a real ***answer***, that he has no attitude of Holier Than Thou, nothing whatever except the sincere desire to be helpful; that there are no fees to pay, no axes to grind, no people to please, no lectures to be endured -- these are the conditions we have found most effective.(p.18)
• It is the purpose of this book to ***answer*** such questions specifically.(p.20)
• Perhaps there never will be a full ***answer*** to these questions.(p.22)
• We cannot ***answer*** the riddle.(p.22)
• We told him what we knew of alcoholism and the ***answer*** we had found.(p.35)
• "Then they outlined the spiritual ***answer*** and program of action which a hundred of them had followed successfully.(p.42)
• While pondering the ***answer*** he felt as though he lived in hell.(p.56)
• The right ***answer*** will come, if we want it.(p.69)
• If we can ***answer*** to our satisfaction, we then look at Step Six.(p.76)
• If you ***answer*** these questions satisfactorily, you need have no apprehension.(p.102)
• His case presents additional questions which we shall try to ***answer*** for you.(p.110)
• The only ***answer*** I could make was that if the man followed the usual pattern, he would go on a bigger bust than ever.(p.138)
• Ask him if he thinks he has the ***answer***.(p.144)
• The practical ***answer*** is that since these things have happened among us, they can happen with you.(p.153)
• Many an alcoholic who entered there came away with an ***answer***.(p.160)
• My wife became deeply interested and it was her interest that sustained mine, though I at no time sensed that it might be an ***answer*** to my liquor problem.(p.178)
• But if you really and truly want to quit drinking liquor for good and all, and sincerely feel that you must have some help, we know that we have an ***answer*** for you.(p.181)
• I was trying to find the ***answer***.(p.191)
• I thought, "I think I have the ***answer***."(p.191)
• You're never going to want another drink, are you?"; and this ***answer*** of his is very important to those of us who are victims of alcoholism.(p.206)
• He said Paul would have to ***answer*** for himself.(p.207)
• I never left the church, but I was a fringe member, and the thought simply never occurred to me that through the exercise of what I had I might find the ***answer*** to my problem, simply because I wouldn't admit that I had a problem.(p.214)
• I was an intellectual and I needed an intellectual ***answer***, not an emotional one.(p.227)
• Beer and wine were not the ***answer***.(p.230)
• His own business was practically gone, he told me, when he discovered the ***answer***.(p.236)
• If that was all, then I was a little doubtful that it was the ***answer*** I was looking for.(p.236)
• They did not seem to be getting an ***answer***, for here I was staying sober and selling lots of auto polish, on which they were making one thousand per cent profit.(p.247)
• When the day of their return was almost upon me, and suicide was the only ***answer*** I had been able to think of, I went into Ralph's room one evening and told him the truth.(p.278)
• The most accurate ***answer*** I can give you is this: Fear has never again ruled my life since that day in September, 1938, when I found that a Power greater than myself could not only restore me to sanity but could keep me both sober and sane.(p.285)
• Their ***answer*** was always the same: If they should need it at any time they would surely get in touch with me.(p.293)
• Why he bothered with me as long as he did I shall never know, for he knew there was no ***answer*** for me in medicine and he, like all doctors of his day, had been taught that the alcoholic was incurable and should be ignored.(p.307)
• They had a hunch that there must be an ***answer*** for these apparently hopeless ones, somewhere.(p.307)
• Few doctors will tell a hopeless patient that there is no ***answer*** for him or for her.(p.307)
• In describing his suffering, his fears, his many years of groping for some ***answer*** to that which always seemed to remain unanswerable, he could have been describing me, and nothing short of experience and knowledge could have afforded him that much insight!(p.309)
• The seventeen who now tell their experiences ***answer*** that question.(p.315)
• (Now I know the ***answer*** -- wrong.)(p.317)
• I got so that I hid quite a bit of the time, wouldn't ***answer*** the phone, and stayed by myself as much as I could.(p.324)
• There's only one ***answer*** -- liquid comfort.(p.331)
• I thought that was my ***answer***.(p.338)
• So that wasn't my ***answer*** either.(p.339)
• The ***answer*** came to him by mail.(p.342)
• I tried every gimmick that there was to get some peace of mind, but it was not until I was brought to my alcoholic knees, when I was brought to a group in my own community with the butcher, the baker, the carpenter and the mechanic, who were able to give me the Twelve Steps, that I was finally given some semblance of an ***answer*** to the last half of the First Step.(p.349)
• I had been unhappy, lonely, and scared for so long that the discovery of liquor seemed to be the ***answer*** to all my problems.(p.353)
• But it began to be an awfully painful ***answer*** as hangovers, blackouts, trouble, and remorse set in.(p.353)
• Soon I was to discover the ***answer***.(p.362)
• So, with mixed feelings of humiliation, anger, and fear, I decided to look for an ***answer***.(p.371)

• Within thirty minutes I knew A.A. was the ***answer*** for me.(p.378)
• The ***answer*** came to me very simply in the first step of the Twelve Steps of A.A.(p.379)
• The questions he asked me that I didn't ***answer*** honestly, I thought were none of his business.(p.388)
• I had to go through extreme alcoholism to find my ***answer***.(p.400)
• He was the dream prince, the ***answer***.(p.403)
• I began, here and now, to fear the ***answer*** to the question -- what is the matter with me?(p.406)
• She was endlessly patient as we looked together for an ***answer***.(p.409)
• I am no longer interested in living in a palace, because palace living was not the ***answer*** for me.(p.416)
• Many times in the intervening years I have thanked God for that man, a man who had the courage to admit failure, a man who had the humility to confess that all the hard-won learning of his profession could not turn up the ***answer***.(p.436)
• She cried a bit and went to bed; that was the only ***answer*** to problems that she had left.(p.440)
• The ***answer*** came right back: I'd give him something to pep him up.(p.441)
• When I stopped living in the problem and began living in the ***answer***, the problem went away.(p.449)
• And acceptance is the ***answer*** to all my problems today.(p.449)
• Acceptance has been the ***answer*** to my marital problems.(p.450)
• If I focus on a problem, the problem increases; if I focus on the ***answer***, the ***answer*** increases.(p.451)
• I figured that perhaps if I went ahead with that marriage, which I was sure was right for me, that would be the ***answer*** to my drinking problem.(p.465)
• Can't remember the ***answer*** to the first.(p.499)
• Does that ***answer*** your question?"(p.504)
• "Yes, it does," I ***answer***.(p.504)
• My wife hears my voice and knows I have found the ***answer*** to life.(p.505)
• After I had made my third report, I stepped down town, met some of the old crowd, and of course you know the ***answer***.(p.510)
• Fear of rejection and its ensuing pain were not to be risked, and I turned away from myself once more for the ***answer***, this time to the drinks I had always refused before, and in alcohol I found a false courage.(p.546)

answered

• Each inquiry was painstakingly ***answered***; pamphlets and books were sent out.(p.xviii)
• My friend promised when these things were done I would enter upon a new relationship with my Creator; that I would have the elements of a way of living which ***answered*** all my problems.(p.13)
• We hope this book has ***answered*** some of them.(p.108)
• He ***answered*** by wiring that I could stay there until I earned enough to get home.(p.357)
• I remember finding myself in the middle of the night in the doctors' parking lot at the hospital with one foot in the car and one foot on the ground, not knowing which was the lead foot; finding myself hanging up the telephone – then realizing I had gotten out of bed, ***answered*** the phone, turned on the light, and carried on a conversation with a patient.(p.441)

answering

• Avoid ***answering*** these inquiries as much as you can.(p.115)
• Handling customers, dealers, insurance people, dictation, telephoning, directing new employees, ***answering*** to superiors, and all the rest of it.(p.299)
• It pays daily in more harmonious relations with my fellow men, in ever clearer insight into the true meaning of life, and in the ***answering*** love and gratitude wherever and whenever I have been the instrument of God's will in the lives of others.(p.394)

answers

• We are often surprised how the right ***answers*** come after we have tried this for a while.(p.86)
• The ***answers*** will come, if your own house is in order.(p.164)
• He knew all the ***answers***, and certainly not because he had picked them up in his reading.(p.180)
• I had no ***answers***, and I dared not ask.(p.223)
• I know enough of the ***answers*** to get by.(p.499)
• "I went out of here nine days ago saying that I was going to be honest, and I wasn't," he ***answers***.(p.503)
• "Well," he ***answers***, "You've probably tried praying like I have.(p.504)
• The "12 Traditions" of Alcoholics Anonymous are, we A.A.'s believe, the best ***answers*** that our experience has yet given to those ever urgent questions, "How can A.A. best function?" and, "How can A.A. best stay whole and so survive?"(p.563)

antagonism

• Many of us have been so touchy that even casual reference to spiritual things made us bristle with ***antagonism***.(p.48)
• Dishonest thinking, prejudice, ego, ***antagonism*** toward anyone and everyone who dares to cross him, vanity and a critical attitude are character defects that gradually creep in and become a part of his life.(p.380)

ante

• I remember telling them too that it was going to be awfully tough, because I did some other things, smoked cigarettes and played penny ***ante*** poker, sometimes bet on the horse races and they said, "Don't you think you're having more trouble with this drinking than with anything else at the present time?(p.190)

antenna

• In January 1938, I had the opportunity to go to northern Vermont to manage a small daytime radio station that was up against it financially, and was about to fold its ***antenna***.(p.359)

anti-religious

• Some of us have been violently ***anti-religious***.(p.45)

anti-social

• Yet let him drink for a day, and he frequently becomes disgustingly and even dangerously ***anti-social***.(p.21)

anticipating

• Forgive me – I cannot write further about this latest turn of events, ***anticipating*** seeing the family I deserted so long ago.(p.463)

anticipation

• Some of the things which used to stop me in my tracks from fear still make me nervous in the ***anticipation*** of their doing, but once I kick myself into doing them nervousness disappears and I enjoy myself.(p.285)
• In time, I found myself looking forward to each new day with pleasurable ***anticipation***.(p.311)

anticipatory

• The remorse would turn inside out, and become ***anticipatory*** pleasure.(p.408)

antics

• Nearly always, these ***antics*** indicate nothing more than temporary conditions.(p.141)

antipathy

• The word God still aroused a certain ***antipathy***.(p.12)

antisocial

• If my personality is inadequate, ***antisocial***, or full of kinks and I alter it with alcohol or any chemical, bingo!(p.458)

anuder

• When the policeman released me to my stupefied and exasperated friend at four in the morning, I went to my traveling bag and groped until I found – well, let the officer speak: "Ah," said the policeman, "he's got ***anuder*** pair, t'ank God!"(p.538)

anxieties

• We cast off the burdens of the past and the ***anxieties*** of the future, as we begin to live in the present, one day at a time.(p.560)

anxiety

• Broken promises, humiliation, hopelessness, worry, ***anxiety*** -- but still not enough.(p.377)
• Inside, I went right on being a mass of unlovely self-pity, queasy ***anxiety*** and sickening self-debasement.(p.400)
• But for some time, it was difficult to keep from taking a pill when I had an appropriate symptom, such as a cough, pain, ***anxiety***, insomnia, a muscle spasm, or an upset stomach.(p.448)
• In my late teens I became aware of emotions I'd not counted on; restlessness, ***anxiety***, fear and insecurity.(p.545)

anxious

• He soon indicated he was ***anxious*** to see us.(p.40)
• We say this because we are very ***anxious*** that we talk to the right person.(p.74)
• Sometimes a new man is ***anxious*** to proceed at once, and you may be tempted to let him do so.(p.95)
• That is why we are ***anxious*** that you understand, and that you avoid these unnecessary difficulties.(p.121)
• The doctor proved to be able and exceedingly ***anxious*** to adopt any workable method of handling the situation.(p.163)
• The doctor, a young man, immediately took fire with the idea, and while he did not convince the son, he turned over two prospects who were ***anxious*** for the program.(p.294)
• I am ***anxious*** to get home after dark.(p.303)
• I was down to my shorts, unaware of wrong-doing, before the ambulance got there and hauled me off to a hospital from which ***anxious*** friends rescued me, later that night.(p.537)

anybody

• Besides, we have stopped fighting ***anybody*** or anything.(p.103)
• I said, "Sure, yes, ***anybody*** can do that, for twenty-four hours."(p.188)
• An offer of appreciation for not having had a drink for those few months and then and there, without ***anybody*** promising me anything or threatening me, I made a solemn vow that never so long as I lived would I take another drink.(p.200)
• And I think we calculated, or I did, that there wasn't ***anybody*** who knew that I wasn't drinking.(p.202)
• I was kind of shocked about ***anybody*** talking about themselves the way he did, and my impression was that the guy was a little "touched."(p.216)
• If it isn't anything that's going to help you or ***anybody*** else, why should you become involved in it, and get all disturbed about it?"(p.273)
• I was as defiant as ***anybody*** could be because I was scared.(p.391)
• I don't want ***anybody*** ever to look at me like that again.(p.391)
• How could ***anybody*** forget a drink?(p.407)
• ***Anybody*** who had my problem was beneath contempt!(p.412)
• I was, so far as ***anybody*** could tell, quite a lad.(p.432)
• Aside from being a common drunk, I had a very serious pill affliction and all the garbage that goes with it -- lying, stealing, cheating ***anybody*** and everybody, conning the people I could, and staying clear of the ones I couldn't.(p.478)
• She had been warned numerous times, not only by her family but by my own mother, that I was a hopeless drunk, that there wasn't anything ***anybody*** could do with me, that I'd never stop, and that eventually I'd break her heart.(p.513)
• I got a job by myself which suited me down to the ground, because there was nobody really to interfere with what I did, one way or the other, and I usually had my nerves in good trim when ***anybody*** was coming around to inspect.(p.519)
• It was their open night meeting, but of course I thought they were all alcoholics; I couldn't imagine why ***anybody*** else would want to go there, and my first reaction was, well, I've come to something that's not for me.(p.524)
• In time I concluded that the reason I was hurt was because I loved my parents, and I concluded too that if I never allowed myself to love ***anybody*** or anything I could never be hurt again.(p.545)
• It became second nature for me to remove myself from anything or ***anybody*** I found myself growing fond of.(p.545)
• I wasn't afraid of anything or ***anybody*** after I learned about drinking, for it seemed right from the beginning that with liquor I could always retire to my little private world where nobody could get at me to hurt me.(p.547)

anybody's

• The trial lasted about a week, and whether or not I was going to the death house was ***anybody's*** guess.(p.508)

anyhow

• Or "What's the use ***anyhow***?"(p.24)
• And who could comprehend a Supreme Being ***anyhow***?(p.46)
• He saw that he had to place the outcome in God's hands or he would soon start drinking again, and all would be lost ***anyhow***.(p.80)
• "Sure I would," replied Bill, "Maybe it won't do any good, but I'd like to see you both, ***anyhow***.(p.189)
• ***Anyhow***, I recognized the fact that I couldn't drink like normal people, but I tried hard and kept on trying for twenty-two years.(p.196)
• My thoughts went round and round with "What's it all about ***anyhow***?(p.244)
• "***Anyhow***, I'm on the wagon now," I said.(p.257)
• And, ***anyhow***, if I went on for ten or a hundred times as long I couldn't even begin to tell you all that A.A. has meant to me.(p.274)
• But I was in such deep trouble that I decided to try A.A. ***anyhow***.(p.319)
• I could not identify myself with the people with whom I found myself and there was no understand-

ing, and I can't stand confinement ***anyhow***.(p.387)
• ***Anyhow***, after Christmas my husband gave me a cocker spaniel who is, I think, just as notorious in A.A. as I am.(p.388)
• It looked as if the war would be over any day, but I had to go ***anyhow***.(p.425)
• ***Anyhow***, on the 24th, after drinking all day on the 23rd, I must have decided I wanted to see my wife and have some kind of reconciliation or at least talk with her.(p.491)
• ***Anyhow***, he started talking about himself.(p.494)

anyone

• We are not allied with any particular faith, sect or denomination, nor do we oppose ***anyone***.(p.xiv)
• It brings misunderstanding, fierce resentment, financial insecurity, disgusted friends and employers, warped lives of blameless children, sad wives and parents — ***anyone*** can increase the list.(p.18)
• This should suggest a useful program for ***anyone*** concerned with a drinking problem.(p.19)
• We have no desire to convince ***anyone*** that there is only one way by which faith can be acquired.(p.28)
• If ***anyone*** who is showing inability to control his drinking can do the right-about-face and drink like a gentleman, our hats are off to him.(p.31)
• If ***anyone*** questions whether he has entered this dangerous area, let him try leaving liquor alone for one year.(p.34)
• We never apologize to ***anyone*** for depending upon our Creator.(p.68)
• We must remember that ten or twenty years of drunkenness would make a skeptic out of ***anyone***.(p.83)
• As God's people we stand on our feet; we don't crawl before ***anyone***.(p.83)
• We discuss them with someone immediately and make amends quickly if we have harmed ***anyone***.(p.84)
• And we have ceased fighting anything or ***anyone*** -- even alcohol.(p.84)
• Burn the idea into the consciousness of every man that he can get well regardless of ***anyone***.(p.98)
• These things will come to pass naturally and in good time provided, however, the alcoholic continues to demonstrate that he can be sober, considerate, and helpful, regardless of what ***anyone*** says or does.(p.99)
• But some of us think we should not serve liquor to ***anyone***.(p.102)
• Experience shows that such an attitude is not helpful to ***anyone***.(p.103)
• Do not ask that he do it for you or ***anyone*** else.(p.112)
• Though he is now a most effective member of Alcoholics Anonymous, he still smokes and drinks coffee, but neither his wife or ***anyone*** else stands in judgment.(p.135)
• You cannot see why it should be to ***anyone*** else, save the spineless and stupid.(p.139)
• In addition to these casual get-togethers, it became customary to set apart one night a week for a meeting to be attended by ***anyone*** or everyone interested in a spiritual way of life.(p.159)
• My whole life seemed to be centered around doing what I wanted to do, without regard for the rights, wishes, or privileges of ***anyone*** else; a state of mind which became more and more predominant as the years passed.(p.172)
• Had ***anyone*** undertaken to explain to me what the A.A. movement was, what its real function was, I probably would have been set back several years and I doubt if I would have survived at all.(p.216)
• Sitting in a Second Avenue bar, accepting drinks from ***anyone*** who offered, after my small stake was gone; or sitting at home alone, with the inevitable glass in my hand, I would remember, and remembering, I would drink faster, seeking speedy oblivion.(p.225)
• People have wars and kill each other; they struggle and cut each other's throats for success and what does ***anyone*** get out of it?(p.244)
• When I told them six weeks, they were polite and said that they would contact me in case they had ***anyone*** with an alcoholic problem.(p.293)
• How I had arrived at this tragic impasse I could not have explained to ***anyone***.(p.304)
• Certainly now, ***anyone*** would have agreed that only a miracle could prevent my final breakdown.(p.306)
• I can't afford resentments against ***anyone***, because they are the build-up of another drunk.(p.325)
• I just didn't give a whoop about myself or ***anyone*** else.(p.325)
• I never thought I could be useful to ***anyone*** except my husband and my children and perhaps a few friends.(p.326)
• The second one said, "Don't feel that you stop drinking for ***anyone*** other than yourself," and this hit me between the eyes.(p.346)
• We did, and spent a month boozing it up, popping pills, and smoking marijuana; taking shelter where we could, which included a veterinary hospital one night; accepting meals from ***anyone***; actually begging; stealing anything we were in need of, which was about everything.(p.354)
• I didn't say a word to ***anyone*** about my lapse.(p.364)
• I tried to hide my drinking by going places where I was unlikely to see ***anyone*** I knew.(p.375)
• Resenting ***anyone*** and everyone who might interfere with my personal plans and ways of doing things, I was full of self pity, especially for any interference with my drinking.(p.376)
• We think we can drink to excess without ***anyone*** knowing it.(p.376)
• Over a period of time he has built up self pity, resentments toward ***anyone*** or anything that interferes with his drinking.(p.380)
• Dishonest thinking, prejudice, ego, antagonism toward ***anyone*** and everyone who dares to cross him, vanity and a critical attitude are character defects that gradually creep in and become a part of his life.(p.380)
• I drank alone or with someone, ***anyone*** who would stay and drink with me.(p.406)
• Never in my entire life had ***anyone*** asked me "Are you one of us?"(p.413)
• No one could have told me then that I had not earned all my success, nor could ***anyone*** have told me that I was an alcoholic and a drug addict.(p.418)
• Today I have all that ***anyone*** could ask.(p.431)
• If there ever was ***anyone*** who came to A.A. by mistake, it was I.(p.439)
• I happened to be the best diagnostician I knew at the time, and certainly I knew my case better than ***anyone*** else.(p.444)
• Now I own perhaps the most costly pair of moccasins ***anyone*** has ever seen, and they help me remember where I've been.)(p.445)
• And if I don't know what's good for me, then I don't know what's good or bad for you or for ***anyone***.(p.450)
• There were doctors and psychiatrists there who tried to help me, but at that point I wasn't having help from ***anyone***.(p.468)
• But by listening and talking to these A.A.'s — talking to them as I had never talked to ***anyone*** in my whole life, I saw that it was my life that was unmanageable — not just my drinking.(p.471)
• If ***anyone*** had told me I would be enjoying a hockey game with my husband and my brother without being all boozed up, I would not have believed it.(p.481)
• Mother was of the old school and figured that ***anyone*** I associated with should be of the proper type.(p.484)
• Then he asks me if I am willing to right all the wrongs I have ever done to ***anyone***, no matter how wrong I thought the others were.(p.503)
• I do not fix ***anyone***, but I am getting part of a tremendous education and I have made some new friends.(p.506)
• I don't know ***anyone*** in the program."(p.510)
• It was no use talking of putting myself into a home, a hospital, or of going to see a doctor again, or of going to see a priest or ***anyone*** else.(p.523)
• I remember the day when I decided to drink myself to death quietly, without bothering ***anyone***, because I was tired of having been a dependable, trustworthy person for about thirty-nine years without having received what I thought was a proper reward for my virtue.(p.531)
• My proud southern blood would have boiled if ***anyone*** had named me such a despicable thing.(p.532)
• What a revelation of ego and arrogance still remaining in me -- as if ***anyone***, instinct and training apart, likes to be in jail or in an alcoholic ward or fired from his job.(p.536)
• While an A.A. group may cooperate with ***anyone***, such cooperation ought never go so far as affiliation or endorsement, actual or implied.(p.566)

anyone's

• We do not want to be the arbiter of ***anyone's*** sex conduct.(p.69)
• I couldn't keep up with any of my other friends, and I wouldn't go to ***anyone's*** house unless I knew they drank as heavily as I did.(p.324)
• They prove to almost ***anyone's*** satisfaction that it's never too late to try Alcoholics Anonymous.(p.455)
• I hope I haven't hurt ***anyone's*** feelings, but maybe we could all grow and change.(p.529)

anything

• You may rely absolutely on ***anything*** they say about themselves.(p.xxiv)
• ***Anything*** is better than the way you were."(p.14)
• If what we have learned and felt and seen means ***anything*** at all, it means that all of us, whatever our race, creed, or color are the children of a living Creator with whom we may form a relationship upon simple and understandable terms as soon as we are willing and honest enough to try.(p.28)
• We think few, to whom this book will appeal, can stay dry ***anything*** like a year.(p.34)
• How can such a lack of proportion, of the ability to think straight, be called ***anything*** else?(p.37)
• How could a Supreme Being have ***anything*** to do with it all?(p.46)
• Our friend's gorge rose as he bitterly cried out: "If there is a God, He certainly hasn't done ***anything*** for me!"(p.56)
• No one among us has been able to maintain ***anything*** like perfect adherence to these principles.(p.60)
• It destroys more alcoholics than ***anything*** else.(p.64)
• It may be one of our own family, but we cannot disclose ***anything*** to our wives or our parents which will hurt them and make them unhappy.(p.74)
• Carefully reading the first five proposals we ask if we have omitted ***anything***, for we are building an arch through which we shall walk a free man at last.(p.75)
• We must not shrink at ***anything***.(p.79)
• How could she be ***anything*** else?(p.81)
• To his wife, he remarked, "Don't see ***anything*** the matter here, Ma.(p.82)
• And we have ceased fighting ***anything*** or anyone -- even alcohol.(p.84)
• Neither should the family hysterically plead with him to do ***anything***, nor should they tell him much about you.(p.90)
• In that case he is going to wonder how you can add ***anything*** to what he already knows.(p.93)
• Tell him that if he wants to get well you will do ***anything*** to help.(p.95)
• When we look back, we realize that the things which came to us when we put ourselves in God's hands were better than ***anything*** we could have planned.(p.100)
• We would not even do the cause of temperate drinking any good, for not one drinker in a thousand likes to be told ***anything*** about alcohol by one who hates it.(p.103)
• Besides, we have stopped fighting anybody or ***anything***.(p.103)
• If he gets the idea that you are a nag or a killjoy, your chance of accomplishing ***anything*** useful may be zero.(p.111)
• He may be ***anything*** but that.(p.115)
• Since the home has suffered more than ***anything*** else, it is well that a man exert himself there.(p.127)
• He is unable to focus on ***anything*** else.(p.128)
• During those first days of convalescence, this will do more to insure his sobriety than ***anything*** else.(p.129)
• He will be less likely to drink again, and ***anything*** is preferable to that.(p.130)
• Will he take every necessary step, submit to ***anything*** to get well, to stop drinking forever?(p.142)
• If he feels free to discuss his problems with you, if he knows you understand and will not be upset by ***anything*** he wishes to say, he will probably be off to a fast start.(p.144)
• In fact, he may say almost ***anything*** if he has accepted our solution which, as you know, demands rigorous honesty.(p.145)
• Inwardly he would give ***anything*** to take half a dozen drinks and get away with them.(p.152)
• He would do ***anything***, he said, but that.(p.155)
• "God ought to be able to do ***anything***."(p.158)
• On the third day the lawyer gave his life to the care and direction of his Creator, and said he was perfectly willing to do ***anything*** necessary.(p.158)
• They were deeply religious people, much shocked by their son's refusal to have ***anything*** to do with the church.(p.158)
• I read everything I could find, and talked to everyone who I thought knew ***anything*** about it.(p.178)
• It must be remembered that I had read a great deal and talked to everyone who knew, or thought they knew ***anything*** about the subject of alcoholism.(p.180)
• It did help to certain extent, since I got in places where I could not obtain ***anything*** to drink, and so broke the habitual drinking.(p.183)
• I thought of what liquor had done to me, the opportunities that I had discarded, the abilities that had

been given me and how I had wasted them, and I finally came to the conclusion, that if I didn't want to quit, I certainly ought to want to, and that I was willing to do ***anything*** in the world to stop drinking.(p.186)
• So, after reviewing these things and realizing what liquor had cost me, I went to this Higher Power which, to me was God, without any reservation, and admitted that I was completely powerless over alcohol, and that I was willing to do ***anything*** in the world to get rid of the problem.(p.187)
• I remember telling them too that it was going to be awfully tough, because I did some other things, smoked cigarettes and played penny ante poker, sometimes bet on the horse races and they said, "Don't you think you're having more trouble with this drinking than with ***anything*** else at the present time?(p.190)
• Right then I determined that never so long as I lived would I have ***anything*** more to do with martinis.(p.195)
• I think it was probably more than a year before I had ***anything*** more to do with liquor.(p.195)
• I early discovered that if I drank ***anything***, I was not accountable for what happened.(p.196)
• I didn't remember ***anything*** that had happened.(p.196)
• I would put off doing ***anything*** that I could until the next day and, consequently, everything would pile up and then there would be the blackout.(p.197)
• So in spite of ***anything*** that I might do, I prospered, being one of only two brokers in the rubber center of the world.(p.197)
• To my mind, drinking didn't have ***anything*** to do with not going through with things.(p.198)
• An offer of appreciation for not having had a drink for those few months and then and there, without anybody promising me ***anything*** or threatening me, I made a solemn vow that never so long as I lived would I take another drink.(p.200)
• I think the longest drunk I was ever on was eleven days, but usually only two days with a complete blackout for a day, and then backing off by drinking as long as I could get ***anything***.(p.203)
• They suffered from my conduct without saying ***anything***, but the reason for this was I still managed to hang onto a very substantial practice.(p.215)
• As far as my home was concerned, I did not see then, though of course I can see now, that it was ***anything*** but a happy situation for my wife.(p.215)
• My children had lost respect for me and, in fact, it was only after three or four years of sobriety that any of them ever said ***anything*** to me to indicate that I had recouped even a little of their respect.(p.215)
• I realized that there wasn't ***anything*** I could say to place myself in a more favorable light with my children, that it was going to be a matter of time; for I also understood the intolerance of young people towards deficiencies in their elders.(p.220)
• She gave no sign of recognizing ***anything*** wrong, but what had I been doing for those lost five hours?(p.223)
• With a creeping insidiousness, drink had become more important than ***anything*** else.(p.226)
• But I hardly tasted ***anything*** for two years and started in business for myself, founding a mattress factory which is today an important industrial enterprise in our city.(p.232)
• He had no desire to know ***anything***, except whether I was definite about my desire to quit drinking.(p.235)
• Had he come two or three days later I think I would have thrown him out, but he hit when I was open for ***anything***.(p.239)
• If ***anything***, he had known all of them even better and more often than I.(p.239)
• At our weekly meeting I was a menace to serenity those first few months, for I took every opportunity to lambaste the "spiritual angle" as we called it, or ***anything*** else that had any tinge of theology.(p.246)
• I had never known him to be ***anything*** but a good healthy pagan with a propensity for getting into liquor jams and scrapes.(p.257)
• But they didn't do ***anything*** for me to build up my ego.(p.262)
• He hardly ever went to ***anything*** like that without me.(p.263)
• They didn't give me ***anything*** to eat.(p.264)
• I thought, "No matter how crazy they are I'll do ***anything*** they say to do."(p.267)
• That was our last drink of ***anything*** alcoholic.(p.267)
• I didn't know that ***anything*** was ever done for them in a medical way.(p.267)
• I don't think that there was ***anything*** said about religion.(p.268)
• I didn't know ***anything*** about the Sermon on the Mount.(p.268)
• I knew then that I hadn't made a complete surrender, because I tried to bargain with the God I had found, and I said, "***Anything*** but that!(p.271)
• If it isn't ***anything*** that's going to help you or anybody else, why should you become involved in it, and get all disturbed about it?"(p.273)
• Never in sixteen years have I dodged ***anything*** because I was afraid of it.(p.285)
• Being an alcoholic, I couldn't dream of doing ***anything*** by halves!(p.286)
• I could not wait to tell him that I wanted help, that if these men in Akron had ***anything*** I wanted it, and would do ***anything*** to get it.(p.289)
• In the summer of 1938, almost a year from the time I made my original contact with Akron, the man for whom I was working and who knew about the program, approached me and asked if I could do ***anything*** about one of his salesmen who was drinking very heavily.(p.294)
• Also, I have no fear of ***anything***.(p.303)
• I'd brazen ***anything*** out.(p.324)
• If I had been sincere in what I thought I wanted more than ***anything*** else in life – a sober husband and a happy, contented home – I would have gone on the wagon with him.(p.324)
• He'll never read in his "sweetness and light" senior-citizen publications ***anything*** but the joys of lolling in the rocking chair, angling on the riverbank, or bowling on the green.(p.330)
• I couldn't do ***anything*** without it.(p.337)
• I was willing to try ***anything***.(p.340)
• I went on the wagon more to placate my wife than ***anything*** else.(p.344)
• And then I thought to myself: "Imagine an alcoholic admitting ***anything***!"(p.349)
• We can handle ***anything***.(p.350)
• I never robbed my family of ***anything***.(p.351)
• So I went to my wife and asked her, wasn't there something that she and I could do to somehow get together, and she turned on her heel and looked me squarely in the eye, and said, "You don't care ***anything*** about my problem," and I could have smacked her, but I said to myself, "Grab on to your serenity!"(p.351)
• So I went to her and said, "There's only one thing I want in my whole life, and I don't want any commendation; I don't want any credit; I don't want ***anything*** from you or Janey for the rest of your life except one thing; and that is, the opportunity to do ***anything*** you want always, and I would like to start off by doing the dishes."(p.351)
• We did, and spent a month boozing it up, popping pills, and smoking marijuana; taking shelter where we could, which included a veterinary hospital one night; accepting meals from anyone; actually begging; stealing ***anything*** we were in need of, which was about everything.(p.354)
• I wouldn't give it up or trade it for ***anything***.(p.355)
• I didn't particularly like it, but I loved the effects, and managed for the next twenty-five years to drink ***anything*** and everything, either handed to me or purchased, at the slightest excuse.(p.357)
• And deep in my heart I really meant what I said because I loved her more than ***anything*** else in the world, yes – even more than liquor.(p.362)
• I was going to prove to her that liquor wasn't necessary in my life, and above all that I still loved her more than ***anything*** else in the world and that I wanted her back.(p.362)
• Of course, more than ***anything*** else I had let myself down, but I didn't realize how much then – as I do now.(p.364)
• I haven't written ***anything*** about that part of my story, but I believe in a Greater Power which I call God and I ask for His wisdom and guidance daily.(p.366)
• Try ***anything***.(p.377)
• This suggestion had been made before on a number of occasions, but like all alcoholics I wanted to handle my problem my own way, which really meant I didn't want ***anything*** to interfere with my drinking.(p.378)
• Over a period of time he has built up self pity, resentments toward anyone or ***anything*** that interferes with his drinking.(p.380)
• To me this meant telling my associates that I had joined Alcoholics Anonymous; that I didn't know what was expected of me by A.A., but that whatever it was, it was the most important thing in life for me; that sobriety meant more to me than ***anything*** in this world.(p.382)
• It was so important that it must come ahead of ***anything***.(p.382)
• I knew that I wanted to try A.A. and if that didn't work, I didn't think ***anything*** would.(p.384)
• But I couldn't enjoy ***anything***; I was scared to death.(p.385)
• In six years of worry, I hadn't learned ***anything***.(p.387)
• About this time, at Christmas, after being under this doctor's care, we decided that there wasn't ***anything*** more to do.(p.388)
• The only time my dog would have ***anything*** to do with me was when I had a hangover, and when I was so sick he was the only one who would have ***anything*** to do with me at all.(p.390)
• So when he came for me, as he walked down the stairs, I could see him through the bars, and he was signing for me; I looked at him and said, "Don't you sign ***anything*** in this place!"(p.391)
• So please accept these humble calculations as, if ***anything***, an underestimation.(p.396)
• Like most statistics, it doesn't prove ***anything*** -- just satisfies a little curiosity engendered by the wail "Oh, those initiation fees" that prompted this investigation.(p.399)
• My personality, from the time I can remember ***anything***, was the perfect set-up for an alcoholic career.(p.400)
• If I had not become an active alcoholic and joined A.A., I might never have found my own identity or become a part of ***anything***.(p.417)
• I didn't give a whoop about ***anything*** scholastic.(p.423)
• There wasn't much I could do about it, and I didn't want to do ***anything*** anyway.(p.427)
• Dear God, I'll do ***anything***!(p.430)
• Were I to revert to drinking, even now, I wouldn't give ***anything*** for these four years in A.A.(p.430)
• "You've got to space your drinks and take plenty of water in between," or "coat the stomach with a little olive oil," or "drink ***anything*** but those damn martinis."(p.433)
• Right from the start, I felt that they weren't doing ***anything*** for me, but they sure were helping Max.(p.447)
• And when I place more value on my serenity and sobriety than on ***anything*** else, I can maintain them at a higher level -- at least for the time being.(p.452)
• When I didn't have ***anything*** else to do -- a dull evening at home -- I'd sneak a few drinks upstairs in my room, and that began to be a habit.(p.464)
• And there didn't seem to be ***anything*** to do about it.)(p.465)
• Instead, I started going to a nice private sanitarium which, after the first visit, turned out to be more like a country club than ***anything*** else.(p.468)
• I realized that I was trying to pin everything on an individual – not the book or the group or the Higher Power, or ***anything*** else.(p.472)
• I feel that I have been restored to health and sanity these past years not through my own efforts nor as a result of ***anything*** I may have done, but because I've come to believe -- to really believe – that alone I can do nothing.(p.473)
• The only time that I have ever seen my mother take ***anything*** alcoholic was around Christmas time, when she would drink some eggnog or light wine.(p.484)
• I don't know ***anything*** about the bottles."(p.488)
• She continued to watch me, although she didn't say ***anything***.(p.493)
• She didn't say ***anything*** about A.A. or getting me a sponsor at that time, but she did ask about Vi, and I told her Vi was working and how she could locate her.(p.494)
• She never mentioned ***anything*** about my whiskey drinking because if she had I would have told her, "No" right then.(p.494)
• I knew my wife didn't because I had been sincere in all my promises to her as well as to my mother and to my close friends, but the urge to take that drink was more powerful than ***anything*** else.(p.494)
• I don't seem to remember ***anything***.(p.499)
• "Don't say ***anything***," I say to her.(p.502)
• I might go out West on a ranch where I couldn't get ***anything*** to drink.(p.502)
• ***Anything*** to get my mind from myself.(p.502)
• I told him that I believe in electricity and other forces of nature, but as for a God, if there is one, He has never done ***anything*** for me.(p.503)
• "I'll do ***anything***," I reply.(p.503)
• When you've been in a jam you've said, 'God, please do this or that,' and if it turned out your way that was the last of it, and if it didn't you've said 'There isn't any God' or 'He doesn't do ***anything*** for me.'(p.504)
• I've made a mess of things and can't do ***anything*** about it.(p.504)

• You take me, and all my troubles, and do ***anything*** you want with me.'(p.504)
• I will not go out and I will not enter into ***anything***.(p.506)
• There was no time off for so-called good behavior, first-timers, or ***anything*** else.(p.509)
• I rounded up a few more of my friends and off we went to the meeting, not for ***anything*** we would gain from it as much as to make a burlesque out of it.(p.509)
• It wasn't ***anything*** strange to me, and I knew if I wanted to stay on the outside, that would be the spot for me.(p.510)
• She had been warned numerous times, not only by her family but by my own mother, that I was a hopeless drunk, that there wasn't ***anything*** anybody could do with me, that I'd never stop, and that eventually I'd break her heart.(p.513)
• Oh yes, I get the dry jitters once in a while, but that isn't ***anything*** to worry about.(p.516)
• Before I step out and do ***anything***, I stop and check it over first, and then let my conscience be my guide.(p.516)
• When I look back, I can't see ***anything*** that would have predisposed me towards being either a neurotic or a drunk.(p.517)
• There was nothing in my school life that I can look back on which was responsible for ***anything*** that happened afterwards.(p.517)
• Up to that time, drinking didn't really mean ***anything*** to me at all.(p.518)
• It didn't worry me very much, because at that time I could shut off for a couple of months without taking a drink or even wanting one, and without feeling that I was giving ***anything*** up.(p.518)
• But that didn't mean ***anything*** to me.(p.521)
• I stayed there just long enough to work up a real good resentment against the doctor in charge, who I didn't think was doing ***anything*** at all except collecting fees, and I left there fully determined that I'd never put myself in the power of medical people again.(p.521)
• I had no work to do and I was at an age where it seemed too late to start ***anything*** new.(p.522)
• I was intensely unhappy the whole time, but I didn't seem to be able to do ***anything*** about it, and the worst part to me was the realization that all this was going to happen again and again until I died.(p.522)
• I couldn't think of ***anything*** at all to do.(p.523)
• Providentially, this was a Monday might when the Dublin Group met in those days, and my family agreed that if A.A. could do ***anything*** for me at all, that I'd be allowed to stay on at home on probation.(p.523)
• I always blamed my drinking on being poor, or on ***anything*** other than the truth – that I liked what booze did for me, that when I had a drink I was as big and had as much as the next person.(p.526)
• I felt that I didn't have ***anything*** to live for, so I tried suicide many times.(p.528)
• They tell me that I killed a man during that period, but I can't remember ***anything***.(p.528)
• Repeated year on end, they are horrible -- frightening and degrading, a chronicle of tragedy which may be greater because the individual undergoing the tragedy, myself, knew what was happening, and yet refused to do ***anything*** to stop it.(p.538)
• I say, "refused to do ***anything*** to stop it."(p.539)
• I was not capable of ***anything*** better.(p.540)
• I have not had a drink of ***anything*** alcoholic since that ten-day binge.(p.541)
• In time I concluded that the reason I was hurt was because I loved my parents, and I concluded too that if I never allowed myself to love anybody or ***anything*** I could never be hurt again.(p.545)
• It became second nature for me to remove myself from ***anything*** or anybody I found myself growing fond of.(p.545)
• The only kind of security I knew ***anything*** about at that time was material security and I decided that all these intruders would vanish immediately if I only had a lot of money.(p.545)
• I wasn't afraid of ***anything*** or anybody after I learned about drinking, for it seemed right from the beginning that with liquor I could always retire to my little private world where nobody could get at me to hurt me.(p.547)
• I realize now that this phase of my development had been arrested by my obsession with self, and my egocentricity had reached such proportions that adjustment to ***anything*** outside my personal control was impossible for me.(p.547)
• The only reality I was able to face had been forced upon me by its very repetition – I had to drink; and I didn't know there was ***anything*** in the world that could be done about it.(p.548)
• The people who came knew immediately I was in no condition to absorb ***anything*** of the program, and I was put in a sanitarium to be defogged so that I could make a sober decision about this for myself.(p.549)
• Society can do ***anything*** it chooses to do with me when I am drunk and I can't lift a finger to stop it, for I forfeit my rights through the simple expedient of becoming a menace to myself and to the people around me.(p.549)

anyway

• I failed to persuade my broker friends to send me out looking over factories and managements, but my wife and I decided to go ***anyway***.(p.2)
• Telling them what we are trying to do, we make no bones about our drinking; they usually know it ***anyway***, whether we think so or not.(p.78)
• I was able to rationalize it ***anyway***.(p.198)
• Partially so, ***anyway***.(p.263)
• One of them was that I would try to get a group started in Chicago; the second was that I would have to return to Akron to attend meetings at least every two months until I did get a group started in Chicago; third, I decided I must place this program above everything else, even my family, because if I did not maintain my sobriety I would lose my family ***anyway***.(p.292)
• I became a drunk ***anyway***, but I was scared to death to take that morning drink.(p.323)
• There wasn't much I could do about it, and I didn't want to do anything ***anyway***.(p.427)
• I'll be honest ***anyway***.(p.506)
• Even when you don't really want it for them, and your prayers are only words and you don't mean it, go ahead and do it ***anyway***.(p.552)

anywhere

• He can go ***anywhere*** on this earth where other free men may go without disaster, provided he remains willing to maintain a certain simple attitude.(p.26)
• Your job now is to be at the place where you may be of maximum helpfulness to others, so never hesitate to go ***anywhere*** if you can be helpful.(p.102)
• If he is conscientiously following the program of recovery he can go ***anywhere*** your business may call him.(p.147)
• But at no time have I been ***anywhere*** near yielding.(p.181)
• I have already done it, and I am willing to do it again here in the presence of you or I am willing to say it any place, ***anywhere*** in the world from now on and not be ashamed of it."(p.190)
• There were, at that time, in the neighborhood of twelve or thirteen Cleveland members who had been sober ***anywhere*** from a year and a half to a couple of months.(p.219)
• I was soon broke, this time without trainfare to go ***anywhere***.(p.252)
• Indeed, I was beginning to see that I would require implicit faith, like a small child, if I was going to get ***anywhere***.(p.259)
• I never was concerned any more, ***anywhere*** he went.(p.263)
• We had not gotten ***anywhere***.(p.406)

apart

• Would there be schisms which would split A.A. ***apart***?(p.xix)
• This phenomenon, as we have suggested, may be the manifestation of an allergy which differentiates these people, and sets them ***apart*** as a distinct entity.(p.xxviii)
• As to two of you men, whose stories I have heard, there is no doubt in my mind that you were 100% hopeless, ***apart*** from divine help.(p.43)
• Sometimes it is to the best interests of all concerned that a couple remain ***apart***.(p.99)
• In addition to these casual get-togethers, it became customary to set ***apart*** one night a week for a meeting to be attended by anyone or everyone interested in a spiritual way of life.(p.159)
• It fell ***apart*** in the twenties.(p.197)
• After a couple of days in dollar hotels and one night in the pokey, I finally landed on my mother's doorstep -- shaking ***apart***, with several days' beard and, of course, broke as usual.(p.238)
• Science could take my mind ***apart*** expertly, but it couldn't seem to put it together again.(p.435)
• What a revelation of ego and arrogance still remaining in me -- as if anyone, instinct and training ***apart***, likes to be in jail or in an alcoholic ward or fired from his job.(p.536)
• Instead of drinking in fancy bars and clubs, I had to carry a bottle of vodka in my briefcase, duck into public toilets, and gulp from the bottle, trembling, in order to keep from falling ***apart***.(p.557)
• Secondary aids to A.A., such as clubs or hospitals which require much property or administration, ought to be incorporated and so set ***apart*** that, if necessary, they can be freely discarded by the groups.(p.566)

apartment

• There were many unhappy scenes in our sumptuous ***apartment***.(p.3)
• I optioned a piece of land just off East Market Street to put up a three-hundred suite ***apartment***.(p.198)
• First, my new wife had walked out, bag, baggage and furniture; then the ***apartment*** landlord had thrown me out of the empty ***apartment*** and the finish was the loss of another job.(p.238)
• I had some financial success through no ability of my own and, when jobless and almost wiped out in 1930, I began to trade and sell my collection; much of the proceeds went to keep my ***apartment*** stocked with liquor and almost every night saw me helpless to bed.(p.255)
• After finding every bottle that I had hidden around the ***apartment***, she took away my pants, my shoes, my money and my keys, threw them under the bed in the back bedroom and slip-locked our door.(p.288)
• Then when we got back to the ***apartment***, he was willing to wait two or three days until I got my health back to be paid off for the liquor and fare.(p.289)
• I had bottles hidden all over the ***apartment***.(p.324)
• I reached a stage where I couldn't go into my ***apartment*** without a drink.(p.324)
• (My addiction bloomed within a small ***apartment*** I shared with my wife, a heart patient.)(p.329)
• I paced back and forth in the ***apartment*** with the cold sweats.(p.338)
• A duplex ***apartment*** isn't any place to raise a dog.(p.388)
• I rented a beautiful ***apartment*** on the banks of the Seine in the winter, and a chalet in Switzerland in the summer.(p.405)
• I had a tiny trust fund, and I moved into a small ***apartment*** where I learned to cook, keep house, and do the things that normal people do.(p.409)
• The ***apartment*** was charming; the shelves were full of books, many of which I myself owned.(p.413)
• I fix up a little ***apartment*** over the garage with books and drinking water.(p.506)
• I shall not drink until I get back to the ***apartment***.(p.506)

apathy

• If they sense these things, they will not take so seriously his periods of crankiness, depression, or ***apathy***, which will disappear when there is tolerance, love, and spiritual understanding.(p.127)

apex

• I do feel, though, that the fact that I finally grew up to a point where I could even tackle such a job is the ***apex*** of the story of a man who spent eighteen years running away from life.(p.286)
• Everybody did, in the set which I regarded as the ***apex*** of civilization.(p.433)

apiece

• They were doing very well – at least a fifth ***apiece*** a day, except on dad's days off when they did some serious drinking.(p.425)

apologize

• We never ***apologize*** to anyone for depending upon our Creator.(p.68)
• We never ***apologize*** for God.(p.68)
• You will no longer be self-conscious or feel that you must ***apologize*** as though your husband were a weak character.(p.115)

apologized

• I sat down on the side of one of their beds, and I started to weep, and I couldn't stop, and I was so startled, and I ***apologized*** again and again for it.(p.272)

apology

• Do we owe an ***apology***?(p.86)

appalling

• I began to wonder, for such an ***appalling*** lack of perspective seemed near being just that.(p.5)
• Of course, there is such a thing as incompatibility, but in nearly every instance the alcoholic only seems to be unloving and inconsiderate; it is usually because he is warped and sickened that he says and does these ***appalling*** things.(p.108)
• The insidiousness of alcoholism is an ***appalling*** thing.(p.432)

appallingly

• And how ***appallingly*** true for the alcoholic!(p.14)

apparent

• The first thing ***apparent*** was that this world and its

people were often quite wrong.(p.65)
• When the time for living together has come, it will be ***apparent*** to both parties.(p.99)
• Time after time, this ***apparent*** calamity has been a boon to us, for it opened up a path which led to the discovery of God.(p.116)
• Of course, we had talked over quite a number of the failings that I had and made a sort of an inventory, which wasn't too difficult, because I had an awful lot of things wrong that were very ***apparent*** to me, because I knew all about them.(p.190)
• Soon, it became ***apparent*** that my schooling was interfering with my drinking.(p.354)
• But success brought increased social activities and I realized that many of my friends enjoyed a social drink with no ***apparent*** harm to themselves or others.(p.374)
• Cunning, baffling, powerful -- the gradual creeping up of the frequency and quantity of alcohol, and what it does to a person is ***apparent*** to everyone but the person involved.(p.375)
• Over the years, as I thought about Max, her good qualities grew and grew, and we married, and all these qualities became more and more ***apparent*** to me, and we were happier and happier.(p.450)
• The only thing this changed, however, was my surroundings, and it was soon ***apparent*** that I could have the same uncomfortable emotions with an unlimited checking account that I could on a working girl's salary.(p.545)

apparently
• I ***apparently*** was willing to subdue these personality disturbances in a tremendous drive to succeed.(p.211)
• He waited until I was completely sober and the day before I was to head back for Chicago, he told me of a small group of men in Akron who ***apparently*** had the same problem that I had but were doing something about it.(p.289)
• They had a hunch that there must be an answer for these ***apparently*** hopeless ones, somewhere.(p.307)
• The doctor, ***apparently*** realizing that one thing that I certainly needed was sleep, left a bottle of sleeping pills there and in my drunken state I took them all, instead of the one or two he had prescribed.(p.465)
• From that time on, fear was with me because I realized that not only would I not remember what happened to me while I was drinking, but ***apparently*** I couldn't control what happened.(p.465)
• The only importance in all of this lies in the fact that at twenty-three I was just as sick as I was at thirty three, when I came into A.A., but at that time I ***apparently*** had no place to go because I had no drinking problem.(p.546)
• ***Apparently*** I'd grown physically at the customary rate of speed, and I had acquired an average amount of intellectual training in the intervening years, but there had been no emotional maturity at all.(p.547)

appeal
• Frothy emotional ***appeal*** seldom suffices.(p.xxvi)
• Men have cried out to me in sincere and despairing ***appeal***: "Doctor, I cannot go on like this!(p.xxvii)
• We think few, to whom this book will ***appeal***, can stay dry anything like a year.(p.34)
• I learned that it was something of a spiritual nature, which did not ***appeal*** to me very much, but I thought it could do no harm.(p.178)
• But, although I was a good Catholic, the monastic life had little ***appeal*** for me.(p.230)
• I did work of all kinds after school and during vacations, trying to find that which would ***appeal*** most as a goal for a life work.(p.373)

appealed
• Finally, in desperation, my family ***appealed*** to a doctor for advice and he suggested A.A.(p.549)

appealing
• However, I had phoned New York from the farm, ***appealing*** for help, and there in the station to meet us were two A.A.'s, John and Bud.(p.415)

appeals
• It is important that we remain anonymous because we are too few, at present to handle the overwhelming number of personal ***appeals*** which may result from this publication.(p.xiii)

appear
• This man and over one hundred others ***appear*** to have recovered.(p.xxiii)
• These facts ***appear*** to be of extreme medical importance; because of the extraordinary possibilities of rapid growth inherent in this group they may mark a new epoch in the annals of alcoholism.(p.xxiii)
• If any feel that as psychiatrists directing a hospital for alcoholics we ***appear*** somewhat sentimental, let them stand with us a while on the firing line, see the tragedies, the despairing wives, the little children; let the solving of these problems become a part of their daily work, and even of their sleeping moments, and the most cynical will not wonder that we have accepted and encouraged this movement.(p.xxvi)
• Then he begins to ***appear*** at hospitals and sanitariums.(p.22)
• They ***appear*** to be in the nature of huge emotional displacements and rearrangements.(p.27)
• Neither does there ***appear*** to be any kind of treatment which will make alcoholics of our kind like other men.(p.30)
• We seldom had friends at our homes, never knowing how or when the men of the house would ***appear***.(p.105)
• This time I seemed to be already awake, sitting upright in a big easy chair, in the middle of an animated conversation with a perfectly strange young woman, who didn't ***appear*** to think it strange.(p.222)

appearance
• With the ***appearance*** of the new book a great deal began to happen.(p.xvii)
• To all ***appearance*** he is a stable, well balanced individual.(p.39)
• It wasn't necessary to report to the office in person every day, and when I did go in, it was just to make an ***appearance*** and bounce right out again.(p.300)
• I cared nothing about my personal ***appearance***.(p.337)

appearances
• It is being constantly revealed, as mankind studies the material world, that outward ***appearances*** are not inward reality at all.(p.48)

appeared
• The first edition ***appeared*** in April 1939, and in the following sixteen years, more than 300,000 copies went into circulation.(p.xi)
• This is the Foreword as it ***appeared*** in the first printing of the first edition in 1939(p.xiii)
• In a matter of fact way he told how two men had ***appeared*** in court, persuading the judge to suspend his commitment.(p.9)
• At that time I was not aware of the almost unlimited supply the government made it possible for us doctors to obtain, neither had I any knowledge of the bootlegger who soon ***appeared*** on the horizon.(p.175)
• They spoke with great freedom from embarrassment, which I could never do, and they seemed very much at ease on all occasions and ***appeared*** very healthy.(p.178)
• After the book ***appeared*** we all became very busy in our efforts to save all and sundry, but I was still actually on the fringes of A.A.(p.248)
• Whenever we went out she ***appeared*** to go out of her way to keep me from having more than one drink.(p.376)
• Then two bulbs ***appeared***.(p.498)
• Angry bruises ***appeared*** mysteriously all over my body.(p.558)

appears
• He had also been greatly helped by the late Dr. William D. Silkworth, a New York specialist in alcoholism who is now accounted no less than a medical saint by A.A. members, and whose story of the early days of our Society ***appears*** in the next pages.(p.xvi)
• The basic principles of the A.A. program, it ***appears***, hold good for individuals with many different lifestyles, just as the program has brought recovery to those of many different nationalities.(p.xxii)
• In the following chapter, there ***appears*** an explanation of alcoholism, as we understand it, then a chapter addressed to the agnostic.(p.28)
• He is violent, or ***appears*** definitely insane when drunk.(p.110)
• My father-in-law ***appears***.(p.501)

appendices
• The second edition added the ***appendices***, the Twelve Traditions, and the directions for getting in touch with A.A.(p.xi)
• *APPENDICES*(p.563)

appetite
• My experience in the hospital I considered to be terrific because Dr. Bob told me very quickly that medicine would have very little to do with it, outside of trying to restore my ***appetite*** for food.(p.217)

applaud
• We went at once to the country, my wife to ***applaud*** while I started out to overtake Walter Hagen.(p.3)

applause
• Here was love, ***applause***, war; moments sublime with intervals hilarious.(p.1)
• For the next few years fortune threw money and ***applause*** my way.(p.3)

applecart
• I would follow certain drinking schedules or diets faithfully for a few days, and then somewhere along the line would over-train and upset the ***applecart***.(p.361)

application
• We doctors have realized for a long time that some form of moral psychology was of urgent importance to alcoholics, but its ***application*** presented difficulties beyond our conception.(p.xxv)
• Many years ago one of the leading contributors to this book came under our care in this hospital and while here he acquired some ideas which he put into practical ***application*** at once.(p.xxv)
• It would be wonderful were I able to tell you that my confidence in God and my ***application*** of the Twelve Steps to my daily living have utterly banished fear.(p.284)
• Instead of wanting to escape some perplexing problem, we experience a thrill of challenge in the opportunity it affords for another ***application*** of A.A. techniques, and we find ourselves tackling it with surprising vigor.(p.311)
• They suggested that I study the A.A. book and try to take the Twelve Steps according to the explanation in the Book, for it was their opinion that the ***application*** of these principles in our daily lives will get us sober and keep us sober.(p.550)

applied
• Admit that he probably knows more about it than you do, but call to his attention the fact that however deep his faith and knowledge, he could not have ***applied*** it or he would not drink.(p.93)
• He did things much better than I did because he ***applied*** himself and learned how to do them, and I never ***applied*** myself.(p.194)
• I ***applied*** for a publicity job and got it.(p.254)
• I ***applied*** for photo school at Pensacola Air Base and made it.(p.426)
• And when this six month school was over I ***applied*** for duty in Hawaii and pulled it.(p.426)
• Now I had to face up to the fact that knowledge of this sort, ***applied*** to my individual case, was not power.(p.435)
• Only through being beaten down by my own misery would I ever have accepted the term "alcoholic" as ***applied*** to myself.(p.436)

applies
• This ***applies***, too, to other spiritual expressions which you find in this book.(p.47)
• But what we have said ***applies*** quite as much to women.(p.104)
• The same principle ***applies*** in dealing with the children.(p.115)
• The word "alcoholic" does not turn me off any more; in fact, it is music to my ears when it ***applies*** to me.(p.463)

apply
• What with our ultra-modern standards, our scientific approach to everything, we are perhaps not well equipped to ***apply*** the powers of good that lie outside our synthetic knowledge.(p.xxv)
• Some of you are thinking: "Yes, what you tell us is true, but it doesn't fully ***apply***.(p.38)
• We had to ask ourselves why we shouldn't ***apply*** to our human problems this same readiness to change our point of view.(p.52)
• What they say will ***apply*** to nearly everyone bound by ties of blood or affections to an alcoholic.(p.104)
• The same principles which ***apply*** to husband number one should be practiced.(p.112)
• As our husbands began to ***apply*** spiritual principles in their lives, we began to see the desirability of doing so too.(p.116)
• I can remember well thinking that I would quit drinking, really go to work hard, ***apply*** myself eight hours a day, five days a week, make a lot of money, and then I could start drinking again.(p.199)
• It is, however, only the first of a series of miracles which have followed one after another as a result of my trying to ***apply*** to my daily life the principles embodies in our Twelve Steps.(p.280)

applying
• My personal definition, which I submit as ***applying*** only to myself (although everyone is welcome to it who wants it), includes every waking activity of the human being; to have a creative attitude towards things is a more exact meaning, to live and to deal with other human beings creatively, which to me means seeing the God in them, and respecting and worshipping this God.(p.535)

appointed
• Our friends thought a lunacy commission should be ***appointed***.(p.3)
• Those of us belonging to a religious denomination which requires confession must, and of course, will want to go to the properly ***appointed*** authority whose duty it is to receive it.(p.74)
• I have been ***appointed*** to the faculty of my old school, to teach in my new field.(p.541)

appointment
• They took a drink a day or so prior to the date, and then the phenomenon of craving at once became paramount to all other interests so that the important ***appointment*** was not met.(p.xxvii)
• There was more than one occasion when I got up in the morning with just enough money for coffee and toast and the bus fare to carry me to my first ***appointment***.(p.283)
• In those days, I was doing a staff ***appointment*** in the army headquarters in New Delhi.(p.343)
• Then he called Marty and made and ***appointment*** for me.(p.413)

appointments
• The slightest disposition on your part to guide his ***appointments*** or his affairs so he will not be tempted will be noticed.(p.120)

appraisal
• But I have a fortune in friendships, courage, self assurance and honest ***appraisal*** of my own abilities.(p.296)

appraise
• No outsider can ***appraise*** such an intimate situation.(p.82)

appreciate
• Your husband may come to ***appreciate*** your reasonableness and patience.(p.111)
• If the family will ***appreciate*** that dad's current behavior is but a phase of his development, all will be well.(p.129)
• He will ***appreciate*** knowing you are not bothering your head about him, that you are not suspicious nor are you trying to run his life so he will be shielded from temptation to drink.(p.146)
• If I could, that was wonderful, that was just fine, and they would very much ***appreciate*** a person who had that kind of power, but they were looking for a man that knew he had a problem, and knew that he couldn't handle it himself and needed outside help.(p.186)
• He is a real friend but I do not ***appreciate*** him.(p.501)

appreciated
• I rather ***appreciated*** your ideas about the subtle insanity which precedes the first drink, but I was confident it could not happen to me after what I had learned.(p.40)
• Can it be ***appreciated*** that he has been a victim of crooked thinking, directly caused by the action of alcohol on his brain?(p.140)
• You might say you ***appreciated*** his abilities, would like to keep him, but cannot if he continues to drink.(p.141)

appreciation
• I fancied myself a leader, for had not the men of my battery given me a special token of ***appreciation***?(p.1)
• An offer of ***appreciation*** for not having had a drink for those few months and then and there, without anybody promising me anything or threatening me, I made a solemn vow that never so long as I lived would I take another drink.(p.200)
• Philosophy, faith, a sense of humor (they could laugh at themselves), clear-cut objectives, ***appreciation*** -- and most especially ***appreciation*** and sympathetic understanding for their fellow man.(p.310)
• I seem to get no sympathy for my illness and have no ***appreciation*** of the love behind the gift.(p.501)
• If he were still sober, chances are that very quickly I put him down as a Philistine with no ***appreciation*** of literary genius; and then I went on to another bar to find a new victim.(p.537)

appreciative
• I think our profession must take ***appreciative*** cognizance of this great therapeutic weapon.(p.571)

apprehended
• Three weeks after an armed robbery in which one person received a superficial flesh wound (I could have killed someone!), I was ***apprehended***.(p.460)

apprehension
• If you answer these questions satisfactorily, you need have no ***apprehension***.(p.102)
• As soon as his sobriety begins to be taken as a matter of course, the family may look at their strange new dad with ***apprehension***, then with irritation.(p.128)

apprentice
• I was always interested in mechanics and after having about twenty miscellaneous jobs, lasting from one day to two weeks, I obtained a job as a toolmaker ***apprentice***.(p.211)

apprenticed
• Very early I became ***apprenticed*** to harness-making and acquired considerable knowledge of upholstering.(p.230)

apprenticeship
• I finished my ***apprenticeship*** and was moved into the drafting department.(p.211)
• When I got back to Germany I settled down to finish my ***apprenticeship***, drinking the wine of the country as usual.(p.231)

approach
• What with our ultra-modern standards, our scientific ***approach*** to everything, we are perhaps not well equipped to apply the powers of good that lie outside our synthetic knowledge.(p.xxv)
• Many types do not respond to the ordinary psychological ***approach***.(p.xxvii)
• I expressed my entire willingness to ***approach*** these individuals, admitting my wrong.(p.13)
• That the man who is making the ***approach*** has had the same difficulty, that he obviously knows what he is talking about, that his whole deportment shouts at the new prospect that he is a man with a real answer, that he has no attitude of Holier Than Thou, nothing whatever except the sincere desire to be helpful; that there are no fees to pay, no axes to grind, no people to please, no lectures to be endured -- these are the conditions we have found most effective.(p.18)
• After such an ***approach*** many take up their beds and walk again.(p.19)
• Though not a religious person, I have profound respect for the spiritual ***approach*** in such cases as yours.(p.43)
• Our own conception, however inadequate, was sufficient to make the ***approach*** and to effect a contact with Him.(p.46)
• Whether we agree with a particular ***approach*** or conception seems to make little difference.(p.50)
• We agnostically inclined would not feel satisfied with a proposal which does not lend itself to reasonable ***approach*** and interpretation.(p.53)
• To some people we need not, and probably should not emphasize the spiritual feature on our first ***approach***.(p.76)
• It is seldom wise to ***approach*** an individual, who still smarts from our injustice to him, and announce that we have gone religious.(p.77)
• The question of how to ***approach*** the man we hated will arise.(p.77)
• You need this information to put yourself in his place, to see how you would like him to ***approach*** you if the tables were turned.(p.90)
• ***Approach*** through a doctor or an institution is a better bet.(p.91)
• If he thinks he can do the job in some other way, or prefers some other spiritual ***approach***, encourage him to follow his own conscience.(p.95)
• We have no monopoly on God; we merely have an ***approach*** that worked with us.(p.95)
• If this kind of ***approach*** does not catch your husband's interest, it may be best to drop the subject, but after a friendly talk your husband will usually revive the topic himself.(p.112)
• Suppose an ***approach*** is made something like this:(p.141)
• Perhaps you are not quite in sympathy with the ***approach*** we suggest.(p.144)
• We think this method of ***approach*** will accomplish several things.(p.148)
• The other day an ***approach*** was made to the vice president of a large industrial concern.(p.148)
• They will ***approach*** still other sick ones and fellowships of Alcoholics Anonymous may spring up in each city and hamlet, havens for those who must find a way out.(p.153)
• In the chapter "Working With Others" you gathered an idea of how we ***approach*** and aid others to health.(p.153)
• The very practical ***approach*** to his problems, the absence of intolerance of any kind, the informality, the genuine democracy, the uncanny understanding which these people had were irresistible.(p.160)
• Every few days this doctor suggests our ***approach*** to one of his patients.(p.162)
• But this was a man who had experienced many years of frightful drinking, who had had most all the drunkard's experiences known to man, but who had been cured by the very means I had been trying to employ, that is to say the spiritual ***approach***.(p.180)
• A complete change takes place in our ***approach*** to life.(p.311)
• "The American Public Health Association presents a Lasker Group Award for 1951 to Alcoholics Anonymous in recognition of its unique and highly successful ***approach*** to that age-old public health and social problem, alcoholism . . .(p.573)
• Speaking at a dinner given by John D. Rockefeller Jr. to introduce Alcoholics Anonymous to some of his friends, Dr. Harry Emerson Fosdick remarked: "I think that psychologically speaking there is a point of advantage in the ***approach*** that is being made in this movement that cannot be duplicated.(p.574)

approached
• More often than not, it is imperative that a man's brain be cleared before he is ***approached***, as he has then a better chance of understanding and accepting what we have to offer.(p.xxiv)
• When, therefore, we were ***approached*** by those in whom the problem had been solved, there was nothing left for us but to pick up the simple kit of spiritual tools laid at our feet.(p.25)
• One night, when confined in a hospital, he was ***approached*** by an acholic who had known a spiritual experience.(p.56)
• Most people ***approached*** in this way will be glad to help; they will be honored by our confidence.(p.75)
• ***Approached*** in this way, the most ruthless creditor will sometimes surprise us.(p.78)
• Many a distracted wife has visited this house to find loving and understanding companionship among women who knew her problem, to hear from the lips of their husbands what had happened to them, to be advised how her own wayward mate might be hospitalized and ***approached*** when next he stumbled.(p.160)
• Some of them may sink and perhaps never get up, but if our experience is a criterion, more than half of those ***approached*** will become fellows of Alcoholics Anonymous.(p.163)
• I was forty-nine and a half years old when I was first ***approached*** about the Akron Group.(p.215)
• In the summer of 1938, almost a year from the time I made my original contact with Akron, the man for whom I was working and who knew about the program, ***approached*** me and asked if I could do anything about one of his salesmen who was drinking very heavily.(p.294)
• I ***approached*** several ministers and all of them thought it was a very good idea, but they never relinquished any space.(p.495)

approaches
• When people presented us with spiritual ***approaches***, how frequently did we all say, "I wish I had what that man has.(p.47)
• In our personal stories you will find a wide variation in the way each teller ***approaches*** and conceives of the Power which is greater than himself.(p.50)

approaching
• I went back to law school, and doubled up on the courses because I was then ***approaching*** thirty years of age and I wanted to get through as quickly as possible.(p.212)
• Until I took Social Security and a pension at the age of sixty-eight, after forty years in motion-picture-studio public relations, I had successfully hidden even any hints of ***approaching*** alcoholism.(p.327)

appropriate
• But for some time, it was difficult to keep from taking a pill when I had an ***appropriate*** symptom, such as a cough, pain, anxiety, insomnia, a muscle spasm, or an upset stomach.(p.448)

approval
• Dr. Harry Emerson Fosdick, the noted clergyman, reviewed it with ***approval***.(p.xvii)
• His action met widespread ***approval***, and today his is one of the most trusted citizens of his town.(p.80)
• Some of us sought out sordid places, hoping to find understanding companionship and ***approval***.(p.151)
• But as the years go by, the stretch becomes unbearable; and the man with the grown-up brain and the childish emotions -- vanity, self-interest, false pride, jealousy, longing for social ***approval***, to name few -- becomes a prime candidate for alcohol.(p.534)
• Since Dr. Silkworth's first endorsement of Alcoholics Anonymous, medical societies and physicians throughout the world have set their ***approval*** upon us.(p.571)

approve
• It is important that he be able to keep a confidence; that he fully understand and ***approve*** what we are driving at; that he will not try to change our plan.(p.74)

• Another principle we observe carefully is that we do not relate intimate experiences of another person unless we are sure he would ***approve***.(p.125)
• They can hardly fail to ***approve*** these simple principles, though the head of the house still fails somewhat in practicing them.(p.130)

approves
• There is something spiritual about an art museum or a symphony, and the Catholic Church ***approves*** of our use of them.(p.574)

approximately
• After reading this book, a junior executive can go to such a man and say ***approximately*** this, "Look here, Ed.(p.147)
• I had bought a piece of ground in Cuyahoga Falls and cut it into lots and had a profit of ***approximately*** $40,000 and that was a lot of money in those days.(p.194)
• Everything in the world a man could possibly want, and I was driving from Akron to Cleveland, having just been to the bank and discovered that I had ***approximately*** $5,000.(p.200)
• I succeeded in this attempt for ***approximately*** fifteen months with only a couple of slips.(p.343)
• After all, upon coming out of a week-long or ten-day drunk, it was hard enough to figure up just how much that one drunk cost, let alone trying to calculate the cost of ***approximately*** twenty-five years of active alcoholism.(p.396)
• I don't think I actually started to drink pathologically until ***approximately*** 1935.(p.487)

April
• The first edition appeared in ***April*** 1939, and in the following sixteen years, more than 300,000 copies went into circulation.(p.xi)
• I went into the hospital in ***April***, 1939.(p.217)
• That was on the 28th of ***April***, 1947.(p.523)
• Since I joined on that ***April*** night, A.A. has done more for me than just stop me from drinking; it has brought me back to life again.(p.524)

apropos
• We have three little mottoes which are ***apropos***.(p.135)

apt
• I am very ***apt*** to get into quite an uproar for a day or two before starting, but I do start, and once started, I have a swell time.(p.285)

aptitudes
• He often possesses special abilities, skills, and ***aptitudes***, and has a promising career ahead of him.(p.21)

arbiter
• We do not want to be the ***arbiter*** of anyone's sex conduct.(p.69)

arch
• Most good ideas are simple, and this concept was the keystone of the new and triumphant ***arch*** through which we passed to freedom.(p.62)
• Carefully reading the first five proposals we ask if we have omitted anything, for we are building an ***arch*** through which we shall walk a free man at last.(p.75)

area
• If anyone questions whether he has entered this dangerous ***area***, let him try leaving liquor alone for one year.(p.34)
• When I had been in the hospital ten days, Sister Ignatia, who has played such a part in the development of A.A. in this ***area***, stuck her head in the door one morning and announced, looking at me quizzically, that they might be able to make something human out of my face after all.(p.205)
• We now live in the West and are very fortunate in our ***area*** A.A.; it is good, simple and friendly, and our one desire is to stay in A.A. and not on it.(p.250)
• From a single member in the Chicago ***area***, commuting to Akron, we now exceed six thousand.(p.295)
• He told me that eventually he hoped such a group would develop in the Chicago ***area***, but that so far this had not been started.(p.309)
• And then we went up the side of a hill where we have a little barbecue ***area*** to make the fire for the barbecue, and on the way up, I thought to myself – I'll go back down to the kitchen and refill this drink.(p.347)
• The small group may elect its secretary, the large group its rotating committee, and the groups of a large metropolitan ***area*** their central or intergroup committee, which often employs a full-time secretary.(p.567)

areas
• Most important, A.A. has enabled me to go back and start growing up all over again in all ***areas*** of my life.(p.420)

aren't
• But we ***aren't*** a glum lot.(p.132)
• You're just a martyr, ***aren't*** you?"(p.322)
• ***Aren't*** we all?(p.328)
• All hidden drunks ***aren't*** at home in housewives' dresses.(p.328)
• They have contributed fantastic amounts of time and work to our problem, but they ***aren't*** able, it seems, to arrest either your alcoholism or mine.(p.352)
• In this program there ***aren't*** any half way measures.(p.516)

argue
• Under no condition do we criticize such a person or ***argue***.(p.77)
• We never ***argue*** this question.(p.102)
• It is of little use to ***argue*** and only makes the impasse worse.(p.126)
• If he does not ***argue*** about religion, he will make new friends and is sure to find new avenues of usefulness and pleasure.(p.132)
• We used to ***argue*** about our differing ideas, but we can't ***argue*** about our feelings.(p.451)

argued
• Why, he ***argued***, should he lose the remainder of his business, only to bring still more suffering to his family by foolishly admitting his plight to people from whom he made his livelihood?(p.155)

argument
• Nothing would please us so much as to write a book which would contain no basis for contention or ***argument***.(p.19)
• We avoid retaliation or ***argument***.(p.67)
• ***Argument*** and fault-finding are to be avoided like the plague.(p.98)
• Unless they actually need protection from their father, it is best not to take sides in any ***argument*** he has with them while drinking.(p.115)
• These family talks will be constructive if they can be carried on without heated ***argument***, self-pity, self-justification or resentful criticism.(p.127)
• Dad may feel that for years his drinking has placed him on the wrong side of every ***argument***, but now he has become a superior person with God on his side.(p.129)
• After much ***argument*** they allowed me to return and take my exams, all of which I passed creditably.(p.173)

argumentative
• Alcoholics being the ***argumentative*** lot that we are, the A.A. membership will undoubtedly come up with a few who will dispute these figures.(p.399)

arguments
• We read wordy books and indulge in windy ***arguments***, thinking we believe this universe needs no God to explain it.(p.49)
• In the course of drunken ***arguments***, I found my own views and sense of responsibility as a citizen.(p.410)
• "There is a principle which is a bar against all information, which is proof against all ***arguments*** and which cannot fail to keep a man in everlasting ignorance – that principle is contempt prior to investigation."(p.570)

arise
• There are many situations which ***arise*** out of the phenomenon of craving which cause men to make the supreme sacrifice rather than continue to fight.(p.xxviii)
• They ***arise*** out of ourselves, and the alcoholic is an extreme example of self-will run riot, though he usually doesn't think so.(p.62)
• The question of how to approach the man we hated will ***arise***.(p.77)
• When a discussion does ***arise***, you might suggest he read this book or at least the chapter on alcoholism.(p.111)
• In either case certain family problems will ***arise***.(p.126)
• When he renews interest in such things, a feeling of jealousy may ***arise***.(p.131)
• The first definite indications of an alcoholic pattern began to ***arise*** when I would go to New York on business and disappear, and wind up in Philadelphia or Boston for two or three day periods.(p.213)

arises
• Here difficulty ***arises*** with agnostics.(p.45)
• Beginning with such complaints, a barrier ***arises***.(p.126)

arising
• Wherever men are gathered together in business there will be rivalries and, ***arising*** out of these, a certain amount of office politics.(p.145)

Arizona
• Next, I was sent to ***Arizona***, where my drinking picked up some more, and I started having blackouts, and I was thrown in jail for speeding and drunken driving.(p.318)

arm
• Within a week after leaving the hospital a fast-moving trolley car breaks his ***arm***.(p.38)
• So I didn't have a beer one night, and as I drove home I was breaking my ***arm*** patting myself on the back because I had proved I could lick liquor.(p.203)
• Need I say that in a very short time I was walking along a prairie highway with ***arm*** extended and thumb pointed?(p.255)
• He sent to New York for a copy, and after reading it he tucked it under his ***arm*** and called on me.(p.307)

armed
• But the ex-problem drinker who has found this solution, who is properly ***armed*** with facts about himself, can generally win the entire confidence of another alcoholic in a few hours.(p.18)
• Three weeks after an ***armed*** robbery in which one person received a superficial flesh wound (I could have killed someone!), I was apprehended.(p.460)

armies
• I belonged to one of the Irish families who, more or less traditionally, sent their boys to the British ***armies***.(p.517)

Armistice
• Then came the insidious insanity of that first drink, and on ***Armistice*** Day 1935, I was off again.(p.8)
• We heard by wireless on the 5th that the ***Armistice*** would be signed the next day (this was a premature report) so I had a couple of cognacs to celebrate; then I hopped a truck and went AWOL.(p.242)
• It was November 11th and bells were ringing and whistles blowing for the real ***Armistice***.(p.242)
• I had run away from school to join the army in World War I, but missed it by one day since the ***Armistice*** was signed the very day I landed in Atlanta to sign up with Uncle Sam.(p.357)
• The ***Armistice*** is signed on the 11th and the draft is called off.(p.499)

armor
• My inability to accept the harsh realities of life had resulted in a disillusioned cynic, clothed in protective ***armor*** against the world's misunderstanding.(p.226)
• That ***armor*** had turned into prison walls, locking me in loneliness – and fear.(p.226)

armored
• An ***armored*** car could not have brought the pay envelopes home.(p.105)

arms
• I welcomed him with open ***arms***.(p.263)
• While I sought the comforting ***arms*** of alcohol, I knew this was a sign of weakness on the part of a longtime-successful old codger with white hair, the image of dignity.(p.331)
• I blinked slowly as I shifted my gaze to my ***arms***.(p.422)
• If you give us a try, you will see that we are really human beings, and we will welcome you with open ***arms*** and hearts.(p.529)
• I awoke next day with tubes in both ***arms***.(p.558)
• A.A. led me gently from this fantasizing to embrace reality with open ***arms***.(p.561)

army
• I left the university in the latter part of my senior year and enlisted in the ***army***.(p.183)
• I can remember that in my childhood, he was ill at ease with the children because he attempted to assert an ***army*** discipline that had been ground into him during his three and a half years of ***army*** service.(p.210)
• In the spring of 1917, in order to beat being fired from school, I became "patriotic" and joined the ***Army***.(p.241)
• I had been to OTC the previous summer so I went into the ***Army*** as a sergeant, but I came out a private, and you really have to be unusual to do that.(p.241)
• In the ***Army***, I became a periodic alcoholic -- the periods always coming whenever I could make the opportunity.(p.241)
• My last bout in the ***Army*** lasted from November 5th to 11th, 1918.(p.242)
• Since I didn't do well in school, I quit and joined the ***Army*** at age seventeen.(p.317)
• For this officer in the Indian ***Army***, going on the wagon was not enough; attempts at control failed.(p.342)
• I eventually became a schoolmaster, but gave up that profession to join the Indian ***Army***.(p.342)

• The *army* made a difference to me.(p.343)
• In those days, I was doing a staff appointment in the *army* headquarters in New Delhi.(p.343)
• This was my first long vacation of sixty days since I had joined the *army*.(p.343)
• I had run away from school to join the *army* in World War I, but missed it by one day since the Armistice was signed the very day I landed in Atlanta to sign up with Uncle Sam.(p.357)
• In fact I was afraid to try it for fear that I would wind up like many examples I had seen of excessive drinking in the *Army*.(p.374)
• At age twenty-one, I enlisted in the Navy for two reasons: (1) to avoid being drafted into the *Army*, and (2) out of a burst of patriotic fervor inspired by the advent of World War II and as the result of an all-night drinking binge which found me sitting on the doorstep of the Navy recruiting office when the chief petty officer arrived to open for business at nine o'clock Monday morning.(p.398)
• I felt like a gangster's moll about to be interviewed by the Salvation *Army*.(p.413)
• I enlisted in the Navy to escape the *Army* draft.(p.425)
• When I was twenty-one, my cousin come home from U.S. *Army* on leave.(p.474)
• I join Canadian *Army*, but could not run away from problem.(p.474)
• So that pattern continued until I went into the *Army*.(p.513)
• The *Army* drinking alone covered a lot of territory.(p.513)
• But I came out of the *Army* just as big a drunk as when I went in, if not worse, because now I had a lot more resentments.(p.513)
• I should say there was less drinking in the *Army* than I thought at that time.(p.518)
• Strangely enough, right through to the end of my twenty-six years in the *Army*, I was still being offered very good and important jobs in spite of the fact that my superiors must have known that I wasn't thoroughly reliable.(p.519)
• About three months after that, my record reached home and I got a letter telling me I was retired from the *Army*, they put it very kindly, on medical grounds.(p.521)
• In part, it was a feeling of intense shame at having to leave the *Army* during the war, but mostly it was resentment that this kind of thing should happen to me for, strange as it may seem, up to then I still thought I could control drinking.(p.521)

arose

• He added that occasionally in the night a vague craving *arose* which would be satisfied by candy.(p.134)
• Whenever a situation *arose* that fast talk wouldn't explain away, I simply withdrew.(p.214)
• All my troubles *arose* when I was thrown socially among groups of people.(p.486)

around

• It was fun to carom *around* the exclusive course which had inspired such awe in me as a lad.(p.4)
• Quicksand stretched *around* me in all directions.(p.8)
• He is the fellow who goes to bed so intoxicated he ought to sleep the clock *around*.(p.21)
• The prosaic steel girder is a mass of electrons whirling *around* each other at incredible speed.(p.48)
• He commences to look *around* in the night clubs, or their equivalent, for something besides liquor.(p.81)
• This means a new attitude and spirit all *around*.(p.99)
• sometimes they were so inaccessible that it seemed as though a great wall had been built *around* them.(p.107)
• Use your energies to promote a better understanding all *around*.(p.115)
• We think the business fabric is shot through with a situation which might be helped by better understanding all *around*.(p.137)
• My whole life seemed to be centered *around* doing what I wanted to do, without regard for the rights, wishes, or privileges of anyone else; a state of mind which became more and more predominant as the years passed.(p.172)
• There my drinking became so much worse that the boys in the fraternity house where I lived felt forced to send for my father, who made a long journey in the vain endeavor to get me straightened *around*.(p.174)
• This would lessen my chances of smuggling some home that evening, which in turn would mean a night of futile tossing *around* in bed followed by a morning of unbearable jitters.(p.176)
• I remember that my father kept whiskey *around* the house for medical purposes and entertainment, and I would drink from this when no one was about and then water it to keep my parents from knowing I was drinking.(p.183)
• So, after hearing some more of my story, he turned *around* and said to Doc – I don't think he knew I heard him, but I did – he said, "Well, I believe he's worth saving and working on."(p.185)
• Another time, I had gone *around* to Max R. trying to get a job driving one of his trucks.(p.200)
• The people in the group hadn't been *around* that day; part of my family was in Florida and the rest of them weren't speaking to me, so I spent a very lonesome day and by evening I was feeling very sorry for myself.(p.207)
• Terrified, I looked *around*.(p.222)
• I was doing well in business, and in going *around* town I was frequently invited to have a drink in a speakeasy.(p.233)
• Beer was too bulky and it couldn't be kept in a jug under the counter ready to be dumped when John Law came *around*.(p.233)
• Imagine my surprise when I read in a page one "box" that I had been taken from the theater unconscious *around* noon that day, removed by ambulance to a hospital and stomach-pumped and then released.(p.244)
• So I drank all three beers, one after the other, said "I'll be seeing you, boys," and went *around* the corner for a bottle.(p.247)
• I had completely forgotten the January 8th when I found the fellowship, and I spent the next four days wandering *around* New England half drunk, by which I mean I couldn't get drunk and I couldn't get sober.(p.247)
• *Around* this time our big A.A. book was being written and it all became much simpler; we had a definite formula which some sixty of us agreed was the middle course for all alcoholics who wanted sobriety, and that formula has not been changed one iota down through the years.(p.248)
• Then I got a very good position in Philadelphia and quickly found I would need a few fellow alcoholics *around* me if I was to stay sober.(p.249)
• As I look back on the events of two months, I can clearly see that I had been circling *around*, half-afraid of encountering the remedy for my situation, half wanting it, deferring fulfillment of my promise to get in touch with the doctor I had heard about.(p.258)
• The next time vacation time rolled *around* that was a bitter lesson to us.(p.265)
• I paced the floor with a bath towel *around* my shoulders, the perspiration running off me.(p.268)
• Now, if you've got a Bible *around* . . ."(p.268)
• Three more months of being up and *around* the house for brief periods and in bed the rest of the time.(p.275)
• He told me that it was imperative that I walk *around* the entire block, cost me what it might in mental agony.(p.276)
• I shut myself in my room, which began to go *around* in circles.(p.279)
• It ran something like this: If I go *around* shouting from the rooftops about my alcoholism, it might very possibly prevent me from getting a good job.(p.282)
• That same year, my wife became fed up with my drinking *around* the house and called my dad in Akron to come and pick me up.(p.288)
• After finding every bottle that I had hidden *around* the apartment, she took away my pants, my shoes, my money and my keys, threw them under the bed in the back bedroom and slip-locked our door.(p.288)
• And still by the time I was thirty years old I was being pushed *around* with a compulsion to drink that was completely beyond my control.(p.305)
• I heard voices when no one was *around*, and I saw things that weren't there.(p.319)
• He used to wonder, when he'd spot one of my bottles *around* the house, just how he could have overlooked that particular bottle.(p.325)
• My home at that time was a place to mill *around* in.(p.337)
• She was doing fine, she was up and *around*, and that day her husband phoned me and said, "Doctor, thanks very much for curing my wife," and I thanked him for his felicitations, and he hung up.(p.350)
• My parents' car had a strong attraction to fences, and one night I blacked out and drove the car down a bank, ramming the steel fence *around* someone's backyard.(p.353)
• By the time I figured out what had happened, I saw two flashing red lights atop squad cars, sedately coming *around* the corner.(p.353)
• I got *around* this by joining the local Rotary Club, and through this association with the business men of the community my little station began to grow.(p.360)
• When our meeting night came *around* the next evening, I went -- "for her sake" I told her.(p.365)
• I woke up in this bare room with nothing *around* me but bars; they wouldn't let me smoke and treated me, well, like I was nuts.(p.387)
• My father, as I have said, was very indulgent and loved me dearly, and knew how to get *around* me.(p.389)
• I guess there are plenty of other graduates of this treatment *around*.(p.389)
• But Frank turned *around* and looked at me and said, "Esther, remember you're in jail and not at home."(p.391)
• I took two or three drinks so my eyes could focus, and I could see that horrible picture of the awful drunk on the first page; he couldn't get the drink to his mouth, he had a towel *around* his hand and he needed a shave.(p.391)
• The only other occasionally limiting factor was that I might run out of money before the next payday rolled *around*.(p.398)
• But at this time, I began gravitating toward the really hard drinkers, hanging *around* with them more and more.(p.404)
• On our honeymoon in Egypt, he cuffed me *around* quite a bit, and subsequently hit me some more.(p.405)
• Finally my new friends told me, one by one, that I could not come *around* any more.(p.410)
• The bartender, a tough Irishman, came *around* and "gave me the elbow," which means that he raised his elbow and smacked me in the face.(p.411)
• I lost it many times and mom and dad would drive me *around* until I found it.(p.429)
• I didn't feel I could lie in bed and squirt the stuff in my veins while my kids and wife stood *around* watching me, so I kept the drug in my bag and the bag in the car and the car in the garage.(p.442)
• If they were *around*, I always found a need for them – especially the pills.(p.443)
• Today, I find I can't work my A.A. program while taking pills, nor may I even have them *around* for dire emergencies only.(p.443)
• After I had been *around* A.A. for seven months, tapering off alcohol and pills, not finding the program working very well, I was finally able to say, "Okay, God.(p.448)
• But it was the other way *around*.(p.452)
• So we turned *around* and started back to Washington.(p.467)
• As an indication of just how confused and mixed up I was, just as soon as I could I left the office and hurried *around* to tell other patients that I was getting better.(p.470)
• They build you up with a lot of false hopes and promises, and rush you *around* here and there and then, all of a sudden, it's gone."(p.472)
• So I wasn't just tinkering *around* with it -- I had to get in with both feet.(p.480)
• We are aware of the nice things *around* us, things we never noticed before in our drunken stupor.(p.481)
• The only time that I have ever seen my mother take anything alcoholic was *around* Christmas time, when she would drink some eggnog or light wine.(p.484)
• This was *around* 1935, and it was about this time that I actually started drinking.(p.486)
• I'd go into my home with a bottle, and I remember clearly how I would look *around* to see if Vi was watching.(p.487)
• I had to put up a three hundred dollar bond because he was carrying the same summons *around* in his pocket for me.(p.491)
• *Around* eight or nine o'clock there came two big detectives and a policeman to arrest me for assault; and I was the most amazed person in the world when they said I had assaulted someone, and especially that I had assaulted my wife.(p.492)
• When I had known her years before she was rather slender, but at this time she weighed as much as she does now, which is up *around* in the two hundreds or very close to it.(p.493)
• It was *around* noon, a day or two later, when the telephone rang and it was Ella.(p.494)
• The wind is rising and howls *around* the house.(p.497)
• I mope *around* the house.(p.506)
• So instead of going near A.A., I just browsed *around* for that first month.(p.510)
• I started prowling *around* with a couple of these A.A. boys, which kept me pretty busy and kept my mind off of down town.(p.511)
• Yes, we find it rather confusing, but as we get *around* and get to know people in the group, they lead the way and all we have to do is to follow.(p.512)
• You hit the street about ten minutes to eight, and

you walk ***around*** the block, God knows how many times, waiting for that joint to open.(p.514)
- I got a job by myself which suited me down to the ground, because there was nobody really to interfere with what I did, one way or the other, and I usually had my nerves in good trim when anybody was coming ***around*** to inspect.(p.519)
- I was not able to hold a job – no one wants a drunk ***around***.(p.526)
- It's time to stop finding excuses for drinking and getting into trouble, because now there is a way out, and if you want what we have, try coming ***around*** and giving the program a chance.(p.530)
- I looked ***around*** me at people who seemed happy and tried to analyze their happiness, and it seemed to me that without exception these people had something or somebody they loved very much.(p.546)
- I was drunk for sixty days ***around*** the clock and it was my intention, literally, to drink myself to death.(p.549)
- Society can do anything it chooses to do with me when I am drunk and I can't lift a finger to stop it, for I forfeit my rights through the simple expedient of becoming a menace to myself and to the people ***around*** me.(p.549)
- I became so weak, I could barely drag myself ***around***.(p.558)

arouse
- Did we unjustifiably ***arouse*** jealousy, suspicion or bitterness?(p.69)
- You will be handicapped if you ***arouse*** it.(p.89)

aroused
- The word God still ***aroused*** a certain antipathy.(p.12)

arouses
- Long experience with alcoholic excuses naturally ***arouses*** suspicion.(p.146)

arousing
- There is no use ***arousing*** any prejudice he may have against certain theological terms and conceptions about which he may already be confused.(p.93)
- You should warn against ***arousing*** resentment or jealousy.(p.100)
- They can urge action without ***arousing*** hostility.(p.113)

arraigned
- I was immediately arrested, ***arraigned*** in Homicide Court, held without bail, and remanded to the old Tombs Prison to await trial.(p.508)

arraignment
- The next morning I went up for ***arraignment***.(p.492)

arrange
- Each person is like an actor who wants to run the whole show; is forever trying to ***arrange*** the lights, the ballet, the scenery and the rest of the players in his own way.(p.60)
- We do not tire so easily, for we are not burning up energy foolishly as we did when we were trying to ***arrange*** life to suit ourselves.(p.88)
- We never, never try to ***arrange*** a man's life so as to shield him from temptation.(p.120)
- Is not each trying to ***arrange*** the family show to his liking?(p.122)
- In large cities, groups often maintain local offices where alcoholics or their families may ***arrange*** for interviews or hospitalization.(p.575)

arranged
- Oddly enough, the dentist who started A.A. in Amarillo, Tex., benevolently ***arranged*** my admission to dental college.(p.419)
- He ***arranged*** for me to see a local psychiatrist, who quickly decided I should be in the mental-health unit of our local hospital.(p.445)

arrangement
- They also were held in some sort of strap ***arrangement***.(p.422)
- So I went down to talk to the District Attorney, and the ***arrangement*** was made that I would go home to stay with my mother, and that meant Vi and I were separated.(p.491)

arrangements
- If his ***arrangements*** would only stay put, if only people would do as he wished, the show would be great.(p.60)
- In trying to make these ***arrangements*** our actor may sometimes be quite virtuous.(p.61)
- ***Arrangements*** were also made with the chief psychiatrist of a large public hospital to select still others from the stream of misery which flows through that institution.(p.163)
- I made ***arrangements*** to enter the hospital three days later and promptly went out and got stiff for three days.(p.302)
- She makes the ***arrangements***, but I will not go.(p.502)

arranging
- ***Arranging*** the best deal we can we let these people know we are sorry.(p.78)

arrears
- It was the usual situation: home in jeopardy, wife ill, children distracted, bills in ***arrears*** and standing damaged.(p.155)

arrest
- She is indignant about it, and has a warrant out for our ***arrest***.(p.79)
- She went to court and got an order for his ***arrest***.(p.79)
- They have contributed fantastic amounts of time and work to our problem, but they aren't able, it seems, to ***arrest*** either your alcoholism or mine.(p.352)
- Around eight or nine o'clock there came two big detectives and a policeman to ***arrest*** me for assault; and I was the most amazed person in the world when they said I had assaulted someone, and especially that I had assaulted my wife.(p.492)

arrested
- I was ***arrested*** and taken to jail where I was beaten up by two or three fellows who were already in there and whom I tried to boss.(p.204)
- As ***arrested*** alcoholics, we must have a program for living that allows for limitless expansion.(p.311)
- I get ***arrested***.(p.475)
- I get ***arrested*** again.(p.475)
- Finally, I was ***arrested*** and got six months for drugs.(p.480)
- There is no cure for alcoholism, but it can be ***arrested*** in the program of A.A.(p.480)
- I was immediately ***arrested***, arraigned in Homicide Court, held without bail, and remanded to the old Tombs Prison to await trial.(p.508)
- I realize now that this phase of my development had been ***arrested*** by my obsession with self, and my egocentricity had reached such proportions that adjustment to anything outside my personal control was impossible for me.(p.547)

arresting
- Then he told me there was a handful of people in Akron and New York who had worked out a technique for ***arresting*** their alcoholism.(p.308)

arrestment
- He asked me to read the book "Alcoholics Anonymous," and then he wanted me to talk with a man who was experiencing success with his own ***arrestment***.(p.308)
- Keeping one foot in front of the other is essential for maintaining our ***arrestment***.(p.311)
- I told her that I was an alcoholic, victim of a disease, that there was no cure, only ***arrestment*** through total abstinence.(p.333)

arrival
- For weeks after my ***arrival*** I was feted and entertained in the already large colony of Alsatians in the city, and among the Germans in their saloons and clubs.(p.231)
- Now, with the ***arrival*** at retirement, it was gone.(p.329)
- It was my second ***arrival*** in New York.(p.513)

arrive
- The tragic truth is that if the man be a real alcoholic, the happy day may not ***arrive***.(p.23)
- Eventually I would ***arrive*** home for a late supper for which, of course, I had absolutely no relish.(p.299)

arrived
- I had ***arrived***.(p.3)
- This tragic situation has already ***arrived*** in practically every case long before it is suspected.(p.24)
- ***Arrived*** at this point, we were squarely confronted with the question of faith.(p.53)
- He just ***arrived*** in D.T.'s.(p.188)
- When I was about forty-seven, after indulging in all kinds of self-deception to control my drinking, I ***arrived*** at a period when I felt convinced I had to have so much alcohol every day and that the real problem was to control how much.(p.214)
- I resented it of course, and I offered Clarence his commission, whatever it might be, if he would please not bother me because I had ***arrived*** at the conclusion that he was a solicitor for some alcoholic institute.(p.216)
- Jackie ***arrived*** about seven in the evening and talked until three a.m.(p.239)
- I ***arrived*** drunk, but I promised my wife I would keep sober, and I knew I could get work if I did.(p.256)
- I ***arrived*** at the stage where I couldn't quite make it to the office some mornings.(p.299)
- How I had ***arrived*** at this tragic impasse I could not have explained to anyone.(p.304)
- I was certainly a complete surprise when I ***arrived*** at her family's home, but because I ***arrived*** on the wings of a tropical hurricane there wasn't much she could do but let me in.(p.364)
- Luck was with me for I made my train, but I ***arrived*** home the next morning with a new kind of hangover.(p.364)
- The only drawback was, I always knew how I ***arrived*** there, but somehow, between the rest room, the rinse, and the fluff-dry, I never knew when or how I got home.(p.370)
- The time for decision had ***arrived***, and it was a relief to say "Yes" when my family said they would call Alcoholics Anonymous for me.(p.378)
- At age twenty-one, I enlisted in the Navy for two reasons: (1) to avoid being drafted into the Army, and (2) out of a burst of patriotic fervor inspired by the advent of World War II and as the result of an all-night drinking binge which found me sitting on the doorstep of the Navy recruiting office when the chief petty officer ***arrived*** to open for business at nine o'clock Monday morning.(p.398)
- I was listed in "Who's Who in America" as an American who, by distinguished achievement, had ***arrived***.(p.432)
- On another occasion I ***arrived*** home covered with blood.(p.435)
- They sent me up with an attendant, and the attendant and I both ***arrived*** at the Egyptian Hospital rather the worse for wear.(p.521)
- When I ***arrived*** back in Dublin, I had no friends left.(p.522)
- I was taking Benzedrine and paraldehyde quite impartially during the day then, and by the time I ***arrived*** at my first A.A. meeting, I was pretty drunk and certainly doped up to the eyes and completely jittery.(p.523)
- When I ***arrived*** at The Country Shop, which was a restaurant where they met in Dublin, I found about thirty-five or forty people in the room.(p.524)
- Despite my wife's entreaties to take it easy that day, I ***arrived*** home in bad shape.(p.557)

arrives
- If we do a good job of living today, and if tomorrow comes for us, then the chances are we will do a good job when it ***arrives*** -- so why worry about it?(p.382)

arriving
- Hence the two men set to work almost frantically upon alcoholics ***arriving*** in the ward of the Akron City Hospital.(p.xvii)
- I have been drinking while the baby was ***arriving***.(p.502)

arrogance
- What a revelation of ego and ***arrogance*** still remaining in me – as if anyone, instinct and training apart, likes to be in jail or in an alcoholic ward or fired from his job.(p.536)

arrogant
- The last two years of my drinking my entire personality changed to a cynical, intolerant and ***arrogant*** person completely different from my normal self.(p.376)
- I am still ***arrogant***, egocentric, self-righteous, with no humility, even phony at times, but I'm trying to be a better person and help my fellowman.(p.463)

art
- I studied ***art***; I desperately endeavored to create an interest in many things, in a new place among new people.(p.305)
- This phase was right down my alley; I had my master's degree in the ***art*** of making "whoopee."(p.359)
- Doing our best, living each day to the fullest is the ***art*** of living.(p.382)
- He had not developed this ***art*** and had no recourse but his fists.(p.405)
- Could they discuss literature or ***art***?(p.412)
- There is something spiritual about an ***art*** museum or a symphony, and the Catholic Church approves of our use of them.(p.574)

article
- Then Jack Alexander wrote a feature ***article*** in the Saturday Evening Post and placed such a compelling picture of A.A. before the general public that alcoholics in need of help really deluged us.(p.xviii)
- I think I actually read more contempt than was really there because just a week before someone had sent him the Saturday Evening Post ***article*** on A.A., and there was some glimmer of hope in

it for him.(p.391)
• The next morning he came into my room and said, "Esther, I'm not going to lecture you any more, but I want you to read this ***article***.(p.391)
• I only know that it first reached me through that Saturday Evening Post ***article***.(p.392)
• I had learned an awful lot about myself in that one little ***article***.(p.393)
• There are so many to whom I feel deeply grateful; to my husband (and best critic), whose generous love, compassion and understanding have helped me along the way; to those before me in A.A. who inspired the first ***article*** I read, and the friend who sent that ***article*** to Frank; to Ruth for her personal note, and the first A.A. to talk to me; to my Bishop, whose loving and believing spirit inspired me; and to all the members of the Houston Group who were so patient, kind and helpful -- and to countless others.(p.393)
• Even the Jack Alexander Saturday Evening Post ***article*** hadn't been written, and there was only a tiny group of people in Washington.(p.469)
• During the day a friend of mine brought me some magazines to take to a hospital group I was interested in, and I looked through them and a "banner" across the front of one featured an ***article*** by a prominent clergyman in which I caught the word "resentment."(p.552)
• I sold my first ***article*** to a national magazine while still an undergraduate.(p.555)

articles
• But I cannot accept as surely true the many ***articles*** of faith which are so plain to him."(p.47)
• The movie racket had kept me too long from writing those novels, ***articles***, short stories, and scripts on which I had copious notes.(p.330)

artificial
• It had been so many years since I had not relied on some ***artificial*** crutch, either alcohol or sedatives.(p.310)

artist
• I was club-man, athlete, ***artist***, musician, author, editor, aircraft pilot and world traveller.(p.432)

arts
• With nothing but a liberal ***arts*** education, very definitely estranged from my family and already married, soon after graduation from college I became a bookmaker's clerk on the British racing circuits, far better off financially than the average professional man.(p.251)
• I'd been on the board of governors of the Academy of Motion Picture ***Arts*** and Sciences for six years.(p.328)
• To create: Everyone does it, some at the instinct level, others in the ***arts***.(p.535)

ascertained
• We have admitted certain defects; we have ***ascertained*** in a rough way what the trouble is; we have put our finger on the weak items in our personal inventory.(p.72)

ascribed
• Federal Theatre in Texas gave me an administrative job which I held for a year, only because I worked hard and productively when I worked, and because my very tolerant chief ***ascribed*** my frequent lapses to a bohemian temperament.(p.256)

ash
• I also made use of old trunks and chests, the old can container, and even the ***ash*** container.(p.176)

ashamed
• It was his first experience of this kind, and he was much ***ashamed*** of it.(p.39)
• I have already done it, and I am willing to do it again here in the presence of you or I am willing to say it any place, anywhere in the world from now on and not be ***ashamed*** of it."(p.190)
• One morning after a terrific drinking bout, I was in a little bar near our house, and I shook so that I was very much ***ashamed***, because I was getting the shakes worse and worse.(p.266)
• I sipped the drink off the bar because I couldn't hold it in my hand, but I was still a lady, believe it or not, and I was deeply ***ashamed***.(p.266)
• I try to live today so that tomorrow I won't be ***ashamed*** when I wake up in the morning.(p.325)
• Bruised, and deadly ***ashamed***, I told no one.(p.406)
• They did not seem ***ashamed*** to be with us, these strangers.(p.415)
• Why, I wasn't even ***ashamed*** of my skinny legs!(p.498)
• Finally, I got so lowdown, I was ***ashamed*** of my friends' seeing me, so I went to the worst joints I could find.(p.527)

ashes
• Then, under one provocation or another, the aggrieved one would unearth the old affair and angrily cast its ***ashes*** about.(p.124)

ashore
• But somehow, we couldn't quite step ***ashore***.(p.53)

Asia
• Some are just now taking shape in ***Asia***.(p.xv)

aside
• Yet all reasons for not drinking were easily pushed ***aside*** in favor of the foolish idea that he could take whiskey if only he mixed it with milk!(p.36)
• We found that as soon as we were able to lay ***aside*** prejudice and express even a willingness to believe in a Power greater than ourselves, we commenced to get results, even though it was impossible for any of us to fully define or comprehend that Power, which is God.(p.46)
• Though some of us resisted, we found no great difficulty in casting ***aside*** such feelings.(p.48)
• We, who have traveled this dubious path, beg you to lay ***aside*** prejudice, even against organized religion.(p.49)
• Leaving ***aside*** the drink question, they tell why living was so unsatisfactory.(p.51)
• Father may have laid ***aside*** for years all normal activities -- clubs, civic duties, sports.(p.131)
• ***Aside*** from fellowship and sociability, the prime object was to provide a time and place where new people might bring their problems.(p.160)
• Help which you once continually rejected, suggestions once turned ***aside*** are finally accepted in desperation.(p.377)
• ***Aside*** from being a common drunk, I had a very serious pill affliction and all the garbage that goes with it -- lying, stealing, cheating anybody and everybody, conning the people I could, and staying clear of the ones I couldn't.(p.478)

ask
• Very earnestly we ***ask*** the press also, to observe this request, for otherwise we shall be greatly handicapped.(p.xiii)
• For a moment I was alarmed, and called my friend, the doctor, to ***ask*** if I were still sane.(p.14)
• If you ***ask*** him why he started on that last bender, the chances are he will offer you any one of a hundred alibis.(p.23)
• Next day we would ***ask*** ourselves, in all earnestness and sincerity, how it could have happened.(p.37)
• We needed to ***ask*** ourselves but one short question.(p.47)
• The reader may still ***ask*** why he should believe in a Power greater than himself.(p.48)
• We had to ***ask*** ourselves why we shouldn't apply to our human problems this same readiness to change our point of view.(p.52)
• We ***ask*** Him to remove our fear and direct our attention to what He would have us be.(p.68)
• In meditation, we ***ask*** God what we should do about each specific matter.(p.69)
• Carefully reading the first five proposals we ***ask*** if we have omitted anything, for we are building an arch through which we shall walk a free man at last.(p.75)
• If we still cling to something we will not let go, we ***ask*** God to help us be willing.(p.76)
• If we haven't the will to do this, we ***ask*** until it comes.(p.76)
• Reminding ourselves that we have decided to go to any length to find a spiritual experience we ***ask*** that we be given strength and direction to do the right thing, no matter what the personal consequences may be.(p.79)
• When these crop up, we ***ask*** God at once to remove them.(p.84)
• After making our review we ***ask*** God's forgiveness and inquire what corrective measures should be taken.(p.86)
• Before we begin, we ***ask*** God to direct our thinking, especially asking that it be divorced from self-pity, dishonest or self-seeking motives.(p.86)
• Here we ***ask*** God for inspiration, an intuitive thought or a decision.(p.86)
• We ***ask*** especially for freedom from self-will, and are careful to make no request for ourselves only.(p.87)
• We may ***ask*** for ourselves, however, if others will be helped.(p.87)
• If circumstances warrant, we ***ask*** our wives or friends to join us in morning meditation.(p.87)
• As we go through the day we pause, when agitated or doubtful, and ***ask*** for the right thought or action.(p.87)
• Then let his family or a friend ***ask*** him if he wants to quit for good and if he would go to any extreme to do so.(p.90)
• Let him ***ask*** you that question, if he will.(p.93)
• If he is sincerely interested and wants to see you again, ***ask*** him to read this book in the interval.(p.95)
• ***Ask*** them to remember, when they are impatient, the blessed fact of his sobriety.(p.100)
• ***Ask*** any woman who has sent her husband to distant places on the theory he would escape the alcohol problem.(p.101)
• Therefore, ***ask*** yourself on each occasion, "Have I any good social, business, or personal reason for going to this place?(p.101)
• If you do this thoroughly, few people will ***ask*** you to drink.(p.102)
• We began to ***ask*** medical advice as the sprees got closer together.(p.106)
• But after his next binge, ***ask*** him if he would really like to get over drinking for good.(p.112)
• Do not ***ask*** that he do it for you or anyone else.(p.112)
• If you think he will be shy of a spiritual remedy, ***ask*** him to look at the chapter on alcoholism.(p.112)
• ***Ask*** him what you should do if he places you in such a position again.(p.116)
• Cheer him up and ***ask*** him how you can be still more helpful.(p.120)
• Little by little, mother and children will see they ***ask*** too much, and father will see he gives too little.(p.127)
• You ***ask***, because many alcoholics, being warped and drugged, do not want to quit.(p.142)
• ***Ask*** him if he thinks he has the answer.(p.144)
• "How is that to come about?" you ***ask***.(p.152)
• ***Ask*** Him in your morning meditation what you can do each day for the man who is still sick.(p.164)
• The next thing they wanted to know was would I be willing to go to this Higher Power and ***ask*** for help, calmly and without any reservations.(p.186)
• The very simple program they advised me to follow was that I should ***ask*** to know God's will for me for that one day, and then, to the best of my ability, to follow that, and at night to express my gratefulness to God for the things that had happened to me during the day.(p.208)
• I'd waked up in strange rooms before, fully dressed on a bed or a couch; I'd waked up in my own room, in or on my own bed, not knowing what hour or day it was, afraid to ***ask*** . . . but this was different.(p.222)
• It must have been a long time since I had my last drink -- but I didn't dare ***ask*** this stranger for one.(p.223)
• I had no answers, and I dared not ***ask***.(p.223)
• The name on it was unfamiliar and I had to ***ask*** the way to Grand Central.(p.223)
• I remembered my loud resolution to find him and ***ask*** him to help me get into that "Asylum" he had written about.(p.224)
• My wife made several attempts to get me to stop and I had the usual visits from persons who would always ***ask*** me "Why?" -- as if I knew!(p.254)
• On my trips back to Akron to get my spirits recharged and to work with other alcoholics, I would ***ask*** Dr. Bob about this delay and wonder just what was wrong with me.(p.293)
• I soon was to ***ask*** myself, "What living?"(p.329)
• I had to give him a story and ***ask*** him the same question over and over again, "Well, now, how many will that bottle serve?"(p.336)
• I had given her everything a wife could ***ask*** for.(p.362)
• I haven't written anything about that part of my story, but I believe in a Greater Power which I call God and I ***ask*** for His wisdom and guidance daily.(p.366)
• Up to my early thirties, when my drinking had become a major problem, I lived in large houses, with servants and all the luxuries that I could possibly ***ask*** for.(p.401)
• Today I have all that anyone could ***ask***.(p.431)
• The neurologist in charge of my case didn't think to ***ask*** me whether I drank, and I didn't think to tell him.(p.444)
• The girl had explained them to me four times, and I was too embarrassed to ***ask*** her again.(p.445)
• The psychiatrist, who had generally been ignoring me, now became quite interested; every day, he would ***ask*** me all kinds of questions about the A.A. meetings.(p.446)
• "How?" they ***ask*** me.(p.477)
• ***Ask*** him about it.(p.488)
• She didn't say anything about A.A. or getting me a sponsor at that time, but she did ***ask*** about Vi, and I told her Vi was working and how she could

locate her.(p.494)
• "Have a drink?" I ***ask***.(p.501)
• "What are you doing here then?" I ***ask***.(p.503)
• "I must ***ask*** you a question," I say to the man.(p.504)
• Each time I would make a report to the parole officer he would ***ask*** me, "Have you been to an A.A. meeting yet?"(p.510)
• I ***ask*** the forgiveness of the reader; and from now on I shall try to write with the humility I honestly pray for.)(p.536)
• I had even borrowed money from her, over her protest: "Bob, please don't ***ask*** me to lend you money -- you're the only one who hasn't."(p.540)
• I choose to believe that the Power greater than ourselves we ***ask*** for help, wrapped my shivering body in loving warmth and strength which has never left me.(p.541)
• If you will ***ask*** in prayer for everything you want for yourself to be given to them, you will be free.(p.552)
• ***Ask*** for their health, their prosperity, their happiness, and you will be free.(p.552)
• Sometimes I have to ***ask*** first for the willingness, but it too always comes.(p.552)

askance

• We looked ***askance*** at many individuals who claimed to be godly.(p.46)

asked

• There was, therefore, a sense of real satisfaction when I was ***asked*** to contribute a few words on a subject which is covered in such masterly detail in these pages.(p.xxv)
• The cheery voice of an old school friend ***asked*** if he might come over.(p.8)
• You may already have ***asked*** yourself why it is that all of us became so very ill from drinking.(p.20)
• So he returned to this doctor, whom he admired, and ***asked*** him point-blank why he could not recover.(p.26)
• We ***asked*** him to tell us exactly how it happened.(p.36)
• They grinned, which I didn't like so much, and then ***asked*** me if I thought myself alcoholic and if I were really licked this time.(p.42)
• We ***asked*** ourselves this: Are not some of us just as biased and unreasonable about the realm of the material?(p.51)
• But later, alone in his room, he ***asked*** himself this question: "Is it possible that all the religious people I have known are wrong?"(p.56)
• We ***asked*** His protection and care with complete abandon.(p.59)
• 7.Humbly ***asked*** Him to remove our shortcomings.(p.59)
• We ***asked*** ourselves why we were angry.(p.64)
• We ***asked*** God to help us show them the same tolerance, pity, and patience that we would cheerfully grant a sick friend.(p.67)
• We ***asked*** ourselves why we had them.(p.68)
• We ***asked*** God to mold our ideals and help us to live up to them.(p.69)
• If we have obtained permission, have consulted with others, ***asked*** God to help and the drastic step is indicated we must not shrink.(p.80)
• ***Asked*** why they commenced to drink again, they would reply with some silly excuse, or none.(p.107)
• The next question they ***asked*** was, "You can quit twenty-four hours can't you?"(p.188)
• Straightway, Bob called Akron's City Hospital and ***asked*** for the nurse on the receiving ward.(p.188)
• We boys drove out in somebody's car and went to the bar on the way do the dining room and I, in an effort to impress the other boys that I was city-bred, having lived in Scranton and Cleveland, ***asked*** them if they didn't want a drink.(p.194)
• He had known something of my drinking pattern, and he ***asked*** me what I was doing about it.(p.200)
• I went downstairs and there was the grizzly old veteran police officer in charge of the property desk, and as he gave me the stuff, he ***asked***, "Are you going out in the street that way?"(p.204)
• They ***asked*** me if I would take some medicine, and I promised that I would if they got me a drink.(p.206)
• The afternoon that I was to leave the hospital, he came in to see me and ***asked*** me if I were willing to attempt to follow the program.(p.218)
• That day I gave my will to God and ***asked*** to be directed.(p.237)
• I had not ***asked*** for help and seriously doubt that I would have, but Fitz, an old school friend of mine, had persuaded Jackie to call on me.(p.238)
• I heard my son-in-law coming upstairs, and I ***asked*** him where dad was.(p.263)
• Well, I wasn't sure I did, and it was awful foggy, and I wept and ***asked*** her what she thought I ought to do about it.(p.273)
• I shut my eyes and ***asked*** for help.(p.285)
• She ***asked*** him to do something about me because she couldn't.(p.288)
• I would at least have ***asked*** for a quarter!(p.289)
• We went over these at great length and then he finally ***asked*** me if I wanted these defects of character removed.(p.292)
• I went to a minister and a doctor that I still knew and they, in turn, ***asked*** me how long I had been sober.(p.293)
• In the summer of 1938, almost a year from the time I made my original contact with Akron, the man for whom I was working and who knew about the program, approached me and ***asked*** if I could do anything about one of his salesmen who was drinking very heavily.(p.294)
• He ***asked*** me to read the book "Alcoholics Anonymous," and then he wanted me to talk with a man who was experiencing success with his own arrestment.(p.308)
• The doctor ***asked*** about my drinking, but I wouldn't talk to him.(p.319)
• When I'm ***asked*** to go out on a call, I go.(p.340)
• And the last sentence was "We ***asked*** His protection and care with complete abandon."(p.349)
• Now they ***asked*** us to make a decision!(p.350)
• So I went to my wife and ***asked*** her, wasn't there something that she and I could do to somehow get together, and she turned on her heel and looked me squarely in the eye, and said, "You don't care anything about my problem," and I could have smacked her, but I said to myself, "Grab on to your serenity!"(p.351)
• After several months of acquaintance I ***asked*** her to marry me, but was politely refused.(p.359)
• I ***asked*** this question weekly for the next couple of years.(p.359)
• Once again I ***asked*** my girl to marry me and join me in this new venture.(p.359)
• I attended my weekly meetings with regularity, reread the Big Book, attended other group meetings, gave leads when ***asked*** to and did some Twelve Step work whenever I was called upon to do so.(p.365)
• If I were ***asked*** what in my opinion was the most important factor in being successful in this program, besides following the Twelve Steps, I would say Honesty.(p.367)
• He ***asked*** if I would cooperate with him after I went home, and if I would have a trained nurse stay with me for at least two weeks.(p.387)
• I know now that I ***asked*** questions and told him what I wanted to learn, but I told him only what I wanted to believe about myself.(p.388)
• The questions he ***asked*** me that I didn't answer honestly, I thought were none of his business.(p.388)
• I was shaking so, I ***asked*** my husband to write the letter for me, but he said no.(p.392)
• It was the first time in my life that I could not get a lift out of what I was drinking; and so one Friday night, at five minutes to six, I had half a water glass of warm gin, and that is when I first ***asked*** God to help me.(p.393)
• Other girls whom I had known all my life ***asked*** for one weak scotch after dinner.(p.406)
• She ***asked*** me to read it.(p.412)
• "Why don't you just go down and see Mr. W.?" she ***asked***.(p.412)
• Never in my entire life had anyone ***asked*** me "Are you one of us?"(p.413)
• He ***asked*** me if I had any spiritual belief, and when I said No, he suggested that I keep an open mind.(p.413)
• He ***asked*** how I felt.(p.422)
• The doctor sat down beside the bed and ***asked*** me how I felt.(p.423)
• It became progressively harder to get up in the morning, until one day I ***asked*** myself what I would do for a patient who felt this rotten.(p.441)
• Finally, she ***asked***, "Do you realize he's on the staff of this hospital?"(p.445)
• One day as I sat there in the hospital, my psychiatrist walked up behind me and ***asked***, "How'd you like to talk to the man from A.A.?"(p.446)
• So, for no better reason than to fool him, I ***asked*** Frank to take me to a meeting every night.(p.447)
• On the day before Christmas I telephoned him and told him I was sober and ***asked*** him to come home.(p.467)
• The same doctor who had sent me to the psycho had ***asked*** my husband, "Why don't you send her to this Alcoholics Anonymous?"(p.469)
• A policeman came to the door and ***asked*** for James S., but there wasn't any James S. there.(p.491)
• I'd been home about a week or ten days when one of my friends ***asked*** if I could repair one of his electrical outlets.(p.493)
• She ***asked*** me if I would let someone come up and talk to me concerning a business deal.(p.494)
• I ***asked*** her just what this deal was, but she wouldn't say.(p.494)
• She ***asked*** me one other thing.(p.494)
• She ***asked*** me if I would try to be sober if I possibly could.(p.494)
• Pioneer A.A., minister's son, and southern farmer, he ***asked***, "Who am I to say there is no God?"(p.497)
• I go to see a man I had been ***asked*** to visit and tell him my story.(p.505)
• After the meeting was over and we had returned to the cell block again, I was ***asked*** how I was impressed.(p.510)
• She ***asked*** me, was I going to do this to her all over again?(p.510)
• I ***asked*** God for help.(p.515)
• It was the first time that I had ***asked*** for help sincerely and honestly.(p.515)
• I went in there and ***asked*** him honestly if he could give me a cure.(p.515)
• I went to hospitals, I went to retreats and doctors, and finally my mother ***asked*** me to go and see a specialist of her own choosing.(p.522)
• "Bob," he ***asked*** quietly, "do you want to live or die?"(p.540)
• In my prayers that morning I ***asked*** God to point out to me some way to be free of this resentment.(p.552)

askew

• But my life, even sober, was all ***askew*** and so were my emotions.(p.414)

asking

• In no time I was beating on the bar ***asking*** myself how it happened.(p.6)
• I was to sit quietly when in doubt, ***asking*** only for direction and strength to meet my problems as He would have me.(p.13)
• If your are an alcoholic who wants to get over it, you may already be ***asking*** -- "What do I have to do?"(p.20)
• Do not let any prejudice you may have against spiritual terms deter you from honestly ***asking*** yourself what they mean to you.(p.47)
• We suggested he write his first wife admitting his faults and ***asking*** forgiveness.(p.79)
• So we clean house with the family, ***asking*** each morning in meditation that our Creator show us the way of patience, tolerance, kindliness and love.(p.83)
• Before we begin, we ask God to direct our thinking, especially ***asking*** that it be divorced from self-pity, dishonest or self-seeking motives.(p.86)
• You can easily find some by ***asking*** a few doctors, ministers, priests or hospitals.(p.89)
• I then began ***asking*** a lot of questions of both my brother and Dr. Bob about how this thing worked, and I suppose I was becoming more glassy-eyed all the while, for eventually I said to Bob, "You're all dried up.(p.206)
• When I said yes, we both knelt at his desk and prayed, each of us ***asking*** to have these defects taken away.(p.292)
• I never could quite get the knack of it and kept ***asking*** myself, "What's a nice guy like me doing in a place like this?"(p.445)
• I have to discard my "rights," as well as my expectations, by ***asking*** myself, "How important is it, really?(p.452)
• We lived just a few doors from the First Baptist Church and when they had funerals I remember very often ***asking*** my mother whether the person was good or bad and whether they were going to heaven or hell.(p.483)
• If something does come along that sort of upsets me, instead of walking in and throwing a buck at the barman and ***asking*** for a drink, I walk into a telephone booth, drop a dime in the box, and call somebody who was so kind as to give me his name and telephone number to meet such an emergency.(p.511)

asks

• "You think you are hopeless, don't you?" he ***asks***.(p.503)
• Then he ***asks*** me if I believe in a power greater than myself, whether I call that power God, Allah, Confucius, Prime Cause, Divine Mind, or any other name.(p.503)
• Then he ***asks*** me if I am willing to right all the wrongs I have ever done to anyone, no matter how wrong I thought the others were.(p.503)

asleep

• I would be half ***asleep*** and half awake, and in the morning, I would be both tired and stupid.(p.440)

• The longer the drinking continued, the shorter the time the alcohol would keep me ***asleep;*** I would have to drink myself back to sleep again and again throughout the night.(p.441)

• That's the stuff used when the oral surgeon puts the needle in your vein and says, "Count to ten," and before you get to two, you're ***asleep***.(p.442)

• In the garage, I would put the needle in my vein and then try to figure out exactly how much medication to inject to overcome the pep pills while adding to the sleeping pills while ignoring the tranquilizers, in order to get just enough to be able to pull out the needle, jerk the tourniquet, throw it in the car, slam the car door shut, run down the hall, and fall in bed before I fell ***asleep***.(p.442)

• And then my waiting until I was sure he was ***asleep,*** and stealing money from him to replenish the supply.(p.466)

aspect

• This short word somehow touches about every ***aspect*** of our lives.(p.67)

• We have been dealing with alcohol in its worst ***aspect***.(p.132)

• That was one ***aspect*** of it, and a true one.(p.532)

• There was the physical ***aspect;*** to be the youngest and the runt of the brood of children, to have to wear glasses very early and so to be teased, to be bookish and bored in school because the captain of the football team could not translate Virgil and yet was the school god while you, you, you little shrimp, were the school egghead, junior size and an early model.(p.533)

aspects

• I have published a book covering certain ***aspects*** of this field which has been well-reviewed and which is helping other people.(p.541)

aspirin

• I didn't know whether I had told him to rush to the hospital and I'd meet him there, or to take two ***aspirin*** and call me in the morning.(p.441)

assail

• The doctor who came to see me almost at once did not ***assail*** me with any new doctrines; he made sure that I had a need and that I wanted to have that need filled, and little by little I learned how my need could be met.(p.258)

assault

• Around eight or nine o'clock there came two big detectives and a policeman to arrest me for ***assault;*** and I was the most amazed person in the world when they said I had assaulted someone, and especially that I had assaulted my wife.(p.492)

assaulted

• Around eight or nine o'clock there came two big detectives and a policeman to arrest me for assault; and I was the most amazed person in the world when they said I had ***assaulted*** someone, and especially that I had ***assaulted*** my wife.(p.492)

assert

• In a vague way their families and friends sense that these drinkers are abnormal, but everybody hopefully awaits the day when the sufferer will rouse himself from his lethargy and ***assert*** his power of will.(p.23)

• Even when he wanted to ***assert*** himself he could not, for his drinking placed him constantly in the wrong.(p.130)

• Father, coming suddenly to life again, often begins to ***assert*** himself.(p.131)

• I can remember that in my childhood, he was ill at ease with the children because he attempted to ***assert*** an army discipline that had been ground into him during his three and a half years of army service.(p.210)

asserting

• I remembered ***asserting*** that I was going to do something about this, that I couldn't go on . . .(p.224)

assessment

• It has taught me that success and failure are never final, and that neither count for very much in the final ***assessment*** of any man who has done his best.(p.525)

asset

• The alcoholic's past thus becomes the principal ***asset*** of the family and frequently it is almost the only one!(p.124)

• He has since become famous and distinguished, an ***asset*** to his country.(p.403)

• He has so much understanding, a real ***asset*** in sharing sobriety.(p.481)

assets

• Today the remarkable unity of A.A. is one of the greatest ***assets*** that our Society has.(p.xix)

• We grow by our willingness to face and rectify errors and convert them into ***assets***.(p.124)

• And then my thinking became calculation as to how much longer I had to live, how long the ***assets*** would last.(p.215)

assigned

• War fever ran high in the New England town to which we new, young officers from Plattsburg were ***assigned,*** and we were flattered when the first citizens took us to their homes, making us feel heroic.(p.1)

• I was ***assigned*** to keep media guests happy at a Halloween party given by a major star in his plush home.(p.328)

assignment

• Probably only a few readers of this story will be able, from personal experiences of their own, to understand the exhilaration and sense of accomplishment which I felt after finishing this seemingly simple ***assignment***.(p.276)

assigns

• We are in the world to play the role He ***assigns***.(p.68)

assist

• They will be only too glad to ***assist*** you.(p.89)

assistance

• Occasionally, they will offer ***assistance***.(p.78)

• If he is, you might try to help him about getting a job, or give him a little financial ***assistance***.(p.96)

• The minute we put our work on a service plane, the alcoholic commences to rely upon our ***assistance*** rather than upon God.(p.98)

• You may wonder why, since I was having all this trouble, and was having to seek the ***assistance*** of others, A.A. hadn't come into the picture.(p.469)

• I have no ***assistance*** and am working nights, Saturdays and Sundays.(p.500)

• My wife's parents come to our ***assistance***.(p.501)

assistant

• I was at one time ***assistant*** manager of a corporation department employing sixty-six hundred men.(p.136)

assisted

• In his prodigy of service, he was well ***assisted*** by Sister Ignatia at St. Thomas Hospital in Akron, Ohio, one of the greatest friends our Fellowship will ever know.(p.171)

associated

• Shortly after that, my brother, who had then become ***associated*** with a group of people and had stopped drinking, urged me to attend meetings with him.(p.205)

• Even then he went into no great detail about how he and a crowd of alcoholics, with whom he ***associated***, had mastered their difficulty.(p.235)

• I always feel that our God Consciousness was a steady growth after we became ***associated*** with A.A.(p.270)

• By this time I had become ***associated*** with the fast growing and fascinating business of broadcasting.(p.358)

• At a women's halfway house, I became ***associated*** with Alcoholics Anonymous and became aware of alcoholism as a disease, not just a "weakness."(p.371)

• I'm sure my ideas as to what life should be like were quite different from that of the average person with whom I ***associated***.(p.483)

• Mother was of the old school and figured that anyone I ***associated*** with should be of the proper type.(p.484)

• In emphasizing alcoholism as an illness, the social stigma ***associated*** with this condition is being blotted out . . .(p.573)

associates

• It was fortunate, for my old business ***associates*** remained skeptical for a year and a half, during which I found little work.(p.15)

• Can he talk frankly with you so long as he does not bear business tales or criticize his ***associates***?(p.145)

• I had to adapt to new associations and ***associates***, and it seemed to be the smart thing to drink and smoke.(p.287)

• I will never know all the people I hurt, all the friends I abused, the humiliation of my family, the worry of my business ***associates***, or how far reaching it was.(p.376)

• To me this meant telling my ***associates*** that I had joined Alcoholics Anonymous; that I didn't know what was expected of me by A.A., but that whatever it was, it was the most important thing in life for me; that sobriety meant more to me than anything in this world.(p.382)

• Above all, I am grateful to A.A. for my sobriety, which means so much to my family, friends and business ***associates***, because God and A.A. were able to do for me something I was unable to do for myself.(p.383)

• My ***associates***, and all the wits and literary lights I so much admired, also drank.(p.433)

• My alcoholic ***associates*** fired me, took control, and ran the enterprise into bankruptcy.(p.437)

• I also began visiting bars after work, with my older ***associates***.(p.555)

associating

• Through A.A., many receive the needed change and awakening just by trying to live by A.A. principles and ***associating*** with A.A. people.(p.459)

association

• I didn't have any need of such an ***association***!(p.206)

• And we loved every minute of that ***association***.(p.270)

• I got around this by joining the local Rotary Club, and through this ***association*** with the business men of the community my little station began to grow.(p.360)

• After a few meetings I decided to drive to Florida unannounced to see my wife and tell her about my new found friends and ***association***.(p.364)

• There was the necessity for sticking to a job I hated, a dull, repetitive job performed in ***association*** with other men I had nothing in common with . . . performed for years on end, because the money was needed at home.(p.532)

• Dr. Foster Kennedy, neurologist: "This organization of Alcoholics Anonymous calls on two of the greatest reservoirs of power known to man, religion and that instinct for ***association*** with one's fellows . . . the 'herd instinct.'(p.571)

• Dr. W.W. Bauer, broadcasting under the auspices of The American Medical ***Association*** in 1946, over the NBC network, said, in part: "Alcoholics Anonymous are no crusaders; not a temperance society.(p.572)

• The American Psychiatric ***Association*** requested, in 1949, that a paper be prepared by one of the older members of Alcoholics Anonymous to be read at the Association's annual meeting of that year.(p.572)

• "The American Public Health ***Association*** presents a Lasker Group Award for 1951 to Alcoholics Anonymous in recognition of its unique and highly successful approach to that age-old public health and social problem, alcoholism . . .(p.573)

association's

• The American Psychiatric Association requested, in 1949, that a paper be prepared by one of the older members of Alcoholics Anonymous to be read at the ***Association's*** annual meeting of that year.(p.572)

associations

• This should be an entirely personal affair which each one decides for himself in the light of past ***associations***, or his present choice.(p.28)

• I had to adapt to new ***associations*** and associates, and it seemed to be the smart thing to drink and smoke.(p.287)

• These so-called intergroup ***associations*** are found under the listing "A.A." or "Alcoholics Anonymous" in telephone directories.(p.575)

assorted

• One man and his wife placed their large home at the disposal of this strangely ***assorted*** crowd.(p.160)

assume

• Never avoid these responsibilities, but be sure you are doing the right thing if you ***assume*** them.(p.97)

• ***Assume*** on the other hand that father has, at the outset, a stirring spiritual experience.(p.128)

• Hangovers began to ***assume*** monstrous proportions and the morning drink became an urgent necessity.(p.226)

• Here was something requiring a greater willingness to ***assume*** responsibility, and take a larger degree of cooperation and "give and take" than even business requires of one.(p.286)

assumed

• My drinking ***assumed*** more serious proportions, continuing all day and almost every night.(p.3)

• That was great news to us, for we had ***assumed*** we could not make use of spiritual principles unless we accepted many things on faith which seemed difficult to believe.(p.47)

• There was the father one lost respect for at the age of eleven, because the father broke his solemn word in a circumstance where you, eleven years old, had ***assumed*** guilt when you were innocent; but the father would not believe you, no matter what; and to ease his suffering you "confessed" and were "forgiven," only – months later – to have your "guilt" brought up – only he and you knew what he was talking bout -- brought up in front of the stern grandmother.(p.533)

assuming
• We are ***assuming***, of course, that the reader desires to stop.(p.34)
• ***Assuming*** we are spiritually fit, we can do all sorts of things alcoholics are not supposed to do.(p.100)
• With God's help I am able, for one day at a time, to carry business responsibilities which, not many years ago, I would not have dreamed of ***assuming***.(p.284)

assumption
• Simply because it is impossible to explain what we see, feel, direct, and use, without a reasonable ***assumption*** as a starting point.(p.48)
• When, however, the perfectly logical ***assumption*** is suggested that underneath the material world and life as we see it, there is an All Powerful, Guiding, Creative Intelligence, right there our perverse streak comes to the surface and we laboriously set out to convince ourselves it isn't so.(p.49)

assumptions
• Everybody nowadays, believes in scores of ***assumptions*** for which there is good evidence, but no perfect visual proof.(p.48)

assurance
• My talent for leadership, I imagined, would place me at the head of vast enterprises which I would manage with the utmost ***assurance***.(p.1)
• Under these conditions we can employ our mental faculties with ***assurance***, for after all God gave us brains to use.(p.86)
• Here, while in a hospital bed, men with clear eyes, happy faces, and a look of ***assurance*** and purposefulness about them, came to see me and told me their stories.(p.279)
• But I have a fortune in friendships, courage, self ***assurance*** and honest appraisal of my own abilities.(p.296)
• I have self confidence and ***assurance*** that cannot be confused with the cockiness I once possessed.(p.303)

assure
• Following his physical rehabilitation, he had a talk with me in which he frankly stated he thought the treatment a waste of effort, unless I could ***assure*** him, which no one ever had, that in the future he would have the "will power" to resist the impulse to drink.(p.xxix)
• As soon as a man can say that he does believe, or is willing to believe, we emphatically ***assure*** him that he is on his way.(p.47)
• I won't go into detail about that, but I can ***assure*** you it's no fun.(p.469)

assured
• Next he can be ***assured*** that you do not intend to lecture, moralize, or condemn; that if this was done formerly, it was because of misunderstanding.(p.142)
• I remembered going through what my sister ***assured*** me was my nightly procedure of trying to find Willie Seabrook's name in the telephone book.(p.224)
• Weeks would go by without further trouble, and I'd be ***assured*** I'd at last hit on the right formula.(p.433)
• At noon on Christmas Day I called my family in New York, wished them a Merry Christmas, and ***assured*** them everything was fine with me.(p.467)

astonished
• Certain drinkers, who would be greatly insulted if called alcoholics, are ***astonished*** at their inability to stop.(p.33)
• I was ***astonished*** and deeply moved.(p.415)

astonishing
• The persistence of this illusion is ***astonishing***.(p.30)

astonishingly
• These allergic types can never safely use alcohol in any form at all; and once having formed the habit and found they cannot break it, once having lost their self-confidence, their reliance upon things human, their problems pile up on them and become ***astonishingly*** difficult to solve.(p.xxvi)

astonishment
• New groups started up and it was found, to the ***astonishment*** of everyone, that A.A.'s message could be transmitted in the mail as well as by word of mouth.(p.xviii)

astounded
• Naturally, in spite of my good intentions, in spite of my protected life behind sanitarium walls, I several times got drunk, and was ***astounded*** . . . and badly shaken.(p.227)

astray
• I was an honor graduate in high school, and I was a "good boy" to whom mothers pointed when their sons went ***astray***.(p.419)

astronomers
• My intellectual heroes, the chemists the ***astronomers***, even the evolutionists, suggested vast laws and forces at work.(p.10)

astronomical
• Others came near putting Galileo to death for his ***astronomical*** heresies.(p.51)

asylum
• She would soon have to give me over to the undertaker or the ***asylum***.(p.7)
• On leaving the ***asylum*** he came into contact with us.(p.35)
• He knew he faced another trip to the ***asylum*** if he kept on.(p.35)
• Thus started one more journey to the ***asylum*** for Jim.(p.36)
• He shuts himself up in an ***asylum***, hoping to mend his ways.(p.38)
• I remembered my loud resolution to find him and ask him to help me get into that "***Asylum***" he had written about.(p.224)
• People didn't behave this way outside of an ***asylum***.(p.306)
• I had never been inside of an insane ***asylum*** and I really thought I was going to a private hospital.(p.387)
• Vi was very kind and explained to the jury that I was basically a fine fellow and a good husband, but that I drank too much and that she thought I had lost my mind and felt that I should be committed to an ***asylum***.(p.492)
• The insane ***asylum*** lies ahead.(p.502)

asylums
• I have seen men come out of ***asylums*** and resume a vital place in the lives of their families and communities.(p.15)
• Here are some of the methods we have tried: Drinking beer only, limiting the number of drinks, never drinking alone, never drinking in the morning, drinking only at home, never having it in the house, never drinking during business hours, drinking only at parties, switching from scotch to brandy, drinking only natural wines, agreeing to resign if ever drunk on the job, taking a trip, not taking a trip, swearing off forever (with and without a solemn oath), taking more physical exercise, reading inspirational books, going to health farms and sanitariums, accepting voluntary commitment to ***asylums*** -- we could increase the list ad infinitum.(p.31)
• It may mean sharing your money and your home, counseling frantic wives and relatives, innumerable trips to police courts, sanitariums, hospitals, jails and ***asylums***.(p.97)
• Since this book was first published, A.A. has released thousands of alcoholics from ***asylums*** and hospitals of every kind.(p.114)
• Most of these fortunate ones have had little or no acquaintance with delirium, with hospitals, ***asylums***, and jails.(p.315)
• Many tried everything – hospitals, special treatments, sanitariums, ***asylums***, and jails.(p.455)

asymmetrical
• Bill was tall, grey haired, with the kind of ***asymmetrical*** good looks and pleasant easy manner that inspire confidence in the shaken and afraid.(p.413)

ate
• He ***ate*** his olive and I ***ate*** mine.(p.195)
• I ***ate*** up every bit of it, because I wanted to find out how to stay sober.(p.273)
• I never enjoyed any meal, but I ***ate*** my lunch at noon for two reasons; first, to help me get out of the fog of the night before and, second, to furnish some measure of nourishment.(p.299)

atheist
• I was not an ***atheist***.(p.10)
• To one who feels he is an ***atheist*** or agnostic such an experience seems impossible, but to continue as he is means disaster, especially if he is an alcoholic of the hopeless variety.(p.44)
• In this book you will read the experience of a man who thought he was an ***atheist***.(p.55)
• If the man be agnostic or ***atheist***, make it emphatic that he does not have to agree with your conception of God.(p.93)
• If you think you are an ***atheist***, an agnostic, a skeptic, or have any other form of intellectual pride which keeps you from accepting what is in this book, I feel sorry for you.(p.181)

atheists
• But cheer up, something like half of us thought we were ***atheists*** or agnostics.(p.44)
• Instead of regarding ourselves as intelligent agents, spearheads of God's ever advancing Creation, we agnostics and ***atheists*** chose to believe that our human intelligence was the last word, the alpha and the omega, the beginning and end of all.(p.49)
• We agnostics and ***atheists*** were sticking to the idea that self-sufficiency would solve our problems.(p.52)

athlete
• I was club-man, ***athlete***, artist, musician, author, editor, aircraft pilot and world traveller.(p.432)

athletic
• I was strong and healthy and quite ***athletic***.(p.305)

athletics
• I was very much interested in ***athletics***, and because of this and parental influence, I didn't drink or smoke in either grade or high school.(p.287)
• I was raised like the majority of American boys, coming from a family of modest circumstances, attending public schools, having the social life of a small midwestern town, with part-time work and some ***athletics***.(p.373)

Atlanta
• I had run away from school to join the army in World War I, but missed it by one day since the Armistice was signed the very day I landed in ***Atlanta*** to sign up with Uncle Sam.(p.357)

Atlantic City
• This dry spell lasted for about three weeks; then I went to ***Atlantic City*** to attend several days' meeting of a national society of which I was a member.(p.179)
• As part of this promotion, they sent me to their national convention in ***Atlantic City*** to tell the big wheels how I'd done it.(p.243)

atmosphere
• These can then be discussed in an ***atmosphere*** of helpfulness and friendliness.(p.99)
• Or am I expecting to steal a little vicarious pleasure from the ***atmosphere*** of such places?"(p.101)
• When you have carefully explained to such people that he is a sick person, you will have created a new ***atmosphere***.(p.115)
• The expression on the faces of the women, that indefinable something in the eyes of the men, the stimulating and electric ***atmosphere*** of the place, conspired to let him know that here was haven at last.(p.160)
• When I walked into the friendly ***atmosphere*** of my first A.A. meeting, I knew I was where I belonged.(p.355)
• The ***atmosphere*** of "eat, drink, and be merry" prevails and I absorb it.(p.499)
• In this ***atmosphere*** the alcoholic often overcomes his excessive concentration upon himself.(p.572)

atop
• By the time I figured out what had happened, I saw two flashing red lights ***atop*** squad cars, sedately coming around the corner.(p.353)

attached
• Luckily, the garage was ***attached*** to the house.(p.442)

attachment
• Because of the employee's special ability, or of his own strong personal ***attachment*** to him, the employer has sometimes kept such a man at work long beyond a reasonable period.(p.137)

attack
• Shortly after I came to this conclusion, I was importuned by another well-known patent law firm to help them out on some trial work because their trial man had had a heart ***attack*** and had been forbidden to go into the courtroom.(p.220)
• I foresaw another heart ***attack***.(p.333)
• While I was at Pensacola my dad became dangerously ill and almost died of pneumonia plus a heart ***attack***.(p.426)
• Father says grace, which delays my ***attack*** on the buckwheat cakes and sausage.(p.497)

attacked
• Good generalship may decide that the problem be ***attacked*** on the flank rather than risk a face-to-face combat.(p.82)

attained
• The periods of sobriety ***attained*** by these thirteen A.A.'s range from fifteen to forty-six years.(p.169)

attainment
• Every reasonable desire was possible of ***attainment*** for me.(p.304)

attempt
• Every ***attempt*** failed.(p.33)
• We ***attempt*** to sweep away the debris which has accumulated out of our effort to live on self-will and run

the show ourselves.(p.76)
• It is important for him to realize that your ***attempt*** to pass this on to him plays a vital part in your own recovery.(p.94)
• ***Attempt*** instead, to put yourself in his place.(p.111)
• He may either plunge into a frantic ***attempt*** to get on his feet in business, or he may be so enthralled by his new life that he talks or thinks of little else.(p.125)
• Seeing your ***attempt*** to understand and help, some men will try to take advantage of your kindness.(p.141)
• There was always one more ***attempt*** -- and one more failure.(p.151)
• But they were much disgusted and told me they would ***attempt*** to struggle along without my presence.(p.173)
• The afternoon that I was to leave the hospital, he came in to see me and asked me if I were willing to ***attempt*** to follow the program.(p.218)
• I would make a feeble ***attempt*** at eating supper, but I never met with any howling success.(p.299)
• I was sent to a psychiatrist, for they didn't think it was normal for me to want to kill my platoon sergeant or to ***attempt*** suicide twice.(p.318)
• I succeeded in this ***attempt*** for approximately fifteen months with only a couple of slips.(p.343)
• In an ***attempt*** to get over that feeling, there was a quick onslaught of a greater number of drinks, and then all was lost.(p.346)
• So did the waterboy on the high school football team ***attempt*** to revenge himself on the big brother who was the star quarterback; for I was the waterboy and my brother was the star quarterback, innocent of everything except the fact that he was a star quarterback.(p.537)

attempted

• Then, gathering all his forces, he ***attempted*** to stop altogether and found he could not.(p.32)
• Next we launched out on a course of vigorous action, the first step of which is a personal housecleaning, which many of us had never ***attempted***.(p.63)
• After three years of this, I wound up in the local hospital where they ***attempted*** to help me, but I would get my friends to smuggle me a quart, or I would steal the alcohol about the building, so that I got rapidly worse.(p.175)
• Now I ***attempted*** to quit.(p.199)
• I can remember that in my childhood, he was ill at ease with the children because he ***attempted*** to assert an army discipline that had been ground into him during his three and a half years of army service.(p.210)
• I ***attempted*** nearly two years ago to make some amends and contact my children, but it wasn't God's time yet.(p.463)
• I felt very sorry for myself and ***attempted*** suicide on many occasions, making sure there was always somebody within reaching distance to see that I didn't finish the job.(p.478)
• In the meantime I had been indicted for the second crime, ***attempted*** murder.(p.508)

attempts

• Therefore, it is not surprising that our drinking careers have been characterized by countless vain ***attempts*** to prove we could drink like other people.(p.30)
• These ***attempts*** to do the impossible have always failed.(p.101)
• I had to persist in my ***attempts*** to get straightened out enough to be able to use the drinks I needed, without their turning on me.(p.227)
• My wife made several ***attempts*** to get me to stop and I had the usual visits from persons who would always ask me "Why?" -- as if I knew!(p.254)
• For this officer in the Indian Army, going on the wagon was not enough; ***attempts*** at control failed.(p.342)
• But my ***attempts*** at community service ended in a drunken and abusive row with a fellow volunteer.(p.410)
• My life there was a nightmare of periodic binges on alcohol and pills, adultery, unhappy hours at the dental office, seeing my wife give birth to our second child and have several miscarriages, living in a turbulent household, and making continual ***attempts*** to be the respectable dentist, husband, father, and community leader.(p.419)
• Three ***attempts*** to enlist in the service, and three failures because of being skinny.(p.499)

attend

• If we belong to a religious denomination which requires a definite morning devotion, we ***attend*** to that also.(p.87)
• If it is a happy occasion, try to increase the pleasure of those there; if a business occasion, go and ***attend*** to your business enthusiastically.(p.102)
• We suggest you draw the book to the attention of the doctor who is to ***attend*** your patient during treatment.(p.144)
• This dry spell lasted for about three weeks; then I went to Atlantic City to ***attend*** several days' meeting of a national society of which I was a member.(p.179)
• Shortly after that, my brother, who had then become associated with a group of people and had stopped drinking, urged me to ***attend*** meetings with him.(p.205)
• Then and then only, after a thorough indoctrination by eight or nine individuals, was I allowed to ***attend*** my first meeting.(p.291)
• One of them was that I would try to get a group started in Chicago; the second was that I would have to return to Akron to ***attend*** meetings at least every two months until I did get a group started in Chicago; third, I decided I must place this program above everything else, even my family, because if I did not maintain my sobriety I would lose my family anyway.(p.292)
• One is that I don't remember too many of them, as I was one of those drunks who could be on his feet and ***attend*** a meeting or a party, engage in a conversation with people and do things that any nearly normal person would do, and the next day not remember a thing about where I was, what I did, whom I saw, or how I got home.(p.301)
• He had tried everything from having me ***attend*** daily mass at six a.m. to performing the most menial labor for his charity patients.(p.306)
• Doctors were advised to ***attend*** patients who could be benefited by medicine.(p.307)
• I promised my two sponsors that I would ***attend*** their meeting the next Tuesday evening.(p.363)
• However, one thing I am certain of: Inmates in prison who ***attend*** A.A. have their chances of remaining free greatly enhanced -- this is a proved fact.(p.458)
• However, I still would not ***attend*** A.A. in prison.(p.461)
• Shortly thereafter, I was selected, with eight other inmates out of the 10,000 in the state's prisons at that time, to ***attend*** a school designed to take former "management problems" like me and convert them into paracounselors.(p.462)
• My visits to that sanitarium went on for nearly three years, until in March of 1944, my father died and I was too drunk to ***attend*** his funeral.(p.469)
• He went into the religious side and told me that I didn't ***attend*** church as regularly as I should, and that he felt, more or less, that this was responsible for my trouble.(p.489)
• But the more meetings you ***attend***, the more people you meet at these meetings, the clearer the Steps become.(p.516)

attendance

• We are greatly indebted to the doctor in ***attendance*** there, for he, although it might prejudice his own work, has told us of his belief in ours.(p.162)
• I had always been a good Catholic, possibly not so devoted as I should have been, but fairly regular in my ***attendance*** at services.(p.234)
• Most of my ***attendance*** there was when people would come in from the outside.(p.510)

attendant

• If hundreds of experiences have shown him that one drink means another debacle with all its ***attendant*** suffering and humiliation, why is it he takes that one drink?(p.22)
• They sent me up with an ***attendant***, and the ***attendant*** and I both arrived at the Egyptian Hospital rather the worse for wear.(p.521)

attended

• In late 1934 I ***attended*** a patient who, though he had been a competent businessman of good earning capacity, was an alcoholic of a type I had come to regard as hopeless.(p.xxiii)
• He ***attended*** church school, where he became rebellious at what he thought an overdose of religious education.(p.56)
• He ***attended*** church for the first time in many years.(p.80)
• In addition to these casual get-togethers, it became customary to set apart one night a week for a meeting to be ***attended*** by anyone or everyone interested in a spiritual way of life.(p.159)
• I ***attended*** their meetings every Sunday and Wednesday for about nine months.(p.202)
• If there was a lecture on the subject within a hundred miles of Akron, I ***attended***.(p.202)
• I had ***attended*** several of these meetings before I discovered that all those who were there were not alcoholics.(p.218)
• For there were of course periods of clear realization of what I had become, ***attended*** by memories of what I had been, what I had expected to be.(p.224)
• My parents had some vague idea of making a priest out of me and for some years I ***attended*** the Franciscan school at Basle, Switzerland, just across the border, about six miles from my home.(p.230)
• Until I was thirteen I ***attended*** public schools, with regular promotions and average grades.(p.240)
• While I went along with all that was done and ***attended*** the meetings, I never took an active job of leadership until February 1940.(p.249)
• By the time I was twenty-one I had six years of life in foreign countries, spoke three languages fluently, and had ***attended*** college for two years.(p.275)
• I have never ***attended*** an A.A. meeting, so it is essentially the literature that has kept me on the A.A. program.(p.342)
• I will never forget the first meeting that I ***attended***.(p.347)
• In the various schools I ***attended***, it was always a case of just getting by.(p.357)
• We ***attended*** meetings together, and mutually enjoyed our new found friends.(p.364)
• I ***attended*** my weekly meetings with regularity, reread the Big Book, ***attended*** other group meetings, gave leads when asked to and did some Twelve Step work whenever I was called upon to do so.(p.365)
• We visited most of that day and ***attended*** a meeting that night.(p.378)
• Nor have I ***attended*** them with a feeling of just doing my duty.(p.381)
• I ***attended*** meetings, I talked to my folks, I talked to younger people they had gotten in contact with to sponsor me.(p.430)
• It is true that the doctors and nurses in the various institutions I ***attended*** knew too.(p.470)
• I rebelled, and from that time on I don't think I ***attended*** church more than a dozen times.(p.489)
• So I ***attended*** as many meetings as possible.(p.516)
• I ***attended*** my first A.A. meeting eight years ago, and it is with deep gratitude that I'm able to say I've not had a drink since that time, and that I take no sedation or narcotics, for this program is to me one of complete sobriety and I no longer need to escape reality.(p.549)

attending

• But life among Alcoholics Anonymous is more than ***attending*** gatherings and visiting hospitals.(p.161)
• ***Attending*** his fourth or fifth meeting was an old friend I had not seen for twenty years.(p.365)
• I was raised like the majority of American boys, coming from a family of modest circumstances, ***attending*** public schools, having the social life of a small midwestern town, with part-time work and some athletics.(p.373)
• ***Attending*** meetings has never been a chore to me.(p.381)
• A "spiritual experience" to me meant ***attending*** meetings, seeing a group of people, all there for the purpose of helping each other; hearing the Twelve Steps and the Twelve Traditions read at a meeting, and hearing the Lord's Prayer, which in an A.A. meeting has such great meaning -- "Thy will be done, not mine."(p.381)
• I was ***attending*** a convention in Chicago and carousing day and night.(p.558)
• I acquired a sponsor and began ***attending*** meetings, but continued to drink.(p.559)

attends

• And with such good effect that the doctor agreed to a test among his patients and certain other alcoholics from a clinic which he ***attends***.(p.163)

attention

• My ***attention*** was caught by a doggerel on an old tombstone:(p.1)
• If a sufficiently strong reason -- ill health, falling in love, change of environment, or the warning of a doctor -- becomes operative, this man can also stop or moderate, although he may find it difficult and troublesome and may even need medical ***attention***.(p.21)
• If you draw this fallacious reasoning to the ***attention*** of an alcoholic, he will laugh it off, or become irritated and refuse to talk.(p.23)
• His ***attention*** to my wife.(p.65)
• We ask Him to remove our fear and direct our ***attention*** to what He would have us be.(p.68)
• If he says yes, then his ***attention*** should be drawn to you as a person who has recovered.(p.90)
• Keep his ***attention*** focussed mainly on your personal experience.(p.92)
• Admit that he probably knows more about it than you do, but call to his ***attention*** the fact that however

deep his faith and knowledge, he could not have applied it or he would not drink.(p.93)
• Still another difficulty is that you may become jealous of the *attention* he bestows on other people, especially alcoholics.(p.119)
• It will do little good if you point that out and urge more *attention* for yourself.(p.119)
• The problems of the community might engage *attention*.(p.131)
• Though you are providing him with the best possible medical *attention*, he should understand that he must undergo a change of heart.(p.143)
• We suggest you draw the book to the *attention* of the doctor who is to attend your patient during treatment.(p.144)
• It is not to be expected that an alcoholic employee will receive a disproportionate amount of time and *attention*.(p.149)
• As far as I know that was the first time I had ever paid any *attention* to that word.(p.187)
• It took me a year, or a year and a half to get to feeling physically well, and it was rather tough, but I soon found folks whose friendship I had once had, and I found, after I had been sober for quite some little time, that these people began to act like they had in previous years, before I had gotten so bad, so that I didn't pay too awful much *attention* to financial gains.(p.190)
• I seemed to react by developing a streak of varying meanness, which would cause me to do things to create excitement and to get *attention*.(p.211)
• And then I'd say, "God, don't pay any *attention* to me.(p.324)
• I was the center of *attention*, just what my sick ego craved.(p.407)
• We had a minor campaign or two and that helped distract *attention* from my drinking.(p.519)

attentions
• And just as we were being convinced of their heartlessness, they would surprise us with fresh resolves and new *attentions*.(p.107)

attic
• I climb to my room in the *attic*.(p.497)

attitude
• That the man who is making the approach has had the same difficulty, that he obviously knows what he is talking about, that his whole deportment shouts at the new prospect that he is a man with a real answer, that he has no *attitude* of Holier Than Thou, nothing whatever except the sincere desire to be helpful; that there are no fees to pay, no axes to grind, no people to please, no lectures to be endured -- these are the conditions we have found most effective.(p.18)
• The great fact is just this, and nothing less: That we have had deep and effective spiritual experiences which have revolutionized our whole *attitude* toward life, toward our fellows and toward God's universe.(p.25)
• He can go anywhere on this earth where other free men may go without disaster, provided he remains willing to maintain a certain simple *attitude*.(p.26)
• They flatly declare that since they have come to believe in a Power greater than themselves, to take a certain *attitude* toward that Power, and to do certain simple things, there has been a revolutionary change in their way of living and thinking.(p.50)
• With this *attitude* you cannot fail.(p.55)
• We have been trying to get a new *attitude*, a new relationship with our Creator, and to discover the obstacle in our path.(p.72)
• It may be he has done us more harm than we have done him and, though we may have acquired a better *attitude* toward him, we are still not too keen about admitting our faults.(p.77)
• Our whole *attitude* and outlook upon life will change.(p.84)
• We will see that our new *attitude* toward liquor has been given us without any thought or effort on our part.(p.85)
• It works, if we have the proper *attitude* and work at it.(p.86)
• This means a new *attitude* and spirit all around.(p.99)
• Experience shows that such an *attitude* is not helpful to anyone.(p.103)
• Some day we hope that Alcoholics Anonymous will help the public to a better realization of the gravity of the alcoholic problem, but we shall be of little use if our *attitude* is one of bitterness or hostility.(p.103)
• We urge you to try our program, for nothing will be so helpful to your husband as the radically changed *attitude* toward him which God will show you how to have.(p.117)
• The alcoholic, his wife, his children, his "in-laws," each one is likely to have fixed ideas about the family's *attitude* toward himself or herself.(p.122)
• A firm *attitude* at this point has helped many of us.(p.142)
• To get over drinking will require a transformation of thought and *attitude*.(p.143)
• While on the subject of confidence, can you adopt the *attitude* that so far as you are concerned this will be a strictly personal matter, that his alcoholic derelictions, the treatment about to be undertaken, will never be discussed without his consent?(p.143)
• You are betting, of course, that your changed *attitude* plus the contents of this book will turn the trick.(p.144)
• With this kind of employee such an *attitude* will command undying loyalty.(p.145)
• Perhaps this is a typical *attitude*.(p.149)
• They have a new *attitude*, and they have been saved from a living death.(p.150)
• When the others saw my altered *attitude* they took me back in, but for me they had to make it tough; if they hadn't I don't think I ever would have stuck it out.(p.248)
• My defiant *attitude* became worse.(p.265)
• Several months later dad was back in Chicago to pick me up again, but this time my *attitude* was entirely different.(p.289)
• He laid great stress on the progression of his *attitude* toward life and people, and most of his attitudes had been very similar to mine.(p.290)
• Mentally, the fears and tensions, the complete change in *attitude* and outlook, bewildered me.(p.378)
• Dishonest thinking, prejudice, ego, antagonism toward anyone and everyone who dares to cross him, vanity and a critical *attitude* are character defects that gradually creep in and become a part of his life.(p.380)
• That was my *attitude* toward A.A. at that time.(p.510)
• My personal definition, which I submit as applying only to myself (although everyone is welcome to it who wants it), includes every waking activity of the human being; to have a creative *attitude* towards things is a more exact meaning, to live and to deal with other human beings creatively, which to me means seeing the God in them, and respecting and worshipping this God.(p.535)
• I was immersed in self-pity and resentment, and the only people who would support this *attitude* or who I felt understood me at all were the people I met in bars and the ones who drank as I did.(p.547)
• He can only be defeated by an *attitude* of intolerance or belligerent denial.(p.570)

attitudes
• Most of us sense that real tolerance of other people's shortcomings and viewpoints and a respect for their opinions are *attitudes* which make us more useful to others.(p.19)
• Ideas, emotions, and *attitudes* which were once the guiding forces of the lives of these men are suddenly cast to one side, and a completely new set of conceptions and motives begin to dominate them.(p.27)
• Our women folk have suggested certain *attitudes* a wife may take with the husband who is recovering.(p.122)
• In telling newcomers how to change their lives and *attitudes*, all of a sudden I found I was doing a little changing myself.(p.249)
• I had been too self-sufficient to write a moral inventory, but I discovered in pointing out to the new man his wrong *attitudes* and actions that I was really taking my own inventory, and that if I expected him to change I would have to work on myself too.(p.249)
• He laid great stress on the progression of his attitude toward life and people, and most of his *attitudes* had been very similar to mine.(p.290)
• I need to concentrate not so much on what needs to be changed in the world as on what needs to be changed in me and in my *attitudes*.(p.449)
• For example, we are told in A.A. that we cannot afford resentments and self-pity, so we learn to avoid these festering mental *attitudes*.(p.560)

attorney
• I had gone to an *attorney* to see about getting a divorce during that year.(p.263)
• An *attorney* sat at the side of the bed where I was lying, and he sat on the edge of his chair and looked as innocent as a baby.(p.268)
• In a few days an *attorney* called on me and explained that something would have to be done as she couldn't face returning to me as I was.(p.377)
• It wasn't until later that he told me he was an *attorney*.(p.446)
• I went back to my mother's for a few days until things cooled off, because the District *Attorney* had put out a summons for me to come to see him in his office.(p.491)
• So I went down to talk to the District *Attorney*, and the arrangement was made that I would go home to stay with my mother, and that meant Vi and I were separated.(p.491)

attracted
• Alcoholics are being *attracted* from far and near.(p.161)
• About the time of the beer experiment I was thrown in with a crowd of people who *attracted* me because of their seeming poise, health, and happiness.(p.178)

attraction
• Our public relations were to be based upon *attraction* rather than promotion.(p.xix)
• My parents' car had a strong *attraction* to fences, and one night I blacked out and drove the car down a bank, ramming the steel fence around someone's backyard.(p.353)
• It made me feel quite grown-up and mature, and I think another added *attraction* was the fact that so far as my family was concerned, it was forbidden, and it had a special *attraction* for that reason.(p.464)
• Eleven -- Our public relations policy is based on *attraction* rather than promotion; we need always maintain personal anonymity at the level of press, radio and films.(p.564)
• Our public relations should be guided by the principle of *attraction* rather than promotion.(p.567)

attractive
• He has so *attractive* a personality that he makes friends with everyone.(p.39)
• Down the lobby a door opened into an *attractive* bar.(p.154)
• How can a person with a fine family, an *attractive* home, an excellent position and high standing in an important city become an alcoholic?(p.373)
• She was *attractive*; she was like the friends I had once had.(p.414)
• They were a couple of normal, sober, *attractive* men.(p.415)
• This really makes for an *attractive* woman!(p.479)

attributes
• That is one of man's magnificent *attributes*.(p.53)
• More than these *attributes*, they seemed to be happy.(p.178)

attuned
• Being wrecked in the same vessel, being restored and united under one God, with hearts and minds *attuned* to the welfare of others, the things which matter so much to some people no longer signify much to them.(p.161)

audience
• New programing was beginning to build an *audience*, but sponsors were pretty scarce.(p.360)

auditorium
• They were having a large A.A. meeting in the prison *auditorium*.(p.460)

augury
• Many of our friends encourage us by saying that this is but a beginning, only the *augury* of a much larger future ahead.(p.xv)

aunt
• At the age of sixteen, I was invited to spend the summer with an *aunt* and I, very delightedly, accepted the invitation.(p.261)
• When I came to my *aunt*, she knew that I had had an unhappy childhood, and she said, "Now, Ethel, you're welcome to have boy friends in our home, but there are two boys in this town that I don't want you to date, and one of them comes from a very fine family, one of the best.(p.262)
• My *aunt* had sharp words for me about drinking.(p.474)

aunt's
• I stay with him at *aunt's* house in Maine.(p.474)

auspices
• Dr. W.W. Bauer, broadcasting under the *auspices* of The American Medical Association in 1946, over the NBC network, said, in part: "Alcoholics Anonymous are no crusaders; not a temperance society.(p.572)

Australia
• A.A. has flourishing communities in the British Isles, the Scandinavian countries, South Africa, South America, Mexico, Alaska, *Australia* and Hawaii.(p.xv)
• I wanted to roam again and through relatives got a supercargo job on an Australian packet which allowed me to visit my people in *Australia* where I was born.(p.252)

Australian
• I wanted to roam again and through relatives got a

supercargo job on an *Australian* packet which allowed me to visit my people in Australia where I was born.(p.252)

authentication
• For them, we hope these pages will prove so convincing that no further *authentication* will be necessary.(p.xiii)

author
• Barleycorn's wringer squeezed this *author* – but he escaped quite whole.(p.432)
• I was club-man, athlete, artist, musician, *author*, editor, aircraft pilot and world traveller.(p.432)
• I, a man of steel, with very high ideals, well brought up, an honor student and the recipient of scholarships and prizes, a boy wonder in business – I, Bob, the *author* of this essay, looked and saw that the universe was beneath my contempt, and that to remove myself from it was the only thing of dignity a man could do.(p.531)
• There was the over-weening ambition to be the world's greatest *author*, when – at thirty-nine -- I had nothing of importance to say to the world.(p.534)
• Actually, of course, I wanted someone to listen to me, because when I had a few martinis inside, I became the great *author* I longed to be; and the right listener was in for some pretty highflown theories of literature and of genius.(p.536)

authorities
• Perhaps we have committed a criminal offense which might land us in jail if it were known to the *authorities*.(p.78)
• (1939) The *authorities* were much concerned.(p.163)
• I think the Commanding Officer was rather tired of this particular chicken coming back to roost so often because he very soon wrote in to the medical *authorities* to tell them that they had to get me into hospital, to be thoroughly examined for drinking.(p.520)
• Within a month, the police, the hospital *authorities*, several kind strangers, most of my friends, all of my close relatives, and a few adepts at rolling a drunk and removing his wrist watch and wallet had been involved.(p.532)

authority
• Those of us belonging to a religious denomination which requires confession must, and of course, will want to go to the properly appointed *authority* whose duty it is to receive it.(p.74)
• It wasn't very long until I had developed a pretty good brew with uniformity and plenty of *authority*.(p.232)
• I had never, since the believing days of childhood, been able to conceive an *authority* directing the universe.(p.259)
• Two – For our group purpose there is but one ultimate *authority* -- a loving God as He may express Himself in our group conscience.(p.564)
• 2. – For our group purpose there is but one ultimate *authority* -- a loving God as He may express Himself in our group conscience.(p.565)
• 4. – With respect to its own affairs, each A.A group should be responsible to no other *authority* than its own conscience.(p.565)
• 6. – Problems of money, property, and *authority* may easily divert us from our primary spiritual aim.(p.565)
• Experience has often warned us that nothing can so surely destroy our spiritual heritage as futile disputes over property, money, and *authority*.(p.566)
• They derive no real *authority* from their titles; they do not govern.(p.567)

authorized
• They are *authorized* by the groups to handle our over-all public relations and they guarantee the integrity of our principal newspaper, the A.A. Grapevine.(p.567)

authors
• My alcoholism-prone mind, however, reminded me that all great *authors* had needed a stimulus to build up inspiration and inventiveness before each day's work.(p.331)

auto
• They did not seem to be getting an answer, for here I was staying sober and selling lots of *auto* polish, on which they were making one thousand per cent profit.(p.247)
• So I rocked along my merry independent way until June, when I went out selling *auto* polish in New England.(p.247)

automatically
• We react sanely and normally, and we will find that this has happened *automatically*.(p.84)
• Then getting and staying honest with other people will come *automatically*.(p.482)

automobile
• He inherited a lucrative *automobile* agency.(p.35)
• I didn't want to jeopardize the lives of innocent people by driving an *automobile* while intoxicated, but I did.(p.199)
• I had an *automobile*.(p.200)
• There had been some occasions – there was an *automobile* wreck, for instance – when I had police escort home but not to jail, all of which, instead of doing me a favor, did me harm because I was then full of self-esteem as to the progress I had made both professionally and financially.(p.213)
• Bill and Hank had just taken over a small *automobile* polishing company and they offered me a job -- ten dollars a week and keep at Hank's house.(p.246)
• After being fired, I lined up with a new finance company that was just starting in business, and took the position of business promotion man, contacting *automobile* dealers.(p.300)
• I went to jail for the second time during this period for being drunk in an *automobile*.(p.549)

automobiles
• I had every advantage a child could have, private schools (several of them), dancing schools, two colleges, coon skin coats, *automobiles*, a listing in the social register and all the rest.(p.357)

automotive
• Offered the job of advertising manager for an eastern *automotive* company, I moved to Philadelphia to begin life anew.(p.254)

autonomous
• It was thought that no alcoholic man or woman could be excluded from our Society; that our leaders might serve but never govern; that each group was to be *autonomous* and there was to be no professional class of therapy.(p.xix)
• Four -- Each group should be *autonomous* except in matters affecting other groups or A.A. as a whole.(p.564)

autumn
• Immediately on her return we began to have formal meetings once a week, in the *autumn* of 1939, and we have continued to do this and to expand ever since.(p.295)

avail
• At a certain point in the drinking of every alcoholic, he passes into a state where the most powerful desire to stop drinking is of absolutely no *avail*.(p.24)
• I fought and struggled, but to no *avail*.(p.466)

available
• Notwithstanding the great necessity for discussing ourselves with someone, it may be one is so situated that there is no suitable person *available*.(p.74)
• Let him know you are *available* if he wishes to make a decision and tell his story, but do not insist upon it if he prefers to consult someone else.(p.96)
• He thought all alcoholics should constantly have chocolate *available* for its quick energy value at times of fatigue.(p.133)
• However, due to financial difficulties the whole printing was, for a while, held up and the book received no publicity, nor, of course, was it *available* in the stores, even if one knew it existed.(p.307)
• They told me to go to meetings, and I still do at every *available* opportunity, whether I am at home or in some other city.(p.381)
• I'm fortunate because I live in an era when A.A. is *available*, and I'm able to take advantage of it.(p.512)
• But not for long; now, for five Friday nights in a row, I went to jail, picked up sodden with beer (which I always disliked, but which was the only drink *available*); in jail five consecutive Friday nights in the town where I had grown up, where I had been an honor student in high school, where a kindly uncle, bailing me out, said, "Bob, our family just doesn't do this sort of thing."(p.539)
• (This address is now *available* in pamphlet form at nominal cost through most A.A. groups or from Box 459, Grand Central Station, New York, NY 10163, under the title "Three Talks to Medical Societies by Bill W." – formerly called "Bill on Alcoholism" and earlier "Alcoholism the Illness.")(p.572)

availed
• Half measures *availed* us nothing.(p.59)
• And then it went on to say: "Half measures *availed* us nothing.(p.349)
• "Complete abandon"; "Half measures *availed* us nothing"; "Thoroughly follow our path"; "Completely give oneself to this simple program" – rang in my swelled head.(p.349)

avenue
• Sitting in a Second *Avenue* bar, accepting drinks from anyone who offered, after my small stake was gone; or sitting at home alone, with the inevitable glass in my hand, I would remember, and remembering, I would drink faster, seeking speedy oblivion.(p.225)
• I was living in a small room on West 53rd Street right off Fifth *Avenue*, when I met a young lady who eventually was responsible for altering my entire way of living.(p.359)

avenues
• If he does not argue about religion, he will make new friends and is sure to find new *avenues* of usefulness and pleasure.(p.132)
• He had a desperate desire to stop, but saw no way out, for he had earnestly tried many *avenues* of escape.(p.155)

average
• We believe, and so suggested a few years ago, that the action of alcohol on these chronic alcoholics is a manifestation of an allergy; that the phenomenon of craving is limited to this class and never occurs in the *average* temperate drinker.(p.xxvi)
• We are *average* Americans.(p.17)
• One of these men, staff member of a world-renowned hospital, recently made this statement to some of us: "What you say about the general hopelessness of the *average* alcoholic's plight is, in my opinion, correct.(p.43)
• Their chances are less than *average*.(p.58)
• He will perceive that his spiritual growth is lopsided, that for an *average* man like himself, a spiritual life which does not include his family obligations may not be so perfect after all.(p.129)
• The general moral standard was, as I recall it, far above the *average*.(p.171)
• Both father and mother were considerably above the *average* in intelligence.(p.172)
• Until I was thirteen I attended public schools, with regular promotions and *average* grades.(p.240)
• Very rarely do I miss the meetings of my neighborhood A.A. group, and my *average* has never been less than two meetings a week.(p.249)
• With nothing but a liberal arts education, very definitely estranged from my family and already married, soon after graduation from college I became a bookmaker's clerk on the British racing circuits, far better off financially than the *average* professional man.(p.251)
• I grew up in a small town outside Akron, Ohio, where the life was typical of any *average* small town.(p.287)
• After holding good positions, making better than an *average* income for over ten years, I was in debt, had no clothes to speak of, no money, no friends, and no one any longer tolerating me but my wife.(p.301)
• He further explained that alcohol was no respecter of sex or background, but that most of the alcoholics he had encountered had better than *average* minds and abilities.(p.308)
• They were neither poor nor wealthy, but far better off than the *average* couple.(p.357)
• Saying these sprees were limited to one a week (they were not), and saying that the *average* spree was ten of these drinks (sometimes more, sometimes less), we come up with the first boring statistic: two-fifty per week out of twelve dollars.(p.397)
• For an estimate of salary from the twenty-one a month to start with, to over $400 per month upon my retirement after twenty years in the Navy, I believe that an *average* income of $2,000 a year over this period is low, but as I stated earlier, an underestimate is best.(p.399)
• Evening cocktails were as standard as morning coffee, and I suppose my *average* daily consumption ran a little more or less than a pint.(p.433)
• Our shoes are not better than the *average* hobo's, and if we are fortunate enough to have a pair of stockings on, nobody notices the runs in them, because of our dazzling beauty and our dirty feet.(p.479)
• I was born in a little town in Virginia in an *average* religious home.(p.483)
• I'm sure my ideas as to what life should be like were quite different from that of the *average* person with whom I associated.(p.483)
• On the other hand, I believe that I've always been medically inclined, though I have never been able to see medicine quite as the *average* person sees it.(p.485)
• From that point on, it's just the *average* drinker's story.(p.488)
• My drinking pattern isn't very different from the *average* you find in A.A.(p.512)
• In my own generation I stuck out, I can see that now, as being a very much heavier drinker than the *average* man.(p.518)
• Apparently I'd grown physically at the customary

rate of speed, and I had acquired an *average* amount of intellectual training in the intervening years, but there had been no emotional maturity at all.(p.547)

averages

• By the law of *averages*, some efforts came out well.(p.331)

aversion

• However, here I probably took my first step towards my coming alcoholism by developing a terrific *aversion* to all churches and established religions.(p.240)

avert

• With it you can *avert* death and misery for them.(p.124)

aviation

• I was transferred to Kaneohe Bay, across the hump to the windward side of Oahu, to the *aviation* base.(p.426)

avid

• Regaining my health, I became an *avid* jogger, sailor, and skier.(p.559)

avocation

• We would like it understood that our alcoholic work is an *avocation*.(p.xiii)

• An old *avocation*, the collecting of first editions, rare books and Americana, fascinated me between times.(p.255)

avoid

• I had had some success at speculation, so we had a little money, but we once worked on a farm for a month to *avoid* drawing on our small capital.(p.3)

• Had you offered yourselves as patients at this hospital, I would not have taken you, if I had been able to *avoid* it.(p.43)

• At first some of us tried to *avoid* the issue, hoping against hope we were not true alcoholics.(p.44)

• We *avoid* retaliation or argument.(p.67)

• We *avoid* hysterical thinking or advice.(p.70)

• Trying to *avoid* this humbling experience, they have turned to easier methods.(p.72)

• When possible, *avoid* meeting a man through his family.(p.91)

• Never *avoid* these responsibilities, but be sure you are doing the right thing if you assume them.(p.97)

• People have said we must not go where liquor is served; we must not have it in our homes; we must shun friends who drink; we must *avoid* moving pictures which show drinking scenes; we must not go into bars; our friends must hide their bottles if we go to their houses; we mustn't think or be reminded about alcohol at all.(p.100)

• So our rule is not to *avoid* a place where there is drinking, if we have a legitimate reason for being there.(p.101)

• *Avoid* urging him to follow our program.(p.113)

• You *avoid* the subject of drinking, even with your own parents.(p.114)

• *Avoid* answering these inquiries as much as you can.(p.115)

• If your husband is trying to live on a spiritual basis, he will also be doing everything in his power to *avoid* disagreement or contention.(p.118)

• That is why we are anxious that you understand, and that you *avoid* these unnecessary difficulties.(p.121)

• *Avoid* then, the deliberate manufacture of misery, but if trouble comes, cheerfully capitalize it as an opportunity to demonstrate His omnipotence.(p.133)

• Somehow I had always managed to *avoid* D.T.'s.(p.238)

• During that first year, however, I managed to make both ends meet, and to *avoid* ever going back to my old habit pattern of borrowing money when I could not earn it.(p.283)

• At age twenty-one, I enlisted in the Navy for two reasons: (1) to *avoid* being drafted into the Army, and (2) out of a burst of patriotic fervor inspired by the advent of World War II and as the result of an all-night drinking binge which found me sitting on the doorstep of the Navy recruiting office when the chief petty officer arrived to open for business at nine o'clock Monday morning.(p.398)

• The last time I drank, when I was twenty-nine, I drank for only four days, yet I threatened to kill my children; I beat my wife at home and on the church steps; I mistreated a child in my office; and I ran to a hospital for mental illness to *avoid* jail.(p.418)

• For example, we are told in A.A. that we cannot afford resentments and self-pity, so we learn to *avoid* these festering mental attitudes.(p.560)

• We think A.A. ought to *avoid* sensational advertising.(p.567)

avoidance

• About that period, too, came increasing procrastination and the *avoidance* of responsibilities.(p.197)

avoided

• But we don't delay if it can be *avoided*.(p.83)

• Argument and fault-finding are to be *avoided* like the plague.(p.98)

• Suppose we tell you some of the obstacles a family will meet; suppose we suggest how they may be *avoided* -- even converted to good use for others.(p.123)

• This sort of thing can be *avoided*.(p.126)

• I *avoided* them rather than explain why they weren't seeing me.(p.203)

• I had *avoided* a drink this time.(p.203)

• The sacred word was broken and you never trusted your father again, and *avoided* him.(p.533)

• My children *avoided* me.(p.558)

avoiding

• We are not fighting it, neither are we *avoiding* temptation.(p.85)

• Often you must carry the burden of *avoiding* them or keeping them under control.(p.117)

• This practice enables us to lend a hand, at the same time *avoiding* certain alluring distractions of the road, about which any traveling man can inform you.(p.162)

• Pretty soon, I wasn't going at all, and was *avoiding* those people who had been so kind to me.(p.203)

• I noticed that I was *avoiding* all my social friends except for my bridge.(p.324)

• Always we'd emerge with a new formula for *avoiding* future trouble.(p.433)

avoids

• Unlike the drinking driver, he *avoids* facing judges.(p.330)

await

• I was immediately arrested, arraigned in Homicide Court, held without bail, and remanded to the old Tombs Prison to *await* trial.(p.508)

awaiting

• I visit a friend who is *awaiting* orders.(p.499)

awaits

• In a vague way their families and friends sense that these drinkers are abnormal, but everybody hopefully *awaits* the day when the sufferer will rouse himself from his lethargy and assert his power of will.(p.23)

awake

• Morning after morning I would *awake* sick and with terrible jitters, but there was always a flask of liquor sitting on the table beside my bed.(p.183)

• Away from my office two or three weeks at a time; horrible days and nights when I would lie on the floor of my home, lying *awake* and reaching over to get the bottle, taking a drink and going back into oblivion.(p.184)

• Bill then related how he had lain *awake* nearly all night.(p.189)

• This time I seemed to be already *awake*, sitting upright in a big easy chair, in the middle of an animated conversation with a perfectly strange young woman, who didn't appear to think it strange.(p.222)

• So I stayed *awake*.(p.268)

• I would be half asleep and half *awake*, and in the morning, I would be both tired and stupid.(p.440)

awaken

• Both of you will *awaken* to a new sense of responsibility for others.(p.119)

awakened

• I painfully *awakened* each time, mentally, physically, and spiritually sick.(p.457)

awakening

• 12.Having had a spiritual *awakening* as the result of these steps, we tried to carry this message to alcoholics, and to practice these principles in all our affairs.(p.60)

• On *awakening* let us think about the twenty-four hours ahead.(p.86)

• Momentarily we did -- then would come oblivion and the awful *awakening* to face the hideous Four Horsemen -- Terror, Bewilderment, Frustration, Despair.(p.151)

• A spiritual *awakening* soon came to mean trying each day to be a little more thoughtful, more considerate, a little more courteous to those with whom I came in contact.(p.381)

• My spiritual *awakening* in A.A. finally resulted in my joining a church some years ago.(p.417)

• Sobriety and a plan for living that produces a personality change and a spiritual *awakening* are imperative.(p.459)

• Through A.A., many receive the needed change and *awakening* just by trying to live by A.A. principles and associating with A.A. people.(p.459)

• The terms "spiritual experience" and "spiritual *awakening*" are used many times in this book which, upon careful reading, shows that the personality change sufficient to bring about recovery from alcoholism has manifested itself among us in many different forms.(p.569)

award

• My guild had elected me president twice and later given me a "man of the year" *award*.(p.328)

• In 1951 the Lasker *Award* was given Alcoholics Anonymous.(p.573)

• "The American Public Health Association presents a Lasker Group *Award* for 1951 to Alcoholics Anonymous in recognition of its unique and highly successful approach to that age-old public health and social problem, alcoholism . . .(p.573)

awarded

• *Awarded* a scholarship to a famous old Eastern college, I began to drink at the end of my freshman year, and by junior year, I had to transfer to an easier state university to keep my grades up.(p.419)

aware

• We are *aware* that these matters are, from their very nature, controversial.(p.19)

• He is worried at times, and is becoming *aware* that he cannot drink like other people.(p.109)

• Painfully *aware* of being somehow abnormal, the man did not fully realize what it meant to be alcoholic.(p.155)

• At that time I was not *aware* of the almost unlimited supply the government made it possible for us doctors to obtain, neither had I any knowledge of the bootlegger who soon appeared on the horizon.(p.175)

• I was *aware* of symptoms of impending dependence, and I told myself I had gotten out of the rat race just in time to head off any booze problem.(p.327)

• I was keenly *aware* that my all-important security, which I had been constantly afraid of losing for four decades, no longer was endangered.(p.329)

• At a women's halfway house, I became associated with Alcoholics Anonymous and became *aware* of alcoholism as a disease, not just a "weakness."(p.371)

• It helped me a great deal to become convinced that alcoholism was a disease, not a moral issue; that I had been drinking as a result of a compulsion, even though I had not been *aware* of the compulsion at the time; and that sobriety was not a matter of willpower.(p.448)

• We are *aware* of the nice things around us, things we never noticed before in our drunken stupor.(p.481)

• In my late teens I became *aware* of emotions I'd not counted on; restlessness, anxiety, fear and insecurity.(p.545)

• Quite often friends of the newcomer are *aware* of the difference long before he is himself.(p.569)

awareness

• It has brought about a revelation of self, the discovery of an inner being, an *awareness* of God.(p.355)

• Most of us think this *awareness* of a Power greater than ourselves is the essence of spiritual experience.(p.570)

away

• I ruthlessly faced my sins and became willing to have my new-found Friend take them *away*, root and branch.(p.13)

• If he can afford it, he may have liquor concealed all over his house to be certain no one gets his entire supply *away* from him to throw down the waterpipe.(p.22)

• We know that while the alcoholic keeps *away* from drink, as he may do for months or years, he reacts much like other men.(p.22)

• Is not our age characterized by the ease with which we discard old ideas for new, by the complete readiness with which we throw *away* the theory or gadget which does not work for something new which does?(p.52)

• If our testimony helps sweep *away* prejudice, enables you to think honestly, encourages you to search diligently within yourself, then, if you wish, you can join us on the Broad Highway.(p.55)

• The barriers he had built through the years were swept *away*.(p.56)

• His alcoholic problem was taken *away*.(p.56)

• Take *away* my difficulties, that victory over them may bear witness to those I would help of Thy Power, Thy Love, and Thy Way of life.(p.63)

• We could not wish them *away* any more than alcohol.(p.66)

• We attempt to sweep *away* the debris which has accumulated out of our effort to live on self-will and run

the show ourselves.(p.76)
• We don't use this as an excuse for shying *away* from the subject of God.(p.77)
• Sometimes the man we are calling upon admits his own fault, so feuds of years' standing melt *away* in an hour.(p.78)
• If he opened that old affair, he was afraid it would destroy the reputation of his partner, disgrace his family and take *away* his means of livelihood.(p.80)
• Self-seeking will slip *away*.(p.84)
• Go or stay *away*, whichever seems best.(p.102)
• But for every man who drinks others are involved -- the wife who trembles in fear of the next debauch; the mother and father who see their son wasting *away*.(p.104)
• We have run *away*.(p.105)
• Don't let him get *away* with it.(p.108)
• His friends have slipped *away*, his home is a near-wreck and he cannot hold a position.(p.110)
• Maybe you have already been obliged to put him *away*.(p.110)
• If not, it had better be found out right *away*.(p.120)
• Cessation of drinking is but the first step *away* from a highly strained, abnormal condition.(p.122)
• It will take time to clear *away* the wreck.(p.123)
• He may not see at once that he has barely scratched a limitless lode which will pay dividends only if he mines it for the rest of his life and insists on giving *away* the entire product.(p.129)
• If he says yes, does he really mean it, or down inside does he think he is fooling you, and that after rest and treatment he will be able to get *away* with a few drinks now and then?(p.142)
• He may, for example, reveal that he has padded his expense account or that he has planned to take your best customers *away* from you.(p.145)
• If you take it, your past will be forgotten and the fact that you went *away* for treatment will not be mentioned.(p.147)
• Inwardly he would give anything to take half a dozen drinks and get *away* with them.(p.152)
• With a shiver, he turned *away* and walked down the lobby to the church directory.(p.154)
• Many an alcoholic who entered there came *away* with an answer.(p.160)
• A community thirty miles *away* has fifteen fellows of Alcoholics Anonymous.(p.161)
• Clear *away* the wreckage of your past.(p.164)
• All have now passed *away* from natural causes, having maintained complete sobriety.(p.169)
• *Away* from my office two or three weeks at a time; horrible days and nights when I would lie on the floor of my home, lying awake and reaching over to get the bottle, taking a drink and going back into oblivion.(p.184)
• We're not up here trying to take any of your rights or privileges *away* from you, but we have a program whereby we think we can stay sober.(p.186)
• I lost money, and then just fooled *away* a large part of that profit.(p.194)
• I could work a deal up to where all I had to do was to go ahead with it; all the planning had been done, all the financing had been done, but then I'd say "Nuts to it!" and walk *away*.(p.197)
• I told him I'd take the medicine and I would take it, but I hadn't told him when, and thereupon I got *away* with the third drink.(p.206)
• Whenever a situation arose that fast talk wouldn't explain *away*, I simply withdrew.(p.214)
• The interne came along with a glassful of bleached lightning that put me *away* for about fifteen hours.(p.217)
• From far *away*, as if in a delirium, I heard my own voice – calling someone "Dorothy," talking of dress shops, of jobs . . . the words came clearer . . . this sound of my own voice frightened me as it came closer . . . and suddenly, there I was, talking of I knew not what, to someone I'd never seen before this very moment.(p.222)
• Cold chills started chasing up and down my spine; my teeth were chattering; my hands were shaking so I tucked them under me to keep them from flying *away*.(p.222)
• I had them hidden *away* in the house and all over my shop in careful concealment.(p.233)
• My wife wrote *away* for advertised cures for the liquor habit and gave them to me in coffee.(p.235)
• Sniffing at emotional religion, I walked *away*.(p.256)
• Right *away*, I saw it was the same outfit this other guy told me about, and then again hope died.(p.267)
• He said, "Let's put the Big Book *away* again, and when you read it again, turn to the back and read some of the stories.(p.269)
• I often think how that could have turned some people *away*, because there were no other women alcoholics there then.(p.269)
• He talked about his wife taking his little boy *away* from him because of his drinking, and how he got back together with them through A.A., and we began feeling grateful right then that all these things hadn't been taken from us.(p.270)
• I used to think I was cowardly because when things came out pertaining to the program that troubled me, I said to her many times, "Annie, am I being a coward because I lay those things *away* on the shelf and skip it?"(p.273)
• He spent eighteen years in running *away*; and then found he didn't have to run.(p.275)
• I could not expect to keep what I had gained unless I gave it *away*.(p.282)
• I, carried *away* with the desire to serve A.A., gave what was probably one of the first radio broadcasts about A.A., living through a case of mike fright and feeling like a million dollars when it was all over.(p.283)
• I have faced life instead of running *away* from it.(p.285)
• It was therefore not extraordinary that I should shy *away* from any serious thought of marriage for a great many years after joining A.A.(p.286)
• I do feel, though, that the fact that I finally grew up to a point where I could even tackle such a job is the apex of the story of a man who spent eighteen years running *away* from life.(p.286)
• They went into a huddle and dad explained that he simply took my pants, shoes and money *away*, so that I could get no liquor and had to sober up.(p.288)
• After finding every bottle that I had hidden around the apartment, she took *away* my pants, my shoes, my money and my keys, threw them under the bed in the back bedroom and slip-locked our door.(p.288)
• When I said yes, we both knelt at his desk and prayed, each of us asking to have these defects taken *away*.(p.292)
• That was my lesson, that one could not take the moral inventory and then file it *away*; that the alcoholic has to continue to take inventory every day if he expects to get well and stay well.(p.293)
• Upon leaving the office in the evening, my first stop would be a saloon about a block *away*.(p.298)
• This would get me feeling fit, and then I would start for home and fireside, thirteen miles *away*.(p.299)
• Even some of the saloon-keepers, where I had spent so much time and money, requested that I stay *away* from their places.(p.301)
• I moved a thousand miles *away* from home to Chicago and a new environment.(p.305)
• And all the while my fear fed a growing conviction that before long it would be necessary for me to be put *away* in some institution.(p.306)
• Either they die of acute alcoholism or they develop wet brains and have to be put *away* permanently."(p.308)
• I walked *away* from that girl grinding my teeth and cursing under my breath.(p.322)
• As my son, our second child, came along, and as he became school age and was *away* at school most of the time, something happened.(p.323)
• *Away* down deep, I was motivated into dishonest behavior because I was a people-pleaser.(p.328)
• Nobody could take *away* my retirement income.(p.329)
• My writing career was described in the couplet "Alcohol gave me wings to fly,/And then it took *away* the sky."(p.331)
• And of course a half empty bottle wasn't worth keeping, so I finished it up and naturally had to get more in right *away* for the people who "might come in unexpectedly."(p.336)
• Toward five o'clock, helter-skelter, I'd get everything put *away* and try to get supper on the table, and after supper I'd finish the job up and knock myself out.(p.337)
• On the second, I knew – as I know now – that if I remained *away* from the first drink, then I had not to worry about the hundredth one.(p.344)
• Without hesitation, I did the only logical thing -- ran *away* from home.(p.354)
• And the only one who can take it *away* from me is me – by taking that first drink.(p.355)
• This man faced the last ditch when his wife's voice from 1,300 miles *away* sent him to A.A.(p.356)
• I had run *away* from school to join the army in World War I, but missed it by one day since the Armistice was signed the very day I landed in Atlanta to sign up with Uncle Sam.(p.357)
• Like all alcoholics endeavoring to run *away* from themselves and their environment, I decided to go to New York.(p.358)
• The challenge intrigued me; also it was another opportunity to run *away* from myself and the "fast life of the big city."(p.359)
• I kept *away* from liquor and eagerly waited.(p.363)
• She said she cut this clipping from the paper at about ten on the same night, and at the same time as I called A.A. in Pittsburgh -- some 1300 miles *away*.(p.367)
• We soon resumed our marriage, even moved *away* from the street of sad memories and found a new home.(p.371)
• I knew this, and right *away* I got furious and would not even talk to the doctor in the place.(p.387)
• But now, with His help and grace, this child of His has paid his initiation fee for good, as long as he remembers to stay *away* from that first drink (the one that does all the damage) one day at a time.(p.399)
• At eighteen I ran *away* from home.(p.401)
• I think I had the physical allergy right *away*.(p.402)
• He saw that I was unsettled, living *away* from my family and renting houses here and there.(p.403)
• I was accepting help with one hand and pushing it *away* with the other.(p.407)
• It combined running *away* from my world, and drinking all I wanted to.(p.407)
• She was duly sent to school, *away* from me.(p.409)
• Only A.A. kept me from running *away*.(p.420)
• I ran *away* for the second time, with another lad.(p.424)
• I wanted to get as far *away* from home as possible.(p.426)
• When I stopped living in the problem and began living in the answer, the problem went *away*.(p.449)
• I can tell her she ought not to think a certain way, but I certainly can't take *away* her right to feel however she does feel.(p.451)
• Same thing when I let lye and water eat *away* at four of my toes and my foot for five hours.(p.458)
• Finally, I threw *away* all my books and decided never to return to A.A.(p.460)
• If I failed, they would throw *away* the key, and I would never get out again.(p.461)
• Then I remember him coming into my room one night with a friend, and telling me to get dressed -- we were going *away*.(p.466)
• On one occasion when I was serving time in my favorite drying-out place while I was having a session with the psychiatrist, she left my case history on her desk when she was called *away* from the room.(p.470)
• She realized that, and the way I felt, and so for my own good she gradually began to pull *away*.(p.472)
• I join Canadian Army, but could not run *away* from problem.(p.474)
• Tell him I want to get *away* from bottle and misery.(p.475)
• Then, of course, there are always the wrinkled slacks, which have been slept in and are so dirty, they could walk *away* by themselves.(p.479)
• I had not recognized her, but as soon as she said who she was I remembered her right *away*.(p.493)
• It has flown *away*.(p.497)
• Those that understand me are far *away*.(p.505)
• The fear and the insane idea are taken *away*.(p.505)
• I want to sell the place and move *away*.(p.506)
• He finally passed *away*, and the fear of him left me.(p.508)
• Finally, he was drinking to keep *away* those little men, and those strange voices, and the organ music that came out of the walls.(p.512)
• I was drinking to keep *away* the shakes, drinking to keep *away* those little men and those strange voices and the organ music that comes out of the walls.(p.514)
• It passes *away*.(p.516)
• They weren't quite so up-to-date on my history and I got *away* with about four years with them.(p.520)
• The Commanding Officer only spoke to me when he wanted to tell me exactly who I was and what I was and how little I counted in the scheme of things and how glad he would be if I went *away*.(p.520)
• Poor, black, totally ruled by alcohol, she felt shut *away* from any life worth living.(p.526)
• I got out on bail right *away*, but when I went to trial, the judge gave me thirty days.(p.528)
• Only, having found them, I threw them *away*, and ordered another extra dry martini.(p.533)
• One by one, the understanding friends dropped *away*.(p.538)
• I went back home, to a job of manual labor where for a little while I was able to keep *away* from alcohol.(p.539)

• But I remembered the years of agony preceding the binge, I remembered the years I had thrown ***away***.(p.540)
• Fear of rejection and its ensuing pain were not to be risked, and I turned ***away*** from myself once more for the answer, this time to the drinks I had always refused before, and in alcohol I found a false courage.(p.546)
• I've had many spiritual experiences since I've been in the program, many that I didn't recognize right ***away***, for I'm slow to learn and they take many guises.(p.551)
• I found myself being lifted onto a stretcher and whisked ***away*** in an ambulance to a strange hospital.(p.558)

awe

• It was fun to carom around the exclusive course which had inspired such ***awe*** in me as a lad.(p.4)
• There was a feeling of ***awe*** and wonder, but it was fleeting and soon lost.(p.46)

awful

• Momentarily we did – then would come oblivion and the ***awful*** awakening to face the hideous Four Horsemen -- Terror, Bewilderment, Frustration, Despair.(p.151)
• Of course, we had talked over quite a number of the failings that I had and made a sort of an inventory, which wasn't too difficult, because I had an ***awful*** lot of things wrong that were very apparent to me, because I knew all about them.(p.190)
• It took me a year, or a year and a half to get to feeling physically well, and it was rather tough, but I soon found folks whose friendship I had once had, and I found, after I had been sober for quite some little time, that these people began to act like they had in previous years, before I had gotten so bad, so that I didn't pay too ***awful*** much attention to financial gains.(p.190)
• That is the way Jackie found me, lying on a cot in my skivvies, with hot and cold sweats, pounding heart and that ***awful*** itchy scratchiness all over.(p.238)
• Well, I wasn't sure I did, and it was ***awful*** foggy, and I wept and asked her what she thought I ought to do about it.(p.273)
• There is no more "aloneness," with that ***awful*** ache, so deep in the heart of every alcoholic that nothing, before, could ever reach it.(p.312)
• I took two or three drinks so my eyes could focus, and I could see that horrible picture of the ***awful*** drunk on the first page; he couldn't get the drink to his mouth, he had a towel around his hand and he needed a shave.(p.391)
• I had learned an ***awful*** lot about myself in that one little article.(p.393)
• Well, I'm willing, if it will curb this ***awful*** desire to drink, this fear of not having a drink, this feeling of always being alone, scared, deserted, sick.(p.430)
• The trip back was completed in one of those dead, ***awful*** silences.(p.467)
• There was that ***awful*** alcoholic loneliness.(p.467)
• To this day I can't hear that song without remembering that ***awful*** Christmas.(p.468)

awfully

• I remember telling them too that it was going to be ***awfully*** tough, because I did some other things, smoked cigarettes and played penny ante poker, sometimes bet on the horse races and they said, "Don't you think you're having more trouble with this drinking than with anything else at the present time?(p.190)
• I think it's ***awfully*** hard on people, especially if they're new people, to hear these long drawn out talks.(p.273)
• But it began to be an ***awfully*** painful answer as hangovers, blackouts, trouble, and remorse set in.(p.353)
• I sure had been working ***awfully*** hard of late.(p.360)
• They were ***awfully*** good about not cutting me off.(p.409)

awfulness

• For always, over and above everything else, was the ***awfulness*** of the lack of meaning in life.(p.535)

awoke

• One morning, after I had been on a binge for a couple of days, I ***awoke*** to find my brother and Doctor Bob in my room talking to me about not drinking.(p.206)
• Because it affected me so strenuously, they felt that hospitalization was indicated and I ***awoke*** in a hospital.(p.207)
• An hour later I ***awoke*** to a new world.(p.280)
• I don't mean that I went to bed one night a normal drinker, and ***awoke*** the next morning an alcoholic.(p.464)
• When I ***awoke*** in the middle of the night with shakes and sweats and fears, I would hear my wife weeping quietly in bed beside me.(p.558)
• I ***awoke*** next day with tubes in both arms.(p.558)

AWOL

• We heard by wireless on the 5th that the Armistice would be signed the next day (this was a premature report) so I had a couple of cognacs to celebrate; then I hopped a truck and went ***AWOL***.(p.242)

axes

• That the man who is making the approach has had the same difficulty, that he obviously knows what he is talking about, that his whole depórtment shouts at the new prospect that he is a man with a real answer, that he has no attitude of Holier Than Thou, nothing whatever except the sincere desire to be helpful; that there are no fees to pay, no ***axes*** to grind, no people to please, no lectures to be endured -- these are the conditions we have found most effective.(p.18)

Bb

babe

• I was thirty-two, a ***babe*** in Boozeville.(p.328)

babies

• I had two ***babies***.(p.335)

baby

• My wife traveled with me, but with a ***baby*** coming I decided to settle in a large city where I got a job with a commission agent which is a polite term for a hand-book operator.(p.251)

• Saying goodbye to my wife and ***baby***, I was treading Manhattan's streets in a little more than a week.(p.252)

• An attorney sat at the side of the bed where I was lying, and he sat on the edge of his chair and looked as innocent as a ***baby***.(p.268)

• The birth of a ***baby*** boy did nothing toward staying the downward spiral.(p.278)

• When she finally took the ***baby*** and left, I locked myself in the house and stayed drunk for a month.(p.278)

• I sleep like a ***baby***, and never give a thought to such a thing as insomnia.(p.303)

• When I was called upon for a few words I had to tell my friends that I wasn't one year old in A.A. that evening but only a "nine month ***baby***."(p.366)

• When I was a ***baby***, my mother brought me to America, and I never again saw my father.(p.401)

• But we have a ***baby*** who, if you'll pardon a little post-alcoholic sentimentality, is right out of Heaven.(p.438)

• I think the thing that galled me was that just after Easter I had drawn my salary for two weeks' work and had decided that I was going to send some money to Vi; and above all else I was going to send my ***baby*** daughter an Easter outfit.(p.493)

• My wife and new ***baby*** are fortunately staying with relatives.(p.500)

• I have been drinking while the ***baby*** was arriving.(p.502)

bachelor

• I moved into a "***bachelor*** hall."(p.277)

• However, I must have felt, deep down inside myself, that living the selfish life of a ***bachelor*** was only half living.(p.286)

back

• They believe in themselves, and still more in the Power which pulls chronic alcoholics ***back*** from the gates of death.(p.xxv)

• I went ***back*** to the bar.(p.4)

• As I drank, the old fierce determination to win came ***back***.(p.4)

• There were flights from city to country and ***back***, as my wife and I sought escape.(p.6)

• That war-time day in old Winchester Cathedral came ***back*** again.(p.10)

• This sometimes nearly drove me ***back*** to drink, but I soon found that when all other measures failed, work with another alcoholic would save the day.(p.15)

• ***Back*** of them is a world of ignorance and misunderstanding.(p.20)

• As we look ***back***, we feel we had gone on drinking many years beyond the point where we could quit on our will power.(p.34)

• But the day he comes out he races in front of a fire engine, which breaks his ***back***.(p.38)

• One day we were told that he was ***back*** in the hospital.(p.40)

• The story he told is most instructive, for here was a chap absolutely convinced he had to stop drinking, who had no excuse for drinking, who exhibited splendid judgment and determination in all his other concerns, yet was flat on his ***back*** nevertheless.(p.40)

• I would not go ***back*** to it even if I could."(p.43)

• We went ***back*** through our lives.(p.65)

• We turned ***back*** to the list, for it held the key to the future.(p.66)

• Let no alcoholic say he cannot recover unless he has his family ***back***.(p.99)

• In some cases the wife will never come ***back*** for one reason or another.(p.99)

• We have seen others slip when the family came ***back*** too soon.(p.100)

• When we look ***back***, we realize that the things which came to us when we put ourselves in God's hands were better than anything we could have planned.(p.100)

• Now you are getting ***back*** into the social life of this world.(p.102)

• Our friends have counseled chucking the men and we have done so with finality, only to be ***back*** in a little while hoping, always hoping.(p.105)

• As animals on a treadmill, we have patiently and wearily climbed, falling ***back*** in exhaustion after each futile effort to reach solid ground.(p.107)

• Let's now go ***back*** to husband number one.(p.110)

• Show him these things in yourself and they will be reflected ***back*** to you from him.(p.118)

• The good old days will soon be ***back***, they think.(p.123)

• Sometimes they demand that dad bring them ***back*** instantly!(p.123)

• I seemed to be able to snap ***back*** the next morning better than most of my fellow drinkers, who were cursed (or perhaps blessed) with a great deal of morning-after nausea.(p.172)

• Many mornings I have gone to classes, and even though fully prepared, would turn and walk ***back*** to the fraternity house because of my jitters, not daring to enter the classroom for fear of making a scene should I be called on for recitation.(p.173)

• I was, of course, soon on the carpet and the upshot was that I had to go ***back*** for two more quarters and remain absolutely dry, if I wished to graduate.(p.174)

• Finally my father had to send a doctor out from my home town who managed to get me ***back*** there in some way, and I was in bed about two months before I could venture out of the house.(p.175)

• I drank with moderation at first, but it took me only a relatively short time to drift ***back*** into the old habits which had wound up so disastrously before.(p.175)

• I used to put eight or twelve ounce bottles of alcohol in a fur lined glove and toss it onto the ***back*** airing porch when winter days got dark enough.(p.176)

• My bootlegger had hidden alcohol at the ***back*** steps where I could get it at my convenience.(p.176)

• When beer first came ***back***, I thought that I was safe.(p.177)

• Away from my office two or three weeks at a time; horrible days and nights when I would lie on the floor of my home, lying awake and reaching over to get the bottle, taking a drink and going ***back*** into oblivion.(p.184)

• They left this with me to think over, and I lay there on that hospital bed and went ***back*** over and reviewed my life.(p.186)

• So, when they came ***back***, I told them.(p.187)

• I said, "Yes, Doc, I would like to quit, at least for five, six, or eight months, until I get things straightened up, and begin to get the respect of my wife and some other people ***back***, and get my finances fixed up and so on."(p.187)

• Then I remember when the boys came ***back***, that I told them, "I have gone to this Higher Power and I have told Him that I am willing to put His world first, above everything.(p.190)

• I spent most of my time trying to get ***back*** these friendships, and to make some recompense towards my wife, whom I had hurt a lot.(p.191)

• Of course, as time went on, and I began to get my health ***back*** and began to be so I didn't have to hide from people all the time, it's just been wonderful.(p.192)

• He wouldn't give me any money for the groceries, but he did take me across the street and buy me a bag of candy, which I later took ***back*** and traded for a loaf of bread.(p.193)

• When I was sixteen years old, my mother remarried and I was given the opportunity of going ***back*** to school.(p.193)

• I went into the high school grades, but having missed all the intermediate grades, I didn't get along too well, so I developed the habit of going ***back*** to school just long enough for the football season and then quitting.(p.193)

• I could take one drink and get right ***back*** on the wagon.(p.202)

• And I continued to drink, on and off then, until every dollar I had in the world was gone again and I was right ***back*** living at my sister's, getting my cigarettes by calling her grocer and telling him to put in a couple of cartons with her order, exactly as I had before I started to work at Max's.(p.202)

• So I didn't have a beer one night, and as I drove home I was breaking my arm patting myself on the ***back*** because I had proved I could lick liquor.(p.203)

• So Paul was dispatched and brought ***back*** a pint.(p.206)

• As I look ***back***, all the brothers developed personality problems.(p.210)

• I went ***back*** to law school, and doubled up on the courses because I was then approaching thirty years of age and I wanted to get through as quickly as possible.(p.212)

• In fact, as I look ***back***, I have often thought that they probably concluded that they would put up with me for a couple of years, that I couldn't live much longer, and that they would inherit whatever was left of the practice.(p.215)

• Had anyone undertaken to explain to me what the A.A. movement was, what its real function was, I probably would have been set ***back*** several years and I doubt if I would have survived at all.(p.216)

• It took three-quarters of an hour and two changes to get there – ***back*** to my starting point.(p.223)

• That went on for two more months before I landed in a hospital and started my slow fight ***back*** to normalcy.(p.224)

• When I look ***back*** on that last horrible year of constant drinking I wonder how I survived it either physically or mentally.(p.224)

• When I got ***back*** to Germany I settled down to finish my apprenticeship, drinking the wine of the country as usual.(p.231)

• I was eased out of the business I had founded and was reduced to doing general upholstery in a small shop at the ***back*** of my house.(p.233)

• ***Back*** at camp, all was forgiven because it was the End, but in the light of what I have since learned I know I was a confirmed alcoholic at nineteen.(p.242)

• With the war over, and ***back*** in Baltimore with the folks, there were several small jobs for three years and then I went to work soliciting as one of the first ten employees of a new national finance company.(p.242)

• My next job was in sales promotion for an oil company in Mississippi where I promptly became high man and got lots of pats on the ***back***.(p.242)

• After the oil job blew up, I went ***back*** to Baltimore and mother, my first wife having said a permanent "Goodbye."(p.243)

• As long as things were tough and the job a challenge I could always manage to hold on pretty well, but as soon as I learned the combination, got the puzzle under control and the boss to pat me on the ***back***, I was gone again.(p.243)

• Evidently I had gone right ***back*** to the movie with a bottle, stayed there several hours and started home with no recollection of what had happened.(p.244)

• Just give me a good front and a couple of bucks and I'd be right ***back*** in the big time.(p.246)

• I tried to contact the boys in New York, but telegrams bounced right ***back*** and when I finally got Hank on the telephone he fired me right then.(p.247)

• Peddling off my polish samples for expenses, I crawled ***back*** to New York a few days later in a very chastened frame of mind.(p.248)

• When the others saw my altered attitude they took me ***back*** in, but for me they had to make it tough; if they hadn't I don't think I ever would have stuck it out.(p.248)

• Tom Sharkey's brawling bar on 14th Street and the famous wine-room at the ***back*** were headquarters for me.(p.251)

• I was soon ***back*** in Liverpool.(p.252)

• Drifting ***back*** to Ohio, I landed on a small newspaper and later was impressed into the direction of boy-welfare work at the local "Y."(p.253)

• As I look ***back*** on the events of two months, I can clearly see that I had been circling around, half-afraid of encountering the remedy for my situation, half wanting it, deferring fulfillment of my promise to get in touch with the doctor I had heard about.(p.258)

• As soon as I could get up and walk I started to drink again and kept it up until my friend of the hospital, who, in his first try at the new way of life had stubbed his toe in Chicago but had come ***back*** to the town to take counsel and make a new start, picked me up and got me into a hospital.(p.258)

• I look ***back*** and remember these things because they made me very unhappy, and added to my feeling of inferiority at never being the same as other people.(p.261)

• Finally, it got so bad that I left him and went ***back*** home and took my two children with me.(p.262)

• I looked much older than I was, I was always large,

and I went **back** to work in this job.(p.262)
• He had taken up light work, and he had a safety valve and a pair of spurs and the clothes on his **back**, and that was all.(p.263)
• He got a job and went **back** to work.(p.263)
• As I look **back**, I was very broken up about it.(p.263)
• And another thing, it's a wonder they didn't throw us **back** in because I could become very dignified and sarcastic.(p.264)
• He said, "Let's put the Big Book away again, and when you read it again, turn to the **back** and read some of the stories.(p.269)
• He talked about his wife taking his little boy away from him because of his drinking, and how he got **back** together with them through A.A., and we began feeling grateful right then that all these things hadn't been taken from us.(p.270)
• I remember sometime, it was possibly six months after we had been going steadily to King School, that we were coming home from a meeting and saw a car along the way, and a fellow in **back** drinking a bottle of beer.(p.271)
• Fear froze me in my tracks, but the instant I turned **back** toward home this paralyzing fear left me.(p.276)
• When I reached a point directly **back** of our house, where I could have cut through a friend's garden, I was almost overpowered by the desire to get home, but I made the whole journey.(p.276)
• The details of the long road **back** to something resembling normal living -- the first short streetcar ride, the purchase of a used bike which enabled me to widen the narrow horizon of life, the first trip downtown – I will not dwell on.(p.276)
• It is well over sixteen years since I came **back** to life.(p.280)
• During that first year, however, I managed to make both ends meet, and to avoid ever going **back** to my old habit pattern of borrowing money when I could not earn it.(p.283)
• This was the beginning of five years of bounding **back** and forth between my home in Chicago and Akron to sober up.(p.288)
• After finding every bottle that I had hidden around the apartment, she took away my pants, my shoes, my money and my keys, threw them under the bed in the **back** bedroom and slip-locked our door.(p.288)
• I jimmied the front door so that I could get **back** in, and walked out.(p.288)
• Then when we got **back** to the apartment, he was willing to wait two or three days until I got my health **back** to be paid off for the liquor and fare.(p.289)
• He waited until I was completely sober and the day before I was to head **back** for Chicago, he told me of a small group of men in Akron who apparently had the same problem that I had but were doing something about it.(p.289)
• He said they were sober, happy and had their self-respect **back** as well as the respect of their neighbors.(p.289)
• But I had my health **back** and besides, I reasoned, they were much worse than I would ever be.(p.289)
• Several months later dad was **back** in Chicago to pick me up again, but this time my attitude was entirely different.(p.289)
• He was happy, getting a kick out of life and people, and beginning to get his medical practice **back** again.(p.290)
• As I look **back** on that first evening I realize that I began to hope, then, for the first time; and I felt that if he could regain these things, perhaps it would be possible for me too.(p.290)
• The day before I was due to go **back** to Chicago, a Wednesday and Dr. Bob's afternoon off, he had me down to the office and we spent three or four hours formally going through the Six-Step program as it was at that time.(p.291)
• The next day I went **back** to Chicago and started a vigorous campaign among my so-called friends or drinking companions.(p.293)
• On my trips **back** to Akron to get my spirits recharged and to work with other alcoholics, I would ask Dr. Bob about this delay and wonder just what was wrong with me.(p.293)
• At that time, I was living out of town, so I moved **back** to the home town and made a connection in a responsible position with one of the larger companies in the finance business.(p.298)
• I had a tough pull **back** to normal good health.(p.310)
• Finally, I reenlisted to go **back** to Nam.(p.318)
• When I was released from the hospital, I went **back** to my unit, and nothing had changed.(p.319)
• I still couldn't make it through the nights without drinking, so I went **back** into the hospital, this time to a rehabilitation center.(p.320)
• As we walked **back** through the hall, I, for the first time in my life, said to another human being, "I'm having trouble with my drinking, too."(p.321)
• We had a small child, and I loved her dearly, so that held me **back** quite a bit in my drinking career.(p.322)
• In the old days I hated to wake up and look **back** at what last night was like.(p.325)
• How hurt I was when editors bounced **back** my ideas quickly and my best friends opined that my output needed a lot of rewriting.(p.331)
• I'd just take a couple or three barbiturates to get **back** to sleep -- eating my alcohol.(p.333)
• Whatever it was, it brushed all the heavy burdens off my **back**.(p.334)
• When alcohol took me over, my bar was my kitchen, my living room, my bedroom, the **back** bathroom, and the two hampers.(p.335)
• I paced **back** and forth in the apartment with the cold sweats.(p.338)
• But I had to get **back** to that first drink somehow.(p.339)
• He had come **back**, however, and he was on this program.(p.346)
• In my stupid way I went up to see him with the idea in the **back** of my mind that I would investigate Alcoholics Anonymous from a medical standpoint.(p.346)
• And then we went up the side of a hill where we have a little barbecue area to make the fire for the barbecue, and on the way up, I thought to myself – I'll go **back** down to the kitchen and refill this drink.(p.347)
• Looking **back**, it is surprising to me now that I managed to keep working and have enough money to squander at the various spots in the big city.(p.358)
• Once again I was **back** in the big time operations, and along with them, big shot complexes.(p.361)
• I was going to prove to her that liquor wasn't necessary in my life, and above all that I still loved her more than anything else in the world and that I wanted her **back**.(p.362)
• We came **back** to Pittsburgh as happy as a bride and groom.(p.364)
• I went **back** to my group meetings, but not wholeheartedly, and I often skipped them with the excuse that I was too tired.(p.364)
• While I was in Florida trying to convince my wife with all the A.A. literature that she should come **back** to me, she went over to her desk and picked up a clipping she had taken from the St. Petersburg Times about A.A.(p.366)
• Emma ran out to the kitchen and came **back** with a water glass full of bourbon and made me drink it down.(p.385)
• I had no feeling of security, and I knew that I had done a very stupid thing, so I went **back** to Texas and remarried my ex-husband.(p.386)
• That went on for about three years, and then we moved **back** to Texas again.(p.386)
• He hesitated to send me **back** to that hospital.(p.388)
• But somewhere during that time, I remembered going **back** on the bunk and crying my eyes out.(p.390)
• So I wrote this letter in very shaky handwriting, and in just one week came **back** a letter with A.A. literature from New York.(p.392)
• He said, "Wait until I get **back** and I will go with you to see this man."(p.393)
• A retired Navy man looks **back** over twenty years of drinking, to add up his A.A. "initiation fee."(p.396)
• In the **back** of my mind, I probably thought, "They won't take me as drunk as I am."(p.398)
• We came **back** East and met both families.(p.402)
• Others have come **back**, others I have lost.(p.404)
• I returned from Europe a while after that encounter, and I never went **back**.(p.406)
• A load weighing a thousand pounds came off my **back**.(p.414)
• On the train going **back**, Anne's one idea was to get to the nearest bar.(p.415)
• When I went **back** to my hometown to go into private practice, I experienced another brief lull in my addiction to alcohol and drugs.(p.420)
• In A.A., I have had to be torn down and then put **back** together differently.(p.420)
• Most important, A.A. has enabled me to go **back** and start growing up all over again in all areas of my life.(p.420)
• I remembered **back** to high school when I was fifteen.(p.423)
• ***Back*** home again!(p.424)
• I was escorted **back** to San Diego next morning -- by the Shore Patrol, but I was discharged on schedule.(p.428)
• I thought, "If this is A.A. why not go **back** to drinking, kill myself with booze in the next three years the doctor had given me, and call it a bad job?"(p.430)
• I'd claw my way **back** to "respectability" and stay there – until the inevitable next time.(p.432)
• I crawled **back** to my analyst, not so much because I had faith in him, but because I had nowhere else to turn.(p.435)
• With a problem like that, I couldn't go **back** to sleep.(p.441)
• The longer the drinking continued, the shorter the time the alcohol would keep me asleep; I would have to drink myself **back** to sleep again and again throughout the night.(p.441)
• If it was one minute before five, I'd drink myself **back** to sleep.(p.441)
• The answer came right **back**: I'd give him something to pep him up.(p.441)
• One night, I had to put myself **back** to sleep three times, and then I finally decided to give it up.(p.443)
• One has to be pretty sick to do that, and perhaps one has to be even sicker to come **back** every day for a new list, as she did.(p.446)
• We sat in the **back** and talked only to each other.(p.447)
• And we found ourselves **back** in prison, where our personalities became even more warped.(p.459)
• Ten days of this treatment the first time knocked me from 200 pounds to 130, and I seldom stayed out of the hole long enough to gain **back** my weight.(p.460)
• I left California and came **back** to my native state.(p.460)
• Fortunately, I received only fifteen-twenty years, and I went **back** to my alma mater (where I had spent so much time in the hole).(p.461)
• I go **back** to my old alma mater occasionally to give A.A. talks, and -- just think! -- the warden is my friend.(p.462)
• So we turned around and started **back** to Washington.(p.467)
• The trip **back** was completed in one of those dead, awful silences.(p.467)
• I went out to a restaurant, found a booth way **back** in the rear, and started drinking.(p.467)
• And then I went **back** home to live with my parents, and the merry-go-round started again – only this time I didn't have to worry about waking up behind bars in a psychiatric ward.(p.468)
• Actually it had, way **back** in 1940.(p.469)
• In my screwed up mind I kept thinking I could have gone to A.A. way **back** there in 1940, and perhaps saved my marriage and home.(p.469)
• And A.A. took this wreck of a woman and brought her **back** to life.(p.470)
• And I landed right smack **back** in that sanitarium that I had gone to so often.(p.472)
• I really do believe it is much harder for a woman to gain **back** her self-respect than it is for a man.(p.480)
• Men are supposed to be tough and rugged to start with, but if a woman becomes that way, it is pretty hard to get **back** the niceties of womanhood.(p.480)
• Since then, I have never been **back** to heroin.(p.480)
• Of course, when father finally came to Virginia to work his way through school, he resented the southern "cracker," as he often called them, so much that he didn't even go **back** to his mother's funeral.(p.486)
• At that time the repeal whiskies were **back**, and I'd go to the store and buy my whiskey and take it to my office and put it under the desk, first in one place and then in another, and there soon was an accumulation of empty bottles.(p.488)
• The following day, Saturday, he came **back** and said, "Jim, I owe you for that prescription last night.(p.488)
• Then I decided that I'd go **back** to Washington, which I did.(p.490)
• I went **back** to my mother's for a few days until things cooled off, because the District Attorney had put out a summons for me to come to see him in his office.(p.491)
• He came **back** several times.(p.491)
• I sometimes gave it to my mother and then I'd go **back** and hound her for it.(p.491)
• I worked in the steel mill for possibly two months, and then I became disgusted with myself and decided to go **back** home.(p.492)
• I just gathered up this and that alcoholic, because, in the **back** of my mind, I wanted to save all the world.(p.496)
• A wasp is crawling up the **back** of the lady in front of me.(p.497)
• Now **back** to the exam.(p.499)
• I go **back** to the hotel and get more gin.(p.501)
• One man comes **back**, closing the door behind him.(p.503)
• I crawl **back** into bed and sleep like a child.(p.504)

• I shall not drink until I get ***back*** to the apartment.(p.506)
• I ***back*** up to the door and go into the house.(p.506)
• An ailment developed in one of my eyes, and I was transferred ***back*** to Sing Sing and operated upon.(p.509)
• However, my two friends kept coaxing and cajoling to get me ***back*** again.(p.510)
• I remember the day I came ***back*** to New York.(p.513)
• I had just come off a good one, and I went ***back*** on to the next one.(p.514)
• I knew it, and I turned for help to someone upon whom I had turned my ***back*** for many years.(p.515)
• I went ***back*** to the old family doctor who had helped me the first time I had the D.T.'s.(p.515)
• When I look ***back***, I can't see anything that would have predisposed me towards being either a neurotic or a drunk.(p.517)
• There was nothing in my school life that I can look ***back*** on which was responsible for anything that happened afterwards.(p.517)
• When I came ***back***, I told the priest, the Chaplain of the place, exactly what I thought of him and he didn't like it.(p.517)
• I buttonholed him after dinner and gave him a few tips on how to run his colony better and the result of that was about a fortnight or so later I was shipped ***back*** to my regiment.(p.520)
• At the end of that time, they shipped me ***back*** to my regiment again.(p.520)
• I think the Commanding Officer was rather tired of this particular chicken coming ***back*** to roost so often because he very soon wrote in to the medical authorities to tell them that they had to get me into hospital, to be thoroughly examined for drinking.(p.520)
• I was never to be allowed ***back***.(p.521)
• I stopped off just to have one drink to see if it tasted the same on the way ***back*** to London, and that night I was carried ***back*** to bed again.(p.522)
• So I decided I'd go ***back*** and live in Ireland to try the geography cure.(p.522)
• When I arrived ***back*** in Dublin, I had no friends left.(p.522)
• But if I came ***back*** in the usual state, then I'd have to go off for good the next day.(p.523)
• I had been using paraldehyde more or less like ordinary drink for the last six years though, occasionally, I'd bounce ***back*** to phenobarbital and things like that.(p.524)
• Since I joined on that April night, A.A. has done more for me than just stop me from drinking; it has brought me ***back*** to life again.(p.524)
• It has brought me ***back*** to a realization of my Maker and my duties to Him.(p.525)
• In time, I began to go out and forget the way ***back*** home.(p.527)
• He said if I came ***back*** again, they would send me to the state hospital.(p.528)
• When my thirty days were up, I started ***back*** on my rounds.(p.528)
• Was I the disloyal sort who would turn his ***back*** on this, my last and truest friend?(p.539)
• I went ***back*** home, to a job of manual labor where for a little while I was able to keep away from alcohol.(p.539)
• ***Back*** to the big city, for another year of precarious living, paid for largely by one or two friends I still had not milked dry or worn to exhaustion with demands on their bounty.(p.540)
• The doc and I went ***back*** into the house.(p.541)
• It wasn't strong enough, so I added a shot of vodka -- and was right ***back*** to worse trouble than before.(p.556)
• Each time, I went ***back*** to drinking -- even smuggling a bottle of vodka into the hospital as soon as the blood transfusions had ceased.(p.558)
• While there, I read the Big Book and the Grapevine and began the slow road ***back*** to health and sanity through the recovery program of A.A.(p.559)
• By learning -- through practicing the Twelve Steps and through sharing at meetings -- how to cope with the problems that we looked to booze to solve, ***back*** in our drinking days.(p.560)
• Even among those who occasionally land ***back*** in here again, we observe a profound change in personality.(p.572)

backfired

• As long as it eased situations socially, it helped just fine, but somewhere along the line, it ***backfired***.(p.386)

background

• Get an idea of his behavior, his problems, his ***background***, the seriousness of his condition, and his religious leanings.(p.90)
• This was the ***background*** that made me willing to listen on January 8th.(p.245)
• I come from a very poor family in material things, with a fine Christian mother, but with no religious ***background***.(p.261)
• He further explained that alcohol was no respecter of sex or ***background***, but that most of the alcoholics he had encountered had better than average minds and abilities.(p.308)
• The Higher Power to whom I had turned, and who had sustained me, had once again been thrust into the ***background***, while my emotions were running my life and, as always, my emotions ran me to the bottle.(p.472)

backgrounds

• All sections of this country and many of its occupations are represented, as well as many political, economic, social, and religious ***backgrounds***.(p.17)

backing

• To duplicate, with such ***backing***, what we have accomplished is only a matter of willingness, patience and labor.(p.163)
• I think the longest drunk I was ever on was eleven days, but usually only two days with a complete blackout for a day, and then ***backing*** off by drinking as long as I could get anything.(p.203)

backs

• No monkeys on our ***backs***.(p.329)

backwards

• Then, one day in A.A., I was told that I had the lenses in my glasses ***backwards***; "the courage to change" in the Serenity Prayer meant, not that I should change my marriage, but rather that I should change myself and learn to accept my spouse as she was.(p.451)

backyard

• My parents' car had a strong attraction to fences, and one night I blacked out and drove the car down a bank, ramming the steel fence around someone's ***backyard***.(p.353)

bad

• We hope no one will consider these self-revealing accounts in ***bad*** taste.(p.29)
• It may be worth a ***bad*** case of jitters if you get a full knowledge of your condition.(p.32)
• Commencing to drink after a period of sobriety, we are in a short time as ***bad*** as ever.(p.33)
• We first saw Fred about a year ago in a hospital where he had gone to recover from a ***bad*** case of jitters.(p.39)
• My old manner of life was by no means a ***bad*** one, but I would not exchange its best moments for the worst I have now.(p.43)
• When ready, we say something like this: "My Creator, I am now willing that you should have all of me, good and ***bad***.(p.76)
• When your husband is ***bad***, you become a trembling recluse, wishing the telephone had never been invented.(p.115)
• Though it is infinitely better that he have no relapse at all, as has been true with many of our men, it is by no means a ***bad*** thing in some cases.(p.120)
• Everybody knows that those in ***bad*** health, and those who seldom play, do not laugh much.(p.132)
• But these scrapes can generally be charged, no matter how ***bad***, to the abnormal action of alcohol on his mind.(p.140)
• Can you charge this off as you would a ***bad*** account and start fresh with him?(p.145)
• How can they rise out of such misery, ***bad*** repute and hopelessness?(p.153)
• This went from ***bad*** to worse until Sophomore spring when, after a prolonged period of drinking, I made up my mind that I could not complete my course, so I packed my grip and went South to spend a month on a large farm owned by a friend of mine.(p.173)
• Of course, the result was very ***bad***, and that ended the beer experiment.(p.178)
• That wasn't so ***bad***, to tell it to another drunk.(p.185)
• They said, "We've got some ***bad*** news for you.(p.187)
• It was ***bad*** news for us, and it will probably be ***bad*** news for you.(p.187)
• It took me a year, or a year and a half to get to feeling physically well, and it was rather tough, but I soon found folks whose friendship I had once had, and I found, after I had been sober for quite some little time, that these people began to act like they had in previous years, before I had gotten so ***bad***, so that I didn't pay too awful much attention to financial gains.(p.190)
• On Sunday when I came to, it was a ***bad***, wet, snowy day in February, 1937, and Paul and Doc and a lot of other fellows were in Cleveland on business.(p.207)
• All during Prohibition, every alcoholic felt that he made the best hooch, regardless of how ***bad*** it was.(p.213)
• I had had no hospitalization up to this time because I would not call doctors when I was getting over a ***bad*** one.(p.217)
• Finally, it got so ***bad*** that I left him and went back home and took my two children with me.(p.262)
• I had ***bad*** nervous headaches, particularly at the base of my neck.(p.277)
• After a particularly ***bad*** Christmas and New Year's holiday, dad picked me up again early in January, 1937, to go through the usual sobering up routine.(p.289)
• I could not possibly be that ***bad***.(p.289)
• At the moral inventory, he brought up some of my ***bad*** personality traits or character defects, such as selfishness, conceit, jealousy, carelessness, intolerance, ill-temper, sarcasm and resentments.(p.292)
• One morning when I was feeling really ***bad***, I was put on K.P. and the head cook wanted me to go out and scrub the garbage cans.(p.317)
• If ever I got that ***bad*** . . .(p.332)
• I had forgotten "If I ever I get that ***bad***, I'll try A.A."(p.333)
• For the next couple of hours a terrible battle went on between the good gremlins and the ***bad*** ones, one faction urging me to tell the truth, the other telling me to sit tight and say nothing.(p.366)
• Gradually the quantity increased, the occasions for a drink came more frequently; a hard day, worries and pressure, ***bad*** news, good news -- there were more and more reasons for a drink.(p.374)
• I wasn't entirely immoral; I wasn't ***bad***; I wasn't vicious.(p.392)
• I spent eighteen hundred dollars fixing up that car in the first year I was home, after four ***bad*** smashups.(p.429)
• I thought, "If this is A.A. why not go back to drinking, kill myself with booze in the next three years the doctor had given me, and call it a ***bad*** job?"(p.430)
• And should I have more ***bad*** times, I know that I'll never again have to go through them alone.(p.438)
• A.A. and acceptance have taught me that there is a bit of good in the worst of us and a bit of ***bad*** in the best of us; that we are all children of God and we each have a right to be here.(p.449)
• And if I don't know what's good for me, then I don't know what's good or ***bad*** for you or for anyone.(p.450)
• When I focus on what's good today, I have a good day, and when I focus on what's ***bad***, I have a ***bad*** day.(p.451)
• I thought that was ***bad*** until I hit the hole at a prison camp; it was just wide enough and long enough to lie down in.(p.459)
• I was one of those ***bad*** cons nobody can reach.(p.460)
• It was in Washington, D.C. that this transition took place, and that the really ***bad*** part of alcoholism began happening.(p.465)
• Things went from ***bad*** to worse, and since I had finally and completely failed at the job of being a wife and a mother, my marriage ended.(p.468)
• My husband interrupted, "She's ***bad*** enough now without getting mixed up with a bunch of drunks."(p.469)
• I want to stop this ***bad*** life, but where to turn?(p.475)
• Call friend in A.A. when ***bad*** thoughts come.(p.477)
• We lived just a few doors from the First Baptist Church and when they had funerals I remember very often asking my mother whether the person was good or ***bad*** and whether they were going to heaven or hell.(p.483)
• During the years 1930 to 1935, due to the Depression and its aftermath, business went from ***bad*** to worse.(p.486)
• For the first couple of years it wasn't too ***bad*** because the momentum kept things going.(p.486)
• Things had just gone from ***bad*** to worse.(p.487)
• There came a time when she spoke to me about it, and I would say that I had a ***bad*** cold or that I wasn't feeling well.(p.487)
• Matters got worse all the time until finally they got so ***bad*** that I was reinvestigated by the Government.(p.490)
• Then I had my first ***bad*** stomach hemorrhage.(p.490)

- Father is an Episcopal minister and his work takes him over long drives on ***bad*** roads.(p.497)
- This wasn't so ***bad*** after all.(p.498)
- The man is in ***bad*** mental shape certainly.(p.503)
- Finances are in ***bad*** shape.(p.506)
- I rolled along with the mob this way, that way and the other way, but in those years nothing really ***bad*** happened to me.(p.508)
- Things got so ***bad***, I was afraid to go on the street, so I turned to Mothers' Aid.(p.527)
- Despite my wife's entreaties to take it easy that day, I arrived home in ***bad*** shape.(p.557)
- Soon my drinking was as ***bad*** as ever -- all day long every day.(p.557)

bad-intentioned
- We realize some men are thoroughly ***bad-intentioned***, that no amount of patience will make any difference.(p.108)

bade
- The sheriff ***bade*** us goodbye very happily.(p.424)

badly
- He may have the habit ***badly*** enough to gradually impair him physically and mentally.(p.20)
- Most alcoholics have to be pretty ***badly*** mangled before they really commence to solve their problems.(p.43)
- Now about health: A body ***badly*** burned by alcohol does not often recover overnight nor do twisted thinking and depression vanish in a twinkling.(p.133)
- From a business standpoint, his trip came off ***badly***.(p.153)
- Most of the time therefore, I did not take the morning drink which I craved so ***badly***, but instead would fill up on large doses of sedatives to quiet the jitters, which distressed me terribly.(p.176)
- Wishing to be polite, though I felt very ***badly***, I said, "Let's make the call," and extracted from my wife a promise that we would not stay over fifteen minutes.(p.179)
- I spend a great deal of time passing on what I learned to others who want and need it ***badly***.(p.180)
- I was bounding along and not doing too ***badly***.(p.204)
- I was ***badly*** beaten.(p.204)
- My physical health was ***badly*** shaken, but I began to pick up.(p.220)
- Naturally, in spite of my good intentions, in spite of my protected life behind sanitarium walls, I several times got drunk, and was astounded . . . and ***badly*** shaken.(p.227)
- We need them so ***badly*** even if you can only give one day, or perhaps two days?"(p.326)
- I wanted so ***badly*** to see the picture as it was in her mind.(p.355)
- One of the things I needed ***badly*** was business for the station.(p.360)
- They sent me the regular letter they send to everybody else, but along with it, Ruth Hock, the nonalcoholic secretary, wrote a longhand note because she could see from the letter that I really needed help ***badly***.(p.392)
- This physician, the originator of A.A.'s first black group, but ***badly*** caught in the toils, tells of his release and of how freedom came as he worked among his own people.(p.483)
- I'm grateful because that Higher Power led me to A.A. a little over three years ago, when I needed it very ***badly***.(p.512)
- The Abyssinian war broke out just as things were going very ***badly*** for me, and I went off to Egypt on a job there.(p.519)
- Too often, I would overdo it and behave ***badly*** at the very time I wanted to be at my best!(p.556)
- The doctor pronounced it a ***badly*** enlarged liver and said I had to quit drinking.(p.557)

baffle
- We will intuitively know how to handle situations which used to ***baffle*** us.(p.84)

baffled
- Once this malady has a real hold, they are a ***baffled*** lot.(p.23)
- Once confused and ***baffled*** by the seeming futility of existence they show the underlying reasons why they were making heavy going of life.(p.50)
- Tell him how ***baffled*** you were, how you finally learned that you were sick.(p.92)
- Up to that time, I was so completely ***baffled*** by my behavior that I had never really stopped to think at all.(p.392)

baffling
- More ***baffling*** still, he could give himself no satisfactory explanation for his fall.(p.26)
- This is the ***baffling*** feature of alcoholism as we know it -- this utter inability to leave it alone, no matter how great the necessity or the wish.(p.34)
- Remember that we deal with alcohol -- cunning, ***baffling***, powerful!(p.58)
- It was so ***baffling***, so heartbreaking.(p.107)
- Cunning, ***baffling***, powerful -- the gradual creeping up of the frequency and quantity of alcohol, and what it does to a person is apparent to everyone but the person involved.(p.375)
- The ***baffling*** problem of getting drunk when I had every intention of staying sober was simplified.(p.379)
- The other side of the coin was sinister, ***baffling***.(p.432)

bag
- He wouldn't give me any money for the groceries, but he did take me across the street and buy me a ***bag*** of candy, which I later took back and traded for a loaf of bread.(p.193)
- First, my new wife had walked out, ***bag***, baggage and furniture; then the apartment landlord had thrown me out of the empty apartment and the finish was the loss of another job.(p.238)
- That night she too had new hope because I had made sure she would know what I was doing about my drinking by packing every bit of A.A. literature I could put my hands on right on top so she couldn't help but see it when she opened my ***bag***.(p.364)
- I didn't feel I could lie in bed and squirt the stuff in my veins while my kids and wife stood around watching me, so I kept the drug in my ***bag*** and the ***bag*** in the car and the car in the garage.(p.442)
- My husband helped me into the house, packed himself a ***bag***, and gave me some money.(p.467)
- I pack my ***bag*** and leave.(p.505)
- When the policeman released me to my stupefied and exasperated friend at four in the morning, I went to my traveling ***bag*** and groped until I found -- well, let the officer speak: "Ah," said the policeman, "he's got anuder pair, t'ank God!"(p.538)

baggage
- First, my new wife had walked out, bag, ***baggage*** and furniture; then the apartment landlord had thrown me out of the empty apartment and the finish was the loss of another job.(p.238)

baggy
- My tweed suit, once a very good one, was shapeless and ***baggy*** with bare places worn in the elbows from leaning on the bar.(p.411)

bags
- I would have to return to New York and pick up my bills and ***bags***.(p.213)

bail
- I was immediately arrested, arraigned in Homicide Court, held without ***bail***, and remanded to the old Tombs Prison to await trial.(p.508)
- I got out on ***bail*** right away, but when I went to trial, the judge gave me thirty days.(p.528)

bailing
- But not for long; now, for five Friday nights in a row, I went to jail, picked up sodden with beer (which I always disliked, but which was the only drink available); in jail five consecutive Friday nights in the town where I had grown up, where I had been an honor student in high school, where a kindly uncle, ***bailing*** me out, said, "Bob, our family just doesn't do this sort of thing."(p.539)

baker
- I recall, as I walked into that meeting, saying to myself, "Here I am, a fellow of the American College of Surgeons, a Fellow of the International College of Surgeons, a diplomate of one of the great specialty boards in these United States, a member of the American Psychiatric Society, and I have to go to the butcher, the ***baker*** and the carpenter to help make a man out of me!"(p.347)
- I tried every gimmick that there was to get some peace of mind, but it was not until I was brought to my alcoholic knees, when I was brought to a group in my own community with the butcher, the ***baker***, the carpenter and the mechanic, who were able to give me the Twelve Steps, that I was finally given some semblance of an answer to the last half of the First Step.(p.349)

bakery
- At the other side of the table sat one of the carpenters in our community, and at the further end of the table sat the man who ran the ***bakery***, while on one side sat my friend who was a mechanic.(p.347)

balance
- I honestly doubted whether, on ***balance***, the religions of mankind had done any good.(p.11)
- He said he had finally learned that drinking was a fatal illness made up of an allergy plus an obsession, and once the drinking had passed from habit to obsession, we were completely hopeless, and could look forward only to spending the ***balance*** of our lives in mental institutions or to death.(p.290)
- In the next two or three days the ***balance*** of this handful of men contacted me, encouraged me, and told me how they were trying to live this program of recovery and the fun they were having doing it.(p.291)
- That discovery so intrigued me, that I stayed on that diet almost entirely for the ***balance*** of my extensive drinking life.(p.298)
- I clung to the outfit for the ***balance*** of my time, and finally I was released, after having spent twenty years and nine months behind bars.(p.510)

balanced
- He is often perfectly sensible and well ***balanced*** concerning everything except liquor, but in that respect he is incredibly dishonest and selfish.(p.21)
- To all appearance he is a stable, well ***balanced*** individual.(p.39)
- Father will necessarily spend much time with other alcoholics, but this activity should be ***balanced***.(p.131)

balked
- At some of these we ***balked***.(p.58)

ball
- But did not we, ourselves, set the ***ball*** rolling?(p.67)
- So he inquired, what did our friend have on the ***ball***?(p.163)
- Eventually, there would be a ***ball*** game, or a show, or some sort of special occasion to celebrate and I would turn up drunk.(p.196)
- When I finally returned to Detroit to find work and to learn to stand on my own feet, the ***ball*** was already rolling, however slowly.(p.282)

balls
- During my first year out of college I had endless dates, and went to countless dances, ***balls*** and dinner parties.(p.275)

balmy
- They suspect father is a bit ***balmy***!(p.128)
- I had thought that I was completely different from other people, that I was beginning to become a little ***balmy***, even to the point of withdrawing more and more from society and wanting to be alone with my bottle.(p.290)

Baltimore
- My early life was spent in ***Baltimore*** where my father was a physician and a grain merchant.(p.240)
- With the war over, and back in ***Baltimore*** with the folks, there were several small jobs for three years and then I went to work soliciting as one of the first ten employees of a new national finance company.(p.242)
- After the oil job blew up, I went back to ***Baltimore*** and mother, my first wife having said a permanent "Goodbye."(p.243)

balustrades
- After my last binge I came home and smashed my dining room furniture to splinters, kicked out six windows and two ***balustrades***.(p.435)

band
- I was married and divorced again before I was twenty-three years old, this time to a prominent ***band*** leader -- a man that many women wanted.(p.546)

bang
- I really started drinking with a ***bang***.(p.323)

banged
- He had gone through the windshields of cars a couple of times and was pretty well ***banged*** up.(p.510)

banished
- It would be wonderful were I able to tell you that my confidence in God and my application of the Twelve Steps to my daily living have utterly ***banished*** fear.(p.284)

bank
- One day he told me about an executive of the same ***bank*** who, from his description, was undoubtedly alcoholic.(p.138)
- I felt this was inevitable and wondered if the ***bank*** was doing the man an injustice.(p.138)
- Everything in the world a man could possibly want, and I was driving from Akron to Cleveland, having just been to the ***bank*** and discovered that I had approximately $5,000.(p.200)
- My parents' car had a strong attraction to fences, and one night I blacked out and drove the car down a ***bank***, ramming the steel fence around someone's backyard.(p.353)
- It was I who had to tell the ***bank***, after a certain time, to refuse all further deposits.(p.409)
- I borrowed five hundred dollars from the ***bank*** and

three hundred from the loan shop, and I drank that up pretty fast.(p.490)
• The doctor bills are heavy and the ***bank*** account is low.(p.501)

bankbook
• I had turned eighteen during the trip, and I despondently returned home by jet (on Daddy's ***bankbook***) to a pair of miserable, hurt parents.(p.354)

banker
• The local ***banker*** watched me whirl fat checks in and out of his till with amused skepticism.(p.4)
• If he is not interested in your solution, if he expects you to act only as a ***banker*** for his financial difficulties or a nurse for his sprees, you may have to drop him until he changes his mind.(p.95)
• I wanted to throw up my hands in discouragement, for I saw that I had failed to help my ***banker*** friend understand.(p.138)

banker's
• Alcohol was a looming cloud in this ***banker's*** bright sky.(p.373)

banking
• Here, for instance, is a typical example: An officer of one of the largest ***banking*** institutions in America knows I no longer drink.(p.138)

bankroll
• Again I spent my ***bankroll***, by no means as thick as the one I had when I first saw the skyline of Gotham.(p.252)

bankruptcy
• Friends who have reasoned with him after a spree which has brought him to the point of divorce or ***bankruptcy*** are mystified when he walks directly into a saloon.(p.35)
• My divorce coincided with my father's ***bankruptcy***, and I went to work, casting off all allegiances and responsibilities to any other than myself.(p.225)
• My alcoholic associates fired me, took control, and ran the enterprise into ***bankruptcy***.(p.437)
• After all, it was self (you, me) that stood in our own way, that ran the show and ran ourselves into ***bankruptcy***, that hurt the ones we loved.(p.459)

banks
• In time I became an officer and director of one of the largest commercial ***banks*** in the country.(p.374)
• I rented a beautiful apartment on the ***banks*** of the Seine in the winter, and a chalet in Switzerland in the summer.(p.405)

banner
• During the day a friend of mine brought me some magazines to take to a hospital group I was interested in, and I looked through them and a "***banner***" across the front of one featured an article by a prominent clergyman in which I caught the word "resentment."(p.552)

banquet
• When I was eighteen, at the end of high school, the high school team had a ***banquet*** at a well-known roadhouse outside of Akron.(p.194)
• At that particular time, the boys put me on a shutter and took me out to the shed, and I lay in the car while they enjoyed their ***banquet***.(p.195)

Baptist
• We lived just a few doors from the First ***Baptist*** Church and when they had funerals I remember very often asking my mother whether the person was good or bad and whether they were going to heaven or hell.(p.483)

baptized
• (My mother and father were Catholics and I had been ***baptized***, but at the end of my instructions for Confirmation I had not gone to church, and then when my mother remarried, she married a Protestant and the whole religious angle was forgotten.(p.201)

bar
• After one of those days of inferno, I wobbled from a hotel ***bar*** to a brokerage office.(p.4)
• I went back to the ***bar***.(p.4)
• In no time I was beating on the ***bar*** asking myself how it happened.(p.6)
• How often have some of us begun to drink in this nonchalant way, and after the third or fourth, pounded on the ***bar*** and said to ourselves, "For God's sake, how did I ever get started again?"(p.24)
• On the way I felt hungry so I stopped at a roadside place where they have a ***bar***.(p.36)
• When I returned to the hotel it struck me a highball would be fine before going to bed, so I stepped into the ***bar*** and had one.(p.41)
• If you are with a person who wants to eat in a ***bar***, by all means go along.(p.102)
• Down the lobby a door opened into an attractive ***bar***.(p.154)
• Music and gay chatter still floated to him from the ***bar***.(p.154)
• I drank all I dared in the ***bar***, and then went to my room to finish the job.(p.179)
• We boys drove out in somebody's car and went to the ***bar*** on the way do the dining room and I, in an effort to impress the other boys that I was city-bred, having lived in Scranton and Cleveland, asked them if they didn't want a drink.(p.194)
• I didn't even know what a martini looked like, but I had heard a man down the ***bar*** order one.(p.194)
• I kept watching the man down the ***bar*** to see what he did with a contraption like that, and he just smelled of his drink and set it down again, so I did the same.(p.195)
• I went into a ***bar***, and there I got into a fight.(p.204)
• This experience sent me to law school where I went at night and which course I completed in less than three years, taking the highest state ***bar*** examinations and passing them.(p.212)
• As a matter of fact, I had two children at the time I was admitted to the ***bar***.(p.212)
• There wasn't a ***bar*** in sight, but I found the subway station.(p.223)
• Sitting in a Second Avenue ***bar***, accepting drinks from anyone who offered, after my small stake was gone; or sitting at home alone, with the inevitable glass in my hand, I would remember, and remembering, I would drink faster, seeking speedy oblivion.(p.225)
• My next conscious memory was in ***Bar*** le Duc, many miles from base.(p.242)
• Tom Sharkey's brawling ***bar*** on 14th Street and the famous wine-room at the back were headquarters for me.(p.251)
• In my mind's eye I saw Broadway again and Tom Sharkey's ***bar***; the roar of the subway was in my ears.(p.252)
• One morning after a terrific drinking bout, I was in a little ***bar*** near our house, and I shook so that I was very much ashamed, because I was getting the shakes worse and worse.(p.266)
• I sipped the drink off the ***bar*** because I couldn't hold it in my hand, but I was still a lady, believe it or not, and I was deeply ashamed.(p.266)
• Time went on and the drinking got worse and worse, and I was in another barroom, down the road the other way, a small one, and I took my glass – that morning I'd been able to lift it from the ***bar*** – and I said to the woman behind the ***bar***, "I wish I might never take another drop of that stuff.(p.266)
• Finally, one morning, I got up and got in the car and cried all the way down to the M.'s – the people who owned the ***bar*** -- and told her I was licked and wanted help.(p.267)
• On my ride to the nearest ***bar***, I sold the driver on how misunderstood I was by my wife and what an unreasonable person she was.(p.288)
• By the time we reached the ***bar***, he was willing to buy me a quart with his own money.(p.288)
• I called her every night from a local ***bar***, and often she was not at home.(p.318)
• There was a ***bar***, and what I tasted spelled sheer heaven.(p.328)
• When alcohol took me over, my ***bar*** was my kitchen, my living room, my bedroom, the back bathroom, and the two hampers.(p.335)
• It didn't take long for me to fall in with a fast crowd who had their lunch in the men's ***bar*** of a leading hotel.(p.361)
• There was one Village ***bar*** in particular for which I formed an obsession.(p.410)
• An obstreperous woman in a ***bar*** is a nuisance, and they wanted no trouble with the police.(p.410)
• I stopped at the cashier's any hour of the night on the way to the ***bar*** and cashed a check.(p.410)
• My tweed suit, once a very good one, was shapeless and baggy with bare places worn in the elbows from leaning on the ***bar***.(p.411)
• Once, in a strange gin mill, I stole a bottle from behind the ***bar***.(p.411)
• On the train going back, Anne's one idea was to get to the nearest ***bar***.(p.415)
• At night I tended ***bar***.(p.426)
• When I got out of there, I lasted about fifteen minutes at home, before I headed for the drugstore and more pills, and then the ***bar***.(p.479)
• I knew I wasn't capable of keeping the bulk of the money myself, so I gave it to a white fellow who owned the ***bar*** which I frequented.(p.493)
• I'd visit one ***bar*** after another, having one martini in each, and in each hoping to find someone interesting to talk to.(p.536)
• If he were still sober, chances are that very quickly I put him down as a Philistine with no appreciation of literary genius; and then I went on to another ***bar*** to find a new victim.(p.537)
• Still another friend and temporary host received me at four in the morning from the charge of a policeman who had found me "going to bed" in a garage far from the last place I could remember having been, a fashionable ***bar*** and restaurant in the theatrical district of New York, to which I had repaired after my date for that evening, a charming lady of the theatre who had refused my company for obvious reasons.(p.538)
• In my mind's eye, I played and replayed scenes in which I was plucked magically from the ***bar*** where I stood nursing a drink, and was instantly exalted to some position of power and prestige.(p.560)
• "There is a principle which is a ***bar*** against all information, which is proof against all arguments and which cannot fail to keep a man in everlasting ignorance – that principle is contempt prior to investigation."(p.570)

Bar le Duc
• My next conscious memory was in ***Bar le Duc***, many miles from base.(p.242)

barbecue
• And then we went up the side of a hill where we have a little ***barbecue*** area to make the fire for the ***barbecue***, and on the way up, I thought to myself – I'll go back down to the kitchen and refill this drink.(p.347)

barbershop
• In the basement were to be dry-cleaning facilities, a ***barbershop***, a pool room, a grocery shop and everything.(p.198)

barbiturates
• I would use ***barbiturates***.(p.217)
• In fact, the last three years of my drinking was a routine of ***barbiturates*** in the morning, so that I could stop shaking enough to shave, and then alcohol beginning about four-thirty or five o'clock, with a struggle not to take a drink at noon or during the day, because I had the idea that if I took one drink, I would smell as though I had had a pint.(p.217)
• I'd just take a couple or three ***barbiturates*** to get back to sleep -- eating my alcohol.(p.333)

bare
• I was unwilling to ***bare*** my secrets to those who might display scorn.(p.331)
• I woke up in this ***bare*** room with nothing around me but bars; they wouldn't let me smoke and treated me, well, like I was nuts.(p.387)
• My tweed suit, once a very good one, was shapeless and baggy with ***bare*** places worn in the elbows from leaning on the bar.(p.411)
• In a prison in my native state, I spent eleven months in solitary confinement, bouncing in and out of the "hole" (a ***bare*** concrete-and-steel cubicle) about five times during those eleven months.(p.459)

barely
• He may not see at once that he has ***barely*** scratched a limitless lode which will pay dividends only if he mines it for the rest of his life and insists on giving away the entire product.(p.129)
• I stayed sober during the trip except for an occasional bottle of beer because funds ***barely*** met expenses.(p.255)
• One night I ***barely*** made my downtown club; if I'd had to go another fifty feet I'd have collapsed in the gutter.(p.435)
• My practice at that juncture was just ***barely*** getting us a living.(p.488)
• I became so weak, I could ***barely*** drag myself around.(p.558)

barflies
• At the Laundromat, I was undisturbed by ***barflies*** with questionable and unwanted intentions.(p.369)
• I despised the other ***barflies*** and, naturally, they loathed me.(p.410)
• I said it over and over, boring my fellow ***barflies***.(p.412)

barfly
• Waitress by day, ***barfly*** by night, she drifted down the years into jail.(p.478)

bargain
• I very early came to see that there had to be a continual renewal for that simple deal with God; that I had perpetually to keep the ***bargain***.(p.237)
• I knew then that I hadn't made a complete surrender, because I tried to ***bargain*** with the God I had found, and I said, "Anything but that!(p.271)
• Having made that ***bargain***, I immediately began to feel I'd been trapped into it and I went out and had some drinks – four glasses of gin, I remember.(p.523)

Barleycorn
- In three months John ***Barleycorn*** had me kicked out.(p.254)
- I have been of a very religious outlook all my life, but that made no difference once John ***Barleycorn*** got the better of me.(p.343)
- In this I was greatly aided and abetted by one John ***Barleycorn***.(p.358)
- And so I met John ***Barleycorn***.(p.498)
- Good old John ***Barleycorn***!(p.499)

Barleycorn's
- ***Barleycorn's*** wringer squeezed this author -- but he escaped quite whole.(p.432)

barman
- If something does come along that sort of upsets me, instead of walking in and throwing a buck at the ***barman*** and asking for a drink, I walk into a telephone booth, drop a dime in the box, and call somebody who was so kind as to give me his name and telephone number to meet such an emergency.(p.511)

barn
- The patient had made his own diagnosis, and deciding his situation hopeless, had hidden in a deserted ***barn*** determined to die.(p.xxix)
- A couple of hired hands were cleaning out the ***barn*** on the farm and I would ride to and fro on the sled, and while they were loading I would drink hard cider out of a barrel in the ***barn***.(p.183)
- I come to on a pile of hay in a ***barn***.(p.502)

barracks
- Military service was compulsory and I did my stretch with the class of my age, goose-stepping in German ***barracks*** and taking part in the Boxer Rebellion in China, my first time at any great distance from home.(p.230)
- I stayed in the ***barracks*** all day, "making out guard schedules," and getting mildly plastered from the jug under my desk.(p.426)
- I talked the Old Man into letting me live in the photo lab instead of the ***barracks***, and for eighteen months nothing interfered with my drinking.(p.426)

barred
- So I was ***barred*** from the plant for ten days, and during that ten day period I was drunk twice, showing how little control these restraints had on me.(p.205)

barrel
- After two weeks of drinking, he had placed his toe on the trigger of a loaded shotgun -- the ***barrel*** in his mouth.(p.137)
- A couple of hired hands were cleaning out the barn on the farm and I would ride to and fro on the sled, and while they were loading I would drink hard cider out of a ***barrel*** in the barn.(p.183)

barrier
- Beginning with such complaints, a ***barrier*** arises.(p.126)
- She knew that at that time any suggestion she made about my drinking would only build up a ***barrier***, a consideration for which I am ever grateful.(p.216)

barriers
- The ***barriers*** he had built through the years were swept away.(p.56)
- ***Barriers*** which have sprung up between you and your friends will disappear with the growth of sympathetic understanding.(p.115)

barroom
- Step over to the nearest ***barroom*** and try some controlled drinking.(p.31)
- Time went on and the drinking got worse and worse, and I was in another ***barroom***, down the road the other way, a small one, and I took my glass -- that morning I'd been able to lift it from the bar -- and I said to the woman behind the bar, "I wish I might never take another drop of that stuff.(p.266)
- He brought many people into A.A. through his ***barroom***.)(p.267)
- I learned that a person just can't find a job hanging in a dive or ***barroom*** all day and all night, as jobs don't seem to turn up in those places.(p.300)
- No jail booking, drunk-driving citation, ***barroom*** fight, or even a tumble off a barstool.(p.327)

barrooms
- From the top of the heap in a few years he had skidded to becoming a shuffling customer, still entering the better ***barrooms*** but welcomed by neither mine host nor his patrons.(p.236)
- Young and able to travel with the best of them, I managed to hold my job and keep my end up in the ***barrooms***.(p.252)
- I had missed them myself from the ***barrooms*** of the town.(p.258)

bars
- Sometimes a small deal would net a few hundred dollars, and I would pay my bills at the ***bars*** and delicatessens.(p.5)
- People have said we must not go where liquor is served; we must not have it in our homes; we must shun friends who drink; we must avoid moving pictures which show drinking scenes; we must not go into ***bars***; our friends must hide their bottles if we go to their houses; we mustn't think or be reminded about alcohol at all.(p.100)
- That includes ***bars***, nightclubs, dances, receptions, weddings, even plain ordinary whoopee parties.(p.101)
- I wanted "ripe" prospects and I didn't feel that I would get very far chasing individual drunks in and out of ***bars***.(p.281)
- I could let down the ***bars***.(p.329)
- I do recall lying on a cold cement floor and shredding into little bits several pieces of stolen identification cards, and washing my face in the toilet bowl trying to sober up, and screaming hysterically while clinging to ***bars*** too high to see out of, and cursing everyone that came near me.(p.354)
- Rehearsals then became a part of the pattern, stopping at ***bars*** on the way to or from the place where drinks were to be served.(p.375)
- I woke up in this bare room with nothing around me but ***bars***; they wouldn't let me smoke and treated me, well, like I was nuts.(p.387)
- As I said before, I don't like to be fenced in, and with those ***bars*** you don't get hotel service.(p.390)
- So when he came for me, as he walked down the stairs, I could see him through the ***bars***, and he was signing for me; I looked at him and said, "Don't you sign anything in this place!"(p.391)
- At this time, the price of booze in the ***bars*** was fifteen cents a shot and ten cents a beer.(p.397)
- I went to ***bars*** alone to drink.(p.410)
- She too had gone to cheap ***bars*** to drink.(p.414)
- I went to several Village ***bars***, and drank cokes or tea.(p.414)
- There were gold ***bars*** on his shoulders.(p.422)
- I would drink all night in ***bars***, come home about five a.m., down a good big glass of whiskey straight, and tumble into bed.(p.428)
- And then I went back home to live with my parents, and the merry-go-round started again -- only this time I didn't have to worry about waking up behind ***bars*** in a psychiatric ward.(p.468)
- From a Canadian reservation to overseas ***bars*** to New England lockups, an Indian traveled a long trail that finally led him home to A.A.(p.474)
- I clung to the outfit for the balance of my time, and finally I was released, after having spent twenty years and nine months behind ***bars***.(p.510)
- There are no color ***bars*** in A.A.(p.529)
- I remember how horrible jails are, how dreadful a thing it is to be behind steel ***bars***.(p.542)
- I was immersed in self-pity and resentment, and the only people who would support this attitude or who I felt understood me at all were the people I met in ***bars*** and the ones who drank as I did.(p.547)
- I also began visiting ***bars*** after work, with my older associates.(p.555)
- Our courtship was mainly in ***bars*** and night spots when my ship was in New York.(p.555)
- Instead of drinking in fancy ***bars*** and clubs, I had to carry a bottle of vodka in my briefcase, duck into public toilets, and gulp from the bottle, trembling, in order to keep from falling apart.(p.557)

barstool
- No jail booking, drunk-driving citation, barroom fight, or even a tumble off a ***barstool***.(p.327)

barstools
- They got so they moved their ***barstools*** when they saw me coming.(p.411)

bartender
- Age and the law were still against me, but laws were not as strictly enforced in those days as they are now, and I discovered that as long as I had the green blood, there was always a way to get alcohol, either from a nondiscriminatory ***bartender*** or from an older friend who would be glad to purchase the joy juice for the privilege of sharing it.(p.397)
- The ***bartender***, a tough Irishman, came around and "gave me the elbow," which means that he raised his elbow and smacked me in the face.(p.411)
- Luckily a friend was with me, who dragged me out, screaming and cursing, while the ***bartender*** threatened to call the police.(p.411)
- While waiting to depart I was selected -- by giving a CPO five dollars -- to be ***bartender*** in the Navy Chief's Club.(p.426)
- I began sneaking drinks when playing ***bartender*** for guests.(p.556)

bartenders
- The ***bartenders*** took care of me, not out of brotherly love, but through enlightened self-interest.(p.410)
- I suspect that those ***bartenders*** would wait until I shot my wad, then call a cab and send me home.(p.410)
- The ***bartenders*** too, treated me with contempt.(p.411)
- To wear expensive clothes, to have ***bartenders*** know what to serve me before I ordered, to be recognized by headwaiters and shown to the best table, to play gin rummy for high stakes with the insouciance of a riverboat gambler -- these were the enduring values in life, I thought.(p.556)

base
- One set of voices cry that sex is a lust of our lower nature, a ***base*** necessity of procreation.(p.68)
- My next conscious memory was in Bar le Duc, many miles from ***base***.(p.242)
- I had bad nervous headaches, particularly at the ***base*** of my neck.(p.277)
- I applied for photo school at Pensacola Air ***Base*** and made it.(p.426)
- I was transferred to Kaneohe Bay, across the hump to the windward side of Oahu, to the aviation ***base***.(p.426)
- I seldom left the ***base*** any more except once in a while when I felt the need of talking to some girl.(p.427)
- I was supposed to come home on a troop ship, but I talked the ***base*** commander into flying me home.(p.428)

based
- Our public relations were to be ***based*** upon attraction rather than promotion.(p.xix)
- Sometimes they hurt us, seemingly without provocation, but we invariably find that at some time in the past we have made decisions ***based*** on self which later placed us in a position to be hurt.(p.62)
- But what we have related is ***based*** upon experience, some of it painful.(p.121)
- The family may be possessed by the idea that future happiness can be ***based*** only upon forgetfulness of the past.(p.123)
- This is ***based***, really, on the Sermon on the Mount.(p.268)
- For me, A.A. is a synthesis of all the philosophy I've ever read, all of the positive, good philosophy, all of it ***based*** on love.(p.542)
- I thought that life was a pretty simple thing; you simply made a plan for your life, ***based*** upon what you wanted, and then you needed only the courage to go after it.(p.545)
- Eleven -- Our public relations policy is ***based*** on attraction rather than promotion; we need always maintain personal anonymity at the level of press, radio and films.(p.564)
- Historians may one day recognize Alcoholics Anonymous to have been a great venture in social pioneering which forged a new instrument for social action; a new therapy ***based*** on the kinship of common suffering; one having a vast potential for the myriad other ills of mankind."(p.573)

basement
- In the ***basement*** were to be dry-cleaning facilities, a barbershop, a pool room, a grocery shop and everything.(p.198)
- I was in a large, dark, rather poorly furnished room -- the living room of a ***basement*** flat.(p.222)

basic
- Because this book has become the ***basic*** text for our Society and has helped such large numbers of alcoholic men and women to recover, there exists a sentiment against any radical changes being made in it.(p.xi)
- And besides, there were scattered alcoholics who had picked up the ***basic*** ideas in Akron or New York and were trying to form A.A. groups in other cities.(p.xvii)
- The ***basic*** principles of the A.A. program, it appears, hold good for individuals with many different life-styles, just as the program has brought recovery to those of many different nationalities.(p.xxii)
- We were having trouble with personal relationships, we couldn't control our emotional natures, we were a prey to misery and depression, we couldn't make a living, we had a feeling of uselessness, we were full of fear, we were unhappy, we couldn't seem to be of real help to other people -- was not a ***basic*** solution of these bedevilments more important than whether we should see newsreels of lunar flight?(p.52)

• What is his ***basic*** trouble?(p.61)
• While I was in ***basic***, I got high off booze almost every night.(p.317)
• Somehow, I made it through ***basic*** and then laid off the booze for about three months, because I was in school at night.(p.317)
• They are not ideas of resignation but of the recognition of certain ***basic*** facts of living.(p.382)
• Had I been able to explain to a psychiatrist the feeling of futility, loneliness and lack of purpose that had come with my deep sense of personal failure at this second divorce, I seriously doubt that the good doctor could have convinced me that my ***basic*** problem was a spiritual hunger, but A.A. has shown me this was the truth.(p.546)

basically
• So our troubles, we think, are ***basically*** of our own making.(p.62)
• She, more than the others, showed me what ailed me ***basically***, why I was immature and insecure.(p.409)
• I think that was ***basically*** the thing that started me drinking in 1935.(p.487)
• Vi was very kind and explained to the jury that I was ***basically*** a fine fellow and a good husband, but that I drank too much and that she thought I had lost my mind and felt that I should be committed to an asylum.(p.492)

basis
• This has become the ***basis*** of a rapidly growing fellowship of these men and their families.(p.xxiii)
• Nothing would please us so much as to write a book which would contain no ***basis*** for contention or argument.(p.19)
• Whether such a person can quit upon a nonspiritual ***basis*** depends upon the extent to which he has already lost the power to choose whether he will drink or not.(p.34)
• But the actual or potential alcoholic, with hardly an exception, will be absolutely unable to stop drinking on the ***basis*** of self-knowledge.(p.39)
• To be doomed to an alcoholic death or to live on a spiritual ***basis*** are not always easy alternatives to face.(p.44)
• But after a while we had to face the fact that we must find a spiritual ***basis*** of life – or else.(p.44)
• Instead, we looked at the human defects of these people, and sometimes used their shortcomings as a ***basis*** of wholesale condemnation.(p.50)
• On that ***basis*** we are almost always in collision with something or somebody, even though our motives are good.(p.60)
• For we are now on a different ***basis***; the ***basis*** of trusting and relying upon God.(p.68)
• As we look over the list of business acquaintances and friends we have hurt, we may feel diffident about going to some of them on a spiritual ***basis***.(p.76)
• He subsequently denied having received the money and used the incident as a ***basis*** for discrediting the man.(p.80)
• The most incompatible people discover they have a ***basis*** upon which they can meet.(p.99)
• If their old relationship is to be resumed it must be on a better ***basis***, since the former did not work.(p.99)
• If your husband is trying to live on a spiritual ***basis***, he will also be doing everything in his power to avoid disagreement or contention.(p.118)
• Perhaps your husband will make a fair start on the new ***basis***, but just as things are going beautifully he dismays you by coming home drunk.(p.120)
• As each member of a resentful family begins to see his short comings and admits them to the others, he lays a ***basis*** for helpful discussion.(p.127)
• Whether the family goes on a spiritual ***basis*** or not, the alcoholic member has to if he would recover.(p.135)
• Being on a radically different ***basis*** of life, he will never take advantage of the situation.(p.146)
• A spiritual experience, he conceded, was absolutely necessary, but the price seemed high upon the ***basis*** suggested.(p.155)
• Understanding our work, he can do this with an eye to selecting those who are willing and able to recover on a spiritual ***basis***.(p.162)
• He went on talking and told me that he had found the plan has a ***basis*** of love, and the practice of Christ's injunction, "Love thy neighbor as thyself."(p.236)
• I have my A.A. friends, and I have become reacquainted with my old friends on a new ***basis***.(p.416)
• The Episcopal magazine, The Living Church, observes editorially: "The ***basis*** of the technique of Alcoholics Anonymous is the truly Christian principle that a man cannot help himself except by helping others.(p.574)

basketball
• A busload of ***basketball*** players had been passing and saw the flames.(p.424)
• During recess we were playing ***basketball*** and I had accidentally tripped a fellow just a little larger than I was.(p.484)
• He took the ***basketball*** and smashed me in the face with it.(p.484)

Basle
• My parents had some vague idea of making a priest out of me and for some years I attended the Franciscan school at ***Basle***, Switzerland, just across the border, about six miles from my home.(p.230)

bat
• He even went to ***bat*** for me before the court martial that inevitably followed and, as a result, I drew only thirty days – fifteen in solitary.(p.428)

bath
• I paced the floor with a ***bath*** towel around my shoulders, the perspiration running off me.(p.268)
• To me, taking a ***bath*** was just being in a place with a bottle where I could drink in privacy.(p.337)

bathing
• (We don't have much time for ***bathing*** in our crowded schedule.)(p.479)

bathroom
• This problem was soon solved, however, as I began to take my bottle along with me and hide it in the ***bathroom*** or in the shrubbery outside.(p.184)
• Sometimes I would lie on the ***bathroom*** floor, deathly sick, praying I would die, and praying to God as I always had prayed to Him when I was drinking: "Dear God, get me out of this one and I'll never do it again."(p.324)
• When alcohol took me over, my bar was my kitchen, my living room, my bedroom, the back ***bathroom***, and the two hampers.(p.335)
• I staggered to the ***bathroom***.(p.498)

bathrooms
• I had no need to hide in closets, ***bathrooms***, or garages.(p.332)

bathtub
• "***Bathtub***" gin, two bottles a day, and often three, got to be routine.(p.5)

battalion
• I talked to the first sergeant and the ***battalion*** commander, and they got me in contact with an A.A. member.(p.319)
• However, I kept that job in Egypt and Palestine for about two years, and then I changed over to the other ***battalion*** in my regiment.(p.520)

battery
• I fancied myself a leader, for had not the men of my ***battery*** given me a special token of appreciation?(p.1)

battle
• The courage to do ***battle*** was not there.(p.6)
• For the next couple of hours a terrible ***battle*** went on between the good gremlins and the bad ones, one faction urging me to tell the truth, the other telling me to sit tight and say nothing.(p.366)
• Each ***battle*** has ended in defeat.(p.502)

battle-grounds
• Our homes have been ***battle-grounds*** many an evening.(p.105)

Bauer
• Dr. W.W. ***Bauer***, broadcasting under the auspices of The American Medical Association in 1946, over the NBC network, said, in part: "Alcoholics Anonymous are no crusaders; not a temperance society.(p.572)

bay
• It didn't say I had to finally live on skid row and drink ***bay*** rum, canned heat or lemon extract.(p.379)
• I was transferred to Kaneohe ***Bay***, across the hump to the windward side of Oahu, to the aviation base.(p.426)

beach
• Many retirees embrace alcoholism while secluded in motor trailers, rest homes, leisure-world bungalows, mountain cabins, or ***beach*** cottages, or even in penthouses, on yachts, and inside Palm Springs cabanas.(p.329)

beaches
• ***Beaches***, parties, dances, movies – everything.(p.425)

beam
• Had I tried honestly and sincerely to practice the Twelve Steps I would have seen from my continuous moral inventory that I was getting off the ***beam*** – I would have found that there were some active resentments in my life, a terrific amount of self-pity.(p.471)

beams
• If my wife was planning to go out in the afternoon, I would get a large supply of liquor and smuggle it home and hide it in the coal bin, the clothes chute, over door jambs, over ***beams*** in the cellar and in cracks in the cellar tile.(p.176)

bear
• Take away my difficulties, that victory over them may ***bear*** witness to those I would help of Thy Power, Thy Love, and Thy Way of life.(p.63)
• Can he talk frankly with you so long as he does not ***bear*** business tales or criticize his associates?(p.145)
• They ***bear*** witness that release from alcoholism can really be permanent.(p.169)
• This was my introduction to this "understanding fellowship" although it was to be more than a year later before our Society was to ***bear*** the name, Alcoholics Anonymous.(p.239)
• I can't ***bear*** to be here when you lose the respect of others, and above all – when you lose your own self respect."(p.362)
• I can't ***bear*** to be here when you lose the respect of others, and above all when you lose your own self respect."(p.363)
• So please ***bear*** in mind, and I would like to emphasize, that this is a very rough estimate.(p.399)
• The two years I spent there, I was incorrigible, and the records ***bear*** this out.(p.458)
• I ***bear*** a few scars on my face from these fights, which I always lost, because the "stick" existed only in my mind.(p.537)

bearable
• And even though he continues to drink, the family will find life more ***bearable***.(p.97)

beard
• After a couple of days in dollar hotels and one night in the pokey, I finally landed on my mother's doorstep -- shaking apart, with several days' ***beard*** and, of course, broke as usual.(p.238)

bearing
• I'd get so fed up with drinking all alone and ***bearing*** the burden of guilt all by myself, that I'd egg him on to drink, to get started again.(p.325)
• It was nothing to my own inner distress, my self-reproach, and my self-loathing, for was I not ***bearing*** out all the horrible things I had always suspected of myself?(p.404)
• I don't know whether she was a pacifist or whether she just thought that in the event of another war it would have some ***bearing*** on my joining up.(p.484)

beat
• There is the obsession that somehow, someday, they will ***beat*** the game.(p.23)
• It finally ***beat*** us into a state of reasonableness.(p.48)
• If you still think you are strong enough to ***beat*** the game alone, that is your affair.(p.181)
• In the spring of 1917, in order to ***beat*** being fired from school, I became "patriotic" and joined the Army.(p.241)
• I have stood listening to street-corner preachers tell how they ***beat*** the game.(p.256)
• And, believe me, I thank God that I found out about A.A. before I had to ***beat*** my brains out -- before I had been hospitalized, jailed or lost a job.(p.367)
• The last time I drank, when I was twenty-nine, I drank for only four days, yet I threatened to kill my children; I ***beat*** my wife at home and on the church steps; I mistreated a child in my office; and I ran to a hospital for mental illness to avoid jail.(p.418)
• I ***beat*** him to it.(p.424)
• Pearl Harbor was a breeze of nine months, a gay Hawaiian paradise, drinking under the palms, listening to the surf ***beat*** on the shore, a bottle of whiskey near at hand.(p.426)
• I learned what a devastating effect it can have on a child to coddle him and build him up, and then turn and ***beat*** him savagely, as had happened to me.(p.434)

beat-up
• Mind you, I had absolutely nothing to show for that eighteen years, except a ***beat-up*** car that I hadn't even paid for, but I was doing all right.(p.478)
• I would wake to find myself in some ***beat-up*** rooming house, where roaches were crawling over everything.(p.527)

beaten
• He's just ***beaten*** up a couple of nurses.(p.156)
• I was arrested and taken to jail where I was ***beaten*** up by two or three fellows who were already in there and whom I tried to boss.(p.204)

• I was badly *beaten.*(p.204)
• During this time, I had been threatened, *beaten,* kissed, praised and damned alternately by relatives, family, friends and strangers, but of course it all went for naught.(p.300)
• A people-pleaser *beaten* down?(p.331)
• Only through being *beaten* down by my own misery would I ever have accepted the term "alcoholic" as applied to myself.(p.436)
• You see, I am a five-time loser, which means five felony convictions (not including the cases *beaten*).(p.457)
• In each new place, I was the new kid – a skinny, shy kid – to be tested and *beaten* up.(p.555)

beating

• In no time I was *beating* on the bar asking myself how it happened.(p.6)
• They acted on me like the *beating* of a club.(p.195)
• They phoned my husband that I was in jail and in such terrible shape that they didn't know what I would do to myself; and they realized that jail was no place for me, but that he was to wait a while before he got me, because at the time they called him to come over for me I was *beating* a tin cup against the wall.(p.390)

beats

• They sound like the philosophy of the man who, having a headache, *beats* himself on the head with a hammer so that he can't feel the ache.(p.23)

beautiful

• And he then said a *beautiful* prayer.(p.219)
• There was a young fellow who led the meeting and that was a *beautiful* thing to me.(p.270)
• My sponsor used to say to me, "If I could only paint you a picture of how *beautiful* life can be without booze . . ."(p.355)
• It was the first of many such experiences that became the only cause of harsh words, tears and heartaches in an otherwise truly *beautiful* marriage.(p.361)
• I went to many meetings and met many *beautiful* people.(p.371)
• Even when I was old enough to know better, I dreamed about being as *beautiful* as Venus, as pure as the Madonna and as brilliant as the President of the United States is supposed to be.(p.400)
• I rented a *beautiful* apartment on the banks of the Seine in the winter, and a chalet in Switzerland in the summer.(p.405)
• I was not *beautiful* or good, as I had yearned to be.(p.411)
• I had just begun a dental practice in a *beautiful* new office.(p.418)
• A.A. has given me a new wife, a *beautiful* stepdaughter, a new practice, a new home, and a new relationship with my four children.(p.420)
• (I am pleased to state, however, that I had gone to only a very few A.A. meetings before I was able to make a really *beautiful* pair of moccasins -- and half a wallet.(p.445)
• Oh, I was *beautiful* in those days!(p.479)
• We are so *beautiful* that it is never too much trouble to get some poor stranger to buy us a drink.(p.479)
• It is so *beautiful* to get up in the morning not being hung-over and being able to remember where we were the night before.(p.481)
• As the sober days grew into sober months and then into sober years, a new and *beautiful* life began to emerge from the shambles of my former existence.(p.559)
• And I found it *beautiful*!(p.561)

beautifully

• Perhaps your husband will make a fair start on the new basis, but just as things are going *beautifully* he dismays you by coming home drunk.(p.120)
• We complement each other *beautifully,* as he is a born salesman and my taste is for finance and management.(p.284)
• I was at a *beautifully* set dinner table.(p.285)

beauty

• We missed the reality and *beauty* of the forest because we were diverted by the ugliness of some of its trees.(p.50)
• I returned to my home in Lucknow, India, at the end of November last year from a vacation in one of the most famous *beauty* spots in our country, a mountain resort 6,800 feet up, with a wonderful lake.(p.342)
• Prior to our marriage, when she was a shy, scrawny adolescent, I was able to see things in her that others couldn't necessarily see -- things like *beauty,* charm, gaiety, a gift for being easy to talk to, a sense of humor, and many other fine qualities.(p.450)
• Then A.A. showed her the *beauty* of normal living, in a whole family reborn.(p.478)
• If our hair is half-bleached (with dark roots), poker-straight, and not combed, this adds to our *beauty.*(p.479)
• Our shoes are not better than the average hobo's, and if we are fortunate enough to have a pair of stockings on, nobody notices the runs in them, because of our dazzling *beauty* and our dirty feet.(p.479)

became

• Their very first case, a desperate one, recovered immediately and *became* A.A. number three.(p.xvii)
• Another reason for the wide acceptance of A.A. was the ministration of friends -- friends in medicine, religion, and the press, together with innumerable others who *became* our able and persistent advocates.(p.xx)
• They took a drink a day or so prior to the date, and then the phenomenon of craving at once *became* paramount to all other interests so that the important appointment was not met.(p.xxvii)
• My work took me about Wall street and little by little I *became* interested in the market.(p.2)
• Many people lost money – but some *became* very rich.(p.2)
• The remonstrances of my friends terminated in a row and I *became* a lone wolf.(p.3)
• I *became* an unwelcome hanger-on at brokerage places.(p.5)
• Liquor ceased to be a luxury; it *became* a necessity.(p.5)
• The house was taken over by the mortgage holder, my mother-in-law died, and my wife and father-in-law *became* ill.(p.5)
• Everyone *became* resigned to the certainty that I would have to be shut up somewhere, or would stumble along to a miserable end.(p.8)
• When they talked of a God personal to me, who was love, superhuman strength and direction, I *became* irritated and my mind snapped shut against such a theory.(p.10)
• I ruthlessly faced my sins and *became* willing to have my new-found Friend take them away, root and branch.(p.13)
• You may already have asked yourself why it is that all of us *became* so very ill from drinking.(p.20)
• In a few years he *became* so violent when intoxicated that he had to be committed.(p.35)
• Faced with alcoholic destruction, we soon *became* as open minded on spiritual matters as we tried to be on other questions.(p.48)
• When we *became* alcoholics, crushed by a self-imposed crisis we could not postpone or evade, we had to fearlessly face the proposition that either God is everything or else He is nothing.(p.53)
• He attended church school, where he *became* rebellious at what he thought an overdose of religious education.(p.56)
• 8.Made a list of all persons we had harmed, and *became* willing to make amends to them all.(p.59)
• Established on such a footing we *became* less and less interested in ourselves, our little plans and designs.(p.63)
• More and more we *became* interested in seeing what we could contribute to life.(p.63)
• As we felt new power flow in, as we enjoyed peace of mind, as we discovered we could face life successfully, as we *became* conscious of His presence, we began to lose our fear of today, tomorrow or the hereafter.(p.63)
• Though once like number two he *became* worse.(p.109)
• Liquor incapacitated father for so many years that mother *became* head of the house.(p.130)
• Thus mother, through no fault of her own, *became* accustomed to wearing the family trousers.(p.131)
• What irony – I *became* an alcoholic myself!(p.137)
• As we *became* subjects of King Alcohol, shivering denizens of his mad realm, the chilling vapor that is loneliness settled down.(p.151)
• Though they knew they must help other alcoholics if they would remain sober, that motive *became* secondary.(p.159)
• In addition to these casual get-togethers, it *became* customary to set apart one night a week for a meeting to be attended by anyone or everyone interested in a spiritual way of life.(p.159)
• Outsiders *became* interested.(p.160)
• My whole life seemed to be centered around doing what I wanted to do, without regard for the rights, wishes, or privileges of anyone else; a state of mind which *became* more and more predominant as the years passed.(p.172)
• On account of my enormous capacity for beer, I was elected to membership in one of the drinking societies, and soon *became* one of the leading spirits.(p.173)
• There my drinking *became* so much worse that the boys in the fraternity house where I lived felt forced to send for my father, who made a long journey in the vain endeavor to get me straightened around.(p.174)
• Sometimes I would bring it in my pockets, but they were inspected, and that *became* too risky.(p.176)
• During all this time we *became* more or less ostracized by our friends.(p.177)
• My wife *became* deeply interested and it was her interest that sustained mine, though I at no time sensed that it might be an answer to my liquor problem.(p.178)
• The first time that I *became* intoxicated I was eight years old.(p.182)
• As time went on my drinking *became* progressively worse.(p.184)
• They came in and began to give me instruction in the program which later *became* known as Alcoholics Anonymous.(p.185)
• Naturally, what little restraint I had exercised before was gone now, and my drinking *became* worse.(p.199)
• I immediately *became* unconscious.(p.207)
• In the fall of the graduating year, I *became* involved in some litigation over the ownership of inventions and patents.(p.212)
• I *became* a specialist in making elderberry blossom wine.(p.213)
• These periods *became* more frequent and I resolved that when I *became* forty, which was very shortly, I was going on the wagon.(p.213)
• This pattern deepened and *became* worse.(p.214)
• I *became* a constant drinker with a terrific fight to control the amount of my consumption each day.(p.214)
• And then my thinking *became* calculation as to how much longer I had to live, how long the assets would last.(p.215)
• But then the story *became* my own.(p.225)
• Hangovers began to assume monstrous proportions and the morning drink *became* an urgent necessity.(p.226)
• Very early I *became* apprenticed to harness-making and acquired considerable knowledge of upholstering.(p.230)
• I *became* a periodic drinker.(p.233)
• My "periodics" *became* more frequent until I reached the point where I wanted to devote all my time to drinking, working as little as possible, and then only when the necessity of my family demanded it.(p.234)
• There were four of us children, and although both of my brothers later *became* alcoholic -- one died of alcoholism -- my sister has never taken a drink in her life.(p.240)
• At this school we had Bible readings before each meal, and church services four times on Sunday, and I *became* so rebellious at this that I swore I would never join or go to any church except for weddings or funerals.(p.240)
• In the spring of 1917, in order to beat being fired from school, I *became* "patriotic" and joined the Army.(p.241)
• In the Army, I *became* a periodic alcoholic – the periods always coming whenever I could make the opportunity.(p.241)
• My next job was in sales promotion for an oil company in Mississippi where I promptly *became* high man and got lots of pats on the back.(p.242)
• Around this time our big A.A. book was being written and it all *became* much simpler; we had a definite formula which some sixty of us agreed was the middle course for all alcoholics who wanted sobriety, and that formula has not been changed one iota down through the years.(p.248)
• After the book appeared we all *became* very busy in our efforts to save all and sundry, but I was still actually on the fringes of A.A.(p.248)
• With nothing but a liberal arts education, very definitely estranged from my family and already married, soon after graduation from college I *became* a bookmaker's clerk on the British racing circuits, far better off financially than the average professional man.(p.251)
• I again *became* a reporter on a Pittsburgh daily.(p.254)
• Every encouragement was given me with frequent salary increases, but the sober times between "periods" *became* shorter.(p.254)
• Returning to the town I had left three months before, I *became* editor of a monthly magazine, soon had additional publicity and advertising accounts and the money rolled in.(p.254)
• These vacations *became* quite something, and he always had two weeks vacation the first two weeks of every September.(p.264)
• I hated myself worse and worse, and as I hated

myself I ***became*** more defiant towards everything and everybody.(p.265)

• My defiant attitude ***became*** worse.(p.265)

• I always feel that our God Consciousness was a steady growth after we ***became*** associated with A.A.(p.270)

• My pattern of drinking ***became*** very different from theirs.(p.277)

• This gave me the freedom to do A.A. work, and to rest for periods of two or three days when I ***became*** too exhausted to carry on.(p.283)

• That same year, my wife ***became*** fed up with my drinking around the house and called my dad in Akron to come and pick me up.(p.288)

• In the meantime, another doctor in Evanston ***became*** convinced that the program had possibilities, and turned over a woman to us to do something about.(p.295)

• Strangely enough, I ***became*** acquainted with the "hilarious life" just at the time in my own life when I was beginning really to settle down to a common-sense, sane domesticity.(p.297)

• My wife ***became*** pregnant and the doctor recommended the use of port or ale . . . so . . . I bought a six gallon crock and a few bottles, listened to advice from amateur brewmeisters, and was off on my beer manufacturing career on a small scale (for the time being).(p.297)

• I cannot remember just when I ***became*** the victim of insomnia, but I do know that the last year and a half I never went to bed sober a single night.(p.299)

• But the firm ***became*** violently ill with my drunkenness and their course of treatment was to remove their ulcer, in the form of me, from the payroll, amid much fanfare and very personal and slighting remarks and insinuations.(p.300)

• Finally this company also ***became*** involved and I was once more looking for a job.(p.300)

• I ***became*** convinced of that because I spent most of my time there and nary a job turned up.(p.300)

• As my son, our second child, came along, and as he ***became*** school age and was away at school most of the time, something happened.(p.323)

• I ***became*** a drunk anyway, but I was scared to death to take that morning drink.(p.323)

• When I found this impossible, I ***became*** scared for the first time.(p.333)

• I ***became*** one of the most active women in the community, what with P.T.A., other community organizations and drives.(p.339)

• I ***became*** a Jekyll-and-Hyde person.(p.339)

• Because I found that everything I turned to ***became*** a substitute for drink.(p.339)

• I eventually ***became*** a schoolmaster, but gave up that profession to join the Indian Army.(p.342)

• In a short time, it ***became*** uncontrolled drinking.(p.343)

• It only ***became*** another excuse to drink.(p.354)

• Soon, it ***became*** apparent that my schooling was interfering with my drinking.(p.354)

• Every day ***became*** that much harder to live through, and I began to take a look at myself.(p.354)

• It wasn't long before I ***became*** a five o'clock alcoholic.(p.360)

• It was the first of many such experiences that ***became*** the only cause of harsh words, tears and heartaches in an otherwise truly beautiful marriage.(p.361)

• When I hear the more rugged stories of alcoholics who ***became*** sicker than I did with this affliction, I humbly thank God for showing me "the handwriting on the wall."(p.367)

• At a women's halfway house, I ***became*** associated with Alcoholics Anonymous and ***became*** aware of alcoholism as a disease, not just a "weakness."(p.371)

• In time I ***became*** an officer and director of one of the largest commercial banks in the country.(p.374)

• The cocktail hour ***became*** a daily routine.(p.374)

• When it ***became*** noticeable to the point of comment, I devised ways of sneaking drinks on the side.(p.375)

• Rehearsals then ***became*** a part of the pattern, stopping at bars on the way to or from the place where drinks were to be served.(p.375)

• Drink planning ***became*** more important than any other plans.(p.375)

• To wake up at home, not knowing how I got there, and to realize I had driven my car, ***became*** torture.(p.375)

• It now ***became*** necessary to have noon drinks; at first just two, then gradually more.(p.375)

• Then I ***became*** careless and returned sometimes when I shouldn't have.(p.376)

• Finally our invitations ***became*** fewer and fewer as friends had more experience with my drinking pattern.(p.377)

• Her father ***became*** both mother and father to her.(p.402)

• Here, also, I had good friends, but I ***became*** more and more separated from them.(p.406)

• But I was not able to make use of this knowledge until after I ***became*** sober.(p.409)

• I ***became*** a menace, the fish-wife, the common scold.(p.410)

• John and Bud ***became*** my friends.(p.415)

• While I was at Pensacola my dad ***became*** dangerously ill and almost died of pneumonia plus a heart attack.(p.426)

• But I never ***became*** a morning drinker.(p.441)

• It ***became*** progressively harder to get up in the morning, until one day I asked myself what I would do for a patient who felt this rotten.(p.441)

• The psychiatrist, who had generally been ignoring me, now ***became*** quite interested; every day, he would ask me all kinds of questions about the A.A. meetings.(p.446)

• But it quickly ***became*** obvious that he had this childish notion instead: If he could get me to go to enough meetings while in the hospital, I would continue to go after he let me out.(p.447)

• Over the years, as I thought about Max, her good qualities grew and grew, and we married, and all these qualities ***became*** more and more apparent to me, and we were happier and happier.(p.450)

• Every defect I pointed out to her ***became*** greater and greater.(p.450)

• And we found ourselves back in prison, where our personalities ***became*** even more warped.(p.459)

• After a while I really did enjoy drinking and what it did to me, and I ***became*** dependent upon it for every occasion.(p.464)

• In the light of subsequent events it ***became*** evident that I took their advice far too literally, for, after some months of happy sobriety I drank again.(p.471)

• After our first child came my parents both ***became*** allies, but in later days, after I ***became*** an alcoholic, they both turned against me.(p.485)

• But when things ***became*** crucial, everything started going haywire and I started going haywire with them.(p.486)

• I said that she told me she was going to the movies, and I ***became*** foolishly disturbed about it and, as things snowballed, I decided to go out and get drunk.(p.487)

• I worked in the steel mill for possibly two months, and then I ***became*** disgusted with myself and decided to go back home.(p.492)

• At first they were rather amusing, but a little later on they ***became*** serious.(p.513)

• I don't know when I ***became*** an alcoholic, but I do believe I ***became*** one because I drank too much too often.(p.526)

• That was the day, that was the decision, I know now, when I crossed over the line and ***became*** an active alcoholic.(p.531)

• Actually, of course, I wanted someone to listen to me, because when I had a few martinis inside, I ***became*** the great author I longed to be; and the right listener was in for some pretty highflown theories of literature and of genius.(p.536)

• It ***became*** second nature for me to remove myself from anything or anybody I found myself growing fond of.(p.545)

• In my late teens I ***became*** aware of emotions I'd not counted on; restlessness, anxiety, fear and insecurity.(p.545)

• It ***became*** more and more necessary to escape from myself, for my remorse and shame and humiliation when I was sober were almost unbearable.(p.547)

• An honor student in college, I ***became*** editor of the yearbook.(p.555)

• My values ***became*** distorted.(p.556)

• Of course, the more I drank, the more unrealistic my expectations ***became*** and the poorer my performance, and the gap widened.(p.557)

• I ***became*** so weak, I could barely drag myself around.(p.558)

• The relationship between my wife and me was restored to a love and happiness that we had not known even before my alcoholism ***became*** acute.(p.559)

• Regaining my health, I ***became*** an avid jogger, sailor, and skier.(p.559)

because

• ***Because*** this book has become the basic text for our Society and has helped such large numbers of alcoholic men and women to recover, there exists a sentiment against any radical changes being made in it.(p.xi)

• It is important that we remain anonymous ***because*** we are too few, at present to handle the overwhelming number of personal appeals which may result from this publication.(p.xiii)

• These facts appear to be of extreme medical importance; ***because*** of the extraordinary possibilities of rapid growth inherent in this group they may mark a new epoch in the annals of alcoholism.(p.xxiii)

• It did not satisfy us to be told that we could not control our drinking just ***because*** we were maladjusted to life, that we were in full flight from reality, or were outright mental defectives.(p.xxiv)

• Men and women drink essentially ***because*** they like the effect produced by alcohol.(p.xxvi)

• This we did ***because*** we honestly wanted to, and were willing to make the effort.(p.25)

• We have heard of few instances where people, who showed definite signs of alcoholism, were able to stop for a long period ***because*** of an overpowering desire to do so.(p.32)

• We doubt if many of them can do it, ***because*** none will really want to stop, and hardly one of them, ***because*** of the peculiar mental twist already acquired, will find he can win out.(p.33)

• That may be true of certain nonalcoholic people who, though drinking foolishly and heavily at the present time, are able to stop or moderate, ***because*** their brains and bodies have not been damaged as ours were.(p.39)

• Perhaps we rejected this particular conception ***because*** it seemed inadequate.(p.45)

• Simply ***because*** it is impossible to explain what we see, feel, direct, and use, without a reasonable assumption as a starting point.(p.48)

• We missed the reality and beauty of the forest ***because*** we were diverted by the ugliness of some of its trees.(p.50)

• Wasn't it ***because*** self-reliance failed us?(p.68)

• We say this ***because*** we are very anxious that we talk to the right person.(p.74)

• ***Because*** of resentment and drinking, he had not paid alimony to his first wife.(p.79)

• Ministers and doctors are competent and you can learn much from them if you wish, but it happens that ***because*** of your own drinking experience you can be uniquely useful to other alcoholics.(p.89)

• But you may talk to him about the hopelessness of alcoholism ***because*** you offer a solution.(p.92)

• Don't start to withdraw again just ***because*** your friends drink liquor.(p.102)

• Of course, there is such a thing as incompatibility, but in nearly every instance the alcoholic only seems to be unloving and inconsiderate; it is usually ***because*** he is warped and sickened that he says and does these appalling things.(p.108)

• Is it not ***because*** each wants to play the lead?(p.122)

• Here were three exceptional men lost to this world ***because*** I did not understand alcoholism as I do now.(p.137)

• ***Because*** of the employee's special ability, or of his own strong personal attachment to him, the employer has sometimes kept such a man at work long beyond a reasonable period.(p.137)

• Next he can be assured that you do not intend to lecture, moralize, or condemn; that if this was done formerly, it was ***because*** of misunderstanding.(p.142)

• You ask, ***because*** many alcoholics, being warped and drugged, do not want to quit.(p.142)

• It boils right down to this: No man should be fired just ***because*** he is alcoholic.(p.148)

• But what about his responsibilities — his family and the men who would die ***because*** they would not know how to get well, ah -- yes, those other alcoholics?(p.154)

• Many mornings I have gone to classes, and even though fully prepared, would turn and walk back to the fraternity house ***because*** of my jitters, not daring to enter the classroom for fear of making a scene should I be called on for recitation.(p.173)

• I was between Scylla and Charybdis now, ***because*** if I did not drink my stomach tortured me, and if I did, my nerves did the same thing.(p.175)

• The water tank on the toilet I never used, ***because*** that looked too easy.(p.176)

• We could not be invited out ***because*** I would surely get tight and my wife dared not invite people in for the same reason.(p.177)

• About the time of the beer experiment I was thrown in with a crowd of people who attracted me ***because*** of their seeming poise, health, and happiness.(p.178)

• He knew all the answers, and certainly not ***because*** he had picked them up in his reading.(p.180)

• However, after two or three trials, I found this was not satisfactory ***because*** they did not serve enough to satisfy me.(p.184)

• Before very long we began to relate some incidents

of our drinking and, naturally, pretty soon, I realized both of them knew what they were talking about ***because*** you can see things and smell things when you're drunk, that you can't other times, and, if I had thought they didn't know what they were talking about, I wouldn't have been willing to talk to them at all.(p.185)

• I had no trouble there ***because*** I had never actually ceased to believe in God, and had tried lots of times to get help but hadn't succeeded.(p.186)

• I remember telling them too that it was going to be awfully tough, ***because*** I did some other things, smoked cigarettes and played penny ante poker, sometimes bet on the horse races and they said, "Don't you think you're having more trouble with this drinking than with anything else at the present time?(p.190)

• Of course, we had talked over quite a number of the failings that I had and made a sort of an inventory, which wasn't too difficult, ***because*** I had an awful lot of things wrong that were very apparent to me, ***because*** I knew all about them.(p.190)

• I still go to meetings, ***because*** I like to go.(p.192)

• There was always a tremendous drive and ambition to become a great guy, ***because*** I think I recognized inwardly that I didn't have any special talents.(p.194)

• He did things much better than I did ***because*** he applied himself and learned how to do them, and I never applied myself.(p.194)

• I can remember occasions when friends recommended me for positions or business opportunities that I wouldn't take ***because*** I felt that at some future date I'd get drunk and they would be hurt.(p.198)

• Long since I had come to believe I was insane ***because*** I did so many things I didn't want to do.(p.199)

• That was the reverse of my former pattern of fearing to go to work ***because*** I might drink!(p.199)

• I came to the conclusion it was ***because*** I hadn't been drunk.(p.200)

• And I hadn't been drunk ***because*** I hadn't taken a drink.(p.200)

• I was picked up at two-thirty that morning with my car smashed up by a street-car ***because*** I had run into a big concrete safety zone, and the street-car had run into me, and they took me out through the roof -- there's where I lost the suit.(p.202)

• The circumstances under which I reached these people were very odd ***because*** I was led there through things that I said when I couldn't even remember speaking.(p.202)

• Then, I started to miss meetings ***because*** it was raining or snowing or something else.(p.203)

• So I didn't have a beer one night, and as I drove home I was breaking my arm patting myself on the back ***because*** I had proved I could lick liquor.(p.203)

• The next day, they called me in for an examination, and the doctor wouldn't let me continue working and pardoned me from the plant for ten days ***because*** he said my eye had been injured.(p.205)

• I got two drinks, each of them a quarter of that pint, in me, and was talking along with these people, but I felt that sooner or later they were going to have me cornered ***because*** they were smarter than I was and the drink was beginning to take effect; but as I reached for the third drink Bob said, "Listen, Buster, you promised to take some medicine if we got you a drink.(p.206)

• ***Because*** it affected me so strenuously, they felt that hospitalization was indicated and I awoke in a hospital.(p.207)

• Then he started to talk to me about his drinking experiences, what his drinking had cost him, how much he had drunk and where, things like that, and I remember I was quite bored ***because*** I had never seen the guy before and had no interest at all in what, where and when he drank.(p.208)

• I knew I could quit ***because*** he had quit; he hadn't had a drink for over a year.(p.208)

• He was released, relieved from his alcoholism and was happy and contented ***because*** of it.(p.208)

• I can remember that in my childhood, he was ill at ease with the children ***because*** he attempted to assert an army discipline that had been ground into him during his three and a half years of army service.(p.210)

• I went to five grade schools, primarily ***because*** I was expelled for my conduct, but I eventually graduated from the eighth grade.(p.211)

• I went back to law school, and doubled up on the courses ***because*** I was then approaching thirty years of age and I wanted to get through as quickly as possible.(p.212)

• There had been some occasions – there was an automobile wreck, for instance -- when I had police escort home but not to jail, all of which, instead of doing me a favor, did me harm ***because*** I was then full of self-esteem as to the progress I had made both professionally and financially.(p.213)

• I realized that I had a problem, although my realization was not very deep ***because*** my own conceit wouldn't admit that I had any personality problems.(p.214)

• I never left the church, but I was a fringe member, and the thought simply never occurred to me that through the exercise of what I had I might find the answer to my problem, simply ***because*** I wouldn't admit that I had a problem.(p.214)

• I resented it of course, and I offered Clarence his commission, whatever it might be, if he would please not bother me ***because*** I had arrived at the conclusion that he was a solicitor for some alcoholic institute.(p.216)

• My experience in the hospital I considered to be terrific ***because*** Dr. Bob told me very quickly that medicine would have very little to do with it, outside of trying to restore my appetite for food.(p.217)

• I had had no hospitalization up to this time ***because*** I would not call doctors when I was getting over a bad one.(p.217)

• In fact, the last three years of my drinking was a routine of barbiturates in the morning, so that I could stop shaking enough to shave, and then alcohol beginning about four-thirty or five o'clock, with a struggle not to take a drink at noon or during the day, ***because*** I had the idea that if I took one drink, I would smell as though I had had a pint.(p.217)

• I believe every member of the Akron Group did come to see me, which impressed me terrifically, not so much ***because*** of the stories they told, but ***because*** they would take the time to come and talk to me without even knowing who I was.(p.218)

• That was an experience that I have never forgotten, and many times in my own work with A.A. newcomers I feel kind of guilty ***because*** I haven't done the same thing.(p.219)

• Professionally, after I was sober for a month or so I realized that I should school myself to dissolve the partnership I was in ***because*** I felt that I would never regain the respect of my partners no matter how long I was sober, and that I would be at a disadvantage.(p.220)

• Shortly after I came to this conclusion, I was importuned by another well-known patent law firm to help them out on some trial work ***because*** their trial man had had a heart attack and had been forbidden to go into the courtroom.(p.220)

• Having regard for the law of the land, I resigned myself to the will of the national legislators and quit drinking altogether, not ***because*** I had found it harmful, but ***because*** I couldn't get what I was accustomed to drink.(p.232)

• My customers lost confidence in me to the point where I retained what business I had only ***because*** I was a well-trained and reputedly fine craftsman.(p.234)

• "Best in the business, when he's sober," my customers would say, and I still had a following who would give me work though they deplored my habits, ***because*** they knew the job would be well done when they eventually got it.(p.234)

• And, ***because*** as I have discovered since, it is part of the "treatment" that these men be sent to see and talk with alcoholics who want to quit, he kept them busy.(p.235)

• Back at camp, all was forgiven ***because*** it was the End, but in the light of what I have since learned I know I was a confirmed alcoholic at nineteen.(p.242)

• Despite all this, I did like these new friends ***because***, again, they were like me.(p.245)

• My family would have nothing to do with me, in fact couldn't ***because*** I couldn't spare any of my money, which I needed for drink, to support them.(p.255)

• I stayed sober during the trip except for an occasional bottle of beer ***because*** funds barely met expenses.(p.255)

• Federal Theatre in Texas gave me an administrative job which I held for a year, only ***because*** I worked hard and productively when I worked, and ***because*** my very tolerant chief ascribed my frequent lapses to a bohemian temperament.(p.256)

• As he talked I gathered vaguely, (***because*** he was a faltering beginner then, just as I am now) that to be relieved of alcoholism I would have to be different.(p.257)

• I was deprived of many of the things that we feel are important in life, such as education particularly, ***because*** of my father's drinking.(p.261)

• I remember starting to city school, coming from a country school, and wanting so very, very much to be like the other girls and trying flour on my face for powder ***because*** I wasn't able to have any real powder.(p.261)

• I look back and remember these things ***because*** they made me very unhappy, and added to my feeling of inferiority at never being the same as other people.(p.261)

• But he's in all sorts of scrapes ***because*** he drinks too much."(p.262)

• I felt that his family were accepting me ***because*** it was good sense.(p.262)

• I was still bitter ***because*** I felt that drink had completely ruined my childhood and my married life, and I hated everything pertaining to it.(p.262)

• And another thing, it's a wonder they didn't throw us back in ***because*** I could become very dignified and sarcastic.(p.264)

• If I'd had a gun I'd have shot the horns right off the thing, ***because*** it made me raving mad.(p.265)

• One morning after a terrific drinking bout, I was in a little bar near our house, and I shook so that I was very much ashamed, ***because*** I was getting the shakes worse and worse.(p.266)

• I sipped the drink off the bar ***because*** I couldn't hold it in my hand, but I was still a lady, believe it or not, and I was deeply ashamed.(p.266)

• I'll get you the password, and I can find out where they meet ***because*** I know a guy that belongs.(p.266)

• One of our gifts from the family was a very lovely Bible, but we'd let the bulldog chew it ***because*** we weren't too interested in it.(p.268)

• I didn't know what they were going to do ***because*** he didn't tell us much.(p.269)

• I often think how that could have turned some people away, ***because*** there were no other women alcoholics there then.(p.269)

• He talked about his wife taking his little boy away from him ***because*** of his drinking, and how he got back together with them through A.A., and we began feeling grateful right then that all these things hadn't been taken from us.(p.270)

• I'd like to say here how important it was to us then that we do all the little things that people said were important, ***because*** later when Russ was so sick that I had to hold him up, they had a meeting out at the house.(p.270)

• Russ used to be very much pleased ***because*** he'd say, "I think Dr. Bob thoroughly enjoys coming out here.(p.271)

• We were so mad at her ***because*** she talked to him that way.(p.271)

• In the spiritual strength I had found, ***because*** of A.A., I felt that I had made a complete surrender, that I had really turned my life over that summer.(p.271)

• I knew then that I hadn't made a complete surrender, ***because*** I tried to bargain with the God I had found, and I said, "Anything but that!(p.271)

• Before the end finally came, I had, I guess made the surrender ***because*** I finally had been able to say that I would not mind too much.(p.272)

• I ate up every bit of it, ***because*** I wanted to find out how to stay sober.(p.273)

• I used to think I was cowardly ***because*** when things came out pertaining to the program that troubled me, I said to her many times, "Annie, am I being a coward ***because*** I lay those things away on the shelf and skip it?"(p.273)

• At least three of those four years must have been a living hell for my wife, ***because*** she had to watch the man she loved disintegrate morally, mentally and financially.(p.277)

• He it was who convinced me, ***because*** his own conviction was so real, that a Power greater than myself could help me in the crises of life, and that the means of communicating with this Power was simple prayer.(p.279)

• Out of this maelstrom just two coherent thoughts came to the surface; one, a drink would mean homelessness and death; two, I could no longer relieve the pressure of fear by starting home, as was once my habitual solution to this problem, ***because*** I no longer had a home.(p.279)

• After six months of sobriety I saw the picture in a different light: Detroit was the place I had to return to, not only ***because*** I must face the mess I had made there, but ***because*** it was there that I could be of the most service to A.A.(p.281)

• While there, two or three more "cash customers" (as Dr. Bob used to call them – probably ***because*** they had so little cash) were shipped in to us from Detroit.(p.282)

• But – supposing that just one man died ***because*** I had, for selfish reasons, kept my mouth shut?(p.282)

• I lived through a week of the fidgets ***because*** I had agreed to address a group of alcoholic inmates in one of our state mental hospitals.(p.283)

• Never in sixteen years have I dodged anything ***because*** I was afraid of it.(p.285)

• I learned early in my A.A. life that I could not afford to fondle such thoughts, as you might fondle

a pet, ***because*** this particular pet could grow into a monster.(p.285)
• I was very much interested in athletics, and ***because*** of this and parental influence, I didn't drink or smoke in either grade or high school.(p.287)
• She asked him to do something about me ***because*** she couldn't.(p.288)
• One of them was that I would try to get a group started in Chicago; the second was that I would have to return to Akron to attend meetings at least every two months until I did get a group started in Chicago; third, I decided I must place this program above everything else, even my family, ***because*** if I did not maintain my sobriety I would lose my family anyway.(p.292)
• In the spring of 1939, the Big Book was printed, and we had two inquiries from the New York office ***because*** of a fifteen-minute radio talk that was made.(p.294)
• I became convinced of that ***because*** I spent most of my time there and nary a job turned up.(p.300)
• Alone in the relative safety of my home ***because*** I knew I dare not risk the danger of blacking out in some public place or at the wheel of a car.(p.306)
• Some of us struggle with these people ***because*** we know that they are really very sick, but we also know that short of some miracle, we are not going to help them except temporarily, and that they will inevitably get worse and worse until one of two things happens.(p.308)
• "We watch the alcoholic performing in a position of responsibility and we know that ***because*** he is drinking heavily and daily he has cut his capacities by fifty per cent, and still he seems able to do a satisfactory job.(p.308)
• I have had my share of problems, heartaches and disappointments, ***because*** that is life, but also I have known a great deal of joy, and a peace that is the handmaiden of an inner freedom, I have a wealth of friends and, with my A.A. friends, an unusual quality of fellowship.(p.312)
• They sum it up like this: "We didn't wait to hit bottom ***because***, thank God, we could see the bottom.(p.315)
• Somehow, I made it through basic and then laid off the booze for about three months, ***because*** I was in school at night.(p.317)
• "It can't be my drinking," I thought, "***because*** I can stop any time I want to.(p.318)
• Other days, I had to miss work ***because*** I was still too drunk to stand up.(p.318)
• Once I did have a slip – tried drinking again – but the A.A.'s tell me not to worry about yesterday, ***because*** nobody can change it, and not to worry about tomorrow, ***because*** it hasn't come yet.(p.320)
• I was being very cagey, ***because*** I knew that if I did take one or two, I might want to take five or six or seven or eight.(p.323)
• I needed a drink, but I was afraid to take a morning drink, ***because*** I didn't want to be a drunk.(p.323)
• And then I'd fight with him ***because*** he had started!(p.325)
• I can't afford resentments against anyone, ***because*** they are the build-up of another drunk.(p.325)
• Through studied sneaky-drinking, I'd become a senior citizen without having lost a day's work ***because*** of booze.(p.327)
• I had suppressed tendencies to overindulge and thus reveal my "moral weakness," ***because*** false pride was so dominant.(p.327)
• Away down deep, I was motivated into dishonest behavior ***because*** I was a people-pleaser.(p.328)
• ***Because*** it was only through feeling defeat and feeling failure, the inability to cope with my life and with alcohol, that I was able to surrender and accept the fact that I had this disease, and that I had to learn to live again without alcohol.(p.335)
• I knew nothing about alcoholism or the D.T.'s, but when I woke up on this last morning of my son's illness, I taped the keyhole on my door ***because*** "everyone was out there."(p.338)
• ***Because*** I found that everything I turned to became a substitute for drink.(p.339)
• One said, "Don't feel that you are a martyr ***because*** you stopped drinking," and this hit me between the eyes.(p.346)
• With these new and enlightening doors opening up to me, I was able to make the eventual decision to stop drinking, a day at a time – ***because*** I, too, was an alcoholic.(p.355)
• Lucky ***because*** my excessive drinking never got me in jail, or hospitalized, nor did it ever cost me a job.(p.356)
• By persistence and salesmanship I managed to see more and more of my new friend, and ***because*** of her sympathetic nature she tolerated my company.(p.359)
• And deep in my heart I really meant what I said ***because*** I loved her more than anything else in the world, yes – even more than liquor.(p.362)
• Even I couldn't understand it, ***because*** I did love her so.(p.362)
• Her parting words were "I am not leaving you ***because*** I don't love you; it's ***because*** I do love you.(p.362)
• Looking directly at me was a large oil painting of my wife, and her very words seemed to shout at me -- "I am not leaving you ***because*** I don't love you; it's ***because*** I do love you.(p.363)
• I was certainly a complete surprise when I arrived at her family's home, but ***because*** I arrived on the wings of a tropical hurricane there wasn't much she could do but let me in.(p.364)
• That night she too had new hope ***because*** I had made sure she would know what I was doing about my drinking by packing every bit of A.A. literature I could put my hands on right on top so she couldn't help but see it when she opened my bag.(p.364)
• I had no qualms, ***because*** I felt the source of a drinking problem was all in how weak one was, and I wasn't like my dad (I thought).(p.370)
• It left us dazed, ***because*** he had seemed so indestructible.(p.370)
• I couldn't drink at home, ***because*** my husband frowned upon this.(p.370)
• With that, he told me to leave, ***because*** I was unfit as a mother, a wife, and a laundress.(p.371)
• A year later, while we were on a vacation trip she packed up to go home ***because*** of my excessive drinking, and I talked her out of it with the promise I would go on the wagon for at least a year.(p.377)
• The allergy I could understand ***because*** I am allergic to certain pollens.(p.380)
• Making amends is sometimes doing what we are capable of doing but failed to do ***because*** of alcohol; carrying out community responsibilities such as Community Funds, Red Cross, educational and religious activities in proportion to our abilities and energy.(p.381)
• Above all, I am grateful to A.A. for my sobriety, which means so much to my family, friends and business associates, ***because*** God and A.A. were able to do for me something I was unable to do for myself.(p.383)
• So I was used to it, but I didn't know what the effect of alcohol was ***because*** I always had wine, usually with dinner, but always with a lot of ice and about two tablespoons of sugar in it.(p.385)
• For some reason I can't remember, it finally dawned on me that I had a problem, and yet nobody was very critical about it except my family, and that was only ***because*** I decided, after seven years of marriage, that I would divorce my husband.(p.386)
• He called me that ***because*** I was drinking too much.(p.387)
• ***Because*** of this state of confusion and frustration I had hysterics on the seventeenth day for the first and only time in my life.(p.387)
• Frank had to go to New York, but ***because*** I had a dog, we had a duplex, and I thought – if only we had a house!(p.388)
• So I located a house, and I thought we ought to move into it immediately, but Frank was horrified, ***because*** he never knew what was going to happen to me.(p.388)
• He said that ***because*** of my drinking, he shouldn't leave, but that he had to go to New York for two weeks.(p.388)
• Then he said I couldn't possibly move on the first of February ***because*** I couldn't stay in that place by myself.(p.388)
• I wouldn't go to hospitals ***because*** I wanted my dog there, so I had to have a trained nurse.(p.390)
• I couldn't walk, having it in a cast, and the doctor left the cast on three weeks longer than was necessary ***because*** he never found me sober enough to take it off.(p.390)
• The cop must have seen the condition that I was in ***because*** he decided to take me home.(p.390)
• They phoned my husband that I was in jail and in such terrible shape that they didn't know what I would do to myself; and they realized that jail was no place for me, but that he was to wait a while before he got me, ***because*** at the time they called him to come over for me I was beating a tin cup against the wall.(p.390)
• I was as defiant as anybody could be ***because*** I was scared.(p.391)
• I think I actually read more contempt than was really there ***because*** just a week before someone had sent him the Saturday Evening Post article on A.A., and there was some glimmer of hope in it for him.(p.391)
• But Frank was frightened to death to give it to me, ***because*** I resented everything he said and did.(p.391)
• Today, ***because*** of A.A.'s growth during the intervening years, it is of course much bigger than it was then.(p.392)
• They sent me the regular letter they send to everybody else, but along with it, Ruth Hock, the nonalcoholic secretary, wrote a longhand note ***because*** she could see from the letter that I really needed help badly.(p.392)
• To me, A.A. is within the reach of every alcoholic, ***because*** it can be achieved in any walk of life and ***because*** the achievement is not ours but God's.(p.395)
• The statement fascinates me ***because*** of its simple verity.(p.396)
• It is bound to be rough, ***because*** who can say exactly how much of that green blood -- commonly known as money – was dissipated on dissipation?(p.396)
• Eighteen will be used as the starting point, ***because*** my drinking before was limited by age, the law, and money.(p.397)
• I saw him recently and he told me that he had always felt guilty, ***because***, after our separation, I had become a serious alcoholic.(p.403)
• In the morning, ***because*** I was young and healthy, my remorse was worse than my hangover.(p.404)
• In the first year there were episodes such as kicking Priscilla in the shins, getting the lock changed on the desk in the A.A. Club, ***because*** I, as secretary, didn't want the Intergroup secretary "interfering," and taking an older woman member out to lunch for the express purpose of informing her that she was "a phony."(p.416)
• I am no longer interested in living in a palace, ***because*** palace living was not the answer for me.(p.416)
• My friendships are meaningful, loving and interesting ***because*** I am sober.(p.416)
• I came to A.A. simply ***because*** there were no other doors of help open to me in my hometown.(p.420)
• ***Because*** A.A. really works for me!(p.421)
• Mom and I drank every waking moment ***because*** we felt so sorry for dad.(p.426)
• I took it easy, ***because*** they didn't know about me.(p.428)
• I crawled back to my analyst, not so much ***because*** I had faith in him, but ***because*** I had nowhere else to turn.(p.435)
• Max hadn't gotten that way ***because*** I didn't care.(p.440)
• But I thought it was ***because*** my responsibilities were increasing.(p.441)
• I never in my life took a tranquilizer, sedative, or pep pill ***because*** I was a pillhead.(p.443)
• I always took it ***because*** I had the symptom that only that pill would relieve.(p.443)
• When I am disturbed, it is ***because*** I find some person, place, thing, or situation – some fact of my life -- unacceptable to me, and I can find no serenity until I accept that person, place, thing, or situation as being exactly the way it is supposed to be at this moment.(p.449)
• And I was always glad to point it out, ***because*** I knew you wanted perfection, just as I did.(p.449)
• Then I went on my first week-long bender of solitary drinking, locked up in a hotel room, ***because*** my family opposed my coming marriage.(p.464)
• From that time on, fear was with me ***because*** I realized that not only would I not remember what happened to me while I was drinking, but apparently I couldn't control what happened.(p.465)
• This time I didn't put up any fight ***because*** I knew why they were there and where I was going, the psychopathic ward of the City Hospital, where I had been once before.(p.468)
• Was it ***because*** they told me in A.A. that I was an alcoholic?(p.470)
• A.A. didn't teach me I was an alcoholic; rather it taught me that ***because*** I was an alcoholic my life had become unmanageable.(p.470)
• In other words, the kindest doctor in the whole world, and I had one such, couldn't help me ***because*** I always felt, "You can't know about me – you can't possibly know – you don't even drink!"(p.471)
• They were always there ***because*** of a nervous breakdown, or for a "rest cure" – any reason except ***because*** of drinking.(p.471)
• With their help I also saw that certainly, ***because*** of some of the things I had done during the years, I was bordering on insanity, and so, facing the record, I tried to believe that a Power greater than I could and would restore me to sanity.(p.471)
• I feel that I have been restored to health and sanity these past years not through my own efforts nor as a result of anything I may have done, but ***because*** I've

come to believe -- to really believe -- that alone I can do nothing.(p.473)

• I felt very lonely and hurt, *because* nobody understood me.(p.478)

• Our shoes are not better than the average hobo's, and if we are fortunate enough to have a pair of stockings on, nobody notices the runs in them, *because* of our dazzling beauty and our dirty feet.(p.479)

• A couple of years later, we lost our elder brother in a house fire, *because* of pills and booze.(p.480)

• This means a great deal to me, *because* I had always figured that nobody cared.(p.481)

• Honesty is the easiest word for me to understand *because* it is the exact opposite of what I've been doing all my life.(p.482)

• About this time an incident took place in grade school that I have never forgotten *because* it made me realize that I was actually a physical coward.(p.484)

• I had quite a heartache about her then *because* she wasn't the type of girl that my mother wanted me to marry.(p.485)

• I do surgery *because* that's something that you can see; it's more tangible.(p.485)

• Father, through the years, had built up a very good mail order business *because*, at that time, there wasn't too much money in medicine.(p.485)

• I don't think I suffered too much as far as the racial situation was concerned *because* I was born into it and knew nothing other than that.(p.485)

• Economic conditions had a great deal to do with it, *because* I've often heard my father say that his mother would take one of the old time flour sacks and cut a hole through the bottom and two corners of it and there you'd have a gown.(p.486)

• For the first couple of years it wasn't too bad *because* the momentum kept things going.(p.486)

• I thought, "I know you didn't pay me, *because* you didn't get a prescription."(p.488)

• Fear gripped me then, *because* I could remember nothing about it.(p.489)

• I rebelled against this, *because* just about the time that I was getting ready to leave high school, a revelation came to me about God and it made things very complicated for me.(p.489)

• Then I went South, *because* they told me that the particular county I was going to in North Carolina was a dry county.(p.489)

• Nevertheless, I stayed sober there about six months, *because* I knew that Vi was to come later and bring the children.(p.490)

• I went back to my mother's for a few days until things cooled off, *because* the District Attorney had put out a summons for me to come to see him in his office.(p.491)

• I had to put up a three hundred dollar bond *because* he was carrying the same summons around in his pocket for me.(p.491)

• She never mentioned anything about my whiskey drinking *because* if she had I would have told her, "No" right then.(p.494)

• I knew my wife didn't *because* I had been sincere in all my promises to her as well as to my mother and to my close friends, but the urge to take that drink was more powerful than anything else.(p.494)

• Even when we were paying that two dollars a night, they often paid it for us *because* our collection was so small.(p.496)

• I just gathered up this and that alcoholic, *because*, in the back of my mind, I wanted to save all the world.(p.496)

• Three attempts to enlist in the service, and three failures *because* of being skinny.(p.499)

• We buy a gallon of "corn" *because* it is so cheap.(p.500)

• One evening I decided to go *because* two of those friends were to speak.(p.509)

• I'm fortunate *because* I live in an era when A.A. is available, and I'm able to take advantage of it.(p.512)

• I'm grateful *because* that Higher Power led me to A.A. a little over three years ago, when I needed it very badly.(p.512)

• When we first come into A.A., many of us are confused *because* as a general rule we're at the end of our respective ropes, and we don't know what to do.(p.512)

• It was a thorn in my side, *because* I knew it was the truth, and I hated to hear the truth, especially about myself.(p.513)

• But I came out of the Army just as big a drunk as when I went in, if not worse, *because* now I had a lot more resentments.(p.513)

• For me, it was a little different *because* I couldn't help thinking about the past, and I saw the future more or less mirrored in the past.(p.513)

• *Because* as I sat on that bed, I knew that I was in a terrible spot and didn't know how to get out of it.(p.515)

• Of course I really didn't have to worry on that score, *because* I wasn't the type that got half drunk.(p.515)

• *Because*, thank God, since I came into this program I haven't had any trouble.(p.516)

• It didn't worry me very much, *because* at that time I could shut off for a couple of months without taking a drink or even wanting one, and without feeling that I was giving anything up.(p.518)

• I got a job by myself which suited me down to the ground, *because* there was nobody really to interfere with what I did, one way or the other, and I usually had my nerves in good trim when anybody was coming around to inspect.(p.519)

• India lent itself to drinking then, if you were disposed to drink, *because* you lived in bungalows; you didn't live all together as you do at home in an Officer's Mess.(p.519)

• I left *because* I had a contretemps with the Governor.(p.520)

• But on the other hand, I was terribly fortunate *because* that should have been a court martial offense and I should have been out on my ear.(p.520)

• I lasted at that for four months chiefly on alcohol, *because* I never seemed to find any time to eat.(p.520)

• I think the Commanding Officer was rather tired of this particular chicken coming back to roost so often *because* he very soon wrote in to the medical authorities to tell them that they had to get me into hospital, to be thoroughly examined for drinking.(p.520)

• Finally, my mother came and said she had kept me at home for six years *because* she thought she could help me, but that now she had come to the conclusion that I wasn't even worth trying to help.(p.523)

• I don't know when I became an alcoholic, but I do believe I became one *because* I drank too much too often.(p.526)

• I don't remember any of them getting put out in the winter *because* they didn't pay their rent.(p.527)

• *Because* I had been drunk, the judge gave me only a twelve-year sentence in prison.(p.528)

• I just want to say that you don't have to be afraid, *because* no one at any A.A. meeting will bite you.(p.529)

• I have not seen a black face but mine since I've been here, and if I didn't look in the mirror, I wouldn't know that I was black, *because* these people treat me as one of them, which I am.(p.530)

• It's time to stop finding excuses for drinking and getting into trouble, *because* now there is a way out, and if you want what we have, try coming around and giving the program a chance.(p.530)

• I remember the day when I decided to drink myself to death quietly, without bothering anyone, *because* I was tired of having been a dependable, trustworthy person for about thirty-nine years without having received what I thought was a proper reward for my virtue.(p.531)

• There was the necessity for sticking to a job I hated, a dull, repetitive job performed in association with other men I had nothing in common with . . . performed for years on end, *because* the money was needed at home.(p.532)

• There was the physical aspect; to be the youngest and the runt of the brood of children, to have to wear glasses very early and so to be teased, to be bookish and bored in school *because* the captain of the football team could not translate Virgil and yet was the school god while you, you, you little shrimp, were the school egghead, junior size and an early model.(p.533)

• There was the father one lost respect for at the age of eleven, *because* the father broke his solemn word in a circumstance where you, eleven years old, had assumed guilt when you were innocent; but the father would not believe you, no matter what; and to ease his suffering you "confessed" and were "forgiven," only -- months later -- to have your "guilt" brought up -- only he and you knew what he was talking bout -- brought up in front of the stern grandmother.(p.533)

• Actually, of course, I wanted someone to listen to me, *because* when I had a few martinis inside, I became the great author I longed to be; and the right listener was in for some pretty highflown theories of literature and of genius.(p.536)

• Brandishing my "motto," which was "A little man with a stick is equal to a big man," sometimes I varied the literary lecture by a fight with a big man, selected solely *because* he was big and I was little.(p.537)

• I bear a few scars on my face from these fights, which I always lost, *because* the "stick" existed only in my mind.(p.537)

• Need I add that such was the case *because* I had no money to provide a roof over my head?(p.538)

• Still, I had had funds sufficient to get plastered *because* that, of course, was more important than paying my own way.(p.538)

• Repeated year on end, they are horrible -- frightening and degrading, a chronicle of tragedy which may be greater *because* the individual undergoing the tragedy, myself, knew what was happening, and yet refused to do anything to stop it.(p.538)

• In time I concluded that the reason I was hurt was *because* I loved my parents, and I concluded too that if I never allowed myself to love anybody or anything I could never be hurt again.(p.545)

• The only importance in all of this lies in the fact that at twenty-three I was just as sick as I was at thirty three, when I came into A.A., but at that time I apparently had no place to go *because* I had no drinking problem.(p.546)

• And *because* it works for me, it will work for all of us.(p.552)

• As another great man says, "The only real freedom a human being can ever know is doing what you ought to do *because* you want to do it."(p.553)

• By twenty-nine, I was having trouble coping with life *because* of my drinking.(p.555)

• Above all, I was suffering inner pain *because* my performance and my accomplishments in life failed to live up to my own expectations of myself.(p.557)

• And it had gone underground now, *because* everyone knew I shouldn't be drinking.(p.557)

• *Because* the "long form" is more explicit and of possible historic value, it is also reproduced.(p.563)

• Most of our experiences are what the psychologist William James calls the "educational variety" *because* they develop slowly over a period of time.(p.569)

become

• Because this book has *become* the basic text for our Society and has helped such large numbers of alcoholic men and women to recover, there exists a sentiment against any radical changes being made in it.(p.xi)

• A.A. had *become* a national institution.(p.xviii)

• Though none of these principles had the force of rules or laws, they had *become* so widely accepted by 1950 that they were confirmed by our first International Conference held at Cleveland.(p.xix)

• This has *become* the basis of a rapidly growing fellowship of these men and their families.(p.xxiii)

• These allergic types can never safely use alcohol in any form at all; and once having formed the habit and found they cannot break it, once having lost their self-confidence, their reliance upon things human, their problems pile up on them and *become* astonishingly difficult to solve.(p.xxvi)

• If any feel that as psychiatrists directing a hospital for alcoholics we appear somewhat sentimental, let them stand with us a while on the firing line, see the tragedies, the despairing wives, the little children; let the solving of these problems *become* a part of their daily work, and even of their sleeping moments, and the most cynical will not wonder that we have accepted and encouraged this movement.(p.xxvi)

• However, he did *become* "sold" on the ideas contained in this book.(p.xxx)

• Common sense would thus *become* uncommon sense.(p.13)

• He may start off as a moderate drinker; he may or may not *become* a continuous hard drinker; but at some stage of his drinking career he begins to lose all control of his liquor consumption, once he starts to drink.(p.21)

• What has *become* of the common sense and will power that he still sometimes displays with respect to other matters?(p.22)

• If you draw this fallacious reasoning to the attention of an alcoholic, he will laugh it off, or *become* irritated and refuse to talk.(p.23)

• 1.We admitted we were powerless over alcohol -- that our lives had *become* unmanageable.(p.59)

• To some extent we have *become* God-conscious.(p.85)

• We *become* much more efficient.(p.88)

• Even though your protege may not have entirely admitted his condition, he has *become* very curious to know how you got well.(p.92)

• If you leave such a person alone, he may soon *become* convinced that he cannot recover by himself.(p.96)

• What had *become* of their judgment, their common sense, their will power?(p.107)

• Of those who keep on, a good number will *become* true alcoholics after a while.(p.109)

• When they *become* too dangerous, we think the kind thing is to lock them up, but of course a good doctor should always be consulted.(p.114)

• When your husband is bad, you *become* a trembling recluse, wishing the telephone had never been invented.(p.115)

• Still another difficulty is that you may *become* jealous of the attention he bestows on other people, especially alcoholics.(p.119)
• We find the more one member of the family demands that the others concede to him, the more resentful they *become*.(p.122)
• It is possible to dig up past misdeeds so they *become* a blight, a veritable plague.(p.124)
• Giving, rather than getting, will *become* the guiding principle.(p.128)
• Dad may feel that for years his drinking has placed him on the wrong side of every argument, but now he has *become* a superior person with God on his side.(p.129)
• Drinking occasionally, and understanding your own reactions, it is possible for you to *become* quite sure of many things which, so far as the alcoholic is concerned, are not always so.(p.139)
• It may seem incredible that these men are to *become* happy, respected, and useful once more.(p.153)
• He too, has *become* a respected and useful member of his community.(p.158)
• This couple has since *become* so fascinated that they have dedicated their home to the work.(p.160)
• Some of them may sink and perhaps never get up, but if our experience is a criterion, more than half of those approached will *become* fellows of Alcoholics Anonymous.(p.163)
• Yet, as my record shows, I did *become* an extremely serious case.(p.182)
• There was always a tremendous drive and ambition to *become* a great guy, because I think I recognized inwardly that I didn't have any special talents.(p.194)
• It had long since *become* a serious problem.(p.197)
• Shortly after that, my brother, who had then *become* associated with a group of people and had stopped drinking, urged me to attend meetings with him.(p.205)
• For there were of course periods of clear realization of what I had *become*, attended by memories of what I had been, what I had expected to be.(p.224)
• With a creeping insidiousness, drink had *become* more important than anything else.(p.226)
• I was born in Europe, in Alsace to be exact, shortly after it had *become* German, and practically grew up with the "good Rhine wine" of song and story.(p.230)
• But each drink after the "first" seemed to *become* less effective and after three or four they all seemed like water.(p.241)
• Routine jobs bored me, but I would take on the toughest one I could find, work day and night until I had it under control; then it would *become* tedious and I'd lose all interest in it.(p.243)
• After being dry two weeks and sticking close to Jackie, all of a sudden I found I had *become* the sponsor of my sponsor, for he was suddenly taken drunk.(p.245)
• In my early twenties the hardships of hobo life did not discourage me, but I had no wish to *become* just a tramp.(p.253)
• Today I have Someone who will always hear me; I have a warm fellowship among men who understand my problems; I have tasks to do and am glad to do them, to see others who are alcoholics and to help them in any way I can to *become* sober men.(p.260)
• And another thing, it's a wonder they didn't throw us back in because I could *become* very dignified and sarcastic.(p.264)
• If it isn't anything that's going to help you or anybody else, why should you *become* involved in it, and get all disturbed about it?"(p.273)
• Liquor had *become* a crutch on the one hand and a means of retreat from life on the other.(p.277)
• I had thought that I was completely different from other people, that I was beginning to *become* a little balmy, even to the point of withdrawing more and more from society and wanting to be alone with my bottle.(p.290)
• I was caught in a cycle of alcohol and sedation that was proving inescapable and consciousness had *become* intolerable.(p.304)
• However, this isn't as rough as it sounds, as we do *become* grateful for the necessity that makes us toe the line, for we find that we are more than compensated for a consistent effort by the countless dividends we receive.(p.311)
• They saw that they had *become* actual or potential alcoholics, even though no serious harm had yet been done.(p.315)
• They realized that in the end alcoholism could be a mortal as cancer; certainly no sane man would wait for a malignant growth to *become* fatal before seeking help.(p.315)
• Through studied sneaky-drinking, I'd *become* a senior citizen without having lost a day's work because of booze.(p.327)
• A square from ultra-dry Kansas, I did not taste grog until I had finished college, done a stint on newspapers, married, *become* a father, and been in studio publicity two years.(p.328)
• He may even read in a newspaper that one out of every seven drinkers will *become* alcoholic, but he rarely is told that it holds true for all ages -- or that the tolerance to alcohol (and other drugs) decreases steadily, year after year, in the bodies of all persons.(p.330)
• I'd lived too long and *become* a loser, dependent on booze.(p.333)
• I should have realized that alcohol was getting hold of me when I started to *become* secretive in my drinking.(p.336)
• I spent five and a half years in psychoanalysis and proceeded to *become* a drunk.(p.349)
• A.A. has *become* a way of life and living for me.(p.355)
• By this time I had *become* associated with the fast growing and fascinating business of broadcasting.(p.358)
• With rare foresight he realized it could *become* a tornado.(p.373)
• How can a person with a fine family, an attractive home, an excellent position and high standing in an important city *become* an alcoholic?(p.373)
• By now it had *become* difficult to visualize a life without alcohol.(p.378)
• "We admitted we were powerless over alcohol -- that our lives had *become* unmanageable."(p.379)
• It did say, "admitted I was powerless over alcohol; that my life had *become* unmanageable."(p.379)
• Most certainly I was powerless over alcohol, and for me, my life had *become* unmanageable.(p.379)
• Dishonest thinking, prejudice, ego, antagonism toward anyone and everyone who dares to cross him, vanity and a critical attitude are character defects that gradually creep in and *become* a part of his life.(p.380)
• These thoughts *become* part of our daily lives.(p.382)
• Up to my early thirties, when my drinking had *become* a major problem, I lived in large houses, with servants and all the luxuries that I could possibly ask for.(p.401)
• I only saw that I had not *become* Mrs. Shakespeare.(p.403)
• He has since *become* famous and distinguished, an asset to his country.(p.403)
• I saw him recently and he told me that he had always felt guilty, because, after our separation, I had *become* a serious alcoholic.(p.403)
• My tongue had *become* increasingly skilled at venomous home truths.(p.405)
• The remorse would turn inside out, and *become* anticipatory pleasure.(p.408)
• What I had secretly believed myself to be all along, this I had *become*.(p.411)
• Priscilla, an A.A. who, like Marty, has *become* one of my greatest friends, decided that I was a stubborn case.(p.414)
• All the people involved in these flare-ups took it with remarkable grace, have teased me about it since, and have *become* good friends of mine.(p.416)
• I have my A.A. friends, and I have *become* reacquainted with my old friends on a new basis.(p.416)
• If I had not *become* an active alcoholic and joined A.A., I might never have found my own identity or *become* a part of anything.(p.417)
• To this day, I am amazed at how many of my problems -- most of which had nothing to do with drinking, I believed -- have *become* manageable or have simply disappeared since I quit drinking.(p.448)
• It helped me a great deal to *become* convinced that alcoholism was a disease, not a moral issue; that I had been drinking as a result of a compulsion, even though I had not been aware of the compulsion at the time; and that sobriety was not a matter of will-power.(p.448)
• The idea behind it is that, having taken the treatment, your system is so "conditioned" that the mere sight or smell or taste of alcohol produces a violent reaction, and you *become* ill.(p.469)
• A.A. didn't teach me I was an alcoholic; rather it taught me that because I was an alcoholic my life had *become* unmanageable.(p.470)
• My mother had been recently converted and, actually, had *become* a religious fanatic.(p.483)
• I *become* a teacher in a boys' school.(p.500)
• When I am through speaking, the whole idea has *become* absurd.(p.507)
• My life had *become* unmanageable due to the excessive use of alcohol.(p.515)
• But the more meetings you attend, the more people you meet at these meetings, the clearer the Steps *become*.(p.516)
• For me, A.A. has *become* a way of life.(p.516)
• He survived to *become* a mainstay of A.A. in Eire.(p.517)
• I wandered, craving peace, from one spot to another of youthful happy memory, and loathed the man I had *become*.(p.539)
• I could not face the boy and youth I was in the reality of the contemptible man I had *become*.(p.540)
• The less you think of yourself the more of a person you *become*.(p.542)
• I had no problem admitting I was powerless over alcohol, and I certainly agreed that my life had *become* unmanageable.(p.550)
• I had fed it, fanned it and nurtured it as one might a delicate child, and it had *become* as much a part of me as my breathing.(p.551)

becomes

• If a sufficiently strong reason -- ill health, falling in love, change of environment, or the warning of a doctor -- *becomes* operative, this man can also stop or moderate, although he may find it difficult and troublesome and may even need medical attention.(p.21)
• Yet let him drink for a day, and he frequently *becomes* disgustingly and even dangerously anti-social.(p.21)
• Our so-called will power *becomes* practically nonexistent.(p.24)
• He *becomes*, on the next occasion, still more demanding or gracious, as the case may be.(p.61)
• He *becomes* angry, indignant, self-pitying.(p.61)
• What used to be the hunch or the occasional inspiration gradually *becomes* a working part of the mind.(p.87)
• Even though your husband *becomes* unbearable and you have to leave him temporarily, you should, if you can, go without rancor.(p.111)
• Sometimes he will be so interested that he *becomes* really neglectful.(p.119)
• The alcoholic's past thus *becomes* the principal asset of the family and frequently it is almost the only one!(p.124)
• He *becomes* still less communicative.(p.126)
• He *becomes* a religious enthusiast.(p.128)
• It *becomes* vital, also, that others not know of our defeats, nor suspect our loss of confidence.(p.331)
• The more I focus my mind on its defects -- late start, long drunkalogues, cigarette smoke -- the worse the meeting *becomes*.(p.451)
• Men are supposed to be tough and rugged to start with, but if a woman *becomes* that way, it is pretty hard to get back the niceties of womanhood.(p.480)
• I learn that when we act upon the highest conception of honesty which is given us, our sense of honesty *becomes* more acute.(p.507)
• But as the years go by, the stretch *becomes* unbearable; and the man with the grown-up brain and the childish emotions -- vanity, self-interest, false pride, jealousy, longing for social approval, to name few -- *becomes* a prime candidate for alcohol.(p.534)

becoming

• We were in a position where life was *becoming* impossible, and if we had passed into the region from which there is no return through human aid we had but two alternatives: One was to go on to the bitter end, blotting out the consciousness of our intolerable situation as best we could; and the other, to accept spiritual help.(p.25)
• In the early days of our drinking we occasionally remained sober for a year or more, *becoming* serious drinkers again later.(p.34)
• In this way you can set them on the right track without *becoming* critical of them.(p.100)
• He is worried at times, and is *becoming* aware that he cannot drink like other people.(p.109)
• It thickened, ever *becoming* blacker.(p.151)
• I then began asking a lot of questions of both my brother and Dr. Bob about how this thing worked, and I suppose I was *becoming* more glassy-eyed all the while, for eventually I said to Bob, "You're all dried up.(p.206)
• From the top of the heap in a few years he had skidded to *becoming* a shuffling customer, still entering the better barrooms but welcomed by neither mine host nor his patrons.(p.236)
• What about those fears which once paralyzed me to the point of my *becoming* a semi-hermit?(p.284)
• She realized what she was *becoming*.(p.335)
• I went on, realizing what I was *becoming*, hating myself for it, bitter, blaming life, blaming everything else but the fact that I should turn about and do something about my drinking.(p.337)

- I achieved recognized and national standing in my profession, as well as ***becoming*** a director in many important institutions having to do with the civic life of a large city.(p.374)
- It seemed to me my wife was ***becoming*** more intolerant and narrow minded all the time.(p.376)
- Cold sweats, jumpy nerves and lack of sleep were ***becoming*** intolerable.(p.378)
- My first analyst said, "You are ***becoming*** more and more of an alcoholic," and sent me to another analyst.(p.407)
- I was ***becoming*** a solitary drinker, but I didn't care.(p.426)
- With all this, it was ***becoming*** increasingly hard to maintain my front of distinction and respectability to the world.(p.435)
- But I am to learn later that it began with my desire for material success ***becoming*** greater than my interest in the welfare of my fellow man.(p.507)
- Society can do anything it chooses to do with me when I am drunk and I can't lift a finger to stop it, for I forfeit my rights through the simple expedient of ***becoming*** a menace to myself and to the people around me.(p.549)
- There is something spiritual about A.A. too, and Catholic participation in it almost invariably results in poor Catholics ***becoming*** better Catholics."(p.574)

bed

- I wondered whether I dared hide a full bottle of gin near the head of our ***bed***.(p.8)
- He is the fellow who goes to ***bed*** so intoxicated he ought to sleep the clock around.(p.21)
- When I returned to the hotel it struck me a highball would be fine before going to ***bed***, so I stepped into the bar and had one.(p.41)
- This man recounts that he tumbled out of ***bed*** to his knees.(p.56)
- Two days later, a future fellow of Alcoholics Anonymous stared glassily at the strangers beside his ***bed***.(p.157)
- The man in the ***bed*** was told of the acute poisoning from which he suffered, how it deteriorates the body of an alcoholic and warps his mind.(p.157)
- Finally my father had to send a doctor out from my home town who managed to get me back there in some way, and I was in ***bed*** about two months before I could venture out of the house.(p.175)
- This would lessen my chances of smuggling some home that evening, which in turn would mean a night of futile tossing around in ***bed*** followed by a morning of unbearable jitters.(p.176)
- He came and got me home and to ***bed***, gave me a few drinks that night, and one bottle of beer the next morning.(p.179)
- Morning after morning I would awake sick and with terrible jitters, but there was always a flask of liquor sitting on the table beside my ***bed***.(p.183)
- During the first six months of 1935, I was hospitalized eight times for intoxication and shackled to the ***bed*** two or three days before I even knew where I was.(p.184)
- They left this with me to think over, and I lay there on that hospital ***bed*** and went back over and reviewed my life.(p.186)
- (At this point, the Editors intrude just long enough to supplement Bill D.'s account, that of the man on the ***bed***, with that of Bill W., the man who sat by the side of the ***bed***.)(p.188)
- Bill lay on his hospital ***bed*** and looked at us in wonder.(p.188)
- I'd waked up in strange rooms before, fully dressed on a ***bed*** or a couch; I'd waked up in my own room, in or on my own ***bed***, not knowing what hour or day it was, afraid to ask . . . but this was different.(p.222)
- And as I fumed helplessly and planned to get good and drunk and show them, my eye caught a sentence in the book lying open on my ***bed***: "We cannot live with anger."(p.228)
- I had some financial success through no ability of my own and, when jobless and almost wiped out in 1930, I began to trade and sell my collection; much of the proceeds went to keep my apartment stocked with liquor and almost every night saw me helpless to ***bed***.(p.255)
- I lay across the ***bed*** on my stomach with nothing but pain and sickness.(p.267)
- An attorney sat at the side of the ***bed*** where I was lying, and he sat on the edge of his chair and looked as innocent as a baby.(p.268)
- When we went to ***bed*** my sides ached, and I said to my husband, "I thought I would never laugh again, but I have laughed."(p.269)
- Russ lived a year longer than they expected him to live, and in that year he was in ***bed*** for at least six months.(p.272)
- Three months in ***bed***.(p.275)
- Three more months of being up and around the house for brief periods and in ***bed*** the rest of the time.(p.275)
- But – I also stayed up week nights after they had retired and drank myself into ***bed***.(p.277)
- Instead, he got dressed, took me out, bought me three or four double shots and put me to ***bed***.(p.278)
- Here, while in a hospital ***bed***, men with clear eyes, happy faces, and a look of assurance and purposefulness about them, came to see me and told me their stories.(p.279)
- I lay down on the ***bed*** and slept like a child.(p.280)
- After finding every bottle that I had hidden around the apartment, she took away my pants, my shoes, my money and my keys, threw them under the ***bed*** in the back bedroom and slip-locked our door.(p.288)
- I can still remember very distinctly getting into Akron at eleven p.m. and routing this same Howard out of ***bed*** to do something about me.(p.290)
- The last day of my drinking career, I drank twenty-two of them between ten and twelve a.m. and I shall never know how many more followed them until I was poured into ***bed*** that night.(p.298)
- I cannot remember just when I became the victim of insomnia, but I do know that the last year and a half I never went to ***bed*** sober a single night.(p.299)
- I had a mortal fear of going to ***bed*** and tossing all night.(p.299)
- I usually passed out when I hit the ***bed***.(p.319)
- No matter how often I had gone into and come out of alcoholic lows during the day, the pattern bounced me out of ***bed*** each night about 2:00 a.m., shaking and hurting in the agitation that always follows a drug's sedation.(p.332)
- The horrors of increasing hangover sickness to occupy the entire day; nausea, dry heaves, the rocking ***bed***, the nightmare-filled mind.(p.408)
- Slowly I realized I was in ***bed*** and that the objects were my feet, encased in a harness affair.(p.422)
- At one end of the ***bed***, near the foot, was a printed card, and beneath that was a charted graph.(p.422)
- I opened my eyes again and a shadow fell across the ***bed***.(p.422)
- The doctor sat down beside the ***bed*** and asked me how I felt.(p.423)
- The doctor was still sitting beside my ***bed***.(p.427)
- I would drink all night in bars, come home about five a.m., down a good big glass of whiskey straight, and tumble into ***bed***.(p.428)
- She cried a bit and went to ***bed***; that was the only answer to problems that she had left.(p.440)
- Then I found the solution: At the end of study time, I would drink two beers, jump in ***bed***, sleep real fast, and wake up smart.(p.440)
- I remember finding myself in the middle of the night in the doctors' parking lot at the hospital with one foot in the car and one foot on the ground, not knowing which was the lead foot; finding myself hanging up the telephone – then realizing I had gotten out of ***bed***, answered the phone, turned on the light, and carried on a conversation with a patient.(p.441)
- Eventually, I was taking forty-five milligrams of the long-acting Benzedrine and forty-five of the short-acting just to get out of ***bed*** in the morning.(p.442)
- I didn't feel I could lie in ***bed*** and squirt the stuff in my veins while my kids and wife stood around watching me, so I kept the drug in my bag and the bag in the car and the car in the garage.(p.442)
- In the garage, I would put the needle in my vein and then try to figure out exactly how much medication to inject to overcome the pep pills while adding to the sleeping pills while ignoring the tranquilizers, in order to get just enough to be able to pull out the needle, jerk the tourniquet, throw it in the car, slam the car door shut, run down the hall, and fall in ***bed*** before I fell asleep.(p.442)
- When we got home, I got a bottle of Scotch and went to ***bed***.(p.445)
- I don't mean that I went to ***bed*** one night a normal drinker, and awoke the next morning an alcoholic.(p.464)
- When I got home my mouth was very painful, so I got an ice-bag and went to ***bed***.(p.466)
- The next day the ice-bag and I were still in ***bed*** -- but we had a bottle too!(p.466)
- My pattern of drinking at that time had reached the point where once I really started, I would retire to my ***bed*** and drink myself into oblivion.(p.466)
- But I can remember in post graduate days, and during interneship, that very often I'd go to a patient's ***bed*** and start a process of elimination and then, very often, I'd wind up guessing.(p.485)
- Then I left and went home to ***bed***.(p.492)
- I'll go to ***bed***.(p.500)
- Yet I am fairly steady when I go to ***bed***.(p.500)
- I drink and go to ***bed***; I take a few the next morning and go see my mother once more.(p.501)
- She puts me to ***bed*** and gives me a hypodermic.(p.501)
- I get in ***bed*** and turn out the light.(p.503)
- I get out of ***bed*** and go to the man's room.(p.504)
- I return to ***bed***.(p.504)
- I tumble out of ***bed*** onto my knees.(p.504)
- I crawl back into ***bed*** and sleep like a child.(p.504)
- It's no ***bed*** of roses, but somehow or other I've been able to make it, through the kindness of people in A.A.(p.511)
- Because as I sat on that ***bed***, I knew that I was in a terrible spot and didn't know how to get out of it.(p.515)
- I stopped off just to have one drink to see if it tasted the same on the way back to London, and that night I was carried back to ***bed*** again.(p.522)
- When sleep overtook me, my practice was to undress and go to ***bed***, wherever.(p.537)
- Still another friend and temporary host received me at four in the morning from the charge of a policeman who had found me "going to ***bed***" in a garage far from the last place I could remember having been, a fashionable bar and restaurant in the theatrical district of New York, to which I had repaired after my date for that evening, a charming lady of the theatre who had refused my company for obvious reasons.(p.538)
- After my very first drink – a tiny glass of sherry my father gave me to celebrate the New Year when I was thirteen -- I went up to ***bed***, dizzy with exhilaration and excitement, and I prayed I wouldn't drink any more!(p.554)
- When I awoke in the middle of the night with shakes and sweats and fears, I would hear my wife weeping quietly in ***bed*** beside me.(p.558)

bed-time

- ***Bed-time*** comes.(p.497)

bedevilments

- We were having trouble with personal relationships, we couldn't control our emotional natures, we were a prey to misery and depression, we couldn't make a living, we had a feeling of uselessness, we were full of fear, we were unhappy, we couldn't seem to be of real help to other people – was not a basic solution of these ***bedevilments*** more important than whether we should see newsreels of lunar flight?(p.52)

bedraggled

- We, who were dirty, ***bedraggled*** and in ski clothes.(p.415)

bedroom

- But it took six more months of work and disappointments before a group of three men got together in my rooming house ***bedroom*** for their first A.A. meeting.(p.282)
- After finding every bottle that I had hidden around the apartment, she took away my pants, my shoes, my money and my keys, threw them under the bed in the back ***bedroom*** and slip-locked our door.(p.288)
- When alcohol took me over, my bar was my kitchen, my living room, my ***bedroom***, the back bathroom, and the two hampers.(p.335)
- (I am looking at it now in my ***bedroom*** -- a copy that was presented to me a couple of years ago by the A.A. group in that same prison.)(p.461)

beds

- After such an approach many take up their ***beds*** and walk again.(p.19)
- I sat down on the side of one of their ***beds***, and I started to weep, and I couldn't stop, and I was so startled, and I apologized again and again for it.(p.272)
- Hidden old-drunks can pass out on their ***beds*** and snooze unreproached, under the guise of taking those vital retirement-age naps.(p.330)

bedside

- I felt it certainly must be very depressing to her that I should sit there by her ***bedside*** and cry.(p.272)
- This was such a new thought that I got all sorts of books on Higher Powers, and I put a Bible by my ***bedside***, and I put a Bible in my car.(p.348)
- On our honeymoon, we had iced champagne by the ***bedside*** day and night.(p.555)

beer

- "Here lies a Hampshire Grenadier Who caught his death Drinking cold small ***beer***.(p.1)
- A tumbler full of gin followed by half a dozen bottles of ***beer*** would be required if I were to eat any breakfast.(p.5)
- "Why don't you try ***beer*** and wine?"(p.20)

• The almost certain consequences that follow taking even a glass of ***beer*** do not crowd into the mind to deter us.(p.24)
• Here are some of the methods we have tried: Drinking ***beer*** only, limiting the number of drinks, never drinking alone, never drinking in the morning, drinking only at home, never having it in the house, never drinking during business hours, drinking only at parties, switching from scotch to brandy, drinking only natural wines, agreeing to resign if ever drunk on the job, taking a trip, not taking a trip, swearing off forever (with and without a solemn oath), taking more physical exercise, reading inspirational books, going to health farms and sanitariums, accepting voluntary commitment to asylums -- we could increase the list ad infinitum.(p.31)
• If he temporizes and still thinks he can ever drink again, even ***beer***, he might as well be discharged after the next bender which, if an alcoholic, he is almost certain to have.(p.142)
• No ***beer*** or liquor was sold in the neighborhood, except at the State liquor agency where perhaps one might procure a pint if he could convince the agent that he really needed it.(p.171)
• On account of my enormous capacity for ***beer***, I was elected to membership in one of the drinking societies, and soon became one of the leading spirits.(p.173)
• For the benefit of those experimentally inclined, I should mention the so-called ***beer*** experiment.(p.177)
• When ***beer*** first came back, I thought that I was safe.(p.177)
• It was harmless; nobody ever got drunk on ***beer***.(p.177)
• It then occurred to me that after one was all smelled up with ***beer*** nobody could tell what had been drunk, so I began to fortify my ***beer*** with straight alcohol.(p.178)
• Of course, the result was very bad, and that ended the ***beer*** experiment.(p.178)
• About the time of the ***beer*** experiment I was thrown in with a crowd of people who attracted me because of their seeming poise, health, and happiness.(p.178)
• He came and got me home and to bed, gave me a few drinks that night, and one bottle of ***beer*** the next morning.(p.179)
• They looked at one another queerly and, finally, one of them allowed he'd have a ***beer*** and they all followed him, each of them saying he'd have a ***beer*** too.(p.194)
• At the end of fifteen months, I tried the ***beer*** experiment.(p.203)
• After drinking one glass of ***beer*** at the end of my work period for about five days, I thought I'd better find out whether I really had the stuff licked.(p.203)
• So I didn't have a ***beer*** one night, and as I drove home I was breaking my arm patting myself on the back because I had proved I could lick liquor.(p.203)
• ***Beer*** and wine were not the answer.(p.230)
• I early decided that the wine of America was very inferior stuff and took up ***beer*** instead.(p.231)
• There I sat in the evenings, enjoying with my friends our memories of the "old country," singing the old songs we all knew, playing simple card games for drinks and consuming great quantities of ***beer***.(p.231)
• I missed the old social times, of course, but had no definite craving even for ***beer***.(p.232)
• ***Beer*** was too bulky and it couldn't be kept in a jug under the counter ready to be dumped when John Law came around.(p.233)
• I stayed sober during the trip except for an occasional bottle of ***beer*** because funds barely met expenses.(p.255)
• He came with two cans of ***beer***.(p.267)
• That nasty little can of ***beer***!(p.267)
• I remember sometime, it was possibly six months after we had been going steadily to King School, that we were coming home from a meeting and saw a car along the way, and a fellow in back drinking a bottle of ***beer***.(p.271)
• So I told dad that I would lick it on my own, that I would drink nothing for a month and after that only ***beer***.(p.289)
• My wife became pregnant and the doctor recommended the use of port or ale . . . so . . . I bought a six gallon crock and a few bottles, listened to advice from amateur brewmeisters, and was off on my ***beer*** manufacturing career on a small scale (for the time being).(p.297)
• Somehow or other, I must have misunderstood the doctor's instructions, for I not only made the ***beer*** for my wife, I also drank it for her.(p.297)
• That being the case, it didn't take me long to figure out that my meager manufacturing facilities were entirely inadequate to the manufacture of ***beer*** for social and domestic consumption.(p.297)
• We were having card parties with limburger and ***beer*** quite regularly.(p.297)
• Eventually, of course, what with all the hilarity that could be provoked with a few gallons of ***beer***, there seemed to be no need of bridge or poker playing for entertainment.(p.297)
• The parties waxed more liquid and hilarious as time went on, and eventually I discovered that a little shot of liquor now and then between beers had the tendency to put me in a whacky mood much quicker than having to down several quarts of ***beer*** to obtain the same effect.(p.298)
• The inevitable result of this discovery was that I soon learned that ***beer*** made a very good chaser for whiskey.(p.298)
• I got along fairly well with my party drinking for quite some time, but eventually I began to visit ***beer*** joints in between parties.(p.298)
• I tried the ***beer*** diet, the wine diet, timing, measuring, and spacing of drinks.(p.305)
• I switched to ***beer***.(p.339)
• I had always hated ***beer***, but now I grew to love it, bottle after bottle of it, warm or cold.(p.339)
• Near the Laundromat, I would buy one bottle of pop and a few bottles of ***beer*** or wine, and go into the rest room, empty the pop bottle, refill it with the booze, and proceed to do my laundering.(p.370)
• So I went down to him quite a few times a month and had him shoot me full of the stuff; and then I went across the street to a little drug store to take a glass of ***beer*** or two beers, and then stopped at the liquor store to get myself a pint and go home.(p.389)
• At this time, the price of booze in the bars was fifteen cents a shot and ten cents a ***beer***.(p.397)
• I found out fast that the cheapest way to get drunk was on shots with ***beer*** chasers at two bits a crack.(p.397)
• I graduated from shots and ***beer*** chasers to Scotch and sodas.(p.398)
• (It was the ***beer*** and cheap whiskey that was making me so sick.(p.398)
• They introduced me to ***beer*** in the morning to kill hangovers.(p.407)
• Drink only ***beer*** or wine.(p.408)
• I remembered having had a little drink of whiskey with a can of warm ***beer*** as a chaser.(p.422)
• I also kept ***beer***.(p.423)
• At fifteen I was strictly a ***beer*** drinker.(p.423)
• One night I was sitting in the lab alone with a fifth and a case of ***beer*** listening to dreamy Hawaiian music on the radio.(p.427)
• I swung, I swore, I started throwing ***beer*** cans at the advancing hordes of pineapple faces.(p.427)
• That night we drink ***beer*** at taverns.(p.474)
• Went overseas on ***beer***.(p.475)
• Soon I drink ***beer***.(p.475)
• I wander to a stable and drink five bottles of ***beer***.(p.502)
• But not for long; now, for five Friday nights in a row, I went to jail, picked up sodden with ***beer*** (which I always disliked, but which was the only drink available); in jail five consecutive Friday nights in the town where I had grown up, where I had been an honor student in high school, where a kindly uncle, bailing me out, said, "Bob, our family just doesn't do this sort of thing."(p.539)
• I also began to drink at fraternity parties and ***beer*** busts.(p.555)

beers

• Then I got into the habit of having ***beers***, and decided that a drink of whiskey was not any worse; so I would get the one drink of whiskey but, on second thought, I decided that as long as I was only going to have one, I might as well make it a double-header.(p.203)
• At that time I could go into any saloon, have one or two ***beers***, walk out and forget about it.(p.231)
• You can all remember that in the first few months after the change, a great many men, who had formerly been used to a few ***beers*** every day or an occasional drink of whiskey, simply quit all alcoholic drinks.(p.232)
• We ordered sandwiches and one man said, "Three ***beers***."(p.247)
• After a bit, the other man said "Three ***beers***."(p.247)
• Then it was my turn -- I ordered "Three ***beers***," but this time it was different, I had a cash investment of thirty cents and, on a ten dollar a week salary, that's a big thing.(p.247)
• So I drank all three ***beers***, one after the other, said "I'll be seeing you, boys," and went around the corner for a bottle.(p.247)
• The parties waxed more liquid and hilarious as time went on, and eventually I discovered that a little shot of liquor now and then between ***beers*** had the tendency to put me in a whacky mood much quicker than having to down several quarts of beer to obtain the same effect.(p.298)
• So I went down to him quite a few times a month and had him shoot me full of the stuff; and then I went across the street to a little drug store to take a glass of beer or two ***beers***, and then stopped at the liquor store to get myself a pint and go home.(p.389)
• Then I found the solution: At the end of study time, I would drink two ***beers***, jump in bed, sleep real fast, and wake up smart.(p.440)
• I'll just take a few ***beers*** now and then.(p.502)

Beery

• This worked nicely until my wife and I went to see Wallace ***Beery*** in "Tugboat Annie," after which the pant-leg and stocking racket were out!(p.177)
• So I'd sit up, watch old Wallace ***Beery*** movies on all-night TV, and drink.(p.441)

befall

• You may be afraid your husband will lose his position; you are thinking of the disgrace and hard times which will ***befall*** you and the children.(p.116)

befell

• The head of the house ought to remember that he is mainly to blame for what ***befell*** his home.(p.127)
• The most terrible blow of my life ***befell*** me after I'd found sobriety through A.A.(p.437)

befogged

• Though we work out our solution on the spiritual as well as an altruistic plane, we favor hospitalization for the alcoholic who is very jittery or ***befogged***.(p.xxiv)

before

• But when the broker gave him Dr. Silkworth's description of alcoholism and its hopelessness, the physician began to pursue the spiritual remedy for his malady with a willingness he had never ***before*** been able to muster.(p.xvi)
• It was now time, the struggling groups thought, to place their message and unique experience ***before*** the world.(p.xvii)
• Then Jack Alexander wrote a feature article in the Saturday Evening Post and placed such a compelling picture of A.A. ***before*** the general public that alcoholics in need of help really deluged us.(p.xviii)
• More often than not, it is imperative that a man's brain be cleared ***before*** he is approached, as he has then a better chance of understanding and accepting what we have to offer.(p.xxiv)
• Of course an alcoholic ought to be freed from his physical craving for liquor, and this often requires a definite hospital procedure, ***before*** psychological measures can be of maximum benefit.(p.xxv)
• I talked with him for some time, but was not able to bring myself to feel that I had known him ***before***.(p.xxix)
• ***Before*** then, I had written lots of sweet promises, but my wife happily observed that this time I meant business.(p.5)
• Again I swayed dizzily ***before*** an open window, or the medicine cabinet where there was poison, cursing myself for a weakling.(p.6)
• Now I was to plunge into the dark, joining that endless procession of sots who had gone on ***before***.(p.8)
• How dark it is ***before*** the dawn!(p.8)
• I would need it ***before*** daylight.(p.8)
• Childhood memories rose ***before*** me.(p.10)
• I could almost hear the sound of the preacher's voice as I sat, on still Sundays, way over there on the hillside; there was that proffered temperance pledge I never signed; my grandfather's good natured contempt of some church folk and their doings; his insistence that the spheres really had their music; but his denial of the preacher's right to tell him how he must listen; his fearlessness as he spoke of these things just ***before*** he died; these recollections welled up from the past.(p.10)
• But my friend sat ***before*** me, and he made the point-blank declaration that God had done for him what he could not do for himself.(p.11)
• A much more important demonstration of our principles lies ***before*** us in our respective homes, occupations and affairs.(p.19)
• ***Before*** going into a detailed discussion, it may be well to summarize some points as we see them.(p.20)
• It may cause him to die a few years ***before*** his time.(p.21)
• Yet early next morning he searches madly for the bottle he misplaced the night ***before***.(p.21)
• This tragic situation has already arrived in practically every case long ***before*** it is suspected.(p.24)
• I had been out of town ***before*** during this particular dry spell, so there was nothing new about that.(p.41)

• When I returned to the hotel it struck me a highball would be fine ***before*** going to bed, so I stepped into the bar and had one.(p.41)
• They had said that though I did raise a defense, it would one day give way ***before*** some trivial reason for having a drink.(p.42)
• I have since been brought into a way of living infinitely more satisfying and, I hope, more useful than the life I lived ***before***.(p.42)
• Most alcoholics have to be pretty badly mangled ***before*** they really commence to solve their problems.(p.43)
• This world of ours has made more material progress in the last century than in all the millenniums which went ***before***.(p.51)
• Had not all efforts at flight failed ***before***?(p.51)
• Our description of the alcoholic, the chapter to the agnostic, and our personal adventures ***before*** and after make clear three pertinent ideas:(p.60)
• We thought well ***before*** taking this step making sure we were ready; that we could at last abandon ourselves utterly to Him.(p.63)
• We placed them ***before*** us in black and white.(p.67)
• Rightly and naturally, we think well ***before*** we choose the person or persons with whom to take this intimate and confidential step.(p.74)
• ***Before*** taking drastic action which might implicate other people we secure their consent.(p.80)
• After consulting with his wife and partner he came to the conclusion that it was better to take those risks than to stand ***before*** his Creator guilty of such ruinous slander.(p.80)
• As God's people we stand on our feet; we don't crawl ***before*** anyone.(p.83)
• If we are painstaking about this phase of our development, we will be amazed ***before*** we are half way through.(p.83)
• ***Before*** we begin, we ask God to direct our thinking, especially asking that it be divorced from self-pity, dishonest or self-seeking motives.(p.86)
• The men who cry for money and shelter ***before*** conquering alcohol, are on the wrong track.(p.98)
• But be sure you are on solid spiritual ground ***before*** you start and that your motive in going is thoroughly good.(p.102)
• Today most of our men are better husbands and fathers than ever ***before***.(p.108)
• Especially when he has ***before*** him a way to stop his drinking and abuse if he really wants to pay the price.(p.108)
• You have passed happy evenings together chatting and drinking ***before*** your fire.(p.110)
• They expect him to give them the nice times they used to have ***before*** he drank so much, and to show his contrition for what they suffered.(p.126)
• I had discharged him for drinking six weeks ***before***.(p.137)
• Four days ***before*** he had hanged himself in his woodshed.(p.137)
• You, as a business man, want to know the necessities ***before*** considering the result.(p.140)
• Of course he couldn't drink, but why not sit hopefully at a table, a bottle of ginger ale ***before*** him?(p.154)
• I was always in a ward ***before***."(p.157)
• Finally my father had to send a doctor out from my home town who managed to get me back there in some way, and I was in bed about two months ***before*** I could venture out of the house.(p.175)
• I drank with moderation at first, but it took me only a relatively short time to drift back into the old habits which had wound up so disastrously ***before***.(p.175)
• Occasionally, I would yield to the morning craving, but if I did, it would be only a few hours ***before*** I would be quite unfit for work.(p.176)
• It was not long ***before*** I was drinking at least a case and a half a day.(p.177)
• It was the day ***before*** Mother's Day and I had come home plastered, carrying a big potted plant which I set down on the table and forthwith went upstairs and passed out.(p.179)
• ***Before*** my drinking had cut me down completely, I achieved a considerable measure of success, having been a City Councilman for five years and a financial director of Kenmore, a suburb later taken into the city itself.(p.182)
• During the first six months of 1935, I was hospitalized eight times for intoxication and shackled to the bed two or three days ***before*** I even knew where I was.(p.184)
• ***Before*** very long we began to relate some incidents of our drinking and, naturally, pretty soon, I realized both of them knew what they were talking about because you can see things and smell things when you're drunk, that you can't other times, and, if I had thought they didn't know what they were talking about, I wouldn't have been willing to talk to them at all.(p.185)
• Two days ***before*** this, Dr. Bob had said to me, "If you and I are going to stay sober, we had better get busy."(p.188)
• ***Before*** our visit was over, Bill suddenly turned to his wife and said, "Go fetch my clothes, dear.(p.189)
• It took me a year, or a year and a half to get to feeling physically well, and it was rather tough, but I soon found folks whose friendship I had once had, and I found, after I had been sober for quite some little time, that these people began to act like they had in previous years, ***before*** I had gotten so bad, so that I didn't pay too awful much attention to financial gains.(p.190)
• I think it was probably more than a year ***before*** I had anything more to do with liquor.(p.195)
• Naturally, what little restraint I had exercised ***before*** was gone now, and my drinking became worse.(p.199)
• I drove towards Cleveland wondering why I found myself in such a changed set of conditions as compared with those of six months ***before***.(p.200)
• And I continued to drink, on and off then, until every dollar I had in the world was gone again and I was right back living at my sister's, getting my cigarettes by calling her grocer and telling him to put in a couple of cartons with her order, exactly as I had ***before*** I started to work at Max's.(p.202)
• So having licked it, there was no reason why I shouldn't have a drink, and I stopped in ***before*** I got home and had one.(p.203)
• Then I started drinking again, with possibly a little more restraint, periods a little bit longer than they had been ***before***, but substantially the same pattern.(p.203)
• I'll never forget, he never even hesitated and I had never seen him ***before*** in my life.(p.207)
• Then he started to talk to me about his drinking experiences, what his drinking had cost him, how much he had drunk and where, things like that, and I remember I was quite bored because I had never seen the guy ***before*** and had no interest at all in what, where and when he drank.(p.208)
• I remember well one fellow, Joe, walking nearly three miles through slush, wet and snow to come to the hospital to see a man that he had never seen ***before*** in his life, and that impressed me very much.(p.208)
• There were only seven or eight people in the group ***before*** me and they all visited me during my period in the hospital.(p.208)
• In other words, I fired the client ***before*** the client fired me.(p.214)
• I had attended several of these meetings ***before*** I discovered that all those who were there were not alcoholics.(p.218)
• In my own experience I was so jubilant at finding myself sober, and I had so many things to catch up on, that a month went by ***before*** the thought even occurred to me.(p.219)
• From far away, as if in a delirium, I heard my own voice – calling someone "Dorothy," talking of dress shops, of jobs . . . the words came clearer . . . this sound of my own voice frightened me as it came closer . . . and suddenly, there I was, talking of I knew not what, to someone I'd never seen ***before*** this very moment.(p.222)
• I'd waked up in strange rooms ***before***, fully dressed on a bed or a couch; I'd waked up in my own room, in or on my own bed, not knowing what hour or day it was, afraid to ask . . . but this was different.(p.222)
• In any case I must get out of here ***before*** I let slip my abysmal ignorance of how I came to be here, and she realized that I was stark, staring mad.(p.223)
• I remember looking longingly at the window as an easier solution, and shuddering at the memory of that other window, three years ***before***, and the six agonizing months in a London hospital ward.(p.224)
• That went on for two more months ***before*** I landed in a hospital and started my slow fight back to normalcy.(p.224)
• It wasn't very long ***before*** home-brewing was an institution and men began to search feverishly for old recipe books on wine-making.(p.232)
• It wasn't long ***before*** the bootlegger was an established institution in this, as in other towns.(p.233)
• ***Before*** long I had a definite taste for hard liquor, knew nausea and headaches I had never known ***before***, but as in the old days, I suffered them out.(p.233)
• Unlike many other Catholics who frequently take pledges for definite periods – a year, two years or for good, I never had any desire to "take a pledge" ***before*** the priest.(p.234)
• This last real merry-go-round had started the day ***before*** Christmas and I had really accomplished a lot in those fourteen days.(p.238)
• Many of these same things had happened to me many times ***before***, but this time they had all descended together.(p.238)
• We had played this game ***before***.(p.238)
• Little more of our talk stayed in my memory, but I do know I slept the rest of that night while ***before*** I had never known what a real night's sleep was.(p.239)
• This was my introduction to this "understanding fellowship" although it was to be more than a year later ***before*** our Society was to bear the name, Alcoholics Anonymous.(p.239)
• I like to think I was fairly normal ***before*** alcohol took over.(p.240)
• At this school we had Bible readings ***before*** each meal, and church services four times on Sunday, and I became so rebellious at this that I swore I would never join or go to any church except for weddings or funerals.(p.240)
• In the eight years ***before*** A.A. found me, I had over forty jobs -- selling and travelling -- one thing after another, and the same old routine.(p.244)
• Three months ***before*** I met Jackie I had made my second feeble try at suicide.(p.245)
• We checked into the home of Hank, the man who had fired me eleven years ***before*** in Mississippi, and there I met Bill, our founder.(p.245)
• My loneliness was worse than it had ever been ***before***, for now even my own kind had turned against me.(p.247)
• For a long time the only Higher Power I could concede was the power of the group, but this was far more than I had ever recognized ***before***, and it was at least a beginning.(p.248)
• Returning to the town I had left three months ***before***, I became editor of a monthly magazine, soon had additional publicity and advertising accounts and the money rolled in.(p.254)
• A friend who knew I would soon be broke mounted guard over me when I left my job of writing the histories of Texas cities and put me aboard a bus for the town I had left almost five years ***before***.(p.256)
• I had been drinking heavily from one state of semi-coma to another and it was several days ***before*** I got "defogged," but subconsciously I was in earnest about wanting to quit liquor forever.(p.258)
• We always started out on the Saturday ***before*** Labor Day.(p.264)
• So, on that Saturday ***before*** Labor Day, I got drunk and set the house on fire -- so we didn't have to paint it.(p.265)
• I think that was the last vacation ***before*** sobriety.(p.265)
• The next morning his wife came dragging him in ***before*** Russ went to work, while I was getting breakfast.(p.271)
• ***Before*** the end finally came, I had, I guess made the surrender because I finally had been able to say that I would not mind too much.(p.272)
• ***Before*** I stop – I always was a great talker – I want to say that nobody will ever know how I miss Annie's advice about things.(p.273)
• Long ***before*** I had any real opportunity to give, I had to learn the equally important lesson of receiving graciously.(p.281)
• We spent two days there together ***before*** he returned to New York.(p.281)
• But it took six more months of work and disappointments ***before*** a group of three men got together in my rooming house bedroom for their first A.A. meeting.(p.282)
• His road lay clear ***before*** me, and I'd better quit rationalizing myself into any detours.(p.282)
• It took five years of A.A. living, and a substantial improvement in my health, ***before*** I could take a full-time office job where someone else was boss.(p.283)
• I am very apt to get into quite an uproar for a day or two ***before*** starting, but I do start, and once started, I have a swell time.(p.285)
• My wife could not understand the next morning why I was drunker than the night ***before*** when she took my bottles.(p.289)
• He waited until I was completely sober and the day ***before*** I was to head back for Chicago, he told me of a small group of men in Akron who apparently had the same problem that I had but were doing something about it.(p.289)
• The day ***before*** I was due to go back to Chicago, a Wednesday and Dr. Bob's afternoon off, he had me down to the office and we spent three or four hours formally going through the Six-Step program as it was at that time.(p.291)
• Needless to say, it was a year or more ***before*** they did contact me.(p.293)
• Doctors told me ***before*** I stopped that I had only three years at the outside to live.(p.295)

• I never enjoyed any meal, but I ate my lunch at noon for two reasons; first, to help me get out of the fog of the night ***before*** and, second, to furnish some measure of nourishment.(p.299)
• How many times I swore off in the morning and got drunk ***before*** sunset I don't know.(p.300)
• Indeed, I was always well on my way ***before*** I would undertake to go visiting at all.(p.301)
• I had never seen him ***before***, and at the time hoped I would never see him again.(p.302)
• Mentally . . . I know where I was last night, the night ***before***, and the nights ***before*** that.(p.303)
• It wasn't long ***before*** any party without drinks was a dud for me.(p.305)
• And all the while my fear fed a growing conviction that ***before*** long it would be necessary for me to be put away in some institution.(p.306)
• They would travel miles and stay up all night with someone they had never laid eyes on ***before*** and think nothing of it.(p.310)
• There is no more "aloneness," with that awful ache, so deep in the heart of every alcoholic that nothing, ***before***, could ever reach it.(p.312)
• They realized that in the end alcoholism could be a mortal as cancer; certainly no sane man would wait for a malignant growth to become fatal ***before*** seeking help.(p.315)
• It wasn't long ***before*** I quit caring how I looked or what my job performance was.(p.318)
• The same as ***before***, I stayed drunk pretty much of the time.(p.318)
• I was still woozy from the night ***before***.(p.323)
• My alcoholism-prone mind, however, reminded me that all great authors had needed a stimulus to build up inspiration and inventiveness ***before*** each day's work.(p.331)
• Since I started out eager for early-day efforts, that meant guzzling ***before*** noon.(p.331)
• How full it has kept my retirement years -- the five I've lived since the first two lost in traveling a rocky road to hell, ***before*** I made a U-turn.(p.334)
• It wasn't long ***before*** I was drinking all day.(p.336)
• I'd go into an organization, and it wasn't long ***be-fore*** I was on the committee, then I was chairman of the committee; and if I was in a group, I'd soon be treasurer or secretary of the group.(p.339)
• I made more money the last year of my drinking than I ever made ***before*** in my whole life.(p.345)
• When a few drinks made me feel good ***before*** I went over that line, those same drinks now made me wretched.(p.346)
• And I gave him some idea of what you do, and so I made my first Twelfth Step call ***before*** I ever came into the program.(p.347)
• The satisfaction I got from giving him a little of what I had read in those pamphlets far surpassed any feeling that I had ever had ***before*** in helping patients.(p.347)
• It started when I joined a few of the men for cocktails ***before*** the noonday Rotary luncheon.(p.360)
• ***Before*** long I was at the luncheon meeting an hour ***before*** the others, that old and familiar trademark of every alcoholic.(p.360)
• It wasn't long ***before*** I became a five o'clock alcoholic.(p.360)
• It was to be short lived, for on the day ***before*** Christmas I completely disillusioned my wife and ruined our first Christmas by coming home from the Rotary lunch dead drunk.(p.361)
• By hook or crook I usually managed to sober up ***be-fore*** I reached home, but always "terribly tired" from a "hard day's work," and just having to have one or two ***before*** dinner.(p.361)
• They told me their stories, which were much more rugged than mine -- yet what they said made sense, and the way they put it was easy for me to understand, with an understanding I had never had ***be-fore***.(p.363)
• I stayed on in Florida for three weeks, enjoying our reunion, a new found health and a deeper love than I had ever experienced ***before***.(p.364)
• I tried a few drinks my last night in the city ***before*** coming home.(p.364)
• A whole new world of happiness and love began to unfold ***before*** my eyes, a truly new way of living.(p.365)
• And, believe me, I thank God that I found out about A.A. ***before*** I had to beat my brains out -- ***before*** I had been hospitalized, jailed or lost a job.(p.367)
• It was fun at first, since I never had indulged ***be-fore***.(p.370)
• ***Before*** too long, my husband (who seemed to prefer his shirts dirty) put his foot down, declaring that our family might have the cleanest clothes in town, but that I hadn't been out of the same old dirty slacks and blouse for a week.(p.371)
• Slowly, my life seemed to unfold ***before*** me, shedding insights on childhood resentments, jealousies, and fears that had mushroomed in adulthood, and also on the self-pity that I had wallowed in at every opportunity.(p.371)
• Two years ***before*** I joined A.A. my wife took a long trip during which she wrote me she just couldn't return unless I did something about my drinking.(p.377)
• This suggestion had been made ***before*** on a number of occasions, but like all alcoholics I wanted to handle my problem my own way, which really meant I didn't want anything to interfere with my drinking.(p.378)
• "First Things First": solving our immediate problems ***before*** we try to solve all the others and get muddled in our thinking and doing.(p.382)
• As I grow in A.A., I realize that a person with as much self-will as I had, as hard a head and as diseased an ego, had to try everything that I could think of, butting my head against every stone wall ***before*** I was ready to come in.(p.384)
• You didn't carry a little orchid up the aisle in those days; you carried a great big bouquet, like a funeral spray, and you didn't have your picture taken until just ***before*** you went to the church.(p.385)
• As I said ***before***, I don't like to be fenced in, and with those bars you don't get hotel service.(p.390)
• They phoned my husband that I was in jail and in such terrible shape that they didn't know what I would do to myself; and they realized that jail was no place for me, but that he was to wait a while ***before*** he got me, because at the time they called him to come over for me I was beating a tin cup against the wall.(p.390)
• I think I actually read more contempt than was really there because just a week ***before*** someone had sent him the Saturday Evening Post article on A.A., and there was some glimmer of hope in it for him.(p.391)
• There are so many to whom I feel deeply grateful; to my husband (and best critic), whose generous love, compassion and understanding have helped me along the way; to those ***before*** me in A.A. who inspired the first article I read, and the friend who sent that article to Frank; to Ruth for her personal note, and the first A.A. to talk to me; to my Bishop, whose loving and believing spirit inspired me; and to all the members of the Houston Group who were so patient, kind and helpful -- and to countless others.(p.393)
• It has made life a thousand times easier and simpler than did the endless compromises and conflicts by which I lived ***before***.(p.394)
• In all these ways I've experienced, in ever growing measure and beyond all expectations and rewards, a joy which I had never ***before*** imagined.(p.395)
• Eighteen will be used as the starting point, because my drinking ***before*** was limited by age, the law, and money.(p.397)
• Where have we heard this ***before***?)(p.398)
• The only other occasionally limiting factor was that I might run out of money ***before*** the next payday rolled around.(p.398)
• When the overcast lifted, the stars were there as ***be-fore***.(p.400)
• My alcoholic problem began long ***before*** I drank.(p.400)
• ***Before*** I started to drink seriously, I tried a couple of other escapes.(p.401)
• Like most sick people ***before*** me, I was implacably selfish, and chronically self-centered.(p.401)
• They said I was so funny, and told me, with shrieks of laughter, what I'd done the night ***before***.(p.407)
• It had never occurred to me ***before*** that I could live simply and be independent of my family.(p.409)
• We were to go up to our A.A. farm in Kent, and I spent the evening ***before*** riding herd on Anne.(p.415)
• I had never had the physical courage to shake it out ***before***.(p.415)
• Drinking conditions at home were even worse than ***before***.(p.424)
• I planned to stay home the night ***before*** I left, but my folks got so drunk I walked off early in the evening and spent the night with my girl, getting very drunk myself.(p.425)
• I tried to control her drinking by pouring her whiskey down the sink ***before*** I'd leave for the night, to get drunker myself.(p.426)
• My past had slipped ***before*** me in a twinkling.(p.427)
• He even went to bat for me ***before*** the court martial that inevitably followed and, as a result, I drew only thirty days -- fifteen in solitary.(p.428)
• I spent the time in a nearby tavern, was loaded on the ship, went to sleep ***before*** take-off, and the next thing I knew someone was shaking me and telling me we were over San Diego.(p.428)
• When I try to reconstruct what my life was like "***be-fore***," I see a coin with two faces.(p.432)
• If pressed further, all I can do is follow the psalmist who said it long, long ***before*** me: "Be still, and know that I am God."(p.437)
• My work is on a much deeper and more significant level than it ever was ***before***, and I am today a fairly creative, relatively sane human being.(p.438)
• If it was one minute ***before*** five, I'd drink myself back to sleep.(p.441)
• That's the stuff used when the oral surgeon puts the needle in your vein and says, "Count to ten," and ***be-fore*** you get to two, you're asleep.(p.442)
• In the garage, I would put the needle in my vein and then try to figure out exactly how much medication to inject to overcome the pep pills while adding to the sleeping pills while ignoring the tranquilizers, in order to get just enough to be able to pull out the needle, jerk the tourniquet, throw it in the car, slam the car door shut, run down the hall, and fall in bed ***before*** I fell asleep.(p.442)
• Both times, my reaction was that I had had nothing to drink the night ***before***, so obviously alcohol had nothing to do with it.(p.444)
• (I am pleased to state, however, that I had gone to only a very few A.A. meetings ***before*** I was able to make a really beautiful pair of moccasins -- and half a wallet.(p.445)
• It was precisely a year ***before*** I spoke at an A.A. meeting.(p.447)
• When a big, healthy-looking young fellow stood up there and said, "I'm a success today if I don't drink today," I thought, "Man, I've got a thousand things to do today ***before*** I can brag about not taking a drink, for God's sake!"(p.447)
• ***Before*** A.A., I judged myself by my intentions, while the world was judging me by my actions.(p.450)
• There, I received several soda crackers and water daily, and ***before*** I could have my third-day meal (again the only meal in ten days), I had to drink a glass of castor oil or mineral oil, depending on the cruelty of the person who was doing the dispensing.(p.459)
• They hadn't mentioned the living hell ***before*** death.(p.461)
• Only a few days ***before*** Christmas I went to the dentist for a periodic checkup.(p.465)
• On the day ***before*** Christmas I telephoned him and told him I was sober and asked him to come home.(p.467)
• This time I didn't put up any fight because I knew why they were there and where I was going, the psychopathic ward of the City Hospital, where I had been once ***before***.(p.468)
• They say call friend ***before*** I buy drink.(p.476)
• He planted many seeds, and it will be many moons ***before*** another rises to walk in his shoes."(p.476)
• Knowing that he was sober, I timed it just right, so I could do the slashing just ***before*** he hit the steps.(p.479)
• When I got out of there, I lasted about fifteen minutes at home, ***before*** I headed for the drugstore and more pills, and then the bar.(p.479)
• For me, my sobriety comes ***before*** his or even ***before*** my feeling for him.(p.481)
• It is so beautiful to get up in the morning not being hung-over and being able to remember where we were the night ***before***.(p.481)
• We are aware of the nice things around us, things we never noticed ***before*** in our drunken stupor.(p.481)
• In the first place, she had been married ***before***; I was her second husband.(p.485)
• Finally, I broke the last one hundred dollar bill the Saturday ***before*** I left.(p.493)
• When I had known her years ***before*** she was rather slender, but at this time she weighed as much as she does now, which is up around in the two hundreds or very close to it.(p.493)
• After he'd talked half an hour, I still wanted him to hurry up and get out so I could go and get some whiskey ***before*** the liquor store closed.(p.494)
• It is not long ***before*** he drives up in the buggy.(p.497)
• "Let your light so shine ***before*** men that they may see your good works --."(p.497)
• I wish I were dead, as I have often wished ***be-fore***.(p.502)
• Some men and women come to visit my friend of the night ***before***.(p.504)
• I have never seen people that joyous ***before***.(p.504)
• Anger possesses me, anger such as I have never felt ***before***.(p.505)

- However, *before* the meeting got started, a group from the outside came in unexpectedly.(p.509)
- I had an advantage in having an idea of what A.A. was about *before* coming out on the street.(p.510)
- We must learn to walk *before* we can run.(p.516)
- *Before* I step out and do anything, I stop and check it over first, and then let my conscience be my guide.(p.516)
- I was afraid to drink *before* the meeting.(p.526)
- You were thirty-five *before* you understood your father's horrible anguish, and forgave him, and loved him again.(p.533)
- I was down to my shorts, unaware of wrong-doing, *before* the ambulance got there and hauled me off to a hospital from which anxious friends rescued me, later that night.(p.537)
- All of my family and loved ones, all of my friends, are nearer and dearer to me than ever *before* and I have literally dozens of new friends who say they cannot believe that a short eight years ago I was ready for the scrap heap.(p.541)
- The mental twists that led up to my drinking began many years *before* I ever took a drink for I am one of those whose history proves conclusively that my drinking was "a symptom of a deeper trouble."(p.544)
- I was married and divorced again *before* I was twenty-three years old, this time to a prominent band leader -- a man that many women wanted.(p.546)
- Fear of rejection and its ensuing pain were not to be risked, and I turned away from myself once more for the answer, this time to the drinks I had always refused *before*, and in alcohol I found a false courage.(p.546)
- One of the truly great things A.A. has taught me is that reality too has two sides; I had only known the grim side *before* the program, but now I had a chance to learn about the pleasant side as well.(p.550)
- It's been true in my case, nor could I quarrel with "restore us to sanity," for my actions drunk or sober, *before* A.A., were not those of a sane person.(p.550)
- It wasn't strong enough, so I added a shot of vodka -- and was right back to worse trouble than *before*.(p.556)
- To wear expensive clothes, to have bartenders know what to serve me *before* I ordered, to be recognized by headwaiters and shown to the best table, to play gin rummy for high stakes with the insouciance of a riverboat gambler -- these were the enduring values in life, I thought.(p.556)
- The relationship between my wife and me was restored to a love and happiness that we had not known even *before* my alcoholism became acute.(p.559)
- I have learned how to relate to people; *before* A.A., I could never do that comfortably without alcohol.(p.559)
- Twelve -- Anonymity is the spiritual foundation of all our Traditions, ever reminding us to place principles *before* personalities.(p.564)
- It reminds us that we are to place principles *before* personalities; that we are actually to practice a genuine humility.(p.568)
- Quite often friends of the newcomer are aware of the difference long *before* he is himself.(p.569)

beforehand

- The next meeting I went to, I didn't have any drinks *beforehand*.(p.319)

beg

- We, who have traveled this dubious path, *beg* you to lay aside prejudice, even against organized religion.(p.49)
- With all the earnestness at our command, we *beg* of you to be fearless and thorough from the very start.(p.58)
- Time after time I would *beg* forgiveness on bended knees, with tears rolling down my cheeks, and promise I would never again drink too much.(p.362)

began

- But when the broker gave him Dr. Silkworth's description of alcoholism and its hopelessness, the physician *began* to pursue the spiritual remedy for his malady with a willingness he had never before been able to muster.(p.xvi)
- The fledgling society, which had been nameless, now *began* to be called Alcoholics Anonymous, from the title of its own book.(p.xvii)
- With the appearance of the new book a great deal *began* to happen.(p.xvii)
- But great numbers of these -- about two out of three -- *began* to return as time passed.(p.xx)
- I *began* to be jittery in the morning.(p.3)
- My wife *began* to work in a department store, coming home exhausted to find me drunk.(p.4)
- This went on endlessly, and I *began* to waken very early in the morning shaking violently.(p.5)
- I *began* to wonder, for such an appalling lack of perspective seemed near being just that.(p.5)
- Some time passed, and confidence *began* to be replaced by cock-sureness.(p.5)
- It *began* to look as though religious people were right after all.(p.11)
- His family was re-assembled, and he *began* to work as a salesman for the business he had lost through drinking.(p.35)
- We now see that when we *began* to drink deliberately, instead of casually, there was little serious or effective thought during the period of premeditation of what the terrific consequences might be.(p.37)
- I had no trouble refusing drinks, and *began* to wonder if I had not been making too hard work of a simple matter.(p.40)
- As soon as we admitted the possible existence of a Creative Intelligence, a Spirit of the Universe underlying the totality of things, we *began* to be possessed of a new sense of power and direction, provided we took other simple steps.(p.46)
- When others showed us that "God-sufficiency" worked with them, we *began* to feel like those who had insisted the Wrights would never fly.(p.52)
- As we felt new power flow in, as we enjoyed peace of mind, as we discovered we could face life successfully, as we became conscious of His presence, we *began* to lose our fear of today, tomorrow or the hereafter.(p.63)
- We *began* to see that the world and its people really dominated us.(p.66)
- We *began* to ask medical advice as the sprees got closer together.(p.106)
- As our husbands *began* to apply spiritual principles in their lives, we *began* to see the desirability of doing so too.(p.116)
- It then occurred to me that after one was all smelled up with beer nobody could tell what had been drunk, so I *began* to fortify my beer with straight alcohol.(p.178)
- My wife and I belonged to some bridge clubs and they *began* to make wine and serve it.(p.184)
- This problem was soon solved, however, as I *began* to take my bottle along with me and hide it in the bathroom or in the shrubbery outside.(p.184)
- They came in and *began* to give me instruction in the program which later became known as Alcoholics Anonymous.(p.185)
- Before very long we *began* to relate some incidents of our drinking and, naturally, pretty soon, I realized both of them knew what they were talking about because you can see things and smell things when you're drunk, that you can't other times, and, if I had thought they didn't know what they were talking about, I wouldn't have been willing to talk to them at all.(p.185)
- It took me a year, or a year and a half to get to feeling physically well, and it was rather tough, but I soon found folks whose friendship I had once had, and I found, after I had been sober for quite some little time, that these people *began* to act like they had in previous years, before I had gotten so bad, so that I didn't pay too awful much attention to financial gains.(p.190)
- Of course, as time went on, and I *began* to get my health back and *began* to be so I didn't have to hide from people all the time, it's just been wonderful.(p.192)
- I then *began* asking a lot of questions of both my brother and Dr. Bob about how this thing worked, and I suppose I was becoming more glassy-eyed all the while, for eventually I said to Bob, "You're all dried up.(p.206)
- My drinking career *began* about four years after I had moved up into partnership and had joined certain clubs, societies and so fourth, and during which period we had Prohibition.(p.213)
- The first definite indications of an alcoholic pattern *began* to arise when I would go to New York on business and disappear, and wind up in Philadelphia or Boston for two or three day periods.(p.213)
- That was skeptically received by me when I first heard it, but after some twenty-eight or thirty fellows had come to see me, and pretty nearly all of them had said the same thing, I *began* to believe it.(p.219)
- My physical health was badly shaken, but I *began* to pick up.(p.220)
- Hangovers *began* to assume monstrous proportions and the morning drink became an urgent necessity.(p.226)
- As the treatment progressed I *began* to get a picture of myself, of the temperament that had caused me so much trouble.(p.226)
- The feeling of impending disaster that had haunted me for years *began* to dissolve as I put into practice more and more of the Twelve Steps.(p.229)
- It wasn't very long before home-brewing was an institution and men *began* to search feverishly for old recipe books on wine-making.(p.232)
- Successful home-brewers among my friends *began* to invite me to their homes.(p.232)
- I *began* to bring bottles in.(p.233)
- I had never doubted the existence of the Supreme Being, but now I *began* to absent myself from my church where I had formerly been a member of the choir.(p.234)
- So I *began* to pray; to place my problems in God's hands.(p.237)
- And I *began* putting into practice what I was learning every day.(p.237)
- That job *began* a series of brief working spells, each one ending in a "drunk" and the urge to travel.(p.253)
- I had some financial success through no ability of my own and, when jobless and almost wiped out in 1930, I *began* to trade and sell my collection; much of the proceeds went to keep my apartment stocked with liquor and almost every night saw me helpless to bed.(p.255)
- I even *began* to go the rounds of churches.(p.255)
- I *began* to know the inside of jails and workhouses.(p.255)
- When it was closed through Washington edict I *began* with Federal Writers in San Antonio.(p.256)
- He introduced himself and *began* to tell me about a bunch of some sixty former drinkers and drunkards who met once a week, and he invited me to go with him to the next meeting.(p.257)
- I *began* to read the Bible daily and to go over a simple devotional exercise as a way to begin each day.(p.259)
- Gradually I *began* to understand.(p.259)
- He talked about his wife taking his little boy away from him because of his drinking, and how he got back together with them through A.A., and we *began* feeling grateful right then that all these things hadn't been taken from us.(p.270)
- I shut myself in my room, which *began* to go around in circles.(p.279)
- Such thinking usually *began* with thoughts of the pleasant drinking of my youth.(p.285)
- As I look back on that first evening I realize that I *began* to hope, then, for the first time; and I felt that if he could regain these things, perhaps it would be possible for me too.(p.290)
- Immediately on her return we *began* to have formal meetings once a week, in the autumn of 1939, and we have continued to do this and to expand ever since.(p.295)
- I got along fairly well with my party drinking for quite some time, but eventually I *began* to visit beer joints in between parties.(p.298)
- My new duties were extremely confining and my liquor consumption *began* to increase.(p.298)
- I *began* making the rounds of the doctors in the hope that one of them might find some cure for my accumulating ailments, preferably something that could be removed surgically.(p.305)
- In learning to practice these steps in my daily living I *began* to acquire faith and a philosophy to live by.(p.311)
- Whole new vistas were opened and life *began* to take on color and interest.(p.311)
- I *began* taking drinks in the morning to get started.(p.318)
- After a time, my mind *began* to clear of the fog that had covered it.(p.320)
- Hauling her to the divan, I sat with her and *began* to talk, frantically but clearly -- and making sense.(p.333)
- I *began* to have to have supplies on hand for the people who "might come in."(p.336)
- Nevertheless, I *began* to try to live without alcohol.(p.338)
- But it *began* to be an awfully painful answer as hangovers, blackouts, trouble, and remorse set in.(p.353)
- It was then that I *began* to hate myself, and drank primarily to ease my conscience and forget.(p.354)
- Every day became that much harder to live through, and I *began* to take a look at myself.(p.354)
- I got around this by joining the local Rotary Club, and through this association with the business men of the community my little station *began* to grow.(p.360)
- I *began* hitting the bottle again, and with it self-pity, resentment, loneliness and remorse set in deeply.(p.362)
- In other words, I *began* contributing, and so, naturally, I *began* to get something more.(p.365)
- A whole new world of happiness and love *began* to unfold before my eyes, a truly new way of living.(p.365)

• I disliked being different so, ultimately, I ***began*** to join them occasionally.(p.374)
• Then I ***began*** to have blackouts and that was a constant worry.(p.375)
• I promised, but within two months, I ***began*** again.(p.377)
• My alcoholic problem ***began*** long before I drank.(p.400)
• But at this time, I ***began*** gravitating toward the really hard drinkers, hanging around with them more and more.(p.404)
• I ***began***, here and now, to fear the answer to the question -- what is the matter with me?(p.406)
• At this stage, I ***began*** a daily mental routine.(p.408)
• In my cups I ***began*** to say, "I can't stop."(p.412)
• I, who had feared questions, now ***began*** trying to interrupt and tell my story.(p.414)
• Not understanding the twenty-four hour plan, or not wanting to, I ***began*** drinking and was off-again on-again, during that first month.(p.414)
• Awarded a scholarship to a famous old Eastern college, I ***began*** to drink at the end of my freshman year, and by junior year, I had to transfer to an easier state university to keep my grades up.(p.419)
• I depended on optimism and ambition to live in society; when I ***began*** to tire, I had to depend on chemicals instead to keep going.(p.420)
• Against my better judgment, I went to a meeting with him that night, and a strange thing ***began*** to happen.(p.446)
• Eventually, the psychiatrist discharged me from the hospital, and Max and I ***began*** going to meetings ourselves.(p.447)
• When I stopped living in the problem and ***began*** living in the answer, the problem went away.(p.449)
• But then, as I drank more and more, the alcohol seemed to affect my vision: Instead of continuing to see what was good about my wife, I ***began*** to see her defects.(p.450)
• I ***began*** to sleep, to relax, to accept my plight.(p.461)
• I count my sobriety date from the day I ***began*** going to A.A. in prison, not from the date of my last drink.(p.462)
• When I didn't have anything else to do -- a dull evening at home -- I'd sneak a few drinks upstairs in my room, and that ***began*** to be a habit.(p.464)
• It was in Washington, D.C. that this transition took place, and that the really bad part of alcoholism ***began*** happening.(p.465)
• She realized that, and the way I felt, and so for my own good she gradually ***began*** to pull away.(p.472)
• The electric light ***began*** to move.(p.498)
• But I am to learn later that it ***began*** with my desire for material success becoming greater than my interest in the welfare of my fellow man.(p.507)
• I ***began*** drinking as a kid, shortly after I reached my fourteenth birthday.(p.508)
• When I landed of course I hit a gin mill, and with three or four good shots under my belt the world ***began*** to go into that rosy glow.(p.513)
• Having made that bargain, I immediately ***began*** to feel I'd been trapped into it and I went out and had some drinks -- four glasses of gin, I remember.(p.523)
• But when she ***began*** a prison sentence, a door opened.(p.526)
• In time, I ***began*** to go out and forget the way back home.(p.527)
• The mental twists that led up to my drinking ***began*** many years before I ever took a drink for I am one of those whose history proves conclusively that my drinking was "a symptom of a deeper trouble."(p.544)
• As I said earlier, self-pity and resentment were my constant companions and my inventory ***began*** to look like a thirty-three year diary, for I seemed to have a resentment against everybody I had ever known.(p.551)
• I also ***began*** to drink at fraternity parties and beer busts.(p.555)
• Regarded as something of a "boy wonder," I ***began*** to see myself that way.(p.555)
• I also ***began*** visiting bars after work, with my older associates.(p.555)
• I ***began*** sneaking drinks when playing bartender for guests.(p.556)
• The early promise of the "boy wonder" faded, and my career ***began*** to drift.(p.556)
• Suddenly, I ***began*** vomiting and losing rectally great quantities of blood.(p.558)
• I acquired a sponsor and ***began*** attending meetings, but continued to drink.(p.559)
• While there, I read the Big Book and the Grapevine and ***began*** the slow road back to health and sanity through the recovery program of A.A.(p.559)
• As the sober days grew into sober months and then into sober years, a new and beautiful life ***began*** to emerge from the shambles of my former existence.(p.559)

begged

• He ***begged*** the doctor to tell him the whole truth, and he got it.(p.26)
• We have prayed, we have ***begged***, we have been patient.(p.105)

begging

• We did, and spent a month boozing it up, popping pills, and smoking marijuana; taking shelter where we could, which included a veterinary hospital one night; accepting meals from anyone; actually ***begging***; stealing anything we were in need of, which was about everything.(p.354)

begin

• Yet it is our great hope that all those who have as yet found no answer may ***begin*** to find one in the pages of this book and will presently join us on the highroad to a new freedom.(p.xxi)
• Ideas, emotions, and attitudes which were once the guiding forces of the lives of these men are suddenly cast to one side, and a completely new set of conceptions and motives ***begin*** to dominate them.(p.27)
• That was growth, but if we wished to grow we had to ***begin*** somewhere.(p.47)
• We ***begin*** to feel the nearness of our Creator.(p.75)
• We may have had certain spiritual beliefs, but now we ***begin*** to have a spiritual experience.(p.75)
• Before we ***begin***, we ask God to direct our thinking, especially asking that it be divorced from self-pity, dishonest or self-seeking motives.(p.86)
• If you are satisfied that he is a real alcoholic, ***begin*** to dwell on the hopeless feature of the malady.(p.92)
• We believe and hope it contains all you will need to ***begin***.(p.163)
• I said, "Yes, Doc, I would like to quit, at least for five, six, or eight months, until I get things straightened up, and ***begin*** to get the respect of my wife and some other people back, and get my finances fixed up and so on."(p.187)
• Offered the job of advertising manager for an eastern automotive company, I moved to Philadelphia to ***begin*** life anew.(p.254)
• I began to read the Bible daily and to go over a simple devotional exercise as a way to ***begin*** each day.(p.259)
• We couldn't ***begin*** to."(p.269)
• And, anyhow, if I went on for ten or a hundred times as long I couldn't even ***begin*** to tell you all that A.A. has meant to me.(p.274)
• In so simple a manner did my morning drinking ***begin***.(p.331)
• When we ***begin*** to do things like that with alcohol, something's gone wrong.(p.336)
• Of course, an inmate must ***begin*** living the A.A. way "inside," if he is to stand a chance "outside."(p.458)
• I can't ***begin*** to tell you of all the benefits I have derived from this new way of living.(p.481)
• I ***begin*** to see I am not the person I had thought myself, that I had judged myself by comparing myself to others, and always to my own advantage.(p.504)
• I ***begin*** to play God.(p.506)
• But I would always wake up in the psychiatric ward to ***begin*** another long treatment.(p.528)
• In A.A. we can ***begin*** again no matter how late it may be.(p.543)
• We cast off the burdens of the past and the anxieties of the future, as we ***begin*** to live in the present, one day at a time.(p.560)

beginner

• As he talked I gathered vaguely, (because he was a faltering ***beginner*** then, just as I am now) that to be relieved of alcoholism I would have to be different.(p.257)

beginning

• Many of our friends encourage us by saying that this is but a ***beginning***, only the augury of a much larger future ahead.(p.xv)
• In reality that was the ***beginning*** of my last debauch.(p.8)
• Nothing more was required of me to make my ***beginning***.(p.12)
• We feel that elimination of our drinking is but a ***beginning***.(p.19)
• He made a ***beginning***.(p.35)
• But even in this type of ***beginning*** we are obliged to admit that our justification for a spree was insanely insufficient in the light of what always happened.(p.37)
• Instead of regarding ourselves as intelligent agents, spearheads of God's ever advancing Creation, we agnostics and atheists chose to believe that our human intelligence was the last word, the alpha and the omega, the ***beginning*** and end of all.(p.49)
• This was only a ***beginning***, though if honestly and humbly made, an effect, sometimes a very great one, was felt at once.(p.63)
• If you have already made a decision, and an inventory of your grosser handicaps, you have made a good ***beginning***.(p.71)
• Remember it was agreed at the ***beginning*** we would go to any lengths for victory over alcohol.(p.76)
• Maybe he is ***beginning*** to lose his friends.(p.109)
• The chances are he will not for, like yourself, he is just ***beginning*** his development.(p.118)
• At the ***beginning*** of recovery a man will take, as a rule, one of two directions.(p.125)
• ***Beginning*** with such complaints, a barrier arises.(p.126)
• At the very ***beginning***, the couple ought to frankly face the fact that each will have to yield here and there if the family is going to play an effective part in the new life.(p.131)
• ***Beginning*** with the story of "Dr. Bob," a co-founder of A.A., there are here presented three groups of personal histories.(p.165)
• During these years, I drank as much as my purse permitted, still without paying too great a penalty, although I was ***beginning*** to have morning jitters at times.(p.173)
• By this time I was ***beginning*** to pay very dearly physically and, in hope of relief, voluntarily incarcerated myself at least a dozen times in one of the local sanitariums.(p.174)
• I got two drinks, each of them a quarter of that pint, in me, and was talking along with these people, but I felt that sooner or later they were going to have me cornered because they were smarter than I was and the drink was ***beginning*** to take effect; but as I reached for the third drink Bob said, "Listen, Buster, you promised to take some medicine if we got you a drink.(p.206)
• In fact, the last three years of my drinking was a routine of barbiturates in the morning, so that I could stop shaking enough to shave, and then alcohol ***beginning*** about four-thirty or five o'clock, with a struggle not to take a drink at noon or during the day, because I had the idea that if I took one drink, I would smell as though I had had a pint.(p.217)
• That was the ***beginning*** of a new life, a fuller life, a happier life than I had ever known or believed possible.(p.228)
• For a long time the only Higher Power I could concede was the power of the group, but this was far more than I had ever recognized before, and it was at least a ***beginning***.(p.248)
• Indeed, I was ***beginning*** to see that I would require implicit faith, like a small child, if I was going to get anywhere.(p.259)
• This was the ***beginning*** of an unending series of such experiences.(p.276)
• This was the ***beginning*** of five years of bounding back and forth between my home in Chicago and Akron to sober up.(p.288)
• I had thought that I was completely different from other people, that I was ***beginning*** to become a little balmy, even to the point of withdrawing more and more from society and wanting to be alone with my bottle.(p.290)
• He was happy, getting a kick out of life and people, and ***beginning*** to get his medical practice back again.(p.290)
• Strangely enough, I became acquainted with the "hilarious life" just at the time in my own life when I was ***beginning*** really to settle down to a common-sense, sane domesticity.(p.297)
• New programing was ***beginning*** to build an audience, but sponsors were pretty scarce.(p.360)
• It also was the ***beginning*** of another cycle in my drinking.(p.360)
• How easy it was, in the ***beginning***, to forget that those binges ever happened!(p.433)
• He didn't seem too much at ease in the ***beginning***.(p.494)
• Of course, it wasn't very much of a meeting in the ***beginning***; most of the time it was just Vi and myself.(p.495)
• For you learned that he had been guilty of the thing he had accused you of, and his guilt had brought suffering to his entire family; and he thought he saw his young son ***beginning*** his own tragic pattern.(p.533)
• If I write with the air of one who has discovered the obvious, which is to say, the eternal truths which have been offered to us since the ***beginning***, forgive my callowness; I had to find these things out for myself.(p.536)
• I wasn't afraid of anything or anybody after I learned about drinking, for it seemed right from the ***beginning*** that with liquor I could always retire to my

little private world where nobody could get at me to hurt me.(p.547)

• The A.A. members who sponsored me told me in the ***beginning*** that I would not only find a way to live without having a drink, but that I would find a way to live without wanting to drink, if I would do these simple things.(p.550)

• A.A. taught me that willingness to believe was enough for a ***beginning***.(p.550)

beginnings

• All told, promising ***beginnings*** have been made in some 50 foreign countries and U.S. possessions.(p.xv)

begins

• Each day, somewhere in the world, recovery ***begins*** when one alcoholic talks with another alcoholic, sharing experience, strength, and hope.(p.xxii)

• He may start off as a moderate drinker; he may or may not become a continuous hard drinker; but at some stage of his drinking career he ***begins*** to lose all control of his liquor consumption, once he starts to drink.(p.21)

• As matters grow worse, he ***begins*** to use a combination of high-powered sedative and liquor to quiet his nerves so he can go to work.(p.22)

• Then he ***begins*** to appear at hospitals and sanitariums.(p.22)

• He ***begins*** to think life doesn't treat him right.(p.61)

• The husband ***begins*** to feel lonely, sorry for himself.(p.81)

• But when he gets over the spree, he ***begins*** to think once more how he can drink moderately next time.(p.109)

• As each member of a resentful family ***begins*** to see his short comings and admits them to the others, he lays a basis for helpful discussion.(p.127)

• As soon as his sobriety ***begins*** to be taken as a matter of course, the family may look at their strange new dad with apprehension, then with irritation.(p.128)

• Father, coming suddenly to life again, often ***begins*** to assert himself.(p.131)

• So the story of my introduction into A.A. ***begins*** with the activities of my wife.(p.216)

begotten

• Our loyalty and the desire that our husbands hold up their heads and be like other men have ***begotten*** all sorts of predicaments.(p.105)

begrudged

• I would have ***begrudged*** the time or money for alcohol.(p.374)

begs

• She ***begs*** me to go to a hospital for alcoholics which has been recommended.(p.502)

begun

• How often have some of us ***begun*** to drink in this nonchalant way, and after the third or fourth, pounded on the bar and said to ourselves, "For God's sake, how did I ever get started again?"(p.24)

• We have ***begun*** to comprehend their futility and their fatality.(p.70)

• We have ***begun*** to learn tolerance, patience and good will toward all men, even our enemies, for we look on them as sick people.(p.70)

• If we have carefully followed directions, we have ***begun*** to sense the flow of His Spirit into us.(p.85)

• We have ***begun*** to develop this vital sixth sense.(p.85)

• He has ***begun*** to try, with or without your cooperation, various means of moderating or staying dry.(p.109)

• Maybe the doctor has been called in, and the weary round of sanitariums and hospitals has ***begun***.(p.110)

• Seed has started to sprout in a new soil, but growth has only ***begun***.(p.117)

• He had ***begun*** to have a spiritual experience.(p.158)

• This was in Virginia, where I had rented a house with stables and a swimming pool, and the fall fox hunting had ***begun***.(p.404)

• I had just ***begun*** a dental practice in a beautiful new office.(p.418)

• I had ***begun*** to drink in the early years of pharmacy school, in order to get to sleep.(p.440)

• I hadn't been drinking much about that time, for I had ***begun*** to realize that there was something abnormal about my drinking, although as yet, I didn't realize that it was so out of control.(p.465)

• I have ***begun*** again.(p.543)

• As soon as I had made a few friends and had ***begun*** to feel accepted, we moved again.(p.555)

behalf

• Our activities in ***behalf*** of women who drink are on the increase.(p.104)

• A year later, after I completed the course in contracts, I quit the law school, and undertook some engineering work for a patent law firm on ***behalf*** of clients who were in difficulties and who desired to keep their troubles from their own engineering department.(p.212)

behave

• Why does he ***behave*** like this?(p.22)

• He is like the retired business man who lolls in the Florida sunshine in the winter complaining of the sad state of the nation; the minister who sighs over the sins of the twentieth century; politicians and reformers who are sure all would be Utopia if the rest of the world would only ***behave***; the outlaw safe cracker who thinks society has wronged him; and the alcoholic who has lost all and is locked up.(p.61)

• People didn't ***behave*** this way outside of an asylum.(p.306)

• During this time, you are supposed to ***behave*** yourself, but I took a little wine-tasting tour through France, all by my lone, with car and chauffeur.(p.405)

• Too often, I would overdo it and ***behave*** badly at the very time I wanted to be at my best!(p.556)

behaved

• Had we fully understood the nature of the alcoholic illness, we might have ***behaved*** differently.(p.107)

• I wasn't the only person in the world who felt and ***behaved*** like this!(p.227)

• I realized that there were other people in this world who ***behaved*** and acted as I did, and that I was a sick person, that I was suffering from an actual disease.(p.392)

• He was well ***behaved***, and idealistic where women were concerned.(p.403)

behavior

• My incredible ***behavior*** in the face of a desperate desire to stop was explained.(p.7)

• This is by no means a comprehensive picture of the true alcoholic, as our ***behavior*** patterns vary.(p.22)

• Our ***behavior*** is as absurd and incomprehensible with respect to the first drink as that of an individual with a passion, say, for jay-walking.(p.37)

• Our ***behavior*** will convince them more than our words.(p.83)

• Get an idea of his ***behavior***, his problems, his background, the seriousness of his condition, and his religious leanings.(p.90)

• If the family will appreciate that dad's current ***behavior*** is but a phase of his development, all will be well.(p.129)

• Away down deep, I was motivated into dishonest ***behavior*** because I was a people-pleaser.(p.328)

• Up to that time, I was so completely baffled by my ***behavior*** that I had never really stopped to think at all.(p.392)

• Now it was semi-blackouts every night, outrageous ***behavior***, passing out in some friend's Village studio or not knowing how I got home.(p.407)

• I was an alcoholic, with a recognizable ***behavior*** pattern.(p.414)

• How exciting to learn the inward mysteries that govern the ***behavior*** of people, how wonderful to know, at last, all about myself!(p.434)

• There go my good intentions, fear of consequences, will to care, responsibility for my ***behavior***.(p.458)

• There was no time off for so-called good ***behavior***, first-timers, or anything else.(p.509)

• It had to be or I could not have justified my erratic ***behavior*** as I did.(p.551)

• I've been benefited from a dictionary definition I found that reads: "rationalization is giving a socially acceptable reason for socially unacceptable ***behavior***, and socially unacceptable ***behavior*** is a form of insanity."(p.551)

beheld

• And then, with a better motive, had we not worshipfully ***beheld*** the sunset, the sea, or a flower?(p.54)

behind

• By late 1937, the number of members having substantial sobriety time ***behind*** them was sufficient to convince the membership that a new light had entered the dark world of the alcoholic.(p.xvii)

• Liquor caught up with me much faster than I came up ***behind*** Walter.(p.3)

• He now returned home, leaving ***behind*** his first acquaintance, the lawyer and the devil-may-care chap.(p.159)

• Naturally, in spite of my good intentions, in spite of my protected life ***behind*** sanitarium walls, I several times got drunk, and was astounded . . . and badly shaken.(p.227)

• Time went on and the drinking got worse and worse, and I was in another barroom, down the road the other way, a small one, and I took my glass – that morning I'd been able to lift it from the bar -- and I said to the woman ***behind*** the bar, "I wish I might never take another drop of that stuff.(p.266)

• This was drinking in sheer desperation, alone and locked ***behind*** my own door.(p.306)

• I could hide my alcoholic stupor ***behind*** pretense.(p.332)

• Hiding ***behind*** a newspaper, magazine, or book, I really saw nothing, but simulated deep interest.(p.332)

• Here I am down at my office ***behind*** my desk and there she is out at the hospital.(p.350)

• As these words are written at fifty-three years of age, with over nine years of A.A. ***behind*** me, with all its wonderful teachings, I haven't the slightest doubt about being an alcoholic.(p.356)

• I got ***behind*** in my rent, but never in my drinking.(p.358)

• I entered the house, opened a new bottle of whiskey and sat down to drink myself into the right frame of mind to get in my car, start the motor and close the garage door ***behind*** me.(p.363)

• With ten years of A.A. ***behind*** me, I was able to tell him that I'd have been alcoholic, no matter what; that I had been a sick person, unfit for marriage.(p.403)

• Once, in a strange gin mill, I stole a bottle from ***behind*** the bar.(p.411)

• So I sat down with me and went over the facts ***behind*** the convulsions: personality changes, daily headaches, sense of impending doom, sense of impending insanity.(p.444)

• One day as I sat there in the hospital, my psychiatrist walked up ***behind*** me and asked, "How'd you like to talk to the man from A.A.?"(p.446)

• And then I went back home to live with my parents, and the merry-go-round started again – only this time I didn't have to worry about waking up ***behind*** bars in a psychiatric ward.(p.468)

• The idea ***behind*** it is that, having taken the treatment, your system is so "conditioned" that the mere sight or smell or taste of alcohol produces a violent reaction, and you become ill.(p.469)

• I seem to get no sympathy for my illness and have no appreciation of the love ***behind*** the gift.(p.501)

• One man comes back, closing the door ***behind*** him.(p.503)

• I clung to the outfit for the balance of my time, and finally I was released, after having spent twenty years and nine months ***behind*** bars.(p.510)

• I got married to the girl I'd left ***behind***.(p.513)

• I remember how horrible jails are, how dreadful a thing it is to be ***behind*** steel bars.(p.542)

behoove

• So it doesn't ***behoove*** me to squawk about it for, after all, nobody ever had to throw me down and pour liquor down my throat.(p.181)

being

• Because this book has become the basic text for our Society and has helped such large numbers of alcoholic men and women to recover, there exists a sentiment against any radical changes ***being*** made in it.(p.xi)

• ***Being*** mostly business or professional folk, we could not well carry on our occupations in such an event.(p.xiii)

• While the internal difficulties of our adolescent period were ***being*** ironed out, public acceptance of A.A. grew by leaps and bounds.(p.xix)

• Alcohol ***being*** no respecter of persons, we are an accurate cross section of America, and in distant lands, the same democratic evening-up process is now going on.(p.xx)

• Later, he requested the privilege of ***being*** allowed to tell his story to other patients here and with some misgiving, we consented.(p.xxv)

• On the other hand – and strange as this may seem to those who do not understand -- once a psychic change has occurred, the very same person who seemed doomed, who had so many problems he despaired of ever solving them, suddenly finds himself easily able to control his desire for alcohol, the only effort necessary ***being*** that required to follow a few simple rules.(p.xxvii)

• There is the type who always believes that after ***being*** entirely free from alcohol for a period of time he can take a drink without danger.(p.xxviii)

• I began to wonder, for such an appalling lack of perspective seemed near ***being*** just that.(p.5)

• It was only a matter of ***being*** willing to believe in a Power greater than myself.(p.12)

• I vaguely sensed I was not ***being*** any too smart, but felt reassured as I was taking the whiskey on a full stomach.(p.36)

• I have a shadowy recollection of ***being*** in an airplane bound for New York, and of finding a friendly taxicab driver at the landing field instead of my wife.(p.41)

• Except in a few rare cases, neither he nor any other human *being* can provide such a defense.(p.43)

• How could a Supreme *Being* have anything to do with it all?(p.46)

• And who could comprehend a Supreme *Being* anyhow?(p.46)

• It is *being* constantly revealed, as mankind studies the material world, that outward appearances are not inward reality at all.(p.48)

• Those who do not recover are people who cannot or will not completely give themselves to this simple program, usually men and women who are constitutionally incapable of *being* honest with themselves.(p.58)

• 5.Admitted to God, to ourselves, and to another human *being* the exact nature of our wrongs.(p.59)

• *Being* convinced, we were at Step Three, which is that we decided to turn our will and our life over to God as we understood Him.(p.60)

• *Being* all powerful, He provided what we needed, if we kept close to Him and performed His work well.(p.63)

• *Being* convinced that self, manifested in various ways, was what had defeated us, we considered its common manifestations.(p.64)

• God save me from *being* angry.(p.67)

• If we do, we destroy our chance of *being* helpful.(p.67)

• That *being* so you have swallowed and digested some big chunks of truth about yourself.(p.71)

• This requires action on our part, which, when completed, will mean that we have admitted to God, to ourselves, and to another human *being* the exact nature of our defects.(p.72)

• We have emphasized willingness as *being* indispensable.(p.76)

• Why lay ourselves open to *being* branded fanatics or religious bores?(p.77)

• We ought to sit down with the family and frankly analyze the past as we now see it, *being* very careful not to criticize them.(p.83)

• We should be sensible, tactful, considerate and humble without *being* servile or scraping.(p.83)

• They are *being* fulfilled among us – sometimes quickly, sometimes slowly.(p.84)

• *Being* still inexperienced and having just made conscious contact with God, it is not probable that we are going to be inspired at all times.(p.87)

• He will feel he can deal with you without *being* nagged by his family.(p.91)

• If he is in a serious mood dwell on the trouble liquor has caused you, *being* careful not to moralize or lecture.(p.91)

• You may spoil your chance of *being* helpful if you do.(p.100)

• So our rule is not to avoid a place where there is drinking, if we have a legitimate reason for *being* there.(p.101)

• And just as we were *being* convinced of their heartlessness, they would surprise us with fresh resolves and new attentions.(p.107)

• *Being* certain he wants to stop, you can go to him with this volume as joyfully as though you had struck oil.(p.113)

• We thought, on the whole, we were pretty good women, capable of *being* nicer if our husbands stopped drinking.(p.116)

• *Being* possessed of a spiritual experience, the alcoholic will find he has much in common with these people, though he may differ with them on many matters.(p.131)

• She sees she was wrong to make a burning issue out of such a matter when his more serious ailments were *being* rapidly cured.(p.135)

• Say that you believe he is a gravely ill person, with this qualification -- *being* perhaps fatally ill, does he want to get well?(p.142)

• You ask, because many alcoholics, *being* warped and drugged, do not want to quit.(p.142)

• *Being* somewhat weakened, and faced with physical and mental readjustment to a life which knows no alcohol, he may overdo.(p.146)

• *Being* on a radically different basis of life, he will never take advantage of the situation.(p.146)

• Now and then a serious drinker, *being* dry at the moment says, "I don't miss it at all.(p.151)

• Painfully aware of *being* somehow abnormal, the man did not fully realize what it meant to be alcoholic.(p.155)

• *Being* intrigued, however, he invited our friend to his home.(p.155)

• Alcoholics are *being* attracted from far and near.(p.161)

• *Being* a large place, we think that some day its Fellowship will number many hundreds.(p.161)

• *Being* wrecked in the same vessel, *being* restored and united under one God, with hearts and minds attuned to the welfare of others, the things which matter so much to some people no longer signify much to them.(p.161)

• Not *being* a man of means, I knew that if I did not stay sober enough to earn money, I would run out of liquor.(p.175)

• At a comparatively early age, I can remember *being* jealous of my brother.(p.194)

• So in spite of anything that I might do, I prospered, *being* one of only two brokers in the rubber center of the world.(p.197)

• I don't know whether I drank to cover up *being* a failure, or whether I drank and then missed the deals.(p.198)

• Of course, it was always my aim to have my own way without *being* caught.(p.210)

• *Being* intensely interested in the work, I changed my conduct sufficiently to master the job.(p.211)

• I was supporting myself through all this education by *being* a toolmaker and a draftsman.(p.212)

• And *being* a big-shot man of my word, I said, "Well, if I said so, then I'll go."(p.217)

• In four or five days I would be hunting all over the place, at home and in my workshop, for the bottles I had destroyed, cursing myself for *being* a fool.(p.234)

• I had never doubted the existence of the Supreme *Being*, but now I began to absent myself from my church where I had formerly been a member of the choir.(p.234)

• In a few sentences he made God seem personal to me, explained Him as a *being* who was interested in me, the alcoholic, and that all I needed to do was to be willing to follow His way; that as long as I followed it I would be able to overcome my desire for liquor.(p.236)

• In the spring of 1917, in order to beat *being* fired from school, I became "patriotic" and joined the Army.(p.241)

• After *being* dry two weeks and sticking close to Jackie, all of a sudden I found I had become the sponsor of my sponsor, for he was suddenly taken drunk.(p.245)

• Around this time our big A.A. book was *being* written and it all became much simpler; we had a definite formula which some sixty of us agreed was the middle course for all alcoholics who wanted sobriety, and that formula has not been changed one iota down through the years.(p.248)

• I don't think the boys were completely convinced of my personality change, for they fought shy of including my story in the book, so my only contribution to their literary efforts was my firm conviction, *being* still a theological rebel, that the word God should be qualified with the phrase "as we understand him" -- for that was the only way I could accept spirituality.(p.248)

• I myself could see deterioration in my work from *being* physically and mentally affected by liquor, although I had not yet reached the point where all I wanted was more to drink.(p.254)

• Always, in between, there were intervals of *being* broke, riding freights and hitch-hiking interminable distances from one big town to another in three states.(p.255)

• I look back and remember these things because they made me very unhappy, and added to my feeling of inferiority at never *being* the same as other people.(p.261)

• Of course, this year we decided on staying home and *being* sensible, doing a little drinking, and painting the house.(p.265)

• I used to think I was cowardly because when things came out pertaining to the program that troubled me, I said to her many times, "Annie, am I *being* a coward because I lay those things away on the shelf and skip it?"(p.273)

• She said, "I feel you're just *being* wise.(p.273)

• Three more months of *being* up and around the house for brief periods and in bed the rest of the time.(p.275)

• Immediately a great feeling of peace descended upon me, intermingled with a feeling of *being* suffused with a quiet strength.(p.280)

• *Being* an alcoholic, I couldn't dream of doing anything by halves!(p.286)

• It was a period of binges coming closer and closer together and *being* of longer duration.(p.288)

• Neither one of the two was interested for himself, one *being* a mother who wanted to do something for her son.(p.294)

• My wife became pregnant and the doctor recommended the use of port or ale . . . so . . . I bought a six gallon crock and a few bottles, listened to advice from amateur brewmeisters, and was off on my beer manufacturing career on a small scale (for the time *being*).(p.297)

• That *being* the case, it didn't take me long to figure out that my meager manufacturing facilities were entirely inadequate to the manufacture of beer for social and domestic consumption.(p.297)

• Up to this point I had spent six years in the business and had enjoyed the reputation of *being* very successful.(p.298)

• After *being* fired, I lined up with a new finance company that was just starting in business, and took the position of business promotion man, contacting automobile dealers.(p.300)

• After *being* in the hospital for several days, a plan of living was outlined to me.(p.302)

• A little more than fifteen years ago, through a long and calamitous series of shattering experiences, I found myself *being* helplessly propelled toward total destruction.(p.304)

• And still by the time I was thirty years old I was *being* pushed around with a compulsion to drink that was completely beyond my control.(p.305)

• It is a way of life, and the challenge contained in its principles is great enough to keep any human *being* striving for as long as he lives.(p.311)

• Now there is a sense of belonging, of *being* wanted and needed and loved.(p.312)

• All of them were so nice to me that I figured I must be careful – they were bound to want something, *being* that nice.(p.319)

• As we walked back through the hall, I, for the first time in my life, said to another human *being*, "I'm having trouble with my drinking, too."(p.321)

• I was *being* very cagey, because I knew that if I did take one or two, I might want to take five or six or seven or eight.(p.323)

• I was "too important" to show any indication of *being* a drunk.(p.328)

• To me, taking a bath was just *being* in a place with a bottle where I could drink in privacy.(p.337)

• It has brought about a revelation of self, the discovery of an inner *being*, an awareness of God.(p.355)

• As these words are written at fifty-three years of age, with over nine years of A.A. behind me, with all its wonderful teachings, I haven't the slightest doubt about *being* an alcoholic.(p.356)

• As a matter of fact, when I came into Alcoholics Anonymous I was close to *being* at the peak of my career.(p.356)

• I had no trouble at all in *being* elected to the two drinking societies at my college.(p.357)

• If I were asked what in my opinion was the most important factor in *being* successful in this program, besides following the Twelve Steps, I would say Honesty.(p.367)

• I saw at last that I had the same disease my father had, only I was *being* given a chance to live, not die.(p.371)

• I disliked *being* different so, ultimately, I began to join them occasionally.(p.374)

• It was frightening that drink was *being* substituted for more and more of the things I really enjoyed doing.(p.374)

• Just *being* sober will be making amends to many we have hurt by our drunken actions.(p.381)

• About this time, at Christmas, after *being* under this doctor's care, we decided that there wasn't anything more to do.(p.388)

• At age twenty-one, I enlisted in the Navy for two reasons: (1) to avoid *being* drafted into the Army, and (2) out of a burst of patriotic fervor inspired by the advent of World War II and as the result of an all-night drinking binge which found me sitting on the doorstep of the Navy recruiting office when the chief petty officer arrived to open for business at nine o'clock Monday morning.(p.398)

• Two weeks later found me *being* sworn in, and the first payday in the Navy made me realize I had found a home.(p.398)

• My first pay was ten dollars, pay for recruits at that time *being* twenty-one dollars per month.(p.398)

• Alcoholics *being* the argumentative lot that we are, the A.A. membership will undoubtedly come up with a few who will dispute these figures.(p.399)

• Even when I was old enough to know better, I dreamed about *being* as beautiful as Venus, as pure as the Madonna and as brilliant as the President of the United States is supposed to be.(p.400)

• Inside, I went right on *being* a mass of unlovely self-pity, queasy anxiety and sickening self-debasement.(p.400)

• My child was *being* exposed to all this.(p.408)

• Then came my tour in the U.S. Navy, part of it ***being*** two years in the Philippines.(p.419)
• Well, I'm willing, if it will curb this awful desire to drink, this fear of not having a drink, this feeling of always ***being*** alone, scared, deserted, sick.(p.430)
• Only through ***being*** beaten down by my own misery would I ever have accepted the term "alcoholic" as applied to myself.(p.436)
• My work is on a much deeper and more significant level than it ever was before, and I am today a fairly creative, relatively sane human ***being***.(p.438)
• Not only did I not think that ***being*** an alcoholic was a good idea, I didn't even feel that I had all that much of a drinking problem!(p.439)
• I didn't like ***being*** on the nut ward, and I particularly didn't like ***being*** forced to ice cookies on Christmas Eve.(p.444)
• I interpreted "sober" as meaning "drinking but not ***being*** drunk."(p.447)
• When I am disturbed, it is because I find some person, place, thing, or situation -- some fact of my life -- unacceptable to me, and I can find no serenity until I accept that person, place, thing, or situation as ***being*** exactly the way it is supposed to be at this moment.(p.449)
• Prior to our marriage, when she was a shy, scrawny adolescent, I was able to see things in her that others couldn't necessarily see -- things like beauty, charm, gaiety, a gift for ***being*** easy to talk to, a sense of humor, and many other fine qualities.(p.450)
• And when I place more value on my serenity and sobriety than on anything else, I can maintain them at a higher level -- at least for the time ***being***.(p.452)
• He and his wife more than accepted me; he listened to all my woes; both of them treated me as a human ***being***.(p.462)
• ***Being*** dry is not ***being*** sober.(p.462)
• Things went from bad to worse, and since I had finally and completely failed at the job of ***being*** a wife and a mother, my marriage ended.(p.468)
• Aside from ***being*** a common drunk, I had a very serious pill affliction and all the garbage that goes with it -- lying, stealing, cheating anybody and everybody, conning the people I could, and staying clear of the ones I couldn't.(p.478)
• It is so beautiful to get up in the morning not ***being*** hung-over and ***being*** able to remember where we were the night before.(p.481)
• If anyone had told me I would be enjoying a hockey game with my husband and my brother without ***being*** all boozed up, I would not have believed it.(p.481)
• He wanted to give me the very best and he thought that nothing but ***being*** a doctor would suffice.(p.485)
• ***Being*** an alcoholic, slick, and having some good sense left, I survived the investigation.(p.490)
• Within about ten days I got locked up for ***being*** drunk and this same policeman was in the station house as I was ***being*** booked.(p.491)
• Very often we rode to and from work together, but ***being*** separated really galled me deep down.(p.491)
• A case of measles saved me from ***being*** kicked out during my Sophomore year.(p.499)
• Three attempts to enlist in the service, and three failures because of ***being*** skinny.(p.499)
• When I look back, I can't see anything that would have predisposed me towards ***being*** either a neurotic or a drunk.(p.517)
• In my own generation I stuck out, I can see that now, as ***being*** a very much heavier drinker than the average man.(p.518)
• Strangely enough, right through to the end of my twenty-six years in the Army, I was still ***being*** offered very good and important jobs in spite of the fact that my superiors must have known that I wasn't thoroughly reliable.(p.519)
• My mind was too screwy to be able to understand much of what was ***being*** said.(p.524)
• I always blamed my drinking on ***being*** poor, or on anything other than the truth -- that I liked what booze did for me, that when I had a drink I was as big and had as much as the next person.(p.526)
• Today, I thank my Higher Power for giving me another chance at life and A.A. and ***being*** able to try and help some other alcoholic.(p.529)
• All they care about is that I am a human ***being*** and that I want to stay sober.(p.529)
• There was the love affair which was ridiculous -- "imagine that midget ***being*** able to fall in love!" -- and my head knew it while my heart pumped real, genuine anguish, for it hurt like hell, and since it was first love, things have never been quite the same.(p.534)
• There was the sense of ***being*** "misunderstood," when as a matter of fact by my middle twenties I was quite popular, although I hadn't grown much bigger physically.(p.534)
• For a while, for a long time, we can endure the intellect's ***being*** ahead of the emotions, which is the import of Millay's couplet.(p.534)
• To my way of thinking, that is a definition of alcoholism; a state of ***being*** in which the emotions have failed to grow to the stature of the intellect.(p.535)
• My personal definition, which I submit as applying only to myself (although everyone is welcome to it who wants it), includes every waking activity of the human ***being***; to have a creative attitude towards things is a more exact meaning, to live and to deal with other human beings creatively, which to me means seeing the God in them, and respecting and worshipping this God.(p.535)
• For a little while, I was the great man I wanted to be, and thought myself entitled to be just by reason of ***being***.(p.537)
• I have had the joy of seeing many a human ***being***, down and out, learn to stand straight again, and to proceed under his own power to happiness in life.(p.541)
• A happy man is not likely to do harm to another human ***being***.(p.542)
• I have seen that there is only one law, the law of love, and there are only two sins; the first is to interfere with the growth of another human ***being***, and the second is to interfere with one's own growth.(p.542)
• My mother went to a nearby city to go to work, and my father, ***being*** an alcoholic, simply went.(p.544)
• My grandparents were strangers to me and I remember ***being*** lonely, and terrified and hurt.(p.545)
• I grew up believing that one had to be totally self-sufficient, for one never dared to depend on another human ***being***.(p.545)
• I went to jail for the second time during this period for ***being*** drunk in an automobile.(p.549)
• As another great man says, "The only real freedom a human ***being*** can ever know is doing what you ought to do because you want to do it."(p.553)
• I remember ***being*** dragged, drink in hand, from beneath the grand piano, where I had hidden, to be locked in my room in disgrace.(p.557)
• I found myself ***being*** lifted onto a stretcher and whisked away in an ambulance to a strange hospital.(p.558)
• In emphasizing alcoholism as an illness, the social stigma associated with this condition is ***being*** blotted out . . .(p.573)
• Speaking at a dinner given by John D. Rockefeller Jr. to introduce Alcoholics Anonymous to some of his friends, Dr. Harry Emerson Fosdick remarked: "I think that psychologically speaking there is a point of advantage in the approach that is ***being*** made in this movement that cannot be duplicated.(p.574)

beings

• If you give us a try, you will see that we are really human ***beings***, and we will welcome you with open arms and hearts.(p.529)
• My personal definition, which I submit as applying only to myself (although everyone is welcome to it who wants it), includes every waking activity of the human being; to have a creative attitude towards things is a more exact meaning, to live and to deal with other human ***beings*** creatively, which to me means seeing the God in them, and respecting and worshipping this God.(p.535)
• I hope I have been able to impart to you, the reader, at least a bit of what I know; the joy of living, the irresistible power of divine love and its healing strength, and the fact that we, as sentient ***beings***, have the knowledge to choose between good and evil, and, choosing good, are made happy.(p.543)

belief

• Though he could not accept all the tenets of the Oxford Groups, he was convinced of the need for moral inventory, confession of personality defects, restitution to those harmed, helpfulness to others, and the necessity of ***belief*** in and dependence upon God.(p.xvi)
• In our ***belief***, any picture of the alcoholic which leaves out this physical factor is incomplete.(p.xxiv)
• ***Belief*** in the power of God, plus enough willingness, honesty and humility to establish and maintain the new order of things, were the essential requirements.(p.13)
• Then he fell victim to a ***belief*** which practically every alcoholic has -- that his long period of sobriety and self-discipline had qualified him to drink as other men.(p.32)
• The consciousness of your ***belief*** is sure to come to you.(p.55)
• In our ***belief*** any scheme of combating alcoholism which proposes to shield the sick man from temptation is doomed to failure.(p.101)
• We cannot subscribe to the ***belief*** that this life is a vale of tears, though it once was just that for many of us.(p.133)
• We are greatly indebted to the doctor in attendance there, for he, although it might prejudice his own work, has told us of his ***belief*** in ours.(p.162)
• She was tolerant beyond all ***belief***.(p.361)
• In meeting me casually, I don't think my strong ***belief*** in "The Man Upstairs" shows, but I have no other explanation for the many good things that have happened to me since I have been in A.A. -- they came to me from a Greater Power.(p.367)
• They meant patience, tolerance and humility, and above all the ***belief*** that a Power greater than myself could help.(p.381)
• He asked me if I had any spiritual ***belief***, and when I said No, he suggested that I keep an open mind.(p.413)

beliefs

• Those having religious affiliations will find here nothing disturbing to their ***beliefs*** or ceremonies.(p.28)
• We used to amuse ourselves by cynically dissecting spiritual ***beliefs*** and practices when we might have observed that many spiritually-minded persons of all races, colors, and creeds were demonstrating a degree of stability, happiness and usefulness which we should have sought ourselves.(p.49)
• We may have had certain spiritual ***beliefs***, but now we begin to have a spiritual experience.(p.75)
• My new friends made fun of God and all the orthodox ***beliefs***.(p.408)

believe

• If you have a drinking problem, we hope that you may pause in reading one of the forty-four personal stories and think: "Yes, that happened to me"; or, more important, "Yes, I've felt like that"; or most important, "Yes, I ***believe*** this program can work for me, too."(p.xii)
• We of Alcoholics Anonymous ***believe*** that the reader will be interested in the medical estimate of the plan of recovery described in this book.(p.xxiii)
• In this statement he confirms what we who have suffered alcoholic torture must ***believe*** -- that the body of the alcoholic is quite as abnormal as his mind.(p.xxiv)
• They ***believe*** in themselves, and still more in the Power which pulls chronic alcoholics back from the gates of death.(p.xxv)
• We ***believe***, and so suggested a few years ago, that the action of alcohol on these chronic alcoholics is a manifestation of an allergy; that the phenomenon of craving is limited to this class and never occurs in the average temperate drinker.(p.xxvi)
• I do not hold with those who ***believe*** that alcoholism is entirely a problem of mental control.(p.xxvii)
• I simply had to ***believe*** in a Spirit of the Universe, who knew neither time nor limitation.(p.10)
• It was only a matter of being willing to ***believe*** in a Power greater than myself.(p.12)
• An illness of this sort -- and we have come to ***believe*** it an illness --involves those about us in a way no other human sickness can.(p.18)
• But we saw that it really worked in others, and we had come to ***believe*** in the hopelessness and futility of life as we had been living it.(p.25)
• If you are as seriously alcoholic as we were, we ***believe*** there is no middle-of-the-road solution.(p.25)
• Our hope is that many alcoholic men and women, desperately in need, will see these pages, and we ***believe*** that it is only by fully disclosing ourselves and our problems that they will be persuaded to say, "Yes, I am one of them too; I must have this thing."(p.29)
• Despite all we can say, many who are real alcoholics are not going to ***believe*** they are in that class.(p.31)
• Though there is no way of proving it, we ***believe*** that early in our drinking careers most of us could have stopped drinking.(p.32)
• Fred would not ***believe*** himself an alcoholic, much less accept a spiritual remedy for his problem.(p.39)
• Let him tell you about it: "I was much impressed with what you fellows said about alcoholism, and I frankly did not ***believe*** it would be possible for me to drink again.(p.40)
• That means we have written a book which we ***believe*** to be spiritual as well as moral.(p.45)
• We found that as soon as we were able to lay aside prejudice and express even a willingness to ***believe*** in a Power greater than ourselves, we commenced to get results, even though it was impossible for any of us to fully define or comprehend that Power, which is God.(p.46)
• It is open, we ***believe***, to all men.(p.46)
• "Do I now ***believe***, or am I even willing to ***believe***, that there is a Power greater than myself?"(p.47)
• As soon as a man can say that he does ***believe***, or is willing to ***believe***, we emphatically assure him that he is on his way.(p.47)

• That was great news to us, for we had assumed we could not make use of spiritual principles unless we accepted many things on faith which seemed difficult to ***believe***.(p.47)
• I'm sure it would work if I could only ***believe*** as he believes.(p.47)
• The reader may still ask why he should ***believe*** in a Power greater than himself.(p.48)
• We read wordy books and indulge in windy arguments, thinking we ***believe*** this universe needs no God to explain it.(p.49)
• Instead of regarding ourselves as intelligent agents, spearheads of God's ever advancing Creation, we agnostics and atheists chose to ***believe*** that our human intelligence was the last word, the alpha and the omega, the beginning and end of all.(p.49)
• They flatly declare that since they have come to ***believe*** in a Power greater than themselves, to take a certain attitude toward that Power, and to do certain simple things, there has been a revolutionary change in their way of living and thinking.(p.50)
• Hence we are at pains to tell why we think our present faith is reasonable, why we think it more sane and logical to ***believe*** than not to ***believe***, why we say our former thinking was soft and mushy when we threw up our hands in doubt and said, "We don't know."(p.53)
• For did we not ***believe*** in our own reasoning?(p.53)
• Circumstances made him willing to ***believe***.(p.57)
• 2.Came to ***believe*** that a Power greater than ourselves could restore us to sanity.(p.59)
• If we are sorry for what we have done, and have the honest desire to let God take us to better things, we ***believe*** we will be forgiven and will have learned our lesson.(p.70)
• Yet, we ***believe*** we can make some definite and valuable suggestions.(p.86)
• The main thing is that he be willing to ***believe*** in a Power greater than himself and that he live by spiritual principles.(p.93)
• At first, some of us did not ***believe*** we needed this help.(p.116)
• God, they ***believe***, almost owes this recompense on a long overdue account.(p.123)
• We have come to ***believe*** He would like us to keep our heads in the clouds with Him, but that our feet ought to be firmly planted on earth.(p.130)
• He simply could not ***believe*** that his brother-executive suffered from a serious illness.(p.138)
• Say that you ***believe*** he is a gravely ill person, with this qualification – being perhaps fatally ill, does he want to get well?(p.142)
• We ***believe*** a man should be thoroughly probed on these points.(p.142)
• If you propose such a procedure to him, it may be necessary to advance the cost of treatment, but we ***believe*** it should be made plain that any expense will later be deducted from his pay.(p.143)
• But alcoholism – well, they just don't ***believe*** they have it.(p.149)
• We ***believe*** that managers of large enterprises often have little idea how prevalent this problem is.(p.149)
• We ***believe*** and hope it contains all you will need to begin.(p.163)
• Those who ***believe*** their drinking to be hopeless may again find hope in these thirteen impressive tales.(p.167)
• Without this proof the expectant purchaser would be forced to depart empty handed with none of what I later came to ***believe*** was the great panacea for all human ills.(p.171)
• Never once in my life have I had a headache, which fact leads me to ***believe*** that I was an alcoholic almost from the start.(p.172)
• I used to get terribly upset when I saw my friends drink and knew I could not, but I schooled myself to ***believe*** that though I once had the same privilege, I had abused it so frightfully that it was withdrawn.(p.181)
• That was worth a lot even though I did not ***believe*** it.(p.185)
• So, after hearing some more of my story, he turned around and said to Doc -- I don't think he knew I heard him, but I did – he said, "Well, I ***believe*** he's worth saving and working on."(p.185)
• I had no trouble there because I had never actually ceased to ***believe*** in God, and had tried lots of times to get help but hadn't succeeded.(p.186)
• I was at one time a deacon in the church and I still ***believe*** in God.(p.189)
• But I guess He doesn't ***believe*** much in me."(p.189)
• Don't you ***believe*** you are going to have all you can do to get rid of that?"(p.190)
• Long since I had come to ***believe*** I was insane because I did so many things I didn't want to do.(p.199)
• He said, "So long as I'm thinking as I'm thinking now, and so long as I'm doing the things I'm doing now, I don't ***believe*** I'll ever take another drink."(p.206)
• I do not recollect the specific conversation that went on but I ***believe*** I did challenge Bill to tell me something about A.A. and I do recall one other thing: I wanted to know what this was that worked so many wonders, and hanging over the mantel was a picture of Gethsemane and Bill pointed to it and said, "There it is," which didn't make much sense to me.(p.216)
• I ***believe*** every member of the Akron Group did come to see me, which impressed me terrifically, not so much because of the stories they told, but because they would take the time to come and talk to me without even knowing who I was.(p.218)
• That was skeptically received by me when I first heard it, but after some twenty-eight or thirty fellows had come to see me, and pretty nearly all of them had said the same thing, I began to ***believe*** it.(p.219)
• I ***believe*** though that it helped my family tremendously to have the A.A. meetings every week in my own home.(p.220)
• When my doctor told me I should never touch a drink again, I couldn't afford to ***believe*** him.(p.226)
• I ***believe*** that my once over-weening self-will has finally found its proper place, for I can say many times daily, "Thy will be done, not mine" . . . and mean it.(p.229)
• Even that first night I blacked out, which leads me to ***believe*** that I was an alcoholic from my very first drink.(p.241)
• When I started to tell the boys how we did it in New York and all about the spiritual part of the program, I found they would not ***believe*** me unless I was practicing what I preached.(p.249)
• In those days my system was always to drink up my last pay check and ***believe*** that necessity would bring the next job.(p.256)
• But I don't ***believe*** now that it was with any deep feeling of resentment that I said to him, "The children are raised, and if this is the way you want it, this is the way we'll have it.(p.263)
• It would stop out in front of our house, and I still ***believe*** those people sent it!(p.265)
• I sipped the drink off the bar because I couldn't hold it in my hand, but I was still a lady, ***believe*** it or not, and I was deeply ashamed.(p.266)
• I ***believe*** the sociologists would call it "upper middle class."(p.275)
• I had been brought up to ***believe*** this, and I had shown during my teens considerable enterprise and imagination about earning money.(p.275)
• Some of these were hard to ***believe***, but it did not require a giant brain to perceive that they had something I could use.(p.279)
• Looking at him it was hard to ***believe*** he had ever been as I was then.(p.309)
• However, as he unfolded his story for me, I could not help but ***believe*** him.(p.309)
• My first drinking spree was on corn liquor and I was allergic to it, ***believe*** me.(p.322)
• I ***believe*** that the release from people-pleasing restrictions gives retirees more motivation to drink than boredom does.(p.329)
• I don't ***believe***, when I started, that I even had in mind the thought that I was drinking.(p.336)
• And ***believe*** me, an alcoholic cannot fight alcohol.(p.338)
• I heard one very ill woman say that she didn't ***believe*** in the surrender part of the A.A. program.(p.340)
• I had been brought up to ***believe*** in God, but I know that until I found this A.A. program, I had never found or known faith in the reality of God, the reality of His power that is now with me in everything I do.(p.341)
• I don't ***believe*** it."(p.356)
• Many times have I heard the above expressions since I have been in A.A., and many times I have had to reply "Definitely I am an alcoholic, and while it may be hard for you to ***believe***, it is not hard for me, for I have learned many things about alcohol and myself that would, perhaps, be difficult for you to understand."(p.356)
• It was hard for her to ***believe*** in my love by my actions.(p.362)
• I haven't written anything about that part of my story, but I ***believe*** in a Greater Power which I call God and I ask for His wisdom and guidance daily.(p.366)
• And, ***believe*** me, I thank God that I found out about A.A. before I had to beat my brains out – before I had been hospitalized, jailed or lost a job.(p.367)
• I ***believe*** the first time I ever realized what alcohol would do for me was at my own wedding.(p.385)
• I know now that I asked questions and told him what I wanted to learn, but I told him only what I wanted to ***believe*** about myself.(p.388)
• So I ***believe*** that twenty percent is a very conservative estimate of the amount of income I blew.(p.399)
• For an estimate of salary from the twenty-one a month to start with, to over $400 per month upon my retirement after twenty years in the Navy, I ***believe*** that an average income of $2,000 a year over this period is low, but as I stated earlier, an underestimate is best.(p.399)
• I think now that a God, in whom I did not ***believe***, was looking after me.(p.412)
• With their help I also saw that certainly, because of some of the things I had done during the years, I was bordering on insanity, and so, facing the record, I tried to ***believe*** that a Power greater than I could and would restore me to sanity.(p.471)
• I feel that I have been restored to health and sanity these past years not through my own efforts nor as a result of anything I may have done, but because I've come to ***believe*** -- to really ***believe*** -- that alone I can do nothing.(p.473)
• I have come to ***believe*** that my illness is spiritual as well as physical and mental, and I know that for help in the spiritual sphere I have to turn to a Higher Power.(p.473)
• Came to ***believe***.(p.476)
• I really do ***believe*** it is much harder for a woman to gain back her self-respect than it is for a man.(p.480)
• I like to ***believe*** that I may have helped him, too.(p.481)
• I don't ***believe*** this program would work for me if I didn't get honest with myself about everything.(p.482)
• For that reason, I ***believe***, I married at a much younger age than I would have, had it not been for my home training.(p.485)
• On the other hand, I ***believe*** that I've always been medically inclined, though I have never been able to see medicine quite as the average person sees it.(p.485)
• At this point I ***believe*** I had only been intoxicated on maybe three or four occasions, and certainly whiskey was no problem to me.(p.487)
• But as he continued to talk, I realized that this was the first time I had met a person who had the same problems I did and who, I sincerely ***believe***, understood me as an individual.(p.494)
• Then he asks me if I ***believe*** in a power greater than myself, whether I call that power God, Allah, Confucius, Prime Cause, Divine Mind, or any other name.(p.503)
• I told him that I ***believe*** in electricity and other forces of nature, but as for a God, if there is one, He has never done anything for me.(p.503)
• I ***believe*** in God.(p.504)
• I tell them of the peace, and that I ***believe*** in God.(p.505)
• It's like the fellow who came in A.A., and his sponsor said to him, "Listen, buddy, do you ***believe*** in a Higher Power?"(p.512)
• In any case, I made myself ***believe*** that, so I just drifted about, existing on my retired pay, drinking, and living at home.(p.522)
• I don't know when I became an alcoholic, but I do ***believe*** I became one because I drank too much too often.(p.526)
• So many wonderful things have happened to me that at times I can't ***believe*** this is me.(p.529)
• There was the father one lost respect for at the age of eleven, because the father broke his solemn word in a circumstance where you, eleven years old, had assumed guilt when you were innocent; but the father would not ***believe*** you, no matter what; and to ease his suffering you "confessed" and were "forgiven," only – months later – to have your "guilt" brought up – only he and you knew what he was talking bout -- brought up in front of the stern grandmother.(p.533)
• I choose to ***believe*** that the Power greater than ourselves we ask for help, wrapped my shivering body in loving warmth and strength which has never left me.(p.541)
• All of my family and loved ones, all of my friends, are nearer and dearer to me than ever before and I have literally dozens of new friends who say they cannot ***believe*** that a short eight years ago I was ready for the scrap heap.(p.541)
• I've heard it said many times in A.A., "There is just one good drunk in every alcoholic's life, and that's the one that brings us into A.A.," and I ***believe*** it.(p.549)
• I ***believe*** this, and I ***believe*** too that it is equally impossible to practice these principles to the best of our ability, a day at a time, and still drink, for I don't think the two things are compatible.(p.550)

• A.A. taught me that willingness to ***believe*** was enough for a beginning.(p.550)
• The "12 Traditions" of Alcoholics Anonymous are, we A.A.'s ***believe***, the best answers that our experience has yet given to those ever urgent questions, "How can A.A. best function?" and, "How can A.A. best stay whole and so survive?"(p.563)
• 12. – And finally, we of Alcoholics Anonymous ***believe*** that the principle of anonymity has immense spiritual significance.(p.567)

believed

• He frankly admitted and ***believed*** that for him there was no hope.(p.xxix)
• I had always ***believed*** in a Power greater than myself.(p.10)
• At long last I saw, I felt, I ***believed***.(p.12)
• Above all, he ***believed*** he had acquired such a profound knowledge of the inner workings of his mind and its hidden springs that relapse was unthinkable.(p.26)
• Most of us have ***believed*** that if we remained sober for a long stretch, we could thereafter drink normally.(p.33)
• But we ***believed*** in life – of course we did.(p.54)
• We have ***believed*** them when no one else could or would.(p.105)
• The next question, they wanted to know was if I ***believed*** in a Higher Power.(p.186)
• That was the beginning of a new life, a fuller life, a happier life than I had ever known or ***believed*** possible.(p.228)
• My brilliant agnosticism vanished, and I saw for the first time that those who really ***believed***, or at least honestly tried to find a Power greater than themselves, were much more composed and contented than I had ever been, and they seemed to have a degree of happiness which I had never known.(p.247)
• And I ***believed*** him.(p.263)
• As many times as he would tell me that, I still ***believed*** him.(p.263)
• I would hang on to sobriety for short intervals, but always there would come the tide of an overpowering necessity to drink and, as I was engulfed in it, I felt such a sense of panic that I really ***believed*** I would die if I didn't get that drink inside.(p.306)
• Also, I ***believed*** I was the image of all domestic virtues, secluded in my washday (any day) refuge.(p.369)
• What I had secretly ***believed*** myself to be all along, this I had become.(p.411)
• Second, you wouldn't have ***believed*** me even if I had told you."(p.436)
• To this day, I am amazed at how many of my problems -- most of which had nothing to do with drinking, I ***believed*** -- have become manageable or have simply disappeared since I quit drinking.(p.448)
• If anyone had told me I would be enjoying a hockey game with my husband and my brother without being all boozed up, I would not have ***believed*** it.(p.481)
• When I had heard about it, it meant nothing but just two letters to me, but some friends of mine in the institution were very active in the program and really ***believed*** in it.(p.509)
• It seems only fitting that when I did finally fall in love it was with an alcoholic, and for the next ten years I progressed as rapidly as is humanly possible into what I ***believed*** to be hopeless alcoholism.(p.547)

believes

• There is the type who always ***believes*** that after being entirely free from alcohol for a period of time he can take a drink without danger.(p.xxviii)
• I'm sure it would work if I could only believe as he ***believes***.(p.47)
• Everybody ***believes*** them without a murmur of doubt.(p.48)
• Everybody nowadays, ***believes*** in scores of assumptions for which there is good evidence, but no perfect visual proof.(p.48)
• Every one of them has gained access to, and ***believes*** in, a Power greater than himself.(p.50)
• Young when she joined, this A.A. ***believes*** her serious drinking was the result of even deeper defects.(p.544)

believing

• Seeing is ***believing*** to most families who have lived with a drinker.(p.135)
• I had never, since the ***believing*** days of childhood, been able to conceive an authority directing the universe.(p.259)
• There are so many to whom I feel deeply grateful; to my husband (and best critic), whose generous love, compassion and understanding have helped me along the way; to those before me in A.A. who inspired the first article I read, and the friend who sent that article to Frank; to Ruth for her personal note, and the first A.A. to talk to me; to my Bishop, whose loving and ***believing*** spirit inspired me; and to all the members of the Houston Group who were so patient, kind and helpful -- and to countless others.(p.393)
• I grew up ***believing*** that one had to be totally self-sufficient, for one never dared to depend on another human being.(p.545)

belittle

• Try to remember that though God has wrought miracles among us, we should never ***belittle*** a good doctor or psychiatrist.(p.133)

bell

• I said, "All right, call me a cab," as though I was talking to a ***bell*** boy.(p.204)
• The word "thoroughly" rang a ***bell***.(p.349)
• If there is something in my story that rings a ***bell*** with you, then do something – now!(p.368)

belladonna

• Under the so-called ***belladonna*** treatment my brain cleared.(p.7)

Bellaire

• One year we got as far as ***Bellaire***, Ohio.(p.264)
• One Sunday afternoon, the only time I ever got picked up for drunken driving, I got picked up in ***Bellaire***.(p.264)
• As we left, and they were escorting us across the bridge into Wheeling, I, with great dignity and sarcasm, told them if their wives were ever visiting in Akron, and they, too, were looking for their route sign as I was, that I hoped I could extend to them the hospitality that had been shown to me in ***Bellaire***.(p.264)

bellboy

• I return to the hotel where I am staying and get gin from the ***bellboy***.(p.501)

belle

• The glittering society ***belle***, the modern Shakespeare, the happy wife, the loving and beloved.(p.411)
• *BELLE* OF THE BAR(p.478)

belligerent

• He can only be defeated by an attitude of intolerance or ***belligerent*** denial.(p.570)

bells

• It was November 11th and ***bells*** were ringing and whistles blowing for the real Armistice.(p.242)

belong

• If we ***belong*** to a religious denomination which requires a definite morning devotion, we attend to that also.(p.87)
• Your prospect may ***belong*** to a religious denomination.(p.93)
• I was sure I wouldn't ***belong*** in an A.A. group -- they were all old men, I thought, and all skid-row bums.(p.319)
• I ***belong*** to more medical societies and honor societies than men ten to twenty years my senior.(p.345)
• (I ***belong*** to the American Psychiatric Society, but I don't practice psychiatry as such.(p.347)
• It doesn't ***belong*** to me.(p.351)
• I just didn't ***belong*** here.(p.439)

belonged

• My wife and I ***belonged*** to some bridge clubs and they began to make wine and serve it.(p.184)
• When I walked into the friendly atmosphere of my first A.A. meeting, I knew I was where I ***belonged***.(p.355)
• I ***belonged*** to one of the Irish families who, more or less traditionally, sent their boys to the British armies.(p.517)

belonging

• Those of us ***belonging*** to a religious denomination which requires confession must, and of course, will want to go to the properly appointed authority whose duty it is to receive it.(p.74)
• Now there is a sense of ***belonging***, of being wanted and needed and loved.(p.312)
• Never had I felt a sense of ***belonging***.(p.413)

belongs

• I'll get you the password, and I can find out where they meet because I know a guy that ***belongs***.(p.266)

beloved

• The glittering society belle, the modern Shakespeare, the happy wife, the loving and ***beloved***.(p.411)
• I promised on the grave of a ***beloved*** sister that I would stop drinking.(p.539)

below

• Of course, we all fall much ***below*** this standard many times.(p.99)
• We worked in five ***below*** zero weather, fixing on an elm tree a wrought iron device which modestly proclaimed that he was indeed a country doctor.(p.540)

belt

• Like a gaunt prospector, ***belt*** drawn in over the last ounce of food, our pick struck gold.(p.128)
• When I landed of course I hit a gin mill, and with three or four good shots under my ***belt*** the world began to go into that rosy glow.(p.513)

belts

• They wanted me to make leather ***belts***, of all things!(p.445)
• Had I gone to school all those years just to sit and make leather ***belts***?(p.445)
• When I was faced with a special challenge or social event – such as an important business presentation or a dinner party – I had to fortify myself with a couple of ***belts***.(p.556)

bench

• Tasting the best of burgundy at a famous restaurant one night, landed me passed out on a park ***bench*** in the public square.(p.405)

bend

• At the end of about four months, I not only had good looking clothes –and I might say that at the time I first talked to Max I didn't have a suit of clothes I could ***bend*** over in real sudden; now I had six suits of clothes.(p.200)

bended

• Time after time I would beg forgiveness on ***bended*** knees, with tears rolling down my cheeks, and promise I would never again drink too much.(p.362)

bender

• Then I went on a prodigious ***bender***, and that chance vanished.(p.5)
• If you ask him why he started on that last ***bender***, the chances are he will offer you any one of a hundred alibis.(p.23)
• Of an evening, you can go on a mild ***bender***, get up in the morning, shake your head and go to business.(p.139)
• If he temporizes and still thinks he can ever drink again, even beer, he might as well be discharged after the next ***bender*** which, if an alcoholic, he is almost certain to have.(p.142)
• Some time later, and just as he thought he was getting control of his liquor situation, he went on a roaring ***bender***.(p.155)
• He knew too well that didn't mean a thing, just as I knew in my heart that it would be only a question of time -- a few days, a week, or even a month, it was inevitable -- till I would be off on another ***bender***.(p.257)
• A fellow A.A., called Anne, who had helped me, went on a terrible ***bender***.(p.414)
• Her idea of fun on a ***bender*** was to hit sailors and insult cops.(p.414)
• Then I went on my first week-long ***bender*** of solitary drinking, locked up in a hotel room, because my family opposed my coming marriage.(p.464)

benders

• By 1932, I was going on two or three day ***benders***.(p.288)

beneath

• Anybody who had my problem was ***beneath*** contempt!(p.412)
• At one end of the bed, near the foot, was a printed card, and ***beneath*** that was a charted graph.(p.422)
• I, a man of steel, with very high ideals, well brought up, an honor student and the recipient of scholarships and prizes, a boy wonder in business -- I, Bob, the author of this essay, looked and saw that the universe was ***beneath*** my contempt, and that to remove myself from it was the only thing of dignity a man could do.(p.531)
• I remember being dragged, drink in hand, from ***beneath*** the grand piano, where I had hidden, to be locked in my room in disgrace.(p.557)

benefactor

• The section called "The Doctor's Opinion" has been kept intact, just as it was originally written in 1939 by the late Dr. William D. Silkworth, our Society's great medical ***benefactor***.(p.xi)

beneficial

• We may kill a future opportunity to carry a ***beneficial*** message.(p.77)
• It is harder to go to an enemy than to a friend, but we find it much more ***beneficial*** to us.(p.77)
• Many of us have noticed a tendency to eat sweets and have found this practice ***beneficial***.(p.134)

benefit

• Of course an alcoholic ought to be freed from his physical craving for liquor, and this often requires a

definite hospital procedure, before psychological measures can be of maximum ***benefit***.(p.xxv)
• No matter how far down the scale we have gone, we will see how our experience can ***benefit*** others.(p.84)
• Still you may say: "But I will not have the ***benefit*** of contact with you who write this book."(p.164)
• For the ***benefit*** of those experimentally inclined, I should mention the so-called beer experiment.(p.177)
• I know now that sixty per cent of the time I drank alone without ***benefit*** of customers.(p.287)
• It was very impressive and I wish that every A.A. could have the ***benefit*** of this type of sponsorship today.(p.292)
• Alas for us men toward whom Shaw hurled his cry, "Must a Christ be crucified in every generation for the ***benefit*** of those who have no imagination?"(p.536)

benefited

• Doctors were advised to attend patients who could be ***benefited*** by medicine.(p.307)
• I've been ***benefited*** from a dictionary definition I found that reads: "rationalization is giving a socially acceptable reason for socially unacceptable behavior, and socially unacceptable behavior is a form of insanity."(p.551)

benefits

• It is impossible to put on paper all the ***benefits*** I have derived . . . physical, mental, domestic, spiritual, and monetary.(p.302)
• I can't begin to tell you of all the ***benefits*** I have derived from this new way of living.(p.481)

benevolent

• I suppose the psychiatrist might say, "This is ***benevolent*** interpersonal relations.(p.352)

benevolently

• Oddly enough, the dentist who started A.A. in Amarillo, Tex., ***benevolently*** arranged my admission to dental college.(p.419)

Benzedrine

• Eventually, I was taking forty-five milligrams of the long-acting ***Benzedrine*** and forty-five of the short-acting just to get out of bed in the morning.(p.442)
• I was taking ***Benzedrine*** and paraldehyde quite impartially during the day then, and by the time I arrived at my first A.A. meeting, I was pretty drunk and certainly doped up to the eyes and completely jittery.(p.523)

beset

• Soon A.A. was ***beset*** by these very problems on every side and in every group.(p.xix)
• Too many economic and social problems would ***beset*** me there.(p.281)

beside

• Two days later, a future fellow of Alcoholics Anonymous stared glassily at the strangers ***beside*** his bed.(p.157)
• Morning after morning I would awake sick and with terrible jitters, but there was always a flask of liquor sitting on the table ***beside*** my bed.(p.183)
• A corpsman stood ***beside*** him.(p.422)
• The doctor sat down ***beside*** the bed and asked me how I felt.(p.423)
• The doctor was still sitting ***beside*** my bed.(p.427)
• I talk to the stranger in the seat ***beside*** me.(p.505)
• When I awoke in the middle of the night with shakes and sweats and fears, I would hear my wife weeping quietly in bed ***beside*** me.(p.558)

besides

• And ***besides***, we are sure that our way of living has its advantages for all.(p.xiii)
• And ***besides***, there were scattered alcoholics who had picked up the basic ideas in Akron or New York and were trying to form A.A. groups in other cities.(p.xvii)
• ***Besides***, my gin would last longer than his preaching.(p.9)
• ***Besides*** a seeming inability to accept much on faith, we often found ourselves handicapped by obstinacy, sensitiveness, and unreasoning prejudice.(p.47)
• He commences to look around in the night clubs, or their equivalent, for something ***besides*** liquor.(p.81)
• ***Besides***, we have stopped fighting anybody or anything.(p.103)
• ***Besides***, how could he understand?(p.227)
• But I had my health back and ***besides***, I reasoned, they were much worse than I would ever be.(p.289)
• If I were asked what in my opinion was the most important factor in being successful in this program, ***besides*** following the Twelve Steps, I would say Honesty.(p.367)
• ***Besides***, I couldn't understand the instructions.(p.445)
• ***Besides***, I can only live today.(p.463)
• I actually wanted a drink, ***besides*** feeling that I had to have a drink.(p.488)

best

• Perhaps I can ***best*** answer this by relating one of my experiences.(p.xxix)
• We had long talks when I would still her foreboding by telling her that men of genius conceived their ***best*** projects when drunk; that the most majestic constructions of philosophic thought were so derived.(p.2)
• ***Best*** of all, I met a kind doctor who explained that though certainly selfish and foolish, I had been seriously ill, bodily and mentally.(p.7)
• Then he had, in effect, been raised from the dead, suddenly taken from the scrap heap to a level of life better than the ***best*** he had ever known!(p.11)
• We were in a position where life was becoming impossible, and if we had passed into the region from which there is no return through human aid we had but two alternatives: One was to go on to the bitter end, blotting out the consciousness of our intolerable situation as ***best*** we could; and the other, to accept spiritual help.(p.25)
• He had consulted the ***best*** known American psychiatrists.(p.26)
• My old manner of life was by no means a bad one, but I would not exchange its ***best*** moments for the worst I have now.(p.43)
• Students of ancient history tell us that the intellect of men in those days was equal to the ***best*** of today.(p.51)
• Was it not true that the ***best*** mathematical minds had proved man could never fly?(p.51)
• Neither is reason, as most of us use it, entirely dependable, though it emanate from our ***best*** minds.(p.54)
• Is he not, even in his ***best*** moments, a producer of confusion rather than harmony?(p.61)
• We found it very desirable to take this spiritual step with an understanding person, such as our wife, ***best*** friend or spiritual adviser.(p.63)
• The ***best*** reason first: If we skip this vital step, we may not overcome drinking.(p.72)
• Arranging the ***best*** deal we can we let these people know we are sorry.(p.78)
• Though there may be justifiable exceptions, and though we wish to lay down no rule of any sort, we have often found this the ***best*** course to take.(p.81)
• "How can I ***best*** serve Thee -- Thy will (not mine) be done."(p.85)
• Sometimes it is to the ***best*** interests of all concerned that a couple remain apart.(p.99)
• Go or stay away, whichever seems ***best***.(p.102)
• If this kind of approach does not catch your husband's interest, it may be ***best*** to drop the subject, but after a friendly talk your husband will usually revive the topic himself.(p.112)
• Unless they actually need protection from their father, it is ***best*** not to take sides in any argument he has with them while drinking.(p.115)
• He left us a note saying you were the ***best*** boss he ever had, and that you were not to blame in any way."(p.136)
• It was the obituary of one of the ***best*** salesmen I ever had.(p.137)
• I had been obliged to discharge him for drinking, though he was brilliant, alert, and one of the ***best*** organizers I have ever known.(p.137)
• And we, who have imposed on the ***best*** of employers, can scarcely blame them if they have been short with us.(p.138)
• This may seem severe, but it is usually the ***best*** course.(p.142)
• Though you are providing him with the ***best*** possible medical attention, he should understand that he must undergo a change of heart.(p.143)
• When the man is presented with this volume it is ***best*** that no one tell him he must abide by its suggestions.(p.144)
• He may, for example, reveal that he has padded his expense account or that he has planned to take your ***best*** customers away from you.(p.145)
• Perhaps the ***best*** way of treating you to a glimpse of your future will be to describe the growth of the fellowship among us.(p.153)
• After high school came four years in one of the ***best*** colleges in the country where drinking seemed to be a major extra-curricular activity.(p.172)
• Each day I would try to find out what His will was, and try to follow that, rather than trying to get Him to always agree that the things I thought of myself were the things ***best*** for me.(p.187)
• It was in the next two or three days after I had first met Doc and Bill, that I finally came to a decision to turn my will over to God and to go along with this program the ***best*** that I could.(p.189)
• The very simple program they advised me to follow was that I should ask to know God's will for me for that one day, and then, to the ***best*** of my ability, to follow that, and at night to express my gratefulness to God for the things that had happened to me during the day.(p.208)
• All during Prohibition, every alcoholic felt that he made the ***best*** hooch, regardless of how bad it was.(p.213)
• The ***best*** boarding schools and a finishing school in Europe had fitted me for the conventional role of debutante and young matron.(p.225)
• "***Best*** in the business, when he's sober," my customers would say, and I still had a following who would give me work though they deplored my habits, because they knew the job would be well done when they eventually got it.(p.234)
• Young and able to travel with the ***best*** of them, I managed to hold my job and keep my end up in the barrooms.(p.252)
• When I came to my aunt, she knew that I had had an unhappy childhood, and she said, "Now, Ethel, you're welcome to have boy friends in our home, but there are two boys in this town that I don't want you to date, and one of them comes from a very fine family, one of the ***best***.(p.262)
• To the ***best*** of my recollection I was completely free from any abnormal fears.(p.275)
• A complete checkup at one of the ***best*** hospitals revealed nothing.(p.276)
• I had the ***best*** schools, summer camps, resort vacations and travel.(p.304)
• It explained so much I had not understood about myself and, ***best*** of all, it promised recovery if I would do a few simple things and be willing to have the desire to drink removed.(p.309)
• How hurt I was when editors bounced back my ideas quickly and my ***best*** friends opined that my output needed a lot of rewriting.(p.331)
• ***Best*** that they not be found after I'd had my last drink on earth.(p.333)
• Since I gave my will over to A.A., whatever A.A. has wanted of me I've tried to do to the ***best*** of my ability.(p.340)
• Doing our ***best***, living each day to the fullest is the art of living.(p.382)
• There are so many to whom I feel deeply grateful; to my husband (and ***best*** critic), whose generous love, compassion and understanding have helped me along the way; to those before me in A.A. who inspired the first article I read, and the friend who sent that article to Frank; to Ruth for her personal note, and the first A.A. to talk to me; to my Bishop, whose loving and believing spirit inspired me; and to all the members of the Houston Group who were so patient, kind and helpful -- and to countless others.(p.393)
• For an estimate of salary from the twenty-one a month to start with, to over $400 per month upon my retirement after twenty years in the Navy, I believe that an average income of $2,000 a year over this period is low, but as I stated earlier, an underestimate is ***best***.(p.399)
• They did the ***best*** they knew how as far as I was concerned.(p.401)
• My family always bought the ***best***, and the embassies were flowing.(p.402)
• Tasting the ***best*** of burgundy at a famous restaurant one night, landed me passed out on a park bench in the public square.(p.405)
• This new analyst was a woman doctor, one of the ***best*** in the country.(p.409)
• I happened to be the ***best*** diagnostician I knew at the time, and certainly I knew my case better than anyone else.(p.444)
• A.A. and acceptance have taught me that there is a bit of good in the worst of us and a bit of bad in the ***best*** of us; that we are all children of God and we each have a right to be here.(p.449)
• Today, I find it's the ***best*** thing that has ever happened to me.(p.450)
• So I'm better off if I don't give advice, don't figure I know what's ***best***, and just accept life on life's terms, as it is today -- especially my own life, as it actually is.(p.450)
• Perhaps the ***best*** thing of all for me is to remember that my serenity is inversely proportional to my expectations.(p.452)
• We are told to practice the Twelve Steps and Twelve Traditions to the ***best*** of our ability every day, one day at a time.(p.481)
• He is my ***best*** teacher; without him, I am sure I would never have made the progress I have.(p.481)
• He wanted to give me the very ***best*** and he thought

that nothing but being a doctor would suffice.(p.485)
• My only hope was to try and get through what was left of life as ***best*** I could, but I could never visualize doing that without drinking.(p.522)
• It has taught me that I can ***best*** keep my sobriety by sharing it out with others; that I must bring that sobriety to others who need it, in my own interest.(p.524)
• It has taught me that success and failure are never final, and that neither count for very much in the final assessment of any man who has done his ***best***.(p.525)
• I would wait for the mailman each month, like any good mother, but as soon as he handed me my check, I put on my ***best*** dress and went looking for my alcoholic friend.(p.527)
• No, it can ***best*** be explained in a little phrase I coined and sang to myself: "What happened to Bob?(p.532)
• I don't care too much about personal fame or glory, and I want only enough money to enable me to do the work I feel I can perhaps do ***best***.(p.542)
• I believe this, and I believe too that it is equally impossible to practice these principles to the ***best*** of our ability, a day at a time, and still drink, for I don't think the two things are compatible.(p.550)
• To wear expensive clothes, to have bartenders know what to serve me before I ordered, to be recognized by headwaiters and shown to the ***best*** table, to play gin rummy for high stakes with the insouciance of a riverboat gambler – these were the enduring values in life, I thought.(p.556)
• Too often, I would overdo it and behave badly at the very time I wanted to be at my ***best***!(p.556)
• The "12 Traditions" of Alcoholics Anonymous are, we A.A.'s believe, the ***best*** answers that our experience has yet given to those ever urgent questions, "How can A.A. ***best*** function?" and, "How can A.A. ***best*** stay whole and so survive?"(p.563)
• Rotating leadership is the ***best***.(p.567)
• Dr. G. Kirby Collier, psychiatrist: "I have felt that A.A. is a group unto themselves and their ***best*** results can be had under their own guidance, as a result of their philosophy.(p.571)

bestows

• Still another difficulty is that you may become jealous of the attention he ***bestows*** on other people, especially alcoholics.(p.119)

bet

• Show any longshoreman a Sunday supplement describing a proposal to explore the moon by means of a rocket and he will say, "I ***bet*** they do it – maybe not so long either."(p.52)
• Approach through a doctor or an institution is a better ***bet***.(p.91)
• I remember telling them too that it was going to be awfully tough, because I did some other things, smoked cigarettes and played penny ante poker, sometimes ***bet*** on the horse races and they said, "Don't you think you're having more trouble with this drinking than with anything else at the present time?(p.190)
• And I thought, "I ***bet*** he's a sissy.(p.268)
• I ***bet*** he never drank."(p.268)
• You ***bet*** your life!(p.500)

bets

• My job was to collect ***bets*** and betting-slips in the business section, a lucrative spot.(p.251)

better

• We think this account of our experiences will help everyone to ***better*** understand the alcoholic.(p.xiii)
• More often than not, it is imperative that a man's brain be cleared before he is approached, as he has then a ***better*** chance of understanding and accepting what we have to offer.(p.xxiv)
• He had plenty of money left and thought I had ***better*** go to Canada.(p.4)
• As the whisky rose to my head I told myself I would manage ***better*** next time, but I might as well get good and drunk then.(p.6)
• Then he had, in effect, been raised from the dead, suddenly taken from the scrap heap to a level of life ***better*** than the best he had ever known!(p.11)
• But you had ***better*** hang on to it.(p.14)
• Anything is ***better*** than the way you were."(p.14)
• Over any considerable period we get worse, never ***better***.(p.30)
• If a mere code of morals or a ***better*** philosophy of life were sufficient to overcome alcoholism, many of us would have recovered long ago.(p.44)
• And then, with a ***better*** motive, had we not worshipfully beheld the sunset, the sea, or a flower?(p.54)
• Relieve me of the bondage of self, that I may ***better*** do Thy will.(p.63)
• But it is ***better*** to meet God alone than with one who might misunderstand.(p.63)
• Perhaps there is a ***better*** way – we think so.(p.68)
• If we are sorry for what we have done, and have the honest desire to let God take us to ***better*** things, we believe we will be forgiven and will have learned our lesson.(p.70)
• We thank God from the bottom of our heart that we know Him ***better***.(p.75)
• It may be he has done us more harm than we have done him and, though we may have acquired a ***better*** attitude toward him, we are still not too keen about admitting our faults.(p.77)
• After consulting with his wife and partner he came to the conclusion that it was ***better*** to take those risks than to stand before his Creator guilty of such ruinous slander.(p.80)
• It is ***better***, however, that one does not needlessly name a person upon whom she can vent jealously.(p.82)
• ***Better*** men than we are using it constantly.(p.85)
• What could we have done ***better***?(p.86)
• The family may object to this, but unless he is in a dangerous physical condition, it is ***better*** to risk it.(p.90)
• Approach through a doctor or an institution is a ***better*** bet.(p.91)
• When your man is ***better***, the doctor might suggest a visit from you.(p.91)
• You will thus get a ***better*** idea of how you ought to proceed.(p.91)
• If his own doctor is willing to tell him that he is alcoholic, so much the ***better***.(p.92)
• When dealing with such a person, you had ***better*** use everyday language to describe spiritual principles.(p.93)
• The more hopeless he feels, the ***better***.(p.94)
• Should they accept and practice spiritual principles, there is a much ***better*** chance that the head of the family will recover.(p.97)
• If their old relationship is to be resumed it must be on a ***better*** basis, since the former did not work.(p.99)
• When we look back, we realize that the things which came to us when we put ourselves in God's hands were ***better*** than anything we could have planned.(p.100)
• But if you are shaky, you had ***better*** work with another alcoholic instead!(p.102)
• Some day we hope that Alcoholics Anonymous will help the public to a ***better*** realization of the gravity of the alcoholic problem, but we shall be of little use if our attitude is one of bitterness or hostility.(p.103)
• You can see that he really does love you with his ***better*** self.(p.108)
• Today most of our men are ***better*** husbands and fathers than ever before.(p.108)
• If you are positive he is one of this type you may feel you had ***better*** leave.(p.108)
• He admits this is true, but is positive that he will do ***better***.(p.109)
• You think he ought to know the subject ***better***, as everyone should have a clear understanding of the risk he takes if he drinks too much.(p.112)
• In some cases it may be ***better*** to let someone outside of the family present the book.(p.113)
• Use your energies to promote a ***better*** understanding all around.(p.115)
• We have elsewhere remarked how much ***better*** life is when lived on a spiritual plane.(p.116)
• A ***better*** way of life will emerge when they are overcome.(p.117)
• You will lose the old life to find one much ***better***.(p.120)
• Though it is infinitely ***better*** that he have no relapse at all, as has been true with many of our men, it is by no means a bad thing in some cases.(p.120)
• If not, it had ***better*** be found out right away.(p.120)
• We find it ***better*** when possible, to stick to our own stories.(p.125)
• He may tell mother, who has been religious all her life, that she doesn't know what it's all about, and that she had ***better*** get his brand of spirituality while there is yet time.(p.128)
• Father feels he has struck something ***better*** than gold.(p.129)
• Nothing will help the man who is off on a spiritual tangent so much as the wife who adopts a sane spiritual program, making a ***better*** practical use of it.(p.130)
• We think the business fabric is shot through with a situation which might be helped by ***better*** understanding all around.(p.137)
• Even when you understand the malady ***better***, you may feel this feeling rising.(p.139)
• If you are sure your man does not want to stop, he may as well be discharged, the sooner the ***better***.(p.141)
• Your man will fare ***better*** if placed in such physical condition that he can think straight and no longer craves liquor.(p.143)
• It is ***better*** for him to feel fully responsible.(p.143)
• An alcoholic who has recovered, but holds a relatively unimportant job, can talk to a man with a ***better*** position.(p.146)
• So, for one reason or another, they cover these men, hoping matters will take a turn for the ***better***.(p.147)
• Feel ***better***.(p.151)
• Work ***better***.(p.151)
• Having a ***better*** time."(p.151)
• I seemed to be able to snap back the next morning ***better*** than most of my fellow drinkers, who were cursed (or perhaps blessed) with a great deal of morning-after nausea.(p.172)
• When I got the fog out of my brain, I decided that quitting school was very foolish and that I had ***better*** return and continue my work.(p.173)
• And they both laughed very heartily, and said, "That's ***better*** than you've been doing, isn't it?"(p.187)
• Two days before this, Dr. Bob had said to me, "If you and I are going to stay sober, we had ***better*** get busy."(p.188)
• Then Dr. Bob said, "Well, Bill, maybe you'll feel ***better*** tomorrow.(p.189)
• He did things much ***better*** than I did because he applied himself and learned how to do them, and I never applied myself.(p.194)
• And we stood there for twenty minutes, telling each other how much ***better*** we were, how much ***better*** we looked, how much ***better*** off we were financially, mentally, physically, morally, and in every way, shape and manner.(p.201)
• After drinking one glass of beer at the end of my work period for about five days, I thought I'd ***better*** find out whether I really had the stuff licked.(p.203)
• I had found friends, understanding friends who often knew what I was thinking and feeling ***better*** than I knew myself, and didn't allow me to retreat into my prison of loneliness and fear over a fancied slight or hurt.(p.228)
• From the top of the heap in a few years he had skidded to becoming a shuffling customer, still entering the ***better*** barrooms but welcomed by neither mine host nor his patrons.(p.236)
• If anything, he had known all of them even ***better*** and more often than I.(p.239)
• With nothing but a liberal arts education, very definitely estranged from my family and already married, soon after graduation from college I became a bookmaker's clerk on the British racing circuits, far ***better*** off financially than the average professional man.(p.251)
• Successive Monday morning hangovers, which despite mid-week resolutions to do ***better***, came with unfailing regularity, eventually caused me to quit my job.(p.254)
• She said, "Well, you ***better*** talk to Jack."(p.266)
• A year later I was able to buy a Model T roadster and take a ***better*** job with a downtown printer.(p.276)
• His road lay clear before me, and I'd ***better*** quit rationalizing myself into any detours.(p.282)
• Once dad came all the way to Florida to sober me up, after a hotel manager called him and said that if he wanted to see me alive he ***better*** get there fast.(p.288)
• After holding good positions, making ***better*** than an average income for over ten years, I was in debt, had no clothes to speak of, no money, no friends, and no one any longer tolerating me but my wife.(p.301)
• He further explained that alcohol was no respecter of sex or background, but that most of the alcoholics he had encountered had ***better*** than average minds and abilities.(p.308)
• I felt ***better*** mentally and physically.(p.320)
• Half a mother was ***better*** than no mother at all.(p.337)
• I have been of a very religious outlook all my life, but that made no difference once John Barleycorn got the ***better*** of me.(p.343)
• They were neither poor nor wealthy, but far ***better*** off than the average couple.(p.357)
• All I can remember about the Roaring Twenties is that I drank a great deal, thought I was having a grand time, managed to get to Europe for a few weeks, was very proud of the dozens of speak-easy cards entitling me to an entree in the ***better*** joints between Cleveland and New York, took on a wife, and built a home in a fashionable suburb of Cleveland.(p.358)
• My salesmanship was still good, for in the fall of

1938 she called me from Salt Lake and finally agreed to take me on for ***better*** or for worse.(p.360)
• I said I was okay, but if it would make her feel ***better*** I would go "as tired as I was after the strenuous holidays."(p.365)
• Even when I was old enough to know ***better***, I dreamed about being as beautiful as Venus, as pure as the Madonna and as brilliant as the President of the United States is supposed to be.(p.400)
• Things were no ***better*** with the family, so I moved to New York.(p.406)
• I'd ***better*** taper off.(p.408)
• I want to write ***better*** and sell more.(p.417)
• I happened to be the best diagnostician I knew at the time, and certainly I knew my case ***better*** than anyone else.(p.444)
• So, for no ***better*** reason than to make him happy, I agreed.(p.446)
• Against my ***better*** judgment, I went to a meeting with him that night, and a strange thing began to happen.(p.446)
• So, for no ***better*** reason than to fool him, I asked Frank to take me to a meeting every night.(p.447)
• The people of A.A. had something that looked much ***better*** than what I had, but I was afraid to let go of what I had in order to try something new; there was a certain sense of security in the familiar.(p.448)
• I am saying that I know ***better*** than God.(p.449)
• So I'm ***better*** off if I don't give advice, don't figure I know what's best, and just accept life on life's terms, as it is today -- especially my own life, as it actually is.(p.450)
• But when I try to see what I can add to the meeting, rather than what I can get out of it, and when I focus my mind on what's good about it, rather than what's wrong with it, the meeting keeps getting ***better*** and ***better***.(p.451)
• When we deal in feelings, we tend to come to know ourselves and each other much ***better***.(p.451)
• I am still arrogant, egocentric, self-righteous, with no humility, even phony at times, but I'm trying to be a ***better*** person and help my fellowman.(p.463)
• I had decided I was no good – never would be any good, and the sooner I could drink myself out of this life, the ***better***.(p.468)
• As an indication of just how confused and mixed up I was, just as soon as I could I left the office and hurried around to tell other patients that I was getting ***better***.(p.470)
• Our shoes are not ***better*** than the average hobo's, and if we are fortunate enough to have a pair of stockings on, nobody notices the runs in them, because of our dazzling beauty and our dirty feet.(p.479)
• I feel much ***better***!(p.505)
• The days have grown into a little ***better*** than four years of sobriety.(p.511)
• I buttonholed him after dinner and gave him a few tips on how to run his colony ***better*** and the result of that was about a fortnight or so later I was shipped back to my regiment.(p.520)
• Perhaps a ***better*** way of saying it is that, on that day, with that decision, I no longer fought drinking as an escape.(p.531)
• I was not capable of anything ***better***.(p.540)
• Hopeless now, I felt it would be ***better*** for my wife, my children, and everyone in my life if I went ahead and died.(p.558)
• We feel it ***better*** to let our friends recommend us.(p.567)
• There is something spiritual about A.A. too, and Catholic participation in it almost invariably results in poor Catholics becoming ***better*** Catholics."(p.574)

betting

• You are ***betting***, of course, that your changed attitude plus the contents of this book will turn the trick.(p.144)

betting-slips

• My job was to collect bets and ***betting-slips*** in the business section, a lucrative spot.(p.251)

between

• Sixteen years have elapsed ***between*** our first printing of this book and the presentation in 1955 of our second edition.(p.xv)
• The spark that was to flare into the first A.A. group was struck at Akron, Ohio, in June 1935, during a talk ***between*** a New York stockbroker and an Akron physician.(p.xv)
• We hope we have made clear the distinction ***between*** the alcoholic and the non-alcoholic.(p.44)
• We could not prove life in the sense that you can prove a straight line is the shortest distance ***between*** two points, yet, there it was.(p.54)
• That often makes the difference ***between*** failure and success.(p.98)
• Barriers which have sprung up ***between*** you and your friends will disappear with the growth of sympathetic understanding.(p.115)
• We have found nothing incompatible ***between*** a powerful spiritual experience and a life of sane and happy usefulness.(p.130)
• As to them, his policy is undoubtedly sound, but he did not distinguish ***between*** such people and the alcoholic.(p.149)
• There is a good bit of travel ***between*** East and West and we foresee a great increase in this helpful interchange.(p.162)
• I was ***between*** Scylla and Charybdis now, because if I did not drink my stomach tortured me, and if I did, my nerves did the same thing.(p.175)
• ***Between*** classes I would run down to the wash room, take enough to steady my nerves and then go on to the next class.(p.183)
• I figured the only difference ***between*** me and a millionaire was that I hadn't the strength, or that he got the breaks and I didn't.(p.197)
• The differences ***between*** my father and my sisters, who were school teachers, made an excellent environment for the type of child I was – that is, slick and cute enough to take advantage of any adult quarrel.(p.210)
• I kept myself so busy that outside of some school and group parties, I didn't go overboard on drinking very much ***between*** the ages of twenty-five and thirty.(p.213)
• Every encouragement was given me with frequent salary increases, but the sober times ***between*** "periods" became shorter.(p.254)
• An old avocation, the collecting of first editions, rare books and Americana, fascinated me ***between*** times.(p.255)
• Always, in ***between***, there were intervals of being broke, riding freights and hitch-hiking interminable distances from one big town to another in three states.(p.255)
• This was the beginning of five years of bounding back and forth ***between*** my home in Chicago and Akron to sober up.(p.288)
• The parties waxed more liquid and hilarious as time went on, and eventually I discovered that a little shot of liquor now and then ***between*** beers had the tendency to put me in a whacky mood much quicker than having to down several quarts of beer to obtain the same effect.(p.298)
• The last day of my drinking career, I drank twenty-two of them ***between*** ten and twelve a.m. and I shall never know how many more followed them until I was poured into bed that night.(p.298)
• I got along fairly well with my party drinking for quite some time, but eventually I began to visit beer joints in ***between*** parties.(p.298)
• ***Between*** the ages of twenty-five and thirty I tried everything.(p.305)
• The difference ***between*** the two vacations was this:(p.344)
• One said, "Don't feel that you are a martyr because you stopped drinking," and this hit me ***between*** the eyes.(p.346)
• The second one said, "Don't feel that you stop drinking for anyone other than yourself," and this hit me ***between*** the eyes.(p.346)
• All I can remember about the Roaring Twenties is that I drank a great deal, thought I was having a grand time, managed to get to Europe for a few weeks, was very proud of the dozens of speak-easy cards entitling me to an entree in the better joints ***between*** Cleveland and New York, took on a wife, and built a home in a fashionable suburb of Cleveland.(p.358)
• For the next couple of hours a terrible battle went on ***between*** the good gremlins and the bad ones, one faction urging me to tell the truth, the other telling me to sit tight and say nothing.(p.366)
• The only drawback was, I always knew how I arrived there, but somehow, ***between*** the rest room, the rinse, and the fluff-dry, I never knew when or how I got home.(p.370)
• "You've got to space your drinks and take plenty of water in ***between***," or "coat the stomach with a little olive oil," or "drink anything but those damn martinis."(p.433)
• Intervals ***between*** binges were, at first, eight months.(p.434)
• In seven years the intervals ***between*** them decreased from eight months to ten days!(p.434)
• The line ***between*** a heavy drinker and an alcoholic is not always clear.(p.436)
• But what a difference there is ***between*** going through hell without a power greater than one's self, and with it!(p.437)
• There was a long discussion ***between*** my husband, my sister and her husband.(p.466)
• But there happened to be a liquor store ***between*** the post office and the mill, and I stopped to get that one drink.(p.493)
• In fact, I couldn't have told you the difference ***between*** sherry and brandy.(p.518)
• I hope I have been able to impart to you, the reader, at least a bit of what I know; the joy of living, the irresistible power of divine love and its healing strength, and the fact that we, as sentient beings, have the knowledge to choose ***between*** good and evil, and, choosing good, are made happy.(p.543)
• I had only to reflect on the contrast ***between*** the plans I made so many years ago for my life with what really happened to know I couldn't manage my life drunk or sober.(p.550)
• The relationship ***between*** my wife and me was restored to a love and happiness that we had not known even before my alcoholism became acute.(p.559)
• We are taught to differentiate ***between*** our wants (which are never satisfied) and our needs (which are always provided for).(p.560)
• To those now in its fold, Alcoholics Anonymous has made the difference ***between*** misery and sobriety, and often the difference ***between*** life and death.(p.563)

beverage

• I came of good stock, of men and women who drank wine all their lives as a ***beverage***, and while they occasionally got drunk at special celebrations, they were up and about their business the next day.(p.231)

Beverly Hills

• You tell that dumb cat-and-dog doctor he's not a ***Beverly Hills*** psychiatrist.(p.440)

bewail

• Then we have the voices who cry for sex and more sex; who ***bewail*** the institution of marriage; who think that most of the troubles of the race are traceable to sex causes.(p.69)

bewildered

• Mentally, the fears and tensions, the complete change in attitude and outlook, ***bewildered*** me.(p.378)

bewilderment

• Momentarily we did – then would come oblivion and the awful awakening to face the hideous Four Horsemen – Terror, ***Bewilderment***, Frustration, Despair.(p.151)
• ***Bewilderment***, fear, and resentment moved into my life.(p.556)

beyond

• We doctors have realized for a long time that some form of moral psychology was of urgent importance to alcoholics, but its application presented difficulties ***beyond*** our conception.(p.xxv)
• These men were not drinking to escape; they were drinking to overcome a craving ***beyond*** their mental control.(p.xxviii)
• When this sort of thinking is fully established in an individual with alcoholic tendencies, he has probably placed himself ***beyond*** human aid, and unless locked up, may die or go permanently insane.(p.24)
• Potential female alcoholics often turn into the real thing and are gone ***beyond*** recall in a few years.(p.33)
• As we look back, we feel we had gone on drinking many years ***beyond*** the point where we could quit on our will power.(p.34)
• We were bothered with the thought that faith and dependence upon a Power ***beyond*** ourselves was somewhat weak, even cowardly.(p.45)
• They often forget father was ***beyond*** human aid.(p.128)
• The others must be convinced of his new status ***beyond*** the shadow of a doubt.(p.135)
• Because of the employee's special ability, or of his own strong personal attachment to him, the employer has sometimes kept such a man at work long ***beyond*** a reasonable period.(p.137)
• The mental state of the sick alcoholic is ***beyond*** description.(p.244)
• And still by the time I was thirty years old I was being pushed around with a compulsion to drink that was completely ***beyond*** my control.(p.305)
• Two years later, a month ***beyond*** age seventy, I was crying for help from A.A.(p.327)
• It was a month ***beyond*** my seventieth birthday.(p.333)
• Finally I didn't care, I was ***beyond*** caring.(p.337)
• She was tolerant ***beyond*** all belief.(p.361)
• We rationalize and excuse our conduct ***beyond*** all reason.(p.376)
• In all these ways I've experienced, in ever growing measure and ***beyond*** all expectations and rewards, a

joy which I had never before imagined.(p.395)
• Then too, we view with much concern those A.A. treasuries which continue, ***beyond*** prudent reserves, to accumulate funds for no stated A.A. purpose.(p.566)

bias
• When this happens, they can be invited to join in morning meditation and then they can take part in the daily discussion without rancor or ***bias***.(p.134)

biased
• We asked ourselves this: Are not some of us just as ***biased*** and unreasonable about the realm of the material?(p.51)

Bible
• There is another meaning for the Hebrew word that in the King James version of the ***Bible*** is translated "salvation."(p.228)
• At this school we had ***Bible*** readings before each meal, and church services four times on Sunday, and I became so rebellious at this that I swore I would never join or go to any church except for weddings or funerals.(p.240)
• I noticed a ***Bible*** on his table and it amazed me.(p.257)
• I began to read the ***Bible*** daily and to go over a simple devotional exercise as a way to begin each day.(p.259)
• Now, if you've got a ***Bible*** around . . ."(p.268)
• One of our gifts from the family was a very lovely ***Bible***, but we'd let the bulldog chew it because we weren't too interested in it.(p.268)
• This was such a new thought that I got all sorts of books on Higher Powers, and I put a ***Bible*** by my bedside, and I put a ***Bible*** in my car.(p.348)
• And I put a ***Bible*** in my locker at the hospital.(p.348)
• And I put a ***Bible*** in my desk.(p.348)

bidding
• Grant me strength, as I go out from here, to do your ***bidding***.(p.76)

big
• All changes made over the years in the ***Big*** Book (A.A. members' fond nickname for this volume) have had the same purpose: to represent the current membership of Alcoholics Anonymous more accurately, and thereby to reach more alcoholics.(p.xii)
• That being so you have swallowed and digested some ***big*** chunks of truth about yourself.(p.71)
• The family may feel they hold a mortgage on dad, so ***big*** that no equity should be left for outsiders.(p.131)
• Among many employers nowadays, we think of one member who has spent much of his life in the world of ***big*** business.(p.136)
• It was the day before Mother's Day and I had come home plastered, carrying a ***big*** potted plant which I set down on the table and forthwith went upstairs and passed out.(p.179)
• I looked up and there were two great ***big*** fellows over six foot tall, very likable looking.(p.185)
• A ***big*** event of any kind precipitated heavy drinking.(p.197)
• I was prone to do everything on a ***big*** scale.(p.197)
• I was always able to skate along the fringe of ***big*** money.(p.197)
• With the ***big*** companies, and with the amount of money we could have gotten and the promises I had, it could have been done.(p.198)
• I worked along until I had really ***big*** names in rubber on a tentative contract, and then I neglected to go through with it.(p.198)
• My ***big*** job was to keep other people from finding it out.(p.199)
• I was picked up at two-thirty that morning with my car smashed up by a street-car because I had run into a ***big*** concrete safety zone, and the street-car had run into me, and they took me out through the roof -- there's where I lost the suit.(p.202)
• My only thought that day was getting a drink, and how to get rid of those clowns was my ***big*** problem.(p.206)
• It was getting pretty dark and I hadn't turned on any lights, when some ***big*** fellow stepped inside the door and flipped on the light switch.(p.207)
• This time I seemed to be already awake, sitting upright in a ***big*** easy chair, in the middle of an animated conversation with a perfectly strange young woman, who didn't appear to think it strange.(p.222)
• Oddly enough, the ***big*** shot who fired me from this company was one of the first men I met when I later joined the New York A.A. Group.(p.242)
• As part of this promotion, they sent me to their national convention in Atlantic City to tell the ***big*** wheels how I'd done it.(p.243)
• The ***Big*** Shot?(p.243)
• They had also been periodic ***big*** shots who had goofed out repeatedly at the wrong time, and they also knew how to split one paper match into three separate matches.(p.245)
• Just give me a good front and a couple of bucks and I'd be right back in the ***big*** time.(p.246)
• Then it was my turn – I ordered "Three beers," but this time it was different, I had a cash investment of thirty cents and, on a ten dollar a week salary, that's a ***big*** thing.(p.247)
• Around this time our ***big*** A.A. book was being written and it all became much simpler; we had a definite formula which some sixty of us agreed was the middle course for all alcoholics who wanted sobriety, and that formula has not been changed one iota down through the years.(p.248)
• My boss, in his way, was "***big*** business."(p.251)
• Following a ***big*** drunk on that sheet, where I was doing leg-work and rewrite, a feeling of nostalgia made me buy a ticket for Liverpool and I returned to Britain.(p.252)
• Always, in between, there were intervals of being broke, riding freights and hitch-hiking interminable distances from one ***big*** town to another in three states.(p.255)
• The ***big*** thing was that these men were all sober and evidently had something I didn't have.(p.259)
• I had the ***Big*** Book ("Alcoholics Anonymous") that had been brought to me.(p.268)
• Paul S. had just called me, and I remember he stressed reading the ***Big*** Book.(p.269)
• He said, "Let's put the ***Big*** Book away again, and when you read it again, turn to the back and read some of the stories.(p.269)
• We had ***big*** picnics out at the house with A.A.(p.270)
• The ***big*** A.A. book had not been written and there was no literature except various religious pamphlets.(p.291)
• In the spring of 1939, the ***Big*** Book was printed, and we had two inquiries from the New York office because of a fifteen-minute radio talk that was made.(p.294)
• No more snoops or ***big*** shots breathing down our necks.(p.329)
• Not wishing to disturb my wife, I slumped in a ***big*** red-leather chair and suffered.(p.332)
• I sat up in the ***big*** red chair, suddenly thinking, "My God, with my kind of lousy luck, I might not die soon!(p.333)
• Studied the ***Big*** Book again.(p.344)
• And I put a ***Big*** Book by my night stand, and I put a "Twelve Steps and Twelve Tradition" in my locker at the hospital, and I got books by Emmet Fox, and I got books by God-knows-who, and I got to reading all these things.(p.348)
• Why don't you go home and get the ***Big*** Book and open it at page fifty-eight and see what it says?"(p.349)
• I got the ***Big*** Book and I read it, and this is what it said: "Rarely have we seen a person fail who has thoroughly followed our path."(p.349)
• Looking back, it is surprising to me now that I managed to keep working and have enough money to squander at the various spots in the ***big*** city.(p.358)
• The challenge intrigued me; also it was another opportunity to run away from myself and the "fast life of the ***big*** city."(p.359)
• Once again I was back in the ***big*** time operations, and along with them, ***big*** shot complexes.(p.361)
• I attended my weekly meetings with regularity, reread the ***Big*** Book, attended other group meetings, gave leads when asked to and did some Twelve Step work whenever I was called upon to do so.(p.365)
• I had thrown off a ***big*** lie that had been burdening me down for months.(p.366)
• Dad's image for me was that of a ***big*** Irish oilman who came up through the school of hard knocks and so had to be a two-fisted drinker.(p.369)
• The night that I was married I had a ***big*** church wedding.(p.385)
• You didn't carry a little orchid up the aisle in those days; you carried a great ***big*** bouquet, like a funeral spray, and you didn't have your picture taken until just before you went to the church.(p.385)
• I dropped a two-quart water bottle on my ***big*** toe.(p.390)
• I accepted a ***big*** tax-free income from the family, but I didn't like it when they told me how to live.(p.405)
• For three generations, my family had had a charge account in one of the ***big*** New York hotels.(p.410)
• In those days there was only one ***big*** meeting a week in New York.(p.414)
• Now, I am ***big*** and weak, but Anne was bigger than I and strong.(p.414)
• School was getting to be on
• I would drink all night in b
five a.m., down a good ***big*** gl
and tumble into bed.(p.428)
• We got on the plane and im
fight over whether I'd drink t
• Each with the other as a wit
Step out loud – just as it says
• Very shortly, I realized tha
when this ***big*** clown came bo
most shouting, "My name is
holic, ha-ha-ha!"(p.446)
• When a ***big***, healthy-lookin
there and said, "I'm a success
today," I thought, "Man, I've
do today before I can brag ab
for God's sake!"(p.447)
• I wanted to talk about my
drinking seemed a small one.
• It is painful to grow, and wi
vilian" A.A. companion, ***big***
survived that critical year of
• When he speak from heart,
• Tall Man now see Great Spi
sky.(p.476)
• Some of us always rememb
it comes to a drink, but somev
seem to have forgotten about
teeth.(p.479)
• I thought that this would be
• Around eight or nine o'cloc
tectives and a policeman to ar
was the most amazed person
said I had assaulted someone,
had assaulted my wife.(p.492)
• But I came out of the Army
when I went in, if not worse,
more resentments.(p.513)
• But I knew that they knew
grounds were, and that they h
against my name.(p.521)
• I always blamed my drinkin
anything other than the truth
booze did for me, that when I
and had as much as the next p
• Brandishing my "motto," wh
with a stick is equal to a ***big*** m
the literary lecture by a fight w
solely because he was ***big*** and
• So did the waterboy on the h
team attempt to revenge hims
who was the star quarterback;
and my brother was the star q
everything except the fact tha
back.(p.537)
• Back to the ***big*** city, for anoth
living, paid for largely by one
had not milked dry or worn to
mands on their bounty.(p.540)
• While there, I read the ***Big*** B
and began the slow road back
through the recovery program

big-shot
• And being a ***big-shot*** man of
if I said so, then I'll go."(p.217)

big-hearted
• After the trial, I got ***big-heart***
should do something in paym
me; so I left Washington and v
work.(p.492)

bigger
• If the alcoholic tries to shield
ceed for a time, but he usually
explosion than ever.(p.101)
• The only answer I could ma
followed the usual pattern, he
bust than ever.(p.138)
• Here he is powerless, unma
something ***bigger*** than he is, a
whole business over to someo
• Today, because of A.A.'s gro
vening years, it is of course mu
then.(p.392)
• Now, I am big and weak, bu
I and strong.(p.414)
• They got ***bigger*** and ***bigger*** a
as if they were going to fall an
• There was the sense of being
when as a matter of fact by my
quite popular, although I hadr
physically.(p.534)

biggest
• The man who was going to t
biggest branches come Monda

• I would get in the ***biggest*** dither about something.(p.273)
• I know the ***biggest*** word for me in A.A. is "honesty."(p.482)
• I thought, well, now that I've been put out for drinking, I'll just show them that they were completely wrong, so I went off on the ***biggest*** bout I had been on up to then, involving about a fortnight's blackout.(p.521)
• I was trying to remember where it came from, when two of the ***biggest*** cops I ever saw walked in and took me to jail.(p.528)

bike
• The details of the long road back to something resembling normal living -- the first short streetcar ride, the purchase of a used ***bike*** which enabled me to widen the narrow horizon of life, the first trip downtown -- I will not dwell on.(p.276)

bill
• A remorseful mumbling that we are sorry won't fill the ***bill*** at all.(p.83)
• The ***bill*** collectors, the sheriffs, the angry taxi drivers, the policemen, the bums, the pals, and even the ladies they sometimes brought home -- our husbands thought we were so inhospitable.(p.106)
• One dismal afternoon he paced a hotel lobby wondering how his ***bill*** was to be paid.(p.154)
• This man's wife had been suffering for a couple of months and when he came in he owed me a little ***bill***.(p.488)
• Finally, I broke the last one hundred dollar ***bill*** the Saturday before I left.(p.493)
• I got out of that ***bill*** one pair of shoes, and the rest of that money was blown.(p.493)

Bill
• ***Bill*** W., co-founder of A.A., died January 24, 1971.(p.16)
• We of ALCOHOLICS ANONYMOUS, know thousands of men and women who were once just as hopeless as ***Bill***.(p.17)
• So, at the time Dr. Bob and ***Bill*** came along I had about run out my strength.(p.182)
• (I knew afterwards that the two who came in were ***Bill*** W. and Doctor Bob.)(p.185)
• After a while, ***Bill*** said, "Well, now, you've been talking a good long time, let me talk a minute or two."(p.185)
• (At this point, the Editors intrude just long enough to supplement ***Bill*** D.'s account, that of the man on the bed, with that of ***Bill*** W., the man who sat by the side of the bed.)(p.188)
• Says ***Bill*** W.:(p.188)
• Nineteen years ago last summer, Dr. Bob and I saw him (***Bill*** D.) for the first time.(p.188)
• ***Bill*** lay on his hospital bed and looked at us in wonder.(p.188)
• ***Bill*** didn't seem too impressed.(p.188)
• Then Dr. Bob said, "Well, ***Bill***, maybe you'll feel better tomorrow.(p.189)
• "Sure I would," replied ***Bill***, "Maybe it won't do any good, but I'd like to see you both, anyhow.(p.189)
• Looking in later we found ***Bill*** with his wife, Henrietta.(p.189)
• ***Bill*** then related how he had lain awake nearly all night.(p.189)
• Before our visit was over, ***Bill*** suddenly turned to his wife and said, "Go fetch my clothes, dear.(p.189)
• ***Bill*** D. walked out of that hospital a free man never to drink again.(p.189)
• (***Bill*** D. now continues his story.)(p.189)
• It was in the next two or three days after I had first met Doc and ***Bill***, that I finally came to a decision to turn my will over to God and to go along with this program the best that I could.(p.189)
• I know there was even more, something that I hadn't got, and I remember one day, a week or two after I had come out of the hospital, ***Bill*** was over to my house talking to my wife and me.(p.191)
• ***Bill*** looked across at my wife, and said to her, "Henrietta, the Lord has been so wonderful to me, curing me of this terrible disease, that I just want to keep talking about it and telling people."(p.191)
• ***Bill*** was very, very grateful that he had been released from this terrible thing and he had given God the credit for having done it, and he's so grateful about it he wants to tell other people about it.(p.191)
• The man turned out to be ***Bill*** D., a very early member of A.A., and I couldn't tell you a word of what he said.(p.208)
• One evening I had gone out after dinner to take on a couple of double-headers and stayed a little later than usual, and when I came home Clarence was sitting on the davenport with ***Bill*** W.(p.216)
• I do not recollect the specific conversation that went on but I believe I did challenge ***Bill*** to tell me something about A.A. and I do recall one other thing: I wanted to know what this was that worked so many wonders, and hanging over the mantel was a picture of Gethsemane and ***Bill*** pointed to it and said, "There it is," which didn't make much sense to me.(p.216)
• There was also some conversation about Dr. Bob and I must have said that I would go down to Akron with ***Bill*** in the morning.(p.217)
• ***Bill*** bought me a drink or two on the way, and Dorothy S. came with us, and the three of us went over to the City Hospital.(p.217)
• ***Bill*** left me at the elevator and said, "Your room is so and so," and I didn't see him again for six months.(p.217)
• We checked into the home of Hank, the man who had fired me eleven years before in Mississippi, and there I met ***Bill***, our founder.(p.245)
• ***Bill*** had then been dry three years and Hank, two.(p.245)
• ***Bill*** and Hank had just taken over a small automobile polishing company and they offered me a job -- ten dollars a week and keep at Hank's house.(p.246)
• The example which they and ***Bill*** W., whose visits to Akron were fairly frequent, set me of service to their fellow men imbued me with a great desire to emulate them.(p.281)
• In the spring of 1939, ***Bill*** stopped off in Akron on his way to Detroit on business.(p.281)
• This first meeting was held in the living room of a home and was led by ***Bill*** D., the first man that ***Bill*** W. and Dr. Bob had worked with successfully.(p.291)
• The words of Dr. Bob and ***Bill*** are with me all the time.(p.395)
• Dr. Bob said, "Love and service keep us dry," and ***Bill*** said, "Always we must remember that our first duty is face-to-face help for the alcoholic who still suffers."(p.395)
• Perhaps it was He who sent my analyst to a psychiatrist's meeting at which ***Bill*** spoke.(p.412)
• Having heard ***Bill*** speak, she was instantly sold.(p.412)
• ***Bill*** was tall, grey haired, with the kind of asymmetrical good looks and pleasant easy manner that inspire confidence in the shaken and afraid.(p.413)
• Marty came in, looking clean, neat, well-dressed and, like ***Bill***, she was neither a bloated wreck nor a reformer.(p.413)
• (This address is now available in pamphlet form at nominal cost through most A.A. groups or from Box 459, Grand Central Station, New York, NY 10163, under the title "Three Talks to Medical Societies by ***Bill*** W." -- formerly called "***Bill*** on Alcoholism" and earlier "Alcoholism the Illness.")(p.572)

Bill's
• "***Bill's*** Story," "Doctor Bob's Nightmare," and one other personal history from the first edition were retained intact; three were edited and one of these was retitled; new versions of two stories were written with new titles; thirty completely new stories were added; and the story section was divided into three parts, under the same headings that are used now.(p.xi)
• ***BILL'S*** STORY(p.1)
• There was one meeting a week at ***Bill's*** home in Brooklyn, and we all took turns there spouting off about how we had changed our lives overnight, how many drunks we had saved and straightened out, and last, but not least, how God had touched each of us personally on the shoulder.(p.246)

billboarded
• Only a few knew of it at first but, within a short time, it was ***billboarded*** throughout the entire company.(p.145)

billet
• At Great Lakes Boot Camp I latched onto a soft ***billet***.(p.425)

billion
• This company now does a volume of over three ***billion*** dollars annually.(p.242)

bills
• Sometimes a small deal would net a few hundred dollars, and I would pay my ***bills*** at the bars and delicatessens.(p.5)
• It was the usual situation: home in jeopardy, wife ill, children distracted, ***bills*** in arrears and standing damaged.(p.155)
• Consequently, my labor ***bills*** ran up.(p.194)
• I would have to return to New York and pick up my ***bills*** and bags.(p.213)
• I'd work like mad for three or four weeks without a single drink, save my money, pay a few ***bills*** and then "reward" myself with alcohol.(p.244)
• The doctor ***bills*** are heavy and the bank account is low.(p.501)

bin
• If my wife was planning to go out in the afternoon, I would get a large supply of liquor and smuggle it home and hide it in the coal ***bin***, the clothes chute, over door jambs, over beams in the cellar and in cracks in the cellar tile.(p.176)

bind
• An A.A. group can ***bind*** itself to no one.(p.566)

binds
• The feeling of having shared in a common peril is one element in the powerful cement which ***binds*** us.(p.17)

Bing
• All afternoon I sat there and drank and played ***Bing*** Crosby's recording of "Silent Night" over and over again on the juke box.(p.467)

binge
• Sometimes it is wise to wait till he goes on a ***binge***.(p.90)
• But after his next ***binge***, ask him if he would really like to get over drinking for good.(p.112)
• One morning, after I had been on a ***binge*** for a couple of days, I awoke to find my brother and Doctor Bob in my room talking to me about not drinking.(p.206)
• At age twenty-one, I enlisted in the Navy for two reasons: (1) to avoid being drafted into the Army, and (2) out of a burst of patriotic fervor inspired by the advent of World War II and as the result of an all-night drinking ***binge*** which found me sitting on the doorstep of the Navy recruiting office when the chief petty officer arrived to open for business at nine o'clock Monday morning.(p.398)
• Even on my rare (at first) ***binge*** nights it never ran much over a quart.(p.433)
• The ***binge*** had been just "one of those things."(p.433)
• After my last ***binge*** I came home and smashed my dining room furniture to splinters, kicked out six windows and two balustrades.(p.435)
• My last ***binge*** followed the previous one by two weeks.(p.514)
• It paid for a ten-day ***binge*** which was the end of my drinking days.(p.540)
• I did not remember much of the ten-day ***binge***.(p.540)
• But I remembered the years of agony preceding the ***binge***, I remembered the years I had thrown away.(p.540)
• I have not had a drink of anything alcoholic since that ten-day ***binge***.(p.541)

binges
• It was a period of ***binges*** coming closer and closer together and being of longer duration.(p.288)
• My life there was a nightmare of periodic ***binges*** on alcohol and pills, adultery, unhappy hours at the dental office, seeing my wife give birth to our second child and have several miscarriages, living in a turbulent household, and making continual attempts to be the respectable dentist, husband, father, and community leader.(p.419)
• My ***binges*** were one-night stands only.(p.432)
• How easy it was, in the beginning, to forget that those ***binges*** ever happened!(p.433)
• Intervals between ***binges*** were, at first, eight months.(p.434)
• My daily alcoholic consumption remained about the same through all this, with perhaps a slight increase, and my ***binges*** remained one-nighters.(p.434)
• The ***binges*** were longer.(p.514)

bingo
• Then I turned two company cars over in a short time and ***Bingo*** -- fired again.(p.242)
• If my personality is inadequate, antisocial, or full of kinks and I alter it with alcohol or any chemical, ***bingo***!(p.458)

birds
• Had not people said God had reserved this privilege to the ***birds***?(p.51)
• He said something about God or a Higher Power, but I brushed that off -- that was for the ***birds***, not for me.(p.239)

Birmingham
• I went to work in ***Birmingham*** for a newspaper at fifteen dollars a week.(p.357)

birth
• The ***birth*** of our Society dates from his first day of permanent sobriety, June 10, 1935.(p.171)
• The ***birth*** of a baby boy did nothing toward staying the downward spiral.(p.278)

• The *birth* of a daughter filled me with new fears.(p.402)
• My life there was a nightmare of periodic binges on alcohol and pills, adultery, unhappy hours at the dental office, seeing my wife give *birth* to our second child and have several miscarriages, living in a turbulent household, and making continual attempts to be the respectable dentist, husband, father, and community leader.(p.419)

birthday

• It was a month beyond my seventieth *birthday*.(p.333)
• One night at the dinner table my wife said that tonight was my first *birthday* in A.A., and that the group would have the usual ice cream and cake for the "one year man."(p.365)
• I had no trouble making the right decision when I saw my wife open her purse at the meeting that night and deposit a cute little angel in the middle of my *birthday* cake.(p.366)
• The final decision came when my daughter, following a drunk which ruined my wife's *birthday*, said, "It's Alcoholics Anonymous -- or else!"(p.378)
• For my seventh A.A. *birthday*, my program-oriented, Al-Anon wife had my moccasins bronzed.(p.445)
• The November following, I took a few days off after pay day to celebrate my *birthday* on the 25th of the month.(p.491)
• I began drinking as a kid, shortly after I reached my fourteenth *birthday*.(p.508)

Bishop

• There are so many to whom I feel deeply grateful; to my husband (and best critic), whose generous love, compassion and understanding have helped me along the way; to those before me in A.A. who inspired the first article I read, and the friend who sent that article to Frank; to Ruth for her personal note, and the first A.A. to talk to me; to my *Bishop*, whose loving and believing spirit inspired me; and to all the members of the Houston Group who were so patient, kind and helpful -- and to countless others.(p.393)

bit

• Fear sobered me for a *bit*.(p.8)
• We can only clear the ground a *bit*.(p.55)
• Nevertheless, with a person we dislike, we take the *bit* in our teeth.(p.77)
• They suspect father is a *bit* balmy!(p.128)
• That won't hurt him a *bit*, even though he does not go for this remedy.(p.144)
• After a *bit*, he said, "The way you fellows put this spiritual stuff makes sense.(p.159)
• There is a good *bit* of travel between East and West and we foresee a great increase in this helpful interchange.(p.162)
• Then I started drinking again, with possibly a little more restraint, periods a little *bit* longer than they had been before, but substantially the same pattern.(p.203)
• Paul measured the medicine out, but he figured that with my track record that little *bit* wouldn't be enough, so he doubled it and added a few drops more and then gave it to me.(p.207)
• Father was a very well-integrated person, and while mother was highstrung and a *bit* selfish and demanding, our home life was reasonably harmonious.(p.240)
• That is where I had my first drink and I still remember it, for every "first" drink afterwards did exactly the same trick – I could feel it go right through every *bit* of my body and down to my very toes.(p.241)
• After a *bit*, the other man said "Three beers."(p.247)
• I ate up every *bit* of it, because I wanted to find out how to stay sober.(p.273)
• Acceptance of things as they are has replaced the old impatient champing at the *bit* to conquer the world.(p.295)
• We had a small child, and I loved her dearly, so that held me back quite a *bit* in my drinking career.(p.322)
• I got so that I hid quite a *bit* of the time, wouldn't answer the phone, and stayed by myself as much as I could.(p.324)
• I was sure those who needed a *bit* of the hair of the dog really were alcoholics.(p.332)
• I read, studied, and meditated on every *bit* of A.A. literature in my possession.(p.344)
• That night she too had new hope because I had made sure she would know what I was doing about my drinking by packing every *bit* of A.A. literature I could put my hands on right on top so she couldn't help but see it when she opened my bag.(p.364)
• I was a little *bit* knocked out.(p.402)
• On our honeymoon in Egypt, he cuffed me around quite a *bit*, and subsequently hit me some more.(p.405)
• Every day, I feel a little *bit* more useful, more happy and more free.(p.417)
• I was drinking quite a *bit* of whiskey now.(p.425)
• She cried a *bit* and went to bed; that was the only answer to problems that she had left.(p.440)
• I cried a *bit* and then mixed me another drink.(p.440)
• A.A. and acceptance have taught me that there is a *bit* of good in the worst of us and a *bit* of bad in the best of us; that we are all children of God and we each have a right to be here.(p.449)
• That really stopped me for a little *bit*.(p.510)
• That gave me my first *bit* of hope.(p.524)
• Since, perhaps, suicide was a *bit* too drastic (actually, I was afraid), dry martinis were chosen as the slow, pleasant, private, gradual instrument of self-destruction.(p.531)
• I hope I have been able to impart to you, the reader, at least a *bit* of what I know; the joy of living, the irresistible power of divine love and its healing strength, and the fact that we, as sentient beings, have the knowledge to choose between good and evil, and, choosing good, are made happy.(p.543)

bite

• I just want to say that you don't have to be afraid, because no one at any A.A. meeting will *bite* you.(p.529)

biting

• I've stuck pretty close to A.A. ever since then, taken it day by day, not *biting* off more than I can chew.(p.511)

bits

• I do recall lying on a cold cement floor and shredding into little *bits* several pieces of stolen identification cards, and washing my face in the toilet bowl trying to sober up, and screaming hysterically while clinging to bars too high to see out of, and cursing everyone that came near me.(p.354)
• I found out fast that the cheapest way to get drunk was on shots with beer chasers at two *bits* a crack.(p.397)

bitter

• No words can tell of the loneliness and despair I found in that *bitter* morass of self-pity.(p.8)
• We were in a position where life was becoming impossible, and if we had passed into the region from which there is no return through human aid we had but two alternatives: One was to go on to the *bitter* end, blotting out the consciousness of our intolerable situation as best we could; and the other, to accept spiritual help.(p.25)
• This is a point we wish to emphasize and re-emphasize, to smash home upon our alcoholic readers as it has been revealed to us out of *bitter* experience.(p.39)
• We have been driven to maudlin sympathy, to *bitter* resentment.(p.104)
• I was still *bitter* because I felt that drink had completely ruined my childhood and my married life, and I hated everything pertaining to it.(p.262)
• The next time vacation time rolled around that was a *bitter* lesson to us.(p.265)
• I went on, realizing what I was becoming, hating myself for it, *bitter*, blaming life, blaming everything else but the fact that I should turn about and do something about my drinking.(p.337)
• I was *bitter*, living in hate.(p.338)
• I was an agitator, a troublemaker, and many men as *bitter* as I was followed me.(p.458)
• But the difference lay in the fact that the A.A.'s knew from their own *bitter* experience.(p.471)

bitterly

• Our friend's gorge rose as he *bitterly* cried out: "If there is a God, He certainly hasn't done anything for me!"(p.56)
• *Bitterly* discouraged, he found himself in a strange place, discredited and almost broke.(p.154)
• I was *bitterly* unhappy.(p.226)

bitterly-hated

• While drinking, he accepted a sum of money from a *bitterly-hated* business rival, giving him no receipt for it.(p.80)

bitterness

• I have seen hundreds of families set their feet in the path that really goes somewhere; have seen the most impossible domestic situations righted; feuds and *bitterness* of all sorts wiped out.(p.15)
• Did we unjustifiably arouse jealousy, suspicion or *bitterness*?(p.69)
• Some day we hope that Alcoholics Anonymous will help the public to a better realization of the gravity of the alcoholic problem, but we shall be of little use if our attitude is one of *bitterness* or hostility.(p.103)
• Do it every day for two weeks and you will find you have come to mean it and to want it [illegible] you will realize that where you used to feel [illegible] and resentment and hatred, you now fee[illegible] ate understanding and love."(p.552)

black

• We placed them before us in *black* and whi[illegible]
• I had a broken nose, a fractured cheekbone, [illegible] *black* from the lower part of my face up [illegible] hair.(p.204)
• I was *black* and blue, with my lips all swolle[illegible] when they roused us to go into court in the mo[illegible] ing.(p.204)
• They knew what to do about those *black* [illegible] that yawned ready to swallow me when [illegible] pressed, or nervous.(p.229)
• Now came the *black* and endless dismal night.(p.410)
• Then I *black* out and get home four days later.(p.475)
• Last time in jail, I have two *black* eyes.(p.475)
• This physician, the originator of A.A.'s [illegible] group, but badly caught in the toils, tells [illegible] and of how freedom came as he worked among [illegible] own people.(p.483)
• But I knew that they knew what the medical [illegible] grounds were, and that they had put a big [illegible] against my name.(p.521)
• Poor, *black*, totally ruled by alcohol, she [illegible] away from any life worth living.(p.526)
• Now I had gotten to the place where I would [illegible] up with *black* eyes and not know where I got [illegible] wake up with a lot of money and not know w[illegible] got it.(p.528)
• Since I have been in A.A., I have more friends [illegible] ever had in my life – friends who care about [illegible] my welfare, friends who don't care that I am [illegible] and that I have been in prison.(p.52[illegible])
• I have not seen a *black* face but mine since I['ve been] here, and if I didn't look in the mirror, I would[n't] know that I was *black*, because these people [illegible] as one of them, which I am.(p.530)

blacked

• Had *blacked* the eyes of two nurses, and now had him strapped down tight.(p.18[illegible])
• Even that first night I *blacked* out, which lea[illegible] to believe that I was an alcoholic from my very [illegible] drink.(p.241)
• Every time I *blacked* out, and that was every[illegible] drank, there was always that gnawing fear "W[illegible] I do this time?"(p.244)
• My parents' car had a strong attraction for [illegible] and one night I *blacked* out and drove the car [illegible] bank, ramming the steel fence around someone's yard.(p.353)
• That first night I *blacked* out at a large dinner party.(p.404)
• I completely *blacked* out.(p.468)

blacker

• It thickened, ever becoming *blacker*.(p.1[illegible])

blacking

• Alone in the relative safety of my home [illegible] knew I dare not risk the danger of *blacking* out [illegible] some public place or at the wheel of a car.(p.[illegible])

blacklisted

• I was the fair-haired boy all right, but two ye[ars] later I was *blacklisted* as an irresponsible drunk.(p.242)

blackout

• *Blackout* drinking at once.(p.195)
• Another *blackout*.(p.196)
• I would put off doing anything that I could [illegible] next day and, consequently, everything would [illegible] and then there would be the *blackout*.(p.1[illegible])
• I think the longest drunk I was ever on was [illegible] days, but usually only two days with a comple[te] *blackout* for a day, and then backing off b[illegible] as long as I could get anything.(p.20[illegible])
• Instant *blackout* was what it was, and it seem[illegible] lightful.(p.442)
• This career girl preferred solitary drinking, [illegible] *blackout* kind, often hoping she'd stay that wa[y] keeps.(p.464)
• First time I have *blackout*, but not last.(p.[illegible]7[illegible])
• It was the first *blackout* I had to recognize as [a] *blackout*.(p.489)
• I thought, well, now that I've been put out fo[r drink]ing, I'll just show them that they were completely wrong, so I went off on the biggest bout I [ha]d up to then, involving about a fortnight's *blackout*.(p.521)
• It was a total *blackout*.(p.528)

blackouts
• Next, I was sent to Arizona, where my drinking picked up some more, and I started having ***blackouts***, and I was thrown in jail for speeding and drunken driving.(p.318)
• But it began to be an awfully painful answer as hangovers, ***blackouts***, trouble, and remorse set in.(p.353)
• Then I began to have ***blackouts*** and that was a constant worry.(p.375)
• Then many ***blackouts*** for next two years.(p.475)
• As I progressed and gained in capacity, I had ***blackouts***.(p.512)
• I suffered frequent ***blackouts***.(p.558)

blame
• Admitting he may be somewhat at fault, he is sure that other people are more to ***blame***.(p.61)
• Where were we to ***blame***?(p.67)
• If he gets drunk, don't ***blame*** yourself.(p.120)
• Father knows he is to ***blame***; it may take him many seasons of hard work to be restored financially, but he shouldn't be reproached.(p.123)
• The head of the house ought to remember that he is mainly to ***blame*** for what befell his home.(p.127)
• He left us a note saying you were the best boss he ever had, and that you were not to ***blame*** in any way."(p.136)
• And we, who have imposed on the best of employers, can scarcely ***blame*** them if they have been short with us.(p.138)
• I thought to myself, "Well, she is going to tell me this is the end," and I certainly couldn't ***blame*** her and did not intend to try to justify myself.(p.184)
• Nor could I ***blame*** my dilemma on my childhood environment.(p.304)
• It shows nothing or no one to ***blame*** for alcoholism.(p.373)
• I can't ***blame*** him.(p.405)
• I ***blame*** my wife and children.(p.505)

blamed
• I told the doctor my parents' drinking history and ***blamed*** them.(p.428)
• This was the only time in my life that I'd ever known my mother to be almost pitiless, but she couldn't be ***blamed*** for that.(p.523)
• I always ***blamed*** my drinking on being poor, or on anything other than the truth – that I liked what booze did for me, that when I had a drink I was as big and had as much as the next person.(p.526)

blameless
• It brings misunderstanding, fierce resentment, financial insecurity, disgusted friends and employers, warped lives of ***blameless*** children, sad wives and parents -- anyone can increase the list.(p.18)

blaming
• I went on, realizing what I was becoming, hating myself for it, bitter, ***blaming*** life, ***blaming*** everything else but the fact that I should turn about and do something about my drinking.(p.337)

blank
• I saw that will power and self-knowledge would not help in those strange mental ***blank*** spots.(p.42)
• I passed in at least three absolutely ***blank*** books.(p.174)

blanket
• "Joykiller, nag, wet ***blanket***" – that's what they said.(p.106)
• Say you do not want to be a wet ***blanket***; that you only want him to take care of his health.(p.112)

blankets
• We gave up our positions and off we roared on a motorcycle, the sidecar stuffed with tent, ***blankets***, a change of clothes, and three huge volumes of a financial reference service.(p.2)
• I crawl under a pile of ***blankets*** and blow out the candle.(p.497)
• The war leaves me with a pair of ***blankets***, a toilet kit, a sweater knit by my sister, and a still greater inferiority.(p.499)

blanks
• "***Blanks***" were more frequent, and I seldom knew how I'd got home.(p.226)

blast
• I was hit by an icy ***blast***.(p.288)

blazed
• The Twelve Steps that summarize the program may be called los Doce Pasos in one country, los Douze Etapes in another, but they trace exactly the same path to recovery that was ***blazed*** by the earliest members of Alcoholics Anonymous.(p.xxii)
• My torch ***blazed*** madly and the pew caught fire.(p.424)

bleached
• The interne came along with a glassful of ***bleached*** lightning that put me away for about fifteen hours.(p.217)

bleak
• Near the end of that ***bleak*** November, I sat drinking in my kitchen.(p.8)
• It is a cold, ***bleak*** day in November.(p.502)

bless
• But ***bless*** his heart, let him rant!(p.9)
• So to you out there -- who may soon be with us -- we say "Good luck and God ***bless*** you!"(p.121)
• May God ***bless*** you and keep you -- until then.(p.164)
• My Quaker mother-in-law, ***bless*** her heart, used to set the Christmas pudding ablaze with lumps of sugar dipped in rubbing alcohol.(p.402)
• God ***bless*** all you people in A.A. and especially you fellows in prison.(p.463)

blessed
• Ask them to remember, when they are impatient, the ***blessed*** fact of his sobriety.(p.100)
• I seemed to be able to snap back the next morning better than most of my fellow drinkers, who were cursed (or perhaps ***blessed***) with a great deal of morning-after nausea.(p.172)
• However, I threw myself into Twelve Step work, and what I feared would be a calamity turned out to be the most ***blessed*** of blessings.(p.394)

blessing
• Maybe it will prove a ***blessing***!(p.116)
• Firing such an individual may prove a ***blessing*** to him.(p.141)
• It is a most wonderful ***blessing*** to be relieved of the terrible curse with which I was afflicted.(p.180)
• Out of those forty years as a movie press agent came one ***blessing*** that granted me a blind faith in the program.(p.334)
• Clergymen of practically every denomination have given A.A. their ***blessing***.(p.574)

blessings
• When resentful thoughts come, try to pause and count your ***blessings***.(p.119)
• For all of these ***blessings***, I thank Him.(p.303)
• Today, I'm counting my ***blessings*** instead of my troubles.(p.355)
• However, I threw myself into Twelve Step work, and what I feared would be a calamity turned out to be the most blessed of ***blessings***.(p.394)
• This to the end that our great ***blessings*** may never spoil us; that we shall forever live in thankful contemplation of Him who presides over us all.(p.568)

blew
• I felt lifted up, as though the great clean wind of a mountain top ***blew*** through and through.(p.14)
• He tossed off half of his martini; I tossed off half of mine and it nearly ***blew*** the top of my head off.(p.195)
• After the oil job ***blew*** up, I went back to Baltimore and mother, my first wife having said a permanent "Goodbye."(p.243)
• So I believe that twenty percent is a very conservative estimate of the amount of income I ***blew***.(p.399)
• We started to light matches to see, but the draft ***blew*** them out.(p.424)

blight
• It is possible to dig up past misdeeds so they become a ***blight***, a veritable plague.(p.124)

blind
• Few people really are, for that means ***blind*** faith in the strange proposition that this universe originated in a cipher and aimlessly rushes nowhere.(p.10)
• How ***blind*** I had been.(p.13)
• And even if they did not love their families, how could they be so ***blind*** about themselves?(p.107)
• I got my first introduction to "riding the rods and making a ***blind***."(p.252)
• Out of those forty years as a movie press agent came one blessing that granted me a ***blind*** faith in the program.(p.334)
• Alcohol wrings the guts out of life, eats into the brain in such a way as to make the alcoholic ***blind*** to the truth.(p.457)
• Tall Man was ***blind***, but soon he see.(p.476)

blindness
• My mother lived on for five years after I joined A.A., the last two in complete ***blindness***.(p.525)

blinked
• I ***blinked*** slowly as I shifted my gaze to my arms.(p.422)

bliss
• My wife loved to drink, and we tied on many a hooter in the name of marital ***bliss***.(p.433)

bloated
• I was fat, ***bloated***, dirty and unkempt.(p.411)
• Marty came in, looking clean, neat, well-dressed and, like Bill, she was neither a ***bloated*** wreck nor a reformer.(p.413)

block
• Half a ***block*** from the house, I tried to turn the corner.(p.276)
• He told me that it was imperative that I walk around the entire ***block***, cost me what it might in mental agony.(p.276)
• Upon leaving the office in the evening, my first stop would be a saloon about a ***block*** away.(p.298)
• When he left I walked with him to the streetcar line, which was just about a half a ***block***, but there were two liquor stores, one on each corner from my home.(p.495)
• After the meeting was over and we had returned to the cell ***block*** again, I was asked how I was impressed.(p.510)
• You hit the street about ten minutes to eight, and you walk around the ***block***, God knows how many times, waiting for that joint to open.(p.514)

blocked
• We hope you are convinced now that God can remove whatever self-will has ***blocked*** you off from Him.(p.71)

blocking
• Though our decision was a vital and crucial step, it could have little permanent effect unless at once followed by a strenuous effort to face, and to be rid of, the things in ourselves which had been ***blocking*** us.(p.64)

blocks
• Somehow I got out of there and walked five ***blocks*** past brownstone houses.(p.223)
• It was February with snow and ice on the ground and I had a four ***blocks*** walk to the nearest cab stand, but I made it.(p.288)
• The church was just three ***blocks*** from our home.(p.385)

blonde
• I teamed up with a cute little ***blonde*** with whom I was working at the office, and for about a year we were inseparable.(p.425)

blood
• What they say will apply to nearly everyone bound by ties of ***blood*** or affections to an alcoholic.(p.104)
• I had white trousers on, white shoes and a white shirt that was streaked with ***blood***.(p.204)
• It is bound to be rough, because who can say exactly how much of that green ***blood*** -- commonly known as money – was dissipated on dissipation?(p.396)
• Age and the law were still against me, but laws were not as strictly enforced in those days as they are now, and I discovered that as long as I had the green ***blood***, there was always a way to get alcohol, either from a nondiscriminatory bartender or from an older friend who would be glad to purchase the joy juice for the privilege of sharing it.(p.397)
• On another occasion I arrived home covered with ***blood***.(p.435)
• The closest I came to a psychiatrist during that time was an interne who came to take ***blood*** tests.(p.492)
• My proud southern ***blood*** would have boiled if anyone had named me such a despicable thing.(p.532)
• Suddenly, I began vomiting and losing rectally great quantities of ***blood***.(p.558)
• Each time, I went back to drinking – even smuggling a bottle of vodka into the hospital as soon as the ***blood*** transfusions had ceased.(p.558)

bloomed
• (My addiction ***bloomed*** within a small apartment I shared with my wife, a heart patient.)(p.329)
• Somewhat faded, she nevertheless ***bloomed*** afresh.(p.384)

blossom
• I became a specialist in making elderberry ***blossom*** wine.(p.213)

blotted
• But soon the sense of His presence had been ***blotted*** out by worldly clamors, mostly those within myself.(p.12)
• In emphasizing alcoholism as an illness, the social stigma associated with this condition is being ***blotted*** out . . .(p.573)

blotting

• We were in a position where life was becoming impossible, and if we had passed into the region from which there is no return through human aid we had but two alternatives: One was to go on to the bitter end, ***blotting*** out the consciousness of our intolerable situation as best we could; and the other, to accept spiritual help.(p.25)

blouse

• I know that one of the outfits I had was a skirt and a very funny looking ***blouse*** that my mother had picked up at a rummage sale.(p.261)

• Before too long, my husband (who seemed to prefer his shirts dirty) put his foot down, declaring that our family might have the cleanest clothes in town, but that I hadn't been out of the same old dirty slacks and ***blouse*** for a week.(p.371)

blow

• It was a devastating ***blow*** to my pride.(p.7)

• It was a crushing ***blow***.(p.42)

• It was a terrible ***blow*** at the time and I thought he was pretty much of a heel, but of course it was the finest thing he could have done for me under the circumstances.(p.357)

• I felt this was the final ***blow***.(p.370)

• The most terrible ***blow*** of my life befell me after I'd found sobriety through A.A.(p.437)

• I crawl under a pile of blankets and ***blow*** out the candle.(p.497)

• For to have accepted the reasons and to have acted on them would have been too great a ***blow*** to my ego, which was as great, in reverse, as my body was small.(p.534)

blowin'

• Ain't it grand the wind stopped ***blowin'***?"(p.82)

blowing

• It was November 11th and bells were ringing and whistles ***blowing*** for the real Armistice.(p.242)

blown

• I got out of that bill one pair of shoes, and the rest of that money was ***blown***.(p.493)

blue

• I was black and ***blue***, with my lips all swollen, when they roused us to go into court in the morning.(p.204)

• I am ***blue*** and unhappy.(p.505)

• I am ***blue*** again.(p.506)

bluntly

• It was my "secret garden" – ***bluntly***, it was my retreat from life, and I didn't want to give it up.(p.534)

blurry

• It was a pretty ***blurry*** night.(p.353)

board

• He has just returned from a three-months leave of absence, has taken a cure, looks fine, and to clinch the matter, the ***board*** of directors told him this was his last chance."(p.138)

• After I was on the drafting ***board*** about two years I decided I wanted a technical education.(p.211)

• I'd been on the ***board*** of governors of the Academy of Motion Picture Arts and Sciences for six years.(p.328)

• But my ***board***, room, and clothing were free, and I could spend the whole ten bucks on booze.(p.398)

• My wife was in the Junior League, and I was on the ***board*** of directors of the local center for the mentally retarded.(p.418)

• I gaze at the ***board*** with its questions.(p.499)

• At that very time, he was a nonalcoholic trustee on the General Service ***Board*** of Alcoholics Anonymous!(p.559)

• And no group, regional committee, or individual should ever take any action that might greatly affect A.A. as a whole without conferring with the trustees of the General Service ***Board***.(p.565)

• The trustees of the General Service ***Board*** are, in effect, our A.A. General Service Committee.(p.567)

• The General Service ***Board*** of A.A. (the trustees) administers A.A.'s General Service Office, A.A. World Services, Inc., and our monthly magazine, the A.A. Grapevine.(p.575)

boarding

• The best ***boarding*** schools and a finishing school in Europe had fitted me for the conventional role of debutante and young matron.(p.225)

• At thirteen I was packed off to a very fine Protestant ***boarding*** school in Virginia where I stayed four years, graduating without any special achievements.(p.240)

boards

• I recall, as I walked into that meeting, saying to myself, "Here I am, a fellow of the American College of Surgeons, a Fellow of the International College of Surgeons, a diplomate of one of the great specialty ***boards*** in these United States, a member of the American Psychiatric Society, and I have to go to the butcher, the baker and the carpenter to help make a man out of me!"(p.347)

• Nine – A.A., as such, ought never be organized; but we may create service ***boards*** or committees directly responsible to those they serve.(p.564)

bob

• However, on a couple of other occasions, Clarence seemed to ***bob*** up at the last saloon that I would stop at on the way home every day.(p.216)

• That age of the flapper and the "It" girl, speakeasies and the hip flask, the boyish ***bob*** and the drugstore cowboy, John Held Jr. and F. Scott Fitzgerald, all generously sprinkled with a patent pseudo-sophistication.(p.304)

Bob

• Beginning with the story of "Dr. ***Bob***," a co-founder of A.A., there are here presented three groups of personal histories.(p.165)

• Dr. ***Bob*** and the twelve men and women who here tell their stories were among the early members of A.A.'s first groups.(p.169)

• So, at the time Dr. ***Bob*** and Bill came along I had about run out my strength.(p.182)

• (I knew afterwards that the two who came in were Bill W. and Doctor ***Bob***.)(p.185)

• Nineteen years ago last summer, Dr. ***Bob*** and I saw him (Bill D.) for the first time.(p.188)

• Two days before this, Dr. ***Bob*** had said to me, "If you and I are going to stay sober, we had better get busy."(p.188)

• Straightway, ***Bob*** called Akron's City Hospital and asked for the nurse on the receiving ward.(p.188)

• Knowing ***Bob*** of old, she jokingly replied, "Well, Doctor, I suppose you've already tried it yourself?"(p.188)

• After prescribing medicines, Dr. ***Bob*** ordered, "Put him in a private room.(p.188)

• Then Dr. ***Bob*** said, "Well, Bill, maybe you'll feel better tomorrow.(p.189)

• Twenty-two years later, Doctor ***Bob*** told me that what I had done was like turning a switch and setting up a demand for more alcohol in my system.(p.195)

• One morning, after I had been on a binge for a couple of days, I awoke to find my brother and Doctor ***Bob*** in my room talking to me about not drinking.(p.206)

• I got two drinks, each of them a quarter of that pint, in me, and was talking along with these people, but I felt that sooner or later they were going to have me cornered because they were smarter than I was and the drink was beginning to take effect; but as I reached for the third drink ***Bob*** said, "Listen, Buster, you promised to take some medicine if we got you a drink.(p.206)

• I then began asking a lot of questions of both my brother and Dr. ***Bob*** about how this thing worked, and I suppose I was becoming more glassy-eyed all the while, for eventually I said to ***Bob***, "You're all dried up.(p.206)

• So Paul repeated substantially what Dr. ***Bob*** had said.(p.207)

• A few minutes later, Dr. ***Bob*** left, leaving with my brother some medicine I should get.(p.207)

• There was also some conversation about Dr. ***Bob*** and I must have said that I would go down to Akron with Bill in the morning.(p.217)

• My experience in the hospital I considered to be terrific because Dr. ***Bob*** told me very quickly that medicine would have very little to do with it, outside of trying to restore my appetite for food.(p.217)

• Dr. ***Bob*** did not lay out the whole program.(p.218)

• In fact, I never lost my faith, since I had been prepared by some conversations toward the end of my sojourn in the hospital with Dr. ***Bob***, conversations pretty much along spiritual lines.(p.218)

• Dr. ***Bob*** often said that it was a record for what he felt was a typical alcoholic.(p.263)

• I think his entry into A.A. was through spending some hours with Dr. ***Bob*** at his office.(p.267)

• Dr. ***Bob*** was in Florida, but Jack didn't know that.(p.267)

• Russ used to be very much pleased because he'd say, "I think Dr. ***Bob*** thoroughly enjoys coming out here.(p.271)

• The next day he turned me over to a couple who, although neither was an alcoholic, knew Dr. ***Bob*** and were willing to drive me to Akron where they would turn me over to his care.(p.278)

• So I was driven to Akron the very next day by these Good Samaritans, and turned over to Dr. ***Bob*** and the then tiny Akron Group.(p.279)

• Dr. ***Bob*** dwelt at length on how prayer had given him release, time and time again, from the nearly overpowering compulsion to take a drink.(p.279)

• When I got out of the hospital, I was invited to stay with Dr. ***Bob*** and his dear wife, Anne.(p.279)

• Poor health and a complete lack of money necessitated my remaining with Dr. ***Bob*** and Anne for very close to a year.(p.280)

• While there, two or three more "cash customers" (as Dr. ***Bob*** used to call them -- probably because they had so little cash) were shipped in to us from Detroit.(p.282)

• This first meeting was held in the living room of a home and was led by Bill D., the first man that Bill W. and Dr. ***Bob*** had worked with successfully.(p.291)

• I spent a great deal of time with Dr. ***Bob***, whenever he had the time to spare, and in the homes of two or three other people, trying to see how the family lived the program.(p.291)

• Dr. ***Bob*** led me through all of these steps.(p.292)

• Dr. ***Bob*** always emphasized the religious angle very strongly, and I think it helped.(p.292)

• Dr. ***Bob*** then led me through the restitution step, in which I made a list of all of the persons I had harmed, and worked out ways and means of slowly making restitution.(p.292)

• On my trips back to Akron to get my spirits recharged and to work with other alcoholics, I would ask Dr. ***Bob*** about this delay and wonder just what was wrong with me.(p.293)

• The words of Dr. ***Bob*** and Bill are with me all the time.(p.395)

• Dr. ***Bob*** said, "Love and service keep us dry," and Bill said, "Always we must remember that our first duty is face-to-face help for the alcoholic who still suffers."(p.395)

• Dr. ***Bob*** tells about keeping it simple and not to louse it up.(p.395)

• I, a man of steel, with very high ideals, well brought up, an honor student and the recipient of scholarships and prizes, a boy wonder in business – I, ***Bob***, the author of this essay, looked and saw that the universe was beneath my contempt, and that to remove myself from it was the only thing of dignity a man could do.(p.531)

• No, it can best be explained in a little phrase I coined and sang to myself: "What happened to ***Bob***?(p.532)

• ***Bob*** found alcohol!"(p.532)

• And having sung that phrase, I'd chuckle with amusement, turning into irony turning into self-contempt turning into self-pity, at the sad fate of ***Bob***, that wonderful, poor little motherless boy who was so smart in school and who grew up to accept responsibility so early and so fast and who staggered under his burdens without a whimper until the time came when he thought he was too good for this world and so he ought to be out of it.(p.532)

• Poor ***Bob***!(p.532)

• But not for long; now, for five Friday nights in a row, I went to jail, picked up sodden with beer (which I always disliked, but which was the only drink available); in jail five consecutive Friday nights in the town where I had grown up, where I had been an honor student in high school, where a kindly uncle, bailing me out, said, "***Bob***, our family just doesn't do this sort of thing."(p.539)

• I had even borrowed money from her, over her protest: "***Bob***, please don't ask me to lend you money -- you're the only one who hasn't."(p.540)

• "***Bob***," he asked quietly, "do you want to live or die?"(p.540)

Bob's

• "Bill's Story," "Doctor ***Bob's*** Nightmare," and one other personal history from the first edition were retained intact; three were edited and one of these was retitled; new versions of two stories were written with new titles; thirty completely new stories were added; and the story section was divided into three parts, under the same headings that are used now.(p.xi)

• DOCTOR ***BOB'S*** NIGHTMARE(p.171)

• The day before I was due to go back to Chicago, a Wednesday and Dr. ***Bob's*** afternoon off, he had me down to the office and we spent three or four hours formally going through the Six-Step program as it was at that time.(p.291)

bodies

• But we are sure that our ***bodies*** were sickened as well.(p.xxiv)

• We think it no concern of ours what religious ***bodies*** our members identify themselves with as individuals.(p.28)

• Not all of us join religious ***bodies***, but most of us favor such memberships.(p.28)

• That may be true of certain nonalcoholic people who, though drinking foolishly and heavily at the

present time, are able to stop or moderate, because their brains and ***bodies*** have not been damaged as ours were.(p.39)
• These tiny ***bodies*** are governed by precise laws, and these laws hold true throughout the material world.(p.49)
• If not members of religious ***bodies,*** we sometimes select and memorize a few set prayers which emphasize the principles we have been discussing.(p.87)
• But we have seen remarkable transformations in our ***bodies.***(p.133)
• Most of them give freely of themselves, that their fellows may enjoy sound minds and ***bodies.***(p.133)
• He may even read in a newspaper that one out of every seven drinkers will become alcoholic, but he rarely is told that it holds true for all ages – or that the tolerance to alcohol (and other drugs) decreases steadily, year after year, in the ***bodies*** of all persons.(p.330)
• Somehow our ***bodies*** had reached the point where we could no longer absorb alcohol in our systems.(p.380)

bodily

• Best of all, I met a kind doctor who explained that though certainly selfish and foolish, I had been seriously ill, ***bodily*** and mentally.(p.7)
• The curve of my declining moral and ***bodily*** health fell off like a ski-jump.(p.7)
• We are equally positive that once he takes any alcohol whatever into his system, something happens, both in the ***bodily*** and mental sense, which makes it virtually impossible for him to stop.(p.22)
• No person likes to think he is ***bodily*** and mentally different from his fellows.(p.30)
• I was taken out of the house and put ***bodily*** into a waiting car with nothing on but a robe and gown.(p.466)

body

• We, of Alcoholics Anonymous, are more than one hundred men and women who have recovered from a seemingly hopeless state of mind and ***body.***(p.xiii)
• In this statement he confirms what we who have suffered alcoholic torture must believe – that the ***body*** of the alcoholic is quite as abnormal as his mind.(p.xxiv)
• The mind and ***body*** are marvelous mechanisms, for mine endured this agony two more years.(p.6)
• Doubtless you are curious to discover how and why, in the face of expert opinion to the contrary, we have recovered from a hopeless condition of mind and ***body.***(p.20)
• Therefore, the main problem of the alcoholic centers in his mind, rather than in his ***body.***(p.23)
• Talk about the conditions of ***body*** and mind which accompany it.(p.92)
• Though the family has no religious connections, they may wish to make contact with or take membership in a religious ***body.***(p.131)
• Now about health: A ***body*** badly burned by alcohol does not often recover overnight nor do twisted thinking and depression vanish in a twinkling.(p.133)
• Whatever the method, its object is to thoroughly clear mind and ***body*** of the effects of alcohol.(p.143)
• The man in the bed was told of the acute poisoning from which he suffered, how it deteriorates the ***body*** of an alcoholic and warps his mind.(p.157)
• That is where I had my first drink and I still remember it, for every "first" drink afterwards did exactly the same trick -- I could feel it go right through every bit of my ***body*** and down to my very toes.(p.241)
• But, of course," he continued, "eventually the alcoholic loses all of his capacities as his disease gets progressively worse, and this is a tragedy that is painful to watch; the disintegration of a sound mind and ***body.***"(p.308)
• After that I sat for a week, a ***body*** in a chair, a mind off in space.(p.338)
• I was president of my grammar school student ***body.***(p.345)
• I was president of all my classes in high school and in my last year I was president of that student ***body.***(p.345)
• I was president of each class in the University, and president of that student ***body.***(p.345)
• The explanation that alcoholism was a disease of a two fold nature, an allergy of the ***body*** and an obsession of the mind, cleared up a number of puzzling questions for me.(p.380)
• But when I cracked my leg with a sixteen-pound sledgehammer in the rock hole, I was fighting the system, using my ***body.***(p.458)
• At least, my ***body*** went.(p.526)
• For to have accepted the reasons and to have acted on them would have been too great a blow to my ego, which was as great, in reverse, as my ***body*** was small.(p.534)
• I choose to believe that the Power greater than ourselves we ask for help, wrapped my shivering ***body*** in loving warmth and strength which has never left me.(p.541)
• Angry bruises appeared mysteriously all over my ***body.***(p.558)

bodyguard

• In the doctor's judgment he was utterly hopeless; he could never regain his position in society and he would have to place himself under lock and key or hire a ***bodyguard*** if he expected to live long.(p.26)
• He does not need a ***bodyguard*** nor is he confined.(p.26)

bogged

• But his venture wound up in a law suit and ***bogged*** down completely.(p.154)

bohemian

• Federal Theatre in Texas gave me an administrative job which I held for a year, only because I worked hard and productively when I worked, and because my very tolerant chief ascribed my frequent lapses to a ***bohemian*** temperament.(p.256)
• This I would do by going completely "***bohemian***" for a night, getting drunk and rolling home with the dawn.(p.432)

Bohemians

• I had met a bunch of gay young ***Bohemians*** who lived in the Village, and were sowing their wild oats.(p.407)

boiled

• I've prayed to God on hangover mornings and sworn that I'd never touch another drop but by nine o'clock I'd be ***boiled*** as an owl."(p.158)
• My proud southern blood would have ***boiled*** if anyone had named me such a despicable thing.(p.532)

boils

• It ***boils*** right down to this: No man should be fired just because he is alcoholic.(p.148)

bologna

• I would rather have stayed in jail except I didn't like ***bologna*** and cold potatoes for breakfast.(p.425)

bolsterer

• Formerly, in the acute mental and physical pain during the remorseful periods succeeding each drunk, I found my recollection of the misery I had gone through a ***bolsterer*** of resolution and afterward, perhaps, a deterrent for a time.(p.260)

bolted

• While I was taking inventory in the cold-storage locker one Sunday, a wooden sign ***bolted*** to the inside door stopped me in my tracks.(p.461)

bond

• I had contracted for half of it, at least verbally, and the contractors were taking half of the second mortgage ***bond.***(p.198)
• I had to put up a three hundred dollar ***bond*** because he was carrying the same summons around in his pocket for me.(p.491)

bondage

• Relieve me of the ***bondage*** of self, that I may better do Thy will.(p.63)
• FREEDOM FROM ***BONDAGE***(p.544)
• This great experience that released me from the ***bondage*** of hatred and replaced it with love is really just another affirmation of the truth I know: I get everything I need in Alcoholics Anonymous – everything I need I get – and when I get what I need I invariably find that it was just what I wanted all the time.(p.553)

bone

• An exceptional man, he remained ***bone*** dry for twenty-five years and retired at the age of fifty-five, after a successful and happy business career.(p.32)

bones

• Telling them what we are trying to do, we make no ***bones*** about our drinking; they usually know it anyway, whether we think so or not.(p.78)

bonfire

• My broken home and broken heart fanned my smoldering self-pity into a fair-sized ***bonfire*** and this kept me well supplied with reasons for having another drink, and then another.(p.305)

booby-hatch

• So I got drunker and drunker, and then, suddenly, I woke up in the ***booby-hatch.***(p.387)

book

• This is the third edition of the ***book*** "Alcoholics Anonymous."(p.xi)
• Because this ***book*** has become the basic text for our Society and has helped such large numbers of alcoholic men and women to recover, there exists a sentiment against any radical changes being made in it.(p.xi)
• All changes made over the years in the Big ***Book*** (A.A. members' fond nickname for this volume) have had the same purpose: to represent the current membership of Alcoholics Anonymous more accurately, and thereby to reach more alcoholics.(p.xii)
• To show other alcoholics precisely how we have recovered is the main purpose of this ***book.***(p.xiii)
• We shall be interested to hear from those who are getting results from this ***book,*** particularly from those who have commenced work with other alcoholics.(p.xiv)
• Since the original Foreword to this ***book*** was written in 1939, a wholesale miracle has taken place.(p.xv)
• Sixteen years have elapsed between our first printing of this ***book*** and the presentation in 1955 of our second edition.(p.xv)
• The fledgling society, which had been nameless, now began to be called Alcoholics Anonymous, from the title of its own ***book.***(p.xvii)
• With the appearance of the new ***book*** a great deal began to happen.(p.xvii)
• News of this got on the world wires; inquiries poured in again and many people went to the bookstores to get the ***book*** "Alcoholics Anonymous."(p.xviii)
• This was the substance of A.A.'s Twelve Traditions, which are stated in full on page 564 of this ***book.***(p.xix)
• Some of the recommendations of A.A.'s early medical and religious friends will be found further on in this ***book.***(p.xx)
• Yet it is our great hope that all those who have as yet found no answer may begin to find one in the pages of this ***book*** and will presently join us on the highroad to a new freedom.(p.xxi)
• We of Alcoholics Anonymous believe that the reader will be interested in the medical estimate of the plan of recovery described in this ***book.***(p.xxiii)
• The subject presented in this ***book*** seems to me to be of paramount importance to those afflicted with alcoholic addiction.(p.xxv)
• Many years ago one of the leading contributors to this ***book*** came under our care in this hospital and while here he acquired some ideas which he put into practical application at once.(p.xxv)
• The classification of alcoholics seems most difficult, and in much detail is outside the scope of this ***book.***(p.xxviii)
• He accepted the plan outlined in this ***book.***(p.xxix)
• However, he did become "sold" on the ideas contained in this ***book.***(p.xxx)
• I earnestly advise every alcoholic to read this ***book*** through, and though perhaps he came to scoff, he may remain to pray.(p.xxx)
• This is the great news this ***book*** carries to those who suffer from alcoholism.(p.17)
• Nothing would please us so much as to write a ***book*** which would contain no basis for contention or argument.(p.19)
• It is the purpose of this ***book*** to answer such questions specifically.(p.20)
• The distinguished American psychologist, William James, in his ***book*** "Varieties of Religious Experience," indicates a multitude of ways in which men have discovered God.(p.28)
• We think few, to whom this ***book*** will appeal, can stay dry anything like a year.(p.34)
• Well, that's exactly what this ***book*** is about.(p.45)
• That means we have written a ***book*** which we believe to be spiritual as well as moral.(p.45)
• This applies, too, to other spiritual expressions which you find in this ***book.***(p.47)
• In this ***book*** you will read the experience of a man who thought he was an atheist.(p.55)
• In this ***book*** you read again and again that faith did for us what we could not do for ourselves.(p.70)
• Taking this ***book*** down from our shelf we turn to the page which contains the twelve steps.(p.75)
• You might place this ***book*** where he can see it in the interval.(p.90)
• Don't, at this stage, refer to this ***book,*** unless he has seen it and wishes to discuss it.(p.92)
• If he shows interest, lend him your copy of this ***book.***(p.94)
• If he is sincerely interested and wants to see you again, ask him to read this ***book*** in the interval.(p.95)
• With few exceptions, our ***book*** thus far has spoken of men.(p.104)
• We hope this ***book*** has answered some of them.(p.108)

• When a discussion does arise, you might suggest he read this ***book*** or at least the chapter on alcoholism.(p.111)
• Show him your copy of this ***book*** and tell him what you have found out about alcoholism.(p.112)
• Show him that as alcoholics, the writers of the ***book*** understand.(p.112)
• Sooner or later, you are likely to find him reading the ***book*** once more.(p.113)
• He may not share your enthusiasm, but he is practically sure to read the ***book*** and he may go for the program at once.(p.113)
• Talk about his condition or this ***book*** only when he raises the issue.(p.113)
• In some cases it may be better to let someone outside of the family present the ***book***.(p.113)
• In any event, try to have your husband read this ***book***.(p.114)
• Since this ***book*** was first published, A.A. has released thousands of alcoholics from asylums and hospitals of every kind.(p.114)
• We do not like the thought that the contents of a ***book*** or the work of another alcoholic has accomplished in a few weeks that for which we struggled for years.(p.118)
• If there is no Al-Anon listing in your local telephone ***book***, you may obtain further information on Al-Anon Family Groups by writing to its World Service Office: Box 182, Madison Square Station, New York, NY 10159.(p.121)
• One of the many doctors who had the opportunity of reading this ***book*** in manuscript form told us that the use of sweets was often helpful, of course depending upon a doctor's advice.(p.133)
• Had they fired me first, and had they then taken steps to see that I was presented with the solution contained in this ***book***, I might have returned to them six months later, a well man.(p.141)
• Whether you mention this ***book*** is a matter for your discretion.(p.142)
• To return to the subject matter of this ***book***: It contains full suggestions by which the employee may solve his problem.(p.143)
• We suggest you draw the ***book*** to the attention of the doctor who is to attend your patient during treatment.(p.144)
• If the ***book*** is read the moment the patient is able, while acutely depressed, realization of his condition may come to him.(p.144)
• You are betting, of course, that your changed attitude plus the contents of this ***book*** will turn the trick.(p.144)
• Meanwhile, we are sure a great deal can be accomplished by the use of the ***book*** alone.(p.144)
• If your organization is a large one, your junior executives might be provided with this ***book***.(p.147)
• After reading this ***book***, a junior executive can go to such a man and say approximately this, "Look here, Ed.(p.147)
• Your junior executive may not agree with the contents of our ***book***.(p.148)
• Our hope is that when this chip of a ***book*** is launched on the world tide of alcoholism, defeated drinkers will seize upon it, to follow its suggestions.(p.153)
• And so can you, though you be but one man with this ***book*** in your hand.(p.162)
• Still you may say: "But I will not have the benefit of contact with you who write this ***book***."(p.164)
• Our ***book*** is meant to be suggestive only.(p.164)
• If you think you are an atheist, an agnostic, a skeptic, or have any other form of intellectual pride which keeps you from accepting what is in this ***book***, I feel sorry for you.(p.181)
• I had to look in the telephone ***book*** later to find out who these people were.(p.196)
• I remembered going through what my sister assured me was my nightly procedure of trying to find Willie Seabrook's name in the telephone ***book***.(p.224)
• That was the point at which my doctor gave me the ***book*** "Alcoholics Anonymous" to read.(p.227)
• And so on and on, for several weeks, while I grudgingly plowed through some more of the offending ***book***, and felt more and more hopeless about myself.(p.227)
• And as I fumed helplessly and planned to get good and drunk and show them, my eye caught a sentence in the ***book*** lying open on my bed: "We cannot live with anger."(p.228)
• Around this time our big A.A. ***book*** was being written and it all became much simpler; we had a definite formula which some sixty of us agreed was the middle course for all alcoholics who wanted sobriety, and that formula has not been changed one iota down through the years.(p.248)
• I don't think the boys were completely convinced of my personality change, for they fought shy of including my story in the ***book***, so my only contribution to their literary efforts was my firm conviction, being still a theological rebel, that the word God should be qualified with the phrase "as we understand him" -- for that was the only way I could accept spirituality.(p.248)
• After the ***book*** appeared we all became very busy in our efforts to save all and sundry, but I was still actually on the fringes of A.A.(p.248)
• One evening, the ***book***, after checking up, was very definitely in the red for plenty through a piece of studied carelessness on my part, and my boss, very shrewd and able, fired me with a parting statement to the effect that once was enough.(p.251)
• My last venture, a ***book*** shop, was hastened to closed doors by my steady intoxication.(p.255)
• I had the Big ***Book*** ("Alcoholics Anonymous") that had been brought to me.(p.268)
• Paul S. had just called me, and I remember he stressed reading the Big ***Book***.(p.269)
• He said, "Let's put the Big ***Book*** away again, and when you read it again, turn to the back and read some of the stories.(p.269)
• The big A.A. ***book*** had not been written and there was no literature except various religious pamphlets.(p.291)
• In the spring of 1939, the Big ***Book*** was printed, and we had two inquiries from the New York office because of a fifteen-minute radio talk that was made.(p.294)
• And then, in the spring of 1939, a very remarkable ***book*** was rolled off a New York press with the title "Alcoholics Anonymous."(p.307)
• However, due to financial difficulties the whole printing was, for a while, held up and the ***book*** received no publicity, nor, of course, was it available in the stores, even if one knew it existed.(p.307)
• But somehow my good doctor heard of this ***book*** and also he learned a little about the people responsible for its publication.(p.307)
• He asked me to read the ***book*** "Alcoholics Anonymous," and then he wanted me to talk with a man who was experiencing success with his own arrestment.(p.308)
• I stayed up all night reading that ***book***.(p.309)
• By this time, with the doctor's explanation, the revelations contained in the ***book***, and the hope-inspiring interview with Mr. T., I was ready and willing to go into the interior of the African jungles, if that was what it took, for me to find what these people had.(p.309)
• Hiding behind a newspaper, magazine, or ***book***, I really saw nothing, but simulated deep interest.(p.332)
• Studied the Big ***Book*** again.(p.344)
• And I put a Big ***Book*** by my night stand, and I put a "Twelve Steps and Twelve Tradition" in my locker at the hospital, and I got books by Emmet Fox, and I got books by God-knows-who, and I got to reading all these things.(p.348)
• Why don't you go home and get the Big ***Book*** and open it at page fifty-eight and see what it says?"(p.349)
• I got the Big ***Book*** and I read it, and this is what it said: "Rarely have we seen a person fail who has thoroughly followed our path."(p.349)
• I had read and heard a little about A.A. and so, groping for the phone ***book***, I found the A.A. number and with hope in my heart eagerly telephoned.(p.363)
• I attended my weekly meetings with regularity, reread the Big ***Book***, attended other group meetings, gave leads when asked to and did some Twelve Step work whenever I was called upon to do so.(p.365)
• Study the A.A. ***book*** -- don't just read it.(p.381)
• The ***book*** was published, but the reading public said -- So what?(p.403)
• I did not see that the ***book*** dripped with self-pity.(p.403)
• She read this ***book*** that you are reading now.(p.412)
• I read the ***book*** and God leapt at me from every page.(p.412)
• I returned the ***book*** to my analyst and shook my head.(p.412)
• Something in the ***book*** had reached me after all.(p.412)
• I was skipping classes about two days a week and doing no ***book*** work whatever.(p.423)
• Moreover, I am deeply convinced that so long as I continue to strive, in my bumbling way, toward the principles I first encountered in the earlier chapters of this ***book***, this remarkable power will continue to flow through me.(p.437)
• Each with the other as a witness, we took the Third Step out loud -- just as it says in the Big ***Book***.(p.446)
• I realized that I was trying to pin everything on an individual -- not the ***book*** or the group or the Higher Power, or anything else.(p.472)
• So I concentrated and studied the ***book*** during that time, and I liked a lot of the things it said in there.(p.472)
• Here was a ***book*** that said I could do something that all these doctors and priests and ministers and psychiatrists that I'd been going to for years couldn't do!(p.473)
• I pick up a ***book*** and try to read, but I cannot concentrate.(p.503)
• I have published a ***book*** covering certain aspects of this field which has been well-reviewed and which is helping other people.(p.541)
• They said if you want to know how this program works, take the first word of your question -- the H is for honesty, the O is for open-mindedness and the W is for willingness; these our ***Book*** calls the essentials of recovery.(p.550)
• They suggested that I study the A.A. ***book*** and try to take the Twelve Steps according to the explanation in the ***Book***, for it was their opinion that the application of these principles in our daily lives will get us sober and keep us sober.(p.550)
• While there, I read the Big ***Book*** and the Grapevine and began the slow road back to health and sanity through the recovery program of A.A.(p.559)
• The terms "spiritual experience" and "spiritual awakening" are used many times in this ***book*** which, upon careful reading, shows that the personality change sufficient to bring about recovery from alcoholism has manifested itself among us in many different forms.(p.569)

booked

• Within about ten days I got locked up for being drunk and this same policeman was in the station house as I was being ***booked***.(p.491)

bookies

• I knew I was through among the English "***bookies***."(p.251)

booking

• No jail ***booking***, drunk-driving citation, barroom fight, or even a tumble off a barstool.(p.327)

bookish

• There was the physical aspect; to be the youngest and the runt of the brood of children, to have to wear glasses very early and so to be teased, to be ***bookish*** and bored in school because the captain of the football team could not translate Virgil and yet was the school god while you, you, you little shrimp, were the school egghead, junior size and an early model.(p.533)

bookmaker's

• With nothing but a liberal arts education, very definitely estranged from my family and already married, soon after graduation from college I became a ***bookmaker's*** clerk on the British racing circuits, far better off financially than the average professional man.(p.251)

books

• Each inquiry was painstakingly answered; pamphlets and ***books*** were sent out.(p.xviii)
• Here are some of the methods we have tried: Drinking beer only, limiting the number of drinks, never drinking alone, never drinking in the morning, drinking only at home, never having it in the house, never drinking during business hours, drinking only at parties, switching from scotch to brandy, drinking only natural wines, agreeing to resign if ever drunk on the job, taking a trip, not taking a trip, swearing off forever (with and without a solemn oath), taking more physical exercise, reading inspirational ***books***, going to health farms and sanitariums, accepting voluntary commitment to asylums -- we could increase the list ad infinitum.(p.31)
• We read wordy ***books*** and indulge in windy arguments, thinking we believe this universe needs no God to explain it.(p.49)
• There are many helpful ***books*** also.(p.87)
• I passed in at least three absolutely blank ***books***.(p.174)
• To go into a gathering of people was the sort of thing that all my life, from the time I left my private world of ***books*** and dreams to meet the real world of people and parties and jobs, had left me feeling an uncomfortable outsider, needing the warming stimulus of drinks to join in.(p.228)
• It wasn't very long before home-brewing was an institution and men began to search feverishly for old recipe ***books*** on wine-making.(p.232)
• An old avocation, the collecting of first editions, rare ***books*** and Americana, fascinated me between times.(p.255)
• Loading a car with good old ***books*** to sell to collectors, librarians, universities and historical societies, I started out to travel the country.(p.255)

• This was such a new thought that I got all sorts of ***books*** on Higher Powers, and I put a Bible by my bedside, and I put a Bible in my car.(p.348)
• And I put a Big Book by my night stand, and I put a "Twelve Steps and Twelve Tradition" in my locker at the hospital, and I got ***books*** by Emmet Fox, and I got ***books*** by God-knows-who, and I got to reading all these things.(p.348)
• The apartment was charming; the shelves were full of ***books***, many of which I myself owned.(p.413)
• The other pupils kept ***books***, pencils, paper, gym equipment and such stuff in their lockers.(p.423)
• Finally, I threw away all my ***books*** and decided never to return to A.A.(p.460)
• I am working hard on the ***books*** of a subsidiary company of a large corporation.(p.500)
• I, and the ***books*** of my division, have been transferred to the head office.(p.500)
• I fix up a little apartment over the garage with ***books*** and drinking water.(p.506)
• I read self-help ***books***.(p.555)

bookstore

• When I hit Houston, Texas, I found employment in a large ***bookstore***.(p.255)
• I managed to maintain myself with odd jobs, did ten weeks in a social rescue institution, and at length wound up in a second-hand ***bookstore*** in an adjacent town as manager.(p.257)

bookstores

• News of this got on the world wires; inquiries poured in again and many people went to the ***bookstores*** to get the book "Alcoholics Anonymous."(p.xviii)

boom

• The great ***boom*** of the late twenties was seething and swelling.(p.3)
• Akron was really on the ***boom*** in those days, 1919-1920; expansion was terrific.(p.198)

boomerang

• Out of this alloy of drink and speculation, I commenced to forge the weapon that one day would turn in its flight like a ***boomerang*** and all but cut me to ribbons.(p.2)
• Maine newsletter (***Boomerang***) say: "With tireless devotion and humility, this venerable Indian gentleman traveled thousands of miles humbly pleading for sobriety.(p.476)

boon

• Time after time, this apparent calamity has been a ***boon*** to us, for it opened up a path which led to the discovery of God.(p.116)

boost

• I found I could ***boost*** my income by figuring out a lot of cute little tricks that the boss wouldn't be likely to notice – filching money from the Coke machine, short-sticking the customers on oil, and selling oil I'd drained out of other cars.(p.423)

boot

• At Great Lakes ***Boot*** Camp I latched onto a soft billet.(p.425)

booth

• Selecting a church at random from the directory, he stepped into a ***booth*** and lifted the receiver.(p.155)
• I went out to a restaurant, found a ***booth*** way back in the rear, and started drinking.(p.467)
• If something does come along that sort of upsets me, instead of walking in and throwing a buck at the barman and asking for a drink, I walk into a telephone ***booth***, drop a dime in the box, and call somebody who was so kind as to give me his name and telephone number to meet such an emergency.(p.511)

bootleg

• We went into a ***bootleg*** joint and I don't remember leaving that place.(p.202)

bootlegger

• At that time I was not aware of the almost unlimited supply the government made it possible for us doctors to obtain, neither had I any knowledge of the ***bootlegger*** who soon appeared on the horizon.(p.175)
• My ***bootlegger*** had hidden alcohol at the back steps where I could get it at my convenience.(p.176)
• It wasn't long before the ***bootlegger*** was an established institution in this, as in other towns.(p.233)
• I call the ***bootlegger*** and fill up my charred keg.(p.501)

bootleggers

• I condoned my domestic brewing along with the ***bootleggers*** and their business.(p.233)

booze

• Then he added, "He sure didn't do much for me when I was trying to fight this ***booze*** racket alone."(p.158)
• I was startled to learn he had only been off the ***booze*** a month or so himself when he brought me the message!(p.245)
• While I was in basic, I got high off ***booze*** almost every night.(p.317)
• Somehow, I made it through basic and then laid off the ***booze*** for about three months, because I was in school at night.(p.317)
• An alcoholic can't lay off the ***booze*** – right?(p.317)
• Through studied sneaky-drinking, I'd become a senior citizen without having lost a day's work because of ***booze***.(p.327)
• I was aware of symptoms of impending dependence, and I told myself I had gotten out of the rat race just in time to head off any ***booze*** problem.(p.327)
• I felt disgraced and humiliated – a man who couldn't hold ***booze*** -- a social disaster.(p.328)
• That, of course, was a shot of ***booze***.(p.331)
• I'd lived too long and become a loser, dependent on ***booze***.(p.333)
• My sponsor used to say to me, "If I could only paint you a picture of how beautiful life can be without ***booze*** . . ."(p.355)
• When I was nineteen, I married a fine man who had never known an insecure moment in his life, let alone the trials and tribulations of ***booze***.(p.369)
• Near the Laundromat, I would buy one bottle of pop and a few bottles of beer or wine, and go into the rest room, empty the pop bottle, refill it with the ***booze***, and proceed to do my laundering.(p.370)
• At this time, the price of ***booze*** in the bars was fifteen cents a shot and ten cents a beer.(p.397)
• After a few more estimates as to income and expenditures for ***booze*** over a few sample years, taken at random, I conclude that this twenty per cent stayed fairly constant.(p.398)
• But my board, room, and clothing were free, and I could spend the whole ten bucks on ***booze***.(p.398)
• I thought, "If this is A.A. why not go back to drinking, kill myself with ***booze*** in the next three years the doctor had given me, and call it a bad job?"(p.430)
• Whatever the root of my unhappiness might turn out to be, I thought, it could not possibly be ***booze***.(p.433)
• We got on the plane and immediately had a big fight over whether I'd drink the free ***booze***.(p.444)
• We went to ***booze*** joint in Maine.(p.475)
• A couple of years later, we lost our elder brother in a house fire, because of pills and ***booze***.(p.480)
• I always blamed my drinking on being poor, or on anything other than the truth – that I liked what ***booze*** did for me, that when I had a drink I was as big and had as much as the next person.(p.526)
• By learning -- through practicing the Twelve Steps and through sharing at meetings – how to cope with the problems that we looked to ***booze*** to solve, back in our drinking days.(p.560)

boozed

• If anyone had told me I would be enjoying a hockey game with my husband and my brother without being all ***boozed*** up, I would not have believed it.(p.481)

Boozeville

• I was thirty-two, a babe in ***Boozeville***.(p.328)

boozing

• We did, and spent a month ***boozing*** it up, popping pills, and smoking marijuana; taking shelter where we could, which included a veterinary hospital one night; accepting meals from anyone; actually begging; stealing anything we were in need of, which was about everything.(p.354)

border

• My parents had some vague idea of making a priest out of me and for some years I attended the Franciscan school at Basle, Switzerland, just across the ***border***, about six miles from my home.(p.230)
• Having passed over the ***border*** line, the next five years were filled with fear, failure and frustration.(p.465)

bordering

• Heartsickness, shame, and fear, fear ***bordering*** on panic, and no complete escape any longer except in oblivion.(p.306)
• With their help I also saw that certainly, because of some of the things I had done during the years, I was ***bordering*** on insanity, and so, facing the record, I tried to believe that a Power greater than I could and would restore me to sanity.(p.471)

bore

• This determination ***bore*** fruit in the spring of 1939 by the publication of this volume.(p.xvii)
• I was staring at an inch of the tape which ***bore*** the inscription XYZ-32.(p.4)
• Never was I to pray for myself, except as my requests ***bore*** on my usefulness to others.(p.13)
• School was getting to be one big ***bore***.(p.423)

bored

• Then he started to talk to me about his drinking experiences, what his drinking had cost him, how much he had drunk and where, things like that, and I remember I was quite ***bored*** because I had never seen the guy before and had no interest at all in what, where and when he drank.(p.208)
• Routine jobs ***bored*** me, but I would take on the toughest one I could find, work day and night until I had it under control; then it would become tedious and I'd lose all interest in it.(p.243)
• I don't ever remember that I was ***bored*** myself when we first came in, and they came out to the house and talked to us about these things.(p.273)
• When I retired, I said I'd never be ***bored***.(p.334)
• There was the physical aspect; to be the youngest and the runt of the brood of children, to have to wear glasses very early and so to be teased, to be bookish and ***bored*** in school because the captain of the football team could not translate Virgil and yet was the school god while you, you, you little shrimp, were the school egghead, junior size and an early model.(p.533)

boredom

• It means release from care, ***boredom*** and worry.(p.151)
• There you will find release from care, ***boredom*** and worry.(p.152)
• I don't remember much of what he said, but I did realize that here was another guy exactly like me; he had been in the same laughing academies and the same jails, known the same loss of jobs, same frustrations, same ***boredom*** and the same loneliness.(p.239)
• I believe that the release from people-pleasing restrictions gives retirees more motivation to drink than ***boredom*** does.(p.329)
• ***Boredom*** sets up every retiree for two chief dangers: obesity and alcoholism.(p.330)
• ***Boredom*** was no worry to me when I went out to pasture.(p.330)
• He was close to tears in describing his ***boredom*** without an activity.(p.334)

bores

• Why lay ourselves open to being branded fanatics or religious ***bores***?(p.77)

boring

• If not irritable, he may seem dull and ***boring***, not gay and affectionate as the family would like him to be.(p.126)
• But am I to be consigned to a life where I shall be stupid, ***boring*** and glum, like some righteous people I see?(p.152)
• It was never ***boring***, but I developed a feeling of deep insecurity.(p.369)
• Drunkalogues and statistics can be ***boring***, but it is necessary to delve a little into each in order to come up with some kind of rough estimate.(p.396)
• Saying these sprees were limited to one a week (they were not), and saying that the average spree was ten of these drinks (sometimes more, sometimes less), we come up with the first ***boring*** statistic: two-fifty per week out of twelve dollars.(p.397)
• I said it over and over, ***boring*** my fellow barflies.(p.412)

born

• They are not at fault; they seem to have been ***born*** that way.(p.58)
• I was ***born*** in a small New England village of about seven thousand souls.(p.171)
• One of five children, I was ***born*** on a Kentucky farm in Carlyle County.(p.182)
• Down in the pit of his depression, new hope had somehow been ***born***.(p.189)
• I was ***born*** in Cleveland, Ohio, in 1889, the last child of a family of eight children.(p.210)
• I was ***born*** in Europe, in Alsace to be exact, shortly after it had become German, and practically grew up with the "good Rhine wine" of song and story.(p.230)
• I wanted to roam again and through relatives got a supercargo job on an Australian packet which allowed me to visit my people in Australia where I was ***born***.(p.252)
• It was no momentary emotionalism ***born*** of self-pity in a maudlin condition.(p.258)
• With the bravery ***born*** of desperation, and abetted by alcohol, I married a young and lovely girl.(p.277)
• We complement each other beautifully, as he is a ***born*** salesman and my taste is for finance and management.(p.284)
• Thus, A.A. was ***born*** in Chicago.(p.287)

• I was *born* in Cleveland, Ohio, the only child of a prominent dentist, and a very proud mother.(p.357)
• I was *born* in a castle -- the family home, in Europe.(p.400)
• I was *born* a Maliseet Indian on reservation in Canada.(p.474)
• I was *born* in a little town in Virginia in an average religious home.(p.483)
• I don't think I suffered too much as far as the racial situation was concerned because I was *born* into it and knew nothing other than that.(p.485)
• And there a tremendous hope is *born*.(p.504)

borrowed

• I *borrowed* five hundred dollars from the bank and three hundred from the loan shop, and I drank that up pretty fast.(p.490)
• I had even *borrowed* money from her, over her protest: "Bob, please don't ask me to lend you money -- you're the only one who hasn't."(p.540)
• On another small *borrowed* sum, I went up into the country to the home of a doctor I had known since boyhood.(p.540)

borrowing

• During that first year, however, I managed to make both ends meet, and to avoid ever going back to my old habit pattern of *borrowing* money when I could not earn it.(p.283)

boss

• If there was a Devil, he seemed the *Boss* Universal, and he certainly had me.(p.11)
• I had a few words with the *boss*, but nothing serious.(p.36)
• He left us a note saying you were the best *boss* he ever had, and that you were not to blame in any way."(p.136)
• I was arrested and taken to jail where I was beaten up by two or three fellows who were already in there and whom I tried to *boss*.(p.204)
• I'd show 'em who was *boss*!(p.243)
• As long as things were tough and the job a challenge I could always manage to hold on pretty well, but as soon as I learned the combination, got the puzzle under control and the *boss* to pat me on the back, I was gone again.(p.243)
• My *boss*, in his way, was "big business."(p.251)
• One evening, the book, after checking up, was very definitely in the red for plenty through a piece of studied carelessness on my part, and my *boss*, very shrewd and able, fired me with a parting statement to the effect that once was enough.(p.251)
• I was my own *boss*.(p.283)
• It took five years of A.A. living, and a substantial improvement in my health, before I could take a full-time office job where someone else was *boss*.(p.283)
• Every breadwinner, whether trying to impress a *boss* or to hold customers in his own business, is fettered by people-pleasing.(p.329)
• The Great *Boss* has given me diagnostic and surgical talent, and He has loaned it to me to use for the rest of my life.(p.350)
• I found I could boost my income by figuring out a lot of cute little tricks that the *boss* wouldn't be likely to notice – filching money from the Coke machine, short-sticking the customers on oil, and selling oil I'd drained out of other cars.(p.423)
• I fled, finally, after having been fired from my job by a *boss* who wept a little (since I had worked hard) as he gave notice for me to clear out.(p.539)

Boston

• Men who had liquor shipped in from *Boston* or New York by express were looked upon with great distrust and disfavor by most of the good townspeople.(p.171)
• The next three years I spent in *Boston*, Chicago, and Montreal in the employ of a large manufacturing concern, selling railway supplies, gas engines of all sorts, and many other items of heavy hardware.(p.172)
• The first definite indications of an alcoholic pattern began to arise when I would go to New York on business and disappear, and wind up in Philadelphia or *Boston* for two or three day periods.(p.213)

both

• Therefore, the first portion of this volume, describing the A.A. recovery program, has been left untouched in the course of revisions made for *both* the second and the third editions.(p.xi)
• Next day found me drinking *both* gin and sedative.(p.7)
• We are equally positive that once he takes any alcohol whatever into his system, something happens, *both* in the bodily and mental sense, which makes it virtually impossible for him to stop.(p.22)
• He tells you he has decided to stop jay-walking for good, but in a few weeks he breaks *both* legs.(p.38)
• I had to concede *both* propositions.(p.42)
• It may be that *both* will decide that the way of good sense and loving kindness is to let by-gones be by-gones.(p.82)
• When the time for living together has come, it will be apparent to *both* parties.(p.99)
• *Both* you and the new man must walk day by day in the path of spiritual progress.(p.100)
• Perhaps you *both* like parties which would be dull without liquor.(p.110)
• You might suggest that you *both* take an interest in them.(p.112)
• The faith and sincerity of *both* you and your husband will be put to the test.(p.117)
• If you *both* show a willingness to remedy your own defects, there will be little need to criticize each other.(p.118)
• *Both* of you will awaken to a new sense of responsibility for others.(p.119)
• *Both* father and the family are mistaken, though each side may have some justification.(p.126)
• If your decision is yes, whether the reason be humanitarian or business or *both*, then the following suggestions may be helpful.(p.140)
• We all had to place recovery above everything, for without recovery we would have lost *both* home and business.(p.143)
• There is a real interest, *both* humanitarian and business, in the well-being of employees.(p.149)
• *Both* saw that they must keep spiritually active.(p.156)
• At this *both* the visitors burst into a laugh.(p.157)
• My father was a professional man of recognized ability and *both* my father and mother were most active in church affairs.(p.171)
• *Both* father and mother were considerably above the average in intelligence.(p.172)
• This I did, and proved myself satisfactory to the faculty, *both* in deportment and scholastically.(p.174)
• I think I must have been thoroughly scared by what had happened, or by the doctor, or probably *both*, so that I did not touch a drink again until the country went dry.(p.175)
• This was no fault of my father or mother, as they were *both* very much opposed to drinking.(p.182)
• Before very long we began to relate some incidents of our drinking and, naturally, pretty soon, I realized *both* of them knew what they were talking about because you can see things and smell things when you're drunk, that you can't other times, and, if I had thought they didn't know what they were talking about, I wouldn't have been willing to talk to them at all.(p.185)
• And they *both* laughed very heartily, and said, "That's better than you've been doing, isn't it?"(p.187)
• "Sure I would," replied Bill, "Maybe it won't do any good, but I'd like to see you *both*, anyhow.(p.189)
• I'm so grateful for *both* the program and the people in it that I still want to go, and then probably the most wonderful thing that I learned from the program -- I've seen this in the 'A.A. Grapevine' a lot of times, and I've had people say it to me personally, and I've heard people get up in meetings and make the same statement: The statement is, "I came into A.A. solely for the purpose of sobriety, but it has been through A.A. that I have found God."(p.192)
• And then we *both* realized we should go.(p.201)
• I then began asking a lot of questions of *both* my brother and Dr. Bob about how this thing worked, and I suppose I was becoming more glassy-eyed all the while, for eventually I said to Bob, "You're all dried up.(p.206)
• There had been some occasions -- there was an automobile wreck, for instance -- when I had police escort home but not to jail, all of which, instead of doing me a favor, did me harm because I was then full of self-esteem as to the progress I had made *both* professionally and financially.(p.213)
• I went to *both* Catholic and public schools.(p.214)
• My family lived in very prosperous circumstances, and while *both* my parents drank, sometimes too much, neither was an alcoholic.(p.240)
• There were four of us children, and although *both* of my brothers later became alcoholic – one died of alcoholism -- my sister has never taken a drink in her life.(p.240)
• However, I made an SOS call to the New York Group, whom I hadn't met yet, and they suggested we *both* come there.(p.245)
• My parents died, *both* in the same year, leaving me, a sheltered and somewhat immature man, on my own.(p.277)
• The ensuing nine years were the Depression years, *both* nationally and personally.(p.277)
• During that first year, however, I managed to make *both* ends meet, and to avoid ever going back to my old habit pattern of borrowing money when I could not earn it.(p.283)
• The most accurate answer I can give you is this: Fear has never again ruled my life since that day in September, 1938, when I found that a Power greater than myself could not only restore me to sanity but could keep me *both* sober and sane.(p.285)
• The adjustments in such a case are difficult and take time, but we *both* feel that they are certainly worth it.(p.286)
• We are *both* depending upon God and our use of the A.A. program to help us make a success of this joint undertaking.(p.286)
• When I said yes, we *both* knelt at his desk and prayed, each of us asking to have these defects taken away.(p.292)
• Such has been my privilege, *both* nationally and in my home city.(p.295)
• To be sure, this had been a dizzy and confused interval, but most everyone else I knew had emerged from it with *both* feet on the ground and a fair amount of adult maturity.(p.304)
• Letting go of everything at once was *both* painful and terrifying.(p.311)
• This girl and her husband are *both* in A.A., and she said to me, "Oh, but you're not the alcoholic; it's your husband."(p.322)
• I had not yet lost my job or family, even though *both* were on the verge of going.(p.379)
• Meetings are *both* relaxing and refreshing to me after a hard day.(p.381)
• We came back East and met *both* families.(p.402)
• Her father became *both* mother and father to her.(p.402)
• Through going to meetings and listening, and occasionally speaking, through doing Twelve Step work, whereby in helping others you are *both* the teacher and the student, by making many wonderful A.A. friends, I have been taught all the things in life that are worth having.(p.416)
• They *both* drank like fish.(p.424)
• Meanwhile, I was getting worse, *both* as regards my inward misery and my drinking.(p.434)
• I would be half asleep and half awake, and in the morning, I would be *both* tired and stupid.(p.440)
• *Both* times, my reaction was that I had had nothing to drink the night before, so obviously alcohol had nothing to do with it.(p.444)
• The people there insisted on putting me in a ward, when Max and I *both* knew I ought to have a private room.(p.445)
• He and his wife more than accepted me; he listened to all my woes; *both* of them treated me as a human being.(p.462)
• We *both* happy.(p.476)
• Any time I tried to kill myself, I was either drunk or pilled-up or *both* -- usually the last.(p.479)
• So I wasn't just tinkering around with it -- I had to get in with *both* feet.(p.480)
• After our first child came my parents *both* became allies, but in later days, after I became an alcoholic, they *both* turned against me.(p.485)
• We were now *both* working in the same agency.(p.490)
• Nevertheless, we continued to work together and I continued to drink, but I guess, deep down within her heart as well as within mine, we *both* knew I couldn't stop drinking.(p.490)
• I put Charlie on the car and when I left him I passed *both* of those liquor stores without even thinking about them.(p.495)
• *Both* he and old Maud are glad to get home.(p.497)
• God has been good to me *both* in my drinking and in my sobriety.(p.516)
• And I jumped in with *both* feet.(p.516)
• They sent me up with an attendant, and the attendant and I *both* arrived at the Egyptian Hospital rather the worse for wear.(p.521)
• I awoke next day with tubes in *both* arms.(p.558)
• We learn how to level out the emotional wings that got us into trouble *both* when we were up and when we were down.(p.560)

bother

• That didn't seem to *bother* me so I tried another."(p.36)
• I resented it of course, and I offered Clarence his commission, whatever it might be, if he would please not *bother* me because I had arrived at the conclusion that he was a solicitor for some alcoholic institute.(p.216)
• It didn't *bother* me any more whether George was drinking or not.(p.324)

• She told me not to *bother* going "for her sake"; she told me in a nice way that it didn't make any difference to her – and that really scared me – so I went.(p.365)
• My mother's heartbreak, or the unpleasant publicity I had caused did not *bother* my pretty head.(p.401)

bothered

• We were *bothered* with the thought that faith and dependence upon a Power beyond ourselves was somewhat weak, even cowardly.(p.45)
• I could never be *bothered* with the follow-through and would invariably reward myself for my efforts with that "first" drink.(p.243)
• I don't feel *bothered* about liquor."(p.257)
• Why he *bothered* with me as long as he did I shall never know, for he knew there was no answer for me in medicine and he, like all doctors of his day, had been taught that the alcoholic was incurable and should be ignored.(p.307)
• The only thing that *bothered* me was a queasy feeling I had in the pit of my stomach.(p.418)

bothering

• He will appreciate knowing you are not *bothering* your head about him, that you are not suspicious nor are you trying to run his life so he will be shielded from temptation to drink.(p.146)
• I remember the day when I decided to drink myself to death quietly, without *bothering* anyone, because I was tired of having been a dependable, trustworthy person for about thirty-nine years without having received what I thought was a proper reward for my virtue.(p.531)

bothers

• The only thing that *bothers* me is that there are only about five Negroes in A.A. in my city.(p.529)

bottle

• I wondered whether I dared hide a full *bottle* of gin near the head of our bed.(p.8)
• Yet early next morning he searches madly for the *bottle* he misplaced the night before.(p.21)
• Out came his carpet slippers and a *bottle*.(p.32)
• His only chance for sobriety would be some place like the Greenland Ice Cap, and even there an Eskimo might turn up with a *bottle* of scotch and ruin everything!(p.101)
• Of course he couldn't drink, but why not sit hopefully at a table, a *bottle* of ginger ale before him?(p.154)
• He came and got me home and to bed, gave me a few drinks that night, and one *bottle* of beer the next morning.(p.179)
• This problem was soon solved, however, as I began to take my *bottle* along with me and hide it in the bathroom or in the shrubbery outside.(p.184)
• Away from my office two or three weeks at a time; horrible days and nights when I would lie on the floor of my home, lying awake and reaching over to get the *bottle*, taking a drink and going back into oblivion.(p.184)
• One of the earliest memories that I have is of a *bottle* sitting on his desk with a skull and crossbones and marked "Poison."(p.193)
• I'd only had two with her, but I'd managed four in the fifteen minutes I'd waited for her, and of course I'd had the usual uncounted swigs from the *bottle* as I painfully got up and did my slow spasmodic dressing.(p.223)
• I remembered filling the peroxide *bottle* in my medicine chest with gin, in case my sister found the *bottle* I hid under the mattress.(p.224)
• And I remembered the creeping horror of the interminable night, in which I slept for short spells and woke up dripping with cold sweat and shaken with utter despair, to drink hastily from my *bottle* and mercifully pass out again, "You're mad, you're mad, you're mad!" pounded through my brain with each returning ray of consciousness, and I drowned the refrain with drink.(p.224)
• Many things happened; business trials, little worries, and feelings of general despondency came near driving me to the *bottle*, but I made progress.(p.237)
• Many alcoholics have learned they can bring their *bottle* to a cheap movie theater and drink, sleep, wake up and drink again in the darkness.(p.244)
• Evidently I had gone right back to the movie with a *bottle*, stayed there several hours and started home with no recollection of what had happened.(p.244)
• So I drank all three beers, one after the other, said "I'll be seeing you, boys," and went around the corner for a *bottle*.(p.247)
• Lots of times, vain-gloriously, I used to take the *bottle* out, look at it and say, "I've got you licked."(p.253)
• The strain of overwork led me to the *bottle* again.(p.254)
• I stayed sober during the trip except for an occasional *bottle* of beer because funds barely met expenses.(p.255)
• I remember sometime, it was possibly six months after we had been going steadily to King School, that we were coming home from a meeting and saw a car along the way, and a fellow in back drinking a *bottle* of beer.(p.271)
• After finding every *bottle* that I had hidden around the apartment, she took away my pants, my shoes, my money and my keys, threw them under the bed in the back bedroom and slip-locked our door.(p.288)
• I had thought that I was completely different from other people, that I was beginning to become a little balmy, even to the point of withdrawing more and more from society and wanting to be alone with my *bottle*.(p.290)
• In return for a *bottle* and a hangover, we have been given the Keys of the Kingdom.(p.312)
• We got along fine for about two weeks, until she told me where to go and to take my damn *bottle* with me.(p.318)
• So I took my *bottle* and went and drowned my sorrows.(p.318)
• When I came home again, the only thing I had left to love was the *bottle*.(p.318)
• We got engaged, and we were happy – Jean with me, and me with the *bottle* and Jean.(p.318)
• He used to wonder, when he'd spot one of my bottles around the house, just how he could have overlooked that particular *bottle*.(p.325)
• So long as a retiree woos his *bottle* at home, he stays out of public trouble.(p.330)
• Three months later, he hated the game and found solace in the *bottle*.(p.330)
• Yet I recently recalled that each morning I used to talk to the *bottle* when I took it down from the closet.(p.332)
• And of course a half empty *bottle* wasn't worth keeping, so I finished it up and naturally had to get more in right away for the people who "might come in unexpectedly."(p.336)
• But I was always the unexpected person who had to finish the *bottle*.(p.336)
• I couldn't go to one wine store and look the man honestly in the face and buy a *bottle*, as I used to do when I had parties and entertained and did normal drinking.(p.336)
• I had to give him a story and ask him the same question over and over again, "Well, now, how many will that *bottle* serve?"(p.336)
• I wanted him to be sure that I wasn't the one who was going to drink the whole *bottle*.(p.336)
• To me, taking a bath was just being in a place with a *bottle* where I could drink in privacy.(p.337)
• I had always hated beer, but now I grew to love it, *bottle* after *bottle* of it, warm or cold.(p.339)
• I surrendered once to the *bottle*, and I couldn't do these things.(p.340)
• I began hitting the *bottle* again, and with it self-pity, resentment, loneliness and remorse set in deeply.(p.362)
• I entered the house, opened a new *bottle* of whiskey and sat down to drink myself into the right frame of mind to get in my car, start the motor and close the garage door behind me.(p.363)
• We had some people in, and I was making drinks in the kitchen, when I suddenly decided to hoist the *bottle* for a quick one.(p.365)
• I had just raised the *bottle* to my lips when my wife opened the door and froze me completely in my tracks with "Happy New Year, dear."(p.365)
• Near the Laundromat, I would buy one *bottle* of pop and a few bottles of beer or wine, and go into the rest room, empty the pop *bottle*, refill it with the booze, and proceed to do my laundering.(p.370)
• The next steps were *bottle* hiding, and excuses for trips in order to drink without restraint.(p.375)
• I dropped a two-quart water *bottle* on my big toe.(p.390)
• Once, in a strange gin mill, I stole a *bottle* from behind the bar.(p.411)
• This was fine, but it was just an extra dividend, for I'd made connections by this time and was buying a *bottle* a day from the cook.(p.426)
• Pearl Harbor was a breeze of nine months, a gay Hawaiian paradise, drinking under the palms, listening to the surf beat on the shore, a *bottle* of whiskey near at hand.(p.426)
• I'd lost my car again, pawned my wallet and all identification papers for a *bottle*, and gotten home somehow.(p.429)
• When we got home, I got a *bottle* of Scotch and went to bed.(p.445)
• The doctor, apparently realizing that one thing that I certainly needed was sleep, left a *bottle* of sleeping pills there and in my drunken state I took them all, instead of the one or two he had prescribed.(p.465)
• The next day the ice-bag and I were still in bed -- but we had a *bottle* too!(p.466)
• Finally they stopped and bought me a *bottle*; they knew so well that would keep me quiet.(p.466)
• The Higher Power to whom I had turned, and who had sustained me, had once again been thrust into the background, while my emotions were running my life and, as always, my emotions ran me to the *bottle*.(p.472)
• He had *bottle* of hard stuff.(p.474)
• He gave me many drinks from *bottle*.(p.474)
• Tell him I want to get away from *bottle* and misery.(p.475)
• He old, sick, want to be alone with *bottle*.(p.476)
• This sober Indian say to sick, red-eyed alcoholic who want good medicine: "Put cork in *bottle*.(p.477)
• I'd go into my home with a *bottle*, and I remember clearly how I would look around to see if Vi was watching.(p.487)
• The next morning I carried another prescription to this man's house and exchanged it for the *bottle* his wife had.(p.489)
• I took that *bottle* of medicine and gave it to a very good friend of mine who was a pharmacist and had it analyzed, and the *bottle* was perfectly all right.(p.489)
• I reach for the *bottle* which I just got from George, the elevator boy.(p.500)
• I sneak downstairs and get a *bottle* of whiskey from the cellaret.(p.501)
• I thought if they smelled whiskey on my breath, they would lock me up, and I couldn't live without my *bottle*.(p.526)
• I never was a "secret" drinker, and I never kept a *bottle* at home.(p.536)
• He had a shot of brandy against the cold and passed me the *bottle*.(p.541)
• When I was criticized or reprimanded, the *bottle* was my refuge and comfort.(p.556)
• Instead of drinking in fancy bars and clubs, I had to carry a *bottle* of vodka in my briefcase, duck into public toilets, and gulp from the *bottle*, trembling, in order to keep from falling apart.(p.557)
• Each time, I went back to drinking – even smuggling a *bottle* of vodka into the hospital as soon as the blood transfusions had ceased.(p.558)
• I have learned to deal with disappointments and problems that once would have sent me right to the *bottle*.(p.559)

bottles

• "Bathtub" gin, two *bottles* a day, and often three, got to be routine.(p.5)
• A tumbler full of gin followed by half a dozen *bottles* of beer would be required if I were to eat any breakfast.(p.5)
• So two *bottles*, and -- oblivion.(p.6)
• People have said we must not go where liquor is served; we must not have it in our homes; we must shun friends who drink; we must avoid moving pictures which show drinking scenes; we must not go into bars; our friends must hide their *bottles* if we go to their houses; we mustn't think or be reminded about alcohol at all.(p.100)
• *Bottles* were only a symbol.(p.103)
• I knew everyone would buy a few *bottles*, or cases, of liquor as their exchequers permitted, and that it would soon be gone.(p.175)
• I used to put eight or twelve ounce *bottles* of alcohol in a fur lined glove and toss it onto the back airing porch when winter days got dark enough.(p.176)
• I used also to put it up in four ounce *bottles* and stick several in my stocking tops.(p.177)
• I began to bring *bottles* in.(p.233)
• With a great deal of determination, I would throw out full pints – pour them out and smash the *bottles* -- firmly resolved never to take another drink of the stuff.(p.234)
• In four or five days I would be hunting all over the place, at home and in my workshop, for the *bottles* I had destroyed, cursing myself for being a fool.(p.234)
• My wife could not understand the next morning why I was drunker than the night before when she took my *bottles*.(p.289)
• My wife became pregnant and the doctor recommended the use of port or ale . . . so . . . I bought a six gallon crock and a few *bottles*, listened to advice from amateur brewmeisters, and was off on my beer manufacturing career on a small scale (for the time being).(p.297)
• As time went on, I found that it was customary to open a few *bottles* whenever visitors dropped in.(p.297)

• I had ***bottles*** hidden all over the apartment.(p.324)
• He used to wonder, when he'd spot one of my ***bottles*** around the house, just how he could have overlooked that particular bottle.(p.325)
• She hid her ***bottles*** in clothes hampers and dresser drawers.(p.335)
• Near the Laundromat, I would buy one bottle of pop and a few ***bottles*** of beer or wine, and go into the rest room, empty the pop bottle, refill it with the booze, and proceed to do my laundering.(p.370)
• At that time the repeal whiskies were back, and I'd go to the store and buy my whiskey and take it to my office and put it under the desk, first in one place and then in another, and there soon was an accumulation of empty ***bottles***.(p.488)
• My brother-in-law was living with us at that time and I said to Vi, "Maybe the ***bottles*** are brother's.(p.488)
• I don't know anything about the ***bottles***."(p.488)
• I wander to a stable and drink five ***bottles*** of beer.(p.502)

bottom

• Did not Professor Langley's flying machine go to the ***bottom*** of the Potomac River?(p.51)
• We thank God from the ***bottom*** of our heart that we know Him better.(p.75)
• I was willing to admit to myself that I had hit ***bottom***, that I had gotten hold of something that I didn't know how to handle by myself.(p.187)
• I offered them a drink, and they came to the ***bottom*** of the stairs and the good woman fainted, just looking at me.(p.205)
• This newsman covered life from top to ***bottom***; but he ended up, safely enough, in the middle.(p.251)
• The A.A. program showed me the way to come down to earth, start from the ***bottom*** and work up.(p.284)
• They sum it up like this: "We didn't wait to hit ***bottom*** because, thank God, we could see the ***bottom***.(p.315)
• Actually, the ***bottom*** came up and hit us.(p.315)
• I think that is when I hit ***bottom***.(p.391)
• I hit my ***bottom***.(p.461)
• Economic conditions had a great deal to do with it, because I've often heard my father say that his mother would take one of the old time flour sacks and cut a hole through the ***bottom*** and two corners of it and there you'd have a gown.(p.486)
• I am in the ***bottom*** of hell.(p.504)

bought

• I drank all the scotch they had on the train and ***bought*** several quarts on my way to the hotel.(p.179)
• I ***bought*** some more liquor on the way to the depot.(p.179)
• I had ***bought*** a piece of ground in Cuyahoga Falls and cut it into lots and had a profit of approximately $40,000 and that was a lot of money in those days.(p.194)
• I went over and ***bought*** a jug of hard cider and a gallon of wine that I gave these fellows to drink.(p.195)
• Bill ***bought*** me a drink or two on the way, and Dorothy S. came with us, and the three of us went over to the City Hospital.(p.217)
• Instead, he got dressed, took me out, ***bought*** me three or four double shots and put me to bed.(p.278)
• My wife became pregnant and the doctor recommended the use of port or ale . . . so . . . I ***bought*** a six gallon crock and a few bottles, listened to advice from amateur brewmeisters, and was off on my beer manufacturing career on a small scale (for the time being).(p.297)
• My family always ***bought*** the best, and the embassies were flowing.(p.402)
• Finally they stopped and ***bought*** me a bottle; they knew so well that would keep me quiet.(p.466)
• The cops had picked her up, and she told them she had ***bought*** it from me.(p.528)
• (There was a time, for about three months, when I ***bought*** a ten-dollar wrist watch every pay day – that is every two weeks.(p.532)

bounce

• It wasn't necessary to report to the office in person every day, and when I did go in, it was just to make an appearance and ***bounce*** right out again.(p.300)
• I had been using paraldehyde more or less like ordinary drink for the last six years though, occasionally, I'd ***bounce*** back to phenobarbital and things like that.(p.524)

bounced

• I tried to contact the boys in New York, but telegrams ***bounced*** right back and when I finally got Hank on the telephone he fired me right then.(p.247)
• How hurt I was when editors ***bounced*** back my ideas quickly and my best friends opined that my output needed a lot of rewriting.(p.331)
• No matter how often I had gone into and come out of alcoholic lows during the day, the pattern ***bounced*** me out of bed each night about 2:00 a.m., shaking and hurting in the agitation that always follows a drug's sedation.(p.332)

bouncing

• In a prison in my native state, I spent eleven months in solitary confinement, ***bouncing*** in and out of the "hole" (a bare concrete-and-steel cubicle) about five times during those eleven months.(p.459)

bound

• I have a shadowy recollection of being in an airplane ***bound*** for New York, and of finding a friendly taxicab driver at the landing field instead of my wife.(p.41)
• What they say will apply to nearly everyone ***bound*** by ties of blood or affections to an alcoholic.(p.104)
• You will be ***bound*** to them with new and wonderful ties, for you will escape disaster together and you will commence shoulder to shoulder your common journey.(p.152)
• All of them were so nice to me that I figured I must be careful – they were ***bound*** to want something, being that nice.(p.319)
• It is ***bound*** to be rough, because who can say exactly how much of that green blood – commonly known as money -- was dissipated on dissipation?(p.396)

bounding

• I was ***bounding*** along and not doing too badly.(p.204)
• This was the beginning of five years of ***bounding*** back and forth between my home in Chicago and Akron to sober up.(p.288)
• Very shortly, I realized that had been a mistake -- when this big clown came ***bounding*** into the room, almost shouting, "My name is Frank, and I'm an alcoholic, ha-ha-ha!"(p.446)

bounds

• While the internal difficulties of our adolescent period were being ironed out, public acceptance of A.A. grew by leaps and ***bounds***.(p.xix)
• Joy at our release from a lifetime of frustration knew no ***bounds***.(p.128)

bounty

• Back to the big city, for another year of precarious living, paid for largely by one or two friends I still had not milked dry or worn to exhaustion with demands on their ***bounty***.(p.540)

bouquet

• You didn't carry a little orchid up the aisle in those days; you carried a great big ***bouquet***, like a funeral spray, and you didn't have your picture taken until just before you went to the church.(p.385)
• As self-conscious as I was, I had to pose for those pictures, holding this huge ***bouquet***.(p.385)

bourbon

• Emma ran out to the kitchen and came back with a water glass full of ***bourbon*** and made me drink it down.(p.385)
• As I started down the aisle, that ***bourbon*** went right through me.(p.385)

bout

• Sometimes these excuses have a certain plausibility, but none of them really makes sense in the light of the havoc an alcoholic's drinking ***bout*** creates.(p.23)
• They should wait for the end of his next drinking ***bout***.(p.90)
• When drinking, or getting over a ***bout***, an alcoholic, sometimes the model of honesty when normal, will do incredible things.(p.140)
• Sometimes, after sobering up after a ***bout*** of several weeks, I would righteously resolve to quit.(p.233)
• My last ***bout*** in the Army lasted from November 5th to 11th, 1918.(p.242)
• One morning after a terrific drinking ***bout***, I was in a little bar near our house, and I shook so that I was very much ashamed, because I was getting the shakes worse and worse.(p.266)
• But as I came out of this second ***bout*** with D.T.'s I knew I was licked.(p.429)
• I thought, well, now that I've been put out for drinking, I'll just show them that they were completely wrong, so I went off on the biggest ***bout*** I had been on up to then, involving about a fortnight's blackout.(p.521)
• As I say, this specialist put a scare in me for about a fortnight or three weeks, then I started my last ***bout*** which went on and off for about three months.(p.523)
• There was the father one lost respect for at the age of eleven, because the father broke his solemn word in a circumstance where you, eleven years old, had assumed guilt when you were innocent; but the father would not believe you, no matter what; and to ease his suffering you "confessed" and were "forgiven," only – months later – to have your "guilt" brought up – only he and you knew what he was talking ***bout*** -- brought up in front of the stern grandmother.(p.533)

bouts

• He was very nervous in the morning after these ***bouts*** and quieted himself with more liquor.(p.32)
• He is remorseful after serious drinking ***bouts*** and tells you he wants to stop.(p.109)

bowl

• I do recall lying on a cold cement floor and shredding into little bits several pieces of stolen identification cards, and washing my face in the toilet ***bowl*** trying to sober up, and screaming hysterically while clinging to bars too high to see out of, and cursing everyone that came near me.(p.354)
• I would pull out early, and go to the hunt breakfast and the flowing ***bowl*** of milk-punch.(p.404)

bowling

• He'll never read in his "sweetness and light" senior-citizen publications anything but the joys of lolling in the rocking chair, angling on the riverbank, or ***bowling*** on the green.(p.330)
• The other kids would light out for the hamburger huts or ice cream parlors, the pizza joints or ***bowling*** alleys, after football games and dances.(p.423)

box

• If there is no Al-Anon listing in your local telephone book, you may obtain further information on Al-Anon Family Groups by writing to its World Service Office: ***Box*** 182, Madison Square Station, New York, NY 10159.(p.121)
• Imagine my surprise when I read in a page one "***box***" that I had been taken from the theater unconscious around noon that day, removed by ambulance to a hospital and stomach-pumped and then released.(p.244)
• I know that when Frank came home, I said, "I want to try this thing," and he said, "There's a post office ***box*** to write to in New York."(p.392)
• All afternoon I sat there and drank and played Bing Crosby's recording of "Silent Night" over and over again on the juke ***box***.(p.467)
• If something does come along that sort of upsets me, instead of walking in and throwing a buck at the barman and asking for a drink, I walk into a telephone booth, drop a dime in the ***box***, and call somebody who was so kind as to give me his name and telephone number to meet such an emergency.(p.511)
• (This address is now available in pamphlet form at nominal cost through most A.A. groups or from ***Box*** 459, Grand Central Station, New York, NY 10163, under the title "Three Talks to Medical Societies by Bill W." -- formerly called "Bill on Alcoholism" and earlier "Alcoholism the Illness.")(p.572)
• If you cannot find A.A. in your locality, a letter addressed to Alcoholics Anonymous, ***Box*** 459, Grand Central Station, New York, NY 10163, U.S.A., will receive a prompt reply from this world center, referring you to the nearest A.A. group.(p.575)
• Should you be the relative or friend of an alcoholic who shows no immediate interest in A.A., it is suggested that you write the Al-Anon Family Groups, Inc., ***Box*** 182, Madison Square Station, New York, NY 10159, U.S.A.(p.575)

boxer

• Military service was compulsory and I did my stretch with the class of my age, goose-stepping in German barracks and taking part in the ***Boxer*** Rebellion in China, my first time at any great distance from home.(p.230)

boy

• Yes, the old ***boy*** was on fire all right.(p.9)
• We know our friend is like a ***boy*** whistling in the dark to keep up his spirits.(p.152)
• We had two children, a ***boy*** and a girl, and when the ***boy*** was about twelve, we broke up the marriage.(p.199)
• I said, "All right, call me a cab," as though I was talking to a bell ***boy***.(p.204)
• By that time, I had one ***boy*** in college, another a senior in high school, and a daughter about twelve years old.(p.215)
• I was the fair-haired ***boy*** all right, but two years later I was blacklisted as an irresponsible drunk.(p.242)
• ***Boy***, what a circle of confused idealists!(p.246)
• When I came to my aunt, she knew that I had had an unhappy childhood, and she said, "Now, Ethel, you're welcome to have ***boy*** friends in our home, but there are two boys in this town that I don't want you to date, and one of them comes from a

very fine family, one of the best.(p.262)
• He talked about his wife taking his little ***boy*** away from him because of his drinking, and how he got back together with them through A.A., and we began feeling grateful right then that all these things hadn't been taken from us.(p.270)
• The birth of a baby ***boy*** did nothing toward staying the downward spiral.(p.278)
• While working in an office, there was some semblance of restraint, but, oh ***boy***, when I got on the outside with this new company without supervision, did I go to town!(p.300)
• The doctor prescribed brandy for the ***boy*** to help him through the night when he coughed, a teaspoon of brandy.(p.338)
• A "good ***boy***" reached adulthood and success without achieving maturity or fulfillment.(p.418)
• I was an honor graduate in high school, and I was a "good ***boy***" to whom mothers pointed when their sons went astray.(p.419)
• Perhaps the single flicker of decency that shone through the fog of my drinking days was a clumsy affection for my two children, a ***boy*** and a girl.(p.437)
• Was altar ***boy*** at church on reservation.(p.474)
• We had two girls and a ***boy*** at that time.(p.490)
• "Well," said the older ***boy***, "do you?"(p.498)
• I reach for the bottle which I just got from George, the elevator ***boy***.(p.500)
• How's the ***boy***?(p.500)
• At this point, I was no longer the wise ***boy***.(p.515)
• But I pointed out to him that as I was the first British ***boy*** who had been to the school, it wouldn't be a very good advertisement for him, so I got over that all right.(p.518)
• I, a man of steel, with very high ideals, well brought up, an honor student and the recipient of scholarships and prizes, a ***boy*** wonder in business -- I, Bob, the author of this essay, looked and saw that the universe was beneath my contempt, and that to remove myself from it was the only thing of dignity a man could do.(p.531)
• And having sung that phrase, I'd chuckle with amusement, turning into irony turning into self-contempt turning into self-pity, at the sad fate of Bob, that wonderful, poor little motherless ***boy*** who was so smart in school and who grew up to accept responsibility so early and so fast and who staggered under his burdens without a whimper until the time came when he thought he was too good for this world and so he ought to be out of it.(p.532)
• I could not face the ***boy*** and youth I was in the reality of the contemptible man I had become.(p.540)
• Regarded as something of a "***boy*** wonder," I began to see myself that way.(p.555)
• The early promise of the "***boy*** wonder" faded, and my career began to drift.(p.556)

boy-welfare
• Drifting back to Ohio, I landed on a small newspaper and later was impressed into the direction of ***boy-welfare*** work at the local "Y."(p.253)

boyfriend
• I was always able to get a ***boyfriend*** who had a drinking joint or sold whiskey, but it didn't last long.(p.526)

boyhood
• On another small borrowed sum, I went up into the country to the home of a doctor I had known since ***boyhood***.(p.540)

boyish
• That age of the flapper and the "It" girl, speakeasies and the hip flask, the ***boyish*** bob and the drugstore cowboy, John Held Jr. and F. Scott Fitzgerald, all generously sprinkled with a patent pseudo-sophistication.(p.304)

boys
• There my drinking became so much worse that the ***boys*** in the fraternity house where I lived felt forced to send for my father, who made a long journey in the vain endeavor to get me straightened around.(p.174)
• Then I remember when the ***boys*** came back, that I told them, "I have gone to this Higher Power and I have told Him that I am willing to put His world first, above everything.(p.190)
• We ***boys*** drove out in somebody's car and went to the bar on the way do the dining room and I, in an effort to impress the other ***boys*** that I was city-bred, having lived in Scranton and Cleveland, asked them if they didn't want a drink.(p.194)
• At that particular time, the ***boys*** put me on a shutter and took me out to the shed, and I lay in the car while they enjoyed their banquet.(p.195)
• In sports I made the track and tennis teams; I got along well with the other ***boys*** and had a fairly large circle of acquaintances but no intimate friends.(p.240)
• So I drank all three beers, one after the other, said "I'll be seeing you, ***boys***," and went around the corner for a bottle.(p.247)
• I tried to contact the ***boys*** in New York, but telegrams bounced right back and when I finally got Hank on the telephone he fired me right then.(p.247)
• I don't think the ***boys*** were completely convinced of my personality change, for they fought shy of including my story in the book, so my only contribution to their literary efforts was my firm conviction, being still a theological rebel, that the word God should be qualified with the phrase "as we understand him" -- for that was the only way I could accept spirituality.(p.248)
• When I started to tell the ***boys*** how we did it in New York and all about the spiritual part of the program, I found they would not believe me unless I was practicing what I preached.(p.249)
• When I came to my aunt, she knew that I had had an unhappy childhood, and she said, "Now, Ethel, you're welcome to have boy friends in our home, but there are two ***boys*** in this town that I don't want you to date, and one of them comes from a very fine family, one of the best.(p.262)
• I was raised like the majority of American ***boys***, coming from a family of modest circumstances, attending public schools, having the social life of a small midwestern town, with part-time work and some athletics.(p.373)
• That was when all the ***boys*** and Esther got drunk and the wives didn't.(p.386)
• The ***boys*** at the Post Office used to bring me my jugs; mail couldn't be opened for inspection at the gate.(p.426)
• I have two wonderful little ***boys***.(p.431)
• By grace of God I stop, think two things: This would kill good mother and father; then remember ***boys*** talk about Indian fellow who been sober three years.(p.475)
• About then too, I realized that my point of view on the opposite sex wasn't entirely like that of most of the ***boys*** I knew.(p.484)
• I had never had a drink, but I had seen enough merriment in the ***boys*** who were drinking to be interested.(p.498)
• Other ***boys*** came in.(p.498)
• The faces of the other ***boys*** grew dim.(p.498)
• I like the ***boys*** and we have lots of fun, in class and out.(p.500)
• I started prowling around with a couple of these A.A. ***boys***, which kept me pretty busy and kept my mind off of down town.(p.511)
• I have my brilliant moments yet, but whenever the ***boys*** catch me at it they tell me so very plainly.(p.512)
• A lot of the ***boys*** had tears in their eyes, they were so happy to be home.(p.513)
• I belonged to one of the Irish families who, more or less traditionally, sent their ***boys*** to the British armies.(p.517)
• I would never admit that I was drinking too much, or spending money that I should have used to buy food for my two little ***boys***.(p.526)
• Once I started drinking, I didn't care that the rent wasn't paid, or that there was no food in the house, or that my ***boys*** needed shoes.(p.527)

boys'
• I become a teacher in a ***boys'*** school.(p.500)

bra
• And we usually have some kind of grimy sweater that we think we look sexy in, even if we weigh ninety-five pounds soaking wet and are not wearing a ***bra***.(p.479)

bracket
• Why should this happen to me – hadn't I provided a good home – wasn't I making a good living -- didn't I just get a substantial raise that had put me in the upper ***bracket*** class?(p.362)

bracketed
• Notice that the word "fear" is ***bracketed*** alongside the difficulties with Mr. Brown, Mrs. Jones, the employer, and the wife.(p.67)

brag
• I really felt sorry for him; the only thing in life he had to ***brag*** about was the fact that he was an alcoholic.(p.446)
• When a big, healthy-looking young fellow stood up there and said, "I'm a success today if I don't drink today," I thought, "Man, I've got a thousand things to do today before I can ***brag*** about not taking a drink, for God's sake!"(p.447)

brain
• More often than not, it is imperative that a man's ***brain*** be cleared before he is approached, as he has then a better chance of understanding and accepting what we have to offer.(p.xxiv)
• Following the elimination of alcohol, there was found to be no permanent ***brain*** injury.(p.xxix)
• My ***brain*** raced uncontrollably and there was a terrible sense of impending calamity.(p.6)
• Under the so-called belladonna treatment my ***brain*** cleared.(p.7)
• My weary and despairing wife was informed that it would all end with heart failure during delirium tremens, or I would develop a wet ***brain***, perhaps within a year.(p.7)
• Can it be appreciated that he has been a victim of crooked thinking, directly caused by the action of alcohol on his ***brain***?(p.140)
• I well remember the shock I received when a prominent doctor in Chicago told me of cases where pressure of the spinal fluid actually ruptured the ***brain***.(p.140)
• Who wouldn't be, with such a fevered ***brain***?(p.140)
• When I got the fog out of my ***brain***, I decided that quitting school was very foolish and that I had better return and continue my work.(p.173)
• My ***brain*** whirled.(p.223)
• And I remembered the creeping horror of the interminable night, in which I slept for short spells and woke up dripping with cold sweat and shaken with utter despair, to drink hastily from my bottle and mercifully pass out again, "You're mad, you're mad, you're mad!" pounded through my ***brain*** with each returning ray of consciousness, and I drowned the refrain with drink.(p.224)
• Some of these were hard to believe, but it did not require a giant ***brain*** to perceive that they had something I could use.(p.279)
• Suddenly, it was obvious to me: I had a ***brain*** tumor and would die, and everyone would be sorry for me.(p.444)
• Alcohol wrings the guts out of life, eats into the ***brain*** in such a way as to make the alcoholic blind to the truth.(p.457)
• I was very fortunate indeed not to have suffered any ***brain*** damage.(p.480)
• But somehow or other, with my old alcoholic ***brain***, sitting there in that chair, I kept saying to myself, "I wonder if it'll work?(p.515)
• But as the years go by, the stretch becomes unbearable; and the man with the grown-up ***brain*** and the childish emotions – vanity, self-interest, false pride, jealousy, longing for social approval, to name few -- becomes a prime candidate for alcohol.(p.534)

brains
• That may be true of certain nonalcoholic people who, though drinking foolishly and heavily at the present time, are able to stop or moderate, because their ***brains*** and bodies have not been damaged as ours were.(p.39)
• Under these conditions we can employ our mental faculties with assurance, for after all God gave us ***brains*** to use.(p.86)
• Either they die of acute alcoholism or they develop wet ***brains*** and have to be put away permanently."(p.308)
• And, believe me, I thank God that I found out about A.A. before I had to beat my ***brains*** out – before I had been hospitalized, jailed or lost a job.(p.367)
• I was going to be sent to the Indian Civil Service, which, in those days, meant that people thought you had a certain amount of ***brains***.(p.517)
• I thought that if these kind of ordinary people can do it, a man of my ***brains*** ought to find it much more easy, and I joined.(p.524)
• An ambitious playwright, he let his ***brains*** get so far ahead of his emotions that he collapsed into suicidal drinking.(p.531)

brainstorm
• The grouch and the ***brainstorm*** were not for us.(p.66)

brakes
• I did not know that I had no power over alcohol, that I, alone and unaided, could not stop; that I was on a downgrade, tearing along at full speed with all my ***brakes*** gone, and that the end would be a total smash-up, death or insanity.(p.408)

branch
• I ruthlessly faced my sins and became willing to have my new-found Friend take them away, root and ***branch***.(p.13)
• I re-organized their city sales policy and eighteen months later, when I was thirty, they offered me the ***branch*** managership.(p.243)

branches
• The man who was going to take over one of their biggest ***branches*** come Monday?(p.243)

brand
- He changes his ***brand*** or his environment.(p.xxviii)
- And be careful not to ***brand*** him as an alcoholic.(p.92)
- He may tell mother, who has been religious all her life, that she doesn't know what it's all about, and that she had better get his ***brand*** of spirituality while there is yet time.(p.128)
- These men had found something ***brand*** new in life.(p.159)
- Thus I found myself in the middle of a ***brand*** new group.(p.249)

branded
- Why lay ourselves open to being ***branded*** fanatics or religious bores?(p.77)

brandishing
- ***Brandishing*** my "motto," which was "A little man with a stick is equal to a big man," sometimes I varied the literary lecture by a fight with a big man, selected solely because he was big and I was little.(p.537)

brandy
- Here are some of the methods we have tried: Drinking beer only, limiting the number of drinks, never drinking alone, never drinking in the morning, drinking only at home, never having it in the house, never drinking during business hours, drinking only at parties, switching from scotch to ***brandy***, drinking only natural wines, agreeing to resign if ever drunk on the job, taking a trip, not taking a trip, swearing off forever (with and without a solemn oath), taking more physical exercise, reading inspirational books, going to health farms and sanitariums, accepting voluntary commitment to asylums -- we could increase the list ad infinitum.(p.31)
- We all have them, and I thought a little ***brandy*** or a little wine now and then could certainly hurt no one.(p.336)
- The doctor prescribed ***brandy*** for the boy to help him through the night when he coughed, a teaspoon of ***brandy***.(p.338)
- Well, of course that was all I needed — to switch from wine to ***brandy*** for three weeks.(p.338)
- A British officer, this Irishman — that is, until ***brandy*** "retired" him.(p.517)
- In fact, I couldn't have told you the difference between sherry and ***brandy***.(p.518)
- He had a shot of ***brandy*** against the cold and passed me the bottle.(p.541)

brat
- All of which could turn out but one thing — a very popular, but spoiled, ***brat***.(p.357)
- I was nothing more than a spoiled, indulged, and talented ***brat***.(p.418)

bravery
- With the ***bravery*** born of desperation, and abetted by alcohol, I married a young and lovely girl.(p.277)

brawl
- I found a job; then lost it as the result of a ***brawl*** with a taxi driver.(p.4)
- Drunk and causing a ***brawl***, they said.(p.428)

brawling
- Tom Sharkey's ***brawling*** bar on 14th Street and the famous wine-room at the back were headquarters for me.(p.251)

brazen
- I couldn't look them straight in the eyes, although I was always a self-possessed ***brazen*** sort of person.(p.323)
- I'd ***brazen*** anything out.(p.324)

bread
- He wouldn't give me any money for the groceries, but he did take me across the street and buy me a bag of candy, which I later took back and traded for a loaf of ***bread***.(p.193)
- Each ten-day period in the dark hole, I was fed ***bread*** and water daily, with one full meal on the third day only.(p.459)
- I learned the true meaning of ***bread*** cast upon the waters.(p.541)

breadwinner
- Every ***breadwinner***, whether trying to impress a boss or to hold customers in his own business, is fettered by people-pleasing.(p.329)

break
- These allergic types can never safely use alcohol in any form at all; and once having formed the habit and found they cannot ***break*** it, once having lost their self-confidence, their reliance upon things human, their problems pile up on them and become astonishingly difficult to solve.(p.xxvi)
- We know but few instances where we have given these doctors a fair ***break***.(p.73)
- How could I continually ***break*** my promises?(p.362)
- A lucky ***break***, at least some will call it lucky, was in store for me at my group that night.(p.365)
- "I've got to stop if I want to live," I told myself, and if I don't want to ***break*** my parents' hearts and maybe jeopardize their own carefully built up and hard-fought-for sobriety.(p.429)
- There would be times when the life of respectability and achievement seemed insufferably dull -- I had to ***break*** out.(p.432)
- The worst of prison treatment couldn't ***break*** this tough con.(p.457)
- Take many pledges, but ***break*** them.(p.475)
- She had been warned numerous times, not only by her family but by my own mother, that I was a hopeless drunk, that there wasn't anything anybody could do with me, that I'd never stop, and that eventually I'd ***break*** her heart.(p.513)
- For the only problems I have now are those I create when I ***break*** out in a rash of self-will.(p.551)

breakdown
- When I entered a sanitarium for prolonged and intensive psychiatric treatment, I was convinced that I was having a serious mental ***breakdown***.(p.226)
- I underwent a shattering nervous ***breakdown***.(p.275)
- Certainly now, anyone would have agreed that only a miracle could prevent my final ***breakdown***.(p.306)
- They were always there because of a nervous ***breakdown***, or for a "rest cure" — any reason except because of drinking.(p.471)

breakfast
- A tumbler full of gin followed by half a dozen bottles of beer would be required if I were to eat any ***breakfast***.(p.5)
- I would reach over and get this and take a shot and in a few moments get up and take another, shave and eat my ***breakfast***, slip a half pint of liquor in my hip pocket, and go on to school.(p.183)
- The next morning his wife came dragging him in before Russ went to work, while I was getting ***breakfast***.(p.271)
- I would pull out early, and go to the hunt ***breakfast*** and the flowing bowl of milk-punch.(p.404)
- I would rather have stayed in jail except I didn't like bologna and cold potatoes for ***breakfast***.(p.425)

breaking
- I was self conscious and ill at ease most of the time, my health was at the ***breaking*** point, and I was thoroughly miserable.(p.178)
- So I didn't have a beer one night, and as I drove home I was ***breaking*** my arm patting myself on the back because I had proved I could lick liquor.(p.203)
- Tragedies during those years that were caused by my drinking, such as the ***breaking*** up of my marriage, the death of my child, other things — had little restraining effect.(p.465)
- I now conceive the psychiatrist's job to be the task of ***breaking*** down the patient's inner resistance so that which is inside him will flower, as under the activity of the A.A. program."(p.571)

breaks
- Within a week after leaving the hospital a fast-moving trolley car ***breaks*** his arm.(p.38)
- He tells you he has decided to stop jay-walking for good, but in a few weeks he ***breaks*** both legs.(p.38)
- But the day he comes out he races in front of a fire engine, which ***breaks*** his back.(p.38)
- I figured the only difference between me and a millionaire was that I hadn't the strength, or that he got the ***breaks*** and I didn't.(p.197)

breath
- Mercifully, no one could guess that I was to have no real employment for five years, or hardly draw a sober ***breath***.(p.4)
- I put on thirty pounds of weight in about two months, looked like a pig, and was uncomfortable from shortness of ***breath***.(p.177)
- I walked away from that girl grinding my teeth and cursing under my ***breath***.(p.322)
- I thought if they smelled whiskey on my ***breath***, they would lock me up, and I couldn't live without my bottle.(p.526)

breathing
- In the long ago past I used to start at the top as president or treasurer and end up with the sheriff ***breathing*** down my neck.(p.284)
- No more snoops or big shots ***breathing*** down our necks.(p.329)
- I had fed it, fanned it and nurtured it as one might a delicate child, and it had become as much a part of me as my ***breathing***.(p.551)

breeze
- Pearl Harbor was a ***breeze*** of nine months, a gay Hawaiian paradise, drinking under the palms, listening to the surf beat on the shore, a bottle of whiskey near at hand.(p.426)

brew
- It wasn't very long until I had developed a pretty good ***brew*** with uniformity and plenty of authority.(p.232)
- From that point on, I secured crocks of ten gallon capacity and really took quite an active interest in the manufacture of home ***brew***.(p.297)
- (No home ***brew*** as an inducement).(p.303)

brewery
- They owned this joint, she ran it, and he sold for a ***brewery***.(p.267)

brewing
- I condoned my domestic ***brewing*** along with the bootleggers and their business.(p.233)

brewmeister
- HOME ***BREWMEISTER***(p.297)

brewmeisters
- My wife became pregnant and the doctor recommended the use of port or ale . . . so . . . I bought a six gallon crock and a few bottles, listened to advice from amateur ***brewmeisters***, and was off on my beer manufacturing career on a small scale (for the time being).(p.297)

bricks
- The drive was long and cold but he was thankful for the hot ***bricks*** which some thoughtful person had given him for his feet.(p.497)

bride
- Proud of my little station and of my new ***bride*** I settled down to a happy married life.(p.361)
- We came back to Pittsburgh as happy as a ***bride*** and groom.(p.364)
- I also wanted to be the queen of society, with a glittering salon, the ***bride*** of a dream prince and the mother of a happy brood.(p.400)

bridge
- Some of us had already walked far over the ***Bridge*** of Reason toward the desired shore of faith.(p.53)
- He had stepped from ***bridge*** to shore.(p.56)
- My wife and I belonged to some ***bridge*** clubs and they began to make wine and serve it.(p.184)
- As we left, and they were escorting us across the ***bridge*** into Wheeling, I, with great dignity and sarcasm, told them if their wives were ever visiting in Akron, and they, too, were looking for their route sign as I was, that I hoped I could extend to them the hospitality that had been shown to me in Bellaire.(p.264)
- Eventually, of course, what with all the hilarity that could be provoked with a few gallons of beer, there seemed to be no need of ***bridge*** or poker playing for entertainment.(p.297)
- I was accused of it many times when I went to play ***bridge*** in the afternoon, but I really never did take a morning drink.(p.323)
- I noticed that I was avoiding all my social friends except for my ***bridge***.(p.324)
- I would walk up and down under the 59th Street ***bridge***, trying to get up the nerve to go up there and jump.(p.411)
- Then went on ***bridge*** to jump.(p.475)
- Four alcoholics play ***bridge*** in a smoke-filled room.(p.502)

Bridgeport
- After six months, we move to ***Bridgeport***, Conn.(p.476)

brief
- In that ***brief*** space, Alcoholics Anonymous has mushroomed into nearly 6,000 groups whose membership is far above 150,000 recovered alcoholics.(p.xv)
- For a ***brief*** moment, I had needed and wanted God.(p.12)
- All of us felt at times that we were regaining control, but such intervals -- usually ***brief*** — were inevitably followed by still less control, which led in time to pitiful and incomprehensible demoralization.(p.30)
- In some instances there has been ***brief*** recovery, followed always by a still worse relapse.(p.31)
- Save for a few ***brief*** moments of temptation the thought of drink has never returned; and at such times a great revulsion has risen up in him.(p.57)
- Here is a ***brief*** account:(p.153)
- That job began a series of ***brief*** working spells, each one ending in a "drunk" and the urge to travel.(p.253)
- Three more months of being up and around the house for ***brief*** periods and in bed the rest of the time.(p.275)

• When I went back to my hometown to go into private practice, I experienced another ***brief*** lull in my addiction to alcohol and drugs.(p.420)
• I'd gladly do it anonymously, as I have done this ***brief*** account of my struggle with alcohol -- merely to present certain ideas for the consideration of the reader.(p.542)

briefcase
• Instead of drinking in fancy bars and clubs, I had to carry a bottle of vodka in my ***briefcase***, duck into public toilets, and gulp from the bottle, trembling, in order to keep from falling apart.(p.557)

bright
• He uses his gifts to build up a ***bright*** outlook for his family and himself, and then pulls the structure down on his head by a senseless series of sprees.(p.21)
• Frequent contact with newcomers and with each other is the ***bright*** spot of our lives.(p.89)
• He and his family can be a ***bright*** spot in such congregations.(p.132)
• Alcohol was a looming cloud in this banker's ***bright*** sky.(p.373)
• They were ***bright*** and well read, they held various political views.(p.410)

brilliant
• I had been obliged to discharge him for drinking, though he was ***brilliant***, alert, and one of the best organizers I have ever known.(p.137)
• Is he not usually ***brilliant***, fast-thinking, imaginative and likeable?(p.139)
• My ***brilliant*** agnosticism vanished, and I saw for the first time that those who really believed, or at least honestly tried to find a Power greater than themselves, were much more composed and contented than I had ever been, and they seemed to have a degree of happiness which I had never known.(p.247)
• Even when I was old enough to know better, I dreamed about being as beautiful as Venus, as pure as the Madonna and as ***brilliant*** as the President of the United States is supposed to be.(p.400)
• My family, on my mother's side, was ***brilliant***, gifted and charming.(p.401)
• He was ***brilliant*** and ambitious.(p.403)
• This good and gentle man, a ***brilliant*** research doctor, got nowhere with me fast.(p.407)
• I also thought I was a ***brilliant*** drunk.(p.512)
• I have my ***brilliant*** moments yet, but whenever the boys catch me at it they tell me so very plainly.(p.512)

brimming
• From a trembling, despairing nervous wreck, had emerged a man ***brimming*** over with self-reliance and contentment.(p.xxix)

bring
• I talked with him for some time, but was not able to ***bring*** myself to feel that I had known him before.(p.xxix)
• We shall ***bring*** to the task our combined experience and knowledge.(p.19)
• We are unable, at certain times, to ***bring*** into our consciousness with sufficient force the memory of the suffering and humiliation of even a week or a month ago.(p.24)
• What a state of mental goose-flesh that used to ***bring*** on!(p.54)
• We must be willing to make amends where we have done harm, provided that we do not ***bring*** about still more harm in so doing.(p.69)
• Think of what you can ***bring*** to it.(p.102)
• Try to have him ***bring*** up the subject himself.(p.111)
• Sometimes they demand that dad ***bring*** them back instantly!(p.123)
• We think each family which has been relieved owes something to those who have not, and when the occasion requires, each member of it should be only too willing to ***bring*** former mistakes, no matter how grievous, out of their hiding places.(p.124)
• He may ***bring*** new hope and new courage to many a priest, minister, or rabbi, who gives his all to minister to our troubled world.(p.132)
• Why not ***bring*** him into contact with some of our alcoholic crowd?(p.138)
• Why, he argued, should he lose the remainder of his business, only to ***bring*** still more suffering to his family by foolishly admitting his plight to people from whom he made his livelihood?(p.155)
• They experienced a few distressing failures, but in those cases they made an effort to ***bring*** the man's family into a spiritual way of living, thus relieving much worry and suffering.(p.159)
• Aside from fellowship and sociability, the prime object was to provide a time and place where new people might ***bring*** their problems.(p.160)
• Sometimes I would ***bring*** it in my pockets, but they were inspected, and that became too risky.(p.176)
• I began to ***bring*** bottles in.(p.233)
• Many alcoholics have learned they can ***bring*** their bottle to a cheap movie theater and drink, sleep, wake up and drink again in the darkness.(p.244)
• In those days my system was always to drink up my last pay check and believe that necessity would ***bring*** the next job.(p.256)
• We had always encouraged our children to ***bring*** their friends home at any time, but after a few experiences with a drunken father they eliminated home as a place to entertain friends.(p.376)
• The following spring she left me one day without giving me any idea of where she had gone, hoping this would ***bring*** me to my senses.(p.377)
• There may be many reasons which ***bring*** one to A.A. for the first time, but the lasting one must be to want sobriety and the A.A. way of living for oneself.(p.379)
• But it did not take long for the pressures of living to ***bring*** out my immaturity and my insecurity.(p.420)
• The boys at the Post Office used to ***bring*** me my jugs; mail couldn't be opened for inspection at the gate.(p.426)
• But now I change if it ***bring*** good life.(p.475)
• Nevertheless, I stayed sober there about six months, because I knew that Vi was to come later and ***bring*** the children.(p.490)
• It has taught me that I can best keep my sobriety by sharing it out with others; that I must ***bring*** that sobriety to others who need it, in my own interest.(p.524)
• I am hoping that writing this may ***bring*** some poor, mixed-up soul into the program.(p.530)
• A.A. has taught me that I will have peace of mind in exact proportion to the peace of mind I ***bring*** into the lives of other people, and it has taught me the true meaning of the admonition "happy are ye who know these things and do them."(p.551)
• The terms "spiritual experience" and "spiritual awakening" are used many times in this book which, upon careful reading, shows that the personality change sufficient to ***bring*** about recovery from alcoholism has manifested itself among us in many different forms.(p.569)

bringing
• Unfortunately for me, I was the only child, which perhaps engendered the selfishness which played such an important part in ***bringing*** on my alcoholism.(p.172)

brings
• It ***brings*** misunderstanding, fierce resentment, financial insecurity, disgusted friends and employers, warped lives of blameless children, sad wives and parents -- anyone can increase the list.(p.18)
• This ***brings*** us to the Fifth Step in the program of recovery mentioned in the preceding chapter.(p.72)
• This ***brings*** to mind a story about one of our friends.(p.80)
• This thought ***brings*** us to Step Ten, which suggests we continue to take personal inventory and continue to set right any new mistakes as we go along.(p.84)
• Some crisis ***brings*** you to a point of making a decision to do something about your drinking problem.(p.377)
• I've heard it said many times in A.A., "There is just one good drunk in every alcoholic's life, and that's the one that ***brings*** us into A.A.," and I believe it.(p.549)

bristle
• Many of us have been so touchy that even casual reference to spiritual things made us ***bristle*** with antagonism.(p.48)

Britain
• Following a big drunk on that sheet, where I was doing leg-work and rewrite, a feeling of nostalgia made me buy a ticket for Liverpool and I returned to ***Britain***.(p.252)

British
• A.A. has flourishing communities in the ***British*** Isles, the Scandinavian countries, South Africa, South America, Mexico, Alaska, Australia and Hawaii.(p.xv)
• With nothing but a liberal arts education, very definitely estranged from my family and already married, soon after graduation from college I became a bookmaker's clerk on the ***British*** racing circuits, far better off financially than the average professional man.(p.251)
• A ***British*** officer, this Irishman — that is, until brandy "retired" him.(p.517)
• I belonged to one of the Irish families who, more or less traditionally, sent their boys to the ***British*** armies.(p.517)
• But I pointed out to him that as I was the first ***British*** boy who had been to the school, it wouldn't be a very good advertisement for him, so I got over that all right.(p.518)
• I had two years at Dublin University, and then in 1916, I got a nomination for Sandhurst, the ***British*** Military College.(p.518)

British Isles
• A.A. has flourishing communities in the ***British Isles***, the Scandinavian countries, South Africa, South America, Mexico, Alaska, Australia and Hawaii.(p.xv)

broad
• To us, the Realm of Spirit is ***broad***, roomy, all inclusive; never exclusive or forbidding to those who earnestly seek.(p.46)
• If our testimony helps sweep away prejudice, enables you to think honestly, encourages you to search diligently within yourself, then, if you wish, you can join us on the ***Broad*** Highway.(p.55)
• We feel we are on the ***Broad*** Highway, walking hand in hand with the Spirit of the Universe.(p.75)

broadcast
• Our names and pictures as A.A. members ought not be ***broadcast***, filmed, or publicly printed.(p.567)

broadcasting
• By this time I had become associated with the fast growing and fascinating business of ***broadcasting***.(p.358)
• Dr. W.W. Bauer, ***broadcasting*** under the auspices of The American Medical Association in 1946, over the NBC network, said, in part: "Alcoholics Anonymous are no crusaders; not a temperance society.(p.572)

broadcasts
• I, carried away with the desire to serve A.A., gave what was probably one of the first radio ***broadcasts*** about A.A., living through a case of mike fright and feeling like a million dollars when it was all over.(p.283)

Broadway
• In my mind's eye I saw ***Broadway*** again and Tom Sharkey's bar; the roar of the subway was in my ears.(p.252)

broke
• Abruptly in October 1929 hell ***broke*** loose on the New York stock exchange.(p.4)
• This time we stayed ***broke***.(p.4)
• A business which takes no regular inventory usually goes ***broke***.(p.64)
• He may be ***broke*** and homeless.(p.96)
• Bitterly discouraged, he found himself in a strange place, discredited and almost ***broke***.(p.154)
• It did help to certain extent, since I got in places where I could not obtain anything to drink, and so ***broke*** the habitual drinking.(p.183)
• We had two children, a boy and a girl, and when the boy was about twelve, we ***broke*** up the marriage.(p.199)
• I agreed with him and told him in no uncertain terms that I never ***broke*** my word in my life.(p.206)
• How it finally ***broke*** a Southerner's obstinacy and destined this salesman to start A.A. at Philadelphia.(p.238)
• After a couple of days in dollar hotels and one night in the pokey, I finally landed on my mother's doorstep -- shaking apart, with several days' beard and, of course, ***broke*** as usual.(p.238)
• Then ***broke*** again, hiding out in cheap hotels all over the country, one night jail stands here and there, and always that horrible feeling "What's the use -- nothing is worth while."(p.244)
• I was soon ***broke***, this time without trainfare to go anywhere.(p.252)
• Always, in between, there were intervals of being ***broke***, riding freights and hitch-hiking interminable distances from one big town to another in three states.(p.255)
• A friend who knew I would soon be ***broke*** mounted guard over me when I left my job of writing the histories of Texas cities and put me aboard a bus for the town I had left almost five years before.(p.256)
• I made promises to myself, my family and friends -- and ***broke*** them.(p.375)
• After I came to A.A., I was divorced by my wife; I lost my practice; I was legally restrained from seeing my children; I went ***broke***; and the dental society threatened me with the loss of my license.(p.420)
• We ***broke*** open a window and got inside.(p.424)
• We pulled up in front of my sister's house just as dawn ***broke***.(p.466)
• I almost ***broke*** down and cried when I talked with them but I didn't.(p.467)
• And when she ***broke*** a luncheon date with me one Saturday, after I had been in A.A. for about three months, I said, "I'll show her!(p.472)

• I was just about ***broke***.(p.491)
• Finally, I ***broke*** the last one hundred dollar bill the Saturday before I left.(p.493)
• The Abyssinian war ***broke*** out just as things were going very badly for me, and I went off to Egypt on a job there.(p.519)
• Then Hitler's war ***broke*** out, and again, I was given a really important job on the Suez Canal, dealing with military shipping.(p.520)
• There was the father one lost respect for at the age of eleven, because the father ***broke*** his solemn word in a circumstance where you, eleven years old, had assumed guilt when you were innocent; but the father would not believe you, no matter what; and to ease his suffering you "confessed" and were "forgiven," only – months later – to have your "guilt" brought up – only he and you knew what he was talking bout -- brought up in front of the stern grandmother.(p.533)

broken
• Trembling, I stepped from the hospital a ***broken*** man.(p.8)
• Hearts are ***broken***.(p.82)
• I had a ***broken*** nose, a fractured cheekbone, and was black from the lower part of my face up into my hair.(p.204)
• As I look back, I was very ***broken*** up about it.(p.263)
• My ***broken*** home and ***broken*** heart fanned my smoldering self-pity into a fair-sized bonfire and this kept me well supplied with reasons for having another drink, and then another.(p.305)
• But the saddest, and thus the most consoling, drifted through from the country-music station – stories of ***broken*** hearts, wasted lives, lost loves, sung plaintively.(p.332)
• ***Broken*** promises, humiliation, hopelessness, worry, anxiety – but still not enough.(p.377)
• However, after I heard a few stories of jails, sanitariums, ***broken*** homes and skid row, I wondered if I really was an alcoholic.(p.378)
• Incalculable are the intangible initiation fees that A.A. members have paid: the sick, sick hangovers, the remorse, guilt, ***broken*** homes, jails, and institutions, and the mental anguish in general that has been generated over the years.(p.399)
• The sacred word was ***broken*** and you never trusted your father again, and avoided him.(p.533)

broker
• Six months earlier, the ***broker*** had been relieved of his drink obsession by a sudden spiritual experience, following a meeting with an alcoholic friend who had been in contact with the Oxford Groups of that day.(p.xv)
• From this doctor, the ***broker*** had learned the grave nature of alcoholism.(p.xvi)
• Prior to his journey to Akron, the ***broker*** had worked hard with many alcoholics on the theory that only an alcoholic could help an alcoholic, but he had succeeded only in keeping sober himself.(p.xvi)
• The ***broker*** had gone to Akron on a business venture which had collapsed, leaving him greatly in fear that he might start drinking again.(p.xvi)
• But when the ***broker*** gave him Dr. Silkworth's description of alcoholism and its hopelessness, the physician began to pursue the spiritual remedy for his malady with a willingness he had never before been able to muster.(p.xvi)
• When the ***broker*** returned to New York in the fall of 1935, the first A.A. group had actually been formed, though no one realized it at the time.(p.xvii)
• I failed to persuade my ***broker*** friends to send me out looking over factories and managements, but my wife and I decided to go anyway.(p.2)
• At the end of this selling of lots, just prior to World War I, I got into the crude rubber business, and six months later there was only one ***broker*** and myself left in Akron.(p.197)

brokerage
• After one of those days of inferno, I wobbled from a hotel bar to a ***brokerage*** office.(p.4)
• I became an unwelcome hanger-on at ***brokerage*** places.(p.5)
• I switched into real estate ***brokerage*** and property management work.(p.277)

brokers
• So in spite of anything that I might do, I prospered, being one of only two ***brokers*** in the rubber center of the world.(p.197)

bronzed
• For my seventh A.A. birthday, my program-oriented, Al-Anon wife had my moccasins ***bronzed***.(p.445)

brood
• I also wanted to be the queen of society, with a glittering salon, the bride of a dream prince and the mother of a happy ***brood***.(p.400)
• There was the physical aspect; to be the youngest and the runt of the ***brood*** of children, to have to wear glasses very early and so to be teased, to be bookish and bored in school because the captain of the football team could not translate Virgil and yet was the school god while you, you, you little shrimp, were the school egghead, junior size and an early model.(p.533)

Brooklyn
• I had been in the remote reaches of ***Brooklyn***.(p.224)
• I went trembling into a house in ***Brooklyn*** filled with strangers . . . and I found I had come home at last, to my own kind.(p.228)
• There was one meeting a week at Bill's home in ***Brooklyn***, and we all took turns there spouting off about how we had changed our lives overnight, how many drunks we had saved and straightened out, and last, but not least, how God had touched each of us personally on the shoulder.(p.246)

broomstick
• I tried to conduct a kangaroo court and hit them with a ***broomstick***.(p.204)

brother
• My secretary returned to say that it was not Mr. B---- on the phone; it was Mr. B----'s ***brother***, and he wished to give me a message.(p.136)
• At a comparatively early age, I can remember being jealous of my ***brother***.(p.194)
• Shortly after that, my ***brother***, who had then become associated with a group of people and had stopped drinking, urged me to attend meetings with him.(p.205)
• One morning, after I had been on a binge for a couple of days, I awoke to find my ***brother*** and Doctor Bob in my room talking to me about not drinking.(p.206)
• I then began asking a lot of questions of both my ***brother*** and Dr. Bob about how this thing worked, and I suppose I was becoming more glassy-eyed all the while, for eventually I said to Bob, "You're all dried up.(p.206)
• A few minutes later, Dr. Bob left, leaving with my ***brother*** some medicine I should get.(p.207)
• Unlike his skid-row ***brother***, he isn't heckled for sleeping in alleys or doorways.(p.330)
• About two days later I was called by a friend of mine from Nevada City – he's a ***brother*** of my wife's closest friend.(p.347)
• We always had cordials after dinner and I know my sister and my ***brother*** and I loved creme de menthe.(p.384)
• My ***brother*** and me find work on turnpike in Maine.(p.475)
• So I jump quick from First Step to Twelfth Step to help my ***brother***, living with me.(p.476)
• Two years later, my ***brother*** take Tall Man to first A.A. meeting.(p.476)
• A couple of years later, we lost our elder ***brother*** in a house fire, because of pills and booze.(p.480)
• If anyone had told me I would be enjoying a hockey game with my husband and my ***brother*** without being all boozed up, I would not have believed it.(p.481)
• Her ***brother*** had been a drinker and had died in a State Hospital for the insane.(p.498)
• So did the waterboy on the high school football team attempt to revenge himself on the big ***brother*** who was the star quarterback; for I was the waterboy and my ***brother*** was the star quarterback, innocent of everything except the fact that he was a star quarterback.(p.537)

brother-executive
• He simply could not believe that his ***brother-executive*** suffered from a serious illness.(p.138)

brother-in-law
• She had a hairdresser who used to tell her about a ***brother-in-law*** who had been quite a drinker and about some doctor in Akron who had straightened him out.(p.216)
• Once, I phoned my ***brother-in-law*** and told him I was going to take a handful of pills (in fact, I already had) and I would slash my wrists if he didn't come over to stop me.(p.479)
• My ***brother-in-law*** was living with us at that time and I said to Vi, "Maybe the bottles are brother's.(p.488)

brother's
• My brother-in-law was living with us at that time and I said to Vi, "Maybe the bottles are ***brother's***.(p.488)

Brotherhood
• Judging from what I had seen in Europe and since, the power of God in human affairs was negligible, the ***Brotherhood*** of Man a grim jest.(p.11)

brotherly
• We have a way out on which we can absolutely agree, and upon which we can join in ***brotherly*** and harmonious action.(p.17)
• The bartenders took care of me, not out of ***brotherly*** love, but through enlightened self-interest.(p.410)

brothers
• I had four ***brothers*** and three sisters.(p.210)
• As I look back, all the ***brothers*** developed personality problems.(p.210)
• There were four of us children, and although both of my ***brothers*** later became alcoholic – one died of alcoholism -- my sister has never taken a drink in her life.(p.240)

brothers'
• Even in the present century, American newspapers were afraid to print an account of the Wright ***brothers'*** first successful flight at Kitty Hawk.(p.51)
• The Wright ***brothers'*** almost childish faith that they could build a machine which would fly was the mainspring of their accomplishment.(p.52)

brought
• This ***brought*** a rush of 800 frantic inquiries into the little New York office which meanwhile had been established.(p.xviii)
• The basic principles of the A.A. program, it appears, hold good for individuals with many different lifestyles, just as the program has ***brought*** recovery to those of many different nationalities.(p.xxii)
• About one year prior to this experience a man was ***brought*** in to be treated for chronic alcoholism.(p.xxix)
• When I need a mental uplift, I often think of another case ***brought*** in by a physician prominent in New York.(p.xxix)
• He was rescued by a searching party, and, in desperate condition, ***brought*** to me.(p.xxix)
• The exercise of an option ***brought*** in more money, leaving us with a profit of several thousand dollars for that year.(p.3)
• Friends who have reasoned with him after a spree which has ***brought*** him to the point of divorce or bankruptcy are mystified when he walks directly into a saloon.(p.35)
• I have since been ***brought*** into a way of living infinitely more satisfying and, I hope, more useful than the life I lived before.(p.42)
• To others, the word "God" ***brought*** up a particular idea of Him with which someone had tried to impress them during childhood.(p.45)
• The outlines and the promise of the New Land had ***brought*** lustre to tired eyes and fresh courage to flagging spirits.(p.53)
• We were grateful that Reason had ***brought*** us so far.(p.53)
• Without knowing it, had we not been ***brought*** to where we stood by a certain kind of faith?(p.53)
• Post-war disillusionment, ever more serious alcoholism, impending mental and physical collapse, ***brought*** him to the point of self-destruction.(p.56)
• It set in motion trains of circumstances which ***brought*** us misfortune we felt we didn't deserve.(p.67)
• An armored car could not have ***brought*** the pay envelopes home.(p.105)
• The bill collectors, the sheriffs, the angry taxi drivers, the policemen, the bums, the pals, and even the ladies they sometimes ***brought*** home – our husbands thought we were so inhospitable.(p.106)
• Your husband will be the first to say it was your devotion and care which ***brought*** him to the point where he could have a spiritual experience.(p.118)
• He ***brought*** the quart out and I took a good swig.(p.205)
• So Paul was dispatched and ***brought*** back a pint.(p.206)
• In fact, on one occasion, I was picked up by the police and ***brought*** home.(p.211)
• Why had "Dorothy" ***brought*** me here?(p.223)
• He ***brought*** in many of our original members, yet he himself could not make it and died of alcoholism.(p.239)
• I was startled to learn he had only been off the booze a month or so himself when he ***brought*** me the message!(p.245)
• And I said, "Well, they ***brought*** a pitcher of coffee, and a sandwich wrapped up for me."(p.264)
• He ***brought*** many people into A.A. through his barroom.)(p.267)
• Jack ***brought*** the Saturday Post with Jack Alexander's story.(p.268)
• I had the Big Book ("Alcoholics Anonymous") that had been ***brought*** to me.(p.268)

• His wife was cussing him, raving at him, "I just ***brought*** him over to show you what kind of a guy he is!(p.271)
• I had been ***brought*** up to believe this, and I had shown during my 'teens considerable enterprise and imagination about earning money.(p.275)
• This office job ***brought*** me face to face with a problem which I had sidestepped all my adult life, lack of training.(p.284)
• Seven years of work in this field ***brought*** an opportunity to affiliate myself actively with one of my clients, a fellow A.A.(p.284)
• At the moral inventory, he ***brought*** up some of my bad personality traits or character defects, such as selfishness, conceit, jealousy, carelessness, intolerance, ill-temper, sarcasm and resentments.(p.292)
• I had been ***brought*** up to believe in God, but I know that until I found this A.A. program, I had never found or known faith in the reality of God, the reality of His power that is now with me in everything I do.(p.341)
• I tried every gimmick that there was to get some peace of mind, but it was not until I was ***brought*** to my alcoholic knees, when I was ***brought*** to a group in my own community with the butcher, the baker, the carpenter and the mechanic, who were able to give me the Twelve Steps, that I was finally given some semblance of an answer to the last half of the First Step.(p.349)
• It has ***brought*** about a revelation of self, the discovery of an inner being, an awareness of God.(p.355)
• But success ***brought*** increased social activities and I realized that many of my friends enjoyed a social drink with no apparent harm to themselves or others.(p.374)
• I was unhappy myself and I had ***brought*** unhappiness to all who cared for me.(p.378)
• When I was a baby, my mother ***brought*** me to America, and I never again saw my father.(p.401)
• Imagine my surprise when I came to, in Europe, and discovered I had ***brought*** myself along!(p.405)
• All these things together ***brought*** me into A.A.(p.415)
• The doctor said I'd been ***brought*** into the hospital like a madman, crying, raving, ranting, swearing, completely in the throes of delirium tremens.(p.427)
• And A.A. took this wreck of a woman and ***brought*** her back to life.(p.470)
• Finally, he ***brought*** in the angle of whiskey.(p.494)
• However, a verdict was ***brought*** in of murder in the second degree.(p.508)
• They ***brought*** me in and of course, they hadn't very much trouble in finding that I was alcoholic.(p.521)
• Since I joined on that April night, A.A. has done more for me than just stop me from drinking; it has ***brought*** me back to life again.(p.524)
• It has ***brought*** me back to a realization of my Maker and my duties to Him.(p.525)
• I, a man of steel, with very high ideals, well ***brought*** up, an honor student and the recipient of scholarships and prizes, a boy wonder in business -- I, Bob, the author of this essay, looked and saw that the universe was beneath my contempt, and that to remove myself from it was the only thing of dignity a man could do.(p.531)
• There was the father one lost respect for at the age of eleven, because the father broke his solemn word in a circumstance where you, eleven years old, had assumed guilt when you were innocent; but the father would not believe you, no matter what; and to ease his suffering you "confessed" and were "forgiven," only – months later – to have your "guilt" ***brought*** up – only he and you knew what he was talking bout -- ***brought*** up in front of the stern grandmother.(p.533)
• For you learned that he had been guilty of the thing he had accused you of, and his guilt had ***brought*** suffering to his entire family; and he thought he saw his young son beginning his own tragic pattern.(p.533)
• During the day a friend of mine ***brought*** me some magazines to take to a hospital group I was interested in, and I looked through them and a "banner" across the front of one featured an article by a prominent clergyman in which I caught the word "resentment."(p.552)
• He finally realizes that he has undergone a profound alteration in his reaction to life; that such a change could hardly have been ***brought*** about by himself alone.(p.569)

Brown
• Mr. ***Brown***(p.65)
• ***Brown*** may get my job at the office.(p.65)
• Likes ***Brown***.(p.65)
• Notice that the word "fear" is bracketed alongside the difficulties with Mr. ***Brown***, Mrs. Jones, the employer, and the wife.(p.67)

brownstone
• Somehow I got out of there and walked five blocks past ***brownstone*** houses.(p.223)

browsed
• So instead of going near A.A., I just ***browsed*** around for that first month.(p.510)

bruised
• ***Bruised***, and deadly ashamed, I told no one.(p.406)

bruises
• Most of the time I was covered with ***bruises*** from "running into doors."(p.411)
• Angry ***bruises*** appeared mysteriously all over my body.(p.558)

brushed
• He said something about God or a Higher Power, but I ***brushed*** that off -- that was for the birds, not for me.(p.239)
• Whatever it was, it ***brushed*** all the heavy burdens off my back.(p.334)

brushes
• I had had no ***brushes*** with the law, though I should have had many.(p.379)

Bub
• I said, "Look, ***Bub***, if I want those lights on, I'll turn them on."(p.207)

buck
• I thought, "Aha, he's passing the ***buck***.(p.413)
• If something does come along that sort of upsets me, instead of walking in and throwing a ***buck*** at the barman and asking for a drink, I walk into a telephone booth, drop a dime in the box, and call somebody who was so kind as to give me his name and telephone number to meet such an emergency.(p.511)

buckle
• At this time, however, she had an opportunity to go to Salt Lake City on a new project for the government, but she did promise me that if I would curtail my drinking and ***buckle*** down to hard work she would give serious consideration to my latest proposal and maybe join me at a later date when I got settled.(p.359)

bucks
• But I didn't do a thing about giving them any part of the seven ***bucks*** I had in my pocket.(p.197)
• Just give me a good front and a couple of ***bucks*** and I'd be right back in the big time.(p.246)
• But my board, room, and clothing were free, and I could spend the whole ten ***bucks*** on booze.(p.398)

buckwheat
• Father says grace, which delays my attack on the ***buckwheat*** cakes and sausage.(p.497)

Bud
• However, I had phoned New York from the farm, appealing for help, and there in the station to meet us were two A.A.'s, John and ***Bud***.(p.415)
• John and ***Bud*** became my friends.(p.415)

Buddhists
• By personal religious affiliation, we include Catholics, Protestants, Jews, Hindus, and a sprinkling of Moslems and ***Buddhists***.(p.xx)

buddy
• It's like the fellow who came in A.A., and his sponsor said to him, "Listen, ***buddy***, do you believe in a Higher Power?"(p.512)

budget
• I was never drunk on the job, never missed a day's work, was seldom rendered totally ineffective by a hangover and kept my liquor expenses well within my adequate ***budget***.(p.433)

Buffalo
• Quebec, Toronto, ***Buffalo***, and finally Pittsburgh, were the scenes of man-sized drunks until I had gone through my readjusted discharge pay, a fair sum.(p.253)

buggy
• It is not long before he drives up in the ***buggy***.(p.497)

build
• Upon a foundation of complete willingness I might ***build*** what I saw in my friend.(p.12)
• He uses his gifts to ***build*** up a bright outlook for his family and himself, and then pulls the structure down on his head by a senseless series of sprees.(p.21)
• The Wright brothers' almost childish faith that they could ***build*** a machine which would fly was the mainspring of their accomplishment.(p.52)
• Many of us said to our Maker, as we understood Him: "God, I offer myself to Thee -- to ***build*** with me and to do with me as Thou wilt.(p.63)
• She knew that at that time any suggestion she made about my drinking would only ***build*** up a barrier, a consideration for which I am ever grateful.(p.216)
• But they didn't do anything for me to ***build*** up my ego.(p.262)
• My alcoholism-prone mind, however, reminded me that all great authors had needed a stimulus to ***build*** up inspiration and inventiveness before each day's work.(p.331)
• New programing was beginning to ***build*** an audience, but sponsors were pretty scarce.(p.360)
• Slowly a pile of pineapples started to ***build*** up on the table.(p.427)
• I learned what a devastating effect it can have on a child to coddle him and ***build*** him up, and then turn and beat him savagely, as had happened to me.(p.434)
• All Twelve Steps of A.A. are designed to kill the old self (deflate the old ego) and ***build*** a new, free self.(p.459)
• They ***build*** you up with a lot of false hopes and promises, and rush you around here and there and then, all of a sudden, it's gone."(p.472)
• ***Build*** houses for some cops – ha-ha.(p.475)
• I have been allowed to ***build*** an entirely new career in a field I had never worked in.(p.541)

build-up
• I can't afford resentments against anyone, because they are the ***build-up*** of another drunk.(p.325)

building
• Carefully reading the first five proposals we ask if we have omitted anything, for we are ***building*** an arch through which we shall walk a free man at last.(p.75)
• After three years of this, I wound up in the local hospital where they attempted to help me, but I would get my friends to smuggle me a quart, or I would steal the alcohol about the ***building***, so that I got rapidly worse.(p.175)
• Forced to detrain from an empty gondola on the other side of Chicago by a terrific rainstorm which drenched me to the skin, I hit the first factory ***building*** I saw for a job.(p.253)
• On Wednesday night Jack M. said, "You meet me at the Ohio Edison ***Building***, and I will take you to the meeting."(p.269)
• I had been far too busy ***building***, protecting, and maintaining an image of respectability and all the other business pluses.(p.327)
• He always thought that maybe I was safer in a ***building*** where there were other people.(p.388)
• Vi was taking care of me and I was devoting all my time to the ***building*** of that group.(p.496)

buildings
• Though old ***buildings*** will eventually be replaced by finer ones, the new structures will take years to complete.(p.123)

built
• It has been repeatedly proven among us that upon this simple cornerstone a wonderfully effective spiritual structure can be ***built***.(p.47)
• The barriers he had ***built*** through the years were swept away.(p.56)
• sometimes they were so inaccessible that it seemed as though a great wall had been ***built*** around them.(p.107)
• I always ***built*** up in my own mind the great things that I was going to do, and in fact I accomplished about fifty percent of them and then lost interest.(p.193)
• With that profit, I ***built*** a number of houses, but then I neglected them.(p.194)
• Not far from where I lived they ***built*** a new technical high school and one of the teachers sold me on the idea that I needed a little mechanical drawing if I were going to be a good toolmaker.(p.211)
• We ***built*** up a splendid life.(p.263)
• All I can remember about the Roaring Twenties is that I drank a great deal, thought I was having a grand time, managed to get to Europe for a few weeks, was very proud of the dozens of speak-easy cards entitling me to an entree in the better joints between Cleveland and New York, took on a wife, and ***built*** a home in a fashionable suburb of Cleveland.(p.358)
• Over a period of time he has ***built*** up self pity, resentments toward anyone or anything that interferes with his drinking.(p.380)
• "I've got to stop if I want to live," I told myself, and if I don't want to break my parents' hearts and maybe jeopardize their own carefully ***built*** up and hard-fought-for sobriety.(p.429)
• It was a fantastic structure, ***built*** on a crumbling foundation.(p.435)
• Father, through the years, had ***built*** up a very good

mail order business because, at that time, there wasn't too much money in medicine.(p.485)
• In that short period he *built* within me something that I had long since lost, which was hope.(p.495)

bulbs
• Then two *bulbs* appeared.(p.498)

bulk
• I knew I wasn't capable of keeping the *bulk* of the money myself, so I gave it to a white fellow who owned the bar which I frequented.(p.493)

bulky
• Beer was too *bulky* and it couldn't be kept in a jug under the counter ready to be dumped when John Law came around.(p.233)

bull
• One morning he took the *bull* by the horns and set out to tell those he feared what his trouble had been.(p.156)

bulldog
• One of our gifts from the family was a very lovely Bible, but we'd let the *bulldog* chew it because we weren't too interested in it.(p.268)

bum
• Then he came into town on the *bum*.(p.263)

bumbling
• Moreover, I am deeply convinced that so long as I continue to strive, in my *bumbling* way, toward the principles I first encountered in the earlier chapters of this book, this remarkable power will continue to flow through me.(p.437)

bums
• The bill collectors, the sheriffs, the angry taxi drivers, the policemen, the *bums*, the pals, and even the ladies they sometimes brought home -- our husbands thought we were so inhospitable.(p.106)
• I went to a meeting to see for myself this group of freaks or *bums* who had done this thing.(p.228)
• I was sure I wouldn't belong in an A.A. group -- they were all old men, I thought, and all skid-row *bums*.(p.319)

bunch
• That is, it was sort of a mixed *bunch* of Oxford Groupers, who were interested in the alcoholic problem, and of alcoholics themselves.(p.218)
• He introduced himself and began to tell me about a *bunch* of some sixty former drinkers and drunkards who met once a week, and he invited me to go with him to the next meeting.(p.257)
• But they are the craziest *bunch*!(p.266)
• To go north into the empty pine country and shoot myself, or to go south in the faint hope that a *bunch* of strangers might help me with my drinking problem.(p.278)
• I had met a *bunch* of gay young Bohemians who lived in the Village, and were sowing their wild oats.(p.407)
• So the doctor said, "I really don't know too much about it, but they tell me it is a *bunch* of drunks who get together . . ."(p.469)
• My husband interrupted, "She's bad enough now without getting mixed up with a *bunch* of drunks."(p.469)

bungalows
• Many retirees embrace alcoholism while secluded in motor trailers, rest homes, leisure-world *bungalows*, mountain cabins, or beach cottages, or even in penthouses, on yachts, and inside Palm Springs cabanas.(p.329)
• India lent itself to drinking then, if you were disposed to drink, because you lived in *bungalows*; you didn't live all together as you do at home in an Officer's Mess.(p.519)

bunk
• But somewhere during that time, I remembered going back on the *bunk* and crying my eyes out.(p.390)

burden
• Often you must carry the *burden* of avoiding them or keeping them under control.(p.117)
• But those of us who have tried to shoulder the entire *burden* and trouble of others find we are soon overcome by them.(p.132)
• And this, as I said, certainly gave me a lot of confidence, seemed to take a lot of the *burden* off me.(p.190)
• Sometimes during that year I rebelled inwardly at what seemed like lost time, and at having to be a *burden* to these good people whose means were limited.(p.281)
• I'd get so fed up with drinking all alone and bearing the *burden* of guilt all by myself, that I'd egg him on to drink, to get started again.(p.325)

burdened
• I wasn't *burdened* with parental guidance and I didn't want any.(p.424)

burdening
• I had thrown off a big lie that had been *burdening* me down for months.(p.366)

burdens
• Whatever it was, it brushed all the heavy *burdens* off my back.(p.334)
• No one individual can carry all the *burdens* of the world.(p.382)
• And having sung that phrase, I'd chuckle with amusement, turning into irony turning into self-contempt turning into self-pity, at the sad fate of Bob, that wonderful, poor little motherless boy who was so smart in school and who grew up to accept responsibility so early and so fast and who staggered under his *burdens* without a whimper until the time came when he thought he was too good for this world and so he ought to be out of it.(p.532)
• We cast off the *burdens* of the past and the anxieties of the future, as we begin to live in the present, one day at a time.(p.560)

bureau
• One day I went to Washington to present some accounting evidence to a government *bureau*.(p.40)
• I checked into my hotel room and then noticed a placard tucked under the glass on the *bureau* stating "There will be positively NO drinking at this convention" signed by the president of the company.(p.243)
• I stayed so sober that I used to keep a quart of medicinal whiskey in my *bureau* which I used to taper off the occasional newspaper alcoholics who were sent to see me.(p.253)

burgundy
• Tasting the best of *burgundy* at a famous restaurant one night, landed me passed out on a park bench in the public square.(p.405)

buried
• (Russ was *buried* on Friday, and on Sunday afternoon Hilda S. had invited me there to dinner Sunday night, and I didn't think I could do it.(p.272)

burlesque
• I rounded up a few more of my friends and off we went to the meeting, not for anything we would gain from it as much as to make a *burlesque* out of it.(p.509)

burn
• The alcoholic may say to himself in the most casual way, "It won't *burn* me this time, so here's how!"(p.24)
• A drunk may smash the furniture in your home, or *burn* a mattress.(p.97)
• *Burn* the idea into the consciousness of every man that he can get well regardless of anyone.(p.98)

burned
• We were "*burned* up."(p.65)
• Now about health: A body badly *burned* by alcohol does not often recover overnight nor do twisted thinking and depression vanish in a twinkling.(p.133)

burning
• We do not tire so easily, for we are not *burning* up energy foolishly as we did when we were trying to arrange life to suit ourselves.(p.88)
• She sees she was wrong to make a *burning* issue out of such a matter when his more serious ailments were being rapidly cured.(p.135)

burnings
• The wars which had been fought, the *burnings* and chicanery that religious dispute had facilitated, made me sick.(p.11)

burnt
• I'd hear them on the phone having prayer meetings and so forth, that sort of talk over the phone, and it completely *burnt* me up.(p.265)
• And we went down through the valley, and I remembered reading about the Ku Klux Klan and how they *burnt* crosses, and I thought, "God alone knows what we are getting into this time!"(p.269)

burst
• Then came the night when the physical and mental torture was so hellish I feared I would *burst* through my window, sash and all.(p.6)
• The real significance of my experience in the Cathedral *burst* upon me.(p.12)
• Outsiders are sometimes shocked when we *burst* into merriment over a seemingly tragic experience out of the past.(p.132)
• At this both the visitors *burst* into a laugh.(p.157)
• Finally, out of his hope, there *burst* conviction.(p.189)
• At age twenty-one, I enlisted in the Navy for two reasons: (1) to avoid being drafted into the Army, and (2) out of a *burst* of patriotic fervor inspired by the advent of World War II and as the result of an all-night drinking binge which found me sitting on the doorstep of the Navy recruiting office when the chief petty officer arrived to open for business at nine o'clock Monday morning.(p.398)

bury
• The first impulse will be to *bury* these skeletons in a dark closet and padlock the door.(p.123)

bus
• He walked to the hospital to save *bus* fare and did it gladly in order to be helpful to an individual he had never even seen.(p.208)
• A friend who knew I would soon be broke mounted guard over me when I left my job of writing the histories of Texas cities and put me aboard a *bus* for the town I had left almost five years before.(p.256)
• There was more than one occasion when I got up in the morning with just enough money for coffee and toast and the *bus* fare to carry me to my first appointment.(p.283)

buses
• During the first three months I carried on all these activities without a car, depending entirely on *buses* and streetcars -- I, who had always to have a car at my immediate command.(p.283)

business
• Being mostly *business* or professional folk, we could not well carry on our occupations in such an event.(p.xiii)
• The broker had gone to Akron on a *business* venture which had collapsed, leaving him greatly in fear that he might start drinking again.(p.xvi)
• I have had many men who had, for example, worked a period of months on some problem or *business* deal which was to be settled on a certain date, favorable to them.(p.xxvii)
• I studied economics and *business* as well as law.(p.2)
• *Business* and financial leaders were my heroes.(p.2)
• Then I got a promising *business* opportunity.(p.5)
• Before then, I had written lots of sweet promises, but my wife happily observed that this time I meant *business*.(p.5)
• It was fortunate, for my old *business* associates remained skeptical for a year and a half, during which I found little work.(p.15)
• *Business* and professional men have regained their standing.(p.15)
• A certain American *business* man had ability, good sense, and high character.(p.26)
• Here are some of the methods we have tried: Drinking beer only, limiting the number of drinks, never drinking alone, never drinking in the morning, drinking only at home, never having it in the house, never drinking during *business* hours, drinking only at parties, switching from scotch to brandy, drinking only natural wines, agreeing to resign if ever drunk on the job, taking a trip, not taking a trip, swearing off forever (with and without a solemn oath), taking more physical exercise, reading inspirational books, going to health farms and sanitariums, accepting voluntary commitment to asylums -- we could increase the list ad infinitum.(p.31)
• He was ambitious to succeed in *business*, but saw that he would get nowhere if he drank at all.(p.32)
• He made up his mind that until he had been successful in *business* and had retired, he would not touch another drop.(p.32)
• An exceptional man, he remained bone dry for twenty-five years and retired at the age of fifty-five, after a successful and happy *business* career.(p.32)
• His family was re-assembled, and he began to work as a salesman for the *business* he had lost through drinking.(p.35)
• If ever there was a successful *business* man, it is Fred.(p.39)
• "In this frame of mind, I went about my *business* and for a time all was well.(p.40)
• My *business* came off well, I was pleased and knew my partners would be too.(p.41)
• *Business* failure, insanity, fatal illness, suicide -- these calamities in his immediate family embittered and depressed him.(p.56)
• He is like the retired *business* man who lolls in the Florida sunshine in the winter complaining of the sad state of the nation; the minister who sighs over the sins of the twentieth century; politicians and reformers who are sure all would be Utopia if the rest of the world would only behave; the outlaw safe cracker who thinks society has wronged him; and the alcoholic who has lost all and is locked up.(p.61)

• A *business* which takes no regular inventory usually goes broke.(p.64)
• If the owner of the *business* is to be successful, he cannot fool himself about values.(p.64)
• But with the alcoholic, whose hope is the maintenance and growth of a spiritual experience, this *business* of resentment is infinitely grave.(p.66)
• As we look over the list of *business* acquaintances and friends we have hurt, we may feel diffident about going to some of them on a spiritual basis.(p.76)
• While drinking, he accepted a sum of money from a bitterly-hated *business* rival, giving him no receipt for it.(p.80)
• It may mean the loss of many nights' sleep, great interference with your pleasures, interruptions to your *business*.(p.97)
• Therefore, ask yourself on each occasion, "Have I any good social, *business*, or personal reason for going to this place?(p.101)
• If it is a happy occasion, try to increase the pleasure of those there; if a *business* occasion, go and attend to your *business* enthusiastically.(p.102)
• He is positive he can handle his liquor, that it does him no harm, that drinking is necessary in his *business*.(p.109)
• His *business* may suffer somewhat.(p.109)
• Perhaps he can still tend to *business* fairly well.(p.109)
• If he is already committed to an institution, but can convince you and your doctor that he means *business*, give him a chance to try our method, unless the doctor thinks his mental condition too abnormal or dangerous.(p.114)
• But the head of the house has spent years in pulling down the structures of *business*, romance, friendship, health -- these things are now ruined or damaged.(p.123)
• He may either plunge into a frantic attempt to get on his feet in *business*, or he may be so enthralled by his new life that he talks or thinks of little else.(p.125)
• Though some of his manifestations are alarming and disagreeable, we think dad will be on a firmer foundation than the man who is placing *business* or professional success ahead of spiritual development.(p.129)
• Among many employers nowadays, we think of one member who has spent much of his life in the world of big *business*.(p.136)
• His present views ought to prove exceptionally useful to *business* men everywhere.(p.136)
• My downfall cost the *business* community unknown thousands of dollars, for it takes real money to train a man for an executive position.(p.137)
• We think the *business* fabric is shot through with a situation which might be helped by better understanding all around.(p.137)
• Of an evening, you can go on a mild bender, get up in the morning, shake your head and go to *business*.(p.139)
• If your decision is yes, whether the reason be humanitarian or *business* or both, then the following suggestions may be helpful.(p.140)
• You, as a *business* man, want to know the necessities before considering the result.(p.140)
• He wants to quit drinking and you want to help him, even if it be only a matter of good *business*.(p.141)
• We all had to place recovery above everything, for without recovery we would have lost both home and *business*.(p.143)
• Can he talk frankly with you so long as he does not bear *business* tales or criticize his associates?(p.145)
• Wherever men are gathered together in *business* there will be rivalries and, arising out of these, a certain amount of office politics.(p.145)
• He may wish to do a lot for other alcoholics and something of the sort may come up during *business* hours.(p.146)
• If he is conscientiously following the program of recovery he can go anywhere your *business* may call him.(p.147)
• If you are sure he doesn't mean *business*, there is no doubt you should discharge him.(p.147)
• There is a real interest, both humanitarian and *business*, in the well-being of employees.(p.149)
• We, who have collectively seen a great deal of *business* life, at least from the alcoholic angle, had to smile at this gentleman's sincere opinion.(p.149)
• From a *business* standpoint, his trip came off badly.(p.153)
• Why, he argued, should he lose the remainder of his *business*, only to bring still more suffering to his family by foolishly admitting his plight to people from whom he made his livelihood?(p.155)
• He trembled as he went about, for this might mean ruin, particularly to a person in his line of *business*.(p.156)
• I'm ready to do *business*.(p.159)
• No one is too discredited or has sunk too low to be welcomed cordially – if he means *business*.(p.161)
• There I took up the *business* of drinking with much greater earnestness than I had previously shown.(p.173)
• My home life is ideal and my *business* is as good as can be expected in these uncertain times.(p.180)
• It's none of our *business* about your drinking.(p.186)
• Of course, by this time, my *business* was practically non-existent.(p.190)
• I was married at the age of nineteen to a grand girl and had good *business* prospects.(p.194)
• At the end of this selling of lots, just prior to World War I, I got into the crude rubber *business*, and six months later there was only one broker and myself left in Akron.(p.197)
• I can remember occasions when friends recommended me for positions or *business* opportunities that I wouldn't take because I felt that at some future date I'd get drunk and they would be hurt.(p.198)
• On Sunday when I came to, it was a bad, wet, snowy day in February, 1937, and Paul and Doc and a lot of other fellows were in Cleveland on *business*.(p.207)
• The first definite indications of an alcoholic pattern began to arise when I would go to New York on *business* and disappear, and wind up in Philadelphia or Boston for two or three day periods.(p.213)
• I had my own *business*, successful enough for me to indulge most of my desires.(p.225)
• I have something to contribute to humanity, since I am peculiarly qualified, as a fellow-sufferer, to give aid and comfort to those who have stumbled and fallen over this *business* of meeting life.(p.229)
• I came of good stock, of men and women who drank wine all their lives as a beverage, and while they occasionally got drunk at special celebrations, they were up and about their *business* the next day.(p.231)
• But I hardly tasted anything for two years and started in *business* for myself, founding a mattress factory which is today an important industrial enterprise in our city.(p.232)
• I was doing well in *business*, and in going around town I was frequently invited to have a drink in a speakeasy.(p.233)
• I condoned my domestic brewing along with the bootleggers and their *business*.(p.233)
• More and more I formed the habit of doing some of my *business* in the speakeasy, and after a time I did not need that as an excuse.(p.233)
• I was eased out of the *business* I had founded and was reduced to doing general upholstery in a small shop at the back of my house.(p.233)
• My wife upbraided me often and plenty when she saw that my "periodics" were gradually losing me what *business* I could get.(p.233)
• My customers lost confidence in me to the point where I retained what *business* I had only because I was a well-trained and reputedly fine craftsman.(p.234)
• "Best in the *business*, when he's sober," my customers would say, and I still had a following who would give me work though they deplored my habits, because they knew the job would be well done when they eventually got it.(p.234)
• His own *business* was practically gone, he told me, when he discovered the answer.(p.236)
• Many things happened; *business* trials, little worries, and feelings of general despondency came near driving me to the bottle, but I made progress.(p.237)
• Haven't I been successful, haven't I accomplished extraordinary things in *business*?(p.245)
• We were all set to put DuPont out of *business*.(p.246)
• My job was to collect bets and betting-slips in the *business* section, a lucrative spot.(p.251)
• My boss, in his way, was "big *business*."(p.251)
• I thanked him, pleaded *business* engagements and promised I'd go with him at some future date.(p.257)
• There were *business* men, professional men, and factory workers.(p.258)
• There was a man watching, and I turned to him and said with a defiant air I carried with me all the time, "If I don't quit this I'm going to have to join that alcoholic *business* they're talking about."(p.266)
• I entered the *business* world with every confidence that success lay ahead of me.(p.275)
• In the spring of 1939, Bill stopped off in Akron on his way to Detroit on *business*.(p.281)
• With this specialized training, and a liberal *business* education in the school of hard knocks, I was able to set up shop some two years later as an independent accountant.(p.284)
• So much for my *business* life.(p.284)
• Obviously I have overcome fear to a sufficient degree to think in terms of success in *business*.(p.284)
• With God's help I am able, for one day at a time, to carry *business* responsibilities which, not many years ago, I would not have dreamed of assuming.(p.284)
• Here was something requiring a greater willingness to assume responsibility, and take a larger degree of cooperation and "give and take" than even *business* requires of one.(p.286)
• At that time, I was living out of town, so I moved back to the home town and made a connection in a responsible position with one of the larger companies in the finance *business*.(p.298)
• Up to this point I had spent six years in the *business* and had enjoyed the reputation of being very successful.(p.298)
• After being fired, I lined up with a new finance company that was just starting in *business*, and took the position of *business* promotion man, contacting automobile dealers.(p.300)
• I really worked for several weeks, and having had a fairly wide acquaintance with the dealer trade, it was not difficult for me to line up enough of them to give me a very substantial volume of *business* with a minimum of effort.(p.300)
• By this time, my chances of getting lined up in my chosen *business* were shot.(p.301)
• Finally, an old *business* acquaintance of mine, whom I hadn't seen for several years offered me a job.(p.301)
• Seldom had any of these lost either health, *business*, family, or friends.(p.315)
• I had been far too busy building, protecting, and maintaining an image of respectability and all the other *business* pluses.(p.327)
• Every breadwinner, whether trying to impress a boss or to hold customers in his own *business*, is fettered by people-pleasing.(p.329)
• No more *business* pressures.(p.329)
• So when the children were in school from nine to three, I started up a nice little *business* and was fairly successful in it.(p.339)
• We've got to turn the whole *business* over to some joker we can't even see!(p.350)
• Here he is powerless, unmanageable, in the grip of something bigger than he is, and he's got to turn the whole *business* over to someone else!(p.350)
• By this time I had become associated with the fast growing and fascinating *business* of broadcasting.(p.358)
• It was also my job to entertain the owners of these stations when they came East on *business* -- or the pretense of *business*.(p.359)
• One of the things I needed badly was *business* for the station.(p.360)
• I got around this by joining the local Rotary Club, and through this association with the *business* men of the community my little station began to grow.(p.360)
• My *business* reputation had reached from Vermont to Pennsylvania, but, thank goodness, my drinking reputation had not.(p.361)
• As my father climbed the ladder of success in the oil-field *business*, his drinking also climbed.(p.369)
• As I later found out through Alcoholics Anonymous, alcohol is no respecter of economic status, social and *business* standing or intelligence.(p.373)
• After that came marriage, getting started in *business*, and a family.(p.373)
• I will never know all the people I hurt, all the friends I abused, the humiliation of my family, the worry of my *business* associates, or how far reaching it was.(p.376)
• I liked the description of the alcoholic as a person who had found that alcohol is interfering with his social or *business* life.(p.380)
• Above all, I am grateful to A.A. for my sobriety, which means so much to my family, friends and *business* associates, because God and A.A. were able to do for me something I was unable to do for myself.(p.383)
• The questions he asked me that I didn't answer honestly, I thought were none of his *business*.(p.388)
• At age twenty-one, I enlisted in the Navy for two reasons: (1) to avoid being drafted into the Army, and (2) out of a burst of patriotic fervor inspired by the advent of World War II and as the result of an all-night drinking binge which found me sitting on the doorstep of the Navy recruiting office when the chief petty officer arrived to open for *business* at nine o'clock Monday morning.(p.398)
• What we do with it is our own *business*; how we

use it is up to us individually.(p.473)
• Father, through the years, had built up a very good mail order ***business*** because, at that time, there wasn't too much money in medicine.(p.485)
• During the years 1930 to 1935, due to the Depression and its aftermath, ***business*** went from bad to worse.(p.486)
• I had my own medical practice in Washington at that time, but the practice slackened and the mail order ***business*** started to fall off.(p.486)
• I got to the place where I'd look forward to the week-end's drinking and pacify myself by saying that the week-ends were mine, that it didn't interfere with my family or with my ***business*** if I drank on the week-ends.(p.488)
• She asked me if I would let someone come up and talk to me concerning a ***business*** deal.(p.494)
• The day is over and ***business*** has been not so good.(p.500)
• She really meant ***business*** this time.(p.523)
• I, a man of steel, with very high ideals, well brought up, an honor student and the recipient of scholarships and prizes, a boy wonder in ***business*** – I, Bob, the author of this essay, looked and saw that the universe was beneath my contempt, and that to remove myself from it was the only thing of dignity a man could do.(p.531)
• And it was nobody's ***business***, nobody's but mine.(p.532)
• When I was faced with a special challenge or social event -- such as an important ***business*** presentation or a dinner party – I had to fortify myself with a couple of belts.(p.556)
• An A.A. group, as such, should never go into ***business***.(p.566)

business-getters
• The third man who came to see me had been one of the greatest ***business-getters*** his company had ever employed.(p.235)

businessman
• In late 1934 I attended a patient who, though he had been a competent ***businessman*** of good earning capacity, was an alcoholic of a type I had come to regard as hopeless.(p.xxiii)

businessmen
• ***Businessmen***, traveling out of existing groups, were referred to these prospective newcomers.(p.xviii)

busload
• A ***busload*** of basketball players had been passing and saw the flames.(p.424)

bust
• The only answer I could make was that if the man followed the usual pattern, he would go on a bigger ***bust*** than ever.(p.138)

Buster
• I got two drinks, each of them a quarter of that pint, in me, and was talking along with these people, but I felt that sooner or later they were going to have me cornered because they were smarter than I was and the drink was beginning to take effect; but as I reached for the third drink Bob said, "Listen, ***Buster***, you promised to take some medicine if we got you a drink.(p.206)

busts
• I also began to drink at fraternity parties and beer ***busts***.(p.555)

busy
• During these two years I was kept so ***busy*** that I hardly left the hospital at all.(p.174)
• Two days before this, Dr. Bob had said to me, "If you and I are going to stay sober, we had better get ***busy***."(p.188)
• I kept myself so ***busy*** that outside of some school and group parties, I didn't go overboard on drinking very much between the ages of twenty-five and thirty.(p.213)
• And, because as I have discovered since, it is part of the "treatment" that these men be sent to see and talk with alcoholics who want to quit, he kept them ***busy***.(p.235)
• After the book appeared we all became very ***busy*** in our efforts to save all and sundry, but I was still actually on the fringes of A.A.(p.248)
• I had been far too ***busy*** building, protecting, and maintaining an image of respectability and all the other business pluses.(p.327)
• Creativity at the typewriter would keep me ***busy*** and alert, I said.(p.331)
• My work kept me ***busy*** the first few months on the new job.(p.360)
• "Keep ***busy***; always have something constructive to do."(p.373)
• The drive to get ahead, to succeed, kept me too ***busy*** for many years to have any great experience with social life.(p.374)
• I was too ***busy*** devising excuses to be out with drinking pals.(p.376)
• I was so ***busy*** keeping her out of trouble, and so scared she'd swing on me, that I had my last two drinks that night.(p.415)
• Following an injection I would have to keep one hand ***busy*** scratching my constantly itching nose and would also have sudden uncontrollable urges to vomit.(p.442)
• I started prowling around with a couple of these A.A. boys, which kept me pretty ***busy*** and kept my mind off of down town.(p.511)

butcher
• At one end of the table sat our community ***butcher***.(p.347)
• I recall, as I walked into that meeting, saying to myself, "Here I am, a fellow of the American College of Surgeons, a Fellow of the International College of Surgeons, a diplomate of one of the great specialty boards in these United States, a member of the American Psychiatric Society, and I have to go to the ***butcher***, the baker and the carpenter to help make a man out of me!"(p.347)
• I went to Clark, the community ***butcher***, and I said, "Clark, what is the matter with me?(p.348)
• I tried every gimmick that there was to get some peace of mind, but it was not until I was brought to my alcoholic knees, when I was brought to a group in my own community with the ***butcher***, the baker, the carpenter and the mechanic, who were able to give me the Twelve Steps, that I was finally given some semblance of an answer to the last half of the First Step.(p.349)

butlers
• A house in Virginia, during the fox hunting season; a little chalet in Switzerland during the summer or a place on Long Island – each house complete with cooks, ***butlers*** and maids.(p.403)

butting
• As I grow in A.A., I realize that a person with as much self-will as I had, as hard a head and as diseased an ego, had to try everything that I could think of, ***butting*** my head against every stone wall before I was ready to come in.(p.384)

buttonholed
• I ***buttonholed*** him after dinner and gave him a few tips on how to run his colony better and the result of that was about a fortnight or so later I was shipped back to my regiment.(p.520)

buy
• Stocks were at the low point of 1932, and I had somehow formed a group to ***buy***.(p.5)
• Every means of solving his problem which money could ***buy*** was at his disposal.(p.32)
• I knew everyone would ***buy*** a few bottles, or cases, of liquor as their exchequers permitted, and that it would soon be gone.(p.175)
• When he was uptown – we were living in the little town of Moscow – I went up to try to get some money from him to ***buy*** groceries.(p.193)
• He wouldn't give me any money for the groceries, but he did take me across the street and ***buy*** me a bag of candy, which I later took back and traded for a loaf of bread.(p.193)
• I felt having gotten married, I was an adult and one of the first things I did was to ***buy*** two cases of whiskey with no idea of drinking it.(p.196)
• My idea was to have all the companies pool their funds and ***buy*** rubber when rubber was cheap and then put it in a pool.(p.198)
• When rubber reached a certain low point, they would draw on the rubber out of the pool and ***buy***.(p.198)
• I'll ***buy*** you one drink, and if you suggest a second one, I'll poke you right in the nose."(p.201)
• Following a big drunk on that sheet, where I was doing leg-work and rewrite, a feeling of nostalgia made me ***buy*** a ticket for Liverpool and I returned to Britain.(p.252)
• Now on a new job I was always thinking about payday and how much liquor I could ***buy*** and the pleasure I could have.(p.255)
• We always tried to ***buy*** him a drink, and he always told us he had liquor trouble -- couldn't drink.)(p.266)
• A year later I was able to ***buy*** a Model T roadster and take a better job with a downtown printer.(p.276)
• By the time we reached the bar, he was willing to ***buy*** me a quart with his own money.(p.288)
• I couldn't go to one wine store and look the man honestly in the face and ***buy*** a bottle, as I used to do when I had parties and entertained and did normal drinking.(p.336)
• Near the Laundromat, I would ***buy*** one bottle of pop and a few bottles of beer or wine, and go into the rest room, empty the pop bottle, refill it with the booze, and proceed to do my laundering.(p.370)
• Cops now sick of me, so they ***buy*** me one-way ticket to Canada.(p.475)
• They say call friend before I ***buy*** drink.(p.476)
• We are so beautiful that it is never too much trouble to get some poor stranger to ***buy*** us a drink.(p.479)
• At that time the repeal whiskies were back, and I'd go to the store and ***buy*** my whiskey and take it to my office and put it under the desk, first in one place and then in another, and there soon was an accumulation of empty bottles.(p.488)
• I took the last to ***buy*** my railroad ticket.(p.493)
• Thinking only of two or three dollars to ***buy*** some whiskey, I did the job and that's how I met Ella G., who was responsible for my coming into A.A.(p.493)
• We ***buy*** a gallon of "corn" because it is so cheap.(p.500)
• I would never admit that I was drinking too much, or spending money that I should have used to ***buy*** food for my two little boys.(p.526)

buying
• This was fine, but it was just an extra dividend, for I'd made connections by this time and was ***buying*** a bottle a day from the cook.(p.426)
• I'm ***buying*** my home.(p.431)

by-gones
• It may be that both will decide that the way of good sense and loving kindness is to let ***by-gones*** be ***by-gones***.(p.82)

by-paths
• There will be alluring shortcuts and ***by-paths*** down which they may wander and lose their way.(p.123)

by-product
• Now, for me, and to my satisfaction, I know the purpose of life: The purpose of life is to create and the ***by-product*** is happiness.(p.535)

Cc

cab
• He said, "Well, why don't you take a ***cab***?"(p.204)
• I said, "All right, call me a ***cab***," as though I was talking to a bell boy.(p.204)
• He did call me a ***cab*** and when I got into the ***cab***, I said, "Drive me to a liquor store."(p.204)
• It was February with snow and ice on the ground and I had a four blocks walk to the nearest ***cab*** stand, but I made it.(p.288)
• I suspect that those bartenders would wait until I shot my wad, then call a ***cab*** and send me home.(p.410)

cabanas
• Many retirees embrace alcoholism while secluded in motor trailers, rest homes, leisure-world bungalows, mountain cabins, or beach cottages, or even in penthouses, on yachts, and inside Palm Springs ***cabanas***.(p.329)

cabinet
• Again I swayed dizzily before an open window, or the medicine ***cabinet*** where there was poison, cursing myself for a weakling.(p.6)

cabins
• Many retirees embrace alcoholism while secluded in motor trailers, rest homes, leisure-world bungalows, mountain ***cabins***, or beach cottages, or even in penthouses, on yachts, and inside Palm Springs cabanas.(p.329)

cache
• I was gathering that ***cache*** for disposal when my wife woke up and caught me at it.(p.333)

cadet
• I remember in my first year in high school, that mother suggested that I do not join the ***cadet*** unit.(p.484)

cafe
• One day I walked into a ***cafe*** to telephone.(p.6)

cagey
• I was being very ***cagey***, because I knew that if I did take one or two, I might want to take five or six or seven or eight.(p.323)

cajoling
• However, my two friends kept coaxing and ***cajoling*** to get me back again.(p.510)

cake
• So he got me a cup of coffee, and a piece of ***cake***, and sat me down and said, "Why, there's nothing wrong with you.(p.348)
• One night at the dinner table my wife said that tonight was my first birthday in A.A., and that the group would have the usual ice cream and ***cake*** for the "one year man."(p.365)
• I had no trouble making the right decision when I saw my wife open her purse at the meeting that night and deposit a cute little angel in the middle of my birthday ***cake***.(p.366)

cakes
• Father says grace, which delays my attack on the buckwheat ***cakes*** and sausage.(p.497)

calamities
• Business failure, insanity, fatal illness, suicide -- these ***calamities*** in his immediate family embittered and depressed him.(p.56)

calamitous
• A little more than fifteen years ago, through a long and ***calamitous*** series of shattering experiences, I found myself being helplessly propelled toward total destruction.(p.304)

calamity
• My brain raced uncontrollably and there was a terrible sense of impending ***calamity***.(p.6)
• We looked upon this world of warring individuals, warring theological systems, and inexplicable ***calamity***, with deep skepticism.(p.46)
• It may be obscured by ***calamity***, by pomp, by worship of other things, but in some form or other it is there.(p.55)
• Just to the extent that we do as we think He would have us, and humbly rely on Him, does He enable us to match ***calamity*** with serenity.(p.68)
• Time after time, this apparent ***calamity*** has been a boon to us, for it opened up a path which led to the discovery of God.(p.116)
• However, I threw myself into Twelve Step work, and what I feared would be a ***calamity*** turned out to be the most blessed of blessings.(p.394)
• What is much more important to me, A.A. has taught me that through this simple program I may experience a change in this reaction pattern that will indeed allow me to "match ***calamity*** with serenity."(p.544)

calculate
• After all, upon coming out of a week-long or ten-day drunk, it was hard enough to figure up just how much that one drunk cost, let alone trying to ***calculate*** the cost of approximately twenty-five years of active alcoholism.(p.396)
• Only God as we understand Him can ***calculate*** these.(p.399)

calculated
• And I think we ***calculated***, or I did, that there wasn't anybody who knew that I wasn't drinking.(p.202)

calculating
• *CALCULATING* THE COSTS(p.396)

calculation
• And then my thinking became ***calculation*** as to how much longer I had to live, how long the assets would last.(p.215)
• With cold ***calculation*** I set about to marry a fortune, and I did.(p.545)

calculations
• So please accept these humble ***calculations*** as, if anything, an underestimation.(p.396)

caldron
• This immediately precipitates us into a seething ***caldron*** of debate.(p.xxviii)

California
• I left ***California*** and came back to my native state.(p.460)

call
• I was soon to be catapulted into what I like to ***call*** the fourth dimension of existence.(p.8)
• Our first example is a friend we shall ***call*** Jim.(p.35)
• Whatever the precise definition of the word may be, we ***call*** this plain insanity.(p.37)
• Our actor is self-centered -- ego-centric, as people like to ***call*** it nowadays.(p.61)
• ***Call*** on him while he is still jittery.(p.91)
• Admit that he probably knows more about it than you do, but ***call*** to his attention the fact that however deep his faith and knowledge, he could not have applied it or he would not drink.(p.93)
• You should not be offended if he wants to ***call*** it off, for he has helped you more than you have helped him.(p.94)
• Sometimes you will have to ***call*** a doctor and administer sedatives under his direction.(p.97)
• If he is conscientiously following the program of recovery he can go anywhere your business may ***call*** him.(p.147)
• His ***call*** to the clergyman led him presently to a certain resident of the town, who, though formerly able and respected, was then nearing the nadir of alcoholic despair.(p.155)
• Wishing to be polite, though I felt very badly, I said, "Let's make the ***call***," and extracted from my wife a promise that we would not stay over fifteen minutes.(p.179)
• I said, "All right, ***call*** me a cab," as though I was talking to a bell boy.(p.204)
• He did ***call*** me a cab and when I got into the cab, I said, "Drive me to a liquor store."(p.204)
• He said, "No, ***call*** the nurse."(p.208)
• I had had no hospitalization up to this time because I would not ***call*** doctors when I was getting over a bad one.(p.217)
• I had not asked for help and seriously doubt that I would have, but Fitz, an old school friend of mine, had persuaded Jackie to ***call*** on me.(p.238)
• The lesson of his death still remains with me, yet I often wonder what would have happened if somebody else had made that first ***call*** on me.(p.239)
• However, I made an SOS ***call*** to the New York Group, whom I hadn't met yet, and they suggested we both come there.(p.245)
• In June, 1945, with another member, I made my first -- and only -- Twelfth Step ***call*** on a female alcoholic and a year later I married her.(p.249)
• I was scared to death to ***call*** a doctor.(p.267)
• I believe the sociologists would ***call*** it "upper middle class."(p.275)
• While there, two or three more "cash customers" (as Dr. Bob used to ***call*** them -- probably because they had so little cash) were shipped in to us from Detroit.(p.282)
• That ***call*** marked the turning point in my life.(p.307)
• Perhaps I could find freedom and peace and be able once again to ***call*** my soul my own.(p.309)
• Nothing in their lives took precedence over their response to a ***call*** for help from some alcoholic in need.(p.310)
• When I came home from Nam, I met a girl I'll ***call*** Karen.(p.318)
• But I met a real wonderful girl I'll ***call*** Jean.(p.318)
• She took me by the hand and introduced me to the girl that I'm very proud to ***call*** my sponsor.(p.321)
• When I'm asked to go out on a ***call***, I go.(p.340)
• And I gave him some idea of what you do, and so I made my first Twelfth Step ***call*** before I ever came into the program.(p.347)
• I was told that someone would ***call*** on me shortly, to sit tight and not take another drink.(p.363)
• A lucky break, at least some will ***call*** it lucky, was in store for me at my group that night.(p.365)
• I haven't written anything about that part of my story, but I believe in a Greater Power which I ***call*** God and I ask for His wisdom and guidance daily.(p.366)
• You will recall that I said the time that I got the idea out of a clear sky to ***call*** A.A. on a certain night was at about ten.(p.366)
• The time for decision had arrived, and it was a relief to say "Yes" when my family said they would ***call*** Alcoholics Anonymous for me.(p.378)
• That Power I chose to ***call*** God.(p.381)
• The only thing that I could do would be to ***call*** the doctor to help sober me up.(p.389)
• There was no one I could ***call***.(p.392)
• I stayed drunk from Monday until Friday, and I ***call*** that my spill into A.A.(p.393)
• I suspect that those bartenders would wait until I shot my wad, then ***call*** a cab and send me home.(p.410)
• Luckily a friend was with me, who dragged me out, screaming and cursing, while the bartender threatened to ***call*** the police.(p.411)
• I thought, "If this is A.A. why not go back to drinking, kill myself with booze in the next three years the doctor had given me, and ***call*** it a bad job?"(p.430)
• I didn't know whether I had told him to rush to the hospital and I'd meet him there, or to take two aspirin and ***call*** me in the morning.(p.441)
• Cops say for me to ***call*** them, they get me out.(p.475)
• Next two years, I ***call*** them many times.(p.475)
• They say ***call*** friend before I buy drink.(p.476)
• ***Call*** friend in A.A. when bad thoughts come.(p.477)
• The grand fellow who at my ***call*** made me a hail-fellow-well-met, who gave me such a fine voice, as we sang "Hail, hail, the gang's all here," and "Sweet Adeline," who gave me freedom from fear and feelings of inferiority.(p.498)
• I ***call*** the bootlegger and fill up my charred keg.(p.501)
• Then he asks me if I believe in a power greater than myself, whether I ***call*** that power God, Allah, Confucius, Prime Cause, Divine Mind, or any other name.(p.503)
• I ***call*** my wife into a room where we can talk privately.(p.506)
• If something does come along that sort of upsets me, instead of walking in and throwing a buck at the barman and asking for a drink, I walk into a telephone booth, drop a dime in the box, and ***call*** somebody who was so kind as to give me his name and telephone number to meet such an emergency.(p.511)
• I suppose I had reached my spiritual gutter that night, but I have never had what you could ***call*** a real urge to drink again.(p.524)
• Any two or three alcoholics gathered together for sobriety may ***call*** themselves an A.A. group, provided that, as a group, they have no other affiliation.(p.565)
• Our more religious members ***call*** it "God-consciousness."(p.570)

called
• The section ***called*** "The Doctor's Opinion" has been

kept intact, just as it was originally written in 1939 by the late Dr. William D. Silkworth, our Society's great medical benefactor.(p.xi)
• The fledgling society, which had been nameless, now began to be *called* Alcoholics Anonymous, from the title of its own book.(p.xvii)
• In the fall of 1939, Fulton Oursler, then editor of Liberty, printed a piece in his magazine, *called* "Alcoholics and God."(p.xviii)
• The Twelve Steps that summarize the program may be *called* los Doce Pasos in one country, los Douze Etapes in another, but they trace exactly the same path to recovery that was blazed by the earliest members of Alcoholics Anonymous.(p.xxii)
• One year later he *called* to see me, and I experienced a very strange sensation.(p.xxix)
• His alcoholic problem was so complex, and his depression so great, that we felt his only hope would be through what we then *called* "moral psychology," and we doubted if even that would have any effect.(p.xxix)
• For a moment I was alarmed, and *called* my friend, the doctor, to ask if I were still sane.(p.14)
• Here and there, once in a while, alcoholics have had what are *called* vital spiritual experiences.(p.27)
• Certain drinkers, who would be greatly insulted if *called* alcoholics, are astonished at their inability to stop.(p.33)
• How can such a lack of proportion, of the ability to think straight, be *called* anything else?(p.37)
• In the prize ring, this would be *called* leading with the chin.(p.77)
• He would probably be insulted if he were *called* an alcoholic.(p.109)
• Maybe the doctor has been *called* in, and the weary round of sanitariums and hospitals has begun.(p.110)
• Not long afterward he had *called* me from Hartford on two successive days, so drunk he could hardly speak.(p.136)
• One day they *called* up the head nurse of a local hospital.(p.156)
• Many mornings I have gone to classes, and even though fully prepared, would turn and walk back to the fraternity house because of my jitters, not daring to enter the classroom for fear of making a scene should I be *called* on for recitation.(p.173)
• About this time a lady *called* up my wife one Saturday afternoon, saying she wanted me to come over that evening to meet a friend of hers who might help me.(p.179)
• The next day she *called* again.(p.179)
• At the time, I *called* it patriotism.(p.183)
• Straightway, Bob *called* Akron's City Hospital and asked for the nurse on the receiving ward.(p.188)
• They *called* a doctor and it happened that they *called* one I knew.(p.205)
• The next day, they *called* me in for an examination, and the doctor wouldn't let me continue working and pardoned me from the plant for ten days because he said my eye had been injured.(p.205)
• My wife didn't tell me this, but one Sunday afternoon when Mary was trying to get the cobwebs out of my mind, Clarence and his sister-in-law, the hairdresser, *called* at the house.(p.216)
• At our weekly meeting I was a menace to serenity those first few months, for I took every opportunity to lambaste the "spiritual angle" as we *called* it, or anything else that had any tinge of theology.(p.246)
• While there I was *called* to the hospital in my home town to see a former partner who had insisted that I visit him.(p.257)
• They *called* the Mayor in so we wouldn't have to stay in there over the holiday.(p.264)
• Paul S. had just *called* me, and I remember he stressed reading the Big Book.(p.269)
• I hadn't been in too long when one of the men's wives *called* me one Sunday and told me she didn't think I had any part of the program.(p.273)
• I didn't think I was going to get drunk right then, but I remember how comforting it was when I *called* Anne and told her.(p.273)
• That same year, my wife became fed up with my drinking around the house and *called* my dad in Akron to come and pick me up.(p.288)
• Once dad came all the way to Florida to sober me up, after a hotel manager *called* him and said that if he wanted to see me alive he better get there fast.(p.288)
• He sent to New York for a copy, and after reading it he tucked it under his arm and *called* on me.(p.307)
• I *called* her every night from a local bar, and often she was not at home.(p.318)
• I *called* my husband up and told him to come home.(p.338)
• About two days later I was *called* by a friend of mine from Nevada City – he's a brother of my wife's closest friend.(p.347)
• Out of sheer despair, she *called* for help.(p.353)
• Thank God I knew of A.A., so I *called*.(p.355)
• My salesmanship was still good, for in the fall of 1938 she *called* me from Salt Lake and finally agreed to take me on for better or for worse.(p.360)
• I attended my weekly meetings with regularity, reread the Big Book, attended other group meetings, gave leads when asked to and did some Twelve Step work whenever I was *called* upon to do so.(p.365)
• When I was *called* upon for a few words I had to tell my friends that I wasn't one year old in A.A. that evening but only a "nine month baby."(p.366)
• She said she cut this clipping from the paper at about ten on the same night, and at the same time as I *called* A.A. in Pittsburgh -- some 1300 miles away.(p.367)
• In a few days an attorney *called* on me and explained that something would have to be done as she couldn't face returning to me as I was.(p.377)
• Early the next morning a man whose name I knew well, a lawyer, *called* on me.(p.378)
• He *called* me that because I was drinking too much.(p.387)
• So I *called* my father and he said, "Yes," he'd come out and stay with me for that time.(p.389)
• They phoned my husband that I was in jail and in such terrible shape that they didn't know what I would do to myself; and they realized that jail was no place for me, but that he was to wait a while before he got me, because at the time they *called* him to come over for me I was beating a tin cup against the wall.(p.390)
• So I got a half pint and at midnight that night, I *called* the number I had been given, but the man who had started the group was in the hospital so I didn't know what to do.(p.393)
• Once, when I *called* my analyst, and told her I was contemplating death, she came over and tried to get me into a sanitarium.(p.411)
• Then he *called* Marty and made and appointment for me.(p.413)
• A fellow A.A., *called* Anne, who had helped me, went on a terrible bender.(p.414)
• The folks *called* a doctor and he knocked me out with sedatives.(p.429)
• A week after my decision to join A.A., she *called* it quits.(p.430)
• How could such a man possibly be *called* an alcoholic?(p.433)
• However, I've heard of an organization *called* Alcoholics Anonymous that has had some success with people like you.(p.436)
• The next day, Max *called* the neurologist and told him about the Mayo psychiatrist's opinion.(p.445)
• At noon on Christmas Day I *called* my family in New York, wished them a Merry Christmas, and assured them everything was fine with me.(p.467)
• On one occasion when I was serving time in my favorite drying-out place while I was having a session with the psychiatrist, she left my case history on her desk when she was *called* away from the room.(p.470)
• During these seven years a thing *called* the Twenty-four Hour Program —a gadget I used to think was only a snare to trap the newcomer -- has come to mean much to me, not only as regards my drinking but in the whole pattern of my life.(p.473)
• Of course, when father finally came to Virginia to work his way through school, he resented the southern "cracker," as he often *called* them, so much that he didn't even go back to his mother's funeral.(p.486)
• The Armistice is signed on the 11th and the draft is *called* off.(p.499)
• I remained there for about ten months, and then I was sent to a place *called* Wallkill, a so-called rehabilitation center.(p.509)
• (This address is now available in pamphlet form at nominal cost through most A.A. groups or from Box 459, Grand Central Station, New York, NY 10163, under the title "Three Talks to Medical Societies by Bill W." – formerly *called* "Bill on Alcoholism" and earlier "Alcoholism the Illness.")(p.572)

calling

• Sometimes the man we are *calling* upon admits his own fault, so feuds of years' standing melt away in an hour.(p.78)
• And I continued to drink, on and off then, until every dollar I had in the world was gone again and I was right back living at my sister's, getting my cigarettes by *calling* her grocer and telling him to put in a couple of cartons with her order, exactly as I had before I started to work at Max's.(p.202)
• From far away, as if in a delirium, I heard my own voice – *calling* someone "Dorothy," talking of dress shops, of jobs . . . the words came clearer . . . this sound of my own voice frightened me as it came closer . . . and suddenly, there I was, talking of I knew not what, to someone I'd never seen before this very moment.(p.222)
• So I spent much of my time *calling* on the people who I felt would logically come in contact with alcoholic cases, doctors, ministers, lawyers and the personnel men in industry.(p.281)

callous

• How could men who loved their wives and children be so unthinking, so *callous*, so cruel?(p.107)

callowness

• If I write with the air of one who has discovered the obvious, which is to say, the eternal truths which have been offered to us since the beginning, forgive my *callowness*; I had to find these things out for myself.(p.536)

calls

• When his wife next *calls* saying he is sick, you might jump to the conclusion he is drunk.(p.146)
• A man *calls* me on the phone.(p.506)
• They said if you want to know how this program works, take the first word of your question – the H is for honesty, the O is for open-mindedness and the W is for willingness; these our Book *calls* the essentials of recovery.(p.550)
• Most of our experiences are what the psychologist William James *calls* the "educational variety" because they develop slowly over a period of time.(p.569)
• Dr. Foster Kennedy, neurologist: "This organization of Alcoholics Anonymous *calls* on two of the greatest reservoirs of power known to man, religion and that instinct for association with one's fellows . . . the 'herd instinct.'(p.571)

calm

• If our manner is *calm*, frank, and open, we will be gratified with the result.(p.78)
• She maintains a perfect *calm*.(p.507)

calmly

• The next thing they wanted to know was would I be willing to go to this Higher Power and ask for help, *calmly* and without any reservations.(p.186)

camaraderie

• We are like the passengers of a great liner the moment after rescue from shipwreck when *camaraderie*, joyousness and democracy pervade the vessel from steerage to Captain's table.(p.17)

came

• Of alcoholics who *came* to A.A. and really tried, 50% got sober at once and remained that way; 25% sobered up after some relapses, and among the remainder, those who stayed on with A.A. showed improvement.(p.xx)
• Other thousands *came* to a few A.A. meetings and at first decided they didn't want the program.(p.xx)
• Many years ago one of the leading contributors to this book *came* under our care in this hospital and while here he acquired some ideas which he put into practical application at once.(p.xxv)
• I earnestly advise every alcoholic to read this book through, and though perhaps he *came* to scoff, he may remain to pray.(p.xxx)
• Liquor caught up with me much faster than I *came* up behind Walter.(p.3)
• As I drank, the old fierce determination to win *came* back.(p.4)
• Shortly afterward I *came* home drunk.(p.5)
• Then *came* the night when the physical and mental torture was so hellish I feared I would burst through my window, sash and all.(p.6)
• A doctor *came* with a heavy sedative.(p.6)
• But it was not, for the frightful day *came* when I drank once more.(p.7)
• Then *came* the insidious insanity of that first drink, and on Armistice Day 1935, I was off again.(p.8)
• That war-time day in old Winchester Cathedral *came* back again.(p.10)
• A new world *came* into view.(p.12)
• There had been a humble willingness to have Him with me – and He *came*.(p.12)
• While I lay in the hospital the thought *came* that there were thousands of hopeless alcoholics who might be glad to have what had been so freely given me.(p.14)
• Out *came* his carpet slippers and a bottle.(p.32)
• On leaving the asylum he *came* into contact with us.(p.35)
• This is his story: "I *came* to work on Tuesday morning.(p.36)
• Far from admitting he was an alcoholic, he told himself he *came* to the hospital to rest his nerves.(p.39)
• My business *came* off well, I was pleased and knew

my partners would be too.(p.41)
• As I crossed the threshold of the dining room, the thought *came* to mind that it would be nice to have a couple of cocktails with dinner.(p.41)
• Then *came* the hospital with unbearable mental and physical suffering.(p.41)
• "Two of the members of Alcoholics Anonymous *came* to see me.(p.42)
• They show how the change *came* over them.(p.51)
• Others *came* near putting Galileo to death for his astronomical heresies.(p.51)
• Then, like a thunderbolt, a great thought *came*.(p.56)
• After consulting with his wife and partner he *came* to the conclusion that it was better to take those risks than to stand before his Creator guilty of such ruinous slander.(p.80)
• He is like the farmer who *came* up out of his cyclone cellar to find his home ruined.(p.82)
• We have seen others slip when the family *came* back too soon.(p.100)
• When we look back, we realize that the things which *came* to us when we put ourselves in God's hands were better than anything we could have planned.(p.100)
• We *came* to live almost alone.(p.105)
• One day my secretary *came* in saying that Mr. B---- insisted on speaking with me.(p.136)
• I still expected a plea for clemency, but these words *came* through the receiver: "I just wanted to tell you Paul jumped from a hotel window in Hartford last Saturday.(p.136)
• Still another experience: A woman's voice *came* faintly over long distance from Virginia.(p.137)
• From a business standpoint, his trip *came* off badly.(p.153)
• At midnight he *came* home exhausted, but very happy.(p.156)
• His wife *came*, scarcely daring to be hopeful, though she thought she saw something different about her husband already.(p.158)
• He *came* through an acquaintance who had heard the good news.(p.158)
• Many an alcoholic who entered there *came* away with an answer.(p.160)
• Without this proof the expectant purchaser would be forced to depart empty handed with none of what I later *came* to believe was the great panacea for all human ills.(p.171)
• After high school *came* four years in one of the best colleges in the country where drinking seemed to be a major extra-curricular activity.(p.172)
• When beer first *came* back, I thought that I was safe.(p.177)
• He *came* and got me home and to bed, gave me a few drinks that night, and one bottle of beer the next morning.(p.179)
• My wife, a Kentucky girl, *came* with me to Akron where I completed my course in law at the Akron Law School.(p.182)
• So, at the time Dr. Bob and Bill *came* along I had about run out my strength.(p.182)
• Then Prohibition *came* into effect, and the facts that the stuff obtainable was so horrible and sometimes deadly, and that I had married and had a job which I had to look after, helped me for a period of some three or four years, although I would get drunk every time I could get hold of enough to drink to get started.(p.183)
• On June 26, 1935, I *came* to in the hospital and to say I was discouraged is to put it mildly.(p.184)
• They *came* in and began to give me instruction in the program which later became known as Alcoholics Anonymous.(p.185)
• (I knew afterwards that the two who *came* in were Bill W. and Doctor Bob.)(p.185)
• I thought of what liquor had done to me, the opportunities that I had discarded, the abilities that had been given me and how I had wasted them, and I finally *came* to the conclusion, that if I didn't want to quit, I certainly ought to want to, and that I was willing to do anything in the world to stop drinking.(p.186)
• So, when they *came* back, I told them.(p.187)
• Then *came* a great joy.(p.189)
• It was in the next two or three days after I had first met Doc and Bill, that I finally *came* to a decision to turn my will over to God and to go along with this program the best that I could.(p.189)
• Then I remember when the boys *came* back, that I told them, "I have gone to this Higher Power and I have told Him that I am willing to put His world first, above everything.(p.190)
• I'm so grateful for both the program and the people in it that I still want to go, and then probably the most wonderful thing that I learned from the program -- I've seen this in the 'A.A. Grapevine' a lot of times, and I've had people say it to me personally, and I've heard people get up in meetings and make the same statement: The statement is, "I *came* into A.A. solely for the purpose of sobriety, but it has been through A.A. that I have found God."(p.192)
• I *came* to Cleveland with the deeds to these lots and to pick up my money.(p.196)
• About that period, too, *came* increasing procrastination and the avoidance of responsibilities.(p.197)
• I quite naturally *came* to the conclusion that I must be insane.(p.199)
• I *came* to the conclusion it was because I hadn't been drunk.(p.200)
• To show you the point to which this obsession went, there *came* an occasion when I had spent a most delightful week-end, and at nine o'clock on Sunday night I was on my way home, and I thought I would get a drink.(p.204)
• I offered them a drink, and they *came* to the bottom of the stairs and the good woman fainted, just looking at me.(p.205)
• He *came* in and took a look at me and sent me to the hospital.(p.205)
• On Sunday when I *came* to, it was a bad, wet, snowy day in February, 1937, and Paul and Doc and a lot of other fellows were in Cleveland on business.(p.207)
• The next day, others from the group *came* in to see me.(p.208)
• Forty *came* and went and then the resolution was advanced to forty-one, forty-two, and so on in the usual pattern.(p.214)
• One evening I had gone out after dinner to take on a couple of double-headers and stayed a little later than usual, and when I *came* home Clarence was sitting on the davenport with Bill W.(p.216)
• The next morning, my wife *came* into my room and wakened me and said, "That man is downstairs and he said you said you'd go to Akron."(p.217)
• Bill bought me a drink or two on the way, and Dorothy S. *came* with us, and the three of us went over to the City Hospital.(p.217)
• The interne *came* along with a glassful of bleached lightning that put me away for about fifteen hours.(p.217)
• The afternoon that I was to leave the hospital, he *came* in to see me and asked me if I were willing to attempt to follow the program.(p.218)
• One of the things that *came* up repeatedly in the stories they told me was that once they had accepted the program, they never had a desire to take a drink.(p.219)
• Shortly after I *came* to this conclusion, I was importuned by another well-known patent law firm to help them out on some trial work because their trial man had had a heart attack and had been forbidden to go into the courtroom.(p.220)
• From far away, as if in a delirium, I heard my own voice -- calling someone "Dorothy," talking of dress shops, of jobs . . . the words *came* clearer . . . this sound of my own voice frightened me as it *came* closer . . . and suddenly, there I was, talking of I knew not what, to someone I'd never seen before this very moment.(p.222)
• In any case I must get out of here before I let slip my abysmal ignorance of how I *came* to be here, and she realized that I was stark, staring mad.(p.223)
• I *came* directly to a growing industrial city in the middle west, where I have lived practically ever since.(p.231)
• I *came* of good stock, of men and women who drank wine all their lives as a beverage, and while they occasionally got drunk at special celebrations, they were up and about their business the next day.(p.231)
• Prohibition *came*.(p.232)
• Beer was too bulky and it couldn't be kept in a jug under the counter ready to be dumped when John Law *came* around.(p.233)
• An alcoholic who was a doctor *came* to see me.(p.235)
• The third man who *came* to see me had been one of the greatest business-getters his company had ever employed.(p.235)
• I very early *came* to see that there had to be a continual renewal for that simple deal with God; that I had perpetually to keep the bargain.(p.237)
• Many things happened; business trials, little worries, and feelings of general despondency *came* near driving me to the bottle, but I made progress.(p.237)
• The age-old question in A.A. is which *came* first, the neurosis or the alcoholism.(p.240)
• I am one of the lads who *came* out of the service with a lower rank than when I went in.(p.241)
• I had been to OTC the previous summer so I went into the Army as a sergeant, but I *came* out a private, and you really have to be unusual to do that.(p.241)
• Then *came* a sales job with a national tire company.(p.243)
• After the tire job *came* the thirties, the Depression and the down hill road.(p.244)
• My wife *came* over from Scotland and we started housekeeping in a large Ohio city.(p.254)
• Successive Monday morning hangovers, which despite mid-week resolutions to do better, *came* with unfailing regularity, eventually caused me to quit my job.(p.254)
• Some days later, after he had been discharged, a stranger *came* into my shop in the nearby town.(p.257)
• The time *came* just a week later.(p.258)
• The doctor who *came* to see me almost at once did not assail me with any new doctrines; he made sure that I had a need and that I wanted to have that need filled, and little by little I learned how my need could be met.(p.258)
• Singly and in groups of two or three, they *came* to visit me.(p.258)
• When I *came* to my aunt, she knew that I had had an unhappy childhood, and she said, "Now, Ethel, you're welcome to have boy friends in our home, but there are two boys in this town that I don't want you to date, and one of them comes from a very fine family, one of the best.(p.262)
• Then he *came* into town on the bum.(p.263)
• Mrs. M. said she would send Jack over as quick as he *came* in.(p.267)
• He *came* with two cans of beer.(p.267)
• And Jim G. had such a wonderful sense of humor, and when he *came* I was in tears, and I told him, "I want to do this, but I can't.(p.269)
• So we *came* to King School.(p.269)
• The next morning his wife *came* dragging him in before Russ went to work, while I was getting breakfast.(p.271)
• Before the end finally *came*, I had, I guess made the surrender because I finally had been able to say that I would not mind too much.(p.272)
• I don't ever remember that I was bored myself when we first *came* in, and they *came* out to the house and talked to us about these things.(p.273)
• I used to think I was cowardly because when things *came* out pertaining to the program that troubled me, I said to her many times, "Annie, am I being a coward because I lay those things away on the shelf and skip it?"(p.273)
• I *came* from a good family.(p.275)
• Spring *came*.(p.276)
• Here, while in a hospital bed, men with clear eyes, happy faces, and a look of assurance and purposefulness about them, *came* to see me and told me their stories.(p.279)
• Out of this maelstrom just two coherent thoughts *came* to the surface; one, a drink would mean homelessness and death; two, I could no longer relieve the pressure of fear by starting home, as was once my habitual solution to this problem, because I no longer had a home.(p.279)
• Finally, and I shall never know how much later it was, one clear thought *came* to me: Try prayer.(p.280)
• It is well over sixteen years since I *came* back to life.(p.280)
• Once dad *came* all the way to Florida to sober me up, after a hotel manager called him and said that if he wanted to see me alive he better get there fast.(p.288)
• A few months later one of the men who had been in touch with the group in Akron *came* to Chicago to live, and then there were three of us who continued to have informal meetings quite regularly.(p.294)
• Things eventually *came* to the point where I had no friends.(p.301)
• Seeing this danger, they *came* to A.A.(p.315)
• Actually, the bottom *came* up and hit us.(p.315)
• When I *came* home from Nam, I met a girl I'll call Karen.(p.318)
• When I *came* home again, the only thing I had left to love was the bottle.(p.318)
• And when my husband found A.A., I *came* to the second meeting with him.(p.321)
• As my son, our second child, *came* along, and as he became school age and was away at school most of the time, something happened.(p.323)
• By the law of averages, some efforts *came* out well.(p.331)
• In succession *came* "What Made Milwaukee Famous Made a Loser Out of Me" and "I'm Drinking

My Christmas Dinner All Alone."(p.332)
• The word "insanity" *came* through clearly -- and repugnantly.(p.332)
• Out of those forty years as a movie press agent *came* one blessing that granted me a blind faith in the program.(p.334)
• I never knew which *came* first, the thinking or the drinking.(p.337)
• But there *came* a point when I could no longer live with it.(p.337)
• And that *came* after a three-weeks' illness of my son.(p.338)
• The answer *came* to him by mail.(p.342)
• It was here I *came* to know properly what alcohol was.(p.343)
• The reply *came*, putting me in touch by mail with my sponsor in New Delhi.(p.343)
• The thought *came* to me -- This is the last one!(p.347)
• And as that thought *came* to me, it was as though someone had reached down and taken a heavy overcoat off my shoulders, for that was the last one.(p.347)
• And I gave him some idea of what you do, and so I made my first Twelfth Step call before I ever *came* into the program.(p.347)
• And then a silly, simple thought *came* to me.(p.351)
• I do recall lying on a cold cement floor and shredding into little bits several pieces of stolen identification cards, and washing my face in the toilet bowl trying to sober up, and screaming hysterically while clinging to bars too high to see out of, and cursing everyone that *came* near me.(p.354)
• And with this *came* the only real freedom, the freedom of truth.(p.355)
• As a matter of fact, when I *came* into Alcoholics Anonymous I was close to being at the peak of my career.(p.356)
• I was active and did well, however, in school publications, dramatics (which *came* in handy during my drinking career), and Greek letter societies.(p.357)
• Prohibition *came* along, and with it my first taste of moonshine.(p.357)
• It was also my job to entertain the owners of these stations when they *came* East on business -- or the pretense of business.(p.359)
• In 1940 another good opportunity *came* up and we moved to Pittsburgh where I was to manage two radio stations under the same ownership.(p.361)
• A few hours later I *came* out of a complete stupor in our living room with a flash of sanity.(p.363)
• We *came* back to Pittsburgh as happy as a bride and groom.(p.364)
• When our meeting night *came* around the next evening, I went -- "for her sake" I told her.(p.365)
• My first spiritual experience in A.A. *came* quite early to me.(p.366)
• It was the first she had heard or read about it and she said she had considered sending it to me or trying to have someone in Pittsburgh send it to me so I wouldn't know where it *came* from.(p.366)
• In meeting me casually, I don't think my strong belief in "The Man Upstairs" shows, but I have no other explanation for the many good things that have happened to me since I have been in A.A. -- they *came* to me from a Greater Power.(p.367)
• Dad's image for me was that of a big Irish oilman who *came* up through the school of hard knocks and so had to be a two-fisted drinker.(p.369)
• The ambition to succeed was instilled in me by my Scandinavian parents who *came* to this country where opportunities were so great.(p.373)
• After that *came* marriage, getting started in business, and a family.(p.373)
• Gradually the quantity increased, the occasions for a drink *came* more frequently; a hard day, worries and pressure, bad news, good news -- there were more and more reasons for a drink.(p.374)
• It was at this stage of my life that resentments *came* in.(p.376)
• The final decision *came* when my daughter, following a drunk which ruined my wife's birthday, said, "It's Alcoholics Anonymous -- or else!"(p.378)
• The answer *came* to me very simply in the first step of the Twelve Steps of A.A.(p.379)
• A spiritual awakening soon *came* to mean trying each day to be a little more thoughtful, more considerate, a little more courteous to those with whom I *came* in contact.(p.381)
• I didn't know that when I *came* into A.A.(p.384)
• I *came* from a family where alcohol was socially acceptable.(p.384)
• Emma ran out to the kitchen and *came* back with a water glass full of bourbon and made me drink it down.(p.385)
• Or he would leave on a trip and by the time he *came* home, I'd be passed out.(p.386)
• I know that I was terribly screwed up inside, but I *came* out much worse.(p.387)
• So when he *came* for me, as he walked down the stairs, I could see him through the bars, and he was signing for me; I looked at him and said, "Don't you sign anything in this place!"(p.391)
• The next morning he *came* into my room and said, "Esther, I'm not going to lecture you any more, but I want you to read this article.(p.391)
• It was such a feeling of relief that I wanted to know more about it and with that, I think for the first time, *came* the realization that there was something horribly, horribly wrong with me.(p.392)
• I know that when Frank *came* home, I said, "I want to try this thing," and he said, "There's a post office box to write to in New York."(p.392)
• So I wrote this letter in very shaky handwriting, and in just one week *came* back a letter with A.A. literature from New York.(p.392)
• We *came* back East and met both families.(p.402)
• Imagine my surprise when I *came* to, in Europe, and discovered I had brought myself along!(p.405)
• I *came* to and found a man leaning over me.(p.405)
• For, after those daily self-punishing sessions with myself, after the vows to stop, I would change entirely as evening *came* on.(p.408)
• Now *came* the black and endless dismal night.(p.410)
• The bartender, a tough Irishman, *came* around and "gave me the elbow," which means that he raised his elbow and smacked me in the face.(p.411)
• Once, when I called my analyst, and told her I was contemplating death, she *came* over and tried to get me into a sanitarium.(p.411)
• Marty *came* in, looking clean, neat, well-dressed and, like Bill, she was neither a bloated wreck nor a reformer.(p.413)
• A load weighing a thousand pounds *came* off my back.(p.414)
• I had been on the wagon when I *came* to A.A. and this sobriety-tension eventually popped.(p.414)
• I tried the church and psychiatry and finally *came* to A.A.(p.418)
• Then *came* my tour in the U.S. Navy, part of it being two years in the Philippines.(p.419)
• I *came* to A.A. simply because there were no other doors of help open to me in my hometown.(p.420)
• After I *came* to A.A., I was divorced by my wife; I lost my practice; I was legally restrained from seeing my children; I went broke; and the dental society threatened me with the loss of my license.(p.420)
• Two fuzzy objects *came* into focus.(p.422)
• Then it *came* to me.(p.422)
• The end *came* next year.(p.429)
• But as I *came* out of this second bout with D.T.'s I knew I was licked.(p.429)
• That is how I *came* into A.A.(p.430)
• I *came* to understand the intricate processes of projection, by which we cast into our adult world the images of the horrors of our childhood.(p.434)
• After my last binge I *came* home and smashed my dining room furniture to splinters, kicked out six windows and two balustrades.(p.435)
• If there ever was anyone who *came* to A.A. by mistake, it was I.(p.439)
• The answer *came* right back: I'd give him something to pep him up.(p.441)
• Very shortly, I realized that had been a mistake -- when this big clown *came* bounding into the room, almost shouting, "My name is Frank, and I'm an alcoholic, ha-ha-ha!"(p.446)
• I had already given up all the narcotics, most of the pills, and some of the alcohol when I first *came* to A.A.(p.448)
• I would rather talk about the good things A.A. has taught me; I feel that hitting on just a few sordid points should be sufficient to let those of you in institutions know where I *came* from.(p.459)
• I left California and *came* back to my native state.(p.460)
• Eventually the day *came* when I was dependent upon it even when there wasn't any occasion.(p.464)
• (I think my first feeling of fear *came* with my first week's solitary drinking, locked up in that hotel room.(p.465)
• It *came* about in this way.(p.472)
• When I first *came* into A.A., the woman who was my sponsor was the first woman I had ever met who admitted that she was an alcoholic.(p.472)
• *Came* home.(p.475)
• *Came* to believe.(p.476)
• When I *came* into A.A., I had no intention of quitting drinking -- I figured I was doing all right.(p.478)
• This physician, the originator of A.A.'s first black group, but badly caught in the toils, tells of his release and of how freedom *came* as he worked among his own people.(p.483)
• After our first child *came* my parents both became allies, but in later days, after I became an alcoholic, they both turned against me.(p.485)
• Of course, when father finally *came* to Virginia to work his way through school, he resented the southern "cracker," as he often called them, so much that he didn't even go back to his mother's funeral.(p.486)
• She *came* in for her dinner.(p.487)
• A very good friend of mine who owned a drug store across the street from us, *came* by only about two hours later and said that he had seen Vi down town.(p.487)
• There *came* a time when she spoke to me about it, and I would say that I had a bad cold or that I wasn't feeling well.(p.487)
• But the week-ends stretched on into Mondays and the time soon *came* when I drank every day.(p.488)
• That year, on a Friday night, a man whom I had known for years *came* to my office.(p.488)
• This man's wife had been suffering for a couple of months and when he *came* in he owed me a little bill.(p.488)
• The following day, Saturday, he *came* back and said, "Jim, I owe you for that prescription last night.(p.488)
• I had a long talk with a psychiatrist, but nothing *came* of that, and I had also, just about that time, talked with a minister for whom I had a great deal of respect.(p.489)
• I rebelled against this, because just about the time that I was getting ready to leave high school, a revelation *came* to me about God and it made things very complicated for me.(p.489)
• The thought *came* to me that if God, as my mother said, was a vengeful God, he couldn't be a loving God.(p.489)
• A policeman *came* to the door and asked for James S., but there wasn't any James S. there.(p.491)
• He *came* back several times.(p.491)
• Around eight or nine o'clock there *came* two big detectives and a policeman to arrest me for assault; and I was the most amazed person in the world when they said I had assaulted someone, and especially that I had assaulted my wife.(p.492)
• The closest I *came* to a psychiatrist during that time was an interne who *came* to take blood tests.(p.492)
• They *came*, many of them, and stuck by us and told us how to hold meetings.(p.495)
• Other boys *came* in.(p.498)
• However, before the meeting got started, a group from the outside *came* in unexpectedly.(p.509)
• Finally, he was drinking to keep away those little men, and those strange voices, and the organ music that *came* out of the walls.(p.512)
• After I *came* in I found I wasn't an exceptional drunk.(p.512)
• It's like the fellow who *came* in A.A., and his sponsor said to him, "Listen, buddy, do you believe in a Higher Power?"(p.512)
• That and the morning drink *came* very early in my drinking career.(p.513)
• But I *came* out of the Army just as big a drunk as when I went in, if not worse, because now I had a lot more resentments.(p.513)
• I remember the day I *came* back to New York.(p.513)
• I wasn't a happy man that morning, but I'm happy now that it *came* about.(p.515)
• The realization *came* to me that I had to stop drinking, that I had to find a way.(p.515)
• Because, thank God, since I *came* into this program I haven't had any trouble.(p.516)
• When I *came* back, I told the priest, the Chaplain of the place, exactly what I thought of him and he didn't like it.(p.517)
• When I *came* home to ordinary garrison life in England, I found that I was drinking rather more than most people of may age.(p.518)
• Finally, my mother *came* and said she had kept me at home for six years because she thought she could help me, but that now she had come to the conclusion that I wasn't even worth trying to help.(p.523)
• But if I *came* back in the usual state, then I'd have to go off for good the next day.(p.523)
• Then the time *came* when I couldn't afford whiskey, so I turned to wine.(p.527)
• He said if I *came* back again, they would send me to the state hospital.(p.528)

• I was trying to remember where it *came* from, when two of the biggest cops I ever saw walked in and took me to jail.(p.528)
• It *came* out that I had sold a woman a fur coat.(p.528)
• I had rejected A.A. on the outside, but now it *came* to me in prison.(p.528)
• And having sung that phrase, I'd chuckle with amusement, turning into irony turning into self-contempt turning into self-pity, at the sad fate of Bob, that wonderful, poor little motherless boy who was so smart in school and who grew up to accept responsibility so early and so fast and who staggered under his burdens without a whimper until the time *came* when he thought he was too good for this world and so he ought to be out of it.(p.532)
• The only importance in all of this lies in the fact that at twenty-three I was just as sick as I was at thirty three, when I *came* into A.A., but at that time I apparently had no place to go because I had no drinking problem.(p.546)
• The people who *came* knew immediately I was in no condition to absorb anything of the program, and I was put in a sanitarium to be defogged so that I could make a sober decision about this for myself.(p.549)
• With deep shame *came* the knowledge too that I had lived with no sense of social obligation nor had I known the meaning of moral responsibility to my fellow men.(p.549)
• Then the drinks *came* more frequently, but carefully spaced out.(p.557)

camp

• Back at *camp*, all was forgiven because it was the End, but in the light of what I have since learned I know I was a confirmed alcoholic at nineteen.(p.242)
• At Great Lakes Boot *Camp* I latched onto a soft billet.(p.425)
• I served time in four penitentiaries and several prison camps, including a maximum-security *camp*.(p.457)
• I thought that was bad until I hit the hole at a prison *camp*; it was just wide enough and long enough to lie down in.(p.459)
• I am to go to *camp* on November 13th.(p.499)

campaign

• He entered a political *campaign*, making speeches, frequenting men's gathering places of all sorts, often staying up all night.(p.158)
• The next day I went back to Chicago and started a vigorous *campaign* among my so-called friends or drinking companions.(p.293)
• We had a minor *campaign* or two and that helped distract attention from my drinking.(p.519)

camps

• I had the best schools, summer *camps*, resort vacations and travel.(p.304)
• I served time in four penitentiaries and several prison *camps*, including a maximum-security camp.(p.457)

can't

• Why *can't* he?"(p.20)
• "That fellow *can't* handle his liquor."(p.20)
• Why *can't* he stay on the water wagon?(p.22)
• They sound like the philosophy of the man who, having a headache, beats himself on the head with a hammer so that he *can't* feel the ache.(p.23)
• I *can't* go through with it."(p.60)
• I *can't* understand it."(p.157)
• From what you tell me, I know more than ever I *can't* stop."(p.157)
• Before very long we began to relate some incidents of our drinking and, naturally, pretty soon, I realized both of them knew what they were talking about because you can see things and smell things when you're drunk, that you *can't* other times, and, if I had thought they didn't know what they were talking about, I wouldn't have been willing to talk to them at all.(p.185)
• The next question they asked was, "You can quit twenty-four hours *can't* you?"(p.188)
• Looking sadder than ever, he wearily ventured, "Well this is wonderful for you fellows, but it *can't* be for me.(p.188)
• But he discovered that there are some gentlemen who *can't* drink.(p.210)
• "You *can't* win unless you try God's way."(p.236)
• When you have a hangover and *can't* even sit still, try to read small print!(p.268)
• I was reading it for all that was in it, and I said to Russ, "We *can't* do this.(p.269)
• And Jim G. had such a wonderful sense of humor, and when he came I was in tears, and I told him, "I want to do this, but I *can't*.(p.269)
• I *can't* express what A.A. meant to us during that year.(p.272)
• You *can't* lose, and maybe God will help you -- just maybe, mind you.(p.280)
• I learned that a person just *can't* find a job hanging in a dive or barroom all day and all night, as jobs don't seem to turn up in those places.(p.300)
• An alcoholic *can't* lay off the booze – right?(p.317)
• "It *can't* be my drinking," I thought, "because I can stop any time I want to.(p.318)
• "I'm not crazy," I thought, "and I *can't* be an alcoholic -- I'm too young."(p.319)
• I *can't* afford resentments against anyone, because they are the build-up of another drunk.(p.325)
• I said, "I *can't* find my middle road in life.(p.340)
• I *can't* find it.(p.340)
• No one likes to admit that they're a drunk, that they *can't* control this thing.(p.340)
• And then one ill-defined day, one day that I *can't* recall, I stepped across the line that alcoholics know so well, and from that day on drinking was miserable.(p.346)
• We've got to turn the whole business over to some joker we *can't* even see!(p.350)
• What can He do for us that we *can't* do for ourselves?"(p.350)
• I *can't* bear to be here when you lose the respect of others, and above all – when you lose your own self respect."(p.362)
• I *can't* bear to be here when you lose the respect of others, and above all when you lose your own self respect."(p.363)
• I *can't* remember a dinner at home that we didn't have white wine or claret on the table.(p.384)
• For some reason I *can't* remember, it finally dawned on me that I had a problem, and yet nobody was very critical about it except my family, and that was only because I decided, after seven years of marriage, that I would divorce my husband.(p.386)
• I could not identify myself with the people with whom I found myself and there was no understanding, and I *can't* stand confinement anyhow.(p.387)
• (I *can't* know how much others of our Fellowship have paid financially and, even more important, mentally and physically.)(p.396)
• I *can't* blame him.(p.405)
• In my cups I began to say, "I *can't* stop."(p.412)
• Except for one short slip, during the first eight months, which was an angry "the world *can't* do this to me" reaction to a personal tragedy in my life, I have been sober for twelve years.(p.416)
• I *can't* control my drinking any more.(p.423)
• Now I know I *can't* live without A.A.(p.430)
• Today, I find I *can't* work my A.A. program while taking pills, nor may I even have them around for dire emergencies only.(p.443)
• I *can't* say, "Thy will be done," and take a pill.(p.443)
• I *can't* say, "I'm powerless over alcohol, but solid alcohol is okay."(p.443)
• I *can't* say, "God could restore me to sanity, but until He does, I'll control myself – with pills."(p.443)
• We used to argue about our differing ideas, but we *can't* argue about our feelings.(p.451)
• I can tell her she ought not to think a certain way, but I certainly *can't* take away her right to feel however she does feel.(p.451)
• Yet prisoners often *can't* identify with many A.A. members' drinking stories.(p.458)
• To this day I *can't* hear that song without remembering that awful Christmas.(p.468)
• In other words, the kindest doctor in the whole world, and I had one such, couldn't help me because I always felt, "You *can't* know about me – you *can't* possibly know – you don't even drink!"(p.471)
• She *can't* do that to me!"(p.472)
• I *can't* begin to tell you of all the benefits I have derived from this new way of living.(p.481)
• *Can't* remember the answer to the first.(p.499)
• I *can't* think.(p.499)
• I look for liquor and *can't* find any.(p.502)
• It rings in my head; I *can't* get rid of it.(p.504)
• I've made a mess of things and *can't* do anything about it.(p.504)
• When I look back, I *can't* see anything that would have predisposed me towards being either a neurotic or a drunk.(p.517)
• They tell me that I killed a man during that period, but I *can't* remember anything.(p.528)
• So many wonderful things have happened to me that at times I *can't* believe this is me.(p.529)
• Society can do anything it chooses to do with me when I am drunk and I *can't* lift a finger to stop it, for I forfeit my rights through the simple expedient of becoming a menace to myself and to the people around me.(p.549)

Canada

• Groups are to be found in each of the United States and all of the provinces of *Canada*.(p.xv)
• Surveys of groups in the United States and *Canada* indicate that A.A. is reaching out, not only to more and more people, but to a wider and wider range.(p.xxii)
• He had plenty of money left and thought I had better go to *Canada*.(p.4)
• Then I started traveling, with the United States and *Canada* as my territory, and with so much freedom and with an unlimited expense account, I was soon drinking every night and kidding myself that it was all part of the job.(p.287)
• I was born a Maliseet Indian on reservation in *Canada*.(p.474)
• Cops now sick of me, so they buy me one-way ticket to *Canada*.(p.475)
• Year later, I go to *Canada* to carry message to Tall Man, but he not listen to son.(p.476)
• In the United States and *Canada*, most towns and cities have A.A. groups.(p.575)

Canadian

• Curious about it, feeling I was missing something, absolutely without any illusions about the aftermath, with no pronounced feeling of patriotism, I joined up with a *Canadian* regiment, serving a little over two years.(p.253)
• From a *Canadian* reservation to overseas bars to New England lockups, an Indian traveled a long trail that finally led him home to A.A.(p.474)
• I join *Canadian* Army, but could not run away from problem.(p.474)

canal

• I had three or four very uncomfortable months with my regiment then on the Suez *Canal*.(p.520)
• Then Hitler's war broke out, and again, I was given a really important job on the Suez *Canal*, dealing with military shipping.(p.520)

cancer

• If a person has *cancer* all are sorry for him and no one is angry or hurt.(p.18)
• I was suffering from an actual disease that had a name and symptoms like diabetes or *cancer* or TB -- and a disease was respectable, not a moral stigma!(p.227)
• They realized that in the end alcoholism could be a mortal as *cancer*, certainly no sane man would wait for a malignant growth to become fatal before seeking help.(p.315)
• Mother has been dying of *cancer* for a long time.(p.501)

candidate

• Your *candidate* may give reasons why he need not follow all of the program.(p.94)
• But as the years go by, the stretch becomes unbearable; and the man with the grown-up brain and the childish emotions – vanity, self-interest, false pride, jealousy, longing for social approval, to name few – becomes a prime *candidate* for alcohol.(p.534)

candidly

• I thought I had done that until Russ' second collapse, and the doctor told me very *candidly* that he wasn't long for this world.(p.271)

candle

• I crawl under a pile of blankets and blow out the *candle*.(p.497)

candy

• He added that occasionally in the night a vague craving arose which would be satisfied by *candy*.(p.134)
• He wouldn't give me any money for the groceries, but he did take me across the street and buy me a bag of *candy*, which I later took back and traded for a loaf of bread.(p.193)

canned

• It didn't say I had to finally live on skid row and drink bay rum, *canned* heat or lemon extract.(p.379)

cannot

• It explains many things for which we *cannot* otherwise account.(p.xxiv)
• These allergic types can never safely use alcohol in any form at all; and once having formed the habit and found they *cannot* break it, once having lost their self-confidence, their reliance upon things human, their problems pile up on them and become astonishingly difficult to solve.(p.xxvi)
• The sensation is so elusive that, while they admit it is injurious, they *cannot* after a time differentiate the

true from the false.(p.xxvi)
• Men have cried out to me in sincere and despairing appeal: "Doctor, I *cannot* go on like this!(p.xxvii)
• I must stop, but I *cannot*!(p.xxvii)
• There is the type of man who is unwilling to admit that he *cannot* take a drink.(p.xxviii)
• All these, and many others, have one symptom in common: they *cannot* start drinking without developing the phenomenon of craving.(p.xxviii)
• Then comes the day when he simply *cannot* make it and gets drunk all over again.(p.22)
• We *cannot* answer the riddle.(p.22)
• So many want to stop but *cannot*.(p.25)
• We admit we have some of these symptoms, but we have not gone to the extremes you fellows did, nor are we likely to, for we understand ourselves so well after what you have told us that such things *cannot* happen again.(p.38)
• But I *cannot* accept as surely true the many articles of faith which are so plain to him."(p.47)
• With this attitude you *cannot* fail.(p.55)
• Those who do not recover are people who *cannot* or will not completely give themselves to this simple program, usually men and women who are constitutionally incapable of being honest with themselves.(p.58)
• If the owner of the business is to be successful, he *cannot* fool himself about values.(p.64)
• We *cannot* be helpful to all people, but at least God will show us how to take a kindly and tolerant view of each and every one.(p.67)
• If we *cannot* or would rather not do this, we search our acquaintance for a close-mouthed, understanding friend.(p.74)
• It may be one of our own family, but we *cannot* disclose anything to our wives or our parents which will hurt them and make them unhappy.(p.74)
• More than that we *cannot* do; we have no right to go further.(p.81)
• Some people *cannot* be seen — we send them an honest letter.(p.83)
• We find it a waste of time to keep chasing a man who *cannot* or will not work with you.(p.96)
• If you leave such a person alone, he may soon become convinced that he *cannot* recover by himself.(p.96)
• He clamors for this or that, claiming he *cannot* master alcohol until his material needs are cared for.(p.98)
• Let no alcoholic say he *cannot* recover unless he has his family back.(p.99)
• An alcoholic who *cannot* meet them, still has an alcoholic mind; there is something the matter with his spiritual status.(p.101)
• He is worried at times, and is becoming aware that he *cannot* drink like other people.(p.109)
• His friends have slipped away, his home is a near-wreck and he *cannot* hold a position.(p.110)
• He admits he *cannot* drink like other people, but does not see why.(p.110)
• He may have come to the point where he desperately wants to stop but *cannot*.(p.110)
• Some men have been so impaired by alcohol that they *cannot* stop.(p.114)
• Some men *cannot* or will not get over alcoholism.(p.114)
• As non-denominational people, we *cannot* make up others' minds for them.(p.132)
• We *cannot* subscribe to the belief that this life is a vale of tears, though it once was just that for many of us.(p.133)
• They *cannot* seem to forgive and forget.(p.134)
• You *cannot* see why it should be to anyone else, save the spineless and stupid.(p.139)
• You might say you appreciated his abilities, would like to keep him, but *cannot* if he continues to drink.(p.141)
• The employer *cannot* play favorites, but he can always defend a man from needless provocation and unfair criticism.(p.146)
• But if you *cannot* or will not stop drinking, I think you ought to resign."(p.148)
• If he *cannot* or does not want to stop, he should be discharged.(p.148)
• At the same time you will feel no reluctance to rid yourself of those who *cannot* or will not stop.(p.148)
• He *cannot* picture life without alcohol.(p.152)
• We *cannot* be sure.(p.164)
• But obviously you *cannot* transmit something you haven't got.(p.164)
• Why they should be subjected to the tortures we inflict upon them, I *cannot* explain.(p.178)
• And as I fumed helplessly and planned to get good and drunk and show them, my eye caught a sentence in the book lying open on my bed: "We *cannot* live with anger."(p.228)
• I *cannot* say, however, that I acquired any craving for hard liquor as a result.(p.231)
• I *cannot* say that my taste for liquor has entirely disappeared.(p.259)
• I *cannot* remember just when I became the victim of insomnia, but I do know that the last year and a half I never went to bed sober a single night.(p.299)
• I have self confidence and assurance that *cannot* be confused with the cockiness I once possessed.(p.303)
• We do not, *cannot*, out-grow this plan.(p.311)
• And believe me, an alcoholic *cannot* fight alcohol.(p.338)
• "Grant us the serenity to accept the things we *cannot* change, courage to change the things we can, and the wisdom to know the difference."(p.382)
• I *cannot* sit by and watch you destroy yourself."(p.391)
• An alcoholic *cannot* accept the news that he's an alcoholic unless there is a meaningful explanation given, and an offer of help, such as you get in A.A.(p.406)
• Until I could accept my alcoholism, I could not stay sober; unless I accept life completely on life's terms, I *cannot* be happy.(p.449)
• Forgive me — I *cannot* write further about this latest turn of events, anticipating seeing the family I deserted so long ago.(p.463)
• I *cannot* sleep.(p.501)
• I *cannot* stand it.(p.501)
• I tell my wife I *cannot* stop drinking.(p.502)
• I pick up a book and try to read, but I *cannot* concentrate.(p.503)
• But I *cannot* sleep.(p.503)
• I am learning that I *cannot* have my own way as I used to.(p.505)
• I *cannot* understand.(p.506)
• I *cannot* see the cause of this temptation now.(p.507)
• It has made me understand that I must be one of my world, that I *cannot* exist in any happiness as a rebel by myself.(p.524)
• All of my family and loved ones, all of my friends, are nearer and dearer to me than ever before and I have literally dozens of new friends who say they *cannot* believe that a short eight years ago I was ready for the scrap heap.(p.541)
• For example, we are told in A.A. that we *cannot* afford resentments and self-pity, so we learn to avoid these festering mental attitudes.(p.560)
• We are granted "the serenity to accept the things we *cannot* change" -- and thus lose our quickness to anger and our sensitivity to criticism.(p.560)
• "There is a principle which is a bar against all information, which is proof against all arguments and which *cannot* fail to keep a man in everlasting ignorance — that principle is contempt prior to investigation."(p.570)
• Dr. John F. Stouffer, Chief Psychiatrist, Philadelphia General Hospital, citing his experience with A.A., said: "The alcoholics we get here at Philadelphia General are mostly those who *cannot* afford private treatment, and A.A. is by far the greatest thing we have been able to offer them.(p.572)
• The Episcopal magazine, The Living Church, observes editorially: "The basis of the technique of Alcoholics Anonymous is the truly Christian principle that a man *cannot* help himself except by helping others.(p.574)
• Speaking at a dinner given by John D. Rockefeller Jr. to introduce Alcoholics Anonymous to some of his friends, Dr. Harry Emerson Fosdick remarked: "I think that psychologically speaking there is a point of advantage in the approach that is being made in this movement that *cannot* be duplicated.(p.574)
• If you *cannot* find A.A. in your locality, a letter addressed to Alcoholics Anonymous, Box 459, Grand Central Station, New York, NY 10163, U.S.A., will receive a prompt reply from this world center, referring you to the nearest A.A. group.(p.575)

cans
• He came with two *cans* of beer.(p.267)
• One morning when I was feeling really bad, I was put on K.P. and the head cook wanted me to go out and scrub the garbage *cans*.(p.317)
• I halfway washed them, and he told me to do them again, and I did, and he yelled at me to do them again, and I picked up one of the *cans* and threw it at him and told him to do them himself.(p.317)
• I swung, I swore, I started throwing beer *cans* at the advancing hordes of pineapple faces.(p.427)

canteens
• Soon found wet *canteens* serve drinks to Indians in uniform.(p.474)

cap
• His only chance for sobriety would be some place like the Greenland Ice *Cap*, and even there an Eskimo might turn up with a bottle of scotch and ruin everything!(p.101)

capability
• I had the time, I certainly had the *capability*, but I never did a thing.(p.326)

capable
• We thought, on the whole, we were pretty good women, *capable* of being nicer if our husbands stopped drinking.(p.116)
• By the time I had completed law school I had picked up some experience in patent law, for I remained with the patent law firm and worked too in Washington where they found that I was a *capable* infringement investigator.(p.213)
• Making amends is sometimes doing what we are *capable* of doing but failed to do because of alcohol; carrying out community responsibilities such as Community Funds, Red Cross, educational and religious activities in proportion to our abilities and energy.(p.381)
• I knew I wasn't *capable* of keeping the bulk of the money myself, so I gave it to a white fellow who owned the bar which I frequented.(p.493)
• I was not *capable* of anything better.(p.540)
• Most emphatically we wish to say that any alcoholic *capable* of honestly facing his problems in the light of our experience can recover, provided he does not close his mind to all spiritual concepts.(p.570)

capacities
• "We watch the alcoholic performing in a position of responsibility and we know that because he is drinking heavily and daily he has cut his *capacities* by fifty per cent, and still he seems able to do a satisfactory job.(p.308)
• But, of course," he continued, "eventually the alcoholic loses all of his *capacities* as his disease gets progressively worse, and this is a tragedy that is painful to watch; the disintegration of a sound mind and body."(p.308)
• I suspect that if it is wisely handled — and it seems to be in wise and prudent hands — there are doors of opportunity ahead of this project that may surpass our *capacities* to imagine."(p.574)

capacity
• In late 1934 I attended a patient who, though he had been a competent businessman of good earning *capacity*, was an alcoholic of a type I had come to regard as hopeless.(p.xxiii)
• I, who had thought so well of myself and my abilities, of my *capacity* to surmount obstacles, was cornered at last.(p.8)
• It was impossible to say we had no *capacity* for faith, or love, or worship.(p.54)
• There are those, too, who suffer from grave emotional and mental disorders, but many of them do recover if they have the *capacity* to be honest.(p.58)
• On account of my enormous *capacity* for beer, I was elected to membership in one of the drinking societies, and soon became one of the leading spirits.(p.173)
• My husband was an alcoholic -- I had only contempt for those without my own amazing *capacity* -- the outcome was inevitable.(p.225)
• It's only natural that we don't have the *capacity* to change, but we ought not to criticize those who have, There's another thing I would stress.(p.273)
• From that point on, I secured crocks of ten gallon *capacity* and really took quite an active interest in the manufacture of home brew.(p.297)
• I could no longer gage my *capacity* and it might be the second or the tenth drink that would erase my consciousness.(p.306)
• As I progressed and gained in *capacity*, I had blackouts.(p.512)
• I didn't have the courage to love; I was not even sure I had the *capacity*.(p.546)

capital
• I had had some success at speculation, so we had a little money, but we once worked on a farm for a month to avoid drawing on our small *capital*.(p.3)
• I couldn't stomach religion, and I didn't like the mention of God or any of the other *capital* letters.(p.227)

capitalize
• Instead, you will *capitalize* them.(p.117)
• Avoid then, the deliberate manufacture of misery, but if trouble comes, cheerfully *capitalize* it as an opportunity to demonstrate His omnipotence.(p.133)

capitulated
• Impressed by those who visited him at the hospital,

he *capitulated* entirely when, later, in an upper room of this house, he heard the story of some man whose experience closely tallied with his own.(p.160)

caps

• At one time, I was using twenty *caps* a day; I nearly died half a dozen times on the street.(p.480)

captain

• I thought I was the *captain* of my soul.(p.408)

• There was the physical aspect; to be the youngest and the runt of the brood of children, to have to wear glasses very early and so to be teased, to be bookish and bored in school because the *captain* of the football team could not translate Virgil and yet was the school god while you, you, you little shrimp, were the school egghead, junior size and an early model.(p.533)

Captain's

• We are like the passengers of a great liner the moment after rescue from shipwreck when camaraderie, joyousness and democracy pervade the vessel from steerage to *Captain's* table.(p.17)

car

• Then I decided to drive into the country and see one of my prospects for a *car*.(p.36)

• I also had the notion that I might find a customer for a *car* at this place, which was familiar for I had been going to it for years.(p.36)

• Within a week after leaving the hospital a fast-moving trolley *car* breaks his arm.(p.38)

• An armored *car* could not have brought the pay envelopes home.(p.105)

• Stepping into his *car*, he made the rounds of people he had hurt.(p.156)

• We boys drove out in somebody's *car* and went to the bar on the way do the dining room and I, in an effort to impress the other boys that I was city-bred, having lived in Scranton and Cleveland, asked them if they didn't want a drink.(p.194)

• At that particular time, the boys put me on a shutter and took me out to the shed, and I lay in the *car* while they enjoyed their banquet.(p.195)

• I was picked up at two-thirty that morning with my *car* smashed up by a street-car because I had run into a big concrete safety zone, and the street-car had run into me, and they took me out through the roof -- there's where I lost the suit.(p.202)

• I lost the *car*, of course.(p.202)

• We drove my *car* and I left it down in the yard.(p.217)

• Loading a *car* with good old books to sell to collectors, librarians, universities and historical societies, I started out to travel the country.(p.255)

• Finally, one morning, I got up and got in the *car* and cried all the way down to the M.'s – the people who owned the bar -- and told her I was licked and wanted help.(p.267)

• I remember sometime, it was possibly six months after we had been going steadily to King School, that we were coming home from a meeting and saw a *car* along the way, and a fellow in back drinking a bottle of beer.(p.271)

• During the first three months I carried on all these activities without a *car*, depending entirely on buses and streetcars – I, who had always to have a *car* at my immediate command.(p.283)

• Alone in the relative safety of my home because I knew I dare not risk the danger of blacking out in some public place or at the wheel of a *car*.(p.306)

• I still had a wife and family, a home and a *car*, my driver's license, and a proper amount of insurance.(p.327)

• This was such a new thought that I got all sorts of books on Higher Powers, and I put a Bible by my bedside, and I put a Bible in my *car*.(p.348)

• My parents' *car* had a strong attraction to fences, and one night I blacked out and drove the *car* down a bank, ramming the steel fence around someone's backyard.(p.353)

• I entered the house, opened a new bottle of whiskey and sat down to drink myself into the right frame of mind to get in my *car*, start the motor and close the garage door behind me.(p.363)

• Very soon after I lost Mother, my five-year-old little girl was killed by a neighbor's *car*.(p.370)

• I was living in constant fear that I would get caught while driving a *car*, so I used taxis part of the time.(p.375)

• To wake up at home, not knowing how I got there, and to realize I had driven my *car*, became torture.(p.375)

• I got right into the *car* and they drove me over, and just as soon as I got to the church they started the wedding.(p.385)

• A patrol *car* passed.(p.390)

• During this time, you are supposed to behave yourself, but I took a little wine-tasting tour through France, all by my lone, with *car* and chauffeur.(p.405)

• Sometimes I'd make it home and go to sleep at the wheel of my *car*, for all the neighbors to see next morning as they left for work.(p.429)

• I paid nine hundred dollars for a second hand *car* on my return.(p.429)

• I spent eighteen hundred dollars fixing up that *car* in the first year I was home, after four bad smash-ups.(p.429)

• I'd lost my *car* again, pawned my wallet and all identification papers for a bottle, and gotten home somehow.(p.429)

• I remember finding myself in the middle of the night in the doctors' parking lot at the hospital with one foot in the *car* and one foot on the ground, not knowing which was the lead foot; finding myself hanging up the telephone – then realizing I had gotten out of bed, answered the phone, turned on the light, and carried on a conversation with a patient.(p.441)

• I didn't feel I could lie in bed and squirt the stuff in my veins while my kids and wife stood around watching me, so I kept the drug in my bag and the bag in the *car* and the *car* in the garage.(p.442)

• In the garage, I would put the needle in my vein and then try to figure out exactly how much medication to inject to overcome the pep pills while adding to the sleeping pills while ignoring the tranquilizers, in order to get just enough to be able to pull out the needle, jerk the tourniquet, throw it in the *car*, slam the *car* door shut, run down the hall, and fall in bed before I fell asleep.(p.442)

• I was taken out of the house and put bodily into a waiting *car* with nothing on but a robe and gown.(p.466)

• On the way I tried, and I mean really tried, to throw myself out of the *car*.(p.466)

• I was too weak and exhausted to even try to throw myself out of the *car*.(p.467)

• Mind you, I had absolutely nothing to show for that eighteen years, except a beat-up *car* that I hadn't even paid for, but I was doing all right.(p.478)

• I put Charlie on the *car* and when I left him I passed both of those liquor stores without even thinking about them.(p.495)

• She had looked for me last evening after I left the *car* and wandered off into the night.(p.502)

• Maybe a drink – I put on my hat and dash off in the *car*.(p.505)

• I get in the *car* and drive off.(p.506)

card

• There I sat in the evenings, enjoying with my friends our memories of the "old country," singing the old songs we all knew, playing simple *card* games for drinks and consuming great quantities of beer.(p.231)

• At the end of a year, the children got a *card* from their father, which I still have and cherish.(p.262)

• We were having *card* parties with limburger and beer quite regularly.(p.297)

• At one end of the bed, near the foot, was a printed *card*, and beneath that was a charted graph.(p.422)

• I couldn't focus enough to make out the chart, but the *card* contained two words -- "ACUTE ALCOHOLISM."(p.422)

cards

• Gone are time *cards* to punch, alarm clocks to obey, nosey rumor-mongers and talebearers to evade.(p.329)

• I do recall lying on a cold cement floor and shredding into little bits several pieces of stolen identification *cards*, and washing my face in the toilet bowl trying to sober up, and screaming hysterically while clinging to bars too high to see out of, and cursing everyone that came near me.(p.354)

• All I can remember about the Roaring Twenties is that I drank a great deal, thought I was having a grand time, managed to get to Europe for a few weeks, was very proud of the dozens of speak-easy *cards* entitling me to an entree in the better joints between Cleveland and New York, took on a wife, and built a home in a fashionable suburb of Cleveland.(p.358)

• We weren't even permitted to play *cards* in our home, but father would give us just a little toddy with whiskey and sugar and warm water now and then.(p.484)

care

• Many years ago one of the leading contributors to this book came under our *care* in this hospital and while here he acquired some ideas which he put into practical application at once.(p.xxv)

• I placed myself unreservedly under His *care* and direction.(p.13)

• Then he had gone to Europe, placing himself in the *care* of a celebrated physician (the psychiatrist, Dr. Jung) who prescribed for him.(p.26)

• We asked His protection and *care* with complete abandon.(p.59)

• 3.Made a decision to turn our will and our lives over to the *care* of God as we understood Him.(p.59)

• Perhaps we are mixed up with women in a fashion we wouldn't *care* to have advertised.(p.80)

• We usually conclude the period of meditation with a prayer that we be shown all through the day what our next step is to be, that we be given whatever we need to take *care* of such problems.(p.87)

• When working with a man and his family, you should take *care* not to participate in their quarrels.(p.100)

• Say you do not want to be a wet blanket; that you only want him to take *care* of his health.(p.112)

• Your husband will be the first to say it was your devotion and *care* which brought him to the point where he could have a spiritual experience.(p.118)

• If that is so we are sorry, for we ourselves don't always *care* for people who lecture us.(p.121)

• What about his talk that God will take *care* of them?(p.128)

• It means release from *care*, boredom and worry.(p.151)

• There you will find release from *care*, boredom and worry.(p.152)

• On the third day the lawyer gave his life to the *care* and direction of his Creator, and said he was perfectly willing to do anything necessary.(p.158)

• The next day he turned me over to a couple who, although neither was an alcoholic, knew Dr. Bob and were willing to drive me to Akron where they would turn me over to his *care*.(p.278)

• I didn't *care* to go visiting unless the parties we might visit had plenty of liquor on hand and I could get drunk.(p.301)

• No one seemed to *care* if I made it or not.(p.319)

• I didn't *care* what I looked like, I didn't *care* what I did.(p.337)

• Finally I didn't *care*, I was beyond caring.(p.337)

• And the last sentence was "We asked His protection and *care* with complete abandon."(p.349)

• The Third Step said: "Made a decision to turn our will and our lives over to the *care* of God as we understood Him."(p.350)

• So I went to my wife and asked her, wasn't there something that she and I could do to somehow get together, and she turned on her heel and looked me squarely in the eye, and said, "You don't *care* anything about my problem," and I could have smacked her, but I said to myself, "Grab on to your serenity!"(p.351)

• About this time, at Christmas, after being under this doctor's *care*, we decided that there wasn't anything more to do.(p.388)

• The short tours could be taken *care* of by sneaking enough whiskey aboard ship so that it could be rationed out until another supply could be laid in.(p.398)

• The bartenders took *care* of me, not out of brotherly love, but through enlightened self-interest.(p.410)

• I was becoming a solitary drinker, but I didn't *care*.(p.426)

• Max hadn't gotten that way because I didn't *care*.(p.440)

• Max still works with me in the office, but we have turned our wills and our lives and our work over to the *care* of God.(p.446)

• And life keeps getting simpler and easier as we try to reverse my old idea, by taking *care* of the internal environment via the Twelve Steps, and letting the external environment take *care* of itself.)(p.446)

• There go my good intentions, fear of consequences, will to *care*, responsibility for my behavior.(p.458)

• He said he didn't *care* what I did with the money, but there was going to be no more until I was completely sober.(p.467)

• Some of us always remember our big mouths when it comes to a drink, but somewhere along the line, we seem to have forgotten about taking *care* of our teeth.(p.479)

• Vi was taking *care* of me and I was devoting all my time to the building of that group.(p.496)

• Once I started drinking, I didn't *care* that the rent wasn't paid, or that there was no food in the house, or that my boys needed shoes.(p.527)

• Since I have been in A.A., I have more friends than I ever had in my life -- friends who *care* about me and my welfare, friends who don't *care* that I am black and that I have been in prison.(p.529)

• All they *care* about is that I am a human being and that I want to stay sober.(p.529)

• I don't *care* too much about personal fame or glory, and I want only enough money to enable me to do the work I feel I can perhaps do best.(p.542)
• Maybe I wouldn't be able to hold any job, or maybe (and this was my greatest fear) I wouldn't *care* whether I had a job or not.(p.548)

cared

• He had come to pass his experience along to me -- if I *cared* to have it.(p.9)
• He clamors for this or that, claiming he cannot master alcohol until his material needs are *cared* for.(p.98)
• He told me that there were some other fellows that had tried this with success, and if I *cared* to see any of them he'd have them come in to see me.(p.218)
• Friends invited me to stay on for as long as I *cared* to.(p.281)
• I *cared* nothing about my personal appearance.(p.337)
• I was unhappy myself and I had brought unhappiness to all who *cared* for me.(p.378)
• Indeed, it seemed that I *cared* too much.(p.440)
• This means a great deal to me, because I had always figured that nobody *cared*.(p.481)

career

• He may start off as a moderate drinker; he may or may not become a continuous hard drinker; but at some stage of his drinking *career* he begins to lose all control of his liquor consumption, once he starts to drink.(p.21)
• He often possesses special abilities, skills, and aptitudes, and has a promising *career* ahead of him.(p.21)
• An exceptional man, he remained bone dry for twenty-five years and retired at the age of fifty-five, after a successful and happy business *career*.(p.32)
• If he is not communicative, give him a sketch of your drinking *career* up to the time you quit.(p.91)
• Now and then the family will be plagued by spectres from the past, for the drinking *career* of almost every alcoholic has been marked by escapades, funny, humiliating, shameful or tragic.(p.123)
• My drinking *career* began about four years after I had moved up into partnership and had joined certain clubs, societies and so fourth, and during which period we had Prohibition.(p.213)
• My wife became pregnant and the doctor recommended the use of port or ale . . . so . . . I bought a six gallon crock and a few bottles, listened to advice from amateur brewmeisters, and was off on my beer manufacturing *career* on a small scale (for the time being).(p.297)
• The last day of my drinking *career*, I drank twenty-two of them between ten and twelve a.m. and I shall never know how many more followed them until I was poured into bed that night.(p.298)
• Three years after I started on my drinking *career*, I lost my first job.(p.298)
• We had a small child, and I loved her dearly, so that held me back quite a bit in my drinking *career*.(p.322)
• My drinking *career* started late.(p.328)
• My writing *career* was described in the couplet "Alcohol gave me wings to fly,/And then it took away the sky."(p.331)
• As a matter of fact, when I came into Alcoholics Anonymous I was close to being at the peak of my *career*.(p.356)
• I was active and did well, however, in school publications, dramatics (which came in handy during my drinking *career*), and Greek letter societies.(p.357)
• Then my father fell down a flight of stairs on one of his lost weekends, at the peak of his *career*, and died.(p.370)
• My drinking did not start until after I was thirty-five, and a fairly successful *career* had been established.(p.374)
• It is an endless *career*.(p.394)
• My drinking *career* extended from age eighteen to forty-three.(p.397)
• My personality, from the time I can remember anything, was the perfect set-up for an alcoholic *career*.(p.400)
• A few stood by me, at least in their hearts, throughout the whole of my drinking *career*.(p.404)
• This *career* girl preferred solitary drinking, the blackout kind, often hoping she'd stay that way for keeps.(p.464)
• That and the morning drink came very early in my drinking *career*.(p.513)
• THE *CAREER* OFFICER(p.517)
• I have been allowed to build an entirely new *career* in a field I had never worked in.(p.541)
• Upon graduation, I ventured to New York to pursue my writing *career*.(p.555)
• The early promise of the "boy wonder" faded, and my *career* began to drift.(p.556)

careers

• Therefore, it is not surprising that our drinking *careers* have been characterized by countless vain attempts to prove we could drink like other people.(p.30)
• Though there is no way of proving it, we believe that early in our drinking *careers* most of us could have stopped drinking.(p.32)

careful

• On through the years this conduct continues, accompanied by his continual promises to be *careful* or to keep off the streets altogether.(p.38)
• We ought to sit down with the family and frankly analyze the past as we now see it, being very *careful* not to criticize them.(p.83)
• But we must be *careful* not to drift into worry, remorse or morbid reflection, for that would diminish our usefulness to others.(p.86)
• We ask especially for freedom from self-will, and are *careful* to make no request for ourselves only.(p.87)
• We are *careful* never to pray for our own selfish ends.(p.87)
• If he is in a serious mood dwell on the trouble liquor has caused you, being *careful* not to moralize or lecture.(p.91)
• And be *careful* not to brand him as an alcoholic.(p.92)
• We are *careful* never to show intolerance or hatred of drinking as an institution.(p.103)
• But be *careful* not to be resentful about the last time he did so.(p.116)
• Just be *careful* not to disagree in a resentful or critical spirit.(p.117)
• I had them hidden away in the house and all over my shop in *careful* concealment.(p.233)
• My drinking was never the spaced doses of the *careful* tippler; it was always gluttonous.(p.254)
• All of them were so nice to me that I figured I must be *careful* -- they were bound to want something, being that nice.(p.319)
• I was afraid, and I had made my mind up that I would never get drunk, so I was watchful and *careful*.(p.322)
• But I was a *careful* and cunning alcoholic, and this didn't happen very often.(p.399)
• The terms "spiritual experience" and "spiritual awakening" are used many times in this book which, upon *careful* reading, shows that the personality change sufficient to bring about recovery from alcoholism has manifested itself among us in many different forms.(p.569)

carefully

• On each of these occasions we worked with him, reviewing *carefully* what had happened.(p.35)
• "As soon as I regained my ability to think, I went *carefully* over that evening in Washington.(p.41)
• When we were finished we considered it *carefully*.(p.65)
• Returning home we find a place where we can be quiet for an hour *carefully* reviewing what we have done.(p.75)
• *Carefully* reading the first five proposals we ask if we have omitted anything, for we are building an arch through which we shall walk a free man at last.(p.75)
• If we have *carefully* followed directions, we have begun to sense the flow of His Spirit into us.(p.85)
• When you have *carefully* explained to such people that he is a sick person, you will have created a new atmosphere.(p.115)
• Another principle we observe *carefully* is that we do not relate intimate experiences of another person unless we are sure he would approve.(p.125)
• Members of a family should watch such matters *carefully*, for one careless, inconsiderate remark has been known to raise the very devil.(p.125)
• "I've got to stop if I want to live," I told myself, and if I don't want to break my parents' hearts and maybe jeopardize their own *carefully* built up and hard-fought-for sobriety.(p.429)
• People seemed to be *carefully* dressed, too happy, too normal.(p.524)
• Then the drinks came more frequently, but *carefully* spaced out.(p.557)

careless

• Members of a family should watch such matters carefully, for one *careless*, inconsiderate remark has been known to raise the very devil.(p.125)
• Then I became *careless* and returned sometimes when I shouldn't have.(p.376)
• I was full of *careless* chatter.(p.402)

carelessly

• I had commenced to drink as *carelessly* as though the cocktails were ginger ale.(p.41)

carelessness

• One evening, the book, after checking up, was very definitely in the red for plenty through a piece of studied *carelessness* on my part, and my boss, very shrewd and able, fired me with a parting statement to the effect that once was enough.(p.251)
• At the moral inventory, he brought up some of my bad personality traits or character defects, such as selfishness, conceit, jealousy, *carelessness*, intolerance, ill-temper, sarcasm and resentments.(p.292)

cares

• You should be described to him as one of a fellowship who, as part of their own recovery, try to help others and who will be glad to talk to him if he *cares* to see you.(p.90)
• He also *cares*; he really *cares*.(p.481)

caring

• It wasn't long before I quit *caring* how I looked or what my job performance was.(p.318)
• Finally I didn't care, I was beyond *caring*.(p.337)

Carlyle

• One of five children, I was born on a Kentucky farm in *Carlyle* County.(p.182)

carom

• It was fun to *carom* around the exclusive course which had inspired such awe in me as a lad.(p.4)

carousal

• I stayed sober for four years except for a one-night *carousal* in Chicago.(p.253)

carousing

• I was attending a convention in Chicago and *carousing* day and night.(p.558)

carpenter

• I recall, as I walked into that meeting, saying to myself, "Here I am, a fellow of the American College of Surgeons, a Fellow of the International College of Surgeons, a diplomate of one of the great specialty boards in these United States, a member of the American Psychiatric Society, and I have to go to the butcher, the baker and the *carpenter* to help make a man out of me!"(p.347)
• I tried every gimmick that there was to get some peace of mind, but it was not until I was brought to my alcoholic knees, when I was brought to a group in my own community with the butcher, the baker, the *carpenter* and the mechanic, who were able to give me the Twelve Steps, that I was finally given some semblance of an answer to the last half of the First Step.(p.349)

carpenters

• At the other side of the table sat one of the *carpenters* in our community, and at the further end of the table sat the man who ran the bakery, while on one side sat my friend who was a mechanic.(p.347)

carpet

• Out came his *carpet* slippers and a bottle.(p.32)
• I was, of course, soon on the *carpet* and the upshot was that I had to go back for two more quarters and remain absolutely dry, if I wished to graduate.(p.174)
• There was a red plush *carpet* to welcome me, but even so it wasn't easy.(p.430)

carried

• Nine of the stories in Part II ("They Stopped in Time") are *carried* over from the second edition; eight new stories have been added.(p.xii)
• These family talks will be constructive if they can be *carried* on without heated argument, self-pity, self-justification or resentful criticism.(p.127)
• The two friends spoke of their spiritual experience and told him about the course of action they *carried* out.(p.157)
• To 1950, the year of his death, he *carried* the A.A. message to more than 5,000 alcoholic men and women, and to all these he gave his medical services without thought of charge.(p.171)
• On the return trip, after two or three loads, I passed out and had to be *carried* to the house.(p.183)
• There was a man watching, and I turned to him and said with a defiant air I *carried* with me all the time, "If I don't quit this I'm going to have to join that alcoholic business they're talking about."(p.266)
• I *carried* out his instructions.(p.276)
• During the first three months I *carried* on all these activities without a car, depending entirely on buses and streetcars – I, who had always to have a car at my immediate command.(p.283)
• I, *carried* away with the desire to serve A.A., gave what was probably one of the first radio broadcasts about A.A., living through a case of mike fright and

feeling like a million dollars when it was all over.(p.283)
• The program was *carried* on entirely by word of mouth.(p.291)
• You didn't carry a little orchid up the aisle in those days; you *carried* a great big bouquet, like a funeral spray, and you didn't have your picture taken until just before you went to the church.(p.385)
• Many of them *carried* a flask and sandwich case, strapped to their saddles so they could stay out all day.(p.404)
• These things were *carried* out in moments of less severe hangover or short stretches on the wagon.(p.409)
• Once or twice, during my early drinking, I *carried* it over into the second day, and only once, that I can remember, did it continue into the third.(p.432)
• I remember finding myself in the middle of the night in the doctors' parking lot at the hospital with one foot in the car and one foot on the ground, not knowing which was the lead foot; finding myself hanging up the telephone – then realizing I had gotten out of bed, answered the phone, turned on the light, and *carried* on a conversation with a patient.(p.441)
• The next morning I *carried* another prescription to this man's house and exchanged it for the bottle his wife had.(p.489)
• I stopped off just to have one drink to see if it tasted the same on the way back to London, and that night I was *carried* back to bed again.(p.522)

carries
• This is the great news this book *carries* to those who suffer from alcoholism.(p.17)

carry
• Being mostly business or professional folk, we could not well *carry* on our occupations in such an event.(p.xiii)
• He suddenly realized that in order to save himself he must *carry* his message to another alcoholic.(p.xvi)
• With a certain satisfaction I reflected there was enough gin concealed about the house to *carry* me through that night and the next day.(p.8)
• 11.Sought through prayer and meditation to improve our conscious contact with God as we understood Him, praying only for knowledge of His will for us and the power to *carry* that out.(p.59)
• 12.Having had a spiritual awakening as the result of these steps, we tried to *carry* this message to alcoholics, and to practice these principles in all our affairs.(p.60)
• We may kill a future opportunity to *carry* a beneficial message.(p.77)
• Every day is a day when we must *carry* the vision of God's will into all of our activities.(p.85)
• This is our twelfth suggestion: *Carry* this message to other alcoholics!(p.89)
• We often need it to *carry* green recruits through a severe hangover.(p.102)
• Often you must *carry* the burden of avoiding them or keeping them under control.(p.117)
• We women *carry* with us a picture of the ideal man, the sort of chap we would like our husbands to be.(p.118)
• We try not to indulge in cynicism over the state of the nations, nor do we *carry* the world's troubles on our shoulders.(p.132)
• This gave me the freedom to do A.A. work, and to rest for periods of two or three days when I became too exhausted to *carry* on.(p.283)
• There was more than one occasion when I got up in the morning with just enough money for coffee and toast and the bus fare to *carry* me to my first appointment.(p.283)
• With God's help I am able, for one day at a time, to *carry* business responsibilities which, not many years ago, I would not have dreamed of assuming.(p.284)
• I just wanted to live to a certain age, *carry* through with what I felt was my job with the children, and after that – no matter.(p.337)
• No one individual can *carry* all the burdens of the world.(p.382)
• You didn't *carry* a little orchid up the aisle in those days; you carried a great big bouquet, like a funeral spray, and you didn't have your picture taken until just before you went to the church.(p.385)
• But she couldn't *carry* me forever.(p.472)
• *Carry* this message to other alcoholics.(p.473)
• Year later, I go to Canada to *carry* message to Tall Man, but he not listen to son.(p.476)
• Start group on reservation and *carry* message, help start other groups all over Maritimes and New England.(p.476)
• I keep it simple; go to many meetings; *carry* message to those who listen.(p.476)
• I think I am very lucky that there are people like A.A.'s and an A.A. program to hang on to and *carry* me through.(p.511)
• Instead of drinking in fancy bars and clubs, I had to *carry* a bottle of vodka in my briefcase, duck into public toilets, and gulp from the bottle, trembling, in order to keep from falling apart.(p.557)
• Five – Each group has but one primary purpose -- to *carry* its message to the alcoholic who still suffers.(p.564)
• If there is none nearby, you will be invited to *carry* on a correspondence which will do much to insure your sobriety no matter how isolated you are.(p.575)

carrying
• In this way he was slyly *carrying* tales.(p.145)
• It was the day before Mother's Day and I had come home plastered, *carrying* a big potted plant which I set down on the table and forthwith went upstairs and passed out.(p.179)
• Making amends is sometimes doing what we are capable of doing but failed to do because of alcohol; *carrying* out community responsibilities such as Community Funds, Red Cross, educational and religious activities in proportion to our abilities and energy.(p.381)
• I had to put up a three hundred dollar bond because he was *carrying* the same summons around in his pocket for me.(p.491)
• 5. – Each Alcoholics Anonymous group ought to be a spiritual entity having but one primary purpose -- that of *carrying* its message to the alcoholic who still suffers.(p.565)
• We think that each group should soon achieve this ideal; that any public solicitation of funds using the name of Alcoholics Anonymous is highly dangerous, whether by groups, clubs, hospitals, or other outside agencies; that acceptance of large gifts from any source, or of contributions *carrying* any obligation whatever, is unwise.(p.566)

cars
• Then I turned two company *cars* over in a short time and Bingo -- fired again.(p.242)
• "Well," I said to dad, when the A.A. people kept coming with these lovely *cars* and looked so nice, "I suppose the neighbors say, 'Now those old fools must have up and died, but where's the hearse?'"(p.269)
• By the time I figured out what had happened, I saw two flashing red lights atop squad *cars*, sedately coming around the corner.(p.353)
• I found I could boost my income by figuring out a lot of cute little tricks that the boss wouldn't be likely to notice – filching money from the Coke machine, short-sticking the customers on oil, and selling oil I'd drained out of other *cars*.(p.423)
• He had gone through the windshields of *cars* a couple of times and was pretty well banged up.(p.510)

cart
• I would gather up all my soiled clothes, as much as I could cram into a grocery *cart*, and be off.(p.370)

cartons
• And I continued to drink, on and off then, until every dollar I had in the world was gone again and I was right back living at my sister's, getting my cigarettes by calling her grocer and telling him to put in a couple of *cartons* with her order, exactly as I had before I started to work at Max's.(p.202)

case
• Their very first *case*, a desperate one, recovered immediately and became A.A. number three.(p.xvii)
• He had but partially recovered from a gastric hemorrhage and seemed to be a *case* of pathological mental deterioration.(p.xxix)
• When I need a mental uplift, I often think of another *case* brought in by a physician prominent in New York.(p.xxix)
• This tragic situation has already arrived in practically every *case* long before it is suspected.(p.24)
• I have never seen one single *case* recover, where that state of mind existed to the extent that it does in you."(p.27)
• This hope, however, was destroyed by the doctor's telling him that while his religious convictions were very good, in his *case* they did not spell the necessary vital spiritual experience.(p.27)
• It may be worth a bad *case* of jitters if you get a full knowledge of your condition.(p.32)
• This *case* contains a powerful lesson.(p.33)
• You may think this an extreme *case*.(p.37)
• We first saw Fred about a year ago in a hospital where he had gone to recover from a bad *case* of jitters.(p.39)
• If that be the *case*, you may be suffering from an illness which only a spiritual experience will conquer.(p.44)
• This Power has in each *case* accomplished the miraculous, the humanly impossible.(p.50)
• He becomes, on the next occasion, still more demanding or gracious, as the *case* may be.(p.61)
• In that *case* he is going to wonder how you can add anything to what he already knows.(p.93)
• But point out that we alcoholics have much in common and that you would like, in any *case*, to be friendly.(p.95)
• His *case* presents additional questions which we shall try to answer for you.(p.110)
• In either *case* certain family problems will arise.(p.126)
• Their services are often indispensable in treating a newcomer and in following his *case* afterward.(p.133)
• Here is a *case* in point: One of our friends is a heavy smoker and coffee drinker.(p.135)
• I know, in my own particular *case*, that nothing my company could have done would have stopped me for, so long as I was able to hold my position, I could not possibly realize how serious my situation was.(p.141)
• In another *case*, an alcoholic was sent to a hospital for treatment.(p.145)
• In *case* he does stumble, even once, you will have to decide whether to let him go.(p.147)
• It was not long before I was drinking at least a *case* and a half a day.(p.177)
• My *case* is rather unusual in one respect.(p.182)
• Yet, as my record shows, I did become an extremely serious *case*.(p.182)
• My *case* is so terrible that I'm scared to go out of this hospital at all.(p.188)
• I said, "In that *case*, there's no use of wasting this," and I got the last of that pint.(p.207)
• I then entered *Case* School and worked while I went to school and finished there.(p.212)
• In any *case* I must get out of here before I let slip my abysmal ignorance of how I came to be here, and she realized that I was stark, staring mad.(p.223)
• I remembered filling the peroxide bottle in my medicine chest with gin, in *case* my sister found the bottle I hid under the mattress.(p.224)
• He was a man of considerable means and he might have done what many men would have done in such a *case*.(p.278)
• Nothing has ever to this day equalled the thrill of that first *case*.(p.282)
• I, carried away with the desire to serve A.A., gave what was probably one of the first radio broadcasts about A.A., living through a *case* of mike fright and feeling like a million dollars when it was all over.(p.283)
• The adjustments in such a *case* are difficult and take time, but we both feel that they are certainly worth it.(p.286)
• When I told them six weeks, they were polite and said that they would contact me in *case* they had anyone with an alcoholic problem.(p.293)
• That being the *case*, it didn't take me long to figure out that my meager manufacturing facilities were entirely inadequate to the manufacture of beer for social and domestic consumption.(p.297)
• I had to have it with me at night, in *case* I woke up and needed that drink.(p.337)
• In the various schools I attended, it was always a *case* of just getting by.(p.357)
• And I still felt it was a weakness – plus, in her *case*, adverse circumstances.(p.370)
• There was a doctor in our church congregation who was interested in my *case*, and he thought it was a vitamin deficiency.(p.389)
• Many of them carried a flask and sandwich *case*, strapped to their saddles so they could stay out all day.(p.404)
• Priscilla, an A.A. who, like Marty, has become one of my greatest friends, decided that I was a stubborn *case*.(p.414)
• One night I was sitting in the lab alone with a fifth and a *case* of beer listening to dreamy Hawaiian music on the radio.(p.427)
• Now I had to face up to the fact that knowledge of this sort, applied to my individual *case*, was not power.(p.435)
• It wasn't until just lately that, in your *case*, I could draw it.(p.436)
• The neurologist in charge of my *case* didn't think to ask me whether I drank, and I didn't think to tell him.(p.444)
• I happened to be the best diagnostician I knew at the time, and certainly I knew my *case* better than anyone else.(p.444)
• On one occasion when I was serving time in my favorite drying-out place while I was having a session

with the psychiatrist, she left my ***case*** history on her desk when she was called away from the room.(p.470)
• A ***case*** of measles saved me from being kicked out during my Sophomore year.(p.499)
• In any ***case***, I made myself believe that, so I just drifted about, existing on my retired pay, drinking, and living at home.(p.522)
• Need I add that such was the ***case*** because I had no money to provide a roof over my head?(p.538)
• It's been true in my ***case***, nor could I quarrel with "restore us to sanity," for my actions drunk or sober, before A.A., were not those of a sane person.(p.550)

cases
• We should like to be helpful to such ***cases***.(p.xiv)
• I personally know scores of ***cases*** who were of the type with whom other methods had failed completely.(p.xxiii)
• The ***cases*** we have followed through have been most interesting; in fact, many of them are amazing.(p.xxv)
• In nearly all ***cases***, their ideals must be grounded in a power greater than themselves, if they are to re-create their lives.(p.xxvi)
• Exceptions to ***cases*** such as yours have been occurring since early times.(p.27)
• They cited ***cases*** out of their own experience by the dozen.(p.42)
• Though not a religious person, I have profound respect for the spiritual approach in such ***cases*** as yours.(p.43)
• For most ***cases***, there is virtually no other solution."(p.43)
• Except in a few rare ***cases***, neither he nor any other human being can provide such a defense.(p.43)
• In most ***cases*** it was found that our self-esteem, our pocketbooks, our ambitions, our personal relationships (including sex) were hurt or threatened.(p.64)
• In nine ***cases*** out of ten the unexpected happens.(p.78)
• Perhaps there are some ***cases*** where the utmost frankness is demanded.(p.82)
• And there may be a valid reason for postponement in some ***cases***.(p.83)
• In some ***cases*** the wife will never come back for one reason or another.(p.99)
• In some ***cases*** it may be better to let someone outside of the family present the book.(p.113)
• Sometimes there are ***cases*** where alcoholism is complicated by other disorders.(p.114)
• Though it is infinitely better that he have no relapse at all, as has been true with many of our men, it is by no means a bad thing in some ***cases***.(p.120)
• In most ***cases***, the alcoholic survived this ordeal without relapse, but not always.(p.125)
• We do not know of many ***cases*** where this difficulty lasted long.(p.134)
• I well remember the shock I received when a prominent doctor in Chicago told me of ***cases*** where pressure of the spinal fluid actually ruptured the brain.(p.140)
• Your understanding treatment of their ***cases*** will pay dividends.(p.141)
• In some ***cases*** it will, and in others it may not.(p.144)
• The use of spiritual principles in such ***cases*** was not so well understood as it is now.(p.156)
• They experienced a few distressing failures, but in those ***cases*** they made an effort to bring the man's family into a spiritual way of living, thus relieving much worry and suffering.(p.159)
• I knew everyone would buy a few bottles, or ***cases***, of liquor as their exchequers permitted, and that it would soon be gone.(p.175)
• I felt having gotten married, I was an adult and one of the first things I did was to buy two ***cases*** of whiskey with no idea of drinking it.(p.196)
• So I spent much of my time calling on the people who I felt would logically come in contact with alcoholic ***cases***, doctors, ministers, lawyers and the personnel men in industry.(p.281)
• But the money I had saved up went for ***cases*** of liquor.(p.409)
• You see, I am a five-time loser, which means five felony convictions (not including the ***cases*** beaten).(p.457)

cash
• She paid me in ***cash***.(p.196)
• Then it was my turn -- I ordered "Three beers," but this time it was different, I had a ***cash*** investment of thirty cents and, on a ten dollar a week salary, that's a big thing.(p.247)
• While there, two or three more "***cash*** customers" (as Dr. Bob used to call them -- probably because they had so little ***cash***) were shipped in to us from Detroit.(p.282)

cashed
• I stopped at the cashier's any hour of the night on the way to the bar and ***cashed*** a check.(p.410)

cashier's
• I stopped at the ***cashier's*** any hour of the night on the way to the bar and cashed a check.(p.410)

cast
• Ideas, emotions, and attitudes which were once the guiding forces of the lives of these men are suddenly ***cast*** to one side, and a completely new set of conceptions and motives begin to dominate them.(p.27)
• Now these are about to be ***cast*** out.(p.72)
• Then, under one provocation or another, the aggrieved one would unearth the old affair and angrily ***cast*** its ashes about.(p.124)
• I couldn't walk, having it in a ***cast***, and the doctor left the ***cast*** on three weeks longer than was necessary because he never found me sober enough to take it off.(p.390)
• I came to understand the intricate processes of projection, by which we ***cast*** into our adult world the images of the horrors of our childhood.(p.434)
• I learned the true meaning of bread ***cast*** upon the waters.(p.541)
• We ***cast*** off the burdens of the past and the anxieties of the future, as we begin to live in the present, one day at a time.(p.560)

casting
• Though some of us resisted, we found no great difficulty in ***casting*** aside such feelings.(p.48)
• My divorce coincided with my father's bankruptcy, and I went to work, ***casting*** off all allegiances and responsibilities to any other than myself.(p.225)

castle
• I was born in a ***castle*** -- the family home, in Europe.(p.400)

castor
• There, I received several soda crackers and water daily, and before I could have my third-day meal (again the only meal in ten days), I had to drink a glass of ***castor*** oil or mineral oil, depending on the cruelty of the person who was doing the dispensing.(p.459)

casual
• The alcoholic may say to himself in the most ***casual*** way, "It won't burn me this time, so here's how!"(p.24)
• Many of us have been so touchy that even ***casual*** reference to spiritual things made us bristle with antagonism.(p.48)
• In addition to these ***casual*** get-togethers, it became customary to set apart one night a week for a meeting to be attended by anyone or everyone interested in a spiritual way of life.(p.159)
• Where once I had ***casual*** acquaintances, all of whom were fair weather friends, I now have a host of friends who accept me for what I am.(p.296)

casually
• We now see that when we began to drink deliberately, instead of ***casually***, there was little serious or effective thought during the period of premeditation of what the terrific consequences might be.(p.37)
• In meeting me ***casually***, I don't think my strong belief in "The Man Upstairs" shows, but I have no other explanation for the many good things that have happened to me since I have been in A.A. -- they came to me from a Greater Power.(p.367)

casualties
• Slight ***casualties***, complicated however by a long and serious illness, were my only mishaps.(p.253)

cat-and-dog
• You tell that dumb ***cat-and-dog*** doctor he's not a Beverly Hills psychiatrist.(p.440)

catalyst
• It was to be my lifesaver -- the final ***catalyst***.(p.461)

catapulted
• I was soon to be ***catapulted*** into what I like to call the fourth dimension of existence.(p.8)

catch
• If this kind of approach does not ***catch*** your husband's interest, it may be best to drop the subject, but after a friendly talk your husband will usually revive the topic himself.(p.112)
• In my own experience I was so jubilant at finding myself sober, and I had so many things to ***catch*** up on, that a month went by before the thought even occurred to me.(p.219)
• I have my brilliant moments yet, but whenever the boys ***catch*** me at it they tell me so very plainly.(p.512)

categories
• The problem with which you struggle usually falls within one of four ***categories***:(p.108)

cathedral
• I visited Winchester ***Cathedral***.(p.1)
• That war-time day in old Winchester ***Cathedral*** came back again.(p.10)
• The real significance of my experience in the ***Cathedral*** burst upon me.(p.12)

Catholic
• Insofar as religion was concerned, I had a ***Catholic*** training in my youth.(p.214)
• I went to both ***Catholic*** and public schools.(p.214)
• I resolved that if I were going to continue with the ***Catholic*** Church, I was going to know the roots of the doctrine, since those roots had caused me some confusion.(p.221)
• In summing up, I can say that A.A. had made me, I hope, a real ***Catholic***.(p.221)
• But, although I was a good ***Catholic***, the monastic life had little appeal for me.(p.230)
• I had always been a good ***Catholic***, possibly not so devoted as I should have been, but fairly regular in my attendance at services.(p.234)
• There is something spiritual about an art museum or a symphony, and the ***Catholic*** Church approves of our use of them.(p.574)
• There is something spiritual about A.A. too, and ***Catholic*** participation in it almost invariably results in poor Catholics becoming better Catholics."(p.574)

Catholicism
• I had accepted ***Catholicism*** somewhat as an inheritance.(p.220)

Catholics
• By personal religious affiliation, we include ***Catholics***, Protestants, Jews, Hindus, and a sprinkling of Moslems and Buddhists.(p.xx)
• (My mother and father were ***Catholics*** and I had been baptized, but at the end of my instructions for Confirmation I had not gone to church, and then when my mother remarried, she married a Protestant and the whole religious angle was forgotten.(p.201)
• Unlike many other ***Catholics*** who frequently take pledges for definite periods -- a year, two years or for good, I never had any desire to "take a pledge" before the priest.(p.234)
• There is something spiritual about A.A. too, and Catholic participation in it almost invariably results in poor ***Catholics*** becoming better ***Catholics***."(p.574)

caught
• My attention was ***caught*** by a doggerel on an old tombstone:(p.1)
• "Here lies a Hampshire Grenadier Who ***caught*** his death Drinking cold small beer.(p.1)
• Liquor ***caught*** up with me much faster than I came up behind Walter.(p.3)
• But drinking ***caught*** up with me again and my generous friend had to let me go.(p.4)
• Of course, it was always my aim to have my own way without being ***caught***.(p.210)
• And as I fumed helplessly and planned to get good and drunk and show them, my eye ***caught*** a sentence in the book lying open on my bed: "We cannot live with anger."(p.228)
• However, it finally ***caught*** up with me, and when it did, I was a mental, physical, and nervous wreck.(p.299)
• I was ***caught*** in a cycle of alcohol and sedation that was proving inescapable and consciousness had become intolerable.(p.304)
• I was gathering that cache for disposal when my wife woke up and ***caught*** me at it.(p.333)
• When I did make it home in 1920, I re-entered school and ***caught*** up with my class in a few short months -- I actually did a year's work in three months, proving much to the disgust of my dad that I could do it when I wanted to.(p.358)
• I was living in constant fear that I would get ***caught*** while driving a car, so I used taxis part of the time.(p.375)
• My torch blazed madly and the pew ***caught*** fire.(p.424)
• This physician, the originator of A.A.'s first black group, but badly ***caught*** in the toils, tells of his release and of how freedom came as he worked among his own people.(p.483)
• During the day a friend of mine brought me some magazines to take to a hospital group I was interested in, and I looked through them and a "banner" across the front of one featured an article by a prominent clergyman in which I ***caught*** the word "resentment."(p.552)

cause

• There are many situations which arise out of the phenomenon of craving which *cause* men to make the supreme sacrifice rather than continue to fight.(p.xxviii)

• It may *cause* him to die a few years before his time.(p.21)

• It seems to *cause* more trouble.(p.68)

• Nor are we afraid of disclosing our alcoholism on the theory it may *cause* financial harm.(p.78)

• We would not even do the *cause* of temperate drinking any good, for not one drinker in a thousand likes to be told anything about alcohol by one who hates it.(p.103)

• Your desire to protect him should not *cause* you to lie to people when they have a right to know where he is and what he is doing.(p.115)

• Therefore, you probably need fresh interests and a great *cause* to live for as much as your husband.(p.119)

• I seemed to react by developing a streak of varying meanness, which would *cause* me to do things to create excitement and to get attention.(p.211)

• It was the first of many such experiences that became the only *cause* of harsh words, tears and heartaches in an otherwise truly beautiful marriage.(p.361)

• Then he asks me if I believe in a power greater than myself, whether I call that power God, Allah, Confucius, Prime *Cause*, Divine Mind, or any other name.(p.503)

• I cannot see the *cause* of this temptation now.(p.507)

caused

• Here was the threat of commitment, the loss of family and position, to say nothing of that intense mental and physical suffering which drinking always *caused* him.(p.36)

• First, we searched out the flaws in our make-up which *caused* our failure.(p.64)

• If he is in a serious mood dwell on the trouble liquor has *caused* you, being careful not to moralize or lecture.(p.91)

• Can it be appreciated that he has been a victim of crooked thinking, directly *caused* by the action of alcohol on his brain?(p.140)

• All the other people that had talked to me wanted to help me, and my pride prevented me from listening to them, and *caused* only resentment on my part, but I felt as if I would be a real stinker if I did not listen to a couple of fellows for a short time, if that would cure them.(p.185)

• I resolved that if I were going to continue with the Catholic Church, I was going to know the roots of the doctrine, since those roots had *caused* me some confusion.(p.221)

• As the treatment progressed I began to get a picture of myself, of the temperament that had *caused* me so much trouble.(p.226)

• But I can remember, in my teens, that there were a few characters who *caused* the village heads to nod pityingly and sometimes in anger as they paused to say, "That sot, Henri" and "Ce pauvre Jules," who drank too much.(p.230)

• Successive Monday morning hangovers, which despite mid-week resolutions to do better, came with unfailing regularity, eventually *caused* me to quit my job.(p.254)

• Now my drinking was limited by only one factor, the enforced periods of dryness *caused* by lengthy tours at sea.(p.398)

• My mother's heartbreak, or the unpleasant publicity I had *caused* did not bother my pretty head.(p.401)

• Tragedies during those years that were *caused* by my drinking, such as the breaking up of my marriage, the death of my child, other things – had little restraining effect.(p.465)

• This *caused* the rather cryptic comment from one of my A.A. friends, when I told my story after coming into the program, that I had always been a cinch for the program, for I had always been interested in mankind, but that I was just taking them one man at a time.(p.548)

• I also got into my first disciplinary trouble *caused* by drinking, on two separate occasions.(p.555)

causes

• So we had to get down to *causes* and conditions.(p.64)

• Then we have the voices who cry for sex and more sex; who bewail the institution of marriage; who think that most of the troubles of the race are traceable to sex *causes*.(p.69)

• All have now passed away from natural *causes*, having maintained complete sobriety.(p.169)

• Through my efforts to get down to "*causes* and conditions," I stand convinced that my emotional illness has been present from my earliest recollection.(p.544)

causing

• Alcoholism may be *causing* your organization considerable damage in its waste of time, men and reputation.(p.148)

• Drunk and *causing* a brawl, they said.(p.428)

• I know there are some alcoholics who seem terribly, terribly grown-up, but I think that they are trying to make themselves think they are grown-up, and the strain of their effort is what is *causing* them to drink -- a sense of inadequacy, a childish vanity to be the most popular, the most sought after, the mostest of the most.(p.535)

caution

• Although I did drink, it always was with *caution* -- unless I was alone.(p.328)

cautious

• This lady was *cautious*.(p.321)

• Furthermore, I knew that I was looked upon as a city slicker from New York, and I had to be pretty *cautious* among small town, conservative Yankees.(p.360)

ce

• But I can remember, in my teens, that there were a few characters who caused the village heads to nod pityingly and sometimes in anger as they paused to say, "That sot, Henri" and "*Ce* pauvre Jules," who drank too much.(p.230)

cease

• There was a tremendous urge to *cease* forever.(p.34)

ceased

• Liquor *ceased* to be a luxury; it became a necessity.(p.5)

• And we have *ceased* fighting anything or anyone -- even alcohol.(p.84)

• I had no trouble there because I had never actually *ceased* to believe in God, and had tried lots of times to get help but hadn't succeeded.(p.186)

• By this time I had *ceased* to be the life of the party.(p.410)

• Each time, I went back to drinking – even smuggling a bottle of vodka into the hospital as soon as the blood transfusions had *ceased*.(p.558)

celebrate

• Eventually, there would be a ball game, or a show, or some sort of special occasion to *celebrate* and I would turn up drunk.(p.196)

• We heard by wireless on the 5th that the Armistice would be signed the next day (this was a premature report) so I had a couple of cognacs to *celebrate*; then I hopped a truck and went AWOL.(p.242)

• The November following, I took a few days off after pay day to *celebrate* my birthday on the 25th of the month.(p.491)

• After my very first drink – a tiny glass of sherry my father gave me to *celebrate* the New Year when I was thirteen -- I went up to bed, dizzy with exhilaration and excitement, and I prayed I wouldn't drink any more!(p.554)

celebrated

• Then he had gone to Europe, placing himself in the care of a *celebrated* physician (the psychiatrist, Dr. Jung) who prescribed for him.(p.26)

• As a *celebrated* American statesman put it, "Let's look at the record."(p.50)

celebrations

• I came of good stock, of men and women who drank wine all their lives as a beverage, and while they occasionally got drunk at special *celebrations*, they were up and about their business the next day.(p.231)

cell

• I spent the next three days in a *cell*.(p.424)

• After the meeting was over and we had returned to the *cell* block again, I was asked how I was impressed.(p.510)

cellar

• He is like the farmer who came up out of his cyclone *cellar* to find his home ruined.(p.82)

• If my wife was planning to go out in the afternoon, I would get a large supply of liquor and smuggle it home and hide it in the coal bin, the clothes chute, over door jambs, over beams in the *cellar* and in cracks in the *cellar* tile.(p.176)

• So I filled the *cellar* full, with the permission of my good wife.(p.177)

cellaret

• I sneak downstairs and get a bottle of whiskey from the *cellaret*.(p.501)

cement

• The feeling of having shared in a common peril is one element in the powerful *cement* which binds us.(p.17)

• Have we skimped on the *cement* put into the foundation?(p.75)

• I do recall lying on a cold *cement* floor and shredding into little bits several pieces of stolen identification cards, and washing my face in the toilet bowl trying to sober up, and screaming hysterically while clinging to bars too high to see out of, and cursing everyone that came near me.(p.354)

cent

• At present, our membership is increasing at the rate of about seven per *cent* a year.(p.xx)

• My efficiency as a professional man was probably reduced to twenty-five per *cent* of what it should have been.(p.215)

• They did not seem to be getting an answer, for here I was staying sober and selling lots of auto polish, on which they were making one thousand per *cent* profit.(p.247)

• I know now that sixty per *cent* of the time I drank alone without benefit of customers.(p.287)

• "We watch the alcoholic performing in a position of responsibility and we know that because he is drinking heavily and daily he has cut his capacities by fifty per *cent*, and still he seems able to do a satisfactory job.(p.308)

• And we wonder how much further this man could go if his alcoholic problem could be removed and he could throw one hundred per *cent* of his abilities into action.(p.308)

• I cooperated with that man one hundred per *cent*!(p.388)

• To keep it in round figures, let's say twenty per *cent* of my income went for giggle gurgles.(p.397)

• After a few more estimates as to income and expenditures for booze over a few sample years, taken at random, I conclude that this twenty per *cent* stayed fairly constant.(p.398)

• $2,000 a year for twenty-five years is $50,000, twenty per *cent* of which is $10,000.(p.399)

center

• So in spite of anything that I might do, I prospered, being one of only two brokers in the rubber *center* of the world.(p.197)

• That had been in the *center* of New York, on noisy 42nd Street . . . this was obviously a quiet residential section.(p.223)

• I had tried to be the *center* of my own little world, whereas God was the *center* of a vast universe of which I was perhaps an essential, but a very tiny, part.(p.280)

• I still couldn't make it through the nights without drinking, so I went back into the hospital, this time to a rehabilitation *center*.(p.320)

• I was the *center* of attention, just what my sick ego craved.(p.407)

• My wife was in the Junior League, and I was on the board of directors of the local *center* for the mentally retarded.(p.418)

• I remained there for about ten months, and then I was sent to a place called Wallkill, a so-called rehabilitation *center*.(p.509)

• At New York, U.S.A., Alcoholics Anonymous maintains its international service *center*.(p.575)

• If you cannot find A.A. in your locality, a letter addressed to Alcoholics Anonymous, Box 459, Grand Central Station, New York, NY 10163, U.S.A., will receive a prompt reply from this world *center*, referring you to the nearest A.A. group.(p.575)

centered

• My whole life seemed to be *centered* around doing what I wanted to do, without regard for the rights, wishes, or privileges of anyone else; a state of mind which became more and more predominant as the years passed.(p.172)

• I went to meetings, I spent a lot of time at the clubroom, but it was all *centered* in this one woman.(p.472)

centers

• There was to be the least possible organization, even in our service *centers*.(p.xix)

• Therefore, the main problem of the alcoholic *centers* in his mind, rather than in his body.(p.23)

• Little clusters of twos and threes and fives of us have sprung up in other communities, through contact with our two larger *centers*.(p.162)

• Eight – Alcoholics Anonymous should remain forever nonprofessional, but our service *centers* may employ special workers.(p.564)

central

• The *central* fact of our lives today is the absolute certainty that our Creator has entered into our hearts and lives in a way which is indeed miraculous.(p.25)

• The name on it was unfamiliar and I had to ask the

way to Grand *Central*.(p.223)
• There was no *central* heating, and this was the dead of winter.(p.415)
• The small group may elect its secretary, the large group its rotating committee, and the groups of a large metropolitan area their *central* or intergroup committee, which often employs a full-time secretary.(p.567)
• (This address is now available in pamphlet form at nominal cost through most A.A. groups or from Box 459, Grand *Central* Station, New York, NY 10163, under the title "Three Talks to Medical Societies by Bill W." – formerly called "Bill on Alcoholism" and earlier "Alcoholism the Illness.")(p.572)
• If you cannot find A.A. in your locality, a letter addressed to Alcoholics Anonymous, Box 459, Grand *Central* Station, New York, NY 10163, U.S.A., will receive a prompt reply from this world center, referring you to the nearest A.A. group.(p.575)

cents
• Then it was my turn – I ordered "Three beers," but this time it was different, I had a cash investment of thirty *cents* and, on a ten dollar a week salary, that's a big thing.(p.247)
• At this time, the price of booze in the bars was fifteen *cents* a shot and ten *cents* a beer.(p.397)

century
• Nevertheless, the twentieth *century* readily accepts theories of all kinds, provided they are firmly grounded in fact.(p.48)
• This world of ours has made more material progress in the last *century* than in all the millenniums which went before.(p.51)
• Even in the present *century*, American newspapers were afraid to print an account of the Wright brothers' first successful flight at Kitty Hawk.(p.51)
• He is like the retired business man who lolls in the Florida sunshine in the winter complaining of the sad state of the nation; the minister who sighs over the sins of the twentieth *century*; politicians and reformers who are sure all would be Utopia if the rest of the world would only behave; the outlaw safe cracker who thinks society has wronged him; and the alcoholic who has lost all and is locked up.(p.61)

ceremonies
• Those having religious affiliations will find here nothing disturbing to their beliefs or *ceremonies*.(p.28)

certain
• In the course of his third treatment he acquired *certain* ideas concerning a possible means of recovery.(p.xxiii)
• I have had many men who had, for example, worked a period of months on some problem or business deal which was to be settled on a *certain* date, favorable to them.(p.xxvii)
• It went into *certain* securities, then cheap and rather unpopular.(p.2)
• With a *certain* satisfaction I reflected there was enough gin concealed about the house to carry me through that night and the next day.(p.8)
• The word God still aroused a *certain* antipathy.(p.12)
• For if an alcoholic failed to perfect and enlarge his spiritual life through work and self-sacrifice for others, he could not survive the *certain* trials and low spots ahead.(p.14)
• Then we have a *certain* type of hard drinker.(p.20)
• If he can afford it, he may have liquor concealed all over his house to be *certain* no one gets his entire supply away from him to throw down the waterpipe.(p.22)
• We are not sure why, once a *certain* point is reached, little can be done for him.(p.22)
• Sometimes these excuses have a *certain* plausibility, but none of them really makes sense in the light of the havoc an alcoholic's drinking bout creates.(p.23)
• At a *certain* point in the drinking of every alcoholic, he passes into a state where the most powerful desire to stop drinking is of absolutely no avail.(p.24)
• We are unable, at *certain* times, to bring into our consciousness with sufficient force the memory of the suffering and humiliation of even a week or a month ago.(p.24)
• The almost *certain* consequences that follow taking even a glass of beer do not crowd into the mind to deter us.(p.24)
• A *certain* American business man had ability, good sense, and high character.(p.26)
• He can go anywhere on this earth where other free men may go without disaster, provided he remains willing to maintain a *certain* simple attitude.(p.26)
• *Certain* drinkers, who would be greatly insulted if called alcoholics, are astonished at their inability to stop.(p.33)
• That may be true of *certain* nonalcoholic people who, though drinking foolishly and heavily at the present time, are able to stop or moderate, because their brains and bodies have not been damaged as ours were.(p.39)
• Once more: The alcoholic at *certain* times has no effective mental defense against the first drink.(p.43)
• They flatly declare that since they have come to believe in a Power greater than themselves, to take a *certain* attitude toward that Power, and to do *certain* simple things, there has been a revolutionary change in their way of living and thinking.(p.50)
• Without knowing it, had we not been brought to where we stood by a *certain* kind of faith?(p.53)
• If you have decided you want what we have and are willing to go to any length to get it – then you are ready to take *certain* steps.(p.58)
• We have admitted *certain* defects; we have ascertained in a rough way what the trouble is; we have put our finger on the weak items in our personal inventory.(p.72)
• Time after time newcomers have tried to keep to themselves *certain* facts about their lives.(p.72)
• He wants to enjoy a *certain* reputation, but knows in his heart he doesn't deserve it.(p.73)
• Coming to his senses, he is revolted at *certain* episodes he vaguely remembers.(p.73)
• We may have had *certain* spiritual beliefs, but now we begin to have a spiritual experience.(p.75)
• There is no use arousing any prejudice he may have against *certain* theological terms and conceptions about which he may already be confused.(p.93)
• Be *certain* he will be welcomed by your family, and that he is not trying to impose upon you for money, connections, or shelter.(p.96)
• His drinking may be constant or it may be heavy only on *certain* occasions.(p.109)
• Being *certain* he wants to stop, you can go to him with this volume as joyfully as though you had struck oil.(p.113)
• Defeat seemed *certain*.(p.113)
• Our women folk have suggested *certain* attitudes a wife may take with the husband who is recovering.(p.122)
• In either case *certain* family problems will arise.(p.126)
• Even if he displays a *certain* amount of neglect and irresponsibility towards the family, it is well to let him go as far as he likes in helping other alcoholics.(p.129)
• If he temporizes and still thinks he can ever drink again, even beer, he might as well be discharged after the next bender which, if an alcoholic, he is almost *certain* to have.(p.142)
• For most alcoholics who are drinking, or who are just getting over a spree, a *certain* amount of physical treatment is desirable, even imperative.(p.142)
• Wherever men are gathered together in business there will be rivalries and, arising out of these, a *certain* amount of office politics.(p.145)
• Years ago, in 1935, one of our number made a journey to a *certain* western city.(p.153)
• His call to the clergyman led him presently to a *certain* resident of the town, who, though formerly able and respected, was then nearing the nadir of alcoholic despair.(p.155)
• This practice enables us to lend a hand, at the same time avoiding *certain* alluring distractions of the road, about which any traveling man can inform you.(p.162)
• He got in touch with a prominent psychiatrist who had undertaken *certain* responsibilities for the mental health of the community.(p.163)
• And with such good effect that the doctor agreed to a test among his patients and *certain* other alcoholics from a clinic which he attends.(p.163)
• It did help to *certain* extent, since I got in places where I could not obtain anything to drink, and so broke the habitual drinking.(p.183)
• Their talk and action had instilled me with a *certain* amount of confidence, although I was not too absolutely *certain*.(p.189)
• When rubber reached a *certain* low point, they would draw on the rubber out of the pool and buy.(p.198)
• I didn't like having to come home at a *certain* time; I didn't like this, I didn't like that, and I think the poor girl actually divorced me to help me stop drinking!(p.199)
• My drinking career began about four years after I had moved up into partnership and had joined *certain* clubs, societies and so fourth, and during which period we had Prohibition.(p.213)
• They had that *certain* something that seemed to glow, a peace and a serenity combined with happiness.(p.290)
• I just wanted to live to a *certain* age, carry through with what I felt was my job with the children, and after that – no matter.(p.337)
• I would follow *certain* drinking schedules or diets faithfully for a few days, and then somewhere along the line would over-train and upset the applecart.(p.361)
• You will recall that I said the time that I got the idea out of a clear sky to call A.A. on a *certain* night was at about ten.(p.366)
• The allergy I could understand because I am allergic to *certain* pollens.(p.380)
• Some of my family are allergic to *certain* foods.(p.380)
• They are not ideas of resignation but of the recognition of *certain* basic facts of living.(p.382)
• It was I who had to tell the bank, after a *certain* time, to refuse all further deposits.(p.409)
• The people of A.A. had something that looked much better than what I had, but I was afraid to let go of what I had in order to try something new; there was a *certain* sense of security in the familiar.(p.448)
• I can tell her she ought not to think a *certain* way, but I certainly can't take away her right to feel however she does feel.(p.451)
• However, one thing I am *certain* of: Inmates in prison who attend A.A. have their chances of remaining free greatly enhanced – this is a proved fact.(p.458)
• I was going to be sent to the Indian Civil Service, which, in those days, meant that people thought you had a *certain* amount of brains.(p.517)
• I have published a book covering *certain* aspects of this field which has been well-reviewed and which is helping other people.(p.541)
• I'd gladly do it anonymously, as I have done this brief account of my struggle with alcohol -- merely to present *certain* ideas for the consideration of the reader.(p.542)

certainly
• Best of all, I met a kind doctor who explained that though *certainly* selfish and foolish, I had been seriously ill, bodily and mentally.(p.7)
• *Certainly* I was interested.(p.10)
• If there was a Devil, he seemed the Boss Universal, and he *certainly* had me.(p.11)
• We have not lost everything in life through drinking and we *certainly* do not intend to.(p.38)
• Our friend's gorge rose as he bitterly cried out: "If there is a God, He *certainly* hasn't done anything for me!"(p.56)
• *Certainly* he must keep sober, for there will be no home if he doesn't.(p.82)
• He knew all the answers, and *certainly* not because he had picked them up in his reading.(p.180)
• I thought to myself, "Well, she is going to tell me this is the end," and I *certainly* couldn't blame her and did not intend to try to justify myself.(p.184)
• I thought of what liquor had done to me, the opportunities that I had discarded, the abilities that had been given me and how I had wasted them, and I finally came to the conclusion, that if I didn't want to quit, I *certainly* ought to want to, and that I was willing to do anything in the world to stop drinking.(p.186)
• That *certainly* was real disheartening news, at the time.(p.188)
• You *certainly* know what you are talking about."(p.189)
• And this, as I said, *certainly* gave me a lot of confidence, seemed to take a lot of the burden off me.(p.190)
• I said, "I'm *certainly* not going to stay in here!"(p.204)
• I couldn't afford to be found with those people, but I said I would *certainly* pay his dues if it would keep him from drinking.(p.205)
• *Certainly*, at that time I was one of those who "can take it or leave it alone."(p.231)
• I had all the usual experiences of the alcoholic, for I was *certainly* one by this time.(p.233)
• And Russ didn't tell me he'd stop drinking, and he *certainly* didn't stop.(p.262)
• I felt it *certainly* must be very depressing to her that I should sit there by her bedside and cry.(p.272)
• The adjustments in such a case are difficult and take time, but we both feel that they are *certainly* worth it.(p.286)
• *Certainly* now, anyone would have agreed that only a miracle could prevent my final breakdown.(p.306)
• They realized that in the end alcoholism could be a mortal as cancer; *certainly* no sane man would wait for a malignant growth to become fatal

before seeking help.(p.315)
• I had the time, I ***certainly*** had the capability, but I never did a thing.(p.326)
• We all have them, and I thought a little brandy or a little wine now and then could ***certainly*** hurt no one.(p.336)
• I ***certainly*** wasn't my shy, quiet self that night -- as I was informed the next morning.(p.353)
• I ***certainly*** was, as far as my living standard was concerned.(p.356)
• I was ***certainly*** a complete surprise when I arrived at her family's home, but because I arrived on the wings of a tropical hurricane there wasn't much she could do but let me in.(p.364)
• I don't know what I expected, but I most ***certainly*** didn't visualize a group of people talking about their drinking problems, making light of their personal tragedies and at the same time enjoying themselves.(p.378)
• Most ***certainly*** I was powerless over alcohol, and for me, my life had become unmanageable.(p.379)
• ***Certainly,*** when I was in my cups, I was not just drunk, I was crazy.(p.408)
• I happened to be the best diagnostician I knew at the time, and ***certainly*** I knew my case better than anyone else.(p.444)
• I can tell her she ought not to think a certain way, but I ***certainly*** can't take away her right to feel however she does feel.(p.451)
• The doctor, apparently realizing that one thing that I ***certainly*** needed was sleep, left a bottle of sleeping pills there and in my drunken state I took them all, instead of the one or two he had prescribed.(p.465)
• With their help I also saw that ***certainly,*** because of some of the things I had done during the years, I was bordering on insanity, and so, facing the record, I tried to believe that a Power greater than I could and would restore me to sanity.(p.471)
• At this point I believe I had only been intoxicated on maybe three or four occasions, and ***certainly*** whiskey was no problem to me.(p.487)
• He can ***certainly*** be depended on.(p.499)
• The man is in bad mental shape ***certainly.***(p.503)
• She ***certainly*** wasn't in the dark about my drinking.(p.513)
• I was taking Benzedrine and paraldehyde quite impartially during the day then, and by the time I arrived at my first A.A. meeting, I was pretty drunk and ***certainly*** doped up to the eyes and completely jittery.(p.523)
• It was impossible for me to say at this point, "Maybe there is something wrong with my philosophy," and I ***certainly*** couldn't say, "Maybe there is something wrong with me."(p.545)
• I had no problem admitting I was powerless over alcohol, and I ***certainly*** agreed that my life had become unmanageable.(p.550)

certainty
• Everyone became resigned to the ***certainty*** that I would have to be shut up somewhere, or would stumble along to a miserable end.(p.8)
• To Christ I conceded the ***certainty*** of a great man, not too closely followed by those who claimed Him.(p.11)
• The central fact of our lives today is the absolute ***certainty*** that our Creator has entered into our hearts and lives in a way which is indeed miraculous.(p.25)
• It poured over and through him with the ***certainty*** and majesty of a great tide at flood.(p.56)

certificate
• She got a medical ***certificate*** so that I should not have to join it.(p.484)

cessation
• ***Cessation*** of drinking is but the first step away from a highly strained, abnormal condition.(p.122)
• Mere ***cessation*** from drinking is not enough for an alcoholic while the need for that drink goes on.(p.339)

chains
• I wore stripes and ***chains.***(p.460)
• There is really nothing to dressing with ***chains*** and shackles on, once you learn the technique of pulling inside-out pants through the shackles.(p.460)

chair
• He then pulled up his ***chair*** with one of his knees touching mine and said, "Will you pray with me for your success?"(p.218)
• This time I seemed to be already awake, sitting upright in a big easy ***chair,*** in the middle of an animated conversation with a perfectly strange young woman, who didn't appear to think it strange.(p.222)
• An attorney sat at the side of the bed where I was lying, and he sat on the edge of his ***chair*** and looked as innocent as a baby.(p.268)
• My wife accompanied me on my visit and the doctor really told me some things that in my state of jitters nearly knocked me out of the ***chair.***(p.302)
• He'll never read in his "sweetness and light" senior-citizen publications anything but the joys of lolling in the rocking ***chair,*** angling on the riverbank, or bowling on the green.(p.330)
• Not wishing to disturb my wife, I slumped in a big red-leather ***chair*** and suffered.(p.332)
• I sat up in the big red ***chair,*** suddenly thinking, "My God, with my kind of lousy luck, I might not die soon!(p.333)
• After that I sat for a week, a body in a ***chair,*** a mind off in space.(p.338)
• But somehow or other, with my old alcoholic brain, sitting there in that ***chair,*** I kept saying to myself, "I wonder if it'll work?(p.515)

chairman
• I'd go into an organization, and it wasn't long before I was on the committee, then I was ***chairman*** of the committee; and if I was in a group, I'd soon be treasurer or secretary of the group.(p.339)

chairs
• But I don't remember that any of them ever went to sleep in joints and woke up with no shoes on in the winter, or fell out of ***chairs.***(p.527)

chalet
• A house in Virginia, during the fox hunting season; a little ***chalet*** in Switzerland during the summer or a place on Long Island -- each house complete with cooks, butlers and maids.(p.403)
• I rented a beautiful apartment on the banks of the Seine in the winter, and a ***chalet*** in Switzerland in the summer.(p.405)

challenge
• I do not recollect the specific conversation that went on but I believe I did ***challenge*** Bill to tell me something about A.A. and I do recall one other thing: I wanted to know what this was that worked so many wonders, and hanging over the mantel was a picture of Gethsemane and Bill pointed to it and said, "There it is," which didn't make much sense to me.(p.216)
• As long as things were tough and the job a ***challenge*** I could always manage to hold on pretty well, but as soon as I learned the combination, got the puzzle under control and the boss to pat me on the back, I was gone again.(p.243)
• Once again, there was the ***challenge*** of a tough job, but this time I was determined to follow through.(p.248)
• It is a way of life, and the ***challenge*** contained in its principles is great enough to keep any human being striving for as long as he lives.(p.311)
• Instead of wanting to escape some perplexing problem, we experience a thrill of ***challenge*** in the opportunity it affords for another application of A.A. techniques, and we find ourselves tackling it with surprising vigor.(p.311)
• The ***challenge*** intrigued me; also it was another opportunity to run away from myself and the "fast life of the big city."(p.359)
• When I was faced with a special ***challenge*** or social event -- such as an important business presentation or a dinner party -- I had to fortify myself with a couple of belts.(p.556)

challenges
• But my thinking was still confused, and I was still unable to deal with the ***challenges*** of everyday living without help.(p.558)

champagne
• On our honeymoon, we had iced ***champagne*** by the bedside day and night.(p.555)

champing
• Acceptance of things as they are has replaced the old impatient ***champing*** at the bit to conquer the world.(p.295)

Champlain
• At three-thirty the next morning, I was in ***Champlain*** Street Station, in jail for driving while intoxicated and insulting an officer; and the suit of which I was so proud was in such shape that the turnkey had to get me a pair of trousers to go into court in the next morning.(p.201)

chance
• More often than not, it is imperative that a man's brain be cleared before he is approached, as he has then a better ***chance*** of understanding and accepting what we have to offer.(p.xxiv)
• Then I went on a prodigious bender, and that ***chance*** vanished.(p.5)
• If he is a real alcoholic and very far advanced, there is scant ***chance*** of success.(p.34)
• It is not by ***chance*** we were given the power to reason, to examine the evidence of our senses, and to draw conclusions.(p.53)
• If we do, we destroy our ***chance*** of being helpful.(p.67)
• Small wonder many in the medical profession have a low opinion of alcoholics and their ***chance*** for recovery!(p.73)
• But insist that if he is severely afflicted, there may be little ***chance*** he can recover by himself.(p.92)
• Give him a ***chance*** to think it over.(p.95)
• He often says that if he had continued to work on them, he might have deprived many others, who have since recovered, of their ***chance.***(p.96)
• Should they accept and practice spiritual principles, there is a much better ***chance*** that the head of the family will recover.(p.97)
• You may spoil your ***chance*** of being helpful if you do.(p.100)
• His only ***chance*** for sobriety would be some place like the Greenland Ice Cap, and even there an Eskimo might turn up with a bottle of scotch and ruin everything!(p.101)
• If he gets the idea that you are a nag or a killjoy, your ***chance*** of accomplishing anything useful may be zero.(p.111)
• If he is already committed to an institution, but can convince you and your doctor that he means business, give him a ***chance*** to try our method, unless the doctor thinks his mental condition too abnormal or dangerous.(p.114)
• The slightest sign of fear or intolerance may lessen your husband's ***chance*** of recovery.(p.120)
• I had warned him several times that he had but one more ***chance.***(p.136)
• He has just returned from a three-months leave of absence, has taken a cure, looks fine, and to clinch the matter, the board of directors told him this was his last ***chance.***"(p.138)
• He might have a ***chance.***(p.138)
• Naturally this sort of thing decreased the man's ***chance*** of recovery.(p.145)
• If, on the contrary, you are sure he is doing his utmost, you may wish to give him another ***chance.***(p.147)
• If he wants to stop, he should be afforded a real ***chance.***(p.148)
• We think we are sensible when we urge that you stop this waste and give your worthwhile man a ***chance.***(p.148)
• I really had a ***chance*** to see myself from a non-drinking point of view.(p.245)
• I have served on only one committee in the past nine years, for I feel that I had my ***chance*** the first few years and that newer members should fill the jobs.(p.250)
• Having no one else to turn to, I was willing to give Him a ***chance,*** although with considerable doubt.(p.280)
• I saw at last that I had the same disease my father had, only I was being given a ***chance*** to live, not die.(p.371)
• She still had her husband, her home, and a ***chance*** to help start A.A. in Texas.(p.384)
• Of course, an inmate must begin living the A.A. way "inside," if he is to stand a ***chance*** "outside."(p.458)
• I know I will be grateful for a ***chance*** to make amends to everybody I have hurt in the past.(p.482)
• So I went to an A.A. meeting the first ***chance*** I got, and I listened.(p.511)
• ANOTHER ***CHANCE***(p.526)
• Today, I thank my Higher Power for giving me another ***chance*** at life and A.A. and being able to try and help some other alcoholic.(p.529)
• It's time to stop finding excuses for drinking and getting into trouble, because now there is a way out, and if you want what we have, try coming around and giving the program a ***chance.***(p.530)
• One of the truly great things A.A. has taught me is that reality too has two sides; I had only known the grim side before the program, but now I had a ***chance*** to learn about the pleasant side as well.(p.550)

chances
• If you ask him why he started on that last bender, the ***chances*** are he will offer you any one of a hundred alibis.(p.23)
• Their ***chances*** are less than average.(p.58)
• The ***chances*** are that we have domestic troubles.(p.80)
• Their defects may be glaring, but the ***chances*** are that our own actions are partly responsible.(p.83)
• The ***chances*** are he would.(p.112)
• If your husband is otherwise a normal individual, your ***chances*** are good at this stage.(p.113)

• The *chances* are he will not for, like yourself, he is just beginning his development.(p.118)
• This would lessen my *chances* of smuggling some home that evening, which in turn would mean a night of futile tossing around in bed followed by a morning of unbearable jitters.(p.176)
• By this time, my *chances* of getting lined up in my chosen business were shot.(p.301)
• If we do a good job of living today, and if tomorrow comes for us, then the *chances* are we will do a good job when it arrives – so why worry about it?(p.382)
• However, one thing I am certain of: Inmates in prison who attend A.A. have their *chances* of remaining free greatly enhanced – this is a proved fact.(p.458)
• If he were still sober, *chances* are that very quickly I put him down as a Philistine with no appreciation of literary genius; and then I went on to another bar to find a new victim.(p.537)

change

• But the chief *change* was in the section of personal stories, which was expanded to reflect the Fellowship's growth.(p.xi)
• This is repeated over and over, and unless this person can experience an entire psychic *change* there is very little hope of his recovery.(p.xxvii)
• On the other hand – and strange as this may seem to those who do not understand -- once a psychic *change* has occurred, the very same person who seemed doomed, who had so many problems he despaired of ever solving them, suddenly finds himself easily able to control his desire for alcohol, the only effort necessary being that required to follow a few simple rules.(p.xxvii)
• One feels that something more than human power is needed to produce the essential psychic *change*.(p.xxvii)
• We gave up our positions and off we roared on a motorcycle, the sidecar stuffed with tent, blankets, a *change* of clothes, and three huge volumes of a financial reference service.(p.2)
• If a sufficiently strong reason – ill health, falling in love, *change* of environment, or the warning of a doctor – becomes operative, this man can also stop or moderate, although he may find it difficult and troublesome and may even need medical attention.(p.21)
• They flatly declare that since they have come to believe in a Power greater than themselves, to take a certain attitude toward that Power, and to do certain simple things, there has been a revolutionary *change* in their way of living and thinking.(p.50)
• They show how the *change* came over them.(p.51)
• We had to ask ourselves why we shouldn't apply to our human problems this same readiness to *change* our point of view.(p.52)
• His *change* of heart was dramatic, convincing, and moving.(p.55)
• It is important that he be able to keep a confidence; that he fully understand and approve what we are driving at; that he will not try to *change* our plan.(p.74)
• They will *change* in time.(p.83)
• Our whole attitude and outlook upon life will *change*.(p.84)
• Let your friends know they are not to *change* their habits on your account.(p.102)
• Though you are providing him with the best possible medical attention, he should understand that he must undergo a *change* of heart.(p.143)
• I wanted to learn to stand on my own feet, not to *change* one prop for another, and an intangible and dubious one at that.(p.227)
• You can all remember that in the first few months after the *change*, a great many men, who had formerly been used to a few beers every day or an occasional drink of whiskey, simply quit all alcoholic drinks.(p.232)
• I don't think the boys were completely convinced of my personality *change*, for they fought shy of including my story in the book, so my only contribution to their literary efforts was my firm conviction, being still a theological rebel, that the word God should be qualified with the phrase "as we understand him" -- for that was the only way I could accept spirituality.(p.248)
• Then I found that as I gave in to this spiritual or personality *change* I was getting a little more serenity.(p.249)
• In telling newcomers how to *change* their lives and attitudes, all of a sudden I found I was doing a little changing myself.(p.249)
• I had been too self-sufficient to write a moral inventory, but I discovered in pointing out to the new man his wrong attitudes and actions that I was really taking my own inventory, and that if I expected him to *change* I would have to work on myself too.(p.249)
• This *change* had been a long, slow process for me, but through these latter years the dividends have been tremendous.(p.249)
• It's only natural that we don't have the capacity to *change*, but we ought not to criticize those who have, There's another thing I would stress.(p.273)
• My thinking about drinking had undergone a great *change*.(p.277)
• This represents another great *change* for me.(p.284)
• I was without power to *change* the course my life had taken.(p.304)
• A complete *change* takes place in our approach to life.(p.311)
• Once I did have a slip – tried drinking again – but the A.A.'s tell me not to worry about yesterday, because nobody can *change* it, and not to worry about tomorrow, because it hasn't come yet.(p.320)
• What I needed was a *change*, mental relaxation, getting out and doing something.(p.338)
• Mentally, the fears and tensions, the complete *change* in attitude and outlook, bewildered me.(p.378)
• "Grant us the serenity to accept the things we cannot *change*, courage to *change* the things we can, and the wisdom to know the difference."(p.382)
• We moved once more, to Houston; my husband thought maybe a *change* of environment would help and I'd be all right.(p.389)
• For, after those daily self-punishing sessions with myself, after the vows to stop, I would *change* entirely as evening came on.(p.408)
• Then, one day in A.A., I was told that I had the lenses in my glasses backwards; "the courage to *change*" in the Serenity Prayer meant, not that I should *change* my marriage, but rather that I should *change* myself and learn to accept my spouse as she was.(p.451)
• Sobriety and a plan for living that produces a personality *change* and a spiritual awakening are imperative.(p.459)
• Through A.A., many receive the needed *change* and awakening just by trying to live by A.A. principles and associating with A.A. people.(p.459)
• Soon *change* to hard stuff.(p.475)
• So I *change* counties in Maine.(p.475)
• But now I *change* if it bring good life.(p.475)
• We can have this new way of life – learning to live with our sickness and to be happy and content -- if we are willing to *change* our way of thinking and be honest, first with ourselves, then with others.(p.480)
• But after I passed through the gates I took a *change* of heart and mind.(p.510)
• Then a *change* in management took place in the regiment and the new O.C. didn't like me very much and I didn't like him, and he started to lie in wait for me.(p.519)
• I hope I haven't hurt anyone's feelings, but maybe we could all grow and *change*.(p.529)
• What is much more important to me, A.A. has taught me that through this simple program I may experience a *change* in this reaction pattern that will indeed allow me to "match calamity with serenity."(p.544)
• We are granted "the serenity to accept the things we cannot *change*" – and thus lose our quickness to anger and our sensitivity to criticism.(p.560)
• The terms "spiritual experience" and "spiritual awakening" are used many times in this book which, upon careful reading, shows that the personality *change* sufficient to bring about recovery from alcoholism has manifested itself among us in many different forms.(p.569)
• Though it was not our intention to create such an impression, many alcoholics have nevertheless concluded that in order to recover they must acquire an immediate and overwhelming "God-consciousness" followed at once by a vast *change* in feeling and outlook.(p.569)
• He finally realizes that he has undergone a profound alteration in his reaction to life; that such a *change* could hardly have been brought about by himself alone.(p.569)
• Even among those who occasionally land back in here again, we observe a profound *change* in personality.(p.572)

changed

• We urge you to try our program, for nothing will be so helpful to your husband as the radically *changed* attitude toward him which God will show you how to have.(p.117)
• You are betting, of course, that your *changed* attitude plus the contents of this book will turn the trick.(p.144)
• I drove towards Cleveland wondering why I found myself in such a *changed* set of conditions as compared with those of six months before.(p.200)
• Being intensely interested in the work, I *changed* my conduct sufficiently to master the job.(p.211)
• There was one meeting a week at Bill's home in Brooklyn, and we all took turns there spouting off about how we had *changed* our lives overnight, how many drunks we had saved and straightened out, and last, but not least, how God had touched each of us personally on the shoulder.(p.246)
• Around this time our big A.A. book was being written and it all became much simpler; we had a definite formula which some sixty of us agreed was the middle course for all alcoholics who wanted sobriety, and that formula has not been *changed* one iota down through the years.(p.248)
• We old-timers who get scattered and separated and then witness the construction of services to get in more people and to make this thing function, we think that A.A. has *changed*, but the root of it hasn't.(p.272)
• Suddenly all this *changed*.(p.275)
• All this *changed* when I was thirty years old.(p.277)
• Nothing had *changed* and yet everything had *changed*.(p.280)
• All of this *changed* when I went to college.(p.287)
• When I was released from the hospital, I went back to my unit, and nothing had *changed*.(p.319)
• Now the picture has *changed* completely.(p.325)
• It has *changed* my thinking entirely, about everything I do.(p.325)
• The last two years of my drinking my entire personality *changed* to a cynical, intolerant and arrogant person completely different from my normal self.(p.376)
• I was so happy over getting home that I *changed* overnight, but not enough.(p.387)
• It has *changed* not simply one department of my life – it has *changed* my whole life.(p.394)
• In the first year there were episodes such as kicking Priscilla in the shins, getting the lock *changed* on the desk in the A.A. Club, because I, as secretary, didn't want the Intergroup secretary "interfering," and taking an older woman member out to lunch for the express purpose of informing her that she was "a phony."(p.416)
• I need to concentrate not so much on what needs to be *changed* in the world as on what needs to be *changed* in me and in my attitudes.(p.449)
• But with the first drink, our good intentions dissolved; our personalities *changed*.(p.458)
• In fact it has been only within the last fifteen years that I *changed* from a fairly normal, controlled drinker into an alcoholic.(p.464)
• Of course, in my day, times had *changed*; she just hadn't *changed* with the times.(p.484)
• However, I kept that job in Egypt and Palestine for about two years, and then I *changed* over to the other battalion in my regiment.(p.520)
• Simply, yes it did end; for I had *changed* my mind about alcohol, and it stayed *changed*.(p.541)
• The only thing this *changed*, however, was my surroundings, and it was soon apparent that I could have the same uncomfortable emotions with an unlimited checking account that I could on a working girl's salary.(p.545)
• I thought this would give me ego-strength, make me feel wanted and secure, and alleviate my fears, but again nothing *changed* inside me.(p.546)
• In fact, I *changed* schools every year until high school.(p.555)

changes

• Because this book has become the basic text for our Society and has helped such large numbers of alcoholic men and women to recover, there exists a sentiment against any radical *changes* being made in it.(p.xi)
• All *changes* made over the years in the Big Book (A.A. members' fond nickname for this volume) have had the same purpose: to represent the current membership of Alcoholics Anonymous more accurately, and thereby to reach more alcoholics.(p.xii)
• He *changes* his brand or his environment.(p.xxviii)
• If he is not interested in your solution, if he expects you to act only as a banker for his financial difficulties or a nurse for his sprees, you may have to drop him until he *changes* his mind.(p.95)
• There will be other profound *changes* in the household.(p.130)
• It took three-quarters of an hour and two *changes* to get there – back to my starting point.(p.223)
• So I sat down with me and went over the facts behind the convulsions: personality *changes*, daily headaches, sense of impending doom, sense of impending insanity.(p.444)
• Intake of alcohol *changes* one's personality -- even the healthy personality.(p.458)
• Yet it is true that our first printing gave many read-

ers the impression that these personality *changes*, or religious experiences, must be in the nature of sudden and spectacular upheavals.(p.569)
• In the first few chapters a number of sudden revolutionary *changes* are described.(p.569)

changing
• In telling newcomers how to change their lives and attitudes, all of a sudden I found I was doing a little *changing* myself.(p.249)
• I give a great deal of credit to Doc and Anne for *changing* our life.(p.270)

channel
• The amount of will power exercised to control my drinking during working hours, diverted into a constructive *channel*, would have made me President, and the thing that made the will power possible was the knowledge that as soon as my day was finished I could drink myself into oblivion.(p.548)

channels
• Instead of developing new *channels* of activity for themselves, mother and children demand that he stay home and make up the deficiency.(p.131)

chaos
• Panic, confusion and *chaos* were supreme.(p.279)

chap
• One poor *chap* committed suicide in my home.(p.16)
• Up to this point you would label him as a foolish *chap* having queer ideas of fun.(p.37)
• The story he told is most instructive, for here was a *chap* absolutely convinced he had to stop drinking, who had no excuse for drinking, who exhibited splendid judgment and determination in all his other concerns, yet was flat on his back nevertheless.(p.40)
• We women carry with us a picture of the ideal man, the sort of *chap* we would like our husbands to be.(p.118)
• "Oh no," said my friend, "this *chap* is either through with liquor, or he is minus a job.(p.138)
• You may be at a loss to understand how such a seemingly above-board *chap* could be so involved.(p.140)
• But he's a grand *chap* when he's sober, though he's been in here eight times in the last six months.(p.156)
• He now returned home, leaving behind his first acquaintance, the lawyer and the devil-may-care *chap*.(p.159)
• I went to the sanitarium where this *chap* was incarcerated and found to my surprise that he was interested.(p.294)

Chaplain
• When I came back, I told the priest, the *Chaplain* of the place, exactly what I thought of him and he didn't like it.(p.517)

chapter
• There is the manic-depressive type, who is, perhaps, the least understood by his friends, and about whom a whole *chapter* could be written.(p.xxviii)
• *Chapter* 1(p.1)
• *Chapter* 2(p.17)
• In the following *chapter*, there appears an explanation of alcoholism, as we understand it, then a *chapter* addressed to the agnostic.(p.28)
• *Chapter* 3(p.30)
• *Chapter* 4(p.44)
• *Chapter* 5(p.58)
• Our description of the alcoholic, the *chapter* to the agnostic, and our personal adventures before and after make clear three pertinent ideas:(p.60)
• *Chapter* 6(p.72)
• This brings us to the Fifth Step in the program of recovery mentioned in the preceding *chapter*.(p.72)
• The next *chapter* is entirely devoted to Step Twelve.(p.88)
• *Chapter* 7(p.89)
• We suggest you do this as we have done it in the *chapter* on alcoholism.(p.92)
• *Chapter* 8(p.104)
• An alcoholic of this temperament may be quick to use this *chapter* as a club over your head.(p.108)
• When a discussion does arise, you might suggest he read this book or at least the *chapter* on alcoholism.(p.111)
• If you think he will be shy of a spiritual remedy, ask him to look at the *chapter* on alcoholism.(p.112)
• The fellowship of Al-Anon Family Groups was formed about thirteen years after this *chapter* was written.(p.121)
• *Chapter* 9(p.122)
• *Chapter* 10(p.136)
• Of course, this *chapter* refers to alcoholics, sick people, deranged men.(p.149)
• *Chapter* 11(p.151)
• In the *chapter* "Working With Others" you gathered an idea of how we approach and aid others to health.(p.153)

chapters
• In the preceding *chapters* you have learned something of alcoholism.(p.44)
• If this presents difficulty, re-reading *chapters* two and three, where the alcoholic sickness is discussed at length might be worth while.(p.140)
• The first *chapters* were a revelation to me.(p.227)
• Moreover, I am deeply convinced that so long as I continue to strive, in my bumbling way, toward the principles I first encountered in the earlier *chapters* of this book, this remarkable power will continue to flow through me.(p.437)
• In the first few *chapters* a number of sudden revolutionary changes are described.(p.569)

character
• A certain American business man had ability, good sense, and high *character*.(p.26)
• Many of us felt that we had plenty of *character*.(p.34)
• It never occurred to him that perhaps he could not do so, in spite of *character* and standing.(p.39)
• 6.Were entirely ready to have God remove all these defects of *character*.(p.59)
• To the outer world he presents his stage *character*.(p.73)
• We pocket our pride and go to it, illuminating every twist of *character*, every dark cranny of the past.(p.75)
• I pray that you now remove from me every single defect of *character* which stands in the way of my usefulness to you and my fellows.(p.76)
• You should point out that his defects of *character* are not going to disappear over night.(p.100)
• You will no longer be self-conscious or feel that you must apologize as though your husband were a weak *character*.(p.115)
• We all had hundreds of *character* traits, of fears and phobias, likes and dislikes, in common.(p.229)
• At the moral inventory, he brought up some of my bad personality traits or *character* defects, such as selfishness, conceit, jealousy, carelessness, intolerance, ill-temper, sarcasm and resentments.(p.292)
• We went over these at great length and then he finally asked me if I wanted these defects of *character* removed.(p.292)
• Dishonest thinking, prejudice, ego, antagonism toward anyone and everyone who dares to cross him, vanity and a critical attitude are *character* defects that gradually creep in and become a part of his life.(p.380)
• It took me some time to realize that the Twelve Steps of A.A. were designed to help correct these defects of *character* and so help remove the obsession to drink.(p.380)
• I learn more of that foundation stone of *character*, which is honesty.(p.507)

characteristic
• To us it is not far-fetched, for this kind of thinking has been *characteristic* of every single one of us.(p.37)

characterized
• Therefore, it is not surprising that our drinking careers have been *characterized* by countless vain attempts to prove we could drink like other people.(p.30)
• Is not our age *characterized* by the ease with which we discard old ideas for new, by the complete readiness with which we throw away the theory or gadget which does not work for something new which does?(p.52)
• 11. -- Our relations with the general public should be *characterized* by personal anonymity.(p.567)

characters
• But I can remember, in my teens, that there were a few *characters* who caused the village heads to nod pityingly and sometimes in anger as they paused to say, "That sot, Henri" and "Ce pauvre Jules," who drank too much.(p.230)

charge
• Can you *charge* this off as you would a bad account and start fresh with him?(p.145)
• To 1950, the year of his death, he carried the A.A. message to more than 5,000 alcoholic men and women, and to all these he gave his medical services without thought of *charge*.(p.171)
• I went downstairs and there was the grizzly old veteran police officer in *charge* of the property desk, and as he gave me the stuff, he asked, "Are you going out in the street that way?"(p.204)
• For three generations, my family had had a *charge* account in one of the big New York hotels.(p.410)
• The neurologist in *charge* of my case didn't think to ask me whether I drank, and I didn't think to tell him.(p.444)
• I woke up in jail, sick, withdrawing from alcohol and speed, already a four-time loser, and now with a fifth felony *charge* against me.(p.460)
• I stayed there just long enough to work up a real good resentment against the doctor in *charge*, who I didn't think was doing anything at all except collecting fees, and I left there fully determined that I'd never put myself in the power of medical people again.(p.521)
• Still another friend and temporary host received me at four in the morning from the *charge* of a policeman who had found me "going to bed" in a garage far from the last place I could remember having been, a fashionable bar and restaurant in the theatrical district of New York, to which I had repaired after my date for that evening, a charming lady of the theatre who had refused my company for obvious reasons.(p.538)

charged
• But these scrapes can generally be *charged*, no matter how bad, to the abnormal action of alcohol on his mind.(p.140)

charity
• For the type of alcoholic who is able and willing to get well, little *charity*, in the ordinary sense of the word, is needed or wanted.(p.97)
• He had tried everything from having me attend daily mass at six a.m. to performing the most menial labor for his *charity* patients.(p.306)
• It continues to try to teach me the real *charity*, the *charity* that gives time and good will and service, and not just money.(p.525)

Charleston
• So, sometimes we'd end up in *Charleston*, West Virginia, or here or there, drinking all along the way.(p.264)

Charlie
• About seven that evening my sponsor walked in, *Charlie* G.(p.494)
• After *Charlie* had talked a while, I knew that this man had something.(p.495)
• I put *Charlie* on the car and when I left him I passed both of those liquor stores without even thinking about them.(p.495)
• It was *Charlie* and three or four others.(p.495)
• Then *Charlie* or someone in the group suggested that we try to get a place in a church or hall to hold meetings.(p.495)
• I haven't mentioned it, but *Charlie*, my sponsor, was white, and when we got our group started we got help from other white groups in Washington.(p.495)
• Good old *Charlie*!(p.500)

charm
• I was immediately impressed with his graciousness and *charm*.(p.309)
• Prior to our marriage, when she was a shy, scrawny adolescent, I was able to see things in her that others couldn't necessarily see -- things like beauty, *charm*, gaiety, a gift for being easy to talk to, a sense of humor, and many other fine qualities.(p.450)

charming
• This man has a *charming* wife and family.(p.35)
• So six months ago I acquired a ready made family consisting of one *charming* wife, four grown children to whom I am devoted, and three grandchildren.(p.286)
• My family, on my mother's side, was brilliant, gifted and *charming*.(p.401)
• The apartment was *charming*; the shelves were full of books, many of which I myself owned.(p.413)
• And she was a *charming*, delightful, lovely person.(p.472)
• Still another friend and temporary host received me at four in the morning from the charge of a policeman who had found me "going to bed" in a garage far from the last place I could remember having been, a fashionable bar and restaurant in the theatrical district of New York, to which I had repaired after my date for that evening, a *charming* lady of the theatre who had refused my company for obvious reasons.(p.538)

charred
• I call the bootlegger and fill up my *charred* keg.(p.501)
• But I do not wait for the *charred* keg to work.(p.501)

chart
• I couldn't focus enough to make out the *chart*, but

the card contained two words -- "ACUTE ALCOHOLISM."(p.422)

charted
• At one end of the bed, near the foot, was a printed card, and beneath that was a *charted* graph.(p.422)

chartered
• There was that time we had *chartered* an airplane to complete a jag!(p.9)

Charybdis
• I was between Scylla and *Charybdis* now, because if I did not drink my stomach tortured me, and if I did, my nerves did the same thing.(p.175)

chaser
• The inevitable result of this discovery was that I soon learned that beer made a very good *chaser* for whiskey.(p.298)
• I remembered having had a little drink of whiskey with a can of warm beer as a *chaser*.(p.422)

chasers
• I found out fast that the cheapest way to get drunk was on shots with beer *chasers* at two bits a crack.(p.397)
• I graduated from shots and beer *chasers* to Scotch and sodas.(p.398)

chasing
• We find it a waste of time to keep *chasing* a man who cannot or will not work with you.(p.96)
• Cold chills started *chasing* up and down my spine; my teeth were chattering; my hands were shaking so I tucked them under me to keep them from flying away.(p.222)
• I wanted "ripe" prospects and I didn't feel that I would get very far *chasing* individual drunks in and out of bars.(p.281)

chastened
• Peddling off my polish samples for expenses, I crawled back to New York a few days later in a very *chastened* frame of mind.(p.248)

chat
• It might be well to have a long *chat* with him on his return.(p.143)

chatter
• Music and gay *chatter* still floated to him from the bar.(p.154)
• I was full of careless *chatter*.(p.402)

chattered
• Everyone spent in thousands and *chattered* in millions.(p.3)

chattering
• Cold chills started chasing up and down my spine; my teeth were *chattering*; my hands were shaking so I tucked them under me to keep them from flying away.(p.222)

chatting
• You have passed happy evenings together *chatting* and drinking before your fire.(p.110)
• She was *chatting* on, pleasantly and comfortably.(p.222)

chauffeur
• During this time, you are supposed to behave yourself, but I took a little wine-tasting tour through France, all by my lone, with car and *chauffeur*.(p.405)

cheap
• It went into certain securities, then *cheap* and rather unpopular.(p.2)
• My idea was to have all the companies pool their funds and buy rubber when rubber was *cheap* and then put it in a pool.(p.198)
• Then broke again, hiding out in *cheap* hotels all over the country, one night jail stands here and there, and always that horrible feeling "What's the use -- nothing is worth while."(p.244)
• Many alcoholics have learned they can bring their bottle to a *cheap* movie theater and drink, sleep, wake up and drink again in the darkness.(p.244)
• (It was the beer and *cheap* whiskey that was making me so sick.(p.398)
• She too had gone to *cheap* bars to drink.(p.414)
• We buy a gallon of "corn" because it is so *cheap*.(p.500)

cheaper
• I think whiskey was *cheaper* there than it was in Washington.(p.490)

cheapest
• I found out fast that the *cheapest* way to get drunk was on shots with beer chasers at two bits a crack.(p.397)

cheating
• Aside from being a common drunk, I had a very serious pill affliction and all the garbage that goes with it -- lying, stealing, *cheating* anybody and everybody, conning the people I could, and staying clear of the ones I couldn't.(p.478)

check
• Our sound reasoning failed to hold us in *check*.(p.37)
• He sometimes drinks in the morning and through the day also, to hold his nervousness in *check*.(p.109)
• When I got home I had to give him a *check* for the taxi fare.(p.205)
• In those days my system was always to drink up my last pay *check* and believe that necessity would bring the next job.(p.256)
• I stopped at the cashier's any hour of the night on the way to the bar and cashed a *check*.(p.410)
• Before I step out and do anything, I stop and *check* it over first, and then let my conscience be my guide.(p.516)
• I would wait for the mailman each month, like any good mother, but as soon as he handed me my *check*, I put on my best dress and went looking for my alcoholic friend.(p.527)
• Then I would go home full of remorse, and wonder what I was going to do until I got my next *check*.(p.527)

checked
• I did not want to disgrace myself so I then *checked* out.(p.179)
• I *checked* into my hotel room and then noticed a placard tucked under the glass on the bureau stating "There will be positively NO drinking at this convention" signed by the president of the company.(p.243)
• We *checked* into the home of Hank, the man who had fired me eleven years before in Mississippi, and there I met Bill, our founder.(p.245)
• It was with grim foreboding and advanced jitters that I *checked* in at the hospital.(p.302)

checking
• The *checking* account melted like snow in June.(p.106)
• One evening, the book, after *checking* up, was very definitely in the red for plenty through a piece of studied carelessness on my part, and my boss, very shrewd and able, fired me with a parting statement to the effect that once was enough.(p.251)
• The only thing this changed, however, was my surroundings, and it was soon apparent that I could have the same uncomfortable emotions with an unlimited *checking* account that I could on a working girl's salary.(p.545)

checks
• The local banker watched me whirl fat *checks* in and out of his till with amused skepticism.(p.4)

checkup
• A complete *checkup* at one of the best hospitals revealed nothing.(p.276)
• Only a few days before Christmas I went to the dentist for a periodic *checkup*.(p.465)

cheekbone
• I had a broken nose, a fractured *cheekbone*, and was black from the lower part of my face up into my hair.(p.204)

cheeks
• Time after time I would beg forgiveness on bended knees, with tears rolling down my *cheeks*, and promise I would never again drink too much.(p.362)

cheer
• But *cheer* up, something like half of us thought we were atheists or agnostics.(p.44)
• *Cheer* him up and ask him how you can be still more helpful.(p.120)

cheerfully
• We asked God to help us show them the same tolerance, pity, and patience that we would *cheerfully* grant a sick friend.(p.67)
• *Cheerfully* see him through more sprees.(p.113)
• Avoid then, the deliberate manufacture of misery, but if trouble comes, *cheerfully* capitalize it as an opportunity to demonstrate His omnipotence.(p.133)

cheerfulness
• So we think *cheerfulness* and laughter make for usefulness.(p.132)

cheery
• The *cheery* voice of an old school friend asked if he might come over.(p.8)

chemical
• Today, I feel I have used up my right to *chemical* peace of mind.(p.448)
• If my personality is inadequate, antisocial, or full of kinks and I alter it with alcohol or any *chemical*, bingo!(p.458)

chemicals
• I depended on optimism and ambition to live in society; when I began to tire, I had to depend on *chemicals* instead to keep going.(p.420)
• I wasn't able to quit *chemicals* as long as they were in the house.(p.443)
• Giving up alcohol alone was not enough for me; I've had to give up all mood-and mind-affecting *chemicals* in order to stay sober and comfortable.(p.443)
• Still later, even alcohol and *chemicals* together could not lift me.(p.457)
• We do this by going to many A.A. meetings with an open mind and a desire to live the good-feeling life without *chemicals* -- liquid or otherwise.(p.459)

chemist
• At least, so the *chemist* said.(p.54)

chemists
• My intellectual heroes, the *chemists* the astronomers, even the evolutionists, suggested vast laws and forces at work.(p.10)

cherish
• At the end of a year, the children got a card from their father, which I still have and *cherish*.(p.262)
• And over my A.A. years I have made many real, honest, sincere friendships that I shall always *cherish*.(p.296)

cherished
• It is the most natural thing in the world, once his liquor problem is solved, to feel that he will now measure up to that *cherished* vision.(p.118)

chest
• I remembered filling the peroxide bottle in my medicine *chest* with gin, in case my sister found the bottle I hid under the mattress.(p.224)

chests
• I also made use of old trunks and *chests*, the old can container, and even the ash container.(p.176)

chew
• One of our gifts from the family was a very lovely Bible, but we'd let the bulldog *chew* it because we weren't too interested in it.(p.268)
• I've stuck pretty close to A.A. ever since then, taken it day by day, not biting off more than I can *chew*.(p.511)

Chicago
• I well remember the shock I received when a prominent doctor in *Chicago* told me of cases where pressure of the spinal fluid actually ruptured the brain.(p.140)
• The next three years I spent in Boston, *Chicago*, and Montreal in the employ of a large manufacturing concern, selling railway supplies, gas engines of all sorts, and many other items of heavy hardware.(p.172)
• I found, however, that when I would leave Akron to go to *Chicago*, I would get drunk.(p.197)
• Forced to detrain from an empty gondola on the other side of *Chicago* by a terrific rainstorm which drenched me to the skin, I hit the first factory building I saw for a job.(p.253)
• I stayed sober for four years except for a one-night carousal in *Chicago*.(p.253)
• As soon as I could get up and walk I started to drink again and kept it up until my friend of the hospital, who, in his first try at the new way of life had stubbed his toe in *Chicago* but had come back to the town to take counsel and make a new start, picked me up and got me into a hospital.(p.258)
• Thus, A.A. was born in *Chicago*.(p.287)
• In 1930, I moved to *Chicago*.(p.287)
• This was the beginning of five years of bounding back and forth between my home in *Chicago* and Akron to sober up.(p.288)
• He waited until I was completely sober and the day before I was to head back for *Chicago*, he told me of a small group of men in Akron who apparently had the same problem that I had but were doing something about it.(p.289)
• Several months later dad was back in *Chicago* to pick me up again, but this time my attitude was entirely different.(p.289)
• The day before I was due to go back to *Chicago*, a Wednesday and Dr. Bob's afternoon off, he had me down to the office and we spent three or four hours formally going through the Six-Step program as it was at that time.(p.291)
• One of them was that I would try to get a group started in *Chicago*; the second was that I would have to return to Akron to attend meetings at least every two months until I did get a group started in *Chicago*; third, I decided I must place this program above everything else, even my family, because if I did not

maintain my sobriety I would lose my family anyway.(p.292)
• The next day I went back to *Chicago* and started a vigorous campaign among my so-called friends or drinking companions.(p.293)
• A few months later one of the men who had been in touch with the group in Akron came to *Chicago* to live, and then there were three of us who continued to have informal meetings quite regularly.(p.294)
• From a single member in the *Chicago* area, commuting to Akron, we now exceed six thousand.(p.295)
• This worldly lady helped to develop A.A. in *Chicago* and thus passed her keys to many.(p.304)
• I moved a thousand miles away from home to *Chicago* and a new environment.(p.305)
• He told me that eventually he hoped such a group would develop in the *Chicago* area, but that so far this had not been started.(p.309)
• Shortly after I returned to *Chicago*, my doctor, encouraged by the results of my contact with A.A., sent us two more of his alcoholic patients.(p.310)
• I was working for a *Chicago* firm that represented several large radio stations.(p.358)
• Indeed, she had known my cousin in *Chicago*.(p.414)
• We got to Omaha, from my home in *Chicago*.(p.424)
• We were identified and I was put on a train for *Chicago*.(p.424)
• I was attending a convention in *Chicago* and carousing day and night.(p.558)

chicanery
• The wars which had been fought, the burnings and *chicanery* that religious dispute had facilitated, made me sick.(p.11)

chicken
• I think the Commanding Officer was rather tired of this particular *chicken* coming back to roost so often because he very soon wrote in to the medical authorities to tell them that they had to get me into hospital, to be thoroughly examined for drinking.(p.520)

chief
• But the *chief* change was in the section of personal stories, which was expanded to reflect the Fellowship's growth.(p.xi)
• A well-known doctor, *chief* physician at a nationally prominent hospital specializing in alcoholic and drug addiction, gave Alcoholics Anonymous this letter:(p.xxiii)
• Arrangements were also made with the *chief* psychiatrist of a large public hospital to select still others from the stream of misery which flows through that institution.(p.163)
• Federal Theatre in Texas gave me an administrative job which I held for a year, only because I worked hard and productively when I worked, and because my very tolerant *chief* ascribed my frequent lapses to a bohemian temperament.(p.256)
• Boredom sets up every retiree for two *chief* dangers: obesity and alcoholism.(p.330)
• At age twenty-one, I enlisted in the Navy for two reasons: (1) to avoid being drafted into the Army, and (2) out of a burst of patriotic fervor inspired by the advent of World War II and as the result of an all-night drinking binge which found me sitting on the doorstep of the Navy recruiting office when the *chief* petty officer arrived to open for business at nine o'clock Monday morning.(p.398)
• He forgot to mention that I was the *chief* critic.(p.449)
• But I wanted a cosmos, a universe all my own which I had created and where I reigned as *chief* top reigner and ruler over everyone else.(p.535)
• Dr. John F. Stouffer, *Chief* Psychiatrist, Philadelphia General Hospital, citing his experience with A.A., said: "The alcoholics we get here at Philadelphia General are mostly those who cannot afford private treatment, and A.A. is by far the greatest thing we have been able to offer them.(p.572)

chief's
• While waiting to depart I was selected -- by giving a CPO five dollars -- to be bartender in the Navy *Chief's* Club.(p.426)

chiefly
• I lasted at that for four months *chiefly* on alcohol, because I never seemed to find any time to eat.(p.520)

child
• Actually we were fooling ourselves, for deep down in every man, woman, and *child*, is the fundamental idea of God.(p.55)
• A doctor said to us, "Years of living with an alcoholic is almost sure to make any wife or *child* neurotic.(p.122)
• By force of circumstances, she was often obliged to treat father as a sick or wayward *child*.(p.130)
• Unfortunately for me, I was the only *child*, which perhaps engendered the selfishness which played such an important part in bringing on my alcoholism.(p.172)
• I was born in Cleveland, Ohio, in 1889, the last *child* of a family of eight children.(p.210)
• The differences between my father and my sisters, who were school teachers, made an excellent environment for the type of *child* I was -- that is, slick and cute enough to take advantage of any adult quarrel.(p.210)
• My oldest *child* sometimes sat in on the meetings.(p.220)
• Indeed, I was beginning to see that I would require implicit faith, like a small *child*, if I was going to get anywhere.(p.259)
• I lay down on the bed and slept like a *child*.(p.280)
• We had a small *child*, and I loved her dearly, so that held me back quite a bit in my drinking career.(p.322)
• As my son, our second *child*, came along, and as he became school age and was away at school most of the time, something happened.(p.323)
• I was born in Cleveland, Ohio, the only *child* of a prominent dentist, and a very proud mother.(p.357)
• I had every advantage a *child* could have, private schools (several of them), dancing schools, two colleges, coon skin coats, automobiles, a listing in the social register and all the rest.(p.357)
• But now, with His help and grace, this *child* of His has paid his initiation fee for good, as long as he remembers to stay away from that first drink (the one that does all the damage) one day at a time.(p.399)
• He got half custody of our *child*, but later kept her during most of the school terms.(p.402)
• But he noticed that I was not a good mother to my *child*, that I relegated her to nurses when she was with me.(p.403)
• My *child* was being exposed to all this.(p.408)
• My poor *child* could not know this.(p.409)
• She did all she could to help this situation and to protect my *child*.(p.409)
• The last time I drank, when I was twenty-nine, I drank for only four days, yet I threatened to kill my children; I beat my wife at home and on the church steps; I mistreated a *child* in my office; and I ran to a hospital for mental illness to avoid jail.(p.418)
• My life there was a nightmare of periodic binges on alcohol and pills, adultery, unhappy hours at the dental office, seeing my wife give birth to our second *child* and have several miscarriages, living in a turbulent household, and making continual attempts to be the respectable dentist, husband, father, and community leader.(p.419)
• Educated *child* of the scientific age that I was, I had complete faith in the science of the mind.(p.434)
• I learned what a devastating effect it can have on a *child* to coddle him and build him up, and then turn and beat him savagely, as had happened to me.(p.434)
• Tragedies during those years that were caused by my drinking, such as the breaking up of my marriage, the death of my *child*, other things -- had little restraining effect.(p.465)
• After our first *child* came my parents both became allies, but in later days, after I became an alcoholic, they both turned against me.(p.485)
• We have another *child*.(p.501)
• I crawl back into bed and sleep like a *child*.(p.504)
• And, as a *child* is a part of his father, so do I now want to be a part of God.(p.535)
• And I am sure they would be right as far as they go, but A.A. has taught me I am the result of the way I reacted to what happened to me as a *child*.(p.544)
• I am an only *child*, and when I was seven years old my parents separated very abruptly.(p.544)
• I had never had a *child* and this had been a satisfactory excuse many times for my drinking.(p.548)
• I had fed it, fanned it and nurtured it as one might a delicate *child*, and it had become as much a part of me as my breathing.(p.551)
• I was raised in Kansas, the only *child* of loving parents who just drank socially.(p.554)

childhood
• *Childhood* memories rose before me.(p.10)
• To others, the word "God" brought up a particular idea of Him with which someone had tried to impress them during *childhood*.(p.45)
• From *childhood* through high school I was more or less forced to go to church, Sunday School and evening service, Monday night Christian Endeavor and sometimes to Wednesday evening prayer meeting.(p.172)
• There were no *childhood* episodes of unhappiness to account for my alcoholism.(p.182)
• I can remember that in my *childhood*, he was ill at ease with the children because he attempted to assert an army discipline that had been ground into him during his three and a half years of army service.(p.210)
• I had never, since the believing days of *childhood*, been able to conceive an authority directing the universe.(p.259)
• Mine was far from a happy *childhood*.(p.261)
• When I came to my aunt, she knew that I had had an unhappy *childhood*, and she said, "Now, Ethel, you're welcome to have boy friends in our home, but there are two boys in this town that I don't want you to date, and one of them comes from a very fine family, one of the best.(p.262)
• I was still bitter because I felt that drink had completely ruined my *childhood* and my married life, and I hated everything pertaining to it.(p.262)
• Nor could I blame my dilemma on my *childhood* environment.(p.304)
• My *childhood* was shrouded in the fumes of alcohol.(p.369)
• Slowly, my life seemed to unfold before me, shedding insights on *childhood* resentments, jealousies, and fears that had mushroomed in adulthood, and also on the self-pity that I had wallowed in at every opportunity.(p.371)
• I came to understand the intricate processes of projection, by which we cast into our adult world the images of the horrors of our *childhood*.(p.434)
• The medical profession would probably tell me I was conditioned for alcoholism by the things that happened to me in my *childhood*.(p.544)

childish
• The Wright brothers' almost *childish* faith that they could build a machine which would fly was the mainspring of their accomplishment.(p.52)
• But it quickly became obvious that he had this *childish* notion instead: If he could get me to go to enough meetings while in the hospital, I would continue to go after he let me out.(p.447)
• But as the years go by, the stretch becomes unbearable; and the man with the grown-up brain and the *childish* emotions -- vanity, self-interest, false pride, jealousy, longing for social approval, to name few -- becomes a prime candidate for alcohol.(p.534)
• I know there are some alcoholics who seem terribly, terribly grown-up, but I think that they are trying to make themselves think they are grown-up, and the strain of their effort is what is causing them to drink -- a sense of inadequacy, a *childish* vanity to be the most popular, the most sought after, the mostest of the most.(p.535)

childishness
• Those of us who have spent much time in the world of spiritual make-believe have eventually seen the *childishness* of it.(p.130)

children
• If any feel that as psychiatrists directing a hospital for alcoholics we appear somewhat sentimental, let them stand with us a while on the firing line, see the tragedies, the despairing wives, the little *children*; let the solving of these problems become a part of their daily work, and even of their sleeping moments, and the most cynical will not wonder that we have accepted and encouraged this movement.(p.xxvi)
• It brings misunderstanding, fierce resentment, financial insecurity, disgusted friends and employers, warped lives of blameless *children*, sad wives and parents -- anyone can increase the list.(p.18)
• If what we have learned and felt and seen means anything at all, it means that all of us, whatever our race, creed, or color are the *children* of a living Creator with whom we may form a relationship upon simple and understandable terms as soon as we are willing and honest enough to try.(p.28)
• His income is good, he has a fine home, is happily married and the father of promising *children* of college age.(p.39)
• He is the Father, and we are His *children*.(p.62)
• We have tried to hold the love of our *children* for their father.(p.106)
• They struck the *children*, kicked out door panels, smashed treasured crockery, and ripped the keys out of pianos.(p.106)
• Perhaps at this point we got a divorce and took the *children* home to father and mother.(p.106)
• How could men who loved their wives and *children* be so unthinking, so callous, so cruel?(p.107)
• Is it right to let him ruin your life and the lives of your *children*?(p.108)
• Be determined that your husband's drinking is not going to spoil your relations with your *children* or your friends.(p.111)
• The wives and *children* of such men suffer horribly,

but not more than the men themselves.(p.114)
- You do not know what to tell the *children.*(p.115)
- The same principle applies in dealing with the *children.*(p.115)
- You may be afraid your husband will lose his position; you are thinking of the disgrace and hard times which will befall you and the *children.*(p.116)
- Alateen, for teen-aged *children* of alcoholics, is a part of Al-Anon.(p.121)
- The alcoholic, his wife, his *children,* his "in-laws," each one is likely to have fixed ideas about the family's attitude toward himself or herself.(p.122)
- He may take small interest in the *children* and may show irritation when reproved for his delinquencies.(p.126)
- Sometimes mother and *children* don't think so.(p.126)
- Little by little, mother and *children* will see they ask too much, and father will see he gives too little.(p.127)
- Instead of developing new channels of activity for themselves, mother and *children* demand that he stay home and make up the deficiency.(p.131)
- The alcoholic may find it hard to re-establish friendly relations with his *children.*(p.134)
- The *children* are sometimes dominated by a pathetic hardness and cynicism.(p.134)
- It was the usual situation: home in jeopardy, wife ill, *children* distracted, bills in arrears and standing damaged.(p.155)
- I used to promise my wife, my friends, and my *children* that I would drink no more -- promises which seldom kept me sober even through the day, though I was very sincere when I made them.(p.177)
- One of five *children,* I was born on a Kentucky farm in Carlyle County.(p.182)
- I was the oldest of three *children,* and my father was an alcoholic.(p.193)
- We had two *children,* a boy and a girl, and when the boy was about twelve, we broke up the marriage.(p.199)
- I didn't want to neglect my *children.*(p.199)
- I was born in Cleveland, Ohio, in 1889, the last child of a family of eight *children.*(p.210)
- I can remember that in my childhood, he was ill at ease with the *children* because he attempted to assert an army discipline that had been ground into him during his three and a half years of army service.(p.210)
- As a matter of fact, I had two *children* at the time I was admitted to the bar.(p.212)
- My *children* had lost respect for me and, in fact, it was only after three or four years of sobriety that any of them ever said anything to me to indicate that I had recouped even a little of their respect.(p.215)
- I realized that there wasn't anything I could say to place myself in a more favorable light with my *children,* that it was going to be a matter of time; for I also understood the intolerance of young people towards deficiencies in their elders.(p.220)
- There were four of us *children,* and although both of my brothers later became alcoholic – one died of alcoholism – my sister has never taken a drink in her life.(p.240)
- I had none of these things that *children* should have to make them happy.(p.261)
- Finally, it got so bad that I left him and went back home and took my two *children* with me.(p.262)
- I kept my *children* with me.(p.262)
- At the end of a year, the *children* got a card from their father, which I still have and cherish.(p.262)
- But I don't believe now that it was with any deep feeling of resentment that I said to him, "The *children* are raised, and if this is the way you want it, this is the way we'll have it.(p.263)
- They made me feel as if I were a part of their family, and so did their *children.*(p.281)
- So six months ago I acquired a ready made family consisting of one charming wife, four grown *children* to whom I am devoted, and three grandchildren.(p.286)
- I was married at twenty, had two *children* and was divorced at twenty-three.(p.305)
- Many women who have reached the stage that I had reached in my drinking have lost husbands, *children,* homes, everything they hold dear.(p.323)
- I didn't think my *children* knew about it, but I found out they did.(p.324)
- I never thought I could be useful to anyone except my husband and my *children* and perhaps a few friends.(p.326)
- I just wanted to live to a certain age, carry through with what I felt was my job with the *children,* and after that – no matter.(p.337)
- My husband, my *children* saw the other side of me.(p.339)
- So when the *children* were in school from nine to three, I started up a nice little business and was fairly successful in it.(p.339)
- He and I had a large family – six *children,* to be exact.(p.370)
- We had always encouraged our *children* to bring their friends home at any time, but after a few experiences with a drunken father they eliminated home as a place to entertain friends.(p.376)
- I had a lovely wife and three *children.*(p.418)
- In less than two years, I lost my practice, my home, my wife, and my *children.*(p.418)
- The last time I drank, when I was twenty-nine, I drank for only four days, yet I threatened to kill my *children;* I beat my wife at home and on the church steps; I mistreated a child in my office; and I ran to a hospital for mental illness to avoid jail.(p.418)
- After I came to A.A., I was divorced by my wife; I lost my practice; I was legally restrained from seeing my *children;* I went broke; and the dental society threatened me with the loss of my license.(p.420)
- A.A. has given me a new wife, a beautiful step-daughter, a new practice, a new home, and a new relationship with my four *children.*(p.420)
- Perhaps the single flicker of decency that shone through the fog of my drinking days was a clumsy affection for my two *children,* a boy and a girl.(p.437)
- A.A. and acceptance have taught me that there is a bit of good in the worst of us and a bit of bad in the best of us; that we are all *children* of God and we each have a right to be here.(p.449)
- On the contrary, the hardest place to work this program has been in my own home, with my own *children* and, finally, with Max.(p.451)
- I attempted nearly two years ago to make some amends and contact my *children,* but it wasn't God's time yet.(p.463)
- I will be fifty years old next month, haven't seen my son or daughter yet, nor my daughter's two *children,* my grandchildren; but I am grateful.(p.463)
- Oldest of thirteen *children.*(p.474)
- She was very possessive with us *children.*(p.483)
- Nevertheless, I stayed sober there about six months, because I knew that Vi was to come later and bring the *children.*(p.490)
- I blame my wife and *children.*(p.505)
- There was the physical aspect; to be the youngest and the runt of the brood of *children,* to have to wear glasses very early and so to be teased, to be bookish and bored in school because the captain of the football team could not translate Virgil and yet was the school god while you, you, you little shrimp, were the school egghead, junior size and an early model.(p.533)
- I want to be one of His *children,* a member of the human race.(p.535)
- About this time, I met a man who had three motherless *children* and it seemed that might be a solution to my problem.(p.548)
- It seemed logical to me that if I married this man and took the responsibility for these *children* that they would keep me sober.(p.548)
- The *children* kept me sober for darn near three weeks, and then I went on (please God) my last drunk.(p.549)
- My *children* avoided me.(p.558)
- Hopeless now, I felt it would be better for my wife, my *children,* and everyone in my life if I went ahead and died.(p.558)
- As our *children* grew up, I was able to be a father to them when they most needed one.(p.559)

children's
- I said, "Well, I stood it to keep the home together, and for the *children's* sake."(p.322)

chilling
- As we became subjects of King Alcohol, shivering denizens of his mad realm, the *chilling* vapor that is loneliness settled down.(p.151)

chills
- Cold *chills* started chasing up and down my spine; my teeth were chattering; my hands were shaking so I tucked them under me to keep them from flying away.(p.222)

chin
- In the prize ring, this would be called leading with the *chin.*(p.77)

China
- Military service was compulsory and I did my stretch with the class of my age, goose-stepping in German barracks and taking part in the Boxer Rebellion in *China,* my first time at any great distance from home.(p.230)

chip
- Our hope is that when this *chip* of a book is launched on the world tide of alcoholism, defeated drinkers will seize upon it, to follow its suggestions.(p.153)

chocolate
- He thought all alcoholics should constantly have *chocolate* available for its quick energy value at times of fatigue.(p.133)

choice
- The fact is that most alcoholics, for reasons yet obscure, have lost the power of *choice* in drink.(p.24)
- This should be an entirely personal affair which each one decides for himself in the light of past associations, or his present *choice.*(p.28)
- What was our *choice* to be?(p.53)
- The *choice* was limited.(p.278)
- Remember, now you have a *choice.*(p.463)
- But now all *choice* was gone.(p.558)

choir
- I had never doubted the existence of the Supreme Being, but now I began to absent myself from my church where I had formerly been a member of the *choir.*(p.234)
- I was one of the star singers in the *choir* and one of the leading violins in the orchestra.(p.517)

choked
- It irritated my nostrils; I *choked,* I didn't like it.(p.195)
- I gulped it down and *choked.*(p.498)

chokes
- And this *chokes* the alcoholic.(p.350)

choose
- He said, "Why don't you *choose* your own conception of God?"(p.12)
- Whether such a person can quit upon a nonspiritual basis depends upon the extent to which he has already lost the power to *choose* whether he will drink or not.(p.34)
- Rightly and naturally, we think well before we *choose* the person or persons with whom to take this intimate and confidential step.(p.74)
- He can *choose* any conception he likes, provided it makes sense to him.(p.93)
- I *choose* to believe that the Power greater than ourselves we ask for help, wrapped my shivering body in loving warmth and strength which has never left me.(p.541)
- I hope I have been able to impart to you, the reader, at least a bit of what I know; the joy of living, the irresistible power of divine love and its healing strength, and the fact that we, as sentient beings, have the knowledge to *choose* between good and evil, and, choosing good, are made happy.(p.543)

chooses
- Society can do anything it *chooses* to do with me when I am drunk and I can't lift a finger to stop it, for I forfeit my rights through the simple expedient of becoming a menace to myself and to the people around me.(p.549)

choosing
- I went to hospitals, I went to retreats and doctors, and finally my mother asked me to go and see a specialist of her own *choosing.*(p.522)
- I hope I have been able to impart to you, the reader, at least a bit of what I know; the joy of living, the irresistible power of divine love and its healing strength, and the fact that we, as sentient beings, have the knowledge to choose between good and evil, and, *choosing* good, are made happy.(p.543)

chore
- Attending meetings has never been a *chore* to me.(p.381)

chose
- Instead of regarding ourselves as intelligent agents, spearheads of God's ever advancing Creation, we agnostics and atheists *chose* to believe that our human intelligence was the last word, the alpha and the omega, the beginning and end of all.(p.49)
- That Power I *chose* to call God.(p.381)

chosen
- Suppose we fall short of the *chosen* ideal and stumble?(p.70)
- They were earnest and obviously trying to help me on the road I had *chosen.*(p.259)
- By this time, my chances of getting lined up in my *chosen* business were shot.(p.301)
- I couldn't have *chosen* more loving and conscientious parents.(p.304)
- I continued to advance in my *chosen* field.(p.433)
- Since, perhaps, suicide was a bit too drastic (actually, I was afraid), dry martinis were *chosen* as the slow, pleasant, private, gradual instrument

of self-destruction.(p.531)

Christ

• To *Christ* I conceded the certainty of a great man, not too closely followed by those who claimed Him.(p.11)

• Alas for us men toward whom Shaw hurled his cry, "Must a *Christ* be crucified in every generation for the benefit of those who have no imagination?"(p.536)

Christ's

• He went on talking and told me that he had found the plan has a basis of love, and the practice of *Christ's* injunction, "Love thy neighbor as thyself."(p.236)

Christian

• From childhood through high school I was more or less forced to go to church, Sunday School and evening service, Monday night *Christian* Endeavor and sometimes to Wednesday evening prayer meeting.(p.172)

• In 1932, some friends of mine advised me that I might try *Christian* Science, which had done a lot for some of their friends.(p.202)

• I told somebody that I was going down to get *Christian* Science and they took me down, but I don't remember saying that.(p.202)

• This *Christian* Science experience with a sobriety of fifteen months was in 1932.(p.203)

• During the latter part of the *Christian* Science experience I had gotten a job and was working at Firestone.(p.203)

• But I had never been a flippant, wise-cracking sneerer at the few persons I had met who had impressed me as *Christian* men and women, or at any institution whose sincerity of purpose I could see.(p.259)

• I come from a very poor family in material things, with a fine *Christian* mother, but with no religious background.(p.261)

• The Episcopal magazine, The Living Church, observes editorially: "The basis of the technique of Alcoholics Anonymous is the truly *Christian* principle that a man cannot help himself except by helping others.(p.574)

Christmas

• This last real merry-go-round had started the day before *Christmas* and I had really accomplished a lot in those fourteen days.(p.238)

• After a particularly bad *Christmas* and New Year's holiday, dad picked me up again early in January, 1937, to go through the usual sobering up routine.(p.289)

• In succession came "What Made Milwaukee Famous Made a Loser Out of Me" and "I'm Drinking My *Christmas* Dinner All Alone."(p.332)

• At Christmastime next year, I convinced my wife that I had alcohol under control and that I would do controlled drinking over *Christmas* and the New Year.(p.343)

• It was to be short lived, for on the day before *Christmas* I completely disillusioned my wife and ruined our first *Christmas* by coming home from the Rotary lunch dead drunk.(p.361)

• About this time, at *Christmas*, after being under this doctor's care, we decided that there wasn't anything more to do.(p.388)

• Anyhow, after *Christmas* my husband gave me a cocker spaniel who is, I think, just as notorious in A.A. as I am.(p.388)

• My Quaker mother-in-law, bless her heart, used to set the *Christmas* pudding ablaze with lumps of sugar dipped in rubbing alcohol.(p.402)

• I didn't like being on the nut ward, and I particularly didn't like being forced to ice cookies on *Christmas* Eve.(p.444)

• And that was how Max and I and our two daughters spent *Christmas* Day, eight years ago.(p.444)

• The last *Christmas* I spent in Washington, fourteen years ago, comes to mind.(p.465)

• Only a few days before *Christmas* I went to the dentist for a periodic checkup.(p.465)

• On the day before *Christmas* I telephoned him and told him I was sober and asked him to come home.(p.467)

• At noon on *Christmas* Day I called my family in New York, wished them a Merry *Christmas*, and assured them everything was fine with me.(p.467)

• It was the one redeeming act of that *Christmas*.(p.467)

• To this day I can't hear that song without remembering that awful *Christmas*.(p.468)

• The only time that I have ever seen my mother take anything alcoholic was around *Christmas* time, when she would drink some eggnog or light wine.(p.484)

• My mother resented it so that the first *Christmas* after our marriage, she didn't even invite us to dinner.(p.485)

• My father was and still is a minister, and I was afraid that I might run into him, or that someone might tell him where I was, and I could still remember what he had done to me when I got drunk one *Christmas* when I was very young.(p.527)

Christmastime

• At *Christmastime* next year, I convinced my wife that I had alcohol under control and that I would do controlled drinking over Christmas and the New Year.(p.343)

chronic

• They believe in themselves, and still more in the Power which pulls *chronic* alcoholics back from the gates of death.(p.xxv)

• We believe, and so suggested a few years ago, that the action of alcohol on these *chronic* alcoholics is a manifestation of an allergy; that the phenomenon of craving is limited to this class and never occurs in the average temperate drinker.(p.xxvi)

• Much has been written pro and con, but among physicians, the general opinion seems to be that most *chronic* alcoholics are doomed.(p.xxviii)

• About one year prior to this experience a man was brought in to be treated for *chronic* alcoholism.(p.xxix)

• The doctor said: "You have the mind of a *chronic* alcoholic.(p.27)

• You know the deteriorating effects, the disintegrating effects of *chronic* wine-drinking.(p.337)

• Yes, I even knew I was a "*chronic* alcoholic."(p.470)

• Only they had been scratched out and over them was written, "*Chronic* Alcoholic."(p.470)

• I had been promoted from a periodic drinker to a *chronic* alcoholic!(p.470)

chronically

• Like most sick people before me, I was implacably selfish, and *chronically* self-centered.(p.401)

chronicle

• Repeated year on end, they are horrible -- frightening and degrading, a *chronicle* of tragedy which may be greater because the individual undergoing the tragedy, myself, knew what was happening, and yet refused to do anything to stop it.(p.538)

chucking

• Our friends have counseled *chucking* the men and we have done so with finality, only to be back in a little while hoping, always hoping.(p.105)

chuckle

• And having sung that phrase, I'd *chuckle* with amusement, turning into irony turning into self-contempt turning into self-pity, at the sad fate of Bob, that wonderful, poor little motherless boy who was so smart in school and who grew up to accept responsibility so early and so fast and who staggered under his burdens without a whimper until the time came when he thought he was too good for this world and so he ought to be out of it.(p.532)

chunks

• That being so you have swallowed and digested some big *chunks* of truth about yourself.(p.71)

church

• I could almost hear the sound of the preacher's voice as I sat, on still Sundays, way over there on the hillside; there was that proffered temperance pledge I never signed; my grandfather's good natured contempt of some *church* folk and their doings; his insistence that the spheres really had their music; but his denial of the preacher's right to tell him how he must listen; his fearlessness as he spoke of these things just before he died; these recollections welled up from the past.(p.10)

• Upon hearing this, our friend was somewhat relieved, for he reflected that after all, he was a good *church* member.(p.27)

• He attended *church* school, where he became rebellious at what he thought an overdose of religious education.(p.56)

• He attended *church* for the first time in many years.(p.80)

• With a shiver, he turned away and walked down the lobby to the *church* directory.(p.154)

• Selecting a *church* at random from the directory, he stepped into a booth and lifted the receiver.(p.155)

• He interrupted: "I used to be strong for the *church*, but that won't fix it.(p.157)

• He has helped other men recover, and is a power in the *church* from which he was long absent.(p.158)

• They were deeply religious people, much shocked by their son's refusal to have anything to do with the *church*.(p.158)

• My father was a professional man of recognized ability and both my father and mother were most active in *church* affairs.(p.171)

• From childhood through high school I was more or less forced to go to *church*, Sunday School and evening service, Monday night Christian Endeavor and sometimes to Wednesday evening prayer meeting.(p.172)

• This had the effect of making me resolve that when I was free from parental domination, I would never again darken the doors of a *church*.(p.172)

• I was at one time a deacon in the *church* and I still believe in God.(p.189)

• (My mother and father were Catholics and I had been baptized, but at the end of my instructions for Confirmation I had not gone to *church*, and then when my mother remarried, she married a Protestant and the whole religious angle was forgotten.(p.201)

• So I started to investigate Science through some friends of mine who were Readers in the *church*.(p.202)

• I never left the *church*, but I was a fringe member, and the thought simply never occurred to me that through the exercise of what I had I might find the answer to my problem, simply because I wouldn't admit that I had a problem.(p.214)

• I resolved that if I were going to continue with the Catholic *Church*, I was going to know the roots of the doctrine, since those roots had caused me some confusion.(p.221)

• I had never doubted the existence of the Supreme Being, but now I began to absent myself from my *church* where I had formerly been a member of the choir.(p.234)

• I knew somehow that it meant more than just going to *church* and living a moral life.(p.236)

• My *church* taught that.(p.236)

• At this school we had Bible readings before each meal, and *church* services four times on Sunday, and I became so rebellious at this that I swore I would never join or go to any *church* except for weddings or funerals.(p.240)

• I was an honest agnostic, but definitely not a hater of the *church* or its adherents.(p.256)

• The night that I was married I had a big *church* wedding.(p.385)

• Scared that my dress wasn't going to fit right, that the *church* wasn't going to be filled, that I'd fall flat on my face walking up the aisle; in fact, I was afraid I wasn't going to be a prima donna in the place where I should be.(p.385)

• You didn't carry a little orchid up the aisle in those days; you carried a great big bouquet, like a funeral spray, and you didn't have your picture taken until just before you went to the *church*.(p.385)

• The *church* was just three blocks from our home.(p.385)

• I got right into the car and they drove me over, and just as soon as I got to the *church* they started the wedding.(p.385)

• There was a doctor in our *church* congregation who was interested in my case, and he thought it was a vitamin deficiency.(p.389)

• My spiritual awakening in A.A. finally resulted in my joining a *church* some years ago.(p.417)

• I consider that I was taking the Eleventh Step when I joined this *church*.(p.417)

• Many good A.A.'s never join a *church*, and do not need to.(p.417)

• I tried the *church* and psychiatry and finally came to A.A.(p.418)

• The last time I drank, when I was twenty-nine, I drank for only four days, yet I threatened to kill my children; I beat my wife at home and on the *church* steps; I mistreated a child in my office; and I ran to a hospital for mental illness to avoid jail.(p.418)

• A return to the United States proved effective as a geographical cure, and a period of sobriety ensued, with the help of the *church*.(p.419)

• We spotted a *church* in a small town.(p.424)

• Was altar boy at *church* on reservation.(p.474)

• I went to *church* on Easter Sunday with my husband, and it didn't hurt at all.(p.482)

• (And the *church* walls haven't tumbled down yet.)(p.482)

• We lived just a few doors from the First Baptist *Church* and when they had funerals I remember very often asking my mother whether the person was good or bad and whether they were going to heaven or hell.(p.483)

• He went into the religious side and told me that I didn't attend *church* as regularly as I should, and that he felt, more or less, that this was responsible for my trouble.(p.489)

• I rebelled, and from that time on I don't think I attended *church* more than a dozen times.(p.489)

• Then Charlie or someone in the group suggested

that we try to get a place in a *church* or hall to hold meetings.(p.495)
• I am in *church*.(p.497)
• And if I had been able to turn to the *church* at that time I'm sure they could not have convinced me my sickness was within myself, nor could they have shown me the need for self-analysis that A.A. has shown me is vital if I am to survive.(p.546)
• There is something spiritual about an art museum or a symphony, and the Catholic *Church* approves of our use of them.(p.574)
• The Episcopal magazine, The Living *Church*, observes editorially: "The basis of the technique of Alcoholics Anonymous is the truly Christian principle that a man cannot help himself except by helping others.(p.574)

church-goer
• In those days, I trusted no *church-goer*, and thought A.A. was for weaklings.(p.460)

churches
• At one end of the room stood a glass covered directory of local *churches*.(p.154)
• The town was well supplied with *churches* and schools in which I pursued my early educational activities.(p.171)
• However, here I probably took my first step towards my coming alcoholism by developing a terrific aversion to all *churches* and established religions.(p.240)
• I even began to go the rounds of *churches*.(p.255)

churchgoing
• What had happened to the shy, lonely, *churchgoing* wallflower?(p.355)

churchman
• Though I had been only a nominal *churchman*, their proposals were not, intellectually, hard to swallow.(p.42)

chute
• If my wife was planning to go out in the afternoon, I would get a large supply of liquor and smuggle it home and hide it in the coal bin, the clothes *chute*, over door jambs, over beams in the cellar and in cracks in the cellar tile.(p.176)

cider
• A couple of hired hands were cleaning out the barn on the farm and I would ride to and fro on the sled, and while they were loading I would drink hard *cider* out of a barrel in the barn.(p.183)
• I went over and bought a jug of hard *cider* and a gallon of wine that I gave these fellows to drink.(p.195)
• Wine and hard *cider*.(p.196)

cigarette
• He took a couple of puffs of a *cigarette* and I took a couple of puffs of my *cigarette*.(p.195)
• I wanted a *cigarette* and room service, which I didn't get.(p.390)
• The more I focus my mind on its defects -- late start, long drunkalogues, *cigarette* smoke -- the worse the meeting becomes.(p.451)

cigarettes
• I remember telling them too that it was going to be awfully tough, because I did some other things, smoked *cigarettes* and played penny ante poker, sometimes bet on the horse races and they said, "Don't you think you're having more trouble with this drinking than with anything else at the present time?(p.190)
• And I continued to drink, on and off then, until every dollar I had in the world was gone again and I was right back living at my sister's, getting my *cigarettes* by calling her grocer and telling him to put in a couple of cartons with her order, exactly as I had before I started to work at Max's.(p.202)

cinch
• This caused the rather cryptic comment from one of my A.A. friends, when I told my story after coming into the program, that I had always been a *cinch* for the program, for I had always been interested in mankind, but that I was just taking them one man at a time.(p.548)

Cincinnati
• I remember one instance when he took off and went down to *Cincinnati* and was gone a week on a drunk.(p.262)

cipher
• Few people really are, for that means blind faith in the strange proposition that this universe originated in a *cipher* and aimlessly rushes nowhere.(p.10)

circle
• Each day my friend's simple talk in our kitchen multiplies itself in a widening *circle* of peace on earth and good will to men.(p.16)
• In sports I made the track and tennis teams; I got along well with the other boys and had a fairly large *circle* of acquaintances but no intimate friends.(p.240)
• Boy, what a *circle* of confused idealists!(p.246)

circles
• I shut myself in my room, which began to go around in *circles*.(p.279)

circling
• As I look back on the events of two months, I can clearly see that I had been *circling* around, half-afraid of encountering the remedy for my situation, half wanting it, deferring fulfillment of my promise to get in touch with the doctor I had heard about.(p.258)

circuits
• With nothing but a liberal arts education, very definitely estranged from my family and already married, soon after graduation from college I became a bookmaker's clerk on the British racing *circuits*, far better off financially than the average professional man.(p.251)

circulation
• The first edition appeared in April 1939, and in the following sixteen years, more than 300,000 copies went into *circulation*.(p.xi)

circumstance
• There was the father one lost respect for at the age of eleven, because the father broke his solemn word in a *circumstance* where you, eleven years old, had assumed guilt when you were innocent; but the father would not believe you, no matter what; and to ease his suffering you "confessed" and were "forgiven," only -- months later -- to have your "guilt" brought up -- only he and you knew what he was talking bout -- brought up in front of the stern grandmother.(p.533)

circumstances
• And in no *circumstances* should we give endorsements, make alliances, or enter public controversies.(p.xix)
• In some *circumstances* we have gone out deliberately to get drunk, feeling ourselves justified by nervousness, anger, worry, depression, jealousy or the like.(p.37)
• *Circumstances* made him willing to believe.(p.57)
• It set in motion trains of *circumstances* which brought us misfortune we felt we didn't deserve.(p.67)
• If *circumstances* warrant, we ask our wives or friends to join us in morning meditation.(p.87)
• Follow the dictates of a Higher Power and you will presently live in a new and wonderful world, no matter what your present *circumstances*!(p.100)
• We feel that each family, in the light of their own *circumstances*, ought to decide for themselves.(p.103)
• By force of *circumstances*, she was often obliged to treat father as a sick or wayward child.(p.130)
• So let each family play together or separately, as much as their *circumstances* warrant.(p.132)
• This resolution I kept steadfastly for the next forty years, except when *circumstances* made it seem unwise to absent myself.(p.172)
• The *circumstances* under which I reached these people were very odd because I was led there through things that I said when I couldn't even remember speaking.(p.202)
• My family lived in very prosperous *circumstances*, and while both my parents drank, sometimes too much, neither was an alcoholic.(p.240)
• Oddly enough, the *circumstances* and surroundings were pleasant.(p.285)
• It was a terrible blow at the time and I thought he was pretty much of a heel, but of course it was the finest thing he could have done for me under the *circumstances*.(p.357)
• Neither of these *circumstances* was very helpful to my type since I had not learned to face realities.(p.358)
• And I still felt it was a weakness -- plus, in her case, adverse *circumstances*.(p.370)
• I was raised like the majority of American boys, coming from a family of modest *circumstances*, attending public schools, having the social life of a small midwestern town, with part-time work and some athletics.(p.373)
• There was the economic fear which made me too timid to take any action which might improve my *circumstances*.(p.534)

cirrhosis
• After his death, my mother soon picked up drinking where Dad left off, and in a very short time she died of *cirrhosis* of the liver.(p.370)
• The enlargement of my liver degenerated into *cirrhosis*.(p.557)

citation
• No jail booking, drunk-driving *citation*, barroom fight, or even a tumble off a barstool.(p.327)
• The *citation* reads in part as follows:(p.573)

cited
• They *cited* cases out of their own experience by the dozen.(p.42)

cities
• And besides, there were scattered alcoholics who had picked up the basic ideas in Akron or New York and were trying to form A.A. groups in other *cities*.(p.xvii)
• Those of us who live in large *cities* are overcome by the reflection that close by hundreds are dropping into oblivion every day.(p.19)
• Under only slightly different conditions, the same thing is taking place in many eastern *cities*.(p.161)
• A friend who knew I would soon be broke mounted guard over me when I left my job of writing the histories of Texas *cities* and put me aboard a bus for the town I had left almost five years before.(p.256)
• In the United States and Canada, most towns and *cities* have A.A. groups.(p.575)
• In large *cities*, groups often maintain local offices where alcoholics or their families may arrange for interviews or hospitalization.(p.575)

citing
• Dr. John F. Stouffer, Chief Psychiatrist, Philadelphia General Hospital, *citing* his experience with A.A., said: "The alcoholics we get here at Philadelphia General are mostly those who cannot afford private treatment, and A.A. is by far the greatest thing we have been able to offer them.(p.572)

citizen
• A few months after I made my original trip to Akron I was feeling pretty cocky, and I didn't think my wife was treating me with proper respect, now that I was an outstanding *citizen*.(p.293)
• Through studied sneaky-drinking, I'd become a senior *citizen* without having lost a day's work because of booze.(p.327)
• In the course of drunken arguments, I found my own views and sense of responsibility as a *citizen*.(p.410)

citizens
• War fever ran high in the New England town to which we new, young officers from Plattsburg were assigned, and we were flattered when the first *citizens* took us to their homes, making us feel heroic.(p.1)
• His action met widespread approval, and today his is one of the most trusted *citizens* of his town.(p.80)

citizenship
• I had a family to be proud of, actively sharing in the responsibilities of good *citizenship*.(p.374)

city
• Hence the two men set to work almost frantically upon alcoholics arriving in the ward of the Akron *City* Hospital.(p.xvii)
• There were flights from *city* to country and back, as my wife and I sought escape.(p.6)
• In one western *city* and its environs there are one thousand of us and our families.(p.15)
• They will approach still other sick ones and fellowships of Alcoholics Anonymous may spring up in each *city* and hamlet, havens for those who must find a way out.(p.153)
• Years ago, in 1935, one of our number made a journey to a certain western *city*.(p.153)
• Then, in this eastern *city*, there are informal meetings such as we have described to you, where you may now see scores of members.(p.162)
• He had lived there but a few weeks when he found that the place probably contained more alcoholics per square mile than any *city* in the country.(p.163)
• When a few men in this *city* have found themselves, and have discovered the joy of helping others to face life again, there will be no stopping until everyone in that town has had his opportunity to recover -- if he can and will.(p.163)
• I conducted myself so creditably that I was able to secure a much coveted internship in a western *city*, where I spent two years.(p.174)
• This dry spell lasted for about three weeks; then I went to Atlantic *City* to attend several days' meeting of a national society of which I was a member.(p.179)
• Before my drinking had cut me down completely, I achieved a considerable measure of success, having been a *City* Councilman for five years and a financial director of Kenmore, a suburb later taken into the *city* itself.(p.182)
• Straightway, Bob called Akron's *City* Hospital and asked for the nurse on the receiving ward.(p.188)
• Bill bought me a drink or two on the way, and Dorothy S. came with us, and the three of us went over to

the *City* Hospital.(p.217)
• I came directly to a growing industrial *city* in the middle west, where I have lived practically ever since.(p.231)
• For weeks after my arrival I was feted and entertained in the already large colony of Alsatians in the *city*, and among the Germans in their saloons and clubs.(p.231)
• But I hardly tasted anything for two years and started in business for myself, founding a mattress factory which is today an important industrial enterprise in our *city*.(p.232)
• I re-organized their *city* sales policy and eighteen months later, when I was thirty, they offered me the branch managership.(p.243)
• As part of this promotion, they sent me to their national convention in Atlantic *City* to tell the big wheels how I'd done it.(p.243)
• My wife traveled with me, but with a baby coming I decided to settle in a large *city* where I got a job with a commission agent which is a polite term for a handbook operator.(p.251)
• My wife came over from Scotland and we started housekeeping in a large Ohio *city*.(p.254)
• FROM FARM TO *CITY*(p.261)
• I remember starting to *city* school, coming from a country school, and wanting so very, very much to be like the other girls and trying flour on my face for powder because I wasn't able to have any real powder.(p.261)
• Now I was in a strange house, in a strange *city*, and fear gripped me.(p.279)
• I, who had never made a speech in my life and who would have been frightened sick at the prospect, stood up in front of Rotary groups in different parts of the *city* and talked about Alcoholics Anonymous.(p.283)
• Such has been my privilege, both nationally and in my home *city*.(p.295)
• Just at this time my wife heard of a doctor in another *city* who had been very successful with drunks.(p.301)
• The physical skid row in any *city* is miserable.(p.345)
• About two days later I was called by a friend of mine from Nevada *City* -- he's a brother of my wife's closest friend.(p.347)
• Looking back, it is surprising to me now that I managed to keep working and have enough money to squander at the various spots in the big *city*.(p.358)
• The challenge intrigued me; also it was another opportunity to run away from myself and the "fast life of the big *city*."(p.359)
• At this time, however, she had an opportunity to go to Salt Lake *City* on a new project for the government, but she did promise me that if I would curtail my drinking and buckle down to hard work she would give serious consideration to my latest proposal and maybe join me at a later date when I got settled.(p.359)
• Furthermore, I knew that I was looked upon as a *city* slicker from New York, and I had to be pretty cautious among small town, conservative Yankees.(p.360)
• I tried a few drinks my last night in the *city* before coming home.(p.364)
• How can a person with a fine family, an attractive home, an excellent position and high standing in an important *city* become an alcoholic?(p.373)
• I achieved recognized and national standing in my profession, as well as becoming a director in many important institutions having to do with the civic life of a large *city*.(p.374)
• They told me to go to meetings, and I still do at every available opportunity, whether I am at home or in some other *city*.(p.381)
• I was going to sue the *city* for what they did to me.(p.391)
• This time I didn't put up any fight because I knew why they were there and where I was going, the psychopathic ward of the *City* Hospital, where I had been once before.(p.468)
• I am on a train headed for a *city*.(p.505)
• Maybe a few drinks when I get to the *city* will help.(p.505)
• The only thing that bothers me is that there are only about five Negroes in A.A. in my *city*.(p.529)
• Back to the big *city*, for another year of precarious living, paid for largely by one or two friends I still had not milked dry or worn to exhaustion with demands on their bounty.(p.540)
• My mother went to a nearby *city* to go to work, and my father, being an alcoholic, simply went.(p.544)

city-bred
• We boys drove out in somebody's car and went to the bar on the way do the dining room and I, in an effort to impress the other boys that I was *city-bred*, having lived in Scranton and Cleveland, asked them if they didn't want a drink.(p.194)

civic
• Father may have laid aside for years all normal activities -- clubs, *civic* duties, sports.(p.131)
• I achieved recognized and national standing in my profession, as well as becoming a director in many important institutions having to do with the *civic* life of a large city.(p.374)
• I had been elected president of a *civic* club.(p.418)

civil
• My father was a railroad man and a *Civil* War veteran.(p.210)
• I was going to be sent to the Indian *Civil* Service, which, in those days, meant that people thought you had a certain amount of brains.(p.517)

civilian
• It is painful to grow, and without the help of my "*civilian*" A.A. companion, big Gene, I might not have survived that critical year of adjustment.(p.462)
• I was a *civilian* now.(p.521)

civilization
• Everybody did, in the set which I regarded as the apex of *civilization*.(p.433)

claim
• We *claim* spiritual progress rather than spiritual perfection.(p.60)
• But I will never be totally honest -- that would make me perfect, and none of us can *claim* to be perfect.(p.482)

claimed
• To Christ I conceded the certainty of a great man, not too closely followed by those who *claimed* Him.(p.11)
• We looked askance at many individuals who *claimed* to be godly.(p.46)
• Far from expecting praise for their deeds, they *claimed* the performance a privilege and insisted that they invariably received more than they gave.(p.310)

claiming
• He clamors for this or that, *claiming* he cannot master alcohol until his material needs are cared for.(p.98)

clamors
• But soon the sense of His presence had been blotted out by worldly *clamors*, mostly those within myself.(p.12)
• He *clamors* for this or that, claiming he cannot master alcohol until his material needs are cared for.(p.98)

clang
• Our friend felt as though the gates of hell had closed on him with a *clang*.(p.27)

Clarence
• My wife didn't tell me this, but one Sunday afternoon when Mary was trying to get the cobwebs out of my mind, *Clarence* and his sister-in-law, the hairdresser, called at the house.(p.216)
• I was introduced to them and *Clarence* proceeded to put on his Twelve Step work.(p.216)
• However, on a couple of other occasions, *Clarence* seemed to bob up at the last saloon that I would stop at on the way home every day.(p.216)
• I resented it of course, and I offered *Clarence* his commission, whatever it might be, if he would please not bother me because I had arrived at the conclusion that he was a solicitor for some alcoholic institute.(p.216)
• One evening I had gone out after dinner to take on a couple of double-headers and stayed a little later than usual, and when I came home *Clarence* was sitting on the davenport with Bill W.(p.216)

claret
• I can't remember a dinner at home that we didn't have white wine or *claret* on the table.(p.384)

Clark
• I went to *Clark*, the community butcher, and I said, "*Clark*, what is the matter with me?(p.348)

class
• It was thought that no alcoholic man or woman could be excluded from our Society; that our leaders might serve but never govern; that each group was to be autonomous and there was to be no professional *class* of therapy.(p.xix)
• We believe, and so suggested a few years ago, that the action of alcohol on these chronic alcoholics is a manifestation of an allergy; that the phenomenon of craving is limited to this *class* and never occurs in the average temperate drinker.(p.xxvi)
• Many who once were in this *class* are now among our members.(p.28)
• Despite all we can say, many who are real alcoholics are not going to believe they are in that *class*.(p.31)
• As a *class*, alcoholics are energetic people.(p.146)
• They explained their need and inquired if she had a first *class* alcoholic prospect.(p.156)
• Between classes I would run down to the wash room, take enough to steady my nerves and then go on to the next *class*.(p.183)
• Military service was compulsory and I did my stretch with the *class* of my age, goose-stepping in German barracks and taking part in the Boxer Rebellion in China, my first time at any great distance from home.(p.230)
• I believe the sociologists would call it "upper middle *class*."(p.275)
• I was president of each *class* in the University, and president of that student body.(p.345)
• When I did make it home in 1920, I re-entered school and caught up with my *class* in a few short months -- I actually did a year's work in three months, proving much to the disgust of my dad that I could do it when I wanted to.(p.358)
• Why should this happen to me -- hadn't I provided a good home -- wasn't I making a good living -- didn't I just get a substantial raise that had put me in the upper bracket *class*?(p.362)
• After nine months of training, all the rest of my *class* was paroled and I went to work in the Department of Corrections.(p.462)
• I like the boys and we have lots of fun, in *class* and out.(p.500)

classed
• Sometimes we think fear ought to be *classed* with stealing.(p.67)

classes
• Many mornings I have gone to *classes*, and even though fully prepared, would turn and walk back to the fraternity house because of my jitters, not daring to enter the classroom for fear of making a scene should I be called on for recitation.(p.173)
• Between *classes* I would run down to the wash room, take enough to steady my nerves and then go on to the next class.(p.183)
• I was president of all my *classes* in high school and in my last year I was president of that student body.(p.345)
• I was skipping *classes* about two days a week and doing no book work whatever.(p.423)

classification
• The *classification* of alcoholics seems most difficult, and in much detail is outside the scope of this book.(p.xxviii)
• You would suppose that men in the fourth *classification* would be quite hopeless, but that is not so.(p.113)

classroom
• Many mornings I have gone to classes, and even though fully prepared, would turn and walk back to the fraternity house because of my jitters, not daring to enter the *classroom* for fear of making a scene should I be called on for recitation.(p.173)

clattered
• The ticker still *clattered*.(p.4)

claw
• I'd *claw* my way back to "respectability" and stay there -- until the inevitable next time.(p.432)

clean
• I felt lifted up, as though the great *clean* wind of a mountain top blew through and through.(p.14)
• So we *clean* house with the family, asking each morning in meditation that our Creator show us the way of patience, tolerance, kindliness and love.(p.83)
• The only condition is that he trust in God and *clean* house.(p.98)
• Marty came in, looking *clean*, neat, well-dressed and, like Bill, she was neither a bloated wreck nor a reformer.(p.413)
• I start to *clean* up the debris.(p.502)
• Similarly, we rid ourselves of guilt and remorse as we "*clean* out the garbage" from our minds through the Fourth and Fifth Steps of our recovery program.(p.560)

cleaned
• We vigorously commenced this way of living as we *cleaned* up the past.(p.84)

cleanest
• Before too long, my husband (who seemed to prefer his shirts dirty) put his foot down, declaring that our family might have the *cleanest* clothes in town, but that I hadn't been out of the same old dirty slacks and blouse for a week.(p.371)

cleaning
- *Cleaning* up old scrapes, helping to settle family differences, explaining the disinherited son to his irate parents, lending money and securing jobs for each other, when justified -- these are everyday occurrences.(p.161)
- A couple of hired hands were *cleaning* out the barn on the farm and I would ride to and fro on the sled, and while they were loading I would drink hard cider out of a barrel in the barn.(p.183)

clear
- We hope we have made *clear* the distinction between the alcoholic and the non-alcoholic.(p.44)
- We can only *clear* the ground a bit.(p.55)
- Our description of the alcoholic, the chapter to the agnostic, and our personal adventures before and after make *clear* three pertinent ideas:(p.60)
- Make it *clear* that he is not under pressure, that he needn't see you again if he doesn't want to.(p.94)
- You think he ought to know the subject better, as everyone should have a *clear* understanding of the risk he takes if he drinks too much.(p.112)
- It will take time to *clear* away the wreck.(p.123)
- But it is *clear* that we made our own misery.(p.133)
- Whatever the method, its object is to thoroughly *clear* mind and body of the effects of alcohol.(p.143)
- *Clear* away the wreckage of your past.(p.164)
- I had run into him, and he looked real prosperous; his face and eyes looked *clear* and he started to compliment me on my good front and how well I looked, and I said, "I haven't had a drink for nine months."(p.201)
- For there were of course periods of *clear* realization of what I had become, attended by memories of what I had been, what I had expected to be.(p.224)
- So it is *clear* that I never had any fun out of drinking – I would be the soberest-seeming one in the crowd and all of a sudden I would be the drunkest.(p.241)
- Here, while in a hospital bed, men with *clear* eyes, happy faces, and a look of assurance and purposefulness about them, came to see me and told me their stories.(p.279)
- Finally, and I shall never know how much later it was, one *clear* thought came to me: Try prayer.(p.280)
- His road lay *clear* before me, and I'd better quit rationalizing myself into any detours.(p.282)
- After a time, my mind began to *clear* of the fog that had covered it.(p.320)
- I could never be sure I'd have a *clear* head and hands that were willing to do some work.(p.326)
- I had to sleep, I had to *clear* my mind and free it from worry, and I had to relax.(p.336)
- Thank God that in spite of my heavy drinking my mind was *clear* enough to make a decision then and there.(p.363)
- You will recall that I said the time that I got the idea out of a *clear* sky to call A.A. on a certain night was at about ten.(p.366)
- The line between a heavy drinker and an alcoholic is not always *clear*.(p.436)
- Aside from being a common drunk, I had a very serious pill affliction and all the garbage that goes with it -- lying, stealing, cheating anybody and everybody, conning the people I could, and staying *clear* of the ones I couldn't.(p.478)
- I fled, finally, after having been fired from my job by a boss who wept a little (since I had worked hard) as he gave notice for me to *clear* out.(p.539)

clear-cut
- Further on, *clear-cut* directions are given showing how we recovered.(p.29)
- These give a fair cross section of our membership and a *clear-cut* idea of what has actually happened in their lives.(p.29)
- Philosophy, faith, a sense of humor (they could laugh at themselves), *clear-cut* objectives, appreciation – and most especially appreciation and sympathetic understanding for their fellow man.(p.310)

cleared
- More often than not, it is imperative that a man's brain be *cleared* before he is approached, as he has then a better chance of understanding and accepting what we have to offer.(p.xxiv)
- Under the so-called belladonna treatment my brain *cleared*.(p.7)
- Our thought-life will be placed on a much higher plane when our thinking is *cleared* of wrong motives.(p.86)
- The explanation that alcoholism was a disease of a two fold nature, an allergy of the body and an obsession of the mind, *cleared* up a number of puzzling questions for me.(p.380)

clearer
- From far away, as if in a delirium, I heard my own voice – calling someone "Dorothy," talking of dress shops, of jobs . . . the words came *clearer* . . . this sound of my own voice frightened me as it came closer . . . and suddenly, there I was, talking of I knew not what, to someone I'd never seen before this very moment.(p.222)
- It pays daily in more harmonious relations with my fellow men, in ever *clearer* insight into the true meaning of life, and in the answering love and gratitude wherever and whenever I have been the instrument of God's will in the lives of others.(p.394)
- But the more meetings you attend, the more people you meet at these meetings, the *clearer* the Steps become.(p.516)

clearing
- This is a world *clearing* house for the Al-Anon Family Groups, composed largely of the wives, husbands and friends of A.A. members.(p.575)

clearly
- There were times when I got to drinking, and I had been warned by Firestone that they wouldn't stand for this much longer, so, *clearly*, they were conscious of the fact that I drank too much and too often.(p.204)
- As I look back on the events of two months, I can *clearly* see that I had been circling around, half-afraid of encountering the remedy for my situation, half wanting it, deferring fulfillment of my promise to get in touch with the doctor I had heard about.(p.258)
- I can think *clearly* and am helped much in my thinking and judgment by my spiritual development which grows daily.(p.303)
- The word "insanity" came through *clearly* -- and repugnantly.(p.332)
- Hauling her to the divan, I sat with her and began to talk, frantically but *clearly* -- and making sense.(p.333)
- I'd go into my home with a bottle, and I remember *clearly* how I would look around to see if Vi was watching.(p.487)
- This question so insulted the emotions that *clearly* there was only one thing to do, go and get drunk again, and put that enquiring mind in its proper place, which was oblivion.(p.537)

clears
- We'll be down as soon as he *clears* up."(p.188)

clemency
- I still expected a plea for *clemency*, but these words came through the receiver: "I just wanted to tell you Paul jumped from a hotel window in Hartford last Saturday.(p.136)

clergy
- And the *clergy* have tried hard to help us, but we haven't been helped.(p.352)
- And the psychiatrist has had thousands of couches, and has put you and me on them many, many times, but he hasn't helped us very much, though he has tried hard; and we owe the *clergy* and the doctor and the psychiatrist a deep debt of gratitude, but they haven't helped our alcoholism, except in a rare few instances.(p.352)

clergyman
- Dr. Harry Emerson Fosdick, the noted *clergyman*, reviewed it with approval.(p.xvii)
- He would phone a *clergyman*.(p.154)
- His call to the *clergyman* led him presently to a certain resident of the town, who, though formerly able and respected, was then nearing the nadir of alcoholic despair.(p.155)
- During the day a friend of mine brought me some magazines to take to a hospital group I was interested in, and I looked through them and a "banner" across the front of one featured an article by a prominent *clergyman* in which I caught the word "resentment."(p.552)

clergymen
- *Clergymen* of practically every denomination have given A.A. their blessing.(p.574)

clerk
- With nothing but a liberal arts education, very definitely estranged from my family and already married, soon after graduation from college I became a bookmaker's *clerk* on the British racing circuits, far better off financially than the average professional man.(p.251)

Cleveland
- Though none of these principles had the force of rules or laws, they had become so widely accepted by 1950 that they were confirmed by our first International Conference held at *Cleveland*.(p.xix)
- We boys drove out in somebody's car and went to the bar on the way do the dining room and I, in an effort to impress the other boys that I was city-bred, having lived in Scranton and *Cleveland*, asked them if they didn't want a drink.(p.194)
- I sold three lots to an elderly lady in *Cleveland*.(p.196)
- I came to *Cleveland* with the deeds to these lots and to pick up my money.(p.196)
- The next morning I woke up in jail in *Cleveland* and the jailor had $1,175 of my money in an envelope.(p.196)
- Everything in the world a man could possibly want, and I was driving from Akron to *Cleveland*, having just been to the bank and discovered that I had approximately $5,000.(p.200)
- I drove towards *Cleveland* wondering why I found myself in such a changed set of conditions as compared with those of six months before.(p.200)
- So I was driving to *Cleveland* when I made this solemn promise never to drink again.(p.201)
- On Sunday when I came to, it was a bad, wet, snowy day in February, 1937, and Paul and Doc and a lot of other fellows were in *Cleveland* on business.(p.207)
- I was born in *Cleveland*, Ohio, in 1889, the last child of a family of eight children.(p.210)
- That was in *Cleveland*.(p.211)
- There were, at that time, in the neighborhood of twelve or thirteen *Cleveland* members who had been sober anywhere from a year and a half to a couple of months.(p.219)
- It was finally decided to undertake the organization of a *Cleveland* group and toward the end of May, 1939, the first meeting was held in *Cleveland* in my home.(p.219)
- At that meeting, there were a number of Akron people and all the *Cleveland* people.(p.219)
- So I went to Akron, and also to *Cleveland*, and I met more recovered alcoholics.(p.310)
- I was born in *Cleveland*, Ohio, the only child of a prominent dentist, and a very proud mother.(p.357)
- All I can remember about the Roaring Twenties is that I drank a great deal, thought I was having a grand time, managed to get to Europe for a few weeks, was very proud of the dozens of speak-easy cards entitling me to an entree in the better joints between *Cleveland* and New York, took on a wife, and built a home in a fashionable suburb of *Cleveland*.(p.358)
- She was studying fashion design, was living in the same rooming house, and was from my home town of *Cleveland*.(p.359)

Cleveland's
- An originator of *Cleveland's* Group No. 3, this one fought Prohibition in vain.(p.297)

client
- In other words, I fired the *client* before the *client* fired me.(p.214)
- I did not reflect that half the office was composed of A.A. members, and that I was as unexciting as any *client* in any office.(p.413)

clients
- A year later, after I completed the course in contracts, I quit the law school, and undertook some engineering work for a patent law firm on behalf of *clients* who were in difficulties and who desired to keep their troubles from their own engineering department.(p.212)
- In 1924, I had acquired enough *clients* of my own so that the firm made me a junior partner.(p.213)
- Seven years of work in this field brought an opportunity to affiliate myself actively with one of my *clients*, a fellow A.A.(p.284)

climb
- I would like to sketch for you the highlights of these sixteen years of a slow but steady and satisfying upward *climb*.(p.280)
- *Climb* on water wagon for few months.(p.475)
- I *climb* to my room in the attic.(p.497)

climbed
- As animals on a treadmill, we have patiently and wearily *climbed*, falling back in exhaustion after each futile effort to reach solid ground.(p.107)
- As my father *climbed* the ladder of success in the oilfield business, his drinking also *climbed*.(p.369)

clinch
- He has just returned from a three-months leave of absence, has taken a cure, looks fine, and to *clinch* the matter, the board of directors told him this was his last chance."(p.138)

cling
- If we still *cling* to something we will not let go, we ask God to help us be willing.(p.76)
- *Cling* to the thought that, in God's hands, the dark

past is the greatest possession you have -- the key to life and happiness for others.(p.124)

clinging

• I do recall lying on a cold cement floor and shredding into little bits several pieces of stolen identification cards, and washing my face in the toilet bowl trying to sober up, and screaming hysterically while *clinging* to bars too high to see out of, and cursing everyone that came near me.(p.354)

clings

• He *clings* to the notion that he will yet find a way to do so.(p.110)

clinic

• And with such good effect that the doctor agreed to a test among his patients and certain other alcoholics from a *clinic* which he attends.(p.163)

• As a result, he couldn't figure out why I had the convulsions, and he decided to send me to the Mayo *Clinic*.(p.444)

• The Mayo *Clinic* seemed like a good place to have my diagnosis confirmed.(p.444)

clipping

• Another time, as I opened a letter which lay on my desk, a newspaper *clipping* fell out.(p.136)

• While I was in Florida trying to convince my wife with all the A.A. literature that she should come back to me, she went over to her desk and picked up a *clipping* she had taken from the St. Petersburg Times about A.A.(p.366)

• But for some reason -- she just didn't know why -- she just had to hold onto that *clipping*, with its thin hope.(p.367)

• She said she cut this *clipping* from the paper at about ten on the same night, and at the same time as I called A.A. in Pittsburgh -- some 1300 miles away.(p.367)

clock

• He is the fellow who goes to bed so intoxicated he ought to sleep the *clock* around.(p.21)

• I was drunk for sixty days around the *clock* and it was my intention, literally, to drink myself to death.(p.549)

clocks

• Gone are time cards to punch, alarm *clocks* to obey, nosey rumor-mongers and talebearers to evade.(p.329)

close

• By the *close* of 1941, A.A. numbered 8,000 members.(p.xviii)

• Those of us who live in large cities are overcome by the reflection that *close* by hundreds are dropping into oblivion every day.(p.19)

• Being all powerful, He provided what we needed, if we kept *close* to Him and performed His work well.(p.63)

• Though it is entirely separate from Alcoholics Anonymous, it uses the general principles of the A.A. program as a guide for husbands, wives, relatives, friends, and others *close* to alcoholics.(p.121)

• After being dry two weeks and sticking *close* to Jackie, all of a sudden I found I had become the sponsor of my sponsor, for he was suddenly taken drunk.(p.245)

• I ended up, homeless, jobless, penniless and rudderless, as the problem guest of a *close* friend whose family was out of town.(p.278)

• Poor health and a complete lack of money necessitated my remaining with Dr. Bob and Anne for very *close* to a year.(p.280)

• He was *close* to tears in describing his boredom without an activity.(p.334)

• As a matter of fact, when I came into Alcoholics Anonymous I was *close* to being at the peak of my career.(p.356)

• I entered the house, opened a new bottle of whiskey and sat down to drink myself into the right frame of mind to get in my car, start the motor and *close* the garage door behind me.(p.363)

• When I had known her years before she was rather slender, but at this time she weighed as much as she does now, which is up around in the two hundreds or very *close* to it.(p.493)

• I knew my wife didn't because I had been sincere in all my promises to her as well as to my mother and to my *close* friends, but the urge to take that drink was more powerful than anything else.(p.494)

• I've stuck pretty *close* to A.A. ever since then, taken it day by day, not biting off more than I can chew.(p.511)

• But I've never come *close* to that first drink.(p.516)

• Within a month, the police, the hospital authorities, several kind strangers, most of my friends, all of my *close* relatives, and a few adepts at rolling a drunk and removing his wrist watch and wallet had been involved.(p.532)

• But individual welfare follows *close* afterward.(p.565)

• Most emphatically we wish to say that any alcoholic capable of honestly facing his problems in the light of our experience can recover, provided he does not *close* his mind to all spiritual concepts.(p.570)

close-mouthed

• If we cannot or would rather not do this, we search our acquaintance for a *close-mouthed*, understanding friend.(p.74)

closed

• It was eight o'clock -- five hours after the market *closed*.(p.4)

• Our friend felt as though the gates of hell had *closed* on him with a clang.(p.27)

• My last venture, a book shop, was hastened to *closed* doors by my steady intoxication.(p.255)

• When it was *closed* through Washington edict I began with Federal Writers in San Antonio.(p.256)

• They opened with a little prayer, and I thought it was very fine that we stood, all of us together, and *closed* with the Lord's Prayer.(p.270)

• When we *closed* the meeting with the Lord's Prayer, Russ said, "Mother, help me stand."(p.270)

• The meeting lasted an hour and *closed* with the Lord's Prayer.(p.291)

• After it was *closed* we all retired to the kitchen and had coffee and doughnuts and more discussion until the small hours of the morning.(p.291)

• I went to *closed* meetings and open meetings.(p.340)

• What healed those tissues, those tissues that I *closed*, what healed them?(p.351)

• I *closed* my eyes and tried to think.(p.422)

• After he'd talked half an hour, I still wanted him to hurry up and get out so I could go and get some whiskey before the liquor store *closed*.(p.494)

• Offices *closed* up and workers discharged.(p.500)

closely

• To Christ I conceded the certainty of a great man, not too *closely* followed by those who claimed Him.(p.11)

• That was natural, but let us think a little more *closely*.(p.53)

• Impressed by those who visited him at the hospital, he capitulated entirely when, later, in an upper room of this house, he heard the story of some man whose experience *closely* tallied with his own.(p.160)

closer

• We began to ask medical advice as the sprees got *closer* together.(p.106)

• His friends feel *closer* over a highball.(p.110)

• In the first flush of spiritual experience they forgave each other and drew *closer* together.(p.124)

• From far away, as if in a delirium, I heard my own voice -- calling someone "Dorothy," talking of dress shops, of jobs . . . the words came clearer . . . this sound of my own voice frightened me as it came *closer* . . . and suddenly, there I was, talking of I knew not what, to someone I'd never seen before this very moment.(p.222)

• It was a period of binges coming *closer* and *closer* together and being of longer duration.(p.288)

closest

• About two days later I was called by a friend of mine from Nevada City -- he's a brother of my wife's *closest* friend.(p.347)

• The *closest* I came to a psychiatrist during that time was an interne who came to take blood tests.(p.492)

• Edward Dowling, S.J., of the Queen's Work staff says, "Alcoholics Anonymous is natural; it is natural at the point where nature comes *closest* to the supernatural, namely in humiliations and in consequent humility.(p.574)

closet

• The first impulse will be to bury these skeletons in a dark *closet* and padlock the door.(p.123)

• We families of Alcoholics Anonymous keep few skeletons in the *closet*.(p.125)

• Yet I recently recalled that each morning I used to talk to the bottle when I took it down from the *closet*.(p.332)

closets

• I had no need to hide in *closets*, bathrooms, or garages.(p.332)

closing

• One man comes back, *closing* the door behind him.(p.503)

• I had a habit of getting up just prior to the *closing* time of the saloons, about two or three o'clock in the morning.(p.514)

clothed

• My inability to accept the harsh realities of life had resulted in a disillusioned cynic, *clothed* in protective armor against the world's misunderstanding.(p.226)

clothes

• We gave up our positions and off we roared on a motorcycle, the sidecar stuffed with tent, blankets, a change of *clothes*, and three huge volumes of a financial reference service.(p.2)

• That afternoon he put on his *clothes* and walked from the hospital a free man.(p.158)

• If my wife was planning to go out in the afternoon, I would get a large supply of liquor and smuggle it home and hide it in the coal bin, the *clothes* chute, over door jambs, over beams in the cellar and in cracks in the cellar tile.(p.176)

• Before our visit was over, Bill suddenly turned to his wife and said, "Go fetch my *clothes*, dear.(p.189)

• At the end of about four months, I not only had good looking *clothes* --and I might say that at the time I first talked to Max I didn't have a suit of *clothes* I could bend over in real sudden; now I had six suits of *clothes*.(p.200)

• Mother would take me in only if I would stay locked in a small storeroom and give her my *clothes* and shoes.(p.238)

• There I was, unshaven, *clothes* torn and dirty with no recollection of wandering all over France but, of course, a hero to the local French.(p.242)

• He had taken up light work, and he had a safety valve and a pair of spurs and the *clothes* on his back, and that was all.(p.263)

• After holding good positions, making better than an average income for over ten years, I was in debt, had no *clothes* to speak of, no money, no friends, and no one any longer tolerating me but my wife.(p.301)

• She hid her bottles in *clothes* hampers and dresser drawers.(p.335)

• I would gather up all my soiled *clothes*, as much as I could cram into a grocery cart, and be off.(p.370)

• Before too long, my husband (who seemed to prefer his shirts dirty) put his foot down, declaring that our family might have the cleanest *clothes* in town, but that I hadn't been out of the same old dirty slacks and blouse for a week.(p.371)

• I still wash *clothes*, lots of them, but I no longer lose them at the Laundromat.(p.372)

• Anne and I went up in ski *clothes* and fur coats, and it was so cold we slept in them.(p.415)

• We, who were dirty, bedraggled and in ski *clothes*.(p.415)

• Pack my *clothes* and put me on train.(p.475)

• No *clothes*, no money, no home, no real friends to speak of, mentally and physically pooped, but I was doing all right!(p.478)

• Later, I found out that I went into stores and stole *clothes*, then sold them.(p.528)

• I had no money -- well, maybe a dime -- and only the *clothes* I stood in.(p.540)

• To wear expensive *clothes*, to have bartenders know what to serve me before I ordered, to be recognized by headwaiters and shown to the best table, to play gin rummy for high stakes with the insouciance of a riverboat gambler -- these were the enduring values in life, I thought.(p.556)

clothing

• But my board, room, and *clothing* were free, and I could spend the whole ten bucks on booze.(p.398)

cloud

• It was the end of a perfect day, not a *cloud* on the horizon.(p.41)

• And the first thing you know I was lifted right out of the A.A. group, and I floated higher, and higher, and even higher, until I was way up on a pink *cloud* which is known as Pink Seven, and I felt miserable again.(p.348)

• "Well," he said, "you've been sober, but you've been floating way up on a *cloud* somewhere.(p.349)

• Alcohol was a looming *cloud* in this banker's bright sky.(p.373)

clouds

• We have come to believe He would like us to keep our heads in the *clouds* with Him, but that our feet ought to be firmly planted on earth.(p.130)

clown

• Very shortly, I realized that had been a mistake -- when this big *clown* came bounding into the room, almost shouting, "My name is Frank, and I'm an alcoholic, ha-ha-ha!"(p.446)

clowning

• I had enough decency so that I dismissed the idea of doing any *clowning*, and I did listen.(p.509)

clowns
• My only thought that day was getting a drink, and how to get rid of those *clowns* was my big problem.(p.206)

club
• An alcoholic of this temperament may be quick to use this chapter as a *club* over your head.(p.108)
• They acted on me like the beating of a *club*.(p.195)
• Fond of singing, I joined a German singing society which had good *club* headquarters.(p.231)
• I got around this by joining the local Rotary *Club*, and through this association with the business men of the community my little station began to grow.(p.360)
• A few times at meetings, I have heard this statement: "Members of A.A. have paid the highest initiation fee of any *club* members in the world."(p.396)
• In the first year there were episodes such as kicking Priscilla in the shins, getting the lock changed on the desk in the A.A. *Club*, because I, as secretary, didn't want the Intergroup secretary "interfering," and taking an older woman member out to lunch for the express purpose of informing her that she was "a phony."(p.416)
• I had been elected president of a civic *club*.(p.418)
• While waiting to depart I was selected -- by giving a CPO five dollars -- to be bartender in the Navy Chief's *Club*.(p.426)
• One night I barely made my downtown *club*; if I'd had to go another fifty feet I'd have collapsed in the gutter.(p.435)
• Instead, I started going to a nice private sanitarium which, after the first visit, turned out to be more like a country *club* than anything else.(p.468)

club-man
• I was *club-man*, athlete, artist, musician, author, editor, aircraft pilot and world traveller.(p.432)

clubroom
• I went to meetings, I spent a lot of time at the *clubroom*, but it was all centered in this one woman.(p.472)

clubs
• He commences to look around in the night *clubs*, or their equivalent, for something besides liquor.(p.81)
• Father may have laid aside for years all normal activities -- *clubs*, civic duties, sports.(p.131)
• I would sometimes hide out in one of the *clubs* of which I was a member, and had the habit at times of registering at a hotel under a fictitious name.(p.176)
• My wife and I belonged to some bridge *clubs* and they began to make wine and serve it.(p.184)
• My drinking career began about four years after I had moved up into partnership and had joined certain *clubs*, societies and so fourth, and during which period we had Prohibition.(p.213)
• For weeks after my arrival I was feted and entertained in the already large colony of Alsatians in the city, and among the Germans in their saloons and *clubs*.(p.231)
• I moved in a gay crowd in the various "pubs" and sporting *clubs*.(p.251)
• Instead of drinking in fancy bars and *clubs*, I had to carry a bottle of vodka in my briefcase, duck into public toilets, and gulp from the bottle, trembling, in order to keep from falling apart.(p.557)
• Secondary aids to A.A., such as *clubs* or hospitals which require much property or administration, ought to be incorporated and so set apart that, if necessary, they can be freely discarded by the groups.(p.566)
• For *clubs*, A.A. managers are usually preferred.(p.566)
• We think that each group should soon achieve this ideal; that any public solicitation of funds using the name of Alcoholics Anonymous is highly dangerous, whether by groups, *clubs*, hospitals, or other outside agencies; that acceptance of large gifts from any source, or of contributions carrying any obligation whatever, is unwise.(p.566)

clumsy
• Perhaps the single flicker of decency that shone through the fog of my drinking days was a *clumsy* affection for my two children, a boy and a girl.(p.437)

clung
• I *clung* to the outfit for the balance of my time, and finally I was released, after having spent twenty years and nine months behind bars.(p.510)

clusters
• Little *clusters* of twos and threes and fives of us have sprung up in other communities, through contact with our two larger centers.(p.162)

clutches
• This escapade also ended up in the *clutches* of the law, and my friend was institutionalized for eight months.(p.354)

co-founder
• Bill W., *co-founder* of A.A., died January 24, 1971.(p.16)
• Beginning with the story of "Dr. Bob," a *co-founder* of A.A., there are here presented three groups of personal histories.(p.165)
• A *co-founder* of Alcoholics Anonymous.(p.171)

co-operation
• I tried psychiatry, but of course I gave the psychiatrist no *co-operation*.(p.375)

coal
• If my wife was planning to go out in the afternoon, I would get a large supply of liquor and smuggle it home and hide it in the *coal* bin, the clothes chute, over door jambs, over beams in the cellar and in cracks in the cellar tile.(p.176)

coast
• I went out to the West *Coast*, waited on table, washed dishes and sold newspaper subscriptions.(p.401)

coat
• I acquired the impeccable *coat* of tan one sees upon the well-to-do.(p.4)
• I loved my father dearly and I adored my dog, and I'd gotten this new house and Frank had just given me a new fur *coat* and I was thrilled to death.(p.389)
• "You've got to space your drinks and take plenty of water in between," or "*coat* the stomach with a little olive oil," or "drink anything but those damn martinis."(p.433)
• It came out that I had sold a woman a fur *coat*.(p.528)

coats
• I had every advantage a child could have, private schools (several of them), dancing schools, two colleges, coon skin *coats*, automobiles, a listing in the social register and all the rest.(p.357)
• Anne and I went up in ski clothes and fur *coats*, and it was so cold we slept in them.(p.415)

coaxing
• However, my two friends kept *coaxing* and cajoling to get me back again.(p.510)

cobwebs
• My wife didn't tell me this, but one Sunday afternoon when Mary was trying to get the *cobwebs* out of my mind, Clarence and his sister-in-law, the hairdresser, called at the house.(p.216)

cock-sureness
• Some time passed, and confidence began to be replaced by *cock-sureness*.(p.5)

cocker
• Anyhow, after Christmas my husband gave me a *cocker* spaniel who is, I think, just as notorious in A.A. as I am.(p.388)

cockiness
• I have self confidence and assurance that cannot be confused with the *cockiness* I once possessed.(p.303)

cockpit
• I don't know why I didn't fall out of the open *cockpit* of some of those planes I flew in while taking aerial pictures.(p.426)

cocktail
• I ordered a *cocktail* and my meal.(p.41)
• Then I ordered another *cocktail*.(p.41)
• I had long since given up any pretense of the "social" *cocktail* hour.(p.306)
• The *cocktail* hour became a daily routine.(p.374)
• After every *cocktail* party or dinner party she would say she couldn't understand how I could get in such a drunken stupor on one drink.(p.377)
• I lived in New Orleans where, at that time, *cocktail* parties, dances and night spots were almost the order of the day -- or rather the night.(p.384)

cocktails
• As I crossed the threshold of the dining room, the thought came to mind that it would be nice to have a couple of *cocktails* with dinner.(p.41)
• I had commenced to drink as carelessly as though the *cocktails* were ginger ale.(p.41)
• Almost simultaneously, I discovered that *cocktails* in the late afternoon and highballs in the evening relieved the many tensions of the day.(p.277)
• It started when I joined a few of the men for *cocktails* before the noonday Rotary luncheon.(p.360)
• Why did I have to have at least three *cocktails* to sit through dinner?(p.406)
• Evening *cocktails* were as standard as morning coffee, and I suppose my average daily consumption ran a little more or less than a pint.(p.433)

cocky
• When it made us *cocky*, it was worse.(p.68)
• We are neither *cocky* nor are we afraid.(p.85)
• A few months after I made my original trip to Akron I was feeling pretty *cocky*, and I didn't think my wife was treating me with proper respect, now that I was an outstanding citizen.(p.293)

coddle
• I learned what a devastating effect it can have on a child to *coddle* him and build him up, and then turn and beat him savagely, as had happened to me.(p.434)

code
• If a mere *code* of morals or a better philosophy of life were sufficient to overcome alcoholism, many of us would have recovered long ago.(p.44)
• Love and tolerance of others is our *code*.(p.84)

codeine
• I never got much effect out of *codeine* and Percodan and the tranquilizers.(p.442)

codes
• But we found that such *codes* and philosophies did not save us, no matter how much we tried.(p.45)

codger
• While I sought the comforting arms of alcohol, I knew this was a sign of weakness on the part of a longtime-successful old *codger* with white hair, the image of dignity.(p.331)

coffee
• Here is a case in point: One of our friends is a heavy smoker and *coffee* drinker.(p.135)
• Though he is now a most effective member of Alcoholics Anonymous, he still smokes and drinks *coffee*, but neither his wife or anyone else stands in judgment.(p.135)
• My wife wrote away for advertised cures for the liquor habit and gave them to me in *coffee*.(p.235)
• Instead, over *coffee* cups, this man and his wife told me what had been done for them.(p.259)
• And I said, "Well, they brought a pitcher of *coffee*, and a sandwich wrapped up for me."(p.264)
• There was more than one occasion when I got up in the morning with just enough money for *coffee* and toast and the bus fare to carry me to my first appointment.(p.283)
• After it was closed we all retired to the kitchen and had *coffee* and doughnuts and more discussion until the small hours of the morning.(p.291)
• Every evening we would meet at the home of one of the members and have *coffee* and doughnuts and spend a social evening.(p.291)
• So he got me a cup of *coffee*, and a piece of cake, and sat me down and said, "Why, there's nothing wrong with you.(p.348)
• Evening cocktails were as standard as morning *coffee*, and I suppose my average daily consumption ran a little more or less than a pint.(p.433)
• I set it down and made myself a cup of *coffee*.(p.541)

cognac
• My four years of abstinence had something to do with it, but soldiering is a tough enough game for a sober man, and I had no yen for full-pack slogging through mud with a *cognac* or vin rouge hangover.(p.253)

cognacs
• We heard by wireless on the 5th that the Armistice would be signed the next day (this was a premature report) so I had a couple of *cognacs* to celebrate; then I hopped a truck and went AWOL.(p.242)

cognizance
• I think our profession must take appreciative *cognizance* of this great therapeutic weapon.(p.571)

coherent
• Out of this maelstrom just two *coherent* thoughts came to the surface; one, a drink would mean homelessness and death; two, I could no longer relieve the pressure of fear by starting home, as was once my habitual solution to this problem, because I no longer had a home.(p.279)

coin
• When I try to reconstruct what my life was like "before," I see a *coin* with two faces.(p.432)
• The other side of the *coin* was sinister, baffling.(p.432)

coincided
• My divorce *coincided* with my father's bankruptcy, and I went to work, casting off all allegiances and responsibilities to any other than myself.(p.225)

coined
• No, it can best be explained in a little phrase I

coined and sang to myself: "What happened to Bob?(p.532)

Coke

• I found I could boost my income by figuring out a lot of cute little tricks that the boss wouldn't be likely to notice – filching money from the *Coke* machine, short-sticking the customers on oil, and selling oil I'd drained out of other cars.(p.423)

cokes

• I went to several Village bars, and drank *cokes* or tea.(p.414)

cold

• "Here lies a Hampshire Grenadier Who caught his death Drinking *cold* small beer.(p.1)

• *Cold* chills started chasing up and down my spine; my teeth were chattering; my hands were shaking so I tucked them under me to keep them from flying away.(p.222)

• And I remembered the creeping horror of the interminable night, in which I slept for short spells and woke up dripping with *cold* sweat and shaken with utter despair, to drink hastily from my bottle and mercifully pass out again, "You're mad, you're mad, you're mad!" pounded through my brain with each returning ray of consciousness, and I drowned the refrain with drink.(p.224)

• That is the way Jackie found me, lying on a cot in my skivvies, with hot and *cold* sweats, pounding heart and that awful itchy scratchiness all over.(p.238)

• I paced back and forth in the apartment with the *cold* sweats.(p.338)

• I had always hated beer, but now I grew to love it, bottle after bottle of it, warm or *cold*.(p.339)

• I do recall lying on a *cold* cement floor and shredding into little bits several pieces of stolen identification cards, and washing my face in the toilet bowl trying to sober up, and screaming hysterically while clinging to bars too high to see out of, and cursing everyone that came near me.(p.354)

• *Cold* sweats, jumpy nerves and lack of sleep were becoming intolerable.(p.378)

• Anne and I went up in ski clothes and fur coats, and it was so *cold* we slept in them.(p.415)

• We headed out of town walking – no money, *cold* and hungry.(p.424)

• I would rather have stayed in jail except I didn't like bologna and *cold* potatoes for breakfast.(p.425)

• There came a time when she spoke to me about it, and I would say that I had a bad *cold* or that I wasn't feeling well.(p.487)

• The drive was long and *cold* but he was thankful for the hot bricks which some thoughtful person had given him for his feet.(p.497)

• It is *cold* so there is no delay.(p.497)

• Cotton struck the skids and collections went *cold*.(p.500)

• It is a *cold*, bleak day in November.(p.502)

• I had to stop *cold*.(p.514)

• He had a shot of brandy against the *cold* and passed me the bottle.(p.541)

• With *cold* calculation I set about to marry a fortune, and I did.(p.545)

cold-blooded

• It is a *cold-blooded* idea.(p.506)

cold-storage

• While I was taking inventory in the *cold-storage* locker one Sunday, a wooden sign bolted to the inside door stopped me in my tracks.(p.461)

cold-turkey

• I simply did not have the pep to do hard, "*cold-turkey*" selling.(p.277)

collapse

• I hardly dared cross the street, lest I *collapse* and be run down by an early morning truck, for it was scarcely daylight.(p.6)

• In the face of *collapse* and despair, in the face of the total failure of their human resources, they found that a new power, peace, happiness, and sense of direction flowed into them.(p.50)

• Post-war disillusionment, ever more serious alcoholism, impending mental and physical *collapse*, brought him to the point of self-destruction.(p.56)

• I thought I had done that until Russ' second *collapse*, and the doctor told me very candidly that he wasn't long for this world.(p.271)

• Was I having a nervous *collapse*?(p.319)

collapsed

• The broker had gone to Akron on a business venture which had *collapsed*, leaving him greatly in fear that he might start drinking again.(p.xvi)

• Then I *collapsed*.(p.427)

• One night I barely made my downtown club; if I'd had to go another fifty feet I'd have *collapsed* in the gutter.(p.435)

• As might have been predicted, my teetering tower of worldly success *collapsed*.(p.437)

• An ambitious playwright, he let his brains get so far ahead of his emotions that he *collapsed* into suicidal drinking.(p.531)

colleagues

• My health is good and I have regained my self-respect and the respect of my *colleagues*.(p.180)

collect

• My job was to *collect* bets and betting-slips in the business section, a lucrative spot.(p.251)

collecting

• An old avocation, the *collecting* of first editions, rare books and Americana, fascinated me between times.(p.255)

• I have had experience in selling, *collecting*, and accounting, and am on my way up the ladder.(p.500)

• I stayed there just long enough to work up a real good resentment against the doctor in charge, who I didn't think was doing anything at all except *collecting* fees, and I left there fully determined that I'd never put myself in the power of medical people again.(p.521)

collection

• I had some financial success through no ability of my own and, when jobless and almost wiped out in 1930, I began to trade and sell my *collection*; much of the proceeds went to keep my apartment stocked with liquor and almost every night saw me helpless to bed.(p.255)

• Even when we were paying that two dollars a night, they often paid it for us because our *collection* was so small.(p.496)

collections

• Cotton struck the skids and *collections* went cold.(p.500)

collective

• Under the skilled guidance of an expert practitioner I wallowed in the world's individual and *collective* mental agony.(p.434)

collectively

• We, who have *collectively* seen a great deal of business life, at least from the alcoholic angle, had to smile at this gentleman's sincere opinion.(p.149)

collectors

• The bill *collectors*, the sheriffs, the angry taxi drivers, the policemen, the bums, the pals, and even the ladies they sometimes brought home – our husbands thought we were so inhospitable.(p.106)

• Loading a car with good old books to sell to *collectors*, librarians, universities and historical societies, I started out to travel the country.(p.255)

college

• His income is good, he has a fine home, is happily married and the father of promising children of *college* age.(p.39)

• This was an engineering *college*.(p.212)

• By that time, I had one boy in *college*, another a senior in high school, and a daughter about twelve years old.(p.215)

• The first year in *college* I just got by in my studies, and that year I majored in poker and drinking.(p.241)

• With nothing but a liberal arts education, very definitely estranged from my family and already married, soon after graduation from *college* I became a bookmaker's clerk on the British racing circuits, far better off financially than the average professional man.(p.251)

• Some *college* friends got me jobs when I finally had to go to work, but I didn't stick to them.(p.251)

• By the time I was twenty-one I had six years of life in foreign countries, spoke three languages fluently, and had attended *college* for two years.(p.275)

• During my first year out of *college* I had endless dates, and went to countless dances, balls and dinner parties.(p.275)

• All of this changed when I went to *college*.(p.287)

• I confined drinking to weekends, and drank normally in *college* and for several years thereafter.(p.287)

• A square from ultra-dry Kansas, I did not taste grog until I had finished *college*, done a stint on newspapers, married, become a father, and been in studio publicity two years.(p.328)

• I finished high school here in an American-sponsored Methodist public school, know as Philander Smith *College*.(p.342)

• I recall, as I walked into that meeting, saying to myself, "Here I am, a fellow of the American *College* of Surgeons, a Fellow of the International *College* of Surgeons, a diplomate of one of the great specialty boards in these United States, a member of the American Psychiatric Society, and I have to go to the butcher, the baker and the carpenter to help make a man out of me!"(p.347)

• I had no trouble at all in being elected to the two drinking societies at my *college*.(p.357)

• Awarded a scholarship to a famous old Eastern *college*, I began to drink at the end of my freshman year, and by junior year, I had to transfer to an easier state university to keep my grades up.(p.419)

• Oddly enough, the dentist who started A.A. in Amarillo, Tex., benevolently arranged my admission to dental *college*.(p.419)

• Fear, love of dentistry, and an imitation of my father's periodic drinking pattern took me through dental *college* soberly, except for the few parties and vacations in those four years.(p.419)

• It was my ex-wife, and she said my twenty-seven-year-old son, who has completed his Marine Corps training and graduated from *college*, wanted to see me privately, was getting married in three months, and wanted me at the wedding.(p.462)

• I am in another fellow's room at *college*.(p.497)

• I had two years at Dublin University, and then in 1916, I got a nomination for Sandhurst, the British Military *College*.(p.518)

• But I did, when I reached *college* age.(p.554)

• An honor student in *college*, I became editor of the yearbook.(p.555)

colleges

• After high school came four years in one of the best *colleges* in the country where drinking seemed to be a major extra-curricular activity.(p.172)

• I had every advantage a child could have, private schools (several of them), dancing schools, two *colleges*, coon skin coats, automobiles, a listing in the social register and all the rest.(p.357)

Collier

• Dr. G. Kirby *Collier*, psychiatrist: "I have felt that A.A. is a group unto themselves and their best results can be had under their own guidance, as a result of their philosophy.(p.571)

collision

• On that basis we are almost always in *collision* with something or somebody, even though our motives are good.(p.60)

colony

• For weeks after my arrival I was feted and entertained in the already large *colony* of Alsatians in the city, and among the Germans in their saloons and clubs.(p.231)

• I buttonholed him after dinner and gave him a few tips on how to run his *colony* better and the result of that was about a fortnight or so later I was shipped back to my regiment.(p.520)

color

• If what we have learned and felt and seen means anything at all, it means that all of us, whatever our race, creed, or *color* are the children of a living Creator with whom we may form a relationship upon simple and understandable terms as soon as we are willing and honest enough to try.(p.28)

• Whole new vistas were opened and life began to take on *color* and interest.(p.311)

• They had *color* in their faces, sparkle in their eyes and love in their hearts.(p.428)

• There are no *color* bars in A.A.(p.529)

colored

• That was the next meeting, and the first meeting of a *colored* group in A.A., so far as I know.(p.495)

colorful

• For most normal folks, drinking means conviviality, companionship and *colorful* imagination.(p.151)

colors

• We used to amuse ourselves by cynically dissecting spiritual beliefs and practices when we might have observed that many spiritually-minded persons of all races, *colors*, and creeds were demonstrating a degree of stability, happiness and usefulness which we should have sought ourselves.(p.49)

Columbus

• Some of the contemporaries of *Columbus* thought a round earth preposterous.(p.51)

coma

• The next three years saw me in sanitariums, once in a ten day *coma*, from which I very nearly did not recover, in and out of hospitals or confined at home with day and night nurses.(p.306)

combat

• Good generalship may decide that the problem be attacked on the flank rather than risk a face-to-face *combat.*(p.82)

combating
• It relieved me somewhat to learn that in alcoholics the will is amazingly weakened when it comes to *combating* liquor, though it often remains strong in other respects.(p.7)
• In our belief any scheme of *combating* alcoholism which proposes to shield the sick man from temptation is doomed to failure.(p.101)

combed
• If our hair is half-bleached (with dark roots), poker-straight, and not *combed*, this adds to our beauty.(p.479)

combination
• This *combination* soon landed me on the rocks.(p.7)
• As matters grow worse, he begins to use a *combination* of high-powered sedative and liquor to quiet his nerves so he can go to work.(p.22)
• As long as things were tough and the job a challenge I could always manage to hold on pretty well, but as soon as I learned the *combination*, got the puzzle under control and the boss to pat me on the back, I was gone again.(p.243)
• This happy *combination* of pleasant work and alcohol lasted for five years.(p.277)
• In recent years I have had the happy *combination* of time and money to travel occasionally.(p.285)
• This *combination* nearly threw me.(p.430)

combined
• We shall bring to the task our *combined* experience and knowledge.(p.19)
• They had that certain something that seemed to glow, a peace and a serenity *combined* with happiness.(p.290)
• It *combined* running away from my world, and drinking all I wanted to.(p.407)
• He now said that we had a physical allergy *combined* with a mental obsession, and he explained this so that I saw for the first time how this could be.(p.413)

come
• Convincing testimony must surely *come* from the medical men who have had experience with the sufferings of our members and have witnessed our return to health.(p.xxiii)
• In late 1934 I attended a patient who, though he had been a competent businessman of good earning capacity, was an alcoholic of a type I had *come* to regard as hopeless.(p.xxiii)
• The unselfishness of these men as we have *come* to know them, the entire absence of profit motive, and their community spirit, is indeed inspiring to one who has labored long and wearily in this alcoholic field.(p.xxv)
• It hadn't even *come* to mind.(p.5)
• The cheery voice of an old school friend asked if he might *come* over.(p.8)
• "*Come*, what's all this about?" I queried.(p.9)
• He had *come* to pass his experience along to me -- if I cared to have it.(p.9)
• I have seen men *come* out of asylums and resume a vital place in the lives of their families and communities.(p.15)
• An illness of this sort -- and we have *come* to believe it an illness --involves those about us in a way no other human sickness can.(p.18)
• But we saw that it really worked in others, and we had *come* to believe in the hopelessness and futility of life as we had been living it.(p.25)
• I now remembered what my alcoholic friends had told me, how they prophesied that if I had an alcoholic mind, the time and place would *come* -- I would drink again.(p.41)
• His defense must *come* from a Higher Power.(p.43)
• They flatly declare that since they have *come* to believe in a Power greater than themselves, to take a certain attitude toward that Power, and to do certain simple things, there has been a revolutionary change in their way of living and thinking.(p.50)
• The consciousness of your belief is sure to *come* to you.(p.55)
• But He has *come* to all who have honestly sought Him.(p.57)
• The show doesn't *come* off very well.(p.61)
• The right answer will *come*, if we want it.(p.69)
• The feeling that the drink problem has disappeared will often *come* strongly.(p.75)
• We are often surprised how the right answers *come* after we have tried this for a while.(p.86)
• We *come* to rely upon it.(p.87)
• If he is to find God, the desire must *come* from within.(p.95)
• These things will *come* to pass naturally and in good time provided, however, the alcoholic continues to demonstrate that he can be sober, considerate, and helpful, regardless of what anyone says or does.(p.99)
• When the time for living together has *come*, it will be apparent to both parties.(p.99)
• In some cases the wife will never *come* back for one reason or another.(p.99)
• He may have *come* to the point where he desperately wants to stop but cannot.(p.110)
• Your husband may *come* to appreciate your reasonableness and patience.(p.111)
• This experience may *come* to you.(p.116)
• When resentful thoughts *come*, try to pause and count your blessings.(p.119)
• Make him feel absolutely free to *come* and go as he likes.(p.120)
• We have *come* to believe He would like us to keep our heads in the clouds with Him, but that our feet ought to be firmly planted on earth.(p.130)
• If the book is read the moment the patient is able, while acutely depressed, realization of his condition may *come* to him.(p.144)
• He may wish to do a lot for other alcoholics and something of the sort may *come* up during business hours.(p.146)
• Momentarily we did -- then would *come* oblivion and the awful awakening to face the hideous Four Horsemen -- Terror, Bewilderment, Frustration, Despair.(p.151)
• "How is that to *come* about?" you ask.(p.152)
• Should you wish them above all else, and be willing to make use of our experience, we are sure they will *come*.(p.153)
• They had seen miracles, and one was to *come* to them.(p.161)
• The answers will *come*, if your own house is in order.(p.164)
• See to it that your relationship with Him is right, and great events will *come* to pass for you and countless others.(p.164)
• About this time a lady called up my wife one Saturday afternoon, saying she wanted me to *come* over that evening to meet a friend of hers who might help me.(p.179)
• It was the day before Mother's Day and I had *come* home plastered, carrying a big potted plant which I set down on the table and forthwith went upstairs and passed out.(p.179)
• The question which might naturally *come* into your mind would be: "What did the man do or say that was different from what others had done or said?"(p.180)
• Each of the seven times that I had left this hospital in the last six months, I had *come* out fully determined in my own mind that I would not get drunk again -- for at least six or eight months.(p.184)
• I wasn't afraid that the program wouldn't work, but I still was doubtful whether I would be able to hang on to the program, but I did *come* to the conclusion that I was willing to put everything I had into it, with God's power, and that I wanted to do just that.(p.189)
• I know there was even more, something that I hadn't got, and I remember one day, a week or two after I had *come* out of the hospital, Bill was over to my house talking to my wife and me.(p.191)
• I didn't like having to *come* home at a certain time; I didn't like this, I didn't like that, and I think the poor girl actually divorced me to help me stop drinking!(p.199)
• Long since I had *come* to believe I was insane because I did so many things I didn't want to do.(p.199)
• I told him that I had not had a drink for ninety days and that I had *come* to the conclusion that I was one of those individuals who couldn't drink.(p.200)
• I remember well one fellow, Joe, walking nearly three miles through slush, wet and snow to *come* to the hospital to see a man that he had never seen before in his life, and that impressed me very much.(p.208)
• He told me that there were some other fellows that had tried this with success, and if I cared to see any of them he'd have them *come* in to see me.(p.218)
• I believe every member of the Akron Group did *come* to see me, which impressed me terrifically, not so much because of the stories they told, but because they would take the time to *come* and talk to me without even knowing who I was.(p.218)
• That was skeptically received by me when I first heard it, but after some twenty-eight or thirty fellows had *come* to see me, and pretty nearly all of them had said the same thing, I began to believe it.(p.219)
• I went trembling into a house in Brooklyn filled with strangers . . . and I found I had *come* home at last, to my own kind.(p.228)
• It is: "to *come* home."(p.228)
• Had he *come* two or three days later I think I would have thrown him out, but he hit when I was open for anything.(p.239)
• The man who was going to take over one of their biggest branches *come* Monday?(p.243)
• However, I made an SOS call to the New York Group, whom I hadn't met yet, and they suggested we both *come* there.(p.245)
• In conclusion, I can only say that whatever growth or understanding has *come* to me, I have no wish to graduate.(p.249)
• She had just *come* in and was scheduled to sail in two days.(p.252)
• As soon as I could get up and walk I started to drink again and kept it up until my friend of the hospital, who, in his first try at the new way of life had stubbed his toe in Chicago but had *come* back to the town to take counsel and make a new start, picked me up and got me into a hospital.(p.258)
• I *come* from a very poor family in material things, with a fine Christian mother, but with no religious background.(p.261)
• So I spent much of my time calling on the people who I felt would logically *come* in contact with alcoholic cases, doctors, ministers, lawyers and the personnel men in industry.(p.281)
• The A.A. program showed me the way to *come* down to earth, start from the bottom and work up.(p.284)
• It is undoubtedly too soon for me to say how much of a success I shall be as a husband in time to *come*.(p.286)
• That same year, my wife became fed up with my drinking around the house and called my dad in Akron to *come* and pick me up.(p.288)
• Above all, I have gained the greatest thing accorded to any man, the love and understanding of a gracious God, who has lifted me from the alcoholic scrap-heap to a position of trust where I have been able to reap the rich rewards that *come* from showing a little love for others and from serving them as I can.(p.296)
• My wife is glad to see me *come* in.(p.303)
• I would hang on to sobriety for short intervals, but always there would *come* the tide of an overpowering necessity to drink and, as I was engulfed in it, I felt such a sense of panic that I really believed I would die if I didn't get that drink inside.(p.306)
• Once I did have a slip -- tried drinking again -- but the A.A.'s tell me not to worry about yesterday, because nobody can change it, and not to worry about tomorrow, because it hasn't *come* yet.(p.320)
• I did try, for a day or two, but something always would *come* up that would throw me.(p.324)
• No matter how often I had gone into and *come* out of alcoholic lows during the day, the pattern bounced me out of bed each night about 2:00 a.m., shaking and hurting in the agitation that always follows a drug's sedation.(p.332)
• I began to have to have supplies on hand for the people who "might *come* in."(p.336)
• And of course a half empty bottle wasn't worth keeping, so I finished it up and naturally had to get more in right away for the people who "might *come* in unexpectedly."(p.336)
• I called my husband up and told him to *come* home.(p.338)
• The people who would have *come* to help me were just the people I would have nothing to do with.(p.338)
• But when we *come* into A.A., we can face our problem honestly and openly.(p.340)
• He had *come* back, however, and he was on this program.(p.346)
• And he said, "Earle, why don't you *come* on over and let me talk to you for a minute."(p.348)
• I didn't know how to be a father; I don't know how to *come* home and work week-ends like other husbands; I don't know how to entertain my family.(p.351)
• As usual, I ran out of money, and, as usual, I wired my father for funds to *come* home.(p.357)
• While I was in Florida trying to convince my wife with all the A.A. literature that she should *come* back to me, she went over to her desk and picked up a clipping she had taken from the St. Petersburg Times about A.A.(p.366)
• It was so important that it must *come* ahead of anything.(p.382)
• As I grow in A.A., I realize that a person with as much self-will as I had, as hard a head and as diseased an ego, had to try everything that I could think of, butting my head against every stone wall before I was ready to *come* in.(p.384)
• Frank, my husband, would *come* home day after day and find me passed out.(p.386)

• He said, "If your father will *come* out and stay with you, you can have the house."(p.389)
• So I called my father and he said, "Yes," he'd *come* out and stay with me for that time.(p.389)
• He even had the people *come* out, and tell me what kind of room I was going to have, and that he could *come* and see me, and that the dog could *come* and see me.(p.389)
• They phoned my husband that I was in jail and in such terrible shape that they didn't know what I would do to myself; and they realized that jail was no place for me, but that he was to wait a while before he got me, because at the time they called him to *come* over for me I was beating a tin cup against the wall.(p.390)
• Drunkalogues and statistics can be boring, but it is necessary to delve a little into each in order to *come* up with some kind of rough estimate.(p.396)
• Saying these sprees were limited to one a week (they were not), and saying that the average spree was ten of these drinks (sometimes more, sometimes less), we *come* up with the first boring statistic: two-fifty per week out of twelve dollars.(p.397)
• Alcoholics being the argumentative lot that we are, the A.A. membership will undoubtedly *come* up with a few who will dispute these figures.(p.399)
• Others have *come* back, others I have lost.(p.404)
• Finally my new friends told me, one by one, that I could not *come* around any more.(p.410)
• The personality rehabilitation did not *come* overnight.(p.416)
• Truth and sincerity do not *come* easily to me.(p.420)
• Didn't I *come* from a family of drinkers?(p.427)
• I was supposed to *come* home on a troop ship, but I talked the base commander into flying me home.(p.428)
• I would drink all night in bars, *come* home about five a.m., down a good big glass of whiskey straight, and tumble into bed.(p.428)
• Or maybe I'd *come* home wild drunk, singing and raving about what a fine place home was and what grand parents I had since they joined A.A.(p.428)
• After a day or two of grovelling remorse I'd *come* up with an explanation.(p.433)
• I think He's on hand to see all of us through whatever may *come* to us.(p.437)
• One has to be pretty sick to do that, and perhaps one has to be even sicker to *come* back every day for a new list, as she did.(p.446)
• When we deal in feelings, we tend to *come* to know ourselves and each other much better.(p.451)
• X-rays showed that a couple of teeth had to *come* out.(p.465)
• On the day before Christmas I telephoned him and told him I was sober and asked him to *come* home.(p.467)
• You may wonder why, since I was having all this trouble, and was having to seek the assistance of others, A.A. hadn't *come* into the picture.(p.469)
• During these seven years a thing called the Twenty-four Hour Program —a gadget I used to think was only a snare to trap the newcomer — has *come* to mean much to me, not only as regards my drinking but in the whole pattern of my life.(p.473)
• I feel that I have been restored to health and sanity these past years not through my own efforts nor as a result of anything I may have done, but because I've *come* to believe — to really believe — that alone I can do nothing.(p.473)
• I have *come* to believe that my illness is spiritual as well as physical and mental, and I know that for help in the spiritual sphere I have to turn to a Higher Power.(p.473)
• When I was twenty-one, my cousin *come* home from U.S. Army on leave.(p.474)
• Two weeks later, he *come* to A.A. meeting.(p.476)
• Call friend in A.A. when bad thoughts *come*.(p.477)
• Once, I phoned my brother-in-law and told him I was going to take a handful of pills (in fact, I already had) and I would slash my wrists if he didn't *come* over to stop me.(p.479)
• It never entered my head that I would have been pushing up the daisies if he had decided not to *come*.(p.479)
• He did *come*, and I landed in the funny farm for a while.(p.479)
• You see how much work some of us have to do on ourselves when we finally *come* into A.A.!(p.480)
• Then getting and staying honest with other people will *come* automatically.(p.482)
• My father had *come* out of the South and had suffered a great deal down there.(p.485)
• Nevertheless, I stayed sober there about six months, because I knew that Vi was to *come* later and bring the children.(p.490)
• I went back to my mother's for a few days until things cooled off, because the District Attorney had put out a summons for me to *come* to see him in his office.(p.491)
• She asked me if I would let someone *come* up and talk to me concerning a business deal.(p.494)
• But, finally, we got one or two to *come* in and stick and from there, of course, we started to grow.(p.495)
• My wife's parents *come* to our assistance.(p.501)
• I drink steadily, I *come* to at three in the morning.(p.501)
• I *come* to on a pile of hay in a barn.(p.502)
• Some men and women *come* to visit my friend of the night before.(p.504)
• Strength has *come* from weakness.(p.507)
• That was still to *come*.(p.508)
• Most of my attendance there was when people would *come* in from the outside.(p.510)
• If something does *come* along that sort of upsets me, instead of walking in and throwing a buck at the barman and asking for a drink, I walk into a telephone booth, drop a dime in the box, and call somebody who was so kind as to give me his name and telephone number to meet such an emergency.(p.511)
• When we first *come* into A.A., many of us are confused because as a general rule we're at the end of our respective ropes, and we don't know what to do.(p.512)
• I had just *come* off a good one, and I went back on to the next one.(p.514)
• That thought had *come* to me many, many times.(p.515)
• But I've never *come* close to that first drink.(p.516)
• When you *come* in here, you find the understanding that you need.(p.516)
• Finally, my mother came and said she had kept me at home for six years because she thought she could help me, but that now she had *come* to the conclusion that I wasn't even worth trying to help.(p.523)
• It was their open night meeting, but of course I thought they were all alcoholics; I couldn't imagine why anybody else would want to go there, and my first reaction was, well, I've *come* to something that's not for me.(p.524)
• I thought if the cops did *come* to the hospital, the doctors would tell them I was crazy and didn't know what I was doing.(p.528)
• The helpful family finally said, over long distance, that there would be no more money and that I could not *come* home.(p.538)
• At fifty-four, I have had *come* true for me the old wish, "If only I could live my life over, knowing what I know."(p.543)
• Had I been able to explain to a psychiatrist the feeling of futility, loneliness and lack of purpose that had *come* with my deep sense of personal failure at this second divorce, I seriously doubt that the good doctor could have convinced me that my basic problem was a spiritual hunger, but A.A. has shown me this was the truth.(p.546)
• By this time I was such a past master at kidding myself that I had convinced myself I had sat out a war and waited for this man to *come* home and, as my resentment and self-pity grew, so did my alcoholic problem.(p.548)
• Do it every day for two weeks and you will find you have *come* to mean it and to want it for them, and you will realize that where you used to feel bitterness and resentment and hatred, you now feel compassionate understanding and love."(p.552)
• To do that, I had *come* to A.A. to learn how to handle sobriety -- which is what I could not handle in the first place.(p.554)
• I have *come* to realize that the name of the game is not so much to stop drinking as to stay sober.(p.559)
• One -- Our common welfare should *come* first; personal recovery depends upon A.A. unity.(p.564)
• Dr. Harry M. Tiebout, psychiatrist: "As a psychiatrist, I have thought a great deal about the relationship of my specialty to A.A. and I have *come* to the conclusion that our particular function can very often lie in preparing the way for the patient to accept any sort of treatment or outside help.(p.571)

comes

• They are restless, irritable and discontented, unless they can again experience the sense of ease and comfort which *comes* at once by taking a few drinks -- drinks which they see others taking with impunity.(p.xxvi)
• It relieved me somewhat to learn that in alcoholics the will is amazingly weakened when it *comes* to combating liquor, though it often remains strong in other respects.(p.7)
• God *comes* to most men gradually, but His impact on me was sudden and profound.(p.14)
• Then *comes* the day when he simply cannot make it and gets drunk all over again.(p.22)
• But the day he *comes* out he races in front of a fire engine, which breaks his back.(p.38)
• When, however, the perfectly logical assumption is suggested that underneath the material world and life as we see it, there is an All Powerful, Guiding, Creative Intelligence, right there our perverse streak *comes* to the surface and we laboriously set out to convince ourselves it isn't so.(p.49)
• If we haven't the will to do this, we ask until it *comes*.(p.76)
• It just *comes*!(p.85)
• This means trouble, unless the family watches for these tendencies in each other and *comes* to a friendly agreement about them.(p.131)
• Avoid then, the deliberate manufacture of misery, but if trouble *comes*, cheerfully capitalize it as an opportunity to demonstrate His omnipotence.(p.133)
• One instance *comes* to mind in which a malicious individual was always making friendly little jokes about an alcoholic's drinking exploits.(p.145)
• When I came to my aunt, she knew that I had had an unhappy childhood, and she said, "Now, Ethel, you're welcome to have boy friends in our home, but there are two boys in this town that I don't want you to date, and one of them *comes* from a very fine family, one of the best.(p.262)
• Haunting me through each day's stupor -- and there were eighteen or nineteen such days in this man's home — was the thought: "Where do I go when his family *comes* home?"(p.278)
• Surrender to me has meant the ability to run my home, to face my responsibilities as they should be faced, to take life as it *comes* to me day by day, and work my problems out.(p.340)
• When the time *comes* to solve them, God will give me strength for that day.(p.341)
• There *comes* a time when you don't want to live and are afraid to die.(p.377)
• If we do a good job of living today, and if tomorrow *comes* for us, then the chances are we will do a good job when it arrives — so why worry about it?(p.382)
• I think that no one *comes* to A.A. until he's tried everything else.(p.384)
• Now *comes* the questionnaire."(p.413)
• The last Christmas I spent in Washington, fourteen years ago, *comes* to mind.(p.465)
• Some of us always remember our big mouths when it *comes* to a drink, but somewhere along the line, we seem to have forgotten about taking care of our teeth.(p.479)
• For me, my sobriety *comes* before his or even before my feeling for him.(p.481)
• Bed-time *comes*.(p.497)
• Morning *comes*.(p.500)
• Her father *comes* to sit with me.(p.501)
• One man *comes* back, closing the door behind him.(p.503)
• Suddenly a thought *comes*.(p.503)
• Then *comes* a thought that is like a Voice.(p.504)
• But slowly a great peace *comes* to me.(p.504)
• She *comes* to New York.(p.505)
• I was drinking to keep away the shakes, drinking to keep away those little men and those strange voices and the organ music that *comes* out of the walls.(p.514)
• Sometimes I have to ask first for the willingness, but it too always *comes*.(p.552)
• Hence our common welfare *comes* first.(p.565)
• Edward Dowling, S.J., of the Queen's Work staff says, "Alcoholics Anonymous is natural; it is natural at the point where nature *comes* closest to the supernatural, namely in humiliations and in consequent humility.(p.574)

comfort

• They are restless, irritable and discontented, unless they can again experience the sense of ease and *comfort* which comes at once by taking a few drinks -- drinks which they see others taking with impunity.(p.xxvi)
• We hope this volume will inform and *comfort* those who are, or who may be affected.(p.18)
• And, accepting, I felt a new inner *comfort*, and the willingness and strength to do something about the traits I couldn't live with.(p.229)
• I have something to contribute to humanity, since I am peculiarly qualified, as a fellow-sufferer, to give aid and *comfort* to those who have stumbled and fallen over this business of meeting life.(p.229)
• I can actually take my problems to Him and He gives me *comfort*, peace, and happiness.(p.303)
• There's only one answer — liquid *comfort*.(p.331)
• Things weren't going as I thought they should, for

my greater enjoyment, ***comfort*** and fame; therefore, if the universe wouldn't play my way, I wouldn't play at all.(p.531)
• When I was criticized or reprimanded, the bottle was my refuge and ***comfort***.(p.556)

comfortable
• In that I was correct: I couldn't be ***comfortable*** with any kind of people without drinking.(p.227)
• Giving up alcohol alone was not enough for me; I've had to give up all mood-and mind-affecting chemicals in order to stay sober and ***comfortable***.(p.443)
• In the hospital, I hung on to the idea I'd had most of my life: that if I could just control the external environment, the internal environment would then be ***comfortable***.(p.445)

comfortably
• She was chatting on, pleasantly and ***comfortably***.(p.222)
• I'd been sitting ***comfortably*** in a restaurant with Rita, drinking my sixth martini and hoping the waiter would forget about the lunch order – at least long enough for me to have a couple more.(p.223)
• From a monetary standpoint . . . in the past few years, I have reduced my reckless debts to almost nothing, and have had money to get along on ***comfortably***.(p.303)
• I have learned how to relate to people; before A.A., I could never do that ***comfortably*** without alcohol.(p.559)

comforted
• We could wish to be moral, we could wish to be philosophically ***comforted***, in fact, we could will these things with all our might, but the needed power wasn't there.(p.45)
• We ***comforted*** each other.(p.265)

comforter
• I had to cope with the demands of everyday living without my ***comforter***, my anesthetic, my crutch.(p.557)

comforting
• So it was ***comforting*** to learn that we could commence at a simpler level.(p.47)
• I didn't think I was going to get drunk right then, but I remember how ***comforting*** it was when I called Anne and told her.(p.273)
• While I sought the ***comforting*** arms of alcohol, I knew this was a sign of weakness on the part of a longtime-successful old codger with white hair, the image of dignity.(p.331)

comic
• Our struggles with them are variously strenuous, ***comic*** and tragic.(p.16)

coming
• My wife began to work in a department store, ***coming*** home exhausted to find me drunk.(p.4)
• It was years since I could remember his ***coming*** to New York in that condition.(p.9)
• His ***coming*** was an oasis in the dreary desert of futility.(p.9)
• ***Coming*** to his senses, he is revolted at certain episodes he vaguely remembers.(p.73)
• Perhaps your husband will make a fair start on the new basis, but just as things are going beautifully he dismays you by ***coming*** home drunk.(p.120)
• A man may criticize or laugh at himself and it will affect others favorably, but criticism or ridicule ***coming*** from another often produces the contrary effect.(p.125)
• Father, ***coming*** suddenly to life again, often begins to assert himself.(p.131)
• ***Coming*** up to final exams I went on a particularly strenuous spree.(p.174)
• The year after ***coming*** out, I married.(p.225)
• However, here I probably took my first step towards my ***coming*** alcoholism by developing a terrific aversion to all churches and established religions.(p.240)
• In the Army, I became a periodic alcoholic – the periods always ***coming*** whenever I could make the opportunity.(p.241)
• My wife traveled with me, but with a baby ***coming*** I decided to settle in a large city where I got a job with a commission agent which is a polite term for a handbook operator.(p.251)
• ***Coming*** out of a pub near the Cunard pier I saw the Lusitania standing out in the middle of the Mersey.(p.252)
• I remember starting to city school, ***coming*** from a country school, and wanting so very, very much to be like the other girls and trying flour on my face for powder because I wasn't able to have any real powder.(p.261)
• I heard my son-in-law ***coming*** upstairs, and I asked him where dad was.(p.263)
• He had a very peculiar look on his face, and he said, "He's ***coming***."(p.263)
• He was ***coming***, on his hands and knees, up the stairs.(p.263)
• Men from A.A. started ***coming*** out to the house the next day.(p.268)
• "Well," I said to dad, when the A.A. people kept ***coming*** with these lovely cars and looked so nice, "I suppose the neighbors say, 'Now those old fools must have up and died, but where's the hearse?'"(p.269)
• Russ used to be very much pleased because he'd say, "I think Dr. Bob thoroughly enjoys ***coming*** out here.(p.271)
• I remember sometime, it was possibly six months after we had been going steadily to King School, that we were ***coming*** home from a meeting and saw a car along the way, and a fellow in back drinking a bottle of beer.(p.271)
• It was a period of binges ***coming*** closer and closer together and being of longer duration.(p.288)
• I could feel fear ***coming*** into my life.(p.323)
• But I felt a fear ***coming*** into my life, and I couldn't cope with it.(p.324)
• Where were all those words ***coming*** from?(p.333)
• By the time I figured out what had happened, I saw two flashing red lights atop squad cars, sedately ***coming*** around the corner.(p.353)
• It was to be short lived, for on the day before Christmas I completely disillusioned my wife and ruined our first Christmas by ***coming*** home from the Rotary lunch dead drunk.(p.361)
• I tried a few drinks my last night in the city before ***coming*** home.(p.364)
• I was raised like the majority of American boys, ***coming*** from a family of modest circumstances, attending public schools, having the social life of a small midwestern town, with part-time work and some athletics.(p.373)
• After all, upon ***coming*** out of a week-long or ten-day drunk, it was hard enough to figure up just how much that one drunk cost, let alone trying to calculate the cost of approximately twenty-five years of active alcoholism.(p.396)
• They got so they moved their barstools when they saw me ***coming***.(p.411)
• Then I went on my first week-long bender of solitary drinking, locked up in a hotel room, because my family opposed my ***coming*** marriage.(p.464)
• Then I remember him ***coming*** into my room one night with a friend, and telling me to get dressed – we were going away.(p.466)
• The next recollection I have is of my husband ***coming*** into my room (later found out it was on New Year's Eve) accompanied by two policemen.(p.468)
• Sly and crafty, I thought now I'll find out what they think of me here, what they "have on" me, what I've said ***coming*** in here drunk.(p.470)
• When they saw me ***coming***, they locked up the silverware and everything else of value.(p.478)
• Thinking only of two or three dollars to buy some whiskey, I did the job and that's how I met Ella G., who was responsible for my ***coming*** into A.A.(p.493)
• I had an advantage in having an idea of what A.A. was about before ***coming*** out on the street.(p.510)
• The first had been as a youngster ***coming*** out from Ireland.(p.513)
• Somehow or other I was ***coming*** face to face with myself, and I didn't like it.(p.513)
• I got a job by myself which suited me down to the ground, because there was nobody really to interfere with what I did, one way or the other, and I usually had my nerves in good trim when anybody was ***coming*** around to inspect.(p.519)
• I think the Commanding Officer was rather tired of this particular chicken ***coming*** back to roost so often because he very soon wrote in to the medical authorities to tell them that they had to get me into hospital, to be thoroughly examined for drinking.(p.520)
• I would embarrass everyone by ***coming*** in drunk or passing out.(p.526)
• It's time to stop finding excuses for drinking and getting into trouble, because now there is a way out, and if you want what we have, try ***coming*** around and giving the program a chance.(p.530)
• Inside, though, I was scared to death, for I knew that the time was ***coming*** (and it couldn't be too remote) when I would be unable to hold that job.(p.548)
• This caused the rather cryptic comment from one of my A.A. friends, when I told my story after ***coming*** into the program, that I had always been a cinch for the program, for I had always been interested in mankind, but that I was just taking them one man at a time.(p.548)

comings
• As each member of a resentful family begins to see his short ***comings*** and admits them to the others, he lays a basis for helpful discussion.(p.127)

command
• With all the earnestness at our ***command***, we beg of you to be fearless and thorough from the very start.(p.58)
• With this kind of employee such an attitude will ***command*** undying loyalty.(p.145)
• I told him with all the sincerity at my ***command*** that I did.(p.235)
• During the first three months I carried on all these activities without a car, depending entirely on buses and streetcars – I, who had always to have a car at my immediate ***command***.(p.283)
• Then I had about six months on a small island in ***command*** of the troops there.(p.520)

commander
• He turned me in to the company ***commander***, but I got off the hook, and that was all that mattered.(p.317)
• I talked to the first sergeant and the battalion ***commander***, and they got me in contact with an A.A. member.(p.319)
• I was supposed to come home on a troop ship, but I talked the base ***commander*** into flying me home.(p.428)
• Later, I went to sea, serving as a gunnery officer on a destroyer escort and emerging a lieutenant ***commander***.(p.555)

commanding
• The ***Commanding*** Officer only spoke to me when he wanted to tell me exactly who I was and what I was and how little I counted in the scheme of things and how glad he would be if I went away.(p.520)
• I think the ***Commanding*** Officer was rather tired of this particular chicken coming back to roost so often because he very soon wrote in to the medical authorities to tell them that they had to get me into hospital, to be thoroughly examined for drinking.(p.520)

commence
• Most alcoholics have to be pretty badly mangled before they really ***commence*** to solve their problems.(p.43)
• At the start, this was all we needed to ***commence*** spiritual growth, to effect our first conscious relation with God as we understood Him.(p.47)
• So it was comforting to learn that we could ***commence*** at a simpler level.(p.47)
• At once, we ***commence*** to outgrow fear.(p.68)
• When he sees you know all about the drinking game, ***commence*** to describe yourself as an alcoholic.(p.91)
• You will be bound to them with new and wonderful ties, for you will escape disaster together and you will ***commence*** shoulder to shoulder your common journey.(p.152)

commenced
• We shall be interested to hear from those who are getting results from this book, particularly from those who have ***commenced*** work with other alcoholics.(p.xiv)
• As part of his rehabilitation he ***commenced*** to present his conceptions to other alcoholics, impressing upon them that they must do likewise with still others.(p.xxiii)
• Out of this alloy of drink and speculation, I ***commenced*** to forge the weapon that one day would turn in its flight like a boomerang and all but cut me to ribbons.(p.2)
• We ***commenced*** to make many fast friends and a fellowship has grown up among us of which it is a wonderful thing to feel a part.(p.15)
• He has ***commenced*** to accomplish those things for us which we could never do by ourselves.(p.25)
• I had ***commenced*** to drink as carelessly as though the cocktails were ginger ale.(p.41)
• We found that as soon as we were able to lay aside prejudice and express even a willingness to believe in a Power greater than ourselves, we ***commenced*** to get results, even though it was impossible for any of us to fully define or comprehend that Power, which is God.(p.46)
• We have ***commenced*** to see their terrible destructiveness.(p.70)
• He had ***commenced*** our way of life, had secured a position, and was getting his head above water.(p.79)
• We vigorously ***commenced*** this way of living as we cleaned up the past.(p.84)
• Asked why they ***commenced*** to drink again, they would reply with some silly excuse, or none.(p.107)
• Seeing this, and meaning to be helpful, his wife ***commenced*** to admonish him about it.(p.135)

commences
• He *commences* to look around in the night clubs, or their equivalent, for something besides liquor.(p.81)
• The minute we put our work on a service plane, the alcoholic *commences* to rely upon our assistance rather than upon God.(p.98)
commencing
• *Commencing* to drink after a period of sobriety, we are in a short time as bad as ever.(p.33)
commendable
• He had a *commendable* World War record.(p.35)
commendation
• So I went to her and said, "There's only one thing I want in my whole life, and I don't want any *commendation;* I don't want any credit; I don't want anything from you or Janey for the rest of your life except one thing; and that is, the opportunity to do anything you want always, and I would like to start off by doing the dishes."(p.351)
comment
• His *comment* was, "Very interesting.(p.138)
• When it became noticeable to the point of *comment,* I devised ways of sneaking drinks on the side.(p.375)
• This caused the rather cryptic *comment* from one of my A.A. friends, when I told my story after coming into the program, that I had always been a cinch for the program, for I had always been interested in mankind, but that I was just taking them one man at a time.(p.548)
comments
• Following are excerpts from the *comments* of doctors present at the annual meeting of the Medical Society of the State of New York where a paper on A.A. was read:(p.571)
commercial
• Taking a *commercial* inventory is a fact-finding and a fact-facing process.(p.64)
• In time I became an officer and director of one of the largest *commercial* banks in the country.(p.374)
commission
• Our friends thought a lunacy *commission* should be appointed.(p.3)
• I resented it of course, and I offered Clarence his *commission,* whatever it might be, if he would please not bother me because I had arrived at the conclusion that he was a solicitor for some alcoholic institute.(p.216)
• My wife traveled with me, but with a baby coming I decided to settle in a large city where I got a job with a *commission* agent which is a polite term for a handbook operator.(p.251)
commissioned
• After training, I was *commissioned* as a first lieutenant.(p.342)
• Then I joined the Navy and was *commissioned* as an ensign to write speeches for admirals.(p.555)
commit
• I was not fit to be on the loose, and there was no one to *commit* me.(p.412)
commitment
• In a matter of fact way he told how two men had appeared in court, persuading the judge to suspend his *commitment.*(p.9)
• Here are some of the methods we have tried: Drinking beer only, limiting the number of drinks, never drinking alone, never drinking in the morning, drinking only at home, never having it in the house, never drinking during business hours, drinking only at parties, switching from scotch to brandy, drinking only natural wines, agreeing to resign if ever drunk on the job, taking a trip, not taking a trip, swearing off forever (with and without a solemn oath), taking more physical exercise, reading inspirational books, going to health farms and sanitariums, accepting voluntary *commitment* to asylums -- we could increase the list ad infinitum.(p.31)
• Here was the threat of *commitment,* the loss of family and position, to say nothing of that intense mental and physical suffering which drinking always caused him.(p.36)
• Most of us have entered the final stage with its *commitment* to health resorts, sanitariums, hospitals, and jails.(p.107)
committed
• Rumor had it that he had been *committed* for alcoholic insanity.(p.9)
• One poor chap *committed* suicide in my home.(p.16)
• In a few years he became so violent when intoxicated that he had to be *committed.*(p.35)
• She *committed* her husband for drinking.(p.65)
• Perhaps we have *committed* a criminal offense which might land us in jail if it were known to the authorities.(p.78)
• Doctors may shake their heads and advise you to have him *committed.*(p.110)
• If he is already *committed* to an institution, but can convince you and your doctor that he means business, give him a chance to try our method, unless the doctor thinks his mental condition too abnormal or dangerous.(p.114)
• For years we have been working with alcoholics *committed* to institutions.(p.114)
• Perhaps you have a husband who is at large, but who should be *committed.*(p.114)
• It is estimated that two-thirds of the men in prison were under the influence of alcohol and/or drugs when they *committed* their offenses.(p.458)
• Then I *committed* my last offense.(p.460)
• Vi was very kind and explained to the jury that I was basically a fine fellow and a good husband, but that I drank too much and that she thought I had lost my mind and felt that I should be *committed* to an asylum.(p.492)
committee
• I have served on only one *committee* in the past nine years, for I feel that I had my chance the first few years and that newer members should fill the jobs.(p.250)
• I'd go into an organization, and it wasn't long before I was on the *committee,* then I was chairman of the *committee;* and if I was in a group, I'd soon be treasurer or secretary of the group.(p.339)
• And no group, regional *committee,* or individual should ever take any action that might greatly affect A.A. as a whole without conferring with the trustees of the General Service Board.(p.565)
• The small group may elect its secretary, the large group its rotating *committee,* and the groups of a large metropolitan area their central or intergroup *committee,* which often employs a full-time secretary.(p.567)
• The trustees of the General Service Board are, in effect, our A.A. General Service *Committee.*(p.567)
committees
• Nine – A.A., as such, ought never be organized; but we may create service boards or *committees* directly responsible to those they serve.(p.564)
commodities
• His wife is one of those persons who really feels there is something rather sinful about these *commodities,* so she nagged, and her intolerance finally threw him into a fit of anger.(p.135)
common
• All these, and many others, have one symptom in *common:* they cannot start drinking without developing the phenomenon of craving.(p.xxviii)
• *Common* sense would thus become uncommon sense.(p.13)
• The feeling of having shared in a *common* peril is one element in the powerful cement which binds us.(p.17)
• The tremendous fact for every one of us is that we have discovered a *common* solution.(p.17)
• What has become of the *common* sense and will power that he still sometimes displays with respect to other matters?(p.22)
• Being convinced that self, manifested in various ways, was what had defeated us, we considered its *common* manifestations.(p.64)
• When it will serve any good purpose, we are willing to announce our convictions with tact and *common* sense.(p.77)
• That's a *common* form of trouble too.(p.79)
• We are dealing only with general principles *common* to most denominations.(p.94)
• But point out that we alcoholics have much in *common* and that you would like, in any case, to be friendly.(p.95)
• What had become of their judgment, their *common* sense, their will power?(p.107)
• All members of the family should meet upon the *common* ground of tolerance, understanding and love.(p.122)
• Being possessed of a spiritual experience, the alcoholic will find he has much in *common* with these people, though he may differ with them on many matters.(p.131)
• You will be bound to them with new and wonderful ties, for you will escape disaster together and you will commence shoulder to shoulder your *common* journey.(p.152)
• We all had hundreds of character traits, of fears and phobias, likes and dislikes, in *common.*(p.229)
• My daily consumption of wine was about a quart, but that was *common* where I lived.(p.230)
• The same old routines seemed to be *common* to us all.(p.246)
• What we had in *common* was alcohol.(p.405)
• I became a menace, the fish-wife, the *common* scold.(p.410)
• What intellectual interests could we have in *common?*(p.412)
• Loneliness, great physical and mental agony – these were the *common* lot.(p.455)
• Aside from being a *common* drunk, I had a very serious pill affliction and all the garbage that goes with it -- lying, stealing, cheating anybody and everybody, conning the people I could, and staying clear of the ones I couldn't.(p.478)
• There was the necessity for sticking to a job I hated, a dull, repetitive job performed in association with other men I had nothing in *common* with . . . performed for years on end, because the money was needed at home.(p.532)
• One – Our *common* welfare should come first; personal recovery depends upon A.A. unity.(p.564)
• Hence our *common* welfare comes first.(p.565)
• On such issues our *common* welfare is paramount.(p.565)
• Historians may one day recognize Alcoholics Anonymous to have been a great venture in social pioneering which forged a new instrument for social action; a new therapy based on the kinship of *common* suffering; one having a vast potential for the myriad other ills of mankind."(p.573)
common-sense
• Strangely enough, I became acquainted with the "hilarious life" just at the time in my own life when I was beginning really to settle down to a *common-sense,* sane domesticity.(p.297)
commonly
• It is bound to be rough, because who can say exactly how much of that green blood – *commonly* known as money – was dissipated on dissipation?(p.396)
commonplace
• Now these are *commonplace* observations on drinkers which we hear all the time.(p.20)
communicate
• Today, Max and I try to *communicate* what we feel, rather than what we think.(p.451)
communicating
• He it was who convinced me, because his own conviction was so real, that a Power greater than myself could help me in the crises of life, and that the means of *communicating* with this Power was simple prayer.(p.279)
communicative
• If he is not *communicative,* give him a sketch of your drinking career up to the time you quit.(p.91)
• He becomes still less *communicative.*(p.126)
communities
• Already," continues the early text, "twos and threes and fives of us have sprung up in other *communities.*"(p.xv)
• A.A. has flourishing *communities* in the British Isles, the Scandinavian countries, South Africa, South America, Mexico, Alaska, Australia and Hawaii.(p.xv)
• I have seen men come out of asylums and resume a vital place in the lives of their families and *communities.*(p.15)
• Little clusters of twos and threes and fives of us have sprung up in other *communities,* through contact with our two larger centers.(p.162)
community
• The unselfishness of these men as we have come to know them, the entire absence of profit motive, and their *community* spirit, is indeed inspiring to one who has labored long and wearily in this alcoholic field.(p.xxv)
• The problems of the *community* might engage attention.(p.131)
• My downfall cost the business *community* unknown thousands of dollars, for it takes real money to train a man for an executive position.(p.137)
• You are going to meet these new friends in your own *community.*(p.152)
• As we shall see, he now means a great deal to his *community,* and the major liabilities of thirty years of hard drinking have been repaired in four.(p.156)
• He too, has become a respected and useful member of his *community.*(p.158)
• A *community* thirty miles away has fifteen fellows of Alcoholics Anonymous.(p.161)
• We know of an A.A. member who was living in a large *community.*(p.163)
• He got in touch with a prominent psychiatrist who

had undertaken certain responsibilities for the mental health of the ***community***.(p.163)

- I became one of the most active women in the ***community***, what with P.T.A., other ***community*** organizations and drives.(p.339)
- At one end of the table sat our ***community*** butcher.(p.347)
- At the other side of the table sat one of the carpenters in our ***community***, and at the further end of the table sat the man who ran the bakery, while on one side sat my friend who was a mechanic.(p.347)
- I went to Clark, the ***community*** butcher, and I said, "Clark, what is the matter with me?(p.348)
- We have here in this ***community*** an organization which helps people, and this organization is known as Alcoholics Anonymous.(p.348)
- I tried every gimmick that there was to get some peace of mind, but it was not until I was brought to my alcoholic knees, when I was brought to a group in my own ***community*** with the butcher, the baker, the carpenter and the mechanic, who were able to give me the Twelve Steps, that I was finally given some semblance of an answer to the last half of the First Step.(p.349)
- I got around this by joining the local Rotary Club, and through this association with the business men of the ***community*** my little station began to grow.(p.360)
- Making amends is sometimes doing what we are capable of doing but failed to do because of alcohol; carrying out ***community*** responsibilities such as ***Community*** Funds, Red Cross, educational and religious activities in proportion to our abilities and energy.(p.381)
- But my attempts at ***community*** service ended in a drunken and abusive row with a fellow volunteer.(p.410)
- My life there was a nightmare of periodic binges on alcohol and pills, adultery, unhappy hours at the dental office, seeing my wife give birth to our second child and have several miscarriages, living in a turbulent household, and making continual attempts to be the respectable dentist, husband, father, and ***community*** leader.(p.419)
- Why am I alive, free, a respected member of my ***community***?(p.421)

commuting

- From a single member in the Chicago area, ***commuting*** to Akron, we now exceed six thousand.(p.295)

companies

- My idea was to have all the ***companies*** pool their funds and buy rubber when rubber was cheap and then put it in a pool.(p.198)
- With the big ***companies***, and with the amount of money we could have gotten and the promises I had, it could have been done.(p.198)
- As a draftsman, I worked for several large ***companies*** and gained a variety of experience.(p.211)
- At that time, I was living out of town, so I moved back to the home town and made a connection in a responsible position with one of the larger ***companies*** in the finance business.(p.298)

companion

- It is painful to grow, and without the help of my "civilian" A.A. ***companion***, big Gene, I might not have survived that critical year of adjustment.(p.462)

companions

- These are not pleasant ***companions***.(p.104)
- The next day I went back to Chicago and started a vigorous campaign among my so-called friends or drinking ***companions***.(p.293)
- As I said earlier, self-pity and resentment were my constant ***companions*** and my inventory began to look like a thirty-three year diary, for I seemed to have a resentment against everybody I had ever known.(p.551)

companionship

- For the first time, he lived in conscious ***companionship*** with his Creator.(p.56)
- They need your ***companionship*** and your help.(p.111)
- You have been starving for his ***companionship***, yet he spends long hours helping other men and their families.(p.119)
- For most normal folks, drinking means conviviality, ***companionship*** and colorful imagination.(p.151)
- Some of us sought out sordid places, hoping to find understanding ***companionship*** and approval.(p.151)
- In there he would find ***companionship*** and release.(p.154)
- Many a distracted wife has visited this house to find loving and understanding ***companionship*** among women who knew her problem, to hear from the lips of their husbands what had happened to them, to be advised how her own wayward mate might be hospitalized and approached when next he stumbled.(p.160)
- It took the help, understanding and wonderful ***companionship*** that was given so freely to me by my "exalkie" friends.(p.311)
- Her influence and ***companionship*** managed to lessen my drinking to some degree.(p.359)

company

- I took a night law course, and obtained employment as investigator for a surety ***company***.(p.2)
- She wanted to know if her husband's ***company*** insurance was still in force.(p.137)
- I know, in my own particular case, that nothing my ***company*** could have done would have stopped me for, so long as I was able to hold my position, I could not possibly realize how serious my situation was.(p.141)
- Only a few knew of it at first but, within a short time, it was billboarded throughout the entire ***company***.(p.145)
- But the policy of this ***company*** is not to interfere with the habits of our employees.(p.148)
- This same ***company*** spends millions for research every year.(p.149)
- There is ***company*** insurance.(p.149)
- That ***company*** may harbor many actual or potential alcoholics.(p.149)
- Today I own a little ***company***.(p.149)
- Every ***company*** in the country, except Firestone, was reorganized at that time.(p.197)
- The school then obtained a job for me in the drafting department of another ***company***.(p.211)
- The third man who came to see me had been one of the greatest business-getters his ***company*** had ever employed.(p.235)
- With the war over, and back in Baltimore with the folks, there were several small jobs for three years and then I went to work soliciting as one of the first ten employees of a new national finance ***company***.(p.242)
- This ***company*** now does a volume of over three billion dollars annually.(p.242)
- My next job was in sales promotion for an oil ***company*** in Mississippi where I promptly became high man and got lots of pats on the back.(p.242)
- Then I turned two ***company*** cars over in a short time and Bingo -- fired again.(p.242)
- Oddly enough, the big shot who fired me from this ***company*** was one of the first men I met when I later joined the New York A.A. Group.(p.242)
- Then came a sales job with a national tire ***company***.(p.243)
- I checked into my hotel room and then noticed a placard tucked under the glass on the bureau stating "There will be positively NO drinking at this convention" signed by the president of the ***company***.(p.243)
- No one in that ***company*** saw me again – ten days later I wired my resignation.(p.243)
- Bill and Hank had just taken over a small automobile polishing ***company*** and they offered me a job -- ten dollars a week and keep at Hank's house.(p.246)
- Offered the job of advertising manager for an eastern automotive ***company***, I moved to Philadelphia to begin life anew.(p.254)
- In the two succeeding years I held ten different jobs ranging from newspaper copy-desk and rewrite, to traffic director for an oil field equipment ***company***.(p.255)
- After being fired, I lined up with a new finance ***company*** that was just starting in business, and took the position of business promotion man, contacting automobile dealers.(p.300)
- While working in an office, there was some semblance of restraint, but, oh boy, when I got on the outside with this new ***company*** without supervision, did I go to town!(p.300)
- Finally this ***company*** also became involved and I was once more looking for a job.(p.300)
- He turned me in to the ***company*** commander, but I got off the hook, and that was all that mattered.(p.317)
- By persistence and salesmanship I managed to see more and more of my new friend, and because of her sympathetic nature she tolerated my ***company***.(p.359)
- Above all, he noticed that I drank a good deal, often got tight in his ***company*** and told him naughty stories.(p.403)
- I am working hard on the books of a subsidiary ***company*** of a large corporation.(p.500)
- Still another friend and temporary host received me at four in the morning from the charge of a policeman who had found me "going to bed" in a garage far from the last place I could remember having been, a fashionable bar and restaurant in the theatrical district of New York, to which I had repaired after my date for that evening, a charming lady of the theatre who had refused my ***company*** for obvious reasons.(p.538)
- I landed a good job with a ***company*** publication and was moonlighting on other magazines.(p.555)
- My ***company*** advanced me rapidly, once my reliability was established again.(p.559)

comparatively

- At a ***comparatively*** early age, I can remember being jealous of my brother.(p.194)

compared

- I drove towards Cleveland wondering why I found myself in such a changed set of conditions as ***compared*** with those of six months before.(p.200)
- How important is it ***compared*** to my serenity, my emotional sobriety?"(p.452)

comparing

- I begin to see I am not the person I had thought myself, that I had judged myself by ***comparing*** myself to others, and always to my own advantage.(p.504)

compassion

- There are so many to whom I feel deeply grateful; to my husband (and best critic), whose generous love, ***compassion*** and understanding have helped me along the way; to those before me in A.A. who inspired the first article I read, and the friend who sent that article to Frank; to Ruth for her personal note, and the first A.A. to talk to me; to my Bishop, whose loving and believing spirit inspired me; and to all the members of the Houston Group who were so patient, kind and helpful -- and to countless others.(p.393)

compassionate

- Do it every day for two weeks and you will find you have come to mean it and to want it for them, and you will realize that where you used to feel bitterness and resentment and hatred, you now feel ***compassionate*** understanding and love."(p.552)

compatible

- I believe this, and I believe too that it is equally impossible to practice these principles to the best of our ability, a day at a time, and still drink, for I don't think the two things are ***compatible***.(p.550)

compelling

- Then Jack Alexander wrote a feature article in the Saturday Evening Post and placed such a ***compelling*** picture of A.A. before the general public that alcoholics in need of help really deluged us.(p.xviii)

compensate

- I tried to ***compensate*** with impossible dreams and ambitions, which were simply early forms of escape.(p.400)

compensated

- However, this isn't as rough as it sounds, as we do become grateful for the necessity that makes us toe the line, for we find that we are more than ***compensated*** for a consistent effort by the countless dividends we receive.(p.311)

compensation

- And all this, of course, is, in the popular modern jargon, "***compensation***" for immaturity.(p.535)

compensations

- It is a way of life that pays as it goes, every step of the way, in ***compensations*** that have been wonderfully rich and rewarding.(p.394)

competent

- In late 1934 I attended a patient who, though he had been a ***competent*** businessman of good earning capacity, was an alcoholic of a type I had come to regard as hopeless.(p.xxiii)
- Highly ***competent*** psychiatrists who have dealt with us have found it sometimes impossible to persuade an alcoholic to discuss his situation without reserve.(p.18)
- Ministers and doctors are ***competent*** and you can learn much from them if you wish, but it happens that because of your own drinking experience you can be uniquely useful to other alcoholics.(p.89)
- In ***competent*** hands, this seldom takes long nor is it very expensive.(p.143)

complain

- If you cooperate, rather than ***complain***, you will find that his excess enthusiasm will tone down.(p.119)
- Mother may ***complain*** of inattention.(p.126)
- When I ***complain*** about me or about you, I am complaining about God's handiwork.(p.449)

complaining

- He is like the retired business man who lolls in the Florida sunshine in the winter ***complaining*** of the sad state of the nation; the minister who sighs over the sins of the twentieth century; politicians and reformers who are sure all would be Utopia if the rest of the world would only behave; the outlaw safe cracker who thinks society has wronged him; and the alcoholic who has lost all and is locked up.(p.61)

• When I complain about me or about you, I am *complaining* about God's handiwork.(p.449)

complaints

• Beginning with such *complaints*, a barrier arises.(p.126)

complement

• We *complement* each other beautifully, as he is a born salesman and my taste is for finance and management.(p.284)

complete

• There was that time we had chartered an airplane to *complete* a jag!(p.9)

• Like myself, he had admitted *complete* defeat.(p.11)

• Upon a foundation of *complete* willingness I might build what I saw in my friend.(p.12)

• There is a *complete* failure of the kind of defense that keeps one from putting his hand on a hot stove.(p.24)

• But in most fields our generation has witnessed *complete* liberation of our thinking.(p.52)

• Is not our age characterized by the ease with which we discard old ideas for new, by the *complete* readiness with which we throw away the theory or gadget which does not work for something new which does?(p.52)

• We asked His protection and care with *complete* abandon.(p.59)

• If that is so, this step may be postponed, only however, if we hold ourselves in *complete* readiness to go through with it at the first opportunity.(p.74)

• Though old buildings will eventually be replaced by finer ones, the new structures will take years to *complete*.(p.123)

• All have now passed away from natural causes, having maintained *complete* sobriety.(p.169)

• This went from bad to worse until Sophomore spring when, after a prolonged period of drinking, I made up my mind that I could not *complete* my course, so I packed my grip and went South to spend a month on a large farm owned by a friend of mine.(p.173)

• I think the longest drunk I was ever on was eleven days, but usually only two days with a *complete* blackout for a day, and then backing off by drinking as long as I could get anything.(p.203)

• Here I was, thirty-nine years old and a *complete* washout.(p.238)

• In the spiritual strength I had found, because of A.A., I felt that I had made a *complete* surrender, that I had really turned my life over that summer.(p.271)

• I knew then that I hadn't made a *complete* surrender, because I tried to bargain with the God I had found, and I said, "Anything but that!(p.271)

• A *complete* checkup at one of the best hospitals revealed nothing.(p.276)

• Poor health and a *complete* lack of money necessitated my remaining with Dr. Bob and Anne for very close to a year.(p.280)

• Heartsickness, shame, and fear, fear bordering on panic, and no *complete* escape any longer except in oblivion.(p.306)

• A *complete* change takes place in our approach to life.(p.311)

• This, plus mounting emotional disturbances, convinced them that compulsive alcoholism already had them; that *complete* ruin would be only a question of time.(p.315)

• And the last sentence was "We asked His protection and care with *complete* abandon."(p.349)

• "*Complete* abandon"; "Half measures availed us nothing"; "Thoroughly follow our path"; "Completely give oneself to this simple program" – rang in my swelled head.(p.349)

• A few hours later I came out of a *complete* stupor in our living room with a flash of sanity.(p.363)

• I was certainly a *complete* surprise when I arrived at her family's home, but because I arrived on the wings of a tropical hurricane there wasn't much she could do but let me in.(p.364)

• Mentally, the fears and tensions, the *complete* change in attitude and outlook, bewildered me.(p.378)

• A house in Virginia, during the fox hunting season; a little chalet in Switzerland during the summer or a place on Long Island -- each house *complete* with cooks, butlers and maids.(p.403)

• Educated child of the scientific age that I was, I had *complete* faith in the science of the mind.(p.434)

• My mother lived on for five years after I joined A.A., the last two in *complete* blindness.(p.525)

• The only way existence was possible was through rationalizing every sober moment and drinking myself into *complete* oblivion as often as I could.(p.547)

• I attended my first A.A. meeting eight years ago, and it is with deep gratitude that I'm able to say I've not had a drink since that time, and that I take no sedation or narcotics, for this program is to me one of *complete* sobriety and I no longer need to escape reality.(p.549)

completed

• By the time I had *completed* the course, I knew the law was not for me.(p.2)

• This requires action on our part, which, when *completed*, will mean that we have admitted to God, to ourselves, and to another human being the exact nature of our defects.(p.72)

• We think the reason is that they never *completed* their housecleaning.(p.73)

• We have then *completed* Step Seven.(p.76)

• My wife, a Kentucky girl, came with me to Akron where I *completed* my course in law at the Akron Law School.(p.182)

• This experience sent me to law school where I went at night and which course I *completed* in less than three years, taking the highest state bar examinations and passing them.(p.212)

• A year later, after I *completed* the course in contracts, I quit the law school, and undertook some engineering work for a patent law firm on behalf of clients who were in difficulties and who desired to keep their troubles from their own engineering department.(p.212)

• By the time I had *completed* law school I had picked up some experience in patent law, for I remained with the patent law firm and worked too in Washington where they found that I was a capable infringement investigator.(p.213)

• I had *completed* a three-year tour in the Navy.(p.418)

• It was my ex-wife, and she said my twenty-seven-year-old son, who has *completed* his Marine Corps training and graduated from college, wanted to see me privately, was getting married in three months, and wanted me at the wedding.(p.462)

• The trip back was *completed* in one of those dead, awful silences.(p.467)

• During the course of that drinking, I had shot and killed one person and almost *completed* the job on a second one.(p.508)

completely

• "Bill's Story," "Doctor Bob's Nightmare," and one other personal history from the first edition were retained intact; three were edited and one of these was retitled; new versions of two stories were written with new titles; thirty *completely* new stories were added; and the story section was divided into three parts, under the same headings that are used now.(p.xi)

• I personally know scores of cases who were of the type with whom other methods had failed *completely*.(p.xxiii)

• Ideas, emotions, and attitudes which were once the guiding forces of the lives of these men are suddenly cast to one side, and a *completely* new set of conceptions and motives begin to dominate them.(p.27)

• Those who do not recover are people who cannot or will not *completely* give themselves to this simple program, usually men and women who are constitutionally incapable of being honest with themselves.(p.58)

• Four: You may have a husband of whom you *completely* despair.(p.110)

• But his venture wound up in a law suit and bogged down *completely*.(p.154)

• Goes off his head *completely* when he's drinking.(p.156)

• Before my drinking had cut me down *completely*, I achieved a considerable measure of success, having been a City Councilman for five years and a financial director of Kenmore, a suburb later taken into the city itself.(p.182)

• So, after reviewing these things and realizing what liquor had cost me, I went to this Higher Power which, to me was God, without any reservation, and admitted that I was *completely* powerless over alcohol, and that I was willing to do anything in the world to get rid of the problem.(p.187)

• I had *completely* forgotten the January 8th when I found the fellowship, and I spent the next four days wandering around New England half drunk, by which I mean I couldn't get drunk and I couldn't get sober.(p.247)

• I don't think the boys were *completely* convinced of my personality change, for they fought shy of including my story in the book, so my only contribution to their literary efforts was my firm conviction, being still a theological rebel, that the word God should be qualified with the phrase "as we understand him" -- for that was the only way I could accept spirituality.(p.248)

• I was still bitter because I felt that drink had *completely* ruined my childhood and my married life, and I hated everything pertaining to it.(p.262)

• I'd hear them on the phone having prayer meetings and so forth, that sort of talk over the phone, and it *completely* burnt me up.(p.265)

• To the best of my recollection I was *completely* free from any abnormal fears.(p.275)

• Those three weeks left me *completely* exhausted and I had to return to Akron for three more months of rest.(p.282)

• He waited until I was *completely* sober and the day before I was to head back for Chicago, he told me of a small group of men in Akron who apparently had the same problem that I had but were doing something about it.(p.289)

• I was *completely* licked by alcohol.(p.290)

• He said he had finally learned that drinking was a fatal illness made up of an allergy plus an obsession, and once the drinking had passed from habit to obsession, we were *completely* hopeless, and could look forward only to spending the balance of our lives in mental institutions or to death.(p.290)

• I had thought that I was *completely* different from other people, that I was beginning to become a little balmy, even to the point of withdrawing more and more from society and wanting to be alone with my bottle.(p.290)

• And still by the time I was thirty years old I was being pushed around with a compulsion to drink that was *completely* beyond my control.(p.305)

• Now the picture has changed *completely*.(p.325)

• It finally got such a hold on me that I was *completely* at my wits' end, not knowing what the result would be.(p.343)

• "Complete abandon"; "Half measures availed us nothing"; "Thoroughly follow our path"; "*Completely* give oneself to this simple program" – rang in my swelled head.(p.349)

• It was to be short lived, for on the day before Christmas I *completely* disillusioned my wife and ruined our first Christmas by coming home from the Rotary lunch dead drunk.(p.361)

• I had just raised the bottle to my lips when my wife opened the door and froze me *completely* in my tracks with "Happy New Year, dear."(p.365)

• The last two years of my drinking my entire personality changed to a cynical, intolerant and arrogant person *completely* different from my normal self.(p.376)

• Up to that time, I was so *completely* baffled by my behavior that I had never really stopped to think at all.(p.392)

• I *completely* forgot myself in trying vainly to help Anne, whose misery I understood.(p.415)

• The doctor said I'd been brought into the hospital like a madman, crying, raving, ranting, swearing, *completely* in the throes of delirium tremens.(p.427)

• This I would do by going *completely* "bohemian" for a night, getting drunk and rolling home with the dawn.(p.432)

• By early July, I had tapered off alcohol *completely*, and I got off all pills in the ensuing few months.(p.448)

• Until I could accept my alcoholism, I could not stay sober; unless I accept life *completely* on life's terms, I cannot be happy.(p.449)

• He said he didn't care what I did with the money, but there was going to be no more until I was *completely* sober.(p.467)

• He said he was finally and *completely* through -- that he never wanted to see me again.(p.467)

• I *completely* blacked out.(p.468)

• Things went from bad to worse, and since I had finally and *completely* failed at the job of being a wife and a mother, my marriage ended.(p.468)

• I thought, well, now that I've been put out for drinking, I'll just show them that they were *completely* wrong, so I went off on the biggest bout I had been on up to then, involving about a fortnight's blackout.(p.521)

• I was taking Benzedrine and paraldehyde quite impartially during the day then, and by the time I arrived at my first A.A. meeting, I was pretty drunk and certainly doped up to the eyes and *completely* jittery.(p.523)

complex

• His alcoholic problem was so *complex*, and his depression so great, that we felt his only hope would be through what we then called "moral psychology," and we doubted if even that would have any effect.(p.xxix)

complexes

• Once again I was back in the big time operations, and along with them, big shot *complexes*.(p.361)

complexities

• It's the last thing I ever heard him say, and I think

there are some of us who, at times, try to read extra messages and ***complexities*** into the Steps.(p.395)

complicate

• But drinking does ***complicate*** sex relations in the home.(p.81)

complicated

• Sometimes there are cases where alcoholism is ***complicated*** by other disorders.(p.114)

• Slight casualties, ***complicated*** however by a long and serious illness, were my only mishaps.(p.253)

• I rebelled against this, because just about the time that I was getting ready to leave high school, a revelation came to me about God and it made things very ***complicated*** for me.(p.489)

complication

• If we have no such ***complication***, there is plenty we should do at home.(p.82)

complications

• It is not good for him, and it sometimes creates serious ***complications*** in a family.(p.97)

• A good doctor or psychiatrist can tell you whether these ***complications*** are serious.(p.114)

compliment

• I had run into him, and he looked real prosperous; his face and eyes looked clear and he started to ***compliment*** me on my good front and how well I looked, and I said, "I haven't had a drink for nine months."(p.201)

composed

• At that time the group in New York was ***composed*** of about twelve men who were working on the principle of every drunk for himself; we had no real formula and no name.(p.246)

• My brilliant agnosticism vanished, and I saw for the first time that those who really believed, or at least honestly tried to find a Power greater than themselves, were much more ***composed*** and contented than I had ever been, and they seemed to have a degree of happiness which I had never known.(p.247)

• I did not reflect that half the office was ***composed*** of A.A. members, and that I was as unexciting as any client in any office.(p.413)

• This is a world clearing house for the Al-Anon Family Groups, ***composed*** largely of the wives, husbands and friends of A.A. members.(p.575)

comprehend

• Many do not ***comprehend*** that the alcoholic is a very sick person.(p.xiii)

• And who could ***comprehend*** a Supreme Being anyhow?(p.46)

• We found that as soon as we were able to lay aside prejudice and express even a willingness to believe in a Power greater than ourselves, we commenced to get results, even though it was impossible for any of us to fully define or ***comprehend*** that Power, which is God.(p.46)

• We have begun to ***comprehend*** their futility and their fatality.(p.70)

• We will ***comprehend*** the word serenity and we will know peace.(p.83)

• I wasn't able to ***comprehend*** it.(p.489)

comprehensive

• This is by no means a ***comprehensive*** picture of the true alcoholic, as our behavior patterns vary.(p.22)

compromises

• It has made life a thousand times easier and simpler than did the endless ***compromises*** and conflicts by which I lived before.(p.394)

compulsion

• Dr. Bob dwelt at length on how prayer had given him release, time and time again, from the nearly overpowering ***compulsion*** to take a drink.(p.279)

• Only once did I suffer from a nearly overpowering ***compulsion*** to take a drink.(p.285)

• And still by the time I was thirty years old I was being pushed around with a ***compulsion*** to drink that was completely beyond my control.(p.305)

• She of course didn't realize how cunning an alcoholic can be and the lengths to which he will go in finding ways to satisfy the ***compulsion*** for more and more drinks after having had the first one.(p.377)

• When the ***compulsion*** to drink left, it was relatively easy to stay off alcohol.(p.448)

• It helped me a great deal to become convinced that alcoholism was a disease, not a moral issue; that I had been drinking as a result of a ***compulsion***, even though I had not been aware of the ***compulsion*** at the time; and that sobriety was not a matter of will-power.(p.448)

• From that moment on, I have not had a single ***compulsion*** to drink.(p.449)

compulsive

• This, plus mounting emotional disturbances, convinced them that ***compulsive*** alcoholism already had them; that complete ruin would be only a question of time.(p.315)

compulsory

• Military service was ***compulsory*** and I did my stretch with the class of my age, goose-stepping in German barracks and taking part in the Boxer Rebellion in China, my first time at any great distance from home.(p.230)

comrades

• So I indulged with my ***comrades*** in everything the Far East had to offer.(p.231)

con

• Much has been written pro and ***con***, but among physicians, the general opinion seems to be that most chronic alcoholics are doomed.(p.xxviii)

• The worst of prison treatment couldn't break this tough ***con***.(p.457)

conceal

• Your man has probably been trying to ***conceal*** a number of scrapes, perhaps pretty messy ones.(p.140)

concealed

• With a certain satisfaction I reflected there was enough gin ***concealed*** about the house to carry me through that night and the next day.(p.8)

• If he can afford it, he may have liquor ***concealed*** all over his house to be certain no one gets his entire supply away from him to throw down the waterpipe.(p.22)

concealment

• I had them hidden away in the house and all over my shop in careful ***concealment***.(p.233)

concede

• We learned that we had to fully ***concede*** to our innermost selves that we were alcoholics.(p.30)

• I had to ***concede*** both propositions.(p.42)

• We find the more one member of the family demands that the others ***concede*** to him, the more resentful they become.(p.122)

• If you ***concede*** that your employee is ill, can he be forgiven for what he has done in the past?(p.140)

• For a long time the only Higher Power I could ***concede*** was the power of the group, but this was far more than I had ever recognized before, and it was at least a beginning.(p.248)

conceded

• To Christ I ***conceded*** the certainty of a great man, not too closely followed by those who claimed Him.(p.11)

• He was interested and ***conceded*** that he had some of the symptoms, but he was a long way from admitting that he could do nothing about it himself.(p.40)

• A spiritual experience, he ***conceded***, was absolutely necessary, but the price seemed high upon the basis suggested.(p.155)

conceit

• I realized that I had a problem, although my realization was not very deep because my own ***conceit*** wouldn't admit that I had any personality problems.(p.214)

• At the moral inventory, he brought up some of my bad personality traits or character defects, such as selfishness, ***conceit***, jealousy, carelessness, intolerance, ill-temper, sarcasm and resentments.(p.292)

conceive

• I had never, since the believing days of childhood, been able to ***conceive*** an authority directing the universe.(p.259)

• I now ***conceive*** the psychiatrist's job to be the task of breaking down the patient's inner resistance so that which is inside him will flower, as under the activity of the A.A. program."(p.571)

conceived

• We had long talks when I would still her foreboding by telling her that men of genius ***conceived*** their best projects when drunk; that the most majestic constructions of philosophic thought were so derived.(p.2)

conceives

• In our personal stories you will find a wide variation in the way each teller approaches and ***conceives*** of the Power which is greater than himself.(p.50)

concentrate

• He should ***concentrate*** on his own spiritual demonstration.(p.98)

• They said, "Let's forget about those other things, that is, trying to eliminate them all at once, and ***concentrate*** on the drink."(p.190)

• I need to ***concentrate*** not so much on what needs to be changed in the world as on what needs to be changed in me and in my attitudes.(p.449)

• I ***concentrate*** on one of the questions.(p.499)

• I pick up a book and try to read, but I cannot ***concentrate***.(p.503)

concentrated

• So I ***concentrated*** and studied the book during that time, and I liked a lot of the things it said in there.(p.472)

• Then I was sent out to India and from then on drinking just increased and increased, and I started having two or three day spells instead of just the ordinary ***concentrated*** one day.(p.519)

concentration

• In this atmosphere the alcoholic often overcomes his excessive ***concentration*** upon himself.(p.572)

concept

• Most good ideas are simple, and this ***concept*** was the keystone of the new and triumphant arch through which we passed to freedom.(p.62)

conception

• We doctors have realized for a long time that some form of moral psychology was of urgent importance to alcoholics, but its application presented difficulties beyond our ***conception***.(p.xxv)

• He said, "Why don't you choose your own ***conception*** of God?"(p.12)

• Perhaps we rejected this particular ***conception*** because it seemed inadequate.(p.45)

• Much to our relief, we discovered we did not need to consider another's ***conception*** of God.(p.46)

• Our own ***conception***, however inadequate, was sufficient to make the approach and to effect a contact with Him.(p.46)

• When, therefore, we speak to you of God, we mean your own ***conception*** of God.(p.47)

• So we used our own ***conception***, however limited it was.(p.47)

• Actually, we used to have no reasonable ***conception*** whatever.(p.49)

• Whether we agree with a particular approach or ***conception*** seems to make little difference.(p.50)

• If the man be agnostic or atheist, make it emphatic that he does not have to agree with your ***conception*** of God.(p.93)

• He can choose any ***conception*** he likes, provided it makes sense to him.(p.93)

• I learn that when we act upon the highest ***conception*** of honesty which is given us, our sense of honesty becomes more acute.(p.507)

• With few exceptions our members find that they have tapped an unsuspected inner resource which they presently identify with their own ***conception*** of a Power greater than themselves.(p.569)

conceptions

• As part of his rehabilitation he commenced to present his ***conceptions*** to other alcoholics, impressing upon them that they must do likewise with still others.(p.xxiii)

• I could go for such ***conceptions*** as Creative Intelligence, Universal Mind or Spirit of Nature but I resisted the thought of a Czar of the Heavens, however loving His sway might be.(p.12)

• Ideas, emotions, and attitudes which were once the guiding forces of the lives of these men are suddenly cast to one side, and a completely new set of ***conceptions*** and motives begin to dominate them.(p.27)

• It meant I would have to throw several lifelong ***conceptions*** out of the window.(p.42)

• There is no use arousing any prejudice he may have against certain theological terms and ***conceptions*** about which he may already be confused.(p.93)

concepts

• Most emphatically we wish to say that any alcoholic capable of honestly facing his problems in the light of our experience can recover, provided he does not close his mind to all spiritual ***concepts***.(p.570)

concern

• To whom it may ***concern***:(p.xxiii)

• We think it no ***concern*** of ours what religious bodies our members identify themselves with as individuals.(p.28)

• I remember I felt irritated that I had to be a salesman for a ***concern*** I once owned.(p.36)

• If he means to right his past wrongs, why all this ***concern*** for everyone in the world but his family?(p.128)

• The other day an approach was made to the vice president of a large industrial ***concern***.(p.148)

• The next three years I spent in Boston, Chicago, and Montreal in the employ of a large manufacturing ***concern***, selling railway supplies, gas engines of all sorts, and many other items of heavy hardware.(p.172)

• But when its plans *concern* the welfare of neighboring groups also, those groups ought to be consulted.(p.565)
• Then too, we view with much *concern* those A.A. treasuries which continue, beyond prudent reserves, to accumulate funds for no stated A.A. purpose.(p.566)

concerned

• Thus was I convinced that God is *concerned* with us humans when we want Him enough.(p.12)
• This should suggest a useful program for anyone *concerned* with a drinking problem.(p.19)
• Whatever our protestations, are not most of us *concerned* with ourselves, our resentments, or our self-pity?(p.62)
• Though his family be at fault in many respects, he should not be *concerned* about that.(p.98)
• Sometimes it is to the best interests of all *concerned* that a couple remain apart.(p.99)
• So far as we are *concerned*, there is nothing obligatory about it.(p.132)
• Drinking occasionally, and understanding your own reactions, it is possible for you to become quite sure of many things which, so far as the alcoholic is *concerned*, are not always so.(p.139)
• While on the subject of confidence, can you adopt the attitude that so far as you are *concerned* this will be a strictly personal matter, that his alcoholic derelictions, the treatment about to be undertaken, will never be discussed without his consent?(p.143)
• By no means do we offer it as the last word on this subject, but so far as we are *concerned*, it has worked with us.(p.144)
• (1939) The authorities were much *concerned*.(p.163)
• Insofar as religion was *concerned*, I had a Catholic training in my youth.(p.214)
• As far as my home was *concerned*, I did not see then, though of course I can see now, that it was anything but a happy situation for my wife.(p.215)
• I found in the fall of 1939, that I was not mentally impaired, so far as trial work was *concerned*, and thereafter took up where I had left off when I was about forty-five years old.(p.220)
• I never was *concerned* any more, anywhere he went.(p.263)
• I certainly was, as far as my living standard was *concerned*.(p.356)
• They did the best they knew how as far as I was *concerned*.(p.401)
• He was well behaved, and idealistic where women were *concerned*.(p.403)
• It made me feel quite grown-up and mature, and I think another added attraction was the fact that so far as my family was *concerned*, it was forbidden, and it had a special attraction for that reason.(p.464)
• I don't think I suffered too much as far as the racial situation was *concerned* because I was born into it and knew nothing other than that.(p.485)
• As far as school was *concerned*, I made fair grades throughout.(p.486)
• But his life was unmentioned, so far as I was *concerned*.(p.498)

concerning

• In the course of his third treatment he acquired certain ideas *concerning* a possible means of recovery.(p.xxiii)
• I forgot the strong warnings and the prejudices of my people *concerning* drink.(p.1)
• He is often perfectly sensible and well balanced *concerning* everything except liquor, but in that respect he is incredibly dishonest and selfish.(p.21)
• She asked me if I would let someone come up and talk to me *concerning* a business deal.(p.494)
• *Concerning* such matters they can express no views whatever.(p.567)

concerns

• The story he told is most instructive, for here was a chap absolutely convinced he had to stop drinking, who had no excuse for drinking, who exhibited splendid judgment and determination in all his other *concerns*, yet was flat on his back nevertheless.(p.40)

conclude

• To *conclude* that others were wrong was as far as most of us ever got.(p.66)
• We usually *conclude* the period of meditation with a prayer that we be shown all through the day what our next step is to be, that we be given whatever we need to take care of such problems.(p.87)
• After a few more estimates as to income and expenditures for booze over a few sample years, taken at random, I *conclude* that this twenty per cent stayed fairly constant.(p.398)

concluded

• We have *concluded* to publish an anonymous volume setting forth the problem as we see it.(p.19)
• In fact, as I look back, I have often thought that they probably *concluded* that they would put up with me for a couple of years, that I couldn't live much longer, and that they would inherit whatever was left of the practice.(p.215)
• In time I *concluded* that the reason I was hurt was because I loved my parents, and I *concluded* too that if I never allowed myself to love anybody or anything I could never be hurt again.(p.545)
• Though it was not our intention to create such an impression, many alcoholics have nevertheless *concluded* that in order to recover they must acquire an immediate and overwhelming "God-consciousness" followed at once by a vast change in feeling and outlook.(p.569)

conclusion

• After consulting with his wife and partner he came to the *conclusion* that it was better to take those risks than to stand before his Creator guilty of such ruinous slander.(p.80)
• Let him draw his own *conclusion*.(p.92)
• When his wife next calls saying he is sick, you might jump to the *conclusion* he is drunk.(p.146)
• I thought of what liquor had done to me, the opportunities that I had discarded, the abilities that had been given me and how I had wasted them, and I finally came to the *conclusion*, that if I didn't want to quit, I certainly ought to want to, and that I was willing to do anything in the world to stop drinking.(p.186)
• I wasn't afraid that the program wouldn't work, but I still was doubtful whether I would be able to hang on to the program, but I did come to the *conclusion* that I was willing to put everything I had into it, with God's power, and that I wanted to do just that.(p.189)
• I quite naturally came to the *conclusion* that I must be insane.(p.199)
• I told him that I had not had a drink for ninety days and that I had come to the *conclusion* that I was one of those individuals who couldn't drink.(p.200)
• I came to the *conclusion* it was because I hadn't been drunk.(p.200)
• I resented it of course, and I offered Clarence his commission, whatever it might be, if he would please not bother me because I had arrived at the *conclusion* that he was a solicitor for some alcoholic institute.(p.216)
• Shortly after I came to this *conclusion*, I was importuned by another well-known patent law firm to help them out on some trial work because their trial man had had a heart attack and had been forbidden to go into the courtroom.(p.220)
• In *conclusion*, I can only say that whatever growth or understanding has come to me, I have no wish to graduate.(p.249)
• Finally, my mother came and said she had kept me at home for six years because she thought she could help me, but that now she had come to the *conclusion* that I wasn't even worth trying to help.(p.523)
• Happily for everyone, this *conclusion* is erroneous.(p.569)
• Dr. Harry M. Tiebout, psychiatrist: "As a psychiatrist, I have thought a great deal about the relationship of my specialty to A.A. and I have come to the *conclusion* that our particular function can very often lie in preparing the way for the patient to accept any sort of treatment or outside help.(p.571)

conclusions

• Many doctors and psychiatrists agree with our *conclusions*.(p.43)
• It is not by chance we were given the power to reason, to examine the evidence of our senses, and to draw *conclusions*.(p.53)

conclusively

• The mental twists that led up to my drinking began many years before I ever took a drink for I am one of those whose history proves *conclusively* that my drinking was "a symptom of a deeper trouble."(p.544)

concrete

• I was picked up at two-thirty that morning with my car smashed up by a street-car because I had run into a big *concrete* safety zone, and the street-car had run into me, and they took me out through the roof -- there's where I lost the suit.(p.202)
• There was a *concrete* program, designed to secure the greatest possible inner security for us long-time escapists.(p.229)

concrete-and-steel

• In a prison in my native state, I spent eleven months in solitary confinement, bouncing in and out of the "hole" (a bare *concrete-and-steel* cubicle) about five times during those eleven months.(p.459)

condemn

• Try not to *condemn* your alcoholic husband no matter what he says or does.(p.108)
• The opposite may happen should the family *condemn* and criticize.(p.129)
• Next he can be assured that you do not intend to lecture, moralize, or *condemn*; that if this was done formerly, it was because of misunderstanding.(p.142)

condemnation

• Instead, we looked at the human defects of these people, and sometimes used their shortcomings as a basis of wholesale *condemnation*.(p.50)

condensed

• This is a *condensed* version of the original "long form" A.A. Traditions as first printed in 1946.(p.563)

condition

• He was rescued by a searching party, and, in desperate *condition*, brought to me.(p.xxix)
• It was years since I could remember his coming to New York in that *condition*.(p.9)
• Doubtless you are curious to discover how and why, in the face of expert opinion to the contrary, we have recovered from a hopeless *condition* of mind and body.(p.20)
• His physical and mental *condition* were unusually good.(p.26)
• It may be worth a bad case of jitters if you get a full knowledge of your *condition*.(p.32)
• He agreed he was a real alcoholic and in a serious *condition*.(p.35)
• For a few days he was depressed about his *condition*.(p.39)
• They piled on me heaps of evidence to the effect that an alcoholic mentality, such as I had exhibited in Washington, was a hopeless *condition*.(p.42)
• But the moment I made up my mind to go through with the process, I had the curious feeling that my alcoholic *condition* was relieved, as in fact it proved to be.(p.42)
• Under no *condition* do we criticize such a person or argue.(p.77)
• That is how we react so long as we keep in fit spiritual *condition*.(p.85)
• What we really have is a daily reprieve contingent on the maintenance of our spiritual *condition*.(p.85)
• Get an idea of his behavior, his problems, his background, the seriousness of his *condition*, and his religious leanings.(p.90)
• The family may object to this, but unless he is in a dangerous physical *condition*, it is better to risk it.(p.90)
• Show him, from your own experience, how the queer mental *condition* surrounding that first drink prevents normal functioning of the will power.(p.92)
• Even though your protege may not have entirely admitted his *condition*, he has become very curious to know how you got well.(p.92)
• The only *condition* is that he trust in God and clean house.(p.98)
• Talk about his *condition* or this book only when he raises the issue.(p.113)
• If he is already committed to an institution, but can convince you and your doctor that he means business, give him a chance to try our method, unless the doctor thinks his mental *condition* too abnormal or dangerous.(p.114)
• Cessation of drinking is but the first step away from a highly strained, abnormal *condition*.(p.122)
• This is a *condition* which, in ordinary life, would produce untold grief; there might be scandalous gossip, laughter at the expense of other people, and a tendency to take advantage of intimate information.(p.125)
• There should be no hesitancy in consulting a doctor or psychologist if the *condition* persists.(p.134)
• Your man will fare better if placed in such physical *condition* that he can think straight and no longer craves liquor.(p.143)
• If the book is read the moment the patient is able, while acutely depressed, realization of his *condition* may come to him.(p.144)
• We hope the doctor will tell the patient the truth about his *condition*, whatever that happens to be.(p.144)
• For the great majority of us, however, that *condition* didn't last.(p.232)
• It was no momentary emotionalism born of self-pity in a maudlin *condition*.(p.258)
• I wasn't nearly in the *condition* I had been in many times to be picked up.(p.264)
• (That *condition* was a distinct handicap to me in trying to vindicate myself with the not so

patient wife.)(p.301)
• So the doctor let me go home on one *condition*.(p.387)
• The cop must have seen the *condition* that I was in because he decided to take me home.(p.390)
• To cut a long story short, I spent seven years and ten thousand dollars on my psychiatric adventure, and emerged in worse *condition* than ever.(p.434)
• But it didn't *condition* this girl's thinking.(p.469)
• Her mother is in a critical *condition* at a hospital.(p.501)
• The people who came knew immediately I was in no *condition* to absorb anything of the program, and I was put in a sanitarium to be defogged so that I could make a sober decision about this for myself.(p.549)
• In emphasizing alcoholism as an illness, the social stigma associated with this *condition* is being blotted out . . .(p.573)

conditioned

• They held consultations and discussions, and finally decided to give me the "*Conditioned* Reflex" treatment.(p.469)
• The idea behind it is that, having taken the treatment, your system is so "*conditioned*" that the mere sight or smell or taste of alcohol produces a violent reaction, and you become ill.(p.469)
• The medical profession would probably tell me I was *conditioned* for alcoholism by the things that happened to me in my childhood.(p.544)

conditions

• That the man who is making the approach has had the same difficulty, that he obviously knows what he is talking about, that his whole deportment shouts at the new prospect that he is a man with a real answer, that he has no attitude of Holier Than Thou, nothing whatever except the sincere desire to be helpful; that there are no fees to pay, no axes to grind, no people to please, no lectures to be endured – these are the *conditions* we have found most effective.(p.18)
• So we had to get down to causes and *conditions*.(p.64)
• Under these *conditions* we can employ our mental faculties with assurance, for after all God gave us brains to use.(p.86)
• Under these *conditions* your prospect will see he is under no pressure.(p.91)
• Talk about the *conditions* of body and mind which accompany it.(p.92)
• Occasionally you will have to meet such *conditions*.(p.97)
• We meet these *conditions* every day.(p.101)
• Under these *conditions* we naturally made mistakes.(p.107)
• We know women who are unafraid, even happy under these *conditions*.(p.111)
• You draw more and more into yourself and you think everyone is talking about *conditions* at your home.(p.114)
• Nearly always, these antics indicate nothing more than temporary *conditions*.(p.141)
• Under only slightly different *conditions*, the same thing is taking place in many eastern cities.(p.161)
• I drove towards Cleveland wondering why I found myself in such a changed set of *conditions* as compared with those of six months before.(p.200)
• Drinking *conditions* at home were even worse than before.(p.424)
• Economic *conditions* had a great deal to do with it, because I've often heard my father say that his mother would take one of the old time flour sacks and cut a hole through the bottom and two corners of it and there you'd have a gown.(p.486)
• Through my efforts to get down to "causes and *conditions*," I stand convinced that my emotional illness has been present from my earliest recollection.(p.544)

condoned

• I *condoned* my domestic brewing along with the bootleggers and their business.(p.233)

conduct

• On through the years this *conduct* continues, accompanied by his continual promises to be careful or to keep off the streets altogether.(p.38)
• We do not want to be the arbiter of anyone's sex *conduct*.(p.69)
• We reviewed our own *conduct* over the years past.(p.69)
• If we are not sorry, and our *conduct* continues to harm others, we are quite sure to drink.(p.70)
• We have listed the people we have hurt by our *conduct*, and are willing to straighten out the past if we can.(p.70)
• I tried to *conduct* a kangaroo court and hit them with a broomstick.(p.204)
• I went to five grade schools, primarily because I was expelled for my *conduct*, but I eventually graduated from the eighth grade.(p.211)
• Being intensely interested in the work, I changed my *conduct* sufficiently to master the job.(p.211)
• They suffered from my *conduct* without saying anything, but the reason for this was I still managed to hang onto a very substantial practice.(p.215)
• We rationalize and excuse our *conduct* beyond all reason.(p.376)

conducted

• I *conducted* myself so creditably that I was able to secure a much coveted internship in a western city, where I spent two years.(p.174)

conference

• Though none of these principles had the force of rules or laws, they had become so widely accepted by 1950 that they were confirmed by our first International *Conference* held at Cleveland.(p.xix)
• When I protested, his lawyer, my lawyer, and my third and last analyst had a *conference*.(p.409)

conferences

• My experience has been active: three meetings a week, many tapes, many A.A. *conferences*, much work on the Twelve Steps, and much work with other alcoholics and their families.(p.420)

conferring

• And no group, regional committee, or individual should ever take any action that might greatly affect A.A. as a whole without *conferring* with the trustees of the General Service Board.(p.565)

confess

• Many times in the intervening years I have thanked God for that man, a man who had the courage to admit failure, a man who had the humility to *confess* that all the hard-won learning of his profession could not turn up the answer.(p.436)

confessed

• There was the father one lost respect for at the age of eleven, because the father broke his solemn word in a circumstance where you, eleven years old, had assumed guilt when you were innocent; but the father would not believe you, no matter what; and to ease his suffering you "*confessed*" and were "forgiven," only – months later – to have your "guilt" brought up – only he and you knew what he was talking bout -- brought up in front of the stern grandmother.(p.533)

confessing

• We go to him in a helpful and forgiving spirit, *confessing* our former ill feeling and expressing our regret.(p.77)

confession

• Though he could not accept all the tenets of the Oxford Groups, he was convinced of the need for moral inventory, *confession* of personality defects, restitution to those harmed, helpfulness to others, and the necessity of belief in and dependence upon God.(p.xvi)
• Almost none of us liked the self-searching, the leveling of our pride, the *confession* of shortcomings which the process requires for its successful consummation.(p.25)
• Those of us belonging to a religious denomination which requires *confession* must, and of course, will want to go to the properly appointed authority whose duty it is to receive it.(p.74)

confidence

• Some time passed, and *confidence* began to be replaced by cock-sureness.(p.5)
• There was utter *confidence*.(p.14)
• But the ex-problem drinker who has found this solution, who is properly armed with facts about himself, can generally win the entire *confidence* of another alcoholic in a few hours.(p.18)
• Though experience had made him skeptical, he finished his treatment with unusual *confidence*.(p.26)
• Did we not have *confidence* in our ability to think?(p.54)
• It is important that he be able to keep a *confidence*; that he fully understand and approve what we are driving at; that he will not try to change our plan.(p.74)
• Most people approached in this way will be glad to help; they will be honored by our *confidence*.(p.75)
• We have already admitted this in *confidence* to another person, but we are sure we would be imprisoned or lose our job if it were known.(p.78)
• You can secure their *confidence* when others fail.(p.89)
• Show him you have *confidence* in his power to stop or moderate.(p.112)
• We make this recommendation with some *confidence*.(p.114)
• Family *confidence* in dad is rising high.(p.123)
• Can you have every *confidence* in his ability to recover?(p.143)
• While on the subject of *confidence*, can you adopt the attitude that so far as you are concerned this will be a strictly personal matter, that his alcoholic derelictions, the treatment about to be undertaken, will never be discussed without his consent?(p.143)
• Their talk and action had instilled me with a certain amount of *confidence*, although I was not too absolutely certain.(p.189)
• And this, as I said, certainly gave me a lot of *confidence*, seemed to take a lot of the burden off me.(p.190)
• My customers lost *confidence* in me to the point where I retained what business I had only because I was a well-trained and reputedly fine craftsman.(p.234)
• I entered the business world with every *confidence* that success lay ahead of me.(p.275)
• It would be wonderful were I able to tell you that my *confidence* in God and my application of the Twelve Steps to my daily living have utterly banished fear.(p.284)
• I have self *confidence* and assurance that cannot be confused with the cockiness I once possessed.(p.303)
• It becomes vital, also, that others not know of our defeats, nor suspect our loss of *confidence*.(p.331)
• Bill was tall, grey haired, with the kind of asymmetrical good looks and pleasant easy manner that inspire *confidence* in the shaken and afraid.(p.413)
• I have achieved the inner *confidence* to write quite unlike Shakespeare, and I have sold a good deal of what I've written.(p.416)

confident

• I rather appreciated your ideas about the subtle insanity which precedes the first drink, but I was *confident* it could not happen to me after what I had learned.(p.40)
• Yet he was happy, relaxed, *confident* and laughing.(p.239)

confidential

• Rightly and naturally, we think well before we choose the person or persons with whom to take this intimate and *confidential* step.(p.74)

confine

• The judge said that if she felt that way he would *confine* me for thirty days' examination and observation.(p.492)

confined

• He does not need a bodyguard nor is he *confined*.(p.26)
• One night, when *confined* in a hospital, he was approached by an acholic who had known a spiritual experience.(p.56)
• I refused to join any fraternity, as I wanted to be a free lance, and that year my drinking was *confined* to one-night stands, once or twice a week.(p.241)
• I *confined* drinking to weekends, and drank normally in college and for several years thereafter.(p.287)
• The next three years saw me in sanitariums, once in a ten day coma, from which I very nearly did not recover, in and out of hospitals or *confined* at home with day and night nurses.(p.306)

confinement

• I could not identify myself with the people with whom I found myself and there was no understanding, and I can't stand *confinement* anyhow.(p.387)
• In a prison in my native state, I spent eleven months in solitary *confinement*, bouncing in and out of the "hole" (a bare concrete-and-steel cubicle) about five times during those eleven months.(p.459)

confining

• My new duties were extremely *confining* and my liquor consumption began to increase.(p.298)

confirm

• The experience of any alcoholic will abundantly *confirm* this.(p.23)

confirmation

• (My mother and father were Catholics and I had been baptized, but at the end of my instructions for *Confirmation* I had not gone to church, and then when my mother remarried, she married a Protestant and the whole religious angle was forgotten.(p.201)

confirmed

• Though none of these principles had the force of rules or laws, they had become so widely accepted by 1950 that they were *confirmed* by our first International Conference held at Cleveland.(p.xix)
• These stark and ugly facts have been *confirmed* by legions of alcoholics throughout history.(p.24)
• Back at camp, all was forgiven because it was the

End, but in the light of what I have since learned I know I was a *confirmed* alcoholic at nineteen.(p.242)
• The Mayo Clinic seemed like a good place to have my diagnosis *confirmed.*(p.444)

confirms
• In this statement he *confirms* what we who have suffered alcoholic torture must believe – that the body of the alcoholic is quite as abnormal as his mind.(p.xxiv)

conflict
• We think that such a view is self-centered and in direct *conflict* with the new way of living.(p.124)

conflicts
• It has made life a thousand times easier and simpler than did the endless compromises and *conflicts* by which I lived before.(p.394)

conformity
• Nor ought A.A. membership ever depend upon money or *conformity.*(p.565)

confronted
• Arrived at this point, we were squarely *confronted* with the question of faith.(p.53)
• When I woke up sober, my handiwork *confronted* me.(p.435)

Confucius
• Then he asks me if I believe in a power greater than myself, whether I call that power God, Allah, *Confucius*, Prime Cause, Divine Mind, or any other name.(p.503)

confuse
• A.A.'s Twelve Steps may *confuse* you when you read them over.(p.516)

confused
• Once *confused* and baffled by the seeming futility of existence they show the underlying reasons why they were making heavy going of life.(p.50)
• There is no use arousing any prejudice he may have against certain theological terms and conceptions about which he may already be *confused.*(p.93)
• Boy, what a circle of *confused* idealists!(p.246)
• I have self confidence and assurance that cannot be *confused* with the cockiness I once possessed.(p.303)
• To be sure, this had been a dizzy and *confused* interval, but most everyone else I knew had emerged from it with both feet on the ground and a fair amount of adult maturity.(p.304)
• As someone in A.A. said to me once upon a time, there is nothing worse than a *confused* psychiatrist.(p.347)
• As an indication of just how *confused* and mixed up I was, just as soon as I could I left the office and hurried around to tell other patients that I was getting better.(p.470)
• When we first come into A.A., many of us are *confused* because as a general rule we're at the end of our respective ropes, and we don't know what to do.(p.512)
• But my thinking was still *confused,* and I was still unable to deal with the challenges of everyday living without help.(p.558)

confusing
• Yes, we find it rather *confusing,* but as we get around and get to know people in the group, they lead the way and all we have to do is to follow.(p.512)

confusion
• Is he not, even in his best moments, a producer of *confusion* rather than harmony?(p.61)
• I resolved that if I were going to continue with the Catholic Church, I was going to know the roots of the doctrine, since those roots had caused me some *confusion.*(p.221)
• Panic, *confusion* and chaos were supreme.(p.279)
• Twenty-seven years of *confusion* is what my early married life was.(p.325)
• Because of this state of *confusion* and frustration I had hysterics on the seventeenth day for the first and only time in my life.(p.387)

congenial
• We were the most *congenial* drinkers you ever saw.(p.264)

congregation
• There was a doctor in our church *congregation* who was interested in my case, and he thought it was a vitamin deficiency.(p.389)

congregations
• He and his family can be a bright spot in such *congregations.*(p.132)

Conn.
• After six months, we move to Bridgeport, *Conn.*(p.476)

connected
• He advised me to enter the particular hospital with which he was *connected* and I readily agreed.(p.302)

Connecticut
• When counties run out, I move to *Connecticut.*(p.475)
• Then I find jails in *Connecticut*, too.(p.475)

connection
• We put them on paper, even though we had no resentment in *connection* with them.(p.68)
• Though we have no religious *connection,* we may still do well to talk with someone ordained by an established religion.(p.74)
• In this *connection,* can you remain undisturbed if the man proceeds to tell you shocking things?(p.145)
• At that time, I was living out of town, so I moved back to the home town and made a *connection* in a responsible position with one of the larger companies in the finance business.(p.298)

connections
• Be certain he will be welcomed by your family, and that he is not trying to impose upon you for money, *connections*, or shelter.(p.96)
• Though the family has no religious *connections,* they may wish to make contact with or take membership in a religious body.(p.131)
• My dad, who was a newspaper man and had some *connections*, had meantime put a stop on me, and I guess that report went all over the country.(p.424)
• This was fine, but it was just an extra dividend, for I'd made *connections* by this time and was buying a bottle a day from the cook.(p.426)

conning
• Aside from being a common drunk, I had a very serious pill affliction and all the garbage that goes with it -- lying, stealing, cheating anybody and everybody, *conning* the people I could, and staying clear of the ones I couldn't.(p.478)

conquer
• If that be the case, you may be suffering from an illness which only a spiritual experience will *conquer.*(p.44)
• Acceptance of things as they are has replaced the old impatient champing at the bit to *conquer* the world.(p.295)

conquering
• The men who cry for money and shelter before *conquering* alcohol, are on the wrong track.(p.98)

conquest
• Only thirty years later the *conquest* of the air was almost an old story and airplane travel was in full swing.(p.52)

cons
• I was one of those bad *cons* nobody can reach.(p.460)

conscience
• If he thinks he can do the job in some other way, or prefers some other spiritual approach, encourage him to follow his own *conscience.*(p.95)
• Each individual should consult his own *conscience.*(p.132)
• It was then that I began to hate myself, and drank primarily to ease my *conscience* and forget.(p.354)
• My new friends had a social *conscience.*(p.410)
• Before I step out and do anything, I stop and check it over first, and then let my *conscience* be my guide.(p.516)
• Two – For our group purpose there is but one ultimate authority – a loving God as He may express Himself in our group *conscience.*(p.564)
• 2. – For our group purpose there is but one ultimate authority -- a loving God as He may express Himself in our group *conscience.*(p.565)
• 4. – With respect to its own affairs, each A.A group should be responsible to no other authority than its own *conscience.*(p.565)

consciences
• No prickling *consciences* to needle us with guilt feelings.(p.329)

conscientious
• I couldn't have chosen more loving and *conscientious* parents.(p.304)

conscientiously
• If he is *conscientiously* following the program of recovery he can go anywhere your business may call him.(p.147)

conscious
• At the start, this was all we needed to commence spiritual growth, to effect our first *conscious* relation with God as we understood Him.(p.47)
• For the first time, he lived in *conscious* companionship with his Creator.(p.56)
• 11.Sought through prayer and meditation to improve our *conscious* contact with God as we understood Him, praying only for knowledge of His will for us and the power to carry that out.(p.59)
• As we felt new power flow in, as we enjoyed peace of mind, as we discovered we could face life successfully, as we became *conscious* of His presence, we began to lose our fear of today, tomorrow or the hereafter.(p.63)
• Being still inexperienced and having just made *conscious* contact with God, it is not probable that we are going to be inspired at all times.(p.87)
• I was self *conscious* and ill at ease most of the time, my health was at the breaking point, and I was thoroughly miserable.(p.178)
• My marriage was happy and, as I have said, I never had any of the reasons, *conscious* or unconscious, which are often given for drinking.(p.182)
• There were times when I got to drinking, and I had been warned by Firestone that they wouldn't stand for this much longer, so, clearly, they were *conscious* of the fact that I drank too much and too often.(p.204)
• My next *conscious* memory was in Bar le Duc, many miles from base.(p.242)
• I needed it, and I knew I was drinking too much, but I wasn't *conscious* of the fact that I should stop.(p.336)
• I don't think that I was *conscious* of what had happened to me, but I think that it registered subconsciously.(p.386)

consciously
• So I *consciously* thought.)(p.196)

consciousness
• We are unable, at certain times, to bring into our *consciousness* with sufficient force the memory of the suffering and humiliation of even a week or a month ago.(p.24)
• We were in a position where life was becoming impossible, and if we had passed into the region from which there is no return through human aid we had but two alternatives: One was to go on to the bitter end, blotting out the *consciousness* of our intolerable situation as best we could; and the other, to accept spiritual help.(p.25)
• When many hundreds of people are able to say that the *consciousness* of the Presence of God is today the most important fact of their lives, they present a powerful reason why one should have faith.(p.51)
• The *consciousness* of your belief is sure to come to you.(p.55)
• Burn the idea into the *consciousness* of every man that he can get well regardless of anyone.(p.98)
• This dream world has been replaced by a great sense of purpose, accompanied by a growing *consciousness* of the power of God in our lives.(p.130)
• I regained *consciousness* on Sunday.(p.207)
• And I remembered the creeping horror of the interminable night, in which I slept for short spells and woke up dripping with cold sweat and shaken with utter despair, to drink hastily from my bottle and mercifully pass out again, "You're mad, you're mad, you're mad!" pounded through my brain with each returning ray of *consciousness*, and I drowned the refrain with drink.(p.224)
• I always feel that our God *Consciousness* was a steady growth after we became associated with A.A.(p.270)
• I was caught in a cycle of alcohol and sedation that was proving inescapable and *consciousness* had become intolerable.(p.304)
• I could no longer gage my capacity and it might be the second or the tenth drink that would erase my *consciousness.*(p.306)
• Gradually *consciousness* returned enough to let me know I was in a hospital.(p.422)

consent
• Before taking drastic action which might implicate other people we secure their *consent.*(p.80)
• While on the subject of confidence, can you adopt the attitude that so far as you are concerned this will be a strictly personal matter, that his alcoholic derelictions, the treatment about to be undertaken, will never be discussed without his *consent?*(p.143)

consented
• Later, he requested the privilege of being allowed to tell his story to other patients here and with some misgiving, we *consented.*(p.xxv)
• He *consented*, however, to go the hospital, where he occupied the very room recently vacated by the lawyer.(p.159)

consequences
• The almost certain *consequences* that follow taking

even a glass of beer do not crowd into the mind to deter us.(p.24)
• We have sometimes reflected more than Jim did upon the *consequences.*(p.37)
• We now see that when we began to drink deliberately, instead of casually, there was little serious or effective thought during the period of premeditation of what the terrific *consequences* might be.(p.37)
• This time I had not thought of the *consequences* at all.(p.41)
• Reminding ourselves that we have decided to go to any length to find a spiritual experience we ask that we be given strength and direction to do the right thing, no matter what the personal *consequences* may be.(p.79)
• No one could live such an irresponsible, immature life as I had without *consequences.*(p.420)
• A.A. made it possible for me to face the *consequences* of my past actions.(p.420)
• There go my good intentions, fear of *consequences,* will to care, responsibility for my behavior.(p.458)

consequent

• Edward Dowling, S.J., of the Queen's Work staff says, "Alcoholics Anonymous is natural; it is natural at the point where nature comes closest to the supernatural, namely in humiliations and in *consequent* humility.(p.574)

consequently

• *Consequently,* I could not get into any trouble.(p.174)
• *Consequently,* my labor bills ran up.(p.194)
• I would put off doing anything that I could until the next day and, *consequently,* everything would pile up and then there would be the blackout.(p.197)

conservative

• Furthermore, I knew that I was looked upon as a city slicker from New York, and I had to be pretty cautious among small town, *conservative* Yankees.(p.360)
• So I believe that twenty percent is a very *conservative* estimate of the amount of income I blew.(p.399)

conservatively

• By March 1976, when this edition went to the printer, the total worldwide membership of Alcoholics Anonymous was *conservatively* estimated at more than 1,000,000, with almost 28,000 groups meeting in over 90 countries.(p.xxii)

consider

• We hope no one will *consider* these self-revealing accounts in bad taste.(p.29)
• Much to our relief, we discovered we did not need to *consider* another's conception of God.(p.46)
• We *consider* our plans for the day.(p.86)
• I *consider* that I was taking the Eleventh Step when I joined this church.(p.417)
• After nearly eight years of sobriety in A.A., I still can set down such thoughts, "against my instinct and training," showing that I still *consider* myself a "special" person, entitled to special privileges.(p.536)

considerable

• These things were true to some extent, in fact, to a *considerable* extent with some of us.(p.xxiv)
• Though the aggregate of recoveries resulting from psychiatric effort is *considerable,* we physicians must admit we have made little impression upon the problem as a whole.(p.xxvii)
• Over any *considerable* period we get worse, never better.(p.30)
• Though you may be able to stop for a *considerable* period, you may yet be a potential alcoholic.(p.34)
• Alcoholism may be causing your organization *considerable* damage in its waste of time, men and reputation.(p.148)
• I had some money, all the time in the world, and *considerable* stomach trouble.(p.174)
• Before my drinking had cut me down completely, I achieved a *considerable* measure of success, having been a City Councilman for five years and a financial director of Kenmore, a suburb later taken into the city itself.(p.182)
• In other words, I was always safe from the discipline of my father, and having developed along that line, I had *considerable* difficulty in school.(p.210)
• Very early I became apprenticed to harness-making and acquired *considerable* knowledge of upholstering.(p.230)
• I had been brought up to believe this, and I had shown during my 'teens *considerable* enterprise and imagination about earning money.(p.275)
• He was a man of *considerable* means and he might have done what many men would have done in such a case.(p.278)
• Having no one else to turn to, I was willing to give Him a chance, although with *considerable* doubt.(p.280)
• We think, therefore, that any *considerable* property of genuine use to A.A. should be separately incorporated and managed, thus dividing the material from the spiritual.(p.565)

considerably

• Opinions vary *considerably* as to why the alcoholic reacts differently from normal people.(p.22)
• Both father and mother were *considerably* above the average in intelligence.(p.172)

considerate

• He may be kind, *considerate,* patient, generous; even modest and self-sacrificing.(p.61)
• The rule is we must be hard on ourself, but always *considerate* of others.(p.74)
• We should be sensible, tactful, *considerate* and humble without being servile or scraping.(p.83)
• These things will come to pass naturally and in good time provided, however, the alcoholic continues to demonstrate that he can be sober, *considerate,* and helpful, regardless of what anyone says or does.(p.99)
• A spiritual awakening soon came to mean trying each day to be a little more thoughtful, more *considerate,* a little more courteous to those with whom I came in contact.(p.381)

consideration

• New acquaintances who know nothing of alcoholism might be made and thoughtful *consideration* given their needs.(p.131)
• Should he have the same *consideration* as other ailing employees?(p.140)
• She knew that at that time any suggestion she made about my drinking would only build up a barrier, a *consideration* for which I am ever grateful.(p.216)
• At this time, however, she had an opportunity to go to Salt Lake City on a new project for the government, but she did promise me that if I would curtail my drinking and buckle down to hard work she would give serious *consideration* to my latest proposal and maybe join me at a later date when I got settled.(p.359)
• I'd gladly do it anonymously, as I have done this brief account of my struggle with alcohol -- merely to present certain ideas for the *consideration* of the reader.(p.542)
• Any therapeutic or philosophic procedure which can prove a recovery rate of 50% to 60% must merit our *consideration.*"(p.571)

considerations

• He may demand that the family find God in a hurry, or exhibit amazing indifference to them and say he is above worldly *considerations.*(p.128)

considered

• Being convinced that self, manifested in various ways, was what had defeated us, we *considered* its common manifestations.(p.64)
• When we were finished we *considered* it carefully.(p.65)
• My experience in the hospital I *considered* to be terrific because Dr. Bob told me very quickly that medicine would have very little to do with it, outside of trying to restore my appetite for food.(p.217)
• I feel that one of the things that I still have to guard against is that I used to be set in my way about what I *considered* the old-time A.A.(p.272)
• I have always *considered* myself one of the lucky members of our fraternity.(p.356)
• It was the first she had heard or read about it and she said she had *considered* sending it to me or trying to have someone in Pittsburgh send it to me so I wouldn't know where it came from.(p.366)
• It hurt to be *considered* a kid.(p.423)

considering

• You, as a business man, want to know the necessities before *considering* the result.(p.140)

consigned

• But am I to be *consigned* to a life where I shall be stupid, boring and glum, like some righteous people I see?(p.152)

consist

• Of course, I had no hint or intimation as to what the treatment was to *consist* of.(p.302)

consisted

• This *consisted* of walking the floor for three or four days and nights until I could take nourishment.(p.289)
• The meeting *consisted* of perhaps eight or nine alcoholics and seven or eight wives.(p.291)

consistent

• However, this isn't as rough as it sounds, as we do become grateful for the necessity that makes us toe the line, for we find that we are more than compensated for a *consistent* effort by the countless dividends we receive.(p.311)

consisting

• So six months ago I acquired a ready made family *consisting* of one charming wife, four grown children to whom I am devoted, and three grandchildren.(p.286)

consolation

• This was the only period when I didn't drink, but that was hardly any *consolation.*(p.480)

console

• He may seek someone else to *console* him – not always another man.(p.111)

consoling

• But the saddest, and thus the most *consoling,* drifted through from the country-music station – stories of broken hearts, wasted lives, lost loves, sung plaintively.(p.332)

conspired

• The expression on the faces of the women, that indefinable something in the eyes of the men, the stimulating and electric atmosphere of the place, *conspired* to let him know that here was haven at last.(p.160)

constant

• Our very lives, as ex-problem drinkers, depend upon our *constant* thought of others and how we may help meet their needs.(p.20)
• He is under *constant* fear and tension – that makes for more drinking.(p.73)
• His drinking may be *constant* or it may be heavy only on certain occasions.(p.109)
• He told how he lived in *constant* worry about those who might find out about his alcoholism.(p.155)
• I became a *constant* drinker with a terrific fight to control the amount of my consumption each day.(p.214)
• When I look back on that last horrible year of *constant* drinking I wonder how I survived it either physically or mentally.(p.224)
• I was living in *constant* fear that I would get caught while driving a car, so I used taxis part of the time.(p.375)
• Then I began to have blackouts and that was a *constant* worry.(p.375)
• After a few more estimates as to income and expenditures for booze over a few sample years, taken at random, I conclude that this twenty per cent stayed fairly *constant.*(p.398)
• As I said earlier, self-pity and resentment were my *constant* companions and my inventory began to look like a thirty-three year diary, for I seemed to have a resentment against everybody I had ever known.(p.551)

constantly

• It is being *constantly* revealed, as mankind studies the material world, that outward appearances are not inward reality at all.(p.48)
• These are thoughts which must go with us *constantly.*(p.85)
• Better men than we are using it *constantly.*(p.85)
• We *constantly* remind ourselves we are no longer running the show, humbly saying to ourselves many times each day "Thy will be done."(p.87)
• Even when he wanted to assert himself he could not, for his drinking placed him *constantly* in the wrong.(p.130)
• He thought all alcoholics should *constantly* have chocolate available for its quick energy value at times of fatigue.(p.133)
• Seeing much of each other, scarce an evening passed that someone's home did not shelter a little gathering of men and women, happy in their release, and *constantly* thinking how they might present their discovery to some newcomer.(p.159)
• God will *constantly* disclose more to you and to us.(p.164)
• It was not known to me as a group, but I later learned that my wife had known about it for nine months and had prayed *constantly* that I would stumble into Akron some way or another.(p.215)
• I was keenly aware that my all-important security, which I had been *constantly* afraid of losing for four decades, no longer was endangered.(p.329)
• Following an injection I would have to keep one hand busy scratching my *constantly* itching nose and would also have sudden uncontrollable urges to vomit.(p.442)

consternation

• To his *consternation,* he found himself drunk half a dozen times in rapid succession.(p.35)

constitutionally

• Those who do not recover are people who cannot or will not completely give themselves to this simple program, usually men and women who are

constitutionally incapable of being honest with themselves.(p.58)

constructed
• Were not these things the tissue out of which our lives were ***constructed***?(p.54)

construction
• We old-timers who get scattered and separated and then witness the ***construction*** of services to get in more people and to make this thing function, we think that A.A. has changed, but the root of it hasn't.(p.272)

constructions
• We had long talks when I would still her foreboding by telling her that men of genius conceived their best projects when drunk; that the most majestic ***constructions*** of philosophic thought were so derived.(p.2)

constructive
• To be vital, faith must be accompanied by self sacrifice and unselfish, ***constructive*** action.(p.93)
• These family talks will be ***constructive*** if they can be carried on without heated argument, self-pity, self-justification or resentful criticism.(p.127)
• "Keep busy; always have something ***constructive*** to do."(p.373)
• I resented this, but I did nothing ***constructive*** about it.(p.402)
• But I have not seen yet that I should do some ***constructive*** acts of love without expecting any return.(p.505)
• The amount of will power exercised to control my drinking during working hours, diverted into a ***constructive*** channel, would have made me President, and the thing that made the will power possible was the knowledge that as soon as my day was finished I could drink myself into oblivion.(p.548)

constructively
• When we retire at night, we ***constructively*** review our day.(p.86)

consult
• Let him know you are available if he wishes to make a decision and tell his story, but do not insist upon it if he prefers to ***consult*** someone else.(p.96)
• Each individual should ***consult*** his own conscience.(p.132)
• Unfortunately, I had no desire to ***consult*** my priest about my drinking.(p.234)

consultation
• It seemed to me I needed a ***consultation*** first.(p.444)

consultations
• They held ***consultations*** and discussions, and finally decided to give me the "Conditioned Reflex" treatment.(p.469)

consulted
• He had ***consulted*** the best known American psychiatrists.(p.26)
• If we have obtained permission, have ***consulted*** with others, asked God to help and the drastic step is indicated we must not shrink.(p.80)
• When they become too dangerous, we think the kind thing is to lock them up, but of course a good doctor should always be ***consulted***.(p.114)
• But when its plans concern the welfare of neighboring groups also, those groups ought to be ***consulted***.(p.565)

consulting
• After ***consulting*** with his wife and partner he came to the conclusion that it was better to take those risks than to stand before his Creator guilty of such ruinous slander.(p.80)
• There should be no hesitancy in ***consulting*** a doctor or psychologist if the condition persists.(p.134)

consumed
• This work ***consumed*** a period of about two-thirds of a year, and worked out successfully so I decided to follow patent law.(p.212)

consuming
• There I sat in the evenings, enjoying with my friends our memories of the "old country," singing the old songs we all knew, playing simple card games for drinks and ***consuming*** great quantities of beer.(p.231)

consummation
• Almost none of us liked the self-searching, the leveling of our pride, the confession of shortcomings which the process requires for its successful ***consummation***.(p.25)

consumption
• He may start off as a moderate drinker; he may or may not become a continuous hard drinker; but at some stage of his drinking career he begins to lose all control of his liquor ***consumption***, once he starts to drink.(p.21)
• Although, during this period I was not addicted to any pattern of alcohol ***consumption***, when I did drink the drinking was pretty wild.(p.212)
• I became a constant drinker with a terrific fight to control the amount of my ***consumption*** each day.(p.214)
• My daily ***consumption*** of wine was about a quart, but that was common where I lived.(p.230)
• That being the case, it didn't take me long to figure out that my meager manufacturing facilities were entirely inadequate to the manufacture of beer for social and domestic ***consumption***.(p.297)
• My new duties were extremely confining and my liquor ***consumption*** began to increase.(p.298)
• She had not known the extent of my ***consumption***.(p.333)
• Evening cocktails were as standard as morning coffee, and I suppose my average daily ***consumption*** ran a little more or less than a pint.(p.433)
• My daily alcoholic ***consumption*** remained about the same through all this, with perhaps a slight increase, and my binges remained one-nighters.(p.434)

contact
• Six months earlier, the broker had been relieved of his drink obsession by a sudden spiritual experience, following a meeting with an alcoholic friend who had been in ***contact*** with the Oxford Groups of that day.(p.xv)
• On leaving the asylum he came into ***contact*** with us.(p.35)
• Our own conception, however inadequate, was sufficient to make the approach and to effect a ***contact*** with Him.(p.46)
• 11.Sought through prayer and meditation to improve our conscious ***contact*** with God as we understood Him, praying only for knowledge of His will for us and the power to carry that out.(p.59)
• Being still inexperienced and having just made conscious ***contact*** with God, it is not probable that we are going to be inspired at all times.(p.87)
• Frequent ***contact*** with newcomers and with each other is the bright spot of our lives.(p.89)
• Though the family has no religious connections, they may wish to make ***contact*** with or take membership in a religious body.(p.131)
• Why not bring him into ***contact*** with some of our alcoholic crowd?(p.138)
• As our work spreads and our numbers increase, we hope your employees may be put in personal ***contact*** with some of us.(p.144)
• Little clusters of twos and threes and fives of us have sprung up in other communities, through ***contact*** with our two larger centers.(p.162)
• Still you may say: "But I will not have the benefit of ***contact*** with you who write this book."(p.164)
• So I had never had any lasting ***contact*** with any kind of religion.)(p.201)
• I tried to ***contact*** the boys in New York, but telegrams bounced right back and when I finally got Hank on the telephone he fired me right then.(p.247)
• So I spent much of my time calling on the people who I felt would logically come in ***contact*** with alcoholic cases, doctors, ministers, lawyers and the personnel men in industry.(p.281)
• When I told them six weeks, they were polite and said that they would ***contact*** me in case they had anyone with an alcoholic problem.(p.293)
• Needless to say, it was a year or more before they did ***contact*** me.(p.293)
• In the summer of 1938, almost a year from the time I made my original ***contact*** with Akron, the man for whom I was working and who knew about the program, approached me and asked if I could do anything about one of his salesmen who was drinking very heavily.(p.294)
• He had been dry for two and a half years and had been maintaining his ***contact*** with a group of recovered alcoholics in Akron.(p.309)
• ***Contact*** with this group was extremely important to him.(p.309)
• Shortly after I returned to Chicago, my doctor, encouraged by the results of my ***contact*** with A.A., sent us two more of his alcoholic patients.(p.310)
• I talked to the first sergeant and the battalion commander, and they got me in ***contact*** with an A.A. member.(p.319)
• A spiritual awakening soon came to mean trying each day to be a little more thoughtful, more considerate, a little more courteous to those with whom I came in ***contact***.(p.381)
• I attended meetings, I talked to my folks, I talked to younger people they had gotten in ***contact*** with to sponsor me.(p.430)
• I attempted nearly two years ago to make some amends and ***contact*** my children, but it wasn't God's time yet.(p.463)

contacted
• Following his discharge, we ***contacted*** him.(p.139)
• In the next two or three days the balance of this handful of men ***contacted*** me, encouraged me, and told me how they were trying to live this program of recovery and the fun they were having doing it.(p.291)

contacting
• After being fired, I lined up with a new finance company that was just starting in business, and took the position of business promotion man, ***contacting*** automobile dealers.(p.300)
• In such places, A.A. can be located through the local telephone directory, newspaper office, or police station, or by ***contacting*** local priests or ministers.(p.575)

contacts
• Alcoholics who have derided religious people will be helped by such ***contacts***.(p.131)
• You must always be willing and continue to make ***contacts***."(p.293)

contain
• Nothing would please us so much as to write a book which would ***contain*** no basis for contention or argument.(p.19)

contained
• However, he did become "sold" on the ideas ***contained*** in this book.(p.xxx)
• Had they fired me first, and had they then taken steps to see that I was presented with the solution ***contained*** in this book, I might have returned to them six months later, a well man.(p.141)
• He had lived there but a few weeks when he found that the place probably ***contained*** more alcoholics per square mile than any city in the country.(p.163)
• By this time, with the doctor's explanation, the revelations ***contained*** in the book, and the hope-inspiring interview with Mr. T., I was ready and willing to go into the interior of the African jungles, if that was what it took, for me to find what these people had.(p.309)
• It is a way of life, and the challenge ***contained*** in its principles is great enough to keep any human being striving for as long as he lives.(p.311)
• I couldn't focus enough to make out the chart, but the card ***contained*** two words -- "ACUTE ALCOHOLISM."(p.422)

container
• I also made use of old trunks and chests, the old can ***container***, and even the ash ***container***.(p.176)

contains
• This case ***contains*** a powerful lesson.(p.33)
• Taking this book down from our shelf we turn to the page which ***contains*** the twelve steps.(p.75)
• To return to the subject matter of this book: It ***contains*** full suggestions by which the employee may solve his problem.(p.143)
• To you, some of the ideas which it ***contains*** are novel.(p.144)
• We believe and hope it ***contains*** all you will need to begin.(p.163)
• That couplet ***contains*** most of my reasons for drinking.(p.534)

contemplating
• Somewhere in one of the conversations, I mentioned that I was ***contemplating*** forming a new firm.(p.220)
• Once, when I called my analyst, and told her I was ***contemplating*** death, she came over and tried to get me into a sanitarium.(p.411)

contemplation
• This to the end that our great blessings may never spoil us; that we shall forever live in thankful ***contemplation*** of Him who presides over us all.(p.568)

contemporaries
• Some of the ***contemporaries*** of Columbus thought a round earth preposterous.(p.51)

contempt
• I could almost hear the sound of the preacher's voice as I sat, on still Sundays, way over there on the hillside; there was that proffered temperance pledge I never signed; my grandfather's good natured ***contempt*** of some church folk and their doings; his insistence that the spheres really had their music; but his denial of the preacher's right to tell him how he must listen; his fearlessness as he spoke of these things just before he died; these recollections welled up from the past.(p.10)
• My husband was an alcoholic -- I had only ***contempt*** for those without my own amazing capacity -- the outcome was inevitable.(p.225)

- Where derision, *contempt* and pity were once shown me, I now enjoy the respect of many people.(p.296)
- The *contempt* and disgust that was in his face and thoughts!(p.391)
- I think I actually read more *contempt* than was really there because just a week before someone had sent him the Saturday Evening Post article on A.A., and there was some glimmer of hope in it for him.(p.391)
- The bartenders too, treated me with *contempt*.(p.411)
- Anybody who had my problem was beneath *contempt*!(p.412)
- I, a man of steel, with very high ideals, well brought up, an honor student and the recipient of scholarships and prizes, a boy wonder in business -- I, Bob, the author of this essay, looked and saw that the universe was beneath my *contempt*, and that to remove myself from it was the only thing of dignity a man could do.(p.531)
- "There is a principle which is a bar against all information, which is proof against all arguments and which cannot fail to keep a man in everlasting ignorance -- that principle is *contempt* prior to investigation."(p.570)

contemptible
- I could not face the boy and youth I was in the reality of the *contemptible* man I had become.(p.540)

content
- We can have this new way of life – learning to live with our sickness and to be happy and *content* – if we are willing to change our way of thinking and be honest, first with ourselves, then with others.(p.480)

contented
- He was released, relieved from his alcoholism and was happy and *contented* because of it.(p.208)
- Like most immigrants I wanted to be somebody and have something and I was very happy and *contented* as I felt success crown my efforts.(p.232)
- My brilliant agnosticism vanished, and I saw for the first time that those who really believed, or at least honestly tried to find a Power greater than themselves, were much more composed and *contented* than I had ever been, and they seemed to have a degree of happiness which I had never known.(p.247)
- If I had been sincere in what I thought I wanted more than anything else in life – a sober husband and a happy, *contented* home – I would have gone on the wagon with him.(p.324)

contention
- Nothing would please us so much as to write a book which would contain no basis for *contention* or argument.(p.19)
- If your husband is trying to live on a spiritual basis, he will also be doing everything in his power to avoid disagreement or *contention*.(p.118)

contentions
- Were our *contentions* true, it would follow that life originated out of nothing, and proceeds nowhere.(p.49)

contentment
- From a trembling, despairing nervous wreck, had emerged a man brimming over with self-reliance and *contentment*.(p.xxix)
- Try for inner *contentment*.(p.382)
- Today I think of life in terms of happiness, *contentment*, freedom from fear and despair, sane thinking, ability to face problems as they occur, the opportunity to help other alcoholics and to be decent.(p.430)

contents
- We do not like the thought that the *contents* of a book or the work of another alcoholic has accomplished in a few weeks that for which we struggled for years.(p.118)
- You are betting, of course, that your changed attitude plus the *contents* of this book will turn the trick.(p.144)
- Your junior executive may not agree with the *contents* of our book.(p.148)

contingent
- What we really have is a daily reprieve *contingent* on the maintenance of our spiritual condition.(p.85)

continual
- On through the years this conduct continues, accompanied by his *continual* promises to be careful or to keep off the streets altogether.(p.38)
- I very early came to see that there had to be a *continual* renewal for that simple deal with God; that I had perpetually to keep the bargain.(p.237)
- My life there was a nightmare of periodic binges on alcohol and pills, adultery, unhappy hours at the dental office, seeing my wife give birth to our second child and have several miscarriages, living in a turbulent household, and making *continual* attempts to be the respectable dentist, husband, father, and community leader.(p.419)

continually
- How could I *continually* break my promises?(p.362)
- Help which you once *continually* rejected, suggestions once turned aside are finally accepted in desperation.(p.377)
- So I don't just take the inventory at night – I take it *continually* throughout the day.(p.516)

continuance
- I looked so terrible in the court that the judge suggested that I get a *continuance* and let me sign all the papers to go to a hospital and to a doctor.(p.204)

continue
- There are many situations which arise out of the phenomenon of craving which cause men to make the supreme sacrifice rather than *continue* to fight.(p.xxviii)
- To one who feels he is an atheist or agnostic such an experience seems impossible, but to *continue* as he is means disaster, especially if he is an alcoholic of the hopeless variety.(p.44)
- This thought brings us to Step Ten, which suggests we *continue* to take personal inventory and *continue* to set right any new mistakes as we go along.(p.84)
- It should *continue* for our lifetime.(p.84)
- *Continue* to watch for selfishness, dishonesty, resentment, and fear.(p.84)
- *Continue* to speak of alcoholism as an illness, a fatal malady.(p.92)
- You should *continue* to be friendly to them.(p.97)
- Let the alcoholic *continue* his program day by day.(p.99)
- Then perhaps he will be interested enough to *continue*.(p.113)
- When I got the fog out of my brain, I decided that quitting school was very foolish and that I had better return and *continue* my work.(p.173)
- The next day, they called me in for an examination, and the doctor wouldn't let me *continue* working and pardoned me from the plant for ten days because he said my eye had been injured.(p.205)
- I resolved that if I were going to *continue* with the Catholic Church, I was going to know the roots of the doctrine, since those roots had caused me some confusion.(p.221)
- You must always be willing and *continue* to make contacts."(p.293)
- That was my lesson, that one could not take the moral inventory and then file it away; that the alcoholic has to *continue* to take inventory every day if he expects to get well and stay well.(p.293)
- With increasing guilt and never-ending depression, I was too weak to *continue* this day-by-day suicide.(p.355)
- I *continue* to be surprised by the people I meet who say, "You haven't had a drink for a long time, have you?"(p.376)
- It was important to me to see what alcohol had done to me and would *continue* to do if I didn't have help.(p.379)
- Once or twice, during my early drinking, I carried it over into the second day, and only once, that I can remember, did it *continue* into the third.(p.432)
- Moreover, I am deeply convinced that so long as I *continue* to strive, in my bumbling way, toward the principles I first encountered in the earlier chapters of this book, this remarkable power will *continue* to flow through me.(p.437)
- But it quickly became obvious that he had this childish notion instead: If he could get me to go to enough meetings while in the hospital, I would *continue* to go after he let me out.(p.447)
- I suddenly remembered one of my first A.A. meetings, where I heard, "If you are an alcoholic and if you *continue* to drink, the end is death or insanity."(p.461)
- My husband eventually returned, but it was not long until we realized we could not *continue* our marriage.(p.547)
- A.A. must *continue* to live or most of us will surely die.(p.565)
- Then too, we view with much concern those A.A. treasuries which *continue*, beyond prudent reserves, to accumulate funds for no stated A.A. purpose.(p.566)

continued
- This work at Akron *continued* through the summer of 1935.(p.xvii)
- The usual outcome was that people *continued* to wrong us and we stayed sore.(p.66)
- He often says that if he had *continued* to work on them, he might have deprived many others, who have since recovered, of their chance.(p.96)
- This *continued* until I enrolled in our state university and, at the end of four years, I realized that I was a drunk.(p.183)
- That *continued* through my entire life.(p.193)
- And I *continued* to drink, on and off then, until every dollar I had in the world was gone again and I was right back living at my sister's, getting my cigarettes by calling her grocer and telling him to put in a couple of cartons with her order, exactly as I had before I started to work at Max's.(p.202)
- My sobriety *continued* for another six months.(p.203)
- It has *continued* to work now for nearly eighteen years.(p.209)
- This *continued* until I was twenty-seven.(p.287)
- A few months later one of the men who had been in touch with the group in Akron came to Chicago to live, and then there were three of us who *continued* to have informal meetings quite regularly.(p.294)
- Immediately on her return we began to have formal meetings once a week, in the autumn of 1939, and we have *continued* to do this and to expand ever since.(p.295)
- Fifteen of those years I would not have enjoyed had I *continued* drinking.(p.295)
- For about one year, prior to this time, there was one doctor who had *continued* to struggle with me.(p.306)
- But, of course," he *continued*, "eventually the alcoholic loses all of his capacities as his disease gets progressively worse, and this is a tragedy that is painful to watch; the disintegration of a sound mind and body."(p.308)
- When I got out of the hospital, I *continued* making the meetings.(p.320)
- I *continued* to advance in my chosen field.(p.433)
- The longer the drinking *continued*, the shorter the time the alcohol would keep me asleep; I would have to drink myself back to sleep again and again throughout the night.(p.441)
- I *continued* to drink.(p.490)
- Nevertheless, we *continued* to work together and I *continued* to drink, but I guess, deep down within her heart as well as within mine, we both knew I couldn't stop drinking.(p.490)
- I *continued* to work and *continued* to go to lunch with Vi, and none of our acquaintances on the job knew that we had separated.(p.491)
- She *continued* to watch me, although she didn't say anything.(p.493)
- He *continued* to talk and I to listen.(p.494)
- But as he *continued* to talk, I realized that this was the first time I had met a person who had the same problems I did and who, I sincerely believe, understood me as an individual.(p.494)
- "That isn't the way," he *continued*.(p.504)
- So that pattern *continued* until I went into the Army.(p.513)
- I acquired a sponsor and began attending meetings, but *continued* to drink.(p.559)

continues
- Already," *continues* the early text, "twos and threes and fives of us have sprung up in other communities."(p.xv)
- On through the years this conduct *continues*, accompanied by his continual promises to be careful or to keep off the streets altogether.(p.38)
- If we are not sorry, and our conduct *continues* to harm others, we are quite sure to drink.(p.70)
- And even though he *continues* to drink, the family will find life more bearable.(p.97)
- These things will come to pass naturally and in good time provided, however, the alcoholic *continues* to demonstrate that he can be sober, considerate, and helpful, regardless of what anyone says or does.(p.99)
- It is possible to have a full and useful life, though your husband *continues* to drink.(p.111)
- You might say you appreciated his abilities, would like to keep him, but cannot if he *continues* to drink.(p.141)
- (Bill D. now *continues* his story.)(p.189)
- It *continues* to try to teach me the real charity, the charity that gives time and good will and service, and not just money.(p.525)

continuing
- My drinking assumed more serious proportions, *continuing* all day and almost every night.(p.3)
- But then, as I drank more and more, the alcohol seemed to affect my vision: Instead of *continuing* to see what was good about my wife, I began to see her defects.(p.450)

continuous
- Though my drinking was not yet *continuous*, it

disturbed my wife.(p.2)
• He may start off as a moderate drinker; he may or may not become a ***continuous*** hard drinker; but at some stage of his drinking career he begins to lose all control of his liquor consumption, once he starts to drink.(p.21)
• Had I tried honestly and sincerely to practice the Twelve Steps I would have seen from my ***continuous*** moral inventory that I was getting off the beam -- I would have found that there were some active resentments in my life, a terrific amount of self-pity.(p.471)
• Therefore, no society of men and women ever had more urgent need for ***continuous*** effectiveness and permanent unity.(p.563)

contract
• I worked along until I had really big names in rubber on a tentative ***contract***, and then I neglected to go through with it.(p.198)
• This duty together with my weekly meetings with my fellow alcoholics, and my daily renewal of the ***contract*** I originally made with God, have kept me sober when nothing else ever did.(p.237)

contracted
• In 1929 I ***contracted*** golf fever.(p.3)
• I had ***contracted*** for half of it, at least verbally, and the contractors were taking half of the second mortgage bond.(p.198)

contractors
• I had contracted for half of it, at least verbally, and the ***contractors*** were taking half of the second mortgage bond.(p.198)

contracts
• During the day, looking over the ***contracts*** and money in my pocket, I found that I had sold six lots that I couldn't even remember, and didn't even know the people I had sold them to.(p.196)
• The law school experience was not inspired by a desire to follow patent law, which has been my profession since: I went to law school primarily to learn the law of ***contracts*** following my own experience with litigation.(p.212)
• A year later, after I completed the course in ***contracts***, I quit the law school, and undertook some engineering work for a patent law firm on behalf of clients who were in difficulties and who desired to keep their troubles from their own engineering department.(p.212)

contradict
• Do not ***contradict*** such views.(p.94)

contraption
• I kept watching the man down the bar to see what he did with a ***contraption*** like that, and he just smelled of his drink and set it down again, so I did the same.(p.195)

contrary
• Despite ***contrary*** indications, I had little doubt that a mighty purpose and rhythm underlay all.(p.10)
• Doubtless you are curious to discover how and why, in the face of expert opinion to the ***contrary***, we have recovered from a hopeless condition of mind and body.(p.20)
• A man may criticize or laugh at himself and it will affect others favorably, but criticism or ridicule coming from another often produces the ***contrary*** effect.(p.125)
• If, on the ***contrary***, you are sure he is doing his utmost, you may wish to give him another chance.(p.147)
• On the ***contrary***, the hardest place to work this program has been in my own home, with my own children and, finally, with Max.(p.451)

contrast
• And the ***contrast*** was pretty shattering.(p.225)
• I had only to reflect on the ***contrast*** between the plans I made so many years ago for my life with what really happened to know I couldn't manage my life drunk or sober.(p.550)

contretemps
• I left because I had a ***contretemps*** with the Governor.(p.520)

contribute
• There was, therefore, a sense of real satisfaction when I was asked to ***contribute*** a few words on a subject which is covered in such masterly detail in these pages.(p.xxv)
• More and more we became interested in seeing what we could ***contribute*** to life.(p.63)
• I have something to ***contribute*** to humanity, since I am peculiarly qualified, as a fellow-sufferer, to give aid and comfort to those who have stumbled and fallen over this business of meeting life.(p.229)

contributed
• We feel, after many years of experience, that we have found nothing which has ***contributed*** more to the rehabilitation of these men than the altruistic movement now growing up among them.(p.xxvi)
• They have ***contributed*** fantastic amounts of time and work to our problem, but they aren't able, it seems, to arrest either your alcoholism or mine.(p.352)

contributing
• In other words, I began ***contributing***, and so, naturally, I began to get something more.(p.365)

contribution
• I don't think the boys were completely convinced of my personality change, for they fought shy of including my story in the book, so my only ***contribution*** to their literary efforts was my firm conviction, being still a theological rebel, that the word God should be qualified with the phrase "as we understand him" -- for that was the only way I could accept spirituality.(p.248)

contributions
• There were to be no fees or dues; our expenses were to be met by our own voluntary ***contributions***.(p.xix)
• Seven -- Every A.A. group ought to be fully self-supporting, declining outside ***contributions***.(p.564)
• 7. -- The A.A. groups themselves ought to be fully supported by the voluntary ***contributions*** of their own members.(p.566)
• We think that each group should soon achieve this ideal; that any public solicitation of funds using the name of Alcoholics Anonymous is highly dangerous, whether by groups, clubs, hospitals, or other outside agencies; that acceptance of large gifts from any source, or of ***contributions*** carrying any obligation whatever, is unwise.(p.566)
• They are the custodians of our A.A. Tradition and the receivers of voluntary A.A. ***contributions*** by which we maintain our A.A. General Service Office at New York.(p.567)

contributors
• Many years ago one of the leading ***contributors*** to this book came under our care in this hospital and while here he acquired some ideas which he put into practical application at once.(p.xxv)

contrition
• They expect him to give them the nice times they used to have before he drank so much, and to show his ***contrition*** for what they suffered.(p.126)

control
• It did not satisfy us to be told that we could not ***control*** our drinking just because we were maladjusted to life, that we were in full flight from reality, or were outright mental defectives.(p.xxiv)
• On the other hand -- and strange as this may seem to those who do not understand -- once a psychic change has occurred, the very same person who seemed doomed, who had so many problems he despaired of ever solving them, suddenly finds himself easily able to ***control*** his desire for alcohol, the only effort necessary being that required to follow a few simple rules.(p.xxvii)
• I do not hold with those who believe that alcoholism is entirely a problem of mental ***control***.(p.xxvii)
• These men were not drinking to escape; they were drinking to overcome a craving beyond their mental ***control***.(p.xxviii)
• Nevertheless, I still thought I could ***control*** the situation, and there were periods of sobriety which renewed my wife's hope.(p.5)
• He may start off as a moderate drinker; he may or may not become a continuous hard drinker; but at some stage of his drinking career he begins to lose all ***control*** of his liquor consumption, once he starts to drink.(p.21)
• Here is the fellow who has been puzzling you, especially in his lack of ***control***.(p.21)
• He has lost ***control***.(p.23)
• Yet he had no ***control*** whatever over alcohol.(p.26)
• The idea that somehow, someday he will ***control*** and enjoy his drinking is the great obsession of every abnormal drinker.(p.30)
• We alcoholics are men and women who have lost the ability to ***control*** our drinking.(p.30)
• We know that no real alcoholic ever recovers ***control***.(p.30)
• All of us felt at times that we were regaining ***control***, but such intervals -- usually brief -- were inevitably followed by still less ***control***, which led in time to pitiful and incomprehensible demoralization.(p.30)
• If anyone who is showing inability to ***control*** his drinking can do the right-about-face and drink like a gentleman, our hats are off to him.(p.31)
• Once he started, he had no ***control*** whatever.(p.32)
• We were having trouble with personal relationships, we couldn't ***control*** our emotional natures, we were a prey to misery and depression, we couldn't make a living, we had a feeling of uselessness, we were full of fear, we were unhappy, we couldn't seem to be of real help to other people -- was not a basic solution of these bedevilments more important than whether we should see newsreels of lunar flight?(p.52)
• If he sticks to the ideas that he can still ***control*** his drinking, tell him that possibly he can -- if he is not too alcoholic.(p.92)
• Two: Your husband is showing lack of ***control***, for he is unable to stay on the water wagon even when he wants to.(p.109)
• Often you must carry the burden of avoiding them or keeping them under ***control***.(p.117)
• Whenever you want to, you ***control*** your drinking.(p.139)
• There was an insistent yearning to enjoy life as we once did and a heartbreaking obsession that some new miracle of ***control*** would enable us to do it.(p.151)
• Some time later, and just as he thought he was getting ***control*** of his liquor situation, he went on a roaring bender.(p.155)
• So I was barred from the plant for ten days, and during that ten day period I was drunk twice, showing how little ***control*** these restraints had on me.(p.205)
• I became a constant drinker with a terrific fight to ***control*** the amount of my consumption each day.(p.214)
• When I was about forty-seven, after indulging in all kinds of self-deception to ***control*** my drinking, I arrived at a period when I felt convinced I had to have so much alcohol every day and that the real problem was to ***control*** how much.(p.214)
• As long as things were tough and the job a challenge I could always manage to hold on pretty well, but as soon as I learned the combination, got the puzzle under ***control*** and the boss to pat me on the back, I was gone again.(p.243)
• Routine jobs bored me, but I would take on the toughest one I could find, work day and night until I had it under ***control***; then it would become tedious and I'd lose all interest in it.(p.243)
• My drinking habits increased in spite of my struggle for ***control***.(p.305)
• And still by the time I was thirty years old I was being pushed around with a compulsion to drink that was completely beyond my ***control***.(p.305)
• Nevertheless, there were a few doctors who saw alcoholism as a disease and felt that the alcoholic was a victim of something over which he had no ***control***.(p.307)
• They realized that repeated lack of drinking ***control***, when they really wanted ***control***, was the fatal symptom that spelled problem drinking.(p.315)
• Now, no longer under pressure, I could safely guard against loss of ***control***.(p.327)
• No one likes to admit that they're a drunk, that they can't ***control*** this thing.(p.340)
• For this officer in the Indian Army, going on the wagon was not enough; attempts at ***control*** failed.(p.342)
• At Christmastime next year, I convinced my wife that I had alcohol under ***control*** and that I would do controlled drinking over Christmas and the New Year.(p.343)
• The surprise to me is the fact that I didn't know that they knew my drinking had gotten out of ***control***.(p.376)
• I can't ***control*** my drinking any more.(p.423)
• I tried to ***control*** her drinking by pouring her whiskey down the sink before I'd leave for the night, to get drunker myself.(p.426)
• My alcoholic associates fired me, took ***control***, and ran the enterprise into bankruptcy.(p.437)
• I can't say, "God could restore me to sanity, but until He does, I'll ***control*** myself -- with pills."(p.443)
• In the hospital, I hung on to the idea I'd had most of my life: that if I could just ***control*** the external environment, the internal environment would then be comfortable.(p.445)
• From that time on, fear was with me because I realized that not only would I not remember what happened to me while I was drinking, but apparently I couldn't ***control*** what happened.(p.465)
• I hadn't been drinking much about that time, for I had begun to realize that there was something abnormal about my drinking, although as yet, I didn't realize that it was so out of ***control***.(p.465)
• At first, like everybody else, I could keep ***control*** when I drank, but if I did start to drink, even in those days, I was always one of the last to leave the party.(p.518)

• In part, it was a feeling of intense shame at having to leave the Army during the war, but mostly it was resentment that this kind of thing should happen to me for, strange as it may seem, up to then I still thought I could *control* drinking.(p.521)
• I realize now that this phase of my development had been arrested by my obsession with self, and my egocentricity had reached such proportions that adjustment to anything outside my personal *control* was impossible for me.(p.547)
• The amount of will power exercised to *control* my drinking during working hours, diverted into a constructive channel, would have made me President, and the thing that made the will power possible was the knowledge that as soon as my day was finished I could drink myself into oblivion.(p.548)
• But I was trying frantically to *control* it.(p.557)

controlled

• Step over to the nearest barroom and try some *controlled* drinking.(p.31)
• At Christmastime next year, I convinced my wife that I had alcohol under control and that I would do *controlled* drinking over Christmas and the New Year.(p.343)
• In fact it has been only within the last fifteen years that I changed from a fairly normal, *controlled* drinker into an alcoholic.(p.464)

controls

• It *controls* me.(p.423)

controversial

• We are aware that these matters are, from their very nature, *controversial*.(p.19)
• 10. – No A.A. group or member should ever, in such a way as to implicate A.A., express any opinion on outside *controversial* issues -- particularly those of politics, alcohol reform, or sectarian religion.(p.567)

controversies

• And in no circumstances should we give endorsements, make alliances, or enter public *controversies*.(p.xix)

controversy

• We want to stay out of this *controversy*.(p.69)
• The proceeding was shot through with much hard feeling and *controversy*.(p.154)
• Ten – Alcoholics Anonymous has no opinion on outside issues; hence the A.A. name ought never be drawn into public *controversy*.(p.564)

convalescence

• During those first days of *convalescence*, this will do more to insure his sobriety than anything else.(p.129)

convalescing

• The family must realize that dad, though marvelously improved, is still *convalescing*.(p.127)

convenience

• My bootlegger had hidden alcohol at the back steps where I could get it at my *convenience*.(p.176)

convenient

• For myself, I had adopted those parts which seemed *convenient* and not too difficult; the rest I disregarded.(p.11)

convention

• As part of this promotion, they sent me to their national *convention* in Atlantic City to tell the big wheels how I'd done it.(p.243)
• I checked into my hotel room and then noticed a placard tucked under the glass on the bureau stating "There will be positively NO drinking at this *convention*" signed by the president of the company.(p.243)
• The only salesman invited to talk at the *convention*?(p.243)
• I'm writing this during an A.A. *convention*, where I have spent the weekend with nothing but white people.(p.529)
• I was attending a *convention* in Chicago and carousing day and night.(p.558)

conventional

• We are not an organization in the *conventional* sense of the word.(p.xiii)
• The best boarding schools and a finishing school in Europe had fitted me for the *conventional* role of debutante and young matron.(p.225)
• My story has a happy ending, but not of the *conventional* kind.(p.437)

conversation

• Let us tell you the rest of the *conversation* our friend had with his doctor.(p.27)
• At first engage in general *conversation*.(p.91)
• If you do stay, let him steer the *conversation* in any direction he likes.(p.95)
• I do not recollect the specific *conversation* that went on but I believe I did challenge Bill to tell me something about A.A. and I do recall one other thing: I wanted to know what this was that worked so many wonders, and hanging over the mantel was a picture of Gethsemane and Bill pointed to it and said, "There it is," which didn't make much sense to me.(p.216)
• There was also some *conversation* about Dr. Bob and I must have said that I would go down to Akron with Bill in the morning.(p.217)
• This time I seemed to be already awake, sitting upright in a big easy chair, in the middle of an animated *conversation* with a perfectly strange young woman, who didn't appear to think it strange.(p.222)
• One is that I don't remember too many of them, as I was one of those drunks who could be on his feet and attend a meeting or a party, engage in a *conversation* with people and do things that any nearly normal person would do, and the next day not remember a thing about where I was, what I did, whom I saw, or how I got home.(p.301)
• Ribaldry was the substance of the *conversation*, and I set out to be the funniest and most ribald of them all.(p.407)
• I remember finding myself in the middle of the night in the doctors' parking lot at the hospital with one foot in the car and one foot on the ground, not knowing which was the lead foot; finding myself hanging up the telephone – then realizing I had gotten out of bed, answered the phone, turned on the light, and carried on a *conversation* with a patient.(p.441)

conversations

• In fact, I never lost my faith, since I had been prepared by some *conversations* toward the end of my sojourn in the hospital with Dr. Bob, *conversations* pretty much along spiritual lines.(p.218)
• Somewhere in one of the *conversations*, I mentioned that I was contemplating forming a new firm.(p.220)
• Most of my *conversations* were meaningless to everyone but me.(p.319)

convert

• We grow by our willingness to face and rectify errors and *convert* them into assets.(p.124)
• Shortly thereafter, I was selected, with eight other inmates out of the 10,000 in the state's prisons at that time, to attend a school designed to take former "management problems" like me and *convert* them into paracounselors.(p.462)

converted

• Suppose we tell you some of the obstacles a family will meet; suppose we suggest how they may be avoided – even *converted* to good use for others.(p.123)
• My mother had been recently *converted* and, actually, had become a religious fanatic.(p.483)

convicted

• If we do not do so, we shall stand *convicted* of emotional sterility and of having lost the faith that moves mountains, without which medicine can do little."(p.571)

conviction

• But out of this frightening and at first disrupting experience the *conviction* grew that A.A.'s had to hang together or die separately.(p.xix)
• This process snuffed out the last flicker of *conviction* that I could do the job myself.(p.42)
• In a few seconds he was overwhelmed by a *conviction* of the Presence of God.(p.56)
• Finally, out of his hope, there burst *conviction*.(p.189)
• I don't think the boys were completely convinced of my personality change, for they fought shy of including my story in the book, so my only contribution to their literary efforts was my firm *conviction*, being still a theological rebel, that the word God should be qualified with the phrase "as we understand him" -- for that was the only way I could accept spirituality.(p.248)
• No *conviction* was necessary to establish my status as a miserable failure at managing my own life.(p.259)
• He it was who convinced me, because his own *conviction* was so real, that a Power greater than myself could help me in the crises of life, and that the means of communicating with this Power was simple prayer.(p.279)
• And all the while my fear fed a growing *conviction* that before long it would be necessary for me to be put away in some institution.(p.306)
• He was serving time on his fifth felony *conviction* when a miracle happened.(p.457)

convictions

• This hope, however, was destroyed by the doctor's telling him that while his religious *convictions* were very good, in his case they did not spell the necessary vital spiritual experience.(p.27)
• Surprisingly enough, we find such *convictions* no great obstacle to a spiritual experience.(p.28)
• Many of us had moral and philosophical *convictions* galore, but we could not live up to them even though we would have liked to.(p.62)
• When it will serve any good purpose, we are willing to announce our *convictions* with tact and common sense.(p.77)
• Don't raise such issues, no matter what your own *convictions* are.(p.93)
• But he will be curious to learn why his own *convictions* have not worked and why yours seem to work so well.(p.93)
• One more suggestion: Whether the family has spiritual *convictions* or not, they may do well to examine the principles by which the alcoholic member is trying to live.(p.130)
• You see, I am a five-time loser, which means five felony *convictions* (not including the cases beaten).(p.457)

convince

• By late 1937, the number of members having substantial sobriety time behind them was sufficient to *convince* the membership that a new light had entered the dark world of the alcoholic.(p.xvii)
• We have no desire to *convince* anyone that there is only one way by which faith can be acquired.(p.28)
• When, however, the perfectly logical assumption is suggested that underneath the material world and life as we see it, there is an All Powerful, Guiding, Creative Intelligence, right there our perverse streak comes to the surface and we laboriously set out to *convince* ourselves it isn't so.(p.49)
• Our behavior will *convince* them more than our words.(p.83)
• If he is already committed to an institution, but can *convince* you and your doctor that he means business, give him a chance to try our method, unless the doctor thinks his mental condition too abnormal or dangerous.(p.114)
• It may *convince* your husband he wants to stop drinking forever.(p.116)
• No beer or liquor was sold in the neighborhood, except at the State liquor agency where perhaps one might procure a pint if he could *convince* the agent that he really needed it.(p.171)
• The doctor, a young man, immediately took fire with the idea, and while he did not *convince* the son, he turned over two prospects who were anxious for the program.(p.294)
• While I was in Florida trying to *convince* my wife with all the A.A. literature that she should come back to me, she went over to her desk and picked up a clipping she had taken from the St. Petersburg Times about A.A.(p.366)
• It was not difficult to *convince* myself that my unhappiness was the fault of the man I had married, and I divorced him at the end of a year.(p.545)

convinced

• Though he could not accept all the tenets of the Oxford Groups, he was *convinced* of the need for moral inventory, confession of personality defects, restitution to those harmed, helpfulness to others, and the necessity of belief in and dependence upon God.(p.xvi)
• Thus was I *convinced* that God is concerned with us humans when we want Him enough.(p.12)
• We are *convinced* to a man that alcoholics of our type are in the grip of a progressive illness.(p.30)
• The story he told is most instructive, for here was a chap absolutely *convinced* he had to stop drinking, who had no excuse for drinking, who exhibited splendid judgment and determination in all his other concerns, yet was flat on his back nevertheless.(p.40)
• Being *convinced*, we were at Step Three, which is that we decided to turn our will and our life over to God as we understood Him.(p.60)
• The first requirement is that we be *convinced* that any life run on self-will can hardly be a success.(p.60)
• Being *convinced* that self, manifested in various ways, was what had defeated us, we considered its common manifestations.(p.64)
• We hope you are *convinced* now that God can remove whatever self-will has blocked you off from Him.(p.71)
• If you leave such a person alone, he may soon become *convinced* that he cannot recover by himself.(p.96)
• And just as we were being *convinced* of their heartlessness, they would surprise us with fresh resolves and new attentions.(p.107)
• We are *convinced* that a spiritual mode of living is a most powerful health restorative.(p.133)
• The others must be *convinced* of his new status

beyond the shadow of a doubt.(p.135)
• "Who is *convinced* against his will is of the same opinion still."(p.193)
• The successful demonstration I had made of my life problems in other respects *convinced* me that some day I was going to be able to drink like a gentleman.(p.214)
• When I was about forty-seven, after indulging in all kinds of self-deception to control my drinking, I arrived at a period when I felt *convinced* I had to have so much alcohol every day and that the real problem was to control how much.(p.214)
• When I entered a sanitarium for prolonged and intensive psychiatric treatment, I was *convinced* that I was having a serious mental breakdown.(p.226)
• I don't think the boys were completely *convinced* of my personality change, for they fought shy of including my story in the book, so my only contribution to their literary efforts was my firm conviction, being still a theological rebel, that the word God should be qualified with the phrase "as we understand him" -- for that was the only way I could accept spirituality.(p.248)
• He it was who *convinced* me, because his own conviction was so real, that a Power greater than myself could help me in the crises of life, and that the means of communicating with this Power was simple prayer.(p.279)
• The three of us did not feel up to the job, and after a few meetings we *convinced* the prospects that they too should go to Akron where they could see an older group in action.(p.295)
• In the meantime, another doctor in Evanston became *convinced* that the program had possibilities, and turned over a woman to us to do something about.(p.295)
• I became *convinced* of that because I spent most of my time there and nary a job turned up.(p.300)
• This, plus mounting emotional disturbances, *convinced* them that compulsive alcoholism already had them; that complete ruin would be only a question of time.(p.315)
• At Christmastime next year, I *convinced* my wife that I had alcohol under control and that I would do controlled drinking over Christmas and the New Year.(p.343)
• I was told that I must want sobriety for my own sake and I am *convinced* this is true.(p.379)
• Moreover, I am deeply *convinced* that so long as I continue to strive, in my bumbling way, toward the principles I first encountered in the earlier chapters of this book, this remarkable power will continue to flow through me.(p.437)
• It helped me a great deal to become *convinced* that alcoholism was a disease, not a moral issue; that I had been drinking as a result of a compulsion, even though I had not been aware of the compulsion at the time; and that sobriety was not a matter of willpower.(p.448)
• Through my efforts to get down to "causes and conditions," I stand *convinced* that my emotional illness has been present from my earliest recollection.(p.544)
• Had I been able to explain to a psychiatrist the feeling of futility, loneliness and lack of purpose that had come with my deep sense of personal failure at this second divorce, I seriously doubt that the good doctor could have *convinced* me that my basic problem was a spiritual hunger, but A.A. has shown me this was the truth.(p.546)
• And if I had been able to turn to the church at that time I'm sure they could not have *convinced* me my sickness was within myself, nor could they have shown me the need for self-analysis that A.A. has shown me is vital if I am to survive.(p.546)
• By this time I was such a past master at kidding myself that I had *convinced* myself I had sat out a war and waited for this man to come home and, as my resentment and self-pity grew, so did my alcoholic problem.(p.548)

convinces
• Wait until repeated stumbling *convinces* him he must act, for the more you hurry him the longer his recovery may be delayed.(p.113)

convincing
• For them, we hope these pages will prove so *convincing* that no further authentication will be necessary.(p.xiii)
• *Convincing* testimony must surely come from the medical men who have had experience with the sufferings of our members and have witnessed our return to health.(p.xxiii)
• But for the grace of God, there would have been thousands more *convincing* demonstrations.(p.25)
• His change of heart was dramatic, *convincing*, and moving.(p.55)
• Of course I kept her posted on how well the station was doing and wrote *convincing* letters of how well I was doing with the liquor problem.(p.360)

conviviality
• For most normal folks, drinking means *conviviality*, companionship and colorful imagination.(p.151)

convulsion
• On each occasion, I had a *convulsion* on Sunday morning.(p.444)

convulsions
• As a result, he couldn't figure out why I had the *convulsions*, and he decided to send me to the Mayo Clinic.(p.444)
• So I sat down with me and went over the facts behind the *convulsions*: personality changes, daily headaches, sense of impending doom, sense of impending insanity.(p.444)

cook
• One morning when I was feeling really bad, I was put on K.P. and the head *cook* wanted me to go out and scrub the garbage cans.(p.317)
• The servant he turned to was our old *cook*, and she liked to drink.(p.385)
• I had a tiny trust fund, and I moved into a small apartment where I learned to *cook*, keep house, and do the things that normal people do.(p.409)
• This was fine, but it was just an extra dividend, for I'd made connections by this time and was buying a bottle a day from the *cook*.(p.426)

cooked
• They *cooked* up a plan whereby she didn't have to be molested by me if she didn't want to be.(p.491)

cookies
• I didn't like being on the nut ward, and I particularly didn't like being forced to ice *cookies* on Christmas Eve.(p.444)

cooks
• A house in Virginia, during the fox hunting season; a little chalet in Switzerland during the summer or a place on Long Island -- each house complete with *cooks*, butlers and maids.(p.403)

cooled
• I went back to my mother's for a few days until things *cooled* off, because the District Attorney had put out a summons for me to come to see him in his office.(p.491)

coon
• I had every advantage a child could have, private schools (several of them), dancing schools, two colleges, *coon* skin coats, automobiles, a listing in the social register and all the rest.(p.357)

cooperate
• Neither does A.A. take any particular medical point of view, though we *cooperate* widely with the men of medicine as well as with the men of religion.(p.xx)
• So *cooperate*; never criticize.(p.89)
• If you *cooperate*, rather than complain, you will find that his excess enthusiasm will tone down.(p.119)
• I wanted help, and I tried to *cooperate*.(p.226)
• He asked if I would *cooperate* with him after I went home, and if I would have a trained nurse stay with me for at least two weeks.(p.387)
• While an A.A. group may *cooperate* with anyone, such cooperation ought never go so far as affiliation or endorsement, actual or implied.(p.566)

cooperated
• I *cooperated* with that man one hundred per cent!(p.388)

cooperates
• If the family *cooperates*, dad will soon see that he is suffering from a distortion of values.(p.129)

cooperation
• He has begun to try, with or without your *cooperation*, various means of moderating or staying dry.(p.109)
• If he is enthusiastic your *cooperation* will mean a great deal.(p.113)
• Here was something requiring a greater willingness to assume responsibility, and take a larger degree of *cooperation* and "give and take" than even business requires of one.(p.286)
• While an A.A. group may cooperate with anyone, such *cooperation* ought never go so far as affiliation or endorsement, actual or implied.(p.566)

cop
• The *cop* must have seen the condition that I was in because he decided to take me home.(p.390)

cope
• But I felt a fear coming into my life, and I couldn't *cope* with it.(p.324)
• Because it was only through feeling defeat and feeling failure, the inability to *cope* with my life and with alcohol, that I was able to surrender and accept the fact that I had this disease, and that I had to learn to live again without alcohol.(p.335)
• Indeed, I had to drink now to live, to *cope* with the demands of everyday existence.(p.556)
• I had to *cope* with the demands of everyday living without my comforter, my anesthetic, my crutch.(p.557)
• By learning -- through practicing the Twelve Steps and through sharing at meetings -- how to *cope* with the problems that we looked to booze to solve, back in our drinking days.(p.560)

copies
• The first edition appeared in April 1939, and in the following sixteen years, more than 300,000 *copies* went into circulation.(p.xi)
• The second edition, published in 1955, reached a total of more than 1,150,000 *copies*.(p.xi)

coping
• By twenty-nine, I was having trouble *coping* with life because of my drinking.(p.555)

copious
• The movie racket had kept me too long from writing those novels, articles, short stories, and scripts on which I had *copious* notes.(p.330)

cops
• Her idea of fun on a bender was to hit sailors and insult *cops*.(p.414)
• Build houses for some *cops* -- ha-ha.(p.475)
• *Cops* say for me to call them, they get me out.(p.475)
• *Cops* now sick of me, so they buy me one-way ticket to Canada.(p.475)
• I thought if the *cops* did come to the hospital, the doctors would tell them I was crazy and didn't know what I was doing.(p.528)
• I was trying to remember where it came from, when two of the biggest *cops* I ever saw walked in and took me to jail.(p.528)
• The *cops* had picked her up, and she told them she had bought it from me.(p.528)

copy
• If he shows interest, lend him your *copy* of this book.(p.94)
• Show him your *copy* of this book and tell him what you have found out about alcoholism.(p.112)
• He sent to New York for a *copy*, and after reading it he tucked it under his arm and called on me.(p.307)
• (I am looking at it now in my bedroom -- a *copy* that was presented to me a couple of years ago by the A.A. group in that same prison.)(p.461)

copy-desk
• In the two succeeding years I held ten different jobs ranging from newspaper *copy-desk* and rewrite, to traffic director for an oil field equipment company.(p.255)

cordially
• Without saying so, they may *cordially* hate him for what he has done to them and to their mother.(p.134)
• No one is too discredited or has sunk too low to be welcomed *cordially* -- if he means business.(p.161)

cordials
• We always had *cordials* after dinner and I know my sister and my brother and I loved creme de menthe.(p.384)

core
• In spite of the great increase in the size and the span of this Fellowship, at its *core* it remains simple and personal.(p.xxii)

cork
• This sober Indian say to sick, red-eyed alcoholic who want good medicine: "Put *cork* in bottle.(p.477)

corker
• She replied, "Yes, we've got a *corker*.(p.156)

corn
• My first drinking spree was on *corn* liquor and I was allergic to it, believe me.(p.322)
• We buy a gallon of "*corn*" because it is so cheap.(p.500)

corner
• So I drank all three beers, one after the other, said "I'll be seeing you, boys," and went around the *corner* for a bottle.(p.247)
• Half a block from the house, I tried to turn the *corner*.(p.276)
• By the time I figured out what had happened, I saw two flashing red lights atop squad cars, sedately coming around the *corner*.(p.353)
• The one thing I can remember now was that Vi was on the *corner* of 8th and L, and I remember vividly

that she had an envelope in her hand.(p.492)
• When he left I walked with him to the streetcar line, which was just about a half a block, but there were two liquor stores, one on each *corner* from my home.(p.495)

cornered
• I, who had thought so well of myself and my abilities, of my capacity to surmount obstacles, was *cornered* at last.(p.8)
• I got two drinks, each of them a quarter of that pint, in me, and was talking along with these people, but I felt that sooner or later they were going to have me *cornered* because they were smarter than I was and the drink was beginning to take effect; but as I reached for the third drink Bob said, "Listen, Buster, you promised to take some medicine if we got you a drink.(p.206)

corners
• I also talked A.A. to every friend who would listen, at lunch, at dinner, on street *corners*.(p.282)
• Economic conditions had a great deal to do with it, because I've often heard my father say that his mother would take one of the old time flour sacks and cut a hole through the bottom and two *corners* of it and there you'd have a gown.(p.486)

cornerstone
• It has been repeatedly proven among us that upon this simple *cornerstone* a wonderfully effective spiritual structure can be built.(p.47)
• Thus was our friend's *cornerstone* fixed in place.(p.56)

corporation
• I was at one time assistant manager of a *corporation* department employing sixty-six hundred men.(p.136)
• I am working hard on the books of a subsidiary company of a large *corporation*.(p.500)

corps
• It was my ex-wife, and she said my twenty-seven-year-old son, who has completed his Marine *Corps* training and graduated from college, wanted to see me privately, was getting married in three months, and wanted me at the wedding.(p.462)

corpsman
• A *corpsman* stood beside him.(p.422)
• The doctor motioned to the *corpsman* to undo my straitjacket and leg restraints.(p.422)

correct
• One of these men, staff member of a world-renowned hospital, recently made this statement to some of us: "What you say about the general hopelessness of the average alcoholic's plight is, in my opinion, *correct*.(p.43)
• In that I was *correct*: I couldn't be comfortable with any kind of people without drinking.(p.227)
• It took me some time to realize that the Twelve Steps of A.A. were designed to help *correct* these defects of character and so help remove the obsession to drink.(p.380)

correctional
• One would have to understand the *correctional* machinery to see what a miracle this really was.(p.462)

corrections
• After nine months of training, all the rest of my class was paroled and I went to work in the Department of *Corrections*.(p.462)
• Then I, too, went to work as a counselor in *Corrections*.(p.462)

corrective
• After making our review we ask God's forgiveness and inquire what *corrective* measures should be taken.(p.86)

correspondence
• I enrolled in a *correspondence* school which taught nothing but accounting.(p.284)
• If there is none nearby, you will be invited to carry on a *correspondence* which will do much to insure your sobriety no matter how isolated you are.(p.575)

corroding
• It was an evil and *corroding* thread; the fabric of our existence was shot through with it.(p.67)

cosmos
• But I wanted a *cosmos*, a universe all my own which I had created and where I reigned as chief top reigner and ruler over everyone else.(p.535)

cost
• My downfall *cost* the business community unknown thousands of dollars, for it takes real money to train a man for an executive position.(p.137)
• If you propose such a procedure to him, it may be necessary to advance the *cost* of treatment, but we believe it should be made plain that any expense will later be deducted from his pay.(p.143)
• Their *cost* of production is figured to a fine decimal point.(p.149)
• So, after reviewing these things and realizing what liquor had *cost* me, I went to this Higher Power which, to me was God, without any reservation, and admitted that I was completely powerless over alcohol, and that I was willing to do anything in the world to get rid of the problem.(p.187)
• Then he started to talk to me about his drinking experiences, what his drinking had *cost* him, how much he had drunk and where, things like that, and I remember I was quite bored because I had never seen the guy before and had no interest at all in what, where and when he drank.(p.208)
• He told me that it was imperative that I walk around the entire block, *cost* me what it might in mental agony.(p.276)
• Lucky because my excessive drinking never got me in jail, or hospitalized, nor did it ever *cost* me a job.(p.356)
• After all, upon coming out of a week-long or ten-day drunk, it was hard enough to figure up just how much that one drunk *cost*, let alone trying to calculate the *cost* of approximately twenty-five years of active alcoholism.(p.396)
• (This address is now available in pamphlet form at nominal *cost* through most A.A. groups or from Box 459, Grand Central Station, New York, NY 10163, under the title "Three Talks to Medical Societies by Bill W." – formerly called "Bill on Alcoholism" and earlier "Alcoholism the Illness.")(p.572)

costing
• He might be shocked if he knew how much alcoholism is *costing* his organization a year.(p.149)

costly
• Now I own perhaps the most *costly* pair of moccasins anyone has ever seen, and they help me remember where I've been.)(p.445)

costs
• CALCULATING THE *COSTS*(p.396)

cot
• That is the way Jackie found me, lying on a *cot* in my skivvies, with hot and cold sweats, pounding heart and that awful itchy scratchiness all over.(p.238)

cottages
• Many retirees embrace alcoholism while secluded in motor trailers, rest homes, leisure-world bungalows, mountain cabins, or beach *cottages*, or even in penthouses, on yachts, and inside Palm Springs cabanas.(p.329)

cotton
• Perhaps they created the impression that he is to be wrapped in *cotton* wool and placed on a pedestal.(p.122)
• *Cotton* struck the skids and collections went cold.(p.500)

couch
• I'd waked up in strange rooms before, fully dressed on a bed or a *couch*; I'd waked up in my own room, in or on my own bed, not knowing what hour or day it was, afraid to ask . . . but this was different.(p.222)

couches
• And the psychiatrist has had thousands of *couches*, and has put you and me on them many, many times, but he hasn't helped us very much, though he has tried hard; and we owe the clergy and the doctor and the psychiatrist a deep debt of gratitude, but they haven't helped our alcoholism, except in a rare few instances.(p.352)

cough
• But for some time, it was difficult to keep from taking a pill when I had an appropriate symptom, such as a *cough*, pain, anxiety, insomnia, a muscle spasm, or an upset stomach.(p.448)

coughed
• The doctor prescribed brandy for the boy to help him through the night when he *coughed*, a teaspoon of brandy.(p.338)

couldn't
• "Suddenly the thought crossed my mind that if I were to put an ounce of whiskey in my milk it *couldn't* hurt me on a full stomach.(p.36)
• We were having trouble with personal relationships, we *couldn't* control our emotional natures, we were a prey to misery and depression, we *couldn't* make a living, we had a feeling of uselessness, we were full of fear, we were unhappy, we *couldn't* seem to be of real help to other people – was not a basic solution of these bedevilments more important than whether we should see newsreels of lunar flight?(p.52)
• We *couldn't* duck the issue.(p.53)
• But somehow, we *couldn't* quite step ashore.(p.53)
• Of course we *couldn't*.(p.54)
• Of course he *couldn't* drink, but why not sit hopefully at a table, a bottle of ginger ale before him?(p.154)
• I *couldn't* do that."(p.163)
• I thought to myself, "Well, she is going to tell me this is the end," and I certainly *couldn't* blame her and did not intend to try to justify myself.(p.184)
• If I could, that was wonderful, that was just fine, and they would very much appreciate a person who had that kind of power, but they were looking for a man that knew he had a problem, and knew that he *couldn't* handle it himself and needed outside help.(p.186)
• During the day, looking over the contracts and money in my pocket, I found that I had sold six lots that I *couldn't* even remember, and didn't even know the people I had sold them to.(p.196)
• I decided that I *couldn't* drink.(p.196)
• Anyhow, I recognized the fact that I *couldn't* drink like normal people, but I tried hard and kept on trying for twenty-two years.(p.196)
• I told him that I had not had a drink for ninety days and that I had come to the conclusion that I was one of those individuals who *couldn't* drink.(p.200)
• The circumstances under which I reached these people were very odd because I was led there through things that I said when I *couldn't* even remember speaking.(p.202)
• I *couldn't* afford to be found with those people, but I said I would certainly pay his dues if it would keep him from drinking.(p.205)
• The man turned out to be Bill D., a very early member of A.A., and I *couldn't* tell you a word of what he said.(p.208)
• I could not see why I *couldn't* drink like a gentleman, and that was my primary ambition – until I landed in A.A.(p.214)
• In fact, as I look back, I have often thought that they probably concluded that they would put up with me for a couple of years, that I *couldn't* live much longer, and that they would inherit whatever was left of the practice.(p.215)
• I remembered asserting that I was going to do something about this, that I *couldn't* go on . . .(p.224)
• When my doctor told me I should never touch a drink again, I *couldn't* afford to believe him.(p.226)
• And I was sure that I *couldn't* be with people who drank, without drinking.(p.227)
• In that I was correct: I *couldn't* be comfortable with any kind of people without drinking.(p.227)
• I *couldn't* stomach religion, and I didn't like the mention of God or any of the other capital letters.(p.227)
• And, accepting, I felt a new inner comfort, and the willingness and strength to do something about the traits I *couldn't* live with.(p.229)
• Having regard for the law of the land, I resigned myself to the will of the national legislators and quit drinking altogether, not because I had found it harmful, but because I *couldn't* get what I was accustomed to drink.(p.232)
• Beer was too bulky and it *couldn't* be kept in a jug under the counter ready to be dumped when John Law came around.(p.233)
• I had completely forgotten the January 8th when I found the fellowship, and I spent the next four days wandering around New England half drunk, by which I mean I *couldn't* get drunk and I *couldn't* get sober.(p.247)
• I *couldn't* stand the pace.(p.254)
• My family would have nothing to do with me, in fact *couldn't* because I *couldn't* spare any of my money, which I needed for drink, to support them.(p.255)
• I sipped the drink off the bar because I *couldn't* hold it in my hand, but I was still a lady, believe it or not, and I was deeply ashamed.(p.266)
• We always tried to buy him a drink, and he always told us he had liquor trouble – *couldn't* drink.)(p.266)
• And I'd try, but I *couldn't* even see the letters.(p.268)
• We *couldn't* begin to."(p.269)
• I sat down on the side of one of their beds, and I started to weep, and I *couldn't* stop, and I was so startled, and I apologized again and again for it.(p.272)
• And, anyhow, if I went on for ten or a hundred times as long I *couldn't* even begin to tell you all that A.A. has meant to me.(p.274)
• Being an alcoholic, I *couldn't* dream of doing anything by halves!(p.286)
• She asked him to do something about me because she *couldn't*.(p.288)
• I *couldn't* sleep.(p.299)

• I arrived at the stage where I ***couldn't*** quite make it to the office some mornings.(p.299)
• Well . . . I had a job, and I really wanted desperately to stop drinking, but ***couldn't***, so I readily agreed to visit the doctor she recommended.(p.301)
• I ***couldn't*** have chosen more loving and conscientious parents.(p.304)
• I ***couldn't*** stop drinking.(p.306)
• But he ***couldn't*** be an alcoholic at his age, could he?(p.317)
• I ***couldn't*** think straight any more.(p.319)
• I ***couldn't*** remember what had been said five minutes ago.(p.319)
• I realized I ***couldn't*** quit.(p.319)
• But I ***couldn't*** go on with it either.(p.319)
• I ***couldn't*** trust them.(p.319)
• I ***couldn't*** admit that I was.(p.319)
• I still ***couldn't*** make it through the nights without drinking, so I went back into the hospital, this time to a rehabilitation center.(p.320)
• I ***couldn't*** face people.(p.323)
• I ***couldn't*** look them straight in the eyes, although I was always a self-possessed brazen sort of person.(p.323)
• But I felt a fear coming into my life, and I ***couldn't*** cope with it.(p.324)
• I ***couldn't*** keep up with any of my other friends, and I wouldn't go to anyone's house unless I knew they drank as heavily as I did.(p.324)
• I thought I was losing my mind when I realized that I ***couldn't*** stop drinking.(p.324)
• I reached a stage where I ***couldn't*** go into my apartment without a drink.(p.324)
• I felt disgraced and humiliated -- a man who ***couldn't*** hold booze -- a social disaster.(p.328)
• But I ***couldn't*** help thinking, "You poor guy.(p.334)
• I ***couldn't*** go to one wine store and look the man honestly in the face and buy a bottle, as I used to do when I had parties and entertained and did normal drinking.(p.336)
• I ***couldn't*** live without it.(p.337)
• I ***couldn't*** do anything without it.(p.337)
• I ***couldn't*** live with it any more.(p.338)
• The first time was when I knew I ***couldn't*** live with alcohol.(p.340)
• But this second time, I found I ***couldn't*** live normally without it, and I was licked worse than ever.(p.340)
• I ***couldn't*** do it among my relatives, I ***couldn't*** do it among my friends.(p.340)
• I surrendered once to the bottle, and I ***couldn't*** do these things.(p.340)
• I ***couldn't*** practice medicine without the Great Physician.(p.351)
• Even I ***couldn't*** understand it, because I did love her so.(p.362)
• In the very early spring of 1944, my frustrated wife ***couldn't*** take it any longer.(p.362)
• That night she too had new hope because I had made sure she would know what I was doing about my drinking by packing every bit of A.A. literature I could put my hands on right on top so she ***couldn't*** help but see it when she opened my bag.(p.364)
• I ***couldn't*** drink at home, because my husband frowned upon this.(p.370)
• After every cocktail party or dinner party she would say she ***couldn't*** understand how I could get in such a drunken stupor on one drink.(p.377)
• Two years before I joined A.A. my wife took a long trip during which she wrote me she just ***couldn't*** return unless I did something about my drinking.(p.377)
• In a few days an attorney called on me and explained that something would have to be done as she ***couldn't*** face returning to me as I was.(p.377)
• Physically I ***couldn't*** take it any more.(p.378)
• I ***couldn't*** afford the luxury of prejudice.(p.383)
• But I ***couldn't*** enjoy anything; I was scared to death.(p.385)
• I put my poor mother and father through agonies but, finally, I ***couldn't*** stand living with them and having them watch everything I did.(p.386)
• Then he said I ***couldn't*** possibly move on the first of February because I ***couldn't*** stay in that place by myself.(p.388)
• I ***couldn't*** walk, having it in a cast, and the doctor left the cast on three weeks longer than was necessary because he never found me sober enough to take it off.(p.390)
• When he picked me up, I must have gotten sassy and told him that he ***couldn't*** do that, so he took my dog home and took me to jail!(p.390)
• My husband ***couldn't*** tell whether I wanted to do something about my drinking.(p.391)
• I took two or three drinks so my eyes could focus, and I could see that horrible picture of the awful drunk on the first page; he ***couldn't*** get the drink to his mouth, he had a towel around his hand and he needed a shave.(p.391)
• In spite of knowing that my drunkenness was a symptom of the things that were wrong with me, and that I could never drink again, I thought I ***couldn't*** yet give it up, although I was going to try.(p.393)
• ***Couldn't*** I drink less?(p.404)
• ***Couldn't*** I stop, after a few?(p.404)
• I ***couldn't*** get a word in edgewise!(p.414)
• I ***couldn't*** focus enough to make out the chart, but the card contained two words -- "ACUTE ALCOHOLISM."(p.422)
• I ***couldn't*** recall.(p.422)
• The boys at the Post Office used to bring me my jugs; mail ***couldn't*** be opened for inspection at the gate.(p.426)
• And I'd proved I ***couldn't*** handle it, time and again.(p.429)
• Science could take my mind apart expertly, but it ***couldn't*** seem to put it together again.(p.435)
• "First, I ***couldn't*** be sure.(p.436)
• With a problem like that, I ***couldn't*** go back to sleep.(p.441)
• The pep pills affected my hearing at times: I ***couldn't*** listen fast enough to hear what I was saying.(p.442)
• Still, I ***couldn't*** turn my mouth off.(p.442)
• As a result, he ***couldn't*** figure out why I had the convulsions, and he decided to send me to the Mayo Clinic.(p.444)
• Besides, I ***couldn't*** understand the instructions.(p.445)
• Prior to our marriage, when she was a shy, scrawny adolescent, I was able to see things in her that others ***couldn't*** necessarily see -- things like beauty, charm, gaiety, a gift for being easy to talk to, a sense of humor, and many other fine qualities.(p.450)
• The worst of prison treatment ***couldn't*** break this tough con.(p.457)
• But, of course, I ***couldn't*** die.(p.457)
• From that time on, fear was with me because I realized that not only would I not remember what happened to me while I was drinking, but apparently I ***couldn't*** control what happened.(p.465)
• In other words, the kindest doctor in the whole world, and I had one such, ***couldn't*** help me because I always felt, "You can't know about me -- you can't possibly know -- you don't even drink!"(p.471)
• But she ***couldn't*** carry me forever.(p.472)
• Here was a book that said I could do something that all these doctors and priests and ministers and psychiatrists that I'd been going to for years ***couldn't*** do!(p.473)
• Aside from being a common drunk, I had a very serious pill affliction and all the garbage that goes with it -- lying, stealing, cheating anybody and everybody, conning the people I could, and staying clear of the ones I ***couldn't***.(p.478)
• But I knew at that point that I ***couldn't*** stop and I knew that I was a danger to myself and to others.(p.489)
• The thought came to me that if God, as my mother said, was a vengeful God, he ***couldn't*** be a loving God.(p.489)
• Nevertheless, we continued to work together and I continued to drink, but I guess, deep down within her heart as well as within mine, we both knew I ***couldn't*** stop drinking.(p.490)
• Indeed, without their aid we ***couldn't*** possibly have gone on.(p.496)
• I might go out West on a ranch where I ***couldn't*** get anything to drink.(p.502)
• I ***couldn't*** tell you how I got there.(p.510)
• For me, it was a little different because I ***couldn't*** help thinking about the past, and I saw the future more or less mirrored in the past.(p.513)
• In fact, I ***couldn't*** have told you the difference between sherry and brandy.(p.518)
• I ***couldn't*** understand myself.(p.522)
• I ***couldn't*** see that there was any way out of it, and I got absolutely despairing.(p.522)
• I ***couldn't*** think of anything at all to do.(p.523)
• This was the only time in my life that I'd ever known my mother to be almost pitiless, but she ***couldn't*** be blamed for that.(p.523)
• It was their open night meeting, but of course I thought they were all alcoholics; I ***couldn't*** imagine why anybody else would want to go there, and my first reaction was, well, I've come to something that's not for me.(p.524)
• Then it got to the place I ***couldn't*** drink without getting in jail.(p.526)
• I ***couldn't*** wait until the meeting was over to get a drink.(p.526)
• I thought if they smelled whiskey on my breath, they would lock me up, and I ***couldn't*** live without my bottle.(p.526)
• Then the time came when I ***couldn't*** afford whiskey, so I turned to wine.(p.527)
• It was impossible for me to say at this point, "Maybe there is something wrong with my philosophy," and I certainly ***couldn't*** say, "Maybe there is something wrong with me."(p.545)
• Inside, though, I was scared to death, for I knew that the time was coming (and it ***couldn't*** be too remote) when I would be unable to hold that job.(p.548)
• I had only to reflect on the contrast between the plans I made so many years ago for my life with what really happened to know I ***couldn't*** manage my life drunk or sober.(p.550)
• I ***couldn't*** face food.(p.558)

council

• He's now in A.A. and works as a volunteer for the local alcoholism ***council***.(p.330)

councilman

• Before my drinking had cut me down completely, I achieved a considerable measure of success, having been a City ***Councilman*** for five years and a financial director of Kenmore, a suburb later taken into the city itself.(p.182)

counsel

• ***Counsel*** with persons is often desirable, but we let God be the final judge.(p.69)
• They need the ***counsel*** and love of a woman who has gone through what you have.(p.119)
• As soon as I could get up and walk I started to drink again and kept it up until my friend of the hospital, who, in his first try at the new way of life had stubbed his toe in Chicago but had come back to the town to take ***counsel*** and make a new start, picked me up and got me into a hospital.(p.258)

counseled

• Our friends have ***counseled*** chucking the men and we have done so with finality, only to be back in a little while hoping, always hoping.(p.105)

counseling

• It may mean sharing your money and your home, ***counseling*** frantic wives and relatives, innumerable trips to police courts, sanitariums, hospitals, jails and asylums.(p.97)
• We define professionalism as the occupation of ***counseling*** alcoholics for fees or hire.(p.566)

counselor

• Then I, too, went to work as a ***counselor*** in Corrections.(p.462)
• Now, I have been an alcoholism ***counselor*** for over a year and am off parole.(p.462)

count

• But they often suspect they are down for the ***count***.(p.23)
• When resentful thoughts come, try to pause and ***count*** your blessings.(p.119)
• That's the stuff used when the oral surgeon puts the needle in your vein and says, "***Count*** to ten," and before you get to two, you're asleep.(p.442)
• I ***count*** my sobriety date from the day I began going to A.A. in prison, not from the date of my last drink.(p.462)
• It has taught me that success and failure are never final, and that neither ***count*** for very much in the final assessment of any man who has done his best.(p.525)

counted

• Nothing ***counted*** but thoroughness and honesty.(p.65)
• The Commanding Officer only spoke to me when he wanted to tell me exactly who I was and what I was and how little I ***counted*** in the scheme of things and how glad he would be if I went away.(p.520)
• In my late teens I became aware of emotions I'd not ***counted*** on; restlessness, anxiety, fear and insecurity.(p.545)

countenance

• Social distinctions, petty rivalries and jealousies -- these are laughed out of ***countenance***.(p.161)

counter

• Beer was too bulky and it couldn't be kept in a jug under the ***counter*** ready to be dumped when John Law came around.(p.233)

counteracted

• The liquor ***counteracted*** the help I was getting.(p.407)

counties

- So I change *counties* in Maine.(p.475)
- When *counties* run out, I move to Connecticut.(p.475)

counting

- I always wanted to drink too much, so I was watchful, always watchful, *counting* my drinks.(p.322)
- Today, I'm *counting* my blessings instead of my troubles.(p.355)

countless

- Therefore, it is not surprising that our drinking careers have been characterized by *countless* vain attempts to prove we could drink like other people.(p.30)
- See to it that your relationship with Him is right, and great events will come to pass for you and *countless* others.(p.164)
- He kept the faith; therefore, he and *countless* others found a new life.(p.182)
- I get my greatest thrill of accomplishment from the knowledge that I have played a part in the new happiness achieved by *countless* others like myself.(p.229)
- During my first year out of college I had endless dates, and went to *countless* dances, balls and dinner parties.(p.275)
- However, this isn't as rough as it sounds, as we do become grateful for the necessity that makes us toe the line, for we find that we are more than compensated for a consistent effort by the *countless* dividends we receive.(p.311)
- There are so many to whom I feel deeply grateful; to my husband (and best critic), whose generous love, compassion and understanding have helped me along the way; to those before me in A.A. who inspired the first article I read, and the friend who sent that article to Frank; to Ruth for her personal note, and the first A.A. to talk to me; to my Bishop, whose loving and believing spirit inspired me; and to all the members of the Houston Group who were so patient, kind and helpful – and to *countless* others.(p.393)

countries

- A.A. has flourishing communities in the British Isles, the Scandinavian *countries*, South Africa, South America, Mexico, Alaska, Australia and Hawaii.(p.xv)
- All told, promising beginnings have been made in some 50 foreign *countries* and U.S. possessions.(p.xv)
- By March 1976, when this edition went to the printer, the total worldwide membership of Alcoholics Anonymous was conservatively estimated at more than 1,000,000, with almost 28,000 groups meeting in over 90 *countries*.(p.xxii)
- By the time I was twenty-one I had six years of life in foreign *countries*, spoke three languages fluently, and had attended college for two years.(p.275)
- At a large party in Geneva, with people from many *countries* represented, the kind of party that is "protocol" in the extreme, I swayed, laughed hysterically, made naughty remarks in an unhushed voice, and was finally led from the scene.(p.406)

country

- The Twelve Steps that summarize the program may be called los Doce Pasos in one *country*, los Douze Etapes in another, but they trace exactly the same path to recovery that was blazed by the earliest members of Alcoholics Anonymous.(p.xxii)
- I say this after many years' experience as Medical Director of one of the oldest hospitals in the *country* treating alcoholic and drug addiction.(p.xxv)
- We went at once to the *country*, my wife to applaud while I started out to overtake Walter Hagen.(p.3)
- There were flights from city to *country* and back, as my wife and I sought escape.(p.6)
- All sections of this *country* and many of its occupations are represented, as well as many political, economic, social, and religious backgrounds.(p.17)
- Then I decided to drive into the *country* and see one of my prospects for a car.(p.36)
- He had lived there but a few weeks when he found that the place probably contained more alcoholics per square mile than any city in the *country*.(p.163)
- After high school came four years in one of the best colleges in the *country* where drinking seemed to be a major extra-curricular activity.(p.172)
- After many painful discussions, they finally gave me my credits and I migrated to another of the leading universities of the *country* and entered as a Junior that fall.(p.173)
- I think I must have been thoroughly scared by what had happened, or by the doctor, or probably both, so that I did not touch a drink again until the *country* went dry.(p.175)
- Every company in the *country*, except Firestone, was reorganized at that time.(p.197)
- When I got back to Germany I settled down to finish my apprenticeship, drinking the wine of the *country* as usual.(p.231)
- There I sat in the evenings, enjoying with my friends our memories of the "old *country*," singing the old songs we all knew, playing simple card games for drinks and consuming great quantities of beer.(p.231)
- Then broke again, hiding out in cheap hotels all over the *country*, one night jail stands here and there, and always that horrible feeling "What's the use -- nothing is worth while."(p.244)
- Loading a car with good old books to sell to collectors, librarians, universities and historical societies, I started out to travel the *country*.(p.255)
- We moved in from the *country* at the age when girls want all sorts of nice things.(p.261)
- I remember starting to city school, coming from a *country* school, and wanting so very, very much to be like the other girls and trying flour on my face for powder because I wasn't able to have any real powder.(p.261)
- To go north into the empty pine *country* and shoot myself, or to go south in the faint hope that a bunch of strangers might help me with my drinking problem.(p.278)
- I returned to my home in Lucknow, India, at the end of November last year from a vacation in one of the most famous beauty spots in our *country*, a mountain resort 6,800 feet up, with a wonderful lake.(p.342)
- The ambition to succeed was instilled in me by my Scandinavian parents who came to this *country* where opportunities were so great.(p.373)
- In time I became an officer and director of one of the largest commercial banks in the *country*.(p.374)
- He has since become famous and distinguished, an asset to his *country*.(p.403)
- This new analyst was a woman doctor, one of the best in the *country*.(p.409)
- My dad, who was a newspaper man and had some connections, had meantime put a stop on me, and I guess that report went all over the *country*.(p.424)
- Instead, I started going to a nice private sanitarium which, after the first visit, turned out to be more like a *country* club than anything else.(p.468)
- My father, a Negro, was a *country* physician.(p.483)
- I was there about three weeks, and then I got restless and started to tramp across the *country*, here and there, until I finally wound up in Pennsylvania, in a steel mill.(p.492)
- When I arrived at The *Country* Shop, which was a restaurant where they met in Dublin, I found about thirty-five or forty people in the room.(p.524)
- On another small borrowed sum, I went up into the *country* to the home of a doctor I had known since boyhood.(p.540)
- We worked in five below zero weather, fixing on an elm tree a wrought iron device which modestly proclaimed that he was indeed a *country* doctor.(p.540)
- During this time, our *country* was at war.(p.547)

country-music

- But the saddest, and thus the most consoling, drifted through from the *country-music* station -- stories of broken hearts, wasted lives, lost loves, sung plaintively.(p.332)

counts

- I would never have tried, but mother *counts* on it so.(p.499)

county

- My next move was to take up the study of medicine, entering one of the largest universities in the *county*.(p.173)
- One of five children, I was born on a Kentucky farm in Carlyle *County*.(p.182)
- After a few months there, I went to *County* Mental Health as an alcoholism worker.(p.462)
- Then I went South, because they told me that the particular *county* I was going to in North Carolina was a dry *county*.(p.489)
- I would meet some new faces and be in a dry *county*.(p.490)
- I had replied, "Uncle, give the judge ten dollars, or I'll have to work it out on the *county* road."(p.539)

couple

- As I crossed the threshold of the dining room, the thought came to mind that it would be nice to have a *couple* of cocktails with dinner.(p.41)
- If there be divorce or separation, there should be no undue haste for the *couple* to get together.(p.99)
- Sometimes it is to the best interests of all concerned that a *couple* remain apart.(p.99)
- At the very beginning, the *couple* ought to frankly face the fact that each will have to yield here and there if the family is going to play an effective part in the new life.(p.131)
- He's just beaten up a *couple* of nurses.(p.156)
- This *couple* has since become so fascinated that they have dedicated their home to the work.(p.160)
- I soon discovered that a *couple* of drinks would alleviate my gastric distress, at least for a few hours at a time, so it was not at all difficult for me to return to my former excessive indulgence.(p.174)
- I stayed about town a *couple* of months more and then returned to resume my practice.(p.175)
- I had a *couple* of shorter talks with this man afterward, and stopped drinking abruptly.(p.179)
- A *couple* of hired hands were cleaning out the barn on the farm and I would ride to and fro on the sled, and while they were loading I would drink hard cider out of a barrel in the barn.(p.183)
- She told me that she had been talking to a *couple* of fellows about drinking.(p.184)
- I resented this very much, until she informed me that they were a *couple* of drunks just as I was.(p.184)
- All the other people that had talked to me wanted to help me, and my pride prevented me from listening to them, and caused only resentment on my part, but I felt as if I would be a real stinker if I did not listen to a *couple* of fellows for a short time, if that would cure them.(p.185)
- He took a *couple* of puffs of a cigarette and I took a *couple* of puffs of my cigarette.(p.195)
- I could get through an evening with just a *couple* of snorts.(p.196)
- And I continued to drink, on and off then, until every dollar I had in the world was gone again and I was right back living at my sister's, getting my cigarettes by calling her grocer and telling him to put in a *couple* of cartons with her order, exactly as I had before I started to work at Max's.(p.202)
- One morning, after I had been on a binge for a *couple* of days, I awoke to find my brother and Doctor Bob in my room talking to me about not drinking.(p.206)
- In fact, as I look back, I have often thought that they probably concluded that they would put up with me for a *couple* of years, that I couldn't live much longer, and that they would inherit whatever was left of the practice.(p.215)
- However, on a *couple* of other occasions, Clarence seemed to bob up at the last saloon that I would stop at on the way home every day.(p.216)
- One evening I had gone out after dinner to take on a *couple* of double-headers and stayed a little later than usual, and when I came home Clarence was sitting on the davenport with Bill W.(p.216)
- There were, at that time, in the neighborhood of twelve or thirteen Cleveland members who had been sober anywhere from a year and a half to a *couple* of months.(p.219)
- I'd been sitting comfortably in a restaurant with Rita, drinking my sixth martini and hoping the waiter would forget about the lunch order – at least long enough for me to have a *couple* more.(p.223)
- After a *couple* of days in dollar hotels and one night in the pokey, I finally landed on my mother's doorstep -- shaking apart, with several days' beard and, of course, broke as usual.(p.238)
- We heard by wireless on the 5th that the Armistice would be signed the next day (this was a premature report) so I had a *couple* of cognacs to celebrate; then I hopped a truck and went AWOL.(p.242)
- Just give me a good front and a *couple* of bucks and I'd be right back in the big time.(p.246)
- The next day he turned me over to a *couple* who, although neither was an alcoholic, knew Dr. Bob and were willing to drive me to Akron where they would turn me over to his care.(p.278)
- So I suggested that he take a trip to Akron for a *couple* of weeks, which he did, living with one of the A.A. families there.(p.294)
- I'd just take a *couple* or three barbiturates to get back to sleep -- eating my alcohol.(p.333)
- I succeeded in this attempt for approximately fifteen months with only a *couple* of slips.(p.343)
- They were neither poor nor wealthy, but far better off than the average *couple*.(p.357)
- High living, a great many fair weather friends, the 1929 stock market crash, and a *couple* of years of Depression, soon relieved me one by one of my worldly goods including my wife.(p.358)
- I asked this question weekly for the next *couple* of years.(p.359)
- Sure enough in a *couple* of hours two men were at my door and for the first time I heard some facts about liquor and my problem that sounded sensible to me.(p.363)
- For the next *couple* of hours a terrible battle went on between the good gremlins and the bad ones, one faction urging me to tell the truth, the other telling me to sit tight and say nothing.(p.366)

- Before I started to drink seriously, I tried a *couple* of other escapes.(p.401)
- There were a *couple* of good things.(p.409)
- They were a *couple* of normal, sober, attractive men.(p.415)
- He and mom smuggled in a *couple* of pints to me.(p.425)
- I nearly reverted to my old, incorrigible self -- had trouble with a *couple* of other prisoners, was planning an escape.(p.461)
- (I am looking at it now in my bedroom – a copy that was presented to me a *couple* of years ago by the A.A. group in that same prison.)(p.461)
- X-rays showed that a *couple* of teeth had to come out.(p.465)
- On the day set for the extractions, on my way to the dentist's I felt a little nervous, so I had a *couple* of drinks, and after the teeth were out I was very nervous, so I had a few more.(p.466)
- Then in a *couple* of hours, when there was still no word from my husband and no sign of him, I had the feeling we alcoholics all know.(p.467)
- A *couple* of years later, we lost our elder brother in a house fire, because of pills and booze.(p.480)
- For the first *couple* of years it wasn't too bad because the momentum kept things going.(p.486)
- This man's wife had been suffering for a *couple* of months and when he came in he owed me a little bill.(p.488)
- He had gone through the windshields of cars a *couple* of times and was pretty well banged up.(p.510)
- I started prowling around with a *couple* of these A.A. boys, which kept me pretty busy and kept my mind off of down town.(p.511)
- It didn't worry me very much, because at that time I could shut off for a *couple* of months without taking a drink or even wanting one, and without feeling that I was giving anything up.(p.518)
- I was there for another *couple* of months and then, after a few more adventures in the East, I was shipped home.(p.521)
- When I was faced with a special challenge or social event – such as an important business presentation or a dinner party – I had to fortify myself with a *couple* of belts.(p.556)

couples

- *Couples* are occasionally dismayed to find that when drinking is stopped the man tends to be impotent.(p.134)
- One hundred for unmarried women at one end, one hundred for men at the other, and one hundred for married *couples* in the middle.(p.198)

couplet

- My writing career was described in the *couplet* "Alcohol gave me wings to fly,/And then it took away the sky."(p.331)
- That *couplet* contains most of my reasons for drinking.(p.534)
- For a while, for a long time, we can endure the intellect's being ahead of the emotions, which is the import of Millay's *couplet*.(p.534)

courage

- The *courage* to do battle was not there.(p.6)
- The outlines and the promise of the New Land had brought lustre to tired eyes and fresh *courage* to flagging spirits.(p.53)
- The verdict of the ages is that faith means *courage*.(p.68)
- All men of faith have *courage*.(p.68)
- Your new *courage*, good nature and lack of self-consciousness will do wonders for you socially.(p.115)
- He may bring new hope and new *courage* to many a priest, minister, or rabbi, who gives his all to minister to our troubled world.(p.132)
- Unless he took some drinks, he might not have the *courage* to scrape an acquaintance and would have a lonely week-end.(p.154)
- How my wife kept her faith and *courage* during all those years, I'll never know, but she did.(p.178)
- *Courage* to face each day has replaced the fears and uncertainties of earlier years.(p.295)
- But I have a fortune in friendships, *courage*, self assurance and honest appraisal of my own abilities.(p.296)
- By now I wanted to die, but had lost the *courage* even to take my life.(p.306)
- "Grant us the serenity to accept the things we cannot change, *courage* to change the things we can, and the wisdom to know the difference."(p.382)
- Showing all the *courage* and ingenuity that I had not used in a positive way, I covered my tracks and hid from my family so successfully that they did not find me for months.(p.401)
- With more physical *courage* than I had possessed, she had twice tried to take her life.(p.414)
- I had never had the physical *courage* to shake it out before.(p.415)
- Many times in the intervening years I have thanked God for that man, a man who had the *courage* to admit failure, a man who had the humility to confess that all the hard-won learning of his profession could not turn up the answer.(p.436)
- Here was power to live to the end of any given day, power to have the *courage* to face the next day, power to have friends, power to help people, power to be sane, power to stay sober.(p.436)
- Then, one day in A.A., I was told that I had the lenses in my glasses backwards; "the *courage* to change" in the Serenity Prayer meant, not that I should change my marriage, but rather that I should change myself and learn to accept my spouse as she was.(p.451)
- I thought that life was a pretty simple thing; you simply made a plan for your life, based upon what you wanted, and then you needed only the *courage* to go after it.(p.545)
- I didn't have the *courage* to love; I was not even sure I had the capacity.(p.546)
- Fear of rejection and its ensuing pain were not to be risked, and I turned away from myself once more for the answer, this time to the drinks I had always refused before, and in alcohol I found a false *courage*.(p.546)

courageous

- A man so involved often feels very remorseful at times, especially if he is married to a loyal and *courageous* girl who has literally gone through hell for him.(p.81)

course

- Therefore, the first portion of this volume, describing the A.A. recovery program, has been left untouched in the *course* of revisions made for both the second and the third editions.(p.xi)
- In the *course* of his third treatment he acquired certain ideas concerning a possible means of recovery.(p.xxiii)
- As laymen, our opinion as to its soundness may, of *course*, mean little.(p.xxiv)
- Of *course* an alcoholic ought to be freed from his physical craving for liquor, and this often requires a definite hospital procedure, before psychological measures can be of maximum benefit.(p.xxv)
- There are, of *course*, the psychopaths who are emotionally unstable.(p.xxviii)
- I took a night law *course*, and obtained employment as investigator for a surety company.(p.2)
- Potential alcoholic that I was, I nearly failed my law *course*.(p.2)
- By the time I had completed the *course*, I knew the law was not for me.(p.2)
- It was fun to carom around the exclusive *course* which had inspired such awe in me as a lad.(p.4)
- Of *course* he would have dinner, and then I could drink openly with him.(p.9)
- Of *course* I would!(p.12)
- We are assuming, of *course*, that the reader desires to stop.(p.34)
- And it means, of *course*, that we are going to talk about God.(p.45)
- Of *course* it was.(p.52)
- Did not these feelings, after all, determine the *course* of our existence?(p.54)
- But we believed in life – of *course* we did.(p.54)
- Of *course* we couldn't.(p.54)
- The wording was, of *course*, quite optional so long as we expressed the idea, voicing it without reservation.(p.63)
- Next we launched out on a *course* of vigorous action, the first step of which is a personal housecleaning, which many of us had never attempted.(p.63)
- This was our *course*: We realized that the people who wronged us were perhaps spiritually sick.(p.66)
- Those of us belonging to a religious denomination which requires confession must, and of *course*, will want to go to the properly appointed authority whose duty it is to receive it.(p.74)
- Of *course*, we sometimes encounter people who do not understand alcoholics.(p.74)
- Of *course* she did not, and the whole situation has long since been adjusted.(p.79)
- Though there may be justifiable exceptions, and though we wish to lay down no rule of any sort, we have often found this the best *course* to take.(p.81)
- We may not be able to determine which *course* to take.(p.86)
- Of *course*, we all fall much below this standard many times.(p.99)
- Of *course*, there is such a thing as incompatibility, but in nearly every instance the alcoholic only seems to be unloving and inconsiderate; it is usually because he is warped and sickened that he says and does these appalling things.(p.108)
- When they become too dangerous, we think the kind thing is to lock them up, but of *course* a good doctor should always be consulted.(p.114)
- If you and your husband find a solution for the pressing problem of drink you are, of *course*, going to be very happy.(p.117)
- As soon as his sobriety begins to be taken as a matter of *course*, the family may look at their strange new dad with apprehension, then with irritation.(p.128)
- One of the many doctors who had the opportunity of reading this book in manuscript form told us that the use of sweets was often helpful, of *course* depending upon a doctor's advice.(p.133)
- Of *course* our friend was wrong – dead wrong.(p.135)
- Of *course* that isn't so, and such people often may impose on you.(p.141)
- This may seem severe, but it is usually the best *course*.(p.142)
- After satisfying yourself that your man wants to recover and that he will go to any extreme to do so, you may suggest a definite *course* of action.(p.142)
- The matter of physical treatment should, of *course*, be referred to your own doctor.(p.143)
- You are betting, of *course*, that your changed attitude plus the contents of this book will turn the trick.(p.144)
- After your man has gone along without drinking for a few months, you may be able to make use of his services with other employees who are giving you the alcoholic run-around – provided, of *course*, they are willing to have a third party in the picture.(p.146)
- Of *course*, this chapter refers to alcoholics, sick people, deranged men.(p.149)
- Of *course* he couldn't drink, but why not sit hopefully at a table, a bottle of ginger ale before him?(p.154)
- He had, of *course*, the familiar alcoholic obsession that few knew of his drinking.(p.155)
- The two friends spoke of their spiritual experience and told him about the *course* of action they carried out.(p.157)
- This went from bad to worse until Sophomore spring when, after a prolonged period of drinking, I made up my mind that I could not complete my *course*, so I packed my grip and went South to spend a month on a large farm owned by a friend of mine.(p.173)
- I was, of *course*, soon on the carpet and the upshot was that I had to go back for two more quarters and remain absolutely dry, if I wished to graduate.(p.174)
- Of *course*, the result was very bad, and that ended the beer experiment.(p.178)
- My wife, a Kentucky girl, came with me to Akron where I completed my *course* in law at the Akron Law School.(p.182)
- But, of *course*, this all went up the spout with my increased drinking.(p.182)
- Which of *course* was true.(p.187)
- Of *course*, we had talked over quite a number of the failings that I had and made a sort of an inventory, which wasn't too difficult, because I had an awful lot of things wrong that were very apparent to me, because I knew all about them.(p.190)
- Of *course*, by this time, my business was practically non-existent.(p.190)
- Of *course*, as time went on, and I began to get my health back and began to be so I didn't have to hide from people all the time, it's just been wonderful.(p.192)
- Of *course* he did.(p.193)
- I lost the car, of *course*.(p.202)
- Of *course*, it was always my aim to have my own way without being caught.(p.210)
- I did not have a high school education so I went to night school to take the full high school *course*, which I finished in two years and nine months.(p.211)
- This experience sent me to law school where I went at night and which *course* I completed in less than three years, taking the highest state bar examinations and passing them.(p.212)
- A year later, after I completed the *course* in contracts, I quit the law school, and undertook some engineering work for a patent law firm on behalf of clients who were in difficulties and who desired to keep their troubles from their own engineering department.(p.212)
- As far as my home was concerned, I did not see then, though of *course* I can see now, that it was anything but a happy situation for my wife.(p.215)

• I resented it of *course*, and I offered Clarence his commission, whatever it might be, if he would please not bother me because I had arrived at the conclusion that he was a solicitor for some alcoholic institute.(p.216)
• I'd only had two with her, but I'd managed four in the fifteen minutes I'd waited for her, and of *course* I'd had the usual uncounted swigs from the bottle as I painfully got up and did my slow spasmodic dressing.(p.223)
• For there were of *course* periods of clear realization of what I had become, attended by memories of what I had been, what I had expected to be.(p.224)
• I missed the old social times, of *course*, but had no definite craving even for beer.(p.232)
• After a couple of days in dollar hotels and one night in the pokey, I finally landed on my mother's doorstep -- shaking apart, with several days' beard and, of *course*, broke as usual.(p.238)
• There I was, unshaven, clothes torn and dirty with no recollection of wandering all over France but, of *course*, a hero to the local French.(p.242)
• Around this time our big A.A. book was being written and it all became much simpler; we had a definite formula which some sixty of us agreed was the middle *course* for all alcoholics who wanted sobriety, and that formula has not been changed one iota down through the years.(p.248)
• Of *course* I didn't keep sober.(p.257)
• Of *course*, this year we decided on staying home and being sensible, doing a little drinking, and painting the house.(p.265)
• We had meetings at each other's homes and, of *course*, that was a grand place for people to get together out there; they seemed to think so too.(p.270)
• Of *course*, the latter ultimately killed the former, but of this, more anon.(p.277)
• Here was a tall, rugged, highly educated Yankee talking in a matter of *course* way about God and prayer.(p.279)
• Eventually, of *course*, what with all the hilarity that could be provoked with a few gallons of beer, there seemed to be no need of bridge or poker playing for entertainment.(p.297)
• Eventually I would arrive home for a late supper for which, of *course*, I had absolutely no relish.(p.299)
• But the firm became violently ill with my drunkenness and their *course* of treatment was to remove their ulcer, in the form of me, from the payroll, amid much fanfare and very personal and slighting remarks and insinuations.(p.300)
• During this time, I had been threatened, beaten, kissed, praised and damned alternately by relatives, family, friends and strangers, but of *course* it all went for naught.(p.300)
• He mentioned lies and deceptions in the *course* of his story in the presence of the one person in the world I wouldn't want to know such things.(p.302)
• Of *course*, I had no hint or intimation as to what the treatment was to consist of.(p.302)
• I was without power to change the *course* my life had taken.(p.304)
• Of *course* the doctors found nothing.(p.305)
• However, due to financial difficulties the whole printing was, for a while, held up and the book received no publicity, nor, of *course*, was it available in the stores, even if one knew it existed.(p.307)
• But, of *course*," he continued, "eventually the alcoholic loses all of his capacities as his disease gets progressively worse, and this is a tragedy that is painful to watch; the disintegration of a sound mind and body."(p.308)
• That, of *course*, was a shot of booze.(p.331)
• That fear, of *course*, necessitated a program of hidden alcoholism.(p.331)
• And of *course* a half empty bottle wasn't worth keeping, so I finished it up and naturally had to get more in right away for the people who "might come in unexpectedly."(p.336)
• Well, of *course* that was all I needed – to switch from wine to brandy for three weeks.(p.338)
• The regular flow of all the literature, which I keep meticulously and which, of *course*, I study, has been wonderful.(p.342)
• It was a terrible blow at the time and I thought he was pretty much of a heel, but of *course* it was the finest thing he could have done for me under the circumstances.(p.357)
• Of *course* I kept her posted on how well the station was doing and wrote convincing letters of how well I was doing with the liquor problem.(p.360)
• Of *course*, it didn't work.(p.364)
• Of *course*, more than anything else I had let myself down, but I didn't realize how much then – as I do now.(p.364)
• I tried psychiatry, but of *course* I gave the psychiatrist no co-operation.(p.375)
• She of *course* didn't realize how cunning an alcoholic can be and the lengths to which he will go in finding ways to satisfy the compulsion for more and more drinks after having had the first one.(p.377)
• It was a shock of *course*, but I promised to stop and she returned.(p.377)
• Today, because of A.A.'s growth during the intervening years, it is of *course* much bigger than it was then.(p.392)
• In the *course* of drunken arguments, I found my own views and sense of responsibility as a citizen.(p.410)
• I'd thought of it in an offhand way, of *course*.(p.429)
• Of *course* I drank.(p.433)
• Of *course*, I had problems, all sort of problems.(p.439)
• Of *course*, I was still drinking at the time.(p.447)
• But, of *course*, I couldn't die.(p.457)
• Of *course*, an inmate must begin living the A.A. way "inside," if he is to stand a chance "outside."(p.458)
• Of *course* I had the sensitive, hurt feelings of the alcoholic.(p.472)
• Then, of *course*, there are always the wrinkled slacks, which have been slept in and are so dirty, they could walk away by themselves.(p.479)
• Of *course*, in my day, times had changed; she just hadn't changed with the times.(p.484)
• Of *course*, when father finally came to Virginia to work his way through school, he resented the southern "cracker," as he often called them, so much that he didn't even go back to his mother's funeral.(p.486)
• I started inquiring where I could get a drink and, of *course*, I found that it wasn't hard.(p.490)
• Of *course* the kid never got the Easter outfit.(p.493)
• Of *course*, it wasn't very much of a meeting in the beginning; most of the time it was just Vi and myself.(p.495)
• But, finally, we got one or two to come in and stick and from there, of *course*, we started to grow.(p.495)
• During the *course* of that drinking, I had shot and killed one person and almost completed the job on a second one.(p.508)
• After I had made my third report, I stepped down town, met some of the old crowd, and of *course* you know the answer.(p.510)
• When I landed of *course* I hit a gin mill, and with three or four good shots under my belt the world began to go into that rosy glow.(p.513)
• Of *course* I really didn't have to worry on that score, because I wasn't the type that got half drunk.(p.515)
• The war was on and it was a fairly short *course*, about eight months.(p.518)
• They brought me in and of *course*, they hadn't very much trouble in finding that I was alcoholic.(p.521)
• It was their open night meeting, but of *course* I thought they were all alcoholics; I couldn't imagine why anybody else would want to go there, and my first reaction was, well, I've come to something that's not for me.(p.524)
• And all this, of *course*, is, in the popular modern jargon, "compensation" for immaturity.(p.535)
• Actually, of *course*, I wanted someone to listen to me, because when I had a few martinis inside, I became the great author I longed to be; and the right listener was in for some pretty highflown theories of literature and of genius.(p.536)
• Still, I had had funds sufficient to get plastered because that, of *course*, was more important than paying my own way.(p.538)
• It had provided me with excuses for my lack of education, my marital failures, personal failures, inadequacy, and of *course*, my alcoholism and, though I really thought I had been willing to part with it, now I knew I was reluctant to let it go.(p.552)
• Of *course*, the more I drank, the more unrealistic my expectations became and the poorer my performance, and the gap widened.(p.557)
• A.A. can, of *course*, mean just as much to uncounted alcoholics not yet reached.(p.563)

courses
• I went back to law school, and doubled up on the *courses* because I was then approaching thirty years of age and I wanted to get through as quickly as possible.(p.212)
• So I enrolled at the university for night *courses* in religion, and I pursued those *courses* for a year.(p.221)

court
• In a matter of fact way he told how two men had appeared in *court*, persuading the judge to suspend his commitment.(p.9)
• She went to *court* and got an order for his arrest.(p.79)
• At three-thirty the next morning, I was in Champlain Street Station, in jail for driving while intoxicated and insulting an officer; and the suit of which I was so proud was in such shape that the turnkey had to get me a pair of trousers to go into *court* in the next morning.(p.201)
• I tried to conduct a kangaroo *court* and hit them with a broomstick.(p.204)
• I was black and blue, with my lips all swollen, when they roused us to go into *court* in the morning.(p.204)
• I looked so terrible in the *court* that the judge suggested that I get a continuance and let me sign all the papers to go to a hospital and to a doctor.(p.204)
• I lost my driver's license, was made a ward of the *court*, and was put on probation (not to mention the fact that I might have killed three friends and myself).(p.354)
• He even went to bat for me before the *court* martial that inevitably followed and, as a result, I drew only thirty days – fifteen in solitary.(p.428)
• So she went to *court* and talked it over with the judge.(p.491)
• I was immediately arrested, arraigned in Homicide *Court*, held without bail, and remanded to the old Tombs Prison to await trial.(p.508)
• But on the other hand, I was terribly fortunate because that should have been a *court* martial offense and I should have been out on my ear.(p.520)

courteous
• A spiritual awakening soon came to mean trying each day to be a little more thoughtful, more considerate, a little more *courteous* to those with whom I came in contact.(p.381)

courteously
• From this job and the next one with another printer I was *courteously* dismissed.(p.277)

courtroom
• Shortly after I came to this conclusion, I was importuned by another well-known patent law firm to help them out on some trial work because their trial man had had a heart attack and had been forbidden to go into the *courtroom*.(p.220)

courts
• It may mean sharing your money and your home, counseling frantic wives and relatives, innumerable trips to police *courts*, sanitariums, hospitals, jails and asylums.(p.97)

courtship
• Our *courtship* was mainly in bars and night spots when my ship was in New York.(p.555)

cousin
• Indeed, she had known my *cousin* in Chicago.(p.414)
• When I was twenty-one, my *cousin* come home from U.S. Army on leave.(p.474)

cover
• So, for one reason or another, they *cover* these men, hoping matters will take a turn for the better.(p.147)
• I don't know whether I drank to *cover* up being a failure, or whether I drank and then missed the deals.(p.198)
• My father was alive, and I had to do as he wanted, so I drank under *cover*.(p.508)

covered
• There was, therefore, a sense of real satisfaction when I was asked to contribute a few words on a subject which is *covered* in such masterly detail in these pages.(p.xxv)
• We *covered* the whole eastern United States in a year.(p.3)
• At one end of the room stood a glass *covered* directory of local churches.(p.154)
• This newsman *covered* life from top to bottom; but he ended up, safely enough, in the middle.(p.251)
• I'd wake up *covered* with sweat.(p.319)
• After a time, my mind began to clear of the fog that had *covered* it.(p.320)
• Showing all the courage and ingenuity that I had not used in a positive way, I *covered* my tracks and hid from my family so successfully that they did not find me for months.(p.401)
• Most of the time I was *covered* with bruises from "running into doors."(p.411)
• On another occasion I arrived home *covered* with blood.(p.435)
• The Army drinking alone *covered* a lot of territory.(p.513)
• I was up to international standards in one particular game, and that again *covered* quite a lot of my sins.(p.519)
• He didn't have to lie in wait very long, but fortu-

nately by that time, I had acquired friends upstairs and they *covered* me for quite a time.(p.519)
• My serious drinking *covered* about seven years.(p.536)

covering
• He will have no further reason for *covering* up an alcoholic employee.(p.148)
• If reasons for *covering* up are strong enough, secrets can be hidden from the world.(p.327)
• I have published a book *covering* certain aspects of this field which has been well-reviewed and which is helping other people.(p.541)

coveted
• I conducted myself so creditably that I was able to secure a much *coveted* internship in a western city, where I spent two years.(p.174)

coward
• I used to think I was cowardly because when things came out pertaining to the program that troubled me, I said to her many times, "Annie, am I being a *coward* because I lay those things away on the shelf and skip it?"(p.273)
• About this time an incident took place in grade school that I have never forgotten because it made me realize that I was actually a physical *coward*.(p.484)

cowardly
• We were bothered with the thought that faith and dependence upon a Power beyond ourselves was somewhat weak, even *cowardly*.(p.45)
• I used to think I was *cowardly* because when things came out pertaining to the program that troubled me, I said to her many times, "Annie, am I being a coward because I lay those things away on the shelf and skip it?"(p.273)

cowboy
• That age of the flapper and the "It" girl, speakeasies and the hip flask, the boyish bob and the drugstore *cowboy*, John Held Jr. and F. Scott Fitzgerald, all generously sprinkled with a patent pseudo-sophistication.(p.304)

CPO
• While waiting to depart I was selected -- by giving a *CPO* five dollars -- to be bartender in the Navy Chief's Club.(p.426)

crack
• I found out fast that the cheapest way to get drunk was on shots with beer chasers at two bits a *crack*.(p.397)

crack-pot
• When he left I thought, what is this *crack-pot* thing?(p.391)

crack-up
• Then the *crack-up*.(p.500)

cracked
• So that was it -- last summer an alcoholic crackpot; now, I suspected, a little *cracked* about religion.(p.9)
• But when I *cracked* my leg with a sixteen-pound sledgehammer in the rock hole, I was fighting the system, using my body.(p.458)

cracker
• He is like the retired business man who lolls in the Florida sunshine in the winter complaining of the sad state of the nation; the minister who sighs over the sins of the twentieth century; politicians and reformers who are sure all would be Utopia if the rest of the world would only behave; the outlaw safe *cracker* who thinks society has wronged him; and the alcoholic who has lost all and is locked up.(p.61)
• Of course, when father finally came to Virginia to work his way through school, he resented the southern "*cracker*," as he often called them, so much that he didn't even go back to his mother's funeral.(p.486)

crackers
• There, I received several soda *crackers* and water daily, and before I could have my third-day meal (again the only meal in ten days), I had to drink a glass of castor oil or mineral oil, depending on the cruelty of the person who was doing the dispensing.(p.459)

crackpot
• So that was it -- last summer an alcoholic *crackpot*; now, I suspected, a little cracked about religion.(p.9)

cracks
• If my wife was planning to go out in the afternoon, I would get a large supply of liquor and smuggle it home and hide it in the coal bin, the clothes chute, over door jambs, over beams in the cellar and in *cracks* in the cellar tile.(p.176)

craftsman
• My customers lost confidence in me to the point where I retained what business I had only because I was a well-trained and reputedly fine *craftsman*.(p.234)

crafty
• Sly and *crafty*, I thought now I'll find out what they think of me here, what they "have on" me, what I've said coming in here drunk.(p.470)

cram
• I would gather up all my soiled clothes, as much as I could *cram* into a grocery cart, and be off.(p.370)

crankiness
• If they sense these things, they will not take so seriously his periods of *crankiness*, depression, or apathy, which will disappear when there is tolerance, love, and spiritual understanding.(p.127)

cranny
• We pocket our pride and go to it, illuminating every twist of character, every dark *cranny* of the past.(p.75)

crash
• High living, a great many fair weather friends, the 1929 stock market *crash*, and a couple of years of Depression, soon relieved me one by one of my worldly goods including my wife.(p.358)

crashed
• Two of them leaped from the table and *crashed* into my head.(p.427)

crave
• He will show you how to create the fellowship you *crave*.(p.164)

craved
• Most of the time therefore, I did not take the morning drink which I *craved* so badly, but instead would fill up on large doses of sedatives to quiet the jitters, which distressed me terribly.(p.176)
• I was the center of attention, just what my sick ego *craved*.(p.407)

craves
• Your man will fare better if placed in such physical condition that he can think straight and no longer *craves* liquor.(p.143)

craving
• Of course an alcoholic ought to be freed from his physical *craving* for liquor, and this often requires a definite hospital procedure, before psychological measures can be of maximum benefit.(p.xxv)
• We believe, and so suggested a few years ago, that the action of alcohol on these chronic alcoholics is a manifestation of an allergy; that the phenomenon of *craving* is limited to this class and never occurs in the average temperate drinker.(p.xxvi)
• After they have succumbed to the desire again, as so many do, and the phenomenon of *craving* develops, they pass through the well-known stages of a spree, emerging remorseful, with a firm resolution not to drink again.(p.xxvii)
• They took a drink a day or so prior to the date, and then the phenomenon of *craving* at once became paramount to all other interests so that the important appointment was not met.(p.xxvii)
• These men were not drinking to escape; they were drinking to overcome a *craving* beyond their mental control.(p.xxviii)
• There are many situations which arise out of the phenomenon of *craving* which cause men to make the supreme sacrifice rather than continue to fight.(p.xxviii)
• All these, and many others, have one symptom in common: they cannot start drinking without developing the phenomenon of *craving*.(p.xxviii)
• He added that occasionally in the night a vague *craving* arose which would be satisfied by candy.(p.134)
• Occasionally, I would yield to the morning *craving*, but if I did, it would be only a few hours before I would be quite unfit for work.(p.176)
• Unlike most of our crowd, I did not get over my *craving* for liquor much during the first two and one-half years of abstinence.(p.181)
• I cannot say, however, that I acquired any *craving* for hard liquor as a result.(p.231)
• I missed the old social times, of course, but had no definite *craving* even for beer.(p.232)
• Never having enough, always *craving* more, the obsession for alcohol gradually dominated all my activities, particularly while travelling.(p.375)
• I wandered, *craving* peace, from one spot to another of youthful happy memory, and loathed the man I had become.(p.539)

crawl
• As God's people we stand on our feet; we don't *crawl* before anyone.(p.83)
• I *crawl* under a pile of blankets and blow out the candle.(p.497)
• I *crawl* back into bed and sleep like a child.(p.504)

crawled
• Peddling off my polish samples for expenses, I *crawled* back to New York a few days later in a very chastened frame of mind.(p.248)
• I *crawled* back to my analyst, not so much because I had faith in him, but because I had nowhere else to turn.(p.435)

crawling
• A wasp is *crawling* up the back of the lady in front of me.(p.497)
• I would wake to find myself in some beat-up rooming house, where roaches were *crawling* over everything.(p.527)

craziest
• We'd start out on the *craziest* trips.(p.264)
• But they are the *craziest* bunch!(p.266)

crazy
• Was I *crazy*?(p.5)
• Such a man would be *crazy*, wouldn't he?(p.38)
• I thought, "No matter how *crazy* they are I'll do anything they say to do."(p.267)
• "I'm not *crazy*," I thought, "and I can't be an alcoholic -- I'm too young."(p.319)
• A lot of lost dreams, empty futures, and *crazy* things of the past went through my mind.(p.333)
• I was *crazy* about my doctor.(p.387)
• Certainly, when I was in my cups, I was not just drunk, I was *crazy*.(p.408)
• Now my whole thinking was *crazy*.(p.408)
• I once hear people say only Indians *crazy* when drunk.(p.477)
• I thought if the cops did come to the hospital, the doctors would tell them I was *crazy* and didn't know what I was doing.(p.528)

cream
• One night at the dinner table my wife said that tonight was my first birthday in A.A., and that the group would have the usual ice *cream* and cake for the "one year man."(p.365)
• The other kids would light out for the hamburger huts or ice *cream* parlors, the pizza joints or bowling alleys, after football games and dances.(p.423)

create
• He will show you how to *create* the fellowship you crave.(p.164)
• I seemed to react by developing a streak of varying meanness, which would cause me to do things to *create* excitement and to get attention.(p.211)
• I studied art; I desperately endeavored to *create* an interest in many things, in a new place among new people.(p.305)
• Now, for me, and to my satisfaction, I know the purpose of life: The purpose of life is to *create* and the by-product is happiness.(p.535)
• To *create*: Everyone does it, some at the instinct level, others in the arts.(p.535)
• For the only problems I have now are those I *create* when I break out in a rash of self-will.(p.551)
• Nine -- A.A., as such, ought never be organized; but we may *create* service boards or committees directly responsible to those they serve.(p.564)
• Though it was not our intention to *create* such an impression, many alcoholics have nevertheless concluded that in order to recover they must acquire an immediate and overwhelming "God-consciousness" followed at once by a vast change in feeling and outlook.(p.569)

created
• Could we still say the whole thing was nothing but a mass of electrons, *created* out of nothing, meaning nothing, whirling on to a destiny of nothingness?(p.54)
• When you have carefully explained to such people that he is a sick person, you will have *created* a new atmosphere.(p.115)
• Perhaps they *created* the impression that he is to be wrapped in cotton wool and placed on a pedestal.(p.122)
• So I *created* a job for myself selling women's hosiery and men's made-to-order shirts.(p.282)
• After such often-painful vigilance (and numerous phony stints of abstinence), retirement naturally *created* an impulse to live without restraints.(p.328)
• But I wanted a cosmos, a universe all my own which I had *created* and where I reigned as chief top reigner and ruler over everyone else.(p.535)

creates
• Sometimes these excuses have a certain plausibility, but none of them really makes sense in the light of the

CHRIST pg 11 second word

havoc an alcoholic's drinking bout *creates*.(p.23)
• It is not good for him, and it sometimes *creates* serious complications in a family.(p.97)

Creation
• Instead of regarding ourselves as intelligent agents, spearheads of God's ever advancing *Creation*, we agnostics and atheists chose to believe that our human intelligence was the last word, the alpha and the omega, the beginning and end of all.(p.49)

creative
• I could go for such conceptions as *Creative* Intelligence, Universal Mind or Spirit of Nature but I resisted the thought of a Czar of the Heavens, however loving His sway might be.(p.12)
• As soon as we admitted the possible existence of a *Creative* Intelligence, a Spirit of the Universe underlying the totality of things, we began to be possessed of a new sense of power and direction, provided we took other simple steps.(p.46)
• When, however, the perfectly logical assumption is suggested that underneath the material world and life as we see it, there is an All Powerful, Guiding, *Creative* Intelligence, right there our perverse streak comes to the surface and we laboriously set out to convince ourselves it isn't so.(p.49)
• My work is on a much deeper and more significant level than it ever was before, and I am today a fairly *creative*, relatively sane human being.(p.438)
• My personal definition, which I submit as applying only to myself (although everyone is welcome to it who wants it), includes every waking activity of the human being; to have a *creative* attitude towards things is a more exact meaning, to live and to deal with other human beings creatively, which to me means seeing the God in them, and respecting and worshipping this God.(p.535)

creatively
• My personal definition, which I submit as applying only to myself (although everyone is welcome to it who wants it), includes every waking activity of the human being; to have a creative attitude towards things is a more exact meaning, to live and to deal with other human beings *creatively*, which to me means seeing the God in them, and respecting and worshipping this God.(p.535)

creativity
• *Creativity* at the typewriter would keep me busy and alert, I said.(p.331)
• Seated at the typewriter, I faked deep thinking or portrayed *creativity* by key-tapping.(p.332)

Creator
• My friend promised when these things were done I would enter upon a new relationship with my *Creator*; that I would have the elements of a way of living which answered all my problems.(p.13)
• The central fact of our lives today is the absolute certainty that our *Creator* has entered into our hearts and lives in a way which is indeed miraculous.(p.25)
• If what we have learned and felt and seen means anything at all, it means that all of us, whatever our race, creed, or color are the children of a living *Creator* with whom we may form a relationship upon simple and understandable terms as soon as we are willing and honest enough to try.(p.28)
• For the first time, he lived in conscious companionship with his *Creator*.(p.56)
• We never apologize to anyone for depending upon our *Creator*.(p.68)
• We have been trying to get a new attitude, a new relationship with our *Creator*, and to discover the obstacle in our path.(p.72)
• We begin to feel the nearness of our *Creator*.(p.75)
• When ready, we say something like this: "My *Creator*, I am now willing that you should have all of me, good and bad.(p.76)
• After consulting with his wife and partner he came to the conclusion that it was better to take those risks than to stand before his *Creator* guilty of such ruinous slander.(p.80)
• So we clean house with the family, asking each morning in meditation that our *Creator* show us the way of patience, tolerance, kindliness and love.(p.83)
• On the third day the lawyer gave his life to the care and direction of his *Creator*, and said he was perfectly willing to do anything necessary.(p.158)
• They had visioned the Great Reality – their loving and All Powerful *Creator*.(p.161)

creature
• An alcoholic in his cups is an unlovely *creature*.(p.16)

credit
• Bill was very, very grateful that he had been released from this terrible thing and he had given God the *credit* for having done it, and he's so grateful about it he wants to tell other people about it.(p.191)
• I give a great deal of *credit* to Doc and Anne for changing our life.(p.270)
• So I went to her and said, "There's only one thing I want in my whole life, and I don't want any commendation; I don't want any *credit*; I don't want anything from you or Janey for the rest of your life except one thing; and that is, the opportunity to do anything you want always, and I would like to start off by doing the dishes."(p.351)
• However, what I had gained materially on the *credit* side of my ledger, I have since learned was more than offset on the debit side by egotism, resentment and dishonesty.(p.356)
• I take *credit* for nothing.(p.463)

creditably
• After much argument they allowed me to return and take my exams, all of which I passed *creditably*.(p.173)
• I conducted myself so *creditably* that I was able to secure a much coveted internship in a western city, where I spent two years.(p.174)

creditor
• Approached in this way, the most ruthless *creditor* will sometimes surprise us.(p.78)

creditors
• We do not dodge our *creditors*.(p.78)
• We must lose our fear of *creditors* no matter how far we have to go, for we are liable to drink if we are afraid to face them.(p.78)
• But you should not deprive your family or *creditors* of money they should have.(p.96)

credits
• After many painful discussions, they finally gave me my *credits* and I migrated to another of the leading universities of the country and entered as a Junior that fall.(p.173)

creed
• If what we have learned and felt and seen means anything at all, it means that all of us, whatever our race, *creed*, or color are the children of a living Creator with whom we may form a relationship upon simple and understandable terms as soon as we are willing and honest enough to try.(p.28)
• His parishioners are limited in number, but his friends are many, for to him race, *creed*, or social position makes no difference.(p.497)

creeds
• We used to amuse ourselves by cynically dissecting spiritual beliefs and practices when we might have observed that many spiritually-minded persons of all races, colors, and *creeds* were demonstrating a degree of stability, happiness and usefulness which we should have sought ourselves.(p.49)

creep
• Dishonest thinking, prejudice, ego, antagonism toward anyone and everyone who dares to cross him, vanity and a critical attitude are character defects that gradually *creep* in and become a part of his life.(p.380)

creeping
• And I remembered the *creeping* horror of the interminable night, in which I slept for short spells and woke up dripping with cold sweat and shaken with utter despair, to drink hastily from my bottle and mercifully pass out again, "You're mad, you're mad, you're mad!" pounded through my brain with each returning ray of consciousness, and I drowned the refrain with drink.(p.224)
• With a *creeping* insidiousness, drink had become more important than anything else.(p.226)
• Cunning, baffling, powerful – the gradual *creeping* up of the frequency and quantity of alcohol, and what it does to a person is apparent to everyone but the person involved.(p.375)

creme de menthe
• We always had cordials after dinner and I know my sister and my brother and I loved *creme de menthe*.(p.384)

crew
• I had a *crew* of men working there and I wanted them to work Sunday afternoons so that I could sell lots on Sunday.(p.195)
• I was the kid of the *crew*.(p.423)

cried
• Men have *cried* out to me in sincere and despairing appeal: "Doctor, I cannot go on like this!(p.xxvii)
• Our friend's gorge rose as he bitterly *cried* out: "If there is a God, He certainly hasn't done anything for me!"(p.56)
• Finally, one morning, I got up and got in the car and *cried* all the way down to the M.'s -- the people who owned the bar – and told her I was licked and wanted help.(p.267)
• Lying on the divan, "getting in the mood" to write, I *cried* openly or inwardly, as I listened to sad songs.(p.332)
• I read sad poetry, *cried*, drank red wine, wrote sad poetry, and drank some more.(p.405)
• She *cried* a bit and went to bed; that was the only answer to problems that she had left.(p.440)
• I *cried* a bit and then mixed me another drink.(p.440)
• I almost broke down and *cried* when I talked with them but I didn't.(p.467)

crime
• "Ace *crime* photographer," that's me.(p.425)
• I was indicted for the *crime* of murder in the first degree.(p.508)
• For that *crime* I received a minimum of twenty years and a maximum of natural life.(p.508)
• In the meantime I had been indicted for the second *crime*, attempted murder.(p.508)

criminal
• Perhaps we have committed a *criminal* offense which might land us in jail if it were known to the authorities.(p.78)

crises
• He it was who convinced me, because his own conviction was so real, that a Power greater than myself could help me in the *crises* of life, and that the means of communicating with this Power was simple prayer.(p.279)
• *Crises* were emerging rapidly.(p.333)

crisis
• When we became alcoholics, crushed by a self-imposed *crisis* we could not postpone or evade, we had to fearlessly face the proposition that either God is everything or else He is nothing.(p.53)
• It isn't always so sudden with everyone, but I ran into a personal *crisis* which filled me with a raging and righteous anger.(p.228)
• Some *crisis* brings you to a point of making a decision to do something about your drinking problem.(p.377)

criterion
• Some of them may sink and perhaps never get up, but if our experience is a *criterion*, more than half of those approached will become fellows of Alcoholics Anonymous.(p.163)

critic
• There are so many to whom I feel deeply grateful; to my husband (and best *critic*), whose generous love, compassion and understanding have helped me along the way; to those before me in A.A. who inspired the first article I read, and the friend who sent that article to Frank; to Ruth for her personal note, and the first A.A. to talk to me; to my Bishop, whose loving and believing spirit inspired me; and to all the members of the Houston Group who were so patient, kind and helpful -- and to countless others.(p.393)
• He forgot to mention that I was the chief *critic*.(p.449)

critical
• Never was I to be *critical* of them.(p.13)
• In this way you can set them on the right track without becoming *critical* of them.(p.100)
• Be sure you are not *critical* during such a discussion.(p.111)
• Let him see that you want to be helpful rather than *critical*.(p.111)
• Just be careful not to disagree in a resentful or *critical* spirit.(p.117)
• Dishonest thinking, prejudice, ego, antagonism toward anyone and everyone who dares to cross him, vanity and a *critical* attitude are character defects that gradually creep in and become a part of his life.(p.380)
• For some reason I can't remember, it finally dawned on me that I had a problem, and yet nobody was very *critical* about it except my family, and that was only because I decided, after seven years of marriage, that I would divorce my husband.(p.386)
• It is painful to grow, and without the help of my "civilian" A.A. companion, big Gene, I might not have survived that *critical* year of adjustment.(p.462)
• Her mother is in a *critical* condition at a hospital.(p.501)

criticism
• The story of how you and your wife settled your difficulties is worth any amount of *criticism*.(p.100)
• A man may criticize or laugh at himself and it will affect others favorably, but *criticism* or ridicule coming from another often produces the contrary effect.(p.125)
• These family talks will be constructive if they can be

carried on without heated argument, self-pity, self-justification or resentful *criticism.*(p.127)
• If the family persists in *criticism*, this fallacy may take a still greater hold on father.(p.129)
• The employer cannot play favorites, but he can always defend a man from needless provocation and unfair *criticism.*(p.146)
• I had always been oversensitive to *criticism* and was acutely so now.(p.556)
• We are granted "the serenity to accept the things we cannot change" -- and thus lose our quickness to anger and our sensitivity to *criticism.*(p.560)

criticize
• Under no condition do we *criticize* such a person or argue.(p.77)
• We ought to sit down with the family and frankly analyze the past as we now see it, being very careful not to *criticize* them.(p.83)
• So cooperate; never *criticize.*(p.89)
• Your husband will sometimes be unreasonable and you will want to *criticize.*(p.117)
• If you both show a willingness to remedy your own defects, there will be little need to *criticize* each other.(p.118)
• A man may *criticize* or laugh at himself and it will affect others favorably, but criticism or ridicule coming from another often produces the contrary effect.(p.125)
• They *criticize*, pointing out how he is falling down on his spiritual program.(p.126)
• The opposite may happen should the family condemn and *criticize.*(p.129)
• Can he talk frankly with you so long as he does not bear business tales or *criticize* his associates?(p.145)
• It's only natural that we don't have the capacity to change, but we ought not to *criticize* those who have, There's another thing I would stress.(p.273)

criticized
• Then we were severely *criticized* by our husband's parents for desertion.(p.106)
• When I was *criticized* or reprimanded, the bottle was my refuge and comfort.(p.556)

critics
• Even the *critics* kidded me about this one.(p.405)

crock
• My wife became pregnant and the doctor recommended the use of port or ale . . . so . . . I bought a six gallon *crock* and a few bottles, listened to advice from amateur brewmeisters, and was off on my beer manufacturing career on a small scale (for the time being).(p.297)

crockery
• They struck the children, kicked out door panels, smashed treasured *crockery*, and ripped the keys out of pianos.(p.106)

crocks
• From that point on, I secured *crocks* of ten gallon capacity and really took quite an active interest in the manufacture of home brew.(p.297)

crook
• By hook or *crook* I usually managed to sober up before I reached home, but always "terribly tired" from a "hard day's work," and just having to have one or two before dinner.(p.361)

crooked
• Can it be appreciated that he has been a victim of *crooked* thinking, directly caused by the action of alcohol on his brain?(p.140)

crop
• When these *crop* up, we ask God at once to remove them.(p.84)

Crosby's
• All afternoon I sat there and drank and played Bing *Crosby's* recording of "Silent Night" over and over again on the juke box.(p.467)

cross
• Alcohol being no respecter of persons, we are an accurate *cross* section of America, and in distant lands, the same democratic evening-up process is now going on.(p.xx)
• I hardly dared *cross* the street, lest I collapse and be run down by an early morning truck, for it was scarcely daylight.(p.6)
• These give a fair *cross* section of our membership and a clear-cut idea of what has actually happened in their lives.(p.29)
• Dishonest thinking, prejudice, ego, antagonism toward anyone and everyone who dares to *cross* him, vanity and a critical attitude are character defects that gradually creep in and become a part of his life.(p.380)
• Making amends is sometimes doing what we are capable of doing but failed to do because of alcohol; carrying out community responsibilities such as Community Funds, Red *Cross*, educational and religious activities in proportion to our abilities and energy.(p.381)
• I started to *cross* out that last sentence, but decided to let it stand.(p.536)

cross-grained
• And when I get upset, *cross-grained* and out of tune with my fellow man I know that I am out of tune with God.(p.237)

crossbones
• One of the earliest memories that I have is of a bottle sitting on his desk with a skull and *crossbones* and marked "Poison."(p.193)

crossed
• "Suddenly the thought *crossed* my mind that if I were to put an ounce of whiskey in my milk it couldn't hurt me on a full stomach.(p.36)
• As I *crossed* the threshold of the dining room, the thought came to mind that it would be nice to have a couple of cocktails with dinner.(p.41)
• She left, and I sat down and *crossed* my hands, and looked up and said, "For God's sake, help me."(p.351)
• When I *crossed* that line, I don't know.(p.386)
• That was the day, that was the decision, I know now, when I *crossed* over the line and became an active alcoholic.(p.531)

crosses
• And we went down through the valley, and I remembered reading about the Ku Klux Klan and how they burnt *crosses*, and I thought, "God alone knows what we are getting into this time!"(p.269)

crowd
• The almost certain consequences that follow taking even a glass of beer do not *crowd* into the mind to deter us.(p.24)
• Several of our *crowd*, men of thirty or less, had been drinking only a few years, but they found themselves as helpless as those who had been drinking twenty years.(p.33)
• Again, you should not *crowd* him.(p.113)
• Hardly one of our *crowd* now shows any mark of dissipation.(p.133)
• Why not bring him into contact with some of our alcoholic *crowd*?(p.138)
• He could see the gay *crowd* inside.(p.154)
• One man and his wife placed their large home at the disposal of this strangely assorted *crowd.*(p.160)
• He succumbed to that gay *crowd* inside, who laughed at their own misfortunes and understood his.(p.160)
• About the time of the beer experiment I was thrown in with a *crowd* of people who attracted me because of their seeming poise, health, and happiness.(p.178)
• Unlike most of our *crowd*, I did not get over my craving for liquor much during the first two and one-half years of abstinence.(p.181)
• Even then he went into no great detail about how he and a *crowd* of alcoholics, with whom he associated, had mastered their difficulty.(p.235)
• So it is clear that I never had any fun out of drinking -- I would be the soberest-seeming one in the *crowd* and all of a sudden I would be the drunkest.(p.241)
• I moved in a gay *crowd* in the various "pubs" and sporting clubs.(p.251)
• It didn't take long for me to fall in with a fast *crowd* who had their lunch in the men's bar of a leading hotel.(p.361)
• They are a joyous *crowd.*(p.504)
• After I had made my third report, I stepped down town, met some of the old *crowd*, and of course you know the answer.(p.510)
• Then instead of going out with A.A. again I went out with some of the other *crowd*, and off again I went.(p.511)
• I don't miss any of the old *crowd* nor do I miss any of their parties.(p.511)

crowded
• It *crowded* out all else:(p.56)
• My life was fairly well *crowded* and I didn't seem to need any stimulants to keep me going.(p.213)
• (We don't have much time for bathing in our *crowded* schedule.)(p.479)

crown
• Like most immigrants I wanted to be somebody and have something and I was very happy and contented as I felt success *crown* my efforts.(p.232)

crucial
• Though our decision was a vital and *crucial* step, it could have little permanent effect unless at once followed by a strenuous effort to face, and to be rid of, the things in ourselves which had been blocking us.(p.64)
• But when things became *crucial*, everything started going haywire and I started going haywire with them.(p.486)

crucified
• Alas for us men toward whom Shaw hurled his cry, "Must a Christ be *crucified* in every generation for the benefit of those who have no imagination?"(p.536)

crude
• At the end of this selling of lots, just prior to World War I, I got into the *crude* rubber business, and six months later there was only one broker and myself left in Akron.(p.197)

cruel
• How heartbreaking was this discovery; how *cruel* to be told they understood our men as we did not!(p.106)
• How could men who loved their wives and children be so unthinking, so callous, so *cruel*?(p.107)

cruelty
• There, I received several soda crackers and water daily, and before I could have my third-day meal (again the only meal in ten days), I had to drink a glass of castor oil or mineral oil, depending on the *cruelty* of the person who was doing the dispensing.(p.459)

crumbling
• It was a fantastic structure, built on a *crumbling* foundation.(p.435)

crumpled
• The walls *crumpled* -- and the light streamed in.(p.228)

crusade
• You will be most successful with alcoholics if you do not exhibit any passion for *crusade* or reform.(p.95)

crusaders
• Dr. W.W. Bauer, broadcasting under the auspices of The American Medical Association in 1946, over the NBC network, said, in part: "Alcoholics Anonymous are no *crusaders*; not a temperance society.(p.572)

crush
• About this time I got my first *crush* on a girl.(p.425)
• They got bigger and bigger and nearer and nearer, as if they were going to fall and *crush* me.(p.427)

crushed
• When we became alcoholics, *crushed* by a self-imposed crisis we could not postpone or evade, we had to fearlessly face the proposition that either God is everything or else He is nothing.(p.53)

crushing
• It was a *crushing* blow.(p.42)

crutch
• Liquor had become a *crutch* on the one hand and a means of retreat from life on the other.(p.277)
• It had been so many years since I had not relied on some artificial *crutch*, either alcohol or sedatives.(p.310)
• But the feeling was a *crutch*, an excuse.(p.534)
• I had to cope with the demands of everyday living without my comforter, my anesthetic, my *crutch.*(p.557)

crux
• So we shall describe some of the mental states that precede a relapse into drinking, for obviously this is the *crux* of the problem.(p.35)

cry
• One set of voices *cry* that sex is a lust of our lower nature, a base necessity of procreation.(p.68)
• Then we have the voices who *cry* for sex and more sex; who bewail the institution of marriage; who think that most of the troubles of the race are traceable to sex causes.(p.69)
• The men who *cry* for money and shelter before conquering alcohol, are on the wrong track.(p.98)
• I felt it certainly must be very depressing to her that I should sit there by her bedside and *cry.*(p.272)
• When he speak from heart, big men *cry.*(p.476)
• Alas for us men toward whom Shaw hurled his *cry*, "Must a Christ be crucified in every generation for the benefit of those who have no imagination?"(p.536)

crying
• I was *crying*, and I said, "Alice says she knows I don't have any part of the program."(p.273)
• Two years later, a month beyond age seventy, I was *crying* for help from A.A.(p.327)
• But somewhere during that time, I remembered

going back on the bunk and *crying* my eyes out.(p.390)
• The doctor said I'd been brought into the hospital like a madman, *crying*, raving, ranting, swearing, completely in the throes of delirium tremens.(p.427)

cryptic
• This caused the rather *cryptic* comment from one of my A.A. friends, when I told my story after coming into the program, that I had always been a cinch for the program, for I had always been interested in mankind, but that I was just taking them one man at a time.(p.548)

cubicle
• In a prison in my native state, I spent eleven months in solitary confinement, bouncing in and out of the "hole" (a bare concrete-and-steel *cubicle*) about five times during those eleven months.(p.459)

cuffed
• On our honeymoon in Egypt, he *cuffed* me around quite a bit, and subsequently hit me some more.(p.405)

Cunard
• Coming out of a pub near the *Cunard* pier I saw the Lusitania standing out in the middle of the Mersey.(p.252)

cunning
• Remember that we deal with alcohol – *cunning*, baffling, powerful!(p.58)
• *Cunning*, baffling, powerful -- the gradual creeping up of the frequency and quantity of alcohol, and what it does to a person is apparent to everyone but the person involved.(p.375)
• She of course didn't realize how *cunning* an alcoholic can be and the lengths to which he will go in finding ways to satisfy the compulsion for more and more drinks after having had the first one.(p.377)
• But I was a careful and *cunning* alcoholic, and this didn't happen very often.(p.399)

cup
• I was a very young married man, having his whiskey in the cupboard over the sink, and when I helped my wife with the dishes at night I would take a *cup* of tea and spike it with whiskey.(p.196)
• So he got me a *cup* of coffee, and a piece of cake, and sat me down and said, "Why, there's nothing wrong with you.(p.348)
• They phoned my husband that I was in jail and in such terrible shape that they didn't know what I would do to myself; and they realized that jail was no place for me, but that he was to wait a while before he got me, because at the time they called him to come over for me I was beating a tin *cup* against the wall.(p.390)
• I set it down and made myself a *cup* of coffee.(p.541)

cupboard
• I was a very young married man, having his whiskey in the *cupboard* over the sink, and when I helped my wife with the dishes at night I would take a cup of tea and spike it with whiskey.(p.196)
• There was an upper *cupboard* full of empties.(p.333)

cups
• An alcoholic in his *cups* is an unlovely creature.(p.16)
• Instead, over coffee *cups*, this man and his wife told me what had been done for them.(p.259)
• Certainly, when I was in my *cups*, I was not just drunk, I was crazy.(p.408)
• In my *cups* I used to tell them off, giving them lengthy advice on how to lead the right life.(p.410)
• In my *cups* I began to say, "I can't stop."(p.412)

curative
• This *curative* power?(p.352)

curb
• You may have to *curb* his desire to work sixteen hours a day.(p.146)
• Well, I'm willing, if it will *curb* this awful desire to drink, this fear of not having a drink, this feeling of always being alone, scared, deserted, sick.(p.430)

cure
• Another feeling we are very likely to entertain is one of resentment that love and loyalty could not *cure* our husbands of alcoholism.(p.118)
• He has just returned from a three-months leave of absence, has taken a *cure*, looks fine, and to clinch the matter, the board of directors told him this was his last chance."(p.138)
• All the other people that had talked to me wanted to help me, and my pride prevented me from listening to them, and caused only resentment on my part, but I felt as if I would be a real stinker if I did not listen to a couple of fellows for a short time, if that would *cure* them.(p.185)
• He explained that he and a man from New York had a *cure* for alcoholism.(p.188)
• I found my friend was there for alcoholism and now he was insisting that he had found the only *cure*.(p.257)
• I began making the rounds of the doctors in the hope that one of them might find some *cure* for my accumulating ailments, preferably something that could be removed surgically.(p.305)
• And I was able to go on the wagon for long periods of time – once for four years, to *cure* an ulcer.(p.328)
• I told her that I was an alcoholic, victim of a disease, that there was no *cure*, only arrestment through total abstinence.(p.333)
• All I do in a very simple way, is to help Him *cure* my patients.(p.351)
• A return to the United States proved effective as a geographical *cure*, and a period of sobriety ensued, with the help of the church.(p.419)
• It would be a sure *cure* and also an adventure.(p.434)
• They were always there because of a nervous breakdown, or for a "rest *cure*" – any reason except because of drinking.(p.471)
• There is no *cure* for alcoholism, but it can be arrested in the program of A.A.(p.480)
• I went in there and asked him honestly if he could give me a *cure*.(p.515)
• He just looked at me and said, "Pat, for you there isn't any *cure*."(p.515)
• So I decided I'd go back and live in Ireland to try the geography *cure*.(p.522)
• To *cure* my dreadful hangovers, I discovered the morning drink.(p.556)

cure-all
• At last I discovered alcohol as a *cure-all*.(p.277)
• Like many of us who went into the service, I thought it would be a *cure-all*, a new life.(p.513)

cured
• We are not *cured* of alcoholism.(p.85)
• She sees she was wrong to make a burning issue out of such a matter when his more serious ailments were being rapidly *cured*.(p.135)
• But this was a man who had experienced many years of frightful drinking, who had had most all the drunkard's experiences known to man, but who had been *cured* by the very means I had been trying to employ, that is to say the spiritual approach.(p.180)
• And then I scratched my head and said to myself, "What a fantastic thing for a man to say, that I *cured* his wife.(p.350)

cures
• My wife wrote away for advertised *cures* for the liquor habit and gave them to me in coffee.(p.235)
• None of the various *cures* of this kind were any good.(p.235)

curing
• Bill looked across at my wife, and said to her, "Henrietta, the Lord has been so wonderful to me, *curing* me of this terrible disease, that I just want to keep talking about it and telling people."(p.191)
• That sentence, "The Lord has been so wonderful to me, *curing* me of this terrible disease, that I just want to keep telling people about it," has been sort of a golden text for the A.A. program and for me.(p.191)
• She was doing fine, she was up and around, and that day her husband phoned me and said, "Doctor, thanks very much for *curing* my wife," and I thanked him for his felicitations, and he hung up.(p.350)
• I am not even there, and if I was there the only thing I could do would be to give her moral support, and yet he thanks me for *curing* his wife."(p.350)
• I thought to myself – what is *curing* that woman?(p.350)

curiosity
• Like most statistics, it doesn't prove anything -- just satisfies a little *curiosity* engendered by the wail "Oh, those initiation fees" that prompted this investigation.(p.399)
• I got a good non-academic education; my intellectual *curiosity* was encouraged.(p.401)

curious
• Disappointed but *curious*, I wondered what had got into the fellow.(p.9)
• Doubtless you are *curious* to discover how and why, in the face of expert opinion to the contrary, we have recovered from a hopeless condition of mind and body.(p.20)
• But there was always the *curious* mental phenomenon that parallel with our sound reasoning there inevitably ran some insanely trivial excuse for taking the first drink.(p.37)
• But the moment I made up my mind to go through with the process, I had the *curious* feeling that my alcoholic condition was relieved, as in fact it proved to be.(p.42)
• Even though your protege may not have entirely admitted his condition, he has become very *curious* to know how you got well.(p.92)
• But he will be *curious* to learn why his own convictions have not worked and why yours seem to work so well.(p.93)
• *Curious* about it, feeling I was missing something, absolutely without any illusions about the aftermath, with no pronounced feeling of patriotism, I joined up with a Canadian regiment, serving a little over two years.(p.253)

curled
• They told Annabelle to take me under her wing, and I shall never forget how she sort of *curled* up her nose and said, "They tell me you drink too."(p.269)

curls
• I remember in my early youth my mother dressed me just as she did my two sisters, and I wore *curls* until I was six years of age.(p.483)
• At that time I started school and that's how I got rid of the *curls*.(p.483)

current
• All changes made over the years in the Big Book (A.A. members' fond nickname for this volume) have had the same purpose: to represent the *current* membership of Alcoholics Anonymous more accurately, and thereby to reach more alcoholics.(p.xii)
• If the family will appreciate that dad's *current* behavior is but a phase of his development, all will be well.(p.129)

curse
• It is a most wonderful blessing to be relieved of the terrible *curse* with which I was afflicted.(p.180)

cursed
• I seemed to be able to snap back the next morning better than most of my fellow drinkers, who were *cursed* (or perhaps blessed) with a great deal of morning-after nausea.(p.172)

cursing
• Again I swayed dizzily before an open window, or the medicine cabinet where there was poison, *cursing* myself for a weakling.(p.6)
• In four or five days I would be hunting all over the place, at home and in my workshop, for the bottles I had destroyed, *cursing* myself for being a fool.(p.234)
• I walked away from that girl grinding my teeth and *cursing* under my breath.(p.322)
• I do recall lying on a cold cement floor and shredding into little bits several pieces of stolen identification cards, and washing my face in the toilet bowl trying to sober up, and screaming hysterically while clinging to bars too high to see out of, and *cursing* everyone that came near me.(p.354)
• Luckily a friend was with me, who dragged me out, screaming and *cursing*, while the bartender threatened to call the police.(p.411)

curtail
• At this time, however, she had an opportunity to go to Salt Lake City on a new project for the government, but she did promise me that if I would *curtail* my drinking and buckle down to hard work she would give serious consideration to my latest proposal and maybe join me at a later date when I got settled.(p.359)

curtain
• This was the finish, the *curtain*, it seemed to me.(p.7)

curve
• The *curve* of my declining moral and bodily health fell off like a ski-jump.(p.7)

cussing
• His wife was *cussing* him, raving at him, "I just brought him over to show you what kind of a guy he is!(p.271)

custodians
• They are the *custodians* of our A.A. Tradition and the receivers of voluntary A.A. contributions by which we maintain our A.A. General Service Office at New York.(p.567)

custody
• He got half *custody* of our child, but later kept her during most of the school terms.(p.402)

customary
• In addition to these casual get-togethers, it became *customary* to set apart one night a week for a meeting to be attended by anyone or everyone interested in a spiritual way of life.(p.159)
• As time went on, I found that it was *customary* to open a few bottles whenever visitors

dropped in.(p.297)

• Apparently I'd grown physically at the ***customary*** rate of speed, and I had acquired an average amount of intellectual training in the intervening years, but there had been no emotional maturity at all.(p.547)

customer

• I also had the notion that I might find a ***customer*** for a car at this place, which was familiar for I had been going to it for years.(p.36)

• Did she have an alcoholic ***customer*** on whom it could be tried?(p.188)

• Yes, she did have a ***customer*** -- a dandy.(p.188)

• From the top of the heap in a few years he had skidded to becoming a shuffling ***customer***, still entering the better barrooms but welcomed by neither mine host nor his patrons.(p.236)

• On the other hand, I was a marvelous ***customer***.(p.410)

customers

• He may, for example, reveal that he has padded his expense account or that he has planned to take your best ***customers*** away from you.(p.145)

• My ***customers*** lost confidence in me to the point where I retained what business I had only because I was a well-trained and reputedly fine craftsman.(p.234)

• "Best in the business, when he's sober," my ***customers*** would say, and I still had a following who would give me work though they deplored my habits, because they knew the job would be well done when they eventually got it.(p.234)

• After a very good week, two of my ***customers*** took me to lunch on Saturday.(p.247)

• While there, two or three more "cash ***customers***" (as Dr. Bob used to call them -- probably because they had so little cash) were shipped in to us from Detroit.(p.282)

• I know now that sixty per cent of the time I drank alone without benefit of ***customers***.(p.287)

• Handling ***customers***, dealers, insurance people, dictation, telephoning, directing new employees, answering to superiors, and all the rest of it.(p.299)

• Every breadwinner, whether trying to impress a boss or to hold ***customers*** in his own business, is fettered by people-pleasing.(p.329)

• I found I could boost my income by figuring out a lot of cute little tricks that the boss wouldn't be likely to notice – filching money from the Coke machine, short-sticking the ***customers*** on oil, and selling oil I'd drained out of other cars.(p.423)

cut

• Out of this alloy of drink and speculation, I commenced to forge the weapon that one day would turn in its flight like a boomerang and all but ***cut*** me to ribbons.(p.2)

• You would expect him, if he were normal, to ***cut*** it out.(p.38)

• Before my drinking had ***cut*** me down completely, I achieved a considerable measure of success, having been a City Councilman for five years and a financial director of Kenmore, a suburb later taken into the city itself.(p.182)

• I had bought a piece of ground in Cuyahoga Falls and ***cut*** it into lots and had a profit of approximately $40,000 and that was a lot of money in those days.(p.194)

• People have wars and kill each other; they struggle and ***cut*** each other's throats for success and what does anyone get out of it?(p.244)

• When I reached a point directly back of our house, where I could have ***cut*** through a friend's garden, I was almost overpowered by the desire to get home, but I made the whole journey.(p.276)

• "We watch the alcoholic performing in a position of responsibility and we know that because he is drinking heavily and daily he has ***cut*** his capacities by fifty per cent, and still he seems able to do a satisfactory job.(p.308)

• She said she ***cut*** this clipping from the paper at about ten on the same night, and at the same time as I called A.A. in Pittsburgh -- some 1300 miles away.(p.367)

• Years of drinking and general high jinks had ***cut*** her off from old friends.(p.414)

• I ***cut*** my hands, my face, my legs.(p.427)

• I merely wanted to ***cut*** down.(p.429)

• To ***cut*** a long story short, I spent seven years and ten thousand dollars on my psychiatric adventure, and emerged in worse condition than ever.(p.434)

• I was not eligible for parole, until -- with God's help, I'm sure – the governor ***cut*** five years off my sentence.(p.462)

• Economic conditions had a great deal to do with it, because I've often heard my father say that his mother would take one of the old time flour sacks and ***cut*** a hole through the bottom and two corners of it and there you'd have a gown.(p.486)

• My salary has been ***cut***.(p.500)

• I wish I knew a short ***cut*** to maturity.(p.535)

cute

• The differences between my father and my sisters, who were school teachers, made an excellent environment for the type of child I was – that is, slick and ***cute*** enough to take advantage of any adult quarrel.(p.210)

• I had no trouble making the right decision when I saw my wife open her purse at the meeting that night and deposit a ***cute*** little angel in the middle of my birthday cake.(p.366)

• I found I could boost my income by figuring out a lot of ***cute*** little tricks that the boss wouldn't be likely to notice – filching money from the Coke machine, short-sticking the customers on oil, and selling oil I'd drained out of other cars.(p.423)

• I teamed up with a ***cute*** little blonde with whom I was working at the office, and for about a year we were inseparable.(p.425)

cutting

• They were awfully good about not ***cutting*** me off.(p.409)

Cuyahoga

• I had bought a piece of ground in ***Cuyahoga*** Falls and cut it into lots and had a profit of approximately $40,000 and that was a lot of money in those days.(p.194)

cycle

• These observations would be academic and pointless if our friend never took the first drink, thereby setting the terrible ***cycle*** in motion.(p.23)

• THE VICIOUS ***CYCLE***(p.238)

• I was caught in a ***cycle*** of alcohol and sedation that was proving inescapable and consciousness had become intolerable.(p.304)

• It also was the beginning of another ***cycle*** in my drinking.(p.360)

cyclone

• He is like the farmer who came up out of his ***cyclone*** cellar to find his home ruined.(p.82)

cynic

• My inability to accept the harsh realities of life had resulted in a disillusioned ***cynic***, clothed in protective armor against the world's misunderstanding.(p.226)

cynical

• If any feel that as psychiatrists directing a hospital for alcoholics we appear somewhat sentimental, let them stand with us a while on the firing line, see the tragedies, the despairing wives, the little children; let the solving of these problems become a part of their daily work, and even of their sleeping moments, and the most ***cynical*** will not wonder that we have accepted and encouraged this movement.(p.xxvi)

• The last two years of my drinking my entire personality changed to a ***cynical***, intolerant and arrogant person completely different from my normal self.(p.376)

cynically

• We used to amuse ourselves by ***cynically*** dissecting spiritual beliefs and practices when we might have observed that many spiritually-minded persons of all races, colors, and creeds were demonstrating a degree of stability, happiness and usefulness which we should have sought ourselves.(p.49)

cynicism

• We try not to indulge in ***cynicism*** over the state of the nations, nor do we carry the world's troubles on our shoulders.(p.132)

• The children are sometimes dominated by a pathetic hardness and ***cynicism***.(p.134)

Czar

• I could go for such conceptions as Creative Intelligence, Universal Mind or Spirit of Nature but I resisted the thought of a ***Czar*** of the Heavens, however loving His sway might be.(p.12)

Dd

D-Day

• January 8, 1938 – that was my *D-Day;* the place, Washington, D.C.(p.238)

dad

• Family confidence in *dad* is rising high.(p.123)
• Sometimes they demand that *dad* bring them back instantly!(p.123)
• *Dad* may be tired at night and preoccupied by day.(p.126)
• But *dad* doesn't give freely of himself.(p.126)
• The family must realize that *dad,* though marvelously improved, is still convalescing.(p.127)
• As soon as his sobriety begins to be taken as a matter of course, the family may look at their strange new *dad* with apprehension, then with irritation.(p.128)
• *Dad* is not so spiritual after all, they say.(p.128)
• If the family cooperates, *dad* will soon see that he is suffering from a distortion of values.(p.129)
• *Dad* may feel that for years his drinking has placed him on the wrong side of every argument, but now he has become a superior person with God on his side.(p.129)
• Though some of his manifestations are alarming and disagreeable, we think *dad* will be on a firmer foundation than the man who is placing business or professional success ahead of spiritual development.(p.129)
• The family may feel they hold a mortgage on *dad,* so big that no equity should be left for outsiders.(p.131)
• This may hang on for months, long after their mother has accepted *dad*'s new way of living and thinking.(p.134)
• I heard my son-in-law coming upstairs, and I asked him where *dad* was.(p.263)
• "Well," I said to *dad,* when the A.A. people kept coming with these lovely cars and looked so nice, "I suppose the neighbors say, 'Now those old fools must have up and died, but where's the hearse?'"(p.269)
• That same year, my wife became fed up with my drinking around the house and called my *dad* in Akron to come and pick me up.(p.288)
• Once *dad* came all the way to Florida to sober me up, after a hotel manager called him and said that if he wanted to see me alive he better get there fast.(p.288)
• My wife could not understand why I would sober up for *dad* but not for her.(p.288)
• They went into a huddle and *dad* explained that he simply took my pants, shoes and money away, so that I could get no liquor and had to sober up.(p.288)
• After a particularly bad Christmas and New Year's holiday, *dad* picked me up again early in January, 1937, to go through the usual sobering up routine.(p.289)
• So I told *dad* that I would lick it on my own, that I would drink nothing for a month and after that only beer.(p.289)
• Several months later *dad* was back in Chicago to pick me up again, but this time my attitude was entirely different.(p.289)
• When I did make it home in 1920, I re-entered school and caught up with my class in a few short months – I actually did a year's work in three months, proving much to the disgust of my *dad* that I could do it when I wanted to.(p.358)
• I had no qualms, because I felt the source of a drinking problem was all in how weak one was, and I wasn't like my *dad* (I thought).(p.370)
• After his death, my mother soon picked up drinking where *Dad* left off, and in a very short time she died of cirrhosis of the liver.(p.370)
• My *dad,* who was a newspaper man and had some connections, had meantime put a stop on me, and I guess that report went all over the country.(p.424)
• I still think *dad* paid him something to let me go.(p.424)
• I got a job with the newspaper my *dad* worked for.(p.425)

• But my *dad* pulled some strings and got in to see me after three weeks.(p.425)
• While I was at Pensacola my *dad* became dangerously ill and almost died of pneumonia plus a heart attack.(p.426)
• Mom and I drank every waking moment because we felt so sorry for *dad.*(p.426)
• I headed home for the most wonderful experience of all time – meeting my "new" parents – mom and *dad* looked different than I had pictured them.(p.428)
• *Dad* got out a jug for me and poured welcome home drinks.(p.428)
• I lost it many times and mom and *dad* would drive me around until I found it.(p.429)
• *Dad,* due to having spent most of his time in a small Virginia town, didn't have any too much money, and the money he had saved and the property he had acquired were in Washington.(p.486)

dad's

• They may be jealous of a God who has stolen *dad's* affections.(p.128)
• Many of us have experienced *dad's* elation.(p.128)
• If the family will appreciate that *dad's* current behavior is but a phase of his development, all will be well.(p.129)
• In the midst of an understanding and sympathetic family, these vagaries of *dad's* spiritual infancy will quickly disappear.(p.129)
• Though the family does not fully agree with *dad's* spiritual activities, they should let him have his head.(p.129)
• This may hang on for months, long after their mother has accepted *dad's* new way of living and thinking.(p.134)
• *Dad's* image for me was that of a big Irish oilman who came up through the school of hard knocks and so had to be a two-fisted drinker.(p.369)
• They were doing very well – at least a fifth apiece a day, except on *dad's* days off when they did some serious drinking.(p.425)

Daddy's

• I had turned eighteen during the trip, and I despondently returned home by jet (on *Daddy's* bankbook) to a pair of miserable, hurt parents.(p.354)

daily

• If any feel that as psychiatrists directing a hospital for alcoholics we appear somewhat sentimental, let them stand with us a while on the firing line, see the tragedies, the despairing wives, the little children; let the solving of these problems become a part of their *daily* work, and even of their sleeping moments, and the most cynical will not wonder that we have accepted and encouraged this movement.(p.xxvi)
• What we really have is a *daily* reprieve contingent on the maintenance of our spiritual condition.(p.85)
• When this happens, they can be invited to join in morning meditation and then they can take part in the *daily* discussion without rancor or bias.(p.134)
• I believe that my once over-weening self-will has finally found its proper place, for I can say many times *daily,* "Thy will be done, not mine" . . . and mean it.(p.229)
• My *daily* consumption of wine was about a quart, but that was common where I lived.(p.230)
• This duty together with my weekly meetings with my fellow alcoholics, and my *daily* renewal of the contract I originally made with God, have kept me sober when nothing else ever did.(p.237)
• As I go along I seem to get strength *daily* to be able to resist more easily.(p.237)
• We can share in the laughter and tears of our many friends, and most important, we can share our A.A. way of life and are given a *daily* opportunity to help others.(p.249)
• I quit the factory and got a job on a small newspaper, going from that to a Pittsburgh *daily,* long ago defunct.(p.252)
• I again became a reporter on a Pittsburgh *daily.*(p.254)
• I began to read the Bible *daily* and to go over a simple devotional exercise as a way to begin each day.(p.259)
• It was simple, they said, and went on to explain to me in their own language the program of recovery and *daily* living which we know today as the Twelve Steps of A.A.(p.279)
• It is, however, only the first of a series of miracles which have followed one after another as a result of my trying to apply to my *daily* life the principles embodies in our Twelve Steps.(p.280)
• It would be wonderful were I able to tell you that my confidence in God and my application of the Twelve Steps to my *daily* living have utterly banished fear.(p.284)
• When he returned, we had practically *daily* meetings from that time on.(p.294)
• This latest part of my life has had a purpose, not in great things accomplished but in *daily* living.(p.295)
• I have stopped tilting at windmills, and instead have tried to accomplish the little *daily* tasks, unimportant in themselves, but tasks that are an integral part of living fully.(p.295)
• I can think clearly and am helped much in my thinking and judgment by my spiritual development which grows *daily.*(p.303)
• He had tried everything from having me attend *daily* mass at six a.m. to performing the most menial labor for his charity patients.(p.306)
• "We watch the alcoholic performing in a position of responsibility and we know that because he is drinking heavily and *daily* he has cut his capacities by fifty per cent, and still he seems able to do a satisfactory job.(p.308)
• In learning to practice these steps in my *daily* living I began to acquire faith and a philosophy to live by.(p.311)
• They *daily* pass into oblivion, alone or with mates.(p.329)
• I haven't written anything about that part of my story, but I believe in a Greater Power which I call God and I ask for His wisdom and guidance *daily.*(p.366)
• We went out occasionally, and I would take a drink to ease the tensions of *daily* life.(p.370)
• The cocktail hour became a *daily* routine.(p.374)
• These thoughts become part of our *daily* lives.(p.382)
• I know that if I do *daily* what I have done for these last thirteen and a half years, I will stay sober.(p.384)
• It pays *daily* in more harmonious relations with my fellow men, in ever clearer insight into the true meaning of life, and in the answering love and gratitude wherever and whenever I have been the instrument of God's will in the lives of others.(p.394)
• At this stage, I began a *daily* mental routine.(p.408)
• For, after those *daily* self-punishing sessions with myself, after the vows to stop, I would change entirely as evening came on.(p.408)
• Evening cocktails were as standard as morning coffee, and I suppose my average *daily* consumption ran a little more or less than a pint.(p.433)
• My *daily* alcoholic consumption remained about the same through all this, with perhaps a slight increase, and my binges remained one-nighters.(p.434)
• So I sat down with me and went over the facts behind the convulsions: personality changes, *daily* headaches, sense of impending doom, sense of impending insanity.(p.444)
• Each ten-day period in the dark hole, I was fed bread and water *daily,* with one full meal on the third day only.(p.459)
• There, I received several soda crackers and water *daily,* and before I could have my third-day meal (again the only meal in ten days), I had to drink a glass of castor oil or mineral oil, depending on the cruelty of the person who was doing the dispensing.(p.459)
• They suggested that I study the A.A. book and try to take the Twelve Steps according to the explanation in the Book, for it was their opinion that the application of these principles in our *daily* lives will get us sober and keep us sober.(p.550)
• By age twenty-two, I was a *daily* drinker.(p.555)

daisies

• It never entered my head that I would have been pushing up the *daisies* if he had decided not to come.(p.479)

Dallas

• In my second year in A.A. we were transferred to *Dallas.*(p.394)

dam

• It's water over the *dam.*(p.78)

damage

• Now we go out to our fellows and repair the *damage* done in the past.(p.76)
• But we must try to repair the *damage* immediately lest we pay the penalty by a spree.(p.99)
• Let them remember that his drinking wrought all kinds of *damage* that may take long to repair.(p.127)
• Alcoholism may be causing your organization considerable *damage* in its waste of time, men and reputation.(p.148)

• But now, with His help and grace, this child of His has paid his initiation fee for good, as long as he remembers to stay away from that first drink (the one that does all the ***damage***) one day at a time.(p.399)
• I was very fortunate indeed not to have suffered any brain ***damage***.(p.480)
• No one had ever told me it was the first drink that did the ***damage***.(p.514)

damaged
• That may be true of certain nonalcoholic people who, though drinking foolishly and heavily at the present time, are able to stop or moderate, because their brains and bodies have not been ***damaged*** as ours were.(p.39)
• One object is to disclose ***damaged*** or unsalable goods, to get rid of them promptly and without regret.(p.64)
• But the head of the house has spent years in pulling down the structures of business, romance, friendship, health -- these things are now ruined or ***damaged***.(p.123)
• It was the usual situation: home in jeopardy, wife ill, children distracted, bills in arrears and standing ***damaged***.(p.155)

damn
• Said the future Fellow Anonymous: "***Damn*** little to laugh about that I can see."(p.157)
• We got along fine for about two weeks, until she told me where to go and to take my ***damn*** bottle with me.(p.318)
• "You've got to space your drinks and take plenty of water in between," or "coat the stomach with a little olive oil," or "drink anything but those ***damn*** martinis."(p.433)

damned
• Scoffers could scoff and be ***damned***.(p.3)
• During this time, I had been threatened, beaten, kissed, praised and ***damned*** alternately by relatives, family, friends and strangers, but of course it all went for naught.(p.300)

dampen
• We find it a real mistake to ***dampen*** his enthusiasm for alcoholic work.(p.119)

danced
• Men ***danced*** with me at parties.(p.402)

dances
• That includes bars, nightclubs, ***dances***, receptions, weddings, even plain ordinary whoopee parties.(p.101)
• During my first year out of college I had endless dates, and went to countless ***dances***, balls and dinner parties.(p.275)
• I lived in New Orleans where, at that time, cocktail parties, ***dances*** and night spots were almost the order of the day -- or rather the night.(p.384)
• The other kids would light out for the hamburger huts or ice cream parlors, the pizza joints or bowling alleys, after football games and ***dances***.(p.423)
• Beaches, parties, ***dances***, movies -- everything.(p.425)

dancing
• I had every advantage a child could have, private schools (several of them), ***dancing*** schools, two colleges, coon skin coats, automobiles, a listing in the social register and all the rest.(p.357)

dandy
• Yes, she did have a customer -- a ***dandy***.(p.188)
• This one was a ***dandy***.(p.407)

danger
• There is the type who always believes that after being entirely free from alcohol for a period of time he can take a drink without ***danger***.(p.xxviii)
• We are then in much less ***danger*** of excitement, fear, anger, worry, self-pity, or foolish decisions.(p.88)
• We think this person is in ***danger***.(p.109)
• But he must see the ***danger*** of over-concentration on financial success.(p.127)
• Alone in the relative safety of my home because I knew I dare not risk the ***danger*** of blacking out in some public place or at the wheel of a car.(p.306)
• Others may idle in a retrogressive groove without too much ***danger***, but retrogression can spell death for us.(p.311)
• Seeing this ***danger***, they came to A.A.(p.315)
• But I knew at that point that I couldn't stop and I knew that I was a ***danger*** to myself and to others.(p.489)

dangerous
• If anyone questions whether he has entered this ***dangerous*** area, let him try leaving liquor alone for one year.(p.34)
• The family may object to this, but unless he is in a ***dangerous*** physical condition, it is better to risk it.(p.90)
• If he is already committed to an institution, but can convince you and your doctor that he means business, give him a chance to try our method, unless the doctor thinks his mental condition too abnormal or ***dangerous***.(p.114)
• When they become too ***dangerous***, we think the kind thing is to lock them up, but of course a good doctor should always be consulted.(p.114)
• These family dissensions are very ***dangerous***, especially to your husband.(p.117)
• We think it ***dangerous*** if he rushes headlong at his economic problem.(p.126)
• Still physically weak, and sober but a few months, he saw that his predicament was ***dangerous***.(p.154)
• We think that each group should soon achieve this ideal; that any public solicitation of funds using the name of Alcoholics Anonymous is highly ***dangerous***, whether by groups, clubs, hospitals, or other outside agencies; that acceptance of large gifts from any source, or of contributions carrying any obligation whatever, is unwise.(p.566)

dangerously
• Yet let him drink for a day, and he frequently becomes disgustingly and even ***dangerously*** anti-social.(p.21)
• While I was at Pensacola my dad became ***dangerously*** ill and almost died of pneumonia plus a heart attack.(p.426)

dangers
• Why was it, when these ***dangers*** were pointed out that they agreed, and then got drunk again immediately?(p.107)
• Boredom sets up every retiree for two chief ***dangers***: obesity and alcoholism.(p.330)

Dannemora
• I spent about six or seven weeks in Sing Sing, and was finally sent off to ***Dannemora*** in the Adirondacks.(p.509)

dare
• It must have been a long time since I had my last drink -- but I didn't ***dare*** ask this stranger for one.(p.223)
• Alone in the relative safety of my home because I knew I ***dare*** not risk the danger of blacking out in some public place or at the wheel of a car.(p.306)
• I didn't ***dare*** hope I might find for myself all that these people had found, but if I could acquire some small part of their intriguing quality of living -- and sobriety -- that would be enough.(p.310)
• I did not ***dare*** to think.(p.406)

dared
• I hardly ***dared*** cross the street, lest I collapse and be run down by an early morning truck, for it was scarcely daylight.(p.6)
• I wondered whether I ***dared*** hide a full bottle of gin near the head of our bed.(p.8)
• We could not be invited out because I would surely get tight and my wife ***dared*** not invite people in for the same reason.(p.177)
• I drank all I ***dared*** in the bar, and then went to my room to finish the job.(p.179)
• I had no answers, and I ***dared*** not ask.(p.223)
• I grew up believing that one had to be totally self-sufficient, for one never ***dared*** to depend on another human being.(p.545)

dares
• Dishonest thinking, prejudice, ego, antagonism toward anyone and everyone who ***dares*** to cross him, vanity and a critical attitude are character defects that gradually creep in and become a part of his life.(p.380)

daring
• His wife came, scarcely ***daring*** to be hopeful, though she thought she saw something different about her husband already.(p.158)
• Many mornings I have gone to classes, and even though fully prepared, would turn and walk back to the fraternity house because of my jitters, not ***daring*** to enter the classroom for fear of making a scene should I be called on for recitation.(p.173)

dark
• By late 1937, the number of members having substantial sobriety time behind them was sufficient to convince the membership that a new light had entered the ***dark*** world of the alcoholic.(p.xvii)
• Now I was to plunge into the ***dark***, joining that endless procession of sots who had gone on before.(p.8)
• How ***dark*** it is before the dawn!(p.8)
• We pocket our pride and go to it, illuminating every twist of character, every ***dark*** cranny of the past.(p.75)
• This picture may not be as ***dark*** as it looks.(p.110)
• The first impulse will be to bury these skeletons in a ***dark*** closet and padlock the door.(p.123)
• Cling to the thought that, in God's hands, the ***dark*** past is the greatest possession you have -- the key to life and happiness for others.(p.124)
• We know our friend is like a boy whistling in the ***dark*** to keep up his spirits.(p.152)
• I used to put eight or twelve ounce bottles of alcohol in a fur lined glove and toss it onto the back airing porch when winter days got ***dark*** enough.(p.176)
• It was getting pretty ***dark*** and I hadn't turned on any lights, when some big fellow stepped inside the door and flipped on the light switch.(p.207)
• I was in a large, ***dark***, rather poorly furnished room -- the living room of a basement flat.(p.222)
• I am anxious to get home after ***dark***.(p.303)
• Each ten-day period in the ***dark*** hole, I was fed bread and water daily, with one full meal on the third day only.(p.459)
• If our hair is half-bleached (with ***dark*** roots), poker-straight, and not combed, this adds to our beauty.(p.479)
• It is the last day of the following October, a ***dark***, rainy morning.(p.502)
• She certainly wasn't in the ***dark*** about my drinking.(p.513)

darken
• This had the effect of making me resolve that when I was free from parental domination, I would never again ***darken*** the doors of a church.(p.172)

darkening
• A titled lady, she still saw her world ***darkening***.(p.400)

darkness
• Many alcoholics have learned they can bring their bottle to a cheap movie theater and drink, sleep, wake up and drink again in the ***darkness***.(p.244)

darn
• "Oh, some ***darn*** thing they've got here in the paper about it."(p.266)
• And now I am doing the ***darn*** dishes every night!(p.352)
• The children kept me sober for ***darn*** near three weeks, and then I went on (please God) my last drunk.(p.549)

dash
• For a while they would be their old sweet selves, only to ***dash*** the new structure of affection to pieces once more.(p.107)
• Maybe a drink -- I put on my hat and ***dash*** off in the car.(p.505)

date
• I have had many men who had, for example, worked a period of months on some problem or business deal which was to be settled on a certain ***date***, favorable to them.(p.xxvii)
• They took a drink a day or so prior to the ***date***, and then the phenomenon of craving at once became paramount to all other interests so that the important appointment was not met.(p.xxvii)
• I can remember occasions when friends recommended me for positions or business opportunities that I wouldn't take because I felt that at some future ***date*** I'd get drunk and they would be hurt.(p.198)
• I thanked him, pleaded business engagements and promised I'd go with him at some future ***date***.(p.257)
• When I came to my aunt, she knew that I had had an unhappy childhood, and she said, "Now, Ethel, you're welcome to have boy friends in our home, but there are two boys in this town that I don't want you to ***date***, and one of them comes from a very fine family, one of the best.(p.262)
• At this time, however, she had an opportunity to go to Salt Lake City on a new project for the government, but she did promise me that if I would curtail my drinking and buckle down to hard work she would give serious consideration to my latest proposal and maybe join me at a later ***date*** when I got settled.(p.359)
• And Frank did set me up for a meeting every night except Friday, when he thought he might have a ***date*** with his girl friend.(p.447)
• I count my sobriety ***date*** from the day I began going to A.A. in prison, not from the ***date*** of my last drink.(p.462)
• And when she broke a luncheon ***date*** with me one Saturday, after I had been in A.A. for about three months, I said, "I'll show her!(p.472)
• Still another friend and temporary host received me at four in the morning from the charge of a policeman who had found me "going to bed" in a garage far

from the last place I could remember having been, a fashionable bar and restaurant in the theatrical district of New York, to which I had repaired after my *date* for that evening, a charming lady of the theatre who had refused my company for obvious reasons.(p.538)

dates

• The birth of our Society *dates* from his first day of permanent sobriety, June 10, 1935.(p.171)
• A.A.'s Number One Group *dates* from that very day.(p.189)
• During my first year out of college I had endless *dates*, and went to countless dances, balls and dinner parties.(p.275)

daughter

• By that time, I had one boy in college, another a senior in high school, and a *daughter* about twelve years old.(p.215)
• Our oldest *daughter* got married; they were living at our house.(p.263)
• Our other *daughter* was in her last year of high school, and one night the new son-in-law and my husband went out to a prize fight.(p.263)
• It turned out that she had been in high school with my *daughter*.(p.321)
• The final decision came when my *daughter*, following a drunk which ruined my wife's birthday, said, "It's Alcoholics Anonymous -- or else!"(p.378)
• The birth of a *daughter* filled me with new fears.(p.402)
• At the wedding, I hope I will also get to see my *daughter* and their mother.(p.463)
• My *daughter* was one and a half years old when I last saw her.(p.463)
• I will be fifty years old next month, haven't seen my son or *daughter* yet, nor my daughter's two children, my grandchildren; but I am grateful.(p.463)
• My parents were due for the holidays that day, and she didn't want them to find their drunken *daughter* there.(p.467)
• To tell you a small part of what my mother's life must have been like: Three of her kids were in jail that year – two sons and a *daughter*.(p.480)
• I think the thing that galled me was that just after Easter I had drawn my salary for two weeks' work and had decided that I was going to send some money to Vi; and above all else I was going to send my baby *daughter* an Easter outfit.(p.493)

daughter's

• I will be fifty years old next month, haven't seen my son or daughter yet, nor my *daughter's* two children, my grandchildren; but I am grateful.(p.463)

daughters

• We had two *daughters*.(p.262)
• And that was how Max and I and our two *daughters* spent Christmas Day, eight years ago.(p.444)

davenport

• One evening I had gone out after dinner to take on a couple of double-headers and stayed a little later than usual, and when I came home Clarence was sitting on the *davenport* with Bill W.(p.216)

dawn

• How dark it is before the *dawn*!(p.8)
• This I would do by going completely "bohemian" for a night, getting drunk and rolling home with the *dawn*.(p.432)
• We pulled up in front of my sister's house just as *dawn* broke.(p.466)

dawned

• For some reason I can't remember, it finally *dawned* on me that I had a problem, and yet nobody was very critical about it except my family, and that was only because I decided, after seven years of marriage, that I would divorce my husband.(p.386)

day

• Six months earlier, the broker had been relieved of his drink obsession by a sudden spiritual experience, following a meeting with an alcoholic friend who had been in contact with the Oxford Groups of that *day*.(p.xv)
• Each *day*, somewhere in the world, recovery begins when one alcoholic talks with another alcoholic, sharing experience, strength, and hope.(p.xxii)
• They took a drink a *day* or so prior to the date, and then the phenomenon of craving at once became paramount to all other interests so that the important appointment was not met.(p.xxvii)
• Out of this alloy of drink and speculation, I commenced to forge the weapon that one *day* would turn in its flight like a boomerang and all but cut me to ribbons.(p.2)
• I rightly imagined that they would some *day* have a great rise.(p.2)
• That was the last honest manual labor on my part for many a *day*.(p.3)
• My drinking assumed more serious proportions, continuing all *day* and almost every night.(p.3)
• Golf permitted drinking every *day* and every night.(p.3)
• Tomorrow was another *day*.(p.4)
• "Bathtub" gin, two bottles a *day*, and often three, got to be routine.(p.5)
• One *day* I walked into a cafe to telephone.(p.6)
• Next *day* found me drinking both gin and sedative.(p.7)
• But it was not, for the frightful *day* came when I drank once more.(p.7)
• Then came the insidious insanity of that first drink, and on Armistice *Day* 1935, I was off again.(p.8)
• With a certain satisfaction I reflected there was enough gin concealed about the house to carry me through that night and the next *day*.(p.8)
• That war-time *day* in old Winchester Cathedral came back again.(p.10)
• This sometimes nearly drove me back to drink, but I soon found that when all other measures failed, work with another alcoholic would save the *day*.(p.15)
• Faith has to work twenty-four hours a *day* in and through us, or we perish.(p.16)
• Each *day* my friend's simple talk in our kitchen multiplies itself in a widening circle of peace on earth and good will to men.(p.16)
• Those of us who live in large cities are overcome by the reflection that close by hundreds are dropping into oblivion every *day*.(p.19)
• Yet let him drink for a *day*, and he frequently becomes disgustingly and even dangerously anti-social.(p.21)
• Then comes the *day* when he simply cannot make it and gets drunk all over again.(p.22)
• In a vague way their families and friends sense that these drinkers are abnormal, but everybody hopefully awaits the *day* when the sufferer will rouse himself from his lethargy and assert his power of will.(p.23)
• The tragic truth is that if the man be a real alcoholic, the happy *day* may not arrive.(p.23)
• Science may one *day* accomplish this, but it hasn't done so yet.(p.31)
• Some will be drunk the *day* after making their resolutions; most of them within a few weeks.(p.34)
• Next *day* we would ask ourselves, in all earnestness and sincerity, how it could have happened.(p.37)
• But the *day* he comes out he races in front of a fire engine, which breaks his back.(p.38)
• One *day* we were told that he was back in the hospital.(p.40)
• One *day* I went to Washington to present some accounting evidence to a government bureau.(p.40)
• It was the end of a perfect *day*, not a cloud on the horizon.(p.41)
• They had said that though I did raise a defense, it would one *day* give way before some trivial reason for having a drink.(p.42)
• He hopes they will never see the light of *day*.(p.73)
• Every *day* is a *day* when we must carry the vision of God's will into all of our activities.(p.85)
• When we retire at night, we constructively review our *day*.(p.86)
• We consider our plans for the *day*.(p.86)
• In thinking about our *day* we may face indecision.(p.86)
• We usually conclude the period of meditation with a prayer that we be shown all through the *day* what our next step is to be, that we be given whatever we need to take care of such problems.(p.87)
• As we go through the *day* we pause, when agitated or doubtful, and ask for the right thought or action.(p.87)
• We constantly remind ourselves we are no longer running the show, humbly saying to ourselves many times each *day* "Thy will be done."(p.87)
• You have to act the Good Samaritan every *day*, if need be.(p.97)
• Your telephone may jangle at any time of the *day* or night.(p.97)
• Let the alcoholic continue his program *day* by *day*.(p.99)
• Both you and the new man must walk *day* by *day* in the path of spiritual progress.(p.100)
• We meet these conditions every *day*.(p.101)
• Some *day* we hope that Alcoholics Anonymous will help the public to a better realization of the gravity of the alcoholic problem, but we shall be of little use if our attitude is one of bitterness or hostility.(p.103)
• Some of us veered from extreme to extreme, ever hoping that one *day* our loved ones would be themselves once more.(p.105)
• Next *day* they would be themselves again and we would forgive and try to forget.(p.106)
• He sometimes drinks in the morning and through the *day* also, to hold his nervousness in check.(p.109)
• Dad may be tired at night and preoccupied by *day*.(p.126)
• One *day* my secretary came in saying that Mr. B—— insisted on speaking with me.(p.136)
• One *day* he told me about an executive of the same bank who, from his description, was undoubtedly alcoholic.(p.138)
• You may have to curb his desire to work sixteen hours a *day*.(p.146)
• The other *day* an approach was made to the vice president of a large industrial concern.(p.148)
• He will work like the devil and thank you to his dying *day*.(p.149)
• Some *day* he will be unable to imagine life either with alcohol or without it.(p.152)
• One *day* they called up the head nurse of a local hospital.(p.156)
• Next *day* found the prospect more receptive.(p.158)
• On the third *day* the lawyer gave his life to the care and direction of his Creator, and said he was perfectly willing to do anything necessary.(p.158)
• They were willing, by *day* or night, to place a new man in the hospital and visit him afterward.(p.159)
• Being a large place, we think that some *day* its Fellowship will number many hundreds.(p.161)
• Some *day* we hope that every alcoholic who journeys will find a Fellowship of Alcoholics Anonymous at his destination.(p.162)
• Ask Him in your morning meditation what you can do each *day* for the man who is still sick.(p.164)
• The birth of our Society dates from his first *day* of permanent sobriety, June 10, 1935.(p.171)
• My phobia for sleeplessness demanded that I get drunk every night, but in order to get more liquor for the next night, I had to stay sober during the *day*, at least up to four o'clock.(p.177)
• I used to promise my wife, my friends, and my children that I would drink no more – promises which seldom kept me sober even through the *day*, though I was very sincere when I made them.(p.177)
• It was not long before I was drinking at least a case and a half a *day*.(p.177)
• It was the *day* before Mother's *Day* and I had come home plastered, carrying a big potted plant which I set down on the table and forthwith went upstairs and passed out.(p.179)
• The next *day* she called again.(p.179)
• Each *day* I would try to find out what His will was, and try to follow that, rather than trying to get Him to always agree that the things I thought of myself were the things best for me.(p.187)
• A.A.'s Number One Group dates from that very *day*.(p.189)
• I know there was even more, something that I hadn't got, and I remember one *day*, a week or two after I had come out of the hospital, Bill was over to my house talking to my wife and me.(p.191)
• During the *day*, looking over the contracts and money in my pocket, I found that I had sold six lots that I couldn't even remember, and didn't even know the people I had sold them to.(p.196)
• I would put off doing anything that I could until the next *day* and, consequently, everything would pile up and then there would be the blackout.(p.197)
• I can remember well thinking that I would quit drinking, really go to work hard, apply myself eight hours a *day*, five days a week, make a lot of money, and then I could start drinking again.(p.199)
• I think the longest drunk I was ever on was eleven days, but usually only two days with a complete blackout for a *day*, and then backing off by drinking as long as I could get anything.(p.203)
• I drank some more and slept through the *day*.(p.205)
• The next *day*, they called me in for an examination, and the doctor wouldn't let me continue working and pardoned me from the plant for ten days because he said my eye had been injured.(p.205)
• So I was barred from the plant for ten days, and during that ten *day* period I was drunk twice, showing how little control these restraints had on me.(p.205)
• My only thought that *day* was getting a drink, and how to get rid of those clowns was my big problem.(p.206)
• On Sunday when I came to, it was a bad, wet, snowy *day* in February, 1937, and Paul and Doc and a lot of other fellows were in Cleveland on business.(p.207)
• The people in the group hadn't been around that

day; part of my family was in Florida and the rest of them weren't speaking to me, so I spent a very lonesome ***day*** and by evening I was feeling very sorry for myself.(p.207)
• The next ***day***, others from the group came in to see me.(p.208)
• The very simple program they advised me to follow was that I should ask to know God's will for me for that one ***day***, and then, to the best of my ability, to follow that, and at night to express my gratefulness to God for the things that had happened to me during the ***day***.(p.208)
• When I left the hospital I tried this for a ***day*** and it worked, for a week and it worked, and for a month, and it worked -- and then for a year and it still worked.(p.209)
• I was always interested in mechanics and after having about twenty miscellaneous jobs, lasting from one ***day*** to two weeks, I obtained a job as a toolmaker apprentice.(p.211)
• The first definite indications of an alcoholic pattern began to arise when I would go to New York on business and disappear, and wind up in Philadelphia or Boston for two or three ***day*** periods.(p.213)
• I became a constant drinker with a terrific fight to control the amount of my consumption each ***day***.(p.214)
• The successful demonstration I had made of my life problems in other respects convinced me that some ***day*** I was going to be able to drink like a gentleman.(p.214)
• When I was about forty-seven, after indulging in all kinds of self-deception to control my drinking, I arrived at a period when I felt convinced I had to have so much alcohol every ***day*** and that the real problem was to control how much.(p.214)
• After two or three years of effort along this line, I reached the point of actual despair that I ever would be able to drink only a harmless amount each ***day***.(p.215)
• However, on a couple of other occasions, Clarence seemed to bob up at the last saloon that I would stop at on the way home every ***day***.(p.216)
• In fact, the last three years of my drinking was a routine of barbiturates in the morning, so that I could stop shaking enough to shave, and then alcohol beginning about four-thirty or five o'clock, with a struggle not to take a drink at noon or during the ***day***, because I had the idea that if I took one drink, I would smell as though I had had a pint.(p.217)
• I'd waked up in strange rooms before, fully dressed on a bed or a couch; I'd waked up in my own room, in or on my own bed, not knowing what hour or ***day*** it was, afraid to ask . . . but this was different.(p.222)
• I came of good stock, of men and women who drank wine all their lives as a beverage, and while they occasionally got drunk at special celebrations, they were up and about their business the next ***day***.(p.231)
• You can all remember that in the first few months after the change, a great many men, who had formerly been used to a few beers every ***day*** or an occasional drink of whiskey, simply quit all alcoholic drinks.(p.232)
• That ***day*** I gave my will to God and asked to be directed.(p.237)
• And I began putting into practice what I was learning every ***day***.(p.237)
• This last real merry-go-round had started the ***day*** before Christmas and I had really accomplished a lot in those fourteen days.(p.238)
• We heard by wireless on the 5th that the Armistice would be signed the next ***day*** (this was a premature report) so I had a couple of cognacs to celebrate; then I hopped a truck and went AWOL.(p.242)
• Routine jobs bored me, but I would take on the toughest one I could find, work ***day*** and night until I had it under control; then it would become tedious and I'd lose all interest in it.(p.243)
• Imagine my surprise when I read in a page one "box" that I had been taken from the theater unconscious around noon that ***day***, removed by ambulance to a hospital and stomach-pumped and then released.(p.244)
• This we did the next ***day***, and what a trip!(p.245)
• I began to read the Bible daily and to go over a simple devotional exercise as a way to begin each ***day***.(p.259)
• We always started out on the Saturday before Labor ***Day***.(p.264)
• I'm pretty near afraid of Labor ***Day*** yet.(p.264)
• So, on that Saturday before Labor ***Day***, I got drunk and set the house on fire -- so we didn't have to paint it.(p.265)
• He gave my husband one and me one about ten-thirty on the eighth ***day*** of May in 1941.(p.267)
• Men from A.A. started coming out to the house the next ***day***.(p.268)
• Almost simultaneously, I discovered that cocktails in the late afternoon and highballs in the evening relieved the many tensions of the ***day***.(p.277)
• When the ***day*** of their return was almost upon me, and suicide was the only answer I had been able to think of, I went into Ralph's room one evening and told him the truth.(p.278)
• The next ***day*** he turned me over to a couple who, although neither was an alcoholic, knew Dr. Bob and were willing to drive me to Akron where they would turn me over to his care.(p.278)
• So I was driven to Akron the very next ***day*** by these Good Samaritans, and turned over to Dr. Bob and the then tiny Akron Group.(p.279)
• Nothing has ever to this ***day*** equalled the thrill of that first case.(p.282)
• With God's help I am able, for one ***day*** at a time, to carry business responsibilities which, not many years ago, I would not have dreamed of assuming.(p.284)
• The most accurate answer I can give you is this: Fear has never again ruled my life since that ***day*** in September, 1938, when I found that a Power greater than myself could not only restore me to sanity but could keep me both sober and sane.(p.285)
• I am very apt to get into quite an uproar for a ***day*** or two before starting, but I do start, and once started, I have a swell time.(p.285)
• By 1932, I was going on two or three ***day*** benders.(p.288)
• He waited until I was completely sober and the ***day*** before I was to head back for Chicago, he told me of a small group of men in Akron who apparently had the same problem that I had but were doing something about it.(p.289)
• The ***day*** before I was due to go back to Chicago, a Wednesday and Dr. Bob's afternoon off, he had me down to the office and we spent three or four hours formally going through the Six-Step program as it was at that time.(p.291)
• The next ***day*** I went back to Chicago and started a vigorous campaign among my so-called friends or drinking companions.(p.293)
• That was my lesson, that one could not take the moral inventory and then file it away; that the alcoholic has to continue to take inventory every ***day*** if he expects to get well and stay well.(p.293)
• Courage to face each ***day*** has replaced the fears and uncertainties of earlier years.(p.295)
• The last ***day*** of my drinking career, I drank twenty-two of them between ten and twelve a.m. and I shall never know how many more followed them until I was poured into bed that night.(p.298)
• It doesn't pay to be seen in the same place at the same hour every ***day***.(p.299)
• It wasn't necessary to report to the office in person every ***day***, and when I did go in, it was just to make an appearance and bounce right out again.(p.300)
• I learned that a person just can't find a job hanging in a dive or barroom all ***day*** and all night, as jobs don't seem to turn up in those places.(p.300)
• One is that I don't remember too many of them, as I was one of those drunks who could be on his feet and attend a meeting or a party, engage in a conversation with people and do things that any nearly normal person would do, and the next ***day*** not remember a thing about where I was, what I did, whom I saw, or how I got home.(p.301)
• I eat three good meals a ***day*** now, and really enjoy them.(p.303)
• The next three years saw me in sanitariums, once in a ten ***day*** coma, from which I very nearly did not recover, in and out of hospitals or confined at home with ***day*** and night nurses.(p.306)
• Why he bothered with me as long as he did I shall never know, for he knew there was no answer for me in medicine and he, like all doctors of his ***day***, had been taught that the alcoholic was incurable and should be ignored.(p.307)
• But this ***day*** my doctor gave it to me straight and said, "People like you are pretty well known to the medical profession.(p.307)
• The next ***day*** I received a visit from Mr. T., a recovered alcoholic.(p.309)
• In time, I found myself looking forward to each new ***day*** with pleasurable anticipation.(p.311)
• Then one ***day***, whammo!(p.319)
• I did try, for a ***day*** or two, but something always would come up that would throw me.(p.324)
• I try to live our program as it has been outlined to me, one ***day*** at a time.(p.325)
• And unless I had some rosy picture of what was going to happen that ***day***, I wouldn't even feel like getting up in the morning at all.(p.325)
• Now I feel so very grateful not only for my sobriety, which I try to maintain ***day*** by ***day***, but I'm grateful also for the ability to help other people.(p.326)
• I said to her one ***day*** when I met her on the street, "What sort of volunteer work do you do?"(p.326)
• We need them so badly even if you can only give one ***day***, or perhaps two days?"(p.326)
• I was afraid to set even one ***day***.(p.326)
• I am trying now, each ***day***, to make up for all those selfish, thoughtless, foolish things I did in my drinking days.(p.326)
• A friend of mine, a golf nut, rushed out on retirement to play every ***day***.(p.330)
• No matter how often I had gone into and come out of alcoholic lows during the ***day***, the pattern bounced me out of bed each night about 2:00 a.m., shaking and hurting in the agitation that always follows a drug's sedation.(p.332)
• It wasn't long before I was drinking all ***day***.(p.336)
• The only incentive that I had, toward the end, for getting dressed in the morning was to get out and get supplies to help me get my ***day*** started.(p.336)
• Easy does it, first things first, one ***day*** at a time.(p.340)
• Surrender to me has meant the ability to run my home, to face my responsibilities as they should be faced, to take life as it comes to me ***day*** by ***day***, and work my problems out.(p.340)
• That life for me is lived one ***day*** at a time, letting the problems of the future rest with the future.(p.340)
• When the time comes to solve them, God will give me strength for that ***day***.(p.341)
• However, I am an alcoholic, so I always looked forward to the ***day*** when I would be able to drink again.(p.343)
• And then one ill-defined ***day***, one ***day*** that I can't recall, I stepped across the line that alcoholics know so well, and from that ***day*** on drinking was miserable.(p.346)
• On the last ***day*** I was drinking I went up to see a friend who had had a good deal of trouble with alcohol, and whose wife had left him a number of times.(p.346)
• It was a long four or five hour operation, a large surgical procedure, and she was on her ninth or tenth post-operative ***day***.(p.350)
• She was doing fine, she was up and around, and that ***day*** her husband phoned me and said, "Doctor, thanks very much for curing my wife," and I thanked him for his felicitations, and he hung up.(p.350)
• Every ***day*** became that much harder to live through, and I began to take a look at myself.(p.354)
• With these new and enlightening doors opening up to me, I was able to make the eventual decision to stop drinking, a ***day*** at a time -- because I, too, was an alcoholic.(p.355)
• I had run away from school to join the army in World War I, but missed it by one ***day*** since the Armistice was signed the very ***day*** I landed in Atlanta to sign up with Uncle Sam.(p.357)
• It was to be short lived, for on the ***day*** before Christmas I completely disillusioned my wife and ruined our first Christmas by coming home from the Rotary lunch dead drunk.(p.361)
• I got through the holidays all right until New Year's ***Day***.(p.365)
• ANY ***DAY*** WAS WASHDAY(p.369)
• Also, I believed I was the image of all domestic virtues, secluded in my washday (any ***day***) refuge.(p.369)
• Gradually the quantity increased, the occasions for a drink came more frequently; a hard ***day***, worries and pressure, bad news, good news -- there were more and more reasons for a drink.(p.374)
• The following spring she left me one ***day*** without giving me any idea of where she had gone, hoping this would bring me to my senses.(p.377)
• We visited most of that ***day*** and attended a meeting that night.(p.378)
• Meetings are both relaxing and refreshing to me after a hard ***day***.(p.381)
• A spiritual awakening soon came to mean trying each ***day*** to be a little more thoughtful, more considerate, a little more courteous to those with whom I came in contact.(p.381)
• "Twenty-four hours a ***day***."(p.382)
• Today is the ***day***.(p.382)
• Doing our best, living each ***day*** to the fullest is the art of living.(p.382)
• Each ***day*** seems to be so much more productive and satisfying.(p.383)
• I lived in New Orleans where, at that time, cocktail parties, dances and night spots were almost the order of the ***day*** -- or rather the night.(p.384)

• Frank, my husband, would come home ***day*** after ***day*** and find me passed out.(p.386)
• Because of this state of confusion and frustration I had hysterics on the seventeenth ***day*** for the first and only time in my life.(p.387)
• My work with other alcoholics has led me, ***day*** by ***day***, into ever wider and richer experiences.(p.394)
• But now, with His help and grace, this child of His has paid his initiation fee for good, as long as he remembers to stay away from that first drink (the one that does all the damage) one ***day*** at a time.(p.399)
• Many of them carried a flask and sandwich case, strapped to their saddles so they could stay out all ***day***.(p.404)
• The horrors of increasing hangover sickness to occupy the entire ***day***; nausea, dry heaves, the rocking bed, the nightmare-filled mind.(p.408)
• One ***day*** soon, the analyses would reveal why I drank and how to stop.(p.408)
• Every ***day***, I feel a little bit more useful, more happy and more free.(p.417)
• My gratitude to A.A. grows deeper each ***day*** I am sober.(p.420)
• They were doing very well — at least a fifth apiece a ***day***, except on dad's days off when they did some serious drinking.(p.425)
• It looked as if the war would be over any ***day***, but I had to go anyhow.(p.425)
• This was fine, but it was just an extra dividend, for I'd made connections by this time and was buying a bottle a ***day*** from the cook.(p.426)
• I stayed in the barracks all ***day***, "making out guard schedules," and getting mildly plastered from the jug under my desk.(p.426)
• Wasn't I drinking more than a quart every ***day***?(p.427)
• To this ***day*** I haven't been able to decipher what I wrote to them.(p.427)
• Next ***day*** remorse would be on me like a tiger.(p.432)
• Once or twice, during my early drinking, I carried it over into the second ***day***, and only once, that I can remember, did it continue into the third.(p.432)
• After a ***day*** or two of grovelling remorse I'd come up with an explanation.(p.433)
• Here was power to live to the end of any given ***day***, power to have the courage to face the next ***day***, power to have friends, power to help people, power to be sane, power to stay sober.(p.436)
• My new wife and I don't own any property to speak of, and the flashy successes of another ***day*** are no longer mine.(p.438)
• After going to school all ***day***, working in the family drugstore all evening, and then studying until one or two in the morning, I would not be able to sleep soundly, with everything I had been studying going round in my head.(p.440)
• If it was one minute after, I'd stay up and act like a martyr all ***day***.(p.441)
• It became progressively harder to get up in the morning, until one ***day*** I asked myself what I would do for a patient who felt this rotten.(p.441)
• I took more through the ***day*** to increase the high, and more to maintain it; when I overshot the mark, I'd take tranquilizers to level off.(p.442)
• And that was how Max and I and our two daughters spent Christmas ***Day***, eight years ago.(p.444)
• The next ***day***, Max called the neurologist and told him about the Mayo psychiatrist's opinion.(p.445)
• One has to be pretty sick to do that, and perhaps one has to be even sicker to come back every ***day*** for a new list, as she did.(p.446)
• One ***day*** as I sat there in the hospital, my psychiatrist walked up behind me and asked, "How'd you like to talk to the man from A.A.?"(p.446)
• The psychiatrist, who had generally been ignoring me, now became quite interested; every ***day***, he would ask me all kinds of questions about the A.A. meetings.(p.446)
• (Today, there is absolutely nothing in the world more important to me than my keeping this alcoholic sober; not taking a drink is by far the most important thing I do each ***day***.)(p.447)
• And I knew that giving up "one drink for one ***day***" wouldn't really do any good.(p.448)
• To this ***day***, I am amazed at how many of my problems -- most of which had nothing to do with drinking, I believed -- have become manageable or have simply disappeared since I quit drinking.(p.448)
• Then, one ***day*** in A.A., I was told that I had the lenses in my glasses backwards; "the courage to change" in the Serenity Prayer meant, not that I should change my marriage, but rather that I should change myself and learn to accept my spouse as she was.(p.451)
• When I focus on what's good today, I have a good ***day***, and when I focus on what's bad, I have a bad ***day***.(p.451)
• Each ten-day period in the dark hole, I was fed bread and water daily, with one full meal on the third ***day*** only.(p.459)
• I count my sobriety date from the ***day*** I began going to A.A. in prison, not from the date of my last drink.(p.462)
• Eventually the ***day*** came when I was dependent upon it even when there wasn't any occasion.(p.464)
• On the ***day*** set for the extractions, on my way to the dentist's I felt a little nervous, so I had a couple of drinks, and after the teeth were out I was very nervous, so I had a few more.(p.466)
• The next ***day*** the ice-bag and I were still in bed -- but we had a bottle too!(p.466)
• My parents were due for the holidays that ***day***, and she didn't want them to find their drunken daughter there.(p.467)
• On the ***day*** before Christmas I telephoned him and told him I was sober and asked him to come home.(p.467)
• I waited all the rest of that ***day*** and paced the floor all that night.(p.467)
• At noon on Christmas ***Day*** I called my family in New York, wished them a Merry Christmas, and assured them everything was fine with me.(p.467)
• To this ***day*** I can't hear that song without remembering that awful Christmas.(p.468)
• The poorest person has no less and the wealthiest has no more — each of us has but one ***day***.(p.473)
• We all one as Great Spirit walks through A.A. like sun walks through ***day***.(p.474)
• Next thing I know, it was next ***day***.(p.474)
• I hear men say, "One ***day*** not drink.(p.476)
• Just one ***day***."(p.476)
• Waitress by ***day***, barfly by night, she drifted down the years into jail.(p.478)
• At one time, I was using twenty caps a ***day***; I nearly died half a dozen times on the street.(p.480)
• We are told to practice the Twelve Steps and Twelve Traditions to the best of our ability every ***day***, one ***day*** at a time.(p.481)
• It is suggested that we do not try to do a lifetime of repairs in one ***day***.(p.481)
• If I work on it every ***day***, it will be easier to be honest with myself.(p.482)
• Of course, in my ***day***, times had changed; she just hadn't changed with the times.(p.484)
• But the week-ends stretched on into Mondays and the time soon came when I drank every ***day***.(p.488)
• The following ***day***, Saturday, he came back and said, "Jim, I owe you for that prescription last night.(p.488)
• The November following, I took a few days off after pay ***day*** to celebrate my birthday on the 25th of the month.(p.491)
• Anyhow, on the 24th, after drinking all ***day*** on the 23rd, I must have decided I wanted to see my wife and have some kind of reconciliation or at least talk with her.(p.491)
• I got very little out of the two hundred, that I drew on that pay ***day***.(p.493)
• It was around noon, a ***day*** or two later, when the telephone rang and it was Ella.(p.494)
• So I put forth some effort that ***day*** to try to stay sober if I could, though my sobriety was just a daze.(p.494)
• The ***day*** is over and business has been not so good.(p.500)
• It is a cold, bleak ***day*** in November.(p.502)
• It is the last ***day*** of the following October, a dark, rainy morning.(p.502)
• I've stuck pretty close to A.A. ever since then, taken it ***day*** by ***day***, not biting off more than I can chew.(p.511)
• I remember the ***day*** I came back to New York.(p.513)
• I use that "Easy Does It" every ***day***, to slow me down a little.(p.516)
• So I don't just take the inventory at night — I take it continually throughout the ***day***.(p.516)
• Then I was sent out to India and from then on drinking just increased and increased, and I started having two or three ***day*** spells instead of just the ordinary concentrated one ***day***.(p.519)
• But if I came back in the usual state, then I'd have to go off for good the next ***day***.(p.523)
• I was taking Benzedrine and paraldehyde quite impartially during the ***day*** then, and by the time I arrived at my first A.A. meeting, I was pretty drunk and certainly doped up to the eyes and completely jittery.(p.523)
• I remember the ***day*** when I decided to drink myself to death quietly, without bothering anyone, because I was tired of having been a dependable, trustworthy person for about thirty-nine years without having received what I thought was a proper reward for my virtue.(p.531)
• That was the ***day***, that was the decision, I know now, when I crossed over the line and became an active alcoholic.(p.531)
• Perhaps a better way of saying it is that, on that ***day***, with that decision, I no longer fought drinking as an escape.(p.531)
• (There was a time, for about three months, when I bought a ten-dollar wrist watch every pay ***day*** -- that is every two weeks.(p.532)
• On that ***day*** of decision, I didn't acknowledge that I was an alcoholic.(p.532)
• The amount of will power exercised to control my drinking during working hours, diverted into a constructive channel, would have made me President, and the thing that made the will power possible was the knowledge that as soon as my ***day*** was finished I could drink myself into oblivion.(p.548)
• I believe this, and I believe too that it is equally impossible to practice these principles to the best of our ability, a ***day*** at a time, and still drink, for I don't think the two things are compatible.(p.550)
• During the ***day*** a friend of mine brought me some magazines to take to a hospital group I was interested in, and I looked through them and a "banner" across the front of one featured an article by a prominent clergyman in which I caught the word "resentment."(p.552)
• Do it every ***day*** for two weeks and you will find you have come to mean it and to want it for them, and you will realize that where you used to feel bitterness and resentment and hatred, you now feel compassionate understanding and love."(p.552)
• "God willing, we . . . may never again have to deal with drinking, but we have to deal with sobriety every ***day***."(p.554)
• On our honeymoon, we had iced champagne by the bedside ***day*** and night.(p.555)
• Despite my wife's entreaties to take it easy that ***day***, I arrived home in bad shape.(p.557)
• Soon my drinking was as bad as ever — all ***day*** long every ***day***.(p.557)
• I was attending a convention in Chicago and carousing ***day*** and night.(p.558)
• I awoke next ***day*** with tubes in both arms.(p.558)
• God willing, we members of A.A. may never again have to deal with drinking, but we have to deal with sobriety every ***day***.(p.560)
• We cast off the burdens of the past and the anxieties of the future, as we begin to live in the present, one ***day*** at a time.(p.560)
• Learning to depend upon a higher power and absorb himself in his work with other alcoholics, he remains sober ***day*** by ***day***.(p.572)
• Historians may one ***day*** recognize Alcoholics Anonymous to have been a great venture in social pioneering which forged a new instrument for social action; a new therapy based on the kinship of common suffering; one having a vast potential for the myriad other ills of mankind."(p.573)

day-by-day

• With increasing guilt and never-ending depression, I was too weak to continue this ***day-by-day*** suicide.(p.355)

day's

• I lost only a half ***day's*** work during these three years.(p.173)
• When they got through the ***day's*** work, part was left which I proceeded to drink.(p.196)
• Drinking was all in the ***day's*** work.(p.251)
• Haunting me through each ***day's*** stupor — and there were eighteen or nineteen such days in this man's home -- was the thought: "Where do I go when his family comes home?"(p.278)
• Through studied sneaky-drinking, I'd become a senior citizen without having lost a ***day's*** work because of booze.(p.327)
• My alcoholism-prone mind, however, reminded me that all great authors had needed a stimulus to build up inspiration and inventiveness before each ***day's*** work.(p.331)
• By hook or crook I usually managed to sober up before I reached home, but always "terribly tired" from a "hard ***day's*** work," and just having to have one or two before dinner.(p.361)
• I was never drunk on the job, never missed a ***day's*** work, was seldom rendered totally ineffective by a hangover and kept my liquor expenses well within my adequate budget.(p.433)

daylight

• I hardly dared cross the street, lest I collapse and be run down by an early morning truck, for it was scarcely ***daylight***.(p.6)
• I would need it before ***daylight***.(p.8)
• If it was ***daylight***, I would go down alleys to make sure no one saw me.(p.527)

days

• He had also been greatly helped by the late Dr. William D. Silkworth, a New York specialist in alcoholism who is now accounted no less than a medical saint by A.A. members, and whose story of the early ***days*** of our Society appears in the next pages.(p.xvi)
• After one of those ***days*** of inferno, I wobbled from a hotel bar to a brokerage office.(p.4)
• Unmindful of his welfare, I thought only of recapturing the spirit of other ***days***.(p.9)
• In the early ***days*** of our drinking we occasionally remained sober for a year or more, becoming serious drinkers again later.(p.34)
• For a few ***days*** he was depressed about his condition.(p.39)
• The driver escorted me about for several ***days***.(p.41)
• Students of ancient history tell us that the intellect of men in those ***days*** was equal to the best of today.(p.51)
• Perhaps you will want to take the man into your home for a few ***days***.(p.96)
• Why sit with a long face in places where there is drinking, sighing about the good old ***days***.(p.102)
• Then, in ***days***, weeks, or months, a fresh outburst.(p.105)
• The good old ***days*** will soon be back, they think.(p.123)
• During those first ***days*** of convalescence, this will do more to insure his sobriety than anything else.(p.129)
• Not long afterward he had called me from Hartford on two successive ***days***, so drunk he could hardly speak.(p.136)
• Four ***days*** before he had hanged himself in his woodshed.(p.137)
• But not so with us in those last ***days*** of heavy drinking.(p.151)
• Two ***days*** later, a future fellow of Alcoholics Anonymous stared glassily at the strangers beside his bed.(p.157)
• Every few ***days*** this doctor suggests our approach to one of his patients.(p.162)
• This was only a few ***days*** ago at this writing.(p.163)
• I used to put eight or twelve ounce bottles of alcohol in a fur lined glove and toss it onto the back airing porch when winter ***days*** got dark enough.(p.176)
• Away from my office two or three weeks at a time; horrible ***days*** and nights when I would lie on the floor of my home, lying awake and reaching over to get the bottle, taking a drink and going back into oblivion.(p.184)
• During the first six months of 1935, I was hospitalized eight times for intoxication and shackled to the bed two or three ***days*** before I even knew where I was.(p.184)
• Whether you quit six ***days***, months, or years, if you go out and take a drink or two you'll end up in this hospital tied down, just like you have been in these past six months.(p.187)
• Two ***days*** before this, Dr. Bob had said to me, "If you and I are going to stay sober, we had better get busy."(p.188)
• It was in the next two or three ***days*** after I had first met Doc and Bill, that I finally came to a decision to turn my will over to God and to go along with this program the best that I could.(p.189)
• I had bought a piece of ground in Cuyahoga Falls and cut it into lots and had a profit of approximately $40,000 and that was a lot of money in those ***days***.(p.194)
• Akron was really on the boom in those ***days***, 1919-1920; expansion was terrific.(p.198)
• I can remember well thinking that I would quit drinking, really go to work hard, apply myself eight hours a day, five ***days*** a week, make a lot of money, and then I could start drinking again.(p.199)
• I remember one occasion when I did not drink for three hundred and sixty-four ***days***, but I didn't quite make the year.(p.200)
• I told him that I had not had a drink for ninety ***days*** and that I had come to the conclusion that I was one of those individuals who couldn't drink.(p.200)
• On that statement and the fact that I had been sober for ninety ***days***, he gave me a job selling lots in an allotment he had.(p.200)
• After drinking one glass of beer at the end of my work period for about five ***days***, I thought I'd better find out whether I really had the stuff licked.(p.203)
• I think the longest drunk I was ever on was eleven ***days***, but usually only two ***days*** with a complete blackout for a day, and then backing off by drinking as long as I could get anything.(p.203)
• When I had been in the hospital ten ***days***, Sister Ignatia, who has played such a part in the development of A.A. in this area, stuck her head in the door one morning and announced, looking at me quizzically, that they might be able to make something human out of my face after all.(p.205)
• And at the end of fourteen ***days***, they let me out.(p.205)
• Three ***days*** later I went to work.(p.205)
• The next day, they called me in for an examination, and the doctor wouldn't let me continue working and pardoned me from the plant for ten ***days*** because he said my eye had been injured.(p.205)
• So I was barred from the plant for ten ***days***, and during that ten day period I was drunk twice, showing how little control these restraints had on me.(p.205)
• One morning, after I had been on a binge for a couple of ***days***, I awoke to find my brother and Doctor Bob in my room talking to me about not drinking.(p.206)
• That was at the end of eight ***days*** in which I had had no liquor.(p.218)
• Before long I had a definite taste for hard liquor, knew nausea and headaches I had never known before, but as in the old ***days***, I suffered them out.(p.233)
• In four or five ***days*** I would be hunting all over the place, at home and in my workshop, for the bottles I had destroyed, cursing myself for being a fool.(p.234)
• This last real merry-go-round had started the day before Christmas and I had really accomplished a lot in those fourteen ***days***.(p.238)
• After a couple of ***days*** in dollar hotels and one night in the pokey, I finally landed on my mother's doorstep -- shaking apart, with several days' beard and, of course, broke as usual.(p.238)
• Had he come two or three ***days*** later I think I would have thrown him out, but he hit when I was open for anything.(p.239)
• No one in that company saw me again -- ten ***days*** later I wired my resignation.(p.243)
• In those ***days*** we really took each other's inventories firmly and often.(p.245)
• I had completely forgotten the January 8th when I found the fellowship, and I spent the next four ***days*** wandering around New England half drunk, by which I mean I couldn't get drunk and I couldn't get sober.(p.247)
• Peddling off my polish samples for expenses, I crawled back to New York a few ***days*** later in a very chastened frame of mind.(p.248)
• She had just come in and was scheduled to sail in two ***days***.(p.252)
• In those ***days*** my system was always to drink up my last pay check and believe that necessity would bring the next job.(p.256)
• Some ***days*** later, after he had been discharged, a stranger came into my shop in the nearby town.(p.257)
• He knew too well that didn't mean a thing, just as I knew in my heart that it would be only a question of time -- a few ***days***, a week, or even a month, it was inevitable – till I would be off on another bender.(p.257)
• I had been drinking heavily from one state of semi-coma to another and it was several ***days*** before I got "defogged," but subconsciously I was in earnest about wanting to quit liquor forever.(p.258)
• I had never, since the believing ***days*** of childhood, been able to conceive an authority directing the universe.(p.259)
• But in those ***days*** I had no one to whom I might take my troubles.(p.260)
• Haunting me through each day's stupor -- and there were eighteen or nineteen such ***days*** in this man's home – was the thought: "Where do I go when his family comes home?"(p.278)
• We spent two ***days*** there together before he returned to New York.(p.281)
• This gave me the freedom to do A.A. work, and to rest for periods of two or three ***days*** when I became too exhausted to carry on.(p.283)
• Then when we got back to the apartment, he was willing to wait two or three ***days*** until I got my health back to be paid off for the liquor and fare.(p.289)
• This consisted of walking the floor for three or four ***days*** and nights until I could take nourishment.(p.289)
• In the next two or three ***days*** the balance of this handful of men contacted me, encouraged me, and told me how they were trying to live this program of recovery and the fun they were having doing it.(p.291)
• A week later, I had to get an old friend from Akron to spend two ***days*** sobering me up.(p.293)
• I spent several ***days*** with him, but I did not feel adequate to pass the program on to him alone.(p.294)
• I made arrangements to enter the hospital three ***days*** later and promptly went out and got stiff for three ***days***.(p.302)
• After being in the hospital for several ***days***, a plan of living was outlined to me.(p.302)
• Other ***days***, I had to miss work because I was still too drunk to stand up.(p.318)
• In the old ***days*** I hated to wake up and look back at what last night was like.(p.325)
• We need them so badly even if you can only give one day, or perhaps two ***days***?"(p.326)
• I am trying now, each day, to make up for all those selfish, thoughtless, foolish things I did in my drinking ***days***.(p.326)
• I did go to A.A., two ***days*** later, walking in alone.(p.334)
• The encouragement received in the early ***days***, especially from the A.A. General Service Office, made a tremendous difference to my sobriety.(p.342)
• In those ***days***, I was doing a staff appointment in the army headquarters in New Delhi.(p.343)
• This was my first long vacation of sixty ***days*** since I had joined the army.(p.343)
• About two ***days*** later I was called by a friend of mine from Nevada City – he's a brother of my wife's closest friend.(p.347)
• He has loaned it to me and I did my job, but that ended nine ***days*** ago.(p.351)
• I would follow certain drinking schedules or diets faithfully for a few ***days***, and then somewhere along the line would over-train and upset the applecart.(p.361)
• In my drinking ***days***, I found the ideal spot for the alcoholic housewife: the neighborhood Laundromat.(p.369)
• We lived a kind of seesaw existence in the early ***days***.(p.369)
• In a few ***days*** an attorney called on me and explained that something would have to be done as she couldn't face returning to me as I was.(p.377)
• You didn't carry a little orchid up the aisle in those ***days***; you carried a great big bouquet, like a funeral spray, and you didn't have your picture taken until just before you went to the church.(p.385)
• But they kept me there -- I was supposed to stay a month, but they only kept me there seventeen ***days***.(p.387)
• Age and the law were still against me, but laws were not as strictly enforced in those ***days*** as they are now, and I discovered that as long as I had the green blood, there was always a way to get alcohol, either from a nondiscriminatory bartender or from an older friend who would be glad to purchase the joy juice for the privilege of sharing it.(p.397)
• In those ***days***, psychiatry and A.A. had not gotten together as they have since.(p.412)
• In those ***days*** the A.A. Foundation was down in the Wall Street district of New York.(p.413)
• In those ***days*** there was only one big meeting a week in New York.(p.414)
• The farm, in those ***days***, was primitive.(p.415)
• The last time I drank, when I was twenty-nine, I drank for only four ***days***, yet I threatened to kill my children; I beat my wife at home and on the church steps; I mistreated a child in my office; and I ran to a hospital for mental illness to avoid jail.(p.418)
• I was skipping classes about two ***days*** a week and doing no book work whatever.(p.423)
• I spent the next three ***days*** in a cell.(p.424)
• They were doing very well – at least a fifth apiece a day, except on dad's ***days*** off when they did some serious drinking.(p.425)
• I got emergency leave for twenty ***days***.(p.426)
• He even went to bat for me before the court martial that inevitably followed and, as a result, I drew only thirty ***days*** -- fifteen in solitary.(p.428)
• Three ***days*** later I lost my job.(p.430)
• In seven years the intervals between them decreased from eight months to ten ***days***!(p.434)
• Perhaps the single flicker of decency that shone through the fog of my drinking ***days*** was a clumsy affection for my two children, a boy and a girl.(p.437)
• After nine ***days*** of tests at Mayo, I was put in the locked ward – of all places!(p.444)
• Although we enjoyed the laughter in the early ***days***, I heard a lot of things that I thought were stupid.(p.447)
• There, I received several soda crackers and water

daily, and before I could have my third-day meal (again the only meal in ten *days*), I had to drink a glass of castor oil or mineral oil, depending on the cruelty of the person who was doing the dispensing.(p.459)
• Ten *days* of this treatment the first time knocked me from 200 pounds to 130, and I seldom stayed out of the hole long enough to gain back my weight.(p.460)
• In those *days*, I trusted no church-goer, and thought A.A. was for weaklings.(p.460)
• Only a few *days* before Christmas I went to the dentist for a periodic checkup.(p.465)
• I was frightened -- terribly frightened, and in about three *days* I was sober.(p.467)
• After the first two or three *days* you were allowed the run of the place and it was a lot of fun.(p.468)
• This easy method of sobering up would last at least three *days*.(p.468)
• Then I black out and get home four *days* later.(p.475)
• Oh, I was beautiful in those *days*!(p.479)
• After our first child came my parents both became allies, but in later *days*, after I became an alcoholic, they both turned against me.(p.485)
• But I can remember in post graduate *days*, and during interneship, that very often I'd go to a patient's bed and start a process of elimination and then, very often, I'd wind up guessing.(p.485)
• I was out of work for about four *days*.(p.490)
• I went back to my mother's for a few *days* until things cooled off, because the District Attorney had put out a summons for me to come to see him in his office.(p.491)
• Within about ten *days* I got locked up for being drunk and this same policeman was in the station house as I was being booked.(p.491)
• The November following, I took a few *days* off after pay day to celebrate my birthday on the 25th of the month.(p.491)
• I'd been home about a week or ten *days* when one of my friends asked if I could repair one of his electrical outlets.(p.493)
• "I went out of here nine *days* ago saying that I was going to be honest, and I wasn't," he answers.(p.503)
• When I wended my way home four *days* later, on the 27th, there was a detective waiting for me.(p.508)
• The *days* have grown into a little better than four years of sobriety.(p.511)
• I was going to be sent to the Indian Civil Service, which, in those *days*, meant that people thought you had a certain amount of brains.(p.517)
• At first, like everybody else, I could keep control when I drank, but if I did start to drink, even in those *days*, I was always one of the last to leave the party.(p.518)
• They kept me in hospital for two months, and then they sent me up to Egypt, a three *days* journey.(p.521)
• Everybody I had known in the old *days* had gone.(p.522)
• Providentially, this was a Monday might when the Dublin Group met in those *days*, and my family agreed that if A.A. could do anything for me at all, that I'd be allowed to stay on at home on probation.(p.523)
• I got out on bail right away, but when I went to trial, the judge gave me thirty *days*.(p.528)
• When my thirty *days* were up, I started back on my rounds.(p.528)
• It paid for a ten-day binge which was the end of my drinking *days*.(p.540)
• Thank God that those *days* are gone.(p.540)
• I was drunk for sixty *days* around the clock and it was my intention, literally, to drink myself to death.(p.549)
• Within a few *days*, I found myself drying out on a drunk farm.(p.559)
• As the sober *days* grew into sober months and then into sober years, a new and beautiful life began to emerge from the shambles of my former existence.(p.559)
• By learning -- through practicing the Twelve Steps and through sharing at meetings – how to cope with the problems that we looked to booze to solve, back in our drinking *days*.(p.560)
• The *days* add up into weeks, the weeks into months and years."(p.572)

days'

• This dry spell lasted for about three weeks; then I went to Atlantic City to attend several *days'* meeting of a national society of which I was a member.(p.179)
• After a couple of days in dollar hotels and one night in the pokey, I finally landed on my mother's door-step -- shaking apart, with several *days'* beard and, of course, broke as usual.(p.238)
• The judge said that if she felt that way he would confine me for thirty *days'* examination and observation.(p.492)

daytime

• In January 1938, I had the opportunity to go to northern Vermont to manage a small *daytime* radio station that was up against it financially, and was about to fold its antenna.(p.359)

daze

• So I put forth some effort that day to try to stay sober if I could, though my sobriety was just a *daze*.(p.494)

dazed

• Many a man, yet *dazed* from his hospital experience, has stepped over the threshold of that home into freedom.(p.160)
• It left us *dazed*, because he had seemed so indestructible.(p.370)

dazzling

• Our shoes are not better than the average hobo's, and if we are fortunate enough to have a pair of stockings on, nobody notices the runs in them, because of our *dazzling* beauty and our dirty feet.(p.479)

deacon

• I was at one time a *deacon* in the church and I still believe in God.(p.189)
• I was a *deacon* and a Sunday-school teacher.(p.418)

dead

• Then he had, in effect, been raised from the *dead*, suddenly taken from the scrap heap to a level of life better than the best he had ever known!(p.11)
• Faith without works was *dead*, he said.(p.14)
• Then faith would be *dead* indeed.(p.15)
• Though a robust man at retirement, he went to pieces quickly and was *dead* within four years.(p.33)
• Now we need more action, without which we find that "Faith without works is *dead*."(p.76)
• Had this not been so, many of us would have no homes today, would perhaps be *dead*.(p.82)
• Sweet relationships are *dead*.(p.82)
• "Faith without works is *dead*."(p.88)
• Of course our friend was wrong – *dead* wrong.(p.135)
• If she had not, I know I would have been *dead* a long time ago.(p.178)
• It was to be short lived, for on the day before Christmas I completely disillusioned my wife and ruined our first Christmas by coming home from the Rotary lunch *dead* drunk.(p.361)
• But when this happened to me, I declared to friends that I would get drunk, *dead* drunk that very night, and stay drunk for a month.(p.403)
• There was no central heating, and this was the *dead* of winter.(p.415)
• I was living, but I was *dead*.(p.460)
• The trip back was completed in one of those *dead*, awful silences.(p.467)
• It read something like this: "Faith without works is *dead*.(p.473)
• I wish I were *dead*, as I have often wished before.(p.502)

dead-end

• So here, in this dive, this hangout for *dead-end* alcoholics and neurotics, here was I.(p.410)

deadlock

• We went through two years of *deadlock* required by the English divorce laws.(p.405)

deadly

• But just underneath there is *deadly* earnestness.(p.16)
• Never forget that resentment is a *deadly* hazard to an alcoholic.(p.117)
• Then Prohibition came into effect, and the facts that the stuff obtainable was so horrible and sometimes *deadly*, and that I had married and had a job which I had to look after, helped me for a period of some three or four years, although I would get drunk every time I could get hold of enough to drink to get started.(p.183)
• Bruised, and *deadly* ashamed, I told no one.(p.406)

deal

• With the appearance of the new book a great *deal* began to happen.(p.xvii)
• I have had many men who had, for example, worked a period of months on some problem or business *deal* which was to be settled on a certain date, favorable to them.(p.xxvii)
• Sometimes a small *deal* would net a few hundred dollars, and I would pay my bills at the bars and delicatessens.(p.5)
• A man of thirty was doing a great *deal* of spree drinking.(p.32)
• Remember that we *deal* with alcohol – cunning, baffling, powerful!(p.58)
• Arranging the best *deal* we can we let these people know we are sorry.(p.78)
• Don't *deal* with him when he is very drunk, unless he is ugly and the family needs your help.(p.90)
• He will feel he can *deal* with you without being nagged by his family.(p.91)
• Oddly enough, he is often difficult to *deal* with.(p.110)
• If he is enthusiastic your cooperation will mean a great *deal*.(p.113)
• A few of us have had these growing pains and they hurt a great *deal*.(p.124)
• We do talk about each other a great *deal*, but we almost invariably temper such talk by a spirit of love and tolerance.(p.125)
• Meanwhile, we are sure a great *deal* can be accomplished by the use of the book alone.(p.144)
• We, who have collectively seen a great *deal* of business life, at least from the alcoholic angle, had to smile at this gentleman's sincere opinion.(p.149)
• As we shall see, he now means a great *deal* to his community, and the major liabilities of thirty years of hard drinking have been repaired in four.(p.156)
• I seemed to be able to snap back the next morning better than most of my fellow drinkers, who were cursed (or perhaps blessed) with a great *deal* of morning-after nausea.(p.172)
• This had little effect however for I kept on drinking and used a great *deal* more hard liquor than in former years.(p.174)
• It must be remembered that I had read a great *deal* and talked to everyone who knew, or thought they knew anything about the subject of alcoholism.(p.180)
• I spend a great *deal* of time passing on what I learned to others who want and need it badly.(p.180)
• I could work a *deal* up to where all I had to do was to go ahead with it; all the planning had been done, all the financing had been done, but then I'd say "Nuts to it!" and walk away.(p.197)
• At that particular stage, I lost interest in it, sold the option for $5,000 and forgot the whole *deal*.(p.198)
• With a great *deal* of determination, I would throw out full pints – pour them out and smash the bottles -- firmly resolved never to take another drink of the stuff.(p.234)
• I very early came to see that there had to be a continual renewal for that simple *deal* with God; that I had perpetually to keep the bargain.(p.237)
• I give a great *deal* of credit to Doc and Anne for changing our life.(p.270)
• Shortly thereafter, aided by the Depression, I found that I had a great *deal* of spare time and that a little drink in the morning helped.(p.287)
• I spent a great *deal* of time with Dr. Bob, whenever he had the time to spare, and in the homes of two or three other people, trying to see how the family lived the program.(p.291)
• I have had my share of problems, heartaches and disappointments, because that is life, but also I have known a great *deal* of joy, and a peace that is the handmaiden of an inner freedom, I have a wealth of friends and, with my A.A. friends, an unusual quality of fellowship.(p.312)
• On the last day I was drinking I went up to see a friend who had had a good *deal* of trouble with alcohol, and whose wife had left him a number of times.(p.346)
• All I can remember about the Roaring Twenties is that I drank a great *deal*, thought I was having a grand time, managed to get to Europe for a few weeks, was very proud of the dozens of speak-easy cards entitling me to an entree in the better joints between Cleveland and New York, took on a wife, and built a home in a fashionable suburb of Cleveland.(p.358)
• My first meeting gave me a great *deal* of hope and lots of willing ears for my tale of woe and for my questions.(p.364)
• You'll read and hear a great *deal* about the spiritual part of our program.(p.366)
• Above all, he noticed that I drank a good *deal*, often got tight in his company and told him naughty stories.(p.403)
• I have achieved the inner confidence to write quite unlike Shakespeare, and I have sold a good *deal* of what I've written.(p.416)
• It helped me a great *deal* to become convinced that alcoholism was a disease, not a moral issue; that I had been drinking as a result of a compulsion, even though I had not been aware of the compulsion at the time; and that sobriety was not a matter of will-power.(p.448)

• When we ***deal*** in feelings, we tend to come to know ourselves and each other much better.(p.451)
• This means a great ***deal*** to me, because I had always figured that nobody cared.(p.481)
• That hurt and disturbed me a great ***deal***.(p.484)
• My father had come out of the South and had suffered a great ***deal*** down there.(p.485)
• Economic conditions had a great ***deal*** to do with it, because I've often heard my father say that his mother would take one of the old time flour sacks and cut a hole through the bottom and two corners of it and there you'd have a gown.(p.486)
• I had a long talk with a psychiatrist, but nothing came of that, and I had also, just about that time, talked with a minister for whom I had a great ***deal*** of respect.(p.489)
• She asked me if I would let someone come up and talk to me concerning a business ***deal***.(p.494)
• I asked her just what this ***deal*** was, but she wouldn't say.(p.494)
• They taught us a great ***deal*** about Twelve Step work too.(p.496)
• There was a great ***deal*** of difference.(p.513)
• I found a great ***deal*** of friendship in this movement.(p.516)
• Lots of the older people had taken to drinking quite a good ***deal*** more during the war, but the younger generation was, I think, about the same.(p.518)
• My personal definition, which I submit as applying only to myself (although everyone is welcome to it who wants it), includes every waking activity of the human being; to have a creative attitude towards things is a more exact meaning, to live and to ***deal*** with other human beings creatively, which to me means seeing the God in them, and respecting and worshipping this God.(p.535)
• "God willing, we . . . may never again have to ***deal*** with drinking, but we have to ***deal*** with sobriety every day."(p.554)
• But my thinking was still confused, and I was still unable to ***deal*** with the challenges of everyday living without help.(p.558)
• I have learned to ***deal*** with disappointments and problems that once would have sent me right to the bottle.(p.559)
• God willing, we members of A.A. may never again have to ***deal*** with drinking, but we have to ***deal*** with sobriety every day.(p.560)
• Dr. Harry M. Tiebout, psychiatrist: "As a psychiatrist, I have thought a great ***deal*** about the relationship of my specialty to A.A. and I have come to the conclusion that our particular function can very often lie in preparing the way for the patient to accept any sort of treatment or outside help.(p.571)

dealer

• I really worked for several weeks, and having had a fairly wide acquaintance with the ***dealer*** trade, it was not difficult for me to line up enough of them to give me a very substantial volume of business with a minimum of effort.(p.300)

dealers

• Handling customers, ***dealers***, insurance people, dictation, telephoning, directing new employees, answering to superiors, and all the rest of it.(p.299)
• After being fired, I lined up with a new finance company that was just starting in business, and took the position of business promotion man, contacting automobile ***dealers***.(p.300)

dealing

• In ***dealing*** with resentments, we set them on paper.(p.64)
• Keep it always in sight that we are ***dealing*** with that most terrible human emotion – jealousy.(p.82)
• They should be patient, realizing they are ***dealing*** with a sick person.(p.90)
• When ***dealing*** with such a person, you had better use everyday language to describe spiritual principles.(p.93)
• We are ***dealing*** only with general principles common to most denominations.(p.94)
• Sometimes we sensed dimly that we were ***dealing*** with sick men.(p.107)
• The same principle applies in ***dealing*** with the children.(p.115)
• We have been ***dealing*** with alcohol in its worst aspect.(p.132)
• When ***dealing*** with an alcoholic, there may be a natural annoyance that a man could be so weak, stupid and irresponsible.(p.139)
• Can you discard the feeling that you are ***dealing*** only with habit, with stubbornness, or a weak will?(p.140)
• Either you are ***dealing*** with a man who can and will get well or you are not.(p.142)
• Then Hitler's war broke out, and again, I was given a really important job on the Suez Canal, ***dealing*** with military shipping.(p.520)

deals

• I don't know whether I drank to cover up being a failure, or whether I drank and then missed the ***deals***.(p.198)

dealt

• Highly competent psychiatrists who have ***dealt*** with us have found it sometimes impossible to persuade an alcoholic to discuss his situation without reserve.(p.18)

Dean

• I was graduated "summa cum laude" in the eyes of the drinking fraternity, but not in the eyes of the ***Dean***.(p.172)

dear

• Before our visit was over, Bill suddenly turned to his wife and said, "Go fetch my clothes, ***dear***.(p.189)
• When I got out of the hospital, I was invited to stay with Dr. Bob and his ***dear*** wife, Anne.(p.279)
• Many women who have reached the stage that I had reached in my drinking have lost husbands, children, homes, everything they hold ***dear***.(p.323)
• Sometimes I would lie on the bathroom floor, deathly sick, praying I would die, and praying to God as I always had prayed to Him when I was drinking: "***Dear*** God, get me out of this one and I'll never do it again."(p.324)
• And he, poor ***dear***, didn't know what was going on.(p.325)
• I had just raised the bottle to my lips when my wife opened the door and froze me completely in my tracks with "Happy New Year, ***dear***."(p.365)
• Until I reached A.A. my life was a shambles; I was a mess, and I made everybody near and ***dear*** to me miserable.(p.400)
• ***Dear*** God, I'll do anything!(p.430)

dearer

• All of my family and loved ones, all of my friends, are nearer and ***dearer*** to me than ever before and I have literally dozens of new friends who say they cannot believe that a short eight years ago I was ready for the scrap heap.(p.541)

dearly

• By this time I was beginning to pay very ***dearly*** physically and, in hope of relief, voluntarily incarcerated myself at least a dozen times in one of the local sanitariums.(p.174)
• We had a small child, and I loved her ***dearly***, so that held me back quite a bit in my drinking career.(p.322)
• I loved my father ***dearly*** and I adored my dog, and I'd gotten this new house and Frank had just given me a new fur coat and I was thrilled to death.(p.389)
• My father, as I have said, was very indulgent and loved me ***dearly***, and knew how to get around me.(p.389)

death

• He sobered, never to drink again up to the moment of his ***death*** in 1950.(p.xvi)
• They believe in themselves, and still more in the Power which pulls chronic alcoholics back from the gates of ***death***.(p.xxv)
• "Here lies a Hampshire Grenadier Who caught his ***death*** Drinking cold small beer.(p.1)
• The papers reported men jumping to ***death*** from the towers of High Finance.(p.4)
• Many pursue it into the gates of insanity or ***death***.(p.30)
• To be doomed to an alcoholic ***death*** or to live on a spiritual basis are not always easy alternatives to face.(p.44)
• Others came near putting Galileo to ***death*** for his astronomical heresies.(p.51)
• ***Death*** was often near.(p.107)
• With it you can avert ***death*** and misery for them.(p.124)
• They have a new attitude, and they have been saved from a living ***death***.(p.150)
• To 1950, the year of his ***death***, he carried the A.A. message to more than 5,000 alcoholic men and women, and to all these he gave his medical services without thought of charge.(p.171)
• My mother was eighty-nine years old when she died, and I was a full-blown alcoholic at the time of her ***death***.(p.210)
• The lesson of his ***death*** still remains with me, yet I often wonder what would have happened if somebody else had made that first call on me.(p.239)
• I was scared to ***death*** to call a doctor.(p.267)
• Out of this maelstrom just two coherent thoughts came to the surface; one, a drink would mean homelessness and ***death***; two, I could no longer relieve the pressure of fear by starting home, as was once my habitual solution to this problem, because I no longer had a home.(p.279)
• He said he had finally learned that drinking was a fatal illness made up of an allergy plus an obsession, and once the drinking had passed from habit to obsession, we were completely hopeless, and could look forward only to spending the balance of our lives in mental institutions or to ***death***.(p.290)
• Others may idle in a retrogressive groove without too much danger, but retrogression can spell ***death*** for us.(p.311)
• I became a drunk anyway, but I was scared to ***death*** to take that morning drink.(p.323)
• Only ***death*** could wipe out that security.(p.329)
• And retirement is a time for thinking, not of ***death***, but of living – at long last.(p.329)
• Well, at least I could drink myself to ***death***.(p.333)
• ***Death*** seemed the only way out.(p.333)
• My eventual goal was to drink myself to ***death***.(p.353)
• After his ***death***, my mother soon picked up drinking where Dad left off, and in a very short time she died of cirrhosis of the liver.(p.370)
• But I couldn't enjoy anything; I was scared to ***death***.(p.385)
• I loved my father dearly and I adored my dog, and I'd gotten this new house and Frank had just given me a new fur coat and I was thrilled to ***death***.(p.389)
• But Frank was frightened to ***death*** to give it to me, because I resented everything he said and did.(p.391)
• I did not know that I had no power over alcohol, that I, alone and unaided, could not stop; that I was on a downgrade, tearing along at full speed with all my brakes gone, and that the end would be a total smash-up, ***death*** or insanity.(p.408)
• Once, when I called my analyst, and told her I was contemplating ***death***, she came over and tried to get me into a sanitarium.(p.411)
• There are many things worse than dying, but is there any ***death*** worse than the progressive, self-induced, slow suicide of the practicing alcoholic?(p.457)
• The alcoholic suffers ***death*** many times over.(p.457)
• I suddenly remembered one of my first A.A. meetings, where I heard, "If you are an alcoholic and if you continue to drink, the end is ***death*** or insanity."(p.461)
• They hadn't mentioned the living hell before ***death***.(p.461)
• Tragedies during those years that were caused by my drinking, such as the breaking up of my marriage, the ***death*** of my child, other things -- had little restraining effect.(p.465)
• He was in his late fifties, and all that he had undertaken fell upon my shoulders at his ***death*** in 1928.(p.486)
• He kept the money for me, but I worried him to ***death*** for it.(p.493)
• The trial lasted about a week, and whether or not I was going to the ***death*** house was anybody's guess.(p.508)
• I remember the day when I decided to drink myself to ***death*** quietly, without bothering anyone, because I was tired of having been a dependable, trustworthy person for about thirty-nine years without having received what I thought was a proper reward for my virtue.(p.531)
• Inside, though, I was scared to ***death***, for I knew that the time was coming (and it couldn't be too remote) when I would be unable to hold that job.(p.548)
• I was drunk for sixty days around the clock and it was my intention, literally, to drink myself to ***death***.(p.549)
• To those now in its fold, Alcoholics Anonymous has made the difference between misery and sobriety, and often the difference between life and ***death***.(p.563)

deathly

• I was ***deathly*** sick every time I took a drink.(p.322)
• Sometimes I would lie on the bathroom floor, ***deathly*** sick, praying I would die, and praying to God as I always had prayed to Him when I was drinking: "Dear God, get me out of this one and I'll never do it again."(p.324)

debacle

• If hundreds of experiences have shown him that one drink means another ***debacle*** with all its attendant suffering and humiliation, why is it he takes that one drink?(p.22)

debate

• This immediately precipitates us into a seething caldron of ***debate***.(p.xxviii)

debauch
• In reality that was the beginning of my last debauch.(p.8)
• But for every man who drinks others are involved -- the wife who trembles in fear of the next *debauch*; the mother and father who see their son wasting away.(p.104)

debit
• However, what I had gained materially on the credit side of my ledger, I have since learned was more than offset on the *debit* side by egotism, resentment and dishonesty.(p.356)

debris
• We attempt to sweep away the *debris* which has accumulated out of our effort to live on self-will and run the show ourselves.(p.76)
• I start to clean up the *debris*.(p.502)

debt
• 3.Because in so doing I am paying my *debt* to the man who took time to pass it on to me.(p.181)
• After holding good positions, making better than an average income for over ten years, I was in *debt*, had no clothes to speak of, no money, no friends, and no one any longer tolerating me but my wife.(p.301)
• And the psychiatrist has had thousands of couches, and has put you and me on them many, many times, but he hasn't helped us very much, though he has tried hard; and we owe the clergy and the doctor and the psychiatrist a deep *debt* of gratitude, but they haven't helped our alcoholism, except in a rare few instances.(p.352)

debts
• From a monetary standpoint . . . in the past few years, I have reduced my reckless *debts* to almost nothing, and have had money to get along on comfortably.(p.303)
• Not least of my *debts* to A.A. is the knowledge that in that time when she wanted me most, I was there -- and that I wasn't drunk.(p.525)
• There were *debts* totaling nearly ten thousand dollars to be paid off.(p.541)

debutante
• The best boarding schools and a finishing school in Europe had fitted me for the conventional role of *debutante* and young matron.(p.225)
• It was all about Scott Fitzgerald's little lost *debutante*, abused, misunderstood and running wild.(p.402)
• I also wrote another novel, all about Scott Fitzgerald's poor, misbegotten, unloved, tipsy little *debutante*.(p.405)

decade
• For a *decade*, I'd headed up a forty-publicist department.(p.328)

decades
• I was keenly aware that my all-important security, which I had been constantly afraid of losing for four *decades*, no longer was endangered.(p.329)

deceit
• I had worked so long in a profession where fakery, *deceit*, and untruths are tools of trade that I instantly recognized honesty when I heard it, from the mouths of A.A. members.(p.334)

deceiving
• Be satisfied he is not *deceiving* himself or you.(p.142)

decency
• Perhaps the single flicker of *decency* that shone through the fog of my drinking days was a clumsy affection for my two children, a boy and a girl.(p.437)
• I had enough *decency* so that I dismissed the idea of doing any clowning, and I did listen.(p.509)

decent
• Today I think of life in terms of happiness, contentment, freedom from fear and despair, sane thinking, ability to face problems as they occur, the opportunity to help other alcoholics and to be *decent*.(p.430)

decentralized
• I worked for the Government about a year and still maintained my evening office practice when the Government agencies were *decentralized*.(p.489)

deceptions
• He mentioned lies and *deceptions* in the course of his story in the presence of the one person in the world I wouldn't want to know such things.(p.302)

decide
• It will not take long for you to *decide* if you are honest with yourself about it.(p.32)
• When we *decide* who is to hear our story, we waste no time.(p.75)
• It may be that both will *decide* that the way of good sense and loving kindness is to let by-gones be by-gones.(p.82)
• Good generalship may *decide* that the problem be attacked on the flank rather than risk a face-to-face combat.(p.82)
• The family must *decide* these things.(p.90)
• After doing that, he must *decide* for himself whether he wants to go on.(p.95)
• We feel that each family, in the light of their own circumstances, ought to *decide* for themselves.(p.103)
• Let him *decide* for himself.(p.113)
• The man must *decide* for himself.(p.144)
• In case he does stumble, even once, you will have to *decide* whether to let him go.(p.147)
• Seventeen stories may help you *decide* whether you are alcoholic; also, whether A.A. is for you.(p.167)
• We would follow one man's ideas for a while, *decide* he was wrong and switch to another's method.(p.246)

decided
• It was *decided* that all members ought to be anonymous at the level of press, radio, TV and films.(p.xix)
• Other thousands came to a few A.A. meetings and at first *decided* they didn't want the program.(p.xx)
• I failed to persuade my broker friends to send me out looking over factories and managements, but my wife and I *decided* to go anyway.(p.2)
• Then I *decided* to drive into the country and see one of my prospects for a car.(p.36)
• I ordered another sandwich and *decided* to have another glass of milk.(p.36)
• He tells you he has *decided* to stop jay-walking for good, but in a few weeks he breaks both legs.(p.38)
• After dinner I *decided* to take a walk.(p.41)
• If you have *decided* you want what we have and are willing to go to any length to get it -- then you are ready to take certain steps.(p.58)
• Being convinced, we were at Step Three, which is that we *decided* to turn our will and our life over to God as we understood Him.(p.60)
• Next, we *decided* that hereafter in this drama of life, God was going to be our Director.(p.62)
• Reminding ourselves that we have *decided* to go to any length to find a spiritual experience we ask that we be given strength and direction to do the right thing, no matter what the personal consequences may be.(p.79)
• When I got the fog out of my brain, I *decided* that quitting school was very foolish and that I had better return and continue my work.(p.173)
• I *decided* that I couldn't drink.(p.196)
• Then I got into the habit of having beers, and *decided* that a drink of whiskey was not any worse; so I would get the one drink of whiskey but, on second thought, I *decided* that as long as I was only going to have one, I might as well make it a double-header.(p.203)
• So they *decided* that I should have a doctor.(p.205)
• After I was on the drafting board about two years I *decided* I wanted a technical education.(p.211)
• This work consumed a period of about two-thirds of a year, and worked out successfully so I *decided* to follow patent law.(p.212)
• It was finally *decided* to undertake the organization of a Cleveland group and toward the end of May, 1939, the first meeting was held in Cleveland in my home.(p.219)
• Many friends of my family had emigrated to America, so at twenty-four I *decided* that the United States offered me the opportunity I was never likely to find in my native land.(p.231)
• I early *decided* that the wine of America was very inferior stuff and took up beer instead.(p.231)
• I *decided* that if these fellows could make it I would try it myself, and so I did.(p.232)
• During that first week-end I *decided* to stay in New York and take all they gave out with, except the "God stuff."(p.246)
• My wife traveled with me, but with a baby coming I *decided* to settle in a large city where I got a job with a commission agent which is a polite term for a handbook operator.(p.251)
• Of course, this year we *decided* on staying home and being sensible, doing a little drinking, and painting the house.(p.265)
• One time my wife *decided* to try this too.(p.288)
• One of them was that I would try to get a group started in Chicago; the second was that I would have to return to Akron to attend meetings at least every two months until I did get a group started in Chicago; third, I *decided* I must place this program above everything else, even my family, because if I did not maintain my sobriety I would lose my family anyway.(p.292)
• But I was in such deep trouble that I *decided* to try A.A. anyhow.(p.319)
• She *decided* she wouldn't let herself go in her drinking.(p.321)
• I *decided* to quit drinking.(p.333)
• Eight years ago, my wife and I *decided* to spend a vacation in Naini Tal, the mountain resort.(p.343)
• During this vacation, in the months of September and October, I *decided* to go on the water wagon.(p.343)
• Last year, I *decided* on an A.A. vacation in Naini Tal.(p.343)
• So I *decided* that I would go to my first meeting.(p.347)
• Like all alcoholics endeavoring to run away from themselves and their environment, I *decided* to go to New York.(p.358)
• After a few meetings I *decided* to drive to Florida unannounced to see my wife and tell her about my new found friends and association.(p.364)
• We had some people in, and I was making drinks in the kitchen, when I suddenly *decided* to hoist the bottle for a quick one.(p.365)
• So, with mixed feelings of humiliation, anger, and fear, I *decided* to look for an answer.(p.371)
• For some reason I can't remember, it finally dawned on me that I had a problem, and yet nobody was very critical about it except my family, and that was only because I *decided*, after seven years of marriage, that I would divorce my husband.(p.386)
• About this time, at Christmas, after being under this doctor's care, we *decided* that there wasn't anything more to do.(p.388)
• The cop must have seen the condition that I was in because he *decided* to take me home.(p.390)
• He finally *decided* that he did not love me enough, and soon he told me so and said he was engaged to another girl.(p.403)
• Priscilla, an A.A. who, like Marty, has become one of my greatest friends, *decided* that I was a stubborn case.(p.414)
• One night, I had to put myself back to sleep three times, and then I finally *decided* to give it up.(p.443)
• On two occasions, over weekends, I *decided* I would take absolutely nothing.(p.443)
• As a result, he couldn't figure out why I had the convulsions, and he *decided* to send me to the Mayo Clinic.(p.444)
• He arranged for me to see a local psychiatrist, who quickly *decided* I should be in the mental-health unit of our local hospital.(p.445)
• Finally after seven months, I *decided* to try it.(p.448)
• Finally, I threw away all my books and *decided* never to return to A.A.(p.460)
• I had *decided* I was no good -- never would be any good, and the sooner I could drink myself out of this life, the better.(p.468)
• At that point everyone *decided* something drastic had to be done.(p.469)
• They held consultations and discussions, and finally *decided* to give me the "Conditioned Reflex" treatment.(p.469)
• It never entered my head that I would have been pushing up the daisies if he had *decided* not to come.(p.479)
• To get rid of me one evening, she *decided* to go to the movies, she and another friend.(p.487)
• I said that she told me she was going to the movies, and I became foolishly disturbed about it and, as things snowballed, I *decided* to go out and get drunk.(p.487)
• Then I *decided* that I'd go back to Washington, which I did.(p.490)
• She *decided* that she didn't want any more of that.(p.491)
• Anyhow, on the 24th, after drinking all day on the 23rd, I must have *decided* I wanted to see my wife and have some kind of reconciliation or at least talk with her.(p.491)
• I worked in the steel mill for possibly two months, and then I became disgusted with myself and *decided* to go back home.(p.492)
• I think the thing that galled me was that just after Easter I had drawn my salary for two weeks' work and had *decided* that I was going to send some money to Vi; and above all else I was going to send my baby daughter an Easter outfit.(p.493)
• One evening I *decided* to go because two of those friends were to speak.(p.509)
• So I *decided* I'd go back and live in Ireland to try the geography cure.(p.522)
• I remember the day when I *decided* to drink myself to death quietly, without bothering anyone, because I

was tired of having been a dependable, trustworthy person for about thirty-nine years without having received what I thought was a proper reward for my virtue.(p.531)
• I started to cross out that last sentence, but *decided* to let it stand.(p.536)
• The only kind of security I knew anything about at that time was material security and I *decided* that all these intruders would vanish immediately if I only had a lot of money.(p.545)

decides
• This should be an entirely personal affair which each one *decides* for himself in the light of past associations, or his present choice.(p.28)
• He *decides* to exert himself more.(p.61)

deciding
• The patient had made his own diagnosis, and *deciding* his situation hopeless, had hidden in a deserted barn determined to die.(p.xxix)

decimal
• Their cost of production is figured to a fine *decimal* point.(p.149)

decipher
• To this day I haven't been able to *decipher* what I wrote to them.(p.427)

decision
• They are over-remorseful and make many resolutions, but never a *decision*.(p.xxviii)
• He has a positive genius for getting tight at exactly the wrong moment, particularly when some important *decision* must be made or engagement kept.(p.21)
• 3.Made a *decision* to turn our will and our lives over to the care of God as we understood Him.(p.59)
• Though our *decision* was a vital and crucial step, it could have little permanent effect unless at once followed by a strenuous effort to face, and to be rid of, the things in ourselves which had been blocking us.(p.64)
• If you have already made a *decision*, and an inventory of your grosser handicaps, you have made a good beginning.(p.71)
• Here we ask God for inspiration, an intuitive thought or a *decision*.(p.86)
• Let him know you are available if he wishes to make a *decision* and tell his story, but do not insist upon it if he prefers to consult someone else.(p.96)
• If your *decision* is yes, whether the reason be humanitarian or business or both, then the following suggestions may be helpful.(p.140)
• It was in the next two or three days after I had first met Doc and Bill, that I finally came to a *decision* to turn my will over to God and to go along with this program the best that I could.(p.189)
• The only stipulation they made was this: I had to make the *decision* myself.(p.278)
• What *decision*?(p.278)
• The Third Step said: "Made a *decision* to turn our will and our lives over to the care of God as we understood Him."(p.350)
• Now they asked us to make a *decision*!(p.350)
• A TEEN-AGER'S *DECISION*(p.353)
• With these new and enlightening doors opening up to me, I was able to make the eventual *decision* to stop drinking, a day at a time -- because I, too, was an alcoholic.(p.355)
• Thank God that in spite of my heavy drinking my mind was clear enough to make a *decision* then and there.(p.363)
• I had no trouble making the right *decision* when I saw my wife open her purse at the meeting that night and deposit a cute little angel in the middle of my birthday cake.(p.366)
• Some crisis brings you to a point of making a *decision* to do something about your drinking problem.(p.377)
• The final *decision* came when my daughter, following a drunk which ruined my wife's birthday, said, "It's Alcoholics Anonymous -- or else!"(p.378)
• The time for *decision* had arrived, and it was a relief to say "Yes" when my family said they would call Alcoholics Anonymous for me.(p.378)
• A week after my *decision* to join A.A., she called it quits.(p.430)
• I'm twenty-six now and I haven't had a drink since I made my *decision*.(p.430)
• That was the day, that was the *decision*, I know now, when I crossed over the line and became an active alcoholic.(p.531)
• Perhaps a better way of saying it is that, on that day, with that *decision*, I no longer fought drinking as an escape.(p.531)
• On that day of *decision*, I didn't acknowledge that I was an alcoholic.(p.532)
• The people who came knew immediately I was in no condition to absorb anything of the program, and I was put in a sanitarium to be defogged so that I could make a sober *decision* about this for myself.(p.549)

decisions
• Sometimes they hurt us, seemingly without provocation, but we invariably find that at some time in the past we have made *decisions* based on self which later placed us in a position to be hurt.(p.62)
• We are then in much less danger of excitement, fear, anger, worry, self-pity, or foolish *decisions*.(p.88)
• I made several *decisions* at that time.(p.292)

deck
• The Higher Power was on *deck* to see me through, sober.(p.437)

declaration
• But my friend sat before me, and he made the point-blank *declaration* that God had done for him what he could not do for himself.(p.11)

declare
• They flatly *declare* that since they have come to believe in a Power greater than themselves, to take a certain attitude toward that Power, and to do certain simple things, there has been a revolutionary change in their way of living and thinking.(p.50)

declared
• But when this happened to me, I *declared* to friends that I would get drunk, dead drunk that very night, and stay drunk for a month.(p.403)
• My doctor finally *declared* he could no longer be responsible for me, and sent me to a psychiatrist who practiced in the same suite of offices.(p.558)

declaring
• Before too long, my husband (who seemed to prefer his shirts dirty) put his foot down, *declaring* that our family might have the cleanest clothes in town, but that I hadn't been out of the same old dirty slacks and blouse for a week.(p.371)

declining
• The curve of my *declining* moral and bodily health fell off like a ski-jump.(p.7)
• Seven -- Every A.A. group ought to be fully self-supporting, *declining* outside contributions.(p.564)

decreased
• Naturally this sort of thing *decreased* the man's chance of recovery.(p.145)
• In seven years the intervals between them *decreased* from eight months to ten days!(p.434)

decreases
• He may even read in a newspaper that one out of every seven drinkers will become alcoholic, but he rarely is told that it holds true for all ages -- or that the tolerance to alcohol (and other drugs) *decreases* steadily, year after year, in the bodies of all persons.(p.330)

dedicated
• This couple has since become so fascinated that they have *dedicated* their home to the work.(p.160)

deducted
• If you propose such a procedure to him, it may be necessary to advance the cost of treatment, but we believe it should be made plain that any expense will later be *deducted* from his pay.(p.143)

deeds
• I came to Cleveland with the *deeds* to these lots and to pick up my money.(p.196)
• Far from expecting praise for their *deeds*, they claimed the performance a privilege and insisted that they invariably received more than they gave.(p.310)

deep
• The great fact is just this, and nothing less: That we have had *deep* and effective spiritual experiences which have revolutionized our whole attitude toward life, toward our fellows and toward God's universe.(p.25)
• Moreover, he would lose his family for whom he had a *deep* affection.(p.35)
• We looked upon this world of warring individuals, warring theological systems, and inexplicable calamity, with *deep* skepticism.(p.46)
• Actually we were fooling ourselves, for *deep* down in every man, woman, and child, is the fundamental idea of God.(p.55)
• We found the Great Reality *deep* down within us.(p.55)
• It is plain that a life which includes *deep* resentment leads only to futility and unhappiness.(p.66)
• Admit that he probably knows more about it than you do, but call to his attention the fact that however *deep* his faith and knowledge, he could not have applied it or he would not drink.(p.93)
• The power of God goes *deep*!(p.114)
• I realized that I had a problem, although my realization was not very *deep* because my own conceit wouldn't admit that I had any personality problems.(p.214)
• But I don't believe now that it was with any *deep* feeling of resentment that I said to him, "The children are raised, and if this is the way you want it, this is the way we'll have it.(p.263)
• However, I must have felt, *deep* down inside myself, that living the selfish life of a bachelor was only half living.(p.286)
• There is no more "aloneness," with that awful ache, so *deep* in the heart of every alcoholic that nothing, before, could ever reach it.(p.312)
• But I was in such *deep* trouble that I decided to try A.A. anyhow.(p.319)
• Away down *deep*, I was motivated into dishonest behavior because I was a people-pleaser.(p.328)
• Seated at the typewriter, I faked *deep* thinking or portrayed creativity by key-tapping.(p.332)
• Hiding behind a newspaper, magazine, or book, I really saw nothing, but simulated *deep* interest.(p.332)
• *Deep* in my heart was the feeling that maybe I could get some help here.(p.346)
• And the psychiatrist has had thousands of couches, and has put you and me on them many, many times, but he hasn't helped us very much, though he has tried hard; and we owe the clergy and the doctor and the psychiatrist a *deep* debt of gratitude, but they haven't helped our alcoholism, except in a rare few instances.(p.352)
• And *deep* in my heart I really meant what I said because I loved her more than anything else in the world, yes -- even more than liquor.(p.362)
• It was never boring, but I developed a feeling of *deep* insecurity.(p.369)
• So it drove me deeper into the psychosis or neurosis that I had, and that I hated *deep* down in my heart.(p.388)
• He said he never wanted to set foot in the *deep* south again and he didn't.(p.486)
• Nevertheless, we continued to work together and I continued to drink, but I guess, *deep* down within her heart as well as within mine, we both knew I couldn't stop drinking.(p.490)
• Very often we rode to and from work together, but being separated really galled me *deep* down.(p.491)
• Had I been able to explain to a psychiatrist the feeling of futility, loneliness and lack of purpose that had come with my *deep* sense of personal failure at this second divorce, I seriously doubt that the good doctor could have convinced me that my basic problem was a spiritual hunger, but A.A. has shown me this was the truth.(p.546)
• With *deep* shame came the knowledge too that I had lived with no sense of social obligation nor had I known the meaning of moral responsibility to my fellow men.(p.549)
• I attended my first A.A. meeting eight years ago, and it is with *deep* gratitude that I'm able to say I've not had a drink since that time, and that I take no sedation or narcotics, for this program is to me one of complete sobriety and I no longer need to escape reality.(p.549)

deepened
• This pattern *deepened* and became worse.(p.214)

deepening
• The alarming physical and mental symptoms, the *deepening* pall of remorse, depression and inferiority that settled down on our loved ones -- these things terrified and distracted us.(p.106)

deeper
• I stayed on in Florida for three weeks, enjoying our reunion, a new found health and a *deeper* love than I had ever experienced before.(p.364)
• So it drove me *deeper* into the psychosis or neurosis that I had, and that I hated deep down in my heart.(p.388)
• My gratitude to A.A. grows *deeper* each day I am sober.(p.420)
• My work is on a much *deeper* and more significant level than it ever was before, and I am today a fairly creative, relatively sane human being.(p.438)
• Young when she joined, this A.A. believes her serious drinking was the result of even *deeper* defects.(p.544)
• The mental twists that led up to my drinking began many years before I ever took a drink for I am one of those whose history proves conclusively that my drinking was "a symptom of a *deeper* trouble."(p.544)

deeply
• They were *deeply* religious people, much shocked by their son's refusal to have anything

to do with the church.(p.158)
• My wife became *deeply* interested and it was her interest that sustained mine, though I at no time sensed that it might be an answer to my liquor problem.(p.178)
• I sipped the drink off the bar because I couldn't hold it in my hand, but I was still a lady, believe it or not, and I was *deeply* ashamed.(p.266)
• I began hitting the bottle again, and with it self-pity, resentment, loneliness and remorse set in *deeply*.(p.362)
• There are so many to whom I feel *deeply* grateful; to my husband (and best critic), whose generous love, compassion and understanding have helped me along the way; to those before me in A.A. who inspired the first article I read, and the friend who sent that article to Frank; to Ruth for her personal note, and the first A.A. to talk to me; to my Bishop, whose loving and believing spirit inspired me; and to all the members of the Houston Group who were so patient, kind and helpful -- and to countless others.(p.393)
• I was astonished and *deeply* moved.(p.415)
• Moreover, I am *deeply* convinced that so long as I continue to strive, in my bumbling way, toward the principles I first encountered in the earlier chapters of this book, this remarkable power will continue to flow through me.(p.437)

defeat
• Like myself, he had admitted complete *defeat*.(p.11)
• *Defeat* seemed certain.(p.113)
• At one time, the admission that I was and am an alcoholic meant shame, *defeat*, and failure to me.(p.335)
• But in the light of the new understanding that I have found in A.A., I have been able to interpret that *defeat*, and that failure, and that shame, as seeds of victory.(p.335)
• Because it was only through feeling *defeat* and feeling failure, the inability to cope with my life and with alcohol, that I was able to surrender and accept the fact that I had this disease, and that I had to learn to live again without alcohol.(p.335)
• Each battle has ended in *defeat*.(p.502)

defeated
• I had never been able to understand people who said that a problem had them hopelessly *defeated*.(p.42)
• Being convinced that self, manifested in various ways, was what had *defeated* us, we considered its common manifestations.(p.64)
• Our hope is that when this chip of a book is launched on the world tide of alcoholism, *defeated* drinkers will seize upon it, to follow its suggestions.(p.153)
• *Defeated* by alcohol and pills, he found the way to a new life.(p.418)
• He can only be *defeated* by an attitude of intolerance or belligerent denial.(p.570)

defeats
• It becomes vital, also, that others not know of our *defeats*, nor suspect our loss of confidence.(p.331)

defect
• I pray that you now remove from me every single *defect* of character which stands in the way of my usefulness to you and my fellows.(p.76)
• Every *defect* I pointed out to her became greater and greater.(p.450)

defectives
• It did not satisfy us to be told that we could not control our drinking just because we were maladjusted to life, that we were in full flight from reality, or were outright mental *defectives*.(p.xxiv)

defects
• Though he could not accept all the tenets of the Oxford Groups, he was convinced of the need for moral inventory, confession of personality *defects*, restitution to those harmed, helpfulness to others, and the necessity of belief in and dependence upon God.(p.xvi)
• Instead, we looked at the human *defects* of these people, and sometimes used their shortcomings as a basis of wholesale condemnation.(p.50)
• 6.Were entirely ready to have God remove all these *defects* of character.(p.59)
• We have admitted certain *defects*; we have ascertained in a rough way what the trouble is; we have put our finger on the weak items in our personal inventory.(p.72)
• This requires action on our part, which, when completed, will mean that we have admitted to God, to ourselves, and to another human being the exact nature of our *defects*.(p.72)
• This is perhaps difficult – especially discussing our *defects* with another person.(p.72)
• Their *defects* may be glaring, but the chances are that our own actions are partly responsible.(p.83)
• Little by little the family may see their own *defects* and admit them.(p.99)
• You should point out that his *defects* of character are not going to disappear over night.(p.100)
• If you both show a willingness to remedy your own *defects*, there will be little need to criticize each other.(p.118)
• At the moral inventory, he brought up some of my bad personality traits or character *defects*, such as selfishness, conceit, jealousy, carelessness, intolerance, ill-temper, sarcasm and resentments.(p.292)
• We went over these at great length and then he finally asked me if I wanted these *defects* of character removed.(p.292)
• When I said yes, we both knelt at his desk and prayed, each of us asking to have these *defects* taken away.(p.292)
• Dishonest thinking, prejudice, ego, antagonism toward anyone and everyone who dares to cross him, vanity and a critical attitude are character *defects* that gradually creep in and become a part of his life.(p.380)
• It took me some time to realize that the Twelve Steps of A.A. were designed to help correct these *defects* of character and so help remove the obsession to drink.(p.380)
• But then, as I drank more and more, the alcohol seemed to affect my vision: Instead of continuing to see what was good about my wife, I began to see her *defects*.(p.450)
• And the more I focused my mind on her *defects*, the more they grew and multiplied.(p.450)
• The more I focus my mind on its *defects* -- late start, long drunkalogues, cigarette smoke – the worse the meeting becomes.(p.451)
• Young when she joined, this A.A. believes her serious drinking was the result of even deeper *defects*.(p.544)

defend
• The employer cannot play favorites, but he can always *defend* a man from needless provocation and unfair criticism.(p.146)

defense
• We are without *defense* against the first drink.(p.24)
• There is a complete failure of the kind of *defense* that keeps one from putting his hand on a hot stove.(p.24)
• They had said that though I did raise a *defense*, it would one day give way before some trivial reason for having a drink.(p.42)
• Once more: The alcoholic at certain times has no effective mental *defense* against the first drink.(p.43)
• Except in a few rare cases, neither he nor any other human being can provide such a *defense*.(p.43)
• His *defense* must come from a Higher Power.(p.43)

deferring
• As I look back on the events of two months, I can clearly see that I had been circling around, half-afraid of encountering the remedy for my situation, half wanting it, *deferring* fulfillment of my promise to get in touch with the doctor I had heard about.(p.258)

defiant
• All I had left was an iron determination to live my own life in spite of the alien world -- and here I was, an inwardly frightened, outwardly *defiant* woman, who desperately needed a prop to keep going.(p.226)
• I hated myself worse and worse, and as I hated myself I became more *defiant* towards everything and everybody.(p.265)
• My *defiant* attitude became worse.(p.265)
• There was a man watching, and I turned to him and said with a *defiant* air I carried with me all the time, "If I don't quit this I'm going to have to join that alcoholic business they're talking about."(p.266)
• I was as *defiant* as anybody could be because I was scared.(p.391)

deficiencies
• My schoolmate visited me, and I fully acquainted him with my problems and *deficiencies*.(p.13)
• I realized that there wasn't anything I could say to place myself in a more favorable light with my children, that it was going to be a matter of time; for I also understood the intolerance of young people towards *deficiencies* in their elders.(p.220)

deficiency
• You need not remind him of his spiritual *deficiency* - - he will know of it.(p.120)
• Instead of developing new channels of activity for themselves, mother and children demand that he stay home and make up the *deficiency*.(p.131)
• There was a doctor in our church congregation who was interested in my case, and he thought it was a vitamin *deficiency*.(p.389)

define
• We found that as soon as we were able to lay aside prejudice and express even a willingness to believe in a Power greater than ourselves, we commenced to get results, even though it was impossible for any of us to fully *define* or comprehend that Power, which is God.(p.46)
• We *define* professionalism as the occupation of counseling alcoholics for fees or hire.(p.566)

definite
• Of course an alcoholic ought to be freed from his physical craving for liquor, and this often requires a *definite* hospital procedure, before psychological measures can be of maximum benefit.(p.xxv)
• We have heard of few instances where people, who showed *definite* signs of alcoholism, were able to stop for a long period because of an overpowering desire to do so.(p.32)
• We were usually as *definite* as this example:(p.65)
• Yet, we believe we can make some *definite* and valuable suggestions.(p.86)
• If we belong to a religious denomination which requires a *definite* morning devotion, we attend to that also.(p.87)
• After satisfying yourself that your man wants to recover and that he will go to any extreme to do so, you may suggest a *definite* course of action.(p.142)
• The first *definite* indications of an alcoholic pattern began to arise when I would go to New York on business and disappear, and wind up in Philadelphia or Boston for two or three day periods.(p.213)
• I missed the old social times, of course, but had no *definite* craving even for beer.(p.232)
• Before long I had a *definite* taste for hard liquor, knew nausea and headaches I had never known before, but as in the old days, I suffered them out.(p.233)
• Unlike many other Catholics who frequently take pledges for *definite* periods -- a year, two years or for good, I never had any desire to "take a pledge" before the priest.(p.234)
• He had no desire to know anything, except whether I was *definite* about my desire to quit drinking.(p.235)
• Around this time our big A.A. book was being written and it all became much simpler; we had a *definite* formula which some sixty of us agreed was the middle course for all alcoholics who wanted sobriety, and that formula has not been changed one iota down through the years.(p.248)

definitely
• He is violent, or appears *definitely* insane when drunk.(p.110)
• With nothing but a liberal arts education, very *definitely* estranged from my family and already married, soon after graduation from college I became a bookmaker's clerk on the British racing circuits, far better off financially than the average professional man.(p.251)
• One evening, the book, after checking up, was very *definitely* in the red for plenty through a piece of studied carelessness on my part, and my boss, very shrewd and able, fired me with a parting statement to the effect that once was enough.(p.251)
• I was an honest agnostic, but *definitely* not a hater of the church or its adherents.(p.256)
• I'm sure his family felt that it was a marriage that -- well, I was a girl from the wrong side of the tracks -- *definitely*!(p.262)
• Within a year of my return to Detroit, A.A. was a *definitely* established little group of about a dozen members and I too was established in a modest but steady job handling an independent dry-cleaning route of my own.(p.283)
• In all honesty though, I was skeptical, but I wanted so *definitely* to quit drinking that I would have welcomed any sort of physical torture or pain to accomplish the result.(p.302)
• I *definitely* liked it, everything about it, the taste, the effects; and I realize now that a drink did something for me or to me that was different from the way it affected others.(p.305)
• After having a few drinks, I went to a meeting -- and the people there were not all old men and *definitely* not skid-row types!(p.319)
• Many times have I heard the above expressions since I have been in A.A., and many times I have had to reply "*Definitely* I am an alcoholic, and while it may be hard for you to believe, it is not hard for me, for I have learned many things about alcohol and myself that would, perhaps, be difficult for you to understand."(p.356)

definition
• Whatever the precise *definition* of the word may be, we call this plain insanity.(p.37)
• To my way of thinking, that is a *definition* of alcoholism; a state of being in which the emotions have

failed to grow to the stature of the intellect.(p.535)

• My personal ***definition,*** which I submit as applying only to myself (although everyone is welcome to it who wants it), includes every waking activity of the human being; to have a creative attitude towards things is a more exact meaning, to live and to deal with other human beings creatively, which to me means seeing the God in them, and respecting and worshipping this God.(p.535)

• I've been benefited from a dictionary ***definition*** I found that reads: "rationalization is giving a socially acceptable reason for socially unacceptable behavior, and socially unacceptable behavior is a form of insanity."(p.551)

deflate

• All Twelve Steps of A.A. are designed to kill the old self (***deflate*** the old ego) and build a new, free self.(p.459)

deflation

• This involves a process of ***deflation.***(p.122)

• 1.Complete ***deflation.***(p.292)

defogged

• I had been drinking heavily from one state of semi-coma to another and it was several days before I got "***defogged,***" but subconsciously I was in earnest about wanting to quit liquor forever.(p.258)

• The people who came knew immediately I was in no condition to absorb anything of the program, and I was put in a sanitarium to be ***defogged*** so that I could make a sober decision about this for myself.(p.549)

defunct

• I quit the factory and got a job on a small newspaper, going from that to a Pittsburgh daily, long ago ***defunct.***(p.252)

degenerated

• The enlargement of my liver ***degenerated*** into cirrhosis.(p.557)

degradation

• I have told you some of the funny things, but not much of the shame and ***degradation.***(p.390)

degrading

• Repeated year on end, they are horrible -- frightening and ***degrading,*** a chronicle of tragedy which may be greater because the individual undergoing the tragedy, myself, knew what was happening, and yet refused to do anything to stop it.(p.538)

degree

• We used to amuse ourselves by cynically dissecting spiritual beliefs and practices when we might have observed that many spiritually-minded persons of all races, colors, and creeds were demonstrating a ***degree*** of stability, happiness and usefulness which we should have sought ourselves.(p.49)

• My brilliant agnosticism vanished, and I saw for the first time that those who really believed, or at least honestly tried to find a Power greater than themselves, were much more composed and contented than I had ever been, and they seemed to have a ***degree*** of happiness which I had never known.(p.247)

• Obviously I have overcome fear to a sufficient ***degree*** to think in terms of success in business.(p.284)

• Here was something requiring a greater willingness to assume responsibility, and take a larger ***degree*** of cooperation and "give and take" than even business requires of one.(p.286)

• This phase was right down my alley; I had my master's ***degree*** in the art of making "whoopee."(p.359)

• Her influence and companionship managed to lessen my drinking to some ***degree.***(p.359)

• The alcoholic has them to an exaggerated ***degree.***(p.380)

• I was indicted for the crime of murder in the first ***degree.***(p.508)

• However, a verdict was brought in of murder in the second ***degree.***(p.508)

delay

• But we don't ***delay*** if it can be avoided.(p.83)

• On my trips back to Akron to get my spirits recharged and to work with other alcoholics, I would ask Dr. Bob about this ***delay*** and wonder just what was wrong with me.(p.293)

• It is cold so there is no ***delay.***(p.497)

delayed

• Wait until repeated stumbling convinces him he must act, for the more you hurry him the longer his recovery may be ***delayed.***(p.113)

• We were supposed to take off at noon, but were ***delayed*** until six p.m.(p.428)

delays

• Father says grace, which ***delays*** my attack on the buckwheat cakes and sausage.(p.497)

deliberate

• Avoid then, the ***deliberate*** manufacture of misery, but if trouble comes, cheerfully capitalize it as an opportunity to demonstrate His omnipotence.(p.133)

deliberately

• In some circumstances we have gone out ***deliberately*** to get drunk, feeling ourselves justified by nervousness, anger, worry, depression, jealousy or the like.(p.37)

• We now see that when we began to drink ***deliberately,*** instead of casually, there was little serious or effective thought during the period of premeditation of what the terrific consequences might be.(p.37)

• So I set out to get drunk ***deliberately,*** just to teach her what she was missing.(p.293)

• I'd ***deliberately*** smashed a window.(p.435)

delicate

• I had fed it, fanned it and nurtured it as one might a ***delicate*** child, and it had become as much a part of me as my breathing.(p.551)

delicatessens

• Sometimes a small deal would net a few hundred dollars, and I would pay my bills at the bars and ***delicatessens.***(p.5)

delight

• One night, a few weeks after joining the Fellowship, much to my surprise and ***delight*** I saw a familiar but no longer frowning face.(p.371)

delighted

• Once we have taken this step, withholding nothing, we are ***delighted.***(p.75)

delightedly

• At the age of sixteen, I was invited to spend the summer with an aunt and I, very ***delightedly,*** accepted the invitation.(p.261)

delightful

• To show you the point to which this obsession went, there came an occasion when I had spent a most ***delightful*** week-end, and at nine o'clock on Sunday night I was on my way home, and I thought I would get a drink.(p.204)

• Instant blackout was what it was, and it seemed ***delightful.***(p.442)

• And she was a charming, ***delightful,*** lovely person.(p.472)

delinquencies

• He may take small interest in the children and may show irritation when reproved for his ***delinquencies.***(p.126)

delirium

• My weary and despairing wife was informed that it would all end with heart failure during ***delirium*** tremens, or I would develop a wet brain, perhaps within a year.(p.7)

• Treatment seemed wise, for I showed signs of ***delirium*** tremens.(p.13)

• Sometimes there were screaming ***delirium*** and insanity.(p.107)

• Perhaps he has had ***delirium*** tremens.(p.110)

• From far away, as if in a ***delirium,*** I heard my own voice – calling someone "Dorothy," talking of dress shops, of jobs . . . the words came clearer . . . this sound of my own voice frightened me as it came closer . . . and suddenly, there I was, talking of I knew not what, to someone I'd never seen before this very moment.(p.222)

• Most of these fortunate ones have had little or no acquaintance with ***delirium,*** with hospitals, asylums, and jails.(p.315)

• The doctor said I'd been brought into the hospital like a madman, crying, raving, ranting, swearing, completely in the throes of ***delirium*** tremens.(p.427)

delivered

• The message has been ***delivered.***(p.497)

delivering

• Father is ***delivering*** his sermon.(p.497)

deluged

• Then Jack Alexander wrote a feature article in the Saturday Evening Post and placed such a compelling picture of A.A. before the general public that alcoholics in need of help really ***deluged*** us.(p.xviii)

delusion

• The ***delusion*** that we are like other people, or presently may be, has to be smashed.(p.30)

• Is he not a victim of the ***delusion*** that he can wrest satisfaction and happiness out of this world if he only manages well?(p.61)

delve

• Drunkalogues and statistics can be boring, but it is necessary to ***delve*** a little into each in order to come up with some kind of rough estimate.(p.396)

demand

• Sometimes they ***demand*** that dad bring them back instantly!(p.123)

• He may ***demand*** that the family find God in a hurry, or exhibit amazing indifference to them and say he is above worldly considerations.(p.128)

• Instead of developing new channels of activity for themselves, mother and children ***demand*** that he stay home and make up the deficiency.(p.131)

• Twenty-two years later, Doctor Bob told me that what I had done was like turning a switch and setting up a ***demand*** for more alcohol in my system.(p.195)

demanded

• Perhaps there are some cases where the utmost frankness is ***demanded.***(p.82)

• My phobia for sleeplessness ***demanded*** that I get drunk every night, but in order to get more liquor for the next night, I had to stay sober during the day, at least up to four o'clock.(p.177)

• My "periodics" became more frequent until I reached the point where I wanted to devote all my time to drinking, working as little as possible, and then only when the necessity of my family ***demanded*** it.(p.234)

demanding

• He becomes, on the next occasion, still more ***demanding*** or gracious, as the case may be.(p.61)

• Father was a very well-integrated person, and while mother was highstrung and a bit selfish and ***demanding,*** our home life was reasonably harmonious.(p.240)

demands

• They are naturally incapable of grasping and developing a manner of living which ***demands*** rigorous honesty.(p.58)

• We find the more one member of the family ***demands*** that the others concede to him, the more resentful they become.(p.122)

• In fact, he may say almost anything if he has accepted our solution which, as you know, ***demands*** rigorous honesty.(p.145)

• Back to the big city, for another year of precarious living, paid for largely by one or two friends I still had not milked dry or worn to exhaustion with ***demands*** on their bounty.(p.540)

• Indeed, I had to drink now to live, to cope with the ***demands*** of everyday existence.(p.556)

• I had to cope with the ***demands*** of everyday living without my comforter, my anesthetic, my crutch.(p.557)

Demerol

• For the leveling-off process, I just loved intravenous ***Demerol,*** but I found it hard to practice good medicine while shooting morphine.(p.442)

democracy

• We are like the passengers of a great liner the moment after rescue from shipwreck when camaraderie, joyousness and ***democracy*** pervade the vessel from steerage to Captain's table.(p.17)

• The very practical approach to his problems, the absence of intolerance of any kind, the informality, the genuine ***democracy,*** the uncanny understanding which these people had were irresistible.(p.160)

democratic

• Alcohol being no respecter of persons, we are an accurate cross section of America, and in distant lands, the same ***democratic*** evening-up process is now going on.(p.xx)

demonstrate

• And does not science ***demonstrate*** that visual proof is the weakest proof?(p.48)

• Instead we let Him ***demonstrate,*** through us, what He can do.(p.68)

• These things will come to pass naturally and in good time provided, however, the alcoholic continues to ***demonstrate*** that he can be sober, considerate, and helpful, regardless of what anyone says or does.(p.99)

• Avoid then, the deliberate manufacture of misery, but if trouble comes, cheerfully capitalize it as an opportunity to ***demonstrate*** His omnipotence.(p.133)

demonstrated

• We have seen the truth ***demonstrated*** again and again: "Once an alcoholic, always an alcoholic."(p.33)

demonstrating

• My friend had emphasized the absolute necessity of ***demonstrating*** these principles in all my affairs.(p.14)

• We used to amuse ourselves by cynically dissecting spiritual beliefs and practices when we might have observed that many spiritually-minded persons of all races, colors, and creeds were ***demonstrating*** a degree of stability, happiness and usefulness which we should have sought ourselves.(p.49)

demonstration

• A much more important ***demonstration*** of our principles lies before us in our respective homes, occupations and affairs.(p.19)

• He is going to be more interested in a ***demonstration*** of good will than in our talk of spiritual discoveries.(p.77)

• We have made our ***demonstration,*** done our part.(p.78)

• He should concentrate on his own spiritual ***demonstration.***(p.98)

• The successful ***demonstration*** I had made of my life problems in other respects convinced me that some day I was going to be able to drink like a gentleman.(p.214)

demonstrations

• But for the grace of God, there would have been thousands more convincing ***demonstrations.***(p.25)

• For faith in a Power greater than ourselves, and miraculous ***demonstrations*** of that power in human lives, are facts as old as man himself.(p.55)

demoralization

• All of us felt at times that we were regaining control, but such intervals – usually brief – were inevitably followed by still less control, which led in time to pitiful and incomprehensible ***demoralization.***(p.30)

denial

• I could almost hear the sound of the preacher's voice as I sat, on still Sundays, way over there on the hillside; there was that proffered temperance pledge I never signed; my grandfather's good natured contempt of some church folk and their doings; his insistence that the spheres really had their music; but his ***denial*** of the preacher's right to tell him how he must listen; his fearlessness as he spoke of these things just before he died; these recollections welled up from the past.(p.10)

• My family had money – I had never known ***denial*** of any material desire.(p.225)

• We reverted to the old way of life we knew -- a life full of anger, vindictiveness, resentment, fear, dependence, ***denial,*** self-will, irresponsibility.(p.459)

• He can only be defeated by an attitude of intolerance or belligerent ***denial.***(p.570)

denied

• He subsequently ***denied*** having received the money and used the incident as a basis for discrediting the man.(p.80)

denizens

• As we became subjects of King Alcohol, shivering ***denizens*** of his mad realm, the chilling vapor that is loneliness settled down.(p.151)

denomination

• We are not allied with any particular faith, sect or ***denomination,*** nor do we oppose anyone.(p.xiv)

• Those of us belonging to a religious ***denomination*** which requires confession must, and of course, will want to go to the properly appointed authority whose duty it is to receive it.(p.74)

• If we belong to a religious ***denomination*** which requires a definite morning devotion, we attend to that also.(p.87)

• Your prospect may belong to a religious ***denomination.***(p.93)

• We represent no particular faith or ***denomination.***(p.93)

• Clergymen of practically every ***denomination*** have given A.A. their blessing.(p.574)

denominations

• We are dealing only with general principles common to most ***denominations.***(p.94)

denounced

• I had a drunken quarrel with my family, ***denounced*** them, and left them forever.(p.409)

dental

• I had just begun a ***dental*** practice in a beautiful new office.(p.418)

• Oddly enough, the dentist who started A.A. in Amarillo, Tex., benevolently arranged my admission to ***dental*** college.(p.419)

• Fear, love of dentistry, and an imitation of my father's periodic drinking pattern took me through ***dental*** college soberly, except for the few parties and vacations in those four years.(p.419)

• My life there was a nightmare of periodic binges on alcohol and pills, adultery, unhappy hours at the ***dental*** office, seeing my wife give birth to our second child and have several miscarriages, living in a turbulent household, and making continual attempts to be the respectable dentist, husband, father, and community leader.(p.419)

• After I came to A.A., I was divorced by my wife; I lost my practice; I was legally restrained from seeing my children; I went broke; and the ***dental*** society threatened me with the loss of my license.(p.420)

dentist

• I was born in Cleveland, Ohio, the only child of a prominent ***dentist,*** and a very proud mother.(p.357)

• Oddly enough, the ***dentist*** who started A.A. in Amarillo, Tex., benevolently arranged my admission to dental college.(p.419)

• My life there was a nightmare of periodic binges on alcohol and pills, adultery, unhappy hours at the dental office, seeing my wife give birth to our second child and have several miscarriages, living in a turbulent household, and making continual attempts to be the respectable ***dentist,*** husband, father, and community leader.(p.419)

• Only a few days before Christmas I went to the ***dentist*** for a periodic checkup.(p.465)

dentist's

• On the day set for the extractions, on my way to the ***dentist's*** I felt a little nervous, so I had a couple of drinks, and after the teeth were out I was very nervous, so I had a few more.(p.466)

dentistry

• Fear, love of ***dentistry,*** and an imitation of my father's periodic drinking pattern took me through dental college soberly, except for the few parties and vacations in those four years.(p.419)

deny

• To spend too much time on any one situation is to ***deny*** some other alcoholic an opportunity to live and be happy.(p.96)

depart

• Without this proof the expectant purchaser would be forced to ***depart*** empty handed with none of what I later came to believe was the great panacea for all human ills.(p.171)

• While waiting to ***depart*** I was selected -- by giving a CPO five dollars – to be bartender in the Navy Chief's Club.(p.426)

department

• My wife began to work in a ***department*** store, coming home exhausted to find me drunk.(p.4)

• Now we try to put spiritual principles to work in every ***department*** of our lives.(p.116)

• I was at one time assistant manager of a corporation ***department*** employing sixty-six hundred men.(p.136)

• I finished my apprenticeship and was moved into the drafting ***department.***(p.211)

• The school then obtained a job for me in the drafting ***department*** of another company.(p.211)

• A year later, after I completed the course in contracts, I quit the law school, and undertook some engineering work for a patent law firm on behalf of clients who were in difficulties and who desired to keep their troubles from their own engineering ***department.***(p.212)

• For a decade, I'd headed up a forty-publicist ***department.***(p.328)

• It has changed not simply one ***department*** of my life – it has changed my whole life.(p.394)

• They summoned the fire ***department*** and the sheriff.(p.424)

• I liked it and soon moved into the photo ***department*** which was what I wanted to do.(p.425)

• After nine months of training, all the rest of my class was paroled and I went to work in the ***Department*** of Corrections.(p.462)

depend

• Our very lives, as ex-problem drinkers, ***depend*** upon our constant thought of others and how we may help meet their needs.(p.20)

• Something went haywire and I got to ***depend*** on it so I could do nothing without it.(p.386)

• I depended on optimism and ambition to live in society; when I began to tire, I had to ***depend*** on chemicals instead to keep going.(p.420)

• I grew up believing that one had to be totally self-sufficient, for one never dared to ***depend*** on another human being.(p.545)

• Nor ought A.A. membership ever ***depend*** upon money or conformity.(p.565)

• Learning to ***depend*** upon a higher power and absorb himself in his work with other alcoholics, he remains sober day by day.(p.572)

dependable

• Neither is reason, as most of us use it, entirely ***dependable,*** though it emanate from our best minds.(p.54)

• I remember the day when I decided to drink myself to death quietly, without bothering anyone, because I was tired of having been a ***dependable,*** trustworthy person for about thirty-nine years without having received what I thought was a proper reward for my virtue.(p.531)

depended

• I ***depended*** on optimism and ambition to live in society; when I began to tire, I had to depend on chemicals instead to keep going.(p.420)

• He can certainly be ***depended*** on.(p.499)

dependence

• Though he could not accept all the tenets of the Oxford Groups, he was convinced of the need for moral inventory, confession of personality defects, restitution to those harmed, helpfulness to others, and the necessity of belief in and ***dependence*** upon God.(p.xvi)

• We were bothered with the thought that faith and ***dependence*** upon a Power beyond ourselves was somewhat weak, even cowardly.(p.45)

• Some of us have taken very hard knocks to learn this truth: Job or no job -- wife or no wife -- we simply do not stop drinking so long as we place ***dependence*** upon other people ahead of ***dependence*** on God.(p.98)

• I was aware of symptoms of impending ***dependence,*** and I told myself I had gotten out of the rat race just in time to head off any booze problem.(p.327)

• We reverted to the old way of life we knew -- a life full of anger, vindictiveness, resentment, fear, ***dependence,*** denial, self-will, irresponsibility.(p.459)

dependent

• What right had he to involve those ***dependent*** upon him?(p.80)

• Remind the prospect that his recovery is not ***dependent*** upon people.(p.99)

• It is ***dependent*** upon his relationship with God.(p.100)

• I'd lived too long and become a loser, ***dependent*** on booze.(p.333)

• After a while I really did enjoy drinking and what it did to me, and I became ***dependent*** upon it for every occasion.(p.464)

• Eventually the day came when I was ***dependent*** upon it even when there wasn't any occasion.(p.464)

depending

• We never apologize to anyone for ***depending*** upon our Creator.(p.68)

• One of the many doctors who had the opportunity of reading this book in manuscript form told us that the use of sweets was often helpful, of course ***depending*** upon a doctor's advice.(p.133)

• During the first three months I carried on all these activities without a car, ***depending*** entirely on buses and streetcars – I, who had always to have a car at my immediate command.(p.283)

• We are both ***depending*** upon God and our use of the A.A. program to help us make a success of this joint undertaking.(p.286)

• There, I received several soda crackers and water daily, and before I could have my third-day meal (again the only meal in ten days), I had to drink a glass of castor oil or mineral oil, ***depending*** on the cruelty of the person who was doing the dispensing.(p.459)

• ***Depending*** on the stage of drunkenness, eventually I either fought or went to sleep.(p.537)

depends

• Whether such a person can quit upon a nonspiritual basis ***depends*** upon the extent to which he has already lost the power to choose whether he will drink or not.(p.34)

• It ***depends*** on us and on our motives.(p.70)

• One – Our common welfare should come first; personal recovery ***depends*** upon A.A. unity.(p.564)

deplored

• "Best in the business, when he's sober," my customers would say, and I still had a following who would give me work though they ***deplored*** my habits, because they knew the job would be well done when they eventually got it.(p.234)

deportment

• That the man who is making the approach has had the same difficulty, that he obviously knows what he is talking about, that his whole ***deportment*** shouts at the new prospect that he is a man with a real answer, that he has no attitude of Holier Than Thou, nothing whatever except the sincere desire to be helpful; that there are no fees to pay, no axes to grind, no people to please, no lectures to be endured -- these are the conditions we have found most effective.(p.18)

• This I did, and proved myself satisfactory to the faculty, both in ***deportment*** and scholastically.(p.174)

deposit

• I had no trouble making the right decision when I saw my wife open her purse at the meeting that night and ***deposit*** a cute little angel in the middle of my birthday cake.(p.366)

deposits
• It was I who had to tell the bank, after a certain time, to refuse all further ***deposits***.(p.409)

depot
• I bought some more liquor on the way to the ***depot***.(p.179)

depressed
• For a few days he was ***depressed*** about his condition.(p.39)
• Business failure, insanity, fatal illness, suicide -- these calamities in his immediate family embittered and ***depressed*** him.(p.56)
• He may be more receptive when ***depressed***.(p.91)
• If the book is read the moment the patient is able, while acutely ***depressed***, realization of his condition may come to him.(p.144)
• They knew what to do about those black abysses that yawned ready to swallow me when I felt ***depressed***, or nervous.(p.229)
• I tried them mixed, unmixed, drinking only when gay, only when ***depressed***.(p.305)
• But, as it was with drinking, this project will be entered into with enthusiasm and optimism -- and probably wind up the same way, ***depressed***.(p.396)

depressing
• I felt it certainly must be very ***depressing*** to her that I should sit there by her bedside and cry.(p.272)

depression
• His alcoholic problem was so complex, and his ***depression*** so great, that we felt his only hope would be through what we then called "moral psychology," and we doubted if even that would have any effect.(p.xxix)
• In some circumstances we have gone out deliberately to get drunk, feeling ourselves justified by nervousness, anger, worry, ***depression***, jealousy or the like.(p.37)
• We were having trouble with personal relationships, we couldn't control our emotional natures, we were a prey to misery and ***depression***, we couldn't make a living, we had a feeling of uselessness, we were full of fear, we were unhappy, we couldn't seem to be of real help to other people -- was not a basic solution of these bedevilments more important than whether we should see newsreels of lunar flight?(p.52)
• The alarming physical and mental symptoms, the deepening pall of remorse, ***depression*** and inferiority that settled down on our loved ones -- these things terrified and distracted us.(p.106)
• If they sense these things, they will not take so seriously his periods of crankiness, ***depression***, or apathy, which will disappear when there is tolerance, love, and spiritual understanding.(p.127)
• Now about health: A body badly burned by alcohol does not often recover overnight nor do twisted thinking and ***depression*** vanish in a twinkling.(p.133)
• Down in the pit of his ***depression***, new hope had somehow been born.(p.189)
• After the tire job came the thirties, the ***Depression*** and the down hill road.(p.244)
• The ensuing nine years were the ***Depression*** years, both nationally and personally.(p.277)
• The ***Depression*** was still on and jobs were scarce.(p.282)
• Shortly thereafter, aided by the ***Depression***, I found that I had a great deal of spare time and that a little drink in the morning helped.(p.287)
• In this small group, during the ***Depression***, there was no one who was not hard up.(p.291)
• Just three years of drinking pushed a shy, lonely young girl to the depth of ***depression***.(p.353)
• With increasing guilt and never-ending ***depression***, I was too weak to continue this day-by-day suicide.(p.355)
• High living, a great many fair weather friends, the 1929 stock market crash, and a couple of years of ***Depression***, soon relieved me one by one of my worldly goods including my wife.(p.358)
• This was at the height of the ***Depression*** and the end of Prohibition.(p.358)
• During the years 1930 to 1935, due to the ***Depression*** and its aftermath, business went from bad to worse.(p.486)

Depression
• His alcoholic problem was so complex, and his ***depression*** so great, that we felt his only hope would be through what we then called "moral psychology," and we doubted if even that would have any effect.(p.xxix)
• In some circumstances we have gone out deliberately to get drunk, feeling ourselves justified by nervousness, anger, worry, ***depression***, jealousy or the like.(p.37)
• We were having trouble with personal relationships, we couldn't control our emotional natures, we were a prey to misery and ***depression***, we couldn't make a living, we had a feeling of uselessness, we were full of fear, we were unhappy, we couldn't seem to be of real help to other people -- was not a basic solution of these bedevilments more important than whether we should see newsreels of lunar flight?(p.52)
• The alarming physical and mental symptoms, the deepening pall of remorse, ***depression*** and inferiority that settled down on our loved ones -- these things terrified and distracted us.(p.106)
• If they sense these things, they will not take so seriously his periods of crankiness, ***depression***, or apathy, which will disappear when there is tolerance, love, and spiritual understanding.(p.127)
• Now about health: A body badly burned by alcohol does not often recover overnight nor do twisted thinking and ***depression*** vanish in a twinkling.(p.133)
• Down in the pit of his ***depression***, new hope had somehow been born.(p.189)
• After the tire job came the thirties, the ***Depression*** and the down hill road.(p.244)
• The ensuing nine years were the ***Depression*** years, both nationally and personally.(p.277)
• The ***Depression*** was still on and jobs were scarce.(p.282)
• Shortly thereafter, aided by the ***Depression***, I found that I had a great deal of spare time and that a little drink in the morning helped.(p.287)
• In this small group, during the ***Depression***, there was no one who was not hard up.(p.291)
• Just three years of drinking pushed a shy, lonely young girl to the depth of ***depression***.(p.353)
• With increasing guilt and never-ending ***depression***, I was too weak to continue this day-by-day suicide.(p.355)
• High living, a great many fair weather friends, the 1929 stock market crash, and a couple of years of ***Depression***, soon relieved me one by one of my worldly goods including my wife.(p.358)
• This was at the height of the ***Depression*** and the end of Prohibition.(p.358)
• During the years 1930 to 1935, due to the ***Depression*** and its aftermath, business went from bad to worse.(p.486)

deprive
• But you should not ***deprive*** your family or creditors of money they should have.(p.96)

deprived
• He often says that if he had continued to work on them, he might have ***deprived*** many others, who have since recovered, of their chance.(p.96)
• I was ***deprived*** of many of the things that we feel are important in life, such as education particularly, because of my father's drinking.(p.261)

depth
• The message which can interest and hold these alcoholic people must have ***depth*** and weight.(p.xxvi)
• Just three years of drinking pushed a shy, lonely young girl to the ***depth*** of depression.(p.353)

deranged
• Of course, this chapter refers to alcoholics, sick people, ***deranged*** men.(p.149)

derelictions
• While on the subject of confidence, can you adopt the attitude that so far as you are concerned this will be a strictly personal matter, that his alcoholic ***derelictions***, the treatment about to be undertaken, will never be discussed without his consent?(p.143)

derided
• Alcoholics who have ***derided*** religious people will be helped by such contacts.(p.131)

derision
• Where ***derision***, contempt and pity were once shown me, I now enjoy the respect of many people.(p.296)

derive
• They ***derive*** no real authority from their titles; they do not govern.(p.567)

derived
• We had long talks when I would still her foreboding by telling her that men of genius conceived their best projects when drunk; that the most majestic constructions of philosophic thought were so ***derived***.(p.2)
• It is impossible to put on paper all the benefits I have ***derived*** . . . physical, mental, domestic, spiritual, and monetary.(p.302)
• I can't begin to tell you of all the benefits I have ***derived*** from this new way of living.(p.481)

derogatory
• I don't mean that in any sense as a ***derogatory*** statement about psychotherapy; it's a great tool, not too potent, but a great tool.(p.349)

descended
• Many of these same things had happened to me many times before, but this time they had all ***descended*** together.(p.238)
• Immediately a great feeling of peace ***descended*** upon me, intermingled with a feeling of being suffused with a quiet strength.(p.280)

describe
• Figures given in this foreword ***describe*** the Fellowship as it was in 1955(p.xv)
• All of us spend much of our spare time in the sort of effort which we are going to ***describe***.(p.19)
• So we shall ***describe*** some of the mental states that precede a relapse into drinking, for obviously this is the crux of the problem.(p.35)
• When he sees you know all about the drinking game, commence to ***describe*** yourself as an alcoholic.(p.91)
• When dealing with such a person, you had better use everyday language to ***describe*** spiritual principles.(p.93)
• Perhaps the best way of treating you to a glimpse of your future will be to ***describe*** the growth of the fellowship among us.(p.153)

described
• We of Alcoholics Anonymous believe that the reader will be interested in the medical estimate of the plan of recovery ***described*** in this book.(p.xxiii)
• You should be ***described*** to him as one of a fellowship who, as part of their own recovery, try to help others and who will be glad to talk to him if he cares to see you.(p.90)
• This seemed to me like an opportunity to be helpful, so I spent two hours talking about alcoholism, the malady, and ***described*** the symptoms and results as well as I could.(p.138)
• Then, in this eastern city, there are informal meetings such as we have ***described*** to you, where you may now see scores of members.(p.162)
• My writing career was ***described*** in the couplet "Alcohol gave me wings to fly,/And then it took away the sky."(p.331)
• They ***described*** what had happened when they went out and tried drinking again, and I knew they were sincere in saying that it could happen to me.(p.334)
• The next few years in New York can be ***described*** in a very few words.(p.358)
• In the first few chapters a number of sudden revolutionary changes are ***described***.(p.569)
• The A.A. plan is ***described*** by the members themselves as 'self-insurance.'(p.574)

describes
• Each individual, in the personal stories, ***describes*** in his own language and from his own point of view the way he established his relationship with God.(p.29)

describing
• Therefore, the first portion of this volume, ***describing*** the A.A. recovery program, has been left untouched in the course of revisions made for both the second and the third editions.(p.xi)
• Show any longshoreman a Sunday supplement ***describing*** a proposal to explore the moon by means of a rocket and he will say, "I bet they do it -- maybe not so long either."(p.52)
• In ***describing*** his suffering, his fears, his many years of groping for some answer to that which always seemed to remain unanswerable, he could have been ***describing*** me, and nothing short of experience and knowledge could have afforded him that much insight!(p.309)
• He was close to tears in ***describing*** his boredom without an activity.(p.334)

description
• But when the broker gave him Dr. Silkworth's ***description*** of alcoholism and its hopelessness, the physician began to pursue the spiritual remedy for his malady with a willingness he had never before been able to muster.(p.xvi)
• But this ***description*** should identify him roughly.(p.22)
• With many individuals the methods which I employed are successful, but I have never been successful with an alcoholic of your ***description***."(p.27)
• Our ***description*** of the alcoholic, the chapter to the agnostic, and our personal adventures before and after make clear three pertinent ideas:(p.60)
• Suppose, however, that your husband fits the ***description*** of number two.(p.112)

• One day he told me about an executive of the same bank who, from his ***description,*** was undoubtedly alcoholic.(p.138)
• Here was a prospect all right but, by the ***description,*** none too promising.(p.156)
• The mental state of the sick alcoholic is beyond ***description.***(p.244)
• I liked the ***description*** of the alcoholic as a person who had found that alcohol is interfering with his social or business life.(p.380)

desert
• His coming was an oasis in the dreary ***desert*** of futility.(p.9)
• I wanted to live, not in a ***desert,*** but in a normal world; and my idea of a normal world was among people who drank – teetotallers were not included.(p.227)

deserted
• The patient had made his own diagnosis, and deciding his situation hopeless, had hidden in a ***deserted*** barn determined to die.(p.xxix)
• Well, I'm willing, if it will curb this awful desire to drink, this fear of not having a drink, this feeling of always being alone, scared, ***deserted,*** sick.(p.430)
• Forgive me – I cannot write further about this latest turn of events, anticipating seeing the family I ***deserted*** so long ago.(p.463)

desertion
• Then we were severely criticized by our husband's parents for ***desertion.***(p.106)

deserts
• Luck then ***deserts*** him and he is slightly injured several times in succession.(p.38)

deserve
• It set in motion trains of circumstances which brought us misfortune we felt we didn't ***deserve.***(p.67)
• He wants to enjoy a certain reputation, but knows in his heart he doesn't ***deserve*** it.(p.73)
• Nothing that has happened to me do I ***deserve.***(p.463)

design
• It is a ***design*** for living that works in rough going.(p.15)
• A new life has been given us or, if you prefer, "a ***design*** for living" that really works.(p.28)
• Our ***design*** for living is not a one-way street.(p.81)
• She was studying fashion ***design,*** was living in the same rooming house, and was from my home town of Cleveland.(p.359)

designating
• When writing or speaking publicly about alcoholism, we urge each of our Fellowship to omit his personal name, ***designating*** himself instead as "a member of Alcoholics Anonymous."(p.xiii)

designed
• There was a concrete program, ***designed*** to secure the greatest possible inner security for us long-time escapists.(p.229)
• It took me some time to realize that the Twelve Steps of A.A. were ***designed*** to help correct these defects of character and so help remove the obsession to drink.(p.380)
• All Twelve Steps of A.A. are ***designed*** to kill the old self (deflate the old ego) and build a new, free self.(p.459)
• Shortly thereafter, I was selected, with eight other inmates out of the 10,000 in the state's prisons at that time, to attend a school ***designed*** to take former "management problems" like me and convert them into paracounselors.(p.462)

designs
• Established on such a footing we became less and less interested in ourselves, our little plans and ***designs.***(p.63)

desirability
• As our husbands began to apply spiritual principles in their lives, we began to see the ***desirability*** of doing so too.(p.116)

desirable
• We found it very ***desirable*** to take this spiritual step with an understanding person, such as our wife, best friend or spiritual adviser.(p.63)
• Counsel with persons is often ***desirable,*** but we let God be the final judge.(p.69)
• For most alcoholics who are drinking, or who are just getting over a spree, a certain amount of physical treatment is ***desirable,*** even imperative.(p.142)

desire
• The only requirement for membership is an honest ***desire*** to stop drinking.(p.xiv)
• After they have succumbed to the ***desire*** again, as so many do, and the phenomenon of craving develops, they pass through the well-known stages of a spree, emerging remorseful, with a firm resolution not to drink again.(p.xxvii)
• On the other hand – and strange as this may seem to those who do not understand -- once a psychic change has occurred, the very same person who seemed doomed, who had so many problems he despaired of ever solving them, suddenly finds himself easily able to control his ***desire*** for alcohol, the only effort necessary being that required to follow a few simple rules.(p.xxvii)
• My incredible behavior in the face of a desperate ***desire*** to stop was explained.(p.7)
• That the man who is making the approach has had the same difficulty, that he obviously knows what he is talking about, that his whole deportment shouts at the new prospect that he is a man with a real answer, that he has no attitude of Holier Than Thou, nothing whatever except the sincere ***desire*** to be helpful; that there are no fees to pay, no axes to grind, no people to please, no lectures to be endured -- these are the conditions we have found most effective.(p.18)
• At a certain point in the drinking of every alcoholic, he passes into a state where the most powerful ***desire*** to stop drinking is of absolutely no avail.(p.24)
• We have no ***desire*** to convince anyone that there is only one way by which faith can be acquired.(p.28)
• But the difficulty is that few alcoholics have enough ***desire*** to stop while there is yet time.(p.32)
• We have heard of few instances where people, who showed definite signs of alcoholism, were able to stop for a long period because of an overpowering ***desire*** to do so.(p.32)
• If we are sorry for what we have done, and have the honest ***desire*** to let God take us to better things, we believe we will be forgiven and will have learned our lesson.(p.70)
• But our man is sure to be impressed with a sincere ***desire*** to set right the wrong.(p.77)
• Unless one's family expresses a ***desire*** to live upon spiritual principles we think we ought not to urge them.(p.83)
• If he is to find God, the ***desire*** must come from within.(p.95)
• Our loyalty and the ***desire*** that our husbands hold up their heads and be like other men have begotten all sorts of predicaments.(p.105)
• Your ***desire*** to protect him should not cause you to lie to people when they have a right to know where he is and what he is doing.(p.115)
• If you ***desire*** to help it might be well to disregard your own drinking, or lack of it.(p.139)
• You may have to curb his ***desire*** to work sixteen hours a day.(p.146)
• He had a desperate ***desire*** to stop, but saw no way out, for he had earnestly tried many avenues of escape.(p.155)
• I never had any ***desire*** to get drunk.(p.196)
• The law school experience was not inspired by a ***desire*** to follow patent law, which has been my profession since: I went to law school primarily to learn the law of contracts following my own experience with litigation.(p.212)
• One of the things that came up repeatedly in the stories they told me was that once they had accepted the program, they never had a ***desire*** to take a drink.(p.219)
• I've never had a ***desire*** to take a drink.(p.219)
• My family had money -- I had never known denial of any material ***desire.***(p.225)
• I had no ***desire*** whatever to sit down at a table and stay a whole morning or afternoon drinking.(p.231)
• Unfortunately, I had no ***desire*** to consult my priest about my drinking.(p.234)
• Unlike many other Catholics who frequently take pledges for definite periods – a year, two years or for good, I never had any ***desire*** to "take a pledge" before the priest.(p.234)
• He had no ***desire*** to know anything, except whether I was definite about my ***desire*** to quit drinking.(p.235)
• In a few sentences he made God seem personal to me, explained Him as a being who was interested in me, the alcoholic, and that all I needed to do was to be willing to follow His way; that as long as I followed it I would be able to overcome my ***desire*** for liquor.(p.236)
• We now live in the West and are very fortunate in our area A.A.; it is good, simple and friendly, and our one ***desire*** is to stay in A.A. and not on it.(p.250)
• Thank God I had no ***desire*** for a drink when he died.(p.272)
• When I reached a point directly back of our house, where I could have cut through a friend's garden, I was almost overpowered by the ***desire*** to get home, but I made the whole journey.(p.276)
• The example which they and Bill W., whose visits to Akron were fairly frequent, set me of service to their fellow men imbued me with a great ***desire*** to emulate them.(p.281)
• I, carried away with the ***desire*** to serve A.A., gave what was probably one of the first radio broadcasts about A.A., living through a case of mike fright and feeling like a million dollars when it was all over.(p.283)
• I was seized with an almost uncontrollable ***desire*** to reach out for it.(p.285)
• Every reasonable ***desire*** was possible of attainment for me.(p.304)
• It explained so much I had not understood about myself and, best of all, it promised recovery if I would do a few simple things and be willing to have the ***desire*** to drink removed.(p.309)
• I only know that it does – if you ***desire*** it with your whole heart and without reservation.(p.384)
• Well, I'm willing, if it will curb this awful ***desire*** to drink, this fear of not having a drink, this feeling of always being alone, scared, deserted, sick.(p.430)
• For me, pills don't produce the ***desire*** to swallow a pill; they produce the symptoms that require that the pill be taken for relief.(p.443)
• We do this by going to many A.A. meetings with an open mind and a ***desire*** to live the good-feeling life without chemicals -- liquid or otherwise.(p.459)
• But I am to learn later that it began with my ***desire*** for material success becoming greater than my interest in the welfare of my fellow man.(p.507)
• My ***desire*** to be honest with myself made it necessary for me to realize that my thinking was irrational.(p.550)
• Three – The only requirement for A.A. membership is a ***desire*** to stop drinking.(p.564)

desired
• Some of us had already walked far over the Bridge of Reason toward the ***desired*** shore of faith.(p.53)
• A year later, after I completed the course in contracts, I quit the law school, and undertook some engineering work for a patent law firm on behalf of clients who were in difficulties and who ***desired*** to keep their troubles from their own engineering department.(p.212)
• Where preaching and prayers had touched me very little, I immediately ***desired*** further knowledge of these men.(p.235)

desires
• We are assuming, of course, that the reader ***desires*** to stop.(p.34)
• I had my own business, successful enough for me to indulge most of my ***desires.***(p.225)

desk
• Another time, as I opened a letter which lay on my ***desk,*** a newspaper clipping fell out.(p.136)
• One of the earliest memories that I have is of a bottle sitting on his ***desk*** with a skull and crossbones and marked "Poison."(p.193)
• I went downstairs and there was the grizzly old veteran police officer in charge of the property ***desk,*** and as he gave me the stuff, he asked, "Are you going out in the street that way?"(p.204)
• When I said yes, we both knelt at his ***desk*** and prayed, each of us asking to have these defects taken away.(p.292)
• And I put a Bible in my ***desk.***(p.348)
• Here I am down at my office behind my ***desk*** and there she is out at the hospital.(p.350)
• While I was in Florida trying to convince my wife with all the A.A. literature that she should come back to me, she went over to her ***desk*** and picked up a clipping she had taken from the St. Petersburg Times about A.A.(p.366)
• In the first year there were episodes such as kicking Priscilla in the shins, getting the lock changed on the ***desk*** in the A.A. Club, because I, as secretary, didn't want the Intergroup secretary "interfering," and taking an older woman member out to lunch for the express purpose of informing her that she was "a phony."(p.416)
• I stayed in the barracks all day, "making out guard schedules," and getting mildly plastered from the jug under my ***desk.***(p.426)
• On one occasion when I was serving time in my favorite drying-out place while I was having a session with the psychiatrist, she left my case history on her ***desk*** when she was called away from the room.(p.470)
• At that time the repeal whiskies were back, and I'd go to the store and buy my whiskey and take it to my office and put it under the ***desk,*** first in one place and then in another, and there soon was an accumulation of empty bottles.(p.488)

despair
• No words can tell of the loneliness and ***despair*** I found in that bitter morass of self-pity.(p.8)
• Many times I have gone to my old hospital in ***despair.***(p.15)
• In the face of collapse and ***despair,*** in the face of the total failure of their human resources, they found that a new power, peace, happiness, and sense of direction flowed into them.(p.50)
• Four: You may have a husband of whom you completely ***despair.***(p.110)
• Momentarily we did — then would come oblivion and the awful awakening to face the hideous Four Horsemen -- Terror, Bewilderment, Frustration, ***Despair.***(p.151)
• His call to the clergyman led him presently to a certain resident of the town, who, though formerly able and respected, was then nearing the nadir of alcoholic ***despair.***(p.155)
• After two or three years of effort along this line, I reached the point of actual ***despair*** that I ever would be able to drink only a harmless amount each day.(p.215)
• And I remembered the creeping horror of the interminable night, in which I slept for short spells and woke up dripping with cold sweat and shaken with utter ***despair,*** to drink hastily from my bottle and mercifully pass out again, "You're mad, you're mad, you're mad!" pounded through my brain with each returning ray of consciousness, and I drowned the refrain with drink.(p.224)
• First, through mutual pain and ***despair,*** and later through mutual objectives and new-found faith and hope.(p.312)
• Out of sheer ***despair,*** she called for help.(p.353)
• Today I think of life in terms of happiness, contentment, freedom from fear and ***despair,*** sane thinking, ability to face problems as they occur, the opportunity to help other alcoholics and to be decent.(p.430)
• My personality was stretched almost to splitting in the effort; schizophrenia stared me in the face, and one night I was in a suicidal ***despair.***(p.435)
• It is impossible for me to reproduce my ***despair.***(p.435)
• I sank into total ***despair.***(p.461)

despaired
• On the other hand — and strange as this may seem to those who do not understand -- once a psychic change has occurred, the very same person who seemed doomed, who had so many problems he ***despaired*** of ever solving them, suddenly finds himself easily able to control his desire for alcohol, the only effort necessary being that required to follow a few simple rules.(p.xxvii)

despairing
• If any feel that as psychiatrists directing a hospital for alcoholics we appear somewhat sentimental, let them stand with us a while on the firing line, see the tragedies, the ***despairing*** wives, the little children; let the solving of these problems become a part of their daily work, and even of their sleeping moments, and the most cynical will not wonder that we have accepted and encouraged this movement.(p.xxvi)
• Men have cried out to me in sincere and ***despairing*** appeal: "Doctor, I cannot go on like this!(p.xxvii)
• From a trembling, ***despairing*** nervous wreck, had emerged a man brimming over with self-reliance and contentment.(p.xxix)
• My weary and ***despairing*** wife was informed that it would all end with heart failure during delirium tremens, or I would develop a wet brain, perhaps within a year.(p.7)
• I couldn't see that there was any way out of it, and I got absolutely ***despairing.***(p.522)

desperate
• Their very first case, a ***desperate*** one, recovered immediately and became A.A. number three.(p.xvii)
• He was rescued by a searching party, and, in ***desperate*** condition, brought to me.(p.xxix)
• My incredible behavior in the face of a ***desperate*** desire to stop was explained.(p.7)
• What sort of thinking dominates an alcoholic who repeats time after time the ***desperate*** experiment of the first drink?(p.35)
• You are sure to find someone ***desperate*** enough to accept with eagerness what you offer.(p.96)
• He had a ***desperate*** desire to stop, but saw no way out, for he had earnestly tried many avenues of escape.(p.155)
• By one a.m. I was ***desperate.***(p.288)
• Not knowing where I had been or how I got home was making me ***desperate.***(p.375)
• I feel that there is no situation too difficult, none too ***desperate,*** no unhappiness too great to be overcome in this great fellowship — Alcoholics Anonymous.(p.395)

desperately
• Our hope is that many alcoholic men and women, ***desperately*** in need, will see these pages, and we believe that it is only by fully disclosing ourselves and our problems that they will be persuaded to say, "Yes, I am one of them too; I must have this thing."(p.29)
• He may have come to the point where he ***desperately*** wants to stop but cannot.(p.110)
• All I had left was an iron determination to live my own life in spite of the alien world -- and here I was, an inwardly frightened, outwardly defiant woman, who ***desperately*** needed a prop to keep going.(p.226)
• Well . . . I had a job, and I really wanted ***desperately*** to stop drinking, but couldn't, so I readily agreed to visit the doctor she recommended.(p.301)
• I studied art; I ***desperately*** endeavored to create an interest in many things, in a new place among new people.(p.305)
• I was ***desperately*** in earnest to follow through and understand what was expected of me as a member of A.A. and to take each Step of the Twelve as rapidly as possible.(p.382)

desperation
• We, in our turn, sought the same escape with all the ***desperation*** of drowning men.(p.28)
• In ***desperation,*** we have even got tight ourselves -- the drunk to end all drunks.(p.106)
• With the bravery born of ***desperation,*** and abetted by alcohol, I married a young and lovely girl.(p.277)
• This was drinking in sheer ***desperation,*** alone and locked behind my own door.(p.306)
• After my wife had read this to me, I said to her, as I had said many times in ***desperation,*** "I have got to do something."(p.346)
• Help which you once continually rejected, suggestions once turned aside are finally accepted in ***desperation.***(p.377)
• ***DESPERATION*** DRINKING(p.512)
• It is ***desperation*** drinking.(p.514)
• Finally, in ***desperation,*** my family appealed to a doctor for advice and he suggested A.A.(p.549)

despicable
• My proud southern blood would have boiled if anyone had named me such a ***despicable*** thing.(p.532)

despised
• We remembered always that our sex powers were God-given and therefore good, neither to be used lightly or selfishly nor to be ***despised*** and loathed.(p.69)
• I ***despised*** the other barflies and, naturally, they loathed me.(p.410)

despite
• ***Despite*** contrary indications, I had little doubt that a mighty purpose and rhythm underlay all.(p.10)
• ***Despite*** the living example of my friend there remained in me the vestiges of my old prejudice.(p.12)
• ***Despite*** all we can say, many who are real alcoholics are not going to believe they are in that class.(p.31)
• ***Despite*** great opportunities, alcohol nearly ended her life.(p.222)
• ***Despite*** all this, I did like these new friends because, again, they were like me.(p.245)
• Successive Monday morning hangovers, which ***despite*** mid-week resolutions to do better, came with unfailing regularity, eventually caused me to quit my job.(p.254)
• I was terribly impressed by this meeting and the quality of happiness these men displayed, ***despite*** their lack of material means.(p.291)
• So Frank went to New York and ***despite*** all these things, I got drunk.(p.389)
• ***Despite*** my wife's entreaties to take it easy that day, I arrived home in bad shape.(p.557)

despondency
• Many things happened; business trials, little worries, and feelings of general ***despondency*** came near driving me to the bottle, but I made progress.(p.237)

despondently
• I had turned eighteen during the trip, and I ***despondently*** returned home by jet (on Daddy's bankbook) to a pair of miserable, hurt parents.(p.354)

destination
• Our earliest printing voiced the hope "that every alcoholic who journeys will find the Fellowship of Alcoholics Anonymous at his ***destination.***(p.xv)
• Some day we hope that every alcoholic who journeys will find a Fellowship of Alcoholics Anonymous at his ***destination.***(p.162)

destined
• How it finally broke a Southerner's obstinacy and ***destined*** this salesman to start A.A. at Philadelphia.(p.238)

destiny
• Could we still say the whole thing was nothing but a mass of electrons, created out of nothing, meaning nothing, whirling on to a ***destiny*** of nothingness?(p.54)
• We shall be with you in the Fellowship of the Spirit, and you will surely meet some of us as you trudge the Road of Happy ***Destiny.***(p.164)

destitution
• We finally sought employment ourselves as ***destitution*** faced us and our families.(p.106)

destroy
• If we do, we ***destroy*** our chance of being helpful.(p.67)
• If he opened that old affair, he was afraid it would ***destroy*** the reputation of his partner, disgrace his family and take away his means of livelihood.(p.80)
• I cannot sit by and watch you ***destroy*** yourself."(p.391)
• Experience has often warned us that nothing can so surely ***destroy*** our spiritual heritage as futile disputes over property, money, and authority.(p.566)

destroyed
• This hope, however, was ***destroyed*** by the doctor's telling him that while his religious convictions were very good, in his case they did not spell the necessary vital spiritual experience.(p.27)
• In four or five days I would be hunting all over the place, at home and in my workshop, for the bottles I had ***destroyed,*** cursing myself for being a fool.(p.234)

destroyer
• Later, I went to sea, serving as a gunnery officer on a ***destroyer*** escort and emerging a lieutenant commander.(p.555)

destroying
• He thus used his own wrong-doing as a means of ***destroying*** the reputation of another.(p.80)

destroys
• It ***destroys*** more alcoholics than anything else.(p.64)

destruction
• It meant ***destruction*** of self-centeredness.(p.14)
• Faced with alcoholic ***destruction,*** we soon became as open minded on spiritual matters as we tried to be on other questions.(p.48)
• You may be aiding in his ***destruction*** rather than his recovery.(p.97)
• A little more than fifteen years ago, through a long and calamitous series of shattering experiences, I found myself being helplessly propelled toward total ***destruction.***(p.304)
• All found themselves headed for the same ***destruction,*** and it seemed they could to nothing whatever to stop it.(p.455)

destructiveness
• We have commenced to see their terrible ***destructiveness.***(p.70)

detail
• There was, therefore, a sense of real satisfaction when I was asked to contribute a few words on a subject which is covered in such masterly ***detail*** in these pages.(p.xxv)
• The classification of alcoholics seems most difficult, and in much ***detail*** is outside the scope of this book.(p.xxviii)
• If she knows in a general way that we have been wild, should we tell her in ***detail?***(p.81)
• Even then he went into no great ***detail*** about how he and a crowd of alcoholics, with whom he associated, had mastered their difficulty.(p.235)
• I won't go into ***detail*** about that, but I can assure you it's no fun.(p.469)

detailed
• Before going into a ***detailed*** discussion, it may be well to summarize some points as we see them.(p.20)

details
• The ***details*** of the long road back to something resembling normal living -- the first short streetcar ride, the purchase of a used bike which enabled me to widen the narrow horizon of life, the first trip downtown — I will not dwell on.(p.276)
• I have omitted ***details*** of transgressions that I made when drunk for several reasons.(p.301)

detective
• When I wended my way home four days later, on the 27th, there was a ***detective*** waiting for me.(p.508)

detectives

• Around eight or nine o'clock there came two big ***detectives*** and a policeman to arrest me for assault; and I was the most amazed person in the world when they said I had assaulted someone, and especially that I had assaulted my wife.(p.492)

deter

• The almost certain consequences that follow taking even a glass of beer do not crowd into the mind to ***deter*** us.(p.24)

• Do not let any prejudice you may have against spiritual terms ***deter*** you from honestly asking yourself what they mean to you.(p.47)

deteriorated

• It started out as a good marriage, but it ***deteriorated*** over the years as she progressed through the various stages of qualifying for Al-Anon.(p.439)

deteriorates

• The man in the bed was told of the acute poisoning from which he suffered, how it ***deteriorates*** the body of an alcoholic and warps his mind.(p.157)

deteriorating

• You know the ***deteriorating*** effects, the disintegrating effects of chronic wine-drinking.(p.337)

deterioration

• He had but partially recovered from a gastric hemorrhage and seemed to be a case of pathological mental ***deterioration***.(p.xxix)

• I myself could see ***deterioration*** in my work from being physically and mentally affected by liquor, although I had not yet reached the point where all I wanted was more to drink.(p.254)

determination

• This ***determination*** bore fruit in the spring of 1939 by the publication of this volume.(p.xvii)

• As I drank, the old fierce ***determination*** to win came back.(p.4)

• The story he told is most instructive, for here was a chap absolutely convinced he had to stop drinking, who had no excuse for drinking, who exhibited splendid judgment and ***determination*** in all his other concerns, yet was flat on his back nevertheless.(p.40)

• All I had left was an iron ***determination*** to live my own life in spite of the alien world -- and here I was, an inwardly frightened, outwardly defiant woman, who desperately needed a prop to keep going.(p.226)

• With a great deal of ***determination***, I would throw out full pints – pour them out and smash the bottles -- firmly resolved never to take another drink of the stuff.(p.234)

determine

• How then shall we help our readers ***determine***, to their own satisfaction, whether they are one of us?(p.34)

• Did not these feelings, after all, ***determine*** the course of our existence?(p.54)

• We may not be able to ***determine*** which course to take.(p.86)

• God will ***determine*** that, so you must remember that your real reliance is always upon Him.(p.164)

determined

• The patient had made his own diagnosis, and deciding his situation hopeless, had hidden in a deserted barn ***determined*** to die.(p.xxix)

• Be ***determined*** that your husband's drinking is not going to spoil your relations with your children or your friends.(p.111)

• Each of the seven times that I had left this hospital in the last six months, I had come out fully ***determined*** in my own mind that I would not get drunk again -- for at least six or eight months.(p.184)

• Right then I ***determined*** that never so long as I lived would I have anything more to do with martinis.(p.195)

• I ***determined*** that I wouldn't drink.(p.200)

• So, knowing that, I had ***determined*** that so long as I lived I would never take another drink.(p.200)

• Once again, there was the challenge of a tough job, but this time I was ***determined*** to follow through.(p.248)

• I thought it was my duty to keep her from drinking, not knowing that if the other fellow is really ***determined*** to drink there is nothing you can do about it.(p.415)

• I stayed there just long enough to work up a real good resentment against the doctor in charge, who I didn't think was doing anything at all except collecting fees, and I left there fully ***determined*** that I'd never put myself in the power of medical people again.(p.521)

deterrent

• Formerly, in the acute mental and physical pain during the remorseful periods succeeding each drunk, I found my recollection of the misery I had gone through a bolsterer of resolution and afterward, perhaps, a ***deterrent*** for a time.(p.260)

detours

• His road lay clear before me, and I'd better quit rationalizing myself into any ***detours***.(p.282)

detrain

• Forced to ***detrain*** from an empty gondola on the other side of Chicago by a terrific rainstorm which drenched me to the skin, I hit the first factory building I saw for a job.(p.253)

Detroit

• So he started A.A. in ***Detroit***.(p.275)

• After six months of sobriety I saw the picture in a different light: ***Detroit*** was the place I had to return to, not only because I must face the mess I had made there, but because it was there that I could be of the most service to A.A.(p.281)

• In the spring of 1939, Bill stopped off in Akron on his way to ***Detroit*** on business.(p.281)

• While there, two or three more "cash customers" (as Dr. Bob used to call them -- probably because they had so little cash) were shipped in to us from ***Detroit***.(p.282)

• When I finally returned to ***Detroit*** to find work and to learn to stand on my own feet, the ball was already rolling, however slowly.(p.282)

• Within a year of my return to ***Detroit***, A.A. was a definitely established little group of about a dozen members and I too was established in a modest but steady job handling an independent dry-cleaning route of my own.(p.283)

devastating

• It was a ***devastating*** blow to my pride.(p.7)

• How ***devastating***, too, are the subsequent feelings of inadequacy and self-pity.(p.331)

• I learned what a ***devastating*** effect it can have on a child to coddle him and build him up, and then turn and beat him savagely, as had happened to me.(p.434)

develop

• My weary and despairing wife was informed that it would all end with heart failure during delirium tremens, or I would ***develop*** a wet brain, perhaps within a year.(p.7)

• We have begun to ***develop*** this vital sixth sense.(p.85)

• I knew the stuff I was making was a lot stronger than I had been used to, but I never suspected that steady drinking of it might ***develop*** a taste for something even stronger still.(p.233)

• This worldly lady helped to ***develop*** A.A. in Chicago and thus passed her keys to many.(p.304)

• Either they die of acute alcoholism or they ***develop*** wet brains and have to be put away permanently."(p.308)

• He told me that eventually he hoped such a group would ***develop*** in the Chicago area, but that so far this had not been started.(p.309)

• So oldsters are advised to ***develop*** interest, find hobbies.(p.330)

• Most of us did not stay out of prison long enough to run the alcoholic gamut -- to ***develop*** the ongoing kind of alcoholism or alcoholic drinking you hear about in A.A. talks.(p.458)

• Most of our experiences are what the psychologist William James calls the "educational variety" because they ***develop*** slowly over a period of time.(p.569)

developed

• I had ***developed*** a theory that most people lost money in stocks through ignorance of markets.(p.2)

• During the next few years, I ***developed*** two distinct phobias.(p.175)

• I went into the high school grades, but having missed all the intermediate grades, I didn't get along too well, so I ***developed*** the habit of going back to school just long enough for the football season and then quitting.(p.193)

• In other words, I was always safe from the discipline of my father, and having ***developed*** along that line, I had considerable difficulty in school.(p.210)

• As I look back, all the brothers ***developed*** personality problems.(p.210)

• It wasn't very long until I had ***developed*** a pretty good brew with uniformity and plenty of authority.(p.232)

• At twenty-five I had ***developed*** an alcoholic problem.(p.305)

• It was never boring, but I ***developed*** a feeling of deep insecurity.(p.369)

• He had not ***developed*** this art and had no recourse but his fists.(p.405)

• An ailment ***developed*** in one of my eyes, and I was transferred back to Sing Sing and operated upon.(p.509)

• At age forty, I ***developed*** a large lump in my potbelly, and I feared it was a tumor.(p.557)

developing

• All these, and many others, have one symptom in common: they cannot start drinking without ***developing*** the phenomenon of craving.(p.xxviii)

• They are naturally incapable of grasping and ***developing*** a manner of living which demands rigorous honesty.(p.58)

• Instead of ***developing*** new channels of activity for themselves, mother and children demand that he stay home and make up the deficiency.(p.131)

• I seemed to react by ***developing*** a streak of varying meanness, which would cause me to do things to create excitement and to get attention.(p.211)

• However, here I probably took my first step towards my coming alcoholism by ***developing*** a terrific aversion to all churches and established religions.(p.240)

development

• If we are painstaking about this phase of our ***development***, we will be amazed before we are half way through.(p.83)

• The chances are he will not for, like yourself, he is just beginning his ***development***.(p.118)

• If the family will appreciate that dad's current behavior is but a phase of his ***development***, all will be well.(p.129)

• Though some of his manifestations are alarming and disagreeable, we think dad will be on a firmer foundation than the man who is placing business or professional success ahead of spiritual ***development***.(p.129)

• When I had been in the hospital ten days, Sister Ignatia, who has played such a part in the ***development*** of A.A. in this area, stuck her head in the door one morning and announced, looking at me quizzically, that they might be able to make something human out of my face after all.(p.205)

• I can think clearly and am helped much in my thinking and judgment by my spiritual ***development*** which grows daily.(p.303)

• I realize now that this phase of my ***development*** had been arrested by my obsession with self, and my egocentricity had reached such proportions that adjustment to anything outside my personal control was impossible for me.(p.547)

develops

• After they have succumbed to the desire again, as so many do, and the phenomenon of craving ***develops***, they pass through the well-known stages of a spree, emerging remorseful, with a firm resolution not to drink again.(p.xxvii)

device

• We worked in five below zero weather, fixing on an elm tree a wrought iron ***device*** which modestly proclaimed that he was indeed a country doctor.(p.540)

devil

• If there was a ***Devil***, he seemed the Boss Universal, and he certainly had me.(p.11)

• Members of a family should watch such matters carefully, for one careless, inconsiderate remark has been known to raise the very ***devil***.(p.125)

• He will work like the ***devil*** and thank you to his dying day.(p.149)

• "That's a ***devil*** of a way to run an organization," I thought, and I reported Frank to the psychiatrist, who didn't seem perturbed; he just got someone else to take me on Fridays.(p.447)

devil-may-care

• He proved to be a ***devil-may-care*** young fellow whose parents could not make out whether he wanted to stop drinking or not.(p.158)

• He now returned home, leaving behind his first acquaintance, the lawyer and the ***devil-may-care*** chap.(p.159)

devised

• When it became noticeable to the point of comment, I ***devised*** ways of sneaking drinks on the side.(p.375)

devising

• I was too busy ***devising*** excuses to be out with drinking pals.(p.376)

devote

• My "periodics" became more frequent until I reached the point where I wanted to ***devote*** all my time to drinking, working as little as possible, and then only when the necessity of my family demanded it.(p.234)

devoted

• The next chapter is entirely ***devoted*** to Step

Twelve.(p.88)
• They shared their homes, their slender resources, and gladly *devoted* their spare hours to fellow-sufferers.(p.159)
• She was a woman *devoted* to her family and loyal to her husband, but quarrels did not make a happy environment for her.(p.210)
• I had always been a good Catholic, possibly not so *devoted* as I should have been, but fairly regular in my attendance at services.(p.234)
• What philosophy I had was thoroughly paganistic -- all my life was *devoted* to a search for pleasure.(p.256)
• The rest of my time was *devoted* to A.A. spadework.(p.281)
• So six months ago I acquired a ready made family consisting of one charming wife, four grown children to whom I am *devoted*, and three grandchildren.(p.286)
• Many of my neighbors *devoted* time to volunteer work.(p.326)

devoting
• Vi was taking care of me and I was *devoting* all my time to the building of that group.(p.496)

devotion
• If we belong to a religious denomination which requires a definite morning *devotion*, we attend to that also.(p.87)
• Your husband will be the first to say it was your *devotion* and care which brought him to the point where he could have a spiritual experience.(p.118)
• They may not see why their love and *devotion* did not straighten him out.(p.128)
• Maine newsletter (Boomerang) say: "With tireless *devotion* and humility, this venerable Indian gentleman traveled thousands of miles humbly pleading for sobriety.(p.476)

devotional
• I began to read the Bible daily and to go over a simple *devotional* exercise as a way to begin each day.(p.259)

diabetes
• I was suffering from an actual disease that had a name and symptoms like *diabetes* or cancer or TB -- and a disease was respectable, not a moral stigma!(p.227)
• It had a name and symptoms, just like *diabetes* or T.B.(p.392)

diagnose
• We do not like to pronounce any individual as alcoholic, but you can quickly *diagnose* yourself.(p.31)

diagnosed
• I am a young alcoholic with a drug problem, a doctor, the husband of an alcoholic, the son of an alcoholic, and a man once *diagnosed* as a violent manic-depressive.(p.421)

diagnosis
• The patient had made his own *diagnosis*, and deciding his situation hopeless, had hidden in a deserted barn determined to die.(p.xxix)
• I remember, one time, even the dog had a psychiatric *diagnosis*.(p.440)
• The Mayo Clinic seemed like a good place to have my *diagnosis* confirmed.(p.444)
• I think, with him it possibly was a gift -- intuitive *diagnosis*.(p.485)

diagnostic
• The Great Boss has given me *diagnostic* and surgical talent, and He has loaned it to me to use for the rest of my life.(p.350)

diagnostician
• I happened to be the best *diagnostician* I knew at the time, and certainly I knew my case better than anyone else.(p.444)

diary
• As I said earlier, self-pity and resentment were my constant companions and my inventory began to look like a thirty-three year *diary*, for I seemed to have a resentment against everybody I had ever known.(p.551)

dictates
• Follow the *dictates* of a Higher Power and you will presently live in a new and wonderful world, no matter what your present circumstances!(p.100)

dictation
• Handling customers, dealers, insurance people, *dictation*, telephoning, directing new employees, answering to superiors, and all the rest of it.(p.299)

dictionary
• I've been benefited from a *dictionary* definition I found that reads: "rationalization is giving a socially acceptable reason for socially unacceptable behavior, and socially unacceptable behavior is a form of insanity."(p.551)

didn't
• Other thousands came to a few A.A. meetings and at first decided they *didn't* want the program.(p.xx)
• I simply *didn't* know.(p.5)
• I *didn't* like the idea.(p.12)
• That *didn't* seem to bother me so I tried another."(p.36)
• They grinned, which I *didn't* like so much, and then asked me if I thought myself alcoholic and if I were really licked this time.(p.42)
• It *didn't* work.(p.62)
• It set in motion trains of circumstances which brought us misfortune we felt we *didn't* deserve.(p.67)
• Self-reliance was good as far as it went, but it *didn't* go far enough.(p.68)
• Some of us once had great self-confidence, but it *didn't* fully solve the fear problem, or any other.(p.68)
• We'd hardly be human if we *didn't*.(p.69)
• God *didn't* do it.(p.133)
• Then he added, "He sure *didn't* do much for me when I was trying to fight this booze racket alone."(p.158)
• It hadn't worked out that way and I *didn't* know what the matter was and did not know what to do.(p.184)
• Before very long we began to relate some incidents of our drinking and, naturally, pretty soon, I realized both of them knew what they were talking about because you can see things and smell things when you're drunk, that you can't other times, and, if I had thought they *didn't* know what they were talking about, I wouldn't have been willing to talk to them at all.(p.185)
• I thought of what liquor had done to me, the opportunities that I had discarded, the abilities that had been given me and how I had wasted them, and I finally came to the conclusion, that if I *didn't* want to quit, I certainly ought to want to, and that I was willing to do anything in the world to stop drinking.(p.186)
• I was willing to admit to myself that I had hit bottom, that I had gotten hold of something that I *didn't* know how to handle by myself.(p.187)
• Bill *didn't* seem too impressed.(p.188)
• I *didn't* have any.(p.190)
• It took me a year, or a year and a half to get to feeling physically well, and it was rather tough, but I soon found folks whose friendship I had once had, and I found, after I had been sober for quite some little time, that these people began to act like they had in previous years, before I had gotten so bad, so that I *didn't* pay too awful much attention to financial gains.(p.190)
• Of course, as time went on, and I began to get my health back and began to be so I *didn't* have to hide from people all the time, it's just been wonderful.(p.192)
• I went into the high school grades, but having missed all the intermediate grades, I *didn't* get along too well, so I developed the habit of going back to school just long enough for the football season and then quitting.(p.193)
• There was always a tremendous drive and ambition to become a great guy, because I think I recognized inwardly that I *didn't* have any special talents.(p.194)
• We boys drove out in somebody's car and went to the bar on the way do the dining room and I, in an effort to impress the other boys that I was city-bred, having lived in Scranton and Cleveland, asked them if they *didn't* want a drink.(p.194)
• I *didn't* even know what a martini looked like, but I had heard a man down the bar order one.(p.194)
• It irritated my nostrils; I choked, I *didn't* like it.(p.195)
• I *didn't* even like the olive.(p.195)
• I *didn't* know that then.(p.195)
• During the day, looking over the contracts and money in my pocket, I found that I had sold six lots that I couldn't even remember, and *didn't* even know the people I had sold them to.(p.196)
• I *didn't* remember anything that had happened.(p.196)
• But I *didn't* do a thing about giving them any part of the seven bucks I had in my pocket.(p.197)
• I figured the only difference between me and a millionaire was that I hadn't the strength, or that he got the breaks and I *didn't*.(p.197)
• To my mind, drinking *didn't* have anything to do with not going through with things.(p.198)
• I can remember telling the poor little soul that I could probably quit drinking if I wasn't married to her, and told her that, after all, I *didn't* like restraint!(p.199)
• I *didn't* like having to come home at a certain time; I *didn't* like this, I *didn't* like that, and I think the poor girl actually divorced me to help me stop drinking!(p.199)
• Long since I had come to believe I was insane because I did so many things I *didn't* want to do.(p.199)
• I *didn't* want to neglect my children.(p.199)
• I *didn't* want to get into fights, but I did get into fights.(p.199)
• I *didn't* want to jeopardize the lives of innocent people by driving an automobile while intoxicated, but I did.(p.199)
• I remember one occasion when I did not drink for three hundred and sixty-four days, but I *didn't* quite make the year.(p.200)
• At the end of about four months, I not only had good looking clothes --and I might say that at the time I first talked to Max I *didn't* have a suit of clothes I could bend over in real sudden; now I had six suits of clothes.(p.200)
• Whenever this man and I met -- I *didn't* know his name then nor do I know it now -- we would always get drunk.(p.201)
• So I *didn't* have a beer one night, and as I drove home I was breaking my arm patting myself on the back because I had proved I could lick liquor.(p.203)
• I *didn't* drink very long at a time.(p.203)
• I *didn't* have any need of such an association!(p.206)
• I *didn't* go to high school.(p.211)
• I kept myself so busy that outside of some school and group parties, I *didn't* go overboard on drinking very much between the ages of twenty-five and thirty.(p.213)
• My life was fairly well crowded and I *didn't* seem to need any stimulants to keep me going.(p.213)
• My wife *didn't* tell me this, but one Sunday afternoon when Mary was trying to get the cobwebs out of my mind, Clarence and his sister-in-law, the hairdresser, called at the house.(p.216)
• I do not recollect the specific conversation that went on but I believe I did challenge Bill to tell me something about A.A. and I do recall one other thing: I wanted to know what this was that worked so many wonders, and hanging over the mantel was a picture of Gethsemane and Bill pointed to it and said, "There it is," which *didn't* make much sense to me.(p.216)
• She said, "Well, he wouldn't be here if you *didn't* say so."(p.217)
• Bill left me at the elevator and said, "Your room is so and so," and I *didn't* see him again for six months.(p.217)
• This time I seemed to be already awake, sitting upright in a big easy chair, in the middle of an animated conversation with a perfectly strange young woman, who *didn't* appear to think it strange.(p.222)
• My fright was real enough, but it *didn't* account for these violent reactions.(p.222)
• It must have been a long time since I had my last drink -- but I *didn't* dare ask this stranger for one.(p.223)
• Alcohol was that prop, and I *didn't* see how I could live without it.(p.226)
• He wasn't a drinking man, he *didn't* know what it was to need a drink, nor what a drink could do for one in a pinch.(p.227)
• I couldn't stomach religion, and I *didn't* like the mention of God or any of the other capital letters.(p.227)
• I was free, and I *didn't* have to drink to "show them."(p.228)
• I had found friends, understanding friends who often knew what I was thinking and feeling better than I knew myself, and *didn't* allow me to retreat into my prison of loneliness and fear over a fancied slight or hurt.(p.228)
• It *didn't* stop there.(p.229)
• For the great majority of us, however, that condition *didn't* last.(p.232)
• He *didn't* talk like a preacher at all.(p.235)
• Well, there I was, willing to try it, but I *didn't* know how, except in a vague way.(p.236)
• Every man has his problem of this kind, but we *didn't* discuss it very much.(p.236)
• I *didn't* want to be a fake.(p.237)
• Some college friends got me jobs when I finally had to go to work, but I *didn't* stick to them.(p.251)
• But I *didn't* stay long.(p.252)
• Of course I *didn't* keep sober.(p.257)
• He knew too well that *didn't* mean a thing, just as I knew in my heart that it would be only a question of time -- a few days, a week, or even a month, it was inevitable -- till I would be off on another bender.(p.257)
• The big thing was that these men were all sober and

evidently had something I ***didn't*** have.(p.259)
• But they ***didn't*** do anything for me to build up my ego.(p.262)
• And Russ ***didn't*** tell me he'd stop drinking, and he certainly ***didn't*** stop.(p.262)
• I ***didn't*** see him for a year, or even hear from him.(p.262)
• I ***didn't*** realize how I still felt about him.(p.263)
• They ***didn't*** give me anything to eat.(p.264)
• And another thing, it's a wonder they ***didn't*** throw us back in because I could become very dignified and sarcastic.(p.264)
• So, on that Saturday before Labor Day, I got drunk and set the house on fire – so we ***didn't*** have to paint it.(p.265)
• Dr. Bob was in Florida, but Jack ***didn't*** know that.(p.267)
• I ***didn't*** know that anything was ever done for them in a medical way.(p.267)
• Jack ***didn't*** seem to have too much of the spiritual understanding.(p.268)
• I ***didn't*** know anything about the Sermon on the Mount.(p.268)
• I ***didn't*** know what they were going to do because he ***didn't*** tell us much.(p.269)
• At that time they ***didn't*** let us know that people ever had trouble.(p.271)
• We wept and Russ ***didn't*** go to work.(p.271)
• (Russ was buried on Friday, and on Sunday afternoon Hilda S. had invited me there to dinner Sunday night, and I ***didn't*** think I could do it.(p.272)
• I hadn't been in too long when one of the men's wives called me one Sunday and told me she ***didn't*** think I had any part of the program.(p.273)
• She said she ***didn't*** know, but that I sure showed plain enough I ***didn't*** have any part of it.(p.273)
• I ***didn't*** think I was going to get drunk right then, but I remember how comforting it was when I called Anne and told her.(p.273)
• He spent eighteen years in running away; and then found he ***didn't*** have to run.(p.275)
• I wanted "ripe" prospects and I ***didn't*** feel that I would get very far chasing individual drunks in and out of bars.(p.281)
• I was very much interested in athletics, and because of this and parental influence, I ***didn't*** drink or smoke in either grade or high school.(p.287)
• A few months after I made my original trip to Akron I was feeling pretty cocky, and I ***didn't*** think my wife was treating me with proper respect, now that I was an outstanding citizen.(p.293)
• That being the case, it ***didn't*** take me long to figure out that my meager manufacturing facilities were entirely inadequate to the manufacture of beer for social and domestic consumption.(p.297)
• However, as there happened to be several saloons within that distance, I ***didn't*** find it necessary to patronize the same place each evening.(p.298)
• I ***didn't*** care to go visiting unless the parties we might visit had plenty of liquor on hand and I could get drunk.(p.301)
• I would hang on to sobriety for short intervals, but always there would come the tide of an overpowering necessity to drink and, as I was engulfed in it, I felt such a sense of panic that I really believed I would die if I ***didn't*** get that drink inside.(p.306)
• People ***didn't*** behave this way outside of an asylum.(p.306)
• I ***didn't*** dare hope I might find for myself all that these people had found, but if I could acquire some small part of their intriguing quality of living -- and sobriety – that would be enough.(p.310)
• They sum it up like this: "We ***didn't*** wait to hit bottom because, thank God, we could see the bottom.(p.315)
• Since I ***didn't*** do well in school, I quit and joined the Army at age seventeen.(p.317)
• If I could lay off it, that meant I ***didn't*** have to worry about a drinking problem, I thought.(p.317)
• I was sent to a psychiatrist, for they ***didn't*** think it was normal for me to want to kill my platoon sergeant or to attempt suicide twice.(p.318)
• Karen ***didn't*** want to see me any more, and neither did two other girls I'd been going out with.(p.318)
• Everyone was against me -- I'd show them I ***didn't*** need them.(p.318)
• The next meeting I went to, I ***didn't*** have any drinks beforehand.(p.319)
• I ***didn't*** think I was an alcoholic.(p.321)
• Fortunately, I ***didn't*** say a word to George on the way home.(p.322)
• But I wasn't happy, and I ***didn't*** ever let myself go in my drinking.(p.323)
• I needed a drink, but I was afraid to take a morning drink, because I ***didn't*** want to be a drunk.(p.323)
• I ***didn't*** think my children knew about it, but I found out they did.(p.324)
• It ***didn't*** bother me any more whether George was drinking or not.(p.324)
• And he, poor dear, ***didn't*** know what was going on.(p.325)
• I myself ***didn't*** know all the places I had them hidden.(p.325)
• I just ***didn't*** give a whoop about myself or anyone else.(p.325)
• I ***didn't*** care what I looked like, I ***didn't*** care what I did.(p.337)
• Finally I ***didn't*** care, I was beyond caring.(p.337)
• I screamed on the telephone for my mother to get up there; something was going to happen; I ***didn't*** know what, but if she ***didn't*** get there quick, I'd split wide open.(p.338)
• I ***didn't*** know.(p.338)
• If I ***didn't*** have a drink, I had to do something.(p.339)
• As long as I worked, as long as I got out, I ***didn't*** drink.(p.339)
• So that ***didn't*** work.(p.339)
• I heard one very ill woman say that she ***didn't*** believe in the surrender part of the A.A. program.(p.340)
• The second way in which, perhaps, I differ from some other alcoholics is this; many alcoholics state that they ***didn't*** particularly like the taste of alcohol, but that they liked the effect.(p.345)
• I ***didn't***.(p.351)
• I ***didn't*** know how to be a father; I don't know how to come home and work week-ends like other husbands; I don't know how to entertain my family.(p.351)
• Naturally, this experience ***didn't*** stop me.(p.354)
• I had no idea what would happen -- I just knew I ***didn't*** want to live if life was going to go on like it was.(p.355)
• I ***didn't*** particularly like it, but I loved the effects, and managed for the next twenty-five years to drink anything and everything, either handed to me or purchased, at the slightest excuse.(p.357)
• Since the radio station was getting on its feet, it ***didn't*** require so many nights of evening work, and that permitted leisure time for drinking.(p.360)
• It ***didn't*** take long for me to fall in with a fast crowd who had their lunch in the men's bar of a leading hotel.(p.361)
• Why should this happen to me – hadn't I provided a good home – wasn't I making a good living – ***didn't*** I just get a substantial raise that had put me in the upper bracket class?(p.362)
• Of course, it ***didn't*** work.(p.364)
• Of course, more than anything else I had let myself down, but I ***didn't*** realize how much then – as I do now.(p.364)
• I ***didn't*** say a word to anyone about my lapse.(p.364)
• I ***didn't*** take the drink.(p.365)
• She told me not to bother going "for her sake"; she told me in a nice way that it ***didn't*** make any difference to her – and that really scared me – so I went.(p.365)
• But for some reason – she just ***didn't*** know why -- she just had to hold onto that clipping, with its thin hope.(p.367)
• The surprise to me is the fact that I ***didn't*** know that they knew my drinking had gotten out of control.(p.376)
• At the time this ***didn't*** mean much to me.(p.376)
• She of course ***didn't*** realize how cunning an alcoholic can be and the lengths to which he will go in finding ways to satisfy the compulsion for more and more drinks after having had the first one.(p.377)
• This suggestion had been made before on a number of occasions, but like all alcoholics I wanted to handle my problem my own way, which really meant I ***didn't*** want anything to interfere with my drinking.(p.378)
• I don't know what I expected, but I most certainly ***didn't*** visualize a group of people talking about their drinking problems, making light of their personal tragedies and at the same time enjoying themselves.(p.378)
• This ***didn't*** say we had to be in jail, ten, fifty, or one hundred times.(p.379)
• It ***didn't*** say I had to lose my family.(p.379)
• It ***didn't*** say I had to finally live on skid row and drink bay rum, canned heat or lemon extract.(p.379)
• It was important to me to see what alcohol had done to me and would continue to do if I ***didn't*** have help.(p.379)
• It was a great relief to know I ***didn't*** have to drink any more.(p.379)
• To me this meant telling my associates that I had joined Alcoholics Anonymous; that I ***didn't*** know what was expected of me by A.A., but that whatever it was, it was the most important thing in life for me; that sobriety meant more to me than anything in this world.(p.382)
• The fact that A.A. is a spiritual program ***didn't*** scare me or raise any prejudice in my mind.(p.383)
• I ***didn't*** realize I would find so much more, but a new and different outlook on life started opening up almost immediately.(p.383)
• I ***didn't*** know that when I came into A.A.(p.384)
• I knew that I wanted to try A.A. and if that ***didn't*** work, I ***didn't*** think anything would.(p.384)
• I can't remember a dinner at home that we ***didn't*** have white wine or claret on the table.(p.384)
• So I was used to it, but I ***didn't*** know what the effect of alcohol was because I always had wine, usually with dinner, but always with a lot of ice and about two tablespoons of sugar in it.(p.385)
• Drinking it with your meals, you ***didn't*** feel it.(p.385)
• You ***didn't*** carry a little orchid up the aisle in those days; you carried a great big bouquet, like a funeral spray, and you ***didn't*** have your picture taken until just before you went to the church.(p.385)
• That was when all the boys and Esther got drunk and the wives ***didn't***.(p.386)
• Frank found the doctor, but the doctor ***didn't*** want to take an alcoholic.(p.387)
• The questions he asked me that I ***didn't*** answer honestly, I thought were none of his business.(p.388)
• I resented the fact that Frank had done this to me, and I just ***didn't*** know what was going on.(p.388)
• I took that treatment three times and it ***didn't*** work -- at least, for me.(p.389)
• They phoned my husband that I was in jail and in such terrible shape that they ***didn't*** know what I would do to myself; and they realized that jail was no place for me, but that he was to wait a while before he got me, because at the time they called him to come over for me I was beating a tin cup against the wall.(p.390)
• I wanted a cigarette and room service, which I ***didn't*** get.(p.390)
• I ***didn't*** know which way to turn.(p.391)
• So I got a half pint and at midnight that night, I called the number I had been given, but the man who had started the group was in the hospital so I ***didn't*** know what to do.(p.393)
• But I was a careful and cunning alcoholic, and this ***didn't*** happen very often.(p.399)
• I accepted a big tax-free income from the family, but I ***didn't*** like it when they told me how to live.(p.405)
• I ***didn't*** get into a sanitarium either.(p.411)
• In the first year there were episodes such as kicking Priscilla in the shins, getting the lock changed on the desk in the A.A. Club, because I, as secretary, ***didn't*** want the Intergroup secretary "interfering," and taking an older woman member out to lunch for the express purpose of informing her that she was "a phony."(p.416)
• I ***didn't*** reply.(p.422)
• I ***didn't*** graduate to the hard stuff until I was sixteen.(p.423)
• I ***didn't***.(p.423)
• I ***didn't*** give a whoop about anything scholastic.(p.423)
• Home life ***didn't*** mean much to me.(p.424)
• I wanted love and affection but I ***didn't*** get it.(p.424)
• I wasn't burdened with parental guidance and I ***didn't*** want any.(p.424)
• I would rather have stayed in jail except I ***didn't*** like bologna and cold potatoes for breakfast.(p.425)
• She ***didn't*** like it, but I thought it made a man of me.(p.425)
• I don't know why I ***didn't*** fall out of the open cockpit of some of those planes I flew in while taking aerial pictures.(p.426)
• I ***didn't***.(p.426)
• I was becoming a solitary drinker, but I ***didn't*** care.(p.426)
• ***Didn't*** I come from a family of drinkers?(p.427)
• There wasn't much I could do about it, and I ***didn't*** want to do anything anyway.(p.427)
• I took it easy, because they ***didn't*** know about me.(p.428)
• But I ***didn't*** want to stop drinking – not at twenty-two.(p.429)
• That doctor in the Navy hospital told me I wouldn't live five years if I ***didn't*** quit.(p.429)
• But I ***didn't***.(p.430)
• I just ***didn't*** belong here.(p.439)

• Not only did I not think that being an alcoholic was a good idea, I ***didn't*** even feel that I had all that much of a drinking problem!(p.439)
• Max hadn't gotten that way because I ***didn't*** care.(p.440)
• I ***didn't*** know whether I had told him to rush to the hospital and I'd meet him there, or to take two aspirin and call me in the morning.(p.441)
• I ***didn't*** feel I could lie in bed and squirt the stuff in my veins while my kids and wife stood around watching me, so I kept the drug in my bag and the bag in the car and the car in the garage.(p.442)
• The neurologist in charge of my case ***didn't*** think to ask me whether I drank, and I ***didn't*** think to tell him.(p.444)
• I ***didn't*** like being on the nut ward, and I particularly ***didn't*** like being forced to ice cookies on Christmas Eve.(p.444)
• Max won; I ***didn't*** drink it.(p.444)
• "That's a devil of a way to run an organization," I thought, and I reported Frank to the psychiatrist, who ***didn't*** seem perturbed; he just got someone else to take me on Fridays.(p.447)
• It is true that I -- of all people, strange as it may seem, and even though I ***didn't*** give my permission -- really, really am an alcoholic of sorts.(p.448)
• I ***didn't*** even try to understand.(p.460)
• I ***didn't*** know I was an alcoholic and (like most men in prison today) could not relate alcohol to any of my past troubles.(p.460)
• I ***didn't*** like it particularly at first, but I did like the effect I got from it.(p.464)
• When I ***didn't*** have anything else to do -- a dull evening at home -- I'd sneak a few drinks upstairs in my room, and that began to be a habit.(p.464)
• And there ***didn't*** seem to be anything to do about it.)(p.465)
• I hadn't been drinking much about that time, for I had begun to realize that there was something abnormal about my drinking, although as yet, I ***didn't*** realize that it was so out of control.(p.465)
• My parents were due for the holidays that day, and she ***didn't*** want them to find their drunken daughter there.(p.467)
• He said he ***didn't*** care what I did with the money, but there was going to be no more until I was completely sober.(p.467)
• I almost broke down and cried when I talked with them but I ***didn't***.(p.467)
• This time I ***didn't*** put up any fight because I knew why they were there and where I was going, the psychopathic ward of the City Hospital, where I had been once before.(p.468)
• And then I went back home to live with my parents, and the merry-go-round started again -- only this time I ***didn't*** have to worry about waking up behind bars in a psychiatric ward.(p.468)
• I ***didn't*** want help.(p.468)
• But it ***didn't*** condition this girl's thinking.(p.469)
• I honestly ***didn't*** know the difference.(p.470)
• A.A. ***didn't*** teach me I was an alcoholic; rather it taught me that because I was an alcoholic my life had become unmanageable.(p.470)
• So ***didn't*** drink much then.(p.474)
• Even my family ***didn't*** have much use for me.(p.478)
• I felt very sorry for myself and attempted suicide on many occasions, making sure there was always somebody within reaching distance to see that I ***didn't*** finish the job.(p.478)
• Once, I phoned my brother-in-law and told him I was going to take a handful of pills (in fact, I already had) and I would slash my wrists if he ***didn't*** come over to stop me.(p.479)
• This was the only period when I ***didn't*** drink, but that was hardly any consolation.(p.480)
• I went to church on Easter Sunday with my husband, and it ***didn't*** hurt at all.(p.482)
• I don't believe this program would work for me if I ***didn't*** get honest with myself about everything.(p.482)
• That was enough provocation to fight but I ***didn't*** fight, and I realized after recess why I ***didn't***.(p.484)
• My mother resented it so that the first Christmas after our marriage, she ***didn't*** even invite us to dinner.(p.485)
• Of course, when father finally came to Virginia to work his way through school, he resented the southern "cracker," as he often called them, so much that he ***didn't*** even go back to his mother's funeral.(p.486)
• He said he never wanted to set foot in the deep south again and he ***didn't***.(p.486)
• Dad, due to having spent most of his time in a small Virginia town, ***didn't*** have any too much money, and the money he had saved and the property he had acquired were in Washington.(p.486)
• I got to the place where I'd look forward to the week-end's drinking and pacify myself by saying that the week-ends were mine, that it ***didn't*** interfere with my family or with my business if I drank on the week-ends.(p.488)
• I ***didn't*** pay you."(p.488)
• I thought, "I know you ***didn't*** pay me, because you ***didn't*** get a prescription."(p.488)
• He went into the religious side and told me that I ***didn't*** attend church as regularly as I should, and that he felt, more or less, that this was responsible for my trouble.(p.489)
• Vi thought I ***didn't*** want to stop.(p.490)
• She decided that she ***didn't*** want any more of that.(p.491)
• They cooked up a plan whereby she ***didn't*** have to be molested by me if she ***didn't*** want to be.(p.491)
• She continued to watch me, although she ***didn't*** say anything.(p.493)
• She ***didn't*** say anything about A.A. or getting me a sponsor at that time, but she did ask about Vi, and I told her Vi was working and how she could locate her.(p.494)
• He ***didn't*** seem too much at ease in the beginning.(p.494)
• I knew my wife ***didn't*** because I had been sincere in all my promises to her as well as to my mother and to my close friends, but the urge to take that drink was more powerful than anything else.(p.494)
• We ***didn't*** save the world, but we did manage to help some individuals.(p.496)
• I ***didn't*** like it, but I would not say so.(p.498)
• When you've been in a jam you've said, 'God, please do this or that,' and if it turned out your way that was the last of it, and if it ***didn't*** you've said 'There isn't any God' or 'He doesn't do anything for me.'(p.504)
• I ***didn't*** have to worry about him any longer.(p.508)
• Those poor stiffs probably went to a doctor and were told that if they quit they'd live three weeks and if they ***didn't*** they'd die in one."(p.510)
• I ***didn't*** stick at social drinking very long.(p.512)
• Somehow or other I was coming face to face with myself, and I ***didn't*** like it.(p.513)
• However, she had faith and she had hope (things I ***didn't*** have).(p.514)
• One morning I ***didn't*** wake up until after four o'clock.(p.515)
• Because as I sat on that bed, I knew that I was in a terrible spot and ***didn't*** know how to get out of it.(p.515)
• Of course I really ***didn't*** have to worry on that score, because I wasn't the type that got half drunk.(p.515)
• Someone told me, "When you drank, you ***didn't*** get half drunk.(p.516)
• When I came back, I told the priest, the Chaplain of the place, exactly what I thought of him and he ***didn't*** like it.(p.517)
• Up to that time, drinking ***didn't*** really mean anything to me at all.(p.518)
• It ***didn't*** worry me very much, because at that time I could shut off for a couple of months without taking a drink or even wanting one, and without feeling that I was giving anything up.(p.518)
• But as long as you did your work and ***didn't*** disgrace yourself, you were socially acceptable and nobody really intruded on your private life very much.(p.518)
• India lent itself to drinking then, if you were disposed to drink, because you lived in bungalows; you ***didn't*** live all together as you do at home in an Officer's Mess.(p.519)
• Then a change in management took place in the regiment and the new O.C. ***didn't*** like me very much and I ***didn't*** like him, and he started to lie in wait for me.(p.519)
• He ***didn't*** have to lie in wait very long, but fortunately by that time, I had acquired friends upstairs and they covered me for quite a time.(p.519)
• But that ***didn't*** mean anything to me.(p.521)
• I ***didn't*** know what an alcoholic was.(p.521)
• I stayed there just long enough to work up a real good resentment against the doctor in charge, who I ***didn't*** think was doing anything at all except collecting fees, and I left there fully determined that I'd never put myself in the power of medical people again.(p.521)
• I was intensely unhappy the whole time, but I ***didn't*** seem to be able to do anything about it, and the worst part to me was the realization that all this was going to happen again and again until I died.(p.522)
• I was always able to get a boyfriend who had a drinking joint or sold whiskey, but it ***didn't*** last long.(p.526)
• I don't remember any of them getting put out in the winter because they ***didn't*** pay their rent.(p.527)
• Once I started drinking, I ***didn't*** care that the rent wasn't paid, or that there was no food in the house, or that my boys needed shoes.(p.527)
• I felt that I ***didn't*** have anything to live for, so I tried suicide many times.(p.528)
• I thought if the cops did come to the hospital, the doctors would tell them I was crazy and ***didn't*** know what I was doing.(p.528)
• I ***didn't*** want that, so I stopped going to the psycho ward.(p.528)
• I ***didn't*** last long.(p.528)
• I have not seen a black face but mine since I've been here, and if I ***didn't*** look in the mirror, I wouldn't know that I was black, because these people treat me as one of them, which I am.(p.530)
• On that day of decision, I ***didn't*** acknowledge that I was an alcoholic.(p.532)
• But such is my nature that I must know the reason for things and I ***didn't*** stop until I had satisfied myself about the reasons for my drinking.(p.533)
• It was my "secret garden" -- bluntly, it was my retreat from life, and I ***didn't*** want to give it up.(p.534)
• I ***didn't*** have the courage to love; I was not even sure I had the capacity.(p.546)
• I knew it ***didn't*** make any difference where I started, the inevitable end would be skid row.(p.548)
• The only reality I was able to face had been forced upon me by its very repetition -- I had to drink; and I ***didn't*** know there was anything in the world that could be done about it.(p.548)
• I've had many spiritual experiences since I've been in the program, many that I ***didn't*** recognize right away, for I'm slow to learn and they take many guises.(p.551)
• One morning, however, I realized I had to get rid of it, for my reprieve was running out, and if I ***didn't*** get rid of it I was going to get drunk -- and I ***didn't*** want to get drunk any more.(p.552)
• I went on the wagon, with no outside help and with no real difficulty -- except that I ***didn't*** enjoy life without drinking.(p.557)
• And I ***didn't*** like it.(p.557)

die

• But out of this frightening and at first disrupting experience the conviction grew that A.A.'s had to hang together or ***die*** separately.(p.xix)
• The patient had made his own diagnosis, and deciding his situation hopeless, had hidden in a deserted barn determined to ***die***.(p.xxix)
• If he did not work, he would surely drink again, and if he drank, he would surely ***die***.(p.15)
• It may cause him to ***die*** a few years before his time.(p.21)
• When this sort of thinking is fully established in an individual with alcoholic tendencies, he has probably placed himself beyond human aid, and unless locked up, may ***die*** or go permanently insane.(p.24)
• And with us, to drink is to ***die***.(p.66)
• But what about his responsibilities -- his family and the men who would ***die*** because they would not know how to get well, ah -- yes, those other alcoholics?(p.154)
• At two-forty-five that morning I thought I would ***die***.(p.267)
• I would hang on to sobriety for short intervals, but always there would come the tide of an overpowering necessity to drink and, as I was engulfed in it, I felt such a sense of panic that I really believed I would ***die*** if I didn't get that drink inside.(p.306)
• By now I wanted to ***die***, but had lost the courage even to take my life.(p.306)
• Either they ***die*** of acute alcoholism or they develop wet brains and have to be put away permanently."(p.308)
• Sometimes I would lie on the bathroom floor, deathly sick, praying I would ***die***, and praying to God as I always had prayed to Him when I was drinking: "Dear God, get me out of this one and I'll never do it again."(p.324)
• I sat up in the big red chair, suddenly thinking, "My God, with my kind of lousy luck, I might not ***die*** soon!(p.333)
• I saw at last that I had the same disease my father had, only I was being given a chance to live, not ***die***.(p.371)
• There comes a time when you don't want to live and are afraid to ***die***.(p.377)
• I wanted to ***die*** and often I would think of ways.(p.411)

• Suddenly, it was obvious to me: I had a brain tumor and would *die*, and everyone would be sorry for me.(p.444)
• Others wanted to *die*.(p.455)
• For me, as for most alcoholics, it was "Eat, drink, and be merry, for tomorrow you *die*."(p.457)
• But, of course, I couldn't *die*.(p.457)
• Tall Man *die* five years ago, a sober, peaceful, happy man.(p.476)
• Those poor stiffs probably went to a doctor and were told that if they quit they'd live three weeks and if they didn't they'd *die* in one."(p.510)
• "Bob," he asked quietly, "do you want to live or *die*?"(p.540)
• Maybe it was time to *die*.(p.540)
• My doctor warned me that if I kept on, I might have esophageal hemorrhaging and *die*.(p.558)
• We alcoholics see that we must work together and hang together, else most of us will finally *die* alone.(p.563)
• A.A. must continue to live or most of us will surely *die*.(p.565)

died

• The house was taken over by the mortgage holder, my mother-in-law *died*, and my wife and father-in-law became ill.(p.5)
• I could almost hear the sound of the preacher's voice as I sat, on still Sundays, way over there on the hillside; there was that proffered temperance pledge I never signed; my grandfather's good natured contempt of some church folk and their doings; his insistence that the spheres really had their music; but his denial of the preacher's right to tell him how he must listen; his fearlessness as he spoke of these things just before he *died*; these recollections welled up from the past.(p.10)
• Bill W., co-founder of A.A., *died* January 24, 1971.(p.16)
• My father *died* in 1901 when I was eight years old and I was in the second or third grade at school.(p.193)
• My mother was eighty-nine years old when she *died*, and I was a full-blown alcoholic at the time of her death.(p.210)
• He brought in many of our original members, yet he himself could not make it and *died* of alcoholism.(p.239)
• There were four of us children, and although both of my brothers later became alcoholic – one *died* of alcoholism -- my sister has never taken a drink in her life.(p.240)
• But right then the hope *died* that had been in my heart when we read about John D.(p.266)
• Right away, I saw it was the same outfit this other guy told me about, and then again hope *died*.(p.267)
• "Well," I said to dad, when the A.A. people kept coming with these lovely cars and looked so nice, "I suppose the neighbors say, 'Now those old fools must have up and *died*, but where's the hearse?'"(p.269)
• Thank God I had no desire for a drink when he *died*.(p.272)
• My parents *died*, both in the same year, leaving me, a sheltered and somewhat immature man, on my own.(p.277)
• But – supposing that just one man *died* because I had, for selfish reasons, kept my mouth shut?(p.282)
• Then my father fell down a flight of stairs on one of his lost weekends, at the peak of his career, and *died*.(p.370)
• After his death, my mother soon picked up drinking where Dad left off, and in a very short time she *died* of cirrhosis of the liver.(p.370)
• While I was at Pensacola my dad became dangerously ill and almost *died* of pneumonia plus a heart attack.(p.426)
• If it hadn't been for an alert hotel maid, I might have *died* then.(p.465)
• My visits to that sanitarium went on for nearly three years, until in March of 1944, my father *died* and I was too drunk to attend his funeral.(p.469)
• At one time, I was using twenty caps a day; I nearly *died* half a dozen times on the street.(p.480)
• Her brother had been a drinker and had *died* in a State Hospital for the insane.(p.498)
• I was intensely unhappy the whole time, but I didn't seem to be able to do anything about it, and the worst part to me was the realization that all this was going to happen again and again until I *died*.(p.522)
• To learn to live, he nearly *died*.(p.531)
• And when he *died*, you were unmoved.(p.533)
• Hope had *died*, or so I thought.(p.540)
• Hopeless now, I felt it would be better for my wife, my children, and everyone in my life if I went ahead and *died*.(p.558)

dies

• His wife *dies* that night.(p.501)

diet

• One school would allow man no flavor for his fare and the other would have us all on a straight pepper *diet*.(p.69)
• That discovery so intrigued me, that I stayed on that *diet* almost entirely for the balance of my extensive drinking life.(p.298)
• I tried the beer *diet*, the wine *diet*, timing, measuring, and spacing of drinks.(p.305)

dieth

• A good soldier is ne'er forgot Whether he *dieth* by musket Or by pot."(p.1)

diets

• I would follow certain drinking schedules or *diets* faithfully for a few days, and then somewhere along the line would over-train and upset the applecart.(p.361)

differ

• Being possessed of a spiritual experience, the alcoholic will find he has much in common with these people, though he may *differ* with them on many matters.(p.131)
• The second way in which, perhaps, I *differ* from some other alcoholics is this; many alcoholics state that they didn't particularly like the taste of alcohol, but that they liked the effect.(p.345)

difference

• Whether we agree with a particular approach or conception seems to make little *difference*.(p.50)
• That often makes the *difference* between failure and success.(p.98)
• We realize some men are thoroughly bad-intentioned, that no amount of patience will make any *difference*.(p.108)
• We do not mean that you have to agree with your husband whenever there is an honest *difference* of opinion.(p.117)
• Therefore it would make no great *difference*, even if I should do some drinking.(p.175)
• And they said, "No, you have a disease, and it doesn't make any *difference* how long you do without it, after a drink or two you'll end up just like you are now."(p.187)
• I figured the only *difference* between me and a millionaire was that I hadn't the strength, or that he got the breaks and I didn't.(p.197)
• The encouragement received in the early days, especially from the A.A. General Service Office, made a tremendous *difference* to my sobriety.(p.342)
• The army made a *difference* to me.(p.343)
• I have been of a very religious outlook all my life, but that made no *difference* once John Barleycorn got the better of me.(p.343)
• The *difference* between the two vacations was this:(p.344)
• She told me not to bother going "for her sake"; she told me in a nice way that it didn't make any *difference* to her – and that really scared me – so I went.(p.365)
• "Grant us the serenity to accept the things we cannot change, courage to change the things we can, and the wisdom to know the *difference*."(p.382)
• But what a *difference* there is between going through hell without a power greater than one's self, and with it!(p.437)
• I honestly didn't know the *difference*.(p.470)
• But the *difference* lay in the fact that the A.A.'s knew from their own bitter experience.(p.471)
• His parishioners are limited in number, but his friends are many, for to him race, creed, or social position makes no *difference*.(p.497)
• There was a great deal of *difference*.(p.513)
• In fact, I couldn't have told you the *difference* between sherry and brandy.(p.518)
• I knew it didn't make any *difference* where I started, the inevitable end would be skid row.(p.548)
• To those now in its fold, Alcoholics Anonymous has made the *difference* between misery and sobriety, and often the *difference* between life and death.(p.563)
• Quite often friends of the newcomer are aware of the *difference* long before he is himself.(p.569)

differences

• Cleaning up old scrapes, helping to settle family *differences*, explaining the disinherited son to his irate parents, lending money and securing jobs for each other, when justified -- these are everyday occurrences.(p.161)
• The *differences* between my father and my sisters, who were school teachers, made an excellent environment for the type of child I was – that is, slick and cute enough to take advantage of any adult quarrel.(p.210)

different

• The basic principles of the A.A. program, it appears, hold good for individuals with many *different* lifestyles, just as the program has brought recovery to those of many *different* nationalities.(p.xxii)
• He was inexplicably *different*.(p.9)
• He was on a *different* footing.(p.12)
• We see that these expressions refer to people whose reactions are very *different* from ours.(p.20)
• No person likes to think he is bodily and mentally *different* from his fellows.(p.30)
• We were prepared to look at it from an entirely *different* angle.(p.66)
• For we are now on a *different* basis; the basis of trusting and relying upon God.(p.68)
• Should it happen again, regard it in a *different* light.(p.116)
• Overnight, as it were, he is a *different* man.(p.128)
• Being on a radically *different* basis of life, he will never take advantage of the situation.(p.146)
• His wife came, scarcely daring to be hopeful, though she thought she saw something *different* about her husband already.(p.158)
• Under only slightly *different* conditions, the same thing is taking place in many eastern cities.(p.161)
• The question which might naturally come into your mind would be: "What did the man do or say that was *different* from what others had done or said?"(p.180)
• I'd waked up in strange rooms before, fully dressed on a bed or a couch; I'd waked up in my own room, in or on my own bed, not knowing what hour or day it was, afraid to ask . . . but this was *different*.(p.222)
• For me, work was only a *different* means to the same end, to be able to do exactly what I wanted to do.(p.225)
• Then it was my turn – I ordered "Three beers," but this time it was *different*, I had a cash investment of thirty cents and, on a ten dollar a week salary, that's a big thing.(p.247)
• In the two succeeding years I held ten *different* jobs ranging from newspaper copy-desk and rewrite, to traffic director for an oil field equipment company.(p.255)
• As he talked I gathered vaguely, (because he was a faltering beginner then, just as I am now) that to be relieved of alcoholism I would have to be *different*.(p.257)
• My pattern of drinking became very *different* from theirs.(p.277)
• After six months of sobriety I saw the picture in a *different* light: Detroit was the place I had to return to, not only because I must face the mess I had made there, but because it was there that I could be of the most service to A.A.(p.281)
• I, who had never made a speech in my life and who would have been frightened sick at the prospect, stood up in front of Rotary groups in *different* parts of the city and talked about Alcoholics Anonymous.(p.283)
• Several months later dad was back in Chicago to pick me up again, but this time my attitude was entirely *different*.(p.289)
• I had thought that I was completely *different* from other people, that I was beginning to become a little balmy, even to the point of withdrawing more and more from society and wanting to be alone with my bottle.(p.290)
• It was *different* from the meetings now held.(p.291)
• I definitely liked it, everything about it, the taste, the effects; and I realize now that a drink did something for me or to me that was *different* from the way it affected others.(p.305)
• In two ways I may be a little *different* from other alcoholics.(p.345)
• The story is not very *different* from that of thousands of other young men in my generation.(p.373)
• I disliked being *different* so, ultimately, I began to join them occasionally.(p.374)
• The last two years of my drinking my entire personality changed to a cynical, intolerant and arrogant person completely *different* from my normal self.(p.376)
• I didn't realize I would find so much more, but a new and *different* outlook on life started opening up almost immediately.(p.383)
• I headed home for the most wonderful experience of all time – meeting my "new" parents – mom and dad looked *different* than I had pictured them.(p.428)
• I'm sure my ideas as to what life should be like were quite *different* from that of the average person with whom I associated.(p.483)
• On the other hand, I got quite a *different* picture farther south.(p.486)

• But I found that after I got to North Carolina it wasn't any ***different***.(p.490)
• The State was ***different***, but I wasn't .(p.490)
• My drinking pattern isn't very ***different*** from the average you find in A.A.(p.512)
• For me, it was a little ***different*** because I couldn't help thinking about the past, and I saw the future more or less mirrored in the past.(p.513)
• The terms "spiritual experience" and "spiritual awakening" are used many times in this book which, upon careful reading, shows that the personality change sufficient to bring about recovery from alcoholism has manifested itself among us in many ***different*** forms.(p.569)

differentiate

• The sensation is so elusive that, while they admit it is injurious, they cannot after a time ***differentiate*** the true from the false.(p.xxvi)
• We are taught to ***differentiate*** between our wants (which are never satisfied) and our needs (which are always provided for).(p.560)

differentiates

• This phenomenon, as we have suggested, may be the manifestation of an allergy which ***differentiates*** these people, and sets them apart as a distinct entity.(p.xxviii)

differently

• Opinions vary considerably as to why the alcoholic reacts ***differently*** from normal people.(p.22)
• Had we fully understood the nature of the alcoholic illness, we might have behaved ***differently***.(p.107)
• In A.A., I have had to be torn down and then put back together ***differently***.(p.420)
• We all use them ***differently***.(p.516)

differing

• We used to argue about our ***differing*** ideas, but we can't argue about our feelings.(p.451)

difficult

• These allergic types can never safely use alcohol in any form at all; and once having formed the habit and found they cannot break it, once having lost their self-confidence, their reliance upon things human, their problems pile up on them and become astonishingly ***difficult*** to solve.(p.xxvi)
• The classification of alcoholics seems most ***difficult***, and in much detail is outside the scope of this book.(p.xxviii)
• For myself, I had adopted those parts which seemed convenient and not too ***difficult***; the rest I disregarded.(p.11)
• If a sufficiently strong reason -- ill health, falling in love, change of environment, or the warning of a doctor -- becomes operative, this man can also stop or moderate, although he may find it ***difficult*** and troublesome and may even need medical attention.(p.21)
• But it isn't so ***difficult***.(p.44)
• That was great news to us, for we had assumed we could not make use of spiritual principles unless we accepted many things on faith which seemed ***difficult*** to believe.(p.47)
• This is perhaps ***difficult*** -- especially discussing our defects with another person.(p.72)
• In many homes this is a ***difficult*** thing to do, but it must be done if any results are to be expected.(p.98)
• We want to leave you with the feeling that no situation is too ***difficult*** and no unhappiness too great to be overcome.(p.104)
• Oddly enough, he is often ***difficult*** to deal with.(p.110)
• We know these suggestions are sometimes ***difficult*** to follow, but you will save many a heartbreak if you can succeed in observing them.(p.111)
• We know there are ***difficult*** wives and families, but the man who is getting over alcoholism must remember he did much to make them so.(p.127)
• These juniors are often in a ***difficult*** position.(p.147)
• I soon discovered that a couple of drinks would alleviate my gastric distress, at least for a few hours at a time, so it was not at all ***difficult*** for me to return to my former excessive indulgence.(p.174)
• Of course, we had talked over quite a number of the failings that I had and made a sort of an inventory, which wasn't too ***difficult***, because I had an awful lot of things wrong that were very apparent to me, because I knew all about them.(p.190)
• The adjustments in such a case are ***difficult*** and take time, but we both feel that they are certainly worth it.(p.286)
• I really worked for several weeks, and having had a fairly wide acquaintance with the dealer trade, it was not ***difficult*** for me to line up enough of them to give me a very substantial volume of business with a minimum of effort.(p.300)
• Many times have I heard the above expressions since I have been in A.A., and many times I have had to reply "Definitely I am an alcoholic, and while it may be hard for you to believe, it is not hard for me, for I have learned many things about alcohol and myself that would, perhaps, be ***difficult*** for you to understand."(p.356)
• It is not too ***difficult*** nor too easy to grasp.(p.367)
• These words may be ***difficult*** for you to understand now, but be patient and you'll know what I mean.(p.367)
• By now it had become ***difficult*** to visualize a life without alcohol.(p.378)
• I feel that there is no situation too ***difficult***, none too desperate, no unhappiness too great to be overcome in this great fellowship -- Alcoholics Anonymous.(p.395)
• Admitting that I am wrong or that I do not know is ***difficult*** for me.(p.420)
• But for some time, it was ***difficult*** to keep from taking a pill when I had an appropriate symptom, such as a cough, pain, anxiety, insomnia, a muscle spasm, or an upset stomach.(p.448)
• This is ***difficult***, but it is the only way it has worked for me.(p.463)
• It was not ***difficult*** to convince myself that my unhappiness was the fault of the man I had married, and I divorced him at the end of a year.(p.545)

difficulties

• While the internal ***difficulties*** of our adolescent period were being ironed out, public acceptance of A.A. grew by leaps and bounds.(p.xix)
• We doctors have realized for a long time that some form of moral psychology was of urgent importance to alcoholics, but its application presented ***difficulties*** beyond our conception.(p.xxv)
• Take away my ***difficulties***, that victory over them may bear witness to those I would help of Thy Power, Thy Love, and Thy Way of life.(p.63)
• Notice that the word "fear" is bracketed alongside the ***difficulties*** with Mr. Brown, Mrs. Jones, the employer, and the wife.(p.67)
• Make it plain he is under no obligation to you, that you hope only that he will try to help other alcoholics when he escapes his own ***difficulties***.(p.94)
• If he is not interested in your solution, if he expects you to act only as a banker for his financial ***difficulties*** or a nurse for his sprees, you may have to drop him until he changes his mind.(p.95)
• The story of how you and your wife settled your ***difficulties*** is worth any amount of criticism.(p.100)
• That is why we are anxious that you understand, and that you avoid these unnecessary ***difficulties***.(p.121)
• I pointed out that I had had nothing to drink whatever for three years, and this in the face of ***difficulties*** that would have made nine out of ten men drink their heads off.(p.138)
• Plenty of ***difficulties*** presented themselves.(p.156)
• A year later, after I completed the course in contracts, I quit the law school, and undertook some engineering work for a patent law firm on behalf of clients who were in ***difficulties*** and who desired to keep their troubles from their own engineering department.(p.212)
• However, due to financial ***difficulties*** the whole printing was, for a while, held up and the book received no publicity, nor, of course, was it available in the stores, even if one knew it existed.(p.307)
• I got into a lot of financial ***difficulties*** too.(p.490)

difficulty

• The joy of living we really have, even under pressure and ***difficulty***.(p.15)
• That the man who is making the approach has had the same ***difficulty***, that he obviously knows what he is talking about, that his whole deportment shouts at the new prospect that he is a man with a real answer, that he has no attitude of Holier Than Thou, nothing whatever except the sincere desire to be helpful; that there are no fees to pay, no axes to grind, no people to please, no lectures to be endured -- these are the conditions we have found most effective.(p.18)
• But the ***difficulty*** is that few alcoholics have enough desire to stop while there is yet time.(p.32)
• Here ***difficulty*** arises with agnostics.(p.45)
• Though some of us resisted, we found no great ***difficulty*** in casting aside such feelings.(p.48)
• Still another ***difficulty*** is that you may become jealous of the attention he bestows on other people, especially alcoholics.(p.119)
• We do not know of many cases where this ***difficulty*** lasted long.(p.134)
• If this presents ***difficulty***, re-reading chapters two and three, where the alcoholic sickness is discussed at length might be worth while.(p.140)
• In other words, I was always safe from the discipline of my father, and having developed along that line, I had considerable ***difficulty*** in school.(p.210)
• Even then he went into no great detail about how he and a crowd of alcoholics, with whom he associated, had mastered their ***difficulty***.(p.235)
• I went on the wagon, with no outside help and with no real ***difficulty*** -- except that I didn't enjoy life without drinking.(p.557)
• We find that no one need have ***difficulty*** with the spirituality of the program.(p.570)

diffident

• As we look over the list of business acquaintances and friends we have hurt, we may feel ***diffident*** about going to some of them on a spiritual basis.(p.76)

dig

• It is possible to ***dig*** up past misdeeds so they become a blight, a veritable plague.(p.124)

digested

• That being so you have swallowed and ***digested*** some big chunks of truth about yourself.(p.71)

dignified

• And another thing, it's a wonder they didn't throw us back in because I could become very ***dignified*** and sarcastic.(p.264)

dignity

• As we left, and they were escorting us across the bridge into Wheeling, I, with great ***dignity*** and sarcasm, told them if their wives were ever visiting in Akron, and they, too, were looking for their route sign as I was, that I hoped I could extend to them the hospitality that had been shown to me in Bellaire.(p.264)
• While I sought the comforting arms of alcohol, I knew this was a sign of weakness on the part of a longtime-successful old codger with white hair, the image of ***dignity***.(p.331)
• I, a man of steel, with very high ideals, well brought up, an honor student and the recipient of scholarships and prizes, a boy wonder in business -- I, Bob, the author of this essay, looked and saw that the universe was beneath my contempt, and that to remove myself from it was the only thing of ***dignity*** a man could do.(p.531)

digress

• I do not want to ***digress*** into the dynamics of penology.(p.458)

dilemma

• This physician had repeatedly tried spiritual means to resolve his alcoholic ***dilemma*** but had failed.(p.xvi)
• Here was the terrible ***dilemma*** in which our friend found himself when he had the extraordinary experience which as we have already told you, made him a free man.(p.28)
• Lack of power, that was our ***dilemma***.(p.45)
• Nor could I blame my ***dilemma*** on my childhood environment.(p.304)

diligently

• If our testimony helps sweep away prejudice, enables you to think honestly, encourages you to search ***diligently*** within yourself, then, if you wish, you can join us on the Broad Highway.(p.55)

dim

• The faces of the other boys grew ***dim***.(p.498)

dime

• Why, even a year ago, I had seen Howard, an ex-doctor, mooching a ***dime*** for a drink.(p.289)
• If something does come along that sort of upsets me, instead of walking in and throwing a buck at the barman and asking for a drink, I walk into a telephone booth, drop a ***dime*** in the box, and call somebody who was so kind as to give me his name and telephone number to meet such an emergency.(p.511)
• I had no money -- well, maybe a ***dime*** -- and only the clothes I stood in.(p.540)

dimension

• I was soon to be catapulted into what I like to call the fourth ***dimension*** of existence.(p.8)
• We have found much of heaven and we have been rocketed into a fourth ***dimension*** of existence of which we had not even dreamed.(p.25)

diminish

• But we must be careful not to drift into worry, remorse or morbid reflection, for that would ***diminish*** our usefulness to others.(p.86)

diminishing

• Headstrong and willful, I rushed from pleasure to pleasure, and found the returns ***diminishing*** to the vanishing point.(p.226)

dimly

• Sometimes we sensed ***dimly*** that we were dealing

with sick men.(p.107)

dingy

• I wish I were home with the family and not in the *dingy* hotel.(p.500)

dining

• As I crossed the threshold of the *dining* room, the thought came to mind that it would be nice to have a couple of cocktails with dinner.(p.41)

• We boys drove out in somebody's car and went to the bar on the way do the *dining* room and I, in an effort to impress the other boys that I was city-bred, having lived in Scranton and Cleveland, asked them if they didn't want a drink.(p.194)

• After my last binge I came home and smashed my *dining* room furniture to splinters, kicked out six windows and two balustrades.(p.435)

dinner

• In the spring of 1940, John D. Rockefeller, Jr. gave a *dinner* for many of his friends to which he invited A.A. members to tell their stories.(p.xviii)

• Of course he would have *dinner*, and then I could drink openly with him.(p.9)

• I went to my hotel and leisurely dressed for *dinner*.(p.41)

• As I crossed the threshold of the dining room, the thought came to mind that it would be nice to have a couple of cocktails with *dinner*.(p.41)

• After *dinner* I decided to take a walk.(p.41)

• I got tight that night, stayed sober Monday till after the *dinner* and then proceeded to get tight again.(p.179)

• One evening I had gone out after *dinner* to take on a couple of double-headers and stayed a little later than usual, and when I came home Clarence was sitting on the davenport with Bill W.(p.216)

• I left on a Wednesday afternoon, had *dinner* in Akron and then went to a house where I encountered my first meeting.(p.218)

• (Russ was buried on Friday, and on Sunday afternoon Hilda S. had invited me there to *dinner* Sunday night, and I didn't think I could do it.(p.272)

• During my first year out of college I had endless dates, and went to countless dances, balls and *dinner* parties.(p.275)

• I also talked A.A. to every friend who would listen, at lunch, at *dinner*, on street corners.(p.282)

• I was at a beautifully set *dinner* table.(p.285)

• In succession came "What Made Milwaukee Famous Made a Loser Out of Me" and "I'm Drinking My Christmas *Dinner* All Alone."(p.332)

• But I remembered that every night after *dinner* my wife would get up and do the dishes.(p.351)

• By hook or crook I usually managed to sober up before I reached home, but always "terribly tired" from a "hard day's work," and just having to have one or two before *dinner*.(p.361)

• One night at the *dinner* table my wife said that tonight was my first birthday in A.A., and that the group would have the usual ice cream and cake for the "one year man."(p.365)

• After every cocktail party or *dinner* party she would say she couldn't understand how I could get in such a drunken stupor on one drink.(p.377)

• I can't remember a *dinner* at home that we didn't have white wine or claret on the table.(p.384)

• We always had cordials after *dinner* and I know my sister and my brother and I loved creme de menthe.(p.384)

• So I was used to it, but I didn't know what the effect of alcohol was because I always had wine, usually with *dinner*, but always with a lot of ice and about two tablespoons of sugar in it.(p.385)

• That first night I blacked out at a large *dinner* party.(p.404)

• Why did I have to have at least three cocktails to sit through *dinner*?(p.406)

• Other girls whom I had known all my life asked for one weak scotch after *dinner*.(p.406)

• They took Anne and me to *dinner*.(p.415)

• My mother resented it so that the first Christmas after our marriage, she didn't even invite us to *dinner*.(p.485)

• She came in for her *dinner*.(p.487)

• I went to a *dinner* he gave one night, rather drunk.(p.520)

• I buttonholed him after *dinner* and gave him a few tips on how to run his colony better and the result of that was about a fortnight or so later I was shipped back to my regiment.(p.520)

• When I was faced with a special challenge or social event – such as an important business presentation or a *dinner* party – I had to fortify myself with a couple of belts.(p.556)

• Speaking at a *dinner* given by John D. Rockefeller Jr. to introduce Alcoholics Anonymous to some of his friends, Dr. Harry Emerson Fosdick remarked: "I think that psychologically speaking there is a point of advantage in the approach that is being made in this movement that cannot be duplicated.(p.574)

diploma

• He has given me my *diploma*!(p.499)

diplomate

• I recall, as I walked into that meeting, saying to myself, "Here I am, a fellow of the American College of Surgeons, a Fellow of the International College of Surgeons, a *diplomate* of one of the great specialty boards in these United States, a member of the American Psychiatric Society, and I have to go to the butcher, the baker and the carpenter to help make a man out of me!"(p.347)

dipped

• My Quaker mother-in-law, bless her heart, used to set the Christmas pudding ablaze with lumps of sugar *dipped* in rubbing alcohol.(p.402)

dire

• Today, I find I can't work my A.A. program while taking pills, nor may I even have them around for *dire* emergencies only.(p.443)

direct

• Simply because it is impossible to explain what we see, feel, *direct*, and use, without a reasonable assumption as a starting point.(p.48)

• 9.Made *direct* amends to such people wherever possible, except when to do so would injure them or others.(p.59)

• We ask Him to remove our fear and *direct* our attention to what He would have us be.(p.68)

• Before we begin, we ask God to *direct* our thinking, especially asking that it be divorced from self-pity, dishonest or self-seeking motives.(p.86)

• We suggest that you *direct* some of your thought to the wives of his new alcoholic friends.(p.119)

• We think that such a view is self-centered and in *direct* conflict with the new way of living.(p.124)

directed

• That day I gave my will to God and asked to be *directed*.(p.237)

directing

• If any feel that as psychiatrists *directing* a hospital for alcoholics we appear somewhat sentimental, let them stand with us a while on the firing line, see the tragedies, the despairing wives, the little children; let the solving of these problems become a part of their daily work, and even of their sleeping moments, and the most cynical will not wonder that we have accepted and encouraged this movement.(p.xxvi)

• I had never, since the believing days of childhood, been able to conceive an authority *directing* the universe.(p.259)

• Handling customers, dealers, insurance people, dictation, telephoning, *directing* new employees, answering to superiors, and all the rest of it.(p.299)

direction

• When they talked of a God personal to me, who was love, superhuman strength and *direction*, I became irritated and my mind snapped shut against such a theory.(p.10)

• I placed myself unreservedly under His care and *direction*.(p.13)

• I was to sit quietly when in doubt, asking only for *direction* and strength to meet my problems as He would have me.(p.13)

• As soon as we admitted the possible existence of a Creative Intelligence, a Spirit of the Universe underlying the totality of things, we began to be possessed of a new sense of power and *direction*, provided we took other simple steps.(p.46)

• We have learned that whatever the human frailties of various faiths may be, those faiths have given purpose and *direction* to millions.(p.49)

• In the face of collapse and despair, in the face of the total failure of their human resources, they found that a new power, peace, happiness, and sense of *direction* flowed into them.(p.50)

• Reminding ourselves that we have decided to go to any length to find a spiritual experience we ask that we be given strength and *direction* to do the right thing, no matter what the personal consequences may be.(p.79)

• Much has already been said about receiving strength, inspiration, and *direction* from Him who has all knowledge and power.(p.85)

• If you do stay, let him steer the conversation in any *direction* he likes.(p.95)

• Sometimes you will have to call a doctor and administer sedatives under his *direction*.(p.97)

• We realize that we have been giving you much *direction* and advice.(p.121)

• He is not likely to get far in any *direction* if he fails to show unselfishness and love under his own roof.(p.127)

• On the third day the lawyer gave his life to the care and *direction* of his Creator, and said he was perfectly willing to do anything necessary.(p.158)

• "Well," the doctor said, "we have hopes in that *direction*."(p.207)

• They, too, had taken a train to one town and had wakened hundreds of miles in the opposite *direction*, never knowing how they got there.(p.246)

• Drifting back to Ohio, I landed on a small newspaper and later was impressed into the *direction* of boy-welfare work at the local "Y."(p.253)

• A.A. gives us alcoholics *direction* into a way of life without the need for alcohol.(p.340)

directions

• The second edition added the appendices, the Twelve Traditions, and the *directions* for getting in touch with A.A.(p.xi)

• Quicksand stretched around me in all *directions*.(p.8)

• Further on, clear-cut *directions* are given showing how we recovered.(p.29)

• If we have carefully followed *directions*, we have begun to sense the flow of His Spirit into us.(p.85)

• At the beginning of recovery a man will take, as a rule, one of two *directions*.(p.125)

• Mother made all the plans and gave the *directions*.(p.131)

directly

• Never mind the musty past; here sat a miracle *directly* across the kitchen table.(p.11)

• Friends who have reasoned with him after a spree which has brought him to the point of divorce or bankruptcy are mystified when he walks *directly* into a saloon.(p.35)

• Can it be appreciated that he has been a victim of crooked thinking, *directly* caused by the action of alcohol on his brain?(p.140)

• I came *directly* to a growing industrial city in the middle west, where I have lived practically ever since.(p.231)

• When I reached a point *directly* back of our house, where I could have cut through a friend's garden, I was almost overpowered by the desire to get home, but I made the whole journey.(p.276)

• Looking *directly* at me was a large oil painting of my wife, and her very words seemed to shout at me -- "I am not leaving you because I don't love you; it's because I do love you.(p.363)

• I must keep my magic magnifying mind on my acceptance and off my expectations, for my serenity is *directly* proportional to my level of acceptance.(p.452)

• Father had never *directly* spoken to me about drinking but he never drank any, so far as I knew.(p.498)

• Nine – A.A., as such, ought never be organized; but we may create service boards or committees *directly* responsible to those they serve.(p.564)

director

• I say this after many years' experience as Medical *Director* of one of the oldest hospitals in the country treating alcoholic and drug addiction.(p.xxv)

• Next, we decided that hereafter in this drama of life, God was going to be our *Director*.(p.62)

• Before my drinking had cut me down completely, I achieved a considerable measure of success, having been a City Councilman for five years and a financial *director* of Kenmore, a suburb later taken into the city itself.(p.182)

• In the two succeeding years I held ten different jobs ranging from newspaper copy-desk and rewrite, to traffic *director* for an oil field equipment company.(p.255)

• In time I became an officer and *director* of one of the largest commercial banks in the country.(p.374)

• I achieved recognized and national standing in my profession, as well as becoming a *director* in many important institutions having to do with the civic life of a large city.(p.374)

directories

• These so-called intergroup associations are found under the listing "A.A." or "Alcoholics Anonymous" in telephone *directories*.(p.575)

directors

• He has just returned from a three-months leave of absence, has taken a cure, looks fine, and to clinch the matter, the board of *directors* told him this was his last chance."(p.138)

• My wife was in the Junior League, and I was on the board of *directors* of the local center for the mentally retarded.(p.418)

directory
• At one end of the room stood a glass covered ***directory*** of local churches.(p.154)
• With a shiver, he turned away and walked down the lobby to the church ***directory***.(p.154)
• Selecting a church at random from the ***directory***, he stepped into a booth and lifted the receiver.(p.155)
• In such places, A.A. can be located through the local telephone ***directory***, newspaper office, or police station, or by contacting local priests or ministers.(p.575)

dirty
• There I was, unshaven, clothes torn and ***dirty*** with no recollection of wandering all over France but, of course, a hero to the local French.(p.242)
• Before too long, my husband (who seemed to prefer his shirts ***dirty***) put his foot down, declaring that our family might have the cleanest clothes in town, but that I hadn't been out of the same old ***dirty*** slacks and blouse for a week.(p.371)
• I was fat, bloated, ***dirty*** and unkempt.(p.411)
• We, who were ***dirty***, bedraggled and in ski clothes.(p.415)
• Then, of course, there are always the wrinkled slacks, which have been slept in and are so ***dirty***, they could walk away by themselves.(p.479)
• Our shoes are not better than the average hobo's, and if we are fortunate enough to have a pair of stockings on, nobody notices the runs in them, because of our dazzling beauty and our ***dirty*** feet.(p.479)

disadvantage
• Professionally, after I was sober for a month or so I realized that I should school myself to dissolve the partnership I was in because I felt that I would never regain the respect of my partners no matter how long I was sober, and that I would be at a ***disadvantage***.(p.220)

disagree
• Just be careful not to ***disagree*** in a resentful or critical spirit.(p.117)

disagreeable
• Though some of his manifestations are alarming and ***disagreeable***, we think dad will be on a firmer foundation than the man who is placing business or professional success ahead of spiritual development.(p.129)

disagreement
• If your husband is trying to live on a spiritual basis, he will also be doing everything in his power to avoid ***disagreement*** or contention.(p.118)

disagrees
• At proper time and place explain to all your friends why alcohol ***disagrees*** with you.(p.102)

disappear
• That feeling of uselessness and self-pity will ***disappear***.(p.84)
• You should point out that his defects of character are not going to ***disappear*** over night.(p.100)
• Barriers which have sprung up between you and your friends will ***disappear*** with the growth of sympathetic understanding.(p.115)
• If they sense these things, they will not take so seriously his periods of crankiness, depression, or apathy, which will ***disappear*** when there is tolerance, love, and spiritual understanding.(p.127)
• In the midst of an understanding and sympathetic family, these vagaries of dad's spiritual infancy will quickly ***disappear***.(p.129)
• The first definite indications of an alcoholic pattern began to arise when I would go to New York on business and ***disappear***, and wind up in Philadelphia or Boston for two or three day periods.(p.213)

disappeared
• That very night, years ago, it ***disappeared***.(p.56)
• The feeling that the drink problem has ***disappeared*** will often come strongly.(p.75)
• Some of them I had known for years, good two-fisted drinkers who had ***disappeared*** from their former haunts.(p.258)
• I cannot say that my taste for liquor has entirely ***disappeared***.(p.259)
• To this day, I am amazed at how many of my problems -- most of which had nothing to do with drinking, I believed -- have become manageable or have simply ***disappeared*** since I quit drinking.(p.448)

disappears
• Some of the things which used to stop me in my tracks from fear still make me nervous in the anticipation of their doing, but once I kick myself into doing them nervousness ***disappears*** and I enjoy myself.(p.285)

disappointed
• ***Disappointed*** but curious, I wondered what had got into the fellow.(p.9)
• They are all ***disappointed***, and often let him feel it.(p.126)

disappointments
• But it took six more months of work and ***disappointments*** before a group of three men got together in my rooming house bedroom for their first A.A. meeting.(p.282)
• I have had my share of problems, heartaches and ***disappointments***, because that is life, but also I have known a great deal of joy, and a peace that is the handmaiden of an inner freedom, I have a wealth of friends and, with my A.A. friends, an unusual quality of fellowship.(p.312)
• When I encountered ***disappointments*** or frustrations -- as I did more and more frequently -- my solution was to drink.(p.556)
• I have learned to deal with ***disappointments*** and problems that once would have sent me right to the bottle.(p.559)

disaster
• Unlike the feelings of the ship's passengers, however, our joy in escape from ***disaster*** does not subside as we go our individual ways.(p.17)
• He can go anywhere on this earth where other free men may go without ***disaster***, provided he remains willing to maintain a certain simple attitude.(p.26)
• To one who feels he is an atheist or agnostic such an experience seems impossible, but to continue as he is means ***disaster***, especially if he is an alcoholic of the hopeless variety.(p.44)
• You will be bound to them with new and wonderful ties, for you will escape ***disaster*** together and you will commence shoulder to shoulder your common journey.(p.152)
• The feeling of impending ***disaster*** that had haunted me for years began to dissolve as I put into practice more and more of the Twelve Steps.(p.229)
• I felt disgraced and humiliated — a man who couldn't hold booze — a social ***disaster***.(p.328)

disastrously
• I drank with moderation at first, but it took me only a relatively short time to drift back into the old habits which had wound up so ***disastrously*** before.(p.175)

discard
• Is not our age characterized by the ease with which we ***discard*** old ideas for new, by the complete readiness with which we throw away the theory or gadget which does not work for something new which does?(p.52)
• Can you ***discard*** the feeling that you are dealing only with habit, with stubbornness, or a weak will?(p.140)
• I can watch my serenity level rise when I ***discard*** my expectations.(p.452)
• I have to ***discard*** my "rights," as well as my expectations, by asking myself, "How important is it, really?(p.452)

discarded
• I thought of what liquor had done to me, the opportunities that I had ***discarded***, the abilities that had been given me and how I had wasted them, and I finally came to the conclusion, that if I didn't want to quit, I certainly ought to want to, and that I was willing to do anything in the world to stop drinking.(p.186)
• Secondary aids to A.A., such as clubs or hospitals which require much property or administration, ought to be incorporated and so set apart that, if necessary, they can be freely ***discarded*** by the groups.(p.566)

discharge
• I had been obliged to ***discharge*** him for drinking, though he was brilliant, alert, and one of the best organizers I have ever known.(p.137)
• Following his ***discharge***, we contacted him.(p.139)
• If you are sure he doesn't mean business, there is no doubt you should ***discharge*** him.(p.147)
• Quebec, Toronto, Buffalo, and finally Pittsburgh, were the scenes of man-sized drunks until I had gone through my readjusted ***discharge*** pay, a fair sum.(p.253)
• How I was able to ***discharge*** my duties at the office during those horrible mornings, I will never be able to explain.(p.299)

discharged
• I had ***discharged*** him for drinking six weeks before.(p.137)
• If you are sure your man does not want to stop, he may as well be ***discharged***, the sooner the better.(p.141)
• If he temporizes and still thinks he can ever drink again, even beer, he might as well be ***discharged*** after the next bender which, if an alcoholic, he is almost certain to have.(p.142)
• But you should feel under no obligation to keep him on, for your obligation has been well ***discharged*** already.(p.147)
• If he cannot or does not want to stop, he should be ***discharged***.(p.148)
• ***Discharged*** in 1919, I really made up for my dry spell.(p.253)
• Some days later, after he had been ***discharged***, a stranger came into my shop in the nearby town.(p.257)
• Three years later I was ***discharged*** in the same way.(p.425)
• Two months later I was ***discharged***.(p.428)
• I was escorted back to San Diego next morning -- by the Shore Patrol, but I was ***discharged*** on schedule.(p.428)
• Eventually, the psychiatrist ***discharged*** me from the hospital, and Max and I began going to meetings ourselves.(p.447)
• Offices closed up and workers ***discharged***.(p.500)

disciplinary
• I also got into my first ***disciplinary*** trouble caused by drinking, on two separate occasions.(p.555)

discipline
• So we let God ***discipline*** us in the simple way we have just outlined.(p.88)
• I can remember that in my childhood, he was ill at ease with the children because he attempted to assert an army ***discipline*** that had been ground into him during his three and a half years of army service.(p.210)
• In other words, I was always safe from the ***discipline*** of my father, and having developed along that line, I had considerable difficulty in school.(p.210)
• I could ***discipline*** myself but along the way there would be festivities and occasions when I got drunk.(p.211)
• What often takes place in a few months could seldom have been accomplished by years of self ***discipline***.(p.569)

disclose
• Our stories ***disclose*** in a general way what we used to be like, what happened, and what we are like now.(p.58)
• One object is to ***disclose*** damaged or unsalable goods, to get rid of them promptly and without regret.(p.64)
• It may be one of our own family, but we cannot ***disclose*** anything to our wives or our parents which will hurt them and make them unhappy.(p.74)
• God will constantly ***disclose*** more to you and to us.(p.164)

disclosed
• When we drew near to Him He ***disclosed*** Himself to us!(p.57)

disclosing
• Our hope is that many alcoholic men and women, desperately in need, will see these pages, and we believe that it is only by fully ***disclosing*** ourselves and our problems that they will be persuaded to say, "Yes, I am one of them too; I must have this thing."(p.29)
• Nor are we afraid of ***disclosing*** our alcoholism on the theory it may cause financial harm.(p.78)

disconcerted
• Our experience shows that you need not be ***disconcerted***.(p.44)

discontented
• They are restless, irritable and ***discontented***, unless they can again experience the sense of ease and comfort which comes at once by taking a few drinks -- drinks which they see others taking with impunity.(p.xxvi)

discord
• This makes for ***discord*** and unhappiness.(p.122)

discourage
• In my early twenties the hardships of hobo life did not ***discourage*** me, but I had no wish to become just a tramp.(p.253)

discouraged
• Do not be ***discouraged***.(p.60)
• Do not be ***discouraged*** if your prospect does not respond at once.(p.96)
• Bitterly ***discouraged***, he found himself in a strange place, discredited and almost broke.(p.154)
• On June 26, 1935, I came to in the hospital and to say I was ***discouraged*** is to put it mildly.(p.184)

discouragement
- I wanted to throw up my hands in *discouragement,* for I saw that I had failed to help my banker friend understand.(p.138)

discover
- Doubtless you are curious to *discover* how and why, in the face of expert opinion to the contrary, we have recovered from a hopeless condition of mind and body.(p.20)
- It is an effort to *discover* the truth about the stock-in-trade.(p.64)
- We have been trying to get a new attitude, a new relationship with our Creator, and to *discover* the obstacle in our path.(p.72)
- When you *discover* a prospect for Alcoholics Anonymous, find out all you can about him.(p.90)
- The most incompatible people *discover* they have a basis upon which they can meet.(p.99)
- Searching where I have been at fault, it is not hard to *discover* and get right again, for I have proven to myself and to many others who know me that God can keep a man sober if he will let Him.(p.237)
- Soon I was to *discover* the answer.(p.362)

discovered
- As we *discovered* the principles by which the individual alcoholic could live, so we had to evolve principles by which the A.A. groups and A.A. as a whole could survive and function effectively.(p.xix)
- I was part of life at last, and in the midst of the excitement I *discovered* liquor.(p.1)
- I *discovered* many more reasons later on.(p.2)
- The tremendous fact for every one of us is that we have *discovered* a common solution.(p.17)
- The distinguished American psychologist, William James, in his book "Varieties of Religious Experience," indicates a multitude of ways in which men have *discovered* God.(p.28)
- Much to our relief, we *discovered* we did not need to consider another's conception of God.(p.46)
- So, in one way or another, we *discovered* that faith had been involved all the time!(p.54)
- As we felt new power flow in, as we enjoyed peace of mind, as we *discovered* we could face life successfully, as we became conscious of His presence, we began to lose our fear of today, tomorrow or the hereafter.(p.63)
- When a few men in this city have found themselves, and have *discovered* the joy of helping others to face life again, there will be no stopping until everyone in that town has had his opportunity to recover -- if he can and will.(p.163)
- When I reached school, I *discovered* the faculty had other ideas on the subject.(p.173)
- I soon *discovered* that a couple of drinks would alleviate my gastric distress, at least for a few hours at a time, so it was not at all difficult for me to return to my former excessive indulgence.(p.174)
- I early *discovered* that if I drank anything, I was not accountable for what happened.(p.196)
- Everything in the world a man could possibly want, and I was driving from Akron to Cleveland, having just been to the bank and *discovered* that I had approximately $5,000.(p.200)
- But he *discovered* that there are some gentlemen who can't drink.(p.210)
- I had attended several of these meetings before I *discovered* that all those who were there were not alcoholics.(p.218)
- And, because as I have *discovered* since, it is part of the "treatment" that these men be sent to see and talk with alcoholics who want to quit, he kept them busy.(p.235)
- His own business was practically gone, he told me, when he *discovered* the answer.(p.236)
- Much later I *discovered* the elders held many prayer meetings hoping to find a way to give me the heave-ho, but at the same time stay tolerant and spiritual.(p.247)
- I had been too self-sufficient to write a moral inventory, but I *discovered* in pointing out to the new man his wrong attitudes and actions that I was really taking my own inventory, and that if I expected him to change I would have to work on myself too.(p.249)
- Almost simultaneously, I *discovered* that cocktails in the late afternoon and highballs in the evening relieved the many tensions of the day.(p.277)
- At last I *discovered* alcohol as a cure-all.(p.277)
- The parties waxed more liquid and hilarious as time went on, and eventually I *discovered* that a little shot of liquor now and then between beers had the tendency to put me in a whacky mood much quicker than having to down several quarts of beer to obtain the same effect.(p.298)
- In A.A., she *discovered* she had lost nothing and had found everything.(p.335)
- So that's when I *discovered* the Laundromat.(p.370)
- Age and the law were still against me, but laws were not as strictly enforced in those days as they are now, and I *discovered* that as long as I had the green blood, there was always a way to get alcohol, either from a nondiscriminatory bartender or from an older friend who would be glad to purchase the joy juice for the privilege of sharing it.(p.397)
- Imagine my surprise when I came to, in Europe, and *discovered* I had brought myself along!(p.405)
- If I write with the air of one who has *discovered* the obvious, which is to say, the eternal truths which have been offered to us since the beginning, forgive my callowness; I had to find these things out for myself.(p.536)
- To cure my dreadful hangovers, I *discovered* the morning drink.(p.556)

discoveries
- He is going to be more interested in a demonstration of good will than in our talk of spiritual *discoveries*.(p.77)
- You may make some interesting *discoveries.*(p.149)

discovery
- "Quite as important was the *discovery* that spiritual principles would solve all my problems.(p.42)
- How heartbreaking was this *discovery*; how cruel to be told they understood our men as we did not!(p.106)
- Time after time, this apparent calamity has been a boon to us, for it opened up a path which led to the *discovery* of God.(p.116)
- Seeing much of each other, scarce an evening passed that someone's home did not shelter a little gathering of men and women, happy in their release, and constantly thinking how they might present their *discovery* to some newcomer.(p.159)
- The inevitable result of this *discovery* was that I soon learned that beer made a very good chaser for whiskey.(p.298)
- That *discovery* so intrigued me, that I stayed on that diet almost entirely for the balance of my extensive drinking life.(p.298)
- I had been unhappy, lonely, and scared for so long that the *discovery* of liquor seemed to be the answer to all my problems.(p.353)
- It has brought about a revelation of self, the *discovery* of an inner being, an awareness of God.(p.355)
- With that utterance I again made a wonderful *discovery*.(p.366)

discredited
- Bitterly discouraged, he found himself in a strange place, *discredited* and almost broke.(p.154)
- No one is too *discredited* or has sunk too low to be welcomed cordially -- if he means business.(p.161)

discrediting
- He subsequently denied having received the money and used the incident as a basis for *discrediting* the man.(p.80)

discreet
- So innocent, so *discreet*!(p.370)

discretion
- But be sure you use *discretion.*(p.96)
- Whether you mention this book is a matter for your *discretion.*(p.142)

discuss
- Highly competent psychiatrists who have dealt with us have found it sometimes impossible to persuade an alcoholic to *discuss* his situation without reserve.(p.18)
- Many times we talk to a new man and watch his hope rise as we *discuss* his alcoholic problems and explain our fellowship.(p.45)
- We *discuss* them with someone immediately and make amends quickly if we have harmed anyone.(p.84)
- Don't, at this stage, refer to this book, unless he has seen it and wishes to *discuss* it.(p.92)
- While you need not *discuss* your husband at length, you can quietly let your friends know the nature of his illness.(p.115)
- *Discuss* this with him when he is sober and in good spirits.(p.115)
- If he feels free to *discuss* his problems with you, if he knows you understand and will not be upset by anything he wishes to say, he will probably be off to a fast start.(p.144)
- Every man has his problem of this kind, but we didn't *discuss* it very much.(p.236)
- Could they *discuss* literature or art?(p.412)

discussed
- His faults are not *discussed.*(p.78)
- Have we kept something to ourselves which should be *discussed* with another person at once?(p.86)
- These can then be *discussed* in an atmosphere of helpfulness and friendliness.(p.99)
- So we think that unless some good and useful purpose is to be served, past occurrences should not be *discussed.*(p.125)
- If this presents difficulty, re-reading chapters two and three, where the alcoholic sickness is *discussed* at length might be worth while.(p.140)
- While on the subject of confidence, can you adopt the attitude that so far as you are concerned this will be a strictly personal matter, that his alcoholic derelictions, the treatment about to be undertaken, will never be *discussed* without his consent?(p.143)

discussing
- This is perhaps difficult -- especially *discussing* our defects with another person.(p.72)
- We will be more reconciled to *discussing* ourselves with another person when we see good reasons why we should do so.(p.72)
- Notwithstanding the great necessity for *discussing* ourselves with someone, it may be one is so situated that there is no suitable person available.(p.74)
- If not members of religious bodies, we sometimes select and memorize a few set prayers which emphasize the principles we have been *discussing.*(p.87)

discussion
- Of necessity there will have to be *discussion* of matters medical, psychiatric, social, and religious.(p.19)
- Before going into a detailed *discussion,* it may be well to summarize some points as we see them.(p.20)
- Though you have talked with the family, leave them out of the first *discussion.*(p.91)
- He may rebel at the thought of a drastic housecleaning which requires *discussion* with other people.(p.94)
- Be sure you are not critical during such a *discussion.*(p.111)
- When a *discussion* does arise, you might suggest he read this book or at least the chapter on alcoholism.(p.111)
- Next time you and he have a heated *discussion,* no matter what the subject, it should be the privilege of either to smile and say, "This is getting serious.(p.118)
- As each member of a resentful family begins to see his short comings and admits them to the others, he lays a basis for helpful *discussion.*(p.127)
- When this happens, they can be invited to join in morning meditation and then they can take part in the daily *discussion* without rancor or bias.(p.134)
- After it was closed we all retired to the kitchen and had coffee and doughnuts and more *discussion* until the small hours of the morning.(p.291)
- There was a long *discussion* between my husband, my sister and her husband.(p.466)

discussions
- After many painful *discussions,* they finally gave me my credits and I migrated to another of the leading universities of the country and entered as a Junior that fall.(p.173)
- They held consultations and *discussions,* and finally decided to give me the "Conditioned Reflex" treatment.(p.469)

disease
- From it stem all forms of spiritual *disease,* for we have been not only mentally and physically ill, we have been spiritually sick.(p.64)
- And they said, "No, you have a *disease,* and it doesn't make any difference how long you do without it, after a drink or two you'll end up just like you are now."(p.187)
- Bill looked across at my wife, and said to her, "Henrietta, the Lord has been so wonderful to me, curing me of this terrible *disease,* that I just want to keep talking about it and telling people."(p.191)
- That sentence, "The Lord has been so wonderful to me, curing me of this terrible *disease,* that I just want to keep telling people about it," has been sort of a golden text for the A.A. program and for me.(p.191)
- I was suffering from an actual *disease* that had a name and symptoms like diabetes or cancer or TB -- and a *disease* was respectable, not a moral stigma!(p.227)
- Nevertheless, there were a few doctors who saw alcoholism as a *disease* and felt that the alcoholic was a victim of something over which he had no control.(p.307)
- But, of course," he continued, "eventually the alcoholic loses all of his capacities as his *disease* gets progressively worse, and this is a tragedy that is painful to watch; the disintegration of a sound mind and body."(p.308)
- I told her that I was an alcoholic, victim of a *disease,* that there was no cure, only arrestment through total abstinence.(p.333)

• He did not know it was A.A., and it was useless to tell him, for he doesn't have our ***disease***.(p.334)
• Because it was only through feeling defeat and feeling failure, the inability to cope with my life and with alcohol, that I was able to surrender and accept the fact that I had this ***disease***, and that I had to learn to live again without alcohol.(p.335)
• At a women's halfway house, I became associated with Alcoholics Anonymous and became aware of alcoholism as a ***disease***, not just a "weakness."(p.371)
• I saw at last that I had the same ***disease*** my father had, only I was being given a chance to live, not die.(p.371)
• The explanation that alcoholism was a ***disease*** of a two fold nature, an allergy of the body and an obsession of the mind, cleared up a number of puzzling questions for me.(p.380)
• I realized that there were other people in this world who behaved and acted as I did, and that I was a sick person, that I was suffering from an actual ***disease***.(p.392)
• And as her ***disease*** was reaching the terminal stages, she was screaming, "You hate me!(p.439)
• It helped me a great deal to become convinced that alcoholism was a ***disease***, not a moral issue; that I had been drinking as a result of a compulsion, even though I had not been aware of the compulsion at the time; and that sobriety was not a matter of willpower.(p.448)

diseased

• As I grow in A.A., I realize that a person with as much self-will as I had, as hard a head and as ***diseased*** an ego, had to try everything that I could think of, butting my head against every stone wall before I was ready to come in.(p.384)

disfavor

• Men who had liquor shipped in from Boston or New York by express were looked upon with great distrust and ***disfavor*** by most of the good townspeople.(p.171)

disgrace

• If he opened that old affair, he was afraid it would destroy the reputation of his partner, ***disgrace*** his family and take away his means of livelihood.(p.80)
• You may be afraid your husband will lose his position; you are thinking of the ***disgrace*** and hard times which will befall you and the children.(p.116)
• I did not want to ***disgrace*** myself so I then checked out.(p.179)
• He seldom is a ***disgrace***.(p.330)
• But as long as you did your work and didn't ***disgrace*** yourself, you were socially acceptable and nobody really intruded on your private life very much.(p.518)
• I remember being dragged, drink in hand, from beneath the grand piano, where I had hidden, to be locked in my room in ***disgrace***.(p.557)

disgraced

• I felt ***disgraced*** and humiliated — a man who couldn't hold booze — a social disaster.(p.328)

disgust

• When I did make it home in 1920, I re-entered school and caught up with my class in a few short months — I actually did a year's work in three months, proving much to the ***disgust*** of my dad that I could do it when I wanted to.(p.358)
• The contempt and ***disgust*** that was in his face and thoughts!(p.391)

disgusted

• That ***disgusted*** me.(p.4)
• It brings misunderstanding, fierce resentment, financial insecurity, ***disgusted*** friends and employers, warped lives of blameless children, sad wives and parents -- anyone can increase the list.(p.18)
• But they were much ***disgusted*** and told me they would attempt to struggle along without my presence.(p.173)
• She was thoroughly ***disgusted***.(p.288)
• I worked in the steel mill for possibly two months, and then I became ***disgusted*** with myself and decided to go back home.(p.492)

disgusting

• They may be ***disgusting***.(p.140)

disgustingly

• Yet let him drink for a day, and he frequently becomes ***disgustingly*** and even dangerously anti-social.(p.21)

disheartening

• That certainly was real ***disheartening*** news, at the time.(p.188)

dishes

• I was a very young married man, having his whiskey in the cupboard over the sink, and when I helped my wife with the ***dishes*** at night I would take a cup of tea and spike it with whiskey.(p.196)
• But I remembered that every night after dinner my wife would get up and do the ***dishes***.(p.351)
• Well, I could do the ***dishes***.(p.351)
• So I went to her and said, "There's only one thing I want in my whole life, and I don't want any commendation; I don't want any credit; I don't want anything from you or Janey for the rest of your life except one thing; and that is, the opportunity to do anything you want always, and I would like to start off by doing the ***dishes***."(p.351)
• And now I am doing the darn ***dishes*** every night!(p.352)
• I went out to the West Coast, waited on table, washed ***dishes*** and sold newspaper subscriptions.(p.401)
• I was still untrained for any work but washing ***dishes*** and waiting on table.(p.401)

dishonest

• He is often perfectly sensible and well balanced concerning everything except liquor, but in that respect he is incredibly ***dishonest*** and selfish.(p.21)
• On the other hand, he may be mean, egotistical, selfish and ***dishonest***.(p.61)
• Where had we been selfish, ***dishonest***, self-seeking and frightened?(p.67)
• Where had we been selfish, ***dishonest***, or inconsiderate?(p.69)
• Were we resentful, selfish, ***dishonest*** or afraid?(p.86)
• Before we begin, we ask God to direct our thinking, especially asking that it be divorced from self-pity, ***dishonest*** or self-seeking motives.(p.86)
• Away down deep, I was motivated into ***dishonest*** behavior because I was a people-pleaser.(p.328)
• ***Dishonest*** thinking, prejudice, ego, antagonism toward anyone and everyone who dares to cross him, vanity and a critical attitude are character defects that gradually creep in and become a part of his life.(p.380)
• That is how ***dishonest*** I was with myself.(p.388)

dishonesty

• Continue to watch for selfishness, ***dishonesty***, resentment, and fear.(p.84)
• We wives found that, like everybody else, we were afflicted with pride, self-pity, vanity and all the things which go to make up the self-centered person; and we were not above selfishness or ***dishonesty***.(p.116)
• However, what I had gained materially on the credit side of my ledger, I have since learned was more than offset on the debit side by egotism, resentment and ***dishonesty***.(p.356)

disillusioned

• My inability to accept the harsh realities of life had resulted in a ***disillusioned*** cynic, clothed in protective armor against the world's misunderstanding.(p.226)
• It was to be short lived, for on the day before Christmas I completely ***disillusioned*** my wife and ruined our first Christmas by coming home from the Rotary lunch dead drunk.(p.361)

disillusionment

• Post-war ***disillusionment***, ever more serious alcoholism, impending mental and physical collapse, brought him to the point of self-destruction.(p.56)

disinherited

• Cleaning up old scrapes, helping to settle family differences, explaining the ***disinherited*** son to his irate parents, lending money and securing jobs for each other, when justified -- these are everyday occurrences.(p.161)

disintegrate

• At least three of those four years must have been a living hell for my wife, because she had to watch the man she loved ***disintegrate*** morally, mentally and financially.(p.277)

disintegrating

• You know the deteriorating effects, the ***disintegrating*** effects of chronic wine-drinking.(p.337)

disintegration

• But, of course," he continued, "eventually the alcoholic loses all of his capacities as his disease gets progressively worse, and this is a tragedy that is painful to watch; the ***disintegration*** of a sound mind and body."(p.308)

dislike

• Nevertheless, with a person we ***dislike***, we take the bit in our teeth.(p.77)
• In a weak moment he may take your ***dislike*** of his high-stepping friends as one of those insanely trivial excuses to drink.(p.120)

disliked

• I ***disliked*** being different so, ultimately, I began to join them occasionally.(p.374)
• But not for long; now, for five Friday nights in a row, I went to jail, picked up sodden with beer (which I always ***disliked***, but which was the only drink available); in jail five consecutive Friday nights in the town where I had grown up, where I had been an honor student in high school, where a kindly uncle, bailing me out, said, "Bob, our family just doesn't do this sort of thing."(p.539)

dislikes

• We all had hundreds of character traits, of fears and phobias, likes and ***dislikes***, in common.(p.229)

disloyal

• Was I the ***disloyal*** sort who would turn his back on this, my last and truest friend?(p.539)

dismal

• One ***dismal*** afternoon he paced a hotel lobby wondering how his bill was to be paid.(p.154)
• Now came the black and endless ***dismal*** night.(p.410)

dismayed

• Couples are occasionally ***dismayed*** to find that when drinking is stopped the man tends to be impotent.(p.134)

dismays

• Perhaps your husband will make a fair start on the new basis, but just as things are going beautifully he ***dismays*** you by coming home drunk.(p.120)

dismissed

• From this job and the next one with another printer I was courteously ***dismissed***.(p.277)
• I had enough decency so that I ***dismissed*** the idea of doing any clowning, and I did listen.(p.509)

disorders

• There are those, too, who suffer from grave emotional and mental ***disorders***, but many of them do recover if they have the capacity to be honest.(p.58)
• Sometimes there are cases where alcoholism is complicated by other ***disorders***.(p.114)

dispatched

• So Paul was ***dispatched*** and brought back a pint.(p.206)

dispensed

• Eventually, the noon meal was also ***dispensed*** with.(p.299)

dispensing

• There, I received several soda crackers and water daily, and before I could have my third-day meal (again the only meal in ten days), I had to drink a glass of castor oil or mineral oil, depending on the cruelty of the person who was doing the ***dispensing***.(p.459)

displacements

• They appear to be in the nature of huge emotional ***displacements*** and rearrangements.(p.27)

display

• I was unwilling to bare my secrets to those who might ***display*** scorn.(p.331)

displayed

• I was terribly impressed by this meeting and the quality of happiness these men ***displayed***, despite their lack of material means.(p.291)
• I ***displayed*** alcoholic tendencies actually from the age of fourteen, when I started to steal wine from the family jug, siphoning it off one drink at a time so it wouldn't be missed, not drinking it immediately, but saving it until about a pint was accumulated, so that I could get drunk.(p.397)

displays

• What has become of the common sense and will power that he still sometimes ***displays*** with respect to other matters?(p.22)
• Even if he ***displays*** a certain amount of neglect and irresponsibility towards the family, it is well to let him go as far as he likes in helping other alcoholics.(p.129)

disposal

• Every means of solving his problem which money could buy was at his ***disposal***.(p.32)
• When we see a man sinking into the mire that is alcoholism, we give him first aid and place what we have at his ***disposal***.(p.132)
• One man and his wife placed their large home at the ***disposal*** of this strangely assorted crowd.(p.160)
• I was gathering that cache for ***disposal*** when my wife woke up and caught me at it.(p.333)

dispose
• You and your husband will find that you can ***dispose*** of serious problems easier than you can the trivial ones.(p.118)

disposed
• India lent itself to drinking then, if you were ***disposed*** to drink, because you lived in bungalows; you didn't live all together as you do at home in an Officer's Mess.(p.519)

disposition
• His ***disposition*** while drinking resembles his normal nature but little.(p.21)
• He is an intelligent man, normal so far as we can see, except for a nervous ***disposition.***(p.35)
• The slightest ***disposition*** on your part to guide his appointments or his affairs so he will not be tempted will be noticed.(p.120)

disproportionate
• It is not to be expected that an alcoholic employee will receive a ***disproportionate*** amount of time and attention.(p.149)

dispute
• The wars which had been fought, the burnings and chicanery that religious ***dispute*** had facilitated, made me sick.(p.11)
• Starting from a speck on the domestic horizon, great thunderclouds of ***dispute*** may gather.(p.117)
• Alcoholics being the argumentative lot that we are, the A.A. membership will undoubtedly come up with a few who will ***dispute*** these figures.(p.399)

disputes
• Experience has often warned us that nothing can so surely destroy our spiritual heritage as futile ***disputes*** over property, money, and authority.(p.566)

disregard
• Though a situation had not been entirely our fault, we tried to ***disregard*** the other person involved entirely.(p.67)
• But this does not mean that we ***disregard*** human health measures.(p.133)
• If you desire to help it might be well to ***disregard*** your own drinking, or lack of it.(p.139)

disregarded
• For myself, I had adopted those parts which seemed convenient and not too difficult; the rest I ***disregarded.***(p.11)

disrupted
• I think I ***disrupted*** the hospital.(p.388)

disrupting
• But out of this frightening and at first ***disrupting*** experience the conviction grew that A.A.'s had to hang together or die separately.(p.xix)

dissecting
• We used to amuse ourselves by cynically ***dissecting*** spiritual beliefs and practices when we might have observed that many spiritually-minded persons of all races, colors, and creeds were demonstrating a degree of stability, happiness and usefulness which we should have sought ourselves.(p.49)

dissensions
• These family ***dissensions*** are very dangerous, especially to your husband.(p.117)

dissipated
• It is bound to be rough, because who can say exactly how much of that green blood – commonly known as money – was ***dissipated*** on dissipation?(p.396)

dissipation
• Hardly one of our crowd now shows any mark of ***dissipation.***(p.133)
• It is bound to be rough, because who can say exactly how much of that green blood – commonly known as money -- was dissipated on ***dissipation?***(p.396)

dissolve
• Professionally, after I was sober for a month or so I realized that I should school myself to ***dissolve*** the partnership I was in because I felt that I would never regain the respect of my partners no matter how long I was sober, and that I would be at a disadvantage.(p.220)
• The feeling of impending disaster that had haunted me for years began to ***dissolve*** as I put into practice more and more of the Twelve Steps.(p.229)

dissolved
• By the time I was thirty I had found that alcohol ***dissolved*** fear.(p.275)
• But with the first drink, our good intentions ***dissolved;*** our personalities changed.(p.458)

distance
• We could not prove life in the sense that you can prove a straight line is the shortest ***distance*** between two points, yet, there it was.(p.54)
• Still another experience: A woman's voice came faintly over long ***distance*** from Virginia.(p.137)
• Military service was compulsory and I did my stretch with the class of my age, goose-stepping in German barracks and taking part in the Boxer Rebellion in China, my first time at any great ***distance*** from home.(p.230)
• However, as there happened to be several saloons within that ***distance,*** I didn't find it necessary to patronize the same place each evening.(p.298)
• She was intent on her studies, and kept her ***distance.***(p.359)
• I felt very sorry for myself and attempted suicide on many occasions, making sure there was always somebody within reaching ***distance*** to see that I didn't finish the job.(p.478)
• The helpful family finally said, over long ***distance,*** that there would be no more money and that I could not come home.(p.538)

distances
• From surrounding towns, families drive long ***distances*** to be present.(p.161)
• Always, in between, there were intervals of being broke, riding freights and hitch-hiking interminable ***distances*** from one big town to another in three states.(p.255)

distant
• Alcohol being no respecter of persons, we are an accurate cross section of America, and in ***distant*** lands, the same democratic evening-up process is now going on.(p.xx)
• Ask any woman who has sent her husband to ***distant*** places on the theory he would escape the alcohol problem.(p.101)

distinct
• This phenomenon, as we have suggested, may be the manifestation of an allergy which differentiates these people, and sets them apart as a ***distinct*** entity.(p.xxviii)
• During the next few years, I developed two ***distinct*** phobias.(p.175)
• (That condition was a ***distinct*** handicap to me in trying to vindicate myself with the not so patient wife.)(p.301)

distinction
• We hope we have made clear the ***distinction*** between the alcoholic and the non-alcoholic.(p.44)
• With all this, it was becoming increasingly hard to maintain my front of ***distinction*** and respectability to the world.(p.435)

distinctions
• Social ***distinctions,*** petty rivalries and jealousies -- these are laughed out of countenance.(p.161)

distinctly
• I can still remember very ***distinctly*** getting into Akron at eleven p.m. and routing this same Howard out of bed to do something about me.(p.290)

distinguish
• As to them, his policy is undoubtedly sound, but he did not ***distinguish*** between such people and the alcoholic.(p.149)

distinguished
• The ***distinguished*** American psychologist, William James, in his book "Varieties of Religious Experience," indicates a multitude of ways in which men have discovered God.(p.28)
• He has since become famous and ***distinguished,*** an asset to his country.(p.403)
• One, the side I turned to myself and the world, was respectable – even, in some ways, ***distinguished.***(p.432)
• I was listed in "Who's Who in America" as an American who, by ***distinguished*** achievement, had arrived.(p.432)

distorted
• Perhaps your husband has been living in that strange world of alcoholism where everything is ***distorted*** and exaggerated.(p.108)
• My values became ***distorted.***(p.556)

distortion
• If the family cooperates, dad will soon see that he is suffering from a ***distortion*** of values.(p.129)

distract
• We had a minor campaign or two and that helped ***distract*** attention from my drinking.(p.519)

distracted
• The alarming physical and mental symptoms, the deepening pall of remorse, depression and inferiority that settled down on our loved ones -- these things terrified and ***distracted*** us.(p.106)
• It was the usual situation: home in jeopardy, wife ill, children ***distracted,*** bills in arrears and standing damaged.(p.155)
• Many a ***distracted*** wife has visited this house to find loving and understanding companionship among women who knew her problem, to hear from the lips of their husbands what had happened to them, to be advised how her own wayward mate might be hospitalized and approached when next he stumbled.(p.160)

distractions
• This practice enables us to lend a hand, at the same time avoiding certain alluring ***distractions*** of the road, about which any traveling man can inform you.(p.162)

distress
• I soon discovered that a couple of drinks would alleviate my gastric ***distress,*** at least for a few hours at a time, so it was not at all difficult for me to return to my former excessive indulgence.(p.174)
• My old friends showed ***distress.***(p.404)
• It was nothing to my own inner ***distress,*** my self-reproach, and my self-loathing, for was I not bearing out all the horrible things I had always suspected of myself?(p.404)

distressed
• Most of the time therefore, I did not take the morning drink which I craved so badly, but instead would fill up on large doses of sedatives to quiet the jitters, which ***distressed*** me terribly.(p.176)

distressing
• They experienced a few ***distressing*** failures, but in those cases they made an effort to bring the man's family into a spiritual way of living, thus relieving much worry and suffering.(p.159)

district
• In those days the A.A. Foundation was down in the Wall Street ***district*** of New York.(p.413)
• I went back to my mother's for a few days until things cooled off, because the ***District*** Attorney had put out a summons for me to come to see him in his office.(p.491)
• So I went down to talk to the ***District*** Attorney, and the arrangement was made that I would go home to stay with my mother, and that meant Vi and I were separated.(p.491)
• Still another friend and temporary host received me at four in the morning from the charge of a policeman who had found me "going to bed" in a garage far from the last place I could remember having been, a fashionable bar and restaurant in the theatrical ***district*** of New York, to which I had repaired after my date for that evening, a charming lady of the theatre who had refused my company for obvious reasons.(p.538)

distrust
• Men who had liquor shipped in from Boston or New York by express were looked upon with great ***distrust*** and disfavor by most of the good townspeople.(p.171)

disturb
• Not wishing to ***disturb*** my wife, I slumped in a big red-leather chair and suffered.(p.332)

disturbances
• I apparently was willing to subdue these personality ***disturbances*** in a tremendous drive to succeed.(p.211)
• This, plus mounting emotional ***disturbances,*** convinced them that compulsive alcoholism already had them; that complete ruin would be only a question of time.(p.315)

disturbed
• Though my drinking was not yet continuous, it ***disturbed*** my wife.(p.2)
• Though we did not like their symptoms and the way these ***disturbed*** us, they, like ourselves, were sick too.(p.67)
• Maybe you have ***disturbed*** him about the question of alcoholism.(p.94)
• I'm sorry I got ***disturbed.***(p.118)
• If it isn't anything that's going to help you or anybody else, why should you become involved in it, and get all ***disturbed*** about it?"(p.273)
• When I am ***disturbed,*** it is because I find some person, place, thing, or situation – some fact of my life -- unacceptable to me, and I can find no serenity until I accept that person, place, thing, or situation as being exactly the way it is supposed to be at this moment.(p.449)
• That hurt and ***disturbed*** me a great deal.(p.484)
• I said that she told me she was going to the movies, and I became foolishly ***disturbed*** about it and, as things snowballed, I decided to go out

and get drunk.(p.487)

disturbing

• Those having religious affiliations will find here nothing *disturbing* to their beliefs or ceremonies.(p.28)

ditch

• This man faced the last *ditch* when his wife's voice from 1,300 miles away sent him to A.A.(p.356)

dither

• I would get in the biggest *dither* about something.(p.273)

divan

• Lying on the *divan*, "getting in the mood" to write, I cried openly or inwardly, as I listened to sad songs.(p.332)

• Hauling her to the *divan*, I sat with her and began to talk, frantically but clearly – and making sense.(p.333)

dive

• I learned that a person just can't find a job hanging in a *dive* or barroom all day and all night, as jobs don't seem to turn up in those places.(p.300)

• So here, in this *dive*, this hangout for dead-end alcoholics and neurotics, here was I.(p.410)

divert

• Six – An A.A. group ought never endorse, finance or lend the A.A. name to any related facility or outside enterprise, lest problems of money, property and prestige *divert* us from our primary purpose.(p.564)

• 6. – Problems of money, property, and authority may easily *divert* us from our primary spiritual aim.(p.565)

diverted

• We missed the reality and beauty of the forest because we were *diverted* by the ugliness of some of its trees.(p.50)

• The amount of will power exercised to control my drinking during working hours, *diverted* into a constructive channel, would have made me President, and the thing that made the will power possible was the knowledge that as soon as my day was finished I could drink myself into oblivion.(p.548)

divided

• "Bill's Story," "Doctor Bob's Nightmare," and one other personal history from the first edition were retained intact; three were edited and one of these was retitled; new versions of two stories were written with new titles; thirty completely new stories were added; and the story section was *divided* into three parts, under the same headings that are used now.(p.xi)

dividend

• This was fine, but it was just an extra *dividend*, for I'd made connections by this time and was buying a bottle a day from the cook.(p.426)

dividends

• He may not see at once that he has barely scratched a limitless lode which will pay *dividends* only if he mines it for the rest of his life and insists on giving away the entire product.(p.129)

• Your understanding treatment of their cases will pay *dividends*.(p.141)

• This change had been a long, slow process for me, but through these latter years the *dividends* have been tremendous.(p.249)

• However, this isn't as rough as it sounds, as we do become grateful for the necessity that makes us toe the line, for we find that we are more than compensated for a consistent effort by the countless *dividends* we receive.(p.311)

dividing

• We think, therefore, that any considerable property of genuine use to A.A. should be separately incorporated and managed, thus *dividing* the material from the spiritual.(p.565)

divine

• As to two of you men, whose stories I have heard, there is no doubt in my mind that you were 100% hopeless, apart from *divine* help.(p.43)

• And he further said that God could not accept me as a sincere follower of His *Divine* Law unless I was ready to be thoroughly honest about it.(p.236)

• Then he asks me if I believe in a power greater than myself, whether I call that power God, Allah, Confucius, Prime Cause, *Divine* Mind, or any other name.(p.503)

• I hope I have been able to impart to you, the reader, at least a bit of what I know; the joy of living, the irresistible power of *divine* love and its healing strength, and the fact that we, as sentient beings, have the knowledge to choose between good and evil, and, choosing good, are made happy.(p.543)

division

• I, and the books of my *division*, have been transferred to the head office.(p.500)

divorce

• Friends who have reasoned with him after a spree which has brought him to the point of *divorce* or bankruptcy are mystified when he walks directly into a saloon.(p.35)

• Finally, he can no longer work, his wife gets a *divorce* and he is held up to ridicule.(p.38)

• Now, the domestic problem: There may be *divorce*, separation, or just strained relations.(p.98)

• If there be *divorce* or separation, there should be no undue haste for the couple to get together.(p.99)

• Perhaps at this point we got a *divorce* and took the children home to father and mother.(p.106)

• My *divorce* coincided with my father's bankruptcy, and I went to work, casting off all allegiances and responsibilities to any other than myself.(p.225)

• I had gone to an attorney to see about getting a *divorce* during that year.(p.263)

• He said he was through and would seek a *divorce*.(p.371)

• For some reason I can't remember, it finally dawned on me that I had a problem, and yet nobody was very critical about it except my family, and that was only because I decided, after seven years of marriage, that I would *divorce* my husband.(p.386)

• I did *divorce* him in July.(p.386)

• It only took a month to get a *divorce* in Texas.(p.386)

• At the tender age of twenty-three, I got a *divorce*.(p.402)

• We went through two years of deadlock required by the English *divorce* laws.(p.405)

• Had I been able to explain to a psychiatrist the feeling of futility, loneliness and lack of purpose that had come with my deep sense of personal failure at this second *divorce*, I seriously doubt that the good doctor could have convinced me that my basic problem was a spiritual hunger, but A.A. has shown me this was the truth.(p.546)

divorced

• Maybe we are *divorced*, and have remarried but haven't kept up the alimony to number one.(p.79)

• Before we begin, we ask God to direct our thinking, especially asking that it be *divorced* from self-pity, dishonest or self-seeking motives.(p.86)

• I didn't like having to come home at a certain time; I didn't like this, I didn't like that, and I think the poor girl actually *divorced* me to help me stop drinking!(p.199)

• I was *divorced* in 1925 or 1926.(p.199)

• I was married at twenty, had two children and was *divorced* at twenty-three.(p.305)

• After I came to A.A., I was *divorced* by my wife; I lost my practice; I was legally restrained from seeing my children; I went broke; and the dental society threatened me with the loss of my license.(p.420)

• My alcoholic wife took up someone else, *divorced* me, and took with her all my remaining property.(p.437)

• It was not difficult to convince myself that my unhappiness was the fault of the man I had married, and I *divorced* him at the end of a year.(p.545)

• I was married and *divorced* again before I was twenty-three years old, this time to a prominent band leader -- a man that many women wanted.(p.546)

divorcee

• But now I was a young *divorcee*, leading a Washington social life.(p.402)

dizzily

• Again I swayed *dizzily* before an open window, or the medicine cabinet where there was poison, cursing myself for a weakling.(p.6)

dizzy

• To be sure, this had been a *dizzy* and confused interval, but most everyone else I knew had emerged from it with both feet on the ground and a fair amount of adult maturity.(p.304)

• After my very first drink – a tiny glass of sherry my father gave me to celebrate the New Year when I was thirteen -- I went up to bed, *dizzy* with exhilaration and excitement, and I prayed I wouldn't drink any more!(p.554)

doc

• So, after hearing some more of my story, he turned around and said to *Doc* -- I don't think he knew I heard him, but I did – he said, "Well, I believe he's worth saving and working on."(p.185)

• One of the fellows, I think it was *Doc*, said, "Well, you want to quit?"(p.187)

• I said, "Yes, *Doc*, I would like to quit, at least for five, six, or eight months, until I get things straightened up, and begin to get the respect of my wife and some other people back, and get my finances fixed up and so on."(p.187)

• It was in the next two or three days after I had first met *Doc* and Bill, that I finally came to a decision to turn my will over to God and to go along with this program the best that I could.(p.189)

• On Sunday when I came to, it was a bad, wet, snowy day in February, 1937, and Paul and *Doc* and a lot of other fellows were in Cleveland on business.(p.207)

• There was one experience with *Doc* which made a terrific impression upon me.(p.218)

• *Doc* dwelt on the idea that this was an illness, but *Doc* was pretty frank with me.(p.219)

• I give a great deal of credit to *Doc* and Anne for changing our life.(p.270)

• I knew *Doc* and Anne were going to be there, and all of them thought it would be good for me, but the first thing I did was to go to St. Thomas and try to talk to those women.)(p.272)

• After talking with him for a time I heard myself saying, "*Doc*, I think I'm an alcoholic."(p.436)

• "Well, *Doc*," I said, "what are we going to do?"(p.436)

• The *doc* and I went back into the house.(p.541)

doctor

• From this *doctor*, the broker had learned the grave nature of alcoholism.(p.xvi)

• A well-known *doctor*, chief physician at a nationally prominent hospital specializing in alcoholic and drug addiction, gave Alcoholics Anonymous this letter:(p.xxiii)

• The *doctor* writes:(p.xxv)

• Men have cried out to me in sincere and despairing appeal: "*Doctor*, I cannot go on like this!(p.xxvii)

• Faced with this problem, if a *doctor* is honest with himself, he must sometimes feel his own inadequacy.(p.xxvii)

• A *doctor* came with a heavy sedative.(p.6)

• Best of all, I met a kind *doctor* who explained that though certainly selfish and foolish, I had been seriously ill, bodily and mentally.(p.7)

• For a moment I was alarmed, and called my friend, the *doctor*, to ask if I were still sane.(p.14)

• The good *doctor* now sees many men who have such experiences.(p.14)

• Strangely enough, wives, parents and intimate friends usually find us even more unapproachable than do the psychiatrist and the *doctor*.(p.18)

• "The *doctor* told him that if he ever drank again it would kill him, but there he is all lit up again."(p.20)

• If a sufficiently strong reason – ill health, falling in love, change of environment, or the warning of a *doctor* -- becomes operative, this man can also stop or moderate, although he may find it difficult and troublesome and may even need medical attention.(p.21)

• Perhaps he goes to a *doctor* who gives him morphine or some sedative with which to taper off.(p.22)

• So he returned to this *doctor*, whom he admired, and asked him point-blank why he could not recover.(p.26)

• He begged the *doctor* to tell him the whole truth, and he got it.(p.26)

• Let us tell you the rest of the conversation our friend had with his *doctor*.(p.27)

• The *doctor* said: "You have the mind of a chronic alcoholic.(p.27)

• He said to the *doctor*, "Is there no exception?"(p.27)

• "Yes," replied the *doctor*, "there is.(p.27)

• The *doctor* intimated strongly that he might be worse than he realized.(p.39)

• Perhaps our *doctor* or psychologist will be the person.(p.74)

• Approach through a *doctor* or an institution is a better bet.(p.91)

• Let the *doctor*, if he will, tell him he has something in the way of a solution.(p.91)

• When your man is better, the *doctor* might suggest a visit from you.(p.91)

• If his own *doctor* is willing to tell him that he is alcoholic, so much the better.(p.92)

• Sometimes you will have to call a *doctor* and administer sedatives under his direction.(p.97)

• Maybe the *doctor* has been called in, and the weary round of sanitariums and hospitals has begun.(p.110)

• A good *doctor* or psychiatrist can tell you whether these complications are serious.(p.114)

• If he is already committed to an institution, but can convince you and your *doctor* that he means business, give him a chance to try our method, unless the *doctor* thinks his mental condition too abnormal or dangerous.(p.114)

• When they become too dangerous, we think the kind thing is to lock them up, but of course a good ***doctor*** should always be consulted.(p.114)

• A ***doctor*** said to us, "Years of living with an alcoholic is almost sure to make any wife or child neurotic.(p.122)

• Try to remember that though God has wrought miracles among us, we should never belittle a good ***doctor*** or psychiatrist.(p.133)

• There should be no hesitancy in consulting a ***doctor*** or psychologist if the condition persists.(p.134)

• I well remember the shock I received when a prominent ***doctor*** in Chicago told me of cases where pressure of the spinal fluid actually ruptured the brain.(p.140)

• The matter of physical treatment should, of course, be referred to your own ***doctor***.(p.143)

• We suggest you draw the book to the attention of the ***doctor*** who is to attend your patient during treatment.(p.144)

• We hope the ***doctor*** will tell the patient the truth about his condition, whatever that happens to be.(p.144)

• We are greatly indebted to the ***doctor*** in attendance there, for he, although it might prejudice his own work, has told us of his belief in ours.(p.162)

• Every few days this ***doctor*** suggests our approach to one of his patients.(p.162)

• The ***doctor*** proved to be able and exceedingly anxious to adopt any workable method of handling the situation.(p.163)

• And with such good effect that the ***doctor*** agreed to a test among his patients and certain other alcoholics from a clinic which he attends.(p.163)

• Finally my father had to send a ***doctor*** out from my home town who managed to get me back there in some way, and I was in bed about two months before I could venture out of the house.(p.175)

• I think I must have been thoroughly scared by what had happened, or by the ***doctor***, or probably both, so that I did not touch a drink again until the country went dry.(p.175)

• Knowing Bob of old, she jokingly replied, "Well, ***Doctor***, I suppose you've already tried it yourself?"(p.188)

• I looked so terrible in the court that the judge suggested that I get a continuance and let me sign all the papers to go to a hospital and to a ***doctor***.(p.204)

• So they decided that I should have a ***doctor***.(p.205)

• They called a ***doctor*** and it happened that they called one I knew.(p.205)

• The next day, they called me in for an examination, and the ***doctor*** wouldn't let me continue working and pardoned me from the plant for ten days because he said my eye had been injured.(p.205)

• "Well," the ***doctor*** said, "we have hopes in that direction."(p.207)

• She had a hairdresser who used to tell her about a brother-in-law who had been quite a drinker and about some ***doctor*** in Akron who had straightened him out.(p.216)

• When my ***doctor*** told me I should never touch a drink again, I couldn't afford to believe him.(p.226)

• That was the point at which my ***doctor*** gave me the book "Alcoholics Anonymous" to read.(p.227)

• I told my ***doctor*** so in no uncertain terms.(p.227)

• An alcoholic who was a ***doctor*** came to see me.(p.235)

• This ***doctor*** had imparted his knowledge to just a few other men at that time -- not more than four or five -- they now number more than seventy persons.(p.235)

• He had already imbued them with his own spirit until they were ready and willing at all times to go where sent, and as a ***doctor*** he well knew that this mission and duty would strengthen them as it later helped me.(p.235)

• It wasn't very long until my ***doctor*** friend sent me to tell another alcoholic what my experience had been.(p.237)

• As I look back on the events of two months, I can clearly see that I had been circling around, half-afraid of encountering the remedy for my situation, half wanting it, deferring fulfillment of my promise to get in touch with the ***doctor*** I had heard about.(p.258)

• The ***doctor*** who came to see me almost at once did not assail me with any new doctrines; he made sure that I had a need and that I wanted to have that need filled, and little by little I learned how my need could be met.(p.258)

• He said, "There's a ***doctor*** here in Akron.(p.267)

• I was scared to death to call a ***doctor***.(p.267)

• I thought I had done that until Russ' second collapse, and the ***doctor*** told me very candidly that he wasn't long for this world.(p.271)

• I told our family ***doctor***, an understanding man who gave hours of his time trying to help me, about this experience.(p.276)

• A ***doctor*** tipped me off to my first prospect.(p.282)

• I went to a minister and a ***doctor*** that I still knew and they, in turn, asked me how long I had been sober.(p.293)

• I suggested to her that she should see the son's minister or ***doctor***, and that perhaps he would recommend the A.A. program.(p.294)

• The ***doctor***, a young man, immediately took fire with the idea, and while he did not convince the son, he turned over two prospects who were anxious for the program.(p.294)

• In the meantime, another ***doctor*** in Evanston became convinced that the program had possibilities, and turned over a woman to us to do something about.(p.295)

• My wife became pregnant and the ***doctor*** recommended the use of port or ale . . . so . . . I bought a six gallon crock and a few bottles, listened to advice from amateur brewmeisters, and was off on my beer manufacturing career on a small scale (for the time being).(p.297)

• Just at this time my wife heard of a ***doctor*** in another city who had been very successful with drunks.(p.301)

• Well . . . I had a job, and I really wanted desperately to stop drinking, but couldn't, so I readily agreed to visit the ***doctor*** she recommended.(p.301)

• My wife accompanied me on my visit and the ***doctor*** really told me some things that in my state of jitters nearly knocked me out of the chair.(p.302)

• For about one year, prior to this time, there was one ***doctor*** who had continued to struggle with me.(p.306)

• Fortunately for me, my ***doctor*** was one of the enlightened.(p.307)

• But somehow my good ***doctor*** heard of this book and also he learned a little about the people responsible for its publication.(p.307)

• But this day my ***doctor*** gave it to me straight and said, "People like you are pretty well known to the medical profession.(p.307)

• Every ***doctor*** gets his quota of alcoholic patients.(p.308)

• Shortly after I returned to Chicago, my ***doctor***, encouraged by the results of my contact with A.A., sent us two more of his alcoholic patients.(p.310)

• The ***doctor*** asked about my drinking, but I wouldn't talk to him.(p.319)

• The ***doctor*** prescribed brandy for the boy to help him through the night when he coughed, a teaspoon of brandy.(p.338)

• I went to my ***doctor*** again.(p.339)

• She was doing fine, she was up and around, and that day her husband phoned me and said, "***Doctor***, thanks very much for curing my wife," and I thanked him for his felicitations, and he hung up.(p.350)

• And the psychiatrist has had thousands of couches, and has put you and me on them many, many times, but he hasn't helped us very much, though he has tried hard; and we owe the clergy and the ***doctor*** and the psychiatrist a deep debt of gratitude, but they haven't helped our alcoholism, except in a rare few instances.(p.352)

• I suppose the ***doctor*** might say, "This is psychosomatic medicine."(p.352)

• Frank said, "If you'd like to talk to a psychiatrist, I'll see a ***doctor*** and find out who to go to here."(p.387)

• Frank left to find the ***doctor*** and I got drunk.(p.387)

• Frank found the ***doctor***, but the ***doctor*** didn't want to take an alcoholic.(p.387)

• I knew this, and right away I got furious and would not even talk to the ***doctor*** in the place.(p.387)

• So the ***doctor*** let me go home on one condition.(p.387)

• I was crazy about my ***doctor***.(p.387)

• There was a ***doctor*** in our church congregation who was interested in my case, and he thought it was a vitamin deficiency.(p.389)

• The only thing that I could do would be to call the ***doctor*** to help sober me up.(p.389)

• I couldn't walk, having it in a cast, and the ***doctor*** left the cast on three weeks longer than was necessary because he never found me sober enough to take it off.(p.390)

• An American ***doctor*** in Paris said I had an enlarged liver.(p.406)

• This good and gentle man, a brilliant research ***doctor***, got nowhere with me fast.(p.407)

• This new analyst was a woman ***doctor***, one of the best in the country.(p.409)

• I am a young alcoholic with a drug problem, a ***doctor***, the husband of an alcoholic, the son of an alcoholic, and a man once diagnosed as a violent manic-depressive.(p.421)

• This must be the ***doctor***.(p.422)

• The ***doctor*** motioned to the corpsman to undo my straitjacket and leg restraints.(p.422)

• The ***doctor*** sat down beside the bed and asked me how I felt.(p.423)

• The ***doctor*** was still sitting beside my bed.(p.427)

• The ***doctor*** said I'd been brought into the hospital like a madman, crying, raving, ranting, swearing, completely in the throes of delirium tremens.(p.427)

• I told the ***doctor*** my parents' drinking history and blamed them.(p.428)

• The folks called a ***doctor*** and he knocked me out with sedatives.(p.429)

• That ***doctor*** in the Navy hospital told me I wouldn't live five years if I didn't quit.(p.429)

• I thought, "If this is A.A. why not go back to drinking, kill myself with booze in the next three years the ***doctor*** had given me, and call it a bad job?"(p.430)

• ***DOCTOR***, ALCOHOLIC, ADDICT(p.439)

• You tell that dumb cat-and-dog ***doctor*** he's not a Beverly Hills psychiatrist.(p.440)

• The hotel management, knowing that something was wrong, sent for a ***doctor***.(p.465)

• The ***doctor***, apparently realizing that one thing that I certainly needed was sleep, left a bottle of sleeping pills there and in my drunken state I took them all, instead of the one or two he had prescribed.(p.465)

• The same ***doctor*** who had sent me to the psycho had asked my husband, "Why don't you send her to this Alcoholics Anonymous?"(p.469)

• So the ***doctor*** said, "I really don't know too much about it, but they tell me it is a bunch of drunks who get together . . ."(p.469)

• In other words, the kindest ***doctor*** in the whole world, and I had one such, couldn't help me because I always felt, "You can't know about me – you can't possibly know – you don't even drink!"(p.471)

• He wanted to give me the very best and he thought that nothing but being a ***doctor*** would suffice.(p.485)

• The ***doctor*** has told me that if I don't give up inside work, I'll have tuberculosis.(p.500)

• The ***doctor*** bills are heavy and the bank account is low.(p.501)

• Those poor stiffs probably went to a ***doctor*** and were told that if they quit they'd live three weeks and if they didn't they'd die in one."(p.510)

• I went back to the old family ***doctor*** who had helped me the first time I had the D.T.'s.(p.515)

• I stayed there just long enough to work up a real good resentment against the ***doctor*** in charge, who I didn't think was doing anything at all except collecting fees, and I left there fully determined that I'd never put myself in the power of medical people again.(p.521)

• It was no use talking of putting myself into a home, a hospital, or of going to see a ***doctor*** again, or of going to see a priest or anyone else.(p.523)

• But then one good ***doctor*** told me there was nothing wrong with me except drinking too much.(p.528)

• On another small borrowed sum, I went up into the country to the home of a ***doctor*** I had known since boyhood.(p.540)

• We worked in five below zero weather, fixing on an elm tree a wrought iron device which modestly proclaimed that he was indeed a country ***doctor***.(p.540)

• Had I been able to explain to a psychiatrist the feeling of futility, loneliness and lack of purpose that had come with my deep sense of personal failure at this second divorce, I seriously doubt that the good ***doctor*** could have convinced me that my basic problem was a spiritual hunger, but A.A. has shown me this was the truth.(p.546)

• Finally, in desperation, my family appealed to a ***doctor*** for advice and he suggested A.A.(p.549)

• The ***doctor*** pronounced it a badly enlarged liver and said I had to quit drinking.(p.557)

• My ***doctor*** warned me that if I kept on, I might have esophageal hemorrhaging and die.(p.558)

• What my ***doctor*** had warned me about finally happened.(p.558)

• My ***doctor*** finally declared he could no longer be responsible for me, and sent me to a psychiatrist who practiced in the same suite of offices.(p.558)

Doctor

• "Bill's Story," "***Doctor*** Bob's Nightmare," and one other personal history from the first edition were retained intact; three were edited and one of these was retitled; new versions of two stories were written with new titles; thirty completely new stories were added; and the story section was divided into three parts, under the same headings that are used now.(p.xi)

• ***DOCTOR*** BOB'S NIGHTMARE(p.171)
• (I knew afterwards that the two who came in were Bill W. and ***Doctor*** Bob.)(p.185)
• Twenty-two years later, ***Doctor*** Bob told me that what I had done was like turning a switch and setting up a demand for more alcohol in my system.(p.195)
• One morning, after I had been on a binge for a couple of days, I awoke to find my brother and ***Doctor*** Bob in my room talking to me about not drinking.(p.206)

doctor's

• The section called "The ***Doctor's*** Opinion" has been kept intact, just as it was originally written in 1939 by the late Dr. William D. Silkworth, our Society's great medical benefactor.(p.xi)
• THE ***DOCTOR'S*** OPINION(p.xxiii)
• The ***doctor's*** theory that we have an allergy to alcohol interests us.(p.xxiv)
• In the ***doctor's*** judgment he was utterly hopeless; he could never regain his position in society and he would have to place himself under lock and key or hire a bodyguard if he expected to live long.(p.26)
• This hope, however, was destroyed by the ***doctor's*** telling him that while his religious convictions were very good, in his case they did not spell the necessary vital spiritual experience.(p.27)
• One of the many doctors who had the opportunity of reading this book in manuscript form told us that the use of sweets was often helpful, of course depending upon a ***doctor's*** advice.(p.133)
• Somehow or other, I must have misunderstood the ***doctor's*** instructions, for I not only made the beer for my wife, I also drank it for her.(p.297)
• By this time, with the ***doctor's*** explanation, the revelations contained in the book, and the hope-inspiring interview with Mr. T., I was ready and willing to go into the interior of the African jungles, if that was what it took, for me to find what these people had.(p.309)
• About this time, at Christmas, after being under this ***doctor's*** care, we decided that there wasn't anything more to do.(p.388)

doctors

• We ***doctors*** have realized for a long time that some form of moral psychology was of urgent importance to alcoholics, but its application presented difficulties beyond our conception.(p.xxv)
• ***Doctors*** had pronounced him incurable.(p.11)
• Many ***doctors*** and psychiatrists agree with our conclusions.(p.43)
• We know but few instances where we have given these ***doctors*** a fair break.(p.73)
• You can easily find some by asking a few ***doctors***, ministers, priests or hospitals.(p.89)
• Ministers and ***doctors*** are competent and you can learn much from them if you wish, but it happens that because of your own drinking experience you can be uniquely useful to other alcoholics.(p.89)
• ***Doctors*** are rightly loath to tell alcoholic patients the whole story unless it will serve some good purpose.(p.92)
• ***Doctors*** may shake their heads and advise you to have him committed.(p.110)
• God has abundantly supplied this world with fine ***doctors***, psychologists, and practitioners of various kinds.(p.133)
• One of the many ***doctors*** who had the opportunity of reading this book in manuscript form told us that the use of sweets was often helpful, of course depending upon a doctor's advice.(p.133)
• At that time I was not aware of the almost unlimited supply the government made it possible for us ***doctors*** to obtain, neither had I any knowledge of the bootlegger who soon appeared on the horizon.(p.175)
• I had had no hospitalization up to this time because I would not call ***doctors*** when I was getting over a bad one.(p.217)
• So I spent much of my time calling on the people who I felt would logically come in contact with alcoholic cases, ***doctors***, ministers, lawyers and the personnel men in industry.(p.281)
• ***Doctors*** told me before I stopped that I had only three years at the outside to live.(p.295)
• I began making the rounds of the ***doctors*** in the hope that one of them might find some cure for my accumulating ailments, preferably something that could be removed surgically.(p.305)
• Of course the ***doctors*** found nothing.(p.305)
• Why he bothered with me as long as he did I shall never know, for he knew there was no answer for me in medicine and he, like all ***doctors*** of his day, had been taught that the alcoholic was incurable and should be ignored.(p.307)
• ***Doctors*** were advised to attend patients who could be benefited by medicine.(p.307)
• Nevertheless, there were a few ***doctors*** who saw alcoholism as a disease and felt that the alcoholic was a victim of something over which he had no control.(p.307)
• Few ***doctors*** will tell a hopeless patient that there is no answer for him or for her.(p.307)
• Sergeants, ***doctors***, girl friends -- everybody seemed to be picking on him.(p.317)
• ***Doctors*** have been notoriously unsuccessful in helping alcoholics.(p.352)
• There were ***doctors*** and psychiatrists there who tried to help me, but at that point I wasn't having help from anyone.(p.468)
• It is true that the ***doctors*** and nurses in the various institutions I attended knew too.(p.470)
• Here was a book that said I could do something that all these ***doctors*** and priests and ministers and psychiatrists that I'd been going to for years couldn't do!(p.473)
• I went to hospitals, I went to retreats and ***doctors***, and finally my mother asked me to go and see a specialist of her own choosing.(p.522)
• I thought if the cops did come to the hospital, the ***doctors*** would tell them I was crazy and didn't know what I was doing.(p.528)
• The ***doctors*** told me that if I ever took another drink, it might be my last.(p.558)
• Following are excerpts from the comments of ***doctors*** present at the annual meeting of the Medical Society of the State of New York where a paper on A.A. was read:(p.571)

doctors'

• It was a waste of the ***doctors'*** time and the patients' money.(p.307)
• I remember finding myself in the middle of the night in the ***doctors'*** parking lot at the hospital with one foot in the car and one foot on the ground, not knowing which was the lead foot; finding myself hanging up the telephone – then realizing I had gotten out of bed, answered the phone, turned on the light, and carried on a conversation with a patient.(p.441)

doctrine

• I resolved that if I were going to continue with the Catholic Church, I was going to know the roots of the ***doctrine***, since those roots had caused me some confusion.(p.221)

doctrines

• The doctor who came to see me almost at once did not assail me with any new ***doctrines***; he made sure that I had a need and that I wanted to have that need filled, and little by little I learned how my need could be met.(p.258)

dodge

• We do not ***dodge*** our creditors.(p.78)

dodged

• Never in sixteen years have I ***dodged*** anything because I was afraid of it.(p.285)

does

• Neither ***does*** A.A. take any particular medical point of view, though we cooperate widely with the men of medicine as well as with the men of religion.(p.xx)
• Unlike the feelings of the ship's passengers, however, our joy in escape from disaster ***does*** not subside as we go our individual ways.(p.17)
• He ***does*** absurd, incredible, tragic things while drinking.(p.21)
• Why ***does*** he behave like this?(p.22)
• He ***does*** not need a bodyguard nor is he confined.(p.26)
• I have never seen one single case recover, where that state of mind existed to the extent that it ***does*** in you."(p.27)
• Neither ***does*** there appear to be any kind of treatment which will make alcoholics of our kind like other men.(p.30)
• To be gravely affected, one ***does*** not necessarily have to drink a long time nor take the quantities some of us have.(p.33)
• Why ***does*** he?(p.35)
• We found that God ***does*** not make too hard terms with those who seek Him.(p.46)
• As soon as a man can say that he ***does*** believe, or is willing to believe, we emphatically assure him that he is on his way.(p.47)
• And ***does*** not science demonstrate that visual proof is the weakest proof?(p.48)
• Is not our age characterized by the ease with which we discard old ideas for new, by the complete readiness with which we throw away the theory or gadget which ***does*** not work for something new which ***does***?(p.52)
• We agnostically inclined would not feel satisfied with a proposal which ***does*** not lend itself to reasonable approach and interpretation.(p.53)
• Still the play ***does*** not suit him.(p.61)
• Just to the extent that we do as we think He would have us, and humbly rely on Him, ***does*** He enable us to match calamity with serenity.(p.68)
• ***Does*** this mean we are going to get drunk?(p.70)
• The inconsistency is made worse by the things he ***does*** on his sprees.(p.73)
• It should not matter, however, if someone ***does*** throw us out of his office.(p.78)
• But drinking ***does*** complicate sex relations in the home.(p.81)
• If we are sure our wife ***does*** not know, should we tell her?(p.81)
• It is better, however, that one ***does*** not needlessly name a person upon whom she can vent jealously.(p.82)
• It ***does*** not exist for us.(p.85)
• It works – it really ***does***.(p.88)
• If he ***does*** not want to stop drinking, don't waste time trying to persuade him.(p.90)
• If he ***does*** not want to see you, never force yourself upon him.(p.90)
• If the man be agnostic or atheist, make it emphatic that he ***does*** not have to agree with your conception of God.(p.93)
• Tell him you once felt as he ***does***, but you doubt whether you would have made much progress had you not taken action.(p.94)
• Do not be discouraged if your prospect ***does*** not respond at once.(p.96)
• Though an alcoholic ***does*** not respond, there is no reason why you should neglect his family.(p.97)
• These things will come to pass naturally and in good time provided, however, the alcoholic continues to demonstrate that he can be sober, considerate, and helpful, regardless of what anyone says or ***does***.(p.99)
• You can see that he really ***does*** love you with his better self.(p.108)
• Of course, there is such a thing as incompatibility, but in nearly every instance the alcoholic only seems to be unloving and inconsiderate; it is usually because he is warped and sickened that he says and ***does*** these appalling things.(p.108)
• Try not to condemn your alcoholic husband no matter what he says or ***does***.(p.108)
• It may be slowing him up mentally and physically, but he ***does*** not see it.(p.109)
• He is positive he can handle his liquor, that it ***does*** him no harm, that drinking is necessary in his business.(p.109)
• He admits he cannot drink like other people, but ***does*** not see why.(p.110)
• When a discussion ***does*** arise, you might suggest he read this book or at least the chapter on alcoholism.(p.111)
• If this kind of approach ***does*** not catch your husband's interest, it may be best to drop the subject, but after a friendly talk your husband will usually revive the topic himself.(p.112)
• If he ***does*** not, you will probably not have long to wait.(p.113)
• He will perceive that his spiritual growth is lopsided, that for an average man like himself, a spiritual life which ***does*** not include his family obligations may not be so perfect after all.(p.129)
• Though the family ***does*** not fully agree with dad's spiritual activities, they should let him have his head.(p.129)
• If he ***does*** not argue about religion, he will make new friends and is sure to find new avenues of usefulness and pleasure.(p.132)
• Now about health: A body badly burned by alcohol ***does*** not often recover overnight nor do twisted thinking and depression vanish in a twinkling.(p.133)
• But this ***does*** not mean that we disregard human health measures.(p.133)
• Easy ***Does*** It.(p.135)
• When sober, ***does*** he not work hard and have a knack of getting things done?(p.139)
• If you are sure your man ***does*** not want to stop, he may as well be discharged, the sooner the better.(p.141)
• Say that you believe he is a gravely ill person, with this qualification – being perhaps fatally ill, ***does*** he want to get well?(p.142)
• But ***does*** he?(p.142)
• If he says yes, ***does*** he really mean it, or down inside ***does*** he think he is fooling you, and that after rest and treatment he will be able to get away with a few drinks now and then?(p.142)
• That won't hurt him a bit, even though he ***does*** not go for this remedy.(p.144)

- Can he talk frankly with you so long as he ***does*** not bear business tales or criticize his associates?(p.145)
- In case he ***does*** stumble, even once, you will have to decide whether to let him go.(p.147)
- If he cannot or ***does*** not want to stop, he should be discharged.(p.148)
- This company now ***does*** a volume of over three billion dollars annually.(p.242)
- People have wars and kill each other; they struggle and cut each other's throats for success and what ***does*** anyone get out of it?(p.244)
- Our pet slogan is "Easy ***Does*** It."(p.250)
- But how ***does*** one get a prescription for a miracle?(p.306)
- I believe that the release from people-pleasing restrictions gives retirees more motivation to drink than boredom ***does***.(p.329)
- Easy ***does*** it, first things first, one day at a time.(p.340)
- Cunning, baffling, powerful -- the gradual creeping up of the frequency and quantity of alcohol, and what it ***does*** to a person is apparent to everyone but the person involved.(p.375)
- "Easy ***Does*** It."(p.382)
- I only know that it ***does*** -- if you desire it with your whole heart and without reservation.(p.384)
- But now, with His help and grace, this child of His has paid his initiation fee for good, as long as he remembers to stay away from that first drink (the one that ***does*** all the damage) one day at a time.(p.399)
- I'd packed more drinking into seven years than many a heavy drinker ***does*** in a lifetime.(p.429)
- All I want to know is, why ***does*** that dog wet in my lap every time I hold him?"(p.440)
- I can't say, "God could restore me to sanity, but until He ***does***, I'll control myself -- with pills."(p.443)
- I can tell her she ought not to think a certain way, but I certainly can't take away her right to feel however she ***does*** feel.(p.451)
- The word "alcoholic" ***does*** not turn me off any more; in fact, it is music to my ears when it applies to me.(p.463)
- But the older members in A.A. told me, "easy ***does*** it."(p.471)
- (Actually, he ***does*** it solely to get rid of us.)(p.480)
- When I had known her years before she was rather slender, but at this time she weighed as much as she ***does*** now, which is up around in the two hundreds or very close to it.(p.493)
- "How ***does*** prayer fit into this thing?"(p.504)
- ***Does*** that answer your question?"(p.504)
- "Yes, it ***does***," I answer.(p.504)
- She ***does*** not get excited.(p.507)
- If something ***does*** come along that sort of upsets me, instead of walking in and throwing a buck at the barman and asking for a drink, I walk into a telephone booth, drop a dime in the box, and call somebody who was so kind as to give me his name and telephone number to meet such an emergency.(p.511)
- I use that "Easy ***Does*** It" every day, to slow me down a little.(p.516)
- To create: Everyone ***does*** it, some at the instinct level, others in the arts.(p.535)
- I stood off and took a long look at life and the values I found in it: I saw a paradox, that he who loses his life ***does*** indeed find it.(p.542)
- "A.A. ***does*** not teach us how to handle our drinking," he said.(p.554)
- Most emphatically we wish to say that any alcoholic capable of honestly facing his problems in the light of our experience can recover, provided he ***does*** not close his mind to all spiritual concepts.(p.570)

doesn't

- Or perhaps he ***doesn't*** think at all.(p.24)
- Some of you are thinking: "Yes, what you tell us is true, but it ***doesn't*** fully apply.(p.38)
- The show ***doesn't*** come off very well.(p.61)
- He begins to think life ***doesn't*** treat him right.(p.61)
- They arise out of ourselves, and the alcoholic is an extreme example of self-will run riot, though he usually ***doesn't*** think so.(p.62)
- He wants to enjoy a certain reputation, but knows in his heart he ***doesn't*** deserve it.(p.73)
- Certainly he must keep sober, for there will be no home if he ***doesn't***.(p.82)
- Many of us have wasted a lot of time doing that and it ***doesn't*** work.(p.87)
- Make it clear that he is not under pressure, that he needn't see you again if he ***doesn't*** want to.(p.94)
- Perhaps you enjoy drinking with him yourself when he ***doesn't*** go too far.(p.110)
- But dad ***doesn't*** give freely of himself.(p.126)
- He may tell mother, who has been religious all her life, that she ***doesn't*** know what it's all about, and that she had better get his brand of spirituality while there is yet time.(p.128)
- If you are sure he ***doesn't*** mean business, there is no doubt you should discharge him.(p.147)
- So it ***doesn't*** behoove me to squawk about it for, after all, nobody ever had to throw me down and pour liquor down my throat.(p.181)
- And they said, "No, you have a disease, and it ***doesn't*** make any difference how long you do without it, after a drink or two you'll end up just like you are now."(p.187)
- But I guess He ***doesn't*** believe much in me."(p.189)
- It ***doesn't*** take long.(p.242)
- It ***doesn't*** pay to be seen in the same place at the same hour every day.(p.299)
- He did not know it was A.A., and it was useless to tell him, for he ***doesn't*** have our disease.(p.334)
- It ***doesn't*** belong to me.(p.351)
- Like most statistics, it ***doesn't*** prove anything -- just satisfies a little curiosity engendered by the wail "Oh, those initiation fees" that prompted this investigation.(p.399)
- I don't know how I got here this trip, but it ***doesn't*** matter very much.(p.423)
- He ***doesn't*** know me, nor do I know him.(p.463)
- When you've been in a jam you've said, 'God, please do this or that,' and if it turned out your way that was the last of it, and if it didn't you've said 'There isn't any God' or 'He ***doesn't*** do anything for me.'(p.504)
- It ***doesn't*** make sense.(p.504)
- But not for long; now, for five Friday nights in a row, I went to jail, picked up sodden with beer (which I always disliked, but which was the only drink available); in jail five consecutive Friday nights in the town where I had grown up, where I had been an honor student in high school, where a kindly uncle, bailing me out, said, "Bob, our family just ***doesn't*** do this sort of thing."(p.539)

dog

- I was sure those who needed a bit of the hair of the ***dog*** really were alcoholics.(p.332)
- Frank had to go to New York, but because I had a ***dog***, we had a duplex, and I thought -- if only we had a house!(p.388)
- A duplex apartment isn't any place to raise a ***dog***.(p.388)
- I loved my father dearly and I adored my ***dog***, and I'd gotten this new house and Frank had just given me a new fur coat and I was thrilled to death.(p.389)
- He even had the people come out, and tell me what kind of room I was going to have, and that he could come and see me, and that the ***dog*** could come and see me.(p.389)
- I wouldn't go to hospitals because I wanted my ***dog*** there, so I had to have a trained nurse.(p.390)
- The only time my ***dog*** would have anything to do with me was when I had a hangover, and when I was so sick he was the only one who would have anything to do with me at all.(p.390)
- I got into slacks and out I went, weaving with the ***dog***.(p.390)
- When he picked me up, I must have gotten sassy and told him that he couldn't do that, so he took my ***dog*** home and took me to jail!(p.390)
- I remember, one time, even the ***dog*** had a psychiatric diagnosis.(p.440)
- I yelled at Max, "What do you mean, 'The ***dog*** just needs more love'?(p.440)
- All I want to know is, why does that ***dog*** wet in my lap every time I hold him?"(p.440)
- (That ***dog*** hasn't wet my pants once since I joined A.A., and neither have I!)(p.440)

dogged

- For years thereafter he was ***dogged*** by trouble and frustration.(p.56)

doggerel

- My attention was caught by a ***doggerel*** on an old tombstone:(p.1)

doing

- A man of thirty was ***doing*** a great deal of spree drinking.(p.32)
- We must be willing to make amends where we have done harm, provided that we do not bring about still more harm in so ***doing***.(p.69)
- Our former enemies sometimes praise what we are ***doing*** and wish us well.(p.78)
- We will suddenly realize that God is ***doing*** for us what we could not do for ourselves.(p.84)
- Many of us have wasted a lot of time ***doing*** that and it doesn't work.(p.87)
- After ***doing*** that, he must decide for himself whether he wants to go on.(p.95)
- Never avoid these responsibilities, but be sure you are ***doing*** the right thing if you assume them.(p.97)
- Your desire to protect him should not cause you to lie to people when they have a right to know where he is and what he is ***doing***.(p.115)
- As our husbands began to apply spiritual principles in their lives, we began to see the desirability of ***doing*** so too.(p.116)
- If your husband is trying to live on a spiritual basis, he will also be ***doing*** everything in his power to avoid disagreement or contention.(p.118)
- His ways of thinking and ***doing*** are the habit of years.(p.118)
- Inevitably your lives will be fuller for ***doing*** so.(p.120)
- He is striving to recover fortune and reputation and feels he is ***doing*** very well.(p.126)
- Instead of treating the family as he should, he may retreat further into himself and feel he has spiritual justification for so ***doing***.(p.129)
- I felt this was inevitable and wondered if the bank was ***doing*** the man an injustice.(p.138)
- You are not ***doing*** him a favor by keeping him on.(p.141)
- If, on the contrary, you are sure he is ***doing*** his utmost, you may wish to give him another chance.(p.147)
- My whole life seemed to be centered around ***doing*** what I wanted to do, without regard for the rights, wishes, or privileges of anyone else; a state of mind which became more and more predominant as the years passed.(p.172)
- 3.Because in so ***doing*** I am paying my debt to the man who took time to pass it on to me.(p.181)
- And they both laughed very heartily, and said, "That's better than you've been ***doing***, isn't it?"(p.187)
- I would put off ***doing*** anything that I could until the next day and, consequently, everything would pile up and then there would be the blackout.(p.197)
- He had known something of my drinking pattern, and he asked me what I was ***doing*** about it.(p.200)
- I was bounding along and not ***doing*** too badly.(p.204)
- He said, "So long as I'm thinking as I'm thinking now, and so long as I'm ***doing*** the things I'm ***doing*** now, I don't believe I'll ever take another drink."(p.206)
- There had been some occasions -- there was an automobile wreck, for instance -- when I had police escort home but not to jail, all of which, instead of ***doing*** me a favor, did me harm because I was then full of self-esteem as to the progress I had made both professionally and financially.(p.213)
- They probably felt that it was useless, that surely I had enough intelligence to know what I was ***doing***.(p.215)
- She gave no sign of recognizing anything wrong, but what had I been ***doing*** for those lost five hours?(p.223)
- I was ***doing*** very well with that and general upholstering work, and there was every indication that I would be financially independent by the time I reached middle age.(p.232)
- I was ***doing*** well in business, and in going around town I was frequently invited to have a drink in a speakeasy.(p.233)
- More and more I formed the habit of ***doing*** some of my business in the speakeasy, and after a time I did not need that as an excuse.(p.233)
- I was eased out of the business I had founded and was reduced to ***doing*** general upholstery in a small shop at the back of my house.(p.233)
- In telling newcomers how to change their lives and attitudes, all of a sudden I found I was ***doing*** a little changing myself.(p.249)
- Following a big drunk on that sheet, where I was ***doing*** leg-work and rewrite, a feeling of nostalgia made me buy a ticket for Liverpool and I returned to Britain.(p.252)
- "I'm ***doing*** a job I like and it's quiet where I live, practically no temptations.(p.257)
- Of course, this year we decided on staying home and being sensible, ***doing*** a little drinking, and painting the house.(p.265)
- I was supposed to be ***doing*** God's will, not mine.(p.282)
- At long last I am ***doing*** the kind of work I have always wanted to do, but never had the patience and emotional stability to train myself for.(p.284)
- Some of the things which used to stop me in my tracks from fear still make me nervous in the anticipation of their ***doing***, but once I kick myself into ***doing*** them nervousness disappears and I enjoy myself.(p.285)

• Being an alcoholic, I couldn't dream of *doing* anything by halves!(p.286)
• He waited until I was completely sober and the day before I was to head back for Chicago, he told me of a small group of men in Akron who apparently had the same problem that I had but were *doing* something about it.(p.289)
• The next afternoon and evening, two other men visited me and each told me his story and the things that they were *doing* to try to recover from this tragic illness.(p.290)
• In the next two or three days the balance of this handful of men contacted me, encouraged me, and told me how they were trying to live this program of recovery and the fun they were having *doing* it.(p.291)
• What I needed was a change, mental relaxation, getting out and *doing* something.(p.338)
• He knew what I was *doing*, how I was trying.(p.339)
• In those days, I was *doing* a staff appointment in the army headquarters in New Delhi.(p.343)
• You've been *doing* all right."(p.348)
• I said, "What do you think I've been *doing*?"(p.349)
• She was *doing* fine, she was up and around, and that day her husband phoned me and said, "Doctor, thanks very much for curing my wife," and I thanked him for his felicitations, and he hung up.(p.350)
• So I went to her and said, "There's only one thing I want in my whole life, and I don't want any commendation; I don't want any credit; I don't want anything from you or Janey for the rest of your life except one thing; and that is, the opportunity to do anything you want always, and I would like to start off by *doing* the dishes."(p.351)
• And now I am *doing* the darn dishes every night!(p.352)
• Of course I kept her posted on how well the station was *doing* and wrote convincing letters of how well I was *doing* with the liquor problem.(p.360)
• That night she too had new hope because I had made sure she would know what I was *doing* about my drinking by packing every bit of A.A. literature I could put my hands on right on top so she couldn't help but see it when she opened my bag.(p.364)
• It was frightening that drink was being substituted for more and more of the things I really enjoyed *doing*.(p.374)
• Resenting anyone and everyone who might interfere with my personal plans and ways of *doing* things, I was full of self pity, especially for any interference with my drinking.(p.376)
• Nor have I attended them with a feeling of just *doing* my duty.(p.381)
• Making amends is sometimes *doing* what we are capable of *doing* but failed to do because of alcohol; carrying out community responsibilities such as Community Funds, Red Cross, educational and religious activities in proportion to our abilities and energy.(p.381)
• "First Things First": solving our immediate problems before we try to solve all the others and get muddled in our thinking and *doing*.(p.382)
• *Doing* our best, living each day to the fullest is the art of living.(p.382)
• Through going to meetings and listening, and occasionally speaking, through *doing* Twelve Step work, whereby in helping others you are both the teacher and the student, by making many wonderful A.A. friends, I have been taught all the things in life that are worth having.(p.416)
• I was skipping classes about two days a week and *doing* no book work whatever.(p.423)
• Once in a while I stayed home for a night, to see how my folks were *doing*.(p.425)
• They were *doing* very well — at least a fifth apiece a day, except on dad's days off when they did some serious drinking.(p.425)
• I never could quite get the knack of it and kept asking myself, "What's a nice guy like me *doing* in a place like this?"(p.445)
• Right from the start, I felt that they weren't *doing* anything for me, but they sure were helping Max.(p.447)
• There, I received several soda crackers and water daily, and before I could have my third-day meal (again the only meal in ten days), I had to drink a glass of castor oil or mineral oil, depending on the cruelty of the person who was *doing* the dispensing.(p.459)
• When I came into A.A., I had no intention of quitting drinking -- I figured I was *doing* all right.(p.478)
• Mind you, I had absolutely nothing to show for that eighteen years, except a beat-up car that I hadn't even paid for, but I was *doing* all right.(p.478)
• No clothes, no money, no home, no real friends to speak of, mentally and physically pooped, but I was *doing* all right!(p.478)
• Honesty is the easiest word for me to understand because it is the exact opposite of what I've been *doing* all my life.(p.482)
• I don't seem to be able to keep my mind on what I am *doing*.(p.499)
• "What are you *doing* here then?" I ask.(p.503)
• I had enough decency so that I dismissed the idea of *doing* any clowning, and I did listen.(p.509)
• I stayed there just long enough to work up a real good resentment against the doctor in charge, who I didn't think was *doing* anything at all except collecting fees, and I left there fully determined that I'd never put myself in the power of medical people again.(p.521)
• My only hope was to try and get through what was left of life as best I could, but I could never visualize *doing* that without drinking.(p.522)
• I thought if the cops did come to the hospital, the doctors would tell them I was crazy and didn't know what I was *doing*.(p.528)
• Harm is done by sick people, as I was sick, and *doing* dreadful harm to myself and to my loved ones.(p.542)
• That's what I am *doing*, living again, knowing what I know.(p.543)
• As another great man says, "The only real freedom a human being can ever know is *doing* what you ought to do because you want to do it."(p.553)

dollar

• And I continued to drink, on and off then, until every *dollar* I had in the world was gone again and I was right back living at my sister's, getting my cigarettes by calling her grocer and telling him to put in a couple of cartons with her order, exactly as I had before I started to work at Max's.(p.202)
• After a couple of days in *dollar* hotels and one night in the pokey, I finally landed on my mother's doorstep -- shaking apart, with several days' beard and, of course, broke as usual.(p.238)
• Then it was my turn -- I ordered "Three beers," but this time it was different, I had a cash investment of thirty cents and, on a ten *dollar* a week salary, that's a big thing.(p.247)
• In the morning I would wake up with a *dollar* or two.(p.410)
• I had to put up a three hundred *dollar* bond because he was carrying the same summons around in his pocket for me.(p.491)
• Finally, I broke the last one hundred *dollar* bill the Saturday before I left.(p.493)
• A twenty-three million *dollar* surplus wiped out.(p.500)

dollars

• The exercise of an option brought in more money, leaving us with a profit of several thousand *dollars* for that year.(p.3)
• Sometimes a small deal would net a few hundred *dollars*, and I would pay my bills at the bars and delicatessens.(p.5)
• We have spent thousands of *dollars* for examinations.(p.73)
• My downfall cost the business community unknown thousands of *dollars*, for it takes real money to train a man for an executive position.(p.137)
• I can well remember sitting with seven *dollars* in my pocket, planning on giving my family a hundred or two hundred *dollars*, when I made it next year.(p.197)
• I had lost a hundred *dollars* I had in my pocket, and lost a wristwatch too.(p.202)
• This company now does a volume of over three billion *dollars* annually.(p.242)
• Bill and Hank had just taken over a small automobile polishing company and they offered me a job -- ten *dollars* a week and keep at Hank's house.(p.246)
• He took his one hundred and seventeen *dollars* and let us go, and we proceeded.(p.264)
• He might have handed me fifty *dollars* and said that I ought to pull myself together and make a new start.(p.278)
• I, carried away with the desire to serve A.A., gave what was probably one of the first radio broadcasts about A.A., living through a case of mike fright and feeling like a million *dollars* when it was all over.(p.283)
• I went to work in Birmingham for a newspaper at fifteen *dollars* a week.(p.357)
• Monday morning I was feeling just like a million *dollars* -- all I needed was half a pint!(p.393)
• Twelve *dollars* a week.(p.397)
• Saying these sprees were limited to one a week (they were not), and saying that the average spree was ten of these drinks (sometimes more, sometimes less), we come up with the first boring statistic: two-fifty per week out of twelve *dollars*.(p.397)
• My first pay was ten *dollars*, pay for recruits at that time being twenty-one *dollars* per month.(p.398)
• While waiting to depart I was selected -- by giving a CPO five *dollars* -- to be bartender in the Navy Chief's Club.(p.426)
• I paid nine hundred *dollars* for a second hand car on my return.(p.429)
• I spent eighteen hundred *dollars* fixing up that car in the first year I was home, after four bad smash-ups.(p.429)
• To cut a long story short, I spent seven years and ten thousand *dollars* on my psychiatric adventure, and emerged in worse condition than ever.(p.434)
• I was now head of a publishing venture in which nearly a million *dollars* had been invested.(p.435)
• I borrowed five hundred *dollars* from the bank and three hundred from the loan shop, and I drank that up pretty fast.(p.490)
• I guess I had five or ten *dollars* in my pocket.(p.491)
• Thinking only of two or three *dollars* to buy some whiskey, I did the job and that's how I met Ella G., who was responsible for my coming into A.A.(p.493)
• So, finally, I went to the YMCA and they graciously permitted us to use a room at two *dollars* a night.(p.495)
• Even when we were paying that two *dollars* a night, they often paid it for us because our collection was so small.(p.496)
• One morning, I woke up with a thousand *dollars*.(p.528)
• I had replied, "Uncle, give the judge ten *dollars*, or I'll have to work it out on the county road."(p.539)
• There were debts totaling nearly ten thousand *dollars* to be paid off.(p.541)

domestic

• I have seen hundreds of families set their feet in the path that really goes somewhere; have seen the most impossible *domestic* situations righted; feuds and bitterness of all sorts wiped out.(p.15)
• The chances are that we have *domestic* troubles.(p.80)
• Now, the *domestic* problem: There may be divorce, separation, or just strained relations.(p.98)
• If you have been successful in solving your own *domestic* problems, tell the newcomer's family how that was accomplished.(p.100)
• Starting from a speck on the *domestic* horizon, great thunderclouds of dispute may gather.(p.117)
• In the meantime, the *domestic* situation was not getting along too well.(p.199)
• I condoned my *domestic* brewing along with the bootleggers and their business.(p.233)
• That being the case, it didn't take me long to figure out that my meager manufacturing facilities were entirely inadequate to the manufacture of beer for social and *domestic* consumption.(p.297)
• It is impossible to put on paper all the benefits I have derived . . . physical, mental, *domestic*, spiritual, and monetary.(p.302)
• From a *domestic* standpoint, we really have a home now.(p.303)
• Also, I believed I was the image of all *domestic* virtues, secluded in my washday (any day) refuge.(p.369)

domesticity

• Strangely enough, I became acquainted with the "hilarious life" just at the time in my own life when I was beginning really to settle down to a common-sense, sane *domesticity*.(p.297)

dominant

• I had suppressed tendencies to overindulge and thus reveal my "moral weakness," because false pride was so *dominant*.(p.327)

dominate

• Ideas, emotions, and attitudes which were once the guiding forces of the lives of these men are suddenly cast to one side, and a completely new set of conceptions and motives begin to *dominate* them.(p.27)

dominated

• We began to see that the world and its people really *dominated* us.(p.66)
• The children are sometimes *dominated* by a pathetic hardness and cynicism.(p.134)
• Never having enough, always craving more, the obsession for alcohol gradually *dominated* all my activities, particularly while travelling.(p.375)

dominates

• What sort of thinking *dominates* an alcoholic who repeats time after time the desperate experiment of the first drink?(p.35)

domination

• This had the effect of making me resolve that when I was free from parental ***domination,*** I would never again darken the doors of a church.(p.172)

don't

• He said, "Why ***don't*** you choose your own conception of God?"(p.12)
• Finally he shook his head saying, "Something has happened to you I ***don't*** understand.(p.14)
• "Why ***don't*** you drink like a gentleman or quit?"(p.20)
• "Why ***don't*** you try beer and wine?"(p.20)
• Hence we are at pains to tell why we think our present faith is reasonable, why we think it more sane and logical to believe than not to believe, why we say our former thinking was soft and mushy when we threw up our hands in doubt and said, "We ***don't*** know."(p.53)
• We ***don't*** use this as an excuse for shying away from the subject of God.(p.77)
• To his wife, he remarked, "***Don't*** see anything the matter here, Ma.(p.82)
• We ***don't*** worry about them if we can honestly say to ourselves that we would right them if we could.(p.83)
• But we ***don't*** delay if it can be avoided.(p.83)
• As God's people we stand on our feet; we ***don't*** crawl before anyone.(p.83)
• We ***don't*** struggle.(p.86)
• ***Don't*** start out as an evangelist or reformer.(p.89)
• If he does not want to stop drinking, ***don't*** waste time trying to persuade him.(p.90)
• ***Don't*** deal with him when he is very drunk, unless he is ugly and the family needs your help.(p.90)
• ***Don't,*** at this stage, refer to this book, unless he has seen it and wishes to discuss it.(p.92)
• ***Don't*** raise such issues, no matter what your own convictions are.(p.93)
• ***Don't*** start to withdraw again just because your friends drink liquor.(p.102)
• ***Don't*** let him get away with it.(p.108)
• But ***don't*** remind him of this after he has been drinking, for he may be angry.(p.113)
• If he gets drunk, ***don't*** blame yourself.(p.120)
• If that is so we are sorry, for we ourselves ***don't*** always care for people who lecture us.(p.121)
• Sometimes mother and children ***don't*** think so.(p.126)
• I ***don't*** see how you can be of any help to us for, as you see, we ***don't*** have any alcoholic problem."(p.148)
• But alcoholism – well, they just ***don't*** believe they have it.(p.149)
• Now and then a serious drinker, being dry at the moment says, "I ***don't*** miss it at all.(p.151)
• You fellows know your stuff all right, but I ***don't*** see what good it'll do.(p.157)
• So, after hearing some more of my story, he turned around and said to Doc – I ***don't*** think he knew I heard him, but I did – he said, "Well, I believe he's worth saving and working on."(p.185)
• Now, if you ***don't*** want it, we'll not take up your time, and we'll be going and looking for someone else."(p.186)
• You ***don't*** have to sell me religion, either.(p.188)
• I remember telling them too that it was going to be awfully tough, because I did some other things, smoked cigarettes and played penny ante poker, sometimes bet on the horse races and they said, "***Don't*** you think you're having more trouble with this drinking than with anything else at the present time?(p.190)
• ***Don't*** you believe you are going to have all you can do to get rid of that?"(p.190)
• Whether I could have done as well as he, I ***don't*** know.(p.194)
• I ***don't*** know whether I drank to cover up being a failure, or whether I drank and then missed the deals.(p.198)
• We went into a bootleg joint and I ***don't*** remember leaving that place.(p.202)
• I told somebody that I was going down to get Christian Science and they took me down, but I ***don't*** remember saying that.(p.202)
• He said, "Well, why ***don't*** you take a cab?"(p.204)
• He said, "So long as I'm thinking as I'm thinking now, and so long as I'm doing the things I'm doing now, I ***don't*** believe I'll ever take another drink."(p.206)
• He took off his hat and his overcoat, and he said, "You ***don't*** look very good.(p.207)
• I ***don't*** remember much of what he said, but I did realize that here was another guy exactly like me; he had been in the same laughing academies and the same jails, known the same loss of jobs, same frustrations, same boredom and the same loneliness.(p.239)
• When the others saw my altered attitude they took me back in, but for me they had to make it tough; if they hadn't I ***don't*** think I ever would have stuck it out.(p.248)
• I ***don't*** think the boys were completely convinced of my personality change, for they fought shy of including my story in the book, so my only contribution to their literary efforts was my firm conviction, being still a theological rebel, that the word God should be qualified with the phrase "as we understand him" -- for that was the only way I could accept spirituality.(p.248)
• I ***don't*** feel bothered about liquor."(p.257)
• When I came to my aunt, she knew that I had had an unhappy childhood, and she said, "Now, Ethel, you're welcome to have boy friends in our home, but there are two boys in this town that I ***don't*** want you to date, and one of them comes from a very fine family, one of the best.(p.262)
• But I ***don't*** believe now that it was with any deep feeling of resentment that I said to him, "The children are raised, and if this is the way you want it, this is the way we'll have it.(p.263)
• There was a man watching, and I turned to him and said with a defiant air I carried with me all the time, "If I ***don't*** quit this I'm going to have to join that alcoholic business they're talking about."(p.266)
• I ***don't*** think Jack was hospitalized.(p.267)
• I ***don't*** think that there was anything said about religion.(p.268)
• Russ said, "***Don't*** do another thing today but help him.(p.271)
• ***Don't*** do that to me!"(p.272)
• It's only natural that we ***don't*** have the capacity to change, but we ought not to criticize those who have, There's another thing I would stress.(p.273)
• I ***don't*** ever remember that I was bored myself when we first came in, and they came out to the house and talked to us about these things.(p.273)
• I was crying, and I said, "Alice says she knows I ***don't*** have any part of the program."(p.273)
• How many times I swore off in the morning and got drunk before sunset I ***don't*** know.(p.300)
• I learned that a person just can't find a job hanging in a dive or barroom all day and all night, as jobs ***don't*** seem to turn up in those places.(p.300)
• One is that I ***don't*** remember too many of them, as I was one of those drunks who could be on his feet and attend a meeting or a party, engage in a conversation with people and do things that any nearly normal person would do, and the next day not remember a thing about where I was, what I did, whom I saw, or how I got home.(p.301)
• I ***don't*** know what sort of person I was expecting, but I was very agreeably surprised to find Mr. T. a poised, intelligent, well groomed and mannered gentleman.(p.309)
• I just ***don't*** want to."(p.318)
• And then I'd say, "God, ***don't*** pay any attention to me.(p.324)
• She said "Why ***don't*** you do it too?"(p.326)
• I ***don't*** believe, when I started, that I even had in mind the thought that I was drinking.(p.336)
• How I ran my home, I ***don't*** know.(p.337)
• He said, "Why ***don't*** you try Alcoholics Anonymous?"(p.340)
• One said, "***Don't*** feel that you are a martyr because you stopped drinking," and this hit me between the eyes.(p.346)
• The second one said, "***Don't*** feel that you stop drinking for anyone other than yourself," and this hit me between the eyes.(p.346)
• (I belong to the American Psychiatric Society, but I ***don't*** practice psychiatry as such.(p.347)
• I ***don't*** feel right.(p.348)
• And he said, "Earle, why ***don't*** you come on over and let me talk to you for a minute."(p.348)
• Why ***don't*** you join it?"(p.349)
• Why ***don't*** you go home and get the Big Book and open it at page fifty-eight and see what it says?"(p.349)
• I ***don't*** mean that in any sense as a derogatory statement about psychotherapy; it's a great tool, not too potent, but a great tool.(p.349)
• Well, I ***don't*** know who He is, but I've got my own idea.(p.350)
• So I went to my wife and asked her, wasn't there something that she and I could do to somehow get together, and she turned on her heel and looked me squarely in the eye, and said, "You ***don't*** care anything about my problem," and I could have smacked her, but I said to myself, "Grab on to your serenity!"(p.351)
• I didn't know how to be a father; I ***don't*** know how to come home and work week-ends like other husbands; I ***don't*** know how to entertain my family.(p.351)
• So I went to her and said, "There's only one thing I want in my whole life, and I ***don't*** want any commendation; I ***don't*** want any credit; I ***don't*** want anything from you or Janey for the rest of your life except one thing; and that is, the opportunity to do anything you want always, and I would like to start off by doing the dishes."(p.351)
• I ***don't*** know what it is.(p.352)
• I ***don't*** believe it."(p.356)
• Her parting words were "I am not leaving you because I ***don't*** love you; it's because I do love you.(p.362)
• Looking directly at me was a large oil painting of my wife, and her very words seemed to shout at me -- "I am not leaving you because I ***don't*** love you; it's because I do love you.(p.363)
• In meeting me casually, I ***don't*** think my strong belief in "The Man Upstairs" shows, but I have no other explanation for the many good things that have happened to me since I have been in A.A. -- they came to me from a Greater Power.(p.367)
• There comes a time when you ***don't*** want to live and are afraid to die.(p.377)
• I ***don't*** know what I expected, but I most certainly didn't visualize a group of people talking about their drinking problems, making light of their personal tragedies and at the same time enjoying themselves.(p.378)
• Study the A.A. book – ***don't*** just read it.(p.381)
• Yesterday is gone, and we ***don't*** know whether we will be here tomorrow.(p.382)
• I wish I could tell you how and why A.A. works, but I ***don't*** know.(p.384)
• I ***don't*** think that I was conscious of what had happened to me, but I think that it registered subconsciously.(p.386)
• When I crossed that line, I ***don't*** know.(p.386)
• I said, "Well, I ***don't*** know why."(p.387)
• You know those vitamins just ***don't*** keep you sober!(p.389)
• As I said before, I ***don't*** like to be fenced in, and with those bars you ***don't*** get hotel service.(p.390)
• So when he came for me, as he walked down the stairs, I could see him through the bars, and he was signing for me; I looked at him and said, "***Don't*** you sign anything in this place!"(p.391)
• I ***don't*** want anybody ever to look at me like that again.(p.391)
• So he waited another week or two and I ***don't*** think I stayed sober hardly at all.(p.391)
• If you ***don't,*** you will have to go home.(p.391)
• So, as I have said, I ***don't*** know how or why A.A. works.(p.392)
• STARS ***DON'T*** FALL(p.400)
• "Why ***don't*** you just go down and see Mr. W.?" she asked.(p.412)
• I ***don't*** know how I got here this trip, but it doesn't matter very much.(p.423)
• ***Don't*** mince words.(p.423)
• I ***don't*** know why I didn't fall out of the open cockpit of some of those planes I flew in while taking aerial pictures.(p.426)
• Why I wasn't killed or how I got home I ***don't*** know.(p.429)
• "I've got to stop if I want to live," I told myself, and if I ***don't*** want to break my parents' hearts and maybe jeopardize their own carefully built up and hard-fought-for sobriety.(p.429)
• My new wife and I ***don't*** own any property to speak of, and the flashy successes of another day are no longer mine.(p.438)
• At first, she would say, "You ***don't*** love me.(p.439)
• Why ***don't*** you admit it?"(p.439)
• Later, she would say, "You ***don't*** like me.(p.439)
• Why ***don't*** you admit it?"(p.439)
• Why ***don't*** you admit you hate me?"(p.439)
• (Today, we ***don't*** have to live like that any more.)(p.440)
• For me, pills ***don't*** produce the desire to swallow a pill; they produce the symptoms that require that the pill be taken for relief.(p.443)
• (Today, we ***don't*** have to live that way.(p.446)
• When a big, healthy-looking young fellow stood up there and said, "I'm a success today if I ***don't*** drink today," I thought, "Man, I've got a thousand things to do today before I can brag about not taking a drink, for God's sake!"(p.447)
• This proves I ***don't*** know what's good for me.(p.450)
• And if I ***don't*** know what's good for me, then I ***don't*** know what's good or bad for you or

for anyone.(p.450)
• So I'm better off if I ***don't*** give advice, ***don't*** figure I know what's best, and just accept life on life's terms, as it is today -- especially my own life, as it actually is.(p.450)
• I ***don't*** mean that I went to bed one night a normal drinker, and awoke the next morning an alcoholic.(p.464)
• What happened afterwards I ***don't*** know.(p.468)
• The same doctor who had sent me to the psycho had asked my husband, "Why ***don't*** you send her to this Alcoholics Anonymous?"(p.469)
• So the doctor said, "I really ***don't*** know too much about it, but they tell me it is a bunch of drunks who get together . . ."(p.469)
• In other words, the kindest doctor in the whole world, and I had one such, couldn't help me because I always felt, "You can't know about me – you can't possibly know – you ***don't*** even drink!"(p.471)
• To Indians, I say: "***Don't*** be afraid to join A.A.(p.477)
• (We ***don't*** have much time for bathing in our crowded schedule.)(p.479)
• I ***don't*** believe this program would work for me if I didn't get honest with myself about everything.(p.482)
• I ***don't*** know whether it was right or wrong, but at least I know that people weren't thinking the same.(p.484)
• I ***don't*** know whether she was a pacifist or whether she just thought that in the event of another war it would have some bearing on my joining up.(p.484)
• I ***don't*** think I suffered too much as far as the racial situation was concerned because I was born into it and knew nothing other than that.(p.485)
• I ***don't*** think I actually started to drink pathologically until approximately 1935.(p.487)
• I ***don't*** know.(p.488)
• I ***don't*** know anything about the bottles."(p.488)
• I rebelled, and from that time on I ***don't*** think I attended church more than a dozen times.(p.489)
• I ***don't*** remember whether I went by streetcar, whether I walked or went in a taxicab.(p.492)
• I remember talking to her, but what happened after that I ***don't*** know.(p.492)
• I ***don't*** seem to remember anything.(p.499)
• I ***don't*** seem to be able to keep my mind on what I am doing.(p.499)
• If I ***don't*** get started soon, I won't have time to finish.(p.499)
• The doctor has told me that if I ***don't*** give up inside work, I'll have tuberculosis.(p.500)
• "***Don't*** say anything," I say to her.(p.502)
• "You think you are hopeless, ***don't*** you?" he asks.(p.503)
• "There are men on the streets of New York today who were worse than you, and they ***don't*** drink any more."(p.503)
• I'd say, "No, I ***don't*** know where they're at or when they meet.(p.510)
• I ***don't*** know anyone in the program."(p.510)
• I ***don't*** have any regrets.(p.511)
• I ***don't*** miss any of the old crowd nor do I miss any of their parties.(p.511)
• I ***don't*** have any resentments.(p.511)
• I had a rough lot, but I ***don't*** worry about that, after hearing the stories of many others.(p.511)
• When we first come into A.A., many of us are confused because as a general rule we're at the end of our respective ropes, and we ***don't*** know what to do.(p.512)
• So I ***don't*** just take the inventory at night – I take it continually throughout the day.(p.516)
• I ***don't*** know when I became an alcoholic, but I do believe I became one because I drank too much too often.(p.526)
• But I ***don't*** remember that any of them ever went to sleep in joints and woke up with no shoes on in the winter, or fell out of chairs.(p.527)
• I ***don't*** remember any of them getting put out in the winter because they didn't pay their rent.(p.527)
• Since I have been in A.A., I have more friends than I ever had in my life – friends who care about me and my welfare, friends who ***don't*** care that I am black and that I have been in prison.(p.529)
• Even those ***don't*** take part in A.A. functions as I would like to see them do.(p.529)
• I ***don't*** know if it's force of habit or something else that keeps them in one place, but I do know that in A.A. there is much work to do, and none of us can do it standing still.(p.529)
• I just want to say that you ***don't*** have to be afraid, because no one at any A.A. meeting will bite you.(p.529)
• I had even borrowed money from her, over her protest: "Bob, please ***don't*** ask me to lend you money -- you're the only one who hasn't."(p.540)
• I ***don't*** care too much about personal fame or glory, and I want only enough money to enable me to do the work I feel I can perhaps do best.(p.542)
• I believe this, and I believe too that it is equally impossible to practice these principles to the best of our ability, a day at a time, and still drink, for I ***don't*** think the two things are compatible.(p.550)
• Even when you ***don't*** really want it for them, and your prayers are only words and you ***don't*** mean it, go ahead and do it anyway.(p.552)

done

• I honestly doubted whether, on balance, the religions of mankind had ***done*** any good.(p.11)
• But my friend sat before me, and he made the point-blank declaration that God had ***done*** for him what he could not do for himself.(p.11)
• Here was something at work in a human heart which had ***done*** the impossible.(p.11)
• My friend promised when these things were ***done*** I would enter upon a new relationship with my Creator; that I would have the elements of a way of living which answered all my problems.(p.13)
• We shall tell you what we have ***done***.(p.20)
• We are not sure why, once a certain point is reached, little can be ***done*** for him.(p.22)
• Science may one day accomplish this, but it hasn't ***done*** so yet.(p.31)
• Our friend's gorge rose as he bitterly cried out: "If there is a God, He certainly hasn't ***done*** anything for me!"(p.56)
• Thy will be ***done***."(p.67)
• Putting out of our minds the wrongs others had ***done***, we resolutely looked for our own mistakes.(p.67)
• Where were we at fault, what should we have ***done*** instead?(p.69)
• We must be willing to make amends where we have ***done*** harm, provided that we do not bring about still more harm in so doing.(p.69)
• If we are sorry for what we have ***done***, and have the honest desire to let God take us to better things, we believe we will be forgiven and will have learned our lesson.(p.70)
• We think we have ***done*** well enough in admitting these things to ourselves.(p.72)
• Returning home we find a place where we can be quiet for an hour carefully reviewing what we have ***done***.(p.75)
• Now we go out to our fellows and repair the damage ***done*** in the past.(p.76)
• It may be he has ***done*** us more harm than we have ***done*** him and, though we may have acquired a better attitude toward him, we are still not too keen about admitting our faults.(p.77)
• Simply we tell him that we will never get over drinking until we have ***done*** our utmost to straighten out the past.(p.77)
• We have made our demonstration, ***done*** our part.(p.78)
• Most of us have ***done*** that sort of thing.(p.78)
• He felt that he had ***done*** a wrong he could not possibly make right.(p.80)
• We are sorry for what we have ***done*** and, God willing, it shall not be repeated.(p.81)
• "How can I best serve Thee -- Thy will (not mine) be ***done***."(p.85)
• What could we have ***done*** better?(p.86)
• We constantly remind ourselves we are no longer running the show, humbly saying to ourselves many times each day "Thy will be ***done***."(p.87)
• We suggest you do this as we have ***done*** it in the chapter on alcoholism.(p.92)
• In many homes this is a difficult thing to do, but it must be ***done*** if any results are to be expected.(p.98)
• Our friends have counseled chucking the men and we have ***done*** so with finality, only to be back in a little while hoping, always hoping.(p.105)
• We know women who have ***done*** it.(p.114)
• That is where our fellow travelers are, and that is where our work must be ***done***.(p.130)
• Without saying so, they may cordially hate him for what he has ***done*** to them and to their mother.(p.134)
• That he has not always ***done*** so for the alcoholic is easily understood.(p.137)
• But I'm sure this man is ***done*** drinking.(p.138)
• When sober, does he not work hard and have a knack of getting things ***done***?(p.139)
• If you concede that your employee is ill, can he be forgiven for what he has ***done*** in the past?(p.140)
• I know, in my own particular case, that nothing my company could have ***done*** would have stopped me for, so long as I was able to hold my position, I could not possibly realize how serious my situation was.(p.141)
• Next he can be assured that you do not intend to lecture, moralize, or condemn; that if this was ***done*** formerly, it was because of misunderstanding.(p.142)
• He suffered horribly from his sprees, but it seemed as if nothing could be ***done*** for him.(p.159)
• The question which might naturally come into your mind would be: "What did the man do or say that was different from what others had ***done*** or said?"(p.180)
• I thought of what liquor had ***done*** to me, the opportunities that I had discarded, the abilities that had been given me and how I had wasted them, and I finally came to the conclusion, that if I didn't want to quit, I certainly ought to want to, and that I was willing to do anything in the world to stop drinking.(p.186)
• As soon as I had ***done*** that I did feel a great release.(p.189)
• I have already ***done*** it, and I am willing to do it again here in the presence of you or I am willing to say it any place, anywhere in the world from now on and not be ashamed of it."(p.190)
• It would be hard to estimate how much A.A. has ***done*** for me.(p.191)
• Bill was very, very grateful that he had been released from this terrible thing and he had given God the credit for having ***done*** it, and he's so grateful about it he wants to tell other people about it.(p.191)
• Whether I could have ***done*** as well as he, I don't know.(p.194)
• Twenty-two years later, Doctor Bob told me that what I had ***done*** was like turning a switch and setting up a demand for more alcohol in my system.(p.195)
• I could work a deal up to where all I had to do was to go ahead with it; all the planning had been ***done***, all the financing had been ***done***, but then I'd say "Nuts to it!" and walk away.(p.197)
• With the big companies, and with the amount of money we could have gotten and the promises I had, it could have been ***done***.(p.198)
• In 1932, some friends of mine advised me that I might try Christian Science, which had ***done*** a lot for some of their friends.(p.202)
• That was an experience that I have never forgotten, and many times in my own work with A.A. newcomers I feel kind of guilty because I haven't ***done*** the same thing.(p.219)
• I might have ***done*** terrible things, and I wouldn't even know it!(p.223)
• I went to a meeting to see for myself this group of freaks or bums who had ***done*** this thing.(p.228)
• I believe that my once over-weening self-will has finally found its proper place, for I can say many times daily, "Thy will be ***done***, not mine" . . . and mean it.(p.229)
• I would promise to have jobs ***done*** and never do them.(p.234)
• "Best in the business, when he's sober," my customers would say, and I still had a following who would give me work though they deplored my habits, because they knew the job would be well ***done*** when they eventually got it.(p.234)
• As part of this promotion, they sent me to their national convention in Atlantic City to tell the big wheels how I'd ***done*** it.(p.243)
• While I went along with all that was ***done*** and attended the meetings, I never took an active job of leadership until February 1940.(p.249)
• Instead, over coffee cups, this man and his wife told me what had been ***done*** for them.(p.259)
• I'm going in to see him, and see what can be ***done***."(p.267)
• I didn't know that anything was ever ***done*** for them in a medical way.(p.267)
• I could never go and make up to all the people I've ***done*** wrong to."(p.269)
• I thought I had ***done*** that until Russ' second collapse, and the doctor told me very candidly that he wasn't long for this world.(p.271)
• He was a man of considerable means and he might have ***done*** what many men would have ***done*** in such a case.(p.278)
• Here was a man with essentially the same outlook on life, except that he had ***done*** something about it.(p.290)
• A.A. is not a plan for recovery that can be finished and ***done*** with.(p.311)
• They saw that they had become actual or potential alcoholics, even though no serious harm had yet been ***done***.(p.315)

• She told me; it was simple; I could have *done* it very easily.(p.326)
• A square from ultra-dry Kansas, I did not taste grog until I had finished college, *done* a stint on newspapers, married, become a father, and been in studio publicity two years.(p.328)
• And the mops would get out, the vacuum would get out, everything would get out, but nothing would get *done*.(p.337)
• It was a terrible blow at the time and I thought he was pretty much of a heel, but of course it was the finest thing he could have *done* for me under the circumstances.(p.357)
• I had *done* something terrible!(p.364)
• In a few days an attorney called on me and explained that something would have to be *done* as she couldn't face returning to me as I was.(p.377)
• It was important to me to see what alcohol had *done* to me and would continue to do if I didn't have help.(p.379)
• A "spiritual experience" to me meant attending meetings, seeing a group of people, all there for the purpose of helping each other; hearing the Twelve Steps and the Twelve Traditions read at a meeting, and hearing the Lord's Prayer, which in an A.A. meeting has such great meaning – "Thy will be *done*, not mine."(p.381)
• I know that if I do daily what I have *done* for these last thirteen and a half years, I will stay sober.(p.384)
• I had no feeling of security, and I knew that I had *done* a very stupid thing, so I went back to Texas and remarried my ex-husband.(p.386)
• I resented the fact that Frank had *done* this to me, and I just didn't know what was going on.(p.388)
• I wish I could tell you all that A.A. has *done* for me, all that I think and feel about A.A., but it's something that I have experienced and have never been able to put into words.(p.394)
• It has been a fellowship with God and man that has held good wherever I've turned and whatever I've *done*.(p.394)
• Now I had *done* some living but I hadn't learned a thing.(p.402)
• What had I *done*?(p.404)
• Why had I *done* it?(p.406)
• They said I was so funny, and told me, with shrieks of laughter, what I'd *done* the night before.(p.407)
• My growing inward unhappiness was a very real thing, however, and I knew that something would have to be *done* about it.(p.434)
• I can't say, "Thy will be *done*," and take a pill.(p.443)
• Rather, I do whatever is in front of me to be *done*, and I leave the results up to Him; however it turns out, that's God's will for me.(p.452)
• What else can I do except what I have always *done* in the past? -- act as my old self and return to prison.(p.458)
• At that point everyone decided something drastic had to be *done*.(p.469)
• With their help I also saw that certainly, because of some of the things I had *done* during the years, I was bordering on insanity, and so, facing the record, I tried to believe that a Power greater than I could and would restore me to sanity.(p.471)
• I feel that I have been restored to health and sanity these past years not through my own efforts nor as a result of anything I may have *done*, but because I've come to believe -- to really believe – that alone I can do nothing.(p.473)
• Then I said to my wife, "Something has to be *done*."(p.489)
• That's my story of what A.A. has *done* for me.(p.496)
• I told him that I believe in electricity and other forces of nature, but as for a God, if there is one, He has never *done* anything for me.(p.503)
• Then he asks me if I am willing to right all the wrongs I have ever *done* to anyone, no matter how wrong I thought the others were.(p.503)
• Since I joined on that April night, A.A. has *done* more for me than just stop me from drinking; it has brought me back to life again.(p.524)
• It has taught me that success and failure are never final, and that neither count for very much in the final assessment of any man who has *done* his best.(p.525)
• My father was and still is a minister, and I was afraid that I might run into him, or that someone might tell him where I was, and I could still remember what he had *done* to me when I got drunk one Christmas when I was very young.(p.527)
• Sobering up, the mind that was ahead of the emotions would impel the question: What have you written or *done* to be the great man?(p.537)
• Harm is *done* by sick people, as I was sick, and doing dreadful harm to myself and to my loved ones.(p.542)
• I'd gladly do it anonymously, as I have *done* this brief account of my struggle with alcohol -- merely to present certain ideas for the consideration of the reader.(p.542)
• The only reality I was able to face had been forced upon me by its very repetition – I had to drink; and I didn't know there was anything in the world that could be *done* about it.(p.548)
• This was *done*, and the paper was printed in the American Journal of Psychiatry for November, 1949.(p.572)

doom

• So I sat down with me and went over the facts behind the convulsions: personality changes, daily headaches, sense of impending *doom*, sense of impending insanity.(p.444)

doomed

• On the other hand – and strange as this may seem to those who do not understand -- once a psychic change has occurred, the very same person who seemed *doomed*, who had so many problems he despaired of ever solving them, suddenly finds himself easily able to control his desire for alcohol, the only effort necessary being that required to follow a few simple rules.(p.xxvii)
• Much has been written pro and con, but among physicians, the general opinion seems to be that most chronic alcoholics are *doomed*.(p.xxviii)
• To be *doomed* to an alcoholic death or to live on a spiritual basis are not always easy alternatives to face.(p.44)
• Explain that many are *doomed* who never realize their predicament.(p.92)
• In our belief any scheme of combating alcoholism which proposes to shield the sick man from temptation is *doomed* to failure.(p.101)

door

• The *door* opened and he stood there, fresh-skinned and glowing.(p.9)
• We will not regret the past nor wish to shut the *door* on it.(p.83)
• They struck the children, kicked out *door* panels, smashed treasured crockery, and ripped the keys out of pianos.(p.106)
• The first impulse will be to bury these skeletons in a dark closet and padlock the *door*.(p.123)
• Down the lobby a *door* opened into an attractive bar.(p.154)
• I'm afraid to go out the *door*.(p.157)
• If my wife was planning to go out in the afternoon, I would get a large supply of liquor and smuggle it home and hide it in the coal bin, the clothes chute, over *door* jambs, over beams in the cellar and in cracks in the cellar tile.(p.176)
• When I had been in the hospital ten days, Sister Ignatia, who has played such a part in the development of A.A. in this area, stuck her head in the *door* one morning and announced, looking at me quizzically, that they might be able to make something human out of my face after all.(p.205)
• It was getting pretty dark and I hadn't turned on any lights, when some big fellow stepped inside the *door* and flipped on the light switch.(p.207)
• After finding every bottle that I had hidden around the apartment, she took away my pants, my shoes, my money and my keys, threw them under the bed in the back bedroom and slip-locked our *door*.(p.288)
• I jimmied the front *door* so that I could get back in, and walked out.(p.288)
• This was drinking in sheer desperation, alone and locked behind my own *door*.(p.306)
• I knew nothing about alcoholism or the D.T.'s, but when I woke up on this last morning of my son's illness, I taped the keyhole on my *door* because "everyone was out there."(p.338)
• I entered the house, opened a new bottle of whiskey and sat down to drink myself into the right frame of mind to get in my car, start the motor and close the garage *door* behind me.(p.363)
• Sure enough in a couple of hours two men were at my *door* and for the first time I heard some facts about liquor and my problem that sounded sensible to me.(p.363)
• I had just raised the bottle to my lips when my wife opened the *door* and froze me completely in my tracks with "Happy New Year, dear."(p.365)
• But then, when that steel *door* slammed shut, and she was the one that went home, I was amazed.(p.440)
• In the garage, I would put the needle in my vein and then try to figure out exactly how much medication to inject to overcome the pep pills while adding to the sleeping pills while ignoring the tranquilizers, in order to get just enough to be able to pull out the needle, jerk the tourniquet, throw it in the car, slam the car *door* shut, run down the hall, and fall in bed before I fell asleep.(p.442)
• That's when that steel *door* slammed shut, and Max was the one who went home.(p.444)
• While I was taking inventory in the cold-storage locker one Sunday, a wooden sign bolted to the inside *door* stopped me in my tracks.(p.461)
• A policeman came to the *door* and asked for James S., but there wasn't any James S. there.(p.491)
• One man comes back, closing the *door* behind him.(p.503)
• I back up to the *door* and go into the house.(p.506)
• When my mother opened the *door*, I almost fell in on my face.(p.510)
• But when she began a prison sentence, a *door* opened.(p.526)

doors

• This had the effect of making me resolve that when I was free from parental domination, I would never again darken the *doors* of a church.(p.172)
• My last venture, a book shop, was hastened to closed *doors* by my steady intoxication.(p.255)
• With these new and enlightening *doors* opening up to me, I was able to make the eventual decision to stop drinking, a day at a time -- because I, too, was an alcoholic.(p.355)
• Most of the time I was covered with bruises from "running into *doors*."(p.411)
• I came to A.A. simply because there were no other *doors* of help open to me in my hometown.(p.420)
• We lived just a few *doors* from the First Baptist Church and when they had funerals I remember very often asking my mother whether the person was good or bad and whether they were going to heaven or hell.(p.483)
• I suspect that if it is wisely handled – and it seems to be in wise and prudent hands – there are *doors* of opportunity ahead of this project that may surpass our capacities to imagine."(p.574)

doorstep

• After a couple of days in dollar hotels and one night in the pokey, I finally landed on my mother's *doorstep* -- shaking apart, with several days' beard and, of course, broke as usual.(p.238)
• At age twenty-one, I enlisted in the Navy for two reasons: (1) to avoid being drafted into the Army, and (2) out of a burst of patriotic fervor inspired by the advent of World War II and as the result of an all-night drinking binge which found me sitting on the *doorstep* of the Navy recruiting office when the chief petty officer arrived to open for business at nine o'clock Monday morning.(p.398)

doorway

• In the *doorway* stood a lovely young girl who said, "Are you one of us souses, too?"(p.321)

doorways

• Unlike his skid-row brother, he isn't heckled for sleeping in alleys or *doorways*.(p.330)

doped

• I was taking Benzedrine and paraldehyde quite impartially during the day then, and by the time I arrived at my first A.A. meeting, I was pretty drunk and certainly *doped* up to the eyes and completely jittery.(p.523)

Dorothy

• Bill bought me a drink or two on the way, and *Dorothy* S. came with us, and the three of us went over to the City Hospital.(p.217)
• From far away, as if in a delirium, I heard my own voice – calling someone "*Dorothy*," talking of dress shops, of jobs . . . the words came clearer . . . this sound of my own voice frightened me as it came closer . . . and suddenly, there I was, talking of I knew not what, to someone I'd never seen before this very moment.(p.222)
• Why had "*Dorothy*" brought me here?(p.223)

doses

• Most of the time therefore, I did not take the morning drink which I craved so badly, but instead would fill up on large *doses* of sedatives to quiet the jitters, which distressed me terribly.(p.176)
• It was really a horrible nightmare, this earning money, getting liquor, smuggling it home, getting drunk, morning jitters, taking large *doses* of sedatives to make it possible for me to earn more money, and so on ad nauseam.(p.177)
• My drinking was never the spaced *doses* of the careful tippler; it was always gluttonous.(p.254)

double

• More than most people, the alcoholic leads a *double* life.(p.73)
• Instead, he got dressed, took me out, bought me three or four *double* shots and put me to bed.(p.278)

double-header

• Then I got into the habit of having beers, and decided that a drink of whiskey was not any worse; so I would get the one drink of whiskey but, on second thought, I decided that as long as I was only going to have one, I might as well make it a ***double-header***.(p.203)

• So I had one ***double-header*** every night for about two or three weeks.(p.203)

double-headers

• One evening I had gone out after dinner to take on a couple of ***double-headers*** and stayed a little later than usual, and when I came home Clarence was sitting on the davenport with Bill W.(p.216)

doubled

• Paul measured the medicine out, but he figured that with my track record that little bit wouldn't be enough, so he ***doubled*** it and added a few drops more and then gave it to me.(p.207)

• I went back to law school, and ***doubled*** up on the courses because I was then approaching thirty years of age and I wanted to get through as quickly as possible.(p.212)

doubt

• Despite contrary indications, I had little ***doubt*** that a mighty purpose and rhythm underlay all.(p.10)

• I was to sit quietly when in ***doubt***, asking only for direction and strength to meet my problems as He would have me.(p.13)

• If we keep on the way we are going there is little ***doubt*** that much good will result, but the surface of the problem would hardly be scratched.(p.19)

• We ***doubt*** if many of them can do it, because none will really want to stop, and hardly one of them, because of the peculiar mental twist already acquired, will find he can win out.(p.33)

• As to two of you men, whose stories I have heard, there is no ***doubt*** in my mind that you were 100% hopeless, apart from divine help.(p.43)

• We have shared his honest ***doubt*** and prejudice.(p.45)

• Everybody believes them without a murmur of ***doubt***.(p.48)

• We have no reason to ***doubt*** it.(p.49)

• Hence we are at pains to tell why we think our present faith is reasonable, why we think it more sane and logical to believe than not to believe, why we say our former thinking was soft and mushy when we threw up our hands in ***doubt*** and said, "We don't know."(p.53)

• There is ***doubt*** about that.(p.72)

• We ***doubt*** if, in this respect, alcoholics are fundamentally much worse than other people.(p.81)

• Tell him you once felt as he does, but you ***doubt*** whether you would have made much progress had you not taken action.(p.94)

• The others must be convinced of his new status beyond the shadow of a ***doubt***.(p.135)

• There was no ***doubt*** he over-indulged.(p.135)

• If you are sure he doesn't mean business, there is no ***doubt*** you should discharge him.(p.147)

• Had anyone undertaken to explain to me what the A.A. movement was, what its real function was, I probably would have been set back several years and I ***doubt*** if I would have survived at all.(p.216)

• No ***doubt*** I had been an exile too long -- I should go home to America.(p.226)

• I had not asked for help and seriously ***doubt*** that I would have, but Fitz, an old school friend of mine, had persuaded Jackie to call on me.(p.238)

• Having no one else to turn to, I was willing to give Him a chance, although with considerable ***doubt***.(p.280)

• As these words are written at fifty-three years of age, with over nine years of A.A. behind me, with all its wonderful teachings, I haven't the slightest ***doubt*** about being an alcoholic.(p.356)

• Had I been able to explain to a psychiatrist the feeling of futility, loneliness and lack of purpose that had come with my deep sense of personal failure at this second divorce, I seriously ***doubt*** that the good doctor could have convinced me that my basic problem was a spiritual hunger, but A.A. has shown me this was the truth.(p.546)

doubted

• His alcoholic problem was so complex, and his depression so great, that we felt his only hope would be through what we then called "moral psychology," and we ***doubted*** if even that would have any effect.(p.xxix)

• I honestly ***doubted*** whether, on balance, the religions of mankind had done any good.(p.11)

• I had never ***doubted*** the existence of the Supreme Being, but now I began to absent myself from my church where I had formerly been a member of the choir.(p.234)

doubtful

• As we go through the day we pause, when agitated or ***doubtful***, and ask for the right thought or action.(p.87)

• I wasn't afraid that the program wouldn't work, but I still was ***doubtful*** whether I would be able to hang on to the program, but I did come to the conclusion that I was willing to put everything I had into it, with God's power, and that I wanted to do just that.(p.189)

• If that was all, then I was a little ***doubtful*** that it was the answer I was looking for.(p.236)

doubting

• When we saw others solve their problems by a simple reliance upon the Spirit of the Universe, we had to stop ***doubting*** the power of God.(p.52)

doubtless

• ***Doubtless*** you are curious to discover how and why, in the face of expert opinion to the contrary, we have recovered from a hopeless condition of mind and body.(p.20)

doubts

• It sounds simple, but there were obstacles and ***doubts*** to overcome.(p.282)

doughboy

• In the next two years I washed more pans and peeled more potatoes than any other ***doughboy***.(p.241)

doughnuts

• After it was closed we all retired to the kitchen and had coffee and ***doughnuts*** and more discussion until the small hours of the morning.(p.291)

• Every evening we would meet at the home of one of the members and have coffee and ***doughnuts*** and spend a social evening.(p.291)

Dowling

• Edward ***Dowling***, S.J., of the Queen's Work staff says, "Alcoholics Anonymous is natural; it is natural at the point where nature comes closest to the supernatural, namely in humiliations and in consequent humility.(p.574)

down

• I hardly dared cross the street, lest I collapse and be run ***down*** by an early morning truck, for it was scarcely daylight.(p.6)

• Then a mental fog settled ***down***.(p.6)

• He uses his gifts to build up a bright outlook for his family and himself, and then pulls the structure ***down*** on his head by a senseless series of sprees.(p.21)

• If he can afford it, he may have liquor concealed all over his house to be certain no one gets his entire supply away from him to throw ***down*** the waterpipe.(p.22)

• But they often suspect they are ***down*** for the count.(p.23)

• I sat ***down*** at a table and ordered a sandwich and a glass of milk.(p.36)

• Actually we were fooling ourselves, for deep ***down*** in every man, woman, and child, is the fundamental idea of God.(p.55)

• We found the Great Reality deep ***down*** within us.(p.55)

• The principles we have set ***down*** are guides to progress.(p.60)

• So we had to get ***down*** to causes and conditions.(p.64)

• We got this all ***down*** on paper and looked at it.(p.69)

• If we have been thorough about our personal inventory, we have written ***down*** a lot.(p.70)

• Taking this book ***down*** from our shelf we turn to the page which contains the twelve steps.(p.75)

• Though there may be justifiable exceptions, and though we wish to lay ***down*** no rule of any sort, we have often found this the best course to take.(p.81)

• We ought to sit ***down*** with the family and frankly analyze the past as we now see it, being very careful not to criticize them.(p.83)

• No matter how far ***down*** the scale we have gone, we will see how our experience can benefit others.(p.84)

• Never talk ***down*** to an alcoholic from any moral or spiritual hilltop; simply lay out the kit of spiritual tools for his inspection.(p.95)

• Obviously, no rule can be laid ***down***.(p.99)

• The alarming physical and mental symptoms, the deepening pall of remorse, depression and inferiority that settled ***down*** on our loved ones -- these things terrified and distracted us.(p.106)

• You will make mistakes, but if you are in earnest they will not drag you ***down***.(p.117)

• If you cooperate, rather than complain, you will find that his excess enthusiasm will tone ***down***.(p.119)

• Then you and your husband can get right ***down*** to fundamentals.(p.120)

• There will be alluring shortcuts and by-paths ***down*** which they may wander and lose their way.(p.123)

• But the head of the house has spent years in pulling ***down*** the structures of business, romance, friendship, health -- these things are now ruined or damaged.(p.123)

• They criticize, pointing out how he is falling ***down*** on his spiritual program.(p.126)

• If he says yes, does he really mean it, or ***down*** inside does he think he is fooling you, and that after rest and treatment he will be able to get away with a few drinks now and then?(p.142)

• Sometimes we alcoholics have an idea that people are trying to pull us ***down***.(p.145)

• It boils right ***down*** to this: No man should be fired just because he is alcoholic.(p.148)

• Even if you feel your organization has no alcoholic problem, it might pay to take another look ***down*** the line.(p.149)

• As we became subjects of King Alcohol, shivering denizens of his mad realm, the chilling vapor that is loneliness settled ***down***.(p.151)

• But his venture wound up in a law suit and bogged ***down*** completely.(p.154)

• ***Down*** the lobby a door opened into an attractive bar.(p.154)

• With a shiver, he turned away and walked ***down*** the lobby to the church directory.(p.154)

• Understand he was once a well-known lawyer in town, but just now we've got him strapped ***down*** tight."(p.156)

• We'll be ***down***."(p.157)

• It was the day before Mother's Day and I had come home plastered, carrying a big potted plant which I set ***down*** on the table and forthwith went upstairs and passed out.(p.179)

• So it doesn't behoove me to squawk about it for, after all, nobody ever had to throw me ***down*** and pour liquor ***down*** my throat.(p.181)

• Your Heavenly Father will never let you ***down***!(p.181)

• Before my drinking had cut me ***down*** completely, I achieved a considerable measure of success, having been a City Councilman for five years and a financial director of Kenmore, a suburb later taken into the city itself.(p.182)

• Between classes I would run ***down*** to the wash room, take enough to steady my nerves and then go on to the next class.(p.183)

• Whether you quit six days, months, or years, if you go out and take a drink or two you'll end up in this hospital tied ***down***, just like you have been in these past six months.(p.187)

• Had blacked the eyes of two nurses, and now they had him strapped ***down*** tight.(p.188)

• We'll be ***down*** as soon as he clears up."(p.188)

• ***Down*** in the pit of his depression, new hope had somehow been born.(p.189)

• I didn't even know what a martini looked like, but I had heard a man ***down*** the bar order one.(p.194)

• I kept watching the man ***down*** the bar to see what he did with a contraption like that, and he just smelled of his drink and set it ***down*** again, so I did the same.(p.195)

• I told somebody that I was going ***down*** to get Christian Science and they took me ***down***, but I don't remember saying that.(p.202)

• There was also some conversation about Dr. Bob and I must have said that I would go ***down*** to Akron with Bill in the morning.(p.217)

• We drove my car and I left it ***down*** in the yard.(p.217)

• Cold chills started chasing up and ***down*** my spine; my teeth were chattering; my hands were shaking so I tucked them under me to keep them from flying away.(p.222)

• When I got back to Germany I settled ***down*** to finish my apprenticeship, drinking the wine of the country as usual.(p.231)

• I had no desire whatever to sit ***down*** at a table and stay a whole morning or afternoon drinking.(p.231)

• That night for the first time in my life I really let ***down*** my hair and admitted my general loneliness.(p.239)

• That is where I had my first drink and I still remember it, for every "first" drink afterwards did exactly the same trick -- I could feel it go right through every bit of my body and ***down*** to my very toes.(p.241)

• At this time I was holding what drinking I did ***down*** to weekends, but I hadn't had a drink at all in a month.(p.243)

• After the tire job came the thirties, the Depression and the ***down*** hill road.(p.244)
• Around this time our big A.A. book was being written and it all became much simpler; we had a definite formula which some sixty of us agreed was the middle course for all alcoholics who wanted sobriety, and that formula has not been changed one iota ***down*** through the years.(p.248)
• I remember one instance when he took off and went ***down*** to Cincinnati and was gone a week on a drunk.(p.262)
• There was a very religious family that lived ***down*** the road from us, and we were on the same party line.(p.265)
• Time went on and the drinking got worse and worse, and I was in another barroom, ***down*** the road the other way, a small one, and I took my glass -- that morning I'd been able to lift it from the bar -- and I said to the woman behind the bar, "I wish I might never take another drop of that stuff.(p.266)
• Finally, one morning, I got up and got in the car and cried all the way ***down*** to the M.'s -- the people who owned the bar -- and told her I was licked and wanted help.(p.267)
• I drove these three or four miles ***down*** the road only to find that Jack was out.(p.267)
• And we went ***down*** through the valley, and I remembered reading about the Ku Klux Klan and how they burnt crosses, and I thought, "God alone knows what we are getting into this time!"(p.269)
• I sat ***down*** on the side of one of their beds, and I started to weep, and I couldn't stop, and I was so startled, and I apologized again and again for it.(p.272)
• I got ***down*** on my knees for the first time in thirty years.(p.280)
• I lay ***down*** on the bed and slept like a child.(p.280)
• The A.A. program showed me the way to come ***down*** to earth, start from the bottom and work up.(p.284)
• In the long ago past I used to start at the top as president or treasurer and end up with the sheriff breathing ***down*** my neck.(p.284)
• However, I must have felt, deep ***down*** inside myself, that living the selfish life of a bachelor was only half living.(p.286)
• The day before I was due to go back to Chicago, a Wednesday and Dr. Bob's afternoon off, he had me ***down*** to the office and we spent three or four hours formally going through the Six-Step program as it was at that time.(p.291)
• Strangely enough, I became acquainted with the "hilarious life" just at the time in my own life when I was beginning really to settle ***down*** to a common-sense, sane domesticity.(p.297)
• The parties waxed more liquid and hilarious as time went on, and eventually I discovered that a little shot of liquor now and then between beers had the tendency to put me in a whacky mood much quicker than having to ***down*** several quarts of beer to obtain the same effect.(p.298)
• Spiritually . . . I found a Friend who never lets me ***down*** and is ever eager to help.(p.303)
• That was on a hot summer evening, ***down*** in the Greenwich Village Group, and there was a little porch out there in the old meeting place on Sullivan Street, and after the meeting I went out on the steps for some air.(p.321)
• She said "Suppose I put your name ***down*** as a volunteer.(p.326)
• Away ***down*** deep, I was motivated into dishonest behavior because I was a people-pleaser.(p.328)
• I could let ***down*** the bars.(p.329)
• No more snoops or big shots breathing ***down*** our necks.(p.329)
• A people-pleaser beaten ***down***?(p.331)
• Yet I recently recalled that each morning I used to talk to the bottle when I took it ***down*** from the closet.(p.332)
• A.A. has not let me ***down*** there.(p.334)
• Took ***down*** notes for reference purposes.(p.344)
• And then we went up the side of a hill where we have a little barbecue area to make the fire for the barbecue, and on the way up, I thought to myself -- I'll go back ***down*** to the kitchen and refill this drink.(p.347)
• And as that thought came to me, it was as though someone had reached ***down*** and taken a heavy overcoat off my shoulders, for that was the last one.(p.347)
• So he got me a cup of coffee, and a piece of cake, and sat me ***down*** and said, "Why, there's nothing wrong with you.(p.348)
• Here I am ***down*** at my office behind my desk and there she is out at the hospital.(p.350)
• She left, and I sat ***down*** and crossed my hands, and looked up and said, "For God's sake, help me."(p.351)
• My parents' car had a strong attraction to fences, and one night I blacked out and drove the car ***down*** a bank, ramming the steel fence around someone's backyard.(p.353)
• This phase was right ***down*** my alley; I had my master's degree in the art of making "whoopee."(p.359)
• At this time, however, she had an opportunity to go to Salt Lake City on a new project for the government, but she did promise me that if I would curtail my drinking and buckle ***down*** to hard work she would give serious consideration to my latest proposal and maybe join me at a later date when I got settled.(p.359)
• Proud of my little station and of my new bride I settled ***down*** to a happy married life.(p.361)
• Time after time I would beg forgiveness on bended knees, with tears rolling ***down*** my cheeks, and promise I would never again drink too much.(p.362)
• I entered the house, opened a new bottle of whiskey and sat ***down*** to drink myself into the right frame of mind to get in my car, start the motor and close the garage door behind me.(p.363)
• I had not only let my wife ***down*** but also a lot of other wonderful people who had helped me.(p.364)
• Of course, more than anything else I had let myself ***down***, but I didn't realize how much then -- as I do now.(p.364)
• I had thrown off a big lie that had been burdening me ***down*** for months.(p.366)
• Then my father fell ***down*** a flight of stairs on one of his lost weekends, at the peak of his career, and died.(p.370)
• Before too long, my husband (who seemed to prefer his shirts dirty) put his foot ***down***, declaring that our family might have the cleanest clothes in town, but that I hadn't been out of the same old dirty slacks and blouse for a week.(p.371)
• I realized I had been going ***down*** and ***down***.(p.378)
• Emma ran out to the kitchen and came back with a water glass full of bourbon and made me drink it ***down***.(p.385)
• As I started ***down*** the aisle, that bourbon went right through me.(p.385)
• So it drove me deeper into the psychosis or neurosis that I had, and that I hated deep ***down*** in my heart.(p.388)
• So I went ***down*** to him quite a few times a month and had him shoot me full of the stuff; and then I went across the street to a little drug store to take a glass of beer or two beers, and then stopped at the liquor store to get myself a pint and go home.(p.389)
• I fell ***down*** and knocked out my front teeth.(p.390)
• So when he came for me, as he walked ***down*** the stairs, I could see him through the bars, and he was signing for me; I looked at him and said, "Don't you sign anything in this place!"(p.391)
• All of them have since settled ***down*** to jobs and good marriages.(p.407)
• I would walk up and ***down*** under the 59th Street bridge, trying to get up the nerve to go up there and jump.(p.411)
• "Why don't you just go ***down*** and see Mr. W.?" she asked.(p.412)
• In those days the A.A. Foundation was ***down*** in the Wall Street district of New York.(p.413)
• In A.A., I have had to be torn ***down*** and then put back together differently.(p.420)
• The doctor sat ***down*** beside the bed and asked me how I felt.(p.423)
• I tried to control her drinking by pouring her whiskey ***down*** the sink before I'd leave for the night, to get drunker myself.(p.426)
• I would drink all night in bars, come home about five a.m., ***down*** a good big glass of whiskey straight, and tumble into bed.(p.428)
• I merely wanted to cut ***down***.(p.429)
• Or, "My physical plant had got a little run ***down*** and the stuff rushed right to my head."(p.433)
• Only through being beaten ***down*** by my own misery would I ever have accepted the term "alcoholic" as applied to myself.(p.436)
• In the garage, I would put the needle in my vein and then try to figure out exactly how much medication to inject to overcome the pep pills while adding to the sleeping pills while ignoring the tranquilizers, in order to get just enough to be able to pull out the needle, jerk the tourniquet, throw it in the car, slam the car door shut, run ***down*** the hall, and fall in bed before I fell asleep.(p.442)
• So I sat ***down*** with me and went over the facts behind the convulsions: personality changes, daily headaches, sense of impending doom, sense of impending insanity.(p.444)
• But then my "rights" try to move in, and they, too, can force my serenity level ***down***.(p.452)
• I thought that was bad until I hit the hole at a prison camp; it was just wide enough and long enough to lie ***down*** in.(p.459)
• I almost broke ***down*** and cried when I talked with them but I didn't.(p.467)
• Now I slide ***down*** mountain fast.(p.475)
• Waitress by day, barfly by night, she drifted ***down*** the years into jail.(p.478)
• (And the church walls haven't tumbled ***down*** yet.)(p.482)
• My father had come out of the South and had suffered a great deal ***down*** there.(p.485)
• A very good friend of mine who owned a drug store across the street from us, came by only about two hours later and said that he had seen Vi ***down*** town.(p.487)
• Nevertheless, we continued to work together and I continued to drink, but I guess, deep ***down*** within her heart as well as within mine, we both knew I couldn't stop drinking.(p.490)
• So I went ***down*** to talk to the District Attorney, and the arrangement was made that I would go home to stay with my mother, and that meant Vi and I were separated.(p.491)
• Very often we rode to and from work together, but being separated really galled me deep ***down***.(p.491)
• I gulped it ***down*** and choked.(p.498)
• I pour drinks ***down*** my throat.(p.501)
• Halfway ***down*** the driveway a thought strikes me.(p.506)
• After I had made my third report, I stepped ***down*** town, met some of the old crowd, and of course you know the answer.(p.510)
• I started prowling around with a couple of these A.A. boys, which kept me pretty busy and kept my mind off of ***down*** town.(p.511)
• We talked for a while, and then he sent me ***down*** to the Alanon House over on the west side, and there I had my introduction to A.A.(p.515)
• I use that "Easy Does It" every day, to slow me ***down*** a little.(p.516)
• I got a job by myself which suited me ***down*** to the ground, because there was nobody really to interfere with what I did, one way or the other, and I usually had my nerves in good trim when anybody was coming around to inspect.(p.519)
• I was ***down*** in the Sudan by this time.(p.521)
• So I did manage to get myself ***down*** to an A.A. meeting that night.(p.523)
• If it was daylight, I would go ***down*** alleys to make sure no one saw me.(p.527)
• After nearly eight years of sobriety in A.A., I still can set ***down*** such thoughts, "against my instinct and training," showing that I still consider myself a "special" person, entitled to special privileges.(p.536)
• If he were still sober, chances are that very quickly I put him ***down*** as a Philistine with no appreciation of literary genius; and then I went on to another bar to find a new victim.(p.537)
• I was ***down*** to my shorts, unaware of wrong-doing, before the ambulance got there and hauled me off to a hospital from which anxious friends rescued me, later that night.(p.537)
• I set it ***down*** and made myself a cup of coffee.(p.541)
• I have had the joy of seeing many a human being, ***down*** and out, learn to stand straight again, and to proceed under his own power to happiness in life.(p.541)
• Through my efforts to get ***down*** to "causes and conditions," I stand convinced that my emotional illness has been present from my earliest recollection.(p.544)
• We learn how to level out the emotional wings that got us into trouble both when we were up and when we were ***down***.(p.560)
• I now conceive the psychiatrist's job to be the task of breaking ***down*** the patient's inner resistance so that which is inside him will flower, as under the activity of the A.A. program."(p.571)
• This self-insurance has resulted in the restoration of physical, mental and spiritual health and self-respect to hundreds of men and women who would be hopelessly ***down*** and out without its unique but effective therapy."(p.574)

downfall

• My ***downfall*** cost the business community unknown thousands of dollars, for it takes real money to train a man for an executive position.(p.137)

downgrade

• I did not know that I had no power over alcohol, that I, alone and unaided, could not stop; that I was on a ***downgrade***, tearing along at full speed with all my brakes gone, and that the end would be a total smash-up, death or insanity.(p.408)

downs
- In spite of your new-found happiness, there will be ups and *downs*.(p.117)
- Life, including some ups and *downs*, is a lot of fun.(p.417)
- I have my ups and *downs* the same as the rest.(p.511)

downstairs
- I went *downstairs* and there was the grizzly old veteran police officer in charge of the property desk, and as he gave me the stuff, he asked, "Are you going out in the street that way?"(p.204)
- The next morning, my wife came into my room and wakened me and said, "That man is *downstairs* and he said you said you'd go to Akron."(p.217)
- I sneak *downstairs* and get a bottle of whiskey from the cellaret.(p.501)
- I'd get *downstairs* to the gin mill, get enough in to hold me until eight o'clock in the morning, then I'd go out to join that "misery parade" that so many of us know so well.(p.514)

downtown
- When those two years were up, I opened an office *downtown*.(p.174)
- The details of the long road back to something resembling normal living -- the first short streetcar ride, the purchase of a used bike which enabled me to widen the narrow horizon of life, the first trip *downtown* -- I will not dwell on.(p.276)
- A year later I was able to buy a Model T roadster and take a better job with a *downtown* printer.(p.276)
- One night I barely made my *downtown* club; if I'd had to go another fifty feet I'd have collapsed in the gutter.(p.435)

downward
- The birth of a baby boy did nothing toward staying the *downward* spiral.(p.278)

dozen
- A tumbler full of gin followed by half a *dozen* bottles of beer would be required if I were to eat any breakfast.(p.5)
- An all night place supplied me with a *dozen* glasses of ale.(p.6)
- To his consternation, he found himself drunk half a *dozen* times in rapid succession.(p.35)
- They cited cases out of their own experience by the *dozen*.(p.42)
- One of our Fellowship failed entirely with his first half *dozen* prospects.(p.96)
- Inwardly he would give anything to take half a *dozen* drinks and get away with them.(p.152)
- By this time I was beginning to pay very dearly physically and, in hope of relief, voluntarily incarcerated myself at least a *dozen* times in one of the local sanitariums.(p.174)
- Within a year of my return to Detroit, A.A. was a definitely established little group of about a *dozen* members and I too was established in a modest but steady job handling an independent dry-cleaning route of my own.(p.283)
- At one time, I was using twenty caps a day; I nearly died half a *dozen* times on the street.(p.480)
- I rebelled, and from that time on I don't think I attended church more than a *dozen* times.(p.489)

dozens
- All I can remember about the Roaring Twenties is that I drank a great deal, thought I was having a grand time, managed to get to Europe for a few weeks, was very proud of the *dozens* of speak-easy cards entitling me to an entree in the better joints between Cleveland and New York, took on a wife, and built a home in a fashionable suburb of Cleveland.(p.358)
- All of my family and loved ones, all of my friends, are nearer and dearer to me than ever before and I have literally *dozens* of new friends who say they cannot believe that a short eight years ago I was ready for the scrap heap.(p.541)

Dr.
- The section called "The Doctor's Opinion" has been kept intact, just as it was originally written in 1939 by the late *Dr.* William D. Silkworth, our Society's great medical benefactor.(p.xi)
- He had also been greatly helped by the late *Dr.* William D. Silkworth, a New York specialist in alcoholism who is now accounted no less than a medical saint by A.A. members, and whose story of the early days of our Society appears in the next pages.(p.xvi)
- But when the broker gave him *Dr.* Silkworth's description of alcoholism and its hopelessness, the physician began to pursue the spiritual remedy for his malady with a willingness he had never before been able to muster.(p.xvi)
- *Dr.* Harry Emerson Fosdick, the noted clergyman, reviewed it with approval.(p.xvii)
- He is a real *Dr.* Jekyll and Mr. Hyde.(p.21)
- Then he had gone to Europe, placing himself in the care of a celebrated physician (the psychiatrist, *Dr.* Jung) who prescribed for him.(p.26)
- Beginning with the story of "*Dr.* Bob," a co-founder of A.A., there are here presented three groups of personal histories.(p.165)
- *Dr.* Bob and the twelve men and women who here tell their stories were among the early members of A.A.'s first groups.(p.169)
- So, at the time *Dr.* Bob and Bill came along I had about run out my strength.(p.182)
- Nineteen years ago last summer, *Dr.* Bob and I saw him (Bill D.) for the first time.(p.188)
- Two days before this, *Dr.* Bob had said to me, "If you and I are going to stay sober, we had better get busy."(p.188)
- After prescribing medicines, *Dr.* Bob ordered, "Put him in a private room.(p.188)
- Then *Dr.* Bob said, "Well, Bill, maybe you'll feel better tomorrow.(p.189)
- I then began asking a lot of questions of both my brother and *Dr.* Bob about how this thing worked, and I suppose I was becoming more glassy-eyed all the while, for eventually I said to Bob, "You're all dried up.(p.206)
- So Paul repeated substantially what *Dr.* Bob had said.(p.207)
- A few minutes later, *Dr.* Bob left, leaving with my brother some medicine I should get.(p.207)
- There was also some conversation about *Dr.* Bob and I must have said that I would go down to Akron with Bill in the morning.(p.217)
- My experience in the hospital I considered to be terrific because *Dr.* Bob told me very quickly that medicine would have very little to do with it, outside of trying to restore my appetite for food.(p.217)
- *Dr.* Bob did not lay out the whole program.(p.218)
- In fact, I never lost my faith, since I had been prepared by some conversations toward the end of my sojourn in the hospital with *Dr.* Bob, conversations pretty much along spiritual lines.(p.218)
- *Dr.* Bob often said that it was a record for what he felt was a typical alcoholic.(p.263)
- I think his entry into A.A. was through spending some hours with *Dr.* Bob at his office.(p.267)
- *Dr.* Bob was in Florida, but Jack didn't know that.(p.267)
- Russ used to be very much pleased because he'd say, "I think *Dr.* Bob thoroughly enjoys coming out here.(p.271)
- The next day he turned me over to a couple who, although neither was an alcoholic, knew *Dr.* Bob and were willing to drive me to Akron where they would turn me over to his care.(p.278)
- So I was driven to Akron the very next day by these Good Samaritans, and turned over to *Dr.* Bob and the then tiny Akron Group.(p.279)
- *Dr.* Bob dwelt at length on how prayer had given him release, time and time again, from the nearly over-powering compulsion to take a drink.(p.279)
- When I got out of the hospital, I was invited to stay with *Dr.* Bob and his dear wife, Anne.(p.279)
- Poor health and a complete lack of money necessitated my remaining with *Dr.* Bob and Anne for very close to a year.(p.280)
- While there, two or three more "cash customers" (as *Dr.* Bob used to call them -- probably because they had so little cash) were shipped in to us from Detroit.(p.282)
- This first meeting was held in the living room of a home and was led by Bill D., the first man that Bill W. and *Dr.* Bob had worked with successfully.(p.291)
- I spent a great deal of time with *Dr.* Bob, whenever he had the time to spare, and in the homes of two or three other people, trying to see how the family lived the program.(p.291)
- The day before I was due to go back to Chicago, a Wednesday and *Dr.* Bob's afternoon off, he had me down to the office and we spent three or four hours formally going through the Six-Step program as it was at that time.(p.291)
- *Dr.* Bob led me through all of these steps.(p.292)
- *Dr.* Bob always emphasized the religious angle very strongly, and I think it helped.(p.292)
- *Dr.* Bob then led me through the restitution step, in which I made a list of all of the persons I had harmed, and worked out ways and means of slowly making restitution.(p.292)
- On my trips back to Akron to get my spirits recharged and to work with other alcoholics, I would ask *Dr.* Bob about this delay and wonder just what was wrong with me.(p.293)
- The words of *Dr.* Bob and Bill are with me all the time.(p.395)
- *Dr.* Bob said, "Love and service keep us dry," and Bill said, "Always we must remember that our first duty is face-to-face help for the alcoholic who still suffers."(p.395)
- *Dr.* Bob tells about keeping it simple and not to louse it up.(p.395)
- He happened to be, by the grace of God, *Dr.* Harry Tiebout, the psychiatrist who probably knew more about alcoholism than any other in the world.(p.559)
- It was the late *Dr.* Tiebout, then, who persuaded me to seek help through A.A.(p.559)
- Since *Dr.* Silkworth's first endorsement of Alcoholics Anonymous, medical societies and physicians throughout the world have set their approval upon us.(p.571)
- *Dr.* Foster Kennedy, neurologist: "This organization of Alcoholics Anonymous calls on two of the greatest reservoirs of power known to man, religion and that instinct for association with one's fellows . . . the 'herd instinct.'(p.571)
- *Dr.* G. Kirby Collier, psychiatrist: "I have felt that A.A. is a group unto themselves and their best results can be had under their own guidance, as a result of their philosophy.(p.571)
- *Dr.* Harry M. Tiebout, psychiatrist: "As a psychiatrist, I have thought a great deal about the relationship of my specialty to A.A. and I have come to the conclusion that our particular function can very often lie in preparing the way for the patient to accept any sort of treatment or outside help.(p.571)
- *Dr.* W.W. Bauer, broadcasting under the auspices of The American Medical Association in 1946, over the NBC network, said, in part: "Alcoholics Anonymous are no crusaders; not a temperance society.(p.572)
- *Dr.* John F. Stouffer, Chief Psychiatrist, Philadelphia General Hospital, citing his experience with A.A., said: "The alcoholics we get here at Philadelphia General are mostly those who cannot afford private treatment, and A.A. is by far the greatest thing we have been able to offer them.(p.572)
- Speaking at a dinner given by John D. Rockefeller Jr. to introduce Alcoholics Anonymous to some of his friends, *Dr.* Harry Emerson Fosdick remarked: "I think that psychologically speaking there is a point of advantage in the approach that is being made in this movement that cannot be duplicated.(p.574)

drab
- I did six years of newspaper advertising, and trade journal work with many, many drunks of *drab* and dreary hue woven into the pattern of my life.(p.254)

draft
- We started to light matches to see, but the *draft* blew them out.(p.424)
- I enlisted in the Navy to escape the Army *draft*.(p.425)
- I am examined for the *draft* and pass the physical test.(p.499)
- The Armistice is signed on the 11th and the *draft* is called off.(p.499)

drafted
- At age twenty-one, I enlisted in the Navy for two reasons: (1) to avoid being *drafted* into the Army, and (2) out of a burst of patriotic fervor inspired by the advent of World War II and as the result of an all-night drinking binge which found me sitting on the doorstep of the Navy recruiting office when the chief petty officer arrived to open for business at nine o'clock Monday morning.(p.398)

drafting
- I finished my apprenticeship and was moved into the *drafting* department.(p.211)
- The school then obtained a job for me in the *drafting* department of another company.(p.211)
- After I was on the *drafting* board about two years I decided I wanted a technical education.(p.211)

draftsman
- As a *draftsman*, I worked for several large companies and gained a variety of experience.(p.211)
- I was supporting myself through all this education by being a toolmaker and a *draftsman*.(p.212)

drag
- Somehow I managed to *drag* my mattress to a lower floor, lest I suddenly leap.(p.6)
- You will make mistakes, but if you are in earnest they will not *drag* you down.(p.117)
- I became so weak, I could barely *drag* myself around.(p.558)

dragged
- Luckily a friend was with me, who *dragged* me out, screaming and cursing, while the bartender threatened to call the police.(p.411)

• I remember being ***dragged***, drink in hand, from beneath the grand piano, where I had hidden, to be locked in my room in disgrace.(p.557)

dragging

• The next morning his wife came ***dragging*** him in before Russ went to work, while I was getting breakfast.(p.271)

drained

• I found I could boost my income by figuring out a lot of cute little tricks that the boss wouldn't be likely to notice – filching money from the Coke machine, short-sticking the customers on oil, and selling oil I'd ***drained*** out of other cars.(p.423)

drama

• Next, we decided that hereafter in this ***drama*** of life, God was going to be our Director.(p.62)

dramatic

• His change of heart was ***dramatic***, convincing, and moving.(p.55)

dramatics

• I was active and did well, however, in school publications, ***dramatics*** (which came in handy during my drinking career), and Greek letter societies.(p.357)

dramatizing

• When I remark that I have been in jail nine times, and in an alcoholic ward twice, they think I'm kidding, or possibly ***dramatizing*** for the sake of a good yarn.(p.542)

drank

• As I ***drank***, the old fierce determination to win came back.(p.4)

• But it was not, for the frightful day came when I ***drank*** once more.(p.7)

• If he did not work, he would surely drink again, and if he ***drank***, he would surely die.(p.15)

• "The doctor told him that if he ever ***drank*** again it would kill him, but there he is all lit up again."(p.20)

• He was ambitious to succeed in business, but saw that he would get nowhere if he ***drank*** at all.(p.32)

• They expect him to give them the nice times they used to have before he ***drank*** so much, and to show his contrition for what they suffered.(p.126)

• He never ***drank*** again.(p.158)

• During these years, I ***drank*** as much as my purse permitted, still without paying too great a penalty, although I was beginning to have morning jitters at times.(p.173)

• I ***drank*** with moderation at first, but it took me only a relatively short time to drift back into the old habits which had wound up so disastrously before.(p.175)

• I ***drank*** all the scotch they had on the train and bought several quarts on my way to the hotel.(p.179)

• I ***drank*** all I dared in the bar, and then went to my room to finish the job.(p.179)

• I ***drank*** nine martinis in less than an hour.(p.195)

• That was the first time I ever ***drank*** hard liquor.(p.195)

• I early discovered that if I ***drank*** anything, I was not accountable for what happened.(p.196)

• I don't know whether I ***drank*** to cover up being a failure, or whether I ***drank*** and then missed the deals.(p.198)

• I had run into a man I always ***drank*** with.(p.201)

• There were times when I got to drinking, and I had been warned by Firestone that they wouldn't stand for this much longer, so, clearly, they were conscious of the fact that I ***drank*** too much and too often.(p.204)

• I ***drank*** some more and slept through the day.(p.205)

• Then he started to talk to me about his drinking experiences, what his drinking had cost him, how much he had drunk and where, things like that, and I remember I was quite bored because I had never seen the guy before and had no interest at all in what, where and when he ***drank***.(p.208)

• I wanted to live, not in a desert, but in a normal world; and my idea of a normal world was among people who ***drank*** – teetotallers were not included.(p.227)

• And I was sure that I couldn't be with people who ***drank***, without drinking.(p.227)

• Everybody ***drank*** wine.(p.230)

• But I can remember, in my teens, that there were a few characters who caused the village heads to nod pityingly and sometimes in anger as they paused to say, "That sot, Henri" and "Ce pauvre Jules," who ***drank*** too much.(p.230)

• I came of good stock, of men and women who ***drank*** wine all their lives as a beverage, and while they occasionally got drunk at special celebrations, they were up and about their business the next day.(p.231)

• My family lived in very prosperous circumstances, and while both my parents ***drank***, sometimes too much, neither was an alcoholic.(p.240)

• I was never a hilarious drunk; the more I ***drank*** the quieter I got, and the drunker I got the harder I fought to stay sober.(p.241)

• Every time I blacked out, and that was every time I ***drank***, there was always that gnawing fear, "What did I do this time?"(p.244)

• I knew they needed to straighten out their thinking and habits, but I was all right, I just ***drank*** too much.(p.246)

• So I ***drank*** all three beers, one after the other, said "I'll be seeing you, boys," and went around the corner for a bottle.(p.247)

• We ***drank*** with exactly the same accord that we finally accepted A.A.(p.265)

• I bet he never ***drank***."(p.268)

• These men all ***drank*** on Saturday nights, and enjoyed themselves.(p.277)

• But – I also stayed up week nights after they had retired and ***drank*** myself into bed.(p.277)

• I confined drinking to weekends, and ***drank*** normally in college and for several years thereafter.(p.287)

• When I ***drank***, I hid it from my folks out of respect for their feelings.(p.287)

• I know now that sixty per cent of the time I ***drank*** alone without benefit of customers.(p.287)

• Somehow or other, I must have misunderstood the doctor's instructions, for I not only made the beer for my wife, I also ***drank*** it for her.(p.297)

• The last day of my drinking career, I ***drank*** twenty-two of them between ten and twelve a.m. and I shall never know how many more followed them until I was poured into bed that night.(p.298)

• Even so, every time I ***drank***, I seemed to get in trouble.(p.322)

• I couldn't keep up with any of my other friends, and I wouldn't go to anyone's house unless I knew they ***drank*** as heavily as I did.(p.324)

• THE HOUSEWIFE WHO ***DRANK*** AT HOME(p.335)

• I never ***drank*** socially; I ***drank*** as often and as much as I could.(p.353)

• It was then that I began to hate myself, and ***drank*** primarily to ease my conscience and forget.(p.354)

• The more I ***drank***, the worse it got and the more I had to drink.(p.354)

• All I can remember about the Roaring Twenties is that I ***drank*** a great deal, thought I was having a grand time, managed to get to Europe for a few weeks, was very proud of the dozens of speak-easy cards entitling me to an entree in the better joints between Cleveland and New York, took on a wife, and built a home in a fashionable suburb of Cleveland.(p.358)

• The more I thought like this the more I ***drank*** to submerge my sorrows.(p.362)

• I was intolerant of people who ***drank***, particularly those who ***drank*** to an extent that interfered with on-the-job performance.(p.374)

• My alcoholic problem began long before I ***drank***.(p.400)

• Above all, he noticed that I ***drank*** a good deal, often got tight in his company and told him naughty stories.(p.403)

• The people I knew rode hard, and some of them ***drank*** hard.(p.404)

• I read sad poetry, cried, ***drank*** red wine, wrote sad poetry, and ***drank*** some more.(p.405)

• This was an Englishman who, at least at this time, ***drank*** as much as I did.(p.405)

• I ***drank*** and I kept on drinking.(p.406)

• I ***drank*** alone or with someone, anyone who would stay and drink with me.(p.406)

• One day soon, the analyses would reveal why I ***drank*** and how to stop.(p.408)

• I went to several Village bars, and ***drank*** cokes or tea.(p.414)

• The last time I ***drank***, when I was twenty-nine, I ***drank*** for only four days, yet I threatened to kill my children; I beat my wife at home and on the church steps; I mistreated a child in my office; and I ran to a hospital for mental illness to avoid jail.(p.418)

• I neither ***drank*** nor smoked until I was nineteen years old.(p.419)

• They both ***drank*** like fish.(p.424)

• Mom and I ***drank*** every waking moment because we felt so sorry for dad.(p.426)

• Of course I ***drank***.(p.433)

• My associates, and all the wits and literary lights I so much admired, also ***drank***.(p.433)

• I ***drank*** my way through schools and always got honors.(p.441)

• The neurologist in charge of my case didn't think to ask me whether I ***drank***, and I didn't think to tell him.(p.444)

• But then, as I ***drank*** more and more, the alcohol seemed to affect my vision: Instead of continuing to see what was good about my wife, I began to see her defects.(p.450)

• The more I ***drank***, the more she wilted.(p.451)

• All afternoon I sat there and ***drank*** and played Bing Crosby's recording of "Silent Night" over and over again on the juke box.(p.467)

• In the light of subsequent events it became evident that I took their advice far too literally, for, after some months of happy sobriety I ***drank*** again.(p.471)

• I ***drank*** from the age of twelve until I was thirty-two.(p.480)

• I got to the place where I'd look forward to the week-end's drinking and pacify myself by saying that the week-ends were mine, that it didn't interfere with my family or with my business if I ***drank*** on the week-ends.(p.488)

• But the week-ends stretched on into Mondays and the time soon came when I ***drank*** every day.(p.488)

• I borrowed five hundred dollars from the bank and three hundred from the loan shop, and I ***drank*** that up pretty fast.(p.490)

• Vi was very kind and explained to the jury that I was basically a fine fellow and a good husband, but that I ***drank*** too much and that she thought I had lost my mind and felt that I should be committed to an asylum.(p.492)

• Father had never directly spoken to me about drinking but he never ***drank*** any, so far as I knew.(p.498)

• My father was alive, and I had to do as he wanted, so I ***drank*** under cover.(p.508)

• Someone told me, "When you ***drank***, you didn't get half drunk.(p.516)

• I went out and ***drank*** some German wine and it went to my head.(p.517)

• At first, like everybody else, I could keep control when I ***drank***, but if I did start to drink, even in those days, I was always one of the last to leave the party.(p.518)

• I don't know when I became an alcoholic, but I do believe I became one because I ***drank*** too much too often.(p.526)

• As time went on, I ***drank*** more.(p.526)

• Oh, I might drink too much at times – everyone I knew ***drank***.(p.527)

• I was immersed in self-pity and resentment, and the only people who would support this attitude or who I felt understood me at all were the people I met in bars and the ones who ***drank*** as I did.(p.547)

• The last three years of my drinking, I ***drank*** on my job.(p.548)

• That's why I ***drank***.(p.554)

• I was raised in Kansas, the only child of loving parents who just ***drank*** socially.(p.554)

• Of course, the more I ***drank***, the more unrealistic my expectations became and the poorer my performance, and the gap widened.(p.557)

• The more I ***drank***, the more I fantasized everything.(p.560)

drastic

• These were revolutionary and ***drastic*** proposals, but the moment I fully accepted them, the effect was electric.(p.14)

• But the program of action, though entirely sensible, was pretty ***drastic***.(p.42)

• We subjected ourselves to a ***drastic*** self-appraisal.(p.76)

• Before taking ***drastic*** action which might implicate other people we secure their consent.(p.80)

• If we have obtained permission, have consulted with others, asked God to help and the ***drastic*** step is indicated we must not shrink.(p.80)

• He may rebel at the thought of a ***drastic*** housecleaning which requires discussion with other people.(p.94)

• At that point everyone decided something ***drastic*** had to be done.(p.469)

• Since, perhaps, suicide was a bit too ***drastic*** (actually, I was afraid), dry martinis were chosen as the slow, pleasant, private, gradual instrument of self-destruction.(p.531)

drastically

• My ideas about miracles were ***drastically*** revised right then.(p.11)

draw

• Mercifully, no one could guess that I was to have no real employment for five years, or hardly ***draw*** a sober breath.(p.4)

• If you ***draw*** this fallacious reasoning to the attention

of an alcoholic, he will laugh it off, or become irritated and refuse to talk.(p.23)
• It is not by chance we were given the power to reason, to examine the evidence of our senses, and to *draw* conclusions.(p.53)
• Let him *draw* his own conclusion.(p.92)
• You *draw* more and more into yourself and you think everyone is talking about conditions at your home.(p.114)
• We suggest you *draw* the book to the attention of the doctor who is to attend your patient during treatment.(p.144)
• When rubber reached a certain low point, they would *draw* on the rubber out of the pool and buy.(p.198)
• It wasn't until just lately that, in your case, I could *draw* it.(p.436)

drawback
• The only *drawback* was, I always knew how I arrived there, but somehow, between the rest room, the rinse, and the fluff-dry, I never knew when or how I got home.(p.370)

drawers
• She hid her bottles in clothes hampers and dresser *drawers*.(p.335)
• I did my hiding in the hampers and in my dresser *drawers*.(p.336)

drawing
• I had had some success at speculation, so we had a little money, but we once worked on a farm for a month to avoid *drawing* on our small capital.(p.3)
• Not far from where I lived they built a new technical high school and one of the teachers sold me on the idea that I needed a little mechanical *drawing* if I were going to be a good toolmaker.(p.211)
• I proceeded to take up the *drawing* and advanced rapidly in it.(p.211)

drawn
• If he says yes, then his attention should be *drawn* to you as a person who has recovered.(p.90)
• Like a gaunt prospector, belt *drawn* in over the last ounce of food, our pick struck gold.(p.128)
• I think it's awfully hard on people, especially if they're new people, to hear these long *drawn* out talks.(p.273)
• The next two years were simply a long *drawn* out process of less and less work and more and more whiskey.(p.278)
• Well, suicide was a last straw matter, and I had not *drawn* the last straw yet.(p.278)
• I think the thing that galled me was that just after Easter I had *drawn* my salary for two weeks' work and had decided that I was going to send some money to Vi; and above all else I was going to send my baby daughter an Easter outfit.(p.493)
• Ten – Alcoholics Anonymous has no opinion on outside issues; hence the A.A. name ought never be *drawn* into public controversy.(p.564)

dreaded
• A relief, even though I *dreaded* it, feeling that this was the end of everything.(p.378)

dreadful
• I remember how horrible jails are, how *dreadful* a thing it is to be behind steel bars.(p.542)
• Harm is done by sick people, as I was sick, and doing *dreadful* harm to myself and to my loved ones.(p.542)
• To cure my *dreadful* hangovers, I discovered the morning drink.(p.556)

dream
• This *dream* world has been replaced by a great sense of purpose, accompanied by a growing consciousness of the power of God in our lives.(p.130)
• Being an alcoholic, I couldn't *dream* of doing anything by halves!(p.286)
• I also wanted to be the queen of society, with a glittering salon, the bride of a *dream* prince and the mother of a happy brood.(p.400)
• He was the *dream* prince, the answer.(p.403)
• It is all like a *dream*.(p.463)
• I lived in a *dream* world.(p.560)

dreamed
• We have found much of heaven and we have been rocketed into a fourth dimension of existence of which we had not even *dreamed*.(p.25)
• At the end of these thirteen years I never *dreamed* that he'd ever take another drink.(p.263)
• With God's help I am able, for one day at a time, to carry business responsibilities which, not many years ago, I would not have *dreamed* of assuming.(p.284)
• Even when I was old enough to know better, I *dreamed* about being as beautiful as Venus, as pure as the Madonna and as brilliant as the President of the United States is supposed to be.(p.400)
• I, who had *dreamed* these sick dreams, now reaped the nightmare.(p.411)

dreaming
• I think I am *dreaming* and will soon wake up.(p.529)

dreamless
• I fall into a *dreamless* sleep.(p.497)

dreams
• Always at the end of these *dreams* was drinking.(p.199)
• To go into a gathering of people was the sort of thing that all my life, from the time I left my private world of books and *dreams* to meet the real world of people and parties and jobs, had left me feeling an uncomfortable outsider, needing the warming stimulus of drinks to join in.(p.228)
• A lot of lost *dreams*, empty futures, and crazy things of the past went through my mind.(p.333)
• I tried to compensate with impossible *dreams* and ambitions, which were simply early forms of escape.(p.400)
• I, who had dreamed these sick *dreams*, now reaped the nightmare.(p.411)
• Nor were those impossible *dreams* I used to have the things I really wanted.(p.416)

dreamy
• One night I was sitting in the lab alone with a fifth and a case of beer listening to *dreamy* Hawaiian music on the radio.(p.427)

dreary
• His coming was an oasis in the *dreary* desert of futility.(p.9)
• I did six years of newspaper advertising, and trade journal work with many, many drunks of drab and *dreary* hue woven into the pattern of my life.(p.254)

drenched
• Forced to detrain from an empty gondola on the other side of Chicago by a terrific rainstorm which *drenched* me to the skin, I hit the first factory building I saw for a job.(p.253)

dress
• From far away, as if in a delirium, I heard my own voice – calling someone "Dorothy," talking of *dress* shops, of jobs . . . the words came clearer . . . this sound of my own voice frightened me as it came closer . . . and suddenly, there I was, talking of I knew not what, to someone I'd never seen before this very moment.(p.222)
• Scared that my *dress* wasn't going to fit right, that the church wasn't going to be filled, that I'd fall flat on my face walking up the aisle; in fact, I was afraid I wasn't going to be a prima donna in the place where I should be.(p.385)
• I would wait for the mailman each month, like any good mother, but as soon as he handed me my check, I put on my best *dress* and went looking for my alcoholic friend.(p.527)

dressed
• I went to my hotel and leisurely *dressed* for dinner.(p.41)
• I'd waked up in strange rooms before, fully *dressed* on a bed or a couch; I'd waked up in my own room, in or on my own bed, not knowing what hour or day it was, afraid to ask . . . but this was different.(p.222)
• I feared that I wasn't *dressed* like the rest.(p.261)
• Instead, he got *dressed*, took me out, bought me three or four double shots and put me to bed.(p.278)
• The only incentive that I had, toward the end, for getting *dressed* in the morning was to get out and get supplies to help me get my day started.(p.336)
• He was well *dressed*; he was easy going.(p.413)
• Then I remember him coming into my room one night with a friend, and telling me to get *dressed* – we were going away.(p.466)
• I remember in my early youth my mother *dressed* me just as she did my two sisters, and I wore curls until I was six years of age.(p.483)
• People seemed to be carefully *dressed*, too happy, too normal.(p.524)

dresser
• She hid her bottles in clothes hampers and *dresser* drawers.(p.335)
• I did my hiding in the hampers and in my *dresser* drawers.(p.336)

dresses
• All hidden drunks aren't at home in housewives' *dresses*.(p.328)

dressing
• I'd only had two with her, but I'd managed four in the fifteen minutes I'd waited for her, and of course I'd had the usual uncounted swigs from the bottle as I painfully got up and did my slow spasmodic *dressing*.(p.223)
• There is really nothing to *dressing* with chains and shackles on, once you learn the technique of pulling inside-out pants through the shackles.(p.460)

drew
• When we *drew* near to Him He disclosed Himself to us!(p.57)
• In the first flush of spiritual experience they forgave each other and *drew* closer together.(p.124)
• He even went to bat for me before the court martial that inevitably followed and, as a result, I *drew* only thirty days – fifteen in solitary.(p.428)
• I got very little out of the two hundred, that I *drew* on that pay day.(p.493)

dried
• I then began asking a lot of questions of both my brother and Dr. Bob about how this thing worked, and I suppose I was becoming more glassy-eyed all the while, for eventually I said to Bob, "You're all *dried* up.(p.206)
• And I said, "Well, what about Paul, have you got him all *dried* up?"(p.207)

drift
• But we must be careful not to *drift* into worry, remorse or morbid reflection, for that would diminish our usefulness to others.(p.86)
• I drank with moderation at first, but it took me only a relatively short time to *drift* back into the old habits which had wound up so disastrously before.(p.175)
• The early promise of the "boy wonder" faded, and my career began to *drift*.(p.556)

drifted
• But the saddest, and thus the most consoling, *drifted* through from the country-music station – stories of broken hearts, wasted lives, lost loves, sung plaintively.(p.332)
• Waitress by day, barfly by night, she *drifted* down the years into jail.(p.478)
• In any case, I made myself believe that, so I just *drifted* about, existing on my retired pay, drinking, and living at home.(p.522)

drifting
• *Drifting* back to Ohio, I landed on a small newspaper and later was impressed into the direction of boy-welfare work at the local "Y."(p.253)
• The gradual result was that I was *drifting* into making drinking one of the more important parts of my life.(p.519)

drilled
• Another thing that mother *drilled* into me was a very Puritanical point of view as to sex relations and as to motherhood and womanhood.(p.483)

drink
• Six months earlier, the broker had been relieved of his *drink* obsession by a sudden spiritual experience, following a meeting with an alcoholic friend who had been in contact with the Oxford Groups of that day.(p.xv)
• He sobered, never to *drink* again up to the moment of his death in 1950.(p.xvi)
• He never had another *drink*.(p.xvii)
• Men and women *drink* essentially because they like the effect produced by alcohol.(p.xxvi)
• After they have succumbed to the desire again, as so many do, and the phenomenon of craving develops, they pass through the well-known stages of a spree, emerging remorseful, with a firm resolution not to *drink* again.(p.xxvii)
• They took a *drink* a day or so prior to the date, and then the phenomenon of craving at once became paramount to all other interests so that the important appointment was not met.(p.xxvii)
• There is the type of man who is unwilling to admit that he cannot take a *drink*.(p.xxviii)
• There is the type who always believes that after being entirely free from alcohol for a period of time he can take a *drink* without danger.(p.xxviii)
• He had lost everything worthwhile in life and was only living, one might say, to *drink*.(p.xxix)
• Following his physical rehabilitation, he had a talk with me in which he frankly stated he thought the treatment a waste of effort, unless I could assure him, which no one ever had, that in the future he would have the "will power" to resist the impulse to *drink*.(p.xxix)
• He has not had a *drink* for a great many years.(p.xxx)
• I forgot the strong warnings and the prejudices of my people concerning *drink*.(p.1)
• Out of this alloy of *drink* and speculation, I commenced to forge the weapon that one day would turn

in its flight like a boomerang and all but cut me to ribbons.(p.2)
• ***Drink*** was taking an important and exhilarating part in my life.(p.3)
• I saw I could not take so much as one ***drink***.(p.5)
• Someone had pushed a ***drink*** my way, and I had taken it.(p.5)
• Then came the insidious insanity of that first ***drink***, and on Armistice Day 1935, I was off again.(p.8)
• Of course he would have dinner, and then I could ***drink*** openly with him.(p.9)
• I pushed a ***drink*** across the table.(p.9)
• I have not had a ***drink*** since.(p.13)
• If he did not work, he would surely ***drink*** again, and if he drank, he would surely die.(p.15)
• This sometimes nearly drove me back to ***drink***, but I soon found that when all other measures failed, work with another alcoholic would save the day.(p.15)
• They have solved the ***drink*** problem.(p.17)
• "Why don't you ***drink*** like a gentleman or quit?"(p.20)
• He may start off as a moderate drinker; he may or may not become a continuous hard drinker; but at some stage of his drinking career he begins to lose all control of his liquor consumption, once he starts to ***drink***.(p.21)
• Yet let him ***drink*** for a day, and he frequently becomes disgustingly and even dangerously anti-social.(p.21)
• If hundreds of experiences have shown him that one ***drink*** means another debacle with all its attendant suffering and humiliation, why is it he takes that one ***drink***?(p.22)
• We know that while the alcoholic keeps away from ***drink***, as he may do for months or years, he reacts much like other men.(p.22)
• These observations would be academic and pointless if our friend never took the first ***drink***, thereby setting the terrible cycle in motion.(p.23)
• And the truth, strange to say, is usually that he has no more idea why he took that first ***drink*** than you have.(p.23)
• The fact is that most alcoholics, for reasons yet obscure, have lost the power of choice in ***drink***.(p.24)
• We are without defense against the first ***drink***.(p.24)
• How often have some of us begun to ***drink*** in this nonchalant way, and after the third or fourth, pounded on the bar and said to ourselves, "For God's sake, how did I ever get started again?"(p.24)
• Only to have that thought supplanted by "Well, I'll stop with the sixth ***drink***."(p.24)
• Therefore, it is not surprising that our drinking careers have been characterized by countless vain attempts to prove we could ***drink*** like other people.(p.30)
• If anyone who is showing inability to control his drinking can do the right-about-face and ***drink*** like a gentleman, our hats are off to him.(p.31)
• Heaven knows, we have tried hard enough and long enough to ***drink*** like other people!(p.31)
• Try to ***drink*** and stop abruptly.(p.31)
• Then he fell victim to a belief which practically every alcoholic has – that his long period of sobriety and self-discipline had qualified him to ***drink*** as other men.(p.32)
• Most of us have believed that if we remained sober for a long stretch, we could thereafter ***drink*** normally.(p.33)
• Commencing to ***drink*** after a period of sobriety, we are in a short time as bad as ever.(p.33)
• To be gravely affected, one does not necessarily have to ***drink*** a long time nor take the quantities some of us have.(p.33)
• For those who are unable to ***drink*** moderately the question is how to stop altogether.(p.34)
• Whether such a person can quit upon a nonspiritual basis depends upon the extent to which he has already lost the power to choose whether he will ***drink*** or not.(p.34)
• What sort of thinking dominates an alcoholic who repeats time after time the desperate experiment of the first ***drink***?(p.35)
• But there was always the curious mental phenomenon that parallel with our sound reasoning there inevitably ran some insanely trivial excuse for taking the first ***drink***.(p.37)
• We now see that when we began to ***drink*** deliberately, instead of casually, there was little serious or effective thought during the period of premeditation of what the terrific consequences might be.(p.37)
• Our behavior is as absurd and incomprehensible with respect to the first ***drink*** as that of an individual with a passion, say, for jay-walking.(p.37)
• Let him tell you about it: "I was much impressed with what you fellows said about alcoholism, and I frankly did not believe it would be possible for me to ***drink*** again.(p.40)
• I rather appreciated your ideas about the subtle insanity which precedes the first ***drink***, but I was confident it could not happen to me after what I had learned.(p.40)
• Not only had I been off guard, I had made no fight whatever against the first ***drink***.(p.41)
• I had commenced to ***drink*** as carelessly as though the cocktails were ginger ale.(p.41)
• I now remembered what my alcoholic friends had told me, how they prophesied that if I had an alcoholic mind, the time and place would come – I would ***drink*** again.(p.41)
• They had said that though I did raise a defense, it would one day give way before some trivial reason for having a ***drink***.(p.42)
• Once more: The alcoholic at certain times has no effective mental defense against the first ***drink***.(p.43)
• Leaving aside the ***drink*** question, they tell why living was so unsatisfactory.(p.51)
• Save for a few brief moments of temptation the thought of ***drink*** has never returned; and at such times a great revulsion has risen up in him.(p.57)
• Seemingly he could not ***drink*** even if he would.(p.57)
• The insanity of alcohol returns and we ***drink*** again.(p.66)
• And with us, to ***drink*** is to die.(p.66)
• If we are not sorry, and our conduct continues to harm others, we are quite sure to ***drink***.(p.70)
• The feeling that the ***drink*** problem has disappeared will often come strongly.(p.75)
• We must lose our fear of creditors no matter how far we have to go, for we are liable to ***drink*** if we are afraid to face them.(p.78)
• Show him the mental twist which leads to the first ***drink*** of a spree.(p.92)
• Show him, from your own experience, how the queer mental condition surrounding that first ***drink*** prevents normal functioning of the will power.(p.92)
• Admit that he probably knows more about it than you do, but call to his attention the fact that however deep his faith and knowledge, he could not have applied it or he would not ***drink***.(p.93)
• And even though he continues to ***drink***, the family will find life more bearable.(p.97)
• People have said we must not go where liquor is served; we must not have it in our homes; we must shun friends who ***drink***; we must avoid moving pictures which show drinking scenes; we must not go into bars; our friends must hide their bottles if we go to their houses; we mustn't think or be reminded about alcohol at all.(p.100)
• If you do this thoroughly, few people will ask you to ***drink***.(p.102)
• Don't start to withdraw again just because your friends ***drink*** liquor.(p.102)
• Our activities in behalf of women who ***drink*** are on the increase.(p.104)
• We want the wives of Alcoholics Anonymous to address the wives of men who ***drink*** too much.(p.104)
• Asked why they commenced to ***drink*** again, they would reply with some silly excuse, or none.(p.107)
• Why could they not see that ***drink*** meant ruin to them?(p.107)
• He is worried at times, and is becoming aware that he cannot ***drink*** like other people.(p.109)
• But when he gets over the spree, he begins to think once more how he can ***drink*** moderately next time.(p.109)
• He admits he cannot ***drink*** like other people, but does not see why.(p.110)
• He will use that as an excuse to ***drink*** more.(p.111)
• It is possible to have a full and useful life, though your husband continues to ***drink***.(p.111)
• If you and your husband find a solution for the pressing problem of ***drink*** you are, of course, going to be very happy.(p.117)
• In a weak moment he may take your dislike of his high-stepping friends as one of those insanely trivial excuses to ***drink***.(p.120)
• He will be less likely to ***drink*** again, and anything is preferable to that.(p.130)
• Here, for instance, is a typical example: An officer of one of the largest banking institutions in America knows I no longer ***drink***.(p.138)
• I pointed out that I had had nothing to ***drink*** whatever for three years, and this in the face of difficulties that would have made nine out of ten men ***drink*** their heads off.(p.138)
• Those who ***drink*** moderately may be more annoyed with an alcoholic than a total abstainer would be.(p.139)
• If he had these qualities and did not ***drink*** would he be worth retaining?(p.140)
• You might say you appreciated his abilities, would like to keep him, but cannot if he continues to ***drink***.(p.141)
• If he temporizes and still thinks he can ever ***drink*** again, even beer, he might as well be discharged after the next bender which, if an alcoholic, he is almost certain to have.(p.142)
• He will appreciate knowing you are not bothering your head about him, that you are not suspicious nor are you trying to run his life so he will be shielded from temptation to ***drink***.(p.146)
• Of course he couldn't ***drink***, but why not sit hopefully at a table, a bottle of ginger ale before him?(p.154)
• Again it was the old, insidious insanity -- that first ***drink***.(p.154)
• He has not had a ***drink*** since.(p.156)
• I ***drink*** like that."(p.157)
• There was much talk about the mental state preceding the first ***drink***.(p.157)
• I was between Scylla and Charybdis now, because if I did not ***drink*** my stomach tortured me, and if I did, my nerves did the same thing.(p.175)
• I think I must have been thoroughly scared by what had happened, or by the doctor, or probably both, so that I did not touch a ***drink*** again until the country went dry.(p.175)
• Most of the time therefore, I did not take the morning ***drink*** which I craved so badly, but instead would fill up on large doses of sedatives to quiet the jitters, which distressed me terribly.(p.176)
• I used to promise my wife, my friends, and my children that I would ***drink*** no more – promises which seldom kept me sober even through the day, though I was very sincere when I made them.(p.177)
• I could ***drink*** all I wanted of that.(p.177)
• That was June 10, 1935, and that was my last ***drink***.(p.180)
• I used to get terribly upset when I saw my friends ***drink*** and knew I could not, but I schooled myself to believe that though I once had the same privilege, I had abused it so frightfully that it was withdrawn.(p.181)
• It never fails, if you go about it with one half the zeal you have been in the habit of showing when you were getting another ***drink***.(p.181)
• A couple of hired hands were cleaning out the barn on the farm and I would ride to and fro on the sled, and while they were loading I would ***drink*** hard cider out of a barrel in the barn.(p.183)
• I remember that my father kept whiskey around the house for medical purposes and entertainment, and I would ***drink*** from this when no one was about and then water it to keep my parents from knowing I was drinking.(p.183)
• It did help to certain extent, since I got in places where I could not obtain anything to ***drink***, and so broke the habitual drinking.(p.183)
• Then Prohibition came into effect, and the facts that the stuff obtainable was so horrible and sometimes deadly, and that I had married and had a job which I had to look after, helped me for a period of some three or four years, although I would get drunk every time I could get hold of enough to ***drink*** to get started.(p.183)
• So I would refuse to ***drink***.(p.184)
• Away from my office two or three weeks at a time; horrible days and nights when I would lie on the floor of my home, lying awake and reaching over to get the bottle, taking a ***drink*** and going back into oblivion.(p.184)
• The next thing they wanted to know was if I thought I could quit of my own accord, without any help, if I could just walk out of the hospital and never take another ***drink***.(p.186)
• Whether you quit six days, months, or years, if you go out and take a ***drink*** or two you'll end up in this hospital tied down, just like you have been in these past six months.(p.187)
• And they said, "No, you have a disease, and it doesn't make any difference how long you do without it, after a ***drink*** or two you'll end up just like you are now."(p.187)
• Every time I'd start thinking about drinking, I would think of the long, dry years ahead without having a ***drink***; but this idea of twenty-four hours, that it was up to me from then on, was a lot of help.(p.188)
• Bill D. walked out of that hospital a free man never to ***drink*** again.(p.189)
• They said, "Let's forget about those other things, that is, trying to eliminate them all at once, and concentrate on the ***drink***."(p.190)

• At that time, as I remember, he had promised never to take another ***drink***.(p.193)
• We boys drove out in somebody's car and went to the bar on the way do the dining room and I, in an effort to impress the other boys that I was city-bred, having lived in Scranton and Cleveland, asked them if they didn't want a ***drink***.(p.194)
• That was my first ***drink***.(p.195)
• I kept watching the man down the bar to see what he did with a contraption like that, and he just smelled of his ***drink*** and set it down again, so I did the same.(p.195)
• There was nothing about that ***drink*** that I liked.(p.195)
• I had no more reason to ***drink*** those martinis than a jackrabbit.(p.195)
• I went over and bought a jug of hard cider and a gallon of wine that I gave these fellows to ***drink***.(p.195)
• When they got through the day's work, part was left which I proceeded to ***drink***.(p.196)
• I decided that I couldn't ***drink***.(p.196)
• Anyhow, I recognized the fact that I couldn't ***drink*** like normal people, but I tried hard and kept on trying for twenty-two years.(p.196)
• That was the reverse of my former pattern of fearing to go to work because I might ***drink***!(p.199)
• I determined that I wouldn't ***drink***.(p.200)
• I remember one occasion when I did not ***drink*** for three hundred and sixty-four days, but I didn't quite make the year.(p.200)
• I told him that I had not had a ***drink*** for ninety days and that I had come to the conclusion that I was one of those individuals who couldn't ***drink***.(p.200)
• So, knowing that, I had determined that so long as I lived I would never take another ***drink***.(p.200)
• And I hadn't been drunk because I hadn't taken a ***drink***.(p.200)
• An offer of appreciation for not having had a ***drink*** for those few months and then and there, without anybody promising me anything or threatening me, I made a solemn vow that never so long as I lived would I take another ***drink***.(p.200)
• So I was driving to Cleveland when I made this solemn promise never to ***drink*** again.(p.201)
• I had run into him, and he looked real prosperous; his face and eyes looked clear and he started to compliment me on my good front and how well I looked, and I said, "I haven't had a ***drink*** for nine months."(p.201)
• He said, "Well, I haven't had a ***drink*** for three months."(p.201)
• I'll buy you one ***drink***, and if you suggest a second one, I'll poke you right in the nose."(p.201)
• I could take one ***drink*** and get right back on the wagon.(p.202)
• Nobody would know it, so I agreed to have the one ***drink***.(p.202)
• And I continued to ***drink***, on and off then, until every dollar I had in the world was gone again and I was right back living at my sister's, getting my cigarettes by calling her grocer and telling him to put in a couple of cartons with her order, exactly as I had before I started to work at Max's.(p.202)
• I had avoided a ***drink*** this time.(p.203)
• So having licked it, there was no reason why I shouldn't have a ***drink***, and I stopped in before I got home and had one.(p.203)
• Then I got into the habit of having beers, and decided that a ***drink*** of whiskey was not any worse; so I would get the one ***drink*** of whiskey but, on second thought, I decided that as long as I was only going to have one, I might as well make it a double-header.(p.203)
• I didn't ***drink*** very long at a time.(p.203)
• To show you the point to which this obsession went, there came an occasion when I had spent a most delightful week-end, and at nine o'clock on Sunday night I was on my way home, and I thought I would get a ***drink***.(p.204)
• I offered them a ***drink***, and they came to the bottom of the stairs and the good woman fainted, just looking at me.(p.205)
• My only thought that day was getting a ***drink***, and how to get rid of those clowns was my big problem.(p.206)
• They asked me if I would take some medicine, and I promised that I would if they got me a ***drink***.(p.206)
• I got two drinks, each of them a quarter of that pint, in me, and was talking along with these people, but I felt that sooner or later they were going to have me cornered because they were smarter than I was and the ***drink*** was beginning to take effect; but as I reached for the third ***drink*** Bob said, "Listen, Buster, you promised to take some medicine if we got you a ***drink***.(p.206)
• Now we got you the ***drink***, but you haven't taken the medicine."(p.206)
• I told him I'd take the medicine and I would take it, but I hadn't told him when, and thereupon I got away with the third ***drink***.(p.206)
• You're never going to want another ***drink***, are you?"; and this answer of his is very important to those of us who are victims of alcoholism.(p.206)
• He said, "So long as I'm thinking as I'm thinking now, and so long as I'm doing the things I'm doing now, I don't believe I'll ever take another ***drink***."(p.206)
• I'm not going to want another ***drink***?"(p.207)
• He said, "Maybe you need a little ***drink***."(p.208)
• And he got me a ***drink***.(p.208)
• I knew I could quit because he had quit; he hadn't had a ***drink*** for over a year.(p.208)
• HE THOUGHT HE COULD ***DRINK*** LIKE A GENTLEMAN(p.210)
• But he discovered that there are some gentlemen who can't ***drink***.(p.210)
• Although, during this period I was not addicted to any pattern of alcohol consumption, when I did ***drink*** the drinking was pretty wild.(p.212)
• I could not see why I couldn't ***drink*** like a gentleman, and that was my primary ambition – until I landed in A.A.(p.214)
• The successful demonstration I had made of my life problems in other respects convinced me that some day I was going to be able to ***drink*** like a gentleman.(p.214)
• After two or three years of effort along this line, I reached the point of actual despair that I ever would be able to ***drink*** only a harmless amount each day.(p.215)
• Bill bought me a ***drink*** or two on the way, and Dorothy S. came with us, and the three of us went over to the City Hospital.(p.217)
• In fact, the last three years of my drinking was a routine of barbiturates in the morning, so that I could stop shaking enough to shave, and then alcohol beginning about four-thirty or five o'clock, with a struggle not to take a ***drink*** at noon or during the day, because I had the idea that if I took one ***drink***, I would smell as though I had had a pint.(p.217)
• He startled me by informing me that he was an alcoholic, that he had found a way which so far enabled him to live without taking a ***drink***, and that the main idea was to find a way how not to take that first ***drink***.(p.218)
• One of the things that came up repeatedly in the stories they told me was that once they had accepted the program, they never had a desire to take a ***drink***.(p.219)
• I've never had a desire to take a ***drink***.(p.219)
• I knew what they were all right – a ***drink*** would fix them.(p.223)
• It must have been a long time since I had my last ***drink*** -- but I didn't dare ask this stranger for one.(p.223)
• And I remembered the creeping horror of the interminable night, in which I slept for short spells and woke up dripping with cold sweat and shaken with utter despair, to ***drink*** hastily from my bottle and mercifully pass out again, "You're mad, you're mad, you're mad!" pounded through my brain with each returning ray of consciousness, and I drowned the refrain with ***drink***.(p.224)
• Sitting in a Second Avenue bar, accepting drinks from anyone who offered, after my small stake was gone; or sitting at home alone, with the inevitable glass in my hand, I would remember, and remembering, I would ***drink*** faster, seeking speedy oblivion.(p.225)
• Hangovers began to assume monstrous proportions and the morning ***drink*** became an urgent necessity.(p.226)
• With a creeping insidiousness, ***drink*** had become more important than anything else.(p.226)
• When my doctor told me I should never touch a ***drink*** again, I couldn't afford to believe him.(p.226)
• He wasn't a drinking man, he didn't know what it was to need a ***drink***, nor what a ***drink*** could do for one in a pinch.(p.227)
• I was free, and I didn't have to ***drink*** to "show them."(p.228)
• Having regard for the law of the land, I resigned myself to the will of the national legislators and quit drinking altogether, not because I had found it harmful, but because I couldn't get what I was accustomed to ***drink***.(p.232)
• You can all remember that in the first few months after the change, a great many men, who had formerly been used to a few beers every day or an occasional ***drink*** of whiskey, simply quit all alcoholic drinks.(p.232)
• I was doing well in business, and in going around town I was frequently invited to have a ***drink*** in a speakeasy.(p.233)
• Gradually, however, I'd suffer so much that I simply had to have the morning-after ***drink***.(p.233)
• With a great deal of determination, I would throw out full pints – pour them out and smash the bottles -- firmly resolved never to take another ***drink*** of the stuff.(p.234)
• There were four of us children, and although both of my brothers later became alcoholic – one died of alcoholism -- my sister has never taken a ***drink*** in her life.(p.240)
• That is where I had my first ***drink*** and I still remember it, for every "first" ***drink*** afterwards did exactly the same trick -- I could feel it go right through every bit of my body and down to my very toes.(p.241)
• But each ***drink*** after the "first" seemed to become less effective and after three or four they all seemed like water.(p.241)
• Even that first night I blacked out, which leads me to believe that I was an alcoholic from my very first ***drink***.(p.241)
• At this time I was holding what drinking I did down to weekends, but I hadn't had a ***drink*** at all in a month.(p.243)
• I could never be bothered with the follow-through and would invariably reward myself for my efforts with that "first" ***drink***.(p.243)
• I'd work like mad for three or four weeks without a single ***drink***, save my money, pay a few bills and then "reward" myself with alcohol.(p.244)
• Many alcoholics have learned they can bring their bottle to a cheap movie theater and ***drink***, sleep, wake up and ***drink*** again in the darkness.(p.244)
• Yet we all had one really sincere purpose in our hearts and that was not to ***drink***.(p.246)
• I myself could see deterioration in my work from being physically and mentally affected by liquor, although I had not yet reached the point where all I wanted was more to ***drink***.(p.254)
• My family would have nothing to do with me, in fact couldn't because I couldn't spare any of my money, which I needed for ***drink***, to support them.(p.255)
• In those days my system was always to ***drink*** up my last pay check and believe that necessity would bring the next job.(p.256)
• As soon as I could get up and walk I started to ***drink*** again and kept it up until my friend of the hospital, who, in his first try at the new way of life had stubbed his toe in Chicago but had come back to the town to take counsel and make a new start, picked me up and got me into a hospital.(p.258)
• I took my last ***drink*** in 1937.(p.260)
• I was still bitter because I felt that ***drink*** had completely ruined my childhood and my married life, and I hated everything pertaining to it.(p.262)
• He told me that he would never ***drink*** again.(p.263)
• At the end of these thirteen years I never dreamed that he'd ever take another ***drink***.(p.263)
• Where you go, I'll go, and what you ***drink***, I'll ***drink***."(p.263)
• I sipped the ***drink*** off the bar because I couldn't hold it in my hand, but I was still a lady, believe it or not, and I was deeply ashamed.(p.266)
• We always tried to buy him a ***drink***, and he always told us he had liquor trouble – couldn't ***drink***.)(p.266)
• He used to ***drink***, and then he found something that started up in Akron that helped him quit drinking."(p.267)
• That was our last ***drink*** of anything alcoholic.(p.267)
• They told Annabelle to take me under her wing, and I shall never forget how she sort of curled up her nose and said, "They tell me you ***drink*** too."(p.269)
• Thank God I had no desire for a ***drink*** when he died.(p.272)
• Dr. Bob dwelt at length on how prayer had given him release, time and time again, from the nearly over-powering compulsion to take a ***drink***.(p.279)
• Out of this maelstrom just two coherent thoughts came to the surface; one, a ***drink*** would mean homelessness and death; two, I could no longer relieve the pressure of fear by starting home, as was once my habitual solution to this problem, because I no longer had a home.(p.279)
• I have never had a ***drink*** since.(p.280)
• Have I ever wanted a ***drink*** during these years?(p.285)
• Only once did I suffer from a nearly overpowering compulsion to take a ***drink***.(p.285)
• I had been in A.A. a year, and the last thing in my mind was a ***drink***.(p.285)

• There have also been numerous times when I have thought about taking a ***drink***.(p.285)
• I was very much interested in athletics, and because of this and parental influence, I didn't ***drink*** or smoke in either grade or high school.(p.287)
• I had to adapt to new associations and associates, and it seemed to be the smart thing to ***drink*** and smoke.(p.287)
• Shortly thereafter, aided by the Depression, I found that I had a great deal of spare time and that a little ***drink*** in the morning helped.(p.287)
• Why, even a year ago, I had seen Howard, an ex-doctor, mooching a dime for a ***drink***.(p.289)
• So I told dad that I would lick it on my own, that I would ***drink*** nothing for a month and after that only beer.(p.289)
• I definitely liked it, everything about it, the taste, the effects; and I realize now that a ***drink*** did something for me or to me that was different from the way it affected others.(p.305)
• My broken home and broken heart fanned my smoldering self-pity into a fair-sized bonfire and this kept me well supplied with reasons for having another ***drink***, and then another.(p.305)
• And still by the time I was thirty years old I was being pushed around with a compulsion to ***drink*** that was completely beyond my control.(p.305)
• I would hang on to sobriety for short intervals, but always there would come the tide of an overpowering necessity to ***drink*** and, as I was engulfed in it, I felt such a sense of panic that I really believed I would die if I didn't get that ***drink*** inside.(p.306)
• I could no longer gage my capacity and it might be the second or the tenth ***drink*** that would erase my consciousness.(p.306)
• It explained so much I had not understood about myself and, best of all, it promised recovery if I would do a few simple things and be willing to have the desire to ***drink*** removed.(p.309)
• I had to get a ***drink***, and then another ***drink***, and then . . .(p.319)
• And she would never, never take that morning ***drink***!(p.321)
• I was deathly sick every time I took a ***drink***.(p.322)
• The only way I knew to do it was to ***drink*** right along with him.(p.322)
• I always wanted to ***drink*** too much, so I was watchful, always watchful, counting my drinks.(p.322)
• And, unlike many others, I never took a ***drink*** in the morning.(p.323)
• I needed a ***drink***, but I was afraid to take a morning ***drink***, because I didn't want to be a drunk.(p.323)
• I became a drunk anyway, but I was scared to death to take that morning ***drink***.(p.323)
• I was accused of it many times when I went to play bridge in the afternoon, but I really never did take a morning ***drink***.(p.323)
• I never knew it was the first ***drink*** that did it.(p.324)
• I reached a stage where I couldn't go into my apartment without a ***drink***.(p.324)
• I'd get so fed up with drinking all alone and bearing the burden of guilt all by myself, that I'd egg him on to ***drink***, to get started again.(p.325)
• Safely pensioned, with no job to protect, at last he could ***drink*** as he pleased.(p.327)
• Although I did ***drink***, it always was with caution -- unless I was alone.(p.328)
• I believe that the release from people-pleasing restrictions gives retirees more motivation to ***drink*** than boredom does.(p.329)
• We're free at last to do our thing, to live uninhibited lives, to ***drink*** when and how and where we wish, when we want to and when we need to.(p.329)
• Well, at least I could ***drink*** myself to death.(p.333)
• Best that they not be found after I'd had my last ***drink*** on earth.(p.333)
• And I have not had a ***drink*** since that night.(p.334)
• I wanted him to be sure that I wasn't the one who was going to ***drink*** the whole bottle.(p.336)
• If I could only stop thinking, I wouldn't ***drink***.(p.337)
• And yet I had to have that ***drink***.(p.337)
• To me, taking a bath was just being in a place with a bottle where I could ***drink*** in privacy.(p.337)
• I had to have it with me at night, in case I woke up and needed that ***drink***.(p.337)
• If I didn't have a ***drink***, I had to do something.(p.339)
• As long as I worked, as long as I got out, I didn't ***drink***.(p.339)
• But I had to get back to that first ***drink*** somehow.(p.339)
• And when I took that first ***drink***, I was off on the usual merry-go-round.(p.339)
• Because I found that everything I turned to became a substitute for ***drink***.(p.339)
• And when all of life is a substitute for ***drink***, there's no happiness, no peace.(p.339)
• I still had to ***drink***; I still needed that ***drink***.(p.339)
• Mere cessation from drinking is not enough for an alcoholic while the need for that ***drink*** goes on.(p.339)
• It's either all work, or I ***drink***."(p.340)
• However, I am an alcoholic, so I always looked forward to the day when I would be able to ***drink*** again.(p.343)
• On the first, though on the water wagon, I looked forward to my next ***drink***.(p.344)
• On the second, I knew – as I know now – that if I remained away from the first ***drink***, then I had not to worry about the hundredth one.(p.344)
• And then we went up the side of a hill where we have a little barbecue area to make the fire for the barbecue, and on the way up, I thought to myself – I'll go back down to the kitchen and refill this ***drink***.(p.347)
• I had my first ***drink*** when I was fifteen and my alcoholic potential had ripened me to the point of necessary escapism.(p.353)
• My eventual goal was to ***drink*** myself to death.(p.353)
• It only became another excuse to ***drink***.(p.354)
• The more I drank, the worse it got and the more I had to ***drink***.(p.354)
• I'd managed to ***drink*** my way through all my friends.(p.355)
• And the only one who can take it away from me is me – by taking that first ***drink***.(p.355)
• I didn't particularly like it, but I loved the effects, and managed for the next twenty-five years to ***drink*** anything and everything, either handed to me or purchased, at the slightest excuse.(p.357)
• Time after time I would beg forgiveness on bended knees, with tears rolling down my cheeks, and promise I would never again ***drink*** too much.(p.362)
• I entered the house, opened a new bottle of whiskey and sat down to ***drink*** myself into the right frame of mind to get in my car, start the motor and close the garage door behind me.(p.363)
• I was told that someone would call on me shortly, to sit tight and not take another ***drink***.(p.363)
• I didn't take the ***drink***.(p.365)
• Later I told her I had not taken the ***drink*** and that I was all right.(p.365)
• I have had many more reasons to ***drink*** since I have been in A.A. than I had in all the years of my drinking.(p.367)
• We went out occasionally, and I would take a ***drink*** to ease the tensions of daily life.(p.370)
• I couldn't ***drink*** at home, because my husband frowned upon this.(p.370)
• But success brought increased social activities and I realized that many of my friends enjoyed a social ***drink*** with no apparent harm to themselves or others.(p.374)
• At first it was just that -- an occasional ***drink***.(p.374)
• Gradually the quantity increased, the occasions for a ***drink*** came more frequently; a hard day, worries and pressure, bad news, good news – there were more and more reasons for a ***drink***.(p.374)
• It was frightening that ***drink*** was being substituted for more and more of the things I really enjoyed doing.(p.374)
• Golf, hunting and fishing were now merely excuses to ***drink*** excessively.(p.375)
• The next steps were bottle hiding, and excuses for trips in order to ***drink*** without restraint.(p.375)
• ***Drink*** planning became more important than any other plans.(p.375)
• I continue to be surprised by the people I meet who say, "You haven't had a ***drink*** for a long time, have you?"(p.376)
• We think we can ***drink*** to excess without anyone knowing it.(p.376)
• Whenever we went out she appeared to go out of her way to keep me from having more than one ***drink***.(p.376)
• What alcoholic can be satisfied with one ***drink***?(p.377)
• After every cocktail party or dinner party she would say she couldn't understand how I could get in such a drunken stupor on one ***drink***.(p.377)
• After all, I hadn't started to ***drink*** early in life, so I had some stability and maturity to guide me for a while.(p.379)
• It didn't say I had to finally live on skid row and ***drink*** bay rum, canned heat or lemon extract.(p.379)
• It was a great relief to know I didn't have to ***drink*** any more.(p.379)
• The why is not important; the fact is that one ***drink*** will set up a reaction in our system which requires more; that one ***drink*** was too much and one hundred drinks were not enough.(p.380)
• It took me some time to realize that the Twelve Steps of A.A. were designed to help correct these defects of character and so help remove the obsession to ***drink***.(p.380)
• Get her something to ***drink***."(p.385)
• The servant he turned to was our old cook, and she liked to ***drink***.(p.385)
• Emma ran out to the kitchen and came back with a water glass full of bourbon and made me ***drink*** it down.(p.385)
• I had been reading a lot about psychiatry and I thought, "Maybe if I talk to a psychiatrist he can find out what is happening, and then I can ***drink*** like a lady."(p.387)
• I took two or three drinks so my eyes could focus, and I could see that horrible picture of the awful drunk on the first page; he couldn't get the ***drink*** to his mouth, he had a towel around his hand and he needed a shave.(p.391)
• In spite of knowing that my drunkenness was a symptom of the things that were wrong with me, and that I could never ***drink*** again, I thought I couldn't yet give it up, although I was going to try.(p.393)
• I displayed alcoholic tendencies actually from the age of fourteen, when I started to steal wine from the family jug, siphoning it off one ***drink*** at a time so it wouldn't be missed, not drinking it immediately, but saving it until about a pint was accumulated, so that I could get drunk.(p.397)
• Even at that age, I had learned that one ***drink*** was not enough.(p.397)
• But now, with His help and grace, this child of His has paid his initiation fee for good, as long as he remembers to stay away from that first ***drink*** (the one that does all the damage) one day at a time.(p.399)
• Before I started to ***drink*** seriously, I tried a couple of other escapes.(p.401)
• Up to this time it just hadn't occurred to me to ***drink***.(p.402)
• A ***drink*** never gave me a normal, pleasant glow.(p.402)
• Couldn't I ***drink*** less?(p.404)
• Now I hid when I wanted to ***drink***.(p.406)
• I drank alone or with someone, anyone who would stay and ***drink*** with me.(p.406)
• How could anybody forget a ***drink***?(p.407)
• I must ***drink*** less, I would tell myself.(p.408)
• ***Drink*** only beer or wine.(p.408)
• I went to bars alone to ***drink***.(p.410)
• I could not live on that tiny trust fund and still ***drink*** all I wanted to.(p.411)
• I did not resort to semi-prostitution for the price of a ***drink***.(p.412)
• She too had gone to cheap bars to ***drink***.(p.414)
• I thought it was my duty to keep her from drinking, not knowing that if the other fellow is really determined to ***drink*** there is nothing you can do about it.(p.415)
• A.A. taught me how not to ***drink***.(p.416)
• Awarded a scholarship to a famous old Eastern college, I began to ***drink*** at the end of my freshman year, and by junior year, I had to transfer to an easier state university to keep my grades up.(p.419)
• I remembered having had a little ***drink*** of whiskey with a can of warm beer as a chaser.(p.422)
• I smoked as much, tried to ***drink*** as much, and do everything they did, only more so.(p.423)
• All I'd wanted was one more ***drink***.(p.428)
• I would ***drink*** all night in bars, come home about five a.m., down a good big glass of whiskey straight, and tumble into bed.(p.428)
• Well, I'm willing, if it will curb this awful desire to ***drink***, this fear of not having a ***drink***, this feeling of always being alone, scared, deserted, sick.(p.430)
• I'm twenty-six now and I haven't had a ***drink*** since I made my decision.(p.430)
• In all the twenty-five years of my drinking there were only a few occasions when I took a morning ***drink***.(p.432)
• My wife loved to ***drink***, and we tied on many a hooter in the name of marital bliss.(p.433)
• "You've got to space your drinks and take plenty of water in between," or "coat the stomach with a little olive oil," or "***drink*** anything but those damn martinis."(p.433)
• That was seven years ago -- and many A.A. meetings ago – and I haven't had a ***drink*** during those seven years.(p.437)
• "If you had my problems, you'd ***drink***, too" was my feeling.(p.439)
• "If you had my wife, you'd ***drink***, too."(p.439)

- I cried a bit and then mixed me another ***drink***.(p.440)
- I had begun to ***drink*** in the early years of pharmacy school, in order to get to sleep.(p.440)
- Then I found the solution: At the end of study time, I would ***drink*** two beers, jump in bed, sleep real fast, and wake up smart.(p.440)
- "If you had my responsibilities, if you needed the sleep like I do, you'd ***drink*** too."(p.441)
- So I'd sit up, watch old Wallace Beery movies on all-night TV, and ***drink***.(p.441)
- The longer the drinking continued, the shorter the time the alcohol would keep me asleep; I would have to ***drink*** myself back to sleep again and again throughout the night.(p.441)
- If it was one minute before five, I'd ***drink*** myself back to sleep.(p.441)
- Both times, my reaction was that I had had nothing to ***drink*** the night before, so obviously alcohol had nothing to do with it.(p.444)
- Max accepted responsibility for me after I had promised never to ***drink*** again, never to take another pill, never to swear again, and never to talk to girls again.(p.444)
- We got on the plane and immediately had a big fight over whether I'd ***drink*** the free booze.(p.444)
- Max won; I didn't ***drink*** it.(p.444)
- When a big, healthy-looking young fellow stood up there and said, "I'm a success today if I don't ***drink*** today," I thought, "Man, I've got a thousand things to do today before I can brag about not taking a ***drink***, for God's sake!"(p.447)
- (Today, there is absolutely nothing in the world more important to me than my keeping this alcoholic sober; not taking a ***drink*** is by far the most important thing I do each day.)(p.447)
- And I knew that giving up "one ***drink*** for one day" wouldn't really do any good.(p.448)
- When the compulsion to ***drink*** left, it was relatively easy to stay off alcohol.(p.448)
- From that moment on, I have not had a single compulsion to ***drink***.(p.449)
- For me, as for most alcoholics, it was "Eat, ***drink***, and be merry, for tomorrow you die."(p.457)
- But with the first ***drink***, our good intentions dissolved; our personalities changed.(p.458)
- There, I received several soda crackers and water daily, and before I could have my third-day meal (again the only meal in ten days), I had to ***drink*** a glass of castor oil or mineral oil, depending on the cruelty of the person who was doing the dispensing.(p.459)
- I suddenly remembered one of my first A.A. meetings, where I heard, "If you are an alcoholic and if you continue to ***drink***, the end is death or insanity."(p.461)
- I count my sobriety date from the day I began going to A.A. in prison, not from the date of my last ***drink***.(p.462)
- I thought I would be quite happy and never would I ***drink*** too much again.(p.465)
- In fact, sometimes they served as good excuses to ***drink*** more, to forget.(p.465)
- My pattern of drinking at that time had reached the point where once I really started, I would retire to my bed and ***drink*** myself into oblivion.(p.466)
- I had decided I was no good – never would be any good, and the sooner I could ***drink*** myself out of this life, the better.(p.468)
- In other words, the kindest doctor in the whole world, and I had one such, couldn't help me because I always felt, "You can't know about me – you can't possibly know – you don't even ***drink***!"(p.471)
- That was over seven years ago, and thank God and A.A., I haven't had a ***drink*** since.(p.473)
- Had first ***drink*** in young teens, but was scared of my father.(p.474)
- So didn't ***drink*** much then.(p.474)
- Now think I was alcoholic from first ***drink***.(p.474)
- That night we ***drink*** beer at taverns.(p.474)
- Soon I ***drink*** beer.(p.475)
- Then I ***drink*** again, but more miserable.(p.475)
- Last time I ***drink***, I go to room.(p.475)
- Have not take ***drink*** since.(p.476)
- I hear men say, "One day not ***drink***.(p.476)
- They say call friend before I buy ***drink***.(p.476)
- Have not ***drink*** since.(p.476)
- Some of us always remember our big mouths when it comes to a ***drink***, but somewhere along the line, we seem to have forgotten about taking care of our teeth.(p.479)
- We are so beautiful that it is never too much trouble to get some poor stranger to buy us a ***drink***.(p.479)
- This was the only period when I didn't ***drink***, but that was hardly any consolation.(p.480)
- The only time that I have ever seen my mother take anything alcoholic was around Christmas time, when she would ***drink*** some eggnog or light wine.(p.484)
- I don't think I actually started to ***drink*** pathologically until approximately 1935.(p.487)
- I actually wanted a ***drink***, besides feeling that I had to have a ***drink***.(p.488)
- I started inquiring where I could get a ***drink*** and, of course, I found that it wasn't hard.(p.490)
- I continued to ***drink***.(p.490)
- Nevertheless, we continued to work together and I continued to ***drink***, but I guess, deep down within her heart as well as within mine, we both knew I couldn't stop drinking.(p.490)
- But there happened to be a liquor store between the post office and the mill, and I stopped to get that one ***drink***.(p.493)
- I knew my wife didn't because I had been sincere in all my promises to her as well as to my mother and to my close friends, but the urge to take that ***drink*** was more powerful than anything else.(p.494)
- "Freshman," said he to me, "do you ever take a ***drink***?"(p.497)
- I had never had a ***drink***, but I had seen enough merriment in the boys who were drinking to be interested.(p.498)
- I'd ***drink*** like a gentleman after this.(p.498)
- The atmosphere of "eat, ***drink***, and be merry" prevails and I absorb it.(p.499)
- I ***drink*** a lot every night.(p.499)
- A ***drink***?(p.500)
- A little ***drink*** will put me on my feet.(p.500)
- "Have a ***drink***?" I ask.(p.501)
- I ***drink*** and go to bed; I take a few the next morning and go see my mother once more.(p.501)
- I ***drink*** steadily, I come to at three in the morning.(p.501)
- I wander to a stable and ***drink*** five bottles of beer.(p.502)
- I might go out West on a ranch where I couldn't get anything to ***drink***.(p.502)
- "There are men on the streets of New York today who were worse than you, and they don't ***drink*** any more."(p.503)
- Am I willing to be honest with myself about myself and tell someone about myself, and am I willing to think of other people, of their needs instead of myself, in order to get rid of the ***drink*** problem?(p.503)
- Maybe a ***drink*** -- I put on my hat and dash off in the car.(p.505)
- I have forgotten about a ***drink***.(p.505)
- I shall not ***drink*** until I get back to the apartment.(p.506)
- If something does come along that sort of upsets me, instead of walking in and throwing a buck at the barman and asking for a ***drink***, I walk into a telephone booth, drop a dime in the box, and call somebody who was so kind as to give me his name and telephone number to meet such an emergency.(p.511)
- That and the morning ***drink*** came very early in my drinking career.(p.513)
- But at the end of nine months we went to a party one night, and I took the first ***drink***.(p.514)
- No one had ever told me it was the first ***drink*** that did the damage.(p.514)
- But I've never come close to that first ***drink***.(p.516)
- At first, like everybody else, I could keep control when I drank, but if I did start to ***drink***, even in those days, I was always one of the last to leave the party.(p.518)
- It didn't worry me very much, because at that time I could shut off for a couple of months without taking a ***drink*** or even wanting one, and without feeling that I was giving anything up.(p.518)
- India lent itself to drinking then, if you were disposed to ***drink***, because you lived in bungalows; you didn't live all together as you do at home in an Officer's Mess.(p.519)
- I stopped off just to have one ***drink*** to see if it tasted the same on the way back to London, and that night I was carried back to bed again.(p.522)
- I had been using paraldehyde more or less like ordinary ***drink*** for the last six years though, occasionally, I'd bounce back to phenobarbital and things like that.(p.524)
- I suppose I had reached my spiritual gutter that night, but I have never had what you could call a real urge to ***drink*** again.(p.524)
- I always blamed my drinking on being poor, or on anything other than the truth – that I liked what booze did for me, that when I had a ***drink*** I was as big and had as much as the next person.(p.526)
- Then it got to the place I couldn't ***drink*** without getting in jail.(p.526)
- I couldn't wait until the meeting was over to get a ***drink***.(p.526)
- I was afraid to ***drink*** before the meeting.(p.526)
- Oh, I might ***drink*** too much at times -- everyone I knew drank.(p.527)
- I have been home for a year, and have not taken a ***drink*** in four years.(p.529)
- I remember the day when I decided to ***drink*** myself to death quietly, without bothering anyone, because I was tired of having been a dependable, trustworthy person for about thirty-nine years without having received what I thought was a proper reward for my virtue.(p.531)
- I know there are some alcoholics who seem terribly, terribly grown-up, but I think that they are trying to make themselves think they are grown-up, and the strain of their effort is what is causing them to ***drink*** -- a sense of inadequacy, a childish vanity to be the most popular, the most sought after, the mostest of the most.(p.535)
- But not for long; now, for five Friday nights in a row, I went to jail, picked up sodden with beer (which I always disliked, but which was the only ***drink*** available); in jail five consecutive Friday nights in the town where I had grown up, where I had been an honor student in high school, where a kindly uncle, bailing me out, said, "Bob, our family just doesn't do this sort of thing."(p.539)
- From that instant to this, nearly eight years later, I have not had the slightest urge to ***drink***.(p.541)
- I have not had a ***drink*** of anything alcoholic since that ten-day binge.(p.541)
- The mental twists that led up to my drinking began many years before I ever took a ***drink*** for I am one of those whose history proves conclusively that my drinking was "a symptom of a deeper trouble."(p.544)
- The amount of will power exercised to control my drinking during working hours, diverted into a constructive channel, would have made me President, and the thing that made the will power possible was the knowledge that as soon as my day was finished I could ***drink*** myself into oblivion.(p.548)
- The only reality I was able to face had been forced upon me by its very repetition – I had to ***drink***; and I didn't know there was anything in the world that could be done about it.(p.548)
- I was drunk for sixty days around the clock and it was my intention, literally, to ***drink*** myself to death.(p.549)
- I attended my first A.A. meeting eight years ago, and it is with deep gratitude that I'm able to say I've not had a ***drink*** since that time, and that I take no sedation or narcotics, for this program is to me one of complete sobriety and I no longer need to escape reality.(p.549)
- The A.A. members who sponsored me told me in the beginning that I would not only find a way to live without having a ***drink***, but that I would find a way to live without wanting to ***drink***, if I would do these simple things.(p.550)
- I believe this, and I believe too that it is equally impossible to practice these principles to the best of our ability, a day at a time, and still ***drink***, for I don't think the two things are compatible.(p.550)
- After my very first ***drink*** -- a tiny glass of sherry my father gave me to celebrate the New Year when I was thirteen -- I went up to bed, dizzy with exhilaration and excitement, and I prayed I wouldn't ***drink*** any more!(p.554)
- I also began to ***drink*** at fraternity parties and beer busts.(p.555)
- To cure my dreadful hangovers, I discovered the morning ***drink***.(p.556)
- And yet my ability to lie outwardly and to kid myself inwardly grew with every ***drink*** I took.(p.556)
- Indeed, I had to ***drink*** now to live, to cope with the demands of everyday existence.(p.556)
- When I encountered disappointments or frustrations -- as I did more and more frequently -- my solution was to ***drink***.(p.556)
- I remember being dragged, ***drink*** in hand, from beneath the grand piano, where I had hidden, to be locked in my room in disgrace.(p.557)
- So the need to ***drink*** grew still greater.(p.557)
- At first, just one ***drink***, on occasion.(p.557)
- I had to ***drink***.(p.558)
- The doctors told me that if I ever took another ***drink***, it might be my last.(p.558)
- I acquired a sponsor and began attending meetings, but continued to ***drink***.(p.559)
- In my mind's eye, I played and replayed scenes in which I was plucked magically from the bar where I stood nursing a ***drink***, and was instantly exalted to some position of power and prestige.(p.560)

• They know that they must never *drink*.(p.572)

drinker

• We believe, and so suggested a few years ago, that the action of alcohol on these chronic alcoholics is a manifestation of an allergy; that the phenomenon of craving is limited to this class and never occurs in the average temperate *drinker*.(p.xxvi)
• But the ex-problem *drinker* who has found this solution, who is properly armed with facts about himself, can generally win the entire confidence of another alcoholic in a few hours.(p.18)
• Then we have a certain type of hard *drinker*.(p.20)
• He may start off as a moderate *drinker*; he may or may not become a continuous hard *drinker*, but at some stage of his drinking career he begins to lose all control of his liquor consumption, once he starts to drink.(p.21)
• The idea that somehow, someday he will control and enjoy his drinking is the great obsession of every abnormal *drinker*.(p.30)
• Physicians who are familiar with alcoholism agree there is no such thing as making a normal *drinker* out of an alcoholic.(p.31)
• We would not even do the cause of temperate drinking any good, for not one *drinker* in a thousand likes to be told anything about alcohol by one who hates it.(p.103)
• One: Your husband may be only a heavy *drinker*.(p.108)
• Meanwhile you might try to help the wife of another serious *drinker*.(p.112)
• If your husband is a *drinker*, you probably worry over what other people are thinking and you hate to meet your friends.(p.114)
• Then that terrible tension which grips the home of every problem *drinker* will be lessened.(p.115)
• Seeing is believing to most families who have lived with a *drinker*.(p.135)
• Here is a case in point: One of our friends is a heavy smoker and coffee *drinker*.(p.135)
• Whether you are a hard *drinker*, a moderated *drinker* or a teetotaler, you may have some pretty strong opinions, perhaps prejudices.(p.139)
• As a moderate *drinker*, you can take your liquor or leave it alone.(p.139)
• What our friend, the vice president, had in mind was the habitual or whoopee *drinker*.(p.149)
• Now and then a serious *drinker*, being dry at the moment says, "I don't miss it at all.(p.151)
• When he left, I realized from his story that as a *drinker* I was just a panty-waist.(p.208)
• I became a constant *drinker* with a terrific fight to control the amount of my consumption each day.(p.214)
• She had a hairdresser who used to tell her about a brother-in-law who had been quite a *drinker* and about some doctor in Akron who had straightened him out.(p.216)
• THE EUROPEAN *DRINKER*(p.230)
• I became a periodic *drinker*.(p.233)
• I was never a very heavy social *drinker*.(p.335)
• This secret *drinker* favored the local Laundromat as a watering hole.(p.369)
• Dad's image for me was that of a big Irish oilman who came up through the school of hard knocks and so had to be a two-fisted *drinker*.(p.369)
• At fifteen I was strictly a beer *drinker*.(p.423)
• I was becoming a solitary *drinker*, but I didn't care.(p.426)
• I'd packed more drinking into seven years than many a heavy *drinker* does in a lifetime.(p.429)
• The line between a heavy *drinker* and an alcoholic is not always clear.(p.436)
• But I never became a morning *drinker*.(p.441)
• In fact it has been only within the last fifteen years that I changed from a fairly normal, controlled *drinker* into an alcoholic.(p.464)
• I don't mean that I went to bed one night a normal *drinker*, and awoke the next morning an alcoholic.(p.464)
• There at the top of the folder was my name, age and address, and underneath were the words, "Periodic *Drinker*."(p.470)
• I had been promoted from a periodic *drinker* to a chronic alcoholic!(p.470)
• Her brother had been a *drinker* and had died in a State Hospital for the insane.(p.498)
• In my own generation I stuck out, I can see that now, as being a very much heavier *drinker* than the average man.(p.518)
• I never was a "secret" *drinker*, and I never kept a bottle at home.(p.536)
• By age twenty-two, I was a daily *drinker*.(p.555)

drinker's

• The *drinker's* mind is full of uncertainties and insecurities.(p.331)
• From that point on, it's just the average *drinker's* story.(p.488)

drinkers

• But as ex-problem *drinkers*, we can say that his explanation makes good sense.(p.xxiv)
• *Drinkers* are like that.(p.9)
• Our very lives, as ex-problem *drinkers*, depend upon our constant thought of others and how we may help meet their needs.(p.20)
• Now these are commonplace observations on *drinkers* which we hear all the time.(p.20)
• Moderate *drinkers* have little trouble in giving up liquor entirely if they have good reason for it.(p.20)
• Some *drinkers* have excuses with which they are satisfied part of the time.(p.23)
• In a vague way their families and friends sense that these *drinkers* are abnormal, but everybody hopefully awaits the day when the sufferer will rouse himself from his lethargy and assert his power of will.(p.23)
• Certain *drinkers*, who would be greatly insulted if called alcoholics, are astonished at their inability to stop.(p.33)
• In the early days of our drinking we occasionally remained sober for a year or more, becoming serious *drinkers* again later.(p.34)
• Perhaps you are not acquainted with any *drinkers* who want to recover.(p.89)
• *Drinkers* will not stand for it.(p.103)
• *Drinkers* like to help other *drinkers*.(p.112)
• Normal *drinkers* are not so affected, nor can they understand the aberrations of the alcoholic.(p.140)
• They often jeopardize their own positions by trying to help serious *drinkers* who should have been fired long ago, or else given an opportunity to get well.(p.147)
• Unhappy *drinkers* who read this page will understand!(p.151)
• As ex-problem *drinkers*, we smile at such a sally.(p.151)
• Our hope is that when this chip of a book is launched on the world tide of alcoholism, defeated *drinkers* will seize upon it, to follow its suggestions.(p.153)
• I seemed to be able to snap back the next morning better than most of my fellow *drinkers*, who were cursed (or perhaps blessed) with a great deal of morning-after nausea.(p.172)
• My fellow-workers were mostly good Saturday night *drinkers* and I was right with them.(p.252)
• He introduced himself and began to tell me about a bunch of some sixty former *drinkers* and drunkards who met once a week, and he invited me to go with him to the next meeting.(p.257)
• Some of them I had known for years, good two-fisted *drinkers* who had disappeared from their former haunts.(p.258)
• We were the most congenial *drinkers* you ever saw.(p.264)
• He may even read in a newspaper that one out of every seven *drinkers* will become alcoholic, but he rarely is told that it holds true for all ages -- or that the tolerance to alcohol (and other drugs) decreases steadily, year after year, in the bodies of all persons.(p.330)
• But at this time, I began gravitating toward the really hard *drinkers*, hanging around with them more and more.(p.404)
• Didn't I come from a family of *drinkers*?(p.427)

drinking

• If you have a *drinking* problem, we hope that you may pause in reading one of the forty-four personal stories and think: "Yes, that happened to me"; or, more important, "Yes, I've felt like that"; or most important, "Yes, I believe this program can work for me, too."(p.xii)
• The only requirement for membership is an honest desire to stop *drinking*.(p.xiv)
• The broker had gone to Akron on a business venture which had collapsed, leaving him greatly in fear that he might start *drinking* again.(p.xvi)
• It did not satisfy us to be told that we could not control our *drinking* just because we were maladjusted to life, that we were in full flight from reality, or were outright mental defectives.(p.xxiv)
• These men were not *drinking* to escape; they were *drinking* to overcome a craving beyond their mental control.(p.xxviii)
• He plans various ways of *drinking*.(p.xxviii)
• All these, and many others, have one symptom in common: they cannot start *drinking* without developing the phenomenon of craving.(p.xxviii)
• "Here lies a Hampshire Grenadier Who caught his death *Drinking* cold small beer.(p.1)
• Though my *drinking* was not yet continuous, it disturbed my wife.(p.2)
• My *drinking* assumed more serious proportions, continuing all day and almost every night.(p.3)
• Golf permitted *drinking* every day and every night.(p.3)
• But *drinking* caught up with me again and my generous friend had to let me go.(p.4)
• Next day found me *drinking* both gin and sedative.(p.7)
• I could eat little or nothing when *drinking*, and I was forty pounds under weight.(p.7)
• Near the end of that bleak November, I sat *drinking* in my kitchen.(p.8)
• We feel that elimination of our *drinking* is but a beginning.(p.19)
• This should suggest a useful program for anyone concerned with a *drinking* problem.(p.19)
• You may already have asked yourself why it is that all of us became so very ill from *drinking*.(p.20)
• He may start off as a moderate drinker; he may or may not become a continuous hard drinker; but at some stage of his *drinking* career he begins to lose all control of his liquor consumption, once he starts to drink.(p.21)
• He does absurd, incredible, tragic things while *drinking*.(p.21)
• His disposition while *drinking* resembles his normal nature but little.(p.21)
• Sometimes these excuses have a certain plausibility, but none of them really makes sense in the light of the havoc an alcoholic's *drinking* bout creates.(p.23)
• At a certain point in the *drinking* of every alcoholic, he passes into a state where the most powerful desire to stop *drinking* is of absolutely no avail.(p.24)
• Therefore, it is not surprising that our *drinking* careers have been characterized by countless vain attempts to prove we could drink like other people.(p.30)
• The idea that somehow, someday he will control and enjoy his *drinking* is the great obsession of every abnormal drinker.(p.30)
• We alcoholics are men and women who have lost the ability to control our *drinking*.(p.30)
• If anyone who is showing inability to control his *drinking* can do the right-about-face and drink like a gentleman, our hats are off to him.(p.31)
• Here are some of the methods we have tried: *Drinking* beer only, limiting the number of drinks, never *drinking* alone, never *drinking* in the morning, *drinking* only at home, never having it in the house, never *drinking* during business hours, *drinking* only at parties, switching from scotch to brandy, *drinking* only natural wines, agreeing to resign if ever drunk on the job, taking a trip, not taking a trip, swearing off forever (with and without a solemn oath), taking more physical exercise, reading inspirational books, going to health farms and sanitariums, accepting voluntary commitment to asylums -- we could increase the list ad infinitum.(p.31)
• Step over to the nearest barroom and try some controlled *drinking*.(p.31)
• Though there is no way of proving it, we believe that early in our *drinking* careers most of us could have stopped *drinking*.(p.32)
• A man of thirty was doing a great deal of spree *drinking*.(p.32)
• He tried to regulate his *drinking* for a while, making several trips to the hospital meantime.(p.32)
• If we are planning to stop *drinking*, there must be no reservation of any kind, nor any lurking notion that someday we will be immune to alcohol.(p.33)
• Several of our crowd, men of thirty or less, had been *drinking* only a few years, but they found themselves as helpless as those who had been *drinking* twenty years.(p.33)
• As we look back, we feel we had gone on *drinking* many years beyond the point where we could quit on our will power.(p.34)
• In the early days of our *drinking* we occasionally remained sober for a year or more, becoming serious drinkers again later.(p.34)
• So we shall describe some of the mental states that precede a relapse into *drinking*, for obviously this is the crux of the problem.(p.35)
• He did no *drinking* until he was thirty-five.(p.35)
• His family was re-assembled, and he began to work as a salesman for the business he had lost through *drinking*.(p.35)
• I had no intention of *drinking*.(p.36)
• Still no thought of *drinking*.(p.36)
• Here was the threat of commitment, the loss of family and position, to say nothing of that intense mental

and physical suffering which *drinking* always caused him.(p.36)
• Yet all reasons for not *drinking* were easily pushed aside in favor of the foolish idea that he could take whiskey if only he mixed it with milk!(p.36)
• We have not lost everything in life through *drinking* and we certainly do not intend to.(p.38)
• That may be true of certain nonalcoholic people who, though *drinking* foolishly and heavily at the present time, are able to stop or moderate, because their brains and bodies have not been damaged as ours were.(p.39)
• But the actual or potential alcoholic, with hardly an exception, will be absolutely unable to stop *drinking* on the basis of self-knowledge.(p.39)
• He made up his mind to quit *drinking* altogether.(p.39)
• The story he told is most instructive, for here was a chap absolutely convinced he had to stop *drinking*, who had no excuse for *drinking*, who exhibited splendid judgment and determination in all his other concerns, yet was flat on his back nevertheless.(p.40)
• She committed her husband for *drinking*.(p.65)
• Threatens to fire me for *drinking* and padding my expense account.(p.65)
• The best reason first: If we skip this vital step, we may not overcome *drinking*.(p.72)
• He is under constant fear and tension – that makes for more *drinking*.(p.73)
• Simply we tell him that we will never get over *drinking* until we have done our utmost to straighten out the past.(p.77)
• Telling them what we are trying to do, we make no bones about our *drinking*; they usually know it anyway, whether we think so or not.(p.78)
• Our *drinking* has made us slow to pay.(p.78)
• Because of resentment and *drinking*, he had not paid alimony to his first wife.(p.79)
• While *drinking*, he accepted a sum of money from a bitterly-hated business rival, giving him no receipt for it.(p.80)
• He saw that he had to place the outcome in God's hands or he would soon start *drinking* again, and all would be lost anyhow.(p.80)
• But *drinking* does complicate sex relations in the home.(p.81)
• Practical experience shows that nothing will so much insure immunity from *drinking* as intensive work with other alcoholics.(p.89)
• Ministers and doctors are competent and you can learn much from them if you wish, but it happens that because of your own *drinking* experience you can be uniquely useful to other alcoholics.(p.89)
• If he does not want to stop *drinking*, don't waste time trying to persuade him.(p.90)
• They should wait for the end of his next *drinking* bout.(p.90)
• After a while, turn the talk to some phase of *drinking*.(p.91)
• Tell him enough about your *drinking* habits, symptoms, and experiences to encourage him to speak of himself.(p.91)
• If he is not communicative, give him a sketch of your *drinking* career up to the time you quit.(p.91)
• When he sees you know all about the *drinking* game, commence to describe yourself as an alcoholic.(p.91)
• If he sticks to the ideas that he can still control his *drinking*, tell him that possibly he can -- if he is not too alcoholic.(p.92)
• Some of us have taken very hard knocks to learn this truth: Job or no job – wife or no wife -- we simply do not stop *drinking* so long as we place dependence upon other people ahead of dependence on God.(p.98)
• People have said we must not go where liquor is served; we must not have it in our homes; we must shun friends who drink; we must avoid moving pictures which show *drinking* scenes; we must not go into bars; our friends must hide their bottles if we go to their houses; we mustn't think or be reminded about alcohol at all.(p.100)
• So our rule is not to avoid a place where there is *drinking*, if we have a legitimate reason for being there.(p.101)
• Why sit with a long face in places where there is *drinking*, sighing about the good old days.(p.102)
• While you were *drinking*, you were withdrawing from life little by little.(p.102)
• We are careful never to show intolerance or hatred of *drinking* as an institution.(p.103)
• We would not even do the cause of temperate *drinking* any good, for not one drinker in a thousand likes to be told anything about alcohol by one who hates it.(p.103)
• Our men have sworn great solemn oaths that they were through *drinking* forever.(p.105)
• When *drinking*, they were strangers.(p.107)
• Especially when he has before him a way to stop his *drinking* and abuse if he really wants to pay the price.(p.108)
• His *drinking* may be constant or it may be heavy only on certain occasions.(p.109)
• He is positive he can handle his liquor, that it does him no harm, that *drinking* is necessary in his business.(p.109)
• He often gets entirely out of hand when *drinking*.(p.109)
• He is remorseful after serious *drinking* bouts and tells you he wants to stop.(p.109)
• He enjoys *drinking*.(p.110)
• Perhaps you enjoy *drinking* with him yourself when he doesn't go too far.(p.110)
• You have passed happy evenings together chatting and *drinking* before your fire.(p.110)
• Our next thought is that you should never tell him what he must do about his *drinking*.(p.111)
• Be determined that your husband's *drinking* is not going to spoil your relations with your children or your friends.(p.111)
• But after his next binge, ask him if he would really like to get over *drinking* for good.(p.112)
• But don't remind him of this after he has been *drinking*, for he may be angry.(p.113)
• You avoid the subject of *drinking*, even with your own parents.(p.114)
• Unless they actually need protection from their father, it is best not to take sides in any argument he has with them while *drinking*.(p.115)
• It may convince your husband he wants to stop *drinking* forever.(p.116)
• We thought, on the whole, we were pretty good women, capable of being nicer if our husbands stopped *drinking*.(p.116)
• It is probably true that you and your husband have been living too much alone, for *drinking* many times isolates the wife of an alcoholic.(p.119)
• If you are satisfied he really wants to get over *drinking*, you need not be alarmed.(p.120)
• Cessation of *drinking* is but the first step away from a highly strained, abnormal condition.(p.122)
• Now and then the family will be plagued by spectres from the past, for the *drinking* career of almost every alcoholic has been marked by escapades, funny, humiliating, shameful or tragic.(p.123)
• Let them remember that his *drinking* wrought all kinds of damage that may take long to repair.(p.127)
• Dad may feel that for years his *drinking* has placed him on the wrong side of every argument, but now he has become a superior person with God on his side.(p.129)
• Even when he wanted to assert himself he could not, for his *drinking* placed him constantly in the wrong.(p.130)
• *Drinking* isolates most homes from the outside world.(p.131)
• We, who have recovered from serious *drinking*, are miracles of mental health.(p.133)
• Couples are occasionally dismayed to find that when *drinking* is stopped the man tends to be impotent.(p.134)
• Their young minds were impressionable while he was *drinking*.(p.134)
• After two weeks of *drinking*, he had placed his toe on the trigger of a loaded shotgun -- the barrel in his mouth.(p.137)
• I had discharged him for *drinking* six weeks before.(p.137)
• I had been obliged to discharge him for *drinking*, though he was brilliant, alert, and one of the best organizers I have ever known.(p.137)
• But I'm sure this man is done *drinking*.(p.138)
• If you desire to help it might be well to disregard your own *drinking*, or lack of it.(p.139)
• *Drinking* occasionally, and understanding your own reactions, it is possible for you to become quite sure of many things which, so far as the alcoholic is concerned, are not always so.(p.139)
• Whenever you want to, you control your *drinking*.(p.139)
• When *drinking*, or getting over a bout, an alcoholic, sometimes the model of honesty when normal, will do incredible things.(p.140)
• This is not to say that all alcoholics are honest and upright when not *drinking*.(p.141)
• He wants to quit *drinking* and you want to help him, even if it be only a matter of good business.(p.141)
• State that you know about his *drinking*, and that it must stop.(p.141)
• Will he take every necessary step, submit to anything to get well, to stop *drinking* forever?(p.142)
• For most alcoholics who are *drinking*, or who are just getting over a spree, a certain amount of physical treatment is desirable, even imperative.(p.142)
• To get over *drinking* will require a transformation of thought and attitude.(p.143)
• But sometimes our *drinking* will be used politically.(p.145)
• One instance comes to mind in which a malicious individual was always making friendly little jokes about an alcoholic's *drinking* exploits.(p.145)
• After your man has gone along without *drinking* for a few months, you may be able to make use of his services with other employees who are giving you the alcoholic run-around -- provided, of course, they are willing to have a third party in the picture.(p.146)
• Do you want to stop *drinking* or not?(p.147)
• But if you cannot or will not stop *drinking*, I think you ought to resign."(p.148)
• He remarked: "I'm mighty glad you fellows got over your *drinking*.(p.148)
• For most normal folks, *drinking* means conviviality, companionship and colorful imagination.(p.151)
• But not so with us in those last days of heavy *drinking*.(p.151)
• When our friend related his experience, the man agreed that no amount of will power he might muster could stop his *drinking* for long.(p.155)
• He had, of course, the familiar alcoholic obsession that few knew of his *drinking*.(p.155)
• He found himself surprisingly well received, and learned that many knew of his *drinking*.(p.156)
• As we shall see, he now means a great deal to his community, and the major liabilities of thirty years of hard *drinking* have been repaired in four.(p.156)
• Goes off his head completely when he's *drinking*.(p.156)
• For an hour, the two friends told him about their *drinking* experiences.(p.157)
• He proved to be a devil-may-care young fellow whose parents could not make out whether he wanted to stop *drinking* or not.(p.158)
• Those who believe their *drinking* to be hopeless may again find hope in these thirteen impressive tales.(p.167)
• After high school came four years in one of the best colleges in the country where *drinking* seemed to be a major extra-curricular activity.(p.172)
• I was graduated "summa cum laude" in the eyes of the *drinking* fraternity, but not in the eyes of the Dean.(p.172)
• There I took up the business of *drinking* with much greater earnestness than I had previously shown.(p.173)
• On account of my enormous capacity for beer, I was elected to membership in one of the *drinking* societies, and soon became one of the leading spirits.(p.173)
• This went from bad to worse until Sophomore spring when, after a prolonged period of *drinking*, I made up my mind that I could not complete my course, so I packed my grip and went South to spend a month on a large farm owned by a friend of mine.(p.173)
• There my *drinking* became so much worse that the boys in the fraternity house where I lived felt forced to send for my father, who made a long journey in the vain endeavor to get me straightened around.(p.174)
• This had little effect however for I kept on *drinking* and used a great deal more hard liquor than in former years.(p.174)
• Therefore it would make no great difference, even if I should do some *drinking*.(p.175)
• During the subsequent fifteen years I had sense enough never to go to the hospital if I had been *drinking*, and very seldom did I receive patients.(p.176)
• It was not long before I was *drinking* at least a case and a half a day.(p.177)
• I had a couple of shorter talks with this man afterward, and stopped *drinking* abruptly.(p.179)
• But this was a man who had experienced many years of frightful *drinking*, who had had most all the drunkard's experiences known to man, but who had been cured by the very means I had been trying to employ, that is to say the spiritual approach.(p.180)
• But if you really and truly want to quit *drinking* liquor for good and all, and sincerely feel that you must have some help, we know that we have an answer for you.(p.181)
• My marriage was happy and, as I have said, I never had any of the reasons, conscious or unconscious, which are often given for *drinking*.(p.182)
• Before my *drinking* had cut me down completely, I

achieved a considerable measure of success, having been a City Councilman for five years and a financial director of Kenmore, a suburb later taken into the city itself.(p.182)
• But, of course, this all went up the spout with my increased ***drinking***.(p.182)
• This was no fault of my father or mother, as they were both very much opposed to ***drinking***.(p.182)
• I remember that my father kept whiskey around the house for medical purposes and entertainment, and I would drink from this when no one was about and then water it to keep my parents from knowing I was ***drinking***.(p.183)
• It did help to certain extent, since I got in places where I could not obtain anything to drink, and so broke the habitual ***drinking***.(p.183)
• As time went on my ***drinking*** became progressively worse.(p.184)
• She told me that she had been talking to a couple of fellows about ***drinking***.(p.184)
• Then she told me that these two drunks she had been talking to had a plan whereby they thought they could quit ***drinking***, and part of that plan was that they tell it to another drunk.(p.185)
• Before very long we began to relate some incidents of our ***drinking*** and, naturally, pretty soon, I realized both of them knew what they were talking about because you can see things and smell things when you're drunk, that you can't other times, and, if I had thought they didn't know what they were talking about, I wouldn't have been willing to talk to them at all.(p.185)
• They said to me, "Do you want to quit ***drinking***?(p.186)
• It's none of our business about your ***drinking***.(p.186)
• I thought of what liquor had done to me, the opportunities that I had discarded, the abilities that had been given me and how I had wasted them, and I finally came to the conclusion, that if I didn't want to quit, I certainly ought to want to, and that I was willing to do anything in the world to stop ***drinking***.(p.186)
• Every time I'd start thinking about ***drinking***, I would think of the long, dry years ahead without having a drink; but this idea of twenty-four hours, that it was up to me from then on, was a lot of help.(p.188)
• I remember telling them too that it was going to be awfully tough, because I did some other things, smoked cigarettes and played penny ante poker, sometimes bet on the horse races and they said, "Don't you think you're having more trouble with this ***drinking*** than with anything else at the present time?(p.190)
• Blackout ***drinking*** at once.(p.195)
• I had no pleasure out of the ***drinking*** at all.(p.195)
• This was six or eight months after the last ***drinking*** episode.(p.196)
• I felt having gotten married, I was an adult and one of the first things I did was to buy two cases of whiskey with no idea of ***drinking*** it.(p.196)
• A big event of any kind precipitated heavy ***drinking***.(p.197)
• To my mind, ***drinking*** didn't have anything to do with not going through with things.(p.198)
• I can remember telling the poor little soul that I could probably quit ***drinking*** if I wasn't married to her, and told her that, after all, I didn't like restraint!(p.199)
• I didn't like having to come home at a certain time; I didn't like this, I didn't like that, and I think the poor girl actually divorced me to help me stop ***drinking***!(p.199)
• Naturally, what little restraint I had exercised before was gone now, and my ***drinking*** became worse.(p.199)
• I can remember well thinking that I would quit ***drinking***, really go to work hard, apply myself eight hours a day, five days a week, make a lot of money, and then I could start ***drinking*** again.(p.199)
• Always at the end of these dreams was ***drinking***.(p.199)
• He had known something of my ***drinking*** pattern, and he asked me what I was doing about it.(p.200)
• And I think we calculated, or I did, that there wasn't anybody who knew that I wasn't ***drinking***.(p.202)
• I quit ***drinking*** immediately.(p.202)
• After ***drinking*** one glass of beer at the end of my work period for about five days, I thought I'd better find out whether I really had the stuff licked.(p.203)
• I think the longest drunk I was ever on was eleven days, but usually only two days with a complete blackout for a day, and then backing off by ***drinking*** as long as I could get anything.(p.203)
• Then I started ***drinking*** again, with possibly a little more restraint, periods a little bit longer than they had been before, but substantially the same pattern.(p.203)
• There were times when I got to ***drinking***, and I had been warned by Firestone that they wouldn't stand for this much longer, so, clearly, they were conscious of the fact that I drank too much and too often.(p.204)
• Shortly after that, my brother, who had then become associated with a group of people and had stopped ***drinking***, urged me to attend meetings with him.(p.205)
• I couldn't afford to be found with those people, but I said I would certainly pay his dues if it would keep him from ***drinking***.(p.205)
• One morning, after I had been on a binge for a couple of days, I awoke to find my brother and Doctor Bob in my room talking to me about not ***drinking***.(p.206)
• Then he started to talk to me about his ***drinking*** experiences, what his ***drinking*** had cost him, how much he had drunk and where, things like that, and I remember I was quite bored because I had never seen the guy before and had no interest at all in what, where and when he drank.(p.208)
• Although, during this period I was not addicted to any pattern of alcohol consumption, when I did drink the ***drinking*** was pretty wild.(p.212)
• I kept myself so busy that outside of some school and group parties, I didn't go overboard on ***drinking*** very much between the ages of twenty-five and thirty.(p.213)
• My ***drinking*** career began about four years after I had moved up into partnership and had joined certain clubs, societies and so fourth, and during which period we had Prohibition.(p.213)
• When I was about forty-seven, after indulging in all kinds of self-deception to control my ***drinking***, I arrived at a period when I felt convinced I had to have so much alcohol every day and that the real problem was to control how much.(p.214)
• She knew that at that time any suggestion she made about my ***drinking*** would only build up a barrier, a consideration for which I am ever grateful.(p.216)
• In fact, the last three years of my ***drinking*** was a routine of barbiturates in the morning, so that I could stop shaking enough to shave, and then alcohol beginning about four-thirty or five o'clock, with a struggle not to take a drink at noon or during the day, because I had the idea that if I took one drink, I would smell as though I had had a pint.(p.217)
• I'd been sitting comfortably in a restaurant with Rita, ***drinking*** my sixth martini and hoping the waiter would forget about the lunch order – at least long enough for me to have a couple more.(p.223)
• When I look back on that last horrible year of constant ***drinking*** I wonder how I survived it either physically or mentally.(p.224)
• When my friends suggested that I was ***drinking*** too much – they were no longer my friends.(p.226)
• I moved from group to group -- then from place to place – and went on ***drinking***.(p.226)
• And to my surprise, my ***drinking*** grew worse.(p.226)
• He wasn't a ***drinking*** man, he didn't know what it was to need a drink, nor what a drink could do for one in a pinch.(p.227)
• And I was sure that I couldn't be with people who drank, without ***drinking***.(p.227)
• In that I was correct: I couldn't be comfortable with any kind of people without ***drinking***.(p.227)
• When I got back to Germany I settled down to finish my apprenticeship, ***drinking*** the wine of the country as usual.(p.231)
• I had no desire whatever to sit down at a table and stay a whole morning or afternoon ***drinking***.(p.231)
• Having regard for the law of the land, I resigned myself to the will of the national legislators and quit ***drinking*** altogether, not because I had found it harmful, but because I couldn't get what I was accustomed to drink.(p.232)
• I knew the stuff I was making was a lot stronger than I had been used to, but I never suspected that steady ***drinking*** of it might develop a taste for something even stronger still.(p.233)
• I was now forming an entirely new ***drinking*** technique.(p.233)
• My "periodics" became more frequent until I reached the point where I wanted to devote all my time to ***drinking***, working as little as possible, and then only when the necessity of my family demanded it.(p.234)
• Unfortunately, I had no desire to consult my priest about my ***drinking***.(p.234)
• He had no desire to know anything, except whether I was definite about my desire to quit ***drinking***.(p.235)
• Jackie told me about a group of fellows in New York, of whom my old friend Fitz was one, who had the same problem I had, and who by working together to help each other were not now ***drinking*** and were happy like himself.(p.239)
• So it is clear that I never had any fun out of ***drinking*** – I would be the soberest-seeming one in the crowd and all of a sudden I would be the drunkest.(p.241)
• The first year in college I just got by in my studies, and that year I majored in poker and ***drinking***.(p.241)
• I refused to join any fraternity, as I wanted to be a free lance, and that year my ***drinking*** was confined to one-night stands, once or twice a week.(p.241)
• The second year my ***drinking*** was more or less restricted to week-ends, but I was nearly kicked out for scholastic failure.(p.241)
• At this time I was holding what ***drinking*** I did down to weekends, but I hadn't had a drink at all in a month.(p.243)
• I checked into my hotel room and then noticed a placard tucked under the glass on the bureau stating "There will be positively NO ***drinking*** at this convention" signed by the president of the company.(p.243)
• For the last two years of my ***drinking*** I prayed on every drunk that I wouldn't wake up again.(p.245)
• ***Drinking*** was all in the day's work.(p.251)
• My ***drinking*** was never the spaced doses of the careful tippler; it was always gluttonous.(p.254)
• I had been ***drinking*** heavily from one state of semicoma to another and it was several days before I got "defogged," but subconsciously I was in earnest about wanting to quit liquor forever.(p.258)
• I was deprived of many of the things that we feel are important in life, such as education particularly, because of my father's ***drinking***.(p.261)
• And Russ didn't tell me he'd stop ***drinking***, and he certainly didn't stop.(p.262)
• That's when I started ***drinking***.(p.264)
• So, sometimes we'd end up in Charleston, West Virginia, or here or there, ***drinking*** all along the way.(p.264)
• Of course, this year we decided on staying home and being sensible, doing a little ***drinking***, and painting the house.(p.265)
• Russ read a piece in the paper, and he kind of snickered, and said, "See here, where John D. has found something to keep him from ***drinking***!"(p.265)
• One morning after a terrific ***drinking*** bout, I was in a little bar near our house, and I shook so that I was very much ashamed, because I was getting the shakes worse and worse.(p.266)
• Time went on and the ***drinking*** got worse and worse, and I was in another barroom, down the road the other way, a small one, and I took my glass – that morning I'd been able to lift it from the bar -- and I said to the woman behind the bar, "I wish I might never take another drop of that stuff.(p.266)
• He used to drink, and then he found something that started up in Akron that helped him quit ***drinking***."(p.267)
• But he told a story of ***drinking*** that was amazing to me.(p.268)
• He talked about his wife taking his little boy away from him because of his ***drinking***, and how he got back together with them through A.A., and we began feeling grateful right then that all these things hadn't been taken from us.(p.270)
• I remember sometime, it was possibly six months after we had been going steadily to King School, that we were coming home from a meeting and saw a car along the way, and a fellow in back ***drinking*** a bottle of beer.(p.271)
• My pattern of ***drinking*** became very different from theirs.(p.277)
• My thinking about ***drinking*** had undergone a great change.(p.277)
• To go north into the empty pine country and shoot myself, or to go south in the faint hope that a bunch of strangers might help me with my ***drinking*** problem.(p.278)
• Such thinking usually began with thoughts of the pleasant ***drinking*** of my youth.(p.285)
• Instead, I quickly substituted one or another vivid scene from the nightmare of my later ***drinking***.(p.286)
• I confined ***drinking*** to weekends, and drank normally in college and for several years thereafter.(p.287)
• Then I started traveling, with the United States and Canada as my territory, and with so much freedom and with an unlimited expense account, I was soon ***drinking*** every night and kidding myself that it was all part of the job.(p.287)
• That same year, my wife became fed up with my ***drinking*** around the house and called my dad in Akron to come and pick me up.(p.288)
• He said he had finally learned that ***drinking*** was a fatal illness made up of an allergy plus an obsession, and once the ***drinking*** had passed from habit to obsession, we were completely hopeless, and could look

forward only to spending the balance of our lives in mental institutions or to death.(p.290)
• The next day I went back to Chicago and started a vigorous campaign among my so-called friends or *drinking* companions.(p.293)
• In the summer of 1938, almost a year from the time I made my original contact with Akron, the man for whom I was working and who knew about the program, approached me and asked if I could do anything about one of his salesmen who was *drinking* very heavily.(p.294)
• He had been wanting to do something about his *drinking* for a long time, but did not know how.(p.294)
• Fifteen of those years I would not have enjoyed had I continued *drinking*.(p.295)
• That discovery so intrigued me, that I stayed on that diet almost entirely for the balance of my extensive *drinking* life.(p.298)
• The last day of my *drinking* career, I drank twenty-two of them between ten and twelve a.m. and I shall never know how many more followed them until I was poured into bed that night.(p.298)
• I got along fairly well with my party *drinking* for quite some time, but eventually I began to visit beer joints in between parties.(p.298)
• A night or so a week in a joint, and a party or so a week at home or with friends, along with a little lone *drinking*, soon had me preparing for the existence of a top flight drunkard.(p.298)
• Three years after I started on my *drinking* career, I lost my first job.(p.298)
• Well . . . I had a job, and I really wanted desperately to stop *drinking*, but couldn't, so I readily agreed to visit the doctor she recommended.(p.301)
• In all honesty though, I was skeptical, but I wanted so definitely to quit *drinking* that I would have welcomed any sort of physical torture or pain to accomplish the result.(p.302)
• I experienced some of the pleasure of social *drinking* when I was sixteen.(p.305)
• My *drinking* habits increased in spite of my struggle for control.(p.305)
• I tried them mixed, unmixed, *drinking* only when gay, only when depressed.(p.305)
• I couldn't stop *drinking*.(p.306)
• Needless to say, this was not pleasurable *drinking*.(p.306)
• This was *drinking* in sheer desperation, alone and locked behind my own door.(p.306)
• "We watch the alcoholic performing in a position of responsibility and we know that because he is *drinking* heavily and daily he has cut his capacities by fifty per cent, and still he seems able to do a satisfactory job.(p.308)
• Some were *drinking* heavily and there had been occasional serious episodes.(p.315)
• But with many, *drinking* had been little more than a sometimes uncontrollable nuisance.(p.315)
• They realized that repeated lack of *drinking* control, when they really wanted control, was the fatal symptom that spelled problem *drinking*.(p.315)
• I started *drinking* about age thirteen.(p.317)
• But who wasn't after *drinking* that much?(p.317)
• If I could lay off it, that meant I didn't have to worry about a *drinking* problem, I thought.(p.317)
• Next, I was sent to Arizona, where my *drinking* picked up some more, and I started having blackouts, and I was thrown in jail for speeding and drunken driving.(p.318)
• "It can't be my *drinking*," I thought, "because I can stop any time I want to.(p.318)
• The doctor asked about my *drinking*, but I wouldn't talk to him.(p.319)
• I still couldn't make it through the nights without *drinking*, so I went back into the hospital, this time to a rehabilitation center.(p.320)
• Once I did have a slip – tried *drinking* again – but the A.A.'s tell me not to worry about yesterday, because nobody can change it, and not to worry about tomorrow, because it hasn't come yet.(p.320)
• She decided she wouldn't let herself go in her *drinking*.(p.321)
• As we walked back through the hall, I, for the first time in my life, said to another human being, "I'm having trouble with my *drinking*, too."(p.321)
• I started my *drinking* nearly thirty years ago – right after I was married.(p.322)
• My first *drinking* spree was on corn liquor and I was allergic to it, believe me.(p.322)
• I got into terrific trouble with my *drinking*.(p.322)
• We had a small child, and I loved her dearly, so that held me back quite a bit in my *drinking* career.(p.322)
• But I wasn't happy, and I didn't ever let myself go in my *drinking*.(p.323)
• I really started *drinking* with a bang.(p.323)
• Many women who have reached the stage that I had reached in my *drinking* have lost husbands, children, homes, everything they hold dear.(p.323)
• I thought I was losing my mind when I realized that I couldn't stop *drinking*.(p.324)
• It would be a little thing that I'd think was wrong, and off I'd go, *drinking*.(p.324)
• It's surprising, how we think we fool everybody in our *drinking*.(p.324)
• It didn't bother me any more whether George was *drinking* or not.(p.324)
• Sometimes I would lie on the bathroom floor, deathly sick, praying I would die, and praying to God as I always had prayed to Him when I was *drinking*: "Dear God, get me out of this one and I'll never do it again."(p.324)
• I'd get so fed up with *drinking* all alone and bearing the burden of guilt all by myself, that I'd egg him on to drink, to get started again.(p.325)
• I am trying now, each day, to make up for all those selfish, thoughtless, foolish things I did in my *drinking* days.(p.326)
• I had never even been told by a superior that maybe I was *drinking* too much.(p.327)
• My *drinking* career started late.(p.328)
• Then, one night, my whole pattern for *drinking* was set.(p.328)
• Unlike the *drinking* driver, he avoids facing judges.(p.330)
• In so simple a manner did my morning *drinking* begin.(p.331)
• In succession came "What Made Milwaukee Famous Made a Loser Out of Me" and "I'm *Drinking* My Christmas Dinner All Alone."(p.332)
• I decided to quit *drinking*.(p.333)
• They described what had happened when they went out and tried *drinking* again, and I knew they were sincere in saying that it could happen to me.(p.334)
• I don't believe, when I started, that I even had in mind the thought that I was *drinking*.(p.336)
• It wasn't long before I was *drinking* all day.(p.336)
• But the only thing that got started was my *drinking*.(p.336)
• I should have realized that alcohol was getting hold of me when I started to become secretive in my *drinking*.(p.336)
• I couldn't go to one wine store and look the man honestly in the face and buy a bottle, as I used to do when I had parties and entertained and did normal *drinking*.(p.336)
• I needed it, and I knew I was *drinking* too much, but I wasn't conscious of the fact that I should stop.(p.336)
• I wandered from room to room, thinking, *drinking*, *drinking*, thinking.(p.337)
• I never knew which came first, the thinking or the *drinking*.(p.337)
• If I could only stop *drinking*, maybe I wouldn't think.(p.337)
• I went on, realizing what I was becoming, hating myself for it, bitter, blaming life, blaming everything else but the fact that I should turn about and do something about my *drinking*.(p.337)
• I had all kinds of reasons for my *drinking*.(p.338)
• Mere cessation from *drinking* is not enough for an alcoholic while the need for that drink goes on.(p.339)
• At Christmastime next year, I convinced my wife that I had alcohol under control and that I would do controlled *drinking* over Christmas and the New Year.(p.343)
• In a short time, it became uncontrolled *drinking*.(p.343)
• I made more money the last year of my *drinking* than I ever made before in my whole life.(p.345)
• I had a lot of fun *drinking*.(p.346)
• And then one ill-defined day, one day that I can't recall, I stepped across the line that alcoholics know so well, and from that day on *drinking* was miserable.(p.346)
• On the last day I was *drinking* I went up to see a friend who had had a good deal of trouble with alcohol, and whose wife had left him a number of times.(p.346)
• One said, "Don't feel that you are a martyr because you stopped *drinking*," and this hit me between the eyes.(p.346)
• The second one said, "Don't feel that you stop *drinking* for anyone other than yourself," and this hit me between the eyes.(p.346)
• Just three years of *drinking* pushed a shy, lonely young girl to the depth of depression.(p.353)
• Soon, it became apparent that my schooling was interfering with my *drinking*.(p.354)
• With these new and enlightening doors opening up to me, I was able to make the eventual decision to stop *drinking*, a day at a time -- because I, too, was an alcoholic.(p.355)
• Lucky because my excessive *drinking* never got me in jail, or hospitalized, nor did it ever cost me a job.(p.356)
• I was active and did well, however, in school publications, dramatics (which came in handy during my *drinking* career), and Greek letter societies.(p.357)
• I had no trouble at all in being elected to the two *drinking* societies at my college.(p.357)
• *Drinking* – and more *drinking*.(p.358)
• I got behind in my rent, but never in my *drinking*.(p.358)
• Her influence and companionship managed to lessen my *drinking* to some degree.(p.359)
• At this time, however, she had an opportunity to go to Salt Lake City on a new project for the government, but she did promise me that if I would curtail my *drinking* and buckle down to hard work she would give serious consideration to my latest proposal and maybe join me at a later date when I got settled.(p.359)
• It also was the beginning of another cycle in my *drinking*.(p.360)
• Since the radio station was getting on its feet, it didn't require so many nights of evening work, and that permitted leisure time for *drinking*.(p.360)
• My business reputation had reached from Vermont to Pennsylvania, but, thank goodness, my *drinking* reputation had not.(p.361)
• She tried reasoning with me, endeavored to work out various *drinking* schedules, in fact all the tricks were practised faithfully for a short time somewhere along my shaky road to unhappiness.(p.361)
• I would follow certain *drinking* schedules or diets faithfully for a few days, and then somewhere along the line would over-train and upset the applecart.(p.361)
• Thank God that in spite of my heavy *drinking* my mind was clear enough to make a decision then and there.(p.363)
• That night she too had new hope because I had made sure she would know what I was doing about my *drinking* by packing every bit of A.A. literature I could put my hands on right on top so she couldn't help but see it when she opened my bag.(p.364)
• I have had many more reasons to drink since I have been in A.A. than I had in all the years of my *drinking*.(p.367)
• In my *drinking* days, I found the ideal spot for the alcoholic housewife: the neighborhood Laundromat.(p.369)
• There, I could be a proper mother and wife while *drinking* up a storm.(p.369)
• As my father climbed the ladder of success in the oil-field business, his *drinking* also climbed.(p.369)
• I had no qualms, because I felt the source of a *drinking* problem was all in how weak one was, and I wasn't like my dad (I thought).(p.370)
• After his death, my mother soon picked up *drinking* where Dad left off, and in a very short time she died of cirrhosis of the liver.(p.370)
• In fact I was afraid to try it for fear that I would wind up like many examples I had seen of excessive *drinking* in the Army.(p.374)
• My *drinking* did not start until after I was thirty-five, and a fairly successful career had been established.(p.374)
• Short dry spells ended in heavy *drinking*.(p.375)
• I tried to hide my *drinking* by going places where I was unlikely to see anyone I knew.(p.375)
• The last two years of my *drinking* my entire personality changed to a cynical, intolerant and arrogant person completely different from my normal self.(p.376)
• Resenting anyone and everyone who might interfere with my personal plans and ways of doing things, I was full of self pity, especially for any interference with my *drinking*.(p.376)
• The surprise to me is the fact that I didn't know that they knew my *drinking* had gotten out of control.(p.376)
• I was too busy devising excuses to be out with *drinking* pals.(p.376)
• Finally our invitations became fewer and fewer as friends had more experience with my *drinking* pattern.(p.377)
• Two years before I joined A.A. my wife took a long trip during which she wrote me she just couldn't return unless I did something about my *drinking*.(p.377)
• A year later, while we were on a vacation trip she packed up to go home because of my excessive *drink-*

ing, and I talked her out of it with the promise I would go on the wagon for at least a year.(p.377)
• Some crisis brings you to a point of making a decision to do something about your *drinking* problem.(p.377)
• This suggestion had been made before on a number of occasions, but like all alcoholics I wanted to handle my problem my own way, which really meant I didn't want anything to interfere with my *drinking*.(p.378)
• I don't know what I expected, but I most certainly didn't visualize a group of people talking about their *drinking* problems, making light of their personal tragedies and at the same time enjoying themselves.(p.378)
• Over a period of time he has built up self pity, resentments toward anyone or anything that interferes with his *drinking*.(p.380)
• *Drinking* it with your meals, you didn't feel it.(p.385)
• I really started *drinking* then.(p.386)
• He called me that because I was *drinking* too much.(p.387)
• He said that because of my *drinking*, he shouldn't leave, but that he had to go to New York for two weeks.(p.388)
• My husband couldn't tell whether I wanted to do something about my *drinking*.(p.391)
• It was the first time in my life that I could not get a lift out of what I was *drinking*; and so one Friday night, at five minutes to six, I had half a water glass of warm gin, and that is when I first asked God to help me.(p.393)
• A retired Navy man looks back over twenty years of *drinking*, to add up his A.A. "initiation fee."(p.396)
• But, as it was with *drinking*, this project will be entered into with enthusiasm and optimism -- and probably wind up the same way, depressed.(p.396)
• Twenty-five years of *drinking*!(p.397)
• My *drinking* career extended from age eighteen to forty-three.(p.397)
• Eighteen will be used as the starting point, because my *drinking* before was limited by age, the law, and money.(p.397)
• I displayed alcoholic tendencies actually from the age of fourteen, when I started to steal wine from the family jug, siphoning it off one drink at a time so it wouldn't be missed, not *drinking* it immediately, but saving it until about a pint was accumulated, so that I could get drunk.(p.397)
• At age twenty-one, I enlisted in the Navy for two reasons: (1) to avoid being drafted into the Army, and (2) out of a burst of patriotic fervor inspired by the advent of World War II and as the result of an all-night *drinking* binge which found me sitting on the door-step of the Navy recruiting office when the chief petty officer arrived to open for business at nine o'clock Monday morning.(p.398)
• Now my *drinking* was limited by only one factor, the enforced periods of dryness caused by lengthy tours at sea.(p.398)
• Up to my early thirties, when my *drinking* had become a major problem, I lived in large houses, with servants and all the luxuries that I could possibly ask for.(p.401)
• This was where I started my first *drinking* lessons.(p.402)
• A normal person, hit with adversity, can go on a *drinking* spree and then snap out of it.(p.404)
• But whereas my horse was always equipped with a flask, I merely endured the fox hunting so I could start *drinking* at lunch time.(p.404)
• A few stood by me, at least in their hearts, throughout the whole of my *drinking* career.(p.404)
• I drank and I kept on *drinking*.(p.406)
• It combined running away from my world, and *drinking* all I wanted to.(p.407)
• None of them were alcoholics, but at this time they were *drinking* as much as I was.(p.407)
• I would get wildly excited and look forward to another night of *drinking*.(p.408)
• A.A. had to stop my *drinking* first.(p.409)
• Years of *drinking* and general high jinks had cut her off from old friends.(p.414)
• Her luck had been worse than mine, but not her *drinking*.(p.414)
• Not understanding the twenty-four hour plan, or not wanting to, I began *drinking* and was off-again on-again, during that first month.(p.414)
• I thought it was my duty to keep her from *drinking*, not knowing that if the other fellow is really determined to drink there is nothing you can do about it.(p.415)
• Fear, love of dentistry, and an imitation of my father's periodic *drinking* pattern took me through dental college soberly, except for the few parties and vacations in those four years.(p.419)
• I can't control my *drinking* any more.(p.423)
• I tried to mimic the talk, ideas, moods and even the *drinking* the older men.(p.423)
• I had a *drinking* problem on my hands even at that time.(p.424)
• They had been *drinking* for many years and were getting progressively worse.(p.424)
• *Drinking* conditions at home were even worse than before.(p.424)
• I was *drinking* quite a bit of whiskey now.(p.425)
• They were doing very well – at least a fifth apiece a day, except on dad's days off when they did some serious *drinking*.(p.425)
• I tried to control her *drinking* by pouring her whiskey down the sink before I'd leave for the night, to get drunker myself.(p.426)
• Pearl Harbor was a breeze of nine months, a gay Hawaiian paradise, *drinking* under the palms, listening to the surf beat on the shore, a bottle of whiskey near at hand.(p.426)
• I talked the Old Man into letting me live in the photo lab instead of the barracks, and for eighteen months nothing interfered with my *drinking*.(p.426)
• Wasn't I *drinking* more than a quart every day?(p.427)
• I hadn't told them about my *drinking*, but I guess they knew.(p.427)
• I told the doctor my parents' *drinking* history and blamed them.(p.428)
• But I was soon *drinking* as heavily as I had been.(p.428)
• But I didn't want to stop *drinking* -- not at twenty-two.(p.429)
• I'd packed more *drinking* into seven years than many a heavy drinker does in a lifetime.(p.429)
• I thought, "If this is A.A. why not go back to *drinking*, kill myself with booze in the next three years the doctor had given me, and call it a bad job?"(p.430)
• Were I to revert to *drinking*, even now, I wouldn't give anything for these four years in A.A.(p.430)
• In all the twenty-five years of my *drinking* there were only a few occasions when I took a morning drink.(p.432)
• Once or twice, during my early *drinking*, I carried it over into the second day, and only once, that I can remember, did it continue into the third.(p.432)
• Meanwhile, I was getting worse, both as regards my inward misery and my *drinking*.(p.434)
• And I knew that somewhere along the line I'd lost the power to stop *drinking*.(p.436)
• Perhaps the single flicker of decency that shone through the fog of my *drinking* days was a clumsy affection for my two children, a boy and a girl.(p.437)
• Not only did I not think that being an alcoholic was a good idea, I didn't even feel that I had all that much of a *drinking* problem!(p.439)
• And as I went through pharmacy school, graduate school, medical school, internship, residency, and specialty training and, finally, went into practice, my *drinking* kept increasing.(p.441)
• My *drinking* took place after work hours.(p.441)
• The longer the *drinking* continued, the shorter the time the alcohol would keep me asleep; I would have to drink myself back to sleep again and again throughout the night.(p.441)
• I interpreted "sober" as meaning "*drinking* but not being drunk."(p.447)
• Of course, I was still *drinking* at the time.(p.447)
• It seemed that all they talked about at meetings was *drinking, drinking, drinking*.(p.447)
• I wanted to talk about my many big problems; *drinking* seemed a small one.(p.447)
• To this day, I am amazed at how many of my problems -- most of which had nothing to do with *drinking*, I believed – have become manageable or have simply disappeared since I quit *drinking*.(p.448)
• It helped me a great deal to become convinced that alcoholism was a disease, not a moral issue; that I had been *drinking* as a result of a compulsion, even though I had not been aware of the compulsion at the time; and that sobriety was not a matter of will-power.(p.448)
• At last, acceptance proved to be the key to my *drinking* problem.(p.448)
• Yet prisoners often can't identify with many A.A. members' *drinking* stories.(p.458)
• Most of us did not stay out of prison long enough to run the alcoholic gamut -- to develop the ongoing kind of alcoholism or alcoholic *drinking* you hear about in A.A. talks.(p.458)
• This career girl preferred solitary *drinking*, the blackout kind, often hoping she'd stay that way for keeps.(p.464)
• I started *drinking* socially and at parties and proms when I was about twenty years old.(p.464)
• After a while I really did enjoy *drinking* and what it did to me, and I became dependent upon it for every occasion.(p.464)
• Then I went on my first week-long bender of solitary *drinking*, locked up in a hotel room, because my family opposed my coming marriage.(p.464)
• I figured that perhaps if I went ahead with that marriage, which I was sure was right for me, that would be the answer to my *drinking* problem.(p.465)
• (I think my first feeling of fear came with my first week's solitary *drinking*, locked up in that hotel room.(p.465)
• From that time on, fear was with me because I realized that not only would I not remember what happened to me while I was *drinking*, but apparently I couldn't control what happened.(p.465)
• Tragedies during those years that were caused by my *drinking*, such as the breaking up of my marriage, the death of my child, other things – had little restraining effect.(p.465)
• I hadn't been *drinking* much about that time, for I had begun to realize that there was something abnormal about my *drinking*, although as yet, I didn't realize that it was so out of control.(p.465)
• My pattern of *drinking* at that time had reached the point where once I really started, I would retire to my bed and drink myself into oblivion.(p.466)
• I went out to a restaurant, found a booth way back in the rear, and started *drinking*.(p.467)
• Did that stop my *drinking*?(p.468)
• They were always there because of a nervous breakdown, or for a "rest cure" -- any reason except because of *drinking*.(p.471)
• But by listening and talking to these A.A.'s -- talking to them as I had never talked to anyone in my whole life, I saw that it was my life that was unmanageable -- not just my *drinking*.(p.471)
• During these seven years a thing called the Twenty-four Hour Program --a gadget I used to think was only a snare to trap the newcomer -- has come to mean much to me, not only as regards my *drinking* but in the whole pattern of my life.(p.473)
• My aunt had sharp words for me about *drinking*.(p.474)
• When I came into A.A., I had no intention of quitting *drinking* -- I figured I was doing all right.(p.478)
• This was around 1935, and it was about this time that I actually started *drinking*.(p.486)
• I think that was basically the thing that started me *drinking* in 1935.(p.487)
• I started *drinking* alone then.(p.487)
• That went on for maybe two months, and then she got after me again about *drinking*.(p.488)
• I got to the place where I'd look forward to the week-end's *drinking* and pacify myself by saying that the week-ends were mine, that it didn't interfere with my family or with my business if I drank on the week-ends.(p.488)
• Nevertheless, we continued to work together and I continued to drink, but I guess, deep down within her heart as well as within mine, we both knew I couldn't stop *drinking*.(p.490)
• Anyhow, on the 24th, after *drinking* all day on the 23rd, I must have decided I wanted to see my wife and have some kind of reconciliation or at least talk with her.(p.491)
• She never mentioned anything about my whiskey *drinking* because if she had I would have told her, "No" right then.(p.494)
• Father had never directly spoken to me about *drinking* but he never drank any, so far as I knew.(p.498)
• I had never had a drink, but I had seen enough merriment in the boys who were *drinking* to be interested.(p.498)
• I have been *drinking* a lot, but never get drunk.(p.501)
• I have been *drinking* while the baby was arriving.(p.502)
• I have fought hard to stop *drinking*.(p.502)
• I tell my wife I cannot stop *drinking*.(p.502)
• Will I take a young fellow who has been *drinking* for two weeks to live with me?(p.506)
• I fix up a little apartment over the garage with books and *drinking* water.(p.506)
• I began *drinking* as a kid, shortly after I reached my fourteenth birthday.(p.508)
• During the course of that *drinking*, I had shot and killed one person and almost completed the job on a second one.(p.508)
• He had been in and out of Matteawan and many other mental institutions as a result

of his ***drinking***.(p.509)
• DESPERATION ***DRINKING***(p.512)
• He was ***drinking*** to hold on to his job, to hold on to his wife, to hold on to his sanity.(p.512)
• Finally, he was ***drinking*** to keep away those little men, and those strange voices, and the organ music that came out of the walls.(p.512)
• My ***drinking*** pattern isn't very different from the average you find in A.A.(p.512)
• I started ***drinking*** rather early, at the age of sixteen.(p.512)
• I didn't stick at social ***drinking*** very long.(p.512)
• That and the morning drink came very early in my ***drinking*** career.(p.513)
• The Army ***drinking*** alone covered a lot of territory.(p.513)
• She certainly wasn't in the dark about my ***drinking***.(p.513)
• That type of ***drinking*** is not pleasant.(p.514)
• It is desperation ***drinking***.(p.514)
• I was ***drinking*** to keep away the shakes, ***drinking*** to keep away those little men and those strange voices and the organ music that comes out of the walls.(p.514)
• I was ***drinking*** to try to hold on to a job, to try and hold on to my home, to try to hold on to my wife, to try to hold on to my sanity.(p.514)
• The realization came to me that I had to stop ***drinking***, that I had to find a way.(p.515)
• God has been good to me both in my ***drinking*** and in my sobriety.(p.516)
• Up to that time, ***drinking*** didn't really mean anything to me at all.(p.518)
• But as soon as I got out on my own in France, I started ***drinking***.(p.518)
• When I came home to ordinary garrison life in England, I found that I was ***drinking*** rather more than most people of may age.(p.518)
• I should say there was less ***drinking*** in the Army than I thought at that time.(p.518)
• Lots of the older people had taken to ***drinking*** quite a good deal more during the war, but the younger generation was, I think, about the same.(p.518)
• The gradual result was that I was drifting into making ***drinking*** one of the more important parts of my life.(p.519)
• Then I was sent out to India and from then on ***drinking*** just increased and increased, and I started having two or three day spells instead of just the ordinary concentrated one day.(p.519)
• India lent itself to ***drinking*** then, if you were disposed to drink, because you lived in bungalows; you didn't live all together as you do at home in an Officer's Mess.(p.519)
• We had a minor campaign or two and that helped distract attention from my ***drinking***.(p.519)
• I think the Commanding Officer was rather tired of this particular chicken coming back to roost so often because he very soon wrote in to the medical authorities to tell them that they had to get me into hospital, to be thoroughly examined for ***drinking***.(p.520)
• In part, it was a feeling of intense shame at having to leave the Army during the war, but mostly it was resentment that this kind of thing should happen to me for, strange as it may seem, up to then I still thought I could control ***drinking***.(p.521)
• I thought, well, now that I've been put out for ***drinking***, I'll just show them that they were completely wrong, so I went off on the biggest bout I had been on up to then, involving about a fortnight's blackout.(p.521)
• In any case, I made myself believe that, so I just drifted about, existing on my retired pay, ***drinking***, and living at home.(p.522)
• My only hope was to try and get through what was left of life as best I could, but I could never visualize doing that without ***drinking***.(p.522)
• The thought of stopping ***drinking*** just never occurred to me.(p.522)
• But I did understand this eventually, that these people had been through a lot of ***drinking*** experience just as I had, and had managed to make a job of it.(p.524)
• What struck me most was that they all seemed to be quite pleased with having made a job of it and having stopped ***drinking***.(p.524)
• Since I joined on that April night, A.A. has done more for me than just stop me from ***drinking***; it has brought me back to life again.(p.524)
• I always blamed my ***drinking*** on being poor, or on anything other than the truth -- that I liked what booze did for me, that when I had a drink I was as big and had as much as the next person.(p.526)
• I would never admit that I was ***drinking*** too much, or spending money that I should have used to buy food for my two little boys.(p.526)
• I was always able to get a boyfriend who had a ***drinking*** joint or sold whiskey, but it didn't last long.(p.526)
• Once I started ***drinking***, I didn't care that the rent wasn't paid, or that there was no food in the house, or that my boys needed shoes.(p.527)
• But then one good doctor told me there was nothing wrong with me except ***drinking*** too much.(p.528)
• It's time to stop finding excuses for ***drinking*** and getting into trouble, because now there is a way out, and if you want what we have, try coming around and giving the program a chance.(p.530)
• An ambitious playwright, he let his brains get so far ahead of his emotions that he collapsed into suicidal ***drinking***.(p.531)
• Perhaps a better way of saying it is that, on that day, with that decision, I no longer fought ***drinking*** as an escape.(p.531)
• For by thirty-five I had been ***drinking*** for a few years.(p.533)
• Sometimes we are told in A.A. not to try and learn the reasons for our ***drinking***.(p.533)
• But such is my nature that I must know the reason for things and I didn't stop until I had satisfied myself about the reasons for my ***drinking***.(p.533)
• That couplet contains most of my reasons for ***drinking***.(p.534)
• My serious ***drinking*** covered about seven years.(p.536)
• I promised on the grave of a beloved sister that I would stop ***drinking***.(p.539)
• It paid for a ten-day binge which was the end of my ***drinking*** days.(p.540)
• Young when she joined, this A.A. believes her serious ***drinking*** was the result of even deeper defects.(p.544)
• The mental twists that led up to my ***drinking*** began many years before I ever took a drink for I am one of those whose history proves conclusively that my ***drinking*** was "a symptom of a deeper trouble."(p.544)
• The only importance in all of this lies in the fact that at twenty-three I was just as sick as I was at thirty three, when I came into A.A., but at that time I apparently had no place to go because I had no ***drinking*** problem.(p.546)
• I wasn't afraid of anything or anybody after I learned about ***drinking***, for it seemed right from the beginning that with liquor I could always retire to my little private world where nobody could get at me to hurt me.(p.547)
• The only way existence was possible was through rationalizing every sober moment and ***drinking*** myself into complete oblivion as often as I could.(p.547)
• The last three years of my ***drinking***, I drank on my job.(p.548)
• The amount of will power exercised to control my ***drinking*** during working hours, diverted into a constructive channel, would have made me President, and the thing that made the will power possible was the knowledge that as soon as my day was finished I could drink myself into oblivion.(p.548)
• I had never had a child and this had been a satisfactory excuse many times for my ***drinking***.(p.548)
• "God willing, we . . . may never again have to deal with ***drinking***, but we have to deal with sobriety every day."(p.554)
• "A.A. does not teach us how to handle our ***drinking***," he said.(p.554)
• I guess I always knew that the way to handle my ***drinking*** was to quit.(p.554)
• Like most other alcoholics I have known, I did quit ***drinking*** at various times -- once for ten months on my own and during other interludes when I was hospitalized.(p.554)
• It's no great trick to stop ***drinking***; the trick is to stay stopped.(p.554)
• I also got into my first disciplinary trouble caused by ***drinking***, on two separate occasions.(p.555)
• In the last year of my navy service, I was married to a lovely, lively girl, who enjoyed ***drinking***.(p.555)
• By twenty-nine, I was having trouble coping with life because of my ***drinking***.(p.555)
• The doctor pronounced it a badly enlarged liver and said I had to quit ***drinking***.(p.557)
• I went on the wagon, with no outside help and with no real difficulty -- except that I didn't enjoy life without ***drinking***.(p.557)
• So, when my liver had recovered after ten months, I resumed ***drinking***.(p.557)
• Soon my ***drinking*** was as bad as ever -- all day long every day.(p.557)
• And it had gone underground now, because everyone knew I shouldn't be ***drinking***.(p.557)
• Instead of ***drinking*** in fancy bars and clubs, I had to carry a bottle of vodka in my briefcase, duck into public toilets, and gulp from the bottle, trembling, in order to keep from falling apart.(p.557)
• Within two months, I was ***drinking*** again.(p.558)
• Each time, I went back to ***drinking*** -- even smuggling a bottle of vodka into the hospital as soon as the blood transfusions had ceased.(p.558)
• I have come to realize that the name of the game is not so much to stop ***drinking*** as to stay sober.(p.559)
• Alcoholics can stop ***drinking*** in many places and many ways -- but Alcoholics Anonymous offers us a way to stay sober.(p.559)
• God willing, we members of A.A. may never again have to deal with ***drinking***, but we have to deal with sobriety every day.(p.560)
• By learning -- through practicing the Twelve Steps and through sharing at meetings -- how to cope with the problems that we looked to booze to solve, back in our ***drinking*** days.(p.560)
• Three -- The only requirement for A.A. membership is a desire to stop ***drinking***.(p.564)

drinks

• They are restless, irritable and discontented, unless they can again experience the sense of ease and comfort which comes at once by taking a few ***drinks*** -- ***drinks*** which they see others taking with impunity.(p.xxvi)
• Here are some of the methods we have tried: Drinking beer only, limiting the number of ***drinks***, never drinking alone, never drinking in the morning, drinking only at home, never having it in the house, never drinking during business hours, drinking only at parties, switching from scotch to brandy, drinking only natural wines, agreeing to resign if ever drunk on the job, taking a trip, not taking a trip, swearing off forever (with and without a solemn oath), taking more physical exercise, reading inspirational books, going to health farms and sanitariums, accepting voluntary commitment to asylums -- we could increase the list ad infinitum.(p.31)
• I had no trouble refusing ***drinks***, and began to wonder if I had not been making too hard work of a simple matter.(p.40)
• But for every man who ***drinks*** others are involved -- the wife who trembles in fear of the next debauch; the mother and father who see their son wasting away.(p.104)
• When we were invited out, our husbands sneaked so many ***drinks*** that they spoiled the occasion.(p.105)
• He sometimes ***drinks*** in the morning and through the day also, to hold his nervousness in check.(p.109)
• Sometimes he ***drinks*** on the way home from the hospital.(p.110)
• You think he ought to know the subject better, as everyone should have a clear understanding of the risk he takes if he ***drinks*** too much.(p.112)
• While grateful that he ***drinks*** no more, they may not like the idea that God has accomplished the miracle where they failed.(p.128)
• Though he is now a most effective member of Alcoholics Anonymous, he still smokes and ***drinks*** coffee, but neither his wife or anyone else stands in judgment.(p.135)
• If he says yes, does he really mean it, or down inside does he think he is fooling you, and that after rest and treatment he will be able to get away with a few ***drinks*** now and then?(p.142)
• If a man ***drinks*** so much that his job suffers, we fire him.(p.148)
• Inwardly he would give anything to take half a dozen ***drinks*** and get away with them.(p.152)
• Unless he took some ***drinks***, he might not have the courage to scrape an acquaintance and would have a lonely week-end.(p.154)
• Perhaps he could handle, say, three ***drinks*** -- no more!(p.154)
• I soon discovered that a couple of ***drinks*** would alleviate my gastric distress, at least for a few hours at a time, so it was not at all difficult for me to return to my former excessive indulgence.(p.174)
• He came and got me home and to bed, gave me a few ***drinks*** that night, and one bottle of beer the next morning.(p.179)
• I got two ***drinks***, each of them a quarter of that pint, in me, and was talking along with these people, but I felt that sooner or later they were going to have me cornered because they were smarter than I was and the drink was beginning to take effect; but as I reached for the third drink Bob said, "Listen, Buster, you promised to take some medicine if we got you a drink.(p.206)
• Sitting in a Second Avenue bar, accepting ***drinks*** from anyone who offered, after my small stake was gone; or sitting at home alone, with the inevitable glass in my hand, I would remember, and remember-

ing, I would drink faster, seeking speedy oblivion.(p.225)
• I had to persist in my attempts to get straightened out enough to be able to use the ***drinks*** I needed, without their turning on me.(p.227)
• To go into a gathering of people was the sort of thing that all my life, from the time I left my private world of books and dreams to meet the real world of people and parties and jobs, had left me feeling an uncomfortable outsider, needing the warming stimulus of ***drinks*** to join in.(p.228)
• In foreign parts many a soldier who has been abstemious at home learns to use new and potent ***drinks***.(p.230)
• There I sat in the evenings, enjoying with my friends our memories of the "old country," singing the old songs we all knew, playing simple card games for ***drinks*** and consuming great quantities of beer.(p.231)
• You can all remember that in the first few months after the change, a great many men, who had formerly been used to a few beers every day or an occasional drink of whiskey, simply quit all alcoholic ***drinks***.(p.232)
• But he's in all sorts of scrapes because he ***drinks*** too much."(p.262)
• It wasn't long before any party without ***drinks*** was a dud for me.(p.305)
• I tried the beer diet, the wine diet, timing, measuring, and spacing of ***drinks***.(p.305)
• I began taking ***drinks*** in the morning to get started.(p.318)
• After having a few ***drinks***, I went to a meeting -- and the people there were not all old men and definitely not skid-row types!(p.319)
• The next meeting I went to, I didn't have any ***drinks*** beforehand.(p.319)
• I always wanted to drink too much, so I was watchful, always watchful, counting my ***drinks***.(p.322)
• If we were invited to a formal party and I knew they were only going to have one or two ***drinks***, I wouldn't have any.(p.323)
• And sneaking my ***drinks***.(p.324)
• My story happens to be a particular kind of woman's story; the story of the woman who ***drinks*** at home.(p.335)
• But from one or two ***drinks*** of an afternoon or evening, my intake mounted, and mounted fast.(p.336)
• When a few ***drinks*** made me feel good before I went over that line, those same ***drinks*** now made me wretched.(p.346)
• In an attempt to get over that feeling, there was a quick onslaught of a greater number of ***drinks***, and then all was lost.(p.346)
• I tried a few ***drinks*** my last night in the city before coming home.(p.364)
• We had some people in, and I was making ***drinks*** in the kitchen, when I suddenly decided to hoist the bottle for a quick one.(p.365)
• When it became noticeable to the point of comment, I devised ways of sneaking ***drinks*** on the side.(p.375)
• Rehearsals then became a part of the pattern, stopping at bars on the way to or from the place where ***drinks*** were to be served.(p.375)
• It now became necessary to have noon ***drinks***; at first just two, then gradually more.(p.375)
• She of course didn't realize how cunning an alcoholic can be and the lengths to which he will go in finding ways to satisfy the compulsion for more and more ***drinks*** after having had the first one.(p.377)
• The why is not important; the fact is that one drink will set up a reaction in our system which requires more; that one drink was too much and one hundred ***drinks*** were not enough.(p.380)
• I took two or three ***drinks*** so my eyes could focus, and I could see that horrible picture of the awful drunk on the first page; he couldn't get the drink to his mouth, he had a towel around his hand and he needed a shave.(p.391)
• Saying these sprees were limited to one a week (they were not), and saying that the average spree was ten of these ***drinks*** (sometimes more, sometimes less), we come up with the first boring statistic: two-fifty per week out of twelve dollars.(p.397)
• Five or six ***drinks*** and I was terrific.(p.402)
• I was so busy keeping her out of trouble, and so scared she'd swing on me, that I had my last two ***drinks*** that night.(p.415)
• I went to saloons where I could get ***drinks***.(p.423)
• I was released in a week, a week of hell with no ***drinks***.(p.428)
• Dad got out a jug for me and poured welcome home ***drinks***.(p.428)
• "You've got to space your ***drinks*** and take plenty of water in between," or "coat the stomach with a little olive oil," or "drink anything but those damn martinis."(p.433)
• When I didn't have anything else to do – a dull evening at home – I'd sneak a few ***drinks*** upstairs in my room, and that began to be a habit.(p.464)
• On the day set for the extractions, on my way to the dentist's I felt a little nervous, so I had a couple of ***drinks***, and after the teeth were out I was very nervous, so I had a few more.(p.466)
• He gave me many ***drinks*** from bottle.(p.474)
• Soon found wet canteens serve ***drinks*** to Indians in uniform.(p.474)
• Remember only first two ***drinks***.(p.475)
• Not try no ***drinks*** for Lent or for life.(p.476)
• He poured out two ***drinks***.(p.498)
• I pour ***drinks*** down my throat.(p.501)
• Maybe a few ***drinks*** when I get to the city will help.(p.505)
• And as I read, I shall take little ***drinks*** at long intervals.(p.506)
• Having made that bargain, I immediately began to feel I'd been trapped into it and I went out and had some ***drinks*** -- four glasses of gin, I remember.(p.523)
• Fear of rejection and its ensuing pain were not to be risked, and I turned away from myself once more for the answer, this time to the ***drinks*** I had always refused before, and in alcohol I found a false courage.(p.546)
• I began sneaking ***drinks*** when playing bartender for guests.(p.556)
• Then the ***drinks*** came more frequently, but carefully spaced out.(p.557)

dripped

• I did not see that the book ***dripped*** with self-pity.(p.403)

dripping

• And I remembered the creeping horror of the interminable night, in which I slept for short spells and woke up ***dripping*** with cold sweat and shaken with utter despair, to drink hastily from my bottle and mercifully pass out again, "You're mad, you're mad, you're mad!" pounded through my brain with each returning ray of consciousness, and I drowned the refrain with drink.(p.224)

drive

• The ***drive*** for success was on.(p.2)
• Then I decided to ***drive*** into the country and see one of my prospects for a car.(p.36)
• From surrounding towns, families ***drive*** long distances to be present.(p.161)
• There was always a tremendous ***drive*** and ambition to become a great guy, because I think I recognized inwardly that I didn't have any special talents.(p.194)
• He did call me a cab and when I got into the cab, I said, "***Drive*** me to a liquor store."(p.204)
• I apparently was willing to subdue these personality disturbances in a tremendous ***drive*** to succeed.(p.211)
• The next day he turned me over to a couple who, although neither was an alcoholic, knew Dr. Bob and were willing to ***drive*** me to Akron where they would turn me over to his care.(p.278)
• After a few meetings I decided to ***drive*** to Florida unannounced to see my wife and tell her about my new found friends and association.(p.364)
• The ***drive*** to get ahead, to succeed, kept me too busy for many years to have any great experience with social life.(p.374)
• I lost it many times and mom and dad would ***drive*** me around until I found it.(p.429)
• That my own innate selfishness and stubbornness are the evils which, if left unguarded, can ***drive*** me to alcohol.(p.473)
• The ***drive*** was long and cold but he was thankful for the hot bricks which some thoughtful person had given him for his feet.(p.497)
• I get in the car and ***drive*** off.(p.506)

driven

• ***Driven*** by a hundred forms of fear, self-delusion, self-seeking, and self-pity, we step on the toes of our fellows and they retaliate.(p.62)
• We have been ***driven*** to maudlin sympathy, to bitter resentment.(p.104)
• So I was ***driven*** to Akron the very next day by these Good Samaritans, and turned over to Dr. Bob and the then tiny Akron Group.(p.279)
• To wake up at home, not knowing how I got there, and to realize I had ***driven*** my car, became torture.(p.375)

driver

• I found a job; then lost it as the result of a brawl with a taxi ***driver***.(p.4)
• I have a shadowy recollection of being in an airplane bound for New York, and of finding a friendly taxicab ***driver*** at the landing field instead of my wife.(p.41)
• The ***driver*** escorted me about for several days.(p.41)
• On my ride to the nearest bar, I sold the ***driver*** on how misunderstood I was by my wife and what an unreasonable person she was.(p.288)
• Unlike the drinking ***driver***, he avoids facing judges.(p.330)

driver's

• I still had a wife and family, a home and a car, my ***driver's*** license, and a proper amount of insurance.(p.327)
• I lost my ***driver's*** license, was made a ward of the court, and was put on probation (not to mention the fact that I might have killed three friends and myself).(p.354)
• But more important, I would have found that once again I was sitting in the ***driver's*** seat – I was running the show.(p.471)

drivers

• The bill collectors, the sheriffs, the angry taxi ***drivers***, the policemen, the bums, the pals, and even the ladies they sometimes brought home – our husbands thought we were so inhospitable.(p.106)

drives

• I became one of the most active women in the community, what with P.T.A., other community organizations and ***drives***.(p.339)
• Father is an Episcopal minister and his work takes him over long ***drives*** on bad roads.(p.497)
• It is not long before he ***drives*** up in the buggy.(p.497)

driveway

• Halfway down the ***driveway*** a thought strikes me.(p.506)

driving

• It is important that he be able to keep a confidence; that he fully understand and approve what we are ***driving*** at; that he will not try to change our plan.(p.74)
• I didn't want to jeopardize the lives of innocent people by ***driving*** an automobile while intoxicated, but I did.(p.199)
• Another time, I had gone around to Max R. trying to get a job ***driving*** one of his trucks.(p.200)
• Everything in the world a man could possibly want, and I was ***driving*** from Akron to Cleveland, having just been to the bank and discovered that I had approximately $5,000.(p.200)
• So I was ***driving*** to Cleveland when I made this solemn promise never to drink again.(p.201)
• At three-thirty the next morning, I was in Champlain Street Station, in jail for ***driving*** while intoxicated and insulting an officer; and the suit of which I was so proud was in such shape that the turnkey had to get me a pair of trousers to go into court in the next morning.(p.201)
• Many things happened; business trials, little worries, and feelings of general despondency came near ***driving*** me to the bottle, but I made progress.(p.237)
• One Sunday afternoon, the only time I ever got picked up for drunken ***driving***, I got picked up in Bellaire.(p.264)
• Next, I was sent to Arizona, where my drinking picked up some more, and I started having blackouts, and I was thrown in jail for speeding and drunken ***driving***.(p.318)
• I was living in constant fear that I would get caught while ***driving*** a car, so I used taxis part of the time.(p.375)

drop

• He made up his mind that until he had been successful in business and had retired, he would not touch another ***drop***.(p.32)
• If he is not interested in your solution, if he expects you to act only as a banker for his financial difficulties or a nurse for his sprees, you may have to ***drop*** him until he changes his mind.(p.95)
• If this kind of approach does not catch your husband's interest, it may be best to ***drop*** the subject, but after a friendly talk your husband will usually revive the topic himself.(p.112)
• I've prayed to God on hangover mornings and sworn that I'd never touch another ***drop*** but by nine o'clock I'd be boiled as an owl."(p.158)
• Those of us who travel ***drop*** in as often as we can.(p.162)
• I was about twenty-five then, and I had never touched a ***drop***.(p.262)
• Time went on and the drinking got worse and worse, and I was in another barroom, down the road the other way, a small one, and I took my glass – that

morning I'd been able to lift it from the bar -- and I said to the woman behind the bar, "I wish I might never take another ***drop*** of that stuff.(p.266)
• I hunt for my nickel to ***drop*** in the plate so that mine will be seen.(p.497)
• If something does come along that sort of upsets me, instead of walking in and throwing a buck at the barman and asking for a drink, I walk into a telephone booth, ***drop*** a dime in the box, and call somebody who was so kind as to give me his name and telephone number to meet such an emergency.(p.511)

dropped
• My friends had ***dropped*** several million since ten o'clock -- so what?(p.4)
• The scales had ***dropped*** from my eyes and I could see life in its proper perspective.(p.280)
• As time went on, I found that it was customary to open a few bottles whenever visitors ***dropped*** in.(p.297)
• I ***dropped*** a two-quart water bottle on my big toe.(p.390)
• One by one, the understanding friends ***dropped*** away.(p.538)

dropping
• Those of us who live in large cities are overcome by the reflection that close by hundreds are ***dropping*** into oblivion every day.(p.19)

drops
• Paul measured the medicine out, but he figured that with my track record that little bit wouldn't be enough, so he doubled it and added a few ***drops*** more and then gave it to me.(p.207)

drove
• This sometimes nearly ***drove*** me back to drink, but I soon found that when all other measures failed, work with another alcoholic would save the day.(p.15)
• We boys ***drove*** out in somebody's car and went to the bar on the way do the dining room and I, in an effort to impress the other boys that I was city-bred, having lived in Scranton and Cleveland, asked them if they didn't want a drink.(p.194)
• I ***drove*** towards Cleveland wondering why I found myself in such a changed set of conditions as compared with those of six months before.(p.200)
• So I didn't have a beer one night, and as I ***drove*** home I was breaking my arm patting myself on the back because I had proved I could lick liquor.(p.203)
• We ***drove*** to a store in North Hill and I sent him in with what money I had to get a quart.(p.204)
• We ***drove*** my car and I left it down in the yard.(p.217)
• I ***drove*** these three or four miles down the road only to find that Jack was out.(p.267)
• My parents' car had a strong attraction to fences, and one night I blacked out and ***drove*** the car down a bank, ramming the steel fence around someone's backyard.(p.353)
• I got right into the car and they ***drove*** me over, and just as soon as I got to the church they started the wedding.(p.385)
• So it ***drove*** me deeper into the psychosis or neurosis that I had, and that I hated deep down in my heart.(p.388)

drowned
• And I remembered the creeping horror of the interminable night, in which I slept for short spells and woke up dripping with cold sweat and shaken with utter despair, to drink hastily from my bottle and mercifully pass out again, "You're mad, you're mad, you're mad!" pounded through my brain with each returning ray of consciousness, and I ***drowned*** the refrain with drink.(p.224)
• So I took my bottle and went and ***drowned*** my sorrows.(p.318)

drowning
• We, in our turn, sought the same escape with all the desperation of ***drowning*** men.(p.28)

drug
• A well-known doctor, chief physician at a nationally prominent hospital specializing in alcoholic and ***drug*** addiction, gave Alcoholics Anonymous this letter:(p.xxiii)
• I say this after many years' experience as Medical Director of one of the oldest hospitals in the country treating alcoholic and ***drug*** addiction.(p.xxv)
• In one of these there is a well-known hospital for the treatment of alcoholic and ***drug*** addiction.(p.161)
• So I went down to him quite a few times a month and had him shoot me full of the stuff; and then I went across the street to a little ***drug*** store to take a glass of beer or two beers, and then stopped at the liquor store to get myself a pint and go home.(p.389)
• No one could have told me then that I had not earned all my success, nor could anyone have told me that I was an alcoholic and a ***drug*** addict.(p.418)
• I am a young alcoholic with a ***drug*** problem, a doctor, the husband of an alcoholic, the son of an alcoholic, and a man once diagnosed as a violent manic-depressive.(p.421)
• I didn't feel I could lie in bed and squirt the stuff in my veins while my kids and wife stood around watching me, so I kept the ***drug*** in my bag and the bag in the car and the car in the garage.(p.442)
• A very good friend of mine who owned a ***drug*** store across the street from us, came by only about two hours later and said that he had seen Vi down town.(p.487)

drug's
• No matter how often I had gone into and come out of alcoholic lows during the day, the pattern bounced me out of bed each night about 2:00 a.m., shaking and hurting in the agitation that always follows a ***drug's*** sedation.(p.332)

drugged
• You ask, because many alcoholics, being warped and ***drugged***, do not want to quit.(p.142)

drugs
• He may even read in a newspaper that one out of every seven drinkers will become alcoholic, but he rarely is told that it holds true for all ages -- or that the tolerance to alcohol (and other ***drugs***) decreases steadily, year after year, in the bodies of all persons.(p.330)
• When I went back to my hometown to go into private practice, I experienced another brief lull in my addiction to alcohol and ***drugs***.(p.420)
• The physician wasn't hooked, he thought -- he just prescribed ***drugs*** medically indicated for his many ailments.(p.439)
• Later on, it took alcohol fortified with other ***drugs*** to pull me up.(p.457)
• It is estimated that two-thirds of the men in prison were under the influence of alcohol and/or ***drugs*** when they committed their offenses.(p.458)
• Finally, I was arrested and got six months for ***drugs***.(p.480)

drugstore
• That age of the flapper and the "It" girl, speakeasies and the hip flask, the boyish bob and the ***drugstore*** cowboy, John Held Jr. and F. Scott Fitzgerald, all generously sprinkled with a patent pseudo-sophistication.(p.304)
• After going to school all day, working in the family ***drugstore*** all evening, and then studying until one or two in the morning, I would not be able to sleep soundly, with everything I had been studying going round in my head.(p.440)
• When I got out of there, I lasted about fifteen minutes at home, before I headed for the ***drugstore*** and more pills, and then the bar.(p.479)

drugstore-home
• As a physician and pharmacist who had grown up in a ***drugstore-home***, I had a pill for every ill, and I was sick a lot.(p.443)

drunk
• At one of the finals I was too ***drunk*** to think or write.(p.2)
• We had long talks when I would still her foreboding by telling her that men of genius conceived their best projects when ***drunk***; that the most majestic constructions of philosophic thought were so derived.(p.2)
• My wife began to work in a department store, coming home exhausted to find me ***drunk***.(p.4)
• Shortly afterward I came home ***drunk***.(p.5)
• As the whisky rose to my head I told myself I would manage better next time, but I might as well get good and ***drunk*** then.(p.6)
• He is always more or less insanely ***drunk***.(p.21)
• Then comes the day when he simply cannot make it and gets ***drunk*** all over again.(p.22)
• Nevertheless, he was ***drunk*** in a short time.(p.26)
• Here are some of the methods we have tried: Drinking beer only, limiting the number of drinks, never drinking alone, never drinking in the morning, drinking only at home, never having it in the house, never drinking during business hours, drinking only at parties, switching from scotch to brandy, drinking only natural wines, agreeing to resign if ever ***drunk*** on the job, taking a trip, not taking a trip, swearing off forever (with and without a solemn oath), taking more physical exercise, reading inspirational books, going to health farms and sanitariums, accepting voluntary commitment to asylums -- we could increase the list ad infinitum.(p.31)
• Some will be ***drunk*** the day after making their resolutions; most of them within a few weeks.(p.34)
• To his consternation, he found himself ***drunk*** half a dozen times in rapid succession.(p.35)
• Yet he got ***drunk*** again.(p.36)
• In some circumstances we have gone out deliberately to get ***drunk***, feeling ourselves justified by nervousness, anger, worry, depression, jealousy or the like.(p.37)
• Does this mean we are going to get ***drunk***?(p.70)
• Almost invariably they got ***drunk***.(p.72)
• Don't deal with him when he is very ***drunk***, unless he is ugly and the family needs your help.(p.90)
• A ***drunk*** may smash the furniture in your home, or burn a mattress.(p.97)
• In desperation, we have even got tight ourselves -- the ***drunk*** to end all drunks.(p.106)
• Why was it, when these dangers were pointed out that they agreed, and then got ***drunk*** again immediately?(p.107)
• He is violent, or appears definitely insane when ***drunk***.(p.110)
• Perhaps your husband will make a fair start on the new basis, but just as things are going beautifully he dismays you by coming home ***drunk***.(p.120)
• If he gets ***drunk***, don't blame yourself.(p.120)
• He got ***drunk***.(p.135)
• Not long afterward he had called me from Hartford on two successive days, so ***drunk*** he could hardly speak.(p.136)
• When his wife next calls saying he is sick, you might jump to the conclusion he is ***drunk***.(p.146)
• You put me on the spot every time you get ***drunk***.(p.147)
• The last three times, I got ***drunk*** on the way home from here.(p.157)
• My phobia for sleeplessness demanded that I get ***drunk*** every night, but in order to get more liquor for the next night, I had to stay sober during the day, at least up to four o'clock.(p.177)
• It was really a horrible nightmare, this earning money, getting liquor, smuggling it home, getting ***drunk***, morning jitters, taking large doses of sedatives to make it possible for me to earn more money, and so on ad nauseam.(p.177)
• It was harmless; nobody ever got ***drunk*** on beer.(p.177)
• It then occurred to me that after one was all smelled up with beer nobody could tell what had been ***drunk***, so I began to fortify my beer with straight alcohol.(p.178)
• This continued until I enrolled in our state university and, at the end of four years, I realized that I was a ***drunk***.(p.183)
• Then Prohibition came into effect, and the facts that the stuff obtainable was so horrible and sometimes deadly, and that I had married and had a job which I had to look after, helped me for a period of some three or four years, although I would get ***drunk*** every time I could get hold of enough to drink to get started.(p.183)
• Each of the seven times that I had left this hospital in the last six months, I had come out fully determined in my own mind that I would not get ***drunk*** again -- for at least six or eight months.(p.184)
• That wasn't so bad, to tell it to another ***drunk***.(p.185)
• Then she told me that these two drunks she had been talking to had a plan whereby they thought they could quit drinking, and part of that plan was that they tell it to another ***drunk***.(p.185)
• Before very long we began to relate some incidents of our drinking and, naturally, pretty soon, I realized both of them knew what they were talking about because you can see things and smell things when you're ***drunk***, that you can't other times, and, if I had thought they didn't know what they were talking about, I wouldn't have been willing to talk to them at all.(p.185)
• I figured I was just a ***drunk***.(p.187)
• (I might say right here that never in my life did I ever intend to get ***drunk***.(p.196)
• I never had any desire to get ***drunk***.(p.196)
• Eventually, there would be a ball game, or a show, or some sort of special occasion to celebrate and I would turn up ***drunk***.(p.196)
• I found, however, that when I would leave Akron to go to Chicago, I would get ***drunk***.(p.197)
• I can well remember over a long period of years when I thought I was the only person in the world who knew that sooner or later I was going to get ***drunk***.(p.198)
• I can remember occasions when friends recommended me for positions or business opportunities that I wouldn't take because I felt that at some future date I'd get ***drunk*** and they would be hurt.(p.198)
• I came to the conclusion it was because I hadn't been ***drunk***.(p.200)

• And I hadn't been ***drunk*** because I hadn't taken a drink.(p.200)
• Whenever this man and I met – I didn't know his name then nor do I know it now – we would always get ***drunk***.(p.201)
• I think the longest ***drunk*** I was ever on was eleven days, but usually only two days with a complete blackout for a day, and then backing off by drinking as long as I could get anything.(p.203)
• So I was barred from the plant for ten days, and during that ten day period I was ***drunk*** twice, showing how little control these restraints had on me.(p.205)
• Then he started to talk to me about his drinking experiences, what his drinking had cost him, how much he had ***drunk*** and where, things like that, and I remember I was quite bored because I had never seen the guy before and had no interest at all in what, where and when he drank.(p.208)
• I could discipline myself but along the way there would be festivities and occasions when I got ***drunk***.(p.211)
• That night I got very ***drunk***, which was usual, but I remembered everything, which was very unusual.(p.224)
• Naturally, in spite of my good intentions, in spite of my protected life behind sanitarium walls, I several times got ***drunk***, and was astounded . . . and badly shaken.(p.227)
• And as I fumed helplessly and planned to get good and ***drunk*** and show them, my eye caught a sentence in the book lying open on my bed: "We cannot live with anger."(p.228)
• I came of good stock, of men and women who drank wine all their lives as a beverage, and while they occasionally got ***drunk*** at special celebrations, they were up and about their business the next day.(p.231)
• I was never a hilarious ***drunk***; the more I drank the quieter I got, and the drunker I got the harder I fought to stay sober.(p.241)
• I was the fair-haired boy all right, but two years later I was blacklisted as an irresponsible ***drunk***.(p.242)
• For the last two years of my drinking I prayed on every ***drunk*** that I wouldn't wake up again.(p.245)
• After being dry two weeks and sticking close to Jackie, all of a sudden I found I had become the sponsor of my sponsor, for he was suddenly taken ***drunk***.(p.245)
• At that time the group in New York was composed of about twelve men who were working on the principle of every ***drunk*** for himself; we had no real formula and no name.(p.246)
• I had completely forgotten the January 8th when I found the fellowship, and I spent the next four days wandering around New England half ***drunk***, by which I mean I couldn't get ***drunk*** and I couldn't get sober.(p.247)
• Following a big ***drunk*** on that sheet, where I was doing leg-work and rewrite, a feeling of nostalgia made me buy a ticket for Liverpool and I returned to Britain.(p.252)
• That job began a series of brief working spells, each one ending in a "***drunk***" and the urge to travel.(p.253)
• I arrived ***drunk***, but I promised my wife I would keep sober, and I knew I could get work if I did.(p.256)
• An accident while ***drunk*** laid me low for about three weeks.(p.258)
• Formerly, in the acute mental and physical pain during the remorseful periods succeeding each ***drunk***, I found my recollection of the misery I had gone through a bolsterer of resolution and afterward, perhaps, a deterrent for a time.(p.260)
• I remember one instance when he took off and went down to Cincinnati and was gone a week on a ***drunk***.(p.262)
• So, on that Saturday before Labor Day, I got ***drunk*** and set the house on fire -- so we didn't have to paint it.(p.265)
• I thought, "That guy never could have been a ***drunk***."(p.268)
• I didn't think I was going to get ***drunk*** right then, but I remember how comforting it was when I called Anne and told her.(p.273)
• When she finally took the baby and left, I locked myself in the house and stayed ***drunk*** for a month.(p.278)
• So I set out to get ***drunk*** deliberately, just to teach her what she was missing.(p.293)
• How many times I swore off in the morning and got ***drunk*** before sunset I don't know.(p.300)
• Now I was getting ***drunk*** all the time.(p.300)
• I have omitted details of transgressions that I made when ***drunk*** for several reasons.(p.301)
• I didn't care to go visiting unless the parties we might visit had plenty of liquor on hand and I could get ***drunk***.(p.301)
• I was on that job a month and ***drunk*** most of the time.(p.301)
• I got orders to go to Vietnam, and I spent most of the year over there either ***drunk*** or sick with a hangover.(p.317)
• The same as before, I stayed ***drunk*** pretty much of the time.(p.318)
• Other days, I had to miss work because I was still too ***drunk*** to stand up.(p.318)
• I thought my problem was that I had been married to a ***drunk*** for twenty-seven years.(p.321)
• And when I looked at it, I knew I was just as much a ***drunk*** as George was, if not worse.(p.322)
• I was afraid, and I had made my mind up that I would never get ***drunk***, so I was watchful and careful.(p.322)
• I needed a drink, but I was afraid to take a morning drink, because I didn't want to be a ***drunk***.(p.323)
• I became a ***drunk*** anyway, but I was scared to death to take that morning drink.(p.323)
• I can't afford resentments against anyone, because they are the build-up of another ***drunk***.(p.325)
• I was "too important" to show any indication of being a ***drunk***.(p.328)
• I vowed that never again would any important person whom I wished to please and impress ever see me ***drunk***.(p.328)
• No one likes to admit that they're a ***drunk***, that they can't control this thing.(p.340)
• So I thought to myself, I might just as well be ***drunk*** as feel like this.(p.348)
• I spent five and a half years in psychoanalysis and proceeded to become a ***drunk***.(p.349)
• It was to be short lived, for on the day before Christmas I completely disillusioned my wife and ruined our first Christmas by coming home from the Rotary lunch dead ***drunk***.(p.361)
• The final decision came when my daughter, following a ***drunk*** which ruined my wife's birthday, said, "It's Alcoholics Anonymous -- or else!"(p.378)
• The baffling problem of getting ***drunk*** when I had every intention of staying sober was simplified.(p.379)
• Getting ***drunk*** won't solve them.(p.382)
• The only thing I have really to offer you is my own story, telling you just what sort of a ***drunk*** I was.(p.384)
• That was when all the boys and Esther got ***drunk*** and the wives didn't.(p.386)
• Frank left to find the doctor and I got ***drunk***.(p.387)
• I could see no reason why they should have any relationship to this problem of getting ***drunk*** every now and then.(p.388)
• Every time I got ***drunk***, my husband would send me to a nursing home.(p.388)
• So Frank went to New York and despite all these things, I got ***drunk***.(p.389)
• One afternoon, the year after moving to Houston, I got as ***drunk*** as a skunk, and while I do not walk very straight sober, you should see me when I'm ***drunk***!(p.390)
• I was just as ***drunk*** as I could be, getting ready to take an afternoon walk.(p.390)
• Frank was out of town, and I remember that he'd gotten in this one night and found me ***drunk***.(p.391)
• I took two or three drinks so my eyes could focus, and I could see that horrible picture of the awful ***drunk*** on the first page; he couldn't get the drink to his mouth, he had a towel around his hand and he needed a shave.(p.391)
• I stayed ***drunk*** from Monday until Friday, and I call that my spill into A.A.(p.393)
• I never want to forget that last ***drunk*** as long as I live.(p.393)
• After all, upon coming out of a week-long or ten-day ***drunk***, it was hard enough to figure up just how much that one ***drunk*** cost, let alone trying to calculate the cost of approximately twenty-five years of active alcoholism.(p.396)
• I displayed alcoholic tendencies actually from the age of fourteen, when I started to steal wine from the family jug, siphoning it off one drink at a time so it wouldn't be missed, not drinking it immediately, but saving it until about a pint was accumulated, so that I could get ***drunk***.(p.397)
• I had to have enough to get ***drunk*** on, or what was the use?(p.397)
• I found out fast that the cheapest way to get ***drunk*** was on shots with beer chasers at two bits a crack.(p.397)
• In the back of my mind, I probably thought, "They won't take me as ***drunk*** as I am."(p.398)
• But when this happened to me, I declared to friends that I would get ***drunk***, dead ***drunk*** that very night, and stay ***drunk*** for a month.(p.403)
• But I got ***drunk*** that night and stayed ***drunk***, getting increasingly worse until I found A.A. ten years later.(p.404)
• I stayed with them until I got ***drunk*** and had a row with the Paris editor.(p.405)
• ***Drunk*** or sober, I was hectic, unpredictable, irresponsible.(p.406)
• Certainly, when I was in my cups, I was not just ***drunk***, I was crazy.(p.408)
• I was going to get ***drunk*** again – ***Drunk***!(p.408)
• I was, when ***drunk***, just as undisciplined and erratic as ever.(p.410)
• I planned to stay home the night before I left, but my folks got so ***drunk*** I walked off early in the evening and spent the night with my girl, getting very ***drunk*** myself.(p.425)
• I was ***drunk***.(p.425)
• ***Drunk*** and causing a brawl, they said.(p.428)
• Or maybe I'd come home wild ***drunk***, singing and raving about what a fine place home was and what grand parents I had since they joined A.A.(p.428)
• This I would do by going completely "bohemian" for a night, getting ***drunk*** and rolling home with the dawn.(p.432)
• I was never ***drunk*** on the job, never missed a day's work, was seldom rendered totally ineffective by a hangover and kept my liquor expenses well within my adequate budget.(p.433)
• My reaction was that I'd already helped all the patients on the ward, and I still had plenty of problems of my own without trying to help some ***drunk*** from A.A.(p.446)
• I interpreted "sober" as meaning "drinking but not being ***drunk***."(p.447)
• My visits to that sanitarium went on for nearly three years, until in March of 1944, my father died and I was too ***drunk*** to attend his funeral.(p.469)
• Sly and crafty, I thought now I'll find out what they think of me here, what they "have on" me, what I've said coming in here ***drunk***.(p.470)
• And I got ***drunk***.(p.472)
• No ***drunk*** hopeless if he want to follow guide along right trail.(p.477)
• I once hear people say only Indians crazy when ***drunk***.(p.477)
• Aside from being a common ***drunk***, I had a very serious pill affliction and all the garbage that goes with it -- lying, stealing, cheating anybody and everybody, conning the people I could, and staying clear of the ones I couldn't.(p.478)
• Any time I tried to kill myself, I was either ***drunk*** or pilled-up or both – usually the last.(p.479)
• I've never seen him ***drunk*** in my life, although he'd take a shot in the morning and usually one in the evening, and so did I; but for the most part he kept his whiskey in his office.(p.484)
• I said that she told me she was going to the movies, and I became foolishly disturbed about it and, as things snowballed, I decided to go out and get ***drunk***.(p.487)
• That's the first time I was ever really ***drunk*** in my life.(p.487)
• I got ***drunk*** one night in October, went to sleep in the rain and woke up with pneumonia.(p.490)
• Within about ten days I got locked up for being ***drunk*** and this same policeman was in the station house as I was being booked.(p.491)
• As usual I got ***drunk*** and lost the money.(p.491)
• Shouldn't have ***drunk*** so much or so fast.(p.498)
• I get ***drunk***.(p.501)
• I have been drinking a lot, but never get ***drunk***.(p.501)
• I'll get ***drunk***!(p.506)
• I went on a ***drunk***.(p.508)
• After I came in I found I wasn't an exceptional ***drunk***.(p.512)
• I also thought I was a brilliant ***drunk***.(p.512)
• But I came out of the Army just as big a ***drunk*** as when I went in, if not worse, because now I had a lot more resentments.(p.513)
• She had been warned numerous times, not only by her family but by my own mother, that I was a hopeless ***drunk***, that there wasn't anything anybody could do with me, that I'd never stop, and that eventually I'd break her heart.(p.513)
• I was afraid that sometime I would get half ***drunk*** and go through with it.(p.515)
• Of course I really didn't have to worry on that score, because I wasn't the type that got half ***drunk***.(p.515)
• I had ***drunk*** too often and too much.(p.515)
• I was a very fortunate ***drunk***.(p.516)

• Someone told me, "When you drank, you didn't get half *drunk*.(p.516)
• When I look back, I can't see anything that would have predisposed me towards being either a neurotic or a *drunk*.(p.517)
• Then I had a year in Germany at school – that was, incidentally, when I got *drunk* for the first time.(p.517)
• I went to a dinner he gave one night, rather *drunk*.(p.520)
• Just as I was wondering what on earth I could do -- I was too *drunk* even to pack a handkerchief – the memory of an A.A. write-up that I had seen in the Evening Mail flashed across my mind -- and I thought to myself, this is something I haven't tried yet.(p.523)
• I was taking Benzedrine and paraldehyde quite impartially during the day then, and by the time I arrived at my first A.A. meeting, I was pretty *drunk* and certainly doped up to the eyes and completely jittery.(p.523)
• Not least of my debts to A.A. is the knowledge that in that time when she wanted me most, I was there -- and that I wasn't *drunk*.(p.525)
• I was not able to hold a job -- no one wants a *drunk* around.(p.526)
• I would embarrass everyone by coming in *drunk* or passing out.(p.526)
• My father was and still is a minister, and I was afraid that I might run into him, or that someone might tell him where I was, and I could still remember what he had done to me when I got *drunk* one Christmas when I was very young.(p.527)
• Because I had been *drunk*, the judge gave me only a twelve-year sentence in prison.(p.528)
• Within a month, the police, the hospital authorities, several kind strangers, most of my friends, all of my close relatives, and a few adepts at rolling a *drunk* and removing his wrist watch and wallet had been involved.(p.532)
• If the listener were *drunk* enough, the lecture might go on through several martinis, which I was glad to pay for.(p.537)
• I wonder if ever there has been a sillier reason for getting *drunk* all the time.(p.537)
• This question so insulted the emotions that clearly there was only one thing to do, go and get *drunk* again, and put that enquiring mind in its proper place, which was oblivion.(p.537)
• The children kept me sober for darn near three weeks, and then I went on (please God) my last *drunk*.(p.549)
• I've heard it said many times in A.A., "There is just one good *drunk* in every alcoholic's life, and that's the one that brings us into A.A.," and I believe it.(p.549)
• I was *drunk* for sixty days around the clock and it was my intention, literally, to drink myself to death.(p.549)
• I went to jail for the second time during this period for being *drunk* in an automobile.(p.549)
• Society can do anything it chooses to do with me when I am *drunk* and I can't lift a finger to stop it, for I forfeit my rights through the simple expedient of becoming a menace to myself and to the people around me.(p.549)
• I had only to reflect on the contrast between the plans I made so many years ago for my life with what really happened to know I couldn't manage my life *drunk* or sober.(p.550)
• It's been true in my case, nor could I quarrel with "restore us to sanity," for my actions *drunk* or sober, before A.A., were not those of a sane person.(p.550)
• One morning, however, I realized I had to get rid of it, for my reprieve was running out, and if I didn't get rid of it I was going to get *drunk* -- and I didn't want to get *drunk* any more.(p.552)
• Within a few days, I found myself drying out on a *drunk* farm.(p.559)

drunk-driving
• No jail booking, *drunk-driving* citation, barroom fight, or even a tumble off a barstool.(p.327)

drunkalogues
• *Drunkalogues* and statistics can be boring, but it is necessary to delve a little into each in order to come up with some kind of rough estimate.(p.396)
• The more I focus my mind on its defects -- late start, long *drunkalogues*, cigarette smoke -- the worse the meeting becomes.(p.451)

drunkard
• I knew I was a *drunkard*.(p.256)
• A night or so a week in a joint, and a party or so a week at home or with friends, along with a little lone drinking, soon had me preparing for the existence of a top flight *drunkard*.(p.298)
• I would never be like the village *drunkard* at home.(p.498)

drunkard's
• But this was a man who had experienced many years of frightful drinking, who had had most all the *drunkard's* experiences known to man, but who had been cured by the very means I had been trying to employ, that is to say the spiritual approach.(p.180)

drunkards
• There had never been any *drunkards* in my family.(p.231)
• He introduced himself and began to tell me about a bunch of some sixty former drinkers and *drunkards* who met once a week, and he invited me to go with him to the next meeting.(p.257)

drunken
• One Sunday afternoon, the only time I ever got picked up for *drunken* driving, I got picked up in Bellaire.(p.264)
• As a result, I would fall off in a *drunken* stupor every night.(p.299)
• Next, I was sent to Arizona, where my drinking picked up some more, and I started having blackouts, and I was thrown in jail for speeding and *drunken* driving.(p.318)
• We had always encouraged our children to bring their friends home at any time, but after a few experiences with a *drunken* father they eliminated home as a place to entertain friends.(p.376)
• After every cocktail party or dinner party she would say she couldn't understand how I could get in such a *drunken* stupor on one drink.(p.377)
• Just being sober will be making amends to many we have hurt by our *drunken* actions.(p.381)
• I had a *drunken* quarrel with my family, denounced them, and left them forever.(p.409)
• In the course of *drunken* arguments, I found my own views and sense of responsibility as a citizen.(p.410)
• But my attempts at community service ended in a *drunken* and abusive row with a fellow volunteer.(p.410)
• The doctor, apparently realizing that one thing that I certainly needed was sleep, left a bottle of sleeping pills there and in my *drunken* state I took them all, instead of the one or two he had prescribed.(p.465)
• It was obvious even to me, in my *drunken* state, that I wasn't wanted.(p.466)
• My parents were due for the holidays that day, and she didn't want them to find their *drunken* daughter there.(p.467)
• Some *drunken* women really are, you know.(p.479)
• We are aware of the nice things around us, things we never noticed before in our *drunken* stupor.(p.481)
• Mother hated liquor and feared a *drunken* man.(p.498)

drunkenness
• There had been no real infidelity, for loyalty to my wife, helped at times by extreme *drunkenness*, kept me out of those scrapes.(p.3)
• We must remember that ten or twenty years of *drunkenness* would make a skeptic out of anyone.(p.83)
• And it is true that there was no great amount of *drunkenness*.(p.230)
• But the firm became violently ill with my *drunkenness* and their course of treatment was to remove their ulcer, in the form of me, from the payroll, amid much fanfare and very personal and slighting remarks and insinuations.(p.300)
• In spite of knowing that my *drunkenness* was a symptom of the things that were wrong with me, and that I could never drink again, I thought I couldn't yet give it up, although I was going to try.(p.393)
• Depending on the stage of *drunkenness*, eventually I either fought or went to sleep.(p.537)

drunker
• I was never a hilarious drunk; the more I drank the quieter I got, and the *drunker* I got the harder I fought to stay sober.(p.241)
• My wife could not understand the next morning why I was *drunker* than the night before when she took my bottles.(p.289)
• I'd show them -- I'd get *drunker*!(p.319)
• So I got *drunker* and *drunker*, and then, suddenly, I woke up in the booby-hatch.(p.387)
• I tried to control her drinking by pouring her whiskey down the sink before I'd leave for the night, to get *drunker* myself.(p.426)

drunkest
• So it is clear that I never had any fun out of drinking – I would be the soberest-seeming one in the crowd and all of a sudden I would be the *drunkest*.(p.241)

drunks
• In desperation, we have even got tight ourselves -- the drunk to end all *drunks*.(p.106)
• I resented this very much, until she informed me that they were a couple of *drunks* just as I was.(p.184)
• Then she told me that these two *drunks* she had been talking to had a plan whereby they thought they could quit drinking, and part of that plan was that they tell it to another drunk.(p.185)
• At the time, I thought them just a swell pair of screwballs, for they were not only going to save all the *drunks* in the world but also all the so-called normal people!(p.245)
• There was one meeting a week at Bill's home in Brooklyn, and we all took turns there spouting off about how we had changed our lives overnight, how many *drunks* we had saved and straightened out, and last, but not least, how God had touched each of us personally on the shoulder.(p.246)
• Quebec, Toronto, Buffalo, and finally Pittsburgh, were the scenes of man-sized *drunks* until I had gone through my readjusted discharge pay, a fair sum.(p.253)
• I did six years of newspaper advertising, and trade journal work with many, many *drunks* of drab and dreary hue woven into the pattern of my life.(p.254)
• I wanted "ripe" prospects and I didn't feel that I would get very far chasing individual *drunks* in and out of bars.(p.281)
• One is that I don't remember too many of them, as I was one of those *drunks* who could be on his feet and attend a meeting or a party, engage in a conversation with people and do things that any nearly normal person would do, and the next day not remember a thing about where I was, what I did, whom I saw, or how I got home.(p.301)
• Just at this time my wife heard of a doctor in another city who had been very successful with *drunks*.(p.301)
• All hidden *drunks* aren't at home in housewives' dresses.(p.328)
• So the doctor said, "I really don't know too much about it, but they tell me it is a bunch of *drunks* who get together . . ."(p.469)
• My husband interrupted, "She's bad enough now without getting mixed up with a bunch of *drunks*."(p.469)
• I hated that judge for sending me to a place with all those *drunks*.(p.527)

dry
• An exceptional man, he remained bone *dry* for twenty-five years and retired at the age of fifty-five, after a successful and happy business career.(p.32)
• We think few, to whom this book will appeal, can stay *dry* anything like a year.(p.34)
• I had been out of town before during this particular *dry* spell, so there was nothing new about that.(p.41)
• He has begun to try, with or without your cooperation, various means of moderating or staying *dry*.(p.109)
• Now and then a serious drinker, being *dry* at the moment says, "I don't miss it at all.(p.151)
• I was, of course, soon on the carpet and the upshot was that I had to go back for two more quarters and remain absolutely *dry*, if I wished to graduate.(p.174)
• I think I must have been thoroughly scared by what had happened, or by the doctor, or probably both, so that I did not touch a drink again until the country went *dry*.(p.175)
• This *dry* spell lasted for about three weeks; then I went to Atlantic City to attend several days' meeting of a national society of which I was a member.(p.179)
• Every time I'd start thinking about drinking, I would think of the long, *dry* years ahead without having a drink; but this idea of twenty-four hours, that it was up to me from then on, was a lot of help.(p.188)
• I ordered a martini, extra *dry*.(p.194)
• And I said, "Now you want to *dry* me up.(p.207)
• He had also gone all the way through the wringer and had been *dry* two years when I saw him again.(p.243)
• After being *dry* two weeks and sticking close to Jackie, all of a sudden I found I had become the sponsor of my sponsor, for he was suddenly taken drunk.(p.245)
• Bill had then been *dry* three years and Hank, two.(p.245)
• I'd been *dry* three weeks, had the wrinkles out and had sobered up my sponsor all by myself!(p.246)
• Discharged in 1919, I really made up for my *dry* spell.(p.253)
• He stayed "*dry*" for thirteen years!(p.263)
• And he'd been *dry* a year.(p.267)
• He had been *dry* for two and a half years and had

been maintaining his contact with a group of recovered alcoholics in Akron.(p.309)
• Short *dry* spells ended in heavy drinking.(p.375)
• Dr. Bob said, "Love and service keep us *dry,*" and Bill said, "Always we must remember that our first duty is face-to-face help for the alcoholic who still suffers."(p.395)
• The horrors of increasing hangover sickness to occupy the entire day; nausea, *dry* heaves, the rocking bed, the nightmare-filled mind.(p.408)
• Being *dry* is not being sober.(p.462)
• Then I went South, because they told me that the particular county I was going to in North Carolina was a *dry* county.(p.489)
• I would meet some new faces and be in a *dry* county.(p.490)
• Oh yes, I get the *dry* jitters once in a while, but that isn't anything to worry about.(p.516)
• Since, perhaps, suicide was a bit too drastic (actually, I was afraid), *dry* martinis were chosen as the slow, pleasant, private, gradual instrument of self-destruction.(p.531)
• Only, having found them, I threw them away, and ordered another extra *dry* martini.(p.533)
• Back to the big city, for another year of precarious living, paid for largely by one or two friends I still had not milked *dry* or worn to exhaustion with demands on their bounty.(p.540)

dry-cleaning
• In the basement were to be *dry-cleaning* facilities, a barbershop, a pool room, a grocery shop and everything.(p.198)
• Within a year of my return to Detroit, A.A. was a definitely established little group of about a dozen members and I too was established in a modest but steady job handling an independent *dry-cleaning* route of my own.(p.283)

drying
• Within a few days, I found myself *drying* out on a drunk farm.(p.559)

drying-out
• On one occasion when I was serving time in my favorite *drying-out* place while I was having a session with the psychiatrist, she left my case history on her desk when she was called away from the room.(p.470)

dryness
• Now my drinking was limited by only one factor, the enforced periods of *dryness* caused by lengthy tours at sea.(p.398)

dubious
• We, who have traveled this *dubious* path, beg you to lay aside prejudice, even against organized religion.(p.49)
• They may be the *dubious* luxury of normal men, but for alcoholics these things are poison.(p.66)
• I wanted to learn to stand on my own feet, not to change one prop for another, and an intangible and *dubious* one at that.(p.227)

Dublin
• I had two years at *Dublin* University, and then in 1916, I got a nomination for Sandhurst, the British Military College.(p.518)
• When I arrived back in *Dublin,* I had no friends left.(p.522)
• Providentially, this was a Monday might when the *Dublin* Group met in those days, and my family agreed that if A.A. could do anything for me at all, that I'd be allowed to stay on at home on probation.(p.523)
• When I arrived at The Country Shop, which was a restaurant where they met in *Dublin,* I found about thirty-five or forty people in the room.(p.524)

duck
• We couldn't *duck* the issue.(p.53)
• Instead of drinking in fancy bars and clubs, I had to carry a bottle of vodka in my briefcase, *duck* into public toilets, and gulp from the bottle, trembling, in order to keep from falling apart.(p.557)

dud
• It wasn't long before any party without drinks was a *dud* for me.(p.305)

due
• The day before I was *due* to go back to Chicago, a Wednesday and Dr. Bob's afternoon off, he had me down to the office and we spent three or four hours formally going through the Six-Step program as it was at that time.(p.291)
• However, *due* to financial difficulties the whole printing was, for a while, held up and the book received no publicity, nor, of course, was it available in the stores, even if one knew it existed.(p.307)
• My parents were *due* for the holidays that day, and she didn't want them to find their drunken daughter there.(p.467)
• During the years 1930 to 1935, *due* to the Depression and its aftermath, business went from bad to worse.(p.486)
• Dad, *due* to having spent most of his time in a small Virginia town, didn't have any too much money, and the money he had saved and the property he had acquired were in Washington.(p.486)
• My life had become unmanageable *due* to the excessive use of alcohol.(p.515)

dues
• There are no fees or *dues* whatsoever.(p.xiv)
• There were to be no fees or *dues;* our expenses were to be met by our own voluntary contributions.(p.xix)
• I couldn't afford to be found with those people, but I said I would certainly pay his *dues* if it would keep him from drinking.(p.205)

dull
• Perhaps you both like parties which would be *dull* without liquor.(p.110)
• If not irritable, he may seem *dull* and boring, not gay and affectionate as the family would like him to be.(p.126)
• There would be times when the life of respectability and achievement seemed insufferably *dull* – I had to break out.(p.432)
• When I didn't have anything else to do – a *dull* evening at home -- I'd sneak a few drinks upstairs in my room, and that began to be a habit.(p.464)
• There was the necessity for sticking to a job I hated, a *dull,* repetitive job performed in association with other men I had nothing in common with . . . performed for years on end, because the money was needed at home.(p.532)

dulled
• It no longer gave me pleasure – it merely *dulled* the pain -- but I had to have it.(p.226)

duly
• She was *duly* sent to school, away from me.(p.409)

dumb
• For a long time I kept on trying, in a pretty *dumb* way at first, I know, but very earnestly.(p.237)
• You tell that *dumb* cat-and-dog doctor he's not a Beverly Hills psychiatrist.(p.440)

dumped
• Beer was too bulky and it couldn't be kept in a jug under the counter ready to be *dumped* when John Law came around.(p.233)

duplex
• Frank had to go to New York, but because I had a dog, we had a *duplex,* and I thought – if only we had a house!(p.388)
• A *duplex* apartment isn't any place to raise a dog.(p.388)

duplicate
• To *duplicate,* with such backing, what we have accomplished is only a matter of willingness, patience and labor.(p.163)

duplicated
• Speaking at a dinner given by John D. Rockefeller Jr. to introduce Alcoholics Anonymous to some of his friends, Dr. Harry Emerson Fosdick remarked: "I think that psychologically speaking there is a point of advantage in the approach that is being made in this movement that cannot be *duplicated.*(p.574)

DuPont
• We were all set to put *DuPont* out of business.(p.246)

duration
• It was a period of binges coming closer and closer together and being of longer *duration.*(p.288)

during
• The spark that was to flare into the first A.A. group was struck at Akron, Ohio, in June 1935, *during* a talk between a New York stockbroker and an Akron physician.(p.xv)
• My weary and despairing wife was informed that it would all end with heart failure *during* delirium tremens, or I would develop a wet brain, perhaps within a year.(p.7)
• It was fortunate, for my old business associates remained skeptical for a year and a half, *during* which I found little work.(p.15)
• Here are some of the methods we have tried: Drinking beer only, limiting the number of drinks, never drinking alone, never drinking in the morning, drinking only at home, never having it in the house, never drinking *during* business hours, drinking only at parties, switching from scotch to brandy, drinking only natural wines, agreeing to resign if ever drunk on the job, taking a trip, not taking a trip, swearing off forever (with and without a solemn oath), taking more physical exercise, reading inspirational books, going to health farms and sanitariums, accepting voluntary commitment to asylums -- we could increase the list ad infinitum.(p.31)
• I had eaten there many times *during* the months I was sober.(p.36)
• We now see that when we began to drink deliberately, instead of casually, there was little serious or effective thought *during* the period of premeditation of what the terrific consequences might be.(p.37)
• I had been out of town before *during* this particular dry spell, so there was nothing new about that.(p.41)
• To others, the word "God" brought up a particular idea of Him with which someone had tried to impress them *during* childhood.(p.45)
• Be sure you are not critical *during* such a discussion.(p.111)
• *During* those first days of convalescence, this will do more to insure his sobriety than anything else.(p.129)
• We suggest you draw the book to the attention of the doctor who is to attend your patient *during* treatment.(p.144)
• He may wish to do a lot for other alcoholics and something of the sort may come up *during* business hours.(p.146)
• *During* these years, I drank as much as my purse permitted, still without paying too great a penalty, although I was beginning to have morning jitters at times.(p.173)
• I lost only a half day's work *during* these three years.(p.173)
• *During* these two years I was kept so busy that I hardly left the hospital at all.(p.174)
• *During* the next few years, I developed two distinct phobias.(p.175)
• *During* the subsequent fifteen years I had sense enough never to go to the hospital if I had been drinking, and very seldom did I receive patients.(p.176)
• *During* all this time we became more or less ostracized by our friends.(p.177)
• My phobia for sleeplessness demanded that I get drunk every night, but in order to get more liquor for the next night, I had to stay sober *during* the day, at least up to four o'clock.(p.177)
• How my wife kept her faith and courage *during* all those years, I'll never know, but she did.(p.178)
• Unlike most of our crowd, I did not get over my craving for liquor much *during* the first two and one-half years of abstinence.(p.181)
• *During* the first six months of 1935, I was hospitalized eight times for intoxication and shackled to the bed two or three days before I even knew where I was.(p.184)
• *During* the day, looking over the contracts and money in my pocket, I found that I had sold six lots that I couldn't even remember, and didn't even know the people I had sold them to.(p.196)
• *During* the latter part of the Christian Science experience I had gotten a job and was working at Firestone.(p.203)
• So I was barred from the plant for ten days, and *during* that ten day period I was drunk twice, showing how little control these restraints had on me.(p.205)
• There were only seven or eight people in the group before me and they all visited me *during* my period in the hospital.(p.208)
• The very simple program they advised me to follow was that I should ask to know God's will for me for that one day, and then, to the best of my ability, to follow that, and at night to express my gratefulness to God for the things that had happened to me *during* the day.(p.208)
• I can remember that in my childhood, he was ill at ease with the children because he attempted to assert an army discipline that had been ground into him *during* his three and a half years of army service.(p.210)
• Although, *during* this period I was not addicted to any pattern of alcohol consumption, when I did drink the drinking was pretty wild.(p.212)
• My drinking career began about four years after I had moved up into partnership and had joined certain clubs, societies and so fourth, and *during* which period we had Prohibition.(p.213)
• All *during* Prohibition, every alcoholic felt that he made the best hooch, regardless of how bad it was.(p.213)
• In fact, the last three years of my drinking was a routine of barbiturates in the morning, so that I could stop shaking enough to shave, and then alcohol beginning about four-thirty or five o'clock, with a struggle not to take a drink at noon or *during* the day, because I had the idea that if I took one drink, I would smell as though I had had a pint.(p.217)

• *During* that first week-end I decided to stay in New York and take all they gave out with, except the "God stuff."(p.246)
• *During* my visit there, renewing acquaintance with former friends, I soon spent most of my money.(p.252)
• I stayed sober *during* the trip except for an occasional bottle of beer because funds barely met expenses.(p.255)
• Formerly, in the acute mental and physical pain *during* the remorseful periods succeeding each drunk, I found my recollection of the misery I had gone through a bolsterer of resolution and afterward, perhaps, a deterrent for a time.(p.260)
• I had gone to an attorney to see about getting a divorce *during* that year.(p.263)
• I can't express what A.A. meant to us *during* that year.(p.272)
• I had been brought up to believe this, and I had shown *during* my 'teens considerable enterprise and imagination about earning money.(p.275)
• *During* my first year out of college I had endless dates, and went to countless dances, balls and dinner parties.(p.275)
• Sometimes *during* that year I rebelled inwardly at what seemed like lost time, and at having to be a burden to these good people whose means were limited.(p.281)
• *During* my first few months in Akron I was quite sure that I never wanted to see my home town again.(p.281)
• *During* that first year, however, I managed to make both ends meet, and to avoid ever going back to my old habit pattern of borrowing money when I could not earn it.(p.283)
• *During* the first three months I carried on all these activities without a car, depending entirely on buses and streetcars – I, who had always to have a car at my immediate command.(p.283)
• Have I ever wanted a drink *during* these years?(p.285)
• In this small group, *during* the Depression, there was no one who was not hard up.(p.291)
• How I was able to discharge my duties at the office *during* those horrible mornings, I will never be able to explain.(p.299)
• *During* this time, I had been threatened, beaten, kissed, praised and damned alternately by relatives, family, friends and strangers, but of course it all went for naught.(p.300)
• No matter how often I had gone into and come out of alcoholic lows *during* the day, the pattern bounced me out of bed each night about 2:00 a.m., shaking and hurting in the agitation that always follows a drug's sedation.(p.332)
• But *during* a period of particular stress and strain about thirteen years ago, I resorted to alcohol in my home, alone, as a means of temporary release, as a means of getting a little extra sleep.(p.335)
• *During* this vacation, in the months of September and October, I decided to go on the water wagon.(p.343)
• *During* the next three years, I tried often again to give it up, but failed miserably.(p.343)
• Following this, I had a short vacation, *during* which time I read as much literature as my sponsor could send me.(p.343)
• I had turned eighteen *during* the trip, and I despondently returned home by jet (on Daddy's bankbook) to a pair of miserable, hurt parents.(p.354)
• I was active and did well, however, in school publications, dramatics (which came in handy *during* my drinking career), and Greek letter societies.(p.357)
• *During* this time I faithfully was writing my girl in Utah.(p.360)
• *During* three years in A.A., I haven't lost so much as one shirt.(p.372)
• I did work of all kinds after school and *during* vacations, trying to find that which would appeal most as a goal for a life work.(p.373)
• Two years before I joined A.A. my wife took a long trip *during* which she wrote me she just couldn't return unless I did something about my drinking.(p.377)
• But somewhere *during* that time, I remembered going back on the bunk and crying my eyes out.(p.390)
• Today, because of A.A.'s growth *during* the intervening years, it is of course much bigger than it was then.(p.392)
• He got half custody of our child, but later kept her *during* most of the school terms.(p.402)
• A house in Virginia, *during* the fox hunting season; a little chalet in Switzerland *during* the summer or a place on Long Island – each house complete with cooks, butlers and maids.(p.403)
• *During* these years, I did acquire some good friends.(p.404)
• *During* this period I married again.(p.405)
• *During* this time, you are supposed to behave yourself, but I took a little wine-tasting tour through France, all by my lone, with car and chauffeur.(p.405)
• Not understanding the twenty-four hour plan, or not wanting to, I began drinking and was off-again on-again, *during* that first month.(p.414)
• Except for one short slip, *during* the first eight months, which was an angry "the world can't do this to me" reaction to a personal tragedy in my life, I have been sober for twelve years.(p.416)
• *During* my first year there, I married.(p.419)
• I'd heard a lot about A.A. and met a great many A.A.'s *during* that year at home, but I hadn't thought of it for myself.(p.429)
• Once or twice, *during* my early drinking, I carried it over into the second day, and only once, that I can remember, did it continue into the third.(p.432)
• "Then why in God's name haven't you told me so, *during* all these years?"(p.436)
• That was seven years ago -- and many A.A. meetings ago – and I haven't had a drink *during* those seven years.(p.437)
• In a prison in my native state, I spent eleven months in solitary confinement, bouncing in and out of the "hole" (a bare concrete-and-steel cubicle) about five times *during* those eleven months.(p.459)
• *During* the twenty-four hours after running into the Serenity Prayer, I think I took the first three Steps for the first time.(p.461)
• Tragedies *during* those years that were caused by my drinking, such as the breaking up of my marriage, the death of my child, other things – had little restraining effect.(p.465)
• With their help I also saw that certainly, because of some of the things I had done *during* the years, I was bordering on insanity, and so, facing the record, I tried to believe that a Power greater than I could and would restore me to sanity.(p.471)
• So I concentrated and studied the book *during* that time, and I liked a lot of the things it said in there.(p.472)
• *During* these seven years a thing called the Twenty-four Hour Program –a gadget I used to think was only a snare to trap the newcomer -- has come to mean much to me, not only as regards my drinking but in the whole pattern of my life.(p.473)
• *During* recess we were playing basketball and I had accidentally tripped a fellow just a little larger than I was.(p.484)
• But I can remember in post graduate days, and *during* interneship, that very often I'd go to a patient's bed and start a process of elimination and then, very often, I'd wind up guessing.(p.485)
• *During* the years 1930 to 1935, due to the Depression and its aftermath, business went from bad to worse.(p.486)
• The closest I came to a psychiatrist *during* that time was an interne who came to take blood tests.(p.492)
• A case of measles saved me from being kicked out *during* my Sophomore year.(p.499)
• *During* the course of that drinking, I had shot and killed one person and almost completed the job on a second one.(p.508)
• We were married, and *during* the first nine months of that marriage I was sober.(p.514)
• Lots of the older people had taken to drinking quite a good deal more *during* the war, but the younger generation was, I think, about the same.(p.518)
• In part, it was a feeling of intense shame at having to leave the Army *during* the war, but mostly it was resentment that this kind of thing should happen to me for, strange as it may seem, up to then I still thought I could control drinking.(p.521)
• I was taking Benzedrine and paraldehyde quite impartially *during* the day then, and by the time I arrived at my first A.A. meeting, I was pretty drunk and certainly doped up to the eyes and completely jittery.(p.523)
• They tell me that I killed a man *during* that period, but I can't remember anything.(p.528)
• I'm writing this *during* an A.A. convention, where I have spent the weekend with nothing but white people.(p.529)
• *During* this time, our country was at war.(p.547)
• The amount of will power exercised to control my drinking *during* working hours, diverted into a constructive channel, would have made me President, and the thing that made the will power possible was the knowledge that as soon as my day was finished I could drink myself into oblivion.(p.548)
• I went to jail for the second time *during* this period for being drunk in an automobile.(p.549)
• *During* the day a friend of mine brought me some magazines to take to a hospital group I was interested in, and I looked through them and a "banner" across the front of one featured an article by a prominent clergyman in which I caught the word "resentment."(p.552)
• Like most other alcoholics I have known, I did quit drinking at various times -- once for ten months on my own and *during* other interludes when I was hospitalized.(p.554)

duties

• Father may have laid aside for years all normal activities – clubs, civic *duties*, sports.(p.131)
• My new *duties* were extremely confining and my liquor consumption began to increase.(p.298)
• How I was able to discharge my *duties* at the office during those horrible mornings, I will never be able to explain.(p.299)
• It has brought me back to a realization of my Maker and my *duties* to Him.(p.525)

duty

• Those of us belonging to a religious denomination which requires confession must, and of course, will want to go to the properly appointed authority whose *duty* it is to receive it.(p.74)
• 1.Sense of *duty*.(p.181)
• He had already imbued them with his own spirit until they were ready and willing at all times to go where sent, and as a doctor he well knew that this mission and *duty* would strengthen them as it later helped me.(p.235)
• This *duty* together with my weekly meetings with my fellow alcoholics, and my daily renewal of the contract I originally made with God, have kept me sober when nothing else ever did.(p.237)
• Nor have I attended them with a feeling of just doing my *duty*.(p.381)
• Dr. Bob said, "Love and service keep us dry," and Bill said, "Always we must remember that our first *duty* is face-to-face help for the alcoholic who still suffers."(p.395)
• I thought it was my *duty* to keep her from drinking, not knowing that if the other fellow is really determined to drink there is nothing you can do about it.(p.415)
• And when this six month school was over I applied for *duty* in Hawaii and pulled it.(p.426)

dwell

• If he is in a serious mood *dwell* on the trouble liquor has caused you, being careful not to moralize or lecture.(p.91)
• If you are satisfied that he is a real alcoholic, begin to *dwell* on the hopeless feature of the malady.(p.92)
• The details of the long road back to something resembling normal living -- the first short streetcar ride, the purchase of a used bike which enabled me to widen the narrow horizon of life, the first trip downtown – I will not *dwell* on.(p.276)

dwelt

• Doc *dwelt* on the idea that this was an illness, but Doc was pretty frank with me.(p.219)
• Dr. Bob *dwelt* at length on how prayer had given him release, time and time again, from the nearly over-powering compulsion to take a drink.(p.279)

dying

• He will work like the devil and thank you to his *dying* day.(p.149)
• Near you, alcoholics are *dying* helplessly like people in a sinking ship.(p.152)
• As I went in I was *dying* of mortification.(p.413)
• There are many things worse than *dying*, but is there any death worse than the progressive, self-induced, slow suicide of the practicing alcoholic?(p.457)
• Mother has been *dying* of cancer for a long time.(p.501)

dynamics

• I do not want to digress into the *dynamics* of penology.(p.458)

Ee

each

• When writing or speaking publicly about alcoholism, we urge ***each*** of our Fellowship to omit his personal name, designating himself instead as "a member of Alcoholics Anonymous."(p.xiii)
• Groups are to be found in ***each*** of the United States and all of the provinces of Canada.(p.xv)
• ***Each*** inquiry was painstakingly answered; pamphlets and books were sent out.(p.xviii)
• It was thought that no alcoholic man or woman could be excluded from our Society; that our leaders might serve but never govern; that ***each*** group was to be autonomous and there was to be no professional class of therapy.(p.xix)
• ***Each*** day, somewhere in the world, recovery begins when one alcoholic talks with another alcoholic, sharing experience, strength, and hope.(p.xxii)
• ***Each*** day my friend's simple talk in our kitchen multiplies itself in a widening circle of peace on earth and good will to men.(p.16)
• This should be an entirely personal affair which ***each*** one decides for himself in the light of past associations, or his present choice.(p.28)
• ***Each*** individual, in the personal stories, describes in his own language and from his own point of view the way he established his relationship with God.(p.29)
• On ***each*** of these occasions we worked with him, reviewing carefully what had happened.(p.35)
• The prosaic steel girder is a mass of electrons whirling around ***each*** other at incredible speed.(p.48)
• In our personal stories you will find a wide variation in the way ***each*** teller approaches and conceives of the Power which is greater than himself.(p.50)
• They are questions for ***each*** individual to settle for himself.(p.50)
• This Power has in ***each*** case accomplished the miraculous, the humanly impossible.(p.50)
• ***Each*** person is like an actor who wants to run the whole show; is forever trying to arrange the lights, the ballet, the scenery and the rest of the players in his own way.(p.60)
• And do not his actions make ***each*** of them wish to retaliate, snatching all they can get out of the show?(p.61)
• On our grudge list we set opposite ***each*** name our injuries.(p.65)
• We cannot be helpful to all people, but at least God will show us how to take a kindly and tolerant view of ***each*** and every one.(p.67)
• We subjected ***each*** relation to this test -- was it selfish or not?(p.69)
• In meditation, we ask God what we should do about ***each*** specific matter.(p.69)
• To sum up about sex: We earnestly pray for the right ideal, for guidance in ***each*** questionable situation, for sanity, and for the strength to do the right thing.(p.70)
• ***Each*** might pray about it, having the other one's happiness uppermost in mind.(p.82)
• So we clean house with the family, asking ***each*** morning in meditation that our Creator show us the way of patience, tolerance, kindliness and love.(p.83)
• We constantly remind ourselves we are no longer running the show, humbly saying to ourselves many times ***each*** day "Thy will be done."(p.87)
• Frequent contact with newcomers and with ***each*** other is the bright spot of our lives.(p.89)
• Yet we do go to great extremes to provide ***each*** other with these very things, when such action is warranted.(p.98)
• Therefore, ask yourself on ***each*** occasion, "Have I any good social, business, or personal reason for going to this place?(p.101)
• We feel that ***each*** family, in the light of their own circumstances, ought to decide for themselves.(p.103)
• As animals on a treadmill, we have patiently and wearily climbed, falling back in exhaustion after ***each*** futile effort to reach solid ground.(p.107)
• If you both show a willingness to remedy your own defects, there will be little need to criticize ***each*** other.(p.118)
• The alcoholic, his wife, his children, his "in-laws," ***each*** one is likely to have fixed ideas about the family's attitude toward himself or herself.(p.122)
• ***Each*** is interested in having his or her wishes respected.(p.122)
• Is it not because ***each*** wants to play the lead?(p.122)
• Is not ***each*** trying to arrange the family show to his liking?(p.122)
• ***Each*** in his turn may be footsore and may straggle.(p.122)
• We think ***each*** family which has been relieved owes something to those who have not, and when the occasion requires, ***each*** member of it should be only too willing to bring former mistakes, no matter how grievous, out of their hiding places.(p.124)
• In the first flush of spiritual experience they forgave ***each*** other and drew closer together.(p.124)
• We do talk about ***each*** other a great deal, but we almost invariably temper such talk by a spirit of love and tolerance.(p.125)
• Both father and the family are mistaken, though ***each*** side may have some justification.(p.126)
• As ***each*** member of a resentful family begins to see his short comings and admits them to the others, he lays a basis for helpful discussion.(p.127)
• This means trouble, unless the family watches for these tendencies in ***each*** other and comes to a friendly agreement about them.(p.131)
• At the very beginning, the couple ought to frankly face the fact that ***each*** will have to yield here and there if the family is going to play an effective part in the new life.(p.131)
• ***Each*** individual should consult his own conscience.(p.132)
• So let ***each*** family play together or separately, as much as their circumstances warrant.(p.132)
• They will approach still other sick ones and fellowships of Alcoholics Anonymous may spring up in ***each*** city and hamlet, havens for those who must find a way out.(p.153)
• Seeing much of ***each*** other, scarce an evening passed that someone's home did not shelter a little gathering of men and women, happy in their release, and constantly thinking how they might present their discovery to some newcomer.(p.159)
• Cleaning up old scrapes, helping to settle family differences, explaining the disinherited son to his irate parents, lending money and securing jobs for ***each*** other, when justified -- these are everyday occurrences.(p.161)
• Ask Him in your morning meditation what you can do ***each*** day for the man who is still sick.(p.164)
• ***Each*** of the seven times that I had left this hospital in the last six months, I had come out fully determined in my own mind that I would not get drunk again -- for at least six or eight months.(p.184)
• ***Each*** day I would try to find out what His will was, and try to follow that, rather than trying to get Him to always agree that the things I thought of myself were the things best for me.(p.187)
• They looked at one another queerly and, finally, one of them allowed he'd have a beer and they all followed him, ***each*** of them saying he'd have a beer too.(p.194)
• And we stood there for twenty minutes, telling ***each*** other how much better we were, how much better we looked, how much better off we were financially, mentally, physically, morally, and in every way, shape and manner.(p.201)
• I got two drinks, ***each*** of them a quarter of that pint, in me, and was talking along with these people, but I felt that sooner or later they were going to have me cornered because they were smarter than I was and the drink was beginning to take effect; but as I reached for the third drink Bob said, "Listen, Buster, you promised to take some medicine if we got you a drink.(p.206)
• I became a constant drinker with a terrific fight to control the amount of my consumption ***each*** day.(p.214)
• After two or three years of effort along this line, I reached the point of actual despair that I ever would be able to drink only a harmless amount ***each*** day.(p.215)
• And I remembered the creeping horror of the interminable night, in which I slept for short spells and woke up dripping with cold sweat and shaken with utter despair, to drink hastily from my bottle and mercifully pass out again, "You're mad, you're mad, you're mad!" pounded through my brain with ***each*** returning ray of consciousness, and I drowned the refrain with drink.(p.224)
• Jackie told me about a group of fellows in New York, of whom my old friend Fitz was one, who had the same problem I had, and who by working together to help ***each*** other were not now drinking and were happy like himself.(p.239)
• At this school we had Bible readings before ***each*** meal, and church services four times on Sunday, and I became so rebellious at this that I swore I would never join or go to any church except for weddings or funerals.(p.240)
• But ***each*** drink after the "first" seemed to become less effective and after three or four they all seemed like water.(p.241)
• People have wars and kill ***each*** other; they struggle and cut ***each*** other's throats for success and what does anyone get out of it?(p.244)
• In those days we really took ***each*** other's inventories firmly and often.(p.245)
• There was one meeting a week at Bill's home in Brooklyn, and we all took turns there spouting off about how we had changed our lives overnight, how many drunks we had saved and straightened out, and last, but not least, how God had touched ***each*** of us personally on the shoulder.(p.246)
• That job began a series of brief working spells, ***each*** one ending in a "drunk" and the urge to travel.(p.253)
• I began to read the Bible daily and to go over a simple devotional exercise as a way to begin ***each*** day.(p.259)
• Formerly, in the acute mental and physical pain during the remorseful periods succeeding ***each*** drunk, I found my recollection of the misery I had gone through a bolsterer of resolution and afterward, perhaps, a deterrent for a time.(p.260)
• We comforted ***each*** other.(p.265)
• We had meetings at ***each*** other's homes and, of course, that was a grand place for people to get together out there; they seemed to think so too.(p.270)
• Haunting me through ***each*** day's stupor -- and there were eighteen or nineteen such days in this man's home -- was the thought: "Where do I go when his family comes home?"(p.278)
• We complement ***each*** other beautifully, as he is a born salesman and my taste is for finance and management.(p.284)
• The next afternoon and evening, two other men visited me and ***each*** told me his story and the things that they were doing to try to recover from this tragic illness.(p.290)
• When I said yes, we both knelt at his desk and prayed, ***each*** of us asking to have these defects taken away.(p.292)
• Courage to face ***each*** day has replaced the fears and uncertainties of earlier years.(p.295)
• However, as there happened to be several saloons within that distance, I didn't find it necessary to patronize the same place ***each*** evening.(p.298)
• In time, I found myself looking forward to ***each*** new day with pleasurable anticipation.(p.311)
• We have faith in ***each*** other, trust in ***each*** other, and understanding.(p.325)
• I am trying now, ***each*** day, to make up for all those selfish, thoughtless, foolish things I did in my drinking days.(p.326)
• My alcoholism-prone mind, however, reminded me that all great authors had needed a stimulus to build up inspiration and inventiveness before ***each*** day's work.(p.331)
• Yet I recently recalled that ***each*** morning I used to talk to the bottle when I took it down from the closet.(p.332)
• No matter how often I had gone into and come out of alcoholic lows during the day, the pattern bounced me out of bed ***each*** night about 2:00 a.m., shaking and hurting in the agitation that always follows a drug's sedation.(p.332)
• I was president of ***each*** class in the University, and president of that student body.(p.345)
• A "spiritual experience" to me meant attending meetings, seeing a group of people, all there for the purpose of helping ***each*** other; hearing the Twelve Steps and the Twelve Traditions read at a meeting, and hearing the Lord's Prayer, which in an A.A. meeting has such great meaning -- "Thy will be done, not mine."(p.381)
• A spiritual awakening soon came to mean trying ***each*** day to be a little more thoughtful, more considerate, a little more courteous to those with whom I came in contact.(p.381)
• I was desperately in earnest to follow through and understand what was expected of me as a member of A.A. and to take ***each*** Step of the Twelve as rapidly as possible.(p.382)
• Doing our best, living ***each*** day to the fullest is the art of living.(p.382)
• ***Each*** day seems to be so much more productive

and satisfying.(p.383)
• Drunkalogues and statistics can be boring, but it is necessary to delve a little into ***each*** in order to come up with some kind of rough estimate.(p.396)
• A house in Virginia, during the fox hunting season; a little chalet in Switzerland during the summer or a place on Long Island – ***each*** house complete with cooks, butlers and maids.(p.403)
• My gratitude to A.A. grows deeper ***each*** day I am sober.(p.420)
• On ***each*** occasion, I had a convulsion on Sunday morning.(p.444)
• ***Each*** with the other as a witness, we took the Third Step out loud – just as it says in the Big Book.(p.446)
• We sat in the back and talked only to ***each*** other.(p.447)
• (Today, there is absolutely nothing in the world more important to me than my keeping this alcoholic sober; not taking a drink is by far the most important thing I do ***each*** day.)(p.447)
• A.A. and acceptance have taught me that there is a bit of good in the worst of us and a bit of bad in the best of us; that we are all children of God and we ***each*** have a right to be here.(p.449)
• ***Each*** time I told her she was a nothing, she receded a little more into nowhere.(p.450)
• When we deal in feelings, we tend to come to know ourselves and ***each*** other much better.(p.451)
• Eventually, I had to redo ***each*** of the Twelve Steps specifically with Max in mind, from the First, saying, "I am powerless over alcohol, and my homelife is unmanageable by me," to the Twelfth, in which I tried to think of her as a sick Al-Anon and treat her with the love I would give a sick A.A. newcomer.(p.452)
• I painfully awakened ***each*** time, mentally, physically, and spiritually sick.(p.457)
• ***Each*** ten-day period in the dark hole, I was fed bread and water daily, with one full meal on the third day only.(p.459)
• The poorest person has no less and the wealthiest has no more – ***each*** of us has but one day.(p.473)
• When he left I walked with him to the streetcar line, which was just about a half a block, but there were two liquor stores, one on ***each*** corner from my home.(p.495)
• ***Each*** battle has ended in defeat.(p.502)
• ***Each*** time I would make a report to the parole officer he would ask me, "Have you been to an A.A. meeting yet?"(p.510)
• ***Each*** one has its own place.(p.516)
• I would wait for the mailman ***each*** month, like any good mother, but as soon as he handed me my check, I put on my best dress and went looking for my alcoholic friend.(p.527)
• I'd visit one bar after another, having one martini in ***each***, and in ***each*** hoping to find someone interesting to talk to.(p.536)
• In ***each*** new place, I was the new kid – a skinny, shy kid – to be tested and beaten up.(p.555)
• In the next half-year, I experienced two more esophageal hemorrhages, miraculously surviving ***each*** one by a hair.(p.558)
• ***Each*** time, I went back to drinking – even smuggling a bottle of vodka into the hospital as soon as the blood transfusions had ceased.(p.558)
• Four – ***Each*** group should be autonomous except in matters affecting other groups or A.A. as a whole.(p.564)
• Five – ***Each*** group has but one primary purpose -- to carry its message to the alcoholic who still suffers.(p.564)
• 1. – ***Each*** member of Alcoholics Anonymous is but a small part of a great whole.(p.565)
• 4. – With respect to its own affairs, ***each*** A.A group should be responsible to no other authority than its own conscience.(p.565)
• 5. – ***Each*** Alcoholics Anonymous group ought to be a spiritual entity having but one primary purpose -- that of carrying its message to the alcoholic who still suffers.(p.565)
• We think that ***each*** group should soon achieve this ideal; that any public solicitation of funds using the name of Alcoholics Anonymous is highly dangerous, whether by groups, clubs, hospitals, or other outside agencies; that acceptance of large gifts from any source, or of contributions carrying any obligation whatever, is unwise.(p.566)
• 9. – ***Each*** A.A. group needs the least possible organization.(p.567)

eager

• Spiritually . . . I found a Friend who never lets me down and is ever ***eager*** to help.(p.303)
• Since I started out ***eager*** for early-day efforts, that meant guzzling before noon.(p.331)

eagerly

• ***Eagerly*** he pointed to us saying, "These are the fellows I told you about; they are the ones who understand."(p.189)
• I had read and heard a little about A.A. and so, groping for the phone book, I found the A.A. number and with hope in my heart ***eagerly*** telephoned.(p.363)
• I kept away from liquor and ***eagerly*** waited.(p.363)

eagerness

• You are sure to find someone desperate enough to accept with ***eagerness*** what you offer.(p.96)

ear

• I heard a lovely voice, and a sympathetic ***ear*** listened to my plea.(p.363)
• This went in one ***ear*** and out the other.(p.406)
• But on the other hand, I was terribly fortunate because that should have been a court martial offense and I should have been out on my ***ear***.(p.520)

Earle

• He said, "***Earle***?" and I said, "Yes."(p.347)
• And he said, "***Earle***, why don't you come on over and let me talk to you for a minute."(p.348)

earlier

• Six months ***earlier***, the broker had been relieved of his drink obsession by a sudden spiritual experience, following a meeting with an alcoholic friend who had been in contact with the Oxford Groups of that day.(p.xv)
• I remained with them for three weeks, using part of the time in making many amends, which I had had no ***earlier*** opportunity of making.(p.281)
• Courage to face each day has replaced the fears and uncertainties of ***earlier*** years.(p.295)
• Years ***earlier***, I had gone into psychoanalysis to get relief.(p.349)
• For an estimate of salary from the twenty-one a month to start with, to over $400 per month upon my retirement after twenty years in the Navy, I believe that an average income of $2,000 a year over this period is low, but as I stated ***earlier***, an underestimate is best.(p.399)
• In fact, I was taken to A.A. by a woman whom my father had taken to A.A. thirteen years ***earlier***.(p.419)
• Moreover, I am deeply convinced that so long as I continue to strive, in my bumbling way, toward the principles I first encountered in the ***earlier*** chapters of this book, this remarkable power will continue to flow through me.(p.437)
• As I said ***earlier***, self-pity and resentment were my constant companions and my inventory began to look like a thirty-three year diary, for I seemed to have a resentment against everybody I had ever known.(p.551)
• (This address is now available in pamphlet form at nominal cost through most A.A. groups or from Box 459, Grand Central Station, New York, NY 10163, under the title "Three Talks to Medical Societies by Bill W." – formerly called "Bill on Alcoholism" and ***earlier*** "Alcoholism the Illness.")(p.572)

earliest

• Our ***earliest*** printing voiced the hope "that every alcoholic who journeys will find the Fellowship of Alcoholics Anonymous at his destination.(p.xv)
• The Twelve Steps that summarize the program may be called los Doce Pasos in one country, los Douze Etapes in another, but they trace exactly the same path to recovery that was blazed by the ***earliest*** members of Alcoholics Anonymous.(p.xxii)
• One of the ***earliest*** memories that I have is of a bottle sitting on his desk with a skull and crossbones and marked "Poison."(p.193)
• Through my efforts to get down to "causes and conditions," I stand convinced that my emotional illness has been present from my ***earliest*** recollection.(p.544)

early

• Already," continues the ***early*** text, "twos and threes and fives of us have sprung up in other communities."(p.xv)
• He had also been greatly helped by the late Dr. William D. Silkworth, a New York specialist in alcoholism who is now accounted no less than a medical saint by A.A. members, and whose story of the ***early*** days of our Society appears in the next pages.(p.xvi)
• Some of the recommendations of A.A.'s ***early*** medical and religious friends will be found further on in this book.(p.xx)
• This went on endlessly, and I began to waken very ***early*** in the morning shaking violently.(p.5)
• I hardly dared cross the street, lest I collapse and be run down by an ***early*** morning truck, for it was scarcely daylight.(p.6)
• Yet ***early*** next morning he searches madly for the bottle he misplaced the night before.(p.21)
• Exceptions to cases such as yours have been occurring since ***early*** times.(p.27)
• Though there is no way of proving it, we believe that ***early*** in our drinking careers most of us could have stopped drinking.(p.32)
• In the ***early*** days of our drinking we occasionally remained sober for a year or more, becoming serious drinkers again later.(p.34)
• Dr. Bob and the twelve men and women who here tell their stories were among the ***early*** members of A.A.'s first groups.(p.169)
• The town was well supplied with churches and schools in which I pursued my ***early*** educational activities.(p.171)
• At a comparatively ***early*** age, I can remember being jealous of my brother.(p.194)
• I ***early*** discovered that if I drank anything, I was not accountable for what happened.(p.196)
• The man turned out to be Bill D., a very ***early*** member of A.A., and I couldn't tell you a word of what he said.(p.208)
• I very ***early*** sampled the effects of alcohol.(p.211)
• ***Early*** member, she spread the word among women in our pioneering period.(p.222)
• Very ***early*** I became apprenticed to harness-making and acquired considerable knowledge of upholstering.(p.230)
• I ***early*** decided that the wine of America was very inferior stuff and took up beer instead.(p.231)
• We saw very ***early*** that Prohibition wasn't going to work.(p.232)
• I very ***early*** came to see that there had to be a continual renewal for that simple deal with God; that I had perpetually to keep the bargain.(p.237)
• My ***early*** life was spent in Baltimore where my father was a physician and a grain merchant.(p.240)
• In my ***early*** twenties the hardships of hobo life did not discourage me, but I had no wish to become just a tramp.(p.253)
• I learned ***early*** in my A.A. life that I could not afford to fondle such thoughts, as you might fondle a pet, because this particular pet could grow into a monster.(p.285)
• After a particularly bad Christmas and New Year's holiday, dad picked me up again ***early*** in January, 1937, to go through the usual sobering up routine.(p.289)
• Twenty-seven years of confusion is what my ***early*** married life was.(p.325)
• The encouragement received in the ***early*** days, especially from the A.A. General Service Office, made a tremendous difference to my sobriety.(p.342)
• In the very ***early*** spring of 1944, my frustrated wife couldn't take it any longer.(p.362)
• My first spiritual experience in A.A. came quite ***early*** to me.(p.366)
• We lived a kind of seesaw existence in the ***early*** days.(p.369)
• ***Early*** the next morning a man whose name I knew well, a lawyer, called on me.(p.378)
• After all, I hadn't started to drink ***early*** in life, so I had some stability and maturity to guide me for a while.(p.379)
• I tried to compensate with impossible dreams and ambitions, which were simply ***early*** forms of escape.(p.400)
• Up to my ***early*** thirties, when my drinking had become a major problem, I lived in large houses, with servants and all the luxuries that I could possibly ask for.(p.401)
• I would pull out ***early***, and go to the hunt breakfast and the flowing bowl of milk-punch.(p.404)
• I planned to stay home the night before I left, but my folks got so drunk I walked off ***early*** in the evening and spent the night with my girl, getting very drunk myself.(p.425)
• Once or twice, during my ***early*** drinking, I carried it over into the second day, and only once, that I can remember, did it continue into the third.(p.432)
• I had begun to drink in the ***early*** years of pharmacy school, in order to get to sleep.(p.440)
• Although we enjoyed the laughter in the ***early*** days, I heard a lot of things that I thought were stupid.(p.447)
• By ***early*** July, I had tapered off alcohol completely, and I got off all pills in the ensuing few months.(p.448)
• I remember in my ***early*** youth my mother dressed me just as she did my two sisters, and I wore curls until I was six years of age.(p.483)
• I started drinking rather ***early***, at the age of sixteen.(p.512)
• That and the morning drink came very ***early*** in my drinking career.(p.513)
• And having sung that phrase, I'd chuckle with

amusement, turning into irony turning into self-contempt turning into self-pity, at the sad fate of Bob, that wonderful, poor little motherless boy who was so smart in school and who grew up to accept responsibility so ***early*** and so fast and who staggered under his burdens without a whimper until the time came when he thought he was too good for this world and so he ought to be out of it.(p.532)
• There was the physical aspect; to be the youngest and the runt of the brood of children, to have to wear glasses very ***early*** and so to be teased, to be bookish and bored in school because the captain of the football team could not translate Virgil and yet was the school god while you, you, you little shrimp, were the school egghead, junior size and an ***early*** model.(p.533)
• The ***early*** promise of the "boy wonder" faded, and my career began to drift.(p.556)

early-day
• Since I started out eager for ***early-day*** efforts, that meant guzzling before noon.(p.331)

earmarks
• These are the ***earmarks*** of a real alcoholic.(p.109)

earn
• Not being a man of means, I knew that if I did not stay sober enough to ***earn*** money, I would run out of liquor.(p.175)
• It was really a horrible nightmare, this earning money, getting liquor, smuggling it home, getting drunk, morning jitters, taking large doses of sedatives to make it possible for me to ***earn*** more money, and so on ad nauseam.(p.177)
• I still had enough practice to ***earn*** a good living if I would only work, so I resolved that in January of 1940 I would launch a patent law firm of my own.(p.220)
• The fact that I can work again and ***earn*** my living, is important, but secondary.(p.229)
• During that first year, however, I managed to make both ends meet, and to avoid ever going back to my old habit pattern of borrowing money when I could not ***earn*** it.(p.283)

earned
• As soon as I had satisfied that, what I ***earned*** as an upholsterer went for liquor.(p.234)
• Even obvious intoxication is excused by younger people as something "he's ***earned*** the right to do," and they say, "After all, who's he hurting?"(p.330)
• He answered by wiring that I could stay there until I ***earned*** enough to get home.(p.357)
• No one could have told me then that I had not ***earned*** all my success, nor could anyone have told me that I was an alcoholic and a drug addict.(p.418)

earnest
• You will make mistakes, but if you are in ***earnest*** they will not drag you down.(p.117)
• I had been drinking heavily from one state of semi-coma to another and it was several days before I got "defogged," but subconsciously I was in ***earnest*** about wanting to quit liquor forever.(p.258)
• They were ***earnest*** and obviously trying to help me on the road I had chosen.(p.259)
• I was desperately in ***earnest*** to follow through and understand what was expected of me as a member of A.A. and to take each Step of the Twelve as rapidly as possible.(p.382)

earnestly
• Very ***earnestly*** we ask the press also, to observe this request, for otherwise we shall be greatly handicapped.(p.xiii)
• I ***earnestly*** advise every alcoholic to read this book through, and though perhaps he came to scoff, he may remain to pray.(p.xxx)
• To us, the Realm of Spirit is broad, roomy, all inclusive; never exclusive or forbidding to those who ***earnestly*** seek.(p.46)
• To sum up about sex: We ***earnestly*** pray for the right ideal, for guidance in each questionable situation, for sanity, and for the strength to do the right thing.(p.70)
• He had a desperate desire to stop, but saw no way out, for he had ***earnestly*** tried many avenues of escape.(p.155)
• For a long time I kept on trying, in a pretty dumb way at first, I know, but very ***earnestly***.(p.237)

earnestness
• But just underneath there is deadly ***earnestness***.(p.16)
• Next day we would ask ourselves, in all ***earnestness*** and sincerity, how it could have happened.(p.37)
• With all the ***earnestness*** at our command, we beg of you to be fearless and thorough from the very start.(p.58)
• There I took up the business of drinking with much greater ***earnestness*** than I had previously shown.(p.173)

earning
• In late 1934 I attended a patient who, though he had been a competent businessman of good ***earning*** capacity, was an alcoholic of a type I had come to regard as hopeless.(p.xxiii)
• It was really a horrible nightmare, this ***earning*** money, getting liquor, smuggling it home, getting drunk, morning jitters, taking large doses of sedatives to make it possible for me to earn more money, and so on ad nauseam.(p.177)
• Three years later, at twenty-five, I opened and operated their Philadelphia office and was ***earning*** more than I ever have since.(p.242)
• I had been brought up to believe this, and I had shown during my 'teens considerable enterprise and imagination about ***earning*** money.(p.275)

ears
• In my mind's eye I saw Broadway again and Tom Sharkey's bar; the roar of the subway was in my ***ears***.(p.252)
• My first meeting gave me a great deal of hope and lots of willing ***ears*** for my tale of woe and for my questions.(p.364)
• My analyst pricked up her ***ears***.(p.412)
• The word "alcoholic" does not turn me off any more; in fact, it is music to my ***ears*** when it applies to me.(p.463)

earth
• Each day my friend's simple talk in our kitchen multiplies itself in a widening circle of peace on ***earth*** and good will to men.(p.16)
• He can go anywhere on this ***earth*** where other free men may go without disaster, provided he remains willing to maintain a certain simple attitude.(p.26)
• Some of the contemporaries of Columbus thought a round ***earth*** preposterous.(p.51)
• You should not hesitate to visit the most sordid spot on ***earth*** on such an errand.(p.102)
• We have come to believe He would like us to keep our heads in the clouds with Him, but that our feet ought to be firmly planted on ***earth***.(p.130)
• The A.A. program showed me the way to come down to ***earth***, start from the bottom and work up.(p.284)
• Best that they not be found after I'd had my last drink on ***earth***.(p.333)
• Just as I was wondering what on ***earth*** I could do -- I was too drunk even to pack a handkerchief -- the memory of an A.A. write-up that I had seen in the Evening Mail flashed across my mind -- and I thought to myself, this is something I haven't tried yet.(p.523)

ease
• They are restless, irritable and discontented, unless they can again experience the sense of ***ease*** and comfort which comes at once by taking a few drinks -- drinks which they see others taking with impunity.(p.xxvi)
• Is not our age characterized by the ***ease*** with which we discard old ideas for new, by the complete readiness with which we throw away the theory or gadget which does not work for something new which does?(p.52)
• We can be alone at perfect peace and ***ease***.(p.75)
• They spoke with great freedom from embarrassment, which I could never do, and they seemed very much at ***ease*** on all occasions and appeared very healthy.(p.178)
• I was self conscious and ill at ***ease*** most of the time, my health was at the breaking point, and I was thoroughly miserable.(p.178)
• I can remember that in my childhood, he was ill at ***ease*** with the children because he attempted to assert an army discipline that had been ground into him during his three and a half years of army service.(p.210)
• He put me at ***ease*** with his first few words.(p.309)
• It was then that I began to hate myself, and drank primarily to ***ease*** my conscience and forget.(p.354)
• We went out occasionally, and I would take a drink to ***ease*** the tensions of daily life.(p.370)
• Living with fear and tension inevitably results in wanting to ***ease*** that tension, which alcohol seems to do temporarily.(p.380)
• The strange A.A. put me at ***ease***.(p.413)
• He didn't seem too much at ***ease*** in the beginning.(p.494)
• There was the father one lost respect for at the age of eleven, because the father broke his solemn word in a circumstance where you, eleven years old, had assumed guilt when you were innocent; but the father would not believe you, no matter what; and to ***ease*** his suffering you "confessed" and were "forgiven," only -- months later -- to have your "guilt" brought up -- only he and you knew what he was talking bout -- brought up in front of the stern grandmother.(p.533)

eased
• I was ***eased*** out of the business I had founded and was reduced to doing general upholstery in a small shop at the back of my house.(p.233)
• As long as it ***eased*** situations socially, it helped just fine, but somewhere along the line, it backfired.(p.386)

easier
• We thought we could find an ***easier***, softer way.(p.58)
• Trying to avoid this humbling experience, they have turned to ***easier*** methods.(p.72)
• You and your husband will find that you can dispose of serious problems ***easier*** than you can the trivial ones.(p.118)
• I remember looking longingly at the window as an ***easier*** solution, and shuddering at the memory of that other window, three years before, and the six agonizing months in a London hospital ward.(p.224)
• I was trying to find an ***easier***, softer way.(p.378)
• At first it was a shock to realize I was an alcoholic, but the realization that there was hope made it ***easier***.(p.379)
• It has made life a thousand times ***easier*** and simpler than did the endless compromises and conflicts by which I lived before.(p.394)
• Awarded a scholarship to a famous old Eastern college, I began to drink at the end of my freshman year, and by junior year, I had to transfer to an ***easier*** state university to keep my grades up.(p.419)
• And life keeps getting simpler and ***easier*** as we try to reverse my old idea, by taking care of the internal environment via the Twelve Steps, and letting the external environment take care of itself.)(p.446)
• It has gotten progressively ***easier***.(p.448)
• If I work on it every day, it will be ***easier*** to be honest with myself.(p.482)

easiest
• Honesty is the ***easiest*** word for me to understand because it is the exact opposite of what I've been doing all my life.(p.482)
• It meant that I had to give up a lot of the things that I had been accustomed to and that wasn't the ***easiest*** thing in the world for me.(p.487)

easily
• On the other hand -- and strange as this may seem to those who do not understand -- once a psychic change has occurred, the very same person who seemed doomed, who had so many problems he despaired of ever solving them, suddenly finds himself ***easily*** able to control his desire for alcohol, the only effort necessary being that required to follow a few simple rules.(p.xxvii)
• Yet all reasons for not drinking were ***easily*** pushed aside in favor of the foolish idea that he could take whiskey if only he mixed it with milk!(p.36)
• You can ***easily*** see why.(p.87)
• We do not tire so ***easily***, for we are not burning up energy foolishly as we did when we were trying to arrange life to suit ourselves.(p.88)
• You can ***easily*** find some by asking a few doctors, ministers, priests or hospitals.(p.89)
• That he has not always done so for the alcoholic is ***easily*** understood.(p.137)
• As I go along I seem to get strength daily to be able to resist more ***easily***.(p.237)
• She told me; it was simple; I could have done it very ***easily***.(p.326)
• Truth and sincerity do not come ***easily*** to me.(p.420)
• Please do not think it ended so simply and so ***easily***.(p.541)
• 6. -- Problems of money, property, and authority may ***easily*** divert us from our primary spiritual aim.(p.565)

east
• There is a good bit of travel between ***East*** and West and we foresee a great increase in this helpful interchange.(p.162)
• I optioned a piece of land just off ***East*** Market Street to put up a three-hundred suite apartment.(p.198)
• So I indulged with my comrades in everything the Far ***East*** had to offer.(p.231)
• It was also my job to entertain the owners of these stations when they came ***East*** on business -- or the pretense of business.(p.359)
• We came back ***East*** and met both families.(p.402)
• I was there for another couple of months and then, after a few more adventures in the ***East***, I was shipped home.(p.521)

Easter
• I went to church on ***Easter*** Sunday with my husband, and it didn't hurt at all.(p.482)

• I think the thing that galled me was that just after *Easter* I had drawn my salary for two weeks' work and had decided that I was going to send some money to Vi; and above all else I was going to send my baby daughter an *Easter* outfit.(p.493)
• Of course the kid never got the *Easter* outfit.(p.493)

eastern
• We covered the whole *eastern* United States in a year.(p.3)
• Under only slightly different conditions, the same thing is taking place in many *eastern* cities.(p.161)
• Then, in this *eastern* city, there are informal meetings such as we have described to you, where you may now see scores of members.(p.162)
• Offered the job of advertising manager for an *eastern* automotive company, I moved to Philadelphia to begin life anew.(p.254)
• Awarded a scholarship to a famous old *Eastern* college, I began to drink at the end of my freshman year, and by junior year, I had to transfer to an easier state university to keep my grades up.(p.419)

easy
• Simple, but not *easy*; a price had to be paid.(p.14)
• That was not *easy*.(p.42)
• To be doomed to an alcoholic death or to live on a spiritual basis are not always *easy* alternatives to face.(p.44)
• It's so *easy* to get way off the track.(p.68)
• It is *easy* to let up on the spiritual program of action and rest on our laurels.(p.85)
• It would be *easy* to be vague about this matter.(p.86)
• We relax and take it *easy*.(p.86)
• *Easy* Does It.(p.135)
• But life was not *easy* for the two friends.(p.156)
• The water tank on the toilet I never used, because that looked too *easy*.(p.176)
• This time I seemed to be already awake, sitting upright in a big *easy* chair, in the middle of an animated conversation with a perfectly strange young woman, who didn't appear to think it strange.(p.222)
• Our pet slogan is "*Easy* Does It."(p.250)
• I got an *easy*, part-time job selling printing for a small neighborhood printer.(p.276)
• *Easy* does it, first things first, one day at a time.(p.340)
• They told me their stories, which were much more rugged than mine -- yet what they said made sense, and the way they put it was *easy* for me to understand, with an understanding I had never had before.(p.363)
• It is not too difficult nor too *easy* to grasp.(p.367)
• "*Easy* Does It."(p.382)
• There are no *easy* ways to sober up, but that's the most excruciating.(p.389)
• But again, the living was *easy*.(p.401)
• Bill was tall, grey haired, with the kind of asymmetrical good looks and pleasant *easy* manner that inspire confidence in the shaken and afraid.(p.413)
• He was well dressed; he was *easy* going.(p.413)
• I took it *easy*, because they didn't know about me.(p.428)
• There was a red plush carpet to welcome me, but even so it wasn't *easy*.(p.430)
• How *easy* it was, in the beginning, to forget that those binges ever happened!(p.433)
• When the compulsion to drink left, it was relatively *easy* to stay off alcohol.(p.448)
• Prior to our marriage, when she was a shy, scrawny adolescent, I was able to see things in her that others couldn't necessarily see – things like beauty, charm, gaiety, a gift for being *easy* to talk to, a sense of humor, and many other fine qualities.(p.450)
• It hasn't been *easy* to work out this relationship with Max.(p.451)
• This *easy* method of sobering up would last at least three days.(p.468)
• But the older members in A.A. told me, "*easy* does it."(p.471)
• This sound *easy*, so will try.(p.476)
• My last exam and an *easy* one.(p.499)
• I use that "*Easy* Does It" every day, to slow me down a little.(p.516)
• I thought that if these kind of ordinary people can do it, a man of my brains ought to find it much more *easy*, and I joined.(p.524)
• Despite my wife's entreaties to take it *easy* that day, arrived home in bad shape.(p.557)

eat
• A tumbler full of gin followed by half a dozen bottles of beer would be required if I were to *eat* any breakfast.(p.5)
• I could *eat* little or nothing when drinking, and I was forty pounds under weight.(p.7)
• If you are with a person who wants to *eat* in a bar, by all means go along.(p.102)
• Many of us have noticed a tendency to *eat* sweets and have found this practice beneficial.(p.134)
• I would reach over and get this and take a shot and in a few moments get up and take another, shave and *eat* my breakfast, slip a half pint of liquor in my hip pocket, and go on to school.(p.183)
• They didn't give me anything to *eat*.(p.264)
• I *eat* three good meals a day now, and really enjoy them.(p.303)
• But by God, I wouldn't talk or *eat*, either!(p.444)
• For me, as for most alcoholics, it was "*Eat*, drink, and be merry, for tomorrow you die."(p.457)
• Same thing when I let lye and water *eat* away at four of my toes and my foot for five hours.(p.458)
• The atmosphere of "*eat*, drink, and be merry" prevails and I absorb it.(p.499)
• I lasted at that for four months chiefly on alcohol, because I never seemed to find any time to *eat*.(p.520)

eaten
• I had *eaten* there many times during the months I was sober.(p.36)
• They haven't *eaten* me yet!(p.530)

eating
• We were *eating* lunch, and I was listening and trying to find out why they had this release that they seemed to have.(p.191)
• I would make a feeble attempt at *eating* supper, but I never met with any howling success.(p.299)
• I'd just take a couple or three barbiturates to get back to sleep – *eating* my alcohol.(p.333)

eats
• Alcohol wrings the guts out of life, *eats* into the brain in such a way as to make the alcoholic blind to the truth.(p.457)

ebb
• A low *ebb* in the family fortunes necessitated my going to work when I was twenty.(p.275)

echoed
• How that line *echoed* through my mind!(p.333)

economic
• All sections of this country and many of its occupations are represented, as well as many political, *economic*, social, and religious backgrounds.(p.17)
• Fear of people and of *economic* insecurity will leave us.(p.84)
• We think it dangerous if he rushes headlong at his *economic* problem.(p.126)
• Too many *economic* and social problems would beset me there.(p.281)
• As I later found out through Alcoholics Anonymous, alcohol is no respecter of *economic* status, social and business standing or intelligence.(p.373)
• *Economic* conditions had a great deal to do with it, because I've often heard my father say that his mother would take one of the old time flour sacks and cut a hole through the bottom and two corners of it and there you'd have a gown.(p.486)
• There was the *economic* fear which made me too timid to take any action which might improve my circumstances.(p.534)

economics
• I studied *economics* and business as well as law.(p.2)

Ed
• After reading this book, a junior executive can go to such a man and say approximately this, "Look here, *Ed*.(p.147)

edge
• An attorney sat at the side of the bed where I was lying, and he sat on the *edge* of his chair and looked as innocent as a baby.(p.268)

edgewise
• I couldn't get a word in *edgewise*!(p.414)

edict
• When it was closed through Washington *edict* I began with Federal Writers in San Antonio.(p.256)

Edison
• On Wednesday night Jack M. said, "You meet me at the Ohio *Edison* Building, and I will take you to the meeting."(p.269)

edited
• "Bill's Story," "Doctor Bob's Nightmare," and one other personal history from the first edition were retained intact; three were *edited* and one of these was retitled; new versions of two stories were written with new titles; thirty completely new stories were added; and the story section was divided into three parts, under the same headings that are used now.(p.xi)

edition
• This is the third *edition* of the book "Alcoholics Anonymous."(p.xi)
• The first *edition* appeared in April 1939, and in the following sixteen years, more than 300,000 copies went into circulation.(p.xi)
• The second *edition*, published in 1955, reached a total of more than 1,150,000 copies.(p.xi)
• The second *edition* added the appendices, the Twelve Traditions, and the directions for getting in touch with A.A.(p.xi)
• "Bill's Story," "Doctor Bob's Nightmare," and one other personal history from the first *edition* were retained intact; three were edited and one of these was retitled; new versions of two stories were written with new titles; thirty completely new stories were added; and the story section was divided into three parts, under the same headings that are used now.(p.xi)
• In this third *edition*, Part I ("Pioneers of A.A.") stands unchanged.(p.xii)
• Nine of the stories in Part II ("They Stopped in Time") are carried over from the second *edition*; eight new stories have been added.(p.xii)
• FOREWORD TO FIRST *EDITION*(p.xiii)
• This is the Foreword as it appeared in the first printing of the first *edition* in 1939(p.xiii)
• FOREWORD TO SECOND *EDITION*(p.xv)
• Sixteen years have elapsed between our first printing of this book and the presentation in 1955 of our second *edition*.(p.xv)
• FOREWORD TO THE THIRD *EDITION*(p.xxii)
• By March 1976, when this *edition* went to the printer, the total worldwide membership of Alcoholics Anonymous was conservatively estimated at more than 1,000,000, with almost 28,000 groups meeting in over 90 countries.(p.xxii)

editions
• Therefore, the first portion of this volume, describing the A.A. recovery program, has been left untouched in the course of revisions made for both the second and the third *editions*.(p.xi)
• An old avocation, the collecting of first *editions*, rare books and Americana, fascinated me between times.(p.255)

editor
• In the fall of 1939, Fulton Oursler, then *editor* of Liberty, printed a piece in his magazine, called "Alcoholics and God."(p.xviii)
• Returning to the town I had left three months before, I became *editor* of a monthly magazine, soon had additional publicity and advertising accounts and the money rolled in.(p.254)
• I stayed with them until I got drunk and had a row with the Paris *editor*.(p.405)
• I was club-man, athlete, artist, musician, author, *editor*, aircraft pilot and world traveller.(p.432)
• An honor student in college, I became *editor* of the yearbook.(p.555)

editorially
• The Episcopal magazine, The Living Church, observes *editorially*: "The basis of the technique of Alcoholics Anonymous is the truly Christian principle that a man cannot help himself except by helping others.(p.574)

editors
• (At this point, the *Editors* intrude just long enough to supplement Bill D.'s account, that of the man on the bed, with that of Bill W., the man who sat by the side of the bed.)(p.188)
• How hurt I was when *editors* bounced back my ideas quickly and my best friends opined that my output needed a lot of rewriting.(p.331)

Edna
• In my twenties, I found *Edna* St. Vincent Millay's verse:(p.534)

educated
• Here was a tall, rugged, highly *educated* Yankee talking in a matter of course way about God and prayer.(p.279)
• *Educated* child of the scientific age that I was, I had complete faith in the science of the mind.(p.434)
• Had it not been for A.A. in prison. . . I'll never know, but my *educated* guess is that I would not be alive today.(p.457)

education
• He attended church school, where he became rebellious at what he thought an overdose of religious *education*.(p.56)

• His religious ***education*** and training may be far superior to yours.(p.93)
• These work-outs should be regarded as part of your ***education***, for thus you will be learning to live.(p.117)
• After I was on the drafting board about two years I decided I wanted a technical ***education***.(p.211)
• I did not have a high school ***education*** so I went to night school to take the full high school course, which I finished in two years and nine months.(p.211)
• I was supporting myself through all this ***education*** by being a toolmaker and a draftsman.(p.212)
• My ***education*** had been pretty much pagan – science.(p.221)
• With nothing but a liberal arts ***education***, very definitely estranged from my family and already married, soon after graduation from college I became a bookmaker's clerk on the British racing circuits, far better off financially than the average professional man.(p.251)
• I was deprived of many of the things that we feel are important in life, such as ***education*** particularly, because of my father's drinking.(p.261)
• With this specialized training, and a liberal business ***education*** in the school of hard knocks, I was able to set up shop some two years later as an independent accountant.(p.284)
• Then there was wartime service to interrupt my plans, and an ***education*** to be picked up after the war.(p.373)
• I got a good non-academic ***education***; my intellectual curiosity was encouraged.(p.401)
• I do not fix anyone, but I am getting part of a tremendous ***education*** and I have made some new friends.(p.506)
• It had provided me with excuses for my lack of ***education***, my marital failures, personal failures, inadequacy, and of course, my alcoholism and, though I really thought I had been willing to part with it, now I knew I was reluctant to let it go.(p.552)

educational

• The town was well supplied with churches and schools in which I pursued my early ***educational*** activities.(p.171)
• He said the alcoholic seemed to possess a native acuteness and usually excelled in his field, regardless of environmental or ***educational*** advantages.(p.308)
• Making amends is sometimes doing what we are capable of doing but failed to do because of alcohol; carrying out community responsibilities such as Community Funds, Red Cross, ***educational*** and religious activities in proportion to our abilities and energy.(p.381)
• Most of our experiences are what the psychologist William James calls the "***educational*** variety" because they develop slowly over a period of time.(p.569)

Edward

• ***Edward*** Dowling, S.J., of the Queen's Work staff says, "Alcoholics Anonymous is natural; it is natural at the point where nature comes closest to the supernatural, namely in humiliations and in consequent humility.(p.574)

effect

• Men and women drink essentially because they like the ***effect*** produced by alcohol.(p.xxvi)
• Then there are types entirely normal in every respect except in the ***effect*** alcohol has upon them.(p.xxviii)
• His alcoholic problem was so complex, and his depression so great, that we felt his only hope would be through what we then called "moral psychology," and we doubted if even that would have any ***effect***.(p.xxix)
• Then he had, in ***effect***, been raised from the dead, suddenly taken from the scrap heap to a level of life better than the best he had ever known!(p.11)
• These were revolutionary and drastic proposals, but the moment I fully accepted them, the ***effect*** was electric.(p.14)
• They piled on me heaps of evidence to the ***effect*** that an alcoholic mentality, such as I had exhibited in Washington, was a hopeless condition.(p.42)
• Our own conception, however inadequate, was sufficient to make the approach and to ***effect*** a contact with Him.(p.46)
• At the start, this was all we needed to commence spiritual growth, to ***effect*** our first conscious relation with God as we understood Him.(p.47)
• This was only a beginning, though if honestly and humbly made, an ***effect***, sometimes a very great one, was felt at once.(p.63)
• Though our decision was a vital and crucial step, it could have little permanent ***effect*** unless at once followed by a strenuous effort to face, and to be rid of, the things in ourselves which had been blocking us.(p.64)
• If persisted in for a few months, the ***effect*** on a man's family is sure to be great.(p.99)
• Henry Ford once made a wise remark to the ***effect*** that experience is the thing of supreme value in life.(p.124)
• A man may criticize or laugh at himself and it will affect others favorably, but criticism or ridicule coming from another often produces the contrary ***effect***.(p.125)
• And with such good ***effect*** that the doctor agreed to a test among his patients and certain other alcoholics from a clinic which he attends.(p.163)
• This had the ***effect*** of making me resolve that when I was free from parental domination, I would never again darken the doors of a church.(p.172)
• This had little ***effect*** however for I kept on drinking and used a great deal more hard liquor than in former years.(p.174)
• Then Prohibition came into ***effect***, and the facts that the stuff obtainable was so horrible and sometimes deadly, and that I had married and had a job which I had to look after, helped me for a period of some three or four years, although I would get drunk every time I could get hold of enough to drink to get started.(p.183)
• I got two drinks, each of them a quarter of that pint, in me, and was talking along with these people, but I felt that sooner or later they were going to have me cornered because they were smarter than I was and the drink was beginning to take ***effect***; but as I reached for the third drink Bob said, "Listen, Buster, you promised to take some medicine if we got you a drink.(p.206)
• One evening, the book, after checking up, was very definitely in the red for plenty through a piece of studied carelessness on my part, and my boss, very shrewd and able, fired me with a parting statement to the ***effect*** that once was enough.(p.251)
• The parties waxed more liquid and hilarious as time went on, and eventually I discovered that a little shot of liquor now and then between beers had the tendency to put me in a whacky mood much quicker than having to down several quarts of beer to obtain the same ***effect***.(p.298)
• The second way in which, perhaps, I differ from some other alcoholics is this; many alcoholics state that they didn't particularly like the taste of alcohol, but that they liked the ***effect***.(p.345)
• So I was used to it, but I didn't know what the ***effect*** of alcohol was because I always had wine, usually with dinner, but always with a lot of ice and about two tablespoons of sugar in it.(p.385)
• I learned what a devastating ***effect*** it can have on a child to coddle him and build him up, and then turn and beat him savagely, as had happened to me.(p.434)
• I never got much ***effect*** out of codeine and Percodan and the tranquilizers.(p.442)
• I didn't like it particularly at first, but I did like the ***effect*** I got from it.(p.464)
• Tragedies during those years that were caused by my drinking, such as the breaking up of my marriage, the death of my child, other things – had little restraining ***effect***.(p.465)
• He said, in ***effect***: "If you have a resentment you want to be free of, if you will pray for the person or the thing that you resent, you will be free.(p.552)
• The trustees of the General Service Board are, in ***effect***, our A.A. General Service Committee.(p.567)

effective

• That the man who is making the approach has had the same difficulty, that he obviously knows what he is talking about, that his whole deportment shouts at the new prospect that he is a man with a real answer, that he has no attitude of Holier Than Thou, nothing whatever except the sincere desire to be helpful; that there are no fees to pay, no axes to grind, no people to please, no lectures to be endured -- these are the conditions we have found most ***effective***.(p.18)
• The great fact is just this, and nothing less: That we have had deep and ***effective*** spiritual experiences which have revolutionized our whole attitude toward life, toward our fellows and toward God's universe.(p.25)
• We now see that when we began to drink deliberately, instead of casually, there was little serious or ***effective*** thought during the period of premeditation of what the terrific consequences might be.(p.37)
• Once more: The alcoholic at certain times has no ***effective*** mental defense against the first drink.(p.43)
• It has been repeatedly proven among us that upon this simple cornerstone a wonderfully ***effective*** spiritual structure can be built.(p.47)
• At the very beginning, the couple ought to frankly face the fact that each will have to yield here and there if the family is going to play an ***effective*** part in the new life.(p.131)
• Though he is now a most ***effective*** member of Alcoholics Anonymous, he still smokes and drinks coffee, but neither his wife or anyone else stands in judgment.(p.135)
• But each drink after the "first" seemed to become less ***effective*** and after three or four they all seemed like water.(p.241)
• A return to the United States proved ***effective*** as a geographical cure, and a period of sobriety ensued, with the help of the church.(p.419)
• This self-insurance has resulted in the restoration of physical, mental and spiritual health and self-respect to hundreds of men and women who would be hopelessly down and out without its unique but ***effective*** therapy."(p.574)

effectively

• As we discovered the principles by which the individual alcoholic could live, so we had to evolve principles by which the A.A. groups and A.A. as a whole could survive and function ***effectively***.(p.xix)

effectiveness

• None of us makes a sole vocation of this work, nor do we think its ***effectiveness*** would be increased if we did.(p.19)
• Our next function is to grow in understanding and ***effectiveness***.(p.84)
• Therefore, no society of men and women ever had more urgent need for continuous ***effectiveness*** and permanent unity.(p.563)

effects

• Whatever the method, its object is to thoroughly clear mind and body of the ***effects*** of alcohol.(p.143)
• I very early sampled the ***effects*** of alcohol.(p.211)
• I definitely liked it, everything about it, the taste, the ***effects***; and I realize now that a drink did something for me or to me that was different from the way it affected others.(p.305)
• You know the deteriorating ***effects***, the disintegrating ***effects*** of chronic wine-drinking.(p.337)
• I didn't particularly like it, but I loved the ***effects***, and managed for the next twenty-five years to drink anything and everything, either handed to me or purchased, at the slightest excuse.(p.357)

efficiency

• My ***efficiency*** as a professional man was probably reduced to twenty-five per cent of what it should have been.(p.215)

efficient

• We become much more ***efficient***.(p.88)

effort

• On the other hand – and strange as this may seem to those who do not understand -- once a psychic change has occurred, the very same person who seemed doomed, who had so many problems he despaired of ever solving them, suddenly finds himself easily able to control his desire for alcohol, the only ***effort*** necessary being that required to follow a few simple rules.(p.xxvii)
• Though the aggregate of recoveries resulting from psychiatric ***effort*** is considerable, we physicians must admit we have made little impression upon the problem as a whole.(p.xxvii)
• Following his physical rehabilitation, he had a talk with me in which he frankly stated he thought the treatment a waste of ***effort***, unless I could assure him, which no one ever had, that in the future he would have the "will power" to resist the impulse to drink.(p.xxix)
• All of us spend much of our spare time in the sort of ***effort*** which we are going to describe.(p.19)
• This we did because we honestly wanted to, and were willing to make the ***effort***.(p.25)
• Though our decision was a vital and crucial step, it could have little permanent effect unless at once followed by a strenuous ***effort*** to face, and to be rid of, the things in ourselves which had been blocking us.(p.64)
• It is an ***effort*** to discover the truth about the stock-in-trade.(p.64)
• We attempt to sweep away the debris which has accumulated out of our ***effort*** to live on self-will and run the show ourselves.(p.76)
• We will see that our new attitude toward liquor has been given us without any thought or ***effort*** on our part.(p.85)
• As animals on a treadmill, we have patiently and wearily climbed, falling back in exhaustion after each futile ***effort*** to reach solid ground.(p.107)
• They experienced a few distressing failures, but in those cases they made an ***effort*** to bring the man's family into a spiritual way of living, thus relieving much worry and suffering.(p.159)
• We boys drove out in somebody's car and went to the bar on the way do the dining room and I, in an ***effort*** to impress the other boys that I was city-bred,

having lived in Scranton and Cleveland, asked them if they didn't want a drink.(p.194)
• After two or three years of *effort* along this line, I reached the point of actual despair that I ever would be able to drink only a harmless amount each day.(p.215)
• I really worked for several weeks, and having had a fairly wide acquaintance with the dealer trade, it was not difficult for me to line up enough of them to give me a very substantial volume of business with a minimum of *effort*.(p.300)
• However, this isn't as rough as it sounds, as we do become grateful for the necessity that makes us toe the line, for we find that we are more than compensated for a consistent *effort* by the countless dividends we receive.(p.311)
• My personality was stretched almost to splitting in the *effort*; schizophrenia stared me in the face, and one night I was in a suicidal despair.(p.435)
• Here I found an ingredient that had been lacking in any other *effort* I had made to save myself.(p.436)
• So I put forth some *effort* that day to try to stay sober if I could, though my sobriety was just a daze.(p.494)
• I know there are some alcoholics who seem terribly, terribly grown-up, but I think that they are trying to make themselves think they are grown-up, and the strain of their *effort* is what is causing them to drink -- a sense of inadequacy, a childish vanity to be the most popular, the most sought after, the mostest of the most.(p.535)

efforts

• Had not all *efforts* at flight failed before?(p.51)
• You should join in his *efforts* as much as you possibly can.(p.119)
• Like most immigrants I wanted to be somebody and have something and I was very happy and contented as I felt success crown my *efforts*.(p.232)
• I could never be bothered with the follow-through and would invariably reward myself for my *efforts* with that "first" drink.(p.243)
• I don't think the boys were completely convinced of my personality change, for they fought shy of including my story in the book, so my only contribution to their literary *efforts* was my firm conviction, being still a theological rebel, that the word God should be qualified with the phrase "as we understand him" -- for that was the only way I could accept spirituality.(p.248)
• After the book appeared we all became very busy in our *efforts* to save all and sundry, but I was still actually on the fringes of A.A.(p.248)
• I did not need to be told that my *efforts* were and would be unavailing if I did not get help.(p.258)
• Since I started out eager for early-day *efforts*, that meant guzzling before noon.(p.331)
• By the law of averages, some *efforts* came out well.(p.331)
• I feel that I have been restored to health and sanity these past years not through my own *efforts* nor as a result of anything I may have done, but because I've come to believe -- to really believe -- that alone I can do nothing.(p.473)
• Through my *efforts* to get down to "causes and conditions," I stand convinced that my emotional illness has been present from my earliest recollection.(p.544)

egg

• I'd get so fed up with drinking all alone and bearing the burden of guilt all by myself, that I'd *egg* him on to drink, to get started again.(p.325)
• I now had quite a nest *egg*.(p.409)

egghead

• There was the physical aspect; to be the youngest and the runt of the brood of children, to have to wear glasses very early and so to be teased, to be bookish and bored in school because the captain of the football team could not translate Virgil and yet was the school god while you, you, you little shrimp, were the school *egghead*, junior size and an early model.(p.533)

eggnog

• The only time that I have ever seen my mother take anything alcoholic was around Christmas time, when she would drink some *eggnog* or light wine.(p.484)

ego

• But they didn't do anything for me to build up my *ego*.(p.262)
• Dishonest thinking, prejudice, *ego*, antagonism toward anyone and everyone who dares to cross him, vanity and a critical attitude are character defects that gradually creep in and become a part of his life.(p.380)
• As I grow in A.A., I realize that a person with as much self-will as I had, as hard a head and as diseased an *ego*, had to try everything that I could think of, butting my head against every stone wall before I was ready to come in.(p.384)
• I was the center of attention, just what my sick *ego* craved.(p.407)
• I know I do not have to be "queen of them all" to salve a frightened *ego*.(p.416)
• All Twelve Steps of A.A. are designed to kill the old self (deflate the old *ego*) and build a new, free self.(p.459)
• For to have accepted the reasons and to have acted on them would have been too great a blow to my *ego*, which was as great, in reverse, as my body was small.(p.534)
• What a revelation of *ego* and arrogance still remaining in me -- as if anyone, instinct and training apart, likes to be in jail or in an alcoholic ward or fired from his job.(p.536)

ego-centric

• Our actor is self-centered -- *ego-centric*, as people like to call it nowadays.(p.61)

ego-strength

• I thought this would give me *ego-strength*, make me feel wanted and secure, and alleviate my fears, but again nothing changed inside me.(p.546)

egocentric

• I am still arrogant, *egocentric*, self-righteous, with no humility, even phony at times, but I'm trying to be a better person and help my fellowman.(p.463)

egocentricity

• I realize now that this phase of my development had been arrested by my obsession with self, and my *egocentricity* had reached such proportions that adjustment to anything outside my personal control was impossible for me.(p.547)

egoism

• They only thought they had lost their *egoism* and fear; they only thought they had humbled themselves.(p.73)

egotism

• However, what I had gained materially on the credit side of my ledger, I have since learned was more than offset on the debit side by *egotism*, resentment and dishonesty.(p.356)

egotistical

• On the other hand, he may be mean, *egotistical*, selfish and dishonest.(p.61)

Egypt

• Neither can I honestly say that I have forgotten the "fleshpots of *Egypt*."(p.259)
• On our honeymoon in *Egypt*, he cuffed me around quite a bit, and subsequently hit me some more.(p.405)
• The Abyssinian war broke out just as things were going very badly for me, and I went off to *Egypt* on a job there.(p.519)
• However, I kept that job in *Egypt* and Palestine for about two years, and then I changed over to the other battalion in my regiment.(p.520)
• They kept me in hospital for two months, and then they sent me up to *Egypt*, a three days journey.(p.521)

Egyptian

• They sent me up with an attendant, and the attendant and I both arrived at the *Egyptian* Hospital rather the worse for wear.(p.521)

eight

• Nine of the stories in Part II ("They Stopped in Time") are carried over from the second edition; *eight* new stories have been added.(p.xii)
• In Part III ("They Lost Nearly All"), *eight* stories have been retained; five are new.(p.xii)
• It was *eight* o'clock -- five hours after the market closed.(p.4)
• Let's look at Steps *Eight* and Nine.(p.76)
• But he's a grand chap when he's sober, though he's been in here *eight* times in the last six months.(p.156)
• I used to put *eight* or twelve ounce bottles of alcohol in a fur lined glove and toss it onto the back airing porch when winter days got dark enough.(p.176)
• The first time that I became intoxicated I was *eight* years old.(p.182)
• During the first six months of 1935, I was hospitalized *eight* times for intoxication and shackled to the bed two or three days before I even knew where I was.(p.184)
• Each of the seven times that I had left this hospital in the last six months, I had come out fully determined in my own mind that I would not get drunk again -- for at least six or *eight* months.(p.184)
• I said, "Yes, Doc, I would like to quit, at least for five, six, or *eight* months, until I get things straightened up, and begin to get the respect of my wife and some other people back, and get my finances fixed up and so on."(p.187)
• My father died in 1901 when I was *eight* years old and I was in the second or third grade at school.(p.193)
• This was six or *eight* months after the last drinking episode.(p.196)
• I can remember well thinking that I would quit drinking, really go to work hard, apply myself *eight* hours a day, five days a week, make a lot of money, and then I could start drinking again.(p.199)
• There were only seven or *eight* people in the group before me and they all visited me during my period in the hospital.(p.208)
• I was born in Cleveland, Ohio, in 1889, the last child of a family of *eight* children.(p.210)
• That was at the end of *eight* days in which I had had no liquor.(p.218)
• In the *eight* years before A.A. found me, I had over forty jobs -- selling and travelling -- one thing after another, and the same old routine.(p.244)
• That was seven or *eight* years after we were married.(p.262)
• Then and then only, after a thorough indoctrination by *eight* or nine individuals, was I allowed to attend my first meeting.(p.291)
• The meeting consisted of perhaps *eight* or nine alcoholics and seven or *eight* wives.(p.291)
• I was being very cagey, because I knew that if I did take one or two, I might want to take five or six or seven or *eight*.(p.323)
• *Eight* years ago, my wife and I decided to spend a vacation in Naini Tal, the mountain resort.(p.343)
• This escapade also ended up in the clutches of the law, and my friend was institutionalized for *eight* months.(p.354)
• After *eight* months, the family found me.(p.401)
• Except for one short slip, during the first *eight* months, which was an angry "the world can't do this to me" reaction to a personal tragedy in my life, I have been sober for twelve years.(p.416)
• This went on for thirteen weeks, the first *eight* of which I wasn't allowed visitors.(p.425)
• Intervals between binges were, at first, *eight* months.(p.434)
• In seven years the intervals between them decreased from *eight* months to ten days!(p.434)
• And that was how Max and I and our two daughters spent Christmas Day, *eight* years ago.(p.444)
• Shortly thereafter, I was selected, with *eight* other inmates out of the 10,000 in the state's prisons at that time, to attend a school designed to take former "management problems" like me and convert them into paracounselors.(p.462)
• Around *eight* or nine o'clock there came two big detectives and a policeman to arrest me for assault; and I was the most amazed person in the world when they said I had assaulted someone, and especially that I had assaulted my wife.(p.492)
• I'd get downstairs to the gin mill, get enough in to hold me until *eight* o'clock in the morning, then I'd go out to join that "misery parade" that so many of us know so well.(p.514)
• You hit the street about ten minutes to *eight*, and you walk around the block, God knows how many times, waiting for that joint to open.(p.514)
• The war was on and it was a fairly short course, about *eight* months.(p.518)
• After nearly *eight* years of sobriety in A.A., I still can set down such thoughts, "against my instinct and training," showing that I still consider myself a "special" person, entitled to special privileges.(p.536)
• From that instant to this, nearly *eight* years later, I have not had the slightest urge to drink.(p.541)
• It is going strong still, these *eight* years later, and some of its members have been of great influence for good in state-wide A.A. work.(p.541)
• All of my family and loved ones, all of my friends, are nearer and dearer to me than ever before and I have literally dozens of new friends who say they cannot believe that a short *eight* years ago I was ready for the scrap heap.(p.541)
• I attended my first A.A. meeting *eight* years ago, and it is with deep gratitude that I'm able to say I've not had a drink since that time, and that I take no sedation or narcotics, for this program is to me one of complete sobriety and I no longer need to escape reality.(p.549)
• *Eight* -- Alcoholics Anonymous should remain forever nonprofessional, but our service centers may employ special workers.(p.564)

eighteen

• When I was *eighteen*, at the end of high school, the high school team had a banquet at a well-known roadhouse outside of Akron.(p.194)

• It has continued to work now for nearly *eighteen* years.(p.209)
• I was then about *eighteen.*(p.211)
• I re-organized their city sales policy and *eighteen* months later, when I was thirty, they offered me the branch managership.(p.243)
• He spent *eighteen* years in running away; and then found he didn't have to run.(p.275)
• For *eighteen* years, from the age of twenty-one to thirty-nine, fear governed my life.(p.275)
• Haunting me through each day's stupor -- and there were *eighteen* or nineteen such days in this man's home -- was the thought: "Where do I go when his family comes home?"(p.278)
• It went something like this: "God, for *eighteen* years I have been unable to handle this problem.(p.280)
• My wife, a sister member in A.A., had been a widow nine years and I had been single *eighteen* years.(p.286)
• I do feel, though, that the fact that I finally grew up to a point where I could even tackle such a job is the apex of the story of a man who spent *eighteen* years running away from life.(p.286)
• These last *eighteen* years have been the happiest of my life, trite though that statement may seem.(p.295)
• I had turned *eighteen* during the trip, and I despondently returned home by jet (on Daddy's bankbook) to a pair of miserable, hurt parents.(p.354)
• My drinking career extended from age *eighteen* to forty-three.(p.397)
• *Eighteen* will be used as the starting point, because my drinking before was limited by age, the law, and money.(p.397)
• At *eighteen,* I got my first steady job.(p.397)
• At *eighteen* I ran away from home.(p.401)
• I was now nearly *eighteen.*(p.425)
• I talked the Old Man into letting me live in the photo lab instead of the barracks, and for *eighteen* months nothing interfered with my drinking.(p.426)
• I spent *eighteen* hundred dollars fixing up that car in the first year I was home, after four bad smash-ups.(p.429)
• When I had served only *eighteen* months of my sentence, this ex-incorrigible was placed in honor grade.(p.461)
• After all, I had been working for *eighteen* years, slinging hash, and I was managing.(p.478)
• Mind you, I had absolutely nothing to show for that *eighteen* years, except a beat-up car that I hadn't even paid for, but I was doing all right.(p.478)
• I have spent *eighteen* years in that institution.(p.509)

eighteenth
• With the passing of the *Eighteenth* Amendment I felt quite safe.(p.175)

eighth
• I went to five grade schools, primarily because I was expelled for my conduct, but I eventually graduated from the *eighth* grade.(p.211)
• He gave my husband one and me one about ten-thirty on the *eighth* day of May in 1941.(p.267)

eighty
• Now, this house will hardly accommodate its weekly visitors, for they number sixty or *eighty* as a rule.(p.161)

eighty-nine
• My mother was *eighty-nine* years old when she died, and I was a full-blown alcoholic at the time of her death.(p.210)

eighty-two
• She's still alive today at the age of *eighty-two.*(p.511)

Eileen
• I said, "*Eileen,* are you one of those people?"(p.321)

Eire
• He survived to become a mainstay of A.A. in *Eire.*(p.517)

either
• Show any longshoreman a Sunday supplement describing a proposal to explore the moon by means of a rocket and he will say, "I bet they do it – maybe not so long *either.*"(p.52)
• When we became alcoholics, crushed by a self-imposed crisis we could not postpone or evade, we had to fearlessly face the proposition that *either* God is everything or else He is nothing.(p.53)
• God *either* is, or He isn't.(p.53)
• We thought he ought to be willing to do that if necessary, but if he were in jail he could provide nothing for *either* family.(p.79)
• Next time you and he have a heated discussion, no matter what the subject, it should be the privilege of *either* to smile and say, "This is getting serious.(p.118)
• God has *either* removed your husband's liquor problem or He has not.(p.120)
• He may *either* plunge into a frantic attempt to get on his feet in business, or he may be so enthralled by his new life that he talks or thinks of little else.(p.125)
• In *either* case certain family problems will arise.(p.126)
• "Oh no," said my friend, "this chap is *either* through with liquor, or he is minus a job.(p.138)
• *Either* you are dealing with a man who can and will get well or you are not.(p.142)
• Some day he will be unable to imagine life *either* with alcohol or without it.(p.152)
• I did it more and more, and had lots of fun without much grief, *either* physical or financial.(p.172)
• You don't have to sell me religion, *either.*(p.188)
• Naturally, for quite a time, I wasn't too well physically, *either.*(p.190)
• When I look back on that last horrible year of constant drinking I wonder how I survived it *either* physically or mentally.(p.224)
• I never saw *either* of them again.(p.247)
• And I wasn't resentful toward her, *either.*(p.270)
• I was very much interested in athletics, and because of this and parental influence, I didn't drink or smoke in *either* grade or high school.(p.287)
• *Either* they die of acute alcoholism or they develop wet brains and have to be put away permanently."(p.308)
• It had been so many years since I had not relied on some artificial crutch, *either* alcohol or sedatives.(p.310)
• Seldom had any of these lost *either* health, business, family, or friends.(p.315)
• I got orders to go to Vietnam, and I spent most of the year over there *either* drunk or sick with a hangover.(p.317)
• But I couldn't go on with it *either.*(p.319)
• So that wasn't my answer *either.*(p.339)
• It's *either* all work, or I drink."(p.340)
• They have contributed fantastic amounts of time and work to our problem, but they aren't able, it seems, to arrest *either* your alcoholism or mine.(p.352)
• I didn't particularly like it, but I loved the effects, and managed for the next twenty-five years to drink anything and everything, *either* handed to me or purchased, at the slightest excuse.(p.357)
• Age and the law were still against me, but laws were not as strictly enforced in those days as they are now, and I discovered that as long as I had the green blood, there was always a way to get alcohol, *either* from a nondiscriminatory bartender or from an older friend who would be glad to purchase the joy juice for the privilege of sharing it.(p.397)
• But I did not fit into this pattern *either.*(p.402)
• I didn't get into a sanitarium *either.*(p.411)
• Since they could do nothing with Anne *either,* Priscilla suggested that I go and look after Anne.(p.414)
• But by God, I wouldn't talk or eat, *either!*(p.444)
• Any time I tried to kill myself, I was *either* drunk or pilled-up or both – usually the last.(p.479)
• *Either* that or end my life.(p.515)
• When I look back, I can't see anything that would have predisposed me towards being *either* a neurotic or a drunk.(p.517)
• Depending on the stage of drunkenness, eventually I *either* fought or went to sleep.(p.537)

ejected
• My wife and family stood by me for ten weeks and then, quite justifiably, *ejected* me.(p.257)

elapsed
• Sixteen years have *elapsed* between our first printing of this book and the presentation in 1955 of our second edition.(p.xv)

elated
• He and his wife would leave *elated* by the thought of what they could now do for some stricken acquaintance and his family.(p.160)

elation
• Many of us have experienced dad's *elation.*(p.128)

Elba
• I felt like Napoleon returning from *Elba.*(p.4)

elbow
• The bartender, a tough Irishman, came around and "gave me the *elbow,*" which means that he raised his *elbow* and smacked me in the face.(p.411)

elbows
• My tweed suit, once a very good one, was shapeless and baggy with bare places worn in the *elbows* from leaning on the bar.(p.411)

elder
• A couple of years later, we lost our *elder* brother in a house fire, because of pills and booze.(p.480)

elderberry
• I became a specialist in making *elderberry* blossom wine.(p.213)

elderly
• I sold three lots to an *elderly* lady in Cleveland.(p.196)

elders
• I realized that there wasn't anything I could say to place myself in a more favorable light with my children, that it was going to be a matter of time; for I also understood the intolerance of young people towards deficiencies in their *elders.*(p.220)
• Much later I discovered the *elders* held many prayer meetings hoping to find a way to give me the heave-ho, but at the same time stay tolerant and spiritual.(p.247)

elect
• The small group may *elect* its secretary, the large group its rotating committee, and the groups of a large metropolitan area their central or intergroup committee, which often employs a full-time secretary.(p.567)

elected
• On account of my enormous capacity for beer, I was *elected* to membership in one of the drinking societies, and soon became one of the leading spirits.(p.173)
• My guild had *elected* me president twice and later given me a "man of the year" award.(p.328)
• I had no trouble at all in being *elected* to the two drinking societies at my college.(p.357)
• I had been *elected* president of a civic club.(p.418)

electric
• These were revolutionary and drastic proposals, but the moment I fully accepted them, the effect was *electric.*(p.14)
• The expression on the faces of the women, that indefinable something in the eyes of the men, the stimulating and *electric* atmosphere of the place, conspired to let him know that here was haven at last.(p.160)
• The *electric* light began to move.(p.498)

electrical
• I'd been home about a week or ten days when one of my friends asked if I could repair one of his *electrical* outlets.(p.493)
• I went to this friend's shop to repair his *electrical* outlet and I noticed this lady.(p.493)

electricity
• We have numerous theories, for example, about *electricity.*(p.48)
• I told him that I believe in *electricity* and other forces of nature, but as for a God, if there is one, He has never done anything for me.(p.503)

electrons
• The prosaic steel girder is a mass of *electrons* whirling around each other at incredible speed.(p.48)
• Could we still say the whole thing was nothing but a mass of *electrons,* created out of nothing, meaning nothing, whirling on to a destiny of nothingness?(p.54)
• The *electrons* themselves seemed more intelligent than that.(p.54)

element
• The feeling of having shared in a common peril is one *element* in the powerful cement which binds us.(p.17)

elementary
• I went to *elementary* and high school in Washington, D.C. and then to Howard University.(p.486)

elements
• My friend promised when these things were done I would enter upon a new relationship with my Creator; that I would have the *elements* of a way of living which answered all my problems.(p.13)
• Yet its *elements* are simple.(p.57)
• I can only list a few of its *elements.*(p.435)

elevator
• Bill left me at the *elevator* and said, "Your room is so and so," and I didn't see him again for six months.(p.217)
• I reach for the bottle which I just got from George, the *elevator* boy.(p.500)

eleven
• Step *Eleven* suggests prayer and meditation.(p.85)
• We entered her house at exactly five o'clock and it was *eleven* fifteen when we left.(p.179)
• I think the longest drunk I was ever on was *eleven*

days, but usually only two days with a complete blackout for a day, and then backing off by drinking as long as I could get anything.(p.203)
• We checked into the home of Hank, the man who had fired me ***eleven*** years before in Mississippi, and there I met Bill, our founder.(p.245)
• I can still remember very distinctly getting into Akron at ***eleven*** p.m. and routing this same Howard out of bed to do something about me.(p.290)
• I got a job after school pumping gas and worked until ten or ***eleven*** at night.(p.423)
• In a prison in my native state, I spent ***eleven*** months in solitary confinement, bouncing in and out of the "hole" (a bare concrete-and-steel cubicle) about five times during those ***eleven*** months.(p.459)
• There was the father one lost respect for at the age of ***eleven***, because the father broke his solemn word in a circumstance where you, ***eleven*** years old, had assumed guilt when you were innocent; but the father would not believe you, no matter what; and to ease his suffering you "confessed" and were "forgiven," only -- months later -- to have your "guilt" brought up -- only he and you knew what he was talking bout -- brought up in front of the stern grandmother.(p.533)
• ***Eleven*** -- Our public relations policy is based on attraction rather than promotion; we need always maintain personal anonymity at the level of press, radio and films.(p.564)

eleventh

• I consider that I was taking the ***Eleventh*** Step when I joined this church.(p.417)

eligible

• I was not ***eligible*** for parole, until -- with God's help, I'm sure -- the governor cut five years off my sentence.(p.462)

eliminate

• They said, "Let's forget about those other things, that is, trying to ***eliminate*** them all at once, and concentrate on the drink."(p.190)
• By living alone you can pretty much ***eliminate*** grief from you life, but you also ***eliminate*** joy.(p.286)

eliminated

• We had always encouraged our children to bring their friends home at any time, but after a few experiences with a drunken father they ***eliminated*** home as a place to entertain friends.(p.376)
• This ***eliminated*** one of the limiting factors, the financial.(p.397)

elimination

• Following the ***elimination*** of alcohol, there was found to be no permanent brain injury.(p.xxix)
• We feel that ***elimination*** of our drinking is but a beginning.(p.19)
• But I can remember in post graduate days, and during interneship, that very often I'd go to a patient's bed and start a process of ***elimination*** and then, very often, I'd wind up guessing.(p.485)

Ella

• Thinking only of two or three dollars to buy some whiskey, I did the job and that's how I met ***Ella*** G., who was responsible for my coming into A.A.(p.493)
• She was ***Ella*** G.(p.493)
• It was around noon, a day or two later, when the telephone rang and it was ***Ella***.(p.494)
• The following Sunday we met at ***Ella*** G.'s.(p.495)

Ella's

• We held some two or three meetings at ***Ella's*** home and from there we held some two or three at her mother's home.(p.495)

elm

• We worked in five below zero weather, fixing on an ***elm*** tree a wrought iron device which modestly proclaimed that he was indeed a country doctor.(p.540)

else

• How can such a lack of proportion, of the ability to think straight, be called anything ***else***?(p.37)
• But after a while we had to face the fact that we must find a spiritual basis of life -- or ***else***.(p.44)
• Sometimes this was a tedious process; we hope no one ***else*** will be prejudiced for as long as some of us were.(p.48)
• When we became alcoholics, crushed by a self-imposed crisis we could not postpone or evade, we had to fearlessly face the proposition that either God is everything or ***else*** He is nothing.(p.53)
• In one form or another we had been living by faith and little ***else***.(p.54)
• It crowded out all ***else***:(p.56)
• It destroys more alcoholics than anything ***else***.(p.64)
• But they had not learned enough of humility, fearlessness and honesty, in the sense we find it necessary, until they told someone ***else*** all their life story.(p.73)
• Unwilling to be honest with these sympathetic men, we were honest with no one ***else***.(p.73)
• How could she be anything ***else***?(p.81)
• You can help when no one ***else*** can.(p.89)
• Let him know you are available if he wishes to make a decision and tell his story, but do not insist upon it if he prefers to consult someone ***else***.(p.96)
• We have believed them when no one ***else*** could or would.(p.105)
• He may seek someone ***else*** to console him -- not always another man.(p.111)
• Do not ask that he do it for you or anyone ***else***.(p.112)
• We wives found that, like everybody ***else***, we were afflicted with pride, self-pity, vanity and all the things which go to make up the self-centered person; and we were not above selfishness or dishonesty.(p.116)
• If a repetition is to be prevented, place the problem, along with everything ***else***, in God's hands.(p.120)
• He may either plunge into a frantic attempt to get on his feet in business, or he may be so enthralled by his new life that he talks or thinks of little ***else***.(p.125)
• Since the home has suffered more than anything ***else***, it is well that a man exert himself there.(p.127)
• He is unable to focus on anything ***else***.(p.128)
• During those first days of convalescence, this will do more to insure his sobriety than anything ***else***.(p.129)
• Though he is now a most effective member of Alcoholics Anonymous, he still smokes and drinks coffee, but neither his wife or anyone ***else*** stands in judgment.(p.135)
• You cannot see why it should be to anyone ***else***, save the spineless and stupid.(p.139)
• They often jeopardize their own positions by trying to help serious drinkers who should have been fired long ago, or ***else*** given an opportunity to get well.(p.147)
• Should you wish them above all ***else***, and be willing to make use of our experience, we are sure they will come.(p.153)
• My whole life seemed to be centered around doing what I wanted to do, without regard for the rights, wishes, or privileges of anyone ***else***; a state of mind which became more and more predominant as the years passed.(p.172)
• Part of that program is that we take it to someone ***else***, that needs it and wants it.(p.186)
• Now, if you don't want it, we'll not take up your time, and we'll be going and looking for someone ***else***."(p.186)
• I remember telling them too that it was going to be awfully tough, because I did some other things, smoked cigarettes and played penny ante poker, sometimes bet on the horse races and they said, "Don't you think you're having more trouble with this drinking than with anything ***else*** at the present time?(p.190)
• You should go out and take this program to somebody ***else*** that needs it and wants it."(p.190)
• Then, I started to miss meetings because it was raining or snowing or something ***else***.(p.203)
• With a creeping insidiousness, drink had become more important than anything ***else***.(p.226)
• This duty together with my weekly meetings with my fellow alcoholics, and my daily renewal of the contract I originally made with God, have kept me sober when nothing ***else*** ever did.(p.237)
• The lesson of his death still remains with me, yet I often wonder what would have happened if somebody ***else*** had made that first call on me.(p.239)
• At our weekly meeting I was a menace to serenity those first few months, for I took every opportunity to lambaste the "spiritual angle" as we called it, or anything ***else*** that had any tinge of theology.(p.246)
• If it isn't anything that's going to help you or anybody ***else***, why should you become involved in it, and get all disturbed about it?"(p.273)
• Having no one ***else*** to turn to, I was willing to give Him a chance, although with considerable doubt.(p.280)
• I would make a fresh start somewhere ***else***.(p.281)
• It took five years of A.A. living, and a substantial improvement in my health, before I could take a full-time office job where someone ***else*** was boss.(p.283)
• One of them was that I would try to get a group started in Chicago; the second was that I would have to return to Akron to attend meetings at least every two months until I did get a group started in Chicago; third, I decided I must place this program above everything ***else***, even my family, because if I did not maintain my sobriety I would lose my family anyway.(p.292)
• Then I learned something ***else***.(p.300)
• To be sure, this had been a dizzy and confused interval, but most everyone ***else*** I knew had emerged from it with both feet on the ground and a fair amount of adult maturity.(p.304)
• No one ***else*** would have stayed with me.(p.323)
• If I had been sincere in what I thought I wanted more than anything ***else*** in life -- a sober husband and a happy, contented home -- I would have gone on the wagon with him.(p.324)
• I just didn't give a whoop about myself or anyone ***else***.(p.325)
• I went on, realizing what I was becoming, hating myself for it, bitter, blaming life, blaming everything ***else*** but the fact that I should turn about and do something about my drinking.(p.337)
• I went on the wagon more to placate my wife than anything ***else***.(p.344)
• Something ***else*** happened to me.(p.348)
• Here he is powerless, unmanageable, in the grip of something bigger than he is, and he's got to turn the whole business over to someone ***else***!(p.350)
• And deep in my heart I really meant what I said because I loved her more than anything ***else*** in the world, yes -- even more than liquor.(p.362)
• I was going to prove to her that liquor wasn't necessary in my life, and above all that I still loved her more than anything ***else*** in the world and that I wanted her back.(p.362)
• Of course, more than anything ***else*** I had let myself down, but I didn't realize how much then -- as I do now.(p.364)
• I had nowhere ***else*** to go, and I knew something was terribly wrong, and the reason had to lie within myself.(p.371)
• The final decision came when my daughter, following a drunk which ruined my wife's birthday, said, "It's Alcoholics Anonymous -- or ***else***!"(p.378)
• I think that no one comes to A.A. until he's tried everything ***else***.(p.384)
• There was nothing ***else*** left to try.(p.389)
• There was something ***else*** that I could try -- A.A.(p.391)
• They sent me the regular letter they send to everybody ***else***, but along with it, Ruth Hock, the nonalcoholic secretary, wrote a longhand note because she could see from the letter that I really needed help badly.(p.392)
• I crawled back to my analyst, not so much because I had faith in him, but because I had nowhere ***else*** to turn.(p.435)
• My alcoholic wife took up someone ***else***, divorced me, and took with her all my remaining property.(p.437)
• I happened to be the best diagnostician I knew at the time, and certainly I knew my case better than anyone ***else***.(p.444)
• "That's a devil of a way to run an organization," I thought, and I reported Frank to the psychiatrist, who didn't seem perturbed; he just got someone ***else*** to take me on Fridays.(p.447)
• And when I place more value on my serenity and sobriety than on anything ***else***, I can maintain them at a higher level -- at least for the time being.(p.452)
• What ***else*** can I do except what I have always done in the past? -- act as my old self and return to prison.(p.458)
• When I didn't have anything ***else*** to do -- a dull evening at home -- I'd sneak a few drinks upstairs in my room, and that began to be a habit.(p.464)
• Instead, I started going to a nice private sanitarium which, after the first visit, turned out to be more like a country club than anything ***else***.(p.468)
• I realized that I was trying to pin everything on an individual -- not the book or the group or the Higher Power, or anything ***else***.(p.472)
• You can help where no one ***else*** can."(p.473)
• When they saw me coming, they locked up the silverware and everything ***else*** of value.(p.478)
• I think the thing that galled me was that just after Easter I had drawn my salary for two weeks' work and had decided that I was going to send some money to Vi; and above all ***else*** I was going to send my baby daughter an Easter outfit.(p.493)
• I knew my wife didn't because I had been sincere in all my promises to her as well as to my mother and to my close friends, but the urge to take that drink was more powerful than anything ***else***.(p.494)
• There was no time off for so-called good behavior, first-timers, or anything ***else***.(p.509)
• At first, like everybody ***else***, I could keep control when I drank, but if I did start to drink, even in those days, I was always one of the last to leave the party.(p.518)
• It was no use talking of putting myself into a home, a hospital, or of going to see a doctor again, or of

going to see a priest or anyone ***else***.(p.523)
• It was their open night meeting, but of course I thought they were all alcoholics; I couldn't imagine why anybody ***else*** would want to go there, and my first reaction was, well, I've come to something that's not for me.(p.524)
• I don't know if it's force of habit or something ***else*** that keeps them in one place, but I do know that in A.A. there is much work to do, and none of us can do it standing still.(p.529)
• But I wanted a cosmos, a universe all my own which I had created and where I reigned as chief top reigner and ruler over everyone ***else***.(p.535)
• For always, over and above everything ***else***, was the awfulness of the lack of meaning in life.(p.535)
• But one was so outstanding that I like to pass it on whenever I can in the hope that it will help someone ***else*** as it has me.(p.551)
• We alcoholics see that we must work together and hang together, ***else*** most of us will finally die alone.(p.563)

else's
• I took everybody ***else's*** inventory.(p.410)

elsewhere
• We have ***elsewhere*** remarked how much better life is when lived on a spiritual plane.(p.116)

eluding
• I could hardly see at all, and my memory kept ***eluding*** me.(p.353)

elusive
• The sensation is so ***elusive*** that, while they admit it is injurious, they cannot after a time differentiate the true from the false.(p.xxvi)

emanate
• Neither is reason, as most of us use it, entirely dependable, though it ***emanate*** from our best minds.(p.54)

embarrass
• But you must be on guard not to ***embarrass*** or harm your husband.(p.115)
• I would ***embarrass*** everyone by coming in drunk or passing out.(p.526)

embarrassed
• The girl had explained them to me four times, and I was too ***embarrassed*** to ask her again.(p.445)

embarrassment
• Sometimes he is a source of ***embarrassment*** to you and his friends.(p.109)
• We find that most of this ***embarrassment*** is unnecessary.(p.115)
• They spoke with great freedom from ***embarrassment***, which I could never do, and they seemed very much at ease on all occasions and appeared very healthy.(p.178)

embassies
• My family always bought the best, and the ***embassies*** were flowing.(p.402)

embittered
• Business failure, insanity, fatal illness, suicide -- these calamities in his immediate family ***embittered*** and depressed him.(p.56)

embodied
• This and the program of recovery ***embodied*** in the Twelve Steps.(p.311)

embodies
• It is, however, only the first of a series of miracles which have followed one after another as a result of my trying to apply to my daily life the principles ***embodies*** in our Twelve Steps.(p.280)

embrace
• Many retirees ***embrace*** alcoholism while secluded in motor trailers, rest homes, leisure-world bungalows, mountain cabins, or beach cottages, or even in penthouses, on yachts, and inside Palm Springs cabanas.(p.329)
• A.A. led me gently from this fantasizing to ***embrace*** reality with open arms.(p.561)

emerge
• A better way of life will ***emerge*** when they are overcome.(p.117)
• Always we'd ***emerge*** with a new formula for avoiding future trouble.(p.433)
• As the sober days grew into sober months and then into sober years, a new and beautiful life began to ***emerge*** from the shambles of my former existence.(p.559)

emerged
• From a trembling, despairing nervous wreck, had ***emerged*** a man brimming over with self-reliance and contentment.(p.xxix)
• To be sure, this had been a dizzy and confused interval, but most everyone else I knew had ***emerged*** from it with both feet on the ground and a fair amount of adult maturity.(p.304)
• To cut a long story short, I spent seven years and ten thousand dollars on my psychiatric adventure, and ***emerged*** in worse condition than ever.(p.434)

emergencies
• Today, I find I can't work my A.A. program while taking pills, nor may I even have them around for dire ***emergencies*** only.(p.443)

emergency
• I got ***emergency*** leave for twenty days.(p.426)
• If something does come along that sort of upsets me, instead of walking in and throwing a buck at the barman and asking for a drink, I walk into a telephone booth, drop a dime in the box, and call somebody who was so kind as to give me his name and telephone number to meet such an ***emergency***.(p.511)

emerging
• After they have succumbed to the desire again, as so many do, and the phenomenon of craving develops, they pass through the well-known stages of a spree, ***emerging*** remorseful, with a firm resolution not to drink again.(p.xxvii)
• Crises were ***emerging*** rapidly.(p.333)
• Later, I went to sea, serving as a gunnery officer on a destroyer escort and ***emerging*** a lieutenant commander.(p.555)

Emerson
• Dr. Harry ***Emerson*** Fosdick, the noted clergyman, reviewed it with approval.(p.xvii)
• Speaking at a dinner given by John D. Rockefeller Jr. to introduce Alcoholics Anonymous to some of his friends, Dr. Harry ***Emerson*** Fosdick remarked: "I think that psychologically speaking there is a point of advantage in the approach that is being made in this movement that cannot be duplicated.(p.574)

emigrated
• Many friends of my family had ***emigrated*** to America, so at twenty-four I decided that the United States offered me the opportunity I was never likely to find in my native land.(p.231)

eminently
• He will be able to take a position with such a man which is ***eminently*** fair and square.(p.148)

Emma
• ***Emma*** ran out to the kitchen and came back with a water glass full of bourbon and made me drink it down.(p.385)

Emmet
• And I put a Big Book by my night stand, and I put a "Twelve Steps and Twelve Tradition" in my locker at the hospital, and I got books by ***Emmet*** Fox, and I got books by God-knows-who, and I got to reading all these things.(p.348)

emotion
• Keep it always in sight that we are dealing with that most terrible human ***emotion*** -- jealousy.(p.82)

emotional
• Frothy ***emotional*** appeal seldom suffices.(p.xxvi)
• They appear to be in the nature of huge ***emotional*** displacements and rearrangements.(p.27)
• In fact, I have been trying to produce some such ***emotional*** rearrangement within you.(p.27)
• We were having trouble with personal relationships, we couldn't control our ***emotional*** natures, we were a prey to misery and depression, we couldn't make a living, we had a feeling of uselessness, we were full of fear, we were unhappy, we couldn't seem to be of real help to other people -- was not a basic solution of these bedevilments more important than whether we should see newsreels of lunar flight?(p.52)
• There are those, too, who suffer from grave ***emotional*** and mental disorders, but many of them do recover if they have the capacity to be honest.(p.58)
• Unless the reason is understood, there may be an ***emotional*** upset.(p.134)
• I was an intellectual and I needed an intellectual answer, not an ***emotional*** one.(p.227)
• Sniffing at ***emotional*** religion, I walked away.(p.256)
• At long last I am doing the kind of work I have always wanted to do, but never had the patience and ***emotional*** stability to train myself for.(p.284)
• This, plus mounting ***emotional*** disturbances, convinced them that compulsive alcoholism already had them; that complete ruin would be only a question of time.(p.315)
• How important is it compared to my serenity, my ***emotional*** sobriety?"(p.452)
• Through my efforts to get down to "causes and conditions," I stand convinced that my ***emotional*** illness has been present from my earliest recollection.(p.544)
• I never did react normally to any ***emotional*** situation.(p.544)
• Apparently I'd grown physically at the customary rate of speed, and I had acquired an average amount of intellectual training in the intervening years, but there had been no ***emotional*** maturity at all.(p.547)
• We learn how to level out the ***emotional*** wings that got us into trouble both when we were up and when we were down.(p.560)
• If we do not do so, we shall stand convicted of ***emotional*** sterility and of having lost the faith that moves mountains, without which medicine can do little."(p.571)

emotionalism
• It was no momentary ***emotionalism*** born of self-pity in a maudlin condition.(p.258)

emotionally
• There are, of course, the psychopaths who are ***emotionally*** unstable.(p.xxviii)

emotions
• Ideas, ***emotions***, and attitudes which were once the guiding forces of the lives of these men are suddenly cast to one side, and a completely new set of conceptions and motives begin to dominate them.(p.27)
• But my life, even sober, was all askew and so were my ***emotions***.(p.414)
• The Higher Power to whom I had turned, and who had sustained me, had once again been thrust into the background, while my ***emotions*** were running my life and, as always, my ***emotions*** ran me to the bottle.(p.472)
• An ambitious playwright, he let his brains get so far ahead of his ***emotions*** that he collapsed into suicidal drinking.(p.531)
• For a while, for a long time, we can endure the intellect's being ahead of the ***emotions***, which is the import of Millay's couplet.(p.534)
• But as the years go by, the stretch becomes unbearable; and the man with the grown-up brain and the childish ***emotions*** -- vanity, self-interest, false pride, jealousy, longing for social approval, to name few -- becomes a prime candidate for alcohol.(p.534)
• To my way of thinking, that is a definition of alcoholism; a state of being in which the ***emotions*** have failed to grow to the stature of the intellect.(p.535)
• Sobering up, the mind that was ahead of the ***emotions*** would impel the question: What have you written or done to be the great man?(p.537)
• This question so insulted the ***emotions*** that clearly there was only one thing to do, go and get drunk again, and put that enquiring mind in its proper place, which was oblivion.(p.537)
• In my late teens I became aware of ***emotions*** I'd not counted on; restlessness, anxiety, fear and insecurity.(p.545)
• The only thing this changed, however, was my surroundings, and it was soon apparent that I could have the same uncomfortable ***emotions*** with an unlimited checking account that I could on a working girl's salary.(p.545)

emphasize
• This is a point we wish to ***emphasize*** and re-emphasize, to smash home upon our alcoholic readers as it has been revealed to us out of bitter experience.(p.39)
• To some people we need not, and probably should not ***emphasize*** the spiritual feature on our first approach.(p.76)
• If not members of religious bodies, we sometimes select and memorize a few set prayers which ***emphasize*** the principles we have been discussing.(p.87)
• So please bear in mind, and I would like to ***emphasize***, that this is a very rough estimate.(p.399)

emphasized
• My friend had ***emphasized*** the absolute necessity of demonstrating these principles in all my affairs.(p.14)
• We have ***emphasized*** willingness as being indispensable.(p.76)
• Dr. Bob always ***emphasized*** the religious angle very strongly, and I think it helped.(p.292)

emphasizing
• In ***emphasizing*** alcoholism as an illness, the social stigma associated with this condition is being blotted out . . .(p.573)

emphatic
• If the man be agnostic or atheist, make it ***emphatic*** that he does not have to agree with your conception of God.(p.93)

emphatically
• As soon as a man can say that he does believe, or is willing to believe, we ***emphatically*** assure him that he

is on his way.(p.47)
• He should understand that *emphatically.*(p.142)
• Most *emphatically* we wish to say that any alcoholic capable of honestly facing his problems in the light of our experience can recover, provided he does not close his mind to all spiritual concepts.(p.570)

employ
• Under these conditions we can *employ* our mental faculties with assurance, for after all God gave us brains to use.(p.86)
• The next three years I spent in Boston, Chicago, and Montreal in the *employ* of a large manufacturing concern, selling railway supplies, gas engines of all sorts, and many other items of heavy hardware.(p.172)
• But this was a man who had experienced many years of frightful drinking, who had had most all the drunkard's experiences known to man, but who had been cured by the very means I had been trying to *employ*, that is to say the spiritual approach.(p.180)
• Eight – Alcoholics Anonymous should remain forever nonprofessional, but our service centers may *employ* special workers.(p.564)
• But we may *employ* alcoholics where they are going to perform those services for which we might otherwise have to engage nonalcoholics.(p.566)

employed
• With many individuals the methods which I *employed* are successful, but I have never been successful with an alcoholic of your description."(p.27)
• The third man who came to see me had been one of the greatest business-getters his company had ever *employed.*(p.235)

employee
• If you concede that your *employee* is ill, can he be forgiven for what he has done in the past?(p.140)
• To return to the subject matter of this book: It contains full suggestions by which the *employee* may solve his problem.(p.143)
• Whether your *employee* likes it or not, he will learn the grim truth about alcoholism.(p.144)
• With this kind of *employee* such an attitude will command undying loyalty.(p.145)
• He will have no further reason for covering up an alcoholic *employee.*(p.148)
• It is not to be expected that an alcoholic *employee* will receive a disproportionate amount of time and attention.(p.149)

employee's
• Because of the *employee's* special ability, or of his own strong personal attachment to him, the employer has sometimes kept such a man at work long beyond a reasonable period.(p.137)
• On your *employee's* return, talk with him.(p.144)

employees
• To me, this incident illustrates lack of understanding as to what really ails the alcoholic, and lack of knowledge as to what part employers might profitably take in salvaging their sick *employees.*(p.139)
• Should he have the same consideration as other ailing *employees?*(p.140)
• As our work spreads and our numbers increase, we hope your *employees* may be put in personal contact with some of us.(p.144)
• After your man has gone along without drinking for a few months, you may be able to make use of his services with other *employees* who are giving you the alcoholic run-around – provided, of course, they are willing to have a third party in the picture.(p.146)
• But the policy of this company is not to interfere with the habits of our *employees.*(p.148)
• There is a real interest, both humanitarian and business, in the well-being of *employees.*(p.149)
• There are two alcoholic *employees,* who produce as much as five normal salesmen.(p.149)
• With the war over, and back in Baltimore with the folks, there were several small jobs for three years and then I went to work soliciting as one of the first ten *employees* of a new national finance company.(p.242)
• Handling customers, dealers, insurance people, dictation, telephoning, directing new *employees,* answering to superiors, and all the rest of it.(p.299)

employer
• We had a new *Employer.*(p.63)
• My *employer*(p.65)
• Notice that the word "fear" is bracketed alongside the difficulties with Mr. Brown, Mrs. Jones, the *employer,* and the wife.(p.67)
• Frequently, you have felt obliged to tell your husband's *employer* and his friends that he was sick, when as a matter of fact he was tight.(p.115)
• He knows the alcoholic as the *employer* sees him.(p.136)
• Nearly every modern *employer* feels a moral responsibility for the well-being of his help, and he tries to meet these responsibilities.(p.137)
• Because of the employee's special ability, or of his own strong personal attachment to him, the *employer* has sometimes kept such a man at work long beyond a reasonable period.(p.137)
• The *employer* can many times protect the victim from this kind of talk.(p.145)
• The *employer* cannot play favorites, but he can always defend a man from needless provocation and unfair criticism.(p.146)
• A former *employer* of mine said to me a little over ten years ago, "Pat, you seem to be one of those unfortunate people who at least once every six months must go out and roll in the gutter."(p.513)
• My *employer* gave me one warning, then another.(p.558)

employers
• It brings misunderstanding, fierce resentment, financial insecurity, disgusted friends and *employers,* warped lives of blameless children, sad wives and parents -- anyone can increase the list.(p.18)
• TO *EMPLOYERS*(p.136)
• Among many *employers* nowadays, we think of one member who has spent much of his life in the world of big business.(p.136)
• Some *employers* have tried every known remedy.(p.137)
• And we, who have imposed on the best of *employers,* can scarcely blame them if they have been short with us.(p.138)
• To me, this incident illustrates lack of understanding as to what really ails the alcoholic, and lack of knowledge as to what part *employers* might profitably take in salvaging their sick employees.(p.139)

employing
• I was at one time assistant manager of a corporation department *employing* sixty-six hundred men.(p.136)

employment
• I took a night law course, and obtained *employment* as investigator for a surety company.(p.2)
• Mercifully, no one could guess that I was to have no real *employment* for five years, or hardly draw a sober breath.(p.4)
• We finally sought *employment* ourselves as destitution faced us and our families.(p.106)
• When I hit Houston, Texas, I found *employment* in a large bookstore.(p.255)

employs
• The small group may elect its secretary, the large group its rotating committee, and the groups of a large metropolitan area their central or intergroup committee, which often *employs* a full-time secretary.(p.567)

empties
• There was an upper cupboard full of *empties.*(p.333)

empty
• Without this proof the expectant purchaser would be forced to depart *empty* handed with none of what I later came to believe was the great panacea for all human ills.(p.171)
• First, my new wife had walked out, bag, baggage and furniture; then the apartment landlord had thrown me out of the *empty* apartment and the finish was the loss of another job.(p.238)
• Forced to detrain from an *empty* gondola on the other side of Chicago by a terrific rainstorm which drenched me to the skin, I hit the first factory building I saw for a job.(p.253)
• To go north into the *empty* pine country and shoot myself, or to go south in the faint hope that a bunch of strangers might help me with my drinking problem.(p.278)
• A lot of lost dreams, *empty* futures, and crazy things of the past went through my mind.(p.333)
• And of course a half *empty* bottle wasn't worth keeping, so I finished it up and naturally had to get more in right away for the people who "might come in unexpectedly."(p.336)
• Near the Laundromat, I would buy one bottle of pop and a few bottles of beer or wine, and go into the rest room, *empty* the pop bottle, refill it with the booze, and proceed to do my laundering.(p.370)
• At that time the repeal whiskies were back, and I'd go to the store and buy my whiskey and take it to my office and put it under the desk, first in one place and then in another, and there soon was an accumulation of *empty* bottles.(p.488)

emulate
• The example which they and Bill W., whose visits to Akron were fairly frequent, set me of service to their fellow men imbued me with a great desire to *emulate* them.(p.281)

enable
• Its main object is to *enable* you to find a Power greater than yourself which will solve your problem.(p.45)
• Just to the extent that we do as we think He would have us, and humbly rely on Him, does He *enable* us to match calamity with serenity.(p.68)
• There was an insistent yearning to enjoy life as we once did and a heartbreaking obsession that some new miracle of control would *enable* us to do it.(p.151)
• I don't care too much about personal fame or glory, and I want only enough money to *enable* me to do the work I feel I can perhaps do best.(p.542)

enabled
• He startled me by informing me that he was an alcoholic, that he had found a way which so far *enabled* him to live without taking a drink, and that the main idea was to find a way how not to take that first drink.(p.218)
• The details of the long road back to something resembling normal living -- the first short streetcar ride, the purchase of a used bike which *enabled* me to widen the narrow horizon of life, the first trip downtown – I will not dwell on.(p.276)
• The fellowship I found in A.A. *enabled* me to face my problem honestly and squarely.(p.340)
• Most important, A.A. has *enabled* me to go back and start growing up all over again in all areas of my life.(p.420)

enables
• If our testimony helps sweep away prejudice, *enables* you to think honestly, encourages you to search diligently within yourself, then, if you wish, you can join us on the Broad Highway.(p.55)
• This practice *enables* us to lend a hand, at the same time avoiding certain alluring distractions of the road, about which any traveling man can inform you.(p.162)

enacted
• However, as time went on laws were *enacted* that reduced the sentence.(p.509)

encased
• Slowly I realized I was in bed and that the objects were my feet, *encased* in a harness affair.(p.422)

enchanted
• Yet, in other moments, we found ourselves thinking, when *enchanted* by a starlit night, "Who, then, made all this?"(p.46)

encounter
• Of course, we sometimes *encounter* people who do not understand alcoholics.(p.74)
• Some of the snags you will *encounter* are irritation, hurt feeling and resentments.(p.117)
• I returned from Europe a while after that *encounter,* and I never went back.(p.406)

encountered
• I left on a Wednesday afternoon, had dinner in Akron and then went to a house where I *encountered* my first meeting.(p.218)
• He further explained that alcohol was no respecter of sex or background, but that most of the alcoholics he had *encountered* had better than average minds and abilities.(p.308)
• Moreover, I am deeply convinced that so long as I continue to strive, in my bumbling way, toward the principles I first *encountered* in the earlier chapters of this book, this remarkable power will continue to flow through me.(p.437)
• When I *encountered* disappointments or frustrations -- as I did more and more frequently -- my solution was to drink.(p.556)

encountering
• As I look back on the events of two months, I can clearly see that I had been circling around, half-afraid of *encountering* the remedy for my situation, half wanting it, deferring fulfillment of my promise to get in touch with the doctor I had heard about.(p.258)

encounters
• Not only were they at peace with themselves, but they were getting a kick out of life such as one seldom *encounters,* except in the very young.(p.310)

encourage
• Many of our friends *encourage* us by saying that this is but a beginning, only the augury of a much larger future ahead.(p.xv)
• Tell him enough about your drinking habits, symptoms, and experiences to *encourage* him to speak of himself.(p.91)
• If he thinks he can do the job in some other way, or

prefers some other spiritual approach, *encourage* him to follow his own conscience.(p.95)
• You may need to *encourage* him to play once in a while.(p.146)
• I tried to *encourage* a search for some new goal.(p.334)

encouraged

• If any feel that as psychiatrists directing a hospital for alcoholics we appear somewhat sentimental, let them stand with us a while on the firing line, see the tragedies, the despairing wives, the little children; let the solving of these problems become a part of their daily work, and even of their sleeping moments, and the most cynical will not wonder that we have accepted and *encouraged* this movement.(p.xxvi)
• Young people may be *encouraged* by this man's experience to think that they can stop, as he did, on their own will power.(p.33)
• In the next two or three days the balance of this handful of men contacted me, *encouraged* me, and told me how they were trying to live this program of recovery and the fun they were having doing it.(p.291)
• Shortly after I returned to Chicago, my doctor, *encouraged* by the results of my contact with A.A., sent us two more of his alcoholic patients.(p.310)
• We had always *encouraged* our children to bring their friends home at any time, but after a few experiences with a drunken father they eliminated home as a place to entertain friends.(p.376)
• I got a good non-academic education; my intellectual curiosity was *encouraged.*(p.401)

encouragement

• Every *encouragement* was given me with frequent salary increases, but the sober times between "periods" became shorter.(p.254)
• The *encouragement* received in the early days, especially from the A.A. General Service Office, made a tremendous difference to my sobriety.(p.342)

encourages

• If our testimony helps sweep away prejudice, enables you to think honestly, *encourages* you to search diligently within yourself, then, if you wish, you can join us on the Broad Highway.(p.55)

end

• By the *end* of 1939, it was estimated that 800 alcoholics were on their way to recovery.(p.xviii)
• At the *end* of it, my reports to Wall street procured me a position there and the use of a large expense account.(p.3)
• My weary and despairing wife was informed that it would all *end* with heart failure during delirium tremens, or I would develop a wet brain, perhaps within a year.(p.7)
• Everyone became resigned to the certainty that I would have to be shut up somewhere, or would stumble along to a miserable *end.*(p.8)
• Near the *end* of that bleak November, I sat drinking in my kitchen.(p.8)
• We were in a position where life was becoming impossible, and if we had passed into the region from which there is no return through human aid we had but two alternatives: One was to go on to the bitter *end*, blotting out the consciousness of our intolerable situation as best we could; and the other, to accept spiritual help.(p.25)
• It was the *end* of a perfect day, not a cloud on the horizon.(p.41)
• Instead of regarding ourselves as intelligent agents, spearheads of God's ever advancing Creation, we agnostics and atheists chose to believe that our human intelligence was the last word, the alpha and the omega, the beginning and *end* of all.(p.49)
• But this is not an *end* in itself.(p.77)
• Wait for the *end* of the spree, or at least for a lucid interval.(p.90)
• They should wait for the *end* of his next drinking bout.(p.90)
• In desperation, we have even got tight ourselves -- the drunk to *end* all drunks.(p.106)
• He will wish for the *end.*(p.152)
• At one *end* of the room stood a glass covered directory of local churches.(p.154)
• This continued until I enrolled in our state university and, at the *end* of four years, I realized that I was a drunk.(p.183)
• I thought to myself, "Well, she is going to tell me this is the *end*," and I certainly couldn't blame her and did not intend to try to justify myself.(p.184)
• Whether you quit six days, months, or years, if you go out and take a drink or two you'll *end* up in this hospital tied down, just like you have been in these past six months.(p.187)
• And they said, "No, you have a disease, and it doesn't make any difference how long you do without it, after a drink or two you'll *end* up just like you are now."(p.187)
• When I was eighteen, at the *end* of high school, the high school team had a banquet at a well-known roadhouse outside of Akron.(p.194)
• At the *end* of this selling of lots, just prior to World War I, I got into the crude rubber business, and six months later there was only one broker and myself left in Akron.(p.197)
• One hundred for unmarried women at one *end*, one hundred for men at the other, and one hundred for married couples in the middle.(p.198)
• Always at the *end* of these dreams was drinking.(p.199)
• At the *end* of about four months, I not only had good looking clothes --and I might say that at the time I first talked to Max I didn't have a suit of clothes I could bend over in real sudden; now I had six suits of clothes.(p.200)
• (My mother and father were Catholics and I had been baptized, but at the *end* of my instructions for Confirmation I had not gone to church, and then when my mother remarried, she married a Protestant and the whole religious angle was forgotten.(p.201)
• At the *end* of fifteen months, I tried the beer experiment.(p.203)
• After drinking one glass of beer at the *end* of my work period for about five days, I thought I'd better find out whether I really had the stuff licked.(p.203)
• And at the *end* of fourteen days, they let me out.(p.205)
• In fact, I never lost my faith, since I had been prepared by some conversations toward the *end* of my sojourn in the hospital with Dr. Bob, conversations pretty much along spiritual lines.(p.218)
• That was at the *end* of eight days in which I had had no liquor.(p.218)
• It was finally decided to undertake the organization of a Cleveland group and toward the *end* of May, 1939, the first meeting was held in Cleveland in my home.(p.219)
• For me, work was only a different means to the same *end*, to be able to do exactly what I wanted to do.(p.225)
• Back at camp, all was forgiven because it was the *End*, but in the light of what I have since learned I know I was a confirmed alcoholic at nineteen.(p.242)
• Young and able to travel with the best of them, I managed to hold my job and keep my *end* up in the barrooms.(p.252)
• At the *end* of a year, the children got a card from their father, which I still have and cherish.(p.262)
• At the *end* of these thirteen years I never dreamed that he'd ever take another drink.(p.263)
• So, sometimes we'd *end* up in Charleston, West Virginia, or here or there, drinking all along the way.(p.264)
• Before the *end* finally came, I had, I guess made the surrender because I finally had been able to say that I would not mind too much.(p.272)
• In the *end* I had two problems instead of one: Fear and alcohol.(p.275)
• In the long ago past I used to start at the top as president or treasurer and *end* up with the sheriff breathing down my neck.(p.284)
• They realized that in the *end* alcoholism could be a mortal as cancer; certainly no sane man would wait for a malignant growth to become fatal before seeking help.(p.315)
• The only incentive that I had, toward the *end*, for getting dressed in the morning was to get out and get supplies to help me get my day started.(p.336)
• I returned to my home in Lucknow, India, at the *end* of November last year from a vacation in one of the most famous beauty spots in our country, a mountain resort 6,800 feet up, with a wonderful lake.(p.342)
• It finally got such a hold on me that I was completely at my wits' *end*, not knowing what the result would be.(p.343)
• At one *end* of the table sat our community butcher.(p.347)
• At the other side of the table sat one of the carpenters in our community, and at the further *end* of the table sat the man who ran the bakery, while on one side sat my friend who was a mechanic.(p.347)
• This was at the height of the Depression and the *end* of Prohibition.(p.358)
• I would *end* it all, and then, by George, she'd be sorry!(p.363)
• I could *end* my story here, but for the new man I would like to add a few words.(p.366)
• A relief, even though I dreaded it, feeling that this was the *end* of everything.(p.378)
• I did not know that I had no power over alcohol, that I, alone and unaided, could not stop; that I was on a downgrade, tearing along at full speed with all my brakes gone, and that the *end* would be a total smash-up, death or insanity.(p.408)
• Awarded a scholarship to a famous old Eastern college, I began to drink at the *end* of my freshman year, and by junior year, I had to transfer to an easier state university to keep my grades up.(p.419)
• At one *end* of the bed, near the foot, was a printed card, and beneath that was a charted graph.(p.422)
• The *end* came next year.(p.429)
• Here was power to live to the *end* of any given day, power to have the courage to face the next day, power to have friends, power to help people, power to be sane, power to stay sober.(p.436)
• Then I found the solution: At the *end* of study time, I would drink two beers, jump in bed, sleep real fast, and wake up smart.(p.440)
• In the *end*, I had to do the same with alcohol and all pills.(p.443)
• This was the *end* of my world.(p.461)
• I suddenly remembered one of my first A.A. meetings, where I heard, "If you are an alcoholic and if you continue to drink, the *end* is death or insanity."(p.461)
• But the *end* is in sight.(p.499)
• She is near the *end* now and is in a hospital.(p.501)
• She has reached the *end* of her rope.(p.502)
• When we first come into A.A., many of us are confused because as a general rule we're at the *end* of our respective ropes, and we don't know what to do.(p.512)
• But at the *end* of nine months we went to a party one night, and I took the first drink.(p.514)
• Either that or *end* my life.(p.515)
• I was at the *end* of my rope.(p.515)
• Strangely enough, right through to the *end* of my twenty-six years in the Army, I was still being offered very good and important jobs in spite of the fact that my superiors must have known that I wasn't thoroughly reliable.(p.519)
• At the *end* of that time, they shipped me back to my regiment again.(p.520)
• I talked to him for quite a long time and at the *end*, he said, "Well, you're not quite mad enough to be shut up for good yet, but you soon will be if you live long enough."(p.522)
• There was the necessity for sticking to a job I hated, a dull, repetitive job performed in association with other men I had nothing in common with . . . performed for years on *end*, because the money was needed at home.(p.532)
• Repeated year on *end*, they are horrible -- frightening and degrading, a chronicle of tragedy which may be greater because the individual undergoing the tragedy, myself, knew what was happening, and yet refused to do anything to stop it.(p.538)
• It paid for a ten-day binge which was the *end* of my drinking days.(p.540)
• Simply, yes it did *end*; for I had changed my mind about alcohol, and it stayed changed.(p.541)
• They are almost paid; the *end* is in sight.(p.541)
• It was not difficult to convince myself that my unhappiness was the fault of the man I had married, and I divorced him at the *end* of a year.(p.545)
• I knew it didn't make any difference where I started, the inevitable *end* would be skid row.(p.548)
• This to the *end* that our great blessings may never spoil us; that we shall forever live in thankful contemplation of Him who presides over us all.(p.568)

endangered

• I was keenly aware that my all-important security, which I had been constantly afraid of losing for four decades, no longer was *endangered.*(p.329)

endeavor

• From childhood through high school I was more or less forced to go to church, Sunday School and evening service, Monday night Christian *Endeavor* and sometimes to Wednesday evening prayer meeting.(p.172)
• There my drinking became so much worse that the boys in the fraternity house where I lived felt forced to send for my father, who made a long journey in the vain *endeavor* to get me straightened around.(p.174)

endeavored

• I studied art; I desperately *endeavored* to create an interest in many things, in a new place among new people.(p.305)
• She tried reasoning with me, *endeavored* to work out various drinking schedules, in fact all the tricks were practised faithfully for a short time somewhere along my shaky road to unhappiness.(p.361)

endeavoring

• Outline the program of action, explaining how you made a self-appraisal, how you straightened out your past and why you are now *endeavoring* to be helpful to him.(p.94)

• Like all alcoholics *endeavoring* to run away from themselves and their environment, I decided to go to New York.(p.358)

ended

• The flying-blind period *ended* and A.A. entered a new phase of its pioneering time.(p.xvii)

• I knew the man by name, and partly recognized his features, but there all resemblance *ended*.(p.xxix)

• For him, this was the spree that *ended* all sprees.(p.155)

• Of course, the result was very bad, and that *ended* the beer experiment.(p.178)

• Despite great opportunities, alcohol nearly *ended* her life.(p.222)

• This newsman covered life from top to bottom; but he *ended* up, safely enough, in the middle.(p.251)

• I *ended* up, homeless, jobless, penniless and rudderless, as the problem guest of a close friend whose family was out of town.(p.278)

• He has loaned it to me and I did my job, but that *ended* nine days ago.(p.351)

• This escapade also *ended* up in the clutches of the law, and my friend was institutionalized for eight months.(p.354)

• Short dry spells *ended* in heavy drinking.(p.375)

• But my attempts at community service *ended* in a drunken and abusive row with a fellow volunteer.(p.410)

• Max and I had been married for twenty-eight years when I *ended* up in A.A.(p.439)

• So, when it *ended* up at a psycho ward, I wasn't all that surprised.(p.440)

• Things went from bad to worse, and since I had finally and completely failed at the job of being a wife and a mother, my marriage *ended*.(p.468)

• Each battle has *ended* in defeat.(p.502)

• Please do not think it *ended* so simply and so easily.(p.541)

ending

• It was also an *ending*, for never since June 16th, 1938, have I had to walk alone.(p.248)

• That job began a series of brief working spells, each one *ending* in a "drunk" and the urge to travel.(p.253)

• In *ending* my story I like to think about this.(p.417)

• My story has a happy *ending*, but not of the conventional kind.(p.437)

endless

• Now I was to plunge into the dark, joining that *endless* procession of sots who had gone on before.(p.8)

• During my first year out of college I had *endless* dates, and went to countless dances, balls and dinner parties.(p.275)

• It is an *endless* career.(p.394)

• It has made life a thousand times easier and simpler than did the *endless* compromises and conflicts by which I lived before.(p.394)

• Now came the black and *endless* dismal night.(p.410)

• They saved us *endless* time and lost motion.(p.496)

endlessly

• This went on *endlessly*, and I began to waken very early in the morning shaking violently.(p.5)

• She was *endlessly* patient as we looked together for an answer.(p.409)

endorse

• Six -- An A.A. group ought never *endorse*, finance or lend the A.A. name to any related facility or outside enterprise, lest problems of money, property and prestige divert us from our primary purpose.(p.564)

endorsement

• While an A.A. group may cooperate with anyone, such cooperation ought never go so far as affiliation or *endorsement*, actual or implied.(p.566)

• Since Dr. Silkworth's first *endorsement* of Alcoholics Anonymous, medical societies and physicians throughout the world have set their approval upon us.(p.571)

endorsements

• And in no circumstances should we give *endorsements*, make alliances, or enter public controversies.(p.xix)

ends

• We are careful never to pray for our own selfish *ends*.(p.87)

• During that first year, however, I managed to make both *ends* meet, and to avoid ever going back to my old habit pattern of borrowing money when I could not earn it.(p.283)

endure

• I would have three quick strong ones in order to *endure* the evening.(p.407)

• For a while, for a long time, we can *endure* the intellect's being ahead of the emotions, which is the import of Millay's couplet.(p.534)

endured

• The mind and body are marvelous mechanisms, for mine *endured* this agony two more years.(p.6)

• That the man who is making the approach has had the same difficulty, that he obviously knows what he is talking about, that his whole deportment shouts at the new prospect that he is a man with a real answer, that he has no attitude of Holier Than Thou, nothing whatever except the sincere desire to be helpful; that there are no fees to pay, no axes to grind, no people to please, no lectures to be *endured* -- these are the conditions we have found most effective.(p.18)

• But whereas my horse was always equipped with a flask, I merely *endured* the fox hunting so I could start drinking at lunch time.(p.404)

enduring

• *Enduring* all the hangover hells that every alcoholic experiences, I made the usual resolutions.(p.256)

• To wear expensive clothes, to have bartenders know what to serve me before I ordered, to be recognized by headwaiters and shown to the best table, to play gin rummy for high stakes with the insouciance of a riverboat gambler – these were the *enduring* values in life, I thought.(p.556)

enemies

• We have begun to learn tolerance, patience and good will toward all men, even our *enemies*, for we look on them as sick people.(p.70)

• Our former *enemies* sometimes praise what we are doing and wish us well.(p.78)

• The greatest *enemies* of us alcoholics are resentment, jealousy, envy, frustration, and fear.(p.145)

enemy

• It is harder to go to an *enemy* than to a friend, but we find it much more beneficial to us.(p.77)

• I was really scolding my mortal *enemy*, the inner me.(p.408)

energetic

• As a class, alcoholics are *energetic* people.(p.146)

energies

• Use your *energies* to promote a better understanding all around.(p.115)

energy

• We do not tire so easily, for we are not burning up *energy* foolishly as we did when we were trying to arrange life to suit ourselves.(p.88)

• He thought all alcoholics should constantly have chocolate available for its quick *energy* value at times of fatigue.(p.133)

• Making amends is sometimes doing what we are capable of doing but failed to do because of alcohol; carrying out community responsibilities such as Community Funds, Red Cross, educational and religious activities in proportion to our abilities and *energy*.(p.381)

enforced

• Age and the law were still against me, but laws were not as strictly *enforced* in those days as they are now, and I discovered that as long as I had the green blood, there was always a way to get alcohol, either from a nondiscriminatory bartender or from an older friend who would be glad to purchase the joy juice for the privilege of sharing it.(p.397)

• Now my drinking was limited by only one factor, the *enforced* periods of dryness caused by lengthy tours at sea.(p.398)

engage

• At first *engage* in general conversation.(p.91)

• The problems of the community might *engage* attention.(p.131)

• One is that I don't remember too many of them, as I was one of those drunks who could be on his feet and attend a meeting or a party, *engage* in a conversation with people and do things that any nearly normal person would do, and the next day not remember a thing about where I was, what I did, whom I saw, or how I got home.(p.301)

• But we may employ alcoholics where they are going to perform those services for which we might otherwise have to *engage* nonalcoholics.(p.566)

engaged

• He should realize that we are *engaged* upon a life-and-death errand.(p.75)

• We got *engaged*, and we were happy – Jean with me, and me with the bottle and Jean.(p.318)

• He finally decided that he did not love me enough, and soon he told me so and said he was *engaged* to another girl.(p.403)

engagement

• He has a positive genius for getting tight at exactly the wrong moment, particularly when some important decision must be made or *engagement* kept.(p.21)

engagements

• We could make few social *engagements*.(p.105)

• I thanked him, pleaded business *engagements* and promised I'd go with him at some future date.(p.257)

engendered

• Unfortunately for me, I was the only child, which perhaps *engendered* the selfishness which played such an important part in bringing on my alcoholism.(p.172)

• Like most statistics, it doesn't prove anything -- just satisfies a little curiosity *engendered* by the wail "Oh, those initiation fees" that prompted this investigation.(p.399)

engine

• But the day he comes out he races in front of a fire *engine*, which breaks his back.(p.38)

engineering

• This was an *engineering* college.(p.212)

• A year later, after I completed the course in contracts, I quit the law school, and undertook some *engineering* work for a patent law firm on behalf of clients who were in difficulties and who desired to keep their troubles from their own *engineering* department.(p.212)

engines

• The next three years I spent in Boston, Chicago, and Montreal in the employ of a large manufacturing concern, selling railway supplies, gas *engines* of all sorts, and many other items of heavy hardware.(p.172)

England

• War fever ran high in the New *England* town to which we new, young officers from Plattsburg were assigned, and we were flattered when the first citizens took us to their homes, making us feel heroic.(p.1)

• We landed in *England*.(p.1)

• I was born in a small New *England* village of about seven thousand souls.(p.171)

• So I rocked along my merry independent way until June, when I went out selling auto polish in New *England*.(p.247)

• I had completely forgotten the January 8th when I found the fellowship, and I spent the next four days wandering around New *England* half drunk, by which I mean I couldn't get drunk and I couldn't get sober.(p.247)

• From a Canadian reservation to overseas bars to New *England* lockups, an Indian traveled a long trail that finally led him home to A.A.(p.474)

• Start group on reservation and carry message, help start other groups all over Maritimes and New *England*.(p.476)

• When I came home to ordinary garrison life in *England*, I found that I was drinking rather more than most people of may age.(p.518)

English

• I knew I was through among the *English* "bookies."(p.251)

• We went through two years of deadlock required by the *English* divorce laws.(p.405)

Englishman

• This was an *Englishman* who, at least at this time, drank as much as I did.(p.405)

engulfed

• I would hang on to sobriety for short intervals, but always there would come the tide of an overpowering necessity to drink and, as I was *engulfed* in it, I felt such a sense of panic that I really believed I would die if I didn't get that drink inside.(p.306)

engulfs

• It *engulfs* all whose lives touch the sufferer's.(p.18)

enhanced

• However, one thing I am certain of: Inmates in prison who attend A.A. have their chances of remaining free greatly *enhanced* – this is a proved fact.(p.458)

enjoy

• The idea that somehow, someday he will control and *enjoy* his drinking is the great obsession of every abnormal drinker.(p.30)

• He wants to *enjoy* a certain reputation, but knows in his heart he doesn't deserve it.(p.73)

• Perhaps you *enjoy* drinking with him yourself when he doesn't go too far.(p.110)

• Most of them give freely of themselves, that their fel-

lows may *enjoy* sound minds and bodies.(p.133)
• Some of us had this experience, only to *enjoy*, in a few months, a finer intimacy than ever.(p.134)
• There was an insistent yearning to *enjoy* life as we once did and a heartbreaking obsession that some new miracle of control would enable us to do it.(p.151)
• Some of the things which used to stop me in my tracks from fear still make me nervous in the anticipation of their doing, but once I kick myself into doing them nervousness disappears and I *enjoy* myself.(p.285)
• Where derision, contempt and pity were once shown me, I now *enjoy* the respect of many people.(p.296)
• I eat three good meals a day now, and really *enjoy* them.(p.303)
• But I couldn't *enjoy* anything; I was scared to death.(p.385)
• After a while I really did *enjoy* drinking and what it did to me, and I became dependent upon it for every occasion.(p.464)
• For by now I had been exposed once to A.A., but I had treated it as a vaudeville and had taken friends to meetings so that they too could *enjoy* the fascination of the naked revelation of suffering and recovery.(p.539)
• I went on the wagon, with no outside help and with no real difficulty -- except that I didn't *enjoy* life without drinking.(p.557)

enjoyable

• It is no longer *enjoyable.*(p.514)

enjoyed

• Many could recover if they had the opportunity we have *enjoyed.*(p.19)
• As we felt new power flow in, as we *enjoyed* peace of mind, as we discovered we could face life successfully, as we became conscious of His presence, we began to lose our fear of today, tomorrow or the hereafter.(p.63)
• We have *enjoyed* such evenings ourselves; we had a good time.(p.110)
• I have *enjoyed* every moment spent in getting them straightened out.(p.150)
• At that particular time, the boys put me on a shutter and took me out to the shed, and I lay in the car while they *enjoyed* their banquet.(p.195)
• These men all drank on Saturday nights, and *enjoyed* themselves.(p.277)
• I joined their Saturday night parties and *enjoyed* myself too.(p.277)
• Fifteen of those years I would not have *enjoyed* had I continued drinking.(p.295)
• Up to this point I had spent six years in the business and had *enjoyed* the reputation of being very successful.(p.298)
• I never *enjoyed* any meal, but I ate my lunch at noon for two reasons; first, to help me get out of the fog of the night before and, second, to furnish some measure of nourishment.(p.299)
• I *enjoyed* it immensely.(p.346)
• We attended meetings together, and mutually *enjoyed* our new found friends.(p.364)
• But success brought increased social activities and I realized that many of my friends *enjoyed* a social drink with no apparent harm to themselves or others.(p.374)
• It was frightening that drink was being substituted for more and more of the things I really *enjoyed* doing.(p.374)
• I had worked the previous summer on a New York fashion magazine, a job I really *enjoyed.*(p.405)
• Although we *enjoyed* the laughter in the early days, I heard a lot of things that I thought were stupid.(p.447)
• In the last year of my navy service, I was married to a lovely, lively girl, who *enjoyed* drinking.(p.555)

enjoying

• We absolutely insist on *enjoying* life.(p.132)
• There I sat in the evenings, *enjoying* with my friends our memories of the "old country," singing the old songs we all knew, playing simple card games for drinks and consuming great quantities of beer.(p.231)
• I stayed on in Florida for three weeks, *enjoying* our reunion, a new found health and a deeper love than I had ever experienced before.(p.364)
• I don't know what I expected, but I most certainly didn't visualize a group of people talking about their drinking problems, making light of their personal tragedies and at the same time *enjoying* themselves.(p.378)
• If anyone had told me I would be *enjoying* a hockey game with my husband and my brother without being all boozed up, I would not have believed it.(p.481)

enjoyment

• I get so much more *enjoyment* out of living.(p.383)
• Things weren't going as I thought they should, for my greater *enjoyment*, comfort and fame; therefore, if the universe wouldn't play my way, I wouldn't play at all.(p.531)

enjoys

• He *enjoys* himself for a few years in spite of friendly warnings.(p.37)
• He *enjoys* drinking.(p.110)
• Russ used to be very much pleased because he'd say, "I think Dr. Bob thoroughly *enjoys* coming out here.(p.271)

enlarge

• The physician who at our request, gave us this letter, has been kind enough to *enlarge* upon his views in another statement which follows.(p.xxiv)
• For if an alcoholic failed to perfect and *enlarge* his spiritual life through work and self-sacrifice for others, he could not survive the certain trials and low spots ahead.(p.14)
• All went well for a time, but he failed to *enlarge* his spiritual life.(p.35)

enlarged

• An American doctor in Paris said I had an *enlarged* liver.(p.406)
• The doctor pronounced it a badly *enlarged* liver and said I had to quit drinking.(p.557)

enlargement

• The *enlargement* of my liver degenerated into cirrhosis.(p.557)

enlightened

• Fortunately for me, my doctor was one of the *enlightened.*(p.307)
• The bartenders took care of me, not out of brotherly love, but through *enlightened* self-interest.(p.410)

enlightening

• With these new and *enlightening* doors opening up to me, I was able to make the eventual decision to stop drinking, a day at a time -- because I, too, was an alcoholic.(p.355)

enlightenment

• Talking things over with them, great floods of *enlightenment* showed me myself as I really was and I was like them.(p.229)

enlist

• Three attempts to *enlist* in the service, and three failures because of being skinny.(p.499)

enlisted

• I left the university in the latter part of my senior year and *enlisted* in the army.(p.183)
• At age twenty-one, I *enlisted* in the Navy for two reasons: (1) to avoid being drafted into the Army, and (2) out of a burst of patriotic fervor inspired by the advent of World War II and as the result of an all-night drinking binge which found me sitting on the doorstep of the Navy recruiting office when the chief petty officer arrived to open for business at nine o'clock Monday morning.(p.398)
• I *enlisted* in the Navy to escape the Army draft.(p.425)

enormous

• On account of my *enormous* capacity for beer, I was elected to membership in one of the drinking societies, and soon became one of the leading spirits.(p.173)

enough

• The physician who at our request, gave us this letter, has been kind *enough* to enlarge upon his views in another statement which follows.(p.xxiv)
• Although he gives all that is in him, it often is not *enough.*(p.xxvii)
• With a certain satisfaction I reflected there was *enough* gin concealed about the house to carry me through that night and the next day.(p.8)
• Thus was I convinced that God is concerned with us humans when we want Him *enough.*(p.12)
• Belief in the power of God, plus *enough* willingness, honesty and humility to establish and maintain the new order of things, were the essential requirements.(p.13)
• Strangely *enough*, wives, parents and intimate friends usually find us even more unapproachable than do the psychiatrist and the doctor.(p.18)
• A few are fortunate *enough* to be so situated that they can give nearly all their time to the work.(p.19)
• He may have the habit badly *enough* to gradually impair him physically and mentally.(p.20)
• If what we have learned and felt and seen means anything at all, it means that all of us, whatever our race, creed, or color are the children of a living Creator with whom we may form a relationship upon simple and understandable terms as soon as we are willing and honest *enough* to try.(p.28)
• Surprisingly *enough*, we find such convictions no great obstacle to a spiritual experience.(p.28)
• Heaven knows, we have tried hard *enough* and long *enough* to drink like other people!(p.31)
• But the difficulty is that few alcoholics have *enough* desire to stop while there is yet time.(p.32)
• Self-reliance was good as far as it went, but it didn't go far *enough.*(p.68)
• They think we do not have *enough* of it, or that it isn't the right kind.(p.69)
• We think we have done well *enough* in admitting these things to ourselves.(p.72)
• But they had not learned *enough* of humility, fearlessness and honesty, in the sense we find it necessary, until they told someone else all their life story.(p.73)
• We feel a man is unthinking when he says that sobriety is *enough.*(p.82)
• Tell him *enough* about your drinking habits, symptoms, and experiences to encourage him to speak of himself.(p.91)
• You are sure to find someone desperate *enough* to accept with eagerness what you offer.(p.96)
• A kindly act once in a while isn't *enough.*(p.97)
• That is, if he is lucky *enough* to have a home.(p.98)
• Oddly *enough*, he is often difficult to deal with.(p.110)
• Then perhaps he will be interested *enough* to continue.(p.113)
• Not being a man of means, I knew that if I did not stay sober *enough* to earn money, I would run out of liquor.(p.175)
• During the subsequent fifteen years I had sense *enough* never to go to the hospital if I had been drinking, and very seldom did I receive patients.(p.176)
• I used to put eight or twelve ounce bottles of alcohol in a fur lined glove and toss it onto the back airing porch when winter days got dark *enough.*(p.176)
• If you still think you are strong *enough* to beat the game alone, that is your affair.(p.181)
• Between classes I would run down to the wash room, take *enough* to steady my nerves and then go on to the next class.(p.183)
• Then Prohibition came into effect, and the facts that the stuff obtainable was so horrible and sometimes deadly, and that I had married and had a job which I had to look after, helped me for a period of some three or four years, although I would get drunk every time I could get hold of *enough* to drink to get started.(p.183)
• However, after two or three trials, I found this was not satisfactory because they did not serve *enough* to satisfy me.(p.184)
• (At this point, the Editors intrude just long *enough* to supplement Bill D.'s account, that of the man on the bed, with that of Bill W., the man who sat by the side of the bed.)(p.188)
• I went into the high school grades, but having missed all the intermediate grades, I didn't get along too well, so I developed the habit of going back to school just long *enough* for the football season and then quitting.(p.193)
• Paul measured the medicine out, but he figured that with my track record that little bit wouldn't be *enough*, so he doubled it and added a few drops more and then gave it to me.(p.207)
• The differences between my father and my sisters, who were school teachers, made an excellent environment for the type of child I was – that is, slick and cute *enough* to take advantage of any adult quarrel.(p.210)
• In 1924, I had acquired *enough* clients of my own so that the firm made me a junior partner.(p.213)
• They probably felt that it was useless, that surely I had *enough* intelligence to know what I was doing.(p.215)
• In fact, the last three years of my drinking was a routine of barbiturates in the morning, so that I could stop shaking *enough* to shave, and then alcohol beginning about four-thirty or five o'clock, with a struggle not to take a drink at noon or during the day, because I had the idea that if I took one drink, I would smell as though I had had a pint.(p.217)
• He found that I had *enough* faith in the Almighty to be fairly frank.(p.219)
• I still had *enough* practice to earn a good living if I would only work, so I resolved that in January of 1940 I would launch a patent law firm of my own.(p.220)
• My fright was real *enough*, but it didn't account for these violent reactions.(p.222)
• I'd been sitting comfortably in a restaurant with Rita, drinking my sixth martini and hoping the waiter

would forget about the lunch order – at least long ***enough*** for me to have a couple more.(p.223)
• I had my own business, successful ***enough*** for me to indulge most of my desires.(p.225)
• I had to persist in my attempts to get straightened out ***enough*** to be able to use the drinks I needed, without their turning on me.(p.227)
• Oddly ***enough***, the big shot who fired me from this company was one of the first men I met when I later joined the New York A.A. Group.(p.242)
• This newsman covered life from top to bottom; but he ended up, safely ***enough***, in the middle.(p.251)
• One evening, the book, after checking up, was very definitely in the red for plenty through a piece of studied carelessness on my part, and my boss, very shrewd and able, fired me with a parting statement to the effect that once was ***enough***.(p.251)
• Remarkably ***enough***, I was a very abstemious soldier.(p.253)
• My four years of abstinence had something to do with it, but soldiering is a tough ***enough*** game for a sober man, and I had no yen for full-pack slogging through mud with a cognac or vin rouge hangover.(p.253)
• "Well, I'm nuts ***enough*** now," I said to him.(p.266)
• She said she didn't know, but that I sure showed plain ***enough*** I didn't have any part of it.(p.273)
• There was more than one occasion when I got up in the morning with just ***enough*** money for coffee and toast and the bus fare to carry me to my first appointment.(p.283)
• Oddly ***enough***, the circumstances and surroundings were pleasant.(p.285)
• I had few ***enough*** at that time.(p.293)
• Strangely ***enough***, I became acquainted with the "hilarious life" just at the time in my own life when I was beginning really to settle down to a common-sense, sane domesticity.(p.297)
• I really worked for several weeks, and having had a fairly wide acquaintance with the dealer trade, it was not difficult for me to line up ***enough*** of them to give me a very substantial volume of business with a minimum of effort.(p.300)
• I didn't dare hope I might find for myself all that these people had found, but if I could acquire some small part of their intriguing quality of living -- and sobriety – that would be ***enough***.(p.310)
• It is a way of life, and the challenge contained in its principles is great ***enough*** to keep any human being striving for as long as he lives.(p.311)
• If reasons for covering up are strong ***enough***, secrets can be hidden from the world.(p.327)
• That always has been good ***enough*** for me.(p.334)
• Mere cessation from drinking is not ***enough*** for an alcoholic while the need for that drink goes on.(p.339)
• For this officer in the Indian Army, going on the wagon was not ***enough***; attempts at control failed.(p.342)
• He answered by wiring that I could stay there until I earned ***enough*** to get home.(p.357)
• Looking back, it is surprising to me now that I managed to keep working and have ***enough*** money to squander at the various spots in the big city.(p.358)
• Thank God that in spite of my heavy drinking my mind was clear ***enough*** to make a decision then and there.(p.363)
• Sure ***enough*** in a couple of hours two men were at my door and for the first time I heard some facts about liquor and my problem that sounded sensible to me.(p.363)
• Never having ***enough***, always craving more, the obsession for alcohol gradually dominated all my activities, particularly while travelling.(p.375)
• Broken promises, humiliation, hopelessness, worry, anxiety – but still not ***enough***.(p.377)
• The why is not important; the fact is that one drink will set up a reaction in our system which requires more; that one drink was too much and one hundred drinks were not ***enough***.(p.380)
• I was so happy over getting home that I changed overnight, but not ***enough***.(p.387)
• I couldn't walk, having it in a cast, and the doctor left the cast on three weeks longer than was necessary because he never found me sober ***enough*** to take it off.(p.390)
• After all, upon coming out of a week-long or ten-day drunk, it was hard ***enough*** to figure up just how much that one drunk cost, let alone trying to calculate the cost of approximately twenty-five years of active alcoholism.(p.396)
• Even at that age, I had learned that one drink was not ***enough***.(p.397)
• I had to have ***enough*** to get drunk on, or what was the use?(p.397)
• The short tours could be taken care of by sneaking ***enough*** whiskey aboard ship so that it could be rationed out until another supply could be laid in.(p.398)
• Even when I was old ***enough*** to know better, I dreamed about being as beautiful as Venus, as pure as the Madonna and as brilliant as the President of the United States is supposed to be.(p.400)
• He finally decided that he did not love me ***enough***, and soon he told me so and said he was engaged to another girl.(p.403)
• Oddly ***enough***, the dentist who started A.A. in Amarillo, Tex., benevolently arranged my admission to dental college.(p.419)
• Gradually consciousness returned ***enough*** to let me know I was in a hospital.(p.422)
• I couldn't focus ***enough*** to make out the chart, but the card contained two words -- "ACUTE ALCOHOLISM."(p.422)
• The pep pills affected my hearing at times: I couldn't listen fast ***enough*** to hear what I was saying.(p.442)
• In the garage, I would put the needle in my vein and then try to figure out exactly how much medication to inject to overcome the pep pills while adding to the sleeping pills while ignoring the tranquilizers, in order to get just ***enough*** to be able to pull out the needle, jerk the tourniquet, throw it in the car, slam the car door shut, run down the hall, and fall in bed before I fell asleep.(p.442)
• Giving up alcohol alone was not ***enough*** for me; I've had to give up all mood-and mind-affecting chemicals in order to stay sober and comfortable.(p.443)
• So I raised ***enough*** fuss that they finally agreed to let me sign out, against medical advice.(p.444)
• But it quickly became obvious that he had this childish notion instead: If he could get me to go to ***enough*** meetings while in the hospital, I would continue to go after he let me out.(p.447)
• Most of us did not stay out of prison long ***enough*** to run the alcoholic gamut -- to develop the ongoing kind of alcoholism or alcoholic drinking you hear about in A.A. talks.(p.458)
• I thought that was bad until I hit the hole at a prison camp; it was just wide ***enough*** and long ***enough*** to lie down in.(p.459)
• Ten days of this treatment the first time knocked me from 200 pounds to 130, and I seldom stayed out of the hole long ***enough*** to gain back my weight.(p.460)
• My husband interrupted, "She's bad ***enough*** now without getting mixed up with a bunch of drunks."(p.469)
• Our shoes are not better than the average hobo's, and if we are fortunate ***enough*** to have a pair of stockings on, nobody notices the runs in them, because of our dazzling beauty and our dirty feet.(p.479)
• That was ***enough*** provocation to fight but I didn't fight, and I realized after recess why I didn't.(p.484)
• I had never had a drink, but I had seen ***enough*** merriment in the boys who were drinking to be interested.(p.498)
• I know ***enough*** of the answers to get by.(p.499)
• I had ***enough*** decency so that I dismissed the idea of doing any clowning, and I did listen.(p.509)
• I'd get downstairs to the gin mill, get ***enough*** in to hold me until eight o'clock in the morning, then I'd go out to join that "misery parade" that so many of us know so well.(p.514)
• Strangely ***enough***, right through to the end of my twenty-six years in the Army, I was still being offered very good and important jobs in spite of the fact that my superiors must have known that I wasn't thoroughly reliable.(p.519)
• I stayed there just long ***enough*** to work up a real good resentment against the doctor in charge, who I didn't think was doing anything at all except collecting fees, and I left there fully determined that I'd never put myself in the power of medical people again.(p.521)
• I talked to him for quite a long time and at the end, he said, "Well, you're not quite mad ***enough*** to be shut up for good yet, but you soon will be if you live long ***enough***."(p.522)
• If the listener were drunk ***enough***, the lecture might go on through several martinis, which I was glad to pay for.(p.537)
• I myself have been lucky ***enough*** to help out.(p.541)
• I don't care too much about personal fame or glory, and I want only ***enough*** money to enable me to do the work I feel I can perhaps do best.(p.542)
• A.A. taught me that willingness to believe was ***enough*** for a beginning.(p.550)
• It wasn't strong ***enough***, so I added a shot of vodka -- and was right back to worse trouble than before.(p.556)
• Within a week, I was feeling well ***enough*** to go home.(p.558)

enquire
• "What is it?" I ***enquire***.(p.503)

enquiring
• This question so insulted the emotions that clearly there was only one thing to do, go and get drunk again, and put that ***enquiring*** mind in its proper place, which was oblivion.(p.537)

enrolled
• This continued until I ***enrolled*** in our state university and, at the end of four years, I realized that I was a drunk.(p.183)
• So I ***enrolled*** at the university for night courses in religion, and I pursued those courses for a year.(p.221)
• I ***enrolled*** in a correspondence school which taught nothing but accounting.(p.284)

ensign
• Then I joined the Navy and was commissioned as an ***ensign*** to write speeches for admirals.(p.555)

ensued
• A return to the United States proved effective as a geographical cure, and a period of sobriety ***ensued***, with the help of the church.(p.419)

ensuing
• When we do that, we find it solves our problems too; the ***ensuing*** lack of fear, worry and hurt feelings is a wonderful thing.(p.116)
• The ***ensuing*** nine years were the Depression years, both nationally and personally.(p.277)
• By early July, I had tapered off alcohol completely, and I got off all pills in the ***ensuing*** few months.(p.448)
• Fear of rejection and its ***ensuing*** pain were not to be risked, and I turned away from myself once more for the answer, this time to the drinks I had always refused before, and in alcohol I found a false courage.(p.546)

enter
• And in no circumstances should we give endorsements, make alliances, or ***enter*** public controversies.(p.xix)
• My friend promised when these things were done I would ***enter*** upon a new relationship with my Creator; that I would have the elements of a way of living which answered all my problems.(p.13)
• Many mornings I have gone to classes, and even though fully prepared, would turn and walk back to the fraternity house because of my jitters, not daring to ***enter*** the classroom for fear of making a scene should I be called on for recitation.(p.173)
• He advised me to ***enter*** the particular hospital with which he was connected and I readily agreed.(p.302)
• I made arrangements to ***enter*** the hospital three days later and promptly went out and got stiff for three days.(p.302)
• I will not go out and I will not ***enter*** into anything.(p.506)

entered
• By late 1937, the number of members having substantial sobriety time behind them was sufficient to convince the membership that a new light had ***entered*** the dark world of the alcoholic.(p.xvii)
• The flying-blind period ended and A.A. ***entered*** a new phase of its pioneering time.(p.xvii)
• Our Society then ***entered*** a fearsome and exciting adolescent period.(p.xviii)
• The central fact of our lives today is the absolute certainty that our Creator has ***entered*** into our hearts and lives in a way which is indeed miraculous.(p.25)
• If anyone questions whether he has ***entered*** this dangerous area, let him try leaving liquor alone for one year.(p.34)
• We have ***entered*** the world of the Spirit.(p.84)
• Show them that he has ***entered*** upon a period of growth.(p.100)
• Most of us have ***entered*** the final stage with its commitment to health resorts, sanitariums, hospitals, and jails.(p.107)
• He ***entered*** a political campaign, making speeches, frequenting men's gathering places of all sorts, often staying up all night.(p.158)
• Many an alcoholic who ***entered*** there came away with an answer.(p.160)
• After many painful discussions, they finally gave me my credits and I migrated to another of the leading universities of the country and ***entered*** as a Junior that fall.(p.173)
• We ***entered*** her house at exactly five o'clock and it was eleven fifteen when we left.(p.179)
• I then ***entered*** Case School and worked while I went to school and finished there.(p.212)
• When I ***entered*** a sanitarium for prolonged and intensive psychiatric treatment, I was convinced that I

was having a serious mental breakdown.(p.226)
• At seventeen I *entered* the University, really to satisfy my father who wanted me to study medicine there as he had.(p.241)
• I *entered* the business world with every confidence that success lay ahead of me.(p.275)
• I *entered* the house, opened a new bottle of whiskey and sat down to drink myself into the right frame of mind to get in my car, start the motor and close the garage door behind me.(p.363)
• But, as it was with drinking, this project will be *entered* into with enthusiasm and optimism -- and probably wind up the same way, depressed.(p.396)
• It never *entered* my head that I would have been pushing up the daisies if he had decided not to come.(p.479)

enterprise
• Had he been successful in his *enterprise,* he would have been set on his feet financially which at the time, seemed vitally important.(p.153)
• But I hardly tasted anything for two years and started in business for myself, founding a mattress factory which is today an important industrial *enterprise* in our city.(p.232)
• I had been brought up to believe this, and I had shown during my 'teens considerable *enterprise* and imagination about earning money.(p.275)
• My alcoholic associates fired me, took control, and ran the *enterprise* into bankruptcy.(p.437)
• Six – An A.A. group ought never endorse, finance or lend the A.A. name to any related facility or outside *enterprise,* lest problems of money, property and prestige divert us from our primary purpose.(p.564)

enterprises
• My talent for leadership, I imagined, would place me at the head of vast *enterprises* which I would manage with the utmost assurance.(p.1)
• We believe that managers of large *enterprises* often have little idea how prevalent this problem is.(p.149)

entertain
• Another feeling we are very likely to *entertain* is one of resentment that love and loyalty could not cure our husbands of alcoholism.(p.118)
• I didn't know how to be a father; I don't know how to come home and work week-ends like other husbands; I don't know how to *entertain* my family.(p.351)
• It was also my job to *entertain* the owners of these stations when they came East on business – or the pretense of business.(p.359)
• We had always encouraged our children to bring their friends home at any time, but after a few experiences with a drunken father they eliminated home as a place to *entertain* friends.(p.376)

entertained
• For weeks after my arrival I was feted and *entertained* in the already large colony of Alsatians in the city, and among the Germans in their saloons and clubs.(p.231)
• I couldn't go to one wine store and look the man honestly in the face and buy a bottle, as I used to do when I had parties and *entertained* and did normal drinking.(p.336)

entertaining
• But we had to do a lot of *entertaining,* my husband liked to have a good time; I was very young; and I wanted to have a good time too.(p.322)

entertainment
• I remember that my father kept whiskey around the house for medical purposes and *entertainment,* and I would drink from this when no one was about and then water it to keep my parents from knowing I was drinking.(p.183)
• Eventually, of course, what with all the hilarity that could be provoked with a few gallons of beer, there seemed to be no need of bridge or poker playing for *entertainment.*(p.297)

enthralled
• He may either plunge into a frantic attempt to get on his feet in business, or he may be so *enthralled* by his new life that he talks or thinks of little else.(p.125)

enthusiasm
• My wife and I abandoned ourselves with *enthusiasm* to the idea of helping other alcoholics to a solution of their problems.(p.15)
• He may not share your *enthusiasm,* but he is practically sure to read the book and he may go for the program at once.(p.113)
• His reaction may be one of *enthusiasm.*(p.114)
• We find it a real mistake to dampen his *enthusiasm* for alcoholic work.(p.119)
• If you cooperate, rather than complain, you will find that his excess *enthusiasm* will tone down.(p.119)
• The girl was full of *enthusiasm* and she made the trip to Akron too.(p.295)
• His *enthusiasm* and keen interest in A.A. fired my spirits again.(p.365)
• But, as it was with drinking, this project will be entered into with *enthusiasm* and optimism -- and probably wind up the same way, depressed.(p.396)

enthusiast
• He becomes a religious *enthusiast.*(p.128)

enthusiastic
• If he is *enthusiastic* your cooperation will mean a great deal.(p.113)

enthusiastically
• If it is a happy occasion, try to increase the pleasure of those there; if a business occasion, go and attend to your business *enthusiastically.*(p.102)

enthusiasts
• Many alcoholics are *enthusiasts.*(p.125)

entice
• I would take a gulp, then warn the jug not to try to *entice,* lure, or seduce me into having more than one "medicinal" jolt.(p.332)

entire
• The unselfishness of these men as we have come to know them, the *entire* absence of profit motive, and their community spirit, is indeed inspiring to one who has labored long and wearily in this alcoholic field.(p.xxv)
• This is repeated over and over, and unless this person can experience an *entire* psychic change there is very little hope of his recovery.(p.xxvii)
• The only relief we have to suggest is *entire* abstinence.(p.xxviii)
• I expressed my *entire* willingness to approach these individuals, admitting my wrong.(p.13)
• But the ex-problem drinker who has found this solution, who is properly armed with facts about himself, can generally win the *entire* confidence of another alcoholic in a few hours.(p.18)
• If he can afford it, he may have liquor concealed all over his house to be certain no one gets his *entire* supply away from him to throw down the waterpipe.(p.22)
• The *entire* family is, to some extent, ill."(p.122)
• He may not see at once that he has barely scratched a limitless lode which will pay dividends only if he mines it for the rest of his life and insists on giving away the *entire* product.(p.129)
• But those of us who have tried to shoulder the *entire* burden and trouble of others find we are soon overcome by them.(p.132)
• Only a few knew of it at first but, within a short time, it was billboarded throughout the *entire* company.(p.145)
• That continued through my *entire* life.(p.193)
• He told me that it was imperative that I walk around the *entire* block, cost me what it might in mental agony.(p.276)
• I was living in a small room on West 53rd Street right off Fifth Avenue, when I met a young lady who eventually was responsible for altering my *entire* way of living.(p.359)
• The last two years of my drinking my *entire* personality changed to a cynical, intolerant and arrogant person completely different from my normal self.(p.376)
• I was always at odds with the *entire* world, not to say the universe.(p.400)
• The horrors of increasing hangover sickness to occupy the *entire* day; nausea, dry heaves, the rocking bed, the nightmare-filled mind.(p.408)
• Never in my *entire* life had anyone asked me "Are you one of us?"(p.413)
• For you learned that he had been guilty of the thing he had accused you of, and his guilt had brought suffering to his *entire* family; and he thought he saw his young son beginning his own tragic pattern.(p.533)

entirely
• I do not hold with those who believe that alcoholism is *entirely* a problem of mental control.(p.xxvii)
• There is the type who always believes that after being *entirely* free from alcohol for a period of time he can take a drink without danger.(p.xxviii)
• Then there are types *entirely* normal in every respect except in the effect alcohol has upon them.(p.xxviii)
• Moderate drinkers have little trouble in giving up liquor *entirely* if they have good reason for it.(p.20)
• This should be an *entirely* personal affair which each one decides for himself in the light of past associations, or his present choice.(p.28)
• But the program of action, though *entirely* sensible, was pretty drastic.(p.42)
• But his face falls when we speak of spiritual matters, especially when we mention God, for we have reopened a subject which our man thought he had neatly evaded or *entirely* ignored.(p.45)
• With that rejection we imagined we had abandoned the God idea *entirely.*(p.45)
• Afterward, we found ourselves accepting many things which then seemed *entirely* out of reach.(p.47)
• Neither is reason, as most of us use it, *entirely* dependable, though it emanate from our best minds.(p.54)
• 6.Were *entirely* ready to have God remove all these defects of character.(p.59)
• And there often seems no way of *entirely* getting rid of self without His aid.(p.62)
• We were prepared to look at it from an *entirely* different angle.(p.66)
• Though a situation had not been *entirely* our fault, we tried to disregard the other person involved *entirely.*(p.67)
• We must be *entirely* honest with somebody if we expect to live long or happily in this world.(p.73)
• The next chapter is *entirely* devoted to Step Twelve.(p.88)
• Even though your protege may not have *entirely* admitted his condition, he has become very curious to know how you got well.(p.92)
• One of our Fellowship failed *entirely* with his first half dozen prospects.(p.96)
• He often gets *entirely* out of hand when drinking.(p.109)
• Though it is *entirely* separate from Alcoholics Anonymous, it uses the general principles of the A.A. program as a guide for husbands, wives, relatives, friends, and others close to alcoholics.(p.121)
• Impressed by those who visited him at the hospital, he capitulated *entirely* when, later, in an upper room of this house, he heard the story of some man whose experience closely tallied with his own.(p.160)
• I was now forming an *entirely* new drinking technique.(p.233)
• I cannot say that my taste for liquor has *entirely* disappeared.(p.259)
• During the first three months I carried on all these activities without a car, depending *entirely* on buses and streetcars – I, who had always to have a car at my immediate command.(p.283)
• Several months later dad was back in Chicago to pick me up again, but this time my attitude was *entirely* different.(p.289)
• The program was carried on *entirely* by word of mouth.(p.291)
• That being the case, it didn't take me long to figure out that my meager manufacturing facilities were *entirely* inadequate to the manufacture of beer for social and domestic consumption.(p.297)
• That discovery so intrigued me, that I stayed on that diet almost *entirely* for the balance of my extensive drinking life.(p.298)
• It has changed my thinking *entirely,* about everything I do.(p.325)
• I wasn't *entirely* immoral; I wasn't bad; I wasn't vicious.(p.392)
• For, after those daily self-punishing sessions with myself, after the vows to stop, I would change *entirely* as evening came on.(p.408)
• About then too, I realized that my point of view on the opposite sex wasn't *entirely* like that of most of the boys I knew.(p.484)
• I have been allowed to build an *entirely* new career in a field I had never worked in.(p.541)

entitled
• After all -- wasn't I *entitled* to it?(p.360)
• After nearly eight years of sobriety in A.A., I still can set down such thoughts, "against my instinct and training," showing that I still consider myself a "special" person, *entitled* to special privileges.(p.536)
• For a little while, I was the great man I wanted to be, and thought myself *entitled* to be just by reason of being.(p.537)

entitling
• All I can remember about the Roaring Twenties is that I drank a great deal, thought I was having a grand time, managed to get to Europe for a few weeks, was very proud of the dozens of speak-easy cards *entitling* me to an entree in the better joints between Cleveland and New York, took on a wife, and built a home in a fashionable suburb of Cleveland.(p.358)

entity
• This phenomenon, as we have suggested, may be the manifestation of an allergy which differentiates these people, and sets them apart as a distinct *entity.*(p.xxviii)

• 5. – Each Alcoholics Anonymous group ought to be a spiritual ***entity*** having but one primary purpose – that of carrying its message to the alcoholic who still suffers.(p.565)

entreaties
• Despite my wife's ***entreaties*** to take it easy that day, I arrived home in bad shape.(p.557)

entree
• All I can remember about the Roaring Twenties is that I drank a great deal, thought I was having a grand time, managed to get to Europe for a few weeks, was very proud of the dozens of speak-easy cards entitling me to an ***entree*** in the better joints between Cleveland and New York, took on a wife, and built a home in a fashionable suburb of Cleveland.(p.358)

entry
• I think his ***entry*** into A.A. was through spending some hours with Dr. Bob at his office.(p.267)

envelope
• The next morning I woke up in jail in Cleveland and the jailor had $1,175 of my money in an ***envelope***.(p.196)

• The one thing I can remember now was that Vi was on the corner of 8th and L, and I remember vividly that she had an ***envelope*** in her hand.(p.492)

envelopes
• An armored car could not have brought the pay ***envelopes*** home.(p.105)

environment
• He changes his brand or his ***environment***.(p.xxviii)

• If a sufficiently strong reason – ill health, falling in love, change of ***environment***, or the warning of a doctor – becomes operative, this man can also stop or moderate, although he may find it difficult and troublesome and may even need medical attention.(p.21)

• The differences between my father and my sisters, who were school teachers, made an excellent ***environment*** for the type of child I was – that is, slick and cute enough to take advantage of any adult quarrel.(p.210)

• She was a woman devoted to her family and loyal to her husband, but quarrels did not make a happy ***environment*** for her.(p.210)

• Nor could I blame my dilemma on my childhood ***environment***.(p.304)

• I moved a thousand miles away from home to Chicago and a new ***environment***.(p.305)

• Like all alcoholics endeavoring to run away from themselves and their ***environment***, I decided to go to New York.(p.358)

• We moved once more, to Houston; my husband thought maybe a change of ***environment*** would help and I'd be all right.(p.389)

• In the hospital, I hung on to the idea I'd had most of my life: that if I could just control the external ***environment***, the internal ***environment*** would then be comfortable.(p.445)

• And life keeps getting simpler and easier as we try to reverse my old idea, by taking care of the internal ***environment*** via the Twelve Steps, and letting the external ***environment*** take care of itself.)(p.446)

environmental
• He said the alcoholic seemed to possess a native acuteness and usually excelled in his field, regardless of ***environmental*** or educational advantages.(p.308)

environs
• In one western city and its ***environs*** there are one thousand of us and our families.(p.15)

envy
• The greatest enemies of us alcoholics are resentment, jealousy, ***envy***, frustration, and fear.(p.145)

• He said, "How I ***envy*** you for whatever you've found."(p.334)

Episcopal
• Father is an ***Episcopal*** minister and his work takes him over long drives on bad roads.(p.497)

• The ***Episcopal*** magazine, The Living Church, observes editorially: "The basis of the technique of Alcoholics Anonymous is the truly Christian principle that a man cannot help himself except by helping others.(p.574)

episode
• This was six or eight months after the last drinking ***episode***.(p.196)

episodes
• Coming to his senses, he is revolted at certain ***episodes*** he vaguely remembers.(p.73)

• There were no childhood ***episodes*** of unhappiness to account for my alcoholism.(p.182)

• Some were drinking heavily and there had been occasional serious ***episodes***.(p.315)

• After another of my "never again ***episodes***" she packed up and left for her parents' home in Florida.(p.362)

• In the first year there were ***episodes*** such as kicking Priscilla in the shins, getting the lock changed on the desk in the A.A. Club, because I, as secretary, didn't want the Intergroup secretary "interfering," and taking an older woman member out to lunch for the express purpose of informing her that she was "a phony."(p.416)

epoch
• These facts appear to be of extreme medical importance; because of the extraordinary possibilities of rapid growth inherent in this group they may mark a new ***epoch*** in the annals of alcoholism.(p.xxiii)

equal
• Students of ancient history tell us that the intellect of men in those days was ***equal*** to the best of today.(p.51)

• Brandishing my "motto," which was "A little man with a stick is ***equal*** to a big man," sometimes I varied the literary lecture by a fight with a big man, selected solely because he was big and I was little.(p.537)

equalled
• Nothing has ever to this day ***equalled*** the thrill of that first case.(p.282)

equally
• We are ***equally*** positive that once he takes any alcohol whatever into his system, something happens, both in the bodily and mental sense, which makes it virtually impossible for him to stop.(p.22)

• Long before I had any real opportunity to give, I had to learn the ***equally*** important lesson of receiving graciously.(p.281)

• I believe this, and I believe too that it is ***equally*** impossible to practice these principles to the best of our ability, a day at a time, and still drink, for I don't think the two things are compatible.(p.550)

equipment
• In the two succeeding years I held ten different jobs ranging from newspaper copy-desk and rewrite, to traffic director for an oil field ***equipment*** company.(p.255)

• The other pupils kept books, pencils, paper, gym ***equipment*** and such stuff in their lockers.(p.423)

equipped
• What with our ultra-modern standards, our scientific approach to everything, we are perhaps not well ***equipped*** to apply the powers of good that lie outside our synthetic knowledge.(p.xxv)

• But whereas my horse was always ***equipped*** with a flask, I merely endured the fox hunting so I could start drinking at lunch time.(p.404)

equity
• The family may feel they hold a mortgage on dad, so big that no ***equity*** should be left for outsiders.(p.131)

equivalent
• He commences to look around in the night clubs, or their ***equivalent***, for something besides liquor.(p.81)

era
• The times in which I grew up (the Prohibition ***era*** immortalized by Scott Fitzgerald and John Held Jr.) had taught me to be gay with the gayest; my own inner urges led me to outdo them all.(p.225)

• I was a product of the post-war prohibition ***era*** of the roaring '20's.(p.304)

• I'm fortunate because I live in an ***era*** when A.A. is available, and I'm able to take advantage of it.(p.512)

eradicated
• It has never been, by any treatment with which we are familiar, permanently ***eradicated***.(p.xxviii)

erase
• I could no longer gage my capacity and it might be the second or the tenth drink that would ***erase*** my consciousness.(p.306)

errand
• He should realize that we are engaged upon a life-and-death ***errand***.(p.75)

• You should not hesitate to visit the most sordid spot on earth on such an ***errand***.(p.102)

erratic
• The test that it faced was this: Could these large numbers of erstwhile ***erratic*** alcoholics successfully meet and work together?(p.xviii)

• I was, when drunk, just as undisciplined and ***erratic*** as ever.(p.410)

• It had to be or I could not have justified my ***erratic*** behavior as I did.(p.551)

erroneous
• Happily for everyone, this conclusion is ***erroneous***.(p.569)

errors
• We grow by our willingness to face and rectify ***errors*** and convert them into assets.(p.124)

erstwhile
• The test that it faced was this: Could these large numbers of ***erstwhile*** erratic alcoholics successfully meet and work together?(p.xviii)

escapade
• This ***escapade*** also ended up in the clutches of the law, and my friend was institutionalized for eight months.(p.354)

escapades
• If his mood is light, tell him humorous stories of your ***escapades***.(p.91)

• Now and then the family will be plagued by spectres from the past, for the drinking career of almost every alcoholic has been marked by ***escapades***, funny, humiliating, shameful or tragic.(p.123)

escape
• These men were not drinking to ***escape***; they were drinking to overcome a craving beyond their mental control.(p.xxviii)

• There were flights from city to country and back, as my wife and I sought ***escape***.(p.6)

• Unlike the feelings of the ship's passengers, however, our joy in ***escape*** from disaster does not subside as we go our individual ways.(p.17)

• We, in our turn, sought the same ***escape*** with all the desperation of drowning men.(p.28)

• How could we ***escape***?(p.66)

• Ask any woman who has sent her husband to distant places on the theory he would ***escape*** the alcohol problem.(p.101)

• You will be bound to them with new and wonderful ties, for you will ***escape*** disaster together and you will commence shoulder to shoulder your common journey.(p.152)

• He had a desperate desire to stop, but saw no way out, for he had earnestly tried many avenues of ***escape***.(p.155)

• Heartsickness, shame, and fear, fear bordering on panic, and no complete ***escape*** any longer except in oblivion.(p.306)

• Instead of wanting to ***escape*** some perplexing problem, we experience a thrill of challenge in the opportunity it affords for another application of A.A. techniques, and we find ourselves tackling it with surprising vigor.(p.311)

• I tried to compensate with impossible dreams and ambitions, which were simply early forms of ***escape***.(p.400)

• I went to Europe to ***escape*** them, so I thought.(p.405)

• I was really trying, once more, to ***escape*** from myself.(p.405)

• Meanwhile I had found another ***escape***.(p.407)

• I enlisted in the Navy to ***escape*** the Army draft.(p.425)

• I nearly reverted to my old, incorrigible self – had trouble with a couple of other prisoners, was planning an ***escape***.(p.461)

• Perhaps a better way of saying it is that, on that day, with that decision, I no longer fought drinking as an ***escape***.(p.531)

• It became more and more necessary to ***escape*** from myself, for my remorse and shame and humiliation when I was sober were almost unbearable.(p.547)

• I attended my first A.A. meeting eight years ago, and it is with deep gratitude that I'm able to say I've not had a drink since that time, and that I take no sedation or narcotics, for this program is to me one of complete sobriety and I no longer need to ***escape*** reality.(p.549)

escaped
• I wondered how he had ***escaped***.(p.9)

• Barleycorn's wringer squeezed this author – but he ***escaped*** quite whole.(p.432)

escapes
• Make it plain he is under no obligation to you, that you hope only that he will try to help other alcoholics when he ***escapes*** his own difficulties.(p.94)

• Before I started to drink seriously, I tried a couple of other ***escapes***.(p.401)

escapism
• I had my first drink when I was fifteen and my alcoholic potential had ripened me to the point of necessary ***escapism***.(p.353)

escapists
• There was a concrete program, designed to secure the greatest possible inner security for us long-time *escapists*.(p.229)

escort
• There had been some occasions -- there was an automobile wreck, for instance -- when I had police *escort* home but not to jail, all of which, instead of doing me a favor, did me harm because I was then full of self-esteem as to the progress I had made both professionally and financially.(p.213)
• Later, I went to sea, serving as a gunnery officer on a destroyer *escort* and emerging a lieutenant commander.(p.555)

escorted
• The driver *escorted* me about for several days.(p.41)
• I was *escorted* back to San Diego next morning -- by the Shore Patrol, but I was discharged on schedule.(p.428)

escorting
• As we left, and they were *escorting* us across the bridge into Wheeling, I, with great dignity and sarcasm, told them if their wives were ever visiting in Akron, and they, too, were looking for their route sign as I was, that I hoped I could extend to them the hospitality that had been shown to me in Bellaire.(p.264)

Eskimo
• His only chance for sobriety would be some place like the Greenland Ice Cap, and even there an *Eskimo* might turn up with a bottle of scotch and ruin everything!(p.101)

esophageal
• My doctor warned me that if I kept on, I might have *esophageal* hemorrhaging and die.(p.558)
• In the next half-year, I experienced two more *esophageal* hemorrhages, miraculously surviving each one by a hair.(p.558)

especially
• Here is the fellow who has been puzzling you, *especially* in his lack of control.(p.21)
• To one who feels he is an atheist or agnostic such an experience seems impossible, but to continue as he is means disaster, *especially* if he is an alcoholic of the hopeless variety.(p.44)
• But his face falls when we speak of spiritual matters, *especially* when we mention God, for we have reopened a subject which our man thought he had neatly evaded or entirely ignored.(p.45)
• This is perhaps difficult – *especially* discussing our defects with another person.(p.72)
• A man so involved often feels very remorseful at times, *especially* if he is married to a loyal and courageous girl who has literally gone through hell for him.(p.81)
• Before we begin, we ask God to direct our thinking, *especially* asking that it be divorced from self-pity, dishonest or self-seeking motives.(p.86)
• We ask *especially* for freedom from self-will, and are careful to make no request for ourselves only.(p.87)
• *Especially* when he has before him a way to stop his drinking and abuse if he really wants to pay the price.(p.108)
• These family dissensions are very dangerous, *especially* to your husband.(p.117)
• Still another difficulty is that you may become jealous of the attention he bestows on other people, *especially* alcoholics.(p.119)
• I think it's awfully hard on people, *especially* if they're new people, to hear these long drawn out talks.(p.273)
• Philosophy, faith, a sense of humor (they could laugh at themselves), clear-cut objectives, appreciation – and most *especially* appreciation and sympathetic understanding for their fellow man.(p.310)
• There was one girl *especially*, and I'd watch her from my window every morning, leaving faithfully to go to the hospital in the neighborhood.(p.326)
• The encouragement received in the early days, *especially* from the A.A. General Service Office, made a tremendous difference to my sobriety.(p.342)
• Resenting anyone and everyone who might interfere with my personal plans and ways of doing things, I was full of self pity, *especially* for any interference with my drinking.(p.376)
• If they were around, I always found a need for them – *especially* the pills.(p.443)
• So I'm better off if I don't give advice, don't figure I know what's best, and just accept life on life's terms, as it is today – *especially* my own life, as it actually is.(p.450)
• God bless all you people in A.A. and *especially* you fellows in prison.(p.463)
• Around eight or nine o'clock there came two big detectives and a policeman to arrest me for assault; and I was the most amazed person in the world when they said I had assaulted someone, and *especially* that I had assaulted my wife.(p.492)
• It was a thorn in my side, because I knew it was the truth, and I hated to hear the truth, *especially* about myself.(p.513)

essay
• I, a man of steel, with very high ideals, well brought up, an honor student and the recipient of scholarships and prizes, a boy wonder in business -- I, Bob, the author of this *essay*, looked and saw that the universe was beneath my contempt, and that to remove myself from it was the only thing of dignity a man could do.(p.531)

essence
• Most of us think this awareness of a Power greater than ourselves is the *essence* of spiritual experience.(p.570)

essential
• One feels that something more than human power is needed to produce the *essential* psychic change.(p.xxvii)
• Belief in the power of God, plus enough willingness, honesty and humility to establish and maintain the new order of things, were the *essential* requirements.(p.13)
• I had tried to be the center of my own little world, whereas God was the center of a vast universe of which I was perhaps an *essential*, but a very tiny, part.(p.280)
• Keeping one foot in front of the other is *essential* for maintaining our arrestment.(p.311)

essentially
• Men and women drink *essentially* because they like the effect produced by alcohol.(p.xxvi)
• Here was a man with *essentially* the same outlook on life, except that he had done something about it.(p.290)
• I have never attended an A.A. meeting, so it is *essentially* the literature that has kept me on the A.A. program.(p.342)

essentials
• They said if you want to know how this program works, take the first word of your question – the H is for honesty, the O is for open-mindedness and the W is for willingness; these our Book calls the *essentials* of recovery.(p.550)
• Willingness, honesty and open mindedness are the *essentials* of recovery.(p.570)

establish
• Belief in the power of God, plus enough willingness, honesty and humility to *establish* and maintain the new order of things, were the essential requirements.(p.13)
• No conviction was necessary to *establish* my status as a miserable failure at managing my own life.(p.259)

established
• This brought a rush of 800 frantic inquiries into the little New York office which meanwhile had been *established*.(p.xviii)
• When this sort of thinking is fully *established* in an individual with alcoholic tendencies, he has probably placed himself beyond human aid, and unless locked up, may die or go permanently insane.(p.24)
• Each individual, in the personal stories, describes in his own language and from his own point of view the way he *established* his relationship with God.(p.29)
• *Established* on such a footing we became less and less interested in ourselves, our little plans and designs.(p.63)
• Though we have no religious connection, we may still do well to talk with someone ordained by an *established* religion.(p.74)
• It wasn't long before the bootlegger was an *established* institution in this, as in other towns.(p.233)
• However, here I probably took my first step towards my coming alcoholism by developing a terrific aversion to all churches and *established* religions.(p.240)
• Within a year of my return to Detroit, A.A. was a definitely *established* little group of about a dozen members and I too was *established* in a modest but steady job handling an independent dry-cleaning route of my own.(p.283)
• My drinking did not start until after I was thirty-five, and a fairly successful career had been *established*.(p.374)
• A pattern *established* itself.(p.536)
• My company advanced me rapidly, once my reliability was *established* again.(p.559)

estate
• I switched into real *estate* brokerage and property management work.(p.277)

Esther
• By the time all this was over, I was really in a terrific state, and my father taking in things said, "Miss *Esther* is about to faint.(p.385)
• That was when all the boys and *Esther* got drunk and the wives didn't.(p.386)
• So finally, he said to me one morning, "*Esther*, why do you do this?"(p.386)
• But Frank turned around and looked at me and said, "*Esther*, remember you're in jail and not at home."(p.391)
• The next morning he came into my room and said, "*Esther*, I'm not going to lecture you any more, but I want you to read this article.(p.391)

estimate
• We of Alcoholics Anonymous believe that the reader will be interested in the medical *estimate* of the plan of recovery described in this book.(p.xxiii)
• It would be hard to *estimate* how much A.A. has done for me.(p.191)
• However, a rough *estimate* of one alcoholic's initiation fee seemed possible.(p.396)
• Drunkalogues and statistics can be boring, but it is necessary to delve a little into each in order to come up with some kind of rough *estimate*.(p.396)
• So I believe that twenty percent is a very conservative *estimate* of the amount of income I blew.(p.399)
• For an *estimate* of salary from the twenty-one a month to start with, to over $400 per month upon my retirement after twenty years in the Navy, I believe that an average income of $2,000 a year over this period is low, but as I stated earlier, an underestimate is best.(p.399)
• So please bear in mind, and I would like to emphasize, that this is a very rough *estimate*.(p.399)

estimated
• By the end of 1939, it was *estimated* that 800 alcoholics were on their way to recovery.(p.xviii)
• By March 1976, when this edition went to the printer, the total worldwide membership of Alcoholics Anonymous was conservatively *estimated* at more than 1,000,000, with almost 28,000 groups meeting in over 90 countries.(p.xxii)
• It is *estimated* that two-thirds of the men in prison were under the influence of alcohol and/or drugs when they committed their offenses.(p.458)

estimates
• After a few more *estimates* as to income and expenditures for booze over a few sample years, taken at random, I conclude that this twenty per cent stayed fairly constant.(p.398)

estranged
• With nothing but a liberal arts education, very definitely *estranged* from my family and already married, soon after graduation from college I became a bookmaker's clerk on the British racing circuits, far better off financially than the average professional man.(p.251)

eternal
• If I write with the air of one who has discovered the obvious, which is to say, the *eternal* truths which have been offered to us since the beginning, forgive my callowness; I had to find these things out for myself.(p.536)

Ethel
• When I came to my aunt, she knew that I had had an unhappy childhood, and she said, "Now, *Ethel*, you're welcome to have boy friends in our home, but there are two boys in this town that I don't want you to date, and one of them comes from a very fine family, one of the best.(p.262)

Europe
• Judging from what I had seen in *Europe* and since, the power of God in human affairs was negligible, the Brotherhood of Man a grim jest.(p.11)
• Then he had gone to *Europe*, placing himself in the care of a celebrated physician (the psychiatrist, Dr. Jung) who prescribed for him.(p.26)
• The best boarding schools and a finishing school in *Europe* had fitted me for the conventional role of debutante and young matron.(p.225)
• I was born in *Europe*, in Alsace to be exact, shortly after it had become German, and practically grew up with the "good Rhine wine" of song and story.(p.230)
• All I can remember about the Roaring Twenties is that I drank a great deal, thought I was having a grand time, managed to get to *Europe* for a few weeks, was very proud of the dozens of speak-easy cards entitling me to an entree in the better joints between Cleveland and New York, took on a wife, and

built a home in a fashionable suburb of Cleveland.(p.358)
• I was born in a castle – the family home, in ***Europe***.(p.400)
• I went to ***Europe*** to escape them, so I thought.(p.405)
• Imagine my surprise when I came to, in ***Europe***, and discovered I had brought myself along!(p.405)
• I returned from ***Europe*** a while after that encounter, and I never went back.(p.406)

European
• THE ***EUROPEAN*** DRINKER(p.230)

evade
• When we became alcoholics, crushed by a self-imposed crisis we could not postpone or ***evade***, we had to fearlessly face the proposition that either God is everything or else He is nothing.(p.53)
• Gone are time cards to punch, alarm clocks to obey, nosey rumor-mongers and talebearers to ***evade***.(p.329)

evaded
• But his face falls when we speak of spiritual matters, especially when we mention God, for we have reopened a subject which our man thought he had neatly ***evaded*** or entirely ignored.(p.45)

evangelist
• Don't start out as an ***evangelist*** or reformer.(p.89)

Evanston
• In the meantime, another doctor in ***Evanston*** became convinced that the program had possibilities, and turned over a woman to us to do something about.(p.295)

Eve
• I didn't like being on the nut ward, and I particularly didn't like being forced to ice cookies on Christmas ***Eve***.(p.444)
• The next recollection I have is of my husband coming into my room (later found out it was on New Year's ***Eve***) accompanied by two policemen.(p.468)

even
• There was to be the least possible organization, ***even*** in our service centers.(p.xix)
• If any feel that as psychiatrists directing a hospital for alcoholics we appear somewhat sentimental, let them stand with us a while on the firing line, see the tragedies, the despairing wives, the little children; let the solving of these problems become a part of their daily work, and ***even*** of their sleeping moments, and the most cynical will not wonder that we have accepted and encouraged this movement.(p.xxvi)
• His alcoholic problem was so complex, and his depression so great, that we felt his only hope would be through what we then called "moral psychology," and we doubted if ***even*** that would have any effect.(p.xxix)
• It hadn't ***even*** come to mind.(p.5)
• I went to town regularly and ***even*** made a little money.(p.7)
• My intellectual heroes, the chemists the astronomers, ***even*** the evolutionists, suggested vast laws and forces at work.(p.10)
• The joy of living we really have, ***even*** under pressure and difficulty.(p.15)
• Strangely enough, wives, parents and intimate friends usually find us ***even*** more unapproachable than do the psychiatrist and the doctor.(p.18)
• If a sufficiently strong reason – ill health, falling in love, change of environment, or the warning of a doctor – becomes operative, this man can also stop or moderate, although he may find it difficult and troublesome and may ***even*** need medical attention.(p.21)
• Yet let him drink for a day, and he frequently becomes disgustingly and ***even*** dangerously anti-social.(p.21)
• We are unable, at certain times, to bring into our consciousness with sufficient force the memory of the suffering and humiliation of ***even*** a week or a month ago.(p.24)
• The almost certain consequences that follow taking ***even*** a glass of beer do not crowd into the mind to deter us.(p.24)
• We have found much of heaven and we have been rocketed into a fourth dimension of existence of which we had not ***even*** dreamed.(p.25)
• The experiment of quitting for a period of time will be helpful, but we think we can render an ***even*** greater service to alcoholic sufferers and perhaps to the medical fraternity.(p.34)
• But ***even*** in this type of beginning we are obliged to admit that our justification for a spree was insanely insufficient in the light of what always happened.(p.37)
• I would not go back to it ***even*** if I could."(p.43)
• We were bothered with the thought that faith and dependence upon a Power beyond ourselves was somewhat weak, ***even*** cowardly.(p.45)
• We found that as soon as we were able to lay aside prejudice and express ***even*** a willingness to believe in a Power greater than ourselves, we commenced to get results, ***even*** though it was impossible for any of us to fully define or comprehend that Power, which is God.(p.46)
• "Do I now believe, or am I ***even*** willing to believe, that there is a Power greater than myself?"(p.47)
• Many of us have been so touchy that ***even*** casual reference to spiritual things made us bristle with antagonism.(p.48)
• We, who have traveled this dubious path, beg you to lay aside prejudice, ***even*** against organized religion.(p.49)
• ***Even*** in the present century, American newspapers were afraid to print an account of the Wright brothers' first successful flight at Kitty Hawk.(p.51)
• Seemingly he could not drink ***even*** if he would.(p.57)
• ***Even*** so has God restored us all to our right minds.(p.57)
• On that basis we are almost always in collision with something or somebody, ***even*** though our motives are good.(p.60)
• He may be kind, considerate, patient, generous; ***even*** modest and self-sacrificing.(p.61)
• Is he not really a self-seeker ***even*** when trying to be kind?(p.61)
• Is he not, ***even*** in his best moments, a producer of confusion rather than harmony?(p.61)
• Many of us had moral and philosophical convictions galore, but we could not live up to them ***even*** though we would have liked to.(p.62)
• We put them on paper, ***even*** though we had no resentment in connection with them.(p.68)
• We have begun to learn tolerance, patience and good will toward all men, ***even*** our enemies, for we look on them as sick people.(p.70)
• And we have ceased fighting anything or anyone -- ***even*** alcohol.(p.84)
• We have not ***even*** sworn off.(p.85)
• ***Even*** though your protege may not have entirely admitted his condition, he has become very curious to know how you got well.(p.92)
• And ***even*** though he continues to drink, the family will find life more bearable.(p.97)
• His only chance for sobriety would be some place like the Greenland Ice Cap, and ***even*** there an Eskimo might turn up with a bottle of scotch and ruin everything!(p.101)
• That includes bars, nightclubs, dances, receptions, weddings, ***even*** plain ordinary whoopee parties.(p.101)
• We would not ***even*** do the cause of temperate drinking any good, for not one drinker in a thousand likes to be told anything about alcohol by one who hates it.(p.103)
• The bill collectors, the sheriffs, the angry taxi drivers, the policemen, the bums, the pals, and ***even*** the ladies they sometimes brought home – our husbands thought we were so inhospitable.(p.106)
• In desperation, we have ***even*** got tight ourselves -- the drunk to end all drunks.(p.106)
• And ***even*** if they did not love their families, how could they be so blind about themselves?(p.107)
• Two: Your husband is showing lack of control, for he is unable to stay on the water wagon ***even*** when he wants to.(p.109)
• ***Even*** though your husband becomes unbearable and you have to leave him temporarily, you should, if you can, go without rancor.(p.111)
• We know women who are unafraid, ***even*** happy under these conditions.(p.111)
• You avoid the subject of drinking, ***even*** with your own parents.(p.114)
• Suppose we tell you some of the obstacles a family will meet; suppose we suggest how they may be avoided – ***even*** converted to good use for others.(p.123)
• ***Even*** if he displays a certain amount of neglect and irresponsibility towards the family, it is well to let him go as far as he likes in helping other alcoholics.(p.129)
• ***Even*** when he wanted to assert himself he could not, for his drinking placed him constantly in the wrong.(p.130)
• ***Even*** when you understand the malady better, you may feel this feeling rising.(p.139)
• He wants to quit drinking and you want to help him, ***even*** if it be only a matter of good business.(p.141)
• If he temporizes and still thinks he can ever drink again, ***even*** beer, he might as well be discharged after the next bender which, if an alcoholic, he is almost certain to have.(p.142)
• For most alcoholics who are drinking, or who are just getting over a spree, a certain amount of physical treatment is desirable, ***even*** imperative.(p.142)
• That won't hurt him a bit, ***even*** though he does not go for this remedy.(p.144)
• If he is, and is still trying to recover, he will tell you about it ***even*** if it means the loss of his job.(p.146)
• In case he does stumble, ***even*** once, you will have to decide whether to let him go.(p.147)
• ***Even*** if you feel your organization has no alcoholic problem, it might pay to take another look down the line.(p.149)
• Many mornings I have gone to classes, and ***even*** though fully prepared, would turn and walk back to the fraternity house because of my jitters, not daring to enter the classroom for fear of making a scene should I be called on for recitation.(p.173)
• Therefore it would make no great difference, ***even*** if I should do some drinking.(p.175)
• I also made use of old trunks and chests, the old can container, and ***even*** the ash container.(p.176)
• I used to promise my wife, my friends, and my children that I would drink no more – promises which seldom kept me sober ***even*** through the day, though I was very sincere when I made them.(p.177)
• During the first six months of 1935, I was hospitalized eight times for intoxication and shackled to the bed two or three days before I ***even*** knew where I was.(p.184)
• That was worth a lot ***even*** though I did not believe it.(p.185)
• She also told me that I could not pay them ***even*** if I wanted to and had the money, which I did not.(p.185)
• I know there was ***even*** more, something that I hadn't got, and I remember one day, a week or two after I had come out of the hospital, Bill was over to my house talking to my wife and me.(p.191)
• I didn't ***even*** know what a martini looked like, but I had heard a man down the bar order one.(p.194)
• I didn't ***even*** like the olive.(p.195)
• During the day, looking over the contracts and money in my pocket, I found that I had sold six lots that I couldn't ***even*** remember, and didn't ***even*** know the people I had sold them to.(p.196)
• The circumstances under which I reached these people were very odd because I was led there through things that I said when I couldn't ***even*** remember speaking.(p.202)
• I'll never forget, he never ***even*** hesitated and I had never seen him before in my life.(p.207)
• He walked to the hospital to save bus fare and did it gladly in order to be helpful to an individual he had never ***even*** seen.(p.208)
• My children had lost respect for me and, in fact, it was only after three or four years of sobriety that any of them ever said anything to me to indicate that I had recouped ***even*** a little of their respect.(p.215)
• I believe every member of the Akron Group did come to see me, which impressed me terrifically, not so much because of the stories they told, but because they would take the time to come and talk to me without ***even*** knowing who I was.(p.218)
• In my own experience I was so jubilant at finding myself sober, and I had so many things to catch up on, that a month went by before the thought ***even*** occurred to me.(p.219)
• I might have done terrible things, and I wouldn't ***even*** know it!(p.223)
• I missed the old social times, of course, but had no definite craving ***even*** for beer.(p.232)
• I knew the stuff I was making was a lot stronger than I had been used to, but I never suspected that steady drinking of it might develop a taste for something ***even*** stronger still.(p.233)
• I ***even*** got them myself and tried them.(p.235)
• ***Even*** then he went into no great detail about how he and a crowd of alcoholics, with whom he associated, had mastered their difficulty.(p.235)
• If anything, he had known all of them ***even*** better and more often than I.(p.239)
• ***Even*** that first night I blacked out, which leads me to believe that I was an alcoholic from my very first drink.(p.241)
• My loneliness was worse than it had ever been before, for now ***even*** my own kind had turned against me.(p.247)
• I ***even*** began to go the rounds of churches.(p.255)
• He knew too well that didn't mean a thing, just as I knew in my heart that it would be only a question of time -- a few days, a week, or ***even*** a month, it was inevitable – till I would be off on another bender.(p.257)
• I didn't see him for a year, or ***even*** hear from him.(p.262)
• When you have a hangover and can't ***even*** sit still,

try to read small print!(p.268)
• And I'd try, but I couldn't ***even*** see the letters.(p.268)
• And, anyhow, if I went on for ten or a hundred times as long I couldn't ***even*** begin to tell you all that A.A. has meant to me.(p.274)
• Here was something requiring a greater willingness to assume responsibility, and take a larger degree of cooperation and "give and take" than ***even*** business requires of one.(p.286)
• I do feel, though, that the fact that I finally grew up to a point where I could ***even*** tackle such a job is the apex of the story of a man who spent eighteen years running away from life.(p.286)
• Why, ***even*** a year ago, I had seen Howard, an ex-doctor, mooching a dime for a drink.(p.289)
• I had thought that I was completely different from other people, that I was beginning to become a little balmy, ***even*** to the point of withdrawing more and more from society and wanting to be alone with my bottle.(p.290)
• One of them was that I would try to get a group started in Chicago; the second was that I would have to return to Akron to attend meetings at least every two months until I did get a group started in Chicago; third, I decided I must place this program above everything else, ***even*** my family, because if I did not maintain my sobriety I would lose my family anyway.(p.292)
• ***Even*** some of the saloon-keepers, where I had spent so much time and money, requested that I stay away from their places.(p.301)
• By now I wanted to die, but had lost the courage ***even*** to take my life.(p.306)
• With the alcoholic, they could only give temporary relief and in the last stages not ***even*** that.(p.307)
• However, due to financial difficulties the whole printing was, for a while, held up and the book received no publicity, nor, of course, was it available in the stores, ***even*** if one knew it existed.(p.307)
• They saw that they had become actual or potential alcoholics, ***even*** though no serious harm had yet been done.(p.315)
• ***Even*** so, every time I drank, I seemed to get in trouble.(p.322)
• And unless I had some rosy picture of what was going to happen that day, I wouldn't ***even*** feel like getting up in the morning at all.(p.325)
• We need them so badly ***even*** if you can only give one day, or perhaps two days?"(p.326)
• I was afraid to set ***even*** one day.(p.326)
• Until I took Social Security and a pension at the age of sixty-eight, after forty years in motion-picture-studio public relations, I had successfully hidden ***even*** any hints of approaching alcoholism.(p.327)
• I had never ***even*** been told by a superior that maybe I was drinking too much.(p.327)
• No jail booking, drunk-driving citation, barroom fight, or ***even*** a tumble off a barstool.(p.327)
• We ***even*** can be rebels for the first time in our lives.(p.329)
• Many retirees embrace alcoholism while secluded in motor trailers, rest homes, leisure-world bungalows, mountain cabins, or beach cottages, or ***even*** in penthouses, on yachts, and inside Palm Springs cabanas.(p.329)
• ***Even*** obvious intoxication is excused by younger people as something "he's earned the right to do," and they say, "After all, who's he hurting?"(p.330)
• But for him, financial security or ***even*** affluence can be a tragedy.(p.330)
• He may ***even*** read in a newspaper that one out of every seven drinkers will become alcoholic, but he rarely is told that it holds true for all ages -- or that the tolerance to alcohol (and other drugs) decreases steadily, year after year, in the bodies of all persons.(p.330)
• I did some things I liked, and ***even*** sold some.(p.331)
• The unwillingness to admit failure requires ***even*** further friendly intake.(p.331)
• Two nights later, self-pity went ***even*** further.(p.333)
• I don't believe, when I started, that I ***even*** had in mind the thought that I was drinking.(p.336)
• And the first thing you know I was lifted right out of the A.A. group, and I floated higher, and higher, and ***even*** higher, until I was way up on a pink cloud which is known as Pink Seven, and I felt miserable again.(p.348)
• We've got to turn the whole business over to some joker we can't ***even*** see!(p.350)
• I am not ***even*** there, and if I was there the only thing I could do would be to give her moral support, and yet he thanks me for curing his wife."(p.350)
• And deep in my heart I really meant what I said because I loved her more than anything else in the world, yes – ***even*** more than liquor.(p.362)
• ***Even*** I couldn't understand it, because I did love her so.(p.362)
• We soon resumed our marriage, ***even*** moved away from the street of sad memories and found a new home.(p.371)
• A relief, ***even*** though I dreaded it, feeling that this was the end of everything.(p.378)
• I had not yet lost my job or family, ***even*** though both were on the verge of going.(p.379)
• I knew this, and right away I got furious and would not ***even*** talk to the doctor in the place.(p.387)
• He ***even*** had the people come out, and tell me what kind of room I was going to have, and that he could come and see me, and that the dog could come and see me.(p.389)
• (I can't know how much others of our Fellowship have paid financially and, ***even*** more important, mentally and physically.)(p.396)
• ***Even*** at that age, I had learned that one drink was not enough.(p.397)
• ***Even*** when I was old enough to know better, I dreamed about being as beautiful as Venus, as pure as the Madonna and as brilliant as the President of the United States is supposed to be.(p.400)
• ***Even*** then I knew in my heart that I was unfit for the very things I wanted most, a happy marriage, security, a home and love.(p.403)
• ***Even*** the critics kidded me about this one.(p.405)
• But my life, ***even*** sober, was all askew and so were my emotions.(p.414)
• Some ***even*** remain agnostics.)(p.417)
• I tried to mimic the talk, ideas, moods and ***even*** the drinking the older men.(p.423)
• I had a drinking problem on my hands ***even*** at that time.(p.424)
• Drinking conditions at home were ***even*** worse than before.(p.424)
• He ***even*** went to bat for me before the court martial that inevitably followed and, as a result, I drew only thirty days – fifteen in solitary.(p.428)
• There was a red plush carpet to welcome me, but ***even*** so it wasn't easy.(p.430)
• Were I to revert to drinking, ***even*** now, I wouldn't give anything for these four years in A.A.(p.430)
• One, the side I turned to myself and the world, was respectable -- ***even***, in some ways, distinguished.(p.432)
• ***Even*** on my rare (at first) binge nights it never ran much over a quart.(p.433)
• Second, you wouldn't have believed me ***even*** if I had told you."(p.436)
• Never once had my mother ***even*** hinted at the idea that, when I grew up, I might like to be president of A.A.(p.439)
• Not only did I not think that being an alcoholic was a good idea, I didn't ***even*** feel that I had all that much of a drinking problem!(p.439)
• I remember, one time, ***even*** the dog had a psychiatric diagnosis.(p.440)
• Today, I find I can't work my A.A. program while taking pills, nor may I ***even*** have them around for dire emergencies only.(p.443)
• One has to be pretty sick to do that, and perhaps one has to be ***even*** sicker to come back every day for a new list, as she did.(p.446)
• It helped me a great deal to become convinced that alcoholism was a disease, not a moral issue; that I had been drinking as a result of a compulsion, ***even*** though I had not been aware of the compulsion at the time; and that sobriety was not a matter of willpower.(p.448)
• It is true that I -- of all people, strange as it may seem, and ***even*** though I didn't give my permission -- really, really am an alcoholic of sorts.(p.448)
• Still later, ***even*** alcohol and chemicals together could not lift me.(p.457)
• Intake of alcohol changes one's personality – ***even*** the healthy personality.(p.458)
• And we found ourselves back in prison, where our personalities became ***even*** more warped.(p.459)
• I didn't ***even*** try to understand.(p.460)
• I am still arrogant, egocentric, self-righteous, with no humility, ***even*** phony at times, but I'm trying to be a better person and help my fellowman.(p.463)
• Eventually the day came when I was dependent upon it ***even*** when there wasn't any occasion.(p.464)
• It was obvious ***even*** to me, in my drunken state, that I wasn't wanted.(p.466)
• I was too weak and exhausted to ***even*** try to throw myself out of the car.(p.467)
• ***Even*** the Jack Alexander Saturday Evening Post article hadn't been written, and there was only a tiny group of people in Washington.(p.469)
• I ***even*** wanted to – but I wasn't allowed to, so I won't go now.(p.470)
• Yes, I ***even*** knew I was a "chronic alcoholic."(p.470)
• In other words, the kindest doctor in the whole world, and I had one such, couldn't help me because I always felt, "You can't know about me – you can't possibly know – you don't ***even*** drink!"(p.471)
• Mind you, I had absolutely nothing to show for that eighteen years, except a beat-up car that I hadn't ***even*** paid for, but I was doing all right.(p.478)
• ***Even*** my family didn't have much use for me.(p.478)
• And we usually have some kind of grimy sweater that we think we look sexy in, ***even*** if we weigh ninety-five pounds soaking wet and are not wearing a bra.(p.479)
• For me, my sobriety comes before his or ***even*** before my feeling for him.(p.481)
• I found that ***even*** then I had fears and inhibitions.(p.483)
• We weren't ***even*** permitted to play cards in our home, but father would give us just a little toddy with whiskey and sugar and warm water now and then.(p.484)
• My mother resented it so that the first Christmas after our marriage, she didn't ***even*** invite us to dinner.(p.485)
• Of course, when father finally came to Virginia to work his way through school, he resented the southern "cracker," as he often called them, so much that he didn't ***even*** go back to his mother's funeral.(p.486)
• I put Charlie on the car and when I left him I passed both of those liquor stores without ***even*** thinking about them.(p.495)
• ***Even*** when we were paying that two dollars a night, they often paid it for us because our collection was so small.(p.496)
• Why, I wasn't ***even*** ashamed of my skinny legs!(p.498)
• At first, like everybody else, I could keep control when I drank, but if I did start to drink, ***even*** in those days, I was always one of the last to leave the party.(p.518)
• It didn't worry me very much, because at that time I could shut off for a couple of months without taking a drink or ***even*** wanting one, and without feeling that I was giving anything up.(p.518)
• ***Even*** at that he spoke quite often.(p.520)
• Finally, my mother came and said she had kept me at home for six years because she thought she could help me, but that now she had come to the conclusion that I wasn't ***even*** worth trying to help.(p.523)
• Just as I was wondering what on earth I could do -- I was too drunk ***even*** to pack a handkerchief -- the memory of an A.A. write-up that I had seen in the Evening Mail flashed across my mind -- and I thought to myself, this is something I haven't tried yet.(p.523)
• ***Even*** those don't take part in A.A. functions as I would like to see them do.(p.529)
• Once, or ***even*** twice, such incidents might be amusing.(p.538)
• I had ***even*** borrowed money from her, over her protest: "Bob, please don't ask me to lend you money -- you're the only one who hasn't."(p.540)
• Young when she joined, this A.A. believes her serious drinking was the result of ***even*** deeper defects.(p.544)
• I didn't have the courage to love; I was not ***even*** sure I had the capacity.(p.546)
• ***Even*** when you don't really want it for them, and your prayers are only words and you don't mean it, go ahead and do it anyway.(p.552)
• Each time, I went back to drinking – ***even*** smuggling a bottle of vodka into the hospital as soon as the blood transfusions had ceased.(p.558)
• The relationship between my wife and me was restored to a love and happiness that we had not known ***even*** before my alcoholism became acute.(p.559)
• I imagined getting ***even*** for hurts and rejections.(p.560)
• ***Even*** among those who occasionally land back in here again, we observe a profound change in personality.(p.572)

evening

• Then Jack Alexander wrote a feature article in the Saturday ***Evening*** Post and placed such a compelling picture of A.A. before the general public that alcoholics in need of help really deluged us.(p.xviii)
• "As soon as I regained my ability to think, I went carefully over that ***evening*** in Washington.(p.41)
• Our homes have been battle-grounds many an ***evening***.(p.105)
• Of an ***evening***, you can go on a mild bender, get up in the morning, shake your head and go to business.(p.139)
• Seeing much of each other, scarce an ***evening*** passed that someone's home did not shelter a little gathering of men and women, happy in their release, and con-

stantly thinking how they might present their discovery to some newcomer.(p.159)
• From childhood through high school I was more or less forced to go to church, Sunday School and ***evening*** service, Monday night Christian Endeavor and sometimes to Wednesday ***evening*** prayer meeting.(p.172)
• This would lessen my chances of smuggling some home that ***evening***, which in turn would mean a night of futile tossing around in bed followed by a morning of unbearable jitters.(p.176)
• About this time a lady called up my wife one Saturday afternoon, saying she wanted me to come over that ***evening*** to meet a friend of hers who might help me.(p.179)
• I could get through an ***evening*** with just a couple of snorts.(p.196)
• The people in the group hadn't been around that day; part of my family was in Florida and the rest of them weren't speaking to me, so I spent a very lonesome day and by ***evening*** I was feeling very sorry for myself.(p.207)
• One ***evening*** I had gone out after dinner to take on a couple of double-headers and stayed a little later than usual, and when I came home Clarence was sitting on the davenport with Bill W.(p.216)
• Jackie arrived about seven in the ***evening*** and talked until three a.m.(p.239)
• One ***evening***, the book, after checking up, was very definitely in the red for plenty through a piece of studied carelessness on my part, and my boss, very shrewd and able, fired me with a parting statement to the effect that once was enough.(p.251)
• They spent at least an ***evening*** a week in our home out there for weeks and weeks.(p.270)
• Almost simultaneously, I discovered that cocktails in the late afternoon and highballs in the ***evening*** relieved the many tensions of the day.(p.277)
• When the day of their return was almost upon me, and suicide was the only answer I had been able to think of, I went into Ralph's room one ***evening*** and told him the truth.(p.278)
• As I look back on that first ***evening*** I realize that I began to hope, then, for the first time; and I felt that if he could regain these things, perhaps it would be possible for me too.(p.290)
• The next afternoon and ***evening***, two other men visited me and each told me his story and the things that they were doing to try to recover from this tragic illness.(p.290)
• Every ***evening*** we would meet at the home of one of the members and have coffee and doughnuts and spend a social ***evening***.(p.291)
• Upon leaving the office in the ***evening***, my first stop would be a saloon about a block away.(p.298)
• However, as there happened to be several saloons within that distance, I didn't find it necessary to patronize the same place each ***evening***.(p.298)
• That was on a hot summer ***evening***, down in the Greenwich Village Group, and there was a little porch out there in the old meeting place on Sullivan Street, and after the meeting I went out on the steps for some air.(p.321)
• But from one or two drinks of an afternoon or ***evening***, my intake mounted, and mounted fast.(p.336)
• Since the radio station was getting on its feet, it didn't require so many nights of ***evening*** work, and that permitted leisure time for drinking.(p.360)
• I promised my two sponsors that I would attend their meeting the next Tuesday ***evening***.(p.363)
• When our meeting night came around the next ***evening***, I went -- "for her sake" I told her.(p.365)
• When I was called upon for a few words I had to tell my friends that I wasn't one year old in A.A. that ***evening*** but only a "nine month baby."(p.366)
• I think I actually read more contempt than was really there because just a week before someone had sent him the Saturday ***Evening*** Post article on A.A., and there was some glimmer of hope in it for him.(p.391)
• I only know that it first reached me through that Saturday ***Evening*** Post article.(p.392)
• I would have three quick strong ones in order to endure the ***evening***.(p.407)
• For, after those daily self-punishing sessions with myself, after the vows to stop, I would change entirely as ***evening*** came on.(p.408)
• We were to go up to our A.A. farm in Kent, and I spent the ***evening*** before riding herd on Anne.(p.415)
• I planned to stay home the night before I left, but my folks got so drunk I walked off early in the ***evening*** and spent the night with my girl, getting very drunk myself.(p.425)
• ***Evening*** cocktails were as standard as morning coffee, and I suppose my average daily consumption ran a little more or less than a pint.(p.433)
• After going to school all day, working in the family drugstore all ***evening***, and then studying until one or two in the morning, I would not be able to sleep soundly, with everything I had been studying going round in my head.(p.440)
• When I didn't have anything else to do -- a dull ***evening*** at home -- I'd sneak a few drinks upstairs in my room, and that began to be a habit.(p.464)
• Even the Jack Alexander Saturday ***Evening*** Post article hadn't been written, and there was only a tiny group of people in Washington.(p.469)
• I've never seen him drunk in my life, although he'd take a shot in the morning and usually one in the ***evening***, and so did I; but for the most part he kept his whiskey in his office.(p.484)
• To get rid of me one ***evening***, she decided to go to the movies, she and another friend.(p.487)
• I worked for the Government about a year and still maintained my ***evening*** office practice when the Government agencies were decentralized.(p.489)
• About seven that ***evening*** my sponsor walked in, Charlie G.(p.494)
• She had looked for me last ***evening*** after I left the car and wandered off into the night.(p.502)
• One ***evening*** I decided to go because two of those friends were to speak.(p.509)
• Just as I was wondering what on earth I could do -- I was too drunk even to pack a handkerchief -- the memory of an A.A. write-up that I had seen in the ***Evening*** Mail flashed across my mind -- and I thought to myself, this is something I haven't tried yet.(p.523)
• Still another friend and temporary host received me at four in the morning from the charge of a policeman who had found me "going to bed" in a garage far from the last place I could remember having been, a fashionable bar and restaurant in the theatrical district of New York, to which I had repaired after my date for that ***evening***, a charming lady of the theatre who had refused my company for obvious reasons.(p.538)

evening-up

• Alcohol being no respecter of persons, we are an accurate cross section of America, and in distant lands, the same democratic ***evening-up*** process is now going on.(p.xx)

evenings

• You have passed happy ***evenings*** together chatting and drinking before your fire.(p.110)
• We have enjoyed such ***evenings*** ourselves; we had a good time.(p.110)
• This may lead to lonely ***evenings*** for you.(p.111)
• There I sat in the ***evenings***, enjoying with my friends our memories of the "old country," singing the old songs we all knew, playing simple card games for drinks and consuming great quantities of beer.(p.231)
• ***Evenings*** at home were an ordeal.(p.299)

event

• Being mostly business or professional folk, we could not well carry on our occupations in such an ***event***.(p.xiii)
• In any ***event***, try to have your husband read this book.(p.114)
• A big ***event*** of any kind precipitated heavy drinking.(p.197)
• Then occurred the ***event*** that saved me.(p.235)
• If I were alone I would stop at four or five of them, but only one or two in the ***event*** I had my mistrusting wife with me.(p.299)
• I don't know whether she was a pacifist or whether she just thought that in the ***event*** of another war it would have some bearing on my joining up.(p.484)
• When I was faced with a special challenge or social ***event*** -- such as an important business presentation or a dinner party -- I had to fortify myself with a couple of belts.(p.556)

events

• See to it that your relationship with Him is right, and great ***events*** will come to pass for you and countless others.(p.164)
• As I look back on the ***events*** of two months, I can clearly see that I had been circling around, half-afraid of encountering the remedy for my situation, half wanting it, deferring fulfillment of my promise to get in touch with the doctor I had heard about.(p.258)
• Forgive me -- I cannot write further about this latest turn of ***events***, anticipating seeing the family I deserted so long ago.(p.463)
• In the light of subsequent ***events*** it became evident that I took their advice far too literally, for, after some months of happy sobriety I drank again.(p.471)

eventual

• My ***eventual*** goal was to drink myself to death.(p.353)
• With these new and enlightening doors opening up to me, I was able to make the ***eventual*** decision to stop drinking, a day at a time -- because I, too, was an alcoholic.(p.355)

eventually

• Though old buildings will ***eventually*** be replaced by finer ones, the new structures will take years to complete.(p.123)
• Those of us who have spent much time in the world of spiritual make-believe have ***eventually*** seen the childishness of it.(p.130)
• ***Eventually***, there would be a ball game, or a show, or some sort of special occasion to celebrate and I would turn up drunk.(p.196)
• I then began asking a lot of questions of both my brother and Dr. Bob about how this thing worked, and I suppose I was becoming more glassy-eyed all the while, for ***eventually*** I said to Bob, "You're all dried up.(p.206)
• I went to five grade schools, primarily because I was expelled for my conduct, but I ***eventually*** graduated from the eighth grade.(p.211)
• "Best in the business, when he's sober," my customers would say, and I still had a following who would give me work though they deplored my habits, because they knew the job would be well done when they ***eventually*** got it.(p.234)
• Successive Monday morning hangovers, which despite mid-week resolutions to do better, came with unfailing regularity, ***eventually*** caused me to quit my job.(p.254)
• ***Eventually***, of course, what with all the hilarity that could be provoked with a few gallons of beer, there seemed to be no need of bridge or poker playing for entertainment.(p.297)
• The parties waxed more liquid and hilarious as time went on, and ***eventually*** I discovered that a little shot of liquor now and then between beers had the tendency to put me in a whacky mood much quicker than having to down several quarts of beer to obtain the same effect.(p.298)
• I got along fairly well with my party drinking for quite some time, but ***eventually*** I began to visit beer joints in between parties.(p.298)
• ***Eventually*** I would arrive home for a late supper for which, of course, I had absolutely no relish.(p.299)
• ***Eventually***, the noon meal was also dispensed with.(p.299)
• Things ***eventually*** came to the point where I had no friends.(p.301)
• But, of course," he continued, "***eventually*** the alcoholic loses all of his capacities as his disease gets progressively worse, and this is a tragedy that is painful to watch; the disintegration of a sound mind and body."(p.308)
• He told me that ***eventually*** he hoped such a group would develop in the Chicago area, but that so far this had not been started.(p.309)
• I ***eventually*** became a schoolmaster, but gave up that profession to join the Indian Army.(p.342)
• I was living in a small room on West 53rd Street right off Fifth Avenue, when I met a young lady who ***eventually*** was responsible for altering my entire way of living.(p.359)
• I had been on the wagon when I came to A.A. and this sobriety-tension ***eventually*** popped.(p.414)
• ***Eventually***, I was taking forty-five milligrams of the long-acting Benzedrine and forty-five of the short-acting just to get out of bed in the morning.(p.442)
• ***Eventually***, the psychiatrist discharged me from the hospital, and Max and I began going to meetings ourselves.(p.447)
• ***Eventually***, I had to redo each of the Twelve Steps specifically with Max in mind, from the First, saying, "I am powerless over alcohol, and my homelife is unmanageable by me," to the Twelfth, in which I tried to think of her as a sick Al-Anon and treat her with the love I would give a sick A.A. newcomer.(p.452)
• ***Eventually*** the day came when I was dependent upon it even when there wasn't any occasion.(p.464)
• She had been warned numerous times, not only by her family but by my own mother, that I was a hopeless drunk, that there wasn't anything anybody could do with me, that I'd never stop, and that ***eventually*** I'd break her heart.(p.513)
• But I did understand this ***eventually***, that these people had been through a lot of drinking experience just as I had, and had managed to make a job of it.(p.524)
• Depending on the stage of drunkenness, ***eventually*** I either fought or went to sleep.(p.537)
• My husband ***eventually*** returned, but it was not long until we realized we could not continue our marriage.(p.547)

ever

• On the other hand -- and strange as this may seem to those who do not understand -- once a psychic

change has occurred, the very same person who seemed doomed, who had so many problems he despaired of *ever* solving them, suddenly finds himself easily able to control his desire for alcohol, the only effort necessary being that required to follow a few simple rules.(p.xxvii)
• Following his physical rehabilitation, he had a talk with me in which he frankly stated he thought the treatment a waste of effort, unless I could assure him, which no one *ever* had, that in the future he would have the "will power" to resist the impulse to drink.(p.xxix)
• Then he had, in effect, been raised from the dead, suddenly taken from the scrap heap to a level of life better than the best he had *ever* known!(p.11)
• And so it had been *ever* since.(p.13)
• "The doctor told him that if he *ever* drank again it would kill him, but there he is all lit up again."(p.20)
• How often have some of us begun to drink in this nonchalant way, and after the third or fourth, pounded on the bar and said to ourselves, "For God's sake, how did I *ever* get started again?"(p.24)
• We know that no real alcoholic *ever* recovers control.(p.30)
• Here are some of the methods we have tried: Drinking beer only, limiting the number of drinks, never drinking alone, never drinking in the morning, drinking only at home, never having it in the house, never drinking during business hours, drinking only at parties, switching from scotch to brandy, drinking only natural wines, agreeing to resign if *ever* drunk on the job, taking a trip, not taking a trip, swearing off forever (with and without a solemn oath), taking more physical exercise, reading inspirational books, going to health farms and sanitariums, accepting voluntary commitment to asylums -- we could increase the list ad infinitum.(p.31)
• Commencing to drink after a period of sobriety, we are in a short time as bad as *ever*.(p.33)
• If *ever* there was a successful business man, it is Fred.(p.39)
• Instead of regarding ourselves as intelligent agents, spearheads of God's *ever* advancing Creation, we agnostics and atheists chose to believe that our human intelligence was the last word, the alpha and the omega, the beginning and end of all.(p.49)
• Post-war disillusionment, *ever* more serious alcoholism, impending mental and physical collapse, brought him to the point of self-destruction.(p.56)
• To conclude that others were wrong was as far as most of us *ever* got.(p.66)
• If the alcoholic tries to shield himself he may succeed for a time, but he usually winds up with a bigger explosion than *ever*.(p.101)
• Some of us veered from extreme to extreme, *ever* hoping that one day our loved ones would be themselves once more.(p.105)
• Today most of our men are better husbands and fathers than *ever* before.(p.108)
• Some of us had this experience, only to enjoy, in a few months, a finer intimacy than *ever*.(p.134)
• He left us a note saying you were the best boss he *ever* had, and that you were not to blame in any way."(p.136)
• It was the obituary of one of the best salesmen I *ever* had.(p.137)
• I had been obliged to discharge him for drinking, though he was brilliant, alert, and one of the best organizers I have *ever* known.(p.137)
• The only answer I could make was that if the man followed the usual pattern, he would go on a bigger bust than *ever*.(p.138)
• If he temporizes and still thinks he can *ever* drink again, even beer, he might as well be discharged after the next bender which, if an alcoholic, he is almost certain to have.(p.142)
• It thickened, *ever* becoming blacker.(p.151)
• From what you tell me, I know more than *ever* I can't stop."(p.157)
• In his prodigy of service, he was well assisted by Sister Ignatia at St. Thomas Hospital in Akron, Ohio, one of the greatest friends our Fellowship will *ever* know.(p.171)
• It was harmless; nobody *ever* got drunk on beer.(p.177)
• Of far more importance was the fact that he was the first living human with whom I had *ever* talked, who knew what he was talking about in regard to alcoholism from actual experience.(p.180)
• So it doesn't behoove me to squawk about it for, after all, nobody *ever* had to throw me down and pour liquor down my throat.(p.181)
• As far as I know that was the first time I had *ever* paid any attention to that word.(p.187)
• Looking sadder than *ever*, he wearily ventured, "Well this is wonderful for you fellows, but it can't be for me.(p.188)
• That was the first time I *ever* drank hard liquor.(p.195)
• (I might say right here that never in my life did I *ever* intend to get drunk.(p.196)
• I think the longest drunk I was *ever* on was eleven days, but usually only two days with a complete blackout for a day, and then backing off by drinking as long as I could get anything.(p.203)
• He said, "So long as I'm thinking as I'm thinking now, and so long as I'm doing the things I'm doing now, I don't believe I'll *ever* take another drink."(p.206)
• After two or three years of effort along this line, I reached the point of actual despair that I *ever* would be able to drink only a harmless amount each day.(p.215)
• My children had lost respect for me and, in fact, it was only after three or four years of sobriety that any of them *ever* said anything to me to indicate that I had recouped even a little of their respect.(p.215)
• She knew that at that time any suggestion she made about my drinking would only build up a barrier, a consideration for which I am *ever* grateful.(p.216)
• That was the beginning of a new life, a fuller life, a happier life than I had *ever* known or believed possible.(p.228)
• I came directly to a growing industrial city in the middle west, where I have lived practically *ever* since.(p.231)
• The third man who came to see me had been one of the greatest business-getters his company had *ever* employed.(p.235)
• This duty together with my weekly meetings with my fellow alcoholics, and my daily renewal of the contract I originally made with God, have kept me sober when nothing else *ever* did.(p.237)
• Three years later, at twenty-five, I opened and operated their Philadelphia office and was earning more than I *ever* have since.(p.242)
• My loneliness was worse than it had *ever* been before, for now even my own kind had turned against me.(p.247)
• This time it really hurt, more than any hangover *ever* had.(p.247)
• My brilliant agnosticism vanished, and I saw for the first time that those who really believed, or at least honestly tried to find a Power greater than themselves, were much more composed and contented than I had *ever* been, and they seemed to have a degree of happiness which I had never known.(p.247)
• When the others saw my altered attitude they took me back in, but for me they had to make it tough; if they hadn't I don't think I *ever* would have stuck it out.(p.248)
• For a long time the only Higher Power I could concede was the power of the group, but this was far more than I had *ever* recognized before, and it was at least a beginning.(p.248)
• At the end of these thirteen years I never dreamed that he'd *ever* take another drink.(p.263)
• He hardly *ever* went to anything like that without me.(p.263)
• We were the most congenial drinkers you *ever* saw.(p.264)
• We had the grandest time *ever*.(p.264)
• One Sunday afternoon, the only time I *ever* got picked up for drunken driving, I got picked up in Bellaire.(p.264)
• As we left, and they were escorting us across the bridge into Wheeling, I, with great dignity and sarcasm, told them if their wives were *ever* visiting in Akron, and they, too, were looking for their route sign as I was, that I hoped I could extend to them the hospitality that had been shown to me in Bellaire.(p.264)
• I didn't know that anything was *ever* done for them in a medical way.(p.267)
• And I was glad, and I have been *ever* since, that I said that.(p.270)
• At that time they didn't let us know that people *ever* had trouble.(p.271)
• I don't *ever* remember that I was bored myself when we first came in, and they came out to the house and talked to us about these things.(p.273)
• Before I stop -- I always was a great talker -- I want to say that nobody will *ever* know how I miss Annie's advice about things.(p.273)
• Nothing has *ever* to this day equalled the thrill of that first case.(p.282)
• During that first year, however, I managed to make both ends meet, and to avoid *ever* going back to my old habit pattern of borrowing money when I could not earn it.(p.283)
• Have I *ever* wanted a drink during these years?(p.285)
• But I had my health back and besides, I reasoned, they were much worse than I would *ever* be.(p.289)
• Immediately on her return we began to have formal meetings once a week, in the autumn of 1939, and we have continued to do this and to expand *ever* since.(p.295)
• Spiritually . . . I found a Friend who never lets me down and is *ever* eager to help.(p.303)
• Looking at him it was hard to believe he had *ever* been as I was then.(p.309)
• There is no more "aloneness," with that awful ache, so deep in the heart of every alcoholic that nothing, before, could *ever* reach it.(p.312)
• How did you *ever* stand it?"(p.322)
• But I wasn't happy, and I didn't *ever* let myself go in my drinking.(p.323)
• I vowed that never again would any important person whom I wished to please and impress *ever* see me drunk.(p.328)
• If *ever* I got that bad . . .(p.332)
• I had forgotten "If I *ever* I get that bad, I'll try A.A."(p.333)
• But this second time, I found I couldn't live normally without it, and I was licked worse than *ever*.(p.340)
• I made more money the last year of my drinking than I *ever* made before in my whole life.(p.345)
• And I gave him some idea of what you do, and so I made my first Twelfth Step call before I *ever* came into the program.(p.347)
• The satisfaction I got from giving him a little of what I had read in those pamphlets far surpassed any feeling that I had *ever* had before in helping patients.(p.347)
• Lucky because my excessive drinking never got me in jail, or hospitalized, nor did it *ever* cost me a job.(p.356)
• I stayed on in Florida for three weeks, enjoying our reunion, a new found health and a deeper love than I had *ever* experienced before.(p.364)
• I believe the first time I *ever* realized what alcohol would do for me was at my own wedding.(p.385)
• I don't want anybody *ever* to look at me like that again.(p.391)
• It was one of the worst I *ever* had.(p.393)
• My work with other alcoholics has led me, day by day, into *ever* wider and richer experiences.(p.394)
• It pays daily in more harmonious relations with my fellow men, in *ever* clearer insight into the true meaning of life, and in the answering love and gratitude wherever and whenever I have been the instrument of God's will in the lives of others.(p.394)
• In all these ways I've experienced, in *ever* growing measure and beyond all expectations and rewards, a joy which I had never before imagined.(p.395)
• It's the last thing I *ever* heard him say, and I think there are some of us who, at times, try to read extra messages and complexities into the Steps.(p.395)
• I was, when drunk, just as undisciplined and erratic as *ever*.(p.410)
• Nor was I the "worst woman who *ever* lived."(p.414)
• How easy it was, in the beginning, to forget that those binges *ever* happened!(p.433)
• After a month it seemed unlikely that it *ever* really happened.(p.433)
• To cut a long story short, I spent seven years and ten thousand dollars on my psychiatric adventure, and emerged in worse condition than *ever*.(p.434)
• Only through being beaten down by my own misery would I *ever* have accepted the term "alcoholic" as applied to myself.(p.436)
• My work is on a much deeper and more significant level than it *ever* was before, and I am today a fairly creative, relatively sane human being.(p.438)
• If there *ever* was anyone who came to A.A. by mistake, it was I.(p.439)
• Now I own perhaps the most costly pair of moccasins anyone has *ever* seen, and they help me remember where I've been.)(p.445)
• Today, I find it's the best thing that has *ever* happened to me.(p.450)
• When I first came into A.A., the woman who was my sponsor was the first woman I had *ever* met who admitted that she was an alcoholic.(p.472)
• This first story I *ever* write.(p.474)
• I met and married a man in A.A., and I am the happiest I have *ever* been in my life.(p.481)
• The only time that I have *ever* seen my mother take anything alcoholic was around Christmas time, when she would drink some eggnog or light wine.(p.484)
• Vi was the first girl that I *ever* took out.(p.485)
• That's the first time I was *ever* really drunk in my life.(p.487)
• "Freshman," said he to me, "do you *ever*

take a drink?"(p.497)
• Then he asks me if I am willing to right all the wrongs I have ***ever*** done to anyone, no matter how wrong I thought the others were.(p.503)
• I've stuck pretty close to A.A. ***ever*** since then, taken it day by day, not biting off more than I can chew.(p.511)
• No one had ***ever*** told me it was the first drink that did the damage.(p.514)
• This was the only time in my life that I'd ***ever*** known my mother to be almost pitiless, but she couldn't be blamed for that.(p.523)
• But I don't remember that any of them ***ever*** went to sleep in joints and woke up with no shoes on in the winter, or fell out of chairs.(p.527)
• I was trying to remember where it came from, when two of the biggest cops I ***ever*** saw walked in and took me to jail.(p.528)
• Since I have been in A.A., I have more friends than I ***ever*** had in my life -- friends who care about me and my welfare, friends who don't care that I am black and that I have been in prison.(p.529)
• I wonder if ***ever*** there has been a sillier reason for getting drunk all the time.(p.537)
• All of my family and loved ones, all of my friends, are nearer and dearer to me than ***ever*** before and I have literally dozens of new friends who say they cannot believe that a short eight years ago I was ready for the scrap heap.(p.541)
• For me, A.A. is a synthesis of all the philosophy I've ***ever*** read, all of the positive, good philosophy, all of it based on love.(p.542)
• The mental twists that led up to my drinking began many years before I ***ever*** took a drink for I am one of those whose history proves conclusively that my drinking was "a symptom of a deeper trouble."(p.544)
• I was the only person I'd ***ever*** known personally who had ***ever*** been in jail, and I guess it is most significant that the second time was less humiliating that the first had been.(p.549)
• As I said earlier, self-pity and resentment were my constant companions and my inventory began to look like a thirty-three year diary, for I seemed to have a resentment against everybody I had ***ever*** known.(p.551)
• As another great man says, "The only real freedom a human being can ***ever*** know is doing what you ought to do because you want to do it."(p.553)
• When I had been in A.A. only a short while, an oldtimer told me something that has affected my life ***ever*** since.(p.554)
• Soon my drinking was as bad as ***ever*** -- all day long every day.(p.557)
• The doctors told me that if I ***ever*** took another drink, it might be my last.(p.558)
• Therefore, no society of men and women ***ever*** had more urgent need for continuous effectiveness and permanent unity.(p.563)
• The "12 Traditions" of Alcoholics Anonymous are, we A.A.'s believe, the best answers that our experience has yet given to those ***ever*** urgent questions, "How can A.A. best function?" and, "How can A.A. best stay whole and so survive?"(p.563)
• Twelve -- Anonymity is the spiritual foundation of all our Traditions, ***ever*** reminding us to place principles before personalities.(p.564)
• Nor ought A.A. membership ***ever*** depend upon money or conformity.(p.565)
• And no group, regional committee, or individual should ***ever*** take any action that might greatly affect A.A. as a whole without conferring with the trustees of the General Service Board.(p.565)
• 10. -- No A.A. group or member should ***ever***, in such a way as to implicate A.A., express any opinion on outside controversial issues -- particularly those of politics, alcohol reform, or sectarian religion.(p.567)

everlasting

• "There is a principle which is a bar against all information, which is proof against all arguments and which cannot fail to keep a man in ***everlasting*** ignorance -- that principle is contempt prior to investigation."(p.570)

every

• Our earliest printing voiced the hope "that ***every*** alcoholic who journeys will find the Fellowship of Alcoholics Anonymous at his destination.(p.xv)
• Soon A.A. was beset by these very problems on ***every*** side and in ***every*** group.(p.xix)
• Then there are types entirely normal in ***every*** respect except in the effect alcohol has upon them.(p.xxviii)
• I earnestly advise ***every*** alcoholic to read this book through, and though perhaps he came to scoff, he may remain to pray.(p.xxx)
• My drinking assumed more serious proportions, continuing all day and almost ***every*** night.(p.3)
• Golf permitted drinking ***every*** day and ***every*** night.(p.3)
• The tremendous fact for ***every*** one of us is that we have discovered a common solution.(p.17)
• Those of us who live in large cities are overcome by the reflection that close by hundreds are dropping into oblivion ***every*** day.(p.19)
• At a certain point in the drinking of ***every*** alcoholic, he passes into a state where the most powerful desire to stop drinking is of absolutely no avail.(p.24)
• This tragic situation has already arrived in practically ***every*** case long before it is suspected.(p.24)
• The idea that somehow, someday he will control and enjoy his drinking is the great obsession of ***every*** abnormal drinker.(p.30)
• We have tried ***every*** imaginable remedy.(p.31)
• By ***every*** form of self-deception and experimentation, they will try to prove themselves exceptions to the rule, therefore nonalcoholic.(p.31)
• Then he fell victim to a belief which practically ***every*** alcoholic has -- that his long period of sobriety and self-discipline had qualified him to drink as other men.(p.32)
• ***Every*** means of solving his problem which money could buy was at his disposal.(p.32)
• ***Every*** attempt failed.(p.33)
• To us it is not far-fetched, for this kind of thinking has been characteristic of ***every*** single one of us.(p.37)
• He tries ***every*** known means to get the jay-walking idea out of his head.(p.38)
• I felt I had ***every*** right to be self-confident, that it would be only a matter of exercising my will power and keeping on guard.(p.40)
• ***Every*** one of them has gained access to, and believes in, a Power greater than himself.(p.50)
• Actually we were fooling ourselves, for deep down in ***every*** man, woman, and child, is the fundamental idea of God.(p.55)
• We cannot be helpful to all people, but at least God will show us how to take a kindly and tolerant view of each and ***every*** one.(p.67)
• This short word somehow touches about ***every*** aspect of our lives.(p.67)
• We pocket our pride and go to it, illuminating ***every*** twist of character, ***every*** dark cranny of the past.(p.75)
• Can He now take them all -- ***every*** one?(p.76)
• I pray that you now remove from me ***every*** single defect of character which stands in the way of my usefulness to you and my fellows.(p.76)
• ***Every*** day is a day when we must carry the vision of God's will into all of our activities.(p.85)
• You have to act the Good Samaritan ***every*** day, if need be.(p.97)
• Burn the idea into the consciousness of ***every*** man that he can get well regardless of anyone.(p.98)
• We meet these conditions ***every*** day.(p.101)
• ***Every*** new alcoholic looks for this spirit among us and is immensely relieved when he finds we are not witch-burners.(p.103)
• There is ***every*** evidence that women regain their health as readily as men if they try our suggestions.(p.104)
• But for ***every*** man who drinks others are involved -- the wife who trembles in fear of the next debauch; the mother and father who see their son wasting away.(p.104)
• These are some of the questions which race through the mind of ***every*** woman who has an alcoholic husband.(p.108)
• Of course, there is such a thing as incompatibility, but in nearly ***every*** instance the alcoholic only seems to be unloving and inconsiderate; it is usually because he is warped and sickened that he says and does these appalling things.(p.108)
• Since this book was first published, A.A. has released thousands of alcoholics from asylums and hospitals of ***every*** kind.(p.114)
• Then that terrible tension which grips the home of ***every*** problem drinker will be lessened.(p.115)
• Now we try to put spiritual principles to work in ***every*** department of our lives.(p.116)
• Now and then the family will be plagued by spectres from the past, for the drinking career of almost ***every*** alcoholic has been marked by escapades, funny, humiliating, shameful or tragic.(p.123)
• He is straining ***every*** nerve to make up for lost time.(p.126)
• Dad may feel that for years his drinking has placed him on the wrong side of ***every*** argument, but now he has become a superior person with God on his side.(p.129)
• Nearly ***every*** modern employer feels a moral responsibility for the well-being of his help, and he tries to meet these responsibilities.(p.137)
• Some employers have tried ***every*** known remedy.(p.137)
• Will he take ***every*** necessary step, submit to anything to get well, to stop drinking forever?(p.142)
• Can you have ***every*** confidence in his ability to recover?(p.143)
• You put me on the spot ***every*** time you get drunk.(p.147)
• This same company spends millions for research ***every*** year.(p.149)
• I have enjoyed ***every*** moment spent in getting them straightened out.(p.150)
• ***Every*** few days this doctor suggests our approach to one of his patients.(p.162)
• Some day we hope that ***every*** alcoholic who journeys will find a Fellowship of Alcoholics Anonymous at his destination.(p.162)
• My phobia for sleeplessness demanded that I get drunk ***every*** night, but in order to get more liquor for the next night, I had to stay sober during the day, at least up to four o'clock.(p.177)
• I gave the matter much time and study for the next two and a half years, but still got tight ***every*** night nevertheless.(p.178)
• 4.Because ***every*** time I do it I take out a little more insurance for myself against a possible slip.(p.181)
• Then Prohibition came into effect, and the facts that the stuff obtainable was so horrible and sometimes deadly, and that I had married and had a job which I had to look after, helped me for a period of some three or four years, although I would get drunk ***every*** time I could get hold of enough to drink to get started.(p.183)
• ***Every*** time I'd start thinking about drinking, I would think of the long, dry years ahead without having a drink; but this idea of twenty-four hours, that it was up to me from then on, was a lot of help.(p.188)
• It was repulsive to me from ***every*** standpoint.(p.195)
• ***Every*** company in the country, except Firestone, was reorganized at that time.(p.197)
• And we stood there for twenty minutes, telling each other how much better we were, how much better we looked, how much better off we were financially, mentally, physically, morally, and in ***every*** way, shape and manner.(p.201)
• And I continued to drink, on and off then, until ***every*** dollar I had in the world was gone again and I was right back living at my sister's, getting my cigarettes by calling her grocer and telling him to put in a couple of cartons with her order, exactly as I had before I started to work at Max's.(p.202)
• I attended their meetings ***every*** Sunday and Wednesday for about nine months.(p.202)
• So I had one double-header ***every*** night for about two or three weeks.(p.203)
• All during Prohibition, ***every*** alcoholic felt that he made the best hooch, regardless of how bad it was.(p.213)
• When I was about forty-seven, after indulging in all kinds of self-deception to control my drinking, I arrived at a period when I felt convinced I had to have so much alcohol ***every*** day and that the real problem was to control how much.(p.214)
• However, on a couple of other occasions, Clarence seemed to bob up at the last saloon that I would stop at on the way home ***every*** day.(p.216)
• I believe ***every*** member of the Akron Group did come to see me, which impressed me terrifically, not so much because of the stories they told, but because they would take the time to come and talk to me without even knowing who I was.(p.218)
• I believe though that it helped my family tremendously to have the A.A. meetings ***every*** week in my own home.(p.220)
• You can all remember that in the first few months after the change, a great many men, who had formerly been used to a few beers ***every*** day or an occasional drink of whiskey, simply quit all alcoholic drinks.(p.232)
• I was doing very well with that and general upholstering work, and there was ***every*** indication that I would be financially independent by the time I reached middle age.(p.232)
• ***Every*** man has his problem of this kind, but we didn't discuss it very much.(p.236)
• And I began putting into practice what I was learning ***every*** day.(p.237)
• That is where I had my first drink and I still remember it, for ***every*** "first" drink afterwards did exactly the same trick -- I could feel it go right through ***every*** bit of my body and down to my very toes.(p.241)
• ***Every*** time I blacked out, and that was ***every*** time I drank, there was always that gnawing fear, "What did I do this time?"(p.244)
• For the last two years of my drinking I prayed on

every drunk that I wouldn't wake up again.(p.245)
• At that time the group in New York was composed of about twelve men who were working on the principle of *every* drunk for himself; we had no real formula and no name.(p.246)
• At our weekly meeting I was a menace to serenity those first few months, for I took *every* opportunity to lambaste the "spiritual angle" as we called it, or anything else that had any tinge of theology.(p.246)
• *Every* encouragement was given me with frequent salary increases, but the sober times between "periods" became shorter.(p.254)
• I had some financial success through no ability of my own and, when jobless and almost wiped out in 1930, I began to trade and sell my collection; much of the proceeds went to keep my apartment stocked with liquor and almost *every* night saw me helpless to bed.(p.255)
• Enduring all the hangover hells that *every* alcoholic experiences, I made the usual resolutions.(p.256)
• These vacations became quite something, and he always had two weeks vacation the first two weeks of *every* September.(p.264)
• Jack said there was a meeting in Akron *every* Wednesday night and that it was very important that we go.(p.268)
• And we loved *every* minute of that association.(p.270)
• I ate up *every* bit of it, because I wanted to find out how to stay sober.(p.273)
• I entered the business world with *every* confidence that success lay ahead of me.(p.275)
• I also talked A.A. to *every* friend who would listen, at lunch, at dinner, on street corners.(p.282)
• Then I started traveling, with the United States and Canada as my territory, and with so much freedom and with an unlimited expense account, I was soon drinking *every* night and kidding myself that it was all part of the job.(p.287)
• After finding *every* bottle that I had hidden around the apartment, she took away my pants, my shoes, my money and my keys, threw them under the bed in the back bedroom and slip-locked our door.(p.288)
• *Every* evening we would meet at the home of one of the members and have coffee and doughnuts and spend a social evening.(p.291)
• It was very impressive and I wish that *every* A.A. could have the benefit of this type of sponsorship today.(p.292)
• One of them was that I would try to get a group started in Chicago; the second was that I would have to return to Akron to attend meetings at least *every* two months until I did get a group started in Chicago; third, I decided I must place this program above everything else, even my family, because if I did not maintain my sobriety I would lose my family anyway.(p.292)
• That was my lesson, that one could not take the moral inventory and then file it away; that the alcoholic has to continue to take inventory *every* day if he expects to get well and stay well.(p.293)
• It doesn't pay to be seen in the same place at the same hour *every* day.(p.299)
• As a result, I would fall off in a drunken stupor *every* night.(p.299)
• It wasn't necessary to report to the office in person *every* day, and when I did go in, it was just to make an appearance and bounce right out again.(p.300)
• I was given *every* advantage in a well ordered home.(p.304)
• *Every* reasonable desire was possible of attainment for me.(p.304)
• *Every* doctor gets his quota of alcoholic patients.(p.308)
• There is no more "aloneness," with that awful ache, so deep in the heart of *every* alcoholic that nothing, before, could ever reach it.(p.312)
• While I was in basic, I got high off booze almost *every* night.(p.317)
• I called her *every* night from a local bar, and often she was not at home.(p.318)
• I was deathly sick *every* time I took a drink.(p.322)
• Even so, *every* time I drank, I seemed to get in trouble.(p.322)
• There was one girl especially, and I'd watch her from my window *every* morning, leaving faithfully to go to the hospital in the neighborhood.(p.326)
• *Every* breadwinner, whether trying to impress a boss or to hold customers in his own business, is fettered by people-pleasing.(p.329)
• He may even read in a newspaper that one out of *every* seven drinkers will become alcoholic, but he rarely is told that it holds true for all ages -- or that the tolerance to alcohol (and other drugs) decreases steadily, year after year, in the bodies of all persons.(p.330)
• Boredom sets up *every* retiree for two chief dangers: obesity and alcoholism.(p.330)
• A friend of mine, a golf nut, rushed out on retirement to play *every* day.(p.330)
• I said to my husband, "I'm going to try, *every* free moment that I have, to get interested in something outside, get myself over this rut I'm in."(p.338)
• I read, studied, and meditated on *every* bit of A.A. literature in my possession.(p.344)
• I tried *every* gimmick that there was to get some peace of mind, but it was not until I was brought to my alcoholic knees, when I was brought to a group in my own community with the butcher, the baker, the carpenter and the mechanic, who were able to give me the Twelve Steps, that I was finally given some semblance of an answer to the last half of the First Step.(p.349)
• But I remembered that *every* night after dinner my wife would get up and do the dishes.(p.351)
• And now I am doing the darn dishes *every* night!(p.352)
• *Every* day became that much harder to live through, and I began to take a look at myself.(p.354)
• I had *every* advantage a child could have, private schools (several of them), dancing schools, two colleges, coon skin coats, automobiles, a listing in the social register and all the rest.(p.357)
• Before long I was at the luncheon meeting an hour before the others, that old and familiar trademark of *every* alcoholic.(p.360)
• One Saturday noon I staggered home with *every* intention of showing her.(p.362)
• That night she too had new hope because I had made sure she would know what I was doing about my drinking by packing *every* bit of A.A. literature I could put my hands on right on top so she couldn't help but see it when she opened my bag.(p.364)
• (In fact, *every* time I saw him he had a frown on his face.)(p.370)
• Slowly, my life seemed to unfold before me, shedding insights on childhood resentments, jealousies, and fears that had mushroomed in adulthood, and also on the self-pity that I had wallowed in at *every* opportunity.(p.371)
• After *every* cocktail party or dinner party she would say she couldn't understand how I could get in such a drunken stupor on one drink.(p.377)
• The baffling problem of getting drunk when I had *every* intention of staying sober was simplified.(p.379)
• They told me to go to meetings, and I still do at *every* available opportunity, whether I am at home or in some other city.(p.381)
• As I grow in A.A., I realize that a person with as much self-will as I had, as hard a head and as diseased an ego, had to try everything that I could think of, butting my head against *every* stone wall before I was ready to come in.(p.384)
• I could see no reason why they should have any relationship to this problem of getting drunk *every* now and then.(p.388)
• *Every* time I got drunk, my husband would send me to a nursing home.(p.388)
• It is a way of life that pays as it goes, *every* step of the way, in compensations that have been wonderfully rich and rewarding.(p.394)
• To me, A.A. is within the reach of *every* alcoholic, because it can be achieved in any walk of life and because the achievement is not ours but God's.(p.395)
• Now it was semi-blackouts *every* night, outrageous behavior, passing out in some friend's Village studio or not knowing how I got home.(p.407)
• I had to go there *every* night.(p.410)
• I read the book and God leapt at me from *every* page.(p.412)
• *Every* day, I feel a little bit more useful, more happy and more free.(p.417)
• Mom and I drank *every* waking moment because we felt so sorry for dad.(p.426)
• Wasn't I drinking more than a quart *every* day?(p.427)
• All I want to know is, why does that dog wet in my lap *every* time I hold him?"(p.440)
• Therefore, *every* pill was medically indicated at the time it was taken.(p.443)
• As a physician and pharmacist who had grown up in a drugstore-home, I had a pill for *every* ill, and I was sick a lot.(p.443)
• I wore those moccasins *every* night for the next seven years, until they wore out.(p.445)
• One has to be pretty sick to do that, and perhaps one has to be even sicker to come back *every* day for a new list, as she did.(p.446)
• The psychiatrist, who had generally been ignoring me, now became quite interested; *every* day, he would ask me all kinds of questions about the A.A. meetings.(p.446)
• So, for no better reason than to fool him, I asked Frank to take me to a meeting *every* night.(p.447)
• And Frank did set me up for a meeting *every* night except Friday, when he thought he might have a date with his girl friend.(p.447)
• I was always able to see the flaw in *every* person, *every* situation.(p.449)
• *Every* defect I pointed out to her became greater and greater.(p.450)
• Most had taken shattering losses on nearly *every* front of life.(p.455)
• After a while I really did enjoy drinking and what it did to me, and I became dependent upon it for *every* occasion.(p.464)
• At *every* place, I find A.A. group first.(p.476)
• We are told to practice the Twelve Steps and Twelve Traditions to the best of our ability *every* day, one day at a time.(p.481)
• If I work on it *every* day, it will be easier to be honest with myself.(p.482)
• But the week-ends stretched on into Mondays and the time soon came when I drank *every* day.(p.488)
• I drink a lot *every* night.(p.499)
• A former employer of mine said to me a little over ten years ago, "Pat, you seem to be one of those unfortunate people who at least once *every* six months must go out and roll in the gutter."(p.513)
• The old pattern reasserted itself, but it was no longer once *every* six months.(p.514)
• I use that "Easy Does It" *every* day, to slow me down a little.(p.516)
• I hated *every* minute of it.(p.526)
• (There was a time, for about three months, when I bought a ten-dollar wrist watch *every* pay day -- that is *every* two weeks.(p.532)
• "Pity me the heart that is slow to learn What the quick mind sees at *every* turn."(p.534)
• My personal definition, which I submit as applying only to myself (although everyone is welcome to it who wants it), includes *every* waking activity of the human being; to have a creative attitude towards things is a more exact meaning, to live and to deal with other human beings creatively, which to me means seeing the God in them, and respecting and worshipping this God.(p.535)
• Alas for us men toward whom Shaw hurled his cry, "Must a Christ be crucified in *every* generation for the benefit of those who have no imagination?"(p.536)
• The only way existence was possible was through rationalizing *every* sober moment and drinking myself into complete oblivion as often as I could.(p.547)
• I've heard it said many times in A.A., "There is just one good drunk in *every* alcoholic's life, and that's the one that brings us into A.A.," and I believe it.(p.549)
• Do it *every* day for two weeks and you will find you have come to mean it and to want it for them, and you will realize that where you used to feel bitterness and resentment and hatred, you now feel compassionate understanding and love."(p.552)
• It worked for me then, and it has worked for me many times since, and it will work for me *every* time I am willing to work it.(p.552)
• "God willing, we . . . may never again have to deal with drinking, but we have to deal with sobriety *every* day."(p.554)
• In fact, I changed schools *every* year until high school.(p.555)
• And yet my ability to lie outwardly and to kid myself inwardly grew with *every* drink I took.(p.556)
• Soon my drinking was as bad as ever -- all day long *every* day.(p.557)
• I vomited *every* morning.(p.558)
• God willing, we members of A.A. may never again have to deal with drinking, but we have to deal with sobriety *every* day.(p.560)
• Seven -- *Every* A.A. group ought to be fully self-supporting, declining outside contributions.(p.564)
• Clergymen of practically *every* denomination have given A.A. their blessing.(p.574)

everybody

• In a vague way their families and friends sense that these drinkers are abnormal, but *everybody* hopefully awaits the day when the sufferer will rouse himself from his lethargy and assert his power of will.(p.23)
• *Everybody* likes him.(p.35)
• *Everybody* believes them without a murmur of doubt.(p.48)
• *Everybody* nowadays, believes in scores of assumptions for which there is good evidence, but no perfect visual proof.(p.48)
• *Everybody*, including himself, would be pleased.(p.61)
• *Everybody* had given them up.(p.113)

• We wives found that, like *everybody* else, we were afflicted with pride, self-pity, vanity and all the things which go to make up the self-centered person; and we were not above selfishness or dishonesty.(p.116)
• *Everybody* knows that those in bad health, and those who seldom play, do not laugh much.(p.132)
• *Everybody* drank wine.(p.230)
• I hated myself worse and worse, and as I hated myself I became more defiant towards everything and *everybody*.(p.265)
• Sergeants, doctors, girl friends -- *everybody* seemed to be picking on him.(p.317)
• It's surprising, how we think we fool *everybody* in our drinking.(p.324)
• They sent me the regular letter they send to *everybody* else, but along with it, Ruth Hock, the nonalcoholic secretary, wrote a longhand note because she could see from the letter that I really needed help badly.(p.392)
• Until I reached A.A. my life was a shambles; I was a mess, and I made *everybody* near and dear to me miserable.(p.400)
• I took *everybody* else's inventory.(p.410)
• *Everybody* did, in the set which I regarded as the apex of civilization.(p.433)
• Aside from being a common drunk, I had a very serious pill affliction and all the garbage that goes with it -- lying, stealing, cheating anybody and *everybody*, conning the people I could, and staying clear of the ones I couldn't.(p.478)
• I know I will be grateful for a chance to make amends to *everybody* I have hurt in the past.(p.482)
• At first, like *everybody* else, I could keep control when I drank, but if I did start to drink, even in those days, I was always one of the last to leave the party.(p.518)
• *Everybody* I had known in the old days had gone.(p.522)
• As I said earlier, self-pity and resentment were my constant companions and my inventory began to look like a thirty-three year diary, for I seemed to have a resentment against *everybody* I had ever known.(p.551)

everyday

• When dealing with such a person, you had better use *everyday* language to describe spiritual principles.(p.93)
• Cleaning up old scrapes, helping to settle family differences, explaining the disinherited son to his irate parents, lending money and securing jobs for each other, when justified -- these are *everyday* occurrences.(p.161)
• Indeed, I had to drink now to live, to cope with the demands of *everyday* existence.(p.556)
• I had to cope with the demands of *everyday* living without my comforter, my anesthetic, my crutch.(p.557)
• But my thinking was still confused, and I was still unable to deal with the challenges of *everyday* living without help.(p.558)

everyone

• We think this account of our experiences will help *everyone* to better understand the alcoholic.(p.xiii)
• New groups started up and it was found, to the astonishment of *everyone*, that A.A.'s message could be transmitted in the mail as well as by word of mouth.(p.xviii)
• *Everyone* spent in thousands and chattered in millions.(p.3)
• *Everyone* became resigned to the certainty that I would have to be shut up somewhere, or would stumble along to a miserable end.(p.8)
• He has so attractive a personality that he makes friends with *everyone*.(p.39)
• Almost *everyone* knows the reason.(p.51)
• What they say will apply to nearly *everyone* bound by ties of blood or affections to an alcoholic.(p.104)
• You think he ought to know the subject better, as *everyone* should have a clear understanding of the risk he takes if he drinks too much.(p.112)
• You draw more and more into yourself and you think *everyone* is talking about conditions at your home.(p.114)
• *Everyone* knows about the others' alcoholic troubles.(p.125)
• If he means to right his past wrongs, why all this concern for *everyone* in the world but his family?(p.128)
• In addition to these casual get-togethers, it became customary to set apart one night a week for a meeting to be attended by anyone or *everyone* interested in a spiritual way of life.(p.159)
• When a few men in this city have found themselves, and have discovered the joy of helping others to face life again, there will be no stopping until *everyone* in that town has had his opportunity to recover -- if he can and will.(p.163)
• Almost *everyone* seemed to do it.(p.172)
• I knew *everyone* would buy a few bottles, or cases, of liquor as their exchequers permitted, and that it would soon be gone.(p.175)
• I read everything I could find, and talked to *everyone* who I thought knew anything about it.(p.178)
• It must be remembered that I had read a great deal and talked to *everyone* who knew, or thought they knew anything about the subject of alcoholism.(p.180)
• It isn't always so sudden with *everyone*, but I ran into a personal crisis which filled me with a raging and righteous anger.(p.228)
• I was greeted warmly, honestly, and with a true ring of sincerity by *everyone* present.(p.259)
• *Everyone* had my number and wouldn't hire me at any price.(p.301)
• To be sure, this had been a dizzy and confused interval, but most *everyone* else I knew had emerged from it with both feet on the ground and a fair amount of adult maturity.(p.304)
• *Everyone* was against me -- I'd show them I didn't need them.(p.318)
• I got orders to go to Germany, and *everyone* in Germany was against me.(p.318)
• Most of my conversations were meaningless to *everyone* but me.(p.319)
• Then *everyone* would be sorry for me.(p.333)
• I knew nothing about alcoholism or the D.T.'s, but when I woke up on this last morning of my son's illness, I taped the keyhole on my door because "*everyone* was out there."(p.338)
• I do recall lying on a cold cement floor and shredding into little bits several pieces of stolen identification cards, and washing my face in the toilet bowl trying to sober up, and screaming hysterically while clinging to bars too high to see out of, and cursing *everyone* that came near me.(p.354)
• Cunning, baffling, powerful -- the gradual creeping up of the frequency and quantity of alcohol, and what it does to a person is apparent to *everyone* but the person involved.(p.375)
• Resenting anyone and *everyone* who might interfere with my personal plans and ways of doing things, I was full of self pity, especially for any interference with my drinking.(p.376)
• *Everyone* knows it.(p.376)
• The obsession of the mind was a little harder to understand and yet *everyone* has obsessions of various kinds.(p.380)
• Dishonest thinking, prejudice, ego, antagonism toward anyone and *everyone* who dares to cross him, vanity and a critical attitude are character defects that gradually creep in and become a part of his life.(p.380)
• *Everyone* has problems.(p.382)
• Suddenly, it was obvious to me: I had a brain tumor and would die, and *everyone* would be sorry for me.(p.444)
• At that point *everyone* decided something drastic had to be done.(p.469)
• I had found this new "something," and I wanted to give it to *everyone* who had a problem.(p.496)
• *Everyone* laughed loudly.(p.498)
• I would embarrass *everyone* by coming in drunk or passing out.(p.526)
• Oh, I might drink too much at times -- *everyone* I knew drank.(p.527)
• But I wanted a cosmos, a universe all my own which I had created and where I reigned as chief top reigner and ruler over *everyone* else.(p.535)
• To create: *Everyone* does it, some at the instinct level, others in the arts.(p.535)
• My personal definition, which I submit as applying only to myself (although *everyone* is welcome to it who wants it), includes every waking activity of the human being; to have a creative attitude towards things is a more exact meaning, to live and to deal with other human beings creatively, which to me means seeing the God in them, and respecting and worshipping this God.(p.535)
• I wish we did not have to have jails; I wish *everyone* could be in A.A., and if *everyone* were there would be no need for jails, in my opinion.(p.542)
• And it had gone underground now, because *everyone* knew I shouldn't be drinking.(p.557)
• Hopeless now, I felt it would be better for my wife, my children, and *everyone* in my life if I went ahead and died.(p.558)
• Happily for *everyone*, this conclusion is erroneous.(p.569)

everything

• What with our ultra-modern standards, our scientific approach to *everything*, we are perhaps not well equipped to apply the powers of good that lie outside our synthetic knowledge.(p.xxv)
• I have *everything* to live for!(p.xxvii)
• He had lost *everything* worthwhile in life and was only living, one might say, to drink.(p.xxix)
• He is often perfectly sensible and well balanced concerning *everything* except liquor, but in that respect he is incredibly dishonest and selfish.(p.21)
• We have not lost *everything* in life through drinking and we certainly do not intend to.(p.38)
• When we became alcoholics, crushed by a self-imposed crisis we could not postpone or evade, we had to fearlessly face the proposition that either God is *everything* or else He is nothing.(p.53)
• Hence, we saw that reason isn't *everything*.(p.54)
• Above *everything*, we alcoholics must be rid of this selfishness.(p.62)
• His only chance for sobriety would be some place like the Greenland Ice Cap, and even there an Eskimo might turn up with a bottle of scotch and ruin *everything*!(p.101)
• Perhaps your husband has been living in that strange world of alcoholism where *everything* is distorted and exaggerated.(p.108)
• He by no means ruined *everything*.(p.109)
• If your husband is trying to live on a spiritual basis, he will also be doing *everything* in his power to avoid disagreement or contention.(p.118)
• If a repetition is to be prevented, place the problem, along with *everything* else, in God's hands.(p.120)
• We all had to place recovery above *everything*, for without recovery we would have lost both home and business.(p.143)
• I read *everything* I could find, and talked to everyone who I thought knew anything about it.(p.178)
• I wasn't afraid that the program wouldn't work, but I still was doubtful whether I would be able to hang on to the program, but I did come to the conclusion that I was willing to put *everything* I had into it, with God's power, and that I wanted to do just that.(p.189)
• Then I remember when the boys came back, that I told them, "I have gone to this Higher Power and I have told Him that I am willing to put His world first, above *everything*.(p.190)
• I would put off doing anything that I could until the next day and, consequently, *everything* would pile up and then there would be the blackout.(p.197)
• I was prone to do *everything* on a big scale.(p.197)
• In the basement were to be dry-cleaning facilities, a barbershop, a pool room, a grocery shop and *everything*.(p.198)
• *Everything* in the world a man could possibly want, and I was driving from Akron to Cleveland, having just been to the bank and discovered that I had approximately $5,000.(p.200)
• That night I got very drunk, which was usual, but I remembered *everything*, which was very unusual.(p.224)
• So I indulged with my comrades in *everything* the Far East had to offer.(p.231)
• I was still bitter because I felt that drink had completely ruined my childhood and my married life, and I hated *everything* pertaining to it.(p.262)
• I hated myself worse and worse, and as I hated myself I became more defiant towards *everything* and everybody.(p.265)
• Nothing had changed and yet *everything* had changed.(p.280)
• One of them was that I would try to get a group started in Chicago; the second was that I would have to return to Akron to attend meetings at least every two months until I did get a group started in Chicago; third, I decided I must place this program above *everything* else, even my family, because if I did not maintain my sobriety I would lose my family anyway.(p.292)
• I definitely liked it, *everything* about it, the taste, the effects; and I realize now that a drink did something for me or to me that was different from the way it affected others.(p.305)
• Between the ages of twenty-five and thirty I tried *everything*.(p.305)
• He had tried *everything* from having me attend daily mass at six a.m. to performing the most menial labor for his charity patients.(p.306)
• Letting go of *everything* at once was both painful and terrifying.(p.311)
• Many women who have reached the stage that I had reached in my drinking have lost husbands, children, homes, *everything* they hold dear.(p.323)
• It has changed my thinking entirely, about *everything* I do.(p.325)
• In A.A., she discovered she had lost nothing and had found *everything*.(p.335)

• And the mops would get out, the vacuum would get out, *everything* would get out, but nothing would get done.(p.337)
• Toward five o'clock, helter-skelter, I'd get *everything* put away and try to get supper on the table, and after supper I'd finish the job up and knock myself out.(p.337)
• I went on, realizing what I was becoming, hating myself for it, bitter, blaming life, blaming *everything* else but the fact that I should turn about and do something about my drinking.(p.337)
• Because I found that *everything* I turned to became a substitute for drink.(p.339)
• And I took *everything* that A.A. had to give me.(p.340)
• I had been brought up to believe in God, but I know that until I found this A.A. program, I had never found or known faith in the reality of God, the reality of His power that is now with me in *everything* I do.(p.341)
• I owe *everything* to A.A.(p.344)
• First, we all hear at A.A. meetings about those who have lost *everything*, those who have been in jail, those who have been in prison, those who have lost their families, those who have lost their income.(p.345)
• *Everything* that I touched from grammar school on was successful.(p.345)
• Who is this fellow we are supposed to turn *everything* over to?(p.350)
• I gave them *everything*, except the greatest thing in the world, and that is peace of mind.(p.351)
• We did, and spent a month boozing it up, popping pills, and smoking marijuana; taking shelter where we could, which included a veterinary hospital one night; accepting meals from anyone; actually begging; stealing anything we were in need of, which was about *everything*.(p.354)
• I didn't particularly like it, but I loved the effects, and managed for the next twenty-five years to drink anything and *everything*, either handed to me or purchased, at the slightest excuse.(p.357)
• My wonderful wife did *everything* to play along with me.(p.361)
• I did *everything* to make her an alcoholic too.(p.361)
• I had given her *everything* a wife could ask for.(p.362)
• A relief, even though I dreaded it, feeling that this was the end of *everything*.(p.378)
• From the start I liked *everything* about the A.A. program.(p.380)
• I think that no one comes to A.A. until he's tried *everything* else.(p.384)
• As I grow in A.A., I realize that a person with as much self-will as I had, as hard a head and as diseased an ego, had to try *everything* that I could think of, butting my head against every stone wall before I was ready to come in.(p.384)
• I put my poor mother and father through agonies but, finally, I couldn't stand living with them and having them watch *everything* I did.(p.386)
• We had tried *everything*.(p.389)
• But Frank was frightened to death to give it to me, because I resented *everything* he said and did.(p.391)
• I wanted him to love me and make up to me for *everything*.(p.403)
• It hinted to me that *everything* was phony.(p.418)
• I smoked as much, tried to drink as much, and do *everything* they did, only more so.(p.423)
• I was failing in *everything*.(p.424)
• Beaches, parties, dances, movies – *everything*.(p.425)
• After going to school all day, working in the family drugstore all evening, and then studying until one or two in the morning, I would not be able to sleep soundly, with *everything* I had been studying going round in my head.(p.440)
• It was as if I had, rather than a Midas touch which turned *everything* to gold, a magnifying mind that magnified whatever it focused on.(p.450)
• Many tried *everything* -- hospitals, special treatments, sanitariums, asylums, and jails.(p.455)
• I owe *everything* to A.A. and God.(p.463)
• At noon on Christmas Day I called my family in New York, wished them a Merry Christmas, and assured them *everything* was fine with me.(p.467)
• I realized that I was trying to pin *everything* on an individual – not the book or the group or the Higher Power, or anything else.(p.472)
• When they saw me coming, they locked up the silverware and *everything* else of value.(p.478)
• I don't believe this program would work for me if I didn't get honest with myself about *everything*.(p.482)
• But when things became crucial, *everything* started going haywire and I started going haywire with them.(p.486)
• I would wake to find myself in some beat-up rooming house, where roaches were crawling over *everything*.(p.527)
• For always, over and above *everything* else, was the awfulness of the lack of meaning in life.(p.535)
• So did the waterboy on the high school football team attempt to revenge himself on the big brother who was the star quarterback; for I was the waterboy and my brother was the star quarterback, innocent of *everything* except the fact that he was a star quarterback.(p.537)
• If you will ask in prayer for *everything* you want for yourself to be given to them, you will be free.(p.552)
• This great experience that released me from the bondage of hatred and replaced it with love is really just another affirmation of the truth I know: I get *everything* I need in Alcoholics Anonymous – *everything* I need I get – and when I get what I need I invariably find that it was just what I wanted all the time.(p.553)
• The more I drank, the more I fantasized *everything*.(p.560)

everything's
• *Everything's* all wrong and the hell with it."(p.245)

everywhere
• These made their impressions *everywhere*.(p.xx)
• We, who are familiar with the symptoms, see large numbers of potential alcoholics among young people *everywhere*.(p.33)
• They see its significance *everywhere*.(p.69)
• His present views ought to prove exceptionally useful to business men *everywhere*.(p.136)

evidence
• One day I went to Washington to present some accounting *evidence* to a government bureau.(p.40)
• They piled on me heaps of *evidence* to the effect that an alcoholic mentality, such as I had exhibited in Washington, was a hopeless condition.(p.42)
• Everybody nowadays, believes in scores of assumptions for which there is good *evidence*, but no perfect visual proof.(p.48)
• It is not by chance we were given the power to reason, to examine the *evidence* of our senses, and to draw conclusions.(p.53)
• There is every *evidence* that women regain their health as readily as men if they try our suggestions.(p.104)

evident
• Is it not *evident* to all the rest of the players that these are the things he wants?(p.61)
• In the light of subsequent events it became *evident* that I took their advice far too literally, for, after some months of happy sobriety I drank again.(p.471)

evidently
• *Evidently* I had gone right back to the movie with a bottle, stayed there several hours and started home with no recollection of what had happened.(p.244)
• They seemed to be happy in their fashion, they and their little groups of supporters, but always pride of intellect stopped me from seeking what they *evidently* had.(p.256)
• The big thing was that these men were all sober and *evidently* had something I didn't have.(p.259)

evil
• It was an *evil* and corroding thread; the fabric of our existence was shot through with it.(p.67)
• I hope I have been able to impart to you, the reader, at least a bit of what I know; the joy of living, the irresistible power of divine love and its healing strength, and the fact that we, as sentient beings, have the knowledge to choose between good and *evil*, and, choosing good, are made happy.(p.543)

evils
• That my own innate selfishness and stubbornness are the *evils* which, if left unguarded, can drive me to alcohol.(p.473)

evolutionists
• My intellectual heroes, the chemists the astronomers, even the *evolutionists*, suggested vast laws and forces at work.(p.10)

evolve
• As we discovered the principles by which the individual alcoholic could live, so we had to *evolve* principles by which the A.A. groups and A.A. as a whole could survive and function effectively.(p.xix)

ex-alkie
• It took the help, understanding and wonderful companionship that was given so freely to me by my "*ex-alkie*" friends.(p.311)

ex-doctor
• Why, even a year ago, I had seen Howard, an *ex-doctor*, mooching a dime for a drink.(p.289)

ex-husband
• I had no feeling of security, and I knew that I had done a very stupid thing, so I went back to Texas and remarried my *ex-husband*.(p.386)

ex-incorrigible
• When I had served only eighteen months of my sentence, this *ex-incorrigible* was placed in honor grade.(p.461)

ex-problem
• But as *ex-problem* drinkers, we can say that his explanation makes good sense.(p.xxiv)
• But the *ex-problem* drinker who has found this solution, who is properly armed with facts about himself, can generally win the entire confidence of another alcoholic in a few hours.(p.18)
• Our very lives, as *ex-problem* drinkers, depend upon our constant thought of others and how we may help meet their needs.(p.20)
• As *ex-problem* drinkers, we smile at such a sally.(p.151)

ex-wife
• It was my *ex-wife*, and she said my twenty-seven-year-old son, who has completed his Marine Corps training and graduated from college, wanted to see me privately, was getting married in three months, and wanted me at the wedding.(p.462)

exact
• 5.Admitted to God, to ourselves, and to another human being the *exact* nature of our wrongs.(p.59)
• This requires action on our part, which, when completed, will mean that we have admitted to God, to ourselves, and to another human being the *exact* nature of our defects.(p.72)
• I was born in Europe, in Alsace to be *exact*, shortly after it had become German, and practically grew up with the "good Rhine wine" of song and story.(p.230)
• He and I had a large family -- six children, to be *exact*.(p.370)
• Honesty is the easiest word for me to understand because it is the *exact* opposite of what I've been doing all my life.(p.482)
• My personal definition, which I submit as applying only to myself (although everyone is welcome to it who wants it), includes every waking activity of the human being; to have a creative attitude towards things is a more *exact* meaning, to live and to deal with other human beings creatively, which to me means seeing the God in them, and respecting and worshipping this God.(p.535)
• A.A. has taught me that I will have peace of mind in *exact* proportion to the peace of mind I bring into the lives of other people, and it has taught me the true meaning of the admonition "happy are ye who know these things and do them."(p.551)

exactly
• The Twelve Steps that summarize the program may be called los Doce Pasos in one country, los Douze Etapes in another, but they trace *exactly* the same path to recovery that was blazed by the earliest members of Alcoholics Anonymous.(p.xxii)
• He has a positive genius for getting tight at *exactly* the wrong moment, particularly when some important decision must be made or engagement kept.(p.21)
• We asked him to tell us *exactly* how it happened.(p.36)
• We, who have been through the wringer, have to admit if we substituted alcoholism for jay-walking, the illustration would fit us *exactly*.(p.38)
• About half our original fellowship were of *exactly* that type.(p.44)
• Well, that's *exactly* what this book is about.(p.45)
• We did *exactly* the same thing with our lives.(p.64)
• Tell him *exactly* what happened to you.(p.93)
• We entered her house at *exactly* five o'clock and it was eleven fifteen when we left.(p.179)
• And I continued to drink, on and off then, until every dollar I had in the world was gone again and I was right back living at my sister's, getting my cigarettes by calling her grocer and telling him to put in a couple of cartons with her order, *exactly* as I had before I started to work at Max's.(p.202)
• For me, work was only a different means to the same end, to be able to do *exactly* what I wanted to do.(p.225)
• I don't remember much of what he said, but I did realize that here was another guy *exactly* like me; he had been in the same laughing academies and the same jails, known the same loss of jobs, same frustrations, same boredom and the same loneliness.(p.239)
• That is where I had my first drink and I still remem-

ber it, for every "first" drink afterwards did ***exactly*** the same trick -- I could feel it go right through every bit of my body and down to my very toes.(p.241)
• We drank with ***exactly*** the same accord that we finally accepted A.A.(p.265)
• It is bound to be rough, because who can say ***exactly*** how much of that green blood -- commonly known as money -- was dissipated on dissipation?(p.396)
• In the garage, I would put the needle in my vein and then try to figure out ***exactly*** how much medication to inject to overcome the pep pills while adding to the sleeping pills while ignoring the tranquilizers, in order to get just enough to be able to pull out the needle, jerk the tourniquet, throw it in the car, slam the car door shut, run down the hall, and fall in bed before I fell asleep.(p.442)
• When I am disturbed, it is because I find some person, place, thing, or situation -- some fact of my life -- unacceptable to me, and I can find no serenity until I accept that person, place, thing, or situation as being ***exactly*** the way it is supposed to be at this moment.(p.449)
• When I came back, I told the priest, the Chaplain of the place, ***exactly*** what I thought of him and he didn't like it.(p.517)
• The Commanding Officer only spoke to me when he wanted to tell me ***exactly*** who I was and what I was and how little I counted in the scheme of things and how glad he would be if I went away.(p.520)
• I thought I knew ***exactly*** what I wanted out of life and I thought I knew ***exactly*** how to get it.(p.545)

exaggerated
• Perhaps your husband has been living in that strange world of alcoholism where everything is distorted and ***exaggerated***.(p.108)
• The alcoholic has them to an ***exaggerated*** degree.(p.380)

exalted
• In my mind's eye, I played and replayed scenes in which I was plucked magically from the bar where I stood nursing a drink, and was instantly ***exalted*** to some position of power and prestige.(p.560)

exam
• My last ***exam*** and an easy one.(p.499)
• Now back to the ***exam***.(p.499)

examination
• The next day, they called me in for an ***examination***, and the doctor wouldn't let me continue working and pardoned me from the plant for ten days because he said my eye had been injured.(p.205)
• The judge said that if she felt that way he would confine me for thirty days' ***examination*** and observation.(p.492)

examinations
• We have spent thousands of dollars for ***examinations***.(p.73)
• When I went in to write the ***examinations***, my hand trembled so I could not hold a pencil.(p.174)
• This experience sent me to law school where I went at night and which course I completed in less than three years, taking the highest state bar ***examinations*** and passing them.(p.212)

examine
• It is not by chance we were given the power to reason, to ***examine*** the evidence of our senses, and to draw conclusions.(p.53)
• One more suggestion: Whether the family has spiritual convictions or not, they may do well to ***examine*** the principles by which the alcoholic member is trying to live.(p.130)

examined
• I am ***examined*** for the draft and pass the physical test.(p.499)
• I think the Commanding Officer was rather tired of this particular chicken coming back to roost so often because he very soon wrote in to the medical authorities to tell them that they had to get me into hospital, to be thoroughly ***examined*** for drinking.(p.520)

example
• I have had many men who had, for ***example***, worked a period of months on some problem or business deal which was to be settled on a certain date, favorable to them.(p.xxvii)
• Despite the living ***example*** of my friend there remained in me the vestiges of my old prejudice.(p.12)
• Our first ***example*** is a friend we shall call Jim.(p.35)
• We have numerous theories, for ***example***, about electricity.(p.48)
• They arise out of ourselves, and the alcoholic is an extreme ***example*** of self-will run riot, though he usually doesn't think so.(p.62)
• We were usually as definite as this ***example***:(p.65)
• He may be an ***example*** of the truth that faith alone is insufficient.(p.93)
• For ***example***, we know of situations in which the alcoholic or his wife have had love affairs.(p.124)
• Here, for instance, is a typical ***example***: An officer of one of the largest banking institutions in America knows I no longer drink.(p.138)
• He may, for ***example***, reveal that he has padded his expense account or that he has planned to take your best customers away from you.(p.145)
• The ***example*** which they and Bill W., whose visits to Akron were fairly frequent, set me of service to their fellow men imbued me with a great desire to emulate them.(p.281)
• For ***example***, we are told in A.A. that we cannot afford resentments and self-pity, so we learn to avoid these festering mental attitudes.(p.560)

examples
• In fact I was afraid to try it for fear that I would wind up like many ***examples*** I had seen of excessive drinking in the Army.(p.374)

exams
• After much argument they allowed me to return and take my ***exams***, all of which I passed creditably.(p.173)
• Coming up to final ***exams*** I went on a particularly strenuous spree.(p.174)
• Final ***exams*** of my Senior year and I may somehow graduate.(p.499)

exasperated
• When the policeman released me to my stupefied and ***exasperated*** friend at four in the morning, I went to my traveling bag and groped until I found -- well, let the officer speak: "Ah," said the policeman, "he's got anuder pair, t'ank God!"(p.538)

exceed
• From a single member in the Chicago area, commuting to Akron, we now ***exceed*** six thousand.(p.295)

exceedingly
• The doctor proved to be able and ***exceedingly*** anxious to adopt any workable method of handling the situation.(p.163)

excelled
• He said the alcoholic seemed to possess a native acuteness and usually ***excelled*** in his field, regardless of environmental or educational advantages.(p.308)

excellent
• His moral teaching -- most ***excellent***.(p.11)
• The differences between my father and my sisters, who were school teachers, made an ***excellent*** environment for the type of child I was -- that is, slick and cute enough to take advantage of any adult quarrel.(p.210)
• How can a person with a fine family, an attractive home, an ***excellent*** position and high standing in an important city become an alcoholic?(p.373)

except
• Then there are types entirely normal in every respect ***except*** in the effect alcohol has upon them.(p.xxviii)
• Never was I to pray for myself, ***except*** as my requests bore on my usefulness to others.(p.13)
• That the man who is making the approach has had the same difficulty, that he obviously knows what he is talking about, that his whole deportment shouts at the new prospect that he is a man with a real answer, that he has no attitude of Holier Than Thou, nothing whatever ***except*** the sincere desire to be helpful; that there are no fees to pay, no axes to grind, no people to please, no lectures to be endured -- these are the conditions we have found most effective.(p.18)
• He is often perfectly sensible and well balanced concerning everything ***except*** liquor, but in that respect he is incredibly dishonest and selfish.(p.21)
• He is an intelligent man, normal so far as we can see, ***except*** for a nervous disposition.(p.35)
• ***Except*** in a few rare cases, neither he nor any other human being can provide such a defense.(p.43)
• 9.Made direct amends to such people wherever possible, ***except*** when to do so would injure them or others.(p.59)
• No beer or liquor was sold in the neighborhood, ***except*** at the State liquor agency where perhaps one might procure a pint if he could convince the agent that he really needed it.(p.171)
• This resolution I kept steadfastly for the next forty years, ***except*** when circumstances made it seem unwise to absent myself.(p.172)
• Every company in the country, ***except*** Firestone, was reorganized at that time.(p.197)
• He had no desire to know anything, ***except*** whether I was definite about my desire to quit drinking.(p.235)
• Well, there I was, willing to try it, but I didn't know how, ***except*** in a vague way.(p.236)
• At this school we had Bible readings before each meal, and church services four times on Sunday, and I became so rebellious at this that I swore I would never join or go to any church ***except*** for weddings or funerals.(p.240)
• During that first week-end I decided to stay in New York and take all they gave out with, ***except*** the "God stuff."(p.246)
• I stayed sober for four years ***except*** for a one-night carousal in Chicago.(p.253)
• I stayed sober during the trip ***except*** for an occasional bottle of beer because funds barely met expenses.(p.255)
• I wanted to do nothing ***except*** what it pleased me to do when I wanted to do it.(p.256)
• Here was a man with essentially the same outlook on life, ***except*** that he had done something about it.(p.290)
• The big A.A. book had not been written and there was no literature ***except*** various religious pamphlets.(p.291)
• Heartsickness, shame, and fear, fear bordering on panic, and no complete escape any longer ***except*** in oblivion.(p.306)
• Some of us struggle with these people because we know that they are really very sick, but we also know that short of some miracle, we are not going to help them ***except*** temporarily, and that they will inevitably get worse and worse until one of two things happens.(p.308)
• Not only were they at peace with themselves, but they were getting a kick out of life such as one seldom encounters, ***except*** in the very young.(p.310)
• I noticed that I was avoiding all my social friends ***except*** for my bridge.(p.324)
• I never thought I could be useful to anyone ***except*** my husband and my children and perhaps a few friends.(p.326)
• I gave them everything, ***except*** the greatest thing in the world, and that is peace of mind.(p.351)
• So I went to her and said, "There's only one thing I want in my whole life, and I don't want any commendation; I don't want any credit; I don't want anything from you or Janey for the rest of your life ***except*** one thing; and that is, the opportunity to do anything you want always, and I would like to start off by doing the dishes."(p.351)
• And the psychiatrist has had thousands of couches, and has put you and me on them many, many times, but he hasn't helped us very much, though he has tried hard; and we owe the clergy and the doctor and the psychiatrist a deep debt of gratitude, but they haven't helped our alcoholism, ***except*** in a rare few instances.(p.352)
• I knew he was right, ***except*** for that last statement.(p.371)
• For some reason I can't remember, it finally dawned on me that I had a problem, and yet nobody was very critical about it ***except*** my family, and that was only because I decided, after seven years of marriage, that I would divorce my husband.(p.386)
• ***Except*** for one short slip, during the first eight months, which was an angry "the world can't do this to me" reaction to a personal tragedy in my life, I have been sober for twelve years.(p.416)
• Fear, love of dentistry, and an imitation of my father's periodic drinking pattern took me through dental college soberly, ***except*** for the few parties and vacations in those four years.(p.419)
• I would rather have stayed in jail ***except*** I didn't like bologna and cold potatoes for breakfast.(p.425)
• They were doing very well -- at least a fifth apiece a day, ***except*** on dad's days off when they did some serious drinking.(p.425)
• I seldom left the base any more ***except*** once in a while when I felt the need of talking to some girl.(p.427)
• I owe no one -- ***except*** A.A.(p.431)
• And Frank did set me up for a meeting every night ***except*** Friday, when he thought he might have a date with his girl friend.(p.447)
• What else can I do ***except*** what I have always done in the past? -- act as my old self and return to prison.(p.458)
• They were always there because of a nervous breakdown, or for a "rest cure" -- any reason ***except*** because of drinking.(p.471)
• Mind you, I had absolutely nothing to show for that eighteen years, ***except*** a beat-up car that I hadn't even paid for, but I was doing all right.(p.478)
• About that time I had lost practically all my property ***except*** the place we were living in.(p.487)
• I stayed there just long enough to work up a real good resentment against the doctor in charge, who I didn't think was doing anything at all ***except*** collect-

ing fees, and I left there fully determined that I'd never put myself in the power of medical people again.(p.521)
• But then one good doctor told me there was nothing wrong with me *except* drinking too much.(p.528)
• So did the waterboy on the high school football team attempt to revenge himself on the big brother who was the star quarterback; for I was the waterboy and my brother was the star quarterback, innocent of everything *except* the fact that he was a star quarterback.(p.537)
• I went on the wagon, with no outside help and with no real difficulty – *except* that I didn't enjoy life without drinking.(p.557)
• Four -- Each group should be autonomous *except* in matters affecting other groups or A.A. as a whole.(p.564)
• The Episcopal magazine, The Living Church, observes editorially: "The basis of the technique of Alcoholics Anonymous is the truly Christian principle that a man cannot help himself *except* by helping others.(p.574)

exception
• He said to the doctor, "Is there no *exception*?"(p.27)
• But the actual or potential alcoholic, with hardly an *exception*, will be absolutely unable to stop drinking on the basis of self-knowledge.(p.39)
• There is an important *exception* to the foregoing.(p.108)
• I looked around me at people who seemed happy and tried to analyze their happiness, and it seemed to me that without *exception* these people had something or somebody they loved very much.(p.546)

exceptional
• An *exceptional* man, he remained bone dry for twenty-five years and retired at the age of fifty-five, after a successful and happy business career.(p.32)
• Here were three *exceptional* men lost to this world because I did not understand alcoholism as I do now.(p.137)
• After I came in I found I wasn't an *exceptional* drunk.(p.512)

exceptionally
• His present views ought to prove *exceptionally* useful to business men everywhere.(p.136)

exceptions
• *Exceptions* to cases such as yours have been occurring since early times.(p.27)
• By every form of self-deception and experimentation, they will try to prove themselves *exceptions* to the rule, therefore nonalcoholic.(p.31)
• Though there may be justifiable *exceptions*, and though we wish to lay down no rule of any sort, we have often found this the best course to take.(p.81)
• With few *exceptions*, our book thus far has spoken of men.(p.104)
• There are *exceptions*.(p.114)
• The *exceptions* are few.(p.148)
• With few *exceptions* our members find that they have tapped an unsuspected inner resource which they presently identify with their own conception of a Power greater than themselves.(p.569)

excerpts
• Following are *excerpts* from the comments of doctors present at the annual meeting of the Medical Society of the State of New York where a paper on A.A. was read:(p.571)

excess
• If you cooperate, rather than complain, you will find that his *excess* enthusiasm will tone down.(p.119)
• We think we can drink to *excess* without anyone knowing it.(p.376)

excessive
• I soon discovered that a couple of drinks would alleviate my gastric distress, at least for a few hours at a time, so it was not at all difficult for me to return to my former *excessive* indulgence.(p.174)
• Lucky because my *excessive* drinking never got me in jail, or hospitalized, nor did it ever cost me a job.(p.356)
• In fact I was afraid to try it for fear that I would wind up like many examples I had seen of *excessive* drinking in the Army.(p.374)
• A year later, while we were on a vacation trip she packed up to go home because of my *excessive* drinking, and I talked her out of it with the promise I would go on the wagon for at least a year.(p.377)
• My life had become unmanageable due to the *excessive* use of alcohol.(p.515)
• In this atmosphere the alcoholic often overcomes his *excessive* concentration upon himself.(p.572)

excessively
• Golf, hunting and fishing were now merely excuses to drink *excessively*.(p.375)

exchange
• Abruptly in October 1929 hell broke loose on the New York stock *exchange*.(p.4)
• My old manner of life was by no means a bad one, but I would not *exchange* its best moments for the worst I have now.(p.43)

exchanged
• The next morning I carried another prescription to this man's house and *exchanged* it for the bottle his wife had.(p.489)

exchequers
• I knew everyone would buy a few bottles, or cases, of liquor as their *exchequers* permitted, and that it would soon be gone.(p.175)

excited
• I would get wildly *excited* and look forward to another night of drinking.(p.408)
• I planted my first flower garden this year and am actually *excited* to see the results.(p.481)
• If someone had told me last year that I would be *excited* about gardening this year, I would have said he was off his rocker.(p.481)
• She does not get *excited*.(p.507)

excitement
• I was part of life at last, and in the midst of the *excitement* I discovered liquor.(p.1)
• We are then in much less danger of *excitement*, fear, anger, worry, self-pity, or foolish decisions.(p.88)
• I seemed to react by developing a streak of varying meanness, which would cause me to do things to create *excitement* and to get attention.(p.211)
• For greater freedom and *excitement* I went abroad to live.(p.225)
• After my very first drink -- a tiny glass of sherry my father gave me to celebrate the New Year when I was thirteen -- I went up to bed, dizzy with exhilaration and *excitement*, and I prayed I wouldn't drink any more!(p.554)

exciting
• Our Society then entered a fearsome and *exciting* adolescent period.(p.xviii)
• Perhaps he is having a secret and *exciting* affair with "the girl who understands."(p.81)
• How *exciting* to learn the inward mysteries that govern the behavior of people, how wonderful to know, at last, all about myself!(p.434)

exclaimed
• Many of us *exclaimed*, "What an order!(p.60)

excluded
• It was thought that no alcoholic man or woman could be *excluded* from our Society; that our leaders might serve but never govern; that each group was to be autonomous and there was to be no professional class of therapy.(p.xix)

exclusive
• It was fun to carom around the *exclusive* course which had inspired such awe in me as a lad.(p.4)
• To us, the Realm of Spirit is broad, roomy, all inclusive; never *exclusive* or forbidding to those who earnestly seek.(p.46)

excruciating
• There are no easy ways to sober up, but that's the most *excruciating*.(p.389)

excuse
• But there was always the curious mental phenomenon that parallel with our sound reasoning there inevitably ran some insanely trivial *excuse* for taking the first drink.(p.37)
• The story he told is most instructive, for here was a chap absolutely convinced he had to stop drinking, who had no *excuse* for drinking, who exhibited splendid judgment and determination in all his other concerns, yet was flat on his back nevertheless.(p.40)
• But we must not use this as a mere *excuse* to postpone.(p.75)
• We don't use this as an *excuse* for shying away from the subject of God.(p.77)
• Asked why they commenced to drink again, they would reply with some silly *excuse*, or none.(p.107)
• He will use that as an *excuse* to drink more.(p.111)
• More and more I formed the habit of doing some of my business in the speakeasy, and after a time I did not need that as an *excuse*.(p.233)
• Then I would send an *excuse* of illness.(p.299)
• It only became another *excuse* to drink.(p.354)
• I didn't particularly like it, but I loved the effects, and managed for the next twenty-five years to drink anything and everything, either handed to me or purchased, at the slightest *excuse*.(p.357)
• I went back to my group meetings, but not wholeheartedly, and I often skipped them with the *excuse* that I was too tired.(p.364)
• We rationalize and *excuse* our conduct beyond all reason.(p.376)
• But the feeling was a crutch, an *excuse*.(p.534)
• I had never had a child and this had been a satisfactory *excuse* many times for my drinking.(p.548)

excused
• Even obvious intoxication is *excused* by younger people as something "he's earned the right to do," and they say, "After all, who's he hurting?"(p.330)

excuses
• Sometimes these *excuses* have a certain plausibility, but none of them really makes sense in the light of the havoc an alcoholic's drinking bout creates.(p.23)
• Some drinkers have *excuses* with which they are satisfied part of the time.(p.23)
• In a weak moment he may take your dislike of his high-stepping friends as one of those insanely trivial *excuses* to drink.(p.120)
• Long experience with alcoholic *excuses* naturally arouses suspicion.(p.146)
• I used to make *excuses* to try and get George off the wagon.(p.325)
• Golf, hunting and fishing were now merely *excuses* to drink excessively.(p.375)
• The next steps were bottle hiding, and *excuses* for trips in order to drink without restraint.(p.375)
• I was too busy devising *excuses* to be out with drinking pals.(p.376)
• In fact, sometimes they served as good *excuses* to drink more, to forget.(p.465)
• It's time to stop finding *excuses* for drinking and getting into trouble, because now there is a way out, and if you want what we have, try coming around and giving the program a chance.(p.530)
• It had provided me with *excuses* for my lack of education, my marital failures, personal failures, inadequacy, and of course, my alcoholism and, though I really thought I had been willing to part with it, now I knew I was reluctant to let it go.(p.552)

executive
• My downfall cost the business community unknown thousands of dollars, for it takes real money to train a man for an *executive* position.(p.137)
• One day he told me about an *executive* of the same bank who, from his description, was undoubtedly alcoholic.(p.138)
• After reading this book, a junior *executive* can go to such a man and say approximately this, "Look here, Ed.(p.147)
• Your junior *executive* may not agree with the contents of our book.(p.148)

executives
• If your organization is a large one, your junior *executives* might be provided with this book.(p.147)

exempt
• My job was to make out the guard schedules and thus I was *exempt* from ordinary recruit training activities.(p.425)

exercise
• The *exercise* of an option brought in more money, leaving us with a profit of several thousand dollars for that year.(p.3)
• Hydrotherapy and mild *exercise* helped much.(p.7)
• Here are some of the methods we have tried: Drinking beer only, limiting the number of drinks, never drinking alone, never drinking in the morning, drinking only at home, never having it in the house, never drinking during business hours, drinking only at parties, switching from scotch to brandy, drinking only natural wines, agreeing to resign if ever drunk on the job, taking a trip, not taking a trip, swearing off forever (with and without a solemn oath), taking more physical *exercise*, reading inspirational books, going to health farms and sanitariums, accepting voluntary commitment to asylums -- we could increase the list ad infinitum.(p.31)
• We can *exercise* our will power along this line all we wish.(p.85)
• I never left the church, but I was a fringe member, and the thought simply never occurred to me that through the *exercise* of what I had I might find the answer to my problem, simply because I wouldn't admit that I had a problem.(p.214)
• I began to read the Bible daily and to go over a simple devotional *exercise* as a way to begin each day.(p.259)

exercised
• Naturally, what little restraint I had *exercised* before

was gone now, and my drinking became worse.(p.199)
• The amount of will power *exercised* to control my drinking during working hours, diverted into a constructive channel, would have made me President, and the thing that made the will power possible was the knowledge that as soon as my day was finished I could drink myself into oblivion.(p.548)

exercising
• I felt I had every right to be self-confident, that it would be only a matter of *exercising* my will power and keeping on guard.(p.40)

exert
• He decides to *exert* himself more.(p.61)
• Since the home has suffered more than anything else, it is well that a man *exert* himself there.(p.127)

exhausted
• My wife began to work in a department store, coming home *exhausted* to find me drunk.(p.4)
• At midnight he came home *exhausted,* but very happy.(p.156)
• Visits from friends which lasted over fifteen minutes *exhausted* me.(p.275)
• Those three weeks left me completely *exhausted* and I had to return to Akron for three more months of rest.(p.282)
• This gave me the freedom to do A.A. work, and to rest for periods of two or three days when I became too *exhausted* to carry on.(p.283)
• I was too weak and *exhausted* to even try to throw myself out of the car.(p.467)
• I feel *exhausted.*(p.500)

exhaustion
• As animals on a treadmill, we have patiently and wearily climbed, falling back in *exhaustion* after each futile effort to reach solid ground.(p.107)
• Back to the big city, for another year of precarious living, paid for largely by one or two friends I still had not milked dry or worn to *exhaustion* with demands on their bounty.(p.540)

exhibit
• You will be most successful with alcoholics if you do not *exhibit* any passion for crusade or reform.(p.95)
• He may demand that the family find God in a hurry, or *exhibit* amazing indifference to them and say he is above worldly considerations.(p.128)

exhibited
• The story he told is most instructive, for here was a chap absolutely convinced he had to stop drinking, who had no excuse for drinking, who *exhibited* splendid judgment and determination in all his other concerns, yet was flat on his back nevertheless.(p.40)
• They piled on me heaps of evidence to the effect that an alcoholic mentality, such as I had *exhibited* in Washington, was a hopeless condition.(p.42)

exhilarating
• Drink was taking an important and *exhilarating* part in my life.(p.3)

exhilaration
• Probably only a few readers of this story will be able, from personal experiences of their own, to understand the *exhilaration* and sense of accomplishment which I felt after finishing this seemingly simple assignment.(p.276)
• There was the same reward — *exhilaration* at a mission accomplished.(p.283)
• After my very first drink – a tiny glass of sherry my father gave me to celebrate the New Year when I was thirteen -- I went up to bed, dizzy with *exhilaration* and excitement, and I prayed I wouldn't drink any more!(p.554)

exile
• No doubt I had been an *exile* too long -- I should go home to America.(p.226)

exist
• It does not *exist* for us.(p.85)
• It has made me understand that I must be one of my world, that I cannot *exist* in any happiness as a rebel by myself.(p.524)

existed
• I have never seen one single case recover, where that state of mind *existed* to the extent that it does in you."(p.27)
• However, due to financial difficulties the whole printing was, for a while, held up and the book received no publicity, nor, of course, was it available in the stores, even if one knew it *existed.*(p.307)
• I bear a few scars on my face from these fights, which I always lost, because the "stick" *existed* only in my mind.(p.537)

existence
• I was soon to be catapulted into what I like to call the fourth dimension of *existence.*(p.8)
• We have found much of heaven and we have been rocketed into a fourth dimension of *existence* of which we had not even dreamed.(p.25)
• As soon as we admitted the possible *existence* of a Creative Intelligence, a Spirit of the Universe underlying the totality of things, we began to be possessed of a new sense of power and direction, provided we took other simple steps.(p.46)
• Once confused and baffled by the seeming futility of *existence* they show the underlying reasons why they were making heavy going of life.(p.50)
• Did not these feelings, after all, determine the course of our *existence*?(p.54)
• It was an evil and corroding thread; the fabric of our *existence* was shot through with it.(p.67)
• If newcomers could see no joy or fun in our *existence,* they wouldn't want it.(p.132)
• The most satisfactory years of your *existence* lie ahead.(p.152)
• I had never doubted the *existence* of the Supreme Being, but now I began to absent myself from my church where I had formerly been a member of the choir.(p.234)
• All sorts were represented and their relation of experiences and how they had found the only remedy, added to their human *existence* as sober men, laid the foundation of a very necessary faith.(p.258)
• A night or so a week in a joint, and a party or so a week at home or with friends, along with a little lone drinking, soon had me preparing for the *existence* of a top flight drunkard.(p.298)
• Maybe I could find my way out of this agonizing *existence.*(p.309)
• Happy, happy senior-citizen *existence*!(p.329)
• For myself, I have an absolute proof of the *existence* of God.(p.350)
• This to me is the proof of the *existence* of a Somethingness greater than I am.(p.351)
• We lived a kind of seesaw *existence* in the early days.(p.369)
• Four years ago I had nothing but a jumbled, mad *existence.*(p.430)
• The only way *existence* was possible was through rationalizing every sober moment and drinking myself into complete oblivion as often as I could.(p.547)
• Indeed, I had to drink now to live, to cope with the demands of everyday *existence.*(p.556)
• As the sober days grew into sober months and then into sober years, a new and beautiful life began to emerge from the shambles of my former *existence.*(p.559)

existing
• Businessmen, traveling out of *existing* groups, were referred to these prospective newcomers.(p.xviii)
• In any case, I made myself believe that, so I just drifted about, *existing* on my retired pay, drinking, and living at home.(p.522)

exists
• Because this book has become the basic text for our Society and has helped such large numbers of alcoholic men and women to recover, there *exists* a sentiment against any radical changes being made in it.(p.xi)
• But there *exists* among us a fellowship, a friendliness, and an understanding which is indescribably wonderful.(p.17)
• Unfortunately a lot of prejudice *exists.*(p.89)

exonerating
• How could he possibly make a public statement *exonerating* his rival?(p.80)

expand
• Immediately on her return we began to have formal meetings once a week, in the autumn of 1939, and we have continued to do this and to *expand* ever since.(p.295)

expanded
• But the chief change was in the section of personal stories, which was *expanded* to reflect the Fellowship's growth.(p.xi)

expansion
• Akron was really on the boom in those days, 1919-1920; *expansion* was terrific.(p.198)
• As arrested alcoholics, we must have a program for living that allows for limitless *expansion.*(p.311)

expect
• Then only might I *expect* to receive.(p.13)
• You would *expect* him, if he were normal, to cut it out.(p.38)
• We must be entirely honest with somebody if we *expect* to live long or happily in this world.(p.73)
• Yet you must not *expect* too much.(p.118)
• They *expect* him to give them the nice times they used to have before he drank so much, and to show his contrition for what they suffered.(p.126)
• I could not *expect* to keep what I had gained unless I gave it away.(p.282)

expectant
• Without this proof the *expectant* purchaser would be forced to depart empty handed with none of what I later came to believe was the great panacea for all human ills.(p.171)

expectations
• In all these ways I've experienced, in ever growing measure and beyond all *expectations* and rewards, a joy which I had never before imagined.(p.395)
• Perhaps the best thing of all for me is to remember that my serenity is inversely proportional to my *expectations.*(p.452)
• The higher my *expectations* of Max and other people are, the lower is my serenity.(p.452)
• I can watch my serenity level rise when I discard my *expectations.*(p.452)
• I have to discard my "rights," as well as my *expectations,* by asking myself, "How important is it, really?(p.452)
• I must keep my magic magnifying mind on my acceptance and off my *expectations,* for my serenity is directly proportional to my level of acceptance.(p.452)
• Above all, I was suffering inner pain because my performance and my accomplishments in life failed to live up to my own *expectations* of myself.(p.557)
• Of course, the more I drank, the more unrealistic my *expectations* became and the poorer my performance, and the gap widened.(p.557)

expected
• In the doctor's judgment he was utterly hopeless; he could never regain his position in society and he would have to place himself under lock and key or hire a bodyguard if he *expected* to live long.(p.26)
• In many homes this is a difficult thing to do, but it must be done if any results are to be *expected.*(p.98)
• I still *expected* a plea for clemency, but these words came through the receiver: "I just wanted to tell you Paul jumped from a hotel window in Hartford last Saturday.(p.136)
• It is not to be *expected* that an alcoholic employee will receive a disproportionate amount of time and attention.(p.149)
• My home life is ideal and my business is as good as can be *expected* in these uncertain times.(p.180)
• For there were of course periods of clear realization of what I had become, attended by memories of what I had been, what I had *expected* to be.(p.224)
• I had been too self-sufficient to write a moral inventory, but I discovered in pointing out to the new man his wrong attitudes and actions that I was really taking my own inventory, and that if I *expected* him to change I would have to work on myself too.(p.249)
• Russ lived a year longer than they *expected* him to live, and in that year he was in bed for at least six months.(p.272)
• I don't know what I *expected,* but I most certainly didn't visualize a group of people talking about their drinking problems, making light of their personal tragedies and at the same time enjoying themselves.(p.378)
• I was desperately in earnest to follow through and understand what was *expected* of me as a member of A.A. and to take each Step of the Twelve as rapidly as possible.(p.382)
• To me this meant telling my associates that I had joined Alcoholics Anonymous; that I didn't know what was *expected* of me by A.A., but that whatever it was, it was the most important thing in life for me; that sobriety meant more to me than anything in this world.(p.382)
• I had accomplished all the right things that our society *expected,* and I had no real peace of mind nor gratitude.(p.418)

expecting
• Or am I *expecting* to steal a little vicarious pleasure from the atmosphere of such places?"(p.101)
• I don't know what sort of person I was *expecting,* but I was very agreeably surprised to find Mr. T. a poised, intelligent, well groomed and mannered gentleman.(p.309)
• Far from *expecting* praise for their deeds, they claimed the performance a privilege and insisted that they invariably received more than they gave.(p.310)
• But I have not seen yet that I should do some constructive acts of love without *expecting* any return.(p.505)

expects

• If he is not interested in your solution, if he *expects* you to act only as a banker for his financial difficulties or a nurse for his sprees, you may have to drop him until he changes his mind.(p.95)
• Your husband will see at once that he must redouble his spiritual activities if he *expects* to survive.(p.120)
• That was my lesson, that one could not take the moral inventory and then file it away; that the alcoholic has to continue to take inventory every day if he *expects* to get well and stay well.(p.293)

expedient

• Society can do anything it chooses to do with me when I am drunk and I can't lift a finger to stop it, for I forfeit my rights through the simple *expedient* of becoming a menace to myself and to the people around me.(p.549)

expel

• The principal had no alternative but to *expel* me.(p.424)
• He reported to the Headmaster and the Headmaster was going to *expel* me.(p.517)

expelled

• I went to five grade schools, primarily because I was *expelled* for my conduct, but I eventually graduated from the eighth grade.(p.211)

expenditures

• After a few more estimates as to income and *expenditures* for booze over a few sample years, taken at random, I conclude that this twenty per cent stayed fairly constant.(p.398)

expense

• At the end of it, my reports to Wall street procured me a position there and the use of a large *expense* account.(p.3)
• Threatens to fire me for drinking and padding my *expense* account.(p.65)
• We have no right to save our own skin at another person's *expense*.(p.74)
• Maybe it's only a petty offense such as padding the *expense* account.(p.78)
• This is a condition which, in ordinary life, would produce untold grief; there might be scandalous gossip, laughter at the *expense* of other people, and a tendency to take advantage of intimate information.(p.125)
• If you propose such a procedure to him, it may be necessary to advance the cost of treatment, but we believe it should be made plain that any *expense* will later be deducted from his pay.(p.143)
• He may, for example, reveal that he has padded his *expense* account or that he has planned to take your best customers away from you.(p.145)
• Then I started traveling, with the United States and Canada as my territory, and with so much freedom and with an unlimited *expense* account, I was soon drinking every night and kidding myself that it was all part of the job.(p.287)

expenses

• There were to be no fees or dues; our *expenses* were to be met by our own voluntary contributions.(p.xix)
• Peddling off my polish samples for *expenses*, I crawled back to New York a few days later in a very chastened frame of mind.(p.248)
• I stayed sober during the trip except for an occasional bottle of beer because funds barely met *expenses*.(p.255)
• I was never drunk on the job, never missed a day's work, was seldom rendered totally ineffective by a hangover and kept my liquor *expenses* well within my adequate budget.(p.433)

expensive

• In competent hands, this seldom takes long nor is it very *expensive*.(p.143)
• To wear *expensive* clothes, to have bartenders know what to serve me before I ordered, to be recognized by headwaiters and shown to the best table, to play gin rummy for high stakes with the insouciance of a riverboat gambler – these were the enduring values in life, I thought.(p.556)

experience

• Six months earlier, the broker had been relieved of his drink obsession by a sudden spiritual *experience*, following a meeting with an alcoholic friend who had been in contact with the Oxford Groups of that day.(p.xv)
• It was now time, the struggling groups thought, to place their message and unique *experience* before the world.(p.xvii)
• But out of this frightening and at first disrupting *experience* the conviction grew that A.A.'s had to hang together or die separately.(p.xix)
• Each day, somewhere in the world, recovery begins when one alcoholic talks with another alcoholic, sharing *experience*, strength, and hope.(p.xxii)
• Convincing testimony must surely come from the medical men who have had *experience* with the sufferings of our members and have witnessed our return to health.(p.xxiii)
• I say this after many years' *experience* as Medical Director of one of the oldest hospitals in the country treating alcoholic and drug addiction.(p.xxv)
• We feel, after many years of *experience*, that we have found nothing which has contributed more to the rehabilitation of these men than the altruistic movement now growing up among them.(p.xxvi)
• They are restless, irritable and discontented, unless they can again *experience* the sense of ease and comfort which comes at once by taking a few drinks -- drinks which they see others taking with impunity.(p.xxvi)
• This is repeated over and over, and unless this person can *experience* an entire psychic change there is very little hope of his recovery.(p.xxvii)
• About one year prior to this *experience* a man was brought in to be treated for chronic alcoholism.(p.xxix)
• He had come to pass his *experience* along to me -- if I cared to have it.(p.9)
• The real significance of my *experience* in the Cathedral burst upon me.(p.12)
• We shall bring to the task our combined *experience* and knowledge.(p.19)
• The *experience* of any alcoholic will abundantly confirm this.(p.23)
• Though *experience* had made him skeptical, he finished his treatment with unusual confidence.(p.26)
• This hope, however, was destroyed by the doctor's telling him that while his religious convictions were very good, in his case they did not spell the necessary vital spiritual *experience*.(p.27)
• Here was the terrible dilemma in which our friend found himself when he had the extraordinary *experience* which as we have already told you, made him a free man.(p.28)
• The distinguished American psychologist, William James, in his book "Varieties of Religious *Experience*," indicates a multitude of ways in which men have discovered God.(p.28)
• Surprisingly enough, we find such convictions no great obstacle to a spiritual *experience*.(p.28)
• Young people may be encouraged by this man's *experience* to think that they can stop, as he did, on their own will power.(p.33)
• This is a point we wish to emphasize and re-emphasize, to smash home upon our alcoholic readers as it has been revealed to us out of bitter *experience*.(p.39)
• It was his first *experience* of this kind, and he was much ashamed of it.(p.39)
• He was positive that his humiliating *experience*, plus the knowledge he had acquired, would keep him sober the rest of his life.(p.40)
• They cited cases out of their own *experience* by the dozen.(p.42)
• If that be the case, you may be suffering from an illness which only a spiritual *experience* will conquer.(p.44)
• To one who feels he is an atheist or agnostic such an *experience* seems impossible, but to continue as he is means disaster, especially if he is an alcoholic of the hopeless variety.(p.44)
• Our *experience* shows that you need not be disconcerted.(p.44)
• *Experience* has taught us that these are matters about which, for our purpose, we need not be worried.(p.50)
• In this book you will read the *experience* of a man who thought he was an atheist.(p.55)
• One night, when confined in a hospital, he was approached by an acholic who had known a spiritual *experience*.(p.56)
• But with the alcoholic, whose hope is the maintenance and growth of a spiritual *experience*, this business of resentment is infinitely grave.(p.66)
• These are facts out of our *experience*.(p.70)
• Trying to avoid this humbling *experience*, they have turned to easier methods.(p.72)
• We may have had certain spiritual beliefs, but now we begin to have a spiritual *experience*.(p.75)
• Reminding ourselves that we have decided to go to any length to find a spiritual *experience* we ask that we be given strength and direction to do the right thing, no matter what the personal consequences may be.(p.79)
• No matter how far down the scale we have gone, we will see how our *experience* can benefit others.(p.84)
• That is our *experience*.(p.85)
• Practical *experience* shows that nothing will so much insure immunity from drinking as intensive work with other alcoholics.(p.89)
• To watch people recover, to see them help others, to watch loneliness vanish, to see a fellowship grow up about you, to have a host of friends – this is an *experience* you must not miss.(p.89)
• Ministers and doctors are competent and you can learn much from them if you wish, but it happens that because of your own drinking *experience* you can be uniquely useful to other alcoholics.(p.89)
• Show him, from your own *experience*, how the queer mental condition surrounding that first drink prevents normal functioning of the will power.(p.92)
• Keep his attention focussed mainly on your personal *experience*.(p.92)
• Having had the *experience* yourself, you can give him much practical advice.(p.96)
• Our *experience* shows that this is not necessarily so.(p.101)
• To a person who has had *experience* with an alcoholic, this may seem like tempting Providence, but it isn't.(p.101)
• *Experience* shows that such an attitude is not helpful to anyone.(p.103)
• This *experience* may come to you.(p.116)
• Your husband will be the first to say it was your devotion and care which brought him to the point where he could have a spiritual *experience*.(p.118)
• But what we have related is based upon *experience*, some of it painful.(p.121)
• Henry Ford once made a wise remark to the effect that *experience* is the thing of supreme value in life.(p.124)
• In the first flush of spiritual *experience* they forgave each other and drew closer together.(p.124)
• With these we have had *experience* galore.(p.126)
• Assume on the other hand that father has, at the outset, a stirring spiritual *experience*.(p.128)
• We have found nothing incompatible between a powerful spiritual *experience* and a life of sane and happy usefulness.(p.130)
• Being possessed of a spiritual *experience*, the alcoholic will find he has much in common with these people, though he may differ with them on many matters.(p.131)
• Outsiders are sometimes shocked when we burst into merriment over a seemingly tragic *experience* out of the past.(p.132)
• Some of us had this *experience*, only to enjoy, in a few months, a finer intimacy than ever.(p.134)
• Still another *experience*: A woman's voice came faintly over long distance from Virginia.(p.137)
• Long *experience* with alcoholic excuses naturally arouses suspicion.(p.146)
• Should you wish them above all else, and be willing to make use of our *experience*, we are sure they will come.(p.153)
• When our friend related his *experience*, the man agreed that no amount of will power he might muster could stop his drinking for long.(p.155)
• A spiritual *experience*, he conceded, was absolutely necessary, but the price seemed high upon the basis suggested.(p.155)
• The two friends spoke of their spiritual *experience* and told him about the course of action they carried out.(p.157)
• He had begun to have a spiritual *experience*.(p.158)
• Many a man, yet dazed from his hospital *experience*, has stepped over the threshold of that home into freedom.(p.160)
• Impressed by those who visited him at the hospital, he capitulated entirely when, later, in an upper room of this house, he heard the story of some man whose *experience* closely tallied with his own.(p.160)
• Some of them may sink and perhaps never get up, but if our *experience* is a criterion, more than half of those approached will become fellows of Alcoholics Anonymous.(p.163)
• Of far more importance was the fact that he was the first living human with whom I had ever talked, who knew what he was talking about in regard to alcoholism from actual *experience*.(p.180)
• This Christian Science *experience* with a sobriety of fifteen months was in 1932.(p.203)
• During the latter part of the Christian Science *experience* I had gotten a job and was working at Firestone.(p.203)
• Not one *experience* registered with me.(p.208)
• As a draftsman, I worked for several large companies and gained a variety of *experience*.(p.211)
• This *experience* sent me to law school where I went at night and which course I completed in less than three years, taking the highest state bar examinations

and passing them.(p.212)
• The law school *experience* was not inspired by a desire to follow patent law, which has been my profession since: I went to law school primarily to learn the law of contracts following my own *experience* with litigation.(p.212)
• By the time I had completed law school I had picked up some *experience* in patent law, for I remained with the patent law firm and worked too in Washington where they found that I was a capable infringement investigator.(p.213)
• My *experience* in the hospital I considered to be terrific because Dr. Bob told me very quickly that medicine would have very little to do with it, outside of trying to restore my appetite for food.(p.217)
• There was one *experience* with Doc which made a terrific impression upon me.(p.218)
• That was an *experience* that I have never forgotten, and many times in my own work with A.A. newcomers I feel kind of guilty because I haven't done the same thing.(p.219)
• In my own *experience* I was so jubilant at finding myself sober, and I had so many things to catch up on, that a month went by before the thought even occurred to me.(p.219)
• It wasn't very long until my doctor friend sent me to tell another alcoholic what my *experience* had been.(p.237)
• I told our family doctor, an understanding man who gave hours of his time trying to help me, about this *experience*.(p.276)
• For me it was a wonderful *experience*.(p.309)
• In describing his suffering, his fears, his many years of groping for some answer to that which always seemed to remain unanswerable, he could have been describing me, and nothing short of *experience* and knowledge could have afforded him that much insight!(p.309)
• Instead of wanting to escape some perplexing problem, we *experience* a thrill of challenge in the opportunity it affords for another application of A.A. techniques, and we find ourselves tackling it with surprising vigor.(p.311)
• Spiritual *experience*?(p.334)
• Naturally, this *experience* didn't stop me.(p.354)
• My first spiritual *experience* in A.A. came quite early to me.(p.366)
• The drive to get ahead, to succeed, kept me too busy for many years to have any great *experience* with social life.(p.374)
• Finally our invitations became fewer and fewer as friends had more *experience* with my drinking pattern.(p.377)
• A "spiritual *experience*" to me meant attending meetings, seeing a group of people, all there for the purpose of helping each other; hearing the Twelve Steps and the Twelve Traditions read at a meeting, and hearing the Lord's Prayer, which in an A.A. meeting has such great meaning – "Thy will be done, not mine."(p.381)
• My *experience* has been active: three meetings a week, many tapes, many A.A. conferences, much work on the Twelve Steps, and much work with other alcoholics and their families.(p.420)
• I headed home for the most wonderful *experience* of all time -- meeting my "new" parents -- mom and dad looked different than I had pictured them.(p.428)
• Through A.A., we can *experience* freedom from self.(p.459)
• But the difference lay in the fact that the A.A.'s knew from their own bitter *experience*.(p.471)
• I have had *experience* in selling, collecting, and accounting, and am on my way up the ladder.(p.500)
• But I did understand this eventually, that these people had been through a lot of drinking *experience* just as I had, and had managed to make a job of it.(p.524)
• What is much more important to me, A.A. has taught me that through this simple program I may *experience* a change in this reaction pattern that will indeed allow me to "match calamity with serenity."(p.544)
• This great *experience* that released me from the bondage of hatred and replaced it with love is really just another affirmation of the truth I know: I get everything I need in Alcoholics Anonymous – everything I need I get – and when I get what I need I invariably find that it was just what I wanted all the time.(p.553)
• The "12 Traditions" of Alcoholics Anonymous are, we A.A.'s believe, the best answers that our *experience* has yet given to those ever urgent questions, "How can A.A. best function?" and, "How can A.A. best stay whole and so survive?"(p.563)
• Our A.A. *experience* has taught us that:(p.565)
• *Experience* has often warned us that nothing can so surely destroy our spiritual heritage as futile disputes over property, money, and authority.(p.566)
• The terms "spiritual *experience*" and "spiritual awakening" are used many times in this book which, upon careful reading, shows that the personality change sufficient to bring about recovery from alcoholism has manifested itself among us in many different forms.(p.569)
• Most of us think this awareness of a Power greater than ourselves is the essence of spiritual *experience*.(p.570)
• Most emphatically we wish to say that any alcoholic capable of honestly facing his problems in the light of our *experience* can recover, provided he does not close his mind to all spiritual concepts.(p.570)
• Dr. John F. Stouffer, Chief Psychiatrist, Philadelphia General Hospital, citing his *experience* with A.A., said: "The alcoholics we get here at Philadelphia General are mostly those who cannot afford private treatment, and A.A. is by far the greatest thing we have been able to offer them.(p.572)

experienced

• One year later he called to see me, and I *experienced* a very strange sensation.(p.xxix)
• Many of us have *experienced* dad's elation.(p.128)
• They *experienced* a few distressing failures, but in those cases they made an effort to bring the man's family into a spiritual way of living, thus relieving much worry and suffering.(p.159)
• But this was a man who had *experienced* many years of frightful drinking, who had had most all the drunkard's experiences known to man, but who had been cured by the very means I had been trying to employ, that is to say the spiritual approach.(p.180)
• I *experienced* some of the pleasure of social drinking when I was sixteen.(p.305)
• I stayed on in Florida for three weeks, enjoying our reunion, a new found health and a deeper love than I had ever *experienced* before.(p.364)
• I wish I could tell you all that A.A. has done for me, all that I think and feel about A.A., but it's something that I have *experienced* and have never been able to put into words.(p.394)
• In all these ways I've *experienced*, in ever growing measure and beyond all expectations and rewards, a joy which I had never before imagined.(p.395)
• I *experienced* my first real guilt and shame.(p.404)
• When I went back to my hometown to go into private practice, I *experienced* another brief lull in my addiction to alcohol and drugs.(p.420)
• In the next half-year, I *experienced* two more esophageal hemorrhages, miraculously surviving each one by a hair.(p.558)
• All such representatives are to be guided in the spirit of service, for true leaders in A.A. are but trusted and *experienced* servants of the whole.(p.567)

experiences

• We think this account of our *experiences* will help everyone to better understand the alcoholic.(p.xiii)
• Perhaps I can best answer this by relating one of my *experiences*.(p.xxix)
• The good doctor now sees many men who have such *experiences*.(p.14)
• If hundreds of *experiences* have shown him that one drink means another debacle with all its attendant suffering and humiliation, why is it he takes that one drink?(p.22)
• The great fact is just this, and nothing less: That we have had deep and effective spiritual *experiences* which have revolutionized our whole attitude toward life, toward our fellows and toward God's universe.(p.25)
• Here and there, once in a while, alcoholics have had what are called vital spiritual *experiences*.(p.27)
• These are followed by forty-three personal *experiences*.(p.29)
• Yes, we of agnostic temperament have had these thoughts and *experiences*.(p.46)
• Tell him enough about your drinking habits, symptoms, and *experiences* to encourage him to speak of himself.(p.91)
• Another principle we observe carefully is that we do not relate intimate *experiences* of another person unless we are sure he would approve.(p.125)
• For an hour, the two friends told him about their drinking *experiences*.(p.157)
• I will not take space to relate all my hospital or sanitarium *experiences*.(p.177)
• But this was a man who had experienced many years of frightful drinking, who had had most all the drunkard's *experiences* known to man, but who had been cured by the very means I had been trying to employ, that is to say the spiritual approach.(p.180)
• Then he started to talk to me about his drinking *experiences*, what his drinking had cost him, how much he had drunk and where, things like that, and I remember I was quite bored because I had never seen the guy before and had no interest at all in what, where and when he drank.(p.208)
• I had all the usual *experiences* of the alcoholic, for I was certainly one by this time.(p.233)
• Enduring all the hangover hells that every alcoholic *experiences*, I made the usual resolutions.(p.256)
• All sorts were represented and their relation of *experiences* and how they had found the only remedy, added to their human existence as sober men, laid the foundation of a very necessary faith.(p.258)
• This was the beginning of an unending series of such *experiences*.(p.276)
• Probably only a few readers of this story will be able, from personal *experiences* of their own, to understand the exhilaration and sense of accomplishment which I felt after finishing this seemingly simple assignment.(p.276)
• A little more than fifteen years ago, through a long and calamitous series of shattering *experiences*, I found myself being helplessly propelled toward total destruction.(p.304)
• And, as the years go by, working together, sharing our *experiences* with one another, and also sharing a mutual trust, understanding and love – without strings, without obligation – we acquire relationships that are unique and priceless.(p.312)
• The seventeen who now tell their *experiences* answer that question.(p.315)
• It was the first of many such *experiences* that became the only cause of harsh words, tears and heartaches in an otherwise truly beautiful marriage.(p.361)
• We had always encouraged our children to bring their friends home at any time, but after a few *experiences* with a drunken father they eliminated home as a place to entertain friends.(p.376)
• Could I be an alcoholic without some of the hair-raising *experiences* I had heard of in meetings?(p.379)
• My work with other alcoholics has led me, day by day, into ever wider and richer *experiences*.(p.394)
• A young veteran tells how a few rough *experiences* pushed him into A.A. – and how he was therefore spared years of suffering.(p.422)
• I've had many spiritual *experiences* since I've been in the program, many that I didn't recognize right away, for I'm slow to learn and they take many guises.(p.551)
• Yet it is true that our first printing gave many readers the impression that these personality changes, or religious *experiences*, must be in the nature of sudden and spectacular upheavals.(p.569)
• Most of our *experiences* are what the psychologist William James calls the "educational variety" because they develop slowly over a period of time.(p.569)

experiencing

• He asked me to read the book "Alcoholics Anonymous," and then he wanted me to talk with a man who was *experiencing* success with his own arrestment.(p.308)

experiment

• The *experiment* of quitting for a period of time will be helpful, but we think we can render an even greater service to alcoholic sufferers and perhaps to the medical fraternity.(p.34)
• What sort of thinking dominates an alcoholic who repeats time after time the desperate *experiment* of the first drink?(p.35)
• The *experiment* went so well that I ordered another whiskey and poured it into more milk.(p.36)
• For the benefit of those experimentally inclined, I should mention the so-called beer *experiment*.(p.177)
• Of course, the result was very bad, and that ended the beer *experiment*.(p.178)
• About the time of the beer *experiment* I was thrown in with a crowd of people who attracted me because of their seeming poise, health, and happiness.(p.178)
• At the end of fifteen months, I tried the beer *experiment*.(p.203)
• I thought this was a good time to *experiment* with liquor.(p.364)

experimentally

• For the benefit of those *experimentally* inclined, I should mention the so-called beer experiment.(p.177)

experimentation

• By every form of self-deception and *experimentation*, they will try to prove themselves exceptions to the rule, therefore nonalcoholic.(p.31)

expert

• Doubtless you are curious to discover how and why, in the face of *expert* opinion to the contrary, we have recovered from a hopeless condition of mind and body.(p.20)
• Under the skilled guidance of an *expert* practitioner I wallowed in the world's individual and collective

mental agony.(p.434)

expertly

• Science could take my mind apart *expertly*, but it couldn't seem to put it together again.(p.435)

explain

• Many times we talk to a new man and watch his hope rise as we discuss his alcoholic problems and *explain* our fellowship.(p.45)
• Simply because it is impossible to *explain* what we see, feel, direct, and use, without a reasonable assumption as a starting point.(p.48)
• We read wordy books and indulge in windy arguments, thinking we believe this universe needs no God to *explain* it.(p.49)
• We *explain* to our partner what we are about to do and why we have to do it.(p.75)
• *Explain* that many are doomed who never realize their predicament.(p.92)
• At proper time and place *explain* to all your friends why alcohol disagrees with you.(p.102)
• Whenever possible, let your husband *explain*.(p.115)
• At this point, it might be well to *explain* alcoholism, the illness.(p.142)
• Why they should be subjected to the tortures we inflict upon them, I cannot *explain*.(p.178)
• I avoided them rather than *explain* why they weren't seeing me.(p.203)
• Whenever a situation arose that fast talk wouldn't *explain* away, I simply withdrew.(p.214)
• Had anyone undertaken to *explain* to me what the A.A. movement was, what its real function was, I probably would have been set back several years and I doubt if I would have survived at all.(p.216)
• It was simple, they said, and went on to *explain* to me in their own language the program of recovery and daily living which we know today as the Twelve Steps of A.A.(p.279)
• How I was able to discharge my duties at the office during those horrible mornings, I will never be able to *explain*.(p.299)
• Had I been able to *explain* to a psychiatrist the feeling of futility, loneliness and lack of purpose that had come with my deep sense of personal failure at this second divorce, I seriously doubt that the good doctor could have convinced me that my basic problem was a spiritual hunger, but A.A. has shown me this was the truth.(p.546)

explained

• Best of all, I met a kind doctor who *explained* that though certainly selfish and foolish, I had been seriously ill, bodily and mentally.(p.7)
• My incredible behavior in the face of a desperate desire to stop was *explained*.(p.7)
• When your prospect has made such reparation as he can to his family, and has thoroughly *explained* to them the new principles by which he is living, he should proceed to put those principles into action at home.(p.98)
• When you have carefully *explained* to such people that he is a sick person, you will have created a new atmosphere.(p.115)
• They *explained* their need and inquired if she had a first class alcoholic prospect.(p.156)
• He *explained* that he and a man from New York had a cure for alcoholism.(p.188)
• I *explained* to my sister that some of the people he was meeting with had been in hospitals.(p.205)
• In a few sentences he made God seem personal to me, *explained* Him as a being who was interested in me, the alcoholic, and that all I needed to do was to be willing to follow His way; that as long as I followed it I would be able to overcome my desire for liquor.(p.236)
• They went into a huddle and dad *explained* that he simply took my pants, shoes and money away, so that I could get no liquor and had to sober up.(p.288)
• However, he *explained* to me that he had been just such a rummy as I, only for a much longer period of time.(p.302)
• How I had arrived at this tragic impasse I could not have *explained* to anyone.(p.304)
• He further *explained* that alcohol was no respecter of sex or background, but that most of the alcoholics he had encountered had better than average minds and abilities.(p.308)
• It *explained* so much I had not understood about myself and, best of all, it promised recovery if I would do a few simple things and be willing to have the desire to drink removed.(p.309)
• In a few days an attorney called on me and *explained* that something would have to be done as she couldn't face returning to me as I was.(p.377)
• He now said that we had a physical allergy combined with a mental obsession, and he *explained* this so that I saw for the first time how this could be.(p.413)
• The girl had *explained* them to me four times, and I was too embarrassed to ask her again.(p.445)
• Vi was very kind and *explained* to the jury that I was basically a fine fellow and a good husband, but that I drank too much and that she thought I had lost my mind and felt that I should be committed to an asylum.(p.492)
• Since it was wartime, I *explained* to the somewhat startled shopkeeper that I had many friends in the service whom I was remembering with a watch.(p.532)
• No, it can best be *explained* in a little phrase I coined and sang to myself: "What happened to Bob?(p.532)

explaining

• Outline the program of action, *explaining* how you made a self-appraisal, how you straightened out your past and why you are now endeavoring to be helpful to him.(p.94)
• Cleaning up old scrapes, helping to settle family differences, *explaining* the disinherited son to his irate parents, lending money and securing jobs for each other, when justified -- these are everyday occurrences.(p.161)

explains

• It *explains* many things for which we cannot otherwise account.(p.xxiv)

explanation

• But as ex-problem drinkers, we can say that his *explanation* makes good sense.(p.xxiv)
• More baffling still, he could give himself no satisfactory *explanation* for his fall.(p.26)
• In the following chapter, there appears an *explanation* of alcoholism, as we understand it, then a chapter addressed to the agnostic.(p.28)
• After the sermon, he quietly got up and made an *explanation*.(p.80)
• By this time, with the doctor's *explanation*, the revelations contained in the book, and the hope-inspiring interview with Mr. T., I was ready and willing to go into the interior of the African jungles, if that was what it took, for me to find what these people had.(p.309)
• In meeting me casually, I don't think my strong belief in "The Man Upstairs" shows, but I have no other *explanation* for the many good things that have happened to me since I have been in A.A. -- they came to me from a Greater Power.(p.367)
• The *explanation* that alcoholism was a disease of a two fold nature, an allergy of the body and an obsession of the mind, cleared up a number of puzzling questions for me.(p.380)
• An alcoholic cannot accept the news that he's an alcoholic unless there is a meaningful *explanation* given, and an offer of help, such as you get in A.A.(p.406)
• After a day or two of grovelling remorse I'd come up with an *explanation*.(p.433)
• With no *explanation* at all, I was taken from my home in Florida to my grandparents' home in the middle west.(p.544)
• They suggested that I study the A.A. book and try to take the Twelve Steps according to the *explanation* in the Book, for it was their opinion that the application of these principles in our daily lives will get us sober and keep us sober.(p.550)

explicit

• Because the "long form" is more *explicit* and of possible historic value, it is also reproduced.(p.563)

explodes

• Sometimes he *explodes* over a trifle.(p.126)

exploits

• One instance comes to mind in which a malicious individual was always making friendly little jokes about an alcoholic's drinking *exploits*.(p.145)

explore

• Show any longshoreman a Sunday supplement describing a proposal to *explore* the moon by means of a rocket and he will say, "I bet they do it – maybe not so long either."(p.52)

explosion

• If the alcoholic tries to shield himself he may succeed for a time, but he usually winds up with a bigger *explosion* than ever.(p.101)

explosions

• I shall learn this after some more *explosions*.(p.506)

exposed

• My child was being *exposed* to all this.(p.408)
• For by now I had been *exposed* once to A.A., but I had treated it as a vaudeville and had taken friends to meetings so that they too could enjoy the fascination of the naked revelation of suffering and recovery.(p.539)

express

• We found that as soon as we were able to lay aside prejudice and *express* even a willingness to believe in a Power greater than ourselves, we commenced to get results, even though it was impossible for any of us to fully define or comprehend that Power, which is God.(p.46)
• If possible *express* a lack of hard feeling toward him.(p.142)
• Men who had liquor shipped in from Boston or New York by *express* were looked upon with great distrust and disfavor by most of the good townspeople.(p.171)
• The very simple program they advised me to follow was that I should ask to know God's will for me for that one day, and then, to the best of my ability, to follow that, and at night to *express* my gratefulness to God for the things that had happened to me during the day.(p.208)
• I can't *express* what A.A. meant to us during that year.(p.272)
• In the first year there were episodes such as kicking Priscilla in the shins, getting the lock changed on the desk in the A.A. Club, because I, as secretary, didn't want the Intergroup secretary "interfering," and taking an older woman member out to lunch for the *express* purpose of informing her that she was "a phony."(p.416)
• Two – For our group purpose there is but one ultimate authority – a loving God as He may *express* Himself in our group conscience.(p.564)
• 2. – For our group purpose there is but one ultimate authority -- a loving God as He may *express* Himself in our group conscience.(p.565)
• 10. – No A.A. group or member should ever, in such a way as to implicate A.A., *express* any opinion on outside controversial issues – particularly those of politics, alcohol reform, or sectarian religion.(p.567)
• Concerning such matters they can *express* no views whatever.(p.567)

expressed

• When the thought was *expressed* that there might be a God personal to me this feeling was intensified.(p.12)
• I *expressed* my entire willingness to approach these individuals, admitting my wrong.(p.13)
• The wording was, of course, quite optional so long as we *expressed* the idea, voicing it without reservation.(p.63)
• I had never heard of the remedy *expressed* in just this language.(p.236)

expresses

• Unless one's family *expresses* a desire to live upon spiritual principles we think we ought not to urge them.(p.83)

expressing

• We go to him in a helpful and forgiving spirit, confessing our former ill feeling and *expressing* our regret.(p.77)

expression

• The *expression* on the faces of the women, that indefinable something in the eyes of the men, the stimulating and electric atmosphere of the place, conspired to let him know that here was haven at last.(p.160)
• I heard for the first time an *expression* which I was to grow to loathe: "There is nothing organically wrong."(p.276)

expressions

• We see that these *expressions* refer to people whose reactions are very different from ours.(p.20)
• This applies, too, to other spiritual *expressions* which you find in this book.(p.47)
• Many times have I heard the above *expressions* since I have been in A.A., and many times I have had to reply "Definitely I am an alcoholic, and while it may be hard for you to believe, it is not hard for me, for I have learned many things about alcohol and myself that would, perhaps, be difficult for you to understand."(p.356)
• There are many short phrases and *expressions* in A.A. which make sound sense.(p.382)

extend

• As we left, and they were escorting us across the bridge into Wheeling, I, with great dignity and sarcasm, told them if their wives were ever visiting in Akron, and they, too, were looking for their route sign as I was, that I hoped I could *extend* to them the hospitality that had been shown to me in Bellaire.(p.264)

extended

• My migrations *extended* for over a year as

far west as Omaha.(p.253)
• Need I say that in a very short time I was walking along a prairie highway with arm *extended* and thumb pointed?(p.255)
• My drinking career *extended* from age eighteen to forty-three.(p.397)

extensive
• That discovery so intrigued me, that I stayed on that diet almost entirely for the balance of my *extensive* drinking life.(p.298)

extent
• These things were true to some *extent*, in fact, to a considerable *extent* with some of us.(p.xxiv)
• I have never seen one single case recover, where that state of mind existed to the *extent* that it does in you."(p.27)
• Whether such a person can quit upon a nonspiritual basis depends upon the *extent* to which he has already lost the power to choose whether he will drink or not.(p.34)
• To the precise *extent* that we permit these, do we squander the hours that might have been worth while.(p.66)
• Just to the *extent* that we do as we think He would have us, and humbly rely on Him, does He enable us to match calamity with serenity.(p.68)
• To some *extent* we have become God-conscious.(p.85)
• The entire family is, to some *extent*, ill."(p.122)
• To some *extent* this is already true.(p.162)
• It did help to certain *extent*, since I got in places where I could not obtain anything to drink, and so broke the habitual drinking.(p.183)
• She had not known the *extent* of my consumption.(p.333)
• I was intolerant of people who drank, particularly those who drank to an *extent* that interfered with on-the-job performance.(p.374)

external
• There was no material or *external* reason for this.(p.400)
• In the hospital, I hung on to the idea I'd had most of my life: that if I could just control the *external* environment, the internal environment would then be comfortable.(p.445)
• And life keeps getting simpler and easier as we try to reverse my old idea, by taking care of the internal environment via the Twelve Steps, and letting the *external* environment take care of itself.)(p.446)

extra
• I ordered a martini, *extra* dry.(p.194)
• But during a period of particular stress and strain about thirteen years ago, I resorted to alcohol in my home, alone, as a means of temporary release, as a means of getting a little *extra* sleep.(p.335)
• It's the last thing I ever heard him say, and I think there are some of us who, at times, try to read *extra* messages and complexities into the Steps.(p.395)
• This was fine, but it was just an *extra* dividend, for I'd made connections by this time and was buying a bottle a day from the cook.(p.426)
• Only, having found them, I threw them away, and ordered another *extra* dry martini.(p.533)

extra-curricular
• After high school came four years in one of the best colleges in the country where drinking seemed to be a major *extra-curricular* activity.(p.172)

extract
• It didn't say I had to finally live on skid row and drink bay rum, canned heat or lemon *extract*.(p.379)

extracted
• Wishing to be polite, though I felt very badly, I said, "Let's make the call," and *extracted* from my wife a promise that we would not stay over fifteen minutes.(p.179)

extractions
• On the day set for the *extractions*, on my way to the dentist's I felt a little nervous, so I had a couple of drinks, and after the teeth were out I was very nervous, so I had a few more.(p.466)

extraordinary
• These facts appear to be of extreme medical importance; because of the *extraordinary* possibilities of rapid growth inherent in this group they may mark a new epoch in the annals of alcoholism.(p.xxiii)
• Here was the terrible dilemma in which our friend found himself when he had the *extraordinary* experience which as we have already told you, made him a free man.(p.28)
• Haven't I been successful, haven't I accomplished *extraordinary* things in business?(p.245)
• It was therefore not *extraordinary* that I should shy away from any serious thought of marriage for a great many years after joining A.A.(p.286)
• *Extraordinary* people!(p.310)

extravagant
• Are these *extravagant* promises?(p.84)

extreme
• These facts appear to be of *extreme* medical importance; because of the extraordinary possibilities of rapid growth inherent in this group they may mark a new epoch in the annals of alcoholism.(p.xxiii)
• There had been no real infidelity, for loyalty to my wife, helped at times by *extreme* drunkenness, kept me out of those scrapes.(p.3)
• You may think this an *extreme* case.(p.37)
• They arise out of ourselves, and the alcoholic is an *extreme* example of self-will run riot, though he usually doesn't think so.(p.62)
• Then let his family or a friend ask him if he wants to quit for good and if he would go to any *extreme* to do so.(p.90)
• Some of us veered from *extreme* to *extreme*, ever hoping that one day our loved ones would be themselves once more.(p.105)
• After satisfying yourself that your man wants to recover and that he will go to any *extreme* to do so, you may suggest a definite course of action.(p.142)
• I had to go through *extreme* alcoholism to find my answer.(p.400)
• At a large party in Geneva, with people from many countries represented, the kind of party that is "protocol" in the *extreme*, I swayed, laughed hysterically, made naughty remarks in an unhushed voice, and was finally led from the scene.(p.406)

extremely
• Yet, as my record shows, I did become an *extremely* serious case.(p.182)
• My new duties were *extremely* confining and my liquor consumption began to increase.(p.298)
• Contact with this group was *extremely* important to him.(p.309)
• I was an *extremely* sensitive person and so self-conscious that I hurt all over.(p.385)
• My wife is *extremely* unhappy.(p.501)

extremes
• We admit we have some of these symptoms, but we have not gone to the *extremes* you fellows did, nor are we likely to, for we understand ourselves so well after what you have told us that such things cannot happen again.(p.38)
• Here we find human opinions running to *extremes* -- absurd *extremes*, perhaps.(p.68)
• Yet we do go to great *extremes* to provide each other with these very things, when such action is warranted.(p.98)
• They run to *extremes*.(p.125)

exultantly
• But for the next years, I worked hard and *exultantly* in A.A.(p.541)

eye
• We can look the world in the *eye*.(p.75)
• Understanding our work, he can do this with an *eye* to selecting those who are willing and able to recover on a spiritual basis.(p.162)
• The next day, they called me in for an examination, and the doctor wouldn't let me continue working and pardoned me from the plant for ten days because he said my *eye* had been injured.(p.205)
• And as I fumed helplessly and planned to get good and drunk and show them, my *eye* caught a sentence in the book lying open on my bed: "We cannot live with anger."(p.228)
• In my mind's *eye* I saw Broadway again and Tom Sharkey's bar; the roar of the subway was in my ears.(p.252)
• So I went to my wife and asked her, wasn't there something that she and I could do to somehow get together, and she turned on her heel and looked me squarely in the *eye*, and said, "You don't care anything about my problem," and I could have smacked her, but I said to myself, "Grab on to your serenity!"(p.351)
• My *eye* would be glued to that glass.(p.407)
• In my mind's *eye*, I played and replayed scenes in which I was plucked magically from the bar where I stood nursing a drink, and was instantly exalted to some position of power and prestige.(p.560)

eyes
• There was something about his *eyes*.(p.9)
• Scales of pride and prejudice fell from my *eyes*.(p.12)
• The outlines and the promise of the New Land had brought lustre to tired *eyes* and fresh courage to flagging spirits.(p.53)
• The expression on the faces of the women, that indefinable something in the *eyes* of the men, the stimulating and electric atmosphere of the place, conspired to let him know that here was haven at last.(p.160)
• I was graduated "summa cum laude" in the *eyes* of the drinking fraternity, but not in the *eyes* of the Dean.(p.172)
• Had blacked the *eyes* of two nurses, and now they had him strapped down tight.(p.188)
• I had run into him, and he looked real prosperous; his face and *eyes* looked clear and he started to compliment me on my good front and how well I looked, and I said, "I haven't had a drink for nine months."(p.201)
• Here, while in a hospital bed, men with clear *eyes*, happy faces, and a look of assurance and purposefulness about them, came to see me and told me their stories.(p.279)
• The scales had dropped from my *eyes* and I could see life in its proper perspective.(p.280)
• I shut my *eyes* and asked for help.(p.285)
• They would travel miles and stay up all night with someone they had never laid *eyes* on before and think nothing of it.(p.310)
• I couldn't look them straight in the *eyes*, although I was always a self-possessed brazen sort of person.(p.323)
• One said, "Don't feel that you are a martyr because you stopped drinking," and this hit me between the *eyes*.(p.346)
• The second one said, "Don't feel that you stop drinking for anyone other than yourself," and this hit me between the *eyes*.(p.346)
• A whole new world of happiness and love began to unfold before my *eyes*, a truly new way of living.(p.365)
• But somewhere during that time, I remembered going back on the bunk and crying my *eyes* out.(p.390)
• I took two or three drinks so my *eyes* could focus, and I could see that horrible picture of the awful drunk on the first page; he couldn't get the drink to his mouth, he had a towel around his hand and he needed a shave.(p.391)
• My *eyes* opened onto a hazy world.(p.422)
• I closed my *eyes* and tried to think.(p.422)
• I opened my *eyes* again and a shadow fell across the bed.(p.422)
• They had color in their faces, sparkle in their *eyes* and love in their hearts.(p.428)
• Last time in jail, I have two black *eyes*.(p.475)
• An ailment developed in one of my *eyes*, and I was transferred back to Sing Sing and operated upon.(p.509)
• A lot of the boys had tears in their *eyes*, they were so happy to be home.(p.513)
• I was taking Benzedrine and paraldehyde quite impartially during the day then, and by the time I arrived at my first A.A. meeting, I was pretty drunk and certainly doped up to the *eyes* and completely jittery.(p.523)
• Now I had gotten to the place where I would wake up with black *eyes* and not know where I got them, or wake up with a lot of money and not know where I got it.(p.528)

Ff

fabric

• It was an evil and corroding thread; the *fabric* of our existence was shot through with it.(p.67)

• We think the business *fabric* is shot through with a situation which might be helped by better understanding all around.(p.137)

facade

• The need to uphold a *facade* had been irksome.(p.328)

face

• My incredible behavior in the *face* of a desperate desire to stop was explained.(p.7)

• Doubtless you are curious to discover how and why, in the *face* of expert opinion to the contrary, we have recovered from a hopeless condition of mind and body.(p.20)

• To be doomed to an alcoholic death or to live on a spiritual basis are not always easy alternatives to *face*.(p.44)

• But after a while we had to *face* the fact that we must find a spiritual basis of life -- or else.(p.44)

• But his *face* falls when we speak of spiritual matters, especially when we mention God, for we have re-opened a subject which our man thought he had neatly evaded or entirely ignored.(p.45)

• In the *face* of collapse and despair, in the *face* of the total failure of their human resources, they found that a new power, peace, happiness, and sense of direction flowed into them.(p.50)

• When we became alcoholics, crushed by a self-imposed crisis we could not postpone or evade, we had to fearlessly *face* the proposition that either God is everything or else He is nothing.(p.53)

• As we felt new power flow in, as we enjoyed peace of mind, as we discovered we could *face* life successfully, as we became conscious of His presence, we began to lose our fear of today, tomorrow or the hereafter.(p.63)

• Though our decision was a vital and crucial step, it could have little permanent effect unless at once followed by a strenuous effort to *face*, and to be rid of, the things in ourselves which had been blocking us.(p.64)

• We must lose our fear of creditors no matter how far we have to go, for we are liable to drink if we are afraid to *face* them.(p.78)

• We may lose our position or reputation or *face* jail, but we are willing.(p.79)

• In thinking about our day we may *face* indecision.(p.86)

• Why sit with a long *face* in places where there is drinking, sighing about the good old days.(p.102)

• The foregoing pages (though addressed only to wives) indicate the problems such people may *face*.(p.121)

• We grow by our willingness to *face* and rectify errors and convert them into assets.(p.124)

• At the very beginning, the couple ought to frankly *face* the fact that each will have to yield here and there if the family is going to play an effective part in the new life.(p.131)

• I pointed out that I had had nothing to drink whatever for three years, and this in the *face* of difficulties that would have made nine out of ten men drink their heads off.(p.138)

• Momentarily we did -- then would come oblivion and the awful awakening to *face* the hideous Four Horsemen -- Terror, Bewilderment, Frustration, Despair.(p.151)

• He saw that he would have to *face* his problems squarely that God might give him mastery.(p.155)

• Hopelessness was written large on the man's *face* as he replied, "Oh, but that's no use.(p.157)

• When a few men in this city have found themselves, and have discovered the joy of helping others to *face* life again, there will be no stopping until everyone in that town has had his opportunity to recover -- if he can and will.(p.163)

• I had run into him, and he looked real prosperous; his *face* and eyes looked clear and he started to compliment me on my good front and how well I looked, and I said, "I haven't had a drink for nine months."(p.201)

• I had a broken nose, a fractured cheekbone, and was black from the lower part of my *face* up into my hair.(p.204)

• When I had been in the hospital ten days, Sister Ignatia, who has played such a part in the development of A.A. in this area, stuck her head in the door one morning and announced, looking at me quizzically, that they might be able to make something human out of my *face* after all.(p.205)

• I remember starting to city school, coming from a country school, and wanting so very, very much to be like the other girls and trying flour on my *face* for powder because I wasn't able to have any real powder.(p.261)

• He had a very peculiar look on his *face*, and he said, "He's coming."(p.263)

• After six months of sobriety I saw the picture in a different light: Detroit was the place I had to return to, not only because I must *face* the mess I had made there, but because it was there that I could be of the most service to A.A.(p.281)

• This office job brought me *face* to *face* with a problem which I had sidestepped all my adult life, lack of training.(p.284)

• Courage to *face* each day has replaced the fears and uncertainties of earlier years.(p.295)

• I couldn't *face* people.(p.323)

• I never could *face* it the next morning.(p.325)

• I couldn't go to one wine store and look the man honestly in the *face* and buy a bottle, as I used to do when I had parties and entertained and did normal drinking.(p.336)

• The fellowship I found in A.A. enabled me to *face* my problem honestly and squarely.(p.340)

• But when we come into A.A., we can *face* our problem honestly and openly.(p.340)

• Surrender to me has meant the ability to run my home, to *face* my responsibilities as they should be faced, to take life as it comes to me day by day, and work my problems out.(p.340)

• I do recall lying on a cold cement floor and shredding into little bits several pieces of stolen identification cards, and washing my *face* in the toilet bowl trying to sober up, and screaming hysterically while clinging to bars too high to see out of, and cursing everyone that came near me.(p.354)

• Neither of these circumstances was very helpful to my type since I had not learned to *face* realities.(p.358)

• I've had more problems but, thank God, I have had the teachings of A.A. with which to *face* them.(p.367)

• (In fact, every time I saw him he had a frown on his *face*.)(p.370)

• One night, a few weeks after joining the Fellowship, much to my surprise and delight I saw a familiar but no longer frowning *face*.(p.371)

• In a few days an attorney called on me and explained that something would have to be done as she couldn't *face* returning to me as I was.(p.377)

• Scared that my dress wasn't going to fit right, that the church wasn't going to be filled, that I'd fall flat on my *face* walking up the aisle; in fact, I was afraid I wasn't going to be a prima donna in the place where I should be.(p.385)

• The contempt and disgust that was in his *face* and thoughts!(p.391)

• The bartender, a tough Irishman, came around and "gave me the elbow," which means that he raised his elbow and smacked me in the *face*.(p.411)

• A.A. made it possible for me to *face* the consequences of my past actions.(p.420)

• I cut my hands, my *face*, my legs.(p.427)

• Today I think of life in terms of happiness, contentment, freedom from fear and despair, sane thinking, ability to *face* problems as they occur, the opportunity to help other alcoholics and to be decent.(p.430)

• My personality was stretched almost to splitting in the effort; schizophrenia stared me in the *face*, and one night I was in a suicidal despair.(p.435)

• Now I had to *face* up to the fact that knowledge of this sort, applied to my individual case, was not power.(p.435)

• Here was power to live to the end of any given day, power to have the courage to *face* the next day, power to have friends, power to help people, power to be sane, power to stay sober.(p.436)

• But, by the look on the psychiatrist's *face*, I could tell that it would really make him happy if I agreed.(p.446)

• He took the basketball and smashed me in the *face* with it.(p.484)

• When my mother opened the door, I almost fell in on my *face*.(p.510)

• Somehow or other I was coming *face* to *face* with myself, and I didn't like it.(p.513)

• I have not seen a black *face* but mine since I've been here, and if I didn't look in the mirror, I wouldn't know that I was black, because these people treat me as one of them, which I am.(p.530)

• I bear a few scars on my *face* from these fights, which I always lost, because the "stick" existed only in my mind.(p.537)

• I could not *face* the boy and youth I was in the reality of the contemptible man I had become.(p.540)

• The only reality I was able to *face* had been forced upon me by its very repetition -- I had to drink; and I didn't know there was anything in the world that could be done about it.(p.548)

• I couldn't *face* food.(p.558)

face-to-face

• Good generalship may decide that the problem be attacked on the flank rather than risk a *face-to-face* combat.(p.82)

• Dr. Bob said, "Love and service keep us dry," and Bill said, "Always we must remember that our first duty is *face-to-face* help for the alcoholic who still suffers."(p.395)

faced

• The test that it *faced* was this: Could these large numbers of erstwhile erratic alcoholics successfully meet and work together?(p.xviii)

• *Faced* with this problem, if a doctor is honest with himself, he must sometimes feel his own inadequacy.(p.xxvii)

• I ruthlessly *faced* my sins and became willing to have my new-found Friend take them away, root and branch.(p.13)

• He knew he *faced* another trip to the asylum if he kept on.(p.35)

• *Faced* with alcoholic destruction, we soon became as open minded on spiritual matters as we tried to be on other questions.(p.48)

• We finally sought employment ourselves as destitution *faced* us and our families.(p.106)

• Being somewhat weakened, and *faced* with physical and mental readjustment to a life which knows no alcohol, he may overdo.(p.146)

• I have *faced* life instead of running away from it.(p.285)

• Surrender to me has meant the ability to run my home, to face my responsibilities as they should be *faced*, to take life as it comes to me day by day, and work my problems out.(p.340)

• This man *faced* the last ditch when his wife's voice from 1,300 miles away sent him to A.A.(p.356)

• When I was *faced* with a special challenge or social event -- such as an important business presentation or a dinner party -- I had to fortify myself with a couple of belts.(p.556)

faces

• The expression on the *faces* of the women, that indefinable something in the eyes of the men, the stimulating and electric atmosphere of the place, conspired to let him know that here was haven at last.(p.160)

• Here, while in a hospital bed, men with clear eyes, happy *faces*, and a look of assurance and purposefulness about them, came to see me and told me their stories.(p.279)

• I was knocked to the floor, swinging madly at the *faces* on those pineapples.(p.427)

• I swung, I swore, I started throwing beer cans at the advancing hordes of pineapple *faces*.(p.427)

• They had color in their *faces*, sparkle in their eyes and love in their hearts.(p.428)

• When I try to reconstruct what my life was like "before," I see a coin with two *faces*.(p.432)

• I would meet some new *faces* and be in a dry county.(p.490)

• The *faces* of the other boys grew dim.(p.498)

facilitated

• The wars which had been fought, the burnings and chicanery that religious dispute had *facilitated*, made me sick.(p.11)

facilities

• They have recreational *facilities*.(p.149)

• In the basement were to be dry-cleaning *facilities*, a barbershop, a pool room, a grocery shop and everything.(p.198)

• That being the case, it didn't take me long to figure out that my meager manufacturing *facilities* were entirely inadequate to the manufacture of beer for social and domestic consumption.(p.297)

• Hence such *facilities* ought not to use the A.A.

name.(p.566)

facility

• Six – An A.A. group ought never endorse, finance or lend the A.A. name to any related *facility* or outside enterprise, lest problems of money, property and prestige divert us from our primary purpose.(p.564)

facing

• Unlike the drinking driver, he avoids *facing* judges.(p.330)

• With their help I also saw that certainly, because of some of the things I had done during the years, I was bordering on insanity, and so, *facing* the record, I tried to believe that a Power greater than I could and would restore me to sanity.(p.471)

• Most emphatically we wish to say that any alcoholic capable of honestly *facing* his problems in the light of our experience can recover, provided he does not close his mind to all spiritual concepts.(p.570)

fact

• These things were true to some extent, in *fact*, to a considerable extent with some of us.(p.xxiv)

• The cases we have followed through have been most interesting; in *fact*, many of them are amazing.(p.xxv)

• In a matter of *fact* way he told how two men had appeared in court, persuading the judge to suspend his commitment.(p.9)

• The tremendous *fact* for every one of us is that we have discovered a common solution.(p.17)

• The *fact* is that most alcoholics, for reasons yet obscure, have lost the power of choice in drink.(p.24)

• The great *fact* is just this, and nothing less: That we have had deep and effective spiritual experiences which have revolutionized our whole attitude toward life, toward our fellows and toward God's universe.(p.25)

• The central *fact* of our lives today is the absolute certainty that our Creator has entered into our hearts and lives in a way which is indeed miraculous.(p.25)

• In *fact*, I have been trying to produce some such emotional rearrangement within you.(p.27)

• But the moment I made up my mind to go through with the process, I had the curious feeling that my alcoholic condition was relieved, as in *fact* it proved to be.(p.42)

• But after a while we had to face the *fact* that we must find a spiritual basis of life -- or else.(p.44)

• We could wish to be moral, we could wish to be philosophically comforted, in *fact*, we could will these things with all our might, but the needed power wasn't there.(p.45)

• Nevertheless, the twentieth century readily accepts theories of all kinds, provided they are firmly grounded in *fact*.(p.48)

• When many hundreds of people are able to say that the consciousness of the Presence of God is today the most important *fact* of their lives, they present a powerful reason why one should have faith.(p.51)

• He was as much a *fact* as we were.(p.55)

• In *fact*, his rival was ruined.(p.80)

• Admit that he probably knows more about it than you do, but call to his attention the *fact* that however deep his faith and knowledge, he could not have applied it or he would not drink.(p.93)

• Ask them to remember, when they are impatient, the blessed *fact* of his sobriety.(p.100)

• Frequently, you have felt obliged to tell your husband's employer and his friends that he was sick, when as a matter of *fact* he was tight.(p.115)

• The *fact* is that he should work with other people to maintain his own sobriety.(p.119)

• At the very beginning, the couple ought to frankly face the *fact* that each will have to yield here and there if the family is going to play an effective part in the new life.(p.131)

• In *fact*, he may say almost anything if he has accepted our solution which, as you know, demands rigorous honesty.(p.145)

• If you take it, your past will be forgotten and the *fact* that you went away for treatment will not be mentioned.(p.147)

• This is the Great *Fact* for us.(p.164)

• Never once in my life have I had a headache, which *fact* leads me to believe that I was an alcoholic almost from the start.(p.172)

• Of far more importance was the *fact* that he was the first living human with whom I had ever talked, who knew what he was talking about in regard to alcoholism from actual experience.(p.180)

• In *fact*, I admitted that from now on I was willing to let God take over, instead of me.(p.187)

• I always built up in my own mind the great things that I was going to do, and in *fact* I accomplished about fifty percent of them and then lost interest.(p.193)

• Anyhow, I recognized the *fact* that I couldn't drink like normal people, but I tried hard and kept on trying for twenty-two years.(p.196)

• On that statement and the *fact* that I had been sober for ninety days, he gave me a job selling lots in an allotment he had.(p.200)

• There were times when I got to drinking, and I had been warned by Firestone that they wouldn't stand for this much longer, so, clearly, they were conscious of the *fact* that I drank too much and too often.(p.204)

• In *fact*, on one occasion, I was picked up by the police and brought home.(p.211)

• As a matter of *fact*, I had two children at the time I was admitted to the bar.(p.212)

• In *fact*, as I look back, I have often thought that they probably concluded that they would put up with me for a couple of years, that I couldn't live much longer, and that they would inherit whatever was left of the practice.(p.215)

• My children had lost respect for me and, in *fact*, it was only after three or four years of sobriety that any of them ever said anything to me to indicate that I had recouped even a little of their respect.(p.215)

• In *fact*, the last three years of my drinking was a routine of barbiturates in the morning, so that I could stop shaking enough to shave, and then alcohol beginning about four-thirty or five o'clock, with a struggle not to take a drink at noon or during the day, because I had the idea that if I took one drink, I would smell as though I had had a pint.(p.217)

• In *fact*, I never lost my faith, since I had been prepared by some conversations toward the end of my sojourn in the hospital with Dr. Bob, conversations pretty much along spiritual lines.(p.218)

• In *fact*, after six months of living on food instead of on whiskey, I gained about thirty pounds.(p.220)

• In *fact* I had been in very good shape at one o'clock - - feeling no pain.(p.223)

• The *fact* that I can work again and earn my living, is important, but secondary.(p.229)

• In *fact* I was scared to talk to him about it, for I feared the kind of talk he would give me.(p.234)

• In *fact* his language was perfectly suited to my understanding.(p.235)

• My family would have nothing to do with me, in *fact* couldn't because I couldn't spare any of my money, which I needed for drink, to support them.(p.255)

• I do feel, though, that the *fact* that I finally grew up to a point where I could even tackle such a job is the apex of the story of a man who spent eighteen years running away from life.(p.286)

• I should have lost my husband, and I think that only the *fact* that he was an alcoholic too kept us together.(p.323)

• Because it was only through feeling defeat and feeling failure, the inability to cope with my life and with alcohol, that I was able to surrender and accept the *fact* that I had this disease, and that I had to learn to live again without alcohol.(p.335)

• I needed it, and I knew I was drinking too much, but I wasn't conscious of the *fact* that I should stop.(p.336)

• I went on, realizing what I was becoming, hating myself for it, bitter, blaming life, blaming everything else but the *fact* that I should turn about and do something about my drinking.(p.337)

• I lost my driver's license, was made a ward of the court, and was put on probation (not to mention the *fact* that I might have killed three friends and myself).(p.354)

• As a matter of *fact*, when I came into Alcoholics Anonymous I was close to being at the peak of my career.(p.356)

• She tried reasoning with me, endeavored to work out various drinking schedules, in *fact* all the tricks were practised faithfully for a short time somewhere along my shaky road to unhappiness.(p.361)

• (In *fact*, every time I saw him he had a frown on his face.)(p.370)

• In *fact* I was afraid to try it for fear that I would wind up like many examples I had seen of excessive drinking in the Army.(p.374)

• The surprise to me is the *fact* that I didn't know that they knew my drinking had gotten out of control.(p.376)

• The why is not important; the *fact* is that one drink will set up a reaction in our system which requires more; that one drink was too much and one hundred drinks were not enough.(p.380)

• The *fact* that A.A. is a spiritual program didn't scare me or raise any prejudice in my mind.(p.383)

• Scared that my dress wasn't going to fit right, that the church wasn't going to be filled, that I'd fall flat on my face walking up the aisle; in *fact*, I was afraid I wasn't going to be a prima donna in the place where I should be.(p.385)

• I resented the *fact* that Frank had done this to me, and I just didn't know what was going on.(p.388)

• In *fact*, I was taken to A.A. by a woman whom my father had taken to A.A. thirteen years earlier.(p.419)

• Now I had to face up to the *fact* that knowledge of this sort, applied to my individual case, was not power.(p.435)

• I really felt sorry for him; the only thing in life he had to brag about was the *fact* that he was an alcoholic.(p.446)

• When I am disturbed, it is because I find some person, place, thing, or situation – some *fact* of my life -- unacceptable to me, and I can find no serenity until I accept that person, place, thing, or situation as being exactly the way it is supposed to be at this moment.(p.449)

• However, one thing I am certain of: Inmates in prison who attend A.A. have their chances of remaining free greatly enhanced – this is a proved *fact*.(p.458)

• The word "alcoholic" does not turn me off any more; in *fact*, it is music to my ears when it applies to me.(p.463)

• In *fact* it has been only within the last fifteen years that I changed from a fairly normal, controlled drinker into an alcoholic.(p.464)

• It made me feel quite grown-up and mature, and I think another added attraction was the *fact* that so far as my family was concerned, it was forbidden, and it had a special attraction for that reason.(p.464)

• In *fact*, sometimes they served as good excuses to drink more, to forget.(p.465)

• But the difference lay in the *fact* that the A.A.'s knew from their own bitter experience.(p.471)

• Once, I phoned my brother-in-law and told him I was going to take a handful of pills (in *fact*, I already had) and I would slash my wrists if he didn't come over to stop me.(p.479)

• In *fact*, I couldn't have told you the difference between sherry and brandy.(p.518)

• Strangely enough, right through to the end of my twenty-six years in the Army, I was still being offered very good and important jobs in spite of the *fact* that my superiors must have known that I wasn't thoroughly reliable.(p.519)

• There was the sense of being "misunderstood," when as a matter of *fact* by my middle twenties I was quite popular, although I hadn't grown much bigger physically.(p.534)

• So did the waterboy on the high school football team attempt to revenge himself on the big brother who was the star quarterback; for I was the waterboy and my brother was the star quarterback, innocent of everything except the *fact* that he was a star quarterback.(p.537)

• I hope I have been able to impart to you, the reader, at least a bit of what I know; the joy of living, the irresistible power of divine love and its healing strength, and the *fact* that we, as sentient beings, have the knowledge to choose between good and evil, and, choosing good, are made happy.(p.543)

• The only importance in all of this lies in the *fact* that at twenty-three I was just as sick as I was at thirty three, when I came into A.A., but at that time I apparently had no place to go because I had no drinking problem.(p.546)

• In *fact*, I changed schools every year until high school.(p.555)

fact-facing

• Taking a commercial inventory is a fact-finding and a *fact-facing* process.(p.64)

fact-finding

• Taking a commercial inventory is a *fact-finding* and a fact-facing process.(p.64)

faction

• For the next couple of hours a terrible battle went on between the good gremlins and the bad ones, one *faction* urging me to tell the truth, the other telling me to sit tight and say nothing.(p.366)

factor

• In our belief, any picture of the alcoholic which leaves out this physical *factor* is incomplete.(p.xxiv)

• If I were asked what in my opinion was the most important *factor* in being successful in this program, besides following the Twelve Steps, I would say Honesty.(p.367)

• Now my drinking was limited by only one *factor*, the enforced periods of dryness caused by lengthy tours at sea.(p.398)

• The only other occasionally limiting *factor* was that I might run out of money before the next payday rolled around.(p.398)

factories

• I failed to persuade my broker friends to send me out looking over ***factories*** and managements, but my wife and I decided to go anyway.(p.2)

factors

• This eliminated one of the limiting ***factors***, the financial.(p.397)

factory

• But I hardly tasted anything for two years and started in business for myself, founding a mattress ***factory*** which is today an important industrial enterprise in our city.(p.232)

• Making my way to Pittsburgh, I met other former friends and got a job in a large ***factory*** where piecemakers were making good money.(p.252)

• I quit the ***factory*** and got a job on a small newspaper, going from that to a Pittsburgh daily, long ago defunct.(p.252)

• Forced to detrain from an empty gondola on the other side of Chicago by a terrific rainstorm which drenched me to the skin, I hit the first ***factory*** building I saw for a job.(p.253)

• There were business men, professional men, and ***factory*** workers.(p.258)

facts

• These ***facts*** appear to be of extreme medical importance; because of the extraordinary possibilities of rapid growth inherent in this group they may mark a new epoch in the annals of alcoholism.(p.xxiii)

• But the ex-problem drinker who has found this solution, who is properly armed with ***facts*** about himself, can generally win the entire confidence of another alcoholic in a few hours.(p.18)

• These stark and ugly ***facts*** have been confirmed by legions of alcoholics throughout history.(p.24)

• The practical individual of today is a stickler for ***facts*** and results.(p.48)

• For faith in a Power greater than ourselves, and miraculous demonstrations of that power in human lives, are ***facts*** as old as man himself.(p.55)

• These are ***facts*** out of our experience.(p.70)

• Time after time newcomers have tried to keep to themselves certain ***facts*** about their lives.(p.72)

• Then Prohibition came into effect, and the ***facts*** that the stuff obtainable was so horrible and sometimes deadly, and that I had married and had a job which I had to look after, helped me for a period of some three or four years, although I would get drunk every time I could get hold of enough to drink to get started.(p.183)

• It was hard to reconcile this ghastly present with the simple ***facts*** of the past.(p.225)

• Sure enough in a couple of hours two men were at my door and for the first time I heard some ***facts*** about liquor and my problem that sounded sensible to me.(p.363)

• They are not ideas of resignation but of the recognition of certain basic ***facts*** of living.(p.382)

• So I sat down with me and went over the ***facts*** behind the convulsions: personality changes, daily headaches, sense of impending doom, sense of impending insanity.(p.444)

faculties

• Under these conditions we can employ our mental ***faculties*** with assurance, for after all God gave us brains to use.(p.86)

faculty

• When I reached school, I discovered the ***faculty*** had other ideas on the subject.(p.173)

• This I did, and proved myself satisfactory to the ***faculty***, both in depórtment and scholastically.(p.174)

• I have been appointed to the ***faculty*** of my old school, to teach in my new field.(p.541)

faded

• Somewhat ***faded***, she nevertheless bloomed afresh.(p.384)

• The early promise of the "boy wonder" ***faded***, and my career began to drift.(p.556)

fail

• With this attitude you cannot ***fail***.(p.55)

• Rarely have we seen a person ***fail*** who has thoroughly followed our path.(p.58)

• Rarely do we ***fail*** to make satisfactory progress.(p.78)

• It works when other activities ***fail***.(p.89)

• You can secure their confidence when others ***fail***.(p.89)

• They can hardly ***fail*** to approve these simple principles, though the head of the house still fails somewhat in practicing them.(p.130)

• I knew that I had a helper that I could rely upon, who wouldn't ***fail*** me.(p.189)

• "You've been trying man's ways and they always ***fail***," he told me.(p.236)

• I got the Big Book and I read it, and this is what it said: "Rarely have we seen a person ***fail*** who has thoroughly followed our path."(p.349)

• "There is a principle which is a bar against all information, which is proof against all arguments and which cannot ***fail*** to keep a man in everlasting ignorance – that principle is contempt prior to investigation."(p.570)

failed

• This physician had repeatedly tried spiritual means to resolve his alcoholic dilemma but had ***failed***.(p.xvi)

• I personally know scores of cases who were of the type with whom other methods had ***failed*** completely.(p.xxiii)

• Ominous warning -- which I ***failed*** to heed.(p.1)

• Potential alcoholic that I was, I nearly ***failed*** my law course.(p.2)

• I ***failed*** to persuade my broker friends to send me out looking over factories and managements, but my wife and I decided to go anyway.(p.2)

• His human will had ***failed***.(p.11)

• For if an alcoholic ***failed*** to perfect and enlarge his spiritual life through work and self-sacrifice for others, he could not survive the certain trials and low spots ahead.(p.14)

• This sometimes nearly drove me back to drink, but I soon found that when all other measures ***failed***, work with another alcoholic would save the day.(p.15)

• Every attempt ***failed***.(p.33)

• All went well for a time, but he ***failed*** to enlarge his spiritual life.(p.35)

• Our sound reasoning ***failed*** to hold us in check.(p.37)

• I reasoned I was not so far advanced as most of you fellows, that I had been usually successful in licking my other personal problems, and that I would therefore be successful where you men ***failed***.(p.40)

• Our human resources, as marshalled by the will were not sufficient; they ***failed*** utterly.(p.45)

• Had not all efforts at flight ***failed*** before?(p.51)

• Wasn't it because self-reliance ***failed*** us?(p.68)

• Perhaps your story will help him see where he has ***failed*** to practice the very precepts he knows so well.(p.93)

• One of our Fellowship ***failed*** entirely with his first half dozen prospects.(p.96)

• These attempts to do the impossible have always ***failed***.(p.101)

• While grateful that he drinks no more, they may not like the idea that God has accomplished the miracle where they ***failed***.(p.128)

• I wanted to throw up my hands in discouragement, for I saw that I had ***failed*** to help my banker friend understand.(p.138)

• For this officer in the Indian Army, going on the wagon was not enough; attempts at control ***failed***.(p.342)

• During the next three years, I tried often again to give it up, but ***failed*** miserably.(p.343)

• Alcohol ***failed*** to serve the purpose.(p.346)

• Making amends is sometimes doing what we are capable of doing but ***failed*** to do because of alcohol; carrying out community responsibilities such as Community Funds, Red Cross, educational and religious activities in proportion to our abilities and energy.(p.381)

• I had tried my way and had ***failed***.(p.383)

• If I ***failed***, they would throw away the key, and I would never get out again.(p.461)

• Things went from bad to worse, and since I had finally and completely ***failed*** at the job of being a wife and a mother, my marriage ended.(p.468)

• Why did it work for me when all other agencies had ***failed***?(p.470)

• To my way of thinking, that is a definition of alcoholism; a state of being in which the emotions have ***failed*** to grow to the stature of the intellect.(p.535)

• Above all, I was suffering inner pain because my performance and my accomplishments in life ***failed*** to live up to my own expectations of myself.(p.557)

failing

• I was ***failing*** in everything.(p.424)

failings

• Of course, we had talked over quite a number of the ***failings*** that I had and made a sort of an inventory, which wasn't too difficult, because I had an awful lot of things wrong that were very apparent to me, because I knew all about them.(p.190)

fails

• He is not likely to get far in any direction if he ***fails*** to show unselfishness and love under his own roof.(p.127)

• They can hardly fail to approve these simple principles, though the head of the house still ***fails*** somewhat in practicing them.(p.130)

• It never ***fails***, if you go about it with one half the zeal you have been in the habit of showing when you were getting another drink.(p.181)

failure

• My weary and despairing wife was informed that it would all end with heart ***failure*** during delirium tremens, or I would develop a wet brain, perhaps within a year.(p.7)

• There is a complete ***failure*** of the kind of defense that keeps one from putting his hand on a hot stove.(p.24)

• In the face of collapse and despair, in the face of the total ***failure*** of their human resources, they found that a new power, peace, happiness, and sense of direction flowed into them.(p.50)

• Business ***failure***, insanity, fatal illness, suicide -- these calamities in his immediate family embittered and depressed him.(p.56)

• First, we searched out the flaws in our make-up which caused our ***failure***.(p.64)

• That often makes the difference between ***failure*** and success.(p.98)

• In our belief any scheme of combating alcoholism which proposes to shield the sick man from temptation is doomed to ***failure***.(p.101)

• There was always one more attempt – and one more ***failure***.(p.151)

• I don't know whether I drank to cover up being a ***failure***, or whether I drank and then missed the deals.(p.198)

• The second year my drinking was more or less restricted to week-ends, but I was nearly kicked out for scholastic ***failure***.(p.241)

• No conviction was necessary to establish my status as a miserable ***failure*** at managing my own life.(p.259)

• The unwillingness to admit ***failure*** requires even further friendly intake.(p.331)

• At one time, the admission that I was and am an alcoholic meant shame, defeat, and ***failure*** to me.(p.335)

• But in the light of the new understanding that I have found in A.A., I have been able to interpret that defeat, and that ***failure***, and that shame, as seeds of victory.(p.335)

• Because it was only through feeling defeat and feeling ***failure***, the inability to cope with my life and with alcohol, that I was able to surrender and accept the fact that I had this disease, and that I had to learn to live again without alcohol.(p.335)

• Many times in the intervening years I have thanked God for that man, a man who had the courage to admit ***failure***, a man who had the humility to confess that all the hard-won learning of his profession could not turn up the answer.(p.436)

• Having passed over the border line, the next five years were filled with fear, ***failure*** and frustration.(p.465)

• It has taught me that success and ***failure*** are never final, and that neither count for very much in the final assessment of any man who has done his best.(p.525)

• Had I been able to explain to a psychiatrist the feeling of futility, loneliness and lack of purpose that had come with my deep sense of personal ***failure*** at this second divorce, I seriously doubt that the good doctor could have convinced me that my basic problem was a spiritual hunger, but A.A. has shown me this was the truth.(p.546)

failures

• There were many ***failures***, but there was an occasional heartening success.(p.xvii)

• After several ***failures*** to find others, a fourth turned up.(p.158)

• They experienced a few distressing ***failures***, but in those cases they made an effort to bring the man's family into a spiritual way of living, thus relieving much worry and suffering.(p.159)

• Three attempts to enlist in the service, and three ***failures*** because of being skinny.(p.499)

• It had provided me with excuses for my lack of education, my marital ***failures***, personal ***failures***, inadequacy, and of course, my alcoholism and, though I really thought I had been willing to part with it, now I knew I was reluctant to let it go.(p.552)

faint

• To go north into the empty pine country and shoot myself, or to go south in the ***faint*** hope that a bunch of strangers might help me with my drinking problem.(p.278)

• By the time all this was over, I was really in a terrific state, and my father taking in things said, "Miss Esther is about to ***faint***.(p.385)

fainted
- I offered them a drink, and they came to the bottom of the stairs and the good woman *fainted*, just looking at me.(p.205)

faintly
- Still another experience: A woman's voice came *faintly* over long distance from Virginia.(p.137)

fair
- In all probability, we shall never be able to touch more than a *fair* fraction of the alcohol problem in all its ramifications.(p.xxi)
- These give a *fair* cross section of our membership and a clear-cut idea of what has actually happened in their lives.(p.29)
- We never gave the spiritual side of life a *fair* hearing.(p.50)
- We know but few instances where we have given these doctors a *fair* break.(p.73)
- Perhaps your husband will make a *fair* start on the new basis, but just as things are going beautifully he dismays you by coming home drunk.(p.120)
- Let families realize, as they start their journey, that all will not be *fair* weather.(p.122)
- It isn't *fair* to me or the firm.(p.147)
- He will be able to take a position with such a man which is eminently *fair* and square.(p.148)
- Quebec, Toronto, Buffalo, and finally Pittsburgh, were the scenes of man-sized drunks until I had gone through my readjusted discharge pay, a *fair* sum.(p.253)
- Where once I had casual acquaintances, all of whom were *fair* weather friends, I now have a host of friends who accept me for what I am.(p.296)
- To be sure, this had been a dizzy and confused interval, but most everyone else I knew had emerged from it with both feet on the ground and a *fair* amount of adult maturity.(p.304)
- High living, a great many *fair* weather friends, the 1929 stock market crash, and a couple of years of Depression, soon relieved me one by one of my worldly goods including my wife.(p.358)
- As far as school was concerned, I made *fair* grades throughout.(p.486)

fair-haired
- I was the *fair-haired* boy all right, but two years later I was blacklisted as an irresponsible drunk.(p.242)

fair-sized
- My broken home and broken heart fanned my smoldering self-pity into a *fair-sized* bonfire and this kept me well supplied with reasons for having another drink, and then another.(p.305)

fair-weather
- I made a host of *fair-weather* friends.(p.3)

fairly
- Perhaps he can still tend to business *fairly* well.(p.109)
- My life was *fairly* well crowded and I didn't seem to need any stimulants to keep me going.(p.213)
- He found that I had enough faith in the Almighty to be *fairly* frank.(p.219)
- I had always been a good Catholic, possibly not so devoted as I should have been, but *fairly* regular in my attendance at services.(p.234)
- I like to think I was *fairly* normal before alcohol took over.(p.240)
- In sports I made the track and tennis teams; I got along well with the other boys and had a *fairly* large circle of acquaintances but no intimate friends.(p.240)
- The example which they and Bill W., whose visits to Akron were *fairly* frequent, set me of service to their fellow men imbued me with a great desire to emulate them.(p.281)
- I got along *fairly* well with my party drinking for quite some time, but eventually I began to visit beer joints in between parties.(p.298)
- I really worked for several weeks, and having had a *fairly* wide acquaintance with the dealer trade, it was not difficult for me to line up enough of them to give me a very substantial volume of business with a minimum of effort.(p.300)
- I did stay *fairly* good for a few years.(p.323)
- So when the children were in school from nine to three, I started up a nice little business and was *fairly* successful in it.(p.339)
- My drinking did not start until after I was thirty-five, and a *fairly* successful career had been established.(p.374)
- After a few more estimates as to income and expenditures for booze over a few sample years, taken at random, I conclude that this twenty per cent stayed *fairly* constant.(p.398)
- My work is on a much deeper and more significant level than it ever was before, and I am today a *fairly* creative, relatively sane human being.(p.438)
- In fact it has been only within the last fifteen years that I changed from a *fairly* normal, controlled drinker into an alcoholic.(p.464)
- Yet I am *fairly* steady when I go to bed.(p.500)
- The term was nearly over and we parted on *fairly* friendly terms.(p.518)
- The war was on and it was a *fairly* short course, about eight months.(p.518)

fairness
- In *fairness* we must say that she may understand, but what are we going to do about a thing like that?(p.81)

faith
- We are not allied with any particular *faith*, sect or denomination, nor do we oppose anyone.(p.xiv)
- Few people really are, for that means blind *faith* in the strange proposition that this universe originated in a cipher and aimlessly rushes nowhere.(p.10)
- *Faith* without works was dead, he said.(p.14)
- Then *faith* would be dead indeed.(p.15)
- *Faith* has to work twenty-four hours a day in and through us, or we perish.(p.16)
- We have no desire to convince anyone that there is only one way by which *faith* can be acquired.(p.28)
- We were bothered with the thought that *faith* and dependence upon a Power beyond ourselves was somewhat weak, even cowardly.(p.45)
- That was great news to us, for we had assumed we could not make use of spiritual principles unless we accepted many things on *faith* which seemed difficult to believe.(p.47)
- But I cannot accept as surely true the many articles of *faith* which are so plain to him."(p.47)
- Besides a seeming inability to accept much on *faith*, we often found ourselves handicapped by obstinacy, sensitiveness, and unreasoning prejudice.(p.47)
- People of *faith* have a logical idea of what life is all about.(p.49)
- When many hundreds of people are able to say that the consciousness of the Presence of God is today the most important fact of their lives, they present a powerful reason why one should have *faith*.(p.51)
- The Wright brothers' almost childish *faith* that they could build a machine which would fly was the mainspring of their accomplishment.(p.52)
- Hence we are at pains to tell why we think our present *faith* is reasonable, why we think it more sane and logical to believe than not to believe, why we say our former thinking was soft and mushy when we threw up our hands in doubt and said, "We don't know."(p.53)
- Arrived at this point, we were squarely confronted with the question of *faith*.(p.53)
- Some of us had already walked far over the Bridge of Reason toward the desired shore of *faith*.(p.53)
- Without knowing it, had we not been brought to where we stood by a certain kind of *faith*?(p.53)
- What was that but a sort of *faith*?(p.54)
- So, in one way or another, we discovered that *faith* had been involved all the time!(p.54)
- It was impossible to say we had no capacity for *faith*, or love, or worship.(p.54)
- In one form or another we had been living by *faith* and little else.(p.54)
- Imagine life without *faith*!(p.54)
- For *faith* in a Power greater than ourselves, and miraculous demonstrations of that power in human lives, are facts as old as man himself.(p.55)
- We finally saw that *faith* in some kind of God was a part of our make-up, just as much as the feeling we have for a friend.(p.55)
- The verdict of the ages is that *faith* means courage.(p.68)
- All men of *faith* have courage.(p.68)
- In this book you read again and again that *faith* did for us what we could not do for ourselves.(p.70)
- Now we need more action, without which we find that "*Faith* without works is dead."(p.76)
- "*Faith* without works is dead."(p.88)
- He may be an example of the truth that *faith* alone is insufficient.(p.93)
- To be vital, *faith* must be accompanied by self sacrifice and unselfish, constructive action.(p.93)
- Admit that he probably knows more about it than you do, but call to his attention the fact that however deep his *faith* and knowledge, he could not have applied it or he would not drink.(p.93)
- We represent no particular *faith* or denomination.(p.93)
- The *faith* and sincerity of both you and your husband will be put to the test.(p.117)
- How my wife kept her *faith* and courage during all those years, I'll never know, but she did.(p.178)
- He kept the *faith*; therefore, he and countless others found a new life.(p.182)
- In fact, I never lost my *faith*, since I had been prepared by some conversations toward the end of my sojourn in the hospital with Dr. Bob, conversations pretty much along spiritual lines.(p.218)
- He found that I had enough *faith* in the Almighty to be fairly frank.(p.219)
- All sorts were represented and their relation of experiences and how they had found the only remedy, added to their human existence as sober men, laid the foundation of a very necessary *faith*.(p.258)
- Indeed, I was beginning to see that I would require implicit *faith*, like a small child, if I was going to get anywhere.(p.259)
- But he found that there was a Higher Power which had more *faith* in him than he had in himself.(p.287)
- Philosophy, *faith*, a sense of humor (they could laugh at themselves), clear-cut objectives, appreciation – and most especially appreciation and sympathetic understanding for their fellow man.(p.310)
- In learning to practice these steps in my daily living I began to acquire *faith* and a philosophy to live by.(p.311)
- First, through mutual pain and despair, and later through mutual objectives and new-found *faith* and hope.(p.312)
- We have *faith* in each other, trust in each other, and understanding.(p.325)
- Out of those forty years as a movie press agent came one blessing that granted me a blind *faith* in the program.(p.334)
- I had been brought up to believe in God, but I know that until I found this A.A. program, I had never found or known *faith* in the reality of God, the reality of His power that is now with me in everything I do.(p.341)
- The Twelve Steps, which to me are a spiritual way of living, soon meant honest thinking, not wishful thinking, open mindedness, a willingness to try and a *faith* to accept.(p.381)
- Educated child of the scientific age that I was, I had complete *faith* in the science of the mind.(p.434)
- I'd had absolute *faith* in science, and only in science.(p.435)
- I crawled back to my analyst, not so much because I had *faith* in him, but because I had nowhere else to turn.(p.435)
- It read something like this: "*Faith* without works is dead.(p.473)
- However, she had *faith* and she had hope (things I didn't have).(p.514)
- If we do not do so, we shall stand convicted of emotional sterility and of having lost the *faith* that moves mountains, without which medicine can do little."(p.571)

faithful
- Yes, we had been *faithful*, abjectly *faithful* to the God of Reason.(p.54)

faithfully
- There was one girl especially, and I'd watch her from my window every morning, leaving *faithfully* to go to the hospital in the neighborhood.(p.326)
- During this time I *faithfully* was writing my girl in Utah.(p.360)
- She tried reasoning with me, endeavored to work out various drinking schedules, in fact all the tricks were practised *faithfully* for a short time somewhere along my shaky road to unhappiness.(p.361)
- I would follow certain drinking schedules or diets *faithfully* for a few days, and then somewhere along the line would over-train and upset the applecart.(p.361)

faiths
- We have learned that whatever the human frailties of various *faiths* may be, those *faiths* have given purpose and direction to millions.(p.49)

fake
- I didn't want to be a *fake*.(p.237)

faked
- Seated at the typewriter, I *faked* deep thinking or portrayed creativity by key-tapping.(p.332)

fakery
- I had worked so long in a profession where *fakery*, deceit, and untruths are tools of trade that I instantly recognized honesty when I heard it, from the mouths of A.A. members.(p.334)

fall
- When the broker returned to New York in the *fall* of 1935, the first A.A. group had actually been

formed, though no one realized it at the time.(p.xvii)
• In the *fall* of 1939, Fulton Oursler, then editor of Liberty, printed a piece in his magazine, called "Alcoholics and God."(p.xviii)
• More baffling still, he could give himself no satisfactory explanation for his *fall*.(p.26)
• Suppose we *fall* short of the chosen ideal and stumble?(p.70)
• Our fears *fall* from us.(p.75)
• Of course, we all *fall* much below this standard many times.(p.99)
• After many painful discussions, they finally gave me my credits and I migrated to another of the leading universities of the country and entered as a Junior that *fall*.(p.173)
• In the *fall* of the graduating year, I became involved in some litigation over the ownership of inventions and patents.(p.212)
• I found in the *fall* of 1939, that I was not mentally impaired, so far as trial work was concerned, and thereafter took up where I had left off when I was about forty-five years old.(p.220)
• As a result, I would *fall* off in a drunken stupor every night.(p.299)
• My salesmanship was still good, for in the *fall* of 1938 she called me from Salt Lake and finally agreed to take me on for better or for worse.(p.360)
• It didn't take long for me to *fall* in with a fast crowd who had their lunch in the men's bar of a leading hotel.(p.361)
• Scared that my dress wasn't going to fit right, that the church wasn't going to be filled, that I'd *fall* flat on my face walking up the aisle; in fact, I was afraid I wasn't going to be a prima donna in the place where I should be.(p.385)
• STARS DON'T *FALL*(p.400)
• This was in Virginia, where I had rented a house with stables and a swimming pool, and the *fall* fox hunting had begun.(p.404)
• I don't know why I didn't *fall* out of the open cockpit of some of those planes I flew in while taking aerial pictures.(p.426)
• They got bigger and bigger and nearer and nearer, as if they were going to *fall* and crush me.(p.427)
• It was tottering and it had to *fall*.(p.435)
• In the garage, I would put the needle in my vein and then try to figure out exactly how much medication to inject to overcome the pep pills while adding to the sleeping pills while ignoring the tranquilizers, in order to get just enough to be able to pull out the needle, jerk the tourniquet, throw it in the car, slam the car door shut, run down the hall, and *fall* in bed before I fell asleep.(p.442)
• I had my own medical practice in Washington at that time, but the practice slackened and the mail order business started to *fall* off.(p.486)
• I *fall* into a dreamless sleep.(p.497)
• There was the love affair which was ridiculous -- "imagine that midget being able to *fall* in love!" -- and my head knew it while my heart pumped real, genuine anguish, for it hurt like hell, and since it was first love, things have never been quite the same.(p.534)
• It seems only fitting that when I did finally *fall* in love it was with an alcoholic, and for the next ten years I progressed as rapidly as is humanly possible into what I believed to be hopeless alcoholism.(p.547)

fallacious
• If you draw this *fallacious* reasoning to the attention of an alcoholic, he will laugh it off, or become irritated and refuse to talk.(p.23)

fallacy
• If the family persists in criticism, this *fallacy* may take a still greater hold on father.(p.129)

fallen
• I have something to contribute to humanity, since I am peculiarly qualified, as a fellow-sufferer, to give aid and comfort to those who have stumbled and *fallen* over this business of meeting life.(p.229)

falling
• If a sufficiently strong reason -- ill health, *falling* in love, change of environment, or the warning of a doctor -- becomes operative, this man can also stop or moderate, although he may find it difficult and troublesome and may even need medical attention.(p.21)
• As animals on a treadmill, we have patiently and wearily climbed, *falling* back in exhaustion after each futile effort to reach solid ground.(p.107)
• They criticize, pointing out how he is *falling* down on his spiritual program.(p.126)
• Instead of drinking in fancy bars and clubs, I had to carry a bottle of vodka in my briefcase, duck into public toilets, and gulp from the bottle, trembling, in order to keep from *falling* apart.(p.557)

falls
• But his face *falls* when we speak of spiritual matters, especially when we mention God, for we have reopened a subject which our man thought he had neatly evaded or entirely ignored.(p.45)
• The problem with which you struggle usually *falls* within one of four categories:(p.108)
• Today's life is measured against that of other years and, when it *falls* short, the family may be unhappy.(p.123)
• I had bought a piece of ground in Cuyahoga *Falls* and cut it into lots and had a profit of approximately $40,000 and that was a lot of money in those days.(p.194)

false
• The sensation is so elusive that, while they admit it is injurious, they cannot after a time differentiate the true from the *false*.(p.xxvi)
• I had suppressed tendencies to overindulge and thus reveal my "moral weakness," because *false* pride was so dominant.(p.327)
• They build you up with a lot of *false* hopes and promises, and rush you around here and there and then, all of a sudden, it's gone."(p.472)
• But as the years go by, the stretch becomes unbearable; and the man with the grown-up brain and the childish emotions -- vanity, self-interest, *false* pride, jealousy, longing for social approval, to name few -- becomes a prime candidate for alcohol.(p.534)
• Fear of rejection and its ensuing pain were not to be risked, and I turned away from myself once more for the answer, this time to the drinks I had always refused before, and in alcohol I found a *false* courage.(p.546)

faltering
• As he talked I gathered vaguely, (because he was a *faltering* beginner then, just as I am now) that to be relieved of alcoholism I would have to be different.(p.257)

fame
• Things weren't going as I thought they should, for my greater enjoyment, comfort and *fame*; therefore, if the universe wouldn't play my way, I wouldn't play at all.(p.531)
• I don't care too much about personal *fame* or glory, and I want only enough money to enable me to do the work I feel I can perhaps do best.(p.542)

familiar
• We are all *familiar* with this type.(p.xxviii)
• It has never been, by any treatment with which we are *familiar*, permanently eradicated.(p.xxviii)
• Physicians who are *familiar* with alcoholism agree there is no such thing as making a normal drinker out of an alcoholic.(p.31)
• We, who are *familiar* with the symptoms, see large numbers of potential alcoholics among young people everywhere.(p.33)
• I also had the notion that I might find a customer for a car at this place, which was *familiar* for I had been going to it for years.(p.36)
• He had, of course, the *familiar* alcoholic obsession that few knew of his drinking.(p.155)
• Before long I was at the luncheon meeting an hour before the others, that old and *familiar* trademark of every alcoholic.(p.360)
• One night, a few weeks after joining the Fellowship, much to my surprise and delight I saw a *familiar* but no longer frowning face.(p.371)
• The people of A.A. had something that looked much better than what I had, but I was afraid to let go of what I had in order to try something new; there was a certain sense of security in the *familiar*.(p.448)

families
• This has become the basis of a rapidly growing fellowship of these men and their *families*.(p.xxiii)
• I have seen hundreds of *families* set their feet in the path that really goes somewhere; have seen the most impossible domestic situations righted; feuds and bitterness of all sorts wiped out.(p.15)
• I have seen men come out of asylums and resume a vital place in the lives of their *families* and communities.(p.15)
• In one western city and its environs there are one thousand of us and our *families*.(p.15)
• In a vague way their *families* and friends sense that these drinkers are abnormal, but everybody hopefully awaits the day when the sufferer will rouse himself from his lethargy and assert his power of will.(p.23)
• We have seen men get well whose *families* have not returned at all.(p.100)
• We finally sought employment ourselves as destitution faced us and our *families*.(p.106)
• And even if they did not love their *families*, how could they be so blind about themselves?(p.107)
• You have been starving for his companionship, yet he spends long hours helping other men and their *families*.(p.119)
• Let *families* realize, as they start their journey, that all will not be fair weather.(p.122)
• This painful past may be of infinite value to other *families* still struggling with their problem.(p.124)
• We *families* of Alcoholics Anonymous keep few skeletons in the closet.(p.125)
• We know there are difficult wives and *families*, but the man who is getting over alcoholism must remember he did much to make them so.(p.127)
• Seeing is believing to most *families* who have lived with a drinker.(p.135)
• Suppose now that through you several *families* have adopted this way of life.(p.153)
• From surrounding towns, *families* drive long distances to be present.(p.161)
• So I suggested that he take a trip to Akron for a couple of weeks, which he did, living with one of the A.A. *families* there.(p.294)
• First, we all hear at A.A. meetings about those who have lost everything, those who have been in jail, those who have been in prison, those who have lost their *families*, those who have lost their income.(p.345)
• At times, when I noticed other *families*, I felt something was very wrong with ours.(p.369)
• We came back East and met both *families*.(p.402)
• My experience has been active: three meetings a week, many tapes, many A.A. conferences, much work on the Twelve Steps, and much work with other alcoholics and their *families*.(p.420)
• I belonged to one of the Irish *families* who, more or less traditionally, sent their boys to the British armies.(p.517)
• In large cities, groups often maintain local offices where alcoholics or their *families* may arrange for interviews or hospitalization.(p.575)

family
• He uses his gifts to build up a bright outlook for his *family* and himself, and then pulls the structure down on his head by a senseless series of sprees.(p.21)
• This man has a charming wife and *family*.(p.35)
• His *family* was re-assembled, and he began to work as a salesman for the business he had lost through drinking.(p.35)
• Moreover, he would lose his *family* for whom he had a deep affection.(p.35)
• Here was the threat of commitment, the loss of *family* and position, to say nothing of that intense mental and physical suffering which drinking always caused him.(p.36)
• Business failure, insanity, fatal illness, suicide -- these calamities in his immediate *family* embittered and depressed him.(p.56)
• It may be one of our own *family*, but we cannot disclose anything to our wives or our parents which will hurt them and make them unhappy.(p.74)
• We thought he ought to be willing to do that if necessary, but if he were in jail he could provide nothing for either *family*.(p.79)
• If he opened that old affair, he was afraid it would destroy the reputation of his partner, disgrace his *family* and take away his means of livelihood.(p.80)
• We ought to sit down with the *family* and frankly analyze the past as we now see it, being very careful not to criticize them.(p.83)
• So we clean house with the *family*, asking each morning in meditation that our Creator show us the way of patience, tolerance, kindliness and love.(p.83)
• Unless one's *family* expresses a desire to live upon spiritual principles we think we ought not to urge them.(p.83)
• This advice is given for his *family* also.(p.90)
• The *family* may object to this, but unless he is in a dangerous physical condition, it is better to risk it.(p.90)
• Don't deal with him when he is very drunk, unless he is ugly and the *family* needs your help.(p.90)
• Then let his *family* or a friend ask him if he wants to quit for good and if he would go to any extreme to do so.(p.90)
• Neither should the *family* hysterically plead with him to do anything, nor should they tell him much about you.(p.90)
• The *family* must decide these things.(p.90)
• Usually the *family* should not try to tell your story.(p.91)
• When possible, avoid meeting a man through his *family*.(p.91)
• Though you have talked with the *family*, leave them out of the first discussion.(p.91)

• He will feel he can deal with you without being nagged by his ***family***.(p.91)
• But you should not deprive your ***family*** or creditors of money they should have.(p.96)
• Be certain he will be welcomed by your ***family***, and that he is not trying to impose upon you for money, connections, or shelter.(p.96)
• It is not good for him, and it sometimes creates serious complications in a ***family***.(p.97)
• Though an alcoholic does not respond, there is no reason why you should neglect his ***family***.(p.97)
• The ***family*** should be offered your way of life.(p.97)
• Should they accept and practice spiritual principles, there is a much better chance that the head of the ***family*** will recover.(p.97)
• And even though he continues to drink, the ***family*** will find life more bearable.(p.97)
• When your prospect has made such reparation as he can to his ***family***, and has thoroughly explained to them the new principles by which he is living, he should proceed to put those principles into action at home.(p.98)
• Though his ***family*** be at fault in many respects, he should not be concerned about that.(p.98)
• If persisted in for a few months, the effect on a man's ***family*** is sure to be great.(p.99)
• Little by little the ***family*** may see their own defects and admit them.(p.99)
• After they have seen tangible results, the ***family*** will perhaps want to go along.(p.99)
• Let no alcoholic say he cannot recover unless he has his ***family*** back.(p.99)
• We have seen others slip when the ***family*** came back too soon.(p.100)
• When working with a man and his ***family***, you should take care not to participate in their quarrels.(p.100)
• But urge upon a man's ***family*** that he has been a very sick person and should be treated accordingly.(p.100)
• If you have been successful in solving your own domestic problems, tell the newcomer's ***family*** how that was accomplished.(p.100)
• We feel that each ***family***, in the light of their own circumstances, ought to decide for themselves.(p.103)
• In some cases it may be better to let someone outside of the ***family*** present the book.(p.113)
• These ***family*** dissensions are very dangerous, especially to your husband.(p.117)
• After all, your ***family*** is reunited, alcohol is no longer a problem and you and your husband are working together toward an undreamed-of future.(p.119)
• The fellowship of Al-Anon ***Family*** Groups was formed about thirteen years after this chapter was written.(p.121)
• If there is no Al-Anon listing in your local telephone book, you may obtain further information on Al-Anon ***Family*** Groups by writing to its World Service Office: Box 182, Madison Square Station, New York, NY 10159.(p.121)
• THE ***FAMILY*** AFTERWARD(p.122)
• All members of the ***family*** should meet upon the common ground of tolerance, understanding and love.(p.122)
• We find the more one member of the ***family*** demands that the others concede to him, the more resentful they become.(p.122)
• Is not each trying to arrange the ***family*** show to his liking?(p.122)
• Is he not unconsciously trying to see what he can take from the ***family*** life rather than give?(p.122)
• The entire ***family*** is, to some extent, ill."(p.122)
• Suppose we tell you some of the obstacles a ***family*** will meet; suppose we suggest how they may be avoided -- even converted to good use for others.(p.123)
• The ***family*** of an alcoholic longs for the return of happiness and security.(p.123)
• Today's life is measured against that of other years and, when it falls short, the ***family*** may be unhappy.(p.123)
• ***Family*** confidence in dad is rising high.(p.123)
• But the wise ***family*** will admire him for what he is trying to be, rather than for what he is trying to get.(p.123)
• Now and then the ***family*** will be plagued by specters from the past, for the drinking career of almost every alcoholic has been marked by escapades, funny, humiliating, shameful or tragic.(p.123)
• The ***family*** may be possessed by the idea that future happiness can be based only upon forgetfulness of the past.(p.123)
• The alcoholic's past thus becomes the principal asset of the ***family*** and frequently it is almost the only one!(p.124)
• We think each ***family*** which has been relieved owes something to those who have not, and when the occasion requires, each member of it should be only too willing to bring former mistakes, no matter how grievous, out of their hiding places.(p.124)
• Members of a ***family*** should watch such matters carefully, for one careless, inconsiderate remark has been known to raise the very devil.(p.125)
• In either case certain ***family*** problems will arise.(p.126)
• The ***family*** will be affected also, pleasantly at first, as they feel their money troubles are about to be solved, then not so pleasantly as they find themselves neglected.(p.126)
• If not irritable, he may seem dull and boring, not gay and affectionate as the ***family*** would like him to be.(p.126)
• The ***family*** is mystified.(p.126)
• Both father and the ***family*** are mistaken, though each side may have some justification.(p.126)
• The ***family*** must realize that dad, though marvelously improved, is still convalescing.(p.127)
• As each member of a resentful ***family*** begins to see his short comings and admits them to the others, he lays a basis for helpful discussion.(p.127)
• These ***family*** talks will be constructive if they can be carried on without heated argument, self-pity, self-justification or resentful criticism.(p.127)
• As soon as his sobriety begins to be taken as a matter of course, the ***family*** may look at their strange new dad with apprehension, then with irritation.(p.128)
• He may demand that the ***family*** find God in a hurry, or exhibit amazing indifference to them and say he is above worldly considerations.(p.128)
• When father takes this tack, the ***family*** may react unfavorably.(p.128)
• If he means to right his past wrongs, why all this concern for everyone in the world but his ***family***?(p.128)
• If the ***family*** cooperates, dad will soon see that he is suffering from a distortion of values.(p.129)
• He will perceive that his spiritual growth is lopsided, that for an average man like himself, a spiritual life which does not include his ***family*** obligations may not be so perfect after all.(p.129)
• If the ***family*** will appreciate that dad's current behavior is but a phase of his development, all will be well.(p.129)
• In the midst of an understanding and sympathetic ***family***, these vagaries of dad's spiritual infancy will quickly disappear.(p.129)
• The opposite may happen should the ***family*** condemn and criticize.(p.129)
• If the ***family*** persists in criticism, this fallacy may take a still greater hold on father.(p.129)
• Instead of treating the ***family*** as he should, he may retreat further into himself and feel he has spiritual justification for so doing.(p.129)
• Though the ***family*** does not fully agree with dad's spiritual activities, they should let him have his head.(p.129)
• Even if he displays a certain amount of neglect and irresponsibility towards the ***family***, it is well to let him go as far as he likes in helping other alcoholics.(p.129)
• One more suggestion: Whether the ***family*** has spiritual convictions or not, they may do well to examine the principles by which the alcoholic member is trying to live.(p.130)
• Thus mother, through no fault of her own, became accustomed to wearing the ***family*** trousers.(p.131)
• This means trouble, unless the ***family*** watches for these tendencies in each other and comes to a friendly agreement about them.(p.131)
• The ***family*** may feel they hold a mortgage on dad, so big that no equity should be left for outsiders.(p.131)
• At the very beginning, the couple ought to frankly face the fact that each will have to yield here and there if the ***family*** is going to play an effective part in the new life.(p.131)
• Though the ***family*** has no religious connections, they may wish to make contact with or take membership in a religious body.(p.131)
• He and his ***family*** can be a bright spot in such congregations.(p.132)
• So let each ***family*** play together or separately, as much as their circumstances warrant.(p.132)
• Whether the ***family*** goes on a spiritual basis or not, the alcoholic member has to if he would recover.(p.135)
• But what about his responsibilities -- his ***family*** and the men who would die because they would not know how to get well, ah -- yes, those other alcoholics?(p.154)
• Why, he argued, should he lose the remainder of his business, only to bring still more suffering to his ***family*** by foolishly admitting his plight to people from whom he made his livelihood?(p.155)
• They experienced a few distressing failures, but in those cases they made an effort to bring the man's ***family*** into a spiritual way of living, thus relieving much worry and suffering.(p.159)
• He and his wife would leave elated by the thought of what they could now do for some stricken acquaintance and his ***family***.(p.160)
• Cleaning up old scrapes, helping to settle ***family*** differences, explaining the disinherited son to his irate parents, lending money and securing jobs for each other, when justified -- these are everyday occurrences.(p.161)
• I can well remember sitting with seven dollars in my pocket, planning on giving my ***family*** a hundred or two hundred dollars, when I made it next year.(p.197)
• The people in the group hadn't been around that day; part of my ***family*** was in Florida and the rest of them weren't speaking to me, so I spent a very lonesome day and by evening I was feeling very sorry for myself.(p.207)
• I was born in Cleveland, Ohio, in 1889, the last child of a ***family*** of eight children.(p.210)
• She was a woman devoted to her ***family*** and loyal to her husband, but quarrels did not make a happy environment for her.(p.210)
• I believe though that it helped my ***family*** tremendously to have the A.A. meetings every week in my own home.(p.220)
• My ***family*** had money -- I had never known denial of any material desire.(p.225)
• Many friends of my ***family*** had emigrated to America, so at twenty-four I decided that the United States offered me the opportunity I was never likely to find in my native land.(p.231)
• There had never been any drunkards in my ***family***.(p.231)
• My "periodics" became more frequent until I reached the point where I wanted to devote all my time to drinking, working as little as possible, and then only when the necessity of my ***family*** demanded it.(p.234)
• My ***family*** lived in very prosperous circumstances, and while both my parents drank, sometimes too much, neither was an alcoholic.(p.240)
• With nothing but a liberal arts education, very definitely estranged from my ***family*** and already married, soon after graduation from college I became a bookmaker's clerk on the British racing circuits, far better off financially than the average professional man.(p.251)
• I visited my ***family*** just once in that time.(p.255)
• My ***family*** would have nothing to do with me, in fact couldn't because I couldn't spare any of my money, which I needed for drink, to support them.(p.255)
• My wife and ***family*** stood by me for ten weeks and then, quite justifiably, ejected me.(p.257)
• I come from a very poor ***family*** in material things, with a fine Christian mother, but with no religious background.(p.261)
• I was the oldest in a ***family*** of seven, and my father was an alcoholic.(p.261)
• When I came to my aunt, she knew that I had had an unhappy childhood, and she said, "Now, Ethel, you're welcome to have boy friends in our home, but there are two boys in this town that I don't want you to date, and one of them comes from a very fine ***family***, one of the best.(p.262)
• I'm sure his ***family*** felt that it was a marriage that -- well, I was a girl from the wrong side of the tracks -- definitely!(p.262)
• I felt that his ***family*** were accepting me because it was good sense.(p.262)
• There was a very religious ***family*** that lived down the road from us, and we were on the same party line.(p.265)
• One of our gifts from the ***family*** was a very lovely Bible, but we'd let the bulldog chew it because we weren't too interested in it.(p.268)
• I came from a good ***family***.(p.275)
• A low ebb in the ***family*** fortunes necessitated my going to work when I was twenty.(p.275)
• I told our ***family*** doctor, an understanding man who gave hours of his time trying to help me, about this experience.(p.276)
• I ended up, homeless, jobless, penniless and rudderless, as the problem guest of a close friend whose ***family*** was out of town.(p.278)

• Haunting me through each day's stupor -- and there were eighteen or nineteen such days in this man's home -- was the thought: "Where do I go when his *family* comes home?"(p.278)

• They made me feel as if I were a part of their *family*, and so did their children.(p.281)

• So six months ago I acquired a ready made *family* consisting of one charming wife, four grown children to whom I am devoted, and three grandchildren.(p.286)

• I spent a great deal of time with Dr. Bob, whenever he had the time to spare, and in the homes of two or three other people, trying to see how the *family* lived the program.(p.291)

• One of them was that I would try to get a group started in Chicago; the second was that I would have to return to Akron to attend meetings at least every two months until I did get a group started in Chicago; third, I decided I must place this program above everything else, even my *family*, because if I did not maintain my sobriety I would lose my *family* anyway.(p.292)

• During this time, I had been threatened, beaten, kissed, praised and damned alternately by relatives, *family*, friends and strangers, but of course it all went for naught.(p.300)

• Seldom had any of these lost either health, business, *family*, or friends.(p.315)

• I still had a wife and *family*, a home and a car, my driver's license, and a proper amount of insurance.(p.327)

• I also turned against my *family*, my mother.(p.338)

• Three years and three months of sobriety, without a slip, has meant a lot to me, my wife, and my *family*.(p.342)

• I never robbed my *family* of anything.(p.351)

• I didn't know how to be a father; I don't know how to come home and work week-ends like other husbands; I don't know how to entertain my *family*.(p.351)

• He and I had a large *family* -- six children, to be exact.(p.370)

• Before too long, my husband (who seemed to prefer his shirts dirty) put his foot down, declaring that our *family* might have the cleanest clothes in town, but that I hadn't been out of the same old dirty slacks and blouse for a week.(p.371)

• I'm very active in A.A. work and active at home, too, with my *family*.(p.372)

• How can a person with a fine *family*, an attractive home, an excellent position and high standing in an important city become an alcoholic?(p.373)

• I was raised like the majority of American boys, coming from a *family* of modest circumstances, attending public schools, having the social life of a small midwestern town, with part-time work and some athletics.(p.373)

• After that came marriage, getting started in business, and a *family*.(p.373)

• I had a *family* to be proud of, actively sharing in the responsibilities of good citizenship.(p.374)

• I made promises to myself, my *family* and friends -- and broke them.(p.375)

• I will never know all the people I hurt, all the friends I abused, the humiliation of my *family*, the worry of my business associates, or how far reaching it was.(p.376)

• The time for decision had arrived, and it was a relief to say "Yes" when my *family* said they would call Alcoholics Anonymous for me.(p.378)

• I had not yet lost my job or *family*, even though both were on the verge of going.(p.379)

• It didn't say I had to lose my *family*.(p.379)

• Some of my *family* are allergic to certain foods.(p.380)

• Above all, I am grateful to A.A. for my sobriety, which means so much to my *family*, friends and business associates, because God and A.A. were able to do for me something I was unable to do for myself.(p.383)

• I came from a *family* where alcohol was socially acceptable.(p.384)

• For some reason I can't remember, it finally dawned on me that I had a problem, and yet nobody was very critical about it except my *family*, and that was only because I decided, after seven years of marriage, that I would divorce my husband.(p.386)

• I displayed alcoholic tendencies actually from the age of fourteen, when I started to steal wine from the *family* jug, siphoning it off one drink at a time so it wouldn't be missed, not drinking it immediately, but saving it until about a pint was accumulated, so that I could get drunk.(p.397)

• I was out of step with life, with my *family*, with people in general.(p.400)

• I was born in a castle – the *family* home, in Europe.(p.400)

• My father had a title; there was plenty of means in the *family*.(p.401)

• My *family*, on my mother's side, was brilliant, gifted and charming.(p.401)

• But I did not feel a part of my *family* or a part of the set-up.(p.401)

• Showing all the courage and ingenuity that I had not used in a positive way, I covered my tracks and hid from my *family* so successfully that they did not find me for months.(p.401)

• After eight months, the *family* found me.(p.401)

• My *family* always bought the best, and the embassies were flowing.(p.402)

• He saw that I was unsettled, living away from my *family* and renting houses here and there.(p.403)

• I accepted a big tax-free income from the *family*, but I didn't like it when they told me how to live.(p.405)

• Things were no better with the *family*, so I moved to New York.(p.406)

• It had never occurred to me before that I could live simply and be independent of my *family*.(p.409)

• I had a drunken quarrel with my *family*, denounced them, and left them forever.(p.409)

• For three generations, my *family* had had a charge account in one of the big New York hotels.(p.410)

• Didn't I come from a *family* of drinkers?(p.427)

• After going to school all day, working in the *family* drugstore all evening, and then studying until one or two in the morning, I would not be able to sleep soundly, with everything I had been studying going round in my head.(p.440)

• It seems I should have learned to love my wife and *family* first; the newcomer to A.A., last.(p.451)

• Forgive me – I cannot write further about this latest turn of events, anticipating seeing the *family* I deserted so long ago.(p.463)

• It made me feel quite grown-up and mature, and I think another added attraction was the fact that so far as my *family* was concerned, it was forbidden, and it had a special attraction for that reason.(p.464)

• Then I went on my first week-long bender of solitary drinking, locked up in a hotel room, because my *family* opposed my coming marriage.(p.464)

• At noon on Christmas Day I called my *family* in New York, wished them a Merry Christmas, and assured them everything was fine with me.(p.467)

• Then A.A. showed her the beauty of normal living, in a whole *family* reborn.(p.478)

• Even my *family* didn't have much use for me.(p.478)

• I got to the place where I'd look forward to the week-end's drinking and pacify myself by saying that the week-ends were mine, that it didn't interfere with my *family* or with my business if I drank on the week-ends.(p.488)

• I have a *family* to support and have no time to be looking for another job.(p.500)

• I wish I were home with the *family* and not in the dingy hotel.(p.500)

• Members of my *family* annoy me.(p.505)

• The *family* seems to think of nothing but spending.(p.506)

• She had been warned numerous times, not only by her *family* but by my own mother, that I was a hopeless drunk, that there wasn't anything anybody could do with me, that I'd never stop, and that eventually I'd break her heart.(p.513)

• I went back to the old *family* doctor who had helped me the first time I had the D.T.'s.(p.515)

• Providentially, this was a Monday might when the Dublin Group met in those days, and my *family* agreed that if A.A. could do anything for me at all, that I'd be allowed to stay on at home on probation.(p.523)

• For you learned that he had been guilty of the thing he had accused you of, and his guilt had brought suffering to his entire *family*; and he thought he saw his young son beginning his own tragic pattern.(p.533)

• The helpful *family* finally said, over long distance, that there would be no more money and that I could not come home.(p.538)

• But not for long; now, for five Friday nights in a row, I went to jail, picked up sodden with beer (which I always disliked, but which was the only drink available); in jail five consecutive Friday nights in the town where I had grown up, where I had been an honor student in high school, where a kindly uncle, bailing me out, said, "Bob, our *family* just doesn't do this sort of thing."(p.539)

• All of my *family* and loved ones, all of my friends, are nearer and dearer to me than ever before and I have literally dozens of new friends who say they cannot believe that a short eight years ago I was ready for the scrap heap.(p.541)

• Finally, in desperation, my *family* appealed to a doctor for advice and he suggested A.A.(p.549)

• For instance, the fiftieth wedding anniversary of my wife's parents was the occasion for a huge *family* reunion at our home.(p.556)

• Should you be the relative or friend of an alcoholic who shows no immediate interest in A.A., it is suggested that you write the Al-Anon *Family* Groups, Inc., Box 182, Madison Square Station, New York, NY 10159, U.S.A.(p.575)

• This is a world clearing house for the Al-Anon *Family* Groups, composed largely of the wives, husbands and friends of A.A. members.(p.575)

• This headquarters will give the location of the nearest *family* group and will if you wish, correspond with you about your special problems.(p.575)

family's

• The alcoholic, his wife, his children, his "in-laws," each one is likely to have fixed ideas about the *family's* attitude toward himself or herself.(p.122)

• I was certainly a complete surprise when I arrived at her *family's* home, but because I arrived on the wings of a tropical hurricane there wasn't much she could do but let me in.(p.364)

famous

• Tom Sharkey's brawling bar on 14th Street and the *famous* wine-room at the back were headquarters for me.(p.251)

• I listened to *famous* ministers -- found nothing.(p.255)

• In succession came "What Made Milwaukee *Famous* Made a Loser Out of Me" and "I'm Drinking My Christmas Dinner All Alone."(p.332)

• I returned to my home in Lucknow, India, at the end of November last year from a vacation in one of the most *famous* beauty spots in our country, a mountain resort 6,800 feet up, with a wonderful lake.(p.342)

• They were ambitious, successful, strong and *famous*.(p.401)

• He has since become *famous* and distinguished, an asset to his country.(p.403)

• Tasting the best of burgundy at a *famous* restaurant one night, landed me passed out on a park bench in the public square.(p.405)

• Awarded a scholarship to a *famous* old Eastern college, I began to drink at the end of my freshman year, and by junior year, I had to transfer to an easier state university to keep my grades up.(p.419)

fanatic

• I could see he wasn't a quack or a *fanatic*.(p.413)

• My mother had been recently converted and, actually, had become a religious *fanatic*.(p.483)

• A *fanatic*, I thought to myself, but I was polite.(p.503)

fanatical

• We realize that some people are as *fanatical* about sex as others are loose.(p.70)

fanatics

• Why lay ourselves open to being branded *fanatics* or religious bores?(p.77)

fancied

• I *fancied* myself a leader, for had not the men of my battery given me a special token of appreciation?(p.1)

• In that state, the wrong-doing of others, *fancied* or real, had power to actually kill.(p.66)

• I had found friends, understanding friends who often knew what I was thinking and feeling better than I knew myself, and didn't allow me to retreat into my prison of loneliness and fear over a *fancied* slight or hurt.(p.228)

fancy

• Instead of drinking in *fancy* bars and clubs, I had to carry a bottle of vodka in my briefcase, duck into public toilets, and gulp from the bottle, trembling, in order to keep from falling apart.(p.557)

fanfare

• But the firm became violently ill with my drunkenness and their course of treatment was to remove their ulcer, in the form of me, from the payroll, amid much *fanfare* and very personal and slighting remarks and insinuations.(p.300)

fanned

• My broken home and broken heart *fanned* my smoldering self-pity into a fair-sized bonfire and this kept me well supplied with reasons for having another drink, and then another.(p.305)

• I had fed it, *fanned* it and nurtured it as one might a delicate child, and it had become as much a part of me as my breathing.(p.551)

fantasized

• The more I drank, the more I *fantasized*

everything.(p.560)

fantasizing

• Although my ambition still flickered, it now took the form of *fantasizing*.(p.556)
• Above all, we reject *fantasizing* and accept reality.(p.560)
• A.A. led me gently from this *fantasizing* to embrace reality with open arms.(p.561)

fantastic

• And then I scratched my head and said to myself, "What a *fantastic* thing for a man to say, that I cured his wife.(p.350)
• They have contributed *fantastic* amounts of time and work to our problem, but they aren't able, it seems, to arrest either your alcoholism or mine.(p.352)
• It was a *fantastic* structure, built on a crumbling foundation.(p.435)

far

• In that brief space, Alcoholics Anonymous has mushroomed into nearly 6,000 groups whose membership is *far* above 150,000 recovered alcoholics.(p.xv)
• So *far*, upon the total problem of several million actual and potential alcoholics in the world, we have made only a scratch.(p.xx)
• But that was *far* as I had gone.(p.10)
• If he is a real alcoholic and very *far* advanced, there is scant chance of success.(p.34)
• He is an intelligent man, normal so *far* as we can see, except for a nervous disposition.(p.35)
• *Far* from admitting he was an alcoholic, he told himself he came to the hospital to rest his nerves.(p.39)
• I reasoned I was not so *far* advanced as most of you fellows, that I had been usually successful in licking my other personal problems, and that I would therefore be successful where you men failed.(p.40)
• Some of us had already walked *far* over the Bridge of Reason toward the desired shore of faith.(p.53)
• We were grateful that Reason had brought us so *far*.(p.53)
• To conclude that others were wrong was as *far* as most of us ever got.(p.66)
• Self-reliance was good as *far* as it went, but it didn't go *far* enough.(p.68)
• As fast as he can, he pushes these memories *far* inside himself.(p.73)
• Is our work solid so *far*?(p.75)
• We must lose our fear of creditors no matter how *far* we have to go, for we are liable to drink if we are afraid to face them.(p.78)
• No matter how *far* down the scale we have gone, we will see how our experience can benefit others.(p.84)
• His religious education and training may be *far* superior to yours.(p.93)
• With few exceptions, our book thus *far* has spoken of men.(p.104)
• Many of our husbands were just as *far* gone.(p.110)
• Perhaps you enjoy drinking with him yourself when he doesn't go too *far*.(p.110)
• He is not likely to get *far* in any direction if he fails to show unselfishness and love under his own roof.(p.127)
• Even if he displays a certain amount of neglect and irresponsibility towards the family, it is well to let him go as *far* as he likes in helping other alcoholics.(p.129)
• So *far* as we are concerned, there is nothing obligatory about it.(p.132)
• Drinking occasionally, and understanding your own reactions, it is possible for you to become quite sure of many things which, so *far* as the alcoholic is concerned, are not always so.(p.139)
• But there are many men who want to stop, and with them you can go *far*.(p.141)
• While on the subject of confidence, can you adopt the attitude that so *far* as you are concerned this will be a strictly personal matter, that his alcoholic derelictions, the treatment about to be undertaken, will never be discussed without his consent?(p.143)
• By no means do we offer it as the last word on this subject, but so *far* as we are concerned, it has worked with us.(p.144)
• *Far* from it.(p.149)
• Alcoholics are being attracted from *far* and near.(p.161)
• The general moral standard was, as I recall it, *far* above the average.(p.171)
• Of *far* more importance was the fact that he was the first living human with whom I had ever talked, who knew what he was talking about in regard to alcoholism from actual experience.(p.180)
• As *far* as I know that was the first time I had ever paid any attention to that word.(p.187)
• Not *far* from where I lived they built a new technical high school and one of the teachers sold me on the idea that I needed a little mechanical drawing if I were going to be a good toolmaker.(p.211)
• As *far* as my home was concerned, I did not see then, though of course I can see now, that it was anything but a happy situation for my wife.(p.215)
• He startled me by informing me that he was an alcoholic, that he had found a way which so *far* enabled him to live without taking a drink, and that the main idea was to find a way how not to take that first drink.(p.218)
• I found in the fall of 1939, that I was not mentally impaired, so *far* as trial work was concerned, and thereafter took up where I had left off when I was about forty-five years old.(p.220)
• From *far* away, as if in a delirium, I heard my own voice – calling someone "Dorothy," talking of dress shops, of jobs . . . the words came clearer . . . this sound of my own voice frightened me as it came closer . . . and suddenly, there I was, talking of I knew not what, to someone I'd never seen before this very moment.(p.222)
• So *far*, so good – all according to plan, like thousands of others.(p.225)
• So I indulged with my comrades in everything the *Far* East had to offer.(p.231)
• For a long time the only Higher Power I could concede was the power of the group, but this was *far* more than I had ever recognized before, and it was at least a beginning.(p.248)
• They are *far* more alert and progressive than we floundering fathers were, and the future of our fellowship is in their hands.(p.250)
• With nothing but a liberal arts education, very definitely estranged from my family and already married, soon after graduation from college I became a bookmaker's clerk on the British racing circuits, *far* better off financially than the average professional man.(p.251)
• My migrations extended for over a year as *far* west as Omaha.(p.253)
• Mine was *far* from a happy childhood.(p.261)
• One year we got as *far* as Bellaire, Ohio.(p.264)
• I wanted "ripe" prospects and I didn't feel that I would get very *far* chasing individual drunks in and out of bars.(p.281)
• He told me that eventually he hoped such a group would develop in the Chicago area, but that so *far* this had not been started.(p.309)
• *Far* from expecting praise for their deeds, they claimed the performance a privilege and insisted that they invariably received more than they gave.(p.310)
• I had been *far* too busy building, protecting, and maintaining an image of respectability and all the other business pluses.(p.327)
• The satisfaction I got from giving him a little of what I had read in those pamphlets *far* surpassed any feeling that I had ever had before in helping patients.(p.347)
• I certainly was, as *far* as my living standard was concerned.(p.356)
• They were neither poor nor wealthy, but *far* better off than the average couple.(p.357)
• I will never know all the people I hurt, all the friends I abused, the humiliation of my family, the worry of my business associates, or how *far* reaching it was.(p.376)
• It wasn't how *far* I had gone, but where I was headed.(p.379)
• They did the best they knew how as *far* as I was concerned.(p.401)
• I wanted to get as *far* away from home as possible.(p.426)
• I'd fooled him thus *far*.(p.429)
• I was, so *far* as anybody could tell, quite a lad.(p.432)
• (Today, there is absolutely nothing in the world more important to me than my keeping this alcoholic sober; not taking a drink is by *far* the most important thing I do each day.)(p.447)
• It made me feel quite grown-up and mature, and I think another added attraction was the fact that so *far* as my family was concerned, it was forbidden, and it had a special attraction for that reason.(p.464)
• In the light of subsequent events it became evident that I took their advice *far* too literally, for, after some months of happy sobriety I drank again.(p.471)
• I don't think I suffered too much as *far* as the racial situation was concerned because I was born into it and knew nothing other than that.(p.485)
• As *far* as school was concerned, I made fair grades throughout.(p.486)
• That was the next meeting, and the first meeting of a colored group in A.A., so *far* as I know.(p.495)
• Father had never directly spoken to me about drinking but he never drank any, so *far* as I knew.(p.498)
• But his life was unmentioned, so *far* as I was concerned.(p.498)
• Those that understand me are *far* away.(p.505)
• An ambitious playwright, he let his brains get so *far* ahead of his emotions that he collapsed into suicidal drinking.(p.531)
• Still another friend and temporary host received me at four in the morning from the charge of a policeman who had found me "going to bed" in a garage *far* from the last place I could remember having been, a fashionable bar and restaurant in the theatrical district of New York, to which I had repaired after my date for that evening, a charming lady of the theatre who had refused my company for obvious reasons.(p.538)
• And I am sure they would be right as *far* as they go, but A.A. has taught me I am the result of the way I reacted to what happened to me as a child.(p.544)
• While an A.A. group may cooperate with anyone, such cooperation ought never go so *far* as affiliation or endorsement, actual or implied.(p.566)
• Dr. John F. Stouffer, Chief Psychiatrist, Philadelphia General Hospital, citing his experience with A.A., said: "The alcoholics we get here at Philadelphia General are mostly those who cannot afford private treatment, and A.A. is by *far* the greatest thing we have been able to offer them.(p.572)

far-fetched

• To us it is not *far-fetched*, for this kind of thinking has been characteristic of every single one of us.(p.37)

fare

• One school would allow man no flavor for his *fare* and the other would have us all on a straight pepper diet.(p.69)
• Your man will *fare* better if placed in such physical condition that he can think straight and no longer craves liquor.(p.143)
• When I got home I had to give him a check for the taxi *fare*.(p.205)
• He walked to the hospital to save bus *fare* and did it gladly in order to be helpful to an individual he had never even seen.(p.208)
• My husband said that I said, "Can you imagine them giving us that jail *fare*?"(p.264)
• And he said, "What jail *fare*?"(p.264)
• And he said, "That wasn't jail *fare*.(p.264)
• There was more than one occasion when I got up in the morning with just enough money for coffee and toast and the bus *fare* to carry me to my first appointment.(p.283)
• Then when we got back to the apartment, he was willing to wait two or three days until I got my health back to be paid off for the liquor and *fare*.(p.289)

fared

• Understanding myself now, I *fared* forth in high hope.(p.7)

farm

• I had had some success at speculation, so we had a little money, but we once worked on a *farm* for a month to avoid drawing on our small capital.(p.3)
• This went from bad to worse until Sophomore spring when, after a prolonged period of drinking, I made up my mind that I could not complete my course, so I packed my grip and went South to spend a month on a large *farm* owned by a friend of mine.(p.173)
• One of five children, I was born on a Kentucky *farm* in Carlyle County.(p.182)
• A couple of hired hands were cleaning out the barn on the *farm* and I would ride to and fro on the sled, and while they were loading I would drink hard cider out of a barrel in the barn.(p.183)
• FROM *FARM* TO CITY(p.261)
• We were to go up to our A.A. *farm* in Kent, and I spent the evening before riding herd on Anne.(p.415)
• The *farm*, in those days, was primitive.(p.415)
• However, I had phoned New York from the *farm*, appealing for help, and there in the station to meet us were two A.A.'s, John and Bud.(p.415)
• He did come, and I landed in the funny *farm* for a while.(p.479)
• Within a few days, I found myself drying out on a drunk *farm*.(p.559)

farmer

• He is like the *farmer* who came up out of his cyclone cellar to find his home ruined.(p.82)
• Pioneer A.A., minister's son, and southern *farmer*, he asked, "Who am I to say there is no God?"(p.497)

farms

• Here are some of the methods we have tried: Drinking beer only, limiting the number of drinks, never drinking alone, never drinking in the morning, drinking only at home, never having it in the house, never drinking during business hours, drinking only at parties, switching from scotch to brandy, drinking only natural wines, agreeing to resign if ever drunk on the job, taking a trip, not taking a trip, swearing off forever (with and without a solemn oath), taking more physical exercise, reading inspirational books, going to health *farms* and sanitariums, accepting voluntary commitment to asylums -- we could increase the list ad infinitum.(p.31)

farther

- On the other hand, I got quite a different picture *farther* south.(p.486)

fascinated

- This couple has since become so *fascinated* that they have dedicated their home to the work.(p.160)
- An old avocation, the collecting of first editions, rare books and Americana, *fascinated* me between times.(p.255)
- The story of Alcoholics Anonymous *fascinated* me.(p.258)

fascinates

- The statement *fascinates* me because of its simple verity.(p.396)

fascinating

- By this time I had become associated with the fast growing and *fascinating* business of broadcasting.(p.358)
- To be sure, I learned many *fascinating* things, and many things that were to prove helpful later.(p.434)

fascination

- For by now I had been exposed once to A.A., but I had treated it as a vaudeville and had taken friends to meetings so that they too could enjoy the *fascination* of the naked revelation of suffering and recovery.(p.539)

fashion

- Perhaps we are mixed up with women in a *fashion* we wouldn't care to have advertised.(p.80)
- They seemed to be happy in their *fashion*, they and their little groups of supporters, but always pride of intellect stopped me from seeking what they evidently had.(p.256)
- She was studying *fashion* design, was living in the same rooming house, and was from my home town of Cleveland.(p.359)
- I had worked the previous summer on a New York *fashion* magazine, a job I really enjoyed.(p.405)

fashionable

- All I can remember about the Roaring Twenties is that I drank a great deal, thought I was having a grand time, managed to get to Europe for a few weeks, was very proud of the dozens of speak-easy cards entitling me to an entree in the better joints between Cleveland and New York, took on a wife, and built a home in a *fashionable* suburb of Cleveland.(p.358)
- Still another friend and temporary host received me at four in the morning from the charge of a policeman who had found me "going to bed" in a garage far from the last place I could remember having been, a *fashionable* bar and restaurant in the theatrical district of New York, to which I had repaired after my date for that evening, a charming lady of the theatre who had refused my company for obvious reasons.(p.538)

fast

- We commenced to make many *fast* friends and a fellowship has grown up among us of which it is a wonderful thing to feel a part.(p.15)
- As *fast* as he can, he pushes these memories far inside himself.(p.73)
- If he feels free to discuss his problems with you, if he knows you understand and will not be upset by anything he wishes to say, he will probably be off to a *fast* start.(p.144)
- There are the same *fast* friendships, there is the same helpfulness to one another as you find among our western friends.(p.162)
- Whenever a situation arose that *fast* talk wouldn't explain away, I simply withdrew.(p.214)
- Once dad came all the way to Florida to sober me up, after a hotel manager called him and said that if he wanted to see me alive he better get there *fast*.(p.288)
- But from one or two drinks of an afternoon or evening, my intake mounted, and mounted *fast*.(p.336)
- By this time I had become associated with the *fast* growing and fascinating business of broadcasting.(p.358)
- The challenge intrigued me; also it was another opportunity to run away from myself and the "*fast* life of the big city."(p.359)
- It didn't take long for me to fall in with a *fast* crowd who had their lunch in the men's bar of a leading hotel.(p.361)
- I found out *fast* that the cheapest way to get drunk was on shots with beer chasers at two bits a crack.(p.397)
- This good and gentle man, a brilliant research doctor, got nowhere with me *fast*.(p.407)
- Then I found the solution: At the end of study time, I would drink two beers, jump in bed, sleep real *fast*, and wake up smart.(p.440)
- The pep pills affected my hearing at times: I couldn't listen *fast* enough to hear what I was saying.(p.442)
- Now I slide down mountain *fast*.(p.475)
- I borrowed five hundred dollars from the bank and three hundred from the loan shop, and I drank that up pretty *fast*.(p.490)
- Shouldn't have drunk so much or so *fast*.(p.498)
- And having sung that phrase, I'd chuckle with amusement, turning into irony turning into self-contempt turning into self-pity, at the sad fate of Bob, that wonderful, poor little motherless boy who was so smart in school and who grew up to accept responsibility so early and so *fast* and who staggered under his burdens without a whimper until the time came when he thought he was too good for this world and so he ought to be out of it.(p.532)

fast-moving

- He gets a thrill out of skipping in front of *fast-moving* vehicles.(p.37)
- Within a week after leaving the hospital a *fast-moving* trolley car breaks his arm.(p.38)

fast-thinking

- Is he not usually brilliant, *fast-thinking*, imaginative and likeable?(p.139)

faster

- Liquor caught up with me much *faster* than I came up behind Walter.(p.3)
- Sitting in a Second Avenue bar, accepting drinks from anyone who offered, after my small stake was gone; or sitting at home alone, with the inevitable glass in my hand, I would remember, and remembering, I would drink *faster*, seeking speedy oblivion.(p.225)

fat

- The local banker watched me whirl *fat* checks in and out of his till with amused skepticism.(p.4)
- I was *fat*, bloated, dirty and unkempt.(p.411)

fatal

- Business failure, insanity, *fatal* illness, suicide -- these calamities in his immediate family embittered and depressed him.(p.56)
- We found that it is *fatal*.(p.66)
- Continue to speak of alcoholism as an illness, a *fatal* malady.(p.92)
- He said he had finally learned that drinking was a *fatal* illness made up of an allergy plus an obsession, and once the drinking had passed from habit to obsession, we were completely hopeless, and could look forward only to spending the balance of our lives in mental institutions or to death.(p.290)
- They realized that repeated lack of drinking control, when they really wanted control, was the *fatal* symptom that spelled problem drinking.(p.315)
- They realized that in the end alcoholism could be a mortal as cancer; certainly no sane man would wait for a malignant growth to become *fatal* before seeking help.(p.315)
- I knew from my general reading that alcoholism was irreversible and *fatal*.(p.436)

fatality

- We have begun to comprehend their futility and their *fatality*.(p.70)

fatally

- Say that you believe he is a gravely ill person, with this qualification -- being perhaps *fatally* ill, does he want to get well?(p.142)
- I was *fatally* ill.(p.539)

fate

- And having sung that phrase, I'd chuckle with amusement, turning into irony turning into self-contempt turning into self-pity, at the sad *fate* of Bob, that wonderful, poor little motherless boy who was so smart in school and who grew up to accept responsibility so early and so fast and who staggered under his burdens without a whimper until the time came when he thought he was too good for this world and so he ought to be out of it.(p.532)

father

- I must turn in all things the *Father* of Light who presides over us all.(p.14)
- His income is good, he has a fine home, is happily married and the *father* of promising children of college age.(p.39)
- He is the *Father*, and we are His children.(p.62)
- But for every man who drinks others are involved -- the wife who trembles in fear of the next debauch; the mother and *father* who see their son wasting away.(p.104)
- We have tried to hold the love of our children for their *father*.(p.106)
- We have told small tots that *father* was sick, which was much nearer the truth than we realized.(p.106)
- Perhaps at this point we got a divorce and took the children home to *father* and mother.(p.106)
- Unless they actually need protection from their *father*, it is best not to take sides in any argument he has with them while drinking.(p.115)
- They remember when *father* was romantic, thoughtful and successful.(p.123)
- *Father* knows he is to blame; it may take him many seasons of hard work to be restored financially, but he shouldn't be reproached.(p.123)
- Having been neglected and misused in the past, they think *father* owes them more than they are getting.(p.126)
- Both *father* and the family are mistaken, though each side may have some justification.(p.126)
- Little by little, mother and children will see they ask too much, and *father* will see he gives too little.(p.127)
- Assume on the other hand that *father* has, at the outset, a stirring spiritual experience.(p.128)
- When *father* takes this tack, the family may react unfavorably.(p.128)
- They often forget *father* was beyond human aid.(p.128)
- They suspect *father* is a bit balmy!(p.128)
- *Father* feels he has struck something better than gold.(p.129)
- If the family persists in criticism, this fallacy may take a still greater hold on *father*.(p.129)
- Liquor incapacitated *father* for so many years that mother became head of the house.(p.130)
- By force of circumstances, she was often obliged to treat *father* as a sick or wayward child.(p.130)
- When sober, *father* usually obeyed.(p.131)
- *Father*, coming suddenly to life again, often begins to assert himself.(p.131)
- *Father* may have laid aside for years all normal activities -- clubs, civic duties, sports.(p.131)
- *Father* will necessarily spend much time with other alcoholics, but this activity should be balanced.(p.131)
- My *father* was a professional man of recognized ability and both my *father* and mother were most active in church affairs.(p.171)
- Both *father* and mother were considerably above the average in intelligence.(p.172)
- There my drinking became so much worse that the boys in the fraternity house where I lived felt forced to send for my *father*, who made a long journey in the vain endeavor to get me straightened around.(p.174)
- Finally my *father* had to send a doctor out from my home town who managed to get me back there in some way, and I was in bed about two months before I could venture out of the house.(p.175)
- Your Heavenly *Father* will never let you down!(p.181)
- This was no fault of my *father* or mother, as they were both very much opposed to drinking.(p.182)
- I remember that my *father* kept whiskey around the house for medical purposes and entertainment, and I would drink from this when no one was about and then water it to keep my parents from knowing I was drinking.(p.183)
- I was the oldest of three children, and my *father* was an alcoholic.(p.193)
- My *father* died in 1901 when I was eight years old and I was in the second or third grade at school.(p.193)
- (My mother and *father* were Catholics and I had been baptized, but at the end of my instructions for Confirmation I had not gone to church, and then when my mother remarried, she married a Protestant and the whole religious angle was forgotten.(p.201)
- My *father* was a railroad man and a Civil War veteran.(p.210)
- The differences between my *father* and my sisters, who were school teachers, made an excellent environment for the type of child I was -- that is, slick and cute enough to take advantage of any adult quarrel.(p.210)
- In other words, I was always safe from the discipline of my *father*, and having developed along that line, I had considerable difficulty in school.(p.210)
- My early life was spent in Baltimore where my

father was a physician and a grain merchant.(p.240)
• *Father* was a very well-integrated person, and while mother was highstrung and a bit selfish and demanding, our home life was reasonably harmonious.(p.240)
• At seventeen I entered the University, really to satisfy my *father* who wanted me to study medicine there as he had.(p.241)
• But I can remember the urge of the Prodigal Son to return to his *Father.*(p.260)
• I was the oldest in a family of seven, and my *father* was an alcoholic.(p.261)
• At the end of a year, the children got a card from their *father*, which I still have and cherish.(p.262)
• A square from ultra-dry Kansas, I did not taste grog until I had finished college, done a stint on newspapers, married, become a *father*, and been in studio publicity two years.(p.328)
• Shortly after I was starting to work on the program I realized that I was not a good *father;* I wasn't a good husband, but, oh, I was a good provider.(p.351)
• I didn't know how to be a *father;* I don't know how to come home and work week-ends like other husbands; I don't know how to entertain my family.(p.351)
• As usual, I ran out of money, and, as usual, I wired my *father* for funds to come home.(p.357)
• My mother was a lovely, sweet woman, whose only weakness was my *father.*(p.369)
• As my *father* climbed the ladder of success in the oil-field business, his drinking also climbed.(p.369)
• Then my *father* fell down a flight of stairs on one of his lost weekends, at the peak of his career, and died.(p.370)
• I saw at last that I had the same disease my *father* had, only I was being given a chance to live, not die.(p.371)
• We had always encouraged our children to bring their friends home at any time, but after a few experiences with a drunken *father* they eliminated home as a place to entertain friends.(p.376)
• By the time all this was over, I was really in a terrific state, and my *father* taking in things said, "Miss Esther is about to faint.(p.385)
• I put my poor mother and *father* through agonies but, finally, I couldn't stand living with them and having them watch everything I did.(p.386)
• He said, "If your *father* will come out and stay with you, you can have the house."(p.389)
• So I called my *father* and he said, "Yes," he'd come out and stay with me for that time.(p.389)
• I loved my *father* dearly and I adored my dog, and I'd gotten this new house and Frank had just given me a new fur coat and I was thrilled to death.(p.389)
• My *father*, as I have said, was very indulgent and loved me dearly, and knew how to get around me.(p.389)
• My *father* had a title; there was plenty of means in the family.(p.401)
• When I was a baby, my mother brought me to America, and I never again saw my *father.*(p.401)
• Her *father* became both mother and *father* to her.(p.402)
• Her *father*, quite rightly, wanted to put her in a school.(p.409)
• In fact, I was taken to A.A. by a woman whom my *father* had taken to A.A. thirteen years earlier.(p.419)
• I graduated with honors, but could not feel any real responsibility as a *father* or a husband.(p.419)
• My life there was a nightmare of periodic binges on alcohol and pills, adultery, unhappy hours at the dental office, seeing my wife give birth to our second child and have several miscarriages, living in a turbulent household, and making continual attempts to be the respectable dentist, husband, *father*, and community leader.(p.419)
• I was *father*, husband, taxpayer, home owner.(p.432)
• My visits to that sanitarium went on for nearly three years, until in March of 1944, my *father* died and I was too drunk to attend his funeral.(p.469)
• Had first drink in young teens, but was scared of my *father.*(p.474)
• Met *father* (Tall Man) at fork in road -- one way to reservation, other way to State of Maine.(p.475)
• By grace of God I stop, think two things: This would kill good mother and *father;* then remember boys talk about Indian fellow who been sober three years.(p.475)
• My *father*, a Negro, was a country physician.(p.483)
• We weren't even permitted to play cards in our home, but *father* would give us just a little toddy with whiskey and sugar and warm water now and then.(p.484)
• My *father* had come out of the South and had suffered a great deal down there.(p.485)
• That wasn't the way it was with my *father.*(p.485)
• *Father*, through the years, had built up a very good mail order business because, at that time, there wasn't too much money in medicine.(p.485)
• Economic conditions had a great deal to do with it, because I've often heard my *father* say that his mother would take one of the old time flour sacks and cut a hole through the bottom and two corners of it and there you'd have a gown.(p.486)
• Of course, when *father* finally came to Virginia to work his way through school, he resented the southern "cracker," as he often called them, so much that he didn't even go back to his mother's funeral.(p.486)
• My *father* had purchased a restaurant, which he felt would take up some of my spare time, and that's how I met Vi.(p.487)
• My *father* had treated him many years prior to this.(p.488)
• *Father* is an Episcopal minister and his work takes him over long drives on bad roads.(p.497)
• *Father* says grace, which delays my attack on the buckwheat cakes and sausage.(p.497)
• *Father* is delivering his sermon.(p.497)
• *Father* had never directly spoken to me about drinking but he never drank any, so far as I knew.(p.498)
• Her *father* comes to sit with me.(p.501)
• We are staying with my wife's *father.*(p.501)
• Her *father* stays with her.(p.502)
• My *father* was alive, and I had to do as he wanted, so I drank under cover.(p.508)
• My *father* was and still is a minister, and I was afraid that I might run into him, or that someone might tell him where I was, and I could still remember what he had done to me when I got drunk one Christmas when I was very young.(p.527)
• There was the *father* one lost respect for at the age of eleven, because the *father* broke his solemn word in a circumstance where you, eleven years old, had assumed guilt when you were innocent; but the *father* would not believe you, no matter what; and to ease his suffering you "confessed" and were "forgiven," only -- months later -- to have your "guilt" brought up -- only he and you knew what he was talking bout -- brought up in front of the stern grandmother.(p.533)
• The sacred word was broken and you never trusted your *father* again, and avoided him.(p.533)
• And, as a child is a part of his *father*, so do I now want to be a part of God.(p.535)
• My mother went to a nearby city to go to work, and my *father*, being an alcoholic, simply went.(p.544)
• After my very first drink -- a tiny glass of sherry my *father* gave me to celebrate the New Year when I was thirteen -- I went up to bed, dizzy with exhilaration and excitement, and I prayed I wouldn't drink any more!(p.554)
• As our children grew up, I was able to be a *father* to them when they most needed one.(p.559)

father-in-law

• The house was taken over by the mortgage holder, my mother-in-law died, and my wife and *father-in-law* became ill.(p.5)
• My *father-in-law* appears.(p.501)

father's

• My divorce coincided with my *father's* bankruptcy, and I went to work, casting off all allegiances and responsibilities to any other than myself.(p.225)
• I was deprived of many of the things that we feel are important in life, such as education particularly, because of my *father's* drinking.(p.261)
• Fear, love of dentistry, and an imitation of my *father's* periodic drinking pattern took me through dental college soberly, except for the few parties and vacations in those four years.(p.419)
• We had no whiskey in the house, other than my *father's* private stock.(p.484)
• You were thirty-five before you understood your *father's* horrible anguish, and forgave him, and loved him again.(p.533)

fathers

• Today most of our men are better husbands and *fathers* than ever before.(p.108)
• They are far more alert and progressive than we floundering *fathers* were, and the future of our fellowship is in their hands.(p.250)

fatigue

• He thought all alcoholics should constantly have chocolate available for its quick energy value at times of *fatigue.*(p.133)

fault

• They are not at *fault*; they seem to have been born that way.(p.58)
• Admitting he may be somewhat at *fault*, he is sure that other people are more to blame.(p.61)
• Though a situation had not been entirely our *fault*, we tried to disregard the other person involved entirely.(p.67)
• Where were we at *fault*, what should we have done instead?(p.69)
• Sometimes the man we are calling upon admits his own *fault*, so feuds of years' standing melt away in an hour.(p.78)
• Undoubtedly we should admit our *fault.*(p.81)
• Though his family be at *fault* in many respects, he should not be concerned about that.(p.98)
• Thus mother, through no *fault* of her own, became accustomed to wearing the family trousers.(p.131)
• This was no *fault* of my father or mother, as they were both very much opposed to drinking.(p.182)
• Searching where I have been at *fault*, it is not hard to discover and get right again, for I have proven to myself and to many others who know me that God can keep a man sober if he will let Him.(p.237)
• It was not difficult to convince myself that my unhappiness was the *fault* of the man I had married, and I divorced him at the end of a year.(p.545)

fault-finding

• Argument and *fault-finding* are to be avoided like the plague.(p.98)

faults

• When we saw our *faults* we listed them.(p.67)
• It may be he has done us more harm than we have done him and, though we may have acquired a better attitude toward him, we are still not too keen about admitting our *faults.*(p.77)
• His *faults* are not discussed.(p.78)
• We suggested he write his first wife admitting his *faults* and asking forgiveness.(p.79)
• Admit your *faults* to Him and to your fellows.(p.164)
• Suddenly I could accept myself, *faults* and all, as I was -- for weren't we all like that?(p.229)

favor

• Though we work out our solution on the spiritual as well as an altruistic plane, we *favor* hospitalization for the alcoholic who is very jittery or befogged.(p.xxiv)
• Not all of us join religious bodies, but most of us *favor* such memberships.(p.28)
• Yet all reasons for not drinking were easily pushed aside in *favor* of the foolish idea that he could take whiskey if only he mixed it with milk!(p.36)
• You are not doing him a *favor* by keeping him on.(p.141)
• There had been some occasions -- there was an automobile wreck, for instance -- when I had police escort home but not to jail, all of which, instead of doing me a *favor*, did me harm because I was then full of self-esteem as to the progress I had made both professionally and financially.(p.213)

favorable

• I have had many men who had, for example, worked a period of months on some problem or business deal which was to be settled on a certain date, *favorable* to them.(p.xxvii)
• I realized that there wasn't anything I could say to place myself in a more *favorable* light with my children, that it was going to be a matter of time; for I also understood the intolerance of young people towards deficiencies in their elders.(p.220)

favorably

• A man may criticize or laugh at himself and it will affect others *favorably*, but criticism or ridicule coming from another often produces the contrary effect.(p.125)

favored

• This secret drinker *favored* the local Laundromat as a watering hole.(p.369)

favorite

• He should not be made a *favorite.*(p.149)
• On one occasion when I was serving time in my *favorite* drying-out place while I was having a session with the psychiatrist, she left my case history on her desk when she was called away from the room.(p.470)
• I left this home town, then, after I had made a public spectacle of myself in the presence of a revered teacher whose *favorite* pupil I had been.(p.539)

favorites

• The employer cannot play *favorites*, but he can always defend a man from needless provocation and unfair criticism.(p.146)

fear

• The broker had gone to Akron on a business venture which had collapsed, leaving him greatly in *fear*

that he might start drinking again.(p.xvi)
• ***Fear*** sobered me for a bit.(p.8)
• We were having trouble with personal relationships, we couldn't control our emotional natures, we were a prey to misery and depression, we couldn't make a living, we had a feeling of uselessness, we were full of ***fear***, we were unhappy, we couldn't seem to be of real help to other people – was not a basic solution of these bedevilments more important than whether we should see newsreels of lunar flight?(p.52)
• Driven by a hundred forms of ***fear***, self-delusion, self-seeking, and self-pity, we step on the toes of our fellows and they retaliate.(p.62)
• As we felt new power flow in, as we enjoyed peace of mind, as we discovered we could face life successfully, as we became conscious of His presence, we began to lose our ***fear*** of today, tomorrow or the hereafter.(p.63)
• Self-esteem (***fear***).(p.65)
• Self-esteem (***fear***).(p.65)
• Self-esteem (***fear***).(p.65)
• Self-esteem (***fear***).(p.65)
• Self-esteem (***fear***).(p.65)
• Security (***fear***).(p.65)
• Notice that the word "***fear***" is bracketed alongside the difficulties with Mr. Brown, Mrs. Jones, the employer, and the wife.(p.67)
• Sometimes we think ***fear*** ought to be classed with stealing.(p.67)
• Some of us once had great self-confidence, but it didn't fully solve the ***fear*** problem, or any other.(p.68)
• We ask Him to remove our ***fear*** and direct our attention to what He would have us be.(p.68)
• At once, we commence to outgrow ***fear***.(p.68)
• They only thought they had lost their egoism and ***fear***; they only thought they had humbled themselves.(p.73)
• He is under constant ***fear*** and tension – that makes for more drinking.(p.73)
• We must lose our ***fear*** of creditors no matter how far we have to go, for we are liable to drink if we are afraid to face them.(p.78)
• ***Fear*** of people and of economic insecurity will leave us.(p.84)
• Continue to watch for selfishness, dishonesty, resentment, and ***fear***.(p.84)
• We are then in much less danger of excitement, ***fear***, anger, worry, self-pity, or foolish decisions.(p.88)
• But for every man who drinks others are involved -- the wife who trembles in ***fear*** of the next debauch; the mother and father who see their son wasting away.(p.104)
• We have had long rendezvous with hurt pride, frustration, self-pity, misunderstanding and ***fear***.(p.104)
• There is another paralyzing ***fear***.(p.116)
• When we do that, we find it solves our problems too; the ensuing lack of ***fear***, worry and hurt feelings is a wonderful thing.(p.116)
• The slightest sign of ***fear*** or intolerance may lessen your husband's chance of recovery.(p.120)
• The greatest enemies of us alcoholics are resentment, jealousy, envy, frustration, and ***fear***.(p.145)
• ***Fear*** gripped him.(p.154)
• Many mornings I have gone to classes, and even though fully prepared, would turn and walk back to the fraternity house because of my jitters, not daring to enter the classroom for ***fear*** of making a scene should I be called on for recitation.(p.173)
• One was the ***fear*** of not sleeping, and the other was the ***fear*** of running out of liquor.(p.175)
• That armor had turned into prison walls, locking me in loneliness – and ***fear***.(p.226)
• Freedom from anger and ***fear***, freedom to know happiness and love.(p.228)
• I had found friends, understanding friends who often knew what I was thinking and feeling better than I knew myself, and didn't allow me to retreat into my prison of loneliness and ***fear*** over a fancied slight or hurt.(p.228)
• Every time I blacked out, and that was every time I drank, there was always that gnawing ***fear***, "What did I do this time?"(p.244)
• For eighteen years, from the age of twenty-one to thirty-nine, ***fear*** governed my life.(p.275)
• By the time I was thirty I had found that alcohol dissolved ***fear***.(p.275)
• In the end I had two problems instead of one: ***Fear*** and alcohol.(p.275)
• ***Fear*** froze me in my tracks, but the instant I turned back toward home this paralyzing ***fear*** left me.(p.276)
• Now I was in a strange house, in a strange city, and ***fear*** gripped me.(p.279)
• Out of this maelstrom just two coherent thoughts came to the surface; one, a drink would mean homelessness and death; two, I could no longer relieve the pressure of ***fear*** by starting home, as was once my habitual solution to this problem, because I no longer had a home.(p.279)
• Obviously I have overcome ***fear*** to a sufficient degree to think in terms of success in business.(p.284)
• What about my ***fear*** of travel?(p.284)
• It would be wonderful were I able to tell you that my confidence in God and my application of the Twelve Steps to my daily living have utterly banished ***fear***.(p.284)
• The most accurate answer I can give you is this: ***Fear*** has never again ruled my life since that day in September, 1938, when I found that a Power greater than myself could not only restore me to sanity but could keep me both sober and sane.(p.285)
• Some of the things which used to stop me in my tracks from ***fear*** still make me nervous in the anticipation of their doing, but once I kick myself into doing them nervousness disappears and I enjoy myself.(p.285)
• I had a mortal ***fear*** of going to bed and tossing all night.(p.299)
• Also, I have no ***fear*** of anything.(p.303)
• And all the while my ***fear*** fed a growing conviction that before long it would be necessary for me to be put away in some institution.(p.306)
• Heartsickness, shame, and ***fear***, ***fear*** bordering on panic, and no complete escape any longer except in oblivion.(p.306)
• *FEAR* OF ***FEAR***(p.321)
• I could feel ***fear*** coming into my life.(p.323)
• But I felt a ***fear*** coming into my life, and I couldn't cope with it.(p.324)
• That ***fear***, of course, necessitated a program of hidden alcoholism.(p.331)
• So, with mixed feelings of humiliation, anger, and ***fear***, I decided to look for an answer.(p.371)
• In fact I was afraid to try it for ***fear*** that I would wind up like many examples I had seen of excessive drinking in the Army.(p.374)
• I was living in constant ***fear*** that I would get caught while driving a car, so I used taxis part of the time.(p.375)
• Living with ***fear*** and tension inevitably results in wanting to ease that tension, which alcohol seems to do temporarily.(p.380)
• I began, here and now, to ***fear*** the answer to the question -- what is the matter with me?(p.406)
• ***Fear***, love of dentistry, and an imitation of my father's periodic drinking pattern took me through dental college soberly, except for the few parties and vacations in those four years.(p.419)
• Well, I'm willing, if it will curb this awful desire to drink, this ***fear*** of not having a drink, this feeling of always being alone, scared, deserted, sick.(p.430)
• Today I think of life in terms of happiness, contentment, freedom from ***fear*** and despair, sane thinking, ability to face problems as they occur, the opportunity to help other alcoholics and to be decent.(p.430)
• There go my good intentions, ***fear*** of consequences, will to care, responsibility for my behavior.(p.458)
• We reverted to the old way of life we knew -- a life full of anger, vindictiveness, resentment, ***fear***, dependence, denial, self-will, irresponsibility.(p.459)
• (I think my first feeling of ***fear*** came with my first week's solitary drinking, locked up in that hotel room.(p.465)
• From that time on, ***fear*** was with me because I realized that not only would I not remember what happened to me while I was drinking, but apparently I couldn't control what happened.(p.465)
• Having passed over the border line, the next five years were filled with ***fear***, failure and frustration.(p.465)
• It was ***fear***.(p.484)
• The ***fear*** of the loss of Vi and the feeling that, though she had the right to do as she pleased, she should have told me the truth about it, upset me.(p.487)
• ***Fear*** gripped me then, because I could remember nothing about it.(p.489)
• The grand fellow who at my call made me a hail-fellow-well-met, who gave me such a fine voice, as we sang "Hail, hail, the gang's all here," and "Sweet Adeline," who gave me freedom from ***fear*** and feelings of inferiority.(p.498)
• A great ***fear*** seizes me.(p.505)
• The ***fear*** and the insane idea are taken away.(p.505)
• Not a trace of ***fear*** is in me.(p.507)
• He finally passed away, and the ***fear*** of him left me.(p.508)
• There was the economic ***fear*** which made me too timid to take any action which might improve my circumstances.(p.534)
• In my late teens I became aware of emotions I'd not counted on; restlessness, anxiety, ***fear*** and insecurity.(p.545)
• ***Fear*** of rejection and its ensuing pain were not to be risked, and I turned away from myself once more for the answer, this time to the drinks I had always refused before, and in alcohol I found a false courage.(p.546)
• Maybe I wouldn't be able to hold any job, or maybe (and this was my greatest ***fear***) I wouldn't care whether I had a job or not.(p.548)
• Bewilderment, ***fear***, and resentment moved into my life.(p.556)

feared

• Then came the night when the physical and mental torture was so hellish I ***feared*** I would burst through my window, sash and all.(p.6)
• People ***feared*** for my sanity.(p.7)
• One morning he took the bull by the horns and set out to tell those he ***feared*** what his trouble had been.(p.156)
• In fact I was scared to talk to him about it, for I ***feared*** the kind of talk he would give me.(p.234)
• I ***feared*** that I wasn't dressed like the rest.(p.261)
• However, I threw myself into Twelve Step work, and what I ***feared*** would be a calamity turned out to be the most blessed of blessings.(p.394)
• I had already ***feared*** insanity for a long time.(p.408)
• I, who had ***feared*** questions, now began trying to interrupt and tell my story.(p.414)
• Mother hated liquor and ***feared*** a drunken man.(p.498)
• At age forty, I developed a large lump in my potbelly, and I ***feared*** it was a tumor.(p.557)

fearing

• That was the reverse of my former pattern of ***fearing*** to go to work because I might drink!(p.199)

fearless

• With all the earnestness at our command, we beg of you to be ***fearless*** and thorough from the very start.(p.58)
• 4.Made a searching and ***fearless*** moral inventory of ourselves.(p.59)

fearlessly

• When we became alcoholics, crushed by a self-imposed crisis we could not postpone or evade, we had to ***fearlessly*** face the proposition that either God is everything or else He is nothing.(p.53)
• Sometimes we had to search ***fearlessly***, but He was there.(p.55)

fearlessness

• I could almost hear the sound of the preacher's voice as I sat, on still Sundays, way over there on the hillside; there was that proffered temperance pledge I never signed; my grandfather's good natured contempt of some church folk and their doings; his insistence that the spheres really had their music; but his denial of the preacher's right to tell him how he must listen; his ***fearlessness*** as he spoke of these things just before he died; these recollections welled up from the past.(p.10)
• But they had not learned enough of humility, ***fearlessness*** and honesty, in the sense we find it necessary, until they told someone else all their life story.(p.73)

fears

• We reviewed our ***fears*** thoroughly.(p.68)
• Our ***fears*** fall from us.(p.75)
• We all had hundreds of character traits, of ***fears*** and phobias, likes and dislikes, in common.(p.229)
• To the best of my recollection I was completely free from any abnormal ***fears***.(p.275)
• What about those ***fears*** which once paralyzed me to the point of my becoming a semi-hermit?(p.284)
• Courage to face each day has replaced the ***fears*** and uncertainties of earlier years.(p.295)
• Just an unstable woman, undisciplined, poorly adjusted and filled with nameless ***fears***.(p.305)
• In describing his suffering, his ***fears***, his many years of groping for some answer to that which always seemed to remain unanswerable, he could have been describing me, and nothing short of experience and knowledge could have afforded him that much insight!(p.309)
• Slowly, my life seemed to unfold before me, shedding insights on childhood resentments, jealousies, and ***fears*** that had mushroomed in adulthood, and also on the self-pity that I had wallowed in at every opportunity.(p.371)
• Mentally, the ***fears*** and tensions, the complete

change in attitude and outlook, bewildered me.(p.378)
• The birth of a daughter filled me with new *fears*.(p.402)
• I found that even then I had *fears* and inhibitions.(p.483)
• I thought this would give me ego-strength, make me feel wanted and secure, and alleviate my *fears*, but again nothing changed inside me.(p.546)
• Neurotic *fears* plagued me, and I had occasional, uncontrollable tremors.(p.555)
• When I awoke in the middle of the night with shakes and sweats and *fears*, I would hear my wife weeping quietly in bed beside me.(p.558)

fearsome
• Our Society then entered a *fearsome* and exciting adolescent period.(p.xviii)

feature
• Then Jack Alexander wrote a *feature* article in the Saturday Evening Post and placed such a compelling picture of A.A. before the general public that alcoholics in need of help really deluged us.(p.xviii)
• This is the baffling *feature* of alcoholism as we know it -- this utter inability to leave it alone, no matter how great the necessity or the wish.(p.34)
• To some people we need not, and probably should not emphasize the spiritual *feature* on our first approach.(p.76)
• If you are satisfied that he is a real alcoholic, begin to dwell on the hopeless *feature* of the malady.(p.92)
• Stress the spiritual *feature* freely.(p.93)

featured
• During the day a friend of mine brought me some magazines to take to a hospital group I was interested in, and I looked through them and a "banner" across the front of one *featured* an article by a prominent clergyman in which I caught the word "resentment."(p.552)

features
• I knew the man by name, and partly recognized his *features*, but there all resemblance ended.(p.xxix)

February
• On Sunday when I came to, it was a bad, wet, snowy day in *February*, 1937, and Paul and Doc and a lot of other fellows were in Cleveland on business.(p.207)
• While I went along with all that was done and attended the meetings, I never took an active job of leadership until *February* 1940.(p.249)
• It was *February* with snow and ice on the ground and I had a four blocks walk to the nearest cab stand, but I made it.(p.288)
• Then he said I couldn't possibly move on the first of *February* because I couldn't stay in that place by myself.(p.388)

fed
• That same year, my wife became *fed* up with my drinking around the house and called my dad in Akron to come and pick me up.(p.288)
• And all the while my fear *fed* a growing conviction that before long it would be necessary for me to be put away in some institution.(p.306)
• I'd get so *fed* up with drinking all alone and bearing the burden of guilt all by myself, that I'd egg him on to drink, to get started again.(p.325)
• Each ten-day period in the dark hole, I was *fed* bread and water daily, with one full meal on the third day only.(p.459)
• I had *fed* it, fanned it and nurtured it as one might a delicate child, and it had become as much a part of me as my breathing.(p.551)

Federal
• *Federal* Theatre in Texas gave me an administrative job which I held for a year, only because I worked hard and productively when I worked, and because my very tolerant chief ascribed my frequent lapses to a bohemian temperament.(p.256)
• When it was closed through Washington edict I began with *Federal* Writers in San Antonio.(p.256)

fee
• A retired Navy man looks back over twenty years of drinking, to add up his A.A. "initiation *fee*."(p.396)
• A few times at meetings, I have heard this statement: "Members of A.A. have paid the highest initiation *fee* of any club members in the world."(p.396)
• However, a rough estimate of one alcoholic's initiation *fee* seemed possible.(p.396)
• But now, with His help and grace, this child of His has paid his initiation *fee* for good, as long as he remembers to stay away from that first drink (the one that does all the damage) one day at a time.(p.399)

feeble
• Three months before I met Jackie I had made my second *feeble* try at suicide.(p.245)
• I would make a *feeble* attempt at eating supper, but I never met with any howling success.(p.299)

feel
• If any *feel* that as psychiatrists directing a hospital for alcoholics we appear somewhat sentimental, let them stand with us a while on the firing line, see the tragedies, the despairing wives, the little children; let the solving of these problems become a part of their daily work, and even of their sleeping moments, and the most cynical will not wonder that we have accepted and encouraged this movement.(p.xxvi)
• We *feel*, after many years of experience, that we have found nothing which has contributed more to the rehabilitation of these men than the altruistic movement now growing up among them.(p.xxvi)
• Faced with this problem, if a doctor is honest with himself, he must sometimes *feel* his own inadequacy.(p.xxvii)
• I talked with him for some time, but was not able to bring myself to *feel* that I had known him before.(p.xxix)
• War fever ran high in the New England town to which we new, young officers from Plattsburg were assigned, and we were flattered when the first citizens took us to their homes, making us *feel* heroic.(p.1)
• We commenced to make many fast friends and a fellowship has grown up among us of which it is a wonderful thing to *feel* a part.(p.15)
• Most of us *feel* we need look no further for Utopia.(p.16)
• We *feel* that elimination of our drinking is but a beginning.(p.19)
• They sound like the philosophy of the man who, having a headache, beats himself on the head with a hammer so that he can't *feel* the ache.(p.23)
• As we look back, we *feel* we had gone on drinking many years beyond the point where we could quit on our will power.(p.34)
• Simply because it is impossible to explain what we see, *feel*, direct, and use, without a reasonable assumption as a starting point.(p.48)
• When others showed us that "God-sufficiency" worked with them, we began to *feel* like those who had insisted the Wrights would never fly.(p.52)
• We agnostically inclined would not *feel* satisfied with a proposal which does not lend itself to reasonable approach and interpretation.(p.53)
• We begin to *feel* the nearness of our Creator.(p.75)
• We *feel* we are on the Broad Highway, walking hand in hand with the Spirit of the Universe.(p.75)
• As we look over the list of business acquaintances and friends we have hurt, we may *feel* diffident about going to some of them on a spiritual basis.(p.76)
• The husband begins to *feel* lonely, sorry for himself.(p.81)
• We *feel* we ought to say to her that we have no right to involve another person.(p.81)
• We *feel* a man is unthinking when he says that sobriety is enough.(p.82)
• We *feel* as though we had been placed in a position of neutrality -- safe and protected.(p.85)
• He will *feel* he can deal with you without being nagged by his family.(p.91)
• We *feel* that each family, in the light of their own circumstances, ought to decide for themselves.(p.103)
• As wives of Alcoholics Anonymous, we would like you to *feel* that we understand as perhaps few can.(p.104)
• If you are positive he is one of this type you may *feel* you had better leave.(p.108)
• His friends *feel* closer over a highball.(p.110)
• You will no longer be self-conscious or *feel* that you must apologize as though your husband were a weak character.(p.115)
• It is the most natural thing in the world, once his liquor problem is solved, to *feel* that he will now measure up to that cherished vision.(p.118)
• You *feel* he should now be yours.(p.119)
• Make him *feel* absolutely free to come and go as he likes.(p.120)
• The family will be affected also, pleasantly at first, as they *feel* their money troubles are about to be solved, then not so pleasantly as they find themselves neglected.(p.126)
• They are all disappointed, and often let him *feel* it.(p.126)
• Dad may *feel* that for years his drinking has placed him on the wrong side of every argument, but now he has become a superior person with God on his side.(p.129)
• Instead of treating the family as he should, he may retreat further into himself and *feel* he has spiritual justification for so doing.(p.129)
• The family may *feel* they hold a mortgage on dad, so big that no equity should be left for outsiders.(p.131)
• Even when you understand the malady better, you may *feel* this feeling rising.(p.139)
• It is better for him to *feel* fully responsible.(p.143)
• But you should *feel* under no obligation to keep him on, for your obligation has been well discharged already.(p.147)
• At the same time you will *feel* no reluctance to rid yourself of those who cannot or will not stop.(p.148)
• Even if you *feel* your organization has no alcoholic problem, it might pay to take another look down the line.(p.149)
• *Feel* better.(p.151)
• If you think you are an atheist, an agnostic, a skeptic, or have any other form of intellectual pride which keeps you from accepting what is in this book, I *feel* sorry for you.(p.181)
• But if you really and truly want to quit drinking liquor for good and all, and sincerely *feel* that you must have some help, we know that we have an answer for you.(p.181)
• Then Dr. Bob said, "Well, Bill, maybe you'll *feel* better tomorrow.(p.189)
• As soon as I had done that I did *feel* a great release.(p.189)
• I *feel* that is about the most wonderful thing that a person can do.(p.192)
• That was an experience that I have never forgotten, and many times in my own work with A.A. newcomers I *feel* kind of guilty because I haven't done the same thing.(p.219)
• An active member of A.A. since 1939, I *feel* myself a useful member of the human race at last.(p.229)
• That is where I had my first drink and I still remember it, for every "first" drink afterwards did exactly the same trick -- I could *feel* it go right through every bit of my body and down to my very toes.(p.241)
• I have served on only one committee in the past nine years, for I *feel* that I had my chance the first few years and that newer members should fill the jobs.(p.250)
• I don't *feel* bothered about liquor."(p.257)
• I was deprived of many of the things that we *feel* are important in life, such as education particularly, because of my father's drinking.(p.261)
• I always *feel* that our God Consciousness was a steady growth after we became associated with A.A.(p.270)
• I *feel* that one of the things that I still have to guard against is that I used to be set in my way about what I considered the old-time A.A.(p.272)
• She said, "I *feel* you're just being wise.(p.273)
• They made me *feel* as if I were a part of their family, and so did their children.(p.281)
• I wanted "ripe" prospects and I didn't *feel* that I would get very far chasing individual drunks in and out of bars.(p.281)
• The adjustments in such a case are difficult and take time, but we both *feel* that they are certainly worth it.(p.286)
• I do *feel*, though, that the fact that I finally grew up to a point where I could even tackle such a job is the apex of the story of a man who spent eighteen years running away from life.(p.286)
• I spent several days with him, but I did not *feel* adequate to pass the program on to him alone.(p.294)
• The three of us did not *feel* up to the job, and after a few meetings we convinced the prospects that they too should go to Akron where they could see an older group in action.(p.295)
• I *feel* as I did when I was fifteen years younger.(p.303)
• I could *feel* fear coming into my life.(p.323)
• And unless I had some rosy picture of what was going to happen that day, I wouldn't even *feel* like getting up in the morning at all.(p.325)
• Now I *feel* so very grateful not only for my sobriety, which I try to maintain day by day, but I'm grateful also for the ability to help other people.(p.326)
• But then I thought, well, now wait, how will I *feel* next Tuesday?(p.326)
• How will I *feel* next Friday, if I make it a Friday?(p.326)
• How will I *feel* next Saturday morning?(p.326)
• I *feel* so sorry for you.(p.334)
• When a few drinks made me *feel* good before I went over that line, those same drinks now made me wretched.(p.346)
• One said, "Don't *feel* that you are a martyr because you stopped drinking," and this hit me between the eyes.(p.346)

• The second one said, "Don't *feel* that you stop drinking for anyone other than yourself," and this hit me between the eyes.(p.346)
• So I thought to myself, I might just as well be drunk as *feel* like this.(p.348)
• I don't *feel* right.(p.348)
• I have been on this program for three months and I *feel* terrible."(p.348)
• I said I was okay, but if it would make her *feel* better I would go "as tired as I was after the strenuous holidays."(p.365)
• Drinking it with your meals, you didn't *feel* it.(p.385)
• There are so many to whom I *feel* deeply grateful; to my husband (and best critic), whose generous love, compassion and understanding have helped me along the way; to those before me in A.A. who inspired the first article I read, and the friend who sent that article to Frank; to Ruth for her personal note, and the first A.A. to talk to me; to my Bishop, whose loving and believing spirit inspired me; and to all the members of the Houston Group who were so patient, kind and helpful -- and to countless others.(p.393)
• I wish I could tell you all that A.A. has done for me, all that I think and *feel* about A.A., but it's something that I have experienced and have never been able to put into words.(p.394)
• I *feel* that there is no situation too difficult, none too desperate, no unhappiness too great to be overcome in this great fellowship -- Alcoholics Anonymous.(p.395)
• But I did not *feel* a part of my family or a part of the set-up.(p.401)
• Every day, I *feel* a little bit more useful, more happy and more free.(p.417)
• I graduated with honors, but could not *feel* any real responsibility as a father or a husband.(p.419)
• Not only did I not think that being an alcoholic was a good idea, I didn't even *feel* that I had all that much of a drinking problem!(p.439)
• I didn't *feel* I could lie in bed and squirt the stuff in my veins while my kids and wife stood around watching me, so I kept the drug in my bag and the bag in the car and the car in the garage.(p.442)
• Today, I *feel* I have used up my right to chemical peace of mind.(p.448)
• Today, Max and I try to communicate what we *feel*, rather than what we think.(p.451)
• I can tell her she ought not to think a certain way, but I certainly can't take away her right to *feel* however she does *feel*.(p.451)
• I would rather talk about the good things A.A. has taught me; I *feel* that hitting on just a few sordid points should be sufficient to let those of you in institutions know where I came from.(p.459)
• It made me *feel* quite grown-up and mature, and I think another added attraction was the fact that so far as my family was concerned, it was forbidden, and it had a special attraction for that reason.(p.464)
• I *feel* that I have been restored to health and sanity these past years not through my own efforts nor as a result of anything I may have done, but because I've come to believe -- to really believe -- that alone I can do nothing.(p.473)
• Talk and meeting make me *feel* good.(p.476)
• I *feel* Great Spirit at all meetings and when talk to A.A. friends.(p.477)
• I *feel* exhausted.(p.500)
• I *feel* horrible.(p.500)
• Suddenly I *feel* hopeless, unable to go on.(p.502)
• Suddenly I *feel* a wave of utter hopelessness sweep over me.(p.504)
• I *feel* lifted up.(p.504)
• I *feel* much better!(p.505)
• I do not *feel* angry any more.(p.505)
• I *feel* that I can fix them all.(p.506)
• Having made that bargain, I immediately began to *feel* I'd been trapped into it and I went out and had some drinks -- four glasses of gin, I remember.(p.523)
• I don't care too much about personal fame or glory, and I want only enough money to enable me to do the work I *feel* I can perhaps do best.(p.542)
• I thought this would give me ego-strength, make me *feel* wanted and secure, and alleviate my fears, but again nothing changed inside me.(p.546)
• Do it every day for two weeks and you will find you have come to mean it and to want it for them, and you will realize that where you used to *feel* bitterness and resentment and hatred, you now *feel* compassionate understanding and love."(p.552)
• As soon as I had made a few friends and had begun to *feel* accepted, we moved again.(p.555)
• We *feel* it better to let our friends recommend us.(p.567)

feeling

• When the thought was expressed that there might be a God personal to me this *feeling* was intensified.(p.12)
• The *feeling* of having shared in a common peril is one element in the powerful cement which binds us.(p.17)
• In some circumstances we have gone out deliberately to get drunk, *feeling* ourselves justified by nervousness, anger, worry, depression, jealousy or the like.(p.37)
• But the moment I made up my mind to go through with the process, I had the curious *feeling* that my alcoholic condition was relieved, as in fact it proved to be.(p.42)
• There was a *feeling* of awe and wonder, but it was fleeting and soon lost.(p.46)
• We were having trouble with personal relationships, we couldn't control our emotional natures, we were a prey to misery and depression, we couldn't make a living, we had a *feeling* of uselessness, we were full of fear, we were unhappy, we couldn't seem to be of real help to other people -- was not a basic solution of these bedevilments more important than whether we should see newsreels of lunar flight?(p.52)
• We finally saw that faith in some kind of God was a part of our make-up, just as much as the *feeling* we have for a friend.(p.55)
• The *feeling* that the drink problem has disappeared will often come strongly.(p.75)
• We go to him in a helpful and forgiving spirit, confessing our former ill *feeling* and expressing our regret.(p.77)
• That *feeling* of uselessness and self-pity will disappear.(p.84)
• We want to leave you with the *feeling* that no situation is too difficult and no unhappiness too great to be overcome.(p.104)
• Some of the snags you will encounter are irritation, hurt *feeling* and resentments.(p.117)
• Another *feeling* we are very likely to entertain is one of resentment that love and loyalty could not cure our husbands of alcoholism.(p.118)
• When he renews interest in such things, a *feeling* of jealousy may arise.(p.131)
• Even when you understand the malady better, you may feel this *feeling* rising.(p.139)
• Can you discard the *feeling* that you are dealing only with habit, with stubbornness, or a weak will?(p.140)
• If possible express a lack of hard *feeling* toward him.(p.142)
• It is joyous intimacy with friends and a *feeling* that life is good.(p.151)
• The proceeding was shot through with much hard *feeling* and controversy.(p.154)
• It took me a year, or a year and a half to get to *feeling* physically well, and it was rather tough, but I soon found folks whose friendship I had once had, and I found, after I had been sober for quite some little time, that these people began to act like they had in previous years, before I had gotten so bad, so that I didn't pay too awful much attention to financial gains.(p.190)
• The people in the group hadn't been around that day; part of my family was in Florida and the rest of them weren't speaking to me, so I spent a very lonesome day and by evening I was *feeling* very sorry for myself.(p.207)
• How are you *feeling*?"(p.207)
• I'm *feeling* terrible."(p.208)
• In fact I had been in very good shape at one o'clock -- *feeling* no pain.(p.223)
• To go into a gathering of people was the sort of thing that all my life, from the time I left my private world of books and dreams to meet the real world of people and parties and jobs, had left me *feeling* an uncomfortable outsider, needing the warming stimulus of drinks to join in.(p.228)
• I had found friends, understanding friends who often knew what I was thinking and *feeling* better than I knew myself, and didn't allow me to retreat into my prison of loneliness and fear over a fancied slight or hurt.(p.228)
• The *feeling* of impending disaster that had haunted me for years began to dissolve as I put into practice more and more of the Twelve Steps.(p.229)
• Then broke again, hiding out in cheap hotels all over the country, one night jail stands here and there, and always that horrible *feeling* "What's the use -- nothing is worth while."(p.244)
• Following a big drunk on that sheet, where I was doing leg-work and rewrite, a *feeling* of nostalgia made me buy a ticket for Liverpool and I returned to Britain.(p.252)
• Curious about it, *feeling* I was missing something, absolutely without any illusions about the aftermath, with no pronounced *feeling* of patriotism, I joined up with a Canadian regiment, serving a little over two years.(p.253)
• I remember *feeling* that they were all making fun of me.(p.261)
• I look back and remember these things because they made me very unhappy, and added to my *feeling* of inferiority at never being the same as other people.(p.261)
• But I don't believe now that it was with any deep *feeling* of resentment that I said to him, "The children are raised, and if this is the way you want it, this is the way we'll have it.(p.263)
• He talked about his wife taking his little boy away from him because of his drinking, and how he got back together with them through A.A., and we began *feeling* grateful right then that all these things hadn't been taken from us.(p.270)
• Immediately a great *feeling* of peace descended upon me, intermingled with a *feeling* of being suffused with a quiet strength.(p.280)
• I, carried away with the desire to serve A.A., gave what was probably one of the first radio broadcasts about A.A., living through a case of mike fright and *feeling* like a million dollars when it was all over.(p.283)
• In fifteen seconds or less, the *feeling* passed.(p.285)
• A few months after I made my original trip to Akron I was *feeling* pretty cocky, and I didn't think my wife was treating me with proper respect, now that I was an outstanding citizen.(p.293)
• This would get me *feeling* fit, and then I would start for home and fireside, thirteen miles away.(p.299)
• One morning when I was *feeling* really bad, I was put on K.P. and the head cook wanted me to go out and scrub the garbage cans.(p.317)
• Because it was only through *feeling* defeat and *feeling* failure, the inability to cope with my life and with alcohol, that I was able to surrender and accept the fact that I had this disease, and that I had to learn to live again without alcohol.(p.335)
• In an attempt to get over that *feeling*, there was a quick onslaught of a greater number of drinks, and then all was lost.(p.346)
• Deep in my heart was the *feeling* that maybe I could get some help here.(p.346)
• The satisfaction I got from giving him a little of what I had read in those pamphlets far surpassed any *feeling* that I had ever had before in helping patients.(p.347)
• What a wonderful new *feeling*, what a wonderful relief!(p.366)
• It was never boring, but I developed a *feeling* of deep insecurity.(p.369)
• A relief, even though I dreaded it, *feeling* that this was the end of everything.(p.378)
• Nor have I attended them with a *feeling* of just doing my duty.(p.381)
• I had no *feeling* of security, and I knew that I had done a very stupid thing, so I went back to Texas and remarried my ex-husband.(p.386)
• It was such a *feeling* of relief that I wanted to know more about it and with that, I think for the first time, came the realization that there was something horribly, horribly wrong with me.(p.392)
• Monday morning I was *feeling* just like a million dollars -- all I needed was half a pint!(p.393)
• The only thing that bothered me was a queasy *feeling* I had in the pit of my stomach.(p.418)
• Next morning I was sworn in, *feeling* no pain.(p.425)
• Well, I'm willing, if it will curb this awful desire to drink, this fear of not having a drink, this *feeling* of always being alone, scared, deserted, sick.(p.430)
• "If you had my problems, you'd drink, too" was my *feeling*.(p.439)
• (I think my first *feeling* of fear came with my first week's solitary drinking, locked up in that hotel room.(p.465)
• Then in a couple of hours, when there was still no word from my husband and no sign of him, I had the *feeling* we alcoholics all know.(p.467)
• For me, my sobriety comes before his or even before my *feeling* for him.(p.481)
• The fear of the loss of Vi and the *feeling* that, though she had the right to do as she pleased, she should have told me the truth about it, upset me.(p.487)
• There came a time when she spoke to me about it, and I would say that I had a bad cold or that I wasn't *feeling* well.(p.487)
• I actually wanted a drink, besides *feeling* that I had to have a drink.(p.488)

• It didn't worry me very much, because at that time I could shut off for a couple of months without taking a drink or even wanting one, and without *feeling* that I was giving anything up.(p.518)
• In part, it was a *feeling* of intense shame at having to leave the Army during the war, but mostly it was resentment that this kind of thing should happen to me for, strange as it may seem, up to then I still thought I could control drinking.(p.521)
• But the *feeling* was a crutch, an excuse.(p.534)
• Had I been able to explain to a psychiatrist the *feeling* of futility, loneliness and lack of purpose that had come with my deep sense of personal failure at this second divorce, I seriously doubt that the good doctor could have convinced me that my basic problem was a spiritual hunger, but A.A. has shown me this was the truth.(p.546)
• Within a week, I was *feeling* well enough to go home.(p.558)
• Though it was not our intention to create such an impression, many alcoholics have nevertheless concluded that in order to recover they must acquire an immediate and overwhelming "God-consciousness" followed at once by a vast change in *feeling* and outlook.(p.569)

feelings

• Unlike the *feelings* of the ship's passengers, however, our joy in escape from disaster does not subside as we go our individual ways.(p.17)
• Though some of us resisted, we found no great difficulty in casting aside such *feelings*.(p.48)
• How much did these *feelings*, these loves, these worships, have to do with pure reason?(p.54)
• Did not these *feelings*, after all, determine the course of our existence?(p.54)
• For when harboring such *feelings* we shut ourselves off from the sunlight of the Spirit.(p.66)
• When we do that, we find it solves our problems too; the ensuing lack of fear, worry and hurt *feelings* is a wonderful thing.(p.116)
• Many things happened; business trials, little worries, and *feelings* of general despondency came near driving me to the bottle, but I made progress.(p.237)
• When I drank, I hid it from my folks out of respect for their *feelings*.(p.287)
• No prickling consciences to needle us with guilt *feelings*.(p.329)
• How devastating, too, are the subsequent *feelings* of inadequacy and self-pity.(p.331)
• So, with mixed *feelings* of humiliation, anger, and fear, I decided to look for an answer.(p.371)
• We used to argue about our differing ideas, but we can't argue about our *feelings*.(p.451)
• When we deal in *feelings*, we tend to come to know ourselves and each other much better.(p.451)
• Of course I had the sensitive, hurt *feelings* of the alcoholic.(p.472)
• The grand fellow who at my call made me a hail-fellow-well-met, who gave me such a fine voice, as we sang "Hail, hail, the gang's all here," and "Sweet Adeline," who gave me freedom from fear and *feelings* of inferiority.(p.498)
• I had two or three *feelings* about that.(p.521)
• I hope I haven't hurt anyone's *feelings*, but maybe we could all grow and change.(p.529)

feels

• One *feels* that something more than human power is needed to produce the essential psychic change.(p.xxvii)
• To one who *feels* he is an atheist or agnostic such an experience seems impossible, but to continue as he is means disaster, especially if he is an alcoholic of the hopeless variety.(p.44)
• We know how he *feels*.(p.45)
• A man so involved often *feels* very remorseful at times, especially if he is married to a loyal and courageous girl who has literally gone through hell for him.(p.81)
• The more hopeless he *feels*, the better.(p.94)
• He is striving to recover fortune and reputation and *feels* he is doing very well.(p.126)
• Father *feels* he has struck something better than gold.(p.129)
• His wife is one of those persons who really *feels* there is something rather sinful about these commodities, so she nagged, and her intolerance finally threw him into a fit of anger.(p.135)
• Nearly every modern employer *feels* a moral responsibility for the well-being of his help, and he tries to meet these responsibilities.(p.137)
• If he *feels* free to discuss his problems with you, if he knows you understand and will not be upset by anything he wishes to say, he will probably be off to a fast start.(p.144)

fees

• There are no *fees* or dues whatsoever.(p.xiv)
• There were to be no *fees* or dues; our expenses were to be met by our own voluntary contributions.(p.xix)
• That the man who is making the approach has had the same difficulty, that he obviously knows what he is talking about, that his whole deportment shouts at the new prospect that he is a man with a real answer, that he has no attitude of Holier Than Thou, nothing whatever except the sincere desire to be helpful; that there are no *fees* to pay, no axes to grind, no people to please, no lectures to be endured -- these are the conditions we have found most effective.(p.18)
• Like most statistics, it doesn't prove anything -- just satisfies a little curiosity engendered by the wail "Oh, those initiation *fees*" that prompted this investigation.(p.399)
• Incalculable are the intangible initiation *fees* that A.A. members have paid: the sick, sick hangovers, the remorse, guilt, broken homes, jails, and institutions, and the mental anguish in general that has been generated over the years.(p.399)
• I stayed there just long enough to work up a real good resentment against the doctor in charge, who I didn't think was doing anything at all except collecting *fees*, and I left there fully determined that I'd never put myself in the power of medical people again.(p.521)
• We define professionalism as the occupation of counseling alcoholics for *fees* or hire.(p.566)

feet

• On talking to a man there, I would be amazingly lifted up and set on my *feet*.(p.15)
• I have seen hundreds of families set their *feet* in the path that really goes somewhere; have seen the most impossible domestic situations righted; feuds and bitterness of all sorts wiped out.(p.15)
• When, therefore, we were approached by those in whom the problem had been solved, there was nothing left for us but to pick up the simple kit of spiritual tools laid at our *feet*.(p.25)
• As God's people we stand on our *feet*; we don't crawl before anyone.(p.83)
• He may either plunge into a frantic attempt to get on his *feet* in business, or he may be so enthralled by his new life that he talks or thinks of little else.(p.125)
• We have come to believe He would like us to keep our heads in the clouds with Him, but that our *feet* ought to be firmly planted on earth.(p.130)
• Many, we are sure, will rise to their *feet* and march on.(p.153)
• Had he been successful in his enterprise, he would have been set on his *feet* financially which at the time, seemed vitally important.(p.153)
• I wanted to learn to stand on my own *feet*, not to change one prop for another, and an intangible and dubious one at that.(p.227)
• When I finally returned to Detroit to find work and to learn to stand on my own *feet*, the ball was already rolling, however slowly.(p.282)
• One is that I don't remember too many of them, as I was one of those drunks who could be on his *feet* and attend a meeting or a party, engage in a conversation with people and do things that any nearly normal person would do, and the next day not remember a thing about where I was, what I did, whom I saw, or how I got home.(p.301)
• To be sure, this had been a dizzy and confused interval, but most everyone else I knew had emerged from it with both *feet* on the ground and a fair amount of adult maturity.(p.304)
• I returned to my home in Lucknow, India, at the end of November last year from a vacation in one of the most famous beauty spots in our country, a mountain resort 6,800 *feet* up, with a wonderful lake.(p.342)
• Since the radio station was getting on its *feet*, it didn't require so many nights of evening work, and that permitted leisure time for drinking.(p.360)
• Slowly I realized I was in bed and that the objects were my *feet*, encased in a harness affair.(p.422)
• One night I barely made my downtown club; if I'd had to go another fifty *feet* I'd have collapsed in the gutter.(p.435)
• Our shoes are not better than the average hobo's, and if we are fortunate enough to have a pair of stockings on, nobody notices the runs in them, because of our dazzling beauty and our dirty *feet*.(p.479)
• So I wasn't just tinkering around with it -- I had to get in with both *feet*.(p.480)
• The drive was long and cold but he was thankful for the hot bricks which some thoughtful person had given him for his *feet*.(p.497)
• A little drink will put me on my *feet*.(p.500)
• And I jumped in with both *feet*.(p.516)

felicitations

• She was doing fine, she was up and around, and that day her husband phoned me and said, "Doctor, thanks very much for curing my wife," and I thanked him for his *felicitations*, and he hung up.(p.350)

fell

• The curve of my declining moral and bodily health *fell* off like a ski-jump.(p.7)
• Scales of pride and prejudice *fell* from my eyes.(p.12)
• Then he *fell* victim to a belief which practically every alcoholic has -- that his long period of sobriety and self-discipline had qualified him to drink as other men.(p.32)
• Having persevered with the rest of the program, they wondered why they *fell*.(p.73)
• Another time, as I opened a letter which lay on my desk, a newspaper clipping *fell* out.(p.136)
• It *fell* apart in the twenties.(p.197)
• Then my father *fell* down a flight of stairs on one of his lost weekends, at the peak of his career, and died.(p.370)
• I *fell* down and knocked out my front teeth.(p.390)
• He, in turn, kicked me so I *fell* to the ground.(p.406)
• I opened my eyes again and a shadow *fell* across the bed.(p.422)
• In the garage, I would put the needle in my vein and then try to figure out exactly how much medication to inject to overcome the pep pills while adding to the sleeping pills while ignoring the tranquilizers, in order to get just enough to be able to pull out the needle, jerk the tourniquet, throw it in the car, slam the car door shut, run down the hall, and fall in bed before I *fell* asleep.(p.442)
• He was in his late fifties, and all that he had undertaken *fell* upon my shoulders at his death in 1928.(p.486)
• When my mother opened the door, I almost *fell* in on my face.(p.510)
• But I don't remember that any of them ever went to sleep in joints and woke up with no shoes on in the winter, or *fell* out of chairs.(p.527)

fellow

• Disappointed but curious, I wondered what had got into the *fellow*.(p.9)
• "That *fellow* can't handle his liquor."(p.20)
• Here is the *fellow* who has been puzzling you, especially in his lack of control.(p.21)
• He is the *fellow* who goes to bed so intoxicated he ought to sleep the clock around.(p.21)
• That is where our *fellow* travelers are, and that is where our work must be done.(p.130)
• Two days later, a future *fellow* of Alcoholics Anonymous stared glassily at the strangers beside his bed.(p.157)
• Said the future *Fellow* Anonymous: "Damn little to laugh about that I can see."(p.157)
• He proved to be a devil-may-care young *fellow* whose parents could not make out whether he wanted to stop drinking or not.(p.158)
• So our *fellow* worker will soon have friends galore.(p.163)
• I seemed to be able to snap back the next morning better than most of my *fellow* drinkers, who were cursed (or perhaps blessed) with a great deal of morning-after nausea.(p.172)
• It was getting pretty dark and I hadn't turned on any lights, when some big *fellow* stepped inside the door and flipped on the light switch.(p.207)
• I remember well one *fellow*, Joe, walking nearly three miles through slush, wet and snow to come to the hospital to see a man that he had never seen before in his life, and that impressed me very much.(p.208)
• This duty together with my weekly meetings with my *fellow* alcoholics, and my daily renewal of the contract I originally made with God, have kept me sober when nothing else ever did.(p.237)
• And when I get upset, cross-grained and out of tune with my *fellow* man I know that I am out of tune with God.(p.237)
• Then I got a very good position in Philadelphia and quickly found I would need a few *fellow* alcoholics around me if I was to stay sober.(p.249)
• There was a young *fellow* who led the meeting and that was a beautiful thing to me.(p.270)
• I remember sometime, it was possibly six months after we had been going steadily to King School, that we were coming home from a meeting and saw a car along the way, and a *fellow* in back drinking a bottle of beer.(p.271)
• The example which they and Bill W., whose visits to Akron were fairly frequent, set me of service to their *fellow* men imbued me with a great desire

to emulate them.(p.281)
• Seven years of work in this field brought an opportunity to affiliate myself actively with one of my clients, a *fellow* A.A.(p.284)
• Philosophy, faith, a sense of humor (they could laugh at themselves), clear-cut objectives, appreciation – and most especially appreciation and sympathetic understanding for their *fellow* man.(p.310)
• I recall, as I walked into that meeting, saying to myself, "Here I am, a *fellow* of the American College of Surgeons, a *Fellow* of the International College of Surgeons, a diplomate of one of the great specialty boards in these United States, a member of the American Psychiatric Society, and I have to go to the butcher, the baker and the carpenter to help make a man out of me!"(p.347)
• Who is this *fellow* we are supposed to turn everything over to?(p.350)
• It pays daily in more harmonious relations with my *fellow* men, in ever clearer insight into the true meaning of life, and in the answering love and gratitude wherever and whenever I have been the instrument of God's will in the lives of others.(p.394)
• But my attempts at community service ended in a drunken and abusive row with a *fellow* volunteer.(p.410)
• I said it over and over, boring my *fellow* barflies.(p.412)
• A *fellow* A.A., called Anne, who had helped me, went on a terrible bender.(p.414)
• I thought it was my duty to keep her from drinking, not knowing that if the other *fellow* is really determined to drink there is nothing you can do about it.(p.415)
• When a big, healthy-looking young *fellow* stood up there and said, "I'm a success today if I don't drink today," I thought, "Man, I've got a thousand things to do today before I can brag about not taking a drink, for God's sake!"(p.447)
• By grace of God I stop, think two things: This would kill good mother and father; then remember boys talk about Indian *fellow* who been sober three years.(p.475)
• I find Indian *fellow*.(p.475)
• During recess we were playing basketball and I had accidentally tripped a *fellow* just a little larger than I was.(p.484)
• Vi was very kind and explained to the jury that I was basically a fine *fellow* and a good husband, but that I drank too much and that she thought I had lost my mind and felt that I should be committed to an asylum.(p.492)
• I knew I wasn't capable of keeping the bulk of the money myself, so I gave it to a white *fellow* who owned the bar which I frequented.(p.493)
• The grand *fellow* who at my call made me a hail-fellow-well-met, who gave me such a fine voice, as we sang "Hail, hail, the gang's all here," and "Sweet Adeline," who gave me freedom from fear and feelings of inferiority.(p.498)
• Will I take a young *fellow* who has been drinking for two weeks to live with me?(p.506)
• But I am to learn later that it began with my desire for material success becoming greater than my interest in the welfare of my *fellow* man.(p.507)
• It's like the *fellow* who came in A.A., and his sponsor said to him, "Listen, buddy, do you believe in a Higher Power?"(p.512)
• With deep shame came the knowledge too that I had lived with no sense of social obligation nor had I known the meaning of moral responsibility to my *fellow* men.(p.549)

fellow-sufferer

• I have something to contribute to humanity, since I am peculiarly qualified, as a *fellow-sufferer*, to give aid and comfort to those who have stumbled and fallen over this business of meeting life.(p.229)

fellow-sufferers

• They shared their homes, their slender resources, and gladly devoted their spare hours to *fellow-sufferers*.(p.159)

fellow-workers

• My *fellow-workers* were mostly good Saturday night drinkers and I was right with them.(p.252)

fellow's

• I am in another *fellow's* room at college.(p.497)

fellowman

• I am still arrogant, egocentric, self-righteous, with no humility, even phony at times, but I'm trying to be a better person and help my *fellowman*.(p.463)

fellows

• He may be one of the finest *fellows* in the world.(p.21)
• The great fact is just this, and nothing less: That we have had deep and effective spiritual experiences which have revolutionized our whole attitude toward life, toward our *fellows* and toward God's universe.(p.25)
• No person likes to think he is bodily and mentally different from his *fellows*.(p.30)
• We admit we have some of these symptoms, but we have not gone to the extremes you *fellows* did, nor are we likely to, for we understand ourselves so well after what you have told us that such things cannot happen again.(p.38)
• Let him tell you about it: "I was much impressed with what you *fellows* said about alcoholism, and I frankly did not believe it would be possible for me to drink again.(p.40)
• I reasoned I was not so far advanced as most of you *fellows*, that I had been usually successful in licking my other personal problems, and that I would therefore be successful where you men failed.(p.40)
• Driven by a hundred forms of fear, self-delusion, self-seeking, and self-pity, we step on the toes of our *fellows* and they retaliate.(p.62)
• This is the one he likes his *fellows* to see.(p.73)
• I pray that you now remove from me every single defect of character which stands in the way of my usefulness to you and my *fellows*.(p.76)
• Now we go out to our *fellows* and repair the damage done in the past.(p.76)
• We will lose interest in selfish things and gain interest in our *fellows*.(p.84)
• Most of them give freely of themselves, that their *fellows* may enjoy sound minds and bodies.(p.133)
• He remarked: "I'm mighty glad you *fellows* got over your drinking.(p.148)
• High and low, rich and poor, these are future *fellows* of Alcoholics Anonymous.(p.152)
• "Who are you *fellows*, and why this private room?(p.157)
• You *fellows* know your stuff all right, but I don't see what good it'll do.(p.157)
• You *fellows* are somebody.(p.157)
• After a bit, he said, "The way you *fellows* put this spiritual stuff makes sense.(p.159)
• A community thirty miles away has fifteen *fellows* of Alcoholics Anonymous.(p.161)
• Some of them may sink and perhaps never get up, but if our experience is a criterion, more than half of those approached will become *fellows* of Alcoholics Anonymous.(p.163)
• Admit your faults to Him and to your *fellows*.(p.164)
• She told me that she had been talking to a couple of *fellows* about drinking.(p.184)
• All the other people that had talked to me wanted to help me, and my pride prevented me from listening to them, and caused only resentment on my part, but I felt as if I would be a real stinker if I did not listen to a couple of *fellows* for a short time, if that would cure them.(p.185)
• I looked up and there were two great big *fellows* over six foot tall, very likable looking.(p.185)
• One of the *fellows*, I think it was Doc, said, "Well, you want to quit?"(p.187)
• Looking sadder than ever, he wearily ventured, "Well this is wonderful for you *fellows*, but it can't be for me.(p.188)
• Eagerly he pointed to us saying, "These are the *fellows* I told you about; they are the ones who understand."(p.189)
• I went over and bought a jug of hard cider and a gallon of wine that I gave these *fellows* to drink.(p.195)
• I was arrested and taken to jail where I was beaten up by two or three *fellows* who were already in there and whom I tried to boss.(p.204)
• On Sunday when I came to, it was a bad, wet, snowy day in February, 1937, and Paul and Doc and a lot of other *fellows* were in Cleveland on business.(p.207)
• He told me that there were some other *fellows* that had tried this with success, and if I cared to see any of them he'd have them come in to see me.(p.218)
• That was skeptically received by me when I first heard it, but after some twenty-eight or thirty *fellows* had come to see me, and pretty nearly all of them had said the same thing, I began to believe it.(p.219)
• I decided that if these *fellows* could make it I would try it myself, and so I did.(p.232)
• Jackie told me about a group of *fellows* in New York, of whom my old friend Fitz was one, who had the same problem I had, and who by working together to help each other were not now drinking and were happy like himself.(p.239)
• If he and these other *fellows* could do it, so could I.(p.279)
• God bless all you people in A.A. and especially you *fellows* in prison.(p.463)
• Get into the lives of other people, is one thing the *fellows* in New York had said.(p.505)
• Dr. Foster Kennedy, neurologist: "This organization of Alcoholics Anonymous calls on two of the greatest reservoirs of power known to man, religion and that instinct for association with one's *fellows* . . . the 'herd instinct.'(p.571)

fellowship

• When writing or speaking publicly about alcoholism, we urge each of our *Fellowship* to omit his personal name, designating himself instead as "a member of Alcoholics Anonymous."(p.xiii)
• Figures given in this foreword describe the *Fellowship* as it was in 1955(p.xv)
• Our earliest printing voiced the hope "that every alcoholic who journeys will find the *Fellowship* of Alcoholics Anonymous at his destination.(p.xv)
• We had to unify our *Fellowship* or pass off the scene.(p.xix)
• In spite of the great increase in the size and the span of this *Fellowship*, at its core it remains simple and personal.(p.xxii)
• This has become the basis of a rapidly growing *fellowship* of these men and their families.(p.xxiii)
• We commenced to make many fast friends and a *fellowship* has grown up among us of which it is a wonderful thing to feel a part.(p.15)
• We meet frequently so that newcomers may find the *fellowship* they seek.(p.15)
• But there exists among us a *fellowship*, a friendliness, and an understanding which is indescribably wonderful.(p.17)
• About half our original *fellowship* were of exactly that type.(p.44)
• Many times we talk to a new man and watch his hope rise as we discuss his alcoholic problems and explain our *fellowship*.(p.45)
• To watch people recover, to see them help others, to watch loneliness vanish, to see a *fellowship* grow up about you, to have a host of friends – this is an experience you must not miss.(p.89)
• You should be described to him as one of a *fellowship* who, as part of their own recovery, try to help others and who will be glad to talk to him if he cares to see you.(p.90)
• On your first visit tell him about the *Fellowship* of Alcoholics Anonymous.(p.94)
• Offer him friendship and *fellowship*.(p.95)
• One of our *Fellowship* failed entirely with his first half dozen prospects.(p.96)
• The *fellowship* of Al-Anon Family Groups was formed about thirteen years after this chapter was written.(p.121)
• It is a *fellowship* in Alcoholics Anonymous.(p.152)
• Thus we find the *fellowship*, and so will you.(p.152)
• Perhaps the best way of treating you to a glimpse of your future will be to describe the growth of the *fellowship* among us.(p.153)
• So one more was added to the *Fellowship*.(p.159)
• Aside from *fellowship* and sociability, the prime object was to provide a time and place where new people might bring their problems.(p.160)
• Being a large place, we think that some day its *Fellowship* will number many hundreds.(p.161)
• Some day we hope that every alcoholic who journeys will find a *Fellowship* of Alcoholics Anonymous at his destination.(p.162)
• He will show you how to create the *fellowship* you crave.(p.164)
• We shall be with you in the *Fellowship* of the Spirit, and you will surely meet some of us as you trudge the Road of Happy Destiny.(p.164)
• In his prodigy of service, he was well assisted by Sister Ignatia at St. Thomas Hospital in Akron, Ohio, one of the greatest friends our *Fellowship* will ever know.(p.171)
• This was my introduction to this "understanding *fellowship*" although it was to be more than a year later before our Society was to bear the name, Alcoholics Anonymous.(p.239)
• I had completely forgotten the January 8th when I found the *fellowship*, and I spent the next four days wandering around New England half drunk, by which I mean I couldn't get drunk and I couldn't get sober.(p.247)
• They are far more alert and progressive than we floundering fathers were, and the future of our *fellowship* is in their hands.(p.250)
• The hospitality of their home and their fine *fellowship* were freely mine.(p.259)
• Today I have Someone who will always hear me; I have a warm *fellowship* among men who understand my problems; I have tasks to do and am glad to do

them, to see others who are alcoholics and to help them in any way I can to become sober men.(p.260)
• I have had my share of problems, heartaches and disappointments, because that is life, but also I have known a great deal of joy, and a peace that is the handmaiden of an inner freedom, I have a wealth of friends and, with my A.A. friends, an unusual quality of ***fellowship***.(p.312)
• You can never know the pure joy of recovering within the ***Fellowship*** of Alcoholics Anonymous."(p.334)
• The ***fellowship*** I found in A.A. enabled me to face my problem honestly and squarely.(p.340)
• One night, a few weeks after joining the ***Fellowship***, much to my surprise and delight I saw a familiar but no longer frowning face.(p.371)
• It has been a ***fellowship*** with God and man that has held good wherever I've turned and whatever I've done.(p.394)
• I feel that there is no situation too difficult, none too desperate, no unhappiness too great to be overcome in this great ***fellowship*** – Alcoholics Anonymous.(p.395)
• (I can't know how much others of our ***Fellowship*** have paid financially and, even more important, mentally and physically.)(p.396)
• I have lost the ***fellowship***.(p.505)
• I want to get where I can find some alcoholics to help, and where I can have some ***fellowship***.(p.506)

Fellowship's

• But the chief change was in the section of personal stories, which was expanded to reflect the ***Fellowship's*** growth.(p.xi)

fellowships

• They will approach still other sick ones and ***fellowships*** of Alcoholics Anonymous may spring up in each city and hamlet, havens for those who must find a way out.(p.153)

felony

• He was serving time on his fifth ***felony*** conviction when a miracle happened.(p.457)
• You see, I am a five-time loser, which means five ***felony*** convictions (not including the cases beaten).(p.457)
• I woke up in jail, sick, withdrawing from alcohol and speed, already a four-time loser, and now with a fifth ***felony*** charge against me.(p.460)

felt

• If you have a drinking problem, we hope that you may pause in reading one of the forty-four personal stories and think: "Yes, that happened to me"; or, more important, "Yes, I've ***felt*** like that"; or most important, "Yes, I believe this program can work for me, too."(p.xii)
• His alcoholic problem was so complex, and his depression so great, that we ***felt*** his only hope would be through what we then called "moral psychology," and we doubted if even that would have any effect.(p.xxix)
• I ***felt*** like Napoleon returning from Elba.(p.4)
• I have since talked with scores of men who ***felt*** the same way.(p.12)
• At long last I saw, I ***felt***, I believed.(p.12)
• We made a list of people I had hurt or toward whom I ***felt*** resentment.(p.13)
• I ***felt*** lifted up, as though the great clean wind of a mountain top blew through and through.(p.14)
• Our friend ***felt*** as though the gates of hell had closed on him with a clang.(p.27)
• If what we have learned and ***felt*** and seen means anything at all, it means that all of us, whatever our race, creed, or color are the children of a living Creator with whom we may form a relationship upon simple and understandable terms as soon as we are willing and honest enough to try.(p.28)
• All of us ***felt*** at times that we were regaining control, but such intervals – usually brief – were inevitably followed by still less control, which led in time to pitiful and incomprehensible demoralization.(p.30)
• Many of us ***felt*** that we had plenty of character.(p.34)
• I remember I ***felt*** irritated that I had to be a salesman for a concern I once owned.(p.36)
• On the way I ***felt*** hungry so I stopped at a roadside place where they have a bar.(p.36)
• I vaguely sensed I was not being any too smart, but ***felt*** reassured as I was taking the whiskey on a full stomach.(p.36)
• I ***felt*** I had every right to be self-confident, that it would be only a matter of exercising my will power and keeping on guard.(p.40)
• Physically, I ***felt*** fine.(p.41)
• He had ***felt*** only the first nip of the wringer.(p.43)
• While pondering the answer he ***felt*** as though he lived in hell.(p.56)
• As we ***felt*** new power flow in, as we enjoyed peace of mind, as we discovered we could face life successfully, as we became conscious of His presence, we began to lose our fear of today, tomorrow or the hereafter.(p.63)
• This was only a beginning, though if honestly and humbly made, an effect, sometimes a very great one, was ***felt*** at once.(p.63)
• It set in motion trains of circumstances which brought us misfortune we ***felt*** we didn't deserve.(p.67)
• He ***felt*** that he had done a wrong he could not possibly make right.(p.80)
• Tell him you once ***felt*** as he does, but you doubt whether you would have made much progress had you not taken action.(p.94)
• Frequently, you have ***felt*** obliged to tell your husband's employer and his friends that he was sick, when as a matter of fact he was tight.(p.115)
• I ***felt*** this was inevitable and wondered if the bank was doing the man an injustice.(p.138)
• So, you see, there were three alcoholics in that town, who now ***felt*** they had to give to others what they had found, or be sunk.(p.158)
• Many of us have ***felt***, for the first time, the Presence and Power of God within its walls.(p.162)
• There my drinking became so much worse that the boys in the fraternity house where I lived ***felt*** forced to send for my father, who made a long journey in the vain endeavor to get me straightened around.(p.174)
• With the passing of the Eighteenth Amendment I ***felt*** quite safe.(p.175)
• Wishing to be polite, though I ***felt*** very badly, I said, "Let's make the call," and extracted from my wife a promise that we would not stay over fifteen minutes.(p.179)
• All the other people that had talked to me wanted to help me, and my pride prevented me from listening to them, and caused only resentment on my part, but I ***felt*** as if I would be a real stinker if I did not listen to a couple of fellows for a short time, if that would cure them.(p.185)
• I ***felt*** having gotten married, I was an adult and one of the first things I did was to buy two cases of whiskey with no idea of drinking it.(p.196)
• I can remember occasions when friends recommended me for positions or business opportunities that I wouldn't take because I ***felt*** that at some future date I'd get drunk and they would be hurt.(p.198)
• I got two drinks, each of them a quarter of that pint, in me, and was talking along with these people, but I ***felt*** that sooner or later they were going to have me cornered because they were smarter than I was and the drink was beginning to take effect; but as I reached for the third drink Bob said, "Listen, Buster, you promised to take some medicine if we got you a drink.(p.206)
• Because it affected me so strenuously, they ***felt*** that hospitalization was indicated and I awoke in a hospital.(p.207)
• All during Prohibition, every alcoholic ***felt*** that he made the best hooch, regardless of how bad it was.(p.213)
• When I was about forty-seven, after indulging in all kinds of self-deception to control my drinking, I arrived at a period when I ***felt*** convinced I had to have so much alcohol every day and that the real problem was to control how much.(p.214)
• They probably ***felt*** that it was useless, that surely I had enough intelligence to know what I was doing.(p.215)
• Professionally, after I was sober for a month or so I realized that I should school myself to dissolve the partnership I was in because I ***felt*** that I would never regain the respect of my partners no matter how long I was sober, and that I would be at a disadvantage.(p.220)
• I wasn't the only person in the world who ***felt*** and behaved like this!(p.227)
• And so on and on, for several weeks, while I grudgingly plowed through some more of the offending book, and ***felt*** more and more hopeless about myself.(p.227)
• And, accepting, I ***felt*** a new inner comfort, and the willingness and strength to do something about the traits I couldn't live with.(p.229)
• They knew what to do about those black abysses that yawned ready to swallow me when I ***felt*** depressed, or nervous.(p.229)
• Like most immigrants I wanted to be somebody and have something and I was very happy and contented as I ***felt*** success crown my efforts.(p.232)
• I'm sure his family ***felt*** that it was a marriage that -- well, I was a girl from the wrong side of the tracks -- definitely!(p.262)
• I ***felt*** that his family were accepting me because it was good sense.(p.262)
• I was still bitter because I ***felt*** that drink had completely ruined my childhood and my married life, and I hated everything pertaining to it.(p.262)
• I didn't realize how I still ***felt*** about him.(p.263)
• Dr. Bob often said that it was a record for what he ***felt*** was a typical alcoholic.(p.263)
• We talked about it afterwards, and we ***felt*** that there might be some time we'd need it.(p.266)
• In the spiritual strength I had found, because of A.A., I ***felt*** that I had made a complete surrender, that I had really turned my life over that summer.(p.271)
• I ***felt*** it certainly must be very depressing to her that I should sit there by her bedside and cry.(p.272)
• Probably only a few readers of this story will be able, from personal experiences of their own, to understand the exhilaration and sense of accomplishment which I ***felt*** after finishing this seemingly simple assignment.(p.276)
• So I spent much of my time calling on the people who I ***felt*** would logically come in contact with alcoholic cases, doctors, ministers, lawyers and the personnel men in industry.(p.281)
• However, I must have ***felt***, deep down inside myself, that living the selfish life of a bachelor was only half living.(p.286)
• As I look back on that first evening I realize that I began to hope, then, for the first time; and I ***felt*** that if he could regain these things, perhaps it would be possible for me too.(p.290)
• I would hang on to sobriety for short intervals, but always there would come the tide of an overpowering necessity to drink and, as I was engulfed in it, I ***felt*** such a sense of panic that I really believed I would die if I didn't get that drink inside.(p.306)
• Nevertheless, there were a few doctors who saw alcoholism as a disease and ***felt*** that the alcoholic was a victim of something over which he had no control.(p.307)
• I ***felt*** better mentally and physically.(p.320)
• But I ***felt*** a fear coming into my life, and I couldn't cope with it.(p.324)
• And I ***felt*** depleted, whipped.(p.326)
• I ***felt*** disgraced and humiliated -- a man who couldn't hold booze – a social disaster.(p.328)
• I just wanted to live to a certain age, carry through with what I ***felt*** was my job with the children, and after that – no matter.(p.337)
• And the first thing you know I was lifted right out of the A.A. group, and I floated higher, and higher, and even higher, until I was way up on a pink cloud which is known as Pink Seven, and I ***felt*** miserable again.(p.348)
• Here were people who had thought and ***felt*** as I had.(p.355)
• These people were my friends, and I ***felt*** their sincere interest in me.(p.355)
• At times, when I noticed other families, I ***felt*** something was very wrong with ours.(p.369)
• I had no qualms, because I ***felt*** the source of a drinking problem was all in how weak one was, and I wasn't like my dad (I thought).(p.370)
• And I still ***felt*** it was a weakness – plus, in her case, adverse circumstances.(p.370)
• I ***felt*** this was the final blow.(p.370)
• I tried the wagon on numerous occasions but I always ***felt*** unhappy and abused.(p.375)
• I saw him recently and he told me that he had always ***felt*** guilty, because, after our separation, I had become a serious alcoholic.(p.403)
• Never had I ***felt*** a sense of belonging.(p.413)
• I ***felt*** like a gangster's moll about to be interviewed by the Salvation Army.(p.413)
• She said she ***felt*** too horrible inside to be pretty on the outside.(p.415)
• He asked how I ***felt***.(p.422)
• The doctor sat down beside the bed and asked me how I ***felt***.(p.423)
• Mom and I drank every waking moment because we ***felt*** so sorry for dad.(p.426)
• I seldom left the base any more except once in a while when I ***felt*** the need of talking to some girl.(p.427)
• It became progressively harder to get up in the morning, until one day I asked myself what I would do for a patient who ***felt*** this rotten.(p.441)
• I really ***felt*** sorry for him; the only thing in life he had to brag about was the fact that he was an alcoholic.(p.446)
• Right from the start, I ***felt*** that they weren't doing anything for me, but they sure were helping Max.(p.447)
• On the day set for the extractions, on my way to the

dentist's I *felt* a little nervous, so I had a couple of drinks, and after the teeth were out I was very nervous, so I had a few more.(p.466)
• In other words, the kindest doctor in the whole world, and I had one such, couldn't help me because I always *felt*, "You can't know about me – you can't possibly know – you don't even drink!"(p.471)
• She realized that, and the way I *felt*, and so for my own good she gradually began to pull away.(p.472)
• I *felt* very lonely and hurt, because nobody understood me.(p.478)
• I *felt* very sorry for myself and attempted suicide on many occasions, making sure there was always somebody within reaching distance to see that I didn't finish the job.(p.478)
• My father had purchased a restaurant, which he *felt* would take up some of my spare time, and that's how I met Vi.(p.487)
• He went into the religious side and told me that I didn't attend church as regularly as I should, and that he *felt*, more or less, that this was responsible for my trouble.(p.489)
• Vi was very kind and explained to the jury that I was basically a fine fellow and a good husband, but that I drank too much and that she thought I had lost my mind and *felt* that I should be committed to an asylum.(p.492)
• The judge said that if she *felt* that way he would confine me for thirty days' examination and observation.(p.492)
• After the trial, I got big-hearted again and *felt* that I should do something in payment for Vi's kindness to me; so I left Washington and went to Seattle to work.(p.492)
• I guess I *felt*, and he sensed it, that I wanted him to hurry up and say what he had to say and get out.(p.494)
• How sick I *felt*.(p.498)
• Anger possesses me, anger such as I have never *felt* before.(p.505)
• I was in a world that I knew nothing at all about, and I *felt* intensely afraid.(p.521)
• Poor, black, totally ruled by alcohol, she *felt* shut away from any life worth living.(p.526)
• I *felt* that I didn't have anything to live for, so I tried suicide many times.(p.528)
• I was immersed in self-pity and resentment, and the only people who would support this attitude or who I *felt* understood me at all were the people I met in bars and the ones who drank as I did.(p.547)
• Hopeless now, I *felt* it would be better for my wife, my children, and everyone in my life if I went ahead and died.(p.558)
• Dr. G. Kirby Collier, psychiatrist: "I have *felt* that A.A. is a group unto themselves and their best results can be had under their own guidance, as a result of their philosophy.(p.571)

female
• Potential *female* alcoholics often turn into the real thing and are gone beyond recall in a few years.(p.33)
• In June, 1945, with another member, I made my first – and only -- Twelfth Step call on a *female* alcoholic and a year later I married her.(p.249)

fence
• My parents' car had a strong attraction to fences, and one night I blacked out and drove the car down a bank, ramming the steel *fence* around someone's backyard.(p.353)

fenced
• As I said before, I don't like to be *fenced* in, and with those bars you don't get hotel service.(p.390)

fences
• He had to painfully admit that and mend his spiritual *fences*.(p.135)
• My parents' car had a strong attraction to *fences*, and one night I blacked out and drove the car down a bank, ramming the steel fence around someone's backyard.(p.353)

fervor
• At age twenty-one, I enlisted in the Navy for two reasons: (1) to avoid being drafted into the Army, and (2) out of a burst of patriotic *fervor* inspired by the advent of World War II and as the result of an all-night drinking binge which found me sitting on the doorstep of the Navy recruiting office when the chief petty officer arrived to open for business at nine o'clock Monday morning.(p.398)
• I turned to religion with *fervor*.(p.555)

festering
• For example, we are told in A.A. that we cannot afford resentments and self-pity, so we learn to avoid these *festering* mental attitudes.(p.560)

festivities
• I could discipline myself but along the way there would be *festivities* and occasions when I got drunk.(p.211)

fetch
• Before our visit was over, Bill suddenly turned to his wife and said, "Go *fetch* my clothes, dear.(p.189)

feted
• For weeks after my arrival I was *feted* and entertained in the already large colony of Alsatians in the city, and among the Germans in their saloons and clubs.(p.231)

fettered
• In the realm of the material, men's minds were *fettered* by superstition, tradition, and all sorts of fixed ideas.(p.51)
• Every breadwinner, whether trying to impress a boss or to hold customers in his own business, is *fettered* by people-pleasing.(p.329)

feuds
• I have seen hundreds of families set their feet in the path that really goes somewhere; have seen the most impossible domestic situations righted; *feuds* and bitterness of all sorts wiped out.(p.15)
• Sometimes the man we are calling upon admits his own fault, so *feuds* of years' standing melt away in an hour.(p.78)

fever
• War *fever* ran high in the New England town to which we new, young officers from Plattsburg were assigned, and we were flattered when the first citizens took us to their homes, making us feel heroic.(p.1)
• In 1929 I contracted golf *fever*.(p.3)

fevered
• Who wouldn't be, with such a *fevered* brain?(p.140)

feverishly
• It wasn't very long before home-brewing was an institution and men began to search *feverishly* for old recipe books on wine-making.(p.232)

few
• It is important that we remain anonymous because we are too *few*, at present to handle the overwhelming number of personal appeals which may result from this publication.(p.xiii)
• Other thousands came to a *few* A.A. meetings and at first decided they didn't want the program.(p.xx)
• There was, therefore, a sense of real satisfaction when I was asked to contribute a *few* words on a subject which is covered in such masterly detail in these pages.(p.xxv)
• We believe, and so suggested a *few* years ago, that the action of alcohol on these chronic alcoholics is a manifestation of an allergy; that the phenomenon of craving is limited to this class and never occurs in the average temperate drinker.(p.xxvi)
• They are restless, irritable and discontented, unless they can again experience the sense of ease and comfort which comes at once by taking a *few* drinks -- drinks which they see others taking with impunity.(p.xxvi)
• On the other hand – and strange as this may seem to those who do not understand -- once a psychic change has occurred, the very same person who seemed doomed, who had so many problems he despaired of ever solving them, suddenly finds himself easily able to control his desire for alcohol, the only effort necessary being that required to follow a *few* simple rules.(p.xxvii)
• For the next *few* years fortune threw money and applause my way.(p.3)
• Sometimes a small deal would net a *few* hundred dollars, and I would pay my bills at the bars and delicatessens.(p.5)
• *Few* people really are, for that means blind faith in the strange proposition that this universe originated in a cipher and aimlessly rushes nowhere.(p.10)
• But the ex-problem drinker who has found this solution, who is properly armed with facts about himself, can generally win the entire confidence of another alcoholic in a *few* hours.(p.18)
• A *few* are fortunate enough to be so situated that they can give nearly all their time to the work.(p.19)
• It may cause him to die a *few* years before his time.(p.21)
• How true this is, *few* realize.(p.23)
• But the difficulty is that *few* alcoholics have enough desire to stop while there is yet time.(p.32)
• We have heard of *few* instances where people, who showed definite signs of alcoholism, were able to stop for a long period because of an overpowering desire to do so.(p.32)
• Several of our crowd, men of thirty or less, had been drinking only a *few* years, but they found themselves as helpless as those who had been drinking twenty years.(p.33)
• Potential female alcoholics often turn into the real thing and are gone beyond recall in a *few* years.(p.33)
• We think *few*, to whom this book will appeal, can stay dry anything like a year.(p.34)
• Some will be drunk the day after making their resolutions; most of them within a *few* weeks.(p.34)
• In a *few* years he became so violent when intoxicated that he had to be committed.(p.35)
• I had a *few* words with the boss, but nothing serious.(p.36)
• He enjoys himself for a *few* years in spite of friendly warnings.(p.37)
• He tells you he has decided to stop jay-walking for good, but in a *few* weeks he breaks both legs.(p.38)
• For a *few* days he was depressed about his condition.(p.39)
• Except in a *few* rare cases, neither he nor any other human being can provide such a defense.(p.43)
• This happened soon after they wholeheartedly met a *few* simple requirements.(p.50)
• In a *few* seconds he was overwhelmed by a conviction of the Presence of God.(p.56)
• Save for a *few* brief moments of temptation the thought of drink has never returned; and at such times a great revulsion has risen up in him.(p.57)
• We know but *few* instances where we have given these doctors a fair break.(p.73)
• After a *few* years with an alcoholic, a wife gets worn out, resentful and uncommunicative.(p.81)
• If not members of religious bodies, we sometimes select and memorize a *few* set prayers which emphasize the principles we have been discussing.(p.87)
• You can easily find some by asking a *few* doctors, ministers, priests or hospitals.(p.89)
• Perhaps you will want to take the man into your home for a *few* days.(p.96)
• If persisted in for a *few* months, the effect on a man's family is sure to be great.(p.99)
• If you do this thoroughly, *few* people will ask you to drink.(p.102)
• With *few* exceptions, our book thus far has spoken of men.(p.104)
• As wives of Alcoholics Anonymous, we would like you to feel that we understand as perhaps *few* can.(p.104)
• We could make *few* social engagements.(p.105)
• We do not like the thought that the contents of a book or the work of another alcoholic has accomplished in a *few* weeks that for which we struggled for years.(p.118)
• A *few* of us have had these growing pains and they hurt a great deal.(p.124)
• We families of Alcoholics Anonymous keep *few* skeletons in the closet.(p.125)
• Some of us had this experience, only to enjoy, in a *few* months, a finer intimacy than ever.(p.134)
• In only a *few* instances has there been lack of patience and tolerance.(p.137)
• If he says yes, does he really mean it, or down inside does he think he is fooling you, and that after rest and treatment he will be able to get away with a *few* drinks now and then?(p.142)
• Only a *few* knew of it at first but, within a short time, it was billboarded throughout the entire company.(p.145)
• After your man has gone along without drinking for a *few* months, you may be able to make use of his services with other employees who are giving you the alcoholic run-around -- provided, of course, they are willing to have a third party in the picture.(p.146)
• The exceptions are *few*.(p.148)
• Then he will know loneliness such as *few* do.(p.152)
• Still physically weak, and sober but a *few* months, he saw that his predicament was dangerous.(p.154)
• He had, of course, the familiar alcoholic obsession that *few* knew of his drinking.(p.155)
• They experienced a *few* distressing failures, but in those cases they made an effort to bring the man's family into a spiritual way of living, thus relieving much worry and suffering.(p.159)
• Every *few* days this doctor suggests our approach to one of his patients.(p.162)
• He had lived there but a *few* weeks when he found that the place probably contained more alcoholics per square mile than any city in the country.(p.163)
• This was only a *few* days ago at this writing.(p.163)
• When a *few* men in this city have found themselves, and have discovered the joy of helping others to face life again, there will be no stopping until everyone in that town has had his opportunity to recover -- if he can and will.(p.163)

• I soon discovered that a couple of drinks would alleviate my gastric distress, at least for a *few* hours at a time, so it was not at all difficult for me to return to my former excessive indulgence.(p.174)
• I knew everyone would buy a *few* bottles, or cases, of liquor as their exchequers permitted, and that it would soon be gone.(p.175)
• During the next *few* years, I developed two distinct phobias.(p.175)
• Occasionally, I would yield to the morning craving, but if I did, it would be only a *few* hours before I would be quite unfit for work.(p.176)
• This routine went on with *few* interruptions for seventeen years.(p.177)
• He came and got me home and to bed, gave me a *few* drinks that night, and one bottle of beer the next morning.(p.179)
• I would reach over and get this and take a shot and in a *few* moments get up and take another, shave and eat my breakfast, slip a half pint of liquor in my hip pocket, and go on to school.(p.183)
• An offer of appreciation for not having had a drink for those *few* months and then and there, without anybody promising me anything or threatening me, I made a solemn vow that never so long as I lived would I take another drink.(p.200)
• A *few* minutes later, Dr. Bob left, leaving with my brother some medicine I should get.(p.207)
• Paul measured the medicine out, but he figured that with my track record that little bit wouldn't be enough, so he doubled it and added a *few* drops more and then gave it to me.(p.207)
• But I can remember, in my teens, that there were a *few* characters who caused the village heads to nod pityingly and sometimes in anger as they paused to say, "That sot, Henri" and "Ce pauvre Jules," who drank too much.(p.230)
• You can all remember that in the first *few* months after the change, a great many men, who had formerly been used to a *few* beers every day or an occasional drink of whiskey, simply quit all alcoholic drinks.(p.232)
• This doctor had imparted his knowledge to just a *few* other men at that time – not more than four or five -- they now number more than seventy persons.(p.235)
• From the top of the heap in a *few* years he had skidded to becoming a shuffling customer, still entering the better barrooms but welcomed by neither mine host nor his patrons.(p.236)
• In a *few* sentences he made God seem personal to me, explained Him as a being who was interested in me, the alcoholic, and that all I needed to do was to be willing to follow His way; that as long as I followed it I would be able to overcome my desire for liquor.(p.236)
• The first *few* months were hard.(p.237)
• I'd work like mad for three or four weeks without a single drink, save my money, pay a *few* bills and then "reward" myself with alcohol.(p.244)
• At our weekly meeting I was a menace to serenity those first *few* months, for I took every opportunity to lambaste the "spiritual angle" as we called it, or anything else that had any tinge of theology.(p.246)
• Peddling off my polish samples for expenses, I crawled back to New York a *few* days later in a very chastened frame of mind.(p.248)
• Then I got a very good position in Philadelphia and quickly found I would need a *few* fellow alcoholics around me if I was to stay sober.(p.249)
• I have served on only one committee in the past nine years, for I feel that I had my chance the first *few* years and that newer members should fill the jobs.(p.250)
• He knew too well that didn't mean a thing, just as I knew in my heart that it would be only a question of time -- a *few* days, a week, or even a month, it was inevitable – till I would be off on another bender.(p.257)
• But I had never been a flippant, wise-cracking sneerer at the *few* persons I had met who had impressed me as Christian men and women, or at any institution whose sincerity of purpose I could see.(p.259)
• Probably only a *few* readers of this story will be able, from personal experiences of their own, to understand the exhilaration and sense of accomplishment which I felt after finishing this seemingly simple assignment.(p.276)
• During my first *few* months in Akron I was quite sure that I never wanted to see my home town again.(p.281)
• I had *few* enough at that time.(p.293)
• A *few* months after I made my original trip to Akron I was feeling pretty cocky, and I didn't think my wife was treating me with proper respect, now that I was an outstanding citizen.(p.293)
• A *few* months later one of the men who had been in touch with the group in Akron came to Chicago to live, and then there were three of us who continued to have informal meetings quite regularly.(p.294)
• The three of us did not feel up to the job, and after a *few* meetings we convinced the prospects that they too should go to Akron where they could see an older group in action.(p.295)
• Occasionally, it is accorded to a *few* of us to watch something fine grow from a tiny kernel into something of gigantic goodness.(p.295)
• My wife became pregnant and the doctor recommended the use of port or ale . . . so . . . I bought a six gallon crock and a *few* bottles, listened to advice from amateur brewmeisters, and was off on my beer manufacturing career on a small scale (for the time being).(p.297)
• As time went on, I found that it was customary to open a *few* bottles whenever visitors dropped in.(p.297)
• Eventually, of course, what with all the hilarity that could be provoked with a *few* gallons of beer, there seemed to be no need of bridge or poker playing for entertainment.(p.297)
• From a monetary standpoint . . . in the past *few* years, I have reduced my reckless debts to almost nothing, and have had money to get along on comfortably.(p.303)
• Nevertheless, there were a *few* doctors who saw alcoholism as a disease and felt that the alcoholic was a victim of something over which he had no control.(p.307)
• *Few* doctors will tell a hopeless patient that there is no answer for him or for her.(p.307)
• It explained so much I had not understood about myself and, best of all, it promised recovery if I would do a *few* simple things and be willing to have the desire to drink removed.(p.309)
• He put me at ease with his first *few* words.(p.309)
• After having a *few* drinks, I went to a meeting -- and the people there were not all old men and definitely not skid-row types!(p.319)
• I did stay fairly good for a *few* years.(p.323)
• We have only been in A.A. a *few* years, but now we're trying to make up for lost time.(p.325)
• I never thought I could be useful to anyone except my husband and my children and perhaps a *few* friends.(p.326)
• He has *few* worries, fewer warnings.(p.330)
• When a *few* drinks made me feel good before I went over that line, those same drinks now made me wretched.(p.346)
• And the psychiatrist has had thousands of couches, and has put you and me on them many, many times, but he hasn't helped us very much, though he has tried hard; and we owe the clergy and the doctor and the psychiatrist a deep debt of gratitude, but they haven't helped our alcoholism, except in a rare *few* instances.(p.352)
• When I did make it home in 1920, I re-entered school and caught up with my class in a *few* short months – I actually did a year's work in three months, proving much to the disgust of my dad that I could do it when I wanted to.(p.358)
• All I can remember about the Roaring Twenties is that I drank a great deal, thought I was having a grand time, managed to get to Europe for a *few* weeks, was very proud of the dozens of speak-easy cards entitling me to an entree in the better joints between Cleveland and New York, took on a wife, and built a home in a fashionable suburb of Cleveland.(p.358)
• The next *few* years in New York can be described in a very *few* words.(p.358)
• I made little headway in my first *few* meetings with her.(p.359)
• My work kept me busy the first *few* months on the new job.(p.360)
• It started when I joined a *few* of the men for cocktails before the noonday Rotary luncheon.(p.360)
• I would follow certain drinking schedules or diets faithfully for a *few* days, and then somewhere along the line would over-train and upset the applecart.(p.361)
• In a *few* weeks I toed the line.(p.362)
• A *few* hours later I came out of a complete stupor in our living room with a flash of sanity.(p.363)
• After a *few* meetings I decided to drive to Florida unannounced to see my wife and tell her about my new found friends and association.(p.364)
• I tried a *few* drinks my last night in the city before coming home.(p.364)
• When I was called upon for a *few* words I had to tell my friends that I wasn't one year old in A.A. that evening but only a "nine month baby."(p.366)
• I could end my story here, but for the new man I would like to add a *few* words.(p.366)
• Within a *few* months, I was admitted to a state hospital for the mentally ill.(p.370)
• A *few* months after that, I was released and left the world of insanity, only to return to the world of alcoholic insanity.(p.370)
• Near the Laundromat, I would buy one bottle of pop and a *few* bottles of beer or wine, and go into the rest room, empty the pop bottle, refill it with the booze, and proceed to do my laundering.(p.370)
• One night, a *few* weeks after joining the Fellowship, much to my surprise and delight I saw a familiar but no longer frowning face.(p.371)
• We had always encouraged our children to bring their friends home at any time, but after a *few* experiences with a drunken father they eliminated home as a place to entertain friends.(p.376)
• In a *few* days an attorney called on me and explained that something would have to be done as she couldn't face returning to me as I was.(p.377)
• However, after I heard a *few* stories of jails, sanitariums, broken homes and skid row, I wondered if I really was an alcoholic.(p.378)
• So I went down to him quite a *few* times a month and had him shoot me full of the stuff; and then I went across the street to a little drug store to take a glass of beer or two beers, and then stopped at the liquor store to get myself a pint and go home.(p.389)
• So I was in just a *few* hours.(p.390)
• A *few* times at meetings, I have heard this statement: "Members of A.A. have paid the highest initiation fee of any club members in the world."(p.396)
• After a *few* more estimates as to income and expenditures for booze over a *few* sample years, taken at random, I conclude that this twenty per cent stayed fairly constant.(p.398)
• Alcoholics being the argumentative lot that we are, the A.A. membership will undoubtedly come up with a *few* who will dispute these figures.(p.399)
• A *few* stood by me, at least in their hearts, throughout the whole of my drinking career.(p.404)
• Couldn't I stop, after a *few*?(p.404)
• This was how I had looked and acted a *few* short weeks ago.(p.415)
• Fear, love of dentistry, and an imitation of my father's periodic drinking pattern took me through dental college soberly, except for the *few* parties and vacations in those four years.(p.419)
• A young veteran tells how a *few* rough experiences pushed him into A.A. – and how he was therefore spared years of suffering.(p.422)
• In all the twenty-five years of my drinking there were only a *few* occasions when I took a morning drink.(p.432)
• I can only list a *few* of its elements.(p.435)
• (I am pleased to state, however, that I had gone to only a very *few* A.A. meetings before I was able to make a really beautiful pair of moccasins – and half a wallet.(p.445)
• By early July, I had tapered off alcohol completely, and I got off all pills in the ensuing *few* months.(p.448)
• I would rather talk about the good things A.A. has taught me; I feel that hitting on just a *few* sordid points should be sufficient to let those of you in institutions know where I came from.(p.459)
• After a *few* months there, I went to County Mental Health as an alcoholism worker.(p.462)
• When I didn't have anything else to do – a dull evening at home -- I'd sneak a *few* drinks upstairs in my room, and that began to be a habit.(p.464)
• Only a *few* days before Christmas I went to the dentist for a periodic checkup.(p.465)
• On the day set for the extractions, on my way to the dentist's I felt a little nervous, so I had a couple of drinks, and after the teeth were out I was very nervous, so I had a *few* more.(p.466)
• Our language has *few* words to say many things.(p.474)
• Climb on water wagon for *few* months.(p.475)
• We lived just a *few* doors from the First Baptist Church and when they had funerals I remember very often asking my mother whether the person was good or bad and whether they were going to heaven or hell.(p.483)
• I went back to my mother's for a *few* days until things cooled off, because the District Attorney had put out a summons for me to come to see him in his office.(p.491)
• The November following, I took a *few* days off after pay day to celebrate my birthday on the 25th of the month.(p.491)
• I drink and go to bed; I take a *few* the next morning and go see my mother once more.(p.501)

• I'll just take a *few* beers now and then.(p.502)
• Then I find myself thinking about myself, and a *few* things that I had wanted to forget.(p.503)
• Maybe be a *few* drinks when I get to the city will help.(p.505)
• I rounded up a *few* more of my friends and off we went to the meeting, not for anything we would gain from it as much as to make a burlesque out of it.(p.509)
• I buttonholed him after dinner and gave him a *few* tips on how to run his colony better and the result of that was about a fortnight or so later I was shipped back to my regiment.(p.520)
• I was there for another couple of months and then, after a *few* more adventures in the East, I was shipped home.(p.521)
• Within a month, the police, the hospital authorities, several kind strangers, most of my friends, all of my close relatives, and a *few* adepts at rolling a drunk and removing his wrist watch and wallet had been involved.(p.532)
• For by thirty-five I had been drinking for a *few* years.(p.533)
• But as the years go by, the stretch becomes unbearable; and the man with the grown-up brain and the childish emotions – vanity, self-interest, false pride, jealousy, longing for social approval, to name *few* -- becomes a prime candidate for alcohol.(p.534)
• Actually, of course, I wanted someone to listen to me, because when I had a *few* martinis inside, I became the great author I longed to be; and the right listener was in for some pretty highflown theories of literature and of genius.(p.536)
• I bear a *few* scars on my face from these fights, which I always lost, because the "stick" existed only in my mind.(p.537)
• As soon as I had made a *few* friends and had begun to feel accepted, we moved again.(p.555)
• Within a *few* days, I found myself drying out on a drunk farm.(p.559)
• In the first *few* chapters a number of sudden revolutionary changes are described.(p.569)
• What often takes place in a *few* months could seldom have been accomplished by years of self discipline.(p.569)
• With *few* exceptions our members find that they have tapped an unsuspected inner resource which they presently identify with their own conception of a Power greater than themselves.(p.569)

fewer

• He has few worries, *fewer* warnings.(p.330)
• Finally our invitations became *fewer* and *fewer* as friends had more experience with my drinking pattern.(p.377)

fictitious

• I would sometimes hide out in one of the clubs of which I was a member, and had the habit at times of registering at a hotel under a *fictitious* name.(p.176)

fidgets

• I lived through a week of the *fidgets* because I had agreed to address a group of alcoholic inmates in one of our state mental hospitals.(p.283)

field

• The unselfishness of these men as we have come to know them, the entire absence of profit motive, and their community spirit, is indeed inspiring to one who has labored long and wearily in this alcoholic *field*.(p.xxv)
• I have a shadowy recollection of being in an airplane bound for New York, and of finding a friendly taxicab driver at the landing *field* instead of my wife.(p.41)
• In the two succeeding years I held ten different jobs ranging from newspaper copy-desk and rewrite, to traffic director for an oil *field* equipment company.(p.255)
• Seven years of work in this *field* brought an opportunity to affiliate myself actively with one of my clients, a fellow A.A.(p.284)
• He said the alcoholic seemed to possess a native acuteness and usually excelled in his *field*, regardless of environmental or educational advantages.(p.308)
• I continued to advance in my chosen *field*.(p.433)
• I have been allowed to build an entirely new career in a *field* I had never worked in.(p.541)
• I have published a book covering certain aspects of this *field* which has been well-reviewed and which is helping other people.(p.541)
• I have been appointed to the faculty of my old school, to teach in my new *field*.(p.541)

fields

• But in most *fields* our generation has witnessed complete liberation of our thinking.(p.52)

fierce

• As I drank, the old *fierce* determination to win came back.(p.4)
• It brings misunderstanding, *fierce* resentment, financial insecurity, disgusted friends and employers, warped lives of blameless children, sad wives and parents – anyone can increase the list.(p.18)

fifteen

• A community thirty miles away has *fifteen* fellows of Alcoholics Anonymous.(p.161)
• The periods of sobriety attained by these thirteen A.A.'s range from *fifteen* to forty-six years.(p.169)
• During the subsequent *fifteen* years I had sense enough never to go to the hospital if I had been drinking, and very seldom did I receive patients.(p.176)
• Wishing to be polite, though I felt very badly, I said, "Let's make the call," and extracted from my wife a promise that we would not stay over *fifteen* minutes.(p.179)
• We entered her house at exactly five o'clock and it was eleven *fifteen* when we left.(p.179)
• At the end of *fifteen* months, I tried the beer experiment.(p.203)
• This Christian Science experience with a sobriety of *fifteen* months was in 1932.(p.203)
• The interne came along with a glassful of bleached lightning that put me away for about *fifteen* hours.(p.217)
• I'd only had two with her, but I'd managed four in the *fifteen* minutes I'd waited for her, and of course I'd had the usual uncounted swigs from the bottle as I painfully got up and did my slow spasmodic dressing.(p.223)
• Visits from friends which lasted over *fifteen* minutes exhausted me.(p.275)
• In *fifteen* seconds or less, the feeling passed.(p.285)
• *Fifteen* of those years I would not have enjoyed had I continued drinking.(p.295)
• I feel as I did when I was *fifteen* years younger.(p.303)
• A little more than *fifteen* years ago, through a long and calamitous series of shattering experiences, I found myself being helplessly propelled toward total destruction.(p.304)
• The last *fifteen* years of my life have been rich and meaningful.(p.312)
• I succeeded in this attempt for approximately *fifteen* months with only a couple of slips.(p.343)
• I had my first drink when I was *fifteen* and my alcoholic potential had ripened me to the point of necessary escapism.(p.353)
• I went to work in Birmingham for a newspaper at *fifteen* dollars a week.(p.357)
• At this time, the price of booze in the bars was *fifteen* cents a shot and ten cents a beer.(p.397)
• I remembered back to high school when I was *fifteen*.(p.423)
• At *fifteen* I was strictly a beer drinker.(p.423)
• He even went to bat for me before the court martial that inevitably followed and, as a result, I drew only thirty days – *fifteen* in solitary.(p.428)
• In fact it has been only within the last *fifteen* years that I changed from a fairly normal, controlled drinker into an alcoholic.(p.464)
• When I got out of there, I lasted about *fifteen* minutes at home, before I headed for the drugstore and more pills, and then the bar.(p.479)
• I received an additional *fifteen* years for that, making a minimum of thirty-five years and a maximum of natural life.(p.509)

fifteen-minute

• In the spring of 1939, the Big Book was printed, and we had two inquiries from the New York office because of a *fifteen-minute* radio talk that was made.(p.294)

fifteen-twenty

• Fortunately, I received only *fifteen-twenty* years, and I went back to my alma mater (where I had spent so much time in the hole).(p.461)

fifth

• This brings us to the *Fifth* Step in the program of recovery mentioned in the preceding chapter.(p.72)
• I was well into the second *fifth* by this time.(p.347)
• I was living in a small room on West 53rd Street right off *Fifth* Avenue, when I met a young lady who eventually was responsible for altering my entire way of living.(p.359)
• Attending his fourth or *fifth* meeting was an old friend I had not seen for twenty years.(p.365)
• They were doing very well -- at least a *fifth* apiece a day, except on dad's days off when they did some serious drinking.(p.425)
• One night I was sitting in the lab alone with a *fifth* and a case of beer listening to dreamy Hawaiian music on the radio.(p.427)
• He was serving time on his *fifth* felony conviction when a miracle happened.(p.457)
• I woke up in jail, sick, withdrawing from alcohol and speed, already a four-time loser, and now with a *fifth* felony charge against me.(p.460)
• Similarly, we rid ourselves of guilt and remorse as we "clean out the garbage" from our minds through the Fourth and *Fifth* Steps of our recovery program.(p.560)

fifties

• He was in his late *fifties*, and all that he had undertaken fell upon my shoulders at his death in 1928.(p.486)

fiftieth

• For instance, the *fiftieth* wedding anniversary of my wife's parents was the occasion for a huge family reunion at our home.(p.556)

fifty

• I always built up in my own mind the great things that I was going to do, and in fact I accomplished about *fifty* percent of them and then lost interest.(p.193)
• He might have handed me *fifty* dollars and said that I ought to pull myself together and make a new start.(p.278)
• "We watch the alcoholic performing in a position of responsibility and we know that because he is drinking heavily and daily he has cut his capacities by *fifty* per cent, and still he seems able to do a satisfactory job.(p.308)
• This didn't say we had to be in jail, ten, *fifty*, or one hundred times.(p.379)
• One night I barely made my downtown club; if I'd had to go another *fifty* feet I'd have collapsed in the gutter.(p.435)
• I will be *fifty* years old next month, haven't seen my son or daughter yet, nor my daughter's two children, my grandchildren; but I am grateful.(p.463)

fifty-eight

• Why don't you go home and get the Big Book and open it at page *fifty-eight* and see what it says?"(p.349)

fifty-five

• An exceptional man, he remained bone dry for twenty-five years and retired at the age of *fifty-five*, after a successful and happy business career.(p.32)
• But here is a man who at *fifty-five* years found he was just where he had left off at thirty.(p.33)

fifty-four

• At *fifty-four*, I have had come true for me the old wish, "If only I could live my life over, knowing what I know."(p.543)

fifty-three

• As these words are written at *fifty-three* years of age, with over nine years of A.A. behind me, with all its wonderful teachings, I haven't the slightest doubt about being an alcoholic.(p.356)

fight

• There are many situations which arise out of the phenomenon of craving which cause men to make the supreme sacrifice rather than continue to *fight*.(p.xxviii)
• There had been no *fight*.(p.5)
• Not only had I been off guard, I had made no *fight* whatever against the first drink.(p.41)
• You may have to *fight* with him if he is violent.(p.97)
• Then he added, "He sure didn't do much for me when I was trying to *fight* this booze racket alone."(p.158)
• I went into a bar, and there I got into a *fight*.(p.204)
• I became a constant drinker with a terrific *fight* to control the amount of my consumption each day.(p.214)
• That went on for two more months before I landed in a hospital and started my slow *fight* back to normalcy.(p.224)
• Our other daughter was in her last year of high school, and one night the new son-in-law and my husband went out to a prize *fight*.(p.263)
• And then I'd *fight* with him because he had started!(p.325)
• No jail booking, drunk-driving citation, barroom *fight*, or even a tumble off a barstool.(p.327)
• And believe me, an alcoholic cannot *fight* alcohol.(p.338)
• We got on the plane and immediately had a big *fight* over whether I'd drink the free booze.(p.444)
• This time I didn't put up any *fight* because I knew why they were there and where I was going, the psy-

chopathic ward of the City Hospital, where I had been once before.(p.468)

• That was enough provocation to ***fight*** but I didn't ***fight***, and I realized after recess why I didn't.(p.484)

• Brandishing my "motto," which was "A little man with a stick is equal to a big man," sometimes I varied the literary lecture by a ***fight*** with a big man, selected solely because he was big and I was little.(p.537)

fighting

• And we have ceased ***fighting*** anything or anyone -- even alcohol.(p.84)

• We are not ***fighting*** it, neither are we avoiding temptation.(p.85)

• Besides, we have stopped ***fighting*** anybody or anything.(p.103)

• But I only succeeded in ***fighting*** it.(p.338)

• But when I cracked my leg with a sixteen-pound sledgehammer in the rock hole, I was ***fighting*** the system, using my body.(p.458)

fights

• I didn't want to get into ***fights***, but I did get into ***fights***.(p.199)

• We had several ***fights*** and on one or two occasions I struck her with my fist.(p.491)

• I bear a few scars on my face from these ***fights***, which I always lost, because the "stick" existed only in my mind.(p.537)

figure

• That being the case, it didn't take me long to ***figure*** out that my meager manufacturing facilities were entirely inadequate to the manufacture of beer for social and domestic consumption.(p.297)

• It is also stated that we will never be able to ***figure*** out how much we have spent on alcohol.(p.396)

• After all, upon coming out of a week-long or ten-day drunk, it was hard enough to ***figure*** up just how much that one drunk cost, let alone trying to calculate the cost of approximately twenty-five years of active alcoholism.(p.396)

• In the garage, I would put the needle in my vein and then try to ***figure*** out exactly how much medication to inject to overcome the pep pills while adding to the sleeping pills while ignoring the tranquilizers, in order to get just enough to be able to pull out the needle, jerk the tourniquet, throw it in the car, slam the car door shut, run down the hall, and fall in bed before I fell asleep.(p.442)

• As a result, he couldn't ***figure*** out why I had the convulsions, and he decided to send me to the Mayo Clinic.(p.444)

• So I'm better off if I don't give advice, don't ***figure*** I know what's best, and just accept life on life's terms, as it is today -- especially my own life, as it actually is.(p.450)

figured

• Their cost of production is ***figured*** to a fine decimal point.(p.149)

• I ***figured*** I was just a drunk.(p.187)

• I ***figured*** the only difference between me and a millionaire was that I hadn't the strength, or that he got the breaks and I didn't.(p.197)

• Paul measured the medicine out, but he ***figured*** that with my track record that little bit wouldn't be enough, so he doubled it and added a few drops more and then gave it to me.(p.207)

• All of them were so nice to me that I ***figured*** I must be careful – they were bound to want something, being that nice.(p.319)

• I ***figured*** I'd be all right if I could find something I liked to do.(p.339)

• By the time I ***figured*** out what had happened, I saw two flashing red lights atop squad cars, sedately coming around the corner.(p.353)

• I ***figured*** that perhaps if I went ahead with that marriage, which I was sure was right for me, that would be the answer to my drinking problem.(p.465)

• When I came into A.A., I had no intention of quitting drinking -- I ***figured*** I was doing all right.(p.478)

• This means a great deal to me, because I had always ***figured*** that nobody cared.(p.481)

• Mother was of the old school and ***figured*** that anyone I associated with should be of the proper type.(p.484)

figures

• ***Figures*** given in this foreword describe the Fellowship as it was in 1955(p.xv)

• To keep it in round ***figures***, let's say twenty per cent of my income went for giggle gurgles.(p.397)

• Alcoholics being the argumentative lot that we are, the A.A. membership will undoubtedly come up with a few who will dispute these ***figures***.(p.399)

figuring

• I found I could boost my income by ***figuring*** out a lot of cute little tricks that the boss wouldn't be likely to notice – filching money from the Coke machine, short-sticking the customers on oil, and selling oil I'd drained out of other cars.(p.423)

filching

• I found I could boost my income by figuring out a lot of cute little tricks that the boss wouldn't be likely to notice – ***filching*** money from the Coke machine, short-sticking the customers on oil, and selling oil I'd drained out of other cars.(p.423)

file

• That was my lesson, that one could not take the moral inventory and then ***file*** it away; that the alcoholic has to continue to take inventory every day if he expects to get well and stay well.(p.293)

fill

• A remorseful mumbling that we are sorry won't ***fill*** the bill at all.(p.83)

• Most of the time therefore, I did not take the morning drink which I craved so badly, but instead would ***fill*** up on large doses of sedatives to quiet the jitters, which distressed me terribly.(p.176)

• I have served on only one committee in the past nine years, for I feel that I had my chance the first few years and that newer members should ***fill*** the jobs.(p.250)

• I pour out half a tumbler of grain alcohol and ***fill*** it with ginger ale.(p.499)

• I call the bootlegger and ***fill*** up my charred keg.(p.501)

filled

• Your house is ***filled*** with strangers.(p.119)

• So I ***filled*** the cellar full, with the permission of my good wife.(p.177)

• It isn't always so sudden with everyone, but I ran into a personal crisis which ***filled*** me with a raging and righteous anger.(p.228)

• I went trembling into a house in Brooklyn ***filled*** with strangers . . . and I found I had come home at last, to my own kind.(p.228)

• The doctor who came to see me almost at once did not assail me with any new doctrines; he made sure that I had a need and that I wanted to have that need ***filled***, and little by little I learned how my need could be met.(p.258)

• Just an unstable woman, undisciplined, poorly adjusted and ***filled*** with nameless fears.(p.305)

• Scared that my dress wasn't going to fit right, that the church wasn't going to be ***filled***, that I'd fall flat on my face walking up the aisle; in fact, I was afraid I wasn't going to be a prima donna in the place where I should be.(p.385)

• The birth of a daughter ***filled*** me with new fears.(p.402)

• I woke up ***filled*** with secret guilt and shame.(p.407)

• Having passed over the border line, the next five years were ***filled*** with fear, failure and frustration.(p.465)

• I ***filled*** a prescription for him.(p.488)

• A haze ***filled*** the room.(p.498)

• I am ***filled*** with hurt pride and self-pity.(p.501)

filling

• I remembered ***filling*** the peroxide bottle in my medicine chest with gin, in case my sister found the bottle I hid under the mattress.(p.224)

fills

• It ***fills*** the alcoholic with rage.(p.350)

filmed

• Our names and pictures as A.A. members ought not be broadcast, ***filmed***, or publicly printed.(p.567)

films

• It was decided that all members ought to be anonymous at the level of press, radio, TV and ***films***.(p.xix)

• Eleven -- Our public relations policy is based on attraction rather than promotion; we need always maintain personal anonymity at the level of press, radio and ***films***.(p.564)

final

• Counsel with persons is often desirable, but we let God be the ***final*** judge.(p.69)

• Most of us have entered the ***final*** stage with its commitment to health resorts, sanitariums, hospitals, and jails.(p.107)

• Coming up to ***final*** exams I went on a particularly strenuous spree.(p.174)

• Certainly now, anyone would have agreed that only a miracle could prevent my ***final*** breakdown.(p.306)

• I felt this was the ***final*** blow.(p.370)

• The ***final*** decision came when my daughter, following a drunk which ruined my wife's birthday, said, "It's Alcoholics Anonymous -- or else!"(p.378)

• It was to be my lifesaver – the ***final*** catalyst.(p.461)

• ***Final*** exams of my Senior year and I may somehow graduate.(p.499)

• It has taught me that success and failure are never ***final***, and that neither count for very much in the ***final*** assessment of any man who has done his best.(p.525)

finality

• Our friends have counseled chucking the men and we have done so with ***finality***, only to be back in a little while hoping, always hoping.(p.105)

finally

• ***Finally*** he shook his head saying, "Something has happened to you I don't understand.(p.14)

• ***Finally***, he can no longer work, his wife gets a divorce and he is held up to ridicule.(p.38)

• It ***finally*** beat us into a state of reasonableness.(p.48)

• We ***finally*** saw that faith in some kind of God was a part of our make-up, just as much as the feeling we have for a friend.(p.55)

• Tell him how baffled you were, how you ***finally*** learned that you were sick.(p.92)

• We ***finally*** sought employment ourselves as destitution faced us and our families.(p.106)

• His wife is one of those persons who really feels there is something rather sinful about these commodities, so she nagged, and her intolerance ***finally*** threw him into a fit of anger.(p.135)

• I told him he was through – ***finally*** and forever.(p.136)

• After many painful discussions, they ***finally*** gave me my credits and I migrated to another of the leading universities of the country and entered as a Junior that fall.(p.173)

• ***Finally*** my father had to send a doctor out from my home town who managed to get me back there in some way, and I was in bed about two months before I could venture out of the house.(p.175)

• I thought of what liquor had done to me, the opportunities that I had discarded, the abilities that had been given me and how I had wasted them, and I ***finally*** came to the conclusion, that if I didn't want to quit, I certainly ought to want to, and that I was willing to do anything in the world to stop drinking.(p.186)

• ***Finally***, out of his hope, there burst conviction.(p.189)

• It was in the next two or three days after I had first met Doc and Bill, that I ***finally*** came to a decision to turn my will over to God and to go along with this program the best that I could.(p.189)

• They looked at one another queerly and, ***finally***, one of them allowed he'd have a beer and they all followed him, each of them saying he'd have a beer too.(p.194)

• It was ***finally*** decided to undertake the organization of a Cleveland group and toward the end of May, 1939, the first meeting was held in Cleveland in my home.(p.219)

• I believe that my once over-weening self-will has ***finally*** found its proper place, for I can say many times daily, "Thy will be done, not mine" . . . and mean it.(p.229)

• How it ***finally*** broke a Southerner's obstinacy and destined this salesman to start A.A. at Philadelphia.(p.238)

• After a couple of days in dollar hotels and one night in the pokey, I ***finally*** landed on my mother's doorstep -- shaking apart, with several days' beard and, of course, broke as usual.(p.238)

• I tried to contact the boys in New York, but telegrams bounced right back and when I ***finally*** got Hank on the telephone he fired me right then.(p.247)

• Some college friends got me jobs when I ***finally*** had to go to work, but I didn't stick to them.(p.251)

• Quebec, Toronto, Buffalo, and ***finally*** Pittsburgh, were the scenes of man-sized drunks until I had gone through my readjusted discharge pay, a fair sum.(p.253)

• ***Finally***, it got so bad that I left him and went back home and took my two children with me.(p.262)

• That to me was the greatest humiliation, to think that I'd ***finally*** landed in jail.(p.264)

• We drank with exactly the same accord that we ***finally*** accepted A.A.(p.265)

• ***Finally***, one morning, I got up and got in the car and cried all the way down to the M.'s – the people who owned the bar -- and told her I was licked and wanted help.(p.267)

• Before the end ***finally*** came, I had, I guess made the surrender because I ***finally*** had been able to say that I would not mind too much.(p.272)

• When she ***finally*** took the baby and left, I locked myself in the house and stayed drunk for a month.(p.278)

• *Finally,* and I shall never know how much later it was, one clear thought came to me: Try prayer.(p.280)
• When I *finally* returned to Detroit to find work and to learn to stand on my own feet, the ball was already rolling, however slowly.(p.282)
• I do feel, though, that the fact that I *finally* grew up to a point where I could even tackle such a job is the apex of the story of a man who spent eighteen years running away from life.(p.286)
• He said he had *finally* learned that drinking was a fatal illness made up of an allergy plus an obsession, and once the drinking had passed from habit to obsession, we were completely hopeless, and could look forward only to spending the balance of our lives in mental institutions or to death.(p.290)
• We went over these at great length and then he *finally* asked me if I wanted these defects of character removed.(p.292)
• However, it *finally* caught up with me, and when it did, I was a mental, physical, and nervous wreck.(p.299)
• *Finally* this company also became involved and I was once more looking for a job.(p.300)
• *Finally,* an old business acquaintance of mine, whom I hadn't seen for several years offered me a job.(p.301)
• *Finally,* I reenlisted to go back to Nam.(p.318)
• The third time, after almost five years as an S.P. 4, I *finally* made sergeant.(p.318)
• *Finally* I didn't care, I was beyond caring.(p.337)
• It *finally* got such a hold on me that I was completely at my wits' end, not knowing what the result would be.(p.343)
• I tried every gimmick that there was to get some peace of mind, but it was not until I was brought to my alcoholic knees, when I was brought to a group in my own community with the butcher, the baker, the carpenter and the mechanic, who were able to give me the Twelve Steps, that I was *finally* given some semblance of an answer to the last half of the First Step.(p.349)
• My salesmanship was still good, for in the fall of 1938 she called me from Salt Lake and *finally* agreed to take me on for better or for worse.(p.360)
• *Finally* our invitations became fewer and fewer as friends had more experience with my drinking pattern.(p.377)
• Help which you once continually rejected, suggestions once turned aside are *finally* accepted in desperation.(p.377)
• It didn't say I had to *finally* live on skid row and drink bay rum, canned heat or lemon extract.(p.379)
• For some reason I can't remember, it *finally* dawned on me that I had a problem, and yet nobody was very critical about it except my family, and that was only because I decided, after seven years of marriage, that I would divorce my husband.(p.386)
• I put my poor mother and father through agonies but, *finally,* I couldn't stand living with them and having them watch everything I did.(p.386)
• So *finally,* he said to me one morning, "Esther, why do you do this?"(p.386)
• He *finally* decided that he did not love me enough, and soon he told me so and said he was engaged to another girl.(p.403)
• At a large party in Geneva, with people from many countries represented, the kind of party that is "protocol" in the extreme, I swayed, laughed hysterically, made naughty remarks in an unhushed voice, and was *finally* led from the scene.(p.406)
• *Finally* my new friends told me, one by one, that I could not come around any more.(p.410)
• My spiritual awakening in A.A. *finally* resulted in my joining a church some years ago.(p.417)
• I tried the church and psychiatry and *finally* came to A.A.(p.418)
• And as I went through pharmacy school, graduate school, medical school, internship, residency, and specialty training and, *finally,* went into practice, my drinking kept increasing.(p.441)
• One night, I had to put myself back to sleep three times, and then I *finally* decided to give it up.(p.443)
• So I raised enough fuss that they *finally* agreed to let me sign out, against medical advice.(p.444)
• *Finally,* she asked, "Do you realize he's on the staff of this hospital?"(p.445)
• *Finally* after seven months, I decided to try it.(p.448)
• After I had been around A.A. for seven months, tapering off alcohol and pills, not finding the program working very well, I was *finally* able to say, "Okay, God.(p.448)
• On the contrary, the hardest place to work this program has been in my own home, with my own children and, *finally,* with Max.(p.451)
• *Finally,* I threw away all my books and decided never to return to A.A.(p.460)
• *Finally* they stopped and bought me a bottle; they knew so well that would keep me quiet.(p.466)
• He said he was *finally* and completely through -- that he never wanted to see me again.(p.467)
• Things went from bad to worse, and since I had *finally* and completely failed at the job of being a wife and a mother, my marriage ended.(p.468)
• They held consultations and discussions, and *finally* decided to give me the "Conditioned Reflex" treatment.(p.469)
• *Finally,* however, in November of 1944, at long last I went to A.A.(p.470)
• From a Canadian reservation to overseas bars to New England lockups, an Indian traveled a long trail that *finally* led him home to A.A.(p.474)
• You see how much work some of us have to do on ourselves when we *finally* come into A.A.!(p.480)
• *Finally,* I was arrested and got six months for drugs.(p.480)
• Of course, when father *finally* came to Virginia to work his way through school, he resented the southern "cracker," as he often called them, so much that he didn't even go back to his mother's funeral.(p.486)
• Matters got worse all the time until *finally* they got so bad that I was reinvestigated by the Government.(p.490)
• I was there about three weeks, and then I got restless and started to tramp across the country, here and there, until I *finally* wound up in Pennsylvania, in a steel mill.(p.492)
• *Finally,* I broke the last one hundred dollar bill the Saturday before I left.(p.493)
• *Finally* she said, "Isn't your name Jim S.?"(p.493)
• *Finally,* he brought in the angle of whiskey.(p.494)
• So, *finally,* I went to the YMCA and they graciously permitted us to use a room at two dollars a night.(p.495)
• But, *finally,* we got one or two to come in and stick and from there, of course, we started to grow.(p.495)
• He *finally* passed away, and the fear of him left me.(p.508)
• I spent about six or seven weeks in Sing Sing, and was *finally* sent off to Dannemora in the Adirondacks.(p.509)
• I clung to the outfit for the balance of my time, and *finally* I was released, after having spent twenty years and nine months behind bars.(p.510)
• *Finally,* he was drinking to keep away those little men, and those strange voices, and the organ music that came out of the walls.(p.512)
• I went to hospitals, I went to retreats and doctors, and *finally* my mother asked me to go and see a specialist of her own choosing.(p.522)
• *Finally,* my mother came and said she had kept me at home for six years because she thought she could help me, but that now she had come to the conclusion that I wasn't even worth trying to help.(p.523)
• *Finally,* I got so lowdown, I was ashamed of my friends' seeing me, so I went to the worst joints I could find.(p.527)
• The helpful family *finally* said, over long distance, that there would be no more money and that I could not come home.(p.538)
• I fled, *finally,* after having been fired from my job by a boss who wept a little (since I had worked hard) as he gave notice for me to clear out.(p.539)
• It seems only fitting that when I did *finally* fall in love it was with an alcoholic, and for the next ten years I progressed as rapidly as is humanly possible into what I believed to be hopeless alcoholism.(p.547)
• *Finally,* in desperation, my family appealed to a doctor for advice and he suggested A.A.(p.549)
• What my doctor had warned me about *finally* happened.(p.558)
• My doctor *finally* declared he could no longer be responsible for me, and sent me to a psychiatrist who practiced in the same suite of offices.(p.558)
• We alcoholics see that we must work together and hang together, else most of us will *finally* die alone.(p.563)
• 12. -- And *finally,* we of Alcoholics Anonymous believe that the principle of anonymity has immense spiritual significance.(p.567)
• He *finally* realizes that he has undergone a profound alteration in his reaction to life; that such a change could hardly have been brought about by himself alone.(p.569)

finals

• At one of the *finals* I was too drunk to think or write.(p.2)

finance

• The papers reported men jumping to death from the towers of High *Finance.*(p.4)
• With the war over, and back in Baltimore with the folks, there were several small jobs for three years and then I went to work soliciting as one of the first ten employees of a new national *finance* company.(p.242)
• We complement each other beautifully, as he is a born salesman and my taste is for *finance* and management.(p.284)
• At that time, I was living out of town, so I moved back to the home town and made a connection in a responsible position with one of the larger companies in the *finance* business.(p.298)
• After being fired, I lined up with a new *finance* company that was just starting in business, and took the position of business promotion man, contacting automobile dealers.(p.300)
• Six -- An A.A. group ought never endorse, *finance* or lend the A.A. name to any related facility or outside enterprise, lest problems of money, property and prestige divert us from our primary purpose.(p.564)

finances

• I said, "Yes, Doc, I would like to quit, at least for five, six, or eight months, until I get things straightened up, and begin to get the respect of my wife and some other people back, and get my *finances* fixed up and so on."(p.187)
• *Finances* are in bad shape.(p.506)

financial

• Business and *financial* leaders were my heroes.(p.2)
• We gave up our positions and off we roared on a motorcycle, the sidecar stuffed with tent, blankets, a change of clothes, and three huge volumes of a *financial* reference service.(p.2)
• It brings misunderstanding, fierce resentment, *financial* insecurity, disgusted friends and employers, warped lives of blameless children, sad wives and parents -- anyone can increase the list.(p.18)
• Nor are we afraid of disclosing our alcoholism on the theory it may cause *financial* harm.(p.78)
• If he is not interested in your solution, if he expects you to act only as a banker for his *financial* difficulties or a nurse for his sprees, you may have to drop him until he changes his mind.(p.95)
• If he is, you might try to help him about getting a job, or give him a little *financial* assistance.(p.96)
• There was never *financial* security.(p.105)
• But he must see the danger of over-concentration on *financial* success.(p.127)
• Although *financial* recovery is on the way for many of us, we found we could not place money first.(p.127)
• I did it more and more, and had lots of fun without much grief, either physical or *financial.*(p.172)
• Before my drinking had cut me down completely, I achieved a considerable measure of success, having been a City Councilman for five years and a *financial* director of Kenmore, a suburb later taken into the city itself.(p.182)
• It took me a year, or a year and a half to get to feeling physically well, and it was rather tough, but I soon found folks whose friendship I had once had, and I found, after I had been sober for quite some little time, that these people began to act like they had in previous years, before I had gotten so bad, so that I didn't pay too awful much attention to *financial* gains.(p.190)
• I had some *financial* success through no ability of my own and, when jobless and almost wiped out in 1930, I began to trade and sell my collection; much of the proceeds went to keep my apartment stocked with liquor and almost every night saw me helpless to bed.(p.255)
• However, due to *financial* difficulties the whole printing was, for a while, held up and the book received no publicity, nor, of course, was it available in the stores, even if one knew it existed.(p.307)
• But for him, *financial* security or even affluence can be a tragedy.(p.330)
• My *financial* standing had not been impaired.(p.379)
• This eliminated one of the limiting factors, the *financial.*(p.397)
• I got into a lot of *financial* difficulties too.(p.490)
• And, not only that, but they gave us *financial* help.(p.496)

financially

• Father knows he is to blame; it may take him many seasons of hard work to be restored *financially,* but he shouldn't be reproached.(p.123)
• Had he been successful in his enterprise, he would have been set on his feet *financially* which at the time, seemed vitally important.(p.153)
• And we stood there for twenty minutes, telling each other how much better we were, how much better we looked, how much better off we were *financially,* mentally, physically, morally, and in every way, shape and manner.(p.201)

• There had been some occasions -- there was an automobile wreck, for instance -- when I had police escort home but not to jail, all of which, instead of doing me a favor, did me harm because I was then full of self-esteem as to the progress I had made both professionally and ***financially***.(p.213)
• I was doing very well with that and general upholstering work, and there was every indication that I would be ***financially*** independent by the time I reached middle age.(p.232)
• With nothing but a liberal arts education, very definitely estranged from my family and already married, soon after graduation from college I became a bookmaker's clerk on the British racing circuits, far better off ***financially*** than the average professional man.(p.251)
• At least three of those four years must have been a living hell for my wife, because she had to watch the man she loved disintegrate morally, mentally and ***financially***.(p.277)
• In January 1938, I had the opportunity to go to northern Vermont to manage a small daytime radio station that was up against it ***financially***, and was about to fold its antenna.(p.359)
• (I can't know how much others of our Fellowship have paid ***financially*** and, even more important, mentally and physically.)(p.396)
• Their management should be the sole responsibility of those people who ***financially*** support them.(p.566)

financing

• I could work a deal up to where all I had to do was to go ahead with it; all the planning had been done, all the ***financing*** had been done, but then I'd say "Nuts to it!" and walk away.(p.197)

find

• Our earliest printing voiced the hope "that every alcoholic who journeys will ***find*** the Fellowship of Alcoholics Anonymous at his destination.(p.xv)
• Yet it is our great hope that all those who have as yet found no answer may begin to ***find*** one in the pages of this book and will presently join us on the highroad to a new freedom.(p.xxi)
• My wife began to work in a department store, coming home exhausted to ***find*** me drunk.(p.4)
• We meet frequently so that newcomers may ***find*** the fellowship they seek.(p.15)
• Strangely enough, wives, parents and intimate friends usually ***find*** us even more unapproachable than do the psychiatrist and the doctor.(p.18)
• If a sufficiently strong reason – ill health, falling in love, change of environment, or the warning of a doctor – becomes operative, this man can also stop or moderate, although he may ***find*** it difficult and troublesome and may even need medical attention.(p.21)
• Those having religious affiliations will ***find*** here nothing disturbing to their beliefs or ceremonies.(p.28)
• Surprisingly enough, we ***find*** such convictions no great obstacle to a spiritual experience.(p.28)
• We doubt if many of them can do it, because none will really want to stop, and hardly one of them, because of the peculiar mental twist already acquired, will ***find*** he can win out.(p.33)
• I also had the notion that I might ***find*** a customer for a car at this place, which was familiar for I had been going to it for years.(p.36)
• But after a while we had to face the fact that we must ***find*** a spiritual basis of life – or else.(p.44)
• We had to ***find*** a power by which we could live and it had to be a Power greater than ourselves.(p.45)
• But where and how were we to ***find*** this Power?(p.45)
• Its main object is to enable you to ***find*** a Power greater than yourself which will solve your problem.(p.45)
• This applies, too, to other spiritual expressions which you ***find*** in this book.(p.47)
• In our personal stories you will ***find*** a wide variation in the way each teller approaches and conceives of the Power which is greater than himself.(p.50)
• We thought we could ***find*** an easier, softer way.(p.58)
• May you ***find*** Him now!(p.59)
• Sometimes they hurt us, seemingly without provocation, but we invariably ***find*** that at some time in the past we have made decisions based on self which later placed us in a position to be hurt.(p.62)
• Here we ***find*** human opinions running to extremes -- absurd extremes, perhaps.(p.68)
• In actual practice, we usually ***find*** a solitary self-appraisal insufficient.(p.72)
• But they had not learned enough of humility, fearlessness and honesty, in the sense we ***find*** it necessary, until they told someone else all their life story.(p.73)
• We often ***find*** such a person quick to see and understand our problem.(p.74)
• Returning home we ***find*** a place where we can be quiet for an hour carefully reviewing what we have done.(p.75)
• Now we need more action, without which we ***find*** that "Faith without works is dead."(p.76)
• It is harder to go to an enemy than to a friend, but we ***find*** it much more beneficial to us.(p.77)
• Although these reparations take innumerable forms, there are some general principles which we ***find*** guiding.(p.79)
• Reminding ourselves that we have decided to go to any length to ***find*** a spiritual experience we ask that we be given strength and direction to do the right thing, no matter what the personal consequences may be.(p.79)
• He is like the farmer who came up out of his cyclone cellar to ***find*** his home ruined.(p.82)
• We react sanely and normally, and we will ***find*** that this has happened automatically.(p.84)
• Nevertheless, we ***find*** that our thinking will as time passes, be more and more on the plane of inspiration.(p.87)
• You can easily ***find*** some by asking a few doctors, ministers, priests or hospitals.(p.89)
• When you discover a prospect for Alcoholics Anonymous, ***find*** out all you can about him.(p.90)
• If he is to ***find*** God, the desire must come from within.(p.95)
• You are sure to ***find*** someone desperate enough to accept with eagerness what you offer.(p.96)
• We ***find*** it a waste of time to keep chasing a man who cannot or will not work with you.(p.96)
• And even though he continues to drink, the family will ***find*** life more bearable.(p.97)
• He clings to the notion that he will yet ***find*** a way to do so.(p.110)
• Sooner or later, you are likely to ***find*** him reading the book once more.(p.113)
• We ***find*** that most of this embarrassment is unnecessary.(p.115)
• When we do that, we ***find*** it solves our problems too; the ensuing lack of fear, worry and hurt feelings is a wonderful thing.(p.116)
• If you and your husband ***find*** a solution for the pressing problem of drink you are, of course, going to be very happy.(p.117)
• You and your husband will ***find*** that you can dispose of serious problems easier than you can the trivial ones.(p.118)
• We ***find*** it a real mistake to dampen his enthusiasm for alcoholic work.(p.119)
• If you cooperate, rather than complain, you will ***find*** that his excess enthusiasm will tone down.(p.119)
• You will lose the old life to ***find*** one much better.(p.120)
• We ***find*** the more one member of the family demands that the others concede to him, the more resentful they become.(p.122)
• We ***find*** it better when possible, to stick to our own stories.(p.125)
• The family will be affected also, pleasantly at first, as they feel their money troubles are about to be solved, then not so pleasantly as they ***find*** themselves neglected.(p.126)
• He may demand that the family ***find*** God in a hurry, or exhibit amazing indifference to them and say he is above worldly considerations.(p.128)
• Being possessed of a spiritual experience, the alcoholic will ***find*** he has much in common with these people, though he may differ with them on many matters.(p.131)
• If he does not argue about religion, he will make new friends and is sure to ***find*** new avenues of usefulness and pleasure.(p.132)
• But those of us who have tried to shoulder the entire burden and trouble of others ***find*** we are soon overcome by them.(p.132)
• Couples are occasionally dismayed to ***find*** that when drinking is stopped the man tends to be impotent.(p.134)
• The alcoholic may ***find*** it hard to re-establish friendly relations with his children.(p.134)
• Some of us sought out sordid places, hoping to ***find*** understanding companionship and approval.(p.151)
• There you will ***find*** release from care, boredom and worry.(p.152)
• Thus we ***find*** the fellowship, and so will you.(p.152)
• "Where am I to ***find*** these people?"(p.152)
• They will approach still other sick ones and fellowships of Alcoholics Anonymous may spring up in each city and hamlet, havens for those who must ***find*** a way out.(p.153)
• In there he would ***find*** companionship and release.(p.154)
• He told how he lived in constant worry about those who might ***find*** out about his alcoholism.(p.155)
• After several failures to ***find*** others, a fourth turned up.(p.158)
• Many a distracted wife has visited this house to ***find*** loving and understanding companionship among women who knew her problem, to hear from the lips of their husbands what had happened to them, to be advised how her own wayward mate might be hospitalized and approached when next he stumbled.(p.160)
• There are the same fast friendships, there is the same helpfulness to one another as you ***find*** among our western friends.(p.162)
• Some day we hope that every alcoholic who journeys will ***find*** a Fellowship of Alcoholics Anonymous at his destination.(p.162)
• Give freely of what you ***find*** and join us.(p.164)
• Those who believe their drinking to be hopeless may again ***find*** hope in these thirteen impressive tales.(p.167)
• I read everything I could ***find***, and talked to everyone who I thought knew anything about it.(p.178)
• Each day I would try to ***find*** out what His will was, and try to follow that, rather than trying to get Him to always agree that the things I thought of myself were the things best for me.(p.187)
• I was trying to ***find*** the answer.(p.191)
• We were eating lunch, and I was listening and trying to ***find*** out why they had this release that they seemed to have.(p.191)
• I had to look in the telephone book later to ***find*** out who these people were.(p.196)
• After drinking one glass of beer at the end of my work period for about five days, I thought I'd better ***find*** out whether I really had the stuff licked.(p.203)
• One morning, after I had been on a binge for a couple of days, I awoke to ***find*** my brother and Doctor Bob in my room talking to me about not drinking.(p.206)
• I never left the church, but I was a fringe member, and the thought simply never occurred to me that through the exercise of what I had I might ***find*** the answer to my problem, simply because I wouldn't admit that I had a problem.(p.214)
• He startled me by informing me that he was an alcoholic, that he had found a way which so far enabled him to live without taking a drink, and that the main idea was to ***find*** a way how not to take that first drink.(p.218)
• I remembered going through what my sister assured me was my nightly procedure of trying to ***find*** Willie Seabrook's name in the telephone book.(p.224)
• I remembered my loud resolution to ***find*** him and ask him to help me get into that "Asylum" he had written about.(p.224)
• Many friends of my family had emigrated to America, so at twenty-four I decided that the United States offered me the opportunity I was never likely to ***find*** in my native land.(p.231)
• Routine jobs bored me, but I would take on the toughest one I could ***find***, work day and night until I had it under control; then it would become tedious and I'd lose all interest in it.(p.243)
• Much later I discovered the elders held many prayer meetings hoping to ***find*** a way to give me the heave-ho, but at the same time stay tolerant and spiritual.(p.247)
• My brilliant agnosticism vanished, and I saw for the first time that those who really believed, or at least honestly tried to ***find*** a Power greater than themselves, were much more composed and contented than I had ever been, and they seemed to have a degree of happiness which I had never known.(p.247)
• I'll get you the password, and I can ***find*** out where they meet because I know a guy that belongs.(p.266)
• I drove these three or four miles down the road only to ***find*** that Jack was out.(p.267)
• Jack said, "Now you start and go to these meetings, and then you'll ***find*** out all about it."(p.268)
• I ate up every bit of it, because I wanted to ***find*** out how to stay sober.(p.273)
• When I finally returned to Detroit to ***find*** work and to learn to stand on my own feet, the ball was already rolling, however slowly.(p.282)
• However, as there happened to be several saloons within that distance, I didn't ***find*** it necessary to patronize the same place each evening.(p.298)
• I learned that a person just can't ***find*** a job hanging in a dive or barroom all day and all night, as jobs don't seem to turn up in those places.(p.300)
• A very simple plan that I still ***find*** much joy and happiness in following.(p.302)

• I began making the rounds of the doctors in the hope that one of them might *find* some cure for my accumulating ailments, preferably something that could be removed surgically.(p.305)
• Maybe I could *find* my way out of this agonizing existence.(p.309)
• Perhaps I could *find* freedom and peace and be able once again to call my soul my own.(p.309)
• I don't know what sort of person I was expecting, but I was very agreeably surprised to *find* Mr. T. a poised, intelligent, well groomed and mannered gentleman.(p.309)
• By this time, with the doctor's explanation, the revelations contained in the book, and the hope-inspiring interview with Mr. T., I was ready and willing to go into the interior of the African jungles, if that was what it took, for me to *find* what these people had.(p.309)
• I didn't dare hope I might *find* for myself all that these people had found, but if I could acquire some small part of their intriguing quality of living -- and sobriety – that would be enough.(p.310)
• However, this isn't as rough as it sounds, as we do become grateful for the necessity that makes us toe the line, for we *find* that we are more than compensated for a consistent effort by the countless dividends we receive.(p.311)
• Where we used to run from responsibility, we *find* ourselves accepting it with gratitude that we can successfully shoulder it.(p.311)
• Instead of wanting to escape some perplexing problem, we experience a thrill of challenge in the opportunity it affords for another application of A.A. techniques, and we *find* ourselves tackling it with surprising vigor.(p.311)
• So oldsters are advised to develop interest, *find* hobbies.(p.330)
• I figured I'd be all right if I could *find* something I liked to do.(p.339)
• I said, "I can't *find* my middle road in life.(p.340)
• I can't *find* it.(p.340)
• I did work of all kinds after school and during vacations, trying to *find* that which would appeal most as a goal for a life work.(p.373)
• I was trying to *find* an easier, softer way.(p.378)
• I didn't realize I would *find* so much more, but a new and different outlook on life started opening up almost immediately.(p.383)
• I *find* an inner pleasure in simple things.(p.383)
• Frank, my husband, would come home day after day and *find* me passed out.(p.386)
• I had been reading a lot about psychiatry and I thought, "Maybe if I talk to a psychiatrist he can *find* out what is happening, and then I can drink like a lady."(p.387)
• Frank said, "If you'd like to talk to a psychiatrist, I'll see a doctor and *find* out who to go to here."(p.387)
• Frank left to *find* the doctor and I got drunk.(p.387)
• I had to go through extreme alcoholism to *find* my answer.(p.400)
• Showing all the courage and ingenuity that I had not used in a positive way, I covered my tracks and hid from my family so successfully that they did not *find* me for months.(p.401)
• So we rolled old newspapers together and made torches to *find* a good soft pew and get some sleep.(p.424)
• Today, I *find* I can't work my A.A. program while taking pills, nor may I even have them around for dire emergencies only.(p.443)
• At first, I wondered whether he was alcoholic himself, and was sending me to *find* out about A.A.(p.446)
• When I am disturbed, it is because I *find* some person, place, thing, or situation – some fact of my life -- unacceptable to me, and I can *find* no serenity until I accept that person, place, thing, or situation as being exactly the way it is supposed to be at this moment.(p.449)
• Today, I *find* it's the best thing that has ever happened to me.(p.450)
• My parents were due for the holidays that day, and she didn't want them to *find* their drunken daughter there.(p.467)
• Sly and crafty, I thought now I'll *find* out what they think of me here, what they "have on" me, what I've said coming in here drunk.(p.470)
• Then I *find* jails in Connecticut, too.(p.475)
• My brother and me *find* work on turnpike in Maine.(p.475)
• I *find* Indian fellow.(p.475)
• *Find* same A.A., same Spirit.(p.476)
• To *find* work, I have travel much.(p.476)
• At every place, I *find* A.A. group first.(p.476)
• I look for liquor and can't *find* any.(p.502)
• Then I *find* myself thinking about myself, and a few things that I had wanted to forget.(p.503)
• I want to get where I can *find* some alcoholics to help, and where I can have some fellowship.(p.506)
• I must *find* a way to make some money.(p.506)
• My drinking pattern isn't very different from the average you *find* in A.A.(p.512)
• Yes, we *find* it rather confusing, but as we get around and get to know people in the group, they lead the way and all we have to do is to follow.(p.512)
• The realization came to me that I had to stop drinking, that I had to *find* a way.(p.515)
• It was a revelation to me to *find* that there were such people as those I found in Alcoholics Anonymous.(p.515)
• When you come in here, you *find* the understanding that you need.(p.516)
• I lasted at that for four months chiefly on alcohol, because I never seemed to *find* any time to eat.(p.520)
• I thought that if these kind of ordinary people can do it, a man of my brains ought to *find* it much more easy, and I joined.(p.524)
• I would wake to *find* myself in some beat-up rooming house, where roaches were crawling over everything.(p.527)
• Finally, I got so lowdown, I was ashamed of my friends' seeing me, so I went to the worst joints I could *find*.(p.527)
• If I write with the air of one who has discovered the obvious, which is to say, the eternal truths which have been offered to us since the beginning, forgive my callowness; I had to *find* these things out for myself.(p.536)
• I'd visit one bar after another, having one martini in each, and in each hoping to *find* someone interesting to talk to.(p.536)
• If he were still sober, chances are that very quickly I put him down as a Philistine with no appreciation of literary genius; and then I went on to another bar to *find* a new victim.(p.537)
• I stood off and took a long look at life and the values I found in it: I saw a paradox, that he who loses his life does indeed *find* it.(p.542)
• The A.A. members who sponsored me told me in the beginning that I would not only *find* a way to live without having a drink, but that I would *find* a way to live without wanting to drink, if I would do these simple things.(p.550)
• Do it every day for two weeks and you will *find* you have come to mean it and to want it for them, and you will realize that where you used to feel bitterness and resentment and hatred, you now feel compassionate understanding and love."(p.552)
• This great experience that released me from the bondage of hatred and replaced it with love is really just another affirmation of the truth I know: I get everything I need in Alcoholics Anonymous – everything I need I get – and when I get what I need I invariably *find* that it was just what I wanted all the time.(p.553)
• With few exceptions our members *find* that they have tapped an unsuspected inner resource which they presently identify with their own conception of a Power greater than themselves.(p.569)
• We *find* that no one need have difficulty with the spirituality of the program.(p.570)
• If you cannot *find* A.A. in your locality, a letter addressed to Alcoholics Anonymous, Box 459, Grand Central Station, New York, NY 10163, U.S.A., will receive a prompt reply from this world center, referring you to the nearest A.A. group.(p.575)

finding

• I have a shadowy recollection of being in an airplane bound for New York, and of *finding* a friendly taxicab driver at the landing field instead of my wife.(p.41)
• But he had found God – and in *finding* God had found himself.(p.158)
• My big job was to keep other people from *finding* it out.(p.199)
• In my own experience I was so jubilant at *finding* myself sober, and I had so many things to catch up on, that a month went by before the thought even occurred to me.(p.219)
• After *finding* every bottle that I had hidden around the apartment, she took away my pants, my shoes, my money and my keys, threw them under the bed in the back bedroom and slip-locked our door.(p.288)
• She of course didn't realize how cunning an alcoholic can be and the lengths to which he will go in *finding* ways to satisfy the compulsion for more and more drinks after having had the first one.(p.377)
• I remember *finding* myself in the middle of the night in the doctors' parking lot at the hospital with one foot in the car and one foot on the ground, not knowing which was the lead foot; *finding* myself hanging up the telephone – then realizing I had gotten out of bed, answered the phone, turned on the light, and carried on a conversation with a patient.(p.441)
• After I had been around A.A. for seven months, tapering off alcohol and pills, not *finding* the program working very well, I was finally able to say, "Okay, God.(p.448)
• I remember vaguely violent quarrels with my husband, his *finding* my liquor supply time and time again and throwing it out.(p.466)
• They brought me in and of course, they hadn't very much trouble in *finding* that I was alcoholic.(p.521)
• It's time to stop *finding* excuses for drinking and getting into trouble, because now there is a way out, and if you want what we have, try coming around and giving the program a chance.(p.530)

finds

• On the other hand – and strange as this may seem to those who do not understand -- once a psychic change has occurred, the very same person who seemed doomed, who had so many problems he despaired of ever solving them, suddenly *finds* himself easily able to control his desire for alcohol, the only effort necessary being that required to follow a few simple rules.(p.xxvii)
• Every new alcoholic looks for this spirit among us and is immensely relieved when he *finds* we are not witch-burners.(p.103)

fine

• I see him now and then and he is as *fine* a specimen of manhood as one could wish to meet.(p.xxx)
• His income is good, he has a *fine* home, is happily married and the father of promising children of college age.(p.39)
• Physically, I felt *fine*.(p.41)
• When I returned to the hotel it struck me a highball would be *fine* before going to bed, so I stepped into the bar and had one.(p.41)
• God has abundantly supplied this world with *fine* doctors, psychologists, and practitioners of various kinds.(p.133)
• He has just returned from a three-months leave of absence, has taken a cure, looks *fine*, and to clinch the matter, the board of directors told him this was his last chance."(p.138)
• Their cost of production is figured to a *fine* decimal point.(p.149)
• If I could, that was wonderful, that was just *fine*, and they would very much appreciate a person who had that kind of power, but they were looking for a man that knew he had a problem, and knew that he couldn't handle it himself and needed outside help.(p.186)
• My customers lost confidence in me to the point where I retained what business I had only because I was a well-trained and reputedly *fine* craftsman.(p.234)
• At thirteen I was packed off to a very *fine* Protestant boarding school in Virginia where I stayed four years, graduating without any special achievements.(p.240)
• The hospitality of their home and their *fine* fellowship were freely mine.(p.259)
• I come from a very poor family in material things, with a *fine* Christian mother, but with no religious background.(p.261)
• When I came to my aunt, she knew that I had had an unhappy childhood, and she said, "Now, Ethel, you're welcome to have boy friends in our home, but there are two boys in this town that I don't want you to date, and one of them comes from a very *fine* family, one of the best.(p.262)
• They opened with a little prayer, and I thought it was very *fine* that we stood, all of us together, and closed with the Lord's Prayer.(p.270)
• Occasionally, it is accorded to a few of us to watch something *fine* grow from a tiny kernel into something of gigantic goodness.(p.295)
• We got along *fine* for about two weeks, until she told me where to go and to take my damn bottle with me.(p.318)
• She was doing *fine*, she was up and around, and that day her husband phoned me and said, "Doctor, thanks very much for curing my wife," and I thanked him for his felicitations, and he hung up.(p.350)
• When I was nineteen, I married a *fine* man who had never known an insecure moment in his life, let alone the trials and tribulations of booze.(p.369)
• How can a person with a *fine* family, an attractive home, an excellent position and high standing in an important city become an alcoholic?(p.373)
• As long as it eased situations socially, it helped just *fine*, but somewhere along the line, it backfired.(p.386)
• I went into the Navy in *fine* style.(p.425)

• This was *fine*, but it was just an extra dividend, for I'd made connections by this time and was buying a bottle a day from the cook.(p.426)
• I thought it was *fine* for them.(p.427)
• Or maybe I'd come home wild drunk, singing and raving about what a *fine* place home was and what grand parents I had since they joined A.A.(p.428)
• My outward professional life looked *fine*, on the surface.(p.435)
• Prior to our marriage, when she was a shy, scrawny adolescent, I was able to see things in her that others couldn't necessarily see – things like beauty, charm, gaiety, a gift for being easy to talk to, a sense of humor, and many other *fine* qualities.(p.450)
• When I do this, we get along *fine*.(p.452)
• At noon on Christmas Day I called my family in New York, wished them a Merry Christmas, and assured them everything was *fine* with me.(p.467)
• Vi was very kind and explained to the jury that I was basically a *fine* fellow and a good husband, but that I drank too much and that she thought I had lost my mind and felt that I should be committed to an asylum.(p.492)
• The grand fellow who at my call made me a hail-fellow-well-met, who gave me such a *fine* voice, as we sang "Hail, hail, the gang's all here," and "Sweet Adeline," who gave me freedom from fear and feelings of inferiority.(p.498)
• I still want to write a *fine* play and to get it on.(p.542)

finer

• Though old buildings will eventually be replaced by *finer* ones, the new structures will take years to complete.(p.123)
• Some of us had this experience, only to enjoy, in a few months, a *finer* intimacy than ever.(p.134)

finest

• He may be one of the *finest* fellows in the world.(p.21)
• For some reason, we alcoholics seem to have the gift of picking out the world's *finest* women.(p.178)
• It was a terrible blow at the time and I thought he was pretty much of a heel, but of course it was the *finest* thing he could have done for me under the circumstances.(p.357)

finger

• We have admitted certain defects; we have ascertained in a rough way what the trouble is; we have put our *finger* on the weak items in our personal inventory.(p.72)
• Society can do anything it chooses to do with me when I am drunk and I can't lift a *finger* to stop it, for I forfeit my rights through the simple expedient of becoming a menace to myself and to the people around me.(p.549)

fingers

• I used to like to get it on my *fingers* so I could lick them and get another taste.(p.346)

finish

• This was the *finish*, the curtain, it seemed to me.(p.7)
• I drank all I dared in the bar, and then went to my room to *finish* the job.(p.179)
• When I got back to Germany I settled down to *finish* my apprenticeship, drinking the wine of the country as usual.(p.231)
• First, my new wife had walked out, bag, baggage and furniture; then the apartment landlord had thrown me out of the empty apartment and the *finish* was the loss of another job.(p.238)
• But I was always the unexpected person who had to *finish* the bottle.(p.336)
• Toward five o'clock, helter-skelter, I'd get everything put away and try to get supper on the table, and after supper I'd *finish* the job up and knock myself out.(p.337)
• I felt very sorry for myself and attempted suicide on many occasions, making sure there was always somebody within reaching distance to see that I didn't *finish* the job.(p.478)
• If I don't get started soon, I won't have time to *finish*.(p.499)

finished

• I was *finished* and so were many friends.(p.4)
• Though experience had made him skeptical, he *finished* his treatment with unusual confidence.(p.26)
• When we were *finished* we considered it carefully.(p.65)
• I *finished* my apprenticeship and was moved into the drafting department.(p.211)
• I did not have a high school education so I went to night school to take the full high school course, which I *finished* in two years and nine months.(p.211)
• I then entered Case School and worked while I went to school and *finished* there.(p.212)
• A.A. is not a plan for recovery that can be *finished* and done with.(p.311)
• A square from ultra-dry Kansas, I did not taste grog until I had *finished* college, done a stint on newspapers, married, become a father, and been in studio publicity two years.(p.328)
• And of course a half empty bottle wasn't worth keeping, so I *finished* it up and naturally had to get more in right away for the people who "might come in unexpectedly."(p.336)
• I *finished* high school here in an American-sponsored Methodist public school, know as Philander Smith College.(p.342)
• The amount of will power exercised to control my drinking during working hours, diverted into a constructive channel, would have made me President, and the thing that made the will power possible was the knowledge that as soon as my day was *finished* I could drink myself into oblivion.(p.548)

finishing

• The best boarding schools and a *finishing* school in Europe had fitted me for the conventional role of debutante and young matron.(p.225)
• Probably only a few readers of this story will be able, from personal experiences of their own, to understand the exhilaration and sense of accomplishment which I felt after *finishing* this seemingly simple assignment.(p.276)

finite

• We trust infinite God rather than our *finite* selves.(p.68)

fire

• Yes, the old boy was on *fire* all right.(p.9)
• But the day he comes out he races in front of a *fire* engine, which breaks his back.(p.38)
• Threatens to *fire* me for drinking and padding my expense account.(p.65)
• You have passed happy evenings together chatting and drinking before your *fire*.(p.110)
• If a man drinks so much that his job suffers, we *fire* him.(p.148)
• So, on that Saturday before Labor Day, I got drunk and set the house on *fire* -- so we didn't have to paint it.(p.265)
• The doctor, a young man, immediately took *fire* with the idea, and while he did not convince the son, he turned over two prospects who were anxious for the program.(p.294)
• And then we went up the side of a hill where we have a little barbecue area to make the *fire* for the barbecue, and on the way up, I thought to myself -- I'll go back down to the kitchen and refill this drink.(p.347)
• My torch blazed madly and the pew caught *fire*.(p.424)
• They summoned the *fire* department and the sheriff.(p.424)
• A couple of years later, we lost our elder brother in a house *fire*, because of pills and booze.(p.480)

fired

• He has hired and *fired* hundreds of men.(p.136)
• Presently the man did slip and was *fired*.(p.139)
• Had they *fired* me first, and had they then taken steps to see that I was presented with the solution contained in this book, I might have returned to them six months later, a well man.(p.141)
• They often jeopardize their own positions by trying to help serious drinkers who should have been *fired* long ago, or else given an opportunity to get well.(p.147)
• It boils right down to this: No man should be *fired* just because he is alcoholic.(p.148)
• Your imagination will be *fired*.(p.152)
• In other words, I *fired* the client before the client *fired* me.(p.214)
• In the spring of 1917, in order to beat being *fired* from school, I became "patriotic" and joined the Army.(p.241)
• Then I turned two company cars over in a short time and Bingo – *fired* again.(p.242)
• Oddly enough, the big shot who *fired* me from this company was one of the first men I met when I later joined the New York A.A. Group.(p.242)
• We checked into the home of Hank, the man who had *fired* me eleven years before in Mississippi, and there I met Bill, our founder.(p.245)
• I tried to contact the boys in New York, but telegrams bounced right back and when I finally got Hank on the telephone he *fired* me right then.(p.247)
• One evening, the book, after checking up, was very definitely in the red for plenty through a piece of studied carelessness on my part, and my boss, very shrewd and able, *fired* me with a parting statement to the effect that once was enough.(p.251)
• After being *fired*, I lined up with a new finance company that was just starting in business, and took the position of business promotion man, contacting automobile dealers.(p.300)
• His enthusiasm and keen interest in A.A. *fired* my spirits again.(p.365)
• My alcoholic associates *fired* me, took control, and ran the enterprise into bankruptcy.(p.437)
• In those years I was in jail nine times, in an alcoholic ward, overnight, twice; and I was *fired* from three jobs, two of them very good ones.(p.536)
• What a revelation of ego and arrogance still remaining in me – as if anyone, instinct and training apart, likes to be in jail or in an alcoholic ward or *fired* from his job.(p.536)
• I fled, finally, after having been *fired* from my job by a boss who wept a little (since I had worked hard) as he gave notice for me to clear out.(p.539)

fireside

• This would get me feeling fit, and then I would start for home and *fireside*, thirteen miles away.(p.299)

Firestone

• Every company in the country, except *Firestone*, was reorganized at that time.(p.197)
• During the latter part of the Christian Science experience I had gotten a job and was working at *Firestone*.(p.203)
• There were times when I got to drinking, and I had been warned by *Firestone* that they wouldn't stand for this much longer, so, clearly, they were conscious of the fact that I drank too much and too often.(p.204)

firewater

• Never forgot magic in *firewater*.(p.474)

firing

• If any feel that as psychiatrists directing a hospital for alcoholics we appear somewhat sentimental, let them stand with us a while on the *firing* line, see the tragedies, the despairing wives, the little children; let the solving of these problems become a part of their daily work, and even of their sleeping moments, and the most cynical will not wonder that we have accepted and encouraged this movement.(p.xxvi)
• Keep on the *firing* line of life with these motives and God will keep you unharmed.(p.102)
• *Firing* such an individual may prove a blessing to him.(p.141)

firm

• After they have succumbed to the desire again, as so many do, and the phenomenon of craving develops, they pass through the well-known stages of a spree, emerging remorseful, with a *firm* resolution not to drink again.(p.xxvii)
• Fred is partner in a well known accounting *firm*.(p.39)
• A *firm* attitude at this point has helped many of us.(p.142)
• It isn't fair to me or the *firm*.(p.147)
• The *firm* wants to help you get over it, and if you are interested, there is a way out.(p.147)
• A year later, after I completed the course in contracts, I quit the law school, and undertook some engineering work for a patent law *firm* on behalf of clients who were in difficulties and who desired to keep their troubles from their own engineering department.(p.212)
• By the time I had completed law school I had picked up some experience in patent law, for I remained with the patent law *firm* and worked too in Washington where they found that I was a capable infringement investigator.(p.213)
• In 1924, I had acquired enough clients of my own so that the *firm* made me a junior partner.(p.213)
• I still had enough practice to earn a good living if I would only work, so I resolved that in January of 1940 I would launch a patent law *firm* of my own.(p.220)
• Shortly after I came to this conclusion, I was importuned by another well-known patent law *firm* to help them out on some trial work because their trial man had had a heart attack and had been forbidden to go into the courtroom.(p.220)
• Somewhere in one of the conversations, I mentioned that I was contemplating forming a new *firm*.(p.220)
• I don't think the boys were completely convinced of my personality change, for they fought shy of including my story in the book, so my only contribution to their literary efforts was my *firm* conviction, being still a theological rebel, that the word God should be qualified with the phrase "as we understand him" – for that was the only way I

could accept spirituality.(p.248)
• But the ***firm*** became violently ill with my drunkenness and their course of treatment was to remove their ulcer, in the form of me, from the payroll, amid much fanfare and very personal and slighting remarks and insinuations.(p.300)
• I was working for a Chicago ***firm*** that represented several large radio stations.(p.358)

firmer
• Though some of his manifestations are alarming and disagreeable, we think dad will be on a ***firmer*** foundation than the man who is placing business or professional success ahead of spiritual development.(p.129)

firmly
• Nevertheless, the twentieth century readily accepts theories of all kinds, provided they are ***firmly*** grounded in fact.(p.48)
• We have come to believe He would like us to keep our heads in the clouds with Him, but that our feet ought to be ***firmly*** planted on earth.(p.130)
• With a great deal of determination, I would throw out full pints -- pour them out and smash the bottles -- ***firmly*** resolved never to take another drink of the stuff.(p.234)
• In those days we really took each other's inventories ***firmly*** and often.(p.245)

first
• The ***first*** edition appeared in April 1939, and in the following sixteen years, more than 300,000 copies went into circulation.(p.xi)
• Therefore, the ***first*** portion of this volume, describing the A.A. recovery program, has been left untouched in the course of revisions made for both the second and the third editions.(p.xi)
• "Bill's Story," "Doctor Bob's Nightmare," and one other personal history from the ***first*** edition were retained intact; three were edited and one of these was retitled; new versions of two stories were written with new titles; thirty completely new stories were added; and the story section was divided into three parts, under the same headings that are used now.(p.xi)
• FOREWORD TO ***FIRST*** EDITION(p.xiii)
• This is the Foreword as it appeared in the ***first*** printing of the ***first*** edition in 1939(p.xiii)
• Sixteen years have elapsed between our ***first*** printing of this book and the presentation in 1955 of our second edition.(p.xv)
• The spark that was to flare into the ***first*** A.A. group was struck at Akron, Ohio, in June 1935, during a talk between a New York stockbroker and an Akron physician.(p.xv)
• Their very ***first*** case, a desperate one, recovered immediately and became A.A. number three.(p.xvii)
• When the broker returned to New York in the fall of 1935, the ***first*** A.A. group had actually been formed, though no one realized it at the time.(p.xvii)
• But out of this frightening and at ***first*** disrupting experience the conviction grew that A.A.'s had to hang together or die separately.(p.xix)
• Though none of these principles had the force of rules or laws, they had become so widely accepted by 1950 that they were confirmed by our ***first*** International Conference held at Cleveland.(p.xix)
• Other thousands came to a few A.A. meetings and at ***first*** decided they didn't want the program.(p.xx)
• War fever ran high in the New England town to which we new, young officers from Plattsburg were assigned, and we were flattered when the ***first*** citizens took us to their homes, making us feel heroic.(p.1)
• Then came the insidious insanity of that ***first*** drink, and on Armistice Day 1935, I was off again.(p.8)
• I admitted for the ***first*** time that of myself I was nothing; that without Him I was lost.(p.13)
• These observations would be academic and pointless if our friend never took the ***first*** drink, thereby setting the terrible cycle in motion.(p.23)
• And the truth, strange to say, is usually that he has no more idea why he took that ***first*** drink than you have.(p.23)
• We are without defense against the ***first*** drink.(p.24)
• What seemed at ***first*** a flimsy reed, has proved to be the loving and powerful hand of God.(p.28)
• This is the ***first*** step in recovery.(p.30)
• What sort of thinking dominates an alcoholic who repeats time after time the desperate experiment of the ***first*** drink?(p.35)
• Our ***first*** example is a friend we shall call Jim.(p.35)
• But there was always the curious mental phenomenon that parallel with our sound reasoning there inevitably ran some insanely trivial excuse for taking the ***first*** drink.(p.37)
• Our behavior is as absurd and incomprehensible with respect to the ***first*** drink as that of an individual with a passion, say, for jay-walking.(p.37)
• We ***first*** saw Fred about a year ago in a hospital where he had gone to recover from a bad case of jitters.(p.39)
• It was his ***first*** experience of this kind, and he was much ashamed of it.(p.39)
• I rather appreciated your ideas about the subtle insanity which precedes the ***first*** drink, but I was confident it could not happen to me after what I had learned.(p.40)
• Not only had I been off guard, I had made no fight whatever against the ***first*** drink.(p.41)
• He had felt only the ***first*** nip of the wringer.(p.43)
• Once more: The alcoholic at certain times has no effective mental defense against the ***first*** drink.(p.43)
• At ***first*** some of us tried to avoid the issue, hoping against hope we were not true alcoholics.(p.44)
• At the start, this was all we needed to commence spiritual growth, to effect our ***first*** conscious relation with God as we understood Him.(p.47)
• Even in the present century, American newspapers were afraid to print an account of the Wright brothers' ***first*** successful flight at Kitty Hawk.(p.51)
• For the ***first*** time, he lived in conscious companionship with his Creator.(p.56)
• The ***first*** requirement is that we be convinced that any life run on self-will can hardly be a success.(p.60)
• ***First*** of all, we had to quit playing God.(p.62)
• Next we launched out on a course of vigorous action, the ***first*** step of which is a personal housecleaning, which many of us had never attempted.(p.63)
• ***First***, we searched out the flaws in our make-up which caused our failure.(p.64)
• The ***first*** thing apparent was that this world and its people were often quite wrong.(p.65)
• The best reason ***first***: If we skip this vital step, we may not overcome drinking.(p.72)
• If that is so, this step may be postponed, only however, if we hold ourselves in complete readiness to go through with it at the ***first*** opportunity.(p.74)
• Carefully reading the ***first*** five proposals we ask if we have omitted anything, for we are building an arch through which we shall walk a free man at last.(p.75)
• To some people we need not, and probably should not emphasize the spiritual feature on our ***first*** approach.(p.76)
• Because of resentment and drinking, he had not paid alimony to his ***first*** wife.(p.79)
• We suggested he write his ***first*** wife admitting his faults and asking forgiveness.(p.79)
• He attended church for the ***first*** time in many years.(p.80)
• Though you have talked with the family, leave them out of the ***first*** discussion.(p.91)
• At ***first*** engage in general conversation.(p.91)
• Show him the mental twist which leads to the ***first*** drink of a spree.(p.92)
• Show him, from your own experience, how the queer mental condition surrounding that ***first*** drink prevents normal functioning of the will power.(p.92)
• On your ***first*** visit tell him about the Fellowship of Alcoholics Anonymous.(p.94)
• One of our Fellowship failed entirely with his ***first*** half dozen prospects.(p.96)
• The ***first*** principle of success is that you should never be angry.(p.111)
• Since this book was ***first*** published, A.A. has released thousands of alcoholics from asylums and hospitals of every kind.(p.114)
• At ***first***, some of us did not believe we needed this help.(p.116)
• Your husband will be the ***first*** to say it was your devotion and care which brought him to the point where he could have a spiritual experience.(p.118)
• Cessation of drinking is but the ***first*** step away from a highly strained, abnormal condition.(p.122)
• The ***first*** impulse will be to bury these skeletons in a dark closet and padlock the door.(p.123)
• In the ***first*** flush of spiritual experience they forgave each other and drew closer together.(p.124)
• The family will be affected also, pleasantly at ***first***, as they feel their money troubles are about to be solved, then not so pleasantly as they find themselves neglected.(p.126)
• Although financial recovery is on the way for many of us, we found we could not place money ***first***.(p.127)
• During those ***first*** days of convalescence, this will do more to insure his sobriety than anything else.(p.129)
• When we see a man sinking into the mire that is alcoholism, we give him ***first*** aid and place what we have at his disposal.(p.132)
• ***First*** Things ***First***(p.135)
• To him the alcoholic has often seemed a fool of the ***first*** magnitude.(p.137)
• Had they fired me ***first***, and had they then taken steps to see that I was presented with the solution contained in this book, I might have returned to them six months later, a well man.(p.141)
• Only a few knew of it at ***first*** but, within a short time, it was billboarded throughout the entire company.(p.145)
• Again it was the old, insidious insanity -- that ***first*** drink.(p.154)
• They explained their need and inquired if she had a ***first*** class alcoholic prospect.(p.156)
• There was much talk about the mental state preceding the ***first*** drink.(p.157)
• He now returned home, leaving behind his ***first*** acquaintance, the lawyer and the devil-may-care chap.(p.159)
• Many of us have felt, for the ***first*** time, the Presence and Power of God within its walls.(p.162)
• Dr. Bob and the twelve men and women who here tell their stories were among the early members of A.A.'s ***first*** groups.(p.169)
• The birth of our Society dates from his ***first*** day of permanent sobriety, June 10, 1935.(p.171)
• I drank with moderation at ***first***, but it took me only a relatively short time to drift back into the old habits which had wound up so disastrously before.(p.175)
• When beer ***first*** came back, I thought that I was safe.(p.177)
• Of far more importance was the fact that he was the ***first*** living human with whom I had ever talked, who knew what he was talking about in regard to alcoholism from actual experience.(p.180)
• Unlike most of our crowd, I did not get over my craving for liquor much during the ***first*** two and one-half years of abstinence.(p.181)
• Pioneer member of Akron's Group No. 1, the ***first*** A.A. group in the world.(p.182)
• The ***first*** time that I became intoxicated I was eight years old.(p.182)
• During the ***first*** six months of 1935, I was hospitalized eight times for intoxication and shackled to the bed two or three days before I even knew where I was.(p.184)
• As far as I know that was the ***first*** time I had ever paid any attention to that word.(p.187)
• Nineteen years ago last summer, Dr. Bob and I saw him (Bill D.) for the ***first*** time.(p.188)
• It was in the next two or three days after I had ***first*** met Doc and Bill, that I finally came to a decision to turn my will over to God and to go along with this program the best that I could.(p.189)
• Then I remember when the boys came back, that I told them, "I have gone to this Higher Power and I have told Him that I am willing to put His world ***first***, above everything.(p.190)
• That was my ***first*** drink.(p.195)
• That was the ***first*** time I ever drank hard liquor.(p.195)
• I felt having gotten married, I was an adult and one of the ***first*** things I did was to buy two cases of whiskey with no idea of drinking it.(p.196)
• At the end of about four months, I not only had good looking clothes --and I might say that at the time I ***first*** talked to Max I didn't have a suit of clothes I could bend over in real sudden; now I had six suits of clothes.(p.200)
• The ***first*** definite indications of an alcoholic pattern began to arise when I would go to New York on business and disappear, and wind up in Philadelphia or Boston for two or three day periods.(p.213)
• I was forty-nine and a half years old when I was ***first*** approached about the Akron Group.(p.215)
• He startled me by informing me that he was an alcoholic, that he had found a way which so far enabled him to live without taking a drink, and that the main idea was to find a way how not to take that ***first*** drink.(p.218)
• I left on a Wednesday afternoon, had dinner in Akron and then went to a house where I encountered my ***first*** meeting.(p.218)
• That was skeptically received by me when I ***first*** heard it, but after some twenty-eight or thirty fellows had come to see me, and pretty nearly all of them had said the same thing, I began to believe it.(p.219)
• It was finally decided to undertake the organization of a Cleveland group and toward the end of May, 1939, the ***first*** meeting was held in Cleveland in my home.(p.219)
• The ***first*** chapters were a revelation to me.(p.227)
• Military service was compulsory and I did my stretch with the class of my age, goose-stepping in

German barracks and taking part in the Boxer Rebellion in China, my *first* time at any great distance from home.(p.230)

• You can all remember that in the *first* few months after the change, a great many men, who had formerly been used to a few beers every day or an occasional drink of whiskey, simply quit all alcoholic drinks.(p.232)

• For a long time I kept on trying, in a pretty dumb way at *first*, I know, but very earnestly.(p.237)

• The *first* few months were hard.(p.237)

• *First*, my new wife had walked out, bag, baggage and furniture; then the apartment landlord had thrown me out of the empty apartment and the finish was the loss of another job.(p.238)

• That night for the *first* time in my life I really let down my hair and admitted my general loneliness.(p.239)

• The lesson of his death still remains with me, yet I often wonder what would have happened if somebody else had made that *first* call on me.(p.239)

• The age-old question in A.A. is which came *first*, the neurosis or the alcoholism.(p.240)

• However, here I probably took my *first* step towards my coming alcoholism by developing a terrific aversion to all churches and established religions.(p.240)

• That is where I had my *first* drink and I still remember it, for every "*first*" drink afterwards did exactly the same trick -- I could feel it go right through every bit of my body and down to my very toes.(p.241)

• But each drink after the "*first*" seemed to become less effective and after three or four they all seemed like water.(p.241)

• Even that *first* night I blacked out, which leads me to believe that I was an alcoholic from my very *first* drink.(p.241)

• The *first* year in college I just got by in my studies, and that year I majored in poker and drinking.(p.241)

• With the war over, and back in Baltimore with the folks, there were several small jobs for three years and then I went to work soliciting as one of the *first* ten employees of a new national finance company.(p.242)

• Oddly enough, the big shot who fired me from this company was one of the *first* men I met when I later joined the New York A.A. Group.(p.242)

• After the oil job blew up, I went back to Baltimore and mother, my *first* wife having said a permanent "Goodbye."(p.243)

• I could never be bothered with the follow-through and would invariably reward myself for my efforts with that "*first*" drink.(p.243)

• All they talked of that *first* week-end was God, and how they were going to straighten out Jackie's and my life.(p.245)

• During that *first* week-end I decided to stay in New York and take all they gave out with, except the "God stuff."(p.246)

• At our weekly meeting I was a menace to serenity those *first* few months, for I took every opportunity to lambaste the "spiritual angle" as we called it, or anything else that had any tinge of theology.(p.246)

• This was when I really took my *first* good look at myself.(p.247)

• My brilliant agnosticism vanished, and I saw for the *first* time that those who really believed, or at least honestly tried to find a Power greater than themselves, were much more composed and contented than I had ever been, and they seemed to have a degree of happiness which I had never known.(p.247)

• In June, 1945, with another member, I made my *first* -- and only -- Twelfth Step call on a female alcoholic and a year later I married her.(p.249)

• I have served on only one committee in the past nine years, for I feel that I had my chance the *first* few years and that newer members should fill the jobs.(p.250)

• Again I spent my bankroll, by no means as thick as the one I had when I *first* saw the skyline of Gotham.(p.252)

• I got my *first* introduction to "riding the rods and making a blind."(p.252)

• Forced to detrain from an empty gondola on the other side of Chicago by a terrific rainstorm which drenched me to the skin, I hit the *first* factory building I saw for a job.(p.253)

• An old avocation, the collecting of *first* editions, rare books and Americana, fascinated me between times.(p.255)

• As soon as I could get up and walk I started to drink again and kept it up until my friend of the hospital, who, in his *first* try at the new way of life had stubbed his toe in Chicago but had come back to the town to take counsel and make a new start, picked me up and got me into a hospital.(p.258)

• A pioneer woman member of A.A.'s *first* Group.(p.261)

• These vacations became quite something, and he always had two weeks vacation the *first* two weeks of every September.(p.264)

• I knew Doc and Anne were going to be there, and all of them thought it would be good for me, but the *first* thing I did was to go to St. Thomas and try to talk to those women.)(p.272)

• I don't ever remember that I was bored myself when we *first* came in, and they came out to the house and talked to us about these things.(p.273)

• During my *first* year out of college I had endless dates, and went to countless dances, balls and dinner parties.(p.275)

• I heard for the *first* time an expression which I was to grow to loathe: "There is nothing organically wrong."(p.276)

• I went for my *first* walk.(p.276)

• The details of the long road back to something resembling normal living -- the *first* short streetcar ride, the purchase of a used bike which enabled me to widen the narrow horizon of life, the *first* trip downtown -- I will not dwell on.(p.276)

• I got down on my knees for the *first* time in thirty years.(p.280)

• It is, however, only the *first* of a series of miracles which have followed one after another as a result of my trying to apply to my daily life the principles embodies in our Twelve Steps.(p.280)

• During my *first* few months in Akron I was quite sure that I never wanted to see my home town again.(p.281)

• A doctor tipped me off to my *first* prospect.(p.282)

• Nothing has ever to this day equalled the thrill of that *first* case.(p.282)

• But it took six more months of work and disappointments before a group of three men got together in my rooming house bedroom for their *first* A.A. meeting.(p.282)

• There was more than one occasion when I got up in the morning with just enough money for coffee and toast and the bus fare to carry me to my *first* appointment.(p.283)

• During that *first* year, however, I managed to make both ends meet, and to avoid ever going back to my old habit pattern of borrowing money when I could not earn it.(p.283)

• During the *first* three months I carried on all these activities without a car, depending entirely on buses and streetcars -- I, who had always to have a car at my immediate command.(p.283)

• I, carried away with the desire to serve A.A., gave what was probably one of the *first* radio broadcasts about A.A., living through a case of mike fright and feeling like a million dollars when it was all over.(p.283)

• As I look back on that *first* evening I realize that I began to hope, then, for the *first* time; and I felt that if he could regain these things, perhaps it would be possible for me too.(p.290)

• Then and then only, after a thorough indoctrination by eight or nine individuals, was I allowed to attend my *first* meeting.(p.291)

• This *first* meeting was held in the living room of a home and was led by Bill D., the *first* man that Bill W. and Dr. Bob had worked with successfully.(p.291)

• Three years after I started on my drinking career, I lost my *first* job.(p.298)

• Upon leaving the office in the evening, my *first* stop would be a saloon about a block away.(p.298)

• The general procedure was to take four or five shots in the *first* place I stopped at.(p.299)

• I never enjoyed any meal, but I ate my lunch at noon for two reasons; *first*, to help me get out of the fog of the night before and, second, to furnish some measure of nourishment.(p.299)

• From a physical standpoint, I gained sixteen pounds in the *first* two months I was off liquor.(p.303)

• He put me at ease with his *first* few words.(p.309)

• By the latter part of September 1939, we had a nucleus of six and held our *first* official group meeting.(p.310)

• *First*, through mutual pain and despair, and later through mutual objectives and new-found faith and hope.(p.312)

• I talked to the *first* sergeant and the battalion commander, and they got me in contact with an A.A. member.(p.319)

• I sat and listened and heard the *first* speaker say, "I'm an alcoholic."(p.319)

• I found out that the people in all A.A. groups were as nice as the people in the *first* one.(p.320)

• As we walked back through the hall, I, for the *first* time in my life, said to another human being, "I'm having trouble with my drinking, too."(p.321)

• My *first* drinking spree was on corn liquor and I was allergic to it, believe me.(p.322)

• I never knew it was the *first* drink that did it.(p.324)

• We even can be rebels for the *first* time in our lives.(p.329)

• When I found this impossible, I became scared for the *first* time.(p.333)

• How full it has kept my retirement years -- the five I've lived since the *first* two lost in traveling a rocky road to hell, before I made a U-turn.(p.334)

• I never knew which came *first*, the thinking or the drinking.(p.337)

• But I had to get back to that *first* drink somehow.(p.339)

• And when I took that *first* drink, I was off on the usual merry-go-round.(p.339)

• The *first* time was when I knew I couldn't live with alcohol.(p.340)

• Easy does it, *first* things *first*, one day at a time.(p.340)

• After training, I was commissioned as a *first* lieutenant.(p.342)

• This was my *first* long vacation of sixty days since I had joined the army.(p.343)

• On the *first*, though on the water wagon, I looked forward to my next drink.(p.344)

• On the second, I knew -- as I know now -- that if I remained away from the *first* drink, then I had not to worry about the hundredth one.(p.344)

• *First*, we all hear at A.A. meetings about those who have lost everything, those who have been in jail, those who have been in prison, those who have lost their families, those who have lost their income.(p.345)

• And I gave him some idea of what you do, and so I made my *first* Twelfth Step call before I ever came into the program.(p.347)

• So I decided that I would go to my *first* meeting.(p.347)

• I will never forget the *first* meeting that I attended.(p.347)

• And the *first* thing you know I was lifted right out of the A.A. group, and I floated higher, and higher, and even higher, until I was way up on a pink cloud which is known as Pink Seven, and I felt miserable again.(p.348)

• I tried every gimmick that there was to get some peace of mind, but it was not until I was brought to my alcoholic knees, when I was brought to a group in my own community with the butcher, the baker, the carpenter and the mechanic, who were able to give me the Twelve Steps, that I was finally given some semblance of an answer to the last half of the ***First*** Step.(p.349)

• So, after taking the *first* half of the ***First*** Step, and very gingerly admitting myself to Alcoholics Anonymous, something happened.(p.349)

• I had my *first* drink when I was fifteen and my alcoholic potential had ripened me to the point of necessary escapism.(p.353)

• When I walked into the friendly atmosphere of my *first* A.A. meeting, I knew I was where I belonged.(p.355)

• And the only one who can take it away from me is me -- by taking that *first* drink.(p.355)

• Prohibition came along, and with it my *first* taste of moonshine.(p.357)

• I made little headway in my *first* few meetings with her.(p.359)

• My work kept me busy the *first* few months on the new job.(p.360)

• It was to be short lived, for on the day before Christmas I completely disillusioned my wife and ruined our *first* Christmas by coming home from the Rotary lunch dead drunk.(p.361)

• It was the *first* of many such experiences that became the only cause of harsh words, tears and heartaches in an otherwise truly beautiful marriage.(p.361)

• Sure enough in a couple of hours two men were at my door and for the *first* time I heard some facts about liquor and my problem that sounded sensible to me.(p.363)

• My *first* meeting gave me a great deal of hope and lots of willing ears for my tale of woe and for my questions.(p.364)

• One night at the dinner table my wife said that tonight was my *first* birthday in A.A., and that the group would have the usual ice cream and cake for the "one year man."(p.365)

• My *first* spiritual experience in A.A. came quite early to me.(p.366)

• It was the *first* she had heard or read about it and she said she had considered sending it to me or trying

to have someone in Pittsburgh send it to me so I wouldn't know where it came from.(p.366)
• It was fun at *first*, since I never had indulged before.(p.370)
• At *first* it was just that – an occasional drink.(p.374)
• It now became necessary to have noon drinks; at *first* just two, then gradually more.(p.375)
• She of course didn't realize how cunning an alcoholic can be and the lengths to which he will go in finding ways to satisfy the compulsion for more and more drinks after having had the *first* one.(p.377)
• The answer came to me very simply in the *first* step of the Twelve Steps of A.A.(p.379)
• At *first* it was a shock to realize I was an alcoholic, but the realization that there was hope made it easier.(p.379)
• There may be many reasons which bring one to A.A. for the *first* time, but the lasting one must be to want sobriety and the A.A. way of living for oneself.(p.379)
• "*First* Things *First*": solving our immediate problems before we try to solve all the others and get muddled in our thinking and doing.(p.382)
• I believe the *first* time I ever realized what alcohol would do for me was at my own wedding.(p.385)
• Because of this state of confusion and frustration I had hysterics on the seventeenth day for the *first* and only time in my life.(p.387)
• Then he said I couldn't possibly move on the *first* of February because I couldn't stay in that place by myself.(p.388)
• I took two or three drinks so my eyes could focus, and I could see that horrible picture of the awful drunk on the *first* page; he couldn't get the drink to his mouth, he had a towel around his hand and he needed a shave.(p.391)
• But, from the very *first* paragraph on, something happened to me.(p.392)
• It was such a feeling of relief that I wanted to know more about it and with that, I think for the *first* time, came the realization that there was something horribly, horribly wrong with me.(p.392)
• I only know that it *first* reached me through that Saturday Evening Post article.(p.392)
• It was the *first* time in my life that I could not get a lift out of what I was drinking; and so one Friday night, at five minutes to six, I had half a water glass of warm gin, and that is when I *first* asked God to help me.(p.393)
• There are so many to whom I feel deeply grateful; to my husband (and best critic), whose generous love, compassion and understanding have helped me along the way; to those before me in A.A. who inspired the *first* article I read, and the friend who sent that article to Frank; to Ruth for her personal note, and the *first* A.A. to talk to me; to my Bishop, whose loving and believing spirit inspired me; and to all the members of the Houston Group who were so patient, kind and helpful – and to countless others.(p.393)
• Dr. Bob said, "Love and service keep us dry," and Bill said, "Always we must remember that our *first* duty is face-to-face help for the alcoholic who still suffers."(p.395)
• At eighteen, I got my *first* steady job.(p.397)
• Saying these sprees were limited to one a week (they were not), and saying that the average spree was ten of these drinks (sometimes more, sometimes less), we come up with the *first* boring statistic: two-fifty per week out of twelve dollars.(p.397)
• Two weeks later found me being sworn in, and the *first* payday in the Navy made me realize I had found a home.(p.398)
• My *first* pay was ten dollars, pay for recruits at that time being twenty-one dollars per month.(p.398)
• But now, with His help and grace, this child of His has paid his initiation fee for good, as long as he remembers to stay away from that *first* drink (the one that does all the damage) one day at a time.(p.399)
• This was where I started my *first* drinking lessons.(p.402)
• That *first* night I blacked out at a large dinner party.(p.404)
• I experienced my *first* real guilt and shame.(p.404)
• My *first* analyst said, "You are becoming more and more of an alcoholic," and sent me to another analyst.(p.407)
• A.A. had to stop my drinking *first*.(p.409)
• My analyst was one of the *first* to learn of A.A. and to make subsequent use of it in her work.(p.412)
• In a sense, I had taken the *first* step.(p.412)
• He now said that we had a physical allergy combined with a mental obsession, and he explained this so that I saw for the *first* time how this could be.(p.413)
• I went to my *first* meeting with Marty and some other girls.(p.414)
• Not understanding the twenty-four hour plan, or not wanting to, I began drinking and was off-again on-again, during that *first* month.(p.414)
• Except for one short slip, during the *first* eight months, which was an angry "the world can't do this to me" reaction to a personal tragedy in my life, I have been sober for twelve years.(p.416)
• In the *first* year there were episodes such as kicking Priscilla in the shins, getting the lock changed on the desk in the A.A. Club, because I, as secretary, didn't want the Intergroup secretary "interfering," and taking an older woman member out to lunch for the express purpose of informing her that she was "a phony."(p.416)
• During my *first* year there, I married.(p.419)
• About this time I got my *first* crush on a girl.(p.425)
• This went on for thirteen weeks, the *first* eight of which I wasn't allowed visitors.(p.425)
• I spent eighteen hundred dollars fixing up that car in the *first* year I was home, after four bad smash-ups.(p.429)
• Even on my rare (at *first*) binge nights it never ran much over a quart.(p.433)
• Intervals between binges were, at *first*, eight months.(p.434)
• "*First*, I couldn't be sure.(p.436)
• Moreover, I am deeply convinced that so long as I continue to strive, in my bumbling way, toward the principles I *first* encountered in the earlier chapters of this book, this remarkable power will continue to flow through me.(p.437)
• At *first*, she would say, "You don't love me.(p.439)
• It seemed to me I needed a consultation *first*.(p.444)
• At *first*, I wondered whether he was alcoholic himself, and was sending me to find out about A.A.(p.444)
• I had already given up all the narcotics, most of the pills, and some of the alcohol when I *first* came to A.A.(p.448)
• It seems I should have learned to love my wife and family *first*; the newcomer to A.A., last.(p.451)
• Eventually, I had to redo each of the Twelve Steps specifically with Max in mind, from the *First*, saying, "I am powerless over alcohol, and my homelife is unmanageable by me," to the Twelfth, in which I tried to think of her as a sick Al-Anon and treat her with the love I would give a sick A.A. newcomer.(p.452)
• But with the *first* drink, our good intentions dissolved; our personalities changed.(p.458)
• Ten days of this treatment the *first* time knocked me from 200 pounds to 130, and I seldom stayed out of the hole long enough to gain back my weight.(p.460)
• The *first* time I remember seeing or hearing of A.A. was twenty years ago.(p.460)
• Four years later, I was taken to my *first* A.A. meeting out of prison, in Los Angeles.(p.460)
• I suddenly remembered one of my *first* A.A. meetings, where I heard, "If you are an alcoholic and if you continue to drink, the end is death or insanity."(p.461)
• During the twenty-four hours after running into the Serenity Prayer, I think I took the *first* three Steps for the *first* time.(p.461)
• I didn't like it particularly at *first*, but I did like the effect I got from it.(p.464)
• Then I went on my *first* week-long bender of solitary drinking, locked up in a hotel room, because my family opposed my coming marriage.(p.464)
• (I think my *first* feeling of fear came with my *first* week's solitary drinking, locked up in that hotel room.(p.465)
• Instead, I started going to a nice private sanitarium which, after the *first* visit, turned out to be more like a country club than anything else.(p.468)
• After the *first* two or three days you were allowed the run of the place and it was a lot of fun.(p.468)
• Also, after that *first* visit I learned I could refuse to sign myself in unless they gave me a glass of whiskey in one hand and a glass of paraldehyde in the other.(p.468)
• But to another woman, the *first* woman I met in A.A., I could talk.(p.471)
• The other of the Twelve Steps of Alcoholics Anonymous seemed insurmountable to me at *first*.(p.471)
• When I *first* came into A.A., the woman who was my sponsor was the *first* woman I had ever met who admitted that she was an alcoholic.(p.472)
• This *first* story I ever write.(p.474)
• Had *first* drink in young teens, but was scared of my father.(p.474)
• Now think I was alcoholic from *first* drink.(p.474)
• *First* time I have blackout, but not last.(p.474)
• Remember only *first* two drinks.(p.475)
• I go with him to *first* meeting, in small town in Maine.(p.476)
• So I jump quick from *First* Step to Twelfth Step to help my brother, living with me.(p.476)
• Two years later, my brother take Tall Man to *first* A.A. meeting.(p.476)
• At every place, I find A.A. group *first*.(p.476)
• We can have this new way of life – learning to live with our sickness and to be happy and content -- if we are willing to change our way of thinking and be honest, *first* with ourselves, then with others.(p.480)
• He has also taught me that I must help myself *first*; only then may I be able to help others.(p.481)
• I planted my *first* flower garden this year and am actually excited to see the results.(p.481)
• This physician, the originator of A.A.'s *first* black group, but badly caught in the toils, tells of his release and of how freedom came as he worked among his own people.(p.483)
• We lived just a few doors from the *First* Baptist Church and when they had funerals I remember very often asking my mother whether the person was good or bad and whether they were going to heaven or hell.(p.483)
• I remember in my *first* year in high school, that mother suggested that I do not join the cadet unit.(p.484)
• Vi was the *first* girl that I ever took out.(p.485)
• In the *first* place, she had been married before; I was her second husband.(p.485)
• My mother resented it so that the *first* Christmas after our marriage, she didn't even invite us to dinner.(p.485)
• After our *first* child came my parents both became allies, but in later days, after I became an alcoholic, they both turned against me.(p.485)
• For the *first* couple of years it wasn't too bad because the momentum kept things going.(p.486)
• That's the *first* time I was ever really drunk in my life.(p.487)
• At that time the repeal whiskies were back, and I'd go to the store and buy my whiskey and take it to my office and put it under the desk, *first* in one place and then in another, and there soon was an accumulation of empty bottles.(p.488)
• It was the *first* blackout I had to recognize as a blackout.(p.489)
• Then I had my *first* bad stomach hemorrhage.(p.490)
• But as he continued to talk, I realized that this was the *first* time I had met a person who had the same problems I did and who, I sincerely believe, understood me as an individual.(p.494)
• That was the next meeting, and the *first* meeting of a colored group in A.A., so far as I know.(p.495)
• Can't remember the answer to the *first*.(p.499)
• I was indicted for the crime of murder in the *first* degree.(p.508)
• I spent my last seventeen months in Wallkill, and it was there that I *first* got my introduction to A.A.(p.509)
• After hearing the *first* speaker I could tell myself that my own lot was rather mild.(p.509)
• So instead of going near A.A., I just browsed around for that *first* month.(p.510)
• So I went to an A.A. meeting the *first* chance I got, and I listened.(p.511)
• When we *first* come into A.A., many of us are confused because as a general rule we're at the end of our respective ropes, and we don't know what to do.(p.512)
• At *first* they were rather amusing, but a little later on they became serious.(p.513)
• The *first* had been as a youngster coming out from Ireland.(p.513)
• We were married, and during the *first* nine months of that marriage I was sober.(p.514)
• But at the end of nine months we went to a party one night, and I took the *first* drink.(p.514)
• No one had ever told me it was the *first* drink that did the damage.(p.514)
• It was the *first* time that I had asked for help sincerely and honestly.(p.515)
• I went back to the old family doctor who had helped me the *first* time I had the D.T.'s.(p.515)
• It was a revelation when I read that *First* Step.(p.515)
• Then I went to my *first* meeting.(p.516)
• But I've never come close to that *first* drink.(p.516)
• Before I step out and do anything, I stop and check it over *first*, and then let my conscience be my guide.(p.516)
• Then I had a year in Germany at school – that was, incidentally, when I got drunk for the *first* time.(p.517)

• But I pointed out to him that as I was the *first* British boy who had been to the school, it wouldn't be a very good advertisement for him, so I got over that all right.(p.518)
• At *first*, like everybody else, I could keep control when I drank, but if I did start to drink, even in those days, I was always one of the last to leave the party.(p.518)
• That morning was the *first* time I really realized where I'd got to in my life.(p.523)
• I was taking Benzedrine and paraldehyde quite impartially during the day then, and by the time I arrived at my *first* A.A. meeting, I was pretty drunk and certainly doped up to the eyes and completely jittery.(p.523)
• It was their open night meeting, but of course I thought they were all alcoholics; I couldn't imagine why anybody else would want to go there, and my *first* reaction was, well, I've come to something that's not for me.(p.524)
• That gave me my *first* bit of hope.(p.524)
• There was the love affair which was ridiculous -- "imagine that midget being able to fall in love!" -- and my head knew it while my heart pumped real, genuine anguish, for it hurt like hell, and since it was *first* love, things have never been quite the same.(p.534)
• I have seen that there is only one law, the law of love, and there are only two sins; the *first* is to interfere with the growth of another human being, and the second is to interfere with one's own growth.(p.542)
• My husband was soon in uniform and among the *first* to go overseas.(p.547)
• I was the only person I'd ever known personally who had ever been in jail, and I guess it is most significant that the second time was less humiliating that the *first* had been.(p.549)
• It was here that I realized for the *first* time that as a practicing alcoholic I had no rights.(p.549)
• I attended my *first* A.A. meeting eight years ago, and it is with deep gratitude that I'm able to say I've not had a drink since that time, and that I take no sedation or narcotics, for this program is to me one of complete sobriety and I no longer need to escape reality.(p.549)
• They said if you want to know how this program works, take the *first* word of your question -- the H is for honesty, the O is for open-mindedness and the W is for willingness; these our Book calls the essentials of recovery.(p.550)
• Sometimes I have to ask *first* for the willingness, but it too always comes.(p.552)
• After my very *first* drink -- a tiny glass of sherry my father gave me to celebrate the New Year when I was thirteen -- I went up to bed, dizzy with exhilaration and excitement, and I prayed I wouldn't drink any more!(p.554)
• To do that, I had come to A.A. to learn how to handle sobriety -- which is what I could not handle in the *first* place.(p.554)
• I sold my *first* article to a national magazine while still an undergraduate.(p.555)
• I also got into my *first* disciplinary trouble caused by drinking, on two separate occasions.(p.555)
• At *first*, just one drink, on occasion.(p.557)
• This is a condensed version of the original "long form" A.A. Traditions as *first* printed in 1946.(p.563)
• One -- Our common welfare should come *first*; personal recovery depends upon A.A. unity.(p.564)
• Hence our common welfare comes *first*.(p.565)
• Yet it is true that our *first* printing gave many readers the impression that these personality changes, or religious experiences, must be in the nature of sudden and spectacular upheavals.(p.569)
• In the *first* few chapters a number of sudden revolutionary changes are described.(p.569)
• Since Dr. Silkworth's *first* endorsement of Alcoholics Anonymous, medical societies and physicians throughout the world have set their approval upon us.(p.571)

first-timers
• There was no time off for so-called good behavior, *first-timers*, or anything else.(p.509)

fish
• They both drank like *fish*.(p.424)

fish-wife
• I became a menace, the *fish-wife*, the common scold.(p.410)

fishing
• Golf, hunting and *fishing* were now merely excuses to drink excessively.(p.375)

fist
• We had several fights and on one or two occasions I struck her with my *fist*.(p.491)

fists
• He had not developed this art and had no recourse but his *fists*.(p.405)

fit
• We, who have been through the wringer, have to admit if we substituted alcoholism for jay-walking, the illustration would *fit* us exactly.(p.38)
• Our real purpose is to *fit* ourselves to be of maximum service to God and the people about us.(p.77)
• That is how we react so long as we keep in *fit* spiritual condition.(p.85)
• Assuming we are spiritually *fit*, we can do all sorts of things alcoholics are not supposed to do.(p.100)
• His wife is one of those persons who really feels there is something rather sinful about these commodities, so she nagged, and her intolerance finally threw him into a *fit* of anger.(p.135)
• This would get me feeling *fit*, and then I would start for home and fireside, thirteen miles away.(p.299)
• Scared that my dress wasn't going to *fit* right, that the church wasn't going to be filled, that I'd fall flat on my face walking up the aisle; in fact, I was afraid I wasn't going to be a prima donna in the place where I should be.(p.385)
• But I did not *fit* into this pattern either.(p.402)
• I was not *fit* to be on the loose, and there was no one to commit me.(p.412)
• "How does prayer *fit* into this thing?"(p.504)
• I was still very *fit* and good at games.(p.519)

fits
• Suppose, however, that your husband *fits* the description of number two.(p.112)

fitted
• The best boarding schools and a finishing school in Europe had *fitted* me for the conventional role of debutante and young matron.(p.225)

fitting
• It seems only *fitting* that when I did finally fall in love it was with an alcoholic, and for the next ten years I progressed as rapidly as is humanly possible into what I believed to be hopeless alcoholism.(p.547)

Fitz
• I had not asked for help and seriously doubt that I would have, but *Fitz*, an old school friend of mine, had persuaded Jackie to call on me.(p.238)
• Jackie told me about a group of fellows in New York, of whom my old friend *Fitz* was one, who had the same problem I had, and who by working together to help each other were not now drinking and were happy like himself.(p.239)

Fitzgerald
• The times in which I grew up (the Prohibition era immortalized by Scott *Fitzgerald* and John Held Jr.) had taught me to be gay with the gayest; my own inner urges led me to outdo them all.(p.225)
• That age of the flapper and the "It" girl, speakeasies and the hip flask, the boyish bob and the drugstore cowboy, John Held Jr. and F. Scott *Fitzgerald*, all generously sprinkled with a patent pseudo-sophistication.(p.304)

Fitzgerald's
• It was all about Scott *Fitzgerald's* little lost debutante, abused, misunderstood and running wild.(p.402)
• I also wrote another novel, all about Scott *Fitzgerald's* poor, misbegotten, unloved, tipsy little debutante.(p.405)

five
• In Part III ("They Lost Nearly All"), eight stories have been retained; *five* are new.(p.xii)
• It was eight o'clock -- *five* hours after the market closed.(p.4)
• Mercifully, no one could guess that I was to have no real employment for *five* years, or hardly draw a sober breath.(p.4)
• Carefully reading the first *five* proposals we ask if we have omitted anything, for we are building an arch through which we shall walk a free man at last.(p.75)
• There are two alcoholic employees, who produce as much as *five* normal salesmen.(p.149)
• We entered her house at exactly *five* o'clock and it was eleven fifteen when we left.(p.179)
• One of *five* children, I was born on a Kentucky farm in Carlyle County.(p.182)
• Before my drinking had cut me down completely, I achieved a considerable measure of success, having been a City Councilman for *five* years and a financial director of Kenmore, a suburb later taken into the city itself.(p.182)
• I said, "Yes, Doc, I would like to quit, at least for *five*, six, or eight months, until I get things straightened up, and begin to get the respect of my wife and some other people back, and get my finances fixed up and so on."(p.187)
• I can remember well thinking that I would quit drinking, really go to work hard, apply myself eight hours a day, *five* days a week, make a lot of money, and then I could start drinking again.(p.199)
• After drinking one glass of beer at the end of my work period for about *five* days, I thought I'd better find out whether I really had the stuff licked.(p.203)
• I had taken *five* and a half ounces of paraldehyde.(p.207)
• I went to *five* grade schools, primarily because I was expelled for my conduct, but I eventually graduated from the eighth grade.(p.211)
• In fact, the last three years of my drinking was a routine of barbiturates in the morning, so that I could stop shaking enough to shave, and then alcohol beginning about four-thirty or *five* o'clock, with a struggle not to take a drink at noon or during the day, because I had the idea that if I took one drink, I would smell as though I had had a pint.(p.217)
• She gave no sign of recognizing anything wrong, but what had I been doing for those lost *five* hours?(p.223)
• Somehow I got out of there and walked *five* blocks past brownstone houses.(p.223)
• In four or *five* days I would be hunting all over the place, at home and in my workshop, for the bottles I had destroyed, cursing myself for being a fool.(p.234)
• This doctor had imparted his knowledge to just a few other men at that time -- not more than four or *five* -- they now number more than seventy persons.(p.235)
• The new job lasted *five* years.(p.254)
• A friend who knew I would soon be broke mounted guard over me when I left my job of writing the histories of Texas cities and put me aboard a bus for the town I had left almost *five* years before.(p.256)
• In *five* years a good many persons had forgotten that I had been somewhat notorious.(p.256)
• This happy combination of pleasant work and alcohol lasted for *five* years.(p.277)
• It took *five* years of A.A. living, and a substantial improvement in my health, before I could take a full-time office job where someone else was boss.(p.283)
• This was the beginning of *five* years of bounding back and forth between my home in Chicago and Akron to sober up.(p.288)
• The general procedure was to take four or *five* shots in the first place I stopped at.(p.299)
• If I were alone I would stop at four or *five* of them, but only one or two in the event I had my mistrusting wife with me.(p.299)
• The third time, after almost *five* years as an S.P. 4, I finally made sergeant.(p.318)
• I couldn't remember what had been said *five* minutes ago.(p.319)
• I was being very cagey, because I knew that if I did take one or two, I might want to take *five* or six or seven or eight.(p.323)
• How full it has kept my retirement years -- the *five* I've lived since the first two lost in traveling a rocky road to hell, before I made a U-turn.(p.334)
• Toward *five* o'clock, helter-skelter, I'd get everything put away and try to get supper on the table, and after supper I'd finish the job up and knock myself out.(p.337)
• There were *five* people present, including myself.(p.347)
• I spent *five* and a half years in psychoanalysis and proceeded to become a drunk.(p.349)
• It was a long four or *five* hour operation, a large surgical procedure, and she was on her ninth or tenth post-operative day.(p.350)
• It wasn't long before I became a *five* o'clock alcoholic.(p.360)
• I graduated there from a *five* o'clock alcoholic to a noon-day one.(p.361)
• It was the first time in my life that I could not get a lift out of what I was drinking; and so one Friday night, at *five* minutes to six, I had half a water glass of warm gin, and that is when I first asked God to help me.(p.393)
• *Five* or six drinks and I was terrific.(p.402)
• While waiting to depart I was selected -- by giving a CPO *five* dollars -- to be bartender in the Navy Chief's Club.(p.426)
• I would drink all night in bars, come home about *five* a.m., down a good big glass of whiskey straight, and tumble into bed.(p.428)
• That doctor in the Navy hospital told me I wouldn't live *five* years if I didn't quit.(p.429)
• If it was one minute before *five*, I'd drink myself

back to sleep.(p.441)
• You see, I am a five-time loser, which means *five* felony convictions (not including the cases beaten).(p.457)
• Same thing when I let lye and water eat away at four of my toes and my foot for *five* hours.(p.458)
• In a prison in my native state, I spent eleven months in solitary confinement, bouncing in and out of the "hole" (a bare concrete-and-steel cubicle) about *five* times during those eleven months.(p.459)
• For the next *five* years, I was in and out of A.A. in Los Angeles, Phoenix, and San Francisco.(p.460)
• I was not eligible for parole, until -- with God's help, I'm sure – the governor cut *five* years off my sentence.(p.462)
• Having passed over the border line, the next *five* years were filled with fear, failure and frustration.(p.465)
• Tall Man die *five* years ago, a sober, peaceful, happy man.(p.476)
• I'd known her *five* or six months.(p.487)
• I borrowed *five* hundred dollars from the bank and three hundred from the loan shop, and I drank that up pretty fast.(p.490)
• I guess I had *five* or ten dollars in my pocket.(p.491)
• I wander to a stable and drink *five* bottles of beer.(p.502)
• My mother lived on for *five* years after I joined A.A., the last two in complete blindness.(p.525)
• The only thing that bothers me is that there are only about *five* Negroes in A.A. in my city.(p.529)
• But not for long; now, for *five* Friday nights in a row, I went to jail, picked up sodden with beer (which I always disliked, but which was the only drink available); in jail *five* consecutive Friday nights in the town where I had grown up, where I had been an honor student in high school, where a kindly uncle, bailing me out, said, "Bob, our family just doesn't do this sort of thing."(p.539)
• We worked in *five* below zero weather, fixing on an elm tree a wrought iron device which modestly proclaimed that he was indeed a country doctor.(p.540)
• *Five* -- Each group has but one primary purpose -- to carry its message to the alcoholic who still suffers.(p.564)

five-time

• A *FIVE-TIME* LOSER WINS(p.457)
• You see, I am a *five-time* loser, which means five felony convictions (not including the cases beaten).(p.457)

five-year-old

• Very soon after I lost Mother, my *five-year-old* little girl was killed by a neighbor's car.(p.370)

fives

• Already," continues the early text, "twos and threes and *fives* of us have sprung up in other communities."(p.xv)
• Little clusters of twos and threes and *fives* of us have sprung up in other communities, through contact with our two larger centers.(p.162)

fix

• Gin would *fix* that.(p.6)
• Self-knowledge would *fix* it.(p.40)
• Nothing would *fix* me.(p.157)
• He interrupted: "I used to be strong for the church, but that won't *fix* it.(p.157)
• I knew what they were all right – a drink would *fix* them.(p.223)
• I feel that I can *fix* them all.(p.506)
• I do not *fix* anyone, but I am getting part of a tremendous education and I have made some new friends.(p.506)
• I *fix* up a little apartment over the garage with books and drinking water.(p.506)

fixed

• In the realm of the material, men's minds were fettered by superstition, tradition, and all sorts of *fixed* ideas.(p.51)
• Thus was our friend's cornerstone *fixed* in place.(p.56)
• The alcoholic, his wife, his children, his "in-laws," each one is likely to have *fixed* ideas about the family's attitude toward himself or herself.(p.122)
• I said, "Yes, Doc, I would like to quit, at least for five, six, or eight months, until I get things straightened up, and begin to get the respect of my wife and some other people back, and get my finances *fixed* up and so on."(p.187)

fixing

• I spent eighteen hundred dollars *fixing* up that car in the first year I was home, after four bad smash-ups.(p.429)
• We worked in five below zero weather, *fixing* on an elm tree a wrought iron device which modestly proclaimed that he was indeed a country doctor.(p.540)

flagging

• The outlines and the promise of the New Land had brought lustre to tired eyes and fresh courage to *flagging* spirits.(p.53)

flame

• If tempted, we recoil from it as from a hot *flame*.(p.84)

flames

• A busload of basketball players had been passing and saw the *flames*.(p.424)

flank

• Good generalship may decide that the problem be attacked on the *flank* rather than risk a face-to-face combat.(p.82)

flannels

• I found some wool stockings, some white *flannels* that had shrunk to my knees, and an old jacket.(p.288)

flapper

• That age of the *flapper* and the "It" girl, speakeasies and the hip flask, the boyish bob and the drugstore cowboy, John Held Jr. and F. Scott Fitzgerald, all generously sprinkled with a patent pseudo-sophistication.(p.304)

flare

• The spark that was to *flare* into the first A.A. group was struck at Akron, Ohio, in June 1935, during a talk between a New York stockbroker and an Akron physician.(p.xv)

flare-ups

• All the people involved in these *flare-ups* took it with remarkable grace, have teased me about it since, and have become good friends of mine.(p.416)

flash

• A few hours later I came out of a complete stupor in our living room with a *flash* of sanity.(p.363)

flashed

• The thought *flashed* through his mind, "If they can do it, I can do it!"(p.189)
• Just as I was wondering what on earth I could do -- I was too drunk even to pack a handkerchief – the memory of an A.A. write-up that I had seen in the Evening Mail *flashed* across my mind – and I thought to myself, this is something I haven't tried yet.(p.523)

flashing

• By the time I figured out what had happened, I saw two *flashing* red lights atop squad cars, sedately coming around the corner.(p.353)

flashy

• My new wife and I don't own any property to speak of, and the *flashy* successes of another day are no longer mine.(p.438)

flask

• Morning after morning I would awake sick and with terrible jitters, but there was always a *flask* of liquor sitting on the table beside my bed.(p.183)
• That age of the flapper and the "It" girl, speakeasies and the hip *flask*, the boyish bob and the drugstore cowboy, John Held Jr. and F. Scott Fitzgerald, all generously sprinkled with a patent pseudo-sophistication.(p.304)
• Many of them carried a *flask* and sandwich case, strapped to their saddles so they could stay out all day.(p.404)
• But whereas my horse was always equipped with a *flask*, I merely endured the fox hunting so I could start drinking at lunch time.(p.404)

flat

• The story he told is most instructive, for here was a chap absolutely convinced he had to stop drinking, who had no excuse for drinking, who exhibited splendid judgment and determination in all his other concerns, yet was *flat* on his back nevertheless.(p.40)
• I was in a large, dark, rather poorly furnished room -- the living room of a basement *flat*.(p.222)
• Scared that my dress wasn't going to fit right, that the church wasn't going to be filled, that I'd fall *flat* on my face walking up the aisle; in fact, I was afraid I wasn't going to be a prima donna in the place where I should be.(p.385)

flatly

• They *flatly* declare that since they have come to believe in a Power greater than themselves, to take a certain attitude toward that Power, and to do certain simple things, there has been a revolutionary change in their way of living and thinking.(p.50)

flattered

• War fever ran high in the New England town to which we new, young officers from Plattsburg were assigned, and we were *flattered* when the first citizens took us to their homes, making us feel heroic.(p.1)

flavor

• One school would allow man no *flavor* for his fare and the other would have us all on a straight pepper diet.(p.69)

flaw

• I was always able to see the *flaw* in every person, every situation.(p.449)

flaws

• First, we searched out the *flaws* in our make-up which caused our failure.(p.64)

fled

• I *fled*, finally, after having been fired from my job by a boss who wept a little (since I had worked hard) as he gave notice for me to clear out.(p.539)

fledgling

• The *fledgling* society, which had been nameless, now began to be called Alcoholics Anonymous, from the title of its own book.(p.xvii)

fleeting

• There was a feeling of awe and wonder, but it was *fleeting* and soon lost.(p.46)

flesh

• Three weeks after an armed robbery in which one person received a superficial *flesh* wound (I could have killed someone!), I was apprehended.(p.460)

fleshpots

• Neither can I honestly say that I have forgotten the "*fleshpots* of Egypt."(p.259)

flew

• I don't know why I didn't fall out of the open cockpit of some of those planes I *flew* in while taking aerial pictures.(p.426)

flexible

• My hours of work were *flexible* so that returning to the office was not always important.(p.376)

flicker

• This process snuffed out the last *flicker* of conviction that I could do the job myself.(p.42)
• Perhaps the single *flicker* of decency that shone through the fog of my drinking days was a clumsy affection for my two children, a boy and a girl.(p.437)

flickered

• Although my ambition still *flickered*, it now took the form of fantasizing.(p.556)

flight

• It did not satisfy us to be told that we could not control our drinking just because we were maladjusted to life, that we were in full *flight* from reality, or were outright mental defectives.(p.xxiv)
• Out of this alloy of drink and speculation, I commenced to forge the weapon that one day would turn in its *flight* like a boomerang and all but cut me to ribbons.(p.2)
• Even in the present century, American newspapers were afraid to print an account of the Wright brothers' first successful *flight* at Kitty Hawk.(p.51)
• Had not all efforts at *flight* failed before?(p.51)
• We were having trouble with personal relationships, we couldn't control our emotional natures, we were a prey to misery and depression, we couldn't make a living, we had a feeling of uselessness, we were full of fear, we were unhappy, we couldn't seem to be of real help to other people – was not a basic solution of these bedevilments more important than whether we should see newsreels of lunar *flight*?(p.52)
• Yet we had been seeing another kind of *flight*, a spiritual liberation from this world, people who rose above their problems.(p.55)
• A night or so a week in a joint, and a party or so a week at home or with friends, along with a little lone drinking, soon had me preparing for the existence of a top *flight* drunkard.(p.298)
• Then my father fell down a *flight* of stairs on one of his lost weekends, at the peak of his career, and died.(p.370)

flights

• There were *flights* from city to country and back, as my wife and I sought escape.(p.6)

flimsy

• What seemed at first a *flimsy* reed, has proved to be the loving and powerful hand of God.(p.28)

flippant

• But I had never been a *flippant*, wise-cracking sneerer at the few persons I had met who had impressed me as Christian men and women, or at any institution whose sincerity of purpose I could see.(p.259)

flipped

• It was getting pretty dark and I hadn't turned on any lights, when some big fellow stepped inside the door and *flipped* on the light switch.(p.207)

floated

• Music and gay chatter still *floated* to him from the bar.(p.154)

• And the first thing you know I was lifted right out of the A.A. group, and I *floated* higher, and higher, and even higher, until I was way up on a pink cloud which is known as Pink Seven, and I felt miserable again.(p.348)

floating

• "Well," he said, "you've been sober, but you've been *floating* way up on a cloud somewhere.(p.349)

flood

• It poured over and through him with the certainty and majesty of a great tide at *flood*.(p.56)

floods

• Talking things over with them, great *floods* of enlightenment showed me myself as I really was and I was like them.(p.229)

floor

• Somehow I managed to drag my mattress to a lower *floor*, lest I suddenly leap.(p.6)

• Away from my office two or three weeks at a time; horrible days and nights when I would lie on the *floor* of my home, lying awake and reaching over to get the bottle, taking a drink and going back into oblivion.(p.184)

• They roll on the *floor* and holler, and pull their hair."(p.266)

• I paced the *floor* with a bath towel around my shoulders, the perspiration running off me.(p.268)

• This consisted of walking the *floor* for three or four days and nights until I could take nourishment.(p.289)

• Sometimes I would lie on the bathroom *floor*, deathly sick, praying I would die, and praying to God as I always had prayed to Him when I was drinking: "Dear God, get me out of this one and I'll never do it again."(p.324)

• I do recall lying on a cold cement *floor* and shredding into little bits several pieces of stolen identification cards, and washing my face in the toilet bowl trying to sober up, and screaming hysterically while clinging to bars too high to see out of, and cursing everyone that came near me.(p.354)

• I was knocked to the *floor*, swinging madly at the faces on those pineapples.(p.427)

• I waited all the rest of that day and paced the *floor* all that night.(p.467)

floored

• That *floored* me.(p.11)

Florida

• He is like the retired business man who lolls in the *Florida* sunshine in the winter complaining of the sad state of the nation; the minister who sighs over the sins of the twentieth century; politicians and reformers who are sure all would be Utopia if the rest of the world would only behave; the outlaw safe cracker who thinks society has wronged him; and the alcoholic who has lost all and is locked up.(p.61)

• The people in the group hadn't been around that day; part of my family was in *Florida* and the rest of them weren't speaking to me, so I spent a very lonesome day and by evening I was feeling very sorry for myself.(p.207)

• Dr. Bob was in *Florida*, but Jack didn't know that.(p.267)

• Once dad came all the way to *Florida* to sober me up, after a hotel manager called him and said that if he wanted to see me alive he better get there fast.(p.288)

• After another of my "never again episodes" she packed up and left for her parents' home in *Florida*.(p.362)

• After a few meetings I decided to drive to *Florida* unannounced to see my wife and tell her about my new found friends and association.(p.364)

• I stayed on in *Florida* for three weeks, enjoying our reunion, a new found health and a deeper love than I had ever experienced before.(p.364)

• While I was in *Florida* trying to convince my wife with all the A.A. literature that she should come back to me, she went over to her desk and picked up a clipping she had taken from the St. Petersburg Times about A.A.(p.366)

• With no explanation at all, I was taken from my home in *Florida* to my grandparents' home in the middle west.(p.544)

floundered

• For years he had *floundered* from one sanitarium to another.(p.26)

floundering

• They are far more alert and progressive than we *floundering* fathers were, and the future of our fellowship is in their hands.(p.250)

flour

• I remember starting to city school, coming from a country school, and wanting so very, very much to be like the other girls and trying *flour* on my face for powder because I wasn't able to have any real powder.(p.261)

• Economic conditions had a great deal to do with it, because I've often heard my father say that his mother would take one of the old time *flour* sacks and cut a hole through the bottom and two corners of it and there you'd have a gown.(p.486)

flourishing

• A.A. has *flourishing* communities in the British Isles, the Scandinavian countries, South Africa, South America, Mexico, Alaska, Australia and Hawaii.(p.xv)

flow

• As we felt new power *flow* in, as we enjoyed peace of mind, as we discovered we could face life successfully, as we became conscious of His presence, we began to lose our fear of today, tomorrow or the hereafter.(p.63)

• If we have carefully followed directions, we have begun to sense the *flow* of His Spirit into us.(p.85)

• The regular *flow* of all the literature, which I keep meticulously and which, of course, I study, has been wonderful.(p.342)

• Moreover, I am deeply convinced that so long as I continue to strive, in my bumbling way, toward the principles I first encountered in the earlier chapters of this book, this remarkable power will continue to *flow* through me.(p.437)

flowed

• In the face of collapse and despair, in the face of the total failure of their human resources, they found that a new power, peace, happiness, and sense of direction *flowed* into them.(p.50)

flower

• And then, with a better motive, had we not worshipfully beheld the sunset, the sea, or a *flower*?(p.54)

• A *FLOWER* OF THE SOUTH(p.384)

• I planted my first *flower* garden this year and am actually excited to see the results.(p.481)

• I now conceive the psychiatrist's job to be the task of breaking down the patient's inner resistance so that which is inside him will *flower*, as under the activity of the A.A. program."(p.571)

flowing

• My family always bought the best, and the embassies were *flowing*.(p.402)

• I would pull out early, and go to the hunt breakfast and the *flowing* bowl of milk-punch.(p.404)

flown

• It has *flown* away.(p.497)

flows

• Arrangements were also made with the chief psychiatrist of a large public hospital to select still others from the stream of misery which *flows* through that institution.(p.163)

fluently

• By the time I was twenty-one I had six years of life in foreign countries, spoke three languages *fluently*, and had attended college for two years.(p.275)

fluff-dry

• The only drawback was, I always knew how I arrived there, but somehow, between the rest room, the rinse, and the *fluff-dry*, I never knew when or how I got home.(p.370)

fluid

• I well remember the shock I received when a prominent doctor in Chicago told me of cases where pressure of the spinal *fluid* actually ruptured the brain.(p.140)

flush

• In the first *flush* of spiritual experience they forgave each other and drew closer together.(p.124)

fly

• Was it not true that the best mathematical minds had proved man could never *fly*?(p.51)

• The Wright brothers' almost childish faith that they could build a machine which would *fly* was the mainspring of their accomplishment.(p.52)

• When others showed us that "God-sufficiency" worked with them, we began to feel like those who had insisted the Wrights would never *fly*.(p.52)

• What about people who proved that man could never *fly*?(p.55)

• My writing career was described in the couplet "Alcohol gave me wings to *fly*,/And then it took away the sky."(p.331)

flying

• Did not Professor Langley's *flying* machine go to the bottom of the Potomac River?(p.51)

• Cold chills started chasing up and down my spine; my teeth were chattering; my hands were shaking so I tucked them under me to keep them from *flying* away.(p.222)

• I was supposed to come home on a troop ship, but I talked the base commander into *flying* me home.(p.428)

flying-blind

• The *flying-blind* period ended and A.A. entered a new phase of its pioneering time.(p.xvii)

focus

• He is unable to *focus* on anything else.(p.128)

• I took two or three drinks so my eyes could *focus*, and I could see that horrible picture of the awful drunk on the first page; he couldn't get the drink to his mouth, he had a towel around his hand and he needed a shave.(p.391)

• Two fuzzy objects came into *focus*.(p.422)

• I couldn't *focus* enough to make out the chart, but the card contained two words -- "ACUTE ALCOHOLISM."(p.422)

• I can again *focus* on my wife's good qualities and watch them grow and grow and grow.(p.451)

• The more I *focus* my mind on its defects -- late start, long drunkalogues, cigarette smoke — the worse the meeting becomes.(p.451)

• But when I try to see what I can add to the meeting, rather than what I can get out of it, and when I *focus* my mind on what's good about it, rather than what's wrong with it, the meeting keeps getting better and better.(p.451)

• When I *focus* on what's good today, I have a good day, and when I *focus* on what's bad, I have a bad day.(p.451)

• If I *focus* on a problem, the problem increases; if I *focus* on the answer, the answer increases.(p.451)

focused

• It was as if I had, rather than a Midas touch which turned everything to gold, a magnifying mind that magnified whatever it *focused* on.(p.450)

• And the more I *focused* my mind on her defects, the more they grew and multiplied.(p.450)

focussed

• Keep his attention *focussed* mainly on your personal experience.(p.92)

foe

• We are headed for trouble if we do, for alcohol is a subtle *foe*.(p.85)

fog

• Then a mental *fog* settled down.(p.6)

• When I got the *fog* out of my brain, I decided that quitting school was very foolish and that I had better return and continue my work.(p.173)

• I never enjoyed any meal, but I ate my lunch at noon for two reasons; first, to help me get out of the *fog* of the night before and, second, to furnish some measure of nourishment.(p.299)

• After a time, my mind began to clear of the *fog* that had covered it.(p.320)

• Perhaps the single flicker of decency that shone through the *fog* of my drinking days was a clumsy affection for my two children, a boy and a girl.(p.437)

foggy

• Well, I wasn't sure I did, and it was awful *foggy*, and I wept and asked her what she thought I ought to do about it.(p.273)

fold

• In January 1938, I had the opportunity to go to northern Vermont to manage a small daytime radio station that was up against it financially, and was about to *fold* its antenna.(p.359)

• The explanation that alcoholism was a disease of a two *fold* nature, an allergy of the body and an obsession of the mind, cleared up a number of puzzling questions for me.(p.380)

• To those now in its *fold*, Alcoholics Anonymous has made the difference between misery and sobriety, and often the difference between life and death.(p.563)

folder

• He did not take out a *folder* and say, "What is the nature of your problem?"(p.413)

• There at the top of the *folder* was my name, age and address, and underneath were the words, "Periodic Drinker."(p.470)

folk

• Being mostly business or professional *folk*, we could not well carry on our occupations in such an event.(p.xiii)
• I could almost hear the sound of the preacher's voice as I sat, on still Sundays, way over there on the hillside; there was that proffered temperance pledge I never signed; my grandfather's good natured contempt of some church *folk* and their doings; his insistence that the spheres really had their music; but his denial of the preacher's right to tell him how he must listen; his fearlessness as he spoke of these things just before he died; these recollections welled up from the past.(p.10)
• Our women *folk* have suggested certain attitudes a wife may take with the husband who is recovering.(p.122)
• His were good, simple Quaker *folk* who accepted me with love.(p.402)

folks

• For most normal *folks*, drinking means conviviality, companionship and colorful imagination.(p.151)
• I guess the old *folks* were right after all."(p.159)
• It took me a year, or a year and a half to get to feeling physically well, and it was rather tough, but I soon found *folks* whose friendship I had once had, and I found, after I had been sober for quite some little time, that these people began to act like they had in previous years, before I had gotten so bad, so that I didn't pay too awful much attention to financial gains.(p.190)
• At night, I woke up and the *folks* with whom I roomed were home by then.(p.205)
• With the war over, and back in Baltimore with the *folks*, there were several small jobs for three years and then I went to work soliciting as one of the first ten employees of a new national finance company.(p.242)
• When I drank, I hid it from my *folks* out of respect for their feelings.(p.287)
• Once in a while I stayed home for a night, to see how my *folks* were doing.(p.425)
• I planned to stay home the night before I left, but my *folks* got so drunk I walked off early in the evening and spent the night with my girl, getting very drunk myself.(p.425)
• About this time my *folks* found A.A.(p.427)
• Meanwhile the letters from home were telling about how much my *folks* wanted to make up to me for some of the things I'd missed.(p.427)
• The *folks* called a doctor and he knocked me out with sedatives.(p.429)
• And the *folks* said A.A. was for people who wanted to quit, otherwise it wouldn't work.(p.429)
• I attended meetings, I talked to my *folks*, I talked to younger people they had gotten in contact with to sponsor me.(p.430)

follow

• On the other hand -- and strange as this may seem to those who do not understand -- once a psychic change has occurred, the very same person who seemed doomed, who had so many problems he despaired of ever solving them, suddenly finds himself easily able to control his desire for alcohol, the only effort necessary being that required to *follow* a few simple rules.(p.xxvii)
• The almost certain consequences that *follow* taking even a glass of beer do not crowd into the mind to deter us.(p.24)
• Were our contentions true, it would *follow* that life originated out of nothing, and proceeds nowhere.(p.49)
• He will be more likely to *follow* your suggestions.(p.94)
• Your candidate may give reasons why he need not *follow* all of the program.(p.94)
• If he thinks he can do the job in some other way, or prefers some other spiritual approach, encourage him to *follow* his own conscience.(p.95)
• *Follow* the dictates of a Higher Power and you will presently live in a new and wonderful world, no matter what your present circumstances!(p.100)
• We know these suggestions are sometimes difficult to *follow*, but you will save many a heartbreak if you can succeed in observing them.(p.111)
• Avoid urging him to *follow* our program.(p.113)
• Marvelous results often *follow* such a reunion.(p.134)
• Our hope is that when this chip of a book is launched on the world tide of alcoholism, defeated drinkers will seize upon it, to *follow* its suggestions.(p.153)
• Each day I would try to find out what His will was, and try to *follow* that, rather than trying to get Him to always agree that the things I thought of myself were the things best for me.(p.187)
• The very simple program they advised me to *follow* was that I should ask to know God's will for me for that one day, and then, to the best of my ability, to *follow* that, and at night to express my gratefulness to God for the things that had happened to me during the day.(p.208)
• The law school experience was not inspired by a desire to *follow* patent law, which has been my profession since: I went to law school primarily to learn the law of contracts following my own experience with litigation.(p.212)
• This work consumed a period of about two-thirds of a year, and worked out successfully so I decided to *follow* patent law.(p.212)
• The afternoon that I was to leave the hospital, he came in to see me and asked me if I were willing to attempt to *follow* the program.(p.218)
• In a few sentences he made God seem personal to me, explained Him as a being who was interested in me, the alcoholic, and that all I needed to do was to be willing to *follow* His way; that as long as I followed it I would be able to overcome my desire for liquor.(p.236)
• My visitor well knew, that as I tried to *follow* God I would get to studying these things out for myself.(p.236)
• We would *follow* one man's ideas for a while, decide he was wrong and switch to another's method.(p.246)
• Once again, there was the challenge of a tough job, but this time I was determined to *follow* through.(p.248)
• "Complete abandon"; "Half measures availed us nothing"; "Thoroughly *follow* our path"; "Completely give oneself to this simple program" – rang in my swelled head.(p.349)
• I would *follow* certain drinking schedules or diets faithfully for a few days, and then somewhere along the line would over-train and upset the applecart.(p.361)
• I was desperately in earnest to *follow* through and understand what was expected of me as a member of A.A. and to take each Step of the Twelve as rapidly as possible.(p.382)
• If pressed further, all I can do is *follow* the psalmist who said it long, long before me: "Be still, and know that I am God."(p.437)
• No drunk hopeless if he want to *follow* guide along right trail.(p.477)
• Yes, we find it rather confusing, but as we get around and get to know people in the group, they lead the way and all we have to do is to *follow*.(p.512)

follow-through

• I could never be bothered with the *follow-through* and would invariably reward myself for my efforts with that "first" drink.(p.243)

followed

• The cases we have *followed* through have been most interesting; in fact, many of them are amazing.(p.xxv)
• My judgment and ideas were *followed* by many to the tune of paper millions.(p.3)
• A tumbler full of gin *followed* by half a dozen bottles of beer would be required if I were to eat any breakfast.(p.5)
• To Christ I conceded the certainty of a great man, not too closely *followed* by those who claimed Him.(p.11)
• There was a sense of victory, *followed* by such a peace and serenity as I had never known.(p.14)
• These are *followed* by forty-three personal experiences.(p.29)
• All of us felt at times that we were regaining control, but such intervals – usually brief – were inevitably *followed* by still less control, which led in time to pitiful and incomprehensible demoralization.(p.30)
• In some instances there has been brief recovery, *followed* always by a still worse relapse.(p.31)
• "Then they outlined the spiritual answer and program of action which a hundred of them had *followed* successfully.(p.42)
• Rarely have we seen a person fail who has thoroughly *followed* our path.(p.58)
• When we sincerely took such a position, all sorts of remarkable things *followed.*(p.63)
• Though our decision was a vital and crucial step, it could have little permanent effect unless at once *followed* by a strenuous effort to face, and to be rid of, the things in ourselves which had been blocking us.(p.64)
• We have seldom told them the whole truth nor have we *followed* their advice.(p.73)
• If we have carefully *followed* directions, we have begun to sense the flow of His Spirit into us.(p.85)
• For us, material well-being always *followed* spiritual progress; it never preceded.(p.127)
• And but for the intervention of an understanding person, I might have *followed* in their footsteps.(p.137)
• The only answer I could make was that if the man *followed* the usual pattern, he would go on a bigger bust than ever.(p.138)
• This would lessen my chances of smuggling some home that evening, which in turn would mean a night of futile tossing around in bed *followed* by a morning of unbearable jitters.(p.176)
• They looked at one another queerly and, finally, one of them allowed he'd have a beer and they all *followed* him, each of them saying he'd have a beer too.(p.194)
• In a few sentences he made God seem personal to me, explained Him as a being who was interested in me, the alcoholic, and that all I needed to do was to be willing to follow His way; that as long as I *followed* it I would be able to overcome my desire for liquor.(p.236)
• Taking that as a foundation, he reasoned that if a man *followed* that rule he could not be selfish.(p.236)
• Washington, D.C. and news-gathering agency work *followed*, along with many parties.(p.254)
• It is, however, only the first of a series of miracles which have *followed* one after another as a result of my trying to apply to my daily life the principles embodies in our Twelve Steps.(p.280)
• The last day of my drinking career, I drank twenty-two of them between ten and twelve a.m. and I shall never know how many more *followed* them until I was poured into bed that night.(p.298)
• I got the Big Book and I read it, and this is what it said: "Rarely have we seen a person fail who has thoroughly *followed* our path."(p.349)
• He even went to bat for me before the court martial that inevitably *followed* and, as a result, I drew only thirty days – fifteen in solitary.(p.428)
• I was an agitator, a troublemaker, and many men as bitter as I was *followed* me.(p.458)
• My last binge *followed* the previous one by two weeks.(p.514)
• Though it was not our intention to create such an impression, many alcoholics have nevertheless concluded that in order to recover they must acquire an immediate and overwhelming "God-consciousness" *followed* at once by a vast change in feeling and outlook.(p.569)

follower

• And he further said that God could not accept me as a sincere *follower* of His Divine Law unless I was ready to be thoroughly honest about it.(p.236)

following

• The first edition appeared in April 1939, and in the *following* sixteen years, more than 300,000 copies went into circulation.(p.xi)
• Six months earlier, the broker had been relieved of his drink obsession by a sudden spiritual experience, *following* a meeting with an alcoholic friend who had been in contact with the Oxford Groups of that day.(p.xv)
• *Following* the elimination of alcohol, there was found to be no permanent brain injury.(p.xxix)
• *Following* his physical rehabilitation, he had a talk with me in which he frankly stated he thought the treatment a waste of effort, unless I could assure him, which no one ever had, that in the future he would have the "will power" to resist the impulse to drink.(p.xxix)
• By the *following* spring we were living in our accustomed style.(p.4)
• In the *following* chapter, there appears an explanation of alcoholism, as we understand it, then a chapter addressed to the agnostic.(p.28)
• Their services are often indispensable in treating a newcomer and in *following* his case afterward.(p.133)
• *Following* his discharge, we contacted him.(p.139)
• If your decision is yes, whether the reason be humanitarian or business or both, then the *following* suggestions may be helpful.(p.140)
• If he is conscientiously *following* the program of recovery he can go anywhere your business may call him.(p.147)
• *Following* graduation I was offered a pretty good job which I took.(p.212)
• The law school experience was not inspired by a desire to follow patent law, which has been my profession since: I went to law school primarily to learn the law of contracts *following* my own experience with litigation.(p.212)

• "Best in the business, when he's sober," my customers would say, and I still had a *following* who would give me work though they deplored my habits, because they knew the job would be well done when they eventually got it.(p.234)
• *Following* a big drunk on that sheet, where I was doing leg-work and rewrite, a feeling of nostalgia made me buy a ticket for Liverpool and I returned to Britain.(p.252)
• A very simple plan that I still find much joy and happiness in *following*.(p.302)
• *Following* this, I had a short vacation, during which time I read as much literature as my sponsor could send me.(p.343)
• If I were asked what in my opinion was the most important factor in being successful in this program, besides *following* the Twelve Steps, I would say Honesty.(p.367)
• The *following* spring she left me one day without giving me any idea of where she had gone, hoping this would bring me to my senses.(p.377)
• The final decision came when my daughter, *following* a drunk which ruined my wife's birthday, said, "It's Alcoholics Anonymous -- or else!"(p.378)
• *Following* an injection I would have to keep one hand busy scratching my constantly itching nose and would also have sudden uncontrollable urges to vomit.(p.442)
• And so, in those *following* years, whenever A.A. was mentioned I would have no part of it.(p.469)
• The *following* day, Saturday, he came back and said, "Jim, I owe you for that prescription last night.(p.488)
• The November *following*, I took a few days off after pay day to celebrate my birthday on the 25th of the month.(p.491)
• The *following* Sunday we met at Ella G.'s.(p.495)
• It is the last day of the *following* October, a dark, rainy morning.(p.502)
• *Following* are excerpts from the comments of doctors present at the annual meeting of the Medical Society of the State of New York where a paper on A.A. was read:(p.571)

follows

• The physician who at our request, gave us this letter, has been kind enough to enlarge upon his views in another statement which *follows*.(p.xxiv)
• No matter how often I had gone into and come out of alcoholic lows during the day, the pattern bounced me out of bed each night about 2:00 a.m., shaking and hurting in the agitation that always *follows* a drug's sedation.(p.332)
• But individual welfare *follows* close afterward.(p.565)
• The citation reads in part as *follows*:(p.573)

fond

• All changes made over the years in the Big Book (A.A. members' *fond* nickname for this volume) have had the same purpose: to represent the current membership of Alcoholics Anonymous more accurately, and thereby to reach more alcoholics.(p.xii)
• *Fond* of singing, I joined a German singing society which had good club headquarters.(p.231)
• I was very *fond* of music.(p.517)
• It became second nature for me to remove myself from anything or anybody I found myself growing *fond* of.(p.545)

fondle

• I learned early in my A.A. life that I could not afford to *fondle* such thoughts, as you might *fondle* a pet, because this particular pet could grow into a monster.(p.285)

food

• Like a gaunt prospector, belt drawn in over the last ounce of *food*, our pick struck gold.(p.128)
• My experience in the hospital I considered to be terrific because Dr. Bob told me very quickly that medicine would have very little to do with it, outside of trying to restore my appetite for *food*.(p.217)
• In fact, after six months of living on *food* instead of on whiskey, I gained about thirty pounds.(p.220)
• I am going to town to get some liquor and *food*.(p.506)
• I would never admit that I was drinking too much, or spending money that I should have used to buy *food* for my two little boys.(p.526)
• Once I started drinking, I didn't care that the rent wasn't paid, or that there was no *food* in the house, or that my boys needed shoes.(p.527)
• I couldn't face *food*.(p.558)

foods

• Some of my family are allergic to certain *foods*.(p.380)

fool

• If the owner of the business is to be successful, he cannot *fool* himself about values.(p.64)
• To him the alcoholic has often seemed a *fool* of the first magnitude.(p.137)
• In four or five days I would be hunting all over the place, at home and in my workshop, for the bottles I had destroyed, cursing myself for being a *fool*.(p.234)
• It's surprising, how we think we *fool* everybody in our drinking.(p.324)
• So, for no better reason than to *fool* him, I asked Frank to take me to a meeting every night.(p.447)

fooled

• I lost money, and then just *fooled* away a large part of that profit.(p.194)
• That is where we are really *fooled*.(p.376)
• I'd *fooled* him thus far.(p.429)

fooling

• Actually we were *fooling* ourselves, for deep down in every man, woman, and child, is the fundamental idea of God.(p.55)
• If he says yes, does he really mean it, or down inside does he think he is *fooling* you, and that after rest and treatment he will be able to get away with a few drinks now and then?(p.142)
• The only one we are *fooling* is ourselves.(p.376)

foolish

• Best of all, I met a kind doctor who explained that though certainly selfish and *foolish*, I had been seriously ill, bodily and mentally.(p.7)
• Yet all reasons for not drinking were easily pushed aside in favor of the *foolish* idea that he could take whiskey if only he mixed it with milk!(p.36)
• Up to this point you would label him as a *foolish* chap having queer ideas of fun.(p.37)
• Therefore, we are not to be the hasty and *foolish* martyr who would needlessly sacrifice others to save himself from the alcoholic pit.(p.79)
• We are then in much less danger of excitement, fear, anger, worry, self-pity, or *foolish* decisions.(p.88)
• When I got the fog out of my brain, I decided that quitting school was very *foolish* and that I had better return and continue my work.(p.173)
• I am trying now, each day, to make up for all those selfish, thoughtless, *foolish* things I did in my drinking days.(p.326)
• However, knowing me, she thought it was a *foolish* idea, that I wouldn't be interested.(p.367)
• One more *foolish* idea.(p.502)
• Another *foolish* idea.(p.502)

foolishly

• That may be true of certain nonalcoholic people who, though drinking *foolishly* and heavily at the present time, are able to stop or moderate, because their brains and bodies have not been damaged as ours were.(p.39)
• We do not tire so easily, for we are not burning up energy *foolishly* as we did when we were trying to arrange life to suit ourselves.(p.88)
• Why, he argued, should he lose the remainder of his business, only to bring still more suffering to his family by *foolishly* admitting his plight to people from whom he made his livelihood?(p.155)
• I said that she told me she was going to the movies, and I became *foolishly* disturbed about it and, as things snowballed, I decided to go out and get drunk.(p.487)

fools

• He *fools* himself.(p.152)
• "Well," I said to dad, when the A.A. people kept coming with these lovely cars and looked so nice, "I suppose the neighbors say, 'Now those old *fools* must have up and died, but where's the hearse?'"(p.269)

foot

• I looked up and there were two great big fellows over six *foot* tall, very likable looking.(p.185)
• Keeping one *foot* in front of the other is essential for maintaining our arrestment.(p.311)
• Before too long, my husband (who seemed to prefer his shirts dirty) put his *foot* down, declaring that our family might have the cleanest clothes in town, but that I hadn't been out of the same old dirty slacks and blouse for a week.(p.371)
• At one end of the bed, near the *foot*, was a printed card, and beneath that was a charted graph.(p.422)
• I remember finding myself in the middle of the night in the doctors' parking lot at the hospital with one *foot* in the car and one *foot* on the ground, not knowing which was the lead *foot*; finding myself hanging up the telephone -- then realizing I had gotten out of bed, answered the phone, turned on the light, and carried on a conversation with a patient.(p.441)
• Same thing when I let lye and water eat away at four of my toes and my *foot* for five hours.(p.458)
• He said he never wanted to set *foot* in the deep south again and he didn't.(p.486)

football

• I went into the high school grades, but having missed all the intermediate grades, I didn't get along too well, so I developed the habit of going back to school just long enough for the *football* season and then quitting.(p.193)
• The other kids would light out for the hamburger huts or ice cream parlors, the pizza joints or bowling alleys, after *football* games and dances.(p.423)
• There was the physical aspect; to be the youngest and the runt of the brood of children, to have to wear glasses very early and so to be teased, to be bookish and bored in school because the captain of the *football* team could not translate Virgil and yet was the school god while you, you, you little shrimp, were the school egghead, junior size and an early model.(p.533)
• So did the waterboy on the high school *football* team attempt to revenge himself on the big brother who was the star quarterback; for I was the waterboy and my brother was the star quarterback, innocent of everything except the fact that he was a star quarterback.(p.537)

foothills

• The place is Naini Tal, in the *foothills* of the mighty Himalaya Mountains, and it has some very significant memories for me.(p.342)

footing

• He was on a different *footing*.(p.12)
• Established on such a *footing* we became less and less interested in ourselves, our little plans and designs.(p.63)

footsore

• Each in his turn may be *footsore* and may straggle.(p.122)

footsteps

• And but for the intervention of an understanding person, I might have followed in their *footsteps*.(p.137)

forbidden

• Shortly after I came to this conclusion, I was importuned by another well-known patent law firm to help them out on some trial work because their trial man had had a heart attack and had been *forbidden* to go into the courtroom.(p.220)
• It made me feel quite grown-up and mature, and I think another added attraction was the fact that so far as my family was concerned, it was *forbidden*, and it had a special attraction for that reason.(p.464)

forbidding

• To us, the Realm of Spirit is broad, roomy, all inclusive; never exclusive or *forbidding* to those who earnestly seek.(p.46)

force

• Though none of these principles had the *force* of rules or laws, they had become so widely accepted by 1950 that they were confirmed by our first International Conference held at Cleveland.(p.xix)
• We are unable, at certain times, to bring into our consciousness with sufficient *force* the memory of the suffering and humiliation of even a week or a month ago.(p.24)
• If he does not want to see you, never *force* yourself upon him.(p.90)
• By *force* of circumstances, she was often obliged to treat father as a sick or wayward child.(p.130)
• She wanted to know if her husband's company insurance was still in *force*.(p.137)
• But then my "rights" try to move in, and they, too, can *force* my serenity level down.(p.452)
• I don't know if it's *force* of habit or something else that keeps them in one place, but I do know that in A.A. there is much work to do, and none of us can do it standing still.(p.529)

forced

• Without this proof the expectant purchaser would be *forced* to depart empty handed with none of what I later came to believe was the great panacea for all human ills.(p.171)
• From childhood through high school I was more or less *forced* to go to church, Sunday School and evening service, Monday night Christian Endeavor and sometimes to Wednesday evening prayer meeting.(p.172)
• There my drinking became so much worse that the boys in the fraternity house where I lived felt *forced* to send for my father, who made a long journey in the vain endeavor to get me straightened around.(p.174)

• *Forced* to detrain from an empty gondola on the other side of Chicago by a terrific rainstorm which drenched me to the skin, I hit the first factory building I saw for a job.(p.253)
• I didn't like being on the nut ward, and I particularly didn't like being *forced* to ice cookies on Christmas Eve.(p.444)
• The only reality I was able to face had been *forced* upon me by its very repetition – I had to drink; and I didn't know there was anything in the world that could be done about it.(p.548)

forces
• My intellectual heroes, the chemists the astronomers, even the evolutionists, suggested vast laws and *forces* at work.(p.10)
• Ideas, emotions, and attitudes which were once the guiding *forces* of the lives of these men are suddenly cast to one side, and a completely new set of conceptions and motives begin to dominate them.(p.27)
• Then, gathering all his *forces*, he attempted to stop altogether and found he could not.(p.32)
• I told him that I believe in electricity and other *forces* of nature, but as for a God, if there is one, He has never done anything for me.(p.503)

forcibly
• If your man needs hospitalization, he should have it, but not *forcibly* unless he is violent.(p.91)

Ford
• Henry *Ford* once made a wise remark to the effect that experience is the thing of supreme value in life.(p.124)

foreboding
• We had long talks when I would still her *foreboding* by telling her that men of genius conceived their best projects when drunk; that the most majestic constructions of philosophic thought were so derived.(p.2)
• It was with grim *foreboding* and advanced jitters that I checked in at the hospital.(p.302)

foregoing
• There is an important exception to the *foregoing*.(p.108)
• The *foregoing* pages (though addressed only to wives) indicate the problems such people may face.(p.121)
• We intend the *foregoing* as a helpful suggestion only.(p.132)

foreign
• All told, promising beginnings have been made in some 50 *foreign* countries and U.S. possessions.(p.xv)
• Twenty-two, and a veteran of *foreign* wars, I went home at last.(p.1)
• In *foreign* parts many a soldier who has been abstemious at home learns to use new and potent drinks.(p.230)
• By the time I was twenty-one I had six years of life in *foreign* countries, spoke three languages fluently, and had attended college for two years.(p.275)

foresaw
• I *foresaw* another heart attack.(p.333)

foresee
• There is a good bit of travel between East and West and we *foresee* a great increase in this helpful interchange.(p.162)

foresight
• With rare *foresight* he realized it could become a tornado.(p.373)

forest
• We missed the reality and beauty of the *forest* because we were diverted by the ugliness of some of its trees.(p.50)

forever
• I was through *forever*.(p.5)
• Here are some of the methods we have tried: Drinking beer only, limiting the number of drinks, never drinking alone, never drinking in the morning, drinking only at home, never having it in the house, never drinking during business hours, drinking only at parties, switching from scotch to brandy, drinking only natural wines, agreeing to resign if ever drunk on the job, taking a trip, not taking a trip, swearing off *forever* (with and without a solemn oath), taking more physical exercise, reading inspirational books, going to health farms and sanitariums, accepting voluntary commitment to asylums -- we could increase the list ad infinitum.(p.31)
• There was a tremendous urge to cease *forever*.(p.34)
• Each person is like an actor who wants to run the whole show; is *forever* trying to arrange the lights, the ballet, the scenery and the rest of the players in his own way.(p.60)
• Our men have sworn great solemn oaths that they were through drinking *forever*.(p.105)
• In the midst of such pandemonium they may have rushed out threatening to live with the other woman *forever*.(p.106)
• It may convince your husband he wants to stop drinking *forever*.(p.116)
• I told him he was through -- finally and *forever*.(p.136)
• Will he take every necessary step, submit to anything to get well, to stop drinking *forever*?(p.142)
• I had been drinking heavily from one state of semi-coma to another and it was several days before I got "defogged," but subconsciously I was in earnest about wanting to quit liquor *forever*.(p.258)
• I had a drunken quarrel with my family, denounced them, and left them *forever*.(p.409)
• But she couldn't carry me *forever*.(p.472)
• Eight -- Alcoholics Anonymous should remain *forever* nonprofessional, but our service centers may employ special workers.(p.564)
• 8. – Alcoholics Anonymous should remain *forever* nonprofessional.(p.566)
• This to the end that our great blessings may never spoil us; that we shall *forever* live in thankful contemplation of Him who presides over us all.(p.568)

foreword
• *FOREWORD* TO FIRST EDITION(p.xiii)
• This is the *Foreword* as it appeared in the first printing of the first edition in 1939(p.xiii)
• *FOREWORD* TO SECOND EDITION(p.xv)
• Figures given in this *foreword* describe the Fellowship as it was in 1955(p.xv)
• Since the original *Foreword* to this book was written in 1939, a wholesale miracle has taken place.(p.xv)
• *FOREWORD* TO THE THIRD EDITION(p.xxii)

forfeit
• Society can do anything it chooses to do with me when I am drunk and I can't lift a finger to stop it, for I *forfeit* my rights through the simple expedient of becoming a menace to myself and to the people around me.(p.549)

forgave
• In the first flush of spiritual experience they *forgave* each other and drew closer together.(p.124)
• You were thirty-five before you understood your father's horrible anguish, and *forgave* him, and loved him again.(p.533)

forge
• Out of this alloy of drink and speculation, I commenced to *forge* the weapon that one day would turn in its flight like a boomerang and all but cut me to ribbons.(p.2)

forged
• Historians may one day recognize Alcoholics Anonymous to have been a great venture in social pioneering which *forged* a new instrument for social action; a new therapy based on the kinship of common suffering; one having a vast potential for the myriad other ills of mankind."(p.573)

forget
• If we can *forget*, so can she.(p.81)
• Next day they would be themselves again and we would forgive and try to *forget*.(p.106)
• Never *forget* that resentment is a deadly hazard to an alcoholic.(p.117)
• At such moments we *forget* that alcoholism is an illness over which we could not possibly have had any power.(p.118)
• They often *forget* father was beyond human aid.(p.128)
• They cannot seem to forgive and *forget*.(p.134)
• You *forget* that you have just now tapped a source of power much greater than yourself.(p.163)
• They said, "Let's *forget* about those other things, that is, trying to eliminate them all at once, and concentrate on the drink."(p.190)
• I'll never *forget*, he never even hesitated and I had never seen him before in my life.(p.207)
• That I shall never *forget*.(p.208)
• I'd been sitting comfortably in a restaurant with Rita, drinking my sixth martini and hoping the waiter would *forget* about the lunch order – at least long enough for me to have a couple more.(p.223)
• At that time I could go into any saloon, have one or two beers, walk out and *forget* about it.(p.231)
• But I have never thought of that as something to do and then *forget* about.(p.237)
• They told Annabelle to take me under her wing, and I shall never *forget* how she sort of curled up her nose and said, "They tell me you drink too."(p.269)
• I hope that I never *forget* to be grateful.(p.326)
• I will never *forget* the first meeting that I attended.(p.347)
• It was then that I began to hate myself, and drank primarily to ease my conscience and *forget*.(p.354)
• I never want to *forget* that last drunk as long as I live.(p.393)
• Sometimes they'd put it on the mantel, and *forget* it.(p.407)
• How could anybody *forget* a drink?(p.407)
• How easy it was, in the beginning, to *forget* that those binges ever happened!(p.433)
• In fact, sometimes they served as good excuses to drink more, to *forget*.(p.465)
• Then I find myself thinking about myself, and a few things that I had wanted to *forget*.(p.503)
• In time, I began to go out and *forget* the way back home.(p.527)

forgetfulness
• The family may be possessed by the idea that future happiness can be based only upon *forgetfulness* of the past.(p.123)
• I had nothing to put in the place of alcohol, of the *forgetfulness*, of the oblivion, which alcohol provides.(p.539)

forgive
• Next day they would be themselves again and we would *forgive* and try to forget.(p.106)
• They cannot seem to *forgive* and forget.(p.134)
• *Forgive* me – I cannot write further about this latest turn of events, anticipating seeing the family I deserted so long ago.(p.463)
• If I write with the air of one who has discovered the obvious, which is to say, the eternal truths which have been offered to us since the beginning, *forgive* my callowness; I had to find these things out for myself.(p.536)

forgiven
• If we are sorry for what we have done, and have the honest desire to let God take us to better things, we believe we will be *forgiven* and will have learned our lesson.(p.70)
• If you concede that your employee is ill, can he be *forgiven* for what he has done in the past?(p.140)
• Back at camp, all was *forgiven* because it was the End, but in the light of what I have since learned I know I was a confirmed alcoholic at nineteen.(p.242)
• There was the father one lost respect for at the age of eleven, because the father broke his solemn word in a circumstance where you, eleven years old, had assumed guilt when you were innocent; but the father would not believe you, no matter what; and to ease his suffering you "confessed" and were "*forgiven*," only – months later – to have your "guilt" brought up – only he and you knew what he was talking bout -- brought up in front of the stern grandmother.(p.533)

forgiveness
• We suggested he write his first wife admitting his faults and asking *forgiveness*.(p.79)
• After making our review we ask God's *forgiveness* and inquire what corrective measures should be taken.(p.86)
• Time after time I would beg *forgiveness* on bended knees, with tears rolling down my cheeks, and promise I would never again drink too much.(p.362)
• I ask the *forgiveness* of the reader; and from now on I shall try to write with the humility I honestly pray for.)(p.536)

forgiving
• We go to him in a helpful and *forgiving* spirit, confessing our former ill feeling and expressing our regret.(p.77)

forgot
• I *forgot* the strong warnings and the prejudices of my people concerning drink.(p.1)
• A good soldier is ne'er *forgot* Whether he dieth by musket Or by pot."(p.1)
• At that particular stage, I lost interest in it, sold the option for $5,000 and *forgot* the whole deal.(p.198)
• I completely *forgot* myself in trying vainly to help Anne, whose misery I understood.(p.415)
• Or, "I got to talking and *forgot* how many I was taking and it hit me."(p.433)
• He *forgot* to mention that I was the chief critic.(p.449)
• Never *forgot* magic in firewater.(p.474)

forgotten
• Can his past absurdities be *forgotten*?(p.140)
• If you take it, your past will be *forgotten* and the fact that you went away for treatment will not be mentioned.(p.147)
• (My mother and father were Catholics and I had been baptized, but at the end of my instructions for Confirmation I had not gone to church, and then when my mother remarried, she married a Protestant

and the whole religious angle was ***forgotten.***(p.201)
• That was an experience that I have never ***forgotten,*** and many times in my own work with A.A. newcomers I feel kind of guilty because I haven't done the same thing.(p.219)
• I had completely ***forgotten*** the January 8th when I found the fellowship, and I spent the next four days wandering around New England half drunk, by which I mean I couldn't get drunk and I couldn't get sober.(p.247)
• In five years a good many persons had ***forgotten*** that I had been somewhat notorious.(p.256)
• Neither can I honestly say that I have ***forgotten*** the "fleshpots of Egypt."(p.259)
• I had ***forgotten*** "If I ever I get that bad, I'll try A.A."(p.333)
• After three months it was ***forgotten.***(p.434)
• Some of us always remember our big mouths when it comes to a drink, but somewhere along the line, we seem to have ***forgotten*** about taking care of our teeth.(p.479)
• About this time an incident took place in grade school that I have never ***forgotten*** because it made me realize that I was actually a physical coward.(p.484)
• I have ***forgotten*** about a drink.(p.505)

fork

• I learned how to hold a terrapin ***fork.***(p.401)
• Met father (Tall Man) at ***fork*** in road – one way to reservation, other way to State of Maine.(p.475)

form

• And besides, there were scattered alcoholics who had picked up the basic ideas in Akron or New York and were trying to ***form*** A.A. groups in other cities.(p.xvii)
• We doctors have realized for a long time that some ***form*** of moral psychology was of urgent importance to alcoholics, but its application presented difficulties beyond our conception.(p.xxv)
• These allergic types can never safely use alcohol in any ***form*** at all; and once having formed the habit and found they cannot break it, once having lost their self-confidence, their reliance upon things human, their problems pile up on them and become astonishingly difficult to solve.(p.xxvi)
• There is scarcely any ***form*** of trouble and misery which has not been overcome among us.(p.15)
• If what we have learned and felt and seen means anything at all, it means that all of us, whatever our race, creed, or color are the children of a living Creator with whom we may ***form*** a relationship upon simple and understandable terms as soon as we are willing and honest enough to try.(p.28)
• By every ***form*** of self-deception and experimentation, they will try to prove themselves exceptions to the rule, therefore nonalcoholic.(p.31)
• In one ***form*** or another we had been living by faith and little else.(p.54)
• It may be obscured by calamity, by pomp, by worship of other things, but in some ***form*** or other it is there.(p.55)
• That's a common ***form*** of trouble too.(p.79)
• One of the many doctors who had the opportunity of reading this book in manuscript ***form*** told us that the use of sweets was often helpful, of course depending upon a doctor's advice.(p.133)
• If you think you are an atheist, an agnostic, a skeptic, or have any other ***form*** of intellectual pride which keeps you from accepting what is in this book, I feel sorry for you.(p.181)
• But the firm became violently ill with my drunkenness and their course of treatment was to remove their ulcer, in the ***form*** of me, from the payroll, amid much fanfare and very personal and slighting remarks and insinuations.(p.300)
• Again I went into a mild ***form*** of D.T.'s, but with no pineapples this time.(p.429)
• I've been benefited from a dictionary definition I found that reads: "rationalization is giving a socially acceptable reason for socially unacceptable behavior, and socially unacceptable behavior is a ***form*** of insanity."(p.551)
• Although my ambition still flickered, it now took the ***form*** of fantasizing.(p.556)
• On the next page, A.A.'s "12 Traditions" are seen in their so-called "short ***form,***" the ***form*** in general use today.(p.563)
• This is a condensed version of the original "long ***form***" A.A. Traditions as first printed in 1946.(p.563)
• Because the "long ***form***" is more explicit and of possible historic value, it is also reproduced.(p.563)
• THE TWELVE TRADITIONS (The Long ***Form***)(p.565)
• (This address is now available in pamphlet ***form*** at nominal cost through most A.A. groups or from Box 459, Grand Central Station, New York, NY 10163, under the title "Three Talks to Medical Societies by Bill W." – formerly called "Bill on Alcoholism" and earlier "Alcoholism the Illness.")(p.572)

formal

• Immediately on her return we began to have ***formal*** meetings once a week, in the autumn of 1939, and we have continued to do this and to expand ever since.(p.295)
• If we were invited to a ***formal*** party and I knew they were only going to have one or two drinks, I wouldn't have any.(p.323)

formally

• The day before I was due to go back to Chicago, a Wednesday and Dr. Bob's afternoon off, he had me down to the office and we spent three or four hours ***formally*** going through the Six-Step program as it was at that time.(p.291)

formed

• When the broker returned to New York in the fall of 1935, the first A.A. group had actually been ***formed,*** though no one realized it at the time.(p.xvii)
• These allergic types can never safely use alcohol in any form at all; and once having ***formed*** the habit and found they cannot break it, once having lost their self-confidence, their reliance upon things human, their problems pile up on them and become astonishingly difficult to solve.(p.xxvi)
• Stocks were at the low point of 1932, and I had somehow ***formed*** a group to buy.(p.5)
• The fellowship of Al-Anon Family Groups was ***formed*** about thirteen years after this chapter was written.(p.121)
• More and more I ***formed*** the habit of doing some of my business in the speakeasy, and after a time I did not need that as an excuse.(p.233)
• There was one Village bar in particular for which I ***formed*** an obsession.(p.410)

former

• Hence we are at pains to tell why we think our present faith is reasonable, why we think it more sane and logical to believe than not to believe, why we say our ***former*** thinking was soft and mushy when we threw up our hands in doubt and said, "We don't know."(p.53)
• We go to him in a helpful and forgiving spirit, confessing our ***former*** ill feeling and expressing our regret.(p.77)
• Our ***former*** enemies sometimes praise what we are doing and wish us well.(p.78)
• If their old relationship is to be resumed it must be on a better basis, since the ***former*** did not work.(p.99)
• We think each family which has been relieved owes something to those who have not, and when the occasion requires, each member of it should be only too willing to bring ***former*** mistakes, no matter how grievous, out of their hiding places.(p.124)
• Many of us, ***former*** patients, go there to help.(p.162)
• This had little effect however for I kept on drinking and used a great deal more hard liquor than in ***former*** years.(p.174)
• I soon discovered that a couple of drinks would alleviate my gastric distress, at least for a few hours at a time, so it was not at all difficult for me to return to my ***former*** excessive indulgence.(p.174)
• That was the reverse of my ***former*** pattern of fearing to go to work because I might drink!(p.199)
• Making my way to Pittsburgh, I met other ***former*** friends and got a job in a large factory where piecemakers were making good money.(p.252)
• During my visit there, renewing acquaintance with ***former*** friends, I soon spent most of my money.(p.252)
• While there I was called to the hospital in my home town to see a ***former*** partner who had insisted that I visit him.(p.257)
• He introduced himself and began to tell me about a bunch of some sixty ***former*** drinkers and drunkards who met once a week, and he invited me to go with him to the next meeting.(p.257)
• Some of them I had known for years, good two-fisted drinkers who had disappeared from their ***former*** haunts.(p.258)
• That night I was taken home by a ***former*** alcoholic and his wife.(p.259)
• Of course, the latter ultimately killed the ***former,*** but of this, more anon.(p.277)
• Shortly thereafter, I was selected, with eight other inmates out of the 10,000 in the state's prisons at that time, to attend a school designed to take ***former*** "management problems" like me and convert them into paracounselors.(p.462)
• A ***former*** employer of mine said to me a little over ten years ago, "Pat, you seem to be one of those unfortunate people who at least once every six months must go out and roll in the gutter."(p.513)
• As the sober days grew into sober months and then into sober years, a new and beautiful life began to emerge from the shambles of my ***former*** existence.(p.559)

formerly

• Next he can be assured that you do not intend to lecture, moralize, or condemn; that if this was done ***formerly,*** it was because of misunderstanding.(p.142)
• His call to the clergyman led him presently to a certain resident of the town, who, though ***formerly*** able and respected, was then nearing the nadir of alcoholic despair.(p.155)
• You can all remember that in the first few months after the change, a great many men, who had ***formerly*** been used to a few beers every day or an occasional drink of whiskey, simply quit all alcoholic drinks.(p.232)
• I had never doubted the existence of the Supreme Being, but now I began to absent myself from my church where I had ***formerly*** been a member of the choir.(p.234)
• ***Formerly,*** in the acute mental and physical pain during the remorseful periods succeeding each drunk, I found my recollection of the misery I had gone through a bolsterer of resolution and afterward, perhaps, a deterrent for a time.(p.260)
• (This address is now available in pamphlet form at nominal cost through most A.A. groups or from Box 459, Grand Central Station, New York, NY 10163, under the title "Three Talks to Medical Societies by Bill W." – ***formerly*** called "Bill on Alcoholism" and earlier "Alcoholism the Illness.")(p.572)

forming

• Somewhere in one of the conversations, I mentioned that I was contemplating ***forming*** a new firm.(p.220)
• I was now ***forming*** an entirely new drinking technique.(p.233)

forms

• Driven by a hundred ***forms*** of fear, self-delusion, self-seeking, and self-pity, we step on the toes of our fellows and they retaliate.(p.62)
• From it stem all ***forms*** of spiritual disease, for we have been not only mentally and physically ill, we have been spiritually sick.(p.64)
• Although these reparations take innumerable ***forms,*** there are some general principles which we find guiding.(p.79)
• I tried to compensate with impossible dreams and ambitions, which were simply early ***forms*** of escape.(p.400)
• The terms "spiritual experience" and "spiritual awakening" are used many times in this book which, upon careful reading, shows that the personality change sufficient to bring about recovery from alcoholism has manifested itself among us in many different ***forms.***(p.569)

formula

• At that time the group in New York was composed of about twelve men who were working on the principle of every drunk for himself; we had no real ***formula*** and no name.(p.246)
• Around this time our big A.A. book was being written and it all became much simpler; we had a definite ***formula*** which some sixty of us agreed was the middle course for all alcoholics who wanted sobriety, and that ***formula*** has not been changed one iota down through the years.(p.248)
• Always we'd emerge with a new ***formula*** for avoiding future trouble.(p.433)
• Weeks would go by without further trouble, and I'd be assured I'd at last hit on the right ***formula.***(p.433)

forth

• Understanding myself now, I fared ***forth*** in high hope.(p.7)
• We have concluded to publish an anonymous volume setting ***forth*** the problem as we see it.(p.19)
• I'd hear them on the phone having prayer meetings and so ***forth,*** that sort of talk over the phone, and it completely burnt me up.(p.265)
• This was the beginning of five years of bounding back and ***forth*** between my home in Chicago and Akron to sober up.(p.288)
• I paced back and ***forth*** in the apartment with the cold sweats.(p.338)
• So I put ***forth*** some effort that day to try to stay sober if I could, though my sobriety was just a daze.(p.494)

forthwith

• It was the day before Mother's Day and I had come home plastered, carrying a big potted plant which I set down on the table and ***forthwith*** went upstairs and passed out.(p.179)

fortified
- Later on, it took alcohol ***fortified*** with other drugs to pull me up.(p.457)

fortify
- It then occurred to me that after one was all smelled up with beer nobody could tell what had been drunk, so I began to ***fortify*** my beer with straight alcohol.(p.178)
- When I was faced with a special challenge or social event – such as an important business presentation or a dinner party – I had to ***fortify*** myself with a couple of belts.(p.556)

fortnight
- I buttonholed him after dinner and gave him a few tips on how to run his colony better and the result of that was about a ***fortnight*** or so later I was shipped back to my regiment.(p.520)
- That put a scare in me for about a ***fortnight.***(p.522)
- As I say, this specialist put a scare in me for about a ***fortnight*** or three weeks, then I started my last bout which went on and off for about three months.(p.523)

fortnight's
- I thought, well, now that I've been put out for drinking, I'll just show them that they were completely wrong, so I went off on the biggest bout I had been on up to then, involving about a ***fortnight's*** blackout.(p.521)

fortunate
- It was ***fortunate,*** for my old business associates remained skeptical for a year and a half, during which I found little work.(p.15)
- A few are ***fortunate*** enough to be so situated that they can give nearly all their time to the work.(p.19)
- We now live in the West and are very ***fortunate*** in our area A.A.; it is good, simple and friendly, and our one desire is to stay in A.A. and not on it.(p.250)
- Most of these ***fortunate*** ones have had little or no acquaintance with delirium, with hospitals, asylums, and jails.(p.315)
- I have been very ***fortunate*** in many ways.(p.323)
- I repeat, I am one of the ***fortunate*** members of A.A. -- a lucky guy who is very grateful.(p.368)
- Our shoes are not better than the average hobo's, and if we are ***fortunate*** enough to have a pair of stockings on, nobody notices the runs in them, because of our dazzling beauty and our dirty feet.(p.479)
- I was very ***fortunate*** indeed not to have suffered any brain damage.(p.480)
- I'm ***fortunate*** because I live in an era when A.A. is available, and I'm able to take advantage of it.(p.512)
- I was a very ***fortunate*** drunk.(p.516)
- But on the other hand, I was terribly ***fortunate*** because that should have been a court martial offense and I should have been out on my ear.(p.520)

fortunately
- ***Fortunately*** for me, my doctor was one of the enlightened.(p.307)
- ***Fortunately,*** I didn't say a word to George on the way home.(p.322)
- ***Fortunately,*** I received only fifteen-twenty years, and I went back to my alma mater (where I had spent so much time in the hole).(p.461)
- My wife and new baby are ***fortunately*** staying with relatives.(p.500)
- He didn't have to lie in wait very long, but ***fortunately*** by that time, I had acquired friends upstairs and they covered me for quite a time.(p.519)

fortune
- For the next few years ***fortune*** threw money and applause my way.(p.3)
- He is striving to recover ***fortune*** and reputation and feels he is doing very well.(p.126)
- But I have a ***fortune*** in friendships, courage, self assurance and honest appraisal of my own abilities.(p.296)
- With cold calculation I set about to marry a ***fortune,*** and I did.(p.545)

fortunes
- A low ebb in the family ***fortunes*** necessitated my going to work when I was twenty.(p.275)

forty
- I could eat little or nothing when drinking, and I was ***forty*** pounds under weight.(p.7)
- This resolution I kept steadfastly for the next ***forty*** years, except when circumstances made it seem unwise to absent myself.(p.172)
- These periods became more frequent and I resolved that when I became ***forty,*** which was very shortly, I was going on the wagon.(p.213)
- ***Forty*** came and went and then the resolution was advanced to forty-one, forty-two, and so on in the usual pattern.(p.214)
- In the eight years before A.A. found me, I had over ***forty*** jobs -- selling and travelling – one thing after another, and the same old routine.(p.244)
- Until I took Social Security and a pension at the age of sixty-eight, after ***forty*** years in motion-picture-studio public relations, I had successfully hidden even any hints of approaching alcoholism.(p.327)
- Out of those ***forty*** years as a movie press agent came one blessing that granted me a blind faith in the program.(p.334)
- When I arrived at The Country Shop, which was a restaurant where they met in Dublin, I found about thirty-five or ***forty*** people in the room.(p.524)
- At age ***forty,*** I developed a large lump in my potbelly, and I feared it was a tumor.(p.557)

forty-five
- I found in the fall of 1939, that I was not mentally impaired, so far as trial work was concerned, and thereafter took up where I had left off when I was about ***forty-five*** years old.(p.220)
- Eventually, I was taking ***forty-five*** milligrams of the long-acting Benzedrine and ***forty-five*** of the short-acting just to get out of bed in the morning.(p.442)

forty-four
- If you have a drinking problem, we hope that you may pause in reading one of the ***forty-four*** personal stories and think: "Yes, that happened to me"; or, more important, "Yes, I've felt like that"; or most important, "Yes, I believe this program can work for me, too."(p.xii)
- I was ***forty-four*** years old; my life had been wasted.(p.461)

forty-nine
- I was ***forty-nine*** and a half years old when I was first approached about the Akron Group.(p.215)
- I am an Irishman and I was ***forty-nine*** when I joined A.A.(p.517)

forty-one
- Forty came and went and then the resolution was advanced to ***forty-one,*** forty-two, and so on in the usual pattern.(p.214)

forty-publicist
- For a decade, I'd headed up a ***forty-publicist*** department.(p.328)

forty-seven
- When I was about ***forty-seven,*** after indulging in all kinds of self-deception to control my drinking, I arrived at a period when I felt convinced I had to have so much alcohol every day and that the real problem was to control how much.(p.214)

forty-six
- The periods of sobriety attained by these thirteen A.A.'s range from fifteen to ***forty-six*** years.(p.169)
- I had just turned ***forty-six.***(p.540)

forty-three
- These are followed by ***forty-three*** personal experiences.(p.29)
- How ***Forty-Three*** Alcoholics Recovered From Their Malady(p.165)
- My drinking career extended from age eighteen to ***forty-three.***(p.397)

forty-two
- Forty came and went and then the resolution was advanced to forty-one, ***forty-two,*** and so on in the usual pattern.(p.214)

forward
- Here by itself was a great step ***forward.***(p.283)
- He said he had finally learned that drinking was a fatal illness made up of an allergy plus an obsession, and once the drinking had passed from habit to obsession, we were completely hopeless, and could look ***forward*** only to spending the balance of our lives in mental institutions or to death.(p.290)
- In time, I found myself looking ***forward*** to each new day with pleasurable anticipation.(p.311)
- However, I am an alcoholic, so I always looked ***forward*** to the day when I would be able to drink again.(p.343)
- On the first, though on the water wagon, I looked ***forward*** to my next drink.(p.344)
- Then I looked ***forward*** to the week-end of golf and the nineteenth hole.(p.374)
- I would get wildly excited and look ***forward*** to another night of drinking.(p.408)
- I got to the place where I'd look ***forward*** to the week-end's drinking and pacify myself by saying that the week-ends were mine, that it didn't interfere with my family or with my business if I drank on the week-ends.(p.488)

Fosdick
- Dr. Harry Emerson ***Fosdick,*** the noted clergyman, reviewed it with approval.(p.xvii)
- Speaking at a dinner given by John D. Rockefeller Jr. to introduce Alcoholics Anonymous to some of his friends, Dr. Harry Emerson ***Fosdick*** remarked: "I think that psychologically speaking there is a point of advantage in the approach that is being made in this movement that cannot be duplicated.(p.574)

Foster
- Dr. ***Foster*** Kennedy, neurologist: "This organization of Alcoholics Anonymous calls on two of the greatest reservoirs of power known to man, religion and that instinct for association with one's fellows . . . the 'herd instinct.'(p.571)

fought
- The wars which had been ***fought,*** the burnings and chicanery that religious dispute had facilitated, made me sick.(p.11)
- But the more we ***fought*** and tried to have our own way, the worse matters got.(p.66)
- I was never a hilarious drunk; the more I drank the quieter I got, and the drunker I got the harder I ***fought*** to stay sober.(p.241)
- I don't think the boys were completely convinced of my personality change, for they ***fought*** shy of including my story in the book, so my only contribution to their literary efforts was my firm conviction, being still a theological rebel, that the word God should be qualified with the phrase "as we understand him" -- for that was the only way I could accept spirituality.(p.248)
- We never rowed or ***fought.***(p.264)
- An originator of Cleveland's Group No. 3, this one ***fought*** Prohibition in vain.(p.297)
- I ***fought*** and struggled, but to no avail.(p.466)
- I have ***fought*** hard to stop drinking.(p.502)
- Perhaps a better way of saying it is that, on that day, with that decision, I no longer ***fought*** drinking as an escape.(p.531)
- Depending on the stage of drunkenness, eventually I either ***fought*** or went to sleep.(p.537)

found
- Groups are to be ***found*** in each of the United States and all of the provinces of Canada.(p.xv)
- New groups started up and it was ***found,*** to the astonishment of everyone, that A.A.'s message could be transmitted in the mail as well as by word of mouth.(p.xviii)
- Some of the recommendations of A.A.'s early medical and religious friends will be ***found*** further on in this book.(p.xx)
- Yet it is our great hope that all those who have as yet ***found*** no answer may begin to find one in the pages of this book and will presently join us on the highroad to a new freedom.(p.xxi)
- These allergic types can never safely use alcohol in any form at all; and once having formed the habit and ***found*** they cannot break it, once having lost their self-confidence, their reliance upon things human, their problems pile up on them and become astonishingly difficult to solve.(p.xxvi)
- We feel, after many years of experience, that we have ***found*** nothing which has contributed more to the rehabilitation of these men than the altruistic movement now growing up among them.(p.xxvi)
- Following the elimination of alcohol, there was ***found*** to be no permanent brain injury.(p.xxix)
- I ***found*** a job; then lost it as the result of a brawl with a taxi driver.(p.4)
- Next day ***found*** me drinking both gin and sedative.(p.7)
- No words can tell of the loneliness and despair I ***found*** in that bitter morass of self-pity.(p.8)
- It was fortunate, for my old business associates remained skeptical for a year and a half, during which I ***found*** little work.(p.15)
- This sometimes nearly drove me back to drink, but I soon ***found*** that when all other measures failed, work with another alcoholic would save the day.(p.15)
- Highly competent psychiatrists who have dealt with us have ***found*** it sometimes impossible to persuade an alcoholic to discuss his situation without reserve.(p.18)
- But the ex-problem drinker who has ***found*** this solution, who is properly armed with facts about himself, can generally win the entire confidence of another alcoholic in a few hours.(p.18)
- That the man who is making the approach has had the same difficulty, that he obviously knows what he is talking about, that his whole deportment shouts at the new prospect that he is a man with a real answer, that he has no attitude of Holier Than Thou, nothing whatever except the sincere desire to be helpful; that there are no fees to pay, no axes to grind, no people to please, no lectures to be endured -- these are the conditions we have ***found*** most effective.(p.18)

• We have ***found*** much of heaven and we have been rocketed into a fourth dimension of existence of which we had not even dreamed.(p.25)
• Here was the terrible dilemma in which our friend ***found*** himself when he had the extraordinary experience which as we have already told you, made him a free man.(p.28)
• Then, gathering all his forces, he attempted to stop altogether and ***found*** he could not.(p.32)
• But here is a man who at fifty-five years ***found*** he was just where he had left off at thirty.(p.33)
• Several of our crowd, men of thirty or less, had been drinking only a few years, but they ***found*** themselves as helpless as those who had been drinking twenty years.(p.33)
• Yet we ***found*** it impossible.(p.34)
• We told him what we knew of alcoholism and the answer we had ***found***.(p.35)
• To his consternation, he ***found*** himself drunk half a dozen times in rapid succession.(p.35)
• But we ***found*** that such codes and philosophies did not save us, no matter how much we tried.(p.45)
• Yet, in other moments, we ***found*** ourselves thinking, when enchanted by a starlit night, "Who, then, made all this?"(p.46)
• We ***found*** that as soon as we were able to lay aside prejudice and express even a willingness to believe in a Power greater than ourselves, we commenced to get results, even though it was impossible for any of us to fully define or comprehend that Power, which is God.(p.46)
• We ***found*** that God does not make too hard terms with those who seek Him.(p.46)
• Afterward, we ***found*** ourselves accepting many things which then seemed entirely out of reach.(p.47)
• Besides a seeming inability to accept much on faith, we often ***found*** ourselves handicapped by obstinacy, sensitiveness, and unreasoning prejudice.(p.47)
• Though some of us resisted, we ***found*** no great difficulty in casting aside such feelings.(p.48)
• In the face of collapse and despair, in the face of the total failure of their human resources, they ***found*** that a new power, peace, happiness, and sense of direction flowed into them.(p.50)
• We ***found***, too, that we had been worshippers.(p.54)
• We ***found*** the Great Reality deep down within us.(p.55)
• In the last analysis it is only there that He may be ***found***.(p.55)
• We ***found*** it very desirable to take this spiritual step with an understanding person, such as our wife, best friend or spiritual adviser.(p.63)
• In most cases it was ***found*** that our self-esteem, our pocketbooks, our ambitions, our personal relationships (including sex) were hurt or threatened.(p.64)
• We ***found*** that it is fatal.(p.66)
• Though there may be justifiable exceptions, and though we wish to lay down no rule of any sort, we have often ***found*** this the best course to take.(p.81)
• Among us are wives, relatives and friends whose problem has been solved, as well as some who have not yet ***found*** a happy solution.(p.104)
• Show him your copy of this book and tell him what you have ***found*** out about alcoholism.(p.112)
• We wives ***found*** that, like everybody else, we were afflicted with pride, self-pity, vanity and all the things which go to make up the self-centered person; and we were not above selfishness or dishonesty.(p.116)
• If not, it had better be ***found*** out right away.(p.120)
• Although financial recovery is on the way for many of us, we ***found*** we could not place money first.(p.127)
• We have ***found*** nothing incompatible between a powerful spiritual experience and a life of sane and happy usefulness.(p.130)
• Many of us have noticed a tendency to eat sweets and have ***found*** this practice beneficial.(p.134)
• Bitterly discouraged, he ***found*** himself in a strange place, discredited and almost broke.(p.154)
• He ***found*** himself surprisingly well received, and learned that many knew of his drinking.(p.156)
• Next day ***found*** the prospect more receptive.(p.158)
• But he had ***found*** God — and in finding God had ***found*** himself.(p.158)
• So, you see, there were three alcoholics in that town, who now felt they had to give to others what they had ***found***, or be sunk.(p.158)
• These men had ***found*** something brand new in life.(p.159)
• It was transcended by the happiness they ***found*** in giving themselves for others.(p.159)
• He had lived there but a few weeks when he ***found*** that the place probably contained more alcoholics per square mile than any city in the country.(p.163)
• When a few men in this city have ***found*** themselves, and have discovered the joy of helping others to face life again, there will be no stopping until everyone in that town has had his opportunity to recover -- if he can and will.(p.163)
• Today, hundreds of additional A.A. members can be ***found*** who have had no relapse for more than thirty years.(p.169)
• But my friends usually ***found*** me and I would go home if they promised that I should not be scolded.(p.176)
• I ***found*** out later that my wife inspected it frequently.(p.176)
• He kept the faith; therefore, he and countless others ***found*** a new life.(p.182)
• However, after two or three trials, I ***found*** this was not satisfactory because they did not serve enough to satisfy me.(p.184)
• Looking in later we ***found*** Bill with his wife, Henrietta.(p.189)
• It took me a year, or a year and a half to get to feeling physically well, and it was rather tough, but I soon ***found*** folks whose friendship I had once had, and I ***found***, after I had been sober for quite some little time, that these people began to act like they had in previous years, before I had gotten so bad, so that I didn't pay too awful much attention to financial gains.(p.190)
• I'm so grateful for both the program and the people in it that I still want to go, and then probably the most wonderful thing that I learned from the program -- I've seen this in the 'A.A. Grapevine' a lot of times, and I've had people say it to me personally, and I've heard people get up in meetings and make the same statement: The statement is, "I came into A.A. solely for the purpose of sobriety, but it has been through A.A. that I have ***found*** God."(p.192)
• All of a sudden I ***found*** myself guzzling.(p.195)
• During the day, looking over the contracts and money in my pocket, I ***found*** that I had sold six lots that I couldn't even remember, and didn't even know the people I had sold them to.(p.196)
• I ***found***, however, that when I would leave Akron to go to Chicago, I would get drunk.(p.197)
• I drove towards Cleveland wondering why I ***found*** myself in such a changed set of conditions as compared with those of six months before.(p.200)
• I couldn't afford to be ***found*** with those people, but I said I would certainly pay his dues if it would keep him from drinking.(p.205)
• By the time I had completed law school I had picked up some experience in patent law, for I remained with the patent law firm and worked too in Washington where they ***found*** that I was a capable infringement investigator.(p.213)
• He startled me by informing me that he was an alcoholic, that he had ***found*** a way which so far enabled him to live without taking a drink, and that the main idea was to find a way how not to take that first drink.(p.218)
• He ***found*** that I had enough faith in the Almighty to be fairly frank.(p.219)
• I ***found*** in the fall of 1939, that I was not mentally impaired, so far as trial work was concerned, and thereafter took up where I had left off when I was about forty-five years old.(p.220)
• There wasn't a bar in sight, but I ***found*** the subway station.(p.223)
• I remembered filling the peroxide bottle in my medicine chest with gin, in case my sister ***found*** the bottle I hid under the mattress.(p.224)
• Headstrong and willful, I rushed from pleasure to pleasure, and ***found*** the returns diminishing to the vanishing point.(p.226)
• I went trembling into a house in Brooklyn filled with strangers . . . and I ***found*** I had come home at last, to my own kind.(p.228)
• I had ***found*** my salvation.(p.228)
• I had ***found*** friends, understanding friends who often knew what I was thinking and feeling better than I knew myself, and didn't allow me to retreat into my prison of loneliness and fear over a fancied slight or hurt.(p.228)
• I believe that my once over-weening self-will has finally ***found*** its proper place, for I can say many times daily, "Thy will be done, not mine" . . . and mean it.(p.229)
• Having regard for the law of the land, I resigned myself to the will of the national legislators and quit drinking altogether, not because I had ***found*** it harmful, but because I couldn't get what I was accustomed to drink.(p.232)
• He went on talking and told me that he had ***found*** the plan has a basis of love, and the practice of Christ's injunction, "Love thy neighbor as thyself."(p.236)
• That is the way Jackie ***found*** me, lying on a cot in my skivvies, with hot and cold sweats, pounding heart and that awful itchy scratchiness all over.(p.238)
• In the eight years before A.A. ***found*** me, I had over forty jobs -- selling and travelling -- one thing after another, and the same old routine.(p.244)
• Once I ***found*** out.(p.244)
• After being dry two weeks and sticking close to Jackie, all of a sudden I ***found*** I had become the sponsor of my sponsor, for he was suddenly taken drunk.(p.245)
• I had completely forgotten the January 8th when I ***found*** the fellowship, and I spent the next four days wandering around New England half drunk, by which I mean I couldn't get drunk and I couldn't get sober.(p.247)
• Then I got a very good position in Philadelphia and quickly ***found*** I would need a few fellow alcoholics around me if I was to stay sober.(p.249)
• Thus I ***found*** myself in the middle of a brand new group.(p.249)
• When I started to tell the boys how we did it in New York and all about the spiritual part of the program, I ***found*** they would not believe me unless I was practicing what I preached.(p.249)
• Then I ***found*** that as I gave in to this spiritual or personality change I was getting a little more serenity.(p.249)
• In telling newcomers how to change their lives and attitudes, all of a sudden I ***found*** I was doing a little changing myself.(p.249)
• I listened to famous ministers — ***found*** nothing.(p.255)
• When I hit Houston, Texas, I ***found*** employment in a large bookstore.(p.255)
• I ***found*** my friend was there for alcoholism and now he was insisting that he had ***found*** the only cure.(p.257)
• All sorts were represented and their relation of experiences and how they had ***found*** the only remedy, added to their human existence as sober men, laid the foundation of a very necessary faith.(p.258)
• Formerly, in the acute mental and physical pain during the remorseful periods succeeding each drunk, I ***found*** my recollection of the misery I had gone through a bolsterer of resolution and afterward, perhaps, a deterrent for a time.(p.260)
• Russ read a piece in the paper, and he kind of snickered, and said, "See here, where John D. has ***found*** something to keep him from drinking!"(p.265)
• He used to drink, and then he ***found*** something that started up in Akron that helped him quit drinking."(p.267)
• In the spiritual strength I had ***found***, because of A.A., I felt that I had made a complete surrender, that I had really turned my life over that summer.(p.271)
• I knew then that I hadn't made a complete surrender, because I tried to bargain with the God I had ***found***, and I said, "Anything but that!(p.271)
• He spent eighteen years in running away; and then ***found*** he didn't have to run.(p.275)
• By the time I was thirty I had ***found*** that alcohol dissolved fear.(p.275)
• The most accurate answer I can give you is this: Fear has never again ruled my life since that day in September, 1938, when I ***found*** that a Power greater than myself could not only restore me to sanity but could keep me both sober and sane.(p.285)
• But he ***found*** that there was a Higher Power which had more faith in him than he had in himself.(p.287)
• Shortly thereafter, aided by the Depression, I ***found*** that I had a great deal of spare time and that a little drink in the morning helped.(p.287)
• I ***found*** some wool stockings, some white flannels that had shrunk to my knees, and an old jacket.(p.288)
• I went to the sanitarium where this chap was incarcerated and ***found*** to my surprise that he was interested.(p.294)
• As time went on, I ***found*** that it was customary to open a few bottles whenever visitors dropped in.(p.297)
• Spiritually . . . I ***found*** a Friend who never lets me down and is ever eager to help.(p.303)
• A little more than fifteen years ago, through a long and calamitous series of shattering experiences, I ***found*** myself being helplessly propelled toward total destruction.(p.304)
• Of course the doctors ***found*** nothing.(p.305)
• I didn't dare hope I might find for myself all that these people had ***found***, but if I could acquire some small part of their intriguing quality of living -- and sobriety — that would be enough.(p.310)
• In time, I ***found*** myself looking forward to each new day with pleasurable anticipation.(p.311)
• I ***found*** out that the people in all A.A. groups were as nice as the people in the first one.(p.320)

- I also *found* out that all they wanted was to help me get sober and to stay sober themselves.(p.320)
- And when my husband *found* A.A., I came to the second meeting with him.(p.321)
- I didn't think my children knew about it, but I *found* out they did.(p.324)
- Three months later, he hated the game and *found* solace in the bottle.(p.330)
- When I *found* this impossible, I became scared for the first time.(p.333)
- Best that they not be *found* after I'd had my last drink on earth.(p.333)
- He said, "How I envy you for whatever you've *found*."(p.334)
- In A.A., she discovered she had lost nothing and had *found* everything.(p.335)
- But in the light of the new understanding that I have *found* in A.A., I have been able to interpret that defeat, and that failure, and that shame, as seeds of victory.(p.335)
- Because I *found* that everything I turned to became a substitute for drink.(p.339)
- But this second time, I *found* I couldn't live normally without it, and I was licked worse than ever.(p.340)
- The fellowship I *found* in A.A. enabled me to face my problem honestly and squarely.(p.340)
- I had been brought up to believe in God, but I know that until I *found* this A.A. program, I had never *found* or known faith in the reality of God, the reality of His power that is now with me in everything I do.(p.341)
- I had read and heard a little about A.A. and so, groping for the phone book, I *found* the A.A. number and with hope in my heart eagerly telephoned.(p.363)
- After a few meetings I decided to drive to Florida unannounced to see my wife and tell her about my new *found* friends and association.(p.364)
- I stayed on in Florida for three weeks, enjoying our reunion, a new *found* health and a deeper love than I had ever experienced before.(p.364)
- We attended meetings together, and mutually enjoyed our new *found* friends.(p.364)
- He was full of his new *found* life of happiness and sobriety.(p.365)
- And, believe me, I thank God that I *found* out about A.A. before I had to beat my brains out – before I had been hospitalized, jailed or lost a job.(p.367)
- In my drinking days, I *found* the ideal spot for the alcoholic housewife: the neighborhood Laundromat.(p.369)
- We soon resumed our marriage, even moved away from the street of sad memories and *found* a new home.(p.371)
- But what is more important is that I *found* a new life in Alcoholics Anonymous.(p.372)
- As I later *found* out through Alcoholics Anonymous, alcohol is no respecter of economic status, social and business standing or intelligence.(p.373)
- I liked the description of the alcoholic as a person who had *found* that alcohol is interfering with his social or business life.(p.380)
- Frank *found* the doctor, but the doctor didn't want to take an alcoholic.(p.387)
- I could not identify myself with the people with whom I *found* myself and there was no understanding, and I can't stand confinement anyhow.(p.387)
- I couldn't walk, having it in a cast, and the doctor left the cast on three weeks longer than was necessary because he never *found* me sober enough to take it off.(p.390)
- Frank was out of town, and I remember that he'd gotten in this one night and *found* me drunk.(p.391)
- I *found* out fast that the cheapest way to get drunk was on shots with beer chasers at two bits a crack.(p.397)
- At age twenty-one, I enlisted in the Navy for two reasons: (1) to avoid being drafted into the Army, and (2) out of a burst of patriotic fervor inspired by the advent of World War II and as the result of an all-night drinking binge which *found* me sitting on the doorstep of the Navy recruiting office when the chief petty officer arrived to open for business at nine o'clock Monday morning.(p.398)
- Two weeks later *found* me being sworn in, and the first payday in the Navy made me realize I had *found* a home.(p.398)
- After eight months, the family *found* me.(p.401)
- But I got drunk that night and stayed drunk, getting increasingly worse until I *found* A.A. ten years later.(p.404)
- I came to and *found* a man leaning over me.(p.405)
- Meanwhile I had *found* another escape.(p.407)
- In the course of drunken arguments, I *found* my own views and sense of responsibility as a citizen.(p.410)
- I *found* myself nodding my head.(p.413)
- If I had not become an active alcoholic and joined A.A., I might never have *found* my own identity or become a part of anything.(p.417)
- Defeated by alcohol and pills, he *found* the way to a new life.(p.418)
- I *found* I could boost my income by figuring out a lot of cute little tricks that the boss wouldn't be likely to notice – filching money from the Coke machine, short-sticking the customers on oil, and selling oil I'd drained out of other cars.(p.423)
- About this time my folks *found* A.A.(p.427)
- I lost it many times and mom and dad would drive me around until I *found* it.(p.429)
- A friend had *found* help in psychoanalysis.(p.434)
- Here I *found* an ingredient that had been lacking in any other effort I had made to save myself.(p.436)
- The most terrible blow of my life befell me after I'd *found* sobriety through A.A.(p.437)
- Then I *found* the solution: At the end of study time, I would drink two beers, jump in bed, sleep real fast, and wake up smart.(p.440)
- For the leveling-off process, I just loved intravenous Demerol, but I *found* it hard to practice good medicine while shooting morphine.(p.442)
- If they were around, I always *found* a need for them – especially the pills.(p.443)
- All *found* themselves headed for the same destruction, and it seemed they could to nothing whatever to stop it.(p.455)
- And we *found* ourselves back in prison, where our personalities became even more warped.(p.459)
- I went out to a restaurant, *found* a booth way back in the rear, and started drinking.(p.467)
- The next recollection I have is of my husband coming into my room (later *found* out it was on New Year's Eve) accompanied by two policemen.(p.468)
- Had I tried honestly and sincerely to practice the Twelve Steps I would have seen from my continuous moral inventory that I was getting off the beam -- I would have *found* that there were some active resentments in my life, a terrific amount of self-pity.(p.471)
- But more important, I would have *found* that once again I was sitting in the driver's seat – I was running the show.(p.471)
- Soon *found* wet canteens serve drinks to Indians in uniform.(p.474)
- I *found* that even then I had fears and inhibitions.(p.483)
- But I *found* that after I got to North Carolina it wasn't any different.(p.490)
- I started inquiring where I could get a drink and, of course, I *found* that it wasn't hard.(p.490)
- I had *found* this new "something," and I wanted to give it to everyone who had a problem.(p.496)
- My wife hears my voice and knows I have *found* the answer to life.(p.505)
- After I came in I *found* I wasn't an exceptional drunk.(p.512)
- It was a revelation to me to find that there were such people as those I *found* in Alcoholics Anonymous.(p.515)
- I *found* a great deal of friendship in this movement.(p.516)
- When I came home to ordinary garrison life in England, I *found* that I was drinking rather more than most people of may age.(p.518)
- When I arrived at The Country Shop, which was a restaurant where they met in Dublin, I *found* about thirty-five or forty people in the room.(p.524)
- After a while, I *found* that the psycho ward was a good place to hide when I had taken something stolen to the pawnshop.(p.528)
- Later, I *found* out that I went into stores and stole clothes, then sold them.(p.528)
- It was there that I really *found* out what A.A. was.(p.528)
- Bob *found* alcohol!"(p.532)
- Only, having *found* them, I threw them away, and ordered another extra dry martini.(p.533)
- In my twenties, I *found* Edna St. Vincent Millay's verse:(p.534)
- So it was that in alcohol I *found* fulfillment.(p.537)
- Still another friend and temporary host received me at four in the morning from the charge of a policeman who had *found* me "going to bed" in a garage far from the last place I could remember having been, a fashionable bar and restaurant in the theatrical district of New York, to which I had repaired after my date for that evening, a charming lady of the theatre who had refused my company for obvious reasons.(p.538)
- When the policeman released me to my stupefied and exasperated friend at four in the morning, I went to my traveling bag and groped until I *found* – well, let the officer speak: "Ah," said the policeman, "he's got anuder pair, t'ank God!"(p.538)
- I stood off and took a long look at life and the values I *found* in it: I saw a paradox, that he who loses his life does indeed find it.(p.542)
- It became second nature for me to remove myself from anything or anybody I *found* myself growing fond of.(p.545)
- Fear of rejection and its ensuing pain were not to be risked, and I turned away from myself once more for the answer, this time to the drinks I had always refused before, and in alcohol I *found* a false courage.(p.546)
- I've been benefited from a dictionary definition I *found* that reads: "rationalization is giving a socially acceptable reason for socially unacceptable behavior, and socially unacceptable behavior is a form of insanity."(p.551)
- I *found* myself being lifted onto a stretcher and whisked away in an ambulance to a strange hospital.(p.558)
- Within a few days, I *found* myself drying out on a drunk farm.(p.559)
- And I *found* it beautiful!(p.561)
- These so-called intergroup associations are *found* under the listing "A.A." or "Alcoholics Anonymous" in telephone directories.(p.575)

foundation

- Upon a *foundation* of complete willingness I might build what I saw in my friend.(p.12)
- Have we skimped on the cement put into the *foundation*?(p.75)
- Helping others is the *foundation* stone of your recovery.(p.97)
- Though some of his manifestations are alarming and disagreeable, we think dad will be on a firmer *foundation* than the man who is placing business or professional success ahead of spiritual development.(p.129)
- Taking that as a *foundation*, he reasoned that if a man followed that rule he could not be selfish.(p.236)
- All sorts were represented and their relation of experiences and how they had found the only remedy, added to their human existence as sober men, laid the *foundation* of a very necessary faith.(p.258)
- In those days the A.A. *Foundation* was down in the Wall Street district of New York.(p.413)
- It was a fantastic structure, built on a crumbling *foundation*.(p.435)
- I learn more of that *foundation* stone of character, which is honesty.(p.507)
- Twelve -- Anonymity is the spiritual *foundation* of all our Traditions, ever reminding us to place principles before personalities.(p.564)

founded

- I was eased out of the business I had *founded* and was reduced to doing general upholstery in a small shop at the back of my house.(p.233)

founder

- We checked into the home of Hank, the man who had fired me eleven years before in Mississippi, and there I met Bill, our *founder*.(p.245)

founding

- But I hardly tasted anything for two years and started in business for myself, *founding* a mattress factory which is today an important industrial enterprise in our city.(p.232)

four

- For three or *four* months the goose hung high.(p.7)
- Though a robust man at retirement, he went to pieces quickly and was dead within *four* years.(p.33)
- This was Step *Four*.(p.64)
- The problem with which you struggle usually falls within one of *four* categories:(p.108)
- *Four*: You may have a husband of whom you completely despair.(p.110)
- *Four* days before he had hanged himself in his woodshed.(p.137)
- Momentarily we did – then would come oblivion and the awful awakening to face the hideous *Four* Horsemen -- Terror, Bewilderment, Frustration, Despair.(p.151)
- As we shall see, he now means a great deal to his community, and the major liabilities of thirty years of hard drinking have been repaired in *four*.(p.156)
- After high school came *four* years in one of the best colleges in the country where drinking seemed to be a major extra-curricular activity.(p.172)
- I used also to put it up in *four* ounce bottles and stick several in my stocking tops.(p.177)
- My phobia for sleeplessness demanded that I get

drunk every night, but in order to get more liquor for the next night, I had to stay sober during the day, at least up to *four* o'clock.(p.177)

• As I write nearly *four* years have passed.(p.180)

• I do it for *four* reasons:(p.180)

• This continued until I enrolled in our state university and, at the end of *four* years, I realized that I was a drunk.(p.183)

• Then Prohibition came into effect, and the facts that the stuff obtainable was so horrible and sometimes deadly, and that I had married and had a job which I had to look after, helped me for a period of some three or *four* years, although I would get drunk every time I could get hold of enough to drink to get started.(p.183)

• I was moved in as Sales Manager and had *four* men working under me.(p.200)

• At the end of about *four* months, I not only had good looking clothes --and I might say that at the time I first talked to Max I didn't have a suit of clothes I could bend over in real sudden; now I had six suits of clothes.(p.200)

• I had *four* brothers and three sisters.(p.210)

• My drinking career began about *four* years after I had moved up into partnership and had joined certain clubs, societies and so fourth, and during which period we had Prohibition.(p.213)

• My children had lost respect for me and, in fact, it was only after three or *four* years of sobriety that any of them ever said anything to me to indicate that I had recouped even a little of their respect.(p.215)

• I'd only had two with her, but I'd managed *four* in the fifteen minutes I'd waited for her, and of course I'd had the usual uncounted swigs from the bottle as I painfully got up and did my slow spasmodic dressing.(p.223)

• In *four* or five days I would be hunting all over the place, at home and in my workshop, for the bottles I had destroyed, cursing myself for being a fool.(p.234)

• This doctor had imparted his knowledge to just a few other men at that time -- not more than *four* or five -- they now number more than seventy persons.(p.235)

• There were *four* of us children, and although both of my brothers later became alcoholic -- one died of alcoholism -- my sister has never taken a drink in her life.(p.240)

• At thirteen I was packed off to a very fine Protestant boarding school in Virginia where I stayed *four* years, graduating without any special achievements.(p.240)

• At this school we had Bible readings before each meal, and church services *four* times on Sunday, and I became so rebellious at this that I swore I would never join or go to any church except for weddings or funerals.(p.240)

• But each drink after the "first" seemed to become ess effective and after three or *four* they all seemed ike water.(p.241)

• I'd work like mad for three or *four* weeks without a ingle drink, save my money, pay a few bills and then reward" myself with alcohol.(p.244)

• I had completely forgotten the January 8th when I ound the fellowship, and I spent the next *four* days vandering around New England half drunk, by vhich I mean I couldn't get drunk and I couldn't get ober.(p.247)

• I stayed sober for *four* years except for a one-night arousal in Chicago.(p.253)

• My *four* years of abstinence had something to do vith it, but soldiering is a tough enough game for a ober man, and I had no yen for full-pack slogging hrough mud with a cognac or vin rouge hangver.(p.253)

Four months later, I married this guy.(p.262)

I drove these three or *four* miles down the road nly to find that Jack was out.(p.267)

Our marriage lasted *four* years.(p.277)

At least three of those *four* years must have been a ving hell for my wife, because she had to watch the nan she loved disintegrate morally, mentally and financially.(p.277)

Instead, he got dressed, took me out, bought me hree or *four* double shots and put me to bed.(p.278)

So six months ago I acquired a ready made family onsisting of one charming wife, *four* grown children o whom I am devoted, and three grandchilren.(p.286)

It was February with snow and ice on the ground nd I had a *four* blocks walk to the nearest cab stand, ut I made it.(p.288)

This consisted of walking the floor for three or *four* ays and nights until I could take nourishnent.(p.289)

The day before I was due to go back to Chicago, a Vednesday and Dr. Bob's afternoon off, he had me down to the office and we spent three or *four* hours formally going through the Six-Step program as it was at that time.(p.291)

• The general procedure was to take *four* or five shots in the first place I stopped at.(p.299)

• If I were alone I would stop at *four* or five of them, but only one or two in the event I had my mistrusting wife with me.(p.299)

• And I was able to go on the wagon for long periods of time -- once for *four* years, to cure an ulcer.(p.328)

• I was keenly aware that my all-important security, which I had been constantly afraid of losing for *four* decades, no longer was endangered.(p.329)

• It was a long *four* or five hour operation, a large surgical procedure, and she was on her ninth or tenth post-operative day.(p.350)

• The last time I drank, when I was twenty-nine, I drank for only *four* days, yet I threatened to kill my children; I beat my wife at home and on the church steps; I mistreated a child in my office; and I ran to a hospital for mental illness to avoid jail.(p.418)

• Fear, love of dentistry, and an imitation of my father's periodic drinking pattern took me through dental college soberly, except for the few parties and vacations in those *four* years.(p.419)

• A.A. has given me a new wife, a beautiful stepdaughter, a new practice, a new home, and a new relationship with my *four* children.(p.420)

• I spent eighteen hundred dollars fixing up that car in the first year I was home, after *four* bad smashups.(p.429)

• Were I to revert to drinking, even now, I wouldn't give anything for these *four* years in A.A.(p.430)

• *Four* years ago I had nothing but a jumbled, mad existence.(p.430)

• I had sent her to *four* consecutive psychiatrists, and not one of them had gotten me sober.(p.440)

• The girl had explained them to me *four* times, and I was too embarrassed to ask her again.(p.445)

• I served time in *four* penitentiaries and several prison camps, including a maximum-security camp.(p.457)

• Same thing when I let lye and water eat away at *four* of my toes and my foot for five hours.(p.458)

• *Four* years later, I was taken to my first A.A. meeting out of prison, in Los Angeles.(p.460)

• Then I black out and get home *four* days later.(p.475)

• At this point I believe I had only been intoxicated on maybe three or *four* occasions, and certainly whiskey was no problem to me.(p.487)

• I was out of work for about *four* days.(p.490)

• It was Charlie and three or *four* others.(p.495)

• *Four* alcoholics play bridge in a smoke-filled room.(p.502)

• When I wended my way home *four* days later, on the 27th, there was a detective waiting for me.(p.508)

• The days have grown into a little better than *four* years of sobriety.(p.511)

• When I landed of course I hit a gin mill, and with three or *four* good shots under my belt the world began to go into that rosy glow.(p.513)

• One morning I didn't wake up until after *four* o'clock.(p.515)

• Then I went over again to Germany for *four* years on an occupation job.(p.519)

• They weren't quite so up-to-date on my history and I got away with about *four* years with them.(p.520)

• I had three or *four* very uncomfortable months with my regiment then on the Suez Canal.(p.520)

• I lasted at that for *four* months chiefly on alcohol, because I never seemed to find any time to eat.(p.520)

• Having made that bargain, I immediately began to feel I'd been trapped into it and I went out and had some drinks -- *four* glasses of gin, I remember.(p.523)

• I have been home for a year, and have not taken a drink in *four* years.(p.529)

• Still another friend and temporary host received me at *four* in the morning from the charge of a policeman who had found me "going to bed" in a garage far from the last place I could remember having been, a fashionable bar and restaurant in the theatrical district of New York, to which I had repaired after my date for that evening, a charming lady of the theatre who had refused my company for obvious reasons.(p.538)

• When the policeman released me to my stupefied and exasperated friend at *four* in the morning, I went to my traveling bag and groped until I found -- well, let the officer speak: "Ah," said the policeman, "he's got anuder pair, t'ank God!"(p.538)

• *Four* -- Each group should be autonomous except in matters affecting other groups or A.A. as a whole.(p.564)

four-thirty

• In fact, the last three years of my drinking was a routine of barbiturates in the morning, so that I could stop shaking enough to shave, and then alcohol beginning about *four-thirty* or five o'clock, with a struggle not to take a drink at noon or during the day, because I had the idea that if I took one drink, I would smell as though I had had a pint.(p.217)

four-time

• I woke up in jail, sick, withdrawing from alcohol and speed, already a *four-time* loser, and now with a fifth felony charge against me.(p.460)

fourteen

• And at the end of *fourteen* days, they let me out.(p.205)

• This last real merry-go-round had started the day before Christmas and I had really accomplished a lot in those *fourteen* days.(p.238)

• I displayed alcoholic tendencies actually from the age of *fourteen*, when I started to steal wine from the family jug, siphoning it off one drink at a time so it wouldn't be missed, not drinking it immediately, but saving it until about a pint was accumulated, so that I could get drunk.(p.397)

• The last Christmas I spent in Washington, *fourteen* years ago, comes to mind.(p.465)

fourteenth

• I began drinking as a kid, shortly after I reached my *fourteenth* birthday.(p.508)

fourth

• I was soon to be catapulted into what I like to call the *fourth* dimension of existence.(p.8)

• How often have some of us begun to drink in this nonchalant way, and after the third or *fourth*, pounded on the bar and said to ourselves, "For God's sake, how did I ever get started again?"(p.24)

• We have found much of heaven and we have been rocketed into a *fourth* dimension of existence of which we had not even dreamed.(p.25)

• You would suppose that men in the *fourth* classification would be quite hopeless, but that is not so.(p.113)

• After several failures to find others, a *fourth* turned up.(p.158)

• My drinking career began about four years after I had moved up into partnership and had joined certain clubs, societies and so *fourth*, and during which period we had Prohibition.(p.213)

• I was in the *fourth* quarter of my senior year at high school, and my mother was quite sick in the hospital.(p.354)

• Attending his *fourth* or fifth meeting was an old friend I had not seen for twenty years.(p.365)

• Similarly, we rid ourselves of guilt and remorse as we "clean out the garbage" from our minds through the *Fourth* and Fifth Steps of our recovery program.(p.560)

fox

• And I put a Big Book by my night stand, and I put a "Twelve Steps and Twelve Tradition" in my locker at the hospital, and I got books by Emmet *Fox*, and I got books by God-knows-who, and I got to reading all these things.(p.348)

• A house in Virginia, during the *fox* hunting season; a little chalet in Switzerland during the summer or a place on Long Island -- each house complete with cooks, butlers and maids.(p.403)

• This was in Virginia, where I had rented a house with stables and a swimming pool, and the fall *fox* hunting had begun.(p.404)

• But whereas my horse was always equipped with a flask, I merely endured the *fox* hunting so I could start drinking at lunch time.(p.404)

fraction

• In all probability, we shall never be able to touch more than a fair *fraction* of the alcohol problem in all its ramifications.(p.xxi)

fractured

• Presently he is hit again and this time has a *fractured* skull.(p.38)

• I had a broken nose, a *fractured* cheekbone, and was black from the lower part of my face up into my hair.(p.204)

frailties

• We have learned that whatever the human *frailties* of various faiths may be, those faiths have given purpose and direction to millions.(p.49)

frame

• "In this *frame* of mind, I went about my business and for a time all was well.(p.40)

• Peddling off my polish samples for expenses, I crawled back to New York a few days later in a very

chastened *frame* of mind.(p.248)
• I was in a perfectly happy *frame* of mind.(p.285)
• I entered the house, opened a new bottle of whiskey and sat down to drink myself into the right *frame* of mind to get in my car, start the motor and close the garage door behind me.(p.363)

France

• There I was, unshaven, clothes torn and dirty with no recollection of wandering all over *France* but, of course, a hero to the local French.(p.242)
• During this time, you are supposed to behave yourself, but I took a little wine-tasting tour through *France*, all by my lone, with car and chauffeur.(p.405)
• But as soon as I got out on my own in *France*, I started drinking.(p.518)

Franciscan

• My parents had some vague idea of making a priest out of me and for some years I attended the *Franciscan* school at Basle, Switzerland, just across the border, about six miles from my home.(p.230)

frank

• If our manner is calm, *frank*, and open, we will be gratified with the result.(p.78)
• Doc dwelt on the idea that this was an illness, but Doc was pretty *frank* with me.(p.219)
• He found that I had enough faith in the Almighty to be fairly *frank*.(p.219)

Frank

• *Frank*, my husband, would come home day after day and find me passed out.(p.386)
• *Frank* said, "If you'd like to talk to a psychiatrist, I'll see a doctor and find out who to go to here."(p.387)
• *Frank* left to find the doctor and I got drunk.(p.387)
• *Frank* found the doctor, but the doctor didn't want to take an alcoholic.(p.387)
• I resented the fact that *Frank* had done this to me, and I just didn't know what was going on.(p.388)
• *Frank* had to go to New York, but because I had a dog, we had a duplex, and I thought – if only we had a house!(p.388)
• So I located a house, and I thought we ought to move into it immediately, but *Frank* was horrified, because he never knew what was going to happen to me.(p.388)
• I loved my father dearly and I adored my dog, and I'd gotten this new house and *Frank* had just given me a new fur coat and I was thrilled to death.(p.389)
• So *Frank* went to New York and despite all these things, I got drunk.(p.389)
• But *Frank* turned around and looked at me and said, "Esther, remember you're in jail and not at home."(p.391)
• But *Frank* was frightened to death to give it to me, because I resented everything he said and did.(p.391)
• *Frank* was out of town, and I remember that he'd gotten in this one night and found me drunk.(p.391)
• I know that when *Frank* came home, I said, "I want to try this thing," and he said, "There's a post office box to write to in New York."(p.392)
• So *Frank* left town, and by Monday morning I had been sober for that whole week.(p.393)
• There are so many to whom I feel deeply grateful; to my husband (and best critic), whose generous love, compassion and understanding have helped me along the way; to those before me in A.A. who inspired the first article I read, and the friend who sent that article to *Frank*; to Ruth for her personal note, and the first A.A. to talk to me; to my Bishop, whose loving and believing spirit inspired me; and to all the members of the Houston Group who were so patient, kind and helpful -- and to countless others.(p.393)
• Very shortly, I realized that had been a mistake -- when this big clown came bounding into the room, almost shouting, "My name is *Frank*, and I'm an alcoholic, ha-ha-ha!"(p.446)
• So, for no better reason than to fool him, I asked *Frank* to take me to a meeting every night.(p.447)
• And *Frank* did set me up for a meeting every night except Friday, when he thought he might have a date with his girl friend.(p.447)
• "That's a devil of a way to run an organization," I thought, and I reported *Frank* to the psychiatrist, who didn't seem perturbed; he just got someone else to take me on Fridays.(p.447)

frankly

• He *frankly* admitted and believed that for him there was no hope.(p.xxix)
• Following his physical rehabilitation, he had a talk with me in which he *frankly* stated he thought the treatment a waste of effort, unless I could assure him, which no one ever had, that in the future he would have the "will power" to resist the impulse to drink.(p.xxix)
• Let him tell you about it: "I was much impressed with what you fellows said about alcoholism, and I *frankly* did not believe it would be possible for me to drink again.(p.40)
• We ought to sit down with the family and *frankly* analyze the past as we now see it, being very careful not to criticize them.(p.83)
• At the very beginning, the couple ought to *frankly* face the fact that each will have to yield here and there if the family is going to play an effective part in the new life.(p.131)
• He admitted he was overdoing these things, but *frankly* said that he was not ready to stop.(p.135)
• Can he talk *frankly* with you so long as he does not bear business tales or criticize his associates?(p.145)

frankness

• Perhaps there are some cases where the utmost *frankness* is demanded.(p.82)

frantic

• This brought a rush of 800 *frantic* inquiries into the little New York office which meanwhile had been established.(p.xviii)
• It may mean sharing your money and your home, counseling *frantic* wives and relatives, innumerable trips to police courts, sanitariums, hospitals, jails and asylums.(p.97)
• He may either plunge into a *frantic* attempt to get on his feet in business, or he may be so enthralled by his new life that he talks or thinks of little else.(p.125)

frantically

• Hence the two men set to work almost *frantically* upon alcoholics arriving in the ward of the Akron City Hospital.(p.xvii)
• Hauling her to the divan, I sat with her and began to talk, *frantically* but clearly -- and making sense.(p.333)
• But I was trying *frantically* to control it.(p.557)

fraternity

• The experiment of quitting for a period of time will be helpful, but we think we can render an even greater service to alcoholic sufferers and perhaps to the medical *fraternity*.(p.34)
• I was graduated "summa cum laude" in the eyes of the drinking *fraternity*, but not in the eyes of the Dean.(p.172)
• Many mornings I have gone to classes, and even though fully prepared, would turn and walk back to the *fraternity* house because of my jitters, not daring to enter the classroom for fear of making a scene should I be called on for recitation.(p.173)
• There my drinking became so much worse that the boys in the *fraternity* house where I lived felt forced to send for my father, who made a long journey in the vain endeavor to get me straightened around.(p.174)
• I refused to join any *fraternity*, as I wanted to be a free lance, and that year my drinking was confined to one-night stands, once or twice a week.(p.241)
• I have always considered myself one of the lucky members of our *fraternity*.(p.356)
• I also began to drink at *fraternity* parties and beer busts.(p.555)

freaks

• I went to a meeting to see for myself this group of *freaks* or bums who had done this thing.(p.228)

Fred

• *Fred* is partner in a well known accounting firm.(p.39)
• If ever there was a successful business man, it is *Fred*.(p.39)
• We first saw *Fred* about a year ago in a hospital where he had gone to recover from a bad case of jitters.(p.39)
• *Fred* would not believe himself an alcoholic, much less accept a spiritual remedy for his problem.(p.39)
• We heard no more of *Fred* for a while.(p.40)

Fred's

• *Fred's* story speaks for itself.(p.43)

free

• There is the type who always believes that after being entirely *free* from alcohol for a period of time he can take a drink without danger.(p.xxviii)
• But this man still lives, and is a *free* man.(p.26)
• He can go anywhere on this earth where other *free* men may go without disaster, provided he remains willing to maintain a certain simple attitude.(p.26)
• Here was the terrible dilemma in which our friend found himself when he had the extraordinary experience which as we have already told you, made him a *free* man.(p.28)
• If we were to live, we had to be *free* of anger.(p.66)
• Carefully reading the first five proposals we ask if we have omitted anything, for we are building an arch through which we shall walk a *free* man at last.(p.75)
• Make him feel absolutely *free* to come and go as he likes.(p.120)
• We are sure God wants us to be happy, joyous, and *free*.(p.133)
• If he feels *free* to discuss his problems with you, if he knows you understand and will not be upset by anything he wishes to say, he will probably be off to a fast start.(p.144)
• That afternoon he put on his clothes and walked from the hospital a *free* man.(p.158)
• This had the effect of making me resolve that when I was *free* from parental domination, I would never again darken the doors of a church.(p.172)
• Bill D. walked out of that hospital a *free* man never to drink again.(p.189)
• I was *free*, and I didn't have to drink to "show them."(p.228)
• I refused to join any fraternity, as I wanted to be a *free* lance, and that year my drinking was confined to one-night stands, once or twice a week.(p.241)
• To the best of my recollection I was completely *free* from any abnormal fears.(p.275)
• We're *free* at last to do our thing, to live uninhibited lives, to drink when and how and where we wish, when we want to and when we need to.(p.329)
• I had to sleep, I had to clear my mind and *free* it from worry, and I had to relax.(p.336)
• I said to my husband, "I'm going to try, every *free* moment that I have, to get interested in something outside, get myself over this rut I'm in."(p.338)
• I was *free*, white and twenty-one and I had a time for myself.(p.386)
• But my board, room, and clothing were *free*, and I could spend the whole ten bucks on booze.(p.398)
• Every day, I feel a little bit more useful, more happy and more *free*.(p.417)
• Why am I alive, *free*, a respected member of my community?(p.421)
• But if you want to, you're *free* to try them.(p.436)
• We got on the plane and immediately had a big fight over whether I'd drink the *free* booze.(p.444)
• However, one thing I am certain of: Inmates in prison who attend A.A. have their chances of remaining *free* greatly enhanced – this is a proved fact.(p.458)
• All Twelve Steps of A.A. are designed to kill the old self (deflate the old ego) and build a new, *free* self.(p.459)
• I learn that honesty is truth, and that truth shall make us *free*!(p.507)
• She here tells how she was set *free*.(p.544)
• In my prayers that morning I asked God to point out to me some way to be *free* of this resentment.(p.552)
• He said, in effect: "If you have a resentment you want to be *free* of, if you will pray for the person or the thing that you resent, you will be *free*.(p.552)
• If you will ask in prayer for everything you want fo yourself to be given to them, you will be *free*.(p.552)
• Ask for their health, their prosperity, their happiness, and you will be *free*.(p.552)

freed

• Of course an alcoholic ought to be *freed* from his physical craving for liquor, and this often requires a definite hospital procedure, before psychological mea sures can be of maximum benefit.(p.xxv)

freedom

• Yet it is our great hope that all those who have as yet found no answer may begin to find one in the pages of this book and will presently join us on the highroad to a new *freedom*.(p.xxi)
• Most good ideas are simple, and this concept was the keystone of the new and triumphant arch throug which we passed to *freedom*.(p.62)
• We are going to know a new *freedom* and a new happiness.(p.83)
• We ask especially for *freedom* from self-will, and are careful to make no request for ourselves only.(p.87)
• Many a man, yet dazed from his hospital experience, has stepped over the threshold of that home int *freedom*.(p.160)
• They spoke with great *freedom* from embarrassment, which I could never do, and they seemed very much at ease on all occasions and appeared very healthy.(p.178)
• For greater *freedom* and excitement I went abroad to live.(p.225)
• This wasn't "religion" – this was *freedom*!(p.228)
• *Freedom* from anger and fear, *freedom* to know ha piness and love.(p.228)

• This gave me the ***freedom*** to do A.A. work, and to rest for periods of two or three days when I became too exhausted to carry on.(p.283)
• Then I started traveling, with the United States and Canada as my territory, and with so much ***freedom*** and with an unlimited expense account, I was soon drinking every night and kidding myself that it was all part of the job.(p.287)
• Perhaps I could find ***freedom*** and peace and be able once again to call my soul my own.(p.309)
• I have had my share of problems, heartaches and disappointments, because that is life, but also I have known a great deal of joy, and a peace that is the handmaiden of an inner ***freedom***, I have a wealth of friends and, with my A.A. friends, an unusual quality of fellowship.(p.312)
• And with this came the only real ***freedom***, the ***freedom*** of truth.(p.355)
• Today I think of life in terms of happiness, contentment, ***freedom*** from fear and despair, sane thinking, ability to face problems as they occur, the opportunity to help other alcoholics and to be decent.(p.430)
• Through A.A., we can experience ***freedom*** from self.(p.459)
• This physician, the originator of A.A.'s first black group, but badly caught in the toils, tells of his release and of how ***freedom*** came as he worked among his own people.(p.483)
• The grand fellow who at my call made me a hail-fellow-well-met, who gave me such a fine voice, as we sang "Hail, hail, the gang's all here," and "Sweet Adeline," who gave me ***freedom*** from fear and feelings of inferiority.(p.498)
• ***FREEDOM*** FROM BONDAGE(p.544)
• As another great man says, "The only real ***freedom*** a human being can ever know is doing what you ought to do because you want to do it."(p.553)

freely

• While I lay in the hospital the thought came that there were thousands of hopeless alcoholics who might be glad to have what had been so ***freely*** given me.(p.14)
• How then shall we present that which has been so ***freely*** given us?(p.19)
• Stress the spiritual feature ***freely***.(p.93)
• But dad doesn't give ***freely*** of himself.(p.126)
• Most of them give ***freely*** of themselves, that their fellows may enjoy sound minds and bodies.(p.133)
• Give ***freely*** of what you find and join us.(p.164)
• The hospitality of their home and their fine fellowship were ***freely*** mine.(p.259)
• It took the help, understanding and wonderful companionship that was given so ***freely*** to me by my "exalkie" friends.(p.311)
• Secondary aids to A.A., such as clubs or hospitals which require much property or administration, ought to be incorporated and so set apart that, if necessary, they can be ***freely*** discarded by the groups.(p.566)

freights

• Always, in between, there were intervals of being broke, riding ***freights*** and hitch-hiking interminable distances from one big town to another in three states.(p.255)

French

• There I was, unshaven, clothes torn and dirty with no recollection of wandering all over France but, of course, a hero to the local ***French***.(p.242)

frequency

• Cunning, baffling, powerful -- the gradual creeping up of the ***frequency*** and quantity of alcohol, and what it does to a person is apparent to everyone but the person involved.(p.375)
• But they were occurring with alarming ***frequency***.(p.434)

frequent

• ***Frequent*** contact with newcomers and with each other is the bright spot of our lives.(p.89)
• These periods became more ***frequent*** and I resolved that when I became forty, which was very shortly, I was going on the wagon.(p.213)
• "Blanks" were more ***frequent***, and I seldom knew how I'd got home.(p.226)
• My "periodics" became more ***frequent*** until I reached the point where I wanted to devote all my time to drinking, working as little as possible, and then only when the necessity of my family demanded it.(p.234)
• Every encouragement was given me with ***frequent*** salary increases, but the sober times between "periods" became shorter.(p.254)
• Federal Theatre in Texas gave me an administrative job which I held for a year, only because I worked hard and productively when I worked, and because my very tolerant chief ascribed my ***frequent*** lapses to a bohemian temperament.(p.256)
• The example which they and Bill W., whose visits to Akron were fairly ***frequent***, set me of service to their fellow men imbued me with a great desire to emulate them.(p.281)
• I suffered ***frequent*** blackouts.(p.558)
• Among our rapidly growing membership of thousands of alcoholics such transformations, though ***frequent***, are by no means the rule.(p.569)

frequented

• I knew I wasn't capable of keeping the bulk of the money myself, so I gave it to a white fellow who owned the bar which I ***frequented***.(p.493)

frequenting

• He entered a political campaign, making speeches, ***frequenting*** men's gathering places of all sorts, often staying up all night.(p.158)

frequently

• We meet ***frequently*** so that newcomers may find the fellowship they seek.(p.15)
• Yet let him drink for a day, and he ***frequently*** becomes disgustingly and even dangerously anti-social.(p.21)
• When people presented us with spiritual approaches, how ***frequently*** did we all say, "I wish I had what that man has.(p.47)
• ***Frequently***, you have felt obliged to tell your husband's employer and his friends that he was sick, when as a matter of fact he was tight.(p.115)
• The alcoholic's past thus becomes the principal asset of the family and ***frequently*** it is almost the only one!(p.124)
• Men under them are ***frequently*** their friends.(p.147)
• I found out later that my wife inspected it ***frequently***.(p.176)
• I was doing well in business, and in going around town I was ***frequently*** invited to have a drink in a speakeasy.(p.233)
• Unlike many other Catholics who ***frequently*** take pledges for definite periods -- a year, two years or for good, I never had any desire to "take a pledge" before the priest.(p.234)
• Gradually the quantity increased, the occasions for a drink came more ***frequently***; a hard day, worries and pressure, bad news, good news -- there were more and more reasons for a drink.(p.374)
• I passed out ***frequently*** in my home, alone.(p.406)
• We moved ***frequently***.(p.554)
• When I encountered disappointments or frustrations -- as I did more and more ***frequently*** -- my solution was to drink.(p.556)
• Then the drinks came more ***frequently***, but carefully spaced out.(p.557)

fresh

• The outlines and the promise of the New Land had brought lustre to tired eyes and ***fresh*** courage to flagging spirits.(p.53)
• Then, in days, weeks, or months, a ***fresh*** outburst.(p.105)
• And just as we were being convinced of their heartlessness, they would surprise us with ***fresh*** resolves and new attentions.(p.107)
• Therefore, you probably need ***fresh*** interests and a great cause to live for as much as your husband.(p.119)
• Can you charge this off as you would a bad account and start ***fresh*** with him?(p.145)
• I would make a ***fresh*** start somewhere else.(p.281)

fresh-skinned

• The door opened and he stood there, ***fresh-skinned*** and glowing.(p.9)

freshman

• Awarded a scholarship to a famous old Eastern college, I began to drink at the end of my ***freshman*** year, and by junior year, I had to transfer to an easier state university to keep my grades up.(p.419)
• "***Freshman***," said he to me, "do you ever take a drink?"(p.497)

friction

• There is no ***friction*** among us over such matters.(p.28)

Friday

• (Russ was buried on ***Friday***, and on Sunday afternoon Hilda S. had invited me there to dinner Sunday night, and I didn't think I could do it.(p.272)
• How will I feel next ***Friday***, if I make it a ***Friday***?(p.326)
• I stayed drunk from Monday until ***Friday***, and I call that my spill into A.A.(p.393)
• It was the first time in my life that I could not get a lift out of what I was drinking; and so one ***Friday*** night, at five minutes to six, I had half a water glass of warm gin, and that is when I first asked God to help me.(p.393)
• And Frank did set me up for a meeting every night except ***Friday***, when he thought he might have a date with his girl friend.(p.447)
• That year, on a ***Friday*** night, a man whom I had known for years came to my office.(p.488)
• At that time we had our meetings on ***Friday*** nights.(p.495)
• But not for long; now, for five ***Friday*** nights in a row, I went to jail, picked up sodden with beer (which I always disliked, but which was the only drink available); in jail five consecutive ***Friday*** nights in the town where I had grown up, where I had been an honor student in high school, where a kindly uncle, bailing me out, said, "Bob, our family just doesn't do this sort of thing."(p.539)

Fridays

• "That's a devil of a way to run an organization," I thought, and I reported Frank to the psychiatrist, who didn't seem perturbed; he just got someone else to take me on ***Fridays***.(p.447)

friend

• Six months earlier, the broker had been relieved of his drink obsession by a sudden spiritual experience, following a meeting with an alcoholic ***friend*** who had been in contact with the Oxford Groups of that day.(p.xv)
• Next morning I telephoned a ***friend*** in Montreal.(p.4)
• But drinking caught up with me again and my generous ***friend*** had to let me go.(p.4)
• The cheery voice of an old school ***friend*** asked if he might come over.(p.8)
• But my ***friend*** sat before me, and he made the point-blank declaration that God had done for him what he could not do for himself.(p.11)
• I saw that my ***friend*** was much more than inwardly reorganized.(p.11)
• Despite the living example of my ***friend*** there remained in me the vestiges of my old prejudice.(p.12)
• My ***friend*** suggested what then seemed a novel idea.(p.12)
• Upon a foundation of complete willingness I might build what I saw in my ***friend***.(p.12)
• I ruthlessly faced my sins and became willing to have my new-found ***Friend*** take them away, root and branch.(p.13)
• My ***friend*** promised when these things were done I would enter upon a new relationship with my Creator; that I would have the elements of a way of living which answered all my problems.(p.13)
• For a moment I was alarmed, and called my ***friend***, the doctor, to ask if I were still sane.(p.14)
• My ***friend*** had emphasized the absolute necessity of demonstrating these principles in all my affairs.(p.14)
• These observations would be academic and pointless if our ***friend*** never took the first drink, thereby setting the terrible cycle in motion.(p.23)
• Let us tell you the rest of the conversation our ***friend*** had with his doctor.(p.27)
• Our ***friend*** felt as though the gates of hell had closed on him with a clang.(p.27)
• Upon hearing this, our ***friend*** was somewhat relieved, for he reflected that after all, he was a good church member.(p.27)
• Here was the terrible dilemma in which our ***friend*** found himself when he had the extraordinary experience which as we have already told you, made him a free man.(p.28)
• Our first example is a ***friend*** we shall call Jim.(p.35)
• We finally saw that faith in some kind of God was a part of our make-up, just as much as the feeling we have for a ***friend***.(p.55)
• Our ***friend*** was a minister's son.(p.56)
• We found it very desirable to take this spiritual step with an understanding person, such as our wife, best ***friend*** or spiritual adviser.(p.63)
• He's my ***friend***.(p.65)
• We asked God to help us show them the same tolerance, pity, and patience that we would cheerfully grant a sick ***friend***.(p.67)
• If we cannot or would rather not do this, we search our acquaintance for a close-mouthed, understanding ***friend***.(p.74)
• It is harder to go to an enemy than to a ***friend***, but we find it much more beneficial to us.(p.77)
• Then let his family or a ***friend*** ask him if he wants to quit for good and if he would go to any extreme to do so.(p.90)
• You will soon have your ***friend*** admitting he has many, if not all, of the traits of the alcoholic.(p.92)
• If your talk has been sane, quiet and full of human

understanding, you have perhaps made a *friend*.(p.94)
• Unless your *friend* wants to talk further about himself, do not wear out your welcome.(p.95)
• Of course our *friend* was wrong – dead wrong.(p.135)
• "Oh no," said my *friend*, "this chap is either through with liquor, or he is minus a job.(p.138)
• I wanted to throw up my hands in discouragement, for I saw that I had failed to help my banker *friend* understand.(p.138)
• What our *friend*, the vice president, had in mind was the habitual or whoopee drinker.(p.149)
• We know our *friend* is like a boy whistling in the dark to keep up his spirits.(p.152)
• When our *friend* related his experience, the man agreed that no amount of will power he might muster could stop his drinking for long.(p.155)
• Being intrigued, however, he invited our *friend* to his home.(p.155)
• All this time our *friend* of the hotel lobby incident remained in that town.(p.159)
• So he inquired, what did our *friend* have on the ball?(p.163)
• Our *friend* proceeded to tell him.(p.163)
• This went from bad to worse until Sophomore spring when, after a prolonged period of drinking, I made up my mind that I could not complete my course, so I packed my grip and went South to spend a month on a large farm owned by a *friend* of mine.(p.173)
• About this time a lady called up my wife one Saturday afternoon, saying she wanted me to come over that evening to meet a *friend* of hers who might help me.(p.179)
• These good people notified my wife, who sent my newly made *friend* over to get me.(p.179)
• It wasn't very long until my doctor *friend* sent me to tell another alcoholic what my experience had been.(p.237)
• I had not asked for help and seriously doubt that I would have, but Fitz, an old school *friend* of mine, had persuaded Jackie to call on me.(p.238)
• Jackie told me about a group of fellows in New York, of whom my old *friend* Fitz was one, who had the same problem I had, and who by working together to help each other were not now drinking and were happy like himself.(p.239)
• A *friend* who knew I would soon be broke mounted guard over me when I left my job of writing the histories of Texas cities and put me aboard a bus for the town I had left almost five years before.(p.256)
• I found my *friend* was there for alcoholism and now he was insisting that he had found the only cure.(p.257)
• As soon as I could get up and walk I started to drink again and kept it up until my *friend* of the hospital, who, in his first try at the new way of life had stubbed his toe in Chicago but had come back to the town to take counsel and make a new start, picked me up and got me into a hospital.(p.258)
• I ended up, homeless, jobless, penniless and rudderless, as the problem guest of a close *friend* whose family was out of town.(p.278)
• I also talked A.A. to every *friend* who would listen, at lunch, at dinner, on street corners.(p.282)
• A week later, I had to get an old *friend* from Akron to spend two days sobering me up.(p.293)
• Spiritually . . . I found a *Friend* who never lets me down and is ever eager to help.(p.303)
• A *friend* of mine, a golf nut, rushed out on retirement to play every day.(p.330)
• The radio was my good *friend*.(p.332)
• On the last day I was drinking I went up to see a *friend* who had had a good deal of trouble with alcohol, and whose wife had left him a number of times.(p.346)
• This *friend* gave me a pamphlet, and I took it home and had my wife read it to me.(p.346)
• About two days later I was called by a *friend* of mine from Nevada City – he's a brother of my wife's closest *friend*.(p.347)
• At the other side of the table sat one of the carpenters in our community, and at the further end of the table sat the man who ran the bakery, while on one side sat my *friend* who was a mechanic.(p.347)
• This escapade also ended up in the clutches of the law, and my *friend* was institutionalized for eight months.(p.354)
• By persistence and salesmanship I managed to see more and more of my new *friend*, and because of her sympathetic nature she tolerated my company.(p.359)
• Attending his fourth or fifth meeting was an old *friend* I had not seen for twenty years.(p.365)
• There are so many to whom I feel deeply grateful; to my husband (and best critic), whose generous love, compassion and understanding have helped me along the way; to those before me in A.A. who inspired the first article I read, and the *friend* who sent that article to Frank; to Ruth for her personal note, and the first A.A. to talk to me; to my Bishop, whose loving and believing spirit inspired me; and to all the members of the Houston Group who were so patient, kind and helpful -- and to countless others.(p.393)
• Age and the law were still against me, but laws were not as strictly enforced in those days as they are now, and I discovered that as long as I had the green blood, there was always a way to get alcohol, either from a nondiscriminatory bartender or from an older *friend* who would be glad to purchase the joy juice for the privilege of sharing it.(p.397)
• I wore a man's raincoat, turned inside out, a present from a *friend*, for now my funds were low.(p.411)
• Luckily a *friend* was with me, who dragged me out, screaming and cursing, while the bartender threatened to call the police.(p.411)
• A *friend* of Marty's, another A.A. let me in.(p.413)
• A *friend* had found help in psychoanalysis.(p.434)
• And Frank did set me up for a meeting every night except Friday, when he thought he might have a date with his girl *friend*.(p.447)
• This A.A. *friend* took me into his home when he had me out on pass.(p.462)
• I go back to my old alma mater occasionally to give A.A. talks, and -- just think! -- the warden is my *friend*.(p.462)
• Then I remember him coming into my room one night with a *friend*, and telling me to get dressed – we were going away.(p.466)
• They say call *friend* before I buy drink.(p.476)
• Call *friend* in A.A. when bad thoughts come.(p.477)
• To get rid of me one evening, she decided to go to the movies, she and another *friend*.(p.487)
• A very good *friend* of mine who owned a drug store across the street from us, came by only about two hours later and said that he had seen Vi down town.(p.487)
• I took that bottle of medicine and gave it to a very good *friend* of mine who was a pharmacist and had it analyzed, and the bottle was perfectly all right.(p.489)
• I had a very good *friend* who was in the Government service, and I went to him about a job.(p.489)
• I visit a *friend* who is awaiting orders.(p.499)
• He is a real *friend* but I do not appreciate him.(p.501)
• Some men and women come to visit my *friend* of the night before.(p.504)
• I would wait for the mailman each month, like any good mother, but as soon as he handed me my check, I put on my best dress and went looking for my alcoholic *friend*.(p.527)
• Still another *friend* and temporary host received me at four in the morning from the charge of a policeman who had found me "going to bed" in a garage far from the last place I could remember having been, a fashionable bar and restaurant in the theatrical district of New York, to which I had repaired after my date for that evening, a charming lady of the theatre who had refused my company for obvious reasons.(p.538)
• When the policeman released me to my stupefied and exasperated *friend* at four in the morning, I went to my traveling bag and groped until I found -- well, let the officer speak: "Ah," said the policeman, "he's got anuder pair, t'ank God!"(p.538)
• I mentioned that this *friend* was my temporary host.(p.538)
• Was I the disloyal sort who would turn his back on this, my last and truest *friend*?(p.539)
• During the day a *friend* of mine brought me some magazines to take to a hospital group I was interested in, and I looked through them and a "banner" across the front of one featured an article by a prominent clergyman in which I caught the word "resentment."(p.552)
• Should you be the relative or *friend* of an alcoholic who shows no immediate interest in A.A., it is suggested that you write the Al-Anon Family Groups, Inc., Box 182, Madison Square Station, New York, NY 10159, U.S.A.(p.575)

friend's

• Each day my *friend's* simple talk in our kitchen multiplies itself in a widening circle of peace on earth and good will to men.(p.16)
• Our *friend's* gorge rose as he bitterly cried out: "If there is a God, He certainly hasn't done anything for me!"(p.56)
• Thus was our *friend's* cornerstone fixed in place.(p.56)
• I remember nothing from then on until I woke up at a *friend's* house, in a town near home.(p.179)
• When I reached a point directly back of our house, where I could have cut through a *friend's* garden, I was almost overpowered by the desire to get home, but I made the whole journey.(p.276)
• Now it was semi-blackouts every night, outrageous behavior, passing out in some *friend's* Village studio or not knowing how I got home.(p.407)
• I went to this *friend's* shop to repair his electrical outlet and I noticed this lady.(p.493)

friendliness

• But there exists among us a fellowship, a *friendliness*, and an understanding which is indescribably wonderful.(p.17)
• These can then be discussed in an atmosphere of helpfulness and *friendliness*.(p.99)

friendly

• They are often able, intelligent, *friendly* people.(p.xxviii)
• He enjoys himself for a few years in spite of *friendly* warnings.(p.37)
• I have a shadowy recollection of being in an airplane bound for New York, and of finding a *friendly* taxicab driver at the landing field instead of my wife.(p.41)
• *Friendly* hands had stretched out in welcome.(p.53)
• But point out that we alcoholics have much in common and that you would like, in any case, to be *friendly*.(p.95)
• You should continue to be *friendly* to them.(p.97)
• This may lay the groundwork for a *friendly* talk about his alcoholic problem.(p.111)
• If this kind of approach does not catch your husband's interest, it may be best to drop the subject, but after a *friendly* talk your husband will usually revive the topic himself.(p.112)
• This means trouble, unless the family watches for these tendencies in each other and comes to a *friendly* agreement about them.(p.131)
• The alcoholic may find it hard to re-establish *friendly* relations with his children.(p.134)
• One instance comes to mind in which a malicious individual was always making *friendly* little jokes about an alcoholic's drinking exploits.(p.145)
• We now live in the West and are very fortunate in our area A.A.; it is good, simple and *friendly*, and our one desire is to stay in A.A. and not on it.(p.250)
• The unwillingness to admit failure requires even further *friendly* intake.(p.331)
• When I walked into the *friendly* atmosphere of my first A.A. meeting, I knew I was where I belonged.(p.355)
• The term was nearly over and we parted on fairly *friendly* terms.(p.518)

friends

• Many of our *friends* encourage us by saying that this is but a beginning, only the augury of a much larger future ahead.(p.xv)
• In the spring of 1940, John D. Rockefeller, Jr. gave a dinner for many of his *friends* to which he invited A.A. members to tell their stories.(p.xviii)
• Another reason for the wide acceptance of A.A. was the ministration of *friends* – *friends* in medicine, religion, and the press, together with innumerable others who became our able and persistent advocates.(p.xx)
• Some of the recommendations of A.A.'s early medical and religious *friends* will be found further on in this book.(p.xx)
• There is the manic-depressive type, who is, perhaps, the least understood by his *friends*, and about whom a whole chapter could be written.(p.xxviii)
• I failed to persuade my broker *friends* to send me out looking over factories and managements, but my wife and I decided to go anyway.(p.2)
• Our *friends* thought a lunacy commission should be appointed.(p.3)
• I made a host of fair-weather *friends*.(p.3)
• The remonstrances of my *friends* terminated in a row and I became a lone wolf.(p.3)
• I was finished and so were many *friends*.(p.4)
• My *friends* had dropped several million since ten o'clock -- so what?(p.4)
• We commenced to make many fast *friends* and a fellowship has grown up among us of which it is a wonderful thing to feel a part.(p.15)
• It brings misunderstanding, fierce resentment, financial insecurity, disgusted *friends* and employers, warped lives of blameless children, sad wives and parents – anyone can increase the list.(p.18)
• Strangely enough, wives, parents and intimate *friends* usually find us even more unapproachable than do the psychiatrist and the doctor.(p.18)
• In a vague way their families and *friends* sense that these drinkers are abnormal, but everybody hopefully

awaits the day when the sufferer will rouse himself from his lethargy and assert his power of will.(p.23)
• *Friends* who have reasoned with him after a spree which has brought him to the point of divorce or bankruptcy are mystified when he walks directly into a saloon.(p.35)
• He has so attractive a personality that he makes *friends* with everyone.(p.39)
• I now remembered what my alcoholic *friends* had told me, how they prophesied that if I had an alcoholic mind, the time and place would come – I would drink again.(p.41)
• As we look over the list of business acquaintances and *friends* we have hurt, we may feel diffident about going to some of them on a spiritual basis.(p.76)
• This brings to mind a story about one of our *friends*.(p.80)
• If circumstances warrant, we ask our wives or *friends* to join us in morning meditation.(p.87)
• To watch people recover, to see them help others, to watch loneliness vanish, to see a fellowship grow up about you, to have a host of *friends* -- this is an experience you must not miss.(p.89)
• He should not be pushed or prodded by you, his wife, or his *friends*.(p.95)
• People have said we must not go where liquor is served; we must not have it in our homes; we must shun *friends* who drink; we must avoid moving pictures which show drinking scenes; we must not go into bars; our *friends* must hide their bottles if we go to their houses; we mustn't think or be reminded about alcohol at all.(p.100)
• Let your *friends* know they are not to change their habits on your account.(p.102)
• At proper time and place explain to all your *friends* why alcohol disagrees with you.(p.102)
• Don't start to withdraw again just because your *friends* drink liquor.(p.102)
• Some of us still serve it to our *friends* provided they are not alcoholic.(p.102)
• Among us are wives, relatives and *friends* whose problem has been solved, as well as some who have not yet found a happy solution.(p.104)
• Our *friends* have counseled chucking the men and we have done so with finality, only to be back in a little while hoping, always hoping.(p.105)
• We seldom had *friends* at our homes, never knowing how or when the men of the house would appear.(p.105)
• Sometimes he is a source of embarrassment to you and his *friends*.(p.109)
• Maybe he is beginning to lose his *friends*.(p.109)
• His *friends* have slipped away, his home is a near-wreck and he cannot hold a position.(p.110)
• His *friends* feel closer over a highball.(p.110)
• Be determined that your husband's drinking is not going to spoil your relations with your children or your *friends*.(p.111)
• If your husband is a drinker, you probably worry over what other people are thinking and you hate to meet your *friends*.(p.114)
• While you need not discuss your husband at length, you can quietly let your *friends* know the nature of his illness.(p.115)
• Barriers which have sprung up between you and your *friends* will disappear with the growth of sympathetic understanding.(p.115)
• Frequently, you have felt obliged to tell your husband's employer and his *friends* that he was sick, when as a matter of fact he was tight.(p.115)
• We suggest that you direct some of your thought to the wives of his new alcoholic *friends*.(p.119)
In a weak moment he may take your dislike of his high-stepping *friends* as one of those insanely trivial excuses to drink.(p.120)
Though it is entirely separate from Alcoholics Anonymous, it uses the general principles of the A.A. program as a guide for husbands, wives, relatives, *friends*, and others close to alcoholics.(p.121)
If he does not argue about religion, he will make new *friends* and is sure to find new avenues of usefulness and pleasure.(p.132)
Here is a case in point: One of our *friends* is a heavy smoker and coffee drinker.(p.135)
Men under them are frequently their *friends*.(p.147)
It is joyous intimacy with *friends* and a feeling that life is good.(p.151)
You are going to meet these new *friends* in your own community.(p.152)
Among them you will make lifelong *friends*.(p.152)
But life was not easy for the two *friends*.(p.156)
But one of the *friends* said, "Put him in a private room.(p.157)
For an hour, the two *friends* told him about their drinking experiences.(p.157)
• The two *friends* spoke of their spiritual experience and told him about the course of action they carried out.(p.157)
• They knew they had a host of new *friends*; it seemed they had known these strangers always.(p.161)
• There are the same fast friendships, there is the same helpfulness to one another as you find among our western *friends*.(p.162)
• So our fellow worker will soon have *friends* galore.(p.163)
• In his prodigy of service, he was well assisted by Sister Ignatia at St. Thomas Hospital in Akron, Ohio, one of the greatest *friends* our Fellowship will ever know.(p.171)
• After three years of this, I wound up in the local hospital where they attempted to help me, but I would get my *friends* to smuggle me a quart, or I would steal the alcohol about the building, so that I got rapidly worse.(p.175)
• But my *friends* usually found me and I would go home if they promised that I should not be scolded.(p.176)
• During all this time we became more or less ostracized by our *friends*.(p.177)
• I used to promise my wife, my *friends*, and my children that I would drink no more – promises which seldom kept me sober even through the day, though I was very sincere when I made them.(p.177)
• I used to get terribly upset when I saw my *friends* drink and knew I could not, but I schooled myself to believe that though I once had the same privilege, I had abused it so frightfully that it was withdrawn.(p.181)
• I can remember occasions when *friends* recommended me for positions or business opportunities that I wouldn't take because I felt that at some future date I'd get drunk and they would be hurt.(p.198)
• In 1932, some *friends* of mine advised me that I might try Christian Science, which had done a lot for some of their *friends*.(p.202)
• So I started to investigate Science through some *friends* of mine who were Readers in the church.(p.202)
• When my *friends* suggested that I was drinking too much – they were no longer my *friends*.(p.226)
• I had found *friends*, understanding *friends* who often knew what I was thinking and feeling better than I knew myself, and didn't allow me to retreat into my prison of loneliness and fear over a fancied slight or hurt.(p.228)
• Many *friends* of my family had emigrated to America, so at twenty-four I decided that the United States offered me the opportunity I was never likely to find in my native land.(p.231)
• I was warmly welcomed by *friends* of my youth who had preceded me.(p.231)
• There I sat in the evenings, enjoying with my *friends* our memories of the "old country," singing the old songs we all knew, playing simple card games for drinks and consuming great quantities of beer.(p.231)
• Successful home-brewers among my *friends* began to invite me to their homes.(p.232)
• In sports I made the track and tennis teams; I got along well with the other boys and had a fairly large circle of acquaintances but no intimate *friends*.(p.240)
• Despite all this, I did like these new *friends* because, again, they were like me.(p.245)
• We can share in the laughter and tears of our many *friends*, and most important, we can share our A.A. way of life and are given a daily opportunity to help others.(p.249)
• Some college *friends* got me jobs when I finally had to go to work, but I didn't stick to them.(p.251)
• Making my way to Pittsburgh, I met other former *friends* and got a job in a large factory where piecemakers were making good money.(p.252)
• During my visit there, renewing acquaintance with former *friends*, I soon spent most of my money.(p.252)
• When I came to my aunt, she knew that I had had an unhappy childhood, and she said, "Now, Ethel, you're welcome to have boy *friends* in our home, but there are two boys in this town that I don't want you to date, and one of them comes from a very fine family, one of the best.(p.262)
• Visits from *friends* which lasted over fifteen minutes exhausted me.(p.275)
• *Friends* invited me to stay on for as long as I cared to.(p.281)
• If I did not maintain my sobriety, I would have no *friends* left.(p.293)
• The next day I went back to Chicago and started a vigorous campaign among my so-called *friends* or drinking companions.(p.293)
• Where once I had casual acquaintances, all of whom were fair weather *friends*, I now have a host of *friends* who accept me for what I am.(p.296)
• A night or so a week in a joint, and a party or so a week at home or with *friends*, along with a little lone drinking, soon had me preparing for the existence of a top flight drunkard.(p.298)
• During this time, I had been threatened, beaten, kissed, praised and damned alternately by relatives, family, *friends* and strangers, but of course it all went for naught.(p.300)
• Things eventually came to the point where I had no *friends*.(p.301)
• After holding good positions, making better than an average income for over ten years, I was in debt, had no clothes to speak of, no money, no *friends*, and no one any longer tolerating me but my wife.(p.301)
• Our home is always full of *friends* and visitors.(p.303)
• It took the help, understanding and wonderful companionship that was given so freely to me by my "ex-alkie" *friends*.(p.311)
• I have had my share of problems, heartaches and disappointments, because that is life, but also I have known a great deal of joy, and a peace that is the handmaiden of an inner freedom, I have a wealth of *friends* and, with my A.A. *friends*, an unusual quality of fellowship.(p.312)
• Seldom had any of these lost either health, business, family, or *friends*.(p.315)
• Sergeants, doctors, girl *friends* – everybody seemed to be picking on him.(p.317)
• I noticed that I was avoiding all my social *friends* except for my bridge.(p.324)
• I couldn't keep up with any of my other *friends*, and I wouldn't go to anyone's house unless I knew they drank as heavily as I did.(p.324)
• I never thought I could be useful to anyone except my husband and my children and perhaps a few *friends*.(p.326)
• How hurt I was when editors bounced back my ideas quickly and my best *friends* opined that my output needed a lot of rewriting.(p.331)
• I couldn't do it among my relatives, I couldn't do it among my *friends*.(p.340)
• I lost my driver's license, was made a ward of the court, and was put on probation (not to mention the fact that I might have killed three *friends* and myself).(p.354)
• I'd managed to drink my way through all my *friends*.(p.355)
• These people were my *friends*, and I felt their sincere interest in me.(p.355)
• High living, a great many fair weather *friends*, the 1929 stock market crash, and a couple of years of Depression, soon relieved me one by one of my worldly goods including my wife.(p.358)
• After a few meetings I decided to drive to Florida unannounced to see my wife and tell her about my new found *friends* and association.(p.364)
• We attended meetings together, and mutually enjoyed our new found *friends*.(p.364)
• When I was called upon for a few words I had to tell my *friends* that I wasn't one year old in A.A. that evening but only a "nine month baby."(p.366)
• But success brought increased social activities and I realized that many of my *friends* enjoyed a social drink with no apparent harm to themselves or others.(p.374)
• I made promises to myself, my family and *friends* -- and broke them.(p.375)
• I will never know all the people I hurt, all the *friends* I abused, the humiliation of my family, the worry of my business associates, or how far reaching it was.(p.376)
• We had always encouraged our children to bring their *friends* home at any time, but after a few experiences with a drunken father they eliminated home as a place to entertain *friends*.(p.376)
• Finally our invitations became fewer and fewer as *friends* had more experience with my drinking pattern.(p.377)
• Above all, I am grateful to A.A. for my sobriety, which means so much to my family, *friends* and business associates, because God and A.A. were able to do for me something I was unable to do for myself.(p.383)
• I had *friends*.(p.402)
• But when this happened to me, I declared to *friends* that I would get drunk, dead drunk that very night, and stay drunk for a month.(p.403)
• During these years, I did acquire some good *friends*.(p.404)
• My old *friends* showed distress.(p.404)

• My *friends* were understandably hurt and angry.(p.406)
• Here, also, I had good *friends*, but I became more and more separated from them.(p.406)
• My new *friends* made fun of God and all the orthodox beliefs.(p.408)
• I saw that my Village *friends*, all of whom had small jobs, were living happily on about a tenth of my sinecure.(p.409)
• My new *friends* had a social conscience.(p.410)
• Finally my new *friends* told me, one by one, that I could not come around any more.(p.410)
• She was attractive; she was like the *friends* I had once had.(p.414)
• Years of drinking and general high jinks had cut her off from old *friends*.(p.414)
• Priscilla, an A.A. who, like Marty, has become one of my greatest *friends*, decided that I was a stubborn case.(p.414)
• John and Bud became my *friends*.(p.415)
• All the people involved in these flare-ups took it with remarkable grace, have teased me about it since, and have become good *friends* of mine.(p.416)
• Through going to meetings and listening, and occasionally speaking, through doing Twelve Step work, whereby in helping others you are both the teacher and the student, by making many wonderful A.A. *friends*, I have been taught all the things in life that are worth having.(p.416)
• I have my A.A. *friends*, and I have become reacquainted with my old *friends* on a new basis.(p.416)
• Here was power to live to the end of any given day, power to have the courage to face the next day, power to have *friends*, power to help people, power to be sane, power to stay sober.(p.436)
• With my A.A. *friends*, all I can say is that it's a power greater than myself.(p.437)
• I feel Great Spirit at all meetings and when talk to A.A. *friends*.(p.477)
• No clothes, no money, no home, no real *friends* to speak of, mentally and physically pooped, but I was doing all right!(p.478)
• I'd been home about a week or ten days when one of my *friends* asked if I could repair one of his electrical outlets.(p.493)
• I knew my wife didn't because I had been sincere in all my promises to her as well as to my mother and to my close *friends*, but the urge to take that drink was more powerful than anything else.(p.494)
• His parishioners are limited in number, but his *friends* are many, for to him race, creed, or social position makes no difference.(p.497)
• True, I have recently recovered from pneumonia and have an alibi, but my *friends* are in the war or going, and I am not.(p.499)
• I go to the hospital, where I have made *friends* with the night superintendent.(p.501)
• I get out of the hospital and we visit some of these new-found *friends*.(p.505)
• I stay with understanding *friends*.(p.505)
• I do not fix anyone, but I am getting part of a tremendous education and I have made some new *friends*.(p.506)
• When I had heard about it, it meant nothing but just two letters to me, but some *friends* of mine in the institution were very active in the program and really believed in it.(p.509)
• One evening I decided to go because two of those *friends* were to speak.(p.509)
• I rounded up a few more of my *friends* and off we went to the meeting, not for anything we would gain from it as much as to make a burlesque out of it.(p.509)
• However, my two *friends* kept coaxing and cajoling to get me back again.(p.510)
• He didn't have to lie in wait very long, but fortunately by that time, I had acquired *friends* upstairs and they covered me for quite a time.(p.519)
• When I arrived back in Dublin, I had no *friends* left.(p.522)
• Since I have been in A.A., I have more *friends* than I ever had in my life — *friends* who care about me and my welfare, *friends* who don't care that I am black and that I have been in prison.(p.529)
• Within a month, the police, the hospital authorities, several kind strangers, most of my *friends*, all of my close relatives, and a few adepts at rolling a drunk and removing his wrist watch and wallet had been involved.(p.532)
• Since it was wartime, I explained to the somewhat startled shopkeeper that I had many *friends* in the service whom I was remembering with a watch.(p.532)
• I was down to my shorts, unaware of wrong-doing, before the ambulance got there and hauled me off to a hospital from which anxious *friends* rescued me, later that night.(p.537)
• One by one, the understanding *friends* dropped away.(p.538)
• For by now I had been exposed once to A.A., but I had treated it as a vaudeville and had taken *friends* to meetings so that they too could enjoy the fascination of the naked revelation of suffering and recovery.(p.539)
• Back to the big city, for another year of precarious living, paid for largely by one or two *friends* I still had not milked dry or worn to exhaustion with demands on their bounty.(p.540)
• All of my family and loved ones, all of my *friends*, are nearer and dearer to me than ever before and I have literally dozens of new *friends* who say they cannot believe that a short eight years ago I was ready for the scrap heap.(p.541)
• This caused the rather cryptic comment from one of my A.A. *friends*, when I told my story after coming into the program, that I had always been a cinch for the program, for I had always been interested in mankind, but that I was just taking them one man at a time.(p.548)
• As soon as I had made a few *friends* and had begun to feel accepted, we moved again.(p.555)
• We feel it better to let our *friends* recommend us.(p.567)
• Quite often *friends* of the newcomer are aware of the difference long before he is himself.(p.569)
• Speaking at a dinner given by John D. Rockefeller Jr. to introduce Alcoholics Anonymous to some of his *friends*, Dr. Harry Emerson Fosdick remarked: "I think that psychologically speaking there is a point of advantage in the approach that is being made in this movement that cannot be duplicated.(p.574)
• This is a world clearing house for the Al-Anon Family Groups, composed largely of the wives, husbands and *friends* of A.A. members.(p.575)

friends'
• Finally, I got so lowdown, I was ashamed of my *friends'* seeing me, so I went to the worst joints I could find.(p.527)

friendship
• Offer him *friendship* and fellowship.(p.95)
• But the head of the house has spent years in pulling down the structures of business, romance, *friendship*, health -- these things are now ruined or damaged.(p.123)
• It took me a year, or a year and a half to get to feeling physically well, and it was rather tough, but I soon found folks whose *friendship* I had once had, and I found, after I had been sober for quite some little time, that these people began to act like they had in previous years, before I had gotten so bad, so that I didn't pay too awful much attention to financial gains.(p.190)
• I found a great deal of *friendship* in this movement.(p.516)

friendships
• There are the same fast *friendships*, there is the same helpfulness to one another as you find among our western friends.(p.162)
• I spent most of my time trying to get back these *friendships*, and to make some recompense towards my wife, whom I had hurt a lot.(p.191)
• And over my A.A. years I have made many real, honest, sincere *friendships* that I shall always cherish.(p.296)
• But I have a fortune in *friendships*, courage, self assurance and honest appraisal of my own abilities.(p.296)
• My *friendships* are meaningful, loving and interesting because I am sober.(p.416)

fright
• My *fright* was real enough, but it didn't account for these violent reactions.(p.222)
• I, carried away with the desire to serve A.A., gave what was probably one of the first radio broadcasts about A.A., living through a case of mike *fright* and feeling like a million dollars when it was all over.(p.283)

frightened
• Where had we been selfish, dishonest, self-seeking and *frightened*?(p.67)
• From far away, as if in a delirium, I heard my own voice — calling someone "Dorothy," talking of dress shops, of jobs . . . the words came clearer . . . this sound of my own voice *frightened* me as it came closer . . . and suddenly, there I was, talking of I knew not what, to someone I'd never seen before this very moment.(p.222)
• All I had left was an iron determination to live my own life in spite of the alien world -- and here I was, an inwardly *frightened*, outwardly defiant woman, who desperately needed a prop to keep going.(p.226)
• I, who had never made a speech in my life and who would have been *frightened* sick at the prospect, stood up in front of Rotary groups in different parts of the city and talked about Alcoholics Anonymous.(p.283)
• That *frightened* me terribly.(p.324)
• But Frank was *frightened* to death to give it to me, because I resented everything he said and did.(p.391)
• *Frightened* and shamed, I refused, and sobered up temporarily.(p.411)
• I know I do not have to be "queen of them all" to salve a *frightened* ego.(p.416)
• I was *frightened* -- terribly *frightened*, and in about three days I was sober.(p.467)

frightening
• But out of this *frightening* and at first disrupting experience the conviction grew that A.A.'s had to hang together or die separately.(p.xix)
• It was *frightening* that drink was being substituted for more and more of the things I really enjoyed doing.(p.374)
• Repeated year on end, they are horrible — *frightening* and degrading, a chronicle of tragedy which may be greater because the individual undergoing the tragedy, myself, knew what was happening, and yet refused to do anything to stop it.(p.538)

frightful
• But it was not, for the *frightful* day came when I drank once more.(p.7)
• But this was a man who had experienced many years of *frightful* drinking, who had had most all the drunkard's experiences known to man, but who had been cured by the very means I had been trying to employ, that is to say the spiritual approach.(p.180)

frightfully
• I used to get terribly upset when I saw my friends drink and knew I could not, but I schooled myself to believe that though I once had the same privilege, I had abused it so *frightfully* that it was withdrawn.(p.181)

fringe
• I was always able to skate along the *fringe* of big money.(p.197)
• I never left the church, but I was a *fringe* member, and the thought simply never occurred to me that through the exercise of what I had I might find the answer to my problem, simply because I wouldn't admit that I had a problem.(p.214)

fringes
• After the book appeared we all became very busy in our efforts to save all and sundry, but I was still actually on the *fringes* of A.A.(p.248)

fro
• A couple of hired hands were cleaning out the barn on the farm and I would ride to and *fro* on the sled, and while they were loading I would drink hard cider out of a barrel in the barn.(p.183)

front
• He gets a thrill out of skipping in *front* of fast-moving vehicles.(p.37)
• But the day he comes out he races in *front* of a fire engine, which breaks his back.(p.38)
• I had run into him, and he looked real prosperous; his face and eyes looked clear and he started to compliment me on my good *front* and how well I looked, and I said, "I haven't had a drink for nine months."(p.201)
• Just give me a good *front* and a couple of bucks and I'd be right back in the big time.(p.246)
• It would stop out in *front* of our house, and I still believe those people sent it!(p.265)
• I, who had never made a speech in my life and who would have been frightened sick at the prospect, stood up in *front* of Rotary groups in different parts of the city and talked about Alcoholics Anonymous.(p.283)
• I jimmied the *front* door so that I could get back in, and walked out.(p.288)
• Keeping one foot in *front* of the other is essential for maintaining our arrestment.(p.311)
• I fell down and knocked out my *front* teeth.(p.390)
• With all this, it was becoming increasingly hard to maintain my *front* of distinction and respectability to the world.(p.435)
• Rather, I do whatever is in *front* of me to be done, and I leave the results up to Him; however it turns out, that's God's will for me.(p.452)
• Most had taken shattering losses on nearly every *front* of life.(p.455)
• We pulled up in *front* of my sister's house just as dawn broke.(p.466)
• A wasp is crawling up the back of the lady

in *front* of me.(p.497)
• There was the father one lost respect for at the age of eleven, because the father broke his solemn word in a circumstance where you, eleven years old, had assumed guilt when you were innocent; but the father would not believe you, no matter what; and to ease his suffering you "confessed" and were "forgiven," only – months later – to have your "guilt" brought up – only he and you knew what he was talking bout -- brought up in *front* of the stern grandmother.(p.533)
• Once this was in *front* of the Paramount Theatre in Times Square.(p.537)
• During the day a friend of mine brought me some magazines to take to a hospital group I was interested in, and I looked through them and a "banner" across the *front* of one featured an article by a prominent clergyman in which I caught the word "resentment."(p.552)

frothy
• *Frothy* emotional appeal seldom suffices.(p.xxvi)

frown
• (In fact, every time I saw him he had a *frown* on his face.)(p.370)

frowned
• I couldn't drink at home, because my husband *frowned* upon this.(p.370)

frowning
• One night, a few weeks after joining the Fellowship, much to my surprise and delight I saw a familiar but no longer *frowning* face.(p.371)

froze
• Fear *froze* me in my tracks, but the instant I turned back toward home this paralyzing fear left me.(p.276)
• I had just raised the bottle to my lips when my wife opened the door and *froze* me completely in my tracks with "Happy New Year, dear."(p.365)

fruit
• This determination bore *fruit* in the spring of 1939 by the publication of this volume.(p.xvii)

frustrated
• In the very early spring of 1944, my *frustrated* wife couldn't take it any longer.(p.362)

frustrating
• I have never shown any particular talents nor have I had any really *frustrating* ambitions.(p.240)

frustration
• For years thereafter he was dogged by trouble and *frustration*.(p.56)
• We have had long rendezvous with hurt pride, *frustration*, self-pity, misunderstanding and fear.(p.104)
• Joy at our release from a lifetime of *frustration* knew no bounds.(p.128)
• The greatest enemies of us alcoholics are resentment, jealousy, envy, *frustration*, and fear.(p.145)
• Momentarily we did – then would come oblivion and the awful awakening to face the hideous Four Horsemen -- Terror, Bewilderment, *Frustration*, Despair.(p.151)
• Because of this state of confusion and *frustration* I had hysterics on the seventeenth day for the first and only time in my life.(p.387)
• Having passed over the border line, the next five years were filled with fear, failure and *frustration*.(p.465)

frustrations
• I don't remember much of what he said, but I did realize that here was another guy exactly like me; he had been in the same laughing academies and the same jails, known the same loss of jobs, same *frustrations*, same boredom and the same loneliness.(p.239)
• When I encountered disappointments or *frustrations* -- as I did more and more frequently -- my solution was to drink.(p.556)

fulfilled
• They are being *fulfilled* among us – sometimes quickly, sometimes slowly.(p.84)

fulfillment
• As I look back on the events of two months, I can clearly see that I had been circling around, half-afraid of encountering the remedy for my situation, half wanting it, deferring *fulfillment* of my promise to get in touch with the doctor I had heard about.(p.258)
• A "good boy" reached adulthood and success without achieving maturity or *fulfillment*.(p.418)
• So it was that in alcohol I found *fulfillment*.(p.537)
• A.A. has given me serenity of purpose, the opportunity to be of service to God and to the people about me, and I am serene in the infallibility of these principles that provide the *fulfillment* of my purpose.(p.551)

full
• The mushrooming process was in *full* swing.(p.xviii)
• This was the substance of A.A.'s Twelve Traditions, which are stated in *full* on page 564 of this book.(p.xix)
• It did not satisfy us to be told that we could not control our drinking just because we were maladjusted to life, that we were in *full* flight from reality, or were outright mental defectives.(p.xxiv)
• A tumbler *full* of gin followed by half a dozen bottles of beer would be required if I were to eat any breakfast.(p.5)
• I wondered whether I dared hide a *full* bottle of gin near the head of our bed.(p.8)
• Perhaps there never will be a *full* answer to these questions.(p.22)
• It may be worth a bad case of jitters if you get a *full* knowledge of your condition.(p.32)
• "Suddenly the thought crossed my mind that if I were to put an ounce of whiskey in my milk it couldn't hurt me on a *full* stomach.(p.36)
• I vaguely sensed I was not being any too smart, but felt reassured as I was taking the whiskey on a *full* stomach.(p.36)
• Only thirty years later the conquest of the air was almost an old story and airplane travel was in *full* swing.(p.52)
• We were having trouble with personal relationships, we couldn't control our emotional natures, we were a prey to misery and depression, we couldn't make a living, we had a feeling of uselessness, we were *full* of fear, we were unhappy, we couldn't seem to be of real help to other people – was not a basic solution of these bedevilments more important than whether we should see newsreels of lunar flight?(p.52)
• If your talk has been sane, quiet and *full* of human understanding, you have perhaps made a friend.(p.94)
• This world is *full* of people like him.(p.109)
• It is possible to have a *full* and useful life, though your husband continues to drink.(p.111)
• To return to the subject matter of this book: It contains *full* suggestions by which the employee may solve his problem.(p.143)
• You will learn the *full* meaning of "Love thy neighbor as thyself."(p.153)
• So I filled the cellar *full*, with the permission of my good wife.(p.177)
• I did not have a high school education so I went to night school to take the *full* high school course, which I finished in two years and nine months.(p.211)
• There had been some occasions -- there was an automobile wreck, for instance -- when I had police escort home but not to jail, all of which, instead of doing me a favor, did me harm because I was then *full* of self-esteem as to the progress I had made both professionally and financially.(p.213)
• I was willful, *full* of will to do the things I wanted to do and to get the things that I wanted to have.(p.214)
• With a great deal of determination, I would throw out *full* pints – pour them out and smash the bottles -- firmly resolved never to take another drink of the stuff.(p.234)
• The girl was *full* of enthusiasm and she made the trip to Akron too.(p.295)
• Our home is always *full* of friends and visitors.(p.303)
• The drinker's mind is *full* of uncertainties and insecurities.(p.331)
• There was an upper cupboard *full* of empties.(p.333)
• How *full* it has kept my retirement years -- the five I've lived since the first two lost in traveling a rocky road to hell, before I made a U-turn.(p.334)
• He was *full* of his new found life of happiness and sobriety.(p.365)
• Resenting anyone and everyone who might interfere with my personal plans and ways of doing things, I was *full* of self pity, especially for any interference with my drinking.(p.376)
• Emma ran out to the kitchen and came back with a water glass *full* of bourbon and made me drink it down.(p.385)
• So I went down to him quite a few times a month and had him shoot me *full* of the stuff; and then I went across the street to a little drug store to take a glass of beer or two beers, and then stopped at the liquor store to get myself a pint and go home.(p.389)
• I was *full* of careless chatter.(p.402)
• I did not know that I had no power over alcohol, that I, alone and unaided, could not stop; that I was on a downgrade, tearing along at *full* speed with all my brakes gone, and that the end would be a total smash-up, death or insanity.(p.408)
• The apartment was charming; the shelves were *full* of books, many of which I myself owned.(p.413)
• If my personality is inadequate, antisocial, or *full* of kinks and I alter it with alcohol or any chemical, bingo!(p.458)
• We reverted to the old way of life we knew -- a life *full* of anger, vindictiveness, resentment, fear, dependence, denial, self-will, irresponsibility.(p.459)
• Each ten-day period in the dark hole, I was fed bread and water daily, with one *full* meal on the third day only.(p.459)
• If so, A.A. *full* of Indians.(p.477)
• Then I would go home *full* of remorse, and wonder what I was going to do until I got my next check.(p.527)

full-blown
• My mother was eighty-nine years old when she died, and I was a *full-blown* alcoholic at the time of her death.(p.210)
• Much later, when I had progressed to *full-blown* alcoholism, people told me I should quit.(p.554)

full-pack
• My four years of abstinence had something to do with it, but soldiering is a tough enough game for a sober man, and I had no yen for *full-pack* slogging through mud with a cognac or vin rouge hangover.(p.253)

full-time
• It took five years of A.A. living, and a substantial improvement in my health, before I could take a *full-time* office job where someone else was boss.(p.283)
• The small group may elect its secretary, the large group its rotating committee, and the groups of a large metropolitan area their central or intergroup committee, which often employs a *full-time* secretary.(p.567)

fuller
• Inevitably your lives will be *fuller* for doing so.(p.120)
• That was the beginning of a new life, a *fuller* life, a happier life than I had ever known or believed possible.(p.228)

fullest
• Doing our best, living each day to the *fullest* is the art of living.(p.382)

fully
• My schoolmate visited me, and I *fully* acquainted him with my problems and deficiencies.(p.13)
• These were revolutionary and drastic proposals, but the moment I *fully* accepted them, the effect was electric.(p.14)
• When this sort of thinking is *fully* established in an individual with alcoholic tendencies, he has probably placed himself beyond human aid, and unless locked up, may die or go permanently insane.(p.24)
• Our hope is that many alcoholic men and women, desperately in need, will see these pages, and we believe that it is only by *fully* disclosing ourselves and our problems that they will be persuaded to say, "Yes, I am one of them too; I must have this thing."(p.29)
• We learned that we had to *fully* concede to our innermost selves that we were alcoholics.(p.30)
• Some of you are thinking: "Yes, what you tell us is true, but it doesn't *fully* apply.(p.38)
• We found that as soon as we were able to lay aside prejudice and express even a willingness to believe in a Power greater than ourselves, we commenced to get results, even though it was impossible for any of us to *fully* define or comprehend that Power, which is God.(p.46)
• Some of us once had great self-confidence, but it didn't *fully* solve the fear problem, or any other.(p.68)
• It is important that he be able to keep a confidence; that he *fully* understand and approve what we are driving at; that he will not try to change our plan.(p.74)
• There may be some wrongs we can never *fully* right.(p.83)
• The wife should *fully* understand his new way of life.(p.99)
• Had we *fully* understood the nature of the alcoholic illness, we might have behaved differently.(p.107)
• Though the family does not *fully* agree with dad's spiritual activities, they should let him have his head.(p.129)
• It is better for him to feel *fully* responsible.(p.143)
• Painfully aware of being somehow abnormal, the man did not *fully* realize what it meant to be alcoholic.(p.155)
• Many mornings I have gone to classes, and even though *fully* prepared, would turn and walk back to the fraternity house because of my jitters, not daring to enter the classroom for fear of making a scene

should I be called on for recitation.(p.173)
• Each of the seven times that I had left this hospital in the last six months, I had come out *fully* determined in my own mind that I would not get drunk again -- for at least six or eight months.(p.184)
• I'd waked up in strange rooms before, *fully* dressed on a bed or a couch; I'd waked up in my own room, in or on my own bed, not knowing what hour or day it was, afraid to ask . . . but this was different.(p.222)
• I have stopped tilting at windmills, and instead have tried to accomplish the little daily tasks, unimportant in themselves, but tasks that are an integral part of living *fully*.(p.295)
• Now, however, I accepted it *fully*.(p.436)
• I stayed there just long enough to work up a real good resentment against the doctor in charge, who I didn't think was doing anything at all except collecting fees, and I left there *fully* determined that I'd never put myself in the power of medical people again.(p.521)
• Seven -- Every A.A. group ought to be *fully* self-supporting, declining outside contributions.(p.564)
• 7. -- The A.A. groups themselves ought to be *fully* supported by the voluntary contributions of their own members.(p.566)

Fulton

• In the fall of 1939, *Fulton* Oursler, then editor of Liberty, printed a piece in his magazine, called "Alcoholics and God."(p.xviii)

fumed

• And as I *fumed* helplessly and planned to get good and drunk and show them, my eye caught a sentence in the book lying open on my bed: "We cannot live with anger."(p.228)

fumes

• My childhood was shrouded in the *fumes* of alcohol.(p.369)

fun

• It was *fun* to carom around the exclusive course which had inspired such awe in me as a lad.(p.4)
• There is, however, a vast amount of *fun* about it all.(p.16)
• Up to this point you would label him as a foolish chap having queer ideas of *fun*.(p.37)
• If newcomers could see no joy or *fun* in our existence, they wouldn't want it.(p.132)
• I did it more and more, and had lots of *fun* without much grief, either physical or financial.(p.172)
• So it is clear that I never had any *fun* out of drinking -- I would be the soberest-seeming one in the crowd and all of a sudden I would be the drunkest.(p.241)
• I remember feeling that they were all making *fun* of me.(p.261)
• In the next two or three days the balance of this handful of men contacted me, encouraged me, and told me how they were trying to live this program of recovery and the *fun* they were having doing it.(p.291)
• I had a lot of *fun* drinking.(p.346)
• It was *fun* at first, since I never had indulged before.(p.370)
• My new friends made *fun* of God and all the orthodox beliefs.(p.408)
• Her idea of *fun* on a bender was to hit sailors and insult cops.(p.414)
• Life, including some ups and downs, is a lot of *fun*.(p.417)
• After the first two or three days you were allowed the run of the place and it was a lot of *fun*.(p.468)
• I won't go into detail about that, but I can assure you it's no *fun*.(p.469)
• I like the boys and we have lots of *fun*, in class and out.(p.500)

function

• As we discovered the principles by which the individual alcoholic could live, so we had to evolve principles by which the A.A. groups and A.A. as a whole could survive and *function* effectively.(p.xix)
• Our next *function* is to grow in understanding and effectiveness.(p.84)
• Had anyone undertaken to explain to me what the A.A. movement was, what its real *function* was, I probably would have been set back several years and I doubt if I would have survived at all.(p.216)
• We old-timers who get scattered and separated and then witness the construction of services to get in more people and to make this thing *function*, we think that A.A. has changed, but the root of it hasn't.(p.272)
• The "12 Traditions" of Alcoholics Anonymous are, we A.A.'s believe, the best answers that our experience has yet given to those ever urgent questions, "How can A.A. best *function*?" and, "How can A.A. best stay whole and so survive?"(p.563)
• Dr. Harry M. Tiebout, psychiatrist: "As a psychiatrist, I have thought a great deal about the relationship of my specialty to A.A. and I have come to the conclusion that our particular *function* can very often lie in preparing the way for the patient to accept any sort of treatment or outside help.(p.571)

functioning

• Show him, from your own experience, how the queer mental condition surrounding that first drink prevents normal *functioning* of the will power.(p.92)

functions

• Even those don't take part in A.A. *functions* as I would like to see them do.(p.529)

fund

• I had a tiny trust *fund*, and I moved into a small apartment where I learned to cook, keep house, and do the things that normal people do.(p.409)
• I could not live on that tiny trust *fund* and still drink all I wanted to.(p.411)

fundamental

• Actually we were fooling ourselves, for deep down in every man, woman, and child, is the *fundamental* idea of God.(p.55)

fundamentally

• We doubt if, in this respect, alcoholics are *fundamentally* much worse than other people.(p.81)

fundamentals

• Then you and your husband can get right down to *fundamentals*.(p.120)

funds

• My idea was to have all the companies pool their *funds* and buy rubber when rubber was cheap and then put it in a pool.(p.198)
• I stayed sober during the trip except for an occasional bottle of beer because *funds* barely met expenses.(p.255)
• As usual, I ran out of money, and, as usual, I wired my father for *funds* to come home.(p.357)
• Making amends is sometimes doing what we are capable of doing but failed to do because of alcohol; carrying out community responsibilities such as Community *Funds*, Red Cross, educational and religious activities in proportion to our abilities and energy.(p.381)
• I wore a man's raincoat, turned inside out, a present from a friend, for now my *funds* were low.(p.411)
• Still, I had had *funds* sufficient to get plastered because that, of course, was more important than paying my own way.(p.538)
• We think that each group should soon achieve this ideal; that any public solicitation of *funds* using the name of Alcoholics Anonymous is highly dangerous, whether by groups, clubs, hospitals, or other outside agencies; that acceptance of large gifts from any source, or of contributions carrying any obligation whatever, is unwise.(p.566)
• Then too, we view with much concern those A.A. treasuries which continue, beyond prudent reserves, to accumulate *funds* for no stated A.A. purpose.(p.566)

funeral

• You didn't carry a little orchid up the aisle in those days; you carried a great big bouquet, like a *funeral* spray, and you didn't have your picture taken until just before you went to the church.(p.385)
• My visits to that sanitarium went on for nearly three years, until in March of 1944, my father died and I was too drunk to attend his *funeral*.(p.469)
• Of course, when father finally came to Virginia to work his way through school, he resented the southern "cracker," as he often called them, so much that he didn't even go back to his mother's *funeral*.(p.486)

funerals

• At this school we had Bible readings before each meal, and church services four times on Sunday, and I became so rebellious at this that I swore I would never join or go to any church except for weddings or *funerals*.(p.240)
• We lived just a few doors from the First Baptist Church and when they had *funerals* I remember very often asking my mother whether the person was good or bad and whether they were going to heaven or hell.(p.483)

funniest

• Ribaldry was the substance of the conversation, and I set out to be the *funniest* and most ribald of them all.(p.407)

funny

• Now and then the family will be plagued by spectres from the past, for the drinking career of almost every alcoholic has been marked by escapades, *funny*, humiliating, shameful or tragic.(p.123)
• I know that one of the outfits I had was a skirt and a very *funny* looking blouse that my mother had picked up at a rummage sale.(p.261)
• (This was *funny*.(p.267)
• I have told you some of the *funny* things, but not much of the shame and degradation.(p.390)
• They said I was so *funny*, and told me, with shrieks of laughter, what I'd done the night before.(p.407)
• He did come, and I landed in the *funny* farm for a while.(p.479)

fur

• I used to put eight or twelve ounce bottles of alcohol in a *fur* lined glove and toss it onto the back airing porch when winter days got dark enough.(p.176)
• I loved my father dearly and I adored my dog, and I'd gotten this new house and Frank had just given me a new *fur* coat and I was thrilled to death.(p.389)
• Anne and I went up in ski clothes and *fur* coats, and it was so cold we slept in them.(p.415)
• It came out that I had sold a woman a *fur* coat.(p.528)

furious

• She was *furious*.(p.79)
• I knew this, and right away I got *furious* and would not even talk to the doctor in the place.(p.387)

furnish

• I never enjoyed any meal, but I ate my lunch at noon for two reasons; first, to help me get out of the fog of the night before and, second, to *furnish* some measure of nourishment.(p.299)

furnished

• I was in a large, dark, rather poorly *furnished* room -- the living room of a basement flat.(p.222)

furniture

• A drunk may smash the *furniture* in your home, or burn a mattress.(p.97)
• First, my new wife had walked out, bag, baggage and *furniture*; then the apartment landlord had thrown me out of the empty apartment and the finish was the loss of another job.(p.238)
• After my last binge I came home and smashed my dining room *furniture* to splinters, kicked out six windows and two balustrades.(p.435)

further

• For them, we hope these pages will prove so convincing that no *further* authentication will be necessary.(p.xiii)
• Some of the recommendations of A.A.'s early medical and religious friends will be found *further* on in this book.(p.xx)
• Most of us feel we need look no *further* for Utopia.(p.16)
• *Further* on, clear-cut directions are given showing how we recovered.(p.29)
• Many of us thought it necessary to go much *further*.(p.72)
• More than that we cannot do; we have no right to go *further*.(p.81)
• But we must go *further* and that means more action.(p.85)
• Unless your friend wants to talk *further* about himself, do not wear out your welcome.(p.95)
• Three: This husband has gone much *further* than husband number two.(p.109)
• If there is no Al-Anon listing in your local telephone book, you may obtain *further* information on Al-Anon Family Groups by writing to its World Service Office: Box 182, Madison Square Station, New York, NY 10159.(p.121)
• Instead of treating the family as he should, he may retreat *further* into himself and feel he has spiritual justification for so doing.(p.129)
• He will have no *further* reason for covering up an alcoholic employee.(p.148)
• Where preaching and prayers had touched me very little, I immediately desired *further* knowledge of these men.(p.235)
• And he *further* said that God could not accept me as a sincere follower of His Divine Law unless I was ready to be thoroughly honest about it.(p.236)
• He *further* explained that alcohol was no respecter of sex or background, but that most of the alcoholics he had encountered had better than average minds and abilities.(p.308)
• And we wonder how much *further* this man could go if his alcoholic problem could be removed and he could throw one hundred per cent of his abilities into action.(p.308)
• The unwillingness to admit failure requires even *further* friendly intake.(p.331)
• Two nights later, self-pity went even *further*.(p.333)
• At the other side of the table sat one of the carpen-

ters in our community, and at the ***further*** end of the table sat the man who ran the bakery, while on one side sat my friend who was a mechanic.(p.347)
• It was I who had to tell the bank, after a certain time, to refuse all ***further*** deposits.(p.409)
• Weeks would go by without ***further*** trouble, and I'd be assured I'd at last hit on the right formula.(p.433)
• If pressed ***further***, all I can do is follow the psalmist who said it long, long before me: "Be still, and know that I am God."(p.437)
• Forgive me -- I cannot write ***further*** about this latest turn of events, anticipating seeing the family I deserted so long ago.(p.463)

furthermore

• ***Furthermore***, I knew that I was looked upon as a city slicker from New York, and I had to be pretty cautious among small town, conservative Yankees.(p.360)

fuss

• They want him to make a ***fuss*** over them.(p.126)
• So I raised enough ***fuss*** that they finally agreed to let me sign out, against medical advice.(p.444)

futile

• As animals on a treadmill, we have patiently and wearily climbed, falling back in exhaustion after each ***futile*** effort to reach solid ground.(p.107)
• This would lessen my chances of smuggling some home that evening, which in turn would mean a night of ***futile*** tossing around in bed followed by a morning of unbearable jitters.(p.176)
• How ***futile***!(p.332)
• Experience has often warned us that nothing can so surely destroy our spiritual heritage as ***futile*** disputes over property, money, and authority.(p.566)

futility

• His coming was an oasis in the dreary desert of ***futility***.(p.9)
• But we saw that it really worked in others, and we had come to believe in the hopelessness and ***futility*** of life as we had been living it.(p.25)
• Once confused and baffled by the seeming ***futility*** of existence they show the underlying reasons why they were making heavy going of life.(p.50)
• It is plain that a life which includes deep resentment leads only to ***futility*** and unhappiness.(p.66)
• We have begun to comprehend their ***futility*** and their fatality.(p.70)
• It has shown me, through the tragic stories of so many other alcoholics, the utter ***futility*** of self pity.(p.525)
• Had I been able to explain to a psychiatrist the feeling of ***futility***, loneliness and lack of purpose that had come with my deep sense of personal failure at this second divorce, I seriously doubt that the good doctor could have convinced me that my basic problem was a spiritual hunger, but A.A. has shown me this was the truth.(p.546)

future

• Many of our friends encourage us by saying that this is but a beginning, only the augury of a much larger ***future*** ahead.(p.xv)
• Following his physical rehabilitation, he had a talk with me in which he frankly stated he thought the treatment a waste of effort, unless I could assure him, which no one ever had, that in the ***future*** he would have the "will power" to resist the impulse to drink.(p.xxix)
• We turned back to the list, for it held the key to the ***future***.(p.66)
• In this way we tried to shape a sane and sound ideal for our ***future*** sex life.(p.69)
• We may kill a ***future*** opportunity to carry a beneficial message.(p.77)
• He told her what he would try to do in the ***future***.(p.79)
• After all, your family is reunited, alcohol is no longer a problem and you and your husband are working together toward an undreamed-of ***future***.(p.119)
• The family may be possessed by the idea that ***future*** happiness can be based only upon forgetfulness of the past.(p.123)
• High and low, rich and poor, these are ***future*** fellows of Alcoholics Anonymous.(p.152)
• Perhaps the best way of treating you to a glimpse of your ***future*** will be to describe the growth of the fellowship among us.(p.153)
• Two days later, a ***future*** fellow of Alcoholics Anonymous stared glassily at the strangers beside his bed.(p.157)
• Said the ***future*** Fellow Anonymous: "Damn little to laugh about that I can see."(p.157)
• I can remember occasions when friends recommended me for positions or business opportunities that I wouldn't take because I felt that at some ***future*** date I'd get drunk and they would be hurt.(p.198)
• They are far more alert and progressive than we floundering fathers were, and the ***future*** of our fellowship is in their hands.(p.250)
• I thanked him, pleaded business engagements and promised I'd go with him at some ***future*** date.(p.257)
• That life for me is lived one day at a time, letting the problems of the ***future*** rest with the ***future***.(p.340)
• Always we'd emerge with a new formula for avoiding ***future*** trouble.(p.433)
• For me, it was a little different because I couldn't help thinking about the past, and I saw the ***future*** more or less mirrored in the past.(p.513)
• We cast off the burdens of the past and the anxieties of the ***future***, as we begin to live in the present, one day at a time.(p.560)

futures

• A lot of lost dreams, empty ***futures***, and crazy things of the past went through my mind.(p.333)

fuzzy

• Two ***fuzzy*** objects came into focus.(p.422)

Gg

gadget
• Is not our age characterized by the ease with which we discard old ideas for new, by the complete readiness with which we throw away the theory or ***gadget*** which does not work for something new which does?(p.52)
• During these seven years a thing called the Twenty-four Hour Program —a ***gadget*** I used to think was only a snare to trap the newcomer — has come to mean much to me, not only as regards my drinking but in the whole pattern of my life.(p.473)

gage
• I could no longer ***gage*** my capacity and it might be the second or the tenth drink that would erase my consciousness.(p.306)

gaiety
• Prior to our marriage, when she was a shy, scrawny adolescent, I was able to see things in her that others couldn't necessarily see — things like beauty, charm, ***gaiety***, a gift for being easy to talk to, a sense of humor, and many other fine qualities.(p.450)

gain
• We will lose interest in selfish things and ***gain*** interest in our fellows.(p.84)
• Ten days of this treatment the first time knocked me from 200 pounds to 130, and I seldom stayed out of the hole long enough to ***gain*** back my weight.(p.460)
• I really do believe it is much harder for a woman to ***gain*** back her self-respect than it is for a man.(p.480)
• I rounded up a few more of my friends and off we went to the meeting, not for anything we would ***gain*** from it as much as to make a burlesque out of it.(p.509)
• Since I've been home, I have been able to ***gain*** the respect of my two sons again.(p.529)

gained
• Every one of them has ***gained*** access to, and believes in, a Power greater than himself.(p.50)
• As a draftsman, I worked for several large companies and ***gained*** a variety of experience.(p.211)
• In fact, after six months of living on food instead of on whiskey, I ***gained*** about thirty pounds.(p.220)
• I could not expect to keep what I had ***gained*** unless I gave it away.(p.282)
• Do I have to tell you who ***gained*** the most out of all this?(p.283)
• Above all, I have ***gained*** the greatest thing accorded to any man, the love and understanding of a gracious God, who has lifted me from the alcoholic scrap-heap to a position of trust where I have been able to reap the rich rewards that come from showing a little love for others and from serving them as I can.(p.296)
• From a physical standpoint, I ***gained*** sixteen pounds in the first two months I was off liquor.(p.303)
• However, what I had ***gained*** materially on the credit side of my ledger, I have since learned was more than offset on the debit side by egotism, resentment and dishonesty.(p.356)
• As I progressed and ***gained*** in capacity, I had blackouts.(p.512)

gains
• It took me a year, or a year and a half to get to feeling physically well, and it was rather tough, but I soon found folks whose friendship I had once had, and I found, after I had been sober for quite some little time, that these people began to act like they had in previous years, before I had gotten so bad, so that I didn't pay too awful much attention to financial ***gains***.(p.190)

Galileo
• Others came near putting ***Galileo*** to death for his astronomical heresies.(p.51)

gallantly
• She met these responsibilities ***gallantly***.(p.130)

galled
• Very often we rode to and from work together, but being separated really ***galled*** me deep down.(p.491)
• I think the thing that ***galled*** me was that just after Easter I had drawn my salary for two weeks' work and had decided that I was going to send some money to Vi; and above all else I was going to send my baby daughter an Easter outfit.(p.493)

gallon
• I went over and bought a jug of hard cider and a ***gallon*** of wine that I gave these fellows to drink.(p.195)
• My wife became pregnant and the doctor recommended the use of port or ale . . . so . . . I bought a six ***gallon*** crock and a few bottles, listened to advice from amateur brewmeisters, and was off on my beer manufacturing career on a small scale (for the time being).(p.297)
• From that point on, I secured crocks of ten ***gallon*** capacity and really took quite an active interest in the manufacture of home brew.(p.297)
• We buy a ***gallon*** of "corn" because it is so cheap.(p.500)

gallons
• Eventually, of course, what with all the hilarity that could be provoked with a few ***gallons*** of beer, there seemed to be no need of bridge or poker playing for entertainment.(p.297)

galore
• Many of us had moral and philosophical convictions ***galore***, but we could not live up to them even though we would have liked to.(p.62)
• With these we have had experience ***galore***.(p.126)
• So our fellow worker will soon have friends ***galore***.(p.163)

gambler
• To wear expensive clothes, to have bartenders know what to serve me before I ordered, to be recognized by headwaiters and shown to the best table, to play gin rummy for high stakes with the insouciance of a riverboat ***gambler*** -- these were the enduring values in life, I thought.(p.556)

game
• There is the obsession that somehow, someday, they will beat the ***game***.(p.23)
• When he sees you know all about the drinking ***game***, commence to describe yourself as an alcoholic.(p.91)
• He will presently try the old ***game*** again, for he isn't happy about his sobriety.(p.152)
• If you still think you are strong enough to beat the ***game*** alone, that is your affair.(p.181)
• Eventually, there would be a ball ***game***, or a show, or some sort of special occasion to celebrate and I would turn up drunk.(p.196)
• We had played this ***game*** before.(p.238)
• My four years of abstinence had something to do with it, but soldiering is a tough enough ***game*** for a sober man, and I had no yen for full-pack slogging through mud with a cognac or vin rouge hang-over.(p.253)
• I have stood listening to street-corner preachers tell how they beat the ***game***.(p.256)
• Three months later, he hated the ***game*** and found solace in the bottle.(p.330)
• If anyone had told me I would be enjoying a hockey ***game*** with my husband and my brother without being all boozed up, I would not have believed it.(p.481)
• The ***game*** is over and the other three leave.(p.502)
• I was up to international standards in one particular ***game***, and that again covered quite a lot of my sins.(p.519)
• I have come to realize that the name of the ***game*** is not so much to stop drinking as to stay sober.(p.559)

games
• There I sat in the evenings, enjoying with my friends our memories of the "old country," singing the old songs we all knew, playing simple card ***games*** for drinks and consuming great quantities of beer.(p.231)
• The other kids would light out for the hamburger huts or ice cream parlors, the pizza joints or bowling alleys, after football ***games*** and dances.(p.423)
• I liked ***games***.(p.517)
• I was still very fit and good at ***games***.(p.519)
• I was still very good at ***games***.(p.519)

gamut
• Most of us did not stay out of prison long enough to run the alcoholic ***gamut*** -- to develop the ongoing kind of alcoholism or alcoholic drinking you hear about in A.A. talks.(p.458)

gang's
• The grand fellow who at my call made me a hail-fellow-well-met, who gave me such a fine voice, as we sang "Hail, hail, the ***gang's*** all here," and "Sweet Adeline," who gave me freedom from fear and feelings of inferiority.(p.498)

gangster's
• I felt like a ***gangster's*** moll about to be interviewed by the Salvation Army.(p.413)

gap
• Of course, the more I drank, the more unrealistic my expectations became and the poorer my performance, and the ***gap*** widened.(p.557)

garage
• I entered the house, opened a new bottle of whiskey and sat down to drink myself into the right frame of mind to get in my car, start the motor and close the ***garage*** door behind me.(p.363)
• I didn't feel I could lie in bed and squirt the stuff in my veins while my kids and wife stood around watching me, so I kept the drug in my bag and the bag in the car and the car in the ***garage***.(p.442)
• Luckily, the ***garage*** was attached to the house.(p.442)
• In the ***garage***, I would put the needle in my vein and then try to figure out exactly how much medication to inject to overcome the pep pills while adding to the sleeping pills while ignoring the tranquilizers, in order to get just enough to be able to pull out the needle, jerk the tourniquet, throw it in the car, slam the car door shut, run down the hall, and fall in bed before I fell asleep.(p.442)
• I fix up a little apartment over the ***garage*** with books and drinking water.(p.506)
• Still another friend and temporary host received me at four in the morning from the charge of a policeman who had found me "going to bed" in a ***garage*** far from the last place I could remember having been, a fashionable bar and restaurant in the theatrical district of New York, to which I had repaired after my date for that evening, a charming lady of the theatre who had refused my company for obvious reasons.(p.538)

garages
• I had no need to hide in closets, bathrooms, or ***garages***.(p.332)

garbage
• One morning when I was feeling really bad, I was put on K.P. and the head cook wanted me to go out and scrub the ***garbage*** cans.(p.317)
• Aside from being a common drunk, I had a very serious pill affliction and all the ***garbage*** that goes with it -- lying, stealing, cheating anybody and everybody, conning the people I could, and staying clear of the ones I couldn't.(p.478)
• Similarly, we rid ourselves of guilt and remorse as we "clean out the ***garbage***" from our minds through the Fourth and Fifth Steps of our recovery program.(p.560)

garden
• When I reached a point directly back of our house, where I could have cut through a friend's ***garden***, I was almost overpowered by the desire to get home, but I made the whole journey.(p.276)
• I planted my first flower ***garden*** this year and am actually excited to see the results.(p.481)
• It was my "secret ***garden***" — bluntly, it was my retreat from life, and I didn't want to give it up.(p.534)

gardening
• If someone had told me last year that I would be excited about ***gardening*** this year, I would have said he was off his rocker.(p.481)

garrison
• When I came home to ordinary ***garrison*** life in England, I found that I was drinking rather more than most people of may age.(p.518)

gas
• The next three years I spent in Boston, Chicago, and Montreal in the employ of a large manufacturing concern, selling railway supplies, ***gas*** engines of all sorts, and many other items of heavy hardware.(p.172)
• I got a job after school pumping ***gas*** and worked until ten or eleven at night.(p.423)

gasped
• She ***gasped***.(p.333)

gastric
• He had but partially recovered from a ***gastric*** hemorrhage and seemed to be a case of pathological mental deterioration.(p.xxix)
• I soon discovered that a couple of drinks would alleviate my ***gastric*** distress, at least for a few hours at a time, so it was not at all difficult for me to return to my former excessive indulgence.(p.174)

gate
- The boys at the Post Office used to bring me my jugs; mail couldn't be opened for inspection at the *gate*.(p.426)

gates
- They believe in themselves, and still more in the Power which pulls chronic alcoholics back from the *gates* of death.(p.xxv)
- Our friend felt as though the *gates* of hell had closed on him with a clang.(p.27)
- Many pursue it into the *gates* of insanity or death.(p.30)
- But after I passed through the *gates* I took a change of heart and mind.(p.510)

gather
- Starting from a speck on the domestic horizon, great thunderclouds of dispute may *gather*.(p.117)
- I would *gather* up all my soiled clothes, as much as I could cram into a grocery cart, and be off.(p.370)

gathered
- Wherever men are *gathered* together in business there will be rivalries and, arising out of these, a certain amount of office politics.(p.145)
- In the chapter "Working With Others" you *gathered* an idea of how we approach and aid others to health.(p.153)
- As he talked I *gathered* vaguely, (because he was a faltering beginner then, just as I am now) that to be relieved of alcoholism I would have to be different.(p.257)
- I just *gathered* up this and that alcoholic, because, in the back of my mind, I wanted to save all the world.(p.496)
- Any two or three alcoholics *gathered* together for sobriety may call themselves an A.A. group, provided that, as a group, they have no other affiliation.(p.565)

gathering
- Then, *gathering* all his forces, he attempted to stop altogether and found he could not.(p.32)
- He entered a political campaign, making speeches, frequenting men's *gathering* places of all sorts, often staying up all night.(p.158)
- Seeing much of each other, scarce an evening passed that someone's home did not shelter a little *gathering* of men and women, happy in their release, and constantly thinking how they might present their discovery to some newcomer.(p.159)
- To go into a *gathering* of people was the sort of thing that all my life, from the time I left my private world of books and dreams to meet the real world of people and parties and jobs, had left me feeling an uncomfortable outsider, needing the warming stimulus of drinks to join in.(p.228)
- I was *gathering* that cache for disposal when my wife woke up and caught me at it.(p.333)

gatherings
- At these informal *gatherings* one may often see from 50 to 200 persons.(p.16)
- But life among Alcoholics Anonymous is more than attending *gatherings* and visiting hospitals.(p.161)

gaunt
- Like a *gaunt* prospector, belt drawn in over the last ounce of food, our pick struck gold.(p.128)

gave
- But when the broker *gave* him Dr. Silkworth's description of alcoholism and its hopelessness, the physician began to pursue the spiritual remedy for his malady with a willingness he had never before been able to muster.(p.xvi)
- In the spring of 1940, John D. Rockefeller, Jr. *gave* a dinner for many of his friends to which he invited A.A. members to tell their stories.(p.xviii)
- A well-known doctor, chief physician at a nationally prominent hospital specializing in alcoholic and drug addiction, *gave* Alcoholics Anonymous this letter:(p.xxiii)
- The physician who at our request, *gave* us this letter, has been kind enough to enlarge upon his views in another statement which follows.(p.xxiv)
- We *gave* up our positions and off we roared on a motorcycle, the sidecar stuffed with tent, blankets, a change of clothes, and three huge volumes of a financial reference service.(p.2)
- We never *gave* the spiritual side of life a fair hearing.(p.50)
- Under these conditions we can employ our mental faculties with assurance, for after all God *gave* us brains to use.(p.86)
- Mother made all the plans and *gave* the directions.(p.131)
- On the third day the lawyer *gave* his life to the care and direction of his Creator, and said he was perfectly willing to do anything necessary.(p.158)
- To 1950, the year of his death, he carried the A.A. message to more than 5,000 alcoholic men and women, and to all these he *gave* his medical services without thought of charge.(p.171)
- After many painful discussions, they finally *gave* me my credits and I migrated to another of the leading universities of the country and entered as a Junior that fall.(p.173)
- I *gave* the matter much time and study for the next two and a half years, but still got tight every night nevertheless.(p.178)
- He came and got me home and to bed, *gave* me a few drinks that night, and one bottle of beer the next morning.(p.179)
- He *gave* me information about the subject of alcoholism which was undoubtedly helpful.(p.180)
- And this, as I said, certainly *gave* me a lot of confidence, seemed to take a lot of the burden off me.(p.190)
- I went over and bought a jug of hard cider and a gallon of wine that I *gave* these fellows to drink.(p.195)
- On that statement and the fact that I had been sober for ninety days, he *gave* me a job selling lots in an allotment he had.(p.200)
- I went downstairs and there was the grizzly old veteran police officer in charge of the property desk, and as he *gave* me the stuff, he asked, "Are you going out in the street that way?"(p.204)
- Paul measured the medicine out, but he figured that with my track record that little bit wouldn't be enough, so he doubled it and added a few drops more and then *gave* it to me.(p.207)
- She *gave* no sign of recognizing anything wrong, but what had I been doing for those lost five hours?(p.223)
- It no longer *gave* me pleasure -- it merely dulled the pain -- but I had to have it.(p.226)
- That was the point at which my doctor *gave* me the book "Alcoholics Anonymous" to read.(p.227)
- My wife wrote away for advertised cures for the liquor habit and *gave* them to me in coffee.(p.235)
- That day I *gave* my will to God and asked to be directed.(p.237)
- During that first week-end I decided to stay in New York and take all they *gave* out with, except the "God stuff."(p.246)
- Then I found that as I *gave* in to this spiritual or personality change I was getting a little more serenity.(p.249)
- Federal Theatre in Texas *gave* me an administrative job which I held for a year, only because I worked hard and productively when I worked, and because my very tolerant chief ascribed my frequent lapses to a bohemian temperament.(p.256)
- He *gave* my husband one and me one about ten-thirty on the eighth day of May in 1941.(p.267)
- I told our family doctor, an understanding man who *gave* hours of his time trying to help me, about this experience.(p.276)
- I could not expect to keep what I had gained unless I *gave* it away.(p.282)
- This *gave* me the freedom to do A.A. work, and to rest for periods of two or three days when I became too exhausted to carry on.(p.283)
- I, carried away with the desire to serve A.A., *gave* what was probably one of the first radio broadcasts about A.A., living through a case of mike fright and feeling like a million dollars when it was all over.(p.283)
- But this day my doctor *gave* it to me straight and said, "People like you are pretty well known to the medical profession.(p.307)
- Far from expecting praise for their deeds, they claimed the performance a privilege and insisted that they invariably received more than they *gave*.(p.310)
- I started to take A.A. seriously, and A.A. *gave* me a new way of life.(p.320)
- My writing career was described in the couplet "Alcohol *gave* me wings to fly,/And then it took away the sky."(p.331)
- Since I *gave* my will over to A.A., whatever A.A. has wanted of me I've tried to do to the best of my ability.(p.340)
- I eventually became a schoolmaster, but *gave* up that profession to join the Indian Army.(p.342)
- Then I saw an A.A. advertisement in a newspaper, and I wrote to the address it *gave*.(p.343)
- This friend *gave* me a pamphlet, and I took it home and had my wife read it to me.(p.346)
- And I *gave* him some idea of what you do, and so I made my first Twelfth Step call before I ever came into the program.(p.347)
- I *gave* them everything, except the greatest thing in the world, and that is peace of mind.(p.351)
- My first meeting *gave* me a great deal of hope and lots of willing ears for my tale of woe and for my questions.(p.364)
- I attended my weekly meetings with regularity, reread the Big Book, attended other group meetings, *gave* leads when asked to and did some Twelve Step work whenever I was called upon to do so.(p.365)
- I tried psychiatry, but of course I *gave* the psychiatrist no co-operation.(p.375)
- Anyhow, after Christmas my husband *gave* me a cocker spaniel who is, I think, just as notorious in A.A. as I am.(p.388)
- A drink never *gave* me a normal, pleasant glow.(p.402)
- The bartender, a tough Irishman, came around and "*gave* me the elbow," which means that he raised his elbow and smacked me in the face.(p.411)
- My husband helped me into the house, packed himself a bag, and *gave* me some money.(p.467)
- Also, after that first visit I learned I could refuse to sign myself in unless they *gave* me a glass of whiskey in one hand and a glass of paraldehyde in the other.(p.468)
- She *gave* me such hope and inspiration that I set her right up on a pedestal.(p.472)
- He *gave* me many drinks from bottle.(p.474)
- You know the prescription that you *gave* me for my wife last night."(p.488)
- I took that bottle of medicine and *gave* it to a very good friend of mine who was a pharmacist and had it analyzed, and the bottle was perfectly all right.(p.489)
- I sometimes *gave* it to my mother and then I'd go back and hound her for it.(p.491)
- I knew I wasn't capable of keeping the bulk of the money myself, so I *gave* it to a white fellow who owned the bar which I frequented.(p.493)
- And, not only that, but they *gave* us financial help.(p.496)
- The grand fellow who at my call made me a hail-fellow-well-met, who *gave* me such a fine voice, as we sang "Hail, hail, the gang's all here," and "Sweet Adeline," who *gave* me freedom from fear and feelings of inferiority.(p.498)
- I went to a dinner he *gave* one night, rather drunk.(p.520)
- I buttonholed him after dinner and *gave* him a few tips on how to run his colony better and the result of that was about a fortnight or so later I was shipped back to my regiment.(p.520)
- That *gave* me my first bit of hope.(p.524)
- I got out on bail right away, but when I went to trial, the judge *gave* me thirty days.(p.528)
- Because I had been drunk, the judge *gave* me only a twelve-year sentence in prison.(p.528)
- I fled, finally, after having been fired from my job by a boss who wept a little (since I had worked hard) as he *gave* notice for me to clear out.(p.539)
- After my very first drink -- a tiny glass of sherry my father *gave* me to celebrate the New Year when I was thirteen -- I went up to bed, dizzy with exhilaration and excitement, and I prayed I wouldn't drink any more!(p.554)
- My employer *gave* me one warning, then another.(p.558)
- All these things and many, many more, A.A. *gave* me.(p.559)
- Yet it is true that our first printing *gave* many readers the impression that these personality changes, or religious experiences, must be in the nature of sudden and spectacular upheavals.(p.569)

gay
- If not irritable, he may seem dull and boring, not *gay* and affectionate as the family would like him to be.(p.126)
- He could see the *gay* crowd inside.(p.154)
- Music and *gay* chatter still floated to him from the bar.(p.154)
- He succumbed to that *gay* crowd inside, who laughed at their own misfortunes and understood his.(p.160)
- The times in which I grew up (the Prohibition era immortalized by Scott Fitzgerald and John Held Jr.) had taught me to be *gay* with the gayest; my own inner urges led me to outdo them all.(p.225)
- I moved in a *gay* crowd in the various "pubs" and sporting clubs.(p.251)
- I tried them mixed, unmixed, drinking only when *gay*, only when depressed.(p.305)
- I had met a bunch of *gay* young Bohemians who lived in the Village, and were sowing their wild oats.(p.407)
- Pearl Harbor was a breeze of nine months, a *gay* Hawaiian paradise, drinking under the palms, listening to the surf beat on the shore, a bottle of

whiskey near at hand.(p.426)

gayest

• The times in which I grew up (the Prohibition era immortalized by Scott Fitzgerald and John Held Jr.) had taught me to be gay with the *gayest;* my own inner urges led me to outdo them all.(p.225)

gaze

• I blinked slowly as I shifted my *gaze* to my arms.(p.422)

• I *gaze* at the board with its questions.(p.499)

Gene

• It is painful to grow, and without the help of my "civilian" A.A. companion, big *Gene,* I might not have survived that critical year of adjustment.(p.462)

general

• Then Jack Alexander wrote a feature article in the Saturday Evening Post and placed such a compelling picture of A.A. before the *general* public that alcoholics in need of help really deluged us.(p.xviii)

• Much has been written pro and con, but among physicians, the *general* opinion seems to be that most chronic alcoholics are doomed.(p.xxviii)

• One of these men, staff member of a world-renowned hospital, recently made this statement to some of us: "What you say about the *general* hopelessness of the average alcoholic's plight is, in my opinion, correct.(p.43)

• Our stories disclose in a *general* way what we used to be like, what happened, and what we are like now.(p.58)

• Although these reparations take innumerable forms, there are some *general* principles which we find guiding.(p.79)

• If she knows in a *general* way that we have been wild, should we tell her in detail?(p.81)

• At first engage in *general* conversation.(p.91)

• We are dealing only with *general* principles common to most denominations.(p.94)

• Though it is entirely separate from Alcoholics Anonymous, it uses the *general* principles of the A.A. program as a guide for husbands, wives, relatives, friends, and others close to alcoholics.(p.121)

• The *general* moral standard was, as I recall it, far above the average.(p.171)

• I was doing very well with that and *general* upholstering work, and there was every indication that I would be financially independent by the time I reached middle age.(p.232)

• I was eased out of the business I had founded and was reduced to doing *general* upholstery in a small shop at the back of my house.(p.233)

• Many things happened; business trials, little worries, and feelings of *general* despondency came near driving me to the bottle, but I made progress.(p.237)

• That night for the first time in my life I really let down my hair and admitted my *general* loneliness.(p.239)

• The *general* procedure was to take four or five shots in the first place I stopped at.(p.299)

• The encouragement received in the early days, especially from the A.A. *General* Service Office, made a tremendous difference to my sobriety.(p.342)

• It was the A.A. *General* Service Office in New York that I wrote to, and that office has always meant a lot to me.(p.392)

• Incalculable are the intangible initiation fees that A.A. members have paid: the sick, sick hangovers, the remorse, guilt, broken homes, jails, and institutions, and the mental anguish in *general* that has been generated over the years.(p.399)

• I was out of step with life, with my family, with people in *general.*(p.400)

• Years of drinking and *general* high jinks had cut her off from old friends.(p.414)

• I knew from my *general* reading that alcoholism was irreversible and fatal.(p.436)

• When we first come into A.A., many of us are confused because as a *general* rule we're at the end of our respective ropes, and we don't know what to do.(p.512)

• At that very time, he was a nonalcoholic trustee on the *General* Service Board of Alcoholics Anonymous!(p.559)

• On the next page, A.A.'s "12 Traditions" are seen in their so-called "short form," the form in *general* use today.(p.563)

• And no group, regional committee, or individual should ever take any action that might greatly affect A.A. as a whole without conferring with the trustees of the *General* Service Board.(p.565)

• The trustees of the *General* Service Board are, in effect, our A.A. *General* Service Committee.(p.567)

• They are the custodians of our A.A. Tradition and the receivers of voluntary A.A. contributions by which we maintain our A.A. *General* Service Office at New York.(p.567)

• 11. – Our relations with the *general* public should be characterized by personal anonymity.(p.567)

• Dr. John F. Stouffer, Chief Psychiatrist, Philadelphia *General* Hospital, citing his experience with A.A., said: "The alcoholics we get here at Philadelphia *General* are mostly those who cannot afford private treatment, and A.A. is by far the greatest thing we have been able to offer them.(p.572)

• The *General* Service Board of A.A. (the trustees) administers A.A.'s *General* Service Office, A.A. World Services, Inc., and our monthly magazine, the A.A. Grapevine.(p.575)

generally

• But the ex-problem drinker who has found this solution, who is properly armed with facts about himself, can *generally* win the entire confidence of another alcoholic in a few hours.(p.18)

• But these scrapes can *generally* be charged, no matter how bad, to the abnormal action of alcohol on his mind.(p.140)

• The psychiatrist, who had *generally* been ignoring me, now became quite interested; every day, he would ask me all kinds of questions about the A.A. meetings.(p.446)

generalship

• Good *generalship* may decide that the problem be attacked on the flank rather than risk a face-to-face combat.(p.82)

generated

• Incalculable are the intangible initiation fees that A.A. members have paid: the sick, sick hangovers, the remorse, guilt, broken homes, jails, and institutions, and the mental anguish in general that has been *generated* over the years.(p.399)

generation

• But in most fields our *generation* has witnessed complete liberation of our thinking.(p.52)

• The story is not very different from that of thousands of other young men in my *generation.*(p.373)

• UNTO THE SECOND *GENERATION*(p.422)

• Lots of the older people had taken to drinking quite a good deal more during the war, but the younger *generation* was, I think, about the same.(p.518)

• In my own *generation* I stuck out, I can see that now, as being a very much heavier drinker than the average man.(p.518)

• Alas for us men toward whom Shaw hurled his cry, "Must a Christ be crucified in every *generation* for the benefit of those who have no imagination?"(p.536)

generations

• For three *generations,* my family had had a charge account in one of the big New York hotels.(p.410)

generous

• But drinking caught up with me again and my *generous* friend had to let me go.(p.4)

• He may be kind, considerate, patient, *generous;* even modest and self-sacrificing.(p.61)

• There are so many to whom I feel deeply grateful; to my husband (and best critic), whose *generous* love, compassion and understanding have helped me along the way; to those before me in A.A. who inspired the first article I read, and the friend who sent that article to Frank; to Ruth for her personal note, and the first A.A. to talk to me; to my Bishop, whose loving and believing spirit inspired me; and to all the members of the Houston Group who were so patient, kind and helpful -- and to countless others.(p.393)

generously

• I was to share *generously* in the profits.(p.5)

• That age of the flapper and the "It" girl, speakeasies and the hip flask, the boyish bob and the drugstore cowboy, John Held Jr. and F. Scott Fitzgerald, all *generously* sprinkled with a patent pseudo-sophistication.(p.304)

Geneva

• At a large party in *Geneva,* with people from many countries represented, the kind of party that is "protocol" in the extreme, I swayed, laughed hysterically, made naughty remarks in an unhushed voice, and was finally led from the scene.(p.406)

genius

• We had long talks when I would still her foreboding by telling her that men of *genius* conceived their best projects when drunk; that the most majestic constructions of philosophic thought were so derived.(p.2)

• He has a positive *genius* for getting tight at exactly the wrong moment, particularly when some important decision must be made or engagement kept.(p.21)

• Or: If I'm really a *genius,* I must produce a great work, to show why I act like a *genius.*(p.408)

• Actually, of course, I wanted someone to listen to me, because when I had a few martinis inside, I became the great author I longed to be; and the right listener was in for some pretty highflown theories of literature and of *genius.*(p.536)

• If he were still sober, chances are that very quickly I put him down as a Philistine with no appreciation of literary *genius;* and then I went on to another bar to find a new victim.(p.537)

gentle

• This good and *gentle* man, a brilliant research doctor, got nowhere with me fast.(p.407)

gentleman

• "Why don't you drink like a *gentleman* or quit?"(p.20)

• If anyone who is showing inability to control his drinking can do the right-about-face and drink like a *gentleman,* our hats are off to him.(p.31)

• We, who have collectively seen a great deal of business life, at least from the alcoholic angle, had to smile at this *gentleman's* sincere opinion.(p.149)

• HE THOUGHT HE COULD DRINK LIKE A *GENTLEMAN*(p.210)

• I could not see why I couldn't drink like a *gentleman,* and that was my primary ambition -- until I landed in A.A.(p.214)

• The successful demonstration I had made of my life problems in other respects convinced me that some day I was going to be able to drink like a *gentleman.*(p.214)

• I don't know what sort of person I was expecting, but I was very agreeably surprised to find Mr. T. a poised, intelligent, well groomed and mannered *gentleman.*(p.309)

• Maine newsletter (Boomerang) say: "With tireless devotion and humility, this venerable Indian *gentleman* traveled thousands of miles humbly pleading for sobriety.(p.476)

• I'd drink like a *gentleman* after this.(p.498)

gentleman's

• We, who have collectively seen a great deal of business life, at least from the alcoholic angle, had to smile at this *gentleman's* sincere opinion.(p.149)

gentlemen

• But he discovered that there are some *gentlemen* who can't drink.(p.210)

gently

• He said to me, *gently* and simply, "Do you think that you are one of us?"(p.413)

• A.A. led me *gently* from this fantasizing to embrace reality with open arms.(p.561)

genuine

• The very practical approach to his problems, the absence of intolerance of any kind, the informality, the *genuine* democracy, the uncanny understanding which these people had were irresistible.(p.160)

• I had a *genuine* release right from the start.(p.219)

• There was the love affair which was ridiculous -- "imagine that midget being able to fall in love!" -- and my head knew it while my heart pumped real, *genuine* anguish, for it hurt like hell, and since it was first love, things have never been quite the same.(p.534)

• We think, therefore, that any considerable property of *genuine* use to A.A. should be separately incorporated and managed, thus dividing the material from the spiritual.(p.565)

• It reminds us that we are to place principles before personalities; that we are actually to practice a *genuine* humility.(p.568)

geographical

• A return to the United States proved effective as a *geographical* cure, and a period of sobriety ensued, with the help of the church.(p.419)

geography

• So I decided I'd go back and live in Ireland to try the *geography* cure.(p.522)

George

• Fortunately, I didn't say a word to *George* on the way home.(p.322)

• And when I looked at it, I knew I was just as much a drunk as *George* was, if not worse.(p.322)

• I nudged *George* next morning, and I said, "I'm in," and he said, "Oh, I knew you'd make it."(p.322)

• *George* tried many times to go on the wagon.(p.324)

• It didn't bother me any more whether *George* was drinking or not.(p.324)

• I used to make excuses to try and get *George* off the wagon.(p.325)

• I would end it all, and then, by *George,* she'd be sorry!(p.363)

• I reach for the bottle which I just got from *George,* the elevator boy.(p.500)

German

• I was born in Europe, in Alsace to be exact, shortly after it had become *German*, and practically grew up with the "good Rhine wine" of song and story.(p.230)

• Military service was compulsory and I did my stretch with the class of my age, goose-stepping in *German* barracks and taking part in the Boxer Rebellion in China, my first time at any great distance from home.(p.230)

• Fond of singing, I joined a *German* singing society which had good club headquarters.(p.231)

• I went out and drank some *German* wine and it went to my head.(p.517)

Germans

• For weeks after my arrival I was feted and entertained in the already large colony of Alsatians in the city, and among the *Germans* in their saloons and clubs.(p.231)

Germany

• When I got back to *Germany* I settled down to finish my apprenticeship, drinking the wine of the country as usual.(p.231)

• I got orders to go to *Germany*, and everyone in *Germany* was against me.(p.318)

• Then I had a year in *Germany* at school -- that was, incidentally, when I got drunk for the first time.(p.517)

• When the war was over, we had about a year in *Germany*, occupying the place.(p.518)

• Then I went over again to *Germany* for four years on an occupation job.(p.519)

get

• News of this got on the world wires; inquiries poured in again and many people went to the bookstores to *get* the book "Alcoholics Anonymous."(p.xviii)

• As the whisky rose to my head I told myself I would manage better next time, but I might as well *get* good and drunk then.(p.6)

• If your are an alcoholic who wants to *get* over it, you may already be asking -- "What do I have to do?"(p.20)

• How often have some of us begun to drink in this nonchalant way, and after the third or fourth, pounded on the bar and said to ourselves, "For God's sake, how did I ever *get* started again?"(p.24)

• Over any considerable period we *get* worse, never better.(p.30)

• It may be worth a bad case of jitters if you *get* a full knowledge of your condition.(p.32)

• He was ambitious to succeed in business, but saw that he would *get* nowhere if he drank at all.(p.32)

• But try and *get* them to see it!(p.34)

• I just thought I would *get* a sandwich.(p.36)

• In some circumstances we have gone out deliberately to *get* drunk, feeling ourselves justified by nervousness, anger, worry, depression, jealousy or the like.(p.37)

• He tries every known means to *get* the jay-walking idea out of his head.(p.38)

• We found that as soon as we were able to lay aside prejudice and express even a willingness to believe in a Power greater than ourselves, we commenced to *get* results, even though it was impossible for any of us to fully define or comprehend that Power, which is God.(p.46)

• If you have decided you want what we have and are willing to go to any length to *get* it -- then you are ready to take certain steps.(p.58)

• And do not his actions make each of them wish to retaliate, snatching all they can *get* out of the show?(p.61)

• So we had to *get* down to causes and conditions.(p.64)

• One object is to disclose damaged or unsalable goods, to *get* rid of them promptly and without regret.(p.64)

• Brown may *get* my job at the office.(p.65)

• It's so easy to *get* way off the track.(p.68)

• Does this mean we are going to *get* drunk?(p.70)

• We have been trying to *get* a new attitude, a new relationship with our Creator, and to discover the obstacle in our path.(p.72)

• Simply we tell him that we will never *get* over drinking until we have done our utmost to straighten out the past.(p.77)

• *Get* an idea of his behavior, his problems, his background, the seriousness of his condition, and his religious leanings.(p.90)

• You will thus *get* a better idea of how you ought to proceed.(p.91)

• *Get* him to tell some of his.(p.91)

• Tell him that if he wants to *get* well you will do anything to help.(p.95)

• For the type of alcoholic who is able and willing to *get* well, little charity, in the ordinary sense of the word, is needed or wanted.(p.97)

• Burn the idea into the consciousness of every man that he can *get* well regardless of anyone.(p.98)

• If there be divorce or separation, there should be no undue haste for the couple to *get* together.(p.99)

• We have seen men *get* well whose families have not returned at all.(p.100)

• Do not think of what you will *get* out of the occasion.(p.102)

• Don't let him *get* away with it.(p.108)

• But after his next binge, ask him if he would really like to *get* over drinking for good.(p.112)

• Some men cannot or will not *get* over alcoholism.(p.114)

• If you are satisfied he really wants to *get* over drinking, you need not be alarmed.(p.120)

• Then you and your husband can *get* right down to fundamentals.(p.120)

• But the wise family will admire him for what he is trying to be, rather than for what he is trying to *get*.(p.123)

• He may either plunge into a frantic attempt to *get* on his feet in business, or he may be so enthralled by his new life that he talks or thinks of little else.(p.125)

• He is not likely to *get* far in any direction if he fails to show unselfishness and love under his own roof.(p.127)

• He may tell mother, who has been religious all her life, that she doesn't know what it's all about, and that she had better *get* his brand of spirituality while there is yet time.(p.128)

• Of an evening, you can go on a mild bender, *get* up in the morning, shake your head and go to business.(p.139)

• Say that you believe he is a gravely ill person, with this qualification -- being perhaps fatally ill, does he want to *get* well?(p.142)

• Will he take every necessary step, submit to anything to *get* well, to stop drinking forever?(p.142)

• If he says yes, does he really mean it, or down inside does he think he is fooling you, and that after rest and treatment he will be able to *get* away with a few drinks now and then?(p.142)

• Either you are dealing with a man who can and will *get* well or you are not.(p.142)

• To *get* over drinking will require a transformation of thought and attitude.(p.143)

• They often jeopardize their own positions by trying to help serious drinkers who should have been fired long ago, or else given an opportunity to *get* well.(p.147)

• You put me on the spot every time you *get* drunk.(p.147)

• The firm wants to help you *get* over it, and if you are interested, there is a way out.(p.147)

• Inwardly he would give anything to take half a dozen drinks and *get* away with them.(p.152)

• I know I must *get* along without liquor, but how can I?(p.152)

• But what about his responsibilities -- his family and the men who would die because they would not know how to *get* well, ah -- yes, those other alcoholics?(p.154)

• Some of them may sink and perhaps never *get* up, but if our experience is a criterion, more than half of those approached will become fellows of Alcoholics Anonymous.(p.163)

• There my drinking became so much worse that the boys in the fraternity house where I lived felt forced to send for my father, who made a long journey in the vain endeavor to *get* me straightened around.(p.174)

• Consequently, I could not *get* into any trouble.(p.174)

• After three years of this, I wound up in the local hospital where they attempted to help me, but I would *get* my friends to smuggle me a quart, or I would steal the alcohol about the building, so that I got rapidly worse.(p.175)

• Finally my father had to send a doctor out from my home town who managed to *get* me back there in some way, and I was in bed about two months before I could venture out of the house.(p.175)

• If my wife was planning to go out in the afternoon, I would *get* a large supply of liquor and smuggle it home and hide it in the coal bin, the clothes chute, over door jambs, over beams in the cellar and in cracks in the cellar tile.(p.176)

• My bootlegger had hidden alcohol at the back steps where I could *get* it at my convenience.(p.176)

• We could not be invited out because I would surely *get* tight and my wife dared not invite people in for the same reason.(p.177)

• My phobia for sleeplessness demanded that I *get* drunk every night, but in order to *get* more liquor for the next night, I had to stay sober during the day, at least up to four o'clock.(p.177)

• I got tight that night, stayed sober Monday till after the dinner and then proceeded to *get* tight again.(p.179)

• These good people notified my wife, who sent my newly made friend over to *get* me.(p.179)

• Unlike most of our crowd, I did not *get* over my craving for liquor much during the first two and one-half years of abstinence.(p.181)

• I used to *get* terribly upset when I saw my friends drink and knew I could not, but I schooled myself to believe that though I once had the same privilege, I had abused it so frightfully that it was withdrawn.(p.181)

• I would reach over and *get* this and take a shot and in a few moments *get* up and take another, shave and eat my breakfast, slip a half pint of liquor in my hip pocket, and go on to school.(p.183)

• Then Prohibition came into effect, and the facts that the stuff obtainable was so horrible and sometimes deadly, and that I had married and had a job which I had to look after, helped me for a period of some three or four years, although I would *get* drunk every time I could *get* hold of enough to drink to *get* started.(p.183)

• Away from my office two or three weeks at a time; horrible days and nights when I would lie on the floor of my home, lying awake and reaching over to *get* the bottle, taking a drink and going back into oblivion.(p.184)

• Each of the seven times that I had left this hospital in the last six months, I had come out fully determined in my own mind that I would not *get* drunk again -- for at least six or eight months.(p.184)

• I had no trouble there because I had never actually ceased to believe in God, and had tried lots of times to *get* help but hadn't succeeded.(p.186)

• So, after reviewing these things and realizing what liquor had cost me, I went to this Higher Power which, to me was God, without any reservation, and admitted that I was completely powerless over alcohol, and that I was willing to do anything in the world to *get* rid of the problem.(p.187)

• Each day I would try to find out what His will was, and try to follow that, rather than trying to *get* Him to always agree that the things I thought of myself were the things best for me.(p.187)

• I said, "Yes, Doc, I would like to quit, at least for five, six, or eight months, until I *get* things straightened up, and begin to *get* the respect of my wife and some other people back, and *get* my finances fixed up and so on."(p.187)

• Two days before this, Dr. Bob had said to me, "If you and I are going to stay sober, we had better *get* busy."(p.188)

• We're going to *get* up and *get* out of here."(p.189)

• Don't you believe you are going to have all you can do to *get* rid of that?"(p.190)

• It took me a year, or a year and a half to *get* to feeling physically well, and it was rather tough, but I soon found folks whose friendship I had once had, and I found, after I had been sober for quite some little time, that these people began to act like they had in previous years, before I had gotten so bad, so that I didn't pay too awful much attention to financial gains.(p.190)

• I spent most of my time trying to *get* back these friendships, and to make some recompense towards my wife, whom I had hurt a lot.(p.191)

• Of course, as time went on, and I began to *get* my health back and began to be so I didn't have to hide from people all the time, it's just been wonderful.(p.192)

• I'm so grateful for both the program and the people in it that I still want to go, and then probably the most wonderful thing that I learned from the program -- I've seen this in the 'A.A. Grapevine' a lot of times, and I've had people say it to me personally, and I've heard people *get* up in meetings and make the same statement: The statement is, "I came into A.A. solely for the purpose of sobriety, but it has been through A.A. that I have found God."(p.192)

• When he was uptown -- we were living in the little town of Moscow -- I went up to try to *get* some money from him to buy groceries.(p.193)

• I went into the high school grades, but having missed all the intermediate grades, I didn't *get* along too well, so I developed the habit of going back to school just long enough for the football season and then quitting.(p.193)

• (I might say right here that never in my life did I ever intend to *get* drunk.(p.196)

• I never had any desire to *get* drunk.(p.196)

• I could *get* through an evening with just a

couple of snorts.(p.196)
• I found, however, that when I would leave Akron to go to Chicago, I would ***get*** drunk.(p.197)
• I can well remember over a long period of years when I thought I was the only person in the world who knew that sooner or later I was going to ***get*** drunk.(p.198)
• I can remember occasions when friends recommended me for positions or business opportunities that I wouldn't take because I felt that at some future date I'd ***get*** drunk and they would be hurt.(p.198)
• I didn't want to ***get*** into fights, but I did ***get*** into fights.(p.199)
• Another time, I had gone around to Max R. trying to ***get*** a job driving one of his trucks.(p.200)
• At three-thirty the next morning, I was in Champlain Street Station, in jail for driving while intoxicated and insulting an officer; and the suit of which I was so proud was in such shape that the turnkey had to ***get*** me a pair of trousers to go into court in the next morning.(p.201)
• Whenever this man and I met — I didn't know his name then nor do I know it now — we would always ***get*** drunk.(p.201)
• I could take one drink and ***get*** right back on the wagon.(p.202)
• I told somebody that I was going down to ***get*** Christian Science and they took me down, but I don't remember saying that.(p.202)
• Then I got into the habit of having beers, and decided that a drink of whiskey was not any worse; so I would ***get*** the one drink of whiskey but, on second thought, I decided that as long as I was only going to have one, I might as well make it a double-header.(p.203)
• I think the longest drunk I was ever on was eleven days, but usually only two days with a complete blackout for a day, and then backing off by drinking as long as I could ***get*** anything.(p.203)
• To show you the point to which this obsession went, there came an occasion when I had spent a most delightful week-end, and at nine o'clock on Sunday night I was on my way home, and I thought I would ***get*** a drink.(p.204)
• I looked so terrible in the court that the judge suggested that I ***get*** a continuance and let me sign all the papers to go to a hospital and to a doctor.(p.204)
• We drove to a store in North Hill and I sent him in with what money I had to ***get*** a quart.(p.204)
• My only thought that day was getting a drink, and how to ***get*** rid of those clowns was my big problem.(p.206)
• A few minutes later, Dr. Bob left, leaving with my brother some medicine I should ***get***.(p.207)
• I seemed to react by developing a streak of varying meanness, which would cause me to do things to create excitement and to ***get*** attention.(p.211)
• I went back to law school, and doubled up on the courses because I was then approaching thirty years of age and I wanted to ***get*** through as quickly as possible.(p.212)
• I was willful, full of will to do the things I wanted to do and to ***get*** the things that I wanted to have.(p.214)
• My wife didn't tell me this, but one Sunday afternoon when Mary was trying to ***get*** the cobwebs out of my mind, Clarence and his sister-in-law, the hairdresser, called at the house.(p.216)
• I must ***get*** out of here.(p.223)
• In any case I must ***get*** out of here before I let slip my abysmal ignorance of how I came to be here, and she realized that I was stark, staring mad.(p.223)
• It took three-quarters of an hour and two changes to ***get*** there -- back to my starting point.(p.223)
• I remembered my loud resolution to find him and ask him to help me ***get*** into that "Asylum" he had written about.(p.224)
• As the treatment progressed I began to ***get*** a picture of myself, of the temperament that had caused me so much trouble.(p.226)
• I had to persist in my attempts to ***get*** straightened out enough to be able to use the drinks I needed, without their turning on me.(p.227)
• And as I fumed helplessly and planned to ***get*** good and drunk and show them, my eye caught a sentence in the book lying open on my bed: "We cannot live with anger."(p.228)
• I ***get*** my greatest thrill of accomplishment from the knowledge that I have played a part in the new happiness achieved by countless others like myself.(p.229)
• Having regard for the law of the land, I resigned myself to the will of the national legislators and quit drinking altogether, not because I had found it harmful, but because I couldn't ***get*** what I was accustomed to drink.(p.232)
• My wife upbraided me often and plenty when she saw that my "periodics" were gradually losing me what business I could ***get***.(p.233)
• My visitor well knew, that as I tried to follow God I would ***get*** to studying these things out for myself.(p.236)
• As I go along I seem to ***get*** strength daily to be able to resist more easily.(p.237)
• And when I ***get*** upset, cross-grained and out of tune with my fellow man I know that I am out of tune with God.(p.237)
• Searching where I have been at fault, it is not hard to discover and ***get*** right again, for I have proven to myself and to many others who know me that God can keep a man sober if he will let Him.(p.237)
• People have wars and kill each other; they struggle and cut each other's throats for success and what does anyone ***get*** out of it?(p.244)
• What do I ***get*** out of it?(p.245)
• I had completely forgotten the January 8th when I found the fellowship, and I spent the next four days wandering around New England half drunk, by which I mean I couldn't ***get*** drunk and I couldn't ***get*** sober.(p.247)
• My wife made several attempts to ***get*** me to stop and I had the usual visits from persons who would always ask me "Why?" -- as if I knew!(p.254)
• I arrived drunk, but I promised my wife I would keep sober, and I knew I could ***get*** work if I did.(p.256)
• As I look back on the events of two months, I can clearly see that I had been circling around, half-afraid of encountering the remedy for my situation, half wanting it, deferring fulfillment of my promise to ***get*** in touch with the doctor I had heard about.(p.258)
• As soon as I could ***get*** up and walk I started to drink again and kept it up until my friend of the hospital, who, in his first try at the new way of life had stubbed his toe in Chicago but had come back to the town to take counsel and make a new start, picked me up and got me into a hospital.(p.258)
• I did not need to be told that my efforts were and would be unavailing if I did not ***get*** help.(p.258)
• Indeed, I was beginning to see that I would require implicit faith, like a small child, if I was going to ***get*** anywhere.(p.259)
• I'll ***get*** you the password, and I can find out where they meet because I know a guy that belongs.(p.266)
• We had meetings at each other's homes and, of course, that was a grand place for people to ***get*** together out there; they seemed to think so too.(p.270)
• We old-timers who ***get*** scattered and separated and then witness the construction of services to ***get*** in more people and to make this thing function, we think that A.A. has changed, but the root of it hasn't.(p.272)
• I would ***get*** in the biggest dither about something.(p.273)
• I didn't think I was going to ***get*** drunk right then, but I remember how comforting it was when I called Anne and told her.(p.273)
• If it isn't anything that's going to help you or anybody else, why should you become involved in it, and ***get*** all disturbed about it?"(p.273)
• When I reached a point directly back of our house, where I could have cut through a friend's garden, I was almost overpowered by the desire to ***get*** home, but I made the whole journey.(p.276)
• How could I ***get*** it?(p.279)
• I wanted "ripe" prospects and I didn't feel that I would ***get*** very far chasing individual drunks in and out of bars.(p.281)
• I landed him and shipped him by train to Akron, with a pint of whiskey in his pocket to keep him from wanting to ***get*** off the train in Toledo!(p.282)
• I am very apt to ***get*** into quite an uproar for a day or two before starting, but I do start, and once started, I have a swell time.(p.285)
• Once dad came all the way to Florida to sober me up, after a hotel manager called him and said that if he wanted to see me alive he better ***get*** there fast.(p.288)
• They went into a huddle and dad explained that he simply took my pants, shoes and money away, so that I could ***get*** no liquor and had to sober up.(p.288)
• I jimmied the front door so that I could ***get*** back in, and walked out.(p.288)
• I could not wait to tell him that I wanted help, that if these men in Akron had anything I wanted it, and would do anything to ***get*** it.(p.289)
• He was happy, getting a kick out of life and people, and beginning to ***get*** his medical practice back again.(p.290)
• One of them was that I would try to ***get*** a group started in Chicago; the second was that I would have to return to Akron to attend meetings at least every two months until I did ***get*** a group started in Chicago; third, I decided I must place this program above everything else, even my family, because if I did not maintain my sobriety I would lose my family anyway.(p.292)
• Their answer was always the same: If they should need it at any time they would surely ***get*** in touch with me.(p.293)
• On my trips back to Akron to ***get*** my spirits recharged and to work with other alcoholics, I would ask Dr. Bob about this delay and wonder just what was wrong with me.(p.293)
• So I set out to ***get*** drunk deliberately, just to teach her what she was missing.(p.293)
• A week later, I had to ***get*** an old friend from Akron to spend two days sobering me up.(p.293)
• That was my lesson, that one could not take the moral inventory and then file it away; that the alcoholic has to continue to take inventory every day if he expects to ***get*** well and stay well.(p.293)
• This would ***get*** me feeling fit, and then I would start for home and fireside, thirteen miles away.(p.299)
• I never enjoyed any meal, but I ate my lunch at noon for two reasons; first, to help me ***get*** out of the fog of the night before and, second, to furnish some measure of nourishment.(p.299)
• I didn't care to go visiting unless the parties we might visit had plenty of liquor on hand and I could ***get*** drunk.(p.301)
• I am anxious to ***get*** home after dark.(p.303)
• From a monetary standpoint . . . in the past few years, I have reduced my reckless debts to almost nothing, and have had money to ***get*** along on comfortably.(p.303)
• I would hang on to sobriety for short intervals, but always there would come the tide of an overpowering necessity to drink and, as I was engulfed in it, I felt such a sense of panic that I really believed I would die if I didn't ***get*** that drink inside.(p.306)
• But how does one ***get*** a prescription for a miracle?(p.306)
• Some of us struggle with these people because we know that they are really very sick, but we also know that short of some miracle, we are not going to help them except temporarily, and that they will inevitably ***get*** worse and worse until one of two things happens.(p.308)
• I began taking drinks in the morning to ***get*** started.(p.318)
• I'd show them -- I'd ***get*** drunker!(p.319)
• I had to ***get*** a drink, and then another drink, and then . . .(p.319)
• I also found out that all they wanted was to help me ***get*** sober and to stay sober themselves.(p.320)
• I was afraid, and I had made my mind up that I would never ***get*** drunk, so I was watchful and careful.(p.322)
• Even so, every time I drank, I seemed to ***get*** in trouble.(p.322)
• I lied like a trooper to ***get*** out of many scrapes.(p.324)
• Sometimes I would lie on the bathroom floor, deathly sick, praying I would die, and praying to God as I always had prayed to Him when I was drinking: "Dear God, ***get*** me out of this one and I'll never do it again."(p.324)
• I used to make excuses to try and ***get*** George off the wagon.(p.325)
• I'd ***get*** so fed up with drinking all alone and bearing the burden of guilt all by myself, that I'd egg him on to drink, to ***get*** started again.(p.325)
• I'd just take a couple or three barbiturates to ***get*** back to sleep -- eating my alcohol.(p.333)
• I had forgotten "If I ever I ***get*** that bad, I'll try A.A."(p.333)
• The only incentive that I had, toward the end, for getting dressed in the morning was to ***get*** out and ***get*** supplies to help me ***get*** my day started.(p.336)
• And of course a half empty bottle wasn't worth keeping, so I finished it up and naturally had to ***get*** more in right away for the people who "might come in unexpectedly."(p.336)
• And the mops would ***get*** out, the vacuum would ***get*** out, everything would ***get*** out, but nothing would ***get*** done.(p.337)
• Toward five o'clock, helter-skelter, I'd ***get*** everything put away and try to ***get*** supper on the table, and after supper I'd finish the job up and knock myself out.(p.337)
• I screamed on the telephone for my mother to ***get*** up there; something was going to happen; I didn't know what, but if she didn't ***get*** there quick, I'd split wide open.(p.338)
• I thought the two would never ***get*** together.(p.338)
• I said to my husband, "I'm going to try, every free

moment that I have, to ***get*** interested in something outside, ***get*** myself over this rut I'm in."(p.338)
• But I had to ***get*** back to that first drink somehow.(p.339)
• I used to like to ***get*** it on my fingers so I could lick them and ***get*** another taste.(p.346)
• In an attempt to ***get*** over that feeling, there was a quick onslaught of a greater number of drinks, and then all was lost.(p.346)
• Deep in my heart was the feeling that maybe I could ***get*** some help here.(p.346)
• Why don't you go home and ***get*** the Big Book and open it at page fifty-eight and see what it says?"(p.349)
• Years earlier, I had gone into psychoanalysis to ***get*** relief.(p.349)
• I tried every gimmick that there was to ***get*** some peace of mind, but it was not until I was brought to my alcoholic knees, when I was brought to a group in my own community with the butcher, the baker, the carpenter and the mechanic, who were able to give me the Twelve Steps, that I was finally given some semblance of an answer to the last half of the First Step.(p.349)
• So I went to my wife and asked her, wasn't there something that she and I could do to somehow ***get*** together, and she turned on her heel and looked me squarely in the eye, and said, "You don't care anything about my problem," and I could have smacked her, but I said to myself, "Grab on to your serenity!"(p.351)
• But I remembered that every night after dinner my wife would ***get*** up and do the dishes.(p.351)
• He answered by wiring that I could stay there until I earned enough to ***get*** home.(p.357)
• All I can remember about the Roaring Twenties is that I drank a great deal, thought I was having a grand time, managed to ***get*** to Europe for a few weeks, was very proud of the dozens of speak-easy cards entitling me to an entree in the better joints between Cleveland and New York, took on a wife, and built a home in a fashionable suburb of Cleveland.(p.358)
• Why should this happen to me – hadn't I provided a good home – wasn't I making a good living -- didn't I just ***get*** a substantial raise that had put me in the upper bracket class?(p.362)
• I entered the house, opened a new bottle of whiskey and sat down to drink myself into the right frame of mind to ***get*** in my car, start the motor and close the garage door behind me.(p.363)
• In other words, I began contributing, and so, naturally, I began to ***get*** something more.(p.365)
• The drive to ***get*** ahead, to succeed, kept me too busy for many years to have any great experience with social life.(p.374)
• I was living in constant fear that I would ***get*** caught while driving a car, so I used taxis part of the time.(p.375)
• After every cocktail party or dinner party she would say she couldn't understand how I could ***get*** in such a drunken stupor on one drink.(p.377)
• They said "***Get*** active," so I helped whenever I could, and I still do.(p.381)
• "First Things First": solving our immediate problems before we try to solve all the others and ***get*** muddled in our thinking and doing.(p.382)
• I ***get*** so much more enjoyment out of living.(p.383)
• ***Get*** her something to drink."(p.385)
• It only took a month to ***get*** a divorce in Texas.(p.386)
• My father, as I have said, was very indulgent and loved me dearly, and knew how to ***get*** around me.(p.389)
• So I went down to him quite a few times a month and had him shoot me full of the stuff; and then I went across the street to a little drug store to take a glass of beer or two beers, and then stopped at the liquor store to ***get*** myself a pint and go home.(p.389)
• As I said before, I don't like to be fenced in, and with those bars you don't ***get*** hotel service.(p.390)
• I wanted a cigarette and room service, which I didn't ***get***.(p.390)
• I took two or three drinks so my eyes could focus, and I could see that horrible picture of the awful drunk on the first page; he couldn't ***get*** the drink to his mouth, he had a towel around his hand and he needed a shave.(p.391)
• He said, "Wait until I ***get*** back and I will go with you to see this man."(p.393)
• It was the first time in my life that I could not ***get*** a lift out of what I was drinking; and so one Friday night, at five minutes to six, I had half a water glass of warm gin, and that is when I first asked God to help me.(p.393)
• I displayed alcoholic tendencies actually from the age of fourteen, when I started to steal wine from the family jug, siphoning it off one drink at a time so it wouldn't be missed, not drinking it immediately, but saving it until about a pint was accumulated, so that I could ***get*** drunk.(p.397)
• I had to have enough to ***get*** drunk on, or what was the use?(p.397)
• Age and the law were still against me, but laws were not as strictly enforced in those days as they are now, and I discovered that as long as I had the green blood, there was always a way to ***get*** alcohol, either from a nondiscriminatory bartender or from an older friend who would be glad to purchase the joy juice for the privilege of sharing it.(p.397)
• I found out fast that the cheapest way to ***get*** drunk was on shots with beer chasers at two bits a crack.(p.397)
• It took me three psychoanalysts and several years in A.A. to really ***get*** this through my head.(p.401)
• But when this happened to me, I declared to friends that I would ***get*** drunk, dead drunk that very night, and stay drunk for a month.(p.403)
• An alcoholic cannot accept the news that he's an alcoholic unless there is a meaningful explanation given, and an offer of help, such as you ***get*** in A.A.(p.406)
• I would ***get*** wildly excited and look forward to another night of drinking.(p.408)
• I was going to ***get*** drunk again -- Drunk!(p.408)
• I didn't ***get*** into a sanitarium either.(p.411)
• I would walk up and down under the 59th Street bridge, trying to ***get*** up the nerve to go up there and jump.(p.411)
• Once, when I called my analyst, and told her I was contemplating death, she came over and tried to ***get*** me into a sanitarium.(p.411)
• I couldn't ***get*** a word in edgewise!(p.414)
• On the train going back, Anne's one idea was to ***get*** to the nearest bar.(p.415)
• I went to saloons where I could ***get*** drinks.(p.423)
• I wanted love and affection but I didn't ***get*** it.(p.424)
• So we rolled old newspapers together and made torches to find a good soft pew and ***get*** some sleep.(p.424)
• I tried to control her drinking by pouring her whiskey down the sink before I'd leave for the night, to ***get*** drunker myself.(p.426)
• I wanted to ***get*** as far away from home as possible.(p.426)
• But I knew I'd never ***get*** that way.(p.427)
• Then I'd ***get*** a pass to Honolulu.(p.427)
• I had begun to drink in the early years of pharmacy school, in order to ***get*** to sleep.(p.440)
• It became progressively harder to ***get*** up in the morning, until one day I asked myself what I would do for a patient who felt this rotten.(p.441)
• Eventually, I was taking forty-five milligrams of the long-acting Benzedrine and forty-five of the short-acting just to ***get*** out of bed in the morning.(p.442)
• That's the stuff used when the oral surgeon puts the needle in your vein and says, "Count to ten," and before you ***get*** to two, you're asleep.(p.442)
• In the garage, I would put the needle in my vein and then try to figure out exactly how much medication to inject to overcome the pep pills while adding to the sleeping pills while ignoring the tranquilizers, in order to ***get*** just enough to be able to pull out the needle, jerk the tourniquet, throw it in the car, slam the car door shut, run down the hall, and fall in bed before I fell asleep.(p.442)
• But to do so, I had to ***get*** all the stuff out of the house and out of my possession.(p.443)
• I never could quite ***get*** the knack of it and kept asking myself, "What's a nice guy like me doing in a place like this?"(p.445)
• But it quickly became obvious that he had this childish notion instead: If he could ***get*** me to go to enough meetings while in the hospital, I would continue to go after he let me out.(p.447)
• But when I try to see what I can add to the meeting, rather than what I can ***get*** out of it, and when I focus my mind on what's good about it, rather than what's wrong with it, the meeting keeps getting better and better.(p.451)
• When I do this, we ***get*** along fine.(p.452)
• If I failed, they would throw away the key, and I would never ***get*** out again.(p.461)
• At the wedding, I hope I will also ***get*** to see my daughter and their mother.(p.463)
• Then I remember him coming into my room one night with a friend, and telling me to ***get*** dressed -- we were going away.(p.466)
• So the doctor said, "I really don't know too much about it, but they tell me it is a bunch of drunks who ***get*** together . . ."(p.469)
• Then I black out and ***get*** home four days later.(p.475)
• I ***get*** arrested.(p.475)
• I ***get*** arrested again.(p.475)
• Cops say for me to call them, they ***get*** me out.(p.475)
• Tell him I want to ***get*** away from bottle and misery.(p.475)
• ***Get*** sponsor and phone numbers.(p.477)
• We are so beautiful that it is never too much trouble to ***get*** some poor stranger to buy us a drink.(p.479)
• (Actually, he does it solely to ***get*** rid of us.)(p.480)
• Men are supposed to be tough and rugged to start with, but if a woman becomes that way, it is pretty hard to ***get*** back the niceties of womanhood.(p.480)
• So I wasn't just tinkering around with it -- I had to ***get*** in with both feet.(p.480)
• It is so beautiful to ***get*** up in the morning not being hung-over and being able to remember where we were the night before.(p.481)
• I don't believe this program would work for me if I didn't ***get*** honest with myself about everything.(p.482)
• I was able to ***get*** my work out.(p.486)
• To ***get*** rid of me one evening, she decided to go to the movies, she and another friend.(p.487)
• I said that she told me she was going to the movies, and I became foolishly disturbed about it and, as things snowballed, I decided to go out and ***get*** drunk.(p.487)
• I thought, "I know you didn't pay me, because you didn't ***get*** a prescription."(p.488)
• I started inquiring where I could ***get*** a drink and, of course, I found that it wasn't hard.(p.490)
• But there happened to be a liquor store between the post office and the mill, and I stopped to ***get*** that one drink.(p.493)
• I guess I felt, and he sensed it, that I wanted him to hurry up and say what he had to say and ***get*** out.(p.494)
• After he'd talked half an hour, I still wanted him to hurry up and ***get*** out so I could go and ***get*** some whiskey before the liquor store closed.(p.494)
• Then Charlie or someone in the group suggested that we try to ***get*** a place in a church or hall to hold meetings.(p.495)
• Both he and old Maud are glad to ***get*** home.(p.497)
• I ***get*** uneasy.(p.499)
• If I don't ***get*** started soon, I won't have time to finish.(p.499)
• I know enough of the answers to ***get*** by.(p.499)
• I seem to ***get*** no sympathy for my illness and have no appreciation of the love behind the gift.(p.501)
• I ***get*** drunk.(p.501)
• I must ***get*** myself together.(p.501)
• I sneak downstairs and ***get*** a bottle of whiskey from the cellaret.(p.501)
• I have been drinking a lot, but never ***get*** drunk.(p.501)
• I return to the hotel where I am staying and ***get*** gin from the bellboy.(p.501)
• I go back to the hotel and ***get*** more gin.(p.501)
• I must ***get*** out of the room or I shall jump out of the window.(p.501)
• I must ***get*** some liquor.(p.502)
• I might go out West on a ranch where I couldn't ***get*** anything to drink.(p.502)
• Anything to ***get*** my mind from myself.(p.502)
• Am I willing to be honest with myself about myself and tell someone about myself, and am I willing to think of other people, of their needs instead of myself, in order to ***get*** rid of the drink problem?(p.503)
• I ***get*** in bed and turn out the light.(p.503)
• It rings in my head; I can't ***get*** rid of it.(p.504)
• I ***get*** out of bed and go to the man's room.(p.504)
• I ***get*** out of the hospital and we visit some of these new-found friends.(p.505)
• ***Get*** into the lives of other people, is one thing the fellows in New York had said.(p.505)
• Maybe a few drinks when I ***get*** to the city will help.(p.505)
• I want to ***get*** where I can find some alcoholics to help, and where I can have some fellowship.(p.506)
• I'll ***get*** drunk!(p.506)
• I am going to town to ***get*** some liquor and food.(p.506)
• I shall not drink until I ***get*** back to the apartment.(p.506)
• I shall ***get*** myself "mellow" and stay that way.(p.506)
• I ***get*** in the car and drive off.(p.506)

• She does not ***get*** excited.(p.507)
• However, my two friends kept coaxing and cajoling to ***get*** me back again.(p.510)
• Yes, we find it rather confusing, but as we ***get*** around and ***get*** to know people in the group, they lead the way and all we have to do is to follow.(p.512)
• They were harder to ***get*** off.(p.514)
• You no longer ***get*** the kicks.(p.514)
• I'd ***get*** downstairs to the gin mill, ***get*** enough in to hold me until eight o'clock in the morning, then I'd go out to join that "misery parade" that so many of us know so well.(p.514)
• Because as I sat on that bed, I knew that I was in a terrible spot and didn't know how to ***get*** out of it.(p.515)
• I was afraid that sometime I would ***get*** half drunk and go through with it.(p.515)
• Oh yes, I ***get*** the dry jitters once in a while, but that isn't anything to worry about.(p.516)
• Someone told me, "When you drank, you didn't ***get*** half drunk.(p.516)
• I think the Commanding Officer was rather tired of this particular chicken coming back to roost so often because he very soon wrote in to the medical authorities to tell them that they had to ***get*** me into hospital, to be thoroughly examined for drinking.(p.520)
• My only hope was to try and ***get*** through what was left of life as best I could, but I could never visualize doing that without drinking.(p.522)
• I was to pack and go and ***get*** out of their lives for good.(p.523)
• So I did manage to ***get*** myself down to an A.A. meeting that night.(p.523)
• I was always able to ***get*** a boyfriend who had a drinking joint or sold whiskey, but it didn't last long.(p.526)
• I couldn't wait until the meeting was over to ***get*** a drink.(p.526)
• An ambitious playwright, he let his brains ***get*** so far ahead of his emotions that he collapsed into suicidal drinking.(p.531)
• This question so insulted the emotions that clearly there was only one thing to do, go and ***get*** drunk again, and put that enquiring mind in its proper place, which was oblivion.(p.537)
• Still, I had had funds sufficient to ***get*** plastered because that, of course, was more important than paying my own way.(p.538)
• In the nearby little town there was a plumber who once had tried to ***get*** an A.A. group going.(p.541)
• I still want to write a fine play and to ***get*** it on.(p.542)
• The more you give, the more you ***get***.(p.542)
• Through my efforts to ***get*** down to "causes and conditions," I stand convinced that my emotional illness has been present from my earliest recollection.(p.544)
• I thought I knew exactly what I wanted out of life and I thought I knew exactly how to ***get*** it.(p.545)
• I wasn't afraid of anything or anybody after I learned about drinking, for it seemed right from the beginning that with liquor I could always retire to my little private world where nobody could ***get*** at me to hurt me.(p.547)
• They suggested that I study the A.A. book and try to take the Twelve Steps according to the explanation in the Book, for it was their opinion that the application of these principles in our daily lives will ***get*** us sober and keep us sober.(p.550)
• One morning, however, I realized I had to ***get*** rid of it, for my reprieve was running out, and if I didn't ***get*** rid of it I was going to ***get*** drunk -- and I didn't want to ***get*** drunk any more.(p.552)
• This great experience that released me from the bondage of hatred and replaced it with love is really just another affirmation of the truth I know: I ***get*** everything I need in Alcoholics Anonymous -- everything I need I ***get*** -- and when I ***get*** what I need I invariably find that it was just what I wanted all the time.(p.553)
• VI. How to ***Get*** in Touch With A.A.(p.563)
• Dr. John F. Stouffer, Chief Psychiatrist, Philadelphia General Hospital, citing his experience with A.A., said: "The alcoholics we ***get*** here at Philadelphia General are mostly those who cannot afford private treatment, and A.A. is by far the greatest thing we have been able to offer them.(p.572)
• HOW TO ***GET*** IN TOUCH WITH A.A.(p.575)

get-togethers

• In addition to these casual ***get-togethers***, it became customary to set apart one night a week for a meeting to be attended by anyone or everyone interested in a spiritual way of life.(p.159)

Gethsemane

• I do not recollect the specific conversation that went on but I believe I did challenge Bill to tell me something about A.A. and I do recall one other thing: I wanted to know what this was that worked so many wonders, and hanging over the mantel was a picture of ***Gethsemane*** and Bill pointed to it and said, "There it is," which didn't make much sense to me.(p.216)

gets

• If he can afford it, he may have liquor concealed all over his house to be certain no one ***gets*** his entire supply away from him to throw down the waterpipe.(p.22)
• Then comes the day when he simply cannot make it and ***gets*** drunk all over again.(p.22)
• He ***gets*** a thrill out of skipping in front of fast-moving vehicles.(p.37)
• Finally, he can no longer work, his wife ***gets*** a divorce and he is held up to ridicule.(p.38)
• After a few years with an alcoholic, a wife ***gets*** worn out, resentful and uncommunicative.(p.81)
• This he may do after he ***gets*** hurt some more.(p.95)
• He often ***gets*** entirely out of hand when drinking.(p.109)
• But when he ***gets*** over the spree, he begins to think once more how he can drink moderately next time.(p.109)
• If he ***gets*** the idea that you are a nag or a killjoy, your chance of accomplishing anything useful may be zero.(p.111)
• He ***gets*** stirred up about their troubles, but not at all about yours.(p.119)
• If he ***gets*** drunk, don't blame yourself.(p.120)
• Every doctor ***gets*** his quota of alcoholic patients.(p.308)
• But, of course," he continued, "eventually the alcoholic loses all of his capacities as his disease ***gets*** progressively worse, and this is a tragedy that is painful to watch; the disintegration of a sound mind and body."(p.308)
• And so one ***gets*** to thinking to oneself, "Who is this God?(p.350)

getting

• The second edition added the appendices, the Twelve Traditions, and the directions for ***getting*** in touch with A.A.(p.xi)
• We shall be interested to hear from those who are ***getting*** results from this book, particularly from those who have commenced work with other alcoholics.(p.xiv)
• He has a positive genius for ***getting*** tight at exactly the wrong moment, particularly when some important decision must be made or engagement kept.(p.21)
• And there often seems no way of entirely ***getting*** rid of self without His aid.(p.62)
• He had commenced our way of life, had secured a position, and was ***getting*** his head above water.(p.79)
• If he is, you might try to help him about ***getting*** a job, or give him a little financial assistance.(p.96)
• Now you are ***getting*** back into the social life of this world.(p.102)
• Next time you and he have a heated discussion, no matter what the subject, it should be the privilege of either to smile and say, "This is ***getting*** serious.(p.118)
• Having been neglected and misused in the past, they think father owes them more than they are ***getting***.(p.126)
• We know there are difficult wives and families, but the man who is ***getting*** over alcoholism must remember he did much to make them so.(p.127)
• Giving, rather than ***getting***, will become the guiding principle.(p.128)
• When sober, does he not work hard and have a knack of ***getting*** things done?(p.139)
• When drinking, or ***getting*** over a bout, an alcoholic, sometimes the model of honesty when normal, will do incredible things.(p.140)
• For most alcoholics who are drinking, or who are just ***getting*** over a spree, a certain amount of physical treatment is desirable, even imperative.(p.142)
• I have enjoyed every moment spent in ***getting*** them straightened out.(p.150)
• Some time later, and just as he thought he was ***getting*** control of his liquor situation, he went on a roaring bender.(p.155)
• It was really a horrible nightmare, this earning money, ***getting*** liquor, smuggling it home, ***getting*** drunk, morning jitters, taking large doses of sedatives to make it possible for me to earn more money, and so on ad nauseam.(p.177)
• Tuesday I started in the morning, ***getting*** well organized by noon.(p.179)
• It never fails, if you go about it with one half the zeal you have been in the habit of showing when you were ***getting*** another drink.(p.181)
• In the meantime, the domestic situation was not ***getting*** along too well.(p.199)
• And I continued to drink, on and off then, until every dollar I had in the world was gone again and I was right back living at my sister's, ***getting*** my cigarettes by calling her grocer and telling him to put in a couple of cartons with her order, exactly as I had before I started to work at Max's.(p.202)
• My only thought that day was ***getting*** a drink, and how to get rid of those clowns was my big problem.(p.206)
• It was ***getting*** pretty dark and I hadn't turned on any lights, when some big fellow stepped inside the door and flipped on the light switch.(p.207)
• I had had no hospitalization up to this time because I would not call doctors when I was ***getting*** over a bad one.(p.217)
• They did not seem to be ***getting*** an answer, for here I was staying sober and selling lots of auto polish, on which they were making one thousand per cent profit.(p.247)
• Then I found that as I gave in to this spiritual or personality change I was ***getting*** a little more serenity.(p.249)
• The war was ***getting*** along.(p.253)
• I had never known him to be anything but a good healthy pagan with a propensity for ***getting*** into liquor jams and scrapes.(p.257)
• I had gone to an attorney to see about ***getting*** a divorce during that year.(p.263)
• One morning after a terrific drinking bout, I was in a little bar near our house, and I shook so that I was very much ashamed, because I was ***getting*** the shakes worse and worse.(p.266)
• And we went down through the valley, and I remembered reading about the Ku Klux Klan and how they burnt crosses, and I thought, "God alone knows what we are ***getting*** into this time!"(p.269)
• The next morning his wife came dragging him in before Russ went to work, while I was ***getting*** breakfast.(p.271)
• It ran something like this: If I go around shouting from the rooftops about my alcoholism, it might very possibly prevent me from ***getting*** a good job.(p.282)
• I can still remember very distinctly ***getting*** into Akron at eleven p.m. and routing this same Howard out of bed to do something about me.(p.290)
• He was happy, ***getting*** a kick out of life and people, and beginning to get his medical practice back again.(p.290)
• Now I was ***getting*** drunk all the time.(p.300)
• By this time, my chances of ***getting*** lined up in my chosen business were shot.(p.301)
• Not only were they at peace with themselves, but they were ***getting*** a kick out of life such as one seldom encounters, except in the very young.(p.310)
• And unless I had some rosy picture of what was going to happen that day, I wouldn't even feel like ***getting*** up in the morning at all.(p.325)
• Lying on the divan, "***getting*** in the mood" to write, I cried openly or inwardly, as I listened to sad songs.(p.332)
• But during a period of particular stress and strain about thirteen years ago, I resorted to alcohol in my home, alone, as a means of temporary release, as a means of ***getting*** a little extra sleep.(p.335)
• The only incentive that I had, toward the end, for ***getting*** dressed in the morning was to get out and get supplies to help me get my day started.(p.336)
• I should have realized that alcohol was ***getting*** hold of me when I started to become secretive in my drinking.(p.336)
• What I needed was a change, mental relaxation, ***getting*** out and doing something.(p.338)
• In the various schools I attended, it was always a case of just ***getting*** by.(p.357)
• Since the radio station was ***getting*** on its feet, it didn't require so many nights of evening work, and that permitted leisure time for drinking.(p.360)
• After that came marriage, ***getting*** started in business, and a family.(p.373)
• The baffling problem of ***getting*** drunk when I had every intention of staying sober was simplified.(p.379)
• ***Getting*** drunk won't solve them.(p.382)
• When I joined A.A. I did so for the sole purpose of ***getting*** sober and staying sober.(p.383)
• I was so happy over ***getting*** home that I changed overnight, but not enough.(p.387)
• I could see no reason why they should have any relationship to this problem of ***getting*** drunk every now and then.(p.388)
• I was just as drunk as I could be, ***getting*** ready to take an afternoon walk.(p.390)
• But I got drunk that night and stayed drunk, ***getting*** increasingly worse until I found A.A. ten years later.(p.404)

• The liquor counteracted the help I was ***getting.***(p.407)
• I rarely remembered ***getting*** home.(p.410)
• In the first year there were episodes such as kicking Priscilla in the shins, ***getting*** the lock changed on the desk in the A.A. Club, because I, as secretary, didn't want the Intergroup secretary "interfering," and taking an older woman member out to lunch for the express purpose of informing her that she was "a phony."(p.416)
• School was ***getting*** to be one big bore.(p.423)
• They had been drinking for many years and were ***getting*** progressively worse.(p.424)
• I planned to stay home the night before I left, but my folks got so drunk I walked off early in the evening and spent the night with my girl, ***getting*** very drunk myself.(p.425)
• I stayed in the barracks all day, "making out guard schedules," and ***getting*** mildly plastered from the jug under my desk.(p.426)
• This I would do by going completely "bohemian" for a night, ***getting*** drunk and rolling home with the dawn.(p.432)
• Meanwhile, I was ***getting*** worse, both as regards my inward misery and my drinking.(p.434)
• And life keeps ***getting*** simpler and easier as we try to reverse my old idea, by taking care of the internal environment via the Twelve Steps, and letting the external environment take care of itself.)(p.446)
• But when I try to see what I can add to the meeting, rather than what I can get out of it, and when I focus my mind on what's good about it, rather than what's wrong with it, the meeting keeps ***getting*** better and better.(p.451)
• It was my ex-wife, and she said my twenty-seven-year-old son, who has completed his Marine Corps training and graduated from college, wanted to see me privately, was ***getting*** married in three months, and wanted me at the wedding.(p.462)
• My husband interrupted, "She's bad enough now without ***getting*** mixed up with a bunch of drunks."(p.469)
• As an indication of just how confused and mixed up I was, just as soon as I could I left the office and hurried around to tell other patients that I was ***getting*** better.(p.470)
• Had I tried honestly and sincerely to practice the Twelve Steps I would have seen from my continuous moral inventory that I was ***getting*** off the beam -- I would have found that there were some active resentments in my life, a terrific amount of self-pity.(p.471)
• Then ***getting*** and staying honest with other people will come automatically.(p.482)
• My practice at that juncture was just barely ***getting*** us a living.(p.488)
• I rebelled against this, because just about the time that I was ***getting*** ready to leave high school, a revelation came to me about God and it made things very complicated for me.(p.489)
• She didn't say anything about A.A. or ***getting*** me a sponsor at that time, but she did ask about Vi, and I told her Vi was working and how she could locate her.(p.494)
• I do not fix anyone, but I am ***getting*** part of a tremendous education and I have made some new friends.(p.506)
• I had a habit of ***getting*** up just prior to the closing time of the saloons, about two or three o'clock in the morning.(p.514)
• Things were ***getting*** worse and worse.(p.522)
• Then it got to the place I couldn't drink without ***getting*** in jail.(p.526)
• I don't remember any of them ***getting*** put out in the winter because they didn't pay their rent.(p.527)
• It's time to stop finding excuses for drinking and ***getting*** into trouble, because now there is a way out, and if you want what we have, try coming around and giving the program a chance.(p.530)
• I wonder if ever there has been a sillier reason for ***getting*** drunk all the time.(p.537)
• I imagined ***getting*** even for hurts and rejections.(p.560)

ghastly
• It was hard to reconcile this ***ghastly*** present with the simple facts of the past.(p.225)

giant
• Some of these were hard to believe, but it did not require a ***giant*** brain to perceive that they had something I could use.(p.279)

gift
• For some reason, we alcoholics seem to have the ***gift*** of picking out the world's finest women.(p.178)
• Prior to our marriage, when she was a shy, scrawny adolescent, I was able to see things in her that others couldn't necessarily see — things like beauty, charm, gaiety, a ***gift*** for being easy to talk to, a sense of humor, and many other fine qualities.(p.450)
• I think, with him it possibly was a ***gift*** -- intuitive diagnosis.(p.485)
• I seem to get no sympathy for my illness and have no appreciation of the love behind the ***gift.***(p.501)

gifted
• My family, on my mother's side, was brilliant, ***gifted*** and charming.(p.401)

gifts
• He uses his ***gifts*** to build up a bright outlook for his family and himself, and then pulls the structure down on his head by a senseless series of sprees.(p.21)
• One of our ***gifts*** from the family was a very lovely Bible, but we'd let the bulldog chew it because we weren't too interested in it.(p.268)
• We think that each group should soon achieve this ideal; that any public solicitation of funds using the name of Alcoholics Anonymous is highly dangerous, whether by groups, clubs, hospitals, or other outside agencies; that acceptance of large ***gifts*** from any source, or of contributions carrying any obligation whatever, is unwise.(p.566)

gigantic
• Occasionally, it is accorded to a few of us to watch something fine grow from a tiny kernel into something of ***gigantic*** goodness.(p.295)

giggle
• To keep it in round figures, let's say twenty per cent of my income went for ***giggle*** gurgles.(p.397)

gimmick
• I tried every ***gimmick*** that there was to get some peace of mind, but it was not until I was brought to my alcoholic knees, when I was brought to a group in my own community with the butcher, the baker, the carpenter and the mechanic, who were able to give me the Twelve Steps, that I was finally given some semblance of an answer to the last half of the First Step.(p.349)

gin
• "Bathtub" ***gin***, two bottles a day, and often three, got to be routine.(p.5)
• A tumbler full of ***gin*** followed by half a dozen bottles of beer would be required if I were to eat any breakfast.(p.5)
• I could laugh at the ***gin*** mills.(p.6)
• ***Gin*** would fix that.(p.6)
• Next day found me drinking both ***gin*** and sedative.(p.7)
• With a certain satisfaction I reflected there was enough ***gin*** concealed about the house to carry me through that night and the next day.(p.8)
• I wondered whether I dared hide a full bottle of ***gin*** near the head of our bed.(p.8)
• Besides, my ***gin*** would last longer than his preaching.(p.9)
• I remembered filling the peroxide bottle in my medicine chest with ***gin***, in case my sister found the bottle I hid under the mattress.(p.224)
• It was the first time in my life that I could not get a lift out of what I was drinking; and so one Friday night, at five minutes to six, I had half a water glass of warm ***gin***, and that is when I first asked God to help me.(p.393)
• Once, in a strange ***gin*** mill, I stole a bottle from behind the bar.(p.411)
• I return to the hotel where I am staying and get ***gin*** from the bellboy.(p.501)
• I go back to the hotel and get more ***gin.***(p.501)
• When I landed of course I hit a ***gin*** mill, and with three or four good shots under my belt the world began to go into that rosy glow.(p.513)
• I'd get downstairs to the ***gin*** mill, get enough in to hold me until eight o'clock in the morning, then I'd go out to join that "misery parade" that so many of us know so well.(p.514)
• Having made that bargain, I immediately began to feel I'd been trapped into it and I went out and had some drinks — four glasses of ***gin***, I remember.(p.523)
• To wear expensive clothes, to have bartenders know what to serve me before I ordered, to be recognized by headwaiters and shown to the best table, to play ***gin*** rummy for high stakes with the insouciance of a riverboat gambler -- these were the enduring values in life, I thought.(p.556)

ginger
• I had commenced to drink as carelessly as though the cocktails were ***ginger*** ale.(p.41)
• Of course he couldn't drink, but why not sit hopefully at a table, a bottle of ***ginger*** ale before him?(p.154)
• I pour out half a tumbler of grain alcohol and fill it with ***ginger*** ale.(p.499)

gingerly
• So, after taking the first half of the First Step, and very ***gingerly*** admitting myself to Alcoholics Anonymous, something happened.(p.349)

girder
• The prosaic steel ***girder*** is a mass of electrons whirling around each other at incredible speed.(p.48)

girl
• "She's such a sweet ***girl***, I should think he'd stop for her sake."(p.20)
• Perhaps he is having a secret and exciting affair with "the ***girl*** who understands."(p.81)
• A man so involved often feels very remorseful at times, especially if he is married to a loyal and courageous ***girl*** who has literally gone through hell for him.(p.81)
• My wife, a Kentucky ***girl***, came with me to Akron where I completed my course in law at the Akron Law School.(p.182)
• I was married at the age of nineteen to a grand ***girl*** and had good business prospects.(p.194)
• We had two children, a boy and a ***girl***, and when the boy was about twelve, we broke up the marriage.(p.199)
• I didn't like having to come home at a certain time; I didn't like this, I didn't like that, and I think the poor ***girl*** actually divorced me to help me stop drinking!(p.199)
• I'm sure his family felt that it was a marriage that -- well, I was a ***girl*** from the wrong side of the tracks -- definitely!(p.262)
• With the bravery born of desperation, and abetted by alcohol, I married a young and lovely ***girl.***(p.277)
• The ***girl*** was full of enthusiasm and she made the trip to Akron too.(p.295)
• That age of the flapper and the "It" ***girl***, speakeasies and the hip flask, the boyish bob and the drugstore cowboy, John Held Jr. and F. Scott Fitzgerald, all generously sprinkled with a patent pseudo-sophistication.(p.304)
• Sergeants, doctors, ***girl*** friends -- everybody seemed to be picking on him.(p.317)
• When I came home from Nam, I met a ***girl*** I'll call Karen.(p.318)
• But I met a real wonderful ***girl*** I'll call Jean.(p.318)
• In the doorway stood a lovely young ***girl*** who said, "Are you one of us souses, too?"(p.321)
• She took me by the hand and introduced me to the ***girl*** that I'm very proud to call my sponsor.(p.321)
• This ***girl*** and her husband are both in A.A., and she said to me, "Oh, but you're not the alcoholic; it's your husband."(p.322)
• I walked away from that ***girl*** grinding my teeth and cursing under my breath.(p.322)
• There was one ***girl*** especially, and I'd watch her from my window every morning, leaving faithfully to go to the hospital in the neighborhood.(p.326)
• Just three years of drinking pushed a shy, lonely young ***girl*** to the depth of depression.(p.353)
• Once again I asked my ***girl*** to marry me and join me in this new venture.(p.359)
• During this time I faithfully was writing my ***girl*** in Utah.(p.360)
• Very soon after I lost Mother, my five-year-old little ***girl*** was killed by a neighbor's car.(p.370)
• He finally decided that he did not love me enough, and soon he told me so and said he was engaged to another ***girl.***(p.403)
• About this time I got my first crush on a ***girl.***(p.425)
• I planned to stay home the night before I left, but my folks got so drunk I walked off early in the evening and spent the night with my ***girl***, getting very drunk myself.(p.425)
• I seldom left the base any more except once in a while when I felt the need of talking to some ***girl.***(p.427)
• I'd acquired a new ***girl***, a lovely ***girl*** who knew of my problem and had tried to help me.(p.430)
• Perhaps the single flicker of decency that shone through the fog of my drinking days was a clumsy affection for my two children, a boy and a ***girl.***(p.437)
• The ***girl*** had explained them to me four times, and I was too embarrassed to ask her again.(p.445)
• And Frank did set me up for a meeting every night except Friday, when he thought he might have a date with his ***girl*** friend.(p.447)
• This career ***girl*** preferred solitary drinking, the blackout kind, often hoping she'd stay that way for keeps.(p.464)
• Vi was the first ***girl*** that I ever took out.(p.485)
• I had quite a heartache about her then because she wasn't the type of ***girl*** that my mother wanted

me to marry.(p.485)
• One *girl* suggests that I phone her.(p.505)
• I got married to the *girl* I'd left behind.(p.513)
• In the last year of my navy service, I was married to a lovely, lively *girl*, who enjoyed drinking.(p.555)

girl's
• But it didn't condition this *girl's* thinking.(p.469)
• The only thing this changed, however, was my surroundings, and it was soon apparent that I could have the same uncomfortable emotions with an unlimited checking account that I could on a working *girl's* salary.(p.545)

girls
• We moved in from the country at the age when *girls* want all sorts of nice things.(p.261)
• I remember starting to city school, coming from a country school, and wanting so very, very much to be like the other *girls* and trying flour on my face for powder because I wasn't able to have any real powder.(p.261)
• Karen didn't want to see me any more, and neither did two other *girls* I'd been going out with.(p.318)
• Can you picture two *girls* hitchhiking their way to Las Vegas from Washington State?(p.354)
• Other *girls* whom I had known all my life asked for one weak scotch after dinner.(p.406)
• I went to my first meeting with Marty and some other *girls*.(p.414)
• Max accepted responsibility for me after I had promised never to drink again, never to take another pill, never to swear again, and never to talk to *girls* again.(p.444)
• We had two *girls* and a boy at that time.(p.490)

give
• And in no circumstances should we *give* endorsements, make alliances, or enter public controversies.(p.xix)
• She would soon have to *give* me over to the undertaker or the asylum.(p.7)
• What would I not *give* to make amends.(p.8)
• A few are fortunate enough to be so situated that they can *give* nearly all their time to the work.(p.19)
• More baffling still, he could *give* himself no satisfactory explanation for his fall.(p.26)
• These *give* a fair cross section of our membership and a clear-cut idea of what has actually happened in their lives.(p.29)
• They had said that though I did raise a defense, it would one day *give* way before some trivial reason for having a drink.(p.42)
• Those who do not recover are people who cannot or will not completely *give* themselves to this simple program, usually men and women who are constitutionally incapable of being honest with themselves.(p.58)
• If he is not communicative, *give* him a sketch of your drinking career up to the time you quit.(p.91)
• *Give* him an account of the struggles you made to stop.(p.92)
• Your candidate may *give* reasons why he need not follow all of the program.(p.94)
• *Give* him a chance to think it over.(p.95)
• Having had the experience yourself, you can *give* him much practical advice.(p.96)
• If he is, you might try to help him about getting a job, or *give* him a little financial assistance.(p.96)
• It is not the matter of giving that is in question, but when and how to *give*.(p.98)
• If he is already committed to an institution, but can convince you and your doctor that he means business, *give* him a chance to try our method, unless the doctor thinks his mental condition too abnormal or dangerous.(p.114)
• Is he not unconsciously trying to see what he can take from the family life rather than *give*?(p.122)
• They expect him to *give* them the nice times they used to have before he drank so much, and to show his contrition for what they suffered.(p.126)
• But dad doesn't *give* freely of himself.(p.126)
• When we see a man sinking into the mire that is alcoholism, we *give* him first aid and place what we have at his disposal.(p.132)
• Most of them *give* freely of themselves, that their fellows may enjoy sound minds and bodies.(p.133)
• My secretary returned to say that it was not Mr. B---- on the phone; it was Mr. B----'s brother, and he wished to *give* me a message.(p.136)
• If, on the contrary, you are sure he is doing his utmost, you may wish to *give* him another chance.(p.147)
• We think we are sensible when we urge that you stop this waste and *give* your worthwhile man a chance.(p.148)
• Inwardly he would *give* anything to take half a dozen drinks and get away with them.(p.152)
• Then you will know what it means to *give* of yourself that others may survive and rediscover life.(p.153)
• He saw that he would have to face his problems squarely that God might *give* him mastery.(p.155)
• So, you see, there were three alcoholics in that town, who now felt they had to *give* to others what they had found, or be sunk.(p.158)
• *Give* freely of what you find and join us.(p.164)
• They came in and began to *give* me instruction in the program which later became known as Alcoholics Anonymous.(p.185)
• He wouldn't *give* me any money for the groceries, but he did take me across the street and buy me a bag of candy, which I later took back and traded for a loaf of bread.(p.193)
• When I got home I had to *give* him a check for the taxi fare.(p.205)
• I have something to contribute to humanity, since I am peculiarly qualified, as a fellow-sufferer, to *give* aid and comfort to those who have stumbled and fallen over this business of meeting life.(p.229)
• "Best in the business, when he's sober," my customers would say, and I still had a following who would *give* me work though they deplored my habits, because they knew the job would be well done when they eventually got it.(p.234)
• In fact I was scared to talk to him about it, for I feared the kind of talk he would *give* me.(p.234)
• Mother would take me in only if I would stay locked in a small storeroom and *give* her my clothes and shoes.(p.238)
• Just *give* me a good front and a couple of bucks and I'd be right back in the big time.(p.246)
• Much later I discovered the elders held many prayer meetings hoping to find a way to *give* me the heave-ho, but at the same time stay tolerant and spiritual.(p.247)
• They didn't *give* me anything to eat.(p.264)
• I *give* a great deal of credit to Doc and Anne for changing our life.(p.270)
• Having no one else to turn to, I was willing to *give* Him a chance, although with considerable doubt.(p.280)
• Long before I had any real opportunity to *give*, I had to learn the equally important lesson of receiving graciously.(p.281)
• The most accurate answer I can *give* you is this: Fear has never again ruled my life since that day in September, 1938, when I found that a Power greater than myself could not only restore me to sanity but could keep me both sober and sane.(p.285)
• Here was something requiring a greater willingness to assume responsibility, and take a larger degree of cooperation and "*give* and take" than even business requires of one.(p.286)
• I really worked for several weeks, and having had a fairly wide acquaintance with the dealer trade, it was not difficult for me to line up enough of them to *give* me a very substantial volume of business with a minimum of effort.(p.300)
• I sleep like a baby, and never *give* a thought to such a thing as insomnia.(p.303)
• With the alcoholic, they could only *give* temporary relief and in the last stages not even that.(p.307)
• I just didn't *give* a whoop about myself or anyone else.(p.325)
• We need them so badly even if you can only *give* one day, or perhaps two days?"(p.326)
• I had to *give* him a story and ask him the same question over and over again, "Well, now, how many will that bottle serve?"(p.336)
• And I took everything that A.A. had to *give* me.(p.340)
• When the time comes to solve them, God will *give* me strength for that day.(p.341)
• During the next three years, I tried often again to *give* it up, but failed miserably.(p.343)
• "Complete abandon"; "Half measures availed us nothing"; "Thoroughly follow our path"; "Completely *give* oneself to this simple program" -- rang in my swelled head.(p.349)
• I tried every gimmick that there was to get some peace of mind, but it was not until I was brought to my alcoholic knees, when I was brought to a group in my own community with the butcher, the baker, the carpenter and the mechanic, who were able to *give* me the Twelve Steps, that I was finally given some semblance of an answer to the last half of the First Step.(p.349)
• I am not even there, and if I was there the only thing I could do would be to *give* her moral support, and yet he thanks me for curing his wife."(p.350)
• I wouldn't *give* it up or trade it for anything.(p.355)
• At this time, however, she had an opportunity to go to Salt Lake City on a new project for the government, but she did promise me that if I would curtail my drinking and buckle down to hard work she would *give* serious consideration to my latest proposal and maybe join me at a later date when I got settled.(p.359)
• But Frank was frightened to death to *give* it to me, because I resented everything he said and did.(p.391)
• In spite of knowing that my drunkenness was a symptom of the things that were wrong with me, and that I could never drink again, I thought I couldn't yet *give* it up, although I was going to try.(p.393)
• I, who did not know how to *give* love, was head over heels "in love."(p.403)
• My life there was a nightmare of periodic binges on alcohol and pills, adultery, unhappy hours at the dental office, seeing my wife *give* birth to our second child and have several miscarriages, living in a turbulent household, and making continual attempts to be the respectable dentist, husband, father, and community leader.(p.419)
• I didn't *give* a whoop about anything scholastic.(p.423)
• Were I to revert to drinking, even now, I wouldn't *give* anything for these four years in A.A.(p.430)
• The answer came right back: I'd *give* him something to pep him up.(p.441)
• One night, I had to put myself back to sleep three times, and then I finally decided to *give* it up.(p.443)
• Giving up alcohol alone was not enough for me; I've had to *give* up all mood-and mind-affecting chemicals in order to stay sober and comfortable.(p.443)
• It is true that I -- of all people, strange as it may seem, and even though I didn't *give* my permission -- really, really am an alcoholic of sorts.(p.448)
• So I'm better off if I don't *give* advice, don't figure I know what's best, and just accept life on life's terms, as it is today -- especially my own life, as it actually is.(p.450)
• Eventually, I had to redo each of the Twelve Steps specifically with Max in mind, from the First, saying, "I am powerless over alcohol, and my homelife is unmanageable by me," to the Twelfth, in which I tried to think of her as a sick Al-Anon and treat her with the love I would *give* a sick A.A. newcomer.(p.452)
• I go back to my old alma mater occasionally to *give* A.A. talks, and -- just think! -- the warden is my friend.(p.462)
• They held consultations and discussions, and finally decided to *give* me the "Conditioned Reflex" treatment.(p.469)
• We weren't even permitted to play cards in our home, but father would *give* us just a little toddy with whiskey and sugar and warm water now and then.(p.484)
• He wanted to *give* me the very best and he thought that nothing but being a doctor would suffice.(p.485)
• It meant that I had to *give* up a lot of the things that I had been accustomed to and that wasn't the easiest thing in the world for me.(p.487)
• I had found this new "something," and I wanted to *give* it to everyone who had a problem.(p.496)
• The doctor has told me that if I don't *give* up inside work, I'll have tuberculosis.(p.500)
• If something does come along that sort of upsets me, instead of walking in and throwing a buck at the barman and asking for a drink, I walk into a telephone booth, drop a dime in the box, and call somebody who was so kind as to *give* me his name and telephone number to meet such an emergency.(p.511)
• I went in there and asked him honestly if he could *give* me a cure.(p.515)
• If you *give* us a try, you will see that we are really human beings, and we will welcome you with open arms and hearts.(p.529)
• It was my "secret garden" -- bluntly, it was my retreat from life, and I didn't want to *give* it up.(p.534)
• I had replied, "Uncle, *give* the judge ten dollars, or I'll have to work it out on the county road."(p.539)
• The more you *give*, the more you get.(p.542)
• I thought this would *give* me ego-strength, make me feel wanted and secure, and alleviate my fears, but again nothing changed inside me.(p.546)
• This headquarters will *give* the location of the nearest family group and will if you wish, correspond with you about your special problems.(p.575)

given
• Figures *given* in this foreword describe the Fellowship as it was in 1955(p.xv)
• I fancied myself a leader, for had not the men of my battery *given* me a special token of appreciation?(p.1)
• While I lay in the hospital the thought came that there were thousands of hopeless alcoholics who might be glad to have what had been so freely *given* me.(p.14)

• How then shall we present that which has been so freely ***given*** us?(p.19)
• A new life has been ***given*** us or, if you prefer, "a design for living" that really works.(p.28)
• Further on, clear-cut directions are ***given*** showing how we recovered.(p.29)
• We have learned that whatever the human frailties of various faiths may be, those faiths have ***given*** purpose and direction to millions.(p.49)
• It is not by chance we were ***given*** the power to reason, to examine the evidence of our senses, and to draw conclusions.(p.53)
• We know but few instances where we have ***given*** these doctors a fair break.(p.73)
• Reminding ourselves that we have decided to go to any length to find a spiritual experience we ask that we be ***given*** strength and direction to do the right thing, no matter what the personal consequences may be.(p.79)
• We will see that our new attitude toward liquor has been ***given*** us without any thought or effort on our part.(p.85)
• We usually conclude the period of meditation with a prayer that we be shown all through the day what our next step is to be, that we be ***given*** whatever we need to take care of such problems.(p.87)
• This advice is ***given*** for his family also.(p.90)
• Here no specific rule can be ***given***.(p.90)
• Everybody had ***given*** them up.(p.113)
• Showing others who suffer how we were ***given*** help is the very thing which makes life seem so worth while to us now.(p.124)
• New acquaintances who know nothing of alcoholism might be made and thoughtful consideration ***given*** their needs.(p.131)
• We have recovered, and have been ***given*** the power to help others.(p.132)
• They often jeopardize their own positions by trying to help serious drinkers who should have been fired long ago, or else ***given*** an opportunity to get well.(p.147)
• My marriage was happy and, as I have said, I never had any of the reasons, conscious or unconscious, which are often ***given*** for drinking.(p.182)
• I thought of what liquor had done to me, the opportunities that I had discarded, the abilities that had been ***given*** me and how I had wasted them, and I finally came to the conclusion, that if I didn't want to quit, I certainly ought to want to, and that I was willing to do anything in the world to stop drinking.(p.186)
• Bill was very, very grateful that he had been released from this terrible thing and he had ***given*** God the credit for having done it, and he's so grateful about it he wants to tell other people about it.(p.191)
• When I was sixteen years old, my mother remarried and I was ***given*** the opportunity of going back to school.(p.193)
• We can share in the laughter and tears of our many friends, and most important, we can share our A.A. way of life and are ***given*** a daily opportunity to help others.(p.249)
• Every encouragement was ***given*** me with frequent salary increases, but the sober times between "periods" became shorter.(p.254)
• Dr. Bob dwelt at length on how prayer had ***given*** him release, time and time again, from the nearly over-powering compulsion to take a drink.(p.279)
• I was ***given*** every advantage in a well ordered home.(p.304)
• I had long since ***given*** up any pretense of the "social" cocktail hour.(p.306)
• It took the help, understanding and wonderful companionship that was ***given*** so freely to me by my "ex-alkie" friends.(p.311)
• In return for a bottle and a hangover, we have been ***given*** the Keys of the Kingdom.(p.312)
• Among today's incoming A.A. members, many have never reached the advanced stages of alcoholism, though, ***given*** time, all might have.(p.315)
• A.A. has ***given*** us that.(p.325)
• My guild had elected me president twice and later ***given*** me a "man of the year" award.(p.328)
• I was assigned to keep media guests happy at a Halloween party ***given*** by a major star in his plush home.(p.328)
• I tried every gimmick that there was to get some peace of mind, but it was not until I was brought to my alcoholic knees, when I was brought to a group in my own community with the butcher, the baker, the carpenter and the mechanic, who were able to give me the Twelve Steps, that I was finally ***given*** some semblance of an answer to the last half of the First Step.(p.349)
• The Great Boss has ***given*** me diagnostic and surgical talent, and He has loaned it to me to use for the rest of my life.(p.350)
• I had ***given*** her everything a wife could ask for.(p.362)
• I saw at last that I had the same disease my father had, only I was being ***given*** a chance to live, not die.(p.371)
• I loved my father dearly and I adored my dog, and I'd gotten this new house and Frank had just ***given*** me a new fur coat and I was thrilled to death.(p.389)
• So I got a half pint and at midnight that night, I called the number I had been ***given***, but the man who had started the group was in the hospital so I didn't know what to do.(p.393)
• An alcoholic cannot accept the news that he's an alcoholic unless there is a meaningful explanation ***given***, and an offer of help, such as you get in A.A.(p.406)
• A.A. has ***given*** me a new wife, a beautiful step-daughter, a new practice, a new home, and a new relationship with my four children.(p.420)
• I thought, "If this is A.A. why not go back to drinking, kill myself with booze in the next three years the doctor had ***given*** me, and call it a bad job?"(p.430)
• Here was power to live to the end of any ***given*** day, power to have the courage to face the next day, power to have friends, power to help people, power to be sane, power to stay sober.(p.436)
• I had already ***given*** up all the narcotics, most of the pills, and some of the alcohol when I first came to A.A.(p.448)
• It's as though A.A. had ***given*** me a new pair of glasses.(p.450)
• A.A. has ***given*** me a new pair of glasses.(p.451)
• The drive was long and cold but he was thankful for the hot bricks which some thoughtful person had ***given*** him for his feet.(p.497)
• He has ***given*** me my diploma!(p.499)
• I learn that when we act upon the highest conception of honesty which is ***given*** us, our sense of honesty becomes more acute.(p.507)
• Then Hitler's war broke out, and again, I was ***given*** a really important job on the Suez Canal, dealing with military shipping.(p.520)
• A.A. has ***given*** me serenity of purpose, the opportunity to be of service to God and to the people about me, and I am serene in the infallibility of these principles that provide the fulfillment of my purpose.(p.551)
• If you will ask in prayer for everything you want for yourself to be ***given*** to them, you will be free.(p.552)
• The "12 Traditions" of Alcoholics Anonymous are, we A.A.'s believe, the best answers that our experience has yet ***given*** to those ever urgent questions, "How can A.A. best function?" and, "How can A.A. best stay whole and so survive?"(p.563)
• In 1951 the Lasker Award was ***given*** Alcoholics Anonymous.(p.573)
• Clergymen of practically every denomination have ***given*** A.A. their blessing.(p.574)
• Speaking at a dinner ***given*** by John D. Rockefeller Jr. to introduce Alcoholics Anonymous to some of his friends, Dr. Harry Emerson Fosdick remarked: "I think that psychologically speaking there is a point of advantage in the approach that is being made in this movement that cannot be duplicated.(p.574)

gives

• Although he ***gives*** all that is in him, it often is not enough.(p.xxvii)
• Perhaps he goes to a doctor who ***gives*** him morphine or some sedative with which to taper off.(p.22)
• Little by little, mother and children will see they ask too much, and father will see he ***gives*** too little.(p.127)
• He may bring new hope and new courage to many a priest, minister, or rabbi, who ***gives*** his all to minister to our troubled world.(p.132)
• I can actually take my problems to Him and He ***gives*** me comfort, peace, and happiness.(p.303)
• I believe that the release from people-pleasing restrictions ***gives*** retirees more motivation to drink than boredom does.(p.329)
• A.A. ***gives*** us alcoholics direction into a way of life without the need for alcohol.(p.340)
• She puts me to bed and ***gives*** me a hypodermic.(p.501)
• It continues to try to teach me the real charity, the charity that ***gives*** time and good will and service, and not just money.(p.525)

giving

• Moderate drinkers have little trouble in ***giving*** up liquor entirely if they have good reason for it.(p.20)
• While drinking, he accepted a sum of money from a bitterly-hated business rival, ***giving*** him no receipt for it.(p.80)
• It is not the matter of ***giving*** that is in question, but when and how to give.(p.98)
• We realize that we have been ***giving*** you much direction and advice.(p.121)
• ***Giving***, rather than getting, will become the guiding principle.(p.128)
• He may not see at once that he has barely scratched a limitless lode which will pay dividends only if he mines it for the rest of his life and insists on ***giving*** away the entire product.(p.129)
• After your man has gone along without drinking for a few months, you may be able to make use of his services with other employees who are ***giving*** you the alcoholic run-around – provided, of course, they are willing to have a third party in the picture.(p.146)
• Said one of the visitors, "We're ***giving*** you a treatment for alcoholism."(p.157)
• It was transcended by the happiness they found in ***giving*** themselves for others.(p.159)
• I can well remember sitting with seven dollars in my pocket, planning on ***giving*** my family a hundred or two hundred dollars, when I made it next year.(p.197)
• But I didn't do a thing about ***giving*** them any part of the seven bucks I had in my pocket.(p.197)
• My husband said that I said, "Can you imagine them ***giving*** us that jail fare?"(p.264)
• The satisfaction I got from ***giving*** him a little of what I had read in those pamphlets far surpassed any feeling that I had ever had before in helping patients.(p.347)
• The following spring she left me one day without ***giving*** me any idea of where she had gone, hoping this would bring me to my senses.(p.377)
• In my cups I used to tell them off, ***giving*** them lengthy advice on how to lead the right life.(p.410)
• While waiting to depart I was selected – by ***giving*** a CPO five dollars – to be bartender in the Navy Chief's Club.(p.426)
• ***Giving*** up alcohol alone was not enough for me; I've had to give up all mood-and mind-affecting chemicals in order to stay sober and comfortable.(p.443)
• And I knew that ***giving*** up "one drink for one day" wouldn't really do any good.(p.448)
• It didn't worry me very much, because at that time I could shut off for a couple of months without taking a drink or even wanting one, and without feeling that I was ***giving*** anything up.(p.518)
• Today, I thank my Higher Power for ***giving*** me another chance at life and A.A. and being able to try and help some other alcoholic.(p.529)
• It's time to stop finding excuses for drinking and getting into trouble, because now there is a way out, and if you want what we have, try coming around and ***giving*** the program a chance.(p.530)
• I was ***giving*** up the struggle.(p.531)
• I've been benefited from a dictionary definition I found that reads: "rationalization is ***giving*** a socially acceptable reason for socially unacceptable behavior, and socially unacceptable behavior is a form of insanity."(p.551)

glad

• While I lay in the hospital the thought came that there were thousands of hopeless alcoholics who might be ***glad*** to have what had been so freely given me.(p.14)
• Most people approached in this way will be ***glad*** to help; they will be honored by our confidence.(p.75)
• They will be only too ***glad*** to assist you.(p.89)
• You should be described to him as one of a fellowship who, as part of their own recovery, try to help others and who will be ***glad*** to talk to him if he cares to see you.(p.90)
• He remarked: "I'm mighty ***glad*** you fellows got over your drinking.(p.148)
• Today I have Someone who will always hear me; I have a warm fellowship among men who understand my problems; I have tasks to do and am ***glad*** to do them, to see others who are alcoholics and to help them in any way I can to become sober men.(p.260)
• And I was ***glad***, and I have been ever since, that I said that.(p.270)
• My wife is ***glad*** to see me come in.(p.303)
• I'm ***glad*** I had it then.(p.393)
• Age and the law were still against me, but laws were not as strictly enforced in those days as they are now, and I discovered that as long as I had the green blood, there was always a way to get alcohol, either from a nondiscriminatory bartender or from an older friend who would be ***glad*** to purchase the joy juice for the privilege of sharing it.(p.397)
• And I was always ***glad*** to point it out, because I knew you wanted perfection, just as I did.(p.449)

• Both he and old Maud are ***glad*** to get home.(p.497)
• But she is not ***glad*** to see me.(p.502)
• The Commanding Officer only spoke to me when he wanted to tell me exactly who I was and what I was and how little I counted in the scheme of things and how ***glad*** he would be if I went away.(p.520)
• If the listener were drunk enough, the lecture might go on through several martinis, which I was ***glad*** to pay for.(p.537)

gladly

• They shared their homes, their slender resources, and ***gladly*** devoted their spare hours to fellow-sufferers.(p.159)
• He walked to the hospital to save bus fare and did it ***gladly*** in order to be helpful to an individual he had never even seen.(p.208)
• I'd ***gladly*** do it anonymously, as I have done this brief account of my struggle with alcohol -- merely to present certain ideas for the consideration of the reader.(p.542)

glaring

• Their defects may be ***glaring***, but the chances are that our own actions are partly responsible.(p.83)

glass

• The almost certain consequences that follow taking even a ***glass*** of beer do not crowd into the mind to deter us.(p.24)
• I sat down at a table and ordered a sandwich and a ***glass*** of milk.(p.36)
• I ordered another sandwich and decided to have another ***glass*** of milk.(p.36)
• At one end of the room stood a ***glass*** covered directory of local churches.(p.154)
• After drinking one ***glass*** of beer at the end of my work period for about five days, I thought I'd better find out whether I really had the stuff licked.(p.203)
• Sitting in a Second Avenue bar, accepting drinks from anyone who offered, after my small stake was gone; or sitting at home alone, with the inevitable ***glass*** in my hand, I would remember, and remembering, I would drink faster, seeking speedy oblivion.(p.225)
• I checked into my hotel room and then noticed a placard tucked under the ***glass*** on the bureau stating "There will be positively NO drinking at this convention" signed by the president of the company.(p.243)
• Time went on and the drinking got worse and worse, and I was in another barroom, down the road the other way, a small one, and I took my ***glass*** -- that morning I'd been able to lift it from the bar -- and I said to the woman behind the bar, "I wish I might never take another drop of that stuff.(p.266)
• There was a ***glass*** of sherry at my place.(p.285)
• Emma ran out to the kitchen and came back with a water ***glass*** full of bourbon and made me drink it down.(p.385)
• So I went down to him quite a few times a month and had him shoot me full of the stuff; and then I went across the street to a little drug store to take a ***glass*** of beer or two beers, and then stopped at the liquor store to get myself a pint and go home.(p.389)
• It was the first time in my life that I could not get a lift out of what I was drinking; and so one Friday night, at five minutes to six, I had half a water ***glass*** of warm gin, and that is when I first asked God to help me.(p.393)
• My eye would be glued to that ***glass***.(p.407)
• I would drink all night in bars, come home about five a.m., down a good big ***glass*** of whiskey straight, and tumble into bed.(p.428)
• There, I received several soda crackers and water daily, and before I could have my third-day meal (again the only meal in ten days), I had to drink a ***glass*** of castor oil or mineral oil, depending on the cruelty of the person who was doing the dispensing.(p.459)
• Also, after that first visit I learned I could refuse to sign myself in unless they gave me a ***glass*** of whiskey in one hand and a ***glass*** of paraldehyde in the other.(p.468)
• After my very first drink -- a tiny ***glass*** of sherry my father gave me to celebrate the New Year when I was thirteen -- I went up to bed, dizzy with exhilaration and excitement, and I prayed I wouldn't drink any more!(p.554)

glasses

• An all night place supplied me with a dozen ***glasses*** of ale.(p.6)
• It's as though A.A. had given me a new pair of ***glasses***.(p.450)
• Then, one day in A.A., I was told that I had the lenses in my ***glasses*** backwards; "the courage to change" in the Serenity Prayer meant, not that I should change my marriage, but rather that I should change myself and learn to accept my spouse as she was.(p.451)
• A.A. has given me a new pair of ***glasses***.(p.451)
• Having made that bargain, I immediately began to feel I'd been trapped into it and I went out and had some drinks -- four ***glasses*** of gin, I remember.(p.523)
• There was the physical aspect; to be the youngest and the runt of the brood of children, to have to wear ***glasses*** very early and so to be teased, to be bookish and bored in school because the captain of the football team could not translate Virgil and yet was the school god while you, you, you little shrimp, were the school egghead, junior size and an early model.(p.533)
• This time, whoever had rolled me had taken my ***glasses*** as well (they were gold).(p.538)

glassful

• The interne came along with a ***glassful*** of bleached lightning that put me away for about fifteen hours.(p.217)

glassily

• Two days later, a future fellow of Alcoholics Anonymous stared ***glassily*** at the strangers beside his bed.(p.157)

glassy-eyed

• I then began asking a lot of questions of both my brother and Dr. Bob about how this thing worked, and I suppose I was becoming more ***glassy-eyed*** all the while, for eventually I said to Bob, "You're all dried up.(p.206)

glimmer

• I think I actually read more contempt than was really there because just a week before someone had sent him the Saturday Evening Post article on A.A., and there was some ***glimmer*** of hope in it for him.(p.391)

glimpse

• Perhaps the best way of treating you to a ***glimpse*** of your future will be to describe the growth of the fellowship among us.(p.153)

glittering

• I also wanted to be the queen of society, with a ***glittering*** salon, the bride of a dream prince and the mother of a happy brood.(p.400)
• The ***glittering*** society belle, the modern Shakespeare, the happy wife, the loving and beloved.(p.411)

gloom

• ***Gloom*** surrounds me.(p.506)

glorious

• It was a ***glorious*** homecoming.(p.428)

glory

• I don't care too much about personal fame or ***glory***, and I want only enough money to enable me to do the work I feel I can perhaps do best.(p.542)

glove

• I used to put eight or twelve ounce bottles of alcohol in a fur lined ***glove*** and toss it onto the back airing porch when winter days got dark enough.(p.176)

glow

• They had that certain something that seemed to ***glow***, a peace and a serenity combined with happiness.(p.290)
• A drink never gave me a normal, pleasant ***glow***.(p.402)
• A mellow ***glow*** stole over me.(p.498)
• The ***glow*** increased.(p.498)
• When I landed of course I hit a gin mill, and with three or four good shots under my belt the world began to go into that rosy ***glow***.(p.513)

glowing

• The door opened and he stood there, fresh-skinned and ***glowing***.(p.9)

glued

• My eye would be ***glued*** to that glass.(p.407)

glum

• But we aren't a ***glum*** lot.(p.132)
• But am I to be consigned to a life where I shall be stupid, boring and ***glum***, like some righteous people I see?(p.152)

gluttonous

• My drinking was never the spaced doses of the careful tippler; it was always ***gluttonous***.(p.254)

gnawing

• Every time I blacked out, and that was every time I drank, there was always that ***gnawing*** fear, "What did I do this time?"(p.244)

go

• Men have cried out to me in sincere and despairing appeal: "Doctor, I cannot ***go*** on like this!(p.xxvii)
• I failed to persuade my broker friends to send me out looking over factories and managements, but my wife and I decided to ***go*** anyway.(p.2)
• He had plenty of money left and thought I had better ***go*** to Canada.(p.4)
• But drinking caught up with me again and my generous friend had to let me ***go***.(p.4)
• I could ***go*** for such conceptions as Creative Intelligence, Universal Mind or Spirit of Nature but I resisted the thought of a Czar of the Heavens, however loving His sway might be.(p.12)
• Unlike the feelings of the ship's passengers, however, our joy in escape from disaster does not subside as we ***go*** our individual ways.(p.17)
• As matters grow worse, he begins to use a combination of high-powered sedative and liquor to quiet his nerves so he can ***go*** to work.(p.22)
• When this sort of thinking is fully established in an individual with alcoholic tendencies, he has probably placed himself beyond human aid, and unless locked up, may die or ***go*** permanently insane.(p.24)
• We were in a position where life was becoming impossible, and if we had passed into the region from which there is no return through human aid we had but two alternatives: One was to ***go*** on to the bitter end, blotting out the consciousness of our intolerable situation as best we could; and the other, to accept spiritual help.(p.25)
• He can ***go*** anywhere on this earth where other free men may ***go*** without disaster, provided he remains willing to maintain a certain simple attitude.(p.26)
• But the moment I made up my mind to ***go*** through with the process, I had the curious feeling that my alcoholic condition was relieved, as in fact it proved to be.(p.42)
• I would not ***go*** back to it even if I could."(p.43)
• Did not Professor Langley's flying machine ***go*** to the bottom of the Potomac River?(p.51)
• If you have decided you want what we have and are willing to ***go*** to any length to get it -- then you are ready to take certain steps.(p.58)
• Some of us have tried to hold on to our old ideas and the result was nil until we let ***go*** absolutely.(p.58)
• I can't ***go*** through with it."(p.60)
• Self-reliance was good as far as it went, but it didn't ***go*** far enough.(p.68)
• Many of us thought it necessary to ***go*** much further.(p.72)
• Those of us belonging to a religious denomination which requires confession must, and of course, will want to ***go*** to the properly appointed authority whose duty it is to receive it.(p.74)
• If that is so, this step may be postponed, only however, if we hold ourselves in complete readiness to ***go*** through with it at the first opportunity.(p.74)
• We pocket our pride and ***go*** to it, illuminating every twist of character, every dark cranny of the past.(p.75)
• If we still cling to something we will not let ***go***, we ask God to help us be willing.(p.76)
• Grant me strength, as I ***go*** out from here, to do your bidding.(p.76)
• Now we ***go*** out to our fellows and repair the damage done in the past.(p.76)
• Remember it was agreed at the beginning we would ***go*** to any lengths for victory over alcohol.(p.76)
• It is harder to ***go*** to an enemy than to a friend, but we find it much more beneficial to us.(p.77)
• We ***go*** to him in a helpful and forgiving spirit, confessing our former ill feeling and expressing our regret.(p.77)
• We must lose our fear of creditors no matter how far we have to ***go***, for we are liable to drink if we are afraid to face them.(p.78)
• Reminding ourselves that we have decided to ***go*** to any length to find a spiritual experience we ask that we be given strength and direction to do the right thing, no matter what the personal consequences may be.(p.79)
• He said he was perfectly willing to ***go*** to jail if she insisted.(p.79)
• More than that we cannot do; we have no right to ***go*** further.(p.81)
• This thought brings us to Step Ten, which suggests we continue to take personal inventory and continue to set right any new mistakes as we ***go*** along.(p.84)
• These are thoughts which must ***go*** with us constantly.(p.85)
• But we must ***go*** further and that means more action.(p.85)
• As we ***go*** through the day we pause, when agitated or doubtful, and ask for the right thought or action.(p.87)
• Then let his family or a friend ask him if he wants to quit for good and if he would ***go*** to any extreme to do so.(p.90)

- After doing that, he must decide for himself whether he wants to *go* on.(p.95)
- Let it *go* at that.(p.95)
- He has read this volume and says he is prepared to *go* through with the Twelve Steps of the program of recovery.(p.96)
- Yet we do *go* to great extremes to provide each other with these very things, when such action is warranted.(p.98)
- After they have seen tangible results, the family will perhaps want to *go* along.(p.99)
- People have said we must not *go* where liquor is served; we must not have it in our homes; we must shun friends who drink; we must avoid moving pictures which show drinking scenes; we must not *go* into bars; our friends must hide their bottles if we *go* to their houses; we mustn't think or be reminded about alcohol at all.(p.100)
- *Go* or stay away, whichever seems best.(p.102)
- If it is a happy occasion, try to increase the pleasure of those there; if a business occasion, *go* and attend to your business enthusiastically.(p.102)
- If you are with a person who wants to eat in a bar, by all means *go* along.(p.102)
- Your job now is to be at the place where you may be of maximum helpfulness to others, so never hesitate to *go* anywhere if you can be helpful.(p.102)
- Let's now *go* back to husband number one.(p.110)
- Perhaps you enjoy drinking with him yourself when he doesn't *go* too far.(p.110)
- Even though your husband becomes unbearable and you have to leave him temporarily, you should, if you can, *go* without rancor.(p.111)
- Being certain he wants to stop, you can *go* to him with this volume as joyfully as though you had struck oil.(p.113)
- He may not share your enthusiasm, but he is practically sure to read the book and he may *go* for the program at once.(p.113)
- We wives found that, like everybody else, we were afflicted with pride, self-pity, vanity and all the things which *go* to make up the self-centered person; and we were not above selfishness or dishonesty.(p.116)
- *Go* along with your husband if you possibly can.(p.117)
- Make him feel absolutely free to come and *go* as he likes.(p.120)
- Even if he displays a certain amount of neglect and irresponsibility towards the family, it is well to let him *go* as far as he likes in helping other alcoholics.(p.129)
- The only answer I could make was that if the man followed the usual pattern, he would *go* on a bigger bust than ever.(p.138)
- Of an evening, you can *go* on a mild bender, get up in the morning, shake your head and *go* to business.(p.139)
- But there are many men who want to stop, and with them you can *go* far.(p.141)
- After satisfying yourself that your man wants to recover and that he will *go* to any extreme to do so, you may suggest a definite course of action.(p.142)
- That won't hurt him a bit, even though he does not *go* for this remedy.(p.144)
- If he is conscientiously following the program of recovery he can *go* anywhere your business may call him.(p.147)
- In case he does stumble, even once, you will have to decide whether to let him *go*.(p.147)
- After reading this book, a junior executive can *go* to such a man and say approximately this, "Look here, Ed.(p.147)
- I'm afraid to *go* out the door.(p.157)
- He consented, however, to *go* the hospital, where he occupied the very room recently vacated by the lawyer.(p.159)
- Many of us, former patients, *go* there to help.(p.162)
- Some of us are salesmen and *go* about.(p.162)
- From childhood through high school I was more or less forced to *go* to church, Sunday School and evening service, Monday night Christian Endeavor and sometimes to Wednesday evening prayer meeting.(p.172)
- I was, of course, soon on the carpet and the upshot was that I had to *go* back for two more quarters and remain absolutely dry, if I wished to graduate.(p.174)
- During the subsequent fifteen years I had sense enough never to *go* to the hospital if I had been drinking, and very seldom did I receive patients.(p.176)
- But my friends usually found me and I would *go* home if they promised that I should not be scolded.(p.176)
- If my wife was planning to *go* out in the afternoon, I would get a large supply of liquor and smuggle it home and hide it in the coal bin, the clothes chute, over door jambs, over beams in the cellar and in cracks in the cellar tile.(p.176)
- It never fails, if you *go* about it with one half the zeal you have been in the habit of showing when you were getting another drink.(p.181)
- I would reach over and get this and take a shot and in a few moments get up and take another, shave and eat my breakfast, slip a half pint of liquor in my hip pocket, and *go* on to school.(p.183)
- Between classes I would run down to the wash room, take enough to steady my nerves and then *go* on to the next class.(p.183)
- The next thing they wanted to know was would I be willing to *go* to this Higher Power and ask for help, calmly and without any reservations.(p.186)
- Whether you quit six days, months, or years, if you *go* out and take a drink or two you'll end up in this hospital tied down, just like you have been in these past six months.(p.187)
- My case is so terrible that I'm scared to *go* out of this hospital at all.(p.188)
- Before our visit was over, Bill suddenly turned to his wife and said, "*Go* fetch my clothes, dear.(p.189)
- It was in the next two or three days after I had first met Doc and Bill, that I finally came to a decision to turn my will over to God and to *go* along with this program the best that I could.(p.189)
- You should *go* out and take this program to somebody else that needs it and wants it."(p.190)
- I really wanted the program and I wanted to *go* along with it.(p.191)
- I still *go* to meetings, because I like to *go*.(p.192)
- Another reason I *go* is that I'm still grateful for the good years that I've had.(p.192)
- I'm so grateful for both the program and the people in it that I still want to *go*, and then probably the most wonderful thing that I learned from the program -- I've seen this in the 'A.A. Grapevine' a lot of times, and I've had people say it to me personally, and I've heard people get up in meetings and make the same statement: The statement is, "I came into A.A. solely for the purpose of sobriety, but it has been through A.A. that I have found God."(p.192)
- I found, however, that when I would leave Akron to *go* to Chicago, I would get drunk.(p.197)
- I could work a deal up to where all I had to do was to *go* ahead with it; all the planning had been done, all the financing had been done, but then I'd say "Nuts to it!" and walk away.(p.197)
- I worked along until I had really big names in rubber on a tentative contract, and then I neglected to *go* through with it.(p.198)
- I can remember well thinking that I would quit drinking, really *go* to work hard, apply myself eight hours a day, five days a week, make a lot of money, and then I could start drinking again.(p.199)
- That was the reverse of my former pattern of fearing to *go* to work because I might drink!(p.199)
- At three-thirty the next morning, I was in Champlain Street Station, in jail for driving while intoxicated and insulting an officer; and the suit of which I was so proud was in such shape that the turnkey had to get me a pair of trousers to *go* into court in the next morning.(p.201)
- And then we both realized we should *go*.(p.201)
- I was black and blue, with my lips all swollen, when they roused us to *go* into court in the morning.(p.204)
- I looked so terrible in the court that the judge suggested that I get a continuance and let me sign all the papers to *go* to a hospital and to a doctor.(p.204)
- I didn't *go* to high school.(p.211)
- I kept myself so busy that outside of some school and group parties, I didn't *go* overboard on drinking very much between the ages of twenty-five and thirty.(p.213)
- The first definite indications of an alcoholic pattern began to arise when I would *go* to New York on business and disappear, and wind up in Philadelphia or Boston for two or three day periods.(p.213)
- There was also some conversation about Dr. Bob and I must have said that I would *go* down to Akron with Bill in the morning.(p.217)
- The next morning, my wife came into my room and wakened me and said, "That man is downstairs and he said you said you'd *go* to Akron."(p.217)
- And being a big-shot man of my word, I said, "Well, if I said so, then I'll *go*."(p.217)
- Shortly after I came to this conclusion, I was importuned by another well-known patent law firm to help them out on some trial work because their trial man had had a heart attack and had been forbidden to *go* into the courtroom.(p.220)
- I remembered asserting that I was going to do something about this, that I couldn't *go* on . . .(p.224)
- No doubt I had been an exile too long – I should *go* home to America.(p.226)
- To *go* into a gathering of people was the sort of thing that all my life, from the time I left my private world of books and dreams to meet the real world of people and parties and jobs, had left me feeling an uncomfortable outsider, needing the warming stimulus of drinks to join in.(p.228)
- At that time I could *go* into any saloon, have one or two beers, walk out and forget about it.(p.231)
- He had already imbued them with his own spirit until they were ready and willing at all times to *go* where sent, and as a doctor he well knew that this mission and duty would strengthen them as it later helped me.(p.235)
- As I *go* along I seem to get strength daily to be able to resist more easily.(p.237)
- At this school we had Bible readings before each meal, and church services four times on Sunday, and I became so rebellious at this that I swore I would never join or *go* to any church except for weddings or funerals.(p.240)
- That is where I had my first drink and I still remember it, for every "first" drink afterwards did exactly the same trick – I could feel it *go* right through every bit of my body and down to my very toes.(p.241)
- Some college friends got me jobs when I finally had to *go* to work, but I didn't stick to them.(p.251)
- I was soon broke, this time without trainfare to *go* anywhere.(p.252)
- I even began to *go* the rounds of churches.(p.255)
- He introduced himself and began to tell me about a bunch of some sixty former drinkers and drunkards who met once a week, and he invited me to *go* with him to the next meeting.(p.257)
- I thanked him, pleaded business engagements and promised I'd *go* with him at some future date.(p.257)
- I began to read the Bible daily and to *go* over a simple devotional exercise as a way to begin each day.(p.259)
- Where you *go*, I'll *go*, and what you drink, I'll drink."(p.263)
- He took his one hundred and seventeen dollars and let us *go*, and we proceeded.(p.264)
- Jack said there was a meeting in Akron every Wednesday night and that it was very important that we *go*.(p.268)
- Jack said, "Now you start and *go* to these meetings, and then you'll find out all about it."(p.268)
- I could never *go* and make up to all the people I've done wrong to."(p.269)
- We wept and Russ didn't *go* to work.(p.271)
- He wants to *go* to the hospital, and I'm not paying for the hospital again!"(p.271)
- If he thinks he needs to *go* to the hospital, I'll pay for him."(p.271)
- I knew Doc and Anne were going to be there, and all of them thought it would be good for me, but the first thing I did was to *go* to St. Thomas and try to talk to those women.)(p.272)
- Haunting me through each day's stupor -- and there were eighteen or nineteen such days in this man's home – was the thought: "Where do I *go* when his family comes home?"(p.278)
- To *go* north into the empty pine country and shoot myself, or to *go* south in the faint hope that a bunch of strangers might help me with my drinking problem.(p.278)
- I shut myself in my room, which began to *go* around in circles.(p.279)
- It ran something like this: If I *go* around shouting from the rooftops about my alcoholism, it might very possibly prevent me from getting a good job.(p.282)
- After a particularly bad Christmas and New Year's holiday, dad picked me up again early in January, 1937, to *go* through the usual sobering up routine.(p.289)
- The day before I was due to *go* back to Chicago, a Wednesday and Dr. Bob's afternoon off, he had me down to the office and we spent three or four hours formally going through the Six-Step program as it was at that time.(p.291)
- The three of us did not feel up to the job, and after a few meetings we convinced the prospects that they too should *go* to Akron where they could see an older group in action.(p.295)
- While working in an office, there was some semblance of restraint, but, oh boy, when I got on the outside with this new company without supervision, did I *go* to town!(p.300)
- It wasn't necessary to report to the office in person every day, and when I did *go* in, it was just to make an appearance and bounce right out again.(p.300)
- I didn't care to *go* visiting unless the parties we

might visit had plenty of liquor on hand and I could get drunk.(p.301)
• Indeed, I was always well on my way before I would undertake to *go* visiting at all.(p.301)
• And we wonder how much further this man could *go* if his alcoholic problem could be removed and he could throw one hundred per cent of his abilities into action.(p.308)
• By this time, with the doctor's explanation, the revelations contained in the book, and the hope-inspiring interview with Mr. T., I was ready and willing to *go* into the interior of the African jungles, if that was what it took, for me to find what these people had.(p.309)
• Letting *go* of everything at once was both painful and terrifying.(p.311)
• And, as the years *go* by, working together, sharing our experiences with one another, and also sharing a mutual trust, understanding and love – without strings, without obligation – we acquire relationships that are unique and priceless.(p.312)
• One morning when I was feeling really bad, I was put on K.P. and the head cook wanted me to *go* out and scrub the garbage cans.(p.317)
• I got orders to *go* to Vietnam, and I spent most of the year over there either drunk or sick with a hangover.(p.317)
• We got along fine for about two weeks, until she told me where to *go* and to take my damn bottle with me.(p.318)
• Finally, I reenlisted to *go* back to Nam.(p.318)
• From my post, I'd *go* spend weekends with her.(p.318)
• I got orders to *go* to Germany, and everyone in Germany was against me.(p.318)
• But I couldn't *go* on with it either.(p.319)
• She decided she wouldn't let herself *go* in her drinking.(p.321)
• But that night I tried to *go* to sleep.(p.322)
• But I wasn't happy, and I didn't ever let myself *go* in my drinking.(p.323)
• I couldn't keep up with any of my other friends, and I wouldn't *go* to anyone's house unless I knew they drank as heavily as I did.(p.324)
• George tried many times to *go* on the wagon.(p.324)
• It would be a little thing that I'd think was wrong, and off I'd *go*, drinking.(p.324)
• I reached a stage where I couldn't *go* into my apartment without a drink.(p.324)
• There was one girl especially, and I'd watch her from my window every morning, leaving faithfully to *go* to the hospital in the neighborhood.(p.326)
• And I was able to *go* on the wagon for long periods of time – once for four years, to cure an ulcer.(p.328)
• I could *go* on living and hurting ten years longer, or more."(p.333)
• I told her I had to *go* to A.A.(p.334)
• I did *go* to A.A., two days later, walking in alone.(p.334)
• I couldn't *go* to one wine store and look the man honestly in the face and buy a bottle, as I used to do when I had parties and entertained and did normal drinking.(p.336)
• I'd *go* into an organization, and it wasn't long before I was on the committee, then I was chairman of the committee; and if I was in a group, I'd soon be treasurer or secretary of the group.(p.339)
• When I'm asked to *go* out on a call, I *go*.(p.340)
• During this vacation, in the months of September and October, I decided to *go* on the water wagon.(p.343)
• And then we went up the side of a hill where we have a little barbecue area to make the fire for the barbecue, and on the way up, I thought to myself -- I'll *go* back down to the kitchen and refill this drink.(p.347)
• So I decided that I would *go* to my first meeting.(p.347)
• I recall, as I walked into that meeting, saying to myself, "Here I am, a fellow of the American College of Surgeons, a Fellow of the International College of Surgeons, a diplomate of one of the great specialty boards in these United States, a member of the American Psychiatric Society, and I have to *go* to the butcher, the baker and the carpenter to help make a man out of me!"(p.347)
• Why don't you *go* home and get the Big Book and open it at page fifty-eight and see what it says?"(p.349)
• I had no idea what would happen -- I just knew I didn't want to live if life was going to *go* on like it was.(p.355)
• Like all alcoholics endeavoring to run away from themselves and their environment, I decided to *go* to New York.(p.358)
• In January 1938, I had the opportunity to *go* to northern Vermont to manage a small daytime radio station that was up against it financially, and was about to fold its antenna.(p.359)
• At this time, however, she had an opportunity to *go* to Salt Lake City on a new project for the government, but she did promise me that if I would curtail my drinking and buckle down to hard work she would give serious consideration to my latest proposal and maybe join me at a later date when I got settled.(p.359)
• It was strictly a one man operation and I knew I had to tend to my knitting to make a *go* of it.(p.360)
• I said I was okay, but if it would make her feel better I would *go* "as tired as I was after the strenuous holidays."(p.365)
• Near the Laundromat, I would buy one bottle of pop and a few bottles of beer or wine, and *go* into the rest room, empty the pop bottle, refill it with the booze, and proceed to do my laundering.(p.370)
• I had nowhere else to *go*, and I knew something was terribly wrong, and the reason had to lie within myself.(p.371)
• Whenever we went out she appeared to *go* out of her way to keep me from having more than one drink.(p.376)
• She of course didn't realize how cunning an alcoholic can be and the lengths to which he will *go* in finding ways to satisfy the compulsion for more and more drinks after having had the first one.(p.377)
• A year later, while we were on a vacation trip she packed up to *go* home because of my excessive drinking, and I talked her out of it with the promise I would *go* on the wagon for at least a year.(p.377)
• They told me to *go* to meetings, and I still do at every available opportunity, whether I am at home or in some other city.(p.381)
• Frank said, "If you'd like to talk to a psychiatrist, I'll see a doctor and find out who to *go* to here."(p.387)
• I wanted to *go* home.(p.387)
• So the doctor let me *go* home on one condition.(p.387)
• Frank had to *go* to New York, but because I had a dog, we had a duplex, and I thought – if only we had a house!(p.388)
• He said that because of my drinking, he shouldn't leave, but that he had to *go* to New York for two weeks.(p.388)
• So I went down to him quite a few times a month and had him shoot me full of the stuff; and then I went across the street to a little drug store to take a glass of beer or two beers, and then stopped at the liquor store to get myself a pint and *go* home.(p.389)
• I wouldn't *go* to hospitals because I wanted my dog there, so I had to have a trained nurse.(p.390)
• If you will try this thing, I'll *go* along with you.(p.391)
• If you don't, you will have to *go* home.(p.391)
• He said, "Wait until I get back and I will *go* with you to see this man."(p.393)
• I had to *go* through extreme alcoholism to find my answer.(p.400)
• So I married a nice, well-meaning young newspaperman, so as not to have to *go* home.(p.402)
• A normal person, hit with adversity, can *go* on a drinking spree and then snap out of it.(p.404)
• I would pull out early, and *go* to the hunt breakfast and the flowing bowl of milk-punch.(p.404)
• I must *go* on the wagon for a while.(p.408)
• I had to *go* there every night.(p.410)
• I would walk up and down under the 59th Street bridge, trying to get up the nerve to *go* up there and jump.(p.411)
• "Why don't you just *go* down and see Mr. W.?" she asked.(p.412)
• I did not want to *go* and see her, but I went.(p.413)
• Since they could do nothing with Anne either, Priscilla suggested that I *go* and look after Anne.(p.414)
• We were to *go* up to our A.A. farm in Kent, and I spent the evening before riding herd on Anne.(p.415)
• When I went back to my hometown to *go* into private practice, I experienced another brief lull in my addiction to alcohol and drugs.(p.420)
• Most important, A.A. has enabled me to *go* back and start growing up all over again in all areas of my life.(p.420)
• I still think dad paid him something to let me *go*.(p.424)
• It looked as if the war would be over any day, but I had to *go* anyhow.(p.425)
• Sometimes I'd make it home and *go* to sleep at the wheel of my car, for all the neighbors to see next morning as they left for work.(p.429)
• I thought, "If this is A.A. why not *go* back to drinking, kill myself with booze in the next three years the doctor had given me, and call it a bad job?"(p.430)
• Weeks would *go* by without further trouble, and I'd be assured I'd at last hit on the right formula.(p.433)
• One night I barely made my downtown club; if I'd had to *go* another fifty feet I'd have collapsed in the gutter.(p.435)
• I had a lot more hell to *go* through.(p.437)
• And should I have more bad times, I know that I'll never again have to *go* through them alone.(p.438)
• With a problem like that, I couldn't *go* back to sleep.(p.441)
• But it quickly became obvious that he had this childish notion instead: If he could get me to *go* to enough meetings while in the hospital, I would continue to *go* after he let me out.(p.447)
• The people of A.A. had something that looked much better than what I had, but I was afraid to let *go* of what I had in order to try something new; there was a certain sense of security in the familiar.(p.448)
• There *go* my good intentions, fear of consequences, will to care, responsibility for my behavior.(p.458)
• I *go* back to my old alma mater occasionally to give A.A. talks, and -- just think! -- the warden is my friend.(p.462)
• I won't *go* into detail about that, but I can assure you it's no fun.(p.469)
• I even wanted to – but I wasn't allowed to, so I won't *go* now.(p.470)
• Judge say I *go* to jail next time.(p.475)
• Last time I drink, I *go* to room.(p.475)
• I *go* with him to first meeting, in small town in Maine.(p.476)
• Year later, I *go* to Canada to carry message to Tall Man, but he not listen to son.(p.476)
• I keep it simple; *go* to many meetings; carry message to those who listen.(p.476)
• *Go* to A.A. meetings.(p.477)
• But I can remember in post graduate days, and during interneship, that very often I'd *go* to a patient's bed and start a process of elimination and then, very often, I'd wind up guessing.(p.485)
• Of course, when father finally came to Virginia to work his way through school, he resented the southern "cracker," as he often called them, so much that he didn't even *go* back to his mother's funeral.(p.486)
• To get rid of me one evening, she decided to *go* to the movies, she and another friend.(p.487)
• I said that she told me she was going to the movies, and I became foolishly disturbed about it and, as things snowballed, I decided to *go* out and get drunk.(p.487)
• I'd *go* into my home with a bottle, and I remember clearly how I would look around to see if Vi was watching.(p.487)
• At that time the repeal whiskies were back, and I'd *go* to the store and buy my whiskey and take it to my office and put it under the desk, first in one place and then in another, and there soon was an accumulation of empty bottles.(p.488)
• Then I decided that I'd *go* back to Washington, which I did.(p.490)
• So I went down to talk to the District Attorney, and the arrangement was made that I would *go* home to stay with my mother, and that meant Vi and I were separated.(p.491)
• I continued to work and continued to *go* to lunch with Vi, and none of our acquaintances on the job knew that we had separated.(p.491)
• I sometimes gave it to my mother and then I'd *go* back and hound her for it.(p.491)
• I worked in the steel mill for possibly two months, and then I became disgusted with myself and decided to *go* back home.(p.492)
• After he'd talked half an hour, I still wanted him to hurry up and get out so I could *go* and get some whiskey before the liquor store closed.(p.494)
• I *go* to my room.(p.499)
• I am to *go* to camp on November 13th.(p.499)
• I'll *go* to bed.(p.500)
• Yet I am fairly steady when I *go* to bed.(p.500)
• I see her about to *go*.(p.501)
• I drink and *go* to bed; I take a few the next morning and *go* see my mother once more.(p.501)
• I *go* back to the hotel and get more gin.(p.501)
• I *go* to the hospital, where I have made friends with the night superintendent.(p.501)
• She begs me to *go* to a hospital for alcoholics which has been recommended.(p.502)
• I say I will *go*.(p.502)
• She makes the arrangements, but I will not *go*.(p.502)
• Suddenly I feel hopeless, unable to *go* on.(p.502)
• I *go* home.(p.502)

• I might *go* out West on a ranch where I couldn't get anything to drink.(p.502)
• I get out of bed and *go* to the man's room.(p.504)
• I *go* to see a man I had been asked to visit and tell him my story.(p.505)
• I will not *go* out and I will not enter into anything.(p.506)
• I back up to the door and *go* into the house.(p.506)
• They kept harping on it, that I *go*.(p.509)
• One evening I decided to *go* because two of those friends were to speak.(p.509)
• She was the one who really helped me to make a *go* of that twenty years and nine months in prison.(p.511)
• A former employer of mine said to me a little over ten years ago, "Pat, you seem to be one of those unfortunate people who at least once every six months must *go* out and roll in the gutter."(p.513)
• When I landed of course I hit a gin mill, and with three or four good shots under my belt the world began to *go* into that rosy glow.(p.513)
• I'd get downstairs to the gin mill, get enough in to hold me until eight o'clock in the morning, then I'd *go* out to join that "misery parade" that so many of us know so well.(p.514)
• I was afraid that sometime I would get half drunk and *go* through with it.(p.515)
• In here you must *go* all the way too."(p.516)
• So I decided I'd *go* back and live in Ireland to try the geography cure.(p.522)
• I went to hospitals, I went to retreats and doctors, and finally my mother asked me to *go* and see a specialist of her own choosing.(p.522)
• I was to pack and *go* and get out of their lives for good.(p.523)
• But if I came back in the usual state, then I'd have to *go* off for good the next day.(p.523)
• It was their open night meeting, but of course I thought they were all alcoholics; I couldn't imagine why anybody else would want to *go* there, and my first reaction was, well, I've come to something that's not for me.(p.524)
• Things got so bad, I was afraid to *go* on the street, so I turned to Mothers' Aid.(p.527)
• Then I would *go* home full of remorse, and wonder what I was going to do until I got my next check.(p.527)
• In time, I began to *go* out and forget the way back home.(p.527)
• If it was daylight, I would *go* down alleys to make sure no one saw me.(p.527)
• I do think that some of the Negroes here -- and other places, too -- are afraid to *go* to other meetings.(p.529)
• But as the years *go* by, the stretch becomes unbearable; and the man with the grown-up brain and the childish emotions -- vanity, self-interest, false pride, jealousy, longing for social approval, to name few -- becomes a prime candidate for alcohol.(p.534)
• If the listener were drunk enough, the lecture might *go* on through several martinis, which I was glad to pay for.(p.537)
• This question so insulted the emotions that clearly there was only one thing to do, *go* and get drunk again, and put that enquiring mind in its proper place, which was oblivion.(p.537)
• When sleep overtook me, my practice was to undress and *go* to bed, wherever.(p.537)
• And I am sure they would be right as far as they *go*, but A.A. has taught me I am the result of the way I reacted to what happened to me as a child.(p.544)
• My mother went to a nearby city to *go* to work, and my father, being an alcoholic, simply went.(p.544)
• I thought that life was a pretty simple thing; you simply made a plan for your life, based upon what you wanted, and then you needed only the courage to *go* after it.(p.545)
• The only importance in all of this lies in the fact that at twenty-three I was just as sick as I was at thirty three, when I came into A.A., but at that time I apparently had no place to *go* because I had no drinking problem.(p.546)
• So I had no place to *go*.(p.546)
• My husband was soon in uniform and among the first to *go* overseas.(p.547)
• It had provided me with excuses for my lack of education, my marital failures, personal failures, inadequacy, and of course, my alcoholism and, though I really thought I had been willing to part with it, now I knew I was reluctant to let it *go*.(p.552)
• Even when you don't really want it for them, and your prayers are only words and you don't mean it, *go* ahead and do it anyway.(p.552)
• Within a week, I was feeling well enough to *go* home.(p.558)
• An A.A. group, as such, should never *go* into business.(p.566)
• While an A.A. group may cooperate with anyone, such cooperation ought never *go* so far as affiliation or endorsement, actual or implied.(p.566)

goad

• It was worrying my wife a little, but she had the good sense not to take me to task about it or *goad* me into going.(p.364)

goal

• I tried to encourage a search for some new *goal*.(p.334)
• My eventual *goal* was to drink myself to death.(p.353)
• I did work of all kinds after school and during vacations, trying to find that which would appeal most as a *goal* for a life work.(p.373)

God

• Though he could not accept all the tenets of the Oxford Groups, he was convinced of the need for moral inventory, confession of personality defects, restitution to those harmed, helpfulness to others, and the necessity of belief in and dependence upon *God*.(p.xvi)
• In the fall of 1939, Fulton Oursler, then editor of Liberty, printed a piece in his magazine, called "Alcoholics and *God*."(p.xviii)
• When they talked of a *God* personal to me, who was love, superhuman strength and direction, I became irritated and my mind snapped shut against such a theory.(p.10)
• Judging from what I had seen in Europe and since, the power of *God* in human affairs was negligible, the Brotherhood of Man a grim jest.(p.11)
• But my friend sat before me, and he made the point-blank declaration that *God* had done for him what he could not do for himself.(p.11)
• The word *God* still aroused a certain antipathy.(p.12)
• When the thought was expressed that there might be a *God* personal to me this feeling was intensified.(p.12)
• He said, "Why don't you choose your own conception of *God*?"(p.12)
• Thus was I convinced that *God* is concerned with us humans when we want Him enough.(p.12)
• For a brief moment, I had needed and wanted *God*.(p.12)
• There I humbly offered myself to *God*, as I then understood Him, to do with me as He would.(p.13)
• Belief in the power of *God*, plus enough willingness, honesty and humility to establish and maintain the new order of things, were the essential requirements.(p.13)
• *God* comes to most men gradually, but His impact on me was sudden and profound.(p.14)
• But for the grace of *God*, there would have been thousands more convincing demonstrations.(p.25)
• What seemed at first a flimsy reed, has proved to be the loving and powerful hand of *God*.(p.28)
• The distinguished American psychologist, William James, in his book "Varieties of Religious Experience," indicates a multitude of ways in which men have discovered *God*.(p.28)
• Each individual, in the personal stories, describes in his own language and from his own point of view the way he established his relationship with *God*.(p.29)
• And it means, of course, that we are going to talk about *God*.(p.45)
• But his face falls when we speak of spiritual matters, especially when we mention *God*, for we have reopened a subject which our man thought he had neatly evaded or entirely ignored.(p.45)
• To others, the word "*God*" brought up a particular idea of Him with which someone had tried to impress them during childhood.(p.45)
• With that rejection we imagined we had abandoned the *God* idea entirely.(p.45)
• We found that as soon as we were able to lay aside prejudice and express even a willingness to believe in a Power greater than ourselves, we commenced to get results, even though it was impossible for any of us to fully define or comprehend that Power, which is *God*.(p.46)
• Much to our relief, we discovered we did not need to consider another's conception of *God*.(p.46)
• We found that *God* does not make too hard terms with those who seek Him.(p.46)
• When, therefore, we speak to you of *God*, we mean your own conception of *God*.(p.47)
• At the start, this was all we needed to commence spiritual growth, to effect our first conscious relation with *God* as we understood Him.(p.47)
• We read wordy books and indulge in windy arguments, thinking we believe this universe needs no *God* to explain it.(p.49)
• When many hundreds of people are able to say that the consciousness of the Presence of *God* is today the most important fact of their lives, they present a powerful reason why one should have faith.(p.51)
• Had not people said *God* had reserved this privilege to the birds?(p.51)
• When we saw others solve their problems by a simple reliance upon the Spirit of the Universe, we had to stop doubting the power of *God*.(p.52)
• But the *God* idea did.(p.52)
• When we became alcoholics, crushed by a self-imposed crisis we could not postpone or evade, we had to fearlessly face the proposition that either *God* is everything or else He is nothing.(p.53)
• *God* either is, or He isn't.(p.53)
• Yes, we had been faithful, abjectly faithful to the *God* of Reason.(p.54)
• They said *God* made these things possible, and we only smiled.(p.55)
• Actually we were fooling ourselves, for deep down in every man, woman, and child, is the fundamental idea of *God*.(p.55)
• We finally saw that faith in some kind of *God* was a part of our make-up, just as much as the feeling we have for a friend.(p.55)
• Our friend's gorge rose as he bitterly cried out: "If there is a *God*, He certainly hasn't done anything for me!"(p.56)
• "Who are you to say there is no *God*?"(p.56)
• In a few seconds he was overwhelmed by a conviction of the Presence of *God*.(p.56)
• *God* had restored his sanity.(p.57)
• Even so has *God* restored us all to our right minds.(p.57)
• But there is One who has all power -- that One is *God*.(p.59)
• 3.Made a decision to turn our will and our lives over to the care of *God* as we understood Him.(p.59)
• 5.Admitted to *God*, to ourselves, and to another human being the exact nature of our wrongs.(p.59)
• 6.Were entirely ready to have *God* remove all these defects of character.(p.59)
• 11.Sought through prayer and meditation to improve our conscious contact with *God* as we understood Him, praying only for knowledge of His will for us and the power to carry that out.(p.59)
• (c) That *God* could and would if He were sought.(p.60)
• Being convinced, we were at Step Three, which is that we decided to turn our will and our life over to *God* as we understood Him.(p.60)
• *God* makes that possible.(p.62)
• First of all, we had to quit playing *God*.(p.62)
• Next, we decided that hereafter in this drama of life, *God* was going to be our Director.(p.62)
• Many of us said to our Maker, as we understood Him: "*God*, I offer myself to Thee -- to build with me and to do with me as Thou wilt.(p.63)
• But it is better to meet *God* alone than with one who might misunderstand.(p.63)
• We asked *God* to help us show them the same tolerance, pity, and patience that we would cheerfully grant a sick friend.(p.67)
• *God* save me from being angry.(p.67)
• We cannot be helpful to all people, but at least *God* will show us how to take a kindly and tolerant view of each and every one.(p.67)
• For we are now on a different basis; the basis of trusting and relying upon *God*.(p.68)
• We trust infinite *God* rather than our finite selves.(p.68)
• They trust their *God*.(p.68)
• We never apologize for *God*.(p.68)
• We asked *God* to mold our ideals and help us to live up to them.(p.69)
• In meditation, we ask *God* what we should do about each specific matter.(p.69)
• *God* alone can judge our sex situation.(p.69)
• Counsel with persons is often desirable, but we let *God* be the final judge.(p.69)
• If we are sorry for what we have done, and have the honest desire to let *God* take us to better things, we believe we will be forgiven and will have learned our lesson.(p.70)
• We hope you are convinced now that *God* can remove whatever self-will has blocked you off from Him.(p.71)
• This requires action on our part, which, when completed, will mean that we have admitted to *God*, to ourselves, and to another human being the exact nature of our defects.(p.72)

- We thank *God* from the bottom of our heart that we know Him better.(p.75)
- Are we now ready to let *God* remove from us all the things which we have admitted are objectionable?(p.76)
- If we still cling to something we will not let go, we ask *God* to help us be willing.(p.76)
- Our real purpose is to fit ourselves to be of maximum service to *God* and the people about us.(p.77)
- We don't use this as an excuse for shying away from the subject of *God*.(p.77)
- If we have obtained permission, have consulted with others, asked *God* to help and the drastic step is indicated we must not shrink.(p.80)
- We are sorry for what we have done and, *God* willing, it shall not be repeated.(p.81)
- We will suddenly realize that *God* is doing for us what we could not do for ourselves.(p.84)
- When these crop up, we ask *God* at once to remove them.(p.84)
- Before we begin, we ask *God* to direct our thinking, especially asking that it be divorced from self-pity, dishonest or self-seeking motives.(p.86)
- Under these conditions we can employ our mental faculties with assurance, for after all *God* gave us brains to use.(p.86)
- Here we ask *God* for inspiration, an intuitive thought or a decision.(p.86)
- Being still inexperienced and having just made conscious contact with *God*, it is not probable that we are going to be inspired at all times.(p.87)
- So we let *God* discipline us in the simple way we have just outlined.(p.88)
- If the man be agnostic or atheist, make it emphatic that he does not have to agree with your conception of *God*.(p.93)
- If he is to find *God*, the desire must come from within.(p.95)
- We have no monopoly on *God*; we merely have an approach that worked with us.(p.95)
- The minute we put our work on a service plane, the alcoholic commences to rely upon our assistance rather than upon *God*.(p.98)
- Some of us have taken very hard knocks to learn this truth: Job or no job -- wife or no wife -- we simply do not stop drinking so long as we place dependence upon other people ahead of dependence on *God*.(p.98)
- The only condition is that he trust in *God* and clean house.(p.98)
- It is dependent upon his relationship with *God*.(p.100)
- Keep on the firing line of life with these motives and *God* will keep you unharmed.(p.102)
- The power of *God* goes deep!(p.114)
- Time after time, this apparent calamity has been a boon to us, for it opened up a path which led to the discovery of *God*.(p.116)
- If *God* can solve the age-old riddle of alcoholism, He can solve your problems too.(p.116)
- But it was a silly idea that we were too good to need *God*.(p.116)
- We urge you to try our program, for nothing will be so helpful to your husband as the radically changed attitude toward him which *God* will show you how to have.(p.117)
- *God* has either removed your husband's liquor problem or He has not.(p.120)
- So to you out there -- who may soon be with us -- we say "Good luck and *God* bless you!"(p.121)
- *God*, they believe, almost owes this recompense on a long overdue account.(p.123)
- He may demand that the family find *God* in a hurry, or exhibit amazing indifference to them and say he is above worldly considerations.(p.128)
- They may be jealous of a *God* who has stolen dad's affections.(p.128)
- While grateful that he drinks no more, they may not like the idea that *God* has accomplished the miracle where they failed.(p.128)
- What about his talk that *God* will take care of them?(p.128)
- Dad may feel that for years his drinking has placed him on the wrong side of every argument, but now he has become a superior person with *God* on his side.(p.129)
- This dream world has been replaced by a great sense of purpose, accompanied by a growing consciousness of the power of *God* in our lives.(p.130)
- We are sure *God* wants us to be happy, joyous, and free.(p.133)
- *God* didn't do it.(p.133)
- *God* has abundantly supplied this world with fine doctors, psychologists, and practitioners of various kinds.(p.133)
- Try to remember that though *God* has wrought miracles among us, we should never belittle a good doctor or psychiatrist.(p.133)
- His sanity returned and he thanked *God*.(p.154)
- He saw that he would have to face his problems squarely that *God* might give him mastery.(p.155)
- I've prayed to *God* on hangover mornings and sworn that I'd never touch another drop but by nine o'clock I'd be boiled as an owl."(p.158)
- "*God* ought to be able to do anything."(p.158)
- But he had found *God* -- and in finding *God* had found himself.(p.158)
- Being wrecked in the same vessel, being restored and united under one *God*, with hearts and minds attuned to the welfare of others, the things which matter so much to some people no longer signify much to them.(p.161)
- Many of us have felt, for the first time, the Presence and Power of *God* within its walls.(p.162)
- *God* will determine that, so you must remember that your real reliance is always upon Him.(p.164)
- *God* will constantly disclose more to you and to us.(p.164)
- Abandon yourself to *God* as you understand *God*.(p.164)
- May *God* bless you and keep you -- until then.(p.164)
- I had no trouble there because I had never actually ceased to believe in *God*, and had tried lots of times to get help but hadn't succeeded.(p.186)
- So, after reviewing these things and realizing what liquor had cost me, I went to this Higher Power which, to me was *God*, without any reservation, and admitted that I was completely powerless over alcohol, and that I was willing to do anything in the world to get rid of the problem.(p.187)
- In fact, I admitted that from now on I was willing to let *God* take over, instead of me.(p.187)
- I was at one time a deacon in the church and I still believe in *God*.(p.189)
- It was in the next two or three days after I had first met Doc and Bill, that I finally came to a decision to turn my will over to *God* and to go along with this program the best that I could.(p.189)
- Bill was very, very grateful that he had been released from this terrible thing and he had given *God* the credit for having done it, and he's so grateful about it he wants to tell other people about it.(p.191)
- I'm so grateful for both the program and the people in it that I still want to go, and then probably the most wonderful thing that I learned from the program -- I've seen this in the 'A.A. Grapevine' a lot of times, and I've had people say it to me personally, and I've heard people get up in meetings and make the same statement: The statement is, "I came into A.A. solely for the purpose of sobriety, but it has been through A.A. that I have found *God*."(p.192)
- The very simple program they advised me to follow was that I should ask to know God's will for me for that one day, and then, to the best of my ability, to follow that, and at night to express my gratefulness to *God* for the things that had happened to me during the day.(p.208)
- I couldn't stomach religion, and I didn't like the mention of *God* or any of the other capital letters.(p.227)
- In a few sentences he made *God* seem personal to me, explained Him as a being who was interested in me, the alcoholic, and that all I needed to do was to be willing to follow His way; that as long as I followed it I would be able to overcome my desire for liquor.(p.236)
- And he further said that *God* could not accept me as a sincere follower of His Divine Law unless I was ready to be thoroughly honest about it.(p.236)
- My visitor well knew, that as I tried to follow *God* I would get to studying these things out for myself.(p.236)
- That day I gave my will to *God* and asked to be directed.(p.237)
- I very early came to see that there had to be a continual renewal for that simple deal with *God*; that I had perpetually to keep the bargain.(p.237)
- This duty together with my weekly meetings with my fellow alcoholics, and my daily renewal of the contract I originally made with *God*, have kept me sober when nothing else ever did.(p.237)
- And when I get upset, cross-grained and out of tune with my fellow man I know that I am out of tune with *God*.(p.237)
- Searching where I have been at fault, it is not hard to discover and get right again, for I have proven to myself and to many others who know me that *God* can keep a man sober if he will let Him.(p.237)
- He said something about *God* or a Higher Power, but I brushed that off -- that was for the birds, not for me.(p.239)
- All they talked of that first week-end was *God*, and how they were going to straighten out Jackie's and my life.(p.245)
- During that first week-end I decided to stay in New York and take all they gave out with, except the "*God* stuff."(p.246)
- There was one meeting a week at Bill's home in Brooklyn, and we all took turns there spouting off about how we had changed our lives overnight, how many drunks we had saved and straightened out, and last, but not least, how *God* had touched each of us personally on the shoulder.(p.246)
- I don't think the boys were completely convinced of my personality change, for they fought shy of including my story in the book, so my only contribution to their literary efforts was my firm conviction, being still a theological rebel, that the word *God* should be qualified with the phrase "as we understand him" -- for that was the only way I could accept spirituality.(p.248)
- And I still say that as long as I remember that January 8th in Washington, that is how long, by the grace of *God* as I understand Him, I will retain a happy sobriety.(p.250)
- And we went down through the valley, and I remembered reading about the Ku Klux Klan and how they burnt crosses, and I thought, "*God* alone knows what we are getting into this time!"(p.269)
- I always feel that our *God* Consciousness was a steady growth after we became associated with A.A.(p.270)
- I knew then that I hadn't made a complete surrender, because I tried to bargain with the *God* I had found, and I said, "Anything but that!(p.271)
- Thank *God* I had no desire for a drink when he died.(p.272)
- I have thanked *God* many times in the last sixteen years that that was just what he did not do!(p.278)
- Here was a tall, rugged, highly educated Yankee talking in a matter of course way about *God* and prayer.(p.279)
- You can't lose, and maybe *God* will help you -- just maybe, mind you.(p.280)
- It went something like this: "*God*, for eighteen years I have been unable to handle this problem.(p.280)
- I had tried to be the center of my own little world, whereas *God* was the center of a vast universe of which I was perhaps an essential, but a very tiny, part.(p.280)
- It would be wonderful were I able to tell you that my confidence in *God* and my application of the Twelve Steps to my daily living have utterly banished fear.(p.284)
- We are both depending upon *God* and our use of the A.A. program to help us make a success of this joint undertaking.(p.286)
- Above all, I have gained the greatest thing accorded to any man, the love and understanding of a gracious *God*, who has lifted me from the alcoholic scrap-heap to a position of trust where I have been able to reap the rich rewards that come from showing a little love for others and from serving them as I can.(p.296)
- They sum it up like this: "We didn't wait to hit bottom because, thank *God*, we could see the bottom.(p.315)
- Sometimes I would lie on the bathroom floor, deathly sick, praying I would die, and praying to *God* as I always had prayed to Him when I was drinking: "Dear *God*, get me out of this one and I'll never do it again."(p.324)
- And then I'd say, "*God*, don't pay any attention to me.(p.324)
- I sat up in the big red chair, suddenly thinking, "My *God*, with my kind of lousy luck, I might not die soon!(p.333)
- When the time comes to solve them, *God* will give me strength for that day.(p.341)
- I had been brought up to believe in *God*, but I know that until I found this A.A. program, I had never found or known faith in the reality of *God*, the reality of His power that is now with me in everything I do.(p.341)
- Psychiatrist and surgeon, he had lost his way until he realized that *God*, not he, was the Great Healer.(p.345)
- The Third Step said: "Made a decision to turn our will and our lives over to the care of *God* as we understood Him."(p.350)
- And so one gets to thinking to oneself, "Who is this *God*?(p.350)
- For myself, I have an absolute proof of the existence of *God*.(p.350)
- To me it is *God*.(p.352)
- Thank *God* I knew of A.A., so I called.(p.355)

• It has brought about a revelation of self, the discovery of an inner being, an awareness of ***God***.(p.355)
• Thank ***God*** that in spite of my heavy drinking my mind was clear enough to make a decision then and there.(p.363)
• I haven't written anything about that part of my story, but I believe in a Greater Power which I call ***God*** and I ask for His wisdom and guidance daily.(p.366)
• I've had more problems but, thank ***God***, I have had the teachings of A.A. with which to face them.(p.367)
• And, believe me, I thank ***God*** that I found out about A.A. before I had to beat my brains out – before I had been hospitalized, jailed or lost a job.(p.367)
• When I hear the more rugged stories of alcoholics who became sicker than I did with this affliction, I humbly thank ***God*** for showing me "the handwriting on the wall."(p.367)
• That Power I chose to call ***God***.(p.381)
• Above all, I am grateful to A.A. for my sobriety, which means so much to my family, friends and business associates, because ***God*** and A.A. were able to do for me something I was unable to do for myself.(p.383)
• It was the first time in my life that I could not get a lift out of what I was drinking; and so one Friday night, at five minutes to six, I had half a water glass of warm gin, and that is when I first asked ***God*** to help me.(p.393)
• It has been a fellowship with ***God*** and man that has held good wherever I've turned and whatever I've done.(p.394)
• Only ***God*** as we understand Him can calculate these.(p.399)
• My new friends made fun of ***God*** and all the orthodox beliefs.(p.408)
• I think now that a ***God***, in whom I did not believe, was looking after me.(p.412)
• I read the book and ***God*** leapt at me from every page.(p.412)
• Dear ***God***, I'll do anything!(p.430)
• Many times in the intervening years I have thanked ***God*** for that man, a man who had the courage to admit failure, a man who had the humility to confess that all the hard-won learning of his profession could not turn up the answer.(p.436)
• If pressed further, all I can do is follow the psalmist who said it long, long before me: "Be still, and know that I am ***God***."(p.437)
• I can't say, "***God*** could restore me to sanity, but until He does, I'll control myself – with pills."(p.443)
• But by ***God***, I wouldn't talk or eat, either!(p.444)
• Max still works with me in the office, but we have turned our wills and our lives and our work over to the care of ***God***.(p.446)
• After I had been around A.A. for seven months, tapering off alcohol and pills, not finding the program working very well, I was finally able to say, "Okay, ***God***.(p.448)
• A.A. and acceptance have taught me that there is a bit of good in the worst of us and a bit of bad in the best of us; that we are all children of ***God*** and we each have a right to be here.(p.449)
• I am saying that I know better than ***God***.(p.449)
• Acceptance is the key to my relationship with ***God*** today.(p.452)
• Thank ***God*** for A.A.!(p.452)
• (***God*** works through people.)(p.462)
• I thank ***God*** I am to see him this month.(p.463)
• I owe everything to A.A. and ***God***.(p.463)
• ***God*** bless all you people in A.A. and especially you fellows in prison.(p.463)
• That was over seven years ago, and thank ***God*** and A.A., I haven't had a drink since.(p.473)
• ***God*** must watch over me.(p.475)
• By grace of ***God*** I stop, think two things: This would kill good mother and father; then remember boys talk about Indian fellow who been sober three years.(p.475)
• Only ***God*** is.(p.482)
• I rebelled against this, because just about the time that I was getting ready to leave high school, a revelation came to me about ***God*** and it made things very complicated for me.(p.489)
• The thought came to me that if ***God***, as my mother said, was a vengeful ***God***, he couldn't be a loving ***God***.(p.489)
• Pioneer A.A., minister's son, and southern farmer, he asked, "Who am I to say there is no ***God***?"(p.497)
• Then he asks me if I believe in a power greater than myself, whether I call that power ***God***, Allah, Confucius, Prime Cause, Divine Mind, or any other name.(p.503)
• I told him that I believe in electricity and other forces of nature, but as for a ***God***, if there is one, He has never done anything for me.(p.503)
• Can all the worth while people I have known be wrong about ***God***?(p.503)
• "Who are you to say there is no ***God***?"(p.504)
• When you've been in a jam you've said, '***God***, please do this or that,' and if it turned out your way that was the last of it, and if it didn't you've said 'There isn't any ***God***' or 'He doesn't do anything for me.'(p.504)
• "The thing I do is to say '***God*** here I am and here are all my troubles.(p.504)
• I believe in ***God***.(p.504)
• I tell them of the peace, and that I believe in ***God***.(p.505)
• I begin to play ***God***.(p.506)
• Why has ***God*** left me?(p.506)
• You hit the street about ten minutes to eight, and you walk around the block, ***God*** knows how many times, waiting for that joint to open.(p.514)
• I asked ***God*** for help.(p.515)
• ***God*** has been good to me both in my drinking and in my sobriety.(p.516)
• Because, thank ***God***, since I came into this program I haven't had any trouble.(p.516)
• By the grace of ***God***, I only served three years.(p.528)
• There was the physical aspect; to be the youngest and the runt of the brood of children, to have to wear glasses very early and so to be teased, to be bookish and bored in school because the captain of the football team could not translate Virgil and yet was the school ***god*** while you, you, you little shrimp, were the school egghead, junior size and an early model.(p.533)
• Which is only another way of saying, I had to be right all the time, and only ***God*** can be that.(p.535)
• Okay, I wanted to be ***God***.(p.535)
• And, as a child is a part of his father, so do I now want to be a part of ***God***.(p.535)
• My personal definition, which I submit as applying only to myself (although everyone is welcome to it who wants it), includes every waking activity of the human being; to have a creative attitude towards things is a more exact meaning, to live and to deal with other human beings creatively, which to me means seeing the ***God*** in them, and respecting and worshipping this ***God***.(p.535)
• When the policeman released me to my stupefied and exasperated friend at four in the morning, I went to my traveling bag and groped until I found – well, let the officer speak: "Ah," said the policeman, "he's got anuder pair, t'ank ***God***!"(p.538)
• Thank ***God*** that those days are gone.(p.540)
• The children kept me sober for darn near three weeks, and then I went on (please ***God***) my last drunk.(p.549)
• A.A. has given me serenity of purpose, the opportunity to be of service to ***God*** and to the people about me, and I am serene in the infallibility of these principles that provide the fulfillment of my purpose.(p.551)
• In my prayers that morning I asked ***God*** to point out to me some way to be free of this resentment.(p.552)
• "***God*** willing, we . . . may never again have to deal with drinking, but we have to deal with sobriety every day."(p.554)
• He happened to be, by the grace of ***God***, Dr. Harry Tiebout, the psychiatrist who probably knew more about alcoholism than any other in the world.(p.559)
• ***God*** willing, we members of A.A. may never again have to deal with drinking, but we have to deal with sobriety every day.(p.560)
• And with ***God***.(p.561)
• Two – For our group purpose there is but one ultimate authority – a loving ***God*** as He may express Himself in our group conscience.(p.564)
• 2. – For our group purpose there is but one ultimate authority -- a loving ***God*** as He may express Himself in our group conscience.(p.565)

God-conscious

• To some extent we have become ***God-conscious***.(p.85)

God-consciousness

• I was to test my thinking by the new ***God-consciousness*** within.(p.13)
• Though it was not our intention to create such an impression, many alcoholics have nevertheless concluded that in order to recover they must acquire an immediate and overwhelming "***God-consciousness***" followed at once by a vast change in feeling and outlook.(p.569)
• Our more religious members call it "***God-consciousness***."(p.570)

God-given

• We remembered always that our sex powers were ***God-given*** and therefore good, neither to be used lightly or selfishly nor to be despised and loathed.(p.69)

God-knows-who

• And I put a Big Book by my night stand, and I put a "Twelve Steps and Twelve Tradition" in my locker at the hospital, and I got books by Emmet Fox, and I got books by ***God-knows-who***, and I got to reading all these things.(p.348)

God-sufficiency

• When others showed us that "***God-sufficiency***" worked with them, we began to feel like those who had insisted the Wrights would never fly.(p.52)

God's

• How often have some of us begun to drink in this nonchalant way, and after the third or fourth, pounded on the bar and said to ourselves, "For ***God's*** sake, how did I ever get started again?"(p.24)
• The great fact is just this, and nothing less: That we have had deep and effective spiritual experiences which have revolutionized our whole attitude toward life, toward our fellows and toward ***God's*** universe.(p.25)
• Instead of regarding ourselves as intelligent agents, spearheads of ***God's*** ever advancing Creation, we agnostics and atheists chose to believe that our human intelligence was the last word, the alpha and the omega, the beginning and end of all.(p.49)
• We had to have ***God's*** help.(p.62)
• He saw that he had to place the outcome in ***God's*** hands or he would soon start drinking again, and all would be lost anyhow.(p.80)
• As ***God's*** people we stand on our feet; we don't crawl before anyone.(p.83)
• Every day is a day when we must carry the vision of ***God's*** will into all of our activities.(p.85)
• After making our review we ask ***God's*** forgiveness and inquire what corrective measures should be taken.(p.86)
• When we look back, we realize that the things which came to us when we put ourselves in ***God's*** hands were better than anything we could have planned.(p.100)
• If a repetition is to be prevented, place the problem, along with everything else, in ***God's*** hands.(p.120)
• Cling to the thought that, in ***God's*** hands, the dark past is the greatest possession you have -- the key to life and happiness for others.(p.124)
• I wasn't afraid that the program wouldn't work, but I still was doubtful whether I would be able to hang on to the program, but I did come to the conclusion that I was willing to put everything I had into it, with ***God's*** power, and that I wanted to do just that.(p.189)
• The very simple program they advised me to follow was that I should ask to know ***God's*** will for me for that one day, and then, to the best of my ability, to follow that, and at night to express my gratefulness to God for the things that had happened to me during the day.(p.208)
• "You can't win unless you try ***God's*** way."(p.236)
• So I began to pray; to place my problems in ***God's*** hands.(p.237)
• I was supposed to be doing ***God's*** will, not mine.(p.282)
• With ***God's*** help I am able, for one day at a time, to carry business responsibilities which, not many years ago, I would not have dreamed of assuming.(p.284)
• She left, and I sat down and crossed my hands, and looked up and said, "For ***God's*** sake, help me."(p.351)
• It pays daily in more harmonious relations with my fellow men, in ever clearer insight into the true meaning of life, and in the answering love and gratitude wherever and whenever I have been the instrument of ***God's*** will in the lives of others.(p.394)
• To me, A.A. is within the reach of every alcoholic, because it can be achieved in any walk of life and because the achievement is not ours but ***God's***.(p.395)
• "Then why in ***God's*** name haven't you told me so, during all these years?"(p.436)
• When a big, healthy-looking young fellow stood up there and said, "I'm a success today if I don't drink today," I thought, "Man, I've got a thousand things to do today before I can brag about not taking a drink, for ***God's*** sake!"(p.447)
• Nothing, absolutely nothing happens in ***God's*** world by mistake.(p.449)
• When I complain about me or about you, I am complaining about ***God's*** handiwork.(p.449)
• Rather, I do whatever is in front of me to be done, and I leave the results up to Him; however it turns out, that's ***God's*** will for me.(p.452)
• I was not eligible for parole, until – with ***God's***

help, I'm sure -- the governor cut five years off my sentence.(p.462)

• I attempted nearly two years ago to make some amends and contact my children, but it wasn't *God's* time yet.(p.463)

godly

• We looked askance at many individuals who claimed to be ***godly***.(p.46)

goes

• I have seen hundreds of families set their feet in the path that really ***goes*** somewhere; have seen the most impossible domestic situations righted; feuds and bitterness of all sorts wiped out.(p.15)

• But not so with the alcoholic illness, for with it there ***goes*** annihilation of all the things worth while in life.(p.18)

• He is the fellow who ***goes*** to bed so intoxicated he ought to sleep the clock around.(p.21)

• Perhaps he ***goes*** to a doctor who gives him morphine or some sedative with which to taper off.(p.22)

• A business which takes no regular inventory usually ***goes*** broke.(p.64)

• Sometimes it is wise to wait till he ***goes*** on a binge.(p.90)

• The power of God ***goes*** deep!(p.114)

• Whether the family ***goes*** on a spiritual basis or not, the alcoholic member has to if he would recover.(p.135)

• This kind of waste ***goes*** on unabated.(p.137)

• ***Goes*** off his head completely when he's drinking.(p.156)

• Mere cessation from drinking is not enough for an alcoholic while the need for that drink ***goes*** on.(p.339)

• It is a way of life that pays as it ***goes***, every step of the way, in compensations that have been wonderfully rich and rewarding.(p.394)

• Aside from being a common drunk, I had a very serious pill affliction and all the garbage that ***goes*** with it -- lying, stealing, cheating anybody and everybody, conning the people I could, and staying clear of the ones I couldn't.(p.478)

going

• Alcohol being no respecter of persons, we are an accurate cross section of America, and in distant lands, the same democratic evening-up process is now ***going*** on.(p.xx)

• They are always "***going*** on the wagon for keeps."(p.xxviii)

• It is a design for living that works in rough ***going***.(p.15)

• All of us spend much of our spare time in the sort of effort which we are ***going*** to describe.(p.19)

• If we keep on the way we are ***going*** there is little doubt that much good will result, but the surface of the problem would hardly be scratched.(p.19)

• Before ***going*** into a detailed discussion, it may be well to summarize some points as we see them.(p.20)

• Despite all we can say, many who are real alcoholics are not ***going*** to believe they are in that class.(p.31)

• Here are some of the methods we have tried: Drinking beer only, limiting the number of drinks, never drinking alone, never drinking in the morning, drinking only at home, never having it in the house, never drinking during business hours, drinking only at parties, switching from scotch to brandy, drinking only natural wines, agreeing to resign if ever drunk on the job, taking a trip, not taking a trip, swearing off forever (with and without a solemn oath), taking more physical exercise, reading inspirational books, ***going*** to health farms and sanitariums, accepting voluntary commitment to asylums -- we could increase the list ad infinitum.(p.31)

• I also had the notion that I might find a customer for a car at this place, which was familiar for I had been ***going*** to it for years.(p.36)

• When I returned to the hotel it struck me a highball would be fine before ***going*** to bed, so I stepped into the bar and had one.(p.41)

• Perhaps it is ***going*** to be that way with you.(p.44)

• And it means, of course, that we are ***going*** to talk about God.(p.45)

• Once confused and baffled by the seeming futility of existence they show the underlying reasons why they were making heavy ***going*** of life.(p.50)

• Next, we decided that hereafter in this drama of life, God was ***going*** to be our Director.(p.62)

• Does this mean we are ***going*** to get drunk?(p.70)

• As we look over the list of business acquaintances and friends we have hurt, we may feel diffident about ***going*** to some of them on a spiritual basis.(p.76)

• He is ***going*** to be more interested in a demonstration of good will than in our talk of spiritual discoveries.(p.77)

• In fairness we must say that she may understand, but what are we ***going*** to do about a thing like that?(p.81)

• We are ***going*** to know a new freedom and a new happiness.(p.83)

• Being still inexperienced and having just made conscious contact with God, it is not probable that we are ***going*** to be inspired at all times.(p.87)

• In that case he is ***going*** to wonder how you can add anything to what he already knows.(p.93)

• You should point out that his defects of character are not ***going*** to disappear over night.(p.100)

• Therefore, ask yourself on each occasion, "Have I any good social, business, or personal reason for ***going*** to this place?(p.101)

• But be sure you are on solid spiritual ground before you start and that your motive in ***going*** is thoroughly good.(p.102)

• Be determined that your husband's drinking is not ***going*** to spoil your relations with your children or your friends.(p.111)

• If you and your husband find a solution for the pressing problem of drink you are, of course, ***going*** to be very happy.(p.117)

• Perhaps your husband will make a fair start on the new basis, but just as things are ***going*** beautifully he dismays you by coming home drunk.(p.120)

• At the very beginning, the couple ought to frankly face the fact that each will have to yield here and there if the family is ***going*** to play an effective part in the new life.(p.131)

• You are ***going*** to meet these new friends in your own community.(p.152)

• Away from my office two or three weeks at a time; horrible days and nights when I would lie on the floor of my home, lying awake and reaching over to get the bottle, taking a drink and ***going*** back into oblivion.(p.184)

• I thought to myself, "Well, she is ***going*** to tell me this is the end," and I certainly couldn't blame her and did not intend to try to justify myself.(p.184)

• She said, "You are ***going*** to quit."(p.185)

• This was ***going*** to help them to stay sober.(p.185)

• Now, if you don't want it, we'll not take up your time, and we'll be ***going*** and looking for someone else."(p.186)

• Two days before this, Dr. Bob had said to me, "If you and I are ***going*** to stay sober, we had better get busy."(p.188)

• We're ***going*** to get up and get out of here."(p.189)

• I remember telling them too that it was ***going*** to be awfully tough, because I did some other things, smoked cigarettes and played penny ante poker, sometimes bet on the horse races and they said, "Don't you think you're having more trouble with this drinking than with anything else at the present time?(p.190)

• Don't you believe you are ***going*** to have all you can do to get rid of that?"(p.190)

• I always built up in my own mind the great things that I was ***going*** to do, and in fact I accomplished about fifty percent of them and then lost interest.(p.193)

• When I was sixteen years old, my mother remarried and I was given the opportunity of ***going*** back to school.(p.193)

• I went into the high school grades, but having missed all the intermediate grades, I didn't get along too well, so I developed the habit of ***going*** back to school just long enough for the football season and then quitting.(p.193)

• To my mind, drinking didn't have anything to do with not ***going*** through with things.(p.198)

• I can well remember over a long period of years when I thought I was the only person in the world who knew that sooner or later I was ***going*** to get drunk.(p.198)

• I told somebody that I was ***going*** down to get Christian Science and they took me down, but I don't remember saying that.(p.202)

• Pretty soon, I wasn't ***going*** at all, and was avoiding those people who had been so kind to me.(p.203)

• Then I got into the habit of having beers, and decided that a drink of whiskey was not any worse; so I would get the one drink of whiskey but, on second thought, I decided that as long as I was only ***going*** to have one, I might as well make it a double-header.(p.203)

• I went downstairs and there was the grizzly old veteran police officer in charge of the property desk, and as he gave me the stuff, he asked, "Are you ***going*** out in the street that way?"(p.204)

• I said, "I'm certainly not ***going*** to stay in here!"(p.204)

• I got two drinks, each of them a quarter of that pint, in me, and was talking along with these people, but I felt that sooner or later they were ***going*** to have me cornered because they were smarter than I was and the drink was beginning to take effect; but as I reached for the third drink Bob said, "Listen, Buster, you promised to take some medicine if we got you a drink.(p.206)

• You're never ***going*** to want another drink, are you?"; and this answer of his is very important to those of us who are victims of alcoholism.(p.206)

• I'm not ***going*** to want another drink?"(p.207)

• Not far from where I lived they built a new technical high school and one of the teachers sold me on the idea that I needed a little mechanical drawing if I were ***going*** to be a good toolmaker.(p.211)

• My life was fairly well crowded and I didn't seem to need any stimulants to keep me ***going***.(p.213)

• These periods became more frequent and I resolved that when I became forty, which was very shortly, I was ***going*** on the wagon.(p.213)

• The successful demonstration I had made of my life problems in other respects convinced me that some day I was ***going*** to be able to drink like a gentleman.(p.214)

• I realized that there wasn't anything I could say to place myself in a more favorable light with my children, that it was ***going*** to be a matter of time; for I also understood the intolerance of young people towards deficiencies in their elders.(p.220)

• I resolved that if I were ***going*** to continue with the Catholic Church, I was ***going*** to know the roots of the doctrine, since those roots had caused me some confusion.(p.221)

• I remembered ***going*** through what my sister assured me was my nightly procedure of trying to find Willie Seabrook's name in the telephone book.(p.224)

• I remembered asserting that I was ***going*** to do something about this, that I couldn't go on . . .(p.224)

• I had been ***going*** on like that for over a year.(p.224)

• All I had left was an iron determination to live my own life in spite of the alien world -- and here I was, an inwardly frightened, outwardly defiant woman, who desperately needed a prop to keep ***going***.(p.226)

• We saw very early that Prohibition wasn't ***going*** to work.(p.232)

• I was doing well in business, and in ***going*** around town I was frequently invited to have a drink in a speakeasy.(p.233)

• I was ***going*** to straighten up.(p.234)

• I knew somehow that it meant more than just ***going*** to church and living a moral life.(p.236)

• The man who was ***going*** to take over one of their biggest branches come Monday?(p.243)

• At the time, I thought them just a swell pair of screwballs, for they were not only ***going*** to save all the drunks in the world but also all the so-called normal people!(p.245)

• All they talked of that first week-end was God, and how they were ***going*** to straighten out Jackie's and my life.(p.245)

• I quit the factory and got a job on a small newspaper, ***going*** from that to a Pittsburgh daily, long ago defunct.(p.252)

• Indeed, I was beginning to see that I would require implicit faith, like a small child, if I was ***going*** to get anywhere.(p.259)

• She tells how A.A. works when the ***going*** is rough.(p.261)

• There was a man watching, and I turned to him and said with a defiant air I carried with me all the time, "If I don't quit this I'm ***going*** to have to join that alcoholic business they're talking about."(p.266)

• I'm ***going*** in to see him, and see what can be done."(p.267)

• I didn't know what they were ***going*** to do because he didn't tell us much.(p.269)

• I remember sometime, it was possibly six months after we had been ***going*** steadily to King School, that we were coming home from a meeting and saw a car along the way, and a fellow in back drinking a bottle of beer.(p.271)

• She said, "He's not ***going*** to the hospital, whether you pay for it or I pay for it, he's not ***going***!"(p.271)

• I knew Doc and Anne were ***going*** to be there, and all of them thought it would be good for me, but the first thing I did was to go to St. Thomas and try to talk to those women.)(p.272)

• I didn't think I was ***going*** to get drunk right then, but I remember how comforting it was when I called Anne and told her.(p.273)

• If it isn't anything that's ***going*** to help you or anybody else, why should you become involved in it, and get all disturbed about it?"(p.273)

• A low ebb in the family fortunes necessitated my ***going*** to work when I was twenty.(p.275)

• During that first year, however, I managed to make

both ends meet, and to avoid ever ***going*** back to my old habit pattern of borrowing money when I could not earn it.(p.283)
• By 1932, I was ***going*** on two or three day benders.(p.288)
• The day before I was due to go back to Chicago, a Wednesday and Dr. Bob's afternoon off, he had me down to the office and we spent three or four hours formally ***going*** through the Six-Step program as it was at that time.(p.291)
• I had a mortal fear of ***going*** to bed and tossing all night.(p.299)
• She offered me the alternative of ***going*** to see him or her leaving me for good and all.(p.301)
• Some of us struggle with these people because we know that they are really very sick, but we also know that short of some miracle, we are not ***going*** to help them except temporarily, and that they will inevitably get worse and worse until one of two things happens.(p.308)
• Karen didn't want to see me any more, and neither did two other girls I'd been ***going*** out with.(p.318)
• If we were invited to a formal party and I knew they were only ***going*** to have one or two drinks, I wouldn't have any.(p.323)
• And he, poor dear, didn't know what was ***going*** on.(p.325)
• And unless I had some rosy picture of what was ***going*** to happen that day, I wouldn't even feel like getting up in the morning at all.(p.325)
• I wanted him to be sure that I wasn't the one who was ***going*** to drink the whole bottle.(p.336)
• I screamed on the telephone for my mother to get up there; something was ***going*** to happen; I didn't know what, but if she didn't get there quick, I'd split wide open.(p.338)
• And yet, how was I ***going*** to live without it?(p.338)
• I said to my husband, "I'm ***going*** to try, every free moment that I have, to get interested in something outside, get myself over this rut I'm in."(p.338)
• I thought I was ***going*** out of my mind.(p.339)
• I'm not ***going***; A.A. is leading me there.(p.340)
• For this officer in the Indian Army, ***going*** on the wagon was not enough; attempts at control failed.(p.342)
• I had no idea what would happen -- I just knew I didn't want to live if life was ***going*** to go on like it was.(p.355)
• I was ***going*** to prove to her that liquor wasn't necessary in my life, and above all that I still loved her more than anything else in the world and that I wanted her back.(p.362)
• It was worrying my wife a little, but she had the good sense not to take me to task about it or goad me into ***going***.(p.364)
• She told me not to bother ***going*** "for her sake"; she told me in a nice way that it didn't make any difference to her – and that really scared me – so I went.(p.365)
• I tried to hide my drinking by ***going*** places where I was unlikely to see anyone I knew.(p.375)
• I realized I had been ***going*** down and down.(p.378)
• I had not yet lost my job or family, even though both were on the verge of ***going***.(p.379)
• Scared that my dress wasn't ***going*** to fit right, that the church wasn't ***going*** to be filled, that I'd fall flat on my face walking up the aisle; in fact, I was afraid I wasn't ***going*** to be a prima donna in the place where I should be.(p.385)
• I had never been inside of an insane asylum and I really thought I was ***going*** to a private hospital.(p.387)
• I resented the fact that Frank had done this to me, and I just didn't know what was ***going*** on.(p.388)
• So I located a house, and I thought we ought to move into it immediately, but Frank was horrified, because he never knew what was ***going*** to happen to me.(p.388)
• He even had the people come out, and tell me what kind of room I was ***going*** to have, and that he could come and see me, and that the dog could come and see me.(p.389)
• But somewhere during that time, I remembered ***going*** back on the bunk and crying my eyes out.(p.390)
• I was ***going*** to sue the city for what they did to me.(p.391)
• The next morning he came into my room and said, "Esther, I'm not ***going*** to lecture you any more, but I want you to read this article.(p.391)
• In spite of knowing that my drunkenness was a symptom of the things that were wrong with me, and that I could never drink again, I thought I couldn't yet give it up, although I was ***going*** to try.(p.393)
• I was ***going*** to get drunk again -- Drunk!(p.408)
• Nobody was ***going*** to reform me!(p.412)
• I was ***going*** to reform myself!(p.412)
• He was well dressed; he was easy ***going***.(p.413)
• On the train ***going*** back, Anne's one idea was to get to the nearest bar.(p.415)
• John said, "Keep ***going*** to meetings."(p.415)
• Through ***going*** to meetings and listening, and occasionally speaking, through doing Twelve Step work, whereby in helping others you are both the teacher and the student, by making many wonderful A.A. friends, I have been taught all the things in life that are worth having.(p.416)
• I depended on optimism and ambition to live in society; when I began to tire, I had to depend on chemicals instead to keep ***going***.(p.420)
• They got bigger and bigger and nearer and nearer, as if they were ***going*** to fall and crush me.(p.427)
• This I would do by ***going*** completely "bohemian" for a night, getting drunk and rolling home with the dawn.(p.432)
• "Well, Doc," I said, "what are we ***going*** to do?"(p.436)
• But what a difference there is between ***going*** through hell without a power greater than one's self, and with it!(p.437)
• After ***going*** to school all day, working in the family drugstore all evening, and then studying until one or two in the morning, I would not be able to sleep soundly, with everything I had been studying ***going*** round in my head.(p.440)
• Eventually, the psychiatrist discharged me from the hospital, and Max and I began ***going*** to meetings ourselves.(p.447)
• Now, what am I ***going*** to do about it?"(p.449)
• We do this by ***going*** to many A.A. meetings with an open mind and a desire to live the good-feeling life without chemicals -- liquid or otherwise.(p.459)
• I started ***going*** to A.A. in prison at the group's next meeting.(p.461)
• I count my sobriety date from the day I began ***going*** to A.A. in prison, not from the date of my last drink.(p.462)
• Then I remember him coming into my room one night with a friend, and telling me to get dressed -- we were ***going*** away.(p.466)
• He said he didn't care what I did with the money, but there was ***going*** to be no more until I was completely sober.(p.467)
• This time I didn't put up any fight because I knew why they were there and where I was ***going***, the psychopathic ward of the City Hospital, where I had been once before.(p.468)
• Instead, I started ***going*** to a nice private sanitarium which, after the first visit, turned out to be more like a country club than anything else.(p.468)
• Here was a book that said I could do something that all these doctors and priests and ministers and psychiatrists that I'd been ***going*** to for years couldn't do!(p.473)
• Once, I phoned my brother-in-law and told him I was ***going*** to take a handful of pills (in fact, I already had) and I would slash my wrists if he didn't come over to stop me.(p.479)
• We lived just a few doors from the First Baptist Church and when they had funerals I remember very often asking my mother whether the person was good or bad and whether they were ***going*** to heaven or hell.(p.483)
• For the first couple of years it wasn't too bad because the momentum kept things ***going***.(p.486)
• But when things became crucial, everything started ***going*** haywire and I started ***going*** haywire with them.(p.486)
• I said that she told me she was ***going*** to the movies, and I became foolishly disturbed about it and, as things snowballed, I decided to go out and get drunk.(p.487)
• Then I went South, because they told me that the particular county I was ***going*** to in North Carolina was a dry county.(p.489)
• I promised that I was ***going*** to do the right thing.(p.490)
• I think the thing that galled me was that just after Easter I had drawn my salary for two weeks' work and had decided that I was ***going*** to send some money to Vi; and above all else I was ***going*** to send my baby daughter an Easter outfit.(p.493)
• True, I have recently recovered from pneumonia and have an alibi, but my friends are in the war or ***going***, and I am not.(p.499)
• "I am ***going*** to do something."(p.502)
• "I went out of here nine days ago saying that I was ***going*** to be honest, and I wasn't," he answers.(p.503)
• Things are not ***going*** so well at home.(p.505)
• I am ***going*** to town to get some liquor and food.(p.506)
• I'll tell my wife what I am ***going*** to do.(p.506)
• The trial lasted about a week, and whether or not I was ***going*** to the death house was anybody's guess.(p.508)
• So instead of ***going*** near A.A., I just browsed around for that first month.(p.510)
• She asked me, was I ***going*** to do this to her all over again?(p.510)
• Then instead of ***going*** out with A.A. again I went out with some of the other crowd, and off again I went.(p.511)
• I was ***going*** to be sent to the Indian Civil Service, which, in those days, meant that people thought you had a certain amount of brains.(p.517)
• He reported to the Headmaster and the Headmaster was ***going*** to expel me.(p.517)
• The Abyssinian war broke out just as things were ***going*** very badly for me, and I went off to Egypt on a job there.(p.519)
• I was terribly afraid that I was actually ***going*** mad, if I hadn't gone mad already.(p.522)
• I was intensely unhappy the whole time, but I didn't seem to be able to do anything about it, and the worst part to me was the realization that all this was ***going*** to happen again and again until I died.(p.522)
• It was no use talking of putting myself into a home, a hospital, or of ***going*** to see a doctor again, or of ***going*** to see a priest or anyone else.(p.523)
• Then I would go home full of remorse, and wonder what I was ***going*** to do until I got my next check.(p.527)
• I didn't want that, so I stopped ***going*** to the psycho ward.(p.528)
• I am talking about A.A. people, who have gone through some of the same things that you might be ***going*** through now.(p.529)
• Things weren't ***going*** as I thought they should, for my greater enjoyment, comfort and fame; therefore, if the universe wouldn't play my way, I wouldn't play at all.(p.531)
• Still another friend and temporary host received me at four in the morning from the charge of a policeman who had found me "***going*** to bed" in a garage far from the last place I could remember having been, a fashionable bar and restaurant in the theatrical district of New York, to which I had repaired after my date for that evening, a charming lady of the theatre who had refused my company for obvious reasons.(p.538)
• In the nearby little town there was a plumber who once had tried to get an A.A. group ***going***.(p.541)
• It is ***going*** strong still, these eight years later, and some of its members have been of great influence for good in state-wide A.A. work.(p.541)
• One morning, however, I realized I had to get rid of it, for my reprieve was running out, and if I didn't get rid of it I was ***going*** to get drunk – and I didn't want to get drunk any more.(p.552)
• But we may employ alcoholics where they are ***going*** to perform those services for which we might otherwise have to engage nonalcoholics.(p.566)

gold

• Like a gaunt prospector, belt drawn in over the last ounce of food, our pick struck ***gold***.(p.128)
• Father feels he has struck something better than ***gold***.(p.129)
• There were ***gold*** bars on his shoulders.(p.422)
• It was as if I had, rather than a Midas touch which turned everything to ***gold***, a magnifying mind that magnified whatever it focused on.(p.450)
• This time, whoever had rolled me had taken my glasses as well (they were ***gold***).(p.538)

golden

• That sentence, "The Lord has been so wonderful to me, curing me of this terrible disease, that I just want to keep telling people about it," has been sort of a ***golden*** text for the A.A. program and for me.(p.191)
• THOSE *GOLDEN* YEARS(p.327)

golf

• In 1929 I contracted ***golf*** fever.(p.3)
• ***Golf*** permitted drinking every day and every night.(p.3)
• A friend of mine, a ***golf*** nut, rushed out on retirement to play every day.(p.330)
• Then I looked forward to the week-end of ***golf*** and the nineteenth hole.(p.374)
• ***Golf***, hunting and fishing were now merely excuses to drink excessively.(p.375)

gondola

• Forced to detrain from an empty ***gondola*** on the other side of Chicago by a terrific rainstorm which drenched me to the skin, I hit the first factory building I saw for a job.(p.253)

gone

• The broker had *gone* to Akron on a business venture which had collapsed, leaving him greatly in fear that he might start drinking again.(p.xvi)
• A morning paper told me the market had *gone* to hell again.(p.6)
• Now I was to plunge into the dark, joining that endless procession of sots who had *gone* on before.(p.8)
• But that was far as I had *gone*.(p.10)
• Many times I have *gone* to my old hospital in despair.(p.15)
• Then he had *gone* to Europe, placing himself in the care of a celebrated physician (the psychiatrist, Dr. Jung) who prescribed for him.(p.26)
• Potential female alcoholics often turn into the real thing and are *gone* beyond recall in a few years.(p.33)
• As we look back, we feel we had *gone* on drinking many years beyond the point where we could quit on our will power.(p.34)
• In some circumstances we have *gone* out deliberately to get drunk, feeling ourselves justified by nervousness, anger, worry, depression, jealousy or the like.(p.37)
• We admit we have some of these symptoms, but we have not *gone* to the extremes you fellows did, nor are we likely to, for we understand ourselves so well after what you have told us that such things cannot happen again.(p.38)
• We first saw Fred about a year ago in a hospital where he had *gone* to recover from a bad case of jitters.(p.39)
• It is seldom wise to approach an individual, who still smarts from our injustice to him, and announce that we have *gone* religious.(p.77)
• A man so involved often feels very remorseful at times, especially if he is married to a loyal and courageous girl who has literally *gone* through hell for him.(p.81)
• No matter how far down the scale we have *gone*, we will see how our experience can benefit others.(p.84)
• Positions were always in jeopardy or *gone*.(p.105)
• Three: This husband has *gone* much further than husband number two.(p.109)
• Many of our husbands were just as far *gone*.(p.110)
• Without you he would have *gone* to pieces long ago.(p.119)
• They need the counsel and love of a woman who has *gone* through what you have.(p.119)
• After your man has *gone* along without drinking for a few months, you may be able to make use of his services with other employees who are giving you the alcoholic run-around -- provided, of course, they are willing to have a third party in the picture.(p.146)
• The old pleasures were *gone*.(p.151)
• Many mornings I have *gone* to classes, and even though fully prepared, would turn and walk back to the fraternity house because of my jitters, not daring to enter the classroom for fear of making a scene should I be called on for recitation.(p.173)
• I knew everyone would buy a few bottles, or cases, of liquor as their exchequers permitted, and that it would soon be *gone*.(p.175)
• Then I remember when the boys came back, that I told them, "I have *gone* to this Higher Power and I have told Him that I am willing to put His world first, above everything.(p.190)
• Naturally, what little restraint I had exercised before was *gone* now, and my drinking became worse.(p.199)
• Another time, I had *gone* around to Max R. trying to get a job driving one of his trucks.(p.200)
• (My mother and father were Catholics and I had been baptized, but at the end of my instructions for Confirmation I had not *gone* to church, and then when my mother remarried, she married a Protestant and the whole religious angle was forgotten.(p.201)
• And I continued to drink, on and off then, until every dollar I had in the world was *gone* again and I was right back living at my sister's, getting my cigarettes by calling her grocer and telling him to put in a couple of cartons with her order, exactly as I had before I started to work at Max's.(p.202)
• One evening I had *gone* out after dinner to take on a couple of double-headers and stayed a little later than usual, and when I came home Clarence was sitting on the davenport with Bill W.(p.216)
• Sitting in a Second Avenue bar, accepting drinks from anyone who offered, after my small stake was *gone*; or sitting at home alone, with the inevitable glass in my hand, I would remember, and remembering, I would drink faster, seeking speedy oblivion.(p.225)
• His own business was practically *gone*, he told me, when he discovered the answer.(p.236)
• He had also *gone* all the way through the wringer and had been dry two years when I saw him again.(p.243)
• As long as things were tough and the job a challenge I could always manage to hold on pretty well, but as soon as I learned the combination, got the puzzle under control and the boss to pat me on the back, I was *gone* again.(p.243)
• Evidently I had *gone* right back to the movie with a bottle, stayed there several hours and started home with no recollection of what had happened.(p.244)
• Quebec, Toronto, Buffalo, and finally Pittsburgh, were the scenes of man-sized drunks until I had *gone* through my readjusted discharge pay, a fair sum.(p.253)
• Formerly, in the acute mental and physical pain during the remorseful periods succeeding each drunk, I found my recollection of the misery I had *gone* through a bolsterer of resolution and afterward, perhaps, a deterrent for a time.(p.260)
• I remember one instance when he took off and went down to Cincinnati and was *gone* a week on a drunk.(p.262)
• I had *gone* to an attorney to see about getting a divorce during that year.(p.263)
• Somebody must have taken pity on you and *gone* out and got it for you."(p.264)
• That ache is *gone* and never need return again.(p.312)
• If I had been sincere in what I thought I wanted more than anything else in life – a sober husband and a happy, contented home – I would have *gone* on the wagon with him.(p.324)
• Now, with the arrival at retirement, it was *gone*.(p.329)
• *Gone* are time cards to punch, alarm clocks to obey, nosey rumor-mongers and talebearers to evade.(p.329)
• No matter how often I had *gone* into and come out of alcoholic lows during the day, the pattern bounced me out of bed each night about 2:00 a.m., shaking and hurting in the agitation that always follows a drug's sedation.(p.332)
• When we begin to do things like that with alcohol, something's *gone* wrong.(p.336)
• Years earlier, I had *gone* into psychoanalysis to get relief.(p.349)
• The following spring she left me one day without giving me any idea of where she had *gone*, hoping this would bring me to my senses.(p.377)
• It wasn't how far I had *gone*, but where I was headed.(p.379)
• Yesterday is *gone*, and we don't know whether we will be here tomorrow.(p.382)
• I did not know that I had no power over alcohol, that I, alone and unaided, could not stop; that I was on a downgrade, tearing along at full speed with all my brakes *gone*, and that the end would be a total smash-up, death or insanity.(p.408)
• She too had *gone* to cheap bars to drink.(p.414)
• Had I *gone* to school all those years just to sit and make leather belts?(p.445)
• (I am pleased to state, however, that I had *gone* to only a very few A.A. meetings before I was able to make a really beautiful pair of moccasins – and half a wallet.(p.445)
• In my screwed up mind I kept thinking I could have *gone* to A.A. way back there in 1940, and perhaps saved my marriage and home.(p.469)
• They build you up with a lot of false hopes and promises, and rush you around here and there and then, all of a sudden, it's *gone*."(p.472)
• And I landed right smack back in that sanitarium that I had *gone* to so often.(p.472)
• Things had just *gone* from bad to worse.(p.487)
• Indeed, without their aid we couldn't possibly have *gone* on.(p.496)
• He had *gone* through the windshields of cars a couple of times and was pretty well banged up.(p.510)
• Everybody I had known in the old days had *gone*.(p.522)
• I was terribly afraid that I was actually going mad, if I hadn't *gone* mad already.(p.522)
• I would stay out until my money was *gone*.(p.527)
• I am talking about A.A. people, who have *gone* through some of the same things that you might be going through now.(p.529)
• I stumbled agonizedly past the theatre where in years *gone* by a great star had played my play.(p.540)
• Thank God that those days are *gone*.(p.540)
• And it had *gone* underground now, because everyone knew I shouldn't be drinking.(p.557)
• But now all choice was *gone*.(p.558)

goner

• I'm a *goner*.(p.157)

good

• The basic principles of the A.A. program, it appears, hold *good* for individuals with many different lifestyles, just as the program has brought recovery to those of many different nationalities.(p.xxii)
• In late 1934 I attended a patient who, though he had been a competent businessman of *good* earning capacity, was an alcoholic of a type I had come to regard as hopeless.(p.xxiii)
• But as ex-problem drinkers, we can say that his explanation makes *good* sense.(p.xxiv)
• What with our ultra-modern standards, our scientific approach to everything, we are perhaps not well equipped to apply the powers of *good* that lie outside our synthetic knowledge.(p.xxv)
• A *good* soldier is ne'er forgot Whether he dieth by musket Or by pot."(p.1)
• As the whisky rose to my head I told myself I would manage better next time, but I might as well get *good* and drunk then.(p.6)
• I could almost hear the sound of the preacher's voice as I sat, on still Sundays, way over there on the hillside; there was that proffered temperance pledge I never signed; my grandfather's *good* natured contempt of some church folk and their doings; his insistence that the spheres really had their music; but his denial of the preacher's right to tell him how he must listen; his fearlessness as he spoke of these things just before he died; these recollections welled up from the past.(p.10)
• I honestly doubted whether, on balance, the religions of mankind had done any *good*.(p.11)
• The *good* doctor now sees many men who have such experiences.(p.14)
• Each day my friend's simple talk in our kitchen multiplies itself in a widening circle of peace on earth and *good* will to men.(p.16)
• If we keep on the way we are going there is little doubt that much *good* will result, but the surface of the problem would hardly be scratched.(p.19)
• Moderate drinkers have little trouble in giving up liquor entirely if they have *good* reason for it.(p.20)
• A certain American business man had ability, *good* sense, and high character.(p.26)
• His physical and mental condition were unusually *good*.(p.26)
• Upon hearing this, our friend was somewhat relieved, for he reflected that after all, he was a *good* church member.(p.27)
• This hope, however, was destroyed by the doctor's telling him that while his religious convictions were very *good*, in his case they did not spell the necessary vital spiritual experience.(p.27)
• He is a *good* salesman.(p.35)
• He tells you he has decided to stop jay-walking for *good*, but in a few weeks he breaks both legs.(p.38)
• His income is *good*, he has a fine home, is happily married and the father of promising children of college age.(p.39)
• We think there are *good* reasons.(p.48)
• Everybody nowadays, believes in scores of assumptions for which there is *good* evidence, but no perfect visual proof.(p.48)
• On that basis we are almost always in collision with something or somebody, even though our motives are *good*.(p.60)
• Most *good* ideas are simple, and this concept was the keystone of the new and triumphant arch through which we passed to freedom.(p.62)
• Self-reliance was *good* as far as it went, but it didn't go far enough.(p.68)
• We remembered always that our sex powers were God-given and therefore *good*, neither to be used lightly or selfishly nor to be despised and loathed.(p.69)
• We have begun to learn tolerance, patience and *good* will toward all men, even our enemies, for we look on them as sick people.(p.70)
• If you have already made a decision, and an inventory of your grosser handicaps, you have made a *good* beginning.(p.71)
• We will be more reconciled to discussing ourselves with another person when we see *good* reasons why we should do so.(p.72)
• When ready, we say something like this: "My Creator, I am now willing that you should have all of me, *good* and bad.(p.76)
• He is going to be more interested in a demonstration of *good* will than in our talk of spiritual discoveries.(p.77)
• When it will serve any *good* purpose, we are willing to announce our convictions with tact and common sense.(p.77)
• We may be short in our accounts and unable to make *good*.(p.78)

- It is as ***good*** for the wife as for the husband.(p.81)
- It may be that both will decide that the way of ***good*** sense and loving kindness is to let by-gones be by-gones.(p.82)
- ***Good*** generalship may decide that the problem be attacked on the flank rather than risk a face-to-face combat.(p.82)
- But he is yet a long way from making ***good*** to the wife or parents whom for years he has so shockingly treated.(p.82)
- If there is any indication that he wants to stop, have a ***good*** talk with the person most interested in him -- usually his wife.(p.90)
- Then let his family or a friend ask him if he wants to quit for ***good*** and if he would go to any extreme to do so.(p.90)
- Doctors are rightly loath to tell alcoholic patients the whole story unless it will serve some ***good*** purpose.(p.92)
- This is all to the ***good***.(p.94)
- You have to act the ***Good*** Samaritan every day, if need be.(p.97)
- It is not ***good*** for him, and it sometimes creates serious complications in a family.(p.97)
- These things will come to pass naturally and in ***good*** time provided, however, the alcoholic continues to demonstrate that he can be sober, considerate, and helpful, regardless of what anyone says or does.(p.99)
- Therefore, ask yourself on each occasion, "Have I any ***good*** social, business, or personal reason for going to this place?(p.101)
- But be sure you are on solid spiritual ground before you start and that your motive in going is thoroughly ***good***.(p.102)
- Why sit with a long face in places where there is drinking, sighing about the ***good*** old days.(p.102)
- We would not even do the cause of temperate drinking any ***good***, for not one drinker in a thousand likes to be told anything about alcohol by one who hates it.(p.103)
- Of those who keep on, a ***good*** number will become true alcoholics after a while.(p.109)
- We have enjoyed such evenings ourselves; we had a ***good*** time.(p.110)
- Patience and ***good*** temper are most necessary.(p.111)
- But after his next binge, ask him if he would really like to get over drinking for ***good***.(p.112)
- If your husband is otherwise a normal individual, your chances are ***good*** at this stage.(p.113)
- A ***good*** doctor or psychiatrist can tell you whether these complications are serious.(p.114)
- When they become too dangerous, we think the kind thing is to lock them up, but of course a ***good*** doctor should always be consulted.(p.114)
- Your new courage, ***good*** nature and lack of self-consciousness will do wonders for you socially.(p.115)
- Discuss this with him when he is sober and in ***good*** spirits.(p.115)
- We thought, on the whole, we were pretty ***good*** women, capable of being nicer if our husbands stopped drinking.(p.116)
- But it was a silly idea that we were too ***good*** to need God.(p.116)
- He wants to make ***good***.(p.118)
- It will do little ***good*** if you point that out and urge more attention for yourself.(p.119)
- So to you out there -- who may soon be with us -- we say "***Good*** luck and God bless you!"(p.121)
- Suppose we tell you some of the obstacles a family will meet; suppose we suggest how they may be avoided -- even converted to ***good*** use for others.(p.123)
- The ***good*** old days will soon be back, they think.(p.123)
- That is true only if one is willing to turn the past to ***good*** account.(p.124)
- So we think that unless some ***good*** and useful purpose is to be served, past occurrences should not be discussed.(p.125)
- Try to remember that though God has wrought miracles among us, we should never belittle a ***good*** doctor or psychiatrist.(p.133)
- He wants to quit drinking and you want to help him, even if it be only a matter of ***good*** business.(p.141)
- Your man should be on his mettle to make ***good***.(p.146)
- It will permit the rehabilitation of ***good*** men.(p.148)
- It is joyous intimacy with friends and a feeling that life is ***good***.(p.151)
- You fellows know your stuff all right, but I don't see what ***good*** it'll do.(p.157)
- He came through an acquaintance who had heard the ***good*** news.(p.158)
- There is a ***good*** bit of travel between East and West and we foresee a great increase in this helpful interchange.(p.162)
- And with such ***good*** effect that the doctor agreed to a test among his patients and certain other alcoholics from a clinic which he attends.(p.163)
- Men who had liquor shipped in from Boston or New York by express were looked upon with great distrust and disfavor by most of the ***good*** townspeople.(p.171)
- So I filled the cellar full, with the permission of my ***good*** wife.(p.177)
- These ***good*** people notified my wife, who sent my newly made friend over to get me.(p.179)
- My health is ***good*** and I have regained my self-respect and the respect of my colleagues.(p.180)
- My home life is ideal and my business is as ***good*** as can be expected in these uncertain times.(p.180)
- But if you really and truly want to quit drinking liquor for ***good*** and all, and sincerely feel that you must have some help, we know that we have an answer for you.(p.181)
- After a while, Bill said, "Well, now, you've been talking a ***good*** long time, let me talk a minute or two."(p.185)
- "Sure I would," replied Bill, "Maybe it won't do any ***good***, but I'd like to see you both, anyhow.(p.189)
- Another reason I go is that I'm still grateful for the ***good*** years that I've had.(p.192)
- I can also remember that he was a salesman and a very ***good*** one.(p.193)
- I was married at the age of nineteen to a grand girl and had ***good*** business prospects.(p.194)
- At the end of about four months, I not only had ***good*** looking clothes --and I might say that at the time I first talked to Max I didn't have a suit of clothes I could bend over in real sudden; now I had six suits of clothes.(p.200)
- I had run into him, and he looked real prosperous; his face and eyes looked clear and he started to compliment me on my ***good*** front and how well I looked, and I said, "I haven't had a drink for nine months."(p.201)
- He brought the quart out and I took a ***good*** swig.(p.205)
- I offered them a drink, and they came to the bottom of the stairs and the ***good*** woman fainted, just looking at me.(p.205)
- He took off his hat and his overcoat, and he said, "You don't look very ***good***.(p.207)
- Not far from where I lived they built a new technical high school and one of the teachers sold me on the idea that I needed a little mechanical drawing if I were going to be a ***good*** toolmaker.(p.211)
- Following graduation I was offered a pretty ***good*** job which I took.(p.212)
- My reaction to those meetings was ***good***.(p.218)
- I still had enough practice to earn a ***good*** living if I would only work, so I resolved that in January of 1940 I would launch a patent law firm of my own.(p.220)
- In fact I had been in very ***good*** shape at one o'clock -- feeling no pain.(p.223)
- So far, so ***good*** -- all according to plan, like thousands of others.(p.225)
- Naturally, in spite of my ***good*** intentions, in spite of my protected life behind sanitarium walls, I several times got drunk, and was astounded . . . and badly shaken.(p.227)
- And as I fumed helplessly and planned to get ***good*** and drunk and show them, my eye caught a sentence in the book lying open on my bed: "We cannot live with anger."(p.228)
- I was born in Europe, in Alsace to be exact, shortly after it had become German, and practically grew up with the "***good*** Rhine wine" of song and story.(p.230)
- But, although I was a ***good*** Catholic, the monastic life had little appeal for me.(p.230)
- Fond of singing, I joined a German singing society which had ***good*** club headquarters.(p.231)
- I came of ***good*** stock, of men and women who drank wine all their lives as a beverage, and while they occasionally got drunk at special celebrations, they were up and about their business the next day.(p.231)
- It wasn't very long until I had developed a pretty ***good*** brew with uniformity and plenty of authority.(p.232)
- I had always been a ***good*** Catholic, possibly not so devoted as I should have been, but fairly regular in my attendance at services.(p.234)
- Unlike many other Catholics who frequently take pledges for definite periods -- a year, two years or for ***good***, I never had any desire to "take a pledge" before the priest.(p.234)
- None of the various cures of this kind were any ***good***.(p.235)
- Just give me a ***good*** front and a couple of bucks and I'd be right back in the big time.(p.246)
- After a very ***good*** week, two of my customers took me to lunch on Saturday.(p.247)
- This was when I really took my first ***good*** look at myself.(p.247)
- Then I got a very ***good*** position in Philadelphia and quickly found I would need a few fellow alcoholics around me if I was to stay sober.(p.249)
- She has been sober all the way through and for me that has been ***good***.(p.249)
- We now live in the West and are very fortunate in our area A.A.; it is ***good***, simple and friendly, and our one desire is to stay in A.A. and not on it.(p.250)
- With a ***good*** stake I sailed for New York.(p.251)
- Making my way to Pittsburgh, I met other former friends and got a job in a large factory where piecemakers were making ***good*** money.(p.252)
- My fellow-workers were mostly ***good*** Saturday night drinkers and I was right with them.(p.252)
- Loading a car with ***good*** old books to sell to collectors, librarians, universities and historical societies, I started out to travel the country.(p.255)
- In five years a ***good*** many persons had forgotten that I had been somewhat notorious.(p.256)
- I had never known him to be anything but a ***good*** healthy pagan with a propensity for getting into liquor jams and scrapes.(p.257)
- Some of them I had known for years, ***good*** two-fisted drinkers who had disappeared from their former haunts.(p.258)
- They did not show me to my room and wish me a ***good*** night's rest.(p.259)
- I felt that his family were accepting me because it was ***good*** sense.(p.262)
- I knew Doc and Anne were going to be there, and all of them thought it would be ***good*** for me, but the first thing I did was to go to St. Thomas and try to talk to those women.)(p.272)
- I came from a ***good*** family.(p.275)
- So I was driven to Akron the very next day by these ***Good*** Samaritans, and turned over to Dr. Bob and the then tiny Akron Group.(p.279)
- Sometimes during that year I rebelled inwardly at what seemed like lost time, and at having to be a burden to these ***good*** people whose means were limited.(p.281)
- It ran something like this: If I go around shouting from the rooftops about my alcoholism, it might very possibly prevent me from getting a ***good*** job.(p.282)
- I was a ***good*** salesman.(p.289)
- The inevitable result of this discovery was that I soon learned that beer made a very ***good*** chaser for whiskey.(p.298)
- After holding ***good*** positions, making better than an average income for over ten years, I was in debt, had no clothes to speak of, no money, no friends, and no one any longer tolerating me but my wife.(p.301)
- She offered me the alternative of going to see him or her leaving me for ***good*** and all.(p.301)
- I eat three ***good*** meals a day now, and really enjoy them.(p.303)
- But somehow my ***good*** doctor heard of this book and also he learned a little about the people responsible for its publication.(p.307)
- I had a tough pull back to normal ***good*** health.(p.310)
- But we had to do a lot of entertaining, my husband liked to have a ***good*** time; I was very young; and I wanted to have a ***good*** time too.(p.322)
- I did stay fairly ***good*** for a few years.(p.323)
- The radio was my ***good*** friend.(p.332)
- That always has been ***good*** enough for me.(p.334)
- When a few drinks made me feel ***good*** before I went over that line, those same drinks now made me wretched.(p.346)
- On the last day I was drinking I went up to see a friend who had had a ***good*** deal of trouble with alcohol, and whose wife had left him a number of times.(p.346)
- Shortly after I was starting to work on the program I realized that I was not a ***good*** father; I wasn't a ***good*** husband, but, oh, I was a ***good*** provider.(p.351)
- My salesmanship was still ***good***, for in the fall of 1938 she called me from Salt Lake and finally agreed to take me on for better or for worse.(p.360)
- In 1940 another ***good*** opportunity came up and we moved to Pittsburgh where I was to manage two radio stations under the same ownership.(p.361)
- Why should this happen to me -- hadn't I provided a ***good*** home -- wasn't I making a ***good*** living -- didn't

I just get a substantial raise that had put me in the upper bracket class?(p.362)
• I thought this was a *good* time to experiment with liquor.(p.364)
• It was worrying my wife a little, but she had the *good* sense not to take me to task about it or goad me into going.(p.364)
• For the next couple of hours a terrible battle went on between the *good* gremlins and the bad ones, one faction urging me to tell the truth, the other telling me to sit tight and say nothing.(p.366)
• In meeting me casually, I don't think my strong belief in "The Man Upstairs" shows, but I have no other explanation for the many *good* things that have happened to me since I have been in A.A. -- they came to me from a Greater Power.(p.367)
• I had a family to be proud of, actively sharing in the responsibilities of *good* citizenship.(p.374)
• Gradually the quantity increased, the occasions for a drink came more frequently; a hard day, worries and pressure, bad news, *good* news -- there were more and more reasons for a drink.(p.374)
• If we do a *good* job of living today, and if tomorrow comes for us, then the chances are we will do a *good* job when it arrives -- so why worry about it?(p.382)
• It has been a fellowship with God and man that has held *good* wherever I've turned and whatever I've done.(p.394)
• But now, with His help and grace, this child of His has paid his initiation fee for *good*, as long as he remembers to stay away from that first drink (the one that does all the damage) one day at a time.(p.399)
• I got a *good* non-academic education; my intellectual curiosity was encouraged.(p.401)
• His were *good*, simple Quaker folk who accepted me with love.(p.402)
• But he noticed that I was not a *good* mother to my child, that I relegated her to nurses when she was with me.(p.403)
• Above all, he noticed that I drank a *good* deal, often got tight in his company and told him naughty stories.(p.403)
• During these years, I did acquire some *good* friends.(p.404)
• Here, also, I had *good* friends, but I became more and more separated from them.(p.406)
• This *good* and gentle man, a brilliant research doctor, got nowhere with me fast.(p.407)
• All of them have since settled down to jobs and *good* marriages.(p.407)
• There were a couple of *good* things.(p.409)
• They were awfully *good* about not cutting me off.(p.409)
• I was not beautiful or *good*, as I had yearned to be.(p.411)
• My tweed suit, once a very *good* one, was shapeless and baggy with bare places worn in the elbows from leaning on the bar.(p.411)
• Bill was tall, grey haired, with the kind of asymmetrical *good* looks and pleasant easy manner that inspire confidence in the shaken and afraid.(p.413)
• All the people involved in these flare-ups took it with remarkable grace, have teased me about it since, and have become *good* friends of mine.(p.416)
• I have achieved the inner confidence to write quite unlike Shakespeare, and I have sold a *good* deal of what I've written.(p.416)
• Many *good* A.A.'s never join a church, and do not need to.(p.417)
• A "*good* boy" reached adulthood and success without achieving maturity or fulfillment.(p.418)
• I was an honor graduate in high school, and I was a "*good* boy" to whom mothers pointed when their sons went astray.(p.419)
• So we rolled old newspapers together and made torches to find a *good* soft pew and get some sleep.(p.424)
• I would drink all night in bars, come home about five a.m., down a *good* big glass of whiskey straight, and tumble into bed.(p.428)
• I have a *good* job.(p.431)
• Not only did I not think that being an alcoholic was a *good* idea, I didn't even feel that I had all that much of a drinking problem!(p.439)
• It started out as a *good* marriage, but it deteriorated over the years as she progressed through the various stages of qualifying for Al-Anon.(p.439)
• For the leveling-off process, I just loved intravenous Demerol, but I found it hard to practice *good* medicine while shooting morphine.(p.442)
• The Mayo Clinic seemed like a *good* place to have my diagnosis confirmed.(p.444)
• And I knew that giving up "one drink for one day" wouldn't really do any *good*.(p.448)
• A.A. and acceptance have taught me that there is a bit of *good* in the worst of us and a bit of bad in the best of us; that we are all children of God and we each have a right to be here.(p.449)
• This proves I don't know what's *good* for me.(p.450)
• And if I don't know what's *good* for me, then I don't know what's *good* or bad for you or for anyone.(p.450)
• Over the years, as I thought about Max, her *good* qualities grew and grew, and we married, and all these qualities became more and more apparent to me, and we were happier and happier.(p.450)
• But then, as I drank more and more, the alcohol seemed to affect my vision: Instead of continuing to see what was *good* about my wife, I began to see her defects.(p.450)
• I can again focus on my wife's *good* qualities and watch them grow and grow and grow.(p.451)
• But when I try to see what I can add to the meeting, rather than what I can get out of it, and when I focus my mind on what's *good* about it, rather than what's wrong with it, the meeting keeps getting better and better.(p.451)
• When I focus on what's *good* today, I have a *good* day, and when I focus on what's bad, I have a bad day.(p.451)
• When I remember this, I can see I've never had it so *good*.(p.452)
• There go my *good* intentions, fear of consequences, will to care, responsibility for my behavior.(p.458)
• We always, or nearly always, had *good* intentions when we were released from prison.(p.458)
• But with the first drink, our *good* intentions dissolved; our personalities changed.(p.458)
• I would rather talk about the *good* things A.A. has taught me; I feel that hitting on just a few sordid points should be sufficient to let those of you in institutions know where I came from.(p.459)
• I'm talking about the *good* things that have happened.(p.463)
• In fact, sometimes they served as *good* excuses to drink more, to forget.(p.465)
• I had decided I was no *good* -- never would be any *good*, and the sooner I could drink myself out of this life, the better.(p.468)
• She realized that, and the way I felt, and so for my own *good* she gradually began to pull away.(p.472)
• By grace of God I stop, think two things: This would kill *good* mother and father; then remember boys talk about Indian fellow who been sober three years.(p.475)
• But now I change if it bring *good* life.(p.475)
• Talk and meeting make me feel *good*.(p.476)
• This sober Indian say to sick, red-eyed alcoholic who want *good* medicine: "Put cork in bottle.(p.477)
• It is no problem to me now, but this is not *good* management on my part -- just plain *good* luck.(p.480)
• We lived just a few doors from the First Baptist Church and when they had funerals I remember very often asking my mother whether the person was *good* or bad and whether they were going to heaven or hell.(p.483)
• Father, through the years, had built up a very *good* mail order business because, at that time, there wasn't too much money in medicine.(p.485)
• A very *good* friend of mine who owned a drug store across the street from us, came by only about two hours later and said that he had seen Vi down town.(p.487)
• I took that bottle of medicine and gave it to a very *good* friend of mine who was a pharmacist and had it analyzed, and the bottle was perfectly all right.(p.489)
• I had a very *good* friend who was in the Government service, and I went to him about a job.(p.489)
• Being an alcoholic, slick, and having some *good* sense left, I survived the investigation.(p.490)
• Vi was very kind and explained to the jury that I was basically a fine fellow and a *good* husband, but that I drank too much and that she thought I had lost my mind and felt that I should be committed to an asylum.(p.492)
• I approached several ministers and all of them thought it was a very *good* idea, but they never relinquished any space.(p.495)
• "Let your light so shine before men that they may see your *good* works --."(p.497)
• *Good* old John!(p.498)
• *Good* old John Barleycorn!(p.499)
• The day is over and business has been not so *good*.(p.500)
• *Good* old Charlie!(p.500)
• This time I'm off of it for *good*.(p.502)
• There was no time off for so-called *good* behavior, first-timers, or anything else.(p.509)
• When I landed of course I hit a gin mill, and with three or four *good* shots under my belt the world began to go into that rosy glow.(p.513)
• I had just come off a *good* one, and I went back on to the next one.(p.514)
• God has been *good* to me both in my drinking and in my sobriety.(p.516)
• I went to a very *good* public school run by Jesuits.(p.517)
• But I pointed out to him that as I was the first British boy who had been to the school, it wouldn't be a very *good* advertisement for him, so I got over that all right.(p.518)
• Lots of the older people had taken to drinking quite a *good* deal more during the war, but the younger generation was, I think, about the same.(p.518)
• I was still very fit and *good* at games.(p.519)
• I got a job by myself which suited me down to the ground, because there was nobody really to interfere with what I did, one way or the other, and I usually had my nerves in *good* trim when anybody was coming around to inspect.(p.519)
• I was still very *good* at games.(p.519)
• Strangely enough, right through to the end of my twenty-six years in the Army, I was still being offered very *good* and important jobs in spite of the fact that my superiors must have known that I wasn't thoroughly reliable.(p.519)
• I stayed there just long enough to work up a real *good* resentment against the doctor in charge, who I didn't think was doing anything at all except collecting fees, and I left there fully determined that I'd never put myself in the power of medical people again.(p.521)
• I talked to him for quite a long time and at the end, he said, "Well, you're not quite mad enough to be shut up for *good* yet, but you soon will be if you live long enough."(p.522)
• I was to pack and go and get out of their lives for *good*.(p.523)
• But if I came back in the usual state, then I'd have to go off for *good* the next day.(p.523)
• It continues to try to teach me the real charity, the charity that gives time and *good* will and service, and not just money.(p.525)
• I would wait for the mailman each month, like any *good* mother, but as soon as he handed me my check, I put on my best dress and went looking for my alcoholic friend.(p.527)
• After a while, I found that the psycho ward was a *good* place to hide when I had taken something stolen to the pawnshop.(p.528)
• But then one *good* doctor told me there was nothing wrong with me except drinking too much.(p.528)
• And having sung that phrase, I'd chuckle with amusement, turning into irony turning into self-contempt turning into self-pity, at the sad fate of Bob, that wonderful, poor little motherless boy who was so smart in school and who grew up to accept responsibility so early and so fast and who staggered under his burdens without a whimper until the time came when he thought he was too *good* for this world and so he ought to be out of it.(p.532)
• In those years I was in jail nine times, in an alcoholic ward, overnight, twice; and I was fired from three jobs, two of them very *good* ones.(p.536)
• It is going strong still, these eight years later, and some of its members have been of great influence for *good* in state-wide A.A. work.(p.541)
• When I remark that I have been in jail nine times, and in an alcoholic ward twice, they think I'm kidding, or possibly dramatizing for the sake of a *good* yarn.(p.542)
• For me, A.A. is a synthesis of all the philosophy I've ever read, all of the positive, *good* philosophy, all of it based on love.(p.542)
• I hope I have been able to impart to you, the reader, at least a bit of what I know; the joy of living, the irresistible power of divine love and its healing strength, and the fact that we, as sentient beings, have the knowledge to choose between *good* and evil, and, choosing *good*, are made happy.(p.543)
• Had I been able to explain to a psychiatrist the feeling of futility, loneliness and lack of purpose that had come with my deep sense of personal failure at this second divorce, I seriously doubt that the *good* doctor could have convinced me that my basic problem was a spiritual hunger, but A.A. has shown me this was the truth.(p.546)
• I've heard it said many times in A.A., "There is just one *good* drunk in every alcoholic's life, and that's the one that brings us into A.A.," and I believe it.(p.549)
• I landed a *good* job with a company publication and was moonlighting on other magazines.(p.555)

good-feeling

• We do this by going to many A.A. meetings with an

open mind and a desire to live the ***good-feeling*** life without chemicals -- liquid or otherwise.(p.459)

good-natured

• She's a ***good-natured*** soul and said, "I wouldn't worry about it; probably something will happen."(p.346)

goodbye

• After the oil job blew up, I went back to Baltimore and mother, my first wife having said a permanent "***Goodbye***."(p.243)

• Saying ***goodbye*** to my wife and baby, I was treading Manhattan's streets in a little more than a week.(p.252)

• The sheriff bade us ***goodbye*** very happily.(p.424)

goodness

• Occasionally, it is accorded to a few of us to watch something fine grow from a tiny kernel into something of gigantic ***goodness***.(p.295)

• I said, "Oh, ***goodness***, no!(p.321)

• My business reputation had reached from Vermont to Pennsylvania, but, thank ***goodness***, my drinking reputation had not.(p.361)

goods

• One object is to disclose damaged or unsalable ***goods***, to get rid of them promptly and without regret.(p.64)

• My stock of material ***goods*** isn't great.(p.296)

• High living, a great many fair weather friends, the 1929 stock market crash, and a couple of years of Depression, soon relieved me one by one of my worldly ***goods*** including my wife.(p.358)

goofed

• They had also been periodic big shots who had ***goofed*** out repeatedly at the wrong time, and they also knew how to split one paper match into three separate matches.(p.245)

goose

• For three or four months the ***goose*** hung high.(p.7)

goose-flesh

• What a state of mental ***goose-flesh*** that used to bring on!(p.54)

goose-stepping

• Military service was compulsory and I did my stretch with the class of my age, ***goose-stepping*** in German barracks and taking part in the Boxer Rebellion in China, my first time at any great distance from home.(p.230)

gorge

• Our friend's ***gorge*** rose as he bitterly cried out: "If there is a God, He certainly hasn't done anything for me!"(p.56)

gossip

• She's a ***gossip***.(p.65)

• This is a condition which, in ordinary life, would produce untold grief; there might be scandalous ***gossip***, laughter at the expense of other people, and a tendency to take advantage of intimate information.(p.125)

got

• News of this ***got*** on the world wires; inquiries poured in again and many people went to the bookstores to get the book "Alcoholics Anonymous."(p.xviii)

• Of alcoholics who came to A.A. and really tried, 50% ***got*** sober at once and remained that way; 25% sobered up after some relapses, and among the remainder, those who stayed on with A.A. showed improvement.(p.xx)

• "Bathtub" gin, two bottles a day, and often three, ***got*** to be routine.(p.5)

• Gradually things ***got*** worse.(p.5)

• Then I ***got*** a promising business opportunity.(p.5)

• Disappointed but curious, I wondered what had ***got*** into the fellow.(p.9)

• Simply, but smilingly, he said, "I've ***got*** religion."(p.9)

• He begged the doctor to tell him the whole truth, and he ***got*** it.(p.26)

• Yet he ***got*** drunk again.(p.36)

• To conclude that others were wrong was as far as most of us ever ***got***.(p.66)

• But the more we fought and tried to have our own way, the worse matters ***got***.(p.66)

• We ***got*** this all down on paper and looked at it.(p.69)

• Almost invariably they ***got*** drunk.(p.72)

• She went to court and ***got*** an order for his arrest.(p.79)

• After the sermon, he quietly ***got*** up and made an explanation.(p.80)

• Even though your protege may not have entirely admitted his condition, he has become very curious to know how you ***got*** well.(p.92)

• In desperation, we have even ***got*** tight ourselves -- the drunk to end all drunks.(p.106)

• Perhaps at this point we ***got*** a divorce and took the children home to father and mother.(p.106)

• We began to ask medical advice as the sprees ***got*** closer together.(p.106)

• Why was it, when these dangers were pointed out that they agreed, and then ***got*** drunk again immediately?(p.107)

• Yet they ***got*** well.(p.110)

• I'm sorry I ***got*** disturbed.(p.118)

• He ***got*** drunk.(p.135)

• He remarked: "I'm mighty glad you fellows ***got*** over your drinking.(p.148)

• We have shown how we ***got*** out from under.(p.152)

• She replied, "Yes, we've ***got*** a corker.(p.156)

• Understand he was once a well-known lawyer in town, but just now we've ***got*** him strapped down tight."(p.156)

• The last three times, I ***got*** drunk on the way home from here.(p.157)

• He ***got*** in touch with a prominent psychiatrist who had undertaken certain responsibilities for the mental health of the community.(p.163)

• But obviously you cannot transmit something you haven't ***got***.(p.164)

• When I ***got*** the fog out of my brain, I decided that quitting school was very foolish and that I had better return and continue my work.(p.173)

• After three years of this, I wound up in the local hospital where they attempted to help me, but I would get my friends to smuggle me a quart, or I would steal the alcohol about the building, so that I ***got*** rapidly worse.(p.175)

• I used to put eight or twelve ounce bottles of alcohol in a fur lined glove and toss it onto the back airing porch when winter days ***got*** dark enough.(p.176)

• It was harmless; nobody ever ***got*** drunk on beer.(p.177)

• I gave the matter much time and study for the next two and a half years, but still ***got*** tight every night nevertheless.(p.178)

• I ***got*** tight that night, stayed sober Monday till after the dinner and then proceeded to get tight again.(p.179)

• He came and ***got*** me home and to bed, gave me a few drinks that night, and one bottle of beer the next morning.(p.179)

• It did help to certain extent, since I ***got*** in places where I could not obtain anything to drink, and so broke the habitual drinking.(p.183)

• They said, "We've ***got*** some bad news for you.(p.187)

• I know there was even more, something that I hadn't ***got***, and I remember one day, a week or two after I had come out of the hospital, Bill was over to my house talking to my wife and me.(p.191)

• When they ***got*** through the day's work, part was left which I proceeded to drink.(p.196)

• Then I ***got*** married.(p.196)

• At the end of this selling of lots, just prior to World War I, I ***got*** into the crude rubber business, and six months later there was only one broker and myself left in Akron.(p.197)

• I figured the only difference between me and a millionaire was that I hadn't the strength, or that he ***got*** the breaks and I didn't.(p.197)

• So having licked it, there was no reason why I shouldn't have a drink, and I stopped in before I ***got*** home and had one.(p.203)

• Then I ***got*** into the habit of having beers, and decided that a drink of whiskey was not any worse; so I would get the one drink of whiskey but, on second thought, I decided that as long as I was only going to have one, I might as well make it a double-header.(p.203)

• There were times when I ***got*** to drinking, and I had been warned by Firestone that they wouldn't stand for this much longer, so, clearly, they were conscious of the fact that I drank too much and too often.(p.204)

• I went into a bar, and there I ***got*** into a fight.(p.204)

• He did call me a cab and when I ***got*** into the cab, I said, "Drive me to a liquor store."(p.204)

• When I ***got*** home I had to give him a check for the taxi fare.(p.205)

• They asked me if I would take some medicine, and I promised that I would if they ***got*** me a drink.(p.206)

• I ***got*** two drinks, each of them a quarter of that pint, in me, and was talking along with these people, but I felt that sooner or later they were going to have me cornered because they were smarter than I was and the drink was beginning to take effect; but as I reached for the third drink Bob said, "Listen, Buster, you promised to take some medicine if we ***got*** you a drink.(p.206)

• Now we ***got*** you the drink, but you haven't taken the medicine."(p.206)

• I told him I'd take the medicine and I would take it, but I hadn't told him when, and thereupon I ***got*** away with the third drink.(p.206)

• And I said, "Well, what about Paul, have you ***got*** him all dried up?"(p.207)

• I said, "In that case, there's no use of wasting this," and I ***got*** the last of that pint.(p.207)

• I thought he had it is his pocket, so I said, "You ***got*** some?"(p.208)

• And he ***got*** me a drink.(p.208)

• I could discipline myself but along the way there would be festivities and occasions when I ***got*** drunk.(p.211)

• My practice had advanced to the point where it could stand a lot of abuse and it ***got*** it.(p.214)

• I'd only had two with her, but I'd managed four in the fifteen minutes I'd waited for her, and of course I'd had the usual uncounted swigs from the bottle as I painfully ***got*** up and did my slow spasmodic dressing.(p.223)

• Somehow I ***got*** out of there and walked five blocks past brownstone houses.(p.223)

• That night I ***got*** very drunk, which was usual, but I remembered everything, which was very unusual.(p.224)

• "Blanks" were more frequent, and I seldom knew how I'd ***got*** home.(p.226)

• Naturally, in spite of my good intentions, in spite of my protected life behind sanitarium walls, I several times ***got*** drunk, and was astounded . . . and badly shaken.(p.227)

• When I ***got*** back to Germany I settled down to finish my apprenticeship, drinking the wine of the country as usual.(p.231)

• I came of good stock, of men and women who drank wine all their lives as a beverage, and while they occasionally ***got*** drunk at special celebrations, they were up and about their business the next day.(p.231)

• "Best in the business, when he's sober," my customers would say, and I still had a following who would give me work though they deplored my habits, because they knew the job would be well done when they eventually ***got*** it.(p.234)

• I even ***got*** them myself and tried them.(p.235)

• In sports I made the track and tennis teams; I ***got*** along well with the other boys and had a fairly large circle of acquaintances but no intimate friends.(p.240)

• I was never a hilarious drunk; the more I drank the quieter I ***got***, and the drunker I ***got*** the harder I fought to stay sober.(p.241)

• The first year in college I just ***got*** by in my studies, and that year I majored in poker and drinking.(p.241)

• My next job was in sales promotion for an oil company in Mississippi where I promptly became high man and ***got*** lots of pats on the back.(p.242)

• As long as things were tough and the job a challenge I could always manage to hold on pretty well, but as soon as I learned the combination, ***got*** the puzzle under control and the boss to pat me on the back, I was gone again.(p.243)

• They, too, had taken a train to one town and had wakened hundreds of miles in the opposite direction, never knowing how they ***got*** there.(p.246)

• I tried to contact the boys in New York, but telegrams bounced right back and when I finally ***got*** Hank on the telephone he fired me right then.(p.247)

• Then I ***got*** a very good position in Philadelphia and quickly found I would need a few fellow alcoholics around me if I was to stay sober.(p.249)

• My wife traveled with me, but with a baby coming I decided to settle in a large city where I ***got*** a job with a commission agent which is a polite term for a handbook operator.(p.251)

• Some college friends ***got*** me jobs when I finally had to go to work, but I didn't stick to them.(p.251)

• Making my way to Pittsburgh, I met other former friends and ***got*** a job in a large factory where piecemakers were making good money.(p.252)

• I quit the factory and ***got*** a job on a small newspaper, going from that to a Pittsburgh daily, long ago defunct.(p.252)

• I wanted to roam again and through relatives ***got*** a supercargo job on an Australian packet which allowed me to visit my people in Australia where I was born.(p.252)

• I ***got*** my first introduction to "riding the rods and making a blind."(p.252)

• Lots of times, vain-gloriously, I used to take the

bottle out, look at it and say, "I've *got* you licked."(p.253)
• I applied for a publicity job and *got* it.(p.254)
• As soon as I could get up and walk I started to drink again and kept it up until my friend of the hospital, who, in his first try at the new way of life had stubbed his toe in Chicago but had come back to the town to take counsel and make a new start, picked me up and *got* me into a hospital.(p.258)
• I had been drinking heavily from one state of semi-coma to another and it was several days before I *got* "defogged," but subconsciously I was in earnest about wanting to quit liquor forever.(p.258)
• Finally, it *got* so bad that I left him and went back home and took my two children with me.(p.262)
• I *got* a job in the woolen mills in Ravenna – very hard work.(p.262)
• At the end of a year, the children *got* a card from their father, which I still have and cherish.(p.262)
• He *got* a job and went back to work.(p.263)
• Our oldest daughter *got* married; they were living at our house.(p.263)
• We were together all the time, but this night I *got* up and saw it was late.(p.263)
• One year we *got* as far as Bellaire, Ohio.(p.264)
• One Sunday afternoon, the only time I ever *got* picked up for drunken driving, I *got* picked up in Bellaire.(p.264)
• Somebody must have taken pity on you and gone out and *got* it for you."(p.264)
• So, on that Saturday before Labor Day, I *got* drunk and set the house on fire -- so we didn't have to paint it.(p.265)
• "Oh, some darn thing they've *got* here in the paper about it."(p.266)
• Time went on and the drinking *got* worse and worse, and I was in another barroom, down the road the other way, a small one, and I took my glass – that morning I'd been able to lift it from the bar -- and I said to the woman behind the bar, "I wish I might never take another drop of that stuff.(p.266)
• Finally, one morning, I *got* up and *got* in the car and cried all the way down to the M.'s – the people who owned the bar – and told her I was licked and wanted help.(p.267)
• Now, if you've *got* a Bible around . . ."(p.268)
• And then he *got* us to laugh, which was what we needed.(p.269)
• He talked about his wife taking his little boy away from him because of his drinking, and how he *got* back together with them through A.A., and we began feeling grateful right then that all these things hadn't been taken from us.(p.270)
• She talked to me and laughed about it and *got* me all over it.(p.273)
• I *got* an easy, part-time job selling printing for a small neighborhood printer.(p.276)
• Instead, he *got* dressed, took me out, bought me three or four double shots and put me to bed.(p.278)
• When I *got* out of the hospital, I was invited to stay with Dr. Bob and his dear wife, Anne.(p.279)
• I *got* down on my knees for the first time in thirty years.(p.280)
• But it took six more months of work and disappointments before a group of three men *got* together in my rooming house bedroom for their first A.A. meeting.(p.282)
• There was more than one occasion when I *got* up in the morning with just enough money for coffee and toast and the bus fare to carry me to my first appointment.(p.283)
• Then when we *got* back to the apartment, he was willing to wait two or three days until I *got* my health back to be paid off for the liquor and fare.(p.289)
• I *got* along fairly well with my party drinking for quite some time, but eventually I began to visit beer joints in between parties.(p.298)
• How many times I swore off in the morning and *got* drunk before sunset I don't know.(p.300)
• While working in an office, there was some semblance of restraint, but, oh boy, when I *got* on the outside with this new company without supervision, did I go to town!(p.300)
• One is that I don't remember too many of them, as I was one of those drunks who could be on his feet and attend a meeting or a party, engage in a conversation with people and do things that any nearly normal person would do, and the next day not remember a thing about where I was, what I did, whom I saw, or how I *got* home.(p.301)
• I made arrangements to enter the hospital three days later and promptly went out and *got* stiff for three days.(p.302)
• While I was in basic, I *got* high off booze almost every night.(p.317)
• He turned me in to the company commander, but I *got* off the hook, and that was all that mattered.(p.317)
• I *got* orders to go to Vietnam, and I spent most of the year over there either drunk or sick with a hangover.(p.317)
• We *got* along fine for about two weeks, until she told me where to go and to take my damn bottle with me.(p.318)
• We *got* engaged, and we were happy – Jean with me, and me with the bottle and Jean.(p.318)
• I *got* orders to go to Germany, and everyone in Germany was against me.(p.318)
• I talked to the first sergeant and the battalion commander, and they *got* me in contact with an A.A. member.(p.319)
• When I *got* out of the hospital, I continued making the meetings.(p.320)
• I *got* into terrific trouble with my drinking.(p.322)
• I *got* so that I hid quite a bit of the time, wouldn't answer the phone, and stayed by myself as much as I could.(p.324)
• Nobody but me *got* smashed.(p.328)
• If ever I *got* that bad . . .(p.332)
• But the only thing that *got* started was my drinking.(p.336)
• As long as I worked, as long as I *got* out, I didn't drink.(p.339)
• It finally *got* such a hold on me that I was completely at my wits' end, not knowing what the result would be.(p.343)
• I have been of a very religious outlook all my life, but that made no difference once John Barleycorn *got* the better of me.(p.343)
• After my wife had read this to me, I said to her, as I had said many times in desperation, "I have *got* to do something."(p.346)
• The satisfaction I *got* from giving him a little of what I had read in those pamphlets far surpassed any feeling that I had ever had before in helping patients.(p.347)
• This was such a new thought that I *got* all sorts of books on Higher Powers, and I put a Bible by my bedside, and I put a Bible in my car.(p.348)
• And I put a Big Book by my night stand, and I put a "Twelve Steps and Twelve Tradition" in my locker at the hospital, and I *got* books by Emmet Fox, and I *got* books by God-knows-who, and I *got* to reading all these things.(p.348)
• So he *got* me a cup of coffee, and a piece of cake, and sat me down and said, "Why, there's nothing wrong with you.(p.348)
• I *got* the Big Book and I read it, and this is what it said: "Rarely have we seen a person fail who has thoroughly followed our path."(p.349)
• We've *got* to turn the whole business over to some joker we can't even see!(p.350)
• Here he is powerless, unmanageable, in the grip of something bigger than he is, and he's *got* to turn the whole business over to someone else!(p.350)
• Well, I don't know who He is, but I've *got* my own idea.(p.350)
• The more I drank, the worse it *got* and the more I had to drink.(p.354)
• Lucky because my excessive drinking never *got* me in jail, or hospitalized, nor did it ever cost me a job.(p.356)
• I *got* behind in my rent, but never in my drinking.(p.358)
• At this time, however, she had an opportunity to go to Salt Lake City on a new project for the government, but she did promise me that if I would curtail my drinking and buckle down to hard work she would give serious consideration to my latest proposal and maybe join me at a later date when I *got* settled.(p.359)
• I *got* around this by joining the local Rotary Club, and through this association with the business men of the community my little station began to grow.(p.360)
• I *got* through the holidays all right until New Year's Day.(p.365)
• You will recall that I said the time that I *got* the idea out of a clear sky to call A.A. on a certain night was at about ten.(p.366)
• The only drawback was, I always knew how I arrived there, but somehow, between the rest room, the rinse, and the fluff-dry, I never knew when or how I *got* home.(p.370)
• To wake up at home, not knowing how I *got* there, and to realize I had driven my car, became torture.(p.375)
• Not knowing where I had been or how I *got* home was making me desperate.(p.375)
• I *got* right into the car and they drove me over, and just as soon as I *got* to the church they started the wedding.(p.385)
• Something went haywire and I *got* to depend on it so I could do nothing without it.(p.386)
• That was when all the boys and Esther *got* drunk and the wives didn't.(p.386)
• Frank left to find the doctor and I *got* drunk.(p.387)
• So I *got* drunker and drunker, and then, suddenly, I woke up in the booby-hatch.(p.387)
• I knew this, and right away I *got* furious and would not even talk to the doctor in the place.(p.387)
• Every time I *got* drunk, my husband would send me to a nursing home.(p.388)
• So Frank went to New York and despite all these things, I *got* drunk.(p.389)
• One afternoon, the year after moving to Houston, I *got* as drunk as a skunk, and while I do not walk very straight sober, you should see me when I'm drunk!(p.390)
• I *got* into slacks and out I went, weaving with the dog.(p.390)
• They phoned my husband that I was in jail and in such terrible shape that they didn't know what I would do to myself; and they realized that jail was no place for me, but that he was to wait a while before he *got* me, because at the time they called him to come over for me I was beating a tin cup against the wall.(p.390)
• So I *got* a half pint and at midnight that night, I called the number I had been given, but the man who had started the group was in the hospital so I didn't know what to do.(p.393)
• At eighteen, I *got* my first steady job.(p.397)
• I *got* a good non-academic education; my intellectual curiosity was encouraged.(p.401)
• Otherwise I *got* nothing out of it.(p.401)
• At the tender age of twenty-three, I *got* a divorce.(p.402)
• He *got* half custody of our child, but later kept her during most of the school terms.(p.402)
• I *got* a novel written.(p.402)
• Above all, he noticed that I drank a good deal, often *got* tight in his company and told him naughty stories.(p.403)
• But I *got* drunk that night and stayed drunk, getting increasingly worse until I found A.A. ten years later.(p.404)
• I stayed with them until I *got* drunk and had a row with the Paris editor.(p.405)
• This good and gentle man, a brilliant research doctor, *got* nowhere with me fast.(p.407)
• Now it was semi-blackouts every night, outrageous behavior, passing out in some friend's Village studio or not knowing how I *got* home.(p.407)
• They *got* so they moved their barstools when they saw me coming.(p.411)
• But I never *got* into jail.(p.411)
• I *got* off the so-called wagon, and on the twenty-four hour plan.(p.415)
• I don't know how I *got* here this trip, but it doesn't matter very much.(p.423)
• I *got* a job after school pumping gas and worked until ten or eleven at night.(p.423)
• We *got* to Omaha, from my home in Chicago.(p.424)
• We broke open a window and *got* inside.(p.424)
• I *got* a job with the newspaper my dad worked for.(p.425)
• About this time I *got* my first crush on a girl.(p.425)
• I planned to stay home the night before I left, but my folks *got* so drunk I walked off early in the evening and spent the night with my girl, getting very drunk myself.(p.425)
• But my dad pulled some strings and *got* in to see me after three weeks.(p.425)
• I *got* emergency leave for twenty days.(p.426)
• They *got* bigger and bigger and nearer and nearer, as if they were going to fall and crush me.(p.427)
• Dad *got* out a jug for me and poured welcome home drinks.(p.428)
• Why I wasn't killed or how I *got* home I don't know.(p.429)
• "I've *got* to stop if I want to live," I told myself, and if I don't want to break my parents' hearts and maybe jeopardize their own carefully built up and hard-fought-for sobriety.(p.429)
• Or, "My physical plant had *got* a little run down and the stuff rushed right to my head."(p.433)
• Or, "I *got* to talking and forgot how many I was taking and it hit me."(p.433)
• "You've *got* to space your drinks and take plenty of water in between," or "coat the stomach with a little olive oil," or "drink anything but those damn martinis."(p.433)
• The harder I worked with Max, the sicker she *got*.(p.440)

• I drank my way through schools and always *got* honors.(p.441)
• I never *got* much effect out of codeine and Percodan and the tranquilizers.(p.442)
• We *got* on the plane and immediately had a big fight over whether I'd drink the free booze.(p.444)
• When we *got* home, I *got* a bottle of Scotch and went to bed.(p.445)
• And I *got* my private room.(p.445)
• "That's a devil of a way to run an organization," I thought, and I reported Frank to the psychiatrist, who didn't seem perturbed; he just *got* someone else to take me on Fridays.(p.447)
• When a big, healthy-looking young fellow stood up there and said, "I'm a success today if I don't drink today," I thought, "Man, I've *got* a thousand things to do today before I can brag about not taking a drink, for God's sake!"(p.447)
• By early July, I had tapered off alcohol completely, and I *got* off all pills in the ensuing few months.(p.448)
• Now sober for years, they tell us how they *got* well.(p.455)
• I didn't like it particularly at first, but I did like the effect I *got* from it.(p.464)
• When I *got* home my mouth was very painful, so I *got* an ice-bag and went to bed.(p.466)
• And I *got* drunk.(p.472)
• *Got* into no trouble.(p.475)
• When I *got* out of there, I lasted about fifteen minutes at home, before I headed for the drugstore and more pills, and then the bar.(p.479)
• Finally, I was arrested and *got* six months for drugs.(p.480)
• At that time I started school and that's how I *got* rid of the curls.(p.483)
• She *got* a medical certificate so that I should not have to join it.(p.484)
• On the other hand, I *got* quite a different picture farther south.(p.486)
• That went on for maybe two months, and then she *got* after me again about drinking.(p.488)
• I *got* to the place where I'd look forward to the week-end's drinking and pacify myself by saying that the week-ends were mine, that it didn't interfere with my family or with my business if I drank on the week-ends.(p.488)
• He *got* me one.(p.489)
• But I found that after I *got* to North Carolina it wasn't any different.(p.490)
• Matters *got* worse all the time until finally they *got* so bad that I was reinvestigated by the Government.(p.490)
• I *got* into a lot of financial difficulties too.(p.490)
• I *got* drunk one night in October, went to sleep in the rain and woke up with pneumonia.(p.490)
• Within about ten days I *got* locked up for being drunk and this same policeman was in the station house as I was being booked.(p.491)
• As usual I *got* drunk and lost the money.(p.491)
• After the trial, I *got* big-hearted again and felt that I should do something in payment for Vi's kindness to me; so I left Washington and went to Seattle to work.(p.492)
• I was there about three weeks, and then I *got* restless and started to tramp across the country, here and there, until I finally wound up in Pennsylvania, in a steel mill.(p.492)
• Of course the kid never *got* the Easter outfit.(p.493)
• I *got* very little out of the two hundred, that I drew on that pay day.(p.493)
• I *got* out of that bill one pair of shoes, and the rest of that money was blown.(p.493)
• But, finally, we *got* one or two to come in and stick and from there, of course, we started to grow.(p.495)
• I haven't mentioned it, but Charlie, my sponsor, was white, and when we *got* our group started we *got* help from other white groups in Washington.(p.495)
• I reach for the bottle which I just *got* from George, the elevator boy.(p.500)
• I spent my last seventeen months in Wallkill, and it was there that I first *got* my introduction to A.A.(p.509)
• However, before the meeting *got* started, a group from the outside came in unexpectedly.(p.509)
• I couldn't tell you how I *got* there.(p.510)
• So I went to an A.A. meeting the first chance I *got*, and I listened.(p.511)
• And so I *got* to the swearing off process.(p.513)
• I *got* married to the girl I'd left behind.(p.513)
• Of course I really didn't have to worry on that score, because I wasn't the type that *got* half drunk.(p.515)
• And I *got* help.(p.515)
• I *got* along well there.(p.517)
• Then I had a year in Germany at school – that was, incidentally, when I *got* drunk for the first time.(p.517)
• But I pointed out to him that as I was the first British boy who had been to the school, it wouldn't be a very good advertisement for him, so I *got* over that all right.(p.518)
• I had two years at Dublin University, and then in 1916, I *got* a nomination for Sandhurst, the British Military College.(p.518)
• But as soon as I *got* out on my own in France, I started drinking.(p.518)
• I *got* a job by myself which suited me down to the ground, because there was nobody really to interfere with what I did, one way or the other, and I usually had my nerves in good trim when anybody was coming around to inspect.(p.519)
• By and large, I *got* through.(p.519)
• They weren't quite so up-to-date on my history and I *got* away with about four years with them.(p.520)
• About three months after that, my record reached home and I *got* a letter telling me I was retired from the Army, they put it very kindly, on medical grounds.(p.521)
• I couldn't see that there was any way out of it, and I *got* absolutely despairing.(p.522)
• That morning was the first time I really realized where I'd *got* to in my life.(p.523)
• Then it *got* to the place I couldn't drink without getting in jail.(p.526)
• Things *got* so bad, I was afraid to go on the street, so I turned to Mothers' Aid.(p.527)
• Then I would go home full of remorse, and wonder what I was going to do until I *got* my next check.(p.527)
• Finally, I *got* so lowdown, I was ashamed of my friends' seeing me, so I went to the worst joints I could find.(p.527)
• My father was and still is a minister, and I was afraid that I might run into him, or that someone might tell him where I was, and I could still remember what he had done to me when I *got* drunk one Christmas when I was very young.(p.527)
• Now I had gotten to the place where I would wake up with black eyes and not know where I *got* them, or wake up with a lot of money and not know where I *got* it.(p.528)
• I *got* out on bail right away, but when I went to trial, the judge gave me thirty days.(p.528)
• I was down to my shorts, unaware of wrong-doing, before the ambulance *got* there and hauled me off to a hospital from which anxious friends rescued me, later that night.(p.537)
• When the policeman released me to my stupefied and exasperated friend at four in the morning, I went to my traveling bag and groped until I found – well, let the officer speak: "Ah," said the policeman, "he's *got* anuder pair, t'ank God!"(p.538)
• I also *got* into my first disciplinary trouble caused by drinking, on two separate occasions.(p.555)
• I *got* sick of the sweetness and turned to ale.(p.556)
• We learn how to level out the emotional wings that *got* us into trouble both when we were up and when we were down.(p.560)

Gotham

• Again I spent my bankroll, by no means as thick as the one I had when I first saw the skyline of *Gotham*.(p.252)

gotten

• I was willing to admit to myself that I had hit bottom, that I had *gotten* hold of something that I didn't know how to handle by myself.(p.187)
• It took me a year, or a year and a half to get to feeling physically well, and it was rather tough, but I soon found folks whose friendship I had once had, and I found, after I had been sober for quite some little time, that these people began to act like they had in previous years, before I had *gotten* so bad, so that I didn't pay too awful much attention to financial gains.(p.190)
• I felt having *gotten* married, I was an adult and one of the first things I did was to buy two cases of whiskey with no idea of drinking it.(p.196)
• With the big companies, and with the amount of money we could have *gotten* and the promises I had, it could have been done.(p.198)
• During the latter part of the Christian Science experience I had *gotten* a job and was working at Firestone.(p.203)
• I was aware of symptoms of impending dependence, and I told myself I had *gotten* out of the rat race just in time to head off any booze problem.(p.327)
• The surprise to me is the fact that I didn't know that they knew my drinking had *gotten* out of control.(p.376)
• I loved my father dearly and I adored my dog, and I'd *gotten* this new house and Frank had just given me a new fur coat and I was thrilled to death.(p.389)
• When he picked me up, I must have *gotten* sassy and told him that he couldn't do that, so he took my dog home and took me to jail!(p.390)
• Frank was out of town, and I remember that he'd *gotten* in this one night and found me drunk.(p.391)
• We had not *gotten* anywhere.(p.406)
• In those days, psychiatry and A.A. had not *gotten* together as they have since.(p.412)
• I'd lost my car again, pawned my wallet and all identification papers for a bottle, and *gotten* home somehow.(p.429)
• I attended meetings, I talked to my folks, I talked to younger people they had *gotten* in contact with to sponsor me.(p.430)
• Max hadn't *gotten* that way because I didn't care.(p.440)
• I had sent her to four consecutive psychiatrists, and not one of them had *gotten* me sober.(p.440)
• I remember finding myself in the middle of the night in the doctors' parking lot at the hospital with one foot in the car and one foot on the ground, not knowing which was the lead foot; finding myself hanging up the telephone – then realizing I had *gotten* out of bed, answered the phone, turned on the light, and carried on a conversation with a patient.(p.441)
• It has *gotten* progressively easier.(p.448)
• Now I had *gotten* to the place where I would wake up with black eyes and not know where I got them, or wake up with a lot of money and not know where I got it.(p.528)
• Instead, I had *gotten* sicker.(p.539)

govern

• It was thought that no alcoholic man or woman could be excluded from our Society; that our leaders might serve but never *govern*; that each group was to be autonomous and there was to be no professional class of therapy.(p.xix)
• How exciting to learn the inward mysteries that *govern* the behavior of people, how wonderful to know, at last, all about myself!(p.434)
• Our leaders are but trusted servants; they do not *govern*.(p.564)
• They derive no real authority from their titles; they do not *govern*.(p.567)

governed

• These tiny bodies are *governed* by precise laws, and these laws hold true throughout the material world.(p.49)
• For eighteen years, from the age of twenty-one to thirty-nine, fear *governed* my life.(p.275)

government

• One day I went to Washington to present some accounting evidence to a *government* bureau.(p.40)
• At that time I was not aware of the almost unlimited supply the *government* made it possible for us doctors to obtain, neither had I any knowledge of the bootlegger who soon appeared on the horizon.(p.175)
• At this time, however, she had an opportunity to go to Salt Lake City on a new project for the *government*, but she did promise me that if I would curtail my drinking and buckle down to hard work she would give serious consideration to my latest proposal and maybe join me at a later date when I got settled.(p.359)
• I had a very good friend who was in the *Government* service, and I went to him about a job.(p.489)
• I worked for the *Government* about a year and still maintained my evening office practice when the *Government* agencies were decentralized.(p.489)
• She also was in the *government* service.(p.490)
• Matters got worse all the time until finally they got so bad that I was reinvestigated by the *Government*.(p.490)

governor

• I was not eligible for parole, until -- with God's help, I'm sure -- the *governor* cut five years off my sentence.(p.462)
• I left because I had a contretemps with the *Governor*.(p.520)

governors

• I'd been on the board of *governors* of the Academy of Motion Picture Arts and Sciences for six years.(p.328)

gown
• I was taken out of the house and put bodily into a waiting car with nothing on but a robe and *gown.*(p.466)
• Economic conditions had a great deal to do with it, because I've often heard my father say that his mother would take one of the old time flour sacks and cut a hole through the bottom and two corners of it and there you'd have a *gown.*(p.486)

grab
• So I went to my wife and asked her, wasn't there something that she and I could do to somehow get together, and she turned on her heel and looked me squarely in the eye, and said, "You don't care anything about my problem," and I could have smacked her, but I said to myself, "*Grab* on to your serenity!"(p.351)

grace
• But for the *grace* of God, there would have been thousands more convincing demonstrations.(p.25)
• And I still say that as long as I remember that January 8th in Washington, that is how long, by the *grace* of God as I understand Him, I will retain a happy sobriety.(p.250)
• But now, with His help and *grace*, this child of His has paid his initiation fee for good, as long as he remembers to stay away from that first drink (the one that does all the damage) one day at a time.(p.399)
• All the people involved in these flare-ups took it with remarkable *grace*, have teased me about it since, and have become good friends of mine.(p.416)
• By *grace* of God I stop, think two things: This would kill good mother and father; then remember boys talk about Indian fellow who been sober three years.(p.475)
• Father says *grace*, which delays my attack on the buckwheat cakes and sausage.(p.497)
• By the *grace* of God, I only served three years.(p.528)
• He happened to be, by the *grace* of God, Dr. Harry Tiebout, the psychiatrist who probably knew more about alcoholism than any other in the world.(p.559)

gracious
• He becomes, on the next occasion, still more demanding or *gracious*, as the case may be.(p.61)
• Above all, I have gained the greatest thing accorded to any man, the love and understanding of a *gracious* God, who has lifted me from the alcoholic scrap-heap to a position of trust where I have been able to reap the rich rewards that come from showing a little love for others and from serving them as I can.(p.296)

graciously
• Long before I had any real opportunity to give, I had to learn the equally important lesson of receiving *graciously*.(p.281)
• My wife received me *graciously*, although she was living in a one room with kitchen affair.(p.490)
• So, finally, I went to the YMCA and they *graciously* permitted us to use a room at two dollars a night.(p.495)

graciousness
• I was immediately impressed with his *graciousness* and charm.(p.309)

grade
• If he has your will power and guts, he will make the *grade*."(p.138)
• My father died in 1901 when I was eight years old and I was in the second or third *grade* at school.(p.193)
• I went to five *grade* schools, primarily because I was expelled for my conduct, but I eventually graduated from the eighth *grade*.(p.211)
• I was very much interested in athletics, and because of this and parental influence, I didn't drink or smoke in either *grade* or high school.(p.287)
• To the new man I would also like to say that this program is not for sissies for, in my humble opinion, it takes a man to make the *grade*.(p.367)
• When I had served only eighteen months of my sentence, this ex-incorrigible was placed in honor *grade*.(p.461)
• About this time an incident took place in *grade* school that I have never forgotten because it made me realize that I was actually a physical coward.(p.484)

grades
• I went into the high school *grades*, but having missed all the intermediate *grades*, I didn't get along too well, so I developed the habit of going back to school just long enough for the football season and then quitting.(p.193)
• Until I was thirteen I attended public schools, with regular promotions and average *grades*.(p.240)
• Awarded a scholarship to a famous old Eastern college, I began to drink at the end of my freshman year, and by junior year, I had to transfer to an easier state university to keep my *grades* up.(p.419)
• As far as school was concerned, I made fair *grades* throughout.(p.486)

gradual
• Cunning, baffling, powerful – the *gradual* creeping up of the frequency and quantity of alcohol, and what it does to a person is apparent to everyone but the person involved.(p.375)
• The *gradual* result was that I was drifting into making drinking one of the more important parts of my life.(p.519)
• Since, perhaps, suicide was a bit too drastic (actually, I was afraid), dry martinis were chosen as the slow, pleasant, private, *gradual* instrument of self-destruction.(p.531)

gradually
• *Gradually* things got worse.(p.5)
• God comes to most men *gradually*, but His impact on me was sudden and profound.(p.14)
• He may have the habit badly enough to *gradually* impair him physically and mentally.(p.20)
• What used to be the hunch or the occasional inspiration *gradually* becomes a working part of the mind.(p.87)
• *Gradually*, however, I'd suffer so much that I simply had to have the morning-after drink.(p.233)
• My wife upbraided me often and plenty when she saw that my "periodics" were *gradually* losing me what business I could get.(p.233)
• *Gradually* I began to understand.(p.259)
• *Gradually* the quantity increased, the occasions for a drink came more frequently; a hard day, worries and pressure, bad news, good news – there were more and more reasons for a drink.(p.374)
• Never having enough, always craving more, the obsession for alcohol *gradually* dominated all my activities, particularly while travelling.(p.375)
• It now became necessary to have noon drinks; at first just two, then *gradually* more.(p.375)
• Dishonest thinking, prejudice, ego, antagonism toward anyone and everyone who dares to cross him, vanity and a critical attitude are character defects that *gradually* creep in and become a part of his life.(p.380)
• *Gradually* consciousness returned enough to let me know I was in a hospital.(p.422)
• She realized that, and the way I felt, and so for my own good she *gradually* began to pull away.(p.472)

graduate
• I was, of course, soon on the carpet and the upshot was that I had to go back for two more quarters and remain absolutely dry, if I wished to *graduate*.(p.174)
• In conclusion, I can only say that whatever growth or understanding has come to me, I have no wish to *graduate*.(p.249)
• I was an honor *graduate* in high school, and I was a "good boy" to whom mothers pointed when their sons went astray.(p.419)
• I didn't *graduate* to the hard stuff until I was sixteen.(p.423)
• And as I went through pharmacy school, *graduate* school, medical school, internship, residency, and specialty training and, finally, went into practice, my drinking kept increasing.(p.441)
• But I can remember in post *graduate* days, and during interneship, that very often I'd go to a patient's bed and start a process of elimination and then, very often, I'd wind up guessing.(p.485)
• Final exams of my Senior year and I may somehow *graduate*.(p.499)

graduated
• I was *graduated* "summa cum laude" in the eyes of the drinking fraternity, but not in the eyes of the Dean.(p.172)
• I went to five grade schools, primarily because I was expelled for my conduct, but I eventually *graduated* from the eighth grade.(p.211)
• I *graduated* there from a five o'clock alcoholic to a noon-day one.(p.361)
• I *graduated* from shots and beer chasers to Scotch and sodas.(p.398)
• I *graduated* with honors, but could not feel any real responsibility as a father or a husband.(p.419)
• It was my ex-wife, and she said my twenty-seven-year-old son, who has completed his Marine Corps training and *graduated* from college, wanted to see me privately, was getting married in three months, and wanted me at the wedding.(p.462)

graduates
• I guess there are plenty of other *graduates* of this treatment around.(p.389)

graduating
• In the fall of the *graduating* year, I became involved in some litigation over the ownership of inventions and patents.(p.212)
• At thirteen I was packed off to a very fine Protestant boarding school in Virginia where I stayed four years, *graduating* without any special achievements.(p.240)

graduation
• Following *graduation* I was offered a pretty good job which I took.(p.212)
• With nothing but a liberal arts education, very definitely estranged from my family and already married, soon after *graduation* from college I became a bookmaker's clerk on the British racing circuits, far better off financially than the average professional man.(p.251)
• Upon *graduation*, I ventured to New York to pursue my writing career.(p.555)

grain
• My early life was spent in Baltimore where my father was a physician and a *grain* merchant.(p.240)
• I pour out half a tumbler of *grain* alcohol and fill it with ginger ale.(p.499)

grammar
• Everything that I touched from *grammar* school on was successful.(p.345)
• I was president of my *grammar* school student body.(p.345)

grand
• Ain't it *grand* the wind stopped blowin'?"(p.82)
• But he's a *grand* chap when he's sober, though he's been in here eight times in the last six months.(p.156)
• I was married at the age of nineteen to a *grand* girl and had good business prospects.(p.194)
• The name on it was unfamiliar and I had to ask the way to *Grand* Central.(p.223)
• We had meetings at each other's homes and, of course, that was a *grand* place for people to get together out there; they seemed to think so too.(p.270)
• All I can remember about the Roaring Twenties is that I drank a great deal, thought I was having a *grand* time, managed to get to Europe for a few weeks, was very proud of the dozens of speak-easy cards entitling me to an entree in the better joints between Cleveland and New York, took on a wife, and built a home in a fashionable suburb of Cleveland.(p.358)
• Or maybe I'd come home wild drunk, singing and raving about what a fine place home was and what *grand* parents I had since they joined A.A.(p.428)
• The *grand* fellow who at my call made me a hail-fellow-well-met, who gave me such a fine voice, as we sang "Hail, hail, the gang's all here," and "Sweet Adeline," who gave me freedom from fear and feelings of inferiority.(p.498)
• I remember being dragged, drink in hand, from beneath the *grand* piano, where I had hidden, to be locked in my room in disgrace.(p.557)
• (This address is now available in pamphlet form at nominal cost through most A.A. groups or from Box 459, *Grand* Central Station, New York, NY 10163, under the title "Three Talks to Medical Societies by Bill W." -- formerly called "Bill on Alcoholism" and earlier "Alcoholism the Illness.")(p.572)
• If you cannot find A.A. in your locality, a letter addressed to Alcoholics Anonymous, Box 459, *Grand* Central Station, New York, NY 10163, U.S.A., will receive a prompt reply from this world center, referring you to the nearest A.A. group.(p.575)

grandchildren
• So six months ago I acquired a ready made family consisting of one charming wife, four grown children to whom I am devoted, and three *grandchildren*.(p.286)
• I will be fifty years old next month, haven't seen my son or daughter yet, nor my daughter's two children, my *grandchildren*; but I am grateful.(p.463)

grandest
• We had the *grandest* time ever.(p.264)

grandfather's
• I could almost hear the sound of the preacher's voice as I sat, on still Sundays, way over there on the hillside; there was that proffered temperance pledge I never signed; my *grandfather's* good natured contempt of some church folk and their doings; his insistence that the spheres really had their music; but his denial of the preacher's right to tell him how he must listen; his fearlessness as he spoke of these things just before he died; these recollections welled up from the past.(p.10)

grandmother
• There was the father one lost respect for at the age of eleven, because the father broke his solemn word

a circumstance where you, eleven years old, had assumed guilt when you were innocent; but the father would not believe you, no matter what; and to ease his suffering you "confessed" and were "forgiven," only – months later – to have your "guilt" brought up – only he and you knew what he was talking bout -- brought up in front of the stern *grandmother*.(p.533)

grandparents
• My *grandparents* were strangers to me and I remember being lonely, and terrified and hurt.(p.545)

grandparents'
• With no explanation at all, I was taken from my home in Florida to my *grandparents'* home in the middle west.(p.544)

grant
• We asked God to help us show them the same tolerance, pity, and patience that we would cheerfully *grant* a sick friend.(p.67)
• *Grant* me strength, as I go out from here, to do your bidding.(p.76)
• "*Grant* us the serenity to accept the things we cannot change, courage to change the things we can, and the wisdom to know the difference."(p.382)

granted
• Out of those forty years as a movie press agent came one blessing that *granted* me a blind faith in the program.(p.334)
• We are *granted* "the serenity to accept the things we cannot change" -- and thus lose our quickness to anger and our sensitivity to criticism.(p.560)

Grapevine
• I'm so grateful for both the program and the people in it that I still want to go, and then probably the most wonderful thing that I learned from the program -- I've seen this in the 'A.A. *Grapevine*' a lot of times, and I've had people say it to me personally, and I've heard people get up in meetings and make the same statement: The statement is, "I came into A.A. solely for the purpose of sobriety, but it has been through A.A. that I have found God."(p.192)
• While there, I read the Big Book and the *Grapevine* and began the slow road back to health and sanity through the recovery program of A.A.(p.559)
• They are authorized by the groups to handle our over-all public relations and they guarantee the integrity of our principal newspaper, the A.A. *Grapevine*.(p.567)
• The General Service Board of A.A. (the trustees) administers A.A.'s General Service Office, A.A. World Services, Inc., and our monthly magazine, the A.A. *Grapevine*.(p.575)

graph
• At one end of the bed, near the foot, was a printed card, and beneath that was a charted *graph*.(p.422)

grasp
• It is not too difficult nor too easy to *grasp*.(p.367)

grasped
• His roots *grasped* a new soil.(p.12)

grasping
• They are naturally incapable of *grasping* and developing a manner of living which demands rigorous honesty.(p.58)

grateful
• We were *grateful* that Reason had brought us so far.(p.53)
• While *grateful* that he drinks no more, they may not like the idea that God has accomplished the miracle where they failed.(p.128)
• Bill was very, very *grateful* that he had been released from this terrible thing and he had given God the credit for having done it, and he's so *grateful* about it he wants to tell other people about it.(p.191)
• Another reason I go is that I'm still *grateful* for the good years that I've had.(p.192)
• I'm so *grateful* for both the program and the people in it that I still want to go, and then probably the most wonderful thing that I learned from the program -- I've seen this in the 'A.A. Grapevine' a lot of times, and I've had people say it to me personally, and I've heard people get up in meetings and make the same statement: The statement is, "I came into A.A. solely for the purpose of sobriety, but it has been through A.A. that I have found God."(p.192)
• She knew that at that time any suggestion she made about my drinking would only build up a barrier, a consideration for which I am ever *grateful*.(p.216)
• He talked about his wife taking his little boy away from him because of his drinking, and how he got back together with them through A.A., and we began feeling *grateful* right then that all these things hadn't been taken from us.(p.270)
• However, this isn't as rough as it sounds, as we do become *grateful* for the necessity that makes us toe the line, for we find that we are more than compensated for a consistent effort by the countless dividends we receive.(p.311)
• Now I feel so very *grateful* not only for my sobriety, which I try to maintain day by day, but I'm *grateful* also for the ability to help other people.(p.326)
• I hope that I never forget to be *grateful*.(p.326)
• I repeat, I am one of the fortunate members of A.A. -- a lucky guy who is very *grateful*.(p.368)
• Above all, I am *grateful* to A.A. for my sobriety, which means so much to my family, friends and business associates, because God and A.A. were able to do for me something I was unable to do for myself.(p.383)
• There are so many to whom I feel deeply *grateful*; to my husband (and best critic), whose generous love, compassion and understanding have helped me along the way; to those before me in A.A. who inspired the first article I read, and the friend who sent that article to Frank; to Ruth for her personal note, and the first A.A. to talk to me; to my Bishop, whose loving and believing spirit inspired me; and to all the members of the Houston Group who were so patient, kind and helpful -- and to countless others.(p.393)
• I will be fifty years old next month, haven't seen my son or daughter yet, nor my daughter's two children, my grandchildren; but I am *grateful*.(p.463)
• I know I will be *grateful* for a chance to make amends to everybody I have hurt in the past.(p.482)
• I'm *grateful* because that Higher Power led me to A.A. a little over three years ago, when I needed it very badly.(p.512)

gratefulness
• The very simple program they advised me to follow was that I should ask to know God's will for me for that one day, and then, to the best of my ability, to follow that, and at night to express my *gratefulness* to God for the things that had happened to me during the day.(p.208)

gratified
• If our manner is calm, frank, and open, we will be *gratified* with the result.(p.78)

gratify
• But we think that if you persevere, the percentage of successes will *gratify* you.(p.144)

gratitude
• Where we used to run from responsibility, we find ourselves accepting it with *gratitude* that we can successfully shoulder it.(p.311)
• And the psychiatrist has had thousands of couches, and has put you and me on them many, many times, but he hasn't helped us very much, though he has tried hard; and we owe the clergy and the doctor and the psychiatrist a deep debt of *gratitude*, but they haven't helped our alcoholism, except in a rare few instances.(p.352)
• It pays daily in more harmonious relations with my fellow men, in ever clearer insight into the true meaning of life, and in the answering love and *gratitude* wherever and whenever I have been the instrument of God's will in the lives of others.(p.394)
• I had accomplished all the right things that our society expected, and I had no real peace of mind nor *gratitude*.(p.418)
• My *gratitude* to A.A. grows deeper each day I am sober.(p.420)
• I attended my first A.A. meeting eight years ago, and it is with deep *gratitude* that I'm able to say I've not had a drink since that time, and that I take no sedation or narcotics, for this program is to me one of complete sobriety and I no longer need to escape reality.(p.549)

grave
• From this doctor, the broker had learned the *grave* nature of alcoholism.(p.xvi)
• There are those, too, who suffer from *grave* emotional and mental disorders, but many of them do recover if they have the capacity to be honest.(p.58)
• But with the alcoholic, whose hope is the maintenance and growth of a spiritual experience, this business of resentment is infinitely *grave*.(p.66)
• I promised on the *grave* of a beloved sister that I would stop drinking.(p.539)

gravely
• To be *gravely* affected, one does not necessarily have to drink a long time nor take the quantities some of us have.(p.33)
• Say that you believe he is a *gravely* ill person, with this qualification – being perhaps fatally ill, does he want to get well?(p.142)

gravitating
• But at this time, I began *gravitating* toward the really hard drinkers, hanging around with them more and more.(p.404)

gravity
• Some day we hope that Alcoholics Anonymous will help the public to a better realization of the *gravity* of the alcoholic problem, but we shall be of little use if our attitude is one of bitterness or hostility.(p.103)

gray
• Standing there was a *gray* haired man – tall, trim and in uniform.(p.422)

great
• The section called "The Doctor's Opinion" has been kept intact, just as it was originally written in 1939 by the late Dr. William D. Silkworth, our Society's *great* medical benefactor.(p.xi)
• With the appearance of the new book a *great* deal began to happen.(p.xvii)
• But *great* numbers of these -- about two out of three – began to return as time passed.(p.xx)
• Yet it is our *great* hope that all those who have as yet found no answer may begin to find one in the pages of this book and will presently join us on the highroad to a new freedom.(p.xxi)
• In spite of the *great* increase in the size and the span of this Fellowship, at its core it remains simple and personal.(p.xxii)
• His alcoholic problem was so complex, and his depression so *great*, that we felt his only hope would be through what we then called "moral psychology," and we doubted if even that would have any effect.(p.xxix)
• He has not had a drink for a *great* many years.(p.xxx)
• I rightly imagined that they would some day have a *great* rise.(p.2)
• The *great* boom of the late twenties was seething and swelling.(p.3)
• To Christ I conceded the certainty of a *great* man, not too closely followed by those who claimed Him.(p.11)
• He shouted *great* tidings.(p.11)
• But that would be in *great* measure.(p.13)
• I felt lifted up, as though the *great* clean wind of a mountain top blew through and through.(p.14)
• We are like the passengers of a *great* liner the moment after rescue from shipwreck when camaraderie, joyousness and democracy pervade the vessel from steerage to Captain's table.(p.17)
• This is the *great* news this book carries to those who suffer from alcoholism.(p.17)
• The *great* fact is just this, and nothing less: That we have had deep and effective spiritual experiences which have revolutionized our whole attitude toward life, toward our fellows and toward God's universe.(p.25)
• That was a *great* physician's opinion.(p.26)
• Surprisingly enough, we find such convictions no *great* obstacle to a spiritual experience.(p.28)
• The idea that somehow, someday he will control and enjoy his drinking is the *great* obsession of every abnormal drinker.(p.30)
• A man of thirty was doing a *great* deal of spree drinking.(p.32)
• This is the baffling feature of alcoholism as we know it -- this utter inability to leave it alone, no matter how *great* the necessity or the wish.(p.34)
• That was *great* news to us, for we had assumed we could not make use of spiritual principles unless we accepted many things on faith which seemed difficult to believe.(p.47)
• Though some of us resisted, we found no *great* difficulty in casting aside such feelings.(p.48)
• In this respect alcohol was a *great* persuader.(p.48)
• Logic is *great* stuff.(p.53)
• We found the *Great* Reality deep down within us.(p.55)
• Then, like a thunderbolt, a *great* thought came.(p.56)
• It poured over and through him with the certainty and majesty of a *great* tide at flood.(p.56)
• Save for a few brief moments of temptation the thought of drink has never returned; and at such times a *great* revulsion has risen up in him.(p.57)
• If his arrangements would only stay put, if only people would do as he wished, the show would be *great*.(p.60)
• This was only a beginning, though if honestly and humbly made, an effect, sometimes a very *great* one, was felt at once.(p.63)
• Some of us once had *great* self-confidence, but it didn't fully solve the fear problem, or any other.(p.68)
• Notwithstanding the *great* necessity for discussing ourselves with someone, it may be one is so situated that there is no suitable person available.(p.74)
• It may mean the loss of many nights' sleep, *great* interference with your pleasures, interruptions to

your business.(p.97)
• Yet we do go to *great* extremes to provide each other with these very things, when such action is warranted.(p.98)
• If persisted in for a few months, the effect on a man's family is sure to be *great*.(p.99)
• We want to leave you with the feeling that no situation is too difficult and no unhappiness too *great* to be overcome.(p.104)
• Our men have sworn *great* solemn oaths that they were through drinking forever.(p.105)
• sometimes they were so inaccessible that it seemed as though a *great* wall had been built around them.(p.107)
• If he is enthusiastic your cooperation will mean a *great* deal.(p.113)
• Starting from a speck on the domestic horizon, *great* thunderclouds of dispute may gather.(p.117)
• Therefore, you probably need fresh interests and a *great* cause to live for as much as your husband.(p.119)
• A few of us have had these growing pains and they hurt a *great* deal.(p.124)
• We do talk about each other a *great* deal, but we almost invariably temper such talk by a spirit of love and tolerance.(p.125)
• This dream world has been replaced by a *great* sense of purpose, accompanied by a growing consciousness of the power of God in our lives.(p.130)
• Meanwhile, we are sure a *great* deal can be accomplished by the use of the book alone.(p.144)
• We, who have collectively seen a *great* deal of business life, at least from the alcoholic angle, had to smile at this gentleman's sincere opinion.(p.149)
• Never could we recapture the *great* moments of the past.(p.151)
• As we shall see, he now means a *great* deal to his community, and the major liabilities of thirty years of hard drinking have been repaired in four.(p.156)
• They had visioned the *Great* Reality – their loving and All Powerful Creator.(p.161)
• There is a good bit of travel between East and West and we foresee a *great* increase in this helpful interchange.(p.162)
• See to it that your relationship with Him is right, and *great* events will come to pass for you and countless others.(p.164)
• This is the *Great* Fact for us.(p.164)
• Without this proof the expectant purchaser would be forced to depart empty handed with none of what I later came to believe was the *great* panacea for all human ills.(p.171)
• Men who had liquor shipped in from Boston or New York by express were looked upon with *great* distrust and disfavor by most of the good townspeople.(p.171)
• I seemed to be able to snap back the next morning better than most of my fellow drinkers, who were cursed (or perhaps blessed) with a *great* deal of morning-after nausea.(p.172)
• During these years, I drank as much as my purse permitted, still without paying too *great* a penalty, although I was beginning to have morning jitters at times.(p.173)
• This had little effect however for I kept on drinking and used a *great* deal more hard liquor than in former years.(p.174)
• Therefore it would make no *great* difference, even if I should do some drinking.(p.175)
• They spoke with *great* freedom from embarrassment, which I could never do, and they seemed very much at ease on all occasions and appeared very healthy.(p.178)
• It must be remembered that I had read a *great* deal and talked to everyone who knew, or thought they knew anything about the subject of alcoholism.(p.180)
• I spend a *great* deal of time passing on what I learned to others who want and need it badly.(p.180)
• I looked up and there were two *great* big fellows over six foot tall, very likable looking.(p.185)
• Then came a *great* joy.(p.189)
• As soon as I had done that I did feel a *great* release.(p.189)
• I always built up in my own mind the *great* things that I was going to do, and in fact I accomplished about fifty percent of them and then lost interest.(p.193)
• There was always a tremendous drive and ambition to become a *great* guy, because I think I recognized inwardly that I didn't have any special talents.(p.194)
• Despite *great* opportunities, alcohol nearly ended her life.(p.222)
• Talking things over with them, *great* floods of enlightenment showed me myself as I really was and I was like them.(p.229)
• And it is true that there was no *great* amount of drunkenness.(p.230)
• Military service was compulsory and I did my stretch with the class of my age, goose-stepping in German barracks and taking part in the Boxer Rebellion in China, my first time at any *great* distance from home.(p.230)
• There I sat in the evenings, enjoying with my friends our memories of the "old country," singing the old songs we all knew, playing simple card games for drinks and consuming *great* quantities of beer.(p.231)
• You can all remember that in the first few months after the change, a *great* many men, who had formerly been used to a few beers every day or an occasional drink of whiskey, simply quit all alcoholic drinks.(p.232)
• For the *great* majority of us, however, that condition didn't last.(p.232)
• With a *great* deal of determination, I would throw out full pints – pour them out and smash the bottles -- firmly resolved never to take another drink of the stuff.(p.234)
• Even then he went into no *great* detail about how he and a crowd of alcoholics, with whom he associated, had mastered their difficulty.(p.235)
• As we left, and they were escorting us across the bridge into Wheeling, I, with *great* dignity and sarcasm, told them if their wives were ever visiting in Akron, and they, too, were looking for their route sign as I was, that I hoped I could extend to them the hospitality that had been shown to me in Bellaire.(p.264)
• I give a *great* deal of credit to Doc and Anne for changing our life.(p.270)
• Before I stop – I always was a *great* talker – I want to say that nobody will ever know how I miss Annie's advice about things.(p.273)
• My thinking about drinking had undergone a *great* change.(p.277)
• Immediately a *great* feeling of peace descended upon me, intermingled with a feeling of being suffused with a quiet strength.(p.280)
• The example which they and Bill W., whose visits to Akron were fairly frequent, set me of service to their fellow men imbued me with a *great* desire to emulate them.(p.281)
• Here by itself was a *great* step forward.(p.283)
• This represents another *great* change for me.(p.284)
• It was therefore not extraordinary that I should shy away from any serious thought of marriage for a *great* many years after joining A.A.(p.286)
• At any rate the last *great* step toward a well rounded life still lay ahead of me.(p.286)
• Shortly thereafter, aided by the Depression, I found that I had a *great* deal of spare time and that a little drink in the morning helped.(p.287)
• He laid *great* stress on the progression of his attitude toward life and people, and most of his attitudes had been very similar to mine.(p.290)
• I spent a *great* deal of time with Dr. Bob, whenever he had the time to spare, and in the homes of two or three other people, trying to see how the family lived the program.(p.291)
• We went over these at *great* length and then he finally asked me if I wanted these defects of character removed.(p.292)
• This latest part of my life has had a purpose, not in *great* things accomplished but in daily living.(p.295)
• My stock of material goods isn't *great*.(p.296)
• It is a way of life, and the challenge contained in its principles is *great* enough to keep any human being striving for as long as he lives.(p.311)
• I have had my share of problems, heartaches and disappointments, because that is life, but also I have known a *great* deal of joy, and a peace that is the handmaiden of an inner freedom, I have a wealth of friends and, with my A.A. friends, an unusual quality of fellowship.(p.312)
• My alcoholism-prone mind, however, reminded me that all *great* authors had needed a stimulus to build up inspiration and inventiveness before each day's work.(p.331)
• I agreed it was *great* stuff -- for those who needed it.(p.332)
• I had to hide, as a *great* many people in A.A. have had to do.(p.336)
• Psychiatrist and surgeon, he had lost his way until he realized that God, not he, was the *Great* Healer.(p.345)
• I recall, as I walked into that meeting, saying to myself, "Here I am, a fellow of the American College of Surgeons, a Fellow of the International College of Surgeons, a diplomate of one of the *great* specialty boards in these United States, a member of the American Psychiatric Society, and I have to go to the butcher, the baker and the carpenter to help make a man out of me!"(p.347)
• I don't mean that in any sense as a derogatory statement about psychotherapy; it's a *great* tool, not too potent, but a *great* tool.(p.349)
• We are *great* people.(p.350)
• The *Great* Boss has given me diagnostic and surgical talent, and He has loaned it to me to use for the rest of my life.(p.350)
• I couldn't practice medicine without the *Great* Physician.(p.351)
• All I can remember about the Roaring Twenties is that I drank a *great* deal, thought I was having a grand time, managed to get to Europe for a few weeks, was very proud of the dozens of speak-easy cards entitling me to an entree in the better joints between Cleveland and New York, took on a wife, and built a home in a fashionable suburb of Cleveland.(p.358)
• High living, a *great* many fair weather friends, the 1929 stock market crash, and a couple of years of Depression, soon relieved me one by one of my worldly goods including my wife.(p.358)
• My first meeting gave me a *great* deal of hope and lots of willing ears for my tale of woe and for my questions.(p.364)
• You'll read and hear a *great* deal about the spiritual part of our program.(p.366)
• The ambition to succeed was instilled in me by my Scandinavian parents who came to this country where opportunities were so *great*.(p.373)
• The drive to get ahead, to succeed, kept me too busy for many years to have any *great* experience with social life.(p.374)
• It was a *great* relief to know I didn't have to drink any more.(p.379)
• A "spiritual experience" to me meant attending meetings, seeing a group of people, all there for the purpose of helping each other; hearing the Twelve Steps and the Twelve Traditions read at a meeting, and hearing the Lord's Prayer, which in an A.A. meeting has such *great* meaning – "Thy will be done, not mine."(p.381)
• You didn't carry a little orchid up the aisle in those days; you carried a *great* big bouquet, like a funeral spray, and you didn't have your picture taken until just before you went to the church.(p.385)
• I feel that there is no situation too difficult, none too desperate, no unhappiness too *great* to be overcome in this *great* fellowship – Alcoholics Anonymous.(p.395)
• Or: If I'm really a genius, I must produce a *great* work, to show why I act like a genius.(p.408)
• At *Great* Lakes Boot Camp I latched onto a soft billet.(p.425)
• I'd heard a lot about A.A. and met a *great* many A.A.'s during that year at home, but I hadn't thought of it for myself.(p.429)
• It helped me a *great* deal to become convinced that alcoholism was a disease, not a moral issue; that I had been drinking as a result of a compulsion, even though I had not been aware of the compulsion at the time; and that sobriety was not a matter of willpower.(p.448)
• Loneliness, *great* physical and mental agony -- these were the common lot.(p.455)
• We all one as *Great* Spirit walks through A.A. like sun walks through day.(p.474)
• Tall Man now see *Great* Spirit in Big Group in sky.(p.476)
• I feel *Great* Spirit at all meetings and when talk to A.A. friends.(p.477)
• This means a *great* deal to me, because I had always figured that nobody cared.(p.481)
• That hurt and disturbed me a *great* deal.(p.484)
• My father had come out of the South and had suffered a *great* deal down there.(p.485)
• Economic conditions had a *great* deal to do with it, because I've often heard my father say that his mother would take one of the old time flour sacks and cut a hole through the bottom and two corners of it and there you'd have a gown.(p.486)
• I had a long talk with a psychiatrist, but nothing came of that, and I had also, just about that time, talked with a minister for whom I had a *great* deal of respect.(p.489)
• They taught us a *great* deal about Twelve Step work too.(p.496)
• It's *great* to see him.(p.500)
• But slowly a *great* peace comes to me.(p.504)
• A *great* fear seizes me.(p.505)
• There was a *great* deal of difference.(p.513)
• I found a *great* deal of friendship in this movement.(p.516)
• Rather, I embraced it – I must in honesty admit it --

with a ***great*** sense of relief.(p.531)
• For to have accepted the reasons and to have acted on them would have been too ***great*** a blow to my ego, which was as ***great***, in reverse, as my body was small.(p.534)
• Actually, of course, I wanted someone to listen to me, because when I had a few martinis inside, I became the ***great*** author I longed to be; and the right listener was in for some pretty highflown theories of literature and of genius.(p.536)
• For a little while, I was the ***great*** man I wanted to be, and thought myself entitled to be just by reason of being.(p.537)
• Sobering up, the mind that was ahead of the emotions would impel the question: What have you written or done to be the ***great*** man?(p.537)
• I stumbled agonizedly past the theatre where in years gone by a ***great*** star had played my play.(p.540)
• It is going strong still, these eight years later, and some of its members have been of ***great*** influence for good in state-wide A.A. work.(p.541)
• One of the truly ***great*** things A.A. has taught me is that reality too has two sides; I had only known the grim side before the program, but now I had a chance to learn about the pleasant side as well.(p.550)
• As another ***great*** man says, "The only real freedom a human being can ever know is doing what you ought to do because you want to do it."(p.553)
• This ***great*** experience that released me from the bondage of hatred and replaced it with love is really just another affirmation of the truth I know: I get everything I need in Alcoholics Anonymous – everything I need I get – and when I get what I need I invariably find that it was just what I wanted all the time.(p.553)
• It's no ***great*** trick to stop drinking; the trick is to stay stopped.(p.554)
• Suddenly, I began vomiting and losing rectally ***great*** quantities of blood.(p.558)
• 1. – Each member of Alcoholics Anonymous is but a small part of a ***great*** whole.(p.565)
• This to the end that our ***great*** blessings may never spoil us; that we shall forever live in thankful contemplation of Him who presides over us all.(p.568)
• I think our profession must take appreciative cognizance of this ***great*** therapeutic weapon.(p.571)
• Dr. Harry M. Tiebout, psychiatrist: "As a psychiatrist, I have thought a ***great*** deal about the relationship of my specialty to A.A. and I have come to the conclusion that our particular function can very often lie in preparing the way for the patient to accept any sort of treatment or outside help.(p.571)
• Historians may one day recognize Alcoholics Anonymous to have been a ***great*** venture in social pioneering which forged a new instrument for social action; a new therapy based on the kinship of common suffering; one having a vast potential for the myriad other ills of mankind."(p.573)

greater

• In nearly all cases, their ideals must be grounded in a power ***greater*** than themselves, if they are to re-create their lives.(p.xxvi)
• I had always believed in a Power ***greater*** than myself.(p.10)
• It was only a matter of being willing to believe in a Power ***greater*** than myself.(p.12)
• The experiment of quitting for a period of time will be helpful, but we think we can render an even ***greater*** service to alcoholic sufferers and perhaps to the medical fraternity.(p.34)
• We had to find a power by which we could live and it had to be a Power ***greater*** than ourselves.(p.45)
• Its main object is to enable you to find a Power ***greater*** than yourself which will solve your problem.(p.45)
• We found that as soon as we were able to lay aside prejudice and express even a willingness to believe in a Power ***greater*** than ourselves, we commenced to get results, even though it was impossible for any of us to fully define or comprehend that Power, which is God.(p.46)
• "Do I now believe, or am I even willing to believe, that there is a Power ***greater*** than myself?"(p.47)
• The reader may still ask why he should believe in a Power ***greater*** than himself.(p.48)
• In our personal stories you will find a wide variation in the way each teller approaches and conceives of the Power which is ***greater*** than himself.(p.50)
• Every one of them has gained access to, and believes in, a Power ***greater*** than himself.(p.50)
• They flatly declare that since they have come to believe in a Power ***greater*** than themselves, to take a certain attitude toward that Power, and to do certain simple things, there has been a revolutionary change in their way of living and thinking.(p.50)
• For faith in a Power ***greater*** than ourselves, and miraculous demonstrations of that power in human lives, are facts as old as man himself.(p.55)
• 2.Came to believe that a Power ***greater*** than ourselves could restore us to sanity.(p.59)
• The main thing is that he be willing to believe in a Power ***greater*** than himself and that he live by spiritual principles.(p.93)
• If the family persists in criticism, this fallacy may take a still ***greater*** hold on father.(p.129)
• You forget that you have just now tapped a source of power much ***greater*** than yourself.(p.163)
• There I took up the business of drinking with much ***greater*** earnestness than I had previously shown.(p.173)
• For ***greater*** freedom and excitement I went abroad to live.(p.225)
• My brilliant agnosticism vanished, and I saw for the first time that those who really believed, or at least honestly tried to find a Power ***greater*** than themselves, were much more composed and contented than I had ever been, and they seemed to have a degree of happiness which I had never known.(p.247)
• He it was who convinced me, because his own conviction was so real, that a Power ***greater*** than myself could help me in the crises of life, and that the means of communicating with this Power was simple prayer.(p.279)
• The most accurate answer I can give you is this: Fear has never again ruled my life since that day in September, 1938, when I found that a Power ***greater*** than myself could not only restore me to sanity but could keep me both sober and sane.(p.285)
• Here was something requiring a ***greater*** willingness to assume responsibility, and take a larger degree of cooperation and "give and take" than even business requires of one.(p.286)
• In an attempt to get over that feeling, there was a quick onslaught of a ***greater*** number of drinks, and then all was lost.(p.346)
• This to me is the proof of the existence of a Somethingness ***greater*** than I am.(p.351)
• I haven't written anything about that part of my story, but I believe in a ***Greater*** Power which I call God and I ask for His wisdom and guidance daily.(p.366)
• In meeting me casually, I don't think my strong belief in "The Man Upstairs" shows, but I have no other explanation for the many good things that have happened to me since I have been in A.A. -- they came to me from a ***Greater*** Power.(p.367)
• Why did I want increasingly ***greater*** quantities of alcohol?(p.374)
• They meant patience, tolerance and humility, and above all the belief that a Power ***greater*** than myself could help.(p.381)
• With my A.A. friends, all I can say is that it's a power ***greater*** than myself.(p.437)
• But what a difference there is between going through hell without a power ***greater*** than one's self, and with it!(p.437)
• Every defect I pointed out to her became ***greater*** and ***greater***.(p.450)
• With their help I also saw that certainly, because of some of the things I had done during the years, I was bordering on insanity, and so, facing the record, I tried to believe that a Power ***greater*** than I could and would restore me to sanity.(p.471)
• The war leaves me with a pair of blankets, a toilet kit, a sweater knit by my sister, and a still ***greater*** inferiority.(p.499)
• Then he asks me if I believe in a power ***greater*** than myself, whether I call that power God, Allah, Confucius, Prime Cause, Divine Mind, or any other name.(p.503)
• But I am to learn later that it began with my desire for material success becoming ***greater*** than my interest in the welfare of my fellow man.(p.507)
• Things weren't going as I thought they should, for my ***greater*** enjoyment, comfort and fame; therefore, if the universe wouldn't play my way, I wouldn't play at all.(p.531)
• Repeated year on end, they are horrible -- frightening and degrading, a chronicle of tragedy which may be ***greater*** because the individual undergoing the tragedy, myself, knew what was happening, and yet refused to do anything to stop it.(p.538)
• I choose to believe that the Power ***greater*** than ourselves we ask for help, wrapped my shivering body in loving warmth and strength which has never left me.(p.541)
• So the need to drink grew still ***greater***.(p.557)
• With few exceptions our members find that they have tapped an unsuspected inner resource which they presently identify with their own conception of a Power ***greater*** than themselves.(p.569)
• Most of us think this awareness of a Power ***greater*** than ourselves is the essence of spiritual experience.(p.570)

greatest

• Today the remarkable unity of A.A. is one of the ***greatest*** assets that our Society has.(p.xix)
• Cling to the thought that, in God's hands, the dark past is the ***greatest*** possession you have – the key to life and happiness for others.(p.124)
• The ***greatest*** enemies of us alcoholics are resentment, jealousy, envy, frustration, and fear.(p.145)
• In his prodigy of service, he was well assisted by Sister Ignatia at St. Thomas Hospital in Akron, Ohio, one of the ***greatest*** friends our Fellowship will ever know.(p.171)
• There was a concrete program, designed to secure the ***greatest*** possible inner security for us long-time escapists.(p.229)
• I get my ***greatest*** thrill of accomplishment from the knowledge that I have played a part in the new happiness achieved by countless others like myself.(p.229)
• The third man who came to see me had been one of the ***greatest*** business-getters his company had ever employed.(p.235)
• That to me was the ***greatest*** humiliation, to think that I'd finally landed in jail.(p.264)
• Above all, I have gained the ***greatest*** thing accorded to any man, the love and understanding of a gracious God, who has lifted me from the alcoholic scrap-heap to a position of trust where I have been able to reap the rich rewards that come from showing a little love for others and from serving them as I can.(p.296)
• The very person who stood with me through it all and has been my ***greatest*** help was the person that I turned against, my husband.(p.338)
• I gave them everything, except the ***greatest*** thing in the world, and that is peace of mind.(p.351)
• Priscilla, an A.A. who, like Marty, has become one of my ***greatest*** friends, decided that I was a stubborn case.(p.414)
• There was the over-weening ambition to be the world's ***greatest*** author, when – at thirty-nine -- I had nothing of importance to say to the world.(p.534)
• Maybe I wouldn't be able to hold any job, or maybe (and this was my ***greatest*** fear) I wouldn't care whether I had a job or not.(p.548)
• Dr. Foster Kennedy, neurologist: "This organization of Alcoholics Anonymous calls on two of the ***greatest*** reservoirs of power known to man, religion and that instinct for association with one's fellows . . . the 'herd instinct.'(p.571)
• Dr. John F. Stouffer, Chief Psychiatrist, Philadelphia General Hospital, citing his experience with A.A., said: "The alcoholics we get here at Philadelphia General are mostly those who cannot afford private treatment, and A.A. is by far the ***greatest*** thing we have been able to offer them.(p.572)

greatly

• Very earnestly we ask the press also, to observe this request, for otherwise we shall be ***greatly*** handicapped.(p.xiii)
• He had also been ***greatly*** helped by the late Dr. William D. Silkworth, a New York specialist in alcoholism who is now accounted no less than a medical saint by A.A. members, and whose story of the early days of our Society appears in the next pages.(p.xvi)
• The broker had gone to Akron on a business venture which had collapsed, leaving him ***greatly*** in fear that he might start drinking again.(p.xvi)
• Certain drinkers, who would be ***greatly*** insulted if called alcoholics, are astonished at their inability to stop.(p.33)
• We are ***greatly*** indebted to the doctor in attendance there, for he, although it might prejudice his own work, has told us of his belief in ours.(p.162)
• In this I was ***greatly*** aided and abetted by one John Barleycorn.(p.358)
• However, one thing I am certain of: Inmates in prison who attend A.A. have their chances of remaining free ***greatly*** enhanced – this is a proved fact.(p.458)
• And no group, regional committee, or individual should ever take any action that might ***greatly*** affect A.A. as a whole without conferring with the trustees of the General Service Board.(p.565)

Greek

• I was active and did well, however, in school publications, dramatics (which came in handy during my drinking career), and ***Greek*** letter societies.(p.357)

green

• We often need it to carry ***green*** recruits through a severe hangover.(p.102)
• He'll never read in his "sweetness and light" senior-citizen publications anything but the joys of lolling in

the rocking chair, angling on the riverbank, or bowling on the *green.*(p.330)
• It is bound to be rough, because who can say exactly how much of that *green* blood -- commonly known as money -- was dissipated on dissipation?(p.396)
• Age and the law were still against me, but laws were not as strictly enforced in those days as they are now, and I discovered that as long as I had the *green* blood, there was always a way to get alcohol, either from a nondiscriminatory bartender or from an older friend who would be glad to purchase the joy juice for the privilege of sharing it.(p.397)

Greenland
• His only chance for sobriety would be some place like the *Greenland* Ice Cap, and even there an Eskimo might turn up with a bottle of scotch and ruin everything!(p.101)

Greenwich
• That was on a hot summer evening, down in the *Greenwich* Village Group, and there was a little porch out there in the old meeting place on Sullivan Street, and after the meeting I went out on the steps for some air.(p.321)

greeted
• I was *greeted* warmly, honestly, and with a true ring of sincerity by everyone present.(p.259)

gremlins
• For the next couple of hours a terrible battle went on between the good *gremlins* and the bad ones, one faction urging me to tell the truth, the other telling me to sit tight and say nothing.(p.366)

Grenadier
• "Here lies a Hampshire *Grenadier* Who caught his death Drinking cold small beer.(p.1)

grew
• But out of this frightening and at first disrupting experience the conviction *grew* that A.A.'s had to hang together or die separately.(p.xix)
• While the internal difficulties of our adolescent period were being ironed out, public acceptance of A.A. *grew* by leaps and bounds.(p.xix)
• They *grew* in numbers.(p.159)
• The shakes *grew* worse and I looked at my watch -- six o'clock.(p.223)
• The times in which I *grew* up (the Prohibition era immortalized by Scott Fitzgerald and John Held Jr.) had taught me to be gay with the gayest; my own inner urges led me to outdo them all.(p.225)
• And to my surprise, my drinking *grew* worse.(p.226)
• I was born in Europe, in Alsace to be exact, shortly after it had become German, and practically *grew* up with the "good Rhine wine" of song and story.(p.230)
• It went on and *grew* worse and worse.(p.262)
• I do feel, though, that the fact that I finally *grew* up to a point where I could even tackle such a job is the apex of the story of a man who spent eighteen years running away from life.(p.286)
• I *grew* up in a small town outside Akron, Ohio, where the life was typical of any average small town.(p.287)
• I had always hated beer, but now I *grew* to love it, bottle after bottle of it, warm or cold.(p.339)
• Never once had my mother even hinted at the idea that, when I *grew* up, I might like to be president of A.A.(p.439)
• Over the years, as I thought about Max, her good qualities *grew* and *grew,* and we married, and all these qualities became more and more apparent to me, and we were happier and happier.(p.450)
• And the more I focused my mind on her defects, the more they *grew* and multiplied.(p.450)
• The faces of the other boys *grew* dim.(p.498)
• The intervals *grew* shorter.(p.514)
• And having sung that phrase, I'd chuckle with amusement, turning into irony turning into self-contempt turning into self-pity, at the sad fate of Bob, that wonderful, poor little motherless boy who was so smart in school and who *grew* up to accept responsibility so early and so fast and who staggered under his burdens without a whimper until the time came when he thought he was too good for this world and so he ought to be out of it.(p.532)
• I *grew* up believing that one had to be totally self-sufficient, for one never dared to depend on another human being.(p.545)
• By this time I was such a past master at kidding myself that I had convinced myself I had sat out a war and waited for this man to come home and, as my resentment and self-pity *grew,* so did my alcoholic problem.(p.548)
• And yet my ability to lie outwardly and to kid myself inwardly *grew* with every drink I took.(p.556)
• So the need to drink *grew* still greater.(p.557)
• As the sober days *grew* into sober months and then into sober years, a new and beautiful life began to emerge from the shambles of my former existence.(p.559)
• As our children *grew* up, I was able to be a father to them when they most needed one.(p.559)

grey
• Bill was tall, *grey* haired, with the kind of asymmetrical good looks and pleasant easy manner that inspire confidence in the shaken and afraid.(p.413)

grief
• This is a condition which, in ordinary life, would produce untold *grief;* there might be scandalous gossip, laughter at the expense of other people, and a tendency to take advantage of intimate information.(p.125)
• I did it more and more, and had lots of fun without much *grief,* either physical or financial.(p.172)
• By living alone you can pretty much eliminate *grief* from you life, but you also eliminate joy.(p.286)

grievous
• We think each family which has been relieved owes something to those who have not, and when the occasion requires, each member of it should be only too willing to bring former mistakes, no matter how *grievous,* out of their hiding places.(p.124)

grim
• Judging from what I had seen in Europe and since, the power of God in human affairs was negligible, the Brotherhood of Man a *grim* jest.(p.11)
• Whether your employee likes it or not, he will learn the *grim* truth about alcoholism.(p.144)
• It was with *grim* foreboding and advanced jitters that I checked in at the hospital.(p.302)
• One of the truly great things A.A. has taught me is that reality too has two sides; I had only known the *grim* side before the program, but now I had a chance to learn about the pleasant side as well.(p.550)

grimy
• And we usually have some kind of *grimy* sweater that we think we look sexy in, even if we weigh ninety-five pounds soaking wet and are not wearing a bra.(p.479)

grind
• That the man who is making the approach has had the same difficulty, that he obviously knows what he is talking about, that his whole deportment shouts at the new prospect that he is a man with a real answer, that he has no attitude of Holier Than Thou, nothing whatever except the sincere desire to be helpful; that there are no fees to pay, no axes to *grind,* no people to please, no lectures to be endured -- these are the conditions we have found most effective.(p.18)

grinding
• I walked away from that girl *grinding* my teeth and cursing under my breath.(p.322)

grinned
• They *grinned,* which I didn't like so much, and then asked me if I thought myself alcoholic and if I were really licked this time.(p.42)

grip
• The inviting maelstrom of Wall Street had me in its *grip.*(p.2)
• We are convinced to a man that alcoholics of our type are in the *grip* of a progressive illness.(p.30)
• This went from bad to worse until Sophomore spring when, after a prolonged period of drinking, I made up my mind that I could not complete my course, so I packed my *grip* and went South to spend a month on a large farm owned by a friend of mine.(p.173)
• Here he is powerless, unmanageable, in the *grip* of something bigger than he is, and he's got to turn the whole business over to someone else!(p.350)

gripped
• Fear *gripped* him.(p.154)
• Now I was in a strange house, in a strange city, and fear *gripped* me.(p.279)
• Fear *gripped* me then, because I could remember nothing about it.(p.489)

grips
• Then that terrible tension which *grips* the home of every problem drinker will be lessened.(p.115)

grizzly
• I went downstairs and there was the *grizzly* old veteran police officer in charge of the property desk, and as he gave me the stuff, he asked, "Are you going out in the street that way?"(p.204)

grocer
• And I continued to drink, on and off then, until every dollar I had in the world was gone again and I was right back living at my sister's, getting my cigarettes by calling her *grocer* and telling him to put in a couple of cartons with her order, exactly as I had before I started to work at Max's.(p.202)

groceries
• When he was uptown -- we were living in the little town of Moscow -- I went up to try to get some money from him to buy *groceries.*(p.193)
• He wouldn't give me any money for the *groceries,* but he did take me across the street and buy me a bag of candy, which I later took back and traded for a loaf of bread.(p.193)

grocery
• In the basement were to be dry-cleaning facilities, a barbershop, a pool room, a *grocery* shop and everything.(p.198)
• I would gather up all my soiled clothes, as much as I could cram into a *grocery* cart, and be off.(p.370)

grog
• I had, seemingly, just a natural affinity for *grog.*(p.182)
• A square from ultra-dry Kansas, I did not taste *grog* until I had finished college, done a stint on newspapers, married, become a father, and been in studio publicity two years.(p.328)

groom
• We came back to Pittsburgh as happy as a bride and *groom.*(p.364)

groomed
• I don't know what sort of person I was expecting, but I was very agreeably surprised to find Mr. T. a poised, intelligent, well *groomed* and mannered gentleman.(p.309)

groove
• Others may idle in a retrogressive *groove* without too much danger, but retrogression can spell death for us.(p.311)

groped
• When the policeman released me to my stupefied and exasperated friend at four in the morning, I went to my traveling bag and *groped* until I found -- well, let the officer speak: "Ah," said the policeman, "he's got anuder pair, t'ank God!"(p.538)

groping
• In describing his suffering, his fears, his many years of *groping* for some answer to that which always seemed to remain unanswerable, he could have been describing me, and nothing short of experience and knowledge could have afforded him that much insight!(p.309)
• I had read and heard a little about A.A. and so, *groping* for the phone book, I found the A.A. number and with hope in my heart eagerly telephoned.(p.363)

grosser
• If you have already made a decision, and an inventory of your *grosser* handicaps, you have made a good beginning.(p.71)

grouch
• The *grouch* and the brainstorm were not for us.(p.66)

ground
• We can only clear the *ground* a bit.(p.55)
• But be sure you are on solid spiritual *ground* before you start and that your motive in going is thoroughly good.(p.102)
• As animals on a treadmill, we have patiently and wearily climbed, falling back in exhaustion after each futile effort to reach solid *ground.*(p.107)
• All members of the family should meet upon the common *ground* of tolerance, understanding and love.(p.122)
• I had bought a piece of *ground* in Cuyahoga Falls and cut it into lots and had a profit of approximately $40,000 and that was a lot of money in those days.(p.194)
• I can remember that in my childhood, he was ill at ease with the children because he attempted to assert an army discipline that had been *ground* into him during his three and a half years of army service.(p.210)
• It was February with snow and ice on the *ground* and I had a four blocks walk to the nearest cab stand, but I made it.(p.288)
• To be sure, this had been a dizzy and confused interval, but most everyone else I knew had emerged from it with both feet on the *ground* and a fair amount of adult maturity.(p.304)
• He, in turn, kicked me so I fell to the *ground.*(p.406)
• I remember finding myself in the middle of the night in the doctors' parking lot at the hospital with one foot in the car and one foot on the *ground,* not knowing which was the lead foot; finding myself

hanging up the telephone – then realizing I had gotten out of bed, answered the phone, turned on the light, and carried on a conversation with a patient.(p.441)

• I got a job by myself which suited me down to the ***ground***, because there was nobody really to interfere with what I did, one way or the other, and I usually had my nerves in good trim when anybody was coming around to inspect.(p.519)

grounded

• In nearly all cases, their ideals must be ***grounded*** in a power greater than themselves, if they are to re-create their lives.(p.xxvi)

• Nevertheless, the twentieth century readily accepts theories of all kinds, provided they are firmly ***grounded*** in fact.(p.48)

grounds

• About three months after that, my record reached home and I got a letter telling me I was retired from the Army, they put it very kindly, on medical ***grounds***.(p.521)

• But I knew that they knew what the medical ***grounds*** were, and that they had put a big black mark against my name.(p.521)

groundwork

• This may lay the ***groundwork*** for a friendly talk about his alcoholic problem.(p.111)

group

• The spark that was to flare into the first A.A. ***group*** was struck at Akron, Ohio, in June 1935, during a talk between a New York stockbroker and an Akron physician.(p.xv)

• When the broker returned to New York in the fall of 1935, the first A.A. ***group*** had actually been formed, though no one realized it at the time.(p.xvii)

• A second small ***group*** had promptly taken shape at New York.(p.xvii)

• Soon A.A. was beset by these very problems on every side and in every ***group***.(p.xix)

• It was thought that no alcoholic man or woman could be excluded from our Society; that our leaders might serve but never govern; that each ***group*** was to be autonomous and there was to be no professional class of therapy.(p.xix)

• These facts appear to be of extreme medical importance; because of the extraordinary possibilities of rapid growth inherent in this ***group*** they may mark a new epoch in the annals of alcoholism.(p.xxiii)

• Stocks were at the low point of 1932, and I had somehow formed a ***group*** to buy.(p.5)

• This ***group*** of thirteen stories shows that sobriety in A.A. can be lasting.(p.167)

• Pioneer member of Akron's ***Group*** No. 1, the first A.A. ***group*** in the world.(p.182)

• A.A.'s Number One ***Group*** dates from that very day.(p.189)

• Shortly after that, my brother, who had then become associated with a ***group*** of people and had stopped drinking, urged me to attend meetings with him.(p.205)

• The people in the ***group*** hadn't been around that day; part of my family was in Florida and the rest of them weren't speaking to me, so I spent a very lonesome day and by evening I was feeling very sorry for myself.(p.207)

• The next day, others from the ***group*** came in to see me.(p.208)

• There were only seven or eight people in the ***group*** before me and they all visited me during my period in the hospital.(p.208)

• I kept myself so busy that outside of some school and ***group*** parties, I didn't go overboard on drinking very much between the ages of twenty-five and thirty.(p.213)

• I was forty-nine and a half years old when I was first approached about the Akron ***Group***.(p.215)

• It was not known to me as a ***group***, but I later learned that my wife had known about it for nine months and had prayed constantly that I would stumble into Akron some way or another.(p.215)

• I believe every member of the Akron ***Group*** did come to see me, which impressed me terrifically, not so much because of the stories they told, but because they would take the time to come and talk to me without even knowing who I was.(p.218)

• I did not know there was such a thing as ***group*** activity until I left the hospital.(p.218)

• It was finally decided to undertake the organization of a Cleveland ***group*** and toward the end of May, 1939, the first meeting was held in Cleveland in my home.(p.219)

• I moved from ***group*** to ***group*** -- then from place to place -- and went on drinking.(p.226)

• I went to a meeting to see for myself this ***group*** of freaks or bums who had done this thing.(p.228)

• Jackie told me about a ***group*** of fellows in New York, of whom my old friend Fitz was one, who had the same problem I had, and who by working together to help each other were not now drinking and were happy like himself.(p.239)

• Oddly enough, the big shot who fired me from this company was one of the first men I met when I later joined the New York A.A. ***Group***.(p.242)

• However, I made an SOS call to the New York ***Group***, whom I hadn't met yet, and they suggested we both come there.(p.245)

• At that time the ***group*** in New York was composed of about twelve men who were working on the principle of every drunk for himself; we had no real formula and no name.(p.246)

• For a long time the only Higher Power I could concede was the power of the ***group***, but this was far more than I had ever recognized before, and it was at least a beginning.(p.248)

• Thus I found myself in the middle of a brand new ***group***.(p.249)

• Very rarely do I miss the meetings of my neighborhood A.A. ***group***, and my average has never been less than two meetings a week.(p.249)

• A pioneer woman member of A.A.'s first ***Group***.(p.261)

• So I was driven to Akron the very next day by these Good Samaritans, and turned over to Dr. Bob and the then tiny Akron ***Group***.(p.279)

• But it took six more months of work and disappointments before a ***group*** of three men got together in my rooming house bedroom for their first A.A. meeting.(p.282)

• I lived through a week of the fidgets because I had agreed to address a ***group*** of alcoholic inmates in one of our state mental hospitals.(p.283)

• Within a year of my return to Detroit, A.A. was a definitely established little ***group*** of about a dozen members and I too was established in a modest but steady job handling an independent dry-cleaning route of my own.(p.283)

• He waited until I was completely sober and the day before I was to head back for Chicago, he told me of a small ***group*** of men in Akron who apparently had the same problem that I had but were doing something about it.(p.289)

• In this small ***group***, during the Depression, there was no one who was not hard up.(p.291)

• One of them was that I would try to get a ***group*** started in Chicago; the second was that I would have to return to Akron to attend meetings at least every two months until I did get a ***group*** started in Chicago; third, I decided I must place this program above everything else, even my family, because if I did not maintain my sobriety I would lose my family anyway.(p.292)

• A few months later one of the men who had been in touch with the ***group*** in Akron came to Chicago to live, and then there were three of us who continued to have informal meetings quite regularly.(p.294)

• The three of us did not feel up to the job, and after a few meetings we convinced the prospects that they too should go to Akron where they could see an older ***group*** in action.(p.295)

• An originator of Cleveland's ***Group*** No. 3, this one fought Prohibition in vain.(p.297)

• He had been dry for two and a half years and had been maintaining his contact with a ***group*** of recovered alcoholics in Akron.(p.309)

• Contact with this ***group*** was extremely important to him.(p.309)

• He told me that eventually he hoped such a ***group*** would develop in the Chicago area, but that so far this had not been started.(p.309)

• He thought it would be helpful for me to visit the Akron ***group*** and meet many like himself.(p.309)

• By the latter part of September 1939, we had a nucleus of six and held our first official ***group*** meeting.(p.310)

• I was sure I wouldn't belong in an A.A. ***group*** -- they were all old men, I thought, and all skid-row bums.(p.319)

• That was on a hot summer evening, down in the Greenwich Village ***Group***, and there was a little porch out there in the old meeting place on Sullivan Street, and after the meeting I went out on the steps for some air.(p.321)

• I'd go into an organization, and it wasn't long before I was on the committee, then I was chairman of the committee; and if I was in a ***group***, I'd soon be treasurer or secretary of the ***group***.(p.339)

• And the first thing you know I was lifted right out of the A.A. ***group***, and I floated higher, and higher, and even higher, until I was way up on a pink cloud which is known as Pink Seven, and I felt miserable again.(p.348)

• I tried every gimmick that there was to get some peace of mind, but it was not until I was brought to my alcoholic knees, when I was brought to a ***group*** in my own community with the butcher, the baker, the carpenter and the mechanic, who were able to give me the Twelve Steps, that I was finally given some semblance of an answer to the last half of the First Step.(p.349)

• I suppose others would say, "This is ***group*** psychotherapy."(p.352)

• I went back to my ***group*** meetings, but not wholeheartedly, and I often skipped them with the excuse that I was too tired.(p.364)

• A lucky break, at least some will call it lucky, was in store for me at my ***group*** that night.(p.365)

• I attended my weekly meetings with regularity, reread the Big Book, attended other ***group*** meetings, gave leads when asked to and did some Twelve Step work whenever I was called upon to do so.(p.365)

• One night at the dinner table my wife said that tonight was my first birthday in A.A., and that the ***group*** would have the usual ice cream and cake for the "one year man."(p.365)

• I don't know what I expected, but I most certainly didn't visualize a ***group*** of people talking about their drinking problems, making light of their personal tragedies and at the same time enjoying themselves.(p.378)

• A "spiritual experience" to me meant attending meetings, seeing a ***group*** of people, all there for the purpose of helping each other; hearing the Twelve Steps and the Twelve Traditions read at a meeting, and hearing the Lord's Prayer, which in an A.A. meeting has such great meaning – "Thy will be done, not mine."(p.381)

• So I got a half pint and at midnight that night, I called the number I had been given, but the man who had started the ***group*** was in the hospital so I didn't know what to do.(p.393)

• There are so many to whom I feel deeply grateful; to my husband (and best critic), whose generous love, compassion and understanding have helped me along the way; to those before me in A.A. who inspired the first article I read, and the friend who sent that article to Frank; to Ruth for her personal note, and the first A.A. to talk to me; to my Bishop, whose loving and believing spirit inspired me; and to all the members of the Houston ***Group*** who were so patient, kind and helpful -- and to countless others.(p.393)

• So this was a ***group*** of reformers!(p.412)

• The thirteen stories in this ***group*** tell of alcoholism at its miserable worst.(p.455)

• (I am looking at it now in my bedroom – a copy that was presented to me a couple of years ago by the A.A. ***group*** in that same prison.)(p.461)

• Even the Jack Alexander Saturday Evening Post article hadn't been written, and there was only a tiny ***group*** of people in Washington.(p.469)

• I realized that I was trying to pin everything on an individual -- not the book or the ***group*** or the Higher Power, or anything else.(p.472)

• Start ***group*** on reservation and carry message, help start other groups all over Maritimes and New England.(p.476)

• Tall Man now see Great Spirit in Big ***Group*** in sky.(p.476)

• At every place, I find A.A. ***group*** first.(p.476)

• Let ***group*** spirit of love and understanding protect you.(p.477)

• This physician, the originator of A.A.'s first black ***group***, but badly caught in the toils, tells of his release and of how freedom came as he worked among his own people.(p.483)

• That was the next meeting, and the first meeting of a colored ***group*** in A.A., so far as I know.(p.495)

• Then Charlie or someone in the ***group*** suggested that we try to get a place in a church or hall to hold meetings.(p.495)

• I haven't mentioned it, but Charlie, my sponsor, was white, and when we got our ***group*** started we got help from other white groups in Washington.(p.495)

• Vi was taking care of me and I was devoting all my time to the building of that ***group***.(p.496)

• However, before the meeting got started, a ***group*** from the outside came in unexpectedly.(p.509)

• Yes, we find it rather confusing, but as we get around and get to know people in the ***group***, they lead the way and all we have to do is to follow.(p.512)

• I took the advice of people I had heard at meetings, the people in the ***group***.(p.516)

• Providentially, this was a Monday might when the Dublin ***Group*** met in those days, and my family agreed that if A.A. could do anything for me at all, that I'd be allowed to stay on at home on probation.(p.523)

• In the nearby little town there was a plumber who once had tried to get an A.A. *group* going.(p.541)
• I went over and met him, and we two started the *group* up again.(p.541)
• During the day a friend of mine brought me some magazines to take to a hospital *group* I was interested in, and I looked through them and a "banner" across the front of one featured an article by a prominent clergyman in which I caught the word "resentment."(p.552)
• Two -- For our *group* purpose there is but one ultimate authority -- a loving God as He may express Himself in our *group* conscience.(p.564)
• Four -- Each *group* should be autonomous except in matters affecting other groups or A.A. as a whole.(p.564)
• Five -- Each *group* has but one primary purpose -- to carry its message to the alcoholic who still suffers.(p.564)
• Six -- An A.A. *group* ought never endorse, finance or lend the A.A. name to any related facility or outside enterprise, lest problems of money, property and prestige divert us from our primary purpose.(p.564)
• Seven -- Every A.A. *group* ought to be fully self-supporting, declining outside contributions.(p.564)
• 2. -- For our *group* purpose there is but one ultimate authority -- a loving God as He may express Himself in our *group* conscience.(p.565)
• Any two or three alcoholics gathered together for sobriety may call themselves an A.A. *group*, provided that, as a *group*, they have no other affiliation.(p.565)
• 4. -- With respect to its own affairs, each A.A *group* should be responsible to no other authority than its own conscience.(p.565)
• And no *group*, regional committee, or individual should ever take any action that might greatly affect A.A. as a whole without conferring with the trustees of the General Service Board.(p.565)
• 5. -- Each Alcoholics Anonymous *group* ought to be a spiritual entity having but one primary purpose -- that of carrying its message to the alcoholic who still suffers.(p.565)
• An A.A. *group*, as such, should never go into business.(p.566)
• While an A.A. *group* may cooperate with anyone, such cooperation ought never go so far as affiliation or endorsement, actual or implied.(p.566)
• An A.A. *group* can bind itself to no one.(p.566)
• We think that each *group* should soon achieve this ideal; that any public solicitation of funds using the name of Alcoholics Anonymous is highly dangerous, whether by groups, clubs, hospitals, or other outside agencies; that acceptance of large gifts from any source, or of contributions carrying any obligation whatever, is unwise.(p.566)
• 9. -- Each A.A. *group* needs the least possible organization.(p.567)
• The small *group* may elect its secretary, the large *group* its rotating committee, and the groups of a large metropolitan area their central or intergroup committee, which often employs a full-time secretary.(p.567)
• 10. -- No A.A. *group* or member should ever, in such a way as to implicate A.A., express any opinion on outside controversial issues -- particularly those of politics, alcohol reform, or sectarian religion.(p.567)
• Dr. G. Kirby Collier, psychiatrist: "I have felt that A.A. is a *group* unto themselves and their best results can be had under their own guidance, as a result of their philosophy.(p.571)
• "The American Public Health Association presents a Lasker *Group* Award for 1951 to Alcoholics Anonymous in recognition of its unique and highly successful approach to that age-old public health and social problem, alcoholism . . .(p.573)
• If you cannot find A.A. in your locality, a letter addressed to Alcoholics Anonymous, Box 459, Grand Central Station, New York, NY 10163, U.S.A., will receive a prompt reply from this world center, referring you to the nearest A.A. *group*.(p.575)
• This headquarters will give the location of the nearest family *group* and will if you wish, correspond with you about your special problems.(p.575)

group's
• I started going to A.A. in prison at the *group's* next meeting.(p.461)

groupers
• That is, it was sort of a mixed bunch of Oxford *Groupers*, who were interested in the alcoholic problem, and of alcoholics themselves.(p.218)

groups
• In that brief space, Alcoholics Anonymous has mushroomed into nearly 6,000 *groups* whose membership is far above 150,000 recovered alcoholics.(p.xv)
• *Groups* are to be found in each of the United States and all of the provinces of Canada.(p.xv)
• Six months earlier, the broker had been relieved of his drink obsession by a sudden spiritual experience, following a meeting with an alcoholic friend who had been in contact with the Oxford *Groups* of that day.(p.xv)
• Though he could not accept all the tenets of the Oxford *Groups*, he was convinced of the need for moral inventory, confession of personality defects, restitution to those harmed, helpfulness to others, and the necessity of belief in and dependence upon God.(p.xvi)
• And besides, there were scattered alcoholics who had picked up the basic ideas in Akron or New York and were trying to form A.A. *groups* in other cities.(p.xvii)
• It was now time, the struggling *groups* thought, to place their message and unique experience before the world.(p.xvii)
• Businessmen, traveling out of existing *groups*, were referred to these prospective newcomers.(p.xviii)
• New *groups* started up and it was found, to the astonishment of everyone, that A.A.'s message could be transmitted in the mail as well as by word of mouth.(p.xviii)
• As we discovered the principles by which the individual alcoholic could live, so we had to evolve principles by which the A.A. *groups* and A.A. as a whole could survive and function effectively.(p.xix)
• By March 1976, when this edition went to the printer, the total worldwide membership of Alcoholics Anonymous was conservatively estimated at more than 1,000,000, with almost 28,000 *groups* meeting in over 90 countries.(p.xxii)
• Surveys of *groups* in the United States and Canada indicate that A.A. is reaching out, not only to more and more people, but to a wider and wider range.(p.xxii)
• The fellowship of Al-Anon Family *Groups* was formed about thirteen years after this chapter was written.(p.121)
• If there is no Al-Anon listing in your local telephone book, you may obtain further information on Al-Anon Family *Groups* by writing to its World Service Office: Box 182, Madison Square Station, New York, NY 10159.(p.121)
• Beginning with the story of "Dr. Bob," a co-founder of A.A., there are here presented three *groups* of personal histories.(p.165)
• Dr. Bob and the twelve men and women who here tell their stories were among the early members of A.A.'s first *groups*.(p.169)
• They seemed to be happy in their fashion, they and their little *groups* of supporters, but always pride of intellect stopped me from seeking what they evidently had.(p.256)
• Singly and in *groups* of two or three, they came to visit me.(p.258)
• I, who had never made a speech in my life and who would have been frightened sick at the prospect, stood up in front of Rotary *groups* in different parts of the city and talked about Alcoholics Anonymous.(p.283)
• I found out that the people in all A.A. *groups* were as nice as the people in the first one.(p.320)
• Start group on reservation and carry message, help start other *groups* all over Maritimes and New England.(p.476)
• All my troubles arose when I was thrown socially among *groups* of people.(p.486)
• I haven't mentioned it, but Charlie, my sponsor, was white, and when we got our group started we got help from other white *groups* in Washington.(p.495)
• Four -- Each group should be autonomous except in matters affecting other *groups* or A.A. as a whole.(p.564)
• But when its plans concern the welfare of neighboring *groups* also, those *groups* ought to be consulted.(p.565)
• Secondary aids to A.A., such as clubs or hospitals which require much property or administration, ought to be incorporated and so set apart that, if necessary, they can be freely discarded by the *groups*.(p.566)
• 7. -- The A.A. *groups* themselves ought to be fully supported by the voluntary contributions of their own members.(p.566)
• We think that each group should soon achieve this ideal; that any public solicitation of funds using the name of Alcoholics Anonymous is highly dangerous, whether by *groups*, clubs, hospitals, or other outside agencies; that acceptance of large gifts from any source, or of contributions carrying any obligation whatever, is unwise.(p.566)
• The small group may elect its secretary, the large group its rotating committee, and the *groups* of a large metropolitan area their central or intergroup committee, which often employs a full-time secretary.(p.567)
• They are authorized by the *groups* to handle our over-all public relations and they guarantee the integrity of our principal newspaper, the A.A. Grapevine.(p.567)
• The Alcoholics Anonymous *groups* oppose no one.(p.567)
• (This address is now available in pamphlet form at nominal cost through most A.A. *groups* or from Box 459, Grand Central Station, New York, NY 10163, under the title "Three Talks to Medical Societies by Bill W." -- formerly called "Bill on Alcoholism" and earlier "Alcoholism the Illness.")(p.572)
• In the United States and Canada, most towns and cities have A.A. *groups*.(p.575)
• In large cities, *groups* often maintain local offices where alcoholics or their families may arrange for interviews or hospitalization.(p.575)
• Should you be the relative or friend of an alcoholic who shows no immediate interest in A.A., it is suggested that you write the Al-Anon Family *Groups*, Inc., Box 182, Madison Square Station, New York, NY 10159, U.S.A.(p.575)
• This is a world clearing house for the Al-Anon Family *Groups*, composed largely of the wives, husbands and friends of A.A. members.(p.575)

grovelling
• After a day or two of *grovelling* remorse I'd come up with an explanation.(p.433)

grow
• As matters *grow* worse, he begins to use a combination of high-powered sedative and liquor to quiet his nerves so he can go to work.(p.22)
• We are like men who have lost their legs; they never *grow* new ones.(p.30)
• That was growth, but if we wished to *grow* we had to begin somewhere.(p.47)
• Some of us *grow* into it more slowly.(p.57)
• The point is, that we are willing to *grow* along spiritual lines.(p.60)
• Whatever our ideal turns out to be, we must be willing to *grow* toward it.(p.69)
• Our next function is to *grow* in understanding and effectiveness.(p.84)
• To watch people recover, to see them help others, to watch loneliness vanish, to see a fellowship *grow* up about you, to have a host of friends -- this is an experience you must not miss.(p.89)
• We *grow* by our willingness to face and rectify errors and convert them into assets.(p.124)
• Thus we *grow*.(p.162)
• I heard for the first time an expression which I was to *grow* to loathe: "There is nothing organically wrong."(p.276)
• I learned early in my A.A. life that I could not afford to fondle such thoughts, as you might fondle a pet, because this particular pet could *grow* into a monster.(p.285)
• Occasionally, it is accorded to a few of us to watch something fine *grow* from a tiny kernel into something of gigantic goodness.(p.295)
• I got around this by joining the local Rotary Club, and through this association with the business men of the community my little station began to *grow*.(p.360)
• As I *grow* in A.A., I realize that a person with as much self-will as I had, as hard a head and as diseased an ego, had to try everything that I could think of, butting my head against every stone wall before I was ready to come in.(p.384)
• I can again focus on my wife's good qualities and watch them *grow* and *grow* and *grow*.(p.451)
• It is painful to *grow*, and without the help of my "civilian" A.A. companion, big Gene, I might not have survived that critical year of adjustment.(p.462)
• He was old, but now he *grow* young with new life in A.A. and travel all time.(p.476)
• But, finally, we got one or two to come in and stick and from there, of course, we started to *grow*.(p.495)
• I hope I haven't hurt anyone's feelings, but maybe we could all *grow* and change.(p.529)
• To my way of thinking, that is a definition of alcoholism; a state of being in which the emotions have failed to *grow* to the stature of the intellect.(p.535)

growing
• This has become the basis of a rapidly *growing* fellowship of these men and their families.(p.xxiii)
• We feel, after many years of experience, that we have found nothing which has contributed more to the rehabilitation of these men than the altruistic movement now *growing* up among them.(p.xxvi)
• We are *growing* in numbers and power.(p.16)
• A few of us have had these *growing* pains and they hurt a great deal.(p.124)

• This dream world has been replaced by a great sense of purpose, accompanied by a *growing* consciousness of the power of God in our lives.(p.130)
• I came directly to a *growing* industrial city in the middle west, where I have lived practically ever since.(p.231)
• And all the while my fear fed a *growing* conviction that before long it would be necessary for me to be put away in some institution.(p.306)
• By this time I had become associated with the fast *growing* and fascinating business of broadcasting.(p.358)
• In all these ways I've experienced, in ever *growing* measure and beyond all expectations and rewards, a joy which I had never before imagined.(p.395)
• *GROWING* UP ALL OVER AGAIN(p.418)
• I am one of the *growing* number of A.A. members who are second-generation.(p.419)
• Most important, A.A. has enabled me to go back and start *growing* up all over again in all areas of my life.(p.420)
• My *growing* inward unhappiness was a very real thing, however, and I knew that something would have to be done about it.(p.434)
• And they were *growing* uglier.(p.435)
• It became second nature for me to remove myself from anything or anybody I found myself *growing* fond of.(p.545)
• Among our rapidly *growing* membership of thousands of alcoholics such transformations, though frequent, are by no means the rule.(p.569)

grown

• We commenced to make many fast friends and a fellowship has *grown* up among us of which it is a wonderful thing to feel a part.(p.15)
• So six months ago I acquired a ready made family consisting of one charming wife, four *grown* children to whom I am devoted, and three grandchildren.(p.286)
• As a physician and pharmacist who had *grown* up in a drugstore-home, I had a pill for every ill, and I was sick a lot.(p.443)
• The days have *grown* into a little better than four years of sobriety.(p.511)
• There was the sense of being "misunderstood," when as a matter of fact by my middle twenties I was quite popular, although I hadn't *grown* much bigger physically.(p.534)
• But not for long; now, for five Friday nights in a row, I went to jail, picked up sodden with beer (which I always disliked, but which was the only drink available); in jail five consecutive Friday nights in the town where I had *grown* up, where I had been an honor student in high school, where a kindly uncle, bailing me out, said, "Bob, our family just doesn't do this sort of thing."(p.539)
• Apparently I'd *grown* physically at the customary rate of speed, and I had acquired an average amount of intellectual training in the intervening years, but there had been no emotional maturity at all.(p.547)

grown-up

• It made me feel quite *grown-up* and mature, and I think another added attraction was the fact that so far as my family was concerned, it was forbidden, and it had a special attraction for that reason.(p.464)
• But as the years go by, the stretch becomes unbearable; and the man with the *grown-up* brain and the childish emotions – vanity, self-interest, false pride, jealousy, longing for social approval, to name few -- becomes a prime candidate for alcohol.(p.534)
• I know there are some alcoholics who seem terribly, terribly *grown-up*, but I think that they are trying to make themselves think they are *grown-up*, and the strain of their effort is what is causing them to drink -- a sense of inadequacy, a childish vanity to be the most popular, the most sought after, the mostest of the most.(p.535)

grows

• Resentment *grows*.(p.126)
• I can think clearly and am helped much in my thinking and judgment by my spiritual development which *grows* daily.(p.303)
• My gratitude to A.A. *grows* deeper each day I am sober.(p.420)

growth

• But the chief change was in the section of personal stories, which was expanded to reflect the Fellowship's *growth*.(p.xi)
• These facts appear to be of extreme medical importance; because of the extraordinary possibilities of rapid *growth* inherent in this group they may mark a new epoch in the annals of alcoholism.(p.xxiii)
• I saw that *growth* could start from that point.(p.12)
• At the start, this was all we needed to commence spiritual *growth*, to effect our first conscious relation with God as we understood Him.(p.47)
• That was *growth*, but if we wished to grow we had to begin somewhere.(p.47)
• But with the alcoholic, whose hope is the maintenance and *growth* of a spiritual experience, this business of resentment is infinitely grave.(p.66)
• Show them that he has entered upon a period of *growth*.(p.100)
• Barriers which have sprung up between you and your friends will disappear with the *growth* of sympathetic understanding.(p.115)
• Seed has started to sprout in a new soil, but *growth* has only begun.(p.117)
• He will perceive that his spiritual *growth* is lopsided, that for an average man like himself, a spiritual life which does not include his family obligations may not be so perfect after all.(p.129)
• Perhaps the best way of treating you to a glimpse of your future will be to describe the *growth* of the fellowship among us.(p.153)
• In conclusion, I can only say that whatever *growth* or understanding has come to me, I have no wish to graduate.(p.249)
• I always feel that our God Consciousness was a steady *growth* after we became associated with A.A.(p.270)
• They realized that in the end alcoholism could be a mortal as cancer; certainly no sane man would wait for a malignant *growth* to become fatal before seeking help.(p.315)
• Today, because of A.A.'s *growth* during the intervening years, it is of course much bigger than it was then.(p.392)
• I have seen that there is only one law, the law of love, and there are only two sins; the first is to interfere with the *growth* of another human being, and the second is to interfere with one's own *growth*.(p.542)

grudge

• On our *grudge* list we set opposite each name our injuries.(p.65)

grudgingly

• And so on and on, for several weeks, while I *grudgingly* plowed through some more of the offending book, and felt more and more hopeless about myself.(p.227)

guarantee

• They are authorized by the groups to handle our over-all public relations and they *guarantee* the integrity of our principal newspaper, the A.A. Grapevine.(p.567)

guaranteed

• I realize that all I'm *guaranteed* in life is today.(p.473)

guarantees

• They make no *guarantees* and are not always successful.(p.436)

guard

• I felt I had every right to be self-confident, that it would be only a matter of exercising my will power and keeping on *guard*.(p.40)
• Not only had I been off *guard*, I had made no fight whatever against the first drink.(p.41)
• But you must be on *guard* not to embarrass or harm your husband.(p.115)
• A friend who knew I would soon be broke mounted *guard* over me when I left my job of writing the histories of Texas cities and put me aboard a bus for the town I had left almost five years before.(p.256)
• I feel that one of the things that I still have to *guard* against is that I used to be set in my way about what I considered the old-time A.A.(p.272)
• Now, no longer under pressure, I could safely *guard* against loss of control.(p.327)
• My job was to make out the *guard* schedules and thus I was exempt from ordinary recruit training activities.(p.425)
• I stayed in the barracks all day, "making out *guard* schedules," and getting mildly plastered from the jug under my desk.(p.426)

guardhouse

• However, I did manage to keep out of the *guardhouse*.(p.242)

guess

• Mercifully, no one could *guess* that I was to have no real employment for five years, or hardly draw a sober breath.(p.4)
• I *guess* the old folks were right after all."(p.159)
• But I *guess* He doesn't believe much in me."(p.189)
• Before the end finally came, I had, I *guess* made the surrender because I finally had been able to say that I would not mind too much.(p.272)
• I *guess* there are plenty of other graduates of this treatment around.(p.389)
• My dad, who was a newspaper man and had some connections, had meantime put a stop on me, and I *guess* that report went all over the country.(p.424)
• I hadn't told them about my drinking, but I *guess* they knew.(p.427)
• Had it not been for A.A. in prison. . . I'll never know, but my educated *guess* is that I would not be alive today.(p.457)
• *Guess* I'll never be a saint, but whatever I am, I want to be sober and in A.A.(p.463)
• Nevertheless, we continued to work together and I continued to drink, but I *guess*, deep down within her heart as well as within mine, we both knew I couldn't stop drinking.(p.490)
• I *guess* I had five or ten dollars in my pocket.(p.491)
• I *guess* I felt, and he sensed it, that I wanted him to hurry up and say what he had to say and get out.(p.494)
• The trial lasted about a week, and whether or not I was going to the death house was anybody's *guess*.(p.508)
• I was the only person I'd ever known personally who had ever been in jail, and I *guess* it is most significant that the second time was less humiliating that the first had been.(p.549)
• I *guess* I always knew that the way to handle my drinking was to quit.(p.554)

guessing

• But I can remember in post graduate days, and during interneship, that very often I'd go to a patient's bed and start a process of elimination and then, very often, I'd wind up *guessing*.(p.485)

guest

• I ended up, homeless, jobless, penniless and rudderless, as the problem *guest* of a close friend whose family was out of town.(p.278)

guests

• I was assigned to keep media *guests* happy at a Halloween party given by a major star in his plush home.(p.328)
• I began sneaking drinks when playing bartender for *guests*.(p.556)

guidance

• To sum up about sex: We earnestly pray for the right ideal, for *guidance* in each questionable situation, for sanity, and for the strength to do the right thing.(p.70)
• 2.Dependence and *guidance* from a Higher Power.(p.292)
• I haven't written anything about that part of my story, but I believe in a Greater Power which I call God and I ask for His wisdom and *guidance* daily.(p.366)
• I wasn't burdened with parental *guidance* and I didn't want any.(p.424)
• Under the skilled *guidance* of an expert practitioner I wallowed in the world's individual and collective mental agony.(p.434)
• Dr. G. Kirby Collier, psychiatrist: "I have felt that A.A. is a group unto themselves and their best results can be had under their own *guidance*, as a result of their philosophy.(p.571)

guide

• The slightest disposition on your part to *guide* his appointments or his affairs so he will not be tempted will be noticed.(p.120)
• Though it is entirely separate from Alcoholics Anonymous, it uses the general principles of the A.A. program as a *guide* for husbands, wives, relatives, friends, and others close to alcoholics.(p.121)
• After all, I hadn't started to drink early in life, so I had some stability and maturity to *guide* me for a while.(p.379)
• No drunk hopeless if he want to follow *guide* along right trail.(p.477)
• Before I step out and do anything, I stop and check it over first, and then let my conscience be my *guide*.(p.516)

guided

• All such representatives are to be *guided* in the spirit of service, for true leaders in A.A. are but trusted and experienced servants of the whole.(p.567)
• Our public relations should be *guided* by the principle of attraction rather than promotion.(p.567)

guides

• The principles we have set down are *guides* to progress.(p.60)

guiding

• Ideas, emotions, and attitudes which were once the *guiding* forces of the lives of these men are suddenly

cast to one side, and a completely new set of conceptions and motives begin to dominate them.(p.27)
• When, however, the perfectly logical assumption is suggested that underneath the material world and life as we see it, there is an All Powerful, ***Guiding***, Creative Intelligence, right there our perverse streak comes to the surface and we laboriously set out to convince ourselves it isn't so.(p.49)
• Although these reparations take innumerable forms, there are some general principles which we find ***guiding***.(p.79)
• Giving, rather than getting, will become the ***guiding*** principle.(p.128)

guild
• My ***guild*** had elected me president twice and later given me a "man of the year" award.(p.328)

guilt
• I'd get so fed up with drinking all alone and bearing the burden of ***guilt*** all by myself, that I'd egg him on to drink, to get started again.(p.325)
• No prickling consciences to needle us with ***guilt*** feelings.(p.329)
• With increasing ***guilt*** and never-ending depression, I was too weak to continue this day-by-day suicide.(p.355)
• Incalculable are the intangible initiation fees that A.A. members have paid: the sick, sick hangovers, the remorse, ***guilt***, broken homes, jails, and institutions, and the mental anguish in general that has been generated over the years.(p.399)
• I experienced my first real ***guilt*** and shame.(p.404)
• I woke up filled with secret ***guilt*** and shame.(p.407)
• There was the father one lost respect for at the age of eleven, because the father broke his solemn word in a circumstance where you, eleven years old, had assumed ***guilt*** when you were innocent; but the father would not believe you, no matter what; and to ease his suffering you "confessed" and were "forgiven," only -- months later -- to have your "***guilt***" brought up -- only he and you knew what he was talking bout -- brought up in front of the stern grandmother.(p.533)
• For you learned that he had been guilty of the thing he had accused you of, and his ***guilt*** had brought suffering to his entire family; and he thought he saw his young son beginning his own tragic pattern.(p.533)
• Similarly, we rid ourselves of ***guilt*** and remorse as we "clean out the garbage" from our minds through the Fourth and Fifth Steps of our recovery program.(p.560)

guilty
• After consulting with his wife and partner he came to the conclusion that it was better to take those risks than to stand before his Creator ***guilty*** of such ruinous slander.(p.80)
• That was an experience that I have never forgotten, and many times in my own work with A.A. newcomers I feel kind of ***guilty*** because I haven't done the same thing.(p.219)
• I saw him recently and he told me that he had always felt ***guilty***, because, after our separation, I had become a serious alcoholic.(p.403)
• For you learned that he had been ***guilty*** of the thing he had accused you of, and his guilt had brought suffering to his entire family; and he thought he saw his young son beginning his own tragic pattern.(p.533)

guise
• Hidden old-drunks can pass out on their beds and snooze unreproached, under the ***guise*** of taking those vital retirement-age naps.(p.330)

guises
• I've had many spiritual experiences since I've been in the program, many that I didn't recognize right away, for I'm slow to learn and they take many ***guises***.(p.551)

gulp
• I would take a ***gulp***, then warn the jug not to try to entice, lure, or seduce me into having more than one "medicinal" jolt.(p.332)
• Instead of drinking in fancy bars and clubs, I had to carry a bottle of vodka in my briefcase, duck into public toilets, and ***gulp*** from the bottle, trembling, in order to keep from falling apart.(p.557)

gulped
• I ***gulped*** it down and choked.(p.498)

gun
• If I'd had a ***gun*** I'd have shot the horns right off the thing, because it made me raving mad.(p.265)

gunnery
• Later, I went to sea, serving as a ***gunnery*** officer on a destroyer escort and emerging a lieutenant commander.(p.555)

gurgles
• To keep it in round figures, let's say twenty per cent of my income went for giggle ***gurgles***.(p.397)

gusto
• Vacations from school and from work, spelled "travel" to me -- and I travelled with ***gusto***.(p.275)

guts
• If he has your will power and ***guts***, he will make the grade."(p.138)
• I remember very well saying, "There's only one person in the world whose ***guts*** I hate worse than yours, and those're my own."(p.440)
• Alcohol wrings the ***guts*** out of life, eats into the brain in such a way as to make the alcoholic blind to the truth.(p.457)

gutter
• One night I barely made my downtown club; if I'd had to go another fifty feet I'd have collapsed in the ***gutter***.(p.435)
• A former employer of mine said to me a little over ten years ago, "Pat, you seem to be one of those unfortunate people who at least once every six months must go out and roll in the ***gutter***."(p.513)
• I suppose I had reached my spiritual ***gutter*** that night, but I have never had what you could call a real urge to drink again.(p.524)

guy
• There was always a tremendous drive and ambition to become a great ***guy***, because I think I recognized inwardly that I didn't have any special talents.(p.194)
• Then he started to talk to me about his drinking experiences, what his drinking had cost him, how much he had drunk and where, things like that, and I remember I was quite bored because I had never seen the ***guy*** before and had no interest at all in what, where and when he drank.(p.208)
• I was kind of shocked about anybody talking about themselves the way he did, and my impression was that the ***guy*** was a little "touched."(p.216)
• I don't remember much of what he said, but I did realize that here was another ***guy*** exactly like me; he had been in the same laughing academies and the same jails, known the same loss of jobs, same frustrations, same boredom and the same loneliness.(p.239)
• Four months later, I married this ***guy***.(p.262)
• I'll get you the password, and I can find out where they meet because I know a ***guy*** that belongs.(p.266)
• Right away, I saw it was the same outfit this other ***guy*** told me about, and then again hope died.(p.267)
• I thought, "That ***guy*** never could have been a drunk."(p.268)
• His wife was cussing him, raving at him, "I just brought him over to show you what kind of a ***guy*** he is!(p.271)
• But I couldn't help thinking, "You poor ***guy***.(p.334)
• I repeat, I am one of the fortunate members of A.A. -- a lucky ***guy*** who is very grateful.(p.368)
• I never could quite get the knack of it and kept asking myself, "What's a nice ***guy*** like me doing in a place like this?"(p.445)
• For years, I was sure the worst thing that could happen to a nice ***guy*** like me would be that I would turn out to be an alcoholic.(p.449)
• He started telling me how much trouble he had, and I said to myself, "I wonder why this ***guy*** is telling me all his troubles.(p.494)
• And the ***guy*** said, "Heck, yes, I been married to her for years!"(p.512)

guzzling
• All of a sudden I found myself ***guzzling***.(p.195)
• Since I started out eager for early-day efforts, that meant ***guzzling*** before noon.(p.331)

gym
• The other pupils kept books, pencils, paper, ***gym*** equipment and such stuff in their lockers.(p.423)

Hh

H

• They said if you want to know how this program works, take the first word of your question -- the *H* is for honesty, the O is for open-mindedness and the W is for willingness; these our Book calls the essentials of recovery.(p.550)

ha-ha

• Build houses for some cops – ***ha-ha***.(p.475)

ha-ha-ha

• Very shortly, I realized that had been a mistake -- when this big clown came bounding into the room, almost shouting, "My name is Frank, and I'm an alcoholic, ***ha-ha-ha***!"(p.446)

habit

• These allergic types can never safely use alcohol in any form at all; and once having formed the ***habit*** and found they cannot break it, once having lost their self-confidence, their reliance upon things human, their problems pile up on them and become astonishingly difficult to solve.(p.xxvi)

• He may have the ***habit*** badly enough to gradually impair him physically and mentally.(p.20)

• His ways of thinking and doing are the ***habit*** of years.(p.118)

• Can you discard the feeling that you are dealing only with ***habit***, with stubbornness, or a weak will?(p.140)

• I would sometimes hide out in one of the clubs of which I was a member, and had the ***habit*** at times of registering at a hotel under a fictitious name.(p.176)

• It never fails, if you go about it with one half the zeal you have been in the ***habit*** of showing when you were getting another drink.(p.181)

• I went into the high school grades, but having missed all the intermediate grades, I didn't get along too well, so I developed the ***habit*** of going back to school just long enough for the football season and then quitting.(p.193)

• Then I got into the ***habit*** of having beers, and decided that a drink of whiskey was not any worse; so I would get the one drink of whiskey but, on second thought, I decided that as long as I was only going to have one, I might as well make it a double-header.(p.203)

• More and more I formed the ***habit*** of doing some of my business in the speakeasy, and after a time I did not need that as an excuse.(p.233)

• My wife wrote away for advertised cures for the liquor ***habit*** and gave them to me in coffee.(p.235)

• During that first year, however, I managed to make both ends meet, and to avoid ever going back to my old ***habit*** pattern of borrowing money when I could not earn it.(p.283)

• He said he had finally learned that drinking was a fatal illness made up of an allergy plus an obsession, and once the drinking had passed from ***habit*** to obsession, we were completely hopeless, and could look forward only to spending the balance of our lives in mental institutions or to death.(p.290)

When I didn't have anything else to do – a dull evening at home -- I'd sneak a few drinks upstairs in my room, and that began to be a ***habit***.(p.464)

I had a ***habit*** of getting up just prior to the closing time of the saloons, about two or three o'clock in the morning.(p.514)

I don't know if it's force of ***habit*** or something else that keeps them in one place, but I do know that in A.A. there is much work to do, and none of us can do standing still.(p.529)

habits

Selfish and inconsiderate ***habits*** have kept the home in turmoil.(p.82)

Tell him enough about your drinking ***habits***, symptoms, and experiences to encourage him to speak of himself.(p.91)

Let your friends know they are not to change their ***habits*** on your account.(p.102)

• But the policy of this company is not to interfere with the ***habits*** of our employees.(p.148)

• I drank with moderation at first, but it took me only a relatively short time to drift back into the old ***habits*** which had wound up so disastrously before.(p.175)

• "Best in the business, when he's sober," my customers would say, and I still had a following who would give me work though they deplored my ***habits***, because they knew the job would be well done when they eventually got it.(p.234)

• I knew they needed to straighten out their thinking and ***habits***, but I was all right, I just drank too much.(p.246)

• My drinking ***habits*** increased in spite of my struggle for control.(p.305)

habitual

• What our friend, the vice president, had in mind was the ***habitual*** or whoopee drinker.(p.149)

• It did help to certain extent, since I got in places where I could not obtain anything to drink, and so broke the ***habitual*** drinking.(p.183)

• Out of this maelstrom just two coherent thoughts came to the surface; one, a drink would mean homelessness and death; two, I could no longer relieve the pressure of fear by starting home, as was once my ***habitual*** solution to this problem, because I no longer had a home.(p.279)

hadn't

• It ***hadn't*** even come to mind.(p.5)

• It ***hadn't*** worked out that way and I didn't know what the matter was and did not know what to do.(p.184)

• I had no trouble there because I had never actually ceased to believe in God, and had tried lots of times to get help but ***hadn't*** succeeded.(p.186)

• I know there was even more, something that I ***hadn't*** got, and I remember one day, a week or two after I had come out of the hospital, Bill was over to my house talking to my wife and me.(p.191)

• I figured the only difference between me and a millionaire was that I ***hadn't*** the strength, or that he got the breaks and I didn't.(p.197)

• I came to the conclusion it was because I ***hadn't*** been drunk.(p.200)

• And I ***hadn't*** been drunk because I ***hadn't*** taken a drink.(p.200)

• I told him I'd take the medicine and I would take it, but I ***hadn't*** told him when, and thereupon I got away with the third drink.(p.206)

• The people in the group ***hadn't*** been around that day; part of my family was in Florida and the rest of them weren't speaking to me, so I spent a very lonesome day and by evening I was feeling very sorry for myself.(p.207)

• It was getting pretty dark and I ***hadn't*** turned on any lights, when some big fellow stepped inside the door and flipped on the light switch.(p.207)

• I knew I could quit because he had quit; he ***hadn't*** had a drink for over a year.(p.208)

• At this time I was holding what drinking I did down to weekends, but I ***hadn't*** had a drink at all in a month.(p.243)

• However, I made an SOS call to the New York Group, whom I ***hadn't*** met yet, and they suggested we both come there.(p.245)

• When the others saw my altered attitude they took me back in, but for me they had to make it tough; if they ***hadn't*** I don't think I ever would have stuck it out.(p.248)

• He talked about his wife taking his little boy away from him because of his drinking, and how he got back together with them through A.A., and we began feeling grateful right then that all these things ***hadn't*** been taken from us.(p.270)

• I knew then that I ***hadn't*** made a complete surrender, because I tried to bargain with the God I had found, and I said, "Anything but that!(p.271)

• I ***hadn't*** been in too long when one of the men's wives called me one Sunday and told me she didn't think I had any part of the program.(p.273)

• Finally, an old business acquaintance of mine, whom I ***hadn't*** seen for several years offered me a job.(p.301)

• Why should this happen to me – ***hadn't*** I provided a good home – wasn't I making a good living -- didn't I just get a substantial raise that had put me in the upper bracket class?(p.362)

• Before too long, my husband (who seemed to prefer his shirts dirty) put his foot down, declaring that our family might have the cleanest clothes in town, but that I ***hadn't*** been out of the same old dirty slacks and blouse for a week.(p.371)

• After all, I ***hadn't*** started to drink early in life, so I had some stability and maturity to guide me for a while.(p.379)

• In six years of worry, I ***hadn't*** learned anything.(p.387)

• Now I had done some living but I ***hadn't*** learned a thing.(p.402)

• Up to this time it just ***hadn't*** occurred to me to drink.(p.402)

• I ***hadn't*** told them about my drinking, but I guess they knew.(p.427)

• I'd heard a lot about A.A. and met a great many A.A.'s during that year at home, but I ***hadn't*** thought of it for myself.(p.429)

• Max ***hadn't*** gotten that way because I didn't care.(p.440)

• They ***hadn't*** mentioned the living hell before death.(p.461)

• Three weeks ago, my phone rang, and a voice I ***hadn't*** heard in over twenty-three years spoke.(p.462)

• If it ***hadn't*** been for an alert hotel maid, I might have died then.(p.465)

• I ***hadn't*** been drinking much about that time, for I had begun to realize that there was something abnormal about my drinking, although as yet, I didn't realize that it was so out of control.(p.465)

• You may wonder why, since I was having all this trouble, and was having to seek the assistance of others, A.A. ***hadn't*** come into the picture.(p.469)

• At that time there ***hadn't*** been any publicity such as we have now.(p.469)

• Even the Jack Alexander Saturday Evening Post article ***hadn't*** been written, and there was only a tiny group of people in Washington.(p.469)

• Mind you, I had absolutely nothing to show for that eighteen years, except a beat-up car that I ***hadn't*** even paid for, but I was doing all right.(p.478)

• Of course, in my day, times had changed; she just ***hadn't*** changed with the times.(p.484)

• They brought me in and of course, they ***hadn't*** very much trouble in finding that I was alcoholic.(p.521)

• I was terribly afraid that I was actually going mad, if I ***hadn't*** gone mad already.(p.522)

• There was the sense of being "misunderstood," when as a matter of fact by my middle twenties I was quite popular, although I ***hadn't*** grown much bigger physically.(p.534)

Hagen

• We went at once to the country, my wife to applaud while I started out to overtake Walter ***Hagen***.(p.3)

hail

• The grand fellow who at my call made me a hail-fellow-well-met, who gave me such a fine voice, as we sang "***Hail, hail***, the gang's all here," and "Sweet Adeline," who gave me freedom from fear and feelings of inferiority.(p.498)

hail-fellow-well-met

• The grand fellow who at my call made me a ***hail-fellow-well-met***, who gave me such a fine voice, as we sang "Hail, hail, the gang's all here," and "Sweet Adeline," who gave me freedom from fear and feelings of inferiority.(p.498)

hair

• I had a broken nose, a fractured cheekbone, and was black from the lower part of my face up into my ***hair***.(p.204)

• That night for the first time in my life I really let down my ***hair*** and admitted my general loneliness.(p.239)

• They roll on the floor and holler, and pull their ***hair***."(p.266)

• While I sought the comforting arms of alcohol, I knew this was a sign of weakness on the part of a longtime-successful old codger with white ***hair***, the image of dignity.(p.331)

• I was sure those who needed a bit of the ***hair*** of the dog really were alcoholics.(p.332)

• If our ***hair*** is half-bleached (with dark roots), poker-straight, and not combed, this adds to our beauty.(p.479)

• In the next half-year, I experienced two more esophageal hemorrhages, miraculously surviving each one by a ***hair***.(p.558)

hair-raising

• Could I be an alcoholic without some of the ***hair-raising*** experiences I had heard of in meetings?(p.379)

hairdresser

• She had a ***hairdresser*** who used to tell her about a brother-in-law who had been quite a drinker and about some doctor in Akron who had straightened him out.(p.216)

• My wife didn't tell me this, but one Sunday afternoon when Mary was trying to get the cobwebs out of my mind, Clarence and his sister-in-law, the ***hairdresser***, called at the house.(p.216)

haired

• Bill was tall, grey ***haired***, with the kind of asymmetrical good looks and pleasant easy manner that inspire confidence in the shaken and afraid.(p.413)

• Standing there was a gray ***haired*** man -- tall, trim and in uniform.(p.422)

half

• A tumbler full of gin followed by ***half*** a dozen bottles of beer would be required if I were to eat any breakfast.(p.5)

• It was fortunate, for my old business associates remained skeptical for a year and a ***half***, during which I found little work.(p.15)

• To his consternation, he found himself drunk ***half*** a dozen times in rapid succession.(p.35)

• About ***half*** our original fellowship were of exactly that type.(p.44)

• But cheer up, something like ***half*** of us thought we were atheists or agnostics.(p.44)

• ***Half*** measures availed us nothing.(p.59)

• If we are painstaking about this phase of our development, we will be amazed before we are ***half*** way through.(p.83)

• One of our Fellowship failed entirely with his first ***half*** dozen prospects.(p.96)

• Inwardly he would give anything to take ***half*** a dozen drinks and get away with them.(p.152)

• Some of them may sink and perhaps never get up, but if our experience is a criterion, more than ***half*** of those approached will become fellows of Alcoholics Anonymous.(p.163)

• I lost only a ***half*** day's work during these three years.(p.173)

• It was not long before I was drinking at least a case and a ***half*** a day.(p.177)

• I gave the matter much time and study for the next two and a ***half*** years, but still got tight every night nevertheless.(p.178)

• It never fails, if you go about it with one ***half*** the zeal you have been in the habit of showing when you were getting another drink.(p.181)

• I would reach over and get this and take a shot and in a few moments get up and take another, shave and eat my breakfast, slip a ***half*** pint of liquor in my hip pocket, and go on to school.(p.183)

• It took me a year, or a year and a ***half*** to get to feeling physically well, and it was rather tough, but I soon found folks whose friendship I had once had, and I found, after I had been sober for quite some little time, that these people began to act like they had in previous years, before I had gotten so bad, so that I didn't pay too awful much attention to financial gains.(p.190)

• He tossed off ***half*** of his martini; I tossed off ***half*** of mine and it nearly blew the top of my head off.(p.195)

• I had contracted for ***half*** of it, at least verbally, and the contractors were taking ***half*** of the second mortgage bond.(p.198)

• I had taken five and a ***half*** ounces of paraldehyde.(p.207)

• I can remember that in my childhood, he was ill at ease with the children because he attempted to assert an army discipline that had been ground into him during his three and a ***half*** years of army service.(p.210)

• I was forty-nine and a ***half*** years old when I was first approached about the Akron Group.(p.215)

• There were, at that time, in the neighborhood of twelve or thirteen Cleveland members who had been sober anywhere from a year and a ***half*** to a couple of months.(p.219)

• I had completely forgotten the January 8th when I found the fellowship, and I spent the next four days wandering around New England ***half*** drunk, by which I mean I couldn't get drunk and I couldn't get sober.(p.247)

• As I look back on the events of two months, I can clearly see that I had been circling around, half-afraid of encountering the remedy for my situation, ***half*** wanting it, deferring fulfillment of my promise to get in touch with the doctor I had heard about.(p.258)

• We were in A.A. three and a ***half*** years when he was taken from me.(p.270)

• Jack had been sober about a year and a ***half***.(p.271)

• ***Half*** a block from the house, I tried to turn the corner.(p.276)

• However, I must have felt, deep down inside myself, that living the selfish life of a bachelor was only ***half*** living.(p.286)

• I cannot remember just when I became the victim of insomnia, but I do know that the last year and a ***half*** I never went to bed sober a single night.(p.299)

• He had been dry for two and a ***half*** years and had been maintaining his contact with a group of recovered alcoholics in Akron.(p.309)

• And of course a ***half*** empty bottle wasn't worth keeping, so I finished it up and naturally had to get more in right away for the people who "might come in unexpectedly."(p.336)

• ***Half*** a mother was better than no mother at all.(p.337)

• And then it went on to say: "***Half*** measures availed us nothing.(p.349)

• "Complete abandon"; "***Half*** measures availed us nothing"; "Thoroughly follow our path"; "Completely give oneself to this simple program" -- rang in my swelled head.(p.349)

• I spent five and a ***half*** years in psychoanalysis and proceeded to become a drunk.(p.349)

• I tried every gimmick that there was to get some peace of mind, but it was not until I was brought to my alcoholic knees, when I was brought to a group in my own community with the butcher, the baker, the carpenter and the mechanic, who were able to give me the Twelve Steps, that I was finally given some semblance of an answer to the last ***half*** of the First Step.(p.349)

• So, after taking the first ***half*** of the First Step, and very gingerly admitting myself to Alcoholics Anonymous, something happened.(p.349)

• I know that if I do daily what I have done for these last thirteen and a ***half*** years, I will stay sober.(p.384)

• Monday morning I was feeling just like a million dollars -- all I needed was ***half*** a pint!(p.393)

• So I got a ***half*** pint and at midnight that night, I called the number I had been given, but the man who had started the group was in the hospital so I didn't know what to do.(p.393)

• It was the first time in my life that I could not get a lift out of what I was drinking; and so one Friday night, at five minutes to six, I had ***half*** a water glass of warm gin, and that is when I first asked God to help me.(p.393)

• He got ***half*** custody of our child, but later kept her during most of the school terms.(p.402)

• I did not reflect that ***half*** the office was composed of A.A. members, and that I was as unexciting as any client in any office.(p.413)

• I would be ***half*** asleep and ***half*** awake, and in the morning, I would be both tired and stupid.(p.440)

• (I am pleased to state, however, that I had gone to only a very few A.A. meetings before I was able to make a really beautiful pair of moccasins -- and ***half*** a wallet.(p.445)

• I haven't seen my son since he was three and a ***half*** years old.(p.463)

• My daughter was one and a ***half*** years old when I last saw her.(p.463)

• At one time, I was using twenty caps a day; I nearly died ***half*** a dozen times on the street.(p.480)

• After he'd talked ***half*** an hour, I still wanted him to hurry up and get out so I could go and get some whiskey before the liquor store closed.(p.494)

• When he left I walked with him to the streetcar line, which was just about a ***half*** a block, but there were two liquor stores, one on each corner from my home.(p.495)

• I pour out ***half*** a tumbler of grain alcohol and fill it with ginger ale.(p.499)

• On October 28th, I was sent to Sing Sing with a minimum of thirty-three and a ***half*** years to serve out of that thirty-five.(p.509)

• I was afraid that sometime I would get ***half*** drunk and go through with it.(p.515)

• Of course I really didn't have to worry on that score, because I wasn't the type that got ***half*** drunk.(p.515)

• Someone told me, "When you drank, you didn't get ***half*** drunk.(p.516)

• In this program there aren't any ***half*** way measures.(p.516)

half-afraid

• As I look back on the events of two months, I can clearly see that I had been circling around, ***half-afraid*** of encountering the remedy for my situation, half wanting it, deferring fulfillment of my promise to get in touch with the doctor I had heard about.(p.258)

half-bleached

• If our hair is ***half-bleached*** (with dark roots), poker-straight, and not combed, this adds to our beauty.(p.479)

half-truth

• But this is only a ***half-truth***.(p.70)

half-year

• In the next ***half-year***, I experienced two more esophageal hemorrhages, miraculously surviving each one by a hair.(p.558)

halfway

• I ***halfway*** washed them, and he told me to do them again, and I did, and he yelled at me to do them again, and I picked up one of the cans and threw it at him and told him to do them himself.(p.317)

• At a women's ***halfway*** house, I became associated with Alcoholics Anonymous and became aware of alcoholism as a disease, not just a "weakness."(p.371)

• ***Halfway*** down the driveway a thought strikes me.(p.506)

hall

• I moved into a "bachelor ***hall***."(p.277)

• As we walked back through the ***hall***, I, for the first time in my life, said to another human being, "I'm having trouble with my drinking, too."(p.321)

• In the garage, I would put the needle in my vein and then try to figure out exactly how much medication to inject to overcome the pep pills while adding to the sleeping pills while ignoring the tranquilizers, in order to get just enough to be able to pull out the needle, jerk the tourniquet, throw it in the car, slam the car door shut, run down the ***hall***, and fall in bed before I fell asleep.(p.442)

• Then Charlie or someone in the group suggested that we try to get a place in a church or ***hall*** to hold meetings.(p.495)

Halloween

• I was assigned to keep media guests happy at a ***Halloween*** party given by a major star in his plush home.(p.328)

halves

• Being an alcoholic, I couldn't dream of doing anything by ***halves***!(p.286)

hamburger

• The other kids would light out for the ***hamburger*** huts or ice cream parlors, the pizza joints or bowling alleys, after football games and dances.(p.423)

hamlet

• They will approach still other sick ones and fellowships of Alcoholics Anonymous may spring up in each city and ***hamlet***, havens for those who must find a way out.(p.153)

hammer

• They sound like the philosophy of the man who, having a headache, beats himself on the head with a ***hammer*** so that he can't feel the ache.(p.23)

hampers

• She hid her bottles in clothes ***hampers*** and dresser drawers.(p.335)

• When alcohol took me over, my bar was my kitchen, my living room, my bedroom, the back bathroom, and the two ***hampers***.(p.335)

• I did my hiding in the ***hampers*** and in my dresser drawers.(p.336)

Hampshire

• "Here lies a ***Hampshire*** Grenadier Who caught his death Drinking cold small beer.(p.1)

hand

• On the other ***hand*** -- and strange as this may seem to those who do not understand -- once a psychic change has occurred, the very same person who seemed doomed, who had so many problems he despaired of ever solving them, suddenly finds himself easily able to control his desire for alcohol, the only effort necessary being that required to follow a few simple rules.(p.xxvii)

• There is a complete failure of the kind of defense that keeps one from putting his ***hand*** on a hot stove.(p.24)

• What seemed at first a flimsy reed, has proved to be the loving and powerful ***hand*** of God.(p.28)

• On the other ***hand***, he may be mean, egotistical, selfish and dishonest.(p.61)

• We feel we are on the Broad Highway, walking ***hand*** in ***hand*** with the Spirit of the Universe.(p.75)

• If, on the other ***hand***, they took nothing, their self-pity made them killjoys.(p.105)

• He often gets entirely out of ***hand*** when drinking.(p.109)

• The miracle of reconciliation was at ***hand***.(p.124)

• Assume on the other ***hand*** that father has, at the outset, a stirring spiritual experience.(p.128)

• This practice enables us to lend a ***hand***, at the same time avoiding certain alluring distractions of the road, about which any traveling man can inform you.(p.162)

• And so can you, though you be but one man with this book in your ***hand***.(p.162)

• When I went in to write the examinations, my ***hand*** trembled so I could not hold a pencil.(p.174)

• We shook hands, and he hung onto my ***hand*** for a moment and said, "Tell you what I'll do for old times sake.(p.201)

• Sitting in a Second Avenue bar, accepting drinks

from anyone who offered, after my small stake was gone; or sitting at home alone, with the inevitable glass in my ***hand***, I would remember, and remembering, I would drink faster, seeking speedy oblivion.(p.225)
• I sipped the drink off the bar because I couldn't hold it in my ***hand***, but I was still a lady, believe it or not, and I was deeply ashamed.(p.266)
• Liquor had become a crutch on the one ***hand*** and a means of retreat from life on the other.(p.277)
• I didn't care to go visiting unless the parties we might visit had plenty of liquor on ***hand*** and I could get drunk.(p.301)
• She took me by the ***hand*** and introduced me to the girl that I'm very proud to call my sponsor.(p.321)
• I began to have to have supplies on ***hand*** for the people who "might come in."(p.336)
• I took two or three drinks so my eyes could focus, and I could see that horrible picture of the awful drunk on the first page; he couldn't get the drink to his mouth, he had a towel around his ***hand*** and he needed a shave.(p.391)
• I was accepting help with one ***hand*** and pushing it away with the other.(p.407)
• On the other ***hand***, I was a marvelous customer.(p.410)
• Pearl Harbor was a breeze of nine months, a gay Hawaiian paradise, drinking under the palms, listening to the surf beat on the shore, a bottle of whiskey near at ***hand***.(p.426)
• I paid nine hundred dollars for a second ***hand*** car on my return.(p.429)
• I think He's on ***hand*** to see my son through, too.(p.437)
• I think He's on ***hand*** to see all of us through whatever may come to us.(p.437)
• Following an injection I would have to keep one ***hand*** busy scratching my constantly itching nose and would also have sudden uncontrollable urges to vomit.(p.442)
• Also, after that first visit I learned I could refuse to sign myself in unless they gave me a glass of whiskey in one ***hand*** and a glass of paraldehyde in the other.(p.468)
• Take my ***hand***.(p.477)
• On the other ***hand***, I believe that I've always been medically inclined, though I have never been able to see medicine quite as the average person sees it.(p.485)
• On the other ***hand***, I got quite a different picture farther south.(p.486)
• The one thing I can remember now was that Vi was on the corner of 8th and L, and I remember vividly that she had an envelope in her ***hand***.(p.492)
• But on the other ***hand***, I was terribly fortunate because that should have been a court martial offense and I should have been out on my ear.(p.520)
• I remember being dragged, drink in ***hand***, from beneath the grand piano, where I had hidden, to be locked in my room in disgrace.(p.557)

hand-book
• My wife traveled with me, but with a baby coming I decided to settle in a large city where I got a job with a commission agent which is a polite term for a ***hand-book*** operator.(p.251)

handed
• Without this proof the expectant purchaser would be forced to depart empty ***handed*** with none of what I later came to believe was the great panacea for all human ills.(p.171)
• He might have ***handed*** me fifty dollars and said that I ought to pull myself together and make a new start.(p.278)
• I didn't particularly like it, but I loved the effects, and managed for the next twenty-five years to drink anything and everything, either ***handed*** to me or purchased, at the slightest excuse.(p.357)
• I would wait for the mailman each month, like any good mother, but as soon as he ***handed*** me my check, I put on my best dress and went looking for my alcoholic friend.(p.527)

handful
• In the next two or three days the balance of this ***handful*** of men contacted me, encouraged me, and told me how they were trying to live this program of recovery and the fun they were having doing it.(p.291)
• From a mere ***handful*** in Akron we have spread throughout the world.(p.295)
• Then he told me there was a ***handful*** of people in Akron and New York who had worked out a technique for arresting their alcoholism.(p.308)
• Once, I phoned my brother-in-law and told him I was going to take a ***handful*** of pills (in fact, I already had) and I would slash my wrists if he didn't come over to stop me.(p.479)

handicap
• It takes some of us a long time to outgrow that serious ***handicap***.(p.125)
• (That condition was a distinct ***handicap*** to me in trying to vindicate myself with the not so patient wife.)(p.301)

handicapped
• Very earnestly we ask the press also, to observe this request, for otherwise we shall be greatly ***handicapped***.(p.xiii)
• Besides a seeming inability to accept much on faith, we often found ourselves ***handicapped*** by obstinacy, sensitiveness, and unreasoning prejudice.(p.47)
• You will be ***handicapped*** if you arouse it.(p.89)

handicaps
• If you have already made a decision, and an inventory of your grosser ***handicaps***, you have made a good beginning.(p.71)

handiwork
• When I woke up sober, my ***handiwork*** confronted me.(p.435)
• When I complain about me or about you, I am complaining about God's ***handiwork***.(p.449)

handkerchief
• Just as I was wondering what on earth I could do -- I was too drunk even to pack a ***handkerchief*** -- the memory of an A.A. write-up that I had seen in the Evening Mail flashed across my mind -- and I thought to myself, this is something I haven't tried yet.(p.523)

handle
• It is important that we remain anonymous because we are too few, at present to ***handle*** the overwhelming number of personal appeals which may result from this publication.(p.xiii)
• "That fellow can't ***handle*** his liquor."(p.20)
• If these thoughts occur, they are hazy and readily supplanted with the old threadbare idea that this time we shall ***handle*** ourselves like other people.(p.24)
• We will intuitively know how to ***handle*** situations which used to baffle us.(p.84)
• He is positive he can ***handle*** his liquor, that it does him no harm, that drinking is necessary in his business.(p.109)
• Perhaps he could ***handle***, say, three drinks -- no more!(p.154)
• If I could, that was wonderful, that was just fine, and they would very much appreciate a person who had that kind of power, but they were looking for a man that knew he had a problem, and knew that he couldn't ***handle*** it himself and needed outside help.(p.186)
• I was willing to admit to myself that I had hit bottom, that I had gotten hold of something that I didn't know how to ***handle*** by myself.(p.187)
• It went something like this: "God, for eighteen years I have been unable to ***handle*** this problem.(p.280)
• We can ***handle*** anything.(p.350)
• This suggestion had been made before on a number of occasions, but like all alcoholics I wanted to ***handle*** my problem my own way, which really meant I didn't want anything to interfere with my drinking.(p.378)
• And I'd proved I couldn't ***handle*** it, time and again.(p.429)
• But I knew how to ***handle*** it now.(p.498)
• A.A. TAUGHT HIM TO ***HANDLE*** SOBRIETY(p.554)
• "A.A. does not teach us how to ***handle*** our drinking," he said.(p.554)
• "It teaches us how to ***handle*** sobriety."(p.554)
• I guess I always knew that the way to ***handle*** my drinking was to quit.(p.554)
• To do that, I had come to A.A. to learn how to ***handle*** sobriety -- which is what I could not ***handle*** in the first place.(p.554)
• But above all, it taught me how to ***handle*** sobriety.(p.559)
• They are authorized by the groups to ***handle*** our over-all public relations and they guarantee the integrity of our principal newspaper, the A.A. Grapevine.(p.567)

handled
• I suspect that if it is wisely ***handled*** -- and it seems to be in wise and prudent hands -- there are doors of opportunity ahead of this project that may surpass our capacities to imagine."(p.574)

handling
• The doctor proved to be able and exceedingly anxious to adopt any workable method of ***handling*** the situation.(p.163)
• Within a year of my return to Detroit, A.A. was a definitely established little group of about a dozen members and I too was established in a modest but steady job ***handling*** an independent dry-cleaning route of my own.(p.283)
• ***Handling*** customers, dealers, insurance people, dictation, telephoning, directing new employees, answering to superiors, and all the rest of it.(p.299)

handmaiden
• I have had my share of problems, heartaches and disappointments, because that is life, but also I have known a great deal of joy, and a peace that is the ***handmaiden*** of an inner freedom, I have a wealth of friends and, with my A.A. friends, an unusual quality of fellowship.(p.312)

hands
• Hence we are at pains to tell why we think our present faith is reasonable, why we think it more sane and logical to believe than not to believe, why we say our former thinking was soft and mushy when we threw up our ***hands*** in doubt and said, "We don't know."(p.53)
• Friendly ***hands*** had stretched out in welcome.(p.53)
• He saw that he had to place the outcome in God's ***hands*** or he would soon start drinking again, and all would be lost anyhow.(p.80)
• When we look back, we realize that the things which came to us when we put ourselves in God's ***hands*** were better than anything we could have planned.(p.100)
• You may have the reverse situation on your ***hands***.(p.114)
• If a repetition is to be prevented, place the problem, along with everything else, in God's ***hands***.(p.120)
• Cling to the thought that, in God's ***hands***, the dark past is the greatest possession you have -- the key to life and happiness for others.(p.124)
• I wanted to throw up my ***hands*** in discouragement, for I saw that I had failed to help my banker friend understand.(p.138)
• In competent ***hands***, this seldom takes long nor is it very expensive.(p.143)
• A couple of hired ***hands*** were cleaning out the barn on the farm and I would ride to and fro on the sled, and while they were loading I would drink hard cider out of a barrel in the barn.(p.183)
• We shook ***hands***, and he hung onto my hand for a moment and said, "Tell you what I'll do for old times sake.(p.201)
• Cold chills started chasing up and down my spine; my teeth were chattering; my ***hands*** were shaking so I tucked them under me to keep them from flying away.(p.222)
• So I began to pray; to place my problems in God's ***hands***.(p.237)
• They are far more alert and progressive than we floundering fathers were, and the future of our fellowship is in their ***hands***.(p.250)
• He was coming, on his ***hands*** and knees, up the stairs.(p.263)
• I could never be sure I'd have a clear head and ***hands*** that were willing to do some work.(p.326)
• She left, and I sat down and crossed my ***hands***, and looked up and said, "For God's sake, help me."(p.351)
• That night she too had new hope because I had made sure she would know what I was doing about my drinking by packing every bit of A.A. literature I could put my ***hands*** on right on top so she couldn't help but see it when she opened my bag.(p.364)
• I had a drinking problem on my ***hands*** even at that time.(p.424)
• I cut my ***hands***, my face, my legs.(p.427)
• I suspect that if it is wisely handled -- and it seems to be in wise and prudent ***hands*** -- there are doors of opportunity ahead of this project that may surpass our capacities to imagine."(p.574)

handwriting
• When I hear the more rugged stories of alcoholics who became sicker than I did with this affliction, I humbly thank God for showing me "the ***handwriting*** on the wall."(p.367)
• So I wrote this letter in very shaky ***handwriting***, and in just one week came back a letter with A.A. literature from New York.(p.392)

handy
• I was active and did well, however, in school publications, dramatics (which came in ***handy*** during my drinking career), and Greek letter societies.(p.357)

hang
• But out of this frightening and at first disrupting experience the conviction grew that A.A.'s had to ***hang*** together or die separately.(p.xix)
• But you had better ***hang*** on to it.(p.14)
• This may ***hang*** on for months, long after their

mother has accepted dad's new way of living and thinking.(p.134)

• I wasn't afraid that the program wouldn't work, but I still was doubtful whether I would be able to *hang* on to the program, but I did come to the conclusion that I was willing to put everything I had into it, with God's power, and that I wanted to do just that.(p.189)

• They suffered from my conduct without saying anything, but the reason for this was I still managed to *hang* onto a very substantial practice.(p.215)

• I would *hang* on to sobriety for short intervals, but always there would come the tide of an overpowering necessity to drink and, as I was engulfed in it, I felt such a sense of panic that I really believed I would die if I didn't get that drink inside.(p.306)

• Sure I still loved her, but *hang* it all, she was unreasonable!(p.362)

• I think I am very lucky that there are people like A.A.'s and an A.A. program to *hang* on to and carry me through.(p.511)

• We alcoholics see that we must work together and *hang* together, else most of us will finally die alone.(p.563)

hanged

• Four days before he had *hanged* himself in his woodshed.(p.137)

hanger-on

• I became an unwelcome *hanger-on* at brokerage places.(p.5)

hanging

• I do not recollect the specific conversation that went on but I believe I did challenge Bill to tell me something about A.A. and I do recall one other thing: I wanted to know what this was that worked so many wonders, and *hanging* over the mantel was a picture of Gethsemane and Bill pointed to it and said, "There it is," which didn't make much sense to me.(p.216)

• I learned that a person just can't find a job *hanging* in a dive or barroom all day and all night, as jobs don't seem to turn up in those places.(p.300)

• But at this time, I began gravitating toward the really hard drinkers, *hanging* around with them more and more.(p.404)

• I remember finding myself in the middle of the night in the doctors' parking lot at the hospital with one foot in the car and one foot on the ground, not knowing which was the lead foot; finding myself *hanging* up the telephone -- then realizing I had gotten out of bed, answered the phone, turned on the light, and carried on a conversation with a patient.(p.441)

hangout

• So here, in this dive, this *hangout* for dead-end alcoholics and neurotics, here was I.(p.410)

hangover

• We often need it to carry green recruits through a severe *hangover*.(p.102)

• I've prayed to God on *hangover* mornings and sworn that I'd never touch another drop but by nine o'clock I'd be boiled as an owl."(p.158)

• This time it really hurt, more than any *hangover* ever had.(p.247)

• My four years of abstinence had something to do with it, but soldiering is a tough enough game for a sober man, and I had no yen for full-pack slogging through mud with a cognac or vin rouge *hangover*.(p.253)

• Enduring all the *hangover* hells that every alcoholic experiences, I made the usual resolutions.(p.256)

• They'd sit out there and play hymns and I'd be lying in there with a terrific *hangover*.(p.265)

• When you have a *hangover* and can't even sit still, try to read small print!(p.268)

• In return for a bottle and a *hangover*, we have been given the Keys of the Kingdom.(p.312)

• I got orders to go to Vietnam, and I spent most of the year over there either drunk or sick with a *hangover*.(p.317)

• Luck was with me for I made my train, but I arrived home the next morning with a new kind of *hangover*.(p.364)

• The only time my dog would have anything to do with me was when I had a *hangover*, and when I was so sick he was the only one who would have anything to do with me at all.(p.390)

• In the morning, because I was young and healthy, my remorse was worse than my *hangover*.(p.404)

• The horrors of increasing *hangover* sickness to occupy the entire day; nausea, dry heaves, the rocking bed, the nightmare-filled mind.(p.408)

• These things were carried out in moments of less severe *hangover* or short stretches on the wagon.(p.409)

• I was never drunk on the job, never missed a day's work, was seldom rendered totally ineffective by a *hangover* and kept my liquor expenses well within my adequate budget.(p.433)

hangovers

• *Hangovers* began to assume monstrous proportions and the morning drink became an urgent necessity.(p.226)

• Successive Monday morning *hangovers*, which despite mid-week resolutions to do better, came with unfailing regularity, eventually caused me to quit my job.(p.254)

• But it began to be an awfully painful answer as *hangovers*, blackouts, trouble, and remorse set in.(p.353)

• *Hangovers* and remorse were always with me.(p.375)

• Incalculable are the intangible initiation fees that A.A. members have paid: the sick, sick *hangovers*, the remorse, guilt, broken homes, jails, and institutions, and the mental anguish in general that has been generated over the years.(p.399)

• They introduced me to beer in the morning to kill *hangovers*.(p.407)

• They woke up with *hangovers*, but with no remorse.(p.407)

• To cure my dreadful *hangovers*, I discovered the morning drink.(p.556)

Hank

• We checked into the home of *Hank*, the man who had fired me eleven years before in Mississippi, and there I met Bill, our founder.(p.245)

• Bill had then been dry three years and *Hank*, two.(p.245)

• Bill and *Hank* had just taken over a small automobile polishing company and they offered me a job -- ten dollars a week and keep at Hank's house.(p.246)

• I tried to contact the boys in New York, but telegrams bounced right back and when I finally got *Hank* on the telephone he fired me right then.(p.247)

Hank's

• Bill and Hank had just taken over a small automobile polishing company and they offered me a job -- ten dollars a week and keep at *Hank's* house.(p.246)

happen

• With the appearance of the new book a great deal began to *happen*.(p.xvii)

• We admit we have some of these symptoms, but we have not gone to the extremes you fellows did, nor are we likely to, for we understand ourselves so well after what you have told us that such things cannot *happen* again.(p.38)

• I rather appreciated your ideas about the subtle insanity which precedes the first drink, but I was confident it could not *happen* to me after what I had learned.(p.40)

• Well, just that did *happen* and more, for what I had learned of alcoholism did not occur to me at all.(p.42)

• If you persist, remarkable things will *happen*.(p.100)

• Should it *happen* again, regard it in a different light.(p.116)

• The opposite may *happen* should the family condemn and criticize.(p.129)

• The practical answer is that since these things have happened among us, they can *happen* with you.(p.153)

• And unless I had some rosy picture of what was going to *happen* that day, I wouldn't even feel like getting up in the morning at all.(p.325)

• They described what had happened when they went out and tried drinking again, and I knew they were sincere in saying that it could *happen* to me.(p.334)

• I screamed on the telephone for my mother to get up there; something was going to *happen*; I didn't know what, but if she didn't get there quick, I'd split wide open.(p.338)

• She's a good-natured soul and said, "I wouldn't worry about it; probably something will *happen*."(p.346)

• And just then something did *happen*.(p.347)

• I had no idea what would *happen* – I just knew I didn't want to live if life was going to go on like it was.(p.355)

• Why should this *happen* to me – hadn't I provided a good home – wasn't I making a good living – didn't I just get a substantial raise that had put me in the upper bracket class?(p.362)

• So I located a house, and I thought we ought to move into it immediately, but Frank was horrified, because he never knew what was going to *happen* to me.(p.388)

• But I was a careful and cunning alcoholic, and this didn't *happen* very often.(p.399)

• Against my better judgment, I went to a meeting with him that night, and a strange thing began to *happen*.(p.446)

• For years, I was sure the worst thing that could *happen* to a nice guy like me would be that I would turn out to be an alcoholic.(p.449)

• Miracle *happen* all time in A.A.(p.476)

• I say, "Just let it *happen*."(p.477)

• In part, it was a feeling of intense shame at having to leave the Army during the war, but mostly it was resentment that this kind of thing should *happen* to me for, strange as it may seem, up to then I still thought I could control drinking.(p.521)

• I was intensely unhappy the whole time, but I didn't seem to be able to do anything about it, and the worst part to me was the realization that all this was going to *happen* again and again until I died.(p.522)

happened

• If you have a drinking problem, we hope that you may pause in reading one of the forty-four personal stories and think: "Yes, that *happened* to me"; or, more important, "Yes, I've felt like that"; or most important, "Yes, I believe this program can work for me, too."(p.xii)

• In no time I was beating on the bar asking myself how it *happened*.(p.6)

• What had *happened*?(p.9)

• Finally he shook his head saying, "Something has *happened* to you I don't understand.(p.14)

• These give a fair cross section of our membership and a clear-cut idea of what has actually *happened* in their lives.(p.29)

• On each of these occasions we worked with him, reviewing carefully what had *happened*.(p.35)

• We asked him to tell us exactly how it *happened*.(p.36)

• Next day we would ask ourselves, in all earnestness and sincerity, how it could have *happened*.(p.37)

• But even in this type of beginning we are obliged to admit that our justification for a spree was insanely insufficient in the light of what always *happened*.(p.37)

• This *happened* soon after they wholeheartedly met a few simple requirements.(p.50)

• Without that, nothing could have *happened*.(p.52)

• Our stories disclose in a general way what we used to be like, what *happened*, and what we are like now.(p.58)

• This all *happened* years ago.(p.80)

• We react sanely and normally, and we will find that this has *happened* automatically.(p.84)

• Tell him exactly what *happened* to you.(p.93)

• The practical answer is that since these things have *happened* among us, they can happen with you.(p.153)

• Many a distracted wife has visited this house to find loving and understanding companionship among women who knew her problem, to hear from the lips of their husbands what had *happened* to them, to be advised how her own wayward mate might be hospitalized and approached when next he stumbled.(p.160)

• I think I must have been thoroughly scared by what had *happened*, or by the doctor, or probably both, so that I did not touch a drink again until the country went dry.(p.175)

• I early discovered that if I drank anything, I was not accountable for what *happened*.(p.196)

• I didn't remember anything that had *happened*.(p.196)

• They called a doctor and it *happened* that they called one I knew.(p.205)

• The very simple program they advised me to follow was that I should ask to know God's will for me for that one day, and then, to the best of my ability, to follow that, and at night to express my gratefulness to God for the things that had *happened* to me during the day.(p.208)

• What could have *happened*?(p.223)

• Then the miracle *happened* – to me!(p.228)

• Many things *happened*; business trials, little worries, and feelings of general despondency came near driving me to the bottle, but I made progress.(p.237)

• Many of these same things had *happened* to me many times before, but this time they had all descended together.(p.238)

• The lesson of his death still remains with me, yet I often wonder what would have *happened* if somebody else had made that first call on me.(p.239)

• Evidently I had gone right back to the movie with a bottle, stayed there several hours and started home with no recollection of what had *happened*.(p.244)

• However, as there *happened* to be several saloons within that distance, I didn't find it necessary to patronize the same place each evening.(p.298)

• I was trapped, and for the life of me I did not know how or why this had *happened* to me.(p.306)

• What had ***happened***?(p.319)
• As my son, our second child, came along, and as he became school age and was away at school most of the time, something ***happened***.(p.323)
• They described what had ***happened*** when they went out and tried drinking again, and I knew they were sincere in saying that it could happen to me.(p.334)
• Something else ***happened*** to me.(p.348)
• So, after taking the first half of the First Step, and very gingerly admitting myself to Alcoholics Anonymous, something ***happened***.(p.349)
• By the time I figured out what had ***happened***, I saw two flashing red lights atop squad cars, sedately coming around the corner.(p.353)
• What had ***happened*** to the shy, lonely, churchgoing wallflower?(p.355)
• The inevitable always ***happened***.(p.361)
• It had ***happened*** to me and I had to do something about it.(p.363)
• In meeting me casually, I don't think my strong belief in "The Man Upstairs" shows, but I have no other explanation for the many good things that have ***happened*** to me since I have been in A.A. -- they came to me from a Greater Power.(p.367)
• I don't think that I was conscious of what had ***happened*** to me, but I think that it registered subconsciously.(p.386)
• But, from the very first paragraph on, something ***happened*** to me.(p.392)
• But when this ***happened*** to me, I declared to friends that I would get drunk, dead drunk that very night, and stay drunk for a month.(p.403)
• But all these things could have ***happened***.(p.412)
• The sanitarium should have ***happened***.(p.412)
• But now a strange thing ***happened***.(p.412)
• Then something ***happened***.(p.422)
• How easy it was, in the beginning, to forget that those binges ever ***happened***!(p.433)
• After a month it seemed unlikely that it ever really ***happened***.(p.433)
• I learned what a devastating effect it can have on a child to coddle him and build him up, and then turn and beat him savagely, as had ***happened*** to me.(p.434)
• I ***happened*** to be the best diagnostician I knew at the time, and certainly I knew my case better than anyone else.(p.444)
• Today, I find it's the best thing that has ever ***happened*** to me.(p.450)
• He was serving time on his fifth felony conviction when a miracle ***happened***.(p.457)
• Then the miracle ***happened***.(p.461)
• Nothing that has ***happened*** to me do I deserve.(p.463)
• I'm talking about the good things that have ***happened***.(p.463)
• From that time on, fear was with me because I realized that not only would I not remember what ***happened*** to me while I was drinking, but apparently I couldn't control what ***happened***.(p.465)
• What ***happened*** afterwards I don't know.(p.468)
• Then a terrible thing ***happened***.(p.478)
• A peculiar thing ***happened*** in 1940.(p.488)
• Something ***happened***.(p.490)
• I remember talking to her, but what ***happened*** after that I don't know.(p.492)
• What actually ***happened*** was that I had taken a penknife and stabbed Vi three times with it.(p.492)
• But there ***happened*** to be a liquor store between the post office and the mill, and I stopped to get that one drink.(p.493)
• I rolled along with the mob this way, that way and the other way, but in those years nothing really bad ***happened*** to me.(p.508)
• There was nothing in my school life that I can look back on which was responsible for anything that ***happened*** afterwards.(p.517)
• That was one of the worst things that could have ***happened*** to an alcoholic woman.(p.527)
• So many wonderful things have ***happened*** to me that at times I can't believe this is me.(p.529)
• No, it can best be explained in a little phrase I coined and sang to myself: "What ***happened*** to Bob?(p.532)
• As I write these words, it seems incredible that these things should have ***happened*** to me, for they are, truly, against all my instincts and training.(p.536)
• The medical profession would probably tell me I was conditioned for alcoholism by the things that ***happened*** to me in my childhood.(p.544)
• And I am sure they would be right as far as they go, but A.A. has taught me I am the result of the way I reacted to what ***happened*** to me as a child.(p.544)
• I had only to reflect on the contrast between the plans I made so many years ago for my life with what really ***happened*** to know I couldn't manage my life drunk or sober.(p.550)
• What my doctor had warned me about finally ***happened***.(p.558)
• He ***happened*** to be, by the grace of God, Dr. Harry Tiebout, the psychiatrist who probably knew more about alcoholism than any other in the world.(p.559)

happening

• I had been reading a lot about psychiatry and I thought, "Maybe if I talk to a psychiatrist he can find out what is ***happening***, and then I can drink like a lady."(p.387)
• It was in Washington, D.C. that this transition took place, and that the really bad part of alcoholism began ***happening***.(p.465)
• Repeated year on end, they are horrible -- frightening and degrading, a chronicle of tragedy which may be greater because the individual undergoing the tragedy, myself, knew what was ***happening***, and yet refused to do anything to stop it.(p.538)

happens

• We are equally positive that once he takes any alcohol whatever into his system, something ***happens***, both in the bodily and mental sense, which makes it virtually impossible for him to stop.(p.22)
• What usually ***happens***?(p.61)
• In nine cases out of ten the unexpected ***happens***.(p.78)
• Ministers and doctors are competent and you can learn much from them if you wish, but it ***happens*** that because of your own drinking experience you can be uniquely useful to other alcoholics.(p.89)
• When this ***happens***, they can be invited to join in morning meditation and then they can take part in the daily discussion without rancor or bias.(p.134)
• We hope the doctor will tell the patient the truth about his condition, whatever that ***happens*** to be.(p.144)
• Some of us struggle with these people because we know that they are really very sick, but we also know that short of some miracle, we are not going to help them except temporarily, and that they will inevitably get worse and worse until one of two things ***happens***.(p.308)
• My story ***happens*** to be a particular kind of woman's story; the story of the woman who drinks at home.(p.335)
• Nothing, absolutely nothing ***happens*** in God's world by mistake.(p.449)

happier

• That was the beginning of a new life, a fuller life, a ***happier*** life than I had ever known or believed possible.(p.228)
• Over the years, as I thought about Max, her good qualities grew and grew, and we married, and all these qualities became more and more apparent to me, and we were ***happier*** and ***happier***.(p.450)

happiest

• These last eighteen years have been the ***happiest*** of my life, trite though that statement may seem.(p.295)
• They have been the ***happiest*** of my life.(p.430)
• I met and married a man in A.A., and I am the ***happiest*** I have ever been in my life.(p.481)

happily

• Before then, I had written lots of sweet promises, but my wife ***happily*** observed that this time I meant business.(p.5)
• His income is good, he has a fine home, is ***happily*** married and the father of promising children of college age.(p.39)
• We must be entirely honest with somebody if we expect to live long or ***happily*** in this world.(p.73)
• I saw that my Village friends, all of whom had small jobs, were living ***happily*** on about a tenth of my sinecure.(p.409)
• The sheriff bade us goodbye very ***happily***.(p.424)
• ***Happily*** for everyone, this conclusion is erroneous.(p.569)

happiness

• There had been much ***happiness*** after all.(p.8)
• I was to know ***happiness***, peace, and usefulness, in a way of life that is incredibly more wonderful as time passes.(p.8)
• We used to amuse ourselves by cynically dissecting spiritual beliefs and practices when we might have observed that many spiritually-minded persons of all races, colors, and creeds were demonstrating a degree of stability, ***happiness*** and usefulness which we should have sought ourselves.(p.49)
• In the face of collapse and despair, in the face of the total failure of their human resources, they found that a new power, peace, ***happiness***, and sense of direction flowed into them.(p.50)
• Is he not a victim of the delusion that he can wrest satisfaction and ***happiness*** out of this world if he only manages well?(p.61)
• Each might pray about it, having the other one's ***happiness*** uppermost in mind.(p.82)
• We are going to know a new freedom and a new ***happiness***.(p.83)
• In spite of your new-found ***happiness***, there will be ups and downs.(p.117)
• The family of an alcoholic longs for the return of ***happiness*** and security.(p.123)
• The family may be possessed by the idea that future ***happiness*** can be based only upon forgetfulness of the past.(p.123)
• Cling to the thought that, in God's hands, the dark past is the greatest possession you have -- the key to life and ***happiness*** for others.(p.124)
• It was transcended by the ***happiness*** they found in giving themselves for others.(p.159)
• About the time of the beer experiment I was thrown in with a crowd of people who attracted me because of their seeming poise, health, and ***happiness***.(p.178)
• I noticed that the others seemed to have such a release, a ***happiness***, a something that I thought a person ought to have.(p.191)
• Freedom from anger and fear, freedom to know ***happiness*** and love.(p.228)
• I get my greatest thrill of accomplishment from the knowledge that I have played a part in the new ***happiness*** achieved by countless others like myself.(p.229)
• All of us in A.A. know the tremendous ***happiness*** that is in our sobriety, but there are also tragedies.(p.239)
• My brilliant agnosticism vanished, and I saw for the first time that those who really believed, or at least honestly tried to find a Power greater than themselves, were much more composed and contented than I had ever been, and they seemed to have a degree of ***happiness*** which I had never known.(p.247)
• They had that certain something that seemed to glow, a peace and a serenity combined with ***happiness***.(p.290)
• I was terribly impressed by this meeting and the quality of ***happiness*** these men displayed, despite their lack of material means.(p.291)
• A very simple plan that I still find much joy and ***happiness*** in following.(p.302)
• I can actually take my problems to Him and He gives me comfort, peace, and ***happiness***.(p.303)
• And when all of life is a substitute for drink, there's no ***happiness***, no peace.(p.339)
• He was full of his new found life of ***happiness*** and sobriety.(p.365)
• A whole new world of ***happiness*** and love began to unfold before my eyes, a truly new way of living.(p.365)
• Today I think of life in terms of ***happiness***, contentment, freedom from fear and despair, sane thinking, ability to face problems as they occur, the opportunity to help other alcoholics and to be decent.(p.430)
• It has made me understand that I must be one of my world, that I cannot exist in any ***happiness*** as a rebel by myself.(p.524)
• Now, for me, and to my satisfaction, I know the purpose of life: The purpose of life is to create and the by-product is ***happiness***.(p.535)
• I have had the joy of seeing many a human being, down and out, learn to stand straight again, and to proceed under his own power to ***happiness*** in life.(p.541)
• I looked around me at people who seemed happy and tried to analyze their ***happiness***, and it seemed to me that without exception these people had something or somebody they loved very much.(p.546)
• Ask for their health, their prosperity, their ***happiness***, and you will be free.(p.552)
• The relationship between my wife and me was restored to a love and ***happiness*** that we had not known even before my alcoholism became acute.(p.559)

happy

• The tragic truth is that if the man be a real alcoholic, the ***happy*** day may not arrive.(p.23)
• An exceptional man, he remained bone dry for twenty-five years and retired at the age of fifty-five, after a successful and ***happy*** business career.(p.32)
• To spend too much time on any one situation is to deny some other alcoholic an opportunity to live and be ***happy***.(p.96)
• If it is a ***happy*** occasion, try to increase the pleasure of those there; if a business occasion, go and attend to your business enthusiastically.(p.102)
• Among us are wives, relatives and friends whose

problem has been solved, as well as some who have not yet found a ***happy*** solution.(p.104)
• You have passed ***happy*** evenings together chatting and drinking before your fire.(p.110)
• We know women who are unafraid, even ***happy*** under these conditions.(p.111)
• If you and your husband find a solution for the pressing problem of drink you are, of course, going to be very ***happy***.(p.117)
• We have found nothing incompatible between a powerful spiritual experience and a life of sane and ***happy*** usefulness.(p.130)
• We are sure God wants us to be ***happy***, joyous, and free.(p.133)
• He will presently try the old game again, for he isn't ***happy*** about his sobriety.(p.152)
• It may seem incredible that these men are to become ***happy***, respected, and useful once more.(p.153)
• At midnight he came home exhausted, but very ***happy***.(p.156)
• Seeing much of each other, scarce an evening passed that someone's home did not shelter a little gathering of men and women, ***happy*** in their release, and constantly thinking how they might present their discovery to some newcomer.(p.159)
• We shall be with you in the Fellowship of the Spirit, and you will surely meet some of us as you trudge the Road of ***Happy*** Destiny.(p.164)
• More than these attributes, they seemed to be ***happy***.(p.178)
• My parents were well-to-do people and their marriage was a ***happy*** one.(p.182)
• My marriage was ***happy*** and, as I have said, I never had any of the reasons, conscious or unconscious, which are often given for drinking.(p.182)
• The important thing was that he was ***happy***.(p.208)
• He was released, relieved from his alcoholism and was ***happy*** and contented because of it.(p.208)
• She was a woman devoted to her family and loyal to her husband, but quarrels did not make a ***happy*** environment for her.(p.210)
• As far as my home was concerned, I did not see then, though of course I can see now, that it was anything but a ***happy*** situation for my wife.(p.215)
• Like most immigrants I wanted to be somebody and have something and I was very ***happy*** and contented as I felt success crown my efforts.(p.232)
• Yet he was ***happy***, relaxed, confident and laughing.(p.239)
• Jackie told me about a group of fellows in New York, of whom my old friend Fitz was one, who had the same problem I had, and who by working together to help each other were not now drinking and were ***happy*** like himself.(p.239)
• And I still say that as long as I remember that January 8th in Washington, that is how long, by the grace of God as I understand Him, I will retain a ***happy*** sobriety.(p.250)
• They seemed to be ***happy*** in their fashion, they and their little groups of supporters, but always pride of intellect stopped me from seeking what they evidently had.(p.256)
• Mine was far from a ***happy*** childhood.(p.261)
• I had none of these things that children should have to make them ***happy***.(p.261)
• This ***happy*** combination of pleasant work and alcohol lasted for five years.(p.277)
• Here, while in a hospital bed, men with clear eyes, ***happy*** faces, and a look of assurance and purposefulness about them, came to see me and told me their stories.(p.279)
• In recent years I have had the ***happy*** combination of time and money to travel occasionally.(p.285)
• I was in a perfectly ***happy*** frame of mind.(p.285)
• He said they were sober, ***happy*** and had their self-respect back as well as the respect of their neighbors.(p.289)
• He was ***happy***, getting a kick out of life and people, and beginning to get his medical practice back again.(p.290)
• We got engaged, and we were ***happy*** -- Jean with me, and me with the bottle and Jean.(p.318)
• Like I said, I'm a twenty-four-year-old alcoholic -- and I'm ***happy***.(p.320)
• But I wasn't ***happy***, and I didn't ever let myself go in my drinking.(p.323)
• If I had been sincere in what I thought I wanted more than anything else in life -- a sober husband and a ***happy***, contented home -- I would have gone on the wagon with him.(p.324)
• I was assigned to keep media guests ***happy*** at a Halloween party given by a major star in his plush home.(p.328)
• ***Happy, happy*** senior-citizen existence!(p.329)
• But I wasn't ***happy***.(p.339)
• But not ***happy***.(p.339)
• I had never been very ***happy***, but now it was unbearable.(p.355)
• Proud of my little station and of my new bride I settled down to a ***happy*** married life.(p.361)
• We came back to Pittsburgh as ***happy*** as a bride and groom.(p.364)
• I had just raised the bottle to my lips when my wife opened the door and froze me completely in my tracks with "***Happy*** New Year, dear."(p.365)
• I was so ***happy*** over getting home that I changed overnight, but not enough.(p.387)
• I know that I must work at it as long as I live; I know that it is only by working at it that I can stay sober and have a ***happy*** life.(p.394)
• I also wanted to be the queen of society, with a glittering salon, the bride of a dream prince and the mother of a ***happy*** brood.(p.400)
• Even then I knew in my heart that I was unfit for the very things I wanted most, a ***happy*** marriage, security, a home and love.(p.403)
• The glittering society belle, the modern Shakespeare, the ***happy*** wife, the loving and beloved.(p.411)
• Every day, I feel a little bit more useful, more ***happy*** and more free.(p.417)
• My story has a ***happy*** ending, but not of the conventional kind.(p.437)
• But, by the look on the psychiatrist's face, I could tell that it would really make him ***happy*** if I agreed.(p.446)
• So, for no better reason than to make him ***happy***, I agreed.(p.446)
• Until I could accept my alcoholism, I could not stay sober; unless I accept life completely on life's terms, I cannot be ***happy***.(p.449)
• I thought I would be quite ***happy*** and never would I drink too much again.(p.465)
• In the light of subsequent events it became evident that I took their advice far too literally, for, after some months of ***happy*** sobriety I drank again.(p.471)
• We both ***happy***.(p.476)
• Tall Man die five years ago, a sober, peaceful, ***happy*** man.(p.476)
• We can have this new way of life -- learning to live with our sickness and to be ***happy*** and content -- if we are willing to change our way of thinking and be honest, first with ourselves, then with others.(p.480)
• I am ***happy*** in my work.(p.500)
• A lot of the boys had tears in their eyes, they were so ***happy*** to be home.(p.513)
• I wasn't a ***happy*** man that morning, but I'm ***happy*** now that it came about.(p.515)
• I had a very ***happy*** upbringing at home.(p.517)
• People seemed to be carefully dressed, too ***happy***, too normal.(p.524)
• It has made me very ***happy***.(p.525)
• I wandered, craving peace, from one spot to another of youthful ***happy*** memory, and loathed the man I had become.(p.539)
• For I am ***happy***.(p.542)
• I thought I could never be ***happy***.(p.542)
• A ***happy*** man is not likely to do harm to another human being.(p.542)
• I hope I have been able to impart to you, the reader, at least a bit of what I know; the joy of living, the irresistible power of divine love and its healing strength, and the fact that we, as sentient beings, have the knowledge to choose between good and evil, and, choosing good, are made ***happy***.(p.543)
• I looked around me at people who seemed ***happy*** and tried to analyze their happiness, and it seemed to me that without exception these people had something or somebody they loved very much.(p.546)
• A.A. has taught me that I will have peace of mind in exact proportion to the peace of mind I bring into the lives of other people, and it has taught me the true meaning of the admonition "***happy*** are ye who know these things and do them."(p.551)

harbor

• That company may ***harbor*** many actual or potential alcoholics.(p.149)
• Pearl ***Harbor*** was a breeze of nine months, a gay Hawaiian paradise, drinking under the palms, listening to the surf beat on the shore, a bottle of whiskey near at hand.(p.426)

harboring

• For when ***harboring*** such feelings we shut ourselves off from the sunlight of the Spirit.(p.66)

hard

• Prior to his journey to Akron, the broker had worked ***hard*** with many alcoholics on the theory that only an alcoholic could help an alcoholic, but he had succeeded only in keeping sober himself.(p.xvi)
• They made me swallow ***hard***.(p.10)
• That statement hit me ***hard***.(p.12)
• "Lay off the ***hard*** stuff."(p.20)
• Then we have a certain type of ***hard*** drinker.(p.20)
• He may start off as a moderate drinker; he may or may not become a continuous ***hard*** drinker; but at some stage of his drinking career he begins to lose all control of his liquor consumption, once he starts to drink.(p.21)
• Heaven knows, we have tried ***hard*** enough and long enough to drink like other people!(p.31)
• I had no trouble refusing drinks, and began to wonder if I had not been making too ***hard*** work of a simple matter.(p.40)
• Though I had been only a nominal churchman, their proposals were not, intellectually, ***hard*** to swallow.(p.42)
• We found that God does not make too ***hard*** terms with those who seek Him.(p.46)
• The rule is we must be ***hard*** on ourself, but always considerate of others.(p.74)
• Some of us have taken very ***hard*** knocks to learn this truth: Job or no job -- wife or no wife -- we simply do not stop drinking so long as we place dependence upon other people ahead of dependence on God.(p.98)
• You may be unable to do so, no matter how ***hard*** you try.(p.111)
• You may be afraid your husband will lose his position; you are thinking of the disgrace and ***hard*** times which will befall you and the children.(p.116)
• We had to learn these things the ***hard*** way.(p.121)
• Father knows he is to blame; it may take him many seasons of ***hard*** work to be restored financially, but he shouldn't be reproached.(p.123)
• The alcoholic may find it ***hard*** to re-establish friendly relations with his children.(p.134)
• Whether you are a ***hard*** drinker, a moderated drinker or a teetotaler, you may have some pretty strong opinions, perhaps prejudices.(p.139)
• When sober, does he not work ***hard*** and have a knack of getting things done?(p.139)
• If possible express a lack of ***hard*** feeling toward him.(p.142)
• They work ***hard*** and they play ***hard***.(p.146)
• The proceeding was shot through with much ***hard*** feeling and controversy.(p.154)
• As we shall see, he now means a great deal to his community, and the major liabilities of thirty years of ***hard*** drinking have been repaired in four.(p.156)
• This had little effect however for I kept on drinking and used a great deal more ***hard*** liquor than in former years.(p.174)
• A couple of hired hands were cleaning out the barn on the farm and I would ride to and fro on the sled, and while they were loading I would drink ***hard*** cider out of a barrel in the barn.(p.183)
• It would be ***hard*** to estimate how much A.A. has done for me.(p.191)
• That was the first time I ever drank ***hard*** liquor.(p.195)
• I went over and bought a jug of ***hard*** cider and a gallon of wine that I gave these fellows to drink.(p.195)
• Wine and ***hard*** cider.(p.196)
• Anyhow, I recognized the fact that I couldn't drink like normal people, but I tried ***hard*** and kept on trying for twenty-two years.(p.196)
• I can remember well thinking that I would quit drinking, really go to work ***hard***, apply myself eight hours a day, five days a week, make a lot of money, and then I could start drinking again.(p.199)
• My parents were ***hard*** working people.(p.210)
• It was ***hard*** to reconcile this ghastly present with the simple facts of the past.(p.225)
• I cannot say, however, that I acquired any craving for ***hard*** liquor as a result.(p.231)
• Before long I had a definite taste for ***hard*** liquor, knew nausea and headaches I had never known before, but as in the old days, I suffered them out.(p.233)
• The first few months were ***hard***.(p.237)
• Searching where I have been at fault, it is not ***hard*** to discover and get right again, for I have proven to myself and to many others who know me that God can keep a man sober if he will let Him.(p.237)
• Federal Theatre in Texas gave me an administrative job which I held for a year, only because I worked ***hard*** and productively when I worked, and because my very tolerant chief ascribed my frequent lapses to a bohemian temperament.(p.256)
• I got a job in the woolen mills in Ravenna -- very ***hard*** work.(p.262)
• I think it's awfully ***hard*** on people, especially if they're new people, to hear these long drawn out talks.(p.273)

• I simply did not have the pep to do ***hard***, "cold-turkey" selling.(p.277)
• Some of these were ***hard*** to believe, but it did not require a giant brain to perceive that they had something I could use.(p.279)
• With this specialized training, and a liberal business education in the school of ***hard*** knocks, I was able to set up shop some two years later as an independent accountant.(p.284)
• In this small group, during the Depression, there was no one who was not ***hard*** up.(p.291)
• Looking at him it was ***hard*** to believe he had ever been as I was then.(p.309)
• I'd worked ***hard*** to be tops in my profession.(p.328)
• You've been sober for three months, been working ***hard***.(p.348)
• And the clergy have tried ***hard*** to help us, but we haven't been helped.(p.352)
• And the psychiatrist has had thousands of couches, and has put you and me on them many, many times, but he hasn't helped us very much, though he has tried ***hard***; and we owe the clergy and the doctor and the psychiatrist a deep debt of gratitude, but they haven't helped our alcoholism, except in a rare few instances.(p.352)
• Many times have I heard the above expressions since I have been in A.A., and many times I have had to reply "Definitely I am an alcoholic, and while it may be ***hard*** for you to believe, it is not ***hard*** for me, for I have learned many things about alcohol and myself that would, perhaps, be difficult for you to understand."(p.356)
• At this time, however, she had an opportunity to go to Salt Lake City on a new project for the government, but she did promise me that if I would curtail my drinking and buckle down to ***hard*** work she would give serious consideration to my latest proposal and maybe join me at a later date when I got settled.(p.359)
• I sure had been working awfully ***hard*** of late.(p.360)
• By hook or crook I usually managed to sober up before I reached home, but always "terribly tired" from a "***hard*** day's work," and just having to have one or two before dinner.(p.361)
• It was ***hard*** for her to believe in my love by my actions.(p.362)
• Dad's image for me was that of a big Irish oilman who came up through the school of ***hard*** knocks and so had to be a two-fisted drinker.(p.369)
• Gradually the quantity increased, the occasions for a drink came more frequently; a ***hard*** day, worries and pressure, bad news, good news -- there were more and more reasons for a drink.(p.374)
• Meetings are both relaxing and refreshing to me after a ***hard*** day.(p.381)
• As I grow in A.A., I realize that a person with as much self-will as I had, as ***hard*** a head and as diseased an ego, had to try everything that I could think of, butting my head against every stone wall before I was ready to come in.(p.384)
• After all, upon coming out of a week-long or ten-day drunk, it was ***hard*** enough to figure up just how much that one drunk cost, let alone trying to calculate the cost of approximately twenty-five years of active alcoholism.(p.396)
• The people I knew rode ***hard***, and some of them drank ***hard***.(p.404)
• But at this time, I began gravitating toward the really ***hard*** drinkers, hanging around with them more and more.(p.404)
• I didn't graduate to the ***hard*** stuff until I was sixteen.(p.423)
• With all this, it was becoming increasingly ***hard*** to maintain my front of distinction and respectability to the world.(p.435)
• For the leveling-off process, I just loved intravenous Demerol, but I found it ***hard*** to practice good medicine while shooting morphine.(p.442)
• It was ***hard*** to judge the right amount.(p.443)
• He had bottle of ***hard*** stuff.(p.474)
• Soon change to ***hard*** stuff.(p.475)
• Then ***hard*** stuff.(p.475)
• Men are supposed to be tough and rugged to start with, but if a woman becomes that way, it is pretty ***hard*** to get back the niceties of womanhood.(p.480)
• I started inquiring where I could get a drink and, of course, I found that it wasn't ***hard***.(p.490)
• I am working ***hard*** on the books of a subsidiary company of a large corporation.(p.500)
• I have fought ***hard*** to stop drinking.(p.502)
• I fled, finally, after having been fired from my job by a boss who wept a little (since I had worked ***hard***) as he gave notice for me to clear out.(p.539)
• But for the next years, I worked ***hard*** and exultantly in A.A.(p.541)
• I swore off ***hard*** liquor and turned to wine.(p.555)

hard-fought-for
• "I've got to stop if I want to live," I told myself, and if I don't want to break my parents' hearts and maybe jeopardize their own carefully built up and ***hard-fought-for*** sobriety.(p.429)

hard-won
• Many times in the intervening years I have thanked God for that man, a man who had the courage to admit failure, a man who had the humility to confess that all the ***hard-won*** learning of his profession could not turn up the answer.(p.436)

harder
• If sex is very troublesome, we throw ourselves the ***harder*** into helping others.(p.70)
• It is ***harder*** to go to an enemy than to a friend, but we find it much more beneficial to us.(p.77)
• I was never a hilarious drunk; the more I drank the quieter I got, and the drunker I got the ***harder*** I fought to stay sober.(p.241)
• Every day became that much ***harder*** to live through, and I began to take a look at myself.(p.354)
• The obsession of the mind was a little ***harder*** to understand and yet everyone has obsessions of various kinds.(p.380)
• The ***harder*** I worked with Max, the sicker she got.(p.440)
• It became progressively ***harder*** to get up in the morning, until one day I asked myself what I would do for a patient who felt this rotten.(p.441)
• I really do believe it is much ***harder*** for a woman to gain back her self-respect than it is for a man.(p.480)
• They were ***harder*** to get off.(p.514)

hardest
• On the contrary, the ***hardest*** place to work this program has been in my own home, with my own children and, finally, with Max.(p.451)
• Therefore, it will be the ***hardest*** to work on.(p.482)

hardly
• Mercifully, no one could guess that I was to have no real employment for five years, or ***hardly*** draw a sober breath.(p.4)
• I ***hardly*** dared cross the street, lest I collapse and be run down by an early morning truck, for it was scarcely daylight.(p.6)
• If we keep on the way we are going there is little doubt that much good will result, but the surface of the problem would ***hardly*** be scratched.(p.19)
• We doubt if many of them can do it, because none will really want to stop, and ***hardly*** one of them, because of the peculiar mental twist already acquired, will find he can win out.(p.33)
• But the actual or potential alcoholic, with ***hardly*** an exception, will be absolutely unable to stop drinking on the basis of self-knowledge.(p.39)
• The first requirement is that we be convinced that any life run on self-will can ***hardly*** be a success.(p.60)
• We'd ***hardly*** be human if we didn't.(p.69)
• They can ***hardly*** fail to approve these simple principles, though the head of the house still fails somewhat in practicing them.(p.130)
• ***Hardly*** one of our crowd now shows any mark of dissipation.(p.133)
• Not long afterward he had called me from Hartford on two successive days, so drunk he could ***hardly*** speak.(p.136)
• Now, this house will ***hardly*** accommodate its weekly visitors, for they number sixty or eighty as a rule.(p.161)
• During these two years I was kept so busy that I ***hardly*** left the hospital at all.(p.174)
• But I ***hardly*** tasted anything for two years and started in business for myself, founding a mattress factory which is today an important industrial enterprise in our city.(p.232)
• He ***hardly*** ever went to anything like that without me.(p.263)
• I could ***hardly*** see at all, and my memory kept eluding me.(p.353)
• So he waited another week or two and I don't think I stayed sober ***hardly*** at all.(p.391)
• This was the only period when I didn't drink, but that was ***hardly*** any consolation.(p.480)
• He makes no reply, and ***hardly*** seems to see me.(p.501)
• He finally realizes that he has undergone a profound alteration in his reaction to life; that such a change could ***hardly*** have been brought about by himself alone.(p.569)
• You would ***hardly*** recognize them."(p.572)

hardness
• The children are sometimes dominated by a pathetic ***hardness*** and cynicism.(p.134)

hardships
• In my early twenties the ***hardships*** of hobo life did not discourage me, but I had no wish to become just a tramp.(p.253)

hardware
• The next three years I spent in Boston, Chicago, and Montreal in the employ of a large manufacturing concern, selling railway supplies, gas engines of all sorts, and many other items of heavy ***hardware***.(p.172)

harm
• We must be willing to make amends where we have done ***harm***, provided that we do not bring about still more ***harm*** in so doing.(p.69)
• If we are not sorry, and our conduct continues to ***harm*** others, we are quite sure to drink.(p.70)
• It may be he has done us more ***harm*** than we have done him and, though we may have acquired a better attitude toward him, we are still not too keen about admitting our faults.(p.77)
• Nor are we afraid of disclosing our alcoholism on the theory it may cause financial ***harm***.(p.78)
• Permit that and you only ***harm*** him.(p.96)
• He is positive he can handle his liquor, that it does him no ***harm***, that drinking is necessary in his business.(p.109)
• But you must be on guard not to embarrass or ***harm*** your husband.(p.115)
• I learned that it was something of a spiritual nature, which did not appeal to me very much, but I thought it could do no ***harm***.(p.178)
• There had been some occasions -- there was an automobile wreck, for instance -- when I had police escort home but not to jail, all of which, instead of doing me a favor, did me ***harm*** because I was then full of self-esteem as to the progress I had made both professionally and financially.(p.213)
• They saw that they had become actual or potential alcoholics, even though no serious ***harm*** had yet been done.(p.315)
• But success brought increased social activities and I realized that many of my friends enjoyed a social drink with no apparent ***harm*** to themselves or others.(p.374)
• A happy man is not likely to do ***harm*** to another human being.(p.542)
• ***Harm*** is done by sick people, as I was sick, and doing dreadful ***harm*** to myself and to my loved ones.(p.542)

harmed
• Though he could not accept all the tenets of the Oxford Groups, he was convinced of the need for moral inventory, confession of personality defects, restitution to those ***harmed***, helpfulness to others, and the necessity of belief in and dependence upon God.(p.xvi)
• 8.Made a list of all persons we had ***harmed***, and became willing to make amends to them all.(p.59)
• We have a list of all persons we have ***harmed*** and to whom we are willing to make amends.(p.76)
• We discuss them with someone immediately and make amends quickly if we have ***harmed*** anyone.(p.84)
• Dr. Bob then led me through the restitution step, in which I made a list of all of the persons I had ***harmed***, and worked out ways and means of slowly making restitution.(p.292)

harmful
• Having regard for the law of the land, I resigned myself to the will of the national legislators and quit drinking altogether, not because I had found it ***harmful***, but because I couldn't get what I was accustomed to drink.(p.232)

harmless
• It was ***harmless***; nobody ever got drunk on beer.(p.177)
• After two or three years of effort along this line, I reached the point of actual despair that I ever would be able to drink only a ***harmless*** amount each day.(p.215)

harmonious
• We have a way out on which we can absolutely agree, and upon which we can join in brotherly and ***harmonious*** action.(p.17)
• Father was a very well-integrated person, and while mother was highstrung and a bit selfish and demanding, our home life was reasonably ***harmonious***.(p.240)
• It pays daily in more ***harmonious*** relations with my fellow men, in ever clearer insight into the true meaning of life, and in the answering love and gratitude wherever and whenever I have been the instrument of God's will in the lives of others.(p.394)

harmony
• Is he not, even in his best moments, a producer of confusion rather than ***harmony***?(p.61)

harness
• Slowly I realized I was in bed and that the objects were my feet, encased in a ***harness*** affair.(p.422)

harness-making
• Very early I became apprenticed to ***harness-making*** and acquired considerable knowledge of upholstering.(p.230)

harping
• They kept ***harping*** on it, that I go.(p.509)

Harry
• Dr. ***Harry*** Emerson Fosdick, the noted clergyman, reviewed it with approval.(p.xvii)
• He happened to be, by the grace of God, Dr. ***Harry*** Tiebout, the psychiatrist who probably knew more about alcoholism than any other in the world.(p.559)
• Dr. ***Harry*** M. Tiebout, psychiatrist: "As a psychiatrist, I have thought a great deal about the relationship of my specialty to A.A. and I have come to the conclusion that our particular function can very often lie in preparing the way for the patient to accept any sort of treatment or outside help.(p.571)
• Speaking at a dinner given by John D. Rockefeller Jr. to introduce Alcoholics Anonymous to some of his friends, Dr. ***Harry*** Emerson Fosdick remarked: "I think that psychologically speaking there is a point of advantage in the approach that is being made in this movement that cannot be duplicated.(p.574)

harsh
• My inability to accept the ***harsh*** realities of life had resulted in a disillusioned cynic, clothed in protective armor against the world's misunderstanding.(p.226)
• It was the first of many such experiences that became the only cause of ***harsh*** words, tears and heartaches in an otherwise truly beautiful marriage.(p.361)

Hartford
• Not long afterward he had called me from ***Hartford*** on two successive days, so drunk he could hardly speak.(p.136)
• I still expected a plea for clemency, but these words came through the receiver: "I just wanted to tell you Paul jumped from a hotel window in ***Hartford*** last Saturday.(p.136)

hash
• After all, I had been working for eighteen years, slinging ***hash***, and I was managing.(p.478)

hasn't
• Science may one day accomplish this, but it ***hasn't*** done so yet.(p.31)
• Our friend's gorge rose as he bitterly cried out: "If there is a God, He certainly ***hasn't*** done anything for me!"(p.56)
• We old-timers who get scattered and separated and then witness the construction of services to get in more people and to make this thing function, we think that A.A. has changed, but the root of it ***hasn't***.(p.272)
• Once I did have a slip – tried drinking again – but the A.A.'s tell me not to worry about yesterday, because nobody can change it, and not to worry about tomorrow, because it ***hasn't*** come yet.(p.320)
• And the psychiatrist has had thousands of couches, and has put you and me on them many, many times, but he ***hasn't*** helped us very much, though he has tried hard; and we owe the clergy and the doctor and the psychiatrist a deep debt of gratitude, but they haven't helped our alcoholism, except in a rare few instances.(p.352)
• (That dog ***hasn't*** wet my pants once since I joined A.A., and neither have I!)(p.440)
• It ***hasn't*** been easy to work out this relationship with Max.(p.451)
• I had even borrowed money from her, over her protest: "Bob, please don't ask me to lend you money -- you're the only one who ***hasn't***."(p.540)

haste
• Let us make ***haste*** to reassure you.(p.46)
• If there be divorce or separation, there should be no undue ***haste*** for the couple to get together.(p.99)

hastened
• My last venture, a book shop, was ***hastened*** to closed doors by my steady intoxication.(p.255)

hastily
• And I remembered the creeping horror of the interminable night, in which I slept for short spells and woke up dripping with cold sweat and shaken with utter despair, to drink ***hastily*** from my bottle and mercifully pass out again, "You're mad, you're mad, you're mad!" pounded through my brain with each returning ray of consciousness, and I drowned the refrain with drink.(p.224)

hasty
• Therefore, we are not to be the ***hasty*** and foolish martyr who would needlessly sacrifice others to save himself from the alcoholic pit.(p.79)

hat
• He took off his ***hat*** and his overcoat, and he said, "You don't look very good.(p.207)
• Maybe a drink -- I put on my ***hat*** and dash off in the car.(p.505)

hate
• If your husband is a drinker, you probably worry over what other people are thinking and you ***hate*** to meet your friends.(p.114)
• Without saying so, they may cordially ***hate*** him for what he has done to them and to their mother.(p.134)
• I was bitter, living in ***hate***.(p.338)
• It was then that I began to ***hate*** myself, and drank primarily to ease my conscience and forget.(p.354)
• And as her disease was reaching the terminal stages, she was screaming, "You ***hate*** me!(p.439)
• You ***hate*** me!(p.439)
• Why don't you admit you ***hate*** me?"(p.439)
• I remember very well saying, "There's only one person in the world whose guts I ***hate*** worse than yours, and those're my own."(p.440)
• How I ***hate*** that word.(p.499)

hated
• The question of how to approach the man we ***hated*** will arise.(p.77)
• I was still bitter because I felt that drink had completely ruined my childhood and my married life, and I ***hated*** everything pertaining to it.(p.262)
• I ***hated*** myself worse and worse, and as I ***hated*** myself I became more defiant towards everything and everybody.(p.265)
• In the old days I ***hated*** to wake up and look back at what last night was like.(p.325)
• Three months later, he ***hated*** the game and found solace in the bottle.(p.330)
• I had always ***hated*** beer, but now I grew to love it, bottle after bottle of it, warm or cold.(p.339)
• So it drove me deeper into the psychosis or neurosis that I had, and that I ***hated*** deep down in my heart.(p.388)
• Mother ***hated*** liquor and feared a drunken man.(p.498)
• It was a thorn in my side, because I knew it was the truth, and I ***hated*** to hear the truth, especially about myself.(p.513)
• I ***hated*** every minute of it.(p.526)
• I ***hated*** that judge for sending me to a place with all those drunks.(p.527)
• There was the necessity for sticking to a job I ***hated***, a dull, repetitive job performed in association with other men I had nothing in common with . . . performed for years on end, because the money was needed at home.(p.532)

hater
• I was an honest agnostic, but definitely not a ***hater*** of the church or its adherents.(p.256)

hates
• We would not even do the cause of temperate drinking any good, for not one drinker in a thousand likes to be told anything about alcohol by one who ***hates*** it.(p.103)

hating
• I went on, realizing what I was becoming, ***hating*** myself for it, bitter, blaming life, blaming everything else but the fact that I should turn about and do something about my drinking.(p.337)

hatred
• We are careful never to show intolerance or ***hatred*** of drinking as an institution.(p.103)
• Do it every day for two weeks and you will find you have come to mean it and to want it for them, and you will realize that where you used to feel bitterness and resentment and ***hatred***, you now feel compassionate understanding and love."(p.552)
• This great experience that released me from the bondage of ***hatred*** and replaced it with love is really just another affirmation of the truth I know: I get everything I need in Alcoholics Anonymous – everything I need I get – and when I get what I need I invariably find that it was just what I wanted all the time.(p.553)

hats
• If anyone who is showing inability to control his drinking can do the right-about-face and drink like a gentleman, our ***hats*** are off to him.(p.31)

hauled
• I was down to my shorts, unaware of wrong-doing, before the ambulance got there and ***hauled*** me off to a hospital from which anxious friends rescued me, later that night.(p.537)

hauling
• ***Hauling*** her to the divan, I sat with her and began to talk, frantically but clearly – and making sense.(p.333)

haunted
• The feeling of impending disaster that had ***haunted*** me for years began to dissolve as I put into practice more and more of the Twelve Steps.(p.229)

haunting
• ***Haunting*** me through each day's stupor -- and there were eighteen or nineteen such days in this man's home -- was the thought: "Where do I go when his family comes home?"(p.278)

haunts
• Some of them I had known for years, good two-fisted drinkers who had disappeared from their former ***haunts***.(p.258)

haven
• The expression on the faces of the women, that indefinable something in the eyes of the men, the stimulating and electric atmosphere of the place, conspired to let him know that here was ***haven*** at last.(p.160)

haven't
• If we ***haven't*** the will to do this, we ask until it comes.(p.76)
• Maybe we are divorced, and have remarried but ***haven't*** kept up the alimony to number one.(p.79)
• But obviously you cannot transmit something you ***haven't*** got.(p.164)
• I had run into him, and he looked real prosperous; his face and eyes looked clear and he started to compliment me on my good front and how well I looked, and I said, "I ***haven't*** had a drink for nine months."(p.201)
• He said, "Well, I ***haven't*** had a drink for three months."(p.201)
• Now we got you the drink, but you ***haven't*** taken the medicine."(p.206)
• That was an experience that I have never forgotten, and many times in my own work with A.A. newcomers I feel kind of guilty because I ***haven't*** done the same thing.(p.219)
• ***Haven't*** I been successful, ***haven't*** I accomplished extraordinary things in business?(p.245)
• I ***haven't***.(p.260)
• And the clergy have tried hard to help us, but we ***haven't*** been helped.(p.352)
• And the psychiatrist has had thousands of couches, and has put you and me on them many, many times, but he hasn't helped us very much, though he has tried hard; and we owe the clergy and the doctor and the psychiatrist a deep debt of gratitude, but they ***haven't*** helped our alcoholism, except in a rare few instances.(p.352)
• As these words are written at fifty-three years of age, with over nine years of A.A. behind me, with all its wonderful teachings, I ***haven't*** the slightest doubt about being an alcoholic.(p.356)
• I ***haven't*** written anything about that part of my story, but I believe in a Greater Power which I call God and I ask for His wisdom and guidance daily.(p.366)
• During three years in A.A., I ***haven't*** lost so much as one shirt.(p.372)
• I continue to be surprised by the people I meet who say, "You ***haven't*** had a drink for a long time, have you?"(p.376)
• To this day I ***haven't*** been able to decipher what I wrote to them.(p.427)
• I'm twenty-six now and I ***haven't*** had a drink since I made my decision.(p.430)
• "Then why in God's name ***haven't*** you told me so, during all these years?"(p.436)
• That was seven years ago -- and many A.A. meetings ago – and I ***haven't*** had a drink during those seven years.(p.437)
• I ***haven't*** seen my son since he was three and a half years old.(p.463)
• I will be fifty years old next month, ***haven't*** seen my son or my daughter yet, nor my daughter's two children, my grandchildren; but I am grateful.(p.463)
• That was over seven years ago, and thank God and A.A., I ***haven't*** had a drink since.(p.473)
• (And the church walls ***haven't*** tumbled down yet.)(p.482)
• I ***haven't*** mentioned it, but Charlie, my sponsor, was white, and when we got our group started we got help from other white groups in Washington.(p.495)
• Because, thank God, since I came into this program

I ***haven't*** had any trouble.(p.516)

• Just as I was wondering what on earth I could do -- I was too drunk even to pack a handkerchief – the memory of an A.A. write-up that I had seen in the Evening Mail flashed across my mind -- and I thought to myself, this is something I ***haven't*** tried yet.(p.523)

• I hope I ***haven't*** hurt anyone's feelings, but maybe we could all grow and change.(p.529)

• They ***haven't*** eaten me yet!(p.530)

havens

• They will approach still other sick ones and fellowships of Alcoholics Anonymous may spring up in each city and hamlet, ***havens*** for those who must find a way out.(p.153)

having

• By late 1937, the number of members ***having*** substantial sobriety time behind them was sufficient to convince the membership that a new light had entered the dark world of the alcoholic.(p.xvii)

• These allergic types can never safely use alcohol in any form at all; and once ***having*** formed the habit and found they cannot break it, once ***having*** lost their self-confidence, their reliance upon things human, their problems pile up on them and become astonishingly difficult to solve.(p.xxvi)

• The feeling of ***having*** shared in a common peril is one element in the powerful cement which binds us.(p.17)

• They sound like the philosophy of the man who, ***having*** a headache, beats himself on the head with a hammer so that he can't feel the ache.(p.23)

• Those ***having*** religious affiliations will find here nothing disturbing to their beliefs or ceremonies.(p.28)

• Here are some of the methods we have tried: Drinking beer only, limiting the number of drinks, never drinking alone, never drinking in the morning, drinking only at home, never ***having*** it in the house, never drinking during business hours, drinking only at parties, switching from scotch to brandy, drinking only natural wines, agreeing to resign if ever drunk on the job, taking a trip, not taking a trip, swearing off forever (with and without a solemn oath), taking more physical exercise, reading inspirational books, going to health farms and sanitariums, accepting voluntary commitment to asylums -- we could increase the list ad infinitum.(p.31)

• Up to this point you would label him as a foolish chap ***having*** queer ideas of fun.(p.37)

• I remember ***having*** several more that night and plenty the next morning.(p.41)

• They had said that though I did raise a defense, it would one day give way before some trivial reason for ***having*** a drink.(p.42)

• We were ***having*** trouble with personal relationships, we couldn't control our emotional natures, we were a prey to misery and depression, we couldn't make a living, we had a feeling of uselessness, we were full of fear, we were unhappy, we couldn't seem to be of real help to other people – was not a basic solution of these bedevilments more important than whether we should see newsreels of lunar flight?(p.52)

• ***Having*** made our personal inventory, what shall we do about it?(p.72)

• ***Having*** persevered with the rest of the program, they wondered why they fell.(p.73)

• He subsequently denied ***having*** received the money and used the incident as a basis for discrediting the man.(p.80)

• Perhaps he is ***having*** a secret and exciting affair with "the girl who understands."(p.81)

• Each might pray about it, ***having*** the other one's happiness uppermost in mind.(p.82)

• Being still inexperienced and ***having*** just made conscious contact with God, it is not probable that we are going to be inspired at all times.(p.87)

• ***Having*** had the experience yourself, you can give him much practical advice.(p.96)

• Each is interested in ***having*** his or her wishes respected.(p.122)

• ***Having*** been neglected and misused in the past, they think father owes them more than they are getting.(p.126)

• ***Having*** a better time."(p.151)

• All have now passed away from natural causes, ***having*** maintained complete sobriety.(p.169)

• Before my drinking had cut me down completely, I achieved a considerable measure of success, ***having*** been a City Councilman for five years and a financial director of Kenmore, a suburb later taken into the city itself.(p.182)

• Every time I'd start thinking about drinking, I would think of the long, dry years ahead without ***having*** a drink; but this idea of twenty-four hours, that it was up to me from then on, was a lot of help.(p.188)

• I remember telling them too that it was going to be awfully tough, because I did some other things, smoked cigarettes and played penny ante poker, sometimes bet on the horse races and they said, "Don't you think you're ***having*** more trouble with this drinking than with anything else at the present time?(p.190)

• Bill was very, very grateful that he had been released from this terrible thing and he had given God the credit for ***having*** done it, and he's so grateful about it he wants to tell other people about it.(p.191)

• I went into the high school grades, but ***having*** missed all the intermediate grades, I didn't get along too well, so I developed the habit of going back to school just long enough for the football season and then quitting.(p.193)

• We boys drove out in somebody's car and went to the bar on the way do the dining room and I, in an effort to impress the other boys that I was city-bred, ***having*** lived in Scranton and Cleveland, asked them if they didn't want a drink.(p.194)

• I felt ***having*** gotten married, I was an adult and one of the first things I did was to buy two cases of whiskey with no idea of drinking it.(p.196)

• I was a very young married man, ***having*** his whiskey in the cupboard over the sink, and when I helped my wife with the dishes at night I would take a cup of tea and spike it with whiskey.(p.196)

• I didn't like ***having*** to come home at a certain time; I didn't like this, I didn't like that, and I think the poor girl actually divorced me to help me stop drinking!(p.199)

• Everything in the world a man could possibly want, and I was driving from Akron to Cleveland, ***having*** just been to the bank and discovered that I had approximately $5,000.(p.200)

• An offer of appreciation for not ***having*** had a drink for those few months and then and there, without anybody promising me anything or threatening me, I made a solemn vow that never so long as I lived would I take another drink.(p.200)

• So ***having*** licked it, there was no reason why I shouldn't have a drink, and I stopped in before I got home and had one.(p.203)

• Then I got into the habit of ***having*** beers, and decided that a drink of whiskey was not any worse; so I would get the one drink of whiskey but, on second thought, I decided that as long as I was only going to have one, I might as well make it a double-header.(p.203)

• In other words, I was always safe from the discipline of my father, and ***having*** developed along that line, I had considerable difficulty in school.(p.210)

• I was always interested in mechanics and after ***having*** about twenty miscellaneous jobs, lasting from one day to two weeks, I obtained a job as a toolmaker apprentice.(p.211)

• When I entered a sanitarium for prolonged and intensive psychiatric treatment, I was convinced that I was ***having*** a serious mental breakdown.(p.226)

• ***Having*** regard for the law of the land, I resigned myself to the will of the national legislators and quit drinking altogether, not because I had found it harmful, but because I couldn't get what I was accustomed to drink.(p.232)

• After the oil job blew up, I went back to Baltimore and mother, my first wife ***having*** said a permanent "Goodbye."(p.243)

• I'd hear them on the phone ***having*** prayer meetings and so forth, that sort of talk over the phone, and it completely burnt me up.(p.265)

• ***Having*** no one else to turn to, I was willing to give Him a chance, although with considerable doubt.(p.280)

• Sometimes during that year I rebelled inwardly at what seemed like lost time, and at ***having*** to be a burden to these good people whose means were limited.(p.281)

• In the next two or three days the balance of this handful of men contacted me, encouraged me, and told me how they were trying to live this program of recovery and the fun they were ***having*** doing it.(p.291)

• We were ***having*** card parties with limburger and beer quite regularly.(p.297)

• The parties waxed more liquid and hilarious as time went on, and eventually I discovered that a little shot of liquor now and then between beers had the tendency to put me in a whacky mood much quicker than ***having*** to down several quarts of beer to obtain the same effect.(p.298)

• I really worked for several weeks, and ***having*** had a fairly wide acquaintance with the dealer trade, it was not difficult for me to line up enough of them to give me a very substantial volume of business with a minimum of effort.(p.300)

• My broken home and broken heart fanned my smoldering self-pity into a fair-sized bonfire and this kept me well supplied with reasons for ***having*** another drink, and then another.(p.305)

• He had tried everything from ***having*** me attend daily mass at six a.m. to performing the most menial labor for his charity patients.(p.306)

• Next, I was sent to Arizona, where my drinking picked up some more, and I started ***having*** blackouts, and I was thrown in jail for speeding and drunken driving.(p.318)

• Was I ***having*** a nervous collapse?(p.319)

• After ***having*** a few drinks, I went to a meeting -- and the people there were not all old men and definitely not skid-row types!(p.319)

• As we walked back through the hall, I, for the first time in my life, said to another human being, "I'm ***having*** trouble with my drinking, too."(p.321)

• Through studied sneaky-drinking, I'd become a senior citizen without ***having*** lost a day's work because of booze.(p.327)

• I would take a gulp, then warn the jug not to try to entice, lure, or seduce me into ***having*** more than one "medicinal" jolt.(p.332)

• All I can remember about the Roaring Twenties is that I drank a great deal, thought I was ***having*** a grand time, managed to get to Europe for a few weeks, was very proud of the dozens of speak-easy cards entitling me to an entree in the better joints between Cleveland and New York, took on a wife, and built a home in a fashionable suburb of Cleveland.(p.358)

• By hook or crook I usually managed to sober up before I reached home, but always "terribly tired" from a "hard day's work," and just ***having*** to have one or two before dinner.(p.361)

• I was raised like the majority of American boys, coming from a family of modest circumstances, attending public schools, ***having*** the social life of a small midwestern town, with part-time work and some athletics.(p.373)

• I achieved recognized and national standing in my profession, as well as becoming a director in many important institutions ***having*** to do with the civic life of a large city.(p.374)

• Never ***having*** enough, always craving more, the obsession for alcohol gradually dominated all my activities, particularly while travelling.(p.375)

• Whenever we went out she appeared to go out of her way to keep me from ***having*** more than one drink.(p.376)

• She of course didn't realize how cunning an alcoholic can be and the lengths to which he will go in finding ways to satisfy the compulsion for more and more drinks after ***having*** had the first one.(p.377)

• I put my poor mother and father through agonies but, finally, I couldn't stand living with them and ***having*** them watch everything I did.(p.386)

• I couldn't walk, ***having*** it in a cast, and the doctor left the cast on three weeks longer than was necessary because he never found me sober enough to take it off.(p.390)

• ***Having*** heard Bill speak, she was instantly sold.(p.412)

• Through going to meetings and listening, and occasionally speaking, through doing Twelve Step work, whereby in helping others you are both the teacher and the student, by making many wonderful A.A. friends, I have been taught all the things in life that are worth ***having***.(p.416)

• I remembered ***having*** had a little drink of whiskey with a can of warm beer as a chaser.(p.422)

• Well, I'm willing, if it will curb this awful desire to drink, this fear of not ***having*** a drink, this feeling of always being alone, scared, deserted, sick.(p.430)

• They were ***having*** a large A.A. meeting in the prison auditorium.(p.460)

• ***Having*** passed over the border line, the next five years were filled with fear, failure and frustration.(p.465)

• There were doctors and psychiatrists there who tried to help me, but at that point I wasn't ***having*** help from anyone.(p.468)

• The idea behind it is that, ***having*** taken the treatment, your system is so "conditioned" that the mere sight or smell or taste of alcohol produces a violent reaction, and you become ill.(p.469)

• You may wonder why, since I was ***having*** all this trouble, and was ***having*** to seek the assistance of others, A.A. hadn't come into the picture.(p.469)

• On one occasion when I was serving time in my favorite drying-out place while I was ***having*** a session with the psychiatrist, she left my case history on her desk when she was called away from the room.(p.470)

• Dad, due to ***having*** spent most of his time in a small Virginia town, didn't have any too much money, and

the money he had saved and the property he had acquired were in Washington.(p.486)
• Being an alcoholic, slick, and *having* some good sense left, I survived the investigation.(p.490)
• I clung to the outfit for the balance of my time, and finally I was released, after *having* spent twenty years and nine months behind bars.(p.510)
• I had an advantage in *having* an idea of what A.A. was about before coming out on the street.(p.510)
• Then I was sent out to India and from then on drinking just increased and increased, and I started *having* two or three day spells instead of just the ordinary concentrated one day.(p.519)
• In part, it was a feeling of intense shame at *having* to leave the Army during the war, but mostly it was resentment that this kind of thing should happen to me for, strange as it may seem, up to then I still thought I could control drinking.(p.521)
• *Having* made that bargain, I immediately began to feel I'd been trapped into it and I went out and had some drinks – four glasses of gin, I remember.(p.523)
• What struck me most was that they all seemed to be quite pleased with *having* made a job of it and *having* stopped drinking.(p.524)
• I remember the day when I decided to drink myself to death quietly, without bothering anyone, because I was tired of *having* been a dependable, trustworthy person for about thirty-nine years without *having* received what I thought was a proper reward for my virtue.(p.531)
• And *having* sung that phrase, I'd chuckle with amusement, turning into irony turning into self-contempt turning into self-pity, at the sad fate of Bob, that wonderful, poor little motherless boy who was so smart in school and who grew up to accept responsibility so early and so fast and who staggered under his burdens without a whimper until the time came when he thought he was too good for this world and so he ought to be out of it.(p.532)
• Only, *having* found them, I threw them away, and ordered another extra dry martini.(p.533)
• I'd visit one bar after another, *having* one martini in each, and in each hoping to find someone interesting to talk to.(p.536)
• Still another friend and temporary host received me at four in the morning from the charge of a policeman who had found me "going to bed" in a garage far from the last place I could remember *having* been, a fashionable bar and restaurant in the theatrical district of New York, to which I had repaired after my date for that evening, a charming lady of the theatre who had refused my company for obvious reasons.(p.538)
• I fled, finally, after *having* been fired from my job by a boss who wept a little (since I had worked hard) as he gave notice for me to clear out.(p.539)
• The A.A. members who sponsored me told me in the beginning that I would not only find a way to live without *having* a drink, but that I would find a way to live without wanting to drink, if I would do these simple things.(p.550)
• By twenty-nine, I was *having* trouble coping with life because of my drinking.(p.555)
• 5. – Each Alcoholics Anonymous group ought to be a spiritual entity *having* but one primary purpose -- that of carrying its message to the alcoholic who still suffers.(p.565)
• If we do not do so, we shall stand convicted of emotional sterility and of *having* lost the faith that moves mountains, without which medicine can do little."(p.571)
• Historians may one day recognize Alcoholics Anonymous to have been a great venture in social pioneering which forged a new instrument for social action; a new therapy based on the kinship of common suffering; one *having* a vast potential for the myriad other ills of mankind."(p.573)

havoc
• Sometimes these excuses have a certain plausibility, but none of them really makes sense in the light of the *havoc* an alcoholic's drinking bout creates.(p.23)

Hawaii
• A.A. has flourishing communities in the British Isles, the Scandinavian countries, South Africa, South America, Mexico, Alaska, Australia and *Hawaii*.(p.xv)
• The place – *Hawaii*.(p.422)
• And when this six month school was over I applied for duty in *Hawaii* and pulled it.(p.426)

Hawaiian
• Pearl Harbor was a breeze of nine months, a gay *Hawaiian* paradise, drinking under the palms, listening to the surf beat on the shore, a bottle of whiskey near at hand.(p.426)
• One night I was sitting in the lab alone with a fifth and a case of beer listening to dreamy *Hawaiian* music on the radio.(p.427)

hawk
• Even in the present century, American newspapers were afraid to print an account of the Wright brothers' first successful flight at Kitty *Hawk*.(p.51)
• THE NEWS *HAWK*(p.251)

hay
• I come to on a pile of *hay* in a barn.(p.502)

haywire
• Something went *haywire* and I got to depend on it so I could do nothing without it.(p.386)
• But when things became crucial, everything started going *haywire* and I started going *haywire* with them.(p.486)
• Something should have told me then that things were *haywire*.(p.487)

hazard
• Never forget that resentment is a deadly *hazard* to an alcoholic.(p.117)

haze
• A *haze* filled the room.(p.498)

hazy
• If these thoughts occur, they are *hazy* and readily supplanted with the old threadbare idea that this time we shall handle ourselves like other people.(p.24)
• My eyes opened onto a *hazy* world.(p.422)
• The rest of that week is pretty *hazy*.(p.466)

head
• My talent for leadership, I imagined, would place me at the *head* of vast enterprises which I would manage with the utmost assurance.(p.1)
• As the whisky rose to my *head* I told myself I would manage better next time, but I might as well get good and drunk then.(p.6)
• I wondered whether I dared hide a full bottle of gin near the *head* of our bed.(p.8)
• Finally he shook his *head* saying, "Something has happened to you I don't understand.(p.14)
• He uses his gifts to build up a bright outlook for his family and himself, and then pulls the structure down on his *head* by a senseless series of sprees.(p.21)
• They sound like the philosophy of the man who, having a headache, beats himself on the *head* with a hammer so that he can't feel the ache.(p.23)
• He tries every known means to get the jay-walking idea out of his *head*.(p.38)
• He had commenced our way of life, had secured a position, and was getting his *head* above water.(p.79)
• Should they accept and practice spiritual principles, there is a much better chance that the *head* of the family will recover.(p.97)
• An alcoholic of this temperament may be quick to use this chapter as a club over your *head*.(p.108)
• But the *head* of the house has spent years in pulling down the structures of business, romance, friendship, health -- these things are now ruined or damaged.(p.123)
• The *head* of the house ought to remember that he is mainly to blame for what befell his home.(p.127)
• Though the family does not fully agree with dad's spiritual activities, they should let him have his *head*.(p.129)
• They can hardly fail to approve these simple principles, though the *head* of the house still fails somewhat in practicing them.(p.130)
• Liquor incapacitated father for so many years that mother became *head* of the house.(p.130)
• Of an evening, you can go on a mild bender, get up in the morning, shake your *head* and go to business.(p.139)
• He will appreciate knowing you are not bothering your *head* about him, that you are not suspicious nor are you trying to run his life so he will be shielded from temptation to drink.(p.146)
• One day they called up the *head* nurse of a local hospital.(p.156)
• Goes off his *head* completely when he's drinking.(p.156)
• He tossed off half of his martini; I tossed off half of mine and it nearly blew the top of my *head* off.(p.195)
• When I had been in the hospital ten days, Sister Ignatia, who has played such a part in the development of A.A. in this area, stuck her *head* in the door one morning and announced, looking at me quizzically, that they might be able to make something human out of my face after all.(p.205)
• He waited until I was completely sober and the day before I was to *head* back for Chicago, he told me of a small group of men in Akron who apparently had the same problem that I had but were doing something about it.(p.289)
• One morning when I was feeling really bad, I was put on K.P. and the *head* cook wanted me to go out and scrub the garbage cans.(p.317)
• I could never be sure I'd have a clear *head* and hands that were willing to do some work.(p.326)
• I was aware of symptoms of impending dependence, and I told myself I had gotten out of the rat race just in time to *head* off any booze problem.(p.327)
• "Complete abandon"; "Half measures availed us nothing"; "Thoroughly follow our path"; "Completely give oneself to this simple program" – rang in my swelled *head*.(p.349)
• And then I scratched my *head* and said to myself, "What a fantastic thing for a man to say, that I cured his wife.(p.350)
• As I grow in A.A., I realize that a person with as much self-will as I had, as hard a *head* and as diseased an ego, had to try everything that I could think of, butting my *head* against every stone wall before I was ready to come in.(p.384)
• It took me three psychoanalysts and several years in A.A. to really get this through my *head*.(p.401)
• My mother's heartbreak, or the unpleasant publicity I had caused did not bother my pretty *head*.(p.401)
• Instead it was like a tap on the *head* with a small mallet.(p.402)
• I, who did not know how to give love, was *head* over heels "in love."(p.403)
• I returned the book to my analyst and shook my *head*.(p.412)
• I found myself nodding my *head*.(p.413)
• Two of them leaped from the table and crashed into my *head*.(p.427)
• Or, "My physical plant had got a little run down and the stuff rushed right to my *head*."(p.433)
• I was now *head* of a publishing venture in which nearly a million dollars had been invested.(p.435)
• After going to school all day, working in the family drugstore all evening, and then studying until one or two in the morning, I would not be able to sleep soundly, with everything I had been studying going round in my *head*.(p.440)
• It never entered my *head* that I would have been pushing up the daisies if he had decided not to come.(p.479)
• I, and the books of my division, have been transferred to the *head* office.(p.500)
• It rings in my *head*; I can't get rid of it.(p.504)
• I went out and drank some German wine and it went to my *head*.(p.517)
• There was the love affair which was ridiculous -- "imagine that midget being able to fall in love!" -- and my *head* knew it while my heart pumped real, genuine anguish, for it hurt like hell, and since it was first love, things have never been quite the same.(p.534)
• Need I add that such was the case because I had no money to provide a roof over my *head*?(p.538)

headache
• They sound like the philosophy of the man who, having a *headache*, beats himself on the head with a hammer so that he can't feel the ache.(p.23)
• Never once in my life have I had a *headache*, which fact leads me to believe that I was an alcoholic almost from the start.(p.172)

headaches
• Before long I had a definite taste for hard liquor, knew nausea and *headaches* I had never known before, but as in the old days, I suffered them out.(p.233)
• I had bad nervous *headaches*, particularly at the base of my neck.(p.277)
• So I sat down with me and went over the facts behind the convulsions: personality changes, daily *headaches*, sense of impending doom, sense of impending insanity.(p.444)

headed
• We are *headed* for trouble if we do, for alcohol is a subtle foe.(p.85)
• For a decade, I'd *headed* up a forty-publicist department.(p.328)
• It wasn't how far I had gone, but where I was *headed*.(p.379)
• We *headed* out of town walking – no money, cold and hungry.(p.424)
• I *headed* home for the most wonderful experience of all time -- meeting my "new" parents -- mom and dad looked different than I had pictured them.(p.428)
• All found themselves *headed* for the same destruction, and it seemed they could to nothing whatever to stop it.(p.455)
• When I got out of there, I lasted about fifteen minutes at home, before I *headed* for the drugstore and more pills, and then the bar.(p.479)
• I am on a train *headed* for a city.(p.505)

headings
• "Bill's Story," "Doctor Bob's Nightmare," and one

other personal history from the first edition were retained intact; three were edited and one of these was retitled; new versions of two stories were written with new titles; thirty completely new stories were added; and the story section was divided into three parts, under the same ***headings*** that are used now.(p.xi)

headlong
• We think it dangerous if he rushes ***headlong*** at his economic problem.(p.126)

headmaster
• He reported to the ***Headmaster*** and the ***Headmaster*** was going to expel me.(p.517)

headquarters
• Fond of singing, I joined a German singing society which had good club ***headquarters***.(p.231)
• Tom Sharkey's brawling bar on 14th Street and the famous wine-room at the back were ***headquarters*** for me.(p.251)
• In those days, I was doing a staff appointment in the army ***headquarters*** in New Delhi.(p.343)
• This ***headquarters*** will give the location of the nearest family group and will if you wish, correspond with you about your special problems.(p.575)

heads
• Our loyalty and the desire that our husbands hold up their ***heads*** and be like other men have begotten all sorts of predicaments.(p.105)
• Doctors may shake their ***heads*** and advise you to have him committed.(p.110)
• We have come to believe He would like us to keep our ***heads*** in the clouds with Him, but that our feet ought to be firmly planted on earth.(p.130)
• I pointed out that I had had nothing to drink whatever for three years, and this in the face of difficulties that would have made nine out of ten men drink their ***heads*** off.(p.138)
• But I can remember, in my teens, that there were a few characters who caused the village ***heads*** to nod pityingly and sometimes in anger as they paused to say, "That sot, Henri" and "Ce pauvre Jules," who drank too much.(p.230)

headstrong
• ***Headstrong*** and willful, I rushed from pleasure to pleasure, and found the returns diminishing to the vanishing point.(p.226)

headwaiters
• To wear expensive clothes, to have bartenders know what to serve me before I ordered, to be recognized by ***headwaiters*** and shown to the best table, to play gin rummy for high stakes with the insouciance of a riverboat gambler -- these were the enduring values in life, I thought.(p.556)

headway
• I made little ***headway*** in my first few meetings with her.(p.359)

heal
• PHYSICIAN, ***HEAL*** THYSELF!(p.345)

healed
• What ***healed*** those tissues, those tissues that I closed, what ***healed*** them?(p.351)

healer
• Psychiatrist and surgeon, he had lost his way until he realized that God, not he, was the Great ***Healer***.(p.345)

healing
• What is this but a miracle of ***healing***?(p.57)
• I hope I have been able to impart to you, the reader, at least a bit of what I know; the joy of living, the irresistible power of divine love and its ***healing*** strength, and the fact that we, as sentient beings, have the knowledge to choose between good and evil, and, choosing good, are made happy.(p.543)

health
• Convincing testimony must surely come from the medical men who have had experience with the sufferings of our members and have witnessed our return to ***health***.(p.xxiii)
• The curve of my declining moral and bodily ***health*** fell off like a ski-jump.(p.7)
• If a sufficiently strong reason -- ill ***health***, falling in love, change of environment, or the warning of a doctor -- becomes operative, this man can also stop or moderate, although he may find it difficult and troublesome and may even need medical attention.(p.21)
• Here are some of the methods we have tried: Drinking beer only, limiting the number of drinks, never drinking alone, never drinking in the morning, drinking only at home, never having it in the house, never drinking during business hours, drinking only at parties, switching from scotch to brandy, drinking only natural wines, agreeing to resign if ever drunk on the job, taking a trip, not taking a trip, swearing off forever (with and without a solemn oath), taking more physical exercise, reading inspirational books, going to ***health*** farms and sanitariums, accepting voluntary commitment to asylums -- we could increase the list ad infinitum.(p.31)
• There is every evidence that women regain their ***health*** as readily as men if they try our suggestions.(p.104)
• Most of us have entered the final stage with its commitment to ***health*** resorts, sanitariums, hospitals, and jails.(p.107)
• Say you do not want to be a wet blanket; that you only want him to take care of his ***health***.(p.112)
• But the head of the house has spent years in pulling down the structures of business, romance, friendship, ***health*** -- these things are now ruined or damaged.(p.123)
• Everybody knows that those in bad ***health***, and those who seldom play, do not laugh much.(p.132)
• Now about ***health***: A body badly burned by alcohol does not often recover overnight nor do twisted thinking and depression vanish in a twinkling.(p.133)
• We are convinced that a spiritual mode of living is a most powerful ***health*** restorative.(p.133)
• We, who have recovered from serious drinking, are miracles of mental ***health***.(p.133)
• But this does not mean that we disregard human ***health*** measures.(p.133)
• Do not hesitate to take your ***health*** problems to such persons.(p.133)
• In the chapter "Working With Others" you gathered an idea of how we approach and aid others to ***health***.(p.153)
• He got in touch with a prominent psychiatrist who had undertaken certain responsibilities for the mental ***health*** of the community.(p.163)
• About the time of the beer experiment I was thrown in with a crowd of people who attracted me because of their seeming poise, ***health***, and happiness.(p.178)
• I was self conscious and ill at ease most of the time, my ***health*** was at the breaking point, and I was thoroughly miserable.(p.178)
• My ***health*** is good and I have regained my self-respect and the respect of my colleagues.(p.180)
• Of course, as time went on, and I began to get my ***health*** back and began to be so I didn't have to hide from people all the time, it's just been wonderful.(p.192)
• My physical ***health*** was badly shaken, but I began to pick up.(p.220)
• Poor ***health*** and a complete lack of money necessitated my remaining with Dr. Bob and Anne for very close to a year.(p.280)
• My ***health*** was still uncertain.(p.282)
• It took five years of A.A. living, and a substantial improvement in my ***health***, before I could take a full-time office job where someone else was boss.(p.283)
• Then when we got back to the apartment, he was willing to wait two or three days until I got my ***health*** back to be paid off for the liquor and fare.(p.289)
• But I had my ***health*** back and besides, I reasoned, they were much worse than I would ever be.(p.289)
• I had a tough pull back to normal good ***health***.(p.310)
• Seldom had any of these lost either ***health***, business, family, or friends.(p.315)
• I stayed on in Florida for three weeks, enjoying our reunion, a new found ***health*** and a deeper love than I had ever experienced before.(p.364)
• After a few months there, I went to County Mental ***Health*** as an alcoholism worker.(p.462)
• I feel that I have been restored to ***health*** and sanity these past years not through my own efforts nor as a result of anything I may have done, but because I've come to believe -- to really believe -- that alone I can do nothing.(p.473)
• Ask for their ***health***, their prosperity, their happiness, and you will be free.(p.552)
• While there, I read the Big Book and the Grapevine and began the slow road back to ***health*** and sanity through the recovery program of A.A.(p.559)
• Regaining my ***health***, I became an avid jogger, sailor, and skier.(p.559)
• "The American Public ***Health*** Association presents a Lasker Group Award for 1951 to Alcoholics Anonymous in recognition of its unique and highly successful approach to that age-old public ***health*** and social problem, alcoholism . . .(p.573)
• This self-insurance has resulted in the restoration of physical, mental and spiritual ***health*** and self-respect to hundreds of men and women who would be hopelessly down and out without its unique but effective therapy."(p.574)

healthy
• They spoke with great freedom from embarrassment, which I could never do, and they seemed very much at ease on all occasions and appeared very ***healthy***.(p.178)
• I had never known him to be anything but a good ***healthy*** pagan with a propensity for getting into liquor jams and scrapes.(p.257)
• I was strong and ***healthy*** and quite athletic.(p.305)
• In the morning, because I was young and ***healthy***, my remorse was worse than my hangover.(p.404)
• Intake of alcohol changes one's personality -- even the ***healthy*** personality.(p.458)

healthy-looking
• When a big, ***healthy-looking*** young fellow stood up there and said, "I'm a success today if I don't drink today," I thought, "Man, I've got a thousand things to do today before I can brag about not taking a drink, for God's sake!"(p.447)

heap
• Then he had, in effect, been raised from the dead, suddenly taken from the scrap ***heap*** to a level of life better than the best he had ever known!(p.11)
• From the top of the ***heap*** in a few years he had skidded to becoming a shuffling customer, still entering the better barrooms but welcomed by neither mine host nor his patrons.(p.236)
• All of my family and loved ones, all of my friends, are nearer and dearer to me than ever before and I have literally dozens of new friends who say they cannot believe that a short eight years ago I was ready for the scrap ***heap***.(p.541)

heaps
• They piled on me ***heaps*** of evidence to the effect that an alcoholic mentality, such as I had exhibited in Washington, was a hopeless condition.(p.42)

hear
• We shall be interested to ***hear*** from those who are getting results from this book, particularly from those who have commenced work with other alcoholics.(p.xiv)
• I could almost ***hear*** the sound of the preacher's voice as I sat, on still Sundays, way over there on the hillside; there was that proffered temperance pledge I never signed; my grandfather's good natured contempt of some church folk and their doings; his insistence that the spheres really had their music; but his denial of the preacher's right to tell him how he must listen; his fearlessness as he spoke of these things just before he died; these recollections welled up from the past.(p.10)
• Now these are commonplace observations on drinkers which we ***hear*** all the time.(p.20)
• When we decide who is to ***hear*** our story, we waste no time.(p.75)
• Sometimes we ***hear*** an alcoholic say that the only thing he needs to do is to keep sober.(p.82)
• Why not at least afford him an opportunity to ***hear*** my story?(p.138)
• Many a distracted wife has visited this house to find loving and understanding companionship among women who knew her problem, to ***hear*** from the lips of their husbands what had happened to them, to be advised how her own wayward mate might be hospitalized and approached when next he stumbled.(p.160)
• Today I have Someone who will always ***hear*** me; I have a warm fellowship among men who understand my problems; I have tasks to do and am glad to do them, to see others who are alcoholics and to help them in any way I can to become sober men.(p.260)
• I didn't see him for a year, or even ***hear*** from him.(p.262)
• I'd ***hear*** them on the phone having prayer meetings and so forth, that sort of talk over the phone, and it completely burnt me up.(p.265)
• I think it's awfully hard on people, especially if they're new people, to ***hear*** these long drawn out talks.(p.273)
• First, we all ***hear*** at A.A. meetings about those who have lost everything, those who have been in jail, those who have been in prison, those who have lost their families, those who have lost their income.(p.345)
• You'll read and ***hear*** a great deal about the spiritual part of our program.(p.366)
• When I ***hear*** the more rugged stories of alcoholics who became sicker than I did with this affliction, I humbly thank God for showing me "the handwriting on the wall."(p.367)
• I could just ***hear*** their sweet, pious talk.(p.412)
• The pep pills affected my hearing at times: I couldn't listen fast enough to ***hear*** what I was saying.(p.442)

• Most of us did not stay out of prison long enough to run the alcoholic gamut -- to develop the ongoing kind of alcoholism or alcoholic drinking you ***hear*** about in A.A. talks.(p.458)
• To this day I can't ***hear*** that song without remembering that awful Christmas.(p.468)
• I ***hear*** about A.A., but think it religion.(p.475)
• I ***hear*** men say, "One day not drink.(p.476)
• Listen, not just ***hear*** noise.(p.477)
• I once ***hear*** people say only Indians crazy when drunk.(p.477)
• It was a thorn in my side, because I knew it was the truth, and I hated to ***hear*** the truth, especially about myself.(p.513)
• When I awoke in the middle of the night with shakes and sweats and fears, I would ***hear*** my wife weeping quietly in bed beside me.(p.558)

heard

• We have ***heard*** of few instances where people, who showed definite signs of alcoholism, were able to stop for a long period because of an overpowering desire to do so.(p.32)
• We ***heard*** no more of Fred for a while.(p.40)
• As to two of you men, whose stories I have ***heard***, there is no doubt in my mind that you were 100% hopeless, apart from divine help.(p.43)
• He came through an acquaintance who had ***heard*** the good news.(p.158)
• Impressed by those who visited him at the hospital, he capitulated entirely when, later, in an upper room of this house, he ***heard*** the story of some man whose experience closely tallied with his own.(p.160)
• So, after hearing some more of my story, he turned around and said to Doc -- I don't think he knew I ***heard*** him, but I did -- he said, "Well, I believe he's worth saving and working on."(p.185)
• I'm so grateful for both the program and the people in it that I still want to go, and then probably the most wonderful thing that I learned from the program -- I've seen this in the 'A.A. Grapevine' a lot of times, and I've had people say it to me personally, and I've ***heard*** people get up in meetings and make the same statement: The statement is, "I came into A.A. solely for the purpose of sobriety, but it has been through A.A. that I have found God."(p.192)
• I didn't even know what a martini looked like, but I had ***heard*** a man down the bar order one.(p.194)
• That was skeptically received by me when I first ***heard*** it, but after some twenty-eight or thirty fellows had come to see me, and pretty nearly all of them had said the same thing, I began to believe it.(p.219)
• From far away, as if in a delirium, I ***heard*** my own voice -- calling someone "Dorothy," talking of dress shops, of jobs . . . the words came clearer . . . this sound of my own voice frightened me as it came closer . . . and suddenly, there I was, talking of I knew not what, to someone I'd never seen before this very moment.(p.222)
• I had never ***heard*** of the remedy expressed in just this language.(p.236)
• We ***heard*** by wireless on the 5th that the Armistice would be signed the next day (this was a premature report) so I had a couple of cognacs to celebrate; then I hopped a truck and went AWOL.(p.242)
• As I look back on the events of two months, I can clearly see that I had been circling around, half-afraid of encountering the remedy for my situation, half wanting it, deferring fulfillment of my promise to get in touch with the doctor I had ***heard*** about.(p.258)
• I ***heard*** my son-in-law coming upstairs, and I asked him where dad was.(p.263)
• I ***heard*** for the first time an expression which I was to grow to loathe: "There is nothing organically wrong."(p.276)
• Just at this time my wife ***heard*** of a doctor in another city who had been very successful with drunks.(p.301)
• But somehow my good doctor ***heard*** of this book and also he learned a little about the people responsible for its publication.(p.307)
• I ***heard*** voices when no one was around, and I saw things that weren't there.(p.319)
• I sat and listened and ***heard*** the first speaker say, "I'm an alcoholic."(p.319)
• I had worked so long in a profession where fakery, deceit, and untruths are tools of trade that I instantly recognized honesty when I ***heard*** it, from the mouths of A.A. members.(p.334)
• I ***heard*** one very ill woman say that she didn't believe in the surrender part of the A.A. program.(p.340)
• Many times have I ***heard*** the above expressions since I have been in A.A., and many times I have had to reply "Definitely I am an alcoholic, and while it may be hard for you to believe, it is not hard for me, for I have learned many things about alcohol and myself that would, perhaps, be difficult for you to understand."(p.356)
• I had read and ***heard*** a little about A.A. and so, groping for the phone book, I found the A.A. number and with hope in my heart eagerly telephoned.(p.363)
• I ***heard*** a lovely voice, and a sympathetic ear listened to my plea.(p.363)
• Sure enough in a couple of hours two men were at my door and for the first time I ***heard*** some facts about liquor and my problem that sounded sensible to me.(p.363)
• It was the first she had ***heard*** or read about it and she said she had considered sending it to me or trying to have someone in Pittsburgh send it to me so I wouldn't know where it came from.(p.366)
• My sister-in-law took me to a place she had ***heard*** about that helps women like me.(p.371)
• However, after I ***heard*** a few stories of jails, sanitariums, broken homes and skid row, I wondered if I really was an alcoholic.(p.378)
• Could I be an alcoholic without some of the hair-raising experiences I had ***heard*** of in meetings?(p.379)
• It's the last thing I ever ***heard*** him say, and I think there are some of us who, at times, try to read extra messages and complexities into the Steps.(p.395)
• A few times at meetings, I have ***heard*** this statement: "Members of A.A. have paid the highest initiation fee of any club members in the world."(p.396)
• Where have we ***heard*** this before?)(p.398)
• Having ***heard*** Bill speak, she was instantly sold.(p.412)
• We ***heard*** some yells outside.(p.424)
• I'd ***heard*** a lot about A.A. and met a great many A.A.'s during that year at home, but I hadn't thought of it for myself.(p.429)
• After talking with him for a time I ***heard*** myself saying, "Doc, I think I'm an alcoholic."(p.436)
• However, I've ***heard*** of an organization called Alcoholics Anonymous that has had some success with people like you.(p.436)
• Although we enjoyed the laughter in the early days, I ***heard*** a lot of things that I thought were stupid.(p.447)
• I suddenly remembered one of my first A.A. meetings, where I ***heard***, "If you are an alcoholic and if you continue to drink, the end is death or insanity."(p.461)
• Three weeks ago, my phone rang, and a voice I hadn't ***heard*** in over twenty-three years spoke.(p.462)
• Economic conditions had a great deal to do with it, because I've often ***heard*** my father say that his mother would take one of the old time flour sacks and cut a hole through the bottom and two corners of it and there you'd have a gown.(p.486)
• When I had ***heard*** about it, it meant nothing but just two letters to me, but some friends of mine in the institution were very active in the program and really believed in it.(p.509)
• I took the advice of people I had ***heard*** at meetings, the people in the group.(p.516)
• I've ***heard*** it said many times in A.A., "There is just one good drunk in every alcoholic's life, and that's the one that brings us into A.A.," and I believe it.(p.549)

hearing

• Upon ***hearing*** this, our friend was somewhat relieved, for he reflected that after all, he was a good church member.(p.27)
• We never gave the spiritual side of life a fair ***hearing***.(p.50)
• So, after ***hearing*** some more of my story, he turned around and said to Doc -- I don't think he knew I heard him, but I did -- he said, "Well, I believe he's worth saving and working on."(p.185)
• On ***hearing*** that, these people induced me to make the move immediately and join them as a senior partner, which I did.(p.220)
• But after ***hearing*** their stories, I knew that I was, and I admitted it.(p.320)
• A "spiritual experience" to me meant attending meetings, seeing a group of people, all there for the purpose of helping each other; ***hearing*** the Twelve Steps and the Twelve Traditions read at a meeting, and ***hearing*** the Lord's Prayer, which in an A.A. meeting has such great meaning -- "Thy will be done, not mine."(p.381)
• The pep pills affected my ***hearing*** at times: I couldn't listen fast enough to hear what I was saying.(p.442)
• The first time I remember seeing or ***hearing*** of A.A. was twenty years ago.(p.460)
• After ***hearing*** the first speaker I could tell myself that my own lot was rather mild.(p.509)
• I had a rough lot, but I don't worry about that, after ***hearing*** the stories of many others.(p.511)

hears

• My wife ***hears*** my voice and knows I have found the answer to life.(p.505)

hearse

• "Well," I said to dad, when the A.A. people kept coming with these lovely cars and looked so nice, "I suppose the neighbors say, 'Now those old fools must have up and died, but where's the ***hearse***?'"(p.269)

heart

• My weary and despairing wife was informed that it would all end with ***heart*** failure during delirium tremens, or I would develop a wet brain, perhaps within a year.(p.7)
• But bless his ***heart***, let him rant!(p.9)
• Here was something at work in a human ***heart*** which had done the impossible.(p.11)
• His change of ***heart*** was dramatic, convincing, and moving.(p.55)
• He wants to enjoy a certain reputation, but knows in his ***heart*** he doesn't deserve it.(p.73)
• We thank God from the bottom of our ***heart*** that we know Him better.(p.75)
• Do not set your ***heart*** on reforming your husband.(p.111)
• Though you are providing him with the best possible medical attention, he should understand that he must undergo a change of ***heart***.(p.143)
• Shortly after I came to this conclusion, I was importuned by another well-known patent law firm to help them out on some trial work because their trial man had had a ***heart*** attack and had been forbidden to go into the courtroom.(p.220)
• That is the way Jackie found me, lying on a cot in my skivvies, with hot and cold sweats, pounding ***heart*** and that awful itchy scratchiness all over.(p.238)
• He knew too well that didn't mean a thing, just as I knew in my ***heart*** that it would be only a question of time -- a few days, a week, or even a month, it was inevitable -- till I would be off on another bender.(p.257)
• But right then the hope died that had been in my ***heart*** when we read about John D.(p.266)
• My broken home and broken ***heart*** fanned my smoldering self-pity into a fair-sized bonfire and this kept me well supplied with reasons for having another drink, and then another.(p.305)
• There is no more "aloneness," with that awful ache, so deep in the ***heart*** of every alcoholic that nothing, before, could ever reach it.(p.312)
• (My addiction bloomed within a small apartment I shared with my wife, a ***heart*** patient.)(p.329)
• I foresaw another ***heart*** attack.(p.333)
• Deep in my ***heart*** was the feeling that maybe I could get some help here.(p.346)
• With new hope in my ***heart*** and new resolutions I set off for Vermont.(p.360)
• And deep in my ***heart*** I really meant what I said because I loved her more than anything else in the world, yes -- even more than liquor.(p.362)
• I had read and heard a little about A.A. and so, groping for the phone book, I found the A.A. number and with hope in my ***heart*** eagerly telephoned.(p.363)
• I only know that it does -- if you desire it with your whole ***heart*** and without reservation.(p.384)
• So it drove me deeper into the psychosis or neurosis that I had, and that I hated deep down in my ***heart***.(p.388)
• I wanted to try A.A. with my whole ***heart*** and soul.(p.393)
• My Quaker mother-in-law, bless her ***heart***, used to set the Christmas pudding ablaze with lumps of sugar dipped in rubbing alcohol.(p.402)
• Even then I knew in my ***heart*** that I was unfit for the very things I wanted most, a happy marriage, security, a home and love.(p.403)
• While I was at Pensacola my dad became dangerously ill and almost died of pneumonia plus a ***heart*** attack.(p.426)
• When he speak from ***heart***, big men cry.(p.476)
• Nevertheless, we continued to work together and I continued to drink, but I guess, deep down within her ***heart*** as well as within mine, we both knew I couldn't stop drinking.(p.490)
• But after I passed through the gates I took a change of ***heart*** and mind.(p.510)
• She had been warned numerous times, not only by her family but by my own mother, that I was a hopeless drunk, that there wasn't anything anybody could do with me, that I'd never stop, and that eventually I'd break her ***heart***.(p.513)
• "Pity me the ***heart*** that is slow to learn What the quick mind sees at every turn."(p.534)
• There was the love affair which was ridiculous -- "imagine that midget being able to fall in love!" -- and my head knew it while my ***heart*** pumped real, genu-

ine anguish, for it hurt like hell, and since it was first love, things have never been quite the same.(p.534)

heartache

- It quiets the imperious urge, when to yield would mean *heartache*.(p.70)
- I had quite a *heartache* about her then because she wasn't the type of girl that my mother wanted me to marry.(p.485)

heartaches

- I have had my share of problems, *heartaches* and disappointments, because that is life, but also I have known a great deal of joy, and a peace that is the handmaiden of an inner freedom, I have a wealth of friends and, with my A.A. friends, an unusual quality of fellowship.(p.312)
- It was the first of many such experiences that became the only cause of harsh words, tears and *heartaches* in an otherwise truly beautiful marriage.(p.361)

heartbreak

- We know these suggestions are sometimes difficult to follow, but you will save many a *heartbreak* if you can succeed in observing them.(p.111)
- My mother's *heartbreak*, or the unpleasant publicity I had caused did not bother my pretty head.(p.401)

heartbreaking

- People like you are too *heartbreaking*.(p.43)
- How *heartbreaking* was this discovery; how cruel to be told they understood our men as we did not!(p.106)
- It was so baffling, so *heartbreaking*.(p.107)
- There was an insistent yearning to enjoy life as we once did and a *heartbreaking* obsession that some new miracle of control would enable us to do it.(p.151)

heartening

- There were many failures, but there was an occasional *heartening* success.(p.xvii)

heartily

- And they both laughed very *heartily*, and said, "That's better than you've been doing, isn't it?"(p.187)

heartlessness

- And just as we were being convinced of their *heartlessness*, they would surprise us with fresh resolves and new attentions.(p.107)

hearts

- But in their *hearts* they really do not know why they do it.(p.23)
- The central fact of our lives today is the absolute certainty that our Creator has entered into our *hearts* and lives in a way which is indeed miraculous.(p.25)
- *Hearts* are broken.(p.82)
- Being wrecked in the same vessel, being restored and united under one God, with *hearts* and minds attuned to the welfare of others, the things which matter so much to some people no longer signify much to them.(p.161)
- Yet we all had one really sincere purpose in our *hearts* and that was not to drink.(p.246)
- But the saddest, and thus the most consoling, drifted through from the country-music station – stories of broken *hearts*, wasted lives, lost loves, sung plaintively.(p.332)
- A few stood by me, at least in their *hearts*, throughout the whole of my drinking career.(p.404)
- They had color in their faces, sparkle in their eyes and love in their *hearts*.(p.428)
- "I've got to stop if I want to live," I told myself, and if I don't want to break my parents' *hearts* and maybe jeopardize their own carefully built up and hard-fought-for sobriety.(p.429)
- If you give us a try, you will see that we are really human beings, and we will welcome you with open arms and *hearts*.(p.529)

heartsickness

- *Heartsickness*, shame, and fear, fear bordering on panic, and no complete escape any longer except in oblivion.(p.306)

heat

- It didn't say I had to finally live on skid row and drink bay rum, canned *heat* or lemon extract.(p.379)

heated

- Next time you and he have a *heated* discussion, no matter what the subject, it should be the privilege of either to smile and say, "This is getting serious.(p.118)
- These family talks will be constructive if they can be carried on without *heated* argument, self-pity, self-justification or resentful criticism.(p.127)

heating

- There was no central *heating*, and this was the dead of winter.(p.415)

heave-ho

- Much later I discovered the elders held many prayer meetings hoping to find a way to give me the *heave-ho*, but at the same time stay tolerant and spiritual.(p.247)

heaven

- We have found much of *heaven* and we have been rocketed into a fourth dimension of existence of which we had not even dreamed.(p.25)
- *Heaven* knows, we have tried hard enough and long enough to drink like other people!(p.31)
- There was a bar, and what I tasted spelled sheer *heaven*.(p.328)
- But we have a baby who, if you'll pardon a little post-alcoholic sentimentality, is right out of *Heaven*.(p.438)
- We lived just a few doors from the First Baptist Church and when they had funerals I remember very often asking my mother whether the person was good or bad and whether they were going to *heaven* or hell.(p.483)

heavenly

- Your *Heavenly* Father will never let you down!(p.181)

heavens

- I could go for such conceptions as Creative Intelligence, Universal Mind or Spirit of Nature but I resisted the thought of a Czar of the *Heavens*, however loving His sway might be.(p.12)
- My *heavens*!(p.340)

heaves

- The horrors of increasing hangover sickness to occupy the entire day; nausea, dry *heaves*, the rocking bed, the nightmare-filled mind.(p.408)

heavier

- In my own generation I stuck out, I can see that now, as being a very much *heavier* drinker than the average man.(p.518)

heavily

- That may be true of certain nonalcoholic people who, though drinking foolishly and *heavily* at the present time, are able to stop or moderate, because their brains and bodies have not been damaged as ours were.(p.39)
- Perhaps we had been leaning too *heavily* on Reason that last mile and we did not like to lose our support.(p.53)
- I had been drinking *heavily* from one state of semi-coma to another and it was several days before I got "defogged," but subconsciously I was in earnest about wanting to quit liquor forever.(p.258)
- In the summer of 1938, almost a year from the time I made my original contact with Akron, the man for whom I was working and who knew about the program, approached me and asked if I could do anything about one of his salesmen who was drinking very *heavily*.(p.294)
- "We watch the alcoholic performing in a position of responsibility and we know that because he is drinking *heavily* and daily he has cut his capacities by fifty per cent, and still he seems able to do a satisfactory job.(p.308)
- Some were drinking *heavily* and there had been occasional serious episodes.(p.315)
- I couldn't keep up with any of my other friends, and I wouldn't go to anyone's house unless I knew they drank as *heavily* as I did.(p.324)
- But I was soon drinking as *heavily* as I had been.(p.428)

heavy

- A doctor came with a *heavy* sedative.(p.6)
- Once confused and baffled by the seeming futility of existence they show the underlying reasons why they were making *heavy* going of life.(p.50)
- One: Your husband may be only a *heavy* drinker.(p.108)
- His drinking may be constant or it may be *heavy* only on certain occasions.(p.109)
- Here is a case in point: One of our friends is a *heavy* smoker and coffee drinker.(p.135)
- But not so with us in those last days of *heavy* drinking.(p.151)
- The next three years I spent in Boston, Chicago, and Montreal in the employ of a large manufacturing concern, selling railway supplies, gas engines of all sorts, and many other items of *heavy* hardware.(p.172)
- A big event of any kind precipitated *heavy* drinking.(p.197)
- Whatever it was, it brushed all the *heavy* burdens off my back.(p.334)
- I was never a very *heavy* social drinker.(p.335)
- And as that thought came to me, it was as though someone had reached down and taken a *heavy* overcoat off my shoulders, for that was the last one.(p.347)
- Thank God that in spite of my *heavy* drinking my mind was clear enough to make a decision then and there.(p.363)
- Short dry spells ended in *heavy* drinking.(p.375)
- I'd packed more drinking into seven years than many a *heavy* drinker does in a lifetime.(p.429)
- The line between a *heavy* drinker and an alcoholic is not always clear.(p.436)
- The doctor bills are *heavy* and the bank account is low.(p.501)

Hebrew

- There is another meaning for the *Hebrew* word that in the King James version of the Bible is translated "salvation."(p.228)

heck

- *Heck*.(p.428)
- And the guy said, "*Heck*, yes, I been married to her for years!"(p.512)

heckled

- Unlike his skid-row brother, he isn't *heckled* for sleeping in alleys or doorways.(p.330)

hectic

- Drunk or sober, I was *hectic*, unpredictable, irresponsible.(p.406)

heed

- Ominous warning -- which I failed to *heed*.(p.1)

heel

- So I went to my wife and asked her, wasn't there something that she and I could do to somehow get together, and she turned on her *heel* and looked me squarely in the eye, and said, "You don't care anything about my problem," and I could have smacked her, but I said to myself, "Grab on to your serenity!"(p.351)
- It was a terrible blow at the time and I thought he was pretty much of a *heel*, but of course it was the finest thing he could have done for me under the circumstances.(p.357)

heels

- I, who did not know how to give love, was head over *heels* "in love."(p.403)

height

- This was at the *height* of the Depression and the end of Prohibition.(p.358)

held

- Though none of these principles had the force of rules or laws, they had become so widely accepted by 1950 that they were confirmed by our first International Conference *held* at Cleveland.(p.xix)
- But that in itself would never have *held* us together as we are now joined.(p.17)
- Finally, he can no longer work, his wife gets a divorce and he is *held* up to ridicule.(p.38)
- We turned back to the list, for it *held* the key to the future.(p.66)
- It was finally decided to undertake the organization of a Cleveland group and toward the end of May, 1939, the first meeting was *held* in Cleveland in my home.(p.219)
- The times in which I grew up (the Prohibition era immortalized by Scott Fitzgerald and John *Held* Jr.) had taught me to be gay with the gayest; my own inner urges led me to outdo them all.(p.225)
- Much later I discovered the elders *held* many prayer meetings hoping to find a way to give me the heave-ho, but at the same time stay tolerant and spiritual.(p.247)
- In the two succeeding years I *held* ten different jobs ranging from newspaper copy-desk and rewrite, to traffic director for an oil field equipment company.(p.255)
- Federal Theatre in Texas gave me an administrative job which I *held* for a year, only because I worked hard and productively when I worked, and because my very tolerant chief ascribed my frequent lapses to a bohemian temperament.(p.256)
- This first meeting was *held* in the living room of a home and was led by Bill D., the first man that Bill W. and Dr. Bob had worked with successfully.(p.291)
- It was different from the meetings now *held*.(p.291)
- That age of the flapper and the "It" girl, speakeasies and the hip flask, the boyish bob and the drugstore cowboy, John *Held* Jr. and F. Scott Fitzgerald, all generously sprinkled with a patent pseudo-sophistication.(p.304)
- However, due to financial difficulties the whole printing was, for a while, *held* up and the book received no publicity, nor, of course, was it available in the stores, even if one knew it existed.(p.307)
- By the latter part of September 1939, we had a nu-

cleus of six and ***held*** our first official group meeting.(p.310)
• We had a small child, and I loved her dearly, so that ***held*** me back quite a bit in my drinking career.(p.322)
• It has been a fellowship with God and man that has ***held*** good wherever I've turned and whatever I've done.(p.394)
• They were bright and well read, they ***held*** various political views.(p.410)
• They also were ***held*** in some sort of strap arrangement.(p.422)
• They ***held*** consultations and discussions, and finally decided to give me the "Conditioned Reflex" treatment.(p.469)
• We ***held*** some two or three meetings at Ella's home and from there we ***held*** some two or three at her mother's home.(p.495)
• I was immediately arrested, arraigned in Homicide Court, ***held*** without bail, and remanded to the old Tombs Prison to await trial.(p.508)

hell

• Abruptly in October 1929 ***hell*** broke loose on the New York stock exchange.(p.4)
• A morning paper told me the market had gone to ***hell*** again.(p.6)
• Our friend felt as though the gates of ***hell*** had closed on him with a clang.(p.27)
• While pondering the answer he felt as though he lived in ***hell***.(p.56)
• A man so involved often feels very remorseful at times, especially if he is married to a loyal and courageous girl who has literally gone through ***hell*** for him.(p.81)
• Everything's all wrong and the ***hell*** with it."(p.245)
• At least three of those four years must have been a living ***hell*** for my wife, because she had to watch the man she loved disintegrate morally, mentally and financially.(p.277)
• How full it has kept my retirement years -- the five I've lived since the first two lost in traveling a rocky road to ***hell***, before I made a U-turn.(p.334)
• I was released in a week, a week of ***hell*** with no drinks.(p.428)
• I had a lot more ***hell*** to go through.(p.437)
• But what a difference there is between going through ***hell*** without a power greater than one's self, and with it!(p.437)
• They hadn't mentioned the living ***hell*** before death.(p.461)
• We lived just a few doors from the First Baptist Church and when they had funerals I remember very often asking my mother whether the person was good or bad and whether they were going to heaven or ***hell***.(p.483)
• I am in the bottom of ***hell***.(p.504)
• There was the love affair which was ridiculous -- "imagine that midget being able to fall in love!" -- and my head knew it while my heart pumped real, genuine anguish, for it hurt like ***hell***, and since it was first love, things have never been quite the same.(p.534)
• I was in ***hell***.(p.539)

hellish

• Then came the night when the physical and mental torture was so ***hellish*** I feared I would burst through my window, sash and all.(p.6)

hells

• Enduring all the hangover ***hells*** that every alcoholic experiences, I made the usual resolutions.(p.256)

help

• We think this account of our experiences will ***help*** everyone to better understand the alcoholic.(p.xiii)
• Prior to his journey to Akron, the broker had worked hard with many alcoholics on the theory that only an alcoholic could ***help*** an alcoholic, but he had succeeded only in keeping sober himself.(p.xvi)
• Then Jack Alexander wrote a feature article in the Saturday Evening Post and placed such a compelling picture of A.A. before the general public that alcoholics in need of ***help*** really deluged us.(p.xviii)
• You must ***help*** me!"(p.xxvii)
• Perhaps I could ***help*** some of them.(p.14)
• Our very lives, as ex-problem drinkers, depend upon our constant thought of others and how we may ***help*** meet their needs.(p.20)
• We were in a position where life was becoming impossible, and if we had passed into the region from which there is no return through human aid we had but two alternatives: One was to go on to the bitter end, blotting out the consciousness of our intolerable situation as best we could; and the other, to accept spiritual ***help***.(p.25)
• Some of our alcoholic readers may think they can do without spiritual ***help***.(p.27)
• How then shall we ***help*** our readers determine, to their own satisfaction, whether they are one of us?(p.34)
• I saw that will power and self-knowledge would not ***help*** in those strange mental blank spots.(p.42)
• As to two of you men, whose stories I have heard, there is no doubt in my mind that you were 100% hopeless, apart from divine ***help***.(p.43)
• We were having trouble with personal relationships, we couldn't control our emotional natures, we were a prey to misery and depression, we couldn't make a living, we had a feeling of uselessness, we were full of fear, we were unhappy, we couldn't seem to be of real ***help*** to other people -- was not a basic solution of these bedevilments more important than whether we should see newsreels of lunar flight?(p.52)
• Without ***help*** it is too much for us.(p.59)
• We had to have God's ***help***.(p.62)
• Take away my difficulties, that victory over them may bear witness to those I would ***help*** of Thy Power, Thy Love, and Thy Way of life.(p.63)
• We asked God to ***help*** us show them the same tolerance, pity, and patience that we would cheerfully grant a sick friend.(p.67)
• We asked God to mold our ideals and ***help*** us to live up to them.(p.69)
• Most people approached in this way will be glad to ***help***; they will be honored by our confidence.(p.75)
• If we still cling to something we will not let go, we ask God to ***help*** us be willing.(p.76)
• If we have obtained permission, have consulted with others, asked God to ***help*** and the drastic step is indicated we must not shrink.(p.80)
• Then we resolutely turn our thoughts to someone we can ***help***.(p.84)
• You can ***help*** when no one else can.(p.89)
• To watch people recover, to see them ***help*** others, to watch loneliness vanish, to see a fellowship grow up about you, to have a host of friends – this is an experience you must not miss.(p.89)
• Don't deal with him when he is very drunk, unless he is ugly and the family needs your ***help***.(p.90)
• You should be described to him as one of a fellowship who, as part of their own recovery, try to ***help*** others and who will be glad to talk to him if he cares to see you.(p.90)
• Perhaps your story will ***help*** him see where he has failed to practice the very precepts he knows so well.(p.93)
• Make it plain he is under no obligation to you, that you hope only that he will try to ***help*** other alcoholics when he escapes his own difficulties.(p.94)
• Tell him that if he wants to get well you will do anything to ***help***.(p.95)
• If he is, you might try to ***help*** him about getting a job, or give him a little financial assistance.(p.96)
• Some day we hope that Alcoholics Anonymous will ***help*** the public to a better realization of the gravity of the alcoholic problem, but we shall be of little use if our attitude is one of bitterness or hostility.(p.103)
• They need your companionship and your ***help***.(p.111)
• Drinkers like to ***help*** other drinkers.(p.112)
• Meanwhile you might try to ***help*** the wife of another serious drinker.(p.112)
• At first, some of us did not believe we needed this ***help***.(p.116)
• Showing others who suffer how we were given ***help*** is the very thing which makes life seem so worth while to us now.(p.124)
• Nothing will ***help*** the man who is off on a spiritual tangent so much as the wife who adopts a sane spiritual program, making a better practical use of it.(p.130)
• We have recovered, and have been given the power to ***help*** others.(p.132)
• Nearly every modern employer feels a moral responsibility for the well-being of his ***help***, and he tries to meet these responsibilities.(p.137)
• I wanted to throw up my hands in discouragement, for I saw that I had failed to ***help*** my banker friend understand.(p.138)
• If you desire to ***help*** it might be well to disregard your own drinking, or lack of it.(p.139)
• Seeing your attempt to understand and ***help***, some men will try to take advantage of your kindness.(p.141)
• He wants to quit drinking and you want to ***help*** him, even if it be only a matter of good business.(p.141)
• They often jeopardize their own positions by trying to ***help*** serious drinkers who should have been fired long ago, or else given an opportunity to get well.(p.147)
• The firm wants to ***help*** you get over it, and if you are interested, there is a way out.(p.147)
• We hope our suggestions will ***help*** you plug up this sometimes serious leak.(p.148)
• I don't see how you can be of any ***help*** to us for, as you see, we don't have any alcoholic problem."(p.148)
• Though they knew they must ***help*** other alcoholics if they would remain sober, that motive became secondary.(p.159)
• Many of us, former patients, go there to ***help***.(p.162)
• Seventeen stories may ***help*** you decide whether you are alcoholic; also, whether A.A. is for you.(p.167)
• After three years of this, I wound up in the local hospital where they attempted to ***help*** me, but I would get my friends to smuggle me a quart, or I would steal the alcohol about the building, so that I got rapidly worse.(p.175)
• About this time a lady called up my wife one Saturday afternoon, saying she wanted me to come over that evening to meet a friend of hers who might ***help*** me.(p.179)
• But if you really and truly want to quit drinking liquor for good and all, and sincerely feel that you must have some ***help***, we know that we have an answer for you.(p.181)
• It did ***help*** to certain extent, since I got in places where I could not obtain anything to drink, and so broke the habitual drinking.(p.183)
• This was going to ***help*** them to stay sober.(p.185)
• All the other people that had talked to me wanted to ***help*** me, and my pride prevented me from listening to them, and caused only resentment on my part, but I felt as if I would be a real stinker if I did not listen to a couple of fellows for a short time, if that would cure them.(p.185)
• The next thing they wanted to know was if I thought I could quit of my own accord, without any ***help***, if I could just walk out of the hospital and never take another drink.(p.186)
• If I could, that was wonderful, that was just fine, and they would very much appreciate a person who had that kind of power, but they were looking for a man that knew he had a problem, and knew that he couldn't handle it himself and needed outside ***help***.(p.186)
• I had no trouble there because I had never actually ceased to believe in God, and had tried lots of times to get ***help*** but hadn't succeeded.(p.186)
• The next thing they wanted to know was would I be willing to go to this Higher Power and ask for ***help***, calmly and without any reservations.(p.186)
• Every time I'd start thinking about drinking, I would think of the long, dry years ahead without having a drink; but this idea of twenty-four hours, that it was up to me from then on, was a lot of ***help***.(p.188)
• I didn't like having to come home at a certain time; I didn't like this, I didn't like that, and I think the poor girl actually divorced me to ***help*** me stop drinking!(p.199)
• I accepted their ***help***, and it was helpful.(p.202)
• Shortly after I came to this conclusion, I was importuned by another well-known patent law firm to ***help*** them out on some trial work because their trial man had had a heart attack and had been forbidden to go into the courtroom.(p.220)
• I remembered my loud resolution to find him and ask him to ***help*** me get into that "Asylum" he had written about.(p.224)
• I wanted ***help***, and I tried to cooperate.(p.226)
• I had not asked for ***help*** and seriously doubt that I would have, but Fitz, an old school friend of mine, had persuaded Jackie to call on me.(p.238)
• Jackie told me about a group of fellows in New York, of whom my old friend Fitz was one, who had the same problem I had, and who by working together to ***help*** each other were not now drinking and were happy like himself.(p.239)
• We can share in the laughter and tears of our many friends, and most important, we can share our A.A. way of life and are given a daily opportunity to ***help*** others.(p.249)
• I tried to ***help*** myself.(p.255)
• I did not need to be told that my efforts were and would be unavailing if I did not get ***help***.(p.258)
• They were earnest and obviously trying to ***help*** me on the road I had chosen.(p.259)
• Today I have Someone who will always hear me; I have a warm fellowship among men who understand my problems; I have tasks to do and am glad to do them, to see others who are alcoholics and to ***help*** them in any way I can to become sober men.(p.260)
• Finally, one morning, I got up and got in the car and cried all the way down to the M.'s – the people who owned the bar – and told her I was licked and wanted ***help***.(p.267)

• When we closed the meeting with the Lord's Prayer, Russ said, "Mother, ***help*** me stand."(p.270)
• Russ said, "Don't do another thing today but ***help*** him.(p.271)
• If, on Sunday, I could be there, trying to think of something that would ***help*** her with this problem, then we must have something that could work.(p.272)
• If it isn't anything that's going to ***help*** you or anybody else, why should you become involved in it, and get all disturbed about it?"(p.273)
• I told our family doctor, an understanding man who gave hours of his time trying to ***help*** me, about this experience.(p.276)
• To go north into the empty pine country and shoot myself, or to go south in the faint hope that a bunch of strangers might ***help*** me with my drinking problem.(p.278)
• He it was who convinced me, because his own conviction was so real, that a Power greater than myself could ***help*** me in the crises of life, and that the means of communicating with this Power was simple prayer.(p.279)
• You can't lose, and maybe God will ***help*** you -- just maybe, mind you.(p.280)
• With God's ***help*** I am able, for one day at a time, to carry business responsibilities which, not many years ago, I would not have dreamed of assuming.(p.284)
• I shut my eyes and asked for ***help***.(p.285)
• We are both depending upon God and our use of the A.A. program to ***help*** us make a success of this joint undertaking.(p.286)
• I could not wait to tell him that I wanted ***help***, that if these men in Akron had anything I wanted it, and would do anything to get it.(p.289)
• I never enjoyed any meal, but I ate my lunch at noon for two reasons; first, to ***help*** me get out of the fog of the night before and, second, to furnish some measure of nourishment.(p.299)
• Spiritually . . . I found a Friend who never lets me down and is ever eager to ***help***.(p.303)
• Some of us struggle with these people because we know that they are really very sick, but we also know that short of some miracle, we are not going to ***help*** them except temporarily, and that they will inevitably get worse and worse until one of two things happens.(p.308)
• However, as he unfolded his story for me, I could not ***help*** but believe him.(p.309)
• Nothing in their lives took precedence over their response to a call for ***help*** from some alcoholic in need.(p.310)
• It took the ***help***, understanding and wonderful companionship that was given so freely to me by my "ex-alkie" friends.(p.311)
• They realized that in the end alcoholism could be a mortal as cancer; certainly no sane man would wait for a malignant growth to become fatal before seeking ***help***.(p.315)
• I also found out that all they wanted was to ***help*** me get sober and to stay sober themselves.(p.320)
• Now I feel so very grateful not only for my sobriety, which I try to maintain day by day, but I'm grateful also for the ability to ***help*** other people.(p.326)
• But A.A. has shown me that I can ***help*** other alcoholics.(p.326)
• Two years later, a month beyond age seventy, I was crying for ***help*** from A.A.(p.327)
• But I couldn't ***help*** thinking, "You poor guy.(p.334)
• The only incentive that I had, toward the end, for getting dressed in the morning was to get out and get supplies to ***help*** me get my day started.(p.336)
• The doctor prescribed brandy for the boy to ***help*** him through the night when he coughed, a teaspoon of brandy.(p.338)
• The very person who stood with me through it all and has been my greatest ***help*** was the person that I turned against, my husband.(p.338)
• The people who would have come to ***help*** me were just the people I would have nothing to do with.(p.338)
• Deep in my heart was the feeling that maybe I could get some ***help*** here.(p.346)
• I recall, as I walked into that meeting, saying to myself, "Here I am, a fellow of the American College of Surgeons, a Fellow of the International College of Surgeons, a diplomate of one of the great specialty boards in these United States, a member of the American Psychiatric Society, and I have to go to the butcher, the baker and the carpenter to ***help*** make a man out of me!"(p.347)
• All I do in a very simple way, is to ***help*** Him cure my patients.(p.351)
• She left, and I sat down and crossed my hands, and looked up and said, "For God's sake, ***help*** me."(p.351)
• And the clergy have tried hard to ***help*** us, but we haven't been helped.(p.352)
• Out of sheer despair, she called for ***help***.(p.353)
• That night she too had new hope because I had made sure she would know what I was doing about my drinking by packing every bit of A.A. literature I could put my hands on right on top so she couldn't ***help*** but see it when she opened my bag.(p.364)
• ***Help*** which you once continually rejected, suggestions once turned aside are finally accepted in desperation.(p.377)
• It was important to me to see what alcohol had done to me and would continue to do if I didn't have ***help***.(p.379)
• It took me some time to realize that the Twelve Steps of A.A. were designed to ***help*** correct these defects of character and so ***help*** remove the obsession to drink.(p.380)
• They meant patience, tolerance and humility, and above all the belief that a Power greater than myself could ***help***.(p.381)
• She still had her husband, her home, and a chance to ***help*** start A.A. in Texas.(p.384)
• We moved once more, to Houston; my husband thought maybe a change of environment would ***help*** and I'd be all right.(p.389)
• The only thing that I could do would be to call the doctor to ***help*** sober me up.(p.389)
• They sent me the regular letter they send to everybody else, but along with it, Ruth Hock, the nonalcoholic secretary, wrote a longhand note because she could see from the letter that I really needed ***help*** badly.(p.392)
• That personal touch did ***help*** me too.(p.393)
• It was the first time in my life that I could not get a lift out of what I was drinking; and so one Friday night, at five minutes to six, I had half a water glass of warm gin, and that is when I first asked God to ***help*** me.(p.393)
• Dr. Bob said, "Love and service keep us dry," and Bill said, "Always we must remember that our first duty is face-to-face ***help*** for the alcoholic who still suffers."(p.395)
• But now, with His ***help*** and grace, this child of His has paid his initiation fee for good, as long as he remembers to stay away from that first drink (the one that does all the damage) one day at a time.(p.399)
• An alcoholic cannot accept the news that he's an alcoholic unless there is a meaningful explanation given, and an offer of ***help***, such as you get in A.A.(p.406)
• I was accepting ***help*** with one hand and pushing it away with the other.(p.407)
• The liquor counteracted the ***help*** I was getting.(p.407)
• She did all she could to ***help*** this situation and to protect my child.(p.409)
• I completely forgot myself in trying vainly to ***help*** Anne, whose misery I understood.(p.415)
• However, I had phoned New York from the farm, appealing for ***help***, and there in the station to meet us were two A.A.'s, John and Bud.(p.415)
• They were taking the trouble to try and ***help***.(p.415)
• A return to the United States proved effective as a geographical cure, and a period of sobriety ensued, with the ***help*** of the church.(p.419)
• I came to A.A. simply because there were no other doors of ***help*** open to me in my hometown.(p.420)
• He was interested and said he'd ***help*** me all he could.(p.428)
• I'd acquired a new girl, a lovely girl who knew of my problem and had tried to ***help*** me.(p.430)
• Today I think of life in terms of happiness, contentment, freedom from fear and despair, sane thinking, ability to face problems as they occur, the opportunity to ***help*** other alcoholics and to be decent.(p.430)
• A friend had found ***help*** in psychoanalysis.(p.434)
• Here was power to live to the end of any given day, power to have the courage to face the next day, power to have friends, power to ***help*** people, power to be sane, power to stay sober.(p.436)
• Now I own perhaps the most costly pair of moccasins anyone has ever seen, and they ***help*** me remember where I've been.)(p.445)
• My reaction was that I'd already helped all the patients on the ward, and I still had plenty of problems of my own without trying to ***help*** some drunk from A.A.(p.446)
• It is painful to grow, and without the ***help*** of my "civilian" A.A. companion, big Gene, I might not have survived that critical year of adjustment.(p.462)
• I was not eligible for parole, until -- with God's ***help***, I'm sure – the governor cut five years off my sentence.(p.462)
• I am still arrogant, egocentric, self-righteous, with no humility, even phony at times, but I'm trying to be a better person and ***help*** my fellowman.(p.463)
• There were doctors and psychiatrists there who tried to ***help*** me, but at that point I wasn't having ***help*** from anyone.(p.468)
• I didn't want ***help***.(p.468)
• In other words, the kindest doctor in the whole world, and I had one such, couldn't ***help*** me because I always felt, "You can't know about me – you can't possibly know – you don't even drink!"(p.471)
• With their ***help*** I also saw that certainly, because of some of the things I had done during the years, I was bordering on insanity, and so, facing the record, I tried to believe that a Power greater than I could and would restore me to sanity.(p.471)
• You can ***help*** where no one else can."(p.473)
• I have come to believe that my illness is spiritual as well as physical and mental, and I know that for ***help*** in the spiritual sphere I have to turn to a Higher Power.(p.473)
• So I jump quick from First Step to Twelfth Step to ***help*** my brother, living with me.(p.476)
• Start group on reservation and carry message, ***help*** start other groups all over Maritimes and New England.(p.476)
• He has also taught me that I must ***help*** myself first; only then may I be able to ***help*** others.(p.481)
• I thought that this would be a big ***help*** to me.(p.490)
• I haven't mentioned it, but Charlie, my sponsor, was white, and when we got our group started we got ***help*** from other white groups in Washington.(p.495)
• And, not only that, but they gave us financial ***help***.(p.496)
• We didn't save the world, but we did manage to ***help*** some individuals.(p.496)
• Maybe a few drinks when I get to the city will ***help***.(p.505)
• I want to get where I can find some alcoholics to ***help***, and where I can have some fellowship.(p.506)
• For me, it was a little different because I couldn't ***help*** thinking about the past, and I saw the future more or less mirrored in the past.(p.513)
• I knew it, and I turned for ***help*** to someone upon whom I had turned my back for many years.(p.515)
• I asked God for ***help***.(p.515)
• It was the first time that I had asked for ***help*** sincerely and honestly.(p.515)
• And I got ***help***.(p.515)
• Finally, my mother came and said she had kept me at home for six years because she thought she could ***help*** me, but that now she had come to the conclusion that I wasn't even worth trying to ***help***.(p.523)
• Today, I thank my Higher Power for giving me another chance at life and A.A. and being able to try and ***help*** some other alcoholic.(p.529)
• I choose to believe that the Power greater than ourselves we ask for ***help***, wrapped my shivering body in loving warmth and strength which has never left me.(p.541)
• I myself have been lucky enough to ***help*** out.(p.541)
• But one was so outstanding that I like to pass it on whenever I can in the hope that it will ***help*** someone else as it has me.(p.551)
• I went on the wagon, with no outside ***help*** and with no real difficulty -- except that I didn't enjoy life without drinking.(p.557)
• But my thinking was still confused, and I was still unable to deal with the challenges of everyday living without ***help***.(p.558)
• It was the late Dr. Tiebout, then, who persuaded me to seek ***help*** through A.A.(p.559)
• Dr. Harry M. Tiebout, psychiatrist: "As a psychiatrist, I have thought a great deal about the relationship of my specialty to A.A. and I have come to the conclusion that our particular function can very often lie in preparing the way for the patient to accept any sort of treatment or outside ***help***.(p.571)
• They ***help*** others with similar problems . . .(p.572)
• The Episcopal magazine, The Living Church, observes editorially: "The basis of the technique of Alcoholics Anonymous is the truly Christian principle that a man cannot ***help*** himself except by helping others.(p.574)

helped

• Because this book has become the basic text for our Society and has ***helped*** such large numbers of alcoholic men and women to recover, there exists a sentiment against any radical changes being made in it.(p.xi)
• He had also been greatly ***helped*** by the late Dr. William D. Silkworth, a New York specialist in alcoholism who is now accounted no less than a medical saint by A.A. members, and whose story of the early days of our Society appears in the next pages.(p.xvi)

- There had been no real infidelity, for loyalty to my wife, ***helped*** at times by extreme drunkenness, kept me out of those scrapes.(p.3)
- Hydrotherapy and mild exercise ***helped*** much.(p.7)
- We may ask for ourselves, however, if others will be ***helped***.(p.87)
- You should not be offended if he wants to call it off, for he has ***helped*** you more than you have ***helped*** him.(p.94)
- Alcoholics who have derided religious people will be ***helped*** by such contacts.(p.131)
- We think the business fabric is shot through with a situation which might be ***helped*** by better understanding all around.(p.137)
- Without much ado, he accepted the principles and procedure that had ***helped*** us.(p.139)
- A firm attitude at this point has ***helped*** many of us.(p.142)
- He has ***helped*** other men recover, and is a power in the church from which he was long absent.(p.158)
- Then Prohibition came into effect, and the facts that the stuff obtainable was so horrible and sometimes deadly, and that I had married and had a job which I had to look after, ***helped*** me for a period of some three or four years, although I would get drunk every time I could get hold of enough to drink to get started.(p.183)
- I was a very young married man, having his whiskey in the cupboard over the sink, and when I ***helped*** my wife with the dishes at night I would take a cup of tea and spike it with whiskey.(p.196)
- I believe though that it ***helped*** my family tremendously to have the A.A. meetings every week in my own home.(p.220)
- He had already imbued them with his own spirit until they were ready and willing at all times to go where sent, and as a doctor he well knew that this mission and duty would strengthen them as it later ***helped*** me.(p.235)
- They will never know how much their talk with me ***helped***.(p.259)
- He used to drink, and then he found something that started up in Akron that ***helped*** him quit drinking."(p.267)
- Psychiatry might have ***helped***, but psychiatrists had not penetrated the middle west.(p.276)
- Shortly thereafter, aided by the Depression, I found that I had a great deal of spare time and that a little drink in the morning ***helped***.(p.287)
- Dr. Bob always emphasized the religious angle very strongly, and I think it ***helped***.(p.292)
- I know it ***helped*** me.(p.292)
- I can think clearly and am ***helped*** much in my thinking and judgment by my spiritual development which grows daily.(p.303)
- This worldly lady ***helped*** to develop A.A. in Chicago and thus passed her keys to many.(p.304)
- And the clergy have tried hard to help us, but we haven't been ***helped***.(p.352)
- And the psychiatrist has had thousands of couches, and has put you and me on them many, many times, but he hasn't ***helped*** us very much, though he has tried hard; and we owe the clergy and the doctor and the psychiatrist a deep debt of gratitude, but they haven't ***helped*** our alcoholism, except in a rare few instances.(p.352)
- But -- Alcoholics Anonymous has ***helped***.(p.352)
- I had not only let my wife down but also a lot of other wonderful people who had ***helped*** me.(p.364)
- They said "Get active," so I ***helped*** whenever I could, and I still do.(p.381)
- As long as it eased situations socially, it ***helped*** just fine, but somewhere along the line, it backfired.(p.386)
- There are so many to whom I feel deeply grateful; to my husband (and best critic), whose generous love, compassion and understanding have ***helped*** me along the way; to those before me in A.A. who inspired the first article I read, and the friend who sent that article to Frank; to Ruth for her personal note, and the first A.A. to talk to me; to my Bishop, whose loving and believing spirit inspired me; and to all the members of the Houston Group who were so patient, kind and helpful -- and to countless others.(p.393)
- A fellow A.A., called Anne, who had ***helped*** me, went on a terrible bender.(p.414)
- I have been ***helped*** morally, spiritually, mentally and materially through A.A.(p.430)
- My reaction was that I'd already ***helped*** all the patients on the ward, and I still had plenty of problems of my own without trying to help some drunk from A.A.(p.446)
- It ***helped*** me a great deal to become convinced that alcoholism was a disease, not a moral issue; that I had been drinking as a result of a compulsion, even though I had not been aware of the compulsion at the time; and that sobriety was not a matter of willpower.(p.448)
- My husband ***helped*** me into the house, packed himself a bag, and gave me some money.(p.467)
- I like to believe that I may have ***helped*** him, too.(p.481)
- She was the one who really ***helped*** me to make a go of that twenty years and nine months in prison.(p.511)
- I went back to the old family doctor who had ***helped*** me the first time I had the D.T.'s.(p.515)
- We had a minor campaign or two and that ***helped*** distract attention from my drinking.(p.519)

helper

- I knew that I had a ***helper*** that I could rely upon, who wouldn't fail me.(p.189)

helpful

- We simply wish to be ***helpful*** to those who are afflicted.(p.xiv)
- We should like to be ***helpful*** to such cases.(p.xiv)
- That the man who is making the approach has had the same difficulty, that he obviously knows what he is talking about, that his whole deportment shouts at the new prospect that he is a man with a real answer, that he has no attitude of Holier Than Thou, nothing whatever except the sincere desire to be ***helpful***; that there are no fees to pay, no axes to grind, no people to please, no lectures to be endured -- these are the conditions we have found most effective.(p.18)
- The experiment of quitting for a period of time will be ***helpful***, but we think we can render an even greater service to alcoholic sufferers and perhaps to the medical fraternity.(p.34)
- How can I be ***helpful*** to him?(p.67)
- If we do, we destroy our chance of being ***helpful***.(p.67)
- We cannot be ***helpful*** to all people, but at least God will show us how to take a kindly and tolerant view of each and every one.(p.67)
- We go to him in a ***helpful*** and forgiving spirit, confessing our former ill feeling and expressing our regret.(p.77)
- There are many ***helpful*** books also.(p.87)
- To be ***helpful*** is our only aim.(p.89)
- Outline the program of action, explaining how you made a self-appraisal, how you straightened out your past and why you are now endeavoring to be ***helpful*** to him.(p.94)
- These things will come to pass naturally and in good time provided, however, the alcoholic continues to demonstrate that he can be sober, considerate, and ***helpful***, regardless of what anyone says or does.(p.99)
- You may spoil your chance of being ***helpful*** if you do.(p.100)
- Your job now is to be at the place where you may be of maximum helpfulness to others, so never hesitate to go anywhere if you can be ***helpful***.(p.102)
- Experience shows that such an attitude is not ***helpful*** to anyone.(p.103)
- Let him see that you want to be ***helpful*** rather than critical.(p.111)
- We urge you to try our program, for nothing will be so ***helpful*** to your husband as the radically changed attitude toward him which God will show you how to have.(p.117)
- Cheer him up and ask him how you can be still more ***helpful***.(p.120)
- As each member of a resentful family begins to see his short comings and admits them to the others, he lays a basis for ***helpful*** discussion.(p.127)
- We intend the foregoing as a ***helpful*** suggestion only.(p.132)
- One of the many doctors who had the opportunity of reading this book in manuscript form told us that the use of sweets was often ***helpful***, of course depending upon a doctor's advice.(p.133)
- Seeing this, and meaning to be ***helpful***, his wife commenced to admonish him about it.(p.135)
- This seemed to me like an opportunity to be ***helpful***, so I spent two hours talking about alcoholism, the malady, and described the symptoms and results as well as I could.(p.138)
- If your decision is yes, whether the reason be humanitarian or business or both, then the following suggestions may be ***helpful***.(p.140)
- If he speaks of his home situation, you can undoubtedly make ***helpful*** suggestions.(p.145)
- A reasonable amount of latitude will be ***helpful***.(p.146)
- There is a good bit of travel between East and West and we foresee a great increase in this ***helpful*** interchange.(p.162)
- He gave me information about the subject of alcoholism which was undoubtedly ***helpful***.(p.180)
- I accepted their help, and it was ***helpful***.(p.202)
- He walked to the hospital to save bus fare and did it gladly in order to be ***helpful*** to an individual he had never even seen.(p.208)
- Another thing that was ***helpful*** to me.(p.273)
- He thought it would be ***helpful*** for me to visit the Akron group and meet many like himself.(p.309)
- Neither of these circumstances was very ***helpful*** to my type since I had not learned to face realities.(p.358)
- There are so many to whom I feel deeply grateful; to my husband (and best critic), whose generous love, compassion and understanding have helped me along the way; to those before me in A.A. who inspired the first article I read, and the friend who sent that article to Frank; to Ruth for her personal note, and the first A.A. to talk to me; to my Bishop, whose loving and believing spirit inspired me; and to all the members of the Houston Group who were so patient, kind and ***helpful*** -- and to countless others.(p.393)
- To be sure, I learned many fascinating things, and many things that were to prove ***helpful*** later.(p.434)
- The ***helpful*** family finally said, over long distance, that there would be no more money and that I could not come home.(p.538)

helpfulness

- Though he could not accept all the tenets of the Oxford Groups, he was convinced of the need for moral inventory, confession of personality defects, restitution to those harmed, ***helpfulness*** to others, and the necessity of belief in and dependence upon God.(p.xvi)
- These can then be discussed in an atmosphere of ***helpfulness*** and friendliness.(p.99)
- Your job now is to be at the place where you may be of maximum ***helpfulness*** to others, so never hesitate to go anywhere if you can be helpful.(p.102)
- There are the same fast friendships, there is the same ***helpfulness*** to one another as you find among our western friends.(p.162)

helping

- My wife and I abandoned ourselves with enthusiasm to the idea of ***helping*** other alcoholics to a solution of their problems.(p.15)
- If sex is very troublesome, we throw ourselves the harder into ***helping*** others.(p.70)
- Actually, he may be ***helping*** you more than you are ***helping*** him.(p.94)
- ***Helping*** others is the foundation stone of your recovery.(p.97)
- You have been starving for his companionship, yet he spends long hours ***helping*** other men and their families.(p.119)
- Even if he displays a certain amount of neglect and irresponsibility towards the family, it is well to let him go as far as he likes in ***helping*** other alcoholics.(p.129)
- Cleaning up old scrapes, ***helping*** to settle family differences, explaining the disinherited son to his irate parents, lending money and securing jobs for each other, when justified -- these are everyday occurrences.(p.161)
- When a few men in this city have found themselves, and have discovered the joy of ***helping*** others to face life again, there will be no stopping until everyone in that town has had his opportunity to recover -- if he can and will.(p.163)
- The satisfaction I got from giving him a little of what I had read in those pamphlets far surpassed any feeling that I had ever had before in ***helping*** patients.(p.347)
- Doctors have been notoriously unsuccessful in ***helping*** alcoholics.(p.352)
- A "spiritual experience" to me meant attending meetings, seeing a group of people, all there for the purpose of ***helping*** each other; hearing the Twelve Steps and the Twelve Traditions read at a meeting, and hearing the Lord's Prayer, which in an A.A. meeting has such great meaning -- "Thy will be done, not mine."(p.381)
- Through going to meetings and listening, and occasionally speaking, through doing Twelve Step work, whereby in ***helping*** others you are both the teacher and the student, by making many wonderful A.A. friends, I have been taught all the things in life that are worth having.(p.416)
- Right from the start, I felt that they weren't doing anything for me, but they sure were ***helping*** Max.(p.447)
- We all have the same sickness, and in ***helping*** one another, we are able to stay sober.(p.530)
- I have published a book covering certain aspects of this field which has been well-reviewed and which is ***helping*** other people.(p.541)
- The Episcopal magazine, The Living Church, observes editorially: "The basis of the technique of Alcoholics Anonymous is the truly Christian principle that a man cannot help himself except

by ***helping*** others.(p.574)

helpless

• Several of our crowd, men of thirty or less, had been drinking only a few years, but they found themselves as ***helpless*** as those who had been drinking twenty years.(p.33)

• I wasn't ***helpless.***(p.228)

• I had some financial success through no ability of my own and, when jobless and almost wiped out in 1930, I began to trade and sell my collection; much of the proceeds went to keep my apartment stocked with liquor and almost every night saw me ***helpless*** to bed.(p.255)

helplessly

• Near you, alcoholics are dying ***helplessly*** like people in a sinking ship.(p.152)

• And as I fumed ***helplessly*** and planned to get good and drunk and show them, my eye caught a sentence in the book lying open on my bed: "We cannot live with anger."(p.228)

• A little more than fifteen years ago, through a long and calamitous series of shattering experiences, I found myself being ***helplessly*** propelled toward total destruction.(p.304)

helps

• If our testimony ***helps*** sweep away prejudice, enables you to think honestly, encourages you to search diligently within yourself, then, if you wish, you can join us on the Broad Highway.(p.55)

• We have here in this community an organization which ***helps*** people, and this organization is known as Alcoholics Anonymous.(p.348)

• My sister-in-law took me to a place she had heard about that ***helps*** women like me.(p.371)

• I have a lovely wife who understands my problem and ***helps*** me with it.(p.431)

helter-skelter

• Toward five o'clock, ***helter-skelter,*** I'd get everything put away and try to get supper on the table, and after supper I'd finish the job up and knock myself out.(p.337)

hemorrhage

• He had but partially recovered from a gastric ***hemorrhage*** and seemed to be a case of pathological mental deterioration.(p.xxix)

• Then I had my first bad stomach ***hemorrhage.***(p.490)

hemorrhages

• In the next half-year, I experienced two more esophageal ***hemorrhages,*** miraculously surviving each one by a hair.(p.558)

hemorrhaging

• My doctor warned me that if I kept on, I might have esophageal ***hemorrhaging*** and die.(p.558)

hence

• ***Hence*** the two men set to work almost frantically upon alcoholics arriving in the ward of the Akron City Hospital.(p.xvii)

• ***Hence*** we are at pains to tell why we think our present faith is reasonable, why we think it more sane and logical to believe than not to believe, why we say our former thinking was soft and mushy when we threw up our hands in doubt and said, "We don't know."(p.53)

• ***Hence,*** we saw that reason isn't everything.(p.54)

• Ten — Alcoholics Anonymous has no opinion on outside issues; ***hence*** the A.A. name ought never be drawn into public controversy.(p.564)

• ***Hence*** our common welfare comes first.(p.565)

• ***Hence*** we may refuse none who wish to recover.(p.565)

• ***Hence*** such facilities ought not to use the A.A. name.(p.566)

Henri

• But I can remember, in my teens, that there were a few characters who caused the village heads to nod pityingly and sometimes in anger as they paused to say, "That sot, ***Henri***" and "Ce pauvre Jules," who drank too much.(p.230)

Henrietta

• Looking in later we found Bill with his wife, ***Henrietta.***(p.189)

• Bill looked across at my wife, and said to her, "***Henrietta,*** the Lord has been so wonderful to me, curing me of this terrible disease, that I just want to keep talking about it and telling people."(p.191)

Henry

• ***Henry*** Ford once made a wise remark to the effect that experience is the thing of supreme value in life.(p.124)

Herbert

• -***Herbert*** Spencer(p.570)

herd

• We were to go up to our A.A. farm in Kent, and I spent the evening before riding ***herd*** on Anne.(p.415)

• Dr. Foster Kennedy, neurologist: "This organization of Alcoholics Anonymous calls on two of the greatest reservoirs of power known to man, religion and that instinct for association with one's fellows . . . the '***herd*** instinct.'(p.571)

here

• Many years ago one of the leading contributors to this book came under our care in this hospital and while ***here*** he acquired some ideas which he put into practical application at once.(p.xxv)

• Later, he requested the privilege of being allowed to tell his story to other patients ***here*** and with some misgiving, we consented.(p.xxv)

• ***Here*** was love, applause, war; moments sublime with intervals hilarious.(p.1)

• "***Here*** lies a Hampshire Grenadier Who caught his death Drinking cold small beer.(p.1)

• ***Here*** was something at work in a human heart which had done the impossible.(p.11)

• Never mind the musty past; ***here*** sat a miracle directly across the kitchen table.(p.11)

• We have it with us right ***here*** and now.(p.16)

• ***Here*** is the fellow who has been puzzling you, especially in his lack of control.(p.21)

• ***Here*** and there, once in a while, alcoholics have had what are called vital spiritual experiences.(p.27)

• ***Here*** was the terrible dilemma in which our friend found himself when he had the extraordinary experience which as we have already told you, made him a free man.(p.28)

• Those having religious affiliations will find ***here*** nothing disturbing to their beliefs or ceremonies.(p.28)

• ***Here*** are some of the methods we have tried: Drinking beer only, limiting the number of drinks, never drinking alone, never drinking in the morning, drinking only at home, never having it in the house, never drinking during business hours, drinking only at parties, switching from scotch to brandy, drinking only natural wines, agreeing to resign if ever drunk on the job, taking a trip, not taking a trip, swearing off forever (with and without a solemn oath), taking more physical exercise, reading inspirational books, going to health farms and sanitariums, accepting voluntary commitment to asylums -- we could increase the list ad infinitum.(p.31)

• ***Here*** is one.(p.32)

• But ***here*** is a man who at fifty-five years found he was just where he had left off at thirty.(p.33)

• ***Here*** was the threat of commitment, the loss of family and position, to say nothing of that intense mental and physical suffering which drinking always caused him.(p.36)

• The story he told is most instructive, for ***here*** was a chap absolutely convinced he had to stop drinking, who had no excuse for drinking, who exhibited splendid judgment and determination in all his other concerns, yet was flat on his back nevertheless.(p.40)

• ***Here*** difficulty arises with agnostics.(p.45)

• ***Here*** are thousands of men and women, worldly indeed.(p.50)

• ***Here*** are the steps we took, which are suggested as a program of recovery:(p.59)

• ***Here*** we find human opinions running to extremes -- absurd extremes, perhaps.(p.68)

• Grant me strength, as I go out from ***here,*** to do your bidding.(p.76)

• It would have been impressive heroics if he had walked up to the Judge and said, "***Here*** I am."(p.79)

• To his wife, he remarked, "Don't see anything the matter ***here,*** Ma.(p.82)

• ***Here*** we ask God for inspiration, an intuitive thought or a decision.(p.86)

• ***Here*** no specific rule can be given.(p.90)

• At the very beginning, the couple ought to frankly face the fact that each will have to yield ***here*** and there if the family is going to play an effective part in the new life.(p.131)

• ***Here*** is a case in point: One of our friends is a heavy smoker and coffee drinker.(p.135)

• ***Here*** they are:(p.135)

• ***Here*** were three exceptional men lost to this world because I did not understand alcoholism as I do now.(p.137)

• ***Here,*** for instance, is a typical example: An officer of one of the largest banking institutions in America knows I no longer drink.(p.138)

• After reading this book, a junior executive can go to such a man and say approximately this, "Look ***here,*** Ed.(p.147)

• ***Here*** is a brief account:(p.153)

• But he's a grand chap when he's sober, though he's been in ***here*** eight times in the last six months.(p.156)

• ***Here*** was a prospect all right but, by the description, none too promising.(p.156)

• The last three times, I got drunk on the way home from ***here.***(p.157)

• The expression on the faces of the women, that indefinable something in the eyes of the men, the stimulating and electric atmosphere of the place, conspired to let him know that ***here*** was haven at last.(p.160)

• Beginning with the story of "Dr. Bob," a co-founder of A.A., there are ***here*** presented three groups of personal histories.(p.165)

• Dr. Bob and the twelve men and women who ***here*** tell their stories were among the early members of A.A.'s first groups.(p.169)

• We're not up ***here*** trying to take any of your rights or privileges away from you, but we have a program whereby we think we can stay sober.(p.186)

• We're going to get up and get out of ***here.***"(p.189)

• I have already done it, and I am willing to do it again ***here*** in the presence of you or I am willing to say it any place, anywhere in the world from now on and not be ashamed of it."(p.190)

• (I might say right ***here*** that never in my life did I ever intend to get drunk.(p.196)

• I said, "I'm certainly not going to stay in ***here!***"(p.204)

• She said, "Well, he wouldn't be ***here*** if you didn't say so."(p.217)

• I must get out of ***here.***(p.223)

• In any case I must get out of ***here*** before I let slip my abysmal ignorance of how I came to be ***here,*** and she realized that I was stark, staring mad.(p.223)

• Why had "Dorothy" brought me ***here?***(p.223)

• All I had left was an iron determination to live my own life in spite of the alien world — and ***here*** I was, an inwardly frightened, outwardly defiant woman, who desperately needed a prop to keep going.(p.226)

• ***Here*** I was, thirty-nine years old and a complete washout.(p.238)

• I don't remember much of what he said, but I did realize that ***here*** was another guy exactly like me; he had been in the same laughing academies and the same jails, known the same loss of jobs, same frustrations, same boredom and the same loneliness.(p.239)

• However, ***here*** I probably took my first step towards my coming alcoholism by developing a terrific aversion to all churches and established religions.(p.240)

• Then broke again, hiding out in cheap hotels all over the country, one night jail stands ***here*** and there, and always that horrible feeling "What's the use -- nothing is worth while."(p.244)

• They did not seem to be getting an answer, for ***here*** I was staying sober and selling lots of auto polish, on which they were making one thousand per cent profit.(p.247)

• So, sometimes we'd end up in Charleston, West Virginia, or ***here*** or there, drinking all along the way.(p.264)

• Russ read a piece in the paper, and he kind of snickered, and said, "See ***here,*** where John D. has found something to keep him from drinking!"(p.265)

• "Oh, some darn thing they've got ***here*** in the paper about it."(p.266)

• He said, "There's a doctor ***here*** in Akron.(p.267)

• And I said, "Why sure, that's what I'm ***here*** for."(p.270)

• I'd like to say ***here*** how important it was to us then that we do all the little things that people said were important, because later when Russ was so sick that I had to hold him up, they had a meeting out at the house.(p.270)

• Russ used to be very much pleased because he'd say, "I think Dr. Bob thoroughly enjoys coming out ***here.***(p.271)

• ***Here,*** while in a hospital bed, men with clear eyes, happy faces, and a look of assurance and purposefulness about them, came to see me and told me their stories.(p.279)

• ***Here*** was a tall, rugged, highly educated Yankee talking in a matter of course way about God and prayer.(p.279)

• ***Here*** by itself was a great step forward.(p.283)

• ***Here*** was something requiring a greater willingness to assume responsibility, and take a larger degree of cooperation and "give and take" than even business requires of one.(p.286)

• ***Here*** was a man with essentially the same outlook on life, except that he had done something about it.(p.290)

• ***Here*** was hope.(p.309)

• I finished high school ***here*** in an American-sponsored Methodist public school, know as Philander

Smith College.(p.342)
• It was *here* I came to know properly what alcohol was.(p.343)
• Deep in my heart was the feeling that maybe I could get some help *here*.(p.346)
• I recall, as I walked into that meeting, saying to myself, "*Here* I am, a fellow of the American College of Surgeons, a diplomate of one of the great specialty boards in these United States, a member of the American Psychiatric Society, and I have to go to the butcher, the baker and the carpenter to help make a man out of me!"(p.347)
• We have *here* in this community an organization which helps people, and this organization is known as Alcoholics Anonymous.(p.348)
• *Here* he is powerless, unmanageable, in the grip of something bigger than he is, and he's got to turn the whole business over to someone else!(p.350)
• *Here* I am down at my office behind my desk and there she is out at the hospital.(p.350)
• *Here* were people who had thought and felt as I had.(p.355)
• *Here* was the understanding I'd been searching for all my life.(p.355)
• I can't bear to be *here* when you lose the respect of others, and above all -- when you lose your own self respect."(p.362)
• I can't bear to be *here* when you lose the respect of others, and above all when you lose your own self respect."(p.363)
• This was about ten p.m., and the time *here* is important.(p.363)
• I could end my story *here*, but for the new man I would like to add a few words.(p.366)
• Yesterday is gone, and we don't know whether we will be *here* tomorrow.(p.382)
• Frank said, "If you'd like to talk to a psychiatrist, I'll see a doctor and find out who to go to *here*."(p.387)
• He saw that I was unsettled, living away from my family and renting houses *here* and there.(p.403)
• I began, *here* and now, to fear the answer to the question -- what is the matter with me?(p.406)
• *Here*, also, I had good friends, but I became more and more separated from them.(p.406)
• So *here*, in this dive, this hangout for dead-end alcoholics and neurotics, *here* was I.(p.410)
• "Do you know why you're in *here*?" he queried.(p.423)
• I could tell him a lot of reasons why I am *here* in an alky ward at the age of twenty.(p.423)
• I don't know how I got *here* this trip, but it doesn't matter very much.(p.423)
• *Here* was the lost love I'd missed at home.(p.425)
• *Here* I found an ingredient that had been lacking in any other effort I had made to save myself.(p.436)
• *Here* was -- power!(p.436)
• *Here* was power to live to the end of any given day, power to have the courage to face the next day, power to have friends, power to help people, power to be sane, power to stay sober.(p.436)
• I just didn't belong *here*.(p.439)
• A.A. and acceptance have taught me that there is a bit of good in the worst of us and a bit of bad in the best of us; that we are all children of God and we each have a right to be *here*.(p.449)
• Sly and crafty, I thought now I'll find out what they think of me *here*, what they "have on" me, what I've said coming in *here* drunk.(p.470)
• They build you up with a lot of false hopes and promises, and rush you around *here* and there and then, all of a sudden, it's gone."(p.472)
• *Here* was a book that said I could do something that all these doctors and priests and ministers and psychiatrists that I'd been going to for years couldn't do!(p.473)
• I was there about three weeks, and then I got restless and started to tramp across the country, *here* and there, until I finally wound up in Pennsylvania, in a steel mill.(p.492)
• The grand fellow who at my call made me a hail-fellow-well-met, who gave me such a fine voice, as we sang "Hail, hail, the gang's all *here*," and "Sweet Adeline," who gave me freedom from fear and feelings of inferiority.(p.498)
• Well -- well -- look who's *here*!(p.500)
• "What are you doing *here* then?" I ask.(p.503)
• "I went out of *here* nine days ago saying that I was going to be honest, and I wasn't," he answers.(p.503)
• "The thing I do is to say 'God *here* I am and *here* are all my troubles.(p.504)
• In *here* you must go all the way too."(p.516)
• When you come in *here*, you find the understanding that you need.(p.516)
• I do think that some of the Negroes *here* -- and other places, too -- are afraid to go to other meetings.(p.529)
• I have not seen a black face but mine since I've been *here*, and if I didn't look in the mirror, I wouldn't know that I was black, because these people treat me as one of them, which I am.(p.530)
• She *here* tells how she was set free.(p.544)
• It was *here* that I realized for the first time that as a practicing alcoholic I had no rights.(p.549)
• Dr. John F. Stouffer, Chief Psychiatrist, Philadelphia General Hospital, citing his experience with A.A., said: "The alcoholics we get *here* at Philadelphia General are mostly those who cannot afford private treatment, and A.A. is by far the greatest thing we have been able to offer them.(p.572)
• Even among those who occasionally land back in *here* again, we observe a profound change in personality.(p.572)

here's

• The alcoholic may say to himself in the most casual way, "It won't burn me this time, so *here's* how!"(p.24)
• I thought, now *here's* a nice sympathetic soul!(p.322)
• "*Here's* looking at you," said he.(p.498)

hereafter

• Next, we decided that *hereafter* in this drama of life, God was going to be our Director.(p.62)
• As we felt new power flow in, as we enjoyed peace of mind, as we discovered we could face life successfully, as we became conscious of His presence, we began to lose our fear of today, tomorrow or the *hereafter*.(p.63)

heresies

• Others came near putting Galileo to death for his astronomical *heresies*.(p.51)

heritage

• Experience has often warned us that nothing can so surely destroy our spiritual *heritage* as futile disputes over property, money, and authority.(p.566)

hero

• There I was, unshaven, clothes torn and dirty with no recollection of wandering all over France but, of course, a *hero* to the local French.(p.242)

heroes

• Business and financial leaders were my *heroes*.(p.2)
• My intellectual *heroes*, the chemists the astronomers, even the evolutionists, suggested vast laws and forces at work.(p.10)

heroic

• War fever ran high in the New England town to which we new, young officers from Plattsburg were assigned, and we were flattered when the first citizens took us to their homes, making us feel *heroic*.(p.1)

heroics

• It would have been impressive *heroics* if he had walked up to the Judge and said, "Here I am."(p.79)

heroin

• For two years, I was also addicted to *heroin*.(p.480)
• Since then, I have never been back to *heroin*.(p.480)

hesitancy

• There should be no *hesitancy* in consulting a doctor or psychologist if the condition persists.(p.134)

hesitate

• Your job now is to be at the place where you may be of maximum helpfulness to others, so never *hesitate* to go anywhere if you can be helpful.(p.102)
• You should not *hesitate* to visit the most sordid spot on earth on such an errand.(p.102)
• Do not *hesitate* to take your health problems to such persons.(p.133)

hesitated

• I'll never forget, he never even *hesitated* and I had never seen him before in my life.(p.207)
• He *hesitated* to send me back to that hospital.(p.388)
• I *hesitated*.(p.498)

hesitation

• Without *hesitation*, I did the only logical thing -- ran away from home.(p.354)

hid

• I remembered filling the peroxide bottle in my medicine chest with gin, in case my sister found the bottle I *hid* under the mattress.(p.224)
• When I drank, I *hid* it from my folks out of respect for their feelings.(p.287)
• I got so that I *hid* quite a bit of the time, wouldn't answer the phone, and stayed by myself as much as I could.(p.324)
• She *hid* her bottles in clothes hampers and dresser drawers.(p.335)
• Showing all the courage and ingenuity that I had not used in a positive way, I covered my tracks and *hid* from my family so successfully that they did not find me for months.(p.401)
• Now I *hid* when I wanted to drink.(p.406)

hidden

• The patient had made his own diagnosis, and deciding his situation hopeless, had *hidden* in a deserted barn determined to die.(p.xxix)
• Above all, he believed he had acquired such a profound knowledge of the inner workings of his mind and its *hidden* springs that relapse was unthinkable.(p.26)
• My bootlegger had *hidden* alcohol at the back steps where I could get it at my convenience.(p.176)
• I had them *hidden* away in the house and all over my shop in careful concealment.(p.233)
• After finding every bottle that I had *hidden* around the apartment, she took away my pants, my shoes, my money and my keys, threw them under the bed in the back bedroom and slip-locked our door.(p.288)
• I had bottles *hidden* all over the apartment.(p.324)
• I myself didn't know all the places I had them *hidden*.(p.325)
• Until I took Social Security and a pension at the age of sixty-eight, after forty years in motion-picture-studio public relations, I had successfully *hidden* even any hints of approaching alcoholism.(p.327)
• If reasons for covering up are strong enough, secrets can be *hidden* from the world.(p.327)
• All *hidden* drunks aren't at home in housewives' dresses.(p.328)
• *Hidden* old-drunks can pass out on their beds and snooze unreproached, under the guise of taking those vital retirement-age naps.(p.330)
• That fear, of course, necessitated a program of *hidden* alcoholism.(p.331)
• I remember being dragged, drink in hand, from beneath the grand piano, where I had *hidden*, to be locked in my room in disgrace.(p.557)

hide

• I wondered whether I dared *hide* a full bottle of gin near the head of our bed.(p.8)
• People have said we must not go where liquor is served; we must not have it in our homes; we must shun friends who drink; we must avoid moving pictures which show drinking scenes; we must not go into bars; our friends must *hide* their bottles if we go to their houses; we mustn't think or be reminded about alcohol at all.(p.100)
• I would sometimes *hide* out in one of the clubs of which I was a member, and had the habit at times of registering at a hotel under a fictitious name.(p.176)
• If my wife was planning to go out in the afternoon, I would get a large supply of liquor and smuggle it home and *hide* it in the coal bin, the clothes chute, over door jambs, over beams in the cellar and in cracks in the cellar tile.(p.176)
• This problem was soon solved, however, as I began to take my bottle along with me and *hide* it in the bathroom or in the shrubbery outside.(p.184)
• Of course, as time went on, and I began to get my health back and began to be so I didn't have to *hide* from people all the time, it's just been wonderful.(p.192)
• I had no need to *hide* in closets, bathrooms, or garages.(p.332)
• I could *hide* my alcoholic stupor behind pretense.(p.332)
• I had to *hide*, as a great many people in A.A. have had to do.(p.336)
• I tried to *hide* my drinking by going places where I was unlikely to see anyone I knew.(p.375)
• After a while, I found that the psycho ward was a good place to *hide* when I had taken something stolen to the pawnshop.(p.528)

hideous

• Momentarily we did -- then would come oblivion and the awful awakening to face the *hideous* Four Horsemen -- Terror, Bewilderment, Frustration, Despair.(p.151)

hiding

• We think each family which has been relieved owes something to those who have not, and when the occasion requires, each member of it should be only too willing to bring former mistakes, no matter how grievous, out of their *hiding* places.(p.124)
• Then broke again, *hiding* out in cheap hotels all over the country, one night jail stands here and there, and always that horrible feeling "What's the use -- nothing is worth while."(p.244)
• *Hiding* behind a newspaper, magazine, or book, I really saw nothing, but simulated deep interest.(p.332)
• I did my *hiding* in the hampers and in my

dresser drawers.(p.336)
• The next steps were bottle *hiding*, and excuses for trips in order to drink without restraint.(p.375)

high

• War fever ran *high* in the New England town to which we new, young officers from Plattsburg were assigned, and we were flattered when the first citizens took us to their homes, making us feel heroic.(p.1)
• The papers reported men jumping to death from the towers of *High* Finance.(p.4)
• Where had been my *high* resolve?(p.5)
• Understanding myself now, I fared forth in *high* hope.(p.7)
• For three or four months the goose hung *high*.(p.7)
• A certain American business man had ability, good sense, and *high* character.(p.26)
• Family confidence in dad is rising *high*.(p.123)
• *High* and low, rich and poor, these are future fellows of Alcoholics Anonymous.(p.152)
• A spiritual experience, he conceded, was absolutely necessary, but the price seemed *high* upon the basis suggested.(p.155)
• From childhood through *high* school I was more or less forced to go to church, Sunday School and evening service, Monday night Christian Endeavor and sometimes to Wednesday evening prayer meeting.(p.172)
• After *high* school came four years in one of the best colleges in the country where drinking seemed to be a major extra-curricular activity.(p.172)
• I immediately quit school and went to work, and from that time until I was *high* school age there was never a return to school.(p.193)
• I went into the *high* school grades, but having missed all the intermediate grades, I didn't get along too well, so I developed the habit of going back to school just long enough for the football season and then quitting.(p.193)
• When I was eighteen, at the end of *high* school, the *high* school team had a banquet at a well-known roadhouse outside of Akron.(p.194)
• I didn't go to *high* school.(p.211)
• Not far from where I lived they built a new technical *high* school and one of the teachers sold me on the idea that I needed a little mechanical drawing if I were going to be a good toolmaker.(p.211)
• I did not have a *high* school education so I went to night school to take the full *high* school course, which I finished in two years and nine months.(p.211)
• By that time, I had one boy in college, another a senior in *high* school, and a daughter about twelve years old.(p.215)
• My next job was in sales promotion for an oil company in Mississippi where I promptly became *high* man and got lots of pats on the back.(p.242)
• Our other daughter was in her last year of *high* school, and one night the new son-in-law and my husband went out to a prize fight.(p.263)
• I really wasn't very *high*.(p.264)
• I was very much interested in athletics, and because of this and parental influence, I didn't drink or smoke in either grade or *high* school.(p.287)
• While I was in basic, I got *high* off booze almost every night.(p.317)
• It turned out that she had been in *high* school with my daughter.(p.321)
• I finished *high* school here in an American-sponsored Methodist public school, know as Philander Smith College.(p.342)
• I was president of all my classes in *high* school and in my last year I was president of that student body.(p.345)
• I do recall lying on a cold cement floor and shredding into little bits several pieces of stolen identification cards, and washing my face in the toilet bowl trying to sober up, and screaming hysterically while clinging to bars too *high* to see out of, and cursing everyone that came near me.(p.354)
• I was in the fourth quarter of my senior year at *high* school, and my mother was quite sick in the hospital.(p.354)
• *High* living, a great many fair weather friends, the 1929 stock market crash, and a couple of years of Depression, soon relieved me one by one of my worldly goods including my wife.(p.358)
• How can a person with a fine family, an attractive home, an excellent position and *high* standing in an important city become an alcoholic?(p.373)
• Years of drinking and general *high* jinks had cut her off from old friends.(p.414)
• I was an honor graduate in *high* school, and I was a good boy" to whom mothers pointed when their sons went astray.(p.419)
• I remembered back to *high* school when I was fifteen.(p.423)
• I took more through the day to increase the *high*, and more to maintain it; when I overshot the mark, I'd take tranquilizers to level off.(p.442)
• I remember in my first year in *high* school, that mother suggested that I do not join the cadet unit.(p.484)
• I went to elementary and *high* school in Washington, D.C. and then to Howard University.(p.486)
• I rebelled against this, because just about the time that I was getting ready to leave *high* school, a revelation came to me about God and it made things very complicated for me.(p.489)
• I, a man of steel, with very *high* ideals, well brought up, an honor student and the recipient of scholarships and prizes, a boy wonder in business -- I, Bob, the author of this essay, looked and saw that the universe was beneath my contempt, and that to remove myself from it was the only thing of dignity a man could do.(p.531)
• So did the waterboy on the *high* school football team attempt to revenge himself on the big brother who was the star quarterback; for I was the waterboy and my brother was the star quarterback, innocent of everything except the fact that he was a star quarterback.(p.537)
• But not for long; now, for five Friday nights in a row, I went to jail, picked up sodden with beer (which I always disliked, but which was the only drink available); in jail five consecutive Friday nights in the town where I had grown up, where I had been an honor student in *high* school, where a kindly uncle, bailing me out, said, "Bob, our family just doesn't do this sort of thing."(p.539)
• In fact, I changed schools every year until *high* school.(p.555)
• By the time I reached *high* school, I was an over-achiever.(p.555)
• To wear expensive clothes, to have bartenders know what to serve me before I ordered, to be recognized by headwaiters and shown to the best table, to play gin rummy for *high* stakes with the insouciance of a riverboat gambler -- these were the enduring values in life, I thought.(p.556)

high-powered

• As matters grow worse, he begins to use a combination of *high-powered* sedative and liquor to quiet his nerves so he can go to work.(p.22)

high-stepping

• In a weak moment he may take your dislike of his *high-stepping* friends as one of those insanely trivial excuses to drink.(p.120)

highball

• When I returned to the hotel it struck me a *highball* would be fine before going to bed, so I stepped into the bar and had one.(p.41)
• His friends feel closer over a *highball*.(p.110)

highballs

• Almost simultaneously, I discovered that cocktails in the late afternoon and *highballs* in the evening relieved the many tensions of the day.(p.277)

higher

• His defense must come from a *Higher* Power.(p.43)
• Our thought-life will be placed on a much *higher* plane when our thinking is cleared of wrong motives.(p.86)
• Follow the dictates of a *Higher* Power and you will presently live in a new and wonderful world, no matter what your present circumstances!(p.100)
• The next question, they wanted to know was if I believed in a *Higher* Power.(p.186)
• The next thing they wanted to know was would I be willing to go to this *Higher* Power and ask for help, calmly and without any reservations.(p.186)
• So, after reviewing these things and realizing what liquor had cost me, I went to this *Higher* Power which, to me was God, without any reservation, and admitted that I was completely powerless over alcohol, and that I was willing to do anything in the world to get rid of the problem.(p.187)
• Then I remember when the boys came back, that I told them, "I have gone to this *Higher* Power and I have told Him that I am willing to put His world first, above everything.(p.190)
• He said something about God or a *Higher* Power, but I brushed that off -- that was for the birds, not for me.(p.239)
• For a long time the only *Higher* Power I could concede was the power of the group, but this was far more than I had ever recognized before, and it was at least a beginning.(p.248)
• But he found that there was a *Higher* Power which had more faith in him than he had in himself.(p.287)
• 2.Dependence and guidance from a *Higher* Power.(p.292)
• This was such a new thought that I got all sorts of books on *Higher* Powers, and I put a Bible by my bedside, and I put a Bible in my car.(p.348)
• And the first thing you know I was lifted right out of the A.A. group, and I floated *higher*, and *higher*, and even *higher*, until I was way up on a pink cloud which is known as Pink Seven, and I felt miserable again.(p.348)
• The *Higher* Power was on deck to see me through, sober.(p.437)
• The *higher* my expectations of Max and other people are, the lower is my serenity.(p.452)
• And when I place more value on my serenity and sobriety than on anything else, I can maintain them at a *higher* level -- at least for the time being.(p.452)
• The *Higher* Power to whom I had turned, and who had sustained me, had once again been thrust into the background, while my emotions were running my life and, as always, my emotions ran me to the bottle.(p.472)
• I realized that I was trying to pin everything on an individual -- not the book or the group or the *Higher* Power, or anything else.(p.472)
• I have come to believe that my illness is spiritual as well as physical and mental, and I know that for help in the spiritual sphere I have to turn to a *Higher* Power.(p.473)
• I'm grateful because that *Higher* Power led me to A.A. a little over three years ago, when I needed it very badly.(p.512)
• It's like the fellow who came in A.A., and his sponsor said to him, "Listen, buddy, do you believe in a *Higher* Power?"(p.512)
• Today, I thank my *Higher* Power for giving me another chance at life and A.A. and being able to try and help some other alcoholic.(p.529)
• Learning to depend upon a *higher* power and absorb himself in his work with other alcoholics, he remains sober day by day.(p.572)

Higher Power

• His defense must come from a *Higher Power*.(p.43)
• Follow the dictates of a *Higher Power* and you will presently live in a new and wonderful world, no matter what your present circumstances!(p.100)
• The next question, they wanted to know was if I believed in a *Higher Power*.(p.186)
• The next thing they wanted to know was would I be willing to go to this *Higher Power* and ask for help, calmly and without any reservations.(p.186)
• So, after reviewing these things and realizing what liquor had cost me, I went to this *Higher Power* which, to me was God, without any reservation, and admitted that I was completely powerless over alcohol, and that I was willing to do anything in the world to get rid of the problem.(p.187)
• Then I remember when the boys came back, that I told them, "I have gone to this *Higher Power* and I have told Him that I am willing to put His world first, above everything.(p.190)
• He said something about God or a *Higher Power*, but I brushed that off -- that was for the birds, not for me.(p.239)
• For a long time the only *Higher Power* I could concede was the power of the group, but this was far more than I had ever recognized before, and it was at least a beginning.(p.248)
• But he found that there was a *Higher Power* which had more faith in him than he had in himself.(p.287)
• 2.Dependence and guidance from a *Higher Power*.(p.292)
• The *Higher Power* was on deck to see me through, sober.(p.437)
• The *Higher Power* to whom I had turned, and who had sustained me, had once again been thrust into the background, while my emotions were running my life and, as always, my emotions ran me to the bottle.(p.472)
• I realized that I was trying to pin everything on an individual -- not the book or the group or the *Higher Power*, or anything else.(p.472)
• I have come to believe that my illness is spiritual as well as physical and mental, and I know that for help in the spiritual sphere I have to turn to a *Higher Power*.(p.473)
• I'm grateful because that *Higher Power* led me to A.A. a little over three years ago, when I needed it very badly.(p.512)
• It's like the fellow who came in A.A., and his sponsor said to him, "Listen, buddy, do you believe in a *Higher Power*?"(p.512)
• Today, I thank my *Higher Power* for giving me another chance at life and A.A. and being able to try and help some other alcoholic.(p.529)

• Learning to depend upon a ***higher power*** and absorb himself in his work with other alcoholics, he remains sober day by day.(p.572)

highest

• This experience sent me to law school where I went at night and which course I completed in less than three years, taking the ***highest*** state bar examinations and passing them.(p.212)

• A few times at meetings, I have heard this statement: "Members of A.A. have paid the ***highest*** initiation fee of any club members in the world."(p.396)

• I learn that when we act upon the ***highest*** conception of honesty which is given us, our sense of honesty becomes more acute.(p.507)

highflown

• Actually, of course, I wanted someone to listen to me, because when I had a few martinis inside, I became the great author I longed to be; and the right listener was in for some pretty ***highflown*** theories of literature and of genius.(p.536)

highlights

• I would like to sketch for you the ***highlights*** of these sixteen years of a slow but steady and satisfying upward climb.(p.280)

highly

• ***Highly*** competent psychiatrists who have dealt with us have found it sometimes impossible to persuade an alcoholic to discuss his situation without reserve.(p.18)

• Cessation of drinking is but the first step away from a ***highly*** strained, abnormal condition.(p.122)

• Here was a tall, rugged, ***highly*** educated Yankee talking in a matter of course way about God and prayer.(p.279)

• We think that each group should soon achieve this ideal; that any public solicitation of funds using the name of Alcoholics Anonymous is ***highly*** dangerous, whether by groups, clubs, hospitals, or other outside agencies; that acceptance of large gifts from any source, or of contributions carrying any obligation whatever, is unwise.(p.566)

• "The American Public Health Association presents a Lasker Group Award for 1951 to Alcoholics Anonymous in recognition of its unique and ***highly*** successful approach to that age-old public health and social problem, alcoholism . . .(p.573)

highroad

• Yet it is our great hope that all those who have as yet found no answer may begin to find one in the pages of this book and will presently join us on the ***highroad*** to a new freedom.(p.xxi)

highstrung

• Father was a very well-integrated person, and while mother was ***highstrung*** and a bit selfish and demanding, our home life was reasonably harmonious.(p.240)

highway

• If our testimony helps sweep away prejudice, enables you to think honestly, encourages you to search diligently within yourself, then, if you wish, you can join us on the Broad ***Highway***.(p.55)

• We feel we are on the Broad ***Highway***, walking hand in hand with the Spirit of the Universe.(p.75)

• Need I say that in a very short time I was walking along a prairie ***highway*** with arm extended and thumb pointed?(p.255)

hilarious

• Here was love, applause, war; moments sublime with intervals ***hilarious***.(p.1)

• I was never a ***hilarious*** drunk; the more I drank the quieter I got, and the drunker I got the harder I fought to stay sober.(p.241)

• Strangely enough, I became acquainted with the "***hilarious*** life" just at the time in my own life when I was beginning really to settle down to a common-sense, sane domesticity.(p.297)

• The parties waxed more liquid and ***hilarious*** as time went on, and eventually I discovered that a little shot of liquor now and then between beers had the tendency to put me in a whacky mood much quicker than having to down several quarts of beer to obtain the same effect.(p.298)

hilarity

• Eventually, of course, what with all the ***hilarity*** that could be provoked with a few gallons of beer, there seemed to be no need of bridge or poker playing for entertainment.(p.297)

Hilda

• (Russ was buried on Friday, and on Sunday afternoon ***Hilda*** S. had invited me there to dinner Sunday night, and I didn't think I could do it.(p.272)

hill

• We drove to a store in North ***Hill*** and I sent him in with what money I had to get a quart.(p.204)

• After the tire job came the thirties, the Depression and the down ***hill*** road.(p.244)

• And then we went up the side of a ***hill*** where we have a little barbecue area to make the fire for the barbecue, and on the way up, I thought to myself – I'll go back down to the kitchen and refill this drink.(p.347)

hillside

• I could almost hear the sound of the preacher's voice as I sat, on still Sundays, way over there on the ***hillside***; there was that proffered temperance pledge I never signed; my grandfather's good natured contempt of some church folk and their doings; his insistence that the spheres really had their music; but his denial of the preacher's right to tell him how he must listen; his fearlessness as he spoke of these things just before he died; these recollections welled up from the past.(p.10)

hilltop

• Never talk down to an alcoholic from any moral or spiritual ***hilltop***; simply lay out the kit of spiritual tools for his inspection.(p.95)

Himalaya

• The place is Naini Tal, in the foothills of the mighty ***Himalaya*** Mountains, and it has some very significant memories for me.(p.342)

Hindus

• By personal religious affiliation, we include Catholics, Protestants, Jews, ***Hindus***, and a sprinkling of Moslems and Buddhists.(p.xx)

hint

• Of course, I had no ***hint*** or intimation as to what the treatment was to consist of.(p.302)

hinted

• My wife never ***hinted*** that she would leave me.(p.345)

• It ***hinted*** to me that everything was phony.(p.418)

• Never once had my mother even ***hinted*** at the idea that, when I grew up, I might like to be president of A.A.(p.439)

hints

• Until I took Social Security and a pension at the age of sixty-eight, after forty years in motion-picture-studio public relations, I had successfully hidden even any ***hints*** of approaching alcoholism.(p.327)

hip

• I would reach over and get this and take a shot and in a few moments get up and take another, shave and eat my breakfast, slip a half pint of liquor in my ***hip*** pocket, and go on to school.(p.183)

• That age of the flapper and the "It" girl, speakeasies and the ***hip*** flask, the boyish bob and the drugstore cowboy, John Held Jr. and F. Scott Fitzgerald, all generously sprinkled with a patent pseudo-sophistication.(p.304)

hire

• In the doctor's judgment he was utterly hopeless; he could never regain his position in society and he would have to place himself under lock and key or ***hire*** a bodyguard if he expected to live long.(p.26)

• Everyone had my number and wouldn't ***hire*** me at any price.(p.301)

• We define professionalism as the occupation of counseling alcoholics for fees or ***hire***.(p.566)

hired

• He has ***hired*** and fired hundreds of men.(p.136)

• A couple of ***hired*** hands were cleaning out the barn on the farm and I would ride to and fro on the sled, and while they were loading I would drink hard cider out of a barrel in the barn.(p.183)

historians

• ***Historians*** may one day recognize Alcoholics Anonymous to have been a great venture in social pioneering which forged a new instrument for social action; a new therapy based on the kinship of common suffering; one having a vast potential for the myriad other ills of mankind."(p.573)

historic

• Because the "long form" is more explicit and of possible ***historic*** value, it is also reproduced.(p.563)

historical

• Loading a car with good old books to sell to collectors, librarians, universities and ***historical*** societies, I started out to travel the country.(p.255)

histories

• Beginning with the story of "Dr. Bob," a co-founder of A.A., there are here presented three groups of personal ***histories***.(p.165)

• A friend who knew I would soon be broke mounted guard over me when I left my job of writing the ***histories*** of Texas cities and put me aboard a bus for the town I had left almost five years before.(p.256)

history

• "Bill's Story," "Doctor Bob's Nightmare," and one other personal ***history*** from the first edition were retained intact; three were edited and one of these was retitled; new versions of two stories were written with new titles; thirty completely new stories were added; and the story section was divided into three parts, under the same headings that are used now.(p.xi)

• These stark and ugly facts have been confirmed by legions of alcoholics throughout ***history***.(p.24)

• Students of ancient ***history*** tell us that the intellect of men in those days was equal to the best of today.(p.51)

• I told the doctor my parents' drinking ***history*** and blamed them.(p.428)

• On one occasion when I was serving time in my favorite drying-out place while I was having a session with the psychiatrist, she left my case ***history*** on her desk when she was called away from the room.(p.470)

• They weren't quite so up-to-date on my ***history*** and I got away with about four years with them.(p.520)

• The mental twists that led up to my drinking began many years before I ever took a drink for I am one of those whose ***history*** proves conclusively that my drinking was "a symptom of a deeper trouble."(p.544)

hit

• That statement ***hit*** me hard.(p.12)

• Presently he is ***hit*** again and this time has a fractured skull.(p.38)

• I was willing to admit to myself that I had ***hit*** bottom, that I had gotten hold of something that I didn't know how to handle by myself.(p.187)

• I tried to conduct a kangaroo court and ***hit*** them with a broomstick.(p.204)

• But then I ***hit*** a snag.(p.227)

• Had he come two or three days later I think I would have thrown him out, but he ***hit*** when I was open for anything.(p.239)

• Forced to detrain from an empty gondola on the other side of Chicago by a terrific rainstorm which drenched me to the skin, I ***hit*** the first factory building I saw for a job.(p.253)

• When I ***hit*** Houston, Texas, I found employment in a large bookstore.(p.255)

• I was ***hit*** by an icy blast.(p.288)

• They sum it up like this: "We didn't wait to ***hit*** bottom because, thank God, we could see the bottom.(p.315)

• Actually, the bottom came up and ***hit*** us.(p.315)

• I usually passed out when I ***hit*** the bed.(p.319)

• One night, I ***hit*** the jackpot.(p.332)

• One said, "Don't feel that you are a martyr because you stopped drinking," and this ***hit*** me between the eyes.(p.346)

• The second one said, "Don't feel that you stop drinking for anyone other than yourself," and this ***hit*** me between the eyes.(p.346)

• I think that is when I ***hit*** bottom.(p.391)

• A normal person, ***hit*** with adversity, can go on a drinking spree and then snap out of it.(p.404)

• On our honeymoon in Egypt, he cuffed me around quite a bit, and subsequently ***hit*** me some more.(p.405)

• I literally ***hit*** the sawdust.(p.411)

• Her idea of fun on a bender was to ***hit*** sailors and insult cops.(p.414)

• Or, "I got to talking and forgot how many I was taking and it ***hit*** me."(p.433)

• Weeks would go by without further trouble, and I'd be assured I'd at last ***hit*** on the right formula.(p.433)

• I thought that was bad until I ***hit*** the hole at a prison camp; it was just wide enough and long enough to lie down in.(p.459)

• I ***hit*** my bottom.(p.461)

• Knowing that he was sober, I timed it just right, so I could do the slashing just before he ***hit*** the steps.(p.479)

• When I landed of course I ***hit*** a gin mill, and with three or four good shots under my belt the world began to go into that rosy glow.(p.513)

• You ***hit*** the street about ten minutes to eight, and you walk around the block, God knows how many times, waiting for that joint to open.(p.514)

hitch-hiking

• Always, in between, there were intervals of being broke, riding freights and ***hitch-hiking*** interminable distances from one big town to another in three states.(p.255)

hitchhiking

• Can you picture two girls ***hitchhiking*** their way to Las Vegas from Washington State?(p.354)

Hitler's

• Then ***Hitler's*** war broke out, and again, I was given a really important job on the Suez Canal, dealing with military shipping.(p.520)

hitting

• I began ***hitting*** the bottle again, and with it self-pity, resentment, loneliness and remorse set in deeply.(p.362)

• I knew I was ***hitting*** the skids, but what of it?(p.427)

• I would rather talk about the good things A.A. has taught me; I feel that ***hitting*** on just a few sordid points should be sufficient to let those of you in institutions know where I came from.(p.459)

hobbies

• So oldsters are advised to develop interest, find ***hobbies***.(p.330)

hobo

• In my early twenties the hardships of ***hobo*** life did not discourage me, but I had no wish to become just a tramp.(p.253)

hobo's

• Our shoes are not better than the average ***hobo's***, and if we are fortunate enough to have a pair of stockings on, nobody notices the runs in them, because of our dazzling beauty and our dirty feet.(p.479)

hock

• They sent me the regular letter they send to everybody else, but along with it, Ruth ***Hock***, the nonalcoholic secretary, wrote a longhand note because she could see from the letter that I really needed help badly.(p.392)

hockey

• If anyone had told me I would be enjoying a ***hockey*** game with my husband and my brother without being all boozed up, I would not have believed it.(p.481)

hoist

• We had some people in, and I was making drinks in the kitchen, when I suddenly decided to ***hoist*** the bottle for a quick one.(p.365)

hold

• The basic principles of the A.A. program, it appears, ***hold*** good for individuals with many different life-styles, just as the program has brought recovery to those of many different nationalities.(p.xxii)

• The message which can interest and ***hold*** these alcoholic people must have depth and weight.(p.xxvi)

• I do not ***hold*** with those who believe that alcoholism is entirely a problem of mental control.(p.xxvii)

• Once this malady has a real ***hold***, they are a baffled lot.(p.23)

• Our sound reasoning failed to ***hold*** us in check.(p.37)

• These tiny bodies are governed by precise laws, and these laws ***hold*** true throughout the material world.(p.49)

• Some of us have tried to ***hold*** on to our old ideas and the result was nil until we let go absolutely.(p.58)

• If that is so, this step may be postponed, only however, if we ***hold*** ourselves in complete readiness to go through with it at the first opportunity.(p.74)

• Our loyalty and the desire that our husbands ***hold*** up their heads and be like other men have begotten all sorts of predicaments.(p.105)

• We have tried to ***hold*** the love of our children for their father.(p.106)

• He sometimes drinks in the morning and through the day also, to ***hold*** his nervousness in check.(p.109)

• His friends have slipped away, his home is a near-wreck and he cannot ***hold*** a position.(p.110)

• If the family persists in criticism, this fallacy may take a still greater ***hold*** on father.(p.129)

• The family may feel they ***hold*** a mortgage on dad, so big that no equity should be left for outsiders.(p.131)

• I know, in my own particular case, that nothing my company could have done would have stopped me or, so long as I was able to ***hold*** my position, I could not possibly realize how serious my situation was.(p.141)

• When I went in to write the examinations, my hand trembled so I could not ***hold*** a pencil.(p.174)

Then Prohibition came into effect, and the facts that the stuff obtainable was so horrible and sometimes deadly, and that I had married and had a job which I had to look after, helped me for a period of some three or four years, although I would get drunk every time I could get ***hold*** of enough to drink to get started.(p.183)

I was willing to admit to myself that I had hit bottom, that I had gotten ***hold*** of something that I didn't know how to handle by myself.(p.187)

• As long as things were tough and the job a challenge I could always manage to ***hold*** on pretty well, but as soon as I learned the combination, got the puzzle under control and the boss to pat me on the back, I was gone again.(p.243)

• Young and able to travel with the best of them, I managed to ***hold*** my job and keep my end up in the barrooms.(p.252)

• I sipped the drink off the bar because I couldn't ***hold*** it in my hand, but I was still a lady, believe it or not, and I was deeply ashamed.(p.266)

• I'd like to say here how important it was to us then that we do all the little things that people said were important, because later when Russ was so sick that I had to ***hold*** him up, they had a meeting out at the house.(p.270)

• Many women who have reached the stage that I had reached in my drinking have lost husbands, children, homes, everything they ***hold*** dear.(p.323)

• I felt disgraced and humiliated – a man who couldn't ***hold*** booze – a social disaster.(p.328)

• Every breadwinner, whether trying to impress a boss or to ***hold*** customers in his own business, is fettered by people-pleasing.(p.329)

• I should have realized that alcohol was getting ***hold*** of me when I started to become secretive in my drinking.(p.336)

• It finally got such a ***hold*** on me that I was completely at my wits' end, not knowing what the result would be.(p.343)

• But for some reason – she just didn't know why -- she just had to ***hold*** onto that clipping, with its thin hope.(p.367)

• I learned how to ***hold*** a terrapin fork.(p.401)

• All I want to know is, why does that dog wet in my lap every time I ***hold*** him?"(p.440)

• Then Charlie or someone in the group suggested that we try to get a place in a church or hall to ***hold*** meetings.(p.495)

• They came, many of them, and stuck by us and told us how to ***hold*** meetings.(p.495)

• I can ***hold*** a lot now, more than the others.(p.499)

• He was drinking to ***hold*** on to his job, to ***hold*** on to his wife, to ***hold*** on to his sanity.(p.512)

• I was drinking to try to ***hold*** on to a job, to try and ***hold*** on to my home, to try to ***hold*** on to my wife, to try to ***hold*** on to my sanity.(p.514)

• I'd get downstairs to the gin mill, get enough in to ***hold*** me until eight o'clock in the morning, then I'd go out to join that "misery parade" that so many of us know so well.(p.514)

• I was not able to ***hold*** a job – no one wants a drunk around.(p.526)

• Inside, though, I was scared to death, for I knew that the time was coming (and it couldn't be too remote) when I would be unable to ***hold*** that job.(p.548)

• Maybe I wouldn't be able to ***hold*** any job, or maybe (and this was my greatest fear) I wouldn't care whether I had a job or not.(p.548)

holder

• The house was taken over by the mortgage ***holder***, my mother-in-law died, and my wife and father-in-law became ill.(p.5)

holding

• At this time I was ***holding*** what drinking I did down to weekends, but I hadn't had a drink at all in a month.(p.243)

• After ***holding*** good positions, making better than an average income for over ten years, I was in debt, had no clothes to speak of, no money, no friends, and no one any longer tolerating me but my wife.(p.301)

• As self-conscious as I was, I had to pose for those pictures, ***holding*** this huge bouquet.(p.385)

holds

• An alcoholic who has recovered, but ***holds*** a relatively unimportant job, can talk to a man with a better position.(p.146)

• He may even read in a newspaper that one out of every seven drinkers will become alcoholic, but he rarely is told that it ***holds*** true for all ages – or that the tolerance to alcohol (and other drugs) decreases steadily, year after year, in the bodies of all persons.(p.330)

hole

• This secret drinker favored the local Laundromat as a watering ***hole***.(p.369)

• Then I looked forward to the week-end of golf and the nineteenth ***hole***.(p.374)

• But when I cracked my leg with a sixteen-pound sledgehammer in the rock ***hole***, I was fighting the system, using my body.(p.458)

• In a prison in my native state, I spent eleven months in solitary confinement, bouncing in and out of the "***hole***" (a bare concrete-and-steel cubicle) about five times during those eleven months.(p.459)

• Each ten-day period in the dark ***hole***, I was fed bread and water daily, with one full meal on the third day only.(p.459)

• I thought that was bad until I hit the ***hole*** at a prison camp; it was just wide enough and long enough to lie down in.(p.459)

• Ten days of this treatment the first time knocked me from 200 pounds to 130, and I seldom stayed out of the ***hole*** long enough to gain back my weight.(p.460)

• Fortunately, I received only fifteen-twenty years, and I went back to my alma mater (where I had spent so much time in the ***hole***).(p.461)

• Economic conditions had a great deal to do with it, because I've often heard my father say that his mother would take one of the old time flour sacks and cut a ***hole*** through the bottom and two corners of it and there you'd have a gown.(p.486)

holiday

• They called the Mayor in so we wouldn't have to stay in there over the ***holiday***.(p.264)

• After a particularly bad Christmas and New Year's ***holiday***, dad picked me up again early in January, 1937, to go through the usual sobering up routine.(p.289)

holidays

• I got through the ***holidays*** all right until New Year's Day.(p.365)

• I said I was okay, but if it would make her feel better I would go "as tired as I was after the strenuous ***holidays***."(p.365)

• My parents were due for the ***holidays*** that day, and she didn't want them to find their drunken daughter there.(p.467)

holier

• That the man who is making the approach has had the same difficulty, that he obviously knows what he is talking about, that his whole deportment shouts at the new prospect that he is a man with a real answer, that he has no attitude of ***Holier*** Than Thou, nothing whatever except the sincere desire to be helpful; that there are no fees to pay, no axes to grind, no people to please, no lectures to be endured -- these are the conditions we have found most effective.(p.18)

holler

• They roll on the floor and ***holler***, and pull their hair."(p.266)

home

• Twenty-two, and a veteran of foreign wars, I went ***home*** at last.(p.1)

• My wife began to work in a department store, coming ***home*** exhausted to find me drunk.(p.4)

• Shortly afterward I came ***home*** drunk.(p.5)

• One poor chap committed suicide in my ***home***.(p.16)

• Here are some of the methods we have tried: Drinking beer only, limiting the number of drinks, never drinking alone, never drinking in the morning, drinking only at ***home***, never having it in the house, never drinking during business hours, drinking only at parties, switching from scotch to brandy, drinking only natural wines, agreeing to resign if ever drunk on the job, taking a trip, not taking a trip, swearing off forever (with and without a solemn oath), taking more physical exercise, reading inspirational books, going to health farms and sanitariums, accepting voluntary commitment to asylums -- we could increase the list ad infinitum.(p.31)

• This is a point we wish to emphasize and re-emphasize, to smash ***home*** upon our alcoholic readers as it has been revealed to us out of bitter experience.(p.39)

• His income is good, he has a fine ***home***, is happily married and the father of promising children of college age.(p.39)

• We hope it strikes ***home*** to thousands like him.(p.43)

• Returning ***home*** we find a place where we can be quiet for an hour carefully reviewing what we have done.(p.75)

• But drinking does complicate sex relations in the ***home***.(p.81)

• If we have no such complication, there is plenty we should do at ***home***.(p.82)

• Certainly he must keep sober, for there will be no ***home*** if he doesn't.(p.82)

• Selfish and inconsiderate habits have kept the ***home*** in turmoil.(p.82)

• He is like the farmer who came up out of his cyclone cellar to find his ***home*** ruined.(p.82)

• Perhaps you will want to take the man into your ***home*** for a few days.(p.96)

• It may mean sharing your money and your ***home***, counseling frantic wives and relatives, innumerable trips to police courts, sanitariums,

hospitals, jails and asylums.(p.97)
• A drunk may smash the furniture in your ***home,*** or burn a mattress.(p.97)
• When your prospect has made such reparation as he can to his family, and has thoroughly explained to them the new principles by which he is living, he should proceed to put those principles into action at ***home.***(p.98)
• That is, if he is lucky enough to have a ***home.***(p.98)
• An armored car could not have brought the pay envelopes ***home.***(p.105)
• The bill collectors, the sheriffs, the angry taxi drivers, the policemen, the bums, the pals, and even the ladies they sometimes brought ***home*** -- our husbands thought we were so inhospitable.(p.106)
• Perhaps at this point we got a divorce and took the children ***home*** to father and mother.(p.106)
• His friends have slipped away, his ***home*** is a near-wreck and he cannot hold a position.(p.110)
• Sometimes he drinks on the way ***home*** from the hospital.(p.110)
• You draw more and more into yourself and you think everyone is talking about conditions at your ***home.***(p.114)
• Then that terrible tension which grips the ***home*** of every problem drinker will be lessened.(p.115)
• Perhaps your husband will make a fair start on the new basis, but just as things are going beautifully he dismays you by coming ***home*** drunk.(p.120)
• The head of the house ought to remember that he is mainly to blame for what befell his ***home.***(p.127)
• Since the ***home*** has suffered more than anything else, it is well that a man exert himself there.(p.127)
• Instead of developing new channels of activity for themselves, mother and children demand that he stay ***home*** and make up the deficiency.(p.131)
• We all had to place recovery above everything, for without recovery we would have lost both ***home*** and business.(p.143)
• If he speaks of his ***home*** situation, you can undoubtedly make helpful suggestions.(p.145)
• It was the usual situation: ***home*** in jeopardy, wife ill, children distracted, bills in arrears and standing damaged.(p.155)
• Being intrigued, however, he invited our friend to his ***home.***(p.155)
• At midnight he came ***home*** exhausted, but very happy.(p.156)
• The last three times, I got drunk on the way ***home*** from here.(p.157)
• He now returned ***home,*** leaving behind his first acquaintance, the lawyer and the devil-may-care chap.(p.159)
• Seeing much of each other, scarce an evening passed that someone's ***home*** did not shelter a little gathering of men and women, happy in their release, and constantly thinking how they might present their discovery to some newcomer.(p.159)
• One man and his wife placed their large ***home*** at the disposal of this strangely assorted crowd.(p.160)
• This couple has since become so fascinated that they have dedicated their ***home*** to the work.(p.160)
• Many a man, yet dazed from his hospital experience, has stepped over the threshold of that ***home*** into freedom.(p.160)
• Finally my father had to send a doctor out from my ***home*** town who managed to get me back there in some way, and I was in bed about two months before I could venture out of the house.(p.175)
• This would lessen my chances of smuggling some ***home*** that evening, which in turn would mean a night of futile tossing around in bed followed by a morning of unbearable jitters.(p.176)
• But my friends usually found me and I would go ***home*** if they promised that I should not be scolded.(p.176)
• If my wife was planning to go out in the afternoon, I would get a large supply of liquor and smuggle it ***home*** and hide it in the coal bin, the clothes chute, over door jambs, over beams in the cellar and in cracks in the cellar tile.(p.176)
• It was really a horrible nightmare, this earning money, getting liquor, smuggling it ***home,*** getting drunk, morning jitters, taking large doses of sedatives to make it possible for me to earn more money, and so on ad nauseam.(p.177)
• It was the day before Mother's Day and I had come ***home*** plastered, carrying a big potted plant which I set down on the table and forthwith went upstairs and passed out.(p.179)
• I remember nothing from then on until I woke up at a friend's house, in a town near ***home.***(p.179)
• He came and got me ***home*** and to bed, gave me a few drinks that night, and one bottle of beer the next morning.(p.179)
• My ***home*** life is ideal and my business is as good as can be expected in these uncertain times.(p.180)
• Away from my office two or three weeks at a time; horrible days and nights when I would lie on the floor of my ***home,*** lying awake and reaching over to get the bottle, taking a drink and going back into oblivion.(p.184)
• I didn't like having to come ***home*** at a certain time; I didn't like this, I didn't like that, and I think the poor girl actually divorced me to help me stop drinking!(p.199)
• So I didn't have a beer one night, and as I drove ***home*** I was breaking my arm patting myself on the back because I had proved I could lick liquor.(p.203)
• So having licked it, there was no reason why I shouldn't have a drink, and I stopped in before I got ***home*** and had one.(p.203)
• To show you the point to which this obsession went, there came an occasion when I had spent a most delightful week-end, and at nine o'clock on Sunday night I was on my way ***home,*** and I thought I would get a drink.(p.204)
• When I got ***home*** I had to give him a check for the taxi fare.(p.205)
• At night, I woke up and the folks with whom I roomed were ***home*** by then.(p.205)
• In fact, on one occasion, I was picked up by the police and brought ***home.***(p.211)
• There had been some occasions -- there was an automobile wreck, for instance -- when I had police escort ***home*** but not to jail, all of which, instead of doing me a favor, did me harm because I was then full of self-esteem as to the progress I had made both professionally and financially.(p.213)
• As far as my ***home*** was concerned, I did not see then, though of course I can see now, that it was anything but a happy situation for my wife.(p.215)
• However, on a couple of other occasions, Clarence seemed to bob up at the last saloon that I would stop at on the way ***home*** every day.(p.216)
• One evening I had gone out after dinner to take on a couple of double-headers and stayed a little later than usual, and when I came ***home*** Clarence was sitting on the davenport with Bill W.(p.216)
• It was finally decided to undertake the organization of a Cleveland group and toward the end of May, 1939, the first meeting was held in Cleveland in my ***home.***(p.219)
• I believe though that it helped my family tremendously to have the A.A. meetings every week in my own ***home.***(p.220)
• Sitting in a Second Avenue bar, accepting drinks from anyone who offered, after my small stake was gone; or sitting at ***home*** alone, with the inevitable glass in my hand, I would remember, and remembering, I would drink faster, seeking speedy oblivion.(p.225)
• "Blanks" were more frequent, and I seldom knew how I'd got ***home.***(p.226)
• No doubt I had been an exile too long -- I should go ***home*** to America.(p.226)
• I went trembling into a house in Brooklyn filled with strangers . . . and I found I had come ***home*** at last, to my own kind.(p.228)
• It is: "to come ***home.***"(p.228)
• My parents had some vague idea of making a priest out of me and for some years I attended the Franciscan school at Basle, Switzerland, just across the border, about six miles from my ***home.***(p.230)
• Military service was compulsory and I did my stretch with the class of my age, goose-stepping in German barracks and taking part in the Boxer Rebellion in China, my first time at any great distance from ***home.***(p.230)
• In foreign parts many a soldier who has been abstemious at ***home*** learns to use new and potent drinks.(p.230)
• By this time I was married and was paying for a ***home.***(p.232)
• In four or five days I would be hunting all over the place, at ***home*** and in my workshop, for the bottles I had destroyed, cursing myself for being a fool.(p.234)
• Father was a very well-integrated person, and while mother was highstrung and a bit selfish and demanding, our ***home*** life was reasonably harmonious.(p.240)
• I had repaired to one of these one morning with my jug and when I left late in the afternoon, I picked up a newspaper on the way ***home.***(p.244)
• Evidently I had gone right back to the movie with a bottle, stayed there several hours and started ***home*** with no recollection of what had happened.(p.244)
• We checked into the ***home*** of Hank, the man who had fired me eleven years before in Mississippi, and there I met Bill, our founder.(p.245)
• There was one meeting a week at Bill's ***home*** in Brooklyn, and we all took turns there spouting off about how we had changed our lives overnight, how many drunks we had saved and straightened out, and last, but not least, how God had touched each of us personally on the shoulder.(p.246)
• While there I was called to the hospital in my ***home*** town to see a former partner who had insisted that I visit him.(p.257)
• That night I was taken ***home*** by a former alcoholic and his wife.(p.259)
• The hospitality of their ***home*** and their fine fellowship were freely mine.(p.259)
• When I came to my aunt, she knew that I had had an unhappy childhood, and she said, "Now, Ethel, you're welcome to have boy friends in our ***home,*** but there are two boys in this town that I don't want you to date, and one of them comes from a very fine family, one of the best.(p.262)
• Finally, it got so bad that I left him and went back ***home*** and took my two children with me.(p.262)
• Of course, this year we decided on staying ***home*** and being sensible, doing a little drinking, and painting the house.(p.265)
• They spent at least an evening a week in our ***home*** out there for weeks and weeks.(p.270)
• I remember sometime, it was possibly six months after we had been going steadily to King School, that we were coming ***home*** from a meeting and saw a car along the way, and a fellow in back drinking a bottle of beer.(p.271)
• Fear froze me in my tracks, but the instant I turned back toward ***home*** this paralyzing fear left me.(p.276)
• When I reached a point directly back of our house, where I could have cut through a friend's garden, I was almost overpowered by the desire to get ***home,*** but I made the whole journey.(p.276)
• Haunting me through each day's stupor -- and there were eighteen or nineteen such days in this man's ***home*** -- was the thought: "Where do I go when his family comes ***home?***"(p.278)
• Out of this maelstrom just two coherent thoughts came to the surface; one, a drink would mean homelessness and death; two, I could no longer relieve the pressure of fear by starting ***home,*** as was once my habitual solution to this problem, because I no longer had a ***home.***(p.279)
• During my first few months in Akron I was quite sure that I never wanted to see my ***home*** town again.(p.281)
• After I left school, I went to work in Akron, living at ***home*** with my parents.(p.287)
• ***Home*** life was again a restraining influence.(p.287)
• This was the beginning of five years of bounding back and forth between my ***home*** in Chicago and Akron to sober up.(p.288)
• This first meeting was held in the living room of a ***home*** and was led by Bill D., the first man that Bill W. and Dr. Bob had worked with successfully.(p.291)
• Every evening we would meet at the ***home*** of one of the members and have coffee and doughnuts and spend a social evening.(p.291)
• Such has been my privilege, both nationally and in my ***home*** city.(p.295)
• ***HOME*** BREWMEISTER(p.297)
• From that point on, I secured crocks of ten gallon capacity and really took quite an active interest in the manufacture of ***home*** brew.(p.297)
• A night or so a week in a joint, and a party or so a week at ***home*** or with friends, along with a little lone drinking, soon had me preparing for the existence of a top flight drunkard.(p.298)
• At that time, I was living out of town, so I moved back to the ***home*** town and made a connection in a responsible position with one of the larger companies in the finance business.(p.298)
• This would get me feeling fit, and then I would start for ***home*** and fireside, thirteen miles away.(p.299)
• On the way ***home*** numerous places must be passed.(p.299)
• Eventually I would arrive ***home*** for a late supper for which, of course, I had absolutely no relish.(p.299)
• Evenings at ***home*** were an ordeal.(p.299)
• One is that I don't remember too many of them, as I was one of those drunks who could be on his feet and attend a meeting or a party, engage in a conversation with people and do things that any nearly normal person would do, and the next day not remember a thing about where I was, what I did, whom I saw, or how I got ***home.***(p.301)
• From a domestic standpoint, we really have a ***home*** now.(p.303)
• I am anxious to get ***home*** after dark.(p.303)
• Our ***home*** is always full of friends and visitors.(p.303)
• (No ***home*** brew as an inducement).(p.303)

- I was given every advantage in a well ordered ***home***.(p.304)
- My broken ***home*** and broken heart fanned my smoldering self-pity into a fair-sized bonfire and this kept me well supplied with reasons for having another drink, and then another.(p.305)
- I moved a thousand miles away from ***home*** to Chicago and a new environment.(p.305)
- Alone in the relative safety of my ***home*** because I knew I dare not risk the danger of blacking out in some public place or at the wheel of a car.(p.306)
- The next three years saw me in sanitariums, once in a ten day coma, from which I very nearly did not recover, in and out of hospitals or confined at ***home*** with day and night nurses.(p.306)
- When I came ***home*** from Nam, I met a girl I'll call Karen.(p.318)
- When I came ***home*** again, the only thing I had left to love was the bottle.(p.318)
- I called her every night from a local bar, and often she was not at ***home***.(p.318)
- I said, "Well, I stood it to keep the ***home*** together, and for the children's sake."(p.322)
- Fortunately, I didn't say a word to George on the way ***home***.(p.322)
- If I had been sincere in what I thought I wanted more than anything else in life -- a sober husband and a happy, contented ***home*** -- I would have gone on the wagon with him.(p.324)
- I still had a wife and family, a ***home*** and a car, my driver's license, and a proper amount of insurance.(p.327)
- I was assigned to keep media guests happy at a Halloween party given by a major star in his plush ***home***.(p.328)
- All hidden drunks aren't at ***home*** in housewives' dresses.(p.328)
- So long as a retiree woos his bottle at ***home***, he stays out of public trouble.(p.330)
- THE HOUSEWIFE WHO DRANK AT ***HOME***(p.335)
- My story happens to be a particular kind of woman's story; the story of the woman who drinks at ***home***.(p.335)
- I had to be at ***home***.(p.335)
- But during a period of particular stress and strain about thirteen years ago, I resorted to alcohol in my ***home***, alone, as a means of temporary release, as a means of getting a little extra sleep.(p.335)
- My ***home*** at that time was a place to mill around in.(p.337)
- How I ran my ***home***, I don't know.(p.337)
- I called my husband up and told him to come ***home***.(p.338)
- I was a woman, tied to my ***home***.(p.338)
- And it was my ***home*** that suffered.(p.339)
- Surrender to me has meant the ability to run my ***home***, to face my responsibilities as they should be faced, to take life as it comes to me day by day, and work my problems out.(p.340)
- I returned to my ***home*** in Lucknow, India, at the end of November last year from a vacation in one of the most famous beauty spots in our country, a mountain resort 6,800 feet up, with a wonderful lake.(p.342)
- This friend gave me a pamphlet, and I took it ***home*** and had my wife read it to me.(p.346)
- Why don't you go ***home*** and get the Big Book and open it at page fifty-eight and see what it says?"(p.349)
- I didn't know how to be a father; I don't know how to come ***home*** and work week-ends like other husbands; I don't know how to entertain my family.(p.351)
- Without hesitation, I did the only logical thing -- ran away from ***home***.(p.354)
- I had turned eighteen during the trip, and I despondently returned ***home*** by jet (on Daddy's bankbook) to a pair of miserable, hurt parents.(p.354)
- As usual, I ran out of money, and, as usual, I wired my father for funds to come ***home***.(p.357)
- He answered by wiring that I could stay there until I earned enough to get ***home***.(p.357)
- It took me a year to make it ***home***.(p.357)
- When I did make it ***home*** in 1920, I re-entered school and caught up with my class in a few short months -- I actually did a year's work in three months, proving much to the disgust of my dad that I could do it when I wanted to.(p.358)
- All I can remember about the Roaring Twenties is that I drank a great deal, thought I was having a grand time, managed to get to Europe for a few weeks, was very proud of the dozens of speak-easy cards entitling me to an entree in the better joints between Cleveland and New York, took on a wife, and built a ***home*** in a fashionable suburb of Cleveland.(p.358)
- She was studying fashion design, was living in the same rooming house, and was from my ***home*** town of Cleveland.(p.359)
- It was to be short lived, for on the day before Christmas I completely disillusioned my wife and ruined our first Christmas by coming ***home*** from the Rotary lunch dead drunk.(p.361)
- By hook or crook I usually managed to sober up before I reached ***home***, but always "terribly tired" from a "hard day's work," and just having to have one or two before dinner.(p.361)
- After another of my "never again episodes" she packed up and left for her parents' ***home*** in Florida.(p.362)
- Why should this happen to me -- hadn't I provided a good ***home*** -- wasn't I making a good living -- didn't I just get a substantial raise that had put me in the upper bracket class?(p.362)
- One Saturday noon I staggered ***home*** with every intention of showing her.(p.362)
- I was certainly a complete surprise when I arrived at her family's ***home***, but because I arrived on the wings of a tropical hurricane there wasn't much she could do but let me in.(p.364)
- I tried a few drinks my last night in the city before coming ***home***.(p.364)
- Luck was with me for I made my train, but I arrived ***home*** the next morning with a new kind of hangover.(p.364)
- Now, she no longer risks losing her ***home***, her self-respect, or her laundry.(p.369)
- I couldn't drink at ***home***, because my husband frowned upon this.(p.370)
- The only drawback was, I always knew how I arrived there, but somehow, between the rest room, the rinse, and the fluff-dry, I never knew when or how I got ***home***.(p.370)
- We soon resumed our marriage, even moved away from the street of sad memories and found a new ***home***.(p.371)
- I'm very active in A.A. work and active at ***home***, too, with my family.(p.372)
- How can a person with a fine family, an attractive ***home***, an excellent position and high standing in an important city become an alcoholic?(p.373)
- To wake up at ***home***, not knowing how I got there, and to realize I had driven my car, became torture.(p.375)
- Not knowing where I had been or how I got ***home*** was making me desperate.(p.375)
- We had always encouraged our children to bring their friends ***home*** at any time, but after a few experiences with a drunken father they eliminated ***home*** as a place to entertain friends.(p.376)
- A year later, while we were on a vacation trip she packed up to go ***home*** because of my excessive drinking, and I talked her out of it with the promise I would go on the wagon for at least a year.(p.377)
- They told me to go to meetings, and I still do at every available opportunity, whether I am at ***home*** or in some other city.(p.381)
- She still had her husband, her ***home***, and a chance to help start A.A. in Texas.(p.384)
- I can't remember a dinner at ***home*** that we didn't have white wine or claret on the table.(p.384)
- The church was just three blocks from our ***home***.(p.385)
- Then I went ***home***.(p.386)
- Frank, my husband, would come ***home*** day after day and find me passed out.(p.386)
- Or he would leave on a trip and by the time he came ***home***, I'd be passed out.(p.386)
- I wanted to go ***home***.(p.387)
- So the doctor let me go ***home*** on one condition.(p.387)
- He asked if I would cooperate with him after I went ***home***, and if I would have a trained nurse stay with me for at least two weeks.(p.387)
- I was so happy over getting ***home*** that I changed overnight, but not enough.(p.387)
- Every time I got drunk, my husband would send me to a nursing ***home***.(p.388)
- So I went down to him quite a few times a month and had him shoot me full of the stuff; and then I went across the street to a little drug store to take a glass of beer or two beers, and then stopped at the liquor store to get myself a pint and go ***home***.(p.389)
- The cop must have seen the condition that I was in because he decided to take me ***home***.(p.390)
- When he picked me up, I must have gotten sassy and told him that he couldn't do that, so he took my dog ***home*** and took me to jail!(p.390)
- But Frank turned around and looked at me and said, "Esther, remember you're in jail and not at ***home***."(p.391)
- If you don't, you will have to go ***home***.(p.391)
- I know that when Frank came ***home***, I said, "I want to try this thing," and he said, "There's a post office box to write to in New York."(p.392)
- Two weeks later found me being sworn in, and the first payday in the Navy made me realize I had found a ***home***.(p.398)
- I was born in a castle -- the family ***home***, in Europe.(p.400)
- At eighteen I ran away from ***home***.(p.401)
- So I married a nice, well-meaning young newspaper-man, so as not to have to go ***home***.(p.402)
- It was the only real ***home*** she knew.(p.402)
- Even then I knew in my heart that I was unfit for the very things I wanted most, a happy marriage, security, a ***home*** and love.(p.403)
- My tongue had become increasingly skilled at venomous ***home*** truths.(p.405)
- I had already been to one analyst at ***home***.(p.406)
- I passed out frequently in my ***home***, alone.(p.406)
- Now it was semi-blackouts every night, outrageous behavior, passing out in some friend's Village studio or not knowing how I got ***home***.(p.407)
- I rarely remembered getting ***home***.(p.410)
- I suspect that those bartenders would wait until I shot my wad, then call a cab and send me ***home***.(p.410)
- In less than two years, I lost my practice, my ***home***, my wife, and my children.(p.418)
- The last time I drank, when I was twenty-nine, I drank for only four days, yet I threatened to kill my children; I beat my wife at ***home*** and on the church steps; I mistreated a child in my office; and I ran to a hospital for mental illness to avoid jail.(p.418)
- A.A. has given me a new wife, a beautiful stepdaughter, a new practice, a new ***home***, and a new relationship with my four children.(p.420)
- ***Home*** life didn't mean much to me.(p.424)
- We got to Omaha, from my ***home*** in Chicago.(p.424)
- Back ***home*** again!(p.424)
- Drinking conditions at ***home*** were even worse than before.(p.424)
- Here was the lost love I'd missed at ***home***.(p.425)
- Once in a while I stayed ***home*** for a night, to see how my folks were doing.(p.425)
- I planned to stay ***home*** the night before I left, but my folks got so drunk I walked off early in the evening and spent the night with my girl, getting very drunk myself.(p.425)
- I wanted to get as far away from ***home*** as possible.(p.426)
- Meanwhile the letters from ***home*** were telling about how much my folks wanted to make up to me for some of the things I'd missed.(p.427)
- I was supposed to come ***home*** on a troop ship, but I talked the base commander into flying me ***home***.(p.428)
- I headed ***home*** for the most wonderful experience of all time -- meeting my "new" parents -- mom and dad looked different than I had pictured them.(p.428)
- Dad got out a jug for me and poured welcome ***home*** drinks.(p.428)
- I would drink all night in bars, come ***home*** about five a.m., down a good big glass of whiskey straight, and tumble into bed.(p.428)
- Or maybe I'd come ***home*** wild drunk, singing and raving about what a fine place ***home*** was and what grand parents I had since they joined A.A.(p.428)
- Sometimes I'd make it ***home*** and go to sleep at the wheel of my car, for all the neighbors to see next morning as they left for work.(p.429)
- I spent eighteen hundred dollars fixing up that car in the first year I was ***home***, after four bad smash-ups.(p.429)
- Why I wasn't killed or how I got ***home*** I don't know.(p.429)
- I'd lost my car again, pawned my wallet and all identification papers for a bottle, and gotten ***home*** somehow.(p.429)
- I'd heard a lot about A.A. and met a great many A.A.'s during that year at ***home***, but I hadn't thought of it for myself.(p.429)
- I'm buying my ***home***.(p.431)
- I was father, husband, taxpayer, ***home*** owner.(p.432)
- This I would do by going completely "bohemian" for a night, getting drunk and rolling ***home*** with the dawn.(p.432)
- On another occasion I arrived ***home*** covered with blood.(p.435)

• After my last binge I came ***home*** and smashed my dining room furniture to splinters, kicked out six windows and two balustrades.(p.435)
• But then, when that steel door slammed shut, and she was the one that went ***home***, I was amazed.(p.440)
• That's when that steel door slammed shut, and Max was the one who went ***home***.(p.444)
• When we got ***home***, I got a bottle of Scotch and went to bed.(p.445)
• On the contrary, the hardest place to work this program has been in my own ***home***, with my own children and, finally, with Max.(p.451)
• This A.A. friend took me into his ***home*** when he had me out on pass.(p.462)
• When I didn't have anything else to do – a dull evening at ***home*** -- I'd sneak a few drinks upstairs in my room, and that began to be a habit.(p.464)
• When I got ***home*** my mouth was very painful, so I got an ice-bag and went to bed.(p.466)
• On the day before Christmas I telephoned him and told him I was sober and asked him to come ***home***.(p.467)
• And then I went back ***home*** to live with my parents, and the merry-go-round started again – only this time I didn't have to worry about waking up behind bars in a psychiatric ward.(p.468)
• In my screwed up mind I kept thinking I could have gone to A.A. way back there in 1940, and perhaps saved my marriage and ***home***.(p.469)
• From a Canadian reservation to overseas bars to New England lockups, an Indian traveled a long trail that finally led him ***home*** to A.A.(p.474)
• When I was twenty-one, my cousin come ***home*** from U.S. Army on leave.(p.474)
• Came ***home***.(p.475)
• Then I black out and get ***home*** four days later.(p.475)
• No clothes, no money, no ***home***, no real friends to speak of, mentally and physically pooped, but I was doing all right!(p.478)
• When I got out of there, I lasted about fifteen minutes at ***home***, before I headed for the drugstore and more pills, and then the bar.(p.479)
• I was born in a little town in Virginia in an average religious ***home***.(p.483)
• We weren't even permitted to play cards in our ***home***, but father would give us just a little toddy with whiskey and sugar and warm water now and then.(p.484)
• For that reason, I believe, I married at a much younger age than I would have, had it not been for my ***home*** training.(p.485)
• I'd go into my ***home*** with a bottle, and I remember clearly how I would look around to see if Vi was watching.(p.487)
• So I went down to talk to the District Attorney, and the arrangement was made that I would go ***home*** to stay with my mother, and that meant Vi and I were separated.(p.491)
• Then I left and went ***home*** to bed.(p.492)
• I worked in the steel mill for possibly two months, and then I became disgusted with myself and decided to go back ***home***.(p.492)
• I'd been ***home*** about a week or ten days when one of my friends asked if I could repair one of his electrical outlets.(p.493)
• When he left I walked with him to the streetcar line, which was just about a half a block, but there were two liquor stores, one on each corner from my ***home***.(p.495)
• We held some two or three meetings at Ella's ***home*** and from there we held some two or three at her mother's ***home***.(p.495)
• Both he and old Maud are glad to get ***home***.(p.497)
• I would never be like the village drunkard at ***home***.(p.498)
• I wish I were ***home*** with the family and not in the dingy hotel.(p.500)
• I go ***home***.(p.502)
• Could I have myself locked up at ***home***?(p.502)
• I am ***home*** again.(p.505)
• I have left my wife at ***home***, sick, and I have been unkind to her in leaving.(p.505)
• Things are not going so well at ***home***.(p.505)
• I return ***home*** and say I am sorry for my wrong.(p.505)
• When I wended my way ***home*** four days later, on the 27th, there was a detective waiting for me.(p.508)
• I staggered ***home*** next morning.(p.510)
• A lot of the boys had tears in their eyes, they were so happy to be ***home***.(p.513)
• I was drinking to try to hold on to a job, to try and hold on to my ***home***, to try to hold on to my wife, to try to hold on to my sanity.(p.514)
• I had a very happy upbringing at ***home***.(p.517)
• When I came ***home*** to ordinary garrison life in England, I found that I was drinking rather more than most people of may age.(p.518)
• India lent itself to drinking then, if you were disposed to drink, because you lived in bungalows; you didn't live all together as you do at ***home*** in an Officer's Mess.(p.519)
• I was there for another couple of months and then, after a few more adventures in the East, I was shipped ***home***.(p.521)
• About three months after that, my record reached ***home*** and I got a letter telling me I was retired from the Army, they put it very kindly, on medical grounds.(p.521)
• I put myself into a ***home***.(p.521)
• In any case, I made myself believe that, so I just drifted about, existing on my retired pay, drinking, and living at ***home***.(p.522)
• Finally, my mother came and said she had kept me at ***home*** for six years because she thought she could help me, but that now she had come to the conclusion that I wasn't even worth trying to help.(p.523)
• It was no use talking of putting myself into a ***home***, a hospital, or of going to see a doctor again, or of going to see a priest or anyone else.(p.523)
• Providentially, this was a Monday might when the Dublin Group met in those days, and my family agreed that if A.A. could do anything for me at all, that I'd be allowed to stay on at ***home*** on probation.(p.523)
• But to me, whiskey meant more than a ***home*** for my sons.(p.527)
• Then I would go ***home*** full of remorse, and wonder what I was going to do until I got my next check.(p.527)
• In time, I began to go out and forget the way back ***home***.(p.527)
• I have been ***home*** for a year, and have not taken a drink in four years.(p.529)
• Since I've been ***home***, I have been able to gain the respect of my two sons again.(p.529)
• There was the necessity for sticking to a job I hated, a dull, repetitive job performed in association with other men I had nothing in common with . . . performed for years on end, because the money was needed at ***home***.(p.532)
• I never was a "secret" drinker, and I never kept a bottle at ***home***.(p.536)
• The helpful family finally said, over long distance, that there would be no more money and that I could not come ***home***.(p.538)
• I went back ***home***, to a job of manual labor where for a little while I was able to keep away from alcohol.(p.539)
• I left this ***home*** town, then, after I had made a public spectacle of myself in the presence of a revered teacher whose favorite pupil I had been.(p.539)
• On another small borrowed sum, I went up into the country to the ***home*** of a doctor I had known since boyhood.(p.540)
• With no explanation at all, I was taken from my ***home*** in Florida to my grandparents' ***home*** in the middle west.(p.544)
• By this time I was such a past master at kidding myself that I had convinced myself I had sat out a war and waited for this man to come ***home*** and, as my resentment and self-pity grew, so did my alcoholic problem.(p.548)
• For instance, the fiftieth wedding anniversary of my wife's parents was the occasion for a huge family reunion at our ***home***.(p.556)
• Despite my wife's entreaties to take it easy that day, I arrived ***home*** in bad shape.(p.557)
• Within a week, I was feeling well enough to go ***home***.(p.558)

home-brewers

• Successful ***home-brewers*** among my friends began to invite me to their homes.(p.232)

home-brewing

• It wasn't very long before ***home-brewing*** was an institution and men began to search feverishly for old recipe books on wine-making.(p.232)

homecoming

• It was a glorious ***homecoming***.(p.428)

homeless

• He may be broke and ***homeless***.(p.96)
• I ended up, ***homeless***, jobless, penniless and rudderless, as the problem guest of a close friend whose family was out of town.(p.278)

homelessness

• Out of this maelstrom just two coherent thoughts came to the surface; one, a drink would mean ***homelessness*** and death; two, I could no longer relieve the pressure of fear by starting home, as was once my habitual solution to this problem, because I no longer had a home.(p.279)

homelife

• Eventually, I had to redo each of the Twelve Steps specifically with Max in mind, from the First, saying, "I am powerless over alcohol, and my ***homelife*** is unmanageable by me," to the Twelfth, in which I tried to think of her as a sick Al-Anon and treat her with the love I would give a sick A.A. newcomer.(p.452)

homes

• For this there were two principal reasons: the large numbers of recoveries, and reunited ***homes***.(p.xx)
• War fever ran high in the New England town to which we new, young officers from Plattsburg were assigned, and we were flattered when the first citizens took us to their ***homes***, making us feel heroic.(p.1)
• A much more important demonstration of our principles lies before us in our respective ***homes***, occupations and affairs.(p.19)
• Had this not been so, many of us would have no ***homes*** today, would perhaps be dead.(p.82)
• We seldom allow an alcoholic to live in our ***homes*** for long at a time.(p.97)
• In many ***homes*** this is a difficult thing to do, but it must be done if any results are to be expected.(p.98)
• People have said we must not go where liquor is served; we must not have it in our ***homes***; we must shun friends who drink; we must avoid moving pictures which show drinking scenes; we must not go into bars; our friends must hide their bottles if we go to their houses; we mustn't think or be reminded about alcohol at all.(p.100)
• Many of us keep liquor in our ***homes***.(p.102)
• Our ***homes*** have been battle-grounds many an evening.(p.105)
• We seldom had friends at our ***homes***, never knowing how or when the men of the house would appear.(p.105)
• Drinking isolates most ***homes*** from the outside world.(p.131)
• They shared their ***homes***, their slender resources, and gladly devoted their spare hours to fellow-sufferers.(p.159)
• Successful home-brewers among my friends began to invite me to their ***homes***.(p.232)
• We had meetings at each other's ***homes*** and, of course, that was a grand place for people to get together out there; they seemed to think so too.(p.270)
• I spent a great deal of time with Dr. Bob, whenever he had the time to spare, and in the ***homes*** of two or three other people, trying to see how the family lived the program.(p.291)
• Many women who have reached the stage that I had reached in my drinking have lost husbands, children, ***homes***, everything they hold dear.(p.323)
• Many retirees embrace alcoholism while secluded in motor trailers, rest ***homes***, leisure-world bungalows, mountain cabins, or beach cottages, or even in penthouses, on yachts, and inside Palm Springs cabanas.(p.329)
• However, after I heard a few stories of jails, sanitariums, broken ***homes*** and skid row, I wondered if I really was an alcoholic.(p.378)
• Incalculable are the intangible initiation fees that A.A. members have paid: the sick, sick hangovers, the remorse, guilt, broken ***homes***, jails, and institutions, and the mental anguish in general that has been generated over the years.(p.399)

homesick

• I was never ***homesick*** and was always pretty self-sufficient.(p.240)

hometown

• When I went back to my ***hometown*** to go into private practice, I experienced another brief lull in my addiction to alcohol and drugs.(p.420)
• I came to A.A. simply because there were no other doors of help open to me in my ***hometown***.(p.420)

honest

• The only requirement for membership is an ***honest*** desire to stop drinking.(p.xiv)
• Faced with this problem, if a doctor is ***honest*** with himself, he must sometimes feel his own inadequacy.(p.xxvii)
• That was the last ***honest*** manual labor on my part for many a day.(p.3)
• If what we have learned and felt and seen means anything at all, it means that all of us, whatever our race, creed, or color are the children of a living Creator with whom we may form a relationship upon simple and understandable terms as soon as we are willing and ***honest*** enough to try.(p.28)
• It will not take long for you to decide if you are

honest with yourself about it.(p.32)
• We have shared his ***honest*** doubt and prejudice.(p.45)
• Those who do not recover are people who cannot or will not completely give themselves to this simple program, usually men and women who are constitutionally incapable of being ***honest*** with themselves.(p.58)
• There are those, too, who suffer from grave emotional and mental disorders, but many of them do recover if they have the capacity to be ***honest***.(p.58)
• If we are sorry for what we have done, and have the ***honest*** desire to let God take us to better things, we believe we will be forgiven and will have learned our lesson.(p.70)
• Unwilling to be ***honest*** with these sympathetic men, we were ***honest*** with no one else.(p.73)
• We must be entirely ***honest*** with somebody if we expect to live long or happily in this world.(p.73)
• Some people cannot be seen -- we send them an ***honest*** letter.(p.83)
• We do not mean that you have to agree with your husband whenever there is an ***honest*** difference of opinion.(p.117)
• This is not to say that all alcoholics are ***honest*** and upright when not drinking.(p.141)
• For he knows he must be ***honest*** if he would live at all.(p.146)
• And he further said that God could not accept me as a sincere follower of His Divine Law unless I was ready to be thoroughly ***honest*** about it.(p.236)
• I was an ***honest*** agnostic, but definitely not a hater of the church or its adherents.(p.256)
• And over my A.A. years I have made many real, ***honest***, sincere friendships that I shall always cherish.(p.296)
• But I have a fortune in friendships, courage, self assurance and ***honest*** appraisal of my own abilities.(p.296)
• And the most important person to be ***honest*** with is Yourself.(p.368)
• The Twelve Steps, which to me are a spiritual way of living, soon meant ***honest*** thinking, not wishful thinking, open mindedness, a willingness to try and a faith to accept.(p.381)
• We can have this new way of life -- learning to live with our sickness and to be happy and content -- if we are willing to change our way of thinking and be ***honest***, first with ourselves, then with others.(p.480)
• I don't believe this program would work for me if I didn't get ***honest*** with myself about everything.(p.482)
• But I will never be totally ***honest*** -- that would make me perfect, and none of us can claim to be perfect.(p.482)
• If I work on it every day, it will be easier to be ***honest*** with myself.(p.482)
• Then getting and staying ***honest*** with other people will come automatically.(p.482)
• "I went out of here nine days ago saying that I was going to be ***honest***, and I wasn't," he answers.(p.503)
• Am I willing to be ***honest*** with myself about myself and tell someone about myself, and am I willing to think of other people, of their needs instead of myself, in order to get rid of the drink problem?(p.503)
• I'll be ***honest*** anyway.(p.506)
• My desire to be ***honest*** with myself made it necessary for me to realize that my thinking was irrational.(p.550)

honestly

• I ***honestly*** doubted whether, on balance, the religions of mankind had done any good.(p.11)
• This we did because we ***honestly*** wanted to, and were willing to make the effort.(p.25)
• Do not let any prejudice you may have against spiritual terms deter you from ***honestly*** asking yourself what they mean to you.(p.47)
• If our testimony helps sweep away prejudice, enables you to think ***honestly***, encourages you to search diligently within yourself, then, if you wish, you can join us on the Broad Highway.(p.55)
• But He has come to all who have ***honestly*** sought Him.(p.57)
• This was only a beginning, though if ***honestly*** and humbly made, an effect, sometimes a very great one, was felt at once.(p.63)
• We took stock ***honestly***.(p.64)
• We admitted our wrongs ***honestly*** and were willing to set these matters straight.(p.67)
• We don't worry about them if we can ***honestly*** say to ourselves that we would right them if we could.(p.83)
• My brilliant agnosticism vanished, and I saw for the first time that those who really believed, or at least ***honestly*** tried to find a Power greater than themselves, were much more composed and contented than I had ever been, and they seemed to have a degree of happiness which I had never known.(p.247)
• I was greeted warmly, ***honestly***, and with a true ring of sincerity by everyone present.(p.259)
• Neither can I ***honestly*** say that I have forgotten the "fleshpots of Egypt."(p.259)
• I couldn't go to one wine store and look the man ***honestly*** in the face and buy a bottle, as I used to do when I had parties and entertained and did normal drinking.(p.336)
• The fellowship I found in A.A. enabled me to face my problem ***honestly*** and squarely.(p.340)
• But when we come into A.A., we can face our problem ***honestly*** and openly.(p.340)
• The questions he asked me that I didn't answer ***honestly***, I thought were none of his business.(p.388)
• I ***honestly*** didn't know the difference.(p.470)
• Had I tried ***honestly*** and sincerely to practice the Twelve Steps I would have seen from my continuous moral inventory that I was getting off the beam -- I would have found that there were some active resentments in my life, a terrific amount of self-pity.(p.471)
• It was the first time that I had asked for help sincerely and ***honestly***.(p.515)
• I went in there and asked him ***honestly*** if he could give me a cure.(p.515)
• I learned to pray ***honestly***.(p.516)
• I ask the forgiveness of the reader; and from now on I shall try to write with the humility I ***honestly*** pray for.)(p.536)
• Most emphatically we wish to say that any alcoholic capable of ***honestly*** facing his problems in the light of our experience can recover, provided he does not close his mind to all spiritual concepts.(p.570)

honesty

• Belief in the power of God, plus enough willingness, ***honesty*** and humility to establish and maintain the new order of things, were the essential requirements.(p.13)
• They are naturally incapable of grasping and developing a manner of living which demands rigorous ***honesty***.(p.58)
• Nothing counted but thoroughness and ***honesty***.(p.65)
• But they had not learned enough of humility, fearlessness and ***honesty***, in the sense we find it necessary, until they told someone else all their life story.(p.73)
• When drinking, or getting over a bout, an alcoholic, sometimes the model of ***honesty*** when normal, will do incredible things.(p.140)
• In fact, he may say almost anything if he has accepted our solution which, as you know, demands rigorous ***honesty***.(p.145)
• In all ***honesty*** though, I was skeptical, but I wanted so definitely to quit drinking that I would have welcomed any sort of physical torture or pain to accomplish the result.(p.302)
• I had worked so long in a profession where fakery, deceit, and untruths are tools of trade that I instantly recognized ***honesty*** when I heard it, from the mouths of A.A. members.(p.334)
• If I were asked what in my opinion was the most important factor in being successful in this program, besides following the Twelve Steps, I would say ***Honesty***.(p.367)
• I know the biggest word for me in A.A. is "***honesty***."(p.482)
• ***Honesty*** is the easiest word for me to understand because it is the exact opposite of what I've been doing all my life.(p.482)
• I learn more of that foundation stone of character, which is ***honesty***.(p.507)
• I learn that when we act upon the highest conception of ***honesty*** which is given us, our sense of ***honesty*** becomes more acute.(p.507)
• I learn that ***honesty*** is truth, and that truth shall make us free!(p.507)
• Rather, I embraced it -- I must in ***honesty*** admit it -- with a great sense of relief.(p.531)
• They said if you want to know how this program works, take the first word of your question -- the H is for ***honesty***, the O is for open-mindedness and the W is for willingness; these our Book calls the essentials of recovery.(p.550)
• Willingness, ***honesty*** and open mindedness are the essentials of recovery.(p.570)

honeymoon

• On our ***honeymoon*** in Egypt, he cuffed me around quite a bit, and subsequently hit me some more.(p.405)
• On our ***honeymoon***, we had iced champagne by the bedside day and night.(p.555)

Honolulu

• Then I'd get a pass to ***Honolulu***.(p.427)

honor

• I belong to more medical societies and ***honor*** societies than men ten to twenty years my senior.(p.345)
• I was an ***honor*** graduate in high school, and I was a "good boy" to whom mothers pointed when their sons went astray.(p.419)
• When I had served only eighteen months of my sentence, this ex-incorrigible was placed in ***honor*** grade.(p.461)
• I leave the room, which the ***honor*** system allows.(p.499)
• I, a man of steel, with very high ideals, well brought up, an ***honor*** student and the recipient of scholarships and prizes, a boy wonder in business -- I, Bob, the author of this essay, looked and saw that the universe was beneath my contempt, and that to remove myself from it was the only thing of dignity a man could do.(p.531)
• But not for long; now, for five Friday nights in a row, I went to jail, picked up sodden with beer (which I always disliked, but which was the only drink available); in jail five consecutive Friday nights in the town where I had grown up, where I had been an ***honor*** student in high school, where a kindly uncle, bailing me out, said, "Bob, our family just doesn't do this sort of thing."(p.539)
• An ***honor*** student in college, I became editor of the yearbook.(p.555)

honor-grade

• Then I was transferred to the ***honor-grade*** unit, where I spent the most painful year of my life.(p.462)

honored

• Most people approached in this way will be glad to help; they will be ***honored*** by our confidence.(p.75)

honors

• I graduated with ***honors***, but could not feel any real responsibility as a father or a husband.(p.419)
• I drank my way through schools and always got ***honors***.(p.441)

hooch

• All during Prohibition, every alcoholic felt that he made the best ***hooch***, regardless of how bad it was.(p.213)

hook

• He turned me in to the company commander, but I got off the ***hook***, and that was all that mattered.(p.317)
• By ***hook*** or crook I usually managed to sober up before I reached home, but always "terribly tired" from a "hard day's work," and just having to have one or two before dinner.(p.361)

hooked

• The physician wasn't ***hooked***, he thought -- he just prescribed drugs medically indicated for his many ailments.(p.439)

hooter

• My wife loved to drink, and we tied on many a ***hooter*** in the name of marital bliss.(p.433)

hope

• If you have a drinking problem, we ***hope*** that you may pause in reading one of the forty-four personal stories and think: "Yes, that happened to me"; or, more important, "Yes, I've felt like that"; or most important, "Yes, I believe this program can work for me, too."(p.xii)
• For them, we ***hope*** these pages will prove so convincing that no further authentication will be necessary.(p.xiii)
• Our earliest printing voiced the ***hope*** "that every alcoholic who journeys will find the Fellowship of Alcoholics Anonymous at his destination.(p.xv)
• Yet it is our great ***hope*** that all those who have as yet found no answer may begin to find one in the pages of this book and will presently join us on the highroad to a new freedom.(p.xxi)
• Each day, somewhere in the world, recovery begins when one alcoholic talks with another alcoholic, sharing experience, strength, and ***hope***.(p.xxii)
• This is repeated over and over, and unless this person can experience an entire psychic change there is very little ***hope*** of his recovery.(p.xxvii)
• He frankly admitted and believed that for him there was no ***hope***.(p.xxix)
• His alcoholic problem was so complex, and his depression so great, that we felt his only ***hope*** would be through what we then called "moral psychology," and we doubted if even that would have any effect.(p.xxix)
• Nevertheless, I still thought I could control the situation, and there were periods of sobriety which renewed my wife's ***hope***.(p.5)

• Understanding myself now, I fared forth in high ***hope***.(p.7)
• We ***hope*** this volume will inform and comfort those who are, or who may be affected.(p.18)
• This ***hope***, however, was destroyed by the doctor's telling him that while his religious convictions were very good, in his case they did not spell the necessary vital spiritual experience.(p.27)
• We ***hope*** no one will consider these self-revealing accounts in bad taste.(p.29)
• Our ***hope*** is that many alcoholic men and women, desperately in need, will see these pages, and we believe that it is only by fully disclosing ourselves and our problems that they will be persuaded to say, "Yes, I am one of them too; I must have this thing."(p.29)
• I have since been brought into a way of living infinitely more satisfying and, I ***hope***, more useful than the life I lived before.(p.42)
• We ***hope*** it strikes home to thousands like him.(p.43)
• We ***hope*** we have made clear the distinction between the alcoholic and the non-alcoholic.(p.44)
• At first some of us tried to avoid the issue, hoping against ***hope*** we were not true alcoholics.(p.44)
• Many times we talk to a new man and watch his ***hope*** rise as we discuss his alcoholic problems and explain our fellowship.(p.45)
• Sometimes this was a tedious process; we ***hope*** no one else will be prejudiced for as long as some of us were.(p.48)
• But with the alcoholic, whose ***hope*** is the maintenance and growth of a spiritual experience, this business of resentment is infinitely grave.(p.66)
• We ***hope*** you are convinced now that God can remove whatever self-will has blocked you off from Him.(p.71)
• Make it plain he is under no obligation to you, that you ***hope*** only that he will try to help other alcoholics when he escapes his own difficulties.(p.94)
• Some day we ***hope*** that Alcoholics Anonymous will help the public to a better realization of the gravity of the alcoholic problem, but we shall be of little use if our attitude is one of bitterness or hostility.(p.103)
• We ***hope*** this book has answered some of them.(p.108)
• He may bring new ***hope*** and new courage to many a priest, minister, or rabbi, who gives his all to minister to our troubled world.(p.132)
• We ***hope*** the doctor will tell the patient the truth about his condition, whatever that happens to be.(p.144)
• As our work spreads and our numbers increase, we ***hope*** your employees may be put in personal contact with some of us.(p.144)
• We ***hope*** our suggestions will help you plug up this sometimes serious leak.(p.148)
• Our ***hope*** is that when this chip of a book is launched on the world tide of alcoholism, defeated drinkers will seize upon it, to follow its suggestions.(p.153)
• Some day we ***hope*** that every alcoholic who journeys will find a Fellowship of Alcoholics Anonymous at his destination.(p.162)
• We believe and ***hope*** it contains all you will need to begin.(p.163)
• Those who believe their drinking to be hopeless may again find ***hope*** in these thirteen impressive tales.(p.167)
• By this time I was beginning to pay very dearly physically and, in ***hope*** of relief, voluntarily incarcerated myself at least a dozen times in one of the local sanitariums.(p.174)
• Down in the pit of his depression, new ***hope*** had somehow been born.(p.189)
• Finally, out of his ***hope***, there burst conviction.(p.189)
• In summing up, I can say that A.A. had made me, I ***hope***, a real Catholic.(p.221)
• It was a thought that there might be some ***hope*** for us.(p.266)
• But right then the ***hope*** died that had been in my heart when we read about John D.(p.266)
• Right away, I saw it was the same outfit this other guy told me about, and then again ***hope*** died.(p.267)
• To go north into the empty pine country and shoot myself, or to go south in the faint ***hope*** that a bunch of strangers might help me with my drinking problem.(p.278)
• As I look back on that first evening I realize that I began to ***hope***, then, for the first time; and I felt that if he could regain these things, perhaps it would be possible for me too.(p.290)
• I began making the rounds of the doctors in the ***hope*** that one of them might find some cure for my accumulating ailments, preferably something that could be removed surgically.(p.305)
• Here was ***hope***.(p.309)
• I didn't dare ***hope*** I might find for myself all that these people had found, but if I could acquire some small part of their intriguing quality of living -- and sobriety -- that would be enough.(p.310)
• First, through mutual pain and despair, and later through mutual objectives and new-found faith and ***hope***.(p.312)
• I ***hope*** that I never forget to be grateful.(p.326)
• It was the only ***hope*** I had.(p.334)
• With new ***hope*** in my heart and new resolutions I set off for Vermont.(p.360)
• I had read and heard a little about A.A. and so, groping for the phone book, I found the A.A. number and with ***hope*** in my heart eagerly telephoned.(p.363)
• My first meeting gave me a great deal of ***hope*** and lots of willing ears for my tale of woe and for my questions.(p.364)
• That night she too had new ***hope*** because I had made sure she would know what I was doing about my drinking by packing every bit of A.A. literature I could put my hands on right on top so she couldn't help but see it when she opened my bag.(p.364)
• But for some reason -- she just didn't know why -- she just had to hold onto that clipping, with its thin ***hope***.(p.367)
• At first it was a shock to realize I was an alcoholic, but the realization that there was ***hope*** made it easier.(p.379)
• I think I actually read more contempt than was really there because just a week before someone had sent him the Saturday Evening Post article on A.A., and there was some glimmer of ***hope*** in it for him.(p.391)
• At the wedding, I ***hope*** I will also get to see my daughter and their mother.(p.463)
• She gave me such ***hope*** and inspiration that I set her right up on a pedestal.(p.472)
• In that short period he built within me something that I had long since lost, which was ***hope***.(p.495)
• And there a tremendous ***hope*** is born.(p.504)
• However, she had faith and she had ***hope*** (things I didn't have).(p.514)
• My only ***hope*** was to try and get through what was left of life as best I could, but I could never visualize doing that without drinking.(p.522)
• That gave me my first bit of ***hope***.(p.524)
• I ***hope*** I haven't hurt anyone's feelings, but maybe we could all grow and change.(p.529)
• ***Hope*** had died, or so I thought.(p.540)
• I ***hope*** I have been able to impart to you, the reader, at least a bit of what I know; the joy of living, the irresistible power of divine love and its healing strength, and the fact that we, as sentient beings, have the knowledge to choose between good and evil, and, choosing good, are made happy.(p.543)
• But one was so outstanding that I like to pass it on whenever I can in the ***hope*** that it will help someone else as it has me.(p.551)

hope-inspiring

• By this time, with the doctor's explanation, the revelations contained in the book, and the ***hope-inspiring*** interview with Mr. T., I was ready and willing to go into the interior of the African jungles, if that was what it took, for me to find what these people had.(p.309)

hoped

• As we left, and they were escorting us across the bridge into Wheeling, I, with great dignity and sarcasm, told them if their wives were ever visiting in Akron, and they, too, were looking for their route sign as I was, that I ***hoped*** I could extend to them the hospitality that had been shown to me in Bellaire.(p.264)
• I had never seen him before, and at the time ***hoped*** I would never see him again.(p.302)
• He told me that eventually he ***hoped*** such a group would develop in the Chicago area, but that so far this had not been started.(p.309)

hopeful

• You can be quite ***hopeful*** of a situation like this.(p.110)
• His wife came, scarcely daring to be ***hopeful***, though she thought she saw something different about her husband already.(p.158)

hopefully

• In a vague way their families and friends sense that these drinkers are abnormal, but everybody ***hopefully*** awaits the day when the sufferer will rouse himself from his lethargy and assert his power of will.(p.23)
• Of course he couldn't drink, but why not sit ***hopefully*** at a table, a bottle of ginger ale before him?(p.154)

hopeless

• We, of Alcoholics Anonymous, are more than one hundred men and women who have recovered from a seemingly ***hopeless*** state of mind and body.(p.xiii)
• In late 1934 I attended a patient who, though he had been a competent businessman of good earning capacity, was an alcoholic of a type I had come to regard as ***hopeless***.(p.xxiii)
• The patient had made his own diagnosis, and deciding his situation ***hopeless***, had hidden in a deserted barn determined to die.(p.xxix)
• I had to be, for I was ***hopeless***.(p.10)
• While I lay in the hospital the thought came that there were thousands of ***hopeless*** alcoholics who might be glad to have what had been so freely given me.(p.14)
• We of ALCOHOLICS ANONYMOUS, know thousands of men and women who were once just as ***hopeless*** as Bill.(p.17)
• Doubtless you are curious to discover how and why, in the face of expert opinion to the contrary, we have recovered from a ***hopeless*** condition of mind and body.(p.20)
• In the doctor's judgment he was utterly ***hopeless***; he could never regain his position in society and he would have to place himself under lock and key or hire a bodyguard if he expected to live long.(p.26)
• They piled on me heaps of evidence to the effect that an alcoholic mentality, such as I had exhibited in Washington, was a ***hopeless*** condition.(p.42)
• As to two of you men, whose stories I have heard, there is no doubt in my mind that you were 100% ***hopeless***, apart from divine help.(p.43)
• To one who feels he is an atheist or agnostic such an experience seems impossible, but to continue as he is means disaster, especially if he is an alcoholic of the ***hopeless*** variety.(p.44)
• If you are satisfied that he is a real alcoholic, begin to dwell on the ***hopeless*** feature of the malady.(p.92)
• The more ***hopeless*** he feels, the better.(p.94)
• You would suppose that men in the fourth classification would be quite ***hopeless***, but that is not so.(p.113)
• Those who believe their drinking to be ***hopeless*** may again find hope in these thirteen impressive tales.(p.167)
• And so on and on, for several weeks, while I grudgingly plowed through some more of the offending book, and felt more and more ***hopeless*** about myself.(p.227)
• He said he had finally learned that drinking was a fatal illness made up of an allergy plus an obsession, and once the drinking had passed from habit to obsession, we were completely ***hopeless***, and could look forward only to spending the balance of our lives in mental institutions or to death.(p.290)
• They had a hunch that there must be an answer for these apparently ***hopeless*** ones, somewhere.(p.307)
• Few doctors will tell a ***hopeless*** patient that there is no answer for him or for her.(p.307)
• No drunk ***hopeless*** if he want to follow guide along right trail.(p.477)
• Suddenly I feel ***hopeless***, unable to go on.(p.502)
• "You think you are ***hopeless***, don't you?" he asks.(p.503)
• She had been warned numerous times, not only by her family but by my own mother, that I was a ***hopeless*** drunk, that there wasn't anything anybody could do with me, that I'd never stop, and that eventually I'd break her heart.(p.513)
• It seems only fitting that when I did finally fall in love it was with an alcoholic, and for the next ten years I progressed as rapidly as is humanly possible into what I believed to be ***hopeless*** alcoholism.(p.547)
• ***Hopeless*** now, I felt it would be better for my wife, my children, and everyone in my life if I went ahead and died.(p.558)

hopelessly

• I had never been able to understand people who said that a problem had them ***hopelessly*** defeated.(p.42)
• This self-insurance has resulted in the restoration of physical, mental and spiritual health and self-respect to hundreds of men and women who would be ***hopelessly*** down and out without its unique but effective therapy."(p.574)

hopelessness

• But when the broker gave him Dr. Silkworth's description of alcoholism and its ***hopelessness***, the physi cian began to pursue the spiritual remedy for his malady with a willingness he had never before been able to muster.(p.xvi)
• The remorse, horror and ***hopelessness*** of the next morning are unforgettable.(p.6)
• But we saw that it really worked in others, and we

had come to believe in the ***hopelessness*** and futility of life as we had been living it.(p.25)

- One of these men, staff member of a world-renowned hospital, recently made this statement to some of us: "What you say about the general ***hopelessness*** of the average alcoholic's plight is, in my opinion, correct.(p.43)
- But you may talk to him about the ***hopelessness*** of alcoholism because you offer a solution.(p.92)
- How can they rise out of such misery, bad repute and ***hopelessness***?(p.153)
- ***Hopelessness*** was written large on the man's face as he replied, "Oh, but that's no use.(p.157)
- Broken promises, humiliation, ***hopelessness***, worry, anxiety -- but still not enough.(p.377)
- Suddenly I feel a wave of utter ***hopelessness*** sweep over me.(p.504)

hopes

- He ***hopes*** they will never see the light of day.(p.73)
- "Well," the doctor said, "we have ***hopes*** in that direction."(p.207)
- They build you up with a lot of false ***hopes*** and promises, and rush you around here and there and then, all of a sudden, it's gone."(p.472)

hoping

- He shuts himself up in an asylum, ***hoping*** to mend his ways.(p.38)
- At first some of us tried to avoid the issue, ***hoping*** against hope we were not true alcoholics.(p.44)
- Some of us veered from extreme to extreme, ever ***hoping*** that one day our loved ones would be themselves once more.(p.105)
- Our friends have counseled chucking the men and we have done so with finality, only to be back in a little while ***hoping***, always ***hoping***.(p.105)
- So, for one reason or another, they cover these men, ***hoping*** matters will take a turn for the better.(p.147)
- Some of us sought out sordid places, ***hoping*** to find understanding companionship and approval.(p.151)
- I'd been sitting comfortably in a restaurant with Rita, drinking my sixth martini and ***hoping*** the waiter would forget about the lunch order -- at least long enough for me to have a couple more.(p.223)
- Much later I discovered the elders held many prayer meetings ***hoping*** to find a way to give me the heave-ho, but at the same time stay tolerant and spiritual.(p.247)
- The following spring she left me one day without giving me any idea of where she had gone, ***hoping*** this would bring me to my senses.(p.377)
- This career girl preferred solitary drinking, the blackout kind, often ***hoping*** she'd stay that way for keeps.(p.464)
- I am ***hoping*** that writing this may bring some poor, mixed-up soul into the program.(p.530)
- I'd visit one bar after another, having one martini in each, and in each ***hoping*** to find someone interesting to talk to.(p.536)

hopped

- We heard by wireless on the 5th that the Armistice would be signed the next day (this was a premature report) so I had a couple of cognacs to celebrate; then I ***hopped*** a truck and went AWOL.(p.242)

hordes

- I swung, I swore, I started throwing beer cans at the advancing ***hordes*** of pineapple faces.(p.427)

horizon

- It was the end of a perfect day, not a cloud on the ***horizon***.(p.41)
- Starting from a speck on the domestic ***horizon***, great thunderclouds of dispute may gather.(p.117)
- At that time I was not aware of the almost unlimited supply the government made it possible for us doctors to obtain, neither had I any knowledge of the bootlegger who soon appeared on the ***horizon***.(p.175)
- The details of the long road back to something resembling normal living -- the first short streetcar ride, the purchase of a used bike which enabled me to widen the narrow ***horizon*** of life, the first trip downtown -- I will not dwell on.(p.276)

horns

- One morning he took the bull by the ***horns*** and set out to tell those he feared what his trouble had been.(p.156)
- If I'd had a gun I'd have shot the ***horns*** right off the thing, because it made me raving mad.(p.265)

horrible

- It was really a ***horrible*** nightmare, this earning money, getting liquor, smuggling it home, getting drunk, morning jitters, taking large doses of sedatives to make it possible for me to earn more money, and so on ad nauseam.(p.177)
- Then Prohibition came into effect, and the facts that the stuff obtainable was so ***horrible*** and sometimes deadly, and that I had married and had a job which I had to look after, helped me for a period of some three or four years, although I would get drunk every time I could get hold of enough to drink to get started.(p.183)
- Away from my office two or three weeks at a time; ***horrible*** days and nights when I would lie on the floor of my home, lying awake and reaching over to get the bottle, taking a drink and going back into oblivion.(p.184)
- When I look back on that last ***horrible*** year of constant drinking I wonder how I survived it either physically or mentally.(p.224)
- Then broke again, hiding out in cheap hotels all over the country, one night jail stands here and there, and always that ***horrible*** feeling "What's the use -- nothing is worth while."(p.244)
- How I was able to discharge my duties at the office during those ***horrible*** mornings, I will never be able to explain.(p.299)
- I took two or three drinks so my eyes could focus, and I could see that ***horrible*** picture of the awful drunk on the first page; he couldn't get the drink to his mouth, he had a towel around his hand and he needed a shave.(p.391)
- It was nothing to my own inner distress, my self-reproach, and my self-loathing, for was I not bearing out all the ***horrible*** things I had always suspected of myself?(p.404)
- She said she felt too ***horrible*** inside to be pretty on the outside.(p.415)
- I feel ***horrible***.(p.500)
- You were thirty-five before you understood your father's ***horrible*** anguish, and forgave him, and loved him again.(p.533)
- Repeated year on end, they are ***horrible*** -- frightening and degrading, a chronicle of tragedy which may be greater because the individual undergoing the tragedy, myself, knew what was happening, and yet refused to do anything to stop it.(p.538)
- I remember how ***horrible*** jails are, how dreadful a thing it is to be behind steel bars.(p.542)

horribly

- The wives and children of such men suffer ***horribly***, but not more than the men themselves.(p.114)
- He suffered ***horribly*** from his sprees, but it seemed as if nothing could be done for him.(p.159)
- It was such a feeling of relief that I wanted to know more about it and with that, I think for the first time, came the realization that there was something ***horribly, horribly*** wrong with me.(p.392)

horrified

- So I located a house, and I thought we ought to move into it immediately, but Frank was ***horrified***, because he never knew what was going to happen to me.(p.388)

horror

- The remorse, ***horror*** and hopelessness of the next morning are unforgettable.(p.6)
- And I remembered the creeping ***horror*** of the interminable night, in which I slept for short spells and woke up dripping with cold sweat and shaken with utter despair, to drink hastily from my bottle and mercifully pass out again, "You're mad, you're mad, you're mad!" pounded through my brain with each returning ray of consciousness, and I drowned the refrain with drink.(p.224)

horrors

- For his sake, we do recount and almost relive the ***horrors*** of our past.(p.132)
- The ***horrors*** of increasing hangover sickness to occupy the entire day; nausea, dry heaves, the rocking bed, the nightmare-filled mind.(p.408)
- I came to understand the intricate processes of projection, by which we cast into our adult world the images of the ***horrors*** of our childhood.(p.434)

horse

- I remember telling them too that it was going to be awfully tough, because I did some other things, smoked cigarettes and played penny ante poker, sometimes bet on the ***horse*** races and they said, "Don't you think you're having more trouble with this drinking than with anything else at the present time?(p.190)
- But whereas my ***horse*** was always equipped with a flask, I merely endured the fox hunting so I could start drinking at lunch time.(p.404)

horsemen

- Momentarily we did -- then would come oblivion and the awful awakening to face the hideous Four ***Horsemen*** -- Terror, Bewilderment, Frustration, Despair.(p.151)

hosiery

- So I created a job for myself selling women's ***hosiery*** and men's made-to-order shirts.(p.282)

hospital

- Hence the two men set to work almost frantically upon alcoholics arriving in the ward of the Akron City ***Hospital***.(p.xvii)
- A well-known doctor, chief physician at a nationally prominent ***hospital*** specializing in alcoholic and drug addiction, gave Alcoholics Anonymous this letter:(p.xxiii)
- Many years ago one of the leading contributors to this book came under our care in this ***hospital*** and while here he acquired some ideas which he put into practical application at once.(p.xxv)
- Of course an alcoholic ought to be freed from his physical craving for liquor, and this often requires a definite ***hospital*** procedure, before psychological measures can be of maximum benefit.(p.xxv)
- If any feel that as psychiatrists directing a ***hospital*** for alcoholics we appear somewhat sentimental, let them stand with us a while on the firing line, see the tragedies, the despairing wives, the little children; let the solving of these problems become a part of their daily work, and even of their sleeping moments, and the most cynical will not wonder that we have accepted and encouraged this movement.(p.xxvi)
- My bother-in-law is a physician, and through his kindness and that of my mother I was placed in a nationally-known ***hospital*** for the mental and physical rehabilitation of alcoholics.(p.7)
- After a time I returned to the ***hospital***.(p.7)
- Trembling, I stepped from the ***hospital*** a broken man.(p.8)
- At the ***hospital*** I was separated from alcohol for the last time.(p.13)
- While I lay in the ***hospital*** the thought came that there were thousands of hopeless alcoholics who might be glad to have what had been so freely given me.(p.14)
- Many times I have gone to my old ***hospital*** in despair.(p.15)
- In two months he was in a ***hospital***, puzzled and humiliated.(p.32)
- He tried to regulate his drinking for a while, making several trips to the ***hospital*** meantime.(p.32)
- Within a week after leaving the ***hospital*** a fast-moving trolley car breaks his arm.(p.38)
- We first saw Fred about a year ago in a ***hospital*** where he had gone to recover from a bad case of jitters.(p.39)
- Far from admitting he was an alcoholic, he told himself he came to the ***hospital*** to rest his nerves.(p.39)
- One day we were told that he was back in the ***hospital***.(p.40)
- Then came the ***hospital*** with unbearable mental and physical suffering.(p.41)
- One of these men, staff member of a world-renowned ***hospital***, recently made this statement to some of us: "What you say about the general hopelessness of the average alcoholic's plight is, in my opinion, correct.(p.43)
- Had you offered yourselves as patients at this ***hospital***, I would not have taken you, if I had been able to avoid it.(p.43)
- One night, when confined in a ***hospital***, he was approached by an acholic who had known a spiritual experience.(p.56)
- Sometimes he drinks on the way home from the ***hospital***.(p.110)
- In another case, an alcoholic was sent to a ***hospital*** for treatment.(p.145)
- One day they called up the head nurse of a local ***hospital***.(p.156)
- That afternoon he put on his clothes and walked from the ***hospital*** a free man.(p.158)
- He consented, however, to go the ***hospital***, where he occupied the very room recently vacated by the lawyer.(p.159)
- They were willing, by day or night, to place a new man in the ***hospital*** and visit him afterward.(p.159)
- Many a man, yet dazed from his ***hospital*** experience, has stepped over the threshold of that home into freedom.(p.160)
- Impressed by those who visited him at the ***hospital***, he capitulated entirely when, later, in an upper room of this house, he heard the story of some man whose experience closely tallied with his own.(p.160)
- In one of these there is a well-known ***hospital*** for the treatment of alcoholic and drug addiction.(p.161)
- Arrangements were also made with the chief psychiatrist of a large public ***hospital*** to select still others from the stream of misery which flows through that institution.(p.163)

• In his prodigy of service, he was well assisted by Sister Ignatia at St. Thomas ***Hospital*** in Akron, Ohio, one of the greatest friends our Fellowship will ever know.(p.171)

• During these two years I was kept so busy that I hardly left the ***hospital*** at all.(p.174)

• After three years of this, I wound up in the local ***hospital*** where they attempted to help me, but I would get my friends to smuggle me a quart, or I would steal the alcohol about the building, so that I got rapidly worse.(p.175)

• During the subsequent fifteen years I had sense enough never to go to the ***hospital*** if I had been drinking, and very seldom did I receive patients.(p.176)

• I will not take space to relate all my ***hospital*** or sanitarium experiences.(p.177)

• On June 26, 1935, I came to in the ***hospital*** and to say I was discouraged is to put it mildly.(p.184)

• Each of the seven times that I had left this ***hospital*** in the last six months, I had come out fully determined in my own mind that I would not get drunk again -- for at least six or eight months.(p.184)

• The next thing they wanted to know was if I thought I could quit of my own accord, without any help, if I could just walk out of the ***hospital*** and never take another drink.(p.186)

• They left this with me to think over, and I lay there on that ***hospital*** bed and went back over and reviewed my life.(p.186)

• Whether you quit six days, months, or years, if you go out and take a drink or two you'll end up in this ***hospital*** tied down, just like you have been in these past six months.(p.187)

• Bill lay on his ***hospital*** bed and looked at us in wonder.(p.188)

• Straightway, Bob called Akron's City ***Hospital*** and asked for the nurse on the receiving ward.(p.188)

• My case is so terrible that I'm scared to go out of this ***hospital*** at all.(p.188)

• Bill D. walked out of that ***hospital*** a free man never to drink again.(p.189)

• I know there was even more, something that I hadn't got, and I remember one day, a week or two after I had come out of the ***hospital***, Bill was over to my house talking to my wife and me.(p.191)

• I looked so terrible in the court that the judge suggested that I get a continuance and let me sign all the papers to go to a ***hospital*** and to a doctor.(p.204)

• He came in and took a look at me and sent me to the ***hospital***.(p.205)

• When I had been in the ***hospital*** ten days, Sister Ignatia, who has played such a part in the development of A.A. in this area, stuck her head in the door one morning and announced, looking at me quizzically, that they might be able to make something human out of my face after all.(p.205)

• Because it affected me so strenuously, they felt that hospitalization was indicated and I awoke in a ***hospital***.(p.207)

• I remember well one fellow, Joe, walking nearly three miles through slush, wet and snow to come to the ***hospital*** to see a man that he had never seen before in his life, and that impressed me very much.(p.208)

• He walked to the ***hospital*** to save bus fare and did it gladly in order to be helpful to an individual he had never even seen.(p.208)

• There were only seven or eight people in the group before me and they all visited me during my period in the ***hospital***.(p.208)

• When I left the ***hospital*** I tried this for a day and it worked, for a week and it worked, and for a month, and it worked – and then for a year and it still worked.(p.209)

• Bill bought me a drink or two on the way, and Dorothy S. came with us, and the three of us went over to the City ***Hospital***.(p.217)

• I went into the ***hospital*** in April, 1939.(p.217)

• My experience in the ***hospital*** I considered to be terrific because Dr. Bob told me very quickly that medicine would have very little to do with it, outside of trying to restore my appetite for food.(p.217)

• I did not know there was such a thing as group activity until I left the ***hospital***.(p.218)

• In fact, I never lost my faith, since I had been prepared by some conversations toward the end of my sojourn in the ***hospital*** with Dr. Bob, conversations pretty much along spiritual lines.(p.218)

• The afternoon that I was to leave the ***hospital***, he came in to see me and asked me if I were willing to attempt to follow the program.(p.218)

• I remember looking longingly at the window as an easier solution, and shuddering at the memory of that other window, three years before, and the six agonizing months in a London ***hospital*** ward.(p.224)

• That went on for two more months before I landed in a ***hospital*** and started my slow fight back to normalcy.(p.224)

• Imagine my surprise when I read in a page one "box" that I had been taken from the theater unconscious around noon that day, removed by ambulance to a ***hospital*** and stomach-pumped and then released.(p.244)

• While there I was called to the ***hospital*** in my home town to see a former partner who had insisted that I visit him.(p.257)

• As soon as I could get up and walk I started to drink again and kept it up until my friend of the ***hospital***, who, in his first try at the new way of life had stubbed his toe in Chicago but had come back to the town to take counsel and make a new start, picked me up and got me into a ***hospital***.(p.258)

• I left the ***hospital*** on a meeting night.(p.259)

• He wants to go to the ***hospital***, and I'm not paying for the ***hospital*** again!"(p.271)

• If he thinks he needs to go to the ***hospital***, I'll pay for him."(p.271)

• She said, "He's not going to the ***hospital***, whether you pay for it or I pay for it, he's not going!"(p.271)

• There were two women in the St. Thomas ***Hospital*** at that time in a room.(p.272)

• Here, while in a ***hospital*** bed, men with clear eyes, happy faces, and a look of assurance and purposefulness about them, came to see me and told me their stories.(p.279)

• When I got out of the ***hospital***, I was invited to stay with Dr. Bob and his dear wife, Anne.(p.279)

• The ***hospital*** had seemed so safe.(p.279)

• He advised me to enter the particular ***hospital*** with which he was connected and I readily agreed.(p.302)

• I made arrangements to enter the ***hospital*** three days later and promptly went out and got stiff for three days.(p.302)

• It was with grim foreboding and advanced jitters that I checked in at the ***hospital***.(p.302)

• After being in the ***hospital*** for several days, a plan of living was outlined to me.(p.302)

• I was in the ***hospital***, hysterical.(p.319)

• When I was released from the ***hospital***, I went back to my unit, and nothing had changed.(p.319)

• I still couldn't make it through the nights without drinking, so I went back into the ***hospital***, this time to a rehabilitation center.(p.320)

• When I got out of the ***hospital***, I continued making the meetings.(p.320)

• I never went to a ***hospital***.(p.323)

• There was one girl especially, and I'd watch her from my window every morning, leaving faithfully to go to the ***hospital*** in the neighborhood.(p.326)

• And I put a Bible in my locker at the ***hospital***.(p.348)

• And I put a Big Book by my night stand, and I put a "Twelve Steps and Twelve Tradition" in my locker at the ***hospital***, and I got books by Emmet Fox, and I got books by God-knows-who, and I got to reading all these things.(p.348)

• Here I am down at my office behind my desk and there she is out at the ***hospital***.(p.350)

• I was in the fourth quarter of my senior year at high school, and my mother was quite sick in the ***hospital***.(p.354)

• We did, and spent a month boozing it up, popping pills, and smoking marijuana; taking shelter where we could, which included a veterinary ***hospital*** one night; accepting meals from anyone; actually begging; stealing anything we were in need of, which was about everything.(p.354)

• Within a few months, I was admitted to a state ***hospital*** for the mentally ill.(p.370)

• I had never been inside of an insane asylum and I really thought I was going to a private ***hospital***.(p.387)

• He hesitated to send me back to that ***hospital***.(p.388)

• I think I disrupted the ***hospital***.(p.388)

• So I got a half pint and at midnight that night, I called the number I had been given, but the man who had started the group was in the ***hospital*** so I didn't know what to do.(p.393)

• The last time I drank, when I was twenty-nine, I drank for only four days, yet I threatened to kill my children; I beat my wife at home and on the church steps; I mistreated a child in my office; and I ran to a ***hospital*** for mental illness to avoid jail.(p.418)

• Gradually consciousness returned enough to let me know I was in a ***hospital***.(p.422)

• I was in a ***hospital***.(p.422)

• The doctor said I'd been brought into the ***hospital*** like a madman, crying, raving, ranting, swearing, completely in the throes of delirium tremens.(p.427)

• That doctor in the Navy ***hospital*** told me I wouldn't live five years if I didn't quit.(p.429)

• I remember finding myself in the middle of the night in the doctors' parking lot at the ***hospital*** with one foot in the car and one foot on the ground, not knowing which was the lead foot; finding myself hanging up the telephone – then realizing I had gotten out of bed, answered the phone, turned on the light, and carried on a conversation with a patient.(p.441)

• I didn't know whether I had told him to rush to the ***hospital*** and I'd meet him there, or to take two aspirin and call me in the morning.(p.441)

• He arranged for me to see a local psychiatrist, who quickly decided I should be in the mental-health unit of our local ***hospital***.(p.445)

• Finally, she asked, "Do you realize he's on the staff of this ***hospital***?"(p.445)

• In the ***hospital***, I hung on to the idea I'd had most of my life: that if I could just control the external environment, the internal environment would then be comfortable.(p.445)

• One day as I sat there in the ***hospital***, my psychiatrist walked up behind me and asked, "How'd you like to talk to the man from A.A.?"(p.446)

• But it quickly became obvious that he had this childish notion instead: If he could get me to go to enough meetings while in the ***hospital***, I would continue to go after he let me out.(p.447)

• Eventually, the psychiatrist discharged me from the ***hospital***, and Max and I began going to meetings ourselves.(p.447)

• This time I didn't put up any fight because I knew why they were there and where I was going, the psychopathic ward of the City ***Hospital***, where I had been once before.(p.468)

• Her brother had been a drinker and had died in a State ***Hospital*** for the insane.(p.498)

• Her mother is in a critical condition at a ***hospital***.(p.501)

• She is near the end now and is in a ***hospital***.(p.501)

• I go to the ***hospital***, where I have made friends with the night superintendent.(p.501)

• I am at the ***hospital*** to see my wife.(p.501)

• She begs me to go to a ***hospital*** for alcoholics which has been recommended.(p.502)

• I am in the ***hospital*** for alcoholics.(p.502)

• I get out of the ***hospital*** and we visit some of these new-found friends.(p.505)

• I think the Commanding Officer was rather tired of this particular chicken coming back to roost so often because he very soon wrote in to the medical authorities to tell them that they had to get me into ***hospital***, to be thoroughly examined for drinking.(p.520)

• They kept me in ***hospital*** for two months, and then they sent me up to Egypt, a three days journey.(p.521)

• They sent me up with an attendant, and the attendant and I both arrived at the Egyptian ***Hospital*** rather the worse for wear.(p.521)

• It was no use talking of putting myself into a home, a ***hospital***, or of going to see a doctor again, or of going to see a priest or anyone else.(p.523)

• I thought if the cops did come to the ***hospital***, the doctors would tell them I was crazy and didn't know what I was doing.(p.528)

• He said if I came back again, they would send me to the state ***hospital***.(p.528)

• Within a month, the police, the ***hospital*** authorities, several kind strangers, most of my friends, all of my close relatives, and a few adepts at rolling a drunk and removing his wrist watch and wallet had been involved.(p.532)

• I was down to my shorts, unaware of wrong-doing, before the ambulance got there and hauled me off to a ***hospital*** from which anxious friends rescued me, later that night.(p.537)

• During the day a friend of mine brought me some magazines to take to a ***hospital*** group I was interested in, and I looked through them and a "banner" across the front of one featured an article by a prominent clergyman in which I caught the word "resentment."(p.552)

• I found myself being lifted onto a stretcher and whisked away in an ambulance to a strange ***hospital***.(p.558)

• Each time, I went back to drinking – even smuggling a bottle of vodka into the ***hospital*** as soon as the blood transfusions had ceased.(p.558)

• Dr. John F. Stouffer, Chief Psychiatrist, Philadelphia General ***Hospital***, citing his experience with A.A., said: "The alcoholics we get here at Philadelphia General are mostly those who cannot afford private treatment, and A.A. is by far the greatest thing we have been able to offer them.(p.572)

hospitality

- The ***hospitality*** of their home and their fine fellowship were freely mine.(p.259)
- As we left, and they were escorting us across the bridge into Wheeling, I, with great dignity and sarcasm, told them if their wives were ever visiting in Akron, and they, too, were looking for their route sign as I was, that I hoped I could extend to them the ***hospitality*** that had been shown to me in Bellaire.(p.264)

hospitalization

- Though we work out our solution on the spiritual as well as an altruistic plane, we favor ***hospitalization*** for the alcoholic who is very jittery or befogged.(p.xxiv)
- If your man needs ***hospitalization***, he should have it, but not forcibly unless he is violent.(p.91)
- Because it affected me so strenuously, they felt that ***hospitalization*** was indicated and I awoke in a hospital.(p.207)
- I had had no ***hospitalization*** up to this time because I would not call doctors when I was getting over a bad one.(p.217)
- In large cities, groups often maintain local offices where alcoholics or their families may arrange for interviews or ***hospitalization***.(p.575)

hospitalized

- Many a distracted wife has visited this house to find loving and understanding companionship among women who knew her problem, to hear from the lips of their husbands what had happened to them, to be advised how her own wayward mate might be ***hospitalized*** and approached when next he stumbled.(p.160)
- During the first six months of 1935, I was ***hospitalized*** eight times for intoxication and shackled to the bed two or three days before I even knew where I was.(p.184)
- I don't think Jack was ***hospitalized***.(p.267)
- Lucky because my excessive drinking never got me in jail, or ***hospitalized***, nor did it ever cost me a job.(p.356)
- And, believe me, I thank God that I found out about A.A. before I had to beat my brains out – before I had been ***hospitalized***, jailed or lost a job.(p.367)
- Like most other alcoholics I have known, I did quit drinking at various times -- once for ten months on my own and during other interludes when I was ***hospitalized***.(p.554)

hospitals

- I say this after many years' experience as Medical Director of one of the oldest ***hospitals*** in the country treating alcoholic and drug addiction.(p.xxv)
- Then he begins to appear at ***hospitals*** and sanitariums.(p.22)
- You can easily find some by asking a few doctors, ministers, priests or ***hospitals***.(p.89)
- It may mean sharing your money and your home, counseling frantic wives and relatives, innumerable trips to police courts, sanitariums, ***hospitals***, jails and asylums.(p.97)
- Most of us have entered the final stage with its commitment to health resorts, sanitariums, ***hospitals***, and jails.(p.107)
- Maybe the doctor has been called in, and the weary round of sanitariums and ***hospitals*** has begun.(p.110)
- Since this book was first published, A.A. has released thousands of alcoholics from asylums and ***hospitals*** of every kind.(p.114)
- But life among Alcoholics Anonymous is more than attending gatherings and visiting ***hospitals***.(p.161)
- I explained to my sister that some of the people he was meeting with had been in ***hospitals***.(p.205)
- A complete checkup at one of the best ***hospitals*** revealed nothing.(p.276)
- I lived through a week of the fidgets because I had agreed to address a group of alcoholic inmates in one of our state mental ***hospitals***.(p.283)
- The next three years saw me in sanitariums, once in a ten day coma, from which I very nearly did not recover, in and out of ***hospitals*** or confined at home with day and night nurses.(p.306)
- Most of these fortunate ones have had little or no acquaintance with delirium, with ***hospitals***, asylums, and jails.(p.315)
- I wouldn't go to ***hospitals*** because I wanted my dog there, so I had to have a trained nurse.(p.390)
- Many tried everything – ***hospitals***, special treatments, sanitariums, asylums, and jails.(p.455)
- I had been in several ***hospitals*** for alcoholism.(p.460)
- I went to ***hospitals***, I went to retreats and doctors, and finally my mother asked me to go and see a specialist of her own choosing.(p.522)
- Secondary aids to A.A., such as clubs or ***hospitals*** which require much property or administration, ought to be incorporated and so set apart that, if necessary, they can be freely discarded by the groups.(p.566)
- But ***hospitals***, as well as other places of recuperation, ought to be well outside A.A. – and medically supervised.(p.566)
- We think that each group should soon achieve this ideal; that any public solicitation of funds using the name of Alcoholics Anonymous is highly dangerous, whether by groups, clubs, ***hospitals***, or other outside agencies; that acceptance of large gifts from any source, or of contributions carrying any obligation whatever, is unwise.(p.566)

host

- I made a ***host*** of fair-weather friends.(p.3)
- To watch people recover, to see them help others, to watch loneliness vanish, to see a fellowship grow up about you, to have a ***host*** of friends – this is an experience you must not miss.(p.89)
- They knew they had a ***host*** of new friends; it seemed they had known these strangers always.(p.161)
- From the top of the heap in a few years he had skidded to becoming a shuffling customer, still entering the better barrooms but welcomed by neither mine ***host*** nor his patrons.(p.236)
- Where once I had casual acquaintances, all of whom were fair weather friends, I now have a ***host*** of friends who accept me for what I am.(p.296)
- Still another friend and temporary ***host*** received me at four in the morning from the charge of a policeman who had found me "going to bed" in a garage far from the last place I could remember having been, a fashionable bar and restaurant in the theatrical district of New York, to which I had repaired after my date for that evening, a charming lady of the theatre who had refused my company for obvious reasons.(p.538)
- I mentioned that this friend was my temporary ***host***.(p.538)

hostility

- Some day we hope that Alcoholics Anonymous will help the public to a better realization of the gravity of the alcoholic problem, but we shall be of little use if our attitude is one of bitterness or ***hostility***.(p.103)
- They can urge action without arousing ***hostility***.(p.113)

hot

- There is a complete failure of the kind of defense that keeps one from putting his hand on a ***hot*** stove.(p.24)
- If tempted, we recoil from it as from a ***hot*** flame.(p.84)
- That is the way Jackie found me, lying on a cot in my skivvies, with ***hot*** and cold sweats, pounding heart and that awful itchy scratchiness all over.(p.238)
- That was on a ***hot*** summer evening, down in the Greenwich Village Group, and there was a little porch out there in the old meeting place on Sullivan Street, and after the meeting I went out on the steps for some air.(p.321)
- The drive was long and cold but he was thankful for the ***hot*** bricks which some thoughtful person had given him for his feet.(p.497)

hotel

- After one of those days of inferno, I wobbled from a ***hotel*** bar to a brokerage office.(p.4)
- I went to my ***hotel*** and leisurely dressed for dinner.(p.41)
- When I returned to the ***hotel*** it struck me a highball would be fine before going to bed, so I stepped into the bar and had one.(p.41)
- I still expected a plea for clemency, but these words came through the receiver: "I just wanted to tell you Paul jumped from a ***hotel*** window in Hartford last Saturday.(p.136)
- One dismal afternoon he paced a ***hotel*** lobby wondering how his bill was to be paid.(p.154)
- All this time our friend of the ***hotel*** lobby incident remained in that town.(p.159)
- I would sometimes hide out in one of the clubs of which I was a member, and had the habit at times of registering at a ***hotel*** under a fictitious name.(p.176)
- I drank all the scotch they had on the train and bought several quarts on my way to the ***hotel***.(p.179)
- I checked into my ***hotel*** room and then noticed a placard tucked under the glass on the bureau stating "There will be positively NO drinking at this convention" signed by the president of the company.(p.243)
- Once dad came all the way to Florida to sober me up, after a ***hotel*** manager called him and said that if he wanted to see me alive he better get there fast.(p.288)
- It didn't take long for me to fall in with a fast crowd who had their lunch in the men's bar of a leading ***hotel***.(p.361)
- As I said before, I don't like to be fenced in, and with those bars you don't get ***hotel*** service.(p.390)
- Then I went on my first week-long bender of solitary drinking, locked up in a ***hotel*** room, because my family opposed my coming marriage.(p.464)
- (I think my first feeling of fear came with my first week's solitary drinking, locked up in that ***hotel*** room.(p.465)
- The ***hotel*** management, knowing that something was wrong, sent for a doctor.(p.465)
- If it hadn't been for an alert ***hotel*** maid, I might have died then.(p.465)
- I wish I were home with the family and not in the dingy ***hotel***.(p.500)
- I return to the ***hotel*** where I am staying and get gin from the bellboy.(p.501)
- I go back to the ***hotel*** and get more gin.(p.501)

hotels

- After a couple of days in dollar ***hotels*** and one night in the pokey, I finally landed on my mother's doorstep – shaking apart, with several days' beard and, of course, broke as usual.(p.238)
- Then broke again, hiding out in cheap ***hotels*** all over the country, one night jail stands here and there, and always that horrible feeling "What's the use -- nothing is worth while."(p.244)
- For three generations, my family had had a charge account in one of the big New York ***hotels***.(p.410)

hound

- I sometimes gave it to my mother and then I'd go back and ***hound*** her for it.(p.491)

hour

- Returning home we find a place where we can be quiet for an ***hour*** carefully reviewing what we have done.(p.75)
- Sometimes the man we are calling upon admits his own fault, so feuds of years' standing melt away in an ***hour***.(p.78)
- For an ***hour***, the two friends told him about their drinking experiences.(p.157)
- I drank nine martinis in less than an ***hour***.(p.195)
- I'd waked up in strange rooms before, fully dressed on a bed or a couch; I'd waked up in my own room, in or on my own bed, not knowing what ***hour*** or day it was, afraid to ask . . . but this was different.(p.222)
- It took three-quarters of an ***hour*** and two changes to get there – back to my starting point.(p.223)
- An ***hour*** later I awoke to a new world.(p.280)
- The meeting lasted an ***hour*** and closed with the Lord's Prayer.(p.291)
- It doesn't pay to be seen in the same place at the same ***hour*** every day.(p.299)
- I had long since given up any pretense of the "social" cocktail ***hour***.(p.306)
- It was a long four or five ***hour*** operation, a large surgical procedure, and she was on her ninth or tenth post-operative day.(p.350)
- Before long I was at the luncheon meeting an ***hour*** before the others, that old and familiar trademark of every alcoholic.(p.360)
- The cocktail ***hour*** became a daily routine.(p.374)
- I stopped at the cashier's any ***hour*** of the night on the way to the bar and cashed a check.(p.410)
- Not understanding the twenty-four ***hour*** plan, or not wanting to, I began drinking and was off-again on-again, during that first month.(p.414)
- I got off the so-called wagon, and on the twenty-four ***hour*** plan.(p.415)
- And also, on the twenty-four ***hour*** plan, it taught me how to live.(p.416)
- During these seven years a thing called the Twenty-four *Hour* Program --a gadget I used to think was only a snare to trap the newcomer -- has come to mean much to me, not only as regards my drinking but in the whole pattern of my life.(p.473)
- After he'd talked half an ***hour***, I still wanted him to hurry up and get out so I could go and get some whiskey before the liquor store closed.(p.494)

hours

- It was eight o'clock -- five ***hours*** after the market closed.(p.4)
- He talked for ***hours***.(p.10)
- Faith has to work twenty-four ***hours*** a day in and through us, or we perish.(p.16)
- But the ex-problem drinker who has found this solution, who is properly armed with facts about himself, can generally win the entire confidence of another alcoholic in a few ***hours***.(p.18)
- Here are some of the methods we have tried: Drinking beer only, limiting the number of drinks, never

drinking alone, never drinking in the morning, drinking only at home, never having it in the house, never drinking during business *hours*, drinking only at parties, switching from scotch to brandy, drinking only natural wines, agreeing to resign if ever drunk on the job, taking a trip, not taking a trip, swearing off forever (with and without a solemn oath), taking more physical exercise, reading inspirational books, going to health farms and sanitariums, accepting voluntary commitment to asylums -- we could increase the list ad infinitum.(p.31)
• To the precise extent that we permit these, do we squander the *hours* that might have been worth while.(p.66)
• On awakening let us think about the twenty-four *hours* ahead.(p.86)
• You have been starving for his companionship, yet he spends long *hours* helping other men and their families.(p.119)
• This seemed to me like an opportunity to be helpful, so I spent two *hours* talking about alcoholism, the malady, and described the symptoms and results as well as I could.(p.138)
• You may have to curb his desire to work sixteen *hours* a day.(p.146)
• He may wish to do a lot for other alcoholics and something of the sort may come up during business *hours*.(p.146)
• They shared their homes, their slender resources, and gladly devoted their spare *hours* to fellow-sufferers.(p.159)
• I soon discovered that a couple of drinks would alleviate my gastric distress, at least for a few *hours* at a time, so it was not at all difficult for me to return to my former excessive indulgence.(p.174)
• Occasionally, I would yield to the morning craving, but if I did, it would be only a few *hours* before I would be quite unfit for work.(p.176)
• The next question they asked was, "You can quit twenty-four *hours* can't you?"(p.188)
• I said, "Sure, yes, anybody can do that, for twenty-four *hours*."(p.188)
• Just twenty-four *hours* at a time."(p.188)
• Every time I'd start thinking about drinking, I would think of the long, dry years ahead without having a drink; but this idea of twenty-four *hours*, that it was up to me from then on, was a lot of help.(p.188)
• I can remember well thinking that I would quit drinking, really go to work hard, apply myself eight *hours* a day, five days a week, make a lot of money, and then I could start drinking again.(p.199)
• The interne came along with a glassful of bleached lightning that put me away for about fifteen *hours*.(p.217)
• She gave no sign of recognizing anything wrong, but what had I been doing for those lost five *hours*?(p.223)
• Evidently I had gone right back to the movie with a bottle, stayed there several *hours* and started home with no recollection of what had happened.(p.244)
• I think his entry into A.A. was through spending some *hours* with Dr. Bob at his office.(p.267)
• I told our family doctor, an understanding man who gave *hours* of his time trying to help me, about this experience.(p.276)
• He spent two *hours* with me that night telling me his story.(p.290)
• After it was closed we all retired to the kitchen and had coffee and doughnuts and more discussion until the small *hours* of the morning.(p.291)
• The day before I was due to go back to Chicago, a Wednesday and Dr. Bob's afternoon off, he had me down to the office and we spent three or four *hours* formally going through the Six-Step program as it was at that time.(p.291)
• Live twenty-four *hours* at a time, they say.(p.320)
• A few *hours* later I came out of a complete stupor in our living room with a flash of sanity.(p.363)
• Sure enough in a couple of *hours* two men were at my door and for the first time I heard some facts about liquor and my problem that sounded sensible to me.(p.363)
• For the next couple of *hours* a terrible battle went on between the good gremlins and the bad ones, one faction urging me to tell the truth, the other telling me to sit tight and say nothing.(p.366)
• My *hours* of work were flexible so that returning to the office was not always important.(p.376)
• "Twenty-four *hours* a day."(p.382)
• So I was in just a few *hours*.(p.390)
• My life there was a nightmare of periodic binges on alcohol and pills, adultery, unhappy *hours* at the dental office, seeing my wife give birth to our second child and have several miscarriages, living in a turbulent household, and making continual attempts to be the respectable dentist, husband, father, and community leader.(p.419)
• My drinking took place after work *hours*.(p.441)
• Same thing when I let lye and water eat away at four of my toes and my foot for five *hours*.(p.458)
• During the twenty-four *hours* after running into the Serenity Prayer, I think I took the first three Steps for the first time.(p.461)
• Then in a couple of *hours*, when there was still no word from my husband and no sign of him, I had the feeling we alcoholics all know.(p.467)
• A very good friend of mine who owned a drug store across the street from us, came by only about two *hours* later and said that he had seen Vi down town.(p.487)
• The amount of will power exercised to control my drinking during working *hours*, diverted into a constructive channel, would have made me President, and the thing that made the will power possible was the knowledge that as soon as my day was finished I could drink myself into oblivion.(p.548)

house

• The *house* was taken over by the mortgage holder, my mother-in-law died, and my wife and father-in-law became ill.(p.5)
• With a certain satisfaction I reflected there was enough gin concealed about the *house* to carry me through that night and the next day.(p.8)
• If he can afford it, he may have liquor concealed all over his *house* to be certain no one gets his entire supply away from him to throw down the waterpipe.(p.22)
• Here are some of the methods we have tried: Drinking beer only, limiting the number of drinks, never drinking alone, never drinking in the morning, drinking only at home, never having it in the *house*, never drinking during business hours, drinking only at parties, switching from scotch to brandy, drinking only natural wines, agreeing to resign if ever drunk on the job, taking a trip, not taking a trip, swearing off forever (with and without a solemn oath), taking more physical exercise, reading inspirational books, going to health farms and sanitariums, accepting voluntary commitment to asylums -- we could increase the list ad infinitum.(p.31)
• Wants *house* put in her name.(p.65)
• So we clean *house* with the family, asking each morning in meditation that our Creator show us the way of patience, tolerance, kindliness and love.(p.83)
• The only condition is that he trust in God and clean *house*.(p.98)
• We seldom had friends at our homes, never knowing how or when the men of the *house* would appear.(p.105)
• Your *house* is filled with strangers.(p.119)
• But the head of the *house* has spent years in pulling down the structures of business, romance, friendship, health -- these things are now ruined or damaged.(p.123)
• The head of the *house* ought to remember that he is mainly to blame for what befell his home.(p.127)
• They can hardly fail to approve these simple principles, though the head of the *house* still fails somewhat in practicing them.(p.130)
• Liquor incapacitated father for so many years that mother became head of the *house*.(p.130)
• Many a distracted wife has visited this *house* to find loving and understanding companionship among women who knew her problem, to hear from the lips of their husbands what had happened to them, to be advised how her own wayward mate might be hospitalized and approached when next he stumbled.(p.160)
• Impressed by those who visited him at the hospital, he capitulated entirely when, later, in an upper room of this *house*, he heard the story of some man whose experience closely tallied with his own.(p.160)
• Now, this *house* will hardly accommodate its weekly visitors, for they number sixty or eighty as a rule.(p.161)
• The answers will come, if your own *house* is in order.(p.164)
• Many mornings I have gone to classes, and even though fully prepared, would turn and walk back to the fraternity *house* because of my jitters, not daring to enter the classroom for fear of making a scene should I be called on for recitation.(p.173)
• There my drinking became so much worse that the boys in the fraternity *house* where I lived felt forced to send for my father, who made a long journey in the vain endeavor to get me straightened around.(p.174)
• Finally my father had to send a doctor out from my home town who managed to get me back there in some way, and I was in bed about two months before I could venture out of the *house*.(p.175)
• We entered her *house* at exactly five o'clock and it was eleven fifteen when we left.(p.179)
• I remember nothing from then on until I woke up at a friend's *house*, in a town near home.(p.179)
• On the return trip, after two or three loads, I passed out and had to be carried to the *house*.(p.183)
• I remember that my father kept whiskey around the *house* for medical purposes and entertainment, and I would drink from this when no one was about and then water it to keep my parents from knowing I was drinking.(p.183)
• I know there was even more, something that I hadn't got, and I remember one day, a week or two after I had come out of the hospital, Bill was over to my *house* talking to my wife and me.(p.191)
• My wife didn't tell me this, but one Sunday afternoon when Mary was trying to get the cobwebs out of my mind, Clarence and his sister-in-law, the hairdresser, called at the *house*.(p.216)
• I left on a Wednesday afternoon, had dinner in Akron and then went to a *house* where I encountered my first meeting.(p.218)
• I went trembling into a *house* in Brooklyn filled with strangers . . . and I found I had come home at last, to my own kind.(p.228)
• I was eased out of the business I had founded and was reduced to doing general upholstery in a small shop at the back of my *house*.(p.233)
• I had them hidden away in the *house* and all over my shop in careful concealment.(p.233)
• Bill and Hank had just taken over a small automobile polishing company and they offered me a job -- ten dollars a week and keep at Hank's *house*.(p.246)
• Our oldest daughter got married; they were living at our *house*.(p.263)
• Of course, this year we decided on staying home and being sensible, doing a little drinking, and painting the *house*.(p.265)
• So, on that Saturday before Labor Day, I got drunk and set the *house* on fire -- so we didn't have to paint it.(p.265)
• It would stop out in front of our *house*, and I still believe those people sent it!(p.265)
• One morning after a terrific drinking bout, I was in a little bar near our *house*, and I shook so that I was very much ashamed, because I was getting the shakes worse and worse.(p.266)
• Men from A.A. started coming out to the *house* the next day.(p.268)
• I'd like to say here how important it was to us then that we do all the little things that people said were important, because later when Russ was so sick that I had to hold him up, they had a meeting out at the *house*.(p.270)
• We had big picnics out at the *house* with A.A.(p.270)
• I don't ever remember that I was bored myself when we first came in, and they came out to the *house* and talked to us about these things.(p.273)
• Three more months of being up and around the *house* for brief periods and in bed the rest of the time.(p.275)
• Half a block from the *house*, I tried to turn the corner.(p.276)
• When I reached a point directly back of our *house*, where I could have cut through a friend's garden, I was almost overpowered by the desire to get home, but I made the whole journey.(p.276)
• When she finally took the baby and left, I locked myself in the *house* and stayed drunk for a month.(p.278)
• Now I was in a strange *house*, in a strange city, and fear gripped me.(p.279)
• But it took six more months of work and disappointments before a group of three men got together in my rooming *house* bedroom for their first A.A. meeting.(p.282)
• That same year, my wife became fed up with my drinking around the *house* and called my dad in Akron to come and pick me up.(p.288)
• I couldn't keep up with any of my other friends, and I wouldn't go to anyone's *house* unless I knew they drank as heavily as I did.(p.324)
• He used to wonder, when he'd spot one of my bottles around the *house*, just how he could have overlooked that particular bottle.(p.325)
• She was studying fashion design, was living in the same rooming *house*, and was from my home town of Cleveland.(p.359)
• I entered the *house*, opened a new bottle of whiskey and sat down to drink myself into the right frame of mind to get in my car, start the motor and close the garage door behind me.(p.363)
• At a women's halfway *house*, I became associated with Alcoholics Anonymous and became aware of alcoholism as a disease, not just a "weakness."(p.371)
• Frank had to go to New York, but because I had a dog, we had a duplex, and I thought -- if only we

had a *house*!(p.388)
• So I located a *house*, and I thought we ought to move into it immediately, but Frank was horrified, because he never knew what was going to happen to me.(p.388)
• He said, "If your father will come out and stay with you, you can have the *house*."(p.389)
• I loved my father dearly and I adored my dog, and I'd gotten this new *house* and Frank had just given me a new fur coat and I was thrilled to death.(p.389)
• A *house* in Virginia, during the fox hunting season; a little chalet in Switzerland during the summer or a place on Long Island – each *house* complete with cooks, butlers and maids.(p.403)
• This was in Virginia, where I had rented a *house* with stables and a swimming pool, and the fall fox hunting had begun.(p.404)
• I had a tiny trust fund, and I moved into a small apartment where I learned to cook, keep *house*, and do the things that normal people do.(p.409)
• Luckily, the garage was attached to the *house*.(p.442)
• But to do so, I had to get all the stuff out of the *house* and out of my possession.(p.443)
• I wasn't able to quit chemicals as long as they were in the *house*.(p.443)
• I was taken out of the *house* and put bodily into a waiting car with nothing on but a robe and gown.(p.466)
• We pulled up in front of my sister's *house* just as dawn broke.(p.466)
• My husband helped me into the *house*, packed himself a bag, and gave me some money.(p.467)
• I stay with him at aunt's *house* in Maine.(p.474)
• A couple of years later, we lost our elder brother in a *house* fire, because of pills and booze.(p.480)
• We had no whiskey in the *house*, other than my father's private stock.(p.484)
• The next morning I carried another prescription to this man's *house* and exchanged it for the bottle his wife had.(p.489)
• Within about ten days I got locked up for being drunk and this same policeman was in the station *house* as I was being booked.(p.491)
• I was taken to the station *house* and locked up.(p.492)
• The wind is rising and howls around the *house*.(p.497)
• I mope around the *house*.(p.506)
• I back up to the door and go into the *house*.(p.506)
• The trial lasted about a week, and whether or not I was going to the death *house* was anybody's guess.(p.508)
• We talked for a while, and then he sent me down to the Alanon *House* over on the west side, and there I had my introduction to A.A.(p.515)
• Once I started drinking, I didn't care that the rent wasn't paid, or that there was no food in the *house*, or that my boys needed shoes.(p.527)
• I would wake to find myself in some beat-up rooming *house*, where roaches were crawling over everything.(p.527)
• The doc and I went back into the *house*.(p.541)
• This is a world clearing *house* for the Al-Anon Family Groups, composed largely of the wives, husbands and friends of A.A. members.(p.575)

housecleaning

• Next we launched out on a course of vigorous action, the first step of which is a personal *housecleaning*, which many of us had never attempted.(p.63)
• We think the reason is that they never completed their *housecleaning*.(p.73)
• He may rebel at the thought of a drastic *housecleaning* which requires discussion with other people.(p.94)

household

• There will be other profound changes in the *household*.(p.130)
• My life there was a nightmare of periodic binges on alcohol and pills, adultery, unhappy hours at the dental office, seeing my wife give birth to our second child and have several miscarriages, living in a turbulent *household*, and making continual attempts to be the respectable dentist, husband, father, and community leader.(p.419)

housekeeping

• My wife came over from Scotland and we started *housekeeping* in a large Ohio city.(p.254)

houses

• People have said we must not go where liquor is served; we must not have it in our homes; we must shun friends who drink; we must avoid moving pictures which show drinking scenes; we must not go into bars; our friends must hide their bottles if we go to their *houses*; we mustn't think or be reminded about alcohol at all.(p.100)
• With that profit, I built a number of *houses*, but then I neglected them.(p.194)
• Somehow I got out of there and walked five blocks past brownstone *houses*.(p.223)
• Up to my early thirties, when my drinking had become a major problem, I lived in large *houses*, with servants and all the luxuries that I could possibly ask for.(p.401)
• He saw that I was unsettled, living away from my family and renting *houses* here and there.(p.403)
• Build *houses* for some cops – ha-ha.(p.475)

housewife

• THE *HOUSEWIFE* WHO DRANK AT HOME(p.335)
• In my drinking days, I found the ideal spot for the alcoholic *housewife*: the neighborhood Laundromat.(p.369)

housewives'

• All hidden drunks aren't at home in *housewives'* dresses.(p.328)

Houston

• When I hit *Houston*, Texas, I found employment in a large bookstore.(p.255)
• We moved once more, to *Houston*; my husband thought maybe a change of environment would help and I'd be all right.(p.389)
• One afternoon, the year after moving to *Houston*, I got as drunk as a skunk, and while I do not walk very straight sober, you should see me when I'm drunk!(p.390)
• There are so many to whom I feel deeply grateful; to my husband (and best critic), whose generous love, compassion and understanding have helped me along the way; to those before me in A.A. who inspired the first article I read, and the friend who sent that article to Frank; to Ruth for her personal note, and the first A.A. to talk to me; to my Bishop, whose loving and believing spirit inspired me; and to all the members of the *Houston* Group who were so patient, kind and helpful -- and to countless others.(p.393)

how

• To show other alcoholics precisely *how* we have recovered is the main purpose of this book.(p.xiii)
• In no time I was beating on the bar asking myself *how* it happened.(p.6)
• *How* dark it is before the dawn!(p.8)
• I wondered *how* he had escaped.(p.9)
• In a matter of fact way he told *how* two men had appeared in court, persuading the judge to suspend his commitment.(p.9)
• I could almost hear the sound of the preacher's voice as I sat, on still Sundays, way over there on the hillside; there was that proffered temperance pledge I never signed; my grandfather's good natured contempt of some church folk and their doings; his insistence that the spheres really had their music; but his denial of the preacher's right to tell him *how* he must listen; his fearlessness as he spoke of these things just before he died; these recollections welled up from the past.(p.10)
• *How* could there be so much of precise and immutable law and no intelligence?(p.10)
• *How* blind I had been.(p.13)
• And *how* appallingly true for the alcoholic!(p.14)
• *How* then shall we present that which has been so freely given us?(p.19)
• Our very lives, as ex-problem drinkers, depend upon our constant thought of others and *how* we may help meet their needs.(p.20)
• Doubtless you are curious to discover *how* and why, in the face of expert opinion to the contrary, we have recovered from a hopeless condition of mind and body.(p.20)
• *How* many times people have said to us: "I can take it or leave it alone.(p.20)
• *How* true this is, few realize.(p.23)
• The alcoholic may say to himself in the most casual way, "It won't burn me this time, so here's *how*!"(p.24)
• *How* often have some of us begun to drink in this nonchalant way, and after the third or fourth, pounded on the bar and said to ourselves, "For God's sake, *how* did I ever get started again?"(p.24)
• Further on, clear-cut directions are given showing *how* we recovered.(p.29)
• For those who are unable to drink moderately the question is *how* to stop altogether.(p.34)
• This is the baffling feature of alcoholism as we know it -- this utter inability to leave it alone, no matter *how* great the necessity or the wish.(p.34)
• *How* then shall we help our readers determine, to their own satisfaction, whether they are one of us?(p.34)
• We asked him to tell us exactly *how* it happened.(p.36)
• *How* can such a lack of proportion, of the ability to think straight, be called anything else?(p.37)
• Next day we would ask ourselves, in all earnestness and sincerity, *how* it could have happened.(p.37)
• I now remembered what my alcoholic friends had told me, *how* they prophesied that if I had an alcoholic mind, the time and place would come – I would drink again.(p.41)
• But we found that such codes and philosophies did not save us, no matter *how* much we tried.(p.45)
• But where and *how* were we to find this Power?(p.45)
• We know *how* he feels.(p.45)
• *How* could a Supreme Being have anything to do with it all?(p.46)
• When people presented us with spiritual approaches, *how* frequently did we all say, "I wish I had what that man has.(p.47)
• *How* much did these feelings, these loves, these worships, have to do with pure reason?(p.54)
• *HOW* IT WORKS(p.58)
• This is the *how* and why of it.(p.62)
• *How* could we escape?(p.66)
• We saw that these resentments must be mastered, but *how*?(p.66)
• *How* can I be helpful to him?(p.67)
• We cannot be helpful to all people, but at least God will show us *how* to take a kindly and tolerant view of each and every one.(p.67)
• The question of *how* to approach the man we hated will arise.(p.77)
• We must lose our fear of creditors no matter *how* far we have to go, for we are liable to drink if we are afraid to face them.(p.78)
• *How* could he possibly make a public statement exonerating his rival?(p.80)
• *How* could she be anything else?(p.81)
• No matter *how* far down the scale we have gone, we will see *how* our experience can benefit others.(p.84)
• We will intuitively know *how* to handle situations which used to baffle us.(p.84)
• That is *how* we react so long as we keep in fit spiritual condition.(p.85)
• "*How* can I best serve Thee -- Thy will (not mine) be done."(p.85)
• We are often surprised *how* the right answers come after we have tried this for a while.(p.86)
• You need this information to put yourself in his place, to see *how* you would like him to approach you if the tables were turned.(p.90)
• You will thus get a better idea of *how* you ought to proceed.(p.91)
• But say nothing, for the moment, of *how* that was accomplished.(p.91)
• Tell him *how* baffled you were, *how* you finally learned that you were sick.(p.92)
• Show him, from your own experience, *how* the queer mental condition surrounding that first drink prevents normal functioning of the will power.(p.92)
• Even though your protege may not have entirely admitted his condition, he has become very curious to know *how* you got well.(p.92)
• In that case he is going to wonder *how* you can add anything to what he already knows.(p.93)
• Outline the program of action, explaining *how* you made a self-appraisal, *how* you straightened out your past and why you are now endeavoring to be helpful to him.(p.94)
• Suggest *how* important it is that he place the welfare of other people ahead of his own.(p.94)
• Show him *how* they worked with you.(p.95)
• It is not the matter of giving that is in question, but when and *how* to give.(p.98)
• If you have been successful in solving your own domestic problems, tell the newcomer's family *how* that was accomplished.(p.100)
• The story of *how* you and your wife settled your difficulties is worth any amount of criticism.(p.100)
• We seldom had friends at our homes, never knowing *how* or when the men of the house would appear.(p.105)
• *How* heartbreaking was this discovery; *how* cruel to be told they understood our men as we did not!(p.106)
• *How* could men who loved their wives and children be so unthinking, so callous, so cruel?(p.107)
• And even if they did not love their families, *how* could they be so blind about themselves?(p.107)

• But when he gets over the spree, he begins to think once more *how* he can drink moderately next time.(p.109)
• You may be unable to do so, no matter *how* hard you try.(p.111)
• We have elsewhere remarked *how* much better life is when lived on a spiritual plane.(p.116)
• We urge you to try our program, for nothing will be so helpful to your husband as the radically changed attitude toward him which God will show you *how* to have.(p.117)
• You, as well as your husband, ought to think of what you can put into life instead of *how* much you can take out.(p.120)
• Cheer him up and ask him *how* you can be still more helpful.(p.120)
• Suppose we tell you some of the obstacles a family will meet; suppose we suggest *how* they may be avoided — even converted to good use for others.(p.123)
• We think each family which has been relieved owes something to those who have not, and when the occasion requires, each member of it should be only too willing to bring former mistakes, no matter *how* grievous, out of their hiding places.(p.124)
• Showing others who suffer *how* we were given help is the very thing which makes life seem so worth while to us now.(p.124)
• They criticize, pointing out *how* he is falling down on his spiritual program.(p.126)
• You may be at a loss to understand *how* such a seemingly above-board chap could be so involved.(p.140)
• But these scrapes can generally be charged, no matter *how* bad, to the abnormal action of alcohol on his mind.(p.140)
• I know, in my own particular case, that nothing my company could have done would have stopped me for, so long as I was able to hold my position, I could not possibly realize *how* serious my situation was.(p.141)
• I don't see *how* you can be of any help to us for, as you see, we don't have any alcoholic problem."(p.148)
• He might be shocked if he knew *how* much alcoholism is costing his organization a year.(p.149)
• We believe that managers of large enterprises often have little idea *how* prevalent this problem is.(p.149)
• We have shown *how* we got out from under.(p.152)
• I know I must get along without liquor, but *how* can I?(p.152)
• "*How* is that to come about?" you ask.(p.152)
• *How* can they rise out of such misery, bad repute and hopelessness?(p.153)
• In the chapter "Working With Others" you gathered an idea of *how* we approach and aid others to health.(p.153)
• You will want to know more of *how* to proceed from that point.(p.153)
• One dismal afternoon he paced a hotel lobby wondering *how* his bill was to be paid.(p.154)
• But what about his responsibilities — his family and the men who would die because they would not know *how* to get well, ah -- yes, those other alcoholics?(p.154)
• He told *how* he lived in constant worry about those who might find out about his alcoholism.(p.155)
• The man in the bed was told of the acute poisoning from which he suffered, *how* it deteriorates the body of an alcoholic and warps his mind.(p.157)
• Seeing much of each other, scarce an evening passed that someone's home did not shelter a little gathering of men and women, happy in their release, and constantly thinking *how* they might present their discovery to some newcomer.(p.159)
• Many a distracted wife has visited this house to find loving and understanding companionship among women who knew her problem, to hear from the lips of their husbands what had happened to them, to be advised *how* her own wayward mate might be hospitalized and approached when next he stumbled.(p.160)
• *How* could they?(p.161)
• He will show you *how* to create the fellowship you crave.(p.164)
• *How* Forty-Three Alcoholics Recovered From Their Malady(p.165)
• *How* my wife kept her faith and courage during all those years, I'll never know, but she did.(p.178)
• I thought of what liquor had done to me, the opportunities that I had discarded, the abilities that had been given me and *how* I had wasted them, and I finally came to the conclusion, that if I didn't want to quit, I certainly ought to want to, and that I was willing to do anything in the world to stop drinking.(p.186)
• I was willing to admit to myself that I had hit bottom, that I had gotten hold of something that I didn't know *how* to handle by myself.(p.187)
• And they said, "No, you have a disease, and it doesn't make any difference *how* long you do without it, after a drink or two you'll end up just like you are now."(p.187)
• Bill then related *how* he had lain awake nearly all night.(p.189)
• It would be hard to estimate *how* much A.A. has done for me.(p.191)
• He did things much better than I did because he applied himself and learned *how* to do them, and I never applied myself.(p.194)
• I had run into him, and he looked real prosperous; his face and eyes looked clear and he started to compliment me on my good front and *how* well I looked, and I said, "I haven't had a drink for nine months."(p.201)
• And we stood there for twenty minutes, telling each other *how* much better we were, *how* much better we looked, *how* much better off we were financially, mentally, physically, morally, and in every way, shape and manner.(p.201)
• So I was barred from the plant for ten days, and during that ten day period I was drunk twice, showing *how* little control these restraints had on me.(p.205)
• My only thought that day was getting a drink, and *how* to get rid of those clowns was my big problem.(p.206)
• I then began asking a lot of questions of both my brother and Dr. Bob about *how* this thing worked, and I suppose I was becoming more glassy-eyed all the while, for eventually I said to Bob, "You're all dried up.(p.206)
• *How* are you feeling?"(p.207)
• I said, "*How* do you suppose?(p.208)
• Then he started to talk to me about his drinking experiences, what his drinking had cost him, *how* much he had drunk and where, things like that, and I remember I was quite bored because I had never seen the guy before and had no interest at all in what, where and when he drank.(p.208)
• All during Prohibition, every alcoholic felt that he made the best hooch, regardless of *how* bad it was.(p.213)
• When I was about forty-seven, after indulging in all kinds of self-deception to control my drinking, I arrived at a period when I felt convinced I had to have so much alcohol every day and that the real problem was to control *how* much.(p.214)
• And then my thinking became calculation as to *how* much longer I had to live, *how* long the assets would last.(p.215)
• He startled me by informing me that he was an alcoholic, that he had found a way which so far enabled him to live without taking a drink, and that the main idea was to find a way *how* not to take that first drink.(p.218)
• Professionally, after I was sober for a month or so I realized that I should school myself to dissolve the partnership I was in because I felt that I would never regain the respect of my partners no matter *how* long I was sober, and that I would be at a disadvantage.(p.220)
• In any case I must get out of here before I let slip my abysmal ignorance of *how* I came to be here, and she realized that I was stark, staring mad.(p.223)
• *How* had I met her?(p.223)
• When I look back on that last horrible year of constant drinking I wonder *how* I survived it either physically or mentally.(p.224)
• "Blanks" were more frequent, and I seldom knew *how* I'd got home.(p.226)
• Alcohol was that prop, and I didn't see *how* I could live without it.(p.226)
• Besides, *how* could he understand?(p.227)
• Even then he went into no great detail about *how* he and a crowd of alcoholics, with whom he associated, had mastered their difficulty.(p.235)
• Well, there I was, willing to try it, but I didn't know *how*, except in a vague way.(p.236)
• *How* it finally broke a Southerner's obstinacy and destined this salesman to start A.A. at Philadelphia.(p.238)
• So I always say that as long as I remember January 8th that is *how* long I will remain sober.(p.240)
• As part of this promotion, they sent me to their national convention in Atlantic City to tell the big wheels *how* I'd done it.(p.243)
• All they talked of that first week-end was God, and *how* they were going to straighten out Jackie's and my life.(p.245)
• They had also been periodic big shots who had goofed out repeatedly at the wrong time, and they also knew *how* to split one paper match into three separate matches.(p.245)
• They, too, had taken a train to one town and had wakened hundreds of miles in the opposite direction, never knowing *how* they got there.(p.246)
• There was one meeting a week at Bill's home in Brooklyn, and we all took turns there spouting off about *how* we had changed our lives overnight, *how* many drunks we had saved and straightened out, and last, but not least, *how* God had touched each of us personally on the shoulder.(p.246)
• When I started to tell the boys *how* we did it in New York and all about the spiritual part of the program, I found they would not believe me unless I was practicing what I preached.(p.249)
• In telling newcomers *how* to change their lives and attitudes, all of a sudden I found I was doing a little changing myself.(p.249)
• And I still say that as long as I remember that January 8th in Washington, that is *how* long, by the grace of God as I understand Him, I will retain a happy sobriety.(p.250)
• Now on a new job I was always thinking about payday and *how* much liquor I could buy and the pleasure I could have.(p.255)
• I have stood listening to street-corner preachers tell *how* they beat the game.(p.256)
• The doctor who came to see me almost at once did not assail me with any new doctrines; he made sure that I had a need and that I wanted to have that need filled, and little by little I learned *how* my need could be met.(p.258)
• All sorts were represented and their relation of experiences and *how* they had found the only remedy, added to their human existence as sober men, laid the foundation of a very necessary faith.(p.258)
• They will never know *how* much their talk with me helped.(p.259)
• She tells *how* A.A. works when the going is rough.(p.261)
• I didn't realize *how* I still felt about him.(p.263)
• I thought, "No matter *how* crazy they are I'll do anything they say to do."(p.267)
• Russ said, "Mother, if this tells us *how* to do it, you'll have to read it."(p.268)
• No, I was all interested in this part that told you *how* to do it.(p.269)
• And we went down through the valley, and I remembered reading about the Ku Klux Klan and *how* they burnt crosses, and I thought, "God alone knows what we are getting into this time!"(p.269)
• They told Annabelle to take me under her wing, and I shall never forget *how* she sort of curled up her nose and said, "They tell me you drink too."(p.269)
• I often think *how* that could have turned some people away, because there were no other women alcoholics there then.(p.269)
• He talked about his wife taking his little boy away from him because of his drinking, and *how* he got back together with them through A.A., and we began feeling grateful right then that all these things hadn't been taken from us.(p.270)
• I'd like to say here *how* important it was to us then that we do all the little things that people said were important, because later when Russ was so sick that I had to hold him up, they had a meeting out at the house.(p.270)
• I ate up every bit of it, because I wanted to find out *how* to stay sober.(p.273)
• Before I stop -- I always was a great talker -- I want to say that nobody will ever know *how* I miss Annie's advice about things.(p.273)
• I didn't think I was going to get drunk right then, but I remember *how* comforting it was when I called Anne and told her.(p.273)
• *How* could I get it?(p.279)
• Dr. Bob dwelt at length on *how* prayer had given him release, time and time again, from the nearly overpowering compulsion to take a drink.(p.279)
• Finally, and I shall never know *how* much later it was, one clear thought came to me: Try prayer.(p.280)
• It is undoubtedly too soon for me to say *how* much of a success I shall be as a husband in time to come.(p.286)
• On my ride to the nearest bar, I sold the driver on *how* misunderstood I was by my wife and what an unreasonable person she was.(p.288)
• In the next two or three days the balance of this handful of men contacted me, encouraged me, and told me *how* they were trying to live this program of recovery and the fun they were having doing it.(p.291)
• I spent a great deal of time with Dr. Bob, whenever he had the time to spare, and in the homes of two or three other people, trying to see *how* the family lived the program.(p.291)

• I went to a minister and a doctor that I still knew and they, in turn, asked me ***how*** long I had been sober.(p.293)

• He had been wanting to do something about his drinking for a long time, but did not know ***how***.(p.294)

• The last day of my drinking career, I drank twenty-two of them between ten and twelve a.m. and I shall never know ***how*** many more followed them until I was poured into bed that night.(p.298)

• ***How*** I was able to discharge my duties at the office during those horrible mornings, I will never be able to explain.(p.299)

• ***How*** many times I swore off in the morning and got drunk before sunset I don't know.(p.300)

• One is that I don't remember too many of them, as I was one of those drunks who could be on his feet and attend a meeting or a party, engage in a conversation with people and do things that any nearly normal person would do, and the next day not remember a thing about where I was, what I did, whom I saw, or ***how*** I got home.(p.301)

• ***How*** did he know all this?(p.302)

• ***How*** I had arrived at this tragic impasse I could not have explained to anyone.(p.304)

• I was trapped, and for the life of me I did not know ***how*** or why this had happened to me.(p.306)

• But ***how*** does one get a prescription for a miracle?(p.306)

• And we wonder ***how*** much further this man could go if his alcoholic problem could be removed and he could throw one hundred per cent of his abilities into action.(p.308)

• It wasn't long before I quit caring ***how*** I looked or what my job performance was.(p.318)

• She said, "***How*** long have you been married?"(p.322)

• ***How*** did you ever stand it?"(p.322)

• It's surprising, ***how*** we think we fool everybody in our drinking.(p.324)

• He used to wonder, when he'd spot one of my bottles around the house, just ***how*** he could have overlooked that particular bottle.(p.325)

• But then I thought, well, now wait, ***how*** will I feel next Tuesday?(p.326)

• ***How*** will I feel next Friday, if I make it a Friday?(p.326)

• ***How*** will I feel next Saturday morning?(p.326)

• We're free at last to do our thing, to live uninhibited lives, to drink when and ***how*** and where we wish, when we want to and when we need to.(p.329)

• ***How*** hurt I was when editors bounced back my ideas quickly and my best friends opined that my output needed a lot of rewriting.(p.331)

• ***How*** devastating, too, are the subsequent feelings of inadequacy and self-pity.(p.331)

• "I'll Never Smile Again" – ***how*** perfect.(p.332)

• ***How*** futile!(p.332)

• No matter ***how*** often I had gone into and come out of alcoholic lows during the day, the pattern bounced me out of bed each night about 2:00 a.m., shaking and hurting in the agitation that always follows a drug's sedation.(p.332)

• ***How*** that line echoed through my mind!(p.333)

• ***How*** full it has kept my retirement years -- the five I've lived since the first two lost in traveling a rocky road to hell, before I made a U-turn.(p.334)

• He said, "***How*** I envy you for whatever you've found."(p.334)

• I had to give him a story and ask him the same question over and over again, "Well, now, ***how*** many will that bottle serve?"(p.336)

• ***How*** I ran my home, I don't know.(p.337)

• And yet, ***how*** was I going to live without it?(p.338)

• He knew what I was doing, ***how*** I was trying.(p.339)

• I didn't know ***how*** to be a father; I don't know ***how*** to come home and work week-ends like other husbands; I don't know ***how*** to entertain my family.(p.351)

• My sponsor used to say to me, "If I could only paint you a picture of ***how*** beautiful life can be without booze . . ."(p.355)

• Of course I kept her posted on ***how*** well the station was doing and wrote convincing letters of ***how*** well I was doing with the liquor problem.(p.360)

• ***How*** could I continually break my promises?(p.362)

• Of course, more than anything else I had let myself down, but I didn't realize ***how*** much then -- as I do now.(p.364)

• I had no qualms, because I felt the source of a drinking problem was all in ***how*** weak one was, and I wasn't like my dad (I thought).(p.370)

• The only drawback was, I always knew ***how*** I arrived there, but somehow, between the rest room, the rinse, and the fluff-dry, I never knew when or ***how*** I got home.(p.370)

• ***How*** can a person with a fine family, an attractive home, an excellent position and high standing in an important city become an alcoholic?(p.373)

• To wake up at home, not knowing ***how*** I got there, and to realize I had driven my car, became torture.(p.375)

• Not knowing where I had been or ***how*** I got home was making me desperate.(p.375)

• I will never know all the people I hurt, all the friends I abused, the humiliation of my family, the worry of my business associates, or ***how*** far reaching it was.(p.376)

• After every cocktail party or dinner party she would say she couldn't understand ***how*** I could get in such a drunken stupor on one drink.(p.377)

• She of course didn't realize ***how*** cunning an alcoholic can be and the lengths to which he will go in finding ways to satisfy the compulsion for more and more drinks after having had the first one.(p.377)

• It wasn't ***how*** far I had gone, but where I was headed.(p.379)

• I wish I could tell you ***how*** and why A.A. works, but I don't know.(p.384)

• That is ***how*** dishonest I was with myself.(p.388)

• My father, as I have said, was very indulgent and loved me dearly, and knew ***how*** to get around me.(p.389)

• So, as I have said, I don't know ***how*** or why A.A. works.(p.392)

• It is also stated that we will never be able to figure out ***how*** much we have spent on alcohol.(p.396)

• (I can't know ***how*** much others of our Fellowship have paid financially and, even more important, mentally and physically.)(p.396)

• It is bound to be rough, because who can say exactly ***how*** much of that green blood -- commonly known as money -- was dissipated on dissipation?(p.396)

• After all, upon coming out of a week-long or ten-day drunk, it was hard enough to figure up just ***how*** much that one drunk cost, let alone trying to calculate the cost of approximately twenty-five years of active alcoholism.(p.396)

• They did the best they knew ***how*** as far as I was concerned.(p.401)

• I learned ***how*** to hold a terrapin fork.(p.401)

• I, who did not know ***how*** to give love, was head over heels "in love."(p.403)

• I accepted a big tax-free income from the family, but I didn't like it when they told me ***how*** to live.(p.405)

• ***How*** could anybody forget a drink?(p.407)

• Now it was semi-blackouts every night, outrageous behavior, passing out in some friend's Village studio or not knowing ***how*** I got home.(p.407)

• One day soon, the analyses would reveal why I drank and ***how*** to stop.(p.408)

• This too is ***how*** the nest-egg went.(p.410)

• In my cups I used to tell them off, giving them lengthy advice on ***how*** to lead the right life.(p.410)

• He now said that we had a physical allergy combined with a mental obsession, and he explained this so that I saw for the first time ***how*** this could be.(p.413)

• This was ***how*** I had looked and acted a few short weeks ago.(p.415)

• A.A. taught me ***how*** not to drink.(p.416)

• And also, on the twenty-four hour plan, it taught me ***how*** to live.(p.416)

• A young veteran tells ***how*** a few rough experiences pushed him into A.A. -- and ***how*** he was therefore spared years of suffering.(p.422)

• He asked ***how*** I felt.(p.422)

• The doctor sat down beside the bed and asked me ***how*** I felt.(p.423)

• I don't know ***how*** I got here this trip, but it doesn't matter very much.(p.423)

• Once in a while I stayed home for a night, to see ***how*** my folks were doing.(p.425)

• Meanwhile the letters from home were telling about ***how*** much my folks wanted to make up to me for some of the things I'd missed.(p.427)

• Why I wasn't killed or ***how*** I got home I don't know.(p.429)

• But for ***how*** long?(p.429)

• Only show me ***how***."(p.430)

• That is ***how*** I came into A.A.(p.430)

• ***How*** could such a man possibly be called an alcoholic?(p.433)

• ***How*** easy it was, in the beginning, to forget that those binges ever happened!(p.433)

• Or, "I got to talking and forgot ***how*** many I was taking and it hit me."(p.433)

• ***How*** exciting to learn the inward mysteries that govern the behavior of people, ***how*** wonderful to know, at last, all about myself!(p.434)

• In the garage, I would put the needle in my vein and then try to figure out exactly ***how*** much medication to inject to overcome the pep pills while adding to the sleeping pills while ignoring the tranquilizers, in order to get just enough to be able to pull out the needle, jerk the tourniquet, throw it in the car, slam the car door shut, run down the hall, and fall in bed before I fell asleep.(p.442)

• And that was ***how*** Max and I and our two daughters spent Christmas Day, eight years ago.(p.444)

• To this day, I am amazed at ***how*** many of my problems -- most of which had nothing to do with drinking, I believed -- have become manageable or have simply disappeared since I quit drinking.(p.448)

• I have to discard my "rights," as well as my expectations, by asking myself, "***How*** important is it, really?(p.452)

• ***How*** important is it compared to my serenity, my emotional sobriety?"(p.452)

• Now sober for years, they tell us ***how*** they got well.(p.455)

• As an indication of just ***how*** confused and mixed up I was, just as soon as I could I left the office and hurried around to tell other patients that I was getting better.(p.470)

• What we do with it is our own business; ***how*** we use it is up to us individually.(p.473)

• ***How*** he do it?(p.475)

• "***How***?" they ask me.(p.477)

• You see ***how*** much work some of us have to do on ourselves when we finally come into A.A.!(p.480)

• ***How*** wrong I was!(p.481)

• This physician, the originator of A.A.'s first black group, but badly caught in the toils, tells of his release and of ***how*** freedom came as he worked among his own people.(p.483)

• At that time I started school and that's ***how*** I got rid of the curls.(p.483)

• My father had purchased a restaurant, which he felt would take up some of my spare time, and that's ***how*** I met Vi.(p.487)

• I'd go into my home with a bottle, and I remember clearly ***how*** I would look around to see if Vi was watching.(p.487)

• Thinking only of two or three dollars to buy some whiskey, I did the job and that's ***how*** I met Ella G., who was responsible for my coming into A.A.(p.493)

• She didn't say anything about A.A. or getting me a sponsor at that time, but she did ask about Vi, and I told her Vi was working and ***how*** she could locate her.(p.494)

• He started telling me ***how*** much trouble he had, and I said to myself, "I wonder why this guy is telling me all his troubles.(p.494)

• They came, many of them, and stuck by us and told us ***how*** to hold meetings.(p.495)

• ***How*** sick I felt.(p.498)

• But I knew ***how*** to handle it now.(p.498)

• ***How*** I hate that word.(p.499)

• Then he asks me if I am willing to right all the wrongs I have ever done to anyone, no matter ***how*** wrong I thought the others were.(p.503)

• "***How*** does prayer fit into this thing?"(p.504)

• After the meeting was over and we had returned to the cell block again, I was asked ***how*** I was impressed.(p.510)

• I couldn't tell you ***how*** I got there.(p.510)

• You hit the street about ten minutes to eight, and you walk around the block, God knows ***how*** many times, waiting for that joint to open.(p.514)

• Because as I sat on that bed, I knew that I was in a terrible spot and didn't know ***how*** to get out of it.(p.515)

• I buttonholed him after dinner and gave him a few tips on ***how*** to run his colony better and the result of that was about a fortnight or so later I was shipped back to my regiment.(p.520)

• The Commanding Officer only spoke to me when he wanted to tell me exactly who I was and what I was and ***how*** little I counted in the scheme of things and ***how*** glad he would be if I went away.(p.520)

• The truth is, I did not know ***how*** to stop it, nor did I want to, really.(p.539)

• I did not know ***how***.(p.539)

• I remember ***how*** horrible jails are, ***how*** dreadful a thing it is to be behind steel bars.(p.542)

• In A.A. we can begin again no matter ***how*** late it may be.(p.543)

• She here tells ***how*** she was set free.(p.544)

• I thought I knew exactly what I wanted out of life and I thought I knew exactly ***how*** to get it.(p.545)

• They said if you want to know ***how*** this program works, take the first word of your question – the H is for honesty, the O is for open-mindedness and the W is for willingness; these our Book calls the essentials of recovery.(p.550)

• "A.A. does not teach us ***how*** to handle our drinking," he said.(p.554)

• "It teaches us ***how*** to handle sobriety."(p.554)

• To do that, I had come to A.A. to learn ***how*** to handle sobriety -- which is what I could not handle in the first place.(p.554)

• But above all, it taught me ***how*** to handle sobriety.(p.559)

• I have learned ***how*** to relate to people; before A.A., I could never do that comfortably without alcohol.(p.559)

• ***How*** do we do it?(p.560)

• By learning -- through practicing the Twelve Steps and through sharing at meetings – ***how*** to cope with the problems that we looked to booze to solve, back in our drinking days.(p.560)

• We learn ***how*** to level out the emotional wings that got us into trouble both when we were up and when we were down.(p.560)

• VI. ***How*** to Get in Touch With A.A.(p.563)

• The "12 Traditions" of Alcoholics Anonymous are, we A.A.'s believe, the best answers that our experience has yet given to those ever urgent questions, "***How*** can A.A. best function?" and, "***How*** can A.A. best stay whole and so survive?"(p.563)

• ***HOW*** TO GET IN TOUCH WITH A.A.(p.575)

• If there is none nearby, you will be invited to carry on a correspondence which will do much to insure your sobriety no matter ***how*** isolated you are.(p.575)

how'd

• One day as I sat there in the hospital, my psychiatrist walked up behind me and asked, "***How'd*** you like to talk to the man from A.A.?"(p.446)

how's

• ***How's*** the boy?(p.500)

Howard

• Why, even a year ago, I had seen ***Howard***, an ex-doctor, mooching a dime for a drink.(p.289)

• I can still remember very distinctly getting into Akron at eleven p.m. and routing this same ***Howard*** out of bed to do something about me.(p.290)

• I went to elementary and high school in Washington, D.C. and then to ***Howard*** University.(p.486)

however

• ***However***, he did become "sold" on the ideas contained in this book.(p.xxx)

• I could go for such conceptions as Creative Intelligence, Universal Mind or Spirit of Nature but I resisted the thought of a Czar of the Heavens, ***however*** loving His sway might be.(p.12)

• There is, ***however***, a vast amount of fun about it all.(p.16)

• Unlike the feelings of the ship's passengers, ***however***, our joy in escape from disaster does not subside as we go our individual ways.(p.17)

• This hope, ***however***, was destroyed by the doctor's telling him that while his religious convictions were very good, in his case they did not spell the necessary vital spiritual experience.(p.27)

• ***However*** intelligent we may have been in other respects, where alcohol has been involved, we have been strangely insane.(p.38)

• Our own conception, ***however*** inadequate, was sufficient to make the approach and to effect a contact with Him.(p.46)

• So we used our own conception, ***however*** limited it was.(p.47)

• When, ***however***, the perfectly logical assumption is suggested that underneath the material world and life as we see it, there is an All Powerful, Guiding, Creative Intelligence, right there our perverse streak comes to the surface and we laboriously set out to convince ourselves it isn't so.(p.49)

• On one proposition, ***however***, these men and women are strikingly agreed.(p.50)

• If that is so, this step may be postponed, only ***however***, if we hold ourselves in complete readiness to go through with it at the first opportunity.(p.74)

• It should not matter, ***however***, if someone does throw us out of his office.(p.78)

• Usually, ***however***, other people are involved.(p.79)

• It is better, ***however***, that one does not needlessly name a person upon whom she can vent jealously.(p.82)

• We may ask for ourselves, ***however***, if others will be helped.(p.87)

• Admit that he probably knows more about it than you do, but call to his attention the fact that ***however*** deep his faith and knowledge, he could not have applied it or he would not drink.(p.93)

• These things will come to pass naturally and in good time provided, ***however***, the alcoholic continues to demonstrate that he can be sober, considerate, and helpful, regardless of what anyone says or does.(p.99)

• Suppose, ***however***, that your husband fits the description of number two.(p.112)

• Being intrigued, ***however***, he invited our friend to his home.(p.155)

• He consented, ***however***, to go the hospital, where he occupied the very room recently vacated by the lawyer.(p.159)

• This had little effect ***however*** for I kept on drinking and used a great deal more hard liquor than in former years.(p.174)

• ***However***, after two or three trials, I found this was not satisfactory because they did not serve enough to satisfy me.(p.184)

• This problem was soon solved, ***however***, as I began to take my bottle along with me and hide it in the bathroom or in the shrubbery outside.(p.184)

• I found, ***however***, that when I would leave Akron to go to Chicago, I would get drunk.(p.197)

• ***However***, on a couple of other occasions, Clarence seemed to bob up at the last saloon that I would stop at on the way home every day.(p.216)

• I cannot say, ***however***, that I acquired any craving for hard liquor as a result.(p.231)

• For the great majority of us, ***however***, that condition didn't last.(p.232)

• Gradually, ***however***, I'd suffer so much that I simply had to have the morning-after drink.(p.233)

• ***However***, here I probably took my first step towards my coming alcoholism by developing a terrific aversion to all churches and established religions.(p.240)

• ***However***, I did manage to keep out of the guardhouse.(p.242)

• ***However***, I made an SOS call to the New York Group, whom I hadn't met yet, and they suggested we both come there.(p.245)

• Slight casualties, complicated ***however*** by a long and serious illness, were my only mishaps.(p.253)

• It is, ***however***, only the first of a series of miracles which have followed one after another as a result of my trying to apply to my daily life the principles embodies in our Twelve Steps.(p.280)

• When I finally returned to Detroit to find work and to learn to stand on my own feet, the ball was already rolling, ***however*** slowly.(p.282)

• During that first year, ***however***, I managed to make both ends meet, and to avoid ever going back to my old habit pattern of borrowing money when I could not earn it.(p.283)

• ***However***, I must have felt, deep down inside myself, that living the selfish life of a bachelor was only half living.(p.286)

• ***However***, as there happened to be several saloons within that distance, I didn't find it necessary to patronize the same place each evening.(p.298)

• ***However***, it finally caught up with me, and when it did, I was a mental, physical, and nervous wreck.(p.299)

• ***However***, he explained to me that he had been just such a rummy as I, only for a much longer period of time.(p.302)

• ***However***, due to financial difficulties the whole printing was, for a while, held up and the book received no publicity, nor, of course, was it available in the stores, even if one knew it existed.(p.307)

• ***However***, as he unfolded his story for me, I could not help but believe him.(p.309)

• ***However***, this isn't as rough as it sounds, as we do become grateful for the necessity that makes us toe the line, for we find that we are more than compensated for a consistent effort by the countless dividends we receive.(p.311)

• My alcoholism-prone mind, ***however***, reminded me that all great authors had needed a stimulus to build up inspiration and inventiveness before each day's work.(p.331)

• ***However***, I am an alcoholic, so I always looked forward to the day when I would be able to drink again.(p.343)

• He had come back, ***however***, and he was on this program.(p.346)

• ***However***, what I had gained materially on the credit side of my ledger, I have since learned was more than offset on the debit side by egotism, resentment and dishonesty.(p.356)

• I was active and did well, ***however***, in school publications, dramatics (which came in handy during my drinking career), and Greek letter societies.(p.357)

• At this time, ***however***, she had an opportunity to go to Salt Lake City on a new project for the government, but she did promise me that if I would curtail my drinking and buckle down to hard work she would give serious consideration to my latest proposal and maybe join me at a later date when I got settled.(p.359)

• ***However***, knowing me, she thought it was a foolish idea, that I wouldn't be interested.(p.367)

• ***However***, my low had been reached.(p.378)

• ***However***, after I heard a few stories of jails, sanitariums, broken homes and skid row, I wondered if I really was an alcoholic.(p.378)

• ***However***, I threw myself into Twelve Step work, and what I feared would be a calamity turned out to be the most blessed of blessings.(p.394)

• ***However***, a rough estimate of one alcoholic's initiation fee seemed possible.(p.396)

• ***However***, I had phoned New York from the farm, appealing for help, and there in the station to meet us were two A.A.'s, John and Bud.(p.415)

• My growing inward unhappiness was a very real thing, ***however***, and I knew that something would have to be done about it.(p.434)

• Now, ***however***, I accepted it fully.(p.436)

• ***However***, I've heard of an organization called Alcoholics Anonymous that has had some success with people like you.(p.436)

• ***However***, for a period of time I was injecting Pentothal intravenously to put myself to sleep.(p.442)

• (I am pleased to state, ***however***, that I had gone to only a very few A.A. meetings before I was able to make a really beautiful pair of moccasins – and half a wallet.(p.445)

• I can tell her she ought not to think a certain way, but I certainly can't take away her right to feel ***however*** she does feel.(p.451)

• Rather, I do whatever is in front of me to be done, and I leave the results up to Him; ***however*** it turns out, that's God's will for me.(p.452)

• ***However***, one thing I am certain of: Inmates in prison who attend A.A. have their chances of remaining free greatly enhanced – this is a proved fact.(p.458)

• ***However***, I still would not attend A.A. in prison.(p.461)

• Finally, ***however***, in November of 1944, at long last I went to A.A.(p.470)

• ***However***, a verdict was brought in of murder in the second degree.(p.508)

• ***However***, as time went on laws were enacted that reduced the sentence.(p.509)

• ***However***, before the meeting got started, a group from the outside came in unexpectedly.(p.509)

• ***However***, my two friends kept coaxing and cajoling to get me back again.(p.510)

• ***However***, she had faith and she had hope (things I didn't have).(p.514)

• ***However***, I kept that job in Egypt and Palestine for about two years, and then I changed over to the other battalion in my regiment.(p.520)

• The only thing this changed, ***however***, was my surroundings, and it was soon apparent that I could have the same uncomfortable emotions with an unlimited checking account that I could on a working girl's salary.(p.545)

• One morning, ***however***, I realized I had to get rid of it, for my reprieve was running out, and if I didn't get rid of it I was going to get drunk – and I didn't want to get drunk any more.(p.552)

howling

• I would make a feeble attempt at eating supper, but I never met with any ***howling*** success.(p.299)

howls

• The wind is rising and ***howls*** around the house.(p.497)

huddle

• They went into a ***huddle*** and dad explained that he simply took my pants, shoes and money away, so that I could get no liquor and had to sober up.(p.288)

hue

• I did six years of newspaper advertising, and trade journal work with many, many drunks of drab and dreary ***hue*** woven into the pattern of my life.(p.254)

hug

• For a time he may try to ***hug*** the new treasure to himself.(p.129)

huge

• We gave up our positions and off we roared on a motorcycle, the sidecar stuffed with tent, blankets, a change of clothes, and three ***huge*** volumes of a financial reference service.(p.2)

• They appear to be in the nature of *huge* emotional displacements and rearrangements.(p.27)
• As self-conscious as I was, I had to pose for those pictures, holding this *huge* bouquet.(p.385)
• For instance, the fiftieth wedding anniversary of my wife's parents was the occasion for a *huge* family reunion at our home.(p.556)

human

• These allergic types can never safely use alcohol in any form at all; and once having formed the habit and found they cannot break it, once having lost their self-confidence, their reliance upon things *human*, their problems pile up on them and become astonishingly difficult to solve.(p.xxvi)
• One feels that something more than *human* power is needed to produce the essential psychic change.(p.xxvii)
• Judging from what I had seen in Europe and since, the power of God in *human* affairs was negligible, the Brotherhood of Man a grim jest.(p.11)
• His *human* will had failed.(p.11)
• Here was something at work in a *human* heart which had done the impossible.(p.11)
• An illness of this sort – and we have come to believe it an illness –involves those about us in a way no other *human* sickness can.(p.18)
• When this sort of thinking is fully established in an individual with alcoholic tendencies, he has probably placed himself beyond *human* aid, and unless locked up, may die or go permanently insane.(p.24)
• We were in a position where life was becoming impossible, and if we had passed into the region from which there is no return through *human* aid we had but two alternatives: One was to go on to the bitter end, blotting out the consciousness of our intolerable situation as best we could; and the other, to accept spiritual help.(p.25)
• Except in a few rare cases, neither he nor any other *human* being can provide such a defense.(p.43)
• Our *human* resources, as marshalled by the will were not sufficient; they failed utterly.(p.45)
• Instead of regarding ourselves as intelligent agents, spearheads of God's ever advancing Creation, we agnostics and atheists chose to believe that our *human* intelligence was the last word, the alpha and the omega, the beginning and end of all.(p.49)
• We have learned that whatever the *human* frailties of various faiths may be, those faiths have given purpose and direction to millions.(p.49)
• Instead, we looked at the *human* defects of these people, and sometimes used their shortcomings as a basis of wholesale condemnation.(p.50)
• In the face of collapse and despair, in the face of the total failure of their *human* resources, they found that a new power, peace, happiness, and sense of direction flowed into them.(p.50)
• We had to ask ourselves why we shouldn't apply to our *human* problems this same readiness to change our point of view.(p.52)
• For faith in a Power greater than ourselves, and miraculous demonstrations of that power in *human* lives, are facts as old as man himself.(p.55)
• 5.Admitted to God, to ourselves, and to another *human* being the exact nature of our wrongs.(p.59)
• (b) That probably no *human* power could have relieved our alcoholism.(p.60)
• Here we find *human* opinions running to extremes - - absurd extremes, perhaps.(p.68)
• We'd hardly be *human* if we didn't.(p.69)
• This requires action on our part, which, when completed, will mean that we have admitted to God, to ourselves, and to another *human* being the exact nature of our defects.(p.72)
• Keep it always in sight that we are dealing with that most terrible *human* emotion – jealousy.(p.82)
• If your talk has been sane, quiet and full of *human* understanding, you have perhaps made a friend.(p.94)
• They often forget father was beyond *human* aid.(p.128)
• But this does not mean that we disregard *human* health measures.(p.133)
• Without this proof the expectant purchaser would be forced to depart empty handed with none of what I later came to believe was the great panacea for all *human* ills.(p.171)
• Of far more importance was the fact that he was the first living *human* with whom I had ever talked, who knew what he was talking about in regard to alcoholism from actual experience.(p.180)
• When I had been in the hospital ten days, Sister Ignatia, who has played such a part in the development of A.A. in this area, stuck her head in the door one morning and announced, looking at me quizzically, that they might be able to make something *human* out of my face after all.(p.205)
• An active member of A.A. since 1939, I feel myself a useful member of the *human* race at last.(p.229)
• All sorts were represented and their relation of experiences and how they had found the only remedy, added to their *human* existence as sober men, laid the foundation of a very necessary faith.(p.258)
• It is a way of life, and the challenge contained in its principles is great enough to keep any *human* being striving for as long as he lives.(p.311)
• As we walked back through the hall, I, for the first time in my life, said to another *human* being, "I'm having trouble with my drinking, too."(p.321)
• My work is on a much deeper and more significant level than it ever was before, and I am today a fairly creative, relatively sane *human* being.(p.438)
• He and his wife more than accepted me; he listened to all my woes; both of them treated me as a *human* being.(p.462)
• All they care about is that I am a *human* being and that I want to stay sober.(p.529)
• If you give us a try, you will see that we are really *human* beings, and we will welcome you with open arms and hearts.(p.529)
• I want to be one of His children, a member of the *human* race.(p.535)
• My personal definition, which I submit as applying only to myself (although everyone is welcome to it who wants it), includes every waking activity of the *human* being; to have a creative attitude towards things is a more exact meaning, to live and to deal with other *human* beings creatively, which to me means seeing the God in them, and respecting and worshipping this God.(p.535)
• I have had the joy of seeing many a *human* being, down and out, learn to stand straight again, and to proceed under his own power to happiness in life.(p.541)
• A happy man is not likely to do harm to another *human* being.(p.542)
• I have seen that there is only one law, the law of love, and there are only two sins; the first is to interfere with the growth of another *human* being, and the second is to interfere with one's own growth.(p.542)
• I grew up believing that one had to be totally self-sufficient, for one never dared to depend on another *human* being.(p.545)
• As another great man says, "The only real freedom a *human* being can ever know is doing what you ought to do because you want to do it."(p.553)

humanitarian

• If your decision is yes, whether the reason be *humanitarian* or business or both, then the following suggestions may be helpful.(p.140)
• There is a real interest, both *humanitarian* and business, in the well-being of employees.(p.149)

humanity

• I have something to contribute to *humanity*, since I am peculiarly qualified, as a fellow-sufferer, to give aid and comfort to those who have stumbled and fallen over this business of meeting life.(p.229)

humanly

• This Power has in each case accomplished the miraculous, the *humanly* impossible.(p.50)
• It seems only fitting that when I did finally fall in love it was with an alcoholic, and for the next ten years I progressed as rapidly as is *humanly* possible into what I believed to be hopeless alcoholism.(p.547)

humans

• Thus was I convinced that God is concerned with us *humans* when we want Him enough.(p.12)
• But, as with most *humans*, he is more likely to have varied traits.(p.61)

humble

• There had been a *humble* willingness to have Him with me – and He came.(p.12)
• We should be sensible, tactful, considerate and *humble* without being servile or scraping.(p.83)
• To the new man I would also like to say that this program is not for sissies for, in my *humble* opinion, it takes a man to make the grade.(p.367)
• So please accept these *humble* calculations as, if anything, an underestimation.(p.396)

humbled

• They only thought they had lost their egoism and fear; they only thought they had *humbled* themselves.(p.73)

humbling

• Trying to avoid this *humbling* experience, they have turned to easier methods.(p.72)

humbly

• There I *humbly* offered myself to God, as I then understood Him, to do with me as He would.(p.13)
• He *humbly* offered himself to his Maker – then he knew.(p.57)
• This was only a beginning, though if honestly and *humbly* made, an effect, sometimes a very great one, was felt at once.(p.63)
• Just to the extent that we do as we think He would have us, and *humbly* rely on Him, does He enable us to match calamity with serenity.(p.68)
• We constantly remind ourselves we are no longer running the show, *humbly* saying to ourselves many times each day "Thy will be done."(p.87)
• When I hear the more rugged stories of alcoholics who became sicker than I did with this affliction, I *humbly* thank God for showing me "the handwriting on the wall."(p.367)
• Maine newsletter (Boomerang) say: "With tireless devotion and humility, this venerable Indian gentleman traveled thousands of miles *humbly* pleading for sobriety.(p.476)
• But I said *humbly*, "I suppose I want to live."(p.540)

humiliated

• In two months he was in a hospital, puzzled and *humiliated*.(p.32)
• I felt disgraced and *humiliated* -- a man who couldn't hold booze – a social disaster.(p.328)

humiliating

• He was positive that his *humiliating* experience, plus the knowledge he had acquired, would keep him sober the rest of his life.(p.40)
• Now and then the family will be plagued by spectres from the past, for the drinking career of almost every alcoholic has been marked by escapades, funny, *humiliating*, shameful or tragic.(p.123)
• I was the only person I'd ever known personally who had ever been in jail, and I guess it is most significant that the second time was less *humiliating* that the first had been.(p.549)

humiliation

• If hundreds of experiences have shown him that one drink means another debacle with all its attendant suffering and *humiliation*, why is it he takes that one drink?(p.22)
• We are unable, at certain times, to bring into our consciousness with sufficient force the memory of the suffering and *humiliation* of even a week or a month ago.(p.24)
• That to me was the greatest *humiliation*, to think that I'd finally landed in jail.(p.264)
• So, with mixed feelings of *humiliation*, anger, and fear, I decided to look for an answer.(p.371)
• I will never know all the people I hurt, all the friends I abused, the *humiliation* of my family, the worry of my business associates, or how far reaching it was.(p.376)
• Broken promises, *humiliation*, hopelessness, worry, anxiety – but still not enough.(p.377)
• It became more and more necessary to escape from myself, for my remorse and shame and *humiliation* when I was sober were almost unbearable.(p.547)

humiliations

• Edward Dowling, S.J., of the Queen's Work staff says, "Alcoholics Anonymous is natural; it is natural at the point where nature comes closest to the supernatural, namely in *humiliations* and in consequent humility.(p.574)

humility

• Belief in the power of God, plus enough willingness, honesty and *humility* to establish and maintain the new order of things, were the essential requirements.(p.13)
• But they had not learned enough of *humility*, fearlessness and honesty, in the sense we find it necessary, until they told someone else all their life story.(p.73)
• They meant patience, tolerance and *humility*, and above all the belief that a Power greater than myself could help.(p.381)
• Many times in the intervening years I have thanked God for that man, a man who had the courage to admit failure, a man who had the *humility* to confess that all the hard-won learning of his profession could not turn up the answer.(p.436)
• I am still arrogant, egocentric, self-righteous, with no *humility*, even phony at times, but I'm trying to be a better person and help my fellowman.(p.463)
• Maine newsletter (Boomerang) say: "With tireless devotion and *humility*, this venerable Indian gentleman traveled thousands of miles humbly pleading for sobriety.(p.476)
• I ask the forgiveness of the reader; and from now on I shall try to write with the *humility* I honestly pray for.)(p.536)
• It reminds us that we are to place principles before

personalities; that we are actually to practice a genuine ***humility***.(p.568)
• Edward Dowling, S.J., of the Queen's Work staff says, "Alcoholics Anonymous is natural; it is natural at the point where nature comes closest to the supernatural, namely in humiliations and in consequent ***humility***.(p.574)

humor

• And Jim G. had such a wonderful sense of ***humor***, and when he came I was in tears, and I told him, "I want to do this, but I can't.(p.269)
• Philosophy, faith, a sense of ***humor*** (they could laugh at themselves), clear-cut objectives, appreciation – and most especially appreciation and sympathetic understanding for their fellow man.(p.310)
• Prior to our marriage, when she was a shy, scrawny adolescent, I was able to see things in her that others couldn't necessarily see – things like beauty, charm, gaiety, a gift for being easy to talk to, a sense of ***humor***, and many other fine qualities.(p.450)

humorous

• If his mood is light, tell him ***humorous*** stories of your escapades.(p.91)

hump

• I was transferred to Kaneohe Bay, across the ***hump*** to the windward side of Oahu, to the aviation base.(p.426)

hunch

• What used to be the ***hunch*** or the occasional inspiration gradually becomes a working part of the mind.(p.87)
• They had a ***hunch*** that there must be an answer for these apparently hopeless ones, somewhere.(p.307)

hundred

• We, of Alcoholics Anonymous, are more than one ***hundred*** men and women who have recovered from a seemingly hopeless state of mind and body.(p.xiii)
• This man and over one ***hundred*** others appear to have recovered.(p.xxiii)
• Sometimes a small deal would net a few ***hundred*** dollars, and I would pay my bills at the bars and delicatessens.(p.5)
• If you ask him why he started on that last bender, the chances are he will offer you any one of a ***hundred*** alibis.(p.23)
• "Then they outlined the spiritual answer and program of action which a ***hundred*** of them had followed successfully.(p.42)
• Driven by a ***hundred*** forms of fear, self-delusion, self-seeking, and self-pity, we step on the toes of our fellows and they retaliate.(p.62)
• I was at one time assistant manager of a corporation department employing sixty-six ***hundred*** men.(p.136)
• I can well remember sitting with seven dollars in my pocket, planning on giving my family a ***hundred*** or two ***hundred*** dollars, when I made it next year.(p.197)
• One ***hundred*** for unmarried women at one end, one ***hundred*** for men at the other, and one ***hundred*** for married couples in the middle.(p.198)
• I remember one occasion when I did not drink for three ***hundred*** and sixty-four days, but I didn't quite make the year.(p.200)
• I had lost a ***hundred*** dollars I had in my pocket, and lost a wristwatch too.(p.202)
• If there was a lecture on the subject within a ***hundred*** miles of Akron, I attended.(p.202)
• He took his one ***hundred*** and seventeen dollars and let us go, and we proceeded.(p.264)
• And, anyhow, if I went on for ten or a ***hundred*** times as long I couldn't even begin to tell you all that A.A. has meant to me.(p.274)
• If I live to be a ***hundred***, it will always stand out in my mind.(p.292)
• And we wonder how much further this man could go if his alcoholic problem could be removed and he could throw one ***hundred*** per cent of his abilities into action.(p.308)
• This didn't say we had to be in jail, ten, fifty, or one ***hundred*** times.(p.379)
• The why is not important; the fact is that one drink will set up a reaction in our system which requires more; that one drink was too much and one ***hundred*** drinks were not enough.(p.380)
• I cooperated with that man one ***hundred*** per cent!(p.388)
• I paid nine ***hundred*** dollars for a second hand car on my return.(p.429)
• I spent eighteen ***hundred*** dollars fixing up that car in the first year I was home, after four bad smash-ups.(p.429)
• I borrowed five ***hundred*** dollars from the bank and three ***hundred*** from the loan shop, and I drank that up pretty fast.(p.490)
• I had to put up a three ***hundred*** dollar bond because he was carrying the same summons around in his pocket for me.(p.491)
• I got very little out of the two ***hundred***, that I drew on that pay day.(p.493)
• Finally, I broke the last one ***hundred*** dollar bill the Saturday before I left.(p.493)

hundreds

• I have seen ***hundreds*** of families set their feet in the path that really goes somewhere; have seen the most impossible domestic situations righted; feuds and bitterness of all sorts wiped out.(p.15)
• Those of us who live in large cities are overcome by the reflection that close by ***hundreds*** are dropping into oblivion every day.(p.19)
• If ***hundreds*** of experiences have shown him that one drink means another debacle with all its attendant suffering and humiliation, why is it he takes that one drink?(p.22)
• When many ***hundreds*** of people are able to say that the consciousness of the Presence of God is today the most important fact of their lives, they present a powerful reason why one should have faith.(p.51)
• He has hired and fired ***hundreds*** of men.(p.136)
• If you live in a large place, there are ***hundreds***.(p.152)
• Being a large place, we think that some day its Fellowship will number many ***hundreds***.(p.161)
• Today, ***hundreds*** of additional A.A. members can be found who have had no relapse for more than thirty years.(p.169)
• We all had ***hundreds*** of character traits, of fears and phobias, likes and dislikes, in common.(p.229)
• They, too, had taken a train to one town and had wakened ***hundreds*** of miles in the opposite direction, never knowing how they got there.(p.246)
• Therefore, these seventeen A.A.'s, and ***hundreds*** of thousands like them, have been saved years of infinite suffering.(p.315)
• When I had known her years before she was rather slender, but at this time she weighed as much as she does now, which is up around in the two ***hundreds*** or very close to it.(p.493)
• This self-insurance has resulted in the restoration of physical, mental and spiritual health and self-respect to ***hundreds*** of men and women who would be hopelessly down and out without its unique but effective therapy."(p.574)

hundredth

• On the second, I knew – as I know now – that if I remained away from the first drink, then I had not to worry about the ***hundredth*** one.(p.344)

hung

• For three or four months the goose ***hung*** high.(p.7)
• They took inventory all right, but ***hung*** on to some of the worst items in stock.(p.73)
• We shook hands, and he ***hung*** onto my hand for a moment and said, "Tell you what I'll do for old times sake.(p.201)
• She was doing fine, she was up and around, and that day her husband phoned me and said, "Doctor, thanks very much for curing my wife," and I thanked him for his felicitations, and he ***hung*** up.(p.350)
• In the hospital, I ***hung*** on to the idea I'd had most of my life: that if I could just control the external environment, the internal environment would then be comfortable.(p.445)

hung-over

• It is so beautiful to get up in the morning not being ***hung-over*** and being able to remember where we were the night before.(p.481)

hunger

• Had I been able to explain to a psychiatrist the feeling of futility, loneliness and lack of purpose that had come with my deep sense of personal failure at this second divorce, I seriously doubt that the good doctor could have convinced me that my basic problem was a spiritual ***hunger***, but A.A. has shown me this was the truth.(p.546)

hungry

• On the way I felt ***hungry*** so I stopped at a roadside place where they have a bar.(p.36)
• We headed out of town walking – no money, cold and ***hungry***.(p.424)

hunt

• I would pull out early, and go to the ***hunt*** breakfast and the flowing bowl of milk-punch.(p.404)
• I ***hunt*** for my nickel to drop in the plate so that mine will be seen.(p.497)

hunting

• In four or five days I would be ***hunting*** all over the place, at home and in my workshop, for the bottles I had destroyed, cursing myself for being a fool.(p.234)
• Golf, ***hunting*** and fishing were now merely excuses to drink excessively.(p.375)
• A house in Virginia, during the fox ***hunting*** season; a little chalet in Switzerland during the summer or a place on Long Island – each house complete with cooks, butlers and maids.(p.403)
• This was in Virginia, where I had rented a house with stables and a swimming pool, and the fall fox ***hunting*** had begun.(p.404)
• But whereas my horse was always equipped with a flask, I merely endured the fox ***hunting*** so I could start drinking at lunch time.(p.404)

hurled

• Alas for us men toward whom Shaw ***hurled*** his cry, "Must a Christ be crucified in every generation for the benefit of those who have no imagination?"(p.536)

hurricane

• I was certainly a complete surprise when I arrived at her family's home, but because I arrived on the wings of a tropical ***hurricane*** there wasn't much she could do but let me in.(p.364)

hurried

• As an indication of just how confused and mixed up I was, just as soon as I could I left the office and ***hurried*** around to tell other patients that I was getting better.(p.470)

hurry

• Wait until repeated stumbling convinces him he must act, for the more you ***hurry*** him the longer his recovery may be delayed.(p.113)
• He may demand that the family find God in a ***hurry***, or exhibit amazing indifference to them and say he is above worldly considerations.(p.128)
• I guess I felt, and he sensed it, that I wanted him to ***hurry*** up and say what he had to say and get out.(p.494)
• After he'd talked half an hour, I still wanted him to ***hurry*** up and get out so I could go and get some whiskey before the liquor store closed.(p.494)

hurt

• We made a list of people I had ***hurt*** or toward whom I felt resentment.(p.13)
• If a person has cancer all are sorry for him and no one is angry or ***hurt***.(p.18)
• "Suddenly the thought crossed my mind that if I were to put an ounce of whiskey in my milk it couldn't ***hurt*** me on a full stomach.(p.36)
• Sometimes they ***hurt*** us, seemingly without provocation, but we invariably find that at some time in the past we have made decisions based on self which later placed us in a position to be ***hurt***.(p.62)
• In most cases it was found that our self-esteem, our pocketbooks, our ambitions, our personal relationships (including sex) were ***hurt*** or threatened.(p.64)
• Whom had we ***hurt***?(p.69)
• We have listed the people we have ***hurt*** by our conduct, and are willing to straighten out the past if we can.(p.70)
• It may be one of our own family, but we cannot disclose anything to our wives or our parents which will ***hurt*** them and make them unhappy.(p.74)
• As we look over the list of business acquaintances and friends we have ***hurt***, we may feel diffident about going to some of them on a spiritual basis.(p.76)
• This he may do after he gets ***hurt*** some more.(p.95)
• We have had long rendezvous with ***hurt*** pride, frustration, self-pity, misunderstanding and fear.(p.104)
• When we do that, we find it solves our problems too; the ensuing lack of fear, worry and ***hurt*** feelings is a wonderful thing.(p.116)
• Some of the snags you will encounter are irritation, ***hurt*** feeling and resentments.(p.117)
• A few of us have had these growing pains and they ***hurt*** a great deal.(p.124)
• Husbands and wives have sometimes been obliged to separate for a time until new perspective, new victory over ***hurt*** pride could be rewon.(p.125)
• That won't ***hurt*** him a bit, even though he does not go for this remedy.(p.144)
• Stepping into his car, he made the rounds of people he had ***hurt***.(p.156)
• I spent most of my time trying to get back these friendships, and to make some recompense towards my wife, whom I had ***hurt*** a lot.(p.191)
• I can remember occasions when friends recommended me for positions or business opportunities that I wouldn't take because I felt that at some future date I'd get drunk and they would be ***hurt***.(p.198)
• I had found friends, understanding friends who often knew what I was thinking and feeling better than I knew myself, and didn't allow me to retreat

into my prison of loneliness and fear over a fancied slight or ***hurt***.(p.228)
• This time it really ***hurt***, more than any hangover ever had.(p.247)
• How ***hurt*** I was when editors bounced back my ideas quickly and my best friends opined that my output needed a lot of rewriting.(p.331)
• We all have them, and I thought a little brandy or a little wine now and then could certainly ***hurt*** no one.(p.336)
• I had turned eighteen during the trip, and I despondently returned home by jet (on Daddy's bankbook) to a pair of miserable, ***hurt*** parents.(p.354)
• I will never know all the people I ***hurt***, all the friends I abused, the humiliation of my family, the worry of my business associates, or how far reaching it was.(p.376)
• Just being sober will be making amends to many we have ***hurt*** by our drunken actions.(p.381)
• I was an extremely sensitive person and so self-conscious that I ***hurt*** all over.(p.385)
• My friends were understandably ***hurt*** and angry.(p.406)
• It ***hurt*** to be considered a kid.(p.423)
• After all, it was self (you, me) that stood in our own way, that ran the show and ran ourselves into bankruptcy, that ***hurt*** the ones we loved.(p.459)
• Of course I had the sensitive, ***hurt*** feelings of the alcoholic.(p.472)
• I felt very lonely and ***hurt***, because nobody understood me.(p.478)
• I went to church on Easter Sunday with my husband, and it didn't ***hurt*** at all.(p.482)
• I know I will be grateful for a chance to make amends to everybody I have ***hurt*** in the past.(p.482)
• That ***hurt*** and disturbed me a great deal.(p.484)
• I am filled with ***hurt*** pride and self-pity.(p.501)
• I hope I haven't ***hurt*** anyone's feelings, but maybe we could all grow and change.(p.529)
• There was the love affair which was ridiculous -- "imagine that midget being able to fall in love!" -- and my head knew it while my heart pumped real, genuine anguish, for it ***hurt*** like hell, and since it was first love, things have never been quite the same.(p.534)
• My grandparents were strangers to me and I remember being lonely, and terrified and ***hurt***.(p.545)
• In time I concluded that the reason I was ***hurt*** was because I loved my parents, and I concluded too that if I never allowed myself to love anybody or anything I could never be ***hurt*** again.(p.545)
• I wasn't afraid of anything or anybody after I learned about drinking, for it seemed right from the beginning that with liquor I could always retire to my little private world where nobody could get at me to ***hurt*** me.(p.547)

hurting

• Even obvious intoxication is excused by younger people as something "he's earned the right to do," and they say, "After all, who's he ***hurting***?"(p.330)
• No matter how often I had gone into and come out of alcoholic lows during the day, the pattern bounced me out of bed each night about 2:00 a.m., shaking and ***hurting*** in the agitation that always follows a drug's sedation.(p.332)
• I could go on living and ***hurting*** ten years longer, or more."(p.333)

hurts

• I imagined getting even for ***hurts*** and rejections.(p.560)

husband

• She committed her ***husband*** for drinking.(p.65)
• The ***husband*** begins to feel lonely, sorry for himself.(p.81)
• It is as good for the wife as for the ***husband***.(p.81)
• Ask any woman who has sent her ***husband*** to distant places on the theory he would escape the alcohol problem.(p.101)
• These are some of the questions which race through the mind of every woman who has an alcoholic ***husband***.(p.108)
• Perhaps your ***husband*** has been living in that strange world of alcoholism where everything is distorted and exaggerated.(p.108)
• Try not to condemn your alcoholic ***husband*** no matter what he says or does.(p.108)
• One: Your ***husband*** may be only a heavy drinker.(p.108)
• Two: Your ***husband*** is showing lack of control, for he is unable to stay on the water wagon even when he wants to.(p.109)
• Three: This ***husband*** has gone much further than ***husband*** number two.(p.109)
• Four: You may have a ***husband*** of whom you completely despair.(p.110)
• Let's now go back to ***husband*** number one.(p.110)
• Even though your ***husband*** becomes unbearable and you have to leave him temporarily, you should, if you can, go without rancor.(p.111)
• It is possible to have a full and useful life, though your ***husband*** continues to drink.(p.111)
• Do not set your heart on reforming your ***husband***.(p.111)
• Your ***husband*** may come to appreciate your reasonableness and patience.(p.111)
• Your ***husband*** may be willing to talk to one of them.(p.112)
• If this kind of approach does not catch your husband's interest, it may be best to drop the subject, but after a friendly talk your ***husband*** will usually revive the topic himself.(p.112)
• If you act upon these principles, your ***husband*** may stop or moderate.(p.112)
• Suppose, however, that your ***husband*** fits the description of number two.(p.112)
• The same principles which apply to ***husband*** number one should be practiced.(p.112)
• If you have a number three ***husband***, you may be in luck.(p.113)
• If your ***husband*** is otherwise a normal individual, your chances are good at this stage.(p.113)
• In any event, try to have your ***husband*** read this book.(p.114)
• Perhaps you have a ***husband*** who is at large, but who should be committed.(p.114)
• If your ***husband*** is a drinker, you probably worry over what other people are thinking and you hate to meet your friends.(p.114)
• When your ***husband*** is bad, you become a trembling recluse, wishing the telephone had never been invented.(p.115)
• While you need not discuss your ***husband*** at length, you can quietly let your friends know the nature of his illness.(p.115)
• But you must be on guard not to embarrass or harm your ***husband***.(p.115)
• You will no longer be self-conscious or feel that you must apologize as though your ***husband*** were a weak character.(p.115)
• Whenever possible, let your ***husband*** explain.(p.115)
• You may be afraid your ***husband*** will lose his position; you are thinking of the disgrace and hard times which will befall you and the children.(p.116)
• It may convince your ***husband*** he wants to stop drinking forever.(p.116)
• We urge you to try our program, for nothing will be so helpful to your ***husband*** as the radically changed attitude toward him which God will show you how to have.(p.117)
• Go along with your ***husband*** if you possibly can.(p.117)
• If you and your ***husband*** find a solution for the pressing problem of drink you are, of course, going to be very happy.(p.117)
• The faith and sincerity of both you and your ***husband*** will be put to the test.(p.117)
• Your ***husband*** will sometimes be unreasonable and you will want to criticize.(p.117)
• These family dissensions are very dangerous, especially to your ***husband***.(p.117)
• We do not mean that you have to agree with your ***husband*** whenever there is an honest difference of opinion.(p.117)
• You and your ***husband*** will find that you can dispose of serious problems easier than you can the trivial ones.(p.118)
• If your ***husband*** is trying to live on a spiritual basis, he will also be doing everything in his power to avoid disagreement or contention.(p.118)
• Your ***husband*** knows he owes you more than sobriety.(p.118)
• Your ***husband*** will be the first to say it was your devotion and care which brought him to the point where he could have a spiritual experience.(p.118)
• After all, your family is reunited, alcohol is no longer a problem and you and your ***husband*** are working together toward an undreamed-of future.(p.119)
• It is probably true that you and your ***husband*** have been living too much alone, for drinking many times isolates the wife of an alcoholic.(p.119)
• Therefore, you probably need fresh interests and a great cause to live for as much as your ***husband***.(p.119)
• You, as well as your ***husband***, ought to think of what you can put into life instead of how much you can take out.(p.120)
• Perhaps your ***husband*** will make a fair start on the new basis, but just as things are going beautifully he dismays you by coming home drunk.(p.120)
• Your ***husband*** will see at once that he must redouble his spiritual activities if he expects to survive.(p.120)
• Then you and your ***husband*** can get right down to fundamentals.(p.120)
• Our women folk have suggested certain attitudes a wife may take with the ***husband*** who is recovering.(p.122)
• His wife came, scarcely daring to be hopeful, though she thought she saw something different about her ***husband*** already.(p.158)
• She was a woman devoted to her family and loyal to her ***husband***, but quarrels did not make a happy environment for her.(p.210)
• My ***husband*** was an alcoholic -- I had only contempt for those without my own amazing capacity -- the outcome was inevitable.(p.225)
• Our other daughter was in her last year of high school, and one night the new son-in-law and my ***husband*** went out to a prize fight.(p.263)
• My ***husband*** said that I said, "Can you imagine them giving us that jail fare?"(p.264)
• He gave my ***husband*** one and me one about ten-thirty on the eighth day of May in 1941.(p.267)
• When we went to bed my sides ached, and I said to my ***husband***, "I thought I would never laugh again, but I have laughed."(p.269)
• It is undoubtedly too soon for me to say how much of a success I shall be as a ***husband*** in time to come.(p.286)
• And when my ***husband*** found A.A., I came to the second meeting with him.(p.321)
• My ***husband*** is.(p.321)
• This girl and her ***husband*** are both in A.A., and she said to me, "Oh, but you're not the alcoholic; it's your ***husband***."(p.322)
• But we had to do a lot of entertaining, my ***husband*** liked to have a good time; I was very young; and I wanted to have a good time too.(p.322)
• I should have lost my ***husband***, and I think that only the fact that he was an alcoholic too kept us together.(p.323)
• If I had been sincere in what I thought I wanted more than anything else in life -- a sober ***husband*** and a happy, contented home -- I would have gone on the wagon with him.(p.324)
• I never thought I could be useful to anyone except my ***husband*** and my children and perhaps a few friends.(p.326)
• I called my ***husband*** up and told him to come home.(p.338)
• The very person who stood with me through it all and has been my greatest help was the person that I turned against, my ***husband***.(p.338)
• I said to my ***husband***, "I'm going to try, every free moment that I have, to get interested in something outside, get myself over this rut I'm in."(p.338)
• My ***husband***, my children saw the other side of me.(p.339)
• She was doing fine, she was up and around, and that day her ***husband*** phoned me and said, "Doctor, thanks very much for curing my wife," and I thanked him for his felicitations, and he hung up.(p.350)
• Shortly after I was starting to work on the program I realized that I was not a good father; I wasn't a good ***husband***, but, oh, I was a good provider.(p.351)
• I couldn't drink at home, because my ***husband*** frowned upon this.(p.370)
• Before too long, my ***husband*** (who seemed to prefer his shirts dirty) put his foot down, declaring that our family might have the cleanest clothes in town, but that I hadn't been out of the same old dirty slacks and blouse for a week.(p.371)
• It was my ***husband***, and he was learning, too.(p.371)
• She still had her ***husband***, her home, and a chance to help start A.A. in Texas.(p.384)
• For some reason I can't remember, it finally dawned on me that I had a problem, and yet nobody was very critical about it except my family, and that was only because I decided, after seven years of marriage, that I would divorce my ***husband***.(p.386)
• Frank, my ***husband***, would come home day after day and find me passed out.(p.386)
• Every time I got drunk, my ***husband*** would send me to a nursing home.(p.388)
• Anyhow, after Christmas my ***husband*** gave me a cocker spaniel who is, I think, just as notorious in A.A. as I am.(p.388)
• We moved once more, to Houston; my ***husband*** thought maybe a change of environment would help and I'd be all right.(p.389)
• They phoned my ***husband*** that I was in jail and in such terrible shape that they didn't know what I

would do to myself; and they realized that jail was no place for me, but that he was to wait a while before he got me, because at the time they called him to come over for me I was beating a tin cup against the wall.(p.390)
• My ***husband*** couldn't tell whether I wanted to do something about my drinking.(p.391)
• I was shaking so, I asked my ***husband*** to write the letter for me, but he said no.(p.392)
• That was on Saturday and my ***husband*** was leaving town Sunday night.(p.393)
• There are so many to whom I feel deeply grateful; to my ***husband*** (and best critic), whose generous love, compassion and understanding have helped me along the way; to those before me in A.A. who inspired the first article I read, and the friend who sent that article to Frank; to Ruth for her personal note, and the first A.A. to talk to me; to my Bishop, whose loving and believing spirit inspired me; and to all the members of the Houston Group who were so patient, kind and helpful -- and to countless others.(p.393)
• My ***husband*** was made miserable by this, but I had already made him and myself miserable.(p.402)
• I graduated with honors, but could not feel any real responsibility as a father or a ***husband***.(p.419)
• My life there was a nightmare of periodic binges on alcohol and pills, adultery, unhappy hours at the dental office, seeing my wife give birth to our second child and have several miscarriages, living in a turbulent household, and making continual attempts to be the respectable dentist, ***husband***, father, and community leader.(p.419)
• I am a young alcoholic with a drug problem, a doctor, the ***husband*** of an alcoholic, the son of an alcoholic, and a man once diagnosed as a violent manic-depressive.(p.421)
• I was father, ***husband***, taxpayer, home owner.(p.432)
• I remember vaguely violent quarrels with my ***husband***, his finding my liquor supply time and time again and throwing it out.(p.466)
• There was a long discussion between my ***husband***, my sister and her ***husband***.(p.466)
• My ***husband*** helped me into the house, packed himself a bag, and gave me some money.(p.467)
• Then in a couple of hours, when there was still no word from my ***husband*** and no sign of him, I had the feeling we alcoholics all know.(p.467)
• The next recollection I have is of my ***husband*** coming into my room (later found out it was on New Year's Eve) accompanied by two policemen.(p.468)
• The same doctor who had sent me to the psycho had asked my ***husband***, "Why don't you send her to this Alcoholics Anonymous?"(p.469)
• My ***husband*** said, "What is A.A.?"(p.469)
• My ***husband*** interrupted, "She's bad enough now without getting mixed up with a bunch of drunks."(p.469)
• If anyone had told me I would be enjoying a hockey game with my ***husband*** and my brother without being all boozed up, I would not have believed it.(p.481)
• I went to church on Easter Sunday with my ***husband***, and it didn't hurt at all.(p.482)
• In the first place, she had been married before; I was her second ***husband***.(p.485)
• Vi was very kind and explained to the jury that I was basically a fine fellow and a good ***husband***, but that I drank too much and that she thought I had lost my mind and felt that I should be committed to an asylum.(p.492)
• My ***husband*** was soon in uniform and among the first to go overseas.(p.547)
• My ***husband*** eventually returned, but it was not long until we realized we could not continue our marriage.(p.547)

husband's
• Then we were severely criticized by our ***husband's*** parents for desertion.(p.106)
• Be determined that your ***husband's*** drinking is not going to spoil your relations with your children or your friends.(p.111)
• If this kind of approach does not catch your ***husband's*** interest, it may be best to drop the subject, but after a friendly talk your husband will usually revive the topic himself.(p.112)
• Frequently, you have felt obliged to tell your ***husband's*** employer and his friends that he was sick, when as a matter of fact he was tight.(p.115)
• The slightest sign of fear or intolerance may lessen your ***husband's*** chance of recovery.(p.120)
• God has either removed your ***husband's*** liquor problem or He has not.(p.120)
• She wanted to know if her ***husband's*** company insurance was still in force.(p.137)

husbands
• Our loyalty and the desire that our ***husbands*** hold up their heads and be like other men have begotten all sorts of predicaments.(p.105)
• When we were invited out, our ***husbands*** sneaked so many drinks that they spoiled the occasion.(p.105)
• The bill collectors, the sheriffs, the angry taxi drivers, the policemen, the bums, the pals, and even the ladies they sometimes brought home -- our ***husbands*** thought we were so inhospitable.(p.106)
• The unexpected result was that our ***husbands*** seemed to like it.(p.106)
• Today most of our men are better ***husbands*** and fathers than ever before.(p.108)
• Many of our ***husbands*** were just as far gone.(p.110)
• As our ***husbands*** began to apply spiritual principles in their lives, we began to see the desirability of doing so too.(p.116)
• We thought, on the whole, we were pretty good women, capable of being nicer if our ***husbands*** stopped drinking.(p.116)
• We women carry with us a picture of the ideal man, the sort of chap we would like our ***husbands*** to be.(p.118)
• Another feeling we are very likely to entertain is one of resentment that love and loyalty could not cure our ***husbands*** of alcoholism.(p.118)
• Though it is entirely separate from Alcoholics Anonymous, it uses the general principles of the A.A. program as a guide for ***husbands***, wives, relatives, friends, and others close to alcoholics.(p.121)
• ***Husbands*** and wives have sometimes been obliged to separate for a time until new perspective, new victory over hurt pride could be rewon.(p.125)
• Many a distracted wife has visited this house to find loving and understanding companionship among women who knew her problem, to hear from the lips of their ***husbands*** what had happened to them, to be advised how her own wayward mate might be hospitalized and approached when next he stumbled.(p.160)
• Many women who have reached the stage that I had reached in my drinking have lost ***husbands***, children, homes, everything they hold dear.(p.323)
• I didn't know how to be a father; I don't know how to come home and work week-ends like other ***husbands***; I don't know how to entertain my family.(p.351)
• This is a world clearing house for the Al-Anon Family Groups, composed largely of the wives, ***husbands*** and friends of A.A. members.(p.575)

husbands'
• We have told innumerable lies to protect our pride and our ***husbands'*** reputations.(p.105)

huts
• The other kids would light out for the hamburger ***huts*** or ice cream parlors, the pizza joints or bowling alleys, after football games and dances.(p.423)

Hyde
• He is a real Dr. Jekyll and Mr. ***Hyde***.(p.21)

hydrotherapy
• ***Hydrotherapy*** and mild exercise helped much.(p.7)

hymns
• They'd sit out there and play ***hymns*** and I'd be lying in there with a terrific hangover.(p.265)

hypersensitive
• I had been ***hypersensitive***, shy, idealistic.(p.226)
• We "instant perfectionists" also are ***hypersensitive***, alas.(p.331)

hypodermic
• She puts me to bed and gives me a ***hypodermic***.(p.501)

hysterical
• We avoid ***hysterical*** thinking or advice.(p.70)
• We have been ***hysterical***.(p.105)
• I was in the hospital, ***hysterical***.(p.319)

hysterically
• Neither should the family ***hysterically*** plead with him to do anything, nor should they tell him much about you.(p.90)
• I do recall lying on a cold cement floor and shredding into little bits several pieces of stolen identification cards, and washing my face in the toilet bowl trying to sober up, and screaming ***hysterically*** while clinging to bars too high to see out of, and cursing everyone that came near me.(p.354)
• At a large party in Geneva, with people from many countries represented, the kind of party that is "protocol" in the extreme, I swayed, laughed ***hysterically***, made naughty remarks in an unhushed voice, and was finally led from the scene.(p.406)

hysterics
• Because of this state of confusion and frustration I had ***hysterics*** on the seventeenth day for the first and only time in my life.(p.387)

Ii

ice
• His only chance for sobriety would be some place like the Greenland *Ice* Cap, and even there an Eskimo might turn up with a bottle of scotch and ruin everything!(p.101)
• He was on thin *ice*.(p.154)
• It was February with snow and *ice* on the ground and I had a four blocks walk to the nearest cab stand, but I made it.(p.288)
• One night at the dinner table my wife said that tonight was my first birthday in A.A., and that the group would have the usual *ice* cream and cake for the "one year man."(p.365)
• So I was used to it, but I didn't know what the effect of alcohol was because I always had wine, usually with dinner, but always with a lot of *ice* and about two tablespoons of sugar in it.(p.385)
• The other kids would light out for the hamburger huts or *ice* cream parlors, the pizza joints or bowling alleys, after football games and dances.(p.423)
• I didn't like being on the nut ward, and I particularly didn't like being forced to *ice* cookies on Christmas Eve.(p.444)

ice-bag
• When I got home my mouth was very painful, so I got an *ice-bag* and went to bed.(p.466)
• The next day the *ice-bag* and I were still in bed -- but we had a bottle too!(p.466)

iced
• On our honeymoon, we had *iced* champagne by the bedside day and night.(p.555)

icy
• It melted the *icy* intellectual mountain in whose shadow I had lived and shivered many years.(p.12)
• I was hit by an *icy* blast.(p.288)

idea
• I knew, and almost welcomed the *idea*.(p.7)
• They had told of a simple religious *idea* and a practical program of action.(p.9)
• I didn't like the *idea*.(p.12)
• My friend suggested what then seemed a novel *idea*.(p.12)
• My wife and I abandoned ourselves with enthusiasm to the *idea* of helping other alcoholics to a solution of their problems.(p.15)
• And the truth, strange to say, is usually that he has no more *idea* why he took that first drink than you have.(p.23)
• If these thoughts occur, they are hazy and readily supplanted with the old threadbare *idea* that this time we shall handle ourselves like other people.(p.24)
• These give a fair cross section of our membership and a clear-cut *idea* of what has actually happened in their lives.(p.29)
• The *idea* that somehow, someday he will control and enjoy his drinking is the great obsession of every abnormal drinker.(p.30)
• Yet all reasons for not drinking were easily pushed aside in favor of the foolish *idea* that he could take whiskey if only he mixed it with milk!(p.36)
• The insane *idea* won out.(p.37)
• He tries every known means to get the jay-walking *idea* out of his head.(p.38)
• To others, the word "God" brought up a particular *idea* of Him with which someone had tried to impress them during childhood.(p.45)
• With that rejection we imagined we had abandoned the God *idea* entirely.(p.45)
• People of faith have a logical *idea* of what life is all about.(p.49)
• But the God *idea* did.(p.52)
• We agnostics and atheists were sticking to the *idea* that self-sufficiency would solve our problems.(p.52)
• Actually we were fooling ourselves, for deep down in every man, woman, and child, is the fundamental *idea* of God.(p.55)
• The wording was, of course, quite optional so long as we expressed the *idea*, voicing it without reservation.(p.63)
• Get an *idea* of his behavior, his problems, his background, the seriousness of his condition, and his religious leanings.(p.90)
• You will thus get a better *idea* of how you ought to proceed.(p.91)
• Burn the *idea* into the consciousness of every man that he can get well regardless of anyone.(p.98)
• If he gets the *idea* that you are a nag or a killjoy, your chance of accomplishing anything useful may be zero.(p.111)
• But it was a silly *idea* that we were too good to need God.(p.116)
• The family may be possessed by the *idea* that future happiness can be based only upon forgetfulness of the past.(p.123)
• While grateful that he drinks no more, they may not like the *idea* that God has accomplished the miracle where they failed.(p.128)
• Sometimes we alcoholics have an *idea* that people are trying to pull us down.(p.145)
• We believe that managers of large enterprises often have little *idea* how prevalent this problem is.(p.149)
• In the chapter "Working With Others" you gathered an *idea* of how we approach and aid others to health.(p.153)
• Every time I'd start thinking about drinking, I would think of the long, dry years ahead without having a drink; but this *idea* of twenty-four hours, that it was up to me from then on, was a lot of help.(p.188)
• I felt having gotten married, I was an adult and one of the first things I did was to buy two cases of whiskey with no *idea* of drinking it.(p.196)
• My *idea* was to have all the companies pool their funds and buy rubber when rubber was cheap and then put it in a pool.(p.198)
• Not far from where I lived they built a new technical high school and one of the teachers sold me on the *idea* that I needed a little mechanical drawing if I were going to be a good toolmaker.(p.211)
• In fact, the last three years of my drinking was a routine of barbiturates in the morning, so that I could stop shaking enough to shave, and then alcohol beginning about four-thirty or five o'clock, with a struggle not to take a drink at noon or during the day, because I had the *idea* that if I took one drink, I would smell as though I had had a pint.(p.217)
• He startled me by informing me that he was an alcoholic, that he had found a way which so far enabled him to live without taking a drink, and that the main *idea* was to find a way how not to take that first drink.(p.218)
• Doc dwelt on the *idea* that this was an illness, but Doc was pretty frank with me.(p.219)
• I wanted to live, not in a desert, but in a normal world; and my *idea* of a normal world was among people who drank — teetotallers were not included.(p.227)
• My parents had some vague *idea* of making a priest out of me and for some years I attended the Franciscan school at Basle, Switzerland, just across the border, about six miles from my home.(p.230)
• Then I had an *idea*.(p.255)
• My thoughts sometimes turned to the *idea* that there must be a remedy.(p.256)
• The doctor, a young man, immediately took fire with the *idea*, and while he did not convince the son, he turned over two prospects who were anxious for the program.(p.294)
• In my stupid way I went up to see him with the *idea* in the back of my mind that I would investigate Alcoholics Anonymous from a medical standpoint.(p.346)
• And I gave him some *idea* of what you do, and so I made my first Twelfth Step call before I ever came into the program.(p.347)
• Well, I don't know who He is, but I've got my own *idea*.(p.350)
• I had no *idea* what would happen -- I just knew I didn't want to live if life was going to go on like it was.(p.355)
• You will recall that I said the time that I got the *idea* out of a clear sky to call A.A. on a certain night was at about ten.(p.366)
• However, knowing me, she thought it was a foolish *idea*, that I wouldn't be interested.(p.367)
• The following spring she left me one day without giving me any *idea* of where she had gone, hoping this would bring me to my senses.(p.377)
• Her *idea* of fun on a bender was to hit sailors and insult cops.(p.414)
• On the train going back, Anne's one *idea* was to get to the nearest bar.(p.415)
• Never once had my mother even hinted at the *idea* that, when I grew up, I might like to be president of A.A.(p.439)
• Not only did I not think that being an alcoholic was a good *idea*, I didn't even feel that I had all that much of a drinking problem!(p.439)
• In the hospital, I hung on to the *idea* I'd had most of my life: that if I could just control the external environment, the internal environment would then be comfortable.(p.445)
• And life keeps getting simpler and easier as we try to reverse my old *idea*, by taking care of the internal environment via the Twelve Steps, and letting the external environment take care of itself.)(p.446)
• The *idea* behind it is that, having taken the treatment, your system is so "conditioned" that the mere sight or smell or taste of alcohol produces a violent reaction, and you become ill.(p.469)
• I approached several ministers and all of them thought it was a very good *idea*, but they never relinquished any space.(p.495)
• One more foolish *idea*.(p.502)
• Another foolish *idea*.(p.502)
• What a wonderful *idea*!(p.505)
• The fear and the insane *idea* are taken away.(p.505)
• It is a cold-blooded *idea*.(p.506)
• When I am through speaking, the whole *idea* has become absurd.(p.507)
• I had enough decency so that I dismissed the *idea* of doing any clowning, and I did listen.(p.509)
• I had an advantage in having an *idea* of what A.A. was about before coming out on the street.(p.510)

ideal
• We shall do our utmost to achieve that *ideal*.(p.19)
• In this way we tried to shape a sane and sound *ideal* for our future sex life.(p.69)
• Whatever our *ideal* turns out to be, we must be willing to grow toward it.(p.69)
• Suppose we fall short of the chosen *ideal* and stumble?(p.70)
• To sum up about sex: We earnestly pray for the right *ideal*, for guidance in each questionable situation, for sanity, and for the strength to do the right thing.(p.70)
• We women carry with us a picture of the *ideal* man, the sort of chap we would like our husbands to be.(p.118)
• My home life is *ideal* and my business is as good as can be expected in these uncertain times.(p.180)
• In my drinking days, I found the *ideal* spot for the alcoholic housewife: the neighborhood Laundromat.(p.369)
• This was an *ideal* set-up.(p.426)
• We think that each group should soon achieve this *ideal*; that any public solicitation of funds using the name of Alcoholics Anonymous is highly dangerous, whether by groups, clubs, hospitals, or other outside agencies; that acceptance of large gifts from any source, or of contributions carrying any obligation whatever, is unwise.(p.566)

idealistic
• I had been hypersensitive, shy, *idealistic*.(p.226)
• He was well behaved, and *idealistic* where women were concerned.(p.403)

idealists
• Boy, what a circle of confused *idealists*!(p.246)

ideals
• In nearly all cases, their *ideals* must be grounded in a power greater than themselves, if they are to re-create their lives.(p.xxvi)
• We asked God to mold our *ideals* and help us to live up to them.(p.69)
• I, a man of steel, with very high *ideals*, well brought up, an honor student and the recipient of scholarships and prizes, a boy wonder in business -- I, Bob, the author of this essay, looked and saw that the universe was beneath my contempt, and that to remove myself from it was the only thing of dignity a man could do.(p.531)

ideas
• And besides, there were scattered alcoholics who had picked up the basic *ideas* in Akron or New York and were trying to form A.A. groups in other cities.(p.xvii)
• In the course of his third treatment he acquired certain *ideas* concerning a possible means of recovery.(p.xxiii)
• Many years ago one of the leading contributors to this book came under our care in this hospital and while here he acquired some *ideas* which he put into practical application at once.(p.xxv)
• However, he did become "sold" on the *ideas* con-

tained in this book.(p.xxx)
• My judgment and *ideas* were followed by many to the tune of paper millions.(p.3)
• My *ideas* about miracles were drastically revised right then.(p.11)
• *Ideas*, emotions, and attitudes which were once the guiding forces of the lives of these men are suddenly cast to one side, and a completely new set of conceptions and motives begin to dominate them.(p.27)
• Up to this point you would label him as a foolish chap having queer *ideas* of fun.(p.37)
• I rather appreciated your *ideas* about the subtle insanity which precedes the first drink, but I was confident it could not happen to me after what I had learned.(p.40)
• In the realm of the material, men's minds were fettered by superstition, tradition, and all sorts of fixed *ideas*.(p.51)
• Is not our age characterized by the ease with which we discard old *ideas* for new, by the complete readiness with which we throw away the theory or gadget which does not work for something new which does?(p.52)
• Our *ideas* did not work.(p.52)
• Some of us have tried to hold on to our old *ideas* and the result was nil until we let go absolutely.(p.58)
• Our description of the alcoholic, the chapter to the agnostic, and our personal adventures before and after make clear three pertinent *ideas*:(p.60)
• Most good *ideas* are simple, and this concept was the keystone of the new and triumphant arch through which we passed to freedom.(p.62)
• We might pay for this presumption in all sorts of absurd actions and *ideas*.(p.87)
• If he sticks to the *ideas* that he can still control his drinking, tell him that possibly he can – if he is not too alcoholic.(p.92)
• The alcoholic, his wife, his children, his "in-laws," each one is likely to have fixed *ideas* about the family's attitude toward himself or herself.(p.122)
• To you, some of the *ideas* which it contains are novel.(p.144)
• When I reached school, I discovered the faculty had other *ideas* on the subject.(p.173)
• We would follow one man's *ideas* for a while, decide he was wrong and switch to another's method.(p.246)
• How hurt I was when editors bounced back my *ideas* quickly and my best friends opined that my output needed a lot of rewriting.(p.331)
• They are not *ideas* of resignation but of the recognition of certain basic facts of living.(p.382)
• I tried to mimic the talk, *ideas*, moods and even the drinking the older men.(p.423)
• We used to argue about our differing *ideas*, but we can't argue about our feelings.(p.451)
• But Providence had other *ideas*.(p.464)
• I'm sure my *ideas* as to what life should be like were quite different from that of the average person with whom I associated.(p.483)
• I'd gladly do it anonymously, as I have done this brief account of my struggle with alcohol -- merely to present certain *ideas* for the consideration of the reader.(p.542)

identical

• My reaction to this was *identical* in many respects to my reaction to my parents leaving me when I was seven.(p.547)

identification

• I do recall lying on a cold cement floor and shredding into little bits several pieces of stolen *identification* cards, and washing my face in the toilet bowl trying to sober up, and screaming hysterically while clinging to bars too high to see out of, and cursing everyone that came near me.(p.354)
• I'd lost my car again, pawned my wallet and all *identification* papers for a bottle, and gotten home somehow.(p.429)

identified

• I knew why I *identified*.(p.333)
• We were *identified* and I was put on a train for Chicago.(p.424)

identify

• But this description should *identify* him roughly.(p.22)
• We think it no concern of ours what religious bodies our members *identify* themselves with as individuals.(p.28)
• I could not *identify* myself with the people with whom I found myself and there was no understanding, and I can't stand confinement anyhow.(p.387)
• Yet prisoners often can't *identify* with many A.A. members' drinking stories.(p.458)
• With few exceptions our members find that they have tapped an unsuspected inner resource which they presently *identify* with their own conception of a Power greater than themselves.(p.569)

identity

• If I had not become an active alcoholic and joined A.A., I might never have found my own *identity* or become a part of anything.(p.417)

idle

• This is no *idle* talk.(p.302)
• Others may *idle* in a retrogressive groove without too much danger, but retrogression can spell death for us.(p.311)

Ignatia

• In his prodigy of service, he was well assisted by Sister *Ignatia* at St. Thomas Hospital in Akron, Ohio, one of the greatest friends our Fellowship will ever know.(p.171)
• When I had been in the hospital ten days, Sister *Ignatia*, who has played such a part in the development of A.A. in this area, stuck her head in the door one morning and announced, looking at me quizzically, that they might be able to make something human out of my face after all.(p.205)

ignorance

• I had developed a theory that most people lost money in stocks through *ignorance* of markets.(p.2)
• Back of them is a world of *ignorance* and misunderstanding.(p.20)
• Some of them rose out of *ignorance* of alcoholism.(p.107)
• In any case I must get out of here before I let slip my abysmal *ignorance* of how I came to be here, and she realized that I was stark, staring mad.(p.223)
• "There is a principle which is a bar against all information, which is proof against all arguments and which cannot fail to keep a man in everlasting *ignorance* -- that principle is contempt prior to investigation."(p.570)

ignored

• But his face falls when we speak of spiritual matters, especially when we mention God, for we have reopened a subject which our man thought he had neatly evaded or entirely *ignored*.(p.45)
• Why he bothered with me as long as he did I shall never know, for he knew there was no answer for me in medicine and he, like all doctors of his day, had been taught that the alcoholic was incurable and should be *ignored*.(p.307)

ignoring

• In the garage, I would put the needle in my vein and then try to figure out exactly how much medication to inject to overcome the pep pills while adding to the sleeping pills while *ignoring* the tranquilizers, in order to get just enough to be able to pull out the needle, jerk the tourniquet, throw it in the car, slam the car door shut, run down the hall, and fall in bed before I fell asleep.(p.442)
• The psychiatrist, who had generally been *ignoring* me, now became quite interested; every day, he would ask me all kinds of questions about the A.A. meetings.(p.446)

ill

• The house was taken over by the mortgage holder, my mother-in-law died, and my wife and father-in-law became *ill*.(p.5)
• Best of all, I met a kind doctor who explained that though certainly selfish and foolish, I had been seriously *ill*, bodily and mentally.(p.7)
• You may already have asked yourself why it is that all of us became so very *ill* from drinking.(p.20)
• If a sufficiently strong reason – *ill* health, falling in love, change of environment, or the warning of a doctor – becomes operative, this man can also stop or moderate, although he may find it difficult and troublesome and may even need medical attention.(p.21)
• From it stem all forms of spiritual disease, for we have been not only mentally and physically *ill*, we have been spiritually sick.(p.64)
• We go to him in a helpful and forgiving spirit, confessing our former *ill* feeling and expressing our regret.(p.77)
• Remember they are very *ill*.(p.89)
• When he angers you, remember that he is very *ill*.(p.108)
• The entire family is, to some extent, *ill*."(p.122)
• If you concede that your employee is *ill*, can he be forgiven for what he has done in the past?(p.140)
• Say that you believe he is a gravely *ill* person, with this qualification – being perhaps fatally *ill*, does he want to get well?(p.142)
• It was the usual situation: home in jeopardy, wife *ill*, children distracted, bills in arrears and standing damaged.(p.155)
• I was self conscious and *ill* at ease most of the time, my health was at the breaking point, and I was thoroughly miserable.(p.178)
• I can remember that in my childhood, he was *ill* at ease with the children because he attempted to assert an army discipline that had been ground into him during his three and a half years of army service.(p.210)
• But the firm became violently *ill* with my drunkenness and their course of treatment was to remove their ulcer, in the form of me, from the payroll, amid much fanfare and very personal and slighting remarks and insinuations.(p.300)
• I heard one very *ill* woman say that she didn't believe in the surrender part of the A.A. program.(p.340)
• Within a few months, I was admitted to a state hospital for the mentally *ill*.(p.370)
• While I was at Pensacola my dad became dangerously *ill* and almost died of pneumonia plus a heart attack.(p.426)
• As a physician and pharmacist who had grown up in a drugstore-home, I had a pill for every *ill*, and I was sick a lot.(p.443)
• The idea behind it is that, having taken the treatment, your system is so "conditioned" that the mere sight or smell or taste of alcohol produces a violent reaction, and you become *ill*.(p.469)
• I was fatally *ill*.(p.539)

ill-defined

• And then one *ill-defined* day, one day that I can't recall, I stepped across the line that alcoholics know so well, and from that day on drinking was miserable.(p.346)

ill-temper

• At the moral inventory, he brought up some of my bad personality traits or character defects, such as selfishness, conceit, jealousy, carelessness, intolerance, *ill-temper*, sarcasm and resentments.(p.292)

illness

• An *illness* of this sort – and we have come to believe it an *illness* --involves those about us in a way no other human sickness can.(p.18)
• But not so with the alcoholic *illness*, for with it there goes annihilation of all the things worth while in life.(p.18)
• We are convinced to a man that alcoholics of our type are in the grip of a progressive *illness*.(p.30)
• If that be the case, you may be suffering from an *illness* which only a spiritual experience will conquer.(p.44)
• Business failure, insanity, fatal *illness*, suicide -- these calamities in his immediate family embittered and depressed him.(p.56)
• Continue to speak of alcoholism as an *illness*, a fatal malady.(p.92)
• Had we fully understood the nature of the alcoholic *illness*, we might have behaved differently.(p.107)
• While you need not discuss your husband at length, you can quietly let your friends know the nature of his *illness*.(p.115)
• At such moments we forget that alcoholism is an *illness* over which we could not possibly have had any power.(p.118)
• He simply could not believe that his brother-executive suffered from a serious *illness*.(p.138)
• At this point, it might be well to explain alcoholism, the *illness*.(p.142)
• Doc dwelt on the idea that this was an *illness*, but Doc was pretty frank with me.(p.219)
• He pointed out to me that probably it was more of a moral or spiritual *illness* than it was a physical one.(p.219)
• Slight casualties, complicated however by a long and serious *illness*, were my only mishaps.(p.253)
• This was after his *illness*.(p.270)
• He said he had finally learned that drinking was a fatal *illness* made up of an allergy plus an obsession, and once the drinking had passed from habit to obsession, we were completely hopeless, and could look forward only to spending the balance of our lives in mental institutions or to death.(p.290)
• The next afternoon and evening, two other men visited me and each told me his story and the things that they were doing to try to recover from this tragic *illness*.(p.290)
• Then I would send an excuse of *illness*.(p.299)
• And that came after a three-weeks' *illness* of my son.(p.338)
• I knew nothing about alcoholism or the D.T.'s, but when I woke up on this last morning of my son's *illness*, I taped the keyhole on my door because "everyone was out there."(p.338)
• The last time I drank, when I was twenty-nine, I drank for only four days, yet I threatened to kill my

children; I beat my wife at home and on the church steps; I mistreated a child in my office; and I ran to a hospital for mental *illness* to avoid jail.(p.418)
• I have come to believe that my *illness* is spiritual as well as physical and mental, and I know that for help in the spiritual sphere I have to turn to a Higher Power.(p.473)
• I seem to get no sympathy for my *illness* and have no appreciation of the love behind the gift.(p.501)
• Through my efforts to get down to "causes and conditions," I stand convinced that my emotional *illness* has been present from my earliest recollection.(p.544)
• (This address is now available in pamphlet form at nominal cost through most A.A. groups or from Box 459, Grand Central Station, New York, NY 10163, under the title "Three Talks to Medical Societies by Bill W." – formerly called "Bill on Alcoholism" and earlier "Alcoholism the *Illness*.")(p.572)
• In emphasizing alcoholism as an *illness*, the social stigma associated with this condition is being blotted out . . .(p.573)

ills
• Without this proof the expectant purchaser would be forced to depart empty handed with none of what I later came to believe was the great panacea for all human *ills*.(p.171)
• Historians may one day recognize Alcoholics Anonymous to have been a great venture in social pioneering which forged a new instrument for social action; a new therapy based on the kinship of common suffering; one having a vast potential for the myriad other *ills* of mankind."(p.573)

illuminating
• We pocket our pride and go to it, *illuminating* every twist of character, every dark cranny of the past.(p.75)
• A look at the alcoholic in your organization is many times *illuminating*.(p.139)

illusion
• The persistence of this *illusion* is astonishing.(p.30)

illusions
• Curious about it, feeling I was missing something, absolutely without any *illusions* about the aftermath, with no pronounced feeling of patriotism, I joined up with a Canadian regiment, serving a little over two years.(p.253)

illustrate
• To *illustrate*:(p.48)

illustrates
• To me, this incident *illustrates* lack of understanding as to what really ails the alcoholic, and lack of knowledge as to what part employers might profitably take in salvaging their sick employees.(p.139)

illustration
• You may think our *illustration* is too ridiculous.(p.38)
• We, who have been through the wringer, have to admit if we substituted alcoholism for jay-walking, the *illustration* would fit us exactly.(p.38)
• Let us take another *illustration*.(p.39)

image
• "Yes, that's me," said the sick man, "the very *image*.(p.157)
• I had been far too busy building, protecting, and maintaining an *image* of respectability and all the other business pluses.(p.327)
• While I sought the comforting arms of alcohol, I knew this was a sign of weakness on the part of a longtime-successful old codger with white hair, the *image* of dignity.(p.331)
• Also, I believed I was the *image* of all domestic virtues, secluded in my washday (any day) refuge.(p.369)
• Dad's *image* for me was that of a big Irish oilman who came up through the school of hard knocks and so had to be a two-fisted drinker.(p.369)

images
• I came to understand the intricate processes of projection, by which we cast into our adult world the *images* of the horrors of our childhood.(p.434)

imaginable
• We have tried every *imaginable* remedy.(p.31)

imagination
• It stirs his *imagination*.(p.110)
• For most normal folks, drinking means conviviality, companionship and colorful *imagination*.(p.151)
• Your *imagination* will be fired.(p.152)
• I had been brought up to believe this, and I had shown during my 'teens considerable enterprise and *imagination* about earning money.(p.275)
• Alas for us men toward whom Shaw hurled his cry, "Must a Christ be crucified in every generation for the benefit of those who have no *imagination*?"(p.536)

imaginative
• Is he not usually brilliant, fast-thinking, *imaginative* and likeable?(p.139)

imagine
• *Imagine* life without faith!(p.54)
• Some day he will be unable to *imagine* life either with alcohol or without it.(p.152)
• *Imagine* my surprise when I read in a page one "box" that I had been taken from the theater unconscious around noon that day, removed by ambulance to a hospital and stomach-pumped and then released.(p.244)
• My husband said that I said, "Can you *imagine* them giving us that jail fare?"(p.264)
• And then I thought to myself: "*Imagine* an alcoholic admitting anything!"(p.349)
• *Imagine* my surprise when I came to, in Europe, and discovered I had brought myself along!(p.405)
• It was their open night meeting, but of course I thought they were all alcoholics; I couldn't *imagine* why anybody else would want to go there, and my first reaction was, well, I've come to something that's not for me.(p.524)
• There was the love affair which was ridiculous -- "*imagine* that midget being able to fall in love!" – and my head knew it while my heart pumped real, genuine anguish, for it hurt like hell, and since it was first love, things have never been quite the same.(p.534)
• I suspect that if it is wisely handled – and it seems to be in wise and prudent hands – there are doors of opportunity ahead of this project that may surpass our capacities to *imagine*."(p.574)

imagined
• My talent for leadership, I *imagined*, would place me at the head of vast enterprises which I would manage with the utmost assurance.(p.1)
• I rightly *imagined* that they would some day have a great rise.(p.2)
• With that rejection we *imagined* we had abandoned the God idea entirely.(p.45)
• In all these ways I've experienced, in ever growing measure and beyond all expectations and rewards, a joy which I had never before *imagined*.(p.395)
• I *imagined* getting even for hurts and rejections.(p.560)

imbued
• He had already *imbued* them with his own spirit until they were ready and willing at all times to go where sent, and as a doctor he well knew that this mission and duty would strengthen them as it later helped me.(p.235)
• The example which they and Bill W., whose visits to Akron were fairly frequent, set me of service to their fellow men *imbued* me with a great desire to emulate them.(p.281)

imitation
• Fear, love of dentistry, and an *imitation* of my father's periodic drinking pattern took me through dental college soberly, except for the few parties and vacations in those four years.(p.419)

immature
• My parents died, both in the same year, leaving me, a sheltered and somewhat *immature* man, on my own.(p.277)
• She, more than the others, showed me what ailed me basically, why I was *immature* and insecure.(p.409)
• No one could live such an irresponsible, *immature* life as I had without consequences.(p.420)

immaturity
• But it did not take long for the pressures of living to bring out my *immaturity* and my insecurity.(p.420)
• And all this, of course, is, in the popular modern jargon, "compensation" for *immaturity*.(p.535)

immediate
• Business failure, insanity, fatal illness, suicide -- these calamities in his *immediate* family embittered and depressed him.(p.56)
• During the first three months I carried on all these activities without a car, depending entirely on buses and streetcars – I, who had always to have a car at my *immediate* command.(p.283)
• "First Things First": solving our *immediate* problems before we try to solve all the others and get muddled in our thinking and doing.(p.382)
• Though it was not our intention to create such an impression, many alcoholics have nevertheless concluded that in order to recover they must acquire an *immediate* and overwhelming "God-consciousness" followed at once by a vast change in feeling and outlook.(p.569)
• Should you be the relative or friend of an alcoholic who shows no *immediate* interest in A.A., it is suggested that you write the Al-Anon Family Groups, Inc., Box 182, Madison Square Station, New York, NY 10159, U.S.A.(p.575)

immediately
• Their very first case, a desperate one, recovered *immediately* and became A.A. number three.(p.xvii)
• This *immediately* precipitates us into a seething caldron of debate.(p.xxviii)
• We discuss them with someone *immediately* and make amends quickly if we have harmed anyone.(p.84)
• But we must try to repair the damage *immediately* lest we pay the penalty by a spree.(p.99)
• Why was it, when these dangers were pointed out that they agreed, and then got drunk again *immediately*?(p.107)
• I *immediately* quit school and went to work, and from that time until I was high school age there was never a return to school.(p.193)
• I quit drinking *immediately*.(p.202)
• I *immediately* became unconscious.(p.207)
• On hearing that, these people induced me to make the move *immediately* and join them as a senior partner, which I did.(p.220)
• Where preaching and prayers had touched me very little, I *immediately* desired further knowledge of these men.(p.235)
• *Immediately* a great feeling of peace descended upon me, intermingled with a feeling of being suffused with a quiet strength.(p.280)
• The doctor, a young man, *immediately* took fire with the idea, and while he did not convince the son, he turned over two prospects who were anxious for the program.(p.294)
• *Immediately* on her return we began to have formal meetings once a week, in the autumn of 1939, and we have continued to do this and to expand ever since.(p.295)
• I was *immediately* impressed with his graciousness and charm.(p.309)
• To most of us, making amends will take the rest of our lives, but we can start *immediately*.(p.381)
• I didn't realize I would find so much more, but a new and different outlook on life started opening up almost *immediately*.(p.383)
• So I located a house, and I thought we ought to move into it *immediately*, but Frank was horrified, because he never knew what was going to happen to me.(p.388)
• I displayed alcoholic tendencies actually from the age of fourteen, when I started to steal wine from the family jug, siphoning it off one drink at a time so it wouldn't be missed, not drinking it *immediately*, but saving it until about a pint was accumulated, so that I could get drunk.(p.397)
• So I *immediately* started taking and shooting pep pills.(p.442)
• We got on the plane and *immediately* had a big fight over whether I'd drink the free booze.(p.444)
• I was *immediately* arrested, arraigned in Homicide Court, held without bail, and remanded to the old Tombs Prison to await trial.(p.508)
• Having made that bargain, I *immediately* began to feel I'd been trapped into it and I went out and had some drinks – four glasses of gin, I remember.(p.523)
• The only kind of security I knew anything about at that time was material security and I decided that all these intruders would vanish *immediately* if I only had a lot of money.(p.545)
• The people who came knew *immediately* I was in no condition to absorb anything of the program, and I was put in a sanitarium to be defogged so that I could make a sober decision about this for myself.(p.549)
• All but one "responded to the treatment" suggested in the Steps *immediately*, but this one posed a problem.(p.551)
• *Immediately*, it was part of the pattern and part of the problem.(p.556)

immense
• 12. – And finally, we of Alcoholics Anonymous believe that the principle of anonymity has *immense* spiritual significance.(p.567)

immensely
• Every new alcoholic looks for this spirit among us and is *immensely* relieved when he finds we are not witch-burners.(p.103)
• I enjoyed it *immensely*.(p.346)

immersed
• I was *immersed* in self-pity and resentment, and the only people who would support this attitude or who I felt understood me at all were the people I met in bars and the ones who drank as I did.(p.547)

immigrants
• Like most ***immigrants*** I wanted to be somebody and have something and I was very happy and contented as I felt success crown my efforts.(p.232)

immoral
• I wasn't entirely ***immoral;*** I wasn't bad; I wasn't vicious.(p.392)

immortalized
• The times in which I grew up (the Prohibition era ***immortalized*** by Scott Fitzgerald and John Held Jr.) had taught me to be gay with the gayest; my own inner urges led me to outdo them all.(p.225)

immune
• If we are planning to stop drinking, there must be no reservation of any kind, nor any lurking notion that someday we will be ***immune*** to alcohol.(p.33)

immunity
• Practical experience shows that nothing will so much insure ***immunity*** from drinking as intensive work with other alcoholics.(p.89)

immutable
• How could there be so much of precise and ***immutable*** law and no intelligence?(p.10)

impact
• God comes to most men gradually, but His ***impact*** on me was sudden and profound.(p.14)

impair
• He may have the habit badly enough to gradually ***impair*** him physically and mentally.(p.20)

impaired
• Some men have been so ***impaired*** by alcohol that they cannot stop.(p.114)
• I found in the fall of 1939, that I was not mentally ***impaired,*** so far as trial work was concerned, and thereafter took up where I had left off when I was about forty-five years old.(p.220)
• My financial standing had not been ***impaired.***(p.379)

impart
• I hope I have been able to ***impart*** to you, the reader, at least a bit of what I know; the joy of living, the irresistible power of divine love and its healing strength, and the fact that we, as sentient beings, have the knowledge to choose between good and evil, and, choosing good, are made happy.(p.543)

imparted
• This doctor had ***imparted*** his knowledge to just a few other men at that time -- not more than four or five -- they now number more than seventy persons.(p.235)

impartially
• I was taking Benzedrine and paraldehyde quite ***impartially*** during the day then, and by the time I arrived at my first A.A. meeting, I was pretty drunk and certainly doped up to the eyes and completely jittery.(p.523)

impasse
• It is of little use to argue and only makes the ***impasse*** worse.(p.126)
• How I had arrived at this tragic ***impasse*** I could not have explained to anyone.(p.304)

impatient
• Ask them to remember, when they are ***impatient,*** the blessed fact of his sobriety.(p.100)
• Acceptance of things as they are has replaced the old ***impatient*** champing at the bit to conquer the world.(p.295)

impeccable
• I acquired the ***impeccable*** coat of tan one sees upon the well-to-do.(p.4)

impel
• Sobering up, the mind that was ahead of the emotions would ***impel*** the question: What have you written or done to be the great man?(p.537)

impending
• My brain raced uncontrollably and there was a terrible sense of ***impending*** calamity.(p.6)
• Post-war disillusionment, ever more serious alcoholism, ***impending*** mental and physical collapse, brought him to the point of self-destruction.(p.56)
• The feeling of ***impending*** disaster that had haunted me for years began to dissolve as I put into practice more and more of the Twelve Steps.(p.229)
• I was aware of symptoms of ***impending*** dependence, and I told myself I had gotten out of the rat race just in time to head off any booze problem.(p.327)
• So I sat down with me and went over the facts behind the convulsions: personality changes, daily headaches, sense of ***impending*** doom, sense of ***impending*** insanity.(p.444)

imperative
• More often than not, it is ***imperative*** that a man's brain be cleared before he is approached, as he has then a better chance of understanding and accepting what we have to offer.(p.xxiv)
• Particularly was it ***imperative*** to work with others as he had worked with me.(p.14)
• For most alcoholics who are drinking, or who are just getting over a spree, a certain amount of physical treatment is desirable, even ***imperative.***(p.142)
• He told me that it was ***imperative*** that I walk around the entire block, cost me what it might in mental agony.(p.276)
• Sobriety and a plan for living that produces a personality change and a spiritual awakening are ***imperative.***(p.459)

imperious
• It quiets the ***imperious*** urge, when to yield would mean heartache.(p.70)

implacably
• Like most sick people before me, I was ***implacably*** selfish, and chronically self-centered.(p.401)

implicate
• Before taking drastic action which might ***implicate*** other people we secure their consent.(p.80)
• 10. – No A.A. group or member should ever, in such a way as to ***implicate*** A.A., express any opinion on outside controversial issues – particularly those of politics, alcohol reform, or sectarian religion.(p.567)

implicit
• Indeed, I was beginning to see that I would require ***implicit*** faith, like a small child, if I was going to get anywhere.(p.259)

implied
• While an A.A. group may cooperate with anyone, such cooperation ought never go so far as affiliation or endorsement, actual or ***implied.***(p.566)

import
• For a while, for a long time, we can endure the intellect's being ahead of the emotions, which is the ***import*** of Millay's couplet.(p.534)

importance
• These facts appear to be of extreme medical ***importance;*** because of the extraordinary possibilities of rapid growth inherent in this group they may mark a new epoch in the annals of alcoholism.(p.xxiii)
• The subject presented in this book seems to me to be of paramount ***importance*** to those afflicted with alcoholic addiction.(p.xxv)
• We doctors have realized for a long time that some form of moral psychology was of urgent ***importance*** to alcoholics, but its application presented difficulties beyond our conception.(p.xxv)
• Of far more ***importance*** was the fact that he was the first living human with whom I had ever talked, who knew what he was talking about in regard to alcoholism from actual experience.(p.180)
• There was the over-weening ambition to be the world's greatest author, when -- at thirty-nine -- I had nothing of ***importance*** to say to the world.(p.534)
• The only ***importance*** in all of this lies in the fact that at twenty-three I was just as sick as I was at thirty three, when I came into A.A., but at that time I apparently had no place to go because I had no drinking problem.(p.546)

important
• If you have a drinking problem, we hope that you may pause in reading one of the forty-four personal stories and think: "Yes, that happened to me"; or, more ***important,*** "Yes, I've felt like that"; or most ***important,*** "Yes, I believe this program can work for me, too."(p.xii)
• It is ***important*** that we remain anonymous because we are too few, at present to handle the overwhelming number of personal appeals which may result from this publication.(p.xiii)
• They took a drink a day or so prior to the date, and then the phenomenon of craving at once became paramount to all other interests so that the ***important*** appointment was not met.(p.xxvii)
• I'd prove to the world I was ***important.***(p.2)
• Drink was taking an ***important*** and exhilarating part in my life.(p.3)
• A much more ***important*** demonstration of our principles lies before us in our respective homes, occupations and affairs.(p.19)
• He has a positive genius for getting tight at exactly the wrong moment, particularly when some ***important*** decision must be made or engagement kept.(p.21)
• "Quite as ***important*** was the discovery that spiritual principles would solve all my problems.(p.42)
• When many hundreds of people are able to say that the consciousness of the Presence of God is today the most ***important*** fact of their lives, they present a powerful reason why one should have faith.(p.51)
• We were having trouble with personal relationships, we couldn't control our emotional natures, we were a prey to misery and depression, we couldn't make a living, we had a feeling of uselessness, we were full of fear, we were unhappy, we couldn't seem to be of real help to other people – was not a basic solution of these bedevilments more ***important*** than whether we should see newsreels of lunar flight?(p.52)
• It is ***important*** that he be able to keep a confidence; that he fully understand and approve what we are driving at; that he will not try to change our plan.(p.74)
• It is ***important*** for him to realize that your attempt to pass this on to him plays a vital part in your own recovery.(p.94)
• Suggest how ***important*** it is that he place the welfare of other people ahead of his own.(p.94)
• You will note that we made an ***important*** qualification.(p.101)
• There is an ***important*** exception to the foregoing.(p.108)
• This is ***important.***(p.120)
• Had he been successful in his enterprise, he would have been set on his feet financially which at the time, seemed vitally ***important.***(p.153)
• Unfortunately for me, I was the only child, which perhaps engendered the selfishness which played such an ***important*** part in bringing on my alcoholism.(p.172)
• I made a point of knowing ***important*** people.(p.197)
• But more ***important,*** I lost my sobriety.(p.202)
• You're never going to want another drink, are you?"; and this answer of his is very ***important*** to those of us who are victims of alcoholism.(p.206)
• The ***important*** thing was that he was happy.(p.208)
• With a creeping insidiousness, drink had become more ***important*** than anything else.(p.226)
• The fact that I can work again and earn my living, is ***important,*** but secondary.(p.229)
• But I hardly tasted anything for two years and started in business for myself, founding a mattress factory which is today an ***important*** industrial enterprise in our city.(p.232)
• We can share in the laughter and tears of our many friends, and most ***important,*** we can share our A.A. way of life and are given a daily opportunity to help others.(p.249)
• I was deprived of many of the things that we feel are ***important*** in life, such as education particularly, because of my father's drinking.(p.261)
• But it was so ***important*** that we do the things we were told to do!(p.268)
• Jack said there was a meeting in Akron every Wednesday night and that it was very ***important*** that we go.(p.268)
• I'd like to say here how ***important*** it was to us then that we do all the little things that people said were ***important,*** because later when Russ was so sick that I had to hold him up, they had a meeting out at the house.(p.270)
• Long before I had any real opportunity to give, I had to learn the equally ***important*** lesson of receiving graciously.(p.281)
• Contact with this group was extremely ***important*** to him.(p.309)
• The ***important*** thing I lost was my own self-respect.(p.323)
• And "Think" – that one ***important*** word means so much to me.(p.325)
• I was "too ***important***" to show any indication of being a drunk.(p.328)
• I vowed that never again would any ***important*** person whom I wished to please and impress ever see me drunk.(p.328)
• This was about ten p.m., and the time here is ***important.***(p.363)
• If I were asked what in my opinion was the most ***important*** factor in being successful in this program, besides following the Twelve Steps, I would say Honesty.(p.367)
• And the most ***important*** person to be honest with is Yourself.(p.368)
• But what is more ***important*** is that I found a new life in Alcoholics Anonymous.(p.372)
• How can a person with a fine family, an attractive home, an excellent position and high standing in an ***important*** city become an alcoholic?(p.373)
• I achieved recognized and national standing in my profession, as well as becoming a director in many ***important*** institutions having to do with the civic life of a large city.(p.374)
• Drink planning became more ***important*** than any

other plans.(p.375)
• My hours of work were flexible so that returning to the office was not always ***important.***(p.376)
• It was ***important*** to me to see what alcohol had done to me and would continue to do if I didn't have help.(p.379)
• The why is not ***important;*** the fact is that one drink will set up a reaction in our system which requires more; that one drink was too much and one hundred drinks were not enough.(p.380)
• To me this meant telling my associates that I had joined Alcoholics Anonymous; that I didn't know what was expected of me by A.A., but that whatever it was, it was the most ***important*** thing in life for me; that sobriety meant more to me than anything in this world.(p.382)
• It was so ***important*** that it must come ahead of anything.(p.382)
• (I can't know how much others of our Fellowship have paid financially and, even more ***important,*** mentally and physically.)(p.396)
• Most ***important,*** A.A. has enabled me to go back and start growing up all over again in all areas of my life.(p.420)
• (Today, there is absolutely nothing in the world more ***important*** to me than my keeping this alcoholic sober; not taking a drink is by far the most ***important*** thing I do each day.)(p.447)
• I have to discard my "rights," as well as my expectations, by asking myself, "How ***important*** is it, really?(p.452)
• How ***important*** is it compared to my serenity, my emotional sobriety?"(p.452)
• But more ***important,*** I would have found that once again I was sitting in the driver's seat -- I was running the show.(p.471)
• He has taught me that, in our new life, I am the most ***important*** person of all.(p.481)
• The gradual result was that I was drifting into making drinking one of the more ***important*** parts of my life.(p.519)
• Strangely enough, right through to the end of my twenty-six years in the Army, I was still being offered very good and ***important*** jobs in spite of the fact that my superiors must have known that I wasn't thoroughly reliable.(p.519)
• Then Hitler's war broke out, and again, I was given a really ***important*** job on the Suez Canal, dealing with military shipping.(p.520)
• Still, I had had funds sufficient to get plastered because that, of course, was more ***important*** than paying my own way.(p.538)
• What is much more ***important*** to me, A.A. has taught me that through this simple program I may experience a change in this reaction pattern that will indeed allow me to "match calamity with serenity."(p.544)
• When I was faced with a special challenge or social event -- such as an ***important*** business presentation or a dinner party -- I had to fortify myself with a couple of belts.(p.556)

importuned

• Shortly after I came to this conclusion, I was ***importuned*** by another well-known patent law firm to help them out on some trial work because their trial man had had a heart attack and had been forbidden to go into the courtroom.(p.220)

impose

• Be certain he will be welcomed by your family, and that he is not trying to ***impose*** upon you for money, connections, or shelter.(p.96)
• Of course that isn't so, and such people often may ***impose*** on you.(p.141)
• He will not ***impose.***(p.149)

imposed

• And we, who have ***imposed*** on the best of employers, can scarcely blame them if they have been short with us.(p.138)

impossible

• Here was something at work in a human heart which had done the ***impossible.***(p.11)
• I have seen hundreds of families set their feet in the path that really goes somewhere; have seen the most ***impossible*** domestic situations righted; feuds and bitterness of all sorts wiped out.(p.15)
• Highly competent psychiatrists who have dealt with us have found it sometimes ***impossible*** to persuade an alcoholic to discuss his situation without reserve.(p.18)
• We are equally positive that once he takes any alcohol whatever into his system, something happens, both in the bodily and mental sense, which makes it virtually ***impossible*** for him to stop.(p.22)
• We were in a position where life was becoming ***impossible,*** and if we had passed into the region from which there is no return through human aid we had but two alternatives: One was to go on to the bitter end, blotting out the consciousness of our intolerable situation as best we could; and the other, to accept spiritual help.(p.25)
• Yet we found it ***impossible.***(p.34)
• To one who feels he is an atheist or agnostic such an experience seems ***impossible,*** but to continue as he is means disaster, especially if he is an alcoholic of the hopeless variety.(p.44)
• We found that as soon as we were able to lay aside prejudice and express even a willingness to believe in a Power greater than ourselves, we commenced to get results, even though it was ***impossible*** for any of us to fully define or comprehend that Power, which is God.(p.46)
• Simply because it is ***impossible*** to explain what we see, feel, direct, and use, without a reasonable assumption as a starting point.(p.48)
• This Power has in each case accomplished the miraculous, the humanly ***impossible.***(p.50)
• It was ***impossible*** to say we had no capacity for faith, or love, or worship.(p.54)
• These attempts to do the ***impossible*** have always failed.(p.101)
• It would be ***impossible*** for me to pass over this year without mentioning my love for, and my indebtedness to these two wonderful people who are no longer with us.(p.280)
• It is ***impossible*** to put on paper all the benefits I have derived . . . physical, mental, domestic, spiritual, and monetary.(p.302)
• When I found this ***impossible,*** I became scared for the first time.(p.333)
• I tried to compensate with ***impossible*** dreams and ambitions, which were simply early forms of escape.(p.400)
• Nor were those ***impossible*** dreams I used to have the things I really wanted.(p.416)
• It is ***impossible*** for me to reproduce my despair.(p.435)
• It was ***impossible*** for me to say at this point, "Maybe there is something wrong with my philosophy," and I certainly couldn't say, "Maybe there is something wrong with me."(p.545)
• I realize now that this phase of my development had been arrested by my obsession with self, and my egocentricity had reached such proportions that adjustment to anything outside my personal control was ***impossible*** for me.(p.547)
• I believe this, and I believe too that it is equally ***impossible*** to practice these principles to the best of our ability, a day at a time, and still drink, for I don't think the two things are compatible.(p.550)

impotent

• Couples are occasionally dismayed to find that when drinking is stopped the man tends to be ***impotent.***(p.134)

impress

• To others, the word "God" brought up a particular idea of Him with which someone had tried to ***impress*** them during childhood.(p.45)
• We boys drove out in somebody's car and went to the bar on the way do the dining room and I, in an effort to ***impress*** the other boys that I was city-bred, having lived in Scranton and Cleveland, asked them if they didn't want a drink.(p.194)
• I vowed that never again would any important person whom I wished to please and ***impress*** ever see me drunk.(p.328)
• Every breadwinner, whether trying to ***impress*** a boss or to hold customers in his own business, is fettered by people-pleasing.(p.329)

impressed

• Let him tell you about it: "I was much ***impressed*** with what you fellows said about alcoholism, and I frankly did not believe it would be possible for me to drink again.(p.40)
• But our man is sure to be ***impressed*** with a sincere desire to set right the wrong.(p.77)
• ***Impressed*** by those who visited him at the hospital, he capitulated entirely when, later, in an upper room of this house, he heard the story of some man whose experience closely tallied with his own.(p.160)
• Bill didn't seem too ***impressed.***(p.188)
• I remember well one fellow, Joe, walking nearly three miles through slush, wet and snow to come to the hospital to see a man that he had never seen before in his life, and that ***impressed*** me very much.(p.208)
• I believe every member of the Akron Group did come to see me, which ***impressed*** me terrifically, not so much because of the stories they told, but because they would take the time to come and talk to me without even knowing who I was.(p.218)
• The visits from these men ***impressed*** me at once.(p.235)
• Drifting back to Ohio, I landed on a small newspaper and later was ***impressed*** into the direction of boy-welfare work at the local "Y."(p.253)
• But I had never been a flippant, wise-cracking sneerer at the few persons I had met who had ***impressed*** me as Christian men and women, or at any institution whose sincerity of purpose I could see.(p.259)
• I was terribly ***impressed*** by this meeting and the quality of happiness these men displayed, despite their lack of material means.(p.291)
• I was immediately ***impressed*** with his graciousness and charm.(p.309)
• None of this really ***impressed*** me.(p.354)
• After the meeting was over and we had returned to the cell block again, I was asked how I was ***impressed.***(p.510)

impressing

• As part of his rehabilitation he commenced to present his conceptions to other alcoholics, ***impressing*** upon them that they must do likewise with still others.(p.xxiii)

impression

• Though the aggregate of recoveries resulting from psychiatric effort is considerable, we physicians must admit we have made little ***impression*** upon the problem as a whole.(p.xxvii)
• Perhaps they created the ***impression*** that he is to be wrapped in cotton wool and placed on a pedestal.(p.122)
• I was kind of shocked about anybody talking about themselves the way he did, and my ***impression*** was that the guy was a little "touched."(p.216)
• There was one experience with Doc which made a terrific ***impression*** upon me.(p.218)
• Yet it is true that our first printing gave many readers the ***impression*** that these personality changes, or religious experiences, must be in the nature of sudden and spectacular upheavals.(p.569)
• Though it was not our intention to create such an ***impression,*** many alcoholics have nevertheless concluded that in order to recover they must acquire an immediate and overwhelming "God-consciousness" followed at once by a vast change in feeling and outlook.(p.569)

impressionable

• Their young minds were ***impressionable*** while he was drinking.(p.134)

impressions

• These made their ***impressions*** everywhere.(p.xx)

impressive

• It would have been ***impressive*** heroics if he had walked up to the Judge and said, "Here I am."(p.79)
• Those who believe their drinking to be hopeless may again find hope in these thirteen ***impressive*** tales.(p.167)
• It was very ***impressive*** and I wish that every A.A. could have the benefit of this type of sponsorship today.(p.292)

imprisoned

• We have already admitted this in confidence to another person, but we are sure we would be ***imprisoned*** or lose our job if it were known.(p.78)

improve

• 11.Sought through prayer and meditation to ***improve*** our conscious contact with God as we understood Him, praying only for knowledge of His will for us and the power to carry that out.(p.59)
• There was the economic fear which made me too timid to take any action which might ***improve*** my circumstances.(p.534)

improved

• The family must realize that dad, though marvelously ***improved,*** is still convalescing.(p.127)

improvement

• Of alcoholics who came to A.A. and really tried, 50% got sober at once and remained that way; 25% sobered up after some relapses, and among the remainder, those who stayed on with A.A. showed ***improvement.***(p.xx)
• It took five years of A.A. living, and a substantial ***improvement*** in my health, before I could take a full-time office job where someone else was boss.(p.283)

impulse

• Following his physical rehabilitation, he had a talk with me in which he frankly stated he thought the treatment a waste of effort, unless I could assure him, which no one ever had, that in the future he would have the "will power" to resist the

impulse to drink.(p.xxix)
• The first ***impulse*** will be to bury these skeletons in a dark closet and padlock the door.(p.123)
• After such often-painful vigilance (and numerous phony stints of abstinence), retirement naturally created an ***impulse*** to live without restraints.(p.328)

impunity
• They are restless, irritable and discontented, unless they can again experience the sense of ease and comfort which comes at once by taking a few drinks -- drinks which they see others taking with ***impunity***.(p.xxvi)

in-laws
• The alcoholic, his wife, his children, his "***in-laws***," each one is likely to have fixed ideas about the family's attitude toward himself or herself.(p.122)

inability
• If anyone who is showing ***inability*** to control his drinking can do the right-about-face and drink like a gentleman, our hats are off to him.(p.31)
• Certain drinkers, who would be greatly insulted if called alcoholics, are astonished at their ***inability*** to stop.(p.33)
• This is the baffling feature of alcoholism as we know it -- this utter ***inability*** to leave it alone, no matter how great the necessity or the wish.(p.34)
• Besides a seeming ***inability*** to accept much on faith, we often found ourselves handicapped by obstinacy, sensitiveness, and unreasoning prejudice.(p.47)
• My ***inability*** to accept the harsh realities of life had resulted in a disillusioned cynic, clothed in protective armor against the world's misunderstanding.(p.226)
• Because it was only through feeling defeat and feeling failure, the ***inability*** to cope with my life and with alcohol, that I was able to surrender and accept the fact that I had this disease, and that I had to learn to live again without alcohol.(p.335)

inaccessible
• sometimes they were so ***inaccessible*** that it seemed as though a great wall had been built around them.(p.107)

inadequacy
• Faced with this problem, if a doctor is honest with himself, he must sometimes feel his own ***inadequacy***.(p.xxvii)
• How devastating, too, are the subsequent feelings of ***inadequacy*** and self-pity.(p.331)
• I know there are some alcoholics who seem terribly, terribly grown-up, but I think that they are trying to make themselves think they are grown-up, and the strain of their effort is what is causing them to drink -- a sense of ***inadequacy***, a childish vanity to be the most popular, the most sought after, the mostest of the most.(p.535)
• It had provided me with excuses for my lack of education, my marital failures, personal failures, ***inadequacy***, and of course, my alcoholism and, though I really thought I had been willing to part with it, now I knew I was reluctant to let it go.(p.552)

inadequate
• Perhaps we rejected this particular conception because it seemed ***inadequate***.(p.45)
• Our own conception, however ***inadequate***, was sufficient to make the approach and to effect a contact with Him.(p.46)
• That being the case, it didn't take me long to figure out that my meager manufacturing facilities were entirely ***inadequate*** to the manufacture of beer for social and domestic consumption.(p.297)
• If my personality is ***inadequate***, antisocial, or full of kinks and I alter it with alcohol or any chemical, bingo!(p.458)

inattention
• Mother may complain of ***inattention***.(p.126)

Inc.
• The General Service Board of A.A. (the trustees) administers A.A.'s General Service Office, A.A. World Services, ***Inc.***, and our monthly magazine, the A.A. Grapevine.(p.575)
• Should you be the relative or friend of an alcoholic who shows no immediate interest in A.A., it is suggested that you write the Al-Anon Family Groups, ***Inc.***, Box 182, Madison Square Station, New York, NY 10159, U.S.A.(p.575)

incalculable
• ***Incalculable*** are the intangible initiation fees that A.A. members have paid: the sick, sick hangovers, the remorse, guilt, broken homes, jails, and institutions, and the mental anguish in general that has been generated over the years.(p.399)

incapable
• Those who do not recover are people who cannot or will not completely give themselves to this simple program, usually men and women who are constitutionally ***incapable*** of being honest with themselves.(p.58)
• They are naturally ***incapable*** of grasping and developing a manner of living which demands rigorous honesty.(p.58)

incapacitated
• Liquor ***incapacitated*** father for so many years that mother became head of the house.(p.130)

incarcerated
• By this time I was beginning to pay very dearly physically and, in hope of relief, voluntarily ***incarcerated*** myself at least a dozen times in one of the local sanitariums.(p.174)
• I went to the sanitarium where this chap was ***incarcerated*** and found to my surprise that he was interested.(p.294)

incentive
• The only ***incentive*** that I had, toward the end, for getting dressed in the morning was to get out and get supplies to help me get my day started.(p.336)

incessant
• She was also the victim of my scolding and ***incessant*** nagging.(p.408)

incessantly
• We should not talk ***incessantly*** to them about spiritual matters.(p.83)

inch
• I was staring at an ***inch*** of the tape which bore the inscription XYZ-32.(p.4)

incident
• He subsequently denied having received the money and used the ***incident*** as a basis for discrediting the man.(p.80)
• To me, this ***incident*** illustrates lack of understanding as to what really ails the alcoholic, and lack of knowledge as to what part employers might profitably take in salvaging their sick employees.(p.139)
• All this time our friend of the hotel lobby ***incident*** remained in that town.(p.159)
• About this time an ***incident*** took place in grade school that I have never forgotten because it made me realize that I was actually a physical coward.(p.484)
• After this ***incident*** in 1940, I sought some other means of livelihood.(p.489)

incidentally
• Then I had a year in Germany at school -- that was, ***incidentally***, when I got drunk for the first time.(p.517)

incidents
• Before very long we began to relate some ***incidents*** of our drinking and, naturally, pretty soon, I realized both of them knew what they were talking about because you can see things and smell things when you're drunk, that you can't other times, and, if I had thought they didn't know what they were talking about, I wouldn't have been willing to talk to them at all.(p.185)
• Once, or even twice, such ***incidents*** might be amusing.(p.538)

inclined
• We agnostically ***inclined*** would not feel satisfied with a proposal which does not lend itself to reasonable approach and interpretation.(p.53)
• Psychologists are ***inclined*** to agree with us.(p.73)
• For the benefit of those experimentally ***inclined***, I should mention the so-called beer experiment.(p.177)
• On the other hand, I believe that I've always been medically ***inclined***, though I have never been able to see medicine quite as the average person sees it.(p.485)

include
• By personal religious affiliation, we ***include*** Catholics, Protestants, Jews, Hindus, and a sprinkling of Moslems and Buddhists.(p.xx)
• He will perceive that his spiritual growth is lopsided, that for an average man like himself, a spiritual life which does not ***include*** his family obligations may not be so perfect after all.(p.129)
• 3. -- Our membership ought to ***include*** all who suffer from alcoholism.(p.565)

included
• I wanted to live, not in a desert, but in a normal world; and my idea of a normal world was among people who drank -- teetotallers were not ***included***.(p.227)
• We did, and spent a month boozing it up, popping pills, and smoking marijuana; taking shelter where we could, which ***included*** a veterinary hospital one night; accepting meals from anyone; actually begging; stealing anything we were in need of, which was about everything.(p.354)

includes
• It is plain that a life which ***includes*** deep resentment leads only to futility and unhappiness.(p.66)
• That ***includes*** bars, nightclubs, dances, receptions, weddings, even plain ordinary whoopee parties.(p.101)
• My personal definition, which I submit as applying only to myself (although everyone is welcome to it who wants it), ***includes*** every waking activity of the human being; to have a creative attitude towards things is a more exact meaning, to live and to deal with other human beings creatively, which to me means seeing the God in them, and respecting and worshipping this God.(p.535)

including
• Everybody, ***including*** himself, would be pleased.(p.61)
• In most cases it was found that our self-esteem, our pocketbooks, our ambitions, our personal relationships (***including*** sex) were hurt or threatened.(p.64)
• I don't think the boys were completely convinced of my personality change, for they fought shy of ***including*** my story in the book, so my only contribution to their literary efforts was my firm conviction, being still a theological rebel, that the word God should be qualified with the phrase "as we understand him" -- for that was the only way I could accept spirituality.(p.248)
• There were five people present, ***including*** myself.(p.347)
• High living, a great many fair weather friends, the 1929 stock market crash, and a couple of years of Depression, soon relieved me one by one of my worldly goods ***including*** my wife.(p.358)
• What could be more reasonable than that some people, ***including*** myself, were allergic to alcohol?(p.380)
• He himself took me to many of them, ***including*** the ones out of town.(p.416)
• Life, ***including*** some ups and downs, is a lot of fun.(p.417)
• You see, I am a five-time loser, which means five felony convictions (not ***including*** the cases beaten).(p.457)
• I served time in four penitentiaries and several prison camps, ***including*** a maximum-security camp.(p.457)

inclusive
• To us, the Realm of Spirit is broad, roomy, all ***inclusive***; never exclusive or forbidding to those who earnestly seek.(p.46)

income
• His ***income*** is good, he has a fine home, is happily married and the father of promising children of college age.(p.39)
• After holding good positions, making better than an average ***income*** for over ten years, I was in debt, had no clothes to speak of, no money, no friends, and no one any longer tolerating me but my wife.(p.301)
• Nobody could take away my retirement ***income***.(p.329)
• First, we all hear at A.A. meetings about those who have lost everything, those who have been in jail, those who have been in prison, those who have lost their families, those who have lost their ***income***.(p.345)
• To keep it in round figures, let's say twenty per cent of my ***income*** went for giggle gurgles.(p.397)
• After a few more estimates as to ***income*** and expenditures for booze over a few sample years, taken at random, I conclude that this twenty per cent stayed fairly constant.(p.398)
• As ***income*** increased, the price of liquor increased proportionately.(p.398)
• So I believe that twenty percent is a very conservative estimate of the amount of ***income*** I blew.(p.399)
• For an estimate of salary from the twenty-one a month to start with, to over $400 per month upon my retirement after twenty years in the Navy, I believe that an average ***income*** of $2,000 a year over this period is low, but as I stated earlier, an underestimate is best.(p.399)
• I accepted a big tax-free ***income*** from the family, but I didn't like it when they told me how to live.(p.405)
• I found I could boost my ***income*** by figuring out a lot of cute little tricks that the boss wouldn't be likely to notice -- filching money from the Coke machine, short-sticking the customers on oil, and selling oil I'd drained out of other cars.(p.423)

incoming
• Among today's ***incoming*** A.A. members, many have never reached the advanced stages of alcoholism, though, given time, all might have.(p.315)

incompatibility
• Of course, there is such a thing as ***incompatibility***, but in nearly every instance the alcoholic only seems

to be unloving and inconsiderate; it is usually because he is warped and sickened that he says and does these appalling things.(p.108)

incompatible

• The most *incompatible* people discover they have a basis upon which they can meet.(p.99)

• We have found nothing *incompatible* between a powerful spiritual experience and a life of sane and happy usefulness.(p.130)

incomplete

• In our belief, any picture of the alcoholic which leaves out this physical factor is *incomplete*.(p.xxiv)

incomprehensible

• All of us felt at times that we were regaining control, but such intervals – usually brief – were inevitably followed by still less control, which led in time to pitiful and *incomprehensible* demoralization.(p.30)

• Our behavior is as absurd and *incomprehensible* with respect to the first drink as that of an individual with a passion, say, for jay-walking.(p.37)

inconsiderate

• Where had we been selfish, dishonest, or *inconsiderate*?(p.69)

• Selfish and *inconsiderate* habits have kept the home in turmoil.(p.82)

• Of course, there is such a thing as incompatibility, but in nearly every instance the alcoholic only seems to be unloving and *inconsiderate*; it is usually because he is warped and sickened that he says and does these appalling things.(p.108)

• Members of a family should watch such matters carefully, for one careless, *inconsiderate* remark has been known to raise the very devil.(p.125)

inconsistencies

• He will match your mental *inconsistencies* with some of his own.(p.92)

inconsistency

• The *inconsistency* is made worse by the things he does on his sprees.(p.73)

inconsistent

• This may seem *inconsistent*, but we think it is not.(p.98)

incorporated

• We think, therefore, that any considerable property of genuine use to A.A. should be separately *incorporated* and managed, thus dividing the material from the spiritual.(p.565)

• Secondary aids to A.A., such as clubs or hospitals which require much property or administration, ought to be *incorporated* and so set apart that, if necessary, they can be freely discarded by the groups.(p.566)

incorrigible

• The two years I spent there, I was *incorrigible*, and the records bear this out.(p.458)

• I nearly reverted to my old, *incorrigible* self – had trouble with a couple of other prisoners, was planning an escape.(p.461)

increase

• In spite of the great *increase* in the size and the span of this Fellowship, at its core it remains simple and personal.(p.xxii)

• It brings misunderstanding, fierce resentment, financial insecurity, disgusted friends and employers, warped lives of blameless children, sad wives and parents – anyone can *increase* the list.(p.18)

• Here are some of the methods we have tried: Drinking beer only, limiting the number of drinks, never drinking alone, never drinking in the morning, drinking only at home, never having it in the house, never drinking during business hours, drinking only at parties, switching from scotch to brandy, drinking only natural wines, agreeing to resign if ever drunk on the job, taking a trip, not taking a trip, swearing off forever (with and without a solemn oath), taking more physical exercise, reading inspirational books, going to health farms and sanitariums, accepting voluntary commitment to asylums -- we could *increase* the list ad infinitum.(p.31)

• If it is a happy occasion, try to *increase* the pleasure of those there; if a business occasion, go and attend to your business enthusiastically.(p.102)

• Our activities in behalf of women who drink are on the *increase*.(p.104)

• As our work spreads and our numbers *increase*, we hope your employees may be put in personal contact with some of us.(p.144)

• There is a good bit of travel between East and West and we foresee a great *increase* in this helpful interchange.(p.162)

• My new duties were extremely confining and my liquor consumption began to *increase*.(p.298)

• My daily alcoholic consumption remained about the same through all this, with perhaps a slight *increase*, and my binges remained one-nighters.(p.434)

• I took more through the day to *increase* the high, and more to maintain it; when I overshot the mark, I'd take tranquilizers to level off.(p.442)

increased

• None of us makes a sole vocation of this work, nor do we think its effectiveness would be *increased* if we did.(p.19)

• But, of course, this all went up the spout with my *increased* drinking.(p.182)

• My drinking habits *increased* in spite of my struggle for control.(p.305)

• But success brought *increased* social activities and I realized that many of my friends enjoyed a social drink with no apparent harm to themselves or others.(p.374)

• Gradually the quantity *increased*, the occasions for a drink came more frequently; a hard day, worries and pressure, bad news, good news – there were more and more reasons for a drink.(p.374)

• As income *increased*, the price of liquor *increased* proportionately.(p.398)

• The glow *increased*.(p.498)

• Then I was sent out to India and from then on drinking just *increased* and *increased*, and I started having two or three day spells instead of just the ordinary concentrated one day.(p.519)

increases

• Every encouragement was given me with frequent salary *increases*, but the sober times between "periods" became shorter.(p.254)

• If I focus on a problem, the problem *increases*; if I focus on the answer, the answer *increases*.(p.451)

increasing

• At present, our membership is *increasing* at the rate of about seven per cent a year.(p.xx)

• About that period, too, came *increasing* procrastination and the avoidance of responsibilities.(p.197)

• With *increasing* guilt and never-ending depression, I was too weak to continue this day-by-day suicide.(p.355)

• The horrors of *increasing* hangover sickness to occupy the entire day; nausea, dry heaves, the rocking bed, the nightmare-filled mind.(p.408)

• And as I went through pharmacy school, graduate school, medical school, internship, residency, and specialty training and, finally, went into practice, my drinking kept *increasing*.(p.441)

• But I thought it was because my responsibilities were *increasing*.(p.441)

increasingly

• I met all the people I wanted to meet; I saw all the places I wanted to see; I did all the things I wanted to do – and I was *increasingly* miserable.(p.225)

• Why did I want *increasingly* greater quantities of alcohol?(p.374)

• But I got drunk that night and stayed drunk, getting *increasingly* worse until I found A.A. ten years later.(p.404)

• My tongue had become *increasingly* skilled at venomous home truths.(p.405)

• With all this, it was becoming *increasingly* hard to maintain my front of distinction and respectability to the world.(p.435)

incredible

• My *incredible* behavior in the face of a desperate desire to stop was explained.(p.7)

• He does absurd, *incredible*, tragic things while drinking.(p.21)

• The prosaic steel girder is a mass of electrons whirling around each other at *incredible* speed.(p.48)

• When drinking, or getting over a bout, an alcoholic, sometimes the model of honesty when normal, will do *incredible* things.(p.140)

• It may seem *incredible* that these men are to become happy, respected, and useful once more.(p.153)

• As I write these words, it seems *incredible* that these things should have happened to me, for they are, truly, against all my instincts and training.(p.536)

incredibly

• I was to know happiness, peace, and usefulness, in a way of life that is *incredibly* more wonderful as time passes.(p.8)

• He is often perfectly sensible and well balanced concerning everything except liquor, but in that respect he is *incredibly* dishonest and selfish.(p.21)

incurable

• Doctors had pronounced him *incurable*.(p.11)

• Why he bothered with me as long as he did I shall never know, for he knew there was no answer for me in medicine and he, like all doctors of his day, had been taught that the alcoholic was *incurable* and should be ignored.(p.307)

indebted

• We are greatly *indebted* to the doctor in attendance there, for he, although it might prejudice his own work, has told us of his belief in ours.(p.162)

indebtedness

• It would be impossible for me to pass over this year without mentioning my love for, and my *indebtedness* to these two wonderful people who are no longer with us.(p.280)

indecision

• In thinking about our day we may face *indecision*.(p.86)

indeed

• The unselfishness of these men as we have come to know them, the entire absence of profit motive, and their community spirit, is *indeed* inspiring to one who has labored long and wearily in this alcoholic field.(p.xxv)

• Then faith would be dead *indeed*.(p.15)

• The central fact of our lives today is the absolute certainty that our Creator has entered into our hearts and lives in a way which is *indeed* miraculous.(p.25)

• Here are thousands of men and women, worldly *indeed*.(p.50)

• *Indeed*, I was beginning to see that I would require implicit faith, like a small child, if I was going to get anywhere.(p.259)

• *Indeed*, I was always well on my way before I would undertake to go visiting at all.(p.301)

• *Indeed*, she had known my cousin in Chicago.(p.414)

• *Indeed*, it seemed that I cared too much.(p.440)

• I was very fortunate *indeed* not to have suffered any brain damage.(p.480)

• *Indeed*, without their aid we couldn't possibly have gone on.(p.496)

• We worked in five below zero weather, fixing on an elm tree a wrought iron device which modestly proclaimed that he was *indeed* a country doctor.(p.540)

• I stood off and took a long look at life and the values I found in it: I saw a paradox, that he who loses his life does *indeed* find it.(p.542)

• What is much more important to me, A.A. has taught me that through this simple program I may experience a change in this reaction pattern that will *indeed* allow me to "match calamity with serenity."(p.544)

• *Indeed*, I had to drink now to live, to cope with the demands of everyday existence.(p.556)

indefinable

• The expression on the faces of the women, that *indefinable* something in the eyes of the men, the stimulating and electric atmosphere of the place, conspired to let him know that here was haven at last.(p.160)

independent

• I was doing very well with that and general upholstering work, and there was every indication that I would be financially *independent* by the time I reached middle age.(p.232)

• So I rocked along my merry *independent* way until June, when I went out selling auto polish in New England.(p.247)

• Within a year of my return to Detroit, A.A. was a definitely established little group of about a dozen members and I too was established in a modest but steady job handling an *independent* dry-cleaning route of my own.(p.283)

• With this specialized training, and a liberal business education in the school of hard knocks, I was able to set up shop some two years later as an *independent* accountant.(p.284)

• It had never occurred to me before that I could live simply and be *independent* of my family.(p.409)

indescribable

• The *indescribable* torture has me again.(p.501)

indescribably

• But there exists among us a fellowship, a friendliness, and an understanding which is *indescribably* wonderful.(p.17)

indestructible

• It left us dazed, because he had seemed so *indestructible*.(p.370)

India

• I returned to my home in Lucknow, *India*, at the end of November last year from a vacation in one of the most famous beauty spots in our country, a mountain resort 6,800 feet up, with a wonderful lake.(p.342)

• Then I was sent out to *India* and from then on drinking just increased and increased, and I started

having two or three day spells instead of just the ordinary concentrated one day.(p.519)
• *India* lent itself to drinking then, if you were disposed to drink, because you lived in bungalows; you didn't live all together as you do at home in an Officer's Mess.(p.519)

Indian
• For this officer in the *Indian* Army, going on the wagon was not enough; attempts at control failed.(p.342)
• I eventually became a schoolmaster, but gave up that profession to join the *Indian* Army.(p.342)
• From a Canadian reservation to overseas bars to New England lockups, an *Indian* traveled a long trail that finally led him home to A.A.(p.474)
• I proud to be son of Tall Man, American *Indian*, and member of A.A. for many moons.(p.474)
• I was born a Maliseet *Indian* on reservation in Canada.(p.474)
• By grace of God I stop, think two things: This would kill good mother and father; then remember boys talk about *Indian* fellow who been sober three years.(p.475)
• I find *Indian* fellow.(p.475)
• Maine newsletter (Boomerang) say: "With tireless devotion and humility, this venerable *Indian* gentleman traveled thousands of miles humbly pleading for sobriety.(p.476)
• This sober *Indian* say to sick, red-eyed alcoholic who want good medicine: "Put cork in bottle.(p.477)
• I was going to be sent to the *Indian* Civil Service, which, in those days, meant that people thought you had a certain amount of brains.(p.517)

Indiana
• It was a small town -- Liberty, *Indiana*.(p.262)

Indians
• Soon found wet canteens serve drinks to *Indians* in uniform.(p.474)
• To *Indians*, I say: "Don't be afraid to join A.A.(p.477)
• I once hear people say only *Indians* crazy when drunk.(p.477)
• If so, A.A. full of *Indians*.(p.477)

indicate
• Surveys of groups in the United States and Canada *indicate* that A.A. is reaching out, not only to more and more people, but to a wider and wider range.(p.xxii)
• The foregoing pages (though addressed only to wives) *indicate* the problems such people may face.(p.121)
• Nearly always, these antics *indicate* nothing more than temporary conditions.(p.141)
• My children had lost respect for me and, in fact, it was only after three or four years of sobriety that any of them ever said anything to me to *indicate* that I had recouped even a little of their respect.(p.215)

indicated
• It also *indicated* that strenuous work, one alcoholic with another, was vital to permanent recovery.(p.xvii)
• He soon *indicated* he was anxious to see us.(p.40)
• If we have obtained permission, have consulted with others, asked God to help and the drastic step is *indicated* we must not shrink.(p.80)
• Because it affected me so strenuously, they felt that hospitalization was *indicated* and I awoke in a hospital.(p.207)
• The physician wasn't hooked, he thought -- he just prescribed drugs medically *indicated* for his many ailments.(p.439)
• Therefore, every pill was medically *indicated* at the time it was taken.(p.443)

indicates
• The distinguished American psychologist, William James, in his book "Varieties of Religious Experience," *indicates* a multitude of ways in which men have discovered God.(p.28)

indication
• If there is any *indication* that he wants to stop, have a good talk with the person most interested in him -- usually his wife.(p.90)
• I was doing very well with that and general upholstering work, and there was every *indication* that I would be financially independent by the time I reached middle age.(p.232)
• I was "too important" to show any *indication* of being a drunk.(p.328)
• As an *indication* of just how confused and mixed up I was, just as soon as I could I left the office and hurried around to tell other patients that I was getting better.(p.470)

indications
• Despite contrary *indications*, I had little doubt that a mighty purpose and rhythm underlay all.(p.10)
• The first definite *indications* of an alcoholic pattern began to arise when I would go to New York on business and disappear, and wind up in Philadelphia or Boston for two or three day periods.(p.213)

indicted
• I was *indicted* for the crime of murder in the first degree.(p.508)
• In the meantime I had been *indicted* for the second crime, attempted murder.(p.508)

indifference
• He may demand that the family find God in a hurry, or exhibit amazing *indifference* to them and say he is above worldly considerations.(p.128)

indignant
• He becomes angry, *indignant*, self-pitying.(p.61)
• She is *indignant* about it, and has a warrant out for our arrest.(p.79)

indispensable
• We have emphasized willingness as being *indispensable*.(p.76)
• Their services are often *indispensable* in treating a newcomer and in following his case afterward.(p.133)
• But these are *indispensable*.(p.570)

individual
• As we discovered the principles by which the *individual* alcoholic could live, so we had to evolve principles by which the A.A. groups and A.A. as a whole could survive and function effectively.(p.xix)
• Unlike the feelings of the ship's passengers, however, our joy in escape from disaster does not subside as we go our *individual* ways.(p.17)
• When this sort of thinking is fully established in an *individual* with alcoholic tendencies, he has probably placed himself beyond human aid, and unless locked up, may die or go permanently insane.(p.24)
• Each *individual*, in the personal stories, describes in his own language and from his own point of view the way he established his relationship with God.(p.29)
• We do not like to pronounce any *individual* as alcoholic, but you can quickly diagnose yourself.(p.31)
• Our behavior is as absurd and incomprehensible with respect to the first drink as that of an *individual* with a passion, say, for jay-walking.(p.37)
• To all appearance he is a stable, well balanced *individual*.(p.39)
• The practical *individual* of today is a stickler for facts and results.(p.48)
• They are questions for each *individual* to settle for himself.(p.50)
• It is seldom wise to approach an *individual*, who still smarts from our injustice to him, and announce that we have gone religious.(p.77)
• If your husband is otherwise a normal *individual*, your chances are good at this stage.(p.113)
• Each *individual* should consult his own conscience.(p.132)
• Firing such an *individual* may prove a blessing to him.(p.141)
• One instance comes to mind in which a malicious *individual* was always making friendly little jokes about an alcoholic's drinking exploits.(p.145)
• He walked to the hospital to save bus fare and did it gladly in order to be helpful to an *individual* he had never even seen.(p.208)
• I wanted "ripe" prospects and I didn't feel that I would get very far chasing *individual* drunks in and out of bars.(p.281)
• No one *individual* can carry all the burdens of the world.(p.382)
• Under the skilled guidance of an expert practitioner I wallowed in the world's *individual* and collective mental agony.(p.434)
• Now I had to face up to the fact that knowledge of this sort, applied to my *individual* case, was not power.(p.435)
• I realized that I was trying to pin everything on an *individual* -- not the book or the group or the Higher Power, or anything else.(p.472)
• But as he continued to talk, I realized that this was the first time I had met a person who had the same problems I did and who, I sincerely believe, understood me as an *individual*.(p.494)
• Repeated year on end, they are horrible -- frightening and degrading, a chronicle of tragedy which may be greater because the *individual* undergoing the tragedy, myself, knew what was happening, and yet refused to do anything to stop it.(p.538)
• But *individual* welfare follows close afterward.(p.565)
• And no group, regional committee, or *individual* should ever take any action that might greatly affect A.A. as a whole without conferring with the trustees of the General Service Board.(p.565)

individually
• What we do with it is our own business; how we use it is up to us *individually*.(p.473)

individuals
• The basic principles of the A.A. program, it appears, hold good for *individuals* with many different lifestyles, just as the program has brought recovery to those of many different nationalities.(p.xxii)
• I expressed my entire willingness to approach these *individuals*, admitting my wrong.(p.13)
• With many *individuals* the methods which I employed are successful, but I have never been successful with an alcoholic of your description."(p.27)
• We think it no concern of ours what religious bodies our members identify themselves with as *individuals*.(p.28)
• We looked upon this world of warring *individuals*, warring theological systems, and inexplicable calamity, with deep skepticism.(p.46)
• We looked askance at many *individuals* who claimed to be godly.(p.46)
• I told him that I had not had a drink for ninety days and that I had come to the conclusion that I was one of those *individuals* who couldn't drink.(p.200)
• I had no resentments against *individuals* -- the whole world was all wrong.(p.244)
• Then and then only, after a thorough indoctrination by eight or nine *individuals*, was I allowed to attend my first meeting.(p.291)
• We didn't save the world, but we did manage to help some *individuals*.(p.496)

indoctrination
• Then and then only, after a thorough *indoctrination* by eight or nine individuals, was I allowed to attend my first meeting.(p.291)

induced
• On hearing that, these people *induced* me to make the move immediately and join them as a senior partner, which I did.(p.220)

inducement
• (No home brew as an *inducement*).(p.303)

indulge
• We read wordy books and *indulge* in windy arguments, thinking we believe this universe needs no God to explain it.(p.49)
• We try not to *indulge* in cynicism over the state of the nations, nor do we carry the world's troubles on our shoulders.(p.132)
• I had my own business, successful enough for me to *indulge* most of my desires.(p.225)

indulged
• We have *indulged* in spiritual intoxication.(p.128)
• So I *indulged* with my comrades in everything the Far East had to offer.(p.231)
• It was fun at first, since I never had *indulged* before.(p.370)
• I was nothing more than a spoiled, *indulged*, and talented brat.(p.418)

indulgence
• I soon discovered that a couple of drinks would alleviate my gastric distress, at least for a few hours at a time, so it was not at all difficult for me to return to my former excessive *indulgence*.(p.174)

indulgent
• My father, as I have said, was very *indulgent* and loved me dearly, and knew how to get around me.(p.389)

indulging
• When I was about forty-seven, after *indulging* in all kinds of self-deception to control my drinking, I arrived at a period when I felt convinced I had to have so much alcohol every day and that the real problem was to control how much.(p.214)

industrial
• The other day an approach was made to the vice president of a large *industrial* concern.(p.148)
• I came directly to a growing *industrial* city in the middle west, where I have lived practically ever since.(p.231)
• But I hardly tasted anything for two years and started in business for myself, founding a mattress factory which is today an important *industrial* enterprise in our city.(p.232)

industry
• So I spent much of my time calling on the people who I felt would logically come in contact with alcoholic cases, doctors, ministers, lawyers and the personnel men in *industry*.(p.281)

ineffective
- I was never drunk on the job, never missed a day's work, was seldom rendered totally ***ineffective*** by a hangover and kept my liquor expenses well within my adequate budget.(p.433)

inescapable
- I was caught in a cycle of alcohol and sedation that was proving ***inescapable*** and consciousness had become intolerable.(p.304)

inevitable
- I felt this was ***inevitable*** and wondered if the bank was doing the man an injustice.(p.138)
- Sitting in a Second Avenue bar, accepting drinks from anyone who offered, after my small stake was gone; or sitting at home alone, with the ***inevitable*** glass in my hand, I would remember, and remembering, I would drink faster, seeking speedy oblivion.(p.225)
- My husband was an alcoholic -- I had only contempt for those without my own amazing capacity -- the outcome was ***inevitable***.(p.225)
- He knew too well that didn't mean a thing, just as I knew in my heart that it would be only a question of time -- a few days, a week, or even a month, it was ***inevitable*** -- till I would be off on another bender.(p.257)
- The ***inevitable*** result of this discovery was that I soon learned that beer made a very good chaser for whiskey.(p.298)
- The ***inevitable*** always happened.(p.361)
- I'd claw my way back to "respectability" and stay there -- until the ***inevitable*** next time.(p.432)
- I knew it didn't make any difference where I started, the ***inevitable*** end would be skid row.(p.548)

inevitably
- All of us felt at times that we were regaining control, but such intervals -- usually brief -- were ***inevitably*** followed by still less control, which led in time to pitiful and incomprehensible demoralization.(p.30)
- But there was always the curious mental phenomenon that parallel with our sound reasoning there ***inevitably*** ran some insanely trivial excuse for taking the first drink.(p.37)
- ***Inevitably*** your lives will be fuller for doing so.(p.120)
- Some of us struggle with these people because we know that they are really very sick, but we also know that short of some miracle, we are not going to help them except temporarily, and that they will ***inevitably*** get worse and worse until one of two things happens.(p.308)
- Living with fear and tension ***inevitably*** results in wanting to ease that tension, which alcohol seems to do temporarily.(p.380)
- He even went to bat for me before the court martial that ***inevitably*** followed and, as a result, I drew only thirty days -- fifteen in solitary.(p.428)

inexperienced
- Being still ***inexperienced*** and having just made conscious contact with God, it is not probable that we are going to be inspired at all times.(p.87)

inexplicable
- We looked upon this world of warring individuals, warring theological systems, and ***inexplicable*** calamity, with deep skepticism.(p.46)

inexplicably
- He was ***inexplicably*** different.(p.9)

infallibility
- A.A. has given me serenity of purpose, the opportunity to be of service to God and to the people about me, and I am serene in the ***infallibility*** of these principles that provide the fulfillment of my purpose.(p.551)

infancy
- In the midst of an understanding and sympathetic family, these vagaries of dad's spiritual ***infancy*** will quickly disappear.(p.129)

inferior
- I early decided that the wine of America was very ***inferior*** stuff and took up beer instead.(p.231)

inferiorities
- I had no ***inferiorities***.(p.498)

inferiority
- The alarming physical and mental symptoms, the deepening pall of remorse, depression and ***inferiority*** that settled down on our loved ones -- these things terrified and distracted us.(p.106)
- I look back and remember these things because they made me very unhappy, and added to my feeling of ***inferiority*** at never being the same as other people.(p.261)
- The grand fellow who at my call made me a hail-fellow-well-met, who gave me such a fine voice, as we sang "Hail, hail, the gang's all here," and "Sweet Adeline," who gave me freedom from fear and feelings of ***inferiority***.(p.498)
- The war leaves me with a pair of blankets, a toilet kit, a sweater knit by my sister, and a still greater ***inferiority***.(p.499)

inferno
- After one of those days of ***inferno***, I wobbled from a hotel bar to a brokerage office.(p.4)

infidelity
- There had been no real ***infidelity***, for loyalty to my wife, helped at times by extreme drunkenness, kept me out of those scrapes.(p.3)

infinite
- He stood in the Presence of ***Infinite*** Power and Love.(p.56)
- We trust ***infinite*** God rather than our finite selves.(p.68)
- This painful past may be of ***infinite*** value to other families still struggling with their problem.(p.124)
- Therefore, these seventeen A.A.'s, and hundreds of thousands like them, have been saved years of ***infinite*** suffering.(p.315)

infinitely
- I have since been brought into a way of living ***infinitely*** more satisfying and, I hope, more useful than the life I lived before.(p.42)
- But with the alcoholic, whose hope is the maintenance and growth of a spiritual experience, this business of resentment is ***infinitely*** grave.(p.66)
- Though it is ***infinitely*** better that he have no relapse at all, as has been true with many of our men, it is by no means a bad thing in some cases.(p.120)

inflict
- Why they should be subjected to the tortures we ***inflict*** upon them, I cannot explain.(p.178)

influence
- I was very much interested in athletics, and because of this and parental ***influence***, I didn't drink or smoke in either grade or high school.(p.287)
- Home life was again a restraining ***influence***.(p.287)
- Her ***influence*** and companionship managed to lessen my drinking to some degree.(p.359)
- My responsibilities had been a restraining ***influence***.(p.379)
- It is estimated that two-thirds of the men in prison were under the ***influence*** of alcohol and/or drugs when they committed their offenses.(p.458)
- It is going strong still, these eight years later, and some of its members have been of great ***influence*** for good in state-wide A.A. work.(p.541)

inform
- We hope this volume will ***inform*** and comfort those who are, or who may be affected.(p.18)
- This practice enables us to lend a hand, at the same time avoiding certain alluring distractions of the road, about which any traveling man can ***inform*** you.(p.162)

informal
- At these ***informal*** gatherings one may often see from 50 to 200 persons.(p.16)
- Then, in this eastern city, there are ***informal*** meetings such as we have described to you, where you may now see scores of members.(p.162)
- A few months later one of the men who had been in touch with the group in Akron came to Chicago to live, and then there were three of us who continued to have ***informal*** meetings quite regularly.(p.294)

informality
- The very practical approach to his problems, the absence of intolerance of any kind, the ***informality***, the genuine democracy, the uncanny understanding which these people had were irresistible.(p.160)

information
- Thanks for the ***information***."(p.39)
- You need this ***information*** to put yourself in his place, to see how you would like him to approach you if the tables were turned.(p.90)
- If there is no Al-Anon listing in your local telephone book, you may obtain further ***information*** on Al-Anon Family Groups by writing to its World Service Office: Box 182, Madison Square Station, New York, NY 10159.(p.121)
- This is a condition which, in ordinary life, would produce untold grief; there might be scandalous gossip, laughter at the expense of other people, and a tendency to take advantage of intimate ***information***.(p.125)
- He gave me ***information*** about the subject of alcoholism which was undoubtedly helpful.(p.180)
- "There is a principle which is a bar against all ***information***, which is proof against all arguments and which cannot fail to keep a man in everlasting ignorance -- that principle is contempt prior to investigation."(p.570)

informed
- My weary and despairing wife was ***informed*** that it would all end with heart failure during delirium tremens, or I would develop a wet brain, perhaps within a year.(p.7)
- I resented this very much, until she ***informed*** me that they were a couple of drunks just as I was.(p.184)
- I certainly wasn't my shy, quiet self that night -- as I was ***informed*** the next morning.(p.353)

informing
- He startled me by ***informing*** me that he was an alcoholic, that he had found a way which so far enabled him to live without taking a drink, and that the main idea was to find a way how not to take that first drink.(p.218)
- In the first year there were episodes such as kicking Priscilla in the shins, getting the lock changed on the desk in the A.A. Club, because I, as secretary, didn't want the Intergroup secretary "interfering," and taking an older woman member out to lunch for the express purpose of ***informing*** her that she was "a phony."(p.416)

infringement
- By the time I had completed law school I had picked up some experience in patent law, for I remained with the patent law firm and worked too in Washington where they found that I was a capable ***infringement*** investigator.(p.213)

ingenuity
- Showing all the courage and ***ingenuity*** that I had not used in a positive way, I covered my tracks and hid from my family so successfully that they did not find me for months.(p.401)

ingredient
- Here I found an ***ingredient*** that had been lacking in any other effort I had made to save myself.(p.436)

ingredients
- They seemed to have all the ***ingredients*** for successful living.(p.310)

inherent
- These facts appear to be of extreme medical importance; because of the extraordinary possibilities of rapid growth ***inherent*** in this group they may mark a new epoch in the annals of alcoholism.(p.xxiii)

inherit
- In fact, as I look back, I have often thought that they probably concluded that they would put up with me for a couple of years, that I couldn't live much longer, and that they would ***inherit*** whatever was left of the practice.(p.215)

inheritance
- I had accepted Catholicism somewhat as an ***inheritance***.(p.220)

inherited
- He ***inherited*** a lucrative automobile agency.(p.35)
- They ***inherited*** wealth and acquired more.(p.401)

inhibitions
- I found that even then I had fears and ***inhibitions***.(p.483)

inhospitable
- The bill collectors, the sheriffs, the angry taxi drivers, the policemen, the bums, the pals, and even the ladies they sometimes brought home -- our husbands thought we were so ***inhospitable***.(p.106)

initial
- I stayed in Akron two or three weeks on my ***initial*** trip trying to absorb as much of the program and philosophy as possible.(p.291)

initiation
- A retired Navy man looks back over twenty years of drinking, to add up his A.A. "***initiation*** fee."(p.396)
- A few times at meetings, I have heard this statement: "Members of A.A. have paid the highest ***initiation*** fee of any club members in the world."(p.396)
- However, a rough estimate of one alcoholic's ***initiation*** fee seemed possible.(p.396)
- Like most statistics, it doesn't prove anything -- just satisfies a little curiosity engendered by the wail "Oh, those ***initiation*** fees" that prompted this investigation.(p.399)
- Incalculable are the intangible ***initiation*** fees that A.A. members have paid: the sick, sick hangovers, the remorse, guilt, broken homes, jails, and institutions, and the mental anguish in general that has been generated over the years.(p.399)
- But now, with His help and grace, this child of His has paid his ***initiation*** fee for good, as long as he re-

members to stay away from that first drink (the one that does all the damage) one day at a time.(p.399)

inject

• In the garage, I would put the needle in my vein and then try to figure out exactly how much medication to *inject* to overcome the pep pills while adding to the sleeping pills while ignoring the tranquilizers, in order to get just enough to be able to pull out the needle, jerk the tourniquet, throw it in the car, slam the car door shut, run down the hall, and fall in bed before I fell asleep.(p.442)

injecting

• However, for a period of time I was *injecting* Pentothal intravenously to put myself to sleep.(p.442)

injection

• Following an *injection* I would have to keep one hand busy scratching my constantly itching nose and would also have sudden uncontrollable urges to vomit.(p.442)

injunction

• He went on talking and told me that he had found the plan has a basis of love, and the practice of Christ's *injunction*, "Love thy neighbor as thyself."(p.236)

injure

• 9.Made direct amends to such people wherever possible, except when to do so would *injure* them or others.(p.59)

injured

• Luck then deserts him and he is slightly *injured* several times in succession.(p.38)

• The next day, they called me in for an examination, and the doctor wouldn't let me continue working and pardoned me from the plant for ten days because he said my eye had been *injured*.(p.205)

injuries

• On our grudge list we set opposite each name our *injuries*.(p.65)

injurious

• The sensation is so elusive that, while they admit it is *injurious*, they cannot after a time differentiate the true from the false.(p.xxvi)

injury

• Following the elimination of alcohol, there was found to be no permanent brain *injury*.(p.xxix)

injustice

• It is seldom wise to approach an individual, who still smarts from our *injustice* to him, and announce that we have gone religious.(p.77)

• I felt this was inevitable and wondered if the bank was doing the man an *injustice*.(p.138)

inmate

• Of course, an *inmate* must begin living the A.A. way "inside," if he is to stand a chance "outside."(p.458)

inmates

• I lived through a week of the fidgets because I had agreed to address a group of alcoholic *inmates* in one of our state mental hospitals.(p.283)

• However, one thing I am certain of: *Inmates* in prison who attend A.A. have their chances of remaining free greatly enhanced – this is a proved fact.(p.458)

• Shortly thereafter, I was selected, with eight other *inmates* out of the 10,000 in the state's prisons at that time, to attend a school designed to take former "management problems" like me and convert them into paracounselors.(p.462)

innate

• That my own *innate* selfishness and stubbornness are the evils which, if left unguarded, can drive me to alcohol.(p.473)

inner

• Above all, he believed he had acquired such a profound knowledge of the *inner* workings of his mind and its hidden springs that relapse was unthinkable.(p.26)

• The times in which I grew up (the Prohibition era immortalized by Scott Fitzgerald and John Held Jr.) had taught me to be gay with the gayest; my own *inner* urges led me to outdo them all.(p.225)

• And, accepting, I felt a new *inner* comfort, and the willingness and strength to do something about the traits I couldn't live with.(p.229)

• There was a concrete program, designed to secure the greatest possible *inner* security for us long-time escapists.(p.229)

• I have had my share of problems, heartaches and disappointments, because that is life, but also I have known a great deal of joy, and a peace that is the handmaiden of an *inner* freedom, I have a wealth of friends and, with my A.A. friends, an unusual quality of fellowship.(p.312)

• It has brought about a revelation of self, the discovery of an *inner* being, an awareness of God.(p.355)

• Try for *inner* contentment.(p.382)

• I find an *inner* pleasure in simple things.(p.383)

• It was nothing to my own *inner* distress, my self-reproach, and my self-loathing, for was I not bearing out all the horrible things I had always suspected of myself?(p.404)

• I was really scolding my mortal enemy, the *inner* me.(p.408)

• I have achieved the *inner* confidence to write quite unlike Shakespeare, and I have sold a good deal of what I've written.(p.416)

• Above all, I was suffering *inner* pain because my performance and my accomplishments in life failed to live up to my own expectations of myself.(p.557)

• With few exceptions our members find that they have tapped an unsuspected *inner* resource which they presently identify with their own conception of a Power greater than themselves.(p.569)

• I now conceive the psychiatrist's job to be the task of breaking down the patient's *inner* resistance so that which is inside him will flower, as under the activity of the A.A. program."(p.571)

innermost

• We learned that we had to fully concede to our *innermost* selves that we were alcoholics.(p.30)

innocent

• I didn't want to jeopardize the lives of *innocent* people by driving an automobile while intoxicated, but I did.(p.199)

• An attorney sat at the side of the bed where I was lying, and he sat on the edge of his chair and looked as *innocent* as a baby.(p.268)

• So *innocent*, so discreet!(p.370)

• There was the father one lost respect for at the age of eleven, because the father broke his solemn word in a circumstance where you, eleven years old, had assumed guilt when you were *innocent*; but the father would not believe you, no matter what; and to ease his suffering you "confessed" and were "forgiven," only – months later – to have your "guilt" brought up – only he and you knew what he was talking bout -- brought up in front of the stern grandmother.(p.533)

• So did the waterboy on the high school football team attempt to revenge himself on the big brother who was the star quarterback; for I was the waterboy and my brother was the star quarterback, *innocent* of everything except the fact that he was a star quarterback.(p.537)

innumerable

• Another reason for the wide acceptance of A.A. was the ministration of friends -- friends in medicine, religion, and the press, together with *innumerable* others who became our able and persistent advocates.(p.xx)

• Although these reparations take *innumerable* forms, there are some general principles which we find guiding.(p.79)

• It may mean sharing your money and your home, counseling frantic wives and relatives, *innumerable* trips to police courts, sanitariums, hospitals, jails and asylums.(p.97)

• We have told *innumerable* lies to protect our pride and our husbands' reputations.(p.105)

inquire

• After making our review we ask God's forgiveness and *inquire* what corrective measures should be taken.(p.86)

inquired

• They explained their need and *inquired* if she had a first class alcoholic prospect.(p.156)

• So he *inquired*, what did our friend have on the ball?(p.163)

inquiries

• This brought a rush of 800 frantic *inquiries* into the little New York office which meanwhile had been established.(p.xviii)

• News of this got on the world wires; *inquiries* poured in again and many people went to the bookstores to get the book "Alcoholics Anonymous."(p.xviii)

• Avoid answering these *inquiries* as much as you can.(p.115)

• In the spring of 1939, the Big Book was printed, and we had two *inquiries* from the New York office because of a fifteen-minute radio talk that was made.(p.294)

inquiring

• I started *inquiring* where I could get a drink and, of course, I found that it wasn't hard.(p.490)

inquiry

• *Inquiry* by scientific, medical, and religious societies will be welcomed.(p.xiv)

• Each *inquiry* was painstakingly answered; pamphlets and books were sent out.(p.xviii)

• The spirit of modern scientific *inquiry*, research and invention was almost unknown.(p.51)

insane

• When this sort of thinking is fully established in an individual with alcoholic tendencies, he has probably placed himself beyond human aid, and unless locked up, may die or go permanently *insane*.(p.24)

• The *insane* idea won out.(p.37)

• However intelligent we may have been in other respects, where alcohol has been involved, we have been strangely *insane*.(p.38)

• He is violent, or appears definitely *insane* when drunk.(p.110)

• Long since I had come to believe I was *insane* because I did so many things I didn't want to do.(p.199)

• I quite naturally came to the conclusion that I must be *insane*.(p.199)

• I had never been inside of an *insane* asylum and I really thought I was going to a private hospital.(p.387)

• Was I *insane*?(p.406)

• I wasn't *insane*.(p.414)

• Also, I was *insane* at times -- according to society's yardstick.(p.458)

• Her brother had been a drinker and had died in a State Hospital for the *insane*.(p.498)

• The *insane* asylum lies ahead.(p.502)

• The fear and the *insane* idea are taken away.(p.505)

insanely

• He is always more or less *insanely* drunk.(p.21)

• But there was always the curious mental phenomenon that parallel with our sound reasoning there inevitably ran some *insanely* trivial excuse for taking the first drink.(p.37)

• But even in this type of beginning we are obliged to admit that our justification for a spree was *insanely* insufficient in the light of what always happened.(p.37)

• In a weak moment he may take your dislike of his high-stepping friends as one of those *insanely* trivial excuses to drink.(p.120)

insanity

• Then came the insidious *insanity* of that first drink, and on Armistice Day 1935, I was off again.(p.8)

• Rumor had it that he had been committed for alcoholic *insanity*.(p.9)

• Many pursue it into the gates of *insanity* or death.(p.30)

• Whatever the precise definition of the word may be, we call this plain *insanity*.(p.37)

• I rather appreciated your ideas about the subtle *insanity* which precedes the first drink, but I was confident it could not happen to me after what I had learned.(p.40)

• Business failure, *insanity*, fatal illness, suicide -- these calamities in his immediate family embittered and depressed him.(p.56)

• The *insanity* of alcohol returns and we drink again.(p.66)

• Sometimes there were screaming delirium and *insanity*.(p.107)

• Again it was the old, insidious *insanity* -- that first drink.(p.154)

• The word "*insanity*" came through clearly – and repugnantly.(p.332)

• A few months after that, I was released and left the world of *insanity*, only to return to the world of alcoholic *insanity*.(p.370)

• I did not know that I had no power over alcohol, that I, alone and unaided, could not stop; that I was on a downgrade, tearing along at full speed with all my brakes gone, and that the end would be a total smash-up, death or *insanity*.(p.408)

• I had already feared *insanity* for a long time.(p.408)

• So I sat down with me and went over the facts behind the convulsions: personality changes, daily headaches, sense of impending doom, sense of impending *insanity*.(p.444)

• I suddenly remembered one of my first A.A. meetings, where I heard, "If you are an alcoholic and if you continue to drink, the end is death or *insanity*."(p.461)

• With their help I also saw that certainly, because of some of the things I had done during the years, I was bordering on *insanity*, and so, facing the record, I tried to believe that a Power greater than I could and would restore me to sanity.(p.471)

• I laugh at the *insanity* of it.(p.507)

• I've been benefited from a dictionary definition I found that reads: "rationalization is giving a socially acceptable reason for socially unacceptable behavior, and socially unacceptable behavior is a form of *insanity*."(p.551)

inscription
• I was staring at an inch of the tape which bore the *inscription* XYZ-32.(p.4)

insecure
• When I was nineteen, I married a fine man who had never known an *insecure* moment in his life, let alone the trials and tribulations of booze.(p.369)
• She, more than the others, showed me what ailed me basically, why I was immature and *insecure.*(p.409)

insecurities
• The drinker's mind is full of uncertainties and *insecurities.*(p.331)

insecurity
• It brings misunderstanding, fierce resentment, financial *insecurity*, disgusted friends and employers, warped lives of blameless children, sad wives and parents -- anyone can increase the list.(p.18)
• Fear of people and of economic *insecurity* will leave us.(p.84)
• It was never boring, but I developed a feeling of deep *insecurity.*(p.369)
• But it did not take long for the pressures of living to bring out my immaturity and my *insecurity.*(p.420)
• In my late teens I became aware of emotions I'd not counted on; restlessness, anxiety, fear and *insecurity.*(p.545)

inseparable
• I teamed up with a cute little blonde with whom I was working at the office, and for about a year we were *inseparable.*(p.425)

inside
• As fast as he can, he pushes these memories far *inside* himself.(p.73)
• If he says yes, does he really mean it, or down *inside* does he think he is fooling you, and that after rest and treatment he will be able to get away with a few drinks now and then?(p.142)
• He could see the gay crowd *inside.*(p.154)
• He succumbed to that gay crowd *inside*, who laughed at their own misfortunes and understood his.(p.160)
• It was getting pretty dark and I hadn't turned on any lights, when some big fellow stepped *inside* the door and flipped on the light switch.(p.207)
• I began to know the *inside* of jails and workhouses.(p.255)
• However, I must have felt, deep down *inside* myself, that living the selfish life of a bachelor was only half living.(p.286)
• I would hang on to sobriety for short intervals, but always there would come the tide of an overpowering necessity to drink and, as I was engulfed in it, I felt such a sense of panic that I really believed I would die if I didn't get that drink *inside.*(p.306)
• Many retirees embrace alcoholism while secluded in motor trailers, rest homes, leisure-world bungalows, mountain cabins, or beach cottages, or even in penthouses, on yachts, and *inside* Palm Springs cabanas.(p.329)
• But they were all mixed up together, and I was all mixed up *inside.*(p.337)
• I had never been *inside* of an insane asylum and I really thought I was going to a private hospital.(p.387)
• I know that I was terribly screwed up *inside*, but I came out much worse.(p.387)
• *Inside*, I went right on being a mass of unlovely self-pity, queasy anxiety and sickening self-debasement.(p.400)
• The remorse would turn *inside* out, and become anticipatory pleasure.(p.408)
• I wore a man's raincoat, turned *inside* out, a present from a friend, for now my funds were low.(p.411)
• She said she felt too horrible *inside* to be pretty on the outside.(p.415)
• We broke open a window and got *inside.*(p.424)
• Of course, an inmate must begin living the A.A. way "*inside,*" if he is to stand a chance "outside."(p.458)
• While I was taking inventory in the cold-storage locker one Sunday, a wooden sign bolted to the *inside* door stopped me in my tracks.(p.461)
• The doctor has told me that if I don't give up *inside* work, I'll have tuberculosis.(p.500)
• Actually, of course, I wanted someone to listen to me, because when I had a few martinis *inside*, I became the great author I longed to be; and the right listener was in for some pretty highflown theories of literature and of genius.(p.536)
• I thought this would give me ego-strength, make me feel wanted and secure, and alleviate my fears, but again nothing changed *inside* me.(p.546)
• *Inside*, though, I was scared to death, for I knew that the time was coming (and it couldn't be too remote) when I would be unable to hold that job.(p.548)
• I now conceive the psychiatrist's job to be the task of breaking down the patient's inner resistance so that which is *inside* him will flower, as under the activity of the A.A. program."(p.571)

inside-out
• There is really nothing to dressing with chains and shackles on, once you learn the technique of pulling *inside-out* pants through the shackles.(p.460)

insidious
• Then came the *insidious* insanity of that first drink, and on Armistice Day 1935, I was off again.(p.8)
• Again it was the old, *insidious* insanity -- that first drink.(p.154)

insidiousness
• With a creeping *insidiousness*, drink had become more important than anything else.(p.226)
• The *insidiousness* of alcoholism is an appalling thing.(p.432)

insight
• In describing his suffering, his fears, his many years of groping for some answer to that which always seemed to remain unanswerable, he could have been describing me, and nothing short of experience and knowledge could have afforded him that much *insight!*(p.309)
• It pays daily in more harmonious relations with my fellow men, in ever clearer *insight* into the true meaning of life, and in the answering love and gratitude wherever and whenever I have been the instrument of God's will in the lives of others.(p.394)

insights
• Slowly, my life seemed to unfold before me, shedding *insights* on childhood resentments, jealousies, and fears that had mushroomed in adulthood, and also on the self-pity that I had wallowed in at every opportunity.(p.371)

insincere
• You will be making it possible for him to be *insincere.*(p.96)

insinuations
• But the firm became violently ill with my drunkenness and their course of treatment was to remove their ulcer, in the form of me, from the payroll, amid much fanfare and very personal and slighting remarks and *insinuations.*(p.300)

insist
• She may *insist* on knowing all the particulars.(p.81)
• But *insist* that if he is severely afflicted, there may be little chance he can recover by himself.(p.92)
• Let him know you are available if he wishes to make a decision and tell his story, but do not *insist* upon it if he prefers to consult someone else.(p.96)
• We absolutely *insist* on enjoying life.(p.132)

insisted
• When others showed us that "God-sufficiency" worked with them, we began to feel like those who had *insisted* the Wrights would never fly.(p.52)
• He said he was perfectly willing to go to jail if she *insisted.*(p.79)
• One day my secretary came in saying that Mr. B---- *insisted* on speaking with me.(p.136)
• While there I was called to the hospital in my home town to see a former partner who had *insisted* that I visit him.(p.257)
• Far from expecting praise for their deeds, they claimed the performance a privilege and *insisted* that they invariably received more than they gave.(p.310)
• The people there *insisted* on putting me in a ward, when Max and I both knew I ought to have a private room.(p.445)

insistence
• I could almost hear the sound of the preacher's voice as I sat, on still Sundays, way over there on the hillside; there was that proffered temperance pledge I never signed; my grandfather's good natured contempt of some church folk and their doings; his *insistence* that the spheres really had their music; but his denial of the preacher's right to tell him how he must listen; his fearlessness as he spoke of these things just before he died; these recollections welled up from the past.(p.10)

insistent
• There was an *insistent* yearning to enjoy life as we once did and a heartbreaking obsession that some new miracle of control would enable us to do it.(p.151)

insists
• He may not see at once that he has barely scratched a limitless lode which will pay dividends only if he mines it for the rest of his life and *insists* on giving away the entire product.(p.129)

insofar
• *Insofar* as religion was concerned, I had a Catholic training in my youth.(p.214)

insomnia
• I cannot remember just when I became the victim of *insomnia*, but I do know that the last year and a half I never went to bed sober a single night.(p.299)
• I sleep like a baby, and never give a thought to such a thing as *insomnia.*(p.303)
• But for some time, it was difficult to keep from taking a pill when I had an appropriate symptom, such as a cough, pain, anxiety, *insomnia*, a muscle spasm, or an upset stomach.(p.448)

insouciance
• To wear expensive clothes, to have bartenders know what to serve me before I ordered, to be recognized by headwaiters and shown to the best table, to play gin rummy for high stakes with the *insouciance* of a riverboat gambler -- these were the enduring values in life, I thought.(p.556)

inspect
• I got a job by myself which suited me down to the ground, because there was nobody really to interfere with what I did, one way or the other, and I usually had my nerves in good trim when anybody was coming around to *inspect.*(p.519)

inspected
• I found out later that my wife *inspected* it frequently.(p.176)
• Sometimes I would bring it in my pockets, but they were *inspected*, and that became too risky.(p.176)

inspection
• Never talk down to an alcoholic from any moral or spiritual hilltop; simply lay out the kit of spiritual tools for his *inspection.*(p.95)
• The boys at the Post Office used to bring me my jugs; mail couldn't be opened for *inspection* at the gate.(p.426)

inspiration
• Much has already been said about receiving strength, *inspiration*, and direction from Him who has all knowledge and power.(p.85)
• Here we ask God for *inspiration*, an intuitive thought or a decision.(p.86)
• What used to be the hunch or the occasional *inspiration* gradually becomes a working part of the mind.(p.87)
• Nevertheless, we find that our thinking will as time passes, be more and more on the plane of *inspiration.*(p.87)
• My alcoholism-prone mind, however, reminded me that all great authors had needed a stimulus to build up *inspiration* and inventiveness before each day's work.(p.331)
• She gave me such hope and *inspiration* that I set her right up on a pedestal.(p.472)

inspirational
• Here are some of the methods we have tried: Drinking beer only, limiting the number of drinks, never drinking alone, never drinking in the morning, drinking only at home, never having it in the house, never drinking during business hours, drinking only at parties, switching from scotch to brandy, drinking only natural wines, agreeing to resign if ever drunk on the job, taking a trip, not taking a trip, swearing off forever (with and without a solemn oath), taking more physical exercise, reading *inspirational* books, going to health farms and sanitariums, accepting voluntary commitment to asylums -- we could increase the list ad infinitum.(p.31)

inspire
• Bill was tall, grey haired, with the kind of asymmetrical good looks and pleasant easy manner that *inspire* confidence in the shaken and afraid.(p.413)

inspired
• It was fun to carom around the exclusive course which had *inspired* such awe in me as a lad.(p.4)
• Being still inexperienced and having just made conscious contact with God, it is not probable that we are going to be *inspired* at all times.(p.87)
• The law school experience was not *inspired* by a desire to follow patent law, which has been my profession since: I went to law school primarily to learn the law of contracts following my own experience with litigation.(p.212)
• There are so many to whom I feel deeply grateful; to my husband (and best critic), whose generous love, compassion and understanding have helped me along the way; to those before me in A.A. who *inspired* the first article I read, and the friend who sent that article to Frank; to Ruth for her personal note, and the first A.A. to talk to me; to my Bishop, whose

loving and believing spirit ***inspired*** me; and to all the members of the Houston Group who were so patient, kind and helpful -- and to countless others.(p.393)

• At age twenty-one, I enlisted in the Navy for two reasons: (1) to avoid being drafted into the Army, and (2) out of a burst of patriotic fervor ***inspired*** by the advent of World War II and as the result of an all-night drinking binge which found me sitting on the doorstep of the Navy recruiting office when the chief petty officer arrived to open for business at nine o'clock Monday morning.(p.398)

inspiring

• The unselfishness of these men as we have come to know them, the entire absence of profit motive, and their community spirit, is indeed ***inspiring*** to one who has labored long and wearily in this alcoholic field.(p.xxv)

instance

• Of course, there is such a thing as incompatibility, but in nearly every ***instance*** the alcoholic only seems to be unloving and inconsiderate; it is usually because he is warped and sickened that he says and does these appalling things.(p.108)

• Here, for ***instance***, is a typical example: An officer of one of the largest banking institutions in America knows I no longer drink.(p.138)

• One ***instance*** comes to mind in which a malicious individual was always making friendly little jokes about an alcoholic's drinking exploits.(p.145)

• There had been some occasions -- there was an automobile wreck, for ***instance*** -- when I had police escort home but not to jail, all of which, instead of doing me a favor, did me harm because I was then full of self-esteem as to the progress I had made both professionally and financially.(p.213)

• I remember one ***instance*** when he took off and went down to Cincinnati and was gone a week on a drunk.(p.262)

• For ***instance***, the fiftieth wedding anniversary of my wife's parents was the occasion for a huge family reunion at our home.(p.556)

instances

• In some ***instances*** there has been brief recovery, followed always by a still worse relapse.(p.31)

• We have heard of few ***instances*** where people, who showed definite signs of alcoholism, were able to stop for a long period because of an overpowering desire to do so.(p.32)

• We know but few ***instances*** where we have given these doctors a fair break.(p.73)

• In only a few ***instances*** has there been lack of patience and tolerance.(p.137)

• And the psychiatrist has had thousands of couches, and has put you and me on them many, many times, but he hasn't helped us very much, though he has tried hard; and we owe the clergy and the doctor and the psychiatrist a deep debt of gratitude, but they haven't helped our alcoholism, except in a rare few ***instances***.(p.352)

instant

• Fear froze me in my tracks, but the ***instant*** I turned back toward home this paralyzing fear left me.(p.276)

• We "***instant*** perfectionists" also are hypersensitive, alas.(p.331)

• ***Instant*** blackout was what it was, and it seemed delightful.(p.442)

• From that ***instant*** to this, nearly eight years later, I have not had the slightest urge to drink.(p.541)

instantly

• Sometimes they demand that dad bring them back ***instantly***!(p.123)

• I had worked so long in a profession where fakery, deceit, and untruths are tools of trade that I ***instantly*** recognized honesty when I heard it, from the mouths of A.A. members.(p.334)

• Having heard Bill speak, she was ***instantly*** sold.(p.412)

• In my mind's eye, I played and replayed scenes in which I was plucked magically from the bar where I stood nursing a drink, and was ***instantly*** exalted to some position of power and prestige.(p.560)

instead

• When writing or speaking publicly about alcoholism, we urge each of our Fellowship to omit his personal name, designating himself ***instead*** as "a member of Alcoholics Anonymous."(p.xiii)

• We now see that when we began to drink deliberately, ***instead*** of casually, there was little serious or effective thought during the period of premeditation of what the terrific consequences might be.(p.37)

• I have a shadowy recollection of being in an airplane bound for New York, and of finding a friendly taxicab driver at the landing field ***instead*** of my wife.(p.41)

• ***Instead*** of regarding ourselves as intelligent agents, spearheads of God's ever advancing Creation, we agnostics and atheists chose to believe that our human intelligence was the last word, the alpha and the omega, the beginning and end of all.(p.49)

• ***Instead***, we looked at the human defects of these people, and sometimes used their shortcomings as a basis of wholesale condemnation.(p.50)

• ***Instead*** we let Him demonstrate, through us, what He can do.(p.68)

• Where were we at fault, what should we have done ***instead***?(p.69)

• ***Instead***, the problem has been removed.(p.85)

• But if you are shaky, you had better work with another alcoholic ***instead***!(p.102)

• Attempt ***instead***, to put yourself in his place.(p.111)

• ***Instead***, you will capitalize them.(p.117)

• You, as well as your husband, ought to think of what you can put into life ***instead*** of how much you can take out.(p.120)

• ***Instead*** of treating the family as he should, he may retreat further into himself and feel he has spiritual justification for so doing.(p.129)

• ***Instead*** of developing new channels of activity for themselves, mother and children demand that he stay home and make up the deficiency.(p.131)

• Most of the time therefore, I did not take the morning drink which I craved so badly, but ***instead*** would fill up on large doses of sedatives to quiet the jitters, which distressed me terribly.(p.176)

• In fact, I admitted that from now on I was willing to let God take over, ***instead*** of me.(p.187)

• There had been some occasions -- there was an automobile wreck, for instance -- when I had police escort home but not to jail, all of which, ***instead*** of doing me a favor, did me harm because I was then full of self-esteem as to the progress I had made both professionally and financially.(p.213)

• In fact, after six months of living on food ***instead*** of on whiskey, I gained about thirty pounds.(p.220)

• I early decided that the wine of America was very inferior stuff and took up beer ***instead***.(p.231)

• ***Instead*** he told me that some of them wanted to talk to me and would be over to see me.(p.235)

• ***Instead***, over coffee cups, this man and his wife told me what had been done for them.(p.259)

• In the end I had two problems ***instead*** of one: Fear and alcohol.(p.275)

• ***Instead***, he got dressed, took me out, bought me three or four double shots and put me to bed.(p.278)

• I have faced life ***instead*** of running away from it.(p.285)

• ***Instead***, I quickly substituted one or another vivid scene from the nightmare of my later drinking.(p.286)

• I have stopped tilting at windmills, and ***instead*** have tried to accomplish the little daily tasks, unimportant in themselves, but tasks that are an integral part of living fully.(p.295)

• ***Instead*** of wanting to escape some perplexing problem, we experience a thrill of challenge in the opportunity it affords for another application of A.A. techniques, and we find ourselves tackling it with surprising vigor.(p.311)

• Today, I'm counting my blessings ***instead*** of my troubles.(p.355)

• ***Instead*** it was like a tap on the head with a small mallet.(p.402)

• I depended on optimism and ambition to live in society; when I began to tire, I had to depend on chemicals ***instead*** to keep going.(p.420)

• I talked the Old Man into letting me live in the photo lab ***instead*** of the barracks, and for eighteen months nothing interfered with my drinking.(p.426)

• ***Instead***, I had a 5:00 a.m. shutoff time.(p.441)

• But it quickly became obvious that he had this childish notion ***instead***: If he could get me to go to enough meetings while in the hospital, I would continue to go after he let me out.(p.447)

• But then, as I drank more and more, the alcohol seemed to affect my vision: ***Instead*** of continuing to see what was good about my wife, I began to see her defects.(p.450)

• The doctor, apparently realizing that one thing that I certainly needed was sleep, left a bottle of sleeping pills there and in my drunken state I took them all, ***instead*** of the one or two he had prescribed.(p.465)

• ***Instead***, I started going to a nice private sanitarium which, after the first visit, turned out to be more like a country club than anything else.(p.468)

• Am I willing to be honest with myself about myself and tell someone about myself, and am I willing to think of other people, of their needs ***instead*** of myself, in order to get rid of the drink problem?(p.503)

• So ***instead*** of going near A.A., I just browsed around for that first month.(p.510)

• Then ***instead*** of going out with A.A. again I went out with some of the other crowd, and off again I went.(p.511)

• If something does come along that sort of upsets me, ***instead*** of walking in and throwing a buck at the barman and asking for a drink, I walk into a telephone booth, drop a dime in the box, and call somebody who was so kind as to give me his name and telephone number to meet such an emergency.(p.511)

• Then I was sent out to India and from then on drinking just increased and increased, and I started having two or three day spells ***instead*** of just the ordinary concentrated one day.(p.519)

• On one of these trips, the judge must have thought I was worth saving, for ***instead*** of sending me to jail, he sent me to A.A. for one month.(p.526)

• ***Instead***, I had gotten sicker.(p.539)

• ***Instead*** of drinking in fancy bars and clubs, I had to carry a bottle of vodka in my briefcase, duck into public toilets, and gulp from the bottle, trembling, in order to keep from falling apart.(p.557)

instilled

• Their talk and action had ***instilled*** me with a certain amount of confidence, although I was not too absolutely certain.(p.189)

• The ambition to succeed was ***instilled*** in me by my Scandinavian parents who came to this country where opportunities were so great.(p.373)

instinct

• To create: Everyone does it, some at the ***instinct*** level, others in the arts.(p.535)

• What a revelation of ego and arrogance still remaining in me -- as if anyone, ***instinct*** and training apart, likes to be in jail or in an alcoholic ward or fired from his job.(p.536)

• After nearly eight years of sobriety in A.A., I still can set down such thoughts, "against my ***instinct*** and training," showing that I still consider myself a "special" person, entitled to special privileges.(p.536)

• Dr. Foster Kennedy, neurologist: "This organization of Alcoholics Anonymous calls on two of the greatest reservoirs of power known to man, religion and that ***instinct*** for association with one's fellows . . . the 'herd ***instinct***.'(p.571)

instincts

• As I write these words, it seems incredible that these things should have happened to me, for they are, truly, against all my ***instincts*** and training.(p.536)

institute

• I resented it of course, and I offered Clarence his commission, whatever it might be, if he would please not bother me because I had arrived at the conclusion that he was a solicitor for some alcoholic ***institute***.(p.216)

institution

• A.A. had become a national ***institution***.(p.xviii)

• Then we have the voices who cry for sex and more sex; who bewail the ***institution*** of marriage; who think that most of the troubles of the race are traceable to sex causes.(p.69)

• Approach through a doctor or an ***institution*** is a better bet.(p.91)

• We are careful never to show intolerance or hatred of drinking as an ***institution***.(p.103)

• He has been placed in one ***institution*** after another.(p.110)

• If he is already committed to an ***institution***, but can convince you and your doctor that he means business, give him a chance to try our method, unless the doctor thinks his mental condition too abnormal or dangerous.(p.114)

• Arrangements were also made with the chief psychiatrist of a large public hospital to select still others from the stream of misery which flows through that ***institution***.(p.163)

• It wasn't very long before home-brewing was an ***institution*** and men began to search feverishly for old recipe books on wine-making.(p.232)

• It wasn't long before the bootlegger was an established ***institution*** in this, as in other towns.(p.233)

• I managed to maintain myself with odd jobs, did ten weeks in a social rescue ***institution***, and at length wound up in a second-hand bookstore in an adjacent town as manager.(p.257)

• But I had never been a flippant, wise-cracking sneerer at the few persons I had met who had impressed me as Christian men and women, or at any ***institution*** whose sincerity of purpose I could see.(p.259)

• And all the while my fear fed a growing conviction that before long it would be necessary for me to be put away in some ***institution***.(p.306)

• I have spent eighteen years in that ***institution***.(p.509)

• When I had heard about it, it meant nothing but just two letters to me, but some friends of mine in the ***institution*** were very active in the program and really believed in it.(p.509)

institutionalized

• This escapade also ended up in the clutches of the law, and my friend was ***institutionalized*** for eight months.(p.354)

institutions

• We listed people, ***institutions*** or principles with whom we were angry.(p.64)

• For years we have been working with alcoholics committed to ***institutions.***(p.114)

• Here, for instance, is a typical example: An officer of one of the largest banking ***institutions*** in America knows I no longer drink.(p.138)

• He said he had finally learned that drinking was a fatal illness made up of an allergy plus an obsession, and once the drinking had passed from habit to obsession, we were completely hopeless, and could look forward only to spending the balance of our lives in mental ***institutions*** or to death.(p.290)

• I achieved recognized and national standing in my profession, as well as becoming a director in many important ***institutions*** having to do with the civic life of a large city.(p.374)

• Incalculable are the intangible initiation fees that A.A. members have paid: the sick, sick hangovers, the remorse, guilt, broken homes, jails, and ***institutions,*** and the mental anguish in general that has been generated over the years.(p.399)

• I would rather talk about the good things A.A. has taught me; I feel that hitting on just a few sordid points should be sufficient to let those of you in ***institutions*** know where I came from.(p.459)

• It is true that the doctors and nurses in the various ***institutions*** I attended knew too.(p.470)

• He had been in and out of Matteawan and many other mental ***institutions*** as a result of his drinking.(p.509)

instruct

• Let him see that you are not there to ***instruct*** him in religion.(p.93)

instruction

• They came in and began to give me ***instruction*** in the program which later became known as Alcoholics Anonymous.(p.185)

instructions

• (My mother and father were Catholics and I had been baptized, but at the end of my ***instructions*** for Confirmation I had not gone to church, and then when my mother remarried, she married a Protestant and the whole religious angle was forgotten.(p.201)

• I carried out his ***instructions.***(p.276)

• Somehow or other, I must have misunderstood the doctor's ***instructions,*** for I not only made the beer for my wife, I also drank it for her.(p.297)

• Besides, I couldn't understand the ***instructions.***(p.445)

instructive

• The story he told is most ***instructive,*** for here was a chap absolutely convinced he had to stop drinking, who had no excuse for drinking, who exhibited splendid judgment and determination in all his other concerns, yet was flat on his back nevertheless.(p.40)

instrument

• It pays daily in more harmonious relations with my fellow men, in ever clearer insight into the true meaning of life, and in the answering love and gratitude wherever and whenever I have been the ***instrument*** of God's will in the lives of others.(p.394)

• Since, perhaps, suicide was a bit too drastic (actually, I was afraid), dry martinis were chosen as the slow, pleasant, private, gradual ***instrument*** of self-destruction.(p.531)

• Historians may one day recognize Alcoholics Anonymous to have been a great venture in social pioneering which forged a new ***instrument*** for social action; a new therapy based on the kinship of common suffering; one having a vast potential for the myriad other ills of mankind."(p.573)

insufferably

• There would be times when the life of respectability and achievement seemed ***insufferably*** dull – I had to break out.(p.432)

insufficient

• But even in this type of beginning we are obliged to admit that our justification for a spree was insanely ***insufficient*** in the light of what always happened.(p.37)

• In actual practice, we usually find a solitary self-appraisal ***insufficient.***(p.72)

• He may be an example of the truth that faith alone is ***insufficient.***(p.93)

insult

• Her idea of fun on a bender was to hit sailors and ***insult*** cops.(p.414)

insulted

• Certain drinkers, who would be greatly ***insulted*** if called alcoholics, are astonished at their inability to stop.(p.33)

• He would probably be ***insulted*** if he were called an alcoholic.(p.109)

• This question so ***insulted*** the emotions that clearly there was only one thing to do, go and get drunk again, and put that enquiring mind in its proper place, which was oblivion.(p.537)

insulting

• At three-thirty the next morning, I was in Champlain Street Station, in jail for driving while intoxicated and ***insulting*** an officer; and the suit of which I was so proud was in such shape that the turnkey had to get me a pair of trousers to go into court in the next morning.(p.201)

insurance

• She wanted to know if her husband's company ***insurance*** was still in force.(p.137)

• There is company ***insurance.***(p.149)

• 4.Because every time I do it I take out a little more ***insurance*** for myself against a possible slip.(p.181)

• Handling customers, dealers, ***insurance*** people, dictation, telephoning, directing new employees, answering to superiors, and all the rest of it.(p.299)

• I still had a wife and family, a home and a car, my driver's license, and a proper amount of ***insurance.***(p.327)

insure

• Practical experience shows that nothing will so much ***insure*** immunity from drinking as intensive work with other alcoholics.(p.89)

• During those first days of convalescence, this will do more to ***insure*** his sobriety than anything else.(p.129)

• If there is none nearby, you will be invited to carry on a correspondence which will do much to ***insure*** your sobriety no matter how isolated you are.(p.575)

insurmountable

• The other of the Twelve Steps of Alcoholics Anonymous seemed ***insurmountable*** to me at first.(p.471)

intact

• The section called "The Doctor's Opinion" has been kept ***intact,*** just as it was originally written in 1939 by the late Dr. William D. Silkworth, our Society's great medical benefactor.(p.xi)

• "Bill's Story," "Doctor Bob's Nightmare," and one other personal history from the first edition were retained ***intact;*** three were edited and one of these was retitled; new versions of two stories were written with new titles; thirty completely new stories were added; and the story section was divided into three parts, under the same headings that are used now.(p.xi)

intake

• The unwillingness to admit failure requires even further friendly ***intake.***(p.331)

• But from one or two drinks of an afternoon or evening, my ***intake*** mounted, and mounted fast.(p.336)

• ***Intake*** of alcohol changes one's personality -- even the healthy personality.(p.458)

intangible

• I wanted to learn to stand on my own feet, not to change one prop for another, and an ***intangible*** and dubious one at that.(p.227)

• Incalculable are the ***intangible*** initiation fees that A.A. members have paid: the sick, sick hangovers, the remorse, guilt, broken homes, jails, and institutions, and the mental anguish in general that has been generated over the years.(p.399)

integral

• I have stopped tilting at windmills, and instead have tried to accomplish the little daily tasks, unimportant in themselves, but tasks that are an ***integral*** part of living fully.(p.295)

integrity

• They are authorized by the groups to handle our over-all public relations and they guarantee the ***integrity*** of our principal newspaper, the A.A. Grapevine.(p.567)

intellect

• Students of ancient history tell us that the ***intellect*** of men in those days was equal to the best of today.(p.51)

• They seemed to be happy in their fashion, they and their little groups of supporters, but always pride of ***intellect*** stopped me from seeking what they evidently had.(p.256)

• To my way of thinking, that is a definition of alcoholism; a state of being in which the emotions have failed to grow to the stature of the ***intellect.***(p.535)

intellect's

• For a while, for a long time, we can endure the ***intellect's*** being ahead of the emotions, which is the import of Millay's couplet.(p.534)

intellectual

• My ***intellectual*** heroes, the chemists the astronomers, even the evolutionists, suggested vast laws and forces at work.(p.10)

• It melted the icy ***intellectual*** mountain in whose shadow I had lived and shivered many years.(p.12)

• If you think you are an atheist, an agnostic, a skeptic, or have any other form of ***intellectual*** pride which keeps you from accepting what is in this book, I feel sorry for you.(p.181)

• I was an ***intellectual*** and I needed an ***intellectual*** answer, not an emotional one.(p.227)

• I got a good non-academic education; my ***intellectual*** curiosity was encouraged.(p.401)

• What ***intellectual*** interests could we have in common?(p.412)

• Apparently I'd grown physically at the customary rate of speed, and I had acquired an average amount of ***intellectual*** training in the intervening years, but there had been no emotional maturity at all.(p.547)

intellectually

• Though I had been only a nominal churchman, their proposals were not, ***intellectually,*** hard to swallow.(p.42)

• I was sold, ***intellectually.***(p.414)

intelligence

• How could there be so much of precise and immutable law and no ***intelligence?***(p.10)

• I could go for such conceptions as Creative ***Intelligence,*** Universal Mind or Spirit of Nature but I resisted the thought of a Czar of the Heavens, however loving His sway might be.(p.12)

• As soon as we admitted the possible existence of a Creative ***Intelligence,*** a Spirit of the Universe underlying the totality of things, we began to be possessed of a new sense of power and direction, provided we took other simple steps.(p.46)

• When, however, the perfectly logical assumption is suggested that underneath the material world and life as we see it, there is an All Powerful, Guiding, Creative ***Intelligence,*** right there our perverse streak comes to the surface and we laboriously set out to convince ourselves it isn't so.(p.49)

• Instead of regarding ourselves as intelligent agents, spearheads of God's ever advancing Creation, we agnostics and atheists chose to believe that our human ***intelligence*** was the last word, the alpha and the omega, the beginning and end of all.(p.49)

• Both father and mother were considerably above the average in ***intelligence.***(p.172)

• They probably felt that it was useless, that surely I had enough ***intelligence*** to know what I was doing.(p.215)

• As I later found out through Alcoholics Anonymous, alcohol is no respecter of economic status, social and business standing or ***intelligence.***(p.373)

intelligent

• They are often able, ***intelligent,*** friendly people.(p.xxviii)

• He is an ***intelligent*** man, normal so far as we can see, except for a nervous disposition.(p.35)

• However ***intelligent*** we may have been in other respects, where alcohol has been involved, we have been strangely insane.(p.38)

• Instead of regarding ourselves as ***intelligent*** agents, spearheads of God's ever advancing Creation, we agnostics and atheists chose to believe that our human intelligence was the last word, the alpha and the omega, the beginning and end of all.(p.49)

• The electrons themselves seemed more ***intelligent*** than that.(p.54)

• I don't know what sort of person I was expecting, but I was very agreeably surprised to find Mr. T. a poised, ***intelligent,*** well groomed and mannered gentleman.(p.309)

intend

• We have not lost everything in life through drinking and we certainly do not ***intend*** to.(p.38)

• We ***intend*** the foregoing as a helpful suggestion only.(p.132)

• Next he can be assured that you do not ***intend*** to lecture, moralize, or condemn; that if this was done formerly, it was because of misunderstanding.(p.142)

• I thought to myself, "Well, she is going to tell me this is the end," and I certainly couldn't blame her and

did not *intend* to try to justify myself.(p.184)
- (I might say right here that never in my life did I ever *intend* to get drunk.(p.196)
- I tell her quietly what I *intend* to do.(p.507)

intense
- Here was the threat of commitment, the loss of family and position, to say nothing of that *intense* mental and physical suffering which drinking always caused him.(p.36)
- In part, it was a feeling of *intense* shame at having to leave the Army during the war, but mostly it was resentment that this kind of thing should happen to me for, strange as it may seem, up to then I still thought I could control drinking.(p.521)

intensely
- Being *intensely* interested in the work, I changed my conduct sufficiently to master the job.(p.211)
- I was in a world that I knew nothing at all about, and I felt *intensely* afraid.(p.521)
- I was *intensely* unhappy the whole time, but I didn't seem to be able to do anything about it, and the worst part to me was the realization that all this was going to happen again and again until I died.(p.522)

intensified
- When the thought was expressed that there might be a God personal to me this feeling was *intensified*.(p.12)

intensive
- Practical experience shows that nothing will so much insure immunity from drinking as *intensive* work with other alcoholics.(p.89)
- When I entered a sanitarium for prolonged and *intensive* psychiatric treatment, I was convinced that I was having a serious mental breakdown.(p.226)

intent
- She was *intent* on her studies, and kept her distance.(p.359)

intention
- I had no *intention* of drinking.(p.36)
- I told him that I had no other *intention*.(p.218)
- One Saturday noon I staggered home with every *intention* of showing her.(p.362)
- The baffling problem of getting drunk when I had every *intention* of staying sober was simplified.(p.379)
- When I came into A.A., I had no *intention* of quitting drinking – I figured I was doing all right.(p.478)
- I was drunk for sixty days around the clock and it was my *intention*, literally, to drink myself to death.(p.549)
- Though it was not our *intention* to create such an impression, many alcoholics have nevertheless concluded that in order to recover they must acquire an immediate and overwhelming "God-consciousness" followed at once by a vast change in feeling and outlook.(p.569)

intentions
- Naturally, in spite of my good *intentions*, in spite of my protected life behind sanitarium walls, I several times got drunk, and was astounded . . . and badly shaken.(p.227)
- At the Laundromat, I was undisturbed by barflies with questionable and unwanted *intentions*.(p.369)
- Before A.A., I judged myself by my *intentions*, while the world was judging me by my actions.(p.450)
- There go my good *intentions*, fear of consequences, will to care, responsibility for my behavior.(p.458)
- We always, or nearly always, had good *intentions* when we were released from prison.(p.458)
- But with the first drink, our good *intentions* dissolved; our personalities changed.(p.458)

interchange
- There is a good bit of travel between East and West and we foresee a great increase in this helpful *interchange*.(p.162)

interest
- The message which can *interest* and hold these alcoholic people must have depth and weight.(p.xxvi)
- We will lose *interest* in selfish things and gain *interest* in our fellows.(p.84)
- If he shows *interest*, lend him your copy of this book.(p.94)
- You might suggest that you both take an *interest* in them.(p.112)
- If this kind of approach does not catch your husband's *interest*, it may be best to drop the subject, but after a friendly talk your husband will usually revive the topic himself.(p.112)
- He may take small *interest* in the children and may show irritation when reproved for his delinquencies.(p.126)
- When he renews *interest* in such things, a feeling of jealousy may arise.(p.131)
- There is a real *interest*, both humanitarian and business, in the well-being of employees.(p.149)
- My wife became deeply interested and it was her *interest* that sustained mine, though I at no time sensed that it might be an answer to my liquor problem.(p.178)
- I always built up in my own mind the great things that I was going to do, and in fact I accomplished about fifty percent of them and then lost *interest*.(p.193)
- At that particular stage, I lost *interest* in it, sold the option for $5,000 and forgot the whole deal.(p.198)
- Then he started to talk to me about his drinking experiences, what his drinking had cost him, how much he had drunk and where, things like that, and I remember I was quite bored because I had never seen the guy before and had no *interest* at all in what, where and when he drank.(p.208)
- Routine jobs bored me, but I would take on the toughest one I could find, work day and night until I had it under control; then it would become tedious and I'd lose all *interest* in it.(p.243)
- From that point on, I secured crocks of ten gallon capacity and really took quite an active *interest* in the manufacture of home brew.(p.297)
- I studied art; I desperately endeavored to create an *interest* in many things, in a new place among new people.(p.305)
- Whole new vistas were opened and life began to take on color and *interest*.(p.311)
- So oldsters are advised to develop *interest*, find hobbies.(p.330)
- Hiding behind a newspaper, magazine, or book, I really saw nothing, but simulated deep *interest*.(p.332)
- These people were my friends, and I felt their sincere *interest* in me.(p.355)
- His enthusiasm and keen *interest* in A.A. fired my spirits again.(p.365)
- She said, "He has something of *interest*, if you will see him."(p.494)
- But I am to learn later that it began with my desire for material success becoming greater than my *interest* in the welfare of my fellow man.(p.507)
- It has taught me that I can best keep my sobriety by sharing it out with others; that I must bring that sobriety to others who need it, in my own *interest*.(p.524)
- Should you be the relative or friend of an alcoholic who shows no immediate *interest* in A.A., it is suggested that you write the Al-Anon Family Groups, Inc., Box 182, Madison Square Station, New York, NY 10159, U.S.A.(p.575)

interested
- We shall be *interested* to hear from those who are getting results from this book, particularly from those who have commenced work with other alcoholics.(p.xiv)
- We of Alcoholics Anonymous believe that the reader will be *interested* in the medical estimate of the plan of recovery described in this book.(p.xxiii)
- My work took me about Wall street and little by little I became *interested* in the market.(p.2)
- I was shocked, but *interested*.(p.10)
- Certainly I was *interested*.(p.10)
- He was *interested* and conceded that he had some of the symptoms, but he was a long way from admitting that he could do nothing about it himself.(p.40)
- Established on such a footing we became less and less *interested* in ourselves, our little plans and designs.(p.63)
- More and more we became *interested* in seeing what we could contribute to life.(p.63)
- He is going to be more *interested* in a demonstration of good will than in our talk of spiritual discoveries.(p.77)
- We will seldom be *interested* in liquor.(p.84)
- If there is any indication that he wants to stop, have a good talk with the person most *interested* in him -- usually his wife.(p.90)
- If he is not *interested* in your solution, if he expects you to act only as a banker for his financial difficulties or a nurse for his sprees, you may have to drop him until he changes his mind.(p.95)
- If he is sincerely *interested* and wants to see you again, ask him to read this book in the interval.(p.95)
- Then perhaps he will be *interested* enough to continue.(p.113)
- Sometimes he will be so *interested* that he becomes really neglectful.(p.119)
- Each is *interested* in having his or her wishes respected.(p.122)
- I told her to say that I was not *interested*.(p.136)
- The firm wants to help you get over it, and if you are *interested*, there is a way out.(p.147)
- In addition to these casual get-togethers, it became customary to set apart one night a week for a meeting to be attended by anyone or everyone *interested* in a spiritual way of life.(p.159)
- Outsiders became *interested*.(p.160)
- My wife became deeply *interested* and it was her interest that sustained mine, though I at no time sensed that it might be an answer to my liquor problem.(p.178)
- I was always *interested* in mechanics and after having about twenty miscellaneous jobs, lasting from one day to two weeks, I obtained a job as a toolmaker apprentice.(p.211)
- Being intensely *interested* in the work, I changed my conduct sufficiently to master the job.(p.211)
- That is, it was sort of a mixed bunch of Oxford Groupers, who were *interested* in the alcoholic problem, and of alcoholics themselves.(p.218)
- In a few sentences he made God seem personal to me, explained Him as a being who was *interested* in me, the alcoholic, and that all I needed to do was to be willing to follow His way; that as long as I followed it I would be able to overcome my desire for liquor.(p.236)
- One of our gifts from the family was a very lovely Bible, but we'd let the bulldog chew it because we weren't too *interested* in it.(p.268)
- No, I was all *interested* in this part that told you how to do it.(p.269)
- That was the only part I was *interested* in.(p.269)
- I was very much *interested* in athletics, and because of this and parental influence, I didn't drink or smoke in either grade or high school.(p.287)
- I went to the sanitarium where this chap was incarcerated and found to my surprise that he was *interested*.(p.294)
- Neither one of the two was *interested* for himself, one being a mother who wanted to do something for her son.(p.294)
- I said to my husband, "I'm going to try, every free moment that I have, to get *interested* in something outside, get myself over this rut I'm in."(p.338)
- However, knowing me, she thought it was a foolish idea, that I wouldn't be *interested*.(p.367)
- There was a doctor in our church congregation who was *interested* in my case, and he thought it was a vitamin deficiency.(p.389)
- I am no longer *interested* in living in a palace, because palace living was not the answer for me.(p.416)
- He was *interested* and said he'd help me all he could.(p.428)
- The psychiatrist, who had generally been ignoring me, now became quite *interested*; every day, he would ask me all kinds of questions about the A.A. meetings.(p.446)
- I had never had a drink, but I had seen enough merriment in the boys who were drinking to be *interested*.(p.498)
- This caused the rather cryptic comment from one of my A.A. friends, when I told my story after coming into the program, that I had always been a cinch for the program, for I had always been *interested* in mankind, but that I was just taking them one man at a time.(p.548)
- During the day a friend of mine brought me some magazines to take to a hospital group I was *interested* in, and I looked through them and a "banner" across the front of one featured an article by a prominent clergyman in which I caught the word "resentment."(p.552)

interesting
- The cases we have followed through have been most *interesting*; in fact, many of them are amazing.(p.xxv)
- His story is so *interesting* that some of it should be told now.(p.55)
- Thus you may succeed in *interesting* him in alcoholism.(p.112)
- Tell him some of the *interesting* stories you have read.(p.112)
- His comment was, "Very *interesting*.(p.138)
- You may make some *interesting* discoveries.(p.149)
- My friendships are meaningful, loving and *interesting* because I am sober.(p.416)
- I'd visit one bar after another, having one martini in each, and in each hoping to find someone *interesting* to talk to.(p.536)

interests
- The doctor's theory that we have an allergy to alcohol *interests* us.(p.xxiv)
- They took a drink a day or so prior to the date, and then the phenomenon of craving at once became paramount to all other *interests* so that the important appointment was not met.(p.xxvii)

• Sometimes it is to the best *interests* of all concerned that a couple remain apart.(p.99)

• Therefore, you probably need fresh *interests* and a great cause to live for as much as your husband.(p.119)

• What intellectual *interests* could we have in common?(p.412)

interfere

• But the policy of this company is not to *interfere* with the habits of our employees.(p.148)

• Resenting anyone and everyone who might *interfere* with my personal plans and ways of doing things, I was full of self pity, especially for any interference with my drinking.(p.376)

• This suggestion had been made before on a number of occasions, but like all alcoholics I wanted to handle my problem my own way, which really meant I didn't want anything to *interfere* with my drinking.(p.378)

• I got to the place where I'd look forward to the week-end's drinking and pacify myself by saying that the week-ends were mine, that it didn't *interfere* with my family or with my business if I drank on the week-ends.(p.488)

• I got a job by myself which suited me down to the ground, because there was nobody really to *interfere* with what I did, one way or the other, and I usually had my nerves in good trim when anybody was coming around to inspect.(p.519)

• I have seen that there is only one law, the law of love, and there are only two sins; the first is to *interfere* with the growth of another human being, and the second is to *interfere* with one's own growth.(p.542)

interfered

• Was it our self-esteem, our security, our ambitions, our personal, or sex relations, which had been *interfered* with?(p.65)

• I was intolerant of people who drank, particularly those who drank to an extent that *interfered* with on-the-job performance.(p.374)

• I talked the Old Man into letting me live in the photo lab instead of the barracks, and for eighteen months nothing *interfered* with my drinking.(p.426)

interference

• It may mean the loss of many nights' sleep, great *interference* with your pleasures, interruptions to your business.(p.97)

• Resenting anyone and everyone who might interfere with my personal plans and ways of doing things, I was full of self pity, especially for any *interference* with my drinking.(p.376)

interferes

• Over a period of time he has built up self pity, resentments toward anyone or anything that *interferes* with his drinking.(p.380)

interfering

• Soon, it became apparent that my schooling was *interfering* with my drinking.(p.354)

• I liked the description of the alcoholic as a person who had found that alcohol is *interfering* with his social or business life.(p.380)

• In the first year there were episodes such as kicking Priscilla in the shins, getting the lock changed on the desk in the A.A. Club, because I, as secretary, didn't want the Intergroup secretary "*interfering*," and taking an older woman member out to lunch for the express purpose of informing her that she was "a phony."(p.416)

ntergroup

• In the first year there were episodes such as kicking Priscilla in the shins, getting the lock changed on the desk in the A.A. Club, because I, as secretary, didn't want the *Intergroup* secretary "interfering," and taking an older woman member out to lunch for the express purpose of informing her that she was "a phony."(p.416)

The small group may elect its secretary, the large group its rotating committee, and the groups of a large metropolitan area their central or *intergroup* committee, which often employs a full-time secretary.(p.567)

These so-called *intergroup* associations are found under the listing "A.A." or "Alcoholics Anonymous" in telephone directories.(p.575)

nterior

By this time, with the doctor's explanation, the revelations contained in the book, and the hope-inspiring interview with Mr. T., I was ready and willing to go into the *interior* of the African jungles, if that was what it took, for me to find what these people had.(p.309)

nterludes

Like most other alcoholics I have known, I did quit drinking at various times -- once for ten months on my own and during other *interludes* when I was hospitalized.(p.554)

intermediate

• I went into the high school grades, but having missed all the *intermediate* grades, I didn't get along too well, so I developed the habit of going back to school just long enough for the football season and then quitting.(p.193)

interminable

• And I remembered the creeping horror of the *interminable* night, in which I slept for short spells and woke up dripping with cold sweat and shaken with utter despair, to drink hastily from my bottle and mercifully pass out again, "You're mad, you're mad, you're mad!" pounded through my brain with each returning ray of consciousness, and I drowned the refrain with drink.(p.224)

• Always, in between, there were intervals of being broke, riding freights and hitch-hiking *interminable* distances from one big town to another in three states.(p.255)

intermingled

• Immediately a great feeling of peace descended upon me, *intermingled* with a feeling of being suffused with a quiet strength.(p.280)

internal

• While the *internal* difficulties of our adolescent period were being ironed out, public acceptance of A.A. grew by leaps and bounds.(p.xix)

• In the hospital, I hung on to the idea I'd had most of my life: that if I could just control the external environment, the *internal* environment would then be comfortable.(p.445)

• And life keeps getting simpler and easier as we try to reverse my old idea, by taking care of the *internal* environment via the Twelve Steps, and letting the external environment take care of itself.)(p.446)

international

• Though none of these principles had the force of rules or laws, they had become so widely accepted by 1950 that they were confirmed by our first *International* Conference held at Cleveland.(p.xix)

• I recall, as I walked into that meeting, saying to myself, "Here I am, a fellow of the American College of Surgeons, a Fellow of the *International* College of Surgeons, a diplomate of one of the great specialty boards in these United States, a member of the American Psychiatric Society, and I have to go to the butcher, the baker and the carpenter to help make a man out of me!"(p.347)

• I was up to *international* standards in one particular game, and that again covered quite a lot of my sins.(p.519)

• At New York, U.S.A., Alcoholics Anonymous maintains its *international* service center.(p.575)

interne

• The *interne* came along with a glassful of bleached lightning that put me away for about fifteen hours.(p.217)

• The closest I came to a psychiatrist during that time was an *interne* who came to take blood tests.(p.492)

interneship

• But I can remember in post graduate days, and during *interneship*, that very often I'd go to a patient's bed and start a process of elimination and then, very often, I'd wind up guessing.(p.485)

• My *interneship* was in Washington.(p.486)

internship

• I conducted myself so creditably that I was able to secure a much coveted *internship* in a western city, where I spent two years.(p.174)

• And as I went through pharmacy school, graduate school, medical school, *internship*, residency, and specialty training and, finally, went into practice, my drinking kept increasing.(p.441)

interpersonal

• I suppose the psychiatrist might say, "This is benevolent *interpersonal* relations.(p.352)

interpret

• But in the light of the new understanding that I have found in A.A., I have been able to *interpret* that defeat, and that failure, and that shame, as seeds of victory.(p.335)

interpretation

• We agnostically inclined would not feel satisfied with a proposal which does not lend itself to reasonable approach and *interpretation*.(p.53)

interpreted

• I *interpreted* "sober" as meaning "drinking but not being drunk."(p.447)

interrupt

• Then there was wartime service to *interrupt* my plans, and an education to be picked up after the war.(p.373)

• I, who had feared questions, now began trying to *interrupt* and tell my story.(p.414)

interrupted

• My musing was *interrupted* by the telephone.(p.8)

• He *interrupted*: "I used to be strong for the church, but that won't fix it.(p.157)

• My husband *interrupted*, "She's bad enough now without getting mixed up with a bunch of drunks."(p.469)

interruptions

• It may mean the loss of many nights' sleep, great interference with your pleasures, *interruptions* to your business.(p.97)

• This routine went on with few *interruptions* for seventeen years.(p.177)

interval

• Wait for the end of the spree, or at least for a lucid *interval*.(p.90)

• You might place this book where he can see it in the *interval*.(p.90)

• If he is sincerely interested and wants to see you again, ask him to read this book in the *interval*.(p.95)

• To be sure, this had been a dizzy and confused *interval*, but most everyone else I knew had emerged from it with both feet on the ground and a fair amount of adult maturity.(p.304)

intervals

• Here was love, applause, war; moments sublime with *intervals* hilarious.(p.1)

• All of us felt at times that we were regaining control, but such *intervals* -- usually brief -- were inevitably followed by still less control, which led in time to pitiful and incomprehensible demoralization.(p.30)

• Always, in between, there were *intervals* of being broke, riding freights and hitch-hiking interminable distances from one big town to another in three states.(p.255)

• I would hang on to sobriety for short *intervals*, but always there would come the tide of an overpowering necessity to drink and, as I was engulfed in it, I felt such a sense of panic that I really believed I would die if I didn't get that drink inside.(p.306)

• *Intervals* between binges were, at first, eight months.(p.434)

• In seven years the *intervals* between them decreased from eight months to ten days!(p.434)

• And as I read, I shall take little drinks at long *intervals*.(p.506)

• The *intervals* grew shorter.(p.514)

intervening

• Today, because of A.A.'s growth during the *intervening* years, it is of course much bigger than it was then.(p.392)

• Many times in the *intervening* years I have thanked God for that man, a man who had the courage to admit failure, a man who had the humility to confess that all the hard-won learning of his profession could not turn up the answer.(p.436)

• Apparently I'd grown physically at the customary rate of speed, and I had acquired an average amount of intellectual training in the *intervening* years, but there had been no emotional maturity at all.(p.547)

intervention

• And but for the *intervention* of an understanding person, I might have followed in their footsteps.(p.137)

interview

• By this time, with the doctor's explanation, the revelations contained in the book, and the hope-inspiring *interview* with Mr. T., I was ready and willing to go into the interior of the African jungles, if that was what it took, for me to find what these people had.(p.309)

interviewed

• I felt like a gangster's moll about to be *interviewed* by the Salvation Army.(p.413)

interviews

• In large cities, groups often maintain local offices where alcoholics or their families may arrange for *interviews* or hospitalization.(p.575)

intimacy

• Some of us had this experience, only to enjoy, in a few months, a finer *intimacy* than ever.(p.134)

• It is joyous *intimacy* with friends and a feeling that life is good.(p.151)

intimate

• Strangely enough, wives, parents and *intimate* friends usually find us even more unapproachable than do the psychiatrist and the doctor.(p.18)

• Rightly and naturally, we think well before we choose the person or persons with whom to take this ***intimate*** and confidential step.(p.74)
• No outsider can appraise such an ***intimate*** situation.(p.82)
• This is a condition which, in ordinary life, would produce untold grief; there might be scandalous gossip, laughter at the expense of other people, and a tendency to take advantage of ***intimate*** information.(p.125)
• Another principle we observe carefully is that we do not relate ***intimate*** experiences of another person unless we are sure he would approve.(p.125)
• In sports I made the track and tennis teams; I got along well with the other boys and had a fairly large circle of acquaintances but no ***intimate*** friends.(p.240)

intimated

• The doctor ***intimated*** strongly that he might be worse than he realized.(p.39)

intimation

• Of course, I had no hint or ***intimation*** as to what the treatment was to consist of.(p.302)

into

• The first edition appeared in April 1939, and in the following sixteen years, more than 300,000 copies went ***into*** circulation.(p.xi)
• "Bill's Story," "Doctor Bob's Nightmare," and one other personal history from the first edition were retained intact; three were edited and one of these was retitled; new versions of two stories were written with new titles; thirty completely new stories were added; and the story section was divided ***into*** three parts, under the same headings that are used now.(p.xi)
• In that brief space, Alcoholics Anonymous has mushroomed ***into*** nearly 6,000 groups whose membership is far above 150,000 recovered alcoholics.(p.xv)
• The spark that was to flare ***into*** the first A.A. group was struck at Akron, Ohio, in June 1935, during a talk between a New York stockbroker and an Akron physician.(p.xv)
• This brought a rush of 800 frantic inquiries ***into*** the little New York office which meanwhile had been established.(p.xviii)
• Many years ago one of the leading contributors to this book came under our care in this hospital and while here he acquired some ideas which he put ***into*** practical application at once.(p.xxv)
• This immediately precipitates us ***into*** a seething caldron of debate.(p.xxviii)
• It went ***into*** certain securities, then cheap and rather unpopular.(p.2)
• One day I walked ***into*** a cafe to telephone.(p.6)
• Now I was to plunge ***into*** the dark, joining that endless procession of sots who had gone on before.(p.8)
• I was soon to be catapulted ***into*** what I like to call the fourth dimension of existence.(p.8)
• Disappointed but curious, I wondered what had got ***into*** the fellow.(p.9)
• A new world came ***into*** view.(p.12)
• Those of us who live in large cities are overcome by the reflection that close by hundreds are dropping ***into*** oblivion every day.(p.19)
• Before going ***into*** a detailed discussion, it may be well to summarize some points as we see them.(p.20)
• We are equally positive that once he takes any alcohol whatever ***into*** his system, something happens, both in the bodily and mental sense, which makes it virtually impossible for him to stop.(p.22)
• At a certain point in the drinking of every alcoholic, he passes ***into*** a state where the most powerful desire to stop drinking is of absolutely no avail.(p.24)
• We are unable, at certain times, to bring ***into*** our consciousness with sufficient force the memory of the suffering and humiliation of even a week or a month ago.(p.24)
• The almost certain consequences that follow taking even a glass of beer do not crowd ***into*** the mind to deter us.(p.24)
• We have found much of heaven and we have been rocketed ***into*** a fourth dimension of existence of which we had not even dreamed.(p.25)
• The central fact of our lives today is the absolute certainty that our Creator has entered ***into*** our hearts and lives in a way which is indeed miraculous.(p.25)
• We were in a position where life was becoming impossible, and if we had passed ***into*** the region from which there is no return through human aid we had but two alternatives: One was to go on to the bitter end, blotting out the consciousness of our intolerable situation as best we could; and the other, to accept spiritual help.(p.25)
• Many pursue it ***into*** the gates of insanity or death.(p.30)
• Potential female alcoholics often turn ***into*** the real thing and are gone beyond recall in a few years.(p.33)
• So we shall describe some of the mental states that precede a relapse ***into*** drinking, for obviously this is the crux of the problem.(p.35)
• Friends who have reasoned with him after a spree which has brought him to the point of divorce or bankruptcy are mystified when he walks directly ***into*** a saloon.(p.35)
• On leaving the asylum he came ***into*** contact with us.(p.35)
• Then I decided to drive ***into*** the country and see one of my prospects for a car.(p.36)
• I ordered a whiskey and poured it ***into*** the milk.(p.36)
• The experiment went so well that I ordered another whiskey and poured it ***into*** more milk.(p.36)
• When I returned to the hotel it struck me a highball would be fine before going to bed, so I stepped ***into*** the bar and had one.(p.41)
• I have since been brought ***into*** a way of living infinitely more satisfying and, I hope, more useful than the life I lived before.(p.42)
• It finally beat us ***into*** a state of reasonableness.(p.48)
• In the face of collapse and despair, in the face of the total failure of their human resources, they found that a new power, peace, happiness, and sense of direction flowed ***into*** them.(p.50)
• Some of us grow ***into*** it more slowly.(p.57)
• If sex is very troublesome, we throw ourselves the harder ***into*** helping others.(p.70)
• ***INTO*** ACTION(p.72)
• Have we skimped on the cement put ***into*** the foundation?(p.75)
• Every day is a day when we must carry the vision of God's will ***into*** all of our activities.(p.85)
• If we have carefully followed directions, we have begun to sense the flow of His Spirit ***into*** us.(p.85)
• Or were we thinking of what we could do for others, of what we could pack ***into*** the stream of life?(p.86)
• But we must be careful not to drift ***into*** worry, remorse or morbid reflection, for that would diminish our usefulness to others.(p.86)
• Perhaps you will want to take the man ***into*** your home for a few days.(p.96)
• Burn the idea ***into*** the consciousness of every man that he can get well regardless of anyone.(p.98)
• When your prospect has made such reparation as he can to his family, and has thoroughly explained to them the new principles by which he is living, he should proceed to put those principles ***into*** action at home.(p.98)
• People have said we must not go where liquor is served; we must not have it in our homes; we must shun friends who drink; we must avoid moving pictures which show drinking scenes; we must not go ***into*** bars; our friends must hide their bottles if we go to their houses; we mustn't think or be reminded about alcohol at all.(p.100)
• Now you are getting back ***into*** the social life of this world.(p.102)
• You draw more and more ***into*** yourself and you think everyone is talking about conditions at your home.(p.114)
• You, as well as your husband, ought to think of what you can put ***into*** life instead of how much you can take out.(p.120)
• We grow by our willingness to face and rectify errors and convert them ***into*** assets.(p.124)
• He may either plunge ***into*** a frantic attempt to get on his feet in business, or he may be so enthralled by his new life that he talks or thinks of little else.(p.125)
• Instead of treating the family as he should, he may retreat further ***into*** himself and feel he has spiritual justification for so doing.(p.129)
• When we see a man sinking ***into*** the mire that is alcoholism, we give him first aid and place what we have at his disposal.(p.132)
• Outsiders are sometimes shocked when we burst ***into*** merriment over a seemingly tragic experience out of the past.(p.132)
• His wife is one of those persons who really feels there is something rather sinful about these commodities, so she nagged, and her intolerance finally threw him ***into*** a fit of anger.(p.135)
• Why not bring him ***into*** contact with some of our alcoholic crowd?(p.138)
• Down the lobby a door opened ***into*** an attractive bar.(p.154)
• Selecting a church at random from the directory, he stepped ***into*** a booth and lifted the receiver.(p.155)
• Stepping ***into*** his car, he made the rounds of people he had hurt.(p.156)
• At this both the visitors burst ***into*** a laugh.(p.157)
• They experienced a few distressing failures, but in those cases they made an effort to bring the man's family ***into*** a spiritual way of living, thus relieving much worry and suffering.(p.159)
• Many a man, yet dazed from his hospital experience, has stepped over the threshold of that home ***into*** freedom.(p.160)
• Consequently, I could not get ***into*** any trouble.(p.174)
• I drank with moderation at first, but it took me only a relatively short time to drift back ***into*** the old habits which had wound up so disastrously before.(p.175)
• The question which might naturally come ***into*** your mind would be: "What did the man do or say that was different from what others had done or said?"(p.180)
• Before my drinking had cut me down completely, I achieved a considerable measure of success, having been a City Councilman for five years and a financial director of Kenmore, a suburb later taken ***into*** the city itself.(p.182)
• Then Prohibition came ***into*** effect, and the facts that the stuff obtainable was so horrible and sometimes deadly, and that I had married and had a job which I had to look after, helped me for a period of some three or four years, although I would get drunk every time I could get hold of enough to drink to get started.(p.183)
• Away from my office two or three weeks at a time; horrible days and nights when I would lie on the floor of my home, lying awake and reaching over to get the bottle, taking a drink and going back ***into*** oblivion.(p.184)
• I was moved ***into*** another room that morning and there was my wife.(p.184)
• I wasn't afraid that the program wouldn't work, but I still was doubtful whether I would be able to hang on to the program, but I did come to the conclusion that I was willing to put everything I had ***into*** it, with God's power, and that I wanted to do just that.(p.189)
• I'm so grateful for both the program and the people in it that I still want to go, and then probably the most wonderful thing that I learned from the program -- I've seen this in the 'A.A. Grapevine' a lot of times, and I've had people say it to me personally, and I've heard people get up in meetings and make the same statement: The statement is, "I came ***into*** A.A. solely for the purpose of sobriety, but it has been through A.A. that I have found God."(p.192)
• I went ***into*** the high school grades, but having missed all the intermediate grades, I didn't get along too well, so I developed the habit of going back to school just long enough for the football season and then quitting.(p.193)
• I had bought a piece of ground in Cuyahoga Falls and cut it ***into*** lots and had a profit of approximately $40,000 and that was a lot of money in those days.(p.194)
• At the end of this selling of lots, just prior to World War I, I got ***into*** the crude rubber business, and six months later there was only one broker and myself left in Akron.(p.197)
• I didn't want to get ***into*** fights, but I did get ***into*** fights.(p.199)
• At three-thirty the next morning, I was in Champlain Street Station, in jail for driving while intoxicated and insulting an officer; and the suit of which I was so proud was in such shape that the turnkey had to get me a pair of trousers to go ***into*** court in the next morning.(p.201)
• I had run ***into*** a man I always drank with.(p.201)
• I had run ***into*** him, and he looked real prosperous; his face and eyes looked clear and he started to compliment me on my good front and how well I looked, and I said, "I haven't had a drink for nine months."(p.201)
• We went ***into*** a bootleg joint and I don't remember leaving that place.(p.202)
• I was picked up at two-thirty that morning with my car smashed up by a street-car because I had run ***into*** a big concrete safety zone, and the street-car had run ***into*** me, and they took me out through the roof -- there's where I lost the suit.(p.202)
• Then I got ***into*** the habit of having beers, and decided that a drink of whiskey was not any worse; so I would get the one drink of whiskey but, on second thought, I decided that as long as I was only going to have one, I might as well make it a double-header.(p.203)
• I went ***into*** a bar, and there I got ***into*** a fight.(p.204)
• I had a broken nose, a fractured cheekbone, and was black from the lower part of my face up ***into*** my hair.(p.204)
• I was black and blue, with my lips all swollen, when they roused us to go ***into*** court in the morning.(p.204)
• He did call me a cab and when I got ***into*** the cab, I said, "Drive me to a liquor store."(p.204)

• I can remember that in my childhood, he was ill at ease with the children because he attempted to assert an army discipline that had been ground *into* him during his three and a half years of army service.(p.210)

• I finished my apprenticeship and was moved *into* the drafting department.(p.211)

• My drinking career began about four years after I had moved up *into* partnership and had joined certain clubs, societies and so fourth, and during which period we had Prohibition.(p.213)

• It was not known to me as a group, but I later learned that my wife had known about it for nine months and had prayed constantly that I would stumble *into* Akron some way or another.(p.215)

• So the story of my introduction *into* A.A. begins with the activities of my wife.(p.216)

• The next morning, my wife came *into* my room and wakened me and said, "That man is downstairs and he said you said you'd go to Akron."(p.217)

• I went *into* the hospital in April, 1939.(p.217)

• Shortly after I came to this conclusion, I was importuned by another well-known patent law firm to help them out on some trial work because their trial man had had a heart attack and had been forbidden to go *into* the courtroom.(p.220)

• I remembered my loud resolution to find him and ask him to help me get *into* that "Asylum" he had written about.(p.224)

• That armor had turned *into* prison walls, locking me in loneliness – and fear.(p.226)

• It isn't always so sudden with everyone, but I ran *into* a personal crisis which filled me with a raging and righteous anger.(p.228)

• To go *into* a gathering of people was the sort of thing that all my life, from the time I left my private world of books and dreams to meet the real world of people and parties and jobs, had left me feeling an uncomfortable outsider, needing the warming stimulus of drinks to join in.(p.228)

• I went trembling *into* a house in Brooklyn filled with strangers . . . and I found I had come home at last, to my own kind.(p.228)

• I had found friends, understanding friends who often knew what I was thinking and feeling better than I knew myself, and didn't allow me to retreat *into* my prison of loneliness and fear over a fancied slight or hurt.(p.228)

• The feeling of impending disaster that had haunted me for years began to dissolve as I put *into* practice more and more of the Twelve Steps.(p.229)

• At that time I could go *into* any saloon, have one or two beers, walk out and forget about it.(p.231)

• Even then he went *into* no great detail about how he and a crowd of alcoholics, with whom he associated, had mastered their difficulty.(p.235)

• And I began putting *into* practice what I was learning every day.(p.237)

• I had been to OTC the previous summer so I went *into* the Army as a sergeant, but I came out a private, and you really have to be unusual to do that.(p.241)

• I checked *into* my hotel room and then noticed a placard tucked under the glass on the bureau stating "There will be positively NO drinking at this convention" signed by the president of the company.(p.243)

• We checked *into* the home of Hank, the man who had fired me eleven years before in Mississippi, and there I met Bill, our founder.(p.245)

• They had also been periodic big shots who had goofed out repeatedly at the wrong time, and they also knew how to split one paper match *into* three separate matches.(p.245)

• Drifting back to Ohio, I landed on a small newspaper and later was impressed *into* the direction of boy-welfare work at the local "Y."(p.253)

• I did six years of newspaper advertising, and trade journal work with many, many drunks of drab and dreary hue woven *into* the pattern of my life.(p.254)

• I had never known him to be anything but a good healthy pagan with a propensity for getting *into* liquor jams and scrapes.(p.257)

• Some days later, after he had been discharged, a stranger came *into* my shop in the nearby town.(p.257)

• As soon as I could get up and walk I started to drink again and kept it up until my friend of the hospital, who, in his first try at the new way of life had stubbed his toe in Chicago but had come back to the town to take counsel and make a new start, picked me up and got me *into* a hospital.(p.258)

• Then he came *into* town on the bum.(p.263)

• As we left, and they were escorting us across the bridge *into* Wheeling, I, with great dignity and sarcasm, told them if their wives were ever visiting in Akron, and they, too, were looking for their route sign as I was, that I hoped I could extend to them the hospitality that had been shown to me in Bellaire.(p.264)

• I think his entry *into* A.A. was through spending some hours with Dr. Bob at his office.(p.267)

• He brought many people *into* A.A. through his barroom.)(p.267)

• And we went down through the valley, and I remembered reading about the Ku Klux Klan and how they burnt crosses, and I thought, "God alone knows what we are getting *into* this time!"(p.269)

• I switched *into* real estate brokerage and property management work.(p.277)

• I moved *into* a "bachelor hall."(p.277)

• But – I also stayed up week nights after they had retired and drank myself *into* bed.(p.277)

• When the day of their return was almost upon me, and suicide was the only answer I had been able to think of, I went *into* Ralph's room one evening and told him the truth.(p.278)

• To go north *into* the empty pine country and shoot myself, or to go south in the faint hope that a bunch of strangers might help me with my drinking problem.(p.278)

• His road lay clear before me, and I'd better quit rationalizing myself *into* any detours.(p.282)

• Some of the things which used to stop me in my tracks from fear still make me nervous in the anticipation of their doing, but once I kick myself *into* doing them nervousness disappears and I enjoy myself.(p.285)

• I am very apt to get *into* quite an uproar for a day or two before starting, but I do start, and once started, I have a swell time.(p.285)

• I learned early in my A.A. life that I could not afford to fondle such thoughts, as you might fondle a pet, because this particular pet could grow *into* a monster.(p.285)

• They went *into* a huddle and dad explained that he simply took my pants, shoes and money away, so that I could get no liquor and had to sober up.(p.288)

• I can still remember very distinctly getting *into* Akron at eleven p.m. and routing this same Howard out of bed to do something about me.(p.290)

• Occasionally, it is accorded to a few of us to watch something fine grow from a tiny kernel *into* something of gigantic goodness.(p.295)

• The last day of my drinking career, I drank twenty-two of them between ten and twelve a.m. and I shall never know how many more followed them until I was poured *into* bed that night.(p.298)

• My broken home and broken heart fanned my smoldering self-pity *into* a fair-sized bonfire and this kept me well supplied with reasons for having another drink, and then another.(p.305)

• And we wonder how much further this man could go if his alcoholic problem could be removed and he could throw one hundred per cent of his abilities *into* action.(p.308)

• By this time, with the doctor's explanation, the revelations contained in the book, and the hope-inspiring interview with Mr. T., I was ready and willing to go *into* the interior of the African jungles, if that was what it took, for me to find what these people had.(p.309)

• I still couldn't make it through the nights without drinking, so I went back *into* the hospital, this time to a rehabilitation center.(p.320)

• I got *into* terrific trouble with my drinking.(p.322)

• I could feel fear coming *into* my life.(p.323)

• But I felt a fear coming *into* my life, and I couldn't cope with it.(p.324)

• I reached a stage where I couldn't go *into* my apartment without a drink.(p.324)

• Away down deep, I was motivated *into* dishonest behavior because I was a people-pleaser.(p.328)

• They daily pass *into* oblivion, alone or with mates.(p.329)

• I would take a gulp, then warn the jug not to try to entice, lure, or seduce me *into* having more than one "medicinal" jolt.(p.332)

• No matter how often I had gone *into* and come out of alcoholic lows during the day, the pattern bounced me out of bed each night about 2:00 a.m., shaking and hurting in the agitation that always follows a drug's sedation.(p.332)

• I went *into* action.(p.333)

• I'd go *into* an organization, and it wasn't long before I was on the committee, then I was chairman of the committee; and if I was in a group, I'd soon be treasurer or secretary of the group.(p.339)

• But when we come *into* A.A., we can face our problem honestly and openly.(p.340)

• A.A. gives us alcoholics direction *into* a way of life without the need for alcohol.(p.340)

• I was well *into* the second fifth by this time.(p.347)

• And I gave him some idea of what you do, and so I made my first Twelfth Step call before I ever came *into* the program.(p.347)

• I recall, as I walked *into* that meeting, saying to myself, "Here I am, a fellow of the American College of Surgeons, a Fellow of the International College of Surgeons, a diplomate of one of the great specialty boards in these United States, a member of the American Psychiatric Society, and I have to go to the butcher, the baker and the carpenter to help make a man out of me!"(p.347)

• Years earlier, I had gone *into* psychoanalysis to get relief.(p.349)

• I do recall lying on a cold cement floor and shredding *into* little bits several pieces of stolen identification cards, and washing my face in the toilet bowl trying to sober up, and screaming hysterically while clinging to bars too high to see out of, and cursing everyone that came near me.(p.354)

• When I walked *into* the friendly atmosphere of my first A.A. meeting, I knew I was where I belonged.(p.355)

• As a matter of fact, when I came *into* Alcoholics Anonymous I was close to being at the peak of my career.(p.356)

• I entered the house, opened a new bottle of whiskey and sat down to drink myself *into* the right frame of mind to get in my car, start the motor and close the garage door behind me.(p.363)

• It was worrying my wife a little, but she had the good sense not to take me to task about it or goad me *into* going.(p.364)

• I would gather up all my soiled clothes, as much as I could cram *into* a grocery cart, and be off.(p.370)

• Near the Laundromat, I would buy one bottle of pop and a few bottles of beer or wine, and go *into* the rest room, empty the pop bottle, refill it with the booze, and proceed to do my laundering.(p.370)

• I didn't know that when I came *into* A.A.(p.384)

• I got right *into* the car and they drove me over, and just as soon as I got to the church they started the wedding.(p.385)

• So it drove me deeper *into* the psychosis or neurosis that I had, and that I hated deep down in my heart.(p.388)

• So I located a house, and I thought we ought to move *into* it immediately, but Frank was horrified, because he never knew what was going to happen to me.(p.388)

• He talked me *into* taking the Samaritan Treatment.(p.389)

• I got *into* slacks and out I went, weaving with the dog.(p.390)

• The next morning he came *into* my room and said, "Esther, I'm not going to lecture you any more, but I want you to read this article.(p.391)

• I stayed drunk from Monday until Friday, and I call that my spill *into* A.A.(p.393)

• However, I threw myself *into* Twelve Step work, and what I feared would be a calamity turned out to be the most blessed of blessings.(p.394)

• My work with other alcoholics has led me, day by day, *into* ever wider and richer experiences.(p.394)

• I wish I could tell you all that A.A. has done for me, all that I think and feel about A.A., but it's something that I have experienced and have never been able to put *into* words.(p.394)

• It pays daily in more harmonious relations with my fellow men, in ever clearer insight *into* the true meaning of life, and in the answering love and gratitude wherever and whenever I have been the instrument of God's will in the lives of others.(p.394)

• It's the last thing I ever heard him say, and I think there are some of us who, at times, try to read extra messages and complexities *into* the Steps.(p.395)

• Drunkalogues and statistics can be boring, but it is necessary to delve a little *into* each in order to come up with some kind of rough estimate.(p.396)

• But, as it was with drinking, this project will be entered *into* with enthusiasm and optimism – and probably wind up the same way, depressed.(p.396)

• At age twenty-one, I enlisted in the Navy for two reasons: (1) to avoid being drafted *into* the Army, and (2) out of a burst of patriotic fervor inspired by the advent of World War II and as the result of an all-night drinking binge which found me sitting on the doorstep of the Navy recruiting office when the chief petty officer arrived to open for business at nine o'clock Monday morning.(p.398)

• But I did not fit *into* this pattern either.(p.402)

• I had a tiny trust fund, and I moved *into* a small apartment where I learned to cook, keep house, and do the things that normal people do.(p.409)

• Most of the time I was covered with bruises from "running *into* doors."(p.411)

• But I never got *into* jail.(p.411)

• I didn't get *into* a sanitarium either.(p.411)
• Once, when I called my analyst, and told her I was contemplating death, she came over and tried to get me *into* a sanitarium.(p.411)
• All these things together brought me *into* A.A.(p.415)
• When I went back to my hometown to go *into* private practice, I experienced another brief lull in my addiction to alcohol and drugs.(p.420)
• A young veteran tells how a few rough experiences pushed him *into* A.A. – and how he was therefore spared years of suffering.(p.422)
• Two fuzzy objects came *into* focus.(p.422)
• I liked it and soon moved *into* the photo department which was what I wanted to do.(p.425)
• I went *into* the Navy in fine style.(p.425)
• I talked the Old Man *into* letting me live in the photo lab instead of the barracks, and for eighteen months nothing interfered with my drinking.(p.426)
• Two of them leaped from the table and crashed *into* my head.(p.427)
• The doctor said I'd been brought *into* the hospital like a madman, crying, raving, ranting, swearing, completely in the throes of delirium tremens.(p.427)
• I was supposed to come home on a troop ship, but I talked the base commander *into* flying me home.(p.428)
• I would drink all night in bars, come home about five a.m., down a good big glass of whiskey straight, and tumble *into* bed.(p.428)
• Again I went *into* a mild form of D.T.'s, but with no pineapples this time.(p.429)
• I'd packed more drinking *into* seven years than many a heavy drinker does in a lifetime.(p.429)
• That is how I came *into* A.A.(p.430)
• Once or twice, during my early drinking, I carried it over *into* the second day, and only once, that I can remember, did it continue *into* the third.(p.432)
• I came to understand the intricate processes of projection, by which we cast *into* our adult world the images of the horrors of our childhood.(p.434)
• My alcoholic associates fired me, took control, and ran the enterprise *into* bankruptcy.(p.437)
• And as I went through pharmacy school, graduate school, medical school, internship, residency, and specialty training and, finally, went *into* practice, my drinking kept increasing.(p.441)
• Very shortly, I realized that had been a mistake -- when this big clown came bounding *into* the room, almost shouting, "My name is Frank, and I'm an alcoholic, ha-ha-ha!"(p.446)
• Each time I told her she was a nothing, she receded a little more *into* nowhere.(p.450)
• Alcohol wrings the guts out of life, eats *into* the brain in such a way as to make the alcoholic blind to the truth.(p.457)
• I do not want to digress *into* the dynamics of penology.(p.458)
• After all, it was self (you, me) that stood in our own way, that ran the show and ran ourselves *into* bankruptcy, that hurt the ones we loved.(p.459)
• I sank *into* total despair.(p.461)
• During the twenty-four hours after running *into* the Serenity Prayer, I think I took the first three Steps for the first time.(p.461)
• This A.A. friend took me *into* his home when he had me out on pass.(p.462)
• Shortly thereafter, I was selected, with eight other inmates out of the 10,000 in the state's prisons at that time, to attend a school designed to take former "management problems" like me and convert them *into* paracounselors.(p.462)
• In fact it has been only within the last fifteen years that I changed from a fairly normal, controlled drinker *into* an alcoholic.(p.464)
• My pattern of drinking at that time had reached the point where once I really started, I would retire to my bed and drink myself *into* oblivion.(p.466)
• Then I remember him coming *into* my room one night with a friend, and telling me to get dressed – we were going away.(p.466)
• I was taken out of the house and put bodily *into* a waiting car with nothing on but a robe and gown.(p.466)
• My husband helped me *into* the house, packed himself a bag, and gave me some money.(p.467)
• The next recollection I have is of my husband coming *into* my room (later found out it was on New Year's Eve) accompanied by two policemen.(p.468)
• I won't go *into* detail about that, but I can assure you it's no fun.(p.469)
• You may wonder why, since I was having all this trouble, and was having to seek the assistance of others, A.A. hadn't come *into* the picture.(p.469)
• The Higher Power to whom I had turned, and who had sustained me, had once again been thrust *into* the background, while my emotions were running my life and, as always, my emotions ran me to the bottle.(p.472)
• When I first came *into* A.A., the woman who was my sponsor was the first woman I had ever met who admitted that she was an alcoholic.(p.472)
• Got *into* no trouble.(p.475)
• Waitress by day, barfly by night, she drifted down the years *into* jail.(p.478)
• When I came *into* A.A., I had no intention of quitting drinking – I figured I was doing all right.(p.478)
• You see how much work some of us have to do on ourselves when we finally come *into* A.A.!(p.480)
• Another thing that mother drilled *into* me was a very Puritanical point of view as to sex relations and as to motherhood and womanhood.(p.483)
• I don't think I suffered too much as far as the racial situation was concerned because I was born *into* it and knew nothing other than that.(p.485)
• I'd go *into* my home with a bottle, and I remember clearly how I would look around to see if Vi was watching.(p.487)
• But the week-ends stretched on *into* Mondays and the time soon came when I drank every day.(p.488)
• He went *into* the religious side and told me that I didn't attend church as regularly as I should, and that he felt, more or less, that this was responsible for my trouble.(p.489)
• I got *into* a lot of financial difficulties too.(p.490)
• Thinking only of two or three dollars to buy some whiskey, I did the job and that's how I met Ella G., who was responsible for my coming *into* A.A.(p.493)
• I fall *into* a dreamless sleep.(p.497)
• She had looked for me last evening after I left the car and wandered off *into* the night.(p.502)
• "How does prayer fit *into* this thing?"(p.504)
• I crawl back *into* bed and sleep like a child.(p.504)
• Get *into* the lives of other people, is one thing the fellows in New York had said.(p.505)
• I will not go out and I will not enter *into* anything.(p.506)
• I back up to the door and go *into* the house.(p.506)
• I call my wife *into* a room where we can talk privately.(p.506)
• The days have grown *into* a little better than four years of sobriety.(p.511)
• If something does come along that sort of upsets me, instead of walking in and throwing a buck at the barman and asking for a drink, I walk *into* a telephone booth, drop a dime in the box, and call somebody who was so kind as to give me his name and telephone number to meet such an emergency.(p.511)
• When we first come *into* A.A., many of us are confused because as a general rule we're at the end of our respective ropes, and we don't know what to do.(p.512)
• So that pattern continued until I went *into* the Army.(p.513)
• Like many of us who went *into* the service, I thought it would be a cure-all, a new life.(p.513)
• When I landed of course I hit a gin mill, and with three or four good shots under my belt the world began to go *into* that rosy glow.(p.513)
• Because, thank God, since I came *into* this program I haven't had any trouble.(p.516)
• The gradual result was that I was drifting *into* making drinking one of the more important parts of my life.(p.519)
• I think the Commanding Officer was rather tired of this particular chicken coming back to roost so often because he very soon wrote in to the medical authorities to tell them that they had to get me *into* hospital, to be thoroughly examined for drinking.(p.520)
• I put myself *into* a home.(p.521)
• It was no use talking of putting myself *into* a home, a hospital, or of going to see a doctor again, or of going to see a priest or anyone else.(p.523)
• Having made that bargain, I immediately began to feel I'd been trapped *into* it and I went out and had some drinks – four glasses of gin, I remember.(p.523)
• My father was and still is a minister, and I was afraid that I might run *into* him, or that someone might tell him where I was, and I could still remember what he had done to me when I got drunk one Christmas when I was very young.(p.527)
• Later, I found out that I went *into* stores and stole clothes, then sold them.(p.528)
• I am hoping that writing this may bring some poor, mixed-up soul *into* the program.(p.530)
• It's time to stop finding excuses for drinking and getting *into* trouble, because now there is a way out, and if you want what we have, try coming around and giving the program a chance.(p.530)
• An ambitious playwright, he let his brains get so far ahead of his emotions that he collapsed *into* suicidal drinking.(p.531)
• And having sung that phrase, I'd chuckle with amusement, turning *into* irony turning *into* self-contempt turning *into* self-pity, at the sad fate of Bob, that wonderful, poor little motherless boy who was so smart in school and who grew up to accept responsibility so early and so fast and who staggered under his burdens without a whimper until the time came when he thought he was too good for this world and so he ought to be out of it.(p.532)
• On another small borrowed sum, I went up *into* the country to the home of a doctor I had known since boyhood.(p.540)
• The doc and I went back *into* the house.(p.541)
• The only importance in all of this lies in the fact that at twenty-three I was just as sick as I was at thirty three, when I came *into* A.A., but at that time I apparently had no place to go because I had no drinking problem.(p.546)
• It seems only fitting that when I did finally fall in love it was with an alcoholic, and for the next ten years I progressed as rapidly as is humanly possible *into* what I believed to be hopeless alcoholism.(p.547)
• The only way existence was possible was through rationalizing every sober moment and drinking myself *into* complete oblivion as often as I could.(p.547)
• The amount of will power exercised to control my drinking during working hours, diverted *into* a constructive channel, would have made me President, and the thing that made the will power possible was the knowledge that as soon as my day was finished I could drink myself *into* oblivion.(p.548)
• This caused the rather cryptic comment from one of my A.A. friends, when I told my story after coming *into* the program, that I had always been a cinch for the program, for I had always been interested in mankind, but that I was just taking them one man at a time.(p.548)
• I've heard it said many times in A.A., "There is just one good drunk in every alcoholic's life, and that's the one that brings us *into* A.A.," and I believe it.(p.549)
• A.A. has taught me that I will have peace of mind in exact proportion to the peace of mind I bring *into* the lives of other people, and it has taught me the true meaning of the admonition "happy are ye who know these things and do them."(p.551)
• I also got *into* my first disciplinary trouble caused by drinking, on two separate occasions.(p.555)
• Bewilderment, fear, and resentment moved *into* my life.(p.556)
• Instead of drinking in fancy bars and clubs, I had to carry a bottle of vodka in my briefcase, duck *into* public toilets, and gulp from the bottle, trembling, in order to keep from falling apart.(p.557)
• The enlargement of my liver degenerated *into* cirrhosis.(p.557)
• Each time, I went back to drinking – even smuggling a bottle of vodka *into* the hospital as soon as the blood transfusions had ceased.(p.558)
• As the sober days grew *into* sober months and then *into* sober years, a new and beautiful life began to emerge from the shambles of my former existence.(p.559)
• We learn how to level out the emotional wings that got us *into* trouble both when we were up and when we were down.(p.560)
• Ten – Alcoholics Anonymous has no opinion on outside issues; hence the A.A. name ought never be drawn *into* public controversy.(p.564)
• An A.A. group, as such, should never go *into* business.(p.566)
• The days add up *into* weeks, the weeks *into* months and years."(p.572)

intolerable

• We were in a position where life was becoming impossible, and if we had passed into the region from which there is no return through human aid we had but two alternatives: One was to go on to the bitter end, blotting out the consciousness of our *intolerable* situation as best we could; and the other, to accept spiritual help.(p.25)
• I was caught in a cycle of alcohol and sedation that was proving inescapable and consciousness had become *intolerable*.(p.304)
• Cold sweats, jumpy nerves and lack of sleep were becoming *intolerable*.(p.378)

intolerance

• We talked of *intolerance*, while we were intolerant ourselves.(p.50)
• We are careful never to show *intolerance* or hatred of drinking as an institution.(p.103)
• A spirit of *intolerance* might repel alcoholics whose

lives could have been saved, had it not been for such stupidity.(p.103)
• The slightest sign of fear or ***intolerance*** may lessen your husband's chance of recovery.(p.120)
• His wife is one of those persons who really feels there is something rather sinful about these commodities, so she nagged, and her ***intolerance*** finally threw him into a fit of anger.(p.135)
• The very practical approach to his problems, the absence of ***intolerance*** of any kind, the informality, the genuine democracy, the uncanny understanding which these people had were irresistible.(p.160)
• I realized that there wasn't anything I could say to place myself in a more favorable light with my children, that it was going to be a matter of time; for I also understood the ***intolerance*** of young people towards deficiencies in their elders.(p.220)
• At the moral inventory, he brought up some of my bad personality traits or character defects, such as selfishness, conceit, jealousy, carelessness, ***intolerance***, ill-temper, sarcasm and resentments.(p.292)
• He can only be defeated by an attitude of ***intolerance*** or belligerent denial.(p.570)

intolerant

• We talked of intolerance, while we were ***intolerant*** ourselves.(p.50)
• I was ***intolerant*** of people who drank, particularly those who drank to an extent that interfered with on-the-job performance.(p.374)
• The last two years of my drinking my entire personality changed to a cynical, ***intolerant*** and arrogant person completely different from my normal self.(p.376)
• It seemed to me my wife was becoming more ***intolerant*** and narrow minded all the time.(p.376)

intoxicated

• He is seldom mildly ***intoxicated***.(p.21)
• He is the fellow who goes to bed so ***intoxicated*** he ought to sleep the clock around.(p.21)
• In a few years he became so violent when ***intoxicated*** that he had to be committed.(p.35)
• The first time that I became ***intoxicated*** I was eight years old.(p.182)
• I didn't want to jeopardize the lives of innocent people by driving an automobile while ***intoxicated***, but I did.(p.199)
• At three-thirty the next morning, I was in Champlain Street Station, in jail for driving while ***intoxicated*** and insulting an officer; and the suit of which I was so proud was in such shape that the turnkey had to get me a pair of trousers to go into court in the next morning.(p.201)
• At this point I believe I had only been ***intoxicated*** on maybe three or four occasions, and certainly whiskey was no problem to me.(p.487)

intoxication

• We have indulged in spiritual ***intoxication***.(p.128)
• During the first six months of 1935, I was hospitalized eight times for ***intoxication*** and shackled to the bed two or three days before I even knew where I was.(p.184)
• My last venture, a book shop, was hastened to closed doors by my steady ***intoxication***.(p.255)
• Even obvious ***intoxication*** is excused by younger people as something "he's earned the right to do," and they say, "After all, who's he hurting?"(p.330)

intravenous

• For the leveling-off process, I just loved ***intravenous*** Demerol, but I found it hard to practice good medicine while shooting morphine.(p.442)

intravenously

• However, for a period of time I was injecting Pentothal ***intravenously*** to put myself to sleep.(p.442)

intricate

• I came to understand the ***intricate*** processes of projection, by which we cast into our adult world the images of the horrors of our childhood.(p.434)

intrigued

• Being ***intrigued***, however, he invited our friend to his home.(p.155)
• That discovery so ***intrigued*** me, that I stayed on that diet almost entirely for the balance of my extensive drinking life.(p.298)
• The challenge ***intrigued*** me; also it was another opportunity to run away from myself and the "fast life of the big city."(p.359)

intriguing

• I didn't dare hope I might find for myself all that these people had found, but if I could acquire some small part of their ***intriguing*** quality of living – and sobriety – that would be enough.(p.310)

introduce

• Speaking at a dinner given by John D. Rockefeller Jr. to ***introduce*** Alcoholics Anonymous to some of his friends, Dr. Harry Emerson Fosdick remarked: "I think that psychologically speaking there is a point of advantage in the approach that is being made in this movement that cannot be duplicated.(p.574)

introduced

• I was ***introduced*** to them and Clarence proceeded to put on his Twelve Step work.(p.216)
• He ***introduced*** himself and began to tell me about a bunch of some sixty former drinkers and drunkards who met once a week, and he invited me to go with him to the next meeting.(p.257)
• And they ***introduced*** me to Miriam and Annabelle.(p.269)
• She took me by the hand and ***introduced*** me to the girl that I'm very proud to call my sponsor.(p.321)
• I was ***introduced*** as a psychiatrist.(p.347)
• They ***introduced*** me to beer in the morning to kill hangovers.(p.407)

introduction

• So the story of my ***introduction*** into A.A. begins with the activities of my wife.(p.216)
• This was my ***introduction*** to this "understanding fellowship" although it was to be more than a year later before our Society was to bear the name, Alcoholics Anonymous.(p.239)
• I got my first ***introduction*** to "riding the rods and making a blind."(p.252)
• I spent my last seventeen months in Wallkill, and it was there that I first got my ***introduction*** to A.A.(p.509)
• We talked for a while, and then he sent me down to the Alanon House over on the west side, and there I had my ***introduction*** to A.A.(p.515)

intrude

• (At this point, the Editors ***intrude*** just long enough to supplement Bill D.'s account, that of the man on the bed, with that of Bill W., the man who sat by the side of the bed.)(p.188)

intruded

• But as long as you did your work and didn't disgrace yourself, you were socially acceptable and nobody really ***intruded*** on your private life very much.(p.518)

intruders

• The only kind of security I knew anything about at that time was material security and I decided that all these ***intruders*** would vanish immediately if I only had a lot of money.(p.545)

intuitive

• Here we ask God for inspiration, an ***intuitive*** thought or a decision.(p.86)
• I think, with him it possibly was a gift – ***intuitive*** diagnosis.(p.485)

intuitively

• We will ***intuitively*** know how to handle situations which used to baffle us.(p.84)

invariably

• Sometimes they hurt us, seemingly without provocation, but we ***invariably*** find that at some time in the past we have made decisions based on self which later placed us in a position to be hurt.(p.62)
• Almost ***invariably*** they got drunk.(p.72)
• We do talk about each other a great deal, but we almost ***invariably*** temper such talk by a spirit of love and tolerance.(p.125)
• I could never be bothered with the follow-through and would ***invariably*** reward myself for my efforts with that "first" drink.(p.243)
• He would ***invariably*** reply, "When you are right and the time is right, Providence will provide.(p.293)
• Far from expecting praise for their deeds, they claimed the performance a privilege and insisted that they ***invariably*** received more than they gave.(p.310)
• This great experience that released me from the bondage of hatred and replaced it with love is really just another affirmation of the truth I know: I get everything I need in Alcoholics Anonymous – everything I need I get – and when I get what I need I ***invariably*** find that it was just what I wanted all the time.(p.553)
• There is something spiritual about A.A. too, and Catholic participation in it almost ***invariably*** results in poor Catholics becoming better Catholics."(p.574)

invented

• When your husband is bad, you become a trembling recluse, wishing the telephone had never been ***invented***.(p.115)

invention

• The spirit of modern scientific inquiry, research and ***invention*** was almost unknown.(p.51)

inventions

• In the fall of the graduating year, I became involved in some litigation over the ownership of ***inventions*** and patents.(p.212)

inventiveness

• My alcoholism-prone mind, however, reminded me that all great authors had needed a stimulus to build up inspiration and ***inventiveness*** before each day's work.(p.331)

inventories

• In those days we really took each other's ***inventories*** firmly and often.(p.245)

inventory

• Though he could not accept all the tenets of the Oxford Groups, he was convinced of the need for moral ***inventory***, confession of personality defects, restitution to those harmed, helpfulness to others, and the necessity of belief in and dependence upon God.(p.xvi)
• 4.Made a searching and fearless moral ***inventory*** of ourselves.(p.59)
• 10.Continued to take personal ***inventory*** and when we were wrong promptly admitted it.(p.59)
• Therefore, we started upon a personal ***inventory***.(p.64)
• A business which takes no regular ***inventory*** usually goes broke.(p.64)
• Taking a commercial ***inventory*** is a fact-finding and a fact-facing process.(p.64)
• The ***inventory*** was ours, not the other man's.(p.67)
• If we have been thorough about our personal ***inventory***, we have written down a lot.(p.70)
• If you have already made a decision, and an ***inventory*** of your grosser handicaps, you have made a good beginning.(p.71)
• Having made our personal ***inventory***, what shall we do about it?(p.72)
• We have admitted certain defects; we have ascertained in a rough way what the trouble is; we have put our finger on the weak items in our personal ***inventory***.(p.72)
• They took ***inventory*** all right, but hung on to some of the worst items in stock.(p.73)
• We have a written ***inventory*** and we are prepared for a long talk.(p.75)
• We made it when we took ***inventory***.(p.76)
• This thought brings us to Step Ten, which suggests we continue to take personal ***inventory*** and continue to set right any new mistakes as we go along.(p.84)
• Of course, we had talked over quite a number of the failings that I had and made a sort of an ***inventory***, which wasn't too difficult, because I had an awful lot of things wrong that were very apparent to me, because I knew all about them.(p.190)
• I had been too self-sufficient to write a moral ***inventory***, but I discovered in pointing out to the new man his wrong attitudes and actions that I was really taking my own ***inventory***, and that if I expected him to change I would have to work on myself too.(p.249)
• 3.Moral ***inventory***.(p.292)
• At the moral ***inventory***, he brought up some of my bad personality traits or character defects, such as selfishness, conceit, jealousy, carelessness, intolerance, ill-temper, sarcasm and resentments.(p.292)
• That was my lesson, that one could not take the moral ***inventory*** and then file it away; that the alcoholic has to continue to take ***inventory*** every day if he expects to get well and stay well.(p.293)
• I took everybody else's ***inventory***.(p.410)
• While I was taking ***inventory*** in the cold-storage locker one Sunday, a wooden sign bolted to the inside door stopped me in my tracks.(p.461)
• Had I tried honestly and sincerely to practice the Twelve Steps I would have seen from my continuous moral ***inventory*** that I was getting off the beam – I would have found that there were some active resentments in my life, a terrific amount of self-pity.(p.471)
• So I don't just take the ***inventory*** at night – I take it continually throughout the day.(p.516)
• As I said earlier, self-pity and resentment were my constant companions and my ***inventory*** began to look like a thirty-three year diary, for I seemed to have a resentment against everybody I had ever known.(p.551)

inversely

• Perhaps the best thing of all for me is to remember that my serenity is ***inversely*** proportional to my expectations.(p.452)

invested

• I was now head of a publishing venture in which nearly a million dollars had been ***invested***.(p.435)

investigate
• So I started to ***investigate*** Science through some friends of mine who were Readers in the church.(p.202)
• In my stupid way I went up to see him with the idea in the back of my mind that I would ***investigate*** Alcoholics Anonymous from a medical standpoint.(p.346)

investigation
• Like most statistics, it doesn't prove anything -- just satisfies a little curiosity engendered by the wail "Oh, those initiation fees" that prompted this ***investigation.***(p.399)
• Being an alcoholic, slick, and having some good sense left, I survived the ***investigation.***(p.490)
• There might have been some ***investigation.***(p.492)
• "There is a principle which is a bar against all information, which is proof against all arguments and which cannot fail to keep a man in everlasting ignorance -- that principle is contempt prior to ***investigation.***"(p.570)

investigator
• I took a night law course, and obtained employment as ***investigator*** for a surety company.(p.2)
• By the time I had completed law school I had picked up some experience in patent law, for I remained with the patent law firm and worked too in Washington where they found that I was a capable infringement ***investigator.***(p.213)

investment
• Then it was my turn -- I ordered "Three beers," but this time it was different, I had a cash ***investment*** of thirty cents and, on a ten dollar a week salary, that's a big thing.(p.247)

invitation
• At the age of sixteen, I was invited to spend the summer with an aunt and I, very delightedly, accepted the ***invitation.***(p.261)

invitations
• Finally our ***invitations*** became fewer and fewer as friends had more experience with my drinking pattern.(p.377)

invite
• We could not be invited out because I would surely get tight and my wife dared not ***invite*** people in for the same reason.(p.177)
• Successful home-brewers among my friends began to ***invite*** me to their homes.(p.232)
• My mother resented it so that the first Christmas after our marriage, she didn't even ***invite*** us to dinner.(p.485)

invited
• In the spring of 1940, John D. Rockefeller, Jr. gave a dinner for many of his friends to which he ***invited*** A.A. members to tell their stories.(p.xviii)
• When we were ***invited*** out, our husbands sneaked so many drinks that they spoiled the occasion.(p.105)
• When this happens, they can be ***invited*** to join in morning meditation and then they can take part in the daily discussion without rancor or bias.(p.134)
• Being intrigued, however, he ***invited*** our friend to his home.(p.155)
• We could not be ***invited*** out because I would surely get tight and my wife dared not invite people in for the same reason.(p.177)
• I was doing well in business, and in going around town I was frequently ***invited*** to have a drink in a speakeasy.(p.233)
• The only salesman ***invited*** to talk at the convention?(p.243)
• He introduced himself and began to tell me about a bunch of some sixty former drinkers and drunkards who met once a week, and he ***invited*** me to go with him to the next meeting.(p.257)
• At the age of sixteen, I was ***invited*** to spend the summer with an aunt and I, very delightedly, accepted the invitation.(p.261)
• (Russ was buried on Friday, and on Sunday afternoon Hilda S. had ***invited*** me there to dinner Sunday night, and I didn't think I could do it.(p.272)
• When I got out of the hospital, I was ***invited*** to stay with Dr. Bob and his dear wife, Anne.(p.279)
• Friends ***invited*** me to stay on for as long as I cared to.(p.281)
• If we were ***invited*** to a formal party and I knew they were only going to have one or two drinks, I wouldn't have any.(p.323)
• If there is none nearby, you will be ***invited*** to carry on a correspondence which will do much to insure your sobriety no matter how isolated you are.(p.575)

invites
• He ***invites*** me to meet them.(p.504)

inviting
• The ***inviting*** maelstrom of Wall Street had me in its grip.(p.2)

involve
• What right had he to ***involve*** those dependent upon him?(p.80)
• We feel we ought to say to her that we have no right to ***involve*** another person.(p.81)

involved
• However intelligent we may have been in other respects, where alcohol has been ***involved,*** we have been strangely insane.(p.38)
• So, in one way or another, we discovered that faith had been ***involved*** all the time!(p.54)
• Though a situation had not been entirely our fault, we tried to disregard the other person ***involved*** entirely.(p.67)
• Usually, however, other people are ***involved.***(p.79)
• A man so ***involved*** often feels very remorseful at times, especially if he is married to a loyal and courageous girl who has literally gone through hell for him.(p.81)
• But for every man who drinks others are ***involved*** -- the wife who trembles in fear of the next debauch; the mother and father who see their son wasting away.(p.104)
• You may be at a loss to understand how such a seemingly above-board chap could be so ***involved.***(p.140)
• In the fall of the graduating year, I became ***involved*** in some litigation over the ownership of inventions and patents.(p.212)
• If it isn't anything that's going to help you or anybody else, why should you become ***involved*** in it, and get all disturbed about it?"(p.273)
• Finally this company also became ***involved*** and I was once more looking for a job.(p.300)
• Cunning, baffling, powerful -- the gradual creeping up of the frequency and quantity of alcohol, and what it does to a person is apparent to everyone but the person ***involved.***(p.375)
• All the people ***involved*** in these flare-ups took it with remarkable grace, have teased me about it since, and have become good friends of mine.(p.416)
• Within a month, the police, the hospital authorities, several kind strangers, most of my friends, all of my close relatives, and a few adepts at rolling a drunk and removing his wrist watch and wallet had been ***involved.***(p.532)

involves
• This ***involves*** a process of deflation.(p.122)

involving
• I thought, well, now that I've been put out for drinking, I'll just show them that they were completely wrong, so I went off on the biggest bout I had been on up to then, ***involving*** about a fortnight's blackout.(p.521)

inward
• It is being constantly revealed, as mankind studies the material world, that outward appearances are not ***inward*** reality at all.(p.48)
• My growing ***inward*** unhappiness was a very real thing, however, and I knew that something would have to be done about it.(p.434)
• How exciting to learn the ***inward*** mysteries that govern the behavior of people, how wonderful to know, at last, all about myself!(p.434)
• Meanwhile, I was getting worse, both as regards my ***inward*** misery and my drinking.(p.434)

inwardly
• I saw that my friend was much more than ***inwardly*** reorganized.(p.11)
• ***Inwardly*** he would give anything to take half a dozen drinks and get away with them.(p.152)
• There was always a tremendous drive and ambition to become a great guy, because I think I recognized ***inwardly*** that I didn't have any special talents.(p.194)
• All I had left was an iron determination to live my own life in spite of the alien world -- and here I was, an ***inwardly*** frightened, outwardly defiant woman, who desperately needed a prop to keep going.(p.226)
• Sometimes during that year I rebelled ***inwardly*** at what seemed like lost time, and at having to be a burden to these good people whose means were limited.(p.281)
• Lying on the divan, "getting in the mood" to write, I cried openly or ***inwardly,*** as I listened to sad songs.(p.332)
• I was ***inwardly*** unhappy most of the time.(p.432)
• And yet my ability to lie outwardly and to kid myself ***inwardly*** grew with every drink I took.(p.556)

iota
• Around this time our big A.A. book was being written and it all became much simpler; we had a definite formula which some sixty of us agreed was the middle course for all alcoholics who wanted sobriety, and that formula has not been changed one ***iota*** down through the years.(p.248)

irate
• Cleaning up old scrapes, helping to settle family differences, explaining the disinherited son to his ***irate*** parents, lending money and securing jobs for each other, when justified -- these are everyday occurrences.(p.161)

Ireland
• The first had been as a youngster coming out from ***Ireland.***(p.513)
• So I decided I'd go back and live in ***Ireland*** to try the geography cure.(p.522)

Irish
• Dad's image for me was that of a big ***Irish*** oilman who came up through the school of hard knocks and so had to be a two-fisted drinker.(p.369)
• I belonged to one of the ***Irish*** families who, more or less traditionally, sent their boys to the British armies.(p.517)

Irishman
• The bartender, a tough ***Irishman,*** came around and "gave me the elbow," which means that he raised his elbow and smacked me in the face.(p.411)
• A British officer, this ***Irishman*** -- that is, until brandy "retired" him.(p.517)
• I am an ***Irishman*** and I was forty-nine when I joined A.A.(p.517)

irksome
• The need to uphold a facade had been ***irksome.***(p.328)

iron
• All I had left was an ***iron*** determination to live my own life in spite of the alien world -- and here I was, an inwardly frightened, outwardly defiant woman, who desperately needed a prop to keep going.(p.226)
• We worked in five below zero weather, fixing on an elm tree a wrought ***iron*** device which modestly proclaimed that he was indeed a country doctor.(p.540)

ironed
• While the internal difficulties of our adolescent period were being ***ironed*** out, public acceptance of A.A. grew by leaps and bounds.(p.xix)

irony
• What ***irony*** -- I became an alcoholic myself!(p.137)
• And having sung that phrase, I'd chuckle with amusement, turning into ***irony*** turning into self-contempt turning into self-pity, at the sad fate of Bob, that wonderful, poor little motherless boy who was so smart in school and who grew up to accept responsibility so early and so fast and who staggered under his burdens without a whimper until the time came when he thought he was too good for this world and so he ought to be out of it.(p.532)

irrational
• No wonder an alcoholic is strangely ***irrational.***(p.140)
• My desire to be honest with myself made it necessary for me to realize that my thinking was ***irrational.***(p.550)

irresistible
• The very practical approach to his problems, the absence of intolerance of any kind, the informality, the genuine democracy, the uncanny understanding which these people had were ***irresistible.***(p.160)
• I hope I have been able to impart to you, the reader, at least a bit of what I know; the joy of living, the ***irresistible*** power of divine love and its healing strength, and the fact that we, as sentient beings, have the knowledge to choose between good and evil, and, choosing good, are made happy.(p.543)

irresponsibility
• Even if he displays a certain amount of neglect and ***irresponsibility*** towards the family, it is well to let him go as far as he likes in helping other alcoholics.(p.129)
• We reverted to the old way of life we knew -- a life full of anger, vindictiveness, resentment, fear, dependence, denial, self-will, ***irresponsibility.***(p.459)

irresponsible
• When dealing with an alcoholic, there may be a natural annoyance that a man could be so weak, stupid and ***irresponsible.***(p.139)
• I was the fair-haired boy all right, but two years later I was blacklisted as an ***irresponsible*** drunk.(p.242)

• Drunk or sober, I was hectic, unpredictable, ***irresponsible.***(p.406)
• No one could live such an ***irresponsible,*** immature life as I had without consequences.(p.420)

irreversible
• I knew from my general reading that alcoholism was ***irreversible*** and fatal.(p.436)

irritable
• They are restless, ***irritable*** and discontented, unless they can again experience the sense of ease and comfort which comes at once by taking a few drinks -- drinks which they see others taking with impunity.(p.xxvi)
• If not ***irritable,*** he may seem dull and boring, not gay and affectionate as the family would like him to be.(p.126)

irritated
• When they talked of a God personal to me, who was love, superhuman strength and direction, I became ***irritated*** and my mind snapped shut against such a theory.(p.10)
• If you draw this fallacious reasoning to the attention of an alcoholic, he will laugh it off, or become ***irritated*** and refuse to talk.(p.23)
• I remember I felt ***irritated*** that I had to be a salesman for a concern I once owned.(p.36)
• It ***irritated*** my nostrils; I choked, I didn't like it.(p.195)

irritation
• Some of the snags you will encounter are ***irritation,*** hurt feeling and resentments.(p.117)
• He may take small interest in the children and may show ***irritation*** when reproved for his delinquencies.(p.126)
• As soon as his sobriety begins to be taken as a matter of course, the family may look at their strange new dad with apprehension, then with ***irritation.***(p.128)

island
• A house in Virginia, during the fox hunting season; a little chalet in Switzerland during the summer or a place on Long ***Island*** -- each house complete with cooks, butlers and maids.(p.403)
• Then I had about six months on a small ***island*** in command of the troops there.(p.520)

isn't
• It's strong language -- but ***isn't*** it true?(p.38)
• But it ***isn't*** so difficult.(p.44)
• When, however, the perfectly logical assumption is suggested that underneath the material world and life as we see it, there is an All Powerful, Guiding, Creative Intelligence, right there our perverse streak comes to the surface and we laboriously set out to convince ourselves it ***isn't*** so.(p.49)
• God either is, or He ***isn't.***(p.53)
• Hence, we saw that reason ***isn't*** everything.(p.54)
• They think we do not have enough of it, or that it ***isn't*** the right kind.(p.69)
• A kindly act once in a while ***isn't*** enough.(p.97)
• This just ***isn't*** so.(p.99)
• To a person who has had experience with an alcoholic, this may seem like tempting Providence, but it ***isn't.***(p.101)
• Of course that ***isn't*** so, and such people often may impose on you.(p.141)
• It ***isn't*** fair to me or the firm.(p.147)
• He will presently try the old game again, for he ***isn't*** happy about his sobriety.(p.152)
• And they both laughed very heartily, and said, "That's better than you've been doing, ***isn't*** it?"(p.187)
• It ***isn't*** always so sudden with everyone, but I ran into a personal crisis which filled me with a raging and righteous anger.(p.228)
• If it ***isn't*** anything that's going to help you or anybody else, why should you become involved in it, and get all disturbed about it?"(p.273)
• My stock of material goods ***isn't*** great.(p.296)
• However, this ***isn't*** as rough as it sounds, as we do become grateful for the necessity that makes us toe the line, for we find that we are more than compensated for a consistent effort by the countless dividends we receive.(p.311)
• Unlike his skid-row brother, he ***isn't*** heckled for sleeping in alleys or doorways.(p.330)
• A duplex apartment ***isn't*** any place to raise a dog.(p.388)
• Finally she said, "***Isn't*** your name Jim S.?"(p.493)
• When you've been in a jam you've said, 'God, please do this or that,' and if it turned out your way that was the last of it, and if it didn't you've said There ***isn't*** any God' or 'He doesn't do anything for me.'(p.504)
• "That ***isn't*** the way," he continued.(p.504)
• My drinking pattern ***isn't*** very different from the average you find in A.A.(p.512)
• He just looked at me and said, "Pat, for you there ***isn't*** any cure."(p.515)
• Oh yes, I get the dry jitters once in a while, but that ***isn't*** anything to worry about.(p.516)

isolated
• If there is none nearby, you will be invited to carry on a correspondence which will do much to insure your sobriety no matter how ***isolated*** you are.(p.575)

isolates
• It is probably true that you and your husband have been living too much alone, for drinking many times ***isolates*** the wife of an alcoholic.(p.119)
• Drinking ***isolates*** most homes from the outside world.(p.131)

issue
• At first some of us tried to avoid the ***issue,*** hoping against hope we were not true alcoholics.(p.44)
• We couldn't duck the ***issue.***(p.53)
• Talk about his condition or this book only when he raises the ***issue.***(p.113)
• She sees she was wrong to make a burning ***issue*** out of such a matter when his more serious ailments were being rapidly cured.(p.135)
• They never raised the ***issue.***(p.215)
• It helped me a great deal to become convinced that alcoholism was a disease, not a moral ***issue;*** that I had been drinking as a result of a compulsion, even though I had not been aware of the compulsion at the time; and that sobriety was not a matter of willpower.(p.448)

issues
• Don't raise such ***issues,*** no matter what your own convictions are.(p.93)
• Ten -- Alcoholics Anonymous has no opinion on outside ***issues;*** hence the A.A. name ought never be drawn into public controversy.(p.564)
• On such ***issues*** our common welfare is paramount.(p.565)
• 10. -- No A.A. group or member should ever, in such a way as to implicate A.A., express any opinion on outside controversial ***issues*** -- particularly those of politics, alcohol reform, or sectarian religion.(p.567)

itching
• Following an injection I would have to keep one hand busy scratching my constantly ***itching*** nose and would also have sudden uncontrollable urges to vomit.(p.442)

itchy
• That is the way Jackie found me, lying on a cot in my skivvies, with hot and cold sweats, pounding heart and that awful ***itchy*** scratchiness all over.(p.238)

items
• We have admitted certain defects; we have ascertained in a rough way what the trouble is; we have put our finger on the weak ***items*** in our personal inventory.(p.72)
• They took inventory all right, but hung on to some of the worst ***items*** in stock.(p.73)
• The next three years I spent in Boston, Chicago, and Montreal in the employ of a large manufacturing concern, selling railway supplies, gas engines of all sorts, and many other ***items*** of heavy hardware.(p.172)

itself
• Each day my friend's simple talk in our kitchen multiplies ***itself*** in a widening circle of peace on earth and good will to men.(p.16)
• But that in ***itself*** would never have held us together as we are now joined.(p.17)
• Fred's story speaks for ***itself.***(p.43)
• We agnostically inclined would not feel satisfied with a proposal which does not lend ***itself*** to reasonable approach and interpretation.(p.53)
• But this is not an end in ***itself.***(p.77)
• The less people tolerated us, the more we withdrew from society, from life ***itself.***(p.151)
• Before my drinking had cut me down completely, I achieved a considerable measure of success, having been a City Councilman for five years and a financial director of Kenmore, a suburb later taken into the city ***itself.***(p.182)
• Here by ***itself*** was a great step forward.(p.283)
• And life keeps getting simpler and easier as we try to reverse my old idea, by taking care of the internal environment via the Twelve Steps, and letting the external environment take care of ***itself.***)(p.446)
• The old pattern reasserted ***itself,*** but it was no longer once every six months.(p.514)
• India lent ***itself*** to drinking then, if you were disposed to drink, because you lived in bungalows; you didn't live all together as you do at home in an Officer's Mess.(p.519)
• A pattern established ***itself.***(p.536)
• An A.A. group can bind ***itself*** to no one.(p.566)
• The terms "spiritual experience" and "spiritual awakening" are used many times in this book which, upon careful reading, shows that the personality change sufficient to bring about recovery from alcoholism has manifested ***itself*** among us in many different forms.(p.569)

Jj

Jack
• Then *Jack* Alexander wrote a feature article in the Saturday Evening Post and placed such a compelling picture of A.A. before the general public that alcoholics in need of help really deluged us.(p.xviii)
• She said, "Well, you better talk to *Jack*."(p.266)
• (*Jack* was the owner of the place.(p.266)
• I drove these three or four miles down the road only to find that *Jack* was out.(p.267)
• I don't think *Jack* was hospitalized.(p.267)
• Mrs. M. said she would send *Jack* over as quick as he came in.(p.267)
• Dr. Bob was in Florida, but *Jack* didn't know that.(p.267)
• *Jack* brought the Saturday Post with *Jack* Alexander's story.(p.268)
• *Jack* didn't seem to have too much of the spiritual understanding.(p.268)
• *Jack* said there was a meeting in Akron every Wednesday night and that it was very important that we go.(p.268)
• *Jack* said, "Now you start and go to these meetings, and then you'll find out all about it."(p.268)
• On Wednesday night *Jack* M. said, "You meet me at the Ohio Edison Building, and I will take you to the meeting."(p.269)
• And Russ said, "I would have sworn that was *Jack* M."(p.271)
• It had been *Jack* M.(p.271)
• *Jack* had been sober about a year and a half.(p.271)
• Even the *Jack* Alexander Saturday Evening Post article hadn't been written, and there was only a tiny group of people in Washington.(p.469)

jacket
• I found some wool stockings, some white flannels that had shrunk to my knees, and an old *jacket*.(p.288)

Jackie
• That is the way *Jackie* found me, lying on a cot in my skivvies, with hot and cold sweats, pounding heart and that awful itchy scratchiness all over.(p.238)
• I had not asked for help and seriously doubt that I would have, but Fitz, an old school friend of mine, had persuaded *Jackie* to call on me.(p.238)
• *Jackie* arrived about seven in the evening and talked until three a.m.(p.239)
• *Jackie* told me about a group of fellows in New York, of whom my old friend Fitz was one, who had the same problem I had, and who by working together to help each other were not now drinking and were happy like himself.(p.239)
• My sponsor, *Jackie*, was one of these.(p.239)
• Three months before I met *Jackie* I had made my second feeble try at suicide.(p.245)
• After being dry two weeks and sticking close to *Jackie*, all of a sudden I found I had become the sponsor of my sponsor, for he was suddenly taken drunk.(p.245)

Jackie's
• All they talked of that first week-end was God, and how they were going to straighten out *Jackie's* and my life.(p.245)

jackpot
• One night, I hit the *jackpot*.(p.332)

jackrabbit
• I had no more reason to drink those martinis than a *jackrabbit*.(p.195)

jag
• There was that time we had chartered an airplane to complete a *jag*!(p.9)

jail
• Perhaps we have committed a criminal offense which might land us in *jail* if it were known to the authorities.(p.78)
• We may lose our position or reputation or face *jail*, but we are willing.(p.79)
• We thought he ought to be willing to do that if necessary, but if he were in *jail* he could provide nothing for either family.(p.79)
• He said he was perfectly willing to go to *jail* if she insisted.(p.79)
• The next morning I woke up in *jail* in Cleveland and the jailor had $1,175 of my money in an envelope.(p.196)
• At three-thirty the next morning, I was in Champlain Street Station, in *jail* for driving while intoxicated and insulting an officer; and the suit of which I was so proud was in such shape that the turnkey had to get me a pair of trousers to go into court in the next morning.(p.201)
• I was arrested and taken to *jail* where I was beaten up by two or three fellows who were already in there and whom I tried to boss.(p.204)
• There had been some occasions -- there was an automobile wreck, for instance -- when I had police escort home but not to *jail*, all of which, instead of doing me a favor, did me harm because I was then full of self-esteem as to the progress I had made both professionally and financially.(p.213)
• Then broke again, hiding out in cheap hotels all over the country, one night *jail* stands here and there, and always that horrible feeling "What's the use -- nothing is worth while."(p.244)
• They threw us in the *jail*.(p.264)
• That to me was the greatest humiliation, to think that I'd finally landed in *jail*.(p.264)
• My husband said that I said, "Can you imagine them giving us that *jail* fare?"(p.264)
• And he said, "What *jail* fare?"(p.264)
• And he said, "That wasn't *jail* fare.(p.264)
• Next, I was sent to Arizona, where my drinking picked up some more, and I started having blackouts, and I was thrown in *jail* for speeding and drunken driving.(p.318)
• I was never in *jail*.(p.323)
• No *jail* booking, drunk-driving citation, barroom fight, or even a tumble off a barstool.(p.327)
• First, we all hear at A.A. meetings about those who have lost everything, those who have been in *jail*, those who have been in prison, those who have lost their families, those who have lost their income.(p.345)
• Lucky because my excessive drinking never got me in *jail*, or hospitalized, nor did it ever cost me a job.(p.356)
• This didn't say we had to be in *jail*, ten, fifty, or one hundred times.(p.379)
• When he picked me up, I must have gotten sassy and told him that he couldn't do that, so he took my dog home and took me to *jail*!(p.390)
• They phoned my husband that I was in *jail* and in such terrible shape that they didn't know what I would do to myself; and they realized that *jail* was no place for me, but that he was to wait a while before he got me, because at the time they called him to come over for me I was beating a tin cup against the wall.(p.390)
• But Frank turned around and looked at me and said, "Esther, remember you're in *jail* and not at home."(p.391)
• But I never got into *jail*.(p.411)
• The last time I drank, when I was twenty-nine, I drank for only four days, yet I threatened to kill my children; I beat my wife at home and on the church steps; I mistreated a child in my office; and I ran to a hospital for mental illness to avoid *jail*.(p.418)
• I would rather have stayed in *jail* except I didn't like bologna and cold potatoes for breakfast.(p.425)
• I went to Tijuana that night and landed in *jail*.(p.428)
• I woke up in *jail*, sick, withdrawing from alcohol and speed, already a four-time loser, and now with a fifth felony charge against me.(p.460)
• Judge say I go to *jail* next time.(p.475)
• Last time in *jail*, I have two black eyes.(p.475)
• Waitress by day, barfly by night, she drifted down the years into *jail*.(p.478)
• To tell you a small part of what my mother's life must have been like: Three of her kids were in *jail* that year – two sons and a daughter.(p.480)
• Then it got to the place I couldn't drink without getting in *jail*.(p.526)
• On one of these trips, the judge must have thought I was worth saving, for instead of sending me to *jail*, he sent me to A.A. for one month.(p.526)
• I was trying to remember where it came from, when two of the biggest cops I ever saw walked in and took me to *jail*.(p.528)
• In those years I was in *jail* nine times, in an alcoholic ward, overnight, twice; and I was fired from three jobs, two of them very good ones.(p.536)
• What a revelation of ego and arrogance still remaining in me – as if anyone, instinct and training apart, likes to be in *jail* or in an alcoholic ward or fired from his job.(p.536)
• But not for long; now, for five Friday nights in a row, I went to *jail*, picked up sodden with beer (which I always disliked, but which was the only drink available); in *jail* five consecutive Friday nights in the town where I had grown up, where I had been an honor student in high school, where a kindly uncle, bailing me out, said, "Bob, our family just doesn't do this sort of thing."(p.539)
• When I remark that I have been in *jail* nine times, and in an alcoholic ward twice, they think I'm kidding, or possibly dramatizing for the sake of a good yarn.(p.542)
• I went to *jail* for the second time during this period for being drunk in an automobile.(p.549)
• I was the only person I'd ever known personally who had ever been in *jail*, and I guess it is most significant that the second time was less humiliating that the first had been.(p.549)

jailed
• And, believe me, I thank God that I found out about A.A. before I had to beat my brains out – before I had been hospitalized, *jailed* or lost a job.(p.367)

jailor
• The next morning I woke up in jail in Cleveland and the *jailor* had $1,175 of my money in an envelope.(p.196)

jails
• It may mean sharing your money and your home, counseling frantic wives and relatives, innumerable trips to police courts, sanitariums, hospitals, *jails* and asylums.(p.97)
• Most of us have entered the final stage with its commitment to health resorts, sanitariums, hospitals, and *jails*.(p.107)
• I don't remember much of what he said, but I did realize that here was another guy exactly like me; he had been in the same laughing academies and the same *jails*, known the same loss of jobs, same frustrations, same boredom and the same loneliness.(p.239)
• I began to know the inside of *jails* and workhouses.(p.255)
• Most of these fortunate ones have had little or no acquaintance with delirium, with hospitals, asylums, and *jails*.(p.315)
• However, after I heard a few stories of *jails*, sanitariums, broken homes and skid row, I wondered if I really was an alcoholic.(p.378)
• Incalculable are the intangible initiation fees that A.A. members have paid: the sick, sick hangovers, the remorse, guilt, broken homes, *jails*, and institutions, and the mental anguish in general that has been generated over the years.(p.399)
• Many tried everything – hospitals, special treatments, sanitariums, asylums, and *jails*.(p.455)
• Then I find *jails* in Connecticut, too.(p.475)
• I remember how horrible *jails* are, how dreadful a thing it is to be behind steel bars.(p.542)
• I wish we did not have to have *jails*; I wish everyone could be in A.A., and if everyone were there would be no need for *jails*, in my opinion.(p.542)

jam
• When you've been in a *jam* you've said, 'God, please do this or that,' and if it turned out your way that was the last of it, and if it didn't you've said 'There isn't any God' or 'He doesn't do anything for me.'(p.504)

jambs
• If my wife was planning to go out in the afternoon, I would get a large supply of liquor and smuggle it home and hide it in the coal bin, the clothes chute, over door *jambs*, over beams in the cellar and in cracks in the cellar tile.(p.176)

James
• The distinguished American psychologist, William *James*, in his book "Varieties of Religious Experience," indicates a multitude of ways in which men have discovered God.(p.28)
• There is another meaning for the Hebrew word that in the King *James* version of the Bible is translated "salvation."(p.228)
• A policeman came to the door and asked for *James* S., but there wasn't any *James* S. there.(p.491)
• Most of our experiences are what the psychologist William *James* calls the "educational variety" because they develop slowly over a period of time.(p.569)

jams
• I had never known him to be anything but a good healthy pagan with a propensity for getting into li-

quor *jams* and scrapes.(p.257)

Jane
• And I thought, "You're some martyr, *Jane*!(p.322)

Janey
• So I went to her and said, "There's only one thing I want in my whole life, and I don't want any commendation; I don't want any credit; I don't want anything from you or *Janey* for the rest of your life except one thing; and that is, the opportunity to do anything you want always, and I would like to start off by doing the dishes."(p.351)

jangle
• Your telephone may *jangle* at any time of the day or night.(p.97)

January
• Bill W., co-founder of A.A., died *January* 24, 1971.(p.16)
• I still had enough practice to earn a good living if I would only work, so I resolved that in *January* of 1940 I would launch a patent law firm of my own.(p.220)
• *January* 8, 1938 – that was my D-Day; the place, Washington, D.C.(p.238)
• So I always say that as long as I remember *January* 8th that is how long I will remain sober.(p.240)
• This was the background that made me willing to listen on *January* 8th.(p.245)
• I had completely forgotten the *January* 8th when I found the fellowship, and I spent the next four days wandering around New England half drunk, by which I mean I couldn't get drunk and I couldn't get sober.(p.247)
• And I still say that as long as I remember that *January* 8th in Washington, that is how long, by the grace of God as I understand Him, I will retain a happy sobriety.(p.250)
• After a particularly bad Christmas and New Year's holiday, dad picked me up again early in *January*, 1937, to go through the usual sobering up routine.(p.289)
• In *January* 1938, I had the opportunity to go to northern Vermont to manage a small daytime radio station that was up against it financially, and was about to fold its antenna.(p.359)

jargon
• And all this, of course, is, in the popular modern *jargon*, "compensation" for immaturity.(p.535)

jay-walking
• Our behavior is as absurd and incomprehensible with respect to the first drink as that of an individual with a passion, say, for *jay-walking*.(p.37)
• He tells you he has decided to stop *jay-walking* for good, but in a few weeks he breaks both legs.(p.38)
• He tries every known means to get the *jay-walking* idea out of his head.(p.38)
• We, who have been through the wringer, have to admit if we substituted alcoholism for *jay-walking*, the illustration would fit us exactly.(p.38)

jazz
• There was loud talk in the *jazz* places uptown.(p.3)

jealous
• Still another difficulty is that you may become *jealous* of the attention he bestows on other people, especially alcoholics.(p.119)
• They may be *jealous* of a God who has stolen dad's affections.(p.128)
• At a comparatively early age, I can remember being *jealous* of my brother.(p.194)

jealousies
• Social distinctions, petty rivalries and *jealousies* -- these are laughed out of countenance.(p.161)
• Slowly, my life seemed to unfold before me, shedding insights on childhood resentments, *jealousies*, and fears that had mushroomed in adulthood, and also on the self-pity that I had wallowed in at every opportunity.(p.371)

jealously
• It is better, however, that one does not needlessly name a person upon whom she can vent *jealously*.(p.82)

jealousy
• In some circumstances we have gone out deliberately to get drunk, feeling ourselves justified by nervousness, anger, worry, depression, *jealousy* or the like.(p.37)
• Did we unjustifiably arouse *jealousy*, suspicion or bitterness?(p.69)
• Keep it always in sight that we are dealing with that most terrible human emotion -- *jealousy*.(p.82)
• You should warn against arousing resentment or *jealousy*.(p.100)
• When he renews interest in such things, a feeling of *jealousy* may arise.(p.131)
• The greatest enemies of us alcoholics are resentment, *jealousy*, envy, frustration, and fear.(p.145)
• At the moral inventory, he brought up some of my bad personality traits or character defects, such as selfishness, conceit, *jealousy*, carelessness, intolerance, ill-temper, sarcasm and resentments.(p.292)
• But as the years go by, the stretch becomes unbearable; and the man with the grown-up brain and the childish emotions – vanity, self-interest, false pride, *jealousy*, longing for social approval, to name few -- becomes a prime candidate for alcohol.(p.534)

Jean
• But I met a real wonderful girl I'll call *Jean*.(p.318)
• We got engaged, and we were happy – *Jean* with me, and me with the bottle and *Jean*.(p.318)

Jekyll
• He is a real Dr. *Jekyll* and Mr. Hyde.(p.21)

Jekyll-and-Hyde
• I became a *Jekyll-and-Hyde* person.(p.339)

jeopardize
• They often *jeopardize* their own positions by trying to help serious drinkers who should have been fired long ago, or else given an opportunity to get well.(p.147)
• I didn't want to *jeopardize* the lives of innocent people by driving an automobile while intoxicated, but I did.(p.199)
• "I've got to stop if I want to live," I told myself, and if I don't want to break my parents' hearts and maybe *jeopardize* their own carefully built up and hard-fought-for sobriety.(p.429)

jeopardy
• Positions were always in *jeopardy* or gone.(p.105)
• It was the usual situation: home in *jeopardy*, wife ill, children distracted, bills in arrears and standing damaged.(p.155)

jerk
• In the garage, I would put the needle in my vein and then try to figure out exactly how much medication to inject to overcome the pep pills while adding to the sleeping pills while ignoring the tranquilizers, in order to get just enough to be able to pull out the needle, *jerk* the tourniquet, throw it in the car, slam the car door shut, run down the hall, and fall in bed before I fell asleep.(p.442)

jest
• Judging from what I had seen in Europe and since, the power of God in human affairs was negligible, the Brotherhood of Man a grim *jest*.(p.11)

Jesuits
• I went to a very good public school run by *Jesuits*.(p.517)

jet
• I had turned eighteen during the trip, and I despondently returned home by *jet* (on Daddy's bankbook) to a pair of miserable, hurt parents.(p.354)

Jews
• By personal religious affiliation, we include Catholics, Protestants, *Jews*, Hindus, and a sprinkling of Moslems and Buddhists.(p.xx)

Jim
• Our first example is a friend we shall call *Jim*.(p.35)
• Thus started one more journey to the asylum for *Jim*.(p.36)
• We have sometimes reflected more than *Jim* did upon the consequences.(p.37)
• And *Jim* G. had such a wonderful sense of humor, and when he came I was in tears, and I told him, "I want to do this, but I can't.(p.269)
• The following day, Saturday, he came back and said, "*Jim*, I owe you for that prescription last night.(p.488)
• Finally she said, "Isn't your name *Jim* S.?"(p.493)

Jim's
• *JIM'S* STORY(p.483)

jimmied
• I *jimmied* the front door so that I could get back in, and walked out.(p.288)

jinks
• Years of drinking and general high *jinks* had cut her off from old friends.(p.414)

jitters
• It may be worth a bad case of *jitters* if you get a full knowledge of your condition.(p.32)
• We first saw Fred about a year ago in a hospital where he had gone to recover from a bad case of *jitters*.(p.39)
• During these years, I drank as much as my purse permitted, still without paying too great a penalty, although I was beginning to have morning *jitters* at times.(p.173)
• Many mornings I have gone to classes, and even though fully prepared, would turn and walk back to the fraternity house because of my *jitters*, not daring to enter the classroom for fear of making a scene should I be called on for recitation.(p.173)
• Most of the time therefore, I did not take the morning drink which I craved so badly, but instead would fill up on large doses of sedatives to quiet the *jitters*, which distressed me terribly.(p.176)
• This would lessen my chances of smuggling some home that evening, which in turn would mean a night of futile tossing around in bed followed by a morning of unbearable *jitters*.(p.176)
• It was really a horrible nightmare, this earning money, getting liquor, smuggling it home, getting drunk, morning *jitters*, taking large doses of sedatives to make it possible for me to earn more money, and so on ad nauseam.(p.177)
• Morning after morning I would awake sick and with terrible *jitters*, but there was always a flask of liquor sitting on the table beside my bed.(p.183)
• My wife accompanied me on my visit and the doctor really told me some things that in my state of *jitters* nearly knocked me out of the chair.(p.302)
• It was with grim foreboding and advanced *jitters* that I checked in at the hospital.(p.302)
• Oh yes, I get the dry *jitters* once in a while, but that isn't anything to worry about.(p.516)

jittery
• Though we work out our solution on the spiritual as well as an altruistic plane, we favor hospitalization for the alcoholic who is very *jittery* or befogged.(p.xxiv)
• I began to be *jittery* in the morning.(p.3)
• Call on him while he is still *jittery*.(p.91)
• You are saying to yourself: "I'm *jittery* and alone.(p.163)
• I was taking Benzedrine and paraldehyde quite impartially during the day then, and by the time I arrived at my first A.A. meeting, I was pretty drunk and certainly doped up to the eyes and completely *jittery*.(p.523)

job
• I found a *job*; then lost it as the result of a brawl with a taxi driver.(p.4)
• Here are some of the methods we have tried: Drinking beer only, limiting the number of drinks, never drinking alone, never drinking in the morning, drinking only at home, never having it in the house, never drinking during business hours, drinking only at parties, switching from scotch to brandy, drinking only natural wines, agreeing to resign if ever drunk on the *job*, taking a trip, not taking a trip, swearing off forever (with and without a solemn oath), taking more physical exercise, reading inspirational books, going to health farms and sanitariums, accepting voluntary commitment to asylums -- we could increase the list ad infinitum.(p.31)
• This process snuffed out the last flicker of conviction that I could do the *job* myself.(p.42)
• Brown may get my *job* at the office.(p.65)
• We have already admitted this in confidence to another person, but we are sure we would be imprisoned or lose our *job* if it were known.(p.78)
• If he thinks he can do the *job* in some other way, or prefers some other spiritual approach, encourage him to follow his own conscience.(p.95)
• If he is, you might try to help him about getting a *job*, or give him a little financial assistance.(p.96)
• Some of us have taken very hard knocks to learn this truth: *Job* or no *job* -- wife or no wife -- we simply do not stop drinking so long as we place dependence upon other people ahead of dependence on God.(p.98)
• Your *job* now is to be at the place where you may be of maximum helpfulness to others, so never hesitate to go anywhere if you can be helpful.(p.102)
• "Oh no," said my friend, "this chap is either through with liquor, or he is minus a *job*.(p.138)
• An alcoholic who has recovered, but holds a relatively unimportant *job*, can talk to a man with a better position.(p.146)
• If he is, and is still trying to recover, he will tell you about it even if it means the loss of his *job*.(p.146)
• If a man drinks so much that his *job* suffers, we fire him.(p.148)
• I drank all I dared in the bar, and then went to my room to finish the *job*.(p.179)
• Then Prohibition came into effect, and the facts that the stuff obtainable was so horrible and sometimes deadly, and that I had married and had a *job* which I

had to look after, helped me for a period of some three or four years, although I would get drunk every time I could get hold of enough to drink to get started.(p.183)
• My big *job* was to keep other people from finding it out.(p.199)
• Another time, I had gone around to Max R. trying to get a *job* driving one of his trucks.(p.200)
• On that statement and the fact that I had been sober for ninety days, he gave me a *job* selling lots in an allotment he had.(p.200)
• During the latter part of the Christian Science experience I had gotten a *job* and was working at Firestone.(p.203)
• I was always interested in mechanics and after having about twenty miscellaneous jobs, lasting from one day to two weeks, I obtained a *job* as a toolmaker apprentice.(p.211)
• Being intensely interested in the work, I changed my conduct sufficiently to master the *job*.(p.211)
• The school then obtained a *job* for me in the drafting department of another company.(p.211)
• Following graduation I was offered a pretty good *job* which I took.(p.212)
• "Best in the business, when he's sober," my customers would say, and I still had a following who would give me work though they deplored my habits, because they knew the *job* would be well done when they eventually got it.(p.234)
• First, my new wife had walked out, bag, baggage and furniture; then the apartment landlord had thrown me out of the empty apartment and the finish was the loss of another *job*.(p.238)
• My next *job* was in sales promotion for an oil company in Mississippi where I promptly became high man and got lots of pats on the back.(p.242)
• After the oil *job* blew up, I went back to Baltimore and mother, my first wife having said a permanent "Goodbye."(p.243)
• Then came a sales *job* with a national tire company.(p.243)
• As long as things were tough and the *job* a challenge I could always manage to hold on pretty well, but as soon as I learned the combination, got the puzzle under control and the boss to pat me on the back, I was gone again.(p.243)
• After the tire *job* came the thirties, the Depression and the down hill road.(p.244)
• Bill and Hank had just taken over a small automobile polishing company and they offered me a *job* -- ten dollars a week and keep at Hank's house.(p.246)
• Once again, there was the challenge of a tough *job*, but this time I was determined to follow through.(p.248)
• While I went along with all that was done and attended the meetings, I never took an active *job* of leadership until February 1940.(p.249)
• My wife traveled with me, but with a baby coming I decided to settle in a large city where I got a *job* with a commission agent which is a polite term for a handbook operator.(p.251)
• My *job* was to collect bets and betting-slips in the business section, a lucrative spot.(p.251)
• Making my way to Pittsburgh, I met other former friends and got a *job* in a large factory where piecemakers were making good money.(p.252)
• Young and able to travel with the best of them, I managed to hold my *job* and keep my end up in the barrooms.(p.252)
• I quit the factory and got a *job* on a small newspaper, going from that to a Pittsburgh daily, long ago defunct.(p.252)
• I wanted to roam again and through relatives got a supercargo *job* on an Australian packet which allowed me to visit my people in Australia where I was born.(p.252)
• Forced to detrain from an empty gondola on the other side of Chicago by a terrific rainstorm which drenched me to the skin, I hit the first factory building I saw for a *job*.(p.253)
• That *job* began a series of brief working spells, each one ending in a "drunk" and the urge to travel.(p.253)
• I applied for a publicity *job* and got it.(p.254)
• The new *job* lasted five years.(p.254)
• Successive Monday morning hangovers, which despite mid-week resolutions to do better, came with unfailing regularity, eventually caused me to quit my *job*.(p.254)
• Offered the *job* of advertising manager for an eastern automotive company, I moved to Philadelphia to begin life anew.(p.254)
• Now on a new *job* I was always thinking about payday and how much liquor I could buy and the pleasure I could have.(p.255)
• Federal Theatre in Texas gave me an administrative *job* which I held for a year, only because I worked hard and productively when I worked, and because my very tolerant chief ascribed my frequent lapses to a bohemian temperament.(p.256)
• In those days my system was always to drink up my last pay check and believe that necessity would bring the next *job*.(p.256)
• A friend who knew I would soon be broke mounted guard over me when I left my *job* of writing the histories of Texas cities and put me aboard a bus for the town I had left almost five years before.(p.256)
• "I'm doing a *job* I like and it's quiet where I live, practically no temptations.(p.257)
• I got a *job* in the woolen mills in Ravenna – very hard work.(p.262)
• I looked much older than I was, I was always large, and I went back to work in this *job*.(p.262)
• He got a *job* and went back to work.(p.263)
• That was his *job*.(p.267)
• I got an easy, part-time *job* selling printing for a small neighborhood printer.(p.276)
• A year later I was able to buy a Model T roadster and take a better *job* with a downtown printer.(p.276)
• From this *job* and the next one with another printer I was courteously dismissed.(p.277)
• It ran something like this: If I go around shouting from the rooftops about my alcoholism, it might very possibly prevent me from getting a good *job*.(p.282)
• So I created a *job* for myself selling women's hosiery and men's made-to-order shirts.(p.282)
• Within a year of my return to Detroit, A.A. was a definitely established little group of about a dozen members and I too was established in a modest but steady *job* handling an independent dry-cleaning route of my own.(p.283)
• It took five years of A.A. living, and a substantial improvement in my health, before I could take a full-time office *job* where someone else was boss.(p.283)
• This office *job* brought me face to face with a problem which I had sidestepped all my adult life, lack of training.(p.284)
• I do feel, though, that the fact that I finally grew up to a point where I could even tackle such a *job* is the apex of the story of a man who spent eighteen years running away from life.(p.286)
• Then I started traveling, with the United States and Canada as my territory, and with so much freedom and with an unlimited expense account, I was soon drinking every night and kidding myself that it was all part of the *job*.(p.287)
• If I did not maintain my sobriety, I would not have a *job*.(p.293)
• The three of us did not feel up to the *job*, and after a few meetings we convinced the prospects that they too should go to Akron where they could see an older group in action.(p.295)
• Three years after I started on my drinking career, I lost my first *job*.(p.298)
• Finally this company also became involved and I was once more looking for a *job*.(p.300)
• I learned that a person just can't find a *job* hanging in a dive or barroom all day and all night, as jobs don't seem to turn up in those places.(p.300)
• I became convinced of that because I spent most of my time there and nary a *job* turned up.(p.300)
• Finally, an old business acquaintance of mine, whom I hadn't seen for several years offered me a *job*.(p.301)
• I was on that *job* a month and drunk most of the time.(p.301)
• Well . . . I had a *job*, and I really wanted desperately to stop drinking, but couldn't, so I readily agreed to visit the doctor she recommended.(p.301)
• I still have my *job*, and just prior to the writing of this narrative, I received an advancement.(p.303)
• "We watch the alcoholic performing in a position of responsibility and we know that because he is drinking heavily and daily he has cut his capacities by fifty per cent, and still he seems able to do a satisfactory *job*.(p.308)
• It wasn't long before I quit caring how I looked or what my *job* performance was.(p.318)
• I never lost a *job*.(p.323)
• Safely pensioned, with no *job* to protect, at last he could drink as he pleased.(p.327)
• Toward five o'clock, helter-skelter, I'd get everything put away and try to get supper on the table, and after supper I'd finish the *job* up and knock myself out.(p.337)
• I just wanted to live to a certain age, carry through with what I felt was my *job* with the children, and after that – no matter.(p.337)
• He has loaned it to me and I did my *job*, but that ended nine days ago.(p.351)
• Lucky because my excessive drinking never got me in jail, or hospitalized, nor did it ever cost me a *job*.(p.356)
• It was my *job* to sell time on these stations to advertising agencies in New York.(p.359)
• It was also my *job* to entertain the owners of these stations when they came East on business – or the pretense of business.(p.359)
• My work kept me busy the first few months on the new *job*.(p.360)
• And, believe me, I thank God that I found out about A.A. before I had to beat my brains out – before I had been hospitalized, jailed or lost a *job*.(p.367)
• All this while, I wondered whether I could do laundry for the neighbors as a part-time *job*.(p.371)
• I had not yet lost my *job* or family, even though both were on the verge of going.(p.379)
• If we do a good *job* of living today, and if tomorrow comes for us, then the chances are we will do a good *job* when it arrives -- so why worry about it?(p.382)
• At eighteen, I got my first steady *job*.(p.397)
• It did not occur to me that marriage might be a *job*, too.(p.402)
• I had worked the previous summer on a New York fashion magazine, a *job* I really enjoyed.(p.405)
• I got a *job* after school pumping gas and worked until ten or eleven at night.(p.423)
• I got a *job* with the newspaper my dad worked for.(p.425)
• My *job* was to make out the guard schedules and thus I was exempt from ordinary recruit training activities.(p.425)
• Three days later I lost my *job*.(p.430)
• I thought, "If this is A.A. why not go back to drinking, kill myself with booze in the next three years the doctor had given me, and call it a bad *job*?"(p.430)
• I have a good *job*.(p.431)
• I was never drunk on the *job*, never missed a day's work, was seldom rendered totally ineffective by a hangover and kept my liquor expenses well within my adequate budget.(p.433)
• Things went from bad to worse, and since I had finally and completely failed at the *job* of being a wife and a mother, my marriage ended.(p.468)
• I felt very sorry for myself and attempted suicide on many occasions, making sure there was always somebody within reaching distance to see that I didn't finish the *job*.(p.478)
• I had a very good friend who was in the Government service, and I went to him about a *job*.(p.489)
• I continued to work and continued to go to lunch with Vi, and none of our acquaintances on the *job* knew that we had separated.(p.491)
• Thinking only of two or three dollars to buy some whiskey, I did the *job* and that's how I met Ella G., who was responsible for my coming into A.A.(p.493)
• I have a family to support and have no time to be looking for another *job*.(p.500)
• During the course of that drinking, I had shot and killed one person and almost completed the *job* on a second one.(p.508)
• He was drinking to hold on to his *job*, to hold on to his wife, to hold on to his sanity.(p.512)
• I was drinking to try to hold on to a *job*, to try and hold on to my home, to try to hold on to my wife, to try to hold on to my sanity.(p.514)
• Then I went over again to Germany for four years on an occupation *job*.(p.519)
• I got a *job* by myself which suited me down to the ground, because there was nobody really to interfere with what I did, one way or the other, and I usually had my nerves in good trim when anybody was coming around to inspect.(p.519)
• I was alone by myself in that *job* for a long time.(p.519)
• The Abyssinian war broke out just as things were going very badly for me, and I went off to Egypt on a *job* there.(p.519)
• However, I kept that *job* in Egypt and Palestine for about two years, and then I changed over to the other battalion in my regiment.(p.520)
• Then Hitler's war broke out, and again, I was given a really important *job* on the Suez Canal, dealing with military shipping.(p.520)
• But I did understand this eventually, that these people had been through a lot of drinking experience just as I had, and had managed to make a *job* of it.(p.524)
• What struck me most was that they all seemed to be quite pleased with having made a *job* of it and having stopped drinking.(p.524)
• I was not able to hold a *job* -- no one wants a drunk around.(p.526)
• There was the necessity for sticking to a *job* I hated, a dull, repetitive *job* performed in association with

other men I had nothing in common with . . . performed for years on end, because the money was needed at home.(p.532)

• What a revelation of ego and arrogance still remaining in me – as if anyone, instinct and training apart, likes to be in jail or in an alcoholic ward or fired from his *job*.(p.536)

• I fled, finally, after having been fired from my *job* by a boss who wept a little (since I had worked hard) as he gave notice for me to clear out.(p.539)

• I went back home, to a *job* of manual labor where for a little while I was able to keep away from alcohol.(p.539)

• The last three years of my drinking, I drank on my *job*.(p.548)

• Inside, though, I was scared to death, for I knew that the time was coming (and it couldn't be too remote) when I would be unable to hold that *job*.(p.548)

• Maybe I wouldn't be able to hold any *job*, or maybe (and this was my greatest fear) I wouldn't care whether I had a *job* or not.(p.548)

• I landed a good *job* with a company publication and was moonlighting on other magazines.(p.555)

• I now conceive the psychiatrist's *job* to be the task of breaking down the patient's inner resistance so that which is inside him will flower, as under the activity of the A.A. program."(p.571)

jobless

• I had some financial success through no ability of my own and, when *jobless* and almost wiped out in 1930, I began to trade and sell my collection; much of the proceeds went to keep my apartment stocked with liquor and almost every night saw me helpless to bed.(p.255)

• I ended up, homeless, *jobless*, penniless and rudderless, as the problem guest of a close friend whose family was out of town.(p.278)

jobs

• Cleaning up old scrapes, helping to settle family differences, explaining the disinherited son to his irate parents, lending money and securing *jobs* for each other, when justified -- these are everyday occurrences.(p.161)

• I was always interested in mechanics and after having about twenty miscellaneous *jobs*, lasting from one day to two weeks, I obtained a job as a toolmaker apprentice.(p.211)

• From far away, as if in a delirium, I heard my own voice – calling someone "Dorothy," talking of dress shops, of *jobs* . . . the words came clearer . . . this sound of my own voice frightened me as it came closer . . . and suddenly, there I was, talking of I knew not what, to someone I'd never seen before this very moment.(p.222)

• To go into a gathering of people was the sort of thing that all my life, from the time I left my private world of books and dreams to meet the real world of people and parties and *jobs*, had left me feeling an uncomfortable outsider, needing the warming stimulus of drinks to join in.(p.228)

• I would promise to have *jobs* done and never do them.(p.234)

• I don't remember much of what he said, but I did realize that here was another guy exactly like me; he had been in the same laughing academies and the same jails, known the same loss of *jobs*, same frustrations, same boredom and the same loneliness.(p.239)

• With the war over, and back in Baltimore with the folks, there were several small *jobs* for three years and then I went to work soliciting as one of the first ten employees of a new national finance company.(p.242)

• Routine *jobs* bored me, but I would take on the toughest one I could find, work day and night until I had it under control; then it would become tedious and I'd lose all interest in it.(p.243)

• In the eight years before A.A. found me, I had over forty *jobs* -- selling and travelling – one thing after another, and the same old routine.(p.244)

• I have served on only one committee in the past nine years, for I feel that I had my chance the first few years and that newer members should fill the *jobs*.(p.250)

• Some college friends got me *jobs* when I finally had to go to work, but I didn't stick to them.(p.251)

• In the two succeeding years I held ten different *jobs* ranging from newspaper copy-desk and rewrite, to traffic director for an oil field equipment company.(p.255)

• I managed to maintain myself with odd *jobs*, did ten weeks in a social rescue institution, and at length wound up in a second-hand bookstore in an adjacent town as manager.(p.257)

• The Depression was still on and *jobs* were scarce.(p.282)

• I learned that a person just can't find a job hanging in a dive or barroom all day and all night, as *jobs* don't seem to turn up in those places.(p.300)

• All of them have since settled down to *jobs* and good marriages.(p.407)

• I saw that my Village friends, all of whom had small *jobs*, were living happily on about a tenth of my sinecure.(p.409)

• Strangely enough, right through to the end of my twenty-six years in the Army, I was still being offered very good and important *jobs* in spite of the fact that my superiors must have known that I wasn't thoroughly reliable.(p.519)

• In those years I was in jail nine times, in an alcoholic ward, overnight, twice; and I was fired from three *jobs*, two of them very good ones.(p.536)

• I worked when I could – piddling *jobs* I thought them.(p.540)

Joe

• I remember well one fellow, *Joe*, walking nearly three miles through slush, wet and snow to come to the hospital to see a man that he had never seen before in his life, and that impressed me very much.(p.208)

jogger

• Regaining my health, I became an avid *jogger*, sailor, and skier.(p.559)

John

• In the spring of 1940, *John* D. Rockefeller, Jr. gave a dinner for many of his friends to which he invited A.A. members to tell their stories.(p.xviii)

• The times in which I grew up (the Prohibition era immortalized by Scott Fitzgerald and *John* Held Jr.) had taught me to be gay with the gayest; my own inner urges led me to outdo them all.(p.225)

• Beer was too bulky and it couldn't be kept in a jug under the counter ready to be dumped when *John* Law came around.(p.233)

• In three months *John* Barleycorn had me kicked out.(p.254)

• Russ read a piece in the paper, and he kind of snickered, and said, "See here, where *John* D. has found something to keep him from drinking!"(p.265)

• But right then the hope died that had been in my heart when we read about *John* D.(p.266)

• That age of the flapper and the "It" girl, speakeasies and the hip flask, the boyish bob and the drugstore cowboy, *John* Held Jr. and F. Scott Fitzgerald, all generously sprinkled with a patent pseudo-sophistication.(p.304)

• I have been of a very religious outlook all my life, but that made no difference once *John* Barleycorn got the better of me.(p.343)

• In this I was greatly aided and abetted by one *John* Barleycorn.(p.358)

• However, I had phoned New York from the farm, appealing for help, and there in the station to meet us were two A.A.'s, *John* and Bud.(p.415)

• *John* and Bud became my friends.(p.415)

• *John* said, "Keep going to meetings."(p.415)

• And so I met *John* Barleycorn.(p.498)

• Good old *John*!(p.498)

• Good old *John* Barleycorn!(p.499)

• Dr. *John* F. Stouffer, Chief Psychiatrist, Philadelphia General Hospital, citing his experience with A.A., said: "The alcoholics we get here at Philadelphia General are mostly those who cannot afford private treatment, and A.A. is by far the greatest thing we have been able to offer them.(p.572)

• Speaking at a dinner given by *John* D. Rockefeller Jr. to introduce Alcoholics Anonymous to some of his friends, Dr. Harry Emerson Fosdick remarked: "I think that psychologically speaking there is a point of advantage in the approach that is being made in this movement that cannot be duplicated.(p.574)

join

• Yet it is our great hope that all those who have as yet found no answer may begin to find one in the pages of this book and will presently *join* us on the highroad to a new freedom.(p.xxi)

• We have a way out on which we can absolutely agree, and upon which we can *join* in brotherly and harmonious action.(p.17)

• Not all of us *join* religious bodies, but most of us favor such memberships.(p.28)

• If our testimony helps sweep away prejudice, enables you to think honestly, encourages you to search diligently within yourself, then, if you wish, you can *join* us on the Broad Highway.(p.55)

• If circumstances warrant, we ask our wives or friends to *join* us in morning meditation.(p.87)

• You should *join* in his efforts as much as you possibly can.(p.119)

• When this happens, they can be invited to *join* in morning meditation and then they can take part in the daily discussion without rancor or bias.(p.134)

• Give freely of what you find and *join* us.(p.164)

• On hearing that, these people induced me to make the move immediately and *join* them as a senior partner, which I did.(p.220)

• To go into a gathering of people was the sort of thing that all my life, from the time I left my private world of books and dreams to meet the real world of people and parties and jobs, had left me feeling an uncomfortable outsider, needing the warming stimulus of drinks to *join* in.(p.228)

• At this school we had Bible readings before each meal, and church services four times on Sunday, and I became so rebellious at this that I swore I would never *join* or go to any church except for weddings or funerals.(p.240)

• I refused to *join* any fraternity, as I wanted to be a free lance, and that year my drinking was confined to one-night stands, once or twice a week.(p.241)

• There was a man watching, and I turned to him and said with a defiant air I carried with me all the time, "If I don't quit this I'm going to have to *join* that alcoholic business they're talking about."(p.266)

• He said, "Sister, if you think you're a screwball now, all you have to do is *join* up with that.(p.266)

• Why do men and women like these *join* A.A.?(p.315)

• I eventually became a schoolmaster, but gave up that profession to *join* the Indian Army.(p.342)

• Why don't you *join* it?"(p.349)

• I had run away from school to *join* the army in World War I, but missed it by one day since the Armistice was signed the very day I landed in Atlanta to sign up with Uncle Sam.(p.357)

• Once again I asked my girl to marry me and *join* me in this new venture.(p.359)

• At this time, however, she had an opportunity to go to Salt Lake City on a new project for the government, but she did promise me that if I would curtail my drinking and buckle down to hard work she would give serious consideration to my latest proposal and maybe *join* me at a later date when I got settled.(p.359)

• I disliked being different so, ultimately, I began to *join* them occasionally.(p.374)

• Many good A.A.'s never *join* a church, and do not need to.(p.417)

• I'll *join* A.A. if it kills me.(p.430)

• A week after my decision to *join* A.A., she called it quits.(p.430)

• *JOIN* THE TRIBE!(p.474)

• I *join* Canadian Army, but could not run away from problem.(p.474)

• To Indians, I say: "Don't be afraid to *join* A.A.(p.477)

• *Join* the tribe!"(p.477)

• I remember in my first year in high school, that mother suggested that I do not *join* the cadet unit.(p.484)

• She got a medical certificate so that I should not have to *join* it.(p.484)

• I'd get downstairs to the gin mill, get enough in to hold me until eight o'clock in the morning, then I'd go out to *join* that "misery parade" that so many of us know so well.(p.514)

joined

• But that in itself would never have held us together as we are now *joined*.(p.17)

• My drinking career began about four years after I had moved up into partnership and had *joined* certain clubs, societies and so fourth, and during which period we had Prohibition.(p.213)

• Fond of singing, I *joined* a German singing society which had good club headquarters.(p.231)

• In the spring of 1917, in order to beat being fired from school, I became "patriotic" and *joined* the Army.(p.241)

• Oddly enough, the big shot who fired me from this company was one of the first men I met when I later *joined* the New York A.A. Group.(p.242)

• Curious about it, feeling I was missing something, absolutely without any illusions about the aftermath, with no pronounced feeling of patriotism, I *joined* up with a Canadian regiment, serving a little over two years.(p.253)

• I *joined* their Saturday night parties and enjoyed myself too.(p.277)

• Since I didn't do well in school, I quit and *joined* the Army at age seventeen.(p.317)

• This was my first long vacation of sixty days since I had *joined* the army.(p.343)

• It started when I *joined* a few of the men for cocktails before the noonday Rotary luncheon.(p.360)

• Two years before I *joined* A.A. my wife took a long

trip during which she wrote me she just couldn't return unless I did something about my drinking.(p.377)
• To me this meant telling my associates that I had *joined* Alcoholics Anonymous; that I didn't know what was expected of me by A.A., but that whatever it was, it was the most important thing in life for me; that sobriety meant more to me than anything in this world.(p.382)
• When I *joined* A.A. I did so for the sole purpose of getting sober and staying sober.(p.383)
• I consider that I was taking the Eleventh Step when I *joined* this church.(p.417)
• If I had not become an active alcoholic and *joined* A.A., I might never have found my own identity or become a part of anything.(p.417)
• Or maybe I'd come home wild drunk, singing and raving about what a fine place home was and what grand parents I had since they *joined* A.A.(p.428)
• I *joined* A.A. at twenty-two.(p.430)
• (That dog hasn't wet my pants once since I *joined* A.A., and neither have I!)(p.440)
• I am an Irishman and I was forty-nine when I *joined* A.A.(p.517)
• I thought that if these kind of ordinary people can do it, a man of my brains ought to find it much more easy, and I *joined*.(p.524)
• Since I *joined* on that April night, A.A. has done more for me than just stop me from drinking; it has brought me back to life again.(p.524)
• My mother lived on for five years after I *joined* A.A., the last two in complete blindness.(p.525)
• Young when she *joined*, this A.A. believes her serious drinking was the result of even deeper defects.(p.544)
• Then I *joined* the Navy and was commissioned as an ensign to write speeches for admirals.(p.555)

joining
• Now I was to plunge into the dark, *joining* that endless procession of sots who had gone on before.(p.8)
• It was therefore not extraordinary that I should shy away from any serious thought of marriage for a great many years after *joining* A.A.(p.286)
• I got around this by *joining* the local Rotary Club, and through this association with the business men of the community my little station began to grow.(p.360)
• One night, a few weeks after *joining* the Fellowship, much to my surprise and delight I saw a familiar but no longer frowning face.(p.371)
• My spiritual awakening in A.A. finally resulted in my *joining* a church some years ago.(p.417)
• I don't know whether she was a pacifist or whether she just thought that in the event of another war it would have some bearing on my *joining* up.(p.484)

joint
• We went into a bootleg *joint* and I don't remember leaving that place.(p.202)
• They owned this *joint*, she ran it, and he sold for a brewery.(p.267)
• We are both depending upon God and our use of the A.A. program to help us make a success of this *joint* undertaking.(p.286)
• A night or so a week in a *joint*, and a party or so a week at home or with friends, along with a little lone drinking, soon had me preparing for the existence of a top flight drunkard.(p.298)
• We went to booze *joint* in Maine.(p.475)
• You hit the street about ten minutes to eight, and you walk around the block, God knows how many times, waiting for that *joint* to open.(p.514)
• I was always able to get a boyfriend who had a drinking *joint* or sold whiskey, but it didn't last long.(p.526)

joints
• I got along fairly well with my party drinking for quite some time, but eventually I began to visit beer *joints* in between parties.(p.298)
• All I can remember about the Roaring Twenties is that I drank a great deal, thought I was having a grand time, managed to get to Europe for a few weeks, was very proud of the dozens of speak-easy cards entitling me to an entree in the better *joints* between Cleveland and New York, took on a wife, and built a home in a fashionable suburb of Cleveland.(p.358)
• The other kids would light out for the hamburger huts or ice cream parlors, the pizza *joints* or bowling alleys, after football games and dances.(p.423)
• But I don't remember that any of them ever went to sleep in *joints* and woke up with no shoes on in the winter, or fell out of chairs.(p.527)
• Finally, I got so lowdown, I was ashamed of my friends' seeing me, so I went to the worst *joints* I could find.(p.527)

joker
• We've got to turn the whole business over to some *joker* we can't even see!(p.350)

jokes
• One instance comes to mind in which a malicious individual was always making friendly little *jokes* about an alcoholic's drinking exploits.(p.145)

jokingly
• Knowing Bob of old, she *jokingly* replied, "Well, Doctor, I suppose you've already tried it yourself?"(p.188)

jolt
• It may be just the *jolt* he needs.(p.141)
• I would take a gulp, then warn the jug not to try to entice, lure, or seduce me into having more than one "medicinal" *jolt*.(p.332)

Jones
• Mrs. *Jones*(p.65)
• Notice that the word "fear" is bracketed alongside the difficulties with Mr. Brown, Mrs. *Jones*, the employer, and the wife.(p.67)

journal
• I did six years of newspaper advertising, and trade *journal* work with many, many drunks of drab and dreary hue woven into the pattern of my life.(p.254)
• This was done, and the paper was printed in the American *Journal* of Psychiatry for November, 1949.(p.572)

journey
• Prior to his *journey* to Akron, the broker had worked hard with many alcoholics on the theory that only an alcoholic could help an alcoholic, but he had succeeded only in keeping sober himself.(p.xvi)
• Thus started one more *journey* to the asylum for Jim.(p.36)
• Let families realize, as they start their *journey*, that all will not be fair weather.(p.122)
• You will be bound to them with new and wonderful ties, for you will escape disaster together and you will commence shoulder to shoulder your common *journey*.(p.152)
• Years ago, in 1935, one of our number made a *journey* to a certain western city.(p.153)
• There my drinking became so much worse that the boys in the fraternity house where I lived felt forced to send for my father, who made a long *journey* in the vain endeavor to get me straightened around.(p.174)
• When I reached a point directly back of our house, where I could have cut through a friend's garden, I was almost overpowered by the desire to get home, but I made the whole *journey*.(p.276)
• They kept me in hospital for two months, and then they sent me up to Egypt, a three days *journey*.(p.521)

journeys
• Our earliest printing voiced the hope "that every alcoholic who *journeys* will find the Fellowship of Alcoholics Anonymous at his destination.(p.xv)
• Some day we hope that every alcoholic who *journeys* will find a Fellowship of Alcoholics Anonymous at his destination.(p.162)

joy
• The *joy* of living we really have, even under pressure and difficulty.(p.15)
• Unlike the feelings of the ship's passengers, however, our *joy* in escape from disaster does not subside as we go our individual ways.(p.17)
• *Joy* at our release from a lifetime of frustration knew no bounds.(p.128)
• If newcomers could see no *joy* or fun in our existence, they wouldn't want it.(p.132)
• When a few men in this city have found themselves, and have discovered the *joy* of helping others to face life again, there will be no stopping until everyone in that town has had his opportunity to recover -- if he can and will.(p.163)
• Then came a great *joy*.(p.189)
• By living alone you can pretty much eliminate grief from you life, but you also eliminate *joy*.(p.286)
• A very simple plan that I still find much *joy* and happiness in following.(p.302)
• I have had my share of problems, heartaches and disappointments, because that is life, but also I have known a great deal of *joy*, and a peace that is the handmaiden of an inner freedom, I have a wealth of friends and, with my A.A. friends, an unusual quality of fellowship.(p.312)
• You can never know the pure *joy* of recovering within the Fellowship of Alcoholics Anonymous."(p.334)
• In all these ways I've experienced, in ever growing measure and beyond all expectations and rewards, a *joy* which I had never before imagined.(p.395)
• Age and the law were still against me, but laws were not as strictly enforced in those days as they are now, and I discovered that as long as I had the green blood, there was always a way to get alcohol, either from a nondiscriminatory bartender or from an older friend who would be glad to purchase the *joy* juice for the privilege of sharing it.(p.397)
• I have had the *joy* of seeing many a human being, down and out, learn to stand straight again, and to proceed under his own power to happiness in life.(p.541)
• I hope I have been able to impart to you, the reader, at least a bit of what I know; the *joy* of living, the irresistible power of divine love and its healing strength, and the fact that we, as sentient beings, have the knowledge to choose between good and evil, and, choosing good, are made happy.(p.543)

joyfully
• Being certain he wants to stop, you can go to him with this volume as *joyfully* as though you had struck oil.(p.113)

joykiller
• "*Joykiller*, nag, wet blanket" — that's what they said.(p.106)

joyous
• We are sure God wants us to be happy, *joyous*, and free.(p.133)
• It is *joyous* intimacy with friends and a feeling that life is good.(p.151)
• They are a *joyous* crowd.(p.504)
• I have never seen people that *joyous* before.(p.504)

joyousness
• We are like the passengers of a great liner the moment after rescue from shipwreck when camaraderie, *joyousness* and democracy pervade the vessel from steerage to Captain's table.(p.17)

joys
• All the *joys* of retirement lay ahead for this movie publicist.(p.327)
• He'll never read in his "sweetness and light" senior-citizen publications anything but the *joys* of lolling in the rocking chair, angling on the riverbank, or bowling on the green.(p.330)

Jr.
• In the spring of 1940, John D. Rockefeller, *Jr.* gave a dinner for many of his friends to which he invited A.A. members to tell their stories.(p.xviii)
• The times in which I grew up (the Prohibition era immortalized by Scott Fitzgerald and John Held *Jr.*) had taught me to be gay with the gayest; my own inner urges led me to outdo them all.(p.225)
• That age of the flapper and the "It" girl, speakeasies and the hip flask, the boyish bob and the drugstore cowboy, John Held *Jr.* and F. Scott Fitzgerald, all generously sprinkled with a patent pseudo-sophistication.(p.304)
• Speaking at a dinner given by John D. Rockefeller *Jr.* to introduce Alcoholics Anonymous to some of his friends, Dr. Harry Emerson Fosdick remarked: "I think that psychologically speaking there is a point of advantage in the approach that is being made in this movement that cannot be duplicated.(p.574)

jubilant
• In my own experience I was so *jubilant* at finding myself sober, and I had so many things to catch up on, that a month went by before the thought even occurred to me.(p.219)

judge
• In a matter of fact way he told how two men had appeared in court, persuading the *judge* to suspend his commitment.(p.9)
• God alone can *judge* our sex situation.(p.69)
• Counsel with persons is often desirable, but we let God be the final *judge*.(p.69)
• It would have been impressive heroics if he had walked up to the *Judge* and said, "Here I am."(p.79)
• I looked so terrible in the court that the *judge* suggested that I get a continuance and let me sign all the papers to go to a hospital and to a doctor.(p.204)
• It was hard to *judge* the right amount.(p.443)
• *Judge* say I go to jail next time.(p.475)
• So she went to court and talked it over with the *judge*.(p.491)
• The *judge* said that if she felt that way he would confine me for thirty days' examination and observation.(p.492)
• On one of these trips, the *judge* must have thought I was worth saving, for instead of sending me to jail, he sent me to A.A. for one month.(p.526)
• I hated that *judge* for sending me to a place with all those drunks.(p.527)
• I got out on bail right away, but when I went to trial, the *judge* gave me thirty days.(p.528)

• Because I had been drunk, the ***judge*** gave me only a twelve-year sentence in prison.(p.528)
• I had replied, "Uncle, give the ***judge*** ten dollars, or I'll have to work it out on the county road."(p.539)

judged
• Before A.A., I ***judged*** myself by my intentions, while the world was judging me by my actions.(p.450)
• I begin to see I am not the person I had thought myself, that I had ***judged*** myself by comparing myself to others, and always to my own advantage.(p.504)

judges
• Unlike the drinking driver, he avoids facing ***judges.***(p.330)

judging
• ***Judging*** from what I had seen in Europe and since, the power of God in human affairs was negligible, the Brotherhood of Man a grim jest.(p.11)
• Before A.A., I judged myself by my intentions, while the world was ***judging*** me by my actions.(p.450)

judgment
• My ***judgment*** and ideas were followed by many to the tune of paper millions.(p.3)
• In the doctor's ***judgment*** he was utterly hopeless; he could never regain his position in society and he would have to place himself under lock and key or hire a bodyguard if he expected to live long.(p.26)
• The story he told is most instructive, for here was a chap absolutely convinced he had to stop drinking, who had no excuse for drinking, who exhibited splendid ***judgment*** and determination in all his other concerns, yet was flat on his back nevertheless.(p.40)
• What had become of their ***judgment,*** their common sense, their will power?(p.107)
• Though he is now a most effective member of Alcoholics Anonymous, he still smokes and drinks coffee, but neither his wife or anyone else stands in ***judgment.***(p.135)
• I can think clearly and am helped much in my thinking and ***judgment*** by my spiritual development which grows daily.(p.303)
• Against my better ***judgment,*** I went to a meeting with him that night, and a strange thing began to happen.(p.446)

jug
• I went over and bought a ***jug*** of hard cider and a gallon of wine that I gave these fellows to drink.(p.195)
• Beer was too bulky and it couldn't be kept in a ***jug*** under the counter ready to be dumped when John Law came around.(p.233)
• I had repaired to one of these one morning with my ***jug*** and when I left late in the afternoon, I picked up a newspaper on the way home.(p.244)
• I would take a gulp, then warn the ***jug*** not to try to entice, lure, or seduce me into having more than one "medicinal" jolt.(p.332)
• I displayed alcoholic tendencies actually from the age of fourteen, when I started to steal wine from the family ***jug,*** siphoning it off one drink at a time so it wouldn't be missed, not drinking it immediately, but saving it until about a pint was accumulated, so that I could get drunk.(p.397)
• I stayed in the barracks all day, "making out guard schedules," and getting mildly plastered from the ***jug*** under my desk.(p.426)
• Dad got out a ***jug*** for me and poured welcome home drinks.(p.428)

jugs
• The boys at the Post Office used to bring me my ***jugs;*** mail couldn't be opened for inspection at the gate.(p.426)

juice
• Age and the law were still against me, but laws were not as strictly enforced in those days as they are now, and I discovered that as long as I had the green blood, there was always a way to get alcohol, either from a nondiscriminatory bartender or from an older friend who would be glad to purchase the joy ***juice*** for the privilege of sharing it.(p.397)

juke
• All afternoon I sat there and drank and played Bing Crosby's recording of "Silent Night" over and over again on the ***juke*** box.(p.467)

Jules
• But I can remember, in my teens, that there were a few characters who caused the village heads to nod pityingly and sometimes in anger as they paused to say, "That sot, Henri" and "Ce pauvre ***Jules,***" who drank too much.(p.230)

July
• I did divorce him in ***July.***(p.386)
• By early ***July,*** I had tapered off alcohol completely, and I got off all pills in the ensuing few months.(p.448)
• It started ***July*** 23.(p.508)

jumbled
• Four years ago I had nothing but a ***jumbled,*** mad existence.(p.430)

jump
• I would not ***jump.***(p.4)
• When his wife next calls saying he is sick, you might ***jump*** to the conclusion he is drunk.(p.146)
• I would walk up and down under the 59th Street bridge, trying to get up the nerve to go up there and ***jump.***(p.411)
• Then I found the solution: At the end of study time, I would drink two beers, ***jump*** in bed, sleep real fast, and wake up smart.(p.440)
• Then went on bridge to ***jump.***(p.475)
• So I ***jump*** quick from First Step to Twelfth Step to help my brother, living with me.(p.476)
• I must get out of the room or I shall ***jump*** out of the window.(p.501)

jumped
• I still expected a plea for clemency, but these words came through the receiver: "I just wanted to tell you Paul ***jumped*** from a hotel window in Hartford last Saturday.(p.136)
• I ***jumped*** at the suggestion that I accompany him.(p.281)
• The words ***jumped*** out at me.(p.461)
• And I ***jumped*** in with both feet.(p.516)

jumping
• The papers reported men ***jumping*** to death from the towers of High Finance.(p.4)

jumping-off
• He will be at the ***jumping-off*** place.(p.152)

jumpy
• Cold sweats, ***jumpy*** nerves and lack of sleep were becoming intolerable.(p.378)

juncture
• My practice at that ***juncture*** was just barely getting us a living.(p.488)

June
• The spark that was to flare into the first A.A. group was struck at Akron, Ohio, in ***June*** 1935, during a talk between a New York stockbroker and an Akron physician.(p.xv)
• The checking account melted like snow in ***June.***(p.106)
• That was in ***June,*** 1935.(p.158)
• The birth of our Society dates from his first day of permanent sobriety, ***June*** 10, 1935.(p.171)
• That was ***June*** 10, 1935, and that was my last drink.(p.180)
• On ***June*** 26, 1935, I came to in the hospital and to say I was discouraged is to put it mildly.(p.184)
• So I rocked along my merry independent way until ***June,*** when I went out selling auto polish in New England.(p.247)
• It was also an ending, for never since ***June*** 16th, 1938, have I had to walk alone.(p.248)
• In ***June,*** 1945, with another member, I made my first -- and only -- Twelfth Step call on a female alcoholic and a year later I married her.(p.249)

Jung
• Then he had gone to Europe, placing himself in the care of a celebrated physician (the psychiatrist, Dr. ***Jung***) who prescribed for him.(p.26)

jungles
• By this time, with the doctor's explanation, the revelations contained in the book, and the hope-inspiring interview with Mr. T., I was ready and willing to go into the interior of the African ***jungles,*** if that was what it took, for me to find what these people had.(p.309)

junior
• If your organization is a large one, your ***junior*** executives might be provided with this book.(p.147)
• After reading this book, a ***junior*** executive can go to such a man and say approximately this, "Look here, Ed.(p.147)
• Your ***junior*** executive may not agree with the contents of our book.(p.148)
• After many painful discussions, they finally gave me my credits and I migrated to another of the leading universities of the country and entered as a ***Junior*** that fall.(p.173)
• In 1924, I had acquired enough clients of my own so that the firm made me a ***junior*** partner.(p.213)
• My wife was in the ***Junior*** League, and I was on the board of directors of the local center for the mentally retarded.(p.418)
• Awarded a scholarship to a famous old Eastern college, I began to drink at the end of my freshman year, and by ***junior*** year, I had to transfer to an easier state university to keep my grades up.(p.419)
• There was the physical aspect; to be the youngest and the runt of the brood of children, to have to wear glasses very early and so to be teased, to be bookish and bored in school because the captain of the football team could not translate Virgil and yet was the school god while you, you, you little shrimp, were the school egghead, ***junior*** size and an early model.(p.533)

juniors
• These ***juniors*** are often in a difficult position.(p.147)

jury
• Vi was very kind and explained to the ***jury*** that I was basically a fine fellow and a good husband, but that I drank too much and that she thought I had lost my mind and felt that I should be committed to an asylum.(p.492)

just
• The section called "The Doctor's Opinion" has been kept intact, ***just*** as it was originally written in 1939 by the late Dr. William D. Silkworth, our Society's great medical benefactor.(p.xi)
• Some are ***just*** now taking shape in Asia.(p.xv)
• The basic principles of the A.A. program, it appears, hold good for individuals with many different life-styles, ***just*** as the program has brought recovery to those of many different nationalities.(p.xxii)
• It did not satisfy us to be told that we could not control our drinking ***just*** because we were maladjusted to life, that we were in full flight from reality, or were outright mental defectives.(p.xxiv)
• I began to wonder, for such an appalling lack of perspective seemed near being ***just*** that.(p.5)
• I could almost hear the sound of the preacher's voice as I sat, on still Sundays, way over there on the hillside; there was that proffered temperance pledge I never signed; my grandfather's good natured contempt of some church folk and their doings; his insistence that the spheres really had their music; but his denial of the preacher's right to tell him how he must listen; his fearlessness as he spoke of these things ***just*** before he died; these recollections welled up from the past.(p.10)
• With us it is ***just*** like that.(p.15)
• But ***just*** underneath there is deadly earnestness.(p.16)
• We of ALCOHOLICS ANONYMOUS, know thousands of men and women who were once ***just*** as hopeless as Bill.(p.17)
• The great fact is ***just*** this, and nothing less: That we have had deep and effective spiritual experiences which have revolutionized our whole attitude toward life, toward our fellows and toward God's universe.(p.25)
• But here is a man who at fifty-five years found he was ***just*** where he had left off at thirty.(p.33)
• I ***just*** thought I would get a sandwich.(p.36)
• Well, ***just*** that did happen and more, for what I had learned of alcoholism did not occur to me at all.(p.42)
• We asked ourselves this: Are not some of us ***just*** as biased and unreasonable about the realm of the material?(p.51)
• We finally saw that faith in some kind of God was a part of our make-up, ***just*** as much as the feeling we have for a friend.(p.55)
• ***Just*** what do we mean by that, and ***just*** what do we do?(p.60)
• ***Just*** to the extent that we do as we think He would have us, and humbly rely on Him, does He enable us to match calamity with serenity.(p.68)
• It ***just*** comes!(p.85)
• Being still inexperienced and having ***just*** made conscious contact with God, it is not probable that we are going to be inspired at all times.(p.87)
• So we let God discipline us in the simple way we have ***just*** outlined.(p.88)
• Now, the domestic problem: There may be divorce, separation, or ***just*** strained relations.(p.98)
• This ***just*** isn't so.(p.99)
• Don't start to withdraw again ***just*** because your friends drink liquor.(p.102)
• And ***just*** as we were being convinced of their heartlessness, they would surprise us with fresh resolves and new attentions.(p.107)
• He is ***just*** another very sick, unreasonable person.(p.108)
• Many of our husbands were ***just*** as far gone.(p.110)
• ***Just*** would he like to?(p.112)
• ***Just*** be careful not to disagree in a resentful or

critical spirit.(p.117)
• The chances are he will not for, like yourself, he is *just* beginning his development.(p.118)
• Perhaps your husband will make a fair start on the new basis, but *just* as things are going beautifully he dismays you by coming home drunk.(p.120)
• We cannot subscribe to the belief that this life is a vale of tears, though it once was *just* that for many of us.(p.133)
• I still expected a plea for clemency, but these words came through the receiver: "I *just* wanted to tell you Paul jumped from a hotel window in Hartford last Saturday.(p.136)
• He has *just* returned from a three-months leave of absence, has taken a cure, looks fine, and to clinch the matter, the board of directors told him this was his last chance."(p.138)
• It may be *just* the jolt he needs.(p.141)
• For most alcoholics who are drinking, or who are *just* getting over a spree, a certain amount of physical treatment is desirable, even imperative.(p.142)
• It boils right down to this: No man should be fired *just* because he is alcoholic.(p.148)
• But alcoholism -- well, they *just* don't believe they have it.(p.149)
• Some time later, and *just* as he thought he was getting control of his liquor situation, he went on a roaring bender.(p.155)
• He's *just* beaten up a couple of nurses.(p.156)
• Understand he was once a well-known lawyer in town, but *just* now we've got him strapped down tight."(p.156)
• You forget that you have *just* now tapped a source of power much greater than yourself.(p.163)
• I had, seemingly, *just* a natural affinity for grog.(p.182)
• I resented this very much, until she informed me that they were a couple of drunks *just* as I was.(p.184)
• The next thing they wanted to know was if I thought I could quit of my own accord, without any help, if I could *just* walk out of the hospital and never take another drink.(p.186)
• If I could, that was wonderful, that was *just* fine, and they would very much appreciate a person who had that kind of power, but they were looking for a man that knew he had a problem, and knew that he couldn't handle it himself and needed outside help.(p.186)
• Whether you quit six days, months, or years, if you go out and take a drink or two you'll end up in this hospital tied down, *just* like you have been in these past six months.(p.187)
• I figured I was *just* a drunk.(p.187)
• And they said, "No, you have a disease, and it doesn't make any difference how long you do without it, after a drink or two you'll end up *just* like you are now."(p.187)
• *Just* twenty-four hours at a time."(p.188)
• (At this point, the Editors intrude *just* long enough to supplement Bill D.'s account, that of the man on the bed, with that of Bill W., the man who sat by the side of the bed.)(p.188)
• He *just* arrived in D.T.'s.(p.188)
• I wasn't afraid that the program wouldn't work, but I still was doubtful whether I would be able to hang on to the program, but I did come to the conclusion that I was willing to put everything I had into it, with God's power, and that I wanted to do *just* that.(p.189)
• Bill looked across at my wife, and said to her, "Henrietta, the Lord has been so wonderful to me, curing me of this terrible disease, that I *just* want to keep talking about it and telling people."(p.191)
• That sentence, "The Lord has been so wonderful to me, curing me of this terrible disease, that I *just* want to keep telling people about it," has been sort of a golden text for the A.A. program and for me.(p.191)
• Of course, as time went on, and I began to get my health back and began to be so I didn't have to hide from people all the time, it's *just* been wonderful.(p.192)
• I went into the high school grades, but having missed all the intermediate grades, I didn't get along too well, so I developed the habit of going back to school *just* long enough for the football season and then quitting.(p.193)
• I lost money, and then *just* fooled away a large part of that profit.(p.194)
• I kept watching the man down the bar to see what he did with a contraption like that, and he *just* smelled of his drink and set it down again, so I did the same.(p.195)
• I could get through an evening with *just* a couple of snorts.(p.196)
• At the end of this selling of lots, *just* prior to World War I, I got into the crude rubber business, and six months later there was only one broker and myself left in Akron.(p.197)
• I optioned a piece of land *just* off East Market Street to put up a three-hundred suite apartment.(p.198)
• Everything in the world a man could possibly want, and I was driving from Akron to Cleveland, having *just* been to the bank and discovered that I had approximately $5,000.(p.200)
• I offered them a drink, and they came to the bottom of the stairs and the good woman fainted, *just* looking at me.(p.205)
• When he left, I realized from his story that as a drinker I was *just* a panty-waist.(p.208)
• For the next ten years I did *just* that.(p.225)
• My parents had some vague idea of making a priest out of me and for some years I attended the Franciscan school at Basle, Switzerland, *just* across the border, about six miles from my home.(p.230)
• This doctor had imparted his knowledge to *just* a few other men at that time -- not more than four or five -- they now number more than seventy persons.(p.235)
• I had never heard of the remedy expressed in *just* this language.(p.236)
• I knew somehow that it meant more than *just* going to church and living a moral life.(p.236)
• The first year in college I *just* got by in my studies, and that year I majored in poker and drinking.(p.241)
• At the time, I thought them *just* a swell pair of screwballs, for they were not only going to save all the drunks in the world but also all the so-called normal people!(p.245)
• I knew they needed to straighten out their thinking and habits, but I was all right, I *just* drank too much.(p.246)
• *Just* give me a good front and a couple of bucks and I'd be right back in the big time.(p.246)
• Bill and Hank had *just* taken over a small automobile polishing company and they offered me a job -- ten dollars a week and keep at Hank's house.(p.246)
• She had *just* come in and was scheduled to sail in two days.(p.252)
• In my early twenties the hardships of hobo life did not discourage me, but I had no wish to become *just* a tramp.(p.253)
• I visited my family *just* once in that time.(p.255)
• As he talked I gathered vaguely, (because he was a faltering beginner then, *just* as I am now) that to be relieved of alcoholism I would have to be different.(p.257)
• He knew too well that didn't mean a thing, *just* as I knew in my heart that it would be only a question of time -- a few days, a week, or even a month, it was inevitable -- till I would be off on another bender.(p.257)
• The time came *just* a week later.(p.258)
• We *just* loved it.(p.264)
• It was *just* about this time, in 1940, that we met up with A.A.(p.265)
• I thought when people did what we did that they *just* locked them up.(p.267)
• Paul S. had *just* called me, and I remember he stressed reading the Big Book.(p.269)
• His wife was cussing him, raving at him, "I *just* brought him over to show you what kind of a guy he is!(p.271)
• She said, "I feel you're *just* being wise.(p.273)
• I have thanked God many times in the last sixteen years that that was *just* what he did not do!(p.278)
• Out of this maelstrom *just* two coherent thoughts came to the surface; one, a drink would mean homelessness and death; two, I could no longer relieve the pressure of fear by starting home, as was once my habitual solution to this problem, because I no longer had a home.(p.279)
• You can't lose, and maybe God will help you -- *just* maybe, mind you.(p.280)
• But -- supposing that *just* one man died because I had, for selfish reasons, kept my mouth shut?(p.282)
• There was more than one occasion when I got up in the morning with *just* enough money for coffee and toast and the bus fare to carry me to my first appointment.(p.283)
• On my trips back to Akron to get my spirits recharged and to work with other alcoholics, I would ask Dr. Bob about this delay and wonder *just* what was wrong with me.(p.293)
• So I set out to get drunk deliberately, *just* to teach her what she was missing.(p.293)
• Strangely enough, I became acquainted with the "hilarious life" *just* at the time in my own life when I was beginning really to settle down to a common-sense, sane domesticity.(p.297)
• I cannot remember *just* when I became the victim of insomnia, but I do know that the last year and a half I never went to bed sober a single night.(p.299)
• After being fired, I lined up with a new finance company that was *just* starting in business, and took the position of business promotion man, contacting automobile dealers.(p.300)
• It wasn't necessary to report to the office in person every day, and when I did go in, it was *just* to make an appearance and bounce right out again.(p.300)
• I learned that a person *just* can't find a job hanging in a dive or barroom all day and all night, as jobs don't seem to turn up in those places.(p.300)
• *Just* at this time my wife heard of a doctor in another city who had been very successful with drunks.(p.301)
• However, he explained to me that he had been *just* such a rummy as I, only for a much longer period of time.(p.302)
• I still have my job, and *just* prior to the writing of this narrative, I received an advancement.(p.303)
• *Just* an unstable woman, undisciplined, poorly adjusted and filled with nameless fears.(p.305)
• I *just* don't want to."(p.318)
• You're *just* a martyr, aren't you?"(p.322)
• And when I looked at it, I knew I was *just* as much a drunk as George was, if not worse.(p.322)
• He used to wonder, when he'd spot one of my bottles around the house, *just* how he could have overlooked that particular bottle.(p.325)
• I *just* didn't give a whoop about myself or anyone else.(p.325)
• I was aware of symptoms of impending dependence, and I told myself I had gotten out of the rat race *just* in time to head off any booze problem.(p.327)
• I'd *just* take a couple or three barbiturates to get back to sleep -- eating my alcohol.(p.333)
• To me, taking a bath was *just* being in a place with a bottle where I could drink in privacy.(p.337)
• I *just* wanted to live to a certain age, carry through with what I felt was my job with the children, and after that -- no matter.(p.337)
• The people who would have come to help me were *just* the people I would have nothing to do with.(p.338)
• The skid row of success is *just* as miserable.(p.345)
• And *just* then something did happen.(p.347)
• So I thought to myself, I might *just* as well be drunk as feel like this.(p.348)
• But I made my admission *just* the same.(p.350)
• *Just* three years of drinking pushed a shy, lonely young girl to the depth of depression.(p.353)
• I had no idea what would happen -- I *just* knew I didn't want to live if life was going to go on like it was.(p.355)
• In the various schools I attended, it was always a case of *just* getting by.(p.357)
• By hook or crook I usually managed to sober up before I reached home, but always "terribly tired" from a "hard day's work," and *just* having to have one or two before dinner.(p.361)
• Why should this happen to me -- hadn't I provided a good home -- wasn't I making a good living -- didn't I *just* get a substantial raise that had put me in the upper bracket class?(p.362)
• I had *just* raised the bottle to my lips when my wife opened the door and froze me completely in my tracks with "Happy New Year, dear."(p.365)
• But for some reason -- she *just* didn't know why -- she *just* had to hold onto that clipping, with its thin hope.(p.367)
• At a women's halfway house, I became associated with Alcoholics Anonymous and became aware of alcoholism as a disease, not *just* a "weakness."(p.371)
• At first it was *just* that -- an occasional drink.(p.374)
• It now became necessary to have noon drinks; at first *just* two, then gradually more.(p.375)
• Two years before I joined A.A. my wife took a long trip during which she wrote me she *just* couldn't return unless I did something about my drinking.(p.377)
• Study the A.A. book -- don't *just* read it.(p.381)
• Nor have I attended them with a feeling of *just* doing my duty.(p.381)
• *Just* being sober will be making amends to many we have hurt by our drunken actions.(p.381)
• Living *just* for today is a pleasant adventure.(p.383)
• The only thing I have really to offer you is my own story, telling you *just* what sort of a drunk I was.(p.384)
• You didn't carry a little orchid up the aisle in those days; you carried a great big bouquet, like a funeral spray, and you didn't have your picture taken until *just* before you went to the church.(p.385)
• The church was *just* three blocks from our home.(p.385)

• I got right into the car and they drove me over, and *just* as soon as I got to the church they started the wedding.(p.385)
• I walked up that aisle *just* like Mae West in her prime.(p.385)
• As long as it eased situations socially, it helped *just* fine, but somewhere along the line, it back-fired.(p.386)
• I resented the fact that Frank had done this to me, and I *just* didn't know what was going on.(p.388)
• Anyhow, after Christmas my husband gave me a cocker spaniel who is, I think, *just* as notorious in A.A. as I am.(p.388)
• I loved my father dearly and I adored my dog, and I'd gotten this new house and Frank had *just* given me a new fur coat and I was thrilled to death.(p.389)
• You know those vitamins *just* don't keep you sober!(p.389)
• I was *just* as drunk as I could be, getting ready to take an afternoon walk.(p.390)
• So I was in *just* a few hours.(p.390)
• I think I actually read more contempt than was really there because *just* a week before someone had sent him the Saturday Evening Post article on A.A., and there was some glimmer of hope in it for him.(p.391)
• It had a name and symptoms, *just* like diabetes or T.B.(p.392)
• So I wrote this letter in very shaky handwriting, and in *just* one week came back a letter with A.A. literature from New York.(p.392)
• Monday morning I was feeling *just* like a million dollars -- all I needed was half a pint!(p.393)
• After all, upon coming out of a week-long or ten-day drunk, it was hard enough to figure up *just* how much that one drunk cost, let alone trying to calculate the cost of approximately twenty-five years of active alcoholism.(p.396)
• Like most statistics, it doesn't prove anything -- *just* satisfies a little curiosity engendered by the wail "Oh, those initiation fees" that prompted this investigation.(p.399)
• Up to this time it *just* hadn't occurred to me to drink.(p.402)
• *Just* what I wanted.(p.402)
• I was the center of attention, *just* what my sick ego craved.(p.407)
• Certainly, when I was in my cups, I was not *just* drunk, I was crazy.(p.408)
• I was, when drunk, *just* as undisciplined and erratic as ever.(p.410)
• I could *just* hear their sweet, pious talk.(p.412)
• "Why don't you *just* go down and see Mr. W.?" she asked.(p.412)
• I had *just* begun a dental practice in a beautiful new office.(p.418)
• I quit, when I was *just* past sixteen.(p.424)
• This was fine, but it was *just* an extra dividend, for I'd made connections by this time and was buying a bottle a day from the cook.(p.426)
• "The nervous tension had piled up and *just* had to spill over."(p.433)
• The binge had been *just* "one of those things."(p.433)
• It wasn't until *just* lately that, in your case, I could draw it.(p.436)
• The physician wasn't hooked, he thought -- he *just* prescribed drugs medically indicated for his many ailments.(p.439)
• I *just* didn't belong here.(p.439)
• I yelled at Max, "What do you mean, 'The dog *just* needs more love'?(p.440)
• Eventually, I was taking forty-five milligrams of the long-acting Benzedrine and forty-five of the short-acting *just* to get out of bed in the morning.(p.442)
• For the leveling-off process, I *just* loved intravenous Demerol, but I found it hard to practice good medicine while shooting morphine.(p.442)
• In the garage, I would put the needle in my vein and then try to figure out exactly how much medication to inject to overcome the pep pills while adding to the sleeping pills while ignoring the tranquilizers, in order to get *just* enough to be able to pull out the needle, jerk the tourniquet, throw it in the car, slam the car door shut, run down the hall, and fall in bed before I fell asleep.(p.442)
• Had I gone to school all those years *just* to sit and make leather belts?(p.445)
• In the hospital, I hung on to the idea I'd had most of my life: that if I could *just* control the external environment, the internal environment would then be comfortable.(p.445)
• Each with the other as a witness, we took the Third Step out loud -- *just* as it says in the Big Book.(p.446)
• "That's a devil of a way to run an organization," I thought, and I reported Frank to the psychiatrist, who didn't seem perturbed; he *just* got someone else to take me on Fridays.(p.447)
• And I was always glad to point it out, because I knew you wanted perfection, *just* as I did.(p.449)
• So I'm better off if I don't give advice, don't figure I know what's best, and *just* accept life on life's terms, as it is today -- especially my own life, as it actually is.(p.450)
• I never *just* sit and do nothing while waiting for Him to tell me what to do.(p.452)
• Through A.A., many receive the needed change and awakening *just* by trying to live by A.A. principles and associating with A.A. people.(p.459)
• I would rather talk about the good things A.A. has taught me; I feel that hitting on *just* a few sordid points should be sufficient to let those of you in institutions know where I came from.(p.459)
• I thought that was bad until I hit the hole at a prison camp; it was *just* wide enough and long enough to lie down in.(p.459)
• I go back to my old alma mater occasionally to give A.A. talks, and -- *just* think! -- the warden is my friend.(p.462)
• We pulled up in front of my sister's house *just* as dawn broke.(p.466)
• As an indication of *just* how confused and mixed up I was, *just* as soon as I could I left the office and hurried around to tell other patients that I was getting better.(p.470)
• But by listening and talking to these A.A.'s -- talking to them as I had never talked to anyone in my whole life, I saw that it was my life that was unmanageable -- not *just* my drinking.(p.471)
• I thought, "Oh well, these people are *just* like all the people I've known all my life.(p.472)
• *Just* one day."(p.476)
• I say, "*Just* let it happen."(p.477)
• Listen, not *just* hear noise.(p.477)
• Knowing that he was sober, I timed it *just* right, so I could do the slashing *just* before he hit the steps.(p.479)
• So I wasn't *just* tinkering around with it -- I had to get in with both feet.(p.480)
• It is no problem to me now, but this is not good management on my part -- *just* plain good luck.(p.480)
• I remember in my early youth my mother dressed me *just* as she did my two sisters, and I wore curls until I was six years of age.(p.483)
• We lived *just* a few doors from the First Baptist Church and when they had funerals I remember very often asking my mother whether the person was good or bad and whether they were going to heaven or hell.(p.483)
• During recess we were playing basketball and I had accidentally tripped a fellow *just* a little larger than I was.(p.484)
• Of course, in my day, times had changed; she *just* hadn't changed with the times.(p.484)
• We weren't even permitted to play cards in our home, but father would give us *just* a little toddy with whiskey and sugar and warm water now and then.(p.484)
• I don't know whether she was a pacifist or whether she *just* thought that in the event of another war it would have some bearing on my joining up.(p.484)
• Things had *just* gone from bad to worse.(p.487)
• From that point on, it's *just* the average drinker's story.(p.488)
• My practice at that juncture was *just* barely getting us a living.(p.488)
• I had a long talk with a psychiatrist, but nothing came of that, and I had also, *just* about that time, talked with a minister for whom I had a great deal of respect.(p.489)
• I rebelled against this, because *just* about the time that I was getting ready to leave high school, a revelation came to me about God and it made things very complicated for me.(p.489)
• I was *just* about broke.(p.491)
• I think the thing that galled me was that *just* after Easter I had drawn my salary for two weeks' work and had decided that I was going to send some money to Vi; and above all else I was going to send my baby daughter an Easter outfit.(p.493)
• I asked her *just* what this deal was, but she wouldn't say.(p.494)
• So I put forth some effort that day to try to stay sober if I could, though my sobriety was *just* a daze.(p.494)
• When he left I walked with him to the streetcar line, which was *just* about a half a block, but there were two liquor stores, one on each corner from my home.(p.495)
• Of course, it wasn't very much of a meeting in the beginning; most of the time it was *just* Vi and myself.(p.495)
• I *just* gathered up this and that alcoholic, because, in the back of my mind, I wanted to save all the world.(p.496)
• I reach for the bottle which I *just* got from George, the elevator boy.(p.500)
• I'll *just* take a few beers now and then.(p.502)
• When I had heard about it, it meant nothing but *just* two letters to me, but some friends of mine in the institution were very active in the program and really believed in it.(p.509)
• So instead of going near A.A., I *just* browsed around for that first month.(p.510)
• But I came out of the Army *just* as big a drunk as when I went in, if not worse, because now I had a lot more resentments.(p.513)
• I had *just* come off a good one, and I went back on to the next one.(p.514)
• I had a habit of getting up *just* prior to the closing time of the saloons, about two or three o'clock in the morning.(p.514)
• He *just* looked at me and said, "Pat, for you there isn't any cure."(p.515)
• So I don't *just* take the inventory at night -- I take it continually throughout the day.(p.516)
• But that was *just* a mistake.(p.517)
• Then I was sent out to India and from then on drinking *just* increased and increased, and I started having two or three day spells instead of *just* the ordinary concentrated one day.(p.519)
• The Abyssinian war broke out *just* as things were going very badly for me, and I went off to Egypt on a job there.(p.519)
• I thought, well, now that I've been put out for drinking, I'll *just* show them that they were completely wrong, so I went off on the biggest bout I had been on up to then, involving about a fortnight's blackout.(p.521)
• I stayed there *just* long enough to work up a real good resentment against the doctor in charge, who I didn't think was doing anything at all except collecting fees, and I left there fully determined that I'd never put myself in the power of medical people again.(p.521)
• I stopped off *just* to have one drink to see if it tasted the same on the way back to London, and that night I was carried back to bed again.(p.522)
• In any case, I made myself believe that, so I *just* drifted about, existing on my retired pay, drinking, and living at home.(p.522)
• The thought of stopping drinking *just* never occurred to me.(p.522)
• *Just* as I was wondering what on earth I could do -- I was too drunk even to pack a handkerchief -- the memory of an A.A. write-up that I had seen in the Evening Mail flashed across my mind -- and I thought to myself, this is something I haven't tried yet.(p.523)
• But I did understand this eventually, that these people had been through a lot of drinking experience *just* as I had, and had managed to make a job of it.(p.524)
• Since I joined on that April night, A.A. has done more for me than *just* stop me from drinking; it has brought me back to life again.(p.524)
• It continues to try to teach me the real charity, the charity that gives time and good will and service, and not *just* money.(p.525)
• I *just* want to say that you don't have to be afraid, because no one at any A.A. meeting will bite you.(p.529)
• For a little while, I was the great man I wanted to be, and thought myself entitled to be *just* by reason of being.(p.537)
• But not for long; now, for five Friday nights in a row, I went to jail, picked up sodden with beer (which I always disliked, but which was the only drink available); in jail five consecutive Friday nights in the town where I had grown up, where I had been an honor student in high school, where a kindly uncle, bailing me out, said, "Bob, our family *just* doesn't do this sort of thing."(p.539)
• I had *just* turned forty-six.(p.540)
• The only importance in all of this lies in the fact that at twenty-three I was *just* as sick as I was at thirty three, when I came into A.A., but at that time I apparently had no place to go because I had no drinking problem.(p.546)
• This caused the rather cryptic comment from one of my A.A. friends, when I told my story after coming into the program, that I had always been a cinch for the program, for I had always been interested in mankind, but that I was *just* taking them one man at a time.(p.548)

• I've heard it said many times in A.A., "There is ***just*** one good drunk in every alcoholic's life, and that's the one that brings us into A.A.," and I believe it.(p.549)
• This great experience that released me from the bondage of hatred and replaced it with love is really ***just*** another affirmation of the truth I know: I get everything I need in Alcoholics Anonymous – everything I need I get – and when I get what I need I invariably find that it was ***just*** what I wanted all the time.(p.553)
• I was raised in Kansas, the only child of loving parents who ***just*** drank socially.(p.554)
• At first, ***just*** one drink, on occasion.(p.557)
• A.A. can, of course, mean ***just*** as much to uncounted alcoholics not yet reached.(p.563)

justifiable

• Though there may be ***justifiable*** exceptions, and though we wish to lay down no rule of any sort, we have often found this the best course to take.(p.81)

justifiably

• My wife and family stood by me for ten weeks and then, quite ***justifiably***, ejected me.(p.257)

justification

• But even in this type of beginning we are obliged to admit that our ***justification*** for a spree was insanely insufficient in the light of what always happened.(p.37)
• Both father and the family are mistaken, though each side may have some ***justification***.(p.126)
• Instead of treating the family as he should, he may retreat further into himself and feel he has spiritual ***justification*** for so doing.(p.129)

justified

• In some circumstances we have gone out deliberately to get drunk, feeling ourselves ***justified*** by nervousness, anger, worry, depression, jealousy or the like.(p.37)
• Cleaning up old scrapes, helping to settle family differences, explaining the disinherited son to his irate parents, lending money and securing jobs for each other, when ***justified*** – these are everyday occurrences.(p.161)
• It had to be or I could not have ***justified*** my erratic behavior as I did.(p.551)

justify

• I thought to myself, "Well, she is going to tell me this is the end," and I certainly couldn't blame her and did not intend to try to ***justify*** myself.(p.184)

Kk

Kaneohe
• I was transferred to ***Kaneohe*** Bay, across the hump to the windward side of Oahu, to the aviation base.(p.426)

kangaroo
• I tried to conduct a ***kangaroo*** court and hit them with a broomstick.(p.204)

Kansas
• A square from ultra-dry ***Kansas***, I did not taste grog until I had finished college, done a stint on newspapers, married, become a father, and been in studio publicity two years.(p.328)
• I was raised in ***Kansas***, the only child of loving parents who just drank socially.(p.554)

Karen
• When I came home from Nam, I met a girl I'll call ***Karen***.(p.318)
• ***Karen*** didn't want to see me any more, and neither did two other girls I'd been going out with.(p.318)

keen
• It may be he has done us more harm than we have done him and, though we may have acquired a better attitude toward him, we are still not too ***keen*** about admitting our faults.(p.77)
• His enthusiasm and ***keen*** interest in A.A. fired my spirits again.(p.365)

keenly
• I was ***keenly*** aware that my all-important security, which I had been constantly afraid of losing for four decades, no longer was endangered.(p.329)

keep
• If we ***keep*** on the way we are going there is little doubt that much good will result, but the surface of the problem would hardly be scratched.(p.19)
• On through the years this conduct continues, accompanied by his continual promises to be careful or to ***keep*** off the streets altogether.(p.38)
• He was positive that his humiliating experience, plus the knowledge he had acquired, would ***keep*** him sober the rest of his life.(p.40)
• Time after time newcomers have tried to ***keep*** to themselves certain facts about their lives.(p.72)
• It is important that he be able to ***keep*** a confidence; that he fully understand and approve what we are driving at; that he will not try to change our plan.(p.74)
• ***Keep*** it always in sight that we are dealing with that most terrible human emotion – jealousy.(p.82)
• Sometimes we hear an alcoholic say that the only thing he needs to do is to ***keep*** sober.(p.82)
• Certainly he must ***keep*** sober, for there will be no home if he doesn't.(p.82)
• That is how we react so long as we ***keep*** in fit spiritual condition.(p.85)
• ***Keep*** his attention focussed mainly on your personal experience.(p.92)
• We find it a waste of time to ***keep*** chasing a man who cannot or will not work with you.(p.96)
• ***Keep*** on the firing line of life with these motives and God will ***keep*** you unharmed.(p.102)
• Many of us ***keep*** liquor in our homes.(p.102)
• Of those who ***keep*** on, a good number will become true alcoholics after a while.(p.109)
• We families of Alcoholics Anonymous ***keep*** few skeletons in the closet.(p.125)
• We have come to believe He would like us to ***keep*** our heads in the clouds with Him, but that our feet ought to be firmly planted on earth.(p.130)
• You might say you appreciated his abilities, would like to ***keep*** him, but cannot if he continues to drink.(p.141)
• But you should feel under no obligation to ***keep*** him on, for your obligation has been well discharged already.(p.147)
• We know our friend is like a boy whistling in the dark to ***keep*** up his spirits.(p.152)
• Both saw that they must ***keep*** spiritually active.(p.156)
• May God bless you and ***keep*** you -- until then.(p.164)
• I remember that my father kept whiskey around the house for medical purposes and entertainment, and I would drink from this when no one was about and then water it to ***keep*** my parents from knowing I was drinking.(p.183)
• Bill looked across at my wife, and said to her, "Henrietta, the Lord has been so wonderful to me, curing me of this terrible disease, that I just want to ***keep*** talking about it and telling people."(p.191)
• That sentence, "The Lord has been so wonderful to me, curing me of this terrible disease, that I just want to ***keep*** telling people about it," has been sort of a golden text for the A.A. program and for me.(p.191)
• My big job was to ***keep*** other people from finding it out.(p.199)
• I couldn't afford to be found with those people, but I said I would certainly pay his dues if it would ***keep*** him from drinking.(p.205)
• A year later, after I completed the course in contracts, I quit the law school, and undertook some engineering work for a patent law firm on behalf of clients who were in difficulties and who desired to ***keep*** their troubles from their own engineering department.(p.212)
• My life was fairly well crowded and I didn't seem to need any stimulants to ***keep*** me going.(p.213)
• Cold chills started chasing up and down my spine; my teeth were chattering; my hands were shaking so I tucked them under me to ***keep*** them from flying away.(p.222)
• All I had left was an iron determination to live my own life in spite of the alien world -- and here I was, an inwardly frightened, outwardly defiant woman, who desperately needed a prop to ***keep*** going.(p.226)
• I very early came to see that there had to be a continual renewal for that simple deal with God; that I had perpetually to ***keep*** the bargain.(p.237)
• Searching where I have been at fault, it is not hard to discover and get right again, for I have proven to myself and to many others who know me that God can ***keep*** a man sober if he will let Him.(p.237)
• However, I did manage to ***keep*** out of the guardhouse.(p.242)
• Bill and Hank had just taken over a small automobile polishing company and they offered me a job -- ten dollars a week and ***keep*** at Hank's house.(p.246)
• Young and able to travel with the best of them, I managed to hold my job and ***keep*** my end up in the barrooms.(p.252)
• I stayed so sober that I used to ***keep*** a quart of medicinal whiskey in my bureau which I used to taper off the occasional newspaper alcoholics who were sent to see me.(p.253)
• I had some financial success through no ability of my own and, when jobless and almost wiped out in 1930, I began to trade and sell my collection; much of the proceeds went to ***keep*** my apartment stocked with liquor and almost every night saw me helpless to bed.(p.255)
• I arrived drunk, but I promised my wife I would ***keep*** sober, and I knew I could get work if I did.(p.256)
• Of course I didn't ***keep*** sober.(p.257)
• Russ read a piece in the paper, and he kind of snickered, and said, "See here, where John D. has found something to ***keep*** him from drinking!"(p.265)
• I landed him and shipped him by train to Akron, with a pint of whiskey in his pocket to ***keep*** him from wanting to get off the train in Toledo!(p.282)
• I could not expect to ***keep*** what I had gained unless I gave it away.(p.282)
• The most accurate answer I can give you is this: Fear has never again ruled my life since that day in September, 1938, when I found that a Power greater than myself could not only restore me to sanity but could ***keep*** me both sober and sane.(p.285)
• It is a way of life, and the challenge contained in its principles is great enough to ***keep*** any human being striving for as long as he lives.(p.311)
• I said, "Well, I stood it to ***keep*** the home together, and for the children's sake."(p.322)
• I couldn't ***keep*** up with any of my other friends, and I wouldn't go to anyone's house unless I knew they drank as heavily as I did.(p.324)
• I was assigned to ***keep*** media guests happy at a Halloween party given by a major star in his plush home.(p.328)
• Creativity at the typewriter would ***keep*** me busy and alert, I said.(p.331)
• The regular flow of all the literature, which I ***keep*** meticulously and which, of course, I study, has been wonderful.(p.342)
• Looking back, it is surprising to me now that I managed to ***keep*** working and have enough money to squander at the various spots in the big city.(p.358)
• "***Keep*** busy; always have something constructive to do."(p.373)
• Whenever we went out she appeared to go out of her way to ***keep*** me from having more than one drink.(p.376)
• You know those vitamins just don't ***keep*** you sober!(p.389)
• Dr. Bob said, "Love and service ***keep*** us dry," and Bill said, "Always we must remember that our first duty is face-to-face help for the alcoholic who still suffers."(p.395)
• To ***keep*** it in round figures, let's say twenty per cent of my income went for giggle gurgles.(p.397)
• I had a tiny trust fund, and I moved into a small apartment where I learned to cook, ***keep*** house, and do the things that normal people do.(p.409)
• He asked me if I had any spiritual belief, and when I said No, he suggested that I ***keep*** an open mind.(p.413)
• I thought it was my duty to ***keep*** her from drinking, not knowing that if the other fellow is really determined to drink there is nothing you can do about it.(p.415)
• John said, "***Keep*** going to meetings."(p.415)
• Awarded a scholarship to a famous old Eastern college, I began to drink at the end of my freshman year, and by junior year, I had to transfer to an easier state university to ***keep*** my grades up.(p.419)
• I depended on optimism and ambition to live in society; when I began to tire, I had to depend on chemicals instead to ***keep*** going.(p.420)
• The longer the drinking continued, the shorter the time the alcohol would ***keep*** me asleep; I would have to drink myself back to sleep again and again throughout the night.(p.441)
• Following an injection I would have to ***keep*** one hand busy scratching my constantly itching nose and would also have sudden uncontrollable urges to vomit.(p.442)
• Much of my time was spent writing letters, notes, orders, and lists of things for Max, who was also my office nurse, to do to ***keep*** the world running while I was locked up.(p.445)
• But for some time, it was difficult to ***keep*** from taking a pill when I had an appropriate symptom, such as a cough, pain, anxiety, insomnia, a muscle spasm, or an upset stomach.(p.448)
• I must ***keep*** my magic magnifying mind on my acceptance and off my expectations, for my serenity is directly proportional to my level of acceptance.(p.452)
• Finally they stopped and bought me a bottle; they knew so well that would ***keep*** me quiet.(p.466)
• I ***keep*** it simple; go to many meetings; carry message to those who listen.(p.476)
• I don't seem to be able to ***keep*** my mind on what I am doing.(p.499)
• But it takes others to ***keep*** me there.(p.500)
• Finally, he was drinking to ***keep*** away those little men, and those strange voices, and the organ music that came out of the walls.(p.512)
• I was drinking to ***keep*** away the shakes, drinking to ***keep*** away those little men and those strange voices and the organ music that comes out of the walls.(p.514)
• At first, like everybody else, I could ***keep*** control when I drank, but if I did start to drink, even in those days, I was always one of the last to leave the party.(p.518)
• It has taught me that I can best ***keep*** my sobriety by sharing it out with others; that I must bring that sobriety to others who need it, in my own interest.(p.524)
• I went back home, to a job of manual labor where for a little while I was able to ***keep*** away from alcohol.(p.539)
• It seemed logical to me that if I married this man and took the responsibility for these children that they would ***keep*** me sober.(p.548)
• They suggested that I study the A.A. book and try to take the Twelve Steps according to the explanation in the Book, for it was their opinion that the application of these principles in our daily lives will get us sober and ***keep*** us sober.(p.550)
• Instead of drinking in fancy bars and clubs, I had to carry a bottle of vodka in my briefcase, duck into public toilets, and gulp from the bottle, trembling, in order to ***keep*** from falling apart.(p.557)
• "There is a principle which is a bar against all information, which is proof against all arguments and which cannot fail to ***keep*** a man in everlasting igno-

rance – that principle is contempt prior to investigation."(p.570)

keeping

• Prior to his journey to Akron, the broker had worked hard with many alcoholics on the theory that only an alcoholic could help an alcoholic, but he had succeeded only in ***keeping*** sober himself.(p.xvi)

• I felt I had every right to be self-confident, that it would be only a matter of exercising my will power and ***keeping*** on guard.(p.40)

• Often you must carry the burden of avoiding them or ***keeping*** them under control.(p.117)

• You are not doing him a favor by ***keeping*** him on.(p.141)

• ***Keeping*** one foot in front of the other is essential for maintaining our arrestment.(p.311)

• And of course a half empty bottle wasn't worth ***keeping***, so I finished it up and naturally had to get more in right away for the people who "might come in unexpectedly."(p.336)

• Dr. Bob tells about ***keeping*** it simple and not to louse it up.(p.395)

• I was so busy ***keeping*** her out of trouble, and so scared she'd swing on me, that I had my last two drinks that night.(p.415)

• (Today, there is absolutely nothing in the world more important to me than my ***keeping*** this alcoholic sober; not taking a drink is by far the most important thing I do each day.)(p.447)

• I knew I wasn't capable of ***keeping*** the bulk of the money myself, so I gave it to a white fellow who owned the bar which I frequented.(p.493)

keeps

• They are always "going on the wagon for ***keeps***."(p.xxviii)

• We know that while the alcoholic ***keeps*** away from drink, as he may do for months or years, he reacts much like other men.(p.22)

• There is a complete failure of the kind of defense that ***keeps*** one from putting his hand on a hot stove.(p.24)

• If you think you are an atheist, an agnostic, a skeptic, or have any other form of intellectual pride which ***keeps*** you from accepting what is in this book, I feel sorry for you.(p.181)

• And life ***keeps*** getting simpler and easier as we try to reverse my old idea, by taking care of the internal environment via the Twelve Steps, and letting the external environment take care of itself.)(p.446)

• But when I try to see what I can add to the meeting, rather than what I can get out of it, and when I focus my mind on what's good about it, rather than what's wrong with it, the meeting ***keeps*** getting better and better.(p.451)

• This career girl preferred solitary drinking, the blackout kind, often hoping she'd stay that way for ***keeps***.(p.464)

• I don't know if it's force of habit or something else that ***keeps*** them in one place, but I do know that in A.A. there is much work to do, and none of us can do it standing still.(p.529)

keg

• I call the bootlegger and fill up my charred ***keg***.(p.501)

• But I do not wait for the charred ***keg*** to work.(p.501)

Kenmore

• Before my drinking had cut me down completely, I achieved a considerable measure of success, having been a City Councilman for five years and a financial director of ***Kenmore***, a suburb later taken into the city itself.(p.182)

Kennedy

• Dr. Foster ***Kennedy***, neurologist: "This organization of Alcoholics Anonymous calls on two of the greatest reservoirs of power known to man, religion and that instinct for association with one's fellows . . . the 'herd instinct.'(p.571)

Kent

• We were to go up to our A.A. farm in ***Kent***, and I spent the evening before riding herd on Anne.(p.415)

Kentucky

• One of five children, I was born on a ***Kentucky*** farm in Carlyle County.(p.182)

• My wife, a ***Kentucky*** girl, came with me to Akron where I completed my course in law at the Akron Law School.(p.182)

kept

• The section called "The Doctor's Opinion" has been ***kept*** intact, just as it was originally written in 1939 by the late Dr. William D. Silkworth, our Society's great medical benefactor.(p.xi)

• There had been no real infidelity, for loyalty to my wife, helped at times by extreme drunkenness, ***kept*** me out of those scrapes.(p.3)

• He has a positive genius for getting tight at exactly the wrong moment, particularly when some important decision must be made or engagement ***kept***.(p.21)

• He knew he faced another trip to the asylum if he ***kept*** on.(p.35)

• Being all powerful, He provided what we needed, if we ***kept*** close to Him and performed His work well.(p.63)

• Maybe we are divorced, and have remarried but haven't ***kept*** up the alimony to number one.(p.79)

• Selfish and inconsiderate habits have ***kept*** the home in turmoil.(p.82)

• Have we ***kept*** something to ourselves which should be discussed with another person at once?(p.86)

• Because of the employee's special ability, or of his own strong personal attachment to him, the employer has sometimes ***kept*** such a man at work long beyond a reasonable period.(p.137)

• This resolution I ***kept*** steadfastly for the next forty years, except when circumstances made it seem unwise to absent myself.(p.172)

• This had little effect however for I ***kept*** on drinking and used a great deal more hard liquor than in former years.(p.174)

• During these two years I was ***kept*** so busy that I hardly left the hospital at all.(p.174)

• I used to promise my wife, my friends, and my children that I would drink no more – promises which seldom ***kept*** me sober even through the day, though I was very sincere when I made them.(p.177)

• How my wife ***kept*** her faith and courage during all those years, I'll never know, but she did.(p.178)

• He ***kept*** the faith; therefore, he and countless others found a new life.(p.182)

• I remember that my father ***kept*** whiskey around the house for medical purposes and entertainment, and I would drink from this when no one was about and then water it to keep my parents from knowing I was drinking.(p.183)

• I ***kept*** watching the man down the bar to see what he did with a contraption like that, and he just smelled of his drink and set it down again, so I did the same.(p.195)

• Anyhow, I recognized the fact that I couldn't drink like normal people, but I tried hard and ***kept*** on trying for twenty-two years.(p.196)

• I ***kept*** myself so busy that outside of some school and group parties, I didn't go overboard on drinking very much between the ages of twenty-five and thirty.(p.213)

• Beer was too bulky and it couldn't be ***kept*** in a jug under the counter ready to be dumped when John Law came around.(p.233)

• And, because as I have discovered since, it is part of the "treatment" that these men be sent to see and talk with alcoholics who want to quit, he ***kept*** them busy.(p.235)

• For a long time I ***kept*** on trying, in a pretty dumb way at first, I know, but very earnestly.(p.237)

• This duty together with my weekly meetings with my fellow alcoholics, and my daily renewal of the contract I originally made with God, have ***kept*** me sober when nothing else ever did.(p.237)

• But we were staying sober as long as we ***kept*** and talked together.(p.246)

• As soon as I could get up and walk I started to drink again and ***kept*** it up until my friend of the hospital, who, in his first try at the new way of life had stubbed his toe in Chicago but had come back to the town to take counsel and make a new start, picked me up and got me into a hospital.(p.258)

• I ***kept*** my children with me.(p.262)

• "Well," I said to dad, when the A.A. people ***kept*** coming with these lovely cars and looked so nice, "I suppose the neighbors say, 'Now those old fools must have up and died, but where's the hearse?'"(p.269)

• But – supposing that just one man died because I had, for selfish reasons, ***kept*** my mouth shut?(p.282)

• My broken home and broken heart fanned my smoldering self-pity into a fair-sized bonfire and this ***kept*** me well supplied with reasons for having another drink, and then another.(p.305)

• I should have lost my husband, and I think that only the fact that he was an alcoholic too ***kept*** us together.(p.323)

• The movie racket had ***kept*** me too long from writing those novels, articles, short stories, and scripts on which I had copious notes.(p.330)

• How full it has ***kept*** my retirement years – the five I've lived since the first two lost in traveling a rocky road to hell, before I made a U-turn.(p.334)

• I ***kept*** on.(p.337)

• I have never attended an A.A. meeting, so it is essentially the literature that has ***kept*** me on the A.A. program.(p.342)

• I have read systematically since then, and A.A. literature has ***kept*** me sober.(p.343)

• I could hardly see at all, and my memory ***kept*** eluding me.(p.353)

• She was intent on her studies, and ***kept*** her distance.(p.359)

• My work ***kept*** me busy the first few months on the new job.(p.360)

• Of course I ***kept*** her posted on how well the station was doing and wrote convincing letters of how well I was doing with the liquor problem.(p.360)

• I ***kept*** away from liquor and eagerly waited.(p.363)

• The drive to get ahead, to succeed, ***kept*** me too busy for many years to have any great experience with social life.(p.374)

• But they ***kept*** me there – I was supposed to stay a month, but they only ***kept*** me there seventeen days.(p.387)

• He got half custody of our child, but later ***kept*** her during most of the school terms.(p.402)

• I drank and I ***kept*** on drinking.(p.406)

• Only A.A. ***kept*** me from running away.(p.420)

• The other pupils ***kept*** books, pencils, paper, gym equipment and such stuff in their lockers.(p.423)

• I also ***kept*** beer.(p.423)

• I was never drunk on the job, never missed a day's work, was seldom rendered totally ineffective by a hangover and ***kept*** my liquor expenses well within my adequate budget.(p.433)

• And as I went through pharmacy school, graduate school, medical school, internship, residency, and specialty training and, finally, went into practice, my drinking ***kept*** increasing.(p.441)

• I didn't feel I could lie in bed and squirt the stuff in my veins while my kids and wife stood around watching me, so I ***kept*** the drug in my bag and the bag in the car and the car in the garage.(p.442)

• I never could quite get the knack of it and ***kept*** asking myself, "What's a nice guy like me doing in a place like this?"(p.445)

• In my screwed up mind I ***kept*** thinking I could have gone to A.A. way back there in 1940, and perhaps saved my marriage and home.(p.469)

• I've never seen him drunk in my life, although he'd take a shot in the morning and usually one in the evening, and so did I; but for the most part he ***kept*** his whiskey in his office.(p.484)

• For the first couple of years it wasn't too bad because the momentum ***kept*** things going.(p.486)

• He ***kept*** the money for me, but I worried him to death for it.(p.493)

• They ***kept*** harping on it, that I go.(p.509)

• However, my two friends ***kept*** coaxing and cajoling to get me back again.(p.510)

• I started prowling around with a couple of these A.A. boys, which ***kept*** me pretty busy and ***kept*** my mind off of down town.(p.511)

• But somehow or other, with my old alcoholic brain, sitting there in that chair, I ***kept*** saying to myself, "I wonder if it'll work?(p.515)

• However, I ***kept*** that job in Egypt and Palestine for about two years, and then I changed over to the other battalion in my regiment.(p.520)

• They ***kept*** me in hospital for two months, and then they sent me up to Egypt, a three days journey.(p.521)

• Finally, my mother came and said she had ***kept*** me at home for six years because she thought she could help me, but that now she had come to the conclusion that I wasn't even worth trying to help.(p.523)

• I never was a "secret" drinker, and I never ***kept*** a bottle at home.(p.536)

• The children ***kept*** me sober for darn near three weeks, and then I went on (please God) my last drunk.(p.549)

• My doctor warned me that if I ***kept*** on, I might have esophageal hemorrhaging and die.(p.558)

kernel

• Occasionally, it is accorded to a few of us to watch something fine grow from a tiny ***kernel*** into something of gigantic goodness.(p.295)

key

• In the doctor's judgment he was utterly hopeless; he could never regain his position in society and he would have to place himself under lock and ***key*** or hire a bodyguard if he expected to live long.(p.26)

• We turned back to the list, for it held the ***key*** to the future.(p.66)

• Cling to the thought that, in God's hands, the dark past is the greatest possession you have -- the ***key*** to life and happiness for others.(p.124)

• Acceptance was his ***key*** to liberation.(p.439)

• At last, acceptance proved to be the ***key*** to my

drinking problem.(p.448)
• Acceptance is the ***key*** to my relationship with God today.(p.452)
• If I failed, they would throw away the ***key***, and I would never get out again.(p.461)
• Universal respect is the ***key*** to their usefulness.(p.567)

key-tapping
• Seated at the typewriter, I faked deep thinking or portrayed creativity by ***key-tapping***.(p.332)

keyhole
• I knew nothing about alcoholism or the D.T.'s, but when I woke up on this last morning of my son's illness, I taped the ***keyhole*** on my door because "everyone was out there."(p.338)

keys
• They struck the children, kicked out door panels, smashed treasured crockery, and ripped the ***keys*** out of pianos.(p.106)
• After finding every bottle that I had hidden around the apartment, she took away my pants, my shoes, my money and my ***keys***, threw them under the bed in the back bedroom and slip-locked our door.(p.288)
• THE ***KEYS*** OF THE KINGDOM(p.304)
• This worldly lady helped to develop A.A. in Chicago and thus passed her ***keys*** to many.(p.304)
• In return for a bottle and a hangover, we have been given the ***Keys*** of the Kingdom.(p.312)

keystone
• Most good ideas are simple, and this concept was the ***keystone*** of the new and triumphant arch through which we passed to freedom.(p.62)

kick
• Some of the things which used to stop me in my tracks from fear still make me nervous in the anticipation of their doing, but once I ***kick*** myself into doing them nervousness disappears and I enjoy myself.(p.285)
• He was happy, getting a ***kick*** out of life and people, and beginning to get his medical practice back again.(p.290)
• Not only were they at peace with themselves, but they were getting a ***kick*** out of life such as one seldom encounters, except in the very young.(p.310)

kicked
• They struck the children, ***kicked*** out door panels, smashed treasured crockery, and ripped the keys out of pianos.(p.106)
• The second year my drinking was more or less restricted to week-ends, but I was nearly ***kicked*** out for scholastic failure.(p.241)
• In three months John Barleycorn had me ***kicked*** out.(p.254)
• He, in turn, ***kicked*** me so I fell to the ground.(p.406)
• After my last binge I came home and smashed my dining room furniture to splinters, ***kicked*** out six windows and two balustrades.(p.435)
• A case of measles saved me from being ***kicked*** out during my Sophomore year.(p.499)

kicking
• In the first year there were episodes such as ***kicking*** Priscilla in the shins, getting the lock changed on the desk in the A.A. Club, because I, as secretary, didn't want the Intergroup secretary "interfering," and taking an older woman member out to lunch for the express purpose of informing her that she was "a phony."(p.416)

kicks
• You no longer get the ***kicks***.(p.514)

kid
• I was the ***kid*** of the crew.(p.423)
• It hurt to be considered a ***kid***.(p.423)
• Of course the ***kid*** never got the Easter outfit.(p.493)
• I began drinking as a ***kid***, shortly after I reached my fourteenth birthday.(p.508)
• In each new place, I was the new ***kid*** -- a skinny, shy ***kid*** -- to be tested and beaten up.(p.555)
• And yet my ability to lie outwardly and to ***kid*** myself inwardly grew with every drink I took.(p.556)

kidded
• Even the critics ***kidded*** me about this one.(p.405)

kidding
• Then I started traveling, with the United States and Canada as my territory, and with so much freedom and with an unlimited expense account, I was soon drinking every night and ***kidding*** myself that it was all part of the job.(p.287)
• "You ***kidding*** -- you an alcoholic?"(p.356)
• When I remark that I have been in jail nine times, and in an alcoholic ward twice, they think I'm ***kidding***, or possibly dramatizing for the sake of a good yarn.(p.542)
• By this time I was such a past master at ***kidding*** myself that I had convinced myself I had sat out a war and waited for this man to come home and, as my resentment and self-pity grew, so did my alcoholic problem.(p.548)

kids
• They were all ***kids***, most of them younger than I was.(p.407)
• The other ***kids*** would light out for the hamburger huts or ice cream parlors, the pizza joints or bowling alleys, after football games and dances.(p.423)
• I also sent my ***kids*** to psychiatrists.(p.440)
• I didn't feel I could lie in bed and squirt the stuff in my veins while my ***kids*** and wife stood around watching me, so I kept the drug in my bag and the bag in the car and the car in the garage.(p.442)
• To tell you a small part of what my mother's life must have been like: Three of her ***kids*** were in jail that year – two sons and a daughter.(p.480)

kill
• "The doctor told him that if he ever drank again it would ***kill*** him, but there he is all lit up again."(p.20)
• In that state, the wrong-doing of others, fancied or real, had power to actually ***kill***.(p.66)
• We may ***kill*** a future opportunity to carry a beneficial message.(p.77)
• People have wars and ***kill*** each other; they struggle and cut each other's throats for success and what does anyone get out of it?(p.244)
• I was sent to a psychiatrist, for they didn't think it was normal for me to want to ***kill*** my platoon sergeant or to attempt suicide twice.(p.318)
• They introduced me to beer in the morning to ***kill*** hangovers.(p.407)
• The last time I drank, when I was twenty-nine, I drank for only four days, yet I threatened to ***kill*** my children; I beat my wife at home and on the church steps; I mistreated a child in my office; and I ran to a hospital for mental illness to avoid jail.(p.418)
• I thought, "If this is A.A. why not go back to drinking, ***kill*** myself with booze in the next three years the doctor had given me, and call it a bad job?"(p.430)
• All Twelve Steps of A.A. are designed to ***kill*** the old self (deflate the old ego) and build a new, free self.(p.459)
• Think about ***kill*** myself.(p.475)
• By grace of God I stop, think two things: This would ***kill*** good mother and father; then remember boys talk about Indian fellow who been sober three years.(p.475)
• Any time I tried to ***kill*** myself, I was either drunk or pilled-up or both – usually the last.(p.479)
• I am too yellow to ***kill*** myself.(p.502)

killed
• Of course, the latter ultimately ***killed*** the former, but of this, more anon.(p.277)
• I lost my driver's license, was made a ward of the court, and was put on probation (not to mention the fact that I might have ***killed*** three friends and myself).(p.354)
• Very soon after I lost Mother, my five-year-old little girl was ***killed*** by a neighbor's car.(p.370)
• Why I wasn't ***killed*** or how I got home I don't know.(p.429)
• One night my son, when he was only sixteen, was suddenly and tragically ***killed***.(p.437)
• Three weeks after an armed robbery in which one person received a superficial flesh wound (I could have ***killed*** someone!), I was apprehended.(p.460)
• During the course of that drinking, I had shot and ***killed*** one person and almost completed the job on a second one.(p.508)
• They tell me that I ***killed*** a man during that period, but I can't remember anything.(p.528)

killing
• It's ***killing*** me."(p.266)

killjoy
• If he gets the idea that you are a nag or a ***killjoy***, your chance of accomplishing anything useful may be zero.(p.111)

killjoys
• If, on the other hand, they took nothing, their self-pity made them ***killjoys***.(p.105)

kills
• We must, or it ***kills*** us!(p.62)
• I'll join A.A. if it ***kills*** me.(p.430)

kind
• The physician who at our request, gave us this letter, has been ***kind*** enough to enlarge upon his views in another statement which follows.(p.xxiv)
• Best of all, I met a ***kind*** doctor who explained that though certainly selfish and foolish, I had been seriously ill, bodily and mentally.(p.7)
• There is a complete failure of the ***kind*** of defense that keeps one from putting his hand on a hot stove.(p.24)
• Neither does there appear to be any ***kind*** of treatment which will make alcoholics of our ***kind*** like other men.(p.30)
• If we are planning to stop drinking, there must be no reservation of any ***kind***, nor any lurking notion that someday we will be immune to alcohol.(p.33)
• To us it is not far-fetched, for this ***kind*** of thinking has been characteristic of every single one of us.(p.37)
• It was his first experience of this ***kind***, and he was much ashamed of it.(p.39)
• Without knowing it, had we not been brought to where we stood by a certain ***kind*** of faith?(p.53)
• Yet we had been seeing another ***kind*** of flight, a spiritual liberation from this world, people who rose above their problems.(p.55)
• We finally saw that faith in some ***kind*** of God was a part of our make-up, just as much as the feeling we have for a friend.(p.55)
• He may be ***kind***, considerate, patient, generous; even modest and self-sacrificing.(p.61)
• Is he not really a self-seeker even when trying to be ***kind***?(p.61)
• They think we do not have enough of it, or that it isn't the right ***kind***.(p.69)
• Were we ***kind*** and loving toward all?(p.86)
• If this ***kind*** of approach does not catch your husband's interest, it may be best to drop the subject, but after a friendly talk your husband will usually revive the topic himself.(p.112)
• Since this book was first published, A.A. has released thousands of alcoholics from asylums and hospitals of every ***kind***.(p.114)
• When they become too dangerous, we think the ***kind*** thing is to lock them up, but of course a good doctor should always be consulted.(p.114)
• This ***kind*** of waste goes on unabated.(p.137)
• With this ***kind*** of employee such an attitude will command undying loyalty.(p.145)
• The employer can many times protect the victim from this ***kind*** of talk.(p.145)
• The right ***kind*** of man, the ***kind*** who recovers, will not want this sort of thing.(p.149)
• The very practical approach to his problems, the absence of intolerance of any ***kind***, the informality, the genuine democracy, the uncanny understanding which these people had were irresistible.(p.160)
• If I could, that was wonderful, that was just fine, and they would very much appreciate a person who had that ***kind*** of power, but they were looking for a man that knew he had a problem, and knew that he couldn't handle it himself and needed outside help.(p.186)
• A big event of any ***kind*** precipitated heavy drinking.(p.197)
• So I had never had any lasting contact with any ***kind*** of religion.)(p.201)
• Pretty soon, I wasn't going at all, and was avoiding those people who had been so ***kind*** to me.(p.203)
• I was ***kind*** of shocked about anybody talking about themselves the way he did, and my impression was that the guy was a little "touched."(p.216)
• That was an experience that I have never forgotten, and many times in my own work with A.A. newcomers I feel ***kind*** of guilty because I haven't done the same thing.(p.219)
• In that I was correct: I couldn't be comfortable with any ***kind*** of people without drinking.(p.227)
• I went trembling into a house in Brooklyn filled with strangers . . . and I found I had come home at last, to my own ***kind***.(p.228)
• In fact I was scared to talk to him about it, for I feared the ***kind*** of talk he would give me.(p.234)
• None of the various cures of this ***kind*** were any good.(p.235)
• Every man has his problem of this ***kind***, but we didn't discuss it very much.(p.236)
• My loneliness was worse than it had ever been before, for now even my own ***kind*** had turned against me.(p.247)
• Russ read a piece in the paper, and he ***kind*** of snickered, and said, "See here, where John D. has found something to keep him from drinking!"(p.265)
• His wife was cussing him, raving at him, "I just brought him over to show you what ***kind*** of a guy he is!(p.271)
• At long last I am doing the ***kind*** of work I have always wanted to do, but never had the patience and emotional stability to train myself for.(p.284)

- I sat up in the big red chair, suddenly thinking, "My God, with my *kind* of lousy luck, I might not die soon!(p.333)
- My story happens to be a particular *kind* of woman's story; the story of the woman who drinks at home.(p.335)
- Luck was with me for I made my train, but I arrived home the next morning with a new *kind* of hang-over.(p.364)
- We lived a *kind* of seesaw existence in the early days.(p.369)
- He even had the people come out, and tell me what *kind* of room I was going to have, and that he could come and see me, and that the dog could come and see me.(p.389)
- There are so many to whom I feel deeply grateful; to my husband (and best critic), whose generous love, compassion and understanding have helped me along the way; to those before me in A.A. who inspired the first article I read, and the friend who sent that article to Frank; to Ruth for her personal note, and the first A.A. to talk to me; to my Bishop, whose loving and believing spirit inspired me; and to all the members of the Houston Group who were so patient, *kind* and helpful -- and to countless others.(p.393)
- Drunkalogues and statistics can be boring, but it is necessary to delve a little into each in order to come up with some *kind* of rough estimate.(p.396)
- Their telegram was *kind* and nice.(p.401)
- At a large party in Geneva, with people from many countries represented, the *kind* of party that is "protocol" in the extreme, I swayed, laughed hysterically, made naughty remarks in an unhushed voice, and was finally led from the scene.(p.406)
- Bill was tall, grey haired, with the *kind* of asymmetrical good looks and pleasant easy manner that inspire confidence in the shaken and afraid.(p.413)
- They were *kind* when they thought about it, but that wasn't often.(p.424)
- I have *kind* and sympathetic parents.(p.431)
- My story has a happy ending, but not of the conventional *kind*.(p.437)
- Most of us did not stay out of prison long enough to run the alcoholic gamut -- to develop the ongoing *kind* of alcoholism or alcoholic drinking you hear about in A.A. talks.(p.458)
- This career girl preferred solitary drinking, the blackout *kind*, often hoping she'd stay that way for keeps.(p.464)
- And we usually have some *kind* of grimy sweater that we think we look sexy in, even if we weigh ninety-five pounds soaking wet and are not wearing a bra.(p.479)
- Anyhow, on the 24th, after drinking all day on the 23rd, I must have decided I wanted to see my wife and have some *kind* of reconciliation or at least talk with her.(p.491)
- Vi was very *kind* and explained to the jury that I was basically a fine fellow and a good husband, but that I drank too much and that she thought I had lost my mind and felt that I should be committed to an asylum.(p.492)
- If something does come along that sort of upsets me, instead of walking in and throwing a buck at the barman and asking for a drink, I walk into a telephone booth, drop a dime in the box, and call somebody who was so *kind* as to give me his name and telephone number to meet such an emergency.(p.511)
- In part, it was a feeling of intense shame at having to leave the Army during the war, but mostly it was resentment that this *kind* of thing should happen to me for, strange as it may seem, up to then I still thought I could control drinking.(p.521)
- I thought that if these *kind* of ordinary people can do it, a man of my brains ought to find it much more easy, and I joined.(p.524)
- Within a month, the police, the hospital authorities, several *kind* strangers, most of my friends, all of my close relatives, and a few adepts at rolling a drunk and removing his wrist watch and wallet had been involved.(p.532)
- The only *kind* of security I knew anything about at that time was material security and I decided that all these intruders would vanish immediately if I only had a lot of money.(p.545)

kindest

- In other words, the *kindest* doctor in the whole world, and I had one such, couldn't help me because I always felt, "You can't know about me – you can't possibly know – you don't even drink!"(p.471)

kindliness

- So we clean house with the family, asking each morning in meditation that our Creator show us the way of patience, tolerance, *kindliness* and love.(p.83)

kindly

- We cannot be helpful to all people, but at least God will show us how to take a *kindly* and tolerant view of each and every one.(p.67)
- A *kindly* act once in a while isn't enough.(p.97)
- About three months after that, my record reached home and I got a letter telling me I was retired from the Army, they put it very *kindly*, on medical grounds.(p.521)
- But not for long; now, for five Friday nights in a row, I went to jail, picked up sodden with beer (which I always disliked, but which was the only drink available); in jail five consecutive Friday nights in the town where I had grown up, where I had been an honor student in high school, where a *kindly* uncle, bailing me out, said, "Bob, our family just doesn't do this sort of thing."(p.539)

kindness

- My bother-in-law is a physician, and through his *kindness* and that of my mother I was placed in a nationally-known hospital for the mental and physical rehabilitation of alcoholics.(p.7)
- It may be that both will decide that the way of good sense and loving *kindness* is to let by-gones be bygones.(p.82)
- Seeing your attempt to understand and help, some men will try to take advantage of your *kindness*.(p.141)
- After the trial, I got big-hearted again and felt that I should do something in payment for Vi's *kindness* to me; so I left Washington and went to Seattle to work.(p.492)
- It's no bed of roses, but somehow or other I've been able to make it, through the *kindness* of people in A.A.(p.511)

kinds

- Nevertheless, the twentieth century readily accepts theories of all *kinds*, provided they are firmly grounded in fact.(p.48)
- Let them remember that his drinking wrought all *kinds* of damage that may take long to repair.(p.127)
- God has abundantly supplied this world with fine doctors, psychologists, and practitioners of various *kinds*.(p.133)
- When I was about forty-seven, after indulging in all *kinds* of self-deception to control my drinking, I arrived at a period when I felt convinced I had to have so much alcohol every day and that the real problem was to control how much.(p.214)
- I had all *kinds* of reasons for my drinking.(p.338)
- I did work of all *kinds* after school and during vacations, trying to find that which would appeal most as a goal for a life work.(p.373)
- The obsession of the mind was a little harder to understand and yet everyone has obsessions of various *kinds*.(p.380)
- The psychiatrist, who had generally been ignoring me, now became quite interested; every day, he would ask me all *kinds* of questions about the A.A. meetings.(p.446)

king

- As we became subjects of *King* Alcohol, shivering denizens of his mad realm, the chilling vapor that is loneliness settled down.(p.151)
- There is another meaning for the Hebrew word that in the *King* James version of the Bible is translated "salvation."(p.228)
- So we came to *King* School.(p.269)
- We had never missed a Wednesday night at *King* School for a year.(p.270)
- I remember sometime, it was possibly six months after we had been going steadily to *King* School, that we were coming home from a meeting and saw a car along the way, and a fellow in back drinking a bottle of beer.(p.271)

kingdom

- THE KEYS OF THE *KINGDOM*(p.304)
- In return for a bottle and a hangover, we have been given the Keys of the *Kingdom*.(p.312)

kinks

- If my personality is inadequate, antisocial, or full of *kinks* and I alter it with alcohol or any chemical, bingo!(p.458)

kinship

- Historians may one day recognize Alcoholics Anonymous to have been a great venture in social pioneering which forged a new instrument for social action; a new therapy based on the *kinship* of common suffering; one having a vast potential for the myriad other ills of mankind."(p.573)

Kirby

- Dr. G. *Kirby* Collier, psychiatrist: "I have felt that A.A. is a group unto themselves and their best results can be had under their own guidance, as a result of their philosophy.(p.571)

kissed

- In the morning we have *kissed* and made up.(p.105)
- During this time, I had been threatened, beaten, *kissed*, praised and damned alternately by relatives, family, friends and strangers, but of course it all went for naught.(p.300)

kit

- When, therefore, we were approached by those in whom the problem had been solved, there was nothing left for us but to pick up the simple *kit* of spiritual tools laid at our feet.(p.25)
- Never talk down to an alcoholic from any moral or spiritual hilltop; simply lay out the *kit* of spiritual tools for his inspection.(p.95)
- The war leaves me with a pair of blankets, a toilet *kit*, a sweater knit by my sister, and a still greater inferiority.(p.499)

kitchen

- Near the end of that bleak November, I sat drinking in my *kitchen*.(p.8)
- Never mind the musty past; here sat a miracle directly across the *kitchen* table.(p.11)
- Each day my friend's simple talk in our *kitchen* multiplies itself in a widening circle of peace on earth and good will to men.(p.16)
- After it was closed we all retired to the *kitchen* and had coffee and doughnuts and more discussion until the small hours of the morning.(p.291)
- When alcohol took me over, my bar was my *kitchen*, my living room, my bedroom, the back bathroom, and the two hampers.(p.335)
- And then we went up the side of a hill where we have a little barbecue area to make the fire for the barbecue, and on the way up, I thought to myself – I'll go back down to the *kitchen* and refill this drink.(p.347)
- We had some people in, and I was making drinks in the *kitchen*, when I suddenly decided to hoist the bottle for a quick one.(p.365)
- Emma ran out to the *kitchen* and came back with a water glass full of bourbon and made me drink it down.(p.385)
- My wife received me graciously, although she was living in a one room with *kitchen* affair.(p.490)

Kitty Hawk

- Even in the present century, American newspapers were afraid to print an account of the Wright brothers' first successful flight at *Kitty Hawk*.(p.51)

knack

- When sober, does he not work hard and have a *knack* of getting things done?(p.139)
- I never could quite get the *knack* of it and kept asking myself, "What's a nice guy like me doing in a place like this?"(p.445)

knees

- This man recounts that he tumbled out of bed to his *knees*.(p.56)
- He then pulled up his chair with one of his *knees* touching mine and said, "Will you pray with me for your success?"(p.218)
- He was coming, on his hands and *knees*, up the stairs.(p.263)
- I got down on my *knees* for the first time in thirty years.(p.280)
- I found some wool stockings, some white flannels that had shrunk to my *knees*, and an old jacket.(p.288)
- I tried every gimmick that there was to get some peace of mind, but it was not until I was brought to my alcoholic *knees*, when I was brought to a group in my own community with the butcher, the baker, the carpenter and the mechanic, who were able to give me the Twelve Steps, that I was finally given some semblance of an answer to the last half of the First Step.(p.349)
- Time after time I would beg forgiveness on bended *knees*, with tears rolling down my cheeks, and promise I would never again drink too much.(p.362)
- I tumble out of bed onto my *knees*.(p.504)

knelt

- When I said yes, we both *knelt* at his desk and prayed, each of us asking to have these defects taken away.(p.292)

knew

- I *knew* the man by name, and partly recognized his features, but there all resemblance ended.(p.xxix)
- By the time I had completed the course, I *knew* the law was not for me.(p.2)
- I *knew*, and almost welcomed the idea.(p.7)
- I simply had to believe in a Spirit of the Universe, who *knew* neither time nor limitation.(p.10)
- We told him what we *knew* of alcoholism and the

answer we had found.(p.35)
• He *knew* he faced another trip to the asylum if he kept on.(p.35)
• We told him what we *knew* about alcoholism.(p.39)
• My business came off well, I was pleased and *knew* my partners would be too.(p.41)
• I *knew* from that moment that I had an alcoholic mind.(p.42)
• I *knew* then.(p.42)
• He humbly offered himself to his Maker -- then he *knew*.(p.57)
• Joy at our release from a lifetime of frustration *knew* no bounds.(p.128)
• Only a few *knew* of it at first but, within a short time, it was billboarded throughout the entire company.(p.145)
• He might be shocked if he *knew* how much alcoholism is costing his organization a year.(p.149)
• He had, of course, the familiar alcoholic obsession that few *knew* of his drinking.(p.155)
• He found himself surprisingly well received, and learned that many *knew* of his drinking.(p.156)
• Though they *knew* they must help other alcoholics if they would remain sober, that motive became secondary.(p.159)
• Many a distracted wife has visited this house to find loving and understanding companionship among women who *knew* her problem, to hear from the lips of their husbands what had happened to them, to be advised how her own wayward mate might be hospitalized and approached when next he stumbled.(p.160)
• They *knew* they had a host of new friends; it seemed they had known these strangers always.(p.161)
• I *knew* everyone would buy a few bottles, or cases, of liquor as their exchequers permitted, and that it would soon be gone.(p.175)
• Not being a man of means, I *knew* that if I did not stay sober enough to earn money, I would run out of liquor.(p.175)
• I read everything I could find, and talked to everyone who I thought *knew* anything about it.(p.178)
• It must be remembered that I had read a great deal and talked to everyone who *knew*, or thought they *knew* anything about the subject of alcoholism.(p.180)
• Of far more importance was the fact that he was the first living human with whom I had ever talked, who *knew* what he was talking about in regard to alcoholism from actual experience.(p.180)
• He *knew* all the answers, and certainly not because he had picked them up in his reading.(p.180)
• I used to get terribly upset when I saw my friends drink and *knew* I could not, but I schooled myself to believe that though I once had the same privilege, I had abused it so frightfully that it was withdrawn.(p.181)
• During the first six months of 1935, I was hospitalized eight times for intoxication and shackled to the bed two or three days before I even *knew* where I was.(p.184)
• (I *knew* afterwards that the two who came in were Bill W. and Doctor Bob.)(p.185)
• Before very long we began to relate some incidents of our drinking and, naturally, pretty soon, I realized both of them *knew* what they were talking about because you can see things and smell things when you're drunk, that you can't other times, and, if I had thought they didn't know what they were talking about, I wouldn't have been willing to talk to them at all.(p.185)
• So, after hearing some more of my story, he turned around and said to Doc -- I don't think he *knew* I heard him, but I did -- he said, "Well, I believe he's worth saving and working on."(p.185)
• If I could, that was wonderful, that was just fine, and they would very much appreciate a person who had that kind of power, but they were looking for a man that *knew* he had a problem, and *knew* that he couldn't handle it himself and needed outside help.(p.186)
• I *knew* that I had a helper that I could rely upon, who wouldn't fail me.(p.189)
• Of course, we had talked over quite a number of the failings that I had and made a sort of an inventory, which wasn't too difficult, because I had an awful lot of things wrong that were very apparent to me, because I *knew* all about them.(p.190)
• I can well remember over a long period of years when I thought I was the only person in the world who *knew* that sooner or later I was going to get drunk.(p.198)
• And I think we calculated, or I did, that there wasn't anybody who *knew* that I wasn't drinking.(p.202)
• They called a doctor and it happened that they called one I *knew*.(p.205)
• I *knew* I could quit because he had quit; he hadn't had a drink for over a year.(p.208)
• She *knew* that at that time any suggestion she made about my drinking would only build up a barrier, a consideration for which I am ever grateful.(p.216)
• From far away, as if in a delirium, I heard my own voice -- calling someone "Dorothy," talking of dress shops, of jobs . . . the words came clearer . . . this sound of my own voice frightened me as it came closer . . . and suddenly, there I was, talking of I *knew* not what, to someone I'd never seen before this very moment.(p.222)
• I *knew* what they were all right -- a drink would fix them.(p.223)
• "Blanks" were more frequent, and I seldom *knew* how I'd got home.(p.226)
• I had found friends, understanding friends who often *knew* what I was thinking and feeling better than I *knew* myself, and didn't allow me to retreat into my prison of loneliness and fear over a fancied slight or hurt.(p.228)
• They *knew* what to do about those black abysses that yawned ready to swallow me when I felt depressed, or nervous.(p.229)
• There I sat in the evenings, enjoying with my friends our memories of the "old country," singing the old songs we all *knew*, playing simple card games for drinks and consuming great quantities of beer.(p.231)
• I *knew* the stuff I was making was a lot stronger than I had been used to, but I never suspected that steady drinking of it might develop a taste for something even stronger still.(p.233)
• Before long I had a definite taste for hard liquor, *knew* nausea and headaches I had never known before, but as in the old days, I suffered them out.(p.233)
• "Best in the business, when he's sober," my customers would say, and I still had a following who would give me work though they deplored my habits, because they *knew* the job would be well done when they eventually got it.(p.234)
• He had already imbued them with his own spirit until they were ready and willing at all times to go where sent, and as a doctor he well *knew* that this mission and duty would strengthen them as it later helped me.(p.235)
• I *knew* somehow that it meant more than just going to church and living a moral life.(p.236)
• My visitor well *knew*, that as I tried to follow God I would get to studying these things out for myself.(p.236)
• They had also been periodic big shots who had goofed out repeatedly at the wrong time, and they also *knew* how to split one paper match into three separate matches.(p.245)
• I *knew* they needed to straighten out their thinking and habits, but I was all right, I just drank too much.(p.246)
• I *knew* I was through among the English "bookies."(p.251)
• My wife made several attempts to get me to stop and I had the usual visits from persons who would always ask me "Why?" -- as if I *knew*!(p.254)
• I *knew* I was a drunkard.(p.256)
• A friend who *knew* I would soon be broke mounted guard over me when I left my job of writing the histories of Texas cities and put me aboard a bus for the town I had left almost five years before.(p.256)
• I arrived drunk, but I promised my wife I would keep sober, and I *knew* I could get work if I did.(p.256)
• He *knew* too well that didn't mean a thing, just as I *knew* in my heart that it would be only a question of time -- a few days, a week, or even a month, it was inevitable -- till I would be off on another bender.(p.257)
• When I came to my aunt, she *knew* that I had had an unhappy childhood, and she said, "Now, Ethel, you're welcome to have boy friends in our home, but there are two boys in this town that I don't want you to date, and one of them comes from a very fine family, one of the best.(p.262)
• I *knew* then that I hadn't made a complete surrender, because I tried to bargain with the God I had found, and I said, "Anything but that!(p.271)
• I *knew* Doc and Anne were going to be there, and all of them thought it would be good for me, but the first thing I did was to go to St. Thomas and try to talk to those women.)(p.272)
• The next day he turned me over to a couple who, although neither was an alcoholic, *knew* Dr. Bob and were willing to drive me to Akron where they would turn me over to his care.(p.278)
• I went to a minister and a doctor that I still *knew* and they, in turn, asked me how long I had been sober.(p.293)
• In the summer of 1938, almost a year from the time I made my original contact with Akron, the man for whom I was working and who *knew* about the program, approached me and asked if I could do anything about one of his salesmen who was drinking very heavily.(p.294)
• To be sure, this had been a dizzy and confused interval, but most everyone else I *knew* had emerged from it with both feet on the ground and a fair amount of adult maturity.(p.304)
• Alone in the relative safety of my home because I *knew* I dare not risk the danger of blacking out in some public place or at the wheel of a car.(p.306)
• Why he bothered with me as long as he did I shall never know, for he *knew* there was no answer for me in medicine and he, like all doctors of his day, had been taught that the alcoholic was incurable and should be ignored.(p.307)
• However, due to financial difficulties the whole printing was, for a while, held up and the book received no publicity, nor, of course, was it available in the stores, even if one *knew* it existed.(p.307)
• I saw in these people a quality of peace and serenity that I *knew* I must have for myself.(p.310)
• But after hearing their stories, I *knew* that I was, and I admitted it.(p.320)
• And when I looked at it, I *knew* I was just as much a drunk as George was, if not worse.(p.322)
• I nudged George next morning, and I said, "I'm in," and he said, "Oh, I *knew* you'd make it."(p.322)
• The only way I *knew* to do it was to drink right along with him.(p.322)
• If we were invited to a formal party and I *knew* they were only going to have one or two drinks, I wouldn't have any.(p.323)
• I was being very cagey, because I *knew* that if I did take one or two, I might want to take five or six or seven or eight.(p.323)
• I couldn't keep up with any of my other friends, and I wouldn't go to anyone's house unless I *knew* they drank as heavily as I did.(p.324)
• I never *knew* it was the first drink that did it.(p.324)
• I didn't think my children *knew* about it, but I found out they did.(p.324)
• I never *knew*.(p.326)
• While I sought the comforting arms of alcohol, I *knew* this was a sign of weakness on the part of a longtime-successful old codger with white hair, the image of dignity.(p.331)
• I *knew* about A.A.(p.332)
• I *knew* why I identified.(p.333)
• They described what had happened when they went out and tried drinking again, and I *knew* they were sincere in saying that it could happen to me.(p.334)
• I needed it, and I *knew* I was drinking too much, but I wasn't conscious of the fact that I should stop.(p.336)
• I never *knew* which came first, the thinking or the drinking.(p.337)
• I *knew* nothing about alcoholism or the D.T.'s, but when I woke up on this last morning of my son's illness, I taped the keyhole on my door because "everyone was out there."(p.338)
• I *knew* that alcohol and I had to part.(p.338)
• He *knew* what I was doing, how I was trying.(p.339)
• The first time was when I *knew* I couldn't live with alcohol.(p.340)
• On the second, I *knew* -- as I know now -- that if I remained away from the first drink, then I had not to worry about the hundredth one.(p.344)
• And I *knew* this: Once an alcoholic, always an alcoholic.(p.344)
• Thank God I *knew* of A.A., so I called.(p.355)
• I had no idea what would happen -- I just *knew* I didn't want to live if life was going to go on like it was.(p.355)
• When I walked into the friendly atmosphere of my first A.A. meeting, I *knew* I was where I belonged.(p.355)
• It was strictly a one man operation and I *knew* I had to tend to my knitting to make a go of it.(p.360)
• Furthermore, I *knew* that I was looked upon as a city slicker from New York, and I had to be pretty cautious among small town, conservative Yankees.(p.360)
• The only drawback was, I always *knew* how I arrived there, but somehow, between the rest room, the rinse, and the fluff-dry, I never *knew* when or how I got home.(p.370)
• I *knew* he was right, except for that last statement.(p.371)
• I had nowhere else to go, and I *knew* something was terribly wrong, and the reason had to lie

within myself.(p.371)

• I tried to hide my drinking by going places where I was unlikely to see anyone I ***knew***.(p.375)

• The surprise to me is the fact that I didn't know that they ***knew*** my drinking had gotten out of control.(p.376)

• Early the next morning a man whose name I ***knew*** well, a lawyer, called on me.(p.378)

• Within thirty minutes I ***knew*** A.A. was the answer for me.(p.378)

• I ***knew*** that I wanted to try A.A. and if that didn't work, I didn't think anything would.(p.384)

• I had no feeling of security, and I ***knew*** that I had done a very stupid thing, so I went back to Texas and remarried my ex-husband.(p.386)

• I ***knew*** this, and right away I got furious and would not even talk to the doctor in the place.(p.387)

• So I located a house, and I thought we ought to move into it immediately, but Frank was horrified, because he never ***knew*** what was going to happen to me.(p.388)

• My father, as I have said, was very indulgent and loved me dearly, and ***knew*** how to get around me.(p.389)

• They did the best they ***knew*** how as far as I was concerned.(p.401)

• It was the only real home she ***knew***.(p.402)

• Even then I ***knew*** in my heart that I was unfit for the very things I wanted most, a happy marriage, security, a home and love.(p.403)

• The people I ***knew*** rode hard, and some of them drank hard.(p.404)

• Underneath, I ***knew*** this was all wrong.(p.407)

• I ***knew*** I was hitting the skids, but what of it?(p.427)

• But I ***knew*** I'd never get that way.(p.427)

• I hadn't told them about my drinking, but I guess they ***knew***.(p.427)

• I spent the time in a nearby tavern, was loaded on the ship, went to sleep before take-off, and the next thing I ***knew*** someone was shaking me and telling me we were over San Diego.(p.428)

• But as I came out of this second bout with D.T.'s I ***knew*** I was licked.(p.429)

• I'd acquired a new girl, a lovely girl who ***knew*** of my problem and had tried to help me.(p.430)

• My growing inward unhappiness was a very real thing, however, and I ***knew*** that something would have to be done about it.(p.434)

• I ***knew*** from my general reading that alcoholism was irreversible and fatal.(p.436)

• And I ***knew*** that somewhere along the line I'd lost the power to stop drinking.(p.436)

• I happened to be the best diagnostician I ***knew*** at the time, and certainly I ***knew*** my case better than anyone else.(p.444)

• The people there insisted on putting me in a ward, when Max and I both ***knew*** I ought to have a private room.(p.445)

• And I ***knew*** that giving up "one drink for one day" wouldn't really do any good.(p.448)

• And I was always glad to point it out, because I ***knew*** you wanted perfection, just as I did.(p.449)

• We reverted to the old way of life we ***knew*** -- a life full of anger, vindictiveness, resentment, fear, dependence, denial, self-will, irresponsibility.(p.459)

• Yes, I ***knew*** what the Serenity Prayer was -- A.A. had taught me.(p.461)

• Finally they stopped and bought me a bottle; they ***knew*** so well that would keep me quiet.(p.466)

• This time I didn't put up any fight because I ***knew*** why they were there and where I was going, the psychopathic ward of the City Hospital, where I had been once before.(p.468)

• Yes, I even ***knew*** I was a "chronic alcoholic."(p.470)

• It seemed to me that those A.A.'s to whom I talked ***knew*** all about me.(p.470)

• It is true that the doctors and nurses in the various institutions I attended ***knew*** too.(p.470)

• But the difference lay in the fact that the A.A.'s ***knew*** from their own bitter experience.(p.471)

• About then too, I realized that my point of view on the opposite sex wasn't entirely like that of most of the boys I ***knew***.(p.484)

• I don't think I suffered too much as far as the racial situation was concerned because I was born into it and ***knew*** nothing other than that.(p.485)

• But I ***knew*** at that point that I couldn't stop and I ***knew*** that I was a danger to myself and to others.(p.489)

• Nevertheless, I stayed sober there about six months, because I ***knew*** that Vi was to come later and bring the children.(p.490)

• Nevertheless, we continued to work together and I continued to drink, but I guess, deep down within her heart as well as within mine, we both ***knew*** I couldn't stop drinking.(p.490)

• I continued to work and continued to go to lunch with Vi, and none of our acquaintances on the job ***knew*** that we had separated.(p.491)

• I ***knew*** I wasn't capable of keeping the bulk of the money myself, so I gave it to a white fellow who owned the bar which I frequented.(p.493)

• I ***knew*** my wife didn't because I had been sincere in all my promises to her as well as to my mother and to my close friends, but the urge to take that drink was more powerful than anything else.(p.494)

• After Charlie had talked a while, I ***knew*** that this man had something.(p.495)

• Father had never directly spoken to me about drinking but he never drank any, so far as I ***knew***.(p.498)

• But I ***knew*** how to handle it now.(p.498)

• After twenty years in prison for murder, he ***knew*** A.A. was the spot for him . . . if he wanted to stay on the outside.(p.508)

• It wasn't anything strange to me, and I ***knew*** if I wanted to stay on the outside, that would be the spot for me.(p.510)

• It was a thorn in my side, because I ***knew*** it was the truth, and I hated to hear the truth, especially about myself.(p.513)

• Because as I sat on that bed, I ***knew*** that I was in a terrible spot and didn't know how to get out of it.(p.515)

• I ***knew*** it, and I turned for help to someone upon whom I had turned my back for many years.(p.515)

• But I ***knew*** that they ***knew*** what the medical grounds were, and that they had put a big black mark against my name.(p.521)

• I was in a world that I ***knew*** nothing at all about, and I felt intensely afraid.(p.521)

• Oh, I might drink too much at times -- everyone I ***knew*** drank.(p.527)

• There was the father one lost respect for at the age of eleven, because the father broke his solemn word in a circumstance where you, eleven years old, had assumed guilt when you were innocent; but the father would not believe you, no matter what; and to ease his suffering you "confessed" and were "forgiven," only -- months later -- to have your "guilt" brought up -- only he and you ***knew*** what he was talking bout -- brought up in front of the stern grandmother.(p.533)

• There was the love affair which was ridiculous -- "imagine that midget being able to fall in love!" -- and my head ***knew*** it while my heart pumped real, genuine anguish, for it hurt like hell, and since it was first love, things have never been quite the same.(p.534)

• I wish I ***knew*** a short cut to maturity.(p.535)

• Repeated year on end, they are horrible -- frightening and degrading, a chronicle of tragedy which may be greater because the individual undergoing the tragedy, myself, ***knew*** what was happening, and yet refused to do anything to stop it.(p.538)

• I ***knew*** he did.(p.540)

• I thought I ***knew*** exactly what I wanted out of life and I thought I ***knew*** exactly how to get it.(p.545)

• The only kind of security I ***knew*** anything about at that time was material security and I decided that all these intruders would vanish immediately if I only had a lot of money.(p.545)

• Inside, though, I was scared to death, for I ***knew*** that the time was coming (and it couldn't be too remote) when I would be unable to hold that job.(p.548)

• I ***knew*** it didn't make any difference where I started, the inevitable end would be skid row.(p.548)

• The people who came ***knew*** immediately I was in no condition to absorb anything of the program, and I was put in a sanitarium to be defogged so that I could make a sober decision about this for myself.(p.549)

• It had provided me with excuses for my lack of education, my marital failures, personal failures, inadequacy, and of course, my alcoholism and, though I really thought I had been willing to part with it, now I ***knew*** I was reluctant to let it go.(p.552)

• I guess I always ***knew*** that the way to handle my drinking was to quit.(p.554)

• And it had gone underground now, because everyone ***knew*** I shouldn't be drinking.(p.557)

• He happened to be, by the grace of God, Dr. Harry Tiebout, the psychiatrist who probably ***knew*** more about alcoholism than any other in the world.(p.559)

knit

• The war leaves me with a pair of blankets, a toilet kit, a sweater ***knit*** by my sister, and a still greater inferiority.(p.499)

knitting

• It was strictly a one man operation and I knew I had to tend to my ***knitting*** to make a go of it.(p.360)

knock

• Toward five o'clock, helter-skelter, I'd get everything put away and try to get supper on the table, and after supper I'd finish the job up and ***knock*** myself out.(p.337)

knocked

• My wife accompanied me on my visit and the doctor really told me some things that in my state of jitters nearly ***knocked*** me out of the chair.(p.302)

• I fell down and ***knocked*** out my front teeth.(p.390)

• I was a little bit ***knocked*** out.(p.402)

• I was ***knocked*** to the floor, swinging madly at the faces on those pineapples.(p.427)

• The folks called a doctor and he ***knocked*** me out with sedatives.(p.429)

• Ten days of this treatment the first time ***knocked*** me from 200 pounds to 130, and I seldom stayed out of the hole long enough to gain back my weight.(p.460)

knocks

• Some of us have taken very hard ***knocks*** to learn this truth: Job or no job -- wife or no wife -- we simply do not stop drinking so long as we place dependence upon other people ahead of dependence on God.(p.98)

• With this specialized training, and a liberal business education in the school of hard ***knocks***, I was able to set up shop some two years later as an independent accountant.(p.284)

• Dad's image for me was that of a big Irish oilman who came up through the school of hard ***knocks*** and so had to be a two-fisted drinker.(p.369)

know

• I personally ***know*** scores of cases who were of the type with whom other methods had failed completely.(p.xxiii)

• The unselfishness of these men as we have come to ***know*** them, the entire absence of profit motive, and their community spirit, is indeed inspiring to one who has labored long and wearily in this alcoholic field.(p.xxv)

• I simply didn't ***know***.(p.5)

• I was to ***know*** happiness, peace, and usefulness, in a way of life that is incredibly more wonderful as time passes.(p.8)

• We of ALCOHOLICS ANONYMOUS, ***know*** thousands of men and women who were once just as hopeless as Bill.(p.17)

• We ***know*** that while the alcoholic keeps away from drink, as he may do for months or years, he reacts much like other men.(p.22)

• But in their hearts they really do not ***know*** why they do it.(p.23)

• We ***know*** that no real alcoholic ever recovers control.(p.30)

• This is the baffling feature of alcoholism as we ***know*** it -- this utter inability to leave it alone, no matter how great the necessity or the wish.(p.34)

• I ***know*** little of where I went or what I said and did.(p.41)

• We ***know*** how he feels.(p.45)

• Hence we are at pains to tell why we think our present faith is reasonable, why we think it more sane and logical to believe than not to believe, why we say our former thinking was soft and mushy when we threw up our hands in doubt and said, "We don't ***know***."(p.53)

• We ***know*** but few instances where we have given these doctors a fair break.(p.73)

• We thank God from the bottom of our heart that we ***know*** Him better.(p.75)

• Telling them what we are trying to do, we make no bones about our drinking; they usually ***know*** it anyway, whether we think so or not.(p.78)

• Arranging the best deal we can we let these people ***know*** we are sorry.(p.78)

• A man we ***know*** had remarried.(p.79)

• If we are sure our wife does not ***know***, should we tell her?(p.81)

• She will want to ***know*** who the woman is and where she is.(p.81)

• We are going to ***know*** a new freedom and a new happiness.(p.83)

• We will comprehend the word serenity and we will ***know*** peace.(p.83)

• We will intuitively ***know*** how to handle situations which used to baffle us.(p.84)

• We ***know*** you will not want to miss it.(p.89)

• When he sees you ***know*** all about the drinking game, commence to describe yourself as an alcoholic.(p.91)

• Even though your protege may not have entirely admitted his condition, he has become very curious to ***know*** how you got well.(p.92)

• Let him ***know*** you are available if he wishes to

make a decision and tell his story, but do not insist upon it if he prefers to consult someone else.(p.96)
• Let your friends *know* they are not to change their habits on your account.(p.102)
• We *know* all about liquor as a social lubricant.(p.110)
• We *know* women who are unafraid, even happy under these conditions.(p.111)
• We *know* these suggestions are sometimes difficult to follow, but you will save many a heartbreak if you can succeed in observing them.(p.111)
• You think he ought to *know* the subject better, as everyone should have a clear understanding of the risk he takes if he drinks too much.(p.112)
• We *know* women who have done it.(p.114)
• You do not *know* what to tell the children.(p.115)
• While you need not discuss your husband at length, you can quietly let your friends *know* the nature of his illness.(p.115)
• Your desire to protect him should not cause you to lie to people when they have a right to *know* where he is and what he is doing.(p.115)
• And now you *know* that he can stop if he will!(p.116)
• You need not remind him of his spiritual deficiency – he will *know* of it.(p.120)
• For example, we *know* of situations in which the alcoholic or his wife have had love affairs.(p.124)
• We *know* there are difficult wives and families, but the man who is getting over alcoholism must remember he did much to make them so.(p.127)
• He may tell mother, who has been religious all her life, that she doesn't *know* what it's all about, and that she had better get his brand of spirituality while there is yet time.(p.128)
• New acquaintances who *know* nothing of alcoholism might be made and thoughtful consideration given their needs.(p.131)
• We do not *know* of many cases where this difficulty lasted long.(p.134)
• In time they will see that he is a new man and in their own way they will let him *know* it.(p.134)
• She wanted to *know* if her husband's company insurance was still in force.(p.137)
• You, as a business man, want to *know* the necessities before considering the result.(p.140)
• I *know*, in my own particular case, that nothing my company could have done would have stopped me for, so long as I was able to hold my position, I could not possibly realize how serious my situation was.(p.141)
• You now *know* more about alcoholism.(p.141)
• State that you *know* about his drinking, and that it must stop.(p.141)
• In fact, he may say almost anything if he has accepted our solution which, as you *know*, demands rigorous honesty.(p.145)
• You might let them *know* you have no quarrel with the alcoholics of your organization.(p.147)
• We *know* our friend is like a boy whistling in the dark to keep up his spirits.(p.152)
• Then he will *know* loneliness such as few do.(p.152)
• I *know* I must get along without liquor, but how can I?(p.152)
• Then you will *know* what it means to give of yourself that others may survive and rediscover life.(p.153)
• You will want to *know* more of how to proceed from that point.(p.153)
• But what about his responsibilities – his family and the men who would die because they would not *know* how to get well, ah -- yes, those other alcoholics?(p.154)
• You fellows *know* your stuff all right, but I don't see what good it'll do.(p.157)
• From what you tell me, I *know* more than ever I can't stop."(p.157)
• The expression on the faces of the women, that indefinable something in the eyes of the men, the stimulating and electric atmosphere of the place, conspired to let him *know* that here was haven at last.(p.160)
• We *know* what you are thinking.(p.163)
• We *know* of an A.A. member who was living in a large community.(p.163)
• We realize we *know* only a little.(p.164)
• In his prodigy of service, he was well assisted by Sister Ignatia at St. Thomas Hospital in Akron, Ohio, one of the greatest friends our Fellowship will ever *know*.(p.171)
• How my wife kept her faith and courage during all those years, I'll never *know*, but she did.(p.178)
• If she had not, I *know* I would have been dead a long time ago.(p.178)
• But if you really and truly want to quit drinking liquor for good and all, and sincerely feel that you must have some help, we *know* that we have an answer for you.(p.181)
• It hadn't worked out that way and I didn't *know* what the matter was and did not *know* what to do.(p.184)
• Before very long we began to relate some incidents of our drinking and, naturally, pretty soon, I realized both of them knew what they were talking about because you can see things and smell things when you're drunk, that you can't other times, and, if I had thought they didn't *know* what they were talking about, I wouldn't have been willing to talk to them at all.(p.185)
• The next thing they wanted to *know* was if I thought I could quit of my own accord, without any help, if I could just walk out of the hospital and never take another drink.(p.186)
• The next question, they wanted to *know* was if I believed in a Higher Power.(p.186)
• The next thing they wanted to *know* was would I be willing to go to this Higher Power and ask for help, calmly and without any reservations.(p.186)
• I was willing to admit to myself that I had hit bottom, that I had gotten hold of something that I didn't *know* how to handle by myself.(p.187)
• As far as I *know* that was the first time I had ever paid any attention to that word.(p.187)
• You certainly *know* what you are talking about."(p.189)
• I *know* there was even more, something that I hadn't got, and I remember one day, a week or two after I had come out of the hospital, Bill was over to my house talking to my wife and me.(p.191)
• Whether I could have done as well as he, I don't *know*.(p.194)
• I didn't even *know* what a martini looked like, but I had heard a man down the bar order one.(p.194)
• I didn't *know* that then.(p.195)
• During the day, looking over the contracts and money in my pocket, I found that I had sold six lots that I couldn't even remember, and didn't even *know* the people I had sold them to.(p.196)
• I don't *know* whether I drank to cover up being a failure, or whether I drank and then missed the deals.(p.198)
• Whenever this man and I met -- I didn't *know* his name then nor do I *know* it now – we would always get drunk.(p.201)
• Nobody would *know* it, so I agreed to have the one drink.(p.202)
• The very simple program they advised me to follow was that I should ask to *know* God's will for me for that one day, and then, to the best of my ability, to follow that, and at night to express my gratefulness to God for the things that had happened to me during the day.(p.208)
• They probably felt that it was useless, that surely I had enough intelligence to *know* what I was doing.(p.215)
• I do not recollect the specific conversation that went on but I believe I did challenge Bill to tell me something about A.A. and I do recall one other thing: I wanted to *know* what this was that worked so many wonders, and hanging over the mantel was a picture of Gethsemane and Bill pointed to it and said, "There it is," which didn't make much sense to me.(p.216)
• I did not *know* there was such a thing as group activity until I left the hospital.(p.218)
• I resolved that if I were going to continue with the Catholic Church, I was going to *know* the roots of the doctrine, since those roots had caused me some confusion.(p.221)
• I might have done terrible things, and I wouldn't even *know* it!(p.223)
• He wasn't a drinking man, he didn't *know* what it was to need a drink, nor what a drink could do for one in a pinch.(p.227)
• Freedom from anger and fear, freedom to *know* happiness and love.(p.228)
• He had no desire to *know* anything, except whether I was definite about my desire to quit drinking.(p.235)
• Well, there I was, willing to try it, but I didn't *know* how, except in a vague way.(p.236)
• For a long time I kept on trying, in a pretty dumb way at first, I *know*, but very earnestly.(p.237)
• And when I get upset, cross-grained and out of tune with my fellow man I *know* that I am out of tune with God.(p.237)
• Searching where I have been at fault, it is not hard to discover and get right again, for I have proven to myself and to many others who *know* me that God can keep a man sober if he will let Him.(p.237)
• Little more of our talk stayed in my memory, but I do *know* I slept the rest of that night while before I had never known what a real night's sleep was.(p.239)
• All of us in A.A. *know* the tremendous happiness that is in our sobriety, but there are also tragedies.(p.239)
• Back at camp, all was forgiven because it was the End, but in the light of what I have since learned I *know* I was a confirmed alcoholic at nineteen.(p.242)
• I began to *know* the inside of jails and workhouses.(p.255)
• They will never *know* how much their talk with me helped.(p.259)
• I *know* that one of the outfits I had was a skirt and a very funny looking blouse that my mother had picked up at a rummage sale.(p.261)
• I'll get you the password, and I can find out where they meet because I *know* a guy that belongs.(p.266)
• She said to me, "You *know*, he used to own the Merry-Go-Round.(p.267)
• Dr. Bob was in Florida, but Jack didn't *know* that.(p.267)
• I didn't *know* that anything was ever done for them in a medical way.(p.267)
• I didn't *know* anything about the Sermon on the Mount.(p.268)
• I didn't *know* what they were going to do because he didn't tell us much.(p.269)
• At that time they didn't let us *know* that people ever had trouble.(p.271)
• Before I stop -- I always was a great talker – I want to say that nobody will ever *know* how I miss Annie's advice about things.(p.273)
• She said she didn't *know*, but that I sure showed plain enough I didn't have any part of it.(p.273)
• I *know* I've talked too long, but I always do.(p.274)
• It was simple, they said, and went on to explain to me in their own language the program of recovery and daily living which we *know* today as the Twelve Steps of A.A.(p.279)
• Finally, and I shall never *know* how much later it was, one clear thought came to me: Try prayer.(p.280)
• I *know* now that sixty per cent of the time I drank alone without benefit of customers.(p.287)
• I *know* it helped me.(p.292)
• He had been wanting to do something about his drinking for a long time, but did not *know* how.(p.294)
• The last day of my drinking career, I drank twenty-two of them between ten and twelve a.m. and I shall never *know* how many more followed them until I was poured into bed that night.(p.298)
• I cannot remember just when I became the victim of insomnia, but I do *know* that the last year and a half I never went to bed sober a single night.(p.299)
• How many times I swore off in the morning and got drunk before sunset I don't *know*.(p.300)
• He mentioned lies and deceptions in the course of his story in the presence of the one person in the world I wouldn't want to *know* such things.(p.302)
• How did he *know* all this?(p.302)
• Mentally . . . I *know* where I was last night, the night before, and the nights before that.(p.303)
• I was trapped, and for the life of me I did not *know* how or why this had happened to me.(p.306)
• Why he bothered with me as long as he did I shall never *know*, for he knew there was no answer for me in medicine and he, like all doctors of his day, had been taught that the alcoholic was incurable and should be ignored.(p.307)
• Some of us struggle with these people because we *know* that they are really very sick, but we also *know* that short of some miracle, we are not going to help them except temporarily, and that they will inevitably get worse and worse until one of two things happens.(p.308)
• "We watch the alcoholic performing in a position of responsibility and we *know* that because he is drinking heavily and daily he has cut his capacities by fifty per cent, and still he seems able to do a satisfactory job.(p.308)
• I don't *know* what sort of person I was expecting, but I was very agreeably surprised to find Mr. T. a poised, intelligent, well groomed and mannered gentleman.(p.309)
• (Now I *know* the answer – wrong.)(p.317)
• She told me her name, and I said, "I *know* you from somewhere."(p.321)
• She said, "Yes, I *know*.(p.322)
• You *know* I'll do it tomorrow, the very same thing."(p.325)
• And he, poor dear, didn't *know* what was going on.(p.325)
• I myself didn't *know* all the places I had them hidden.(p.325)

• It becomes vital, also, that others not ***know*** of our defeats, nor suspect our loss of confidence.(p.331)
• He did not ***know*** it was A.A., and it was useless to tell him, for he doesn't have our disease.(p.334)
• You can never ***know*** the pure joy of recovering within the Fellowship of Alcoholics Anonymous."(p.334)
• You ***know*** the deteriorating effects, the disintegrating effects of chronic wine-drinking.(p.337)
• How I ran my home, I don't ***know***.(p.337)
• I screamed on the telephone for my mother to get up there; something was going to happen; I didn't ***know*** what, but if she didn't get there quick, I'd split wide open.(p.338)
• I didn't ***know***.(p.338)
• I had been brought up to believe in God, but I ***know*** that until I found this A.A. program, I had never found or known faith in the reality of God, the reality of His power that is now with me in everything I do.(p.341)
• I finished high school here in an American-sponsored Methodist public school, ***know*** as Philander Smith College.(p.342)
• It was here I came to ***know*** properly what alcohol was.(p.343)
• On the second, I knew -- as I ***know*** now -- that if I remained away from the first drink, then I had not to worry about the hundredth one.(p.344)
• And then one ill-defined day, one day that I can't recall, I stepped across the line that alcoholics ***know*** so well, and from that day on drinking was miserable.(p.346)
• And the first thing you ***know*** I was lifted right out of the A.A. group, and I floated higher, and higher, and even higher, until I was way up on a pink cloud which is known as Pink Seven, and I felt miserable again.(p.348)
• Well, I don't ***know*** who He is, but I've got my own idea.(p.350)
• I didn't ***know*** how to be a father; I don't ***know*** how to come home and work week-ends like other husbands; I don't ***know*** how to entertain my family.(p.351)
• I don't ***know*** what it is.(p.352)
• That night she too had new hope because I had made sure she would ***know*** what I was doing about my drinking by packing every bit of A.A. literature I could put my hands on right on top so she couldn't help but see it when she opened my bag.(p.364)
• It was the first she had heard or read about it and she said she had considered sending it to me or trying to have someone in Pittsburgh send it to me so I wouldn't ***know*** where it came from.(p.366)
• But for some reason -- she just didn't ***know*** why -- she just had to hold onto that clipping, with its thin hope.(p.367)
• These words may be difficult for you to understand now, but be patient and you'll ***know*** what I mean.(p.367)
• I will never ***know*** all the people I hurt, all the friends I abused, the humiliation of my family, the worry of my business associates, or how far reaching it was.(p.376)
• The surprise to me is the fact that I didn't ***know*** that they knew my drinking had gotten out of control.(p.376)
• I don't ***know*** what I expected, but I most certainly didn't visualize a group of people talking about their drinking problems, making light of their personal tragedies and at the same time enjoying themselves.(p.378)
• It was a great relief to ***know*** I didn't have to drink any more.(p.379)
• To me this meant telling my associates that I had joined Alcoholics Anonymous; that I didn't ***know*** what was expected of me by A.A., but that whatever it was, it was the most important thing in life for me; that sobriety meant more to me than anything in this world.(p.382)
• Yesterday is gone, and we don't ***know*** whether we will be here tomorrow.(p.382)
• "Grant us the serenity to accept the things we cannot change, courage to change the things we can, and the wisdom to ***know*** the difference."(p.382)
• I ***know*** that if I do daily what I have done for these last thirteen and a half years, I will stay sober.(p.384)
• I didn't ***know*** that when I came into A.A.(p.384)
• I wish I could tell you how and why A.A. works, but I don't ***know***.(p.384)
• I only ***know*** that it does -- if you desire it with your whole heart and without reservation.(p.384)
• We always had cordials after dinner and I ***know*** my sister and my brother and I loved creme de menthe.(p.384)
• So I was used to it, but I didn't ***know*** what the effect of alcohol was because I always had wine, usually with dinner, but always with a lot of ice and about two tablespoons of sugar in it.(p.385)
• When I crossed that line, I don't ***know***.(p.386)
• I said, "Well, I don't ***know*** why."(p.387)
• I ***know*** that I was terribly screwed up inside, but I came out much worse.(p.387)
• I ***know*** now that I asked questions and told him what I wanted to learn, but I told him only what I wanted to believe about myself.(p.388)
• I resented the fact that Frank had done this to me, and I just didn't ***know*** what was going on.(p.388)
• You ***know*** those vitamins just don't keep you sober!(p.389)
• They phoned my husband that I was in jail and in such terrible shape that they didn't ***know*** what I would do to myself; and they realized that jail was no place for me, but that he was to wait a while before he got me, because at the time they called him to come over for me I was beating a tin cup against the wall.(p.390)
• I didn't ***know*** which way to turn.(p.391)
• It was such a feeling of relief that I wanted to ***know*** more about it and with that, I think for the first time, came the realization that there was something horribly, horribly wrong with me.(p.392)
• So, as I have said, I don't ***know*** how or why A.A. works.(p.392)
• I only ***know*** that it first reached me through that Saturday Evening Post article.(p.392)
• I ***know*** that when Frank came home, I said, "I want to try this thing," and he said, "There's a post office box to write to in New York."(p.392)
• So I got a half pint and at midnight that night, I called the number I had been given, but the man who had started the group was in the hospital so I didn't ***know*** what to do.(p.393)
• I ***know*** that I must work at it as long as I live; I ***know*** that it is only by working at it that I can stay sober and have a happy life.(p.394)
• (I can't ***know*** how much others of our Fellowship have paid financially and, even more important, mentally and physically.)(p.396)
• Even when I was old enough to ***know*** better, I dreamed about being as beautiful as Venus, as pure as the Madonna and as brilliant as the President of the United States is supposed to be.(p.400)
• I, who did not ***know*** how to give love, was head over heels "in love."(p.403)
• I did not ***know*** what he meant.(p.406)
• I did not ***know*** that I had no power over alcohol, that I, alone and unaided, could not stop; that I was on a downgrade, tearing along at full speed with all my brakes gone, and that the end would be a total smash-up, death or insanity.(p.408)
• My poor child could not ***know*** this.(p.409)
• I did not ***know*** who this Marty was.(p.413)
• I ***know*** I do not have to be "queen of them all" to salve a frightened ego.(p.416)
• Admitting that I am wrong or that I do not ***know*** is difficult for me.(p.420)
• Gradually consciousness returned enough to let me ***know*** I was in a hospital.(p.422)
• Now I ***know***.(p.422)
• "Do you ***know*** why you're in here?" he queried.(p.423)
• I don't ***know*** how I got here this trip, but it doesn't matter very much.(p.423)
• I don't ***know*** why I didn't fall out of the open cockpit of some of those planes I flew in while taking aerial pictures.(p.426)
• I took it easy, because they didn't ***know*** about me.(p.428)
• Why I wasn't killed or how I got home I don't ***know***.(p.429)
• Now I ***know*** I can't live without A.A.(p.430)
• How exciting to learn the inward mysteries that govern the behavior of people, how wonderful to ***know***, at last, all about myself!(p.434)
• If pressed further, all I can do is follow the psalmist who said it long, long before me: "Be still, and ***know*** that I am God."(p.437)
• And should I have more bad times, I ***know*** that I'll never again have to go through them alone.(p.438)
• All I want to ***know*** is, why does that dog wet in my lap every time I hold him?"(p.440)
• I didn't ***know*** whether I had told him to rush to the hospital and I'd meet him there, or to take two aspirin and call me in the morning.(p.441)
• I am saying that I ***know*** better than God.(p.449)
• This proves I don't ***know*** what's good for me.(p.450)
• And if I don't ***know*** what's good for me, then I don't ***know*** what's good or bad for you or for anyone.(p.450)
• So I'm better off if I don't give advice, don't figure I ***know*** what's best, and just accept life on life's terms, as it is today -- especially my own life, as it actually is.(p.450)
• When we deal in feelings, we tend to come to ***know*** ourselves and each other much better.(p.451)
• Had it not been for A.A. in prison. . . I'll never ***know***, but my educated guess is that I would not be alive today.(p.457)
• I would rather talk about the good things A.A. has taught me; I feel that hitting on just a few sordid points should be sufficient to let those of you in institutions ***know*** where I came from.(p.459)
• I didn't ***know*** I was an alcoholic and (like most men in prison today) could not relate alcohol to any of my past troubles.(p.460)
• He doesn't ***know*** me, nor do I ***know*** him.(p.463)
• Then in a couple of hours, when there was still no word from my husband and no sign of him, I had the feeling we alcoholics all ***know***.(p.467)
• What happened afterwards I don't ***know***.(p.468)
• So the doctor said, "I really don't ***know*** too much about it, but they tell me it is a bunch of drunks who get together . . ."(p.469)
• I honestly didn't ***know*** the difference.(p.470)
• In other words, the kindest doctor in the whole world, and I had one such, couldn't help me because I always felt, "You can't ***know*** about me -- you can't possibly ***know*** -- you don't even drink!"(p.471)
• Well, you ***know*** who I showed.(p.472)
• I have come to believe that my illness is spiritual as well as physical and mental, and I ***know*** that for help in the spiritual sphere I have to turn to a Higher Power.(p.473)
• Next thing I ***know***, it was next day.(p.474)
• Then I ***know*** we walk same trail.(p.476)
• I ***know*** peace.(p.477)
• Some drunken women really are, you ***know***.(p.479)
• I ***know*** the biggest word for me in A.A. is "honesty."(p.482)
• I ***know*** I will be grateful for a chance to make amends to everybody I have hurt in the past.(p.482)
• I don't ***know*** whether it was right or wrong, but at least I ***know*** that people weren't thinking the same.(p.484)
• I don't ***know*** whether she was a pacifist or whether she just thought that in the event of another war it would have some bearing on my joining up.(p.484)
• I don't ***know***.(p.488)
• I don't ***know*** anything about the bottles."(p.488)
• I thought, "I ***know*** you didn't pay me, because you didn't get a prescription."(p.488)
• You ***know*** the prescription that you gave me for my wife last night."(p.488)
• I remember talking to her, but what happened after that I don't ***know***.(p.492)
• That was the next meeting, and the first meeting of a colored group in A.A., so far as I ***know***.(p.495)
• I ***know*** enough of the answers to get by.(p.499)
• Mother must never ***know***.(p.501)
• "I ***know*** it," I reply.(p.503)
• I ***know*** not what I say.(p.504)
• I'd say, "No, I don't ***know*** where they're at or when they meet.(p.510)
• I don't ***know*** anyone in the program."(p.510)
• After I had made my third report, I stepped down town, met some of the old crowd, and of course you ***know*** the answer.(p.510)
• When we first come into A.A., many of us are confused because as a general rule we're at the end of our respective ropes, and we don't ***know*** what to do.(p.512)
• Yes, we find it rather confusing, but as we get around and get to ***know*** people in the group, they lead the way and all we have to do is to follow.(p.512)
• I'd get downstairs to the gin mill, get enough in to hold me until eight o'clock in the morning, then I'd go out to join that "misery parade" that so many of us ***know*** so well.(p.514)
• Because as I sat on that bed, I knew that I was in a terrible spot and didn't ***know*** how to get out of it.(p.515)
• I didn't ***know*** what an alcoholic was.(p.521)
• I don't ***know*** when I became an alcoholic, but I do believe I became one because I drank too much too often.(p.526)
• I thought if the cops did come to the hospital, the doctors would tell them I was crazy and didn't ***know*** what I was doing.(p.528)
• Now I had gotten to the place where I would wake up with black eyes and not ***know*** where I got them, or wake up with a lot of money and not ***know*** where I got it.(p.528)

• I don't ***know*** if it's force of habit or something else that keeps them in one place, but I do ***know*** that in A.A. there is much work to do, and none of us can do it standing still.(p.529)
• I have not seen a black face but mine since I've been, here, and if I didn't look in the mirror, I wouldn't ***know*** that I was black, because these people treat me as one of them, which I am.(p.530)
• That was the day, that was the decision, I ***know*** now, when I crossed over the line and became an active alcoholic.(p.531)
• But such is my nature that I must ***know*** the reason for things and I didn't stop until I had satisfied myself about the reasons for my drinking.(p.533)
• I ***know*** there are some alcoholics who seem terribly, terribly grown-up, but I think that they are trying to make themselves think they are grown-up, and the strain of their effort is what is causing them to drink -- a sense of inadequacy, a childish vanity to be the most popular, the most sought after, the mostest of the most.(p.535)
• Now, for me, and to my satisfaction, I ***know*** the purpose of life: The purpose of life is to create and the by-product is happiness.(p.535)
• The truth is, I did not ***know*** how to stop it, nor did I want to, really.(p.539)
• I did not ***know*** how.(p.539)
• But I ***know*** I'm not.(p.542)
• At fifty-four, I have had come true for me the old wish, "If only I could live my life over, knowing what I ***know***."(p.543)
• That's what I am doing, living again, knowing what I ***know***.(p.543)
• I hope I have been able to impart to you, the reader, at least a bit of what I ***know***; the joy of living, the irresistible power of divine love and its healing strength, and the fact that we, as sentient beings, have the knowledge to choose between good and evil, and, choosing good, are made happy.(p.543)
• The only reality I was able to face had been forced upon me by its very repetition – I had to drink; and I didn't ***know*** there was anything in the world that could be done about it.(p.548)
• They said if you want to ***know*** how this program works, take the first word of your question – the H is for honesty, the O is for open-mindedness and the W is for willingness; these our Book calls the essentials of recovery.(p.550)
• I had only to reflect on the contrast between the plans I made so many years ago for my life with what really happened to ***know*** I couldn't manage my life drunk or sober.(p.550)
• A.A. has taught me that I will have peace of mind in exact proportion to the peace of mind I bring into the lives of other people, and it has taught me the true meaning of the admonition "happy are ye who ***know*** these things and do them."(p.551)
• As another great man says, "The only real freedom a human being can ever ***know*** is doing what you ought to do because you want to do it."(p.553)
• This great experience that released me from the bondage of hatred and replaced it with love is really just another affirmation of the truth I ***know***: I get everything I need in Alcoholics Anonymous – everything I need I get – and when I get what I need I invariably find that it was just what I wanted all the time.(p.553)
• To wear expensive clothes, to have bartenders ***know*** what to serve me before I ordered, to be recognized by headwaiters and shown to the best table, to play gin rummy for high stakes with the insouciance of a riverboat gambler -- these were the enduring values in life, I thought.(p.556)
• They ***know*** that they must never drink.(p.572)

knowing

• Without ***knowing*** it, had we not been brought to where we stood by a certain kind of faith?(p.53)
• She may insist on ***knowing*** all the particulars.(p.81)
• We seldom had friends at our homes, never ***knowing*** how or when the men of the house would appear.(p.105)
• He will appreciate ***knowing*** you are not bothering your head about him, that you are not suspicious nor are you trying to run his life so he will be shielded from temptation to drink.(p.146)
• I remember that my father kept whiskey around the house for medical purposes and entertainment, and I would drink from this when no one was about and then water it to keep my parents from ***knowing*** I was drinking.(p.183)
• ***Knowing*** Bob of old, she jokingly replied, "Well, Doctor, I suppose you've already tried it yourself?"(p.188)
• I made a point of ***knowing*** important people.(p.197)
• So, ***knowing*** that, I had determined that so long as I lived I would never take another drink.(p.200)
• I believe every member of the Akron Group did come to see me, which impressed me terrifically, not so much because of the stories they told, but because they would take the time to come and talk to me without even ***knowing*** who I was.(p.218)
• I'd waked up in strange rooms before, fully dressed on a bed or a couch; I'd waked up in my own room, in or on my own bed, not ***knowing*** what hour or day it was, afraid to ask . . . but this was different.(p.222)
• They, too, had taken a train to one town and had wakened hundreds of miles in the opposite direction, never ***knowing*** how they got there.(p.246)
• It finally got such a hold on me that I was completely at my wits' end, not ***knowing*** what the result would be.(p.343)
• However, ***knowing*** me, she thought it was a foolish idea, that I wouldn't be interested.(p.367)
• To wake up at home, not ***knowing*** how I got there, and to realize I had driven my car, became torture.(p.375)
• Not ***knowing*** where I had been or how I got home was making me desperate.(p.375)
• We think we can drink to excess without anyone ***knowing*** it.(p.376)
• In spite of ***knowing*** that my drunkenness was a symptom of the things that were wrong with me, and that I could never drink again, I thought I couldn't yet give it up, although I was going to try.(p.393)
• Now it was semi-blackouts every night, outrageous behavior, passing out in some friend's Village studio or not ***knowing*** how I got home.(p.407)
• I thought it was my duty to keep her from drinking, not ***knowing*** that if the other fellow is really determined to drink there is nothing you can do about it.(p.415)
• I remember finding myself in the middle of the night in the doctors' parking lot at the hospital with one foot in the car and one foot on the ground, not ***knowing*** which was the lead foot; finding myself hanging up the telephone – then realizing I had gotten out of bed, answered the phone, turned on the light, and carried on a conversation with a patient.(p.441)
• The hotel management, ***knowing*** that something was wrong, sent for a doctor.(p.465)
• ***Knowing*** that he was sober, I timed it just right, so I could do the slashing just before he hit the steps.(p.479)
• At fifty-four, I have had come true for me the old wish, "If only I could live my life over, ***knowing*** what I know."(p.543)
• That's what I am doing, living again, ***knowing*** what I know.(p.543)

knowledge

• What with our ultra-modern standards, our scientific approach to everything, we are perhaps not well equipped to apply the powers of good that lie outside our synthetic ***knowledge***.(p.xxv)
• We shall bring to the task our combined experience and ***knowledge***.(p.19)
• Above all, he believed he had acquired such a profound ***knowledge*** of the inner workings of his mind and its hidden springs that relapse was unthinkable.(p.26)
• It may be worth a bad case of jitters if you get a full ***knowledge*** of your condition.(p.32)
• He had much ***knowledge*** about himself as an alcoholic.(p.36)
• He was positive that his humiliating experience, plus the ***knowledge*** he had acquired, would keep him sober the rest of his life.(p.40)
• 11.Sought through prayer and meditation to improve our conscious contact with God as we understood Him, praying only for ***knowledge*** of His will for us and the power to carry that out.(p.59)
• Much has already been said about receiving strength, inspiration, and direction from Him who has all ***knowledge*** and power.(p.85)
• Admit that he probably knows more about it than you do, but call to his attention the fact that however deep his faith and ***knowledge***, he could not have applied it or he would not drink.(p.93)
• To me, this incident illustrates lack of understanding as to what really ails the alcoholic, and lack of ***knowledge*** as to what part employers might profitably take in salvaging their sick employees.(p.139)
• At that time I was not aware of the almost unlimited supply the government made it possible for us doctors to obtain, neither had I any ***knowledge*** of the bootlegger who soon appeared on the horizon.(p.175)
• I get my greatest thrill of accomplishment from the ***knowledge*** that I have played a part in the new happiness achieved by countless others like myself.(p.229)
• Very early I became apprenticed to harness-making and acquired considerable ***knowledge*** of upholstering.(p.230)
• This doctor had imparted his ***knowledge*** to just a few other men at that time -- not more than four or five -- they now number more than seventy persons.(p.235)
• Where preaching and prayers had touched me very little, I immediately desired further ***knowledge*** of these men.(p.235)
• (This is very useful ***knowledge*** in places where matches are prohibited.)(p.245)
• In describing his suffering, his fears, his many years of groping for some answer to that which always seemed to remain unanswerable, he could have been describing me, and nothing short of experience and ***knowledge*** could have afforded him that much insight!(p.309)
• But I was not able to make use of this ***knowledge*** until after I became sober.(p.409)
• "***Knowledge*** is power," I'd always been taught.(p.435)
• Now I had to face up to the fact that ***knowledge*** of this sort, applied to my individual case, was not power.(p.435)
• Not least of my debts to A.A. is the ***knowledge*** that in that time when she wanted me most, I was there -- and that I wasn't drunk.(p.525)
• I hope I have been able to impart to you, the reader, at least a bit of what I know; the joy of living, the irresistible power of divine love and its healing strength, and the fact that we, as sentient beings, have the ***knowledge*** to choose between good and evil, and, choosing good, are made happy.(p.543)
• The amount of will power exercised to control my drinking during working hours, diverted into a constructive channel, would have made me President, and the thing that made the will power possible was the ***knowledge*** that as soon as my day was finished I could drink myself into oblivion.(p.548)
• With deep shame came the ***knowledge*** too that I had lived with no sense of social obligation nor had I known the meaning of moral responsibility to my fellow men.(p.549)

known

• I talked with him for some time, but was not able to bring myself to feel that I had ***known*** him before.(p.xxix)
• Then he had, in effect, been raised from the dead, suddenly taken from the scrap heap to a level of life better than the best he had ever ***known***!(p.11)
• There was a sense of victory, followed by such a peace and serenity as I had never ***known***.(p.14)
• He had consulted the best ***known*** American psychiatrists.(p.26)
• He tries every ***known*** means to get the jay-walking idea out of his head.(p.38)
• Fred is partner in a well ***known*** accounting firm.(p.39)
• One night, when confined in a hospital, he was approached by an acholic who had ***known*** a spiritual experience.(p.56)
• But later, alone in his room, he asked himself this question: "Is it possible that all the religious people I have ***known*** are wrong?"(p.56)
• Perhaps we have committed a criminal offense which might land us in jail if it were ***known*** to the authorities.(p.78)
• We have already admitted this in confidence to another person, but we are sure we would be imprisoned or lose our job if it were ***known***.(p.78)
• Members of a family should watch such matters carefully, for one careless, inconsiderate remark has been ***known*** to raise the very devil.(p.125)
• I had been obliged to discharge him for drinking, though he was brilliant, alert, and one of the best organizers I have ever ***known***.(p.137)
• Some employers have tried every ***known*** remedy.(p.137)
• They knew they had a host of new friends; it seemed they had ***known*** these strangers always.(p.161)
• But this was a man who had experienced many years of frightful drinking, who had had most all the drunkard's experiences ***known*** to man, but who had been cured by the very means I had been trying to employ, that is to say the spiritual approach.(p.180)
• They came in and began to give me instruction in the program which later became ***known*** as Alcoholics Anonymous.(p.185)
• He had ***known*** something of my drinking pattern, and he asked me what I was doing about it.(p.200)
• It was not ***known*** to me as a group, but I later learned that my wife had ***known*** about it for nine months and had prayed constantly that I would stumble into Akron some way or another.(p.215)
• My family had money – I had never ***known*** denial

of any material desire.(p.225)

• That was the beginning of a new life, a fuller life, a happier life than I had ever ***known*** or believed possible.(p.228)

• Before long I had a definite taste for hard liquor, knew nausea and headaches I had never ***known*** before, but as in the old days, I suffered them out.(p.233)

• I had always ***known*** that, in theory.(p.236)

• I don't remember much of what he said, but I did realize that here was another guy exactly like me; he had been in the same laughing academies and the same jails, ***known*** the same loss of jobs, same frustrations, same boredom and the same loneliness.(p.239)

• If anything, he had ***known*** all of them even better and more often than I.(p.239)

• Little more of our talk stayed in my memory, but I do know I slept the rest of that night while before I had never ***known*** what a real night's sleep was.(p.239)

• My brilliant agnosticism vanished, and I saw for the first time that those who really believed, or at least honestly tried to find a Power greater than themselves, were much more composed and contented than I had ever been, and they seemed to have a degree of happiness which I had never ***known***.(p.247)

• I had never ***known*** him to be anything but a good healthy pagan with a propensity for getting into liquor jams and scrapes.(p.257)

• Some of them I had ***known*** for years, good two-fisted drinkers who had disappeared from their former haunts.(p.258)

• He mentioned two of them that I had ***known*** through the years and suggested that I talk with them.(p.289)

• But this day my doctor gave it to me straight and said, "People like you are pretty well ***known*** to the medical profession.(p.307)

• I have had my share of problems, heartaches and disappointments, because that is life, but also I have ***known*** a great deal of joy, and a peace that is the handmaiden of an inner freedom, I have a wealth of friends and, with my A.A. friends, an unusual quality of fellowship.(p.312)

• She had not ***known*** the extent of my consumption.(p.333)

• I had been brought up to believe in God, but I know that until I found this A.A. program, I had never found or ***known*** faith in the reality of God, the reality of His power that is now with me in everything I do.(p.341)

• And the first thing you know I was lifted right out of the A.A. group, and I floated higher, and higher, and even higher, until I was way up on a pink cloud which is ***known*** as Pink Seven, and I felt miserable again.(p.348)

• We have here in this community an organization which helps people, and this organization is ***known*** as Alcoholics Anonymous.(p.348)

• When I was nineteen, I married a fine man who had never ***known*** an insecure moment in his life, let alone the trials and tribulations of booze.(p.369)

• It is bound to be rough, because who can say exactly how much of that green blood -- commonly ***known*** as money -- was dissipated on dissipation?(p.396)

• Other girls whom I had ***known*** all my life asked for one weak scotch after dinner.(p.406)

• Indeed, she had ***known*** my cousin in Chicago.(p.414)

• No, I had ***known*** that.(p.470)

• I thought, "Oh well, these people are just like all the people I've ***known*** all my life.(p.472)

• I'd ***known*** her five or six months.(p.487)

• That year, on a Friday night, a man whom I had ***known*** for years came to my office.(p.488)

• When I had ***known*** her years before she was rather slender, but at this time she weighed as much as she does now, which is up around in the two hundreds or very close to it.(p.493)

• Can all the worth while people I have ***known*** be wrong about God?(p.503)

• Strangely enough, right through to the end of my twenty-six years in the Army, I was still being offered very good and important jobs in spite of the fact that my superiors must have ***known*** that I wasn't thoroughly reliable.(p.519)

• Everybody I had ***known*** in the old days had gone.(p.522)

• This was the only time in my life that I'd ever ***known*** my mother to be almost pitiless, but she couldn't be blamed for that.(p.523)

• On another small borrowed sum, I went up into the country to the home of a doctor I had ***known*** since boyhood.(p.540)

• I was the only person I'd ever ***known*** personally who had ever been in jail, and I guess it is most significant that the second time was less humiliating that the first had been.(p.549)

• With deep shame came the knowledge too that I had lived with no sense of social obligation nor had I ***known*** the meaning of moral responsibility to my fellow men.(p.549)

• One of the truly great things A.A. has taught me is that reality too has two sides; I had only ***known*** the grim side before the program, but now I had a chance to learn about the pleasant side as well.(p.550)

• As I said earlier, self-pity and resentment were my constant companions and my inventory began to look like a thirty-three year diary, for I seemed to have a resentment against everybody I had ever ***known***.(p.551)

• Like most other alcoholics I have ***known***, I did quit drinking at various times -- once for ten months on my own and during other interludes when I was hospitalized.(p.554)

• The relationship between my wife and me was restored to a love and happiness that we had not ***known*** even before my alcoholism became acute.(p.559)

• Dr. Foster Kennedy, neurologist: "This organization of Alcoholics Anonymous calls on two of the greatest reservoirs of power ***known*** to man, religion and that instinct for association with one's fellows . . . the 'herd instinct.'(p.571)

knows

• He ***knows*** that they are real.(p.14)

• That the man who is making the approach has had the same difficulty, that he obviously ***knows*** what he is talking about, that his whole deportment shouts at the new prospect that he is a man with a real answer, that he has no attitude of Holier Than Thou, nothing whatever except the sincere desire to be helpful; that there are no fees to pay, no axes to grind, no people to please, no lectures to be endured -- these are the conditions we have found most effective.(p.18)

• Heaven ***knows***, we have tried hard enough and long enough to drink like other people!(p.31)

• Almost everyone ***knows*** the reason.(p.51)

• He wants to enjoy a certain reputation, but ***knows*** in his heart he doesn't deserve it.(p.73)

• If she ***knows*** in a general way that we have been wild, should we tell her in detail?(p.81)

• In that case he is going to wonder how you can add anything to what he already ***knows***.(p.93)

• Admit that he probably ***knows*** more about it than you do, but call to his attention the fact that however deep his faith and knowledge, he could not have applied it or he would not drink.(p.93)

• Perhaps your story will help him see where he has failed to practice the very precepts he ***knows*** so well.(p.93)

• He ***knows*** that thousands of men, much like himself, have recovered.(p.113)

• Your husband ***knows*** he owes you more than sobriety.(p.118)

• Father ***knows*** he is to blame; it may take him many seasons of hard work to be restored financially, but he shouldn't be reproached.(p.123)

• Everyone ***knows*** about the others' alcoholic troubles.(p.125)

• Everybody ***knows*** that those in bad health, and those who seldom play, do not laugh much.(p.132)

• He ***knows*** the alcoholic as the employer sees him.(p.136)

• Here, for instance, is a typical example: An officer of one of the largest banking institutions in America ***knows*** I no longer drink.(p.138)

• If he feels free to discuss his problems with you, if he ***knows*** you understand and will not be upset by anything he wishes to say, he will probably be off to a fast start.(p.144)

• Being somewhat weakened, and faced with physical and mental readjustment to a life which ***knows*** no alcohol, he may overdo.(p.146)

• For he ***knows*** he must be honest if he would live at all.(p.146)

• And we went down through the valley, and I remembered reading about the Ku Klux Klan and how they burnt crosses, and I thought, "God alone ***knows*** what we are getting into this time!"(p.269)

• I was crying, and I said, "Alice says she ***knows*** I don't have any part of the program."(p.273)

• Everyone ***knows*** it.(p.376)

• My wife hears my voice and ***knows*** I have found the answer to life.(p.505)

• You hit the street about ten minutes to eight, and you walk around the block, God ***knows*** how many times, waiting for that joint to open.(p.514)

Ku Klux Klan

• And we went down through the valley, and I remembered reading about the ***Ku Klux Klan*** and how they burnt crosses, and I thought, "God alone knows what we are getting into this time!"(p.269)

L1

lab
• I talked the Old Man into letting me live in the photo *lab* instead of the barracks, and for eighteen months nothing interfered with my drinking.(p.426)
• One night I was sitting in the *lab* alone with a fifth and a case of beer listening to dreamy Hawaiian music on the radio.(p.427)

label
• Up to this point you would *label* him as a foolish chap having queer ideas of fun.(p.37)

labor
• That was the last honest manual *labor* on my part for many a day.(p.3)
• To duplicate, with such backing, what we have accomplished is only a matter of willingness, patience and *labor*.(p.163)
• Consequently, my *labor* bills ran up.(p.194)
• We always started out on the Saturday before *Labor* Day.(p.264)
• I'm pretty near afraid of *Labor* Day yet.(p.264)
• So, on that Saturday before *Labor* Day, I got drunk and set the house on fire -- so we didn't have to paint it.(p.265)
• He had tried everything from having me attend daily mass at six a.m. to performing the most menial *labor* for his charity patients.(p.306)
• I went back home, to a job of manual *labor* where for a little while I was able to keep away from alcohol.(p.539)

labored
• The unselfishness of these men as we have come to know them, the entire absence of profit motive, and their community spirit, is indeed inspiring to one who has *labored* long and wearily in this alcoholic field.(p.xxv)

laboriously
• When, however, the perfectly logical assumption is suggested that underneath the material world and life as we see it, there is an All Powerful, Guiding, Creative Intelligence, right there our perverse streak comes to the surface and we *laboriously* set out to convince ourselves it isn't so.(p.49)

lack
• I began to wonder, for such an appalling *lack* of perspective seemed near being just that.(p.5)
• Here is the fellow who has been puzzling you, especially in his *lack* of control.(p.21)
• How can such a *lack* of proportion, of the ability to think straight, be called anything else?(p.37)
• *Lack* of power, that was our dilemma.(p.45)
• Two: Your husband is showing *lack* of control, for he is unable to stay on the water wagon even when he wants to.(p.109)
• Your new courage, good nature and *lack* of self-consciousness will do wonders for you socially.(p.115)
• When we do that, we find it solves our problems too; the ensuing *lack* of fear, worry and hurt feelings is a wonderful thing.(p.116)
• In only a few instances has there been *lack* of patience and tolerance.(p.137)
• To me, this incident illustrates *lack* of understanding as to what really ails the alcoholic, and *lack* of knowledge as to what part employers might profitably take in salvaging their sick employees.(p.139)
• If you desire to help it might be well to disregard your own drinking, or *lack* of it.(p.139)
• If possible express a *lack* of hard feeling toward him.(p.142)
• Poor health and a complete *lack* of money necessitated my remaining with Dr. Bob and Anne for very close to a year.(p.280)
• This office job brought me face to face with a problem which I had sidestepped all my adult life, *lack* of training.(p.284)
• I was terribly impressed by this meeting and the quality of happiness these men displayed, despite their *lack* of material means.(p.291)
• They realized that repeated *lack* of drinking control, when they really wanted control, was the fatal symptom that spelled problem drinking.(p.315)
• Cold sweats, jumpy nerves and *lack* of sleep were becoming intolerable.(p.378)
• For always, over and above everything else, was the awfulness of the *lack* of meaning in life.(p.535)
• Had I been able to explain to a psychiatrist the feeling of futility, loneliness and *lack* of purpose that had come with my deep sense of personal failure at this second divorce, I seriously doubt that the good doctor could have convinced me that my basic problem was a spiritual hunger, but A.A. has shown me this was the truth.(p.546)
• It had provided me with excuses for my *lack* of education, my marital failures, personal failures, inadequacy, and of course, my alcoholism and, though I really thought I had been willing to part with it, now I knew I was reluctant to let it go.(p.552)

lacking
• Here I found an ingredient that had been *lacking* in any other effort I had made to save myself.(p.436)

lad
• It was fun to carom around the exclusive course which had inspired such awe in me as a *lad*.(p.4)
• I ran away for the second time, with another *lad*.(p.424)
• I was, so far as anybody could tell, quite a *lad*.(p.432)

Ladd
• One night, I was struck with the memory of a line Alan *Ladd* used in "Shane," a movie that I'd worked on.(p.333)

ladder
• As my father climbed the *ladder* of success in the oil-field business, his drinking also climbed.(p.369)
• I have had experience in selling, collecting, and accounting, and am on my way up the *ladder*.(p.500)

ladies
• The bill collectors, the sheriffs, the angry taxi drivers, the policemen, the bums, the pals, and even the *ladies* they sometimes brought home -- our husbands thought we were so inhospitable.(p.106)

lads
• I am one of the *lads* who came out of the service with a lower rank than when I went in.(p.241)

lady
• About this time a *lady* called up my wife one Saturday afternoon, saying she wanted me to come over that evening to meet a friend of hers who might help me.(p.179)
• I sold three lots to an elderly *lady* in Cleveland.(p.196)
• I sipped the drink off the bar because I couldn't hold it in my hand, but I was still a *lady*, believe it or not, and I was deeply ashamed.(p.266)
• This worldly *lady* helped to develop A.A. in Chicago and thus passed her keys to many.(p.304)
• This *lady* was cautious.(p.321)
• I was living in a small room on West 53rd Street right off Fifth Avenue, when I met a young *lady* who eventually was responsible for altering my entire way of living.(p.359)
• I had been reading a lot about psychiatry and I thought, "Maybe if I talk to a psychiatrist he can find out what is happening, and then I can drink like a *lady*."(p.387)
• A titled *lady*, she still saw her world darkening.(p.400)
• I went to this friend's shop to repair his electrical outlet and I noticed this *lady*.(p.493)
• A wasp is crawling up the back of the *lady* in front of me.(p.497)
• Still another friend and temporary host received me at four in the morning from the charge of a policeman who had found me "going to bed" in a garage far from the last place I could remember having been, a fashionable bar and restaurant in the theatrical district of New York, to which I had repaired after my date for that evening, a charming *lady* of the theatre who had refused my company for obvious reasons.(p.538)

laid
• When, therefore, we were approached by those in whom the problem had been solved, there was nothing left for us but to pick up the simple kit of spiritual tools *laid* at our feet.(p.25)
• Obviously, no rule can be *laid* down.(p.99)
• Father may have *laid* aside for years all normal activities -- clubs, civic duties, sports.(p.131)
• An accident while drunk *laid* me low for about three weeks.(p.258)
• All sorts were represented and their relation of experiences and how they had found the only remedy, added to their human existence as sober men, *laid* the foundation of a very necessary faith.(p.258)
• He *laid* great stress on the progression of his attitude toward life and people, and most of his attitudes had been very similar to mine.(p.290)
• They would travel miles and stay up all night with someone they had never *laid* eyes on before and think nothing of it.(p.310)
• Somehow, I made it through basic and then *laid* off the booze for about three months, because I was in school at night.(p.317)
• The short tours could be taken care of by sneaking enough whiskey aboard ship so that it could be rationed out until another supply could be *laid* in.(p.398)

lain
• Bill then related how he had *lain* awake nearly all night.(p.189)

lake
• I returned to my home in Lucknow, India, at the end of November last year from a vacation in one of the most famous beauty spots in our country, a mountain resort 6,800 feet up, with a wonderful *lake*.(p.342)
• At this time, however, she had an opportunity to go to Salt *Lake* City on a new project for the government, but she did promise me that if I would curtail my drinking and buckle down to hard work she would give serious consideration to my latest proposal and maybe join me at a later date when I got settled.(p.359)
• My salesmanship was still good, for in the fall of 1938 she called me from Salt *Lake* and finally agreed to take me on for better or for worse.(p.360)

lakes
• At Great *Lakes* Boot Camp I latched onto a soft billet.(p.425)

lambaste
• At our weekly meeting I was a menace to serenity those first few months, for I took every opportunity to *lambaste* the "spiritual angle" as we called it, or anything else that had any tinge of theology.(p.246)

lance
• I refused to join any fraternity, as I wanted to be a free *lance*, and that year my drinking was confined to one-night stands, once or twice a week.(p.241)

land
• The outlines and the promise of the New *Land* had brought lustre to tired eyes and fresh courage to flagging spirits.(p.53)
• Perhaps we have committed a criminal offense which might *land* us in jail if it were known to the authorities.(p.78)
• I optioned a piece of *land* just off East Market Street to put up a three-hundred suite apartment.(p.198)
• Many friends of my family had emigrated to America, so at twenty-four I decided that the United States offered me the opportunity I was never likely to find in my native *land*.(p.231)
• Having regard for the law of the *land*, I resigned myself to the will of the national legislators and quit drinking altogether, not because I had found it harmful, but because I couldn't get what I was accustomed to drink.(p.232)
• Even among those who occasionally *land* back in here again, we observe a profound change in personality.(p.572)

landed
• We *landed* in England.(p.1)
• This combination soon *landed* me on the rocks.(p.7)
• I could not see why I couldn't drink like a gentleman, and that was my primary ambition -- until I *landed* in A.A.(p.214)
• That went on for two more months before I *landed* in a hospital and started my slow fight back to normalcy.(p.224)
• After a couple of days in dollar hotels and one night in the pokey, I finally *landed* on my mother's doorstep -- shaking apart, with several days' beard and, of course, broke as usual.(p.238)
• Drifting back to Ohio, I *landed* on a small newspaper and later was impressed into the direction of boy-welfare work at the local "Y."(p.253)
• That to me was the greatest humiliation, to think that I'd finally *landed* in jail.(p.264)
• I *landed* him and shipped him by train to Akron, with a pint of whiskey in his pocket to keep him from wanting to get off the train in Toledo!(p.282)
• I had run away from school to join the army in World War I, but missed it by one day since the

• Armistice was signed the very day I *landed* in Atlanta to sign up with Uncle Sam.(p.357)
• Tasting the best of burgundy at a famous restaurant one night, *landed* me passed out on a park bench in the public square.(p.405)
• I went to Tijuana that night and *landed* in jail.(p.428)
• And I *landed* right smack back in that sanitarium that I had gone to so often.(p.472)
• He did come, and I *landed* in the funny farm for a while.(p.479)
• When I *landed* of course I hit a gin mill, and with three or four good shots under my belt the world began to go into that rosy glow.(p.513)
• I *landed* a good job with a company publication and was moonlighting on other magazines.(p.555)

landing
• I have a shadowy recollection of being in an airplane bound for New York, and of finding a friendly taxicab driver at the *landing* field instead of my wife.(p.41)

landlord
• First, my new wife had walked out, bag, baggage and furniture; then the apartment *landlord* had thrown me out of the empty apartment and the finish was the loss of another job.(p.238)

lands
• Alcohol being no respecter of persons, we are an accurate cross section of America, and in distant *lands*, the same democratic evening-up process is now going on.(p.xx)

Langley's
• Did not Professor *Langley's* flying machine go to the bottom of the Potomac River?(p.51)

language
• Each individual, in the personal stories, describes in his own *language* and from his own point of view the way he established his relationship with God.(p.29)
• It's strong *language* -- but isn't it true?(p.38)
• When dealing with such a person, you had better use everyday *language* to describe spiritual principles.(p.93)
• In other words, he talked my *language*.(p.180)
• In fact his *language* was perfectly suited to my understanding.(p.235)
• I had never heard of the remedy expressed in just this *language*.(p.236)
• It was simple, they said, and went on to explain to me in their own *language* the program of recovery and daily living which we know today as the Twelve Steps of A.A.(p.279)
• Our *language* has few words to say many things.(p.474)

languages
• By the time I was twenty-one I had six years of life in foreign countries, spoke three *languages* fluently, and had attended college for two years.(p.275)

lap
• All I want to know is, why does that dog wet in my *lap* every time I hold him?"(p.440)

lapse
• I didn't say a word to anyone about my *lapse*.(p.364)
• I had never told a soul about my *lapse* in New York.(p.366)

lapses
• Federal Theatre in Texas gave me an administrative job which I held for a year, only because I worked hard and productively when I worked, and because my very tolerant chief ascribed my frequent *lapses* to a bohemian temperament.(p.256)

large
• Because this book has become the basic text for our Society and has helped such *large* numbers of alcoholic men and women to recover, there exists a sentiment against any radical changes being made in it.(p.xi)
• The test that it faced was this: Could these *large* numbers of erstwhile erratic alcoholics successfully meet and work together?(p.xviii)
• For this there were two principal reasons: the *large* numbers of recoveries, and reunited homes.(p.xx)
• At the end of it, my reports to Wall street procured me a position there and the use of a *large* expense account.(p.3)
• Those of us who live in *large* cities are overcome by the reflection that close by hundreds are dropping into oblivion every day.(p.19)
• We, who are familiar with the symptoms, see *large* numbers of potential alcoholics among young people everywhere.(p.33)
• Perhaps you have a husband who is at *large*, but who should be committed.(p.114)
• If your organization is a *large* one, your junior executives might be provided with this book.(p.147)
• The other day an approach was made to the vice president of a *large* industrial concern.(p.148)
• We believe that managers of *large* enterprises often have little idea how prevalent this problem is.(p.149)
• If you live in a *large* place, there are hundreds.(p.152)
• Hopelessness was written *large* on the man's face as he replied, "Oh, but that's no use.(p.157)
• One man and his wife placed their *large* home at the disposal of this strangely assorted crowd.(p.160)
• Being a *large* place, we think that some day its Fellowship will number many hundreds.(p.161)
• We know of an A.A. member who was living in a *large* community.(p.163)
• Arrangements were also made with the chief psychiatrist of a *large* public hospital to select still others from the stream of misery which flows through that institution.(p.163)
• The next three years I spent in Boston, Chicago, and Montreal in the employ of a *large* manufacturing concern, selling railway supplies, gas engines of all sorts, and many other items of heavy hardware.(p.172)
• This went from bad to worse until Sophomore spring when, after a prolonged period of drinking, I made up my mind that I could not complete my course, so I packed my grip and went South to spend a month on a *large* farm owned by a friend of mine.(p.173)
• Most of the time therefore, I did not take the morning drink which I craved so badly, but instead would fill up on *large* doses of sedatives to quiet the jitters, which distressed me terribly.(p.176)
• If my wife was planning to go out in the afternoon, I would get a *large* supply of liquor and smuggle it home and hide it in the coal bin, the clothes chute, over door jambs, over beams in the cellar and in cracks in the cellar tile.(p.176)
• It was really a horrible nightmare, this earning money, getting liquor, smuggling it home, getting drunk, morning jitters, taking *large* doses of sedatives to make it possible for me to earn more money, and so on ad nauseam.(p.177)
• I lost money, and then just fooled away a *large* part of that profit.(p.194)
• As a draftsman, I worked for several *large* companies and gained a variety of experience.(p.211)
• I was in a *large*, dark, rather poorly furnished room -- the living room of a basement flat.(p.222)
• For weeks after my arrival I was feted and entertained in the already *large* colony of Alsatians in the city, and among the Germans in their saloons and clubs.(p.231)
• In sports I made the track and tennis teams; I got along well with the other boys and had a fairly *large* circle of acquaintances but no intimate friends.(p.240)
• My wife traveled with me, but with a baby coming I decided to settle in a *large* city where I got a job with a commission agent which is a polite term for a handbook operator.(p.251)
• Making my way to Pittsburgh, I met other former friends and got a job in a *large* factory where piecemakers were making good money.(p.252)
• My wife came over from Scotland and we started housekeeping in a *large* Ohio city.(p.254)
• When I hit Houston, Texas, I found employment in a *large* bookstore.(p.255)
• I looked much older than I was, I was always *large*, and I went back to work in this job.(p.262)
• It was a long four or five hour operation, a *large* surgical procedure, and she was on her ninth or tenth post-operative day.(p.350)
• I was working for a Chicago firm that represented several *large* radio stations.(p.358)
• Looking directly at me was a *large* oil painting of my wife, and her very words seemed to shout at me -- "I am not leaving you because I don't love you; it's because I do love you.(p.363)
• He and I had a *large* family -- six children, to be exact.(p.370)
• I achieved recognized and national standing in my profession, as well as becoming a director in many important institutions having to do with the civic life of a *large* city.(p.374)
• Up to my early thirties, when my drinking had become a major problem, I lived in *large* houses, with servants and all the luxuries that I could possibly ask for.(p.401)
• That first night I blacked out at a *large* dinner party.(p.404)
• At a *large* party in Geneva, with people from many countries represented, the kind of party that is "protocol" in the extreme, I swayed, laughed hysterically, made naughty remarks in an unhushed voice, and was finally led from the scene.(p.406)
• They were having a *large* A.A. meeting in the prison auditorium.(p.460)
• (Two *large* red A's stand out in my memory.)(p.460)
• I am working hard on the books of a subsidiary company of a *large* corporation.(p.500)
• By and *large*, I got through.(p.519)
• At age forty, I developed a *large* lump in my potbelly, and I feared it was a tumor.(p.557)
• We think that each group should soon achieve this ideal; that any public solicitation of funds using the name of Alcoholics Anonymous is highly dangerous, whether by groups, clubs, hospitals, or other outside agencies; that acceptance of *large* gifts from any source, or of contributions carrying any obligation whatever, is unwise.(p.566)
• The small group may elect its secretary, the *large* group its rotating committee, and the groups of a *large* metropolitan area their central or intergroup committee, which often employs a full-time secretary.(p.567)
• In *large* cities, groups often maintain local offices where alcoholics or their families may arrange for interviews or hospitalization.(p.575)

largely
• Back to the big city, for another year of precarious living, paid for *largely* by one or two friends I still had not milked dry or worn to exhaustion with demands on their bounty.(p.540)
• This is a world clearing house for the Al-Anon Family Groups, composed *largely* of the wives, husbands and friends of A.A. members.(p.575)

larger
• Many of our friends encourage us by saying that this is but a beginning, only the augury of a much *larger* future ahead.(p.xv)
• Little clusters of twos and threes and fives of us have sprung up in other communities, through contact with our two *larger* centers.(p.162)
• Here was something requiring a greater willingness to assume responsibility, and take a *larger* degree of cooperation and "give and take" than even business requires of one.(p.286)
• At that time, I was living out of town, so I moved back to the home town and made a connection in a responsible position with one of the *larger* companies in the finance business.(p.298)
• During recess we were playing basketball and I had accidentally tripped a fellow just a little *larger* than I was.(p.484)

largest
• Here, for instance, is a typical example: An officer of one of the *largest* banking institutions in America knows I no longer drink.(p.138)
• My next move was to take up the study of medicine, entering one of the *largest* universities in the county.(p.173)
• In time I became an officer and director of one of the *largest* commercial banks in the country.(p.374)

Las Vegas
• Can you picture two girls hitchhiking their way to *Las Vegas* from Washington State?(p.354)

Lasker
• IV. The *Lasker* Award(p.563)
• THE *LASKER* AWARD(p.573)
• In 1951 the *Lasker* Award was given Alcoholics Anonymous.(p.573)
• "The American Public Health Association presents a *Lasker* Group Award for 1951 to Alcoholics Anonymous in recognition of its unique and highly successful approach to that age-old public health and social problem, alcoholism . . .(p.573)

last
• I was part of life at *last*, and in the midst of the excitement I discovered liquor.(p.1)
• Twenty-two, and a veteran of foreign wars, I went home at *last*.(p.1)
• That was the *last* honest manual labor on my part for many a day.(p.3)
• My writhing nerves were stilled at *last*.(p.6)
• I, who had thought so well of myself and my abilities, of my capacity to surmount obstacles, was cornered at *last*.(p.8)
• In reality that was the beginning of my *last* debauch.(p.8)
• So that was it -- *last* summer an alcoholic crackpot; now, I suspected, a little cracked about religion.(p.9)
• Besides, my gin would *last* longer than his preaching.(p.9)
• I stood in the sunlight at *last*.(p.12)
• At long *last* I saw, I felt, I believed.(p.12)

• At the hospital I was separated from alcohol for the *last* time.(p.13)
• If you ask him why he started on that *last* bender, the chances are he will offer you any one of a hundred alibis.(p.23)
• This process snuffed out the *last* flicker of conviction that I could do the job myself.(p.42)
• Instead of regarding ourselves as intelligent agents, spearheads of God's ever advancing Creation, we agnostics and atheists chose to believe that our human intelligence was the *last* word, the alpha and the omega, the beginning and end of all.(p.49)
• This world of ours has made more material progress in the *last* century than in all the millenniums which went before.(p.51)
• Perhaps we had been leaning too heavily on Reason that *last* mile and we did not like to lose our support.(p.53)
• Little or nothing, we saw at *last.*(p.54)
• In the *last* analysis it is only there that He may be found.(p.55)
• We thought well before taking this step making sure we were ready; that we could at *last* abandon ourselves utterly to Him.(p.63)
• Carefully reading the first five proposals we ask if we have omitted anything, for we are building an arch through which we shall walk a free man at *last.*(p.75)
• But be careful not to be resentful about the *last* time he did so.(p.116)
• Like a gaunt prospector, belt drawn in over the *last* ounce of food, our pick struck gold.(p.128)
• I still expected a plea for clemency, but these words came through the receiver: "I just wanted to tell you Paul jumped from a hotel window in Hartford *last* Saturday.(p.136)
• He has just returned from a three-months leave of absence, has taken a cure, looks fine, and to clinch the matter, the board of directors told him this was his *last* chance."(p.138)
• By no means do we offer it as the *last* word on this subject, but so far as we are concerned, it has worked with us.(p.144)
• But not so with us in those *last* days of heavy drinking.(p.151)
• Life will mean something at *last.*(p.152)
• But he's a grand chap when he's sober, though he's been in here eight times in the *last* six months.(p.156)
• The *last* three times, I got drunk on the way home from here.(p.157)
• The expression on the faces of the women, that indefinable something in the eyes of the men, the stimulating and electric atmosphere of the place, conspired to let him know that here was haven at *last.*(p.160)
• That was June 10, 1935, and that was my *last* drink.(p.180)
• Each of the seven times that I had left this hospital in the *last* six months, I had come out fully determined in my own mind that I would not get drunk again -- for at least six or eight months.(p.184)
• Nineteen years ago *last* summer, Dr. Bob and I saw him (Bill D.) for the first time.(p.188)
• This was six or eight months after the *last* drinking episode.(p.196)
• I said, "In that case, there's no use of wasting this," and I got the *last* of that pint.(p.207)
• I was born in Cleveland, Ohio, in 1889, the *last* child of a family of eight children.(p.210)
• And then my thinking became calculation as to how much longer I had to live, how long the assets would *last.*(p.215)
• However, on a couple of other occasions, Clarence seemed to bob up at the *last* saloon that I would stop at on the way home every day.(p.216)
• In fact, the *last* three years of my drinking was a routine of barbiturates in the morning, so that I could stop shaking enough to shave, and then alcohol beginning about four-thirty or five o'clock, with a struggle not to take a drink at noon or during the day, because I had the idea that if I took one drink, I would smell as though I had had a pint.(p.217)
• It must have been a long time since I had my *last* drink -- but I didn't dare ask this stranger for one.(p.223)
• It had been one o'clock when I *last* remember looking.(p.223)
• When I look back on that *last* horrible year of constant drinking I wonder how I survived it either physically or mentally.(p.224)
• I went trembling into a house in Brooklyn filled with strangers . . . and I found I had come home at *last,* to my own kind.(p.228)
• An active member of A.A. since 1939, I feel myself a useful member of the human race at *last.*(p.229)
• For the great majority of us, however, that condition didn't *last.*(p.232)
• And yet, realizing at *last* that liquor really had me, I wanted to quit.(p.234)
• This *last* real merry-go-round had started the day before Christmas and I had really accomplished a lot in those fourteen days.(p.238)
• My *last* bout in the Army lasted from November 5th to 11th, 1918.(p.242)
• For the *last* two years of my drinking I prayed on every drunk that I wouldn't wake up again.(p.245)
• There was one meeting a week at Bill's home in Brooklyn, and we all took turns there spouting off about how we had changed our lives overnight, how many drunks we had saved and straightened out, and *last,* but not least, how God had touched each of us personally on the shoulder.(p.246)
• My *last* venture, a book shop, was hastened to closed doors by my steady intoxication.(p.255)
• In those days my system was always to drink up my *last* pay check and believe that necessity would bring the next job.(p.256)
• I took my *last* drink in 1937.(p.260)
• Our other daughter was in her *last* year of high school, and one night the new son-in-law and my husband went out to a prize fight.(p.263)
• I think that was the *last* vacation before sobriety.(p.265)
• That was our *last* drink of anything alcoholic.(p.267)
• At *last* I discovered alcohol as a cure-all.(p.277)
• I have thanked God many times in the *last* sixteen years that that was just what he did not do!(p.278)
• Well, suicide was a *last* straw matter, and I had not drawn the *last* straw yet.(p.278)
• At long *last* I am doing the kind of work I have always wanted to do, but never had the patience and emotional stability to train myself for.(p.284)
• I had been in A.A. a year, and the *last* thing in my mind was a drink.(p.285)
• At any rate the *last* great step toward a well rounded life still lay ahead of me.(p.286)
• These *last* eighteen years have been the happiest of my life, trite though that statement may seem.(p.295)
• The *last* day of my drinking career, I drank twenty-two of them between ten and twelve a.m. and I shall never know how many more followed them until I was poured into bed that night.(p.298)
• I cannot remember just when I became the victim of insomnia, but I do know that the *last* year and a half I never went to bed sober a single night.(p.299)
• Mentally . . . I know where I was *last* night, the night before, and the nights before that.(p.303)
• With the alcoholic, they could only give temporary relief and in the *last* stages not even that.(p.307)
• The *last* fifteen years of my life have been rich and meaningful.(p.312)
• In the old days I hated to wake up and look back at what *last* night was like.(p.325)
• Safely pensioned, with no job to protect, at *last* he could drink as he pleased.(p.327)
• We're free at *last* to do our thing, to live uninhibited lives, to drink when and how and where we wish, when we want to and when we need to.(p.329)
• And retirement is a time for thinking, not of death, but of living -- at long *last.*(p.329)
• Best that they not be found after I'd had my *last* drink on earth.(p.333)
• I knew nothing about alcoholism or the D.T.'s, but when I woke up on this *last* morning of my son's illness, I taped the keyhole on my door because "everyone was out there."(p.338)
• I returned to my home in Lucknow, India, at the end of November *last* year from a vacation in one of the most famous beauty spots in our country, a mountain resort 6,800 feet up, with a wonderful lake.(p.342)
• *Last* year, I decided on an A.A. vacation in Naini Tal.(p.343)
• I made more money the *last* year of my drinking than I ever made before in my whole life.(p.345)
• I was president of all my classes in high school and in my *last* year I was president of that student body.(p.345)
• On the *last* day I was drinking I went up to see a friend who had had a good deal of trouble with alcohol, and whose wife had left him a number of times.(p.346)
• The thought came to me -- This is the *last* one!(p.347)
• And as that thought came to me, it was as though someone had reached down and taken a heavy overcoat off my shoulders, for that was the *last* one.(p.347)
• And the *last* sentence was "We asked His protection and care with complete abandon."(p.349)
• I tried every gimmick that there was to get some peace of mind, but it was not until I was brought to my alcoholic knees, when I was brought to a group in my own community with the butcher, the baker, the carpenter and the mechanic, who were able to give me the Twelve Steps, that I was finally given some semblance of an answer to the *last* half of the First Step.(p.349)
• This man faced the *last* ditch when his wife's voice from 1,300 miles away sent him to A.A.(p.356)
• I tried a few drinks my *last* night in the city before coming home.(p.364)
• I knew he was right, except for that *last* statement.(p.371)
• I saw at *last* that I had the same disease my father had, only I was being given a chance to live, not die.(p.371)
• The *last* two years of my drinking my entire personality changed to a cynical, intolerant and arrogant person completely different from my normal self.(p.376)
• I know that if I do daily what I have done for these *last* thirteen and a half years, I will stay sober.(p.384)
• I never want to forget that *last* drunk as long as I live.(p.393)
• It's the *last* thing I ever heard him say, and I think there are some of us who, at times, try to read extra messages and complexities into the Steps.(p.395)
• When I protested, his lawyer, my lawyer, and my third and *last* analyst had a conference.(p.409)
• I was so busy keeping her out of trouble, and so scared she'd swing on me, that I had my *last* two drinks that night.(p.415)
• The *last* time I drank, when I was twenty-nine, I drank for only four days, yet I threatened to kill my children; I beat my wife at home and on the church steps; I mistreated a child in my office; and I ran to a hospital for mental illness to avoid jail.(p.418)
• Weeks would go by without further trouble, and I'd be assured I'd at *last* hit on the right formula.(p.433)
• How exciting to learn the inward mysteries that govern the behavior of people, how wonderful to know, at *last,* all about myself!(p.434)
• After my *last* binge I came home and smashed my dining room furniture to splinters, kicked out six windows and two balustrades.(p.435)
• At *last,* acceptance proved to be the key to my drinking problem.(p.448)
• It seems I should have learned to love my wife and family first; the newcomer to A.A., *last.*(p.451)
• Then I committed my *last* offense.(p.460)
• I count my sobriety date from the day I began going to A.A. in prison, not from the date of my *last* drink.(p.462)
• My daughter was one and a half years old when I *last* saw her.(p.463)
• In fact it has been only within the *last* fifteen years that I changed from a fairly normal, controlled drinker into an alcoholic.(p.464)
• The *last* Christmas I spent in Washington, fourteen years ago, comes to mind.(p.465)
• This easy method of sobering up would *last* at least three days.(p.468)
• Finally, however, in November of 1944, at long *last* I went to A.A.(p.470)
• First time I have blackout, but not *last.*(p.474)
• *Last* time in jail, I have two black eyes.(p.475)
• *Last* time I drink, I go to room.(p.475)
• Any time I tried to kill myself, I was either drunk or pilled-up or both -- usually the *last.*(p.479)
• If someone had told me *last* year that I would be excited about gardening this year, I would have said he was off his rocker.(p.481)
• The following day, Saturday, he came back and said, "Jim, I owe you for that prescription *last* night.(p.488)
• You know the prescription that you gave me for my wife *last* night."(p.488)
• Finally, I broke the *last* one hundred dollar bill the Saturday before I left.(p.493)
• I took the *last* to buy my railroad ticket.(p.493)
• At *last*!(p.497)
• My *last* exam and an easy one.(p.499)
• It is the *last* day of the following October, a dark, rainy morning.(p.502)
• She had looked for me *last* evening after I left the car and wandered off into the night.(p.502)
• When you've been in a jam you've said, 'God, please do this or that,' and if it turned out your way that was the *last* of it, and if it didn't you've said 'There isn't any God' or 'He doesn't do anything for me.'(p.504)
• I spent my *last* seventeen months in Wallkill, and it was there that I first got my introduction to A.A.(p.509)

• My *last* binge followed the previous one by two weeks.(p.514)
• At first, like everybody else, I could keep control when I drank, but if I did start to drink, even in those days, I was always one of the *last* to leave the party.(p.518)
• As I say, this specialist put a scare in me for about a fortnight or three weeks, then I started my *last* bout which went on and off for about three months.(p.523)
• I had been using paraldehyde more or less like ordinary drink for the *last* six years though, occasionally, I'd bounce back to phenobarbital and things like that.(p.524)
• My mother lived on for five years after I joined A.A., the *last* two in complete blindness.(p.525)
• I was always able to get a boyfriend who had a drinking joint or sold whiskey, but it didn't *last* long.(p.526)
• I didn't *last* long.(p.528)
• I started to cross out that *last* sentence, but decided to let it stand.(p.536)
• Still another friend and temporary host received me at four in the morning from the charge of a policeman who had found me "going to bed" in a garage far from the *last* place I could remember having been, a fashionable bar and restaurant in the theatrical district of New York, to which I had repaired after my date for that evening, a charming lady of the theatre who had refused my company for obvious reasons.(p.538)
• Was I the disloyal sort who would turn his back on this, my *last* and truest friend?(p.539)
• The *last* three years of my drinking, I drank on my job.(p.548)
• The children kept me sober for darn near three weeks, and then I went on (please God) my *last* drunk.(p.549)
• In the *last* year of my navy service, I was married to a lovely, lively girl, who enjoyed drinking.(p.555)
• The doctors told me that if I ever took another drink, it might be my *last*.(p.558)
• For, at *last*, I was at peace with myself.(p.561)

lasted

• We do not know of many cases where this difficulty *lasted* long.(p.134)
• This dry spell *lasted* for about three weeks; then I went to Atlantic City to attend several days' meeting of a national society of which I was a member.(p.179)
• My last bout in the Army *lasted* from November 5th to 11th, 1918.(p.242)
• The new job *lasted* five years.(p.254)
• Visits from friends which *lasted* over fifteen minutes exhausted me.(p.275)
• This happy combination of pleasant work and alcohol *lasted* for five years.(p.277)
• Our marriage *lasted* four years.(p.277)
• The meeting *lasted* an hour and closed with the Lord's Prayer.(p.291)
• When I got out of there, I *lasted* about fifteen minutes at home, before I headed for the drugstore and more pills, and then the bar.(p.479)
• The trial *lasted* about a week, and whether or not I was going to the death house was anybody's guess.(p.508)
• I *lasted* at that for four months chiefly on alcohol, because I never seemed to find any time to eat.(p.520)

lasting

• This group of thirteen stories shows that sobriety in A.A. can be *lasting*.(p.167)
• So I had never had any *lasting* contact with any kind of religion.)(p.201)
• I was always interested in mechanics and after having about twenty miscellaneous jobs, *lasting* from one day to two weeks, I obtained a job as a toolmaker apprentice.(p.211)
• There may be many reasons which bring one to A.A. for the first time, but the *lasting* one must be to want sobriety and the A.A. way of living for oneself.(p.379)

latched

• At Great Lakes Boot Camp I *latched* onto a soft billet.(p.425)

late

• The section called "The Doctor's Opinion" has been kept intact, just as it was originally written in 1939 by the *late* Dr. William D. Silkworth, our Society's great medical benefactor.(p.xi)
• He had also been greatly helped by the *late* Dr. William D. Silkworth, a New York specialist in alcoholism who is now accounted no less than a medical saint by A.A. members, and whose story of the early days of our Society appears in the next pages.(p.xvi)
• By *late* 1937, the number of members having substantial sobriety time behind them was sufficient to convince the membership that a new light had entered the dark world of the alcoholic.(p.xvii)
• In *late* 1934 I attended a patient who, though he had been a competent businessman of good earning capacity, was an alcoholic of a type I had come to regard as hopeless.(p.xxiii)
• The great boom of the *late* twenties was seething and swelling.(p.3)
• I had repaired to one of these one morning with my jug and when I left *late* in the afternoon, I picked up a newspaper on the way home.(p.244)
• We were together all the time, but this night I got up and saw it was *late*.(p.263)
• Almost simultaneously, I discovered that cocktails in the *late* afternoon and highballs in the evening relieved the many tensions of the day.(p.277)
• Eventually I would arrive home for a *late* supper for which, of course, I had absolutely no relish.(p.299)
• My drinking career started *late*.(p.328)
• I sure had been working awfully hard of *late*.(p.360)
• Marty was *late*.(p.413)
• It was *late* at night.(p.424)
• The more I focus my mind on its defects – *late* start, long drunkalogues, cigarette smoke – the worse the meeting becomes.(p.451)
• They prove to almost anyone's satisfaction that it's never too *late* to try Alcoholics Anonymous.(p.455)
• He was in his *late* fifties, and all that he had undertaken fell upon my shoulders at his death in 1928.(p.486)
• I had no work to do and I was at an age where it seemed too *late* to start anything new.(p.522)
• In A.A. we can begin again no matter how *late* it may be.(p.543)
• In my *late* teens I became aware of emotions I'd not counted on; restlessness, anxiety, fear and insecurity.(p.545)
• It was the *late* Dr. Tiebout, then, who persuaded me to seek help through A.A.(p.559)

lately

• It wasn't until just *lately* that, in your case, I could draw it.(p.436)

later

• *Later*, he requested the privilege of being allowed to tell his story to other patients here and with some misgiving, we consented.(p.xxv)
• One year *later* he called to see me, and I experienced a very strange sensation.(p.xxix)
• I discovered many more reasons *later* on.(p.2)
• In the early days of our drinking we occasionally remained sober for a year or more, becoming serious drinkers again *later*.(p.34)
• Only thirty years *later* the conquest of the air was almost an old story and airplane travel was in full swing.(p.52)
• But *later*, alone in his room, he asked himself this question: "Is it possible that all the religious people I have known are wrong?"(p.56)
• No *later* vicissitude has shaken it.(p.56)
• Sometimes they hurt us, seemingly without provocation, but we invariably find that at some time in the past we have made decisions based on self which *later* placed us in a position to be hurt.(p.62)
• You may spoil a *later* opportunity.(p.90)
• If he has trouble *later*, he is likely to say you rushed him.(p.95)
• Sooner or *later*, you are likely to find him reading the book once more.(p.113)
• Let's talk about it *later*."(p.118)
• Had they fired me first, and had they then taken steps to see that I was presented with the solution contained in this book, I might have returned to them six months *later*, a well man.(p.141)
• If you propose such a procedure to him, it may be necessary to advance the cost of treatment, but we believe it should be made plain that any expense will *later* be deducted from his pay.(p.143)
• Some time *later*, and just as he thought he was getting control of his liquor situation, he went on a roaring bender.(p.155)
• Two days *later*, a future fellow of Alcoholics Anonymous stared glassily at the strangers beside his bed.(p.157)
• A year and six months *later* these three had succeeded with seven more.(p.159)
• Impressed by those who visited him at the hospital, he capitulated entirely when, *later*, in an upper room of this house, he heard the story of some man whose experience closely tallied with his own.(p.160)
• Without this proof the expectant purchaser would be forced to depart empty handed with none of what I *later* came to believe was the great panacea for all human ills.(p.171)
• I found out *later* that my wife inspected it frequently.(p.176)
• Before my drinking had cut me down completely, I achieved a considerable measure of success, having been a City Councilman for five years and a financial director of Kenmore, a suburb *later* taken into the city itself.(p.182)
• *Later*, I realized that I was running from alcohol.(p.183)
• They came in and began to give me instruction in the program which *later* became known as Alcoholics Anonymous.(p.185)
• Looking in *later* we found Bill with his wife, Henrietta.(p.189)
• He wouldn't give me any money for the groceries, but he did take me across the street and buy me a bag of candy, which I *later* took back and traded for a loaf of bread.(p.193)
• Twenty-two years *later*, Doctor Bob told me that what I had done was like turning a switch and setting up a demand for more alcohol in my system.(p.195)
• I had to look in the telephone book *later* to find out who these people were.(p.196)
• At the end of this selling of lots, just prior to World War I, I got into the crude rubber business, and six months *later* there was only one broker and myself left in Akron.(p.197)
• I can well remember over a long period of years when I thought I was the only person in the world who knew that sooner or *later* I was going to get drunk.(p.198)
• Three days *later* I went to work.(p.205)
• I got two drinks, each of them a quarter of that pint, in me, and was talking along with these people, but I felt that sooner or *later* they were going to have me cornered because they were smarter than I was and the drink was beginning to take effect; but as I reached for the third drink Bob said, "Listen, Buster, you promised to take some medicine if we got you a drink.(p.206)
• A few minutes *later*, Dr. Bob left, leaving with my brother some medicine I should get.(p.207)
• A year *later*, after I completed the course in contracts, I quit the law school, and undertook some engineering work for a patent law firm on behalf of clients who were in difficulties and who desired to keep their troubles from their own engineering department.(p.212)
• It was not known to me as a group, but I *later* learned that my wife had known about it for nine months and had prayed constantly that I would stumble into Akron some way or another.(p.215)
• One evening I had gone out after dinner to take on a couple of double-headers and stayed a little *later* than usual, and when I came home Clarence was sitting on the davenport with Bill W.(p.216)
• He had already imbued them with his own spirit until they were ready and willing at all times to go where sent, and as a doctor he well knew that this mission and duty would strengthen them as it *later* helped me.(p.235)
• Had he come two or three days *later* I think I would have thrown him out, but he hit when I was open for anything.(p.239)
• This was my introduction to this "understanding fellowship" although it was to be more than a year *later* before our Society was to bear the name, Alcoholics Anonymous.(p.239)
• There were four of us children, and although both of my brothers *later* became alcoholic -- one died of alcoholism -- my sister has never taken a drink in her life.(p.240)
• Three years *later*, at twenty-five, I opened and operated their Philadelphia office and was earning more than I ever have since.(p.242)
• I was the fair-haired boy all right, but two years *later* I was blacklisted as an irresponsible drunk.(p.242)
• Oddly enough, the big shot who fired me from this company was one of the first men I met when I *later* joined the New York A.A. Group.(p.242)
• I re-organized their city sales policy and eighteen months *later*, when I was thirty, they offered me the branch managership.(p.243)
• No one in that company saw me again – ten days *later* I wired my resignation.(p.243)
• Much *later* I discovered the elders held many prayer meetings hoping to find a way to give me the heave-ho, but at the same time stay tolerant and spiritual.(p.247)
• Peddling off my polish samples for expenses, I crawled back to New York a few days *later* in a very chastened frame of mind.(p.248)
• In June, 1945, with another member, I made my first – and only – Twelfth Step call on a female alcoholic and a year *later* I married her.(p.249)

• Drifting back to Ohio, I landed on a small newspaper and *later* was impressed into the direction of boy-welfare work at the local "Y."(p.253)
• Some days *later*, after he had been discharged, a stranger came into my shop in the nearby town.(p.257)
• The time came just a week *later*.(p.258)
• Four months *later*, I married this guy.(p.262)
• I'd like to say here how important it was to us then that we do all the little things that people said were important, because *later* when Russ was so sick that I had to hold him up, they had a meeting out at the house.(p.270)
• A year *later* I was able to buy a Model T roadster and take a better job with a downtown printer.(p.276)
• Finally, and I shall never know how much *later* it was, one clear thought came to me: Try prayer.(p.280)
• An hour *later* I awoke to a new world.(p.280)
• With this specialized training, and a liberal business education in the school of hard knocks, I was able to set up shop some two years *later* as an independent accountant.(p.284)
• Instead, I quickly substituted one or another vivid scene from the nightmare of my *later* drinking.(p.286)
• Several months *later* dad was back in Chicago to pick me up again, but this time my attitude was entirely different.(p.289)
• A week *later*, I had to get an old friend from Akron to spend two days sobering me up.(p.293)
• A few months *later* one of the men who had been in touch with the group in Akron came to Chicago to live, and then there were three of us who continued to have informal meetings quite regularly.(p.294)
• I made arrangements to enter the hospital three days *later* and promptly went out and got stiff for three days.(p.302)
• First, through mutual pain and despair, and *later* through mutual objectives and new-found faith and hope.(p.312)
• Two years *later*, a month beyond age seventy, I was crying for help from A.A.(p.327)
• My guild had elected me president twice and *later* given me a "man of the year" award.(p.328)
• Three months *later*, he hated the game and found solace in the bottle.(p.330)
• Two nights *later*, self-pity went even further.(p.333)
• I did go to A.A., two days *later*, walking in alone.(p.334)
• About two days *later* I was called by a friend of mine from Nevada City -- he's a brother of my wife's closest friend.(p.347)
• At this time, however, she had an opportunity to go to Salt Lake City on a new project for the government, but she did promise me that if I would curtail my drinking and buckle down to hard work she would give serious consideration to my latest proposal and maybe join me at a *later* date when I got settled.(p.359)
• A few hours *later* I came out of a complete stupor in our living room with a flash of sanity.(p.363)
• *Later* I told her I had not taken the drink and that I was all right.(p.365)
• As I *later* found out through Alcoholics Anonymous, alcohol is no respecter of economic status, social and business standing or intelligence.(p.373)
• A year *later*, while we were on a vacation trip she packed up to go home because of my excessive drinking, and I talked her out of it with the promise I would go on the wagon for at least a year.(p.377)
• Two weeks *later* found me being sworn in, and the first payday in the Navy made me realize I had found a home.(p.398)
• He got half custody of our child, but *later* kept her during most of the school terms.(p.402)
• But I got drunk that night and stayed drunk, getting increasingly worse until I found A.A. ten years *later*.(p.404)
• Three years *later* I was discharged in the same way.(p.425)
• Two months *later* I was discharged.(p.428)
• Three days *later* I lost my job.(p.430)
• To be sure, I learned many fascinating things, and many things that were to prove helpful *later*.(p.434)
• *Later*, she would say, "You don't like me.(p.439)
• It wasn't until *later* that he told me he was an attorney.(p.446)
• *Later* on, it took alcohol fortified with other drugs to pull me up.(p.457)
• Still *later*, even alcohol and chemicals together could not lift me.(p.457)
• Four years *later*, I was taken to my first A.A. meeting out of prison, in Los Angeles.(p.460)
• The next recollection I have is of my husband coming into my room (*later* found out it was on New Year's Eve) accompanied by two policemen.(p.468)
• Then I black out and get home four days *later*.(p.475)
• Two weeks *later*, he come to A.A. meeting.(p.476)
• Year *later*, I go to Canada to carry message to Tall Man, but he not listen to son.(p.476)
• Two years *later*, my brother take Tall Man to first A.A. meeting.(p.476)
• A couple of years *later*, we lost our elder brother in a house fire, because of pills and booze.(p.480)
• *Later* on in life that took its toll.(p.483)
• After our first child came my parents both became allies, but in *later* days, after I became an alcoholic, they both turned against me.(p.485)
• A very good friend of mine who owned a drug store across the street from us, came by only about two hours *later* and said that he had seen Vi down town.(p.487)
• Nevertheless, I stayed sober there about six months, because I knew that Vi was to come *later* and bring the children.(p.490)
• It was around noon, a day or two *later*, when the telephone rang and it was Ella.(p.494)
• But I am to learn *later* that it began with my desire for material success becoming greater than my interest in the welfare of my fellow man.(p.507)
• When I wended my way home four days *later*, on the 27th, there was a detective waiting for me.(p.508)
• At first they were rather amusing, but a little *later* on they became serious.(p.513)
• I buttonholed him after dinner and gave him a few tips on how to run his colony better and the result of that was about a fortnight or so *later* I was shipped back to my regiment.(p.520)
• *Later*, I found out that I went into stores and stole clothes, then sold them.(p.528)
• There was the father one lost respect for at the age of eleven, because the father broke his solemn word in a circumstance where you, eleven years old, had assumed guilt when you were innocent; but the father would not believe you, no matter what; and to ease his suffering you "confessed" and were "forgiven," only -- months *later* -- to have your "guilt" brought up -- only he and you knew what he was talking bout -- brought up in front of the stern grandmother.(p.533)
• I was down to my shorts, unaware of wrong-doing, before the ambulance got there and hauled me off to a hospital from which anxious friends rescued me, *later* that night.(p.537)
• The reason, as I learned *later*, was that I had not worked for A.A.(p.539)
• From that instant to this, nearly eight years *later*, I have not had the slightest urge to drink.(p.541)
• It is going strong still, these eight years *later*, and some of its members have been of great influence for good in state-wide A.A. work.(p.541)
• Much *later*, when I had progressed to full-blown alcoholism, people told me I should quit.(p.554)
• *Later*, I went to sea, serving as a gunnery officer on a destroyer escort and emerging a lieutenant commander.(p.555)

latest

• This *latest* part of my life has had a purpose, not in great things accomplished but in daily living.(p.295)
• At this time, however, she had an opportunity to go to Salt Lake City on a new project for the government, but she did promise me that if I would curtail my drinking and buckle down to hard work she would give serious consideration to my *latest* proposal and maybe join me at a later date when I got settled.(p.359)
• Forgive me -- I cannot write further about this *latest* turn of events, anticipating seeing the family I deserted so long ago.(p.463)

latitude

• A reasonable amount of *latitude* will be helpful.(p.146)

latter

• I left the university in the *latter* part of my senior year and enlisted in the army.(p.183)
• During the *latter* part of the Christian Science experience I had gotten a job and was working at Firestone.(p.203)
• This change had been a long, slow process for me, but through these *latter* years the dividends have been tremendous.(p.249)
• Of course, the *latter* ultimately killed the former, but of this, more anon.(p.277)
• By the *latter* part of September 1939, we had a nucleus of six and held our first official group meeting.(p.310)

laugh

• I could *laugh* at the gin mills.(p.6)
• If you draw this fallacious reasoning to the attention of an alcoholic, he will *laugh* it off, or become irritated and refuse to talk.(p.23)
• We can *laugh* at those who think spirituality the way of weakness.(p.68)
• A man may criticize or *laugh* at himself and it will affect others favorably, but criticism or ridicule coming from another often produces the contrary effect.(p.125)
• But why shouldn't we *laugh*?(p.132)
• Everybody knows that those in bad health, and those who seldom play, do not *laugh* much.(p.132)
• At this both the visitors burst into a *laugh*.(p.157)
• Said the future Fellow Anonymous: "Damn little to *laugh* about that I can see."(p.157)
• And then he got us to *laugh*, which was what we needed.(p.269)
• When we went to bed my sides ached, and I said to my husband, "I thought I would never *laugh* again, but I have laughed."(p.269)
• Philosophy, faith, a sense of humor (they could *laugh* at themselves), clear-cut objectives, appreciation -- and most especially appreciation and sympathetic understanding for their fellow man.(p.310)
• I *laugh* at the insanity of it.(p.507)

laughed

• He succumbed to that gay crowd inside, who *laughed* at their own misfortunes and understood his.(p.160)
• Social distinctions, petty rivalries and jealousies -- these are *laughed* out of countenance.(p.161)
• And they both *laughed* very heartily, and said, "That's better than you've been doing, isn't it?"(p.187)
• When we went to bed my sides ached, and I said to my husband, "I thought I would never laugh again, but I have *laughed*."(p.269)
• She talked to me and *laughed* about it and got me all over it.(p.273)
• At a large party in Geneva, with people from many countries represented, the kind of party that is "protocol" in the extreme, I swayed, *laughed* hysterically, made naughty remarks in an unhushed voice, and was finally led from the scene.(p.406)
• Everyone *laughed* loudly.(p.498)

laughing

• I don't remember much of what he said, but I did realize that here was another guy exactly like me; he had been in the same *laughing* academies and the same jails, known the same loss of jobs, same frustrations, same boredom and the same loneliness.(p.239)
• Yet he was happy, relaxed, confident and *laughing*.(p.239)

laughter

• This is a condition which, in ordinary life, would produce untold grief; there might be scandalous gossip, *laughter* at the expense of other people, and a tendency to take advantage of intimate information.(p.125)
• So we think cheerfulness and *laughter* make for usefulness.(p.132)
• We can share in the *laughter* and tears of our many friends, and most important, we can share our A.A. way of life and are given a daily opportunity to help others.(p.249)
• They said I was so funny, and told me, with shrieks of *laughter*, what I'd done the night before.(p.407)
• Although we enjoyed the *laughter* in the early days, I heard a lot of things that I thought were stupid.(p.447)

launch

• I still had enough practice to earn a good living if I would only work, so I resolved that in January of 1940 I would *launch* a patent law firm of my own.(p.220)

launched

• Next we *launched* out on a course of vigorous action, the first step of which is a personal housecleaning, which many of us had never attempted.(p.63)
• Our hope is that when this chip of a book is *launched* on the world tide of alcoholism, defeated drinkers will seize upon it, to follow its suggestions.(p.153)

laundering

• Near the Laundromat, I would buy one bottle of pop and a few bottles of beer or wine, and go into the rest room, empty the pop bottle, refill it with the booze, and proceed to do my *laundering*.(p.370)

laundress

• With that, he told me to leave, because I was unfit as a mother, a wife, and a *laundress*.(p.371)

laundromat

• This secret drinker favored the local *Laundromat* as

a watering hole.(p.369)
• In my drinking days, I found the ideal spot for the alcoholic housewife: the neighborhood ***Laundromat***.(p.369)
• At the ***Laundromat***, I was undisturbed by barflies with questionable and unwanted intentions.(p.369)
• So that's when I discovered the ***Laundromat***.(p.370)
• Near the ***Laundromat***, I would buy one bottle of pop and a few bottles of beer or wine, and go into the rest room, empty the pop bottle, refill it with the booze, and proceed to do my laundering.(p.370)
• That way, I could spend most of my time at the ***Laundromat***!(p.371)
• I still wash clothes, lots of them, but I no longer lose them at the ***Laundromat***.(p.372)

laundry
• Now, she no longer risks losing her home, her self-respect, or her ***laundry***.(p.369)
• All this while, I wondered whether I could do ***laundry*** for the neighbors as a part-time job.(p.371)

laurels
• It is easy to let up on the spiritual program of action and rest on our ***laurels***.(p.85)

law
• I took a night ***law*** course, and obtained employment as investigator for a surety company.(p.2)
• I studied economics and business as well as ***law***.(p.2)
• Potential alcoholic that I was, I nearly failed my ***law*** course.(p.2)
• By the time I had completed the course, I knew the ***law*** was not for me.(p.2)
• How could there be so much of precise and immutable ***law*** and no intelligence?(p.10)
• But his venture wound up in a ***law*** suit and bogged down completely.(p.154)
• My wife, a Kentucky girl, came with me to Akron where I completed my course in ***law*** at the Akron ***Law*** School.(p.182)
• This experience sent me to ***law*** school where I went at night and which course I completed in less than three years, taking the highest state bar examinations and passing them.(p.212)
• The ***law*** school experience was not inspired by a desire to follow patent ***law***, which has been my profession since: I went to ***law*** school primarily to learn the ***law*** of contracts following my own experience with litigation.(p.212)
• A year later, after I completed the course in contracts, I quit the ***law*** school, and undertook some engineering work for a patent ***law*** firm on behalf of clients who were in difficulties and who desired to keep their troubles from their own engineering department.(p.212)
• This work consumed a period of about two-thirds of a year, and worked out successfully so I decided to follow patent ***law***.(p.212)
• I went back to ***law*** school, and doubled up on the courses because I was then approaching thirty years of age and I wanted to get through as quickly as possible.(p.212)
• I married when I was twenty-eight years old, and started in ***law*** school after I was married.(p.212)
• By the time I had completed ***law*** school I had picked up some experience in patent ***law***, for I remained with the patent ***law*** firm and worked too in Washington where they found that I was a capable infringement investigator.(p.213)
• I still had enough practice to earn a good living if I would only work, so I resolved that in January of 1940 I would launch a patent ***law*** firm of my own.(p.220)
• Shortly after I came to this conclusion, I was importuned by another well-known patent ***law*** firm to help them out on some trial work because their trial man had had a heart attack and had been forbidden to go into the courtroom.(p.220)
• Having regard for the ***law*** of the land, I resigned myself to the will of the national legislators and quit drinking altogether, not because I had found it harmful, but because I couldn't get what I was accustomed to drink.(p.232)
• Beer was too bulky and it couldn't be kept in a jug under the counter ready to be dumped when John ***Law*** came around.(p.233)
• And he further said that God could not accept me as a sincere follower of His Divine ***Law*** unless I was ready to be thoroughly honest about it.(p.236)
• By the ***law*** of averages, some efforts came out well.(p.331)
• This escapade also ended up in the clutches of the ***law***, and my friend was institutionalized for eight months.(p.354)
• I had had no brushes with the ***law***, though I should have had many.(p.379)
• Eighteen will be used as the starting point, because my drinking before was limited by age, the ***law***, and money.(p.397)
• Age and the ***law*** were still against me, but laws were not as strictly enforced in those days as they are now, and I discovered that as long as I had the green blood, there was always a way to get alcohol, either from a nondiscriminatory bartender or from an older friend who would be glad to purchase the joy juice for the privilege of sharing it.(p.397)
• I have seen that there is only one ***law***, the ***law*** of love, and there are only two sins; the first is to interfere with the growth of another human being, and the second is to interfere with one's own growth.(p.542)

laws
• Though none of these principles had the force of rules or ***laws***, they had become so widely accepted by 1950 that they were confirmed by our first International Conference held at Cleveland.(p.xix)
• My intellectual heroes, the chemists the astronomers, even the evolutionists, suggested vast ***laws*** and forces at work.(p.10)
• These tiny bodies are governed by precise ***laws***, and these ***laws*** hold true throughout the material world.(p.49)
• Age and the law were still against me, but ***laws*** were not as strictly enforced in those days as they are now, and I discovered that as long as I had the green blood, there was always a way to get alcohol, either from a nondiscriminatory bartender or from an older friend who would be glad to purchase the joy juice for the privilege of sharing it.(p.397)
• We went through two years of deadlock required by the English divorce ***laws***.(p.405)
• However, as time went on ***laws*** were enacted that reduced the sentence.(p.509)

lawyer
• Understand he was once a well-known ***lawyer*** in town, but just now we've got him strapped down tight."(p.156)
• On the third day the ***lawyer*** gave his life to the care and direction of his Creator, and said he was perfectly willing to do anything necessary.(p.158)
• He consented, however, to go the hospital, where he occupied the very room recently vacated by the ***lawyer***.(p.159)
• He now returned home, leaving behind his first acquaintance, the ***lawyer*** and the devil-may-care chap.(p.159)
• Early the next morning a man whose name I knew well, a ***lawyer***, called on me.(p.378)
• When I protested, his ***lawyer***, my ***lawyer***, and my third and last analyst had a conference.(p.409)

lawyers
• So I spent much of my time calling on the people who I felt would logically come in contact with alcoholic cases, doctors, ministers, ***lawyers*** and the personnel men in industry.(p.281)

lay
• While I ***lay*** in the hospital the thought came that there were thousands of hopeless alcoholics who might be glad to have what had been so freely given me.(p.14)
• "***Lay*** off the hard stuff."(p.20)
• We found that as soon as we were able to ***lay*** aside prejudice and express even a willingness to believe in a Power greater than ourselves, we commenced to get results, even though it was impossible for any of us to fully define or comprehend that Power, which is God.(p.46)
• We, who have traveled this dubious path, beg you to ***lay*** aside prejudice, even against organized religion.(p.49)
• Why ***lay*** ourselves open to being branded fanatics or religious bores?(p.77)
• Though there may be justifiable exceptions, and though we wish to ***lay*** down no rule of any sort, we have often found this the best course to take.(p.81)
• Never talk down to an alcoholic from any moral or spiritual hilltop; simply ***lay*** out the kit of spiritual tools for his inspection.(p.95)
• This may ***lay*** the groundwork for a friendly talk about his alcoholic problem.(p.111)
• Another time, as I opened a letter which ***lay*** on my desk, a newspaper clipping fell out.(p.136)
• They left this with me to think over, and I ***lay*** there on that hospital bed and went back over and reviewed my life.(p.186)
• Bill ***lay*** on his hospital bed and looked at us in wonder.(p.188)
• At that particular time, the boys put me on a shutter and took me out to the shed, and I ***lay*** in the car while they enjoyed their banquet.(p.195)
• Dr. Bob did not ***lay*** out the whole program.(p.218)
• I ***lay*** across the bed on my stomach with nothing but pain and sickness.(p.267)
• I used to think I was cowardly because when things came out pertaining to the program that troubled me, I said to her many times, "Annie, am I being a coward because I ***lay*** those things away on the shelf and skip it?"(p.273)
• I entered the business world with every confidence that success ***lay*** ahead of me.(p.275)
• I ***lay*** down on the bed and slept like a child.(p.280)
• His road ***lay*** clear before me, and I'd better quit rationalizing myself into any detours.(p.282)
• At any rate the last great step toward a well rounded life still ***lay*** ahead of me.(p.286)
• If I could ***lay*** off it, that meant I didn't have to worry about a drinking problem, I thought.(p.317)
• An alcoholic can't ***lay*** off the booze – right?(p.317)
• All the joys of retirement ***lay*** ahead for this movie publicist.(p.327)
• But the difference ***lay*** in the fact that the A.A.'s knew from their own bitter experience.(p.471)

laymen
• As ***laymen***, our opinion as to its soundness may, of course, mean little.(p.xxiv)

lays
• As each member of a resentful family begins to see his short comings and admits them to the others, he ***lays*** a basis for helpful discussion.(p.127)

lead
• We must take the ***lead***.(p.83)
• This may ***lead*** to lonely evenings for you.(p.111)
• Is it not because each wants to play the ***lead***?(p.122)
• In my cups I used to tell them off, giving them lengthy advice on how to ***lead*** the right life.(p.410)
• I remember finding myself in the middle of the night in the doctors' parking lot at the hospital with one foot in the car and one foot on the ground, not knowing which was the ***lead*** foot; finding myself hanging up the telephone – then realizing I had gotten out of bed, answered the phone, turned on the light, and carried on a conversation with a patient.(p.441)
• Yes, we find it rather confusing, but as we get around and get to know people in the group, they ***lead*** the way and all we have to do is to follow.(p.512)

leader
• I fancied myself a ***leader***, for had not the men of my battery given me a special token of appreciation?(p.1)
• My life there was a nightmare of periodic binges on alcohol and pills, adultery, unhappy hours at the dental office, seeing my wife give birth to our second child and have several miscarriages, living in a turbulent household, and making continual attempts to be the respectable dentist, husband, father, and community ***leader***.(p.419)
• I was married and divorced again before I was twenty-three years old, this time to a prominent band ***leader*** -- a man that many women wanted.(p.546)

leaders
• It was thought that no alcoholic man or woman could be excluded from our Society; that our ***leaders*** might serve but never govern; that each group was to be autonomous and there was to be no professional class of therapy.(p.xix)
• Business and financial ***leaders*** were my heroes.(p.2)
• Our ***leaders*** are but trusted servants; they do not govern.(p.564)
• All such representatives are to be guided in the spirit of service, for true ***leaders*** in A.A. are but trusted and experienced servants of the whole.(p.567)

leadership
• Would there be quarrels over membership, ***leadership*** and money?(p.xviii)
• My talent for ***leadership***, I imagined, would place me at the head of vast enterprises which I would manage with the utmost assurance.(p.1)
• While I went along with all that was done and attended the meetings, I never took an active job of ***leadership*** until February 1940.(p.249)
• Rotating ***leadership*** is the best.(p.567)

leading
• Many years ago one of the ***leading*** contributors to this book came under our care in this hospital and while here he acquired some ideas which he put into practical application at once.(p.xxv)
• In the prize ring, this would be called ***leading*** with the chin.(p.77)
• On account of my enormous capacity for beer, I was elected to membership in one of the drinking societies, and soon became one of the ***leading*** spirits.(p.173)
• After many painful discussions, they finally gave

me my credits and I migrated to another of the ***leading*** universities of the country and entered as a Junior that fall.(p.173)
• I'm not going; A.A. is ***leading*** me there.(p.340)
• It didn't take long for me to fall in with a fast crowd who had their lunch in the men's bar of a ***leading*** hotel.(p.361)
• But now I was a young divorcee, ***leading*** a Washington social life.(p.402)
• I was one of the star singers in the choir and one of the ***leading*** violins in the orchestra.(p.517)

leads
• It is plain that a life which includes deep resentment ***leads*** only to futility and unhappiness.(p.66)
• More than most people, the alcoholic ***leads*** a double life.(p.73)
• Show him the mental twist which ***leads*** to the first drink of a spree.(p.92)
• Never once in my life have I had a headache, which fact ***leads*** me to believe that I was an alcoholic almost from the start.(p.172)
• Even that first night I blacked out, which ***leads*** me to believe that I was an alcoholic from my very first drink.(p.241)
• I attended my weekly meetings with regularity, re-read the Big Book, attended other group meetings, gave ***leads*** when asked to and did some Twelve Step work whenever I was called upon to do so.(p.365)

league
• My wife was in the Junior ***League***, and I was on the board of directors of the local center for the mentally retarded.(p.418)

leak
• We hope our suggestions will help you plug up this sometimes serious ***leak***.(p.148)

leaning
• Perhaps we had been ***leaning*** too heavily on Reason that last mile and we did not like to lose our support.(p.53)
• I came to and found a man ***leaning*** over me.(p.405)
• My tweed suit, once a very good one, was shapeless and baggy with bare places worn in the elbows from ***leaning*** on the bar.(p.411)

leanings
• Get an idea of his behavior, his problems, his background, the seriousness of his condition, and his religious ***leanings***.(p.90)

leap
• Somehow I managed to drag my mattress to a lower floor, lest I suddenly ***leap***.(p.6)

leaped
• Two of them ***leaped*** from the table and crashed into my head.(p.427)

leaps
• While the internal difficulties of our adolescent period were being ironed out, public acceptance of A.A. grew by ***leaps*** and bounds.(p.xix)

leapt
• I read the book and God ***leapt*** at me from every page.(p.412)

learn
• It relieved me somewhat to ***learn*** that in alcoholics the will is amazingly weakened when it comes to combating liquor, though it often remains strong in other respects.(p.7)
• So it was comforting to ***learn*** that we could commence at a simpler level.(p.47)
• We have begun to ***learn*** tolerance, patience and good will toward all men, even our enemies, for we look on them as sick people.(p.70)
• Ministers and doctors are competent and you can ***learn*** much from them if you wish, but it happens that because of your own drinking experience you can be uniquely useful to other alcoholics.(p.89)
• But he will be curious to ***learn*** why his own convictions have not worked and why yours seem to work so well.(p.93)
• Some of us have taken very hard knocks to ***learn*** this truth: Job or no job – wife or no wife -- we simply do not stop drinking so long as we place dependence upon other people ahead of dependence on God.(p.98)
• We had to ***learn*** these things the hard way.(p.121)
• Whether your employee likes it or not, he will ***learn*** the grim truth about alcoholism.(p.144)
• You will ***learn*** the full meaning of "Love thy neighbor as thyself."(p.153)
• The law school experience was not inspired by a desire to follow patent law, which has been my profession since: I went to law school primarily to ***learn*** the law of contracts following my own experience with litigation.(p.212)
• I wanted to ***learn*** to stand on my own feet, not to change one prop for another, and an intangible and dubious one at that.(p.227)
• I was startled to ***learn*** he had only been off the booze a month or so himself when he brought me the message!(p.245)
• I was seeking something and I was ready to ***learn***.(p.258)
• Long before I had any real opportunity to give, I had to ***learn*** the equally important lesson of receiving graciously.(p.281)
• When I finally returned to Detroit to find work and to ***learn*** to stand on my own feet, the ball was already rolling, however slowly.(p.282)
• Because it was only through feeling defeat and feeling failure, the inability to cope with my life and with alcohol, that I was able to surrender and accept the fact that I had this disease, and that I had to ***learn*** to live again without alcohol.(p.335)
• I know now that I asked questions and told him what I wanted to ***learn***, but I told him only what I wanted to believe about myself.(p.388)
• My analyst was one of the first to ***learn*** of A.A. and to make subsequent use of it in her work.(p.412)
• How exciting to ***learn*** the inward mysteries that govern the behavior of people, how wonderful to know, at last, all about myself!(p.434)
• Then, one day in A.A., I was told that I had the lenses in my glasses backwards; "the courage to change" in the Serenity Prayer meant, not that I should change my marriage, but rather that I should change myself and ***learn*** to accept my spouse as she was.(p.451)
• There is really nothing to dressing with chains and shackles on, once you ***learn*** the technique of pulling inside-out pants through the shackles.(p.460)
• I shall ***learn*** this after some more explosions.(p.506)
• But I am to ***learn*** later that it began with my desire for material success becoming greater than my interest in the welfare of my fellow man.(p.507)
• I ***learn*** more of that foundation stone of character, which is honesty.(p.507)
• I ***learn*** that when we act upon the highest conception of honesty which is given us, our sense of honesty becomes more acute.(p.507)
• I ***learn*** that honesty is truth, and that truth shall make us free!(p.507)
• We must ***learn*** to walk before we can run.(p.516)
• To ***learn*** to live, he nearly died.(p.531)
• Sometimes we are told in A.A. not to try and ***learn*** the reasons for our drinking.(p.533)
• "Pity me the heart that is slow to ***learn*** What the quick mind sees at every turn."(p.534)
• I have had the joy of seeing many a human being, down and out, ***learn*** to stand straight again, and to proceed under his own power to happiness in life.(p.541)
• One of the truly great things A.A. has taught me is that reality too has two sides; I had only known the grim side before the program, but now I had a chance to ***learn*** about the pleasant side as well.(p.550)
• I've had many spiritual experiences since I've been in the program, many that I didn't recognize right away, for I'm slow to ***learn*** and they take many guises.(p.551)
• To do that, I had come to A.A. to ***learn*** how to handle sobriety -- which is what I could not handle in the first place.(p.554)
• For example, we are told in A.A. that we cannot afford resentments and self-pity, so we ***learn*** to avoid these festering mental attitudes.(p.560)
• We ***learn*** how to level out the emotional wings that got us into trouble both when we were up and when we were down.(p.560)

learned
• From this doctor, the broker had ***learned*** the grave nature of alcoholism.(p.xvi)
• If what we have ***learned*** and felt and seen means anything at all, it means that all of us, whatever our race, creed, or color are the children of a living Creator with whom we may form a relationship upon simple and understandable terms as soon as we are willing and honest enough to try.(p.28)
• We ***learned*** that we had to fully concede to our innermost selves that we were alcoholics.(p.30)
• I rather appreciated your ideas about the subtle insanity which precedes the first drink, but I was confident it could not happen to me after what I had ***learned***.(p.40)
• Well, just that did happen and more, for what I had ***learned*** of alcoholism did not occur to me at all.(p.42)
• In the preceding chapters you have ***learned*** something of alcoholism.(p.44)
• We have ***learned*** that whatever the human frailties of various faiths may be, those faiths have given purpose and direction to millions.(p.49)
• If we are sorry for what we have done, and have the honest desire to let God take us to better things, we believe we will be forgiven and will have ***learned*** our lesson.(p.70)
• But they had not ***learned*** enough of humility, fearlessness and honesty, in the sense we find it necessary, until they told someone else all their life story.(p.73)
• Tell him how baffled you were, how you finally ***learned*** that you were sick.(p.92)
• He found himself surprisingly well received, and ***learned*** that many knew of his drinking.(p.156)
• I ***learned*** that it was something of a spiritual nature, which did not appeal to me very much, but I thought it could do no harm.(p.178)
• I spend a great deal of time passing on what I ***learned*** to others who want and need it badly.(p.180)
• I'm so grateful for both the program and the people in it that I still want to go, and then probably the most wonderful thing that I ***learned*** from the program -- I've seen this in the 'A.A. Grapevine' a lot of times, and I've had people say it to me personally, and I've heard people get up in meetings and make the same statement: The statement is, "I came into A.A. solely for the purpose of sobriety, but it has been through A.A. that I have found God."(p.192)
• He did things much better than I did because he applied himself and ***learned*** how to do them, and I never applied myself.(p.194)
• It was not known to me as a group, but I later ***learned*** that my wife had known about it for nine months and had prayed constantly that I would stumble into Akron some way or another.(p.215)
• Back at camp, all was forgiven because it was the End, but in the light of what I have since ***learned*** I know I was a confirmed alcoholic at nineteen.(p.242)
• As long as things were tough and the job a challenge I could always manage to hold on pretty well, but as soon as I ***learned*** the combination, got the puzzle under control and the boss to pat me on the back, I was gone again.(p.243)
• Many alcoholics have ***learned*** they can bring their bottle to a cheap movie theater and drink, sleep, wake up and drink again in the darkness.(p.244)
• The doctor who came to see me almost at once did not assail me with any new doctrines; he made sure that I had a need and that I wanted to have that need filled, and little by little I ***learned*** how my need could be met.(p.258)
• I ***learned*** early in my A.A. life that I could not afford to fondle such thoughts, as you might fondle a pet, because this particular pet could grow into a monster.(p.285)
• He said he had finally ***learned*** that drinking was a fatal illness made up of an allergy plus an obsession, and once the drinking had passed from habit to obsession, we were completely hopeless, and could look forward only to spending the balance of our lives in mental institutions or to death.(p.290)
• The inevitable result of this discovery was that I soon ***learned*** that beer made a very good chaser for whiskey.(p.298)
• Then I ***learned*** something else.(p.300)
• I ***learned*** that a person just can't find a job hanging in a dive or barroom all day and all night, as jobs don't seem to turn up in those places.(p.300)
• But somehow my good doctor heard of this book and also he ***learned*** a little about the people responsible for its publication.(p.307)
• Many times have I heard the above expressions since I have been in A.A., and many times I have had to reply "Definitely I am an alcoholic, and while it may be hard for you to believe, it is not hard for me, for I have ***learned*** many things about alcohol and myself that would, perhaps, be difficult for you to understand."(p.356)
• However, what I had gained materially on the credit side of my ledger, I have since ***learned*** was more than offset on the debit side by egotism, resentment and dishonesty.(p.356)
• Neither of these circumstances was very helpful to my type since I had not ***learned*** to face realities.(p.358)
• In six years of worry, I hadn't ***learned*** anything.(p.387)
• I had ***learned*** an awful lot about myself in that one little article.(p.393)
• Even at that age, I had ***learned*** that one drink was not enough.(p.397)
• I ***learned*** how to hold a terrapin fork.(p.401)
• Now I had done some living but I hadn't ***learned*** a thing.(p.402)
• I had a tiny trust fund, and I moved into a small apartment where I ***learned*** to cook, keep house, and

do the things that normal people do.(p.409)
• I *learned* a whole new sense of values.(p.409)
• To be sure, I *learned* many fascinating things, and many things that were to prove helpful later.(p.434)
• I *learned* what a devastating effect it can have on a child to coddle him and build him up, and then turn and beat him savagely, as had happened to me.(p.434)
• It seems I should have *learned* to love my wife and family first; the newcomer to A.A., last.(p.451)
• Alcoholism had respected nobody, neither rich nor poor, *learned* nor unlettered.(p.455)
• Also, after that first visit I *learned* I could refuse to sign myself in unless they gave me a glass of whiskey in one hand and a glass of paraldehyde in the other.(p.468)
• I *learned* to pray honestly.(p.516)
• For you *learned* that he had been guilty of the thing he had accused you of, and his guilt had brought suffering to his entire family; and he thought he saw his young son beginning his own tragic pattern.(p.533)
• The reason, as I *learned* later, was that I had not worked for A.A.(p.539)
• I *learned* the true meaning of bread cast upon the waters.(p.541)
• I wasn't afraid of anything or anybody after I *learned* about drinking, for it seemed right from the beginning that with liquor I could always retire to my little private world where nobody could get at me to hurt me.(p.547)
• I thought I had *learned* my lesson.(p.558)
• I have *learned* how to relate to people; before A.A., I could never do that comfortably without alcohol.(p.559)
• I have *learned* to deal with disappointments and problems that once would have sent me right to the bottle.(p.559)

learning

• These work-outs should be regarded as part of your education, for thus you will be *learning* to live.(p.117)
• I have been *learning* something about alcoholism.(p.147)
• And I began putting into practice what I was *learning* every day.(p.237)
• In *learning* to practice these steps in my daily living I began to acquire faith and a philosophy to live by.(p.311)
• It was my husband, and he was *learning*, too.(p.371)
• Many times in the intervening years I have thanked God for that man, a man who had the courage to admit failure, a man who had the humility to confess that all the hard-won *learning* of his profession could not turn up the answer.(p.436)
• We can have this new way of life -- *learning* to live with our sickness and to be happy and content -- if we are willing to change our way of thinking and be honest, first with ourselves, then with others.(p.480)
• I am *learning* that I cannot have my own way as I used to.(p.505)
• By *learning* -- through practicing the Twelve Steps and through sharing at meetings -- how to cope with the problems that we looked to booze to solve, back in our drinking days.(p.560)
• *Learning* to depend upon a higher power and absorb himself in his work with other alcoholics, he remains sober day by day.(p.572)

learns

• In foreign parts many a soldier who has been abstemious at home *learns* to use new and potent drinks.(p.230)

least

• There was to be the *least* possible organization, even in our service centers.(p.xix)
• There is the manic-depressive type, who is, perhaps, the *least* understood by his friends, and about whom a whole chapter could be written.(p.xxviii)
• At *least*, so the chemist said.(p.54)
• We cannot be helpful to all people, but at *least* God will show us how to take a kindly and tolerant view of each and every one.(p.67)
• Wait for the end of the spree, or at *least* for a lucid interval.(p.90)
• When a discussion does arise, you might suggest he read this book or at *least* the chapter on alcoholism.(p.111)
• Why not at *least* afford him an opportunity to hear my story?(p.138)
• But at *least* he will understand the problem and will no longer be misled by ordinary promises.(p.148)
• We, who have collectively seen a great deal of business life, at *least* from the alcoholic angle, had to smile at this gentleman's sincere opinion.(p.149)
• I passed in at *least* three absolutely blank books.(p.174)
• I soon discovered that a couple of drinks would alleviate my gastric distress, at *least* for a few hours at a time, so it was not at all difficult for me to return to my former excessive indulgence.(p.174)
• By this time I was beginning to pay very dearly physically and, in hope of relief, voluntarily incarcerated myself at *least* a dozen times in one of the local sanitariums.(p.174)
• My phobia for sleeplessness demanded that I get drunk every night, but in order to get more liquor for the next night, I had to stay sober during the day, at *least* up to four o'clock.(p.177)
• It was not long before I was drinking at *least* a case and a half a day.(p.177)
• Each of the seven times that I had left this hospital in the last six months, I had come out fully determined in my own mind that I would not get drunk again -- for at *least* six or eight months.(p.184)
• I said, "Yes, Doc, I would like to quit, at *least* for five, six, or eight months, until I get things straightened up, and begin to get the respect of my wife and some other people back, and get my finances fixed up and so on."(p.187)
• I had contracted for half of it, at *least* verbally, and the contractors were taking half of the second mortgage bond.(p.198)
• I'd been sitting comfortably in a restaurant with Rita, drinking my sixth martini and hoping the waiter would forget about the lunch order -- at *least* long enough for me to have a couple more.(p.223)
• There was one meeting a week at Bill's home in Brooklyn, and we all took turns there spouting off about how we had changed our lives overnight, how many drunks we had saved and straightened out, and last, but not *least*, how God had touched each of us personally on the shoulder.(p.246)
• My brilliant agnosticism vanished, and I saw for the first time that those who really believed, or at *least* honestly tried to find a Power greater than themselves, were much more composed and contented than I had ever been, and they seemed to have a degree of happiness which I had never known.(p.247)
• For a long time the only Higher Power I could concede was the power of the group, but this was far more than I had ever recognized before, and it was at *least* a beginning.(p.248)
• They spent at *least* an evening a week in our home out there for weeks and weeks.(p.270)
• Russ lived a year longer than they expected him to live, and in that year he was in bed for at *least* six months.(p.272)
• At *least* three of those four years must have been a living hell for my wife, because she had to watch the man she loved disintegrate morally, mentally and financially.(p.277)
• I would at *least* have asked for a quarter!(p.289)
• One of them was that I would try to get a group started in Chicago; the second was that I would have to return to Akron to attend meetings at *least* every two months until I did get a group started in Chicago; third, I decided I must place this program above everything else, even my family, because if I did not maintain my sobriety I would lose my family anyway.(p.292)
• Well, at *least* I could drink myself to death.(p.333)
• A lucky break, at *least* some will call it lucky, was in store for me at my group that night.(p.365)
• A year later, while we were on a vacation trip she packed up to go home because of my excessive drinking, and I talked her out of it with the promise I would go on the wagon for at *least* a year.(p.377)
• He asked if I would cooperate with him after I went home, and if I would have a trained nurse stay with me for at *least* two weeks.(p.387)
• I took that treatment three times and it didn't work - - at *least*, for me.(p.389)
• A few stood by me, at *least* in their hearts, throughout the whole of my drinking career.(p.404)
• This was an Englishman who, at *least* at this time, drank as much as I did.(p.405)
• Why did I have to have at *least* three cocktails to sit through dinner?(p.406)
• They were doing very well -- at *least* a fifth apiece a day, except on dad's days off when they did some serious drinking.(p.425)
• And when I place more value on my serenity and sobriety than on anything else, I can maintain them at a higher level -- at *least* for the time being.(p.452)
• This easy method of sobering up would last at *least* three days.(p.468)
• I don't know whether it was right or wrong, but at *least* I know that people weren't thinking the same.(p.484)
• Anyhow, on the 24th, after drinking all day on the 23rd, I must have decided I wanted to see my wife and have some kind of reconciliation or at *least* talk with her.(p.491)
• A former employer of mine said to me a little over ten years ago, "Pat, you seem to be one of those unfortunate people who at *least* once every six months must go out and roll in the gutter."(p.513)
• Not *least* of my debts to A.A. is the knowledge that in that time when she wanted me most, I was there -- and that I wasn't drunk.(p.525)
• At *least*, my body went.(p.526)
• I hope I have been able to impart to you, the reader, at *least* a bit of what I know; the joy of living, the irresistible power of divine love and its healing strength, and the fact that we, as sentient beings, have the knowledge to choose between good and evil, and, choosing good, are made happy.(p.543)
• 9. -- Each A.A. group needs the *least* possible organization.(p.567)

leather

• They wanted me to make *leather* belts, of all things!(p.445)
• Had I gone to school all those years just to sit and make *leather* belts?(p.445)

leave

• How many times people have said to us: "I can take it or *leave* it alone.(p.20)
• They can take it or *leave* it alone.(p.20)
• This is the baffling feature of alcoholism as we know it -- this utter inability to *leave* it alone, no matter how great the necessity or the wish.(p.34)
• Fear of people and of economic insecurity will *leave* us.(p.84)
• Though you have talked with the family, *leave* them out of the first discussion.(p.91)
• If you *leave* such a person alone, he may soon become convinced that he cannot recover by himself.(p.96)
• We want to *leave* you with the feeling that no situation is too difficult and no unhappiness too great to be overcome.(p.104)
• Usually we did not *leave*.(p.106)
• If you are positive he is one of this type you may feel you had better *leave*.(p.108)
• Even though your husband becomes unbearable and you have to *leave* him temporarily, you should, if you can, go without rancor.(p.111)
• If he is lukewarm or thinks he is not an alcoholic, we suggest you *leave* him alone.(p.113)
• He has just returned from a three-months *leave* of absence, has taken a cure, looks fine, and to clinch the matter, the board of directors told him this was his last chance."(p.138)
• As a moderate drinker, you can take your liquor or *leave* it alone.(p.139)
• He and his wife would *leave* elated by the thought of what they could now do for some stricken acquaintance and his family.(p.160)
• I found, however, that when I would *leave* Akron to go to Chicago, I would get drunk.(p.197)
• The afternoon that I was to *leave* the hospital, he came in to see me and asked me if I were willing to attempt to follow the program.(p.218)
• Certainly, at that time I was one of those who "can take it or *leave* it alone."(p.231)
• My wife never hinted that she would *leave* me.(p.345)
• On more than one occasion my wife would threaten to *leave* me.(p.362)
• I was scared -- would she *leave* me again?(p.365)
• With that, he told me to *leave*, because I was unfit as a mother, a wife, and a laundress.(p.371)
• Or he would *leave* on a trip and by the time he came home, I'd be passed out.(p.386)
• He said that because of my drinking, he shouldn't *leave*, but that he had to go to New York for two weeks.(p.388)
• I got emergency *leave* for twenty days.(p.426)
• I tried to control her drinking by pouring her whiskey down the sink before I'd *leave* for the night, to get drunker myself.(p.426)
• Rather, I do whatever is in front of me to be done, and I *leave* the results up to Him; however it turns out, that's God's will for me.(p.452)
• We were on our way to New York where he planned to *leave* me with my sister.(p.466)
• When I was twenty-one, my cousin come home from U.S. Army on *leave*.(p.474)
• I rebelled against this, because just about the time that I was getting ready to *leave* high school, a revelation came to me about God and it made things very complicated for me.(p.489)
• I *leave* the room, which the honor system allows.(p.499)
• The game is over and the other three *leave*.(p.502)

• I pack my bag and *leave*.(p.505)
• At first, like everybody else, I could keep control when I drank, but if I did start to drink, even in those days, I was always one of the last to *leave* the party.(p.518)
• In part, it was a feeling of intense shame at having to *leave* the Army during the war, but mostly it was resentment that this kind of thing should happen to me for, strange as it may seem, up to then I still thought I could control drinking.(p.521)

leaves

• In our belief, any picture of the alcoholic which *leaves* out this physical factor is incomplete.(p.xxiv)
• The war *leaves* me with a pair of blankets, a toilet kit, a sweater knit by my sister, and a still greater inferiority.(p.499)
• "Then all of your troubles are over," says the man and *leaves* the room.(p.503)

leaving

• The broker had gone to Akron on a business venture which had collapsed, *leaving* him greatly in fear that he might start drinking again.(p.xvi)
• The exercise of an option brought in more money, *leaving* us with a profit of several thousand dollars for that year.(p.3)
• If anyone questions whether he has entered this dangerous area, let him try *leaving* liquor alone for one year.(p.34)
• On *leaving* the asylum he came into contact with us.(p.35)
• Within a week after *leaving* the hospital a fast-moving trolley car breaks his arm.(p.38)
• *Leaving* aside the drink question, they tell why living was so unsatisfactory.(p.51)
• He now returned home, *leaving* behind his first acquaintance, the lawyer and the devil-may-care chap.(p.159)
• We went into a bootleg joint and I don't remember *leaving* that place.(p.202)
• A few minutes later, Dr. Bob left, *leaving* with my brother some medicine I should get.(p.207)
• My parents died, both in the same year, *leaving* me, a sheltered and somewhat immature man, on my own.(p.277)
• Upon *leaving* the office in the evening, my first stop would be a saloon about a block away.(p.298)
• She offered me the alternative of going to see him or her *leaving* me for good and all.(p.301)
• There was one girl especially, and I'd watch her from my window every morning, *leaving* faithfully to go to the hospital in the neighborhood.(p.326)
• Her parting words were "I am not *leaving* you because I don't love you; it's because I do love you.(p.362)
• Looking directly at me was a large oil painting of my wife, and her very words seemed to shout at me -- "I am not *leaving* you because I don't love you; it's because I do love you.(p.363)
• That was on Saturday and my husband was *leaving* town Sunday night.(p.393)
• I have left my wife at home, sick, and I have been unkind to her in *leaving*.(p.505)
• My reaction to this was identical in many respects to my reaction to my parents *leaving* me when I was seven.(p.547)

lecture

• If he is in a serious mood dwell on the trouble liquor has caused you, being careful not to moralize or *lecture*.(p.91)
• We may have seemed to *lecture*.(p.121)
• If that is so we are sorry, for we ourselves don't always care for people who *lecture* us.(p.121)
• Next he can be assured that you do not intend to *lecture*, moralize, or condemn; that if this was done formerly, it was because of misunderstanding.(p.142)
• If there was a *lecture* on the subject within a hundred miles of Akron, I attended.(p.202)
• The next morning he came into my room and said, "Esther, I'm not going to *lecture* you any more, but I want you to read this article.(p.391)
• If the listener were drunk enough, the *lecture* might go on through several martinis, which I was glad to pay for.(p.537)
• Brandishing my "motto," which was "A little man with a stick is equal to a big man," sometimes I varied the literary *lecture* by a fight with a big man, selected solely because he was big and I was little.(p.537)

lectures

• That the man who is making the approach has had the same difficulty, that he obviously knows what he is talking about, that his whole deportment shouts at the new prospect that he is a man with a real answer, that he has no attitude of Holier Than Thou, nothing whatever except the sincere desire to be helpful; that there are no fees to pay, no axes to grind, no people to please, no *lectures* to be endured -- these are the conditions we have found most effective.(p.18)

led

• All of us felt at times that we were regaining control, but such intervals — usually brief — were inevitably followed by still less control, which *led* in time to pitiful and incomprehensible demoralization.(p.30)
• Time after time, this apparent calamity has been a boon to us, for it opened up a path which *led* to the discovery of God.(p.116)
• His call to the clergyman *led* him presently to a certain resident of the town, who, though formerly able and respected, was then nearing the nadir of alcoholic despair.(p.155)
• The circumstances under which I reached these people were very odd because I was *led* there through things that I said when I couldn't even remember speaking.(p.202)
• The times in which I grew up (the Prohibition era immortalized by Scott Fitzgerald and John Held Jr.) had taught me to be gay with the gayest; my own inner urges *led* me to outdo them all.(p.225)
• The strain of overwork *led* me to the bottle again.(p.254)
• There was a young fellow who *led* the meeting and that was a beautiful thing to me.(p.270)
• This first meeting was held in the living room of a home and was *led* by Bill D., the first man that Bill W. and Dr. Bob had worked with successfully.(p.291)
• Dr. Bob *led* me through all of these steps.(p.292)
• Dr. Bob then *led* me through the restitution step, in which I made a list of all of the persons I had harmed, and worked out ways and means of slowly making restitution.(p.292)
• My work with other alcoholics has *led* me, day by day, into ever wider and richer experiences.(p.394)
• At a large party in Geneva, with people from many countries represented, the kind of party that is "protocol" in the extreme, I swayed, laughed hysterically, made naughty remarks in an unhushed voice, and was finally *led* from the scene.(p.406)
• From a Canadian reservation to overseas bars to New England lockups, an Indian traveled a long trail that finally *led* him home to A.A.(p.474)
• I'm grateful because that Higher Power *led* me to A.A. a little over three years ago, when I needed it very badly.(p.512)
• The mental twists that *led* up to my drinking began many years before I ever took a drink for I am one of those whose history proves conclusively that my drinking was "a symptom of a deeper trouble."(p.544)
• A.A. *led* me gently from this fantasizing to embrace reality with open arms.(p.561)

ledger

• However, what I had gained materially on the credit side of my *ledger*, I have since learned was more than offset on the debit side by egotism, resentment and dishonesty.(p.356)

left

• Therefore, the first portion of this volume, describing the A.A. recovery program, has been *left* untouched in the course of revisions made for both the second and the third editions.(p.xi)
• To me he was a stranger, and so he *left* me.(p.xxix)
• He had plenty of money *left* and thought I had better go to Canada.(p.4)
• When, therefore, we were approached by those in whom the problem had been solved, there was nothing *left* for us but to pick up the simple kit of spiritual tools laid at our feet.(p.25)
• But here is a man who at fifty-five years found he was just where he had *left* off at thirty.(p.33)
• Were nothing *left* but pure reason, it wouldn't be life.(p.54)
• The family may feel they hold a mortgage on dad, so big that no equity should be *left* for outsiders.(p.131)
• He *left* us a note saying you were the best boss he ever had, and that you were not to blame in any way."(p.136)
• During these two years I was kept so busy that I hardly *left* the hospital at all.(p.174)
• We entered her house at exactly five o'clock and it was eleven fifteen when we *left*.(p.179)
• I *left* the university in the latter part of my senior year and enlisted in the army.(p.183)
• Each of the seven times that I had *left* this hospital in the last six months, I had come out fully determined in my own mind that I would not get drunk again -- for at least six or eight months.(p.184)
• They *left* this with me to think over, and I lay there on that hospital bed and went back over and reviewed my life.(p.186)
• When they got through the day's work, part was *left* which I proceeded to drink.(p.196)
• At the end of this selling of lots, just prior to World War I, I got into the crude rubber business, and six months later there was only one broker and myself *left* in Akron.(p.197)
• A few minutes later, Dr. Bob *left*, leaving with my brother some medicine I should get.(p.207)
• When he *left*, I realized from his story that as a drinker I was just a panty-waist.(p.208)
• When I *left* the hospital I tried this for a day and it worked, for a week and it worked, and for a month, and it worked — and then for a year and it still worked.(p.209)
• I never *left* the church, but I was a fringe member, and the thought simply never occurred to me that through the exercise of what I had I might find the answer to my problem, simply because I wouldn't admit that I had a problem.(p.214)
• In fact, as I look back, I have often thought that they probably concluded that they would put up with me for a couple of years, that I couldn't live much longer, and that they would inherit whatever was *left* of the practice.(p.215)
• We drove my car and I *left* it down in the yard.(p.217)
• Bill *left* me at the elevator and said, "Your room is so and so," and I didn't see him again for six months.(p.217)
• I did not know there was such a thing as group activity until I *left* the hospital.(p.218)
• I *left* on a Wednesday afternoon, had dinner in Akron and then went to a house where I encountered my first meeting.(p.218)
• I found in the fall of 1939, that I was not mentally impaired, so far as trial work was concerned, and thereafter took up where I had *left* off when I was about forty-five years old.(p.220)
• All I had *left* was an iron determination to live my own life in spite of the alien world -- and here I was, an inwardly frightened, outwardly defiant woman, who desperately needed a prop to keep going.(p.226)
• To go into a gathering of people was the sort of thing that all my life, from the time I *left* my private world of books and dreams to meet the real world of people and parties and jobs, had *left* me feeling an uncomfortable outsider, needing the warming stimulus of drinks to join in.(p.228)
• I had repaired to one of these one morning with my jug and when I *left* late in the afternoon, I picked up a newspaper on the way home.(p.244)
• Returning to the town I had *left* three months before, I became editor of a monthly magazine, soon had additional publicity and advertising accounts and the money rolled in.(p.254)
• A friend who knew I would soon be broke mounted guard over me when I *left* my job of writing the histories of Texas cities and put me aboard a bus for the town I had *left* almost five years before.(p.256)
• I *left* the hospital on a meeting night.(p.259)
• Finally, it got so bad that I *left* him and went back home and took my two children with me.(p.262)
• As we *left*, and they were escorting us across the bridge into Wheeling, I, with great dignity and sarcasm, told them if their wives were ever visiting in Akron, and they, too, were looking for their route sign as I was, that I hoped I could extend to them the hospitality that had been shown to me in Bellaire.(p.264)
• Fear froze me in my tracks, but the instant I turned back toward home this paralyzing fear *left* me.(p.276)
• When she finally took the baby and *left*, I locked myself in the house and stayed drunk for a month.(p.278)
• Those three weeks *left* me completely exhausted and I had to return to Akron for three more months of rest.(p.282)
• After I *left* school, I went to work in Akron, living at home with my parents.(p.287)
• If I did not maintain my sobriety, I would have no friends *left*.(p.293)
• When I came home again, the only thing I had *left* to love was the bottle.(p.318)
• On the last day I was drinking I went up to see a friend who had had a good deal of trouble with alcohol, and whose wife had *left* him a number of times.(p.346)
• She *left*, and I sat down and crossed my hands, and looked up and said, "For God's sake, help me."(p.351)
• After another of my "never again episodes" she packed up and *left* for her parents' home in Florida.(p.362)
• It *left* us dazed, because he had seemed so indestructible.(p.370)

• After his death, my mother soon picked up drinking where Dad *left* off, and in a very short time she died of cirrhosis of the liver.(p.370)
• A few months after that, I was released and *left* the world of insanity, only to return to the world of alcoholic insanity.(p.370)
• The following spring she *left* me one day without giving me any idea of where she had gone, hoping this would bring me to my senses.(p.377)
• Frank *left* to find the doctor and I got drunk.(p.387)
• There was nothing else *left* to try.(p.389)
• I couldn't walk, having it in a cast, and the doctor *left* the cast on three weeks longer than was necessary because he never found me sober enough to take it off.(p.390)
• When he *left* I thought, what is this crack-pot thing?(p.391)
• So Frank *left* town, and by Monday morning I had been sober for that whole week.(p.393)
• I had a drunken quarrel with my family, denounced them, and *left* them forever.(p.409)
• I planned to stay home the night before I *left*, but my folks got so drunk I walked off early in the evening and spent the night with my girl, getting very drunk myself.(p.425)
• I seldom *left* the base any more except once in a while when I felt the need of talking to some girl.(p.427)
• Sometimes I'd make it home and go to sleep at the wheel of my car, for all the neighbors to see next morning as they *left* for work.(p.429)
• She cried a bit and went to bed; that was the only answer to problems that she had *left*.(p.440)
• When the compulsion to drink *left*, it was relatively easy to stay off alcohol.(p.448)
• I *left* California and came back to my native state.(p.460)
• The doctor, apparently realizing that one thing that I certainly needed was sleep, *left* a bottle of sleeping pills there and in my drunken state I took them all, instead of the one or two he had prescribed.(p.465)
• On one occasion when I was serving time in my favorite drying-out place while I was having a session with the psychiatrist, she *left* my case history on her desk when she was called away from the room.(p.470)
• As an indication of just how confused and mixed up I was, just as soon as I could I *left* the office and hurried around to tell other patients that I was getting better.(p.470)
• That my own innate selfishness and stubbornness are the evils which, if *left* unguarded, can drive me to alcohol.(p.473)
• Being an alcoholic, slick, and having some good sense *left*, I survived the investigation.(p.490)
• Then I *left* and went home to bed.(p.492)
• After the trial, I got big-hearted again and felt that I should do something in payment for Vi's kindness to me; so I *left* Washington and went to Seattle to work.(p.492)
• Finally, I broke the last one hundred dollar bill the Saturday before I *left*.(p.493)
• When he *left* I walked with him to the streetcar line, which was just about a half a block, but there were two liquor stores, one on each corner from my home.(p.495)
• I put Charlie on the car and when I *left* him I passed both of those liquor stores without even thinking about them.(p.495)
• She had looked for me last evening after I *left* the car and wandered off into the night.(p.502)
• I have *left* my wife at home, sick, and I have been unkind to her in leaving.(p.505)
• Why has God *left* me?(p.506)
• He finally passed away, and the fear of him *left* me.(p.508)
• I got married to the girl I'd *left* behind.(p.513)
• I *left* because I had a contretemps with the Governor.(p.520)
• I stayed there just long enough to work up a real good resentment against the doctor in charge, who I didn't think was doing anything at all except collecting fees, and I *left* there fully determined that I'd never put myself in the power of medical people again.(p.521)
• When I arrived back in Dublin, I had no friends *left*.(p.522)
• My only hope was to try and get through what was *left* of life as best I could, but I could never visualize doing that without drinking.(p.522)
• I *left* this home town, then, after I had made a public spectacle of myself in the presence of a revered teacher whose favorite pupil I had been.(p.539)
• I choose to believe that the Power greater than ourselves we ask for help, wrapped my shivering body in loving warmth and strength which has never *left* me.(p.541)

leg
• The doctor motioned to the corpsman to undo my straitjacket and *leg* restraints.(p.422)
• But when I cracked my *leg* with a sixteen-pound sledgehammer in the rock hole, I was fighting the system, using my body.(p.458)

leg-work
• Following a big drunk on that sheet, where I was doing *leg-work* and rewrite, a feeling of nostalgia made me buy a ticket for Liverpool and I returned to Britain.(p.252)

legally
• After I came to A.A., I was divorced by my wife; I lost my practice; I was *legally* restrained from seeing my children; I went broke; and the dental society threatened me with the loss of my license.(p.420)

legions
• These stark and ugly facts have been confirmed by *legions* of alcoholics throughout history.(p.24)

legislators
• Having regard for the law of the land, I resigned myself to the will of the national *legislators* and quit drinking altogether, not because I had found it harmful, but because I couldn't get what I was accustomed to drink.(p.232)

legitimate
• So our rule is not to avoid a place where there is drinking, if we have a *legitimate* reason for being there.(p.101)

legs
• We are like men who have lost their *legs*; they never grow new ones.(p.30)
• He tells you he has decided to stop jay-walking for good, but in a few weeks he breaks both *legs*.(p.38)
• I cut my hands, my face, my *legs*.(p.427)
• Why, I wasn't even ashamed of my skinny *legs*!(p.498)

leisure
• Since the radio station was getting on its feet, it didn't require so many nights of evening work, and that permitted *leisure* time for drinking.(p.360)

leisure-world
• Many retirees embrace alcoholism while secluded in motor trailers, rest homes, *leisure-world* bungalows, mountain cabins, or beach cottages, or even in penthouses, on yachts, and inside Palm Springs cabanas.(p.329)

leisurely
• I went to my hotel and *leisurely* dressed for dinner.(p.41)

lemon
• It didn't say I had to finally live on skid row and drink bay rum, canned heat or *lemon* extract.(p.379)

lend
• We agnostically inclined would not feel satisfied with a proposal which does not *lend* itself to reasonable approach and interpretation.(p.53)
• If he shows interest, *lend* him your copy of this book.(p.94)
• This practice enables us to *lend* a hand, at the same time avoiding certain alluring distractions of the road, about which any traveling man can inform you.(p.162)
• I had even borrowed money from her, over her protest: "Bob, please don't ask me to *lend* you money -- you're the only one who hasn't."(p.540)
• Six -- An A.A. group ought never endorse, finance or *lend* the A.A. name to any related facility or outside enterprise, lest problems of money, property and prestige divert us from our primary purpose.(p.564)

lending
• Cleaning up old scrapes, helping to settle family differences, explaining the disinherited son to his irate parents, *lending* money and securing jobs for each other, when justified -- these are everyday occurrences.(p.161)

length
• If you have decided you want what we have and are willing to go to any *length* to get it -- then you are ready to take certain steps.(p.58)
• Reminding ourselves that we have decided to go to any *length* to find a spiritual experience we ask that we be given strength and direction to do the right thing, no matter what the personal consequences may be.(p.79)
• While you need not discuss your husband at *length*, you can quietly let your friends know the nature of his illness.(p.115)
• If this presents difficulty, re-reading chapters two and three, where the alcoholic sickness is discussed at *length* might be worth while.(p.140)
• At *length* peace stole over him and he slept.(p.189)
• I managed to maintain myself with odd jobs, did ten weeks in a social rescue institution, and at *length* wound up in a second-hand bookstore in an adjacent town as manager.(p.257)
• Dr. Bob dwelt at *length* on how prayer had given him release, time and time again, from the nearly overpowering compulsion to take a drink.(p.279)
• We went over these at great *length* and then he finally asked me if I wanted these defects of character removed.(p.292)

lengths
• Remember it was agreed at the beginning we would go to any *lengths* for victory over alcohol.(p.76)
• She of course didn't realize how cunning an alcoholic can be and the *lengths* to which he will go in finding ways to satisfy the compulsion for more and more drinks after having had the first one.(p.377)

lengthy
• Now my drinking was limited by only one factor, the enforced periods of dryness caused by *lengthy* tours at sea.(p.398)
• In my cups I used to tell them off, giving them *lengthy* advice on how to lead the right life.(p.410)

lenses
• Then, one day in A.A., I was told that I had the *lenses* in my glasses backwards; "the courage to change" in the Serenity Prayer meant, not that I should change my marriage, but rather that I should change myself and learn to accept my spouse as she was.(p.451)

lent
• Not try no drinks for *Lent* or for life.(p.476)
• India *lent* itself to drinking then, if you were disposed to drink, because you lived in bungalows; you didn't live all together as you do at home in an Officer's Mess.(p.519)

less
• He had also been greatly helped by the late Dr. William D. Silkworth, a New York specialist in alcoholism who is now accounted no *less* than a medical saint by A.A. members, and whose story of the early days of our Society appears in the next pages.(p.xvi)
• Seven percent of the A.A.'s surveyed are *less* than 30 years of age -- among them, many in their teens.(p.xxii)
• He is always more or *less* insanely drunk.(p.21)
• The great fact is just this, and nothing *less*: That we have had deep and effective spiritual experiences which have revolutionized our whole attitude toward life, toward our fellows and toward God's universe.(p.25)
• All of us felt at times that we were regaining control, but such intervals -- usually brief -- were inevitably followed by still *less* control, which led in time to pitiful and incomprehensible demoralization.(p.30)
• Several of our crowd, men of thirty or *less*, had been drinking only a few years, but they found themselves as helpless as those who had been drinking twenty years.(p.33)
• Fred would not believe himself an alcoholic, much *less* accept a spiritual remedy for his problem.(p.39)
• Their chances are *less* than average.(p.58)
• Established on such a footing we became *less* and *less* interested in ourselves, our little plans and designs.(p.63)
• We are then in much *less* danger of excitement, fear, anger, worry, self-pity, or foolish decisions.(p.88)
• He becomes still *less* communicative.(p.126)
• He will be *less* likely to drink again, and anything is preferable to that.(p.130)
• The *less* people tolerated us, the more we withdrew from society, from life itself.(p.151)
• From childhood through high school I was more or *less* forced to go to church, Sunday School and evening service, Monday night Christian Endeavor and sometimes to Wednesday evening prayer meeting.(p.172)
• During all this time we became more or *less* ostracized by our friends.(p.177)
• I drank nine martinis in *less* than an hour.(p.195)
• This experience sent me to law school where I went at night and which course I completed in *less* than three years, taking the highest state bar examinations and passing them.(p.212)
• But each drink after the "first" seemed to become *less* effective and after three or four they all seemed like water.(p.241)
• The second year my drinking was more or *less* restricted to week-ends, but I was nearly kicked out for scholastic failure.(p.241)

• Very rarely do I miss the meetings of my neighborhood A.A. group, and my average has never been ***less*** than two meetings a week.(p.249)
• The next two years were simply a long drawn out process of ***less*** and ***less*** work and more and more whiskey.(p.278)
• In fifteen seconds or ***less***, the feeling passed.(p.285)
• Saying these sprees were limited to one a week (they were not), and saying that the average spree was ten of these drinks (sometimes more, sometimes ***less***), we come up with the first boring statistic: two-fifty per week out of twelve dollars.(p.397)
• Couldn't I drink ***less***?(p.404)
• I must drink ***less***, I would tell myself.(p.408)
• These things were carried out in moments of ***less*** severe hangover or short stretches on the wagon.(p.409)
• In ***less*** than two years, I lost my practice, my home, my wife, and my children.(p.418)
• Evening cocktails were as standard as morning coffee, and I suppose my average daily consumption ran a little more or ***less*** than a pint.(p.433)
• I was paroled when I had served ***less*** than three years.(p.462)
• The poorest person has no ***less*** and the wealthiest has no more – each of us has but one day.(p.473)
• He went into the religious side and told me that I didn't attend church as regularly as I should, and that he felt, more or ***less***, that this was responsible for my trouble.(p.489)
• For me, it was a little different because I couldn't help thinking about the past, and I saw the future more or ***less*** mirrored in the past.(p.513)
• I belonged to one of the Irish families who, more or ***less*** traditionally, sent their boys to the British armies.(p.517)
• I should say there was ***less*** drinking in the Army than I thought at that time.(p.518)
• I had been using paraldehyde more or ***less*** like ordinary drink for the last six years though, occasionally, I'd bounce back to phenobarbital and things like that.(p.524)
• The ***less*** you think of yourself the more of a person you become.(p.542)
• I was the only person I'd ever known personally who had ever been in jail, and I guess it is most significant that the second time was ***less*** humiliating that the first had been.(p.549)

lessen

• The slightest sign of fear or intolerance may ***lessen*** your husband's chance of recovery.(p.120)
• This would ***lessen*** my chances of smuggling some home that evening, which in turn would mean a night of futile tossing around in bed followed by a morning of unbearable jitters.(p.176)
• Her influence and companionship managed to ***lessen*** my drinking to some degree.(p.359)

lessened

• Then that terrible tension which grips the home of every problem drinker will be ***lessened***.(p.115)

lesson

• This case contains a powerful ***lesson***.(p.33)
• If we are sorry for what we have done, and have the honest desire to let God take us to better things, we believe we will be forgiven and will have learned our ***lesson***.(p.70)
• The ***lesson*** of his death still remains with me, yet I often wonder what would have happened if somebody else had made that first call on me.(p.239)
• The next time vacation time rolled around that was a bitter ***lesson*** to us.(p.265)
• Long before I had any real opportunity to give, I had to learn the equally important ***lesson*** of receiving graciously.(p.281)
• That was my ***lesson***, that one could not take the moral inventory and then file it away; that the alcoholic has to continue to take inventory every day if he expects to get well and stay well.(p.293)
• It taught me a valuable ***lesson***.(p.294)
• I thought I had learned my ***lesson***.(p.558)

lessons

• This was where I started my first drinking ***lessons***.(p.402)

lest

• I hardly dared cross the street, ***lest*** I collapse and be run down by an early morning truck, for it was scarcely daylight.(p.6)
• Somehow I managed to drag my mattress to a lower floor, ***lest*** I suddenly leap.(p.6)
• But we must try to repair the damage immediately ***lest*** we pay the penalty by a spree.(p.99)
• Six – An A.A. group ought never endorse, finance or lend the A.A. name to any related facility or outside enterprise, ***lest*** problems of money, property and prestige divert us from our primary purpose.(p.564)

let

• If any feel that as psychiatrists directing a hospital for alcoholics we appear somewhat sentimental, ***let*** them stand with us a while on the firing line, see the tragedies, the despairing wives, the little children; ***let*** the solving of these problems become a part of their daily work, and even of their sleeping moments, and the most cynical will not wonder that we have accepted and encouraged this movement.(p.xxvi)
• But drinking caught up with me again and my generous friend had to ***let*** me go.(p.4)
• But bless his heart, ***let*** him rant!(p.9)
• Yet ***let*** him drink for a day, and he frequently becomes disgustingly and even dangerously anti-social.(p.21)
• ***Let*** us tell you the rest of the conversation our friend had with his doctor.(p.27)
• If anyone questions whether he has entered this dangerous area, ***let*** him try leaving liquor alone for one year.(p.34)
• ***Let*** us take another illustration.(p.39)
• ***Let*** him tell you about it: "I was much impressed with what you fellows said about alcoholism, and I frankly did not believe it would be possible for me to drink again.(p.40)
• ***Let*** us make haste to reassure you.(p.46)
• Do not ***let*** any prejudice you may have against spiritual terms deter you from honestly asking yourself what they mean to you.(p.47)
• ***Let*** us have a look at some of them.(p.48)
• That was natural, but ***let*** us think a little more closely.(p.53)
• Some of us have tried to hold on to our old ideas and the result was nil until we ***let*** go absolutely.(p.58)
• Instead we ***let*** Him demonstrate, through us, what He can do.(p.68)
• Counsel with persons is often desirable, but we ***let*** God be the final judge.(p.69)
• If we are sorry for what we have done, and have the honest desire to ***let*** God take us to better things, we believe we will be forgiven and will have learned our lesson.(p.70)
• Are we now ready to ***let*** God remove from us all the things which we have admitted are objectionable?(p.76)
• If we still cling to something we will not ***let*** go, we ask God to help us be willing.(p.76)
• ***Let*** us be reassured.(p.76)
• Arranging the best deal we can we ***let*** these people know we are sorry.(p.78)
• It may be that both will decide that the way of good sense and loving kindness is to ***let*** by-gones be by-gones.(p.82)
• It is easy to ***let*** up on the spiritual program of action and rest on our laurels.(p.85)
• On awakening ***let*** us think about the twenty-four hours ahead.(p.86)
• So we ***let*** God discipline us in the simple way we have just outlined.(p.88)
• Then ***let*** his family or a friend ask him if he wants to quit for good and if he would go to any extreme to do so.(p.90)
• ***Let*** the doctor, if he will, tell him he has something in the way of a solution.(p.91)
• If he wishes to talk, ***let*** him do so.(p.91)
• ***Let*** him draw his own conclusion.(p.92)
• ***Let*** him ask you that question, if he will.(p.93)
• ***Let*** him see that you are not there to instruct him in religion.(p.93)
• If you do stay, ***let*** him steer the conversation in any direction he likes.(p.95)
• Sometimes a new man is anxious to proceed at once, and you may be tempted to ***let*** him do so.(p.95)
• ***Let*** it go at that.(p.95)
• ***Let*** him know you are available if he wishes to make a decision and tell his story, but do not insist upon it if he prefers to consult someone else.(p.96)
• ***Let*** the alcoholic continue his program day by day.(p.99)
• ***Let*** no alcoholic say he cannot recover unless he has his family back.(p.99)
• ***Let*** your friends know they are not to change their habits on your account.(p.102)
• Don't ***let*** him get away with it.(p.108)
• Is it right to ***let*** him ruin your life and the lives of your children?(p.108)
• ***Let*** him see that you want to be helpful rather than critical.(p.111)
• ***Let*** him decide for himself.(p.113)
• In some cases it may be better to ***let*** someone outside of the family present the book.(p.113)
• While you need not discuss your husband at length, you can quietly ***let*** your friends know the nature of his illness.(p.115)
• Whenever possible, ***let*** your husband explain.(p.115)
• Live and ***let*** live is the rule.(p.118)
• ***Let*** families realize, as they start their journey, that all will not be fair weather.(p.122)
• They are all disappointed, and often ***let*** him feel it.(p.126)
• ***Let*** them praise his progress.(p.127)
• ***Let*** them remember that his drinking wrought all kinds of damage that may take long to repair.(p.127)
• Though the family does not fully agree with dad's spiritual activities, they should ***let*** him have his head.(p.129)
• Even if he displays a certain amount of neglect and irresponsibility towards the family, it is well to ***let*** him go as far as he likes in helping other alcoholics.(p.129)
• So ***let*** each family play together or separately, as much as their circumstances warrant.(p.132)
• In time they will see that he is a new man and in their own way they will ***let*** him know it.(p.134)
• Live and ***Let*** Live(p.135)
• But ***let*** him tell you:(p.136)
• In case he does stumble, even once, you will have to decide whether to ***let*** him go.(p.147)
• You might ***let*** them know you have no quarrel with the alcoholics of your organization.(p.147)
• The expression on the faces of the women, that indefinable something in the eyes of the men, the stimulating and electric atmosphere of the place, conspired to ***let*** him know that here was haven at last.(p.160)
• Your Heavenly Father will never ***let*** you down!(p.181)
• After a while, Bill said, "Well, now, you've been talking a good long time, ***let*** me talk a minute or two."(p.185)
• In fact, I admitted that from now on I was willing to ***let*** God take over, instead of me.(p.187)
• I looked so terrible in the court that the judge suggested that I get a continuance and ***let*** me sign all the papers to go to a hospital and to a doctor.(p.204)
• And at the end of fourteen days, they ***let*** me out.(p.205)
• The next day, they called me in for an examination, and the doctor wouldn't ***let*** me continue working and pardoned me from the plant for ten days because he said my eye had been injured.(p.205)
• In any case I must get out of here before I ***let*** slip my abysmal ignorance of how I came to be here, and she realized that I was stark, staring mad.(p.223)
• Searching where I have been at fault, it is not hard to discover and get right again, for I have proven to myself and to many others who know me that God can keep a man sober if he will ***let*** Him.(p.237)
• That night for the first time in my life I really ***let*** down my hair and admitted my general loneliness.(p.239)
• I ***let*** mine sit.(p.247)
• I ***let*** that sit, too.(p.247)
• He took his one hundred and seventeen dollars and ***let*** us go, and we proceeded.(p.264)
• One of our gifts from the family was a very lovely Bible, but we'd ***let*** the bulldog chew it because we weren't too interested in it.(p.268)
• At that time they didn't ***let*** us know that people ever had trouble.(p.271)
• Please ***let*** me turn it over to you."(p.280)
• She decided she wouldn't ***let*** herself go in her drinking.(p.321)
• But I wasn't happy, and I didn't ever ***let*** myself go in my drinking.(p.323)
• I must live and ***let*** live.(p.325)
• I could ***let*** down the bars.(p.329)
• That ***let*** me out.(p.332)
• A.A. has not ***let*** me down there.(p.334)
• And he said, "Earle, why don't you come on over and ***let*** me talk to you for a minute."(p.348)
• But then he said, "***Let*** me say something to you.(p.348)
• I was certainly a complete surprise when I arrived at her family's home, but because I arrived on the wings of a tropical hurricane there wasn't much she could do but ***let*** me in.(p.364)
• I had not only ***let*** my wife down but also a lot of other wonderful people who had helped me.(p.364)
• Of course, more than anything else I had ***let*** myself down, but I didn't realize how much then – as I do now.(p.364)
• When I was nineteen, I married a fine man who had never known an insecure moment in his life, ***let*** alone

the trials and tribulations of booze.(p.369)

• I woke up in this bare room with nothing around me but bars; they wouldn't ***let*** me smoke and treated me, well, like I was nuts.(p.387)

• So the doctor ***let*** me go home on one condition.(p.387)

• After all, upon coming out of a week-long or ten-day drunk, it was hard enough to figure up just how much that one drunk cost, ***let*** alone trying to calculate the cost of approximately twenty-five years of active alcoholism.(p.396)

• A friend of Marty's, another A.A. ***let*** me in.(p.413)

• Gradually consciousness returned enough to ***let*** me know I was in a hospital.(p.422)

• I still think dad paid him something to ***let*** me go.(p.424)

• So I raised enough fuss that they finally agreed to ***let*** me sign out, against medical advice.(p.444)

• But it quickly became obvious that he had this childish notion instead: If he could get me to go to enough meetings while in the hospital, I would continue to go after he ***let*** me out.(p.447)

• The people of A.A. had something that looked much better than what I had, but I was afraid to ***let*** go of what I had in order to try something new; there was a certain sense of security in the familiar.(p.448)

• Same thing when I ***let*** lye and water eat away at four of my toes and my foot for five hours.(p.458)

• I would rather talk about the good things A.A. has taught me; I feel that hitting on just a few sordid points should be sufficient to ***let*** those of you in institutions know where I came from.(p.459)

• I say, "Just ***let*** it happen."(p.477)

• ***Let*** group spirit of love and understanding protect you.(p.477)

• She asked me if I would ***let*** someone come up and talk to me concerning a business deal.(p.494)

• "***Let*** your light so shine before men that they may see your good works –."(p.497)

• I could not ***let*** him think I was a sissy.(p.498)

• Before I step out and do anything, I stop and check it over first, and then ***let*** my conscience be my guide.(p.516)

• An ambitious playwright, he ***let*** his brains get so far ahead of his emotions that he collapsed into suicidal drinking.(p.531)

• I started to cross out that last sentence, but decided to ***let*** it stand.(p.536)

• When the policeman released me to my stupefied and exasperated friend at four in the morning, I went to my traveling bag and groped until I found – well, ***let*** the officer speak: "Ah," said the policeman, "he's got anuder pair, t'ank God!"(p.538)

• It had provided me with excuses for my lack of education, my marital failures, personal failures, inadequacy, and of course, my alcoholism and, though I really thought I had been willing to part with it, now I knew I was reluctant to ***let*** it go.(p.552)

• We feel it better to ***let*** our friends recommend us.(p.567)

<u>let's</u>

• As a celebrated American statesman put it, "***Let's*** look at the record."(p.50)

• ***Let's*** look at Steps Eight and Nine.(p.76)

• ***Let's*** now go back to husband number one.(p.110)

• ***Let's*** talk about it later."(p.118)

• Wishing to be polite, though I felt very badly, I said, "***Let's*** make the call," and extracted from my wife a promise that we would not stay over fifteen minutes.(p.179)

• They said, "***Let's*** forget about those other things, that is, trying to eliminate them all at once, and concentrate on the drink."(p.190)

• He said, "***Let's*** put the Big Book away again, and when you read it again, turn to the back and read some of the stories.(p.269)

• ***Let's*** look at the record."(p.322)

• To keep it in round figures, ***let's*** say twenty per cent of my income went for giggle gurgles.(p.397)

<u>lethargy</u>

• In a vague way their families and friends sense that these drinkers are abnormal, but everybody hopefully awaits the day when the sufferer will rouse himself from his ***lethargy*** and assert his power of will.(p.23)

<u>lets</u>

• Spiritually . . . I found a Friend who never ***lets*** me down and is ever eager to help.(p.303)

<u>letter</u>

• A well-known doctor, chief physician at a nationally prominent hospital specializing in alcoholic and drug addiction, gave Alcoholics Anonymous this ***letter***.(p.xxiii)

• The physician who at our request, gave us this ***letter***, has been kind enough to enlarge upon his views in another statement which follows.(p.xxiv)

• Some people cannot be seen – we send them an honest ***letter***.(p.83)

• Another time, as I opened a ***letter*** which lay on my desk, a newspaper clipping fell out.(p.136)

• I was active and did well, however, in school publications, dramatics (which came in handy during my drinking career), and Greek ***letter*** societies.(p.357)

• I was shaking so, I asked my husband to write the ***letter*** for me, but he said no.(p.392)

• So I wrote this ***letter*** in very shaky handwriting, and in just one week came back a ***letter*** with A.A. literature from New York.(p.392)

• They sent me the regular ***letter*** they send to everybody else, but along with it, Ruth Hock, the nonalcoholic secretary, wrote a longhand note because she could see from the ***letter*** that I really needed help badly.(p.392)

• The ***letter*** from A.A. had said this man would see me -- there weren't any women.(p.393)

• About three months after that, my record reached home and I got a ***letter*** telling me I was retired from the Army, they put it very kindly, on medical grounds.(p.521)

• If you cannot find A.A. in your locality, a ***letter*** addressed to Alcoholics Anonymous, Box 459, Grand Central Station, New York, NY 10163, U.S.A., will receive a prompt reply from this world center, referring you to the nearest A.A. group.(p.575)

<u>letters</u>

• I couldn't stomach religion, and I didn't like the mention of God or any of the other capital ***letters***.(p.227)

• And I'd try, but I couldn't even see the ***letters***.(p.268)

• Of course I kept her posted on how well the station was doing and wrote convincing ***letters*** of how well I was doing with the liquor problem.(p.360)

• They wrote me many long ***letters*** about it.(p.427)

• Meanwhile the ***letters*** from home were telling about how much my folks wanted to make up to me for some of the things I'd missed.(p.427)

• I'd reply and some of my ***letters*** they saved.(p.427)

• Much of my time was spent writing ***letters***, notes, orders, and lists of things for Max, who was also my office nurse, to do to keep the world running while I was locked up.(p.445)

• When I had heard about it, it meant nothing but just two ***letters*** to me, but some friends of mine in the institution were very active in the program and really believed in it.(p.509)

<u>letting</u>

• Sometimes saying very little, but ***letting*** us say.(p.271)

• ***Letting*** go of everything at once was both painful and terrifying.(p.311)

• That life for me is lived one day at a time, ***letting*** the problems of the future rest with the future.(p.340)

• I talked the Old Man into ***letting*** me live in the photo lab instead of the barracks, and for eighteen months nothing interfered with my drinking.(p.426)

• And life keeps getting simpler and easier as we try to reverse my old idea, by taking care of the internal environment via the Twelve Steps, and ***letting*** the external environment take care of itself.)(p.446)

<u>level</u>

• It was decided that all members ought to be anonymous at the ***level*** of press, radio, TV and films.(p.xix)

• Then he had, in effect, been raised from the dead, suddenly taken from the scrap heap to a ***level*** of life better than the best he had ever known!(p.11)

• So it was comforting to learn that we could commence at a simpler ***level***.(p.47)

• My work is on a much deeper and more significant ***level*** than it ever was before, and I am today a fairly creative, relatively sane human being.(p.438)

• I took more through the day to increase the high, and more to maintain it; when I overshot the mark, I'd take tranquilizers to ***level*** off.(p.442)

• I can watch my serenity ***level*** rise when I discard my expectations.(p.452)

• But then my "rights" try to move in, and they, too, can force my serenity ***level*** down.(p.452)

• And when I place more value on my serenity and sobriety than on anything else, I can maintain them at a higher ***level*** -- at least for the time being.(p.452)

• I must keep my magic magnifying mind on my acceptance and off my expectations, for my serenity is directly proportional to my ***level*** of acceptance.(p.452)

• To create: Everyone does it, some at the instinct ***level***, others in the arts.(p.535)

• We learn how to ***level*** out the emotional wings that got us into trouble both when we were up and when we were down.(p.560)

• Eleven -- Our public relations policy is based on attraction rather than promotion; we need always maintain personal anonymity at the ***level*** of press, radio and films.(p.564)

<u>leveling</u>

• Almost none of us liked the self-searching, the ***leveling*** of our pride, the confession of shortcomings which the process requires for its successful consummation.(p.25)

<u>leveling-off</u>

• For the ***leveling-off*** process, I just loved intravenous Demerol, but I found it hard to practice good medicine while shooting morphine.(p.442)

<u>levity</u>

• I suppose some would be shocked at our seeming worldliness and ***levity***.(p.16)

<u>liabilities</u>

• As we shall see, he now means a great deal to his community, and the major ***liabilities*** of thirty years of hard drinking have been repaired in four.(p.156)

<u>liable</u>

• We must lose our fear of creditors no matter how far we have to go, for we are ***liable*** to drink if we are afraid to face them.(p.78)

<u>liberal</u>

• With nothing but a ***liberal*** arts education, very definitely estranged from my family and already married, soon after graduation from college I became a bookmaker's clerk on the British racing circuits, far better off financially than the average professional man.(p.251)

• With this specialized training, and a ***liberal*** business education in the school of hard knocks, I was able to set up shop some two years later as an independent accountant.(p.284)

<u>liberation</u>

• But in most fields our generation has witnessed complete ***liberation*** of our thinking.(p.52)

• Yet we had been seeing another kind of flight, a spiritual ***liberation*** from this world, people who rose above their problems.(p.55)

• Acceptance was his key to ***liberation***.(p.439)

<u>liberty</u>

• In the fall of 1939, Fulton Oursler, then editor of ***Liberty***, printed a piece in his magazine, called "Alcoholics and God."(p.xviii)

• It was a small town – ***Liberty***, Indiana.(p.262)

<u>librarians</u>

• Loading a car with good old books to sell to collectors, ***librarians***, universities and historical societies, I started out to travel the country.(p.255)

<u>license</u>

• I still had a wife and family, a home and a car, my driver's ***license***, and a proper amount of insurance.(p.327)

• I lost my driver's ***license***, was made a ward of the court, and was put on probation (not to mention the fact that I might have killed three friends and myself).(p.354)

• After I came to A.A., I was divorced by my wife; I lost my practice; I was legally restrained from seeing my children; I went broke; and the dental society threatened me with the loss of my ***license***.(p.420)

<u>licensed</u>

• I am a physician, ***licensed*** to practice in a western state.(p.345)

<u>lick</u>

• So I didn't have a beer one night, and as I drove home I was breaking my arm patting myself on the back because I had proved I could ***lick*** liquor.(p.203)

• So I told dad that I would ***lick*** it on my own, that I would drink nothing for a month and after that only beer.(p.289)

• I used to like to get it on my fingers so I could ***lick*** them and get another taste.(p.346)

<u>licked</u>

• They grinned, which I didn't like so much, and then asked me if I thought myself alcoholic and if I were really ***licked*** this time.(p.42)

• After drinking one glass of beer at the end of my work period for about five days, I thought I'd better find out whether I really had the stuff ***licked***.(p.203)

• So having ***licked*** it, there was no reason why I shouldn't have a drink, and I stopped in before I got home and had one.(p.203)

• Lots of times, vain-gloriously, I used to take the bottle out, look at it and say, "I've got you ***licked***."(p.253)

• Finally, one morning, I got up and got in the car and cried all the way down to the M.'s -- the people who owned the bar – and told her I was

licked and wanted help.(p.267)
• I was completely ***licked*** by alcohol.(p.290)
• I was ***licked***.(p.340)
• For the second time, I was ***licked***.(p.340)
• But this second time, I found I couldn't live normally without it, and I was ***licked*** worse than ever.(p.340)
• But as I came out of this second bout with D.T.'s I knew I was ***licked***.(p.429)

licking
• I reasoned I was not so far advanced as most of you fellows, that I had been usually successful in ***licking*** my other personal problems, and that I would therefore be successful where you men failed.(p.40)

lie
• What with our ultra-modern standards, our scientific approach to everything, we are perhaps not well equipped to apply the powers of good that ***lie*** outside our synthetic knowledge.(p.xxv)
• Your desire to protect him should not cause you to ***lie*** to people when they have a right to know where he is and what he is doing.(p.115)
• The most satisfactory years of your existence ***lie*** ahead.(p.152)
• Away from my office two or three weeks at a time; horrible days and nights when I would ***lie*** on the floor of my home, lying awake and reaching over to get the bottle, taking a drink and going back into oblivion.(p.184)
• Sometimes I would ***lie*** on the bathroom floor, deathly sick, praying I would die, and praying to God as I always had prayed to Him when I was drinking: "Dear God, get me out of this one and I'll never do it again."(p.324)
• I had thrown off a big ***lie*** that had been burdening me down for months.(p.366)
• I had nowhere else to go, and I knew something was terribly wrong, and the reason had to ***lie*** within myself.(p.371)
• I didn't feel I could ***lie*** in bed and squirt the stuff in my veins while my kids and wife stood around watching me, so I kept the drug in my bag and the bag in the car and the car in the garage.(p.442)
• I thought that was bad until I hit the hole at a prison camp; it was just wide enough and long enough to ***lie*** down in.(p.459)
• Then a change in management took place in the regiment and the new O.C. didn't like me very much and I didn't like him, and he started to ***lie*** in wait for me.(p.519)
• He didn't have to ***lie*** in wait very long, but fortunately by that time, I had acquired friends upstairs and they covered me for quite a time.(p.519)
• And yet my ability to ***lie*** outwardly and to kid myself inwardly grew with every drink I took.(p.556)
• Dr. Harry M. Tiebout, psychiatrist: "As a psychiatrist, I have thought a great deal about the relationship of my specialty to A.A. and I have come to the conclusion that our particular function can very often ***lie*** in preparing the way for the patient to accept any sort of treatment or outside help.(p.571)

lied
• I ***lied*** like a trooper to get out of many scrapes.(p.324)
• "Once in a while," I ***lied***.(p.498)

lies
• "Here ***lies*** a Hampshire Grenadier Who caught his death Drinking cold small beer.(p.1)
• A much more important demonstration of our principles ***lies*** before us in our respective homes, occupations and affairs.(p.19)
• We have told innumerable ***lies*** to protect our pride and our husbands' reputations.(p.105)
• He mentioned ***lies*** and deceptions in the course of his story in the presence of the one person in the world I wouldn't want to know such things.(p.302)
• The insane asylum ***lies*** ahead.(p.502)
• The only importance in all of this ***lies*** in the fact that at twenty-three I was just as sick as I was at thirty three, when I came into A.A., but at that time I apparently had no place to go because I had no drinking problem.(p.546)

lieutenant
• After training, I was commissioned as a first ***lieutenant***.(p.342)
• Later, I went to sea, serving as a gunnery officer on a destroyer escort and emerging a ***lieutenant*** commander.(p.555)

life
• It did not satisfy us to be told that we could not control our drinking just because we were maladjusted to ***life***, that we were in full flight from reality, or were outright mental defectives.(p.xxiv)
• To them, their alcoholic ***life*** seems the only normal one.(p.xxvi)
• He had lost everything worthwhile in ***life*** and was only living, one might say, to drink.(p.xxix)
• I was part of ***life*** at last, and in the midst of the excitement I discovered liquor.(p.1)
• Drink was taking an important and exhilarating part in my ***life***.(p.3)
• I was to know happiness, peace, and usefulness, in a way of ***life*** that is incredibly more wonderful as time passes.(p.8)
• Then he had, in effect, been raised from the dead, suddenly taken from the scrap heap to a level of ***life*** better than the best he had ever known!(p.11)
• For if an alcoholic failed to perfect and enlarge his spiritual ***life*** through work and self-sacrifice for others, he could not survive the certain trials and low spots ahead.(p.14)
• He could not, or would not, see our way of ***life***.(p.16)
• But not so with the alcoholic illness, for with it there goes annihilation of all the things worth while in ***life***.(p.18)
• But we saw that it really worked in others, and we had come to believe in the hopelessness and futility of ***life*** as we had been living it.(p.25)
• The great fact is just this, and nothing less: That we have had deep and effective spiritual experiences which have revolutionized our whole attitude toward ***life***, toward our fellows and toward God's universe.(p.25)
• We were in a position where ***life*** was becoming impossible, and if we had passed into the region from which there is no return through human aid we had but two alternatives: One was to go on to the bitter end, blotting out the consciousness of our intolerable situation as best we could; and the other, to accept spiritual help.(p.25)
• A new ***life*** has been given us or, if you prefer, "a design for living" that really works.(p.28)
• All went well for a time, but he failed to enlarge his spiritual ***life***.(p.35)
• We have not lost everything in ***life*** through drinking and we certainly do not intend to.(p.38)
• He was positive that his humiliating experience, plus the knowledge he had acquired, would keep him sober the rest of his ***life***.(p.40)
• I have since been brought into a way of living infinitely more satisfying and, I hope, more useful than the ***life*** I lived before.(p.42)
• My old manner of ***life*** was by no means a bad one, but I would not exchange its best moments for the worst I have now.(p.43)
• But after a while we had to face the fact that we must find a spiritual basis of ***life*** – or else.(p.44)
• If a mere code of morals or a better philosophy of ***life*** were sufficient to overcome alcoholism, many of us would have recovered long ago.(p.44)
• When, however, the perfectly logical assumption is suggested that underneath the material world and ***life*** as we see it, there is an All Powerful, Guiding, Creative Intelligence, right there our perverse streak comes to the surface and we laboriously set out to convince ourselves it isn't so.(p.49)
• Were our contentions true, it would follow that ***life*** originated out of nothing, and proceeds nowhere.(p.49)
• People of faith have a logical idea of what ***life*** is all about.(p.49)
• We never gave the spiritual side of ***life*** a fair hearing.(p.50)
• Once confused and baffled by the seeming futility of existence they show the underlying reasons why they were making heavy going of ***life***.(p.50)
• Imagine ***life*** without faith!(p.54)
• Were nothing left but pure reason, it wouldn't be ***life***.(p.54)
• But we believed in ***life*** -- of course we did.(p.54)
• We could not prove ***life*** in the sense that you can prove a straight line is the shortest distance between two points, yet, there it was.(p.54)
• Being convinced, we were at Step Three, which is that we decided to turn our will and our ***life*** over to God as we understood Him.(p.60)
• The first requirement is that we be convinced that any ***life*** run on self-will can hardly be a success.(p.60)
• ***Life*** will be wonderful.(p.61)
• He begins to think ***life*** doesn't treat him right.(p.61)
• Next, we decided that hereafter in this drama of ***life***, God was going to be our Director.(p.62)
• More and more we became interested in seeing what we could contribute to ***life***.(p.63)
• As we felt new power flow in, as we enjoyed peace of mind, as we discovered we could face ***life*** successfully, as we became conscious of His presence, we began to lose our fear of today, tomorrow or the hereafter.(p.63)
• Take away my difficulties, that victory over them may bear witness to those I would help of Thy Power, Thy Love, and Thy Way of ***life***.(p.63)
• It is plain that a ***life*** which includes deep resentment leads only to futility and unhappiness.(p.66)
• In this way we tried to shape a sane and sound ideal for our future sex ***life***.(p.69)
• But they had not learned enough of humility, fearlessness and honesty, in the sense we find it necessary, until they told someone else all their ***life*** story.(p.73)
• More than most people, the alcoholic leads a double ***life***.(p.73)
• He had commenced our way of ***life***, had secured a position, and was getting his head above water.(p.79)
• The spiritual ***life*** is not a theory.(p.83)
• Our whole attitude and outlook upon ***life*** will change.(p.84)
• Or were we thinking of what we could do for others, of what we could pack into the stream of ***life***?(p.86)
• We do not tire so easily, for we are not burning up energy foolishly as we did when we were trying to arrange ***life*** to suit ourselves.(p.88)
• ***Life*** will take on new meaning.(p.89)
• The family should be offered your way of ***life***.(p.97)
• And even though he continues to drink, the family will find ***life*** more bearable.(p.97)
• The wife should fully understand his new way of ***life***.(p.99)
• While you were drinking, you were withdrawing from ***life*** little by little.(p.102)
• Now you are getting back into the social ***life*** of this world.(p.102)
• Keep on the firing line of ***life*** with these motives and God will keep you unharmed.(p.102)
• Is it right to let him ruin your ***life*** and the lives of your children?(p.108)
• It is possible to have a full and useful ***life***, though your husband continues to drink.(p.111)
• But sometimes you must start ***life*** anew.(p.114)
• If such women adopt a spiritual way of ***life*** their road will be smoother.(p.114)
• We have elsewhere remarked how much better ***life*** is when lived on a spiritual plane.(p.116)
• A better way of ***life*** will emerge when they are overcome.(p.117)
• You, as well as your husband, ought to think of what you can put into ***life*** instead of how much you can take out.(p.120)
• You will lose the old ***life*** to find one much better.(p.120)
• We never, never try to arrange a man's ***life*** so as to shield him from temptation.(p.120)
• Is he not unconsciously trying to see what he can take from the family ***life*** rather than give?(p.122)
• Today's ***life*** is measured against that of other years and, when it falls short, the family may be unhappy.(p.123)
• Henry Ford once made a wise remark to the effect that experience is the thing of supreme value in ***life***.(p.124)
• Showing others who suffer how we were given help is the very thing which makes ***life*** seem so worth while to us now.(p.124)
• Cling to the thought that, in God's hands, the dark past is the greatest possession you have -- the key to ***life*** and happiness for others.(p.124)
• This is a condition which, in ordinary ***life***, would produce untold grief; there might be scandalous gossip, laughter at the expense of other people, and a tendency to take advantage of intimate information.(p.125)
• He may either plunge into a frantic attempt to get on his feet in business, or he may be so enthralled by his new ***life*** that he talks or thinks of little else.(p.125)
• He may tell mother, who has been religious all her ***life***, that she doesn't know what it's all about, and that she had better get his brand of spirituality while there is yet time.(p.128)
• He may not see at once that he has barely scratched a limitless lode which will pay dividends only if he mines it for the rest of his ***life*** and insists on giving away the entire product.(p.129)
• He will perceive that his spiritual growth is lopsided, that for an average man like himself, a spiritual ***life*** which does not include his family obligations may not be so perfect after all.(p.129)
• We have found nothing incompatible between a powerful spiritual experience and a ***life*** of sane and happy usefulness.(p.130)

• Father, coming suddenly to *life* again, often begins to assert himself.(p.131)
• At the very beginning, the couple ought to frankly face the fact that each will have to yield here and there if the family is going to play an effective part in the new *life*.(p.131)
• We absolutely insist on enjoying *life*.(p.132)
• We cannot subscribe to the belief that this *life* is a vale of tears, though it once was just that for many of us.(p.133)
• Among many employers nowadays, we think of one member who has spent much of his *life* in the world of big business.(p.136)
• Being somewhat weakened, and faced with physical and mental readjustment to a *life* which knows no alcohol, he may overdo.(p.146)
• Being on a radically different basis of *life*, he will never take advantage of the situation.(p.146)
• He will appreciate knowing you are not bothering your head about him, that you are not suspicious nor are you trying to run his *life* so he will be shielded from temptation to drink.(p.146)
• We, who have collectively seen a great deal of business *life*, at least from the alcoholic angle, had to smile at this gentleman's sincere opinion.(p.149)
• It is joyous intimacy with friends and a feeling that *life* is good.(p.151)
• There was an insistent yearning to enjoy *life* as we once did and a heartbreaking obsession that some new miracle of control would enable us to do it.(p.151)
• The less people tolerated us, the more we withdrew from society, from *life* itself.(p.151)
• He cannot picture *life* without alcohol.(p.152)
• Some day he will be unable to imagine *life* either with alcohol or without it.(p.152)
• But am I to be consigned to a *life* where I shall be stupid, boring and glum, like some righteous people I see?(p.152)
• *Life* will mean something at last.(p.152)
• Then you will know what it means to give of yourself that others may survive and rediscover *life*.(p.153)
• Suppose now that through you several families have adopted this way of *life*.(p.153)
• But *life* was not easy for the two friends.(p.156)
• On the third day the lawyer gave his *life* to the care and direction of his Creator, and said he was perfectly willing to do anything necessary.(p.158)
• These men had found something brand new in *life*.(p.159)
• In addition to these casual get-togethers, it became customary to set apart one night a week for a meeting to be attended by anyone or everyone interested in a spiritual way of *life*.(p.159)
• But *life* among Alcoholics Anonymous is more than attending gatherings and visiting hospitals.(p.161)
• When a few men in this city have found themselves, and have discovered the joy of helping others to face *life* again, there will be no stopping until everyone in that town has had his opportunity to recover -- if he can and will.(p.163)
• Never once in my *life* have I had a headache, which fact leads me to believe that I was an alcoholic almost from the start.(p.172)
• My whole *life* seemed to be centered around doing what I wanted to do, without regard for the rights, wishes, or privileges of anyone else; a state of mind which became more and more predominant as the years passed.(p.172)
• My home *life* is ideal and my business is as good as can be expected in these uncertain times.(p.180)
• He kept the faith; therefore, he and countless others found a new *life*.(p.182)
• They left this with me to think over, and I lay there on that hospital bed and went back over and reviewed my *life*.(p.186)
• That continued through my entire *life*.(p.193)
• (I might say right here that never in my *life* did I ever intend to get drunk.(p.196)
• I agreed with him and told him in no uncertain terms that I never broke my word in my *life*.(p.206)
• I'll never forget, he never even hesitated and I had never seen him before in my *life*.(p.207)
• I remember well one fellow, Joe, walking nearly three miles through slush, wet and snow to come to the hospital to see a man that he had never seen before in his *life*, and that impressed me very much.(p.208)
• My *life* was fairly well crowded and I didn't seem to need any stimulants to keep me going.(p.213)
• The successful demonstration I had made of my *life* problems in other respects convinced me that some day I was going to be able to drink like a gentleman.(p.214)
• Despite great opportunities, alcohol nearly ended her *life*.(p.222)
• My inability to accept the harsh realities of *life* had resulted in a disillusioned cynic, clothed in protective armor against the world's misunderstanding.(p.226)
• All I had left was an iron determination to live my own *life* in spite of the alien world -- and here I was, an inwardly frightened, outwardly defiant woman, who desperately needed a prop to keep going.(p.226)
• Naturally, in spite of my good intentions, in spite of my protected *life* behind sanitarium walls, I several times got drunk, and was astounded . . . and badly shaken.(p.227)
• To go into a gathering of people was the sort of thing that all my *life*, from the time I left my private world of books and dreams to meet the real world of people and parties and jobs, had left me feeling an uncomfortable outsider, needing the warming stimulus of drinks to join in.(p.228)
• That was the beginning of a new *life*, a fuller *life*, a happier *life* than I had ever known or believed possible.(p.228)
• I have something to contribute to humanity, since I am peculiarly qualified, as a fellow-sufferer, to give aid and comfort to those who have stumbled and fallen over this business of meeting *life*.(p.229)
• But, although I was a good Catholic, the monastic *life* had little appeal for me.(p.230)
• I knew somehow that it meant more than just going to church and living a moral *life*.(p.236)
• That night for the first time in my *life* I really let down my hair and admitted my general loneliness.(p.239)
• My early *life* was spent in Baltimore where my father was a physician and a grain merchant.(p.240)
• Father was a very well-integrated person, and while mother was highstrung and a bit selfish and demanding, our home *life* was reasonably harmonious.(p.240)
• There were four of us children, and although both of my brothers later became alcoholic -- one died of alcoholism -- my sister has never taken a drink in her *life*.(p.240)
• All they talked of that first week-end was God, and how they were going to straighten out Jackie's and my *life*.(p.245)
• We can share in the laughter and tears of our many friends, and most important, we can share our A.A. way of *life* and are given a daily opportunity to help others.(p.249)
• This newsman covered *life* from top to bottom; but he ended up, safely enough, in the middle.(p.251)
• In my early twenties the hardships of hobo *life* did not discourage me, but I had no wish to become just a tramp.(p.253)
• Offered the job of advertising manager for an eastern automotive company, I moved to Philadelphia to begin *life* anew.(p.254)
• I did six years of newspaper advertising, and trade journal work with many, many drunks of drab and dreary hue woven into the pattern of my *life*.(p.254)
• What philosophy I had was thoroughly paganistic -- all my *life* was devoted to a search for pleasure.(p.256)
• As soon as I could get up and walk I started to drink again and kept it up until my friend of the hospital, who, in his first try at the new way of *life* had stubbed his toe in Chicago but had come back to the town to take counsel and make a new start, picked me up and got me into a hospital.(p.258)
• No conviction was necessary to establish my status as a miserable failure at managing my own *life*.(p.259)
• I was deprived of many of the things that we feel are important in *life*, such as education particularly, because of my father's drinking.(p.261)
• I was still bitter because I felt that drink had completely ruined my childhood and my married *life*, and I hated everything pertaining to it.(p.262)
• We built up a splendid *life*.(p.263)
• I give a great deal of credit to Doc and Anne for changing our *life*.(p.270)
• In the spiritual strength I had found, because of A.A., I felt that I had made a complete surrender, that I had really turned my *life* over that summer.(p.271)
• For eighteen years, from the age of twenty-one to thirty-nine, fear governed my *life*.(p.275)
• By the time I was twenty-one I had six years of *life* in foreign countries, spoke three languages fluently, and had attended college for two years.(p.275)
• The details of the long road back to something resembling normal living -- the first short streetcar ride, the purchase of a used bike which enabled me to widen the narrow horizon of *life*, the first trip downtown -- I will not dwell on.(p.276)
• Liquor had become a crutch on the one hand and a means of retreat from *life* on the other.(p.277)
• He it was who convinced me, because his own conviction was so real, that a Power greater than myself could help me in the crises of *life*, and that the means of communicating with this Power was simple prayer.(p.279)
• The scales had dropped from my eyes and I could see *life* in its proper perspective.(p.280)
• It is well over sixteen years since I came back to *life*.(p.280)
• It is, however, only the first of a series of miracles which have followed one after another as a result of my trying to apply to my daily *life* the principles embodies in our Twelve Steps.(p.280)
• I, who had never made a speech in my *life* and who would have been frightened sick at the prospect, stood up in front of Rotary groups in different parts of the city and talked about Alcoholics Anonymous.(p.283)
• This office job brought me face to face with a problem which I had sidestepped all my adult *life*, lack of training.(p.284)
• So much for my business *life*.(p.284)
• But what about my social *life*?(p.284)
• The most accurate answer I can give you is this: Fear has never again ruled my *life* since that day in September, 1938, when I found that a Power greater than myself could not only restore me to sanity but could keep me both sober and sane.(p.285)
• I have faced *life* instead of running away from it.(p.285)
• I learned early in my A.A. *life* that I could not afford to fondle such thoughts, as you might fondle a pet, because this particular pet could grow into a monster.(p.285)
• However, I must have felt, deep down inside myself, that living the selfish *life* of a bachelor was only half living.(p.286)
• By living alone you can pretty much eliminate grief from you *life*, but you also eliminate joy.(p.286)
• At any rate the last great step toward a well rounded *life* still lay ahead of me.(p.286)
• I do feel, though, that the fact that I finally grew up to a point where I could even tackle such a job is the apex of the story of a man who spent eighteen years running away from *life*.(p.286)
• I grew up in a small town outside Akron, Ohio, where the *life* was typical of any average small town.(p.287)
• Home *life* was again a restraining influence.(p.287)
• He laid great stress on the progression of his attitude toward *life* and people, and most of his attitudes had been very similar to mine.(p.290)
• Here was a man with essentially the same outlook on *life*, except that he had done something about it.(p.290)
• He was happy, getting a kick out of *life* and people, and beginning to get his medical practice back again.(p.290)
• These last eighteen years have been the happiest of my *life*, trite though that statement may seem.(p.295)
• This latest part of my *life* has had a purpose, not in great things accomplished but in daily living.(p.295)
• Strangely enough, I became acquainted with the "hilarious *life*" just at the time in my own *life* when I was beginning really to settle down to a common-sense, sane domesticity.(p.297)
• That discovery so intrigued me, that I stayed on that diet almost entirely for the balance of my extensive drinking *life*.(p.298)
• That was the turning point of my *life*.(p.302)
• I was without power to change the course my *life* had taken.(p.304)
• I was thirty-three years old and my *life* was spent.(p.304)
• By now I wanted to die, but had lost the courage even to take my *life*.(p.306)
• I was trapped, and for the *life* of me I did not know how or why this had happened to me.(p.306)
• That call marked the turning point in my *life*.(p.307)
• Not only were they at peace with themselves, but they were getting a kick out of *life* such as one seldom encounters, except in the very young.(p.310)
• Whole new vistas were opened and *life* began to take on color and interest.(p.311)
• It is a way of *life*, and the challenge contained in its principles is great enough to keep any human being striving for as long as he lives.(p.311)
• A complete change takes place in our approach to *life*.(p.311)
• The last fifteen years of my *life* have been rich and meaningful.(p.312)
• I have had my share of problems, heartaches and disappointments, because that is *life*, but also I have known a great deal of joy, and a peace that is the handmaiden of an inner freedom, I have

a wealth of friends and, with my A.A. friends, an unusual quality of fellowship.(p.312)
• I started to take A.A. seriously, and A.A. gave me a new way of *life*.(p.320)
• As we walked back through the hall, I, for the first time in my *life*, said to another human being, "I'm having trouble with my drinking, too."(p.321)
• I could feel fear coming into my *life*.(p.323)
• But I felt a fear coming into my *life*, and I couldn't cope with it.(p.324)
• If I had been sincere in what I thought I wanted more than anything else in *life* -- a sober husband and a happy, contented home — I would have gone on the wagon with him.(p.324)
• Twenty-seven years of confusion is what my early married *life* was.(p.325)
• My *life* was always act and react.(p.325)
• It was my line, the story of my *life*.(p.333)
• Because it was only through feeling defeat and feeling failure, the inability to cope with my *life* and with alcohol, that I was able to surrender and accept the fact that I had this disease, and that I had to learn to live again without alcohol.(p.335)
• I went on, realizing what I was becoming, hating myself for it, bitter, blaming *life*, blaming everything else but the fact that I should turn about and do something about my drinking.(p.337)
• And when all of *life* is a substitute for drink, there's no happiness, no peace.(p.339)
• I said, "I can't find my middle road in *life*.(p.340)
• Surrender to me has meant the ability to run my home, to face my responsibilities as they should be faced, to take *life* as it comes to me day by day, and work my problems out.(p.340)
• A.A. gives us alcoholics direction into a way of *life* without the need for alcohol.(p.340)
• That *life* for me is lived one day at a time, letting the problems of the future rest with the future.(p.340)
• It has meant *life*.(p.342)
• I have been of a very religious outlook all my *life*, but that made no difference once John Barleycorn got the better of me.(p.343)
• I made more money the last year of my drinking than I ever made before in my whole *life*.(p.345)
• The Great Boss has given me diagnostic and surgical talent, and He has loaned it to me to use for the rest of my *life*.(p.350)
• So I went to her and said, "There's only one thing I want in my whole *life*, and I don't want any commendation; I don't want any credit; I don't want anything from you or Janey for the rest of your *life* except one thing; and that is, the opportunity to do anything you want always, and I would like to start off by doing the dishes."(p.351)
• I needed alcohol from that night on, and it in turn used me, ruling my *life* for three years.(p.353)
• All my *life*, it seemed, was spent on the outside looking in.(p.353)
• I had no idea what would happen -- I just knew I didn't want to live if *life* was going to go on like it was.(p.355)
• Here was the understanding I'd been searching for all my *life*.(p.355)
• My sponsor used to say to me, "If I could only paint you a picture of how beautiful *life* can be without booze . . ."(p.355)
• A.A. has become a way of *life* and living for me.(p.355)
• The challenge intrigued me; also it was another opportunity to run away from myself and the "fast *life* of the big city."(p.359)
• Proud of my little station and of my new bride I settled down to a happy married *life*.(p.361)
• I was going to prove to her that liquor wasn't necessary in my *life*, and above all that I still loved her more than anything else in the world and that I wanted her back.(p.362)
• He was full of his new found *life* of happiness and sobriety.(p.365)
• When I was nineteen, I married a fine man who had never known an insecure moment in his *life*, let alone the trials and tribulations of booze.(p.369)
• We went out occasionally, and I would take a drink to ease the tensions of daily *life*.(p.370)
• Slowly, my *life* seemed to unfold before me, shedding insights on childhood resentments, jealousies, and fears that had mushroomed in adulthood, and also on the self-pity that I had wallowed in at every opportunity.(p.371)
• But what is more important is that I found a new *life* in Alcoholics Anonymous.(p.372)
• I was raised like the majority of American boys, coming from a family of modest circumstances, attending public schools, having the social *life* of a small midwestern town, with part-time work and some athletics.(p.373)
• I did work of all kinds after school and during vacations, trying to find that which would appeal most as a goal for a *life* work.(p.373)
• The drive to get ahead, to succeed, kept me too busy for many years to have any great experience with social *life*.(p.374)
• I achieved recognized and national standing in my profession, as well as becoming a director in many important institutions having to do with the civic *life* of a large city.(p.374)
• It was at this stage of my *life* that resentments came in.(p.376)
• By now it had become difficult to visualize a *life* without alcohol.(p.378)
• After all, I hadn't started to drink early in *life*, so I had some stability and maturity to guide me for a while.(p.379)
• It did say, "admitted I was powerless over alcohol; that my *life* had become unmanageable."(p.379)
• Most certainly I was powerless over alcohol, and for me, my *life* had become unmanageable.(p.379)
• I liked the description of the alcoholic as a person who had found that alcohol is interfering with his social or business *life*.(p.380)
• Dishonest thinking, prejudice, ego, antagonism toward anyone and everyone who dares to cross him, vanity and a critical attitude are character defects that gradually creep in and become a part of his *life*.(p.380)
• To me this meant telling my associates that I had joined Alcoholics Anonymous; that I didn't know what was expected of me by A.A., but that whatever it was, it was the most important thing in *life* for me; that sobriety meant more to me than anything in this world.(p.382)
• The A.A. way of *life* is the way we always should have tried to live.(p.382)
• I didn't realize I would find so much more, but a new and different outlook on *life* started opening up almost immediately.(p.383)
• Because of this state of confusion and frustration I had hysterics on the seventeenth day for the first and only time in my *life*.(p.387)
• *Life* was pretty miserable.(p.388)
• It was the first time in my *life* that I could not get a lift out of what I was drinking; and so one Friday night, at five minutes to six, I had half a water glass of warm gin, and that is when I first asked God to help me.(p.393)
• I know that I must work at it as long as I live; I know that it is only by working at it that I can stay sober and have a happy *life*.(p.394)
• It has changed not simply one department of my *life* -- it has changed my whole *life*.(p.394)
• It is a way of *life* that pays as it goes, every step of the way, in compensations that have been wonderfully rich and rewarding.(p.394)
• It has made *life* a thousand times easier and simpler than did the endless compromises and conflicts by which I lived before.(p.394)
• It pays daily in more harmonious relations with my fellow men, in ever clearer insight into the true meaning of *life*, and in the answering love and gratitude wherever and whenever I have been the instrument of God's will in the lives of others.(p.394)
• To me, A.A. is within the reach of every alcoholic, because it can be achieved in any walk of *life* and because the achievement is not ours but God's.(p.395)
• I was out of step with *life*, with my family, with people in general.(p.400)
• Until I reached A.A. my *life* was a shambles; I was a mess, and I made everybody near and dear to me miserable.(p.400)
• But now I was a young divorcee, leading a Washington social *life*.(p.402)
• Other girls whom I had known all my *life* asked for one weak scotch after dinner.(p.406)
• This was the *life*!(p.407)
• By this time I had ceased to be the *life* of the party.(p.410)
• In my cups I used to tell them off, giving them lengthy advice on how to lead the right *life*.(p.410)
• Never in my entire *life* had anyone asked me "Are you one of us?"(p.413)
• With more physical courage than I had possessed, she had twice tried to take her *life*.(p.414)
• But my *life*, even sober, was all askew and so were my emotions.(p.414)
• Except for one short slip, during the first eight months, which was an angry "the world can't do this to me" reaction to a personal tragedy in my *life*, I have been sober for twelve years.(p.416)
• Through going to meetings and listening, and occasionally speaking, through doing Twelve Step work, whereby in helping others you are both the teacher and the student, by making many wonderful A.A. friends, I have been taught all the things in *life* that are worth having.(p.416)
• This has been a wonderful thing in my *life*.(p.417)
• *Life*, including some ups and downs, is a lot of fun.(p.417)
• I am a part of A.A. which is a way of *life*.(p.417)
• Defeated by alcohol and pills, he found the way to a new *life*.(p.418)
• My *life* there was a nightmare of periodic binges on alcohol and pills, adultery, unhappy hours at the dental office, seeing my wife give birth to our second child and have several miscarriages, living in a turbulent household, and making continual attempts to be the respectable dentist, husband, father, and community leader.(p.419)
• No one could live such an irresponsible, immature *life* as I had without consequences.(p.420)
• Most important, A.A. has enabled me to go back and start growing up all over again in all areas of my *life*.(p.420)
• Home *life* didn't mean much to me.(p.424)
• It solved their problems and they started living a sane *life* again.(p.427)
• At that time *life* to me was spelled "w-h-i-s-k-e-y."(p.430)
• Today I think of *life* in terms of happiness, contentment, freedom from fear and despair, sane thinking, ability to face problems as they occur, the opportunity to help other alcoholics and to be decent.(p.430)
• They have been the happiest of my *life*.(p.430)
• When I try to reconstruct what my *life* was like "before," I see a coin with two faces.(p.432)
• There would be times when the *life* of respectability and achievement seemed insufferably dull -- I had to break out.(p.432)
• My outward professional *life* looked fine, on the surface.(p.435)
• The most terrible blow of my *life* befell me after I'd found sobriety through A.A.(p.437)
• I never in my *life* took a tranquilizer, sedative, or pep pill because I was a pillhead.(p.443)
• In the hospital, I hung on to the idea I'd had most of my *life*: that if I could just control the external environment, the internal environment would then be comfortable.(p.445)
• And *life* keeps getting simpler and easier as we try to reverse my old idea, by taking care of the internal environment via the Twelve Steps, and letting the external environment take care of itself.)(p.446)
• I really felt sorry for him; the only thing in *life* he had to brag about was the fact that he was an alcoholic.(p.446)
• When I am disturbed, it is because I find some person, place, thing, or situation — some fact of my *life* -- unacceptable to me, and I can find no serenity until I accept that person, place, thing, or situation as being exactly the way it is supposed to be at this moment.(p.449)
• Until I could accept my alcoholism, I could not stay sober; unless I accept *life* completely on life's terms, I cannot be happy.(p.449)
• So I'm better off if I don't give advice, don't figure I know what's best, and just accept *life* on life's terms, as it is today -- especially my own *life*, as it actually is.(p.450)
• Most had taken shattering losses on nearly every front of *life*.(p.455)
• Alcohol wrings the guts out of *life*, eats into the brain in such a way as to make the alcoholic blind to the truth.(p.457)
• We reverted to the old way of *life* we knew -- a *life* full of anger, vindictiveness, resentment, fear, dependence, denial, self-will, irresponsibility.(p.459)
• We do this by going to many A.A. meetings with an open mind and a desire to live the good-feeling *life* without chemicals -- liquid or otherwise.(p.459)
• I was forty-four years old; my *life* had been wasted.(p.461)
• Then I was transferred to the honor-grade unit, where I spent the most painful year of my *life*.(p.462)
• I had decided I was no good — never would be any good, and the sooner I could drink myself out of this *life*, the better.(p.468)
• And A.A. took this wreck of a woman and brought her back to *life*.(p.470)
• A.A. didn't teach me I was an alcoholic; rather it taught me that because I was an alcoholic my *life* had become unmanageable.(p.470)
• But by listening and talking to these A.A.'s — talking to them as I had never talked to anyone in my whole *life*, I saw that it was my *life* that was unmanageable — not just my drinking.(p.471)

• Had I tried honestly and sincerely to practice the Twelve Steps I would have seen from my continuous moral inventory that I was getting off the beam -- I would have found that there were some active resentments in my *life*, a terrific amount of self-pity.(p.471)
• The Higher Power to whom I had turned, and who had sustained me, had once again been thrust into the background, while my emotions were running my *life* and, as always, my emotions ran me to the bottle.(p.472)
• I thought, "Oh well, these people are just like all the people I've known all my *life*.(p.472)
• During these seven years a thing called the Twenty-four Hour Program --a gadget I used to think was only a snare to trap the newcomer -- has come to mean much to me, not only as regards my drinking but in the whole pattern of my *life*.(p.473)
• I realize that all I'm guaranteed in *life* is today.(p.473)
• I want to stop this bad *life*, but where to turn?(p.475)
• But now I change if it bring good *life*.(p.475)
• Not try no drinks for Lent or for *life*.(p.476)
• He was old, but now he grow young with new *life* in A.A. and travel all time.(p.476)
• I wasted twenty years of my *life*, and there is nothing I can do about that, but there is something I can do about now.(p.480)
• To tell you a small part of what my mother's *life* must have been like: Three of her kids were in jail that year -- two sons and a daughter.(p.480)
• We can have this new way of *life* -- learning to live with our sickness and to be happy and content -- if we are willing to change our way of thinking and be honest, first with ourselves, then with others.(p.480)
• I met and married a man in A.A., and I am the happiest I have ever been in my *life*.(p.481)
• He has taught me that, in our new *life*, I am the most important person of all.(p.481)
• Honesty is the easiest word for me to understand because it is the exact opposite of what I've been doing all my *life*.(p.482)
• I'm sure my ideas as to what *life* should be like were quite different from that of the average person with whom I associated.(p.483)
• Later on in *life* that took its toll.(p.483)
• I've never seen him drunk in my *life*, although he'd take a shot in the morning and usually one in the evening, and so did I; but for the most part he kept his whiskey in his office.(p.484)
• That's the first time I was ever really drunk in my *life*.(p.487)
• But his *life* was unmentioned, so far as I was concerned.(p.498)
• You bet your *life*!(p.500)
• My wife hears my voice and knows I have found the answer to *life*.(p.505)
• For that crime I received a minimum of twenty years and a maximum of natural *life*.(p.508)
• I received an additional fifteen years for that, making a minimum of thirty-five years and a maximum of natural *life*.(p.509)
• Like many of us who went into the service, I thought it would be a cure-all, a new *life*.(p.513)
• Either that or end my *life*.(p.515)
• My *life* had become unmanageable due to the excessive use of alcohol.(p.515)
• For me, A.A. has become a way of *life*.(p.516)
• There was nothing in my school *life* that I can look back on which was responsible for anything that happened afterwards.(p.517)
• When I came home to ordinary garrison *life* in England, I found that I was drinking rather more than most people of may age.(p.518)
• But as long as you did your work and didn't disgrace yourself, you were socially acceptable and nobody really intruded on your private *life* very much.(p.518)
• The gradual result was that I was drifting into making drinking one of the more important parts of my *life*.(p.519)
• My only hope was to try and get through what was left of *life* as best I could, but I could never visualize doing that without drinking.(p.522)
• That morning was the first time I really realized where I'd got to in my *life*.(p.523)
• This was the only time in my *life* that I'd ever known my mother to be almost pitiless, but she couldn't be blamed for that.(p.523)
• Since I joined on that April night, A.A. has done more for me than just stop me from drinking; it has brought me back to *life* again.(p.524)
• Poor, black, totally ruled by alcohol, she felt shut away from any *life* worth living.(p.526)
• Today, I thank my Higher Power for giving me another chance at *life* and A.A. and being able to try and help some other alcoholic.(p.529)
• Since I have been in A.A., I have more friends than I ever had in my *life* -- friends who care about me and my welfare, friends who don't care that I am black and that I have been in prison.(p.529)
• HE WHO LOSES HIS *LIFE*(p.531)
• It was my "secret garden" -- bluntly, it was my retreat from *life*, and I didn't want to give it up.(p.534)
• For always, over and above everything else, was the awfulness of the lack of meaning in *life*.(p.535)
• Now, for me, and to my satisfaction, I know the purpose of *life*: The purpose of *life* is to create and the by-product is happiness.(p.535)
• I have had the joy of seeing many a human being, down and out, learn to stand straight again, and to proceed under his own power to happiness in *life*.(p.541)
• I stood off and took a long look at *life* and the values I found in it: I saw a paradox, that he who loses his *life* does indeed find it.(p.542)
• At fifty-four, I have had come true for me the old wish, "If only I could live my *life* over, knowing what I know."(p.543)
• I thought that *life* was a pretty simple thing; you simply made a plan for your *life*, based upon what you wanted, and then you needed only the courage to go after it.(p.545)
• I thought I knew exactly what I wanted out of *life* and I thought I knew exactly how to get it.(p.545)
• I've heard it said many times in A.A., "There is just one good drunk in every alcoholic's *life*, and that's the one that brings us into A.A.," and I believe it.(p.549)
• I had no problem admitting I was powerless over alcohol, and I certainly agreed that my *life* had become unmanageable.(p.550)
• I had only to reflect on the contrast between the plans I made so many years ago for my *life* with what really happened to know I couldn't manage my *life* drunk or sober.(p.550)
• When I had been in A.A. only a short while, an oldtimer told me something that has affected my *life* ever since.(p.554)
• By twenty-nine, I was having trouble coping with *life* because of my drinking.(p.555)
• To wear expensive clothes, to have bartenders know what to serve me before I ordered, to be recognized by headwaiters and shown to the best table, to play gin rummy for high stakes with the insouciance of a riverboat gambler -- these were the enduring values in *life*, I thought.(p.556)
• Bewilderment, fear, and resentment moved into my *life*.(p.556)
• Above all, I was suffering inner pain because my performance and my accomplishments in *life* failed to live up to my own expectations of myself.(p.557)
• I went on the wagon, with no outside help and with no real difficulty -- except that I didn't enjoy *life* without drinking.(p.557)
• Hopeless now, I felt it would be better for my wife, my children, and everyone in my *life* if I went ahead and died.(p.558)
• As the sober days grew into sober months and then into sober years, a new and beautiful *life* began to emerge from the shambles of my former existence.(p.559)
• To those now in its fold, Alcoholics Anonymous has made the difference between misery and sobriety, and often the difference between *life* and death.(p.563)
• He finally realizes that he has undergone a profound alteration in his reaction to *life*; that such a change could hardly have been brought about by himself alone.(p.569)

life-and-death
• He should realize that we are engaged upon a *life-and-death* errand.(p.75)

life-styles
• The basic principles of the A.A. program, it appears, hold good for individuals with many different *life-styles*, just as the program has brought recovery to those of many different nationalities.(p.xxii)

life's
• Until I could accept my alcoholism, I could not stay sober; unless I accept life completely on *life's* terms, I cannot be happy.(p.449)
• So I'm better off if I don't give advice, don't figure I know what's best, and just accept life on *life's* terms, as it is today -- especially my own life, as it actually is.(p.450)

lifelong
• It meant I would have to throw several *lifelong* conceptions out of the window.(p.42)
• Among them you will make *lifelong* friends.(p.152)

lifesaver
• It was to be my *lifesaver* -- the final catalyst.(p.461)

lifesaving
• *LIFESAVING* WORDS(p.342)

lifetime
• It should continue for our *lifetime*.(p.84)
• He can scarcely square the account in his *lifetime*.(p.127)
• Joy at our release from a *lifetime* of frustration knew no bounds.(p.128)
• I'd packed more drinking into seven years than many a heavy drinker does in a *lifetime*.(p.429)
• It is suggested that we do not try to do a *lifetime* of repairs in one day.(p.481)

lift
• Time went on and the drinking got worse and worse, and I was in another barroom, down the road the other way, a small one, and I took my glass -- that morning I'd been able to *lift* it from the bar -- and I said to the woman behind the bar, "I wish I might never take another drop of that stuff.(p.266)
• It was the first time in my life that I could not get a *lift* out of what I was drinking; and so one Friday night, at five minutes to six, I had half a water glass of warm gin, and that is when I first asked God to help me.(p.393)
• Still later, even alcohol and chemicals together could not *lift* me.(p.457)
• Society can do anything it chooses to do with me when I am drunk and I can't *lift* a finger to stop it, for I forfeit my rights through the simple expedient of becoming a menace to myself and to the people around me.(p.549)

lifted
• I felt *lifted* up, as though the great clean wind of a mountain top blew through and through.(p.14)
• On talking to a man there, I would be amazingly *lifted* up and set on my feet.(p.15)
• Selecting a church at random from the directory, he stepped into a booth and *lifted* the receiver.(p.155)
• Above all, I have gained the greatest thing accorded to any man, the love and understanding of a gracious God, who has *lifted* me from the alcoholic scrap-heap to a position of trust where I have been able to reap the rich rewards that come from showing a little love for others and from serving them as I can.(p.296)
• And the first thing you know I was *lifted* right out of the A.A. group, and I floated higher, and higher, and even higher, until I was way up on a pink cloud which is known as Pink Seven, and I felt miserable again.(p.348)
• When the overcast *lifted*, the stars were there as before.(p.400)
• I feel *lifted* up.(p.504)
• I found myself being *lifted* onto a stretcher and whisked away in an ambulance to a strange hospital.(p.558)

light
• By late 1937, the number of members having substantial sobriety time behind them was sufficient to convince the membership that a new *light* had entered the dark world of the alcoholic.(p.xvii)
• I must turn in all things the Father of *Light* who presides over us all.(p.14)
• Sometimes these excuses have a certain plausibility, but none of them really makes sense in the *light* of the havoc an alcoholic's drinking bout creates.(p.23)
• This should be an entirely personal affair which each one decides for himself in the *light* of past associations, or his present choice.(p.28)
• But even in this type of beginning we are obliged to admit that our justification for a spree was insanely insufficient in the *light* of what always happened.(p.37)
• He hopes they will never see the *light* of day.(p.73)
• If his mood is *light*, tell him humorous stories of your escapades.(p.91)
• We feel that each family, in the *light* of their own circumstances, ought to decide for themselves.(p.103)
• Should it happen again, regard it in a different *light*.(p.116)
• It was getting pretty dark and I hadn't turned on any lights, when some big fellow stepped inside the door and flipped on the *light* switch.(p.207)
• I realized that there wasn't anything I could say to place myself in a more favorable *light* with my children, that it was going to be a matter of time; for I also understood the intolerance of young people towards deficiencies in their elders.(p.220)
• The walls crumpled -- and the *light* streamed in.(p.228)
• Back at camp, all was forgiven because it was the End, but in the *light* of what I have since learned I know I was a confirmed alcoholic at nineteen.(p.242)

• He had taken up ***light*** work, and he had a safety valve and a pair of spurs and the clothes on his back, and that was all.(p.263)
• After six months of sobriety I saw the picture in a different ***light***: Detroit was the place I had to return to, not only because I must face the mess I had made there, but because it was there that I could be of the most service to A.A.(p.281)
• He'll never read in his "sweetness and ***light***" senior-citizen publications anything but the joys of lolling in the rocking chair, angling on the riverbank, or bowling on the green.(p.330)
• But in the ***light*** of the new understanding that I have found in A.A., I have been able to interpret that defeat, and that failure, and that shame, as seeds of victory.(p.335)
• I don't know what I expected, but I most certainly didn't visualize a group of people talking about their drinking problems, making ***light*** of their personal tragedies and at the same time enjoying themselves.(p.378)
• The other kids would ***light*** out for the hamburger huts or ice cream parlors, the pizza joints or bowling alleys, after football games and dances.(p.423)
• We started to ***light*** matches to see, but the draft blew them out.(p.424)
• I remember finding myself in the middle of the night in the doctors' parking lot at the hospital with one foot in the car and one foot on the ground, not knowing which was the lead foot; finding myself hanging up the telephone – then realizing I had gotten out of bed, answered the phone, turned on the ***light***, and carried on a conversation with a patient.(p.441)
• In the ***light*** of subsequent events it became evident that I took their advice far too literally, for, after some months of happy sobriety I drank again.(p.471)
• The only time that I have ever seen my mother take anything alcoholic was around Christmas time, when she would drink some eggnog or ***light*** wine.(p.484)
• "Let your ***light*** so shine before men that they may see your good works –."(p.497)
• The electric ***light*** began to move.(p.498)
• I turn on the ***light***.(p.501)
• I get in bed and turn out the ***light***.(p.503)
• Most emphatically we wish to say that any alcoholic capable of honestly facing his problems in the ***light*** of our experience can recover, provided he does not close his mind to all spiritual concepts.(p.570)

lightly

• We remembered always that our sex powers were God-given and therefore good, neither to be used ***lightly*** or selfishly nor to be despised and loathed.(p.69)

lightning

• The interne came along with a glassful of bleached ***lightning*** that put me away for about fifteen hours.(p.217)

lights

• Each person is like an actor who wants to run the whole show; is forever trying to arrange the ***lights***, the ballet, the scenery and the rest of the players in his own way.(p.60)
• It was getting pretty dark and I hadn't turned on any ***lights***, when some big fellow stepped inside the door and flipped on the light switch.(p.207)
• I said, "Look, Bub, if I want those ***lights*** on, I'll turn them on."(p.207)
• By the time I figured out what had happened, I saw two flashing red ***lights*** atop squad cars, sedately coming around the corner.(p.353)
• My associates, and all the wits and literary ***lights*** I so much admired, also drank.(p.433)

likable

• I looked up and there were two great big fellows over six foot tall, very ***likable*** looking.(p.185)

like

• If you have a drinking problem, we hope that you may pause in reading one of the forty-four personal stories and think: "Yes, that happened to me"; or, more important, "Yes, I've felt ***like*** that"; or most important, "Yes, I believe this program can work for me, too."(p.xii)
• We would ***like*** it understood that our alcoholic work is an avocation.(p.xiii)
• We should ***like*** to be helpful to such cases.(p.xiv)
• Men and women drink essentially because they ***like*** the effect produced by alcohol.(p.xxvi)
• Men have cried out to me in sincere and despairing appeal: "Doctor, I cannot go on ***like*** this!(p.xxvii)
• Out of this alloy of drink and speculation, I commenced to forge the weapon that one day would turn in its flight ***like*** a boomerang and all but cut me to ribbons.(p.2)
• I felt ***like*** Napoleon returning from Elba.(p.4)
• The curve of my declining moral and bodily health fell off ***like*** a ski-jump.(p.7)
• I was soon to be catapulted into what I ***like*** to call the fourth dimension of existence.(p.8)
• Drinkers are ***like*** that.(p.9)
• ***Like*** myself, he had admitted complete defeat.(p.11)
• I didn't ***like*** the idea.(p.12)
• With us it is just ***like*** that.(p.15)
• We are ***like*** the passengers of a great liner the moment after rescue from shipwreck when camaraderie, joyousness and democracy pervade the vessel from steerage to Captain's table.(p.17)
• "Why don't you drink ***like*** a gentleman or quit?"(p.20)
• Why does he behave ***like*** this?(p.22)
• We know that while the alcoholic keeps away from drink, as he may do for months or years, he reacts much ***like*** other men.(p.22)
• They sound ***like*** the philosophy of the man who, having a headache, beats himself on the head with a hammer so that he can't feel the ache.(p.23)
• If these thoughts occur, they are hazy and readily supplanted with the old threadbare idea that this time we shall handle ourselves ***like*** other people.(p.24)
• Therefore, it is not surprising that our drinking careers have been characterized by countless vain attempts to prove we could drink ***like*** other people.(p.30)
• The delusion that we are ***like*** other people, or presently may be, has to be smashed.(p.30)
• We are ***like*** men who have lost their legs; they never grow new ones.(p.30)
• Neither does there appear to be any kind of treatment which will make alcoholics of our kind ***like*** other men.(p.30)
• If anyone who is showing inability to control his drinking can do the right-about-face and drink ***like*** a gentleman, our hats are off to him.(p.31)
• Heaven knows, we have tried hard enough and long enough to drink ***like*** other people!(p.31)
• We do not ***like*** to pronounce any individual as alcoholic, but you can quickly diagnose yourself.(p.31)
• We think few, to whom this book will appeal, can stay dry anything ***like*** a year.(p.34)
• In some circumstances we have gone out deliberately to get drunk, feeling ourselves justified by nervousness, anger, worry, depression, jealousy or the ***like***.(p.37)
• They grinned, which I didn't ***like*** so much, and then asked me if I thought myself alcoholic and if I were really licked this time.(p.42)
• We hope it strikes home to thousands ***like*** him.(p.43)
• People ***like*** you are too heartbreaking.(p.43)
• But cheer up, something ***like*** half of us thought we were atheists or agnostics.(p.44)
• When others showed us that "God-sufficiency" worked with them, we began to feel ***like*** those who had insisted the Wrights would never fly.(p.52)
• We still ***like*** it.(p.53)
• Perhaps we had been leaning too heavily on Reason that last mile and we did not ***like*** to lose our support.(p.53)
• Then, ***like*** a thunderbolt, a great thought came.(p.56)
• Our stories disclose in a general way what we used to be ***like***, what happened, and what we are ***like*** now.(p.58)
• No one among us has been able to maintain anything ***like*** perfect adherence to these principles.(p.60)
• Each person is ***like*** an actor who wants to run the whole show; is forever trying to arrange the lights, the ballet, the scenery and the rest of the players in his own way.(p.60)
• Our actor is self-centered -- ego-centric, as people ***like*** to call it nowadays.(p.61)
• He is ***like*** the retired business man who lolls in the Florida sunshine in the winter complaining of the sad state of the nation; the minister who sighs over the sins of the twentieth century; politicians and reformers who are sure all would be Utopia if the rest of the world would only behave; the outlaw safe cracker who thinks society has wronged him; and the alcoholic who has lost all and is locked up.(p.61)
• Though we did not ***like*** their symptoms and the way these disturbed us, they, ***like*** ourselves, were sick too.(p.67)
• When ready, we say something ***like*** this: "My Creator, I am now willing that you should have all of me, good and bad.(p.76)
• In fairness we must say that she may understand, but what are we going to do about a thing ***like*** that?(p.81)
• The alcoholic is ***like*** a tornado roaring his way through the lives of others.(p.82)
• He is ***like*** the farmer who came up out of his cyclone cellar to find his home ruined.(p.82)
• You need this information to put yourself in his place, to see how you would ***like*** him to approach you if the tables were turned.(p.90)
• But point out that we alcoholics have much in common and that you would ***like***, in any case, to be friendly.(p.95)
• Argument and fault-finding are to be avoided ***like*** the plague.(p.98)
• His only chance for sobriety would be some place ***like*** the Greenland Ice Cap, and even there an Eskimo might turn up with a bottle of scotch and ruin everything!(p.101)
• To a person who has had experience with an alcoholic, this may seem ***like*** tempting Providence, but it isn't.(p.101)
• As wives of Alcoholics Anonymous, we would ***like*** you to feel that we understand as perhaps few can.(p.104)
• Our loyalty and the desire that our husbands hold up their heads and be ***like*** other men have begotten all sorts of predicaments.(p.105)
• The checking account melted ***like*** snow in June.(p.106)
• The unexpected result was that our husbands seemed to ***like*** it.(p.106)
• This world is full of people ***like*** him.(p.109)
• He is worried at times, and is becoming aware that he cannot drink ***like*** other people.(p.109)
• Though once ***like*** number two he became worse.(p.109)
• He admits he cannot drink ***like*** other people, but does not see why.(p.110)
• You can be quite hopeful of a situation ***like*** this.(p.110)
• Perhaps you both ***like*** parties which would be dull without liquor.(p.110)
• Drinkers ***like*** to help other drinkers.(p.112)
• But after his next binge, ask him if he would really ***like*** to get over drinking for good.(p.112)
• Just would he ***like*** to?(p.112)
• He knows that thousands of men, much ***like*** himself, have recovered.(p.113)
• Many of Alcoholics Anonymous were ***like*** that.(p.113)
• We wives found that, ***like*** everybody else, we were afflicted with pride, self-pity, vanity and all the things which go to make up the self-centered person; and we were not above selfishness or dishonesty.(p.116)
• We women carry with us a picture of the ideal man, the sort of chap we would ***like*** our husbands to be.(p.118)
• The chances are he will not for, ***like*** yourself, he is just beginning his development.(p.118)
• We do not ***like*** the thought that the contents of a book or the work of another alcoholic has accomplished in a few weeks that for which we struggled for years.(p.118)
• You may not ***like*** some of them.(p.119)
• If not irritable, he may seem dull and boring, not gay and affectionate as the family would ***like*** him to be.(p.126)
• While grateful that he drinks no more, they may not ***like*** the idea that God has accomplished the miracle where they failed.(p.128)
• ***Like*** a gaunt prospector, belt drawn in over the last ounce of food, our pick struck gold.(p.128)
• He will perceive that his spiritual growth is lopsided, that for an average man ***like*** himself, a spiritual life which does not include his family obligations may not be so perfect after all.(p.129)
• We have come to believe He would ***like*** us to keep our heads in the clouds with Him, but that our feet ought to be firmly planted on earth.(p.130)
• This seemed to me ***like*** an opportunity to be helpful, so I spent two hours talking about alcoholism, the malady, and described the symptoms and results as well as I could.(p.138)
• Suppose an approach is made something ***like*** this:(p.141)
• You might say you appreciated his abilities, would ***like*** to keep him, but cannot if he continues to drink.(p.141)
• You act ***like*** one.(p.147)
• He will work ***like*** the devil and thank you to his dying day.(p.149)
• We know our friend is ***like*** a boy whistling in the dark to keep up his spirits.(p.152)
• But am I to be consigned to a life where I shall be stupid, boring and glum, ***like*** some righteous people I see?(p.152)

• Near you, alcoholics are dying helplessly *like* people in a sinking ship.(p.152)
• I drink *like* that."(p.157)
• I put on thirty pounds of weight in about two months, looked *like* a pig, and was uncomfortable from shortness of breath.(p.177)
• I said, "Yes, Doc, I would *like* to quit, at least for five, six, or eight months, until I get things straightened up, and begin to get the respect of my wife and some other people back, and get my finances fixed up and so on."(p.187)
• Whether you quit six days, months, or years, if you go out and take a drink or two you'll end up in this hospital tied down, just *like* you have been in these past six months.(p.187)
• And they said, "No, you have a disease, and it doesn't make any difference how long you do without it, after a drink or two you'll end up just *like* you are now."(p.187)
• Wouldn't you *like* to see us again?"(p.189)
• "Sure I would," replied Bill, "Maybe it won't do any good, but I'd *like* to see you both, anyhow.(p.189)
• It took me a year, or a year and a half to get to feeling physically well, and it was rather tough, but I soon found folks whose friendship I had once had, and I found, after I had been sober for quite some little time, that these people began to act *like* they had in previous years, before I had gotten so bad, so that I didn't pay too awful much attention to financial gains.(p.190)
• I still go to meetings, because I *like* to go.(p.192)
• I meet the people that I *like* to talk to.(p.192)
• I didn't even know what a martini looked *like*, but I had heard a man down the bar order one.(p.194)
• I kept watching the man down the bar to see what he did with a contraption *like* that, and he just smelled of his drink and set it down again, so I did the same.(p.195)
• It irritated my nostrils; I choked, I didn't *like* it.(p.195)
• I didn't even *like* the olive.(p.195)
• Twenty-two years later, Doctor Bob told me that what I had done was *like* turning a switch and setting up a demand for more alcohol in my system.(p.195)
• They acted on me *like* the beating of a club.(p.195)
• Anyhow, I recognized the fact that I couldn't drink *like* normal people, but I tried hard and kept on trying for twenty-two years.(p.196)
• I can remember telling the poor little soul that I could probably quit drinking if I wasn't married to her, and told her that, after all, I didn't *like* restraint!(p.199)
• I didn't *like* having to come home at a certain time; I didn't *like* this, I didn't *like* that, and I think the poor girl actually divorced me to help me stop drinking!(p.199)
• Then he started to talk to me about his drinking experiences, what his drinking had cost him, how much he had drunk and where, things *like* that, and I remember I was quite bored because I had never seen the guy before and had no interest at all in what, where and when he drank.(p.208)
• HE THOUGHT HE COULD DRINK *LIKE* A GENTLEMAN(p.210)
• I could not see why I couldn't drink *like* a gentleman, and that was my primary ambition – until I landed in A.A.(p.214)
• The successful demonstration I had made of my life problems in other respects convinced me that some day I was going to be able to drink *like* a gentleman.(p.214)
• I had been going on *like* that for over a year.(p.224)
• So far, so good -- all according to plan, *like* thousands of others.(p.225)
• I wasn't the only person in the world who felt and behaved *like* this!(p.227)
• I was suffering from an actual disease that had a name and symptoms *like* diabetes or cancer or TB -- and a disease was respectable, not a moral stigma!(p.227)
• I couldn't stomach religion, and I didn't *like* the mention of God or any of the other capital letters.(p.227)
• Talking things over with them, great floods of enlightenment showed me myself as I really was and I was *like* them.(p.229)
• Suddenly I could accept myself, faults and all, as I was -- for weren't we all *like* that?(p.229)
• I get my greatest thrill of accomplishment from the knowledge that I have played a part in the new happiness achieved by countless others *like* myself.(p.229)
• *Like* most immigrants I wanted to be somebody and have something and I was very happy and contented as I felt success crown my efforts.(p.232)
• He didn't talk *like* a preacher at all.(p.235)
• I don't remember much of what he said, but I did realize that here was another guy exactly *like* me; he had been in the same laughing academies and the same jails, known the same loss of jobs, same frustrations, same boredom and the same loneliness.(p.239)
• Jackie told me about a group of fellows in New York, of whom my old friend Fitz was one, who had the same problem I had, and who by working together to help each other were not now drinking and were happy *like* himself.(p.239)
• I *like* to think I was fairly normal before alcohol took over.(p.240)
• But each drink after the "first" seemed to become less effective and after three or four they all seemed *like* water.(p.241)
• I'd work *like* mad for three or four weeks without a single drink, save my money, pay a few bills and then "reward" myself with alcohol.(p.244)
• Despite all this, I did *like* these new friends because, again, they were *like* me.(p.245)
• "I'm doing a job I *like* and it's quiet where I live, practically no temptations.(p.257)
• Indeed, I was beginning to see that I would require implicit faith, *like* a small child, if I was going to get anywhere.(p.259)
• I remember starting to city school, coming from a country school, and wanting so very, very much to be *like* the other girls and trying flour on my face for powder because I wasn't able to have any real powder.(p.261)
• I feared that I wasn't dressed *like* the rest.(p.261)
• He hardly ever went to anything *like* that without me.(p.263)
• I'd *like* to say here how important it was to us then that we do all the little things that people said were important, because later when Russ was so sick that I had to hold him up, they had a meeting out at the house.(p.270)
• It went something *like* this: "God, for eighteen years I have been unable to handle this problem.(p.280)
• I lay down on the bed and slept *like* a child.(p.280)
• I would *like* to sketch for you the highlights of these sixteen years of a slow but steady and satisfying upward climb.(p.280)
• Sometimes during that year I rebelled inwardly at what seemed *like* lost time, and at having to be a burden to these good people whose means were limited.(p.281)
• It ran something *like* this: If I go around shouting from the rooftops about my alcoholism, it might very possibly prevent me from getting a good job.(p.282)
• I, carried away with the desire to serve A.A., gave what was probably one of the first radio broadcasts about A.A., living through a case of mike fright and feeling *like* a million dollars when it was all over.(p.283)
• I sleep *like* a baby, and never give a thought to such a thing as insomnia.(p.303)
• Why he bothered with me as long as he did I shall never know, for he knew there was no answer for me in medicine and he, *like* all doctors of his day, had been taught that the alcoholic was incurable and should be ignored.(p.307)
• But this day my doctor gave it to me straight and said, "People *like* you are pretty well known to the medical profession.(p.307)
• He thought it would be helpful for me to visit the Akron group and meet many *like* himself.(p.309)
• Why do men and women *like* these join A.A.?(p.315)
• Therefore, these seventeen A.A.'s, and hundreds of thousands *like* them, have been saved years of infinite suffering.(p.315)
• They sum it up *like* this: "We didn't wait to hit bottom because, thank God, we could see the bottom.(p.315)
• *Like* I said, I'm a twenty-four-year-old alcoholic -- and I'm happy.(p.320)
• I lied *like* a trooper to get out of many scrapes.(p.324)
• In the old days I hated to wake up and look back at what last night was *like*.(p.325)
• And unless I had some rosy picture of what was going to happen that day, I wouldn't even feel *like* getting up in the morning at all.(p.325)
• When we begin to do things *like* that with alcohol, something's gone wrong.(p.336)
• I didn't care what I looked *like*, I didn't care what I did.(p.337)
• The second way in which, perhaps, I differ from some other alcoholics is this; many alcoholics state that they didn't particularly *like* the taste of alcohol, but that they liked the effect.(p.345)
• I used to *like* to get it on my fingers so I could lick them and get another taste.(p.346)
• So I thought to myself, I might just as well be drunk as feel *like* this.(p.348)
• I didn't know how to be a father; I don't know how to come home and work week-ends *like* other husbands; I don't know how to entertain my family.(p.351)
• So I went to her and said, "There's only one thing I want in my whole life, and I don't want any commendation; I don't want any credit; I don't want anything from you or Janey for the rest of your life except one thing; and that is, the opportunity to do anything you want always, and I would *like* to start off by doing the dishes."(p.351)
• I had no idea what would happen -- I just knew I didn't want to live if life was going to go on *like* it was.(p.355)
• I didn't particularly *like* it, but I loved the effects, and managed for the next twenty-five years to drink anything and everything, either handed to me or purchased, at the slightest excuse.(p.357)
• *Like* all alcoholics endeavoring to run away from themselves and their environment, I decided to go to New York.(p.358)
• The more I thought *like* this the more I drank to submerge my sorrows.(p.362)
• I could end my story here, but for the new man I would *like* to add a few words.(p.366)
• To the new man I would also *like* to say that this program is not for sissies for, in my humble opinion, it takes a man to make the grade.(p.367)
• I had no qualms, because I felt the source of a drinking problem was all in how weak one was, and I wasn't *like* my dad (I thought).(p.370)
• My sister-in-law took me to a place she had heard about that helps women *like* me.(p.371)
• I was raised *like* the majority of American boys, coming from a family of modest circumstances, attending public schools, having the social life of a small midwestern town, with part-time work and some athletics.(p.373)
• In fact I was afraid to try it for fear that I would wind up *like* many examples I had seen of excessive drinking in the Army.(p.374)
• This suggestion had been made before on a number of occasions, but *like* all alcoholics I wanted to handle my problem my own way, which really meant I didn't want anything to interfere with my drinking.(p.378)
• You didn't carry a little orchid up the aisle in those days; you carried a great big bouquet, *like* a funeral spray, and you didn't have your picture taken until just before you went to the church.(p.385)
• I walked up that aisle just *like* Mae West in her prime.(p.385)
• I had been reading a lot about psychiatry and I thought, "Maybe if I talk to a psychiatrist he can find out what is happening, and then I can drink *like* a lady."(p.387)
• Frank said, "If you'd *like* to talk to a psychiatrist, I'll see a doctor and find out who to go to here."(p.387)
• I woke up in this bare room with nothing around me but bars; they wouldn't let me smoke and treated me, well, *like* I was nuts.(p.387)
• As I said before, I don't *like* to be fenced in, and with those bars you don't get hotel service.(p.390)
• I don't want anybody ever to look at me *like* that again.(p.391)
• It had a name and symptoms, just *like* diabetes or T.B.(p.392)
• Monday morning I was feeling just *like* a million dollars – all I needed was half a pint!(p.393)
• So please bear in mind, and I would *like* to emphasize, that this is a very rough estimate.(p.399)
• *Like* most statistics, it doesn't prove anything -- just satisfies a little curiosity engendered by the wail "Oh, those initiation fees" that prompted this investigation.(p.399)
• I had writing ambitions, and nothing would do but that I'd write *like* Shakespeare.(p.400)
• *Like* most sick people before me, I was implacably selfish, and chronically self-centered.(p.401)
• Instead it was *like* a tap on the head with a small mallet.(p.402)
• He did not *like* naughty stories, so I made them naughtier.(p.403)
• I accepted a big tax-free income from the family, but I didn't *like* it when they told me how to live.(p.405)
• Or: If I'm really a genius, I must produce a great work, to show why I act *like* a genius.(p.408)
• I felt *like* a gangster's moll about to be interviewed by the Salvation Army.(p.413)
• Marty came in, looking clean, neat, well-dressed and, *like* Bill, she was neither a bloated wreck nor a reformer.(p.413)
• She was attractive; she was *like* the friends I had

once had.(p.414)
• Priscilla, an A.A. who, *like* Marty, has become one of my greatest friends, decided that I was a stubborn case.(p.414)
• In ending my story I *like* to think about this.(p.417)
• They both drank *like* fish.(p.424)
• I would rather have stayed in jail except I didn't *like* bologna and cold potatoes for breakfast.(p.425)
• She didn't *like* it, but I thought it made a man of me.(p.425)
• The doctor said I'd been brought into the hospital *like* a madman, crying, raving, ranting, swearing, completely in the throes of delirium tremens.(p.427)
• When I try to reconstruct what my life was *like* "before," I see a coin with two faces.(p.432)
• Next day remorse would be on me *like* a tiger.(p.432)
• However, I've heard of an organization called Alcoholics Anonymous that has had some success with people *like* you.(p.436)
• Never in my wildest moments had it occurred to me that I might *like* to be an alcoholic.(p.439)
• Never once had my mother even hinted at the idea that, when I grew up, I might *like* to be president of A.A.(p.439)
• Later, she would say, "You don't *like* me.(p.439)
• (Today, we don't have to live *like* that any more.)(p.440)
• "If you had my responsibilities, if you needed the sleep *like* I do, you'd drink too."(p.441)
• With a problem *like* that, I couldn't go back to sleep.(p.441)
• If it was one minute after, I'd stay up and act *like* a martyr all day.(p.441)
• The Mayo Clinic seemed *like* a good place to have my diagnosis confirmed.(p.444)
• I didn't *like* being on the nut ward, and I particularly didn't *like* being forced to ice cookies on Christmas Eve.(p.444)
• I never could quite get the knack of it and kept asking myself, "What's a nice guy *like* me doing in a place *like* this?"(p.445)
• One day as I sat there in the hospital, my psychiatrist walked up behind me and asked, "How'd you *like* to talk to the man from A.A.?"(p.446)
• For years, I was sure the worst thing that could happen to a nice guy *like* me would be that I would turn out to be an alcoholic.(p.449)
• Prior to our marriage, when she was a shy, scrawny adolescent, I was able to see things in her that others couldn't necessarily see – things *like* beauty, charm, gaiety, a gift for being easy to talk to, a sense of humor, and many other fine qualities.(p.450)
• I didn't know I was an alcoholic and (*like* most men in prison today) could not relate alcohol to any of my past troubles.(p.460)
• Shortly thereafter, I was selected, with eight other inmates out of the 10,000 in the state's prisons at that time, to attend a school designed to take former "management problems" *like* me and convert them into paracounselors.(p.462)
• It is all *like* a dream.(p.463)
• I didn't *like* it particularly at first, but I did *like* the effect I got from it.(p.464)
• Instead, I started going to a nice private sanitarium which, after the first visit, turned out to be more *like* a country club than anything else.(p.468)
• I thought, "Oh well, these people are just *like* all the people I've known all my life.(p.472)
• It read something *like* this: "Faith without works is dead.(p.473)
• We all one as Great Spirit walks through A.A. *like* sun walks through day.(p.474)
• To tell you a small part of what my mother's life must have been *like*: Three of her kids were in jail that year – two sons and a daughter.(p.480)
• I *like* to believe that I may have helped him, too.(p.481)
• I'm sure my ideas as to what life should be *like* were quite different from that of the average person with whom I associated.(p.483)
• About then too, I realized that my point of view on the opposite sex wasn't entirely *like* that of most of the boys I knew.(p.484)
• I would never be *like* the village drunkard at home.(p.498)
• I didn't *like* it, but I would not say so.(p.498)
• I'd drink *like* a gentleman after this.(p.498)
• I *like* the boys and we have lots of fun, in class and out.(p.500)
• Then comes a thought that is *like* a Voice.(p.504)
• "Well," he answers, "You've probably tried praying *like* I have.(p.504)
• I crawl back into bed and sleep *like* a child.(p.504)
• I think I am very lucky that there are people *like* A.A.'s and an A.A. program to hang on to and carry me through.(p.511)
• It's *like* the fellow who came in A.A., and his sponsor said to him, "Listen, buddy, do you believe in a Higher Power?"(p.512)
• *Like* many of us who went into the service, I thought it would be a cure-all, a new life.(p.513)
• Somehow or other I was coming face to face with myself, and I didn't *like* it.(p.513)
• When I came back, I told the priest, the Chaplain of the place, exactly what I thought of him and he didn't *like* it.(p.517)
• At first, *like* everybody else, I could keep control when I drank, but if I did start to drink, even in those days, I was always one of the last to leave the party.(p.518)
• Then a change in management took place in the regiment and the new O.C. didn't *like* me very much and I didn't *like* him, and he started to lie in wait for me.(p.519)
• I had been using paraldehyde more or less *like* ordinary drink for the last six years though, occasionally, I'd bounce back to phenobarbital and things *like* that.(p.524)
• I would wait for the mailman each month, *like* any good mother, but as soon as he handed me my check, I put on my best dress and went looking for my alcoholic friend.(p.527)
• Even those don't take part in A.A. functions as I would *like* to see them do.(p.529)
• There was the love affair which was ridiculous -- "imagine that midget being able to fall in love!" -- and my head knew it while my heart pumped real, genuine anguish, for it hurt *like* hell, and since it was first love, things have never been quite the same.(p.534)
• But one was so outstanding that I *like* to pass it on whenever I can in the hope that it will help someone else as it has me.(p.551)
• As I said earlier, self-pity and resentment were my constant companions and my inventory began to look *like* a thirty-three year diary, for I seemed to have a resentment against everybody I had ever known.(p.551)
• *Like* most other alcoholics I have known, I did quit drinking at various times -- once for ten months on my own and during other interludes when I was hospitalized.(p.554)
• And I didn't *like* it.(p.557)

likeable

• Is he not usually brilliant, fast-thinking, imaginative and *likeable*?(p.139)

liked

• Almost none of us *liked* the self-searching, the leveling of our pride, the confession of shortcomings which the process requires for its successful consummation.(p.25)
• We *liked* it.(p.53)
• We had seen spiritual release, but *liked* to tell ourselves it wasn't true.(p.55)
• Many of us had moral and philosophical convictions galore, but we could not live up to them even though we would have *liked* to.(p.62)
• There was nothing about that drink that I *liked*.(p.195)
• I definitely *liked* it, everything about it, the taste, the effects; and I realize now that a drink did something for me or to me that was different from the way it affected others.(p.305)
• But we had to do a lot of entertaining, my husband *liked* to have a good time; I was very young; and I wanted to have a good time too.(p.322)
• I did some things I *liked*, and even sold some.(p.331)
• I figured I'd be all right if I could find something I *liked* to do.(p.339)
• The second way in which, perhaps, I differ from some other alcoholics is this; many alcoholics state that they didn't particularly like the taste of alcohol, but that they *liked* the effect.(p.345)
• From the start I *liked* everything about the A.A. program.(p.380)
• I *liked* the description of the alcoholic as a person who had found that alcohol is interfering with his social or business life.(p.380)
• The servant he turned to was our old cook, and she *liked* to drink.(p.385)
• I *liked* it and soon moved into the photo department which was what I wanted to do.(p.425)
• So I concentrated and studied the book during that time, and I *liked* a lot of the things it said in there.(p.472)
• I *liked* games.(p.517)
• I always blamed my drinking on being poor, or on anything other than the truth – that I *liked* what booze did for me, that when I had a drink I was as big and had as much as the next person.(p.526)

likely

• We admit we have some of these symptoms, but we have not gone to the extremes you fellows did, nor are we *likely* to, for we understand ourselves so well after what you have told us that such things cannot happen again.(p.38)
• But, as with most humans, he is more *likely* to have varied traits.(p.61)
• He will be more *likely* to follow your suggestions.(p.94)
• If he has trouble later, he is *likely* to say you rushed him.(p.95)
• Sooner or later, you are *likely* to find him reading the book once more.(p.113)
• Another feeling we are very *likely* to entertain is one of resentment that love and loyalty could not cure our husbands of alcoholism.(p.118)
• The alcoholic, his wife, his children, his "in-laws," each one is *likely* to have fixed ideas about the family's attitude toward himself or herself.(p.122)
• He is not *likely* to get far in any direction if he fails to show unselfishness and love under his own roof.(p.127)
• He will be less *likely* to drink again, and anything is preferable to that.(p.130)
• Many friends of my family had emigrated to America, so at twenty-four I decided that the United States offered me the opportunity I was never *likely* to find in my native land.(p.231)
• I was voted the man most *likely* to succeed.(p.345)
• I found I could boost my income by figuring out a lot of cute little tricks that the boss wouldn't be *likely* to notice – filching money from the Coke machine, short-sticking the customers on oil, and selling oil I'd drained out of other cars.(p.423)
• A happy man is not *likely* to do harm to another human being.(p.542)

likes

• No person *likes* to think he is bodily and mentally different from his fellows.(p.30)
• Everybody *likes* him.(p.35)
• *Likes* Brown.(p.65)
• This is the one he *likes* his fellows to see.(p.73)
• He can choose any conception he *likes*, provided it makes sense to him.(p.93)
• If you do stay, let him steer the conversation in any direction he *likes*.(p.95)
• We would not even do the cause of temperate drinking any good, for not one drinker in a thousand *likes* to be told anything about alcohol by one who hates it.(p.103)
• Make him feel absolutely free to come and go as he *likes*.(p.120)
• Even if he displays a certain amount of neglect and irresponsibility towards the family, it is well to let him go as far as he *likes* in helping other alcoholics.(p.129)
• Whether your employee *likes* it or not, he will learn the grim truth about alcoholism.(p.144)
• We all had hundreds of character traits, of fears and phobias, *likes* and dislikes, in common.(p.229)
• No one *likes* to admit that they're a drunk, that they can't control this thing.(p.340)
• What a revelation of ego and arrogance still remaining in me – as if anyone, instinct and training apart, *likes* to be in jail or in an alcoholic ward or fired from his job.(p.536)

likewise

• As part of his rehabilitation he commenced to present his conceptions to other alcoholics, impressing upon them that they must do *likewise* with still others.(p.xxiii)

liking

• Is not each trying to arrange the family show to his *liking*?(p.122)

limburger

• We were having card parties with *limburger* and beer quite regularly.(p.297)

limitation

• I simply had to believe in a Spirit of the Universe, who knew neither time nor *limitation*.(p.10)

limited

• We believe, and so suggested a few years ago, that the action of alcohol on these chronic alcoholics is a manifestation of an allergy; that the phenomenon of craving is *limited* to this class and never occurs in the average temperate drinker.(p.xxvi)
• So we used our own conception, however *limited* it was.(p.47)

• The choice was ***limited***.(p.278)

• Sometimes during that year I rebelled inwardly at what seemed like lost time, and at having to be a burden to these good people whose means were ***limited***.(p.281)

• Eighteen will be used as the starting point, because my drinking before was ***limited*** by age, the law, and money.(p.397)

• Saying these sprees were ***limited*** to one a week (they were not), and saying that the average spree was ten of these drinks (sometimes more, sometimes less), we come up with the first boring statistic: two-fifty per week out of twelve dollars.(p.397)

• Now my drinking was ***limited*** by only one factor, the enforced periods of dryness caused by lengthy tours at sea.(p.398)

• His parishioners are ***limited*** in number, but his friends are many, for to him race, creed, or social position makes no difference.(p.497)

limiting

• Here are some of the methods we have tried: Drinking beer only, ***limiting*** the number of drinks, never drinking alone, never drinking in the morning, drinking only at home, never having it in the house, never drinking during business hours, drinking only at parties, switching from scotch to brandy, drinking only natural wines, agreeing to resign if ever drunk on the job, taking a trip, not taking a trip, swearing off forever (with and without a solemn oath), taking more physical exercise, reading inspirational books, going to health farms and sanitariums, accepting voluntary commitment to asylums -- we could increase the list ad infinitum.(p.31)

• This eliminated one of the ***limiting*** factors, the financial.(p.397)

• The only other occasionally ***limiting*** factor was that I might run out of money before the next payday rolled around.(p.398)

limitless

• He may not see at once that he has barely scratched a ***limitless*** lode which will pay dividends only if he mines it for the rest of his life and insists on giving away the entire product.(p.129)

• As arrested alcoholics, we must have a program for living that allows for ***limitless*** expansion.(p.311)

line

• If any feel that as psychiatrists directing a hospital for alcoholics we appear somewhat sentimental, let them stand with us a while on the firing ***line***, see the tragedies, the despairing wives, the little children; let the solving of these problems become a part of their daily work, and even of their sleeping moments, and the most cynical will not wonder that we have accepted and encouraged this movement.(p.xxvi)

• We could not prove life in the sense that you can prove a straight ***line*** is the shortest distance between two points, yet, there it was.(p.54)

• We can exercise our will power along this ***line*** all we wish.(p.85)

• Keep on the firing ***line*** of life with these motives and God will keep you unharmed.(p.102)

• Even if you feel your organization has no alcoholic problem, it might pay to take another look down the ***line***.(p.149)

• He trembled as he went about, for this might mean ruin, particularly to a person in his ***line*** of business.(p.156)

• In other words, I was always safe from the discipline of my father, and having developed along that ***line***, I had considerable difficulty in school.(p.210)

• After two or three years of effort along this ***line***, I reached the point of actual despair that I ever would be able to drink only a harmless amount each day.(p.215)

• There was a very religious family that lived down the road from us, and we were on the same party ***line***.(p.265)

• I really worked for several weeks, and having had a fairly wide acquaintance with the dealer trade, it was not difficult for me to ***line*** up enough of them to give me a very substantial volume of business with a minimum of effort.(p.300)

• However, this isn't as rough as it sounds, as we do become grateful for the necessity that makes us toe the ***line***, for we find that we are more than compensated for a consistent effort by the countless dividends we receive.(p.311)

• One night, I was struck with the memory of a ***line*** Alan Ladd used in "Shane," a movie that I'd worked on.(p.333)

• How that ***line*** echoed through my mind!(p.333)

• It was my ***line***, the story of my life.(p.333)

• And then one ill-defined day, one day that I can't recall, I stepped across the ***line*** that alcoholics know so well, and from that day on drinking was miserable.(p.346)

• When a few drinks made me feel good before I went over that ***line***, those same drinks now made me wretched.(p.346)

• I would follow certain drinking schedules or diets faithfully for a few days, and then somewhere along the ***line*** would over-train and upset the applecart.(p.361)

• In a few weeks I toed the ***line***.(p.362)

• As long as it eased situations socially, it helped just fine, but somewhere along the ***line***, it backfired.(p.386)

• When I crossed that ***line***, I don't know.(p.386)

• The ***line*** between a heavy drinker and an alcoholic is not always clear.(p.436)

• And I knew that somewhere along the ***line*** I'd lost the power to stop drinking.(p.436)

• Having passed over the border ***line***, the next five years were filled with fear, failure and frustration.(p.465)

• Some of us always remember our big mouths when it comes to a drink, but somewhere along the ***line***, we seem to have forgotten about taking care of our teeth.(p.479)

• When he left I walked with him to the streetcar ***line***, which was just about a half a block, but there were two liquor stores, one on each corner from my home.(p.495)

• That was the day, that was the decision, I know now, when I crossed over the ***line*** and became an active alcoholic.(p.531)

lined

• I used to put eight or twelve ounce bottles of alcohol in a fur ***lined*** glove and toss it onto the back airing porch when winter days got dark enough.(p.176)

• After being fired, I ***lined*** up with a new finance company that was just starting in business, and took the position of business promotion man, contacting automobile dealers.(p.300)

• By this time, my chances of getting ***lined*** up in my chosen business were shot.(p.301)

liner

• We are like the passengers of a great ***liner*** the moment after rescue from shipwreck when camaraderie, joyousness and democracy pervade the vessel from steerage to Captain's table.(p.17)

lines

• The point is, that we are willing to grow along spiritual ***lines***.(p.60)

• In fact, I never lost my faith, since I had been prepared by some conversations toward the end of my sojourn in the hospital with Dr. Bob, conversations pretty much along spiritual ***lines***.(p.218)

• Love has no words to spell or ***lines*** to start and stop.(p.474)

lips

• Many a distracted wife has visited this house to find loving and understanding companionship among women who knew her problem, to hear from the ***lips*** of their husbands what had happened to them, to be advised how her own wayward mate might be hospitalized and approached when next he stumbled.(p.160)

• I was black and blue, with my ***lips*** all swollen, when they roused us to go into court in the morning.(p.204)

• I had just raised the bottle to my ***lips*** when my wife opened the door and froze me completely in my tracks with "Happy New Year, dear."(p.365)

liquid

• The parties waxed more ***liquid*** and hilarious as time went on, and eventually I discovered that a little shot of liquor now and then between beers had the tendency to put me in a whacky mood much quicker than having to down several quarts of beer to obtain the same effect.(p.298)

• There's only one answer -- ***liquid*** comfort.(p.331)

• We do this by going to many A.A. meetings with an open mind and a desire to live the good-feeling life without chemicals -- ***liquid*** or otherwise.(p.459)

liquor

• Of course an alcoholic ought to be freed from his physical craving for ***liquor***, and this often requires a definite hospital procedure, before psychological measures can be of maximum benefit.(p.xxv)

• I was part of life at last, and in the midst of the excitement I discovered ***liquor***.(p.1)

• ***Liquor*** caught up with me much faster than I came up behind Walter.(p.3)

• ***Liquor*** ceased to be a luxury; it became a necessity.(p.5)

• It relieved me somewhat to learn that in alcoholics the will is amazingly weakened when it comes to combating ***liquor***, though it often remains strong in other respects.(p.7)

• "That fellow can't handle his ***liquor***."(p.20)

• Moderate drinkers have little trouble in giving up ***liquor*** entirely if they have good reason for it.(p.20)

• He may start off as a moderate drinker; he may or may not become a continuous hard drinker; but at some stage of his drinking career he begins to lose all control of his ***liquor*** consumption, once he starts to drink.(p.21)

• He is often perfectly sensible and well balanced concerning everything except ***liquor***, but in that respect he is incredibly dishonest and selfish.(p.21)

• If he can afford it, he may have ***liquor*** concealed all over his house to be certain no one gets his entire supply away from him to throw down the waterpipe.(p.22)

• As matters grow worse, he begins to use a combination of high-powered sedative and ***liquor*** to quiet his nerves so he can go to work.(p.22)

• He was very nervous in the morning after these bouts and quieted himself with more ***liquor***.(p.32)

• If anyone questions whether he has entered this dangerous area, let him try leaving ***liquor*** alone for one year.(p.34)

• Our ***liquor*** was but a symptom.(p.64)

• He commences to look around in the night clubs, or their equivalent, for something besides ***liquor***.(p.81)

• We will seldom be interested in ***liquor***.(p.84)

• We will see that our new attitude toward ***liquor*** has been given us without any thought or effort on our part.(p.85)

• If he is in a serious mood dwell on the trouble ***liquor*** has caused you, being careful not to moralize or lecture.(p.91)

• People have said we must not go where ***liquor*** is served; we must not have it in our homes; we must shun friends who drink; we must avoid moving pictures which show drinking scenes; we must not go into bars; our friends must hide their bottles if we go to their houses; we mustn't think or be reminded about alcohol at all.(p.100)

• Don't start to withdraw again just because your friends drink ***liquor***.(p.102)

• Many of us keep ***liquor*** in our homes.(p.102)

• But some of us think we should not serve ***liquor*** to anyone.(p.102)

• Perhaps he spends too much money for ***liquor***.(p.109)

• He is positive he can handle his ***liquor***, that it does him no harm, that drinking is necessary in his business.(p.109)

• Perhaps you both like parties which would be dull without ***liquor***.(p.110)

• We know all about ***liquor*** as a social lubricant.(p.110)

• It is the most natural thing in the world, once his ***liquor*** problem is solved, to feel that he will now measure up to that cherished vision.(p.118)

• God has either removed your husband's ***liquor*** problem or He has not.(p.120)

• ***Liquor*** incapacitated father for so many years that mother became head of the house.(p.130)

• "Oh no," said my friend, "this chap is either through with ***liquor***, or he is minus a job.(p.138)

• As a moderate drinker, you can take your ***liquor*** or leave it alone.(p.139)

• To you, ***liquor*** is no real problem.(p.139)

• Your man will fare better if placed in such physical condition that he can think straight and no longer craves ***liquor***.(p.143)

• I know I must get along without ***liquor***, but how can I?(p.152)

• Some time later, and just as he thought he was getting control of his ***liquor*** situation, he went on a roaring bender.(p.155)

• No beer or ***liquor*** was sold in the neighborhood, except at the State ***liquor*** agency where perhaps one might procure a pint if he could convince the agent that he really needed it.(p.171)

• Men who had ***liquor*** shipped in from Boston or New York by express were looked upon with great distrust and disfavor by most of the good townspeople.(p.171)

• This had little effect however for I kept on drinking and used a great deal more hard ***liquor*** than in former years.(p.174)

• I knew everyone would buy a few bottles, or cases, of ***liquor*** as their exchequers permitted, and that it would soon be gone.(p.175)

• One was the fear of not sleeping, and the other was the fear of running out of ***liquor***.(p.175)

• Not being a man of means, I knew that if I did not stay sober enough to earn money, I would run out of ***liquor***.(p.175)

• If my wife was planning to go out in the afternoon, I would get a large supply of *liquor* and smuggle it home and hide it in the coal bin, the clothes chute, over door jambs, over beams in the cellar and in cracks in the cellar tile.(p.176)
• My phobia for sleeplessness demanded that I get drunk every night, but in order to get more *liquor* for the next night, I had to stay sober during the day, at least up to four o'clock.(p.177)
• It was really a horrible nightmare, this earning money, getting *liquor*, smuggling it home, getting drunk, morning jitters, taking large doses of sedatives to make it possible for me to earn more money, and so on ad nauseam.(p.177)
• My wife became deeply interested and it was her interest that sustained mine, though I at no time sensed that it might be an answer to my *liquor* problem.(p.178)
• I bought some more *liquor* on the way to the depot.(p.179)
• Unlike most of our crowd, I did not get over my craving for *liquor* much during the first two and one-half years of abstinence.(p.181)
• So it doesn't behoove me to squawk about it for, after all, nobody ever had to throw me down and pour *liquor* down my throat.(p.181)
• But if you really and truly want to quit drinking *liquor* for good and all, and sincerely feel that you must have some help, we know that we have an answer for you.(p.181)
• Morning after morning I would awake sick and with terrible jitters, but there was always a flask of *liquor* sitting on the table beside my bed.(p.183)
• I would reach over and get this and take a shot and in a few moments get up and take another, shave and eat my breakfast, slip a half pint of *liquor* in my hip pocket, and go on to school.(p.183)
• I thought of what *liquor* had done to me, the opportunities that I had discarded, the abilities that had been given me and how I had wasted them, and I finally came to the conclusion, that if I didn't want to quit, I certainly ought to want to, and that I was willing to do anything in the world to stop drinking.(p.186)
• So, after reviewing these things and realizing what *liquor* had cost me, I went to this Higher Power which, to me was God, without any reservation, and admitted that I was completely powerless over alcohol, and that I was willing to do anything in the world to get rid of the problem.(p.187)
• That was the first time I ever drank hard *liquor*.(p.195)
• I think it was probably more than a year before I had anything more to do with *liquor*.(p.195)
• So I didn't have a beer one night, and as I drove home I was breaking my arm patting myself on the back because I had proved I could lick *liquor*.(p.203)
• I had proved that *liquor* was not my master.(p.203)
• He did call me a cab and when I got into the cab, I said, "Drive me to a *liquor* store."(p.204)
• That was at the end of eight days in which I had had no *liquor*.(p.218)
• I cannot say, however, that I acquired any craving for hard *liquor* as a result.(p.231)
• Before long I had a definite taste for hard *liquor*, knew nausea and headaches I had never known before, but as in the old days, I suffered them out.(p.233)
• As soon as I had satisfied that, what I earned as an upholsterer went for *liquor*.(p.234)
• And yet, realizing at last that *liquor* really had me, I wanted to quit.(p.234)
• My wife wrote away for advertised cures for the *liquor* habit and gave them to me in coffee.(p.235)
• In a few sentences he made God seem personal to me, explained Him as a being who was interested in me, the alcoholic, and that all I needed to do was to be willing to follow His way; that as long as I followed it I would be able to overcome my desire for *liquor*.(p.236)
• I myself could see deterioration in my work from being physically and mentally affected by *liquor*, although I had not yet reached the point where all I wanted was more to drink.(p.254)
• I had some financial success through no ability of my own and, when jobless and almost wiped out in 1930, I began to trade and sell my collection; much of the proceeds went to keep my apartment stocked with *liquor* and almost every night saw me helpless to bed.(p.255)
• Now on a new job I was always thinking about payday and how much *liquor* I could buy and the pleasure I could have.(p.255)
• I had never known him to be anything but a good healthy pagan with a propensity for getting into *liquor* jams and scrapes.(p.257)
• I don't feel bothered about *liquor*."(p.257)
• I had been drinking heavily from one state of semi-coma to another and it was several days before I got "defogged," but subconsciously I was in earnest about wanting to quit *liquor* forever.(p.258)
• I cannot say that my taste for *liquor* has entirely disappeared.(p.259)
• We always tried to buy him a drink, and he always told us he had *liquor* trouble – couldn't drink.)(p.266)
• *Liquor* relieved these.(p.277)
• *Liquor* had become a crutch on the one hand and a means of retreat from life on the other.(p.277)
• They went into a huddle and dad explained that he simply took my pants, shoes and money away, so that I could get no *liquor* and had to sober up.(p.288)
• Then when we got back to the apartment, he was willing to wait two or three days until I got my health back to be paid off for the *liquor* and fare.(p.289)
• The parties waxed more liquid and hilarious as time went on, and eventually I discovered that a little shot of *liquor* now and then between beers had the tendency to put me in a whacky mood much quicker than having to down several quarts of beer to obtain the same effect.(p.298)
• My new duties were extremely confining and my *liquor* consumption began to increase.(p.298)
• I didn't care to go visiting unless the parties we might visit had plenty of *liquor* on hand and I could get drunk.(p.301)
• From a physical standpoint, I gained sixteen pounds in the first two months I was off *liquor*.(p.303)
• My first drinking spree was on corn *liquor* and I was allergic to it, believe me.(p.322)
• I had to have *liquor*.(p.324)
• I had been unhappy, lonely, and scared for so long that the discovery of *liquor* seemed to be the answer to all my problems.(p.353)
• Of course I kept her posted on how well the station was doing and wrote convincing letters of how well I was doing with the *liquor* problem.(p.360)
• And deep in my heart I really meant what I said because I loved her more than anything else in the world, yes -- even more than *liquor*.(p.362)
• I was going to prove to her that *liquor* wasn't necessary in my life, and above all that I still loved her more than anything else in the world and that I wanted her back.(p.362)
• Sure enough in a couple of hours two men were at my door and for the first time I heard some facts about *liquor* and my problem that sounded sensible to me.(p.363)
• I kept away from *liquor* and eagerly waited.(p.363)
• I thought this was a good time to experiment with *liquor*.(p.364)
• So I went down to him quite a few times a month and had him shoot me full of the stuff; and then I went across the street to a little drug store to take a glass of beer or two beers, and then stopped at the *liquor* store to get myself a pint and go home.(p.389)
• As income increased, the price of *liquor* increased proportionately.(p.398)
• The *liquor* counteracted the help I was getting.(p.407)
• But the money I had saved up went for cases of *liquor*.(p.409)
• I was never drunk on the job, never missed a day's work, was seldom rendered totally ineffective by a hangover and kept my *liquor* expenses well within my adequate budget.(p.433)
• I remember vaguely violent quarrels with my husband, his finding my *liquor* supply time and time again and throwing it out.(p.466)
• But there happened to be a *liquor* store between the post office and the mill, and I stopped to get that one drink.(p.493)
• After he'd talked half an hour, I still wanted him to hurry up and get out so I could go and get some whiskey before the *liquor* store closed.(p.494)
• When he left I walked with him to the streetcar line, which was just about a half a block, but there were two *liquor* stores, one on each corner from my home.(p.495)
• I put Charlie on the car and when I left him I passed both of those *liquor* stores without even thinking about them.(p.495)
• Mother hated *liquor* and feared a drunken man.(p.498)
• I look for *liquor* and can't find any.(p.502)
• I must get some *liquor*.(p.502)
• I am going to town to get some *liquor* and food.(p.506)
• I wasn't afraid of anything or anybody after I learned about drinking, for it seemed right from the beginning that with *liquor* I could always retire to my little private world where nobody could get at me to hurt me.(p.547)
• I swore off hard *liquor* and turned to wine.(p.555)

list

• We made a *list* of people I had hurt or toward whom I felt resentment.(p.13)
• It brings misunderstanding, fierce resentment, financial insecurity, disgusted friends and employers, warped lives of blameless children, sad wives and parents -- anyone can increase the *list*.(p.18)
• Here are some of the methods we have tried: Drinking beer only, limiting the number of drinks, never drinking alone, never drinking in the morning, drinking only at home, never having it in the house, never drinking during business hours, drinking only at parties, switching from scotch to brandy, drinking only natural wines, agreeing to resign if ever drunk on the job, taking a trip, not taking a trip, swearing off forever (with and without a solemn oath), taking more physical exercise, reading inspirational books, going to health farms and sanitariums, accepting voluntary commitment to asylums – we could increase the *list* ad infinitum.(p.31)
• 8.Made a *list* of all persons we had harmed, and became willing to make amends to them all.(p.59)
• On our grudge *list* we set opposite each name our injuries.(p.65)
• We turned back to the *list*, for it held the key to the future.(p.66)
• Referring to our *list* again.(p.67)
• We have a *list* of all persons we have harmed and to whom we are willing to make amends.(p.76)
• As we look over the *list* of business acquaintances and friends we have hurt, we may feel diffident about going to some of them on a spiritual basis.(p.76)
• Dr. Bob then led me through the restitution step, in which I made a *list* of all of the persons I had harmed, and worked out ways and means of slowly making restitution.(p.292)
• I can only *list* a few of its elements.(p.435)
• One has to be pretty sick to do that, and perhaps one has to be even sicker to come back every day for a new *list*, as she did.(p.446)

listed

• We *listed* people, institutions or principles with whom we were angry.(p.64)
• When we saw our faults we *listed* them.(p.67)
• We have *listed* and analyzed our resentments.(p.70)
• We have *listed* the people we have hurt by our conduct, and are willing to straighten out the past if we can.(p.70)
• I was *listed* in "Who's Who in America" as an American who, by distinguished achievement, had arrived.(p.432)

listen

• I could almost hear the sound of the preacher's voice as I sat, on still Sundays, way over there on the hillside; there was that proffered temperance pledge I never signed; my grandfather's good natured contempt of some church folk and their doings; his insistence that the spheres really had their music; but his denial of the preacher's right to tell him how he must *listen*; his fearlessness as he spoke of these things just before he died; these recollections welled up from the past.(p.10)
• All the other people that had talked to me wanted to help me, and my pride prevented me from listening to them, and caused only resentment on my part, but I felt as if I would be a real stinker if I did not *listen* to a couple of fellows for a short time, if that would cure them.(p.185)
• If I could stick to Him and *listen*, I would make it.(p.190)
• I got two drinks, each of them a quarter of that pint, in me, and was talking along with these people, but I felt that sooner or later they were going to have me cornered because they were smarter than I was and the drink was beginning to take effect; but as I reached for the third drink Bob said, "*Listen*, Buster, you promised to take some medicine if we got you a drink.(p.206)
• This was the background that made me willing to *listen* on January 8th.(p.245)
• I also talked A.A. to every friend who would *listen*, at lunch, at dinner, on street corners.(p.282)
• The pep pills affected my hearing at times: I couldn't *listen* fast enough to hear what I was saying.(p.442)
• I not *listen* to old woman.(p.474)
• Year later, I go to Canada to carry message to Tall Man, but he not *listen* to son.(p.476)
• I keep it simple; go to many meetings; carry message to those who *listen*.(p.476)
• *Listen*, not just hear noise.(p.477)
• He continued to talk and I to *listen*.(p.494)
• I had enough decency so that I dismissed the idea

of doing any clowning, and I did *listen*.(p.509)
• It's like the fellow who came in A.A., and his sponsor said to him, "*Listen*, buddy, do you believe in a Higher Power?"(p.512)
• Actually, of course, I wanted someone to *listen* to me, because when I had a few martinis inside, I became the great author I longed to be; and the right listener was in for some pretty highflown theories of literature and of genius.(p.536)

listened
• He *listened* in wonder as I talked.(p.14)
• I *listened* to famous ministers – found nothing.(p.255)
• I *listened* to him, rather tolerantly.(p.257)
• My wife became pregnant and the doctor recommended the use of port or ale . . . so . . . I bought a six gallon crock and a few bottles, *listened* to advice from amateur brewmeisters, and was off on my beer manufacturing career on a small scale (for the time being).(p.297)
• I sat and *listened* and heard the first speaker say, "I'm an alcoholic."(p.319)
• Lying on the divan, "getting in the mood" to write, I cried openly or inwardly, as I *listened* to sad songs.(p.332)
• I heard a lovely voice, and a sympathetic ear *listened* to my plea.(p.363)
• He and his wife more than accepted me; he *listened* to all my woes; both of them treated me as a human being.(p.462)
• So I went to an A.A. meeting the first chance I got, and I *listened*.(p.511)

listener
• Actually, of course, I wanted someone to listen to me, because when I had a few martinis inside, I became the great author I longed to be; and the right *listener* was in for some pretty highflown theories of literature and of genius.(p.536)
• If the *listener* were drunk enough, the lecture might go on through several martinis, which I was glad to pay for.(p.537)

listening
• All the other people that had talked to me wanted to help me, and my pride prevented me from *listening* to them, and caused only resentment on my part, but I felt as if I would be a real stinker if I did not listen to a couple of fellows for a short time, if that would cure them.(p.185)
• We were eating lunch, and I was *listening* and trying to find out why they had this release that they seemed to have.(p.191)
• I have stood *listening* to street-corner preachers tell how they beat the game.(p.256)
• Through going to meetings and *listening*, and occasionally speaking, through doing Twelve Step work, whereby in helping others you are both the teacher and the student, by making many wonderful A.A. friends, I have been taught all the things in life that are worth having.(p.416)
• Pearl Harbor was a breeze of nine months, a gay Hawaiian paradise, drinking under the palms, *listening* to the surf beat on the shore, a bottle of whiskey near at hand.(p.426)
• One night I was sitting in the lab alone with a fifth and a case of beer *listening* to dreamy Hawaiian music on the radio.(p.427)
• But by *listening* and talking to these A.A.'s – talking to them as I had never talked to anyone in my whole life, I saw that it was my life that was unmanageable – not just my drinking.(p.471)

listing
• If there is no Al-Anon *listing* in your local telephone book, you may obtain further information on Al-Anon Family Groups by writing to its World Service Office: Box 182, Madison Square Station, New York, NY 10159.(p.121)
• I had every advantage a child could have, private schools (several of them), dancing schools, two colleges, coon skin coats, automobiles, a *listing* in the social register and all the rest.(p.357)
• These so-called intergroup associations are found under the *listing* "A.A." or "Alcoholics Anonymous" in telephone directories.(p.575)

lists
• Much of my time was spent writing letters, notes, orders, and *lists* of things for Max, who was also my office nurse, to do to keep the world running while I was locked up.(p.445)

lit
• "The doctor told him that if he ever drank again it would kill him, but there he is all *lit* up again."(p.20)

literally
• A man so involved often feels very remorseful at times, especially if he is married to a loyal and courageous girl who has *literally* gone through hell for him.(p.81)
• I *literally* hit the sawdust.(p.411)
• In the light of subsequent events it became evident that I took their advice far too *literally*, for, after some months of happy sobriety I drank again.(p.471)
• All of my family and loved ones, all of my friends, are nearer and dearer to me than ever before and I have *literally* dozens of new friends who say they cannot believe that a short eight years ago I was ready for the scrap heap.(p.541)
• I was drunk for sixty days around the clock and it was my intention, *literally*, to drink myself to death.(p.549)

literary
• I don't think the boys were completely convinced of my personality change, for they fought shy of including my story in the book, so my only contribution to their *literary* efforts was my firm conviction, being still a theological rebel, that the word God should be qualified with the phrase "as we understand him" -- for that was the only way I could accept spirituality.(p.248)
• My associates, and all the wits and *literary* lights I so much admired, also drank.(p.433)
• If he were still sober, chances are that very quickly I put him down as a Philistine with no appreciation of *literary* genius; and then I went on to another bar to find a new victim.(p.537)
• Brandishing my "motto," which was "A little man with a stick is equal to a big man," sometimes I varied the *literary* lecture by a fight with a big man, selected solely because he was big and I was little.(p.537)

literature
• The big A.A. book had not been written and there was no *literature* except various religious pamphlets.(p.291)
• The regular flow of all the *literature*, which I keep meticulously and which, of course, I study, has been wonderful.(p.342)
• I have never attended an A.A. meeting, so it is essentially the *literature* that has kept me on the A.A. program.(p.342)
• Following this, I had a short vacation, during which time I read as much *literature* as my sponsor could send me.(p.343)
• I have read systematically since then, and A.A. *literature* has kept me sober.(p.343)
• I read, studied, and meditated on every bit of A.A. *literature* in my possession.(p.344)
• That night she too had new hope because I had made sure she would know what I was doing about my drinking by packing every bit of A.A. *literature* I could put my hands on right on top so she couldn't help but see it when she opened my bag.(p.364)
• While I was in Florida trying to convince my wife with all the A.A. *literature* that she should come back to me, she went over to her desk and picked up a clipping she had taken from the St. Petersburg Times about A.A.(p.366)
• So I wrote this letter in very shaky handwriting, and in just one week came back a letter with A.A. *literature* from New York.(p.392)
• Could they discuss *literature* or art?(p.412)
• Actually, of course, I wanted someone to listen to me, because when I had a few martinis inside, I became the great author I longed to be; and the right listener was in for some pretty highflown theories of *literature* and of genius.(p.536)

litigation
• In the fall of the graduating year, I became involved in some *litigation* over the ownership of inventions and patents.(p.212)
• The law school experience was not inspired by a desire to follow patent law, which has been my profession since: I went to law school primarily to learn the law of contracts following my own experience with *litigation*.(p.212)

little
• This brought a rush of 800 frantic inquiries into the *little* New York office which meanwhile had been established.(p.xviii)
• As laymen, our opinion as to its soundness may, of course, mean *little*.(p.xxiv)
• If any feel that as psychiatrists directing a hospital for alcoholics we appear somewhat sentimental, let them stand with us a while on the firing line, see the tragedies, the despairing wives, the *little* children; let the solving of these problems become a part of their daily work, and even of their sleeping moments, and the most cynical will not wonder that we have accepted and encouraged this movement.(p.xxvi)
• This is repeated over and over, and unless this person can experience an entire psychic change there is very *little* hope of his recovery.(p.xxvii)
• Though the aggregate of recoveries resulting from psychiatric effort is considerable, we physicians must admit we have made *little* impression upon the problem as a whole.(p.xxvii)
• My work took me about Wall street and *little* by *little* I became interested in the market.(p.2)
• I had had some success at speculation, so we had a *little* money, but we once worked on a farm for a month to avoid drawing on our small capital.(p.3)
• I could eat *little* or nothing when drinking, and I was forty pounds under weight.(p.7)
• I went to town regularly and even made a *little* money.(p.7)
• So that was it -- last summer an alcoholic crackpot; now, I suspected, a *little* cracked about religion.(p.9)
• Despite contrary indications, I had *little* doubt that a mighty purpose and rhythm underlay all.(p.10)
• It was fortunate, for my old business associates remained skeptical for a year and a half, during which I found *little* work.(p.15)
• Until such an understanding is reached, *little* or nothing can be accomplished.(p.18)
• If we keep on the way we are going there is *little* doubt that much good will result, but the surface of the problem would hardly be scratched.(p.19)
• Moderate drinkers have *little* trouble in giving up liquor entirely if they have good reason for it.(p.20)
• His disposition while drinking resembles his normal nature but *little*.(p.21)
• We are not sure why, once a certain point is reached, *little* can be done for him.(p.22)
• We now see that when we began to drink deliberately, instead of casually, there was *little* serious or effective thought during the period of premeditation of what the terrific consequences might be.(p.37)
• I know *little* of where I went or what I said and did.(p.41)
• Whether we agree with a particular approach or conception seems to make *little* difference.(p.50)
• That was natural, but let us think a *little* more closely.(p.53)
• *Little* or nothing, we saw at last.(p.54)
• In one form or another we had been living by faith and *little* else.(p.54)
• Established on such a footing we became less and less interested in ourselves, our *little* plans and designs.(p.63)
• Though our decision was a vital and crucial step, it could have *little* permanent effect unless at once followed by a strenuous effort to face, and to be rid of, the things in ourselves which had been blocking us.(p.64)
• But insist that if he is severely afflicted, there may be *little* chance he can recover by himself.(p.92)
• If he is, you might try to help him about getting a job, or give him a *little* financial assistance.(p.96)
• For the type of alcoholic who is able and willing to get well, *little* charity, in the ordinary sense of the word, is needed or wanted.(p.97)
• *Little* by *little* the family may see their own defects and admit them.(p.99)
• Or am I expecting to steal a *little* vicarious pleasure from the atmosphere of such places?"(p.101)
• While you were drinking, you were withdrawing from life *little* by *little*.(p.102)
• Some day we hope that Alcoholics Anonymous will help the public to a better realization of the gravity of the alcoholic problem, but we shall be of *little* use if our attitude is one of bitterness or hostility.(p.103)
• Our friends have counseled chucking the men and we have done so with finality, only to be back in a *little* while hoping, always hoping.(p.105)
• If you both show a willingness to remedy your own defects, there will be *little* need to criticize each other.(p.118)
• It will do *little* good if you point that out and urge more attention for yourself.(p.119)
• He may either plunge into a frantic attempt to get on his feet in business, or he may be so enthralled by his new life that he talks or thinks of *little* else.(p.125)
• It is of *little* use to argue and only makes the impasse worse.(p.126)
• *Little* by *little*, mother and children will see they ask too much, and father will see he gives too *little*.(p.127)
• We have three *little* mottoes which are apropos.(p.135)
• One instance comes to mind in which a malicious individual was always making friendly *little* jokes about an alcoholic's drinking exploits.(p.145)
• We believe that managers of large enterprises often have *little* idea how prevalent this problem is.(p.149)
• Today I own a *little* company.(p.149)

• Said the future Fellow Anonymous: "Damn *little* to laugh about that I can see."(p.157)
• Seeing much of each other, scarce an evening passed that someone's home did not shelter a *little* gathering of men and women, happy in their release, and constantly thinking how they might present their discovery to some newcomer.(p.159)
• *Little* clusters of twos and threes and fives of us have sprung up in other communities, through contact with our two larger centers.(p.162)
• We realize we know only a *little*.(p.164)
• This had *little* effect however for I kept on drinking and used a great deal more hard liquor than in former years.(p.174)
• 4.Because every time I do it I take out a *little* more insurance for myself against a possible slip.(p.181)
• It took me a year, or a year and a half to get to feeling physically well, and it was rather tough, but I soon found folks whose friendship I had once had, and I found, after I had been sober for quite some *little* time, that these people began to act like they had in previous years, before I had gotten so bad, so that I didn't pay too awful much attention to financial gains.(p.190)
• When he was uptown – we were living in the *little* town of Moscow – I went up to try to get some money from him to buy groceries.(p.193)
• This was a regular occurrence for a *little* while.(p.196)
• I can remember telling the poor *little* soul that I could probably quit drinking if I wasn't married to her, and told her that, after all, I didn't like restraint!(p.199)
• Naturally, what *little* restraint I had exercised before was gone now, and my drinking became worse.(p.199)
• Then I started drinking again, with possibly a *little* more restraint, periods a *little* bit longer than they had been before, but substantially the same pattern.(p.203)
• So I was barred from the plant for ten days, and during that ten day period I was drunk twice, showing how *little* control these restraints had on me.(p.205)
• Paul measured the medicine out, but he figured that with my track record that *little* bit wouldn't be enough, so he doubled it and added a few drops more and then gave it to me.(p.207)
• He said, "Maybe you need a *little* drink."(p.208)
• Not far from where I lived they built a new technical high school and one of the teachers sold me on the idea that I needed a *little* mechanical drawing if I were going to be a good toolmaker.(p.211)
• My children had lost respect for me and, in fact, it was only after three or four years of sobriety that any of them ever said anything to me to indicate that I had recouped even a *little* of their respect.(p.215)
• I was kind of shocked about anybody talking about themselves the way he did, and my impression was that the guy was a *little* "touched."(p.216)
• One evening I had gone out after dinner to take on a couple of double-headers and stayed a *little* later than usual, and when I came home Clarence was sitting on the davenport with Bill W.(p.216)
• My experience in the hospital I considered to be terrific because Dr. Bob told me very quickly that medicine would have very *little* to do with it, outside of trying to restore my appetite for food.(p.217)
• But, although I was a good Catholic, the monastic life had *little* appeal for me.(p.230)
• My "periodics" became more frequent until I reached the point where I wanted to devote all my time to drinking, working as *little* as possible, and then only when the necessity of my family demanded it.(p.234)
• Where preaching and prayers had touched me very *little*, I immediately desired further knowledge of these men.(p.235)
• If that was all, then I was a *little* doubtful that it was the answer I was looking for.(p.236)
• Many things happened; business trials, *little* worries, and feelings of general despondency came near driving me to the bottle, but I made progress.(p.237)
• *Little* more of our talk stayed in my memory, but I do know I slept the rest of that night while before I had never known what a real night's sleep was.(p.239)
• Then I found that as I gave in to this spiritual or personality change I was getting a *little* more serenity.(p.249)
• In telling newcomers how to change their lives and attitudes, all of a sudden I found I was doing a *little* changing myself.(p.249)
• Saying goodbye to my wife and baby, I was treading Manhattan's streets in a *little* more than a week.(p.252)
• Curious about it, feeling I was missing something, absolutely without any illusions about the aftermath, with no pronounced feeling of patriotism, I joined up with a Canadian regiment, serving a *little* over two years.(p.253)
• They seemed to be happy in their fashion, they and their *little* groups of supporters, but always pride of intellect stopped me from seeking what they evidently had.(p.256)
• The doctor who came to see me almost at once did not assail me with any new doctrines; he made sure that I had a need and that I wanted to have that need filled, and *little* by *little* I learned how my need could be met.(p.258)
• Of course, this year we decided on staying home and being sensible, doing a *little* drinking, and painting the house.(p.265)
• One morning after a terrific drinking bout, I was in a *little* bar near our house, and I shook so that I was very much ashamed, because I was getting the shakes worse and worse.(p.266)
• That nasty *little* can of beer!(p.267)
• I had a *little* Testament, which was very small print.(p.268)
• He talked about his wife taking his *little* boy away from him because of his drinking, and how he got back together with them through A.A., and we began feeling grateful right then that all these things hadn't been taken from us.(p.270)
• They opened with a *little* prayer, and I thought it was very fine that we stood, all of us together, and closed with the Lord's Prayer.(p.270)
• I'd like to say here how important it was to us then that we do all the *little* things that people said were important, because later when Russ was so sick that I had to hold him up, they had a meeting out at the house.(p.270)
• Sometimes saying very *little*, but letting us say.(p.271)
• For a *little* while.(p.275)
• I had tried to be the center of my own *little* world, whereas God was the center of a vast universe of which I was perhaps an essential, but a very tiny, part.(p.280)
• While there, two or three more "cash customers" (as Dr. Bob used to call them -- probably because they had so *little* cash) were shipped in to us from Detroit.(p.282)
• Within a year of my return to Detroit, A.A. was a definitely established *little* group of about a dozen members and I too was established in a modest but steady job handling an independent dry-cleaning route of my own.(p.283)
• Shortly thereafter, aided by the Depression, I found that I had a great deal of spare time and that a *little* drink in the morning helped.(p.287)
• I had thought that I was completely different from other people, that I was beginning to become a *little* balmy, even to the point of withdrawing more and more from society and wanting to be alone with my bottle.(p.290)
• I have stopped tilting at windmills, and instead have tried to accomplish the *little* daily tasks, unimportant in themselves, but tasks that are an integral part of living fully.(p.295)
• Above all, I have gained the greatest thing accorded to any man, the love and understanding of a gracious God, who has lifted me from the alcoholic scrap-heap to a position of trust where I have been able to reap the rich rewards that come from showing a *little* love for others and from serving them as I can.(p.296)
• The parties waxed more liquid and hilarious as time went on, and eventually I discovered that a *little* shot of liquor now and then between beers had the tendency to put me in a whacky mood much quicker than having to down several quarts of beer to obtain the same effect.(p.298)
• A night or so a week in a joint, and a party or so a week at home or with friends, along with a *little* lone drinking, soon had me preparing for the existence of a top flight drunkard.(p.298)
• A *little* more than fifteen years ago, through a long and calamitous series of shattering experiences, I found myself being helplessly propelled toward total destruction.(p.304)
• But somehow my good doctor heard of this book and also he learned a *little* about the people responsible for its publication.(p.307)
• Most of these fortunate ones have had *little* or no acquaintance with delirium, with hospitals, asylums, and jails.(p.315)
• But with many, drinking had been *little* more than a sometimes uncontrollable nuisance.(p.315)
• That was on a hot summer evening, down in the Greenwich Village Group, and there was a *little* porch out there in the old meeting place on Sullivan Street, and after the meeting I went out on the steps for some air.(p.321)
• It would be a *little* thing that I'd think was wrong, and off I'd go, drinking.(p.324)
• But during a period of particular stress and strain about thirteen years ago, I resorted to alcohol in my home, alone, as a means of temporary release, as a means of getting a *little* extra sleep.(p.335)
• We all have them, and I thought a *little* brandy or a *little* wine now and then could certainly hurt no one.(p.336)
• So when the children were in school from nine to three, I started up a nice *little* business and was fairly successful in it.(p.339)
• In two ways I may be a *little* different from other alcoholics.(p.345)
• And then we went up the side of a hill where we have a *little* barbecue area to make the fire for the barbecue, and on the way up, I thought to myself -- I'll go back down to the kitchen and refill this drink.(p.347)
• The satisfaction I got from giving him a *little* of what I had read in those pamphlets far surpassed any feeling that I had ever had before in helping patients.(p.347)
• I do recall lying on a cold cement floor and shredding into *little* bits several pieces of stolen identification cards, and washing my face in the toilet bowl trying to sober up, and screaming hysterically while clinging to bars too high to see out of, and cursing everyone that came near me.(p.354)
• I made *little* headway in my first few meetings with her.(p.359)
• I got around this by joining the local Rotary Club, and through this association with the business men of the community my *little* station began to grow.(p.360)
• Proud of my *little* station and of my new bride I settled down to a happy married life.(p.361)
• I had read and heard a *little* about A.A. and so, groping for the phone book, I found the A.A. number and with hope in my heart eagerly telephoned.(p.363)
• It was worrying my wife a *little*, but she had the good sense not to take me to task about it or goad me into going.(p.364)
• I had no trouble making the right decision when I saw my wife open her purse at the meeting that night and deposit a cute *little* angel in the middle of my birthday cake.(p.366)
• Very soon after I lost Mother, my five-year-old *little* girl was killed by a neighbor's car.(p.370)
• The obsession of the mind was a *little* harder to understand and yet everyone has obsessions of various kinds.(p.380)
• A spiritual awakening soon came to mean trying each day to be a *little* more thoughtful, more considerate, a *little* more courteous to those with whom I came in contact.(p.381)
• Relax a *little*.(p.382)
• You didn't carry a *little* orchid up the aisle in those days; you carried a great big bouquet, like a funeral spray, and you didn't have your picture taken until just before you went to the church.(p.385)
• So I went down to him quite a few times a month and had him shoot me full of the stuff; and then I went across the street to a *little* drug store to take a glass of beer or two beers, and then stopped at the liquor store to get myself a pint and go home.(p.389)
• I had learned an awful lot about myself in that one *little* article.(p.393)
• Drunkalogues and statistics can be boring, but it is necessary to delve a *little* into each in order to come up with some kind of rough estimate.(p.396)
• Like most statistics, it doesn't prove anything -- just satisfies a *little* curiosity engendered by the wail "Oh, those initiation fees" that prompted this investigation.(p.399)
• I was a *little* bit knocked out.(p.402)
• It was all about Scott Fitzgerald's *little* lost debutante, abused, misunderstood and running wild.(p.402)
• A house in Virginia, during the fox hunting season; a *little* chalet in Switzerland during the summer or a place on Long Island – each house complete with cooks, butlers and maids.(p.403)
• I also wrote another novel, all about Scott Fitzgerald's poor, misbegotten, unloved, tipsy *little* debutante.(p.405)
• During this time, you are supposed to behave yourself, but I took a *little* wine-tasting tour through France, all by my lone, with car and chauffeur.(p.405)
• Or – this is a *little* too much!(p.408)
• Oh, poor self-centered, sick *little* me.(p.413)
• I tried to wash a *little*, but Anne refused to wash at all.(p.415)
• Every day, I feel a *little* bit more useful, more

happy and more free.(p.417)
• I remembered having had a *little* drink of whiskey with a can of warm beer as a chaser.(p.422)
• I moved about a *little.*(p.423)
• I found I could boost my income by figuring out a lot of cute *little* tricks that the boss wouldn't be likely to notice – filching money from the Coke machine, short-sticking the customers on oil, and selling oil I'd drained out of other cars.(p.423)
• I teamed up with a cute *little* blonde with whom I was working at the office, and for about a year we were inseparable.(p.425)
• I have two wonderful *little* boys.(p.431)
• Evening cocktails were as standard as morning coffee, and I suppose my average daily consumption ran a *little* more or less than a pint.(p.433)
• Or, "My physical plant had got a *little* run down and the stuff rushed right to my head."(p.433)
• "You've got to space your drinks and take plenty of water in between," or "coat the stomach with a *little* olive oil," or "drink anything but those damn martinis."(p.433)
• But we have a baby who, if you'll pardon a *little* post-alcoholic sentimentality, is right out of Heaven.(p.438)
• Each time I told her she was a nothing, she receded a *little* more into nowhere.(p.450)
• Tragedies during those years that were caused by my drinking, such as the breaking up of my marriage, the death of my child, other things – had *little* restraining effect.(p.465)
• On the day set for the extractions, on my way to the dentist's I felt a *little* nervous, so I had a couple of drinks, and after the teeth were out I was very nervous, so I had a few more.(p.466)
• I was born in a *little* town in Virginia in an average religious home.(p.483)
• During recess we were playing basketball and I had accidentally tripped a fellow just a *little* larger than I was.(p.484)
• We weren't even permitted to play cards in our home, but father would give us just a *little* toddy with whiskey and sugar and warm water now and then.(p.484)
• This man's wife had been suffering for a couple of months and when he came in he owed me a *little* bill.(p.488)
• I got very *little* out of the two hundred, that I drew on that pay day.(p.493)
• A *little* drink will put me on my feet.(p.500)
• I fix up a *little* apartment over the garage with books and drinking water.(p.506)
• And as I read, I shall take *little* drinks at long intervals.(p.506)
• That really stopped me for a *little* bit.(p.510)
• The days have grown into a *little* better than four years of sobriety.(p.511)
• Finally, he was drinking to keep away those *little* men, and those strange voices, and the organ music that came out of the walls.(p.512)
• I'm grateful because that Higher Power led me to A.A. a *little* over three years ago, when I needed it very badly.(p.512)
• At first they were rather amusing, but a *little* later on they became serious.(p.513)
• A former employer of mine said to me a *little* over ten years ago, "Pat, you seem to be one of those unfortunate people who at least once every six months must go out and roll in the gutter."(p.513)
• For me, it was a *little* different because I couldn't help thinking about the past, and I saw the future more or less mirrored in the past.(p.513)
• I was drinking to keep away the shakes, drinking to keep away those *little* men and those strange voices and the organ music that comes out of the walls.(p.514)
• I use that "Easy Does It" every day, to slow me down a *little.*(p.516)
• The Commanding Officer only spoke to me when he wanted to tell me exactly who I was and what I was and how *little* I counted in the scheme of things and how glad he would be if I went away.(p.520)
• I would never admit that I was drinking too much, or spending money that I should have used to buy food for my two *little* boys.(p.526)
• No, it can best be explained in a *little* phrase I coined and sang to myself: "What happened to Bob?(p.532)
• And having sung that phrase, I'd chuckle with amusement, turning into irony turning into self-contempt turning into self-pity, at the sad fate of Bob, that wonderful, poor *little* motherless boy who was so smart in school and who grew up to accept responsibility so early and so fast and who staggered under his burdens without a whimper until the time came when he thought he was too good for this world and so he ought to be out of it.(p.532)
• There was the physical aspect; to be the youngest and the runt of the brood of children, to have to wear glasses very early and so to be teased, to be bookish and bored in school because the captain of the football team could not translate Virgil and yet was the school god while you, you, you *little* shrimp, were the school egghead, junior size and an early model.(p.533)
• For a *little* while, I was the great man I wanted to be, and thought myself entitled to be just by reason of being.(p.537)
• Brandishing my "motto," which was "A *little* man with a stick is equal to a big man," sometimes I varied the literary lecture by a fight with a big man, selected solely because he was big and I was *little.*(p.537)
• I fled, finally, after having been fired from my job by a boss who wept a *little* (since I had worked hard) as he gave notice for me to clear out.(p.539)
• I went back home, to a job of manual labor where for a *little* while I was able to keep away from alcohol.(p.539)
• In the nearby *little* town there was a plumber who once had tried to get an A.A. group going.(p.541)
• I wasn't afraid of anything or anybody after I learned about drinking, for it seemed right from the beginning that with liquor I could always retire to my *little* private world where nobody could get at me to hurt me.(p.547)
• If we do not do so, we shall stand convicted of emotional sterility and of having lost the faith that moves mountains, without which medicine can do *little.*"(p.571)

live

• As we discovered the principles by which the individual alcoholic could *live,* so we had to evolve principles by which the A.A. groups and A.A. as a whole could survive and function effectively.(p.xix)
• I have everything to *live* for!(p.xxvii)
• We went to *live* with my wife's parents.(p.4)
• Those of us who *live* in large cities are overcome by the reflection that close by hundreds are dropping into oblivion every day.(p.19)
• In the doctor's judgment he was utterly hopeless; he could never regain his position in society and he would have to place himself under lock and key or hire a bodyguard if he expected to *live* long.(p.26)
• To be doomed to an alcoholic death or to *live* on a spiritual basis are not always easy alternatives to face.(p.44)
• We had to find a power by which we could *live* and it had to be a Power greater than ourselves.(p.45)
• Most people try to *live* by self-propulsion.(p.60)
• Many of us had moral and philosophical convictions galore, but we could not *live* up to them even though we would have liked to.(p.62)
• If we were to *live,* we had to be free of anger.(p.66)
• We asked God to mold our ideals and help us to *live* up to them.(p.69)
• We must be entirely honest with somebody if we expect to *live* long or happily in this world.(p.73)
• We attempt to sweep away the debris which has accumulated out of our effort to *live* on self-will and run the show ourselves.(p.76)
• We have to *live* it.(p.83)
• Unless one's family expresses a desire to *live* upon spiritual principles we think we ought not to urge them.(p.83)
• The main thing is that he be willing to believe in a Power greater than himself and that he *live* by spiritual principles.(p.93)
• To spend too much time on any one situation is to deny some other alcoholic an opportunity to *live* and be happy.(p.96)
• We seldom allow an alcoholic to *live* in our homes for long at a time.(p.97)
• Follow the dictates of a Higher Power and you will presently *live* in a new and wonderful world, no matter what your present circumstances!(p.100)
• We came to *live* almost alone.(p.105)
• In the midst of such pandemonium they may have rushed out threatening to *live* with the other woman forever.(p.106)
• These work-outs should be regarded as part of your education, for thus you will be learning to *live.*(p.117)
• If your husband is trying to *live* on a spiritual basis, he will also be doing everything in his power to avoid disagreement or contention.(p.118)
• *Live* and let *live* is the rule.(p.118)
• Therefore, you probably need fresh interests and a great cause to *live* for as much as your husband.(p.119)
• One more suggestion: Whether the family has spiritual convictions or not, they may do well to examine the principles by which the alcoholic member is trying to *live.*(p.130)
• *Live* and Let *Live*(p.135)
• For he knows he must be honest if he would *live* at all.(p.146)
• If you *live* in a large place, there are hundreds.(p.152)
• And then my thinking became calculation as to how much longer I had to *live,* how long the assets would last.(p.215)
• In fact, as I look back, I have often thought that they probably concluded that they would put up with me for a couple of years, that I couldn't *live* much longer, and that they would inherit whatever was left of the practice.(p.215)
• He startled me by informing me that he was an alcoholic, that he had found a way which so far enabled him to *live* without taking a drink, and that the main idea was to find a way how not to take that first drink.(p.218)
• For greater freedom and excitement I went abroad to *live.*(p.225)
• All I had left was an iron determination to *live* my own life in spite of the alien world -- and here I was, an inwardly frightened, outwardly defiant woman, who desperately needed a prop to keep going.(p.226)
• Alcohol was that prop, and I didn't see how I could *live* without it.(p.226)
• I wanted to *live,* not in a desert, but in a normal world; and my idea of a normal world was among people who drank – teetotallers were not included.(p.227)
• And as I fumed helplessly and planned to get good and drunk and show them, my eye caught a sentence in the book lying open on my bed: "We cannot *live* with anger."(p.228)
• And, accepting, I felt a new inner comfort, and the willingness and strength to do something about the traits I couldn't *live* with.(p.229)
• We now *live* in the West and are very fortunate in our area A.A.; it is good, simple and friendly, and our one desire is to stay in A.A. and not on it.(p.250)
• "I'm doing a job I like and it's quiet where I *live,* practically no temptations.(p.257)
• Russ lived a year longer than they expected him to *live,* and in that year he was in bed for at least six months.(p.272)
• In the next two or three days the balance of this handful of men contacted me, encouraged me, and told me how they were trying to *live* this program of recovery and the fun they were having doing it.(p.291)
• If I *live* to be a hundred, it will always stand out in my mind.(p.292)
• A few months later one of the men who had been in touch with the group in Akron came to Chicago to *live,* and then there were three of us who continued to have informal meetings quite regularly.(p.294)
• Doctors told me before I stopped that I had only three years at the outside to *live.*(p.295)
• In learning to practice these steps in my daily living I began to acquire faith and a philosophy to *live* by.(p.311)
• *Live* twenty-four hours at a time, they say.(p.320)
• I must *live* and let *live.*(p.325)
• I try to *live* our program as it has been outlined to me, one day at a time.(p.325)
• I try to *live* today so that tomorrow I won't be ashamed when I wake up in the morning.(p.325)
• After such often-painful vigilance (and numerous phony stints of abstinence), retirement naturally created an impulse to *live* without restraints.(p.328)
• We're free at last to do our thing, to *live* uninhibited lives, to drink when and how and where we wish, when we want to and when we need to.(p.329)
• What alcoholic can *live* with rejection?(p.331)
• Because it was only through feeling defeat and feeling failure, the inability to cope with my life and with alcohol, that I was able to surrender and accept the fact that I had this disease, and that I had to learn to *live* again without alcohol.(p.335)
• I just wanted to *live* to a certain age, carry through with what I felt was my job with the children, and after that – no matter.(p.337)
• I couldn't *live* without it.(p.337)
• But there came a point when I could no longer *live* with it.(p.337)
• I couldn't *live* with it any more.(p.338)
• And yet, how was I going to *live* without it?(p.338)
• Nevertheless, I began to try to *live* without alcohol.(p.338)
• The first time was when I knew I couldn't *live* with alcohol.(p.340)
• But this second time, I found I couldn't *live* normally without it, and I was licked worse

than ever.(p.340)
• Every day became that much harder to *live* through, and I began to take a look at myself.(p.354)
• I had no idea what would happen -- I just knew I didn't want to *live* if life was going to go on like it was.(p.355)
• I saw at last that I had the same disease my father had, only I was being given a chance to *live,* not die.(p.371)
• There comes a time when you don't want to *live* and are afraid to die.(p.377)
• This was no way to *live.*(p.378)
• It didn't say I had to finally *live* on skid row and drink bay rum, canned heat or lemon extract.(p.379)
• The A.A. way of life is the way we always should have tried to *live.*(p.382)
• I never want to forget that last drunk as long as I *live.*(p.393)
• I know that I must work at it as long as I *live;* I know that it is only by working at it that I can stay sober and have a happy life.(p.394)
• I accepted a big tax-free income from the family, but I didn't like it when they told me how to *live.*(p.405)
• It had never occurred to me before that I could *live* simply and be independent of my family.(p.409)
• I could not *live* on that tiny trust fund and still drink all I wanted to.(p.411)
• And also, on the twenty-four hour plan, it taught me how to *live.*(p.416)
• I depended on optimism and ambition to *live* in society; when I began to tire, I had to depend on chemicals instead to keep going.(p.420)
• No one could *live* such an irresponsible, immature life as I had without consequences.(p.420)
• I talked the Old Man into letting me *live* in the photo lab instead of the barracks, and for eighteen months nothing interfered with my drinking.(p.426)
• That doctor in the Navy hospital told me I wouldn't *live* five years if I didn't quit.(p.429)
• "I've got to stop if I want to *live,*" I told myself, and if I don't want to break my parents' hearts and maybe jeopardize their own carefully built up and hard-fought-for sobriety.(p.429)
• I used to think, "Why *live* without whiskey?"(p.430)
• Now I know I can't *live* without A.A.(p.430)
• Here was power to *live* to the end of any given day, power to have the courage to face the next day, power to have friends, power to help people, power to be sane, power to stay sober.(p.436)
• (Today, we don't have to *live* like that any more.)(p.440)
• (Today, we don't have to *live* that way.(p.446)
• Some went on trying to *live* with alcohol.(p.455)
• Through A.A., many receive the needed change and awakening just by trying to *live* by A.A. principles and associating with A.A. people.(p.459)
• We do this by going to many A.A. meetings with an open mind and a desire to *live* the good-feeling life without chemicals -- liquid or otherwise.(p.459)
• Besides, I can only *live* today.(p.463)
• And then I went back home to *live* with my parents, and the merry-go-round started again -- only this time I didn't have to worry about waking up behind bars in a psychiatric ward.(p.468)
• We can have this new way of life -- learning to *live* with our sickness and to be happy and content -- if we are willing to change our way of thinking and be honest, first with ourselves, then with others.(p.480)
• Will I take a young fellow who has been drinking for two weeks to *live* with me?(p.506)
• Those poor stiffs probably went to a doctor and were told that if they quit they'd *live* three weeks and if they didn't they'd die in one."(p.510)
• I'm fortunate because I *live* in an era when A.A. is available, and I'm able to take advantage of it.(p.512)
• India lent itself to drinking then, if you were disposed to drink, because you lived in bungalows; you didn't *live* all together as you do at home in an Officer's Mess.(p.519)
• So I decided I'd go back and *live* in Ireland to try the geography cure.(p.522)
• I talked to him for quite a long time and at the end, he said, "Well, you're not quite mad enough to be shut up for good yet, but you soon will be if you *live* long enough."(p.522)
• I thought if they smelled whiskey on my breath, they would lock me up, and I couldn't *live* without my bottle.(p.526)
• I felt that I didn't have anything to *live* for, so I tried suicide many times.(p.528)
• To learn to *live,* he nearly died.(p.531)
• My personal definition, which I submit as applying only to myself (although everyone is welcome to it who wants it), includes every waking activity of the human being; to have a creative attitude towards things is a more exact meaning, to *live* and to deal with other human beings creatively, which to me means seeing the God in them, and respecting and worshipping this God.(p.535)
• "Bob," he asked quietly, "do you want to *live* or die?"(p.540)
• But I said humbly, "I suppose I want to *live.*"(p.540)
• At fifty-four, I have had come true for me the old wish, "If only I could *live* my life over, knowing what I know."(p.543)
• The A.A. members who sponsored me told me in the beginning that I would not only find a way to *live* without having a drink, but that I would find a way to *live* without wanting to drink, if I would do these simple things.(p.550)
• Indeed, I had to drink now to *live,* to cope with the demands of everyday existence.(p.556)
• Above all, I was suffering inner pain because my performance and my accomplishments in life failed to *live* up to my own expectations of myself.(p.557)
• We cast off the burdens of the past and the anxieties of the future, as we begin to *live* in the present, one day at a time.(p.560)
• A.A. must continue to *live* or most of us will surely die.(p.565)
• This to the end that our great blessings may never spoil us; that we shall forever *live* in thankful contemplation of Him who presides over us all.(p.568)

lived

• It melted the icy intellectual mountain in whose shadow I had *lived* and shivered many years.(p.12)
• I have since been brought into a way of living infinitely more satisfying and, I hope, more useful than the life I *lived* before.(p.42)
• While pondering the answer he felt as though he *lived* in hell.(p.56)
• For the first time, he *lived* in conscious companionship with his Creator.(p.56)
• We have elsewhere remarked how much better life is when *lived* on a spiritual plane.(p.116)
• Seeing is believing to most families who have *lived* with a drinker.(p.135)
• He told how he *lived* in constant worry about those who might find out about his alcoholism.(p.155)
• He had *lived* there but a few weeks when he found that the place probably contained more alcoholics per square mile than any city in the country.(p.163)
• There my drinking became so much worse that the boys in the fraternity house where I *lived* felt forced to send for my father, who made a long journey in the vain endeavor to get me straightened around.(p.174)
• We boys drove out in somebody's car and went to the bar on the way do the dining room and I, in an effort to impress the other boys that I was city-bred, having *lived* in Scranton and Cleveland, asked them if they didn't want a drink.(p.194)
• Right then I determined that never so long as I *lived* would I have anything more to do with martinis.(p.195)
• So, knowing that, I had determined that so long as I *lived* I would never take another drink.(p.200)
• An offer of appreciation for not having had a drink for those few months and then and there, without anybody promising me anything or threatening me, I made a solemn vow that never so long as I *lived* would I take another drink.(p.200)
• Not far from where I *lived* they built a new technical high school and one of the teachers sold me on the idea that I needed a little mechanical drawing if I were going to be a good toolmaker.(p.211)
• My daily consumption of wine was about a quart, but that was common where I *lived.*(p.230)
• I came directly to a growing industrial city in the middle west, where I have *lived* practically ever since.(p.231)
• My family *lived* in very prosperous circumstances, and while both my parents drank, sometimes too much, neither was an alcoholic.(p.240)
• There was a very religious family that *lived* down the road from us, and we were on the same party line.(p.265)
• Russ *lived* a year longer than they expected him to live, and in that year he was in bed for at least six months.(p.272)
• I *lived* through a week of the fidgets because I had agreed to address a group of alcoholic inmates in one of our state mental hospitals.(p.283)
• I spent a great deal of time with Dr. Bob, whenever he had the time to spare, and in the homes of two or three other people, trying to see how the family *lived* the program.(p.291)
• He'd told a villain, "The trouble is, old man, you've *lived* too long."(p.333)
• I'd *lived* too long and become a loser, dependent on booze.(p.333)
• How full it has kept my retirement years -- the five I've *lived* since the first two lost in traveling a rocky road to hell, before I made a U-turn.(p.334)
• That life for me is *lived* one day at a time, letting the problems of the future rest with the future.(p.340)
• It was to be short *lived,* for on the day before Christmas I completely disillusioned my wife and ruined our first Christmas by coming home from the Rotary lunch dead drunk.(p.361)
• This routine was short *lived* too.(p.362)
• We *lived* a kind of seesaw existence in the early days.(p.369)
• I *lived* in New Orleans where, at that time, cocktail parties, dances and night spots were almost the order of the day -- or rather the night.(p.384)
• It has made life a thousand times easier and simpler than did the endless compromises and conflicts by which I *lived* before.(p.394)
• Up to my early thirties, when my drinking had become a major problem, I *lived* in large houses, with servants and all the luxuries that I could possibly ask for.(p.401)
• I had met a bunch of gay young Bohemians who *lived* in the Village, and were sowing their wild oats.(p.407)
• Nor was I the "worst woman who ever *lived.*"(p.414)
• We *lived* just a few doors from the First Baptist Church and when they had funerals I remember very often asking my mother whether the person was good or bad and whether they were going to heaven or hell.(p.483)
• India lent itself to drinking then, if you were disposed to drink, because you *lived* in bungalows; you didn't live all together as you do at home in an Officer's Mess.(p.519)
• My mother *lived* on for five years after I joined A.A., the last two in complete blindness.(p.525)
• With deep shame came the knowledge too that I had *lived* with no sense of social obligation nor had I known the meaning of moral responsibility to my fellow men.(p.549)
• I *lived* in a dream world.(p.560)

livelihood

• If he opened that old affair, he was afraid it would destroy the reputation of his partner, disgrace his family and take away his means of *livelihood.*(p.80)
• Why, he argued, should he lose the remainder of his business, only to bring still more suffering to his family by foolishly admitting his plight to people from whom he made his *livelihood?*(p.155)
• After this incident in 1940, I sought some other means of *livelihood.*(p.489)

lively

• In the last year of my navy service, I was married to a lovely, *lively* girl, who enjoyed drinking.(p.555)

liver

• After his death, my mother soon picked up drinking where Dad left off, and in a very short time she died of cirrhosis of the *liver.*(p.370)
• An American doctor in Paris said I had an enlarged *liver.*(p.406)
• The doctor pronounced it a badly enlarged *liver* and said I had to quit drinking.(p.557)
• So, when my *liver* had recovered after ten months, I resumed drinking.(p.557)
• The enlargement of my *liver* degenerated into cirrhosis.(p.557)

Liverpool

• Following a big drunk on that sheet, where I was doing leg-work and rewrite, a feeling of nostalgia made me buy a ticket for *Liverpool* and I returned to Britain.(p.252)
• I was soon back in *Liverpool.*(p.252)

lives

• In nearly all cases, their ideals must be grounded in a power greater than themselves, if they are to re-create their *lives.*(p.xxvi)
• I have seen men come out of asylums and resume a vital place in the *lives* of their families and communities.(p.15)
• It engulfs all whose *lives* touch the sufferer's.(p.18)
• It brings misunderstanding, fierce resentment, financial insecurity, disgusted friends and employers, warped *lives* of blameless children, sad wives and parents -- anyone can increase the list.(p.18)
• Our very *lives,* as ex-problem drinkers, depend upon our constant thought of others and how we may help meet their needs.(p.20)
• The central fact of our *lives* today is the absolute certainty that our Creator has entered into our hearts and *lives* in a way which is indeed miraculous.(p.25)

• But this man still *lives*, and is a free man.(p.26)
• Ideas, emotions, and attitudes which were once the guiding forces of the *lives* of these men are suddenly cast to one side, and a completely new set of conceptions and motives begin to dominate them.(p.27)
• These give a fair cross section of our membership and a clear-cut idea of what has actually happened in their *lives*.(p.29)
• When many hundreds of people are able to say that the consciousness of the Presence of God is today the most important fact of their *lives*, they present a powerful reason why one should have faith.(p.51)
• Were not these things the tissue out of which our *lives* were constructed?(p.54)
• For faith in a Power greater than ourselves, and miraculous demonstrations of that power in human *lives*, are facts as old as man himself.(p.55)
• 1.We admitted we were powerless over alcohol -- that our *lives* had become unmanageable.(p.59)
• 3.Made a decision to turn our will and our *lives* over to the care of God as we understood Him.(p.59)
• (a) That we were alcoholic and could not manage our own *lives*.(p.60)
• We did exactly the same thing with our *lives*.(p.64)
• We went back through our *lives*.(p.65)
• This short word somehow touches about every aspect of our *lives*.(p.67)
• Time after time newcomers have tried to keep to themselves certain facts about their *lives*.(p.72)
• At the moment we are trying to put our *lives* in order.(p.77)
• The alcoholic is like a tornado roaring his way through the *lives* of others.(p.82)
• Frequent contact with newcomers and with each other is the bright spot of our *lives*.(p.89)
• A spirit of intolerance might repel alcoholics whose *lives* could have been saved, had it not been for such stupidity.(p.103)
• Is it right to let him ruin your life and the *lives* of your children?(p.108)
• As our husbands began to apply spiritual principles in their *lives*, we began to see the desirability of doing so too.(p.116)
• Now we try to put spiritual principles to work in every department of our *lives*.(p.116)
• Inevitably your *lives* will be fuller for doing so.(p.120)
• This dream world has been replaced by a great sense of purpose, accompanied by a growing consciousness of the power of God in our *lives*.(p.130)
• I didn't want to jeopardize the *lives* of innocent people by driving an automobile while intoxicated, but I did.(p.199)
• I came of good stock, of men and women who drank wine all their *lives* as a beverage, and while they occasionally got drunk at special celebrations, they were up and about their business the next day.(p.231)
• There was one meeting a week at Bill's home in Brooklyn, and we all took turns there spouting off about how we had changed our *lives* overnight, how many drunks we had saved and straightened out, and last, but not least, how God had touched each of us personally on the shoulder.(p.246)
• In telling newcomers how to change their *lives* and attitudes, all of a sudden I found I was doing a little changing myself.(p.249)
• He said he had finally learned that drinking was a fatal illness made up of an allergy plus an obsession, and once the drinking had passed from habit to obsession, we were completely hopeless, and could look forward only to spending the balance of our *lives* in mental institutions or to death.(p.290)
• Nothing in their *lives* took precedence over their response to a call for help from some alcoholic in need.(p.310)
• It is a way of life, and the challenge contained in its principles is great enough to keep any human being striving for as long as he *lives*.(p.311)
• We're free at last to do our thing, to live uninhibited *lives*, to drink when and how and where we wish, when we want to and when we need to.(p.329)
• We even can be rebels for the first time in our *lives*.(p.329)
• But the saddest, and thus the most consoling, drifted through from the country-music station -- stories of broken hearts, wasted *lives*, lost loves, sung plaintively.(p.332)
• The Third Step said: "Made a decision to turn our will and our *lives* over to the care of God as we understood Him."(p.350)
• "We admitted we were powerless over alcohol -- that our *lives* had become unmanageable."(p.379)
• To most of us, making amends will take the rest of our *lives*, but we can start immediately.(p.381)
• These thoughts become part of our daily *lives*.(p.382)
• It pays daily in more harmonious relations with my fellow men, in ever clearer insight into the true meaning of life, and in the answering love and gratitude wherever and whenever I have been the instrument of God's will in the *lives* of others.(p.394)
• Max still works with me in the office, but we have turned our wills and our *lives* and our work over to the care of God.(p.446)
• Get into the *lives* of other people, is one thing the fellows in New York had said.(p.505)
• I was to pack and go and get out of their *lives* for good.(p.523)
• They suggested that I study the A.A. book and try to take the Twelve Steps according to the explanation in the Book, for it was their opinion that the application of these principles in our daily *lives* will get us sober and keep us sober.(p.550)
• A.A. has taught me that I will have peace of mind in exact proportion to the peace of mind I bring into the *lives* of other people, and it has taught me the true meaning of the admonition "happy are ye who know these things and do them."(p.551)

living

• And besides, we are sure that our way of *living* has its advantages for all.(p.xiii)
• He had lost everything worthwhile in life and was only *living*, one might say, to drink.(p.xxix)
• *Living* modestly, my wife and I saved $1,000.(p.2)
• By the following spring we were *living* in our accustomed style.(p.4)
• Despite the *living* example of my friend there remained in me the vestiges of my old prejudice.(p.12)
• My friend promised when these things were done I would enter upon a new relationship with my Creator; that I would have the elements of a way of *living* which answered all my problems.(p.13)
• It is a design for *living* that works in rough going.(p.15)
• The joy of *living* we really have, even under pressure and difficulty.(p.15)
• But we saw that it really worked in others, and we had come to believe in the hopelessness and futility of life as we had been *living* it.(p.25)
• A new life has been given us or, if you prefer, "a design for *living*" that really works.(p.28)
• If what we have learned and felt and seen means anything at all, it means that all of us, whatever our race, creed, or color are the children of a *living* Creator with whom we may form a relationship upon simple and understandable terms as soon as we are willing and honest enough to try.(p.28)
• I have since been brought into a way of *living* infinitely more satisfying and, I hope, more useful than the life I lived before.(p.42)
• They flatly declare that since they have come to believe in a Power greater than themselves, to take a certain attitude toward that Power, and to do certain simple things, there has been a revolutionary change in their way of *living* and thinking.(p.50)
• Leaving aside the drink question, they tell why *living* was so unsatisfactory.(p.51)
• We were having trouble with personal relationships, we couldn't control our emotional natures, we were a prey to misery and depression, we couldn't make a *living*, we had a feeling of uselessness, we were full of fear, we were unhappy, we couldn't seem to be of real help to other people -- was not a basic solution of these bedevilments more important than whether we should see newsreels of lunar flight?(p.52)
• In one form or another we had been *living* by faith and little else.(p.54)
• They are naturally incapable of grasping and developing a manner of *living* which demands rigorous honesty.(p.58)
• Our design for *living* is not a one-way street.(p.81)
• We vigorously commenced this way of *living* as we cleaned up the past.(p.84)
• When your prospect has made such reparation as he can to his family, and has thoroughly explained to them the new principles by which he is *living*, he should proceed to put those principles into action at home.(p.98)
• When the time for *living* together has come, it will be apparent to both parties.(p.99)
• Perhaps your husband has been *living* in that strange world of alcoholism where everything is distorted and exaggerated.(p.108)
• It is probably true that you and your husband have been *living* too much alone, for drinking many times isolates the wife of an alcoholic.(p.119)
• A doctor said to us, "Years of *living* with an alcoholic is almost sure to make any wife or child neurotic.(p.122)
• We think that such a view is self-centered and in direct conflict with the new way of *living*.(p.124)
• We are convinced that a spiritual mode of *living* is a most powerful health restorative.(p.133)
• This may hang on for months, long after their mother has accepted dad's new way of *living* and thinking.(p.134)
• They have a new attitude, and they have been saved from a *living* death.(p.150)
• They experienced a few distressing failures, but in those cases they made an effort to bring the man's family into a spiritual way of *living*, thus relieving much worry and suffering.(p.159)
• We know of an A.A. member who was *living* in a large community.(p.163)
• Of far more importance was the fact that he was the first *living* human with whom I had ever talked, who knew what he was talking about in regard to alcoholism from actual experience.(p.180)
• When he was uptown -- we were *living* in the little town of Moscow -- I went up to try to get some money from him to buy groceries.(p.193)
• And I continued to drink, on and off then, until every dollar I had in the world was gone again and I was right back *living* at my sister's, getting my cigarettes by calling her grocer and telling him to put in a couple of cartons with her order, exactly as I had before I started to work at Max's.(p.202)
• I still had enough practice to earn a good *living* if I would only work, so I resolved that in January of 1940 I would launch a patent law firm of my own.(p.220)
• In fact, after six months of *living* on food instead of on whiskey, I gained about thirty pounds.(p.220)
• I was in a large, dark, rather poorly furnished room -- the *living* room of a basement flat.(p.222)
• The fact that I can work again and earn my *living*, is important, but secondary.(p.229)
• I knew somehow that it meant more than just going to church and *living* a moral life.(p.236)
• Our oldest daughter got married; they were *living* at our house.(p.263)
• The details of the long road back to something resembling normal *living* -- the first short streetcar ride, the purchase of a used bike which enabled me to widen the narrow horizon of life, the first trip downtown -- I will not dwell on.(p.276)
• At least three of those four years must have been a *living* hell for my wife, because she had to watch the man she loved disintegrate morally, mentally and financially.(p.277)
• It was simple, they said, and went on to explain to me in their own language the program of recovery and daily *living* which we know today as the Twelve Steps of A.A.(p.279)
• I, carried away with the desire to serve A.A., gave what was probably one of the first radio broadcasts about A.A., *living* through a case of mike fright and feeling like a million dollars when it was all over.(p.283)
• It took five years of A.A. *living*, and a substantial improvement in my health, before I could take a full-time office job where someone else was boss.(p.283)
• It would be wonderful were I able to tell you that my confidence in God and my application of the Twelve Steps to my daily *living* have utterly banished fear.(p.284)
• However, I must have felt, deep down inside myself, that *living* the selfish life of a bachelor was only half *living*.(p.286)
• By *living* alone you can pretty much eliminate grief from you life, but you also eliminate joy.(p.286)
• After I left school, I went to work in Akron, *living* at home with my parents.(p.287)
• This first meeting was held in the *living* room of a home and was led by Bill D., the first man that Bill W. and Dr. Bob had worked with successfully.(p.291)
• So I suggested that he take a trip to Akron for a couple of weeks, which he did, *living* with one of the A.A. families there.(p.294)
• This latest part of my life has had a purpose, not in great things accomplished but in daily *living*.(p.295)
• I have stopped tilting at windmills, and instead have tried to accomplish the little daily tasks, unimportant in themselves, but tasks that are an integral part of *living* fully.(p.295)
• At that time, I was *living* out of town, so I moved back to the home town and made a connection in a responsible position with one of the larger companies in the finance business.(p.298)
• After being in the hospital for several days, a plan of *living* was outlined to me.(p.302)
• They seemed to have all the ingredients for successful *living*.(p.310)
• I didn't dare hope I might find for myself all that

these people had found, but if I could acquire some small part of their intriguing quality of ***living*** – and sobriety – that would be enough.(p.310)
• In learning to practice these steps in my daily ***living*** I began to acquire faith and a philosophy to live by.(p.311)
• As arrested alcoholics, we must have a program for ***living*** that allows for limitless expansion.(p.311)
• It really wasn't ***living***.(p.326)
• And retirement is a time for thinking, not of death, but of ***living*** -- at long last.(p.329)
• I soon was to ask myself, "What ***living***?"(p.329)
• I could go on ***living*** and hurting ten years longer, or more."(p.333)
• When alcohol took me over, my bar was my kitchen, my ***living*** room, my bedroom, the back bathroom, and the two hampers.(p.335)
• I was bitter, ***living*** in hate.(p.338)
• Well, now I'm ***living*** it and trying to paint it for others.(p.355)
• A.A. has become a way of life and ***living*** for me.(p.355)
• I certainly was, as far as my ***living*** standard was concerned.(p.356)
• High ***living***, a great many fair weather friends, the 1929 stock market crash, and a couple of years of Depression, soon relieved me one by one of my worldly goods including my wife.(p.358)
• I was ***living*** in a small room on West 53rd Street right off Fifth Avenue, when I met a young lady who eventually was responsible for altering my entire way of ***living***.(p.359)
• She was studying fashion design, was ***living*** in the same rooming house, and was from my home town of Cleveland.(p.359)
• Why should this happen to me – hadn't I provided a good home – wasn't I making a good ***living*** -- didn't I just get a substantial raise that had put me in the upper bracket class?(p.362)
• A few hours later I came out of a complete stupor in our ***living*** room with a flash of sanity.(p.363)
• A whole new world of happiness and love began to unfold before my eyes, a truly new way of ***living***.(p.365)
• I was ***living*** in constant fear that I would get caught while driving a car, so I used taxis part of the time.(p.375)
• There may be many reasons which bring one to A.A. for the first time, but the lasting one must be to want sobriety and the A.A. way of ***living*** for oneself.(p.379)
• ***Living*** with fear and tension inevitably results in wanting to ease that tension, which alcohol seems to do temporarily.(p.380)
• The Twelve Steps, which to me are a spiritual way of ***living***, soon meant honest thinking, not wishful thinking, open mindedness, a willingness to try and a faith to accept.(p.381)
• Doing our best, ***living*** each day to the fullest is the art of ***living***.(p.382)
• If we do a good job of ***living*** today, and if tomorrow comes for us, then the chances are we will do a good job when it arrives – so why worry about it?(p.382)
• They are not ideas of resignation but of the recognition of certain basic facts of ***living***.(p.382)
• I get so much more enjoyment out of ***living***.(p.383)
• ***Living*** just for today is a pleasant adventure.(p.383)
• I put my poor mother and father through agonies but, finally, I couldn't stand ***living*** with them and having them watch everything I did.(p.386)
• But again, the ***living*** was easy.(p.401)
• Now I had done some ***living*** but I hadn't learned a thing.(p.402)
• He saw that I was unsettled, ***living*** away from my family and renting houses here and there.(p.403)
• I saw that my Village friends, all of whom had small jobs, were ***living*** happily on about a tenth of my sinecure.(p.409)
• I am no longer interested in ***living*** in a palace, because palace ***living*** was not the answer for me.(p.416)
• My life there was a nightmare of periodic binges on alcohol and pills, adultery, unhappy hours at the dental office, seeing my wife give birth to our second child and have several miscarriages, ***living*** in a turbulent household, and making continual attempts to be the respectable dentist, husband, father, and community leader.(p.419)
• But it did not take long for the pressures of ***living*** to bring out my immaturity and my insecurity.(p.420)
• It solved their problems and they started ***living*** a sane life again.(p.427)
• When I stopped ***living*** in the problem and began ***living*** in the answer, the problem went away.(p.449)
• Of course, an inmate must begin ***living*** the A.A. way "inside," if he is to stand a chance "outside."(p.458)
• Sobriety and a plan for ***living*** that produces a personality change and a spiritual awakening are imperative.(p.459)
• I was ***living***, but I was dead.(p.460)
• They hadn't mentioned the ***living*** hell before death.(p.461)
• So I jump quick from First Step to Twelfth Step to help my brother, ***living*** with me.(p.476)
• Then A.A. showed her the beauty of normal ***living***, in a whole family reborn.(p.478)
• I can't begin to tell you of all the benefits I have derived from this new way of ***living***.(p.481)
• About that time I had lost practically all my property except the place we were ***living*** in.(p.487)
• My brother-in-law was ***living*** with us at that time and I said to Vi, "Maybe the bottles are brother's.(p.488)
• My practice at that juncture was just barely getting us a ***living***.(p.488)
• My wife received me graciously, although she was ***living*** in a one room with kitchen affair.(p.490)
• My wife is in the ***living*** room.(p.502)
• In any case, I made myself believe that, so I just drifted about, existing on my retired pay, drinking, and ***living*** at home.(p.522)
• Poor, black, totally ruled by alcohol, she felt shut away from any life worth ***living***.(p.526)
• Back to the big city, for another year of precarious ***living***, paid for largely by one or two friends I still had not milked dry or worn to exhaustion with demands on their bounty.(p.540)
• That's what I am doing, ***living*** again, knowing what I know.(p.543)
• I hope I have been able to impart to you, the reader, at least a bit of what I know; the joy of ***living***, the irresistible power of divine love and its healing strength, and the fact that we, as sentient beings, have the knowledge to choose between good and evil, and, choosing good, are made happy.(p.543)
• I had to cope with the demands of everyday ***living*** without my comforter, my anesthetic, my crutch.(p.557)
• But my thinking was still confused, and I was still unable to deal with the challenges of everyday ***living*** without help.(p.558)
• The Episcopal magazine, The ***Living*** Church, observes editorially: "The basis of the technique of Alcoholics Anonymous is the truly Christian principle that a man cannot help himself except by helping others.(p.574)

load

• That sure did take a ***load*** off of my mind.(p.188)
• A ***load*** weighing a thousand pounds came off my back.(p.414)

loaded

• After two weeks of drinking, he had placed his toe on the trigger of a ***loaded*** shotgun – the barrel in his mouth.(p.137)
• I spent the time in a nearby tavern, was ***loaded*** on the ship, went to sleep before take-off, and the next thing I knew someone was shaking me and telling me we were over San Diego.(p.428)

loading

• A couple of hired hands were cleaning out the barn on the farm and I would ride to and fro on the sled, and while they were ***loading*** I would drink hard cider out of a barrel in the barn.(p.183)
• ***Loading*** a car with good old books to sell to collectors, librarians, universities and historical societies, I started out to travel the country.(p.255)

loads

• On the return trip, after two or three ***loads***, I passed out and had to be carried to the house.(p.183)

loaf

• He wouldn't give me any money for the groceries, but he did take me across the street and buy me a bag of candy, which I later took back and traded for a ***loaf*** of bread.(p.193)

loan

• I borrowed five hundred dollars from the bank and three hundred from the ***loan*** shop, and I drank that up pretty fast.(p.490)

loaned

• The Great Boss has given me diagnostic and surgical talent, and He has ***loaned*** it to me to use for the rest of my life.(p.350)
• He has ***loaned*** it to me and I did my job, but that ended nine days ago.(p.351)

loath

• Doctors are rightly ***loath*** to tell alcoholic patients the whole story unless it will serve some good purpose.(p.92)

loathe

• I heard for the first time an expression which I was to grow to ***loathe***: "There is nothing organically wrong."(p.276)

loathed

• We remembered always that our sex powers were God-given and therefore good, neither to be used lightly or selfishly nor to be despised and ***loathed***.(p.69)
• I despised the other barflies and, naturally, they ***loathed*** me.(p.410)
• I wandered, craving peace, from one spot to another of youthful happy memory, and ***loathed*** the man I had become.(p.539)

lobby

• One dismal afternoon he paced a hotel ***lobby*** wondering how his bill was to be paid.(p.154)
• Down the ***lobby*** a door opened into an attractive bar.(p.154)
• With a shiver, he turned away and walked down the ***lobby*** to the church directory.(p.154)
• All this time our friend of the hotel ***lobby*** incident remained in that town.(p.159)

local

• The ***local*** banker watched me whirl fat checks in and out of his till with amused skepticism.(p.4)
• If there is no Al-Anon listing in your ***local*** telephone book, you may obtain further information on Al-Anon Family Groups by writing to its World Service Office: Box 182, Madison Square Station, New York, NY 10159.(p.121)
• At one end of the room stood a glass covered directory of ***local*** churches.(p.154)
• One day they called up the head nurse of a ***local*** hospital.(p.156)
• By this time I was beginning to pay very dearly physically and, in hope of relief, voluntarily incarcerated myself at least a dozen times in one of the ***local*** sanitariums.(p.174)
• After three years of this, I wound up in the ***local*** hospital where they attempted to help me, but I would get my friends to smuggle me a quart, or I would steal the alcohol about the building, so that I got rapidly worse.(p.175)
• There I was, unshaven, clothes torn and dirty with no recollection of wandering all over France but, of course, a hero to the ***local*** French.(p.242)
• Drifting back to Ohio, I landed on a small newspaper and later was impressed into the direction of boy-welfare work at the ***local*** "Y."(p.253)
• I called her every night from a ***local*** bar, and often she was not at home.(p.318)
• He's now in A.A. and works as a volunteer for the ***local*** alcoholism council.(p.330)
• I got around this by joining the ***local*** Rotary Club, and through this association with the business men of the community my little station began to grow.(p.360)
• This secret drinker favored the ***local*** Laundromat as a watering hole.(p.369)
• My wife was in the Junior League, and I was on the board of directors of the ***local*** center for the mentally retarded.(p.418)
• He arranged for me to see a ***local*** psychiatrist, who quickly decided I should be in the mental-health unit of our ***local*** hospital.(p.445)
• In such places, A.A. can be located through the ***local*** telephone directory, newspaper office, or police station, or by contacting ***local*** priests or ministers.(p.575)
• In large cities, groups often maintain ***local*** offices where alcoholics or their families may arrange for interviews or hospitalization.(p.575)

locality

• If you cannot find A.A. in your ***locality***, a letter addressed to Alcoholics Anonymous, Box 459, Grand Central Station, New York, NY 10163, U.S.A., will receive a prompt reply from this world center, referring you to the nearest A.A. group.(p.575)

locate

• She didn't say anything about A.A. or getting me a sponsor at that time, but she did ask about Vi, and I told her Vi was working and how she could ***locate*** her.(p.494)

located

• So I ***located*** a house, and I thought we ought to move into it immediately, but Frank was horrified, because he never knew what was going to happen to me.(p.388)
• In such places, A.A. can be ***located*** through the local telephone directory, newspaper office, or police station, or by contacting local priests

or ministers.(p.575)

location

• This headquarters will give the *location* of the nearest family group and will if you wish, correspond with you about your special problems.(p.575)

lock

• Society was about to *lock* him up.(p.11)

• In the doctor's judgment he was utterly hopeless; he could never regain his position in society and he would have to place himself under *lock* and key or hire a bodyguard if he expected to live long.(p.26)

• When they become too dangerous, we think the kind thing is to *lock* them up, but of course a good doctor should always be consulted.(p.114)

• In the first year there were episodes such as kicking Priscilla in the shins, getting the *lock* changed on the desk in the A.A. Club, because I, as secretary, didn't want the Intergroup secretary "interfering," and taking an older woman member out to lunch for the express purpose of informing her that she was "a phony."(p.416)

• Then I shall *lock* myself in and read.(p.506)

• I thought if they smelled whiskey on my breath, they would *lock* me up, and I couldn't live without my bottle.(p.526)

locked

• When this sort of thinking is fully established in an individual with alcoholic tendencies, he has probably placed himself beyond human aid, and unless *locked* up, may die or go permanently insane.(p.24)

• He is like the retired business man who lolls in the Florida sunshine in the winter complaining of the sad state of the nation; the minister who sighs over the sins of the twentieth century; politicians and reformers who are sure all would be Utopia if the rest of the world would only behave; the outlaw safe cracker who thinks society has wronged him; and the alcoholic who has lost all and is *locked* up.(p.61)

• Mother would take me in only if I would stay *locked* in a small storeroom and give her my clothes and shoes.(p.238)

• I thought when people did what we did that they just *locked* them up.(p.267)

• When she finally took the baby and left, I *locked* myself in the house and stayed drunk for a month.(p.278)

• This was drinking in sheer desperation, alone and *locked* behind my own door.(p.306)

• After nine days of tests at Mayo, I was put in the *locked* ward – of all places!(p.444)

• Much of my time was spent writing letters, notes, orders, and lists of things for Max, who was also my office nurse, to do to keep the world running while I was *locked* up.(p.445)

• Then I went on my first week-long bender of solitary drinking, *locked* up in a hotel room, because my family opposed my coming marriage.(p.464)

• (I think my first feeling of fear came with my first week's solitary drinking, *locked* up in that hotel room.(p.465)

• When they saw me coming, they *locked* up the silverware and everything else of value.(p.478)

• Within about ten days I got *locked* up for being drunk and this same policeman was in the station house as I was being booked.(p.491)

• I was taken to the station house and *locked* up.(p.492)

• Could I have myself *locked* up at home?(p.502)

• I remember being dragged, drink in hand, from beneath the grand piano, where I had hidden, to be *locked* in my room in disgrace.(p.557)

locker

• And I put a Bible in my *locker* at the hospital.(p.348)

• And I put a Big Book by my night stand, and I put a "Twelve Steps and Twelve Tradition" in my *locker* at the hospital, and I got books by Emmet Fox, and I got books by God-knows-who, and I got to reading all these things.(p.348)

• While I was taking inventory in the cold-storage *locker* one Sunday, a wooden sign bolted to the inside door stopped me in my tracks.(p.461)

lockers

• We all had *lockers*.(p.423)

• The other pupils kept books, pencils, paper, gym equipment and such stuff in their *lockers*.(p.423)

locking

• That armor had turned into prison walls, *locking* me in loneliness – and fear.(p.226)

lockups

• From a Canadian reservation to overseas bars to New England *lockups*, an Indian traveled a long trail that finally led him home to A.A.(p.474)

lode

• He may not see at once that he has barely scratched a limitless *lode* which will pay dividends only if he mines it for the rest of his life and insists on giving away the entire product.(p.129)

logic

• *Logic* is great stuff.(p.53)

logical

• When, however, the perfectly *logical* assumption is suggested that underneath the material world and life as we see it, there is an All Powerful, Guiding, Creative Intelligence, right there our perverse streak comes to the surface and we laboriously set out to convince ourselves it isn't so.(p.49)

• People of faith have a *logical* idea of what life is all about.(p.49)

• Hence we are at pains to tell why we think our present faith is reasonable, why we think it more sane and *logical* to believe than not to believe, why we say our former thinking was soft and mushy when we threw up our hands in doubt and said, "We don't know."(p.53)

• That was perfectly *logical*.(p.236)

• Without hesitation, I did the only *logical* thing -- ran away from home.(p.354)

• It seemed *logical* to me that if I married this man and took the responsibility for these children that they would keep me sober.(p.548)

logically

• So I spent much of my time calling on the people who I felt would *logically* come in contact with alcoholic cases, doctors, ministers, lawyers and the personnel men in industry.(p.281)

lolling

• He'll never read in his "sweetness and light" senior-citizen publications anything but the joys of *lolling* in the rocking chair, angling on the riverbank, or bowling on the green.(p.330)

lolls

• He is like the retired business man who *lolls* in the Florida sunshine in the winter complaining of the sad state of the nation; the minister who sighs over the sins of the twentieth century; politicians and reformers who are sure all would be Utopia if the rest of the world would only behave; the outlaw safe cracker who thinks society has wronged him; and the alcoholic who has lost all and is locked up.(p.61)

London

• I remember looking longingly at the window as an easier solution, and shuddering at the memory of that other window, three years before, and the six agonizing months in a *London* hospital ward.(p.224)

• I stopped off just to have one drink to see if it tasted the same on the way back to *London*, and that night I was carried back to bed again.(p.522)

lone

• The remonstrances of my friends terminated in a row and I became a *lone* wolf.(p.3)

• A night or so a week in a joint, and a party or so a week at home or with friends, along with a little *lone* drinking, soon had me preparing for the existence of a top flight drunkard.(p.298)

• During this time, you are supposed to behave yourself, but I took a little wine-tasting tour through France, all by my *lone*, with car and chauffeur.(p.405)

loneliness

• No words can tell of the *loneliness* and despair I found in that bitter morass of self-pity.(p.8)

• To watch people recover, to see them help others, to watch *loneliness* vanish, to see a fellowship grow up about you, to have a host of friends – this is an experience you must not miss.(p.89)

• As we became subjects of King Alcohol, shivering denizens of his mad realm, the chilling vapor that is *loneliness* settled down.(p.151)

• Then he will know *loneliness* such as few do.(p.152)

• That armor had turned into prison walls, locking me in *loneliness* -- and fear.(p.226)

• I had found friends, understanding friends who often knew what I was thinking and feeling better than I knew myself, and didn't allow me to retreat into my prison of *loneliness* and fear over a fancied slight or hurt.(p.228)

• I don't remember much of what he said, but I did realize that here was another guy exactly like me; he had been in the same laughing academies and the same jails, known the same loss of jobs, same frustrations, same boredom and the same *loneliness*.(p.239)

• That night for the first time in my life I really let down my hair and admitted my general *loneliness*.(p.239)

• My *loneliness* was worse than it had ever been before, for now even my own kind had turned against me.(p.247)

• I began hitting the bottle again, and with it self-pity, resentment, *loneliness* and remorse set in deeply.(p.362)

• *Loneliness*, great physical and mental agony – these were the common lot.(p.455)

• There was that awful alcoholic *loneliness*.(p.467)

• There was *loneliness*.(p.532)

• Had I been able to explain to a psychiatrist the feeling of futility, *loneliness* and lack of purpose that had come with my deep sense of personal failure at this second divorce, I seriously doubt that the good doctor could have convinced me that my basic problem was a spiritual hunger, but A.A. has shown me this was the truth.(p.546)

lonely

• I was very *lonely* and again turned to alcohol.(p.1)

• The husband begins to feel *lonely*, sorry for himself.(p.81)

• This may lead to *lonely* evenings for you.(p.111)

• Unless he took some drinks, he might not have the courage to scrape an acquaintance and would have a *lonely* week-end.(p.154)

• Just three years of drinking pushed a shy, *lonely* young girl to the depth of depression.(p.353)

• I had been unhappy, *lonely*, and scared for so long that the discovery of liquor seemed to be the answer to all my problems.(p.353)

• What had happened to the shy, *lonely*, churchgoing wallflower?(p.355)

• I felt very *lonely* and hurt, because nobody understood me.(p.478)

• My grandparents were strangers to me and I remember being *lonely*, and terrified and hurt.(p.545)

lonesome

• The people in the group hadn't been around that day; part of my family was in Florida and the rest of them weren't speaking to me, so I spent a very *lonesome* day and by evening I was feeling very sorry for myself.(p.207)

• On non-meeting nights I was *lonesome*, or so I told myself.(p.414)

long

• We doctors have realized for a *long* time that some form of moral psychology was of urgent importance to alcoholics, but its application presented difficulties beyond our conception.(p.xxv)

• The unselfishness of these men as we have come to know them, the entire absence of profit motive, and their community spirit, is indeed inspiring to one who has labored *long* and wearily in this alcoholic field.(p.xxv)

• A *long* time has passed with no return to alcohol.(p.xxix)

• We had *long* talks when I would still her foreboding by telling her that men of genius conceived their best projects when drunk; that the most majestic constructions of philosophic thought were so derived.(p.2)

• At *long* last I saw, I felt, I believed.(p.12)

• This tragic situation has already arrived in practically every case *long* before it is suspected.(p.24)

• In the doctor's judgment he was utterly hopeless; he could never regain his position in society and he would have to place himself under lock and key or hire a bodyguard if he expected to live *long*.(p.26)

• Heaven knows, we have tried hard enough and *long* enough to drink like other people!(p.31)

• It will not take *long* for you to decide if you are honest with yourself about it.(p.32)

• We have heard of few instances where people, who showed definite signs of alcoholism, were able to stop for a *long* period because of an overpowering desire to do so.(p.32)

• Then he fell victim to a belief which practically every alcoholic has – that his *long* period of sobriety and self-discipline had qualified him to drink as other men.(p.32)

• Most of us have believed that if we remained sober for a *long* stretch, we could thereafter drink normally.(p.33)

• To be gravely affected, one does not necessarily have to drink a *long* time nor take the quantities some of us have.(p.33)

• He was interested and conceded that he had some of the symptoms, but he was a *long* way from admitting that he could do nothing about it himself.(p.40)

• If a mere code of morals or a better philosophy of life were sufficient to overcome alcoholism, many of us would have recovered *long* ago.(p.44)

• Sometimes this was a tedious process; we hope no one else will be prejudiced for as *long* as some of us were.(p.48)

• Show any longshoreman a Sunday supplement describing a proposal to explore the moon by means of a

rocket and he will say, "I bet they do it -- maybe not so *long* either."(p.52)
• The wording was, of course, quite optional so *long* as we expressed the idea, voicing it without reservation.(p.63)
• We must be entirely honest with somebody if we expect to live *long* or happily in this world.(p.73)
• We have a written inventory and we are prepared for a *long* talk.(p.75)
• Of course she did not, and the whole situation has *long* since been adjusted.(p.79)
• But he is yet a *long* way from making good to the wife or parents whom for years he has so shockingly treated.(p.82)
• Yes, there is a *long* period of reconstruction ahead.(p.83)
• That is how we react so *long* as we keep in fit spiritual condition.(p.85)
• We seldom allow an alcoholic to live in our homes for *long* at a time.(p.97)
• Some of us have taken very hard knocks to learn this truth: Job or no job -- wife or no wife -- we simply do not stop drinking so *long* as we place dependence upon other people ahead of dependence on God.(p.98)
• Why sit with a *long* face in places where there is drinking, sighing about the good old days.(p.102)
• We have had *long* rendezvous with hurt pride, frustration, self-pity, misunderstanding and fear.(p.104)
• If he does not, you will probably not have *long* to wait.(p.113)
• Without you he would have gone to pieces *long* ago.(p.119)
• You have been starving for his companionship, yet he spends *long* hours helping other men and their families.(p.119)
• God, they believe, almost owes this recompense on a *long* overdue account.(p.123)
• It takes some of us a *long* time to outgrow that serious handicap.(p.125)
• Let them remember that his drinking wrought all kinds of damage that may take *long* to repair.(p.127)
• We do not know of many cases where this difficulty lasted *long*.(p.134)
• This may hang on for months, *long* after their mother has accepted dad's new way of living and thinking.(p.134)
• Not *long* afterward he had called me from Hartford on two successive days, so drunk he could hardly speak.(p.136)
• Still another experience: A woman's voice came faintly over *long* distance from Virginia.(p.137)
• Because of the employee's special ability, or of his own strong personal attachment to him, the employer has sometimes kept such a man at work *long* beyond a reasonable period.(p.137)
• I know, in my own particular case, that nothing my company could have done would have stopped me for, so *long* as I was able to hold my position, I could not possibly realize how serious my situation was.(p.141)
• In competent hands, this seldom takes *long* nor is it very expensive.(p.143)
• It might be well to have a *long* chat with him on his return.(p.143)
• Can he talk frankly with you so *long* as he does not bear business tales or criticize his associates?(p.145)
• *Long* experience with alcoholic excuses naturally arouses suspicion.(p.146)
• They often jeopardize their own positions by trying to help serious drinkers who should have been fired *long* ago, or else given an opportunity to get well.(p.147)
• When our friend related his experience, the man agreed that no amount of will power he might muster could stop his drinking for *long*.(p.155)
• He has helped other men recover, and is a power in the church from which he was *long* absent.(p.158)
• From surrounding towns, families drive *long* distances to be present.(p.161)
• There my drinking became so much worse that the boys in the fraternity house where I lived felt forced to send for my father, who made a *long* journey in the vain endeavor to get me straightened around.(p.174)
• It was not *long* before I was drinking at least a case and a half a day.(p.177)
• If she had not, I know I would have been dead a *long* time ago.(p.178)
• Before very *long* we began to relate some incidents of our drinking and, naturally, pretty soon, I realized both of them knew what they were talking about because you can see things and smell things when you're drunk, that you can't other times, and, if I had thought they didn't know what they were talking about, I wouldn't have been willing to talk to them at all.(p.185)
• After a while, Bill said, "Well, now, you've been talking a good *long* time, let me talk a minute or two."(p.185)
• And they said, "No, you have a disease, and it doesn't make any difference how *long* you do without it, after a drink or two you'll end up just like you are now."(p.187)
• Every time I'd start thinking about drinking, I would think of the *long*, dry years ahead without having a drink; but this idea of twenty-four hours, that it was up to me from then on, was a lot of help.(p.188)
• (At this point, the Editors intrude just *long* enough to supplement Bill D.'s account, that of the man on the bed, with that of Bill W., the man who sat by the side of the bed.)(p.188)
• I went into the high school grades, but having missed all the intermediate grades, I didn't get along too well, so I developed the habit of going back to school just *long* enough for the football season and then quitting.(p.193)
• Right then I determined that never so *long* as I lived would I have anything more to do with martinis.(p.195)
• It had *long* since become a serious problem.(p.197)
• I can well remember over a *long* period of years when I thought I was the only person in the world who knew that sooner or later I was going to get drunk.(p.198)
• *Long* since I had come to believe I was insane because I did so many things I didn't want to do.(p.199)
• So, knowing that, I had determined that so *long* as I lived I would never take another drink.(p.200)
• An offer of appreciation for not having had a drink for those few months and then and there, without anybody promising me anything or threatening me, I made a solemn vow that never so *long* as I lived would I take another drink.(p.200)
• Then I got into the habit of having beers, and decided that a drink of whiskey was not any worse; so I would get the one drink of whiskey but, on second thought, I decided that as *long* as I was only going to have one, I might as well make it a double-header.(p.203)
• I didn't drink very *long* at a time.(p.203)
• I think the longest drunk I was ever on was eleven days, but usually only two days with a complete blackout for a day, and then backing off by drinking as *long* as I could get anything.(p.203)
• He said, "So *long* as I'm thinking as I'm thinking now, and so *long* as I'm doing the things I'm doing now, I don't believe I'll ever take another drink."(p.206)
• And then my thinking became calculation as to how much longer I had to live, how *long* the assets would last.(p.215)
• Professionally, after I was sober for a month or so I realized that I should school myself to dissolve the partnership I was in because I felt that I would never regain the respect of my partners no matter how *long* I was sober, and that I would be at a disadvantage.(p.220)
• It must have been a *long* time since I had my last drink -- but I didn't dare ask this stranger for one.(p.223)
• I'd been sitting comfortably in a restaurant with Rita, drinking my sixth martini and hoping the waiter would forget about the lunch order -- at least *long* enough for me to have a couple more.(p.223)
• No doubt I had been an exile too *long* -- I should go home to America.(p.226)
• It wasn't very *long* before home-brewing was an institution and men began to search feverishly for old recipe books on wine-making.(p.232)
• It wasn't very *long* until I had developed a pretty good brew with uniformity and plenty of authority.(p.232)
• It wasn't *long* before the bootlegger was an established institution in this, as in other towns.(p.233)
• Before *long* I had a definite taste for hard liquor, knew nausea and headaches I had never known before, but as in the old days, I suffered them out.(p.233)
• In a few sentences he made God seem personal to me, explained Him as a being who was interested in me, the alcoholic, and that all I needed to do was to be willing to follow His way; that as *long* as I followed it I would be able to overcome my desire for liquor.(p.236)
• For a *long* time I kept on trying, in a pretty dumb way at first, I know, but very earnestly.(p.237)
• It wasn't very *long* until my doctor friend sent me to tell another alcoholic what my experience had been.(p.237)
• So I always say that as *long* as I remember January 8th that is how *long* I will remain sober.(p.240)
• It doesn't take *long*.(p.242)
• As *long* as things were tough and the job a challenge I could always manage to hold on pretty well, but as soon as I learned the combination, got the puzzle under control and the boss to pat me on the back, I was gone again.(p.243)
• But we were staying sober as *long* as we kept and talked together.(p.246)
• For a *long* time the only Higher Power I could concede was the power of the group, but this was far more than I had ever recognized before, and it was at least a beginning.(p.248)
• This change had been a *long*, slow process for me, but through these latter years the dividends have been tremendous.(p.249)
• And I still say that as *long* as I remember that January 8th in Washington, that is how *long*, by the grace of God as I understand Him, I will retain a happy sobriety.(p.250)
• I quit the factory and got a job on a small newspaper, going from that to a Pittsburgh daily, *long* ago defunct.(p.252)
• But I didn't stay *long*.(p.252)
• Slight casualties, complicated however by a *long* and serious illness, were my only mishaps.(p.253)
• I thought I had done that until Russ' second collapse, and the doctor told me very candidly that he wasn't *long* for this world.(p.271)
• And that woman told me *long* after that was the surest proof to her that this program could work.(p.272)
• I think it's awfully hard on people, especially if they're new people, to hear these *long* drawn out talks.(p.273)
• I hadn't been in too *long* when one of the men's wives called me one Sunday and told me she didn't think I had any part of the program.(p.273)
• I know I've talked too *long*, but I always do.(p.274)
• And, anyhow, if I went on for ten or a hundred times as *long* I couldn't even begin to tell you all that A.A. has meant to me.(p.274)
• The details of the *long* road back to something resembling normal living -- the first short streetcar ride, the purchase of a used bike which enabled me to widen the narrow horizon of life, the first trip downtown -- I will not dwell on.(p.276)
• The next two years were simply a *long* drawn out process of less and less work and more and more whiskey.(p.278)
• *Long* before I had any real opportunity to give, I had to learn the equally important lesson of receiving graciously.(p.281)
• Friends invited me to stay on for as *long* as I cared to.(p.281)
• At *long* last I am doing the kind of work I have always wanted to do, but never had the patience and emotional stability to train myself for.(p.284)
• In the *long* ago past I used to start at the top as president or treasurer and end up with the sheriff breathing down my neck.(p.284)
• I went to a minister and a doctor that I still knew and they, in turn, asked me how *long* I had been sober.(p.293)
• He had been wanting to do something about his drinking for a *long* time, but did not know how.(p.294)
• That being the case, it didn't take me *long* to figure out that my meager manufacturing facilities were entirely inadequate to the manufacture of beer for social and domestic consumption.(p.297)
• A little more than fifteen years ago, through a *long* and calamitous series of shattering experiences, I found myself being helplessly propelled toward total destruction.(p.304)
• It wasn't *long* before any party without drinks was a dud for me.(p.305)
• I had *long* since given up any pretense of the "social" cocktail hour.(p.306)
• And all the while my fear fed a growing conviction that before *long* it would be necessary for me to be put away in some institution.(p.306)
• Why he bothered with me as *long* as he did I shall never know, for he knew there was no answer for me in medicine and he, like all doctors of his day, had been taught that the alcoholic was incurable and should be ignored.(p.307)
• It is a way of life, and the challenge contained in its principles is great enough to keep any human being striving for as *long* as he lives.(p.311)
• It wasn't *long* before I quit caring how I looked or what my job performance was.(p.318)
• She said, "How *long* have you been married?"(p.322)
• And I was able to go on the wagon for *long* periods of time -- once for four years, to cure an ulcer.(p.328)
• And retirement is a time for thinking, not of death,

but of living – at *long* last.(p.329)
• So *long* as a retiree woos his bottle at home, he stays out of public trouble.(p.330)
• The movie racket had kept me too *long* from writing those novels, articles, short stories, and scripts on which I had copious notes.(p.330)
• He'd told a villain, "The trouble is, old man, you've lived too *long*."(p.333)
• I'd lived too *long* and become a loser, dependent on booze.(p.333)
• I had worked so *long* in a profession where fakery, deceit, and untruths are tools of trade that I instantly recognized honesty when I heard it, from the mouths of A.A. members.(p.334)
• Not *long* ago, I was lunching with another retired publicist.(p.334)
• It wasn't *long* before I was drinking all day.(p.336)
• I'd go into an organization, and it wasn't *long* before I was on the committee, then I was chairman of the committee; and if I was in a group, I'd soon be treasurer or secretary of the group.(p.339)
• As *long* as I worked, as *long* as I got out, I didn't drink.(p.339)
• This was my first *long* vacation of sixty days since I had joined the army.(p.343)
• It was a *long* four or five hour operation, a large surgical procedure, and she was on her ninth or tenth post-operative day.(p.350)
• I had been unhappy, lonely, and scared for so *long* that the discovery of liquor seemed to be the answer to all my problems.(p.353)
• Before *long* I was at the luncheon meeting an hour before the others, that old and familiar trademark of every alcoholic.(p.360)
• It wasn't *long* before I became a five o'clock alcoholic.(p.360)
• It didn't take *long* for me to fall in with a fast crowd who had their lunch in the men's bar of a leading hotel.(p.361)
• Before too *long*, my husband (who seemed to prefer his shirts dirty) put his foot down, declaring that our family might have the cleanest clothes in town, but that I hadn't been out of the same old dirty slacks and blouse for a week.(p.371)
• I continue to be surprised by the people I meet who say, "You haven't had a drink for a *long* time, have you?"(p.376)
• Two years before I joined A.A. my wife took a *long* trip during which she wrote me she just couldn't return unless I did something about my drinking.(p.377)
• As *long* as it eased situations socially, it helped just fine, but somewhere along the line, it backfired.(p.386)
• I never want to forget that last drunk as *long* as I live.(p.393)
• I know that I must work at it as *long* as I live; I know that it is only by working at it that I can stay sober and have a happy life.(p.394)
• Age and the law were still against me, but laws were not as strictly enforced in those days as they are now, and I discovered that as *long* as I had the green blood, there was always a way to get alcohol, either from a nondiscriminatory bartender or from an older friend who would be glad to purchase the joy juice for the privilege of sharing it.(p.397)
• But now, with His help and grace, this child of His has paid his initiation fee for good, as *long* as he remembers to stay away from that first drink (the one that does all the damage) one day at a time.(p.399)
• My alcoholic problem began *long* before I drank.(p.400)
• A house in Virginia, during the fox hunting season; a little chalet in Switzerland during the summer or a place on *Long* Island -- each house complete with cooks, butlers and maids.(p.403)
• I had already feared insanity for a *long* time.(p.408)
• But it did not take *long* for the pressures of living to bring out my immaturity and my insecurity.(p.420)
• They wrote me many *long* letters about it.(p.427)
• But for how *long*?(p.429)
• To cut a *long* story short, I spent seven years and ten thousand dollars on my psychiatric adventure, and emerged in worse condition than ever.(p.434)
• Moreover, I am deeply convinced that so *long* as I continue to strive, in my bumbling way, toward the principles I first encountered in the earlier chapters of this book, this remarkable power will continue to flow through me.(p.437)
• If pressed further, all I can do is follow the psalmist who said it *long*, *long* before me: "Be still, and know that I am God."(p.437)
• I wasn't able to quit chemicals as *long* as they were in the house.(p.443)
• The more I focus my mind on its defects -- late start, *long* drunkalogues, cigarette smoke – the worse the meeting becomes.(p.451)
• Most of us did not stay out of prison *long* enough to run the alcoholic gamut -- to develop the ongoing kind of alcoholism or alcoholic drinking you hear about in A.A. talks.(p.458)
• I thought that was bad until I hit the hole at a prison camp; it was just wide enough and *long* enough to lie down in.(p.459)
• Ten days of this treatment the first time knocked me from 200 pounds to 130, and I seldom stayed out of the hole *long* enough to gain back my weight.(p.460)
• Forgive me – I cannot write further about this latest turn of events, anticipating seeing the family I deserted so *long* ago.(p.463)
• There was a *long* discussion between my husband, my sister and her husband.(p.466)
• Temporarily, but not for *long*.(p.468)
• Finally, however, in November of 1944, at *long* last I went to A.A.(p.470)
• From a Canadian reservation to overseas bars to New England lockups, an Indian traveled a *long* trail that finally led him home to A.A.(p.474)
• We talk *long* time.(p.475)
• I had a *long* talk with a psychiatrist, but nothing came of that, and I had also, just about that time, talked with a minister for whom I had a great deal of respect.(p.489)
• In that short period he built within me something that I had *long* since lost, which was hope.(p.495)
• Father is an Episcopal minister and his work takes him over *long* drives on bad roads.(p.497)
• It is not *long* before he drives up in the buggy.(p.497)
• The drive was *long* and cold but he was thankful for the hot bricks which some thoughtful person had given him for his feet.(p.497)
• Mother has been dying of cancer for a *long* time.(p.501)
• And as I read, I shall take little drinks at *long* intervals.(p.506)
• I didn't stick at social drinking very *long*.(p.512)
• That stuck with me for a *long* time.(p.513)
• But as *long* as you did your work and didn't disgrace yourself, you were socially acceptable and nobody really intruded on your private life very much.(p.518)
• I was alone by myself in that job for a *long* time.(p.519)
• He didn't have to lie in wait very *long*, but fortunately by that time, I had acquired friends upstairs and they covered me for quite a time.(p.519)
• I stayed there just *long* enough to work up a real good resentment against the doctor in charge, who I didn't think was doing anything at all except collecting fees, and I left there fully determined that I'd never put myself in the power of medical people again.(p.521)
• I talked to him for quite a *long* time and at the end, he said, "Well, you're not quite mad enough to be shut up for good yet, but you soon will be if you live *long* enough."(p.522)
• I had played all that out *long* ago.(p.523)
• I was always able to get a boyfriend who had a drinking joint or sold whiskey, but it didn't last *long*.(p.526)
• But I would always wake up in the psychiatric ward to begin another *long* treatment.(p.528)
• I didn't last *long*.(p.528)
• The pressures had started *long* ago.(p.533)
• For a while, for a *long* time, we can endure the intellect's being ahead of the emotions, which is the import of Millay's couplet.(p.534)
• The helpful family finally said, over *long* distance, that there would be no more money and that I could not come home.(p.538)
• But not for *long*; now, for five Friday nights in a row, I went to jail, picked up sodden with beer (which I always disliked, but which was the only drink available); in jail five consecutive Friday nights in the town where I had grown up, where I had been an honor student in high school, where a kindly uncle, bailing me out, said, "Bob, our family just doesn't do this sort of thing."(p.539)
• I stood off and took a *long* look at life and the values I found in it: I saw a paradox, that he who loses his life does indeed find it.(p.542)
• My husband eventually returned, but it was not *long* until we realized we could not continue our marriage.(p.547)
• Soon my drinking was as bad as ever – all day *long* every day.(p.557)
• This is a condensed version of the original "*long* form" A.A. Traditions as first printed in 1946.(p.563)
• Because the "*long* form" is more explicit and of possible historic value, it is also reproduced.(p.563)
• THE TWELVE TRADITIONS (The *Long* Form)(p.565)
• Quite often friends of the newcomer are aware of the difference *long* before he is himself.(p.569)

long-acting

• Eventually, I was taking forty-five milligrams of the *long-acting* Benzedrine and forty-five of the short-acting just to get out of bed in the morning.(p.442)

long-time

• There was a concrete program, designed to secure the greatest possible inner security for us *long-time* escapists.(p.229)

longed

• Actually, of course, I wanted someone to listen to me, because when I had a few martinis inside, I became the great author I *longed* to be; and the right listener was in for some pretty highflown theories of literature and of genius.(p.536)

longer

• Besides, my gin would last *longer* than his preaching.(p.9)
• Finally, he can no *longer* work, his wife gets a divorce and he is held up to ridicule.(p.38)
• We constantly remind ourselves we are no *longer* running the show, humbly saying to ourselves many times each day "Thy will be done."(p.87)
• Wait until repeated stumbling convinces him he must act, for the more you hurry him the *longer* his recovery may be delayed.(p.113)
• You will no *longer* be self-conscious or feel that you must apologize as though your husband were a weak character.(p.115)
• After all, your family is reunited, alcohol is no *longer* a problem and you and your husband are working together toward an undreamed-of future.(p.119)
• Here, for instance, is a typical example: An officer of one of the largest banking institutions in America knows I no *longer* drink.(p.138)
• Your man will fare better if placed in such physical condition that he can think straight and no *longer* craves liquor.(p.143)
• But at least he will understand the problem and will no *longer* be misled by ordinary promises.(p.148)
• Being wrecked in the same vessel, being restored and united under one God, with hearts and minds attuned to the welfare of others, the things which matter so much to some people no *longer* signify much to them.(p.161)
• Then I started drinking again, with possibly a little more restraint, periods a little bit *longer* than they had been before, but substantially the same pattern.(p.203)
• There were times when I got to drinking, and I had been warned by Firestone that they wouldn't stand for this much *longer*, so, clearly, they were conscious of the fact that I drank too much and too often.(p.204)
• And then my thinking became calculation as to how much *longer* I had to live, how long the assets would last.(p.215)
• In fact, as I look back, I have often thought that they probably concluded that they would put up with me for a couple of years, that I couldn't live much *longer*, and that they would inherit whatever was left of the practice.(p.215)
• When my friends suggested that I was drinking too much – they were no *longer* my friends.(p.226)
• It no *longer* gave me pleasure – it merely dulled the pain -- but I had to have it.(p.226)
• Russ lived a year *longer* than they expected him to live, and in that year he was in bed for at least six months.(p.272)
• Out of this maelstrom just two coherent thoughts came to the surface; one, a drink would mean homelessness and death; two, I could no *longer* relieve the pressure of fear by starting home, as was once my habitual solution to this problem, because I no *longer* had a home.(p.279)
• It would be impossible for me to pass over this year without mentioning my love for, and my indebtedness to these two wonderful people who are no *longer* with us.(p.280)
• It was a period of binges coming closer and closer together and being of *longer* duration.(p.288)
• After holding good positions, making better than an average income for over ten years, I was in debt, had no clothes to speak of, no money, no friends, and no one any *longer* tolerating me but my wife.(p.301)
• However, he explained to me that he had been just such a rummy as I, only for a much *longer* period of time.(p.302)
• I could no *longer* gage my capacity and it might be the second or the tenth drink that would erase my consciousness.(p.306)
• Heartsickness, shame, and fear, fear bordering on

panic, and no complete escape any ***longer*** except in oblivion.(p.306)
• Now, no ***longer*** under pressure, I could safely guard against loss of control.(p.327)
• I was keenly aware that my all-important security, which I had been constantly afraid of losing for four decades, no ***longer*** was endangered.(p.329)
• I could go on living and hurting ten years ***longer***, or more."(p.333)
• But there came a point when I could no ***longer*** live with it.(p.337)
• In the very early spring of 1944, my frustrated wife couldn't take it any ***longer***.(p.362)
• Now, she no ***longer*** risks losing her home, her self-respect, or her laundry.(p.369)
• One night, a few weeks after joining the Fellowship, much to my surprise and delight I saw a familiar but no ***longer*** frowning face.(p.371)
• I still wash clothes, lots of them, but I no ***longer*** lose them at the Laundromat.(p.372)
• Somehow our bodies had reached the point where we could no ***longer*** absorb alcohol in our systems.(p.380)
• I couldn't walk, having it in a cast, and the doctor left the cast on three weeks ***longer*** than was necessary because he never found me sober enough to take it off.(p.390)
• I am no ***longer*** interested in living in a palace, because palace living was not the answer for me.(p.416)
• My new wife and I don't own any property to speak of, and the flashy successes of another day are no ***longer*** mine.(p.438)
• The ***longer*** the drinking continued, the shorter the time the alcohol would keep me asleep; I would have to drink myself back to sleep again and again throughout the night.(p.441)
• I didn't have to worry about him any ***longer***.(p.508)
• The old pattern reasserted itself, but it was no ***longer*** once every six months.(p.514)
• The binges were ***longer***.(p.514)
• It is no ***longer*** enjoyable.(p.514)
• You no ***longer*** get the kicks.(p.514)
• At this point, I was no ***longer*** the wise boy.(p.515)
• Perhaps a better way of saying it is that, on that day, with that decision, I no ***longer*** fought drinking as an escape.(p.531)
• I no ***longer*** had to pretend.(p.531)
• I attended my first A.A. meeting eight years ago, and it is with deep gratitude that I'm able to say I've not had a drink since that time, and that I take no sedation or narcotics, for this program is to me one of complete sobriety and I no ***longer*** need to escape reality.(p.549)
• My doctor finally declared he could no ***longer*** be responsible for me, and sent me to a psychiatrist who practiced in the same suite of offices.(p.558)
• (She no ***longer*** weeps in the night.)(p.559)

longest
• I think the ***longest*** drunk I was ever on was eleven days, but usually only two days with a complete blackout for a day, and then backing off by drinking as long as I could get anything.(p.203)

longhand
• They sent me the regular letter they send to everybody else, but along with it, Ruth Hock, the nonalcoholic secretary, wrote a ***longhand*** note because she could see from the letter that I really needed help badly.(p.392)

longing
• But as the years go by, the stretch becomes unbearable; and the man with the grown-up brain and the childish emotions – vanity, self-interest, false pride, jealousy, ***longing*** for social approval, to name few -- becomes a prime candidate for alcohol.(p.534)

longingly
• I remember looking ***longingly*** at the window as an easier solution, and shuddering at the memory of that other window, three years before, and the six agonizing months in a London hospital ward.(p.224)

longs
• The family of an alcoholic ***longs*** for the return of happiness and security.(p.123)

longshoreman
• Show any ***longshoreman*** a Sunday supplement describing a proposal to explore the moon by means of a rocket and he will say, "I bet they do it -- maybe not so long either."(p.52)

longtime-successful
• While I sought the comforting arms of alcohol, I knew this was a sign of weakness on the part of a ***longtime-successful*** old codger with white hair, the image of dignity.(p.331)

look
• He had that starry-eyed ***look***.(p.9)
• It began to ***look*** as though religious people were right after all.(p.11)
• Most of us feel we need ***look*** no further for Utopia.(p.16)
• As we ***look*** back, we feel we had gone on drinking many years beyond the point where we could quit on our will power.(p.34)
• Let us have a ***look*** at some of them.(p.48)
• As a celebrated American statesman put it, "Let's ***look*** at the record."(p.50)
• We were prepared to ***look*** at it from an entirely different angle.(p.66)
• We have begun to learn tolerance, patience and good will toward all men, even our enemies, for we ***look*** on them as sick people.(p.70)
• We can ***look*** the world in the eye.(p.75)
• If we can answer to our satisfaction, we then ***look*** at Step Six.(p.76)
• Let's ***look*** at Steps Eight and Nine.(p.76)
• As we ***look*** over the list of business acquaintances and friends we have hurt, we may feel diffident about going to some of them on a spiritual basis.(p.76)
• He commences to ***look*** around in the night clubs, or their equivalent, for something besides liquor.(p.81)
• When we ***look*** back, we realize that the things which came to us when we put ourselves in God's hands were better than anything we could have planned.(p.100)
• If you think he will be shy of a spiritual remedy, ask him to ***look*** at the chapter on alcoholism.(p.112)
• As soon as his sobriety begins to be taken as a matter of course, the family may ***look*** at their strange new dad with apprehension, then with irritation.(p.128)
• A ***look*** at the alcoholic in your organization is many times illuminating.(p.139)
• After reading this book, a junior executive can go to such a man and say approximately this, "***Look*** here, Ed.(p.147)
• Even if you feel your organization has no alcoholic problem, it might pay to take another ***look*** down the line.(p.149)
• Then Prohibition came into effect, and the facts that the stuff obtainable was so horrible and sometimes deadly, and that I had married and had a job which I had to ***look*** after, helped me for a period of some three or four years, although I would get drunk every time I could get hold of enough to drink to get started.(p.183)
• I had to ***look*** in the telephone book later to find out who these people were.(p.196)
• He came in and took a ***look*** at me and sent me to the hospital.(p.205)
• I said, "***Look***, Bub, if I want those lights on, I'll turn them on."(p.207)
• He took off his hat and his overcoat, and he said, "You don't ***look*** very good.(p.207)
• As I ***look*** back, all the brothers developed personality problems.(p.210)
• In fact, as I ***look*** back, I have often thought that they probably concluded that they would put up with me for a couple of years, that I couldn't live much longer, and that they would inherit whatever was left of the practice.(p.215)
• When I ***look*** back on that last horrible year of constant drinking I wonder how I survived it either physically or mentally.(p.224)
• This was when I really took my first good ***look*** at myself.(p.247)
• Lots of times, vain-gloriously, I used to take the bottle out, ***look*** at it and say, "I've got you licked."(p.253)
• As I ***look*** back on the events of two months, I can clearly see that I had been circling around, half-afraid of encountering the remedy for my situation, half wanting it, deferring fulfillment of my promise to get in touch with the doctor I had heard about.(p.258)
• I ***look*** back and remember these things because they made me very unhappy, and added to my feeling of inferiority at never being the same as other people.(p.261)
• He had a very peculiar ***look*** on his face, and he said, "He's coming."(p.263)
• As I ***look*** back, I was very broken up about it.(p.263)
• Here, while in a hospital bed, men with clear eyes, happy faces, and a ***look*** of assurance and purposefulness about them, came to see me and told me their stories.(p.279)
• He said he had finally learned that drinking was a fatal illness made up of an allergy plus an obsession, and once the drinking had passed from habit to obsession, we were completely hopeless, and could ***look*** forward only to spending the balance of our lives in mental institutions or to death.(p.290)
• As I ***look*** back on that first evening I realize that I began to hope, then, for the first time; and I felt that if he could regain these things, perhaps it would be possible for me too.(p.290)
• Let's ***look*** at the record."(p.322)
• I couldn't ***look*** them straight in the eyes, although I was always a self-possessed brazen sort of person.(p.323)
• In the old days I hated to wake up and ***look*** back at what last night was like.(p.325)
• I couldn't go to one wine store and ***look*** the man honestly in the face and buy a bottle, as I used to do when I had parties and entertained and did normal drinking.(p.336)
• Every day became that much harder to live through, and I began to take a ***look*** at myself.(p.354)
• So, with mixed feelings of humiliation, anger, and fear, I decided to ***look*** for an answer.(p.371)
• I don't want anybody ever to ***look*** at me like that again.(p.391)
• I would get wildly excited and ***look*** forward to another night of drinking.(p.408)
• Since they could do nothing with Anne either, Priscilla suggested that I go and ***look*** after Anne.(p.414)
• But, by the ***look*** on the psychiatrist's face, I could tell that it would really make him happy if I agreed.(p.446)
• And we usually have some kind of grimy sweater that we think we ***look*** sexy in, even if we weigh ninety-five pounds soaking wet and are not wearing a bra.(p.479)
• I'd go into my home with a bottle, and I remember clearly how I would ***look*** around to see if Vi was watching.(p.487)
• I got to the place where I'd ***look*** forward to the week-end's drinking and pacify myself by saying that the week-ends were mine, that it didn't interfere with my family or with my business if I drank on the week-ends.(p.488)
• Well – well – ***look*** who's here!(p.500)
• I ***look*** for liquor and can't find any.(p.502)
• When I ***look*** back, I can't see anything that would have predisposed me towards being either a neurotic or a drunk.(p.517)
• There was nothing in my school life that I can ***look*** back on which was responsible for anything that happened afterwards.(p.517)
• I have not seen a black face but mine since I've been here, and if I didn't ***look*** in the mirror, I wouldn't know that I was black, because these people treat me as one of them, which I am.(p.530)
• I stood off and took a long ***look*** at life and the values I found in it: I saw a paradox, that he who loses his life does indeed find it.(p.542)
• As I said earlier, self-pity and resentment were my constant companions and my inventory began to ***look*** like a thirty-three year diary, for I seemed to have a resentment against everybody I had ever known.(p.551)

looked
• He ***looked*** straight at me.(p.9)
• We ***looked*** upon this world of warring individuals, warring theological systems, and inexplicable calamity, with deep skepticism.(p.46)
• We ***looked*** askance at many individuals who claimed to be godly.(p.46)
• Instead, we ***looked*** at the human defects of these people, and sometimes used their shortcomings as a basis of wholesale condemnation.(p.50)
• Putting out of our minds the wrongs others had done, we resolutely ***looked*** for our own mistakes.(p.67)
• We got this all down on paper and ***looked*** at it.(p.69)
• Men who had liquor shipped in from Boston or New York by express were ***looked*** upon with great distrust and disfavor by most of the good townspeople.(p.171)
• The water tank on the toilet I never used, because that ***looked*** too easy.(p.176)
• I put on thirty pounds of weight in about two months, ***looked*** like a pig, and was uncomfortable from shortness of breath.(p.177)
• I ***looked*** up and there were two great big fellows over six foot tall, very likable looking.(p.185)
• Bill lay on his hospital bed and ***looked*** at us in wonder.(p.188)
• Bill ***looked*** across at my wife, and said to her, "Henrietta, the Lord has been so wonderful to me, curing me of this terrible disease, that I just want to keep talking about it and telling people."(p.191)
• They ***looked*** at one another queerly and, finally, one of them allowed he'd have a beer and they all followed him, each of them saying he'd have

a beer too.(p.194)
• I didn't even know what a martini *looked* like, but I had heard a man down the bar order one.(p.194)
• I had run into him, and he *looked* real prosperous; his face and eyes *looked* clear and he started to compliment me on my good front and how well I *looked*, and I said, "I haven't had a drink for nine months."(p.201)
• And we stood there for twenty minutes, telling each other how much better we were, how much better we *looked*, how much better off we were financially, mentally, physically, morally, and in every way, shape and manner.(p.201)
• I *looked* so terrible in the court that the judge suggested that I get a continuance and let me sign all the papers to go to a hospital and to a doctor.(p.204)
• Terrified, I *looked* around.(p.222)
• The shakes grew worse and I *looked* at my watch -- six o'clock.(p.223)
• He *looked* at me quizzically.(p.257)
• I *looked* much older than I was, I was always large, and I went back to work in this job.(p.262)
• An attorney sat at the side of the bed where I was lying, and he sat on the edge of his chair and *looked* as innocent as a baby.(p.268)
• "Well," I said to dad, when the A.A. people kept coming with these lovely cars and *looked* so nice, "I suppose the neighbors say, 'Now those old fools must have up and died, but where's the hearse?'"(p.269)
• It wasn't long before I quit caring how I *looked* or what my job performance was.(p.318)
• And when I *looked* at it, I knew I was just as much a drunk as George was, if not worse.(p.322)
• I didn't care what I *looked* like, I didn't care what I did.(p.337)
• However, I am an alcoholic, so I always *looked* forward to the day when I would be able to drink again.(p.343)
• On the first, though on the water wagon, I *looked* forward to my next drink.(p.344)
• So I went to my wife and asked her, wasn't there something that she and I could do to somehow get together, and she turned on her heel and *looked* me squarely in the eye, and said, "You don't care anything about my problem," and I could have smacked her, but I said to myself, "Grab on to your serenity!"(p.351)
• She left, and I sat down and crossed my hands, and *looked* up and said, "For God's sake, help me."(p.351)
• Furthermore, I knew that I was *looked* upon as a city slicker from New York, and I had to be pretty cautious among small town, conservative Yankees.(p.360)
• Then I *looked* forward to the week-end of golf and the nineteenth hole.(p.374)
• So when he came for me, as he walked down the stairs, I could see him through the bars, and he was signing for me; I *looked* at him and said, "Don't you sign anything in this place!"(p.391)
• But Frank turned around and *looked* at me and said, "Esther, remember you're in jail and not at home."(p.391)
• She was endlessly patient as we *looked* together for an answer.(p.409)
• This was how I had *looked* and acted a few short weeks ago.(p.415)
• I *looked* about the room.(p.422)
• It *looked* as if the war would be over any day, but I had to go anyhow.(p.425)
• I headed home for the most wonderful experience of all time – meeting my "new" parents – mom and dad *looked* different than I had pictured them.(p.428)
• My outward professional life *looked* fine, on the surface.(p.435)
• I *looked* up an A.A. meeting and went there -- alone.(p.436)
• The people of A.A. had something that *looked* much better than what I had, but I was afraid to let go of what I had in order to try something new; there was a certain sense of security in the familiar.(p.448)
• She had *looked* for me last evening after I left the car and wandered off into the night.(p.502)
• She had *looked* for me this morning.(p.502)
• He just *looked* at me and said, "Pat, for you there isn't any cure."(p.515)
• I, a man of steel, with very high ideals, well brought up, an honor student and the recipient of scholarships and prizes, a boy wonder in business -- I, Bob, the author of this essay, *looked* and saw that the universe was beneath my contempt, and that to remove myself from it was the only thing of dignity a man could do.(p.531)
• I *looked* around me at people who seemed happy and tried to analyze their happiness, and it seemed to me that without exception these people had something or somebody they loved very much.(p.546)
• During the day a friend of mine brought me some magazines to take to a hospital group I was interested in, and I *looked* through them and a "banner" across the front of one featured an article by a prominent clergyman in which I caught the word "resentment."(p.552)
• By learning -- through practicing the Twelve Steps and through sharing at meetings – how to cope with the problems that we *looked* to booze to solve, back in our drinking days.(p.560)

looking

• I failed to persuade my broker friends to send me out *looking* over factories and managements, but my wife and I decided to go anyway.(p.2)
• After all, are you not *looking* for results rather than methods?(p.144)
• I looked up and there were two great big fellows over six foot tall, very likable *looking*.(p.185)
• Now, if you don't want it, we'll not take up your time, and we'll be going and *looking* for someone else."(p.186)
• If I could, that was wonderful, that was just fine, and they would very much appreciate a person who had that kind of power, but they were *looking* for a man that knew he had a problem, and knew that he couldn't handle it himself and needed outside help.(p.186)
• *Looking* sadder than ever, he wearily ventured, "Well this is wonderful for you fellows, but it can't be for me.(p.188)
• *Looking* in later we found Bill with his wife, Henrietta.(p.189)
• During the day, *looking* over the contracts and money in my pocket, I found that I had sold six lots that I couldn't even remember, and didn't even know the people I had sold them to.(p.196)
• At the end of about four months, I not only had good *looking* clothes --and I might say that at the time I first talked to Max I didn't have a suit of clothes I could bend over in real sudden; now I had six suits of clothes.(p.200)
• I offered them a drink, and they came to the bottom of the stairs and the good woman fainted, just *looking* at me.(p.205)
• When I had been in the hospital ten days, Sister Ignatia, who has played such a part in the development of A.A. in this area, stuck her head in the door one morning and announced, *looking* at me quizzically, that they might be able to make something human out of my face after all.(p.205)
• It had been one o'clock when I last remember *looking*.(p.223)
• I remember *looking* longingly at the window as an easier solution, and shuddering at the memory of that other window, three years before, and the six agonizing months in a London hospital ward.(p.224)
• If that was all, then I was a little doubtful that it was the answer I was *looking* for.(p.236)
• I know that one of the outfits I had was a skirt and a very funny *looking* blouse that my mother had picked up at a rummage sale.(p.261)
• As we left, and they were escorting us across the bridge into Wheeling, I, with great dignity and sarcasm, told them if their wives were ever visiting in Akron, and they, too, were *looking* for their route sign as I was, that I hoped I could extend to them the hospitality that had been shown to me in Bellaire.(p.264)
• Finally this company also became involved and I was once more *looking* for a job.(p.300)
• *Looking* at him it was hard to believe he had ever been as I was then.(p.309)
• In time, I found myself *looking* forward to each new day with pleasurable anticipation.(p.311)
• All my life, it seemed, was spent on the outside *looking* in.(p.353)
• *Looking* back, it is surprising to me now that I managed to keep working and have enough money to squander at the various spots in the big city.(p.358)
• *Looking* directly at me was a large oil painting of my wife, and her very words seemed to shout at me -- "I am not leaving you because I don't love you; it's because I do love you.(p.363)
• I think now that a God, in whom I did not believe, was *looking* after me.(p.412)
• Marty came in, *looking* clean, neat, well-dressed and, like Bill, she was neither a bloated wreck nor a reformer.(p.413)
• (I am *looking* at it now in my bedroom -- a copy that was presented to me a couple of years ago by the A.A. group in that same prison.)(p.461)
• "Here's *looking* at you," said he.(p.498)
• I have a family to support and have no time to be *looking* for another job.(p.500)
• I would wait for the mailman each month, like any good mother, but as soon as he handed me my check, I put on my best dress and went *looking* for my alcoholic friend.(p.527)

looks

• Every new alcoholic *looks* for this spirit among us and is immensely relieved when he finds we are not witch-burners.(p.103)
• This picture may not be as dark as it *looks*.(p.110)
• He has just returned from a three-months leave of absence, has taken a cure, *looks* fine, and to clinch the matter, the board of directors told him this was his last chance."(p.138)
• A retired Navy man *looks* back over twenty years of drinking, to add up his A.A. "initiation fee."(p.396)
• Bill was tall, grey haired, with the kind of asymmetrical good *looks* and pleasant easy manner that inspire confidence in the shaken and afraid.(p.413)
• He *looks* at me.(p.503)

looming

• Alcohol was a *looming* cloud in this banker's bright sky.(p.373)

loose

• Abruptly in October 1929 hell broke *loose* on the New York stock exchange.(p.4)
• We realize that some people are as fanatical about sex as others are *loose*.(p.70)
• I was not fit to be on the *loose*, and there was no one to commit me.(p.412)

loosened

• My tongue *loosened*.(p.498)

lopsided

• He will perceive that his spiritual growth is *lopsided*, that for an average man like himself, a spiritual life which does not include his family obligations may not be so perfect after all.(p.129)

Lord

• Bill looked across at my wife, and said to her, "Henrietta, the *Lord* has been so wonderful to me, curing me of this terrible disease, that I just want to keep talking about it and telling people."(p.191)
• That sentence, "The *Lord* has been so wonderful to me, curing me of this terrible disease, that I just want to keep telling people about it," has been sort of a golden text for the A.A. program and for me.(p.191)

Lord's

• They opened with a little prayer, and I thought it was very fine that we stood, all of us together, and closed with the *Lord's* Prayer.(p.270)
• When we closed the meeting with the *Lord's* Prayer, Russ said, "Mother, help me stand."(p.270)
• The meeting lasted an hour and closed with the *Lord's* Prayer.(p.291)
• A "spiritual experience" to me meant attending meetings, seeing a group of other people, all there for the purpose of helping each other; hearing the Twelve Steps and the Twelve Traditions read at a meeting, and hearing the *Lord's* Prayer, which in an A.A. meeting has such great meaning – "Thy will be done, not mine."(p.381)

Los Angeles

• Four years later, I was taken to my first A.A. meeting out of prison, in *Los Angeles*.(p.460)
• For the next five years, I was in and out of A.A. in *Los Angeles*, Phoenix, and San Francisco.(p.460)

los Douze Etapes

• The Twelve Steps that summarize the program may be called los Doce Pasos in one country, *los Douze Etapes* in another, but they trace exactly the same path to recovery that was blazed by the earliest members of Alcoholics Anonymous.(p.xxii)

los Doce Pasos

• The Twelve Steps that summarize the program may be called *los Doce Pasos* in one country, los Douze Etapes in another, but they trace exactly the same path to recovery that was blazed by the earliest members of Alcoholics Anonymous.(p.xxii)

lose

• He may start off as a moderate drinker; he may or may not become a continuous hard drinker; but at some stage of his drinking career he begins to *lose* all control of his liquor consumption, once he starts to drink.(p.21)
• Moreover, he would *lose* his family for whom he had a deep affection.(p.35)
• Perhaps we had been leaning too heavily on Reason that last mile and we did not like to *lose* our support.(p.53)
• As we felt new power flow in, as we enjoyed peace of mind, as we discovered we could face life successfully, as we became conscious of His presence, we began to *lose* our fear of today, tomorrow or the hereafter.(p.63)
• We must *lose* our fear of creditors no matter how

far we have to go, for we are liable to drink if we are afraid to face them.(p.78)
• We have already admitted this in confidence to another person, but we are sure we would be imprisoned or *lose* our job if it were known.(p.78)
• We may *lose* our position or reputation or face jail, but we are willing.(p.79)
• We will *lose* interest in selfish things and gain interest in our fellows.(p.84)
• Maybe he is beginning to *lose* his friends.(p.109)
• You may be afraid your husband will *lose* his position; you are thinking of the disgrace and hard times which will befall you and the children.(p.116)
• You will *lose* the old life to find one much better.(p.120)
• There will be alluring shortcuts and by-paths down which they may wander and *lose* their way.(p.123)
• Why, he argued, should he *lose* the remainder of his business, only to bring still more suffering to his family by foolishly admitting his plight to people from whom he made his livelihood?(p.155)
• Routine jobs bored me, but I would take on the toughest one I could find, work day and night until I had it under control; then it would become tedious and I'd *lose* all interest in it.(p.243)
• You can't *lose*, and maybe God will help you -- just maybe, mind you.(p.280)
• One of them was that I would try to get a group started in Chicago; the second was that I would have to return to Akron to attend meetings at least every two months until I did get a group started in Chicago; third, I decided I must place this program above everything else, even my family, because if I did not maintain my sobriety I would *lose* my family anyway.(p.292)
• I can't bear to be here when you *lose* the respect of others, and above all -- when you *lose* your own self respect."(p.362)
• I can't bear to be here when you *lose* the respect of others, and above all when you *lose* your own self respect."(p.363)
• I still wash clothes, lots of them, but I no longer *lose* them at the Laundromat.(p.372)
• It didn't say I had to *lose* my family.(p.379)
• We are granted "the serenity to accept the things we cannot change" -- and thus *lose* our quickness to anger and our sensitivity to criticism.(p.560)

loser

• In succession came "What Made Milwaukee Famous Made a *Loser* Out of Me" and "I'm Drinking My Christmas Dinner All Alone."(p.332)
• I'd lived too long and become a *loser*, dependent on booze.(p.333)
• A FIVE-TIME *LOSER* WINS(p.457)
• You see, I am a five-time *loser*, which means five felony convictions (not including the cases beaten).(p.457)
• I woke up in jail, sick, withdrawing from alcohol and speed, already a four-time *loser*, and now with a fifth felony charge against me.(p.460)

loses

• But, of course," he continued, "eventually the alcoholic *loses* all of his capacities as his disease gets progressively worse, and this is a tragedy that is painful to watch; the disintegration of a sound mind and body."(p.308)
• HE WHO *LOSES* HIS LIFE(p.531)
• I stood off and took a long look at life and the values I found in it: I saw a paradox, that he who *loses* his life does indeed find it.(p.542)

losing

• My wife upbraided me often and plenty when she saw that my "periodics" were gradually *losing* me what business I could get.(p.233)
• I thought I was *losing* my mind when I realized that I couldn't stop drinking.(p.324)
• I was keenly aware that my all-important security, which I had been constantly afraid of *losing* for four decades, no longer was endangered.(p.329)
• Now, she no longer risks *losing* her home, her self-respect, or her laundry.(p.369)
• Suddenly, I began vomiting and *losing* rectally great quantities of blood.(p.558)

loss

• Here was the threat of commitment, the *loss* of family and position, to say nothing of that intense mental and physical suffering which drinking always caused him.(p.36)
• It may mean the *loss* of many nights' sleep, great interference with your pleasures, interruptions to your business.(p.97)
• You may be at a *loss* to understand how such a seemingly above-board chap could be so involved.(p.140)
• If he is, and is still trying to recover, he will tell you about it even if it means the *loss* of his job.(p.146)
• First, my new wife had walked out, bag, baggage and furniture; then the apartment landlord had thrown me out of the empty apartment and the finish was the *loss* of another job.(p.238)
• I don't remember much of what he said, but I did realize that here was another guy exactly like me; he had been in the same laughing academies and the same jails, known the same *loss* of jobs, same frustrations, same boredom and the same loneliness.(p.239)
• Now, no longer under pressure, I could safely guard against *loss* of control.(p.327)
• It becomes vital, also, that others not know of our defeats, nor suspect our *loss* of confidence.(p.331)
• After I came to A.A., I was divorced by my wife; I lost my practice; I was legally restrained from seeing my children; I went broke; and the dental society threatened me with the *loss* of my license.(p.420)
• The fear of the *loss* of Vi and the feeling that, though she had the right to do as she pleased, she should have told me the truth about it, upset me.(p.487)

losses

• Most had taken shattering *losses* on nearly every front of life.(p.455)

lost

• In Part III ("They *Lost* Nearly All"), eight stories have been retained; five are new.(p.xii)
• These allergic types can never safely use alcohol in any form at all; and once having formed the habit and found they cannot break it, once having *lost* their self-confidence, their reliance upon things human, their problems pile up on them and become astonishingly difficult to solve.(p.xxvi)
• He had *lost* everything worthwhile in life and was only living, one might say, to drink.(p.xxix)
• Many people *lost* money -- but some became very rich.(p.2)
• I had developed a theory that most people *lost* money in stocks through ignorance of markets.(p.2)
• I found a job; then *lost* it as the result of a brawl with a taxi driver.(p.4)
• I admitted for the first time that of myself I was nothing; that without Him I was *lost*.(p.13)
• He has *lost* control.(p.23)
• The fact is that most alcoholics, for reasons yet obscure, have *lost* the power of choice in drink.(p.24)
• We alcoholics are men and women who have *lost* the ability to control our drinking.(p.30)
• We are like men who have *lost* their legs; they never grow new ones.(p.30)
• Whether such a person can quit upon a nonspiritual basis depends upon the extent to which he has already *lost* the power to choose whether he will drink or not.(p.34)
• His family was re-assembled, and he began to work as a salesman for the business he had *lost* through drinking.(p.35)
• We have not *lost* everything in life through drinking and we certainly do not intend to.(p.38)
• There was a feeling of awe and wonder, but it was fleeting and soon *lost*.(p.46)
• He is like the retired business man who lolls in the Florida sunshine in the winter complaining of the sad state of the nation; the minister who sighs over the sins of the twentieth century; politicians and reformers who are sure all would be Utopia if the rest of the world would only behave; the outlaw safe cracker who thinks society has wronged him; and the alcoholic who has *lost* all and is locked up.(p.61)
• They only thought they had *lost* their egoism and fear; they only thought they had humbled themselves.(p.73)
• He saw that he had to place the outcome in God's hands or he would soon start drinking again, and all would be *lost* anyhow.(p.80)
• He is straining every nerve to make up for *lost* time.(p.126)
• Here were three exceptional men *lost* to this world because I did not understand alcoholism as I do now.(p.137)
• We all had to place recovery above everything, for without recovery we would have *lost* both home and business.(p.143)
• He *lost* the race by only a narrow margin.(p.158)
• THEY *LOST* NEARLY ALL(p.167)
• I *lost* only a half day's work during these three years.(p.173)
• I always built up in my own mind the great things that I was going to do, and in fact I accomplished about fifty percent of them and then *lost* interest.(p.193)
• I *lost* money, and then just fooled away a large part of that profit.(p.194)
• At that particular stage, I *lost* interest in it, sold the option for $5,000 and forgot the whole deal.(p.198)
• I was picked up at two-thirty that morning with my car smashed up by a street-car because I had run into a big concrete safety zone, and the street-car had run into me, and they took me out through the roof -- there's where I *lost* the suit.(p.202)
• I had *lost* a hundred dollars I had in my pocket, and *lost* a wristwatch too.(p.202)
• I *lost* the car, of course.(p.202)
• But more important, I *lost* my sobriety.(p.202)
• My children had *lost* respect for me and, in fact, it was only after three or four years of sobriety that any of them ever said anything to me to indicate that I had recouped even a little of their respect.(p.215)
• In fact, I never *lost* my faith, since I had been prepared by some conversations toward the end of my sojourn in the hospital with Dr. Bob, conversations pretty much along spiritual lines.(p.218)
• She gave no sign of recognizing anything wrong, but what had I been doing for those *lost* five hours?(p.223)
• My customers *lost* confidence in me to the point where I retained what business I had only because I was a well-trained and reputedly fine craftsman.(p.234)
• Sometimes during that year I rebelled inwardly at what seemed like *lost* time, and at having to be a burden to these good people whose means were limited.(p.281)
• Three years after I started on my drinking career, I *lost* my first job.(p.298)
• By now I wanted to die, but had *lost* the courage even to take my life.(p.306)
• Seldom had any of these *lost* either health, business, family, or friends.(p.315)
• I never *lost* a job.(p.323)
• I should have *lost* my husband, and I think that only the fact that he was an alcoholic too kept us together.(p.323)
• Many women who have reached the stage that I had reached in my drinking have *lost* husbands, children, homes, everything they hold dear.(p.323)
• The important thing I *lost* was my own self-respect.(p.323)
• We have only been in A.A. a few years, but now we're trying to make up for *lost* time.(p.325)
• Through studied sneaky-drinking, I'd become a senior citizen without having *lost* a day's work because of booze.(p.327)
• But the saddest, and thus the most consoling, drifted through from the country-music station -- stories of broken hearts, wasted lives, *lost* loves, sung plaintively.(p.332)
• A lot of *lost* dreams, empty futures, and crazy things of the past went through my mind.(p.333)
• How full it has kept my retirement years -- the five I've lived since the first two *lost* in traveling a rocky road to hell, before I made a U-turn.(p.334)
• In A.A., she discovered she had *lost* nothing and had found everything.(p.335)
• Psychiatrist and surgeon, he had *lost* his way until he realized that God, not he, was the Great Healer.(p.345)
• First, we all hear at A.A. meetings about those who have *lost* everything, those who have been in jail, those who have been in prison, those who have *lost* their families, those who have *lost* their income.(p.345)
• I never *lost* any of it.(p.345)
• In an attempt to get over that feeling, there was a quick onslaught of a greater number of drinks, and then all was *lost*.(p.346)
• I *lost* my driver's license, was made a ward of the court, and was put on probation (not to mention the fact that I might have killed three friends and myself).(p.354)
• And, believe me, I thank God that I found out about A.A. before I had to beat my brains out -- before I had been hospitalized, jailed or *lost* a job.(p.367)
• Then my father fell down a flight of stairs on one of his *lost* weekends, at the peak of his career, and died.(p.370)
• Very soon after I *lost* Mother, my five-year-old little girl was killed by a neighbor's car.(p.370)
• I *lost* a lot of shirts that way, and sometimes I was minus a whole wash.(p.371)
• During three years in A.A., I haven't *lost* so much as one shirt.(p.372)
• I had not yet *lost* my job or family, even though both were on the verge of going.(p.379)
• I *lost* my shyness.(p.402)

• It was all about Scott Fitzgerald's little *lost* debutante, abused, misunderstood and running wild.(p.402)
• Others have come back, others I have *lost*.(p.404)
• In less than two years, I *lost* my practice, my home, my wife, and my children.(p.418)
• After I came to A.A., I was divorced by my wife; I *lost* my practice; I was legally restrained from seeing my children; I went broke; and the dental society threatened me with the loss of my license.(p.420)
• Here was the *lost* love I'd missed at home.(p.425)
• I *lost* it many times and mom and dad would drive me around until I found it.(p.429)
• I'd *lost* my car again, pawned my wallet and all identification papers for a bottle, and gotten home somehow.(p.429)
• Three days later I *lost* my job.(p.430)
• And I knew that somewhere along the line I'd *lost* the power to stop drinking.(p.436)
• THEY *LOST* NEARLY ALL(p.455)
• A couple of years later, we *lost* our elder brother in a house fire, because of pills and booze.(p.480)
• About that time I had *lost* practically all my property except the place we were living in.(p.487)
• As usual I got drunk and *lost* the money.(p.491)
• Vi was very kind and explained to the jury that I was basically a fine fellow and a good husband, but that I drank too much and that she thought I had *lost* my mind and felt that I should be committed to an asylum.(p.492)
• In that short period he built within me something that I had long since *lost*, which was hope.(p.495)
• They saved us endless time and *lost* motion.(p.496)
• I have *lost* the fellowship.(p.505)
• There was the father one *lost* respect for at the age of eleven, because the father broke his solemn word in a circumstance where you, eleven years old, had assumed guilt when you were innocent; but the father would not believe you, no matter what; and to ease his suffering you "confessed" and were "forgiven," only – months later – to have your "guilt" brought up – only he and you knew what he was talking bout -- brought up in front of the stern grandmother.(p.533)
• I bear a few scars on my face from these fights, which I always *lost*, because the "stick" existed only in my mind.(p.537)
• If we do not do so, we shall stand convicted of emotional sterility and of having *lost* the faith that moves mountains, without which medicine can do little."(p.571)

lot

• Once this malady has a real hold, they are a baffled *lot*.(p.23)
• If we have been thorough about our personal inventory, we have written down a *lot*.(p.70)
• Many of us have wasted a *lot* of time doing that and it doesn't work.(p.87)
• Unfortunately a *lot* of prejudice exists.(p.89)
• But we aren't a glum *lot*.(p.132)
• He may wish to do a *lot* for other alcoholics and something of the sort may come up during business hours.(p.146)
• That was worth a *lot* even though I did not believe it.(p.185)
• Every time I'd start thinking about drinking, I would think of the long, dry years ahead without having a drink; but this idea of twenty-four hours, that it was up to me from then on, was a *lot* of help.(p.188)
• And this, as I said, certainly gave me a *lot* of confidence, seemed to take a *lot* of the burden off me.(p.190)
• Of course, we had talked over quite a number of the failings that I had and made a sort of an inventory, which wasn't too difficult, because I had an awful *lot* of things wrong that were very apparent to me, because I knew all about them.(p.190)
• I spent most of my time trying to get back these friendships, and to make some recompense towards my wife, whom I had hurt a *lot*.(p.191)
• I'm so grateful for both the program and the people in it that I still want to go, and then probably the most wonderful thing that I learned from the program -- I've seen this in the 'A.A. Grapevine' a *lot* of times, and I've had people say it to me personally, and I've heard people get up in meetings and make the same statement: The statement is, "I came into A.A. solely for the purpose of sobriety, but it has been through A.A. that I have found God."(p.192)
• I had bought a piece of ground in Cuyahoga Falls and cut it into lots and had a profit of approximately $40,000 and that was a *lot* of money in those days.(p.194)
• I can remember well thinking that I would quit drinking, really go to work hard, apply myself eight hours a day, five days a week, make a *lot* of money, and then I could start drinking again.(p.199)
• In 1932, some friends of mine advised me that I might try Christian Science, which had done a *lot* for some of their friends.(p.202)
• I then began asking a *lot* of questions of both my brother and Dr. Bob about how this thing worked, and I suppose I was becoming more glassy-eyed all the while, for eventually I said to Bob, "You're all dried up.(p.206)
• On Sunday when I came to, it was a bad, wet, snowy day in February, 1937, and Paul and Doc and a *lot* of other fellows were in Cleveland on business.(p.207)
• My practice had advanced to the point where it could stand a *lot* of abuse and it got it.(p.214)
• We went to Akron for about six weeks and we did a *lot* of visiting among the people in Akron.(p.219)
• I knew the stuff I was making was a *lot* stronger than I had been used to, but I never suspected that steady drinking of it might develop a taste for something even stronger still.(p.233)
• This last real merry-go-round had started the day before Christmas and I had really accomplished a *lot* in those fourteen days.(p.238)
• But we had to do a *lot* of entertaining, my husband liked to have a good time; I was very young; and I wanted to have a good time too.(p.322)
• How hurt I was when editors bounced back my ideas quickly and my best friends opined that my output needed a *lot* of rewriting.(p.331)
• A *lot* of lost dreams, empty futures, and crazy things of the past went through my mind.(p.333)
• Three years and three months of sobriety, without a slip, has meant a *lot* to me, my wife, and my family.(p.342)
• I had a *lot* of fun drinking.(p.346)
• I had not only let my wife down but also a *lot* of other wonderful people who had helped me.(p.364)
• I lost a *lot* of shirts that way, and sometimes I was minus a whole wash.(p.371)
• So I was used to it, but I didn't know what the effect of alcohol was because I always had wine, usually with dinner, but always with a *lot* of ice and about two tablespoons of sugar in it.(p.385)
• I had been reading a *lot* about psychiatry and I thought, "Maybe if I talk to a psychiatrist he can find out what is happening, and then I can drink like a lady."(p.387)
• It was the A.A. General Service Office in New York that I wrote to, and that office has always meant a *lot* to me.(p.392)
• I had learned an awful *lot* about myself in that one little article.(p.393)
• Alcoholics being the argumentative *lot* that we are, the A.A. membership will undoubtedly come up with a few who will dispute these figures.(p.399)
• Life, including some ups and downs, is a *lot* of fun.(p.417)
• I could tell him a *lot* of reasons why I am here in an alky ward at the age of twenty.(p.423)
• I found I could boost my income by figuring out a *lot* of cute little tricks that the boss wouldn't be likely to notice – filching money from the Coke machine, short-sticking the customers on oil, and selling oil I'd drained out of other cars.(p.423)
• I'd heard a *lot* about A.A. and met a great many A.A.'s during that year at home, but I hadn't thought of it for myself.(p.429)
• I had a *lot* more hell to go through.(p.437)
• I remember finding myself in the middle of the night in the doctors' parking *lot* at the hospital with one foot in the car and one foot on the ground, not knowing which was the lead foot; finding myself hanging up the telephone – then realizing I had gotten out of bed, answered the phone, turned on the light, and carried on a conversation with a patient.(p.441)
• As a physician and pharmacist who had grown up in a drugstore-home, I had a pill for every ill, and I was sick a *lot*.(p.443)
• Although we enjoyed the laughter in the early days, I heard a *lot* of things that I thought were stupid.(p.447)
• Loneliness, great physical and mental agony – these were the common *lot*.(p.455)
• After the first two or three days you were allowed the run of the place and it was a *lot* of fun.(p.468)
• I went to meetings, I spent a *lot* of time at the clubroom, but it was all centered in this one woman.(p.472)
• They build you up with a *lot* of false hopes and promises, and rush you around here and there and then, all of a sudden, it's gone."(p.472)
• So I concentrated and studied the book during that time, and I liked a *lot* of the things it said in there.(p.472)
• It meant that I had to give up a *lot* of the things that I had been accustomed to and that wasn't the easiest thing in the world for me.(p.487)
• I got into a *lot* of financial difficulties too.(p.490)
• I drink a *lot* every night.(p.499)
• I can hold a *lot* now, more than the others.(p.499)
• I have been drinking a *lot*, but never get drunk.(p.501)
• After hearing the first speaker I could tell myself that my own *lot* was rather mild.(p.509)
• I had a rough *lot*, but I don't worry about that, after hearing the stories of many others.(p.511)
• The Army drinking alone covered a *lot* of territory.(p.513)
• But I came out of the Army just as big a drunk as when I went in, if not worse, because now I had a *lot* more resentments.(p.513)
• A *lot* of the boys had tears in their eyes, they were so happy to be home.(p.513)
• I was up to international standards in one particular game, and that again covered quite a *lot* of my sins.(p.519)
• But I did understand this eventually, that these people had been through a *lot* of drinking experience just as I had, and had managed to make a job of it.(p.524)
• Now I had gotten to the place where I would wake up with black eyes and not know where I got them, or wake up with a *lot* of money and not know where I got it.(p.528)
• The only kind of security I knew anything about at that time was material security and I decided that all these intruders would vanish immediately if I only had a *lot* of money.(p.545)

lots

• Before then, I had written *lots* of sweet promises, but my wife happily observed that this time I meant business.(p.5)
• I did it more and more, and had *lots* of fun without much grief, either physical or financial.(p.172)
• I had no trouble there because I had never actually ceased to believe in God, and had tried *lots* of times to get help but hadn't succeeded.(p.186)
• I had bought a piece of ground in Cuyahoga Falls and cut it into *lots* and had a profit of approximately $40,000 and that was a lot of money in those days.(p.194)
• I was opening up these *lots* that I spoke of.(p.195)
• I had a crew of men working there and I wanted them to work Sunday afternoons so that I could sell *lots* on Sunday.(p.195)
• During the day, looking over the contracts and money in my pocket, I found that I had sold six *lots* that I couldn't even remember, and didn't even know the people I had sold them to.(p.196)
• I sold three *lots* to an elderly lady in Cleveland.(p.196)
• I came to Cleveland with the deeds to these *lots* and to pick up my money.(p.196)
• At the end of this selling of *lots*, just prior to World War I, I got into the crude rubber business, and six months later there was only one broker and myself left in Akron.(p.197)
• On that statement and the fact that I had been sober for ninety days, he gave me a job selling *lots* in an allotment he had.(p.200)
• My next job was in sales promotion for an oil company in Mississippi where I promptly became high man and got *lots* of pats on the back.(p.242)
• They did not seem to be getting an answer, for here I was staying sober and selling *lots* of auto polish, on which they were making one thousand per cent profit.(p.247)
• *Lots* of times, vain-gloriously, I used to take the bottle out, look at it and say, "I've got you licked."(p.253)
• My first meeting gave me a great deal of hope and *lots* of willing ears for my tale of woe and for my questions.(p.364)
• I still wash clothes, *lots* of them, but I no longer lose them at the Laundromat.(p.372)
• I like the boys and we have *lots* of fun, in class and out.(p.500)
• *Lots* of the older people had taken to drinking quite a good deal more during the war, but the younger generation was, I think, about the same.(p.518)

loud

• There was *loud* talk in the jazz places uptown.(p.3)
• I remembered my *loud* resolution to find him and ask him to help me get into that "Asylum" he had written about.(p.224)
• Each with the other as a witness, we took the Third Step out *loud* -- just as it says in the Big Book.(p.446)

loudly

• Everyone laughed *loudly*.(p.498)

louse

• Dr. Bob tells about keeping it simple and not to *louse* it up.(p.395)

lousy

• I sat up in the big red chair, suddenly thinking, "My God, with my kind of *lousy* luck, I might not die soon!(p.333)

love

• Here was *love*, applause, war; moments sublime with intervals hilarious.(p.1)
• When they talked of a God personal to me, who was *love*, superhuman strength and direction, I became irritated and my mind snapped shut against such a theory.(p.10)
• If a sufficiently strong reason – ill health, falling in *love*, change of environment, or the warning of a doctor – becomes operative, this man can also stop or moderate, although he may find it difficult and troublesome and may even need medical attention.(p.21)
• It was impossible to say we had no capacity for faith, or *love*, or worship.(p.54)
• He stood in the Presence of Infinite Power and *Love*.(p.56)
• Take away my difficulties, that victory over them may bear witness to those I would help of Thy Power, Thy *Love*, and Thy Way of life.(p.63)
• So we clean house with the family, asking each morning in meditation that our Creator show us the way of patience, tolerance, kindliness and *love*.(p.83)
• *Love* and tolerance of others is our code.(p.84)
• We have had retaliatory *love* affairs with other men.(p.105)
• We have tried to hold the *love* of our children for their father.(p.106)
• There could be no *love* in such persons, we thought.(p.107)
• And even if they did not *love* their families, how could they be so blind about themselves?(p.107)
• You can see that he really does *love* you with his better self.(p.108)
• Patience, tolerance, understanding and *love* are the watchwords.(p.118)
• Another feeling we are very likely to entertain is one of resentment that *love* and loyalty could not cure our husbands of alcoholism.(p.118)
• They need the counsel and *love* of a woman who has gone through what you have.(p.119)
• All members of the family should meet upon the common ground of tolerance, understanding and *love*.(p.122)
• For example, we know of situations in which the alcoholic or his wife have had *love* affairs.(p.124)
• We do talk about each other a great deal, but we almost invariably temper such talk by a spirit of *love* and tolerance.(p.125)
• If they sense these things, they will not take so seriously his periods of crankiness, depression, or apathy, which will disappear when there is tolerance, *love*, and spiritual understanding.(p.127)
• He is not likely to get far in any direction if he fails to show unselfishness and *love* under his own roof.(p.127)
• They may not see why their *love* and devotion did not straighten him out.(p.128)
• You will learn the full meaning of "*Love* thy neighbor as thyself."(p.153)
• Freedom from anger and fear, freedom to know happiness and *love*.(p.228)
• He went on talking and told me that he had found the plan has a basis of *love*, and the practice of Christ's injunction, "*Love* thy neighbor as thyself."(p.236)
• He said, "Tell Mommy I still *love* her."(p.263)
• It would be impossible for me to pass over this year without mentioning my *love* for, and my indebtedness to these two wonderful people who are no longer with us.(p.280)
• Above all, I have gained the greatest thing accorded to any man, the *love* and understanding of a gracious God, who has lifted me from the alcoholic scrap-heap to a position of trust where I have been able to reap the rich rewards that come from showing a little *love* for others and from serving them as I can.(p.296)
• And, as the years go by, working together, sharing our experiences with one another, and also sharing a mutual trust, understanding and *love* -- without strings, without obligation – we acquire relationships that are unique and priceless.(p.312)
• When I came home again, the only thing I had left to *love* was the bottle.(p.318)
• I said, "I'd *love* to."(p.326)
• I had always hated beer, but now I grew to *love* it, bottle after bottle of it, warm or cold.(p.339)
• It was hard for her to believe in my *love* by my actions.(p.362)
• Even I couldn't understand it, because I did *love* her so.(p.362)
• Her parting words were "I am not leaving you because I don't *love* you; it's because I do *love* you.(p.362)
• Looking directly at me was a large oil painting of my wife, and her very words seemed to shout at me -- "I am not leaving you because I don't *love* you; it's because I do *love* you.(p.363)
• I stayed on in Florida for three weeks, enjoying our reunion, a new found health and a deeper *love* than I had ever experienced before.(p.364)
• A whole new world of happiness and *love* began to unfold before my eyes, a truly new way of living.(p.365)
• There are so many to whom I feel deeply grateful; to my husband (and best critic), whose generous *love*, compassion and understanding have helped me along the way; to those before me in A.A. who inspired the first article I read, and the friend who sent that article to Frank; to Ruth for her personal note, and the first A.A. to talk to me; to my Bishop, whose loving and believing spirit inspired me; and to all the members of the Houston Group who were so patient, kind and helpful -- and to countless others.(p.393)
• It pays daily in more harmonious relations with my fellow men, in ever clearer insight into the true meaning of life, and in the answering *love* and gratitude wherever and whenever I have been the instrument of God's will in the lives of others.(p.394)
• Dr. Bob said, "*Love* and service keep us dry," and Bill said, "Always we must remember that our first duty is face-to-face help for the alcoholic who still suffers."(p.395)
• His were good, simple Quaker folk who accepted me with *love*.(p.402)
• I, who did not know how to give *love*, was head over heels "in *love*."(p.403)
• I wanted him to *love* me and make up to me for everything.(p.403)
• He finally decided that he did not *love* me enough, and soon he told me so and said he was engaged to another girl.(p.403)
• Even then I knew in my heart that I was unfit for the very things I wanted most, a happy marriage, security, a home and *love*.(p.403)
• The bartenders took care of me, not out of brotherly *love*, but through enlightened self-interest.(p.410)
• Fear, *love* of dentistry, and an imitation of my father's periodic drinking pattern took me through dental college soberly, except for the few parties and vacations in those four years.(p.419)
• I wanted *love* and affection but I didn't get it.(p.424)
• Here was the lost *love* I'd missed at home.(p.425)
• They had color in their faces, sparkle in their eyes and *love* in their hearts.(p.428)
• At first, she would say, "You don't *love* me.(p.439)
• I yelled at Max, "What do you mean, 'The dog just needs more *love*'?(p.440)
• It seems I should have learned to *love* my wife and family first; the newcomer to A.A., last.(p.451)
• Eventually, I had to redo each of the Twelve Steps specifically with Max in mind, from the First, saying, "I am powerless over alcohol, and my homelife is unmanageable by me," to the Twelfth, in which I tried to think of her as a sick Al-Anon and treat her with the *love* I would give a sick A.A. newcomer.(p.452)
• *Love* has no words to spell or lines to start and stop.(p.474)
• Words of truth and *love* are strong medicine.(p.476)
• Let group spirit of *love* and understanding protect you.(p.477)
• I seem to get no sympathy for my illness and have no appreciation of the *love* behind the gift.(p.501)
• But I have not seen yet that I should do some constructive acts of *love* without expecting any return.(p.505)
• There was the *love* affair which was ridiculous -- "imagine that midget being able to fall in *love*!" – and my head knew it while my heart pumped real, genuine anguish, for it hurt like hell, and since it was first *love*, things have never been quite the same.(p.534)
• For me, A.A. is a synthesis of all the philosophy I've ever read, all of the positive, good philosophy, all of it based on *love*.(p.542)
• I have seen that there is only one law, the law of *love*, and there are only two sins; the first is to interfere with the growth of another human being, and the second is to interfere with one's own growth.(p.542)
• I hope I have been able to impart to you, the reader, at least a bit of what I know; the joy of living, the irresistible power of divine *love* and its healing strength, and the fact that we, as sentient beings, have the knowledge to choose between good and evil, and, choosing good, are made happy.(p.543)
• In time I concluded that the reason I was hurt was because I loved my parents, and I concluded too that if I never allowed myself to *love* anybody or anything I could never be hurt again.(p.545)
• I didn't have the courage to *love*; I was not even sure I had the capacity.(p.546)
• It seems only fitting that when I did finally fall in *love* it was with an alcoholic, and for the next ten years I progressed as rapidly as is humanly possible into what I believed to be hopeless alcoholism.(p.547)
• Do it every day for two weeks and you will find you have come to mean it and to want it for them, and you will realize that where you used to feel bitterness and resentment and hatred, you now feel compassionate understanding and *love*."(p.552)
• This great experience that released me from the bondage of hatred and replaced it with *love* is really just another affirmation of the truth I know: I get everything I need in Alcoholics Anonymous – everything I need I get – and when I get what I need I invariably find that it was just what I wanted all the time.(p.553)
• The relationship between my wife and me was restored to a *love* and happiness that we had not known even before my alcoholism became acute.(p.559)

loved

• Who of us had not *loved* something or somebody?(p.54)
• Some of us veered from extreme to extreme, ever hoping that one day our *loved* ones would be themselves once more.(p.105)
• The alarming physical and mental symptoms, the deepening pall of remorse, depression and inferiority that settled down on our *loved* ones – these things terrified and distracted us.(p.106)
• How could men who *loved* their wives and children be so unthinking, so callous, so cruel?(p.107)
• I *loved* them, I think, as much as any parent.(p.199)
• We just *loved* it.(p.264)
• And we *loved* every minute of that association.(p.270)
• At least three of those four years must have been a living hell for my wife, because she had to watch the man she *loved* disintegrate morally, mentally and financially.(p.277)
• Now there is a sense of belonging, of being wanted and needed and *loved*.(p.312)
• We had a small child, and I *loved* her dearly, so that held me back quite a bit in my drinking career.(p.322)
• I *loved* alcohol!(p.346)
• I didn't particularly like it, but I *loved* the effects, and managed for the next twenty-five years to drink anything and everything, either handed to me or purchased, at the slightest excuse.(p.357)
• And deep in my heart I really meant what I said because I *loved* her more than anything else in the world, yes – even more than liquor.(p.362)
• I was going to prove to her that liquor wasn't necessary in my life, and above all that I still *loved* her more than anything else in the world and that I wanted her back.(p.362)
• Sure I still *loved* her, but hang it all, she was unreasonable!(p.362)
• We always had cordials after dinner and I know my sister and my brother and I *loved* creme de menthe.(p.384)
• I *loved* my father dearly and I adored my dog, and I'd gotten this new house and Frank had just given me a new fur coat and I was thrilled to death.(p.389)
• My father, as I have said, was very indulgent and *loved* me dearly, and knew how to get around me.(p.389)
• My wife *loved* to drink, and we tied on many a hooter in the name of marital bliss.(p.433)
• For the leveling-off process, I just *loved* intravenous Demerol, but I found it hard to practice good medicine while shooting morphine.(p.442)
• After all, it was self (you, me) that stood in our own way, that ran the show and ran ourselves into bankruptcy, that hurt the ones we *loved*.(p.459)
• You were thirty-five before you understood your father's horrible anguish, and forgave him, and *loved* him again.(p.533)
• All of my family and *loved* ones, all of my friends, are nearer and dearer to me than ever before and I have literally dozens of new friends who say they cannot believe that a short eight years ago I was ready for the scrap heap.(p.541)
• Harm is done by sick people, as I was sick, and

doing dreadful harm to myself and to my *loved* ones.(p.542)
• In time I concluded that the reason I was hurt was because I *loved* my parents, and I concluded too that if I never allowed myself to love anybody or anything I could never be hurt again.(p.545)
• I looked around me at people who seemed happy and tried to analyze their happiness, and it seemed to me that without exception these people had something or somebody they *loved* very much.(p.546)

lovely
• One of our gifts from the family was a very *lovely* Bible, but we'd let the bulldog chew it because we weren't too interested in it.(p.268)
• "Well," I said to dad, when the A.A. people kept coming with these *lovely* cars and looked so nice, "I suppose the neighbors say, 'Now those old fools must have up and died, but where's the hearse?'"(p.269)
• With the bravery born of desperation, and abetted by alcohol, I married a young and *lovely* girl.(p.277)
• In the doorway stood a *lovely* young girl who said, "Are you one of us souses, too?"(p.321)
• I heard a *lovely* voice, and a sympathetic ear listened to my plea.(p.363)
• My mother was a *lovely*, sweet woman, whose only weakness was my father.(p.369)
• I had a *lovely* wife and three children.(p.418)
• I'd acquired a new girl, a *lovely* girl who knew of my problem and had tried to help me.(p.430)
• I have a *lovely* wife who understands my problem and helps me with it.(p.431)
• And she was a charming, delightful, *lovely* person.(p.472)
• In the last year of my navy service, I was married to a *lovely*, lively girl, who enjoyed drinking.(p.555)

loves
• How much did these feelings, these *loves*, these worships, have to do with pure reason?(p.54)
• But the saddest, and thus the most consoling, drifted through from the country-music station – stories of broken hearts, wasted lives, lost *loves*, sung plaintively.(p.332)

loving
• I could go for such conceptions as Creative Intelligence, Universal Mind or Spirit of Nature but I resisted the thought of a Czar of the Heavens, however *loving* His sway might be.(p.12)
• What seemed at first a flimsy reed, has proved to be the *loving* and powerful hand of God.(p.28)
• It may be that both will decide that the way of good sense and *loving* kindness is to let by-gones be bygones.(p.82)
• Were we kind and *loving* toward all?(p.86)
• Many a distracted wife has visited this house to find *loving* and understanding companionship among women who knew her problem, to hear from the lips of their husbands what had happened to them, to be advised how her own wayward mate might be hospitalized and approached when next he stumbled.(p.160)
• They had visioned the Great Reality -- their *loving* and All Powerful Creator.(p.161)
• I couldn't have chosen more *loving* and conscientious parents.(p.304)
• There are so many to whom I feel deeply grateful; to my husband (and best critic), whose generous love, compassion and understanding have helped me along the way; to those before me in A.A. who inspired the first article I read, and the friend who sent that article to Frank; to Ruth for her personal note, and the first A.A. to talk to me; to my Bishop, whose *loving* and believing spirit inspired me; and to all the members of the Houston Group who were so patient, kind and helpful -- and to countless others.(p.393)
• The glittering society belle, the modern Shakespeare, the happy wife, the *loving* and beloved.(p.411)
• My friendships are meaningful, *loving* and interesting because I am sober.(p.416)
• The thought came to me that if God, as my mother said, was a vengeful God, he couldn't be a *loving* God.(p.489)
• I choose to believe that the Power greater than ourselves we ask for help, wrapped my shivering body in *loving* warmth and strength which has never left me.(p.541)
• I was raised in Kansas, the only child of *loving* parents who just drank socially.(p.554)
• Two – For our group purpose there is but one ultimate authority – a *loving* God as He may express Himself in our group conscience.(p.564)
• 2. – For our group purpose there is but one ultimate authority -- a *loving* God as He may express Himself in our group conscience.(p.565)

low
• Stocks were at the *low* point of 1932, and I had somehow formed a group to buy.(p.5)
• For if an alcoholic failed to perfect and enlarge his spiritual life through work and self-sacrifice for others, he could not survive the certain trials and *low* spots ahead.(p.14)
• Small wonder many in the medical profession have a *low* opinion of alcoholics and their chance for recovery!(p.73)
• High and *low*, rich and poor, these are future fellows of Alcoholics Anonymous.(p.152)
• No one is too discredited or has sunk too *low* to be welcomed cordially – if he means business.(p.161)
• When rubber reached a certain *low* point, they would draw on the rubber out of the pool and buy.(p.198)
• An accident while drunk laid me *low* for about three weeks.(p.258)
• A *low* ebb in the family fortunes necessitated my going to work when I was twenty.(p.275)
• However, my *low* had been reached.(p.378)
• For an estimate of salary from the twenty-one a month to start with, to over $400 per month upon my retirement after twenty years in the Navy, I believe that an average income of $2,000 a year over this period is *low*, but as I stated earlier, an underestimate is best.(p.399)
• I wore a man's raincoat, turned inside out, a present from a friend, for now my funds were *low*.(p.411)
• The doctor bills are heavy and the bank account is *low*.(p.501)

lowdown
• Finally, I got so *lowdown*, I was ashamed of my friends' seeing me, so I went to the worst joints I could find.(p.527)

lower
• Somehow I managed to drag my mattress to a *lower* floor, lest I suddenly leap.(p.6)
• One set of voices cry that sex is a lust of our *lower* nature, a base necessity of procreation.(p.68)
• I had a broken nose, a fractured cheekbone, and was black from the *lower* part of my face up into my hair.(p.204)
• I am one of the lads who came out of the service with a *lower* rank than when I went in.(p.241)
• The higher my expectations of Max and other people are, the *lower* is my serenity.(p.452)

lows
• No matter how often I had gone into and come out of alcoholic *lows* during the day, the pattern bounced me out of bed each night about 2:00 a.m., shaking and hurting in the agitation that always follows a drug's sedation.(p.332)

loyal
• A man so involved often feels very remorseful at times, especially if he is married to a *loyal* and courageous girl who has literally gone through hell for him.(p.81)
• She was a woman devoted to her family and *loyal* to her husband, but quarrels did not make a happy environment for her.(p.210)

loyalty
• There had been no real infidelity, for *loyalty* to my wife, helped at times by extreme drunkenness, kept me out of those scrapes.(p.3)
• Our *loyalty* and the desire that our husbands hold up their heads and be like other men have begotten all sorts of predicaments.(p.105)
• Another feeling we are very likely to entertain is one of resentment that love and *loyalty* could not cure our husbands of alcoholism.(p.118)
• With this kind of employee such an attitude will command undying *loyalty*.(p.145)

lubricant
• We know all about liquor as a social *lubricant*.(p.110)

lucid
• Wait for the end of the spree, or at least for a *lucid* interval.(p.90)

luck
• *Luck* then deserts him and he is slightly injured several times in succession.(p.38)
• If you have a number three husband, you may be in *luck*.(p.113)
• So to you out there -- who may soon be with us -- we say "Good *luck* and God bless you!"(p.121)
• I sat up in the big red chair, suddenly thinking, "My God, with my kind of lousy *luck*, I might not die soon!(p.333)
• *Luck* was with me for I made my train, but I arrived home the next morning with a new kind of hangover.(p.364)
• Her *luck* had been worse than mine, but not her drinking.(p.414)
• It is no problem to me now, but this is not good management on my part -- just plain good *luck*.(p.480)

luckily
• *Luckily* a friend was with me, who dragged me out, screaming and cursing, while the bartender threatened to call the police.(p.411)
• *Luckily*, the garage was attached to the house.(p.442)

Lucknow
• I returned to my home in *Lucknow*, India, at the end of November last year from a vacation in one of the most famous beauty spots in our country, a mountain resort 6,800 feet up, with a wonderful lake.(p.342)

lucky
• That is, if he is *lucky* enough to have a home.(p.98)
• I have always considered myself one of the *lucky* members of our fraternity.(p.356)
• *Lucky* because my excessive drinking never got me in jail, or hospitalized, nor did it ever cost me a job.(p.356)
• A *lucky* break, at least some will call it *lucky*, was in store for me at my group that night.(p.365)
• I repeat, I am one of the fortunate members of A.A. -- a *lucky* guy who is very grateful.(p.368)
• I now said a *lucky* and wonderful thing.(p.412)
• I think I am very *lucky* that there are people like A.A.'s and an A.A. program to hang on to and carry me through.(p.511)
• I was *lucky* again.(p.520)
• I myself have been *lucky* enough to help out.(p.541)

lucrative
• He inherited a *lucrative* automobile agency.(p.35)
• My job was to collect bets and betting-slips in the business section, a *lucrative* spot.(p.251)

lukewarm
• If he is *lukewarm* or thinks he is not an alcoholic, we suggest you leave him alone.(p.113)

lull
• When I went back to my hometown to go into private practice, I experienced another brief *lull* in my addiction to alcohol and drugs.(p.420)

lump
• At age forty, I developed a large *lump* in my potbelly, and I feared it was a tumor.(p.557)

lumps
• My Quaker mother-in-law, bless her heart, used to set the Christmas pudding ablaze with *lumps* of sugar dipped in rubbing alcohol.(p.402)

lunacy
• Our friends thought a *lunacy* commission should be appointed.(p.3)

lunar
• We were having trouble with personal relationships, we couldn't control our emotional natures, we were a prey to misery and depression, we couldn't make a living, we had a feeling of uselessness, we were full of fear, we were unhappy, we couldn't seem to be of real help to other people – was not a basic solution of these bedevilments more important than whether we should see newsreels of *lunar* flight?(p.52)

lunch
• We were eating *lunch*, and I was listening and trying to find out why they had this release that they seemed to have.(p.191)
• I'd been sitting comfortably in a restaurant with Rita, drinking my sixth martini and hoping the waiter would forget about the *lunch* order -- at least long enough for me to have a couple more.(p.223)
• After a very good week, two of my customers took me to *lunch* on Saturday.(p.247)
• I also talked A.A. to every friend who would listen, at *lunch*, at dinner, on street corners.(p.282)
• No sale -- no *lunch*.(p.283)
• I never enjoyed any meal, but I ate my *lunch* at noon for two reasons; first, to help me get out of the fog of the night before and, second, to furnish some measure of nourishment.(p.299)
• It was to be short lived, for on the day before Christmas I completely disillusioned my wife and ruined our first Christmas by coming home from the Rotary *lunch* dead drunk.(p.361)
• It didn't take long for me to fall in with a fast crowd who had their *lunch* in the men's bar of a leading hotel.(p.361)
• But whereas my horse was always equipped with a flask, I merely endured the fox hunting so I could start drinking at *lunch* time.(p.404)

• In the first year there were episodes such as kicking Priscilla in the shins, getting the lock changed on the desk in the A.A. Club, because I, as secretary, didn't want the Intergroup secretary "interfering," and taking an older woman member out to ***lunch*** for the express purpose of informing her that she was "a phony."(p.416)
• I continued to work and continued to go to ***lunch*** with Vi, and none of our acquaintances on the job knew that we had separated.(p.491)

luncheon

• It started when I joined a few of the men for cocktails before the noonday Rotary ***luncheon***.(p.360)
• Before long I was at the ***luncheon*** meeting an hour before the others, that old and familiar trademark of every alcoholic.(p.360)
• And when she broke a ***luncheon*** date with me one Saturday, after I had been in A.A. for about three months, I said, "I'll show her!(p.472)

lunching

• Not long ago, I was ***lunching*** with another retired publicist.(p.334)

lure

• I would take a gulp, then warn the jug not to try to entice, ***lure***, or seduce me into having more than one "medicinal" jolt.(p.332)

lurking

• If we are planning to stop drinking, there must be no reservation of any kind, nor any ***lurking*** notion that someday we will be immune to alcohol.(p.33)

Lusitania

• Coming out of a pub near the Cunard pier I saw the ***Lusitania*** standing out in the middle of the Mersey.(p.252)

lust

• One set of voices cry that sex is a ***lust*** of our lower nature, a base necessity of procreation.(p.68)

lustre

• The outlines and the promise of the New Land had brought ***lustre*** to tired eyes and fresh courage to flagging spirits.(p.53)

luxuries

• Up to my early thirties, when my drinking had become a major problem, I lived in large houses, with servants and all the ***luxuries*** that I could possibly ask for.(p.401)

luxury

• Liquor ceased to be a ***luxury***; it became a necessity.(p.5)
• They may be the dubious ***luxury*** of normal men, but for alcoholics these things are poison.(p.66)
• I couldn't afford the ***luxury*** of prejudice.(p.383)

lye

• Same thing when I let ***lye*** and water eat away at four of my toes and my foot for five hours.(p.458)

lying

• Away from my office two or three weeks at a time; horrible days and nights when I would lie on the floor of my home, ***lying*** awake and reaching over to get the bottle, taking a drink and going back into oblivion.(p.184)
• And as I fumed helplessly and planned to get good and drunk and show them, my eye caught a sentence in the book ***lying*** open on my bed: "We cannot live with anger."(p.228)
• That is the way Jackie found me, ***lying*** on a cot in my skivvies, with hot and cold sweats, pounding heart and that awful itchy scratchiness all over.(p.238)
• They'd sit out there and play hymns and I'd be ***lying*** in there with a terrific hangover.(p.265)
• An attorney sat at the side of the bed where I was ***lying***, and he sat on the edge of his chair and looked as innocent as a baby.(p.268)
• ***Lying*** on the divan, "getting in the mood" to write, I cried openly or inwardly, as I listened to sad songs.(p.332)
• I do recall ***lying*** on a cold cement floor and shredding into little bits several pieces of stolen identification cards, and washing my face in the toilet bowl trying to sober up, and screaming hysterically while clinging to bars too high to see out of, and cursing everyone that came near me.(p.354)
• Aside from being a common drunk, I had a very serious pill affliction and all the garbage that goes with it – ***lying***, stealing, cheating anybody and everybody, conning the people I could, and staying clear of the ones I couldn't.(p.478)

Mm

Ma

• To his wife, he remarked, "Don't see anything the matter here, ***Ma***.(p.82)
• He'd always say, "Take me for a ride, ***Ma***."(p.264)

machine

• Did not Professor Langley's flying ***machine*** go to the bottom of the Potomac River?(p.51)
• The Wright brothers' almost childish faith that they could build a ***machine*** which would fly was the mainspring of their accomplishment.(p.52)
• I found I could boost my income by figuring out a lot of cute little tricks that the boss wouldn't be likely to notice – filching money from the Coke ***machine***, short-sticking the customers on oil, and selling oil I'd drained out of other cars.(p.423)

machinery

• One would have to understand the correctional ***machinery*** to see what a miracle this really was.(p.462)

mad

• As we became subjects of King Alcohol, shivering denizens of his ***mad*** realm, the chilling vapor that is loneliness settled down.(p.151)
• In any case I must get out of here before I let slip my abysmal ignorance of how I came to be here, and she realized that I was stark, staring ***mad***.(p.223)
• I was ***mad*** – I must be.(p.223)
• And I remembered the creeping horror of the interminable night, in which I slept for short spells and woke up dripping with cold sweat and shaken with utter despair, to drink hastily from my bottle and mercifully pass out again, "You're ***mad***, you're ***mad***, you're ***mad***!" pounded through my brain with each returning ray of consciousness, and I drowned the refrain with drink.(p.224)
• I wasn't ***mad*** or vicious – I was a sick person.(p.227)
• I'd work like ***mad*** for three or four weeks without a single drink, save my money, pay a few bills and then "reward" myself with alcohol.(p.244)
• If I'd had a gun I'd have shot the horns right off the thing, because it made me raving ***mad***.(p.265)
• We were so ***mad*** at her because she talked to him that way.(p.271)
• Four years ago I had nothing but a jumbled, ***mad*** existence.(p.430)
• I talked to him for quite a long time and at the end, he said, "Well, you're not quite ***mad*** enough to be shut up for good yet, but you soon will be if you live long enough."(p.522)
• I was terribly afraid that I was actually going ***mad***, if I hadn't gone ***mad*** already.(p.522)

made

• Because this book has become the basic text for our Society and has helped such large numbers of alcoholic men and women to recover, there exists a sentiment against any radical changes being ***made*** in it.(p.xi)
• Therefore, the first portion of this volume, describing the A.A. recovery program, has been left untouched in the course of revisions ***made*** for both the second and the third editions.(p.xi)
• All changes ***made*** over the years in the Big Book (A.A. members' fond nickname for this volume) have had the same purpose: to represent the current membership of Alcoholics Anonymous more accurately, and thereby to reach more alcoholics.(p.xii)
• All told, promising beginnings have been ***made*** in some 50 foreign countries and U.S. possessions.(p.xv)
• These ***made*** their impressions everywhere.(p.xx)
• Without such support, A.A. could have ***made*** only the slowest progress.(p.xx)
• So far, upon the total problem of several million actual and potential alcoholics in the world, we have ***made*** only a scratch.(p.xx)
• Though the aggregate of recoveries resulting from psychiatric effort is considerable, we physicians must admit we have ***made*** little impression upon the problem as a whole.(p.xxvii)
• The patient had ***made*** his own diagnosis, and deciding his situation hopeless, had hidden in a deserted barn determined to die.(p.xxix)
• I ***made*** a host of fair-weather friends.(p.3)
• I went to town regularly and even ***made*** a little money.(p.7)
• They ***made*** me swallow hard.(p.10)
• The wars which had been fought, the burnings and chicanery that religious dispute had facilitated, ***made*** me sick.(p.11)
• But my friend sat before me, and he ***made*** the point-blank declaration that God had done for him what he could not do for himself.(p.11)
• We ***made*** a list of people I had hurt or toward whom I felt resentment.(p.13)
• He has a positive genius for getting tight at exactly the wrong moment, particularly when some important decision must be ***made*** or engagement kept.(p.21)
• Though experience had ***made*** him skeptical, he finished his treatment with unusual confidence.(p.26)
• Here was the terrible dilemma in which our friend found himself when he had the extraordinary experience which as we have already told you, ***made*** him a free man.(p.28)
• He ***made*** up his mind that until he had been successful in business and had retired, he would not touch another drop.(p.32)
• He ***made*** a beginning.(p.35)
• He ***made*** up his mind to quit drinking altogether.(p.39)
• Not only had I been off guard, I had ***made*** no fight whatever against the first drink.(p.41)
• But the moment I ***made*** up my mind to go through with the process, I had the curious feeling that my alcoholic condition was relieved, as in fact it proved to be.(p.42)
• One of these men, staff member of a world-renowned hospital, recently ***made*** this statement to some of us: "What you say about the general hopelessness of the average alcoholic's plight is, in my opinion, correct.(p.43)
• We hope we have ***made*** clear the distinction between the alcoholic and the non-alcoholic.(p.44)
• Yet, in other moments, we found ourselves thinking, when enchanted by a starlit night, "Who, then, ***made*** all this?"(p.46)
• Many of us have been so touchy that even casual reference to spiritual things ***made*** us bristle with antagonism.(p.48)
• This world of ours has ***made*** more material progress in the last century than in all the millenniums which went before.(p.51)
• They said God ***made*** these things possible, and we only smiled.(p.55)
• Circumstances ***made*** him willing to believe.(p.57)
• Sometimes they hurt us, seemingly without provocation, but we invariably find that at some time in the past we have ***made*** decisions based on self which later placed us in a position to be hurt.(p.62)
• This was only a beginning, though if honestly and humbly ***made***, an effect, sometimes a very great one, was felt at once.(p.63)
• When it ***made*** us cocky, it was worse.(p.68)
• If you have already ***made*** a decision, and an inventory of your grosser handicaps, you have ***made*** a good beginning.(p.71)
• Having ***made*** our personal inventory, what shall we do about it?(p.72)
• The inconsistency is ***made*** worse by the things he does on his sprees.(p.73)
• We ***made*** it when we took inventory.(p.76)
• We have ***made*** our demonstration, done our part.(p.78)
• Our drinking has ***made*** us slow to pay.(p.78)
• After the sermon, he quietly got up and ***made*** an explanation.(p.80)
• Being still inexperienced and having just ***made*** conscious contact with God, it is not probable that we are going to be inspired at all times.(p.87)
• Give him an account of the struggles you ***made*** to stop.(p.92)
• Outline the program of action, explaining how you ***made*** a self-appraisal, how you straightened out your past and why you are now endeavoring to be helpful to him.(p.94)
• If your talk has been sane, quiet and full of human understanding, you have perhaps ***made*** a friend.(p.94)
• Tell him you once felt as he does, but you doubt whether you would have ***made*** much progress had you not taken action.(p.94)
• When your prospect has ***made*** such reparation as he can to his family, and has thoroughly explained to them the new principles by which he is living, he should proceed to put those principles into action at home.(p.98)
• You will note that we ***made*** an important qualification.(p.101)
• We want to analyze mistakes we have ***made***.(p.104)
• In the morning we have kissed and ***made*** up.(p.105)
• If, on the other hand, they took nothing, their self-pity ***made*** them killjoys.(p.105)
• Under these conditions we naturally ***made*** mistakes.(p.107)
• Henry Ford once ***made*** a wise remark to the effect that experience is the thing of supreme value in life.(p.124)
• Mother ***made*** all the plans and gave the directions.(p.131)
• New acquaintances who know nothing of alcoholism might be ***made*** and thoughtful consideration given their needs.(p.131)
• But it is clear that we ***made*** our own misery.(p.133)
• I pointed out that I had had nothing to drink whatever for three years, and this in the face of difficulties that would have ***made*** nine out of ten men drink their heads off.(p.138)
• Suppose an approach is ***made*** something like this:(p.141)
• If you propose such a procedure to him, it may be necessary to advance the cost of treatment, but we believe it should be ***made*** plain that any expense will later be deducted from his pay.(p.143)
• The other day an approach was ***made*** to the vice president of a large industrial concern.(p.148)
• He should not be ***made*** a favorite.(p.149)
• Years ago, in 1935, one of our number ***made*** a journey to a certain western city.(p.153)
• Why, he argued, should he lose the remainder of his business, only to bring still more suffering to his family by foolishly admitting his plight to people from whom he ***made*** his livelihood?(p.155)
• Stepping into his car, he ***made*** the rounds of people he had hurt.(p.156)
• They experienced a few distressing failures, but in those cases they ***made*** an effort to bring the man's family into a spiritual way of living, thus relieving much worry and suffering.(p.159)
• Arrangements were also ***made*** with the chief psychiatrist of a large public hospital to select still others from the stream of misery which flows through that institution.(p.163)
• This resolution I kept steadfastly for the next forty years, except when circumstances ***made*** it seem unwise to absent myself.(p.172)
• This went from bad to worse until Sophomore spring when, after a prolonged period of drinking, I ***made*** up my mind that I could not complete my course, so I packed my grip and went South to spend a month on a large farm owned by a friend of mine.(p.173)
• There my drinking became so much worse that the boys in the fraternity house where I lived felt forced to send for my father, who ***made*** a long journey in the vain endeavor to get me straightened around.(p.174)
• At that time I was not aware of the almost unlimited supply the government ***made*** it possible for us doctors to obtain, neither had I any knowledge of the bootlegger who soon appeared on the horizon.(p.175)
• I also ***made*** use of old trunks and chests, the old can container, and even the ash container.(p.176)
• I used to promise my wife, my friends, and my children that I would drink no more – promises which seldom kept me sober even through the day, though I was very sincere when I ***made*** them.(p.177)
• These good people notified my wife, who sent my newly ***made*** friend over to get me.(p.179)
• Of course, we had talked over quite a number of the failings that I had and ***made*** a sort of an inventory, which wasn't too difficult, because I had an awful lot of things wrong that were very apparent to me, because I knew all about them.(p.190)
• I can well remember sitting with seven dollars in my pocket, planning on giving my family a hundred or two hundred dollars, when I ***made*** it next year.(p.197)
• I ***made*** a point of knowing important people.(p.197)
• An offer of appreciation for not having had a drink for those few months and then and there, without anybody promising me anything or threatening me, I ***made*** a solemn vow that never so long as I lived would I take another drink.(p.200)
• So I was driving to Cleveland when I ***made*** this solemn promise never to drink again.(p.201)
• The differences between my father and my sisters, who were school teachers, ***made*** an excellent environment for the type of child I was – that is, slick and cute enough to take advantage of any adult quarrel.(p.210)

• Rules were ***made*** for others, but not for me.(p.210)
• In 1924, I had acquired enough clients of my own so that the firm ***made*** me a junior partner.(p.213)
• All during Prohibition, every alcoholic felt that he ***made*** the best hooch, regardless of how bad it was.(p.213)
• There had been some occasions -- there was an automobile wreck, for instance -- when I had police escort home but not to jail, all of which, instead of doing me a favor, did me harm because I was then full of self-esteem as to the progress I had ***made*** both professionally and financially.(p.213)
• The successful demonstration I had ***made*** of my life problems in other respects convinced me that some day I was going to be able to drink like a gentleman.(p.214)
• She knew that at that time any suggestion she ***made*** about my drinking would only build up a barrier, a consideration for which I am ever grateful.(p.216)
• There was one experience with Doc which ***made*** a terrific impression upon me.(p.218)
• In summing up, I can say that A.A. had ***made*** me, I hope, a real Catholic.(p.221)
• In a few sentences he ***made*** God seem personal to me, explained Him as a being who was interested in me, the alcoholic, and that all I needed to do was to be willing to follow His way; that as long as I followed it I would be able to overcome my desire for liquor.(p.236)
• This duty together with my weekly meetings with my fellow alcoholics, and my daily renewal of the contract I originally ***made*** with God, have kept me sober when nothing else ever did.(p.237)
• Many things happened; business trials, little worries, and feelings of general despondency came near driving me to the bottle, but I ***made*** progress.(p.237)
• The lesson of his death still remains with me, yet I often wonder what would have happened if somebody else had ***made*** that first call on me.(p.239)
• In sports I ***made*** the track and tennis teams; I got along well with the other boys and had a fairly large circle of acquaintances but no intimate friends.(p.240)
• Three months before I met Jackie I had ***made*** my second feeble try at suicide.(p.245)
• This was the background that ***made*** me willing to listen on January 8th.(p.245)
• However, I ***made*** an SOS call to the New York Group, whom I hadn't met yet, and they suggested we both come there.(p.245)
• In June, 1945, with another member, I ***made*** my first – and only – Twelfth Step call on a female alcoholic and a year later I married her.(p.249)
• Following a big drunk on that sheet, where I was doing leg-work and rewrite, a feeling of nostalgia ***made*** me buy a ticket for Liverpool and I returned to Britain.(p.252)
• Discharged in 1919, I really ***made*** up for my dry spell.(p.253)
• My wife ***made*** several attempts to get me to stop and I had the usual visits from persons who would always ask me "Why?" – as if I knew!(p.254)
• Enduring all the hangover hells that every alcoholic experiences, I ***made*** the usual resolutions.(p.256)
• The doctor who came to see me almost at once did not assail me with any new doctrines; he ***made*** sure that I had a need and that I wanted to have that need filled, and little by little I learned how my need could be met.(p.258)
• I look back and remember these things because they ***made*** me very unhappy, and added to my feeling of inferiority at never being the same as other people.(p.261)
• If I'd had a gun I'd have shot the horns right off the thing, because it ***made*** me raving mad.(p.265)
• In the spiritual strength I had found, because of A.A., I felt that I had ***made*** a complete surrender, that had really turned my life over that summer.(p.271)
• I knew then that I hadn't ***made*** a complete surrender, because I tried to bargain with the God I had found, and I said, "Anything but that!(p.271)
• Before the end finally came, I had, I guess ***made*** the surrender because I finally had been able to say that I would not mind too much.(p.272)
• When I reached a point directly back of our house, where I could have cut through a friend's garden, I was almost overpowered by the desire to get home, but I ***made*** the whole journey.(p.276)
• The only stipulation they ***made*** was this: I had to make the decision myself.(p.278)
• They ***made*** me feel as if I were a part of their family, and so did their children.(p.281)
• After six months of sobriety I saw the picture in a different light: Detroit was the place I had to return to, not only because I must face the mess I had ***made*** there, but because it was there that I could be of the most service to A.A.(p.281)
• I, who had never ***made*** a speech in my life and who would have been frightened sick at the prospect, stood up in front of Rotary groups in different parts of the city and talked about Alcoholics Anonymous.(p.283)
• Twenty-odd years ago I ***made*** a mess out of my one and only marriage.(p.286)
• So six months ago I acquired a ready ***made*** family consisting of one charming wife, four grown children to whom I am devoted, and three grandchildren.(p.286)
• It was February with snow and ice on the ground and I had a four blocks walk to the nearest cab stand, but I ***made*** it.(p.288)
• He said he had finally learned that drinking was a fatal illness ***made*** up of an allergy plus an obsession, and once the drinking had passed from habit to obsession, we were completely hopeless, and could look forward only to spending the balance of our lives in mental institutions or to death.(p.290)
• Dr. Bob then led me through the restitution step, in which I ***made*** a list of all of the persons I had harmed, and worked out ways and means of slowly making restitution.(p.292)
• I ***made*** several decisions at that time.(p.292)
• A few months after I ***made*** my original trip to Akron I was feeling pretty cocky, and I didn't think my wife was treating me with proper respect, now that I was an outstanding citizen.(p.293)
• In the summer of 1938, almost a year from the time I ***made*** my original contact with Akron, the man for whom I was working and who knew about the program, approached me and asked if I could do anything about one of his salesmen who was drinking very heavily.(p.294)
• In the spring of 1939, the Big Book was printed, and we had two inquiries from the New York office because of a fifteen-minute radio talk that was ***made***.(p.294)
• The girl was full of enthusiasm and she ***made*** the trip to Akron too.(p.295)
• And over my A.A. years I have ***made*** many real, honest, sincere friendships that I shall always cherish.(p.296)
• Somehow or other, I must have misunderstood the doctor's instructions, for I not only ***made*** the beer for my wife, I also drank it for her.(p.297)
• The inevitable result of this discovery was that I soon learned that beer ***made*** a very good chaser for whiskey.(p.298)
• At that time, I was living out of town, so I moved back to the home town and ***made*** a connection in a responsible position with one of the larger companies in the finance business.(p.298)
• I have omitted details of transgressions that I ***made*** when drunk for several reasons.(p.301)
• I ***made*** arrangements to enter the hospital three days later and promptly went out and got stiff for three days.(p.302)
• Somehow, I ***made*** it through basic and then laid off the booze for about three months, because I was in school at night.(p.317)
• The third time, after almost five years as an S.P. 4, I finally ***made*** sergeant.(p.318)
• No one seemed to care if I ***made*** it or not.(p.319)
• I was afraid, and I had ***made*** my mind up that I would never get drunk, so I was watchful and careful.(p.322)
• In succession came "What ***Made*** Milwaukee Famous ***Made*** a Loser Out of Me" and "I'm Drinking My Christmas Dinner All Alone."(p.332)
• How full it has kept my retirement years -- the five I've lived since the first two lost in traveling a rocky road to hell, before I ***made*** a U-turn.(p.334)
• The encouragement received in the early days, especially from the A.A. General Service Office, ***made*** a tremendous difference to my sobriety.(p.342)
• The army ***made*** a difference to me.(p.343)
• I have been of a very religious outlook all my life, but that ***made*** no difference once John Barleycorn got the better of me.(p.343)
• I ***made*** more money the last year of my drinking than I ever ***made*** before in my whole life.(p.345)
• When a few drinks ***made*** me feel good before I went over that line, those same drinks now ***made*** me wretched.(p.346)
• And I gave him some idea of what you do, and so I ***made*** my first Twelfth Step call before I ever came into the program.(p.347)
• But I ***made*** my admission just the same.(p.350)
• The Third Step said: "***Made*** a decision to turn our will and our lives over to the care of God as we understood Him."(p.350)
• I lost my driver's license, was ***made*** a ward of the court, and was put on probation (not to mention the fact that I might have killed three friends and myself).(p.354)
• I ***made*** little headway in my first few meetings with her.(p.359)
• They told me their stories, which were much more rugged than mine – yet what they said ***made*** sense, and the way they put it was easy for me to understand, with an understanding I had never had before.(p.363)
• That night she too had new hope because I had ***made*** sure she would know what I was doing about my drinking by packing every bit of A.A. literature I could put my hands on right on top so she couldn't help but see it when she opened my bag.(p.364)
• Luck was with me for I ***made*** my train, but I arrived home the next morning with a new kind of hangover.(p.364)
• With that utterance I again ***made*** a wonderful discovery.(p.366)
• I ***made*** promises to myself, my family and friends -- and broke them.(p.375)
• This suggestion had been ***made*** before on a number of occasions, but like all alcoholics I wanted to handle my problem my own way, which really meant I didn't want anything to interfere with my drinking.(p.378)
• At first it was a shock to realize I was an alcoholic, but the realization that there was hope ***made*** it easier.(p.379)
• Emma ran out to the kitchen and came back with a water glass full of bourbon and ***made*** me drink it down.(p.385)
• It has ***made*** life a thousand times easier and simpler than did the endless compromises and conflicts by which I lived before.(p.394)
• Two weeks later found me being sworn in, and the first payday in the Navy ***made*** me realize I had found a home.(p.398)
• Until I reached A.A. my life was a shambles; I was a mess, and I ***made*** everybody near and dear to me miserable.(p.400)
• My husband was ***made*** miserable by this, but I had already ***made*** him and myself miserable.(p.402)
• He did not like naughty stories, so I ***made*** them naughtier.(p.403)
• At a large party in Geneva, with people from many countries represented, the kind of party that is "protocol" in the extreme, I swayed, laughed hysterically, ***made*** naughty remarks in an unhushed voice, and was finally led from the scene.(p.406)
• My new friends ***made*** fun of God and all the orthodox beliefs.(p.408)
• Then he called Marty and ***made*** and appointment for me.(p.413)
• A.A. ***made*** it possible for me to face the consequences of my past actions.(p.420)
• So we rolled old newspapers together and ***made*** torches to find a good soft pew and get some sleep.(p.424)
• She didn't like it, but I thought it ***made*** a man of me.(p.425)
• This was fine, but it was just an extra dividend, for I'd ***made*** connections by this time and was buying a bottle a day from the cook.(p.426)
• I applied for photo school at Pensacola Air Base and ***made*** it.(p.426)
• I'm twenty-six now and I haven't had a drink since I ***made*** my decision.(p.430)
• One night I barely ***made*** my downtown club; if I'd had to go another fifty feet I'd have collapsed in the gutter.(p.435)
• Here I found an ingredient that had been lacking in any other effort I had ***made*** to save myself.(p.436)
• It ***made*** me thirsty.(p.447)
• It ***made*** me feel quite grown-up and mature, and I think another added attraction was the fact that so far as my family was concerned, it was forbidden, and it had a special attraction for that reason.(p.464)
• He is my best teacher; without him, I am sure I would never have ***made*** the progress I have.(p.481)
• About this time an incident took place in grade school that I have never forgotten because it ***made*** me realize that I was actually a physical coward.(p.484)
• As far as school was concerned, I ***made*** fair grades throughout.(p.486)
• I rebelled against this, because just about the time that I was getting ready to leave high school, a revelation came to me about God and it ***made*** things very complicated for me.(p.489)
• So I went down to talk to the District Attorney, and the arrangement was ***made*** that I would go home to stay with my mother, and that meant Vi and I were separated.(p.491)
• The grand fellow who at my call ***made*** me a hail-fel-

low-well-met, who gave me such a fine voice, as we sang "Hail, hail, the gang's all here," and "Sweet Adeline," who gave me freedom from fear and feelings of inferiority.(p.498)
- I go to the hospital, where I have *made* friends with the night superintendent.(p.501)
- I've *made* a mess of things and can't do anything about it.(p.504)
- I do not fix anyone, but I am getting part of a tremendous education and I have *made* some new friends.(p.506)
- After I had *made* my third report, I stepped down town, met some of the old crowd, and of course you know the answer.(p.510)
- In any case, I *made* myself believe that, so I just drifted about, existing on my retired pay, drinking, and living at home.(p.522)
- Having *made* that bargain, I immediately began to feel I'd been trapped into it and I went out and had some drinks – four glasses of gin, I remember.(p.523)
- What struck me most was that they all seemed to be quite pleased with having *made* a job of it and having stopped drinking.(p.524)
- It has *made* me understand that I must be one of my world, that I cannot exist in any happiness as a rebel by myself.(p.524)
- It has *made* me very happy.(p.525)
- There was the economic fear which *made* me too timid to take any action which might improve my circumstances.(p.534)
- I left this home town, then, after I had *made* a public spectacle of myself in the presence of a revered teacher whose favorite pupil I had been.(p.539)
- I set it down and *made* myself a cup of coffee.(p.541)
- I hope I have been able to impart to you, the reader, at least a bit of what I know; the joy of living, the irresistible power of divine love and its healing strength, and the fact that we, as sentient beings, have the knowledge to choose between good and evil, and, choosing good, are *made* happy.(p.543)
- I thought that life was a pretty simple thing; you simply *made* a plan for your life, based upon what you wanted, and then you needed only the courage to go after it.(p.545)
- The amount of will power exercised to control my drinking during working hours, diverted into a constructive channel, would have *made* me President, and the thing that *made* the will power possible was the knowledge that as soon as my day was finished I could drink myself into oblivion.(p.548)
- I had only to reflect on the contrast between the plans I *made* so many years ago for my life with what really happened to know I couldn't manage my life drunk or sober.(p.550)
- My desire to be honest with myself *made* it necessary for me to realize that my thinking was irrational.(p.550)
- As soon as I had *made* a few friends and had begun to feel accepted, we moved again.(p.555)
- To those now in its fold, Alcoholics Anonymous has *made* the difference between misery and sobriety, and often the difference between life and death.(p.563)
- Speaking at a dinner given by John D. Rockefeller Jr. to introduce Alcoholics Anonymous to some of his friends, Dr. Harry Emerson Fosdick remarked: "I think that psychologically speaking there is a point of advantage in the approach that is being *made* in this movement that cannot be duplicated.(p.574)

made-to-order
- So I created a job for myself selling women's hosiery and men's *made-to-order* shirts.(p.282)

Madison
- If there is no Al-Anon listing in your local telephone book, you may obtain further information on Al-Anon Family Groups by writing to its World Service Office: Box 182, *Madison* Square Station, New York, NY 10159.(p.121)
- Should you be the relative or friend of an alcoholic who shows no immediate interest in A.A., it is suggested that you write the Al-Anon Family Groups, Inc., Box 182, *Madison* Square Station, New York, NY 10159, U.S.A.(p.575)

madly
- Yet early next morning he searches *madly* for the bottle he misplaced the night before.(p.21)
- My torch blazed *madly* and the pew caught fire.(p.424)
- I was knocked to the floor, swinging *madly* at the faces on those pineapples.(p.427)

madman
- The doctor said I'd been brought into the hospital like a *madman*, crying, raving, ranting, swearing, completely in the throes of delirium tremens.(p.427)

madness
- Sometimes I stole from my wife's slender purse when the morning terror and *madness* were on me.(p.6)

madonna
- Even when I was old enough to know better, I dreamed about being as beautiful as Venus, as pure as the *Madonna* and as brilliant as the President of the United States is supposed to be.(p.400)

Mae
- I walked up that aisle just like *Mae* West in her prime.(p.385)

maelstrom
- The inviting *maelstrom* of Wall Street had me in its grip.(p.2)
- Out of this *maelstrom* just two coherent thoughts came to the surface; one, a drink would mean homelessness and death; two, I could no longer relieve the pressure of fear by starting home, as was once my habitual solution to this problem, because I no longer had a home.(p.279)

magazine
- In the fall of 1939, Fulton Oursler, then editor of Liberty, printed a piece in his *magazine*, called "Alcoholics and God."(p.xviii)
- Returning to the town I had left three months before, I became editor of a monthly *magazine*, soon had additional publicity and advertising accounts and the money rolled in.(p.254)
- Hiding behind a newspaper, *magazine*, or book, I really saw nothing, but simulated deep interest.(p.332)
- I had worked the previous summer on a New York fashion *magazine*, a job I really enjoyed.(p.405)
- I sold my first article to a national *magazine* while still an undergraduate.(p.555)
- The Episcopal *magazine*, The Living Church, observes editorially: "The basis of the technique of Alcoholics Anonymous is the truly Christian principle that a man cannot help himself except by helping others.(p.574)
- The General Service Board of A.A. (the trustees) administers A.A.'s General Service Office, A.A. World Services, Inc., and our monthly *magazine*, the A.A. Grapevine.(p.575)

magazines
- During the day a friend of mine brought me some *magazines* to take to a hospital group I was interested in, and I looked through them and a "banner" across the front of one featured an article by a prominent clergyman in which I caught the word "resentment."(p.552)
- I landed a good job with a company publication and was moonlighting on other *magazines*.(p.555)

magic
- I must keep my *magic* magnifying mind on my acceptance and off my expectations, for my serenity is directly proportional to my level of acceptance.(p.452)
- Never forgot *magic* in firewater.(p.474)

magically
- In my mind's eye, I played and replayed scenes in which I was plucked *magically* from the bar where I stood nursing a drink, and was instantly exalted to some position of power and prestige.(p.560)

magnificent
- That is one of man's *magnificent* attributes.(p.53)

magnified
- It was as if I had, rather than a Midas touch which turned everything to gold, a magnifying mind that *magnified* whatever it focused on.(p.450)

magnifying
- It was as if I had, rather than a Midas touch which turned everything to gold, a *magnifying* mind that magnified whatever it focused on.(p.450)
- I must keep my magic *magnifying* mind on my acceptance and off my expectations, for my serenity is directly proportional to my level of acceptance.(p.452)

magnitude
- To him the alcoholic has often seemed a fool of the first *magnitude*.(p.137)

maid
- If it hadn't been for an alert hotel *maid*, I might have died then.(p.465)

maids
- A house in Virginia, during the fox hunting season; a little chalet in Switzerland during the summer or a place on Long Island – each house complete with cooks, butlers and *maids*.(p.403)

mail
- New groups started up and it was found, to the astonishment of everyone, that A.A.'s message could be transmitted in the *mail* as well as by word of mouth.(p.xviii)
- The answer came to him by *mail*.(p.342)
- The reply came, putting me in touch by *mail* with my sponsor in New Delhi.(p.343)
- The boys at the Post Office used to bring me my jugs; *mail* couldn't be opened for inspection at the gate.(p.426)
- Father, through the years, had built up a very good *mail* order business because, at that time, there wasn't too much money in medicine.(p.485)
- I had my own medical practice in Washington at that time, but the practice slackened and the *mail* order business started to fall off.(p.486)
- Just as I was wondering what on earth I could do -- I was too drunk even to pack a handkerchief – the memory of an A.A. write-up that I had seen in the Evening *Mail* flashed across my mind – and I thought to myself, this is something I haven't tried yet.(p.523)

mailman
- I would wait for the *mailman* each month, like any good mother, but as soon as he handed me my check, I put on my best dress and went looking for my alcoholic friend.(p.527)

main
- To show other alcoholics precisely how we have recovered is the *main* purpose of this book.(p.xiii)
- Therefore, the *main* problem of the alcoholic centers in his mind, rather than in his body.(p.23)
- Its *main* object is to enable you to find a Power greater than yourself which will solve your problem.(p.45)
- The *main* thing is that he be willing to believe in a Power greater than himself and that he live by spiritual principles.(p.93)
- He startled me by informing me that he was an alcoholic, that he had found a way which so far enabled him to live without taking a drink, and that the *main* idea was to find a way how not to take that first drink.(p.218)
- That was her *main* neurotic manifestation.(p.483)

Maine
- I stay with him at aunt's house in *Maine*.(p.474)
- Met father (Tall Man) at fork in road – one way to reservation, other way to State of *Maine*.(p.475)
- We went to booze joint in *Maine*.(p.475)
- So I change counties in *Maine*.(p.475)
- My brother and me find work on turnpike in *Maine*.(p.475)
- I go with him to first meeting, in small town in *Maine*.(p.476)
- *Maine* newsletter (Boomerang) say: "With tireless devotion and humility, this venerable Indian gentleman traveled thousands of miles humbly pleading for sobriety.(p.476)

mainly
- Keep his attention focussed *mainly* on your personal experience.(p.92)
- The head of the house ought to remember that he is *mainly* to blame for what befell his home.(p.127)
- Our courtship was *mainly* in bars and night spots when my ship was in New York.(p.555)

mainspring
- The Wright brothers' almost childish faith that they could build a machine which would fly was the *mainspring* of their accomplishment.(p.52)

mainstay
- He survived to become a *mainstay* of A.A. in Eire.(p.517)

maintain
- Belief in the power of God, plus enough willingness, honesty and humility to establish and *maintain* the new order of things, were the essential requirements.(p.13)
- He can go anywhere on this earth where other free men may go without disaster, provided he remains willing to *maintain* a certain simple attitude.(p.26)
- No one among us has been able to *maintain* anything like perfect adherence to these principles.(p.60)
- The fact is that he should work with other people to *maintain* his own sobriety.(p.119)
- This work is necessary to *maintain* his sobriety.(p.146)
- I managed to *maintain* myself with odd jobs, did ten weeks in a social rescue institution, and at length wound up in a second-hand bookstore in an adjacent town as manager.(p.257)
- One of them was that I would try to get a group started in Chicago; the second was that I would have to return to Akron to attend meetings at least every two months until I did get a group started in Chicago;

third, I decided I must place this program above everything else, even my family, because if I did not ***maintain*** my sobriety I would lose my family anyway.(p.292)
• If I did not ***maintain*** my sobriety, I would not have a job.(p.293)
• If I did not ***maintain*** my sobriety, I would have no friends left.(p.293)
• Now I feel so very grateful not only for my sobriety, which I try to ***maintain*** day by day, but I'm grateful also for the ability to help other people.(p.326)
• With all this, it was becoming increasingly hard to ***maintain*** my front of distinction and respectability to the world.(p.435)
• I took more through the day to increase the high, and more to ***maintain*** it; when I overshot the mark, I'd take tranquilizers to level off.(p.442)
• And when I place more value on my serenity and sobriety than on anything else, I can ***maintain*** them at a higher level -- at least for the time being.(p.452)
• Eleven -- Our public relations policy is based on attraction rather than promotion; we need always ***maintain*** personal anonymity at the level of press, radio and films.(p.564)
• They are the custodians of our A.A. Tradition and the receivers of voluntary A.A. contributions by which we ***maintain*** our A.A. General Service Office at New York.(p.567)
• In large cities, groups often ***maintain*** local offices where alcoholics or their families may arrange for interviews or hospitalization.(p.575)

maintained
• All have now passed away from natural causes, having ***maintained*** complete sobriety.(p.169)
• I worked for the Government about a year and still ***maintained*** my evening office practice when the Government agencies were decentralized.(p.489)

maintaining
• He had been dry for two and a half years and had been ***maintaining*** his contact with a group of recovered alcoholics in Akron.(p.309)
• Keeping one foot in front of the other is essential for ***maintaining*** our arrestment.(p.311)
• I had been far too busy building, protecting, and ***maintaining*** an image of respectability and all the other business pluses.(p.327)

maintains
• She ***maintains*** a perfect calm.(p.507)
• At New York, U.S.A., Alcoholics Anonymous ***maintains*** its international service center.(p.575)

maintenance
• But with the alcoholic, whose hope is the ***maintenance*** and growth of a spiritual experience, this business of resentment is infinitely grave.(p.66)
• What we really have is a daily reprieve contingent on the ***maintenance*** of our spiritual condition.(p.85)
• There are steps of recovery, of ***maintenance***.(p.516)

majestic
• We had long talks when I would still her foreboding by telling her that men of genius conceived their best projects when drunk; that the most ***majestic*** constructions of philosophic thought were so derived.(p.2)

majesty
• It poured over and through him with the certainty and ***majesty*** of a great tide at flood.(p.56)

major
• As we shall see, he now means a great deal to his community, and the ***major*** liabilities of thirty years of hard drinking have been repaired in four.(p.156)
• After high school came four years in one of the best colleges in the country where drinking seemed to be a ***major*** extra-curricular activity.(p.172)
• I was assigned to keep media guests happy at a Halloween party given by a ***major*** star in his plush home.(p.328)
• Up to my early thirties, when my drinking had become a ***major*** problem, I lived in large houses, with servants and all the luxuries that I could possibly ask for.(p.401)
• My ***major*** problems were marital.(p.439)

majored
• The first year in college I just got by in my studies, and that year I ***majored*** in poker and drinking.(p.241)

majority
• The ***majority*** have never returned.(p.114)
• For the great ***majority*** of us, however, that condition didn't last.(p.232)
• I was raised like the ***majority*** of American boys, coming from a family of modest circumstances, attending public schools, having the social life of a small midwestern town, with part-time work and some athletics.(p.373)

make
• And in no circumstances should we give endorsements, ***make*** alliances, or enter public controversies.(p.xix)
• Women now ***make*** up more than one-fourth of the membership; among newer members, the proportion is nearly one-third.(p.xxii)
• There are many situations which arise out of the phenomenon of craving which cause men to ***make*** the supreme sacrifice rather than continue to fight.(p.xxviii)
• They are over-remorseful and ***make*** many resolutions, but never a decision.(p.xxviii)
• What would I not give to ***make*** amends.(p.8)
• Nothing more was required of me to ***make*** my beginning.(p.12)
• We commenced to ***make*** many fast friends and a fellowship has grown up among us of which it is a wonderful thing to feel a part.(p.15)
• Most of us sense that real tolerance of other people's shortcomings and viewpoints and a respect for their opinions are attitudes which ***make*** us more useful to others.(p.19)
• Then comes the day when he simply cannot ***make*** it and gets drunk all over again.(p.22)
• This we did because we honestly wanted to, and were willing to ***make*** the effort.(p.25)
• Neither does there appear to be any kind of treatment which will ***make*** alcoholics of our kind like other men.(p.30)
• Let us ***make*** haste to reassure you.(p.46)
• Our own conception, however inadequate, was sufficient to ***make*** the approach and to effect a contact with Him.(p.46)
• We found that God does not ***make*** too hard terms with those who seek Him.(p.46)
• That was great news to us, for we had assumed we could not ***make*** use of spiritual principles unless we accepted many things on faith which seemed difficult to believe.(p.47)
• Whether we agree with a particular approach or conception seems to ***make*** little difference.(p.50)
• We were having trouble with personal relationships, we couldn't control our emotional natures, we were a prey to misery and depression, we couldn't ***make*** a living, we had a feeling of uselessness, we were full of fear, we were unhappy, we couldn't seem to be of real help to other people -- was not a basic solution of these bedevilments more important than whether we should see newsreels of lunar flight?(p.52)
• 8.Made a list of all persons we had harmed, and became willing to ***make*** amends to them all.(p.59)
• Our description of the alcoholic, the chapter to the agnostic, and our personal adventures before and after ***make*** clear three pertinent ideas:(p.60)
• In trying to ***make*** these arrangements our actor may sometimes be quite virtuous.(p.61)
• And do not his actions ***make*** each of them wish to retaliate, snatching all they can get out of the show?(p.61)
• We must be willing to ***make*** amends where we have done harm, provided that we do not bring about still more harm in so doing.(p.69)
• It may be one of our own family, but we cannot disclose anything to our wives or our parents which will hurt them and ***make*** them unhappy.(p.74)
• Have we tried to ***make*** mortar without sand?(p.75)
• We have a list of all persons we have harmed and to whom we are willing to ***make*** amends.(p.76)
• Rarely do we fail to ***make*** satisfactory progress.(p.78)
• Telling them what we are trying to do, we ***make*** no bones about our drinking; they usually know it anyway, whether we think so or not.(p.78)
• We may be short in our accounts and unable to ***make*** good.(p.78)
• He felt that he had done a wrong he could not possibly ***make*** right.(p.80)
• How could he possibly ***make*** a public statement exonerating his rival?(p.80)
• We must remember that ten or twenty years of drunkenness would ***make*** a skeptic out of anyone.(p.83)
• We discuss them with someone immediately and ***make*** amends quickly if we have harmed anyone.(p.84)
• Yet, we believe we can ***make*** some definite and valuable suggestions.(p.86)
• We ask especially for freedom from self-will, and are careful to ***make*** no request for ourselves only.(p.87)
• ***Make*** use of what they offer.(p.87)
• If the man be agnostic or atheist, ***make*** it emphatic that he does not have to agree with your conception of God.(p.93)
• ***Make*** it plain he is under no obligation to you, that you hope only that he will try to help other alcoholics when he escapes his own difficulties.(p.94)
• ***Make*** it clear that he is not under pressure, that he needn't see you again if he doesn't want to.(p.94)
• Let him know you are available if he wishes to ***make*** a decision and tell his story, but do not insist upon it if he prefers to consult someone else.(p.96)
• We could ***make*** few social engagements.(p.105)
• We realize some men are thoroughly bad-intentioned, that no amount of patience will ***make*** any difference.(p.108)
• We ***make*** this recommendation with some confidence.(p.114)
• We wives found that, like everybody else, we were afflicted with pride, self-pity, vanity and all the things which go to ***make*** up the self-centered person; and we were not above selfishness or dishonesty.(p.116)
• You will ***make*** mistakes, but if you are in earnest they will not drag you down.(p.117)
• He wants to ***make*** good.(p.118)
• Perhaps your husband will ***make*** a fair start on the new basis, but just as things are going beautifully he dismays you by coming home drunk.(p.120)
• ***Make*** him feel absolutely free to come and go as he likes.(p.120)
• A doctor said to us, "Years of living with an alcoholic is almost sure to ***make*** any wife or child neurotic.(p.122)
• He is straining every nerve to ***make*** up for lost time.(p.126)
• They want him to ***make*** a fuss over them.(p.126)
• We know there are difficult wives and families, but the man who is getting over alcoholism must remember he did much to ***make*** them so.(p.127)
• Instead of developing new channels of activity for themselves, mother and children demand that he stay home and ***make*** up the deficiency.(p.131)
• Though the family has no religious connections, they may wish to ***make*** contact with or take membership in a religious body.(p.131)
• If he does not argue about religion, he will ***make*** new friends and is sure to find new avenues of usefulness and pleasure.(p.132)
• As non-denominational people, we cannot ***make*** up others' minds for them.(p.132)
• So we think cheerfulness and laughter ***make*** for usefulness.(p.132)
• She sees she was wrong to ***make*** a burning issue out of such a matter when his more serious ailments were being rapidly cured.(p.135)
• The only answer I could ***make*** was that if the man followed the usual pattern, he would go on a bigger bust than ever.(p.138)
• If he has your will power and guts, he will ***make*** the grade."(p.138)
• If he owes you money you may wish to ***make*** terms.(p.145)
• If he speaks of his home situation, you can undoubtedly ***make*** helpful suggestions.(p.145)
• Your man should be on his mettle to ***make*** good.(p.146)
• After your man has gone along without drinking for a few months, you may be able to ***make*** use of his services with other employees who are giving you the alcoholic run-around -- provided, of course, they are willing to have a third party in the picture.(p.146)
• You may ***make*** some interesting discoveries.(p.149)
• Among them you will ***make*** lifelong friends.(p.152)
• Should you wish them above all else, and be willing to ***make*** use of our experience, we are sure they will come.(p.153)
• He proved to be a devil-may-care young fellow whose parents could not ***make*** out whether he wanted to stop drinking or not.(p.158)
• Therefore it would ***make*** no great difference, even if I should do some drinking.(p.175)
• It was really a horrible nightmare, this earning money, getting liquor, smuggling it home, getting drunk, morning jitters, taking large doses of sedatives to ***make*** it possible for me to earn more money, and so on ad nauseam.(p.177)
• Wishing to be polite, though I felt very badly, I said, "Let's ***make*** the call," and extracted from my wife a promise that we would not stay over fifteen minutes.(p.179)
• My wife and I belonged to some bridge clubs and they began to ***make*** wine and serve it.(p.184)
• And they said, "No, you have a disease, and it doesn't ***make*** any difference how long you do without it, after a drink or two you'll end up just like you

are now."(p.187)
• If I could stick to Him and listen, I would ***make*** it.(p.190)
• I spent most of my time trying to get back these friendships, and to ***make*** some recompense towards my wife, whom I had hurt a lot.(p.191)
• I'm so grateful for both the program and the people in it that I still want to go, and then probably the most wonderful thing that I learned from the program -- I've seen this in the 'A.A. Grapevine' a lot of times, and I've had people say it to me personally, and I've heard people get up in meetings and ***make*** the same statement: The statement is, "I came into A.A. solely for the purpose of sobriety, but it has been through A.A. that I have found God."(p.192)
• I can remember well thinking that I would quit drinking, really go to work hard, apply myself eight hours a day, five days a week, ***make*** a lot of money, and then I could start drinking again.(p.199)
• I remember one occasion when I did not drink for three hundred and sixty-four days, but I didn't quite ***make*** the year.(p.200)
• Then I got into the habit of having beers, and decided that a drink of whiskey was not any worse; so I would get the one drink of whiskey but, on second thought, I decided that as long as I was only going to have one, I might as well ***make*** it a double-header.(p.203)
• When I had been in the hospital ten days, Sister Ignatia, who has played such a part in the development of A.A. in this area, stuck her head in the door one morning and announced, looking at me quizzically, that they might be able to ***make*** something human out of my face after all.(p.205)
• She was a woman devoted to her family and loyal to her husband, but quarrels did not ***make*** a happy environment for her.(p.210)
• I do not recollect the specific conversation that went on but I believe I did challenge Bill to tell me something about A.A. and I do recall one other thing: I wanted to know what this was that worked so many wonders, and hanging over the mantel was a picture of Gethsemane and Bill pointed to it and said, "There it is," which didn't ***make*** much sense to me.(p.216)
• On hearing that, these people induced me to ***make*** the move immediately and join them as a senior partner, which I did.(p.220)
• I decided that if these fellows could ***make*** it I would try it myself, and so I did.(p.232)
• He brought in many of our original members, yet he himself could not ***make*** it and died of alcoholism.(p.239)
• In the Army, I became a periodic alcoholic – the periods always coming whenever I could ***make*** the opportunity.(p.241)
• When the others saw my altered attitude they took me back in, but for me they had to ***make*** it tough; if they hadn't I don't think I ever would have stuck it out.(p.248)
• As soon as I could get up and walk I started to drink again and kept it up until my friend of the hospital, who, in his first try at the new way of life had stubbed his toe in Chicago but had come back to the town to take counsel and ***make*** a new start, picked me up and got me into a hospital.(p.258)
• I had none of these things that children should have to ***make*** them happy.(p.261)
• I could never go and ***make*** up to all the people I've done wrong to."(p.269)
• We old-timers who get scattered and separated and then witness the construction of services to get in more people and to ***make*** this thing function, we think that A.A. has changed, but the root of it hasn't.(p.272)
• He might have handed me fifty dollars and said that I ought to pull myself together and ***make*** a new start.(p.278)
• The only stipulation they made was this: I had to ***make*** the decision myself.(p.278)
• I would ***make*** a fresh start somewhere else.(p.281)
• During that first year, however, I managed to ***make*** both ends meet, and to avoid ever going back to my old habit pattern of borrowing money when I could not earn it.(p.283)
• Some of the things which used to stop me in my tracks from fear still ***make*** me nervous in the anticipation of their doing, but once I kick myself into doing them nervousness disappears and I enjoy myself.(p.285)
• We are both depending upon God and our use of the A.A. program to help us ***make*** a success of this joint undertaking.(p.286)
• You must always be willing and continue to ***make*** contacts."(p.293)
• I would ***make*** a feeble attempt at eating supper, but I never met with any howling success.(p.299)
• I arrived at the stage where I couldn't quite ***make*** it to the office some mornings.(p.299)
• It wasn't necessary to report to the office in person every day, and when I did go in, it was just to ***make*** an appearance and bounce right out again.(p.300)
• I still couldn't ***make*** it through the nights without drinking, so I went back into the hospital, this time to a rehabilitation center.(p.320)
• I nudged George next morning, and I said, "I'm in," and he said, "Oh, I knew you'd ***make*** it."(p.322)
• I used to ***make*** excuses to try and get George off the wagon.(p.325)
• We have only been in A.A. a few years, but now we're trying to ***make*** up for lost time.(p.325)
• How will I feel next Friday, if I ***make*** it a Friday?(p.326)
• I am trying now, each day, to ***make*** up for all those selfish, thoughtless, foolish things I did in my drinking days.(p.326)
• And then we went up the side of a hill where we have a little barbecue area to ***make*** the fire for the barbecue, and on the way up, I thought to myself – I'll go back down to the kitchen and refill this drink.(p.347)
• I recall, as I walked into that meeting, saying to myself, "Here I am, a fellow of the American College of Surgeons, a Fellow of the International College of Surgeons, a diplomate of one of the great specialty boards in these United States, a member of the American Psychiatric Society, and I have to go to the butcher, the baker and the carpenter to help ***make*** a man out of me!"(p.347)
• Now they asked us to ***make*** a decision!(p.350)
• With these new and enlightening doors opening up to me, I was able to ***make*** the eventual decision to stop drinking, a day at a time -- because I, too, was an alcoholic.(p.355)
• It took me a year to ***make*** it home.(p.357)
• When I did ***make*** it home in 1920, I re-entered school and caught up with my class in a few short months – I actually did a year's work in three months, proving much to the disgust of my dad that I could do it when I wanted to.(p.358)
• It was strictly a one man operation and I knew I had to tend to my knitting to ***make*** a go of it.(p.360)
• I did everything to ***make*** her an alcoholic too.(p.361)
• Thank God that in spite of my heavy drinking my mind was clear enough to ***make*** a decision then and there.(p.363)
• I said I was okay, but if it would ***make*** her feel better I would go "as tired as I was after the strenuous holidays."(p.365)
• She told me not to bother going "for her sake"; she told me in a nice way that it didn't ***make*** any difference to her – and that really scared me – so I went.(p.365)
• To the new man I would also like to say that this program is not for sissies for, in my humble opinion, it takes a man to ***make*** the grade.(p.367)
• There are many short phrases and expressions in A.A. which ***make*** sound sense.(p.382)
• I wanted him to love me and ***make*** up to me for everything.(p.403)
• But I was not able to ***make*** use of this knowledge until after I became sober.(p.409)
• My analyst was one of the first to learn of A.A. and to ***make*** subsequent use of it in her work.(p.412)
• I couldn't focus enough to ***make*** out the chart, but the card contained two words -- "ACUTE ALCOHOLISM."(p.422)
• My job was to ***make*** out the guard schedules and thus I was exempt from ordinary recruit training activities.(p.425)
• Meanwhile the letters from home were telling about how much my folks wanted to ***make*** up to me for some of the things I'd missed.(p.427)
• Sometimes I'd ***make*** it home and go to sleep at the wheel of my car, for all the neighbors to see next morning as they left for work.(p.429)
• They ***make*** no guarantees and are not always successful.(p.436)
• They wanted me to ***make*** leather belts, of all things!(p.445)
• Had I gone to school all those years just to sit and ***make*** leather belts?(p.445)
• (I am pleased to state, however, that I had gone to only a very few A.A. meetings before I was able to ***make*** a really beautiful pair of moccasins – and half a wallet.(p.445)
• But, by the look on the psychiatrist's face, I could tell that it would really ***make*** him happy if I agreed.(p.446)
• So, for no better reason than to ***make*** him happy, I agreed.(p.446)
• Alcohol wrings the guts out of life, eats into the brain in such a way as to ***make*** the alcoholic blind to the truth.(p.457)
• I attempted nearly two years ago to ***make*** some amends and contact my children, but it wasn't God's time yet.(p.463)
• Talk and meeting ***make*** me feel good.(p.476)
• But I will never be totally honest – that would ***make*** me perfect, and none of us can claim to be perfect.(p.482)
• I know I will be grateful for a chance to ***make*** amends to everybody I have hurt in the past.(p.482)
• It doesn't ***make*** sense.(p.504)
• I must find a way to ***make*** some money.(p.506)
• I learn that honesty is truth, and that truth shall ***make*** us free!(p.507)
• I rounded up a few more of my friends and off we went to the meeting, not for anything we would gain from it as much as to ***make*** a burlesque out of it.(p.509)
• Each time I would ***make*** a report to the parole officer he would ask me, "Have you been to an A.A. meeting yet?"(p.510)
• She was the one who really helped me to ***make*** a go of that twenty years and nine months in prison.(p.511)
• It's no bed of roses, but somehow or other I've been able to ***make*** it, through the kindness of people in A.A.(p.511)
• But I did understand this eventually, that these people had been through a lot of drinking experience just as I had, and had managed to ***make*** a job of it.(p.524)
• If it was daylight, I would go down alleys to ***make*** sure no one saw me.(p.527)
• I know there are some alcoholics who seem terribly, terribly grown-up, but I think that they are trying to ***make*** themselves think they are grown-up, and the strain of their effort is what is causing them to drink -- a sense of inadequacy, a childish vanity to be the most popular, the most sought after, the mostest of the most.(p.535)
• I thought this would give me ego-strength, ***make*** me feel wanted and secure, and alleviate my fears, but again nothing changed inside me.(p.546)
• I knew it didn't ***make*** any difference where I started, the inevitable end would be skid row.(p.548)
• The people who came knew immediately I was in no condition to absorb anything of the program, and I was put in a sanitarium to be defogged so that I could ***make*** a sober decision about this for myself.(p.549)

make-believe

• Those of us who have spent much time in the world of spiritual ***make-believe*** have eventually seen the childishness of it.(p.130)

make-up

• We finally saw that faith in some kind of God was a part of our ***make-up***, just as much as the feeling we have for a friend.(p.55)
• First, we searched out the flaws in our ***make-up*** which caused our failure.(p.64)

Maker

• He humbly offered himself to his *Maker* -- then he knew.(p.57)
• Many of us said to our *Maker*, as we understood Him: "God, I offer myself to Thee -- to build with me and to do with me as Thou wilt.(p.63)
• It has brought me back to a realization of my *Maker* and my duties to Him.(p.525)

makes

• But as ex-problem drinkers, we can say that his explanation ***makes*** good sense.(p.xxiv)
• None of us ***makes*** a sole vocation of this work, nor do we think its effectiveness would be increased if we did.(p.19)
• We are equally positive that once he takes any alcohol whatever into his system, something happens, both in the bodily and mental sense, which ***makes*** it virtually impossible for him to stop.(p.22)
• Sometimes these excuses have a certain plausibility, but none of them really ***makes*** sense in the light of the havoc an alcoholic's drinking bout creates.(p.23)
• He has so attractive a personality that he ***makes*** friends with everyone.(p.39)
• God ***makes*** that possible.(p.62)
• He is under constant fear and tension -- that ***makes*** for more drinking.(p.73)
• He can choose any conception he likes, provided it ***makes*** sense to him.(p.93)
• That often ***makes*** the difference between failure and success.(p.98)
• This ***makes*** for discord and unhappiness.(p.122)
• Showing others who suffer how we were given help is the very thing which ***makes*** life seem so worth while to us now.(p.124)
• It is of little use to argue and only ***makes*** the impasse worse.(p.126)

• After a bit, he said, "The way you fellows put this spiritual stuff ***makes*** sense.(p.159)
• However, this isn't as rough as it sounds, as we do become grateful for the necessity that ***makes*** us toe the line, for we find that we are more than compensated for a consistent effort by the countless dividends we receive.(p.311)
• This really ***makes*** for an attractive woman!(p.479)
• His parishioners are limited in number, but his friends are many, for to him race, creed, or social position ***makes*** no difference.(p.497)
• He ***makes*** no reply, and hardly seems to see me.(p.501)
• She ***makes*** the arrangements, but I will not go.(p.502)

making

• War fever ran high in the New England town to which we new, young officers from Plattsburg were assigned, and we were flattered when the first citizens took us to their homes, ***making*** us feel heroic.(p.1)
• That the man who is ***making*** the approach has had the same difficulty, that he obviously knows what he is talking about, that his whole deportment shouts at the new prospect that he is a man with a real answer, that he has no attitude of Holier Than Thou, nothing whatever except the sincere desire to be helpful; that there are no fees to pay, no axes to grind, no people to please, no lectures to be endured -- these are the conditions we have found most effective.(p.18)
• Physicians who are familiar with alcoholism agree there is no such thing as ***making*** a normal drinker out of an alcoholic.(p.31)
• He tried to regulate his drinking for a while, ***making*** several trips to the hospital meantime.(p.32)
• Some will be drunk the day after ***making*** their resolutions; most of them within a few weeks.(p.34)
• I had no trouble refusing drinks, and began to wonder if I had not been ***making*** too hard work of a simple matter.(p.40)
• Once confused and baffled by the seeming futility of existence they show the underlying reasons why they were ***making*** heavy going of life.(p.50)
• So our troubles, we think, are basically of our own ***making***.(p.62)
• We thought well before taking this step ***making*** sure we were ready; that we could at last abandon ourselves utterly to Him.(p.63)
• But he is yet a long way from ***making*** good to the wife or parents whom for years he has so shockingly treated.(p.82)
• After ***making*** our review we ask God's forgiveness and inquire what corrective measures should be taken.(p.86)
• Suppose now you are ***making*** your second visit to a man.(p.96)
• You will be ***making*** it possible for him to be insincere.(p.96)
• After all, our problems were of our own ***making***.(p.103)
• Nothing will help the man who is off on a spiritual tangent so much as the wife who adopts a sane spiritual program, ***making*** a better practical use of it.(p.130)
• One instance comes to mind in which a malicious individual was always ***making*** friendly little jokes about an alcoholic's drinking exploits.(p.145)
• He entered a political campaign, ***making*** speeches, frequenting men's gathering places of all sorts, often staying up all night.(p.158)
• This had the effect of ***making*** me resolve that when I was free from parental domination, I would never again darken the doors of a church.(p.172)
• Many mornings I have gone to classes, and even though fully prepared, would turn and walk back to the fraternity house because of my jitters, not daring to enter the classroom for fear of ***making*** a scene should I be called on for recitation.(p.173)
• I became a specialist in ***making*** elderberry blossom wine.(p.213)
• My parents had some vague idea of ***making*** a priest out of me and for some years I attended the Franciscan school at Basle, Switzerland, just across the border, about six miles from my home.(p.230)
• I knew the stuff I was ***making*** was a lot stronger than I had been used to, but I never suspected that steady drinking of it might develop a taste for something even stronger still.(p.233)
• They did not seem to be getting an answer, for here I was staying sober and selling lots of auto polish, on which they were ***making*** one thousand per cent profit.(p.247)
• ***Making*** my way to Pittsburgh, I met other former friends and got a job in a large factory where piecemakers were ***making*** good money.(p.252)
• I got my first introduction to "riding the rods and ***making*** a blind."(p.252)
• I remember feeling that they were all ***making*** fun of me.(p.261)
• I remained with them for three weeks, using part of the time in ***making*** many amends, which I had had no earlier opportunity of ***making***.(p.281)
• Dr. Bob then led me through the restitution step, in which I made a list of all of the persons I had harmed, and worked out ways and means of slowly ***making*** restitution.(p.292)
• I was on the toboggan and really ***making*** time.(p.300)
• After holding good positions, ***making*** better than an average income for over ten years, I was in debt, had no clothes to speak of, no money, no friends, and no one any longer tolerating me but my wife.(p.301)
• I began ***making*** the rounds of the doctors in the hope that one of them might find some cure for my accumulating ailments, preferably something that could be removed surgically.(p.305)
• When I got out of the hospital, I continued ***making*** the meetings.(p.320)
• Hauling her to the divan, I sat with her and began to talk, frantically but clearly – and ***making*** sense.(p.333)
• This phase was right down my alley; I had my master's degree in the art of ***making*** "whoopee."(p.359)
• Why should this happen to me – hadn't I provided a good home -- wasn't I ***making*** a good living -- didn't I just get a substantial raise that had put me in the upper bracket class?(p.362)
• We had some people in, and I was ***making*** drinks in the kitchen, when I suddenly decided to hoist the bottle for a quick one.(p.365)
• I had no trouble ***making*** the right decision when I saw my wife open her purse at the meeting that night and deposit a cute little angel in the middle of my birthday cake.(p.366)
• Not knowing where I had been or how I got home was ***making*** me desperate.(p.375)
• Some crisis brings you to a point of ***making*** a decision to do something about your drinking problem.(p.377)
• I don't know what I expected, but I most certainly didn't visualize a group of people talking about their drinking problems, ***making*** light of their personal tragedies and at the same time enjoying themselves.(p.378)
• To most of us, ***making*** amends will take the rest of our lives, but we can start immediately.(p.381)
• Just being sober will be ***making*** amends to many we have hurt by our drunken actions.(p.381)
• ***Making*** amends is sometimes doing what we are capable of doing but failed to do because of alcohol; carrying out community responsibilities such as Community Funds, Red Cross, educational and religious activities in proportion to our abilities and energy.(p.381)
• (It was the beer and cheap whiskey that was ***making*** me so sick.(p.398)
• Through going to meetings and listening, and occasionally speaking, through doing Twelve Step work, whereby in helping others you are both the teacher and the student, by ***making*** many wonderful A.A. friends, I have been taught all the things in life that are worth having.(p.416)
• My life there was a nightmare of periodic binges on alcohol and pills, adultery, unhappy hours at the dental office, seeing my wife give birth to our second child and have several miscarriages, living in a turbulent household, and ***making*** continual attempts to be the respectable dentist, husband, father, and community leader.(p.419)
• I stayed in the barracks all day, "***making*** out guard schedules," and getting mildly plastered from the jug under my desk.(p.426)
• I felt very sorry for myself and attempted suicide on many occasions, ***making*** sure there was always somebody within reaching distance to see that I didn't finish the job.(p.478)
• I received an additional fifteen years for that, ***making*** a minimum of thirty-five years and a maximum of natural life.(p.509)
• The gradual result was that I was drifting into ***making*** drinking one of the more important parts of my life.(p.519)

maladjusted

• It did not satisfy us to be told that we could not control our drinking just because we were ***maladjusted*** to life, that we were in full flight from reality, or were outright mental defectives.(p.xxiv)

malady

• But when the broker gave him Dr. Silkworth's description of alcoholism and its hopelessness, the physician began to pursue the spiritual remedy for his ***malady*** with a willingness he had never before been able to muster.(p.xvi)
• Once this ***malady*** has a real hold, they are a baffled lot.(p.23)
• When the spiritual ***malady*** is overcome, we straighten out mentally and physically.(p.64)
• If you are satisfied that he is a real alcoholic, begin to dwell on the hopeless feature of the ***malady***.(p.92)
• Continue to speak of alcoholism as an illness, a fatal ***malady***.(p.92)
• This seemed to me like an opportunity to be helpful, so I spent two hours talking about alcoholism, the ***malady***, and described the symptoms and results as well as I could.(p.138)
• Even when you understand the ***malady*** better, you may feel this feeling rising.(p.139)
• How Forty-Three Alcoholics Recovered From Their ***Malady***(p.165)

malicious

• One instance comes to mind in which a ***malicious*** individual was always making friendly little jokes about an alcoholic's drinking exploits.(p.145)

Maliseet

• I was born a ***Maliseet*** Indian on reservation in Canada.(p.474)

mallet

• Instead it was like a tap on the head with a small ***mallet***.(p.402)

man

• It was thought that no alcoholic ***man*** or woman could be excluded from our Society; that our leaders might serve but never govern; that each group was to be autonomous and there was to be no professional class of therapy.(p.xix)
• This ***man*** and over one hundred others appear to have recovered.(p.xxiii)
• There is the type of ***man*** who is unwilling to admit that he cannot take a drink.(p.xxviii)
• About one year prior to this experience a ***man*** was brought in to be treated for chronic alcoholism.(p.xxix)
• I knew the ***man*** by name, and partly recognized his features, but there all resemblance ended.(p.xxix)
• From a trembling, despairing nervous wreck, had emerged a ***man*** brimming over with self-reliance and contentment.(p.xxix)
• Trembling, I stepped from the hospital a broken ***man***.(p.8)
• To Christ I conceded the certainty of a great ***man***, not too closely followed by those who claimed Him.(p.11)
• Judging from what I had seen in Europe and since, the power of God in human affairs was negligible, the Brotherhood of ***Man*** a grim jest.(p.11)
• On talking to a ***man*** there, I would be amazingly lifted up and set on my feet.(p.15)
• That the ***man*** who is making the approach has had the same difficulty, that he obviously knows what he is talking about, that his whole deportment shouts at the new prospect that he is a ***man*** with a real answer, that he has no attitude of Holier Than Thou, nothing whatever except the sincere desire to be helpful; that there are no fees to pay, no axes to grind, no people to please, no lectures to be endured -- these are the conditions we have found most effective.(p.18)
• If a sufficiently strong reason – ill health, falling in love, change of environment, or the warning of a doctor – becomes operative, this ***man*** can also stop or moderate, although he may find it difficult and troublesome and may even need medical attention.(p.21)
• They sound like the philosophy of the ***man*** who, having a headache, beats himself on the head with a hammer so that he can't feel the ache.(p.23)
• The tragic truth is that if the ***man*** be a real alcoholic, the happy day may not arrive.(p.23)
• A certain American business ***man*** had ability, good sense, and high character.(p.26)
• But this ***man*** still lives, and is a free ***man***.(p.26)
• Here was the terrible dilemma in which our friend found himself when he had the extraordinary experience which as we have already told you, made him a free ***man***.(p.28)
• We are convinced to a ***man*** that alcoholics of our type are in the grip of a progressive illness.(p.30)
• A ***man*** of thirty was doing a great deal of spree drinking.(p.32)
• An exceptional ***man***, he remained bone dry for twenty-five years and retired at the age of fifty-five, after a successful and happy business career.(p.32)
• Though a robust ***man*** at retirement, he went to pieces quickly and was dead within four years.(p.33)
• But here is a ***man*** who at fifty-five years found he

was just where he had left off at thirty.(p.33)
• This *man* has a charming wife and family.(p.35)
• He is an intelligent *man*, normal so far as we can see, except for a nervous disposition.(p.35)
• Such a *man* would be crazy, wouldn't he?(p.38)
• If ever there was a successful business *man*, it is Fred.(p.39)
• Many times we talk to a new *man* and watch his hope rise as we discuss his alcoholic problems and explain our fellowship.(p.45)
• But his face falls when we speak of spiritual matters, especially when we mention God, for we have re-opened a subject which our *man* thought he had neatly evaded or entirely ignored.(p.45)
• As soon as a *man* can say that he does believe, or is willing to believe, we emphatically assure him that he is on his way.(p.47)
• When people presented us with spiritual approaches, how frequently did we all say, "I wish I had what that *man* has.(p.47)
• Was it not true that the best mathematical minds had proved *man* could never fly?(p.51)
• What about people who proved that *man* could never fly?(p.55)
• Actually we were fooling ourselves, for deep down in every *man*, woman, and child, is the fundamental idea of God.(p.55)
• For faith in a Power greater than ourselves, and miraculous demonstrations of that power in human lives, are facts as old as *man* himself.(p.55)
• In this book you will read the experience of a *man* who thought he was an atheist.(p.55)
• This *man* recounts that he tumbled out of bed to his knees.(p.56)
• To this *man*, the revelation was sudden.(p.57)
• He is like the retired business *man* who lolls in the Florida sunshine in the winter complaining of the sad state of the nation; the minister who sighs over the sins of the twentieth century; politicians and reformers who are sure all would be Utopia if the rest of the world would only behave; the outlaw safe cracker who thinks society has wronged him; and the alcoholic who has lost all and is locked up.(p.61)
• When a person offended we said to ourselves, "This is a sick *man*.(p.67)
• One school would allow *man* no flavor for his fare and the other would have us all on a straight pepper diet.(p.69)
• Carefully reading the first five proposals we ask if we have omitted anything, for we are building an arch through which we shall walk a free *man* at last.(p.75)
• But our *man* is sure to be impressed with a sincere desire to set right the wrong.(p.77)
• The question of how to approach the *man* we hated will arise.(p.77)
• Sometimes the *man* we are calling upon admits his own fault, so feuds of years' standing melt away in an hour.(p.78)
• A *man* we know had remarried.(p.79)
• He subsequently denied having received the money and used the incident as a basis for discrediting the *man*.(p.80)
• A *man* so involved often feels very remorseful at times, especially if he is married to a loyal and courageous girl who has literally gone through hell for him.(p.81)
• We feel a *man* is unthinking when he says that sobriety is enough.(p.82)
• When possible, avoid meeting a *man* through his family.(p.91)
• If your *man* needs hospitalization, he should have it, but not forcibly unless he is violent.(p.91)
• When your *man* is better, the doctor might suggest a visit from you.(p.91)
• See your *man* alone, if possible.(p.91)
• If the *man* be agnostic or atheist, make it emphatic that he does not have to agree with your conception of God.(p.93)
• Sometimes a new *man* is anxious to proceed at once, and you may be tempted to let him do so.(p.95)
• We find it a waste of time to keep chasing a *man* who cannot or will not work with you.(p.96)
• Suppose now you are making your second visit to a *man*.(p.96)
• Perhaps you will want to take the *man* into your home for a few days.(p.96)
• Burn the idea into the consciousness of every *man* that he can get well regardless of anyone.(p.98)
• The *man* should be sure of his recovery.(p.99)
• Both you and the new *man* must walk day by day in the path of spiritual progress.(p.100)
• When working with a *man* and his family, you should take care not to participate in their quarrels.(p.100)
• In our belief any scheme of combating alcoholism which proposes to shield the sick *man* from temptation is doomed to failure.(p.101)
• But for every *man* who drinks others are involved -- the wife who trembles in fear of the next debauch; the mother and father who see their son wasting away.(p.104)
• He may seek someone else to console him -- not always another *man*.(p.111)
• We women carry with us a picture of the ideal *man*, the sort of chap we would like our husbands to be.(p.118)
• A *man* may criticize or laugh at himself and it will affect others favorably, but criticism or ridicule coming from another often produces the contrary effect.(p.125)
• At the beginning of recovery a *man* will take, as a rule, one of two directions.(p.125)
• Since the home has suffered more than anything else, it is well that a *man* exert himself there.(p.127)
• We know there are difficult wives and families, but the *man* who is getting over alcoholism must remember he did much to make them so.(p.127)
• Overnight, as it were, he is a different *man*.(p.128)
• He will perceive that his spiritual growth is lopsided, that for an average *man* like himself, a spiritual life which does not include his family obligations may not be so perfect after all.(p.129)
• Though some of his manifestations are alarming and disagreeable, we think dad will be on a firmer foundation than the *man* who is placing business or professional success ahead of spiritual development.(p.129)
• Nothing will help the *man* who is off on a spiritual tangent so much as the wife who adopts a sane spiritual program, making a better practical use of it.(p.130)
• When we see a *man* sinking into the mire that is alcoholism, we give him first aid and place what we have at his disposal.(p.132)
• Couples are occasionally dismayed to find that when drinking is stopped the *man* tends to be impotent.(p.134)
• In time they will see that he is a new *man* and in their own way they will let him know it.(p.134)
• My downfall cost the business community unknown thousands of dollars, for it takes real money to train a *man* for an executive position.(p.137)
• Because of the employee's special ability, or of his own strong personal attachment to him, the employer has sometimes kept such a *man* at work long beyond a reasonable period.(p.137)
• But I'm sure this *man* is done drinking.(p.138)
• The only answer I could make was that if the *man* followed the usual pattern, he would go on a bigger bust than ever.(p.138)
• I felt this was inevitable and wondered if the bank was doing the *man* an injustice.(p.138)
• Presently the *man* did slip and was fired.(p.139)
• When dealing with an alcoholic, there may be a natural annoyance that a *man* could be so weak, stupid and irresponsible.(p.139)
• You, as a business *man*, want to know the necessities before considering the result.(p.140)
• Your *man* has probably been trying to conceal a number of scrapes, perhaps pretty messy ones.(p.140)
• If you are sure your *man* does not want to stop, he may as well be discharged, the sooner the better.(p.141)
• Had they fired me first, and had they then taken steps to see that I was presented with the solution contained in this book, I might have returned to them six months later, a well *man*.(p.141)
• Perhaps you have such a *man* in mind.(p.141)
• We believe a *man* should be thoroughly probed on these points.(p.142)
• Either you are dealing with a *man* who can and will get well or you are not.(p.142)
• After satisfying yourself that your *man* wants to recover and that he will go to any extreme to do so, you may suggest a definite course of action.(p.142)
• Your *man* will fare better if placed in such physical condition that he can think straight and no longer craves liquor.(p.143)
• If your *man* accepts your offer, it should be pointed out that physical treatment is but a small part of the picture.(p.143)
• When the *man* is presented with this volume it is best that no one tell him he must abide by its suggestions.(p.144)
• The *man* must decide for himself.(p.144)
• In this connection, can you remain undisturbed if the *man* proceeds to tell you shocking things?(p.145)
• The employer cannot play favorites, but he can always defend a *man* from needless provocation and unfair criticism.(p.146)
• Your *man* should be on his mettle to make good.(p.146)
• After your *man* has gone along without drinking for a few months, you may be able to make use of his services with other employees who are giving you the alcoholic run-around -- provided, of course, they are willing to have a third party in the picture.(p.146)
• An alcoholic who has recovered, but holds a relatively unimportant job, can talk to a *man* with a better position.(p.146)
• Your *man* may be trusted.(p.146)
• After reading this book, a junior executive can go to such a *man* and say approximately this, "Look here, Ed.(p.147)
• If you are an alcoholic, you are a mighty sick *man*.(p.147)
• He will be able to take a position with such a *man* which is eminently fair and square.(p.148)
• It boils right down to this: No *man* should be fired just because he is alcoholic.(p.148)
• We think we are sensible when we urge that you stop this waste and give your worthwhile *man* a chance.(p.148)
• If a *man* drinks so much that his job suffers, we fire him.(p.148)
• The right kind of *man*, the kind who recovers, will not want this sort of thing.(p.149)
• Painfully aware of being somehow abnormal, the *man* did not fully realize what it meant to be alcoholic.(p.155)
• When our friend related his experience, the *man* agreed that no amount of will power he might muster could stop his drinking for long.(p.155)
• The *man* in the bed was told of the acute poisoning from which he suffered, how it deteriorates the body of an alcoholic and warps his mind.(p.157)
• "Yes, that's me," said the sick *man*, "the very image.(p.157)
• That afternoon he put on his clothes and walked from the hospital a free *man*.(p.158)
• They were willing, by day or night, to place a new *man* in the hospital and visit him afterward.(p.159)
• One *man* and his wife placed their large home at the disposal of this strangely assorted crowd.(p.160)
• Many a *man*, yet dazed from his hospital experience, has stepped over the threshold of that home into freedom.(p.160)
• Impressed by those who visited him at the hospital, he capitulated entirely when, later, in an upper room of this house, he heard the story of some *man* whose experience closely tallied with his own.(p.160)
• This practice enables us to lend a hand, at the same time avoiding certain alluring distractions of the road, about which any traveling *man* can inform you.(p.162)
• And so can you, though you be but one *man* with this book in your hand.(p.162)
• Ask Him in your morning meditation what you can do each day for the *man* who is still sick.(p.164)
• My father was a professional *man* of recognized ability and both my father and mother were most active in church affairs.(p.171)
• Not being a *man* of means, I knew that if I did not stay sober enough to earn money, I would run out of liquor.(p.175)
• I had a couple of shorter talks with this *man* afterward, and stopped drinking abruptly.(p.179)
• The question which might naturally come into your mind would be: "What did the *man* do or say that was different from what others had done or said?"(p.180)
• But this was a *man* who had experienced many years of frightful drinking, who had had most all the drunkard's experiences known to *man*, but who had been cured by the very means I had been trying to employ, that is to say the spiritual approach.(p.180)
• 3.Because in so doing I am paying my debt to the *man* who took time to pass it on to me.(p.181)
• If I could, that was wonderful, that was just fine, and they would very much appreciate a person who had that kind of power, but they were looking for a *man* that knew he had a problem, and knew that he couldn't handle it himself and needed outside help.(p.186)
• (At this point, the Editors intrude just long enough to supplement Bill D.'s account, that of the *man* on the bed, with that of Bill W., the *man* who sat by the side of the bed.)(p.188)
• He explained that he and a *man* from New York had a cure for alcoholism.(p.188)
• Bill D. walked out of that hospital a free *man* never to drink again.(p.189)

• But not this ***man***.(p.193)
• I didn't even know what a martini looked like, but I had heard a ***man*** down the bar order one.(p.194)
• I kept watching the ***man*** down the bar to see what he did with a contraption like that, and he just smelled of his drink and set it down again, so I did the same.(p.195)
• I was a very young married ***man***, having his whiskey in the cupboard over the sink, and when I helped my wife with the dishes at night I would take a cup of tea and spike it with whiskey.(p.196)
• Everything in the world a ***man*** could possibly want, and I was driving from Akron to Cleveland, having just been to the bank and discovered that I had approximately $5,000.(p.200)
• I had run into a ***man*** I always drank with.(p.201)
• Whenever this ***man*** and I met – I didn't know his name then nor do I know it now – we would always get drunk.(p.201)
• That was the smartest ***man*** I'd met in months.(p.208)
• The ***man*** turned out to be Bill D., a very early member of A.A., and I couldn't tell you a word of what he said.(p.208)
• I remember well one fellow, Joe, walking nearly three miles through slush, wet and snow to come to the hospital to see a ***man*** that he had never seen before in his life, and that impressed me very much.(p.208)
• My father was a railroad ***man*** and a Civil War veteran.(p.210)
• My efficiency as a professional ***man*** was probably reduced to twenty-five per cent of what it should have been.(p.215)
• The next morning, my wife came into my room and wakened me and said, "That ***man*** is downstairs and he said you said you'd go to Akron."(p.217)
• And being a big-shot ***man*** of my word, I said, "Well, if I said so, then I'll go."(p.217)
• Shortly after I came to this conclusion, I was importuned by another well-known patent law firm to help them out on some trial work because their trial ***man*** had had a heart attack and had been forbidden to go into the courtroom.(p.220)
• He wasn't a drinking ***man***, he didn't know what it was to need a drink, nor what a drink could do for one in a pinch.(p.227)
• The third ***man*** who came to see me had been one of the greatest business-getters his company had ever employed.(p.235)
• Taking that as a foundation, he reasoned that if a ***man*** followed that rule he could not be selfish.(p.236)
• Every ***man*** has his problem of this kind, but we didn't discuss it very much.(p.236)
• And when I get upset, cross-grained and out of tune with my fellow ***man*** I know that I am out of tune with God.(p.237)
• Searching where I have been at fault, it is not hard to discover and get right again, for I have proven to myself and to many others who know me that God can keep a ***man*** sober if he will let Him.(p.237)
• My next job was in sales promotion for an oil company in Mississippi where I promptly became high ***man*** and got lots of pats on the back.(p.242)
• The ***man*** who was going to take over one of their biggest branches come Monday?(p.243)
• We checked into the home of Hank, the ***man*** who had fired me eleven years before in Mississippi, and there I met Bill, our founder.(p.245)
• We ordered sandwiches and one ***man*** said, "Three beers."(p.247)
• After a bit, the other ***man*** said "Three beers."(p.247)
• I had been too self-sufficient to write a moral inventory, but I discovered in pointing out to the new ***man*** his wrong attitudes and actions that I was really taking my own inventory, and that if I expected him to change I would have to work on myself too.(p.249)
• With nothing but a liberal arts education, very definitely estranged from my family and already married, soon after graduation from college I became a bookmaker's clerk on the British racing circuits, far better off financially than the average professional ***man***.(p.251)
• My four years of abstinence had something to do with it, but soldiering is a tough enough game for a sober ***man***, and I had no yen for full-pack slogging through mud with a cognac or vin rouge hangover.(p.253)
• Instead, over coffee cups, this ***man*** and his wife told me what had been done for them.(p.259)
• There was a ***man*** watching, and I turned to him and said with a defiant air I carried with me all the time, 'If I don't quit this I'm going to have to join that alcoholic business they're talking about."(p.266)
• THE *MAN* WHO MASTERED FEAR(p.275)
• I told our family doctor, an understanding ***man*** who gave hours of his time trying to help me, about this experience.(p.276)
• My parents died, both in the same year, leaving me, a sheltered and somewhat immature ***man***, on my own.(p.277)
• At least three of those four years must have been a living hell for my wife, because she had to watch the ***man*** she loved disintegrate morally, mentally and financially.(p.277)
• He was a ***man*** of considerable means and he might have done what many men would have done in such a case.(p.278)
• But – supposing that just one ***man*** died because I had, for selfish reasons, kept my mouth shut?(p.282)
• I do feel, though, that the fact that I finally grew up to a point where I could even tackle such a job is the apex of the story of a ***man*** who spent eighteen years running away from life.(p.286)
• Here was a ***man*** with essentially the same outlook on life, except that he had done something about it.(p.290)
• This first meeting was held in the living room of a home and was led by Bill D., the first ***man*** that Bill W. and Dr. Bob had worked with successfully.(p.291)
• In the summer of 1938, almost a year from the time I made my original contact with Akron, the ***man*** for whom I was working and who knew about the program, approached me and asked if I could do anything about one of his salesmen who was drinking very heavily.(p.294)
• The doctor, a young ***man***, immediately took fire with the idea, and while he did not convince the son, he turned over two prospects who were anxious for the program.(p.294)
• I'm rated as a modestly successful ***man***.(p.296)
• Above all, I have gained the greatest thing accorded to any ***man***, the love and understanding of a gracious God, who has lifted me from the alcoholic scrap-heap to a position of trust where I have been able to reap the rich rewards that come from showing a little love for others and from serving them as I can.(p.296)
• After being fired, I lined up with a new finance company that was just starting in business, and took the position of business promotion ***man***, contacting automobile dealers.(p.300)
• And we wonder how much further this ***man*** could go if his alcoholic problem could be removed and he could throw one hundred per cent of his abilities into action.(p.308)
• He asked me to read the book "Alcoholics Anonymous," and then he wanted me to talk with a ***man*** who was experiencing success with his own arrestment.(p.308)
• This ***man*** could tell me more.(p.308)
• Philosophy, faith, a sense of humor (they could laugh at themselves), clear-cut objectives, appreciation – and most especially appreciation and sympathetic understanding for their fellow ***man***.(p.310)
• They realized that in the end alcoholism could be a mortal as cancer; certainly no sane ***man*** would wait for a malignant growth to become fatal before seeking help.(p.315)
• My guild had elected me president twice and later given me a "***man*** of the year" award.(p.328)
• I felt disgraced and humiliated – a ***man*** who couldn't hold booze – a social disaster.(p.328)
• He'd told a villain, "The trouble is, old ***man***, you've lived too long."(p.333)
• I couldn't go to one wine store and look the ***man*** honestly in the face and buy a bottle, as I used to do when I had parties and entertained and did normal drinking.(p.336)
• I was voted the ***man*** most likely to succeed.(p.345)
• At the other side of the table sat one of the carpenters in our community, and at the further end of the table sat the ***man*** who ran the bakery, while on one side sat my friend who was a mechanic.(p.347)
• I recall, as I walked into that meeting, saying to myself, "Here I am, a fellow of the American College of Surgeons, a Fellow of the International College of Surgeons, a diplomate of one of the great specialty boards in these United States, a member of the American Psychiatric Society, and I have to go to the butcher, the baker and the carpenter to help make a ***man*** out of me!"(p.347)
• And then I scratched my head and said to myself, "What a fantastic thing for a ***man*** to say, that I cured his wife.(p.350)
• This ***man*** faced the last ditch when his wife's voice from 1,300 miles away sent him to A.A.(p.356)
• It was strictly a one ***man*** operation and I knew I had to tend to my knitting to make a go of it.(p.360)
• One night at the dinner table my wife said that tonight was my first birthday in A.A., and that the group would have the usual ice cream and cake for the "one year ***man***."(p.365)
• I could end my story here, but for the new ***man*** I would like to add a few words.(p.366)
• To the new ***man*** I would also like to say that this program is not for sissies for, in my humble opinion, it takes a ***man*** to make the grade.(p.367)
• In meeting me casually, I don't think my strong belief in "The *Man* Upstairs" shows, but I have no other explanation for the many good things that have happened to me since I have been in A.A. -- they came to me from a Greater Power.(p.367)
• When I was nineteen, I married a fine ***man*** who had never known an insecure moment in his life, let alone the trials and tribulations of booze.(p.369)
• Early the next morning a ***man*** whose name I knew well, a lawyer, called on me.(p.378)
• I cooperated with that ***man*** one hundred per cent!(p.388)
• He said, "Wait until I get back and I will go with you to see this ***man***."(p.393)
• (That was the ***man*** the A.A. office had referred me to.)(p.393)
• So I got a half pint and at midnight that night, I called the number I had been given, but the ***man*** who had started the group was in the hospital so I didn't know what to do.(p.393)
• The letter from A.A. had said this ***man*** would see me -- there weren't any women.(p.393)
• It has been a fellowship with God and ***man*** that has held good wherever I've turned and whatever I've done.(p.394)
• A retired Navy ***man*** looks back over twenty years of drinking, to add up his A.A. "initiation fee."(p.396)
• I met a wonderful ***man***.(p.403)
• I came to and found a ***man*** leaning over me.(p.405)
• This good and gentle ***man***, a brilliant research doctor, got nowhere with me fast.(p.407)
• I am a young alcoholic with a drug problem, a doctor, the husband of an alcoholic, the son of an alcoholic, and a ***man*** once diagnosed as a violent manic-depressive.(p.421)
• Standing there was a gray haired ***man*** -- tall, trim and in uniform.(p.422)
• My dad, who was a newspaper ***man*** and had some connections, had meantime put a stop on me, and I guess that report went all over the country.(p.424)
• She didn't like it, but I thought it made a ***man*** of me.(p.425)
• I talked the Old *Man* into letting me live in the photo lab instead of the barracks, and for eighteen months nothing interfered with my drinking.(p.426)
• I was only twenty now, but I was a ***man***.(p.427)
• How could such a ***man*** possibly be called an alcoholic?(p.433)
• Many times in the intervening years I have thanked God for that ***man***, a ***man*** who had the courage to admit failure, a ***man*** who had the humility to confess that all the hard-won learning of his profession could not turn up the answer.(p.436)
• One day as I sat there in the hospital, my psychiatrist walked up behind me and asked, "How'd you like to talk to the ***man*** from A.A.?"(p.446)
• When a big, healthy-looking young fellow stood up there and said, "I'm a success today if I don't drink today," I thought, "*Man*, I've got a thousand things to do today before I can brag about not taking a drink, for God's sake!"(p.447)
• I proud to be son of Tall *Man*, American Indian, and member of A.A. for many moons.(p.474)
• Met father (Tall *Man*) at fork in road – one way to reservation, other way to State of Maine.(p.475)
• Year later, I go to Canada to carry message to Tall *Man*, but he not listen to son.(p.476)
• Two years later, my brother take Tall *Man* to first A.A. meeting.(p.476)
• Tall *Man* was blind, but soon he see.(p.476)
• Tall *Man* die five years ago, a sober, peaceful, happy ***man***.(p.476)
• Tall *Man* now see Great Spirit in Big Group in sky.(p.476)
• I really do believe it is much harder for a woman to gain back her self-respect than it is for a ***man***.(p.480)
• I met and married a ***man*** in A.A., and I am the happiest I have ever been in my life.(p.481)
• A ***man*** wasn't actually mistreated, though if he was he could only resent it.(p.485)
• That year, on a Friday night, a ***man*** whom I had known for years came to my office.(p.488)
• After Charlie had talked a while, I knew that this ***man*** had something.(p.495)
• Mother hated liquor and feared a drunken ***man***.(p.498)
• One ***man*** comes back, closing the door behind him.(p.503)

• "Well, you're not," says the ***man***.(p.503)
• "Then all of your troubles are over," says the ***man*** and leaves the room.(p.503)
• The ***man*** is in bad mental shape certainly.(p.503)
• "I must ask you a question," I say to the ***man***.(p.504)
• I go to see a ***man*** I had been asked to visit and tell him my story.(p.505)
• A ***man*** calls me on the phone.(p.506)
• But I am to learn later that it began with my desire for material success becoming greater than my interest in the welfare of my fellow ***man***.(p.507)
• I wasn't a happy ***man*** that morning, but I'm happy now that it came about.(p.515)
• In my own generation I stuck out, I can see that now, as being a very much heavier drinker than the average ***man***.(p.518)
• I thought that if these kind of ordinary people can do it, a ***man*** of my brains ought to find it much more easy, and I joined.(p.524)
• It has taught me that success and failure are never final, and that neither count for very much in the final assessment of any ***man*** who has done his best.(p.525)
• They tell me that I killed a ***man*** during that period, but I can't remember anything.(p.528)
• I, a ***man*** of steel, with very high ideals, well brought up, an honor student and the recipient of scholarships and prizes, a boy wonder in business -- I, Bob, the author of this essay, looked and saw that the universe was beneath my contempt, and that to remove myself from it was the only thing of dignity a ***man*** could do.(p.531)
• But as the years go by, the stretch becomes unbearable; and the ***man*** with the grown-up brain and the childish emotions – vanity, self-interest, false pride, jealousy, longing for social approval, to name few -- becomes a prime candidate for alcohol.(p.534)
• For a little while, I was the great ***man*** I wanted to be, and thought myself entitled to be just by reason of being.(p.537)
• Sobering up, the mind that was ahead of the emotions would impel the question: What have you written or done to be the great ***man***?(p.537)
• Brandishing my "motto," which was "A little ***man*** with a stick is equal to a big ***man***," sometimes I varied the literary lecture by a fight with a big ***man***, selected solely because he was big and I was little.(p.537)
• I wandered, craving peace, from one spot to another of youthful happy memory, and loathed the ***man*** I had become.(p.539)
• I could not face the boy and youth I was in the reality of the contemptible ***man*** I had become.(p.540)
• A happy ***man*** is not likely to do harm to another human being.(p.542)
• It was not difficult to convince myself that my unhappiness was the fault of the ***man*** I had married, and I divorced him at the end of a year.(p.545)
• I was married and divorced again before I was twenty-three years old, this time to a prominent band leader – a ***man*** that many women wanted.(p.546)
• By this time I was such a past master at kidding myself that I had convinced myself I had sat out a war and waited for this ***man*** to come home and, as my resentment and self-pity grew, so did my alcoholic problem.(p.548)
• About this time, I met a ***man*** who had three motherless children and it seemed that might be a solution to my problem.(p.548)
• It seemed logical to me that if I married this ***man*** and took the responsibility for these children that they would keep me sober.(p.548)
• This caused the rather cryptic comment from one of my A.A. friends, when I told my story after coming into the program, that I had always been a cinch for the program, for I had always been interested in mankind, but that I was just taking them one ***man*** at a time.(p.548)
• As another great ***man*** says, "The only real freedom a human being can ever know is doing what you ought to do because you want to do it."(p.553)
• "There is a principle which is a bar against all information, which is proof against all arguments and which cannot fail to keep a ***man*** in everlasting ignorance – that principle is contempt prior to investigation."(p.570)
• Dr. Foster Kennedy, neurologist: "This organization of Alcoholics Anonymous calls on two of the greatest reservoirs of power known to ***man***, religion and that instinct for association with one's fellows . . . the 'herd instinct.'(p.571)
• The Episcopal magazine, The Living Church, observes editorially: "The basis of the technique of Alcoholics Anonymous is the truly Christian principle that a ***man*** cannot help himself except by helping others.(p.574)

man-sized

• Quebec, Toronto, Buffalo, and finally Pittsburgh, were the scenes of ***man-sized*** drunks until I had gone through my readjusted discharge pay, a fair sum.(p.253)

man's

• More often than not, it is imperative that a ***man's*** brain be cleared before he is approached, as he has then a better chance of understanding and accepting what we have to offer.(p.xxiv)
• Young people may be encouraged by this ***man's*** experience to think that they can stop, as he did, on their own will power.(p.33)
• That is one of ***man's*** magnificent attributes.(p.53)
• The inventory was ours, not the other ***man's***.(p.67)
• If persisted in for a few months, the effect on a ***man's*** family is sure to be great.(p.99)
• But urge upon a ***man's*** family that he has been a very sick person and should be treated accordingly.(p.100)
• We never, never try to arrange a ***man's*** life so as to shield him from temptation.(p.120)
• Naturally this sort of thing decreased the ***man's*** chance of recovery.(p.145)
• Hopelessness was written large on the ***man's*** face as he replied, "Oh, but that's no use.(p.157)
• They experienced a few distressing failures, but in those cases they made an effort to bring the ***man's*** family into a spiritual way of living, thus relieving much worry and suffering.(p.159)
• "You've been trying ***man's*** ways and they always fail," he told me.(p.236)
• We would follow one ***man's*** ideas for a while, decide he was wrong and switch to another's method.(p.246)
• Haunting me through each day's stupor -- and there were eighteen or nineteen such days in this ***man's*** home -- was the thought: "Where do I go when his family comes home?"(p.278)
• I wore a ***man's*** raincoat, turned inside out, a present from a friend, for now my funds were low.(p.411)
• This ***man's*** wife had been suffering for a couple of months and when he came in he owed me a little bill.(p.488)
• The next morning I carried another prescription to this ***man's*** house and exchanged it for the bottle his wife had.(p.489)
• I get out of bed and go to the ***man's*** room.(p.504)

manage

• My talent for leadership, I imagined, would place me at the head of vast enterprises which I would ***manage*** with the utmost assurance.(p.1)
• As the whisky rose to my head I told myself I would ***manage*** better next time, but I might as well get good and drunk then.(p.6)
• (a) That we were alcoholic and could not ***manage*** our own lives.(p.60)
• However, I did ***manage*** to keep out of the guardhouse.(p.242)
• As long as things were tough and the job a challenge I could always ***manage*** to hold on pretty well, but as soon as I learned the combination, got the puzzle under control and the boss to pat me on the back, I was gone again.(p.243)
• In January 1938, I had the opportunity to go to northern Vermont to ***manage*** a small daytime radio station that was up against it financially, and was about to fold its antenna.(p.359)
• In 1940 another good opportunity came up and we moved to Pittsburgh where I was to ***manage*** two radio stations under the same ownership.(p.361)
• We didn't save the world, but we did ***manage*** to help some individuals.(p.496)
• So I did ***manage*** to get myself down to an A.A. meeting that night.(p.523)
• I had only to reflect on the contrast between the plans I made so many years ago for my life with what really happened to know I couldn't ***manage*** my life drunk or sober.(p.550)

manageable

• To this day, I am amazed at how many of my problems -- most of which had nothing to do with drinking, I believed – have become ***manageable*** or have simply disappeared since I quit drinking.(p.448)

managed

• Somehow I ***managed*** to drag my mattress to a lower floor, lest I suddenly leap.(p.6)
• Finally my father had to send a doctor out from my home town who ***managed*** to get me back there in some way, and I was in bed about two months before I could venture out of the house.(p.175)
• They suffered from my conduct without saying anything, but the reason for this was I still ***managed*** to hang onto a very substantial practice.(p.215)
• I'd only had two with her, but I'd ***managed*** four in the fifteen minutes I'd waited for her, and of course I'd had the usual uncounted swigs from the bottle as I painfully got up and did my slow spasmodic dressing.(p.223)
• Somehow I had always ***managed*** to avoid D.T.'s.(p.238)
• Young and able to travel with the best of them, I ***managed*** to hold my job and keep my end up in the barrooms.(p.252)
• I ***managed*** to maintain myself with odd jobs, did ten weeks in a social rescue institution, and at length wound up in a second-hand bookstore in an adjacent town as manager.(p.257)
• During that first year, however, I ***managed*** to make both ends meet, and to avoid ever going back to my old habit pattern of borrowing money when I could not earn it.(p.283)
• Somehow, I ***managed*** to read pieces on alcoholism.(p.332)
• I'd ***managed*** to drink my way through all my friends.(p.355)
• I didn't particularly like it, but I loved the effects, and ***managed*** for the next twenty-five years to drink anything and everything, either handed to me or purchased, at the slightest excuse.(p.357)
• All I can remember about the Roaring Twenties is that I drank a great deal, thought I was having a grand time, ***managed*** to get to Europe for a few weeks, was very proud of the dozens of speak-easy cards entitling me to an entree in the better joints between Cleveland and New York, took on a wife, and built a home in a fashionable suburb of Cleveland.(p.358)
• Looking back, it is surprising to me now that I ***managed*** to keep working and have enough money to squander at the various spots in the big city.(p.358)
• By persistence and salesmanship I ***managed*** to see more and more of my new friend, and because of her sympathetic nature she tolerated my company.(p.359)
• Her influence and companionship ***managed*** to lessen my drinking to some degree.(p.359)
• By hook or crook I usually ***managed*** to sober up before I reached home, but always "terribly tired" from a "hard day's work," and just having to have one or two before dinner.(p.361)
• But I did understand this eventually, that these people had been through a lot of drinking experience just as I had, and had ***managed*** to make a job of it.(p.524)
• We think, therefore, that any considerable property of genuine use to A.A. should be separately incorporated and ***managed***, thus dividing the material from the spiritual.(p.565)

management

• I switched into real estate brokerage and property ***management*** work.(p.277)
• We complement each other beautifully, as he is a born salesman and my taste is for finance and ***management***.(p.284)
• Shortly thereafter, I was selected, with eight other inmates out of the 10,000 in the state's prisons at that time, to attend a school designed to take former "***management*** problems" like me and convert them into paracounselors.(p.462)
• The hotel ***management***, knowing that something was wrong, sent for a doctor.(p.465)
• It is no problem to me now, but this is not good ***management*** on my part – just plain good luck.(p.480)
• Then a change in ***management*** took place in the regiment and the new O.C. didn't like me very much and I didn't like him, and he started to lie in wait for me.(p.519)
• Their ***management*** should be the sole responsibility of those people who financially support them.(p.566)

managements

• I failed to persuade my broker friends to send me out looking over factories and ***managements***, but my wife and I decided to go anyway.(p.2)

manager

• I was at one time assistant ***manager*** of a corporation department employing sixty-six hundred men.(p.136)
• I was moved in as Sales ***Manager*** and had four men working under me.(p.200)
• Offered the job of advertising ***manager*** for an eastern automotive company, I moved to Philadelphia to begin life anew.(p.254)
• I managed to maintain myself with odd jobs, did ten weeks in a social rescue institution, and at length wound up in a second-hand bookstore in an adjacent town as ***manager***.(p.257)
• Once dad came all the way to Florida to sober me up, after a hotel ***manager*** called him and said that if he wanted to see me alive he better get there fast.(p.288)

managers
• We believe that ***managers*** of large enterprises often have little idea how prevalent this problem is.(p.149)
• For clubs, A.A. ***managers*** are usually preferred.(p.566)

managership
• I re-organized their city sales policy and eighteen months later, when I was thirty, they offered me the branch ***managership***.(p.243)

manages
• Is he not a victim of the delusion that he can wrest satisfaction and happiness out of this world if he only ***manages*** well?(p.61)

managing
• No conviction was necessary to establish my status as a miserable failure at ***managing*** my own life.(p.259)
• After all, I had been working for eighteen years, slinging hash, and I was ***managing***.(p.478)

mangled
• Most alcoholics have to be pretty badly ***mangled*** before they really commence to solve their problems.(p.43)

manhandled
• I was not mugged, or ***manhandled***.(p.412)

Manhattan's
• Saying goodbye to my wife and baby, I was treading ***Manhattan's*** streets in a little more than a week.(p.252)

manhood
• I see him now and then and he is as fine a specimen of ***manhood*** as one could wish to meet.(p.xxx)

manic-depressive
• There is the ***manic-depressive*** type, who is, perhaps, the least understood by his friends, and about whom a whole chapter could be written.(p.xxviii)
• I am a young alcoholic with a drug problem, a doctor, the husband of an alcoholic, the son of an alcoholic, and a man once diagnosed as a violent ***manic-depressive***.(p.421)

manifestation
• We believe, and so suggested a few years ago, that the action of alcohol on these chronic alcoholics is a ***manifestation*** of an allergy; that the phenomenon of craving is limited to this class and never occurs in the average temperate drinker.(p.xxvi)
• This phenomenon, as we have suggested, may be the ***manifestation*** of an allergy which differentiates these people, and sets them apart as a distinct entity.(p.xxviii)
• That was her main neurotic ***manifestation***.(p.483)

manifestations
• Being convinced that self, manifested in various ways, was what had defeated us, we considered its common ***manifestations***.(p.64)
• Though some of his ***manifestations*** are alarming and disagreeable, we think dad will be on a firmer foundation than the man who is placing business or professional success ahead of spiritual development.(p.129)

manifested
• Being convinced that self, ***manifested*** in various ways, was what had defeated us, we considered its common manifestations.(p.64)
• The terms "spiritual experience" and "spiritual awakening" are used many times in this book which, upon careful reading, shows that the personality change sufficient to bring about recovery from alcoholism has ***manifested*** itself among us in many different forms.(p.569)

mankind
• I honestly doubted whether, on balance, the religions of ***mankind*** had done any good.(p.11)
• It is being constantly revealed, as ***mankind*** studies the material world, that outward appearances are not inward reality at all.(p.48)
• This caused the rather cryptic comment from one of my A.A. friends, when I told my story after coming into the program, that I had always been a cinch for the program, for I had always been interested in ***mankind***, but that I was just taking them one man at a time.(p.548)
• Historians may one day recognize Alcoholics Anonymous to have been a great venture in social pioneering which forged a new instrument for social action; a new therapy based on the kinship of common suffering; one having a vast potential for the myriad other ills of ***mankind***."(p.573)

manner
• My old ***manner*** of life was by no means a bad one, but I would not exchange its best moments for the worst I have now.(p.43)
• They are naturally incapable of grasping and developing a ***manner*** of living which demands rigorous honesty.(p.58)
• If our ***manner*** is calm, frank, and open, we will be gratified with the result.(p.78)
• And we stood there for twenty minutes, telling each other how much better we were, how much better we looked, how much better off we were financially, mentally, physically, morally, and in every way, shape and ***manner***.(p.201)
• In so simple a ***manner*** did my morning drinking begin.(p.331)
• Bill was tall, grey haired, with the kind of asymmetrical good looks and pleasant easy ***manner*** that inspire confidence in the shaken and afraid.(p.413)

mannered
• I don't know what sort of person I was expecting, but I was very agreeably surprised to find Mr. T. a poised, intelligent, well groomed and ***mannered*** gentleman.(p.309)

mantel
• I do not recollect the specific conversation that went on but I believe I did challenge Bill to tell me something about A.A. and I do recall one other thing: I wanted to know what this was that worked so many wonders, and hanging over the ***mantel*** was a picture of Gethsemane and Bill pointed to it and said, "There it is," which didn't make much sense to me.(p.216)
• Sometimes they'd put it on the ***mantel***, and forget it.(p.407)

manual
• That was the last honest ***manual*** labor on my part for many a day.(p.3)
• I went back home, to a job of ***manual*** labor where for a little while I was able to keep away from alcohol.(p.539)

manufacture
• Avoid then, the deliberate ***manufacture*** of misery, but if trouble comes, cheerfully capitalize it as an opportunity to demonstrate His omnipotence.(p.133)
• That being the case, it didn't take me long to figure out that my meager manufacturing facilities were entirely inadequate to the ***manufacture*** of beer for social and domestic consumption.(p.297)
• From that point on, I secured crocks of ten gallon capacity and really took quite an active interest in the ***manufacture*** of home brew.(p.297)

manufacturing
• The next three years I spent in Boston, Chicago, and Montreal in the employ of a large ***manufacturing*** concern, selling railway supplies, gas engines of all sorts, and many other items of heavy hardware.(p.172)
• My wife became pregnant and the doctor recommended the use of port or ale . . . so . . . I bought a six gallon crock and a few bottles, listened to advice from amateur brewmeisters, and was off on my beer ***manufacturing*** career on a small scale (for the time being).(p.297)
• That being the case, it didn't take me long to figure out that my meager ***manufacturing*** facilities were entirely inadequate to the manufacture of beer for social and domestic consumption.(p.297)

manuscript
• One of the many doctors who had the opportunity of reading this book in ***manuscript*** form told us that the use of sweets was often helpful, of course depending upon a doctor's advice.(p.133)

many
• ***Many*** do not comprehend that the alcoholic is a very sick person.(p.xiii)
• ***Many*** of our friends encourage us by saying that this is but a beginning, only the augury of a much larger future ahead.(p.xv)
• Prior to his journey to Akron, the broker had worked hard with ***many*** alcoholics on the theory that only an alcoholic could help an alcoholic, but he had succeeded only in keeping sober himself.(p.xvi)
• There were ***many*** failures, but there was an occasional heartening success.(p.xvii)
• In the spring of 1940, John D. Rockefeller, Jr. gave a dinner for ***many*** of his friends to which he invited A.A. members to tell their stories.(p.xviii)
• News of this got on the world wires; inquiries poured in again and ***many*** people went to the bookstores to get the book "Alcoholics Anonymous."(p.xviii)
• Seven percent of the A.A.'s surveyed are less than 30 years of age -- among them, ***many*** in their teens.(p.xxii)
• The basic principles of the A.A. program, it appears, hold good for individuals with ***many*** different life-styles, just as the program has brought recovery to those of ***many*** different nationalities.(p.xxii)
• I have specialized in the treatment of alcoholism for ***many*** years.(p.xxiii)
• It explains ***many*** things for which we cannot otherwise account.(p.xxiv)
• I say this after ***many*** years' experience as Medical Director of one of the oldest hospitals in the country treating alcoholic and drug addiction.(p.xxv)
• ***Many*** years ago one of the leading contributors to this book came under our care in this hospital and while here he acquired some ideas which he put into practical application at once.(p.xxv)
• The cases we have followed through have been most interesting; in fact, ***many*** of them are amazing.(p.xxv)
• We feel, after ***many*** years of experience, that we have found nothing which has contributed more to the rehabilitation of these men than the altruistic movement now growing up among them.(p.xxvi)
• After they have succumbed to the desire again, as so ***many*** do, and the phenomenon of craving develops, they pass through the well-known stages of a spree, emerging remorseful, with a firm resolution not to drink again.(p.xxvii)
• On the other hand -- and strange as this may seem to those who do not understand -- once a psychic change has occurred, the very same person who seemed doomed, who had so ***many*** problems he despaired of ever solving them, suddenly finds himself easily able to control his desire for alcohol, the only effort necessary being that required to follow a few simple rules.(p.xxvii)
• ***Many*** types do not respond to the ordinary psychological approach.(p.xxvii)
• I have had ***many*** men who had, for example, worked a period of months on some problem or business deal which was to be settled on a certain date, favorable to them.(p.xxvii)
• There are ***many*** situations which arise out of the phenomenon of craving which cause men to make the supreme sacrifice rather than continue to fight.(p.xxviii)
• They are over-remorseful and make ***many*** resolutions, but never a decision.(p.xxviii)
• All these, and ***many*** others, have one symptom in common: they cannot start drinking without developing the phenomenon of craving.(p.xxviii)
• He has not had a drink for a great ***many*** years.(p.xxx)
• ***Many*** people lost money -- but some became very rich.(p.2)
• I discovered ***many*** more reasons later on.(p.2)
• That was the last honest manual labor on my part for ***many*** a day.(p.3)
• My judgment and ideas were followed by ***many*** to the tune of paper millions.(p.3)
• There were ***many*** unhappy scenes in our sumptuous apartment.(p.3)
• I was finished and so were ***many*** friends.(p.4)
• It melted the icy intellectual mountain in whose shadow I had lived and shivered ***many*** years.(p.12)
• The good doctor now sees ***many*** men who have such experiences.(p.14)
• ***Many*** times I have gone to my old hospital in despair.(p.15)
• We commenced to make ***many*** fast friends and a fellowship has grown up among us of which it is a wonderful thing to feel a part.(p.15)
• All sections of this country and ***many*** of its occupations are represented, as well as ***many*** political, economic, social, and religious backgrounds.(p.17)
• There are ***many***.(p.18)
• After such an approach ***many*** take up their beds and walk again.(p.19)
• ***Many*** could recover if they had the opportunity we have enjoyed.(p.19)
• How ***many*** times people have said to us: "I can take it or leave it alone.(p.20)
• So ***many*** want to stop but cannot.(p.25)
• With ***many*** individuals the methods which I employed are successful, but I have never been successful with an alcoholic of your description."(p.27)
• ***Many*** who once were in this class are now among our members.(p.28)
• Our hope is that ***many*** alcoholic men and women, desperately in need, will see these pages, and we believe that it is only by fully disclosing ourselves and our problems that they will be persuaded to say, "Yes, I am one of them too; I must have this thing."(p.29)
• ***Many*** pursue it into the gates of insanity or death.(p.30)
• Despite all we can say, ***many*** who are real alcoholics are not going to believe they are in that class.(p.31)
• We doubt if ***many*** of them can do it, because none will really want to stop, and hardly one of them, because of the peculiar mental twist already acquired,

will find he can win out.(p.33)
• As we look back, we feel we had gone on drinking *many* years beyond the point where we could quit on our will power.(p.34)
• *Many* of us felt that we had plenty of character.(p.34)
• I had eaten there *many* times during the months I was sober.(p.36)
• *Many* doctors and psychiatrists agree with our conclusions.(p.43)
• If a mere code of morals or a better philosophy of life were sufficient to overcome alcoholism, *many* of us would have recovered long ago.(p.44)
• *Many* times we talk to a new man and watch his hope rise as we discuss his alcoholic problems and explain our fellowship.(p.45)
• We looked askance at *many* individuals who claimed to be godly.(p.46)
• Afterward, we found ourselves accepting *many* things which then seemed entirely out of reach.(p.47)
• That was great news to us, for we had assumed we could not make use of spiritual principles unless we accepted *many* things on faith which seemed difficult to believe.(p.47)
• But I cannot accept as surely true the *many* articles of faith which are so plain to him."(p.47)
• *Many* of us have been so touchy that even casual reference to spiritual things made us bristle with antagonism.(p.48)
• We used to amuse ourselves by cynically dissecting spiritual beliefs and practices when we might have observed that *many* spiritually-minded persons of all races, colors, and creeds were demonstrating a degree of stability, happiness and usefulness which we should have sought ourselves.(p.49)
• When *many* hundreds of people are able to say that the consciousness of the Presence of God is today the most important fact of their lives, they present a powerful reason why one should have faith.(p.51)
• There are those, too, who suffer from grave emotional and mental disorders, but *many* of them do recover if they have the capacity to be honest.(p.58)
• *Many* of us exclaimed, "What an order!(p.60)
• *Many* of us had moral and philosophical convictions galore, but we could not live up to them even though we would have liked to.(p.62)
• *Many* of us said to our Maker, as we understood Him: "God, I offer myself to Thee -- to build with me and to do with me as Thou wilt.(p.63)
• Next we launched out on a course of vigorous action, the first step of which is a personal housecleaning, which *many* of us had never attempted.(p.63)
• *Many* of us needed an overhauling there.(p.68)
• *Many* of us thought it necessary to go much further.(p.72)
• Small wonder *many* in the medical profession have a low opinion of alcoholics and their chance for recovery!(p.73)
• He attended church for the first time in *many* years.(p.80)
• Had this not been so, *many* of us would have no homes today, would perhaps be dead.(p.82)
• *Many* of us have wasted a lot of time doing that and it doesn't work.(p.87)
• There are *many* helpful books also.(p.87)
• We constantly remind ourselves we are no longer running the show, humbly saying to ourselves *many* times each day "Thy will be done."(p.87)
• Explain that *many* are doomed who never realize their predicament.(p.92)
• You will soon have your friend admitting he has *many*, if not all, of the traits of the alcoholic.(p.92)
• He often says that if he had continued to work on them, he might have deprived *many* others, who have since recovered, of their chance.(p.96)
• It may mean the loss of *many* nights' sleep, great interference with your pleasures, interruptions to your business.(p.97)
• Though his family be at fault in *many* respects, he should not be concerned about that.(p.98)
• In *many* homes this is a difficult thing to do, but it must be done if any results are to be expected.(p.98)
• Of course, we all fall much below this standard *many* times.(p.99)
• *Many* of us keep liquor in our homes.(p.102)
• Our homes have been battle-grounds *many* an evening.(p.105)
• When we were invited out, our husbands sneaked so *many* drinks that they spoiled the occasion.(p.105)
• *Many* of our husbands were just as far gone.(p.110)
• We know these suggestions are sometimes difficult to follow, but you will save *many* a heartbreak if you can succeed in observing them.(p.111)
• *Many* of Alcoholics Anonymous were like that.(p.113)
• *Many* of the old problems will still be with you.(p.117)
• It is probably true that you and your husband have been living too much alone, for drinking *many* times isolates the wife of an alcoholic.(p.119)
• Though it is infinitely better that he have no relapse at all, as has been true with *many* of our men, it is by no means a bad thing in some cases.(p.120)
• Father knows he is to blame; it may take him *many* seasons of hard work to be restored financially, but he shouldn't be reproached.(p.123)
• *Many* alcoholics are enthusiasts.(p.125)
• Although financial recovery is on the way for *many* of us, we found we could not place money first.(p.127)
• *Many* of us have experienced dad's elation.(p.128)
• Liquor incapacitated father for so *many* years that mother became head of the house.(p.130)
• Being possessed of a spiritual experience, the alcoholic will find he has much in common with these people, though he may differ with them on *many* matters.(p.131)
• He may bring new hope and new courage to *many* a priest, minister, or rabbi, who gives his all to minister to our troubled world.(p.132)
• We cannot subscribe to the belief that this life is a vale of tears, though it once was just that for *many* of us.(p.133)
• One of the *many* doctors who had the opportunity of reading this book in manuscript form told us that the use of sweets was often helpful, of course depending upon a doctor's advice.(p.133)
• *Many* of us have noticed a tendency to eat sweets and have found this practice beneficial.(p.134)
• We do not know of *many* cases where this difficulty lasted long.(p.134)
• Among *many* employers nowadays, we think of one member who has spent much of his life in the world of big business.(p.136)
• Drinking occasionally, and understanding your own reactions, it is possible for you to become quite sure of *many* things which, so far as the alcoholic is concerned, are not always so.(p.139)
• A look at the alcoholic in your organization is *many* times illuminating.(p.139)
• But there are *many* men who want to stop, and with them you can go far.(p.141)
• A firm attitude at this point has helped *many* of us.(p.142)
• You ask, because *many* alcoholics, being warped and drugged, do not want to quit.(p.142)
• The employer can *many* times protect the victim from this kind of talk.(p.145)
• That company may harbor *many* actual or potential alcoholics.(p.149)
• *Many*, we are sure, will rise to their feet and march on.(p.153)
• There must be *many* such in this town.(p.154)
• He had a desperate desire to stop, but saw no way out, for he had earnestly tried *many* avenues of escape.(p.155)
• He found himself surprisingly well received, and learned that *many* knew of his drinking.(p.156)
• *Many* a distracted wife has visited this house to find loving and understanding companionship among women who knew her problem, to hear from the lips of their husbands what had happened to them, to be advised how her own wayward mate might be hospitalized and approached when next he stumbled.(p.160)
• *Many* a man, yet dazed from his hospital experience, has stepped over the threshold of that home into freedom.(p.160)
• *Many* an alcoholic who entered there came away with an answer.(p.160)
• Being a large place, we think that some day its Fellowship will number *many* hundreds.(p.161)
• Under only slightly different conditions, the same thing is taking place in *many* eastern cities.(p.161)
• *Many* of us have felt, for the first time, the Presence and Power of God within its walls.(p.162)
• *Many* of us, former patients, go there to help.(p.162)
• The next three years I spent in Boston, Chicago, and Montreal in the employ of a large manufacturing concern, selling railway supplies, gas engines of all sorts, and *many* other items of heavy hardware.(p.172)
• *Many* mornings I have gone to classes, and even though fully prepared, would turn and walk back to the fraternity house because of my jitters, not daring to enter the classroom for fear of making a scene should I be called on for recitation.(p.173)
• After *many* painful discussions, they finally gave me my credits and I migrated to another of the leading universities of the country and entered as a Junior that fall.(p.173)
• But this was a man who had experienced *many* years of frightful drinking, who had had most all the drunkard's experiences known to man, but who had been cured by the very means I had been trying to employ, that is to say the spiritual approach.(p.180)
• Long since I had come to believe I was insane because I did so *many* things I didn't want to do.(p.199)
• I do not recollect the specific conversation that went on but I believe I did challenge Bill to tell me something about A.A. and I do recall one other thing: I wanted to know what this was that worked so *many* wonders, and hanging over the mantel was a picture of Gethsemane and Bill pointed to it and said, "There it is," which didn't make much sense to me.(p.216)
• That was an experience that I have never forgotten, and *many* times in my own work with A.A. newcomers I feel kind of guilty because I haven't done the same thing.(p.219)
• In my own experience I was so jubilant at finding myself sober, and I had so *many* things to catch up on, that a month went by before the thought even occurred to me.(p.219)
• I believe that my once over-weening self-will has finally found its proper place, for I can say *many* times daily, "Thy will be done, not mine" . . . and mean it.(p.229)
• In foreign parts *many* a soldier who has been abstemious at home learns to use new and potent drinks.(p.230)
• *Many* friends of my family had emigrated to America, so at twenty-four I decided that the United States offered me the opportunity I was never likely to find in my native land.(p.231)
• You can all remember that in the first few months after the change, a great *many* men, who had formerly been used to a few beers every day or an occasional drink of whiskey, simply quit all alcoholic drinks.(p.232)
• Unlike *many* other Catholics who frequently take pledges for definite periods -- a year, two years or for good, I never had any desire to "take a pledge" before the priest.(p.234)
• I have been sober for *many* years now.(p.237)
• *Many* things happened; business trials, little worries, and feelings of general despondency came near driving me to the bottle, but I made progress.(p.237)
• Searching where I have been at fault, it is not hard to discover and get right again, for I have proven to myself and to *many* others who know me that God can keep a man sober if he will let Him.(p.237)
• *Many* of these same things had happened to me *many* times before, but this time they had all descended together.(p.238)
• He brought in *many* of our original members, yet he himself could not make it and died of alcoholism.(p.239)
• My next conscious memory was in Bar le Duc, *many* miles from base.(p.242)
• *Many* alcoholics have learned they can bring their bottle to a cheap movie theater and drink, sleep, wake up and drink again in the darkness.(p.244)
• There was one meeting a week at Bill's home in Brooklyn, and we all took turns there spouting off about how we had changed our lives overnight, how *many* drunks we had saved and straightened out, and last, but not least, how God had touched each of us personally on the shoulder.(p.246)
• Much later I discovered the elders held *many* prayer meetings hoping to find a way to give me the heave-ho, but at the same time stay tolerant and spiritual.(p.247)
• We can share in the laughter and tears of our *many* friends, and most important, we can share our A.A. way of life and are given a daily opportunity to help others.(p.249)
• Washington, D.C. and news-gathering agency work followed, along with *many* parties.(p.254)
• I did six years of newspaper advertising, and trade journal work with *many*, *many* drunks of drab and dreary hue woven into the pattern of my life.(p.254)
• In five years a good *many* persons had forgotten that I had been somewhat notorious.(p.256)
• I was deprived of *many* of the things that we feel are important in life, such as education particularly, because of my father's drinking.(p.261)
• As *many* times as he would tell me that, I still believed him.(p.263)
• I wasn't nearly in the condition I had been in *many* times to be picked up.(p.264)
• He brought *many* people into A.A. through his barroom.)(p.267)
• I used to think I was cowardly because when things came out pertaining to the program that troubled me, I said to her *many* times, "Annie, am I being a coward

because I lay those things away on the shelf and skip it?"(p.273)
• Almost simultaneously, I discovered that cocktails in the late afternoon and highballs in the evening relieved the *many* tensions of the day.(p.277)
• He was a man of considerable means and he might have done what *many* men would have done in such a case.(p.278)
• I have thanked God *many* times in the last sixteen years that that was just what he did not do!(p.278)
• Too *many* economic and social problems would beset me there.(p.281)
• I remained with them for three weeks, using part of the time in making *many* amends, which I had had no earlier opportunity of making.(p.281)
• With God's help I am able, for one day at a time, to carry business responsibilities which, not *many* years ago, I would not have dreamed of assuming.(p.284)
• It was therefore not extraordinary that I should shy away from any serious thought of marriage for a great *many* years after joining A.A.(p.286)
• Where derision, contempt and pity were once shown me, I now enjoy the respect of *many* people.(p.296)
• And over my A.A. years I have made *many* real, honest, sincere friendships that I shall always cherish.(p.296)
• The last day of my drinking career, I drank twenty-two of them between ten and twelve a.m. and I shall never know how *many* more followed them until I was poured into bed that night.(p.298)
• How *many* times I swore off in the morning and got drunk before sunset I don't know.(p.300)
• One is that I don't remember too *many* of them, as I was one of those drunks who could be on his feet and attend a meeting or a party, engage in a conversation with people and do things that any nearly normal person would do, and the next day not remember a thing about where I was, what I did, whom I saw, or how I got home.(p.301)
• This worldly lady helped to develop A.A. in Chicago and thus passed her keys to *many*.(p.304)
• I studied art; I desperately endeavored to create an interest in *many* things, in a new place among new people.(p.305)
• In describing his suffering, his fears, his *many* years of groping for some answer to that which always seemed to remain unanswerable, he could have been describing me, and nothing short of experience and knowledge could have afforded him that much insight!(p.309)
• He thought it would be helpful for me to visit the Akron group and meet *many* like himself.(p.309)
• It had been so *many* years since I had not relied on some artificial crutch, either alcohol or sedatives.(p.310)
• Among today's incoming A.A. members, *many* have never reached the advanced stages of alcoholism, though, given time, all might have.(p.315)
• But with *many*, drinking had been little more than a sometimes uncontrollable nuisance.(p.315)
• And, unlike *many* others, I never took a drink in the morning.(p.323)
• I was accused of it *many* times when I went to play bridge in the afternoon, but I really never did take a morning drink.(p.323)
• *Many* women who have reached the stage that I had reached in my drinking have lost husbands, children, homes, everything they hold dear.(p.323)
• I have been very fortunate in *many* ways.(p.323)
• I lied like a trooper to get out of *many* scrapes.(p.324)
• George tried *many* times to go on the wagon.(p.324)
• It has taught me so *many* things.(p.325)
• *Many* of my neighbors devoted time to volunteer work.(p.326)
• Retirement rids the potential alcoholic of *many* shackles.(p.329)
• *Many* retirees embrace alcoholism while secluded in motor trailers, rest homes, leisure-world bungalows, mountain cabins, or beach cottages, or even in penthouses, on yachts, and inside Palm Springs cabanas.(p.329)
• I had to give him a story and ask him the same question over and over again, "Well, now, how *many* will that bottle serve?"(p.336)
• I had to hide, as a great *many* people in A.A. have had to do.(p.336)
• The second way in which, perhaps, I differ from some other alcoholics is this; *many* alcoholics state that they didn't particularly like the taste of alcohol, but that they liked the effect.(p.345)
• After my wife had read this to me, I said to her, as I had said *many* times in desperation, "I have got to do something."(p.346)
• And the psychiatrist has had thousands of couches, and has put you and me on them *many, many* times, but he hasn't helped us very much, though he has tried hard; and we owe the clergy and the doctor and the psychiatrist a deep debt of gratitude, but they haven't helped our alcoholism, except in a rare few instances.(p.352)
• *Many* times have I heard the above expressions since I have been in A.A., and *many* times I have had to reply "Definitely I am an alcoholic, and while it may be hard for you to believe, it is not hard for me, for I have learned *many* things about alcohol and myself that would, perhaps, be difficult for you to understand."(p.356)
• Too *many* outside activities to do much studying.(p.357)
• High living, a great *many* fair weather friends, the 1929 stock market crash, and a couple of years of Depression, soon relieved me one by one of my worldly goods including my wife.(p.358)
• Since the radio station was getting on its feet, it didn't require so *many* nights of evening work, and that permitted leisure time for drinking.(p.360)
• It was the first of *many* such experiences that became the only cause of harsh words, tears and heartaches in an otherwise truly beautiful marriage.(p.361)
• I have had *many* more reasons to drink since I have been in A.A. than I had in all the years of my drinking.(p.367)
• In meeting me casually, I don't think my strong belief in "The Man Upstairs" shows, but I have no other explanation for the *many* good things that have happened to me since I have been in A.A. -- they came to me from a Greater Power.(p.367)
• I went to *many* meetings and met *many* beautiful people.(p.371)
• The drive to get ahead, to succeed, kept me too busy for *many* years to have any great experience with social life.(p.374)
• In fact I was afraid to try it for fear that I would wind up like *many* examples I had seen of excessive drinking in the Army.(p.374)
• I achieved recognized and national standing in my profession, as well as becoming a director in *many* important institutions having to do with the civic life of a large city.(p.374)
• But success brought increased social activities and I realized that *many* of my friends enjoyed a social drink with no apparent harm to themselves or others.(p.374)
• I had had no brushes with the law, though I should have had *many*.(p.379)
• There may be *many* reasons which bring one to A.A. for the first time, but the lasting one must be to want sobriety and the A.A. way of living for oneself.(p.379)
• Just being sober will be making amends to *many* we have hurt by our drunken actions.(p.381)
• There are *many* short phrases and expressions in A.A. which make sound sense.(p.382)
• There are so *many* to whom I feel deeply grateful; to my husband (and best critic), whose generous love, compassion and understanding have helped me along the way; to those before me in A.A. who inspired the first article I read, and the friend who sent that article to Frank; to Ruth for her personal note, and the first A.A. to talk to me; to my Bishop, whose loving and believing spirit inspired me; and to all the members of the Houston Group who were so patient, kind and helpful -- and to countless others.(p.393)
• *Many* of them carried a flask and sandwich case, strapped to their saddles so they could stay out all day.(p.404)
• At a large party in Geneva, with people from *many* countries represented, the kind of party that is "protocol" in the extreme, I swayed, laughed hysterically, made naughty remarks in an unhushed voice, and was finally led from the scene.(p.406)
• The apartment was charming; the shelves were full of books, *many* of which I myself owned.(p.413)
• He himself took me to *many* of them, including the ones out of town.(p.416)
• Through going to meetings and listening, and occasionally speaking, through doing Twelve Step work, whereby in helping others you are both the teacher and the student, by making *many* wonderful A.A. friends, I have been taught all the things in life that are worth having.(p.416)
• *Many* good A.A.'s never join a church, and do not need to.(p.417)
• My experience has been active: three meetings a week, *many* tapes, *many* A.A. conferences, much work on the Twelve Steps, and much work with other alcoholics and their families.(p.420)
• They had been drinking for *many* years and were getting progressively worse.(p.424)
• They wrote me *many* long letters about it.(p.427)
• I lost it *many* times and mom and dad would drive me around until I found it.(p.429)
• I'd heard a lot about A.A. and met a great *many* A.A.'s during that year at home, but I hadn't thought of it for myself.(p.429)
• I'd packed more drinking into seven years than *many* a heavy drinker does in a lifetime.(p.429)
• My wife loved to drink, and we tied on *many* a hooter in the name of marital bliss.(p.433)
• Or, "I got to talking and forgot how *many* I was taking and it hit me."(p.433)
• To be sure, I learned *many* fascinating things, and *many* things that were to prove helpful later.(p.434)
• *Many* times in the intervening years I have thanked God for that man, a man who had the courage to admit failure, a man who had the humility to confess that all the hard-won learning of his profession could not turn up the answer.(p.436)
• That was seven years ago -- and *many* A.A. meetings ago -- and I haven't had a drink during those seven years.(p.437)
• The physician wasn't hooked, he thought -- he just prescribed drugs medically indicated for his *many* ailments.(p.439)
• I wanted to talk about my *many* big problems; drinking seemed a small one.(p.447)
• To this day, I am amazed at how *many* of my problems -- most of which had nothing to do with drinking, I believed -- have become manageable or have simply disappeared since I quit drinking.(p.448)
• Prior to our marriage, when she was a shy, scrawny adolescent, I was able to see things in her that others couldn't necessarily see -- things like beauty, charm, gaiety, a gift for being easy to talk to, a sense of humor, and *many* other fine qualities.(p.450)
• *Many* tried everything -- hospitals, special treatments, sanitariums, asylums, and jails.(p.455)
• There are *many* things worse than dying, but is there any death worse than the progressive, self-induced, slow suicide of the practicing alcoholic?(p.457)
• The alcoholic suffers death *many* times over.(p.457)
• I was an agitator, a troublemaker, and *many* men as bitter as I was followed me.(p.458)
• Yet prisoners often can't identify with *many* A.A. members' drinking stories.(p.458)
• Through A.A., *many* receive the needed change and awakening just by trying to live by A.A. principles and associating with A.A. people.(p.459)
• We do this by going to *many* A.A. meetings with an open mind and a desire to live the good-feeling life without chemicals -- liquid or otherwise.(p.459)
• I proud to be son of Tall Man, American Indian, and member of A.A. for *many* moons.(p.474)
• Our language has few words to say *many* things.(p.474)
• He gave me *many* drinks from bottle.(p.474)
• Then *many* blackouts for next two years.(p.475)
• Take *many* pledges, but break them.(p.475)
• Next two years, I call them *many* times.(p.475)
• He planted *many* seeds, and it will be *many* moons before another rises to walk in his shoes."(p.476)
• I keep it simple; go to *many* meetings; carry message to those who listen.(p.476)
• I felt very sorry for myself and attempted suicide on *many* occasions, making sure there was always somebody within reaching distance to see that I didn't finish the job.(p.478)
• My father had treated him *many* years prior to this.(p.488)
• They came, *many* of them, and stuck by us and told us how to hold meetings.(p.495)
• His parishioners are limited in number, but his friends are *many*, for to him race, creed, or social position makes no difference.(p.497)
• He had been in and out of Matteawan and *many* other mental institutions as a result of his drinking.(p.509)
• I had a rough lot, but I don't worry about that, after hearing the stories of *many* others.(p.511)
• When we first come into A.A., *many* of us are confused because as a general rule we're at the end of our respective ropes, and we don't know what to do.(p.512)
• Like *many* of us who went into the service, I thought it would be a cure-all, a new life.(p.513)
• I'd get downstairs to the gin mill, get enough in to hold me until eight o'clock in the morning, then I'd go out to join that "misery parade" that so *many* of us know so well.(p.514)
• You hit the street about ten minutes to eight, and you walk around the block, God knows how *many* times, waiting for that joint to open.(p.514)

• That thought had come to me ***many, many*** times.(p.515)
• I knew it, and I turned for help to someone upon whom I had turned my back for ***many*** years.(p.515)
• So I attended as ***many*** meetings as possible.(p.516)
• It has shown me, through the tragic stories of so ***many*** other alcoholics, the utter futility of self pity.(p.525)
• I felt that I didn't have anything to live for, so I tried suicide ***many*** times.(p.528)
• So ***many*** wonderful things have happened to me that at times I can't believe this is me.(p.529)
• Since it was wartime, I explained to the somewhat startled shopkeeper that I had ***many*** friends in the service whom I was remembering with a watch.(p.532)
• I have had the joy of seeing ***many*** a human being, down and out, learn to stand straight again, and to proceed under his own power to happiness in life.(p.541)
• The mental twists that led up to my drinking began ***many*** years before I ever took a drink for I am one of those whose history proves conclusively that my drinking was "a symptom of a deeper trouble."(p.544)
• I was married and divorced again before I was twenty-three years old, this time to a prominent band leader -- a man that ***many*** women wanted.(p.546)
• My reaction to this was identical in ***many*** respects to my reaction to my parents leaving me when I was seven.(p.547)
• I had never had a child and this had been a satisfactory excuse ***many*** times for my drinking.(p.548)
• I've heard it said ***many*** times in A.A., "There is just one good drunk in every alcoholic's life, and that's the one that brings us into A.A.," and I believe it.(p.549)
• I had only to reflect on the contrast between the plans I made so ***many*** years ago for my life with what really happened to know I couldn't manage my life drunk or sober.(p.550)
• I've had ***many*** spiritual experiences since I've been in the program, ***many*** that I didn't recognize right away, for I'm slow to learn and they take ***many*** guises.(p.551)
• It worked for me then, and it has worked for me ***many*** times since, and it will work for me every time I am willing to work it.(p.552)
• All these things and ***many, many*** more, A.A. gave me.(p.559)
• Alcoholics can stop drinking in ***many*** places and ***many*** ways — but Alcoholics Anonymous offers us a way to stay sober.(p.559)
• The terms "spiritual experience" and "spiritual awakening" are used ***many*** times in this book which, upon careful reading, shows that the personality change sufficient to bring about recovery from alcoholism has manifested itself among us in ***many*** different forms.(p.569)
• Yet it is true that our first printing gave ***many*** readers the impression that these personality changes, or religious experiences, must be in the nature of sudden and spectacular upheavals.(p.569)
• Though it was not our intention to create such an impression, ***many*** alcoholics have nevertheless concluded that in order to recover they must acquire an immediate and overwhelming "God-consciousness" followed at once by a vast change in feeling and outlook.(p.569)

march
• Many, we are sure, will rise to their feet and ***march*** on.(p.153)

March
• By ***March*** 1941, the membership had shot up to 2,000.(p.xviii)
• By ***March*** 1976, when this edition went to the printer, the total worldwide membership of Alcoholics Anonymous was conservatively estimated at more than 1,000,000, with almost 28,000 groups meeting in over 90 countries.(p.xxii)
• My visits to that sanitarium went on for nearly three years, until in ***March*** of 1944, my father died and I was too drunk to attend his funeral.(p.469)

margin
• He lost the race by only a narrow ***margin.***(p.158)

marijuana
• We did, and spent a month boozing it up, popping pills, and smoking ***marijuana;*** taking shelter where we could, which included a veterinary hospital one night; accepting meals from anyone; actually begging; stealing anything we were in need of, which was about everything.(p.354)

marine
• It was my ex-wife, and she said my twenty-seven-year-old son, who has completed his ***Marine*** Corps training and graduated from college, wanted to see me privately, was getting married in three months, and wanted me at the wedding.(p.462)

marital
• My wife loved to drink, and we tied on many a hooter in the name of ***marital*** bliss.(p.433)
• My major problems were ***marital.***(p.439)
• Acceptance has been the answer to my ***marital*** problems.(p.450)
• It had provided me with excuses for my lack of education, my ***marital*** failures, personal failures, inadequacy, and of course, my alcoholism and, though I really thought I had been willing to part with it, now I knew I was reluctant to let it go.(p.552)

Maritimes
• Start group on reservation and carry message, help start other groups all over ***Maritimes*** and New England.(p.476)

mark
• These facts appear to be of extreme medical importance; because of the extraordinary possibilities of rapid growth inherent in this group they may ***mark*** a new epoch in the annals of alcoholism.(p.xxiii)
• Hardly one of our crowd now shows any ***mark*** of dissipation.(p.133)
• I took more through the day to increase the high, and more to maintain it; when I overshot the ***mark,*** I'd take tranquilizers to level off.(p.442)
• But I knew that they knew what the medical grounds were, and that they had put a big black ***mark*** against my name.(p.521)

marked
• Now and then the family will be plagued by spectres from the past, for the drinking career of almost every alcoholic has been ***marked*** by escapades, funny, humiliating, shameful or tragic.(p.123)
• One of the earliest memories that I have is of a bottle sitting on his desk with a skull and crossbones and ***marked*** "Poison."(p.193)
• That call ***marked*** the turning point in my life.(p.307)

market
• My work took me about Wall street and little by little I became interested in the ***market.***(p.2)
• It was eight o'clock — five hours after the ***market*** closed.(p.4)
• A morning paper told me the ***market*** had gone to hell again.(p.6)
• The ***market*** would recover, but I wouldn't.(p.6)
• I optioned a piece of land just off East ***Market*** Street to put up a three-hundred suite apartment.(p.198)
• High living, a great many fair weather friends, the 1929 stock ***market*** crash, and a couple of years of Depression, soon relieved me one by one of my worldly goods including my wife.(p.358)

markets
• I had developed a theory that most people lost money in stocks through ignorance of ***markets.***(p.2)

marriage
• Then we have the voices who cry for sex and more sex; who bewail the institution of ***marriage;*** who think that most of the troubles of the race are traceable to sex causes.(p.69)
• My parents were well-to-do people and their ***marriage*** was a happy one.(p.182)
• My ***marriage*** was happy and, as I have said, I never had any of the reasons, conscious or unconscious, which are often given for drinking.(p.182)
• We had two children, a boy and a girl, and when the boy was about twelve, we broke up the ***marriage.***(p.199)
• I'm sure his family felt that it was a ***marriage*** that -- well, I was a girl from the wrong side of the tracks -- definitely!(p.262)
• Our ***marriage*** lasted four years.(p.277)
• Twenty-odd years ago I made a mess out of my one and only ***marriage.***(p.286)
• It was therefore not extraordinary that I should shy away from any serious thought of ***marriage*** for a great many years after joining A.A.(p.286)
• It was the first of many such experiences that became the only cause of harsh words, tears and heartaches in an otherwise truly beautiful ***marriage.***(p.361)
• We soon resumed our ***marriage,*** even moved away from the street of sad memories and found a new home.(p.371)
• After that came ***marriage,*** getting started in business, and a family.(p.373)
• For some reason I can't remember, it finally dawned on me that I had a problem, and yet nobody was very critical about it except my family, and that was only because I decided, after seven years of ***marriage,*** that I would divorce my husband.(p.386)
• It did not occur to me that ***marriage*** might be a job, too.(p.402)
• With ten years of A.A. behind me, I was able to tell him that I'd have been alcoholic, no matter what; that I had been a sick person, unfit for ***marriage.***(p.403)
• Even then I knew in my heart that I was unfit for the very things I wanted most, a happy ***marriage,*** security, a home and love.(p.403)
• It started out as a good ***marriage,*** but it deteriorated over the years as she progressed through the various stages of qualifying for Al-Anon.(p.439)
• Prior to our ***marriage,*** when she was a shy, scrawny adolescent, I was able to see things in her that others couldn't necessarily see — things like beauty, charm, gaiety, a gift for being easy to talk to, a sense of humor, and many other fine qualities.(p.450)
• Then, one day in A.A., I was told that I had the lenses in my glasses backwards; "the courage to change" in the Serenity Prayer meant, not that I should change my ***marriage,*** but rather that I should change myself and learn to accept my spouse as she was.(p.451)
• Then I went on my first week-long bender of solitary drinking, locked up in a hotel room, because my family opposed my coming ***marriage.***(p.464)
• I figured that perhaps if I went ahead with that ***marriage,*** which I was sure was right for me, that would be the answer to my drinking problem.(p.465)
• Tragedies during those years that were caused by my drinking, such as the breaking up of my ***marriage,*** the death of my child, other things — had little restraining effect.(p.465)
• Things went from bad to worse, and since I had finally and completely failed at the job of being a wife and a mother, my ***marriage*** ended.(p.468)
• In my screwed up mind I kept thinking I could have gone to A.A. way back there in 1940, and perhaps saved my ***marriage*** and home.(p.469)
• My mother resented it so that the first Christmas after our ***marriage,*** she didn't even invite us to dinner.(p.485)
• We were married, and during the first nine months of that ***marriage*** I was sober.(p.514)
• My husband eventually returned, but it was not long until we realized we could not continue our ***marriage.***(p.547)

marriages
• All of them have since settled down to jobs and good ***marriages.***(p.407)

married
• His income is good, he has a fine home, is happily ***married*** and the father of promising children of college age.(p.39)
• A man so involved often feels very remorseful at times, especially if he is ***married*** to a loyal and courageous girl who has literally gone through hell for him.(p.81)
• Could we have been so mistaken in the men we ***married?***(p.107)
• Then Prohibition came into effect, and the facts that the stuff obtainable was so horrible and sometimes deadly, and that I had ***married*** and had a job which I had to look after, helped me for a period of some three or four years, although I would get drunk every time I could get hold of enough to drink to get started.(p.183)
• I was ***married*** at the age of nineteen to a grand girl and had good business prospects.(p.194)
• Then I got ***married.***(p.196)
• I felt having gotten ***married,*** I was an adult and one of the first things I did was to buy two cases of whiskey with no idea of drinking it.(p.196)
• I was a very young ***married*** man, having his whiskey in the cupboard over the sink, and when I helped my wife with the dishes at night I would take a cup of tea and spike it with whiskey.(p.196)
• One hundred for unmarried women at one end, one hundred for men at the other, and one hundred for ***married*** couples in the middle.(p.198)
• I can remember telling the poor little soul that I could probably quit drinking if I wasn't ***married*** to her, and told her that, after all, I didn't like restraint!(p.199)
• (My mother and father were Catholics and I had been baptized, but at the end of my instructions for Confirmation I had not gone to church, and then when my mother remarried, she ***married*** a Protestant and the whole religious angle was forgotten.(p.201)
• I ***married*** when I was twenty-eight years old, and started in law school after I was ***married.***(p.212)
• The year after coming out, I ***married.***(p.225)
• By this time I was ***married*** and was paying for a home.(p.232)
• In June, 1945, with another member, I made my first – and only – Twelfth Step call on a female alcoholic and a year later I ***married*** her.(p.249)
• With nothing but a liberal arts education, very defi-

nitely estranged from my family and already *married*, soon after graduation from college I became a bookmaker's clerk on the British racing circuits, far better off financially than the average professional man.(p.251)
• Four months later, I *married* this guy.(p.262)
• I was sixteen when we were *married* and he was seven years older.(p.262)
• That was seven or eight years after we were *married*.(p.262)
• I was still bitter because I felt that drink had completely ruined my childhood and my *married* life, and I hated everything pertaining to it.(p.262)
• Our oldest daughter got *married*; they were living at our house.(p.263)
• With the bravery born of desperation, and abetted by alcohol, I *married* a young and lovely girl.(p.277)
• I was *married* at twenty, had two children and was divorced at twenty-three.(p.305)
• I thought my problem was that I had been *married* to a drunk for twenty-seven years.(p.321)
• She said, "How long have you been *married*?"(p.322)
• I started my drinking nearly thirty years ago – right after I was *married*.(p.322)
• Twenty-seven years of confusion is what my early *married* life was.(p.325)
• A square from ultra-dry Kansas, I did not taste grog until I had finished college, done a stint on newspapers, *married*, become a father, and been in studio publicity two years.(p.328)
• We were *married* in Montreal in November.(p.361)
• Proud of my little station and of my new bride I settled down to a happy *married* life.(p.361)
• When I was nineteen, I *married* a fine man who had never known an insecure moment in his life, let alone the trials and tribulations of booze.(p.369)
• The night that I was *married* I had a big church wedding.(p.385)
• So I *married* a nice, well-meaning young newspaper-man, so as not to have to go home.(p.402)
• During this period I *married* again.(p.405)
• During my first year there, I *married*.(p.419)
• Max and I had been *married* for twenty-eight years when I ended up in A.A.(p.439)
• Max and I have been *married* now for thirty-five years.(p.450)
• Over the years, as I thought about Max, her good qualities grew and grew, and we *married*, and all these qualities became more and more apparent to me, and we were happier and happier.(p.450)
• It was my ex-wife, and she said my twenty-seven-year-old son, who has completed his Marine Corps training and graduated from college, wanted to see me privately, was getting *married* in three months, and wanted me at the wedding.(p.462)
• I met and *married* a man in A.A., and I am the happiest I have ever been in my life.(p.481)
• For that reason, I believe, I *married* at a much younger age than I would have, had it not been for my home training.(p.485)
• My wife and I have been *married* for some thirty years now.(p.485)
• In the first place, she had been *married* before; I was her second husband.(p.485)
• And the guy said, "Heck, yes, I been *married* to her for years!"(p.512)
• I got *married* to the girl I'd left behind.(p.513)
• We were *married*, and during the first nine months of that marriage I was sober.(p.514)
• It was not difficult to convince myself that my unhappiness was the fault of the man I had *married*, and I divorced him at the end of a year.(p.545)
• I was *married* and divorced again before I was twenty-three years old, this time to a prominent band leader -- a man that many women wanted.(p.546)
• It seemed logical to me that if I *married* this man and took the responsibility for these children that they would keep me sober.(p.548)
• So I *married* again.(p.548)
• In the last year of my navy service, I was *married* to a lovely, lively girl, who enjoyed drinking.(p.555)

marry
• After several months of acquaintance I asked her to *marry* me, but was politely refused.(p.359)
• Once again I asked my girl to *marry* me and join me in this new venture.(p.359)
• I had quite a heartache about her then because she wasn't the type of girl that my mother wanted me to *marry*.(p.485)
• With cold calculation I set about to *marry* a fortune, and I did.(p.545)

marshalled
• Our human resources, as *marshalled* by the will were not sufficient; they failed utterly.(p.45)

martial
• He even went to bat for me before the court *martial* that inevitably followed and, as a result, I drew only thirty days – fifteen in solitary.(p.428)
• But on the other hand, I was terribly fortunate because that should have been a court *martial* offense and I should have been out on my ear.(p.520)

martini
• I ordered a *martini*, extra dry.(p.194)
• I didn't even know what a *martini* looked like, but I had heard a man down the bar order one.(p.194)
• He tossed off half of his *martini*; I tossed off half of mine and it nearly blew the top of my head off.(p.195)
• I'd been sitting comfortably in a restaurant with Rita, drinking my sixth *martini* and hoping the waiter would forget about the lunch order – at least long enough for me to have a couple more.(p.223)
• Only, having found them, I threw them away, and ordered another extra dry *martini*.(p.533)
• I'd visit one bar after another, having one *martini* in each, and in each hoping to find someone interesting to talk to.(p.536)

martinis
• I drank nine *martinis* in less than an hour.(p.195)
• I had no more reason to drink those *martinis* than a jackrabbit.(p.195)
• Right then I determined that never so long as I lived would I have anything more to do with *martinis*.(p.195)
• "You've got to space your drinks and take plenty of water in between," or "coat the stomach with a little olive oil," or "drink anything but those damn *martinis*."(p.433)
• Since, perhaps, suicide was a bit too drastic (actually, I was afraid), dry *martinis* were chosen as the slow, pleasant, private, gradual instrument of self-destruction.(p.531)
• Actually, of course, I wanted someone to listen to me, because when I had a few *martinis* inside, I became the great author I longed to be; and the right listener was in for some pretty highflown theories of literature and of genius.(p.536)
• If the listener were drunk enough, the lecture might go on through several *martinis*, which I was glad to pay for.(p.537)

Marty
• Then he called *Marty* and made and appointment for me.(p.413)
• I did not know who this *Marty* was.(p.413)
• *Marty* was late.(p.413)
• *Marty* came in, looking clean, neat, well-dressed and, like Bill, she was neither a bloated wreck nor a reformer.(p.413)
• *Marty* was smart.(p.414)
• I went to my first meeting with *Marty* and some other girls.(p.414)
• Priscilla, an A.A. who, like *Marty*, has become one of my greatest friends, decided that I was a stubborn case.(p.414)

Marty's
• A friend of *Marty's*, another A.A. let me in.(p.413)

martyr
• Therefore, we are not to be the hasty and foolish *martyr* who would needlessly sacrifice others to save himself from the alcoholic pit.(p.79)
• You're just a *martyr*, aren't you?"(p.322)
• And I thought, "You're some *martyr*, Jane!(p.322)
• One said, "Don't feel that you are a *martyr* because you stopped drinking," and this hit me between the eyes.(p.346)
• If it was one minute after, I'd stay up and act like a *martyr* all day.(p.441)

marvelous
• The mind and body are *marvelous* mechanisms, for mine endured this agony two more years.(p.6)
• *Marvelous* results often follow such a reunion.(p.134)
• I thought it was wonderful, simply *marvelous*, for him.(p.321)
• On the other hand, I was a *marvelous* customer.(p.410)

marvelously
• The family must realize that dad, though *marvelously* improved, is still convalescing.(p.127)

Mary
• My wife didn't tell me this, but one Sunday afternoon when *Mary* was trying to get the cobwebs out of my mind, Clarence and his sister-in-law, the hairdresser, called at the house.(p.216)

mass
• The prosaic steel girder is a *mass* of electrons whirling around each other at incredible speed.(p.48)
• Could we still say the whole thing was nothing but a *mass* of electrons, created out of nothing, meaning nothing, whirling on to a destiny of nothingness?(p.54)
• He had tried everything from having me attend daily *mass* at six a.m. to performing the most menial labor for his charity patients.(p.306)
• Inside, I went right on being a *mass* of unlovely self-pity, queasy anxiety and sickening self-debasement.(p.400)

master
• Alcohol was my *master*.(p.8)
• He clamors for this or that, claiming he cannot *master* alcohol until his material needs are cared for.(p.98)
• I had proved that liquor was not my *master*.(p.203)
• Being intensely interested in the work, I changed my conduct sufficiently to *master* the job.(p.211)
• By this time I was such a past *master* at kidding myself that I had convinced myself I had sat out a war and waited for this man to come home and, as my resentment and self-pity grew, so did my alcoholic problem.(p.548)

master's
• This phase was right down my alley; I had my *master's* degree in the art of making "whoopee."(p.359)

mastered
• We saw that these resentments must be *mastered*, but how?(p.66)
• Even then he went into no great detail about how he and a crowd of alcoholics, with whom he associated, had *mastered* their difficulty.(p.235)
• THE MAN WHO *MASTERED* FEAR(p.275)

masterly
• There was, therefore, a sense of real satisfaction when I was asked to contribute a few words on a subject which is covered in such *masterly* detail in these pages.(p.xxv)

mastery
• He saw that he would have to face his problems squarely that God might give him *mastery*.(p.155)

match
• I had met my *match*.(p.8)
• Just to the extent that we do as we think He would have us, and humbly rely on Him, does He enable us to *match* calamity with serenity.(p.68)
• He will *match* your mental inconsistencies with some of his own.(p.92)
• They had also been periodic big shots who had goofed out repeatedly at the wrong time, and they also knew how to split one paper *match* into three separate matches.(p.245)
• What is much more important to me, A.A. has taught me that through this simple program I may experience a change in this reaction pattern that will indeed allow me to "*match* calamity with serenity."(p.544)

matches
• They had also been periodic big shots who had goofed out repeatedly at the wrong time, and they also knew how to split one paper match into three separate *matches*.(p.245)
• (This is very useful knowledge in places where *matches* are prohibited.)(p.245)
• We started to light *matches* to see, but the draft blew them out.(p.424)

mate
• Many a distracted wife has visited this house to find loving and understanding companionship among women who knew her problem, to hear from the lips of their husbands what had happened to them, to be advised how her own wayward *mate* might be hospitalized and approached when next he stumbled.(p.160)

material
• It is being constantly revealed, as mankind studies the *material* world, that outward appearances are not inward reality at all.(p.48)
• These tiny bodies are governed by precise laws, and these laws hold true throughout the *material* world.(p.49)
• When, however, the perfectly logical assumption is suggested that underneath the *material* world and life as we see it, there is an All Powerful, Guiding, Creative Intelligence, right there our perverse streak comes to the surface and we laboriously set out to convince ourselves it isn't so.(p.49)
• This world of ours has made more *material* prog-

ress in the last century than in all the millenniums which went before.(p.51)
• Yet in ancient times ***material*** progress was painfully slow.(p.51)
• In the realm of the ***material,*** men's minds were fettered by superstition, tradition, and all sorts of fixed ideas.(p.51)
• We asked ourselves this: Are not some of us just as biased and unreasonable about the realm of the ***material?***(p.51)
• He clamors for this or that, claiming he cannot master alcohol until his ***material*** needs are cared for.(p.98)
• For us, ***material*** well-being always followed spiritual progress; it never preceded.(p.127)
• My family had money -- I had never known denial of any ***material*** desire.(p.225)
• I come from a very poor family in ***material*** things, with a fine Christian mother, but with no religious background.(p.261)
• I was terribly impressed by this meeting and the quality of happiness these men displayed, despite their lack of ***material*** means.(p.291)
• My stock of ***material*** goods isn't great.(p.296)
• There was no ***material*** or external reason for this.(p.400)
• But I am to learn later that it began with my desire for ***material*** success becoming greater than my interest in the welfare of my fellow man.(p.507)
• The only kind of security I knew anything about at that time was ***material*** security and I decided that all these intruders would vanish immediately if I only had a lot of money.(p.545)
• We think, therefore, that any considerable property of genuine use to A.A. should be separately incorporated and managed, thus dividing the ***material*** from the spiritual.(p.565)

materialize
• They will always ***materialize*** if we work for them.(p.84)

materially
• However, what I had gained ***materially*** on the credit side of my ledger, I have since learned was more than offset on the debit side by egotism, resentment and dishonesty.(p.356)
• I have been helped morally, spiritually, mentally and ***materially*** through A.A.(p.430)

mates
• They daily pass into oblivion, alone or with ***mates.***(p.329)

mathematical
• Was it not true that the best ***mathematical*** minds had proved man could never fly?(p.51)

mathematics
• Some simple ***mathematics*** and more statistics:(p.399)

matron
• The best boarding schools and a finishing school in Europe had fitted me for the conventional role of debutante and young ***matron.***(p.225)

Matteawan
• He had been in and out of ***Matteawan*** and many other mental institutions as a result of his drinking.(p.509)

matter
• In a ***matter*** of fact way he told how two men had appeared in court, persuading the judge to suspend his commitment.(p.9)
• It was only a ***matter*** of being willing to believe in a Power greater than myself.(p.12)
• This is the baffling feature of alcoholism as we know it -- this utter inability to leave it alone, no ***matter*** how great the necessity or the wish.(p.34)
• I felt I had every right to be self-confident, that it would be only a ***matter*** of exercising my will power and keeping on guard.(p.40)
• I had no trouble refusing drinks, and began to wonder if I had not been making too hard work of a simple ***matter.***(p.40)
• But we found that such codes and philosophies did not save us, no ***matter*** how much we tried.(p.45)
• In meditation, we ask God what we should do about each specific ***matter.***(p.69)
• It should not ***matter,*** however, if someone does throw us out of his office.(p.78)
• We must lose our fear of creditors no ***matter*** how far we have to go, for we are liable to drink if we are afraid to face them.(p.78)
• Reminding ourselves that we have decided to go to any length to find a spiritual experience we ask that we be given strength and direction to do the right thing, no ***matter*** what the personal consequences may be.(p.79)
• To his wife, he remarked, "Don't see anything the ***matter*** here, Ma.(p.82)
• No ***matter*** how far down the scale we have gone, we will see how our experience can benefit others.(p.84)
• This is not an overnight ***matter.***(p.84)
• We shouldn't be shy on this ***matter*** of prayer.(p.85)
• It would be easy to be vague about this ***matter.***(p.86)
• Don't raise such issues, no ***matter*** what your own convictions are.(p.93)
• It is not the ***matter*** of giving that is in question, but when and how to give.(p.98)
• Follow the dictates of a Higher Power and you will presently live in a new and wonderful world, no ***matter*** what your present circumstances!(p.100)
• An alcoholic who cannot meet them, still has an alcoholic mind; there is something the ***matter*** with his spiritual status.(p.101)
• Try not to condemn your alcoholic husband no ***matter*** what he says or does.(p.108)
• You may be unable to do so, no ***matter*** how hard you try.(p.111)
• Frequently, you have felt obliged to tell your husband's employer and his friends that he was sick, when as a ***matter*** of fact he was tight.(p.115)
• Next time you and he have a heated discussion, no ***matter*** what the subject, it should be the privilege of either to smile and say, "This is getting serious.(p.118)
• We think each family which has been relieved owes something to those who have not, and when the occasion requires, each member of it should be only too willing to bring former mistakes, no ***matter*** how grievous, out of their hiding places.(p.124)
• As soon as his sobriety begins to be taken as a ***matter*** of course, the family may look at their strange new dad with apprehension, then with irritation.(p.128)
• She sees she was wrong to make a burning issue out of such a ***matter*** when his more serious ailments were being rapidly cured.(p.135)
• He has just returned from a three-months leave of absence, has taken a cure, looks fine, and to clinch the ***matter,*** the board of directors told him this was his last chance."(p.138)
• But these scrapes can generally be charged, no ***matter*** how bad, to the abnormal action of alcohol on his mind.(p.140)
• He wants to quit drinking and you want to help him, even if it be only a ***matter*** of good business.(p.141)
• Whether you mention this book is a ***matter*** for your discretion.(p.142)
• The ***matter*** of physical treatment should, of course, be referred to your own doctor.(p.143)
• While on the subject of confidence, can you adopt the attitude that so far as you are concerned this will be a strictly personal ***matter,*** that his alcoholic derelictions, the treatment about to be undertaken, will never be discussed without his consent?(p.143)
• To return to the subject ***matter*** of this book: It contains full suggestions by which the employee may solve his problem.(p.143)
• Being wrecked in the same vessel, being restored and united under one God, with hearts and minds attuned to the welfare of others, the things which ***matter*** so much to some people no longer signify much to them.(p.161)
• To duplicate, with such backing, what we have accomplished is only a ***matter*** of willingness, patience and labor.(p.163)
• I gave the ***matter*** much time and study for the next two and a half years, but still got tight every night nevertheless.(p.178)
• It hadn't worked out that way and I didn't know what the ***matter*** was and did not know what to do.(p.184)
• As a ***matter*** of fact, I had two children at the time I was admitted to the bar.(p.212)
• Professionally, after I was sober for a month or so I realized that I should school myself to dissolve the partnership I was in because I felt that I would never regain the respect of my partners no ***matter*** how long I was sober, and that I would be at a disadvantage.(p.220)
• I realized that there wasn't anything I could say to place myself in a more favorable light with my children, that it was going to be a ***matter*** of time; for I also understood the intolerance of young people towards deficiencies in their elders.(p.220)
• I thought, "No ***matter*** how crazy they are I'll do anything they say to do."(p.267)
• Well, suicide was a last straw ***matter,*** and I had not drawn the last straw yet.(p.278)
• Here was a tall, rugged, highly educated Yankee talking in a ***matter*** of course way about God and prayer.(p.279)
• No ***matter*** how often I had gone into and come out of alcoholic lows during the day, the pattern bounced me out of bed each night about 2:00 a.m., shaking and hurting in the agitation that always follows a drug's sedation.(p.332)
• I just wanted to live to a certain age, carry through with what I felt was my job with the children, and after that -- no ***matter.***(p.337)
• I went to Clark, the community butcher, and I said, "Clark, what is the ***matter*** with me?(p.348)
• As a ***matter*** of fact, when I came into Alcoholics Anonymous I was close to being at the peak of my career.(p.356)
• With ten years of A.A. behind me, I was able to tell him that I'd have been alcoholic, no ***matter*** what; that I had been a sick person, unfit for marriage.(p.403)
• I began, here and now, to fear the answer to the question -- what is the ***matter*** with me?(p.406)
• I don't know how I got here this trip, but it doesn't ***matter*** very much.(p.423)
• It helped me a great deal to become convinced that alcoholism was a disease, not a moral issue; that I had been drinking as a result of a compulsion, even though I had not been aware of the compulsion at the time; and that sobriety was not a ***matter*** of willpower.(p.448)
• Then he asks me if I am willing to right all the wrongs I have ever done to anyone, no ***matter*** how wrong I thought the others were.(p.503)
• What is the ***matter?***(p.506)
• There was the father one lost respect for at the age of eleven, because the father broke his solemn word in a circumstance where you, eleven years old, had assumed guilt when you were innocent; but the father would not believe you, no ***matter*** what; and to ease his suffering you "confessed" and were "forgiven," only -- months later -- to have your "guilt" brought up -- only he and you knew what he was talking bout -- brought up in front of the stern grandmother.(p.533)
• There was the sense of being "misunderstood," when as a ***matter*** of fact by my middle twenties I was quite popular, although I hadn't grown much bigger physically.(p.534)
• In A.A. we can begin again no ***matter*** how late it may be.(p.543)
• If there is none nearby, you will be invited to carry on a correspondence which will do much to insure your sobriety no ***matter*** how isolated you are.(p.575)

mattered
• He turned me in to the company commander, but I got off the hook, and that was all that ***mattered.***(p.317)

matters
• I was to right all such ***matters*** to the utmost of my ability.(p.13)
• Of necessity there will have to be discussion of ***matters*** medical, psychiatric, social, and religious.(p.19)
• We are aware that these ***matters*** are, from their very nature, controversial.(p.19)
• As ***matters*** grow worse, he begins to use a combination of high-powered sedative and liquor to quiet his nerves so he can go to work.(p.22)
• What has become of the common sense and will power that he still sometimes displays with respect to other ***matters?***(p.22)
• There is no friction among us over such ***matters.***(p.28)
• But his face falls when we speak of spiritual ***matters,*** especially when we mention God, for we have reopened a subject which our man thought he had neatly evaded or entirely ignored.(p.45)
• Faced with alcoholic destruction, we soon became as open minded on spiritual ***matters*** as we tried to be on other questions.(p.48)
• Experience has taught us that these are ***matters*** about which, for our purpose, we need not be worried.(p.50)
• But the more we fought and tried to have our own way, the worse ***matters*** got.(p.66)
• We admitted our wrongs honestly and were willing to set these ***matters*** straight.(p.67)
• We should not talk incessantly to them about spiritual ***matters.***(p.83)
• But urge them not to be over-anxious, for that might spoil ***matters.***(p.91)
• Members of a family should watch such ***matters*** carefully, for one careless, inconsiderate remark has been known to raise the very devil.(p.125)
• There is talk about spiritual ***matters*** morning, noon and night.(p.128)
• Being possessed of a spiritual experience, the alcoholic will find he has much in common with these people, though he may differ with them on many ***matters.***(p.131)

• So, for one reason or another, they cover these men, hoping ***matters*** will take a turn for the better.(p.147)
• ***Matters*** got worse all the time until finally they got so bad that I was reinvestigated by the Government.(p.490)
• Four – Each group should be autonomous except in ***matters*** affecting other groups or A.A. as a whole.(p.564)
• Concerning such ***matters*** they can express no views whatever.(p.567)

mattress
• Somehow I managed to drag my ***mattress*** to a lower floor, lest I suddenly leap.(p.6)
• A drunk may smash the furniture in your home, or burn a ***mattress***.(p.97)
• I remembered filling the peroxide bottle in my medicine chest with gin, in case my sister found the bottle I hid under the ***mattress***.(p.224)
• But I hardly tasted anything for two years and started in business for myself, founding a ***mattress*** factory which is today an important industrial enterprise in our city.(p.232)

mature
• It made me feel quite grown-up and ***mature***, and I think another added attraction was the fact that so far as my family was concerned, it was forbidden, and it had a special attraction for that reason.(p.464)

maturity
• To be sure, this had been a dizzy and confused interval, but most everyone else I knew had emerged from it with both feet on the ground and a fair amount of adult ***maturity***.(p.304)
• After all, I hadn't started to drink early in life, so I had some stability and ***maturity*** to guide me for a while.(p.379)
• A "good boy" reached adulthood and success without achieving ***maturity*** or fulfillment.(p.418)
• I wish I knew a short cut to ***maturity***.(p.535)
• Apparently I'd grown physically at the customary rate of speed, and I had acquired an average amount of intellectual training in the intervening years, but there had been no emotional ***maturity*** at all.(p.547)

Maud
• Both he and old ***Maud*** are glad to get home.(p.497)

maudlin
• We have been driven to ***maudlin*** sympathy, to bitter resentment.(p.104)
• It was no momentary emotionalism born of self-pity in a ***maudlin*** condition.(p.258)

Max
• Another time, I had gone around to ***Max*** R. trying to get a job driving one of his trucks.(p.200)
• At the end of about four months, I not only had good looking clothes –and I might say that at the time I first talked to ***Max*** I didn't have a suit of clothes I could bend over in real sudden; now I had six suits of clothes.(p.200)
• ***Max*** and I had been married for twenty-eight years when I ended up in A.A.(p.439)
• ***Max*** hadn't gotten that way because I didn't care.(p.440)
• I yelled at ***Max***, "What do you mean, 'The dog just needs more love'?(p.440)
• The harder I worked with ***Max***, the sicker she got.(p.440)
• That's when that steel door slammed shut, and ***Max*** was the one who went home.(p.444)
• ***Max*** accepted responsibility for me after I had promised never to drink again, never to take another pill, never to swear again, and never to talk to girls again.(p.444)
• ***Max*** won; I didn't drink it.(p.444)
• And that was how ***Max*** and I and our two daughters spent Christmas Day, eight years ago.(p.444)
• The next day, ***Max*** called the neurologist and told him about the Mayo psychiatrist's opinion.(p.445)
• The people there insisted on putting me in a ward, when ***Max*** and I both knew I ought to have a private room.(p.445)
• Much of my time was spent writing letters, notes, orders, and lists of things for ***Max***, who was also my office nurse, to do to keep the world running while I was locked up.(p.445)
• ***Max*** still works with me in the office, but we have turned our wills and our lives and our work over to the care of God.(p.446)
• Eventually, the psychiatrist discharged me from the hospital, and ***Max*** and I began going to meetings ourselves.(p.447)
• Right from the start, I felt that they weren't doing anything for me, but they sure were helping ***Max***.(p.447)
• ***Max*** and I have been married now for thirty-five years.(p.450)
• Over the years, as I thought about ***Max***, her good qualities grew and grew, and we married, and all these qualities became more and more apparent to me, and we were happier and happier.(p.450)
• Today, ***Max*** and I try to communicate what we feel, rather than what we think.(p.451)
• It hasn't been easy to work out this relationship with ***Max***.(p.451)
• On the contrary, the hardest place to work this program has been in my own home, with my own children and, finally, with ***Max***.(p.451)
• Eventually, I had to redo each of the Twelve Steps specifically with ***Max*** in mind, from the First, saying, "I am powerless over alcohol, and my homelife is unmanageable by me," to the Twelfth, in which I tried to think of her as a sick Al-Anon and treat her with the love I would give a sick A.A. newcomer.(p.452)
• The higher my expectations of ***Max*** and other people are, the lower is my serenity.(p.452)

Max's
• And I continued to drink, on and off then, until every dollar I had in the world was gone again and I was right back living at my sister's, getting my cigarettes by calling her grocer and telling him to put in a couple of cartons with her order, exactly as I had before I started to work at ***Max's***.(p.202)

maximum
• Of course an alcoholic ought to be freed from his physical craving for liquor, and this often requires a definite hospital procedure, before psychological measures can be of ***maximum*** benefit.(p.xxv)
• Our real purpose is to fit ourselves to be of ***maximum*** service to God and the people about us.(p.77)
• Your job now is to be at the place where you may be of ***maximum*** helpfulness to others, so never hesitate to go anywhere if you can be helpful.(p.102)
• For that crime I received a minimum of twenty years and a ***maximum*** of natural life.(p.508)
• I received an additional fifteen years for that, making a minimum of thirty-five years and a ***maximum*** of natural life.(p.509)

maximum-security
• I served time in four penitentiaries and several prison camps, including a ***maximum-security*** camp.(p.457)

may
• If you have a drinking problem, we hope that you ***may*** pause in reading one of the forty-four personal stories and think: "Yes, that happened to me"; or, more important, "Yes, I've felt like that"; or most important, "Yes, I believe this program can work for me, too."(p.xii)
• It is important that we remain anonymous because we are too few, at present to handle the overwhelming number of personal appeals which ***may*** result from this publication.(p.xiii)
• Yet it is our great hope that all those who have as yet found no answer ***may*** begin to find one in the pages of this book and will presently join us on the highroad to a new freedom.(p.xxi)
• The Twelve Steps that summarize the program ***may*** be called los Doce Pasos in one country, los Douze Etapes in another, but they trace exactly the same path to recovery that was blazed by the earliest members of Alcoholics Anonymous.(p.xxii)
• To whom it ***may*** concern:(p.xxiii)
• These facts appear to be of extreme medical importance; because of the extraordinary possibilities of rapid growth inherent in this group they ***may*** mark a new epoch in the annals of alcoholism.(p.xxiii)
• These men ***may*** well have a remedy for thousands of such situations.(p.xxiv)
• You ***may*** rely absolutely on anything they say about themselves.(p.xxiv)
• As laymen, our opinion as to its soundness ***may***, of course, mean little.(p.xxiv)
• On the other hand -- and strange as this ***may*** seem to those who do not understand -- once a psychic change has occurred, the very same person who seemed doomed, who had so many problems he despaired of ever solving them, suddenly finds himself easily able to control his desire for alcohol, the only effort necessary being that required to follow a few simple rules.(p.xxvii)
• This phenomenon, as we have suggested, ***may*** be the manifestation of an allergy which differentiates these people, and sets them apart as a distinct entity.(p.xxviii)
• I earnestly advise every alcoholic to read this book through, and though perhaps he came to scoff, he ***may*** remain to pray.(p.xxx)
• We meet frequently so that newcomers ***may*** find the fellowship they seek.(p.15)
• At these informal gatherings one ***may*** often see from 50 to 200 persons.(p.16)
• We hope this volume will inform and comfort those who are, or who ***may*** be affected.(p.18)
• Our very lives, as ex-problem drinkers, depend upon our constant thought of others and how we ***may*** help meet their needs.(p.20)
• You ***may*** already have asked yourself why it is that all of us became so very ill from drinking.(p.20)
• If your are an alcoholic who wants to get over it, you ***may*** already be asking -- "What do I have to do?"(p.20)
• Before going into a detailed discussion, it ***may*** be well to summarize some points as we see them.(p.20)
• He ***may*** have the habit badly enough to gradually impair him physically and mentally.(p.20)
• It ***may*** cause him to die a few years before his time.(p.21)
• If a sufficiently strong reason – ill health, falling in love, change of environment, or the warning of a doctor – becomes operative, this man can also stop or moderate, although he ***may*** find it difficult and troublesome and ***may*** even need medical attention.(p.21)
• He ***may*** start off as a moderate drinker; he ***may*** or ***may*** not become a continuous hard drinker; but at some stage of his drinking career he begins to lose all control of his liquor consumption, once he starts to drink.(p.21)
• He ***may*** be one of the finest fellows in the world.(p.21)
• If he can afford it, he ***may*** have liquor concealed all over his house to be certain no one gets his entire supply away from him to throw down the waterpipe.(p.22)
• We know that while the alcoholic keeps away from drink, as he ***may*** do for months or years, he reacts much like other men.(p.22)
• Once in a while he ***may*** tell the truth.(p.23)
• The tragic truth is that if the man be a real alcoholic, the happy day ***may*** not arrive.(p.23)
• The alcoholic ***may*** say to himself in the most casual way, "It won't burn me this time, so here's how!"(p.24)
• When this sort of thinking is fully established in an individual with alcoholic tendencies, he has probably placed himself beyond human aid, and unless locked up, ***may*** die or go permanently insane.(p.24)
• He can go anywhere on this earth where other free men ***may*** go without disaster, provided he remains willing to maintain a certain simple attitude.(p.26)
• Some of our alcoholic readers ***may*** think they can do without spiritual help.(p.27)
• If what we have learned and felt and seen means anything at all, it means that all of us, whatever our race, creed, or color are the children of a living Creator with whom we ***may*** form a relationship upon simple and understandable terms as soon as we are willing and honest enough to try.(p.28)
• The delusion that we are like other people, or presently ***may*** be, has to be smashed.(p.30)
• Science ***may*** one day accomplish this, but it hasn't done so yet.(p.31)
• It ***may*** be worth a bad case of jitters if you get a full knowledge of your condition.(p.32)
• Young people ***may*** be encouraged by this man's experience to think that they can stop, as he did, on their own will power.(p.33)
• Though you ***may*** be able to stop for a considerable period, you ***may*** yet be a potential alcoholic.(p.34)
• Whatever the precise definition of the word ***may*** be, we call this plain insanity.(p.37)
• You ***may*** think this an extreme case.(p.37)
• You ***may*** think our illustration is too ridiculous.(p.38)
• However intelligent we ***may*** have been in other respects, where alcohol has been involved, we have been strangely insane.(p.38)
• That ***may*** be true of certain nonalcoholic people who, though drinking foolishly and heavily at the present time, are able to stop or moderate, because their brains and bodies have not been damaged as ours were.(p.39)
• If that be the case, you ***may*** be suffering from an illness which only a spiritual experience will conquer.(p.44)
• Do not let any prejudice you ***may*** have against spiritual terms deter you from honestly asking yourself what they mean to you.(p.47)
• The reader ***may*** still ask why he should believe in a Power greater than himself.(p.48)
• We have learned that whatever the human frailties of various faiths ***may*** be, those faiths have given purpose and direction to millions.(p.49)
• It ***may*** be obscured by calamity, by pomp, by worship of [illegible]ngs, but in some form or

other it is there.(p.55)
• In the last analysis it is only there that He ***may*** be found.(p.55)
• ***May*** you find Him now!(p.59)
• In trying to make these arrangements our actor ***may*** sometimes be quite virtuous.(p.61)
• He ***may*** be kind, considerate, patient, generous; even modest and self-sacrificing.(p.61)
• On the other hand, he ***may*** be mean, egotistical, selfish and dishonest.(p.61)
• He becomes, on the next occasion, still more demanding or gracious, as the case ***may*** be.(p.61)
• Admitting he ***may*** be somewhat at fault, he is sure that other people are more to blame.(p.61)
• Relieve me of the bondage of self, that I ***may*** better do Thy will.(p.63)
• Take away my difficulties, that victory over them ***may*** bear witness to those I would help of Thy Power, Thy Love, and Thy Way of life.(p.63)
• ***May*** I do Thy will always!"(p.63)
• Brown ***may*** get my job at the office.(p.65)
• They ***may*** be the dubious luxury of normal men, but for alcoholics these things are poison.(p.66)
• The best reason first: If we skip this vital step, we ***may*** not overcome drinking.(p.72)
• Though we have no religious connection, we ***may*** still do well to talk with someone ordained by an established religion.(p.74)
• It ***may*** be one of our own family, but we cannot disclose anything to our wives or our parents which will hurt them and make them unhappy.(p.74)
• Notwithstanding the great necessity for discussing ourselves with someone, it ***may*** be one is so situated that there is no suitable person available.(p.74)
• If that is so, this step ***may*** be postponed, only however, if we hold ourselves in complete readiness to go through with it at the first opportunity.(p.74)
• We ***may*** have had certain spiritual beliefs, but now we begin to have a spiritual experience.(p.75)
• As we look over the list of business acquaintances and friends we have hurt, we ***may*** feel diffident about going to some of them on a spiritual basis.(p.76)
• We ***may*** kill a future opportunity to carry a beneficial message.(p.77)
• It ***may*** be he has done us more harm than we have done him and, though we ***may*** have acquired a better attitude toward him, we are still not too keen about admitting our faults.(p.77)
• Nor are we afraid of disclosing our alcoholism on the theory it ***may*** cause financial harm.(p.78)
• We ***may*** be short in our accounts and unable to make good.(p.78)
• Reminding ourselves that we have decided to go to any length to find a spiritual experience we ask that we be given strength and direction to do the right thing, no matter what the personal consequences ***may*** be.(p.79)
• We ***may*** lose our position or reputation or face jail, but we are willing.(p.79)
• In fairness we must say that she ***may*** understand, but what are we going to do about a thing like that?(p.81)
• She ***may*** insist on knowing all the particulars.(p.81)
• Though there ***may*** be justifiable exceptions, and though we wish to lay down no rule of any sort, we have often found this the best course to take.(p.81)
• It ***may*** be that both will decide that the way of good sense and loving kindness is to let by-gones be bygones.(p.82)
• Good generalship ***may*** decide that the problem be attacked on the flank rather than risk a face-to-face combat.(p.82)
• Their defects ***may*** be glaring, but the chances are that our own actions are partly responsible.(p.83)
• There ***may*** be some wrongs we can never fully right.(p.83)
• And there ***may*** be a valid reason for postponement in some cases.(p.83)
• In thinking about our day we ***may*** face indecision.(p.86)
• We ***may*** not be able to determine which course to take.(p.86)
• We ***may*** ask for ourselves, however, if others will be helped.(p.87)
• Suggestions about these ***may*** be obtained from one's priest, minister, or rabbi.(p.87)
• You ***may*** spoil a later opportunity.(p.90)
• The family ***may*** object to this, but unless he is in a dangerous physical condition, it is better to risk it.(p.90)
• He ***may*** be more receptive when depressed.(p.91)
• But insist that if he is severely afflicted, there ***may*** be little chance he can recover by himself.(p.92)
• But you ***may*** talk to him about the hopelessness of alcoholism because you offer a solution.(p.92)
• Even though your protege ***may*** not have entirely admitted his condition, he has become very curious to know how you got well.(p.92)
• There is no use arousing any prejudice he ***may*** have against certain theological terms and conceptions about which he ***may*** already be confused.(p.93)
• Your prospect ***may*** belong to a religious denomination.(p.93)
• His religious education and training ***may*** be far superior to yours.(p.93)
• He ***may*** be an example of the truth that faith alone is insufficient.(p.93)
• Actually, he ***may*** be helping you more than you are helping him.(p.94)
• Your candidate ***may*** give reasons why he need not follow all of the program.(p.94)
• He ***may*** rebel at the thought of a drastic housecleaning which requires discussion with other people.(p.94)
• Sometimes a new man is anxious to proceed at once, and you ***may*** be tempted to let him do so.(p.95)
• If he is not interested in your solution, if he expects you to act only as a banker for his financial difficulties or a nurse for his sprees, you ***may*** have to drop him until he changes his mind.(p.95)
• This he ***may*** do after he gets hurt some more.(p.95)
• If you leave such a person alone, he ***may*** soon become convinced that he cannot recover by himself.(p.96)
• He ***may*** be broke and homeless.(p.96)
• You ***may*** be aiding in his destruction rather than his recovery.(p.97)
• It ***may*** mean the loss of many nights' sleep, great interference with your pleasures, interruptions to your business.(p.97)
• It ***may*** mean sharing your money and your home, counseling frantic wives and relatives, innumerable trips to police courts, sanitariums, hospitals, jails and asylums.(p.97)
• Your telephone ***may*** jangle at any time of the day or night.(p.97)
• Your wife ***may*** sometimes say she is neglected.(p.97)
• A drunk ***may*** smash the furniture in your home, or burn a mattress.(p.97)
• You ***may*** have to fight with him if he is violent.(p.97)
• Another time you ***may*** have to send for the police or an ambulance.(p.97)
• This ***may*** seem inconsistent, but we think it is not.(p.98)
• Now, the domestic problem: There ***may*** be divorce, separation, or just strained relations.(p.98)
• Little by little the family ***may*** see their own defects and admit them.(p.99)
• You ***may*** spoil your chance of being helpful if you do.(p.100)
• If the alcoholic tries to shield himself he ***may*** succeed for a time, but he usually winds up with a bigger explosion than ever.(p.101)
• To a person who has had experience with an alcoholic, this ***may*** seem like tempting Providence, but it isn't.(p.101)
• Your job now is to be at the place where you ***may*** be of maximum helpfulness to others, so never hesitate to go anywhere if you can be helpful.(p.102)
• In the midst of such pandemonium they ***may*** have rushed out threatening to live with the other woman forever.(p.106)
• An alcoholic of this temperament ***may*** be quick to use this chapter as a club over your head.(p.108)
• If you are positive he is one of this type you ***may*** feel you had better leave.(p.108)
• One: Your husband ***may*** be only a heavy drinker.(p.108)
• His drinking ***may*** be constant or it ***may*** be heavy only on certain occasions.(p.109)
• It ***may*** be slowing him up mentally and physically, but he does not see it.(p.109)
• His business ***may*** suffer somewhat.(p.109)
• He ***may*** have come to the point where he desperately wants to stop but cannot.(p.110)
• Four: You ***may*** have a husband of whom you completely despair.(p.110)
• Doctors ***may*** shake their heads and advise you to have him committed.(p.110)
• This picture ***may*** not be as dark as it looks.(p.110)
• If he gets the idea that you are a nag or a killjoy, your chance of accomplishing anything useful ***may*** be zero.(p.111)
• This ***may*** lead to lonely evenings for you.(p.111)
• He ***may*** seek someone else to console him -- not always another man.(p.111)
• You ***may*** be unable to do so, no matter how hard you try.(p.111)
• Your husband ***may*** come to appreciate your reasonableness and patience.(p.111)
• This ***may*** lay the groundwork for a friendly talk about his alcoholic problem.(p.111)
• Thus you ***may*** succeed in interesting him in alcoholism.(p.112)
• Your husband ***may*** be willing to talk to one of them.(p.112)
• If this kind of approach does not catch your husband's interest, it ***may*** be best to drop the subject, but after a friendly talk your husband will usually revive the topic himself.(p.112)
• This ***may*** take patient waiting, but it will be worth it.(p.112)
• If you act upon these principles, your husband ***may*** stop or moderate.(p.112)
• But don't remind him of this after he has been drinking, for he ***may*** be angry.(p.113)
• Wait until repeated stumbling convinces him he must act, for the more you hurry him the longer his recovery ***may*** be delayed.(p.113)
• If you have a number three husband, you ***may*** be in luck.(p.113)
• He ***may*** not share your enthusiasm, but he is practically sure to read the book and he ***may*** go for the program at once.(p.113)
• In some cases it ***may*** be better to let someone outside of the family present the book.(p.113)
• His reaction ***may*** be one of enthusiasm.(p.114)
• You ***may*** have the reverse situation on your hands.(p.114)
• He ***may*** be anything but that.(p.115)
• You ***may*** be afraid your husband will lose his position; you are thinking of the disgrace and hard times which will befall you and the children.(p.116)
• This experience ***may*** come to you.(p.116)
• Or you ***may*** already have had it several times.(p.116)
• It ***may*** convince your husband he wants to stop drinking forever.(p.116)
• Starting from a speck on the domestic horizon, great thunderclouds of dispute ***may*** gather.(p.117)
• Still another difficulty is that you ***may*** become jealous of the attention he bestows on other people, especially alcoholics.(p.119)
• You ***may*** not like some of them.(p.119)
• The slightest sign of fear or intolerance ***may*** lessen your husband's chance of recovery.(p.120)
• In a weak moment he ***may*** take your dislike of his high-stepping friends as one of those insanely trivial excuses to drink.(p.120)
• We ***may*** have seemed to lecture.(p.121)
• So to you out there -- who ***may*** soon be with us -- we say "Good luck and God bless you!"(p.121)
• The foregoing pages (though addressed only to wives) indicate the problems such people ***may*** face.(p.121)
• If there is no Al-Anon listing in your local telephone book, you ***may*** obtain further information on Al-Anon Family Groups by writing to its World Service Office: Box 182, Madison Square Station, New York, NY 10159.(p.121)
• Our women folk have suggested certain attitudes a wife ***may*** take with the husband who is recovering.(p.122)
• Each in his turn ***may*** be footsore and ***may*** straggle.(p.122)
• There will be alluring shortcuts and by-paths down which they ***may*** wander and lose their way.(p.123)
• Suppose we tell you some of the obstacles a family will meet; suppose we suggest how they ***may*** be avoided – even converted to good use for others.(p.123)
• Today's life is measured against that of other years and, when it falls short, the family ***may*** be unhappy.(p.123)
• Father knows he is to blame; it ***may*** take him many seasons of hard work to be restored financially, but he shouldn't be reproached.(p.123)
• The family ***may*** be possessed by the idea that future happiness can be based only upon forgetfulness of the past.(p.123)
• This painful past ***may*** be of infinite value to other families still struggling with their problem.(p.124)
• A man ***may*** criticize or laugh at himself and it will affect others favorably, but criticism or ridicule coming from another often produces the contrary effect.(p.125)
• He ***may*** either plunge into a frantic attempt to get on his feet in business, or he ***may*** be so enthralled by his new life that he talks or thinks of little else.(p.125)
• Dad ***may*** be tired at night and preoccupied

by day.(p.126)
• He ***may*** take small interest in the children and ***may*** show irritation when reproved for his delinquencies.(p.126)
• If not irritable, he ***may*** seem dull and boring, not gay and affectionate as the family would like him to be.(p.126)
• Mother ***may*** complain of inattention.(p.126)
• Both father and the family are mistaken, though each side ***may*** have some justification.(p.126)
• Let them remember that his drinking wrought all kinds of damage that ***may*** take long to repair.(p.127)
• As soon as his sobriety begins to be taken as a matter of course, the family ***may*** look at their strange new dad with apprehension, then with irritation.(p.128)
• He ***may*** demand that the family find God in a hurry, or exhibit amazing indifference to them and say he is above worldly considerations.(p.128)
• He ***may*** tell mother, who has been religious all her life, that she doesn't know what it's all about, and that she had better get his brand of spirituality while there is yet time.(p.128)
• When father takes this tack, the family ***may*** react unfavorably.(p.128)
• They ***may*** be jealous of a God who has stolen dad's affections.(p.128)
• While grateful that he drinks no more, they ***may*** not like the idea that God has accomplished the miracle where they failed.(p.128)
• They ***may*** not see why their love and devotion did not straighten him out.(p.128)
• For a time he ***may*** try to hug the new treasure to himself.(p.129)
• He ***may*** not see at once that he has barely scratched a limitless lode which will pay dividends only if he mines it for the rest of his life and insists on giving away the entire product.(p.129)
• He will perceive that his spiritual growth is lopsided, that for an average man like himself, a spiritual life which does not include his family obligations ***may*** not be so perfect after all.(p.129)
• The opposite ***may*** happen should the family condemn and criticize.(p.129)
• Dad ***may*** feel that for years his drinking has placed him on the wrong side of every argument, but now he has become a superior person with God on his side.(p.129)
• If the family persists in criticism, this fallacy ***may*** take a still greater hold on father.(p.129)
• Instead of treating the family as he should, he ***may*** retreat further into himself and feel he has spiritual justification for so doing.(p.129)
• One more suggestion: Whether the family has spiritual convictions or not, they ***may*** do well to examine the principles by which the alcoholic member is trying to live.(p.130)
• Father ***may*** have laid aside for years all normal activities – clubs, civic duties, sports.(p.131)
• When he renews interest in such things, a feeling of jealousy ***may*** arise.(p.131)
• The family ***may*** feel they hold a mortgage on dad, so big that no equity should be left for outsiders.(p.131)
• Though the family has no religious connections, they ***may*** wish to make contact with or take membership in a religious body.(p.131)
• Being possessed of a spiritual experience, the alcoholic will find he has much in common with these people, though he ***may*** differ with them on many matters.(p.131)
• He ***may*** bring new hope and new courage to many a priest, minister, or rabbi, who gives his all to minister to our troubled world.(p.132)
• Most of them give freely of themselves, that their fellows ***may*** enjoy sound minds and bodies.(p.133)
• Unless the reason is understood, there ***may*** be an emotional upset.(p.134)
• The alcoholic ***may*** find it hard to re-establish friendly relations with his children.(p.134)
• Without saying so, they ***may*** cordially hate him for what he has done to them and to their mother.(p.134)
• This ***may*** hang on for months, long after their mother has accepted dad's new way of living and thinking.(p.134)
• Whether you are a hard drinker, a moderated drinker or a teetotaler, you ***may*** have some pretty strong opinions, perhaps prejudices.(p.139)
• Those who drink moderately ***may*** be more annoyed with an alcoholic than a total abstainer would be.(p.139)
• When dealing with an alcoholic, there ***may*** be a natural annoyance that a man could be so weak, stupid and irresponsible.(p.139)
• Even when you understand the malady better, you ***may*** feel this feeling rising.(p.139)
• If your decision is yes, whether the reason be humanitarian or business or both, then the following suggestions ***may*** be helpful.(p.140)
• They ***may*** be disgusting.(p.140)
• You ***may*** be at a loss to understand how such a seemingly above-board chap could be so involved.(p.140)
• Of course that isn't so, and such people often ***may*** impose on you.(p.141)
• If you are sure your man does not want to stop, he ***may*** as well be discharged, the sooner the better.(p.141)
• Firing such an individual ***may*** prove a blessing to him.(p.141)
• It ***may*** be just the jolt he needs.(p.141)
• This ***may*** seem severe, but it is usually the best course.(p.142)
• After satisfying yourself that your man wants to recover and that he will go to any extreme to do so, you ***may*** suggest a definite course of action.(p.142)
• If you propose such a procedure to him, it ***may*** be necessary to advance the cost of treatment, but we believe it should be made plain that any expense will later be deducted from his pay.(p.143)
• To return to the subject matter of this book: It contains full suggestions by which the employee ***may*** solve his problem.(p.143)
• If the book is read the moment the patient is able, while acutely depressed, realization of his condition ***may*** come to him.(p.144)
• In some cases it will, and in others it ***may*** not.(p.144)
• As our work spreads and our numbers increase, we hope your employees ***may*** be put in personal contact with some of us.(p.144)
• He ***may***, for example, reveal that he has padded his expense account or that he has planned to take your best customers away from you.(p.145)
• In fact, he ***may*** say almost anything if he has accepted our solution which, as you know, demands rigorous honesty.(p.145)
• If he owes you money you ***may*** wish to make terms.(p.145)
• Being somewhat weakened, and faced with physical and mental readjustment to a life which knows no alcohol, he ***may*** overdo.(p.146)
• You ***may*** have to curb his desire to work sixteen hours a day.(p.146)
• You ***may*** need to encourage him to play once in a while.(p.146)
• He ***may*** wish to do a lot for other alcoholics and something of the sort ***may*** come up during business hours.(p.146)
• After your man has gone along without drinking for a few months, you ***may*** be able to make use of his services with other employees who are giving you the alcoholic run-around – provided, of course, they are willing to have a third party in the picture.(p.146)
• Your man ***may*** be trusted.(p.146)
• If he is conscientiously following the program of recovery he can go anywhere your business ***may*** call him.(p.147)
• If, on the contrary, you are sure he is doing his utmost, you ***may*** wish to give him another chance.(p.147)
• Your junior executive ***may*** not agree with the contents of our book.(p.148)
• Alcoholism ***may*** be causing your organization considerable damage in its waste of time, men and reputation.(p.148)
• That company ***may*** harbor many actual or potential alcoholics.(p.149)
• You ***may*** make some interesting discoveries.(p.149)
• Then you will know what it means to give of yourself that others ***may*** survive and rediscover life.(p.153)
• It ***may*** seem incredible that these men are to become happy, respected, and useful once more.(p.153)
• They will approach still other sick ones and fellowships of Alcoholics Anonymous ***may*** spring up in each city and hamlet, havens for those who must find a way out.(p.153)
• Then, in this eastern city, there are informal meetings such as we have described to you, where you ***may*** now see scores of members.(p.162)
• Some of them ***may*** sink and perhaps never get up, but if our experience is a criterion, more than half of those approached will become fellows of Alcoholics Anonymous.(p.163)
• Still you ***may*** say: "But I will not have the benefit of contact with you who write this book."(p.164)
• ***May*** God bless you and keep you -- until then.(p.164)
• Seventeen stories ***may*** help you decide whether you are alcoholic; also, whether A.A. is for you.(p.167)
• Those who believe their drinking to be hopeless ***may*** again find hope in these thirteen impressive tales.(p.167)
• It has been that way with some, but it has not been with me and ***may*** never be.(p.259)
• These last eighteen years have been the happiest of my life, trite though that statement ***may*** seem.(p.295)
• Others ***may*** idle in a retrogressive groove without too much danger, but retrogression can spell death for us.(p.311)
• He ***may*** even read in a newspaper that one out of every seven drinkers will become alcoholic, but he rarely is told that it holds true for all ages – or that the tolerance to alcohol (and other drugs) decreases steadily, year after year, in the bodies of all persons.(p.330)
• In two ways I ***may*** be a little different from other alcoholics.(p.345)
• Many times have I heard the above expressions since I have been in A.A., and many times I have had to reply "Definitely I am an alcoholic, and while it ***may*** be hard for you to believe, it is not hard for me, for I have learned many things about alcohol and myself that would, perhaps, be difficult for you to understand."(p.356)
• These words ***may*** be difficult for you to understand now, but be patient and you'll know what I mean.(p.367)
• There ***may*** be many reasons which bring one to A.A. for the first time, but the lasting one must be to want sobriety and the A.A. way of living for oneself.(p.379)
• I think He's on hand to see all of us through whatever ***may*** come to us.(p.437)
• Today, I find I can't work my A.A. program while taking pills, nor ***may*** I even have them around for dire emergencies only.(p.443)
• It is true that I – of all people, strange as it ***may*** seem, and even though I didn't give my permission -- really, really am an alcoholic of sorts.(p.448)
• You ***may*** wonder why, since I was having all this trouble, and was having to seek the assistance of others, A.A. hadn't come into the picture.(p.469)
• I feel that I have been restored to health and sanity these past years not through my own efforts nor as a result of anything I ***may*** have done, but because I've come to believe -- to really believe – that alone I can do nothing.(p.473)
• He has also taught me that I must help myself first; only then ***may*** I be able to help others.(p.481)
• I like to believe that I ***may*** have helped him, too.(p.481)
• "Let your light so shine before men that they ***may*** see your good works –."(p.497)
• Final exams of my Senior year and I ***may*** somehow graduate.(p.499)
• A.A.'s Twelve Steps ***may*** confuse you when you read them over.(p.516)
• When I came home to ordinary garrison life in England, I found that I was drinking rather more than most people of ***may*** age.(p.518)
• In part, it was a feeling of intense shame at having to leave the Army during the war, but mostly it was resentment that this kind of thing should happen to me for, strange as it ***may*** seem, up to then I still thought I could control drinking.(p.521)
• I am hoping that writing this ***may*** bring some poor, mixed-up soul into the program.(p.530)
• Repeated year on end, they are horrible -- frightening and degrading, a chronicle of tragedy which ***may*** be greater because the individual undergoing the tragedy, myself, knew what was happening, and yet refused to do anything to stop it.(p.538)
• In A.A. we can begin again no matter how late it ***may*** be.(p.543)
• What is much more important to me, A.A. has taught me that through this simple program I ***may*** experience a change in this reaction pattern that will indeed allow me to "match calamity with serenity."(p.544)
• "God willing, we . . . ***may*** never again have to deal with drinking, but we have to deal with sobriety every day."(p.554)
• God willing, we members of A.A. ***may*** never again have to deal with drinking, but we have to deal with sobriety every day.(p.560)
• Two – For our group purpose there is but one ultimate authority – a loving God as He ***may*** express Himself in our group conscience.(p.564)
• Eight – Alcoholics Anonymous should remain forever nonprofessional, but our service centers ***may*** employ special workers.(p.564)
• Nine – A.A., as such, ought never be organized; but we ***may*** create service boards or committees directly

responsible to those they serve.(p.564)
• 2. – For our group purpose there is but one ultimate authority -- a loving God as He *may* express Himself in our group conscience.(p.565)
• Hence we *may* refuse none who wish to recover.(p.565)
• Any two or three alcoholics gathered together for sobriety *may* call themselves an A.A. group, provided that, as a group, they have no other affiliation.(p.565)
• 6. – Problems of money, property, and authority *may* easily divert us from our primary spiritual aim.(p.565)
• While an A.A. group *may* cooperate with anyone, such cooperation ought never go so far as affiliation or endorsement, actual or implied.(p.566)
• But we *may* employ alcoholics where they are going to perform those services for which we might otherwise have to engage nonalcoholics.(p.566)
• Such special services *may* be well recompensed.(p.566)
• The small group *may* elect its secretary, the large group its rotating committee, and the groups of a large metropolitan area their central or intergroup committee, which often employs a full-time secretary.(p.567)
• This to the end that our great blessings *may* never spoil us; that we shall forever live in thankful contemplation of Him who presides over us all.(p.568)
• Historians *may* one day recognize Alcoholics Anonymous to have been a great venture in social pioneering which forged a new instrument for social action; a new therapy based on the kinship of common suffering; one having a vast potential for the myriad other ills of mankind."(p.573)
• I suspect that if it is wisely handled – and it seems to be in wise and prudent hands – there are doors of opportunity ahead of this project that *may* surpass our capacities to imagine."(p.574)
• In large cities, groups often maintain local offices where alcoholics or their families *may* arrange for interviews or hospitalization.(p.575)

May

• It was finally decided to undertake the organization of a Cleveland group and toward the end of *May*, 1939, the first meeting was held in Cleveland in my home.(p.219)
• He gave my husband one and me one about tenthirty on the ieghth day of *May* in 1941.(p.267)

maybe

• Show any longshoreman a Sunday supplement describing a proposal to explore the moon by means of a rocket and he will say, "I bet they do it – *maybe* not so long either."(p.52)
• *Maybe* it's only a petty offense such as padding the expense account.(p.78)
• *Maybe* we are divorced, and have remarried but haven't kept up the alimony to number one.(p.79)
• *Maybe* you have disturbed him about the question of alcoholism.(p.94)
• *Maybe* he is beginning to lose his friends.(p.109)
• *Maybe* the doctor has been called in, and the weary round of sanitariums and hospitals has begun.(p.110)
• *Maybe* you have already been obliged to put him away.(p.110)
• *Maybe* it will prove a blessing!(p.116)
• "*Maybe* you're right," he said.(p.158)
• Then Dr. Bob said, "Well, Bill, *maybe* you'll feel better tomorrow.(p.189)
• "Sure I would," replied Bill, "*Maybe* it won't do any good, but I'd like to see you both, anyhow.(p.189)
• He said, "*Maybe* you need a little drink."(p.208)
• You can't lose, and *maybe* God will help you -- just *maybe*, mind you.(p.280)
• *Maybe* I could find my way out of this agonizing existence.(p.309)
• I had never even been told by a superior that *maybe* I was drinking too much.(p.327)
• If I could only stop drinking, *maybe* I wouldn't think.(p.337)
• Deep in my heart was the feeling that *maybe* I could get some help here.(p.346)
• At this time, however, she had an opportunity to go to Salt Lake City on a new project for the government, but she did promise me that if I would curtail my drinking and buckle down to hard work she would give serious consideration to my latest proposal and *maybe* join me at a later date when I got settled.(p.359)
• I had been reading a lot about psychiatry and I thought, "*Maybe* if I talk to a psychiatrist he can find out what is happening, and then I can drink like a lady."(p.387)
• He always thought that *maybe* I was safer in a building where there were other people.(p.388)
• We moved once more, to Houston; my husband thought *maybe* a change of environment would help and I'd be all right.(p.389)
• Or *maybe* I'd come home wild drunk, singing and raving about what a fine place home was and what grand parents I had since they joined A.A.(p.428)
• "I've got to stop if I want to live," I told myself, and if I don't want to break my parents' hearts and *maybe* jeopardize their own carefully built up and hard-fought-for sobriety.(p.429)
• At this point I believe I had only been intoxicated on *maybe* three or four occasions, and certainly whiskey was no problem to me.(p.487)
• That went on for *maybe* two months, and then she got after me again about drinking.(p.488)
• My brother-in-law was living with us at that time and I said to Vi, "*Maybe* the bottles are brother's.(p.488)
• *Maybe* a drink – I put on my hat and dash off in the car.(p.505)
• *Maybe* a few drinks when I get to the city will help.(p.505)
• I hope I haven't hurt anyone's feelings, but *maybe* we could all grow and change.(p.529)
• I had no money -- well, *maybe* a dime – and only the clothes I stood in.(p.540)
• *Maybe* it was time to die.(p.540)
• It was impossible for me to say at this point, "*Maybe* there is something wrong with my philosophy," and I certainly couldn't say, "*Maybe* there is something wrong with me."(p.545)
• *Maybe* I wouldn't be able to hold any job, or *maybe* (and this was my greatest fear) I wouldn't care whether I had a job or not.(p.548)

Mayo

• As a result, he couldn't figure out why I had the convulsions, and he decided to send me to the *Mayo* Clinic.(p.444)
• The *Mayo* Clinic seemed like a good place to have my diagnosis confirmed.(p.444)
• After nine days of tests at *Mayo*, I was put in the locked ward – of all places!(p.444)
• The next day, Max called the neurologist and told him about the *Mayo* psychiatrist's opinion.(p.445)

mayor

• They called the *Mayor* in so we wouldn't have to stay in there over the holiday.(p.264)

meager

• That being the case, it didn't take me long to figure out that my *meager* manufacturing facilities were entirely inadequate to the manufacture of beer for social and domestic consumption.(p.297)

meal

• I ordered a cocktail and my *meal*.(p.41)
• At this school we had Bible readings before each *meal*, and church services four times on Sunday, and I became so rebellious at this that I swore I would never join or go to any church except for weddings or funerals.(p.240)
• I never enjoyed any *meal*, but I ate my lunch at noon for two reasons; first, to help me get out of the fog of the night before and, second, to furnish some measure of nourishment.(p.299)
• Eventually, the noon *meal* was also dispensed with.(p.299)
• Each ten-day period in the dark hole, I was fed bread and water daily, with one full *meal* on the third day only.(p.459)
• There, I received several soda crackers and water daily, and before I could have my third-day *meal* (again the only *meal* in ten days), I had to drink a glass of castor oil or mineral oil, depending on the cruelty of the person who was doing the dispensing.(p.459)

meals

• I eat three good *meals* a day now, and really enjoy them.(p.303)
• We did, and spent a month boozing it up, popping pills, and smoking marijuana; taking shelter where we could, which included a veterinary hospital one night; accepting *meals* from anyone; actually begging; stealing anything we were in need of, which was about everything.(p.354)
• Drinking it with your *meals*, you didn't feel it.(p.385)

mean

• As laymen, our opinion as to its soundness may, of course, *mean* little.(p.xxiv)
• When, therefore, we speak to you of God, we *mean* your own conception of God.(p.47)
• Do not let any prejudice you may have against spiritual terms deter you from honestly asking yourself what they *mean* to you.(p.47)
• Just what do we *mean* by that, and just what do we do?(p.60)
• On the other hand, he may be *mean*, egotistical, selfish and dishonest.(p.61)
• Does this *mean* we are going to get drunk?(p.70)
• It quiets the imperious urge, when to yield would *mean* heartache.(p.70)
• This requires action on our part, which, when completed, will *mean* that we have admitted to God, to ourselves, and to another human being the exact nature of our defects.(p.72)
• It may *mean* the loss of many nights' sleep, great interference with your pleasures, interruptions to your business.(p.97)
• It may *mean* sharing your money and your home, counseling frantic wives and relatives, innumerable trips to police courts, sanitariums, hospitals, jails and asylums.(p.97)
• If he is enthusiastic your cooperation will *mean* a great deal.(p.113)
• We do not *mean* that you have to agree with your husband whenever there is an honest difference of opinion.(p.117)
• But this does not *mean* that we disregard human health measures.(p.133)
• If he says yes, does he really *mean* it, or down inside does he think he is fooling you, and that after rest and treatment he will be able to get away with a few drinks now and then?(p.142)
• If you are sure he doesn't *mean* business, there is no doubt you should discharge him.(p.147)
• Life will *mean* something at last.(p.152)
• He trembled as he went about, for this might *mean* ruin, particularly to a person in his line of business.(p.156)
• This would lessen my chances of smuggling some home that evening, which in turn would *mean* a night of futile tossing around in bed followed by a morning of unbearable jitters.(p.176)
• I believe that my once over-weening self-will has finally found its proper place, for I can say many times daily, "Thy will be done, not mine" . . . and *mean* it.(p.229)
• I had completely forgotten the January 8th when I found the fellowship, and I spent the next four days wandering around New England half drunk, by which I *mean* I couldn't get drunk and I couldn't get sober.(p.247)
• He knew too well that didn't *mean* a thing, just as I knew in my heart that it would be only a question of time -- a few days, a week, or even a month, it was inevitable – till I would be off on another bender.(p.257)
• She said, "Do you really *mean* that?"(p.266)
• I *mean* slips.(p.271)
• Out of this maelstrom just two coherent thoughts came to the surface; one, a drink would *mean* homelessness and death; two, I could no longer relieve the pressure of fear by starting home, as was once my habitual solution to this problem, because I no longer had a home.(p.279)
• I don't *mean* that in any sense as a derogatory statement about psychotherapy; it's a great tool, not too potent, but a great tool.(p.349)
• These words may be difficult for you to understand now, but be patient and you'll know what I *mean*.(p.367)
• At the time this didn't *mean* much to me.(p.376)
• A spiritual awakening soon came to *mean* trying each day to be a little more thoughtful, more considerate, a little more courteous to those with whom I came in contact.(p.381)
• Home life didn't *mean* much to me.(p.424)
• I yelled at Max, "What do you *mean*, 'The dog just needs more love'?(p.440)
• I don't *mean* that I went to bed one night a normal drinker, and awoke the next morning an alcoholic.(p.464)
• On the way I tried, and I *mean* really tried, to throw myself out of the car.(p.466)
• During these seven years a thing called the Twenty-four Hour Program –a gadget I used to think was only a snare to trap the newcomer -- has come to *mean* much to me, not only as regards my drinking but in the whole pattern of my life.(p.473)
• Up to that time, drinking didn't really *mean* anything to me at all.(p.518)
• But that didn't *mean* anything to me.(p.521)
• Even when you don't really want it for them, and your prayers are only words and you don't *mean* it, go ahead and do it anyway.(p.552)
• Do it every day for two weeks and you will find you have come to *mean* it and to want it for them, and you will realize that where you used to feel bitterness and resentment and hatred, you now feel compassionate understanding and love."(p.552)
• A.A. can, of course, *mean* just as much to uncounted

alcoholics not yet reached.(p.563)

meaning

• Could we still say the whole thing was nothing but a mass of electrons, created out of nothing, *meaning* nothing, whirling on to a destiny of nothingness?(p.54)
• Life will take on new *meaning*.(p.89)
• Seeing this, and *meaning* to be helpful, his wife commenced to admonish him about it.(p.135)
• You will learn the full *meaning* of "Love thy neighbor as thyself."(p.153)
• There is another *meaning* for the Hebrew word that in the King James version of the Bible is translated "salvation."(p.228)
• A "spiritual experience" to me meant attending meetings, seeing a group of people, all there for the purpose of helping each other; hearing the Twelve Steps and the Twelve Traditions read at a meeting, and hearing the Lord's Prayer, which in an A.A. meeting has such great *meaning* -- "Thy will be done, not mine."(p.381)
• It pays daily in more harmonious relations with my fellow men, in ever clearer insight into the true *meaning* of life, and in the answering love and gratitude wherever and whenever I have been the instrument of God's will in the lives of others.(p.394)
• I interpreted "sober" as *meaning* "drinking but not being drunk."(p.447)
• For always, over and above everything else, was the awfulness of the lack of *meaning* in life.(p.535)
• My personal definition, which I submit as applying only to myself (although everyone is welcome to it who wants it), includes every waking activity of the human being; to have a creative attitude towards things is a more exact *meaning*, to live and to deal with other human beings creatively, which to me means seeing the God in them, and respecting and worshipping this God.(p.535)
• I learned the true *meaning* of bread cast upon the waters.(p.541)
• With deep shame came the knowledge too that I had lived with no sense of social obligation nor had I known the *meaning* of moral responsibility to my fellow men.(p.549)
• A.A. has taught me that I will have peace of mind in exact proportion to the peace of mind I bring into the lives of other people, and it has taught me the true *meaning* of the admonition "happy are ye who know these things and do them."(p.551)

meaningful

• The last fifteen years of my life have been rich and *meaningful*.(p.312)
• An alcoholic cannot accept the news that he's an alcoholic unless there is a *meaningful* explanation given, and an offer of help, such as you get in A.A.(p.406)
• My friendships are *meaningful*, loving and interesting because I am sober.(p.416)

meaningless

• Most of my conversations were *meaningless* to everyone but me.(p.319)

meanness

• I seemed to react by developing a streak of varying *meanness*, which would cause me to do things to create excitement and to get attention.(p.211)

means

• This physician had repeatedly tried spiritual *means* to resolve his alcoholic dilemma but had failed.(p.xvi)
• In the course of his third treatment he acquired certain ideas concerning a possible *means* of recovery.(p.xxiii)
• Few people really are, for that *means* blind faith in the strange proposition that this universe originated in a cipher and aimlessly rushes nowhere.(p.10)
• This is by no *means* a comprehensive picture of the true alcoholic, as our behavior patterns vary.(p.22)
• If hundreds of experiences have shown him that one drink *means* another debacle with all its attendant suffering and humiliation, why is it he takes that one drink?(p.22)
• If what we have learned and felt and seen *means* anything at all, it *means* that all of us, whatever our race, creed, or color are the children of a living Creator with whom we may form a relationship upon simple and understandable terms as soon as we are willing and honest enough to try.(p.28)
• Every *means* of solving his problem which money could buy was at his disposal.(p.32)
• He tries every known *means* to get the jay-walking idea out of his head.(p.38)
• My old manner of life was by no *means* a bad one, but I would not exchange its best moments for the worst I have now.(p.43)
• To one who feels he is an atheist or agnostic such an experience seems impossible, but to continue as he is *means* disaster, especially if he is an alcoholic of the hopeless variety.(p.44)
• That *means* we have written a book which we believe to be spiritual as well as moral.(p.45)
• And it *means*, of course, that we are going to talk about God.(p.45)
• Show any longshoreman a Sunday supplement describing a proposal to explore the moon by *means* of a rocket and he will say, "I bet they do it -- maybe not so long either."(p.52)
• The verdict of the ages is that faith *means* courage.(p.68)
• He thus used his own wrong-doing as a *means* of destroying the reputation of another.(p.80)
• If he opened that old affair, he was afraid it would destroy the reputation of his partner, disgrace his family and take away his *means* of livelihood.(p.80)
• But we must go further and that *means* more action.(p.85)
• This *means* a new attitude and spirit all around.(p.99)
• If you are with a person who wants to eat in a bar, by all *means* go along.(p.102)
• He has begun to try, with or without your cooperation, various *means* of moderating or staying dry.(p.109)
• He by no *means* ruined everything.(p.109)
• If he is already committed to an institution, but can convince you and your doctor that he *means* business, give him a chance to try our method, unless the doctor thinks his mental condition too abnormal or dangerous.(p.114)
• Though it is infinitely better that he have no relapse at all, as has been true with many of our men, it is by no *means* a bad thing in some cases.(p.120)
• Successful readjustment *means* the opposite.(p.122)
• If he *means* to right his past wrongs, why all this concern for everyone in the world but his family?(p.128)
• This *means* trouble, unless the family watches for these tendencies in each other and comes to a friendly agreement about them.(p.131)
• By no *means* do we offer it as the last word on this subject, but so far as we are concerned, it has worked with us.(p.144)
• If he is, and is still trying to recover, he will tell you about it even if it *means* the loss of his job.(p.146)
• For most normal folks, drinking *means* conviviality, companionship and colorful imagination.(p.151)
• It *means* release from care, boredom and worry.(p.151)
• Then you will know what it *means* to give of yourself that others may survive and rediscover life.(p.153)
• As we shall see, he now *means* a great deal to his community, and the major liabilities of thirty years of hard drinking have been repaired in four.(p.156)
• No one is too discredited or has sunk too low to be welcomed cordially – if he *means* business.(p.161)
• Not being a man of *means*, I knew that if I did not stay sober enough to earn money, I would run out of liquor.(p.175)
• But this was a man who had experienced many years of frightful drinking, who had had most all the drunkard's experiences known to man, but who had been cured by the very *means* I had been trying to employ, that is to say the spiritual approach.(p.180)
• For me, work was only a different *means* to the same end, to be able to do exactly what I wanted to do.(p.225)
• Again I spent my bankroll, by no *means* as thick as the one I had when I first saw the skyline of Gotham.(p.252)
• Liquor had become a crutch on the one hand and a *means* of retreat from life on the other.(p.277)
• He was a man of considerable *means* and he might have done what many men would have done in such a case.(p.278)
• He it was who convinced me, because his own conviction was so real, that a Power greater than myself could help me in the crises of life, and that the *means* of communicating with this Power was simple prayer.(p.279)
• Sometimes during that year I rebelled inwardly at what seemed like lost time, and at having to be a burden to these good people whose *means* were limited.(p.281)
• I was terribly impressed by this meeting and the quality of happiness these men displayed, despite their lack of material *means*.(p.291)
• Dr. Bob then led me through the restitution step, in which I made a list of all of the persons I had harmed, and worked out ways and *means* of slowly making restitution.(p.292)
• And "Think" -- that one important word *means* so much to me.(p.325)
• But during a period of particular stress and strain about thirteen years ago, I resorted to alcohol in my home, alone, as a *means* of temporary release, as a *means* of getting a little extra sleep.(p.335)
• Above all, I am grateful to A.A. for my sobriety, which *means* so much to my family, friends and business associates, because God and A.A. were able to do for me something I was unable to do for myself.(p.383)
• My father had a title; there was plenty of *means* in the family.(p.401)
• The bartender, a tough Irishman, came around and "gave me the elbow," which *means* that he raised his elbow and smacked me in the face.(p.411)
• You see, I am a five-time loser, which *means* five felony convictions (not including the cases beaten).(p.457)
• This *means* a great deal to me, because I had always figured that nobody cared.(p.481)
• After this incident in 1940, I sought some other *means* of livelihood.(p.489)
• My personal definition, which I submit as applying only to myself (although everyone is welcome to it who wants it), includes every waking activity of the human being; to have a creative attitude towards things is a more exact meaning, to live and to deal with other human beings creatively, which to me *means* seeing the God in them, and respecting and worshipping this God.(p.535)
• Among our rapidly growing membership of thousands of alcoholics such transformations, though frequent, are by no *means* the rule.(p.569)

meant

• Before then, I had written lots of sweet promises, but my wife happily observed that this time I *meant* business.(p.5)
• It *meant* destruction of self-centeredness.(p.14)
• It *meant* I would have to throw several lifelong conceptions out of the window.(p.42)
• Why could they not see that drink *meant* ruin to them?(p.107)
• Painfully aware of being somehow abnormal, the man did not fully realize what it *meant* to be alcoholic.(p.155)
• Our book is *meant* to be suggestive only.(p.164)
• I knew somehow that it *meant* more than just going to church and living a moral life.(p.236)
• I can't express what A.A. *meant* to us during that year.(p.272)
• And, anyhow, if I went on for ten or a hundred times as long I couldn't even begin to tell you all that A.A. has *meant* to me.(p.274)
• If I could lay off it, that *meant* I didn't have to worry about a drinking problem, I thought.(p.317)
• Since I started out eager for early-day efforts, that *meant* guzzling before noon.(p.331)
• At one time, the admission that I was and am an alcoholic *meant* shame, defeat, and failure to me.(p.335)
• Surrender to me has *meant* the ability to run my home, to face my responsibilities as they should be faced, to take life as it comes to me day by day, and work my problems out.(p.340)
• That's what surrender has *meant* to me.(p.340)
• Three years and three months of sobriety, without a slip, has *meant* a lot to me, my wife, and my family.(p.342)
• It has *meant* life.(p.342)
• And deep in my heart I really *meant* what I said because I loved her more than anything else in the world, yes – even more than liquor.(p.362)
• This suggestion had been made before on a number of occasions, but like all alcoholics I wanted to handle my problem my own way, which really *meant* I didn't want anything to interfere with my drinking.(p.378)
• The Twelve Steps, which to me are a spiritual way of living, soon *meant* honest thinking, not wishful thinking, open mindedness, a willingness to try and a faith to accept.(p.381)
• They *meant* patience, tolerance and humility, and above all the belief that a Power greater than myself could help.(p.381)
• A "spiritual experience" to me *meant* attending meetings, seeing a group of people, all there for the purpose of helping each other; hearing the Twelve Steps and the Twelve Traditions read at a meeting, and hearing the Lord's Prayer, which in an A.A. meeting has such great meaning – "Thy will be done, not mine."(p.381)
• To me this *meant* telling my associates that I had joined Alcoholics Anonymous; that I didn't know what was expected of me by A.A., but that whatever it was, it was the most important thing in life for me; that sobriety *meant* more to

me than anything in this world.(p.382)
• It was the A.A. General Service Office in New York that I wrote to, and that office has always ***meant*** a lot to me.(p.392)
• I did not know what he ***meant***.(p.406)
• Then, one day in A.A., I was told that I had the lenses in my glasses backwards; "the courage to change" in the Serenity Prayer ***meant***, not that I should change my marriage, but rather that I should change myself and learn to accept my spouse as she was.(p.451)
• It ***meant*** that I had to give up a lot of the things that I had been accustomed to and that wasn't the easiest thing in the world for me.(p.487)
• So I went down to talk to the District Attorney, and the arrangement was made that I would go home to stay with my mother, and that ***meant*** Vi and I were separated.(p.491)
• When I had heard about it, it ***meant*** nothing but just two letters to me, but some friends of mine in the institution were very active in the program and really believed in it.(p.509)
• I was going to be sent to the Indian Civil Service, which, in those days, ***meant*** that people thought you had a certain amount of brains.(p.517)
• She really ***meant*** business this time.(p.523)
• But to me, whiskey ***meant*** more than a home for my sons.(p.527)
• I ***meant*** it.(p.539)
• He ***meant*** it.(p.540)
• I ***meant*** it.(p.540)

meantime
• He tried to regulate his drinking for a while, making several trips to the hospital ***meantime***.(p.32)
• In the ***meantime***, the domestic situation was not getting along too well.(p.199)
• In the ***meantime***, another doctor in Evanston became convinced that the program had possibilities, and turned over a woman to us to do something about.(p.295)
• My dad, who was a newspaper man and had some connections, had ***meantime*** put a stop on me, and I guess that report went all over the country.(p.424)
• In the ***meantime*** I had been indicted for the second crime, attempted murder.(p.508)

meanwhile
• This brought a rush of 800 frantic inquiries into the little New York office which ***meanwhile*** had been established.(p.xviii)
• ***Meanwhile*** you might try to help the wife of another serious drinker.(p.112)
• ***Meanwhile***, we are sure a great deal can be accomplished by the use of the book alone.(p.144)
• ***Meanwhile*** I had found another escape.(p.407)
• ***Meanwhile*** the letters from home were telling about how much my folks wanted to make up to me for some of the things I'd missed.(p.427)
• ***Meanwhile***, I was getting worse, both as regards my inward misery and my drinking.(p.434)

measles
• A case of ***measles*** saved me from being kicked out during my Sophomore year.(p.499)

measure
• But that would be in great ***measure***.(p.13)
• It is the most natural thing in the world, once his liquor problem is solved, to feel that he will now ***measure*** up to that cherished vision.(p.118)
• Before my drinking had cut me down completely, I achieved a considerable ***measure*** of success, having been a City Councilman for five years and a financial director of Kenmore, a suburb later taken into the city itself.(p.182)
• I never enjoyed any meal, but I ate my lunch at noon for two reasons; first, to help me get out of the fog of the night before and, second, to furnish some ***measure*** of nourishment.(p.299)
• In all these ways I've experienced, in ever growing ***measure*** and beyond all expectations and rewards, a joy which I had never before imagined.(p.395)

measured
• Today's life is ***measured*** against that of other years and, when it falls short, the family may be unhappy.(p.123)
• Paul ***measured*** the medicine out, but he figured that with my track record that little bit wouldn't be enough, so he doubled it and added a few drops more and then gave it to me.(p.207)

measures
• Of course an alcoholic ought to be freed from his physical craving for liquor, and this often requires a definite hospital procedure, before psychological ***measures*** can be of maximum benefit.(p.xxv)
• This sometimes nearly drove me back to drink, but I soon found that when all other ***measures*** failed, work with another alcoholic would save the day.(p.15)
• Half ***measures*** availed us nothing.(p.59)
• After making our review we ask God's forgiveness and inquire what corrective ***measures*** should be taken.(p.86)
• But this does not mean that we disregard human health ***measures***.(p.133)
• And then it went on to say: "Half ***measures*** availed us nothing.(p.349)
• "Complete abandon"; "Half ***measures*** availed us nothing"; "Thoroughly follow our path"; "Completely give oneself to this simple program" – rang in my swelled head.(p.349)
• In this program there aren't any half way ***measures***.(p.516)

measuring
• I tried the beer diet, the wine diet, timing, ***measuring***, and spacing of drinks.(p.305)

mechanic
• At the other side of the table sat one of the carpenters in our community, and at the further end of the table sat the man who ran the bakery, while on one side sat my friend who was a ***mechanic***.(p.347)
• I tried every gimmick that there was to get some peace of mind, but it was not until I was brought to my alcoholic knees, when I was brought to a group in my own community with the butcher, the baker, the carpenter and the ***mechanic***, who were able to give me the Twelve Steps, that I was finally given some semblance of an answer to the last half of the First Step.(p.349)

mechanical
• Not far from where I lived they built a new technical high school and one of the teachers sold me on the idea that I needed a little ***mechanical*** drawing if I were going to be a good toolmaker.(p.211)

mechanics
• I was always interested in ***mechanics*** and after having about twenty miscellaneous jobs, lasting from one day to two weeks, I obtained a job as a toolmaker apprentice.(p.211)

mechanisms
• The mind and body are marvelous ***mechanisms***, for mine endured this agony two more years.(p.6)

media
• I was assigned to keep ***media*** guests happy at a Halloween party given by a major star in his plush home.(p.328)

medical
• The section called "The Doctor's Opinion" has been kept intact, just as it was originally written in 1939 by the late Dr. William D. Silkworth, our Society's great ***medical*** benefactor.(p.xi)
• Inquiry by scientific, ***medical***, and religious societies will be welcomed.(p.xiv)
• He had also been greatly helped by the late Dr. William D. Silkworth, a New York specialist in alcoholism who is now accounted no less than a ***medical*** saint by A.A. members, and whose story of the early days of our Society appears in the next pages.(p.xvi)
• Some of the recommendations of A.A.'s early ***medical*** and religious friends will be found further on in this book.(p.xx)
• Neither does A.A. take any particular ***medical*** point of view, though we cooperate widely with the men of medicine as well as with the men of religion.(p.xx)
• We of Alcoholics Anonymous believe that the reader will be interested in the ***medical*** estimate of the plan of recovery described in this book.(p.xxiii)
• Convincing testimony must surely come from the ***medical*** men who have had experience with the sufferings of our members and have witnessed our return to health.(p.xxiii)
• These facts appear to be of extreme ***medical*** importance; because of the extraordinary possibilities of rapid growth inherent in this group they may mark a new epoch in the annals of alcoholism.(p.xxiii)
• I say this after many years' experience as ***Medical*** Director of one of the oldest hospitals in the country treating alcoholic and drug addiction.(p.xxv)
• Of necessity there will have to be discussion of matters ***medical***, psychiatric, social, and religious.(p.19)
• If a sufficiently strong reason – ill health, falling in love, change of environment, or the warning of a doctor – becomes operative, this man can also stop or moderate, although he may find it difficult and troublesome and may even need ***medical*** attention.(p.21)
• The experiment of quitting for a period of time will be helpful, but we think we can render an even greater service to alcoholic sufferers and perhaps to the ***medical*** fraternity.(p.34)
• Small wonder many in the ***medical*** profession have a low opinion of alcoholics and their chance for recovery!(p.73)
• We began to ask ***medical*** advice as the sprees got closer together.(p.106)
• Though you are providing him with the best possible ***medical*** attention, he should understand that he must undergo a change of heart.(p.143)
• To 1950, the year of his death, he carried the A.A. message to more than 5,000 alcoholic men and women, and to all these he gave his ***medical*** services without thought of charge.(p.171)
• I remember that my father kept whiskey around the house for ***medical*** purposes and entertainment, and I would drink from this when no one was about and then water it to keep my parents from knowing I was drinking.(p.183)
• I didn't know that anything was ever done for them in a ***medical*** way.(p.267)
• He was happy, getting a kick out of life and people, and beginning to get his ***medical*** practice back again.(p.290)
• But this day my doctor gave it to me straight and said, "People like you are pretty well known to the ***medical*** profession.(p.307)
• The same thing occurred in ***medical*** school.(p.345)
• I belong to more ***medical*** societies and honor societies than men ten to twenty years my senior.(p.345)
• In my stupid way I went up to see him with the idea in the back of my mind that I would investigate Alcoholics Anonymous from a ***medical*** standpoint.(p.346)
• And as I went through pharmacy school, graduate school, ***medical*** school, internship, residency, and specialty training and, finally, went into practice, my drinking kept increasing.(p.441)
• So I raised enough fuss that they finally agreed to let me sign out, against ***medical*** advice.(p.444)
• She got a ***medical*** certificate so that I should not have to join it.(p.484)
• I had my own ***medical*** practice in Washington at that time, but the practice slackened and the mail order business started to fall off.(p.486)
• I think the Commanding Officer was rather tired of this particular chicken coming back to roost so often because he very soon wrote in to the ***medical*** authorities to tell them that they had to get me into hospital, to be thoroughly examined for drinking.(p.520)
• About three months after that, my record reached home and I got a letter telling me I was retired from the Army, they put it very kindly, on ***medical*** grounds.(p.521)
• But I knew that they knew what the ***medical*** grounds were, and that they had put a big black mark against my name.(p.521)
• I stayed there just long enough to work up a real good resentment against the doctor in charge, who I didn't think was doing anything at all except collecting fees, and I left there fully determined that I'd never put myself in the power of ***medical*** people again.(p.521)
• The ***medical*** profession would probably tell me I was conditioned for alcoholism by the things that happened to me in my childhood.(p.544)
• III. The ***Medical*** View on A.A.(p.563)
• THE ***MEDICAL*** VIEW ON A.A.(p.571)
• Since Dr. Silkworth's first endorsement of Alcoholics Anonymous, ***medical*** societies and physicians throughout the world have set their approval upon us.(p.571)
• Following are excerpts from the comments of doctors present at the annual meeting of the ***Medical*** Society of the State of New York where a paper on A.A. was read:(p.571)
• Dr. W.W. Bauer, broadcasting under the auspices of The American ***Medical*** Association in 1946, over the NBC network, said, in part: "Alcoholics Anonymous are no crusaders; not a temperance society.(p.572)
• (This address is now available in pamphlet form at nominal cost through most A.A. groups or from Box 459, Grand Central Station, New York, NY 10163, under the title "Three Talks to ***Medical*** Societies by Bill W." -- formerly called "Bill on Alcoholism" and earlier "Alcoholism the Illness.")(p.572)

medically
• The physician wasn't hooked, he thought -- he just prescribed drugs ***medically*** indicated for his many ailments.(p.439)
• Therefore, every pill was ***medically*** indicated at the time it was taken.(p.443)
• On the other hand, I believe that I've always been ***medically*** inclined, though I have never been able to see medicine quite as the average person sees it.(p.485)
• But hospitals, as well as other places of recuperation, ought to be well outside A.A. -- and

medically supervised.(p.566)

medication

• It was really medicinal that night, that whiskey, and it was a ***medication*** after that.(p.386)

• In the garage, I would put the needle in my vein and then try to figure out exactly how much ***medication*** to inject to overcome the pep pills while adding to the sleeping pills while ignoring the tranquilizers, in order to get just enough to be able to pull out the needle, jerk the tourniquet, throw it in the car, slam the car door shut, run down the hall, and fall in bed before I fell asleep.(p.442)

medicinal

• I stayed so sober that I used to keep a quart of ***medicinal*** whiskey in my bureau which I used to taper off the occasional newspaper alcoholics who were sent to see me.(p.253)

• I would take a gulp, then warn the jug not to try to entice, lure, or seduce me into having more than one "***medicinal***" jolt.(p.332)

• It was really ***medicinal*** that night, that whiskey, and it was a medication after that.(p.386)

medicine

• Another reason for the wide acceptance of A.A. was the ministration of friends -- friends in ***medicine***, religion, and the press, together with innumerable others who became our able and persistent advocates.(p.xx)

• Neither does A.A. take any particular medical point of view, though we cooperate widely with the men of ***medicine*** as well as with the men of religion.(p.xx)

• Again I swayed dizzily before an open window, or the ***medicine*** cabinet where there was poison, cursing myself for a weakling.(p.6)

• My next move was to take up the study of ***medicine***, entering one of the largest universities in the county.(p.173)

• They asked me if I would take some ***medicine***, and I promised that I would if they got me a drink.(p.206)

• I got two drinks, each of them a quarter of that pint, in me, and was talking along with these people, but I felt that sooner or later they were going to have me cornered because they were smarter than I was and the drink was beginning to take effect; but as I reached for the third drink Bob said, "Listen, Buster, you promised to take some ***medicine*** if we got you a drink.(p.206)

• Now we got you the drink, but you haven't taken the ***medicine***."(p.206)

• I told him I'd take the ***medicine*** and I would take it, but I hadn't told him when, and thereupon I got away with the third drink.(p.206)

• A few minutes later, Dr. Bob left, leaving with my brother some ***medicine*** I should get.(p.207)

• Paul measured the ***medicine*** out, but he figured that with my track record that little bit wouldn't be enough, so he doubled it and added a few drops more and then gave it to me.(p.207)

• My experience in the hospital I considered to be terrific because Dr. Bob told me very quickly that ***medicine*** would have very little to do with it, outside of trying to restore my appetite for food.(p.217)

• I remembered filling the peroxide bottle in my ***medicine*** chest with gin, in case my sister found the bottle I hid under the mattress.(p.224)

• At seventeen I entered the University, really to satisfy my father who wanted me to study ***medicine*** there as he had.(p.241)

• Why he bothered with me as long as he did I shall never know, for he knew there was no answer for me in ***medicine*** and he, like all doctors of his day, had been taught that the alcoholic was incurable and should be ignored.(p.307)

• Doctors were advised to attend patients who could be benefited by ***medicine***.(p.307)

• I couldn't practice ***medicine*** without the Great Physician.(p.351)

• I suppose the doctor might say, "This is psychosomatic ***medicine***."(p.352)

• "There's nothing I can do," he said, "and nothing ***medicine*** can do.(p.436)

• For the leveling-off process, I just loved intravenous Demerol, but I found it hard to practice good ***medicine*** while shooting morphine.(p.442)

• Words of truth and love are strong ***medicine***.(p.476)

• This sober Indian say to sick, red-eyed alcoholic who want good ***medicine***: "Put cork in bottle.(p.477)

• On the other hand, I believe that I've always been medically inclined, though I have never been able to see ***medicine*** quite as the average person sees it.(p.485)

• Father, through the years, had built up a very good mail order business because, at that time, there wasn't too much money in ***medicine***.(p.485)

• I took that bottle of ***medicine*** and gave it to a very good friend of mine who was a pharmacist and had it analyzed, and the bottle was perfectly all right.(p.489)

• If we do not do so, we shall stand convicted of emotional sterility and of having lost the faith that moves mountains, without which ***medicine*** can do little."(p.571)

medicines

• After prescribing ***medicines***, Dr. Bob ordered, "Put him in a private room.(p.188)

meditated

• I read, studied, and ***meditated*** on every bit of A.A. literature in my possession.(p.344)

meditation

• 11.Sought through prayer and ***meditation*** to improve our conscious contact with God as we understood Him, praying only for knowledge of His will for us and the power to carry that out.(p.59)

• In ***meditation***, we ask God what we should do about each specific matter.(p.69)

• So we clean house with the family, asking each morning in ***meditation*** that our Creator show us the way of patience, tolerance, kindliness and love.(p.83)

• Step Eleven suggests prayer and ***meditation***.(p.85)

• We usually conclude the period of ***meditation*** with a prayer that we be shown all through the day what our next step is to be, that we be given whatever we need to take care of such problems.(p.87)

• If circumstances warrant, we ask our wives or friends to join us in morning ***meditation***.(p.87)

• When this happens, they can be invited to join in morning ***meditation*** and then they can take part in the daily discussion without rancor or bias.(p.134)

• Ask Him in your morning ***meditation*** what you can do each day for the man who is still sick.(p.164)

meet

• The test that it faced was this: Could these large numbers of erstwhile erratic alcoholics successfully ***meet*** and work together?(p.xviii)

• I see him now and then and he is as fine a specimen of manhood as one could wish to ***meet***.(p.xxx)

• I was to sit quietly when in doubt, asking only for direction and strength to ***meet*** my problems as He would have me.(p.13)

• We ***meet*** frequently so that newcomers may find the fellowship they seek.(p.15)

• Our very lives, as ex-problem drinkers, depend upon our constant thought of others and how we may help ***meet*** their needs.(p.20)

• But it is better to ***meet*** God alone than with one who might misunderstand.(p.63)

• Occasionally you will have to ***meet*** such conditions.(p.97)

• The most incompatible people discover they have a basis upon which they can ***meet***.(p.99)

• We ***meet*** these conditions every day.(p.101)

• An alcoholic who cannot ***meet*** them, still has an alcoholic mind; there is something the matter with his spiritual status.(p.101)

• If your husband is a drinker, you probably worry over what other people are thinking and you hate to ***meet*** your friends.(p.114)

• All members of the family should ***meet*** upon the common ground of tolerance, understanding and love.(p.122)

• Suppose we tell you some of the obstacles a family will ***meet***; suppose we suggest how they may be avoided -- even converted to good use for others.(p.123)

• Nearly every modern employer feels a moral responsibility for the well-being of his help, and he tries to ***meet*** these responsibilities.(p.137)

• You are going to ***meet*** these new friends in your own community.(p.152)

• We shall be with you in the Fellowship of the Spirit, and you will surely ***meet*** some of us as you trudge the Road of Happy Destiny.(p.164)

• About this time a lady called up my wife one Saturday afternoon, saying she wanted me to come over that evening to ***meet*** a friend of hers who might help me.(p.179)

• I ***meet*** the people that I like to talk to.(p.192)

• I met all the people I wanted to ***meet***; I saw all the places I wanted to see; I did all the things I wanted to do -- and I was increasingly miserable.(p.225)

• To go into a gathering of people was the sort of thing that all my life, from the time I left my private world of books and dreams to ***meet*** the real world of people and parties and jobs, had left me feeling an uncomfortable outsider, needing the warming stimulus of drinks to join in.(p.228)

• I'll get you the password, and I can find out where they ***meet*** because I know a guy that belongs.(p.266)

• On Wednesday night Jack M. said, "You ***meet*** me at the Ohio Edison Building, and I will take you to the meeting."(p.269)

• During that first year, however, I managed to make both ends ***meet***, and to avoid ever going back to my old habit pattern of borrowing money when I could not earn it.(p.283)

• Every evening we would ***meet*** at the home of one of the members and have coffee and doughnuts and spend a social evening.(p.291)

• He thought it would be helpful for me to visit the Akron group and ***meet*** many like himself.(p.309)

• I continue to be surprised by the people I ***meet*** who say, "You haven't had a drink for a long time, have you?"(p.376)

• However, I had phoned New York from the farm, appealing for help, and there in the station to ***meet*** us were two A.A.'s, John and Bud.(p.415)

• I didn't know whether I had told him to rush to the hospital and I'd ***meet*** him there, or to take two aspirin and call me in the morning.(p.441)

• I would ***meet*** some new faces and be in a dry county.(p.490)

• He invites me to ***meet*** them.(p.504)

• I'd say, "No, I don't know where they're at or when they ***meet***.(p.510)

• If something does come along that sort of upsets me, instead of walking in and throwing a buck at the barman and asking for a drink, I walk into a telephone booth, drop a dime in the box, and call somebody who was so kind as to give me his name and telephone number to ***meet*** such an emergency.(p.511)

• But the more meetings you attend, the more people you ***meet*** at these meetings, the clearer the Steps become.(p.516)

meeting

• Six months earlier, the broker had been relieved of his drink obsession by a sudden spiritual experience, following a ***meeting*** with an alcoholic friend who had been in contact with the Oxford Groups of that day.(p.xv)

• By March 1976, when this edition went to the printer, the total worldwide membership of Alcoholics Anonymous was conservatively estimated at more than 1,000,000, with almost 28,000 groups ***meeting*** in over 90 countries.(p.xxii)

• When possible, avoid ***meeting*** a man through his family.(p.91)

• In addition to these casual get-togethers, it became customary to set apart one night a week for a ***meeting*** to be attended by anyone or everyone interested in a spiritual way of life.(p.159)

• From childhood through high school I was more or less forced to go to church, Sunday School and evening service, Monday night Christian Endeavor and sometimes to Wednesday evening prayer ***meeting***.(p.172)

• This dry spell lasted for about three weeks; then I went to Atlantic City to attend several days' ***meeting*** of a national society of which I was a member.(p.179)

• I explained to my sister that some of the people he was ***meeting*** with had been in hospitals.(p.205)

• I left on a Wednesday afternoon, had dinner in Akron and then went to a house where I encountered my first ***meeting***.(p.218)

• It was finally decided to undertake the organization of a Cleveland group and toward the end of May, 1939, the first ***meeting*** was held in Cleveland in my home.(p.219)

• At that ***meeting***, there were a number of Akron people and all the Cleveland people.(p.219)

• I went to a ***meeting*** to see for myself this group of freaks or bums who had done this thing.(p.228)

• I have something to contribute to humanity, since I am peculiarly qualified, as a fellow-sufferer, to give aid and comfort to those who have stumbled and fallen over this business of ***meeting*** life.(p.229)

• There was one ***meeting*** a week at Bill's home in Brooklyn, and we all took turns there spouting off about how we had changed our lives overnight, how many drunks we had saved and straightened out, and last, but not least, how God had touched each of us personally on the shoulder.(p.246)

• At our weekly ***meeting*** I was a menace to serenity those first few months, for I took every opportunity to lambaste the "spiritual angle" as we called it, or anything else that had any tinge of theology.(p.246)

• He introduced himself and began to tell me about a bunch of some sixty former drinkers and drunkards who met once a week, and he invited me to go with him to the next ***meeting***.(p.257)

• I left the hospital on a ***meeting*** night.(p.259)

• Jack said there was a ***meeting*** in Akron every Wednesday night and that it was very important that we go.(p.268)

• On Wednesday night Jack M. said, "You meet me at

the Ohio Edison Building, and I will take you to the *meeting*."(p.269)
• There was a young fellow who led the *meeting* and that was a beautiful thing to me.(p.270)
• I'd like to say here how important it was to us then that we do all the little things that people said were important, because later when Russ was so sick that I had to hold him up, they had a *meeting* out at the house.(p.270)
• When we closed the *meeting* with the Lord's Prayer, Russ said, "Mother, help me stand."(p.270)
• I remember sometime, it was possibly six months after we had been going steadily to King School, that we were coming home from a *meeting* and saw a car along the way, and a fellow in back drinking a bottle of beer.(p.271)
• But it took six more months of work and disappointments before a group of three men got together in my rooming house bedroom for their first A.A. *meeting*.(p.282)
• Then and then only, after a thorough indoctrination by eight or nine individuals, was I allowed to attend my first *meeting*.(p.291)
• This first *meeting* was held in the living room of a home and was led by Bill D., the first man that Bill W. and Dr. Bob had worked with successfully.(p.291)
• The *meeting* consisted of perhaps eight or nine alcoholics and seven or eight wives.(p.291)
• The *meeting* lasted an hour and closed with the Lord's Prayer.(p.291)
• I was terribly impressed by this *meeting* and the quality of happiness these men displayed, despite their lack of material means.(p.291)
• One is that I don't remember too many of them, as I was one of those drunks who could be on his feet and attend a *meeting* or a party, engage in a conversation with people and do things that any nearly normal person would do, and the next day not remember a thing about where I was, what I did, whom I saw, or how I got home.(p.301)
• By the latter part of September 1939, we had a nucleus of six and held our first official group *meeting*.(p.310)
• After having a few drinks, I went to a *meeting* – and the people there were not all old men and definitely not skid-row types!(p.319)
• The next *meeting* I went to, I didn't have any drinks beforehand.(p.319)
• And when my husband found A.A., I came to the second *meeting* with him.(p.321)
• Then I went to another *meeting*, and I still thought it was wonderful --for him, but not for me.(p.321)
• That was on a hot summer evening, down in the Greenwich Village Group, and there was a little porch out there in the old *meeting* place on Sullivan Street, and after the *meeting* I went out on the steps for some air.(p.321)
• I have never attended an A.A. *meeting*, so it is essentially the literature that has kept me on the A.A. program.(p.342)
• So I decided that I would go to my first *meeting*.(p.347)
• I will never forget the first *meeting* that I attended.(p.347)
• I recall, as I walked into that *meeting*, saying to myself, "Here I am, a fellow of the American College of Surgeons, a Fellow of the International College of Surgeons, a diplomate of one of the great specialty boards in these United States, a member of the American Psychiatric Society, and I have to go to the butcher, the baker and the carpenter to help make a man out of me!"(p.347)
• When I walked into the friendly atmosphere of my first A.A. *meeting*, I knew I was where I belonged.(p.355)
• Before long I was at the luncheon *meeting* an hour before the others, that old and familiar trademark of every alcoholic.(p.360)
• I promised my two sponsors that I would attend their *meeting* the next Tuesday evening.(p.363)
• My first *meeting* gave me a great deal of hope and lots of willing ears for my tale of woe and for my questions.(p.364)
• When our *meeting* night came around the next evening, I went -- "for her sake" I told her.(p.365)
• Attending his fourth or fifth *meeting* was an old friend I had not seen for twenty years.(p.365)
• I had no trouble making the right decision when I saw my wife open her purse at the *meeting* that night and deposit a cute little angel in the middle of my birthday cake.(p.366)
• In *meeting* me casually, I don't think my strong belief in "The Man Upstairs" shows, but I have no other explanation for the many good things that have happened to me since I have been in A.A. -- they came to me from a Greater Power.(p.367)
• We visited most of that day and attended a *meeting* that night.(p.378)
• A "spiritual experience" to me meant attending meetings, seeing a group of people, all there for the purpose of helping each other; hearing the Twelve Steps and the Twelve Traditions read at a *meeting*, and hearing the Lord's Prayer, which in an A.A. *meeting* has such great meaning -- "Thy will be done, not mine."(p.381)
• Perhaps it was He who sent my analyst to a psychiatrist's *meeting* at which Bill spoke.(p.412)
• I went to my first *meeting* with Marty and some other girls.(p.414)
• In those days there was only one big *meeting* a week in New York.(p.414)
• I headed home for the most wonderful experience of all time – *meeting* my "new" parents -- mom and dad looked different than I had pictured them.(p.428)
• I looked up an A.A. *meeting* and went there -- alone.(p.436)
• Against my better judgment, I went to a *meeting* with him that night, and a strange thing began to happen.(p.446)
• So, for no better reason than to fool him, I asked Frank to take me to a *meeting* every night.(p.447)
• And Frank did set me up for a *meeting* every night except Friday, when he thought he might have a date with his girl friend.(p.447)
• It was precisely a year before I spoke at an A.A. *meeting*.(p.447)
• I can do the same thing with an A.A. *meeting*.(p.451)
• The more I focus my mind on its defects -- late start, long drunkalogues, cigarette smoke – the worse the *meeting* becomes.(p.451)
• But when I try to see what I can add to the *meeting*, rather than what I can get out of it, and when I focus my mind on what's good about it, rather than what's wrong with it, the *meeting* keeps getting better and better.(p.451)
• They were having a large A.A. *meeting* in the prison auditorium.(p.460)
• Four years later, I was taken to my first A.A. *meeting* out of prison, in Los Angeles.(p.460)
• I started going to A.A. in prison at the group's next *meeting*.(p.461)
• He say he take me to A.A. *meeting*.(p.476)
• I go with him to first *meeting*, in small town in Maine.(p.476)
• Talk and *meeting* make me feel good.(p.476)
• Two weeks later, he come to A.A. *meeting*.(p.476)
• Two years later, my brother take Tall Man to first A.A. *meeting*.(p.476)
• That was the next *meeting*, and the first *meeting* of a colored group in A.A., so far as I know.(p.495)
• Of course, it wasn't very much of a *meeting* in the beginning; most of the time it was just Vi and myself.(p.495)
• I rounded up a few more of my friends and off we went to the *meeting*, not for anything we would gain from it as much as to make a burlesque out of it.(p.509)
• However, before the *meeting* got started, a group from the outside came in unexpectedly.(p.509)
• After the *meeting* was over and we had returned to the cell block again, I was asked how I was impressed.(p.510)
• Each time I would make a report to the parole officer he would ask me, "Have you been to an A.A. *meeting* yet?"(p.510)
• So I went to an A.A. *meeting* the first chance I got, and I listened.(p.511)
• Then I went to my first *meeting*.(p.516)
• So I did manage to get myself down to an A.A. *meeting* that night.(p.523)
• I was taking Benzedrine and paraldehyde quite impartially during the day then, and by the time I arrived at my first A.A. *meeting*, I was pretty drunk and certainly doped up to the eyes and completely jittery.(p.523)
• It was their open night *meeting*, but of course I thought they were all alcoholics; I couldn't imagine why anybody else would want to go there, and my first reaction was, well, I've come to something that's not for me.(p.524)
• I couldn't wait until the *meeting* was over to get a drink.(p.526)
• I was afraid to drink before the *meeting*.(p.526)
• I just want to say that you don't have to be afraid, because no one at any A.A. *meeting* will bite you.(p.529)
• I attended my first A.A. *meeting* eight years ago, and it is with deep gratitude that I'm able to say I've not had a drink since that time, and that I take no sedation or narcotics, for this program is to me one of complete sobriety and I no longer need to escape reality.(p.549)
• Following are excerpts from the comments of doctors present at the annual *meeting* of the Medical Society of the State of New York where a paper on A.A. was read:(p.571)
• The American Psychiatric Association requested, in 1949, that a paper be prepared by one of the older members of Alcoholics Anonymous to be read at the Association's annual *meeting* of that year.(p.572)

meetings

• Other thousands came to a few A.A. *meetings* and at first decided they didn't want the program.(p.xx)
• Then, in this eastern city, there are informal *meetings* such as we have described to you, where you may now see scores of members.(p.162)
• I still go to *meetings*, because I like to go.(p.192)
• I'm so grateful for both the program and the people in it that I still want to go, and then probably the most wonderful thing that I learned from the program -- I've seen this in the 'A.A. Grapevine' a lot of times, and I've had people say it to me personally, and I've heard people get up in *meetings* and make the same statement: The statement is, "I came into A.A. solely for the purpose of sobriety, but it has been through A.A. that I have found God."(p.192)
• I attended their *meetings* every Sunday and Wednesday for about nine months.(p.202)
• Then, I started to miss *meetings* because it was raining or snowing or something else.(p.203)
• Shortly after that, my brother, who had then become associated with a group of people and had stopped drinking, urged me to attend *meetings* with him.(p.205)
• Naturally, I wanted no part of any *meetings*.(p.205)
• I had attended several of these *meetings* before I discovered that all those who were there were not alcoholics.(p.218)
• My reaction to those *meetings* was good.(p.218)
• I believe though that it helped my family tremendously to have the A.A. *meetings* every week in my own home.(p.220)
• My oldest child sometimes sat in on the *meetings*.(p.220)
• This duty together with my weekly *meetings* with my fellow alcoholics, and my daily renewal of the contract I originally made with God, have kept me sober when nothing else ever did.(p.237)
• Much later I discovered the elders held many prayer *meetings* hoping to find a way to give me the heave-ho, but at the same time stay tolerant and spiritual.(p.247)
• While I went along with all that was done and attended the *meetings*, I never took an active job of leadership until February 1940.(p.249)
• Very rarely do I miss the *meetings* of my neighborhood A.A. group, and my average has never been less than two *meetings* a week.(p.249)
• I'd hear them on the phone having prayer *meetings* and so forth, that sort of talk over the phone, and it completely burnt me up.(p.265)
• Jack said, "Now you start and go to these *meetings*, and then you'll find out all about it."(p.268)
• We had *meetings* at each other's homes and, of course, that was a grand place for people to get together out there; they seemed to think so too.(p.270)
• It was different from the *meetings* now held.(p.291)
• One of them was that I would try to get a group started in Chicago; the second was that I would have to return to Akron to attend *meetings* at least every two months until I did get a group started in Chicago; third, I decided I must place this program above everything else, even my family, because if I did not maintain my sobriety I would lose my family anyway.(p.292)
• When he returned, we had practically daily *meetings* from that time on.(p.294)
• A few months later one of the men who had been in touch with the group in Akron came to Chicago to live, and then there were three of us who continued to have informal *meetings* quite regularly.(p.294)
• The three of us did not feel up to the job, and after a few *meetings* we convinced the prospects that they too should go to Akron where they could see an older group in action.(p.295)
• Immediately on her return we began to have formal *meetings* once a week, in the autumn of 1939, and we have continued to do this and to expand ever since.(p.295)
• I went to A.A. *meetings* twice a week.(p.320)
• When I got out of the hospital, I continued making the *meetings*.(p.320)
• I went to closed *meetings* and open *meetings*.(p.340)
• First, we all hear at A.A. *meetings* about those who have lost everything, those who have been in jail,

those who have been in prison, those who have lost their families, those who have lost their income.(p.345)
• I made little headway in my first few ***meetings*** with her.(p.359)
• After a few ***meetings*** I decided to drive to Florida unannounced to see my wife and tell her about my new found friends and association.(p.364)
• We attended ***meetings*** together, and mutually enjoyed our new found friends.(p.364)
• I went back to my group ***meetings***, but not wholeheartedly, and I often skipped them with the excuse that I was too tired.(p.364)
• I attended my weekly ***meetings*** with regularity, reread the Big Book, attended other group ***meetings***, gave leads when asked to and did some Twelve Step work whenever I was called upon to do so.(p.365)
• I went to many ***meetings*** and met many beautiful people.(p.371)
• Could I be an alcoholic without some of the hair-raising experiences I had heard of in ***meetings***?(p.379)
• They told me to go to ***meetings***, and I still do at every available opportunity, whether I am at home or in some other city.(p.381)
• Attending ***meetings*** has never been a chore to me.(p.381)
• ***Meetings*** are both relaxing and refreshing to me after a hard day.(p.381)
• A "spiritual experience" to me meant attending ***meetings***, seeing a group of people, all there for the purpose of helping each other; hearing the Twelve Steps and the Twelve Traditions read at a meeting, and hearing the Lord's Prayer, which in an A.A. meeting has such great meaning – "Thy will be done, not mine."(p.381)
• A few times at ***meetings***, I have heard this statement: "Members of A.A. have paid the highest initiation fee of any club members in the world."(p.396)
• John said, "Keep going to ***meetings***."(p.415)
• Through going to ***meetings*** and listening, and occasionally speaking, through doing Twelve Step work, whereby in helping others you are both the teacher and the student, by making many wonderful A.A. friends, I have been taught all the things in life that are worth having.(p.416)
• My experience has been active: three ***meetings*** a week, many tapes, many A.A. conferences, much work on the Twelve Steps, and much work with other alcoholics and their families.(p.420)
• I attended ***meetings***, I talked to my folks, I talked to younger people they had gotten in contact with to sponsor me.(p.430)
• That was seven years ago – and many A.A. ***meetings*** ago – and I haven't had a drink during those seven years.(p.437)
• (I am pleased to state, however, that I had gone to only a very few A.A. ***meetings*** before I was able to make a really beautiful pair of moccasins – and half a wallet.(p.445)
• The psychiatrist, who had generally been ignoring me, now became quite interested; every day, he would ask me all kinds of questions about the A.A. ***meetings***.(p.446)
• But it quickly became obvious that he had this childish notion instead: If he could get me to go to enough ***meetings*** while in the hospital, I would continue to go after he let me out.(p.447)
• Eventually, the psychiatrist discharged me from the hospital, and Max and I began going to ***meetings*** ourselves.(p.447)
• It seemed that all they talked about at ***meetings*** was drinking, drinking, drinking.(p.447)
• We do this by going to many A.A. ***meetings*** with an open mind and a desire to live the good-feeling life without chemicals -- liquid or otherwise.(p.459)
• I suddenly remembered one of my first A.A. ***meetings***, where I heard, "If you are an alcoholic and if you continue to drink, the end is death or insanity."(p.461)
• I went to ***meetings***, I spent a lot of time at the club-room, but it was all centered in this one woman.(p.472)
• I keep it simple; go to many ***meetings***; carry message to those who listen.(p.476)
• I feel Great Spirit at all ***meetings*** and when talk to A.A. friends.(p.477)
• Go to A.A. ***meetings***.(p.477)
• We held some two or three ***meetings*** at Ella's home and from there we held some two or three at her mother's home.(p.495)
• Then Charlie or someone in the group suggested that we try to get a place in a church or hall to hold ***meetings***.(p.495)
• At that time we had our ***meetings*** on Friday nights.(p.495)
• They came, many of them, and stuck by us and told us how to hold ***meetings***.(p.495)
• I took the advice of people I had heard at ***meetings***, the people in the group.(p.516)
• So I attended as many ***meetings*** as possible.(p.516)
• But the more ***meetings*** you attend, the more people you meet at these ***meetings***, the clearer the Steps become.(p.516)
• I do think that some of the Negroes here – and other places, too -- are afraid to go to other ***meetings***.(p.529)
• For by now I had been exposed once to A.A., but I had treated it as a vaudeville and had taken friends to ***meetings*** so that they too could enjoy the fascination of the naked revelation of suffering and recovery.(p.539)
• I acquired a sponsor and began attending ***meetings***, but continued to drink.(p.559)
• By learning -- through practicing the Twelve Steps and through sharing at ***meetings*** -- how to cope with the problems that we looked to booze to solve, back in our drinking days.(p.560)

mellow

• A ***mellow*** glow stole over me.(p.498)
• I shall get myself "***mellow***" and stay that way.(p.506)

melt

• Sometimes the man we are calling upon admits his own fault, so feuds of years' standing ***melt*** away in an hour.(p.78)

melted

• It ***melted*** the icy intellectual mountain in whose shadow I had lived and shivered many years.(p.12)
• The checking account ***melted*** like snow in June.(p.106)

member

• When writing or speaking publicly about alcoholism, we urge each of our Fellowship to omit his personal name, designating himself instead as "a ***member*** of Alcoholics Anonymous."(p.xiii)
• Upon hearing this, our friend was somewhat relieved, for he reflected that after all, he was a good church ***member***.(p.27)
• One of these men, staff ***member*** of a world-renowned hospital, recently made this statement to some of us: "What you say about the general hopelessness of the average alcoholic's plight is, in my opinion, correct.(p.43)
• We find the more one ***member*** of the family demands that the others concede to him, the more resentful they become.(p.122)
• We think each family which has been relieved owes something to those who have not, and when the occasion requires, each ***member*** of it should be only too willing to bring former mistakes, no matter how grievous, out of their hiding places.(p.124)
• As each ***member*** of a resentful family begins to see his short comings and admits them to the others, he lays a basis for helpful discussion.(p.127)
• One more suggestion: Whether the family has spiritual convictions or not, they may do well to examine the principles by which the alcoholic ***member*** is trying to live.(p.130)
• Whether the family goes on a spiritual basis or not, the alcoholic ***member*** has to if he would recover.(p.135)
• Though he is now a most effective ***member*** of Alcoholics Anonymous, he still smokes and drinks coffee, but neither his wife or anyone else stands in judgment.(p.135)
• Among many employers nowadays, we think of one ***member*** who has spent much of his life in the world of big business.(p.136)
• He too, has become a respected and useful ***member*** of his community.(p.158)
• We know of an A.A. ***member*** who was living in a large community.(p.163)
• I would sometimes hide out in one of the clubs of which I was a ***member***, and had the habit at times of registering at a hotel under a fictitious name.(p.176)
• This dry spell lasted for about three weeks; then I went to Atlantic City to attend several days' meeting of a national society of which I was a ***member***.(p.179)
• Pioneer ***member*** of Akron's Group No. 1, the first A.A. group in the world.(p.182)
• The man turned out to be Bill D., a very early ***member*** of A.A., and I couldn't tell you a word of what he said.(p.208)
• I never left the church, but I was a fringe ***member***, and the thought simply never occurred to me that through the exercise of what I had I might find the answer to my problem, simply because I wouldn't admit that I had a problem.(p.214)
• I believe every ***member*** of the Akron Group did come to see me, which impressed me terrifically, not so much because of the stories they told, but because they would take the time to come and talk to me without even knowing who I was.(p.218)
• Early ***member***, she spread the word among women in our pioneering period.(p.222)
• An active ***member*** of A.A. since 1939, I feel myself a useful ***member*** of the human race at last.(p.229)
• I had never doubted the existence of the Supreme Being, but now I began to absent myself from my church where I had formerly been a ***member*** of the choir.(p.234)
• In June, 1945, with another ***member***, I made my first – and only – Twelfth Step call on a female alcoholic and a year later I married her.(p.249)
• A pioneer woman ***member*** of A.A.'s first Group.(p.261)
• My wife, a sister ***member*** in A.A., had been a widow nine years and I had been single eighteen years.(p.286)
• From a single ***member*** in the Chicago area, commuting to Akron, we now exceed six thousand.(p.295)
• I talked to the first sergeant and the battalion commander, and they got me in contact with an A.A. ***member***.(p.319)
• I recall, as I walked into that meeting, saying to myself, "Here I am, a fellow of the American College of Surgeons, a Fellow of the International College of Surgeons, a diplomate of one of the great specialty boards in these United States, a ***member*** of the American Psychiatric Society, and I have to go to the butcher, the baker and the carpenter to help make a man out of me!"(p.347)
• I was desperately in earnest to follow through and understand what was expected of me as a ***member*** of A.A. and to take each Step of the Twelve as rapidly as possible.(p.382)
• In the first year there were episodes such as kicking Priscilla in the shins, getting the lock changed on the desk in the A.A. Club, because I, as secretary, didn't want the Intergroup secretary "interfering," and taking an older woman ***member*** out to lunch for the express purpose of informing her that she was "a phony."(p.416)
• My second wife is a young A.A. ***member***, too, and what a terrific adventure this is for us!(p.420)
• Why am I alive, free, a respected ***member*** of my community?(p.421)
• I proud to be son of Tall Man, American Indian, and ***member*** of A.A. for many moons.(p.474)
• I want to be one of His children, a ***member*** of the human race.(p.535)
• 1. -- Each ***member*** of Alcoholics Anonymous is but a small part of a great whole.(p.565)
• 10. – No A.A. group or ***member*** should ever, in such a way as to implicate A.A., express any opinion on outside controversial issues – particularly those of politics, alcohol reform, or sectarian religion.(p.567)

members

• He had also been greatly helped by the late Dr. William D. Silkworth, a New York specialist in alcoholism who is now accounted no less than a medical saint by A.A. ***members***, and whose story of the early days of our Society appears in the next pages.(p.xvi)
• By late 1937, the number of ***members*** having substantial sobriety time behind them was sufficient to convince the membership that a new light had entered the dark world of the alcoholic.(p.xvii)
• In the spring of 1940, John D. Rockefeller, Jr. gave a dinner for many of his friends to which he invited A.A. ***members*** to tell their stories.(p.xviii)
• By the close of 1941, A.A. numbered 8,000 ***members***.(p.xviii)
• It was decided that all ***members*** ought to be anonymous at the level of press, radio, TV and films.(p.xix)
• Women now make up more than one-fourth of the membership; among newer ***members***, the proportion is nearly one-third.(p.xxii)
• The Twelve Steps that summarize the program may be called los Doce Pasos in one country, los Douze Etapes in another, but they trace exactly the same path to recovery that was blazed by the earliest ***members*** of Alcoholics Anonymous.(p.xxii)
• Convincing testimony must surely come from the medical men who have had experience with the sufferings of our ***members*** and have witnessed our return to health.(p.xxiii)
• We think it no concern of ours what religious bodies our ***members*** identify themselves with as individuals.(p.28)
• Many who once were in this class are now among our ***members***.(p.28)
• "Two of the ***members*** of Alcoholics Anonymous came to see me.(p.42)
• If not ***members*** of religious bodies, we sometimes select and memorize a few set prayers which emphasize

the principles we have been discussing.(p.87)
• All *members* of the family should meet upon the common ground of tolerance, understanding and love.(p.122)
• *Members* of a family should watch such matters carefully, for one careless, inconsiderate remark has been known to raise the very devil.(p.125)
• Then, in this eastern city, there are informal meetings such as we have described to you, where you may now see scores of *members*.(p.162)
• Dr. Bob and the twelve men and women who here tell their stories were among the early *members* of A.A.'s first groups.(p.169)
• Today, hundreds of additional A.A. *members* can be found who have had no relapse for more than thirty years.(p.169)
• There were, at that time, in the neighborhood of twelve or thirteen Cleveland *members* who had been sober anywhere from a year and a half to a couple of months.(p.219)
• He brought in many of our original *members*, yet he himself could not make it and died of alcoholism.(p.239)
• I have served on only one committee in the past nine years, for I feel that I had my chance the first few years and that newer *members* should fill the jobs.(p.250)
• Within a year of my return to Detroit, A.A. was a definitely established little group of about a dozen *members* and I too was established in a modest but steady job handling an independent dry-cleaning route of my own.(p.283)
• Every evening we would meet at the home of one of the *members* and have coffee and doughnuts and spend a social evening.(p.291)
• Among today's incoming A.A. *members*, many have never reached the advanced stages of alcoholism, though, given time, all might have.(p.315)
• I had worked so long in a profession where fakery, deceit, and untruths are tools of trade that I instantly recognized honesty when I heard it, from the mouths of A.A. *members*.(p.334)
• I have always considered myself one of the lucky *members* of our fraternity.(p.356)
• I repeat, I am one of the fortunate *members* of A.A. -- a lucky guy who is very grateful.(p.368)
• There are so many to whom I feel deeply grateful; to my husband (and best critic), whose generous love, compassion and understanding have helped me along the way; to those before me in A.A. who inspired the first article I read, and the friend who sent that article to Frank; to Ruth for her personal note, and the first A.A. to talk to me; to my Bishop, whose loving and believing spirit inspired me; and to all the *members* of the Houston Group who were so patient, kind and helpful -- and to countless others.(p.393)
• A few times at meetings, I have heard this statement: "*Members* of A.A. have paid the highest initiation fee of any club *members* in the world."(p.396)
• Incalculable are the intangible initiation fees that A.A. *members* have paid: the sick, sick hangovers, the remorse, guilt, broken homes, jails, and institutions, and the mental anguish in general that has been generated over the years.(p.399)
• I did not reflect that half the office was composed of A.A. *members*, and that I was as unexciting as any client in any office.(p.413)
• I am one of the growing number of A.A. *members* who are second-generation.(p.419)
• But the older *members* in A.A. told me, "easy does it."(p.471)
• *Members* of my family annoy me.(p.505)
• It is going strong still, these eight years later, and some of its *members* have been of great influence for good in state-wide A.A. work.(p.541)
• The A.A. *members* who sponsored me told me in the beginning that I would not only find a way to live without having a drink, but that I would find a way to live without wanting to drink, if I would do these simple things.(p.550)
• God willing, we *members* of A.A. may never again have to deal with drinking, but we have to deal with sobriety every day.(p.560)
• 7. -- The A.A. groups themselves ought to be fully supported by the voluntary contributions of their own *members*.(p.566)
• Our names and pictures as A.A. *members* ought not be broadcast, filmed, or publicly printed.(p.567)
• With few exceptions our *members* find that they have tapped an unsuspected inner resource which they presently identify with their own conception of a Power greater than themselves.(p.569)
• Our more religious *members* call it "God-consciousness."(p.570)
• The American Psychiatric Association requested, in 1949, that a paper be prepared by one of the older *members* of Alcoholics Anonymous to be read at the Association's annual meeting of that year.(p.572)
• The A.A. plan is described by the *members* themselves as 'self-insurance.'(p.574)
• This is a world clearing house for the Al-Anon Family Groups, composed largely of the wives, husbands and friends of A.A. *members*.(p.575)

members'

• All changes made over the years in the Big Book (A.A. *members'* fond nickname for this volume) have had the same purpose: to represent the current membership of Alcoholics Anonymous more accurately, and thereby to reach more alcoholics.(p.xii)
• Yet prisoners often can't identify with many A.A. *members'* drinking stories.(p.458)

membership

• All changes made over the years in the Big Book (A.A. members' fond nickname for this volume) have had the same purpose: to represent the current *membership* of Alcoholics Anonymous more accurately, and thereby to reach more alcoholics.(p.xii)
• The only requirement for *membership* is an honest desire to stop drinking.(p.xiv)
• In that brief space, Alcoholics Anonymous has mushroomed into nearly 6,000 groups whose *membership* is far above 150,000 recovered alcoholics.(p.xv)
• By late 1937, the number of members having substantial sobriety time behind them was sufficient to convince the *membership* that a new light had entered the dark world of the alcoholic.(p.xvii)
• The *membership* had then reached about 100 men and women.(p.xvii)
• By March 1941, the *membership* had shot up to 2,000.(p.xviii)
• Would there be quarrels over *membership*, leadership and money?(p.xviii)
• At present, our *membership* is increasing at the rate of about seven per cent a year.(p.xx)
• By March 1976, when this edition went to the printer, the total worldwide *membership* of Alcoholics Anonymous was conservatively estimated at more than 1,000,000, with almost 28,000 groups meeting in over 90 countries.(p.xxii)
• Women now make up more than one-fourth of the *membership*; among newer members, the proportion is nearly one-third.(p.xxii)
• These give a fair cross section of our *membership* and a clear-cut idea of what has actually happened in their lives.(p.29)
• Though the family has no religious connections, they may wish to make contact with or take *membership* in a religious body.(p.131)
• On account of my enormous capacity for beer, I was elected to *membership* in one of the drinking societies, and soon became one of the leading spirits.(p.173)
• Alcoholics being the argumentative lot that we are, the A.A. *membership* will undoubtedly come up with a few who will dispute these figures.(p.399)
• Three -- The only requirement for A.A. *membership* is a desire to stop drinking.(p.564)
• 3. -- Our *membership* ought to include all who suffer from alcoholism.(p.565)
• Nor ought A.A. *membership* ever depend upon money or conformity.(p.565)
• Among our rapidly growing *membership* of thousands of alcoholics such transformations, though frequent, are by no means the rule.(p.569)

memberships

• Not all of us join religious bodies, but most of us favor such *memberships*.(p.28)

memories

• Childhood *memories* rose before me.(p.10)
• These *memories* are a nightmare.(p.73)
• As fast as he can, he pushes these *memories* far inside himself.(p.73)
• They were but *memories*.(p.151)
• One of the earliest *memories* that I have is of a bottle sitting on his desk with a skull and crossbones and marked "Poison."(p.193)
• For there were of course periods of clear realization of what I had become, attended by *memories* of what I had been, what I had expected to be.(p.224)
• There I sat in the evenings, enjoying with my friends our *memories* of the "old country," singing the old songs we all knew, playing simple card games for drinks and consuming great quantities of beer.(p.231)
• The place is Naini Tal, in the foothills of the mighty Himalaya Mountains, and it has some very significant *memories* for me.(p.342)
• We soon resumed our marriage, even moved away from the street of sad *memories* and found a new home.(p.371)

memorize

• If not members of religious bodies, we sometimes select and *memorize* a few set prayers which emphasize the principles we have been discussing.(p.87)

memory

• We are unable, at certain times, to bring into our consciousness with sufficient force the *memory* of the suffering and humiliation of even a week or a month ago.(p.24)
• I remember looking longingly at the window as an easier solution, and shuddering at the *memory* of that other window, three years before, and the six agonizing months in a London hospital ward.(p.224)
• Little more of our talk stayed in my *memory*, but I do know I slept the rest of that night while before I had never known what a real night's sleep was.(p.239)
• My next conscious *memory* was in Bar le Duc, many miles from base.(p.242)
• My *memory* slowly returned.(p.320)
• One night, I was struck with the *memory* of a line Alan Ladd used in "Shane," a movie that I'd worked on.(p.333)
• I could hardly see at all, and my *memory* kept eluding me.(p.353)
• (Two large red A's stand out in my *memory*.)(p.460)
• Just as I was wondering what on earth I could do -- I was too drunk even to pack a handkerchief -- the *memory* of an A.A. write-up that I had seen in the Evening Mail flashed across my mind -- and I thought to myself, this is something I haven't tried yet.(p.523)
• I wandered, craving peace, from one spot to another of youthful happy *memory*, and loathed the man I had become.(p.539)

men

• Because this book has become the basic text for our Society and has helped such large numbers of alcoholic *men* and women to recover, there exists a sentiment against any radical changes being made in it.(p.xi)
• We, of Alcoholics Anonymous, are more than one hundred *men* and women who have recovered from a seemingly hopeless state of mind and body.(p.xiii)
• Hence the two *men* set to work almost frantically upon alcoholics arriving in the ward of the Akron City Hospital.(p.xvii)
• The membership had then reached about 100 *men* and women.(p.xvii)
• Neither does A.A. take any particular medical point of view, though we cooperate widely with the *men* of medicine as well as with the *men* of religion.(p.xx)
• Convincing testimony must surely come from the medical *men* who have had experience with the sufferings of our members and have witnessed our return to health.(p.xxiii)
• This has become the basis of a rapidly growing fellowship of these *men* and their families.(p.xxiii)
• These *men* may well have a remedy for thousands of such situations.(p.xxiv)
• The unselfishness of these *men* as we have come to know them, the entire absence of profit motive, and their community spirit, is indeed inspiring to one who has labored long and wearily in this alcoholic field.(p.xxv)
• We feel, after many years of experience, that we have found nothing which has contributed more to the rehabilitation of these *men* than the altruistic movement now growing up among them.(p.xxvi)
• *Men* and women drink essentially because they like the effect produced by alcohol.(p.xxvi)
• *Men* have cried out to me in sincere and despairing appeal: "Doctor, I cannot go on like this!(p.xxvii)
• I have had many *men* who had, for example, worked a period of months on some problem or business deal which was to be settled on a certain date, favorable to them.(p.xxvii)
• These *men* were not drinking to escape; they were drinking to overcome a craving beyond their mental control.(p.xxviii)
• There are many situations which arise out of the phenomenon of craving which cause *men* to make the supreme sacrifice rather than continue to fight.(p.xxviii)
• I fancied myself a leader, for had not the *men* of my battery given me a special token of appreciation?(p.1)
• We had long talks when I would still her foreboding by telling her that *men* of genius conceived their best projects when drunk; that the most majestic constructions of philosophic thought were so derived.(p.2)
• The papers reported *men* jumping to death from the towers of High Finance.(p.4)
• In a matter of fact way he told how two *men* had appeared in court, persuading the judge to suspend his commitment.(p.9)
• I have since talked with scores of *men* who felt the

same way.(p.12)
• God comes to most *men* gradually, but His impact on me was sudden and profound.(p.14)
• The good doctor now sees many *men* who have such experiences.(p.14)
• I have seen *men* come out of asylums and resume a vital place in the lives of their families and communities.(p.15)
• Business and professional *men* have regained their standing.(p.15)
• Each day my friend's simple talk in our kitchen multiplies itself in a widening circle of peace on earth and good will to *men*.(p.16)
• We of ALCOHOLICS ANONYMOUS, know thousands of *men* and women who were once just as hopeless as Bill.(p.17)
• We know that while the alcoholic keeps away from drink, as he may do for months or years, he reacts much like other *men*.(p.22)
• He can go anywhere on this earth where other free *men* may go without disaster, provided he remains willing to maintain a certain simple attitude.(p.26)
• Ideas, emotions, and attitudes which were once the guiding forces of the lives of these *men* are suddenly cast to one side, and a completely new set of conceptions and motives begin to dominate them.(p.27)
• We, in our turn, sought the same escape with all the desperation of drowning *men*.(p.28)
• The distinguished American psychologist, William James, in his book "Varieties of Religious Experience," indicates a multitude of ways in which *men* have discovered God.(p.28)
• Our hope is that many alcoholic *men* and women, desperately in need, will see these pages, and we believe that it is only by fully disclosing ourselves and our problems that they will be persuaded to say, "Yes, I am one of them too; I must have this thing."(p.29)
• We alcoholics are *men* and women who have lost the ability to control our drinking.(p.30)
• We are like *men* who have lost their legs; they never grow new ones.(p.30)
• Neither does there appear to be any kind of treatment which will make alcoholics of our kind like other *men*.(p.30)
• Then he fell victim to a belief which practically every alcoholic has -- that his long period of sobriety and self-discipline had qualified him to drink as other *men*.(p.32)
• Several of our crowd, *men* of thirty or less, had been drinking only a few years, but they found themselves as helpless as those who had been drinking twenty years.(p.33)
• I reasoned I was not so far advanced as most of you fellows, that I had been usually successful in licking my other personal problems, and that I would therefore be successful where you *men* failed.(p.40)
• One of these *men*, staff member of a world-renowned hospital, recently made this statement to some of us: "What you say about the general hopelessness of the average alcoholic's plight is, in my opinion, correct.(p.43)
• As to two of you *men*, whose stories I have heard, there is no doubt in my mind that you were 100% hopeless, apart from divine help.(p.43)
• It is open, we believe, to all *men*.(p.46)
• On one proposition, however, these *men* and women are strikingly agreed.(p.50)
• Here are thousands of *men* and women, worldly indeed.(p.50)
• Students of ancient history tell us that the intellect of *men* in those days was equal to the best of today.(p.51)
• Those who do not recover are people who cannot or will not completely give themselves to this simple program, usually *men* and women who are constitutionally incapable of being honest with themselves.(p.58)
• They may be the dubious luxury of normal *men*, but for alcoholics these things are poison.(p.66)
• All *men* of faith have courage.(p.68)
• We have begun to learn tolerance, patience and good will toward all *men*, even our enemies, for we look on them as sick people.(p.70)
• Unwilling to be honest with these sympathetic *men*, we were honest with no one else.(p.73)
• Better *men* than we are using it constantly.(p.85)
• The *men* who cry for money and shelter before conquering alcohol, are on the wrong track.(p.98)
• We have seen *men* get well whose families have not returned at all.(p.100)
• With few exceptions, our book thus far has spoken of *men*.(p.104)
• There is every evidence that women regain their health as readily as *men* if they try our suggestions.(p.104)
• We want the wives of Alcoholics Anonymous to address the wives of *men* who drink too much.(p.104)
• Our loyalty and the desire that our husbands hold up their heads and be like other *men* have begotten all sorts of predicaments.(p.105)
• We have had retaliatory love affairs with other *men*.(p.105)
• Our friends have counseled chucking the *men* and we have done so with finality, only to be back in a little while hoping, always hoping.(p.105)
• Our *men* have sworn great solemn oaths that they were through drinking forever.(p.105)
• We seldom had friends at our homes, never knowing how or when the *men* of the house would appear.(p.105)
• How heartbreaking was this discovery; how cruel to be told they understood our *men* as we did not!(p.106)
• Sometimes we sensed dimly that we were dealing with sick *men*.(p.107)
• How could *men* who loved their wives and children be so unthinking, so callous, so cruel?(p.107)
• Could we have been so mistaken in the *men* we married?(p.107)
• Today most of our *men* are better husbands and fathers than ever before.(p.108)
• We realize some *men* are thoroughly bad-intentioned, that no amount of patience will make any difference.(p.108)
• He knows that thousands of *men*, much like himself, have recovered.(p.113)
• You would suppose that *men* in the fourth classification would be quite hopeless, but that is not so.(p.113)
• Yet often such *men* had spectacular and powerful recoveries.(p.113)
• Some *men* have been so impaired by alcohol that they cannot stop.(p.114)
• Some *men* cannot or will not get over alcoholism.(p.114)
• The wives and children of such *men* suffer horribly, but not more than the *men* themselves.(p.114)
• You have been starving for his companionship, yet he spends long hours helping other *men* and their families.(p.119)
• Though it is infinitely better that he have no relapse at all, as has been true with many of our *men*, it is by no means a bad thing in some cases.(p.120)
• Alcohol is so sexually stimulating to some *men* that they have over-indulged.(p.134)
• He has hired and fired hundreds of *men*.(p.136)
• His present views ought to prove exceptionally useful to business *men* everywhere.(p.136)
• I was at one time assistant manager of a corporation department employing sixty-six hundred *men*.(p.136)
• Here were three exceptional *men* lost to this world because I did not understand alcoholism as I do now.(p.137)
• I pointed out that I had had nothing to drink whatever for three years, and this in the face of difficulties that would have made nine out of ten *men* drink their heads off.(p.138)
• Seeing your attempt to understand and help, some *men* will try to take advantage of your kindness.(p.141)
• But there are many *men* who want to stop, and with them you can go far.(p.141)
• Wherever *men* are gathered together in business there will be rivalries and, arising out of these, a certain amount of office politics.(p.145)
• *Men* under them are frequently their friends.(p.147)
• So, for one reason or another, they cover these *men*, hoping matters will take a turn for the better.(p.147)
• It will permit the rehabilitation of good *men*.(p.148)
• Alcoholism may be causing your organization considerable damage in its waste of time, *men* and reputation.(p.148)
• Of course, this chapter refers to alcoholics, sick people, deranged *men*.(p.149)
• It may seem incredible that these *men* are to become happy, respected, and useful once more.(p.153)
• But what about his responsibilities -- his family and the *men* who would die because they would not know how to get well, ah -- yes, those other alcoholics?(p.154)
• He has helped other *men* recover, and is a power in the church from which he was long absent.(p.158)
• These *men* had found something brand new in life.(p.159)
• Seeing much of each other, scarce an evening passed that someone's home did not shelter a little gathering of *men* and women, happy in their release, and constantly thinking how they might present their discovery to some newcomer.(p.159)
• The expression on the faces of the women, that indefinable something in the eyes of the *men*, the stimulating and electric atmosphere of the place, conspired to let him know that here was haven at last.(p.160)
• When a few *men* in this city have found themselves, and have discovered the joy of helping others to face life again, there will be no stopping until everyone in that town has had his opportunity to recover -- if he can and will.(p.163)
• Dr. Bob and the twelve *men* and women who here tell their stories were among the early members of A.A.'s first groups.(p.169)
• To 1950, the year of his death, he carried the A.A. message to more than 5,000 alcoholic *men* and women, and to all these he gave his medical services without thought of charge.(p.171)
• *Men* who had liquor shipped in from Boston or New York by express were looked upon with great distrust and disfavor by most of the good townspeople.(p.171)
• I had a crew of *men* working there and I wanted them to work Sunday afternoons so that I could sell lots on Sunday.(p.195)
• One hundred for unmarried women at one end, one hundred for *men* at the other, and one hundred for married couples in the middle.(p.198)
• I was moved in as Sales Manager and had four *men* working under me.(p.200)
• I came of good stock, of *men* and women who drank wine all their lives as a beverage, and while they occasionally got drunk at special celebrations, they were up and about their business the next day.(p.231)
• You can all remember that in the first few months after the change, a great many *men*, who had formerly been used to a few beers every day or an occasional drink of whiskey, simply quit all alcoholic drinks.(p.232)
• It wasn't very long before home-brewing was an institution and *men* began to search feverishly for old recipe books on wine-making.(p.232)
• This doctor had imparted his knowledge to just a few other *men* at that time -- not more than four or five -- they now number more than seventy persons.(p.235)
• And, because as I have discovered since, it is part of the "treatment" that these *men* be sent to see and talk with alcoholics who want to quit, he kept them busy.(p.235)
• The visits from these *men* impressed me at once.(p.235)
• Where preaching and prayers had touched me very little, I immediately desired further knowledge of these *men*.(p.235)
• Oddly enough, the big shot who fired me from this company was one of the first *men* I met when I later joined the New York A.A. Group.(p.242)
• At that time the group in New York was composed of about twelve *men* who were working on the principle of every drunk for himself; we had no real formula and no name.(p.246)
• There were business *men*, professional *men*, and factory workers.(p.258)
• All sorts were represented and their relation of experiences and how they had found the only remedy, added to their human existence as sober *men*, laid the foundation of a very necessary faith.(p.258)
• The big thing was that these *men* were all sober and evidently had something I didn't have.(p.259)
• But I had never been a flippant, wise-cracking sneerer at the few persons I had met who had impressed me as Christian *men* and women, or at any institution whose sincerity of purpose I could see.(p.259)
• Today I have Someone who will always hear me; I have a warm fellowship among *men* who understand my problems; I have tasks to do and am glad to do them, to see others who are alcoholics and to help them in any way I can to become sober *men*.(p.260)
• *Men* from A.A. started coming out to the house the next day.(p.268)
• These *men* all drank on Saturday nights, and enjoyed themselves.(p.277)
• He was a man of considerable means and he might have done what many *men* would have done in such a case.(p.278)
• Here, while in a hospital bed, *men* with clear eyes, happy faces, and a look of assurance and purposefulness about them, came to see me and told me their stories.(p.279)
• The example which they and Bill W., whose visits to Akron were fairly frequent, set me of service to their fellow *men* imbued me with a great desire to emulate them.(p.281)
• So I spent much of my time calling on the people who I felt would logically come in contact with alcoholic cases, doctors, ministers, lawyers and the per-

sonnel *men* in industry.(p.281)

- But it took six more months of work and disappointments before a group of three *men* got together in my rooming house bedroom for their first A.A. meeting.(p.282)
- He waited until I was completely sober and the day before I was to head back for Chicago, he told me of a small group of *men* in Akron who apparently had the same problem that I had but were doing something about it.(p.289)
- I could not wait to tell him that I wanted help, that if these *men* in Akron had anything I wanted it, and would do anything to get it.(p.289)
- The next afternoon and evening, two other *men* visited me and each told me his story and the things that they were doing to try to recover from this tragic illness.(p.290)
- In the next two or three days the balance of this handful of *men* contacted me, encouraged me, and told me how they were trying to live this program of recovery and the fun they were having doing it.(p.291)
- I was terribly impressed by this meeting and the quality of happiness these *men* displayed, despite their lack of material means.(p.291)
- A few months later one of the *men* who had been in touch with the group in Akron came to Chicago to live, and then there were three of us who continued to have informal meetings quite regularly.(p.294)
- Why do *men* and women like these join A.A.?(p.315)
- I was sure I wouldn't belong in an A.A. group -- they were all old *men*, I thought, and all skid-row bums.(p.319)
- After having a few drinks, I went to a meeting -- and the people there were not all old *men* and definitely not skid-row types!(p.319)
- I belong to more medical societies and honor societies than *men* ten to twenty years my senior.(p.345)
- I got around this by joining the local Rotary Club, and through this association with the business *men* of the community my little station began to grow.(p.360)
- It started when I joined a few of the *men* for cocktails before the noonday Rotary luncheon.(p.360)
- Sure enough in a couple of hours two *men* were at my door and for the first time I heard some facts about liquor and my problem that sounded sensible to me.(p.363)
- The story is not very different from that of thousands of other young *men* in my generation.(p.373)
- It pays daily in more harmonious relations with my fellow *men*, in ever clearer insight into the true meaning of life, and in the answering love and gratitude wherever and whenever I have been the instrument of God's will in the lives of others.(p.394)
- *Men* danced with me at parties.(p.402)
- They were a couple of normal, sober, attractive *men*.(p.415)
- I tried to mimic the talk, ideas, moods and even the drinking the older *men*.(p.423)
- Shakespeare said, "All the world's a stage, all the *men* and women merely players."(p.449)
- I was an agitator, a troublemaker, and many *men* as bitter as I was followed me.(p.458)
- It is estimated that two-thirds of the *men* in prison were under the influence of alcohol and/or drugs when they committed their offenses.(p.458)
- I didn't know I was an alcoholic and (like most *men* in prison today) could not relate alcohol to any of my past troubles.(p.460)
- My sponsor say *men* who talk speak truth.(p.476)
- I hear *men* say, "One day not drink.(p.476)
- When he speak from heart, big *men* cry.(p.476)
- *Men* are supposed to be tough and rugged to start with, but if a woman becomes that way, it is pretty hard to get back the niceties of womanhood.(p.480)
- "Let your light so shine before *men* that they may see your good works --."(p.497)
- "There are *men* on the streets of New York today who were worse than you, and they don't drink any more."(p.503)
- Some *men* and women come to visit my friend of the night before.(p.504)
- Finally, he was drinking to keep away those little *men*, and those strange voices, and the organ music that came out of the walls.(p.512)
- I was drinking to keep away the shakes, drinking to keep away those little *men* and those strange voices and the organ music that comes out of the walls.(p.514)
- There was the necessity for sticking to a job I hated, a dull, repetitive job performed in association with other *men* I had nothing in common with . . . performed for years on end, because the money was needed at home.(p.532)
- Alas for us *men* toward whom Shaw hurled his cry, "Must a Christ be crucified in every generation for the benefit of those who have no imagination?"(p.536)
- With deep shame came the knowledge too that I had lived with no sense of social obligation nor had I known the meaning of moral responsibility to my fellow *men*.(p.549)
- Therefore, no society of *men* and women ever had more urgent need for continuous effectiveness and permanent unity.(p.563)
- This self-insurance has resulted in the restoration of physical, mental and spiritual health and self-respect to hundreds of *men* and women who would be hopelessly down and out without its unique but effective therapy."(p.574)

men's

- In the realm of the material, *men's* minds were fettered by superstition, tradition, and all sorts of fixed ideas.(p.51)
- He entered a political campaign, making speeches, frequenting *men's* gathering places of all sorts, often staying up all night.(p.158)
- I hadn't been in too long when one of the *men's* wives called me one Sunday and told me she didn't think I had any part of the program.(p.273)
- So I created a job for myself selling women's hosiery and *men's* made-to-order shirts.(p.282)
- It didn't take long for me to fall in with a fast crowd who had their lunch in the *men's* bar of a leading hotel.(p.361)

menace

- At our weekly meeting I was a *menace* to serenity those first few months, for I took every opportunity to lambaste the "spiritual angle" as we called it, or anything else that had any tinge of theology.(p.246)
- I became a *menace*, the fish-wife, the common scold.(p.410)
- Society can do anything it chooses to do with me when I am drunk and I can't lift a finger to stop it, for I forfeit my rights through the simple expedient of becoming a *menace* to myself and to the people around me.(p.549)

mend

- He shuts himself up in an asylum, hoping to *mend* his ways.(p.38)
- He had to painfully admit that and *mend* his spiritual fences.(p.135)

menial

- He had tried everything from having me attend daily mass at six a.m. to performing the most *menial* labor for his charity patients.(p.306)

mental

- It did not satisfy us to be told that we could not control our drinking just because we were maladjusted to life, that we were in full flight from reality, or were outright *mental* defectives.(p.xxiv)
- I do not hold with those who believe that alcoholism is entirely a problem of *mental* control.(p.xxvii)
- These men were not drinking to escape; they were drinking to overcome a craving beyond their *mental* control.(p.xxviii)
- He had but partially recovered from a gastric hemorrhage and seemed to be a case of pathological *mental* deterioration.(p.xxix)
- When I need a *mental* uplift, I often think of another case brought in by a physician prominent in New York.(p.xxix)
- Then a *mental* fog settled down.(p.6)
- Then came the night when the physical and *mental* torture was so hellish I feared I would burst through my window, sash and all.(p.6)
- My bother-in-law is a physician, and through his kindness and that of my mother I was placed in a nationally-known hospital for the *mental* and physical rehabilitation of alcoholics.(p.7)
- We are equally positive that once he takes any alcohol whatever into his system, something happens, both in the bodily and *mental* sense, which makes it virtually impossible for him to stop.(p.22)
- His physical and *mental* condition were unusually good.(p.26)
- We doubt if many of them can do it, because none will really want to stop, and hardly one of them, because of the peculiar *mental* twist already acquired, will find he can win out.(p.33)
- So we shall describe some of the *mental* states that precede a relapse into drinking, for obviously this is the crux of the problem.(p.35)
- Here was the threat of commitment, the loss of family and position, to say nothing of that intense *mental* and physical suffering which drinking always caused him.(p.36)
- But there was always the curious *mental* phenomenon that parallel with our sound reasoning there inevitably ran some insanely trivial excuse for taking the first drink.(p.37)
- Then came the hospital with unbearable *mental* and physical suffering.(p.41)
- I saw that will power and self-knowledge would not help in those strange *mental* blank spots.(p.42)
- Once more: The alcoholic at certain times has no effective *mental* defense against the first drink.(p.43)
- What a state of *mental* goose-flesh that used to bring on!(p.54)
- Post-war disillusionment, ever more serious alcoholism, impending *mental* and physical collapse, brought him to the point of self-destruction.(p.56)
- There are those, too, who suffer from grave emotional and *mental* disorders, but many of them do recover if they have the capacity to be honest.(p.58)
- Under these conditions we can employ our *mental* faculties with assurance, for after all God gave us brains to use.(p.86)
- Show him the *mental* twist which leads to the first drink of a spree.(p.92)
- He will match your *mental* inconsistencies with some of his own.(p.92)
- Show him, from your own experience, how the queer *mental* condition surrounding that first drink prevents normal functioning of the will power.(p.92)
- The alarming physical and *mental* symptoms, the deepening pall of remorse, depression and inferiority that settled down on our loved ones -- these things terrified and distracted us.(p.106)
- If he is already committed to an institution, but can convince you and your doctor that he means business, give him a chance to try our method, unless the doctor thinks his *mental* condition too abnormal or dangerous.(p.114)
- We, who have recovered from serious drinking, are miracles of *mental* health.(p.133)
- Being somewhat weakened, and faced with physical and *mental* readjustment to a life which knows no alcohol, he may overdo.(p.146)
- There was much talk about the *mental* state preceding the first drink.(p.157)
- He got in touch with a prominent psychiatrist who had undertaken certain responsibilities for the *mental* health of the community.(p.163)
- When I entered a sanitarium for prolonged and intensive psychiatric treatment, I was convinced that I was having a serious *mental* breakdown.(p.226)
- The *mental* state of the sick alcoholic is beyond description.(p.244)
- Formerly, in the acute *mental* and physical pain during the remorseful periods succeeding each drunk, I found my recollection of the misery I had gone through a bolsterer of resolution and afterward, perhaps, a deterrent for a time.(p.260)
- He told me that it was imperative that I walk around the entire block, cost me what it might in *mental* agony.(p.276)
- I lived through a week of the fidgets because I had agreed to address a group of alcoholic inmates in one of our state *mental* hospitals.(p.283)
- He said he had finally learned that drinking was a fatal illness made up of an allergy plus an obsession, and once the drinking had passed from habit to obsession, we were completely hopeless, and could look forward only to spending the balance of our lives in *mental* institutions or to death.(p.290)
- However, it finally caught up with me, and when it did, I was a *mental*, physical, and nervous wreck.(p.299)
- It is impossible to put on paper all the benefits I have derived . . . physical, *mental*, domestic, spiritual, and monetary.(p.302)
- What I needed was a change, *mental* relaxation, getting out and doing something.(p.338)
- Incalculable are the intangible initiation fees that A.A. members have paid: the sick, sick hangovers, the remorse, guilt, broken homes, jails, and institutions, and the *mental* anguish in general that has been generated over the years.(p.399)
- Was my *mental* state more serious than he said?(p.406)
- At this stage, I began a daily *mental* routine.(p.408)
- He now said that we had a physical allergy combined with a *mental* obsession, and he explained this so that I saw for the first time how this could be.(p.413)
- The last time I drank, when I was twenty-nine, I drank for only four days, yet I threatened to kill my children; I beat my wife at home and on the church steps; I mistreated a child in my office; and I ran to a hospital for *mental* illness to avoid jail.(p.418)
- Under the skilled guidance of an expert practitioner I wallowed in the world's individual and collective *mental* agony.(p.434)
- Loneliness, great physical and *mental* agony -- these were the common lot.(p.455)

• After a few months there, I went to County ***Mental*** Health as an alcoholism worker.(p.462)
• I have come to believe that my illness is spiritual as well as physical and ***mental***, and I know that for help in the spiritual sphere I have to turn to a Higher Power.(p.473)
• The man is in bad ***mental*** shape certainly.(p.503)
• He had been in and out of Matteawan and many other ***mental*** institutions as a result of his drinking.(p.509)
• The ***mental*** twists that led up to my drinking began many years before I ever took a drink for I am one of those whose history proves conclusively that my drinking was "a symptom of a deeper trouble."(p.544)
• For example, we are told in A.A. that we cannot afford resentments and self-pity, so we learn to avoid these festering ***mental*** attitudes.(p.560)
• This self-insurance has resulted in the restoration of physical, ***mental*** and spiritual health and self-respect to hundreds of men and women who would be hopelessly down and out without its unique but effective therapy."(p.574)

mental-health
• He arranged for me to see a local psychiatrist, who quickly decided I should be in the ***mental-health*** unit of our local hospital.(p.445)

mentality
• They piled on me heaps of evidence to the effect that an alcoholic ***mentality***, such as I had exhibited in Washington, was a hopeless condition.(p.42)

mentally
• Best of all, I met a kind doctor who explained that though certainly selfish and foolish, I had been seriously ill, bodily and ***mentally***.(p.7)
• He may have the habit badly enough to gradually impair him physically and ***mentally***.(p.20)
• No person likes to think he is bodily and ***mentally*** different from his fellows.(p.30)
• From it stem all forms of spiritual disease, for we have been not only ***mentally*** and physically ill, we have been spiritually sick.(p.64)
• When the spiritual malady is overcome, we straighten out ***mentally*** and physically.(p.64)
• It may be slowing him up ***mentally*** and physically, but he does not see it.(p.109)
• You can see that he is ***mentally*** and physically sick.(p.141)
• And we stood there for twenty minutes, telling each other how much better we were, how much better we looked, how much better off we were financially, ***mentally***, physically, morally, and in every way, shape and manner.(p.201)
• I found in the fall of 1939, that I was not ***mentally*** impaired, so far as trial work was concerned, and thereafter took up where I had left off when I was about forty-five years old.(p.220)
• When I look back on that last horrible year of constant drinking I wonder how I survived it either physically or ***mentally***.(p.224)
• I myself could see deterioration in my work from being physically and ***mentally*** affected by liquor, although I had not yet reached the point where all I wanted was more to drink.(p.254)
• At least three of those four years must have been a living hell for my wife, because she had to watch the man she loved disintegrate morally, ***mentally*** and financially.(p.277)
• ***Mentally*** . . . I know where I was last night, the night before, and the nights before that.(p.303)
• I felt better ***mentally*** and physically.(p.320)
• Within a few months, I was admitted to a state hospital for the ***mentally*** ill.(p.370)
• ***Mentally***, the fears and tensions, the complete change in attitude and outlook, bewildered me.(p.378)
• (I can't know how much others of our Fellowship have paid financially and, even more important, ***mentally*** and physically.)(p.396)
• My wife was in the Junior League, and I was on the board of directors of the local center for the ***mentally*** retarded.(p.418)
• I have been helped morally, spiritually, ***mentally*** and materially through A.A.(p.430)
• I painfully awakened each time, ***mentally***, physically, and spiritually sick.(p.457)
• No clothes, no money, no home, no real friends to speak of, ***mentally*** and physically pooped, but I was doing all right!(p.478)

mention
• But his face falls when we speak of spiritual matters, especially when we ***mention*** God, for we have reopened a subject which our man thought he had neatly evaded or entirely ignored.(p.45)
• Whether you ***mention*** this book is a matter for your discretion.(p.142)
• For the benefit of those experimentally inclined, I should ***mention*** the so-called beer experiment.(p.177)
• I couldn't stomach religion, and I didn't like the ***mention*** of God or any of the other capital letters.(p.227)
• I lost my driver's license, was made a ward of the court, and was put on probation (not to ***mention*** the fact that I might have killed three friends and myself).(p.354)
• He forgot to ***mention*** that I was the chief critic.(p.449)

mentioned
• This brings us to the Fifth Step in the program of recovery ***mentioned*** in the preceding chapter.(p.72)
• If you take it, your past will be forgotten and the fact that you went away for treatment will not be ***mentioned***.(p.147)
• Somewhere in one of the conversations, I ***mentioned*** that I was contemplating forming a new firm.(p.220)
• He ***mentioned*** two of them that I had known through the years and suggested that I talk with them.(p.289)
• He ***mentioned*** lies and deceptions in the course of his story in the presence of the one person in the world I wouldn't want to know such things.(p.302)
• They hadn't ***mentioned*** the living hell before death.(p.461)
• And so, in those following years, whenever A.A. was ***mentioned*** I would have no part of it.(p.469)
• She never ***mentioned*** anything about my whiskey drinking because if she had I would have told her, "No" right then.(p.494)
• I haven't ***mentioned*** it, but Charlie, my sponsor, was white, and when we got our group started we got help from other white groups in Washington.(p.495)
• I ***mentioned*** that this friend was my temporary host.(p.538)

mentioning
• It would be impossible for me to pass over this year without ***mentioning*** my love for, and my indebtedness to these two wonderful people who are no longer with us.(p.280)

merchant
• My early life was spent in Baltimore where my father was a physician and a grain ***merchant***.(p.240)

mercifully
• ***Mercifully***, no one could guess that I was to have no real employment for five years, or hardly draw a sober breath.(p.4)
• And I remembered the creeping horror of the interminable night, in which I slept for short spells and woke up dripping with cold sweat and shaken with utter despair, to drink hastily from my bottle and ***mercifully*** pass out again, "You're mad, you're mad, you're mad!" pounded through my brain with each returning ray of consciousness, and I drowned the refrain with drink.(p.224)

mere
• If a ***mere*** code of morals or a better philosophy of life were sufficient to overcome alcoholism, many of us would have recovered long ago.(p.44)
• But we must not use this as a ***mere*** excuse to postpone.(p.75)
• From a ***mere*** handful in Akron we have spread throughout the world.(p.295)
• ***Mere*** cessation from drinking is not enough for an alcoholic while the need for that drink goes on.(p.339)
• The idea behind it is that, having taken the treatment, your system is so "conditioned" that the ***mere*** sight or smell or taste of alcohol produces a violent reaction, and you become ill.(p.469)

merely
• We have no monopoly on God; we ***merely*** have an approach that worked with us.(p.95)
• It no longer gave me pleasure -- it ***merely*** dulled the pain -- but I had to have it.(p.226)
• I thought he ***merely*** had a "weakness."(p.369)
• Golf, hunting and fishing were now ***merely*** excuses to drink excessively.(p.375)
• But whereas my horse was always equipped with a flask, I ***merely*** endured the fox hunting so I could start drinking at lunch time.(p.404)
• I ***merely*** wanted to cut down.(p.429)
• Shakespeare said, "All the world's a stage, all the men and women ***merely*** players."(p.449)
• I'd gladly do it anonymously, as I have done this brief account of my struggle with alcohol – ***merely*** to present certain ideas for the consideration of the reader.(p.542)

merit
• Any therapeutic or philosophic procedure which can prove a recovery rate of 50% to 60% must ***merit*** our consideration."(p.571)

merriment
• Outsiders are sometimes shocked when we burst into ***merriment*** over a seemingly tragic experience out of the past.(p.132)
• I had never had a drink, but I had seen enough ***merriment*** in the boys who were drinking to be interested.(p.498)

merry
• So I rocked along my ***merry*** independent way until June, when I went out selling auto polish in New England.(p.247)
• For me, as for most alcoholics, it was "Eat, drink, and be ***merry***, for tomorrow you die."(p.457)
• At noon on Christmas Day I called my family in New York, wished them a ***Merry*** Christmas, and assured them everything was fine with me.(p.467)
• The atmosphere of "eat, drink, and be ***merry***" prevails and I absorb it.(p.499)

merry-go-round
• This last real ***merry-go-round*** had started the day before Christmas and I had really accomplished a lot in those fourteen days.(p.238)
• She said to me, "You know, he used to own the ***Merry-Go-Round***.(p.267)
• And the whole ***merry-go-round*** would be on again.(p.325)
• And when I took that first drink, I was off on the usual ***merry-go-round***.(p.339)
• And then I went back home to live with my parents, and the ***merry-go-round*** started again -- only this time I didn't have to worry about waking up behind bars in a psychiatric ward.(p.468)

Mersey
• Coming out of a pub near the Cunard pier I saw the Lusitania standing out in the middle of the ***Mersey***.(p.252)

mess
• After six months of sobriety I saw the picture in a different light: Detroit was the place I had to return to, not only because I must face the ***mess*** I had made there, but because it was there that I could be of the most service to A.A.(p.281)
• Twenty-odd years ago I made a ***mess*** out of my one and only marriage.(p.286)
• Until I reached A.A. my life was a shambles; I was a ***mess***, and I made everybody near and dear to me miserable.(p.400)
• I've made a ***mess*** of things and can't do anything about it.(p.504)
• India lent itself to drinking then, if you were disposed to drink, because you lived in bungalows; you didn't live all together as you do at home in an Officer's ***Mess***.(p.519)

message
• He suddenly realized that in order to save himself he must carry his ***message*** to another alcoholic.(p.xvi)
• It was now time, the struggling groups thought, to place their ***message*** and unique experience before the world.(p.xvii)
• New groups started up and it was found, to the astonishment of everyone, that A.A.'s ***message*** could be transmitted in the mail as well as by word of mouth.(p.xviii)
• The ***message*** which can interest and hold these alcoholic people must have depth and weight.(p.xxvi)
• 12.Having had a spiritual awakening as the result of these steps, we tried to carry this ***message*** to alcoholics, and to practice these principles in all our affairs.(p.60)
• We may kill a future opportunity to carry a beneficial ***message***.(p.77)
• This is our twelfth suggestion: Carry this ***message*** to other alcoholics!(p.89)
• My secretary returned to say that it was not Mr. B---- on the phone; it was Mr. B----'s brother, and he wished to give me a ***message***.(p.136)
• To 1950, the year of his death, he carried the A.A. ***message*** to more than 5,000 alcoholic men and women, and to all these he gave his medical services without thought of charge.(p.171)
• I was startled to learn he had only been off the booze a month or so himself when he brought me the ***message***!(p.245)
• Carry this ***message*** to other alcoholics.(p.473)
• Year later, I go to Canada to carry ***message*** to Tall Man, but he not listen to son.(p.476)
• Start group on reservation and carry ***message***, help start other groups all over Maritimes and New England.(p.476)
• I keep it simple; go to many meetings; carry ***message*** to those who listen.(p.476)

• The ***message*** has been delivered.(p.497)
• Five -- Each group has but one primary purpose -- to carry its ***message*** to the alcoholic who still suffers.(p.564)
• 5. -- Each Alcoholics Anonymous group ought to be a spiritual entity having but one primary purpose -- that of carrying its ***message*** to the alcoholic who still suffers.(p.565)

messages
• It's the last thing I ever heard him say, and I think there are some of us who, at times, try to read extra ***messages*** and complexities into the Steps.(p.395)

messy
• Your man has probably been trying to conceal a number of scrapes, perhaps pretty ***messy*** ones.(p.140)

met
• There were to be no fees or dues; our expenses were to be ***met*** by our own voluntary contributions.(p.xix)
• They took a drink a day or so prior to the date, and then the phenomenon of craving at once became paramount to all other interests so that the important appointment was not ***met***.(p.xxvii)
• Best of all, I ***met*** a kind doctor who explained that though certainly selfish and foolish, I had been seriously ill, bodily and mentally.(p.7)
• I had ***met*** my match.(p.8)
• This happened soon after they wholeheartedly ***met*** a few simple requirements.(p.50)
• His action ***met*** widespread approval, and today his is one of the most trusted citizens of his town.(p.80)
• She ***met*** these responsibilities gallantly.(p.130)
• It was in the next two or three days after I had first ***met*** Doc and Bill, that I finally came to a decision to turn my will over to God and to go along with this program the best that I could.(p.189)
• Whenever this man and I ***met*** -- I didn't know his name then nor do I know it now -- we would always get drunk.(p.201)
• That was the smartest man I'd ***met*** in months.(p.208)
• How had I ***met*** her?(p.223)
• I ***met*** all the people I wanted to meet; I saw all the places I wanted to see; I did all the things I wanted to do -- and I was increasingly miserable.(p.225)
• Oddly enough, the big shot who fired me from this company was one of the first men I ***met*** when I later joined the New York A.A. Group.(p.242)
• Three months before I ***met*** Jackie I had made my second feeble try at suicide.(p.245)
• However, I made an SOS call to the New York Group, whom I hadn't ***met*** yet, and they suggested we both come there.(p.245)
• We checked into the home of Hank, the man who had fired me eleven years before in Mississippi, and there I ***met*** Bill, our founder.(p.245)
• Making my way to Pittsburgh, I ***met*** other former friends and got a job in a large factory where piecemakers were making good money.(p.252)
• I stayed sober during the trip except for an occasional bottle of beer because funds barely ***met*** expenses.(p.255)
• He introduced himself and began to tell me about a bunch of some sixty former drinkers and drunkards who ***met*** once a week, and he invited me to go with him to the next meeting.(p.257)
• The doctor who came to see me almost at once did not assail me with any new doctrines; he made sure that I had a need and that I wanted to have that need filled, and little by little I learned how my need could be ***met***.(p.258)
• But I had never been a flippant, wise-cracking sneerer at the few persons I had ***met*** who had impressed me as Christian men and women, or at any institution whose sincerity of purpose I could see.(p.259)
• It was just about this time, in 1940, that we ***met*** up with A.A.(p.265)
• I would make a feeble attempt at eating supper, but I never ***met*** with any howling success.(p.299)
• So I went to Akron, and also to Cleveland, and I ***met*** more recovered alcoholics.(p.310)
• When I came home from Nam, I ***met*** a girl I'll call Karen.(p.318)
• But I ***met*** a real wonderful girl I'll call Jean.(p.318)
• I said to her one day when I ***met*** her on the street, "What sort of volunteer work do you do?"(p.326)
• I was living in a small room on West 53rd Street right off Fifth Avenue, when I ***met*** a young lady who eventually was responsible for altering my entire way of living.(p.359)
• I went to many meetings and ***met*** many beautiful people.(p.371)
• We came back East and ***met*** both families.(p.402)
• I ***met*** a wonderful man.(p.403)
• I had ***met*** a bunch of gay young Bohemians who lived in the Village, and were sowing their wild oats.(p.407)
• I'd heard a lot about A.A. and ***met*** a great many A.A.'s during that year at home, but I hadn't thought of it for myself.(p.429)
• But to another woman, the first woman I ***met*** in A.A., I could talk.(p.471)
• In all the sanitariums and psycho wards I had never ***met*** a single woman who said she was an alcoholic.(p.471)
• (I've ***met*** some of these same women since in A.A.)(p.471)
• When I first came into A.A., the woman who was my sponsor was the first woman I had ever ***met*** who admitted that she was an alcoholic.(p.472)
• ***Met*** father (Tall Man) at fork in road -- one way to reservation, other way to State of Maine.(p.475)
• I ***met*** and married a man in A.A., and I am the happiest I have ever been in my life.(p.481)
• My father had purchased a restaurant, which he felt would take up some of my spare time, and that's how I ***met*** Vi.(p.487)
• Thinking only of two or three dollars to buy some whiskey, I did the job and that's how I ***met*** Ella G., who was responsible for my coming into A.A.(p.493)
• But as he continued to talk, I realized that this was the first time I had ***met*** a person who had the same problems I did and who, I sincerely believe, understood me as an individual.(p.494)
• The following Sunday we ***met*** at Ella G.'s.(p.495)
• And so I ***met*** John Barleycorn.(p.498)
• After I had made my third report, I stepped down town, ***met*** some of the old crowd, and of course you know the answer.(p.510)
• Providentially, this was a Monday might when the Dublin Group ***met*** in those days, and my family agreed that if A.A. could do anything for me at all, that I'd be allowed to stay on at home on probation.(p.523)
• When I arrived at The Country Shop, which was a restaurant where they ***met*** in Dublin, I found about thirty-five or forty people in the room.(p.524)
• I went over and ***met*** him, and we two started the group up again.(p.541)
• I was immersed in self-pity and resentment, and the only people who would support this attitude or who I felt understood me at all were the people I ***met*** in bars and the ones who drank as I did.(p.547)
• About this time, I ***met*** a man who had three motherless children and it seemed that might be a solution to my problem.(p.548)

method
• If he is already committed to an institution, but can convince you and your doctor that he means business, give him a chance to try our ***method***, unless the doctor thinks his mental condition too abnormal or dangerous.(p.114)
• Whatever the ***method***, its object is to thoroughly clear mind and body of the effects of alcohol.(p.143)
• We think this ***method*** of approach will accomplish several things.(p.148)
• The doctor proved to be able and exceedingly anxious to adopt any workable ***method*** of handling the situation.(p.163)
• We would follow one man's ideas for a while, decide he was wrong and switch to another's ***method***.(p.246)
• This easy ***method*** of sobering up would last at least three days.(p.468)

Methodist
• I finished high school here in an American-sponsored ***Methodist*** public school, know as Philander Smith College.(p.342)

methods
• I personally know scores of cases who were of the type with whom other ***methods*** had failed completely.(p.xxiii)
• With many individuals the ***methods*** which I employed are successful, but I have never been successful with an alcoholic of your description."(p.27)
• Here are some of the ***methods*** we have tried: Drinking beer only, limiting the number of drinks, never drinking alone, never drinking in the morning, drinking only at home, never having it in the house, never drinking during business hours, drinking only at parties, switching from scotch to brandy, drinking only natural wines, agreeing to resign if ever drunk on the job, taking a trip, not taking a trip, swearing off forever (with and without a solemn oath), taking more physical exercise, reading inspirational books, going to health farms and sanitariums, accepting voluntary commitment to asylums -- we could increase the list ad infinitum.(p.31)
• Trying to avoid this humbling experience, they have turned to easier ***methods***.(p.72)
• We have tried these ***methods***.(p.101)
• After all, are you not looking for results rather than ***methods***?(p.144)

meticulously
• The regular flow of all the literature, which I keep ***meticulously*** and which, of course, I study, has been wonderful.(p.342)

metropolitan
• The small group may elect its secretary, the large group its rotating committee, and the groups of a large ***metropolitan*** area their central or intergroup committee, which often employs a full-time secretary.(p.567)

mettle
• Your man should be on his ***mettle*** to make good.(p.146)

Mexico
• A.A. has flourishing communities in the British Isles, the Scandinavian countries, South Africa, South America, ***Mexico***, Alaska, Australia and Hawaii.(p.xv)

mid-week
• Successive Monday morning hangovers, which despite ***mid-week*** resolutions to do better, came with unfailing regularity, eventually caused me to quit my job.(p.254)

Midas
• It was as if I had, rather than a ***Midas*** touch which turned everything to gold, a magnifying mind that magnified whatever it focused on.(p.450)

middle
• One hundred for unmarried women at one end, one hundred for men at the other, and one hundred for married couples in the ***middle***.(p.198)
• This time I seemed to be already awake, sitting upright in a big easy chair, in the ***middle*** of an animated conversation with a perfectly strange young woman, who didn't appear to think it strange.(p.222)
• I came directly to a growing industrial city in the ***middle*** west, where I have lived practically ever since.(p.231)
• I was doing very well with that and general upholstering work, and there was every indication that I would be financially independent by the time I reached ***middle*** age.(p.232)
• Around this time our big A.A. book was being written and it all became much simpler; we had a definite formula which some sixty of us agreed was the ***middle*** course for all alcoholics who wanted sobriety, and that formula has not been changed one iota down through the years.(p.248)
• Thus I found myself in the ***middle*** of a brand new group.(p.249)
• This newsman covered life from top to bottom; but he ended up, safely enough, in the ***middle***.(p.251)
• Coming out of a pub near the Cunard pier I saw the Lusitania standing out in the ***middle*** of the Mersey.(p.252)
• I believe the sociologists would call it "upper ***middle*** class."(p.275)
• Psychiatry might have helped, but psychiatrists had not penetrated the ***middle*** west.(p.276)
• I said, "I can't find my ***middle*** road in life.(p.340)
• I had no trouble making the right decision when I saw my wife open her purse at the meeting that night and deposit a cute little angel in the ***middle*** of my birthday cake.(p.366)
• I remember finding myself in the ***middle*** of the night in the doctors' parking lot at the hospital with one foot in the car and one foot on the ground, not knowing which was the lead foot; finding myself hanging up the telephone -- then realizing I had gotten out of bed, answered the phone, turned on the light, and carried on a conversation with a patient.(p.441)
• There was the sense of being "misunderstood," when as a matter of fact by my ***middle*** twenties I was quite popular, although I hadn't grown much bigger physically.(p.534)
• With no explanation at all, I was taken from my home in Florida to my grandparents' home in the ***middle*** west.(p.544)
• When I awoke in the ***middle*** of the night with shakes and sweats and fears, I would hear my wife weeping quietly in bed beside me.(p.558)

middle-of-the-road
• If you are as seriously alcoholic as we were, we believe there is no ***middle-of-the-road*** solution.(p.25)

midget
• There was the love affair which was ridiculous -- "imagine that ***midget*** being able to fall in love!" -- and my head knew it while my heart pumped real, genu-

ine anguish, for it hurt like hell, and since it was first love, things have never been quite the same.(p.534)

midnight

• At ***midnight*** he came home exhausted, but very happy.(p.156)

• So I got a half pint and at ***midnight*** that night, I called the number I had been given, but the man who had started the group was in the hospital so I didn't know what to do.(p.393)

midst

• I was part of life at last, and in the ***midst*** of the excitement I discovered liquor.(p.1)

• In the ***midst*** of such pandemonium they may have rushed out threatening to live with the other woman forever.(p.106)

• In the ***midst*** of an understanding and sympathetic family, these vagaries of dad's spiritual infancy will quickly disappear.(p.129)

midwestern

• I was raised like the majority of American boys, coming from a family of modest circumstances, attending public schools, having the social life of a small ***midwestern*** town, with part-time work and some athletics.(p.373)

might

• The broker had gone to Akron on a business venture which had collapsed, leaving him greatly in fear that he ***might*** start drinking again.(p.xvi)

• It was thought that no alcoholic man or woman could be excluded from our Society; that our leaders ***might*** serve but never govern; that each group was to be autonomous and there was to be no professional class of therapy.(p.xix)

• He had lost everything worthwhile in life and was only living, one ***might*** say, to drink.(p.xxix)

• As the whisky rose to my head I told myself I would manage better next time, but I ***might*** as well get good and drunk then.(p.6)

• The cheery voice of an old school friend asked if he ***might*** come over.(p.8)

• When the thought was expressed that there ***might*** be a God personal to me this feeling was intensified.(p.12)

• I could go for such conceptions as Creative Intelligence, Universal Mind or Spirit of Nature but I resisted the thought of a Czar of the Heavens, however loving His sway ***might*** be.(p.12)

• Upon a foundation of complete willingness I ***might*** build what I saw in my friend.(p.12)

• Then only ***might*** I expect to receive.(p.13)

• While I lay in the hospital the thought came that there were thousands of hopeless alcoholics who ***might*** be glad to have what had been so freely given me.(p.14)

• They in turn ***might*** work with others.(p.14)

• I also had the notion that I ***might*** find a customer for a car at this place, which was familiar for I had been going to it for years.(p.36)

• We now see that when we began to drink deliberately, instead of casually, there was little serious or effective thought during the period of premeditation of what the terrific consequences ***might*** be.(p.37)

• The doctor intimated strongly that he ***might*** be worse than he realized.(p.39)

• We could wish to be moral, we could wish to be philosophically comforted, in fact, we could will these things with all our ***might***, but the needed power wasn't there.(p.45)

• We used to amuse ourselves by cynically dissecting spiritual beliefs and practices when we ***might*** have observed that many spiritually-minded persons of all races, colors, and creeds were demonstrating a degree of stability, happiness and usefulness which we should have sought ourselves.(p.49)

• But it is better to meet God alone than with one who ***might*** misunderstand.(p.63)

• To the precise extent that we permit these, do we squander the hours that ***might*** have been worth while.(p.66)

• He trembles to think someone ***might*** have observed him.(p.73)

• We ***might*** prejudice them.(p.77)

• Perhaps we have committed a criminal offense which ***might*** land us in jail if it were known to the authorities.(p.78)

• Before taking drastic action which ***might*** implicate other people we secure their consent.(p.80)

• Each ***might*** pray about it, having the other one's happiness uppermost in mind.(p.82)

• We ***might*** pay for this presumption in all sorts of absurd actions and ideas.(p.87)

• You ***might*** place this book where he can see it in the interval.(p.90)

• But urge them not to be over-anxious, for that ***might*** spoil matters.(p.91)

• When your man is better, the doctor ***might*** suggest a visit from you.(p.91)

• He often says that if he had continued to work on them, he ***might*** have deprived many others, who have since recovered, of their chance.(p.96)

• If he is, you ***might*** try to help him about getting a job, or give him a little financial assistance.(p.96)

• His only chance for sobriety would be some place like the Greenland Ice Cap, and even there an Eskimo ***might*** turn up with a bottle of scotch and ruin everything!(p.101)

• A spirit of intolerance ***might*** repel alcoholics whose lives could have been saved, had it not been for such stupidity.(p.103)

• Had we fully understood the nature of the alcoholic illness, we ***might*** have behaved differently.(p.107)

• When a discussion does arise, you ***might*** suggest he read this book or at least the chapter on alcoholism.(p.111)

• You ***might*** suggest that you both take an interest in them.(p.112)

• Meanwhile you ***might*** try to help the wife of another serious drinker.(p.112)

• This is a condition which, in ordinary life, would produce untold grief; there ***might*** be scandalous gossip, laughter at the expense of other people, and a tendency to take advantage of intimate information.(p.125)

• He is not so unbalanced as they ***might*** think.(p.128)

• New acquaintances who know nothing of alcoholism ***might*** be made and thoughtful consideration given their needs.(p.131)

• The problems of the community ***might*** engage attention.(p.131)

• And but for the intervention of an understanding person, I ***might*** have followed in their footsteps.(p.137)

• We think the business fabric is shot through with a situation which ***might*** be helped by better understanding all around.(p.137)

• He ***might*** have a chance.(p.138)

• To me, this incident illustrates lack of understanding as to what really ails the alcoholic, and lack of knowledge as to what part employers ***might*** profitably take in salvaging their sick employees.(p.139)

• If you desire to help it ***might*** be well to disregard your own drinking, or lack of it.(p.139)

• If this presents difficulty, re-reading chapters two and three, where the alcoholic sickness is discussed at length ***might*** be worth while.(p.140)

• Had they fired me first, and had they then taken steps to see that I was presented with the solution contained in this book, I ***might*** have returned to them six months later, a well man.(p.141)

• You ***might*** say you appreciated his abilities, would like to keep him, but cannot if he continues to drink.(p.141)

• At this point, it ***might*** be well to explain alcoholism, the illness.(p.142)

• If he temporizes and still thinks he can ever drink again, even beer, he ***might*** as well be discharged after the next bender which, if an alcoholic, he is almost certain to have.(p.142)

• It ***might*** be well to have a long chat with him on his return.(p.143)

• When his wife next calls saying he is sick, you ***might*** jump to the conclusion he is drunk.(p.146)

• There is another thing you ***might*** wish to do.(p.147)

• If your organization is a large one, your junior executives ***might*** be provided with this book.(p.147)

• You ***might*** let them know you have no quarrel with the alcoholics of your organization.(p.147)

• He ***might*** be shocked if he knew how much alcoholism is costing his organization a year.(p.149)

• Even if you feel your organization has no alcoholic problem, it ***might*** pay to take another look down the line.(p.149)

• Unless he took some drinks, he ***might*** not have the courage to scrape an acquaintance and would have a lonely week-end.(p.154)

• When our friend related his experience, the man agreed that no amount of will power he ***might*** muster could stop his drinking for long.(p.155)

• He told how he lived in constant worry about those who ***might*** find out about his alcoholism.(p.155)

• He saw that he would have to face his problems squarely that God ***might*** give him mastery.(p.155)

• He trembled as he went about, for this ***might*** mean ruin, particularly to a person in his line of business.(p.156)

• Seeing much of each other, scarce an evening passed that someone's home did not shelter a little gathering of men and women, happy in their release, and constantly thinking how they ***might*** present their discovery to some newcomer.(p.159)

• Aside from fellowship and sociability, the prime object was to provide a time and place where new people ***might*** bring their problems.(p.160)

• Many a distracted wife has visited this house to find loving and understanding companionship among women who knew her problem, to hear from the lips of their husbands what had happened to them, to be advised how her own wayward mate ***might*** be hospitalized and approached when next he stumbled.(p.160)

• We are greatly indebted to the doctor in attendance there, for he, although it ***might*** prejudice his own work, has told us of his belief in ours.(p.162)

• No beer or liquor was sold in the neighborhood, except at the State liquor agency where perhaps one ***might*** procure a pint if he could convince the agent that he really needed it.(p.171)

• I sensed they had something I did not have, from which I ***might*** readily profit.(p.178)

• My wife became deeply interested and it was her interest that sustained mine, though I at no time sensed that it ***might*** be an answer to my liquor problem.(p.178)

• About this time a lady called up my wife one Saturday afternoon, saying she wanted me to come over that evening to meet a friend of hers who ***might*** help me.(p.179)

• The question which ***might*** naturally come into your mind would be: "What did the man do or say that was different from what others had done or said?"(p.180)

• (I ***might*** say right here that never in my life did I ever intend to get drunk.(p.196)

• So in spite of anything that I ***might*** do, I prospered, being one of only two brokers in the rubber center of the world.(p.197)

• That was the reverse of my former pattern of fearing to go to work because I ***might*** drink!(p.199)

• At the end of about four months, I not only had good looking clothes --and I ***might*** say that at the time I first talked to Max I didn't have a suit of clothes I could bend over in real sudden; now I had six suits of clothes.(p.200)

• In 1932, some friends of mine advised me that I ***might*** try Christian Science, which had done a lot for some of their friends.(p.202)

• Then I got into the habit of having beers, and decided that a drink of whiskey was not any worse; so I would get the one drink of whiskey but, on second thought, I decided that as long as I was only going to have one, I ***might*** as well make it a double-header.(p.203)

• When I had been in the hospital ten days, Sister Ignatia, who has played such a part in the development of A.A. in this area, stuck her head in the door one morning and announced, looking at me quizzically, that they ***might*** be able to make something human out of my face after all.(p.205)

• I never left the church, but I was a fringe member, and the thought simply never occurred to me that through the exercise of what I had I ***might*** find the answer to my problem, simply because I wouldn't admit that I had a problem.(p.214)

• I resented it of course, and I offered Clarence his commission, whatever it ***might*** be, if he would please not bother me because I had arrived at the conclusion that he was a solicitor for some alcoholic institute.(p.216)

• I ***might*** have done terrible things, and I wouldn't even know it!(p.223)

• I knew the stuff I was making was a lot stronger than I had been used to, but I never suspected that steady drinking of it ***might*** develop a taste for something even stronger still.(p.233)

• But in those days I had no one to whom I ***might*** take my troubles.(p.260)

• We talked about it afterwards, and we felt that there ***might*** be some time we'd need it.(p.266)

• It was a thought that there ***might*** be some hope for us.(p.266)

• Time went on and the drinking got worse and worse, and I was in another barroom, down the road the other way, a small one, and I took my glass -- that morning I'd been able to lift it from the bar -- and I said to the woman behind the bar, "I wish I ***might*** never take another drop of that stuff.(p.266)

• Psychiatry ***might*** have helped, but psychiatrists had not penetrated the middle west.(p.276)

• He told me that it was imperative that I walk around the entire block, cost me what it ***might*** in mental agony.(p.276)

• He was a man of considerable means and he ***might*** have done what many men would have done in

such a case.(p.278)
• He ***might*** have handed me fifty dollars and said that I ought to pull myself together and make a new start.(p.278)
• To go north into the empty pine country and shoot myself, or to go south in the faint hope that a bunch of strangers ***might*** help me with my drinking problem.(p.278)
• It ran something like this: If I go around shouting from the rooftops about my alcoholism, it ***might*** very possibly prevent me from getting a good job.(p.282)
• I learned early in my A.A. life that I could not afford to fondle such thoughts, as you ***might*** fondle a pet, because this particular pet could grow into a monster.(p.285)
• I didn't care to go visiting unless the parties we ***might*** visit had plenty of liquor on hand and I could get drunk.(p.301)
• I began making the rounds of the doctors in the hope that one of them ***might*** find some cure for my accumulating ailments, preferably something that could be removed surgically.(p.305)
• I could no longer gage my capacity and it ***might*** be the second or the tenth drink that would erase my consciousness.(p.306)
• I didn't dare hope I ***might*** find for myself all that these people had found, but if I could acquire some small part of their intriguing quality of living -- and sobriety – that would be enough.(p.310)
• Among today's incoming A.A. members, many have never reached the advanced stages of alcoholism, though, given time, all ***might*** have.(p.315)
• I was being very cagey, because I knew that if I did take one or two, I ***might*** want to take five or six or seven or eight.(p.323)
• I was unwilling to bare my secrets to those who ***might*** display scorn.(p.331)
• I sat up in the big red chair, suddenly thinking, "My God, with my kind of lousy luck, I ***might*** not die soon!(p.333)
• I began to have to have supplies on hand for the people who "***might*** come in."(p.336)
• And of course a half empty bottle wasn't worth keeping, so I finished it up and naturally had to get more in right away for the people who "***might*** come in unexpectedly."(p.336)
• So I thought to myself, I ***might*** just as well be drunk as feel like this.(p.348)
• I suppose the doctor ***might*** say, "This is psychosomatic medicine."(p.352)
• I suppose the psychiatrist ***might*** say, "This is benevolent interpersonal relations.(p.352)
• I lost my driver's license, was made a ward of the court, and was put on probation (not to mention the fact that I ***might*** have killed three friends and myself).(p.354)
• Before too long, my husband (who seemed to prefer his shirts dirty) put his foot down, declaring that our family ***might*** have the cleanest clothes in town, but that I hadn't been out of the same old dirty slacks and blouse for a week.(p.371)
• IT ***MIGHT*** HAVE BEEN WORSE(p.373)
• Resenting anyone and everyone who ***might*** interfere with my personal plans and ways of doing things, I was full of self pity, especially for any interference with my drinking.(p.376)
• The only other occasionally limiting factor was that I ***might*** run out of money before the next payday rolled around.(p.398)
• It did not occur to me that marriage ***might*** be a job, too.(p.402)
• If I had not become an active alcoholic and joined A.A., I ***might*** never have found my own identity or become a part of anything.(p.417)
• Whatever the root of my unhappiness ***might*** turn out to be, I thought, it could not possibly be booze.(p.433)
• It ***might*** work."(p.436)
• As ***might*** have been predicted, my teetering tower of worldly success collapsed.(p.437)
• Never in my wildest moments had it occurred to me that I ***might*** like to be an alcoholic.(p.439)
• Never once had my mother even hinted at the idea that, when I grew up, I ***might*** like to be president of A.A.(p.439)
• And Frank did set me up for a meeting every night except Friday, when he thought he ***might*** have a date with his girl friend.(p.447)
• It is painful to grow, and without the help of my "civilian" A.A. companion, big Gene, I ***might*** not have survived that critical year of adjustment.(p.462)
• If it hadn't been for an alert hotel maid, I ***might*** have died then.(p.465)
• There ***might*** have been some investigation.(p.492)
• I ***might*** go out West on a ranch where I couldn't get anything to drink.(p.502)
• I ***might*** do that.(p.502)
• It ***might*** be true.(p.504)
• Providentially, this was a Monday ***might*** when the Dublin Group met in those days, and my family agreed that if A.A. could do anything for me at all, that I'd be allowed to stay on at home on probation.(p.523)
• Oh, I ***might*** drink too much at times – everyone I knew drank.(p.527)
• My father was and still is a minister, and I was afraid that I ***might*** run into him, or that someone ***might*** tell him where I was, and I could still remember what he had done to me when I got drunk one Christmas when I was very young.(p.527)
• I am talking about A.A. people, who have gone through some of the same things that you ***might*** be going through now.(p.529)
• There was the economic fear which made me too timid to take any action which ***might*** improve my circumstances.(p.534)
• If the listener were drunk enough, the lecture ***might*** go on through several martinis, which I was glad to pay for.(p.537)
• Once, or even twice, such incidents ***might*** be amusing.(p.538)
• About this time, I met a man who had three motherless children and it seemed that ***might*** be a solution to my problem.(p.548)
• I had fed it, fanned it and nurtured it as one ***might*** a delicate child, and it had become as much a part of me as my breathing.(p.551)
• My doctor warned me that if I kept on, I ***might*** have esophageal hemorrhaging and die.(p.558)
• The doctors told me that if I ever took another drink, it ***might*** be my last.(p.558)
• And no group, regional committee, or individual should ever take any action that ***might*** greatly affect A.A. as a whole without conferring with the trustees of the General Service Board.(p.565)
• But we may employ alcoholics where they are going to perform those services for which we ***might*** otherwise have to engage nonalcoholics.(p.566)

mighty
• Despite contrary indications, I had little doubt that a ***mighty*** purpose and rhythm underlay all.(p.10)
• If you are an alcoholic, you are a ***mighty*** sick man.(p.147)
• He remarked: "I'm ***mighty*** glad you fellows got over your drinking.(p.148)
• The place is Naini Tal, in the foothills of the ***mighty*** Himalaya Mountains, and it has some very significant memories for me.(p.342)

migrated
• After many painful discussions, they finally gave me my credits and I ***migrated*** to another of the leading universities of the country and entered as a Junior that fall.(p.173)

migrations
• My ***migrations*** extended for over a year as far west as Omaha.(p.253)

mike
• I, carried away with the desire to serve A.A., gave what was probably one of the first radio broadcasts about A.A., living through a case of ***mike*** fright and feeling like a million dollars when it was all over.(p.283)

mild
• Hydrotherapy and ***mild*** exercise helped much.(p.7)
• Of an evening, you can go on a ***mild*** bender, get up in the morning, shake your head and go to business.(p.139)
• Again I went into a ***mild*** form of D.T.'s, but with no pineapples this time.(p.429)
• After hearing the first speaker I could tell myself that my own lot was rather ***mild***.(p.509)

mildly
• He is seldom ***mildly*** intoxicated.(p.21)
• On June 26, 1935, I came to in the hospital and to say I was discouraged is to put it ***mildly***.(p.184)
• I stayed in the barracks all day, "making out guard schedules," and getting ***mildly*** plastered from the jug under my desk.(p.426)

mile
• Perhaps we had been leaning too heavily on Reason that last ***mile*** and we did not like to lose our support.(p.53)
• He had lived there but a few weeks when he found that the place probably contained more alcoholics per square ***mile*** than any city in the country.(p.163)

miles
• A community thirty ***miles*** away has fifteen fellows of Alcoholics Anonymous.(p.161)
• If there was a lecture on the subject within a hundred ***miles*** of Akron, I attended.(p.202)
• I remember well one fellow, Joe, walking nearly three ***miles*** through slush, wet and snow to come to the hospital to see a man that he had never seen before in his life, and that impressed me very much.(p.208)
• My parents had some vague idea of making a priest out of me and for some years I attended the Franciscan school at Basle, Switzerland, just across the border, about six ***miles*** from my home.(p.230)
• My next conscious memory was in Bar le Duc, many ***miles*** from base.(p.242)
• They, too, had taken a train to one town and had wakened hundreds of ***miles*** in the opposite direction, never knowing how they got there.(p.246)
• I drove these three or four ***miles*** down the road only to find that Jack was out.(p.267)
• This would get me feeling fit, and then I would start for home and fireside, thirteen ***miles*** away.(p.299)
• I moved a thousand ***miles*** away from home to Chicago and a new environment.(p.305)
• They would travel ***miles*** and stay up all night with someone they had never laid eyes on before and think nothing of it.(p.310)
• This man faced the last ditch when his wife's voice from 1,300 ***miles*** away sent him to A.A.(p.356)
• She said she cut this clipping from the paper at about ten on the same night, and at the same time as I called A.A. in Pittsburgh – some 1300 ***miles*** away.(p.367)
• Maine newsletter (Boomerang) say: "With tireless devotion and humility, this venerable Indian gentleman traveled thousands of ***miles*** humbly pleading for sobriety.(p.476)
• I walk ***miles***.(p.501)

military
• ***Military*** service was compulsory and I did my stretch with the class of my age, goose-stepping in German barracks and taking part in the Boxer Rebellion in China, my first time at any great distance from home.(p.230)
• I had two years at Dublin University, and then in 1916, I got a nomination for Sandhurst, the British ***Military*** College.(p.518)
• Then Hitler's war broke out, and again, I was given a really important job on the Suez Canal, dealing with ***military*** shipping.(p.520)

milk
• I sat down at a table and ordered a sandwich and a glass of ***milk***.(p.36)
• I ordered another sandwich and decided to have another glass of ***milk***.(p.36)
• "Suddenly the thought crossed my mind that if I were to put an ounce of whiskey in my ***milk*** it couldn't hurt me on a full stomach.(p.36)
• I ordered a whiskey and poured it into the ***milk***.(p.36)
• The experiment went so well that I ordered another whiskey and poured it into more ***milk***.(p.36)
• Yet all reasons for not drinking were easily pushed aside in favor of the foolish idea that he could take whiskey if only he mixed it with ***milk***!(p.36)

milk-punch
• I would pull out early, and go to the hunt breakfast and the flowing bowl of ***milk-punch***.(p.404)

milked
• Back to the big city, for another year of precarious living, paid for largely by one or two friends I still had not ***milked*** dry or worn to exhaustion with demands on their bounty.(p.540)

mill
• My home at that time was a place to ***mill*** around in.(p.337)
• Once, in a strange gin ***mill***, I stole a bottle from behind the bar.(p.411)
• I was there about three weeks, and then I got restless and started to tramp across the country, here and there, until I finally wound up in Pennsylvania, in a steel ***mill***.(p.492)
• I worked in the steel ***mill*** for possibly two months, and then I became disgusted with myself and decided to go back home.(p.492)
• But there happened to be a liquor store between the post office and the ***mill***, and I stopped to get that one drink.(p.493)
• When I landed of course I hit a gin ***mill***, and with three or four good shots under my belt the world began to go into that rosy glow.(p.513)
• I'd get downstairs to the gin ***mill***, get enough in to hold me until eight o'clock in the morning, then I'd go out to join that "misery parade" that so many of us

know so well.(p.514)

Millay's

• In my twenties, I found Edna St. Vincent *Millay's* verse:(p.534)

• For a while, for a long time, we can endure the intellect's being ahead of the emotions, which is the import of *Millay's* couplet.(p.534)

millenniums

• This world of ours has made more material progress in the last century than in all the *millenniums* which went before.(p.51)

milligrams

• Eventually, I was taking forty-five *milligrams* of the long-acting Benzedrine and forty-five of the short-acting just to get out of bed in the morning.(p.442)

million

• So far, upon the total problem of several *million* actual and potential alcoholics in the world, we have made only a scratch.(p.xx)

• My friends had dropped several *million* since ten o'clock -- so what?(p.4)

• I, carried away with the desire to serve A.A., gave what was probably one of the first radio broadcasts about A.A., living through a case of mike fright and feeling like a *million* dollars when it was all over.(p.283)

• Monday morning I was feeling just like a *million* dollars -- all I needed was half a pint!(p.393)

• I was now head of a publishing venture in which nearly a *million* dollars had been invested.(p.435)

• A twenty-three *million* dollar surplus wiped out.(p.500)

millionaire

• I figured the only difference between me and a *millionaire* was that I hadn't the strength, or that he got the breaks and I didn't.(p.197)

millions

• My judgment and ideas were followed by many to the tune of paper *millions*.(p.3)

• Everyone spent in thousands and chattered in *millions*.(p.3)

• We have learned that whatever the human frailties of various faiths may be, those faiths have given purpose and direction to *millions*.(p.49)

• This same company spends *millions* for research every year.(p.149)

mills

• I could laugh at the gin *mills*.(p.6)

• I got a job in the woolen *mills* in Ravenna -- very hard work.(p.262)

Milwaukee

• In succession came "What Made *Milwaukee* Famous Made a Loser Out of Me" and "I'm Drinking My Christmas Dinner All Alone."(p.332)

mimic

• I tried to *mimic* the talk, ideas, moods and even the drinking the older men.(p.423)

mince

• Don't *mince* words.(p.423)

mind

• We, of Alcoholics Anonymous, are more than one hundred men and women who have recovered from a seemingly hopeless state of *mind* and body.(p.xiii)

• In this statement he confirms what we who have suffered alcoholic torture must believe -- that the body of the alcoholic is quite as abnormal as his *mind*.(p.xxiv)

• It hadn't even come to *mind*.(p.5)

• The *mind* and body are marvelous mechanisms, for mine endured this agony two more years.(p.6)

• When they talked of a God personal to me, who was love, superhuman strength and direction, I became irritated and my *mind* snapped shut against such a theory.(p.10)

• Never *mind* the musty past; here sat a miracle directly across the kitchen table.(p.11)

• I could go for such conceptions as Creative Intelligence, Universal *Mind* or Spirit of Nature but I resisted the thought of a Czar of the Heavens, however loving His sway might be.(p.12)

• Doubtless you are curious to discover how and why, in the face of expert opinion to the contrary, we have recovered from a hopeless condition of *mind* and body.(p.20)

• Therefore, the main problem of the alcoholic centers in his *mind*, rather than in his body.(p.23)

• The almost certain consequences that follow taking even a glass of beer do not crowd into the *mind* to deter us.(p.24)

• Above all, he believed he had acquired such a profound knowledge of the inner workings of his *mind* and its hidden springs that relapse was unthinkable.(p.26)

• The doctor said: "You have the *mind* of a chronic alcoholic.(p.27)

• I have never seen one single case recover, where that state of *mind* existed to the extent that it does in you."(p.27)

• He made up his *mind* that until he had been successful in business and had retired, he would not touch another drop.(p.32)

• "Suddenly the thought crossed my *mind* that if I were to put an ounce of whiskey in my milk it couldn't hurt me on a full stomach.(p.36)

• He made up his *mind* to quit drinking altogether.(p.39)

• "In this frame of *mind*, I went about my business and for a time all was well.(p.40)

• As I crossed the threshold of the dining room, the thought came to *mind* that it would be nice to have a couple of cocktails with dinner.(p.41)

• I now remembered what my alcoholic friends had told me, how they prophesied that if I had an alcoholic *mind*, the time and place would come -- I would drink again.(p.41)

• I knew from that moment that I had an alcoholic *mind*.(p.42)

• But the moment I made up my *mind* to go through with the process, I had the curious feeling that my alcoholic condition was relieved, as in fact it proved to be.(p.42)

• As to two of you men, whose stories I have heard, there is no doubt in my *mind* that you were 100% hopeless, apart from divine help.(p.43)

• As we felt new power flow in, as we enjoyed peace of *mind*, as we discovered we could face life successfully, as we became conscious of His presence, we began to lose our fear of today, tomorrow or the hereafter.(p.63)

• This brings to *mind* a story about one of our friends.(p.80)

• Each might pray about it, having the other one's happiness uppermost in *mind*.(p.82)

• What used to be the hunch or the occasional inspiration gradually becomes a working part of the *mind*.(p.87)

• Talk about the conditions of body and *mind* which accompany it.(p.92)

• If he is not interested in your solution, if he expects you to act only as a banker for his financial difficulties or a nurse for his sprees, you may have to drop him until he changes his *mind*.(p.95)

• An alcoholic who cannot meet them, still has an alcoholic *mind*; there is something the matter with his spiritual status.(p.101)

• These are some of the questions which race through the *mind* of every woman who has an alcoholic husband.(p.108)

• The seed has been planted in his *mind*.(p.113)

• But these scrapes can generally be charged, no matter how bad, to the abnormal action of alcohol on his *mind*.(p.140)

• Perhaps you have such a man in *mind*.(p.141)

• Whatever the method, its object is to thoroughly clear *mind* and body of the effects of alcohol.(p.143)

• One instance comes to *mind* in which a malicious individual was always making friendly little jokes about an alcoholic's drinking exploits.(p.145)

• What our friend, the vice president, had in *mind* was the habitual or whoopee drinker.(p.149)

• The man in the bed was told of the acute poisoning from which he suffered, how it deteriorates the body of an alcoholic and warps his *mind*.(p.157)

• My whole life seemed to be centered around doing what I wanted to do, without regard for the rights, wishes, or privileges of anyone else; a state of *mind* which became more and more predominant as the years passed.(p.172)

• This went from bad to worse until Sophomore spring when, after a prolonged period of drinking, I made up my *mind* that I could not complete my course, so I packed my grip and went South to spend a month on a large farm owned by a friend of mine.(p.173)

• The question which might naturally come into your *mind* would be: "What did the man do or say that was different from what others had done or said?"(p.180)

• Each of the seven times that I had left this hospital in the last six months, I had come out fully determined in my own *mind* that I would not get drunk again -- for at least six or eight months.(p.184)

• That sure did take a load off of my *mind*.(p.188)

• The thought flashed through his *mind*, "If they can do it, I can do it!"(p.189)

• I always built up in my own *mind* the great things that I was going to do, and in fact I accomplished about fifty percent of them and then lost interest.(p.193)

• To my *mind*, drinking didn't have anything to do with not going through with things.(p.198)

• My wife didn't tell me this, but one Sunday afternoon when Mary was trying to get the cobwebs out of my *mind*, Clarence and his sister-in-law, the hairdresser, called at the house.(p.216)

• Peddling off my polish samples for expenses, I crawled back to New York a few days later in a very chastened frame of *mind*.(p.248)

• Before the end finally came, I had, I guess made the surrender because I finally had been able to say that I would not *mind* too much.(p.272)

• You can't lose, and maybe God will help you -- just maybe, *mind* you.(p.280)

• I was in a perfectly happy frame of *mind*.(p.285)

• I had been in A.A. a year, and the last thing in my *mind* was a drink.(p.285)

• If I live to be a hundred, it will always stand out in my *mind*.(p.292)

• But, of course," he continued, "eventually the alcoholic loses all of his capacities as his disease gets progressively worse, and this is a tragedy that is painful to watch; the disintegration of a sound *mind* and body."(p.308)

• After a time, my *mind* began to clear of the fog that had covered it.(p.320)

• I was afraid, and I had made my *mind* up that I would never get drunk, so I was watchful and careful.(p.322)

• I thought I was losing my *mind* when I realized that I couldn't stop drinking.(p.324)

• My alcoholism-prone *mind*, however, reminded me that all great authors had needed a stimulus to build up inspiration and inventiveness before each day's work.(p.331)

• The drinker's *mind* is full of uncertainties and insecurities.(p.331)

• A lot of lost dreams, empty futures, and crazy things of the past went through my *mind*.(p.333)

• How that line echoed through my *mind*!(p.333)

• I don't believe, when I started, that I even had in *mind* the thought that I was drinking.(p.336)

• I had to sleep, I had to clear my *mind* and free it from worry, and I had to relax.(p.336)

• After that I sat for a week, a body in a chair, a *mind* off in space.(p.338)

• I thought I was going out of my *mind*.(p.339)

• In my stupid way I went up to see him with the idea in the back of my *mind* that I would investigate Alcoholics Anonymous from a medical standpoint.(p.346)

• I tried every gimmick that there was to get some peace of *mind*, but it was not until I was brought to my alcoholic knees, when I was brought to a group in my own community with the butcher, the baker, the carpenter and the mechanic, who were able to give me the Twelve Steps, that I was finally given some semblance of an answer to the last half of the First Step.(p.349)

• I gave them everything, except the greatest thing in the world, and that is peace of *mind*.(p.351)

• I wanted so badly to see the picture as it was in her *mind*.(p.355)

• I entered the house, opened a new bottle of whiskey and sat down to drink myself into the right frame of *mind* to get in my car, start the motor and close the garage door behind me.(p.363)

• Thank God that in spite of my heavy drinking my *mind* was clear enough to make a decision then and there.(p.363)

• The explanation that alcoholism was a disease of a two fold nature, an allergy of the body and an obsession of the *mind*, cleared up a number of puzzling questions for me.(p.380)

• The obsession of the *mind* was a little harder to understand and yet everyone has obsessions of various kinds.(p.380)

• The fact that A.A. is a spiritual program didn't scare me or raise any prejudice in my *mind*.(p.383)

• In the back of my *mind*, I probably thought, "They won't take me as drunk as I am."(p.398)

• So please bear in *mind*, and I would like to emphasize, that this is a very rough estimate.(p.399)

• The horrors of increasing hangover sickness to occupy the entire day; nausea, dry heaves, the rocking bed, the nightmare-filled *mind*.(p.408)

• He asked me if I had any spiritual belief, and when I said No, he suggested that I keep an open *mind*.(p.413)

• I had accomplished all the right things that our society expected, and I had no real peace of *mind* nor gratitude.(p.418)

• Educated child of the scientific age that I was, I had complete faith in the science of the ***mind***.(p.434)
• Science could take my ***mind*** apart expertly, but it couldn't seem to put it together again.(p.435)
• Today, I feel I have used up my right to chemical peace of ***mind***.(p.448)
• It was as if I had, rather than a Midas touch which turned everything to gold, a magnifying ***mind*** that magnified whatever it focused on.(p.450)
• And the more I focused my ***mind*** on her defects, the more they grew and multiplied.(p.450)
• The more I focus my ***mind*** on its defects -- late start, long drunkalogues, cigarette smoke -- the worse the meeting becomes.(p.451)
• But when I try to see what I can add to the meeting, rather than what I can get out of it, and when I focus my ***mind*** on what's good about it, rather than what's wrong with it, the meeting keeps getting better and better.(p.451)
• Eventually, I had to redo each of the Twelve Steps specifically with Max in ***mind***, from the First, saying, "I am powerless over alcohol, and my homelife is unmanageable by me," to the Twelfth, in which I tried to think of her as a sick Al-Anon and treat her with the love I would give a sick A.A. newcomer.(p.452)
• I must keep my magic magnifying ***mind*** on my acceptance and off my expectations, for my serenity is directly proportional to my level of acceptance.(p.452)
• We do this by going to many A.A. meetings with an open ***mind*** and a desire to live the good-feeling life without chemicals -- liquid or otherwise.(p.459)
• The last Christmas I spent in Washington, fourteen years ago, comes to ***mind***.(p.465)
• In my screwed up ***mind*** I kept thinking I could have gone to A.A. way back there in 1940, and perhaps saved my marriage and home.(p.469)
• ***Mind*** you, I had absolutely nothing to show for that eighteen years, except a beat-up car that I hadn't even paid for, but I was doing all right.(p.478)
• Vi was very kind and explained to the jury that I was basically a fine fellow and a good husband, but that I drank too much and that she thought I had lost my ***mind*** and felt that I should be committed to an asylum.(p.492)
• I just gathered up this and that alcoholic, because, in the back of my ***mind***, I wanted to save all the world.(p.496)
• I don't seem to be able to keep my ***mind*** on what I am doing.(p.499)
• What a wonderful power he has over the ***mind***!(p.499)
• Anything to get my ***mind*** from myself.(p.502)
• Then he asks me if I believe in a power greater than myself, whether I call that power God, Allah, Confucius, Prime Cause, Divine ***Mind***, or any other name.(p.503)
• But after I passed through the gates I took a change of heart and ***mind***.(p.510)
• I started prowling around with a couple of these A.A. boys, which kept me pretty busy and kept my ***mind*** off of down town.(p.511)
• Just as I was wondering what on earth I could do -- I was too drunk even to pack a handkerchief -- the memory of an A.A. write-up that I had seen in the Evening Mail flashed across my ***mind*** -- and I thought to myself, this is something I haven't tried yet.(p.523)
• My ***mind*** was too screwy to be able to understand much of what was being said.(p.524)
• "Pity me the heart that is slow to learn What the quick ***mind*** sees at every turn."(p.534)
• Sobering up, the ***mind*** that was ahead of the emotions would impel the question: What have you written or done to be the great man?(p.537)
• This question so insulted the emotions that clearly there was only one thing to do, go and get drunk again, and put that enquiring ***mind*** in its proper place, which was oblivion.(p.537)
• I bear a few scars on my face from these fights, which I always lost, because the "stick" existed only in my ***mind***.(p.537)
• Simply, yes it did end; for I had changed my ***mind*** about alcohol, and it stayed changed.(p.541)
• A.A. has taught me that I will have peace of ***mind*** in exact proportion to the peace of ***mind*** I bring into the lives of other people, and it has taught me the true meaning of the admonition "happy are ye who know these things and do them."(p.551)
• Most emphatically we wish to say that any alcoholic capable of honestly facing his problems in the light of our experience can recover, provided he does not close his ***mind*** to all spiritual concepts.(p.570)

mind-affecting

• Giving up alcohol alone was not enough for me; I've had to give up all mood-and ***mind-affecting*** chemicals in order to stay sober and comfortable.(p.443)

mind's

• In my ***mind's*** eye I saw Broadway again and Tom Sharkey's bar; the roar of the subway was in my ears.(p.252)
• In my ***mind's*** eye, I played and replayed scenes in which I was plucked magically from the bar where I stood nursing a drink, and was instantly exalted to some position of power and prestige.(p.560)

minded

• Faced with alcoholic destruction, we soon became as open ***minded*** on spiritual matters as we tried to be on other questions.(p.48)
• It seemed to me my wife was becoming more intolerant and narrow ***minded*** all the time.(p.376)

mindedness

• The Twelve Steps, which to me are a spiritual way of living, soon meant honest thinking, not wishful thinking, open ***mindedness***, a willingness to try and a faith to accept.(p.381)
• Willingness, honesty and open ***mindedness*** are the essentials of recovery.(p.570)

minds

• In the realm of the material, men's ***minds*** were fettered by superstition, tradition, and all sorts of fixed ideas.(p.51)
• Was it not true that the best mathematical ***minds*** had proved man could never fly?(p.51)
• Neither is reason, as most of us use it, entirely dependable, though it emanate from our best ***minds***.(p.54)
• Even so has God restored us all to our right ***minds***.(p.57)
• Putting out of our ***minds*** the wrongs others had done, we resolutely looked for our own mistakes.(p.67)
• As non-denominational people, we cannot make up others' ***minds*** for them.(p.132)
• Most of them give freely of themselves, that their fellows may enjoy sound ***minds*** and bodies.(p.133)
• Their young ***minds*** were impressionable while he was drinking.(p.134)
• Being wrecked in the same vessel, being restored and united under one God, with hearts and ***minds*** attuned to the welfare of others, the things which matter so much to some people no longer signify much to them.(p.161)
• He further explained that alcohol was no respecter of sex or background, but that most of the alcoholics he had encountered had better than average ***minds*** and abilities.(p.308)
• Similarly, we rid ourselves of guilt and remorse as we "clean out the garbage" from our ***minds*** through the Fourth and Fifth Steps of our recovery program.(p.560)

mine

• The mind and body are marvelous mechanisms, for ***mine*** endured this agony two more years.(p.6)
• "How can I best serve Thee -- Thy will (not ***mine***) be done."(p.85)
• This went from bad to worse until Sophomore spring when, after a prolonged period of drinking, I made up my mind that I could not complete my course, so I packed my grip and went South to spend a month on a large farm owned by a friend of ***mine***.(p.173)
• My wife became deeply interested and it was her interest that sustained ***mine***, though I at no time sensed that it might be an answer to my liquor problem.(p.178)
• He tossed off half of his martini; I tossed off half of ***mine*** and it nearly blew the top of my head off.(p.195)
• But I watched him, and he tossed off the rest of his, so I tossed off the rest of ***mine***.(p.195)
• He ate his olive and I ate ***mine***.(p.195)
• In 1932, some friends of ***mine*** advised me that I might try Christian Science, which had done a lot for some of their friends.(p.202)
• So I started to investigate Science through some friends of ***mine*** who were Readers in the church.(p.202)
• He then pulled up his chair with one of his knees touching ***mine*** and said, "Will you pray with me for your success?"(p.218)
• I believe that my once over-weening self-will has finally found its proper place, for I can say many times daily, "Thy will be done, not ***mine***" . . . and mean it.(p.229)
• From the top of the heap in a few years he had skidded to becoming a shuffling customer, still entering the better barrooms but welcomed by neither ***mine*** host nor his patrons.(p.236)
• I had not asked for help and seriously doubt that I would have, but Fitz, an old school friend of ***mine***, had persuaded Jackie to call on me.(p.238)
• I let ***mine*** sit.(p.247)
• The hospitality of their home and their fine fellowship were freely ***mine***.(p.259)
• ***Mine*** was far from a happy childhood.(p.261)
• I was supposed to be doing God's will, not ***mine***.(p.282)
• He laid great stress on the progression of his attitude toward life and people, and most of his attitudes had been very similar to ***mine***.(p.290)
• Finally, an old business acquaintance of ***mine***, whom I hadn't seen for several years offered me a job.(p.301)
• A friend of ***mine***, a golf nut, rushed out on retirement to play every day.(p.330)
• ***Mine*** was the skid row of success.(p.345)
• About two days later I was called by a friend of ***mine*** from Nevada City -- he's a brother of my wife's closest friend.(p.347)
• They have contributed fantastic amounts of time and work to our problem, but they aren't able, it seems, to arrest either your alcoholism or ***mine***.(p.352)
• They told me their stories, which were much more rugged than ***mine*** -- yet what they said made sense, and the way they put it was easy for me to understand, with an understanding I had never had before.(p.363)
• A "spiritual experience" to me meant attending meetings, seeing a group of people, all there for the purpose of helping each other; hearing the Twelve Steps and the Twelve Traditions read at a meeting, and hearing the Lord's Prayer, which in an A.A. meeting has such great meaning -- "Thy will be done, not ***mine***."(p.381)
• Namely, ***mine***.(p.396)
• Her luck had been worse than ***mine***, but not her drinking.(p.414)
• All the people involved in these flare-ups took it with remarkable grace, have teased me about it since, and have become good friends of ***mine***.(p.416)
• My new wife and I don't own any property to speak of, and the flashy successes of another day are no longer ***mine***.(p.438)
• A very good friend of ***mine*** who owned a drug store across the street from us, came by only about two hours later and said that he had seen Vi down town.(p.487)
• I got to the place where I'd look forward to the week-end's drinking and pacify myself by saying that the week-ends were ***mine***, that it didn't interfere with my family or with my business if I drank on the week-ends.(p.488)
• I took that bottle of medicine and gave it to a very good friend of ***mine*** who was a pharmacist and had it analyzed, and the bottle was perfectly all right.(p.489)
• Nevertheless, we continued to work together and I continued to drink, but I guess, deep down within her heart as well as within ***mine***, we both knew I couldn't stop drinking.(p.490)
• I hunt for my nickel to drop in the plate so that ***mine*** will be seen.(p.497)
• When I had heard about it, it meant nothing but just two letters to me, but some friends of ***mine*** in the institution were very active in the program and really believed in it.(p.509)
• A former employer of ***mine*** said to me a little over ten years ago, "Pat, you seem to be one of those unfortunate people who at least once every six months must go out and roll in the gutter."(p.513)
• I have not seen a black face but ***mine*** since I've been here, and if I didn't look in the mirror, I wouldn't know that I was black, because these people treat me as one of them, which I am.(p.530)
• And it was nobody's business, nobody's but ***mine***.(p.532)
• During the day a friend of ***mine*** brought me some magazines to take to a hospital group I was interested in, and I looked through them and a "banner" across the front of one featured an article by a prominent clergyman in which I caught the word "resentment."(p.552)

mineral

• There, I received several soda crackers and water daily, and before I could have my third-day meal (again the only meal in ten days), I had to drink a glass of castor oil or ***mineral*** oil, depending on the cruelty of the person who was doing the dispensing.(p.459)

mines

• He may not see at once that he has barely scratched a limitless lode which will pay dividends only if he ***mines*** it for the rest of his life and insists on giving away the entire product.(p.129)

minimum

• I really worked for several weeks, and having had a fairly wide acquaintance with the dealer trade, it was

not difficult for me to line up enough of them to give me a very substantial volume of business with a ***minimum*** of effort.(p.300)
• For that crime I received a ***minimum*** of twenty years and a maximum of natural life.(p.508)
• I received an additional fifteen years for that, making a ***minimum*** of thirty-five years and a maximum of natural life.(p.509)
• On October 28th, I was sent to Sing Sing with a ***minimum*** of thirty-three and a half years to serve out of that thirty-five.(p.509)

minister
• He is like the retired business man who lolls in the Florida sunshine in the winter complaining of the sad state of the nation; the ***minister*** who sighs over the sins of the twentieth century; politicians and reformers who are sure all would be Utopia if the rest of the world would only behave; the outlaw safe cracker who thinks society has wronged him; and the alcoholic who has lost all and is locked up.(p.61)
• Suggestions about these may be obtained from one's priest, ***minister***, or rabbi.(p.87)
• He may bring new hope and new courage to many a priest, ***minister***, or rabbi, who gives his all to ***minister*** to our troubled world.(p.132)
• I went to a ***minister*** and a doctor that I still knew and they, in turn, asked me how long I had been sober.(p.293)
• I suggested to her that she should see the son's ***minister*** or doctor, and that perhaps he would recommend the A.A. program.(p.294)
• I had a long talk with a psychiatrist, but nothing came of that, and I had also, just about that time, talked with a ***minister*** for whom I had a great deal of respect.(p.489)
• Father is an Episcopal ***minister*** and his work takes him over long drives on bad roads.(p.497)
• My father was and still is a ***minister***, and I was afraid that I might run into him, or that someone might tell him where I was, and I could still remember what he had done to me when I got drunk one Christmas when I was very young.(p.527)

minister's
• Our friend was a ***minister's*** son.(p.56)
• Pioneer A.A., ***minister's*** son, and southern farmer, he asked, "Who am I to say there is no God?"(p.497)

ministers
• With ***ministers***, and world's religions, I parted right there.(p.10)
• You can easily find some by asking a few doctors, ***ministers***, priests or hospitals.(p.89)
• ***Ministers*** and doctors are competent and you can learn much from them if you wish, but it happens that because of your own drinking experience you can be uniquely useful to other alcoholics.(p.89)
• I listened to famous ***ministers*** -- found nothing.(p.255)
• So I spent much of my time calling on the people who I felt would logically come in contact with alcoholic cases, doctors, ***ministers***, lawyers and the personnel men in industry.(p.281)
• Here was a book that said I could do something that all these doctors and priests and ***ministers*** and psychiatrists that I'd been going to for years couldn't do!(p.473)
• I approached several ***ministers*** and all of them thought it was a very good idea, but they never relinquished any space.(p.495)
• In such places, A.A. can be located through the local telephone directory, newspaper office, or police station, or by contacting local priests or ***ministers***.(p.575)

ministration
• Another reason for the wide acceptance of A.A. was the ***ministration*** of friends -- friends in medicine, religion, and the press, together with innumerable others who became our able and persistent advocates.(p.xx)

minor
• We had a ***minor*** campaign or two and that helped distract attention from my drinking.(p.519)

minus
• "Oh no," said my friend, "this chap is either through with liquor, or he is ***minus*** a job.(p.138)
• I lost a lot of shirts that way, and sometimes I was ***minus*** a whole wash.(p.371)

minute
• There had been no more power in him than there was in me at the ***minute***; and this was none at all.(p.11)
• The ***minute*** we put our work on a service plane, the alcoholic commences to rely upon our assistance rather than upon God.(p.98)
• After a while, Bill said, "Well, now, you've been talking a good long time, let me talk a ***minute*** or two."(p.185)
• And we loved every ***minute*** of that association.(p.270)
• And he said, "Earle, why don't you come on over and let me talk to you for a ***minute***."(p.348)
• If it was one ***minute*** before five, I'd drink myself back to sleep.(p.441)
• If it was one ***minute*** after, I'd stay up and act like a martyr all day.(p.441)
• I hated every ***minute*** of it.(p.526)

minutes
• Wishing to be polite, though I felt very badly, I said, "Let's make the call," and extracted from my wife a promise that we would not stay over fifteen ***minutes***.(p.179)
• And we stood there for twenty ***minutes***, telling each other how much better we were, how much better we looked, how much better off we were financially, mentally, physically, morally, and in every way, shape and manner.(p.201)
• A few ***minutes*** later, Dr. Bob left, leaving with my brother some medicine I should get.(p.207)
• I'd only had two with her, but I'd managed four in the fifteen ***minutes*** I'd waited for her, and of course I'd had the usual uncounted swigs from the bottle as I painfully got up and did my slow spasmodic dressing.(p.223)
• Visits from friends which lasted over fifteen ***minutes*** exhausted me.(p.275)
• I couldn't remember what had been said five ***minutes*** ago.(p.319)
• Within thirty ***minutes*** I knew A.A. was the answer for me.(p.378)
• It was the first time in my life that I could not get a lift out of what I was drinking; and so one Friday night, at five ***minutes*** to six, I had half a water glass of warm gin, and that is when I first asked God to help me.(p.393)
• When I got out of there, I lasted about fifteen ***minutes*** at home, before I headed for the drugstore and more pills, and then the bar.(p.479)
• You hit the street about ten ***minutes*** to eight, and you walk around the block, God knows how many times, waiting for that joint to open.(p.514)

miracle
• Since the original Foreword to this book was written in 1939, a wholesale ***miracle*** has taken place.(p.xv)
• Never mind the musty past; here sat a ***miracle*** directly across the kitchen table.(p.11)
• What is this but a ***miracle*** of healing?(p.57)
• That is the ***miracle*** of it.(p.85)
• The ***miracle*** of reconciliation was at hand.(p.124)
• While grateful that he drinks no more, they may not like the idea that God has accomplished the ***miracle*** where they failed.(p.128)
• There was an insistent yearning to enjoy life as we once did and a heartbreaking obsession that some new ***miracle*** of control would enable us to do it.(p.151)
• Then the ***miracle*** happened -- to me!(p.228)
• This alone is a ***miracle***.(p.280)
• Certainly now, anyone would have agreed that only a ***miracle*** could prevent my final breakdown.(p.306)
• But how does one get a prescription for a ***miracle***?(p.306)
• Some of us struggle with these people because we know that they are really very sick, but we also know that short of some ***miracle***, we are not going to help them except temporarily, and that they will inevitably get worse and worse until one of two things happens.(p.308)
• He was serving time on his fifth felony conviction when a ***miracle*** happened.(p.457)
• Then the ***miracle*** happened.(p.461)
• One would have to understand the correctional machinery to see what a ***miracle*** this really was.(p.462)
• ***Miracle*** happen all time in A.A.(p.476)

miracles
• My ideas about ***miracles*** were drastically revised right then.(p.11)
• We, who have recovered from serious drinking, are ***miracles*** of mental health.(p.133)
• Try to remember that though God has wrought ***miracles*** among us, we should never belittle a good doctor or psychiatrist.(p.133)
• The age of ***miracles*** is still with us.(p.153)
• They had seen ***miracles***, and one was to come to them.(p.161)
• It is, however, only the first of a series of ***miracles*** which have followed one after another as a result of my trying to apply to my daily life the principles embodies in our Twelve Steps.(p.280)

miraculous
• The central fact of our lives today is the absolute certainty that our Creator has entered into our hearts and lives in a way which is indeed ***miraculous***.(p.25)
• This Power has in each case accomplished the ***miraculous***, the humanly impossible.(p.50)
• For faith in a Power greater than ourselves, and ***miraculous*** demonstrations of that power in human lives, are facts as old as man himself.(p.55)

miraculously
• In the next half-year, I experienced two more esophageal hemorrhages, ***miraculously*** surviving each one by a hair.(p.558)

mire
• When we see a man sinking into the ***mire*** that is alcoholism, we give him first aid and place what we have at his disposal.(p.132)

Miriam
• And they introduced me to ***Miriam*** and Annabelle.(p.269)

mirror
• I have not seen a black face but mine since I've been here, and if I didn't look in the ***mirror***, I wouldn't know that I was black, because these people treat me as one of them, which I am.(p.530)

mirrored
• For me, it was a little different because I couldn't help thinking about the past, and I saw the future more or less ***mirrored*** in the past.(p.513)

misbegotten
• I also wrote another novel, all about Scott Fitzgerald's poor, ***misbegotten***, unloved, tipsy little debutante.(p.405)

miscarriages
• My life there was a nightmare of periodic binges on alcohol and pills, adultery, unhappy hours at the dental office, seeing my wife give birth to our second child and have several ***miscarriages***, living in a turbulent household, and making continual attempts to be the respectable dentist, husband, father, and community leader.(p.419)

miscellaneous
• I was always interested in mechanics and after having about twenty ***miscellaneous*** jobs, lasting from one day to two weeks, I obtained a job as a toolmaker apprentice.(p.211)

misdeeds
• It is possible to dig up past ***misdeeds*** so they become a blight, a veritable plague.(p.124)

miserable
• Everyone became resigned to the certainty that I would have to be shut up somewhere, or would stumble along to a ***miserable*** end.(p.8)
• I was self conscious and ill at ease most of the time, my health was at the breaking point, and I was thoroughly ***miserable***.(p.178)
• I met all the people I wanted to meet; I saw all the places I wanted to see; I did all the things I wanted to do -- and I was increasingly ***miserable***.(p.225)
• No conviction was necessary to establish my status as a ***miserable*** failure at managing my own life.(p.259)
• The physical skid row in any city is ***miserable***.(p.345)
• The skid row of success is just as ***miserable***.(p.345)
• And then one ill-defined day, one day that I can't recall, I stepped across the line that alcoholics know so well, and from that day on drinking was ***miserable***.(p.346)
• And the first thing you know I was lifted right out of the A.A. group, and I floated higher, and higher, and even higher, until I was way up on a pink cloud which is known as Pink Seven, and I felt ***miserable*** again.(p.348)
• I had turned eighteen during the trip, and I despondently returned home by jet (on Daddy's bankbook) to a pair of ***miserable***, hurt parents.(p.354)
• Life was pretty ***miserable***.(p.388)
• Until I reached A.A. my life was a shambles; I was a mess, and I made everybody near and dear to me ***miserable***.(p.400)
• My husband was made ***miserable*** by this, but I had already made him and myself ***miserable***.(p.402)
• The thirteen stories in this group tell of alcoholism at its ***miserable*** worst.(p.455)
• I stay on wagon for while, but ***miserable***.(p.475)
• Then I drink again, but more ***miserable***.(p.475)

miserably
• During the next three years, I tried often again to give it up, but failed ***miserably***.(p.343)

misery
• There is scarcely any form of trouble and ***misery***

which has not been overcome among us.(p.15)

• We were having trouble with personal relationships, we couldn't control our emotional natures, we were a prey to *misery* and depression, we couldn't make a living, we had a feeling of uselessness, we were full of fear, we were unhappy, we couldn't seem to be of real help to other people – was not a basic solution of these bedevilments more important than whether we should see newsreels of lunar flight?(p.52)

• With it you can avert death and *misery* for them.(p.124)

• But it is clear that we made our own *misery*.(p.133)

• Avoid then, the deliberate manufacture of *misery*, but if trouble comes, cheerfully capitalize it as an opportunity to demonstrate His omnipotence.(p.133)

• How can they rise out of such *misery*, bad repute and hopelessness?(p.153)

• Arrangements were also made with the chief psychiatrist of a large public hospital to select still others from the stream of *misery* which flows through that institution.(p.163)

• Formerly, in the acute mental and physical pain during the remorseful periods succeeding each drunk, I found my recollection of the *misery* I had gone through a bolsterer of resolution and afterward, perhaps, a deterrent for a time.(p.260)

• I completely forgot myself in trying vainly to help Anne, whose *misery* I understood.(p.415)

• Meanwhile, I was getting worse, both as regards my inward *misery* and my drinking.(p.434)

• Only through being beaten down by my own *misery* would I ever have accepted the term "alcoholic" as applied to myself.(p.436)

• Tell him I want to get away from bottle and *misery*.(p.475)

• I'd get downstairs to the gin mill, get enough in to hold me until eight o'clock in the morning, then I'd go out to join that "*misery* parade" that so many of us know so well.(p.514)

• To those now in its fold, Alcoholics Anonymous has made the difference between *misery* and sobriety, and often the difference between life and death.(p.563)

misfortune

• It set in motion trains of circumstances which brought us *misfortune* we felt we didn't deserve.(p.67)

misfortunes

• He succumbed to that gay crowd inside, who laughed at their own *misfortunes* and understood his.(p.160)

misgiving

• Later, he requested the privilege of being allowed to tell his story to other patients here and with some *misgiving*, we consented.(p.xxv)

misgivings

• Probably there are still some *misgivings*.(p.76)

mishaps

• Slight casualties, complicated however by a long and serious illness, were my only *mishaps*.(p.253)

misled

• But at least he will understand the problem and will no longer be *misled* by ordinary promises.(p.148)

misplaced

• Yet early next morning he searches madly for the bottle he *misplaced* the night before.(p.21)

miss

• To watch people recover, to see them help others, to watch loneliness vanish, to see a fellowship grow up about you, to have a host of friends – this is an experience you must not *miss*.(p.89)

• We know you will not want to *miss* it.(p.89)

• Now and then a serious drinker, being dry at the moment says, "I don't *miss* it at all.(p.151)

• Then, I started to *miss* meetings because it was raining or snowing or something else.(p.203)

• Very rarely do I *miss* the meetings of my neighborhood A.A. group, and my average has never been less than two meetings a week.(p.249)

• Before I stop -- I always was a great talker – I want to say that nobody will ever know how I *miss* Annie's advice about things.(p.273)

• Other days, I had to *miss* work because I was still too drunk to stand up.(p.318)

• By the time all this was over, I was really in a terrific state, and my father taking in things said, "*Miss* Esther is about to faint.(p.385)

• I don't *miss* any of the old crowd nor do I *miss* any of their parties.(p.511)

missed

• We *missed* the reality and beauty of the forest because we were diverted by the ugliness of some of its trees.(p.50)

• I went into the high school grades, but having *missed* all the intermediate grades, I didn't get along too well, so I developed the habit of going back to school just long enough for the football season and then quitting.(p.193)

• I don't know whether I drank to cover up being a failure, or whether I drank and then *missed* the deals.(p.198)

• I *missed* the old social times, of course, but had no definite craving even for beer.(p.232)

• I had *missed* them myself from the barrooms of the town.(p.258)

• We had never *missed* a Wednesday night at King School for a year.(p.270)

• I had run away from school to join the army in World War I, but *missed* it by one day since the Armistice was signed the very day I landed in Atlanta to sign up with Uncle Sam.(p.357)

• I displayed alcoholic tendencies actually from the age of fourteen, when I started to steal wine from the family jug, siphoning it off one drink at a time so it wouldn't be *missed*, not drinking it immediately, but saving it until about a pint was accumulated, so that I could get drunk.(p.397)

• Here was the lost love I'd *missed* at home.(p.425)

• Meanwhile the letters from home were telling about how much my folks wanted to make up to me for some of the things I'd *missed*.(p.427)

• I was never drunk on the job, never *missed* a day's work, was seldom rendered totally ineffective by a hangover and kept my liquor expenses well within my adequate budget.(p.433)

• While I was there I realized that I had *missed* something.(p.472)

missing

• Curious about it, feeling I was *missing* something, absolutely without any illusions about the aftermath, with no pronounced feeling of patriotism, I joined up with a Canadian regiment, serving a little over two years.(p.253)

• So I set out to get drunk deliberately, just to teach her what she was *missing*.(p.293)

mission

• He had already imbued them with his own spirit until they were ready and willing at all times to go where sent, and as a doctor he well knew that this *mission* and duty would strengthen them as it later helped me.(p.235)

• There was the same reward -- exhilaration at a *mission* accomplished.(p.283)

Mississippi

• My next job was in sales promotion for an oil company in *Mississippi* where I promptly became high man and got lots of pats on the back.(p.242)

• We checked into the home of Hank, the man who had fired me eleven years before in *Mississippi*, and there I met Bill, our founder.(p.245)

mistake

• This is sometimes a *mistake*.(p.95)

• We have traveled a rocky road, there is no *mistake* about that.(p.104)

• We find it a real *mistake* to dampen his enthusiasm for alcoholic work.(p.119)

• If there ever was anyone who came to A.A. by *mistake*, it was I.(p.439)

• Very shortly, I realized that had been a *mistake* -- when this big clown came bounding into the room, almost shouting, "My name is Frank, and I'm an alcoholic, ha-ha-ha!"(p.446)

• Nothing, absolutely nothing happens in God's world by *mistake*.(p.449)

• But that was just a *mistake*.(p.517)

mistaken

• Could we have been so *mistaken* in the men we married?(p.107)

• Both father and the family are *mistaken*, though each side may have some justification.(p.126)

mistakes

• Putting out of our minds the wrongs others had done, we resolutely looked for our own *mistakes*.(p.67)

• This thought brings us to Step Ten, which suggests we continue to take personal inventory and continue to set right any new *mistakes* as we go along.(p.84)

• We want to analyze *mistakes* we have made.(p.104)

• Under these conditions we naturally made *mistakes*.(p.107)

• You will make *mistakes*, but if you are in earnest they will not drag you down.(p.117)

• We think each family which has been relieved owes something to those who have not, and when the occasion requires, each member of it should be only too willing to bring former *mistakes*, no matter how grievous, out of their hiding places.(p.124)

• Sorry for *mistakes*.(p.474)

mistreated

• The last time I drank, when I was twenty-nine, I drank for only four days, yet I threatened to kill my children; I beat my wife at home and on the church steps; I *mistreated* a child in my office; and I ran to a hospital for mental illness to avoid jail.(p.418)

• A man wasn't actually *mistreated*, though if he was he could only resent it.(p.485)

mistress

• Told my wife of my *mistress*.(p.65)

mistrusting

• If I were alone I would stop at four or five of them, but only one or two in the event I had my *mistrusting* wife with me.(p.299)

misunderstand

• But it is better to meet God alone than with one who might *misunderstand*.(p.63)

misunderstanding

• It brings *misunderstanding*, fierce resentment, financial insecurity, disgusted friends and employers, warped lives of blameless children, sad wives and parents – anyone can increase the list.(p.18)

• Back of them is a world of ignorance and *misunderstanding*.(p.20)

• We have had long rendezvous with hurt pride, frustration, self-pity, *misunderstanding* and fear.(p.104)

• Next he can be assured that you do not intend to lecture, moralize, or condemn; that if this was done formerly, it was because of *misunderstanding*.(p.142)

• My inability to accept the harsh realities of life had resulted in a disillusioned cynic, clothed in protective armor against the world's *misunderstanding*.(p.226)

misunderstands

• *Misunderstands* and nags.(p.65)

misunderstood

• He will tell you he is *misunderstood*.(p.111)

• On my ride to the nearest bar, I sold the driver on how *misunderstood* I was by my wife and what an unreasonable person she was.(p.288)

• Somehow or other, I must have *misunderstood* the doctor's instructions, for I not only made the beer for my wife, I also drank it for her.(p.297)

• It was all about Scott Fitzgerald's little lost debutante, abused, *misunderstood* and running wild.(p.402)

• There was the sense of being "*misunderstood*," when as a matter of fact by my middle twenties I was quite popular, although I hadn't grown much bigger physically.(p.534)

misused

• Having been neglected and *misused* in the past, they think father owes them more than they are getting.(p.126)

mix

• We are people who normally would not *mix*.(p.17)

mixed

• Yet all reasons for not drinking were easily pushed aside in favor of the foolish idea that he could take whiskey if only he *mixed* it with milk!(p.36)

• Perhaps we are *mixed* up with women in a fashion we wouldn't care to have advertised.(p.80)

• That is, it was sort of a *mixed* bunch of Oxford Groupers, who were interested in the alcoholic problem, and of alcoholics themselves.(p.218)

• I tried them *mixed*, unmixed, drinking only when gay, only when depressed.(p.305)

• But they were all *mixed* up together, and I was all *mixed* up inside.(p.337)

• So, with *mixed* feelings of humiliation, anger, and fear, I decided to look for an answer.(p.371)

• I cried a bit and then *mixed* me another drink.(p.440)

• My husband interrupted, "She's bad enough now without getting *mixed* up with a bunch of drunks."(p.469)

• As an indication of just how confused and *mixed* up I was, just as soon as I could I left the office and hurried around to tell other patients that I was getting better.(p.470)

mixed-up

• I am hoping that writing this may bring some poor, *mixed-up* soul into the program.(p.530)

mob

• I rolled along with the *mob* this way, that way and the other way, but in those years nothing really bad happened to me.(p.508)

moccasins

• (I am pleased to state, however, that I had gone to only a very few A.A. meetings before I was able to

make a really beautiful pair of ***moccasins*** -- and half a wallet.(p.445)
• I wore those ***moccasins*** every night for the next seven years, until they wore out.(p.445)
• For my seventh A.A. birthday, my program-oriented, Al-Anon wife had my ***moccasins*** bronzed.(p.445)
• Now I own perhaps the most costly pair of ***moccasins*** anyone has ever seen, and they help me remember where I've been.)(p.445)

mode
• We are convinced that a spiritual ***mode*** of living is a most powerful health restorative.(p.133)

model
• When drinking, or getting over a bout, an alcoholic, sometimes the ***model*** of honesty when normal, will do incredible things.(p.140)
• A year later I was able to buy a ***Model*** T roadster and take a better job with a downtown printer.(p.276)
• There was the physical aspect; to be the youngest and the runt of the brood of children, to have to wear glasses very early and so to be teased, to be bookish and bored in school because the captain of the football team could not translate Virgil and yet was the school god while you, you, you little shrimp, were the school egghead, junior size and an early ***model***.(p.533)

moderate
• ***Moderate*** drinkers have little trouble in giving up liquor entirely if they have good reason for it.(p.20)
• If a sufficiently strong reason – ill health, falling in love, change of environment, or the warning of a doctor – becomes operative, this man can also stop or ***moderate***, although he may find it difficult and troublesome and may even need medical attention.(p.21)
• He may start off as a ***moderate*** drinker; he may or may not become a continuous hard drinker; but at some stage of his drinking career he begins to lose all control of his liquor consumption, once he starts to drink.(p.21)
• That may be true of certain nonalcoholic people who, though drinking foolishly and heavily at the present time, are able to stop or ***moderate***, because their brains and bodies have not been damaged as ours were.(p.39)
• Some will ***moderate*** or stop altogether, and some will not.(p.109)
• Show him you have confidence in his power to stop or ***moderate***.(p.112)
• If you act upon these principles, your husband may stop or ***moderate***.(p.112)
• As a ***moderate*** drinker, you can take your liquor or leave it alone.(p.139)

moderated
• Whether you are a hard drinker, a ***moderated*** drinker or a teetotaler, you may have some pretty strong opinions, perhaps prejudices.(p.139)

moderately
• For those who are unable to drink ***moderately*** the question is how to stop altogether.(p.34)
• But when he gets over the spree, he begins to think once more how he can drink ***moderately*** next time.(p.109)
• Those who drink ***moderately*** may be more annoyed with an alcoholic than a total abstainer would be.(p.139)

moderating
• He has begun to try, with or without your cooperation, various means of ***moderating*** or staying dry.(p.109)

moderation
• I drank with ***moderation*** at first, but it took me only a relatively short time to drift back into the old habits which had wound up so disastrously before.(p.175)
• Most of them prescribed sedatives and advised rest and ***moderation***.(p.305)

modern
• The spirit of ***modern*** scientific inquiry, research and invention was almost unknown.(p.51)
• Nearly every ***modern*** employer feels a moral responsibility for the well-being of his help, and he tries to meet these responsibilities.(p.137)
• The glittering society belle, the ***modern*** Shakespeare, the happy wife, the loving and beloved.(p.411)
• And all this, of course, is, in the popular ***modern*** jargon, "compensation" for immaturity.(p.535)

modest
• He may be kind, considerate, patient, generous; even ***modest*** and self-sacrificing.(p.61)
• Within a year of my return to Detroit, A.A. was a definitely established little group of about a dozen members and I too was established in a ***modest*** but steady job handling an independent dry-cleaning route of my own.(p.283)
• I was raised like the majority of American boys, coming from a family of ***modest*** circumstances, attending public schools, having the social life of a small midwestern town, with part-time work and some athletics.(p.373)

modestly
• Living ***modestly***, my wife and I saved $1,000.(p.2)
• I'm rated as a ***modestly*** successful man.(p.296)
• We worked in five below zero weather, fixing on an elm tree a wrought iron device which ***modestly*** proclaimed that he was indeed a country doctor.(p.540)

mold
• We asked God to ***mold*** our ideals and help us to live up to them.(p.69)

molested
• They cooked up a plan whereby she didn't have to be ***molested*** by me if she didn't want to be.(p.491)

moll
• I felt like a gangster's ***moll*** about to be interviewed by the Salvation Army.(p.413)

mom
• He and ***mom*** smuggled in a couple of pints to me.(p.425)
• ***Mom*** and I drank every waking moment because we felt so sorry for dad.(p.426)
• I headed home for the most wonderful experience of all time – meeting my "new" parents – ***mom*** and dad looked different than I had pictured them.(p.428)
• I lost it many times and ***mom*** and dad would drive me around until I found it.(p.429)
• ***Mom*** has said the only requisite to start is willingness.(p.430)

moment
• He sobered, never to drink again up to the ***moment*** of his death in 1950.(p.xvi)
• For a brief ***moment***, I had needed and wanted God.(p.12)
• These were revolutionary and drastic proposals, but the ***moment*** I fully accepted them, the effect was electric.(p.14)
• For a ***moment*** I was alarmed, and called my friend, the doctor, to ask if I were still sane.(p.14)
• We are like the passengers of a great liner the ***moment*** after rescue from shipwreck when camaraderie, joyousness and democracy pervade the vessel from steerage to Captain's table.(p.17)
• He has a positive genius for getting tight at exactly the wrong ***moment***, particularly when some important decision must be made or engagement kept.(p.21)
• I knew from that ***moment*** that I had an alcoholic mind.(p.42)
• But the ***moment*** I made up my mind to go through with the process, I had the curious feeling that my alcoholic condition was relieved, as in fact it proved to be.(p.42)
• At the ***moment*** we are trying to put our lives in order.(p.77)
• But say nothing, for the ***moment***, of how that was accomplished.(p.91)
• In a weak ***moment*** he may take your dislike of his high-stepping friends as one of those insanely trivial excuses to drink.(p.120)
• If the book is read the ***moment*** the patient is able, while acutely depressed, realization of his condition may come to him.(p.144)
• I have enjoyed every ***moment*** spent in getting them straightened out.(p.150)
• Now and then a serious drinker, being dry at the ***moment*** says, "I don't miss it at all.(p.151)
• We shook hands, and he hung onto my hand for a ***moment*** and said, "Tell you what I'll do for old times sake.(p.201)
• From far away, as if in a delirium, I heard my own voice – calling someone "Dorothy," talking of dress shops, of jobs . . . the words came clearer . . . this sound of my own voice frightened me as it came closer . . . and suddenly, there I was, talking of I knew not what, to someone I'd never seen before this very ***moment***.(p.222)
• I said to my husband, "I'm going to try, every free ***moment*** that I have, to get interested in something outside, get myself over this rut I'm in."(p.338)
• When I was nineteen, I married a fine man who had never known an insecure ***moment*** in his life, let alone the trials and tribulations of booze.(p.369)
• Mom and I drank every waking ***moment*** because we felt so sorry for dad.(p.426)
• From that ***moment*** on, I have not had a single compulsion to drink.(p.449)
• When I am disturbed, it is because I find some person, place, thing, or situation – some fact of my life -- unacceptable to me, and I can find no serenity until I accept that person, place, thing, or situation as being exactly the way it is supposed to be at this ***moment***.(p.449)
• The only way existence was possible was through rationalizing every sober ***moment*** and drinking myself into complete oblivion as often as I could.(p.547)

momentarily
• ***Momentarily*** we did -- then would come oblivion and the awful awakening to face the hideous Four Horsemen -- Terror, Bewilderment, Frustration, Despair.(p.151)

momentary
• It was no ***momentary*** emotionalism born of self-pity in a maudlin condition.(p.258)

moments
• If any feel that as psychiatrists directing a hospital for alcoholics we appear somewhat sentimental, let them stand with us a while on the firing line, see the tragedies, the despairing wives, the little children; let the solving of these problems become a part of their daily work, and even of their sleeping ***moments***, and the most cynical will not wonder that we have accepted and encouraged this movement.(p.xxvi)
• Here was love, applause, war; ***moments*** sublime with intervals hilarious.(p.1)
• My old manner of life was by no means a bad one, but I would not exchange its best ***moments*** for the worst I have now.(p.43)
• Yet, in other ***moments***, we found ourselves thinking, when enchanted by a starlit night, "Who, then, made all this?"(p.46)
• Save for a few brief ***moments*** of temptation the thought of drink has never returned; and at such times a great revulsion has risen up in him.(p.57)
• Is he not, even in his best ***moments***, a producer of confusion rather than harmony?(p.61)
• Our ***moments*** of triumph were short-lived.(p.66)
• At such ***moments*** we forget that alcoholism is an illness over which we could not possibly have had any power.(p.118)
• Never could we recapture the great ***moments*** of the past.(p.151)
• I would reach over and get this and take a shot and in a few ***moments*** get up and take another, shave and eat my breakfast, slip a half pint of liquor in my hip pocket, and go on to school.(p.183)
• These things were carried out in ***moments*** of less severe hangover or short stretches on the wagon.(p.409)
• Never in my wildest ***moments*** had it occurred to me that I might like to be an alcoholic.(p.439)
• I have my brilliant ***moments*** yet, but whenever the boys catch me at it they tell me so very plainly.(p.512)

momentum
• For the first couple of years it wasn't too bad because the ***momentum*** kept things going.(p.486)

Mommy
• He said, "Tell ***Mommy*** I still love her."(p.263)

monastic
• But, although I was a good Catholic, the ***monastic*** life had little appeal for me.(p.230)

Monday
• From childhood through high school I was more or less forced to go to church, Sunday School and evening service, ***Monday*** night Christian Endeavor and sometimes to Wednesday evening prayer meeting.(p.172)
• I got tight that night, stayed sober ***Monday*** till after the dinner and then proceeded to get tight again.(p.179)
• The man who was going to take over one of their biggest branches come ***Monday***?(p.243)
• Successive ***Monday*** morning hangovers, which despite mid-week resolutions to do better, came with unfailing regularity, eventually caused me to quit my job.(p.254)
• So Frank left town, and by ***Monday*** morning I had been sober for that whole week.(p.393)
• ***Monday*** morning I was feeling just like a million dollars – all I needed was half a pint!(p.393)
• I stayed drunk from ***Monday*** until Friday, and I call that my spill into A.A.(p.393)
• At age twenty-one, I enlisted in the Navy for two reasons: (1) to avoid being drafted into the Army, and (2) out of a burst of patriotic fervor inspired by the advent of World War II and as the result of an all-night drinking binge which found me sitting on the doorstep of the Navy recruiting office when the chief petty officer arrived to open for business at nine o'clock ***Monday*** morning.(p.398)
• Providentially, this was a ***Monday*** might when the Dublin Group met in those days, and my family agreed that if A.A. could do anything for me at all,

that I'd be allowed to stay on at home on probation.(p.523)

Mondays

• But the week-ends stretched on into *Mondays* and the time soon came when I drank every day.(p.488)

monetary

• It is impossible to put on paper all the benefits I have derived . . . physical, mental, domestic, spiritual, and *monetary*.(p.302)

• From a *monetary* standpoint . . . in the past few years, I have reduced my reckless debts to almost nothing, and have had money to get along on comfortably.(p.303)

money

• Would there be quarrels over membership, leadership and *money*?(p.xviii)

• Many people lost *money* -- but some became very rich.(p.2)

• I had developed a theory that most people lost *money* in stocks through ignorance of markets.(p.2)

• I had had some success at speculation, so we had a little *money*, but we once worked on a farm for a month to avoid drawing on our small capital.(p.3)

• The exercise of an option brought in more *money*, leaving us with a profit of several thousand dollars for that year.(p.3)

• For the next few years fortune threw *money* and applause my way.(p.3)

• He had plenty of *money* left and thought I had better go to Canada.(p.4)

• I went to town regularly and even made a little *money*.(p.7)

• Every means of solving his problem which *money* could buy was at his disposal.(p.32)

• Had we not variously worshipped people, sentiment, things, *money*, and ourselves?(p.54)

• Most alcoholics owe *money*.(p.78)

• He did, and also sent a small amount of *money*.(p.79)

• While drinking, he accepted a sum of *money* from a bitterly-hated business rival, giving him no receipt for it.(p.80)

• He subsequently denied having received the *money* and used the incident as a basis for discrediting the man.(p.80)

• But you should not deprive your family or creditors of *money* they should have.(p.96)

• Be certain he will be welcomed by your family, and that he is not trying to impose upon you for *money*, connections, or shelter.(p.96)

• It may mean sharing your *money* and your home, counseling frantic wives and relatives, innumerable trips to police courts, sanitariums, hospitals, jails and asylums.(p.97)

• The men who cry for *money* and shelter before conquering alcohol, are on the wrong track.(p.98)

• Perhaps he spends too much *money* for liquor.(p.109)

• Perhaps he will never have much *money* again.(p.123)

• The family will be affected also, pleasantly at first, as they feel their *money* troubles are about to be solved, then not so pleasantly as they find themselves neglected.(p.126)

• Although financial recovery is on the way for many of us, we found we could not place *money* first.(p.127)

• My downfall cost the business community unknown thousands of dollars, for it takes real *money* to train a man for an executive position.(p.137)

• If he owes you *money* you may wish to make terms.(p.145)

• Cleaning up old scrapes, helping to settle family differences, explaining the disinherited son to his irate parents, lending *money* and securing jobs for each other, when justified -- these are everyday occurrences.(p.161)

• I had some *money*, all the time in the world, and considerable stomach trouble.(p.174)

• Not being a man of means, I knew that if I did not stay sober enough to earn *money*, I would run out of liquor.(p.175)

• It was really a horrible nightmare, this earning *money*, getting liquor, smuggling it home, getting drunk, morning jitters, taking large doses of sedatives to make it possible for me to earn more *money*, and so on ad nauseam.(p.177)

• She also told me that I could not pay them even if I wanted to and had the *money*, which I did not.(p.185)

• When he was uptown -- we were living in the little town of Moscow -- I went up to try to get some *money* from him to buy groceries.(p.193)

• He wouldn't give me any *money* for the groceries, but he did take me across the street and buy me a bag of candy, which I later took back and traded for a loaf of bread.(p.193)

• I had bought a piece of ground in Cuyahoga Falls and cut it into lots and had a profit of approximately $40,000 and that was a lot of *money* in those days.(p.194)

• I lost *money*, and then just fooled away a large part of that profit.(p.194)

• During the day, looking over the contracts and *money* in my pocket, I found that I had sold six lots that I couldn't even remember, and didn't even know the people I had sold them to.(p.196)

• I came to Cleveland with the deeds to these lots and to pick up my *money*.(p.196)

• The next morning I woke up in jail in Cleveland and the jailor had $1,175 of my *money* in an envelope.(p.196)

• I was always able to skate along the fringe of big *money*.(p.197)

• With the big companies, and with the amount of *money* we could have gotten and the promises I had, it could have been done.(p.198)

• I can remember well thinking that I would quit drinking, really go to work hard, apply myself eight hours a day, five days a week, make a lot of *money*, and then I could start drinking again.(p.199)

• We drove to a store in North Hill and I sent him in with what *money* I had to get a quart.(p.204)

• My family had *money* -- I had never known denial of any material desire.(p.225)

• I'd work like mad for three or four weeks without a single drink, save my *money*, pay a few bills and then "reward" myself with alcohol.(p.244)

• Making my way to Pittsburgh, I met other former friends and got a job in a large factory where piecemakers were making good *money*.(p.252)

• During my visit there, renewing acquaintance with former friends, I soon spent most of my *money*.(p.252)

• Returning to the town I had left three months before, I became editor of a monthly magazine, soon had additional publicity and advertising accounts and the *money* rolled in.(p.254)

• My family would have nothing to do with me, in fact couldn't because I couldn't spare any of my *money*, which I needed for drink, to support them.(p.255)

• I had been brought up to believe this, and I had shown during my 'teens considerable enterprise and imagination about earning *money*.(p.275)

• Poor health and a complete lack of *money* necessitated my remaining with Dr. Bob and Anne for very close to a year.(p.280)

• There was more than one occasion when I got up in the morning with just enough *money* for coffee and toast and the bus fare to carry me to my first appointment.(p.283)

• During that first year, however, I managed to make both ends meet, and to avoid ever going back to my old habit pattern of borrowing *money* when I could not earn it.(p.283)

• In recent years I have had the happy combination of time and *money* to travel occasionally.(p.285)

• They went into a huddle and dad explained that he simply took my pants, shoes and *money* away, so that I could get no liquor and had to sober up.(p.288)

• After finding every bottle that I had hidden around the apartment, she took away my pants, my shoes, my *money* and my keys, threw them under the bed in the back bedroom and slip-locked our door.(p.288)

• By the time we reached the bar, he was willing to buy me a quart with his own *money*.(p.288)

• After holding good positions, making better than an average income for over ten years, I was in debt, had no clothes to speak of, no *money*, no friends, and no one any longer tolerating me but my wife.(p.301)

• Even some of the saloon-keepers, where I had spent so much time and *money*, requested that I stay away from their places.(p.301)

• From a monetary standpoint . . . in the past few years, I have reduced my reckless debts to almost nothing, and have had *money* to get along on comfortably.(p.303)

• It was a waste of the doctors' time and the patients' *money*.(p.307)

• I made more *money* the last year of my drinking than I ever made before in my whole life.(p.345)

• As usual, I ran out of *money*, and, as usual, I wired my father for funds to come home.(p.357)

• Looking back, it is surprising to me now that I managed to keep working and have enough *money* to squander at the various spots in the big city.(p.358)

• I would have begrudged the time or *money* for alcohol.(p.374)

• It is bound to be rough, because who can say exactly how much of that green blood -- commonly known as *money* -- was dissipated on dissipation?(p.396)

• Eighteen will be used as the starting point, because my drinking before was limited by age, the law, and *money*.(p.397)

• The only other occasionally limiting factor was that I might run out of *money* before the next payday rolled around.(p.398)

• But the *money* I had saved up went for cases of liquor.(p.409)

• I found I could boost my income by figuring out a lot of cute little tricks that the boss wouldn't be likely to notice -- filching *money* from the Coke machine, short-sticking the customers on oil, and selling oil I'd drained out of other cars.(p.423)

• We headed out of town walking -- no *money*, cold and hungry.(p.424)

• And then my waiting until I was sure he was asleep, and stealing *money* from him to replenish the supply.(p.466)

• My husband helped me into the house, packed himself a bag, and gave me some *money*.(p.467)

• He said he didn't care what I did with the *money*, but there was going to be no more until I was completely sober.(p.467)

• No clothes, no *money*, no home, no real friends to speak of, mentally and physically pooped, but I was doing all right!(p.478)

• Father, through the years, had built up a very good mail order business because, at that time, there wasn't too much *money* in medicine.(p.485)

• Dad, due to having spent most of his time in a small Virginia town, didn't have any too much *money*, and the *money* he had saved and the property he had acquired were in Washington.(p.486)

• As usual I got drunk and lost the *money*.(p.491)

• I think the thing that galled me was that just after Easter I had drawn my salary for two weeks' work and had decided that I was going to send some *money* to Vi; and above all else I was going to send my baby daughter an Easter outfit.(p.493)

• I knew I wasn't capable of keeping the bulk of the *money* myself, so I gave it to a white fellow who owned the bar which I frequented.(p.493)

• He kept the *money* for me, but I worried him to death for it.(p.493)

• I got out of that bill one pair of shoes, and the rest of that *money* was blown.(p.493)

• I must find a way to make some *money*.(p.506)

• It continues to try to teach me the real charity, the charity that gives time and good will and service, and not just *money*.(p.525)

• I would never admit that I was drinking too much, or spending *money* that I should have used to buy food for my two little boys.(p.526)

• I would stay out until my *money* was gone.(p.527)

• Now I had gotten to the place where I would wake up with black eyes and not know where I got them, or wake up with a lot of *money* and not know where I got it.(p.528)

• There was the necessity for sticking to a job I hated, a dull, repetitive job performed in association with other men I had nothing in common with . . . performed for years on end, because the *money* was needed at home.(p.532)

• Need I add that such was the case because I had no *money* to provide a roof over my head?(p.538)

• The helpful family finally said, over long distance, that there would be no more *money* and that I could not come home.(p.538)

• I had even borrowed *money* from her, over her protest: "Bob, please don't ask me to lend you *money* -- you're the only one who hasn't."(p.540)

• I took her *money*, though; I had to have it.(p.540)

• I had no *money* -- well, maybe a dime -- and only the clothes I stood in.(p.540)

• I don't care too much about personal fame or glory, and I want only enough *money* to enable me to do the work I feel I can perhaps do best.(p.542)

• The only kind of security I knew anything about at that time was material security and I decided that all these intruders would vanish immediately if I only had a lot of *money*.(p.545)

• Six -- An A.A. group ought never endorse, finance or lend the A.A. name to any related facility or outside enterprise, lest problems of *money*, property and prestige divert us from our primary purpose.(p.564)

• Nor ought A.A. membership ever depend upon *money* or conformity.(p.565)

• 6. -- Problems of *money*, property, and authority may easily divert us from our primary spiritual aim.(p.565)

• Experience has often warned us that nothing can so surely destroy our spiritual heritage as futile disputes over property, *money*, and authority.(p.566)

monkeys

• No *monkeys* on our backs.(p.329)

monopoly

• Upon therapy for the alcoholic himself, we surely have no *monopoly*.(p.xxi)

• We have no *monopoly* on God; we merely have an approach that worked with us.(p.95)

monster

• I learned early in my A.A. life that I could not afford to fondle such thoughts, as you might fondle a pet, because this particular pet could grow into a *monster*.(p.285)

monstrous

• Hangovers began to assume *monstrous* proportions and the morning drink became an urgent necessity.(p.226)

month

• I had had some success at speculation, so we had a little money, but we once worked on a farm for a *month* to avoid drawing on our small capital.(p.3)

• We are unable, at certain times, to bring into our consciousness with sufficient force the memory of the suffering and humiliation of even a week or a *month* ago.(p.24)

• This went from bad to worse until Sophomore spring when, after a prolonged period of drinking, I made up my mind that I could not complete my course, so I packed my grip and went South to spend a *month* on a large farm owned by a friend of mine.(p.173)

• When I left the hospital I tried this for a day and it worked, for a week and it worked, and for a *month*, and it worked – and then for a year and it still worked.(p.209)

• In my own experience I was so jubilant at finding myself sober, and I had so many things to catch up on, that a *month* went by before the thought even occurred to me.(p.219)

• Professionally, after I was sober for a *month* or so I realized that I should school myself to dissolve the partnership I was in because I felt that I would never regain the respect of my partners no matter how long I was sober, and that I would be at a disadvantage.(p.220)

• At this time I was holding what drinking I did down to weekends, but I hadn't had a drink at all in a *month*.(p.243)

• I was startled to learn he had only been off the booze a *month* or so himself when he brought me the message!(p.245)

• He knew too well that didn't mean a thing, just as I knew in my heart that it would be only a question of time -- a few days, a week, or even a *month*, it was inevitable – till I would be off on another bender.(p.257)

• When she finally took the baby and left, I locked myself in the house and stayed drunk for a *month*.(p.278)

• So I told dad that I would lick it on my own, that I would drink nothing for a *month* and after that only beer.(p.289)

• I was on that job a *month* and drunk most of the time.(p.301)

• Two years later, a *month* beyond age seventy, I was crying for help from A.A.(p.327)

• It was a *month* beyond my seventieth birthday.(p.333)

• We did, and spent a *month* boozing it up, popping pills, and smoking marijuana; taking shelter where we could, which included a veterinary hospital one night; accepting meals from anyone; actually begging; stealing anything we were in need of, which was about everything.(p.354)

• When I was called upon for a few words I had to tell my friends that I wasn't one year old in A.A. that evening but only a "nine *month* baby."(p.366)

• It only took a *month* to get a divorce in Texas.(p.386)

• But they kept me there -- I was supposed to stay a *month*, but they only kept me there seventeen days.(p.387)

• So I went down to him quite a few times a *month* and had him shoot me full of the stuff; and then I went across the street to a little drug store to take a glass of beer or two beers, and then stopped at the liquor store to get myself a pint and go home.(p.389)

• My first pay was ten dollars, pay for recruits at that time being twenty-one dollars per *month*.(p.398)

• For an estimate of salary from the twenty-one a *month* to start with, to over $400 per *month* upon my retirement after twenty years in the Navy, I believe that an average income of $2,000 a year over this period is low, but as I stated earlier, an underestimate is best.(p.399)

• But when this happened to me, I declared to friends that I would get drunk, dead drunk that very night, and stay drunk for a *month*.(p.403)

• Not understanding the twenty-four hour plan, or not wanting to, I began drinking and was off-again on-again, during that first *month*.(p.414)

• And when this six *month* school was over I applied for duty in Hawaii and pulled it.(p.426)

• After a *month* it seemed unlikely that it ever really happened.(p.433)

• I thank God I am to see him this *month*.(p.463)

• I will be fifty years old next *month*, haven't seen my son or daughter yet, nor my daughter's two children, my grandchildren; but I am grateful.(p.463)

• The November following, I took a few days off after pay day to celebrate my birthday on the 25th of the *month*.(p.491)

• So instead of going near A.A., I just browsed around for that first *month*.(p.510)

• On one of these trips, the judge must have thought I was worth saving, for instead of sending me to jail, he sent me to A.A. for one *month*.(p.526)

• I would wait for the mailman each *month*, like any good mother, but as soon as he handed me my check, I put on my best dress and went looking for my alcoholic friend.(p.527)

• Within a *month*, the police, the hospital authorities, several kind strangers, most of my friends, all of my close relatives, and a few adepts at rolling a drunk and removing his wrist watch and wallet had been involved.(p.532)

monthly

• Returning to the town I had left three months before, I became editor of a *monthly* magazine, soon had additional publicity and advertising accounts and the money rolled in.(p.254)

• The General Service Board of A.A. (the trustees) administers A.A.'s General Service Office, A.A. World Services, Inc., and our *monthly* magazine, the A.A. Grapevine.(p.575)

months

• Six *months* earlier, the broker had been relieved of his drink obsession by a sudden spiritual experience, following a meeting with an alcoholic friend who had been in contact with the Oxford Groups of that day.(p.xv)

• I have had many men who had, for example, worked a period of *months* on some problem or business deal which was to be settled on a certain date, favorable to them.(p.xxvii)

• For three or four *months* the goose hung high.(p.7)

• That was two *months* ago and the result was self-evident.(p.9)

• We know that while the alcoholic keeps away from drink, as he may do for *months* or years, he reacts much like other men.(p.22)

• In two *months* he was in a hospital, puzzled and humiliated.(p.32)

• I had eaten there many times during the *months* I was sober.(p.36)

• If persisted in for a few *months*, the effect on a man's family is sure to be great.(p.99)

• Then, in days, weeks, or *months*, a fresh outburst.(p.105)

• Some of us had this experience, only to enjoy, in a few *months*, a finer intimacy than ever.(p.134)

• This may hang on for *months*, long after their mother has accepted dad's new way of living and thinking.(p.134)

• Had they fired me first, and had they then taken steps to see that I was presented with the solution contained in this book, I might have returned to them six *months* later, a well man.(p.141)

• After your man has gone along without drinking for a few *months*, you may be able to make use of his services with other employees who are giving you the alcoholic run-around – provided, of course, they are willing to have a third party in the picture.(p.146)

• Still physically weak, and sober but a few *months*, he saw that his predicament was dangerous.(p.154)

• After all, had he not been sober six *months* now?(p.154)

• But he's a grand chap when he's sober, though he's been in here eight times in the last six *months*.(p.156)

• He was there three *months*.(p.159)

• A year and six *months* later these three had succeeded with seven more.(p.159)

• Finally my father had to send a doctor out from my home town who managed to get me back there in some way, and I was in bed about two *months* before I could venture out of the house.(p.175)

• I stayed about town a couple of *months* more and then returned to resume my practice.(p.175)

• I put on thirty pounds of weight in about two *months*, looked like a pig, and was uncomfortable from shortness of breath.(p.177)

• During the first six *months* of 1935, I was hospitalized eight times for intoxication and shackled to the bed two or three days before I even knew where I was.(p.184)

• Each of the seven times that I had left this hospital in the last six *months*, I had come out fully determined in my own mind that I would not get drunk again -- for at least six or eight *months*.(p.184)

• I said, "Yes, Doc, I would like to quit, at least for five, six, or eight *months*, until I get things straightened up, and begin to get the respect of my wife and some other people back, and get my finances fixed up and so on."(p.187)

• Whether you quit six days, *months*, or years, if you go out and take a drink or two you'll end up in this hospital tied down, just like you have been in these past six *months*.(p.187)

• This was six or eight *months* after the last drinking episode.(p.196)

• At the end of this selling of lots, just prior to World War I, I got into the crude rubber business, and six *months* later there was only one broker and myself left in Akron.(p.197)

• At the end of about four *months*, I not only had good looking clothes –and I might say that at the time I first talked to Max I didn't have a suit of clothes I could bend over in real sudden; now I had six suits of clothes.(p.200)

• I drove towards Cleveland wondering why I found myself in such a changed set of conditions as compared with those of six *months* before.(p.200)

• An offer of appreciation for not having had a drink for those few *months* and then and there, without anybody promising me anything or threatening me, I made a solemn vow that never so long as I lived would I take another drink.(p.200)

• I had run into him, and he looked real prosperous; his face and eyes looked clear and he started to compliment me on my good front and how well I looked, and I said, "I haven't had a drink for nine *months*."(p.201)

• He said, "Well, I haven't had a drink for three *months*."(p.201)

• I attended their meetings every Sunday and Wednesday for about nine *months*.(p.202)

• My sobriety continued for another six *months*.(p.203)

• At the end of fifteen *months*, I tried the beer experiment.(p.203)

• This Christian Science experience with a sobriety of fifteen *months* was in 1932.(p.203)

• That was the smartest man I'd met in *months*.(p.208)

• I did not have a high school education so I went to night school to take the full high school course, which I finished in two years and nine *months*.(p.211)

• It was not known to me as a group, but I later learned that my wife had known about it for nine *months* and had prayed constantly that I would stumble into Akron some way or another.(p.215)

• Bill left me at the elevator and said, "Your room is so and so," and I didn't see him again for six *months*.(p.217)

• There were, at that time, in the neighborhood of twelve or thirteen Cleveland members who had been sober anywhere from a year and a half to a couple of *months*.(p.219)

• In fact, after six *months* of living on food instead of on whiskey, I gained about thirty pounds.(p.220)

• I remember looking longingly at the window as an easier solution, and shuddering at the memory of that other window, three years before, and the six agonizing *months* in a London hospital ward.(p.224)

• That went on for two more *months* before I landed in a hospital and started my slow fight back to normalcy.(p.224)

• You can all remember that in the first few *months* after the change, a great many men, who had formerly been used to a few beers every day or an occasional drink of whiskey, simply quit all alcoholic drinks.(p.232)

• The first few *months* were hard.(p.237)

• I re-organized their city sales policy and eighteen *months* later, when I was thirty, they offered me the branch managership.(p.243)

• Three *months* before I met Jackie I had made my second feeble try at suicide.(p.245)

• At our weekly meeting I was a menace to serenity those first few *months*, for I took every opportunity to lambaste the "spiritual angle" as we called it, or anything else that had any tinge of theology.(p.246)

• Returning to the town I had left three *months* before, I became editor of a monthly magazine, soon had additional publicity and advertising accounts and the money rolled in.(p.254)

• In three *months* John Barleycorn had me kicked out.(p.254)
• As I look back on the events of two *months*, I can clearly see that I had been circling around, half-afraid of encountering the remedy for my situation, half wanting it, deferring fulfillment of my promise to get in touch with the doctor I had heard about.(p.258)
• Four *months* later, I married this guy.(p.262)
• I remember sometime, it was possibly six *months* after we had been going steadily to King School, that we were coming home from a meeting and saw a car along the way, and a fellow in back drinking a bottle of beer.(p.271)
• Russ lived a year longer than they expected him to live, and in that year he was in bed for at least six *months*.(p.272)
• Three *months* in bed.(p.275)
• Three more *months* of being up and around the house for brief periods and in bed the rest of the time.(p.275)
• During my first few *months* in Akron I was quite sure that I never wanted to see my home town again.(p.281)
• After six *months* of sobriety I saw the picture in a different light: Detroit was the place I had to return to, not only because I must face the mess I had made there, but because it was there that I could be of the most service to A.A.(p.281)
• Those three weeks left me completely exhausted and I had to return to Akron for three more *months* of rest.(p.282)
• But it took six more *months* of work and disappointments before a group of three men got together in my rooming house bedroom for their first A.A. meeting.(p.282)
• During the first three *months* I carried on all these activities without a car, depending entirely on buses and streetcars – I, who had always to have a car at my immediate command.(p.283)
• So six *months* ago I acquired a ready made family consisting of one charming wife, four grown children to whom I am devoted, and three grandchildren.(p.286)
• Several *months* later dad was back in Chicago to pick me up again, but this time my attitude was entirely different.(p.289)
• One of them was that I would try to get a group started in Chicago; the second was that I would have to return to Akron to attend meetings at least every two *months* until I did get a group started in Chicago; third, I decided I must place this program above everything else, even my family, because if I did not maintain my sobriety I would lose my family anyway.(p.292)
• A few *months* after I made my original trip to Akron I was feeling pretty cocky, and I didn't think my wife was treating me with proper respect, now that I was an outstanding citizen.(p.293)
• A few *months* later one of the men who had been in touch with the group in Akron came to Chicago to live, and then there were three of us who continued to have informal meetings quite regularly.(p.294)
• From a physical standpoint, I gained sixteen pounds in the first two *months* I was off liquor.(p.303)
• Somehow, I made it through basic and then laid off the booze for about three *months*, because I was in school at night.(p.317)
• After about three *months*, no more weekends.(p.318)
• Three *months* later, he hated the game and found solace in the bottle.(p.330)
• Three years and three *months* of sobriety, without a slip, has meant a lot to me, my wife, and my family.(p.342)
• During this vacation, in the *months* of September and October, I decided to go on the water wagon.(p.343)
• I succeeded in this attempt for approximately fifteen *months* with only a couple of slips.(p.343)
• I have been on this program for three *months* and I feel terrible."(p.348)
• You've been sober for three *months*, been working hard.(p.348)
• This escapade also ended up in the clutches of the law, and my friend was institutionalized for eight *months*.(p.354)
• When I did make it home in 1920, I re-entered school and caught up with my class in a few short *months* -- I actually did a year's work in three *months*, proving much to the disgust of my dad that I could do it when I wanted to.(p.358)
• After several *months* of acquaintance I asked her to marry me, but was politely refused.(p.359)
• My work kept me busy the first few *months* on the new job.(p.360)
• I had thrown off a big lie that had been burdening me down for *months*.(p.366)
• Within a few *months*, I was admitted to a state hospital for the mentally ill.(p.370)
• A few *months* after that, I was released and left the world of insanity, only to return to the world of alcoholic insanity.(p.370)
• I promised, but within two *months*, I began again.(p.377)
• Showing all the courage and ingenuity that I had not used in a positive way, I covered my tracks and hid from my family so successfully that they did not find me for *months*.(p.401)
• After eight *months*, the family found me.(p.401)
• Except for one short slip, during the first eight *months*, which was an angry "the world can't do this to me" reaction to a personal tragedy in my life, I have been sober for twelve years.(p.416)
• Pearl Harbor was a breeze of nine *months*, a gay Hawaiian paradise, drinking under the palms, listening to the surf beat on the shore, a bottle of whiskey near at hand.(p.426)
• I talked the Old Man into letting me live in the photo lab instead of the barracks, and for eighteen *months* nothing interfered with my drinking.(p.426)
• Two *months* later I was discharged.(p.428)
• After three *months* it was forgotten.(p.434)
• Intervals between binges were, at first, eight *months*.(p.434)
• In seven years the intervals between them decreased from eight *months* to ten days!(p.434)
• Finally after seven *months*, I decided to try it.(p.448)
• By early July, I had tapered off alcohol completely, and I got off all pills in the ensuing few *months*.(p.448)
• After I had been around A.A. for seven *months*, tapering off alcohol and pills, not finding the program working very well, I was finally able to say, "Okay, God.(p.448)
• In a prison in my native state, I spent eleven *months* in solitary confinement, bouncing in and out of the "hole" (a bare concrete-and-steel cubicle) about five times during those eleven *months*.(p.459)
• When I had served only eighteen *months* of my sentence, this ex-incorrigible was placed in honor grade.(p.461)
• After nine *months* of training, all the rest of my class was paroled and I went to work in the Department of Corrections.(p.462)
• After a few *months* there, I went to County Mental Health as an alcoholism worker.(p.462)
• It was my ex-wife, and she said my twenty-seven-year-old son, who has completed his Marine Corps training and graduated from college, wanted to see me privately, was getting married in three *months*, and wanted me at the wedding.(p.462)
• In the light of subsequent events it became evident that I took their advice far too literally, for, after some *months* of happy sobriety I drank again.(p.471)
• And so for three *months* this one woman was my A.A.(p.472)
• And when she broke a luncheon date with me one Saturday, after I had been in A.A. for about three *months*, I said, "I'll show her!(p.472)
• Climb on water wagon for few *months*.(p.475)
• After six *months*, we move to Bridgeport, Conn.(p.476)
• Finally, I was arrested and got six *months* for drugs.(p.480)
• I'd known her five or six *months*.(p.487)
• That went on for maybe two *months*, and then she got after me again about drinking.(p.488)
• This man's wife had been suffering for a couple of *months* and when he came in he owed me a little bill.(p.488)
• Nevertheless, I stayed sober there about six *months*, because I knew that Vi was to come later and bring the children.(p.490)
• I worked in the steel mill for possibly two *months*, and then I became disgusted with myself and decided to go back home.(p.492)
• I worked at that alone for six *months*.(p.496)
• I remained there for about ten *months*, and then I was sent to a place called Wallkill, a so-called rehabilitation center.(p.509)
• I spent my last seventeen *months* in Wallkill, and it was there that I first got my introduction to A.A.(p.509)
• I clung to the outfit for the balance of my time, and finally I was released, after having spent twenty years and nine *months* behind bars.(p.510)
• She was the one who really helped me to make a go of that twenty years and nine *months* in prison.(p.511)
• I went along pretty well for the next ten *months*.(p.511)
• A former employer of mine said to me a little over ten years ago, "Pat, you seem to be one of those unfortunate people who at least once every six *months* must go out and roll in the gutter."(p.513)
• We were married, and during the first nine *months* of that marriage I was sober.(p.514)
• But at the end of nine *months* we went to a party one night, and I took the first drink.(p.514)
• The old pattern reasserted itself, but it was no longer once every six *months*.(p.514)
• The war was on and it was a fairly short course, about eight *months*.(p.518)
• It didn't worry me very much, because at that time I could shut off for a couple of *months* without taking a drink or even wanting one, and without feeling that I was giving anything up.(p.518)
• Then I had about six *months* on a small island in command of the troops there.(p.520)
• I had three or four very uncomfortable *months* with my regiment then on the Suez Canal.(p.520)
• I lasted at that for four *months* chiefly on alcohol, because I never seemed to find any time to eat.(p.520)
• They kept me in hospital for two *months*, and then they sent me up to Egypt, a three days journey.(p.521)
• I was there for another couple of *months* and then, after a few more adventures in the East, I was shipped home.(p.521)
• About three *months* after that, my record reached home and I got a letter telling me I was retired from the Army, they put it very kindly, on medical grounds.(p.521)
• As I say, this specialist put a scare in me for about a fortnight or three weeks, then I started my last bout which went on and off for about three *months*.(p.523)
• (There was a time, for about three *months*, when I bought a ten-dollar wrist watch every pay day – that is every two weeks.(p.532)
• There was the father one lost respect for at the age of eleven, because the father broke his solemn word in a circumstance where you, eleven years old, had assumed guilt when you were innocent; but the father would not believe you, no matter what; and to ease his suffering you "confessed" and were "forgiven," only – *months* later – to have your "guilt" brought up – only he and you knew what he was talking bout -- brought up in front of the stern grandmother.(p.533)
• Like most other alcoholics I have known, I did quit drinking at various times -- once for ten *months* on my own and during other interludes when I was hospitalized.(p.554)
• So, when my liver had recovered after ten *months*, I resumed drinking.(p.557)
• Within two *months*, I was drinking again.(p.558)
• As the sober days grew into sober *months* and then into sober years, a new and beautiful life began to emerge from the shambles of my former existence.(p.559)
• What often takes place in a few *months* could seldom have been accomplished by years of self discipline.(p.569)
• The days add up into weeks, the weeks into *months* and years."(p.572)

Montreal

• Next morning I telephoned a friend in *Montreal*.(p.4)
• The next three years I spent in Boston, Chicago, and *Montreal* in the employ of a large manufacturing concern, selling railway supplies, gas engines of all sorts, and many other items of heavy hardware.(p.172)
• We were married in *Montreal* in November.(p.361)

mooching

• Why, even a year ago, I had seen Howard, an ex-doctor, *mooching* a dime for a drink.(p.289)

mood

• If he is in a serious *mood* dwell on the trouble liquor has caused you, being careful not to moralize or lecture.(p.91)
• If his *mood* is light, tell him humorous stories of your escapades.(p.91)
• The parties waxed more liquid and hilarious as time went on, and eventually I discovered that a little shot of liquor now and then between beers had the tendency to put me in a whacky *mood* much quicker than having to down several quarts of beer to obtain the same effect.(p.298)
• Lying on the divan, "getting in the *mood*" to write, I cried openly or inwardly, as I listened to sad songs.(p.332)

moods

• I tried to mimic the talk, ideas, *moods* and even the drinking the older men.(p.423)

moon

• Show any longshoreman a Sunday supplement describing a proposal to explore the ***moon*** by means of a rocket and he will say, "I bet they do it -- maybe not so long either."(p.52)

moonlighting

• I landed a good job with a company publication and was ***moonlighting*** on other magazines.(p.555)

moons

• I proud to be son of Tall Man, American Indian, and member of A.A. for many ***moons***.(p.474)

• He planted many seeds, and it will be many ***moons*** before another rises to walk in his shoes."(p.476)

moonshine

• Prohibition came along, and with it my first taste of ***moonshine***.(p.357)

mope

• I ***mope*** around the house.(p.506)

mops

• And the ***mops*** would get out, the vacuum would get out, everything would get out, but nothing would get done.(p.337)

moral

• Though he could not accept all the tenets of the Oxford Groups, he was convinced of the need for ***moral*** inventory, confession of personality defects, restitution to those harmed, helpfulness to others, and the necessity of belief in and dependence upon God.(p.xvi)

• We doctors have realized for a long time that some form of ***moral*** psychology was of urgent importance to alcoholics, but its application presented difficulties beyond our conception.(p.xxv)

• His alcoholic problem was so complex, and his depression so great, that we felt his only hope would be through what we then called "***moral*** psychology," and we doubted if even that would have any effect.(p.xxix)

• The curve of my declining ***moral*** and bodily health fell off like a ski-jump.(p.7)

• His ***moral*** teaching -- most excellent.(p.11)

• We could wish to be ***moral***, we could wish to be philosophically comforted, in fact, we could will these things with all our might, but the needed power wasn't there.(p.45)

• That means we have written a book which we believe to be spiritual as well as ***moral***.(p.45)

• 4.Made a searching and fearless ***moral*** inventory of ourselves.(p.59)

• Many of us had ***moral*** and philosophical convictions galore, but we could not live up to them even though we would have liked to.(p.62)

• Never talk down to an alcoholic from any ***moral*** or spiritual hilltop; simply lay out the kit of spiritual tools for his inspection.(p.95)

• Nearly every modern employer feels a ***moral*** responsibility for the well-being of his help, and he tries to meet these responsibilities.(p.137)

• The general ***moral*** standard was, as I recall it, far above the average.(p.171)

• He pointed out to me that probably it was more of a ***moral*** or spiritual illness than it was a physical one.(p.219)

• I was suffering from an actual disease that had a name and symptoms like diabetes or cancer or TB -- and a disease was respectable, not a ***moral*** stigma!(p.227)

• I knew somehow that it meant more than just going to church and living a ***moral*** life.(p.236)

• I had been too self-sufficient to write a ***moral*** inventory, but I discovered in pointing out to the new man his wrong attitudes and actions that I was really taking my own inventory, and that if I expected him to change I would have to work on myself too.(p.249)

• At the ***moral*** inventory, he brought up some of my bad personality traits or character defects, such as selfishness, conceit, jealousy, carelessness, intolerance, ill-temper, sarcasm and resentments.(p.292)

• That was my lesson, that one could not take the ***moral*** inventory and then file it away; that the alcoholic has to continue to take inventory every day if he expects to get well and stay well.(p.293)

• I had suppressed tendencies to overindulge and thus reveal my "***moral*** weakness," because false pride was so dominant.(p.327)

• I am not even there, and if I was there the only thing I could do would be to give her ***moral*** support, and yet he thanks me for curing his wife."(p.350)

• It helped me a great deal to become convinced that alcoholism was a disease, not a ***moral*** issue; that I had been drinking as a result of a compulsion, even though I had not been aware of the compulsion at the time; and that sobriety was not a matter of will-power.(p.448)

• Had I tried honestly and sincerely to practice the Twelve Steps I would have seen from my continuous ***moral*** inventory that I was getting off the beam -- I would have found that there were some active resentments in my life, a terrific amount of self-pity.(p.471)

• With deep shame came the knowledge too that I had lived with no sense of social obligation nor had I known the meaning of ***moral*** responsibility to my fellow men.(p.549)

moralize

• If he is in a serious mood dwell on the trouble liquor has caused you, being careful not to ***moralize*** or lecture.(p.91)

• Next he can be assured that you do not intend to lecture, ***moralize***, or condemn; that if this was done formerly, it was because of misunderstanding.(p.142)

morally

• And we stood there for twenty minutes, telling each other how much better we were, how much better we looked, how much better off we were financially, mentally, physically, ***morally***, and in every way, shape and manner.(p.201)

• At least three of those four years must have been a living hell for my wife, because she had to watch the man she loved disintegrate ***morally***, mentally and financially.(p.277)

• I have been helped ***morally***, spiritually, mentally and materially through A.A.(p.430)

morals

• If a mere code of ***morals*** or a better philosophy of life were sufficient to overcome alcoholism, many of us would have recovered long ago.(p.44)

• We talked, too, about personal ***morals***.(p.236)

morass

• No words can tell of the loneliness and despair I found in that bitter ***morass*** of self-pity.(p.8)

morbid

• But we must be careful not to drift into worry, remorse or ***morbid*** reflection, for that would diminish our usefulness to others.(p.86)

more

• The first edition appeared in April 1939, and in the following sixteen years, ***more*** than 300,000 copies went into circulation.(p.xi)

• The second edition, published in 1955, reached a total of ***more*** than 1,150,000 copies.(p.xi)

• All changes made over the years in the Big Book (A.A. members' fond nickname for this volume) have had the same purpose: to represent the current membership of Alcoholics Anonymous ***more*** accurately, and thereby to reach ***more*** alcoholics.(p.xii)

• If you have a drinking problem, we hope that you may pause in reading one of the forty-four personal stories and think: "Yes, that happened to me"; or, ***more*** important, "Yes, I've felt like that"; or most important, "Yes, I believe this program can work for me, too."(p.xii)

• We, of Alcoholics Anonymous, are ***more*** than one hundred men and women who have recovered from a seemingly hopeless state of mind and body.(p.xiii)

• ***More*** than 15% of us are women.(p.xx)

• In all probability, we shall never be able to touch ***more*** than a fair fraction of the alcohol problem in all its ramifications.(p.xxi)

• By March 1976, when this edition went to the printer, the total worldwide membership of Alcoholics Anonymous was conservatively estimated at ***more*** than 1,000,000, with almost 28,000 groups meeting in over 90 countries.(p.xxii)

• Surveys of groups in the United States and Canada indicate that A.A. is reaching out, not only to ***more*** and ***more*** people, but to a wider and wider range.(p.xxii)

• Women now make up ***more*** than one-fourth of the membership; among newer members, the proportion is nearly one-third.(p.xxii)

• ***More*** often than not, it is imperative that a man's brain be cleared before he is approached, as he has then a better chance of understanding and accepting what we have to offer.(p.xxiv)

• They believe in themselves, and still ***more*** in the Power which pulls chronic alcoholics back from the gates of death.(p.xxv)

• We feel, after many years of experience, that we have found nothing which has contributed ***more*** to the rehabilitation of these men than the altruistic movement now growing up among them.(p.xxvi)

• One feels that something ***more*** than human power is needed to produce the essential psychic change.(p.xxvii)

• I discovered many ***more*** reasons later on.(p.2)

• The exercise of an option brought in ***more*** money, leaving us with a profit of several thousand dollars for that year.(p.3)

• My drinking assumed ***more*** serious proportions, continuing all day and almost every night.(p.3)

• The mind and body are marvelous mechanisms, for mine endured this agony two ***more*** years.(p.6)

• But it was not, for the frightful day came when I drank once ***more***.(p.7)

• I was to know happiness, peace, and usefulness, in a way of life that is incredibly ***more*** wonderful as time passes.(p.8)

• There had been no ***more*** power in him than there was in me at the minute; and this was none at all.(p.11)

• I saw that my friend was much ***more*** than inwardly reorganized.(p.11)

• Nothing ***more*** was required of me to make my beginning.(p.12)

• Strangely enough, wives, parents and intimate friends usually find us even ***more*** unapproachable than do the psychiatrist and the doctor.(p.18)

• A much ***more*** important demonstration of our principles lies before us in our respective homes, occupations and affairs.(p.19)

• Most of us sense that real tolerance of other people's shortcomings and viewpoints and a respect for their opinions are attitudes which make us ***more*** useful to others.(p.19)

• He is always ***more*** or less insanely drunk.(p.21)

• And the truth, strange to say, is usually that he has no ***more*** idea why he took that first drink than you have.(p.23)

• But for the grace of God, there would have been thousands ***more*** convincing demonstrations.(p.25)

• ***More*** baffling still, he could give himself no satisfactory explanation for his fall.(p.26)

• ***MORE*** ABOUT ALCOHOLISM(p.30)

• Here are some of the methods we have tried: Drinking beer only, limiting the number of drinks, never drinking alone, never drinking in the morning, drinking only at home, never having it in the house, never drinking during business hours, drinking only at parties, switching from scotch to brandy, drinking only natural wines, agreeing to resign if ever drunk on the job, taking a trip, not taking a trip, swearing off forever (with and without a solemn oath), taking ***more*** physical exercise, reading inspirational books, going to health farms and sanitariums, accepting voluntary commitment to asylums -- we could increase the list ad infinitum.(p.31)

• Try it ***more*** than once.(p.31)

• He was very nervous in the morning after these bouts and quieted himself with ***more*** liquor.(p.32)

• In the early days of our drinking we occasionally remained sober for a year or ***more***, becoming serious drinkers again later.(p.34)

• The experiment went so well that I ordered another whiskey and poured it into ***more*** milk.(p.36)

• Thus started one ***more*** journey to the asylum for Jim.(p.36)

• We have sometimes reflected ***more*** than Jim did upon the consequences.(p.37)

• We heard no ***more*** of Fred for a while.(p.40)

• Nothing ***more***.(p.41)

• I remember having several ***more*** that night and plenty the next morning.(p.41)

• Well, just that did happen and ***more***, for what I had learned of alcoholism did not occur to me at all.(p.42)

• I have since been brought into a way of living infinitely ***more*** satisfying and, I hope, ***more*** useful than the life I lived before.(p.42)

• Once ***more***: The alcoholic at certain times has no effective mental defense against the first drink.(p.43)

• This world of ours has made ***more*** material progress in the last century than in all the millenniums which went before.(p.51)

• We were having trouble with personal relationships, we couldn't control our emotional natures, we were a prey to misery and depression, we couldn't make a living, we had a feeling of uselessness, we were full of fear, we were unhappy, we couldn't seem to be of real help to other people -- was not a basic solution of these bedevilments ***more*** important than whether we should see newsreels of lunar flight?(p.52)

• Hence we are at pains to tell why we think our present faith is reasonable, why we think it ***more*** sane and logical to believe than not to believe, why we say our former thinking was soft and mushy when we threw up our hands in doubt and said, "We don't know."(p.53)

• That was natural, but let us think a little ***more*** closely.(p.53)

• The electrons themselves seemed ***more*** intelligent than that.(p.54)

• Post-war disillusionment, ever ***more*** serious alcoholism, impending mental and physical collapse,

brought him to the point of self-destruction.(p.56)
• Some of us grow into it ***more*** slowly.(p.57)
• But, as with most humans, he is ***more*** likely to have varied traits.(p.61)
• He decides to exert himself ***more***.(p.61)
• He becomes, on the next occasion, still ***more*** demanding or gracious, as the case may be.(p.61)
• Admitting he may be somewhat at fault, he is sure that other people are ***more*** to blame.(p.61)
• ***More*** and ***more*** we became interested in seeing what we could contribute to life.(p.63)
• It destroys ***more*** alcoholics than anything else.(p.64)
• But the ***more*** we fought and tried to have our own way, the worse matters got.(p.66)
• We could not wish them away any ***more*** than alcohol.(p.66)
• It seems to cause ***more*** trouble.(p.68)
• Then we have the voices who cry for sex and ***more*** sex; who bewail the institution of marriage; who think that most of the troubles of the race are traceable to sex causes.(p.69)
• We must be willing to make amends where we have done harm, provided that we do not bring about still ***more*** harm in so doing.(p.69)
• We will be ***more*** reconciled to discussing ourselves with another person when we see good reasons why we should do so.(p.72)
• ***More*** than most people, the alcoholic leads a double life.(p.73)
• He is under constant fear and tension – that makes for ***more*** drinking.(p.73)
• Now we need ***more*** action, without which we find that "Faith without works is dead."(p.76)
• He is going to be ***more*** interested in a demonstration of good will than in our talk of spiritual discoveries.(p.77)
• It may be he has done us ***more*** harm than we have done him and, though we may have acquired a better attitude toward him, we are still not too keen about admitting our faults.(p.77)
• It is harder to go to an enemy than to a friend, but we find it much ***more*** beneficial to us.(p.77)
• ***More*** than that we cannot do; we have no right to go further.(p.81)
• Our behavior will convince them ***more*** than our words.(p.83)
• But we must go further and that means ***more*** action.(p.85)
• Nevertheless, we find that our thinking will as time passes, be ***more*** and ***more*** on the plane of inspiration.(p.87)
• We become much ***more*** efficient.(p.88)
• There is action and ***more*** action.(p.88)
• He may be ***more*** receptive when depressed.(p.91)
• Admit that he probably knows ***more*** about it than you do, but call to his attention the fact that however deep his faith and knowledge, he could not have applied it or he would not drink.(p.93)
• Actually, he may be helping you ***more*** than you are helping him.(p.94)
• You should not be offended if he wants to call it off, for he has helped you ***more*** than you have helped him.(p.94)
• The ***more*** hopeless he feels, the better.(p.94)
• He will be ***more*** likely to follow your suggestions.(p.94)
• This he may do after he gets hurt some ***more***.(p.95)
• And even though he continues to drink, the family will find life ***more*** bearable.(p.97)
• Some of us veered from extreme to extreme, ever hoping that one day our loved ones would be themselves once ***more***.(p.105)
• For a while they would be their old sweet selves, only to dash the new structure of affection to pieces once ***more***.(p.107)
• But when he gets over the spree, he begins to think once ***more*** how he can drink moderately next time.(p.109)
• He will use that as an excuse to drink ***more***.(p.111)
• Sooner or later, you are likely to find him reading the book once ***more***.(p.113)
• Wait until repeated stumbling convinces him he must act, for the ***more*** you hurry him the longer his recovery may be delayed.(p.113)
• Cheerfully see him through ***more*** sprees.(p.113)
• The wives and children of such men suffer horribly, but not ***more*** than the men themselves.(p.114)
• You draw ***more*** and ***more*** into yourself and you think everyone is talking about conditions at your home.(p.114)
• Your husband knows he owes you ***more*** than sobriety.(p.118)
• It will do little good if you point that out and urge ***more*** attention for yourself.(p.119)
• Cheer him up and ask him how you can be still ***more*** helpful.(p.120)
• We find the ***more*** one member of the family demands that the others concede to him, the ***more*** resentful they become.(p.122)
• Having been neglected and misused in the past, they think father owes them ***more*** than they are getting.(p.126)
• They should be thankful he is sober and able to be of this world once ***more***.(p.127)
• Since the home has suffered ***more*** than anything else, it is well that a man exert himself there.(p.127)
• While grateful that he drinks no ***more***, they may not like the idea that God has accomplished the miracle where they failed.(p.128)
• During those first days of convalescence, this will do ***more*** to insure his sobriety than anything else.(p.129)
• One ***more*** suggestion: Whether the family has spiritual convictions or not, they may do well to examine the principles by which the alcoholic member is trying to live.(p.130)
• She sees she was wrong to make a burning issue out of such a matter when his ***more*** serious ailments were being rapidly cured.(p.135)
• I had warned him several times that he had but one ***more*** chance.(p.136)
• Those who drink moderately may be ***more*** annoyed with an alcoholic than a total abstainer would be.(p.139)
• Nearly always, these antics indicate nothing ***more*** than temporary conditions.(p.141)
• You now know ***more*** about alcoholism.(p.141)
• There was always one ***more*** attempt -- and one ***more*** failure.(p.151)
• The less people tolerated us, the ***more*** we withdrew from society, from life itself.(p.151)
• Yes, there is a substitute and it is vastly ***more*** than that.(p.152)
• It may seem incredible that these men are to become happy, respected, and useful once ***more***.(p.153)
• You will want to know ***more*** of how to proceed from that point.(p.153)
• Perhaps he could handle, say, three drinks – no ***more***!(p.154)
• Why, he argued, should he lose the remainder of his business, only to bring still ***more*** suffering to his family by foolishly admitting his plight to people from whom he made his livelihood?(p.155)
• From what you tell me, I know ***more*** than ever I can't stop."(p.157)
• Next day found the prospect ***more*** receptive.(p.158)
• So one ***more*** was added to the Fellowship.(p.159)
• A year and six months later these three had succeeded with seven ***more***.(p.159)
• But life among Alcoholics Anonymous is ***more*** than attending gatherings and visiting hospitals.(p.161)
• He had lived there but a few weeks when he found that the place probably contained ***more*** alcoholics per square mile than any city in the country.(p.163)
• Some of them may sink and perhaps never get up, but if our experience is a criterion, ***more*** than half of those approached will become fellows of Alcoholics Anonymous.(p.163)
• God will constantly disclose ***more*** to you and to us.(p.164)
• Today, hundreds of additional A.A. members can be found who have had no relapse for ***more*** than thirty years.(p.169)
• To 1950, the year of his death, he carried the A.A. message to ***more*** than 5,000 alcoholic men and women, and to all these he gave his medical services without thought of charge.(p.171)
• From childhood through high school I was ***more*** or less forced to go to church, Sunday School and evening service, Monday night Christian Endeavor and sometimes to Wednesday evening prayer meeting.(p.172)
• I did it ***more*** and ***more***, and had lots of fun without much grief, either physical or financial.(p.172)
• My whole life seemed to be centered around doing what I wanted to do, without regard for the rights, wishes, or privileges of anyone else; a state of mind which became ***more*** and ***more*** predominant as the years passed.(p.172)
• This had little effect however for I kept on drinking and used a great deal ***more*** hard liquor than in former years.(p.174)
• I was, of course, soon on the carpet and the upshot was that I had to go back for two ***more*** quarters and remain absolutely dry, if I wished to graduate.(p.174)
• I stayed about town a couple of months ***more*** and then returned to resume my practice.(p.175)
• During all this time we became ***more*** or less ostracized by our friends.(p.177)
• My phobia for sleeplessness demanded that I get drunk every night, but in order to get ***more*** liquor for the next night, I had to stay sober during the day, at least up to four o'clock.(p.177)
• It was really a horrible nightmare, this earning money, getting liquor, smuggling it home, getting drunk, morning jitters, taking large doses of sedatives to make it possible for me to earn ***more*** money, and so on ad nauseam.(p.177)
• I used to promise my wife, my friends, and my children that I would drink no ***more*** -- promises which seldom kept me sober even through the day, though I was very sincere when I made them.(p.177)
• ***More*** than these attributes, they seemed to be happy.(p.178)
• I bought some ***more*** liquor on the way to the depot.(p.179)
• Of far ***more*** importance was the fact that he was the first living human with whom I had ever talked, who knew what he was talking about in regard to alcoholism from actual experience.(p.180)
• 4.Because every time I do it I take out a little ***more*** insurance for myself against a possible slip.(p.181)
• So, after hearing some ***more*** of my story, he turned around and said to Doc -- I don't think he knew I heard him, but I did – he said, "Well, I believe he's worth saving and working on."(p.185)
• I remember telling them too that it was going to be awfully tough, because I did some other things, smoked cigarettes and played penny ante poker, sometimes bet on the horse races and they said, "Don't you think you're having ***more*** trouble with this drinking than with anything else at the present time?(p.190)
• I know there was even ***more***, something that I hadn't got, and I remember one day, a week or two after I had come out of the hospital, Bill was over to my house talking to my wife and me.(p.191)
• I was not ***more*** that six at that time.(p.193)
• Twenty-two years later, Doctor Bob told me that what I had done was like turning a switch and setting up a demand for ***more*** alcohol in my system.(p.195)
• I had no ***more*** reason to drink those martinis than a jackrabbit.(p.195)
• Right then I determined that never so long as I lived would I have anything ***more*** to do with martinis.(p.195)
• I think it was probably ***more*** than a year before I had anything ***more*** to do with liquor.(p.195)
• But ***more*** important, I lost my sobriety.(p.202)
• Then I started drinking again, with possibly a little ***more*** restraint, periods a little bit longer than they had been before, but substantially the same pattern.(p.203)
• I drank some ***more*** and slept through the day.(p.205)
• I then began asking a lot of questions of both my brother and Dr. Bob about how this thing worked, and I suppose I was becoming ***more*** glassy-eyed all the while, for eventually I said to Bob, "You're all dried up.(p.206)
• Paul measured the medicine out, but he figured that with my track record that little bit wouldn't be enough, so he doubled it and added a few drops ***more*** and then gave it to me.(p.207)
• These periods became ***more*** frequent and I resolved that when I became forty, which was very shortly, I was going on the wagon.(p.213)
• He pointed out to me that probably it was ***more*** of a moral or spiritual illness than it was a physical one.(p.219)
• I realized that there wasn't anything I could say to place myself in a ***more*** favorable light with my children, that it was going to be a matter of time; for I also understood the intolerance of young people towards deficiencies in their elders.(p.220)
• I'd been sitting comfortably in a restaurant with Rita, drinking my sixth martini and hoping the waiter would forget about the lunch order – at least long enough for me to have a couple ***more***.(p.223)
• That went on for two ***more*** months before I landed in a hospital and started my slow fight back to normalcy.(p.224)
• "Blanks" were ***more*** frequent, and I seldom knew how I'd got home.(p.226)
• With a creeping insidiousness, drink had become ***more*** important than anything else.(p.226)
• And so on and on, for several weeks, while I grudgingly plowed through some ***more*** of the offending book, and felt ***more*** and ***more*** hopeless about myself.(p.227)
• I wasn't alone any ***more***.(p.228)
• The feeling of impending disaster that had haunted me for years began to dissolve as I put into practice ***more*** and ***more*** of the Twelve Steps.(p.229)

• ***More*** and ***more*** I formed the habit of doing some of my business in the speakeasy, and after a time I did not need that as an excuse.(p.233)
• My "periodics" became ***more*** frequent until I reached the point where I wanted to devote all my time to drinking, working as little as possible, and then only when the necessity of my family demanded it.(p.234)
• This doctor had imparted his knowledge to just a few other men at that time -- not ***more*** than four or five -- they now number ***more*** than seventy persons.(p.235)
• I knew somehow that it meant ***more*** than just going to church and living a moral life.(p.236)
• As I go along I seem to get strength daily to be able to resist ***more*** easily.(p.237)
• If anything, he had known all of them even better and ***more*** often than I.(p.239)
• Little ***more*** of our talk stayed in my memory, but I do know I slept the rest of that night while before I had never known what a real night's sleep was.(p.239)
• This was my introduction to this "understanding fellowship" although it was to be ***more*** than a year later before our Society was to bear the name, Alcoholics Anonymous.(p.239)
• I was never a hilarious drunk; the ***more*** I drank the quieter I got, and the drunker I got the harder I fought to stay sober.(p.241)
• The second year my drinking was ***more*** or less restricted to week-ends, but I was nearly kicked out for scholastic failure.(p.241)
• In the next two years I washed ***more*** pans and peeled ***more*** potatoes than any other dough-boy.(p.241)
• Three years later, at twenty-five, I opened and operated their Philadelphia office and was earning ***more*** than I ever have since.(p.242)
• This time it really hurt, ***more*** than any hangover ever had.(p.247)
• My brilliant agnosticism vanished, and I saw for the first time that those who really believed, or at least honestly tried to find a Power greater than themselves, were much ***more*** composed and contented than I had ever been, and they seemed to have a degree of happiness which I had never known.(p.247)
• For a long time the only Higher Power I could concede was the power of the group, but this was far ***more*** than I had ever recognized before, and it was at least a beginning.(p.248)
• Then I found that as I gave in to this spiritual or personality change I was getting a little ***more*** serenity.(p.249)
• They are far ***more*** alert and progressive than we floundering fathers were, and the future of our fellowship is in their hands.(p.250)
• Saying goodbye to my wife and baby, I was treading Manhattan's streets in a little ***more*** than a week.(p.252)
• I myself could see deterioration in my work from being physically and mentally affected by liquor, although I had not yet reached the point where all I wanted was ***more*** to drink.(p.254)
• I never was concerned any ***more***, anywhere he went.(p.263)
• I hated myself worse and worse, and as I hated myself I became ***more*** defiant towards everything and everybody.(p.265)
• He said, "I think this will tell you ***more***.(p.268)
• We old-timers who get scattered and separated and then witness the construction of services to get in ***more*** people and to make this thing function, we think that A.A. has changed, but the root of it hasn't.(p.272)
• Three ***more*** months of being up and around the house for brief periods and in bed the rest of the time.(p.275)
• Of course, the latter ultimately killed the former, but of this, ***more*** anon.(p.277)
• The next two years were simply a long drawn out process of less and less work and ***more*** and ***more*** whiskey.(p.278)
• Those three weeks left me completely exhausted and I had to return to Akron for three ***more*** months of rest.(p.282)
• While there, two or three ***more*** "cash customers" (as Dr. Bob used to call them -- probably because they had so little cash) were shipped in to us from Detroit.(p.282)
• But it took six ***more*** months of work and disappointments before a group of three men got together in my rooming house bedroom for their first A.A. meeting.(p.282)
• There was ***more*** than one occasion when I got up in the morning with just enough money for coffee and toast and the bus fare to carry me to my first appointment.(p.283)
• But he found that there was a Higher Power which had ***more*** faith in him than he had in himself.(p.287)
• I had thought that I was completely different from other people, that I was beginning to become a little balmy, even to the point of withdrawing ***more*** and ***more*** from society and wanting to be alone with my bottle.(p.290)
• After it was closed we all retired to the kitchen and had coffee and doughnuts and ***more*** discussion until the small hours of the morning.(p.291)
• Needless to say, it was a year or ***more*** before they did contact me.(p.293)
• The parties waxed ***more*** liquid and hilarious as time went on, and eventually I discovered that a little shot of liquor now and then between beers had the tendency to put me in a whacky mood much quicker than having to down several quarts of beer to obtain the same effect.(p.298)
• The last day of my drinking career, I drank twenty-two of them between ten and twelve a.m. and I shall never know how many ***more*** followed them until I was poured into bed that night.(p.298)
• Finally this company also became involved and I was once ***more*** looking for a job.(p.300)
• A little ***more*** than fifteen years ago, through a long and calamitous series of shattering experiences, I found myself being helplessly propelled toward total destruction.(p.304)
• I couldn't have chosen ***more*** loving and conscientious parents.(p.304)
• This man could tell me ***more***.(p.308)
• So I went to Akron, and also to Cleveland, and I met ***more*** recovered alcoholics.(p.310)
• Far from expecting praise for their deeds, they claimed the performance a privilege and insisted that they invariably received ***more*** than they gave.(p.310)
• Shortly after I returned to Chicago, my doctor, encouraged by the results of my contact with A.A., sent us two ***more*** of his alcoholic patients.(p.310)
• However, this isn't as rough as it sounds, as we do become grateful for the necessity that makes us toe the line, for we find that we are ***more*** than compensated for a consistent effort by the countless dividends we receive.(p.311)
• There is no ***more*** "aloneness," with that awful ache, so deep in the heart of every alcoholic that nothing, before, could ever reach it.(p.312)
• But with many, drinking had been little ***more*** than a sometimes uncontrollable nuisance.(p.315)
• Next, I was sent to Arizona, where my drinking picked up some ***more***, and I started having blackouts, and I was thrown in jail for speeding and drunken driving.(p.318)
• Karen didn't want to see me any ***more***, and neither did two other girls I'd been going out with.(p.318)
• After about three months, no ***more*** weekends.(p.318)
• I couldn't think straight any ***more***.(p.319)
• If I had been sincere in what I thought I wanted ***more*** than anything else in life -- a sober husband and a happy, contented home -- I would have gone on the wagon with him.(p.324)
• It didn't bother me any ***more*** whether George was drinking or not.(p.324)
• I believe that the release from people-pleasing restrictions gives retirees ***more*** motivation to drink than boredom does.(p.329)
• No ***more*** snoops or big shots breathing down our necks.(p.329)
• No ***more*** business pressures.(p.329)
• I would take a gulp, then warn the jug not to try to entice, lure, or seduce me into having ***more*** than one "medicinal" jolt.(p.332)
• I could go on living and hurting ten years longer, or ***more***."(p.333)
• And of course a half empty bottle wasn't worth keeping, so I finished it up and naturally had to get ***more*** in right away for the people who "might come in unexpectedly."(p.336)
• I couldn't live with it any ***more***.(p.338)
• I went on the wagon ***more*** to placate my wife than anything else.(p.344)
• I made ***more*** money the last year of my drinking than I ever made before in my whole life.(p.345)
• I belong to ***more*** medical societies and honor societies than men ten to twenty years my senior.(p.345)
• The ***more*** I drank, the worse it got and the ***more*** I had to drink.(p.354)
• However, what I had gained materially on the credit side of my ledger, I have since learned was ***more*** than offset on the debit side by egotism, resentment and dishonesty.(p.356)
• Drinking -- and ***more*** drinking.(p.358)
• By persistence and salesmanship I managed to see ***more*** and ***more*** of my new friend, and because of her sympathetic nature she tolerated my company.(p.359)
• On ***more*** than one occasion my wife would threaten to leave me.(p.362)
• And deep in my heart I really meant what I said because I loved her ***more*** than anything else in the world, yes -- even ***more*** than liquor.(p.362)
• I was going to prove to her that liquor wasn't necessary in my life, and above all that I still loved her ***more*** than anything else in the world and that I wanted her back.(p.362)
• The ***more*** I thought like this the ***more*** I drank to submerge my sorrows.(p.362)
• They told me their stories, which were much ***more*** rugged than mine -- yet what they said made sense, and the way they put it was easy for me to understand, with an understanding I had never had before.(p.363)
• Of course, ***more*** than anything else I had let myself down, but I didn't realize how much then -- as I do now.(p.364)
• In other words, I began contributing, and so, naturally, I began to get something ***more***.(p.365)
• I have had many ***more*** reasons to drink since I have been in A.A. than I had in all the years of my drinking.(p.367)
• I've had ***more*** problems but, thank God, I have had the teachings of A.A. with which to face them.(p.367)
• When I hear the ***more*** rugged stories of alcoholics who became sicker than I did with this affliction, I humbly thank God for showing me "the handwriting on the wall."(p.367)
• But what is ***more*** important is that I found a new life in Alcoholics Anonymous.(p.372)
• Gradually the quantity increased, the occasions for a drink came ***more*** frequently; a hard day, worries and pressure, bad news, good news -- there were ***more*** and ***more*** reasons for a drink.(p.374)
• It was frightening that drink was being substituted for ***more*** and ***more*** of the things I really enjoyed doing.(p.374)
• Never having enough, always craving ***more***, the obsession for alcohol gradually dominated all my activities, particularly while travelling.(p.375)
• Drink planning became ***more*** important than any other plans.(p.375)
• It now became necessary to have noon drinks; at first just two, then gradually ***more***.(p.375)
• It seemed to me my wife was becoming ***more*** intolerant and narrow minded all the time.(p.376)
• Whenever we went out she appeared to go out of her way to keep me from having ***more*** than one drink.(p.376)
• She of course didn't realize how cunning an alcoholic can be and the lengths to which he will go in finding ways to satisfy the compulsion for ***more*** and ***more*** drinks after having had the first one.(p.377)
• Finally our invitations became fewer and fewer as friends had ***more*** experience with my drinking pattern.(p.377)
• Physically I couldn't take it any ***more***.(p.378)
• It was a great relief to know I didn't have to drink any ***more***.(p.379)
• What could be ***more*** reasonable than that some people, including myself, were allergic to alcohol?(p.380)
• The why is not important; the fact is that one drink will set up a reaction in our system which requires ***more***; that one drink was too much and one hundred drinks were not enough.(p.380)
• A spiritual awakening soon came to mean trying each day to be a little ***more*** thoughtful, ***more*** considerate, a little ***more*** courteous to those with whom I came in contact.(p.381)
• To me this meant telling my associates that I had joined Alcoholics Anonymous; that I didn't know what was expected of me by A.A., but that whatever it was, it was the most important thing in life for me; that sobriety meant ***more*** to me than anything in this world.(p.382)
• I didn't realize I would find so much ***more***, but a new and different outlook on life started opening up almost immediately.(p.383)
• Each day seems to be so much ***more*** productive and satisfying.(p.383)
• I get so much ***more*** enjoyment out of living.(p.383)
• About this time, at Christmas, after being under this doctor's care, we decided that there wasn't anything ***more*** to do.(p.388)
• We moved once ***more***, to Houston; my husband thought maybe a change of environment would help and I'd be all right.(p.389)
• I think I actually read ***more*** contempt than was really there because just a week before someone had sent him the Saturday Evening Post article on A.A.,

and there was some glimmer of hope in it for him.(p.391)
• The next morning he came into my room and said, "Esther, I'm not going to lecture you any ***more***, but I want you to read this article.(p.391)
• It was such a feeling of relief that I wanted to know ***more*** about it and with that, I think for the first time, came the realization that there was something horribly, horribly wrong with me.(p.392)
• It pays daily in ***more*** harmonious relations with my fellow men, in ever clearer insight into the true meaning of life, and in the answering love and gratitude wherever and whenever I have been the instrument of God's will in the lives of others.(p.394)
• (I can't know how much others of our Fellowship have paid financially and, even ***more*** important, mentally and physically.)(p.396)
• Saying these sprees were limited to one a week (they were not), and saying that the average spree was ten of these drinks (sometimes ***more***, sometimes less), we come up with the first boring statistic: two-fifty per week out of twelve dollars.(p.397)
• After a few ***more*** estimates as to income and expenditures for booze over a few sample years, taken at random, I conclude that this twenty per cent stayed fairly constant.(p.398)
• Some simple mathematics and ***more*** statistics:(p.399)
• They inherited wealth and acquired ***more***.(p.401)
• But at this time, I began gravitating toward the really hard drinkers, hanging around with them ***more*** and ***more***.(p.404)
• I was really trying, once ***more***, to escape from myself.(p.405)
• I read sad poetry, cried, drank red wine, wrote sad poetry, and drank some ***more***.(p.405)
• On our honeymoon in Egypt, he cuffed me around quite a bit, and subsequently hit me some ***more***.(p.405)
• Was my mental state ***more*** serious than he said?(p.406)
• Here, also, I had good friends, but I became ***more*** and ***more*** separated from them.(p.406)
• My first analyst said, "You are becoming ***more*** and ***more*** of an alcoholic," and sent me to another analyst.(p.407)
• She, ***more*** than the others, showed me what ailed me basically, why I was immature and insecure.(p.409)
• Finally my new friends told me, one by one, that I could not come around any ***more***.(p.410)
• With ***more*** physical courage than I had possessed, she had twice tried to take her life.(p.414)
• I, who could never stay on the wagon for ***more*** than a week.(p.416)
• I want to write better and sell ***more***.(p.417)
• Every day, I feel a little bit ***more*** useful, ***more*** happy and ***more*** free.(p.417)
• I was nothing ***more*** than a spoiled, indulged, and talented brat.(p.418)
• I can't control my drinking any ***more***.(p.423)
• I smoked as much, tried to drink as much, and do everything they did, only ***more*** so.(p.423)
• Wasn't I drinking ***more*** than a quart every day?(p.427)
• I seldom left the base any ***more*** except once in a while when I felt the need of talking to some girl.(p.427)
• All I'd wanted was one ***more*** drink.(p.428)
• I'd packed ***more*** drinking into seven years than many a heavy drinker does in a lifetime.(p.429)
• Evening cocktails were as standard as morning coffee, and I suppose my average daily consumption ran a little ***more*** or less than a pint.(p.433)
• I had a lot ***more*** hell to go through.(p.437)
• My work is on a much deeper and ***more*** significant level than it ever was before, and I am today a fairly creative, relatively sane human being.(p.438)
• And should I have ***more*** bad times, I know that I'll never again have to go through them alone.(p.438)
• (Today, we don't have to live like that any ***more***.)(p.440)
• I yelled at Max, "What do you mean, 'The dog just needs ***more*** love'?(p.440)
• I took ***more*** through the day to increase the high, and ***more*** to maintain it; when I overshot the mark, I'd take tranquilizers to level off.(p.442)
• (Today, there is absolutely nothing in the world ***more*** important to me than my keeping this alcoholic sober; not taking a drink is by far the most important thing I do each day.)(p.447)
• Over the years, as I thought about Max, her good qualities grew and grew, and we married, and all these qualities became ***more*** and ***more*** apparent to me, and we were happier and happier.(p.450)
• But then, as I drank ***more*** and ***more***, the alcohol seemed to affect my vision: Instead of continuing to see what was good about my wife, I began to see her defects.(p.450)
• And the ***more*** I focused my mind on her defects, the ***more*** they grew and multiplied.(p.450)
• Each time I told her she was a nothing, she receded a little ***more*** into nowhere.(p.450)
• The ***more*** I drank, the ***more*** she wilted.(p.451)
• The ***more*** I focus my mind on its defects -- late start, long drunkalogues, cigarette smoke -- the worse the meeting becomes.(p.451)
• And when I place ***more*** value on my serenity and sobriety than on anything else, I can maintain them at a higher level -- at least for the time being.(p.452)
• Nothing could pull me out of the abyss but ***more*** alcohol.(p.457)
• And we found ourselves back in prison, where our personalities became even ***more*** warped.(p.459)
• He and his wife ***more*** than accepted me; he listened to all my woes; both of them treated me as a human being.(p.462)
• The word "alcoholic" does not turn me off any ***more***; in fact, it is music to my ears when it applies to me.(p.463)
• In fact, sometimes they served as good excuses to drink ***more***, to forget.(p.465)
• On the day set for the extractions, on my way to the dentist's I felt a little nervous, so I had a couple of drinks, and after the teeth were out I was very nervous, so I had a few ***more***.(p.466)
• He said he didn't care what I did with the money, but there was going to be no ***more*** until I was completely sober.(p.467)
• Instead, I started going to a nice private sanitarium which, after the first visit, turned out to be ***more*** like a country club than anything else.(p.468)
• But ***more*** important, I would have found that once again I was sitting in the driver's seat -- I was running the show.(p.471)
• The poorest person has no less and the wealthiest has no ***more*** -- each of us has but one day.(p.473)
• Then I drink again, but ***more*** miserable.(p.475)
• When I got out of there, I lasted about fifteen minutes at home, before I headed for the drugstore and ***more*** pills, and then the bar.(p.479)
• I do surgery because that's something that you can see; it's ***more*** tangible.(p.485)
• He went into the religious side and told me that I didn't attend church as regularly as I should, and that he felt, ***more*** or less, that this was responsible for my trouble.(p.489)
• I rebelled, and from that time on I don't think I attended church ***more*** than a dozen times.(p.489)
• She decided that she didn't want any ***more*** of that.(p.491)
• I knew my wife didn't because I had been sincere in all my promises to her as well as to my mother and to my close friends, but the urge to take that drink was ***more*** powerful than anything else.(p.494)
• I can hold a lot now, ***more*** than the others.(p.499)
• I drink and go to bed; I take a few the next morning and go see my mother once ***more***.(p.501)
• I go back to the hotel and get ***more*** gin.(p.501)
• There is no use trying any ***more***, for there is nothing to try.(p.502)
• One ***more*** foolish idea.(p.502)
• "There are men on the streets of New York today who were worse than you, and they don't drink any ***more***."(p.503)
• I do not feel angry any ***more***.(p.505)
• I shall learn this after some ***more*** explosions.(p.506)
• I learn ***more*** of that foundation stone of character, which is honesty.(p.507)
• I learn that when we act upon the highest conception of honesty which is given us, our sense of honesty becomes ***more*** acute.(p.507)
• I rounded up a few ***more*** of my friends and off we went to the meeting, not for anything we would gain from it as much as to make a burlesque out of it.(p.509)
• I've stuck pretty close to A.A. ever since then, taken it day by day, not biting off ***more*** than I can chew.(p.511)
• But I came out of the Army just as big a drunk as when I went in, if not worse, because now I had a lot ***more*** resentments.(p.513)
• For me, it was a little different because I couldn't help thinking about the past, and I saw the future ***more*** or less mirrored in the past.(p.513)
• But the ***more*** meetings you attend, the ***more*** people you meet at these meetings, the clearer the Steps become.(p.516)
• I belonged to one of the Irish families who, ***more*** or less traditionally, sent their boys to the British armies.(p.517)
• When I came home to ordinary garrison life in England, I found that I was drinking rather ***more*** than most people of my age.(p.518)
• Lots of the older people had taken to drinking quite a good deal ***more*** during the war, but the younger generation was, I think, about the same.(p.518)
• The gradual result was that I was drifting into making drinking one of the ***more*** important parts of my life.(p.519)
• I was there for another couple of months and then, after a few ***more*** adventures in the East, I was shipped home.(p.521)
• I had been using paraldehyde ***more*** or less like ordinary drink for the last six years though, occasionally, I'd bounce back to phenobarbital and things like that.(p.524)
• I thought that if these kind of ordinary people can do it, a man of my brains ought to find it much ***more*** easy, and I joined.(p.524)
• Since I joined on that April night, A.A. has done ***more*** for me than just stop me from drinking; it has brought me back to life again.(p.524)
• As time went on, I drank ***more***.(p.526)
• But to me, whiskey meant ***more*** than a home for my sons.(p.527)
• Since I have been in A.A., I have ***more*** friends than I ever had in my life -- friends who care about me and my welfare, friends who don't care that I am black and that I have been in prison.(p.529)
• My personal definition, which I submit as applying only to myself (although everyone is welcome to it who wants it), includes every waking activity of the human being; to have a creative attitude towards things is a ***more*** exact meaning, to live and to deal with other human beings creatively, which to me means seeing the God in them, and respecting and worshipping this God.(p.535)
• Still, I had had funds sufficient to get plastered because that, of course, was ***more*** important than paying my own way.(p.538)
• The helpful family finally said, over long distance, that there would be no ***more*** money and that I could not come home.(p.538)
• The ***more*** you give, the ***more*** you get.(p.542)
• The less you think of yourself the ***more*** of a person you become.(p.542)
• What is much ***more*** important to me, A.A. has taught me that through this simple program I may experience a change in this reaction pattern that will indeed allow me to "match calamity with serenity."(p.544)
• Fear of rejection and its ensuing pain were not to be risked, and I turned away from myself once ***more*** for the answer, this time to the drinks I had always refused before, and in alcohol I found a false courage.(p.546)
• It became ***more*** and ***more*** necessary to escape from myself, for my remorse and shame and humiliation when I was sober were almost unbearable.(p.547)
• One morning, however, I realized I had to get rid of it, for my reprieve was running out, and if I didn't get rid of it I was going to get drunk -- and I didn't want to get drunk any ***more***.(p.552)
• After my very first drink -- a tiny glass of sherry my father gave me to celebrate the New Year when I was thirteen -- I went up to bed, dizzy with exhilaration and excitement, and I prayed I wouldn't drink any ***more***!(p.554)
• When I encountered disappointments or frustrations -- as I did ***more*** and ***more*** frequently -- my solution was to drink.(p.556)
• Of course, the ***more*** I drank, the ***more*** unrealistic my expectations became and the poorer my performance, and the gap widened.(p.557)
• Then the drinks came ***more*** frequently, but carefully spaced out.(p.557)
• In the next half-year, I experienced two ***more*** esophageal hemorrhages, miraculously surviving each one by a hair.(p.558)
• He happened to be, by the grace of God, Dr. Harry Tiebout, the psychiatrist who probably knew ***more*** about alcoholism than any other in the world.(p.559)
• All these things and many, many ***more***, A.A. gave me.(p.559)
• The ***more*** I drank, the ***more*** I fantasized everything.(p.560)
• Therefore, no society of men and women ever had ***more*** urgent need for continuous effectiveness and permanent unity.(p.563)
• Because the "long form" is ***more*** explicit and of possible historic value, it is also reproduced.(p.563)
• Our ***more*** religious members call it "God-consciousness."(p.570)

moreover

• *Moreover,* he would lose his family for whom he had a deep affection.(p.35)

• *Moreover,* I am deeply convinced that so long as I continue to strive, in my bumbling way, toward the principles I first encountered in the earlier chapters of this book, this remarkable power will continue to flow through me.(p.437)

morning

• I began to be jittery in the *morning*.(p.3)

• It had been 52 that *morning*.(p.4)

• Next *morning* I telephoned a friend in Montreal.(p.4)

• This went on endlessly, and I began to waken very early in the *morning* shaking violently.(p.5)

• The remorse, horror and hopelessness of the next *morning* are unforgettable.(p.6)

• I hardly dared cross the street, lest I collapse and be run down by an early *morning* truck, for it was scarcely daylight.(p.6)

• A *morning* paper told me the market had gone to hell again.(p.6)

• Sometimes I stole from my wife's slender purse when the *morning* terror and madness were on me.(p.6)

• Yet early next *morning* he searches madly for the bottle he misplaced the night before.(p.21)

• Here are some of the methods we have tried: Drinking beer only, limiting the number of drinks, never drinking alone, never drinking in the *morning*, drinking only at home, never having it in the house, never drinking during business hours, drinking only at parties, switching from scotch to brandy, drinking only natural wines, agreeing to resign if ever drunk on the job, taking a trip, not taking a trip, swearing off forever (with and without a solemn oath), taking more physical exercise, reading inspirational books, going to health farms and sanitariums, accepting voluntary commitment to asylums -- we could increase the list ad infinitum.(p.31)

• He was very nervous in the *morning* after these bouts and quieted himself with more liquor.(p.32)

• This is his story: "I came to work on Tuesday *morning*.(p.36)

• I remember having several more that night and plenty the next *morning*.(p.41)

• So we clean house with the family, asking each *morning* in meditation that our Creator show us the way of patience, tolerance, kindliness and love.(p.83)

• If circumstances warrant, we ask our wives or friends to join us in *morning* meditation.(p.87)

• If we belong to a religious denomination which requires a definite *morning* devotion, we attend to that also.(p.87)

• In the *morning* we have kissed and made up.(p.105)

• He sometimes drinks in the *morning* and through the day also, to hold his nervousness in check.(p.109)

• There is talk about spiritual matters *morning*, noon and night.(p.128)

• When this happens, they can be invited to join in *morning* meditation and then they can take part in the daily discussion without rancor or bias.(p.134)

• Of an evening, you can go on a mild bender, get up in the *morning*, shake your head and go to business.(p.139)

• One *morning* he took the bull by the horns and set out to tell those he feared what his trouble had been.(p.156)

• Ask Him in your *morning* meditation what you can do each day for the man who is still sick.(p.164)

• I seemed to be able to snap back the next *morning* better than most of my fellow drinkers, who were cursed (or perhaps blessed) with a great deal of morning-after nausea.(p.172)

• During these years, I drank as much as my purse permitted, still without paying too great a penalty, although I was beginning to have *morning* jitters at times.(p.173)

• Most of the time therefore, I did not take the *morning* drink which I craved so badly, but instead would fill up on large doses of sedatives to quiet the jitters, which distressed me terribly.(p.176)

• Occasionally, I would yield to the *morning* craving, but if I did, it would be only a few hours before I would be quite unfit for work.(p.176)

• This would lessen my chances of smuggling some home that evening, which in turn would mean a night of futile tossing around in bed followed by a *morning* of unbearable jitters.(p.176)

• It was really a horrible nightmare, this earning money, getting liquor, smuggling it home, getting drunk, *morning* jitters, taking large doses of sedatives to make it possible for me to earn more money, and so on ad nauseam.(p.177)

• Tuesday I started in the *morning*, getting well organized by noon.(p.179)

• He came and got me home and to bed, gave me a few drinks that night, and one bottle of beer the next *morning*.(p.179)

• *Morning* after *morning* I would awake sick and with terrible jitters, but there was always a flask of liquor sitting on the table beside my bed.(p.183)

• I was moved into another room that *morning* and there was my wife.(p.184)

• The next *morning* I woke up in jail in Cleveland and the jailor had $1,175 of my money in an envelope.(p.196)

• At three-thirty the next *morning*, I was in Champlain Street Station, in jail for driving while intoxicated and insulting an officer; and the suit of which I was so proud was in such shape that the turnkey had to get me a pair of trousers to go into court in the next *morning*.(p.201)

• I was picked up at two-thirty that *morning* with my car smashed up by a street-car because I had run into a big concrete safety zone, and the street-car had run into me, and they took me out through the roof -- there's where I lost the suit.(p.202)

• I was black and blue, with my lips all swollen, when they roused us to go into court in the *morning*.(p.204)

• When I had been in the hospital ten days, Sister Ignatia, who has played such a part in the development of A.A. in this area, stuck her head in the door one *morning* and announced, looking at me quizzically, that they might be able to make something human out of my face after all.(p.205)

• One *morning*, after I had been on a binge for a couple of days, I awoke to find my brother and Doctor Bob in my room talking to me about not drinking.(p.206)

• There was also some conversation about Dr. Bob and I must have said that I would go down to Akron with Bill in the *morning*.(p.217)

• The next *morning*, my wife came into my room and wakened me and said, "That man is downstairs and he said you said you'd go to Akron."(p.217)

• In fact, the last three years of my drinking was a routine of barbiturates in the *morning*, so that I could stop shaking enough to shave, and then alcohol beginning about four-thirty or five o'clock, with a struggle not to take a drink at noon or during the day, because I had the idea that if I took one drink, I would smell as though I had had a pint.(p.217)

• Hangovers began to assume monstrous proportions and the *morning* drink became an urgent necessity.(p.226)

• I had no desire whatever to sit down at a table and stay a whole *morning* or afternoon drinking.(p.231)

• I had repaired to one of these one *morning* with my jug and when I left late in the afternoon, I picked up a newspaper on the way home.(p.244)

• Successive Monday *morning* hangovers, which despite mid-week resolutions to do better, came with unfailing regularity, eventually caused me to quit my job.(p.254)

• One *morning* after a terrific drinking bout, I was in a little bar near our house, and I shook so that I was very much ashamed, because I was getting the shakes worse and worse.(p.266)

• Time went on and the drinking got worse and worse, and I was in another barroom, down the road the other way, a small one, and I took my glass -- that *morning* I'd been able to lift it from the bar -- and I said to the woman behind the bar, "I wish I might never take another drop of that stuff.(p.266)

• Finally, one *morning*, I got up and got in the car and cried all the way down to the M.'s -- the people who owned the bar -- and told her I was licked and wanted help.(p.267)

• At two-forty-five that *morning* I thought I would die.(p.267)

• The next *morning* his wife came dragging him in before Russ went to work, while I was getting breakfast.(p.271)

• There was more than one occasion when I got up in the *morning* with just enough money for coffee and toast and the bus fare to carry me to my first appointment.(p.283)

• Shortly thereafter, aided by the Depression, I found that I had a great deal of spare time and that a little drink in the *morning* helped.(p.287)

• My wife could not understand the next *morning* why I was drunker than the night before when she took my bottles.(p.289)

• After it was closed we all retired to the kitchen and had coffee and doughnuts and more discussion until the small hours of the *morning*.(p.291)

• How many times I swore off in the *morning* and got drunk before sunset I don't know.(p.300)

• Usually, the next *morning* I would be quite sick.(p.317)

• One *morning* when I was feeling really bad, I was put on K.P. and the head cook wanted me to go out and scrub the garbage cans.(p.317)

• I began taking drinks in the *morning* to get started.(p.318)

• And she would never, never take that *morning* drink!(p.321)

• I nudged George next *morning*, and I said, "I'm in," and he said, "Oh, I knew you'd make it."(p.322)

• And, unlike many others, I never took a drink in the *morning*.(p.323)

• I needed a drink, but I was afraid to take a *morning* drink, because I didn't want to be a drunk.(p.323)

• I became a drunk anyway, but I was scared to death to take that *morning* drink.(p.323)

• I was accused of it many times when I went to play bridge in the afternoon, but I really never did take a *morning* drink.(p.323)

• I try to live today so that tomorrow I won't be ashamed when I wake up in the *morning*.(p.325)

• I never could face it the next *morning*.(p.325)

• And unless I had some rosy picture of what was going to happen that day, I wouldn't even feel like getting up in the *morning* at all.(p.325)

• There was one girl especially, and I'd watch her from my window every *morning*, leaving faithfully to go to the hospital in the neighborhood.(p.326)

• How will I feel next Saturday *morning*?(p.326)

• In so simple a manner did my *morning* drinking begin.(p.331)

• Yet I recently recalled that each *morning* I used to talk to the bottle when I took it down from the closet.(p.332)

• The only incentive that I had, toward the end, for getting dressed in the *morning* was to get out and get supplies to help me get my day started.(p.336)

• I knew nothing about alcoholism or the D.T.'s, but when I woke up on this last *morning* of my son's illness, I taped the keyhole on my door because "everyone was out there."(p.338)

• I certainly wasn't my shy, quiet self that night -- as I was informed the next *morning*.(p.353)

• Luck was with me for I made my train, but I arrived home the next *morning* with a new kind of hangover.(p.364)

• Early the next *morning* a man whose name I knew well, a lawyer, called on me.(p.378)

• So finally, he said to me one *morning*, "Esther, why do you do this?"(p.386)

• The next *morning* he came into my room and said, "Esther, I'm not going to lecture you any more, but I want you to read this article.(p.391)

• So Frank left town, and by Monday *morning* I had been sober for that whole week.(p.393)

• Monday *morning* I was feeling just like a million dollars -- all I needed was half a pint!(p.393)

• At age twenty-one, I enlisted in the Navy for two reasons: (1) to avoid being drafted into the Army, and (2) out of a burst of patriotic fervor inspired by the advent of World War II and as the result of an all-night drinking binge which found me sitting on the doorstep of the Navy recruiting office when the chief petty officer arrived to open for business at nine o'clock Monday *morning*.(p.398)

• In the *morning*, because I was young and healthy, my remorse was worse than my hangover.(p.404)

• They introduced me to beer in the *morning* to kill hangovers.(p.407)

• In the *morning* I would wake up with a dollar or two.(p.410)

• Next *morning* I was sworn in, feeling no pain.(p.425)

• I was escorted back to San Diego next *morning* -- by the Shore Patrol, but I was discharged on schedule.(p.428)

• Sometimes I'd make it home and go to sleep at the wheel of my car, for all the neighbors to see next *morning* as they left for work.(p.429)

• In all the twenty-five years of my drinking there were only a few occasions when I took a *morning* drink.(p.432)

• Evening cocktails were as standard as *morning* coffee, and I suppose my average daily consumption ran a little more or less than a pint.(p.433)

• After going to school all day, working in the family drugstore all evening, and then studying until one or two in the *morning*, I would not be able to sleep soundly, with everything I had been studying going round in my head.(p.440)

• I would be half asleep and half awake, and in the *morning*, I would be both tired and stupid.(p.440)

• I didn't know whether I had told him to rush to the

hospital and I'd meet him there, or to take two aspirin and call me in the *morning*.(p.441)

• But I never became a *morning* drinker.(p.441)

• It became progressively harder to get up in the *morning*, until one day I asked myself what I would do for a patient who felt this rotten.(p.441)

• Eventually, I was taking forty-five milligrams of the long-acting Benzedrine and forty-five of the short-acting just to get out of bed in the *morning*.(p.442)

• On each occasion, I had a convulsion on Sunday *morning*.(p.444)

• I don't mean that I went to bed one night a normal drinker, and awoke the next *morning* an alcoholic.(p.464)

• It is so beautiful to get up in the *morning* not being hung-over and being able to remember where we were the night before.(p.481)

• I've never seen him drunk in my life, although he'd take a shot in the *morning* and usually one in the evening, and so did I; but for the most part he kept his whiskey in his office.(p.484)

• The next *morning* I carried another prescription to this man's house and exchanged it for the bottle his wife had.(p.489)

• The next *morning* I went up for arraignment.(p.492)

• *Morning* comes.(p.500)

• I drink and go to bed; I take a few the next *morning* and go see my mother once more.(p.501)

• I drink steadily, I come to at three in the *morning*.(p.501)

• It is the last day of the following October, a dark, rainy *morning*.(p.502)

• She had looked for me this *morning*.(p.502)

• I staggered home next *morning*.(p.510)

• That and the *morning* drink came very early in my drinking career.(p.513)

• I had a habit of getting up just prior to the closing time of the saloons, about two or three o'clock in the *morning*.(p.514)

• I'd get downstairs to the gin mill, get enough in to hold me until eight o'clock in the *morning*, then I'd go out to join that "misery parade" that so many of us know so well.(p.514)

• One *morning* I didn't wake up until after four o'clock.(p.515)

• I wasn't a happy man that *morning*, but I'm happy now that it came about.(p.515)

• That *morning* was the first time I really realized where I'd got to in my life.(p.523)

• One *morning*, I woke up with a thousand dollars.(p.528)

• Still another friend and temporary host received me at four in the *morning* from the charge of a policeman who had found me "going to bed" in a garage far from the last place I could remember having been, a fashionable bar and restaurant in the theatrical district of New York, to which I had repaired after my date for that evening, a charming lady of the theatre who had refused my company for obvious reasons.(p.538)

• When the policeman released me to my stupefied and exasperated friend at four in the *morning*, I went to my traveling bag and groped until I found – well, let the officer speak: "Ah," said the policeman, "he's got anuder pair, t'ank God!"(p.538)

• One *morning*, however, I realized I had to get rid of it, for my reprieve was running out, and if I didn't get rid of it I was going to get drunk – and I didn't want to get drunk any more.(p.552)

• In my prayers that *morning* I asked God to point out to me some way to be free of this resentment.(p.552)

• To cure my dreadful hangovers, I discovered the *morning* drink.(p.556)

• I vomited every *morning*.(p.558)

morning-after

• I seemed to be able to snap back the next morning better than most of my fellow drinkers, who were cursed (or perhaps blessed) with a great deal of *morning-after* nausea.(p.172)

• Gradually, however, I'd suffer so much that I simply had to have the *morning-after* drink.(p.233)

mornings

• I've prayed to God on hangover *mornings* and sworn that I'd never touch another drop but by nine o'clock I'd be boiled as an owl."(p.158)

• Many *mornings* I have gone to classes, and even though fully prepared, would turn and walk back to the fraternity house because of my jitters, not daring to enter the classroom for fear of making a scene should I be called on for recitation.(p.173)

• How I was able to discharge my duties at the office during those horrible *mornings*, I will never be able to explain.(p.299)

• I arrived at the stage where I couldn't quite make it to the office some *mornings*.(p.299)

morphine

• Perhaps he goes to a doctor who gives him *morphine* or some sedative with which to taper off.(p.22)

• For the leveling-off process, I just loved intravenous Demerol, but I found it hard to practice good medicine while shooting *morphine*.(p.442)

mortal

• I had a *mortal* fear of going to bed and tossing all night.(p.299)

• They realized that in the end alcoholism could be a *mortal* as cancer; certainly no sane man would wait for a malignant growth to become fatal before seeking help.(p.315)

• I was really scolding my *mortal* enemy, the inner me.(p.408)

mortar

• Have we tried to make *mortar* without sand?(p.75)

mortgage

• The house was taken over by the *mortgage* holder, my mother-in-law died, and my wife and father-in-law became ill.(p.5)

• The family may feel they hold a *mortgage* on dad, so big that no equity should be left for outsiders.(p.131)

• I had contracted for half of it, at least verbally, and the contractors were taking half of the second *mortgage* bond.(p.198)

mortification

• As I went in I was dying of *mortification*.(p.413)

Moscow

• When he was uptown – we were living in the little town of *Moscow* -- I went up to try to get some money from him to buy groceries.(p.193)

Moslems

• By personal religious affiliation, we include Catholics, Protestants, Jews, Hindus, and a sprinkling of *Moslems* and Buddhists.(p.xx)

most

• If you have a drinking problem, we hope that you may pause in reading one of the forty-four personal stories and think: "Yes, that happened to me"; or, more important, "Yes, I've felt like that"; or *most* important, "Yes, I believe this program can work for me, too."(p.xii)

• The cases we have followed through have been *most* interesting; in fact, many of them are amazing.(p.xxv)

• If any feel that as psychiatrists directing a hospital for alcoholics we appear somewhat sentimental, let them stand with us a while on the firing line, see the tragedies, the despairing wives, the little children; let the solving of these problems become a part of their daily work, and even of their sleeping moments, and the *most* cynical will not wonder that we have accepted and encouraged this movement.(p.xxvi)

• The classification of alcoholics seems *most* difficult, and in much detail is outside the scope of this book.(p.xxviii)

• Much has been written pro and con, but among physicians, the general opinion seems to be that *most* chronic alcoholics are doomed.(p.xxviii)

• We had long talks when I would still her foreboding by telling her that men of genius conceived their best projects when drunk; that the *most* majestic constructions of philosophic thought were so derived.(p.2)

• I had developed a theory that *most* people lost money in stocks through ignorance of markets.(p.2)

• His moral teaching – *most* excellent.(p.11)

• God comes to *most* men gradually, but His impact on me was sudden and profound.(p.14)

• I have seen hundreds of families set their feet in the path that really goes somewhere; have seen the *most* impossible domestic situations righted; feuds and bitterness of all sorts wiped out.(p.15)

• *Most* of us feel we need look no further for Utopia.(p.16)

• That the man who is making the approach has had the same difficulty, that he obviously knows what he is talking about, that his whole deportment shouts at the new prospect that he is a man with a real answer, that he has no attitude of Holier Than Thou, nothing whatever except the sincere desire to be helpful; that there are no fees to pay, no axes to grind, no people to please, no lectures to be endured -- these are the conditions we have found *most* effective.(p.18)

• *Most* of us sense that real tolerance of other people's shortcomings and viewpoints and a respect for their opinions are attitudes which make us more useful to others.(p.19)

• At a certain point in the drinking of every alcoholic, he passes into a state where the *most* powerful desire to stop drinking is of absolutely no avail.(p.24)

• The fact is that *most* alcoholics, for reasons yet obscure, have lost the power of choice in drink.(p.24)

• The alcoholic may say to himself in the *most* casual way, "It won't burn me this time, so here's how!"(p.24)

• Not all of us join religious bodies, but *most* of us favor such memberships.(p.28)

• *Most* of us have been unwilling to admit we were real alcoholics.(p.30)

• Though there is no way of proving it, we believe that early in our drinking careers *most* of us could have stopped drinking.(p.32)

• *Most* of us have believed that if we remained sober for a long stretch, we could thereafter drink normally.(p.33)

• Some will be drunk the day after making their resolutions; *most* of them within a few weeks.(p.34)

• The story he told is *most* instructive, for here was a chap absolutely convinced he had to stop drinking, who had no excuse for drinking, who exhibited splendid judgment and determination in all his other concerns, yet was flat on his back nevertheless.(p.40)

• I reasoned I was not so far advanced as *most* of you fellows, that I had been usually successful in licking my other personal problems, and that I would therefore be successful where you men failed.(p.40)

• *Most* alcoholics have to be pretty badly mangled before they really commence to solve their problems.(p.43)

• For *most* cases, there is virtually no other solution."(p.43)

• When many hundreds of people are able to say that the consciousness of the Presence of God is today the *most* important fact of their lives, they present a powerful reason why one should have faith.(p.51)

• But in *most* fields our generation has witnessed complete liberation of our thinking.(p.52)

• Neither is reason, as *most* of us use it, entirely dependable, though it emanate from our best minds.(p.54)

• *Most* people try to live by self-propulsion.(p.60)

• But, as with *most* humans, he is more likely to have varied traits.(p.61)

• Whatever our protestations, are not *most* of us concerned with ourselves, our resentments, or our self-pity?(p.62)

• *Most* good ideas are simple, and this concept was the keystone of the new and triumphant arch through which we passed to freedom.(p.62)

• In *most* cases it was found that our self-esteem, our pocketbooks, our ambitions, our personal relationships (including sex) were hurt or threatened.(p.64)

• To conclude that others were wrong was as far as *most* of us ever got.(p.66)

• Then we have the voices who cry for sex and more sex; who bewail the institution of marriage; who think that *most* of the troubles of the race are traceable to sex causes.(p.69)

• More than *most* people, the alcoholic leads a double life.(p.73)

• *Most* people approached in this way will be glad to help; they will be honored by our confidence.(p.75)

• *Most* alcoholics owe money.(p.78)

• Approached in this way, the *most* ruthless creditor will sometimes surprise us.(p.78)

• *Most* of us have done that sort of thing.(p.78)

• His action met widespread approval, and today his is one of the *most* trusted citizens of his town.(p.80)

• Keep it always in sight that we are dealing with that *most* terrible human emotion – jealousy.(p.82)

• Were we thinking of ourselves *most* of the time?(p.86)

• If there is any indication that he wants to stop, have a good talk with the person *most* interested in him -- usually his wife.(p.90)

• We are dealing only with general principles common to *most* denominations.(p.94)

• You will be *most* successful with alcoholics if you do not exhibit any passion for crusade or reform.(p.95)

• The *most* incompatible people discover they have a basis upon which they can meet.(p.99)

• You should not hesitate to visit the *most* sordid spot on earth on such an errand.(p.102)

• *Most* of us have entered the final stage with its commitment to health resorts, sanitariums, hospitals, and jails.(p.107)

• Today *most* of our men are better husbands and fathers than ever before.(p.108)

• Patience and good temper are *most* necessary.(p.111)

• We find that *most* of this embarrassment is unnecessary.(p.115)

• It is the *most* natural thing in the world, once his liquor problem is solved, to feel that he will now measure up to that cherished vision.(p.118)

• In ***most*** cases, the alcoholic survived this ordeal without relapse, but not always.(p.125)
• Drinking isolates ***most*** homes from the outside world.(p.131)
• We are convinced that a spiritual mode of living is a ***most*** powerful health restorative.(p.133)
• ***Most*** of them give freely of themselves, that their fellows may enjoy sound minds and bodies.(p.133)
• Seeing is believing to ***most*** families who have lived with a drinker.(p.135)
• Though he is now a ***most*** effective member of Alcoholics Anonymous, he still smokes and drinks coffee, but neither his wife or anyone else stands in judgment.(p.135)
• For ***most*** alcoholics who are drinking, or who are just getting over a spree, a certain amount of physical treatment is desirable, even imperative.(p.142)
• For ***most*** normal folks, drinking means conviviality, companionship and colorful imagination.(p.151)
• The ***most*** satisfactory years of your existence lie ahead.(p.152)
• Men who had liquor shipped in from Boston or New York by express were looked upon with great distrust and disfavor by ***most*** of the good townspeople.(p.171)
• My father was a professional man of recognized ability and both my father and mother were ***most*** active in church affairs.(p.171)
• I seemed to be able to snap back the next morning better than ***most*** of my fellow drinkers, who were cursed (or perhaps blessed) with a great deal of morning-after nausea.(p.172)
• ***Most*** of the time therefore, I did not take the morning drink which I craved so badly, but instead would fill up on large doses of sedatives to quiet the jitters, which distressed me terribly.(p.176)
• I was self conscious and ill at ease ***most*** of the time, my health was at the breaking point, and I was thoroughly miserable.(p.178)
• But this was a man who had experienced many years of frightful drinking, who had had ***most*** all the drunkard's experiences known to man, but who had been cured by the very means I had been trying to employ, that is to say the spiritual approach.(p.180)
• It is a ***most*** wonderful blessing to be relieved of the terrible curse with which I was afflicted.(p.180)
• Unlike ***most*** of our crowd, I did not get over my craving for liquor much during the first two and one-half years of abstinence.(p.181)
• I spent ***most*** of my time trying to get back these friendships, and to make some recompense towards my wife, whom I had hurt a lot.(p.191)
• I'm so grateful for both the program and the people in it that I still want to go, and then probably the ***most*** wonderful thing that I learned from the program -- I've seen this in the 'A.A. Grapevine' a lot of times, and I've had people say it to me personally, and I've heard people get up in meetings and make the same statement: The statement is, "I came into A.A. solely for the purpose of sobriety, but it has been through A.A. that I have found God."(p.192)
• I feel that is about the ***most*** wonderful thing that a person can do.(p.192)
• To show you the point to which this obsession went, there came an occasion when I had spent a ***most*** delightful week-end, and at nine o'clock on Sunday night I was on my way home, and I thought I would get a drink.(p.204)
• I had my own business, successful enough for me to indulge ***most*** of my desires.(p.225)
• Like ***most*** immigrants I wanted to be somebody and have something and I was very happy and contented as I felt success crown my efforts.(p.232)
• We can share in the laughter and tears of our many friends, and ***most*** important, we can share our A.A. way of life and are given a daily opportunity to help others.(p.249)
• During my visit there, renewing acquaintance with former friends, I soon spent ***most*** of my money.(p.252)
• We were the ***most*** congenial drinkers you ever saw.(p.264)
• After six months of sobriety I saw the picture in a different light: Detroit was the place I had to return to, not only because I must face the mess I had made there, but because it was there that I could be of the ***most*** service to A.A.(p.281)
• Do I have to tell you who gained the ***most*** out of all this?(p.283)
• The ***most*** accurate answer I can give you is this: Fear has never again ruled my life since that day in September, 1938, when I found that a Power greater than myself could not only restore me to sanity but could keep me both sober and sane.(p.285)
• He laid great stress on the progression of his attitude toward life and people, and ***most*** of his attitudes had been very similar to mine.(p.290)
• I became convinced of that because I spent ***most*** of my time there and nary a job turned up.(p.300)
• I was on that job a month and drunk ***most*** of the time.(p.301)
• To be sure, this had been a dizzy and confused interval, but ***most*** everyone else I knew had emerged from it with both feet on the ground and a fair amount of adult maturity.(p.304)
• ***Most*** of them prescribed sedatives and advised rest and moderation.(p.305)
• He had tried everything from having me attend daily mass at six a.m. to performing the ***most*** menial labor for his charity patients.(p.306)
• He further explained that alcohol was no respecter of sex or background, but that ***most*** of the alcoholics he had encountered had better than average minds and abilities.(p.308)
• Philosophy, faith, a sense of humor (they could laugh at themselves), clear-cut objectives, appreciation -- and ***most*** especially appreciation and sympathetic understanding for their fellow man.(p.310)
• ***Most*** of these fortunate ones have had little or no acquaintance with delirium, with hospitals, asylums, and jails.(p.315)
• I got orders to go to Vietnam, and I spent ***most*** of the year over there either drunk or sick with a hangover.(p.317)
• ***Most*** of my conversations were meaningless to everyone but me.(p.319)
• As my son, our second child, came along, and as he became school age and was away at school ***most*** of the time, something happened.(p.323)
• But the saddest, and thus the ***most*** consoling, drifted through from the country-music station -- stories of broken hearts, wasted lives, lost loves, sung plaintively.(p.332)
• I became one of the ***most*** active women in the community, what with P.T.A., other community organizations and drives.(p.339)
• I returned to my home in Lucknow, India, at the end of November last year from a vacation in one of the ***most*** famous beauty spots in our country, a mountain resort 6,800 feet up, with a wonderful lake.(p.342)
• I was voted the man ***most*** likely to succeed.(p.345)
• If I were asked what in my opinion was the ***most*** important factor in being successful in this program, besides following the Twelve Steps, I would say Honesty.(p.367)
• And the ***most*** important person to be honest with is Yourself.(p.368)
• That way, I could spend ***most*** of my time at the Laundromat!(p.371)
• I did work of all kinds after school and during vacations, trying to find that which would appeal ***most*** as a goal for a life work.(p.373)
• We visited ***most*** of that day and attended a meeting that night.(p.378)
• I don't know what I expected, but I ***most*** certainly didn't visualize a group of people talking about their drinking problems, making light of their personal tragedies and at the same time enjoying themselves.(p.378)
• ***Most*** certainly I was powerless over alcohol, and for me, my life had become unmanageable.(p.379)
• To ***most*** of us, making amends will take the rest of our lives, but we can start immediately.(p.381)
• To me this meant telling my associates that I had joined Alcoholics Anonymous; that I didn't know what was expected of me by A.A., but that whatever it was, it was the ***most*** important thing in life for me; that sobriety meant more to me than anything in this world.(p.382)
• There are no easy ways to sober up, but that's the ***most*** excruciating.(p.389)
• However, I threw myself into Twelve Step work, and what I feared would be a calamity turned out to be the ***most*** blessed of blessings.(p.394)
• Like ***most*** statistics, it doesn't prove anything -- just satisfies a little curiosity engendered by the wail "Oh, those initiation fees" that prompted this investigation.(p.399)
• Like ***most*** sick people before me, I was implacably selfish, and chronically self-centered.(p.401)
• He got half custody of our child, but later kept her during ***most*** of the school terms.(p.402)
• Even then I knew in my heart that I was unfit for the very things I wanted ***most***, a happy marriage, security, a home and love.(p.403)
• They were all kids, ***most*** of them younger than I was.(p.407)
• Ribaldry was the substance of the conversation, and I set out to be the funniest and ***most*** ribald of them all.(p.407)
• ***Most*** of the time I was covered with bruises from "running into doors."(p.411)
• ***Most*** important, A.A. has enabled me to go back and start growing up all over again in all areas of my life.(p.420)
• I did as I pleased ***most*** of the time.(p.424)
• I headed home for the ***most*** wonderful experience of all time -- meeting my "new" parents -- mom and dad looked different than I had pictured them.(p.428)
• I was inwardly unhappy ***most*** of the time.(p.432)
• The ***most*** terrible blow of my life befell me after I'd found sobriety through A.A.(p.437)
• Now I own perhaps the ***most*** costly pair of moccasins anyone has ever seen, and they help me remember where I've been.)(p.445)
• In the hospital, I hung on to the idea I'd had ***most*** of my life: that if I could just control the external environment, the internal environment would then be comfortable.(p.445)
• (Today, there is absolutely nothing in the world more important to me than my keeping this alcoholic sober; not taking a drink is by far the ***most*** important thing I do each day.)(p.447)
• To this day, I am amazed at how many of my problems -- ***most*** of which had nothing to do with drinking, I believed -- have become manageable or have simply disappeared since I quit drinking.(p.448)
• I had already given up all the narcotics, ***most*** of the pills, and some of the alcohol when I first came to A.A.(p.448)
• ***Most*** had taken shattering losses on nearly every front of life.(p.455)
• For me, as for ***most*** alcoholics, it was "Eat, drink, and be merry, for tomorrow you die."(p.457)
• ***Most*** of us did not stay out of prison long enough to run the alcoholic gamut -- to develop the ongoing kind of alcoholism or alcoholic drinking you hear about in A.A. talks.(p.458)
• I didn't know I was an alcoholic and (like ***most*** men in prison today) could not relate alcohol to any of my past troubles.(p.460)
• Then I was transferred to the honor-grade unit, where I spent the ***most*** painful year of my life.(p.462)
• He has taught me that, in our new life, I am the ***most*** important person of all.(p.481)
• I've never seen him drunk in my life, although he'd take a shot in the morning and usually one in the evening, and so did I; but for the ***most*** part he kept his whiskey in his office.(p.484)
• About then too, I realized that my point of view on the opposite sex wasn't entirely like that of ***most*** of the boys I knew.(p.484)
• Dad, due to having spent ***most*** of his time in a small Virginia town, didn't have any too much money, and the money he had saved and the property he had acquired were in Washington.(p.486)
• Around eight or nine o'clock there came two big detectives and a policeman to arrest me for assault; and I was the ***most*** amazed person in the world when they said I had assaulted someone, and especially that I had assaulted my wife.(p.492)
• Of course, it wasn't very much of a meeting in the beginning; ***most*** of the time it was just Vi and myself.(p.495)
• ***Most*** of my attendance there was when people would come in from the outside.(p.510)
• When I came home to ordinary garrison life in England, I found that I was drinking rather more than ***most*** people of may age.(p.518)
• What struck me ***most*** was that they all seemed to be quite pleased with having made a job of it and having stopped drinking.(p.524)
• Not least of my debts to A.A. is the knowledge that in that time when she wanted me ***most***, I was there -- and that I wasn't drunk.(p.525)
• Within a month, the police, the hospital authorities, several kind strangers, ***most*** of my friends, all of my close relatives, and a few adepts at rolling a drunk and removing his wrist watch and wallet had been involved.(p.532)
• That couplet contains ***most*** of my reasons for drinking.(p.534)
• I know there are some alcoholics who seem terribly, terribly grown-up, but I think that they are trying to make themselves think they are grown-up, and the strain of their effort is what is causing them to drink -- a sense of inadequacy, a childish vanity to be the ***most*** popular, the ***most*** sought after, the mostest of the ***most***.(p.535)
• I was the only person I'd ever known personally who had ever been in jail, and I guess it is ***most*** significant that the second time was less humiliating that the first had been.(p.549)
• Like ***most*** other alcoholics I have known, I did quit drinking at various times -- once for ten months on my own and during other interludes

when I was hospitalized.(p.554)
• As our children grew up, I was able to be a father to them when they ***most*** needed one.(p.559)
• We alcoholics see that we must work together and hang together, else ***most*** of us will finally die alone.(p.563)
• A.A. must continue to live or ***most*** of us will surely die.(p.565)
• ***Most*** of our experiences are what the psychologist William James calls the "educational variety" because they develop slowly over a period of time.(p.569)
• ***Most*** of us think this awareness of a Power greater than ourselves is the essence of spiritual experience.(p.570)
• ***Most*** emphatically we wish to say that any alcoholic capable of honestly facing his problems in the light of our experience can recover, provided he does not close his mind to all spiritual concepts.(p.570)
• (This address is now available in pamphlet form at nominal cost through ***most*** A.A. groups or from Box 459, Grand Central Station, New York, NY 10163, under the title "Three Talks to Medical Societies by Bill W." – formerly called "Bill on Alcoholism" and earlier "Alcoholism the Illness.")(p.572)
• In the United States and Canada, ***most*** towns and cities have A.A. groups.(p.575)

mostest

• I know there are some alcoholics who seem terribly, terribly grown-up, but I think that they are trying to make themselves think they are grown-up, and the strain of their effort is what is causing them to drink -- a sense of inadequacy, a childish vanity to be the most popular, the most sought after, the ***mostest*** of the most.(p.535)

mostly

• Being ***mostly*** business or professional folk, we could not well carry on our occupations in such an event.(p.xiii)
• But soon the sense of His presence had been blotted out by worldly clamors, ***mostly*** those within myself.(p.12)
• My fellow-workers were ***mostly*** good Saturday night drinkers and I was right with them.(p.252)
• In part, it was a feeling of intense shame at having to leave the Army during the war, but ***mostly*** it was resentment that this kind of thing should happen to me for, strange as it may seem, up to then I still thought I could control drinking.(p.521)
• Dr. John F. Stouffer, Chief Psychiatrist, Philadelphia General Hospital, citing his experience with A.A., said: "The alcoholics we get here at Philadelphia General are ***mostly*** those who cannot afford private treatment, and A.A. is by far the greatest thing we have been able to offer them.(p.572)

mother

• My bother-in-law is a physician, and through his kindness and that of my ***mother*** I was placed in a nationally-known hospital for the mental and physical rehabilitation of alcoholics.(p.7)
• But for every man who drinks others are involved -- the wife who trembles in fear of the next debauch; the ***mother*** and father who see their son wasting away.(p.104)
• Perhaps at this point we got a divorce and took the children home to father and ***mother***.(p.106)
• ***Mother*** may complain of inattention.(p.126)
• Sometimes ***mother*** and children don't think so.(p.126)
• Little by little, ***mother*** and children will see they ask too much, and father will see he gives too little.(p.127)
• He may tell ***mother***, who has been religious all her life, that she doesn't know what it's all about, and that she had better get his brand of spirituality while there is yet time.(p.128)
• Liquor incapacitated father for so many years that ***mother*** became head of the house.(p.130)
• ***Mother*** made all the plans and gave the directions.(p.131)
• Thus ***mother***, through no fault of her own, became accustomed to wearing the family trousers.(p.131)
• Instead of developing new channels of activity for themselves, ***mother*** and children demand that he stay home and make up the deficiency.(p.131)
• Without saying so, they may cordially hate him for what he has done to them and to their ***mother***.(p.134)
• This may hang on for months, long after their ***mother*** has accepted dad's new way of living and thinking.(p.134)
• My father was a professional man of recognized ability and both my father and ***mother*** were most active in church affairs.(p.171)
• Both father and ***mother*** were considerably above the average in intelligence.(p.172)
• This was no fault of my father or ***mother***, as they were both very much opposed to drinking.(p.182)
• When I was sixteen years old, my ***mother*** remarried and I was given the opportunity of going back to school.(p.193)
• (My ***mother*** and father were Catholics and I had been baptized, but at the end of my instructions for Confirmation I had not gone to church, and then when my ***mother*** remarried, she married a Protestant and the whole religious angle was forgotten.(p.201)
• My ***mother*** was eighty-nine years old when she died, and I was a full-blown alcoholic at the time of her death.(p.210)
• ***Mother*** would take me in only if I would stay locked in a small storeroom and give her my clothes and shoes.(p.238)
• Father was a very well-integrated person, and while ***mother*** was highstrung and a bit selfish and demanding, our home life was reasonably harmonious.(p.240)
• After the oil job blew up, I went back to Baltimore and ***mother***, my first wife having said a permanent "Goodbye."(p.243)
• I come from a very poor family in material things, with a fine Christian ***mother***, but with no religious background.(p.261)
• I know that one of the outfits I had was a skirt and a very funny looking blouse that my ***mother*** had picked up at a rummage sale.(p.261)
• Russ said, "***Mother***, if this tells us how to do it, you'll have to read it."(p.268)
• When we closed the meeting with the Lord's Prayer, Russ said, "***Mother***, help me stand."(p.270)
• Neither one of the two was interested for himself, one being a ***mother*** who wanted to do something for her son.(p.294)
• Half a ***mother*** was better than no ***mother*** at all.(p.337)
• I screamed on the telephone for my ***mother*** to get up there; something was going to happen; I didn't know what, but if she didn't get there quick, I'd split wide open.(p.338)
• I also turned against my family, my ***mother***.(p.338)
• I was in the fourth quarter of my senior year at high school, and my ***mother*** was quite sick in the hospital.(p.354)
• I was born in Cleveland, Ohio, the only child of a prominent dentist, and a very proud ***mother***.(p.357)
• There, I could be a proper ***mother*** and wife while drinking up a storm.(p.369)
• My ***mother*** was a lovely, sweet woman, whose only weakness was my father.(p.369)
• My ***mother*** said so, again and again.(p.369)
• After his death, my ***mother*** soon picked up drinking where Dad left off, and in a very short time she died of cirrhosis of the liver.(p.370)
• Very soon after I lost ***Mother***, my five-year-old little girl was killed by a neighbor's car.(p.370)
• With that, he told me to leave, because I was unfit as a ***mother***, a wife, and a laundress.(p.371)
• I put my poor ***mother*** and father through agonies but, finally, I couldn't stand living with them and having them watch everything I did.(p.386)
• I also wanted to be the queen of society, with a glittering salon, the bride of a dream prince and the ***mother*** of a happy brood.(p.400)
• When I was a baby, my ***mother*** brought me to America, and I never again saw my father.(p.401)
• Her father became both ***mother*** and father to her.(p.402)
• But he noticed that I was not a good ***mother*** to my child, that I relegated her to nurses when she was with me.(p.403)
• Never once had my ***mother*** even hinted at the idea that, when I grew up, I might like to be president of A.A.(p.439)
• At the wedding, I hope I will also get to see my daughter and their ***mother***.(p.463)
• Things went from bad to worse, and since I had finally and completely failed at the job of being a wife and a ***mother***, my marriage ended.(p.468)
• By grace of God I stop, think two things: This would kill good ***mother*** and father; then remember boys talk about Indian fellow who been sober three years.(p.475)
• We survivors are all in A.A. now, and my ***mother*** is in Al-Anon.(p.480)
• I remember in my early youth my ***mother*** dressed me just as she did my two sisters, and I wore curls until I was six years of age.(p.483)
• We lived just a few doors from the First Baptist Church and when they had funerals I remember very often asking my ***mother*** whether the person was good or bad and whether they were going to heaven or hell.(p.483)
• My ***mother*** had been recently converted and, actually, had become a religious fanatic.(p.483)
• Another thing that ***mother*** drilled into me was a very Puritanical point of view as to sex relations and as to motherhood and womanhood.(p.483)
• ***Mother*** was of the old school and figured that anyone I associated with should be of the proper type.(p.484)
• The only time that I have ever seen my ***mother*** take anything alcoholic was around Christmas time, when she would drink some eggnog or light wine.(p.484)
• I remember in my first year in high school, that ***mother*** suggested that I do not join the cadet unit.(p.484)
• I had quite a heartache about her then because she wasn't the type of girl that my ***mother*** wanted me to marry.(p.485)
• My ***mother*** resented it so that the first Christmas after our marriage, she didn't even invite us to dinner.(p.485)
• Economic conditions had a great deal to do with it, because I've often heard my father say that his ***mother*** would take one of the old time flour sacks and cut a hole through the bottom and two corners of it and there you'd have a gown.(p.486)
• The thought came to me that if God, as my ***mother*** said, was a vengeful God, he couldn't be a loving God.(p.489)
• So I went down to talk to the District Attorney, and the arrangement was made that I would go home to stay with my ***mother***, and that meant Vi and I were separated.(p.491)
• I sometimes gave it to my ***mother*** and then I'd go back and hound her for it.(p.491)
• I knew my wife didn't because I had been sincere in all my promises to her as well as to my ***mother*** and to my close friends, but the urge to take that drink was more powerful than anything else.(p.494)
• ***Mother*** hated liquor and feared a drunken man.(p.498)
• I would never have tried, but ***mother*** counts on it so.(p.499)
• Her ***mother*** is in a critical condition at a hospital.(p.501)
• ***Mother*** has been dying of cancer for a long time.(p.501)
• ***Mother*** must never know.(p.501)
• I drink and go to bed; I take a few the next morning and go see my ***mother*** once more.(p.501)
• When my ***mother*** opened the door, I almost fell in on my face.(p.510)
• She had been warned numerous times, not only by her family but by my own ***mother***, that I was a hopeless drunk, that there wasn't anything anybody could do with me, that I'd never stop, and that eventually I'd break her heart.(p.513)
• I went to hospitals, I went to retreats and doctors, and finally my ***mother*** asked me to go and see a specialist of her own choosing.(p.522)
• Finally, my ***mother*** came and said she had kept me at home for six years because she thought she could help me, but that now she had come to the conclusion that I wasn't even worth trying to help.(p.523)
• This was the only time in my life that I'd ever known my ***mother*** to be almost pitiless, but she couldn't be blamed for that.(p.523)
• My ***mother*** lived on for five years after I joined A.A., the last two in complete blindness.(p.525)
• I would wait for the mailman each month, like any good ***mother***, but as soon as he handed me my check, I put on my best dress and went looking for my alcoholic friend.(p.527)
• My ***mother*** went to a nearby city to go to work, and my father, being an alcoholic, simply went.(p.544)
• It was against my ***mother*** and it was twenty-five years old.(p.551)

mother-in-law

• The house was taken over by the mortgage holder, my ***mother-in-law*** died, and my wife and father-in-law became ill.(p.5)
• My Quaker ***mother-in-law***, bless her heart, used to set the Christmas pudding ablaze with lumps of sugar dipped in rubbing alcohol.(p.402)

mother's

• It was the day before ***Mother's*** Day and I had come home plastered, carrying a big potted plant which I set down on the table and forthwith went upstairs and passed out.(p.179)
• After a couple of days in dollar hotels and one night in the pokey, I finally landed on my ***mother's*** doorstep -- shaking apart, with several days' beard and, of course, broke as usual.(p.238)
• My family, on my ***mother's*** side, was brilliant, gifted and charming.(p.401)
• My ***mother's*** heartbreak, or the unpleasant publicity

I had caused did not bother my pretty head.(p.401)
• To tell you a small part of what my ***mother's*** life must have been like: Three of her kids were in jail that year – two sons and a daughter.(p.480)
• Of course, when father finally came to Virginia to work his way through school, he resented the southern "cracker," as he often called them, so much that he didn't even go back to his ***mother's*** funeral.(p.486)
• I went back to my ***mother's*** for a few days until things cooled off, because the District Attorney had put out a summons for me to come to see him in his office.(p.491)
• We held some two or three meetings at Ella's home and from there we held some two or three at her ***mother's*** home.(p.495)

motherhood
• Another thing that mother drilled into me was a very Puritanical point of view as to sex relations and as to ***motherhood*** and womanhood.(p.483)

motherless
• And having sung that phrase, I'd chuckle with amusement, turning into irony turning into self-contempt turning into self-pity, at the sad fate of Bob, that wonderful, poor little ***motherless*** boy who was so smart in school and who grew up to accept responsibility so early and so fast and who staggered under his burdens without a whimper until the time came when he thought he was too good for this world and so he ought to be out of it.(p.532)
• About this time, I met a man who had three ***motherless*** children and it seemed that might be a solution to my problem.(p.548)

mothers
• Passing all understanding is the patience ***mothers*** and wives have had with alcoholics.(p.82)
• I was an honor graduate in high school, and I was a "good boy" to whom ***mothers*** pointed when their sons went astray.(p.419)
• Things got so bad, I was afraid to go on the street, so I turned to ***Mothers'*** Aid.(p.527)

motion
• These observations would be academic and pointless if our friend never took the first drink, thereby setting the terrible cycle in ***motion.***(p.23)
• It set in ***motion*** trains of circumstances which brought us misfortune we felt we didn't deserve.(p.67)
• I'd been on the board of governors of the Academy of ***Motion*** Picture Arts and Sciences for six years.(p.328)
• They saved us endless time and lost ***motion.***(p.496)

motion-picture-studio
• Until I took Social Security and a pension at the age of sixty-eight, after forty years in ***motion-picture-studio*** public relations, I had successfully hidden even any hints of approaching alcoholism.(p.327)

motioned
• The doctor ***motioned*** to the corpsman to undo my straitjacket and leg restraints.(p.422)

motivated
• Away down deep, I was ***motivated*** into dishonest behavior because I was a people-pleaser.(p.328)

motivation
• I believe that the release from people-pleasing restrictions gives retirees more ***motivation*** to drink than boredom does.(p.329)

motive
• The unselfishness of these men as we have come to know them, the entire absence of profit ***motive,*** and their community spirit, is indeed inspiring to one who has labored long and wearily in this alcoholic field.(p.xxv)
• And then, with a better ***motive,*** had we not worshipfully beheld the sunset, the sea, or a flower?(p.54)
• But be sure you are on solid spiritual ground before you start and that your ***motive*** in going is thoroughly good.(p.102)
• Though they knew they must help other alcoholics if they would remain sober, that ***motive*** became secondary.(p.159)

motives
• Ideas, emotions, and attitudes which were once the guiding forces of the lives of these men are suddenly cast to one side, and a completely new set of conceptions and ***motives*** begin to dominate them.(p.27)
• On that basis we are almost always in collision with something or somebody, even though our ***motives*** are good.(p.60)
• It depends on us and on our ***motives.***(p.70)
• Before we begin, we ask God to direct our thinking, especially asking that it be divorced from self-pity, dishonest or self-seeking ***motives.***(p.86)
• Our thought-life will be placed on a much higher plane when our thinking is cleared of wrong ***motives.***(p.86)
• Keep on the firing line of life with these ***motives*** and God will keep you unharmed.(p.102)

motor
• Many retirees embrace alcoholism while secluded in ***motor*** trailers, rest homes, leisure-world bungalows, mountain cabins, or beach cottages, or even in penthouses, on yachts, and inside Palm Springs cabanas.(p.329)
• I entered the house, opened a new bottle of whiskey and sat down to drink myself into the right frame of mind to get in my car, start the ***motor*** and close the garage door behind me.(p.363)

motorcycle
• We gave up our positions and off we roared on a ***motorcycle,*** the sidecar stuffed with tent, blankets, a change of clothes, and three huge volumes of a financial reference service.(p.2)

motto
• Brandishing my "***motto,***" which was "A little man with a stick is equal to a big man," sometimes I varied the literary lecture by a fight with a big man, selected solely because he was big and I was little.(p.537)

mottoes
• We have three little ***mottoes*** which are apropos.(p.135)

mount
• This is based, really, on the Sermon on the ***Mount.***(p.268)
• I didn't know anything about the Sermon on the ***Mount.***(p.268)

mountain
• It melted the icy intellectual ***mountain*** in whose shadow I had lived and shivered many years.(p.12)
• I felt lifted up, as though the great clean wind of a ***mountain*** top blew through and through.(p.14)
• Many retirees embrace alcoholism while secluded in motor trailers, rest homes, leisure-world bungalows, ***mountain*** cabins, or beach cottages, or even in penthouses, on yachts, and inside Palm Springs cabanas.(p.329)
• I returned to my home in Lucknow, India, at the end of November last year from a vacation in one of the most famous beauty spots in our country, a ***mountain*** resort 6,800 feet up, with a wonderful lake.(p.342)
• Eight years ago, my wife and I decided to spend a vacation in Naini Tal, the ***mountain*** resort.(p.343)
• Now I slide down ***mountain*** fast.(p.475)

mountains
• The place is Naini Tal, in the foothills of the mighty Himalaya ***Mountains,*** and it has some very significant memories for me.(p.342)
• If we do not do so, we shall stand convicted of emotional sterility and of having lost the faith that moves ***mountains,*** without which medicine can do little."(p.571)

mounted
• A friend who knew I would soon be broke ***mounted*** guard over me when I left my job of writing the histories of Texas cities and put me aboard a bus for the town I had left almost five years before.(p.256)
• But from one or two drinks of an afternoon or evening, my intake ***mounted,*** and ***mounted*** fast.(p.336)

mounting
• This, plus ***mounting*** emotional disturbances, convinced them that compulsive alcoholism already had them; that complete ruin would be only a question of time.(p.315)

mouth
• New groups started up and it was found, to the astonishment of everyone, that A.A.'s message could be transmitted in the mail as well as by word of ***mouth.***(p.xviii)
• After two weeks of drinking, he had placed his toe on the trigger of a loaded shotgun -- the barrel in his ***mouth.***(p.137)
• But – supposing that just one man died because I had, for selfish reasons, kept my ***mouth*** shut?(p.282)
• The program was carried on entirely by word of ***mouth.***(p.291)
• I took two or three drinks so my eyes could focus, and I could see that horrible picture of the awful drunk on the first page; he couldn't get the drink to his ***mouth,*** he had a towel around his hand and he needed a shave.(p.391)
• I talked out of the side of my ***mouth,*** as they did.(p.423)
• Still, I couldn't turn my ***mouth*** off.(p.442)
• When I got home my ***mouth*** was very painful, so I got an ice-bag and went to bed.(p.466)

mouths
• I had worked so long in a profession where fakery, deceit, and untruths are tools of trade that I instantly recognized honesty when I heard it, from the ***mouths*** of A.A. members.(p.334)
• Some of us always remember our big ***mouths*** when it comes to a drink, but somewhere along the line, we seem to have forgotten about taking care of our teeth.(p.479)

move
• My next ***move*** was to take up the study of medicine, entering one of the largest universities in the county.(p.173)
• On hearing that, these people induced me to make the ***move*** immediately and join them as a senior partner, which I did.(p.220)
• So I located a house, and I thought we ought to ***move*** into it immediately, but Frank was horrified, because he never knew what was going to happen to me.(p.388)
• Then he said I couldn't possibly ***move*** on the first of February because I couldn't stay in that place by myself.(p.388)
• But then my "rights" try to ***move*** in, and they, too, can force my serenity level down.(p.452)
• When counties run out, I ***move*** to Connecticut.(p.475)
• After six months, we ***move*** to Bridgeport, Conn.(p.476)
• The electric light began to ***move.***(p.498)
• I want to sell the place and ***move*** away.(p.506)

moved
• Much ***moved,*** I wandered outside.(p.1)
• I was ***moved*** into another room that morning and there was my wife.(p.184)
• I was ***moved*** in as Sales Manager and had four men working under me.(p.200)
• I finished my apprenticeship and was ***moved*** into the drafting department.(p.211)
• My drinking career began about four years after I had ***moved*** up into partnership and had joined certain clubs, societies and so fourth, and during which period we had Prohibition.(p.213)
• I ***moved*** from group to group -- then from place to place -- and went on drinking.(p.226)
• I ***moved*** in a gay crowd in the various "pubs" and sporting clubs.(p.251)
• Offered the job of advertising manager for an eastern automotive company, I ***moved*** to Philadelphia to begin life anew.(p.254)
• We ***moved*** in from the country at the age when girls want all sorts of nice things.(p.261)
• I ***moved*** into a "bachelor hall."(p.277)
• In 1930, I ***moved*** to Chicago.(p.287)
• At that time, I was living out of town, so I ***moved*** back to the home town and made a connection in a responsible position with one of the larger companies in the finance business.(p.298)
• I ***moved*** a thousand miles away from home to Chicago and a new environment.(p.305)
• In 1940 another good opportunity came up and we ***moved*** to Pittsburgh where I was to manage two radio stations under the same ownership.(p.361)
• We soon resumed our marriage, even ***moved*** away from the street of sad memories and found a new home.(p.371)
• Then we ***moved*** up to Oklahoma.(p.386)
• That went on for about three years, and then we ***moved*** back to Texas again.(p.386)
• We ***moved*** once more, to Houston; my husband thought maybe a change of environment would help and I'd be all right.(p.389)
• Things were no better with the family, so I ***moved*** to New York.(p.406)
• I had a tiny trust fund, and I ***moved*** into a small apartment where I learned to cook, keep house, and do the things that normal people do.(p.409)
• They got so they ***moved*** their barstools when they saw me coming.(p.411)
• I was astonished and deeply ***moved.***(p.415)
• I ***moved*** about a little.(p.423)
• I liked it and soon ***moved*** into the photo department which was what I wanted to do.(p.425)
• We ***moved*** frequently.(p.554)
• As soon as I had made a few friends and had begun to feel accepted, we ***moved*** again.(p.555)
• Bewilderment, fear, and resentment ***moved*** into my life.(p.556)

movement
• If any feel that as psychiatrists directing a hospital for alcoholics we appear somewhat sentimental, let

them stand with us a while on the firing line, see the tragedies, the despairing wives, the little children; let the solving of these problems become a part of their daily work, and even of their sleeping moments, and the most cynical will not wonder that we have accepted and encouraged this ***movement***.(p.xxvi)

• We feel, after many years of experience, that we have found nothing which has contributed more to the rehabilitation of these men than the altruistic ***movement*** now growing up among them.(p.xxvi)

• Had anyone undertaken to explain to me what the A.A. ***movement*** was, what its real function was, I probably would have been set back several years and I doubt if I would have survived at all.(p.216)

• I found a great deal of friendship in this ***movement***.(p.516)

• Speaking at a dinner given by John D. Rockefeller Jr. to introduce Alcoholics Anonymous to some of his friends, Dr. Harry Emerson Fosdick remarked: "I think that psychologically speaking there is a point of advantage in the approach that is being made in this ***movement*** that cannot be duplicated.(p.574)

moves

• My pen ***moves*** rapidly.(p.499)

• If we do not do so, we shall stand convicted of emotional sterility and of having lost the faith that ***moves*** mountains, without which medicine can do little."(p.571)

movie

• Many alcoholics have learned they can bring their bottle to a cheap ***movie*** theater and drink, sleep, wake up and drink again in the darkness.(p.244)

• Evidently I had gone right back to the ***movie*** with a bottle, stayed there several hours and started home with no recollection of what had happened.(p.244)

• All the joys of retirement lay ahead for this ***movie*** publicist.(p.327)

• The ***movie*** racket had kept me too long from writing those novels, articles, short stories, and scripts on which I had copious notes.(p.330)

• One night, I was struck with the memory of a line Alan Ladd used in "Shane," a ***movie*** that I'd worked on.(p.333)

• Out of those forty years as a ***movie*** press agent came one blessing that granted me a blind faith in the program.(p.334)

movies

• Beaches, parties, dances, ***movies*** -- everything.(p.425)

• So I'd sit up, watch old Wallace Beery ***movies*** on all-night TV, and drink.(p.441)

• To get rid of me one evening, she decided to go to the ***movies***, she and another friend.(p.487)

• I said that she told me she was going to the ***movies***, and I became foolishly disturbed about it and, as things snowballed, I decided to go out and get drunk.(p.487)

moving

• His change of heart was dramatic, convincing, and ***moving***.(p.55)

• People have said we must not go where liquor is served; we must not have it in our homes; we must shun friends who drink; we must avoid ***moving*** pictures which show drinking scenes; we must not go into bars; our friends must hide their bottles if we go to their houses; we mustn't think or be reminded about alcohol at all.(p.100)

• One afternoon, the year after ***moving*** to Houston, I got as drunk as a skunk, and while I do not walk very straight sober, you should see me when I'm drunk!(p.390)

Mr.

• He is a real Dr. Jekyll and ***Mr.*** Hyde.(p.21)

• ***Mr.*** Brown(p.65)

• Notice that the word "fear" is bracketed alongside the difficulties with ***Mr.*** Brown, Mrs. Jones, the employer, and the wife.(p.67)

• One day my secretary came in saying that ***Mr.*** B—— insisted on speaking with me.(p.136)

• My secretary returned to say that it was not ***Mr.*** B—— on the phone; it was ***Mr.*** B——'s brother, and he wished to give me a message.(p.136)

• The next day I received a visit from ***Mr.*** T., a recovered alcoholic.(p.309)

• I don't know what sort of person I was expecting, but I was very agreeably surprised to find ***Mr.*** T. a poised, intelligent, well groomed and mannered gentleman.(p.309)

• By this time, with the doctor's explanation, the revelations contained in the book, and the hope-inspiring interview with ***Mr.*** T., I was ready and willing to go into the interior of the African jungles, if that was what it took, for me to find what these people had.(p.309)

• "Why don't you just go down and see ***Mr.*** W.?" she asked.(p.412)

• Thank you, ***Mr.*** Policeman, wherever you are now.(p.538)

Mrs.

• ***Mrs.*** Jones(p.65)

• Notice that the word "fear" is bracketed alongside the difficulties with Mr. Brown, ***Mrs.*** Jones, the employer, and the wife.(p.67)

• ***Mrs.*** M. said she would send Jack over as quick as he came in.(p.267)

• I only saw that I had not become ***Mrs.*** Shakespeare.(p.403)

much

• Many of our friends encourage us by saying that this is but a beginning, only the augury of a ***much*** larger future ahead.(p.xv)

• The classification of alcoholics seems most difficult, and in ***much*** detail is outside the scope of this book.(p.xxviii)

• ***Much*** has been written pro and con, but among physicians, the general opinion seems to be that most chronic alcoholics are doomed.(p.xxviii)

• ***Much*** moved, I wandered outside.(p.1)

• Liquor caught up with me ***much*** faster than I came up behind Walter.(p.3)

• I saw I could not take so ***much*** as one drink.(p.5)

• Hydrotherapy and mild exercise helped ***much***.(p.7)

• There had been ***much*** happiness after all.(p.8)

• How could there be so ***much*** of precise and immutable law and no intelligence?(p.10)

• I saw that my friend was ***much*** more than inwardly reorganized.(p.11)

• A ***much*** more important demonstration of our principles lies before us in our respective homes, occupations and affairs.(p.19)

• All of us spend ***much*** of our spare time in the sort of effort which we are going to describe.(p.19)

• If we keep on the way we are going there is little doubt that ***much*** good will result, but the surface of the problem would hardly be scratched.(p.19)

• Nothing would please us so ***much*** as to write a book which would contain no basis for contention or argument.(p.19)

• We know that while the alcoholic keeps away from drink, as he may do for months or years, he reacts ***much*** like other men.(p.22)

• We have found ***much*** of heaven and we have been rocketed into a fourth dimension of existence of which we had not even dreamed.(p.25)

• He had ***much*** knowledge about himself as an alcoholic.(p.36)

• It was his first experience of this kind, and he was ***much*** ashamed of it.(p.39)

• Fred would not believe himself an alcoholic, ***much*** less accept a spiritual remedy for his problem.(p.39)

• Let him tell you about it: "I was ***much*** impressed with what you fellows said about alcoholism, and I frankly did not believe it would be possible for me to drink again.(p.40)

• They grinned, which I didn't like so ***much***, and then asked me if I thought myself alcoholic and if I were really licked this time.(p.42)

• But we found that such codes and philosophies did not save us, no matter how ***much*** we tried.(p.45)

• ***Much*** to our relief, we discovered we did not need to consider another's conception of God.(p.46)

• Besides a seeming inability to accept ***much*** on faith, we often found ourselves handicapped by obstinacy, sensitiveness, and unreasoning prejudice.(p.47)

• How ***much*** did these feelings, these loves, these worships, have to do with pure reason?(p.54)

• We finally saw that faith in some kind of God was a part of our make-up, just as ***much*** as the feeling we have for a friend.(p.55)

• He was as ***much*** a fact as we were.(p.55)

• Without help it is too ***much*** for us.(p.59)

• Neither could we reduce our self-centeredness ***much*** by wishing or trying on our own power.(p.62)

• Many of us thought it necessary to go ***much*** further.(p.72)

• He is very ***much*** the actor.(p.73)

• It is harder to go to an enemy than to a friend, but we find it ***much*** more beneficial to us.(p.77)

• We doubt if, in this respect, alcoholics are fundamentally ***much*** worse than other people.(p.81)

• ***Much*** has already been said about receiving strength, inspiration, and direction from Him who has all knowledge and power.(p.85)

• Our thought-life will be placed on a ***much*** higher plane when our thinking is cleared of wrong motives.(p.86)

• We are then in ***much*** less danger of excitement, fear, anger, worry, self-pity, or foolish decisions.(p.88)

• We become ***much*** more efficient.(p.88)

• Practical experience shows that nothing will so ***much*** insure immunity from drinking as intensive work with other alcoholics.(p.89)

• Ministers and doctors are competent and you can learn ***much*** from them if you wish, but it happens that because of your own drinking experience you can be uniquely useful to other alcoholics.(p.89)

• Neither should the family hysterically plead with him to do anything, nor should they tell him ***much*** about you.(p.90)

• If his own doctor is willing to tell him that he is alcoholic, so ***much*** the better.(p.92)

• Tell him you once felt as he does, but you doubt whether you would have made ***much*** progress had you not taken action.(p.94)

• But point out that we alcoholics have ***much*** in common and that you would like, in any case, to be friendly.(p.95)

• To spend too ***much*** time on any one situation is to deny some other alcoholic an opportunity to live and be happy.(p.96)

• Having had the experience yourself, you can give him ***much*** practical advice.(p.96)

• Should they accept and practice spiritual principles, there is a ***much*** better chance that the head of the family will recover.(p.97)

• Of course, we all fall ***much*** below this standard many times.(p.99)

• But what we have said applies quite as ***much*** to women.(p.104)

• We want the wives of Alcoholics Anonymous to address the wives of men who drink too ***much***.(p.104)

• We have told small tots that father was sick, which was ***much*** nearer the truth than we realized.(p.106)

• Perhaps he spends too ***much*** money for liquor.(p.109)

• Three: This husband has gone ***much*** further than husband number two.(p.109)

• You think he ought to know the subject better, as everyone should have a clear understanding of the risk he takes if he drinks too ***much***.(p.112)

• He knows that thousands of men, ***much*** like himself, have recovered.(p.113)

• Avoid answering these inquiries as ***much*** as you can.(p.115)

• We have elsewhere remarked how ***much*** better life is when lived on a spiritual plane.(p.116)

• Yet you must not expect too ***much***.(p.118)

• You should join in his efforts as ***much*** as you possibly can.(p.119)

• It is probably true that you and your husband have been living too ***much*** alone, for drinking many times isolates the wife of an alcoholic.(p.119)

• Therefore, you probably need fresh interests and a great cause to live for as ***much*** as your husband.(p.119)

• You, as well as your husband, ought to think of what you can put into life instead of how ***much*** you can take out.(p.120)

• You will lose the old life to find one ***much*** better.(p.120)

• We realize that we have been giving you ***much*** direction and advice.(p.121)

• Perhaps he will never have ***much*** money again.(p.123)

• They expect him to give them the nice times they used to have before he drank so ***much***, and to show his contrition for what they suffered.(p.126)

• We know there are difficult wives and families, but the man who is getting over alcoholism must remember he did ***much*** to make them so.(p.127)

• Little by little, mother and children will see they ask too ***much***, and father will see he gives too little.(p.127)

• Those of us who have spent ***much*** time in the world of spiritual make-believe have eventually seen the childishness of it.(p.130)

• Nothing will help the man who is off on a spiritual tangent so ***much*** as the wife who adopts a sane spiritual program, making a better practical use of it.(p.130)

• Father will necessarily spend ***much*** time with other alcoholics, but this activity should be balanced.(p.131)

• Being possessed of a spiritual experience, the alcoholic will find he has ***much*** in common with these people, though he may differ with them on many matters.(p.131)

• Everybody knows that those in bad health, and those who seldom play, do not laugh ***much***.(p.132)

• So let each family play together or separately, as ***much*** as their circumstances warrant.(p.132)

• Among many employers nowadays, we think of

one member who has spent ***much*** of his life in the world of big business.(p.136)
• Without ***much*** ado, he accepted the principles and procedure that had helped us.(p.139)
• If a man drinks so ***much*** that his job suffers, we fire him.(p.148)
• He might be shocked if he knew how ***much*** alcoholism is costing his organization a year.(p.149)
• There are two alcoholic employees, who produce as ***much*** as five normal salesmen.(p.149)
• The proceeding was shot through with ***much*** hard feeling and controversy.(p.154)
• He wanted so ***much*** to talk with someone, but whom?(p.154)
• There was ***much*** talk about the mental state preceding the first drink.(p.157)
• Then he added, "He sure didn't do ***much*** for me when I was trying to fight this booze racket alone."(p.158)
• They were deeply religious people, ***much*** shocked by their son's refusal to have anything to do with the church.(p.158)
• They experienced a few distressing failures, but in those cases they made an effort to bring the man's family into a spiritual way of living, thus relieving ***much*** worry and suffering.(p.159)
• Seeing ***much*** of each other, scarce an evening passed that someone's home did not shelter a little gathering of men and women, happy in their release, and constantly thinking how they might present their discovery to some newcomer.(p.159)
• Being wrecked in the same vessel, being restored and united under one God, with hearts and minds attuned to the welfare of others, the things which matter so ***much*** to some people no longer signify ***much*** to them.(p.161)
• You forget that you have just now tapped a source of power ***much*** greater than yourself.(p.163)
• (1939) The authorities were ***much*** concerned.(p.163)
• I did it more and more, and had lots of fun without ***much*** grief, either physical or financial.(p.172)
• During these years, I drank as ***much*** as my purse permitted, still without paying too great a penalty, although I was beginning to have morning jitters at times.(p.173)
• There I took up the business of drinking with ***much*** greater earnestness than I had previously shown.(p.173)
• After ***much*** argument they allowed me to return and take my exams, all of which I passed creditably.(p.173)
• But they were ***much*** disgusted and told me they would attempt to struggle along without my presence.(p.173)
• There my drinking became so ***much*** worse that the boys in the fraternity house where I lived felt forced to send for my father, who made a long journey in the vain endeavor to get me straightened around.(p.174)
• I conducted myself so creditably that I was able to secure a ***much*** coveted internship in a western city, where I spent two years.(p.174)
• They spoke with great freedom from embarrassment, which I could never do, and they seemed very ***much*** at ease on all occasions and appeared very healthy.(p.178)
• I learned that it was something of a spiritual nature, which did not appeal to me very ***much***, but I thought it could do no harm.(p.178)
• I gave the matter ***much*** time and study for the next two and a half years, but still got tight every night nevertheless.(p.178)
• Unlike most of our crowd, I did not get over my craving for liquor ***much*** during the first two and one-half years of abstinence.(p.181)
• This was no fault of my father or mother, as they were both very ***much*** opposed to drinking.(p.182)
• I resented this very ***much***, until she informed me that they were a couple of drunks just as I was.(p.184)
• There was not ***much*** of it at that time.(p.185)
• If I could, that was wonderful, that was just fine, and they would very ***much*** appreciate a person who had that kind of power, but they were looking for a man that knew he had a problem, and knew that he couldn't handle it himself and needed outside help.(p.186)
• But I guess He doesn't believe ***much*** in me."(p.189)
• It took me a year, or a year and a half to get to feeling physically well, and it was rather tough, but I soon found folks whose friendship I had once had, and I found, after I had been sober for quite some little time, that these people began to act like they had in previous years, before I had gotten so bad, so that I didn't pay too awful ***much*** attention to financial gains.(p.190)
• It would be hard to estimate how ***much*** A.A. has done for me.(p.191)
• He did things ***much*** better than I did because he applied himself and learned how to do them, and I never applied myself.(p.194)
• I loved them, I think, as ***much*** as any parent.(p.199)
• And we stood there for twenty minutes, telling each other how ***much*** better we were, how ***much*** better we looked, how ***much*** better off we were financially, mentally, physically, morally, and in every way, shape and manner.(p.201)
• There were times when I got to drinking, and I had been warned by Firestone that they wouldn't stand for this ***much*** longer, so, clearly, they were conscious of the fact that I drank too ***much*** and too often.(p.204)
• Then he started to talk to me about his drinking experiences, what his drinking had cost him, how ***much*** he had drunk and where, things like that, and I remember I was quite bored because I had never seen the guy before and had no interest at all in what, where and when he drank.(p.208)
• I remember well one fellow, Joe, walking nearly three miles through slush, wet and snow to come to the hospital to see a man that he had never seen before in his life, and that impressed me very ***much***.(p.208)
• I kept myself so busy that outside of some school and group parties, I didn't go overboard on drinking very ***much*** between the ages of twenty-five and thirty.(p.213)
• When I was about forty-seven, after indulging in all kinds of self-deception to control my drinking, I arrived at a period when I felt convinced I had to have so ***much*** alcohol every day and that the real problem was to control how ***much***.(p.214)
• And then my thinking became calculation as to how ***much*** longer I had to live, how long the assets would last.(p.215)
• In fact, as I look back, I have often thought that they probably concluded that they would put up with me for a couple of years, that I couldn't live ***much*** longer, and that they would inherit whatever was left of the practice.(p.215)
• I do not recollect the specific conversation that went on but I believe I did challenge Bill to tell me something about A.A. and I do recall one other thing: I wanted to know what this was that worked so many wonders, and hanging over the mantel was a picture of Gethsemane and Bill pointed to it and said, "There it is," which didn't make ***much*** sense to me.(p.216)
• I believe every member of the Akron Group did come to see me, which impressed me terrifically, not so ***much*** because of the stories they told, but because they would take the time to come and talk to me without even knowing who I was.(p.218)
• In fact, I never lost my faith, since I had been prepared by some conversations toward the end of my sojourn in the hospital with Dr. Bob, conversations pretty ***much*** along spiritual lines.(p.218)
• My education had been pretty ***much*** pagan — science.(p.221)
• When my friends suggested that I was drinking too ***much*** -- they were no longer my friends.(p.226)
• As the treatment progressed I began to get a picture of myself, of the temperament that had caused me so ***much*** trouble.(p.226)
• But I can remember, in my teens, that there were a few characters who caused the village heads to nod pityingly and sometimes in anger as they paused to say, "That sot, Henri" and "Ce pauvre Jules," who drank too ***much***.(p.230)
• Gradually, however, I'd suffer so ***much*** that I simply had to have the morning-after drink.(p.233)
• Every man has his problem of this kind, but we didn't discuss it very ***much***.(p.236)
• I don't remember ***much*** of what he said, but I did realize that here was another guy exactly like me; he had been in the same laughing academies and the same jails, known the same loss of jobs, same frustrations, same boredom and the same loneliness.(p.239)
• My family lived in very prosperous circumstances, and while both my parents drank, sometimes too ***much***, neither was an alcoholic.(p.240)
• I knew they needed to straighten out their thinking and habits, but I was all right, I just drank too ***much***.(p.246)
• ***Much*** later I discovered the elders held many prayer meetings hoping to find a way to give me the heave-ho, but at the same time stay tolerant and spiritual.(p.247)
• My brilliant agnosticism vanished, and I saw for the first time that those who really believed, or at least honestly tried to find a Power greater than themselves, were ***much*** more composed and contented than I had ever been, and they seemed to have a degree of happiness which I had never known.(p.247)
• Around this time our big A.A. book was being written and it all became ***much*** simpler; we had a definite formula which some sixty of us agreed was the middle course for all alcoholics who wanted sobriety, and that formula has not been changed one iota down through the years.(p.248)
• I had some financial success through no ability of my own and, when jobless and almost wiped out in 1930, I began to trade and sell my collection; ***much*** of the proceeds went to keep my apartment stocked with liquor and almost every night saw me helpless to bed.(p.255)
• Now on a new job I was always thinking about payday and how ***much*** liquor I could buy and the pleasure I could have.(p.255)
• They will never know how ***much*** their talk with me helped.(p.259)
• I remember starting to city school, coming from a country school, and wanting so very, very ***much*** to be like the other girls and trying flour on my face for powder because I wasn't able to have any real powder.(p.261)
• But he's in all sorts of scrapes because he drinks too ***much***."(p.262)
• I looked ***much*** older than I was, I was always large, and I went back to work in this job.(p.262)
• One morning after a terrific drinking bout, I was in a little bar near our house, and I shook so that I was very ***much*** ashamed, because I was getting the shakes worse and worse.(p.266)
• Jack didn't seem to have too ***much*** of the spiritual understanding.(p.268)
• This is too ***much***.(p.269)
• I didn't know what they were going to do because he didn't tell us ***much***.(p.269)
• Russ used to be very ***much*** pleased because he'd say, "I think Dr. Bob thoroughly enjoys coming out here.(p.271)
• Before the end finally came, I had, I guess made the surrender because I finally had been able to say that I would not mind too ***much***.(p.272)
• Finally, and I shall never know how ***much*** later it was, one clear thought came to me: Try prayer.(p.280)
• So I spent ***much*** of my time calling on the people who I felt would logically come in contact with alcoholic cases, doctors, ministers, lawyers and the personnel men in industry.(p.281)
• So ***much*** for my business life.(p.284)
• By living alone you can pretty ***much*** eliminate grief from you life, but you also eliminate joy.(p.286)
• It is undoubtedly too soon for me to say how ***much*** of a success I shall be as a husband in time to come.(p.286)
• I was very ***much*** interested in athletics, and because of this and parental influence, I didn't drink or smoke in either grade or high school.(p.287)
• Then I started traveling, with the United States and Canada as my territory, and with so ***much*** freedom and with an unlimited expense account, I was soon drinking every night and kidding myself that it was all part of the job.(p.287)
• But I had my health back and besides, I reasoned, they were ***much*** worse than I would ever be.(p.289)
• I stayed in Akron two or three weeks on my initial trip trying to absorb as ***much*** of the program and philosophy as possible.(p.291)
• The parties waxed more liquid and hilarious as time went on, and eventually I discovered that a little shot of liquor now and then between beers had the tendency to put me in a whacky mood ***much*** quicker than having to down several quarts of beer to obtain the same effect.(p.298)
• But the firm became violently ill with my drunkenness and their course of treatment was to remove their ulcer, in the form of me, from the payroll, amid ***much*** fanfare and very personal and slighting remarks and insinuations.(p.300)
• Even some of the saloon-keepers, where I had spent so ***much*** time and money, requested that I stay away from their places.(p.301)
• However, he explained to me that he had been just such a rummy as I, only for a ***much*** longer period of time.(p.302)
• A very simple plan that I still find ***much*** joy and happiness in following.(p.302)
• I can think clearly and am helped ***much*** in my thinking and judgment by my spiritual development which grows daily.(p.303)
• And we wonder how ***much*** further this man could go if his alcoholic problem could be removed and he could throw one hundred per cent of his abilities into action.(p.308)
• It explained so ***much*** I had not understood about myself and, best of all, it promised recovery if I would do a few simple things and be willing to have the desire to drink removed.(p.309)

• In describing his suffering, his fears, his many years of groping for some answer to that which always seemed to remain unanswerable, he could have been describing me, and nothing short of experience and knowledge could have afforded him that *much* insight!(p.309)
• Others may idle in a retrogressive groove without too *much* danger, but retrogression can spell death for us.(p.311)
• But who wasn't after drinking that *much*?(p.317)
• The same as before, I stayed drunk pretty *much* of the time.(p.318)
• And when I looked at it, I knew I was just as *much* a drunk as George was, if not worse.(p.322)
• I always wanted to drink too *much*, so I was watchful, always watchful, counting my drinks.(p.322)
• I got so that I hid quite a bit of the time, wouldn't answer the phone, and stayed by myself as *much* as I could.(p.324)
• And "Think" -- that one important word means so *much* to me.(p.325)
• I had never even been told by a superior that maybe I was drinking too *much*.(p.327)
• I needed it, and I knew I was drinking too *much*, but I wasn't conscious of the fact that I should stop.(p.336)
• Following this, I had a short vacation, during which time I read as *much* literature as my sponsor could send me.(p.343)
• She was doing fine, she was up and around, and that day her husband phoned me and said, "Doctor, thanks very *much* for curing my wife," and I thanked him for his felicitations, and he hung up.(p.350)
• And the psychiatrist has had thousands of couches, and has put you and me on them many, many times, but he hasn't helped us very *much*, though he has tried hard; and we owe the clergy and the doctor and the psychiatrist a deep debt of gratitude, but they haven't helped our alcoholism, except in a rare few instances.(p.352)
• I never drank socially; I drank as often and as *much* as I could.(p.353)
• Every day became that *much* harder to live through, and I began to take a look at myself.(p.354)
• Too many outside activities to do *much* studying.(p.357)
• It was a terrible blow at the time and I thought he was pretty *much* of a heel, but of course it was the finest thing he could have done for me under the circumstances.(p.357)
• When I did make it home in 1920, I re-entered school and caught up with my class in a few short months – I actually did a year's work in three months, proving *much* to the disgust of my dad that I could do it when I wanted to.(p.358)
• Time after time I would beg forgiveness on bended knees, with tears rolling down my cheeks, and promise I would never again drink too *much*.(p.362)
• They told me their stories, which were *much* more rugged than mine -- yet what they said made sense, and the way they put it was easy for me to understand, with an understanding I had never had before.(p.363)
• I was certainly a complete surprise when I arrived at her family's home, but because I arrived on the wings of a tropical hurricane there wasn't *much* she could do but let me in.(p.364)
• Of course, more than anything else I had let myself down, but I didn't realize how *much* then -- as I do now.(p.364)
• I would gather up all my soiled clothes, as *much* as I could cram into a grocery cart, and be off.(p.370)
• One night, a few weeks after joining the Fellowship, *much* to my surprise and delight I saw a familiar but no longer frowning face.(p.371)
• During three years in A.A., I haven't lost so *much* as one shirt.(p.372)
• At the time this didn't mean *much* to me.(p.376)
• The why is not important; the fact is that one drink will set up a reaction in our system which requires more; that one drink was too *much* and one hundred drinks were not enough.(p.380)
• I didn't realize I would find so *much* more, but a new and different outlook on life started opening up almost immediately.(p.383)
• Each day seems to be so *much* more productive and satisfying.(p.383)
• I get so *much* more enjoyment out of living.(p.383)
• Above all, I am grateful to A.A. for my sobriety, which means so *much* to my family, friends and business associates, because God and A.A. were able to do for me something I was unable to do for myself.(p.383)
• As I grow in A.A., I realize that a person with as *much* self-will as I had, as hard a head and as diseased an ego, had to try everything that I could think of, butting my head against every stone wall before I was ready to come in.(p.384)
• He called me that because I was drinking too *much*.(p.387)
• I know that I was terribly screwed up inside, but I came out *much* worse.(p.387)
• I have told you some of the funny things, but not *much* of the shame and degradation.(p.390)
• Today, because of A.A.'s growth during the intervening years, it is of course *much* bigger than it was then.(p.392)
• It is also stated that we will never be able to figure out how *much* we have spent on alcohol.(p.396)
• (I can't know how *much* others of our Fellowship have paid financially and, even more important, mentally and physically.)(p.396)
• It is bound to be rough, because who can say exactly how *much* of that green blood – commonly known as money -- was dissipated on dissipation?(p.396)
• After all, upon coming out of a week-long or ten-day drunk, it was hard enough to figure up just how *much* that one drunk cost, let alone trying to calculate the cost of approximately twenty-five years of active alcoholism.(p.396)
• This was an Englishman who, at least at this time, drank as *much* as I did.(p.405)
• None of them were alcoholics, but at this time they were drinking as *much* as I was.(p.407)
• Or – this is a little too *much*!(p.408)
• My experience has been active: three meetings a week, many tapes, many A.A. conferences, *much* work on the Twelve Steps, and *much* work with other alcoholics and their families.(p.420)
• I don't know how I got here this trip, but it doesn't matter very *much*.(p.423)
• I smoked as *much*, tried to drink as *much*, and do everything they did, only more so.(p.423)
• Home life didn't mean *much* to me.(p.424)
• There wasn't *much* I could do about it, and I didn't want to do anything anyway.(p.427)
• Meanwhile the letters from home were telling about how *much* my folks wanted to make up to me for some of the things I'd missed.(p.427)
• My associates, and all the wits and literary lights I so *much* admired, also drank.(p.433)
• Even on my rare (at first) binge nights it never ran *much* over a quart.(p.433)
• I crawled back to my analyst, not so *much* because I had faith in him, but because I had nowhere else to turn.(p.435)
• My work is on a *much* deeper and more significant level than it ever was before, and I am today a fairly creative, relatively sane human being.(p.438)
• Not only did I not think that being an alcoholic was a good idea, I didn't even feel that I had all that *much* of a drinking problem!(p.439)
• Indeed, it seemed that I cared too *much*.(p.440)
• I never got *much* effect out of codeine and Percodan and the tranquilizers.(p.442)
• In the garage, I would put the needle in my vein and then try to figure out exactly how *much* medication to inject to overcome the pep pills while adding to the sleeping pills while ignoring the tranquilizers, in order to get just enough to be able to pull out the needle, jerk the tourniquet, throw it in the car, slam the car door shut, run down the hall, and fall in bed before I fell asleep.(p.442)
• *Much* of my time was spent writing letters, notes, orders, and lists of things for Max, who was also my office nurse, to do to keep the world running while I was locked up.(p.445)
• The people of A.A. had something that looked *much* better than what I had, but I was afraid to let go of what I had in order to try something new; there was a certain sense of security in the familiar.(p.448)
• I need to concentrate not so *much* on what needs to be changed in the world as on what needs to be changed in me and in my attitudes.(p.449)
• When we deal in feelings, we tend to come to know ourselves and each other *much* better.(p.451)
• Fortunately, I received only fifteen-twenty years, and I went back to my alma mater (where I had spent so *much* time in the hole).(p.461)
• I thought I would be quite happy and never would I drink too *much* again.(p.465)
• I hadn't been drinking *much* about that time, for I had begun to realize that there was something abnormal about my drinking, although as yet, I didn't realize that it was so out of control.(p.465)
• So the doctor said, "I really don't know too *much* about it, but they tell me it is a bunch of drunks who get together . . ."(p.469)
• During these seven years a thing called the Twenty-four Hour Program –a gadget I used to think was only a snare to trap the newcomer -- has come to mean *much* to me, not only as regards my drinking but in the whole pattern of my life.(p.473)
• So didn't drink *much* then.(p.474)
• To find work, I have travel *much*.(p.476)
• Even my family didn't have *much* use for me.(p.478)
• (We don't have *much* time for bathing in our crowded schedule.)(p.479)
• We are so beautiful that it is never too *much* trouble to get some poor stranger to buy us a drink.(p.479)
• You see how *much* work some of us have to do on ourselves when we finally come into A.A.!(p.480)
• I really do believe it is *much* harder for a woman to gain back her self-respect than it is for a man.(p.480)
• He has so *much* understanding, a real asset in sharing sobriety.(p.481)
• For that reason, I believe, I married at a *much* younger age than I would have, had it not been for my home training.(p.485)
• Father, through the years, had built up a very good mail order business because, at that time, there wasn't too *much* money in medicine.(p.485)
• I don't think I suffered too *much* as far as the racial situation was concerned because I was born into it and knew nothing other than that.(p.485)
• Of course, when father finally came to Virginia to work his way through school, he resented the southern "cracker," as he often called them, so *much* that he didn't even go back to his mother's funeral.(p.486)
• I never had too *much* trouble in school.(p.486)
• Dad, due to having spent most of his time in a small Virginia town, didn't have any too *much* money, and the money he had saved and the property he had acquired were in Washington.(p.486)
• Vi was very kind and explained to the jury that I was basically a fine fellow and a good husband, but that I drank too *much* and that she thought I had lost my mind and felt that I should be committed to an asylum.(p.492)
• When I had known her years before she was rather slender, but at this time she weighed as *much* as she does now, which is up around in the two hundreds or very close to it.(p.493)
• He didn't seem too *much* at ease in the beginning.(p.494)
• He started telling me how *much* trouble he had, and I said to myself, "I wonder why this guy is telling me all his troubles.(p.494)
• Of course, it wasn't very *much* of a meeting in the beginning; most of the time it was just Vi and myself.(p.495)
• Shouldn't have drunk so *much* or so fast.(p.498)
• I feel *much* better!(p.505)
• I rounded up a few more of my friends and off we went to the meeting, not for anything we would gain from it as *much* as to make a burlesque out of it.(p.509)
• I had drunk too often and too *much*.(p.515)
• It didn't worry me very *much*, because at that time I could shut off for a couple of months without taking a drink or even wanting one, and without feeling that I was giving anything up.(p.518)
• In my own generation I stuck out, I can see that now, as being a very *much* heavier drinker than the average man.(p.518)
• But as long as you did your work and didn't disgrace yourself, you were socially acceptable and nobody really intruded on your private life very *much*.(p.518)
• Then a change in management took place in the regiment and the new O.C. didn't like me very *much* and I didn't like him, and he started to lie in wait for me.(p.519)
• They brought me in and of course, they hadn't very *much* trouble in finding that I was alcoholic.(p.521)
• My mind was too screwy to be able to understand *much* of what was being said.(p.524)
• I thought that if these kind of ordinary people can do it, a man of my brains ought to find it *much* more easy, and I joined.(p.524)
• It has taught me that success and failure are never final, and that neither count for very *much* in the final assessment of any man who has done his best.(p.525)
• I don't know when I became an alcoholic, but I do believe I became one because I drank too *much* too often.(p.526)
• I always blamed my drinking on being poor, or on anything other than the truth – that I liked what booze did for me, that when I had a drink I was as big and had as *much* as the next person.(p.526)
• I would never admit that I was drinking too *much*, or spending money that I should have used to buy food for my two little boys.(p.526)
• Oh, I might drink too *much* at times – everyone I knew drank.(p.527)

• But then one good doctor told me there was nothing wrong with me except drinking too *much*.(p.528)
• I don't know if it's force of habit or something else that keeps them in one place, but I do know that in A.A. there is *much* work to do, and none of us can do it standing still.(p.529)
• There was the sense of being "misunderstood," when as a matter of fact by my middle twenties I was quite popular, although I hadn't grown *much* bigger physically.(p.534)
• I did not remember *much* of the ten-day binge.(p.540)
• I don't care too *much* about personal fame or glory, and I want only enough money to enable me to do the work I feel I can perhaps do best.(p.542)
• What is *much* more important to me, A.A. has taught me that through this simple program I may experience a change in this reaction pattern that will indeed allow me to "match calamity with serenity."(p.544)
• I looked around me at people who seemed happy and tried to analyze their happiness, and it seemed to me that without exception these people had something or somebody they loved very *much*.(p.546)
• I had fed it, fanned it and nurtured it as one might a delicate child, and it had become as *much* a part of me as my breathing.(p.551)
• *Much* later, when I had progressed to full-blown alcoholism, people told me I should quit.(p.554)
• I have come to realize that the name of the game is not so *much* to stop drinking as to stay sober.(p.559)
• A.A. can, of course, mean just as *much* to uncounted alcoholics not yet reached.(p.563)
• Secondary aids to A.A., such as clubs or hospitals which require *much* property or administration, ought to be incorporated and so set apart that, if necessary, they can be freely discarded by the groups.(p.566)
• Then too, we view with *much* concern those A.A. treasuries which continue, beyond prudent reserves, to accumulate funds for no stated A.A. purpose.(p.566)
• If there is none nearby, you will be invited to carry on a correspondence which will do *much* to insure your sobriety no matter how isolated you are.(p.575)

mud

• My four years of abstinence had something to do with it, but soldiering is a tough enough game for a sober man, and I had no yen for full-pack slogging through *mud* with a cognac or vin rouge hangover.(p.253)

muddled

• "First Things First": solving our immediate problems before we try to solve all the others and get *muddled* in our thinking and doing.(p.382)

mugged

• I was not *mugged*, or manhandled.(p.412)

multiplied

• And the more I focused my mind on her defects, the more they grew and *multiplied*.(p.450)

multiplies

• Each day my friend's simple talk in our kitchen *multiplies* itself in a widening circle of peace on earth and good will to men.(p.16)

multitude

• The distinguished American psychologist, William James, in his book "Varieties of Religious Experience," indicates a *multitude* of ways in which men have discovered God.(p.28)

mumbling

• A remorseful *mumbling* that we are sorry won't fill the bill at all.(p.83)

murder

• After twenty years in prison for *murder*, he knew A.A. was the spot for him . . . if he wanted to stay on the outside.(p.508)
• I was indicted for the crime of *murder* in the first degree.(p.508)
• However, a verdict was brought in of *murder* in the second degree.(p.508)
• In the meantime I had been indicted for the second crime, attempted *murder*.(p.508)

murder

• After twenty years in prison for *murder*, he knew A.A. was the spot for him . . . if he wanted to stay on the outside.(p.508)
• I was indicted for the crime of *murder* in the first degree.(p.508)
• However, a verdict was brought in of *murder* in the second degree.(p.508)
• In the meantime I had been indicted for the second crime, attempted *murder*.(p.508)

murmur

• Everybody believes them without a *murmur* of doubt.(p.48)

muscle

• But for some time, it was difficult to keep from taking a pill when I had an appropriate symptom, such as a cough, pain, anxiety, insomnia, a *muscle* spasm, or an upset stomach.(p.448)

museum

• There is something spiritual about an art *museum* or a symphony, and the Catholic Church approves of our use of them.(p.574)

mushroomed

• In that brief space, Alcoholics Anonymous has *mushroomed* into nearly 6,000 groups whose membership is far above 150,000 recovered alcoholics.(p.xv)
• Slowly, my life seemed to unfold before me, shedding insights on childhood resentments, jealousies, and fears that had *mushroomed* in adulthood, and also on the self-pity that I had wallowed in at every opportunity.(p.371)

mushrooming

• The *mushrooming* process was in full swing.(p.xviii)

mushy

• Hence we are at pains to tell why we think our present faith is reasonable, why we think it more sane and logical to believe than not to believe, why we say our former thinking was soft and *mushy* when we threw up our hands in doubt and said, "We don't know."(p.53)

music

• I could almost hear the sound of the preacher's voice as I sat, on still Sundays, way over there on the hillside; there was that proffered temperance pledge I never signed; my grandfather's good natured contempt of some church folk and their doings; his insistence that the spheres really had their *music*; but his denial of the preacher's right to tell him how he must listen; his fearlessness as he spoke of these things just before he died; these recollections welled up from the past.(p.10)
• *Music* and gay chatter still floated to him from the bar.(p.154)
• One night I was sitting in the lab alone with a fifth and a case of beer listening to dreamy Hawaiian *music* on the radio.(p.427)
• The word "alcoholic" does not turn me off any more; in fact, it is *music* to my ears when it applies to me.(p.463)
• Finally, he was drinking to keep away those little men, and those strange voices, and the organ *music* that came out of the walls.(p.512)
• I was drinking to keep away the shakes, drinking to keep away those little men and those strange voices and the organ *music* that comes out of the walls.(p.514)
• I was very fond of *music*.(p.517)

musician

• I was club-man, athlete, artist, *musician*, author, editor, aircraft pilot and world traveller.(p.432)

musing

• My *musing* was interrupted by the telephone.(p.8)

musket

• A good soldier is ne'er forgot Whether he dieth by *musket* Or by pot."(p.1)

must

• He suddenly realized that in order to save himself he *must* carry his message to another alcoholic.(p.xvi)
• Convincing testimony *must* surely come from the medical men who have had experience with the sufferings of our members and have witnessed our return to health.(p.xxiii)
• As part of his rehabilitation he commenced to present his conceptions to other alcoholics, impressing upon them that they *must* do likewise with still others.(p.xxiii)
• In this statement he confirms what we who have suffered alcoholic torture *must* believe -- that the body of the alcoholic is quite as abnormal as his mind.(p.xxiv)
• The message which can interest and hold these alcoholic people *must* have depth and weight.(p.xxvi)
• In nearly all cases, their ideals *must* be grounded in a power greater than themselves, if they are to re-create their lives.(p.xxvi)
• I *must* stop, but I cannot!(p.xxvii)
• You *must* help me!"(p.xxvii)
• Faced with this problem, if a doctor is honest with himself, he *must* sometimes feel his own inadequacy.(p.xxvii)
• Though the aggregate of recoveries resulting from psychiatric effort is considerable, we physicians *must* admit we have made little impression upon the problem as a whole.(p.xxvii)
• I could almost hear the sound of the preacher's voice as I sat, on still Sundays, way over there on the hillside; there was that proffered temperance pledge I never signed; my grandfather's good natured contempt of some church folk and their doings; his insistence that the spheres really had their music; but his denial of the preacher's right to tell him how he *must* listen; his fearlessness as he spoke of these things just before he died; these recollections welled up from the past.(p.10)
• I *must* turn in all things the Father of Light who presides over us all.(p.14)
• "His will power *must* be weak."(p.20)
• He has a positive genius for getting tight at exactly the wrong moment, particularly when some important decision *must* be made or engagement kept.(p.21)
• Our hope is that many alcoholic men and women, desperately in need, will see these pages, and we believe that it is only by fully disclosing ourselves and our problems that they will be persuaded to say, "Yes, I am one of them too; I *must* have this thing."(p.29)
• If we are planning to stop drinking, there *must* be no reservation of any kind, nor any lurking notion that someday we will be immune to alcohol.(p.33)
• His defense *must* come from a Higher Power.(p.43)
• But after a while we had to face the fact that we *must* find a spiritual basis of life – or else.(p.44)
• Above everything, we alcoholics *must* be rid of this selfishness.(p.62)
• We *must*, or it kills us!(p.62)
• We saw that these resentments *must* be mastered, but how?(p.66)
• Whatever our ideal turns out to be, we *must* be willing to grow toward it.(p.69)
• We *must* be willing to make amends where we have done harm, provided that we do not bring about still more harm in so doing.(p.69)
• We *must* be entirely honest with somebody if we expect to live long or happily in this world.(p.73)
• Those of us belonging to a religious denomination which requires confession *must*, and of course, will want to go to the properly appointed authority whose duty it is to receive it.(p.74)
• The rule is we *must* be hard on ourself, but always considerate of others.(p.74)
• But we *must* not use this as a mere excuse to postpone.(p.75)
• We *must* lose our fear of creditors no matter how far we have to go, for we are liable to drink if we are afraid to face them.(p.78)
• We *must* not shrink at anything.(p.79)
• If we have obtained permission, have consulted with others, asked God to help and the drastic step is indicated we *must* not shrink.(p.80)
• In fairness we *must* say that she may understand, but what are we going to do about a thing like that?(p.81)
• Certainly he *must* keep sober, for there will be no home if he doesn't.(p.82)
• We *must* take the lead.(p.83)
• We *must* remember that ten or twenty years of drunkenness would make a skeptic out of anyone.(p.83)
• Every day is a day when we *must* carry the vision of God's will into all of our activities.(p.85)
• These are thoughts which *must* go with us constantly.(p.85)
• But we *must* go further and that means more action.(p.85)
• But we *must* be careful not to drift into worry, remorse or morbid reflection, for that would diminish our usefulness to others.(p.86)
• To watch people recover, to see them help others, to watch loneliness vanish, to see a fellowship grow up about you, to have a host of friends – this is an experience you *must* not miss.(p.89)
• The family *must* decide these things.(p.90)
• To be vital, faith *must* be accompanied by self sacrifice and unselfish, constructive action.(p.93)
• After doing that, he *must* decide for himself whether he wants to go on.(p.95)
• If he is to find God, the desire *must* come from within.(p.95)
• In many homes this is a difficult thing to do, but it *must* be done if any results are to be expected.(p.98)
• But we *must* try to repair the damage immediately lest we pay the penalty by a spree.(p.99)
• If their old relationship is to be resumed it *must* be on a better basis, since the former did not work.(p.99)
• Both you and the new man *must* walk day by day in the path of spiritual progress.(p.100)
• People have said we *must* not go where liquor is

served; we ***must*** not have it in our homes; we ***must*** shun friends who drink; we ***must*** avoid moving pictures which show drinking scenes; we ***must*** not go into bars; our friends ***must*** hide their bottles if we go to their houses; we mustn't think or be reminded about alcohol at all.(p.100)

• Our next thought is that you should never tell him what he ***must*** do about his drinking.(p.111)

• Wait until repeated stumbling convinces him he ***must*** act, for the more you hurry him the longer his recovery may be delayed.(p.113)

• But sometimes you ***must*** start life anew.(p.114)

• But you ***must*** be on guard not to embarrass or harm your husband.(p.115)

• You will no longer be self-conscious or feel that you ***must*** apologize as though your husband were a weak character.(p.115)

• Often you ***must*** carry the burden of avoiding them or keeping them under control.(p.117)

• Yet you ***must*** not expect too much.(p.118)

• Your husband will see at once that he ***must*** redouble his spiritual activities if he expects to survive.(p.120)

• The family ***must*** realize that dad, though marvelously improved, is still convalescing.(p.127)

• But he ***must*** see the danger of over-concentration on financial success.(p.127)

• We know there are difficult wives and families, but the man who is getting over alcoholism ***must*** remember he did much to make them so.(p.127)

• That is where our fellow travelers are, and that is where our work ***must*** be done.(p.130)

• The others ***must*** be convinced of his new status beyond the shadow of a doubt.(p.135)

• State that you know about his drinking, and that it ***must*** stop.(p.141)

• Though you are providing him with the best possible medical attention, he should understand that he ***must*** undergo a change of heart.(p.143)

• When the man is presented with this volume it is best that no one tell him he ***must*** abide by its suggestions.(p.144)

• The man ***must*** decide for himself.(p.144)

• For he knows he ***must*** be honest if he would live at all.(p.146)

• I know I ***must*** get along without liquor, but how can I?(p.152)

• They will approach still other sick ones and fellowships of Alcoholics Anonymous may spring up in each city and hamlet, havens for those who ***must*** find a way out.(p.153)

• There ***must*** be many such in this town.(p.154)

• Both saw that they ***must*** keep spiritually active.(p.156)

• Though they knew they ***must*** help other alcoholics if they would remain sober, that motive became secondary.(p.159)

• God will determine that, so you ***must*** remember that your real reliance is always upon Him.(p.164)

• I think I ***must*** have been thoroughly scared by what had happened, or by the doctor, or probably both, so that I did not touch a drink again until the country went dry.(p.175)

• It ***must*** be remembered that I had read a great deal and talked to everyone who knew, or thought they knew anything about the subject of alcoholism.(p.180)

• But if you really and truly want to quit drinking liquor for good and all, and sincerely feel that you ***must*** have some help, we know that we have an answer for you.(p.181)

• I quite naturally came to the conclusion that I ***must*** be insane.(p.199)

• There was also some conversation about Dr. Bob and I ***must*** have said that I would go down to Akron with Bill in the morning.(p.217)

• It ***must*** have been a long time since I had my last drink -- but I didn't dare ask this stranger for one.(p.223)

• I ***must*** get out of here.(p.223)

• In any case I ***must*** get out of here before I let slip my abysmal ignorance of how I came to be here, and she realized that I was stark, staring mad.(p.223)

• I was mad -- I ***must*** be.(p.223)

• My thoughts sometimes turned to the idea that there ***must*** be a remedy.(p.256)

• Somebody ***must*** have taken pity on you and gone out and got it for you."(p.264)

• "Well," I said to dad, when the A.A. people kept coming with these lovely cars and looked so nice, "I suppose the neighbors say, 'Now those old fools ***must*** have up and died, but where's the hearse?'"(p.269)

• If, on Sunday, I could be there, trying to think of something that would help her with this problem, then we ***must*** have something that could work.(p.272)

• I felt it certainly ***must*** be very depressing to her that I should sit there by her bedside and cry.(p.272)

• I have to tell myself, "Other things are progressing and A.A. ***must*** too."(p.272)

• At least three of those four years ***must*** have been a living hell for my wife, because she had to watch the man she loved disintegrate morally, mentally and financially.(p.277)

• After six months of sobriety I saw the picture in a different light: Detroit was the place I had to return to, not only because I ***must*** face the mess I had made there, but because it was there that I could be of the most service to A.A.(p.281)

• However, I ***must*** have felt, deep down inside myself, that living the selfish life of a bachelor was only half living.(p.286)

• One of them was that I would try to get a group started in Chicago; the second was that I would have to return to Akron to attend meetings at least every two months until I did get a group started in Chicago; third, I decided I ***must*** place this program above everything else, even my family, because if I did not maintain my sobriety I would lose my family anyway.(p.292)

• You ***must*** always be willing and continue to make contacts."(p.293)

• Somehow or other, I ***must*** have misunderstood the doctor's instructions, for I not only made the beer for my wife, I also drank it for her.(p.297)

• On the way home numerous places ***must*** be passed.(p.299)

• They had a hunch that there ***must*** be an answer for these apparently hopeless ones, somewhere.(p.307)

• I saw in these people a quality of peace and serenity that I knew I ***must*** have for myself.(p.310)

• As arrested alcoholics, we ***must*** have a program for living that allows for limitless expansion.(p.311)

• All of them were so nice to me that I figured I ***must*** be careful – they were bound to want something, being that nice.(p.319)

• I ***must*** live and let live.(p.325)

• I was told that I ***must*** want sobriety for my own sake and I am convinced this is true.(p.379)

• There may be many reasons which bring one to A.A. for the first time, but the lasting one ***must*** be to want sobriety and the A.A. way of living for oneself.(p.379)

• It was so important that it ***must*** come ahead of anything.(p.382)

• The cop ***must*** have seen the condition that I was in because he decided to take me home.(p.390)

• When he picked me up, I ***must*** have gotten sassy and told him that he couldn't do that, so he took my dog home and took me to jail!(p.390)

• I know that I ***must*** work at it as long as I live; I know that it is only by working at it that I can stay sober and have a happy life.(p.394)

• Dr. Bob said, "Love and service keep us dry," and Bill said, "Always we ***must*** remember that our first duty is face-to-face help for the alcoholic who still suffers."(p.395)

• I ***must*** drink less, I would tell myself.(p.408)

• Or: If I'm really a genius, I ***must*** produce a great work, to show why I act like a genius.(p.408)

• I ***must*** use self-will, self-control.(p.408)

• I ***must*** go on the wagon for a while.(p.408)

• I also thought that I ***must*** have power over myself.(p.408)

• This ***must*** be the doctor.(p.422)

• I ***must*** keep my magic magnifying mind on my acceptance and off my expectations, for my serenity is directly proportional to my level of acceptance.(p.452)

• Of course, an inmate ***must*** begin living the A.A. way "inside," if he is to stand a chance "outside."(p.458)

• I ***must*** be ready and willing should I never see them.(p.463)

• God ***must*** watch over me.(p.475)

• To tell you a small part of what my mother's life ***must*** have been like: Three of her kids were in jail that year – two sons and a daughter.(p.480)

• She ***must*** have been real proud of us, I'm sure.(p.480)

• He has also taught me that I ***must*** help myself first; only then may I be able to help others.(p.481)

• Anyhow, on the 24th, after drinking all day on the 23rd, I ***must*** have decided I wanted to see my wife and have some kind of reconciliation or at least talk with her.(p.491)

• I ***must*** get myself together.(p.501)

• Mother ***must*** never know.(p.501)

• I ***must*** get out of the room or I shall jump out of the window.(p.501)

• I ***must*** get some liquor.(p.502)

• "I ***must*** ask you a question," I say to the man.(p.504)

• I ***must*** write her.(p.505)

• I ***must*** find a way to make some money.(p.506)

• A former employer of mine said to me a little over ten years ago, "Pat, you seem to be one of those unfortunate people who at least once every six months ***must*** go out and roll in the gutter."(p.513)

• In here you ***must*** go all the way too."(p.516)

• We ***must*** learn to walk before we can run.(p.516)

• Strangely enough, right through to the end of my twenty-six years in the Army, I was still being offered very good and important jobs in spite of the fact that my superiors ***must*** have known that I wasn't thoroughly reliable.(p.519)

• It has made me understand that I ***must*** be one of my world, that I cannot exist in any happiness as a rebel by myself.(p.524)

• It has taught me that I can best keep my sobriety by sharing it out with others; that I ***must*** bring that sobriety to others who need it, in my own interest.(p.524)

• On one of these trips, the judge ***must*** have thought I was worth saving, for instead of sending me to jail, he sent me to A.A. for one month.(p.526)

• Rather, I embraced it – I ***must*** in honesty admit it -- with a great sense of relief.(p.531)

• But such is my nature that I ***must*** know the reason for things and I didn't stop until I had satisfied myself about the reasons for my drinking.(p.533)

• Alas for us men toward whom Shaw hurled his cry, "***Must*** a Christ be crucified in every generation for the benefit of those who have no imagination?"(p.536)

• We alcoholics see that we ***must*** work together and hang together, else most of us will finally die alone.(p.563)

• A.A. ***must*** continue to live or most of us will surely die.(p.565)

• Yet it is true that our first printing gave many readers the impression that these personality changes, or religious experiences, ***must*** be in the nature of sudden and spectacular upheavals.(p.569)

• Though it was not our intention to create such an impression, many alcoholics have nevertheless concluded that in order to recover they ***must*** acquire an immediate and overwhelming "God-consciousness" followed at once by a vast change in feeling and outlook.(p.569)

• I think our profession ***must*** take appreciative cognizance of this great therapeutic weapon.(p.571)

• Any therapeutic or philosophic procedure which can prove a recovery rate of 50% to 60% ***must*** merit our consideration."(p.571)

• They know that they ***must*** never drink.(p.572)

muster

• But when the broker gave him Dr. Silkworth's description of alcoholism and its hopelessness, the physician began to pursue the spiritual remedy for his malady with a willingness he had never before been able to ***muster***.(p.xvi)

• When our friend related his experience, the man agreed that no amount of will power he might ***muster*** could stop his drinking for long.(p.155)

mustn't

• People have said we must not go where liquor is served; we must not have it in our homes; we must shun friends who drink; we must avoid moving pictures which show drinking scenes; we must not go into bars; our friends must hide their bottles if we go to their houses; we ***mustn't*** think or be reminded about alcohol at all.(p.100)

musty

• Never mind the ***musty*** past; here sat a miracle directly across the kitchen table.(p.11)

mutual

• First, through ***mutual*** pain and despair, and later through ***mutual*** objectives and new-found faith and hope.(p.312)

• And, as the years go by, working together, sharing our experiences with one another, and also sharing a ***mutual*** trust, understanding and love – without strings, without obligation – we acquire relationships that are unique and priceless.(p.312)

mutually

• We attended meetings together, and ***mutually*** enjoyed our new found friends.(p.364)

myriad

• Historians may one day recognize Alcoholics Anonymous to have been a great venture in social pioneering which forged a new instrument for social action; a new therapy based on the kinship of common suffering; one having a vast potential for the ***myriad*** other ills of mankind."(p.573)

myself

• I talked with him for some time, but was not able to

bring ***myself*** to feel that I had known him before.(p.xxix)
• I fancied ***myself*** a leader, for had not the men of my battery given me a special token of appreciation?(p.1)
• In no time I was beating on the bar asking ***myself*** how it happened.(p.6)
• As the whisky rose to my head I told ***myself*** I would manage better next time, but I might as well get good and drunk then.(p.6)
• Again I swayed dizzily before an open window, or the medicine cabinet where there was poison, cursing ***myself*** for a weakling.(p.6)
• Understanding ***myself*** now, I fared forth in high hope.(p.7)
• I, who had thought so well of ***myself*** and my abilities, of my capacity to surmount obstacles, was cornered at last.(p.8)
• I had always believed in a Power greater than ***myself***.(p.10)
• For ***myself***, I had adopted those parts which seemed convenient and not too difficult; the rest I disregarded.(p.11)
• Like ***myself***, he had admitted complete defeat.(p.11)
• It was only a matter of being willing to believe in a Power greater than ***myself***.(p.12)
• But soon the sense of His presence had been blotted out by worldly clamors, mostly those within ***myself***.(p.12)
• There I humbly offered ***myself*** to God, as I then understood Him, to do with me as He would.(p.13)
• I placed ***myself*** unreservedly under His care and direction.(p.13)
• I admitted for the first time that of ***myself*** I was nothing; that without Him I was lost.(p.13)
• Never was I to pray for ***myself***, except as my requests bore on my usefulness to others.(p.13)
• They grinned, which I didn't like so much, and then asked me if I thought ***myself*** alcoholic and if I were really licked this time.(p.42)
• This process snuffed out the last flicker of conviction that I could do the job ***myself***.(p.42)
• "Do I now believe, or am I even willing to believe, that there is a Power greater than ***myself***?"(p.47)
• Many of us said to our Maker, as we understood Him: "God, I offer ***myself*** to Thee -- to build with me and to do with me as Thou wilt.(p.63)
• What irony -- I became an alcoholic ***myself***!(p.137)
• This resolution I kept steadfastly for the next forty years, except when circumstances made it seem unwise to absent ***myself***.(p.172)
• This I did, and proved ***myself*** satisfactory to the faculty, both in deportment and scholastically.(p.174)
• I conducted ***myself*** so creditably that I was able to secure a much coveted internship in a western city, where I spent two years.(p.174)
• By this time I was beginning to pay very dearly physically and, in hope of relief, voluntarily incarcerated ***myself*** at least a dozen times in one of the local sanitariums.(p.174)
• I did not want to disgrace ***myself*** so I then checked out.(p.179)
• 4.Because every time I do it I take out a little more insurance for ***myself*** against a possible slip.(p.181)
• I used to get terribly upset when I saw my friends drink and knew I could not, but I schooled ***myself*** to believe that though I once had the same privilege, I had abused it so frightfully that it was withdrawn.(p.181)
• I thought to ***myself***, "Well, she is going to tell me this is the end," and I certainly couldn't blame her and did not intend to try to justify ***myself***.(p.184)
• I was willing to admit to ***myself*** that I had hit bottom, that I had gotten hold of something that I didn't know how to handle by ***myself***.(p.187)
• Each day I would try to find out what His will was, and try to follow that, rather than trying to get Him to always agree that the things I thought of ***myself*** were the things best for me.(p.187)
• He did things much better than I did because he applied himself and learned how to do them, and I never applied ***myself***.(p.194)
• All of a sudden I found ***myself*** guzzling.(p.195)
• At the end of this selling of lots, just prior to World War I, I got into the crude rubber business, and six months later there was only one broker and ***myself*** left in Akron.(p.197)
• I can remember well thinking that I would quit drinking, really go to work hard, apply ***myself*** eight hours a day, five days a week, make a lot of money, and then I could start drinking again.(p.199)
• I drove towards Cleveland wondering why I found ***myself*** in such a changed set of conditions as compared with those of six months before.(p.200)
• So I didn't have a beer one night, and as I drove home I was breaking my arm patting ***myself*** on the back because I had proved I could lick liquor.(p.203)
• The people in the group hadn't been around that day; part of my family was in Florida and the rest of them weren't speaking to me, so I spent a very lonesome day and by evening I was feeling very sorry for ***myself***.(p.207)
• I could discipline ***myself*** but along the way there would be festivities and occasions when I got drunk.(p.211)
• I was supporting ***myself*** through all this education by being a toolmaker and a draftsman.(p.212)
• I kept ***myself*** so busy that outside of some school and group parties, I didn't go overboard on drinking very much between the ages of twenty-five and thirty.(p.213)
• In my own experience I was so jubilant at finding ***myself*** sober, and I had so many things to catch up on, that a month went by before the thought even occurred to me.(p.219)
• Professionally, after I was sober for a month or so I realized that I should school ***myself*** to dissolve the partnership I was in because I felt that I would never regain the respect of my partners no matter how long I was sober, and that I would be at a disadvantage.(p.220)
• I realized that there wasn't anything I could say to place ***myself*** in a more favorable light with my children, that it was going to be a matter of time; for I also understood the intolerance of young people towards deficiencies in their elders.(p.220)
• My divorce coincided with my father's bankruptcy, and I went to work, casting off all allegiances and responsibilities to any other than ***myself***.(p.225)
• As the treatment progressed I began to get a picture of ***myself***, of the temperament that had caused me so much trouble.(p.226)
• And so on and on, for several weeks, while I grudgingly plowed through some more of the offending book, and felt more and more hopeless about ***myself***.(p.227)
• I went to a meeting to see for ***myself*** this group of freaks or bums who had done this thing.(p.228)
• I had found friends, understanding friends who often knew what I was thinking and feeling better than I knew ***myself***, and didn't allow me to retreat into my prison of loneliness and fear over a fancied slight or hurt.(p.228)
• Talking things over with them, great floods of enlightenment showed me ***myself*** as I really was and I was like them.(p.229)
• Suddenly I could accept ***myself***, faults and all, as I was -- for weren't we all like that?(p.229)
• An active member of A.A. since 1939, I feel ***myself*** a useful member of the human race at last.(p.229)
• I get my greatest thrill of accomplishment from the knowledge that I have played a part in the new happiness achieved by countless others like ***myself***.(p.229)
• Having regard for the law of the land, I resigned ***myself*** to the will of the national legislators and quit drinking altogether, not because I had found it harmful, but because I couldn't get what I was accustomed to drink.(p.232)
• But I hardly tasted anything for two years and started in business for ***myself***, founding a mattress factory which is today an important industrial enterprise in our city.(p.232)
• I decided that if these fellows could make it I would try it ***myself***, and so I did.(p.232)
• In four or five days I would be hunting all over the place, at home and in my workshop, for the bottles I had destroyed, cursing ***myself*** for being a fool.(p.234)
• I had never doubted the existence of the Supreme Being, but now I began to absent ***myself*** from my church where I had formerly been a member of the choir.(p.234)
• I even got them ***myself*** and tried them.(p.235)
• My visitor well knew, that as I tried to follow God I would get to studying these things out for ***myself***.(p.236)
• Searching where I have been at fault, it is not hard to discover and get right again, for I have proven to ***myself*** and to many others who know me that God can keep a man sober if he will let Him.(p.237)
• I could never be bothered with the follow-through and would invariably reward ***myself*** for my efforts with that "first" drink.(p.243)
• I'd work like mad for three or four weeks without a single drink, save my money, pay a few bills and then "reward" ***myself*** with alcohol.(p.244)
• I really had a chance to see ***myself*** from a non-drinking point of view.(p.245)
• I'd been dry three weeks, had the wrinkles out and had sobered up my sponsor all by ***myself***!(p.246)
• This was when I really took my first good look at ***myself***.(p.247)
• Thus I found ***myself*** in the middle of a brand new group.(p.249)
• In telling newcomers how to change their lives and attitudes, all of a sudden I found I was doing a little changing ***myself***.(p.249)
• I had been too self-sufficient to write a moral inventory, but I discovered in pointing out to the new man his wrong attitudes and actions that I was really taking my own inventory, and that if I expected him to change I would have to work on ***myself*** too.(p.249)
• I ***myself*** could see deterioration in my work from being physically and mentally affected by liquor, although I had not yet reached the point where all I wanted was more to drink.(p.254)
• I tried to help ***myself***.(p.255)
• I managed to maintain ***myself*** with odd jobs, did ten weeks in a social rescue institution, and at length wound up in a second-hand bookstore in an adjacent town as manager.(p.257)
• I had missed them ***myself*** from the barrooms of the town.(p.258)
• I hated ***myself*** worse and worse, and as I hated ***myself*** I became more defiant towards everything and everybody.(p.265)
• I have to tell ***myself***, "Other things are progressing and A.A. must too."(p.272)
• I don't ever remember that I was bored ***myself*** when we first came in, and they came out to the house and talked to us about these things.(p.273)
• I joined their Saturday night parties and enjoyed ***myself*** too.(p.277)
• But -- I also stayed up week nights after they had retired and drank ***myself*** into bed.(p.277)
• When she finally took the baby and left, I locked ***myself*** in the house and stayed drunk for a month.(p.278)
• He might have handed me fifty dollars and said that I ought to pull ***myself*** together and make a new start.(p.278)
• The only stipulation they made was this: I had to make the decision ***myself***.(p.278)
• To go north into the empty pine country and shoot ***myself***, or to go south in the faint hope that a bunch of strangers might help me with my drinking problem.(p.278)
• He it was who convinced me, because his own conviction was so real, that a Power greater than ***myself*** could help me in the crises of life, and that the means of communicating with this Power was simple prayer.(p.279)
• I shut ***myself*** in my room, which began to go around in circles.(p.279)
• I well remember a session I had with ***myself*** soon after I returned.(p.282)
• His road lay clear before me, and I'd better quit rationalizing ***myself*** into any detours.(p.282)
• So I created a job for ***myself*** selling women's hosiery and men's made-to-order shirts.(p.282)
• Seven years of work in this field brought an opportunity to affiliate ***myself*** actively with one of my clients, a fellow A.A.(p.284)
• At long last I am doing the kind of work I have always wanted to do, but never had the patience and emotional stability to train ***myself*** for.(p.284)
• The most accurate answer I can give you is this: Fear has never again ruled my life since that day in September, 1938, when I found that a Power greater than ***myself*** could not only restore me to sanity but could keep me both sober and sane.(p.285)
• Some of the things which used to stop me in my tracks from fear still make me nervous in the anticipation of their doing, but once I kick ***myself*** into doing them nervousness disappears and I enjoy ***myself***.(p.285)
• However, I must have felt, deep down inside ***myself***, that living the selfish life of a bachelor was only half living.(p.286)
• Then I started traveling, with the United States and Canada as my territory, and with so much freedom and with an unlimited expense account, I was soon drinking every night and kidding ***myself*** that it was all part of the job.(p.287)
• (That condition was a distinct handicap to me in trying to vindicate ***myself*** with the not so patient wife.)(p.301)
• A little more than fifteen years ago, through a long and calamitous series of shattering experiences, I found ***myself*** being helplessly propelled toward total destruction.(p.304)
• It explained so much I had not understood about ***myself*** and, best of all, it promised recovery if I would do a few simple things and be willing to have the desire to drink removed.(p.309)
• I saw in these people a quality of peace and serenity that I knew I must have for ***myself***.(p.310)

• I didn't dare hope I might find for ***myself*** all that these people had found, but if I could acquire some small part of their intriguing quality of living -- and sobriety — that would be enough.(p.310)

• In time, I found ***myself*** looking forward to each new day with pleasurable anticipation.(p.311)

• But I wasn't happy, and I didn't ever let ***myself*** go in my drinking.(p.323)

• I got so that I hid quite a bit of the time, wouldn't answer the phone, and stayed by ***myself*** as much as I could.(p.324)

• I'd get so fed up with drinking all alone and bearing the burden of guilt all by ***myself***, that I'd egg him on to drink, to get started again.(p.325)

• I ***myself*** didn't know all the places I had them hidden.(p.325)

• I just didn't give a whoop about ***myself*** or anyone else.(p.325)

• I was aware of symptoms of impending dependence, and I told ***myself*** I had gotten out of the rat race just in time to head off any booze problem.(p.327)

• I soon was to ask ***myself***, "What living?"(p.329)

• Well, at least I could drink ***myself*** to death.(p.333)

• Toward five o'clock, helter-skelter, I'd get everything put away and try to get supper on the table, and after supper I'd finish the job up and knock ***myself*** out.(p.337)

• I went on, realizing what I was becoming, hating ***myself*** for it, bitter, blaming life, blaming everything else but the fact that I should turn about and do something about my drinking.(p.337)

• I said to my husband, "I'm going to try, every free moment that I have, to get interested in something outside, get ***myself*** over this rut I'm in."(p.338)

• And then we went up the side of a hill where we have a little barbecue area to make the fire for the barbecue, and on the way up, I thought to ***myself*** -- I'll go back down to the kitchen and refill this drink.(p.347)

• There were five people present, including ***myself***.(p.347)

• I recall, as I walked into that meeting, saying to ***myself***, "Here I am, a fellow of the American College of Surgeons, a Fellow of the International College of Surgeons, a diplomate of one of the great specialty boards in these United States, a member of the American Psychiatric Society, and I have to go to the butcher, the baker and the carpenter to help make a man out of me!"(p.347)

• So I thought to ***myself***, I might just as well be drunk as feel like this.(p.348)

• So, after taking the first half of the First Step, and very gingerly admitting ***myself*** to Alcoholics Anonymous, something happened.(p.349)

• And then I thought to ***myself***: "Imagine an alcoholic admitting anything!"(p.349)

• For ***myself***, I have an absolute proof of the existence of God.(p.350)

• And then I scratched my head and said to ***myself***, "What a fantastic thing for a man to say, that I cured his wife.(p.350)

• I thought to ***myself*** -- what is curing that woman?(p.350)

• So I went to my wife and asked her, wasn't there something that she and I could do to somehow get together, and she turned on her heel and looked me squarely in the eye, and said, "You don't care anything about my problem," and I could have smacked her, but I said to ***myself***, "Grab on to your serenity!"(p.351)

• My eventual goal was to drink ***myself*** to death.(p.353)

• I lost my driver's license, was made a ward of the court, and was put on probation (not to mention the fact that I might have killed three friends and ***myself***).(p.354)

• It was then that I began to hate ***myself***, and drank primarily to ease my conscience and forget.(p.354)

• Every day became that much harder to live through, and I began to take a look at ***myself***.(p.354)

• Many times have I heard the above expressions since I have been in A.A., and many times I have had to reply "Definitely I am an alcoholic, and while it may be hard for you to believe, it is not hard for me, for I have learned many things about alcohol and ***myself*** that would, perhaps, be difficult for you to understand."(p.356)

• I have always considered ***myself*** one of the lucky members of our fraternity.(p.356)

• The challenge intrigued me; also it was another opportunity to run away from ***myself*** and the "fast life of the big city."(p.359)

• I entered the house, opened a new bottle of whiskey and sat down to drink ***myself*** into the right frame of mind to get in my car, start the motor and close the garage door behind me.(p.363)

• Of course, more than anything else I had let ***myself*** down, but I didn't realize how much then – as I do now.(p.364)

• I had nowhere else to go, and I knew something was terribly wrong, and the reason had to lie within ***myself***.(p.371)

• I made promises to ***myself***, my family and friends -- and broke them.(p.375)

• I was unhappy ***myself*** and I had brought unhappiness to all who cared for me.(p.378)

• What could be more reasonable than that some people, including ***myself***, were allergic to alcohol?(p.380)

• They meant patience, tolerance and humility, and above all the belief that a Power greater than ***myself*** could help.(p.381)

• Above all, I am grateful to A.A. for my sobriety, which means so much to my family, friends and business associates, because God and A.A. were able to do for me something I was unable to do for ***myself***.(p.383)

• I was free, white and twenty-one and I had a time for ***myself***.(p.386)

• I could not identify ***myself*** with the people with whom I found ***myself*** and there was no understanding, and I can't stand confinement anyhow.(p.387)

• That is how dishonest I was with ***myself***.(p.388)

• I know now that I asked questions and told him what I wanted to learn, but I told him only what I wanted to believe about ***myself***.(p.388)

• Then he said I couldn't possibly move on the first of February because I couldn't stay in that place by ***myself***.(p.388)

• So I went down to him quite a few times a month and had him shoot me full of the stuff; and then I went across the street to a little drug store to take a glass of beer or two beers, and then stopped at the liquor store to get ***myself*** a pint and go home.(p.389)

• They phoned my husband that I was in jail and in such terrible shape that they didn't know what I would do to ***myself***; and they realized that jail was no place for me, but that he was to wait a while before he got me, because at the time they called him to come over for me I was beating a tin cup against the wall.(p.390)

• This was something I had to do all by ***myself***.(p.392)

• I had learned an awful lot about ***myself*** in that one little article.(p.393)

• However, I threw ***myself*** into Twelve Step work, and what I feared would be a calamity turned out to be the most blessed of blessings.(p.394)

• My husband was made miserable by this, but I had already made him and ***myself*** miserable.(p.402)

• It was nothing to my own inner distress, my self-reproach, and my self-loathing, for was I not bearing out all the horrible things I had always suspected of ***myself***?(p.404)

• I was really trying, once more, to escape from ***myself***.(p.405)

• Imagine my surprise when I came to, in Europe, and discovered I had brought ***myself*** along!(p.405)

• I must drink less, I would tell ***myself***.(p.408)

• I also thought that I must have power over ***myself***.(p.408)

• I told ***myself*** that I had power over this thing.(p.408)

• For, after those daily self-punishing sessions with ***myself***, after the vows to stop, I would change entirely as evening came on.(p.408)

• In a sick people's place, ***myself*** among the sickest.(p.410)

• What I had secretly believed ***myself*** to be all along, this I had become.(p.411)

• I was going to reform ***myself***!(p.412)

• I found ***myself*** nodding my head.(p.413)

• The apartment was charming; the shelves were full of books, many of which I ***myself*** owned.(p.413)

• On non-meeting nights I was lonesome, or so I told ***myself***.(p.414)

• I completely forgot ***myself*** in trying vainly to help Anne, whose misery I understood.(p.415)

• I planned to stay home the night before I left, but my folks got so drunk I walked off early in the evening and spent the night with my girl, getting very drunk ***myself***.(p.425)

• I tried to control her drinking by pouring her whiskey down the sink before I'd leave for the night, to get drunker ***myself***.(p.426)

• I'd heard a lot about A.A. and met a great many A.A.'s during that year at home, but I hadn't thought of it for ***myself***.(p.429)

• "I've got to stop if I want to live," I told ***myself***, and if I don't want to break my parents' hearts and maybe jeopardize their own carefully built up and hard-fought-for sobriety.(p.429)

• "I'll do it," I told ***myself***.(p.430)

• I thought, "If this is A.A. why not go back to drinking, kill ***myself*** with booze in the next three years the doctor had given me, and call it a bad job?"(p.430)

• One, the side I turned to ***myself*** and the world, was respectable -- even, in some ways, distinguished.(p.432)

• How exciting to learn the inward mysteries that govern the behavior of people, how wonderful to know, at last, all about ***myself***!(p.434)

• After talking with him for a time I heard ***myself*** saying, "Doc, I think I'm an alcoholic."(p.436)

• I had to admit to ***myself*** that he was right.(p.436)

• Only through being beaten down by my own misery would I ever have accepted the term "alcoholic" as applied to ***myself***.(p.436)

• Here I found an ingredient that had been lacking in any other effort I had made to save ***myself***.(p.436)

• With my A.A. friends, all I can say is that it's a power greater than ***myself***.(p.437)

• I remember finding ***myself*** in the middle of the night in the doctors' parking lot at the hospital with one foot in the car and one foot on the ground, not knowing which was the lead foot; finding ***myself*** hanging up the telephone – then realizing I had gotten out of bed, answered the phone, turned on the light, and carried on a conversation with a patient.(p.441)

• The longer the drinking continued, the shorter the time the alcohol would keep me asleep; I would have to drink ***myself*** back to sleep again and again throughout the night.(p.441)

• If it was one minute before five, I'd drink ***myself*** back to sleep.(p.441)

• It became progressively harder to get up in the morning, until one day I asked ***myself*** what I would do for a patient who felt this rotten.(p.441)

• However, for a period of time I was injecting Pentothal intravenously to put ***myself*** to sleep.(p.442)

• One night, I had to put ***myself*** back to sleep three times, and then I finally decided to give it up.(p.443)

• I can't say, "God could restore me to sanity, but until He does, I'll control ***myself*** -- with pills."(p.443)

• I never could quite get the knack of it and kept asking ***myself***, "What's a nice guy like me doing in a place like this?"(p.445)

• Before A.A., I judged ***myself*** by my intentions, while the world was judging me by my actions.(p.450)

• Then, one day in A.A., I was told that I had the lenses in my glasses backwards; "the courage to change" in the Serenity Prayer meant, not that I should change my marriage, but rather that I should change ***myself*** and learn to accept my spouse as she was.(p.451)

• I have to discard my "rights," as well as my expectations, by asking ***myself***, "How important is it, really?(p.452)

• My pattern of drinking at that time had reached the point where once I really started, I would retire to my bed and drink ***myself*** into oblivion.(p.466)

• On the way I tried, and I mean really tried, to throw ***myself*** out of the car.(p.466)

• I was too weak and exhausted to even try to throw ***myself*** out of the car.(p.467)

• Also, after that first visit I learned I could refuse to sign ***myself*** in unless they gave me a glass of whiskey in one hand and a glass of paraldehyde in the other.(p.468)

• I had decided I was no good – never would be any good, and the sooner I could drink ***myself*** out of this life, the better.(p.468)

• I showed ***myself***.(p.472)

• Think about kill ***myself***.(p.475)

• I felt very sorry for ***myself*** and attempted suicide on many occasions, making sure there was always somebody within reaching distance to see that I didn't finish the job.(p.478)

• Any time I tried to kill ***myself***, I was either drunk or pilled-up or both – usually the last.(p.479)

• He has also taught me that I must help ***myself*** first; only then may I be able to help others.(p.481)

• I don't believe this program would work for me if I didn't get honest with ***myself*** about everything.(p.482)

• If I work on it every day, it will be easier to be honest with ***myself***.(p.482)

• I got to the place where I'd look forward to the week-end's drinking and pacify ***myself*** by saying that the week-ends were mine, that it didn't interfere with my family or with my business if I drank on the week-ends.(p.488)

• But I knew at that point that I couldn't stop and I knew that I was a danger to ***myself*** and to others.(p.489)

• I worked in the steel mill for possibly two months, and then I became disgusted with ***myself*** and decided to go back home.(p.492)

• I knew I wasn't capable of keeping the bulk of the money ***myself***, so I gave it to a white fellow who owned the bar which I frequented.(p.493)
• He started telling me how much trouble he had, and I said to ***myself***, "I wonder why this guy is telling me all his troubles.(p.494)
• Of course, it wasn't very much of a meeting in the beginning; most of the time it was just Vi and ***myself***.(p.495)
• I must get ***myself*** together.(p.501)
• I'll do it all ***myself***.(p.502)
• Could I have ***myself*** locked up at home?(p.502)
• I am too yellow to kill ***myself***.(p.502)
• Anything to get my mind from ***myself***.(p.502)
• A fanatic, I thought to ***myself***, but I was polite.(p.503)
• Then he asks me if I believe in a power greater than ***myself***, whether I call that power God, Allah, Confucius, Prime Cause, Divine Mind, or any other name.(p.503)
• Am I willing to be honest with ***myself*** about ***myself*** and tell someone about ***myself***, and am I willing to think of other people, of their needs instead of ***myself***, in order to get rid of the drink problem?(p.503)
• Then I find ***myself*** thinking about ***myself***, and a few things that I had wanted to forget.(p.503)
• I begin to see I am not the person I had thought ***myself***, that I had judged ***myself*** by comparing ***myself*** to others, and always to my own advantage.(p.504)
• Then I shall lock ***myself*** in and read.(p.506)
• I shall get ***myself*** "mellow" and stay that way.(p.506)
• After hearing the first speaker I could tell ***myself*** that my own lot was rather mild.(p.509)
• It was a thorn in my side, because I knew it was the truth, and I hated to hear the truth, especially about ***myself***.(p.513)
• Somehow or other I was coming face to face with ***myself***, and I didn't like it.(p.513)
• But somehow or other, with my old alcoholic brain, sitting there in that chair, I kept saying to ***myself***, "I wonder if it'll work?(p.515)
• I have to watch ***myself*** all the time.(p.516)
• I got a job by ***myself*** which suited me down to the ground, because there was nobody really to interfere with what I did, one way or the other, and I usually had my nerves in good trim when anybody was coming around to inspect.(p.519)
• I was alone by ***myself*** in that job for a long time.(p.519)
• I put ***myself*** into a home.(p.521)
• I stayed there just long enough to work up a real good resentment against the doctor in charge, who I didn't think was doing anything at all except collecting fees, and I left there fully determined that I'd never put ***myself*** in the power of medical people again.(p.521)
• In any case, I made ***myself*** believe that, so I just drifted about, existing on my retired pay, drinking, and living at home.(p.522)
• I couldn't understand ***myself***.(p.522)
• It was no use talking of putting ***myself*** into a home, a hospital, or of going to see a doctor again, or of going to see a priest or anyone else.(p.523)
• Just as I was wondering what on earth I could do -- I was too drunk even to pack a handkerchief – the memory of an A.A. write-up that I had seen in the Evening Mail flashed across my mind -- and I thought to ***myself***, this is something I haven't tried yet.(p.523)
• So I did manage to get ***myself*** down to an A.A. meeting that night.(p.523)
• It has made me understand that I must be one of my world, that I cannot exist in any happiness as a rebel by ***myself***.(p.524)
• I would wake to find ***myself*** in some beat-up rooming house, where roaches were crawling over everything.(p.527)
• I remember the day when I decided to drink ***myself*** to death quietly, without bothering anyone, because I was tired of having been a dependable, trustworthy person for about thirty-nine years without having received what I thought was a proper reward for my virtue.(p.531)
• I, a man of steel, with very high ideals, well brought up, an honor student and the recipient of scholarships and prizes, a boy wonder in business -- I, Bob, the author of this essay, looked and saw that the universe was beneath my contempt, and that to remove ***myself*** from it was the only thing of dignity a man could do.(p.531)
• No, it can best be explained in a little phrase I coined and sang to ***myself***: "What happened to Bob?(p.532)
• But such is my nature that I must know the reason for things and I didn't stop until I had satisfied ***myself*** about the reasons for my drinking.(p.533)
• My personal definition, which I submit as applying only to ***myself*** (although everyone is welcome to it who wants it), includes every waking activity of the human being; to have a creative attitude towards things is a more exact meaning, to live and to deal with other human beings creatively, which to me means seeing the God in them, and respecting and worshipping this God.(p.535)
• If I write with the air of one who has discovered the obvious, which is to say, the eternal truths which have been offered to us since the beginning, forgive my callowness; I had to find these things out for ***myself***.(p.536)
• After nearly eight years of sobriety in A.A., I still can set down such thoughts, "against my instinct and training," showing that I still consider ***myself*** a "special" person, entitled to special privileges.(p.536)
• For a little while, I was the great man I wanted to be, and thought ***myself*** entitled to be just by reason of being.(p.537)
• Repeated year on end, they are horrible -- frightening and degrading, a chronicle of tragedy which may be greater because the individual undergoing the tragedy, ***myself***, knew what was happening, and yet refused to do anything to stop it.(p.538)
• I left this home town, then, after I had made a public spectacle of ***myself*** in the presence of a revered teacher whose favorite pupil I had been.(p.539)
• I set it down and made ***myself*** a cup of coffee.(p.541)
• I ***myself*** have been lucky enough to help out.(p.541)
• Harm is done by sick people, as I was sick, and doing dreadful harm to ***myself*** and to my loved ones.(p.542)
• In time I concluded that the reason I was hurt was because I loved my parents, and I concluded too that if I never allowed ***myself*** to love anybody or anything I could never be hurt again.(p.545)
• It became second nature for me to remove ***myself*** from anything or anybody I found ***myself*** growing fond of.(p.545)
• It was not difficult to convince ***myself*** that my unhappiness was the fault of the man I had married, and I divorced him at the end of a year.(p.545)
• And if I had been able to turn to the church at that time I'm sure they could not have convinced me my sickness was within ***myself***, nor could they have shown me the need for self-analysis that A.A. has shown me is vital if I am to survive.(p.546)
• Fear of rejection and its ensuing pain were not to be risked, and I turned away from ***myself*** once more for the answer, this time to the drinks I had always refused before, and in alcohol I found a false courage.(p.546)
• It became more and more necessary to escape from ***myself***, for my remorse and shame and humiliation when I was sober were almost unbearable.(p.547)
• The only way existence was possible was through rationalizing every sober moment and drinking ***myself*** into complete oblivion as often as I could.(p.547)
• By this time I was such a past master at kidding ***myself*** that I had convinced ***myself*** I had sat out a war and waited for this man to come home and, as my resentment and self-pity grew, so did my alcoholic problem.(p.548)
• The amount of will power exercised to control my drinking during working hours, diverted into a constructive channel, would have made me President, and the thing that made the will power possible was the knowledge that as soon as my day was finished I could drink ***myself*** into oblivion.(p.548)
• I was drunk for sixty days around the clock and it was my intention, literally, to drink ***myself*** to death.(p.549)
• The people who came knew immediately I was in no condition to absorb anything of the program, and I was put in a sanitarium to be defogged so that I could make a sober decision about this for ***myself***.(p.549)
• Society can do anything it chooses to do with me when I am drunk and I can't lift a finger to stop it, for I forfeit my rights through the simple expedient of becoming a menace to ***myself*** and to the people around me.(p.549)
• My desire to be honest with ***myself*** made it necessary for me to realize that my thinking was irrational.(p.550)
• Regarded as something of a "boy wonder," I began to see ***myself*** that way.(p.555)
• And yet my ability to lie outwardly and to kid ***myself*** inwardly grew with every drink I took.(p.556)
• When I was faced with a special challenge or social event – such as an important business presentation or a dinner party – I had to fortify ***myself*** with a couple of belts.(p.556)
• Above all, I was suffering inner pain because my performance and my accomplishments in life failed to live up to my own expectations of ***myself***.(p.557)
• I became so weak, I could barely drag ***myself*** around.(p.558)
• I found ***myself*** being lifted onto a stretcher and whisked away in an ambulance to a strange hospital.(p.558)
• Within a few days, I found ***myself*** drying out on a drunk farm.(p.559)
• For, at last, I was at peace with ***myself***.(p.561)

mysteries

• How exciting to learn the inward ***mysteries*** that govern the behavior of people, how wonderful to know, at last, all about myself!(p.434)

mysteriously

• Angry bruises appeared ***mysteriously*** all over my body.(p.558)

mystified

• Friends who have reasoned with him after a spree which has brought him to the point of divorce or bankruptcy are ***mystified*** when he walks directly into a saloon.(p.35)
• The family is ***mystified***.(p.126)

Nn

nadir
• His call to the clergyman led him presently to a certain resident of the town, who, though formerly able and respected, was then nearing the *nadir* of alcoholic despair.(p.155)

nag
• "Joykiller, *nag*, wet blanket" – that's what they said.(p.106)
• If he gets the idea that you are a *nag* or a killjoy, your chance of accomplishing anything useful may be zero.(p.111)

nagged
• He will feel he can deal with you without being *nagged* by his family.(p.91)
• His wife is one of those persons who really feels there is something rather sinful about these commodities, so she *nagged*, and her intolerance finally threw him into a fit of anger.(p.135)

nagging
• She was also the victim of my scolding and incessant *nagging*.(p.408)

nags
• Misunderstands and *nags*.(p.65)

Naini Tal
• The place is *Naini Tal*, in the foothills of the mighty Himalaya Mountains, and it has some very significant memories for me.(p.342)
• Eight years ago, my wife and I decided to spend a vacation in *Naini Tal*, the mountain resort.(p.343)
• Last year, I decided on an A.A. vacation in *Naini Tal*.(p.343)

naked
• For by now I had been exposed once to A.A., but I had treated it as a vaudeville and had taken friends to meetings so that they too could enjoy the fascination of the *naked* revelation of suffering and recovery.(p.539)

Nam
• When I came home from *Nam*, I met a girl I'll call Karen.(p.318)
• Finally, I reenlisted to go back to *Nam*.(p.318)

name
• When writing or speaking publicly about alcoholism, we urge each of our Fellowship to omit his personal *name*, designating himself instead as "a member of Alcoholics Anonymous."(p.xiii)
• I knew the man by *name*, and partly recognized his features, but there all resemblance ended.(p.xxix)
• On our grudge list we set opposite each *name* our injuries.(p.65)
• Wants house put in her *name*.(p.65)
• It is better, however, that one does not needlessly *name* a person upon whom she can vent jealously.(p.82)
• I would sometimes hide out in one of the clubs of which I was a member, and had the habit at times of registering at a hotel under a fictitious *name*.(p.176)
• Whenever this man and I met – I didn't know his *name* then nor do I know it now – we would always get drunk.(p.201)
• The *name* on it was unfamiliar and I had to ask the way to Grand Central.(p.223)
• I remembered going through what my sister assured me was my nightly procedure of trying to find Willie Seabrook's *name* in the telephone book.(p.224)
• I was suffering from an actual disease that had a *name* and symptoms like diabetes or cancer or TB -- and a disease was respectable, not a moral stigma!(p.227)
• This was my introduction to this "understanding fellowship" although it was to be more than a year later before our Society was to bear the *name*, Alcoholics Anonymous.(p.239)
• At that time the group in New York was composed of about twelve men who were working on the principle of every drunk for himself; we had no real formula and no *name*.(p.246)
• She told me her *name*, and I said, "I know you from somewhere."(p.321)
• She said "Suppose I put your *name* down as a volunteer.(p.326)
• Early the next morning a man whose *name* I knew well, a lawyer, called on me.(p.378)
• It had a *name* and symptoms, just like diabetes or T.B.(p.392)
• My wife loved to drink, and we tied on many a hooter in the *name* of marital bliss.(p.433)
• "Then why in God's *name* haven't you told me so, during all these years?"(p.436)
• Very shortly, I realized that had been a mistake -- when this big clown came bounding into the room, almost shouting, "My *name* is Frank, and I'm an alcoholic, ha-ha-ha!"(p.446)
• There at the top of the folder was my *name*, age and address, and underneath were the words, "Periodic Drinker."(p.470)
• Finally she said, "Isn't your *name* Jim S.?"(p.493)
• Then he asks me if I believe in a power greater than myself, whether I call that power God, Allah, Confucius, Prime Cause, Divine Mind, or any other *name*.(p.503)
• If something does come along that sort of upsets me, instead of walking in and throwing a buck at the barman and asking for a drink, I walk into a telephone booth, drop a dime in the box, and call somebody who was so kind as to give me his *name* and telephone number to meet such an emergency.(p.511)
• But I knew that they knew what the medical grounds were, and that they had put a big black mark against my *name*.(p.521)
• But as the years go by, the stretch becomes unbearable; and the man with the grown-up brain and the childish emotions – vanity, self-interest, false pride, jealousy, longing for social approval, to *name* few -- becomes a prime candidate for alcohol.(p.534)
• I have come to realize that the *name* of the game is not so much to stop drinking as to stay sober.(p.559)
• Six – An A.A. group ought never endorse, finance or lend the A.A. *name* to any related facility or outside enterprise, lest problems of money, property and prestige divert us from our primary purpose.(p.564)
• Ten – Alcoholics Anonymous has no opinion on outside issues; hence the A.A. *name* ought never be drawn into public controversy.(p.564)
• Hence such facilities ought not to use the A.A. *name*.(p.566)
• We think that each group should soon achieve this ideal; that any public solicitation of funds using the *name* of Alcoholics Anonymous is highly dangerous, whether by groups, clubs, hospitals, or other outside agencies; that acceptance of large gifts from any source, or of contributions carrying any obligation whatever, is unwise.(p.566)

named
• My proud southern blood would have boiled if anyone had *named* me such a despicable thing.(p.532)

nameless
• The fledgling society, which had been *nameless*, now began to be called Alcoholics Anonymous, from the title of its own book.(p.xvii)
• Just an unstable woman, undisciplined, poorly adjusted and filled with *nameless* fears.(p.305)

namely
• *Namely*, mine.(p.396)
• Edward Dowling, S.J., of the Queen's Work staff says, "Alcoholics Anonymous is natural; it is natural at the point where nature comes closest to the supernatural, *namely* in humiliations and in consequent humility.(p.574)

names
• I worked along until I had really big *names* in rubber on a tentative contract, and then I neglected to go through with it.(p.198)
• Our *names* and pictures as A.A. members ought not be broadcast, filmed, or publicly printed.(p.567)

Napoleon
• I felt like *Napoleon* returning from Elba.(p.4)

naps
• Hidden old-drunks can pass out on their beds and snooze unreproached, under the guise of taking those vital retirement-age *naps*.(p.330)

narcotics
• I had already given up all the *narcotics*, most of the pills, and some of the alcohol when I first came to A.A.(p.448)
• I attended my first A.A. meeting eight years ago, and it is with deep gratitude that I'm able to say I've not had a drink since that time, and that I take no sedation or *narcotics*, for this program is to me one of complete sobriety and I no longer need to escape reality.(p.549)

narrative
• I still have my job, and just prior to the writing of this *narrative*, I received an advancement.(p.303)

narrow
• He lost the race by only a *narrow* margin.(p.158)
• The details of the long road back to something resembling normal living -- the first short streetcar ride, the purchase of a used bike which enabled me to widen the *narrow* horizon of life, the first trip downtown – I will not dwell on.(p.276)
• It seemed to me my wife was becoming more intolerant and *narrow* minded all the time.(p.376)

nary
• I became convinced of that because I spent most of my time there and *nary* a job turned up.(p.300)

nasty
• That *nasty* little can of beer!(p.267)

nation
• He is like the retired business man who lolls in the Florida sunshine in the winter complaining of the sad state of the *nation*; the minister who sighs over the sins of the twentieth century; politicians and reformers who are sure all would be Utopia if the rest of the world would only behave; the outlaw safe cracker who thinks society has wronged him; and the alcoholic who has lost all and is locked up.(p.61)

national
• A.A. had become a *national* institution.(p.xviii)
• This dry spell lasted for about three weeks; then I went to Atlantic City to attend several days' meeting of a *national* society of which I was a member.(p.179)
• Having regard for the law of the land, I resigned myself to the will of the *national* legislators and quit drinking altogether, not because I had found it harmful, but because I couldn't get what I was accustomed to drink.(p.232)
• With the war over, and back in Baltimore with the folks, there were several small jobs for three years and then I went to work soliciting as one of the first ten employees of a new *national* finance company.(p.242)
• Then came a sales job with a *national* tire company.(p.243)
• As part of this promotion, they sent me to their *national* convention in Atlantic City to tell the big wheels how I'd done it.(p.243)
• I achieved recognized and *national* standing in my profession, as well as becoming a director in many important institutions having to do with the civic life of a large city.(p.374)
• I sold my first article to a *national* magazine while still an undergraduate.(p.555)

nationalities
• The basic principles of the A.A. program, it appears, hold good for individuals with many different lifestyles, just as the program has brought recovery to those of many different *nationalities*.(p.xxii)

nationally
• A well-known doctor, chief physician at a *nationally* prominent hospital specializing in alcoholic and drug addiction, gave Alcoholics Anonymous this letter:(p.xxiii)
• The ensuing nine years were the Depression years, both *nationally* and personally.(p.277)
• Such has been my privilege, both *nationally* and in my home city.(p.295)

nationally-known
• My bother-in-law is a physician, and through his kindness and that of my mother I was placed in a *nationally-known* hospital for the mental and physical rehabilitation of alcoholics.(p.7)

nations
• We try not to indulge in cynicism over the state of the *nations*, nor do we carry the world's troubles on our shoulders.(p.132)

native
• Many friends of my family had emigrated to America, so at twenty-four I decided that the United States offered me the opportunity I was never likely to find in my *native* land.(p.231)
• He said the alcoholic seemed to possess a *native* acuteness and usually excelled in his field, regardless of environmental or educational advantages.(p.308)
• In a prison in my *native* state, I spent eleven months in solitary confinement, bouncing in and out of the "hole" (a bare concrete-and-steel cubicle) about five times during those eleven months.(p.459)
• I left California and came back to my *native* state.(p.460)

natural
• Here are some of the methods we have tried: Drinking beer only, limiting the number of drinks, never drinking alone, never drinking in the morning, drinking only at home, never having it in the house, never drinking during business hours, drinking only at parties, switching from scotch to brandy, drinking only *natural* wines, agreeing to resign if ever drunk on the job, taking a trip, not taking a trip, swearing off forever (with and without a solemn oath), taking more physical exercise, reading inspirational books, going to health farms and sanitariums, accepting voluntary commitment to asylums -- we could increase the list ad infinitum.(p.31)
• That was *natural*, but let us think a little more closely.(p.53)
• It is the most *natural* thing in the world, once his liquor problem is solved, to feel that he will now measure up to that cherished vision.(p.118)
• When dealing with an alcoholic, there may be a *natural* annoyance that a man could be so weak, stupid and irresponsible.(p.139)
• All have now passed away from *natural* causes, having maintained complete sobriety.(p.169)
• I had, seemingly, just a *natural* affinity for grog.(p.182)
• It's only *natural* that we don't have the capacity to change, but we ought not to criticize those who have, There's another thing I would stress.(p.273)
• For that crime I received a minimum of twenty years and a maximum of *natural* life.(p.508)
• I received an additional fifteen years for that, making a minimum of thirty-five years and a maximum of *natural* life.(p.509)
• Edward Dowling, S.J., of the Queen's Work staff says, "Alcoholics Anonymous is *natural;* it is *natural* at the point where nature comes closest to the supernatural, namely in humiliations and in consequent humility.(p.574)

naturally
• They are *naturally* incapable of grasping and developing a manner of living which demands rigorous honesty.(p.58)
• Rightly and *naturally*, we think well before we choose the person or persons with whom to take this intimate and confidential step.(p.74)
• These things will come to pass *naturally* and in good time provided, however, the alcoholic continues to demonstrate that he can be sober, considerate, and helpful, regardless of what anyone says or does.(p.99)
• Under these conditions we *naturally* made mistakes.(p.107)
• *Naturally* this sort of thing decreased the man's chance of recovery.(p.145)
• Long experience with alcoholic excuses *naturally* arouses suspicion.(p.146)
• The question which might *naturally* come into your mind would be: "What did the man do or say that was different from what others had done or said?"(p.180)
• Before very long we began to relate some incidents of our drinking and, *naturally*, pretty soon, I realized both of them knew what they were talking about because you can see things and smell things when you're drunk, that you can't other times, and, if I had thought they didn't know what they were talking about, I wouldn't have been willing to talk to them at all.(p.185)
• *Naturally*, for quite a time, I wasn't too well physically, either.(p.190)
• *Naturally*, what little restraint I had exercised before was gone now, and my drinking became worse.(p.199)
• I quite *naturally* came to the conclusion that I must be insane.(p.199)
• *Naturally*, I wanted no part of any meetings.(p.205)
• *Naturally*, in spite of my good intentions, in spite of my protected life behind sanitarium walls, I several times got drunk, and was astounded . . . and badly shaken.(p.227)
• After such often-painful vigilance (and numerous phony stints of abstinence), retirement *naturally* created an impulse to live without restraints.(p.328)
• And of course a half empty bottle wasn't worth keeping, so I finished it up and *naturally* had to get more in right away for the people who "might come in unexpectedly."(p.336)
• *Naturally*, this experience didn't stop me.(p.354)
• In other words, I began contributing, and so, *naturally*, I began to get something more.(p.365)
• *Naturally*, I succeeded in nothing.(p.400)
• I despised the other barflies and, *naturally*, they loathed me.(p.410)

nature
• From this doctor, the broker had learned the grave *nature* of alcoholism.(p.xvi)
• I could go for such conceptions as Creative Intelligence, Universal Mind or Spirit of *Nature* but I resisted the thought of a Czar of the Heavens, however loving His sway might be.(p.12)
• We are aware that these matters are, from their very *nature*, controversial.(p.19)
• His disposition while drinking resembles his normal *nature* but little.(p.21)
• They appear to be in the *nature* of huge emotional displacements and rearrangements.(p.27)
• 5.Admitted to God, to ourselves, and to another human being the exact *nature* of our wrongs.(p.59)
• One set of voices cry that sex is a lust of our lower *nature*, a base necessity of procreation.(p.68)
• This requires action on our part, which, when completed, will mean that we have admitted to God, to ourselves, and to another human being the exact *nature* of our defects.(p.72)
• Had we fully understood the *nature* of the alcoholic illness, we might have behaved differently.(p.107)
• While you need not discuss your husband at length, you can quietly let your friends know the *nature* of his illness.(p.115)
• Your new courage, good *nature* and lack of self-consciousness will do wonders for you socially.(p.115)
• I learned that it was something of a spiritual *nature*, which did not appeal to me very much, but I thought it could do no harm.(p.178)
• By persistence and salesmanship I managed to see more and more of my new friend, and because of her sympathetic *nature* she tolerated my company.(p.359)
• The explanation that alcoholism was a disease of a two fold *nature*, an allergy of the body and an obsession of the mind, cleared up a number of puzzling questions for me.(p.380)
• He did not take out a folder and say, "What is the *nature* of your problem?"(p.413)
• I told him that I believe in electricity and other forces of *nature*, but as for a God, if there is one, He has never done anything for me.(p.503)
• But such is my *nature* that I must know the reason for things and I didn't stop until I had satisfied myself about the reasons for my drinking.(p.533)
• It became second *nature* for me to remove myself from anything or anybody I found myself growing fond of.(p.545)
• Yet it is true that our first printing gave many readers the impression that these personality changes, or religious experiences, must be in the *nature* of sudden and spectacular upheavals.(p.569)
• Edward Dowling, S.J., of the Queen's Work staff says, "Alcoholics Anonymous is natural; it is natural at the point where *nature* comes closest to the supernatural, namely in humiliations and in consequent humility.(p.574)

natured
• I could almost hear the sound of the preacher's voice as I sat, on still Sundays, way over there on the hillside; there was that proffered temperance pledge I never signed; my grandfather's good *natured* contempt of some church folk and their doings; his insistence that the spheres really had their music; but his denial of the preacher's right to tell him how he must listen; his fearlessness as he spoke of these things just before he died; these recollections welled up from the past.(p.10)

natures
• We were having trouble with personal relationships, we couldn't control our emotional *natures*, we were a prey to misery and depression, we couldn't make a living, we had a feeling of uselessness, we were full of fear, we were unhappy, we couldn't seem to be of real help to other people -- was not a basic solution of these bedevilments more important than whether we should see newsreels of lunar flight?(p.52)

naught
• During this time, I had been threatened, beaten, kissed, praised and damned alternately by relatives, family, friends and strangers, but of course it all went for *naught*.(p.300)

naughtier
• He did not like naughty stories, so I made them *naughtier*.(p.403)

naughty
• Above all, he noticed that I drank a good deal, often got tight in his company and told him *naughty* stories.(p.403)
• He did not like *naughty* stories, so I made them naughtier.(p.403)
• At a large party in Geneva, with people from many countries represented, the kind of party that is "protocol" in the extreme, I swayed, laughed hysterically, made *naughty* remarks in an unhushed voice, and was finally led from the scene.(p.406)

nausea
• I seemed to be able to snap back the next morning better than most of my fellow drinkers, who were cursed (or perhaps blessed) with a great deal of morning-after *nausea*.(p.172)
• Before long I had a definite taste for hard liquor, knew *nausea* and headaches I had never known before, but as in the old days, I suffered them out.(p.233)
• The horrors of increasing hangover sickness to occupy the entire day; *nausea*, dry heaves, the rocking bed, the nightmare-filled mind.(p.408)

navy
• A retired *Navy* man looks back over twenty years of drinking, to add up his A.A. "initiation fee."(p.396)
• At age twenty-one, I enlisted in the *Navy* for two reasons: (1) to avoid being drafted into the Army, and (2) out of a burst of patriotic fervor inspired by the advent of World War II and as the result of an all-night drinking binge which found me sitting on the doorstep of the *Navy* recruiting office when the chief petty officer arrived to open for business at nine o'clock Monday morning.(p.398)
• Two weeks later found me being sworn in, and the first payday in the *Navy* made me realize I had found a home.(p.398)
• So I spent twenty years in the *Navy*.(p.398)
• For an estimate of salary from the twenty-one a month to start with, to over $400 per month upon my retirement after twenty years in the *Navy*, I believe that an average income of $2,000 a year over this period is low, but as I stated earlier, an underestimate is best.(p.399)
• I had completed a three-year tour in the *Navy*.(p.418)
• Then came my tour in the U.S. *Navy*, part of it being two years in the Philippines.(p.419)
• I'm in the U.S. *Navy*.(p.422)
• I enlisted in the *Navy* to escape the Army draft.(p.425)
• I went into the *Navy* in fine style.(p.425)
• While waiting to depart I was selected -- by giving a CPO five dollars -- to be bartender in the *Navy* Chief's Club.(p.426)
• That doctor in the *Navy* hospital told me I wouldn't live five years if I didn't quit.(p.429)
• Then I joined the *Navy* and was commissioned as an ensign to write speeches for admirals.(p.555)
• In the last year of my *navy* service, I was married to a lovely, lively girl, who enjoyed drinking.(p.555)

NBC
• Dr. W.W. Bauer, broadcasting under the auspices of The American Medical Association in 1946, over the *NBC* network, said, in part: "Alcoholics Anonymous are no crusaders; not a temperance society.(p.572)

ne'er
• A good soldier is *ne'er* forgot Whether he dieth by musket Or by pot."(p.1)

near
• I began to wonder, for such an appalling lack of perspective seemed *near* being just that.(p.5)
• *Near* the end of that bleak November, I sat drinking in my kitchen.(p.8)
• I wondered whether I dared hide a full bottle of gin *near* the head of our bed.(p.8)
• Others came *near* putting Galileo to death for his astronomical heresies.(p.51)
• When we drew *near* to Him He disclosed Himself to us!(p.57)
• Death was often *near*.(p.107)
• *Near* you, alcoholics are dying helplessly like people in a sinking ship.(p.152)
• Alcoholics are being attracted from far and *near*.(p.161)
• I remember nothing from then on until I woke up at a friend's house, in a town *near* home.(p.179)
• But at no time have I been anywhere *near* yielding.(p.181)
• *Near* success, only *near*.(p.197)
• Many things happened; business trials, little worries, and feelings of general despondency came *near* driving me to the bottle, but I made progress.(p.237)
• Coming out of a pub *near* the Cunard pier I saw the Lusitania standing out in the middle of the Mersey.(p.252)
• I'm pretty *near* afraid of Labor Day yet.(p.264)
• One morning after a terrific drinking bout, I was in a little bar *near* our house, and I shook so that I was very much ashamed, because I was getting the shakes worse and worse.(p.266)

• I do recall lying on a cold cement floor and shredding into little bits several pieces of stolen identification cards, and washing my face in the toilet bowl trying to sober up, and screaming hysterically while clinging to bars too high to see out of, and cursing everyone that came ***near*** me.(p.354)
• ***Near*** the Laundromat, I would buy one bottle of pop and a few bottles of beer or wine, and go into the rest room, empty the pop bottle, refill it with the booze, and proceed to do my laundering.(p.370)
• Until I reached A.A. my life was a shambles; I was a mess, and I made everybody ***near*** and dear to me miserable.(p.400)
• At one end of the bed, ***near*** the foot, was a printed card, and beneath that was a charted graph.(p.422)
• Pearl Harbor was a breeze of nine months, a gay Hawaiian paradise, drinking under the palms, listening to the surf beat on the shore, a bottle of whiskey ***near*** at hand.(p.426)
• She is ***near*** the end now and is in a hospital.(p.501)
• So instead of going ***near*** A.A., I just browsed around for that first month.(p.510)
• The children kept me sober for darn ***near*** three weeks, and then I went on (please God) my last drunk.(p.549)

near-wreck

• His friends have slipped away, his home is a ***near-wreck*** and he cannot hold a position.(p.110)

nearby

• Some days later, after he had been discharged, a stranger came into my shop in the ***nearby*** town.(p.257)
• I spent the time in a ***nearby*** tavern, was loaded on the ship, went to sleep before take-off, and the next thing I knew someone was shaking me and telling me we were over San Diego.(p.428)
• In the ***nearby*** little town there was a plumber who once had tried to get an A.A. group going.(p.541)
• My mother went to a ***nearby*** city to go to work, and my father, being an alcoholic, simply went.(p.544)
• If there is none ***nearby***, you will be invited to carry on a correspondence which will do much to insure your sobriety no matter how isolated you are.(p.575)

nearer

• We have told small tots that father was sick, which was much ***nearer*** the truth than we realized.(p.106)
• They got bigger and bigger and ***nearer*** and ***nearer***, as if they were going to fall and crush me.(p.427)
• All of my family and loved ones, all of my friends, are ***nearer*** and dearer to me than ever before and I have literally dozens of new friends who say they cannot believe that a short eight years ago I was ready for the scrap heap.(p.541)

nearest

• Step over to the ***nearest*** barroom and try some controlled drinking.(p.31)
• It was February with snow and ice on the ground and I had a four blocks walk to the ***nearest*** cab stand, but I made it.(p.288)
• On my ride to the ***nearest*** bar, I sold the driver on how misunderstood I was by my wife and what an unreasonable person she was.(p.288)
• On the train going back, Anne's one idea was to get to the ***nearest*** bar.(p.415)
• If you cannot find A.A. in your locality, a letter addressed to Alcoholics Anonymous, Box 459, Grand Central Station, New York, NY 10163, U.S.A., will receive a prompt reply from this world center, referring you to the ***nearest*** A.A. group.(p.575)
• This headquarters will give the location of the ***nearest*** family group and will if you wish, correspond with you about your special problems.(p.575)

nearing

• His call to the clergyman led him presently to a certain resident of the town, who, though formerly able and respected, was then ***nearing*** the nadir of alcoholic despair.(p.155)

nearly

• In Part III ("They Lost *Nearly* All"), eight stories have been retained; five are new.(p.xii)
• In that brief space, Alcoholics Anonymous has mushroomed into ***nearly*** 6,000 groups whose membership is far above 150,000 recovered alcoholics.(p.xv)
• Women now make up more than one-fourth of the membership; among newer members, the proportion is ***nearly*** one-third.(p.xxii)
• In ***nearly*** all cases, their ideals must be grounded in a power greater than themselves, if they are to re-create their lives.(p.xxvi)
• Potential alcoholic that I was, I ***nearly*** failed my law course.(p.2)
• This sometimes ***nearly*** drove me back to drink, but I soon found that when all other measures failed, work with another alcoholic would save the day.(p.15)
• ***Nearly*** all have recovered.(p.17)
• A few are fortunate enough to be so situated that they can give ***nearly*** all their time to the work.(p.19)
• What they say will apply to ***nearly*** everyone bound by ties of blood or affections to an alcoholic.(p.104)
• Of course, there is such a thing as incompatibility, but in ***nearly*** every instance the alcoholic only seems to be unloving and inconsiderate; it is usually because he is warped and sickened that he says and does these appalling things.(p.108)
• ***Nearly*** every modern employer feels a moral responsibility for the well-being of his help, and he tries to meet these responsibilities.(p.137)
• ***Nearly*** always, these antics indicate nothing more than temporary conditions.(p.141)
• THEY LOST ***NEARLY*** ALL(p.167)
• As I write ***nearly*** four years have passed.(p.180)
• Bill then related how he had lain awake ***nearly*** all night.(p.189)
• He tossed off half of his martini; I tossed off half of mine and it ***nearly*** blew the top of my head off.(p.195)
• I remember well one fellow, Joe, walking ***nearly*** three miles through slush, wet and snow to come to the hospital to see a man that he had never seen before in his life, and that impressed me very much.(p.208)
• It has continued to work now for ***nearly*** eighteen years.(p.209)
• That was skeptically received by me when I first heard it, but after some twenty-eight or thirty fellows had come to see me, and pretty ***nearly*** all of them had said the same thing, I began to believe it.(p.219)
• Despite great opportunities, alcohol ***nearly*** ended her life.(p.222)
• The second year my drinking was more or less restricted to week-ends, but I was ***nearly*** kicked out for scholastic failure.(p.241)
• I wasn't ***nearly*** in the condition I had been in many times to be picked up.(p.264)
• Dr. Bob dwelt at length on how prayer had given him release, time and time again, from the ***nearly*** over-powering compulsion to take a drink.(p.279)
• Only once did I suffer from a ***nearly*** overpowering compulsion to take a drink.(p.285)
• One is that I don't remember too many of them, as I was one of those drunks who could be on his feet and attend a meeting or a party, engage in a conversation with people and do things that any ***nearly*** normal person would do, and the next day not remember a thing about where I was, what I did, whom I saw, or how I got home.(p.301)
• My wife accompanied me on my visit and the doctor really told me some things that in my state of jitters ***nearly*** knocked me out of the chair.(p.302)
• The next three years saw me in sanitariums, once in a ten day coma, from which I very ***nearly*** did not recover, in and out of hospitals or confined at home with day and night nurses.(p.306)
• I started my drinking ***nearly*** thirty years ago – right after I was married.(p.322)
• I was now ***nearly*** eighteen.(p.425)
• This combination ***nearly*** threw me.(p.430)
• I was now head of a publishing venture in which ***nearly*** a million dollars had been invested.(p.435)
• THEY LOST ***NEARLY*** ALL(p.455)
• Most had taken shattering losses on ***nearly*** every front of life.(p.455)
• We always, or ***nearly*** always, had good intentions when we were released from prison.(p.458)
• I ***nearly*** reverted to my old, incorrigible self – had trouble with a couple of other prisoners, was planning an escape.(p.461)
• I attempted ***nearly*** two years ago to make some amends and contact my children, but it wasn't God's time yet.(p.463)
• My visits to that sanitarium went on for ***nearly*** three years, until in March of 1944, my father died and I was too drunk to attend his funeral.(p.469)
• At one time, I was using twenty caps a day; I ***nearly*** died half a dozen times on the street.(p.480)
• The term was ***nearly*** over and we parted on fairly friendly terms.(p.518)
• To learn to live, he ***nearly*** died.(p.531)
• After ***nearly*** eight years of sobriety in A.A., I still can set down such thoughts, "against my instinct and training," showing that I still consider myself a "special" person, entitled to special privileges.(p.536)
• From that instant to this, ***nearly*** eight years later, I have not had the slightest urge to drink.(p.541)
• There were debts totaling ***nearly*** ten thousand dollars to be paid off.(p.541)

nearness

• We begin to feel the ***nearness*** of our Creator.(p.75)

neat

• Marty came in, looking clean, ***neat***, well-dressed and, like Bill, she was neither a bloated wreck nor a reformer.(p.413)

neatly

• But his face falls when we speak of spiritual matters, especially when we mention God, for we have reopened a subject which our man thought he had ***neatly*** evaded or entirely ignored.(p.45)

necessarily

• To be gravely affected, one does not ***necessarily*** have to drink a long time nor take the quantities some of us have.(p.33)
• Our experience shows that this is not ***necessarily*** so.(p.101)
• Father will ***necessarily*** spend much time with other alcoholics, but this activity should be balanced.(p.131)
• Prior to our marriage, when she was a shy, scrawny adolescent, I was able to see things in her that others couldn't ***necessarily*** see -- things like beauty, charm, gaiety, a gift for being easy to talk to, a sense of humor, and many other fine qualities.(p.450)

necessary

• For them, we hope these pages will prove so convincing that no further authentication will be ***necessary***.(p.xiii)
• On the other hand -- and strange as this may seem to those who do not understand -- once a psychic change has occurred, the very same person who seemed doomed, who had so many problems he despaired of ever solving them, suddenly finds himself easily able to control his desire for alcohol, the only effort ***necessary*** being that required to follow a few simple rules.(p.xxvii)
• This hope, however, was destroyed by the doctor's telling him that while his religious convictions were very good, in his case they did not spell the ***necessary*** vital spiritual experience.(p.27)
• Many of us thought it ***necessary*** to go much further.(p.72)
• But they had not learned enough of humility, fearlessness and honesty, in the sense we find it ***necessary***, until they told someone else all their life story.(p.73)
• We thought he ought to be willing to do that if ***necessary***, but if he were in jail he could provide nothing for either family.(p.79)
• He is positive he can handle his liquor, that it does him no harm, that drinking is ***necessary*** in his business.(p.109)
• Patience and good temper are most ***necessary***.(p.111)
• Will he take every ***necessary*** step, submit to anything to get well, to stop drinking forever?(p.142)
• If you propose such a procedure to him, it may be ***necessary*** to advance the cost of treatment, but we believe it should be made plain that any expense will later be deducted from his pay.(p.143)
• This work is ***necessary*** to maintain his sobriety.(p.146)
• A spiritual experience, he conceded, was absolutely ***necessary***, but the price seemed high upon the basis suggested.(p.155)
• On the third day the lawyer gave his life to the care and direction of his Creator, and said he was perfectly willing to do anything ***necessary***.(p.158)
• All sorts were represented and their relation of experiences and how they had found the only remedy, added to their human existence as sober men, laid the foundation of a very ***necessary*** faith.(p.258)
• No conviction was ***necessary*** to establish my status as a miserable failure at managing my own life.(p.259)
• However, as there happened to be several saloons within that distance, I didn't find it ***necessary*** to patronize the same place each evening.(p.298)
• It wasn't ***necessary*** to report to the office in person every day, and when I did go in, it was just to make an appearance and bounce right out again.(p.300)
• And all the while my fear fed a growing conviction that before long it would be ***necessary*** for me to be put away in some institution.(p.306)
• I had my first drink when I was fifteen and my alcoholic potential had ripened me to the point of ***necessary*** escapism.(p.353)
• I was going to prove to her that liquor wasn't ***necessary*** in my life, and above all that I still loved her more than anything else in the world and that I wanted her back.(p.362)
• It now became ***necessary*** to have noon drinks; at first just two, then gradually more.(p.375)
• I couldn't walk, having it in a cast, and the doctor left the cast on three weeks longer than was ***necessary***

because he never found me sober enough to take it off.(p.390)
• Drunkalogues and statistics can be boring, but it is ***necessary*** to delve a little into each in order to come up with some kind of rough estimate.(p.396)
• It became more and more ***necessary*** to escape from myself, for my remorse and shame and humiliation when I was sober were almost unbearable.(p.547)
• My desire to be honest with myself made it ***necessary*** for me to realize that my thinking was irrational.(p.550)
• Secondary aids to A.A., such as clubs or hospitals which require much property or administration, ought to be incorporated and so set apart that, if ***necessary***, they can be freely discarded by the groups.(p.566)

necessitated

• A low ebb in the family fortunes ***necessitated*** my going to work when I was twenty.(p.275)
• Poor health and a complete lack of money ***necessitated*** my remaining with Dr. Bob and Anne for very close to a year.(p.280)
• That fear, of course, ***necessitated*** a program of hidden alcoholism.(p.331)

necessities

• You, as a business man, want to know the ***necessities*** before considering the result.(p.140)

necessity

• Though he could not accept all the tenets of the Oxford Groups, he was convinced of the need for moral inventory, confession of personality defects, restitution to those harmed, helpfulness to others, and the ***necessity*** of belief in and dependence upon God.(p.xvi)
• Liquor ceased to be a luxury; it became a ***necessity***.(p.5)
• My friend had emphasized the absolute ***necessity*** of demonstrating these principles in all my affairs.(p.14)
• Of ***necessity*** there will have to be discussion of matters medical, psychiatric, social, and religious.(p.19)
• This is the baffling feature of alcoholism as we know it -- this utter inability to leave it alone, no matter how great the ***necessity*** or the wish.(p.34)
• One set of voices cry that sex is a lust of our lower nature, a base ***necessity*** of procreation.(p.68)
• Notwithstanding the great ***necessity*** for discussing ourselves with someone, it may be one is so situated that there is no suitable person available.(p.74)
• Hangovers began to assume monstrous proportions and the morning drink became an urgent ***necessity***.(p.226)
• My "periodics" became more frequent until I reached the point where I wanted to devote all my time to drinking, working as little as possible, and then only when the ***necessity*** of my family demanded it.(p.234)
• In those days my system was always to drink up my last pay check and believe that ***necessity*** would bring the next job.(p.256)
• I would hang on to sobriety for short intervals, but always there would come the tide of an overpowering ***necessity*** to drink and, as I was engulfed in it, I felt such a sense of panic that I really believed I would die if I didn't get that drink inside.(p.306)
• However, this isn't as rough as it sounds, as we do become grateful for the ***necessity*** that makes us toe the line, for we find that we are more than compensated for a consistent effort by the countless dividends we receive.(p.311)
• There was the ***necessity*** for sticking to a job I hated, a dull, repetitive job performed in association with other men I had nothing in common with . . . performed for years on end, because the money was needed at home.(p.532)

neck

• I had bad nervous headaches, particularly at the base of my ***neck***.(p.277)
• In the long ago past I used to start at the top as president or treasurer and end up with the sheriff breathing down my ***neck***.(p.284)
• I wonder if it will reach her ***neck***.(p.497)

necks

• No more snoops or big shots breathing down our ***necks***.(p.329)

need

• Though he could not accept all the tenets of the Oxford Groups, he was convinced of the ***need*** for moral inventory, confession of personality defects, restitution to those harmed, helpfulness to others, and the necessity of belief in and dependence upon God.(p.xvi)
• Then Jack Alexander wrote a feature article in the Saturday Evening Post and placed such a compelling picture of A.A. before the general public that alcoholics in ***need*** of help really deluged us.(p.xviii)
• When I ***need*** a mental uplift, I often think of another case brought in by a physician prominent in New York.(p.xxix)
• They did not ***need*** to tell me.(p.7)
• I would ***need*** it before daylight.(p.8)
• Most of us feel we ***need*** look no further for Utopia.(p.16)
• If a sufficiently strong reason – ill health, falling in love, change of environment, or the warning of a doctor – becomes operative, this man can also stop or moderate, although he may find it difficult and troublesome and may even ***need*** medical attention.(p.21)
• He does not ***need*** a bodyguard nor is he confined.(p.26)
• Our hope is that many alcoholic men and women, desperately in ***need***, will see these pages, and we believe that it is only by fully disclosing ourselves and our problems that they will be persuaded to say, "Yes, I am one of them too; I must have this thing."(p.29)
• Our experience shows that you ***need*** not be disconcerted.(p.44)
• Much to our relief, we discovered we did not ***need*** to consider another's conception of God.(p.46)
• Experience has taught us that these are matters about which, for our purpose, we [illegible] not be worried.(p.50)
• Now we ***need*** more action, without which we find that "Faith without works is dead."(p.76)
• To some people we ***need*** not, and probably should not emphasize the spiritual feature on our first approach.(p.76)
• We usually conclude the period of meditation with a prayer that we be shown all through the day what our next step is to be, that we be given whatever we ***need*** to take care of such problems.(p.87)
• You ***need*** this information to put yourself in his place, to see how you would like him to approach you if the tables were turned.(p.90)
• Your candidate may give reasons why he ***need*** not follow all of the program.(p.94)
• You have to act the Good Samaritan every day, if ***need*** be.(p.97)
• If you answer these questions satisfactorily, you ***need*** have no apprehension.(p.102)
• We often ***need*** it to carry green recruits through a severe hangover.(p.102)
• They ***need*** your companionship and your help.(p.111)
• While you ***need*** not discuss your husband at length, you can quietly let your friends know the nature of his illness.(p.115)
• Unless they actually ***need*** protection from their father, it is best not to take sides in any argument he has with them while drinking.(p.115)
• But it was a silly idea that we were too good to ***need*** God.(p.116)
• If you both show a willingness to remedy your own defects, there will be little ***need*** to criticize each other.(p.118)
• They ***need*** the counsel and love of a woman who has gone through what you have.(p.119)
• Therefore, you probably ***need*** fresh interests and a great cause to live for as much as your husband.(p.119)
• If you are satisfied he really wants to get over drinking, you ***need*** not be alarmed.(p.120)
• You ***need*** not remind him of his spiritual deficiency - he will know of it.(p.120)
• You may ***need*** to encourage him to play once in a while.(p.146)
• He ***need*** not, and often should not show it to his alcoholic prospect.(p.148)
• They explained their ***need*** and inquired if she had a first class alcoholic prospect.(p.156)
• We believe and hope it contains all you will ***need*** to begin.(p.163)
• I spend a great deal of time passing on what I learned to others who want and ***need*** it badly.(p.180)
• I didn't have any ***need*** of such an association!(p.206)
• He said, "Maybe you ***need*** a little drink."(p.208)
• My life was fairly well crowded and I didn't seem to ***need*** any stimulants to keep me going.(p.213)
• He wasn't a drinking man, he didn't know what it was to ***need*** a drink, nor what a drink could do for one in a pinch.(p.227)
• More and more I formed the habit of doing some of my business in the speakeasy, and after a time I did not ***need*** that as an excuse.(p.233)
• Then I got a very good position in Philadelphia and quickly found I would ***need*** a few fellow alcoholics around me if I was to stay sober.(p.249)
• ***Need*** I say that in a very short time I was walking along a prairie highway with arm extended and thumb pointed?(p.255)
• I did not ***need*** to be told that my efforts were and would be unavailing if I did not get help.(p.258)
• The doctor who came to see me almost at once did not assail me with any new doctrines; he made sure that I had a ***need*** and that I wanted to have that ***need*** filled, and little by little I learned how my ***need*** could be met.(p.258)
• We talked about it afterwards, and we felt that there might be some time we'd ***need*** it.(p.266)
• Their answer was always the same: If they should ***need*** it at any time they would surely get in touch with me.(p.293)
• Eventually, of course, what with all the hilarity that could be provoked with a few gallons of beer, there seemed to be no ***need*** of bridge or poker playing for entertainment.(p.297)
• Nothing in their lives took precedence over their response to a call for help from some alcoholic in ***need***.(p.310)
• That ache is gone and never ***need*** return again.(p.312)
• Everyone was against me -- I'd show them I didn't ***need*** them.(p.318)
• We ***need*** them so badly even if you can only give one day, or perhaps two days?"(p.326)
• The ***need*** to uphold a facade had been irksome.(p.328)
• We're free at last to do our thing, to live uninhibited lives, to drink when and how and where we wish, when we want to and when we ***need*** to.(p.329)
• I had no ***need*** to hide in closets, bathrooms, or garages.(p.332)
• Mere cessation from drinking is not enough for an alcoholic while the ***need*** for that drink goes on.(p.339)
• A.A. gives us alcoholics direction into a way of life without the ***need*** for alcohol.(p.340)
• We did, and spent a month boozing it up, popping pills, and smoking marijuana; taking shelter where we could, which included a veterinary hospital one night; accepting meals from anyone; actually begging; stealing anything we were in ***need*** of, which was about everything.(p.354)
• Many good A.A.'s never join a church, and do not ***need*** to.(p.417)
• I seldom left the base any more except once in a while when I felt the ***need*** of talking to some girl.(p.427)
• If they were around, I always found a ***need*** for them – especially the pills.(p.443)
• I ***need*** to concentrate not so much on what needs to be changed in the world as on what needs to be changed in me and in my attitudes.(p.449)
• When you come in here, you find the understanding that you ***need***.(p.516)
• It has taught me that I can best keep my sobriety by sharing it out with others; that I must bring that sobriety to others who ***need*** it, in my own interest.(p.524)
• ***Need*** I add that such was the case because I had no money to provide a roof over my head?(p.538)
• I wish we did not have to have jails; I wish everyone could be in A.A., and if everyone were there would be no ***need*** for jails, in my opinion.(p.542)
• And if I had been able to turn to the church at that time I'm sure they could not have convinced me my sickness was within myself, nor could they have shown me the ***need*** for self-analysis that A.A. has shown me is vital if I am to survive.(p.546)
• I attended my first A.A. meeting eight years ago, and it is with deep gratitude that I'm able to say I've not had a drink since that time, and that I take no sedation or narcotics, for this program is to me one of complete sobriety and I no longer ***need*** to escape reality.(p.549)
• This great experience that released me from the bondage of hatred and replaced it with love is really just another affirmation of the truth I know: I get everything I ***need*** in Alcoholics Anonymous – everything I ***need*** I get -- and when I get what I ***need*** I invariably find that it was just what I wanted all the time.(p.553)
• So the ***need*** to drink grew still greater.(p.557)
• Therefore, no society of men and women ever had more urgent ***need*** for continuous effectiveness and permanent unity.(p.563)
• Eleven -- Our public relations policy is based on attraction rather than promotion; we ***need*** always maintain personal anonymity at the level of press, radio and films.(p.564)
• There is never ***need*** to praise ourselves.(p.567)
• We find that no one ***need*** have difficulty with the spirituality of the program.(p.570)

needed

• One feels that something more than human power is ***needed*** to produce the essential

psychic change.(p.xxvii)
• For a brief moment, I had ***needed*** and wanted God.(p.12)
• We could wish to be moral, we could wish to be philosophically comforted, in fact, we could will these things with all our might, but the ***needed*** power wasn't there.(p.45)
• At the start, this was all we ***needed*** to commence spiritual growth, to effect our first conscious relation with God as we understood Him.(p.47)
• We ***needed*** to ask ourselves but one short question.(p.47)
• Being all powerful, He provided what we ***needed***, if we kept close to Him and performed His work well.(p.63)
• Many of us ***needed*** an overhauling there.(p.68)
• For the type of alcoholic who is able and willing to get well, little charity, in the ordinary sense of the word, is ***needed*** or wanted.(p.97)
• At first, some of us did not believe we ***needed*** this help.(p.116)
• No beer or liquor was sold in the neighborhood, except at the State liquor agency where perhaps one might procure a pint if he could convince the agent that he really ***needed*** it.(p.171)
• If I could, that was wonderful, that was just fine, and they would very much appreciate a person who had that kind of power, but they were looking for a man that knew he had a problem, and knew that he couldn't handle it himself and ***needed*** outside help.(p.186)
• Not far from where I lived they built a new technical high school and one of the teachers sold me on the idea that I ***needed*** a little mechanical drawing if I were going to be a good toolmaker.(p.211)
• All I had left was an iron determination to live my own life in spite of the alien world -- and here I was, an inwardly frightened, outwardly defiant woman, who desperately ***needed*** a prop to keep going.(p.226)
• I had to persist in my attempts to get straightened out enough to be able to use the drinks I ***needed***, without their turning on me.(p.227)
• I was an intellectual and I ***needed*** an intellectual answer, not an emotional one.(p.227)
• In a few sentences he made God seem personal to me, explained Him as a being who was interested in me, the alcoholic, and that all I ***needed*** to do was to be willing to follow His way; that as long as I followed it I would be able to overcome my desire for liquor.(p.236)
• I knew they ***needed*** to straighten out their thinking and habits, but I was all right, I just drank too much.(p.246)
• My family would have nothing to do with me, in fact couldn't because I couldn't spare any of my money, which I ***needed*** for drink, to support them.(p.255)
• And then he got us to laugh, which was what we ***needed***.(p.269)
• Now there is a sense of belonging, of being wanted and ***needed*** and loved.(p.312)
• I ***needed*** a drink, but I was afraid to take a morning drink, because I didn't want to be a drunk.(p.323)
• My alcoholism-prone mind, however, reminded me that all great authors had ***needed*** a stimulus to build up inspiration and inventiveness before each day's work.(p.331)
• How hurt I was when editors bounced back my ideas quickly and my best friends opined that my output ***needed*** a lot of rewriting.(p.331)
• I agreed it was great stuff -- for those who ***needed*** it.(p.332)
• I was sure those who ***needed*** a bit of the hair of the dog really were alcoholics.(p.332)
• I ***needed*** it, and I knew I was drinking too much, but I wasn't conscious of the fact that I should stop.(p.336)
• I had to have it with me at night, in case I woke up and ***needed*** that drink.(p.337)
• I ***needed*** that alcohol.(p.337)
• Well, of course that was all I ***needed*** -- to switch from wine to brandy for three weeks.(p.338)
• What I ***needed*** was a change, mental relaxation, getting out and doing something.(p.338)
• I still had to drink; I still ***needed*** that drink.(p.339)
• I ***needed*** alcohol from that night on, and it in turn used me, ruling my life for three years.(p.353)
• One of the things I ***needed*** badly was business for the station.(p.360)
• I took two or three drinks so my eyes could focus, and I could see that horrible picture of the awful drunk on the first page; he couldn't get the drink to his mouth, he had a towel around his hand and he ***needed*** a shave.(p.391)
• They sent me the regular letter they send to everybody else, but along with it, Ruth Hock, the nonalcoholic secretary, wrote a longhand note because she could see from the letter that I really ***needed*** help badly.(p.392)
• Monday morning I was feeling just like a million dollars -- all I ***needed*** was half a pint!(p.393)
• They really ***needed*** it.(p.427)
• "If you had my responsibilities, if you ***needed*** the sleep like I do, you'd drink too."(p.441)
• It seemed to me I ***needed*** a consultation first.(p.444)
• Through A.A., many receive the ***needed*** change and awakening just by trying to live by A.A. principles and associating with A.A. people.(p.459)
• The doctor, apparently realizing that one thing that I certainly ***needed*** was sleep, left a bottle of sleeping pills there and in my drunken state I took them all, instead of the one or two he had prescribed.(p.465)
• I'm grateful because that Higher Power led me to A.A. a little over three years ago, when I ***needed*** it very badly.(p.512)
• Once I started drinking, I didn't care that the rent wasn't paid, or that there was no food in the house, or that my boys ***needed*** shoes.(p.527)
• There was the necessity for sticking to a job I hated, a dull, repetitive job performed in association with other men I had nothing in common with . . . performed for years on end, because the money was ***needed*** at home.(p.532)
• I thought that life was a pretty simple thing; you simply made a plan for your life, based upon what you wanted, and then you ***needed*** only the courage to go after it.(p.545)
• As our children grew up, I was able to be a father to them when they most ***needed*** one.(p.559)

needing
• To go into a gathering of people was the sort of thing that all my life, from the time I left my private world of books and dreams to meet the real world of people and parties and jobs, had left me feeling an uncomfortable outsider, ***needing*** the warming stimulus of drinks to join in.(p.228)

needle
• No prickling consciences to ***needle*** us with guilt feelings.(p.329)
• That's the stuff used when the oral surgeon puts the ***needle*** in your vein and says, "Count to ten," and before you get to two, you're asleep.(p.442)
• In the garage, I would put the ***needle*** in my vein and then try to figure out exactly how much medication to inject to overcome the pep pills while adding to the sleeping pills while ignoring the tranquilizers, in order to get just enough to be able to pull out the ***needle***, jerk the tourniquet, throw it in the car, slam the car door shut, run down the hall, and fall in bed before I fell asleep.(p.442)

needless
• The employer cannot play favorites, but he can always defend a man from ***needless*** provocation and unfair criticism.(p.146)
• ***Needless*** to say, it was a year or more before they did contact me.(p.293)
• ***Needless*** to say, this was not pleasurable drinking.(p.306)

needlessly
• Therefore, we are not to be the hasty and foolish martyr who would ***needlessly*** sacrifice others to save himself from the alcoholic pit.(p.79)
• It is better, however, that one does not ***needlessly*** name a person upon whom she can vent jealously.(p.82)
• Tell him you have been worried, though perhaps ***needlessly***.(p.112)

needn't
• Make it clear that he is not under pressure, that he ***needn't*** see you again if he doesn't want to.(p.94)

needs
• Our very lives, as ex-problem drinkers, depend upon our constant thought of others and how we may help meet their ***needs***.(p.20)
• We read wordy books and indulge in windy arguments, thinking we believe this universe ***needs*** no God to explain it.(p.49)
• We think of their ***needs*** and work for them.(p.70)
• Sometimes we hear an alcoholic say that the only thing he ***needs*** to do is to keep sober.(p.82)
• Don't deal with him when he is very drunk, unless he is ugly and the family ***needs*** your help.(p.90)
• If your man ***needs*** hospitalization, he should have it, but not forcibly unless he is violent.(p.91)
• He clamors for this or that, claiming he cannot master alcohol until his material ***needs*** are cared for.(p.98)
• New acquaintances who know nothing of alcoholism might be made and thoughtful consideration given their ***needs***.(p.131)
• It may be just the jolt he ***needs***.(p.141)
• Part of that program is that we take it to someone else, that ***needs*** it and wants it.(p.186)
• You should go out and take this program to somebody else that ***needs*** it and wants it."(p.190)
• If he thinks he ***needs*** to go to the hospital, I'll pay for him."(p.271)
• I yelled at Max, "What do you mean, 'The dog just ***needs*** more love'?(p.440)
• I need to concentrate not so much on what ***needs*** to be changed in the world as on what ***needs*** to be changed in me and in my attitudes.(p.449)
• Am I willing to be honest with myself about myself and tell someone about myself, and am I willing to think of other people, of their ***needs*** instead of myself, in order to get rid of the drink problem?(p.503)
• We are taught to differentiate between our wants (which are never satisfied) and our ***needs*** (which are always provided for).(p.560)
• 9. -- Each A.A. group ***needs*** the least possible organization.(p.567)

neglect
• Though an alcoholic does not respond, there is no reason why you should ***neglect*** his family.(p.97)
• Even if he displays a certain amount of ***neglect*** and irresponsibility towards the family, it is well to let him go as far as he likes in helping other alcoholics.(p.129)
• I didn't want to ***neglect*** my children.(p.199)
• But I did ***neglect*** them.(p.199)

neglected
• Your wife may sometimes say she is ***neglected***.(p.97)
• The family will be affected also, pleasantly at first, as they feel their money troubles are about to be solved, then not so pleasantly as they find themselves ***neglected***.(p.126)
• Having been ***neglected*** and misused in the past, they think father owes them more than they are getting.(p.126)
• With that profit, I built a number of houses, but then I ***neglected*** them.(p.194)
• I worked along until I had really big names in rubber on a tentative contract, and then I ***neglected*** to go through with it.(p.198)

neglectful
• Sometimes he will be so interested that he becomes really ***neglectful***.(p.119)

negligible
• Judging from what I had seen in Europe and since, the power of God in human affairs was ***negligible***, the Brotherhood of Man a grim jest.(p.11)

Negro
• My father, a ***Negro***, was a country physician.(p.483)

Negroes
• The only thing that bothers me is that there are only about five ***Negroes*** in A.A. in my city.(p.529)
• I do think that some of the ***Negroes*** here -- and other places, too -- are afraid to go to other meetings.(p.529)

neighbor
• You will learn the full meaning of "Love thy ***neighbor*** as thyself."(p.153)
• He went on talking and told me that he had found the plan has a basis of love, and the practice of Christ's injunction, "Love thy ***neighbor*** as thyself."(p.236)

neighbor's
• Very soon after I lost Mother, my five-year-old little girl was killed by a ***neighbor's*** car.(p.370)

neighborhood
• No beer or liquor was sold in the ***neighborhood***, except at the State liquor agency where perhaps one might procure a pint if he could convince the agent that he really needed it.(p.171)
• There were, at that time, in the ***neighborhood*** of twelve or thirteen Cleveland members who had been sober anywhere from a year and a half to a couple of months.(p.219)
• Very rarely do I miss the meetings of my ***neighborhood*** A.A. group, and my average has never been less than two meetings a week.(p.249)
• I got an easy, part-time job selling printing for a small ***neighborhood*** printer.(p.276)
• There was one girl especially, and I'd watch her from my window every morning, leaving faithfully to go to the hospital in the ***neighborhood***.(p.326)
• In my drinking days, I found the ideal spot for the alcoholic housewife: the ***neighborhood*** Laundromat.(p.369)

neighboring
• But when its plans concern the welfare of ***neighbor-***

ing groups also, those groups ought to be consulted.(p.565)

neighbors

- "Well," I said to dad, when the A.A. people kept coming with these lovely cars and looked so nice, "I suppose the ***neighbors*** say, 'Now those old fools must have up and died, but where's the hearse?'"(p.269)
- He said they were sober, happy and had their self-respect back as well as the respect of their ***neighbors***.(p.289)
- Many of my ***neighbors*** devoted time to volunteer work.(p.326)
- All this while, I wondered whether I could do laundry for the ***neighbors*** as a part-time job.(p.371)
- Sometimes I'd make it home and go to sleep at the wheel of my car, for all the ***neighbors*** to see next morning as they left for work.(p.429)

neither

- ***Neither*** does A.A. take any particular medical point of view, though we cooperate widely with the men of medicine as well as with the men of religion.(p.xx)
- I simply had to believe in a Spirit of the Universe, who knew ***neither*** time nor limitation.(p.10)
- ***Neither*** does there appear to be any kind of treatment which will make alcoholics of our kind like other men.(p.30)
- ***Neither*** did I have any pressing problems or worries.(p.41)
- Except in a few rare cases, ***neither*** he nor any other human being can provide such a defense.(p.43)
- ***Neither*** is reason, as most of us use it, entirely dependable, though it emanate from our best minds.(p.54)
- ***Neither*** could we reduce our self-centeredness much by wishing or trying on our own power.(p.62)
- We remembered always that our sex powers were God-given and therefore good, ***neither*** to be used lightly or selfishly nor to be despised and loathed.(p.69)
- We are not fighting it, ***neither*** are we avoiding temptation.(p.85)
- We are ***neither*** cocky nor are we afraid.(p.85)
- ***Neither*** should the family hysterically plead with him to do anything, nor should they tell him much about you.(p.90)
- Though he is now a most effective member of Alcoholics Anonymous, he still smokes and drinks coffee, but ***neither*** his wife or anyone else stands in judgment.(p.135)
- At that time I was not aware of the almost unlimited supply the government made it possible for us doctors to obtain, ***neither*** had I any knowledge of the bootlegger who soon appeared on the horizon.(p.175)
- From the top of the heap in a few years he had skidded to becoming a shuffling customer, still entering the better barrooms but welcomed by ***neither*** mine host nor his patrons.(p.236)
- My family lived in very prosperous circumstances, and while both my parents drank, sometimes too much, ***neither*** was an alcoholic.(p.240)
- ***Neither*** can I honestly say that I have forgotten the "fleshpots of Egypt."(p.259)
- The next day he turned me over to a couple who, although ***neither*** was an alcoholic, knew Dr. Bob and were willing to drive me to Akron where they would turn me over to his care.(p.278)
- ***Neither*** one of the two was interested for himself, one being a mother who wanted to do something for her son.(p.294)
- Karen didn't want to see me any more, and ***neither*** did two other girls I'd been going out with.(p.318)
- They were ***neither*** poor nor wealthy, but far better off than the average couple.(p.357)
- ***Neither*** of these circumstances was very helpful to my type since I had not learned to face realities.(p.358)
- ***Neither*** did I.(p.377)
- Marty came in, looking clean, neat, well-dressed and, like Bill, she was ***neither*** a bloated wreck nor a reformer.(p.413)
- I ***neither*** drank nor smoked until I was nineteen years old.(p.419)
- (That dog hasn't wet my pants once since I joined A.A., and ***neither*** have I!)(p.440)
- Alcoholism had respected nobody, ***neither*** rich nor poor, learned nor unlettered.(p.455)
- It has taught me that success and failure are never final, and that ***neither*** count for very much in the final assessment of any man who has done his best.(p.525)

nerve

- He is straining every ***nerve*** to make up for lost time.(p.126)
- I would walk up and down under the 59th Street bridge, trying to get up the ***nerve*** to go up there and jump.(p.411)

nerves

- My writhing ***nerves*** were stilled at last.(p.6)
- As matters grow worse, he begins to use a combination of high-powered sedative and liquor to quiet his ***nerves*** so he can go to work.(p.22)
- Far from admitting he was an alcoholic, he told himself he came to the hospital to rest his ***nerves***.(p.39)
- I was between Scylla and Charybdis now, because if I did not drink my stomach tortured me, and if I did, my ***nerves*** did the same thing.(p.175)
- Between classes I would run down to the wash room, take enough to steady my ***nerves*** and then go on to the next class.(p.183)
- Cold sweats, jumpy ***nerves*** and lack of sleep were becoming intolerable.(p.378)
- I got a job by myself which suited me down to the ground, because there was nobody really to interfere with what I did, one way or the other, and I usually had my ***nerves*** in good trim when anybody was coming around to inspect.(p.519)

nervous

- From a trembling, despairing ***nervous*** wreck, had emerged a man brimming over with self-reliance and contentment.(p.xxix)
- He was very ***nervous*** in the morning after these bouts and quieted himself with more liquor.(p.32)
- He is an intelligent man, normal so far as we can see, except for a ***nervous*** disposition.(p.35)
- They knew what to do about those black abysses that yawned ready to swallow me when I felt depressed, or ***nervous***.(p.229)
- I underwent a shattering ***nervous*** breakdown.(p.275)
- I had bad ***nervous*** headaches, particularly at the base of my neck.(p.277)
- Some of the things which used to stop me in my tracks from fear still make me ***nervous*** in the anticipation of their doing, but once I kick myself into doing them nervousness disappears and I enjoy myself.(p.285)
- However, it finally caught up with me, and when it did, I was a mental, physical, and ***nervous*** wreck.(p.299)
- Was I having a ***nervous*** collapse?(p.319)
- "The ***nervous*** tension had piled up and just had to spill over."(p.433)
- On the day set for the extractions, on my way to the dentist's I felt a little ***nervous***, so I had a couple of drinks, and after the teeth were out I was very ***nervous***, so I had a few more.(p.466)
- They were always there because of a ***nervous*** breakdown, or for a "rest cure" -- any reason except because of drinking.(p.471)

nervousness

- In some circumstances we have gone out deliberately to get drunk, feeling ourselves justified by ***nervousness***, anger, worry, depression, jealousy or the like.(p.37)
- He sometimes drinks in the morning and through the day also, to hold his ***nervousness*** in check.(p.109)
- Some of the things which used to stop me in my tracks from fear still make me nervous in the anticipation of their doing, but once I kick myself into doing them ***nervousness*** disappears and I enjoy myself.(p.285)

nest

- I now had quite a ***nest*** egg.(p.409)

nest-egg

- This too is how the ***nest-egg*** went.(p.410)

net

- Sometimes a small deal would ***net*** a few hundred dollars, and I would pay my bills at the bars and delicatessens.(p.5)

network

- Dr. W.W. Bauer, broadcasting under the auspices of The American Medical Association in 1946, over the NBC ***network***, said, in part: "Alcoholics Anonymous are no crusaders; not a temperance society.(p.572)

neurologist

- The ***neurologist*** in charge of my case didn't think to ask me whether I drank, and I didn't think to tell him.(p.444)
- The next day, Max called the ***neurologist*** and told him about the Mayo psychiatrist's opinion.(p.445)
- Dr. Foster Kennedy, ***neurologist***: "This organization of Alcoholics Anonymous calls on two of the greatest reservoirs of power known to man, religion and that instinct for association with one's fellows . . . the 'herd instinct.'(p.571)

neurosis

- The age-old question in A.A. is which came first, the ***neurosis*** or the alcoholism.(p.240)
- So it drove me deeper into the psychosis or ***neurosis*** that I had, and that I hated deep down in my heart.(p.388)

neurotic

- A doctor said to us, "Years of living with an alcoholic is almost sure to make any wife or child ***neurotic***.(p.122)
- That was her main ***neurotic*** manifestation.(p.483)
- When I look back, I can't see anything that would have predisposed me towards being either a ***neurotic*** or a drunk.(p.517)
- ***Neurotic*** fears plagued me, and I had occasional, uncontrollable tremors.(p.555)

neurotics

- So here, in this dive, this hangout for dead-end alcoholics and ***neurotics***, here was I.(p.410)

neutrality

- We feel as though we had been placed in a position of ***neutrality*** -- safe and protected.(p.85)

Nevada City

- About two days later I was called by a friend of mine from ***Nevada City*** -- he's a brother of my wife's closest friend.(p.347)

never

- But when the broker gave him Dr. Silkworth's description of alcoholism and its hopelessness, the physician began to pursue the spiritual remedy for his malady with a willingness he had ***never*** before been able to muster.(p.xvi)
- He sobered, ***never*** to drink again up to the moment of his death in 1950.(p.xvi)
- He ***never*** had another drink.(p.xvii)
- It was thought that no alcoholic man or woman could be excluded from our Society; that our leaders might serve but ***never*** govern; that each group was to be autonomous and there was to be no professional class of therapy.(p.xix)
- In all probability, we shall ***never*** be able to touch more than a fair fraction of the alcohol problem in all its ramifications.(p.xxi)
- We believe, and so suggested a few years ago, that the action of alcohol on these chronic alcoholics is a manifestation of an allergy; that the phenomenon of craving is limited to this class and ***never*** occurs in the average temperate drinker.(p.xxvi)
- These allergic types can ***never*** safely use alcohol in any form at all; and once having formed the habit and found they cannot break it, once having lost their self-confidence, their reliance upon things human, their problems pile up on them and become astonishingly difficult to solve.(p.xxvi)
- They are over-remorseful and make many resolutions, but ***never*** a decision.(p.xxviii)
- It has ***never*** been, by any treatment with which we are familiar, permanently eradicated.(p.xxviii)
- I could almost hear the sound of the preacher's voice as I sat, on still Sundays, way over there on the hillside; there was that proffered temperance pledge I ***never*** signed; my grandfather's good natured contempt of some church folk and their doings; his insistence that the spheres really had their music; but his denial of the preacher's right to tell him how he must listen; his fearlessness as he spoke of these things just before he died; these recollections welled up from the past.(p.10)
- ***Never*** mind the musty past; here sat a miracle directly across the kitchen table.(p.11)
- ***Never*** was I to be critical of them.(p.13)
- ***Never*** was I to pray for myself, except as my requests bore on my usefulness to others.(p.13)
- There was a sense of victory, followed by such a peace and serenity as I had ***never*** known.(p.14)
- But that in itself would ***never*** have held us together as we are now joined.(p.17)
- Perhaps there ***never*** will be a full answer to these questions.(p.22)
- These observations would be academic and pointless if our friend ***never*** took the first drink, thereby setting the terrible cycle in motion.(p.23)
- He has commenced to accomplish those things for us which we could ***never*** do by ourselves.(p.25)
- In the doctor's judgment he was utterly hopeless; he could ***never*** regain his position in society and he would have to place himself under lock and key or hire a bodyguard if he expected to live long.(p.26)
- I have ***never*** seen one single case recover, where that state of mind existed to the extent that it does in you."(p.27)
- With many individuals the methods which I employed are successful, but I have ***never*** been success-

ful with an alcoholic of your description."(p.27)
• Over any considerable period we get worse, ***never*** better.(p.30)
• We are like men who have lost their legs; they ***never*** grow new ones.(p.30)
• Here are some of the methods we have tried: Drinking beer only, limiting the number of drinks, ***never*** drinking alone, ***never*** drinking in the morning, drinking only at home, ***never*** having it in the house, ***never*** drinking during business hours, drinking only at parties, switching from scotch to brandy, drinking only natural wines, agreeing to resign if ever drunk on the job, taking a trip, not taking a trip, swearing off forever (with and without a solemn oath), taking more physical exercise, reading inspirational books, going to health farms and sanitariums, accepting voluntary commitment to asylums -- we could increase the list ad infinitum.(p.31)
• It ***never*** occurred to him that perhaps he could not do so, in spite of character and standing.(p.39)
• I had ***never*** been able to understand people who said that a problem had them hopelessly defeated.(p.42)
• To us, the Realm of Spirit is broad, roomy, all inclusive; ***never*** exclusive or forbidding to those who earnestly seek.(p.46)
• We ***never*** gave the spiritual side of life a fair hearing.(p.50)
• Was it not true that the best mathematical minds had proved man could ***never*** fly?(p.51)
• When others showed us that "God-sufficiency" worked with them, we began to feel like those who had insisted the Wrights would ***never*** fly.(p.52)
• What about people who proved that man could ***never*** fly?(p.55)
• Save for a few brief moments of temptation the thought of drink has ***never*** returned; and at such times a great revulsion has risen up in him.(p.57)
• Next we launched out on a course of vigorous action, the first step of which is a personal housecleaning, which many of us had ***never*** attempted.(p.63)
• We ***never*** apologize to anyone for depending upon our Creator.(p.68)
• We ***never*** apologize for God.(p.68)
• We think the reason is that they ***never*** completed their housecleaning.(p.73)
• He hopes they will ***never*** see the light of day.(p.73)
• Simply we tell him that we will ***never*** get over drinking until we have done our utmost to straighten out the past.(p.77)
• We are there to sweep off our side of the street realizing that nothing worth while can be accomplished until we do so, ***never*** trying to tell him what he should do.(p.77)
• There may be some wrongs we can ***never*** fully right.(p.83)
• We are careful ***never*** to pray for our own selfish ends.(p.87)
• So cooperate; ***never*** criticize.(p.89)
• If he does not want to see you, ***never*** force yourself upon him.(p.90)
• Explain that many are doomed who ***never*** realize their predicament.(p.92)
• ***Never*** talk down to an alcoholic from any moral or spiritual hilltop; simply lay out the kit of spiritual tools for his inspection.(p.95)
• ***Never*** avoid these responsibilities, but be sure you are doing the right thing if you assume them.(p.97)
• In some cases the wife will ***never*** come back for one reason or another.(p.99)
• Your job now is to be at the place where you may be of maximum helpfulness to others, so ***never*** hesitate to go anywhere if you can be helpful.(p.102)
• We ***never*** argue this question.(p.102)
• We are careful ***never*** to show intolerance or hatred of drinking as an institution.(p.103)
• We seldom had friends at our homes, ***never*** knowing how or when the men of the house would appear.(p.105)
• There was ***never*** financial security.(p.105)
• The first principle of success is that you should ***never*** be angry.(p.111)
• Our next thought is that you should ***never*** tell him what he must do about his drinking.(p.111)
• The majority have ***never*** returned.(p.114)
• When your husband is bad, you become a trembling recluse, wishing the telephone had ***never*** been invented.(p.115)
• ***Never*** forget that resentment is a deadly hazard to an alcoholic.(p.117)
• We ***never***, ***never*** try to arrange a man's life so as to shield him from temptation.(p.120)
• Perhaps he will ***never*** have much money again.(p.123)
• For us, material well-being always followed spiritual progress; it ***never*** preceded.(p.127)
• Try to remember that though God has wrought miracles among us, we should ***never*** belittle a good doctor or psychiatrist.(p.133)
• While on the subject of confidence, can you adopt the attitude that so far as you are concerned this will be a strictly personal matter, that his alcoholic derelictions, the treatment about to be undertaken, will ***never*** be discussed without his consent?(p.143)
• Being on a radically different basis of life, he will ***never*** take advantage of the situation.(p.146)
• ***Never*** could we recapture the great moments of the past.(p.151)
• I've prayed to God on hangover mornings and sworn that I'd ***never*** touch another drop but by nine o'clock I'd be boiled as an owl."(p.158)
• He ***never*** drank again.(p.158)
• Some of them may sink and perhaps ***never*** get up, but if our experience is a criterion, more than half of those approached will become fellows of Alcoholics Anonymous.(p.163)
• This had the effect of making me resolve that when I was free from parental domination, I would ***never*** again darken the doors of a church.(p.172)
• ***Never*** once in my life have I had a headache, which fact leads me to believe that I was an alcoholic almost from the start.(p.172)
• During the subsequent fifteen years I had sense enough ***never*** to go to the hospital if I had been drinking, and very seldom did I receive patients.(p.176)
• The water tank on the toilet I ***never*** used, because that looked too easy.(p.176)
• They spoke with great freedom from embarrassment, which I could ***never*** do, and they seemed very much at ease on all occasions and appeared very healthy.(p.178)
• How my wife kept her faith and courage during all those years, I'll ***never*** know, but she did.(p.178)
• It ***never*** fails, if you go about it with one half the zeal you have been in the habit of showing when you were getting another drink.(p.181)
• Your Heavenly Father will ***never*** let you down!(p.181)
• My marriage was happy and, as I have said, I ***never*** had any of the reasons, conscious or unconscious, which are often given for drinking.(p.182)
• The next thing they wanted to know was if I thought I could quit of my own accord, without any help, if I could just walk out of the hospital and ***never*** take another drink.(p.186)
• I had no trouble there because I had ***never*** actually ceased to believe in God, and had tried lots of times to get help but hadn't succeeded.(p.186)
• Bill D. walked out of that hospital a free man ***never*** to drink again.(p.189)
• At that time, as I remember, he had promised ***never*** to take another drink.(p.193)
• I immediately quit school and went to work, and from that time until I was high school age there was ***never*** a return to school.(p.193)
• He did things much better than I did because he applied himself and learned how to do them, and I ***never*** applied myself.(p.194)
• Right then I determined that ***never*** so long as I lived would I have anything more to do with martinis.(p.195)
• (I might say right here that ***never*** in my life did I ever intend to get drunk.(p.196)
• I ***never*** had any desire to get drunk.(p.196)
• So, knowing that, I had determined that so long as I lived I would ***never*** take another drink.(p.200)
• An offer of appreciation for not having had a drink for those few months and then and there, without anybody promising me anything or threatening me, I made a solemn vow that ***never*** so long as I lived would I take another drink.(p.200)
• So I had ***never*** had any lasting contact with any kind of religion.)(p.201)
• So I was driving to Cleveland when I made this solemn promise ***never*** to drink again.(p.201)
• I agreed with him and told him in no uncertain terms that I ***never*** broke my word in my life.(p.206)
• You're ***never*** going to want another drink, are you?"; and this answer of his is very important to those of us who are victims of alcoholism.(p.206)
• I'll ***never*** forget, he ***never*** even hesitated and I had ***never*** seen him before in my life.(p.207)
• Then he started to talk to me about his drinking experiences, what his drinking had cost him, how much he had drunk and where, things like that, and I remember I was quite bored because I had ***never*** seen the guy before and had no interest at all in what, where and when he drank.(p.208)
• That I shall ***never*** forget.(p.208)
• I remember well one fellow, Joe, walking nearly three miles through slush, wet and snow to come to the hospital to see a man that he had ***never*** seen before in his life, and that impressed me very much.(p.208)
• He walked to the hospital to save bus fare and did it gladly in order to be helpful to an individual he had ***never*** even seen.(p.208)
• I ***never*** left the church, but I was a fringe member, and the thought simply ***never*** occurred to me that through the exercise of what I had I might find the answer to my problem, simply because I wouldn't admit that I had a problem.(p.214)
• They ***never*** raised the issue.(p.215)
• In fact, I ***never*** lost my faith, since I had been prepared by some conversations toward the end of my sojourn in the hospital with Dr. Bob, conversations pretty much along spiritual lines.(p.218)
• That was an experience that I have ***never*** forgotten, and many times in my own work with A.A. newcomers I feel kind of guilty because I haven't done the same thing.(p.219)
• One of the things that came up repeatedly in the stories they told me was that once they had accepted the program, they ***never*** had a desire to take a drink.(p.219)
• I've ***never*** had a desire to take a drink.(p.219)
• Professionally, after I was sober for a month or so I realized that I should school myself to dissolve the partnership I was in because I felt that I would ***never*** regain the respect of my partners no matter how long I was sober, and that I would be at a disadvantage.(p.220)
• From far away, as if in a delirium, I heard my own voice -- calling someone "Dorothy," talking of dress shops, of jobs . . . the words came clearer . . . this sound of my own voice frightened me as it came closer . . . and suddenly, there I was, talking of I knew not what, to someone I'd ***never*** seen before this very moment.(p.222)
• My family had money -- I had ***never*** known denial of any material desire.(p.225)
• When my doctor told me I should ***never*** touch a drink again, I couldn't afford to believe him.(p.226)
• I ***never*** had been.(p.227)
• Many friends of my family had emigrated to America, so at twenty-four I decided that the United States offered me the opportunity I was ***never*** likely to find in my native land.(p.231)
• There had ***never*** been any drunkards in my family.(p.231)
• I knew the stuff I was making was a lot stronger than I had been used to, but I ***never*** suspected that steady drinking of it might develop a taste for something even stronger still.(p.233)
• Before long I had a definite taste for hard liquor, knew nausea and headaches I had ***never*** known before, but as in the old days, I suffered them out.(p.233)
• With a great deal of determination, I would throw out full pints -- pour them out and smash the bottles -- firmly resolved ***never*** to take another drink of the stuff.(p.234)
• I would promise to have jobs done and ***never*** do them.(p.234)
• I had ***never*** doubted the existence of the Supreme Being, but now I began to absent myself from my church where I had formerly been a member of the choir.(p.234)
• Unlike many other Catholics who frequently take pledges for definite periods -- a year, two years or for good, I ***never*** had any desire to "take a pledge" before the priest.(p.234)
• I had ***never*** heard of the remedy expressed in just this language.(p.236)
• But I have ***never*** thought of that as something to do and then forget about.(p.237)
• Little more of our talk stayed in my memory, but I do know I slept the rest of that night while before I had ***never*** known what a real night's sleep was.(p.239)
• There were four of us children, and although both of my brothers later became alcoholic -- one died of alcoholism -- my sister has ***never*** taken a drink in her life.(p.240)
• I have ***never*** shown any particular talents nor have I had any really frustrating ambitions.(p.240)
• I was ***never*** homesick and was always pretty self-sufficient.(p.240)
• At this school we had Bible readings before each meal, and church services four times on Sunday, and I became so rebellious at this that I swore I would ***never*** join or go to any church except for weddings or funerals.(p.240)
• I was ***never*** a hilarious drunk; the more I drank the quieter I got, and the drunker I got the harder I fought to stay sober.(p.241)
• So it is clear that I ***never*** had any fun out of drinking -- I would be the soberest-seeming one in the crowd

and all of a sudden I would be the drunkest.(p.241)
• I could ***never*** be bothered with the follow-through and would invariably reward myself for my efforts with that "first" drink.(p.243)
• They, too, had taken a train to one town and had wakened hundreds of miles in the opposite direction, ***never*** knowing how they got there.(p.246)
• I ***never*** saw either of them again.(p.247)
• My brilliant agnosticism vanished, and I saw for the first time that those who really believed, or at least honestly tried to find a Power greater than themselves, were much more composed and contented than I had ever been, and they seemed to have a degree of happiness which I had ***never*** known.(p.247)
• It was also an ending, for ***never*** since June 16th, 1938, have I had to walk alone.(p.248)
• While I went along with all that was done and attended the meetings, I ***never*** took an active job of leadership until February 1940.(p.249)
• Very rarely do I miss the meetings of my neighborhood A.A. group, and my average has ***never*** been less than two meetings a week.(p.249)
• My drinking was ***never*** the spaced doses of the careful tippler; it was always gluttonous.(p.254)
• I had ***never*** known him to be anything but a good healthy pagan with a propensity for getting into liquor jams and scrapes.(p.257)
• They will ***never*** know how much their talk with me helped.(p.259)
• I had ***never***, since the believing days of childhood, been able to conceive an authority directing the universe.(p.259)
• But I had ***never*** been a flippant, wise-cracking sneerer at the few persons I had met who had impressed me as Christian men and women, or at any institution whose sincerity of purpose I could see.(p.259)
• It has been that way with some, but it has not been with me and may ***never*** be.(p.259)
• I look back and remember these things because they made me very unhappy, and added to my feeling of inferiority at ***never*** being the same as other people.(p.261)
• I was about twenty-five then, and I had ***never*** touched a drop.(p.262)
• He told me that he would ***never*** drink again.(p.263)
• At the end of these thirteen years I ***never*** dreamed that he'd ever take another drink.(p.263)
• I had ***never*** taken one.(p.263)
• I ***never*** was concerned any more, anywhere he went.(p.263)
• We ***never*** rowed or fought.(p.264)
• Time went on and the drinking got worse and worse, and I was in another barroom, down the road the other way, a small one, and I took my glass – that morning I'd been able to lift it from the bar -- and I said to the woman behind the bar, "I wish I might never take another drop of that stuff.(p.266)
• I thought, "That guy ***never*** could have been a drunk."(p.268)
• I bet he ***never*** drank."(p.268)
• I could ***never*** go and make up to all the people I've done wrong to."(p.269)
• When we went to bed my sides ached, and I said to my husband, "I thought I would ***never*** laugh again, but I have laughed."(p.269)
• They told Annabelle to take me under her wing, and I shall ***never*** forget how she sort of curled up her nose and said, "They tell me you drink too."(p.269)
• We had ***never*** missed a Wednesday night at King School for a year.(p.270)
• Finally, and I shall ***never*** know how much later it was, one clear thought came to me: Try prayer.(p.280)
• I have ***never*** had a drink since.(p.280)
• During my first few months in Akron I was quite sure that I ***never*** wanted to see my home town again.(p.281)
• I, who had ***never*** made a speech in my life and who would have been frightened sick at the prospect, stood up in front of Rotary groups in different parts of the city and talked about Alcoholics Anonymous.(p.283)
• At long last I am doing the kind of work I have always wanted to do, but ***never*** had the patience and emotional stability to train myself for.(p.284)
• The most accurate answer I can give you is this: fear has ***never*** again ruled my life since that day in September, 1938, when I found that a Power greater than myself could not only restore me to sanity but could keep me both sober and sane.(p.285)
• ***Never*** in sixteen years have I dodged anything because I was afraid of it.(p.285)
• The last day of my drinking career, I drank twenty-two of them between ten and twelve a.m. and I shall ***never*** know how many more followed them until I was poured into bed that night.(p.298)
• I would make a feeble attempt at eating supper, but I ***never*** met with any howling success.(p.299)
• I ***never*** enjoyed any meal, but I ate my lunch at noon for two reasons; first, to help me get out of the fog of the night before and, second, to furnish some measure of nourishment.(p.299)
• I cannot remember just when I became the victim of insomnia, but I do know that the last year and a half I ***never*** went to bed sober a single night.(p.299)
• How I was able to discharge my duties at the office during those horrible mornings, I will ***never*** be able to explain.(p.299)
• I had ***never*** seen him before, and at the time hoped I would ***never*** see him again.(p.302)
• I sleep like a baby, and ***never*** give a thought to such a thing as insomnia.(p.303)
• Spiritually . . . I found a Friend who ***never*** lets me down and is ever eager to help.(p.303)
• Why he bothered with me as long as he did I shall ***never*** know, for he knew there was no answer for me in medicine and he, like all doctors of his day, had been taught that the alcoholic was incurable and should be ignored.(p.307)
• Until now, I had ***never*** been told that I was an alcoholic.(p.307)
• They would travel miles and stay up all night with someone they had ***never*** laid eyes on before and think nothing of it.(p.310)
• I could ***never*** have accomplished this alone.(p.311)
• That ache is gone and ***never*** need return again.(p.312)
• Among today's incoming A.A. members, many have ***never*** reached the advanced stages of alcoholism, though, given time, all might have.(p.315)
• And she would ***never***, ***never*** take that morning drink!(p.321)
• I was afraid, and I had made my mind up that I would ***never*** get drunk, so I was watchful and careful.(p.322)
• I ***never*** went to a hospital.(p.323)
• I ***never*** lost a job.(p.323)
• I was ***never*** in jail.(p.323)
• And, unlike many others, I ***never*** took a drink in the morning.(p.323)
• I was accused of it many times when I went to play bridge in the afternoon, but I really ***never*** did take a morning drink.(p.323)
• I ***never*** knew it was the first drink that did it.(p.324)
• Sometimes I would lie on the bathroom floor, deathly sick, praying I would die, and praying to God as I always had prayed to Him when I was drinking: "Dear God, get me out of this one and I'll ***never*** do it again."(p.324)
• I ***never*** stopped to think.(p.325)
• I ***never*** could face it the next morning.(p.325)
• I ***never*** thought I could be useful to anyone except my husband and my children and perhaps a few friends.(p.326)
• I ***never*** knew.(p.326)
• I could ***never*** be sure I'd have a clear head and hands that were willing to do some work.(p.326)
• So I ***never*** did any volunteer work.(p.326)
• I had the time, I certainly had the capability, but I ***never*** did a thing.(p.326)
• I hope that I ***never*** forget to be grateful.(p.326)
• I had ***never*** even been told by a superior that maybe I was drinking too much.(p.327)
• I vowed that ***never*** again would any important person whom I wished to please and impress ever see me drunk.(p.328)
• He'll ***never*** read in his "sweetness and light" senior-citizen publications anything but the joys of lolling in the rocking chair, angling on the riverbank, or bowling on the green.(p.330)
• "I'll ***Never*** Smile Again" – how perfect.(p.332)
• When I retired, I said I'd ***never*** be bored.(p.334)
• You can ***never*** know the pure joy of recovering within the Fellowship of Alcoholics Anonymous."(p.334)
• I was ***never*** a very heavy social drinker.(p.335)
• I ***never*** knew which came first, the thinking or the drinking.(p.337)
• I thought the two would ***never*** get together.(p.338)
• I had been brought up to believe in God, but I know that until I found this A.A. program, I had ***never*** found or known faith in the reality of God, the reality of His power that is now with me in everything I do.(p.341)
• I have ***never*** attended an A.A. meeting, so it is essentially the literature that has kept me on the A.A. program.(p.342)
• I ***never*** lost any of it.(p.345)
• I ***never*** was on skid row.(p.345)
• My wife ***never*** hinted that she would leave me.(p.345)
• I will ***never*** forget the first meeting that I attended.(p.347)
• I ***never*** robbed my family of anything.(p.351)
• I ***never*** drank socially; I drank as often and as much as I could.(p.353)
• I had ***never*** been very happy, but now it was unbearable.(p.355)
• Lucky because my excessive drinking ***never*** got me in jail, or hospitalized, nor did it ever cost me a job.(p.356)
• I got behind in my rent, but ***never*** in my drinking.(p.358)
• Time after time I would beg forgiveness on bended knees, with tears rolling down my cheeks, and promise I would ***never*** again drink too much.(p.362)
• After another of my "***never*** again episodes" she packed up and left for her parents' home in Florida.(p.362)
• They told me their stories, which were much more rugged than mine -- yet what they said made sense, and the way they put it was easy for me to understand, with an understanding I had ***never*** had before.(p.363)
• I had ***never*** told a soul about my lapse in New York.(p.366)
• It was ***never*** boring, but I developed a feeling of deep insecurity.(p.369)
• When I was nineteen, I married a fine man who had ***never*** known an insecure moment in his life, let alone the trials and tribulations of booze.(p.369)
• It was fun at first, since I ***never*** had indulged before.(p.370)
• The only drawback was, I always knew how I arrived there, but somehow, between the rest room, the rinse, and the fluff-dry, I ***never*** knew when or how I got home.(p.370)
• ***Never*** having enough, always craving more, the obsession for alcohol gradually dominated all my activities, particularly while travelling.(p.375)
• I will ***never*** know all the people I hurt, all the friends I abused, the humiliation of my family, the worry of my business associates, or how far reaching it was.(p.376)
• Attending meetings has ***never*** been a chore to me.(p.381)
• I had ***never*** been inside of an insane asylum and I really thought I was going to a private hospital.(p.387)
• So I located a house, and I thought we ought to move into it immediately, but Frank was horrified, because he ***never*** knew what was going to happen to me.(p.388)
• I couldn't walk, having it in a cast, and the doctor left the cast on three weeks longer than was necessary because he ***never*** found me sober enough to take it off.(p.390)
• Up to that time, I was so completely baffled by my behavior that I had ***never*** really stopped to think at all.(p.392)
• In spite of knowing that my drunkenness was a symptom of the things that were wrong with me, and that I could ***never*** drink again, I thought I couldn't yet give it up, although I was going to try.(p.393)
• I ***never*** want to forget that last drunk as long as I live.(p.393)
• I wish I could tell you all that A.A. has done for me, all that I think and feel about A.A., but it's something that I have experienced and have ***never*** been able to put into words.(p.394)
• In all these ways I've experienced, in ever growing measure and beyond all expectations and rewards, a joy which I had ***never*** before imagined.(p.395)
• It is also stated that we will ***never*** be able to figure out how much we have spent on alcohol.(p.396)
• When I was a baby, my mother brought me to America, and I ***never*** again saw my father.(p.401)
• A drink ***never*** gave me a normal, pleasant glow.(p.402)
• I returned from Europe a while after that encounter, and I ***never*** went back.(p.406)
• It had ***never*** occurred to me before that I could live simply and be independent of my family.(p.409)
• But I ***never*** got into jail.(p.411)
• ***Never*** in my entire life had anyone asked me "Are you one of us?"(p.413)
• ***Never*** had I felt a sense of belonging.(p.413)
• I had ***never*** had the physical courage to shake it out before.(p.415)
• I, who could ***never*** stay on the wagon for more than a week.(p.416)
• Many good A.A.'s ***never*** join a church, and do not

need to.(p.417)
• If I had not become an active alcoholic and joined A.A., I might *never* have found my own identity or become a part of anything.(p.417)
• But I knew I'd *never* get that way.(p.427)
• I was *never* drunk on the job, *never* missed a day's work, was seldom rendered totally ineffective by a hangover and kept my liquor expenses well within my adequate budget.(p.433)
• Even on my rare (at first) binge nights it *never* ran much over a quart.(p.433)
• And should I have more bad times, I know that I'll *never* again have to go through them alone.(p.438)
• *Never* in my wildest moments had it occurred to me that I might like to be an alcoholic.(p.439)
• *Never* once had my mother even hinted at the idea that, when I grew up, I might like to be president of A.A.(p.439)
• But I *never* became a morning drinker.(p.441)
• I *never* got much effect out of codeine and Percodan and the tranquilizers.(p.442)
• I *never* in my life took a tranquilizer, sedative, or pep pill because I was a pillhead.(p.443)
• Max accepted responsibility for me after I had promised *never* to drink again, *never* to take another pill, *never* to swear again, and *never* to talk to girls again.(p.444)
• I *never* could quite get the knack of it and kept asking myself, "What's a nice guy like me doing in a place like this?"(p.445)
• I *never* just sit and do nothing while waiting for Him to tell me what to do.(p.452)
• When I remember this, I can see I've *never* had it so good.(p.452)
• They prove to almost anyone's satisfaction that it's *never* too late to try Alcoholics Anonymous.(p.455)
• I served twelve years in prison, *never* suspecting that without alcohol I would not have been in prison at all.(p.457)
• Had it not been for A.A. in prison. . . I'll *never* know, but my educated guess is that I would not be alive today.(p.457)
• Finally, I threw away all my books and decided *never* to return to A.A.(p.460)
• If I failed, they would throw away the key, and I would *never* get out again.(p.461)
• I must be ready and willing should I *never* see them.(p.463)
• Guess I'll *never* be a saint, but whatever I am, I want to be sober and in A.A.(p.463)
• I thought I would be quite happy and *never* would I drink too much again.(p.465)
• He said he was finally and completely through -- that he *never* wanted to see me again.(p.467)
• I had decided I was no good – *never* would be any good, and the sooner I could drink myself out of this life, the better.(p.468)
• In all the sanitariums and psycho wards I had *never* met a single woman who said she was an alcoholic.(p.471)
• But by listening and talking to these A.A.'s -- talking to them as I had *never* talked to anyone in my whole life, I saw that it was my life that was unmanageable -- not just my drinking.(p.471)
• *Never* forgot magic in firewater.(p.474)
• It *never* entered my head that I would have been pushing up the daisies if he had decided not to come.(p.479)
• We are so beautiful that it is *never* too much trouble to get some poor stranger to buy us a drink.(p.479)
• Since then, I have *never* been back to heroin.(p.480)
• He is my best teacher; without him, I am sure I would *never* have made the progress I have.(p.481)
• We are aware of the nice things around us, things we *never* noticed before in our drunken stupor.(p.481)
• But I will *never* be totally honest – that would make me perfect, and none of us can claim to be perfect.(p.482)
• About this time an incident took place in grade school that I have *never* forgotten because it made me realize that I was actually a physical coward.(p.484)
• I've *never* seen him drunk in my life, although he'd take a shot in the morning and usually one in the evening, and so did I; but for the most part he kept his whiskey in his office.(p.484)
• On the other hand, I believe that I've always been medically inclined, though I have *never* been able to see medicine quite as the average person sees it.(p.485)
• He said he *never* wanted to set foot in the deep south again and he didn't.(p.486)
• I *never* had too much trouble in school.(p.486)
• Of course the kid *never* got the Easter outfit.(p.493)
• She *never* mentioned anything about my whiskey drinking because if she had I would have told her, "No" right then.(p.494)
• I approached several ministers and all of them thought it was a very good idea, but they *never* relinquished any space.(p.495)
• Father had *never* directly spoken to me about drinking but he *never* drank any, so far as I knew.(p.498)
• I had *never* had a drink, but I had seen enough merriment in the boys who were drinking to be interested.(p.498)
• I would *never* be like the village drunkard at home.(p.498)
• I would *never* have tried, but mother counts on it so.(p.499)
• *Never* in the service!(p.499)
• He *never* says an unkind word.(p.501)
• I have been drinking a lot, but *never* get drunk.(p.501)
• Mother must *never* know.(p.501)
• I told him that I believe in electricity and other forces of nature, but as for a God, if there is one, He has *never* done anything for me.(p.503)
• I have *never* seen people that joyous before.(p.504)
• Anger possesses me, anger such as I have *never* felt before.(p.505)
• She had been warned numerous times, not only by her family but by my own mother, that I was a hopeless drunk, that there wasn't anything anybody could do with me, that I'd *never* stop, and that eventually I'd break her heart.(p.513)
• But I've *never* come close to that first drink.(p.516)
• I lasted at that for four months chiefly on alcohol, because I *never* seemed to find any time to eat.(p.520)
• I was *never* to be allowed back.(p.521)
• I stayed there just long enough to work up a real good resentment against the doctor in charge, who I didn't think was doing anything at all except collecting fees, and I left there fully determined that I'd *never* put myself in the power of medical people again.(p.521)
• My only hope was to try and get through what was left of life as best I could, but I could *never* visualize doing that without drinking.(p.522)
• The thought of stopping drinking just *never* occurred to me.(p.522)
• I suppose I had reached my spiritual gutter that night, but I have *never* had what you could call a real urge to drink again.(p.524)
• It has taught me that success and failure are *never* final, and that neither count for very much in the final assessment of any man who has done his best.(p.525)
• I would *never* admit that I was drinking too much, or spending money that I should have used to buy food for my two little boys.(p.526)
• The sacred word was broken and you *never* trusted your father again, and avoided him.(p.533)
• There was the love affair which was ridiculous -- "imagine that midget being able to fall in love!" -- and my head knew it while my heart pumped real, genuine anguish, for it hurt like hell, and since it was first love, things have *never* been quite the same.(p.534)
• I *never* was a "secret" drinker, and I *never* kept a bottle at home.(p.536)
• I choose to believe that the Power greater than ourselves we ask for help, wrapped my shivering body in loving warmth and strength which has *never* left me.(p.541)
• I have been allowed to build an entirely new career in a field I had *never* worked in.(p.541)
• I thought I could *never* be happy.(p.542)
• I *never* did react normally to any emotional situation.(p.544)
• In time I concluded that the reason I was hurt was because I loved my parents, and I concluded too that if I *never* allowed myself to love anybody or anything I could *never* be hurt again.(p.545)
• I grew up believing that one had to be totally self-sufficient, for one *never* dared to depend on another human being.(p.545)
• I had *never* had a child and this had been a satisfactory excuse many times for my drinking.(p.548)
• "God willing, we . . . may *never* again have to deal with drinking, but we have to deal with sobriety every day."(p.554)
• I have learned how to relate to people; before A.A., I could *never* do that comfortably without alcohol.(p.559)
• God willing, we members of A.A. may *never* again have to deal with drinking, but we have to deal with sobriety every day.(p.560)
• We are taught to differentiate between our wants (which are *never* satisfied) and our needs (which are always provided for).(p.560)
• Six -- An A.A. group ought *never* endorse, finance or lend the A.A. name to any related facility or outside enterprise, lest problems of money, property and prestige divert us from our primary purpose.(p.564)
• Nine – A.A., as such, ought *never* be organized; but we may create service boards or committees directly responsible to those they serve.(p.564)
• Ten – Alcoholics Anonymous has no opinion on outside issues; hence the A.A. name ought *never* be drawn into public controversy.(p.564)
• An A.A. group, as such, should *never* go into business.(p.566)
• While an A.A. group may cooperate with anyone, such cooperation ought *never* go so far as affiliation or endorsement, actual or implied.(p.566)
• But our usual A.A. "12th Step" work is *never* to be paid for.(p.567)
• There is *never* need to praise ourselves.(p.567)
• This to the end that our great blessings may *never* spoil us; that we shall forever live in thankful contemplation of Him who presides over us all.(p.568)
• They know that they must *never* drink.(p.572)

never-ending

• With increasing guilt and *never-ending* depression, I was too weak to continue this day-by-day suicide.(p.355)

nevertheless

• *Nevertheless,* I still thought I could control the situation, and there were periods of sobriety which renewed my wife's hope.(p.5)
• *Nevertheless,* he was drunk in a short time.(p.26)
• The story he told is most instructive, for here was a chap absolutely convinced he had to stop drinking, who had no excuse for drinking, who exhibited splendid judgment and determination in all his other concerns, yet was flat on his back *nevertheless.*(p.40)
• *Nevertheless,* the twentieth century readily accepts theories of all kinds, provided they are firmly grounded in fact.(p.48)
• *Nevertheless,* with a person we dislike, we take the bit in our teeth.(p.77)
• *Nevertheless,* we find that our thinking will as time passes, be more and more on the plane of inspiration.(p.87)
• I gave the matter much time and study for the next two and a half years, but still got tight every night *nevertheless.*(p.178)
• *Nevertheless,* there were a few doctors who saw alcoholism as a disease and felt that the alcoholic was a victim of something over which he had no control.(p.307)
• *Nevertheless,* I began to try to live without alcohol.(p.338)
• Somewhat faded, she *nevertheless* bloomed afresh.(p.384)
• *Nevertheless,* I stayed sober there about six months, because I knew that Vi was to come later and bring the children.(p.490)
• *Nevertheless,* we continued to work together and I continued to drink, but I guess, deep down within her heart as well as within mine, we both knew I couldn't stop drinking.(p.490)
• Though it was not our intention to create such an impression, many alcoholics have *nevertheless* concluded that in order to recover they must acquire an immediate and overwhelming "God-consciousness" followed at once by a vast change in feeling and outlook.(p.569)

new

• "Bill's Story," "Doctor Bob's Nightmare," and one other personal history from the first edition were retained intact; three were edited and one of these was retitled; *new* versions of two stories were written with *new* titles; thirty completely *new* stories were added; and the story section was divided into three parts, under the same headings that are used now.(p.xi)
• Nine of the stories in Part II ("They Stopped in Time") are carried over from the second edition; eight *new* stories have been added.(p.xii)
• In Part III ("They Lost Nearly All"), eight stories have been retained; five are *new*.(p.xii)
• The spark that was to flare into the first A.A. group was struck at Akron, Ohio, in June 1935, during a talk between a *New* York stockbroker and an Akron physician.(p.xv)
• He had also been greatly helped by the late Dr. William D. Silkworth, a *New* York specialist in alcoholism who is now accounted no less than a medical saint by A.A. members, and whose story of the early days of our Society appears in the next pages.(p.xvi)
• When the broker returned to *New* York in the fall of 1935, the first A.A. group had actually been formed, though no one realized it at the time.(p.xvii)
• By late 1937, the number of members having sub-

stantial sobriety time behind them was sufficient to convince the membership that a *new* light had entered the dark world of the alcoholic.(p.xvii)
• A second small group had promptly taken shape at *New* York.(p.xvii)
• And besides, there were scattered alcoholics who had picked up the basic ideas in Akron or *New* York and were trying to form A.A. groups in other cities.(p.xvii)
• The flying-blind period ended and A.A. entered a *new* phase of its pioneering time.(p.xvii)
• With the appearance of the *new* book a great deal began to happen.(p.xvii)
• This brought a rush of 800 frantic inquiries into the little *New* York office which meanwhile had been established.(p.xviii)
• *New* groups started up and it was found, to the astonishment of everyone, that A.A.'s message could be transmitted in the mail as well as by word of mouth.(p.xviii)
• Yet it is our great hope that all those who have as yet found no answer may begin to find one in the pages of this book and will presently join us on the highroad to a *new* freedom.(p.xxi)
• These facts appear to be of extreme medical importance; because of the extraordinary possibilities of rapid growth inherent in this group they may mark a *new* epoch in the annals of alcoholism.(p.xxiii)
• When I need a mental uplift, I often think of another case brought in by a physician prominent in *New* York.(p.xxix)
• War fever ran high in the *New* England town to which we *new*, young officers from Plattsburg were assigned, and we were flattered when the first citizens took us to their homes, making us feel heroic.(p.1)
• Abruptly in October 1929 hell broke loose on the *New* York stock exchange.(p.4)
• It was years since I could remember his coming to *New* York in that condition.(p.9)
• His roots grasped a *new* soil.(p.12)
• A *new* world came into view.(p.12)
• I was to test my thinking by the *new* God-consciousness within.(p.13)
• My friend promised when these things were done I would enter upon a *new* relationship with my Creator; that I would have the elements of a way of living which answered all my problems.(p.13)
• Belief in the power of God, plus enough willingness, honesty and humility to establish and maintain the *new* order of things, were the essential requirements.(p.13)
• That the man who is making the approach has had the same difficulty, that he obviously knows what he is talking about, that his whole deportment shouts at the *new* prospect that he is a man with a real answer, that he has no attitude of Holier Than Thou, nothing whatever except the sincere desire to be helpful; that there are no fees to pay, no axes to grind, no people to please, no lectures to be endured -- these are the conditions we have found most effective.(p.18)
• Ideas, emotions, and attitudes which were once the guiding forces of the lives of these men are suddenly cast to one side, and a completely *new* set of conceptions and motives begin to dominate them.(p.27)
• A *new* life has been given us or, if you prefer, "a design for living" that really works.(p.28)
• We are like men who have lost their legs; they never grow *new* ones.(p.30)
• I had been out of town before during this particular dry spell, so there was nothing *new* about that.(p.41)
• I have a shadowy recollection of being in an airplane bound for *New* York, and of finding a friendly taxicab driver at the landing field instead of my wife.(p.41)
• Many times we talk to a *new* man and watch his hope rise as we discuss his alcoholic problems and explain our fellowship.(p.45)
• As soon as we admitted the possible existence of a Creative Intelligence, a Spirit of the Universe underlying the totality of things, we began to be possessed of a *new* sense of power and direction, provided we took other simple steps.(p.46)
• In the face of collapse and despair, in the face of the total failure of their human resources, they found that a *new* power, peace, happiness, and sense of direction flowed into them.(p.50)
• Is not our age characterized by the ease with which we discard old ideas for *new*, by the complete readiness with which we throw away the theory or gadget which does not work for something *new* which does?(p.52)
• The outlines and the promise of the *New* Land had brought lustre to tired eyes and fresh courage to flagging spirits.(p.53)
• Most good ideas are simple, and this concept was the keystone of the *new* and triumphant arch through which we passed to freedom.(p.62)
• We had a *new* Employer.(p.63)
• As we felt *new* power flow in, as we enjoyed peace of mind, as we discovered we could face life successfully, as we became conscious of His presence, we began to lose our fear of today, tomorrow or the hereafter.(p.63)
• We have been trying to get a *new* attitude, a *new* relationship with our Creator, and to discover the obstacle in our path.(p.72)
• We are going to know a *new* freedom and a *new* happiness.(p.83)
• This thought brings us to Step Ten, which suggests we continue to take personal inventory and continue to set right any *new* mistakes as we go along.(p.84)
• We will see that our *new* attitude toward liquor has been given us without any thought or effort on our part.(p.85)
• Life will take on *new* meaning.(p.89)
• Sometimes a *new* man is anxious to proceed at once, and you may be tempted to let him do so.(p.95)
• When your prospect has made such reparation as he can to his family, and has thoroughly explained to them the *new* principles by which he is living, he should proceed to put those principles into action at home.(p.98)
• The wife should fully understand his *new* way of life.(p.99)
• This means a *new* attitude and spirit all around.(p.99)
• Both you and the *new* man must walk day by day in the path of spiritual progress.(p.100)
• Follow the dictates of a Higher Power and you will presently live in a *new* and wonderful world, no matter what your present circumstances!(p.100)
• Every *new* alcoholic looks for this spirit among us and is immensely relieved when he finds we are not witch-burners.(p.103)
• And just as we were being convinced of their heartlessness, they would surprise us with fresh resolves and *new* attentions.(p.107)
• For a while they would be their old sweet selves, only to dash the *new* structure of affection to pieces once more.(p.107)
• When you have carefully explained to such people that he is a sick person, you will have created a *new* atmosphere.(p.115)
• Your *new* courage, good nature and lack of self-consciousness will do wonders for you socially.(p.115)
• Seed has started to sprout in a *new* soil, but growth has only begun.(p.117)
• We suggest that you direct some of your thought to the wives of his *new* alcoholic friends.(p.119)
• Both of you will awaken to a *new* sense of responsibility for others.(p.119)
• Perhaps your husband will make a fair start on the *new* basis, but just as things are going beautifully he dismays you by coming home drunk.(p.120)
• If there is no Al-Anon listing in your local telephone book, you may obtain further information on Al-Anon Family Groups by writing to its World Service Office: Box 182, Madison Square Station, *New* York, NY 10159.(p.121)
• Though old buildings will eventually be replaced by finer ones, the *new* structures will take years to complete.(p.123)
• We think that such a view is self-centered and in direct conflict with the *new* way of living.(p.124)
• Husbands and wives have sometimes been obliged to separate for a time until *new* perspective, *new* victory over hurt pride could be rewon.(p.125)
• He may either plunge into a frantic attempt to get on his feet in business, or he may be so enthralled by his *new* life that he talks or thinks of little else.(p.125)
• As soon as his sobriety begins to be taken as a matter of course, the family may look at their strange *new* dad with apprehension, then with irritation.(p.128)
• For a time he may try to hug the *new* treasure to himself.(p.129)
• Instead of developing *new* channels of activity for themselves, mother and children demand that he stay home and make up the deficiency.(p.131)
• At the very beginning, the couple ought to frankly face the fact that each will have to yield here and there if the family is going to play an effective part in the *new* life.(p.131)
• *New* acquaintances who know nothing of alcoholism might be made and thoughtful consideration given their needs.(p.131)
• If he does not argue about religion, he will make *new* friends and is sure to find *new* avenues of usefulness and pleasure.(p.132)
• He may bring *new* hope and *new* courage to many a priest, minister, or rabbi, who gives his all to minister to our troubled world.(p.132)
• This may hang on for months, long after their mother has accepted dad's *new* way of living and thinking.(p.134)
• In time they will see that he is a *new* man and in their own way they will let him know it.(p.134)
• The others must be convinced of his *new* status beyond the shadow of a doubt.(p.135)
• They have a *new* attitude, and they have been saved from a living death.(p.150)
• There was an insistent yearning to enjoy life as we once did and a heartbreaking obsession that some *new* miracle of control would enable us to do it.(p.151)
• You are going to meet these *new* friends in your own community.(p.152)
• You will be bound to them with *new* and wonderful ties, for you will escape disaster together and you will commence shoulder to shoulder your common journey.(p.152)
• These men had found something brand *new* in life.(p.159)
• They were willing, by day or night, to place a *new* man in the hospital and visit him afterward.(p.159)
• Aside from fellowship and sociability, the prime object was to provide a time and place where *new* people might bring their problems.(p.160)
• They knew they had a host of *new* friends; it seemed they had known these strangers always.(p.161)
• I was born in a small *New* England village of about seven thousand souls.(p.171)
• Men who had liquor shipped in from Boston or *New* York by express were looked upon with great distrust and disfavor by most of the good townspeople.(p.171)
• He kept the faith; therefore, he and countless others found a *new* life.(p.182)
• He explained that he and a man from *New* York had a cure for alcoholism.(p.188)
• Down in the pit of his depression, *new* hope had somehow been born.(p.189)
• Not far from where I lived they built a *new* technical high school and one of the teachers sold me on the idea that I needed a little mechanical drawing if I were going to be a good toolmaker.(p.211)
• The first definite indications of an alcoholic pattern began to arise when I would go to *New* York on business and disappear, and wind up in Philadelphia or Boston for two or three day periods.(p.213)
• I would have to return to *New* York and pick up my bills and bags.(p.213)
• Somewhere in one of the conversations, I mentioned that I was contemplating forming a *new* firm.(p.220)
• That had been in the center of *New* York, on noisy 42nd Street . . . this was obviously a quiet residential section.(p.223)
• That was the beginning of a *new* life, a fuller life, a happier life than I had ever known or believed possible.(p.228)
• And, accepting, I felt a *new* inner comfort, and the willingness and strength to do something about the traits I couldn't live with.(p.229)
• I get my greatest thrill of accomplishment from the knowledge that I have played a part in the *new* happiness achieved by countless others like myself.(p.229)
• In foreign parts many a soldier who has been abstemious at home learns to use *new* and potent drinks.(p.230)
• I was now forming an entirely *new* drinking technique.(p.233)
• First, my *new* wife had walked out, bag, baggage and furniture; then the apartment landlord had thrown me out of the empty apartment and the finish was the loss of another job.(p.238)
• Jackie told me about a group of fellows in *New* York, of whom my old friend Fitz was one, who had the same problem I had, and who by working together to help each other were not now drinking and were happy like himself.(p.239)
• With the war over, and back in Baltimore with the folks, there were several small jobs for three years and then I went to work soliciting as one of the first ten employees of a *new* national finance company.(p.242)
• Oddly enough, the big shot who fired me from this company was one of the first men I met when I later joined the *New* York A.A. Group.(p.242)
• However, I made an SOS call to the *New* York Group, whom I hadn't met yet, and they suggested we both come there.(p.245)
• Despite all this, I did like these *new* friends because, again, they were like me.(p.245)
• During that first week-end I decided to stay in *New*

York and take all they gave out with, except the "God stuff."(p.246)
• At that time the group in *New* York was composed of about twelve men who were working on the principle of every drunk for himself; we had no real formula and no name.(p.246)
• So I rocked along my merry independent way until June, when I went out selling auto polish in *New* England.(p.247)
• I had completely forgotten the January 8th when I found the fellowship, and I spent the next four days wandering around *New* England half drunk, by which I mean I couldn't get drunk and I couldn't get sober.(p.247)
• I tried to contact the boys in *New* York, but telegrams bounced right back and when I finally got Hank on the telephone he fired me right then.(p.247)
• Peddling off my polish samples for expenses, I crawled back to *New* York a few days later in a very chastened frame of mind.(p.248)
• Thus I found myself in the middle of a brand *new* group.(p.249)
• When I started to tell the boys how we did it in *New* York and all about the spiritual part of the program, I found they would not believe me unless I was practicing what I preached.(p.249)
• I had been too self-sufficient to write a moral inventory, but I discovered in pointing out to the *new* man his wrong attitudes and actions that I was really taking my own inventory, and that if I expected him to change I would have to work on myself too.(p.249)
• With a good stake I sailed for *New* York.(p.251)
• The *new* job lasted five years.(p.254)
• Now on a *new* job I was always thinking about payday and how much liquor I could buy and the pleasure I could have.(p.255)
• As soon as I could get up and walk I started to drink again and kept it up until my friend of the hospital, who, in his first try at the *new* way of life had stubbed his toe in Chicago but had come back to the town to take counsel and make a *new* start, picked me up and got me into a hospital.(p.258)
• The doctor who came to see me almost at once did not assail me with any *new* doctrines; he made sure that I had a need and that I wanted to have that need filled, and little by little I learned how my need could be met.(p.258)
• Our other daughter was in her last year of high school, and one night the *new* son-in-law and my husband went out to a prize fight.(p.263)
• I think it's awfully hard on people, especially if they're *new* people, to hear these long drawn out talks.(p.273)
• He might have handed me fifty dollars and said that I ought to pull myself together and make a *new* start.(p.278)
• An hour later I awoke to a *new* world.(p.280)
• We spent two days there together before he returned to *New* York.(p.281)
• I had to adapt to *new* associations and associates, and it seemed to be the smart thing to drink and smoke.(p.287)
• After a particularly bad Christmas and *New* Year's holiday, dad picked me up again early in January, 1937, to go through the usual sobering up routine.(p.289)
• In the spring of 1939, the Big Book was printed, and we had two inquiries from the *New* York office because of a fifteen-minute radio talk that was made.(p.294)
• My *new* duties were extremely confining and my liquor consumption began to increase.(p.298)
• Handling customers, dealers, insurance people, dictation, telephoning, directing *new* employees, answering to superiors, and all the rest of it.(p.299)
• After being fired, I lined up with a *new* finance company that was just starting in business, and took the position of business promotion man, contacting automobile dealers.(p.300)
• While working in an office, there was some semblance of restraint, but, oh boy, when I got on the outside with this *new* company without supervision, did I go to town!(p.300)
• I moved a thousand miles away from home to Chicago and a *new* environment.(p.305)
• I studied art; I desperately endeavored to create an interest in many things, in a *new* place among *new* people.(p.305)
• And then, in the spring of 1939, a very remarkable book was rolled off a *New* York press with the title "Alcoholics Anonymous."(p.307)
• He sent to *New* York for a copy, and after reading it he tucked it under his arm and called on me.(p.307)
• Then he told me there was a handful of people in Akron and *New* York who had worked out a technique for arresting their alcoholism.(p.308)
• Whole *new* vistas were opened and life began to take on color and interest.(p.311)
• In time, I found myself looking forward to each *new* day with pleasurable anticipation.(p.311)
• I started to take A.A. seriously, and A.A. gave me a *new* way of life.(p.320)
• I tried to encourage a search for some *new* goal.(p.334)
• But in the light of the *new* understanding that I have found in A.A., I have been able to interpret that defeat, and that failure, and that shame, as seeds of victory.(p.335)
• In those days, I was doing a staff appointment in the army headquarters in *New* Delhi.(p.343)
• At Christmastime next year, I convinced my wife that I had alcohol under control and that I would do controlled drinking over Christmas and the *New* Year.(p.343)
• The reply came, putting me in touch by mail with my sponsor in *New* Delhi.(p.343)
• This was such a *new* thought that I got all sorts of books on Higher Powers, and I put a Bible by my bedside, and I put a Bible in my car.(p.348)
• With these *new* and enlightening doors opening up to me, I was able to make the eventual decision to stop drinking, a day at a time -- because I, too, was an alcoholic.(p.355)
• All I can remember about the Roaring Twenties is that I drank a great deal, thought I was having a grand time, managed to get to Europe for a few weeks, was very proud of the dozens of speak-easy cards entitling me to an entree in the better joints between Cleveland and *New* York, took on a wife, and built a home in a fashionable suburb of Cleveland.(p.358)
• Like all alcoholics endeavoring to run away from themselves and their environment, I decided to go to *New* York.(p.358)
• The next few years in *New* York can be described in a very few words.(p.358)
• It was my job to sell time on these stations to advertising agencies in *New* York.(p.359)
• By persistence and salesmanship I managed to see more and more of my *new* friend, and because of her sympathetic nature she tolerated my company.(p.359)
• Once again I asked my girl to marry me and join me in this *new* venture.(p.359)
• At this time, however, she had an opportunity to go to Salt Lake City on a *new* project for the government, but she did promise me that if I would curtail my drinking and buckle down to hard work she would give serious consideration to my latest proposal and maybe join me at a later date when I got settled.(p.359)
• With *new* hope in my heart and *new* resolutions I set off for Vermont.(p.360)
• My work kept me busy the first few months on the *new* job.(p.360)
• Furthermore, I knew that I was looked upon as a city slicker from *New* York, and I had to be pretty cautious among small town, conservative Yankees.(p.360)
• *New* programing was beginning to build an audience, but sponsors were pretty scarce.(p.360)
• Proud of my little station and of my *new* bride I settled down to a happy married life.(p.361)
• I entered the house, opened a *new* bottle of whiskey and sat down to drink myself into the right frame of mind to get in my car, start the motor and close the garage door behind me.(p.363)
• After a few meetings I decided to drive to Florida unannounced to see my wife and tell her about my *new* found friends and association.(p.364)
• That night she too had *new* hope because I had made sure she would know what I was doing about my drinking by packing every bit of A.A. literature I could put my hands on right on top so she couldn't help but see it when she opened my bag.(p.364)
• I stayed on in Florida for three weeks, enjoying our reunion, a *new* found health and a deeper love than I had ever experienced before.(p.364)
• We attended meetings together, and mutually enjoyed our *new* found friends.(p.364)
• In September of this same year I went to *New* York alone.(p.364)
• Luck was with me for I made my train, but I arrived home the next morning with a *new* kind of hangover.(p.364)
• I got through the holidays all right until *New* Year's Day.(p.365)
• I had just raised the bottle to my lips when my wife opened the door and froze me completely in my tracks with "Happy *New* Year, dear."(p.365)
• He was full of his *new* found life of happiness and sobriety.(p.365)
• A whole *new* world of happiness and love began to unfold before my eyes, a truly *new* way of living.(p.365)
• I had never told a soul about my lapse in *New* York.(p.366)
• What a wonderful *new* feeling, what a wonderful relief!(p.366)
• I could end my story here, but for the *new* man I would like to add a few words.(p.366)
• To the *new* man I would also like to say that this program is not for sissies for, in my humble opinion, it takes a man to make the grade.(p.367)
• We soon resumed our marriage, even moved away from the street of sad memories and found a *new* home.(p.371)
• But what is more important is that I found a *new* life in Alcoholics Anonymous.(p.372)
• I didn't realize I would find so much more, but a *new* and different outlook on life started opening up almost immediately.(p.383)
• I lived in *New* Orleans where, at that time, cocktail parties, dances and night spots were almost the order of the day -- or rather the night.(p.384)
• Frank had to go to *New* York, but because I had a dog, we had a duplex, and I thought -- if only we had a house!(p.388)
• He said that because of my drinking, he shouldn't leave, but that he had to go to *New* York for two weeks.(p.388)
• I loved my father dearly and I adored my dog, and I'd gotten this *new* house and Frank had just given me a *new* fur coat and I was thrilled to death.(p.389)
• So Frank went to *New* York and despite all these things, I got drunk.(p.389)
• I know that when Frank came home, I said, "I want to try this thing," and he said, "There's a post office box to write to in *New* York."(p.392)
• It was the A.A. General Service Office in *New* York that I wrote to, and that office has always meant a lot to me.(p.392)
• So I wrote this letter in very shaky handwriting, and in just one week came back a letter with A.A. literature from *New* York.(p.392)
• The birth of a daughter filled me with *new* fears.(p.402)
• I had worked the previous summer on a *New* York fashion magazine, a job I really enjoyed.(p.405)
• Things were no better with the family, so I moved to *New* York.(p.406)
• My *new* friends made fun of God and all the orthodox beliefs.(p.408)
• This *new* analyst was a woman doctor, one of the best in the country.(p.409)
• I learned a whole *new* sense of values.(p.409)
• My *new* friends had a social conscience.(p.410)
• Finally my *new* friends told me, one by one, that I could not come around any more.(p.410)
• For three generations, my family had had a charge account in one of the big *New* York hotels.(p.410)
• In those days the A.A. Foundation was down in the Wall Street district of *New* York.(p.413)
• In those days there was only one big meeting a week in *New* York.(p.414)
• However, I had phoned *New* York from the farm, appealing for help, and there in the station to meet us were two A.A.'s, John and Bud.(p.415)
• I have my A.A. friends, and I have become reacquainted with my old friends on a *new* basis.(p.416)
• Defeated by alcohol and pills, he found the way to a *new* life.(p.418)
• I had just begun a dental practice in a beautiful *new* office.(p.418)
• A.A. has given me a *new* wife, a beautiful stepdaughter, a *new* practice, a *new* home, and a *new* relationship with my four children.(p.420)
• I headed home for the most wonderful experience of all time -- meeting my "*new*" parents -- mom and dad looked different than I had pictured them.(p.428)
• I'd acquired a *new* girl, a lovely girl who knew of my problem and had tried to help me.(p.430)
• Always we'd emerge with a *new* formula for avoiding future trouble.(p.433)
• My *new* wife and I don't own any property to speak of, and the flashy successes of another day are no longer mine.(p.438)
• One has to be pretty sick to do that, and perhaps one has to be even sicker to come back every day for a *new* list, as she did.(p.446)
• The people of A.A. had something that looked much better than what I had, but I was afraid to let go of what I had in order to try something *new*; there was a certain sense of security in the familiar.(p.448)
• It's as though A.A. had given me a *new* pair of glasses.(p.450)

- A.A. has given me a *new* pair of glasses.(p.451)
- All Twelve Steps of A.A. are designed to kill the old self (deflate the old ego) and build a *new*, free self.(p.459)
- We were on our way to *New* York where he planned to leave me with my sister.(p.466)
- At noon on Christmas Day I called my family in *New* York, wished them a Merry Christmas, and assured them everything was fine with me.(p.467)
- The next recollection I have is of my husband coming into my room (later found out it was on *New* Year's Eve) accompanied by two policemen.(p.468)
- From a Canadian reservation to overseas bars to *New* England lockups, an Indian traveled a long trail that finally led him home to A.A.(p.474)
- Start group on reservation and carry message, help start other groups all over Maritimes and *New* England.(p.476)
- He was old, but now he grow young with *new* life in A.A. and travel all time.(p.476)
- We can have this *new* way of life -- learning to live with our sickness and to be happy and content -- if we are willing to change our way of thinking and be honest, first with ourselves, then with others.(p.480)
- I can't begin to tell you of all the benefits I have derived from this *new* way of living.(p.481)
- He has taught me that, in our *new* life, I am the most important person of all.(p.481)
- I would meet some *new* faces and be in a dry county.(p.490)
- I had found this *new* "something," and I wanted to give it to everyone who had a problem.(p.496)
- My wife and *new* baby are fortunately staying with relatives.(p.500)
- "There are men on the streets of *New* York today who were worse than you, and they don't drink any more."(p.503)
- She comes to *New* York.(p.505)
- Get into the lives of other people, is one thing the fellows in *New* York had said.(p.505)
- I do not fix anyone, but I am getting part of a tremendous education and I have made some *new* friends.(p.506)
- Like many of us who went into the service, I thought it would be a cure-all, a *new* life.(p.513)
- I remember the day I came back to *New* York.(p.513)
- It was my second arrival in *New* York.(p.513)
- Then a change in management took place in the regiment and the *new* O.C. didn't like me very much and I didn't like him, and he started to lie in wait for me.(p.519)
- I had no work to do and I was at an age where it seemed too late to start anything *new*.(p.522)
- If he were still sober, chances are that very quickly I put him down as a Philistine with no appreciation of literary genius; and then I went on to another bar to find a *new* victim.(p.537)
- Still another friend and temporary host received me at four in the morning from the charge of a policeman who had found me "going to bed" in a garage far from the last place I could remember having been, a fashionable bar and restaurant in the theatrical district of *New* York, to which I had repaired after my date for that evening, a charming lady of the theatre who had refused my company for obvious reasons.(p.538)
- I have been allowed to build an entirely *new* career in a field I had never worked in.(p.541)
- I have been appointed to the faculty of my old school, to teach in my *new* field.(p.541)
- All of my family and loved ones, all of my friends, are nearer and dearer to me than ever before and I have literally dozens of *new* friends who say they cannot believe that a short eight years ago I was ready for the scrap heap.(p.541)
- After my very first drink -- a tiny glass of sherry my father gave me to celebrate the *New* Year when I was thirteen -- I went up to bed, dizzy with exhilaration and excitement, and I prayed I wouldn't drink any more!(p.554)
- In each *new* place, I was the *new* kid -- a skinny, shy kid -- to be tested and beaten up.(p.555)
- Upon graduation, I ventured to *New* York to pursue my writing career.(p.555)
- Our courtship was mainly in bars and night spots when my ship was in *New* York.(p.555)
- As the sober days grew into sober months and then into sober years, a *new* and beautiful life began to emerge from the shambles of my former existence.(p.559)
- They are the custodians of our A.A. Tradition and the receivers of voluntary A.A. contributions by which we maintain our A.A. General Service Office at *New* York.(p.567)
- Following are excerpts from the comments of doctors present at the annual meeting of the Medical Society of the State of *New* York where a paper on A.A. was read:(p.571)
- (This address is now available in pamphlet form at nominal cost through most A.A. groups or from Box 459, Grand Central Station, *New* York, NY 10163, under the title "Three Talks to Medical Societies by Bill W." -- formerly called "Bill on Alcoholism" and earlier "Alcoholism the Illness.")(p.572)
- Historians may one day recognize Alcoholics Anonymous to have been a great venture in social pioneering which forged a *new* instrument for social action; a *new* therapy based on the kinship of common suffering; one having a vast potential for the myriad other ills of mankind."(p.573)
- At *New* York, U.S.A., Alcoholics Anonymous maintains its international service center.(p.575)
- If you cannot find A.A. in your locality, a letter addressed to Alcoholics Anonymous, Box 459, Grand Central Station, *New* York, NY 10163, U.S.A., will receive a prompt reply from this world center, referring you to the nearest A.A. group.(p.575)
- Should you be the relative or friend of an alcoholic who shows no immediate interest in A.A., it is suggested that you write the Al-Anon Family Groups, Inc., Box 182, Madison Square Station, *New* York, NY 10159, U.S.A.(p.575)

New Delhi

- In those days, I was doing a staff appointment in the army headquarters in *New Delhi*.(p.343)
- The reply came, putting me in touch by mail with my sponsor in *New Delhi*.(p.343)

New England

- War fever ran high in the *New England* town to which we new, young officers from Plattsburg were assigned, and we were flattered when the first citizens took us to their homes, making us feel heroic.(p.1)
- I was born in a small *New England* village of about seven thousand souls.(p.171)
- So I rocked along my merry independent way until June, when I went out selling auto polish in *New England*.(p.247)
- I had completely forgotten the January 8th when I found the fellowship, and I spent the next four days wandering around *New England* half drunk, by which I mean I couldn't get drunk and I couldn't get sober.(p.247)
- From a Canadian reservation to overseas bars to *New England* lockups, an Indian traveled a long trail that finally led him home to A.A.(p.474)
- Start group on reservation and carry message, help start other groups all over Maritimes and *New England*.(p.476)

New Orleans

- I lived in *New Orleans* where, at that time, cocktail parties, dances and night spots were almost the order of the day -- or rather the night.(p.384)

New Year

- At Christmastime next year, I convinced my wife that I had alcohol under control and that I would do controlled drinking over Christmas and the *New Year*.(p.343)
- I had just raised the bottle to my lips when my wife opened the door and froze me completely in my tracks with "Happy *New Year*, dear."(p.365)
- After my very first drink -- a tiny glass of sherry my father gave me to celebrate the *New Year* when I was thirteen -- I went up to bed, dizzy with exhilaration and excitement, and I prayed I wouldn't drink any more!(p.554)

New Year's

- After a particularly bad Christmas and *New Year's* holiday, dad picked me up again early in January, 1937, to go through the usual sobering up routine.(p.289)
- I got through the holidays all right until *New Year's* Day.(p.365)
- The next recollection I have is of my husband coming into my room (later found out it was on *New Year's* Eve) accompanied by two policemen.(p.468)

New York

- The spark that was to flare into the first A.A. group was struck at Akron, Ohio, in June 1935, during a talk between a *New York* stockbroker and an Akron physician.(p.xv)
- He had also been greatly helped by the late Dr. William D. Silkworth, a *New York* specialist in alcoholism who is now accounted no less than a medical saint by A.A. members, and whose story of the early days of our Society appears in the next pages.(p.xvi)
- When the broker returned to *New York* in the fall of 1935, the first A.A. group had actually been formed, though no one realized it at the time.(p.xvii)
- A second small group had promptly taken shape at *New York*.(p.xvii)
- And besides, there were scattered alcoholics who had picked up the basic ideas in Akron or *New York* and were trying to form A.A. groups in other cities.(p.xvii)
- This brought a rush of 800 frantic inquiries into the little *New York* office which meanwhile had been established.(p.xviii)
- When I need a mental uplift, I often think of another case brought in by a physician prominent in *New York*.(p.xxix)
- Abruptly in October 1929 hell broke loose on the *New York* stock exchange.(p.4)
- It was years since I could remember his coming to *New York* in that condition.(p.9)
- I have a shadowy recollection of being in an airplane bound for *New York*, and of finding a friendly taxicab driver at the landing field instead of my wife.(p.41)
- If there is no Al-Anon listing in your local telephone book, you may obtain further information on Al-Anon Family Groups by writing to its World Service Office: Box 182, Madison Square Station, *New York*, NY 10159.(p.121)
- Men who had liquor shipped in from Boston or *New York* by express were looked upon with great distrust and disfavor by most of the good townspeople.(p.171)
- He explained that he and a man from *New York* had a cure for alcoholism.(p.188)
- The first definite indications of an alcoholic pattern began to arise when I would go to *New York* on business and disappear, and wind up in Philadelphia or Boston for two or three day periods.(p.213)
- I would have to return to *New York* and pick up my bills and bags.(p.213)
- That had been in the center of *New York*, on noisy 42nd Street . . . this was obviously a quiet residential section.(p.223)
- Jackie told me about a group of fellows in *New York*, of whom my old friend Fitz was one, who had the same problem I had, and who by working together to help each other were not now drinking and were happy like himself.(p.239)
- Oddly enough, the big shot who fired me from this company was one of the first men I met when I later joined the *New York* A.A. Group.(p.242)
- However, I made an SOS call to the *New York* Group, whom I hadn't met yet, and they suggested we both come there.(p.245)
- During that first week-end I decided to stay in *New York* and take all they gave out with, except the "God stuff."(p.246)
- At that time the group in *New York* was composed of about twelve men who were working on the principle of every drunk for himself; we had no real formula and no name.(p.246)
- I tried to contact the boys in *New York*, but telegrams bounced right back and when I finally got Hank on the telephone he fired me right then.(p.247)
- Peddling off my polish samples for expenses, I crawled back to *New York* a few days later in a very chastened frame of mind.(p.248)
- When I started to tell the boys how we did it in *New York* and all about the spiritual part of the program, I found they would not believe me unless I was practicing what I preached.(p.249)
- With a good stake I sailed for *New York*.(p.251)
- We spent two days there together before he returned to *New York*.(p.281)
- In the spring of 1939, the Big Book was printed, and we had two inquiries from the *New York* office because of a fifteen-minute radio talk that was made.(p.294)
- And then, in the spring of 1939, a very remarkable book was rolled off a *New York* press with the title "Alcoholics Anonymous."(p.307)
- He sent to *New York* for a copy, and after reading it he tucked it under his arm and called on me.(p.307)
- Then he told me there was a handful of people in Akron and *New York* who had worked out a technique for arresting their alcoholism.(p.308)
- All I can remember about the Roaring Twenties is that I drank a great deal, thought I was having a grand time, managed to get to Europe for a few weeks, was very proud of the dozens of speak-easy cards entitling me to an entree in the better joints between Cleveland and *New York*, took on a wife, and built a home in a fashionable suburb of Cleveland.(p.358)
- Like all alcoholics endeavoring to run away from themselves and their environment, I decided to go to *New York*.(p.358)

• The next few years in *New York* can be described in a very few words.(p.358)
• It was my job to sell time on these stations to advertising agencies in *New York*.(p.359)
• Furthermore, I knew that I was looked upon as a city slicker from *New York*, and I had to be pretty cautious among small town, conservative Yankees.(p.360)
• In September of this same year I went to *New York* alone.(p.364)
• I had never told a soul about my lapse in *New York*.(p.366)
• Frank had to go to *New York*, but because I had a dog, we had a duplex, and I thought – if only we had a house!(p.388)
• He said that because of my drinking, he shouldn't leave, but that he had to go to *New York* for two weeks.(p.388)
• So Frank went to *New York* and despite all these things, I got drunk.(p.389)
• I know that when Frank came home, I said, "I want to try this thing," and he said, "There's a post office box to write to in *New York*."(p.392)
• It was the A.A. General Service Office in *New York* that I wrote to, and that office has always meant a lot to me.(p.392)
• So I wrote this letter in very shaky handwriting, and in just one week came back a letter with A.A. literature from *New York*.(p.392)
• I had worked the previous summer on a *New York* fashion magazine, a job I really enjoyed.(p.405)
• Things were no better with the family, so I moved to *New York*.(p.406)
• For three generations, my family had had a charge account in one of the big *New York* hotels.(p.410)
• In those days the A.A. Foundation was down in the Wall Street district of *New York*.(p.413)
• In those days there was only one big meeting a week in *New York*.(p.414)
• However, I had phoned *New York* from the farm, appealing for help, and there in the station to meet us were two A.A.'s, John and Bud.(p.415)
• We were on our way to *New York* where he planned to leave me with my sister.(p.466)
• At noon on Christmas Day I called my family in *New York*, wished them a Merry Christmas, and assured them everything was fine with me.(p.467)
• "There are men on the streets of *New York* today who were worse than you, and they don't drink any more."(p.503)
• She comes to *New York*.(p.505)
• Get into the lives of other people, is one thing the fellows in *New York* had said.(p.505)
• I remember the day I came back to *New York*.(p.513)
• It was my second arrival in *New York*.(p.513)
• Still another friend and temporary host received me at four in the morning from the charge of a policeman who had found me "going to bed" in a garage far from the last place I could remember having been, a fashionable bar and restaurant in the theatrical district of *New York*, to which I had repaired after my date for that evening, a charming lady of the theatre who had refused my company for obvious reasons.(p.538)
• Upon graduation, I ventured to *New York* to pursue my writing career.(p.555)
• Our courtship was mainly in bars and night spots when my ship was in *New York*.(p.555)
• They are the custodians of our A.A. Tradition and the receivers of voluntary A.A. contributions by which we maintain our A.A. General Service Office at *New York*.(p.567)
• Following are excerpts from the comments of doctors present at the annual meeting of the Medical Society of the State of *New York* where a paper on A.A. was read:(p.571)
• (This address is now available in pamphlet form at nominal cost through most A.A. groups or from Box 459, Grand Central Station, *New York*, NY 10163, under the title "Three Talks to Medical Societies by Bill W." – formerly called "Bill on Alcoholism" and earlier "Alcoholism the Illness.")(p.572)
• At *New York*, U.S.A., Alcoholics Anonymous maintains its international service center.(p.575)
• If you cannot find A.A. in your locality, a letter addressed to Alcoholics Anonymous, Box 459, Grand Central Station, *New York*, NY 10163, U.S.A., will receive a prompt reply from this world center, referring you to the nearest A.A. group.(p.575)
• Should you be the relative or friend of an alcoholic who shows no immediate interest in A.A., it is suggested that you write the Al-Anon Family Groups, Inc., Box 182, Madison Square Station, *New York*, NY 10159, U.S.A.(p.575)

new-found

• I ruthlessly faced my sins and became willing to have my *new-found* Friend take them away, root and branch.(p.13)
• In spite of your *new-found* happiness, there will be ups and downs.(p.117)
• First, through mutual pain and despair, and later through mutual objectives and *new-found* faith and hope.(p.312)
• I get out of the hospital and we visit some of these *new-found* friends.(p.505)

newcomer

• Their services are often indispensable in treating a *newcomer* and in following his case afterward.(p.133)
• Seeing much of each other, scarce an evening passed that someone's home did not shelter a little gathering of men and women, happy in their release, and constantly thinking how they might present their discovery to some *newcomer*.(p.159)
• It seems I should have learned to love my wife and family first; the *newcomer* to A.A., last.(p.451)
• Eventually, I had to redo each of the Twelve Steps specifically with Max in mind, from the First, saying, "I am powerless over alcohol, and my homelife is unmanageable by me," to the Twelfth, in which I tried to think of her as a sick Al-Anon and treat her with the love I would give a sick A.A. *newcomer*.(p.452)
• During these seven years a thing called the Twenty-four Hour Program –a gadget I used to think was only a snare to trap the *newcomer* -- has come to mean much to me, not only as regards my drinking but in the whole pattern of my life.(p.473)
• Quite often friends of the *newcomer* are aware of the difference long before he is himself.(p.569)

newcomer's

• If you have been successful in solving your own domestic problems, tell the *newcomer's* family how that was accomplished.(p.100)

newcomers

• Businessmen, traveling out of existing groups, were referred to these prospective *newcomers*.(p.xviii)
• We meet frequently so that *newcomers* may find the fellowship they seek.(p.15)
• Time after time *newcomers* have tried to keep to themselves certain facts about their lives.(p.72)
• Frequent contact with *newcomers* and with each other is the bright spot of our lives.(p.89)
• If *newcomers* could see no joy or fun in our existence, they wouldn't want it.(p.132)
• That was an experience that I have never forgotten, and many times in my own work with A.A. *newcomers* I feel kind of guilty because I haven't done the same thing.(p.219)
• In telling *newcomers* how to change their lives and attitudes, all of a sudden I found I was doing a little changing myself.(p.249)

newer

• Women now make up more than one-fourth of the membership; among *newer* members, the proportion is nearly one-third.(p.xxii)
• I have served on only one committee in the past nine years, for I feel that I had my chance the first few years and that *newer* members should fill the jobs.(p.250)

newly

• These good people notified my wife, who sent my *newly* made friend over to get me.(p.179)

news

• *News* of this got on the world wires; inquiries poured in again and many people went to the bookstores to get the book "Alcoholics Anonymous."(p.xviii)
• This is the great *news* this book carries to those who suffer from alcoholism.(p.17)
• That was great *news* to us, for we had assumed we could not make use of spiritual principles unless we accepted many things on faith which seemed difficult to believe.(p.47)
• He came through an acquaintance who had heard the good *news*.(p.158)
• They said, "We've got some bad *news* for you.(p.187)
• It was bad *news* for us, and it will probably be bad *news* for you.(p.187)
• That certainly was real disheartening *news*, at the time.(p.188)
• THE *NEWS* HAWK(p.251)
• Gradually the quantity increased, the occasions for a drink came more frequently; a hard day, worries and pressure, bad *news*, good *news* – there were more and more reasons for a drink.(p.374)
• An alcoholic cannot accept the *news* that he's an alcoholic unless there is a meaningful explanation given, and an offer of help, such as you get in A.A.(p.406)

news-gathering

• Washington, D.C. and *news-gathering* agency work followed, along with many parties.(p.254)

newsletter

• Maine *newsletter* (Boomerang) say: "With tireless devotion and humility, this venerable Indian gentleman traveled thousands of miles humbly pleading for sobriety.(p.476)

newsman

• This *newsman* covered life from top to bottom; but he ended up, safely enough, in the middle.(p.251)

newspaper

• Another time, as I opened a letter which lay on my desk, a *newspaper* clipping fell out.(p.136)
• I had repaired to one of these one morning with my jug and when I left late in the afternoon, I picked up a *newspaper* on the way home.(p.244)
• I quit the factory and got a job on a small *newspaper*, going from that to a Pittsburgh daily, long ago defunct.(p.252)
• Drifting back to Ohio, I landed on a small *newspaper* and later was impressed into the direction of boy-welfare work at the local "Y."(p.253)
• I stayed so sober that I used to keep a quart of medicinal whiskey in my bureau which I used to taper off the occasional *newspaper* alcoholics who were sent to see me.(p.253)
• I did six years of *newspaper* advertising, and trade journal work with many, many drunks of drab and dreary hue woven into the pattern of my life.(p.254)
• In the two succeeding years I held ten different jobs ranging from *newspaper* copy-desk and rewrite, to traffic director for an oil field equipment company.(p.255)
• He may even read in a *newspaper* that one out of every seven drinkers will become alcoholic, but he rarely is told that it holds true for all ages -- or that the tolerance to alcohol (and other drugs) decreases steadily, year after year, in the bodies of all persons.(p.330)
• Hiding behind a *newspaper*, magazine, or book, I really saw nothing, but simulated deep interest.(p.332)
• Then I saw an A.A. advertisement in a *newspaper*, and I wrote to the address it gave.(p.343)
• I went to work in Birmingham for a *newspaper* at fifteen dollars a week.(p.357)
• I went out to the West Coast, waited on table, washed dishes and sold *newspaper* subscriptions.(p.401)
• My dad, who was a *newspaper* man and had some connections, had meantime put a stop on me, and I guess that report went all over the country.(p.424)
• I got a job with the *newspaper* my dad worked for.(p.425)
• They are authorized by the groups to handle our over-all public relations and they guarantee the integrity of our principal *newspaper*, the A.A. Grapevine.(p.567)
• In such places, A.A. can be located through the local telephone directory, *newspaper* office, or police station, or by contacting local priests or ministers.(p.575)

newspaper-man

• So I married a nice, well-meaning young *newspaperman*, so as not to have to go home.(p.402)

newspapers

• Even in the present century, American *newspapers* were afraid to print an account of the Wright brothers' first successful flight at Kitty Hawk.(p.51)
• A square from ultra-dry Kansas, I did not taste grog until I had finished college, done a stint on *newspapers*, married, become a father, and been in studio publicity two years.(p.328)
• So we rolled old *newspapers* together and made torches to find a good soft pew and get some sleep.(p.424)

newsreels

• We were having trouble with personal relationships, we couldn't control our emotional natures, we were a prey to misery and depression, we couldn't make a living, we had a feeling of uselessness, we were full of fear, we were unhappy, we couldn't seem to be of real help to other people – was not a basic solution of these bedevilments more important than whether we should see *newsreels* of lunar flight?(p.52)

Newsweek

• My opinions were quoted in Time and *Newsweek* with pictures, and I addressed the public by radio and television.(p.435)

next

• He had also been greatly helped by the late Dr. William D. Silkworth, a New York specialist in alcoholism who is now accounted no less than a medical saint by A.A. members, and whose story of the early days of our Society appears in the *next* pages.(p.xvi)

• For the ***next*** few years fortune threw money and applause my way.(p.3)
• ***Next*** morning I telephoned a friend in Montreal.(p.4)
• As the whisky rose to my head I told myself I would manage better ***next*** time, but I might as well get good and drunk then.(p.6)
• The remorse, horror and hopelessness of the ***next*** morning are unforgettable.(p.6)
• ***Next*** day found me drinking both gin and sedative.(p.7)
• With a certain satisfaction I reflected there was enough gin concealed about the house to carry me through that night and the ***next*** day.(p.8)
• Yet early ***next*** morning he searches madly for the bottle he misplaced the night before.(p.21)
• ***Next*** day we would ask ourselves, in all earnestness and sincerity, how it could have happened.(p.37)
• I remember having several more that night and plenty the ***next*** morning.(p.41)
• He becomes, on the ***next*** occasion, still more demanding or gracious, as the case may be.(p.61)
• ***Next***, we decided that hereafter in this drama of life, God was going to be our Director.(p.62)
• ***Next*** we launched out on a course of vigorous action, the first step of which is a personal housecleaning, which many of us had never attempted.(p.63)
• Our ***next*** function is to grow in understanding and effectiveness.(p.84)
• We usually conclude the period of meditation with a prayer that we be shown all through the day what our ***next*** step is to be, that we be given whatever we need to take care of such problems.(p.87)
• The ***next*** chapter is entirely devoted to Step Twelve.(p.88)
• They should wait for the end of his ***next*** drinking bout.(p.90)
• But for every man who drinks others are involved -- the wife who trembles in fear of the ***next*** debauch; the mother and father who see their son wasting away.(p.104)
• ***Next*** day they would be themselves again and we would forgive and try to forget.(p.106)
• But when he gets over the spree, he begins to think once more how he can drink moderately ***next*** time.(p.109)
• Our ***next*** thought is that you should never tell him what he must do about his drinking.(p.111)
• But after his ***next*** binge, ask him if he would really like to get over drinking for good.(p.112)
• ***Next*** time you and he have a heated discussion, no matter what the subject, it should be the privilege of either to smile and say, "This is getting serious.(p.118)
• ***Next*** he can be assured that you do not intend to lecture, moralize, or condemn; that if this was done formerly, it was because of misunderstanding.(p.142)
• If he temporizes and still thinks he can ever drink again, even beer, he might as well be discharged after the ***next*** bender which, if an alcoholic, he is almost certain to have.(p.142)
• When his wife ***next*** calls saying he is sick, you might jump to the conclusion he is drunk.(p.146)
• ***Next*** day found the prospect more receptive.(p.158)
• Many a distracted wife has visited this house to find loving and understanding companionship among women who knew her problem, to hear from the lips of their husbands what had happened to them, to be advised how her own wayward mate might be hospitalized and approached when ***next*** he stumbled.(p.160)
• This resolution I kept steadfastly for the ***next*** forty years, except when circumstances made it seem unwise to absent myself.(p.172)
• I seemed to be able to snap back the ***next*** morning better than most of my fellow drinkers, who were cursed (or perhaps blessed) with a great deal of morning-after nausea.(p.172)
• The ***next*** three years I spent in Boston, Chicago, and Montreal in the employ of a large manufacturing concern, selling railway supplies, gas engines of all sorts, and many other items of heavy hardware.(p.172)
• My ***next*** move was to take up the study of medicine, entering one of the largest universities in the county.(p.173)
• During the ***next*** few years, I developed two distinct phobias.(p.175)
• My phobia for sleeplessness demanded that I get drunk every night, but in order to get more liquor for the ***next*** night, I had to stay sober during the day, at least up to four o'clock.(p.177)
• I gave the matter much time and study for the ***next*** two and a half years, but still got tight every night nevertheless.(p.178)
• The ***next*** day she called again.(p.179)
• He came and got me home and to bed, gave me a few drinks that night, and one bottle of beer the ***next*** morning.(p.179)
• Between classes I would run down to the wash room, take enough to steady my nerves and then go on to the ***next*** class.(p.183)
• The ***next*** thing they wanted to know was if I thought I could quit of my own accord, without any help, if I could just walk out of the hospital and never take another drink.(p.186)
• The ***next*** question, they wanted to know was if I believed in a Higher Power.(p.186)
• The ***next*** thing they wanted to know was would I be willing to go to this Higher Power and ask for help, calmly and without any reservations.(p.186)
• The ***next*** question they asked was, "You can quit twenty-four hours can't you?"(p.188)
• It was in the ***next*** two or three days after I had first met Doc and Bill, that I finally came to a decision to turn my will over to God and to go along with this program the best that I could.(p.189)
• The ***next*** morning I woke up in jail in Cleveland and the jailor had $1,175 of my money in an envelope.(p.196)
• I would put off doing anything that I could until the ***next*** day and, consequently, everything would pile up and then there would be the blackout.(p.197)
• I can well remember sitting with seven dollars in my pocket, planning on giving my family a hundred or two hundred dollars, when I made it ***next*** year.(p.197)
• At three-thirty the ***next*** morning, I was in Champlain Street Station, in jail for driving while intoxicated and insulting an officer; and the suit of which I was so proud was in such shape that the turnkey had to get me a pair of trousers to go into court in the ***next*** morning.(p.201)
• The ***next*** day, they called me in for an examination, and the doctor wouldn't let me continue working and pardoned me from the plant for ten days because he said my eye had been injured.(p.205)
• The ***next*** day, others from the group came in to see me.(p.208)
• The ***next*** morning, my wife came into my room and wakened me and said, "That man is downstairs and he said you said you'd go to Akron."(p.217)
• For the ***next*** ten years I did just that.(p.225)
• I came of good stock, of men and women who drank wine all their lives as a beverage, and while they occasionally got drunk at special celebrations, they were up and about their business the ***next*** day.(p.231)
• In the ***next*** two years I washed more pans and peeled more potatoes than any other doughboy.(p.241)
• We heard by wireless on the 5th that the Armistice would be signed the ***next*** day (this was a premature report) so I had a couple of cognacs to celebrate; then I hopped a truck and went AWOL.(p.242)
• My ***next*** conscious memory was in Bar le Duc, many miles from base.(p.242)
• My ***next*** job was in sales promotion for an oil company in Mississippi where I promptly became high man and got lots of pats on the back.(p.242)
• This we did the ***next*** day, and what a trip!(p.245)
• I had completely forgotten the January 8th when I found the fellowship, and I spent the ***next*** four days wandering around New England half drunk, by which I mean I couldn't get drunk and I couldn't get sober.(p.247)
• In those days my system was always to drink up my last pay check and believe that necessity would bring the ***next*** job.(p.256)
• He introduced himself and began to tell me about a bunch of some sixty former drinkers and drunkards who met once a week, and he invited me to go with him to the ***next*** meeting.(p.257)
• The ***next*** time vacation time rolled around that was a bitter lesson to us.(p.265)
• Men from A.A. started coming out to the house the ***next*** day.(p.268)
• The ***next*** morning his wife came dragging him in before Russ went to work, while I was getting breakfast.(p.271)
• From this job and the ***next*** one with another printer I was courteously dismissed.(p.277)
• The ***next*** two years were simply a long drawn out process of less and less work and more and more whiskey.(p.278)
• The ***next*** day he turned me over to a couple who, although neither was an alcoholic, knew Dr. Bob and were willing to drive me to Akron where they would turn me over to his care.(p.278)
• So I was driven to Akron the very ***next*** day by these Good Samaritans, and turned over to Dr. Bob and the then tiny Akron Group.(p.279)
• My wife could not understand the ***next*** morning why I was drunker than the night before when she took my bottles.(p.289)
• The ***next*** afternoon and evening, two other men visited me and each told me his story and the things that they were doing to try to recover from this tragic illness.(p.290)
• In the ***next*** two or three days the balance of this handful of men contacted me, encouraged me, and told me how they were trying to live this program of recovery and the fun they were having doing it.(p.291)
• The ***next*** day I went back to Chicago and started a vigorous campaign among my so-called friends or drinking companions.(p.293)
• One is that I don't remember too many of them, as I was one of those drunks who could be on his feet and attend a meeting or a party, engage in a conversation with people and do things that any nearly normal person would do, and the ***next*** day not remember a thing about where I was, what I did, whom I saw, or how I got home.(p.301)
• The ***next*** three years saw me in sanitariums, once in a ten day coma, from which I very nearly did not recover, in and out of hospitals or confined at home with day and night nurses.(p.306)
• The ***next*** day I received a visit from Mr. T., a recovered alcoholic.(p.309)
• Usually, the ***next*** morning I would be quite sick.(p.317)
• ***Next***, I was sent to Arizona, where my drinking picked up some more, and I started having blackouts, and I was thrown in jail for speeding and drunken driving.(p.318)
• The ***next*** meeting I went to, I didn't have any drinks beforehand.(p.319)
• I nudged George ***next*** morning, and I said, "I'm in," and he said, "Oh, I knew you'd make it."(p.322)
• I never could face it the ***next*** morning.(p.325)
• But then I thought, well, now wait, how will I feel ***next*** Tuesday?(p.326)
• How will I feel ***next*** Friday, if I make it a Friday?(p.326)
• How will I feel ***next*** Saturday morning?(p.326)
• At Christmastime ***next*** year, I convinced my wife that I had alcohol under control and that I would do controlled drinking over Christmas and the New Year.(p.343)
• During the ***next*** three years, I tried often again to give it up, but failed miserably.(p.343)
• On the first, though on the water wagon, I looked forward to my ***next*** drink.(p.344)
• I certainly wasn't my shy, quiet self that night -- as I was informed the ***next*** morning.(p.353)
• I didn't particularly like it, but I loved the effects, and managed for the ***next*** twenty-five years to drink anything and everything, either handed to me or purchased, at the slightest excuse.(p.357)
• The ***next*** few years in New York can be described in a very few words.(p.358)
• I asked this question weekly for the ***next*** couple of years.(p.359)
• I promised my two sponsors that I would attend their meeting the ***next*** Tuesday evening.(p.363)
• Luck was with me for I made my train, but I arrived home the ***next*** morning with a new kind of hangover.(p.364)
• When our meeting night came around the ***next*** evening, I went -- "for her sake" I told her.(p.365)
• For the ***next*** couple of hours a terrible battle went on between the good gremlins and the bad ones, one faction urging me to tell the truth, the other telling me to sit tight and say nothing.(p.366)
• The ***next*** steps were bottle hiding, and excuses for trips in order to drink without restraint.(p.375)
• Early the ***next*** morning a man whose name I knew well, a lawyer, called on me.(p.378)
• The ***next*** morning he came into my room and said, "Esther, I'm not going to lecture you any more, but I want you to read this article.(p.391)
• The only other occasionally limiting factor was that I might run out of money before the ***next*** payday rolled around.(p.398)
• I spent the ***next*** three days in a cell.(p.424)
• ***Next*** morning I was sworn in, feeling no pain.(p.425)
• I spent the time in a nearby tavern, was loaded on the ship, went to sleep before take-off, and the ***next*** thing I knew someone was shaking me and telling me we were over San Diego.(p.428)
• I was escorted back to San Diego ***next*** morning -- by the Shore Patrol, but I was discharged on schedule.(p.428)

• Sometimes I'd make it home and go to sleep at the wheel of my car, for all the neighbors to see ***next*** morning as they left for work.(p.429)
• The end came ***next*** year.(p.429)
• I thought, "If this is A.A. why not go back to drinking, kill myself with booze in the ***next*** three years the doctor had given me, and call it a bad job?"(p.430)
• ***Next*** day remorse would be on me like a tiger.(p.432)
• I'd claw my way back to "respectability" and stay there – until the inevitable ***next*** time.(p.432)
• Here was power to live to the end of any given day, power to have the courage to face the ***next*** day, power to have friends, power to help people, power to be sane, power to stay sober.(p.436)
• The ***next*** day, Max called the neurologist and told him about the Mayo psychiatrist's opinion.(p.445)
• I wore those moccasins every night for the ***next*** seven years, until they wore out.(p.445)
• For the ***next*** five years, I was in and out of A.A. in Los Angeles, Phoenix, and San Francisco.(p.460)
• I started going to A.A. in prison at the group's ***next*** meeting.(p.461)
• I will be fifty years old ***next*** month, haven't seen my son or daughter yet, nor my daughter's two children, my grandchildren; but I am grateful.(p.463)
• I don't mean that I went to bed one night a normal drinker, and awoke the ***next*** morning an alcoholic.(p.464)
• Having passed over the border line, the ***next*** five years were filled with fear, failure and frustration.(p.465)
• The ***next*** day the ice-bag and I were still in bed -- but we had a bottle too!(p.466)
• The ***next*** recollection I have is of my husband coming into my room (later found out it was on New Year's Eve) accompanied by two policemen.(p.468)
• ***Next*** thing I know, it was ***next*** day.(p.474)
• Then many blackouts for ***next*** two years.(p.475)
• Judge say I go to jail ***next*** time.(p.475)
• ***Next*** two years, I call them many times.(p.475)
• The ***next*** morning I carried another prescription to this man's house and exchanged it for the bottle his wife had.(p.489)
• The ***next*** morning I went up for arraignment.(p.492)
• That was the ***next*** meeting, and the first meeting of a colored group in A.A., so far as I know.(p.495)
• I drink and go to bed; I take a few the ***next*** morning and go see my mother once more.(p.501)
• I staggered home ***next*** morning.(p.510)
• I went along pretty well for the ***next*** ten months.(p.511)
• I had just come off a good one, and I went back on to the ***next*** one.(p.514)
• But if I came back in the usual state, then I'd have to go off for good the ***next*** day.(p.523)
• I always blamed my drinking on being poor, or on anything other than the truth – that I liked what booze did for me, that when I had a drink I was as big and had as much as the ***next*** person.(p.526)
• Then I would go home full of remorse, and wonder what I was going to do until I got my ***next*** check.(p.527)
• But for the ***next*** years, I worked hard and exultantly in A.A.(p.541)
• It seems only fitting that when I did finally fall in love it was with an alcoholic, and for the ***next*** ten years I progressed as rapidly as is humanly possible into what I believed to be hopeless alcoholism.(p.547)
• Over the ***next*** two years, I sickened rapidly.(p.557)
• I awoke ***next*** day with tubes in both arms.(p.558)
• In the ***next*** half-year, I experienced two more esophageal hemorrhages, miraculously surviving each one by a hair.(p.558)
• On the ***next*** page, A.A.'s "12 Traditions" are seen in their so-called "short form," the form in general use today.(p.563)

nice

• As I crossed the threshold of the dining room, the thought came to mind that it would be ***nice*** to have a couple of cocktails with dinner.(p.41)
• They expect him to give them the ***nice*** times they used to have before he drank so much, and to show his contrition for what they suffered.(p.126)
• We moved in from the country at the age when girls want all sorts of ***nice*** things.(p.261)
• "Well," I said to dad, when the A.A. people kept coming with these lovely cars and looked so ***nice***, "I suppose the neighbors say, 'Now those old fools must have up and died, but where's the hearse?'"(p.269)
• All of them were so ***nice*** to me that I figured I must be careful – they were bound to want something, being that ***nice***.(p.319)
• I found out that the people in all A.A. groups were as ***nice*** as the people in the first one.(p.320)
• I thought, now here's a ***nice*** sympathetic soul!(p.322)
• So when the children were in school from nine to three, I started up a ***nice*** little business and was fairly successful in it.(p.339)
• She told me not to bother going "for her sake"; she told me in a ***nice*** way that it didn't make any difference to her – and that really scared me – so I went.(p.365)
• Their telegram was kind and ***nice***.(p.401)
• So I married a ***nice***, well-meaning young newspaperman, so as not to have to go home.(p.402)
• I never could quite get the knack of it and kept asking myself, "What's a ***nice*** guy like me doing in a place like this?"(p.445)
• For years, I was sure the worst thing that could happen to a ***nice*** guy like me would be that I would turn out to be an alcoholic.(p.449)
• Instead, I started going to a ***nice*** private sanitarium which, after the first visit, turned out to be more like a country club than anything else.(p.468)
• We are aware of the ***nice*** things around us, things we never noticed before in our drunken stupor.(p.481)

nicely

• This worked ***nicely*** until my wife and I went to see Wallace Beery in "Tugboat Annie," after which the pant-leg and stocking racket were out!(p.177)

nicer

• We thought, on the whole, we were pretty good women, capable of being ***nicer*** if our husbands stopped drinking.(p.116)

niceties

• Men are supposed to be tough and rugged to start with, but if a woman becomes that way, it is pretty hard to get back the ***niceties*** of womanhood.(p.480)

nickel

• I hunt for my ***nickel*** to drop in the plate so that mine will be seen.(p.497)

nickname

• All changes made over the years in the Big Book (A.A. members' fond ***nickname*** for this volume) have had the same purpose: to represent the current membership of Alcoholics Anonymous more accurately, and thereby to reach more alcoholics.(p.xii)

night

• I took a ***night*** law course, and obtained employment as investigator for a surety company.(p.2)
• My drinking assumed more serious proportions, continuing all day and almost every ***night***.(p.3)
• Golf permitted drinking every day and every ***night***.(p.3)
• An all ***night*** place supplied me with a dozen glasses of ale.(p.6)
• Then came the ***night*** when the physical and mental torture was so hellish I feared I would burst through my window, sash and all.(p.6)
• With a certain satisfaction I reflected there was enough gin concealed about the house to carry me through that ***night*** and the next day.(p.8)
• Yet early next morning he searches madly for the bottle he misplaced the ***night*** before.(p.21)
• I remember having several more that ***night*** and plenty the next morning.(p.41)
• Yet, in other moments, we found ourselves thinking, when enchanted by a starlit ***night***, "Who, then, made all this?"(p.46)
• One ***night***, when confined in a hospital, he was approached by an acholic who had known a spiritual experience.(p.56)
• That very ***night***, years ago, it disappeared.(p.56)
• He commences to look around in the ***night*** clubs, or their equivalent, for something besides liquor.(p.81)
• When we retire at ***night***, we constructively review our day.(p.86)
• Your telephone may jangle at any time of the day or ***night***.(p.97)
• You should point out that his defects of character are not going to disappear over ***night***.(p.100)
• Dad may be tired at ***night*** and preoccupied by day.(p.126)
• There is talk about spiritual matters morning, noon and ***night***.(p.128)
• He added that occasionally in the ***night*** a vague craving arose which would be satisfied by candy.(p.134)
• He entered a political campaign, making speeches, frequenting men's gathering places of all sorts, often staying up all ***night***.(p.158)
• They were willing, by day or ***night***, to place a new man in the hospital and visit him afterward.(p.159)
• In addition to these casual get-togethers, it became customary to set apart one ***night*** a week for a meeting to be attended by anyone or everyone interested in a spiritual way of life.(p.159)
• From childhood through high school I was more or less forced to go to church, Sunday School and evening service, Monday ***night*** Christian Endeavor and sometimes to Wednesday evening prayer meeting.(p.172)
• This would lessen my chances of smuggling some home that evening, which in turn would mean a ***night*** of futile tossing around in bed followed by a morning of unbearable jitters.(p.176)
• My phobia for sleeplessness demanded that I get drunk every ***night***, but in order to get more liquor for the next ***night***, I had to stay sober during the day, at least up to four o'clock.(p.177)
• I gave the matter much time and study for the next two and a half years, but still got tight every ***night*** nevertheless.(p.178)
• I got tight that ***night***, stayed sober Monday till after the dinner and then proceeded to get tight again.(p.179)
• He came and got me home and to bed, gave me a few drinks that ***night***, and one bottle of beer the next morning.(p.179)
• Bill then related how he had lain awake nearly all ***night***.(p.189)
• I was a very young married man, having his whiskey in the cupboard over the sink, and when I helped my wife with the dishes at ***night*** I would take a cup of tea and spike it with whiskey.(p.196)
• So I didn't have a beer one ***night***, and as I drove home I was breaking my arm patting myself on the back because I had proved I could lick liquor.(p.203)
• So I had one double-header every ***night*** for about two or three weeks.(p.203)
• To show you the point to which this obsession went, there came an occasion when I had spent a most delightful week-end, and at nine o'clock on Sunday ***night*** I was on my way home, and I thought I would get a drink.(p.204)
• At ***night***, I woke up and the folks with whom I roomed were home by then.(p.205)
• The very simple program they advised me to follow was that I should ask to know God's will for me for that one day, and then, to the best of my ability, to follow that, and at ***night*** to express my gratefulness to God for the things that had happened to me during the day.(p.208)
• I did not have a high school education so I went to ***night*** school to take the full high school course, which I finished in two years and nine months.(p.211)
• This experience sent me to law school where I went at ***night*** and which course I completed in less than three years, taking the highest state bar examinations and passing them.(p.212)
• So I enrolled at the university for ***night*** courses in religion, and I pursued those courses for a year.(p.221)
• That ***night*** I got very drunk, which was usual, but I remembered everything, which was very unusual.(p.224)
• And I remembered the creeping horror of the interminable ***night***, in which I slept for short spells and woke up dripping with cold sweat and shaken with utter despair, to drink hastily from my bottle and mercifully pass out again, "You're mad, you're mad, you're mad!" pounded through my brain with each returning ray of consciousness, and I drowned the refrain with drink.(p.224)
• After a couple of days in dollar hotels and one ***night*** in the pokey, I finally landed on my mother's doorstep -- shaking apart, with several days' beard and, of course, broke as usual.(p.238)
• That ***night*** for the first time in my life I really let down my hair and admitted my general loneliness.(p.239)
• Little more of our talk stayed in my memory, but I do know I slept the rest of that ***night*** while before I had never known what a real night's sleep was.(p.239)
• Even that first ***night*** I blacked out, which leads me to believe that I was an alcoholic from my very first drink.(p.241)
• Routine jobs bored me, but I would take on the toughest one I could find, work day and ***night*** until I had it under control; then it would become tedious and I'd lose all interest in it.(p.243)
• Then broke again, hiding out in cheap hotels all over the country, one ***night*** jail stands here and there, and always that horrible feeling "What's the use -- nothing is worth while."(p.244)
• My fellow-workers were mostly good Saturday ***night*** drinkers and I was right with them.(p.252)
• I had some financial success through no ability of my own and, when jobless and almost wiped out in 1930, I began to trade and sell my collection; much of

the proceeds went to keep my apartment stocked with liquor and almost every ***night*** saw me helpless to bed.(p.255)

• I left the hospital on a meeting ***night***.(p.259)

• That ***night*** I was taken home by a former alcoholic and his wife.(p.259)

• Our other daughter was in her last year of high school, and one ***night*** the new son-in-law and my husband went out to a prize fight.(p.263)

• We were together all the time, but this ***night*** I got up and saw it was late.(p.263)

• Jack said there was a meeting in Akron every Wednesday ***night*** and that it was very important that we go.(p.268)

• On Wednesday ***night*** Jack M. said, "You meet me at the Ohio Edison Building, and I will take you to the meeting."(p.269)

• We had never missed a Wednesday ***night*** at King School for a year.(p.270)

• (Russ was buried on Friday, and on Sunday afternoon Hilda S. had invited me there to dinner Sunday ***night***, and I didn't think I could do it.(p.272)

• I joined their Saturday ***night*** parties and enjoyed myself too.(p.277)

• Then I started traveling, with the United States and Canada as my territory, and with so much freedom and with an unlimited expense account, I was soon drinking every ***night*** and kidding myself that it was all part of the job.(p.287)

• My wife could not understand the next morning why I was drunker than the ***night*** before when she took my bottles.(p.289)

• He spent two hours with me that ***night*** telling me his story.(p.290)

• The last day of my drinking career, I drank twenty-two of them between ten and twelve a.m. and I shall never know how many more followed them until I was poured into bed that ***night***.(p.298)

• A ***night*** or so a week in a joint, and a party or so a week at home or with friends, along with a little lone drinking, soon had me preparing for the existence of a top flight drunkard.(p.298)

• I never enjoyed any meal, but I ate my lunch at noon for two reasons; first, to help me get out of the fog of the ***night*** before and, second, to furnish some measure of nourishment.(p.299)

• I cannot remember just when I became the victim of insomnia, but I do know that the last year and a half I never went to bed sober a single ***night***.(p.299)

• I had a mortal fear of going to bed and tossing all ***ight***.(p.299)

• As a result, I would fall off in a drunken stupor every ***night***.(p.299)

• I learned that a person just can't find a job hanging n a dive or barroom all day and all ***night***, as jobs lon't seem to turn up in those places.(p.300)

• Mentally . . . I know where I was last ***night***, the ***ight*** before, and the nights before that.(p.303)

• The next three years saw me in sanitariums, once in ten day coma, from which I very nearly did not re-over, in and out of hospitals or confined at home vith day and ***night*** nurses.(p.306)

• I stayed up all ***night*** reading that book.(p.309)

• They would travel miles and stay up all ***night*** with omeone they had never laid eyes on before and think othing of it.(p.310)

While I was in basic, I got high off booze almost very ***night***.(p.317)

Somehow, I made it through basic and then laid off he booze for about three months, because I was in chool at ***night***.(p.317)

I called her every ***night*** from a local bar, and often he was not at home.(p.318)

But that ***night*** I tried to go to sleep.(p.322)

I was still woozy from the ***night*** before.(p.323)

In the old days I hated to wake up and look back at hat last ***night*** was like.(p.325)

Then, one ***night***, my whole pattern for drinking was et.(p.328)

One ***night***, I hit the jackpot.(p.332)

No matter how often I had gone into and come out f alcoholic lows during the day, the pattern bounced e out of bed each ***night*** about 2:00 a.m., shaking and urting in the agitation that always follows a drug's edation.(p.332)

One ***night***, I was struck with the memory of a line lan Ladd used in "Shane," a movie that I'd worked n.(p.333)

And I have not had a drink since that ***night***.(p.334)

I had to have it with me at ***night***, in case I woke up nd needed that drink.(p.337)

The doctor prescribed brandy for the boy to help m through the ***night*** when he coughed, a teaspoon brandy.(p.338)

• And I put a Big Book by my ***night*** stand, and I put a "Twelve Steps and Twelve Tradition" in my locker at the hospital, and I got books by Emmet Fox, and I got books by God-knows-who, and I got to reading all these things.(p.348)

• But I remembered that every ***night*** after dinner my wife would get up and do the dishes.(p.351)

• And now I am doing the darn dishes every ***night***!(p.352)

• I needed alcohol from that ***night*** on, and it in turn used me, ruling my life for three years.(p.353)

• My parents' car had a strong attraction to fences, and one ***night*** I blacked out and drove the car down a bank, ramming the steel fence around someone's backyard.(p.353)

• I certainly wasn't my shy, quiet self that ***night*** – as I was informed the next morning.(p.353)

• It was a pretty blurry ***night***.(p.353)

• We did, and spent a month boozing it up, popping pills, and smoking marijuana; taking shelter where we could, which included a veterinary hospital one ***night***; accepting meals from anyone; actually begging; stealing anything we were in need of, which was about everything.(p.354)

• That ***night*** she too had new hope because I had made sure she would know what I was doing about my drinking by packing every bit of A.A. literature I could put my hands on right on top so she couldn't help but see it when she opened my bag.(p.364)

• I tried a few drinks my last ***night*** in the city before coming home.(p.364)

• When our meeting ***night*** came around the next evening, I went -- "for her sake" I told her.(p.365)

• A lucky break, at least some will call it lucky, was in store for me at my group that ***night***.(p.365)

• One ***night*** at the dinner table my wife said that tonight was my first birthday in A.A., and that the group would have the usual ice cream and cake for the "one year man."(p.365)

• I had no trouble making the right decision when I saw my wife open her purse at the meeting that ***night*** and deposit a cute little angel in the middle of my birthday cake.(p.366)

• You will recall that I said the time that I got the idea out of a clear sky to call A.A. on a certain ***night*** was at about ten.(p.366)

• She said she cut this clipping from the paper at about ten on the same ***night***, and at the same time as I called A.A. in Pittsburgh -- some 1300 miles away.(p.367)

• One ***night***, a few weeks after joining the Fellowship, much to my surprise and delight I saw a familiar but no longer frowning face.(p.371)

• We visited most of that day and attended a meeting that ***night***.(p.378)

• I lived in New Orleans where, at that time, cocktail parties, dances and ***night*** spots were almost the order of the day – or rather the ***night***.(p.384)

• The ***night*** that I was married I had a big church wedding.(p.385)

• It was really medicinal that ***night***, that whiskey, and it was a medication after that.(p.386)

• Frank was out of town, and I remember that he'd gotten in this one ***night*** and found me drunk.(p.391)

• That was on Saturday and my husband was leaving town Sunday ***night***.(p.393)

• So I got a half pint and at midnight that ***night***, I called the number I had been given, but the man who had started the group was in the hospital so I didn't know what to do.(p.393)

• It was the first time in my life that I could not get a lift out of what I was drinking; and so one Friday ***night***, at five minutes to six, I had half a water glass of warm gin, and that is when I first asked God to help me.(p.393)

• But when this happened to me, I declared to friends that I would get drunk, dead drunk that very ***night***, and stay drunk for a month.(p.403)

• But I got drunk that ***night*** and stayed drunk, getting increasingly worse until I found A.A. ten years later.(p.404)

• That first ***night*** I blacked out at a large dinner party.(p.404)

• Tasting the best of burgundy at a famous restaurant one ***night***, landed me passed out on a park bench in the public square.(p.405)

• They said I was so funny, and told me, with shrieks of laughter, what I'd done the ***night*** before.(p.407)

• Now it was semi-blackouts every ***night***, outrageous behavior, passing out in some friend's Village studio or not knowing how I got home.(p.407)

• I would get wildly excited and look forward to another ***night*** of drinking.(p.408)

• Now came the black and endless dismal ***night***.(p.410)

• I had to go there every ***night***.(p.410)

• I stopped at the cashier's any hour of the ***night*** on the way to the bar and cashed a check.(p.410)

• I was so busy keeping her out of trouble, and so scared she'd swing on me, that I had my last two drinks that ***night***.(p.415)

• I got a job after school pumping gas and worked until ten or eleven at ***night***.(p.423)

• It was late at ***night***.(p.424)

• Once in a while I stayed home for a ***night***, to see how my folks were doing.(p.425)

• I planned to stay home the ***night*** before I left, but my folks got so drunk I walked off early in the evening and spent the ***night*** with my girl, getting very drunk myself.(p.425)

• At ***night*** I tended bar.(p.426)

• I tried to control her drinking by pouring her whiskey down the sink before I'd leave for the ***night***, to get drunker myself.(p.426)

• One ***night*** I was sitting in the lab alone with a fifth and a case of beer listening to dreamy Hawaiian music on the radio.(p.427)

• I went to Tijuana that ***night*** and landed in jail.(p.428)

• I would drink all ***night*** in bars, come home about five a.m., down a good big glass of whiskey straight, and tumble into bed.(p.428)

• This I would do by going completely "bohemian" for a ***night***, getting drunk and rolling home with the dawn.(p.432)

• One ***night*** I barely made my downtown club; if I'd had to go another fifty feet I'd have collapsed in the gutter.(p.435)

• My personality was stretched almost to splitting in the effort; schizophrenia stared me in the face, and one ***night*** I was in a suicidal despair.(p.435)

• One ***night*** my son, when he was only sixteen, was suddenly and tragically killed.(p.437)

• I remember finding myself in the middle of the ***night*** in the doctors' parking lot at the hospital with one foot in the car and one foot on the ground, not knowing which was the lead foot; finding myself hanging up the telephone – then realizing I had gotten out of bed, answered the phone, turned on the light, and carried on a conversation with a patient.(p.441)

• The longer the drinking continued, the shorter the time the alcohol would keep me asleep; I would have to drink myself back to sleep again and again throughout the ***night***.(p.441)

• One ***night***, I had to put myself back to sleep three times, and then I finally decided to give it up.(p.443)

• Both times, my reaction was that I had had nothing to drink the ***night*** before, so obviously alcohol had nothing to do with it.(p.444)

• I wore those moccasins every ***night*** for the next seven years, until they wore out.(p.445)

• Against my better judgment, I went to a meeting with him that ***night***, and a strange thing began to happen.(p.446)

• So, for no better reason than to fool him, I asked Frank to take me to a meeting every ***night***.(p.447)

• And Frank did set me up for a meeting every ***night*** except Friday, when he thought he might have a date with his girl friend.(p.447)

• I don't mean that I went to bed one ***night*** a normal drinker, and awoke the next morning an alcoholic.(p.464)

• Then I remember him coming into my room one ***night*** with a friend, and telling me to get dressed -- we were going away.(p.466)

• I waited all the rest of that day and paced the floor all that ***night***.(p.467)

• All afternoon I sat there and drank and played Bing Crosby's recording of "Silent ***Night***" over and over again on the juke box.(p.467)

• That ***night*** we drink beer at taverns.(p.474)

• Waitress by day, barfly by ***night***, she drifted down the years into jail.(p.478)

• It is so beautiful to get up in the morning not being hung-over and being able to remember where we were the ***night*** before.(p.481)

• That year, on a Friday ***night***, a man whom I had known for years came to my office.(p.488)

• The following day, Saturday, he came back and said, "Jim, I owe you for that prescription last ***night***.(p.488)

• You know the prescription that you gave me for my wife last ***night***."(p.488)

• I got drunk one ***night*** in October, went to sleep in the rain and woke up with pneumonia.(p.490)

• So, finally, I went to the YMCA and they graciously permitted us to use a room at two dollars a ***night***.(p.495)

• Even when we were paying that two dollars a ***night***, they often paid it for us because our collection was so small.(p.496)
• I drink a lot every ***night***.(p.499)
• It is ten o'clock of a Saturday ***night***.(p.500)
• His wife dies that ***night***.(p.501)
• I go to the hospital, where I have made friends with the ***night*** superintendent.(p.501)
• She had looked for me last evening after I left the car and wandered off into the ***night***.(p.502)
• Some men and women come to visit my friend of the ***night*** before.(p.504)
• But at the end of nine months we went to a party one ***night***, and I took the first drink.(p.514)
• So I don't just take the inventory at ***night*** – I take it continually throughout the day.(p.516)
• I went to a dinner he gave one ***night***, rather drunk.(p.520)
• I stopped off just to have one drink to see if it tasted the same on the way back to London, and that ***night*** I was carried back to bed again.(p.522)
• So I did manage to get myself down to an A.A. meeting that ***night***.(p.523)
• It was their open ***night*** meeting, but of course I thought they were all alcoholics; I couldn't imagine why anybody else would want to go there, and my first reaction was, well, I've come to something that's not for me.(p.524)
• I suppose I had reached my spiritual gutter that ***night***, but I have never had what you could call a real urge to drink again.(p.524)
• Since I joined on that April ***night***, A.A. has done more for me than just stop me from drinking; it has brought me back to life again.(p.524)
• I was down to my shorts, unaware of wrong-doing, before the ambulance got there and hauled me off to a hospital from which anxious friends rescued me, later that ***night***.(p.537)
• Our courtship was mainly in bars and ***night*** spots when my ship was in New York.(p.555)
• On our honeymoon, we had iced champagne by the bedside day and ***night***.(p.555)
• When I awoke in the middle of the ***night*** with shakes and sweats and fears, I would hear my wife weeping quietly in bed beside me.(p.558)
• I was attending a convention in Chicago and carousing day and ***night***.(p.558)
• (She no longer weeps in the ***night***.)(p.559)

night's

• Little more of our talk stayed in my memory, but I do know I slept the rest of that night while before I had never known what a real ***night's*** sleep was.(p.239)
• They did not show me to my room and wish me a good ***night's*** rest.(p.259)

nightclubs

• That includes bars, ***nightclubs***, dances, receptions, weddings, even plain ordinary whoopee parties.(p.101)

nightly

• I remembered going through what my sister assured me was my ***nightly*** procedure of trying to find Willie Seabrook's name in the telephone book.(p.224)

nightmare

• "Bill's Story," "Doctor Bob's ***Nightmare***," and one other personal history from the first edition were retained intact; three were edited and one of these was retitled; new versions of two stories were written with new titles; thirty completely new stories were added; and the story section was divided into three parts, under the same headings that are used now.(p.xi)
• These memories are a ***nightmare***.(p.73)
• DOCTOR BOB'S ***NIGHTMARE***(p.171)
• It was really a horrible ***nightmare***, this earning money, getting liquor, smuggling it home, getting drunk, morning jitters, taking large doses of sedatives to make it possible for me to earn more money, and so on ad nauseam.(p.177)
• Instead, I quickly substituted one or another vivid scene from the ***nightmare*** of my later drinking.(p.286)
• I, who had dreamed these sick dreams, now reaped the ***nightmare***.(p.411)
• My life there was a ***nightmare*** of periodic binges on alcohol and pills, adultery, unhappy hours at the dental office, seeing my wife give birth to our second child and have several miscarriages, living in a turbulent household, and making continual attempts to be the respectable dentist, husband, father, and community leader.(p.419)

nightmare-filled

• The horrors of increasing hangover sickness to occupy the entire day; nausea, dry heaves, the rocking bed, the ***nightmare-filled*** mind.(p.408)

nights

• Away from my office two or three weeks at a time; horrible days and ***nights*** when I would lie on the floor of my home, lying awake and reaching over to get the bottle, taking a drink and going back into oblivion.(p.184)
• These men all drank on Saturday ***nights***, and enjoyed themselves.(p.277)
• But – I also stayed up week ***nights*** after they had retired and drank myself into bed.(p.277)
• This consisted of walking the floor for three or four days and ***nights*** until I could take nourishment.(p.289)
• Mentally . . . I know where I was last night, the night before, and the ***nights*** before that.(p.303)
• I still couldn't make it through the ***nights*** without drinking, so I went back into the hospital, this time to a rehabilitation center.(p.320)
• Two ***nights*** later, self-pity went even further.(p.333)
• Since the radio station was getting on its feet, it didn't require so many ***nights*** of evening work, and that permitted leisure time for drinking.(p.360)
• On non-meeting ***nights*** I was lonesome, or so I told myself.(p.414)
• Even on my rare (at first) binge ***nights*** it never ran much over a quart.(p.433)
• At that time we had our meetings on Friday ***nights***.(p.495)
• I have no assistance and am working ***nights***, Saturdays and Sundays.(p.500)
• But not for long; now, for five Friday ***nights*** in a row, I went to jail, picked up sodden with beer (which I always disliked, but which was the only drink available); in jail five consecutive Friday ***nights*** in the town where I had grown up, where I had been an honor student in high school, where a kindly uncle, bailing me out, said, "Bob, our family just doesn't do this sort of thing."(p.539)

nights'

• It may mean the loss of many ***nights'*** sleep, great interference with your pleasures, interruptions to your business.(p.97)

nil

• Some of us have tried to hold on to our old ideas and the result was ***nil*** until we let go absolutely.(p.58)

nine

• ***Nine*** of the stories in Part II ("They Stopped in Time") are carried over from the second edition; eight new stories have been added.(p.xii)
• Let's look at Steps Eight and ***Nine***.(p.76)
• In ***nine*** cases out of ten the unexpected happens.(p.78)
• I pointed out that I had had nothing to drink whatever for three years, and this in the face of difficulties that would have made ***nine*** out of ten men drink their heads off.(p.138)
• I've prayed to God on hangover mornings and sworn that I'd never touch another drop but by ***nine*** o'clock I'd be boiled as an owl."(p.158)
• I drank ***nine*** martinis in less than an hour.(p.195)
• I had run into him, and he looked real prosperous; his face and eyes looked clear and he started to compliment me on my good front and how well I looked, and I said, "I haven't had a drink for ***nine*** months."(p.201)
• I attended their meetings every Sunday and Wednesday for about ***nine*** months.(p.202)
• To show you the point to which this obsession went, there came an occasion when I had spent a most delightful week-end, and at ***nine*** o'clock on Sunday night I was on my way home, and I thought I would get a drink.(p.204)
• I did not have a high school education so I went to night school to take the full high school course, which I finished in two years and ***nine*** months.(p.211)
• It was not known to me as a group, but I later learned that my wife had known about it for ***nine*** months and had prayed constantly that I would stumble into Akron some way or another.(p.215)
• I have served on only one committee in the past ***nine*** years, for I feel that I had my chance the first few years and that newer members should fill the jobs.(p.250)
• The ensuing ***nine*** years were the Depression years, both nationally and personally.(p.277)
• My wife, a sister member in A.A., had been a widow ***nine*** years and I had been single eighteen years.(p.286)
• Then and then only, after a thorough indoctrination by eight or ***nine*** individuals, was I allowed to attend my first meeting.(p.291)
• The meeting consisted of perhaps eight or ***nine*** alcoholics and seven or eight wives.(p.291)
• So when the children were in school from ***nine*** to three, I started up a nice little business and was fairly successful in it.(p.339)
• He has loaned it to me and I did my job, but that ended ***nine*** days ago.(p.351)
• As these words are written at fifty-three years of age, with over ***nine*** years of A.A. behind me, with all its wonderful teachings, I haven't the slightest doubt about being an alcoholic.(p.356)
• When I was called upon for a few words I had to tell my friends that I wasn't one year old in A.A. that evening but only a "***nine*** month baby."(p.366)
• At age twenty-one, I enlisted in the Navy for two reasons: (1) to avoid being drafted into the Army, and (2) out of a burst of patriotic fervor inspired by the advent of World War II and as the result of an all-night drinking binge which found me sitting on the doorstep of the Navy recruiting office when the chief petty officer arrived to open for business at ***nine*** o'clock Monday morning.(p.398)
• Pearl Harbor was a breeze of ***nine*** months, a gay Hawaiian paradise, drinking under the palms, listening to the surf beat on the shore, a bottle of whiskey near at hand.(p.426)
• I paid ***nine*** hundred dollars for a second hand car on my return.(p.429)
• After ***nine*** days of tests at Mayo, I was put in the locked ward – of all places!(p.444)
• After ***nine*** months of training, all the rest of my class was paroled and I went to work in the Department of Corrections.(p.462)
• Around eight or ***nine*** o'clock there came two big detectives and a policeman to arrest me for assault; and I was the most amazed person in the world when they said I had assaulted someone, and especially that I had assaulted my wife.(p.492)
• "I went out of here ***nine*** days ago saying that I was going to be honest, and I wasn't," he answers.(p.503)
• I clung to the outfit for the balance of my time, and finally I was released, after having spent twenty years and ***nine*** months behind bars.(p.510)
• She was the one who really helped me to make a go of that twenty years and ***nine*** months in prison.(p.511)
• We were married, and during the first ***nine*** months of that marriage I was sober.(p.514)
• But at the end of ***nine*** months we went to a party one night, and I took the first drink.(p.514)
• In those years I was in jail ***nine*** times, in an alcoholic ward, overnight, twice; and I was fired from three jobs, two of them very good ones.(p.536)
• When I remark that I have been in jail ***nine*** times, and in an alcoholic ward twice, they think I'm kidding, or possibly dramatizing for the sake of a good yarn.(p.542)
• ***Nine*** -- A.A., as such, ought never be organized; but we may create service boards or committees directly responsible to those they serve.(p.564)

nineteen

• ***Nineteen*** years ago last summer, Dr. Bob and I saw him (Bill D.) for the first time.(p.188)
• I was married at the age of ***nineteen*** to a grand girl and had good business prospects.(p.194)
• (As I've said, I was ***nineteen***.)(p.196)
• Back at camp, all was forgiven because it was the End, but in the light of what I have since learned I know I was a confirmed alcoholic at ***nineteen***.(p.242)
• Haunting me through each day's stupor -- and there were eighteen or ***nineteen*** such days in this man's home -- was the thought: "Where do I go when his family comes home?"(p.278)
• When I was ***nineteen***, I married a fine man who had never known an insecure moment in his life, let alone the trials and tribulations of booze.(p.369)
• I neither drank nor smoked until I was ***nineteen*** years old.(p.419)

nineteenth

• Then I looked forward to the week-end of golf and the ***nineteenth*** hole.(p.374)

ninety

• I told him that I had not had a drink for ***ninety*** days and that I had come to the conclusion that I was one of those individuals who couldn't drink.(p.200)
• On that statement and the fact that I had been sober for ***ninety*** days, he gave me a job selling lots in an allotment he had.(p.200)

ninety-five

• And we usually have some kind of grimy sweater that we think we look sexy in, even if we weigh ***ninety-five*** pounds soaking wet and are not wearing a bra.(p.479)

ninth

• It was a long four or five hour operation, a large surgical procedure, and she was on her ***ninth*** or tenth post-operative day.(p.350)

No. 1
• Pioneer member of Akron's Group *No. 1*, the first A.A. group in the world.(p.182)

No. 3
• An originator of Cleveland's Group *No. 3*, this one fought Prohibition in vain.(p.297)

nobody
• I was once, but I'm a ***nobody*** now.(p.157)
• It was harmless; ***nobody*** ever got drunk on beer.(p.177)
• It then occurred to me that after one was all smelled up with beer ***nobody*** could tell what had been drunk, so I began to fortify my beer with straight alcohol.(p.178)
• So it doesn't behoove me to squawk about it for, after all, ***nobody*** ever had to throw me down and pour liquor down my throat.(p.181)
• ***Nobody*** would know it, so I agreed to have the one drink.(p.202)
• Before I stop -- I always was a great talker -- I want to say that ***nobody*** will ever know how I miss Annie's advice about things.(p.273)
• Once I did have a slip -- tried drinking again -- but the A.A.'s tell me not to worry about yesterday, because ***nobody*** can change it, and not to worry about tomorrow, because it hasn't come yet.(p.320)
• ***Nobody*** but me got smashed.(p.328)
• ***Nobody*** could take away my retirement income.(p.329)
• For some reason I can't remember, it finally dawned on me that I had a problem, and yet ***nobody*** was very critical about it except my family, and that was only because I decided, after seven years of marriage, that I would divorce my husband.(p.386)
• ***Nobody*** was going to reform me!(p.412)
• Alcoholism had respected ***nobody***, neither rich nor poor, learned nor unlettered.(p.455)
• I was one of those bad cons ***nobody*** can reach.(p.460)
• I felt very lonely and hurt, because ***nobody*** understood me.(p.478)
• Our shoes are not better than the average hobo's, and if we are fortunate enough to have a pair of stockings on, ***nobody*** notices the runs in them, because of our dazzling beauty and our dirty feet.(p.479)
• This means a great deal to me, because I had always figured that ***nobody*** cared.(p.481)
• But as long as you did your work and didn't disgrace yourself, you were socially acceptable and ***nobody*** really intruded on your private life very much.(p.518)
• I got a job by myself which suited me down to the ground, because there was ***nobody*** really to interfere with what I did, one way or the other, and I usually had my nerves in good trim when anybody was coming around to inspect.(p.519)
• I wasn't afraid of anything or anybody after I learned about drinking, for it seemed right from the beginning that with liquor I could always retire to my little private world where ***nobody*** could get at me to hurt me.(p.547)

nobody's
• And it was ***nobody's*** business, ***nobody's*** but mine.(p.532)

nod
• But I can remember, in my teens, that there were a few characters who caused the village heads to ***nod*** pityingly and sometimes in anger as they paused to say, "That sot, Henri" and "Ce pauvre Jules," who drank too much.(p.230)

nodding
• I found myself ***nodding*** my head.(p.413)

noise
• Listen, not just hear ***noise***.(p.477)

noisy
• That had been in the center of New York, on ***noisy*** 42nd Street . . . this was obviously a quiet residential section.(p.223)

nominal
• Though I had been only a ***nominal*** churchman, their proposals were not, intellectually, hard to swallow.(p.42)
• (This address is now available in pamphlet form at ***nominal*** cost through most A.A. groups or from Box 459, Grand Central Station, New York, NY 10163, under the title "Three Talks to Medical Societies by Bill W." -- formerly called "Bill on Alcoholism" and earlier "Alcoholism the Illness.")(p.572)

nomination
• I had two years at Dublin University, and then in 1916, I got a ***nomination*** for Sandhurst, the British Military College.(p.518)

non-alcoholic
• We hope we have made clear the distinction between the alcoholic and the ***non-alcoholic***.(p.44)

non-academic
• I got a good ***non-academic*** education; my intellectual curiosity was encouraged.(p.401)

non-denominational
• As ***non-denominational*** people, we cannot make up others' minds for them.(p.132)

non-drinking
• I really had a chance to see myself from a ***non-drinking*** point of view.(p.245)

non-existent
• Of course, by this time, my business was practically ***non-existent***.(p.190)

non-meeting
• On ***non-meeting*** nights I was lonesome, or so I told myself.(p.414)

nonalcoholic
• This seemed to prove that one alcoholic could affect another as no ***nonalcoholic*** could.(p.xvi)
• By every form of self-deception and experimentation, they will try to prove themselves exceptions to the rule, therefore ***nonalcoholic***.(p.31)
• That may be true of certain ***nonalcoholic*** people who, though drinking foolishly and heavily at the present time, are able to stop or moderate, because their brains and bodies have not been damaged as ours were.(p.39)
• They sent me the regular letter they send to everybody else, but along with it, Ruth Hock, the ***nonalcoholic*** secretary, wrote a longhand note because she could see from the letter that I really needed help badly.(p.392)
• At that very time, he was a ***nonalcoholic*** trustee on the General Service Board of Alcoholics Anonymous!(p.559)

nonalcoholics
• But we may employ alcoholics where they are going to perform those services for which we might otherwise have to engage ***nonalcoholics***.(p.566)

nonchalant
• How often have some of us begun to drink in this ***nonchalant*** way, and after the third or fourth, pounded on the bar and said to ourselves, "For God's sake, how did I ever get started again?"(p.24)

nondiscriminatory
• Age and the law were still against me, but laws were not as strictly enforced in those days as they are now, and I discovered that as long as I had the green blood, there was always a way to get alcohol, either from a ***nondiscriminatory*** bartender or from an older friend who would be glad to purchase the joy juice for the privilege of sharing it.(p.397)

none
• Though ***none*** of these principles had the force of rules or laws, they had become so widely accepted by 1950 that they were confirmed by our first International Conference held at Cleveland.(p.xix)
• There had been no more power in him than there was in me at the minute; and this was ***none*** at all.(p.11)
• ***None*** of us makes a sole vocation of this work, nor do we think its effectiveness would be increased if we did.(p.19)
• Sometimes these excuses have a certain plausibility, but ***none*** of them really makes sense in the light of the havoc an alcoholic's drinking bout creates.(p.23)
• Almost ***none*** of us liked the self-searching, the leveling of our pride, the confession of shortcomings which the process requires for its successful consummation.(p.25)
• We doubt if many of them can do it, because ***none*** will really want to stop, and hardly one of them, because of the peculiar mental twist already acquired, will find he can win out.(p.33)
• Asked why they commenced to drink again, they would reply with some silly excuse, or ***none***.(p.107)
• Here was a prospect all right but, by the description, ***none*** too promising.(p.156)
• Without this proof the expectant purchaser would be forced to depart empty handed with ***none*** of what I later came to believe was the great panacea for all human ills.(p.171)
• It's ***none*** of our business about your drinking.(p.186)
• ***None*** of the various cures of this kind were any good.(p.235)
• I had ***none*** of these things that children should have to make them happy.(p.261)
• ***None*** of this really impressed me.(p.354)
• The questions he asked me that I didn't answer honestly, I thought were ***none*** of his business.(p.388)
• I feel that there is no situation too difficult, ***none*** too desperate, no unhappiness too great to be overcome in this great fellowship -- Alcoholics Anonymous.(p.395)
• ***None*** of them were alcoholics, but at this time they were drinking as much as I was.(p.407)
• But I will never be totally honest -- that would make me perfect, and ***none*** of us can claim to be perfect.(p.482)
• I continued to work and continued to go to lunch with Vi, and ***none*** of our acquaintances on the job knew that we had separated.(p.491)
• I don't know if it's force of habit or something else that keeps them in one place, but I do know that in A.A. there is much work to do, and ***none*** of us can do it standing still.(p.529)
• Hence we may refuse ***none*** who wish to recover.(p.565)
• If there is ***none*** nearby, you will be invited to carry on a correspondence which will do much to insure your sobriety no matter how isolated you are.(p.575)

nonexistent
• Our so-called will power becomes practically ***nonexistent***.(p.24)

nonprofessional
• Eight -- Alcoholics Anonymous should remain forever ***nonprofessional***, but our service centers may employ special workers.(p.564)
• 8. -- Alcoholics Anonymous should remain forever ***nonprofessional***.(p.566)

nonsense
• ***Nonsense***.(p.98)

nonspiritual
• Whether such a person can quit upon a ***nonspiritual*** basis depends upon the extent to which he has already lost the power to choose whether he will drink or not.(p.34)

noon
• There is talk about spiritual matters morning, ***noon*** and night.(p.128)
• Tuesday I started in the morning, getting well organized by ***noon***.(p.179)
• In fact, the last three years of my drinking was a routine of barbiturates in the morning, so that I could stop shaking enough to shave, and then alcohol beginning about four-thirty or five o'clock, with a struggle not to take a drink at ***noon*** or during the day, because I had the idea that if I took one drink, I would smell as though I had had a pint.(p.217)
• Imagine my surprise when I read in a page one "box" that I had been taken from the theater unconscious around ***noon*** that day, removed by ambulance to a hospital and stomach-pumped and then released.(p.244)
• I never enjoyed any meal, but I ate my lunch at ***noon*** for two reasons; first, to help me get out of the fog of the night before and, second, to furnish some measure of nourishment.(p.299)
• Eventually, the ***noon*** meal was also dispensed with.(p.299)
• Since I started out eager for early-day efforts, that meant guzzling before ***noon***.(p.331)
• One Saturday ***noon*** I staggered home with every intention of showing her.(p.362)
• It now became necessary to have ***noon*** drinks; at first just two, then gradually more.(p.375)
• We were supposed to take off at ***noon***, but were delayed until six p.m.(p.428)
• At ***noon*** on Christmas Day I called my family in New York, wished them a Merry Christmas, and assured them everything was fine with me.(p.467)
• It was around ***noon***, a day or two later, when the telephone rang and it was Ella.(p.494)

noon-day
• I graduated there from a five o'clock alcoholic to a ***noon-day*** one.(p.361)

noonday
• It started when I joined a few of the men for cocktails before the ***noonday*** Rotary luncheon.(p.360)

nor
• We are not allied with any particular faith, sect or denomination, ***nor*** do we oppose anyone.(p.xiv)
• I simply had to believe in a Spirit of the Universe, who knew neither time ***nor*** limitation.(p.10)
• None of us makes a sole vocation of this work, ***nor*** do we think its effectiveness would be increased if we did.(p.19)
• He does not need a bodyguard ***nor*** is he confined.(p.26)
• If we are planning to stop drinking, there must be no reservation of any kind, ***nor*** any lurking notion

that someday we will be immune to alcohol.(p.33)
• To be gravely affected, one does not necessarily have to drink a long time ***nor*** take the quantities some of us have.(p.33)
• We admit we have some of these symptoms, but we have not gone to the extremes you fellows did, ***nor*** are we likely to, for we understand ourselves so well after what you have told us that such things cannot happen again.(p.38)
• Except in a few rare cases, neither he ***nor*** any other human being can provide such a defense.(p.43)
• We remembered always that our sex powers were God-given and therefore good, neither to be used lightly or selfishly ***nor*** to be despised and loathed.(p.69)
• We have seldom told them the whole truth ***nor*** have we followed their advice.(p.73)
• ***Nor*** are we afraid of disclosing our alcoholism on the theory it may cause financial harm.(p.78)
• We will not regret the past ***nor*** wish to shut the door on it.(p.83)
• We are neither cocky ***nor*** are we afraid.(p.85)
• Neither should the family hysterically plead with him to do anything, ***nor*** should they tell him much about you.(p.90)
• We try not to indulge in cynicism over the state of the nations, ***nor*** do we carry the world's troubles on our shoulders.(p.132)
• Now about health: A body badly burned by alcohol does not often recover overnight ***nor*** do twisted thinking and depression vanish in a twinkling.(p.133)
• Normal drinkers are not so affected, ***nor*** can they understand the aberrations of the alcoholic.(p.140)
• In competent hands, this seldom takes long ***nor*** is it very expensive.(p.143)
• He will appreciate knowing you are not bothering your head about him, that you are not suspicious ***nor*** are you trying to run his life so he will be shielded from temptation to drink.(p.146)
• Whenever this man and I met – I didn't know his name then ***nor*** do I know it now – we would always get drunk.(p.201)
• He wasn't a drinking man, he didn't know what it was to need a drink, ***nor*** what a drink could do for one in a pinch.(p.227)
• From the top of the heap in a few years he had skidded to becoming a shuffling customer, still entering the better barrooms but welcomed by neither mine host ***nor*** his patrons.(p.236)
• I have never shown any particular talents ***nor*** have I had any really frustrating ambitions.(p.240)
• ***Nor*** could I blame my dilemma on my childhood environment.(p.304)
• However, due to financial difficulties the whole printing was, for a while, held up and the book received no publicity, ***nor***, of course, was it available in the stores, even if one knew it existed.(p.307)
• It becomes vital, also, that others not know of our defeats, ***nor*** suspect our loss of confidence.(p.331)
• Lucky because my excessive drinking never got me in jail, or hospitalized, ***nor*** did it ever cost me a job.(p.356)
• They were neither poor ***nor*** wealthy, but far better off than the average couple.(p.357)
• It is not too difficult ***nor*** too easy to grasp.(p.367)
• ***Nor*** have I attended them with a feeling of just doing my duty.(p.381)
• Marty came in, looking clean, neat, well-dressed and, like Bill, she was neither a bloated wreck ***nor*** a reformer.(p.413)
• ***Nor*** was I the "worst woman who ever lived."(p.414)
• ***Nor*** were those impossible dreams I used to have the things I really wanted.(p.416)
• No one could have told me then that I had not earned all my success, ***nor*** could anyone have told me that I was an alcoholic and a drug addict.(p.418)
• I had accomplished all the right things that our society expected, and I had no real peace of mind ***nor*** gratitude.(p.418)
• I neither drank ***nor*** smoked until I was nineteen years old.(p.419)
• Today, I find I can't work my A.A. program while taking pills, ***nor*** may I even have them around for dire emergencies only.(p.443)
• Alcoholism had respected nobody, neither rich ***nor*** poor, learned ***nor*** unlettered.(p.455)
• He doesn't know me, ***nor*** do I know him.(p.463)
• I will be fifty years old next month, haven't seen my son or daughter yet, ***nor*** my daughter's two children, my grandchildren; but I am grateful.(p.463)
• I feel that I have been restored to health and sanity these past years not through my own efforts ***nor*** as a result of anything I may have done, but because I've come to believe -- to really believe – that alone I can do nothing.(p.473)
• I don't miss any of the old crowd ***nor*** do I miss any of their parties.(p.511)
• The truth is, I did not know how to stop it, ***nor*** did I want to, really.(p.539)
• And if I had been able to turn to the church at that time I'm sure they could not have convinced me my sickness was within myself, ***nor*** could they have shown me the need for self-analysis that A.A. has shown me is vital if I am to survive.(p.546)
• With deep shame came the knowledge too that I had lived with no sense of social obligation ***nor*** had I known the meaning of moral responsibility to my fellow men.(p.549)
• It's been true in my case, ***nor*** could I quarrel with "restore us to sanity," for my actions drunk or sober, before A.A., were not those of a sane person.(p.550)
• ***Nor*** ought A.A. membership ever depend upon money or conformity.(p.565)

normal

• To them, their alcoholic life seems the only ***normal*** one.(p.xxvi)
• Then there are types entirely ***normal*** in every respect except in the effect alcohol has upon them.(p.xxviii)
• His disposition while drinking resembles his ***normal*** nature but little.(p.21)
• Opinions vary considerably as to why the alcoholic reacts differently from ***normal*** people.(p.22)
• Physicians who are familiar with alcoholism agree there is no such thing as making a ***normal*** drinker out of an alcoholic.(p.31)
• He is an intelligent man, ***normal*** so far as we can see, except for a nervous disposition.(p.35)
• You would expect him, if he were ***normal***, to cut it out.(p.38)
• They may be the dubious luxury of ***normal*** men, but for alcoholics these things are poison.(p.66)
• Show him, from your own experience, how the queer mental condition surrounding that first drink prevents ***normal*** functioning of the will power.(p.92)
• If your husband is otherwise a ***normal*** individual, your chances are good at this stage.(p.113)
• Father may have laid aside for years all ***normal*** activities – clubs, civic duties, sports.(p.131)
• ***Normal*** drinkers are not so affected, nor can they understand the aberrations of the alcoholic.(p.140)
• When drinking, or getting over a bout, an alcoholic, sometimes the model of honesty when ***normal***, will do incredible things.(p.140)
• There are two alcoholic employees, who produce as much as five ***normal*** salesmen.(p.149)
• For most ***normal*** folks, drinking means conviviality, companionship and colorful imagination.(p.151)
• Anyhow, I recognized the fact that I couldn't drink like ***normal*** people, but I tried hard and kept on trying for twenty-two years.(p.196)
• I wanted to live, not in a desert, but in a ***normal*** world; and my idea of a ***normal*** world was among people who drank – teetotallers were not included.(p.227)
• I like to think I was fairly ***normal*** before alcohol took over.(p.240)
• At the time, I thought them just a swell pair of screwballs, for they were not only going to save all the drunks in the world but also all the so-called ***normal*** people!(p.245)
• The details of the long road back to something resembling ***normal*** living – the first short streetcar ride, the purchase of a used bike which enabled me to widen the narrow horizon of life, the first trip downtown – I will not dwell on.(p.276)
• One is that I don't remember too many of them, as I was one of those drunks who could be on his feet and attend a meeting or a party, engage in a conversation with people and do things that any nearly ***normal*** person would do, and the next day not remember a thing about where I was, what I did, whom I saw, or how I got home.(p.301)
• I had a tough pull back to ***normal*** good health.(p.310)
• I was sent to a psychiatrist, for they didn't think it was ***normal*** for me to want to kill my platoon sergeant or to attempt suicide twice.(p.318)
• I couldn't go to one wine store and look the man honestly in the face and buy a bottle, as I used to do when I had parties and entertained and did ***normal*** drinking.(p.336)
• The last two years of my drinking my entire personality changed to a cynical, intolerant and arrogant person completely different from my ***normal*** self.(p.376)
• A drink never gave me a ***normal***, pleasant glow.(p.402)
• A ***normal*** person, hit with adversity, can go on a drinking spree and then snap out of it.(p.404)
• I had a tiny trust fund, and I moved into a small apartment where I learned to cook, keep house, and do the things that ***normal*** people do.(p.409)
• They were a couple of ***normal***, sober, attractive men.(p.415)
• In fact it has been only within the last fifteen years that I changed from a fairly ***normal***, controlled drinker into an alcoholic.(p.464)
• I don't mean that I went to bed one night a ***normal*** drinker, and awoke the next morning an alcoholic.(p.464)
• Then A.A. showed her the beauty of ***normal*** living, in a whole family reborn.(p.478)
• People seemed to be carefully dressed, too happy, too ***normal***.(p.524)

normalcy

• That went on for two more months before I landed in a hospital and started my slow fight back to ***normalcy***.(p.224)

normally

• We are people who ***normally*** would not mix.(p.17)
• Most of us have believed that if we remained sober for a long stretch, we could thereafter drink ***normally***.(p.33)
• We react sanely and ***normally***, and we will find that this has happened automatically.(p.84)
• I confined drinking to weekends, and drank ***normally*** in college and for several years thereafter.(p.287)
• But this second time, I found I couldn't live ***normally*** without it, and I was licked worse than ever.(p.340)
• I never did react ***normally*** to any emotional situation.(p.544)

north

• We drove to a store in ***North*** Hill and I sent him in with what money I had to get a quart.(p.204)
• To go ***north*** into the empty pine country and shoot myself, or to go south in the faint hope that a bunch of strangers might help me with my drinking problem.(p.278)
• Then I went South, because they told me that the particular county I was going to in ***North*** Carolina was a dry county.(p.489)
• But I found that after I got to ***North*** Carolina it wasn't any different.(p.490)

North Carolina

• Then I went South, because they told me that the particular county I was going to in ***North Carolina*** was a dry county.(p.489)
• But I found that after I got to ***North Carolina*** it wasn't any different.(p.490)

northern

• In January 1938, I had the opportunity to go to ***northern*** Vermont to manage a small daytime radio station that was up against it financially, and was about to fold its antenna.(p.359)

nose

• I'll buy you one drink, and if you suggest a second one, I'll poke you right in the ***nose***."(p.201)
• I had a broken ***nose***, a fractured cheekbone, and was black from the lower part of my face up into my hair.(p.204)
• They told Annabelle to take me under her wing, and I shall never forget how she sort of curled up her ***nose*** and said, "They tell me you drink too."(p.269)
• Following an injection I would have to keep one hand busy scratching my constantly itching ***nose*** and would also have sudden uncontrollable urges to vomit.(p.442)

nosebleeds

• I had severe ***nosebleeds***.(p.558)

nosey

• Gone are time cards to punch, alarm clocks to obey, ***nosey*** rumor-mongers and talebearers to evade.(p.329)

nostalgia

• Following a big drunk on that sheet, where I was doing leg-work and rewrite, a feeling of ***nostalgia*** made me buy a ticket for Liverpool and I returned to Britain.(p.252)

nostrils

• It irritated my ***nostrils***; I choked, I didn't like it.(p.195)

note

• You will ***note*** that we made an important qualification.(p.101)
• He left us a ***note*** saying you were the best boss he ever had, and that you were not to blame in any way."(p.136)
• They sent me the regular letter they send to every-

body else, but along with it, Ruth Hock, the nonalcoholic secretary, wrote a longhand ***note*** because she could see from the letter that I really needed help badly.(p.392)

• There are so many to whom I feel deeply grateful; to my husband (and best critic), whose generous love, compassion and understanding have helped me along the way; to those before me in A.A. who inspired the first article I read, and the friend who sent that article to Frank; to Ruth for her personal ***note***, and the first A.A. to talk to me; to my Bishop, whose loving and believing spirit inspired me; and to all the members of the Houston Group who were so patient, kind and helpful -- and to countless others.(p.393)

noted

• Dr. Harry Emerson Fosdick, the ***noted*** clergyman, reviewed it with approval.(p.xvii)

notes

• The movie racket had kept me too long from writing those novels, articles, short stories, and scripts on which I had copious ***notes***.(p.330)

• Took down ***notes*** for reference purposes.(p.344)

• Much of my time was spent writing letters, ***notes***, orders, and lists of things for Max, who was also my office nurse, to do to keep the world running while I was locked up.(p.445)

nothing

• We feel, after many years of experience, that we have found ***nothing*** which has contributed more to the rehabilitation of these men than the altruistic movement now growing up among them.(p.xxvi)

• I could eat little or ***nothing*** when drinking, and I was forty pounds under weight.(p.7)

• ***Nothing*** more was required of me to make my beginning.(p.12)

• I admitted for the first time that of myself I was ***nothing***; that without Him I was lost.(p.13)

• Until such an understanding is reached, little or ***nothing*** can be accomplished.(p.18)

• That the man who is making the approach has had the same difficulty, that he obviously knows what he is talking about, that his whole deportment shouts at the new prospect that he is a man with a real answer, that he has no attitude of Holier Than Thou, ***nothing*** whatever except the sincere desire to be helpful; that there are no fees to pay, no axes to grind, no people to please, no lectures to be endured -- these are the conditions we have found most effective.(p.18)

• ***Nothing*** would please us so much as to write a book which would contain no basis for contention or argument.(p.19)

• When, therefore, we were approached by those in whom the problem had been solved, there was ***nothing*** left for us but to pick up the simple kit of spiritual tools laid at our feet.(p.25)

• The great fact is just this, and ***nothing*** less: That we have had deep and effective spiritual experiences which have revolutionized our whole attitude toward life, toward our fellows and toward God's universe.(p.25)

• Those having religious affiliations will find here ***nothing*** disturbing to their beliefs or ceremonies.(p.28)

• I had a few words with the boss, but ***nothing*** serious.(p.36)

• Here was the threat of commitment, the loss of family and position, to say ***nothing*** of that intense mental and physical suffering which drinking always caused him.(p.36)

• He was interested and conceded that he had some of the symptoms, but he was a long way from admitting that he could do ***nothing*** about it himself.(p.40)

• I had been out of town before during this particular dry spell, so there was ***nothing*** new about that.(p.41)

• ***Nothing*** more.(p.41)

• Were our contentions true, it would follow that life originated out of ***nothing***, and proceeds nowhere.(p.49)

• Without that, ***nothing*** could have happened.(p.52)

• When we became alcoholics, crushed by a self-imposed crisis we could not postpone or evade, we had to fearlessly face the proposition that either God is everything or else He is ***nothing***.(p.53)

• Little or ***nothing***, we saw at last.(p.54)

• Were ***nothing*** left but pure reason, it wouldn't be life.(p.54)

• Could we still say the whole thing was ***nothing*** but a mass of electrons, created out of ***nothing***, meaning ***nothing***, whirling on to a destiny of nothingness?(p.54)

• Half measures availed us ***nothing***.(p.59)

• ***Nothing*** counted but thoroughness and honesty.(p.65)

• Once we have taken this step, withholding ***nothing***, we are delighted.(p.75)

• We are there to sweep off our side of the street realizing that ***nothing*** worth while can be accomplished until we do so, never trying to tell him what he should do.(p.77)

• We thought he ought to be willing to do that if necessary, but if he were in jail he could provide ***nothing*** for either family.(p.79)

• Practical experience shows that ***nothing*** will so much insure immunity from drinking as intensive work with other alcoholics.(p.89)

• But say ***nothing***, for the moment, of how that was accomplished.(p.91)

• If, on the other hand, they took ***nothing***, their self-pity made them killjoys.(p.105)

• We urge you to try our program, for ***nothing*** will be so helpful to your husband as the radically changed attitude toward him which God will show you how to have.(p.117)

• We have found ***nothing*** incompatible between a powerful spiritual experience and a life of sane and happy usefulness.(p.130)

• ***Nothing*** will help the man who is off on a spiritual tangent so much as the wife who adopts a sane spiritual program, making a better practical use of it.(p.130)

• New acquaintances who know ***nothing*** of alcoholism might be made and thoughtful consideration given their needs.(p.131)

• So far as we are concerned, there is ***nothing*** obligatory about it.(p.132)

• I pointed out that I had had ***nothing*** to drink whatever for three years, and this in the face of difficulties that would have made nine out of ten men drink their heads off.(p.138)

• There was ***nothing*** to do but wait.(p.139)

• Nearly always, these antics indicate ***nothing*** more than temporary conditions.(p.141)

• I know, in my own particular case, that ***nothing*** my company could have done would have stopped me for, so long as I was able to hold my position, I could not possibly realize how serious my situation was.(p.141)

• ***Nothing*** would fix me.(p.157)

• He suffered horribly from his sprees, but it seemed as if ***nothing*** could be done for him.(p.159)

• I remember ***nothing*** from then on until I woke up at a friend's house, in a town near home.(p.179)

• There was ***nothing*** about that drink that I liked.(p.195)

• This duty together with my weekly meetings with my fellow alcoholics, and my daily renewal of the contract I originally made with God, have kept me sober when ***nothing*** else ever did.(p.237)

• ***Nothing*** had worked.(p.238)

• Then broke again, hiding out in cheap hotels all over the country, one night jail stands here and there, and always that horrible feeling "What's the use -- ***nothing*** is worth while."(p.244)

• With ***nothing*** but a liberal arts education, very definitely estranged from my family and already married, soon after graduation from college I became a bookmaker's clerk on the British racing circuits, far better off financially than the average professional man.(p.251)

• I listened to famous ministers – found ***nothing***.(p.255)

• My family would have ***nothing*** to do with me, in fact couldn't because I couldn't spare any of my money, which I needed for drink, to support them.(p.255)

• I wanted to do ***nothing*** except what it pleased me to do when I wanted to do it.(p.256)

• I lay across the bed on my stomach with ***nothing*** but pain and sickness.(p.267)

• A complete checkup at one of the best hospitals revealed ***nothing***.(p.276)

• I heard for the first time an expression which I was to grow to loathe: "There is ***nothing*** organically wrong."(p.276)

• The birth of a baby boy did ***nothing*** toward staying the downward spiral.(p.278)

• ***Nothing*** had changed and yet everything had changed.(p.280)

• ***Nothing*** has ever to this day equalled the thrill of that first case.(p.282)

• I enrolled in a correspondence school which taught ***nothing*** but accounting.(p.284)

• So I told dad that I would lick it on my own, that I would drink ***nothing*** for a month and after that only beer.(p.289)

• From a monetary standpoint . . . in the past few years, I have reduced my reckless debts to almost ***nothing***, and have had money to get along on comfortably.(p.303)

• Of course the doctors found ***nothing***.(p.305)

• ***Nothing*** worked.(p.305)

• In describing his suffering, his fears, his many years of groping for some answer to that which always seemed to remain unanswerable, he could have been describing me, and ***nothing*** short of experience and knowledge could have afforded him that much insight!(p.309)

• ***Nothing*** in their lives took precedence over their response to a call for help from some alcoholic in need.(p.310)

• They would travel miles and stay up all night with someone they had never laid eyes on before and think ***nothing*** of it.(p.310)

• There is no more "aloneness," with that awful ache, so deep in the heart of every alcoholic that ***nothing***, before, could ever reach it.(p.312)

• When I was released from the hospital, I went back to my unit, and ***nothing*** had changed.(p.319)

• Hiding behind a newspaper, magazine, or book, I really saw ***nothing***, but simulated deep interest.(p.332)

• In A.A., she discovered she had lost ***nothing*** and had found everything.(p.335)

• And the mops would get out, the vacuum would get out, everything would get out, but ***nothing*** would get done.(p.337)

• I cared ***nothing*** about my personal appearance.(p.337)

• I knew ***nothing*** about alcoholism or the D.T.'s, but when I woke up on this last morning of my son's illness, I taped the keyhole on my door because "everyone was out there."(p.338)

• The people who would have come to help me were just the people I would have ***nothing*** to do with.(p.338)

• As someone in A.A. said to me once upon a time, there is ***nothing*** worse than a confused psychiatrist.(p.347)

• So he got me a cup of coffee, and a piece of cake, and sat me down and said, "Why, there's ***nothing*** wrong with you.(p.348)

• And then it went on to say: "Half measures availed us ***nothing***.(p.349)

• "Complete abandon"; "Half measures availed us ***nothing***"; "Thoroughly follow our path"; "Completely give oneself to this simple program" – rang in my swelled head.(p.349)

• For the next couple of hours a terrible battle went on between the good gremlins and the bad ones, one faction urging me to tell the truth, the other telling me to sit tight and say ***nothing***.(p.366)

• It shows ***nothing*** or no one to blame for alcoholism.(p.373)

• The allergy we could do ***nothing*** about.(p.380)

• Something went haywire and I got to depend on it so I could do ***nothing*** without it.(p.386)

• I woke up in this bare room with ***nothing*** around me but bars; they wouldn't let me smoke and treated me, well, like I was nuts.(p.387)

• There was ***nothing*** else left to try.(p.389)

• I had writing ambitions, and ***nothing*** would do but that I'd write like Shakespeare.(p.400)

• Naturally, I succeeded in ***nothing***.(p.400)

• Otherwise I got ***nothing*** out of it.(p.401)

• I resented this, but I did ***nothing*** constructive about it.(p.402)

• It was ***nothing*** to my own inner distress, my self-reproach, and my self-loathing, for was I not bearing out all the horrible things I had always suspected of myself?(p.404)

• He also said, "You are an alcoholic and there's ***nothing*** I can do for you."(p.406)

• Since they could do ***nothing*** with Anne either, Priscilla suggested that I go and look after Anne.(p.414)

• I thought it was my duty to keep her from drinking, not knowing that if the other fellow is really determined to drink there is ***nothing*** you can do about it.(p.415)

• I was ***nothing*** more than a spoiled, indulged, and talented brat.(p.418)

• I talked the Old Man into letting me live in the photo lab instead of the barracks, and for eighteen months ***nothing*** interfered with my drinking.(p.426)

• Four years ago I had ***nothing*** but a jumbled, mad existence.(p.430)

• "There's ***nothing*** I can do," he said, "and ***nothing*** medicine can do.(p.436)

• On two occasions, over weekends, I decided I would take absolutely ***nothing***.(p.443)

• Both times, my reaction was that I had had ***nothing*** to drink the night before, so obviously alcohol had ***nothing*** to do with it.(p.444)

• (Today, there is absolutely ***nothing*** in the world

more important to me than my keeping this alcoholic sober; not taking a drink is by far the most important thing I do each day.)(p.447)

• To this day, I am amazed at how many of my problems -- most of which had ***nothing*** to do with drinking, I believed -- have become manageable or have simply disappeared since I quit drinking.(p.448)

• ***Nothing***, absolutely ***nothing*** happens in God's world by mistake.(p.449)

• Each time I told her she was a ***nothing***, she receded a little more into nowhere.(p.450)

• I never just sit and do ***nothing*** while waiting for Him to tell me what to do.(p.452)

• ***Nothing*** worked.(p.455)

• All found themselves headed for the same destruction, and it seemed they could to ***nothing*** whatever to stop it.(p.455)

• ***Nothing*** could pull me out of the abyss but more alcohol.(p.457)

• There is really ***nothing*** to dressing with chains and shackles on, once you learn the technique of pulling inside-out pants through the shackles.(p.460)

• ***Nothing*** that has happened to me do I deserve.(p.463)

• I take credit for ***nothing***.(p.463)

• I was taken out of the house and put bodily into a waiting car with ***nothing*** on but a robe and gown.(p.466)

• I feel that I have been restored to health and sanity these past years not through my own efforts nor as a result of anything I may have done, but because I've come to believe -- to really believe -- that alone I can do ***nothing***.(p.473)

• Mind you, I had absolutely ***nothing*** to show for that eighteen years, except a beat-up car that I hadn't even paid for, but I was doing all right.(p.478)

• I wasted twenty years of my life, and there is ***nothing*** I can do about that, but there is something I can do about now.(p.480)

• He wanted to give me the very best and he thought that ***nothing*** but being a doctor would suffice.(p.485)

• I don't think I suffered too much as far as the racial situation was concerned because I was born into it and knew ***nothing*** other than that.(p.485)

• He could do ***nothing*** about it.(p.486)

• Fear gripped me then, because I could remember ***nothing*** about it.(p.489)

• I had a long talk with a psychiatrist, but ***nothing*** came of that, and I had also, just about that time, talked with a minister for whom I had a great deal of respect.(p.489)

• There is no use trying any more, for there is ***nothing*** to try.(p.502)

• ***Nothing*** seems to be working out right.(p.505)

• ***Nothing*** is right.(p.506)

• The family seems to think of ***nothing*** but spending.(p.506)

• She says ***nothing***.(p.507)

• I rolled along with the mob this way, that way and the other way, but in those years ***nothing*** really bad happened to me.(p.508)

• When I had heard about it, it meant ***nothing*** but just two letters to me, but some friends of mine in the institution were very active in the program and really believed in it.(p.509)

• There was ***nothing*** in my school life that I can look back on which was responsible for anything that happened afterwards.(p.517)

• I was in a world that I knew ***nothing*** at all about, and I felt intensely afraid.(p.521)

• But then one good doctor told me there was ***nothing*** wrong with me except drinking too much.(p.528)

• I'm writing this during an A.A. convention, where I have spent the weekend with ***nothing*** but white people.(p.529)

• There was the necessity for sticking to a job I hated, a dull, repetitive job performed in association with other men I had ***nothing*** in common with . . . performed for years on end, because the money was needed at home.(p.532)

• There was the over-weening ambition to be the world's greatest author, when -- at thirty-nine -- I had ***nothing*** of importance to say to the world.(p.534)

• I had ***nothing*** to put in the place of alcohol, of the forgetfulness, of the oblivion, which alcohol provides.(p.539)

• I thought this would give me ego-strength, make me feel wanted and secure, and alleviate my fears, but again ***nothing*** changed inside me.(p.546)

• Experience has often warned us that ***nothing*** can so surely destroy our spiritual heritage as futile disputes over property, money, and authority.(p.566)

nothingness

• Could we still say the whole thing was nothing but a mass of electrons, created out of nothing, meaning nothing, whirling on to a destiny of ***nothingness***?(p.54)

notice

• ***Notice*** that the word "fear" is bracketed alongside the difficulties with Mr. Brown, Mrs. Jones, the employer, and the wife.(p.67)

• I found I could boost my income by figuring out a lot of cute little tricks that the boss wouldn't be likely to ***notice*** -- filching money from the Coke machine, short-sticking the customers on oil, and selling oil I'd drained out of other cars.(p.423)

• I fled, finally, after having been fired from my job by a boss who wept a little (since I had worked hard) as he gave ***notice*** for me to clear out.(p.539)

noticeable

• When it became ***noticeable*** to the point of comment, I devised ways of sneaking drinks on the side.(p.375)

noticed

• The slightest disposition on your part to guide his appointments or his affairs so he will not be tempted will be ***noticed***.(p.120)

• Many of us have ***noticed*** a tendency to eat sweets and have found this practice beneficial.(p.134)

• I ***noticed*** that the others seemed to have such a release, a happiness, a something that I thought a person ought to have.(p.191)

• I checked into my hotel room and then ***noticed*** a placard tucked under the glass on the bureau stating "There will be positively NO drinking at this convention" signed by the president of the company.(p.243)

• I ***noticed*** a Bible on his table and it amazed me.(p.257)

• I ***noticed*** that I was avoiding all my social friends except for my bridge.(p.324)

• At times, when I ***noticed*** other families, I felt something was very wrong with ours.(p.369)

• But he ***noticed*** that I was not a good mother to my child, that I relegated her to nurses when she was with me.(p.403)

• Above all, he ***noticed*** that I drank a good deal, often got tight in his company and told him naughty stories.(p.403)

• We are aware of the nice things around us, things we never ***noticed*** before in our drunken stupor.(p.481)

• I went to this friend's shop to repair his electrical outlet and I ***noticed*** this lady.(p.493)

notices

• Our shoes are not better than the average hobo's, and if we are fortunate enough to have a pair of stockings on, nobody ***notices*** the runs in them, because of our dazzling beauty and our dirty feet.(p.479)

notified

• These good people ***notified*** my wife, who sent my newly made friend over to get me.(p.179)

notion

• If we are planning to stop drinking, there must be no reservation of any kind, nor any lurking ***notion*** that someday we will be immune to alcohol.(p.33)

• I also had the ***notion*** that I might find a customer for a car at this place, which was familiar for I had been going to it for years.(p.36)

• He clings to the ***notion*** that he will yet find a way to do so.(p.110)

• But it quickly became obvious that he had this childish ***notion*** instead: If he could get me to go to enough meetings while in the hospital, I would continue to go after he let me out.(p.447)

notorious

• In five years a good many persons had forgotten that I had been somewhat ***notorious***.(p.256)

• Anyhow, after Christmas my husband gave me a cocker spaniel who is, I think, just as ***notorious*** in A.A. as I am.(p.388)

notoriously

• Doctors have been ***notoriously*** unsuccessful in helping alcoholics.(p.352)

notwithstanding

• ***Notwithstanding*** the great necessity for discussing ourselves with someone, it may be one is so situated that there is no suitable person available.(p.74)

nourishment

• This consisted of walking the floor for three or four days and nights until I could take ***nourishment***.(p.289)

• I never enjoyed any meal, but I ate my lunch at noon for two reasons; first, to help me get out of the fog of the night before and, second, to furnish some measure of ***nourishment***.(p.299)

novel

• My friend suggested what then seemed a ***novel*** idea.(p.12)

• To you, some of the ideas which it contains are ***novel***.(p.144)

• I got a ***novel*** written.(p.402)

• I also wrote another ***novel***, all about Scott Fitzgerald's poor, misbegotten, unloved, tipsy little debutante.(p.405)

novels

• The movie racket had kept me too long from writing those ***novels***, articles, short stories, and scripts on which I had copious notes.(p.330)

November

• Near the end of that bleak ***November***, I sat drinking in my kitchen.(p.8)

• My last bout in the Army lasted from ***November*** 5th to 11th, 1918.(p.242)

• It was ***November*** 11th and bells were ringing and whistles blowing for the real Armistice.(p.242)

• I returned to my home in Lucknow, India, at the end of ***November*** last year from a vacation in one of the most famous beauty spots in our country, a mountain resort 6,800 feet up, with a wonderful lake.(p.342)

• We were married in Montreal in ***November***.(p.361)

• Finally, however, in ***November*** of 1944, at long last I went to A.A.(p.470)

• The ***November*** following, I took a few days off after pay day to celebrate my birthday on the 25th of the month.(p.491)

• I am to go to camp on ***November*** 13th.(p.499)

• It is a cold, bleak day in ***November***.(p.502)

• This was done, and the paper was printed in the American Journal of Psychiatry for ***November***, 1949.(p.572)

now

• "Bill's Story," "Doctor Bob's Nightmare," and one other personal history from the first edition were retained intact; three were edited and one of these was retitled; new versions of two stories were written with new titles; thirty completely new stories were added; and the story section was divided into three parts, under the same headings that are used ***now***.(p.xi)

• Some are just ***now*** taking shape in Asia.(p.xv)

• He had also been greatly helped by the late Dr. William D. Silkworth, a New York specialist in alcoholism who is ***now*** accounted no less than a medical saint by A.A. members, and whose story of the early days of our Society appears in the next pages.(p.xvi)

• It was ***now*** time, the struggling groups thought, to place their message and unique experience before the world.(p.xvii)

• The fledgling society, which had been nameless, ***now*** began to be called Alcoholics Anonymous, from the title of its own book.(p.xvii)

• Alcohol being no respecter of persons, we are an accurate cross section of America, and in distant lands, the same democratic evening-up process is ***now*** going on.(p.xx)

• Women ***now*** make up more than one-fourth of the membership; among newer members, the proportion is nearly one-third.(p.xxii)

• We feel, after many years of experience, that we have found nothing which has contributed more to the rehabilitation of these men than the altruistic movement ***now*** growing up among them.(p.xxvi)

• I see him ***now*** and then and he is as fine a specimen of manhood as one could wish to meet.(p.xxx)

• ***Now*** I had what it takes!(p.6)

• No -- not ***now***.(p.6)

• Understanding myself ***now***, I fared forth in high hope.(p.7)

• ***Now*** I was to plunge into the dark, joining that endless procession of sots who had gone on before.(p.8)

• But that was over ***now***.(p.8)

• So that was it -- last summer an alcoholic crackpot; ***now***, I suspected, a little cracked about religion.(p.9)

• The good doctor ***now*** sees many men who have such experiences.(p.14)

• We have it with us right here and ***now***.(p.16)

• But that in itself would never have held us together as we are ***now*** joined.(p.17)

• ***Now*** these are commonplace observations on drinkers which we hear all the time.(p.20)

• Many who once were in this class are ***now*** among our members.(p.28)

• We ***now*** see that when we began to drink deliberately, instead of casually, there was little serious or effective thought during the period of premeditation of what the terrific consequences might be.(p.37)

• I ***now*** remembered what my alcoholic friends had told me, how they prophesied that if I had an alcoholic mind, the time and place would come -- I would drink again.(p.41)

• My old manner of life was by no means a bad one, but I would not exchange its best moments for the

worst I have ***now***.(p.43)
• "Do I ***now*** believe, or am I even willing to believe, that there is a Power greater than myself?"(p.47)
• His story is so interesting that some of it should be told ***now***.(p.55)
• Our stories disclose in a general way what we used to be like, what happened, and what we are like ***now***.(p.58)
• May you find Him ***now***!(p.59)
• We are ***now*** at Step Three.(p.63)
• For we are ***now*** on a different basis; the basis of trusting and relying upon God.(p.68)
• ***Now*** about sex.(p.68)
• We hope you are convinced ***now*** that God can remove whatever self-will has blocked you off from Him.(p.71)
• ***Now*** these are about to be cast out.(p.72)
• We may have had certain spiritual beliefs, but ***now*** we begin to have a spiritual experience.(p.75)
• Are we ***now*** ready to let God remove from us all the things which we have admitted are objectionable?(p.76)
• Can He ***now*** take them all -- every one?(p.76)
• When ready, we say something like this: "My Creator, I am ***now*** willing that you should have all of me, good and bad.(p.76)
• I pray that you ***now*** remove from me every single defect of character which stands in the way of my usefulness to you and my fellows.(p.76)
• ***Now*** we need more action, without which we find that "Faith without works is dead."(p.76)
• ***Now*** we go out to our fellows and repair the damage done in the past.(p.76)
• We ought to sit down with the family and frankly analyze the past as we ***now*** see it, being very careful not to criticize them.(p.83)
• Outline the program of action, explaining how you made a self-appraisal, how you straightened out your past and why you are ***now*** endeavoring to be helpful to him.(p.94)
• Suppose ***now*** you are making your second visit to a man.(p.96)
• ***Now***, the domestic problem: There may be divorce, separation, or just strained relations.(p.98)
• ***Now*** you are getting back into the social life of this world.(p.102)
• Your job ***now*** is to be at the place where you may be of maximum helpfulness to others, so never hesitate to go anywhere if you can be helpful.(p.102)
• Let's ***now*** go back to husband number one.(p.110)
• And ***now*** you know that he can stop if he will!(p.116)
• ***Now*** we try to put spiritual principles to work in every department of our lives.(p.116)
• It is the most natural thing in the world, once his liquor problem is solved, to feel that he will ***now*** measure up to that cherished vision.(p.118)
• You feel he should ***now*** be yours.(p.119)
• But the head of the house has spent years in pulling down the structures of business, romance, friendship, health -- these things are ***now*** ruined or damaged.(p.123)
• ***Now*** and then the family will be plagued by spectres from the past, for the drinking career of almost every alcoholic has been marked by escapades, funny, humiliating, shameful or tragic.(p.123)
• Showing others who suffer how we were given help is the very thing which makes life seem so worth while to us ***now***.(p.124)
• Dad may feel that for years his drinking has placed him on the wrong side of every argument, but ***now*** he has become a superior person with God on his side.(p.129)
• ***Now*** about health: A body badly burned by alcohol does not often recover overnight nor do twisted thinking and depression vanish in a twinkling.(p.133)
• Hardly one of our crowd ***now*** shows any mark of dissipation.(p.133)
• Though he is ***now*** a most effective member of Alcoholics Anonymous, he still smokes and drinks coffee, but neither his wife or anyone else stands in judgment.(p.135)
• Here were three exceptional men lost to this world because I did not understand alcoholism as I do ***now***.(p.137)
• You ***now*** know more about alcoholism.(p.141)
• If he says yes, does he really mean it, or down inside does he think he is fooling you, and that after rest and treatment he will be able to get away with a few drinks ***now*** and then?(p.142)
• ***Now*** and then a serious drinker, being dry at the moment says, "I don't miss it at all.(p.151)
• Suppose ***now*** that through you several families have adopted this way of life.(p.153)
• After all, had he not been sober six months ***now***?(p.154)
• As we shall see, he ***now*** means a great deal to his community, and the major liabilities of thirty years of hard drinking have been repaired in four.(p.156)
• Understand he was once a well-known lawyer in town, but just ***now*** we've got him strapped down tight."(p.156)
• The use of spiritual principles in such cases was not so well understood as it is ***now***.(p.156)
• I was once, but I'm a nobody ***now***.(p.157)
• So, you see, there were three alcoholics in that town, who ***now*** felt they had to give to others what they had found, or be sunk.(p.158)
• He ***now*** returned home, leaving behind his first acquaintance, the lawyer and the devil-may-care chap.(p.159)
• He and his wife would leave elated by the thought of what they could ***now*** do for some stricken acquaintance and his family.(p.160)
• ***Now***, this house will hardly accommodate its weekly visitors, for they number sixty or eighty as a rule.(p.161)
• Then, in this eastern city, there are informal meetings such as we have described to you, where you may ***now*** see scores of members.(p.162)
• You forget that you have just ***now*** tapped a source of power much greater than yourself.(p.163)
• All have ***now*** passed away from natural causes, having maintained complete sobriety.(p.169)
• I was between Scylla and Charybdis ***now***, because if I did not drink my stomach tortured me, and if I did, my nerves did the same thing.(p.175)
• After a while, Bill said, "Well, ***now***, you've been talking a good long time, let me talk a minute or two."(p.185)
• ***Now***, if you don't want it, we'll not take up your time, and we'll be going and looking for someone else."(p.186)
• In fact, I admitted that from ***now*** on I was willing to let God take over, instead of me.(p.187)
• And they said, "No, you have a disease, and it doesn't make any difference how long you do without it, after a drink or two you'll end up just like you are ***now***."(p.187)
• Had blacked the eyes of two nurses, and ***now*** they had him strapped down tight.(p.188)
• ***Now*** he was sure.(p.189)
• (Bill D. ***now*** continues his story.)(p.189)
• I have already done it, and I am willing to do it again here in the presence of you or I am willing to say it any place, anywhere in the world from ***now*** on and not be ashamed of it."(p.190)
• Naturally, what little restraint I had exercised before was gone ***now***, and my drinking became worse.(p.199)
• ***Now*** I attempted to quit.(p.199)
• At the end of about four months, I not only had good looking clothes --and I might say that at the time I first talked to Max I didn't have a suit of clothes I could bend over in real sudden; ***now*** I had six suits of clothes.(p.200)
• Whenever this man and I met -- I didn't know his name then nor do I know it ***now*** -- we would always get drunk.(p.201)
• ***Now*** we got you the drink, but you haven't taken the medicine."(p.206)
• He said, "So long as I'm thinking as I'm thinking ***now***, and so long as I'm doing the things I'm doing ***now***, I don't believe I'll ever take another drink."(p.206)
• And I said, "***Now*** you want to dry me up.(p.207)
• It has continued to work ***now*** for nearly eighteen years.(p.209)
• As far as my home was concerned, I did not see then, though of course I can see ***now***, that it was anything but a happy situation for my wife.(p.215)
• I was ***now*** forming an entirely new drinking technique.(p.233)
• I had never doubted the existence of the Supreme Being, but ***now*** I began to absent myself from my church where I had formerly been a member of the choir.(p.234)
• This doctor had imparted his knowledge to just a few other men at that time -- not more than four or five -- they ***now*** number more than seventy persons.(p.235)
• I have been sober for many years ***now***.(p.237)
• Jackie told me about a group of fellows in New York, of whom my old friend Fitz was one, who had the same problem I had, and who by working together to help each other were not ***now*** drinking and were happy like himself.(p.239)
• This company ***now*** does a volume of over three billion dollars annually.(p.242)
• My loneliness was worse than it had ever been before, for ***now*** even my own kind had turned against me.(p.247)
• We ***now*** live in the West and are very fortunate in our area A.A.; it is good, simple and friendly, and our one desire is to stay in A.A. and not on it.(p.250)
• ***Now*** on a new job I was always thinking about payday and how much liquor I could buy and the pleasure I could have.(p.255)
• I found my friend was there for alcoholism and ***now*** he was insisting that he had found the only cure.(p.257)
• As he talked I gathered vaguely, (because he was a faltering beginner then, just as I am ***now***) that to be relieved of alcoholism I would have to be different.(p.257)
• "Anyhow, I'm on the wagon ***now***," I said.(p.257)
• When I came to my aunt, she knew that I had had an unhappy childhood, and she said, "***Now***, Ethel, you're welcome to have boy friends in our home, but there are two boys in this town that I don't want you to date, and one of them comes from a very fine family, one of the best.(p.262)
• But I don't believe ***now*** that it was with any deep feeling of resentment that I said to him, "The children are raised, and if this is the way you want it, this is the way we'll have it.(p.263)
• He said, "Sister, if you think you're a screwball ***now***, all you have to do is join up with that.(p.266)
• "Well, I'm nuts enough ***now***," I said to him.(p.266)
• ***Now***, if you've got a Bible around . . ."(p.268)
• Jack said, "***Now*** you start and go to these meetings, and then you'll find out all about it."(p.268)
• "Well," I said to dad, when the A.A. people kept coming with these lovely cars and looked so nice, "I suppose the neighbors say, '***Now*** those old fools must have up and died, but where's the hearse?'"(p.269)
• ***Now*** I was in a strange house, in a strange city, and fear gripped me.(p.279)
• It was different from the meetings ***now*** held.(p.291)
• A few months after I made my original trip to Akron I was feeling pretty cocky, and I didn't think my wife was treating me with proper respect, ***now*** that I was an outstanding citizen.(p.293)
• From a single member in the Chicago area, commuting to Akron, we ***now*** exceed six thousand.(p.295)
• Where derision, contempt and pity were once shown me, I ***now*** enjoy the respect of many people.(p.296)
• Where once I had casual acquaintances, all of whom were fair weather friends, I ***now*** have a host of friends who accept me for what I am.(p.296)
• The parties waxed more liquid and hilarious as time went on, and eventually I discovered that a little shot of liquor ***now*** and then between beers had the tendency to put me in a whacky mood much quicker than having to down several quarts of beer to obtain the same effect.(p.298)
• ***Now*** I was getting drunk all the time.(p.300)
• I eat three good meals a day ***now***, and really enjoy them.(p.303)
• From a domestic standpoint, we really have a home ***now***.(p.303)
• I definitely liked it, everything about it, the taste, the effects; and I realize ***now*** that a drink did something for me or to me that was different from the way it affected others.(p.305)
• By ***now*** I wanted to die, but had lost the courage even to take my life.(p.306)
• Certainly ***now***, anyone would have agreed that only a miracle could prevent my final breakdown.(p.306)
• Until ***now***, I had never been told that I was an alcoholic.(p.307)
• ***Now*** there is a sense of belonging, of being wanted and needed and loved.(p.312)
• The seventeen who ***now*** tell their experiences answer that question.(p.315)
• (***Now*** I know the answer -- wrong.)(p.317)
• I thought, ***now*** here's a nice sympathetic soul!(p.322)
• We have only been in A.A. a few years, but ***now*** we're trying to make up for lost time.(p.325)
• ***Now*** the picture has changed completely.(p.325)
• ***Now*** I feel so very grateful not only for my sobriety, which I try to maintain day by day, but I'm grateful also for the ability to help other people.(p.326)
• But then I thought, well, ***now*** wait, how will I feel next Tuesday?(p.326)
• I am trying ***now***, each day, to make up for all those selfish, thoughtless, foolish things I did in my drinking days.(p.326)
• ***Now***, no longer under pressure, I could safely guard against loss of control.(p.327)

• *Now*, with the arrival at retirement, it was gone.(p.329)
• He's *now* in A.A. and works as a volunteer for the local alcoholism council.(p.330)
• We all have them, and I thought a little brandy or a little wine *now* and then could certainly hurt no one.(p.336)
• I had to give him a story and ask him the same question over and over again, "Well, *now*, how many will that bottle serve?"(p.336)
• I had always hated beer, but *now* I grew to love it, bottle after bottle of it, warm or cold.(p.339)
• I had been brought up to believe in God, but I know that until I found this A.A. program, I had never found or known faith in the reality of God, the reality of His power that is *now* with me in everything I do.(p.341)
• When a few drinks made me feel good before I went over that line, those same drinks *now* made me wretched.(p.346)
• *Now* they asked us to make a decision!(p.350)
• And *now* I am doing the darn dishes every night!(p.352)
• I had never been very happy, but *now* it was unbearable.(p.355)
• Well, *now* I'm living it and trying to paint it for others.(p.355)
• Looking back, it is surprising to me *now* that I managed to keep working and have enough money to squander at the various spots in the big city.(p.358)
• Of course, more than anything else I had let myself down, but I didn't realize how much then – as I do *now*.(p.364)
• *Now* I was on the spot.(p.366)
• These words may be difficult for you to understand *now*, but be patient and you'll know what I mean.(p.367)
• If there is something in my story that rings a bell with you, then do something – *now*!(p.368)
• *Now*, she no longer risks losing her home, her self-respect, or her laundry.(p.369)
• Golf, hunting and fishing were *now* merely excuses to drink excessively.(p.375)
• It *now* became necessary to have noon drinks; at first just two, then gradually more.(p.375)
• By *now* it had become difficult to visualize a life without alcohol.(p.378)
• I could see no reason why they should have any relationship to this problem of getting drunk every *now* and then.(p.388)
• Age and the law were still against me, but laws were not as strictly enforced in those days as they are *now*, and I discovered that as long as I had the green blood, there was always a way to get alcohol, either from a nondiscriminatory bartender or from an older friend who would be glad to purchase the joy juice for the privilege of sharing it.(p.397)
• *Now* my drinking was limited by only one factor, the enforced periods of dryness caused by lengthy tours at sea.(p.398)
• But *now*, with His help and grace, this child of His has paid his initiation fee for good, as long as he remembers to stay away from that first drink (the one that does all the damage) one day at a time.(p.399)
• *Now* I had done some living but I hadn't learned a thing.(p.402)
• But *now* I was a young divorcee, leading a Washington social life.(p.402)
• I was *now* with the Paris office.(p.405)
• I began, here and *now*, to fear the answer to the question -- what is the matter with me?(p.406)
• *Now* I hid when I wanted to drink.(p.406)
• *Now* it was semi-blackouts every night, outrageous behavior, passing out in some friend's Village studio or not knowing how I got home.(p.407)
• *Now* my whole thinking was crazy.(p.408)
• I *now* had quite a nest egg.(p.409)
• *Now* came the black and endless dismal night.(p.410)
• I, who had dreamed these sick dreams, *now* reaped the nightmare.(p.411)
• I wore a man's raincoat, turned inside out, a present from a friend, for *now* my funds were low.(p.411)
• I think *now* that a God, in whom I did not believe, was looking after me.(p.412)
• She read this book that you are reading *now*.(p.412)
• But *now* a strange thing happened.(p.412)
• I *now* said a lucky and wonderful thing.(p.412)
• He *now* said that we had a physical allergy combined with a mental obsession, and he explained this so that I saw for the first time how this could be.(p.413)
• *Now* comes the questionnaire."(p.413)
• I, who had feared questions, *now* began trying to interrupt and tell my story.(p.414)
• *Now*, I am big and weak, but Anne was bigger than I and strong.(p.414)
• *Now* I know.(p.422)
• I was drinking quite a bit of whiskey *now*.(p.425)
• I was *now* nearly eighteen.(p.425)
• I was only twenty *now*, but I was a man.(p.427)
• I'm twenty-six *now* and I haven't had a drink since I made my decision.(p.430)
• Were I to revert to drinking, even *now*, I wouldn't give anything for these four years in A.A.(p.430)
• *Now* I know I can't live without A.A.(p.430)
• I was *now* head of a publishing venture in which nearly a million dollars had been invested.(p.435)
• *Now* I had to face up to the fact that knowledge of this sort, applied to my individual case, was not power.(p.435)
• *Now*, however, I accepted it fully.(p.436)
• *Now* I own perhaps the most costly pair of moccasins anyone has ever seen, and they help me remember where I've been.)(p.445)
• The psychiatrist, who had generally been ignoring me, *now* became quite interested; every day, he would ask me all kinds of questions about the A.A. meetings.(p.446)
• *Now*, what am I going to do about it?"(p.449)
• Max and I have been married *now* for thirty-five years.(p.450)
• *Now* sober for years, they tell us how they got well.(p.455)
• I woke up in jail, sick, withdrawing from alcohol and speed, already a four-time loser, and *now* with a fifth felony charge against me.(p.460)
• (I am looking at it *now* in my bedroom — a copy that was presented to me a couple of years ago by the A.A. group in that same prison.)(p.461)
• *Now*, I have been an alcoholism counselor for over a year and am off parole.(p.462)
• Remember, *now* you have a choice.(p.463)
• At that time there hadn't been any publicity such as we have *now*.(p.469)
• My husband interrupted, "She's bad enough *now* without getting mixed up with a bunch of drunks."(p.469)
• I even wanted to – but I wasn't allowed to, so I won't go *now*.(p.470)
• Sly and crafty, I thought *now* I'll find out what they think of me here, what they "have on" me, what I've said coming in here drunk.(p.470)
• *Now* think I was alcoholic from first drink.(p.474)
• *Now* I slide down mountain fast.(p.475)
• Cops *now* sick of me, so they buy me one-way ticket to Canada.(p.475)
• But *now* I change if it bring good life.(p.475)
• He was old, but *now* he grow young with new life in A.A. and travel all time.(p.476)
• Tall Man *now* see Great Spirit in Big Group in sky.(p.476)
• I wasted twenty years of my life, and there is nothing I can do about that, but there is something I can do about *now*.(p.480)
• It is no problem to me *now*, but this is not good management on my part -- just plain good luck.(p.480)
• We survivors are all in A.A. *now*, and my mother is in Al-Anon.(p.480)
• I realize that *now*.(p.483)
• We weren't even permitted to play cards in our home, but father would give us just a little toddy with whiskey and sugar and warm water *now* and then.(p.484)
• My wife and I have been married for some thirty years *now*.(p.485)
• We were *now* both working in the same agency.(p.490)
• The one thing I can remember *now* was that Vi was on the corner of 8th and L, and I remember vividly that she had an envelope in her hand.(p.492)
• When I had known her years before she was rather slender, but at this time she weighed as much as she does *now*, which is up around in the two hundreds or very close to it.(p.493)
• But I knew how to handle it *now*.(p.498)
• *Now* back to the exam.(p.499)
• I can hold a lot *now*, more than the others.(p.499)
• She is near the end *now* and is in a hospital.(p.501)
• I'll just take a few beers *now* and then.(p.502)
• I cannot see the cause of this temptation *now*.(p.507)
• But I came out of the Army just as big a drunk as when I went in, if not worse, because *now* I had a lot more resentments.(p.513)
• I wasn't a happy man that morning, but I'm happy *now* that it came about.(p.515)
• In my own generation I stuck out, I can see that *now*, as being a very much heavier drinker than the average man.(p.518)
• I thought, well, *now* that I've been put out for drinking, I'll just show them that they were completely wrong, so I went off on the biggest bout I had been on up to then, involving about a fortnight's black-out.(p.521)
• I was a civilian *now*.(p.521)
• Finally, my mother came and said she had kept me at home for six years because she thought she could help me, but that *now* she had come to the conclusion that I wasn't even worth trying to help.(p.523)
• *Now* I had gotten to the place where I would wake up with black eyes and not know where I got them, or wake up with a lot of money and not know where I got it.(p.528)
• I had rejected A.A. on the outside, but *now* it came to me in prison.(p.528)
• I am talking about A.A. people, who have gone through some of the same things that you might be going through *now*.(p.529)
• It's time to stop finding excuses for drinking and getting into trouble, because *now* there is a way out, and if you want what we have, try coming around and giving the program a chance.(p.530)
• And, as a child is a part of his father, so do I *now* want to be a part of God.(p.535)
• *Now*, for me, and to my satisfaction, I know the purpose of life: The purpose of life is to create and the by-product is happiness.(p.535)
• I ask the forgiveness of the reader; and from *now* on I shall try to write with the humility I honestly pray for.)(p.536)
• Thank you, Mr. Policeman, wherever you are *now*.(p.538)
• But not for long; *now*, for five Friday nights in a row, I went to jail, picked up sodden with beer (which I always disliked, but which was the only drink available); in jail five consecutive Friday nights in the town where I had grown up, where I had been an honor student in high school, where a kindly uncle, bailing me out, said, "Bob, our family just doesn't do this sort of thing."(p.539)
• For by *now* I had been exposed once to A.A., but I had treated it as a vaudeville and had taken friends to meetings so that they too could enjoy the fascination of the naked revelation of suffering and recovery.(p.539)
• I realize *now* that this phase of my development had been arrested by my obsession with self, and my egocentricity had reached such proportions that adjustment to anything outside my personal control was impossible for me.(p.547)
• One of the truly great things A.A. has taught me is that reality too has two sides; I had only known the grim side before the program, but *now* I had a chance to learn about the pleasant side as well.(p.550)
• For the only problems I have *now* are those I create when I break out in a rash of self-will.(p.551)
• It had provided me with excuses for my lack of education, my marital failures, personal failures, inadequacy, and of course, my alcoholism and, though I really thought I had been willing to part with it, *now* I knew I was reluctant to let it go.(p.552)
• Do it every day for two weeks and you will find you have come to mean it and to want it for them, and you will realize that where you used to feel bitterness and resentment and hatred, you *now* feel compassionate understanding and love."(p.552)
• Although my ambition still flickered, it *now* took the form of fantasizing.(p.556)
• Indeed, I had to drink *now* to live, to cope with the demands of everyday existence.(p.556)
• I had always been oversensitive to criticism and was acutely so *now*.(p.556)
• And it had gone underground *now*, because everyone knew I shouldn't be drinking.(p.557)
• But *now* all choice was gone.(p.558)
• Hopeless *now*, I felt it would be better for my wife, my children, and everyone in my life if I went ahead and died.(p.558)
• To those *now* in its fold, Alcoholics Anonymous has made the difference between misery and sobriety, and often the difference between life and death.(p.563)
• I *now* conceive the psychiatrist's job to be the task of breaking down the patient's inner resistance so that which is inside him will flower, as under the activity of the A.A. program."(p.571)
• (This address is *now* available in pamphlet form at nominal cost through most A.A. groups or from Box 459, Grand Central Station, New York, NY 10163, under the title "Three Talks to Medical Societies by Bill W." -- formerly called "Bill on Alcoholism" and earlier "Alcoholism the Illness.")(p.572)

nowadays

• Everybody ***nowadays***, believes in scores of assumptions for which there is good evidence, but no perfect visual proof.(p.48)

• Our actor is self-centered -- ego-centric, as people like to call it ***nowadays***.(p.61)

• Among many employers ***nowadays***, we think of one member who has spent much of his life in the world of big business.(p.136)

nowhere

• Few people really are, for that means blind faith in the strange proposition that this universe originated in a cipher and aimlessly rushes ***nowhere***.(p.10)

• He was ambitious to succeed in business, but saw that he would get ***nowhere*** if he drank at all.(p.32)

• Were our contentions true, it would follow that life originated out of nothing, and proceeds ***no-where***.(p.49)

• I had ***nowhere*** else to go, and I knew something was terribly wrong, and the reason had to lie within myself.(p.371)

• This good and gentle man, a brilliant research doctor, got ***nowhere*** with me fast.(p.407)

• I crawled back to my analyst, not so much because I had faith in him, but because I had ***nowhere*** else to turn.(p.435)

• Each time I told her she was a nothing, she receded a little more into ***nowhere***.(p.450)

nucleus

• By the latter part of September 1939, we had a ***nu-cleus*** of six and held our first official group meeting.(p.310)

nudged

• I ***nudged*** George next morning, and I said, "I'm in," and he said, "Oh, I knew you'd make it."(p.322)

nuisance

• But with many, drinking had been little more than a sometimes uncontrollable ***nuisance***.(p.315)

• An obstreperous woman in a bar is a ***nuisance***, and they wanted no trouble with the police.(p.410)

number

• It is important that we remain anonymous because we are too few, at present to handle the overwhelming ***number*** of personal appeals which may result from this publication.(p.xiii)

• Their very first case, a desperate one, recovered immediately and became A.A. ***number*** three.(p.xvii)

• By late 1937, the ***number*** of members having substantial sobriety time behind them was sufficient to convince the membership that a new light had entered the dark world of the alcoholic.(p.xvii)

• Here are some of the methods we have tried: Drinking beer only, limiting the ***number*** of drinks, never drinking alone, never drinking in the morning, drinking only at home, never having it in the house, never drinking during business hours, drinking only at parties, switching from scotch to brandy, drinking only natural wines, agreeing to resign if ever drunk on the job, taking a trip, not taking a trip, swearing off forever (with and without a solemn oath), taking more physical exercise, reading inspirational books, going to health farms and sanitariums, accepting voluntary commitment to asylums -- we could increase the list ad infinitum.(p.31)

• Resentment is the "***number*** one" offender.(p.64)

• Maybe we are divorced, and have remarried but haven't kept up the alimony to ***number*** one.(p.79)

• Of those who keep on, a good ***number*** will become true alcoholics after a while.(p.109)

• Three: This husband has gone much further than husband ***number*** two.(p.109)

• Though once like ***number*** two he became worse.(p.109)

• Let's now go back to husband ***number*** one.(p.110)

• Suppose, however, that your husband fits the description of ***number*** two.(p.112)

• The same principles which apply to husband ***num-ber*** one should be practiced.(p.112)

• If you have a ***number*** three husband, you may be in luck.(p.113)

• Your man has probably been trying to conceal a ***number*** of scrapes, perhaps pretty messy ones.(p.140)

• Years ago, in 1935, one of our ***number*** made a journey to a certain western city.(p.153)

• Now, this house will hardly accommodate its weekly visitors, for they ***number*** sixty or eighty as a rule.(p.161)

• Being a large place, we think that some day its Fellowship will ***number*** many hundreds.(p.161)

• Six years ago one of our ***number*** was a patient there.(p.162)

• ALCOHOLIC ANONYMOUS ***NUMBER*** THREE(p.182)

• A.A.'s ***Number*** One Group dates from that very day.(p.189)

• Of course, we had talked over quite a ***number*** of the failings that I had and made a sort of an inventory, which wasn't too difficult, because I had an awful lot of things wrong that were very apparent to me, because I knew all about them.(p.190)

• With that profit, I built a ***number*** of houses, but then I neglected them.(p.194)

• At that meeting, there were a ***number*** of Akron people and all the Cleveland people.(p.219)

• This doctor had imparted his knowledge to just a few other men at that time -- not more than four or five -- they now ***number*** more than seventy persons.(p.235)

• Everyone had my ***number*** and wouldn't hire me at any price.(p.301)

• In an attempt to get over that feeling, there was a quick onslaught of a greater ***number*** of drinks, and then all was lost.(p.346)

• On the last day I was drinking I went up to see a friend who had had a good deal of trouble with alcohol, and whose wife had left him a ***number*** of times.(p.346)

• I had read and heard a little about A.A. and so, groping for the phone book, I found the A.A. ***number*** and with hope in my heart eagerly telephoned.(p.363)

• This suggestion had been made before on a ***number*** of occasions, but like all alcoholics I wanted to handle my problem my own way, which really meant I didn't want anything to interfere with my drinking.(p.378)

• The explanation that alcoholism was a disease of a two fold nature, an allergy of the body and an obsession of the mind, cleared up a ***number*** of puzzling questions for me.(p.380)

• So I got a half pint and at midnight that night, I called the ***number*** I had been given, but the man who had started the group was in the hospital so I didn't know what to do.(p.393)

• I am one of the growing ***number*** of A.A. members who are second-generation.(p.419)

• His parishioners are limited in ***number***, but his friends are many, for to him race, creed, or social position makes no difference.(p.497)

• If something does come along that sort of upsets me, instead of walking in and throwing a buck at the barman and asking for a drink, I walk into a telephone booth, drop a dime in the box, and call somebody who was so kind as to give me his name and telephone ***number*** to meet such an emergency.(p.511)

• In the first few chapters a ***number*** of sudden revolutionary changes are described.(p.569)

numbered

• By the close of 1941, A.A. ***numbered*** 8,000 members.(p.xviii)

numbers

• Because this book has become the basic text for our Society and has helped such large ***numbers*** of alcoholic men and women to recover, there exists a sentiment against any radical changes being made in it.(p.xi)

• The test that it faced was this: Could these large ***numbers*** of erstwhile erratic alcoholics successfully meet and work together?(p.xviii)

• For this there were two principal reasons: the large ***numbers*** of recoveries, and reunited homes.(p.xx)

• But great ***numbers*** of these -- about two out of three - - began to return as time passed.(p.xx)

• We are growing in ***numbers*** and power.(p.16)

• We, who are familiar with the symptoms, see large ***numbers*** of potential alcoholics among young people everywhere.(p.33)

• As our work spreads and our ***numbers*** increase, we hope your employees may be put in personal contact with some of us.(p.144)

• They grew in ***numbers***.(p.159)

• Get sponsor and phone ***numbers***.(p.477)

numerous

• We have ***numerous*** theories, for example, about electricity.(p.48)

• There have also been ***numerous*** times when I have thought about taking a drink.(p.285)

• On the way home ***numerous*** places must be passed.(p.299)

• After such often-painful vigilance (and ***numerous*** phony stints of abstinence), retirement naturally created an impulse to live without restraints.(p.328)

• I tried the wagon on ***numerous*** occasions but I always felt unhappy and abused.(p.375)

• She had been warned ***numerous*** times, not only by her family but by my own mother, that I was a hopeless drunk, that there wasn't anything anybody could do with me, that I'd never stop, and that eventually I'd break her heart.(p.513)

nurse

• If he is not interested in your solution, if he expects you to act only as a banker for his financial difficulties or a ***nurse*** for his sprees, you may have to drop him until he changes his mind.(p.95)

• One day they called up the head ***nurse*** of a local hospital.(p.156)

• Straightway, Bob called Akron's City Hospital and asked for the ***nurse*** on the receiving ward.(p.188)

• He said, "No, call the ***nurse***."(p.208)

• He asked if I would cooperate with him after I went home, and if I would have a trained ***nurse*** stay with me for at least two weeks.(p.387)

• I wouldn't go to hospitals because I wanted my dog there, so I had to have a trained ***nurse***.(p.390)

• Much of my time was spent writing letters, notes, orders, and lists of things for Max, who was also my office ***nurse***, to do to keep the world running while I was locked up.(p.445)

nurses

• He's just beaten up a couple of ***nurses***.(p.156)

• Had blacked the eyes of two ***nurses***, and now they had him strapped down tight.(p.188)

• The next three years saw me in sanitariums, once in a ten day coma, from which I very nearly did not recover, in and out of hospitals or confined at home with day and night ***nurses***.(p.306)

• But he noticed that I was not a good mother to my child, that I relegated her to ***nurses*** when she was with me.(p.403)

• It is true that the doctors and ***nurses*** in the various institutions I attended knew too.(p.470)

nursing

• Every time I got drunk, my husband would send me to a ***nursing*** home.(p.388)

• In my mind's eye, I played and replayed scenes in which I was plucked magically from the bar where I stood ***nursing*** a drink, and was instantly exalted to some position of power and prestige.(p.560)

nurtured

• I had fed it, fanned it and ***nurtured*** it as one might a delicate child, and it had become as much a part of me as my breathing.(p.551)

nut

• She's a ***nut*** -- she snubbed me.(p.65)

• A friend of mine, a golf ***nut***, rushed out on retirement to play every day.(p.330)

• I didn't like being on the ***nut*** ward, and I particularly didn't like being forced to ice cookies on Christmas Eve.(p.444)

• Time went by very, very slowly on my second ***nut*** ward.(p.445)

nuts

• I could work a deal up to where all I had to do was to go ahead with it; all the planning had been done, all the financing had been done, but then I'd say "***Nuts*** to it!" and walk away.(p.197)

• "Well, I'm ***nuts*** enough now," I said to him.(p.266)

• I woke up in this bare room with nothing around me but bars; they wouldn't let me smoke and treated me, well, like I was ***nuts***.(p.387)

NY

• If there is no Al-Anon listing in your local telephone book, you may obtain further information on Al-Anon Family Groups by writing to its World Service Office: Box 182, Madison Square Station, New York, ***NY*** 10159.(p.121)

• (This address is now available in pamphlet form at nominal cost through most A.A. groups or from Box 459, Grand Central Station, New York, ***NY*** 10163, under the title "Three Talks to Medical Societies by Bill W." -- formerly called "Bill on Alcoholism" and earlier "Alcoholism the Illness.")(p.572)

• If you cannot find A.A. in your locality, a letter addressed to Alcoholics Anonymous, Box 459, Grand Central Station, New York, ***NY*** 10163, U.S.A., will receive a prompt reply from this world center, referring you to the nearest A.A. group.(p.575)

• Should you be the relative or friend of an alcoholic who shows no immediate interest in A.A., it is suggested that you write the Al-Anon Family Groups, Inc., Box 182, Madison Square Station, New York, ***NY*** 10159, U.S.A.(p.575)

Oo

O
• They said if you want to know how this program works, take the first word of your question – the H is for honesty, the *O* is for open-mindedness and the W is for willingness; these our Book calls the essentials of recovery.(p.550)

O.C.
• Then a change in management took place in the regiment and the new *O.C.* didn't like me very much and I didn't like him, and he started to lie in wait for me.(p.519)

O.K.
• I said, "*O.K.*"(p.412)

o'clock
• It was eight *o'clock* -- five hours after the market closed.(p.4)
• My friends had dropped several million since ten *o'clock* -- so what?(p.4)
• I've prayed to God on hangover mornings and sworn that I'd never touch another drop but by nine *o'clock* I'd be boiled as an owl."(p.158)
• My phobia for sleeplessness demanded that I get drunk every night, but in order to get more liquor for the next night, I had to stay sober during the day, at least up to four *o'clock*.(p.177)
• We entered her house at exactly five *o'clock* and it was eleven fifteen when we left.(p.179)
• To show you the point to which this obsession went, there came an occasion when I had spent a most delightful week-end, and at nine *o'clock* on Sunday night I was on my way home, and I thought I would get a drink.(p.204)
• In fact, the last three years of my drinking was a routine of barbiturates in the morning, so that I could stop shaking enough to shave, and then alcohol beginning about four-thirty or five *o'clock*, with a struggle not to take a drink at noon or during the day, because I had the idea that if I took one drink, I would smell as though I had had a pint.(p.217)
• The shakes grew worse and I looked at my watch -- six *o'clock*.(p.223)
• It had been one *o'clock* when I last remember looking.(p.223)
• In fact I had been in very good shape at one *o'clock* -- feeling no pain.(p.223)
• Toward five *o'clock*, helter-skelter, I'd get everything put away and try to get supper on the table, and after supper I'd finish the job up and knock myself out.(p.337)
• It wasn't long before I became a five *o'clock* alcoholic.(p.360)
• I graduated there from a five *o'clock* alcoholic to a noon-day one.(p.361)
• At age twenty-one, I enlisted in the Navy for two reasons: (1) to avoid being drafted into the Army, and (2) out of a burst of patriotic fervor inspired by the advent of World War II and as the result of an all-night drinking binge which found me sitting on the doorstep of the Navy recruiting office when the chief petty officer arrived to open for business at nine *o'clock* Monday morning.(p.398)
• Around eight or nine *o'clock* there came two big detectives and a policeman to arrest me for assault; and I was the most amazed person in the world when they said I had assaulted someone, and especially that I had assaulted my wife.(p.492)
• It is ten *o'clock* of a Saturday night.(p.500)
• I had a habit of getting up just prior to the closing time of the saloons, about two or three *o'clock* in the morning.(p.514)
• I'd get downstairs to the gin mill, get enough in to hold me until eight *o'clock* in the morning, then I'd go out to join that "misery parade" that so many of us know so well.(p.514)
• One morning I didn't wake up until after four *o'clock*.(p.515)

Oahu
• I was transferred to Kaneohe Bay, across the hump to the windward side of *Oahu*, to the aviation base.(p.426)

oasis
• His coming was an *oasis* in the dreary desert of futility.(p.9)
• The very thing – an *oasis*!(p.9)

oath
• Here are some of the methods we have tried: Drinking beer only, limiting the number of drinks, never drinking alone, never drinking in the morning, drinking only at home, never having it in the house, never drinking during business hours, drinking only at parties, switching from scotch to brandy, drinking only natural wines, agreeing to resign if ever drunk on the job, taking a trip, not taking a trip, swearing off forever (with and without a solemn *oath*), taking more physical exercise, reading inspirational books, going to health farms and sanitariums, accepting voluntary commitment to asylums -- we could increase the list ad infinitum.(p.31)

oaths
• Our men have sworn great solemn *oaths* that they were through drinking forever.(p.105)

oats
• I had met a bunch of gay young Bohemians who lived in the Village, and were sowing their wild *oats*.(p.407)

obesity
• Boredom sets up every retiree for two chief dangers: *obesity* and alcoholism.(p.330)

obey
• Gone are time cards to punch, alarm clocks to *obey*, nosey rumor-mongers and talebearers to evade.(p.329)

obeyed
• When sober, father usually *obeyed*.(p.131)

obituary
• It was the *obituary* of one of the best salesmen I ever had.(p.137)

object
• Its main *object* is to enable you to find a Power greater than yourself which will solve your problem.(p.45)
• One *object* is to disclose damaged or unsalable goods, to get rid of them promptly and without regret.(p.64)
• The family may *object* to this, but unless he is in a dangerous physical condition, it is better to risk it.(p.90)
• Whatever the method, its *object* is to thoroughly clear mind and body of the effects of alcohol.(p.143)
• Aside from fellowship and sociability, the prime *object* was to provide a time and place where new people might bring their problems.(p.160)

objectionable
• Are we now ready to let God remove from us all the things which we have admitted are *objectionable*?(p.76)

objective
• I had an *objective*.(p.211)

objectives
• Philosophy, faith, a sense of humor (they could laugh at themselves), clear-cut *objectives*, appreciation – and most especially appreciation and sympathetic understanding for their fellow man.(p.310)
• First, through mutual pain and despair, and later through mutual *objectives* and new-found faith and hope.(p.312)

objects
• Two fuzzy *objects* came into focus.(p.422)
• Slowly I realized I was in bed and that the *objects* were my feet, encased in a harness affair.(p.422)

obligation
• Make it plain he is under no *obligation* to you, that you hope only that he will try to help other alcoholics when he escapes his own difficulties.(p.94)
• But you should feel under no *obligation* to keep him on, for your *obligation* has been well discharged already.(p.147)
• And, as the years go by, working together, sharing our experiences with one another, and also sharing a mutual trust, understanding and love – without strings, without *obligation* -- we acquire relationships that are unique and priceless.(p.312)
• With deep shame came the knowledge too that I had lived with no sense of social *obligation* nor had I known the meaning of moral responsibility to my fellow men.(p.549)
• We think that each group should soon achieve this ideal; that any public solicitation of funds using the name of Alcoholics Anonymous is highly dangerous, whether by groups, clubs, hospitals, or other outside agencies; that acceptance of large gifts from any source, or of contributions carrying any *obligation* whatever, is unwise.(p.566)

obligations
• He will perceive that his spiritual growth is lopsided, that for an average man like himself, a spiritual life which does not include his family *obligations* may not be so perfect after all.(p.129)

obligatory
• So far as we are concerned, there is nothing *obligatory* about it.(p.132)

obliged
• But even in this type of beginning we are *obliged* to admit that our justification for a spree was insanely insufficient in the light of what always happened.(p.37)
• Maybe you have already been *obliged* to put him away.(p.110)
• Frequently, you have felt *obliged* to tell your husband's employer and his friends that he was sick, when as a matter of fact he was tight.(p.115)
• Husbands and wives have sometimes been *obliged* to separate for a time until new perspective, new victory over hurt pride could be rewon.(p.125)
• By force of circumstances, she was often *obliged* to treat father as a sick or wayward child.(p.130)
• I had been *obliged* to discharge him for drinking, though he was brilliant, alert, and one of the best organizers I have ever known.(p.137)

oblivion
• So two bottles, and – *oblivion*.(p.6)
• Those of us who live in large cities are overcome by the reflection that close by hundreds are dropping into *oblivion* every day.(p.19)
• Momentarily we did -- then would come *oblivion* and the awful awakening to face the hideous Four Horsemen -- Terror, Bewilderment, Frustration, Despair.(p.151)
• Away from my office two or three weeks at a time; horrible days and nights when I would lie on the floor of my home, lying awake and reaching over to get the bottle, taking a drink and going back into *oblivion*.(p.184)
• Sitting in a Second Avenue bar, accepting drinks from anyone who offered, after my small stake was gone; or sitting at home alone, with the inevitable glass in my hand, I would remember, and remembering, I would drink faster, seeking speedy *oblivion*.(p.225)
• Heartsickness, shame, and fear, fear bordering on panic, and no complete escape any longer except in *oblivion*.(p.306)
• They daily pass into *oblivion*, alone or with mates.(p.329)
• My pattern of drinking at that time had reached the point where once I really started, I would retire to my bed and drink myself into *oblivion*.(p.466)
• This question so insulted the emotions that clearly there was only one thing to do, go and get drunk again, and put that enquiring mind in its proper place, which was *oblivion*.(p.537)
• I had nothing to put in the place of alcohol, of the forgetfulness, of the *oblivion*, which alcohol provides.(p.539)
• The only way existence was possible was through rationalizing every sober moment and drinking myself into complete *oblivion* as often as I could.(p.547)
• The amount of will power exercised to control my drinking during working hours, diverted into a constructive channel, would have made me President, and the thing that made the will power possible was the knowledge that as soon as my day was finished I could drink myself into *oblivion*.(p.548)

obscure
• The fact is that most alcoholics, for reasons yet *obscure*, have lost the power of choice in drink.(p.24)

obscured
• It may be *obscured* by calamity, by pomp, by worship of other things, but in some form or other it is there.(p.55)

observation
• The judge said that if she felt that way he would confine me for thirty days' examination and *observation*.(p.492)
• There was no *observation*.(p.492)

observations
• Now these are commonplace *observations* on drinkers which we hear all the time.(p.20)
• These *observations* would be academic and pointless if our friend never took the first drink, thereby set-

ting the terrible cycle in motion.(p.23)

observe

• Very earnestly we ask the press also, to ***observe*** this request, for otherwise we shall be greatly handicapped.(p.xiii)

• Another principle we ***observe*** carefully is that we do not relate intimate experiences of another person unless we are sure he would approve.(p.125)

• Even among those who occasionally land back in here again, we ***observe*** a profound change in personality.(p.572)

observed

• Before then, I had written lots of sweet promises, but my wife happily ***observed*** that this time I meant business.(p.5)

• We used to amuse ourselves by cynically dissecting spiritual beliefs and practices when we might have ***observed*** that many spiritually-minded persons of all races, colors, and creeds were demonstrating a degree of stability, happiness and usefulness which we should have sought ourselves.(p.49)

• He trembles to think someone might have ***observed*** him.(p.73)

observes

• The Episcopal magazine, The Living Church, ***observes*** editorially: "The basis of the technique of Alcoholics Anonymous is the truly Christian principle that a man cannot help himself except by helping others.(p.574)

observing

• We know these suggestions are sometimes difficult to follow, but you will save many a heartbreak if you can succeed in ***observing*** them.(p.111)

obsession

• Six months earlier, the broker had been relieved of his drink ***obsession*** by a sudden spiritual experience, following a meeting with an alcoholic friend who had been in contact with the Oxford Groups of that day.(p.xv)

• There is the ***obsession*** that somehow, someday, they will beat the game.(p.23)

• The idea that somehow, someday he will control and enjoy his drinking is the great ***obsession*** of every abnormal drinker.(p.30)

• There was an insistent yearning to enjoy life as we once did and a heartbreaking ***obsession*** that some new miracle of control would enable us to do it.(p.151)

• He had, of course, the familiar alcoholic ***obsession*** that few knew of his drinking.(p.155)

• To show you the point to which this ***obsession*** went, there came an occasion when I had spent a most delightful week-end, and at nine o'clock on Sunday night I was on my way home, and I thought I would get a drink.(p.204)

• He said he had finally learned that drinking was a fatal illness made up of an allergy plus an ***obsession***, and once the drinking had passed from habit to ***obsession***, we were completely hopeless, and could look forward only to spending the balance of our lives in mental institutions or to death.(p.290)

• Never having enough, always craving more, the ***obsession*** for alcohol gradually dominated all my activities, particularly while travelling.(p.375)

• The explanation that alcoholism was a disease of a two fold nature, an allergy of the body and an ***obsession*** of the mind, cleared up a number of puzzling questions for me.(p.380)

• The ***obsession*** of the mind was a little harder to understand and yet everyone has obsessions of various kinds.(p.380)

• It took me some time to realize that the Twelve Steps of A.A. were designed to help correct these defects of character and so help remove the ***obsession*** to drink.(p.380)

• There was one Village bar in particular for which I formed an ***obsession***.(p.410)

• He now said that we had a physical allergy combined with a mental ***obsession***, and he explained this so that I saw for the first time how this could be.(p.413)

• I realize now that this phase of my development had been arrested by my ***obsession*** with self, and my egocentricity had reached such proportions that adjustment to anything outside my personal control was impossible for me.(p.547)

obsessions

• The obsession of the mind was a little harder to understand and yet everyone has ***obsessions*** of various kinds.(p.380)

obstacle

• Surprisingly enough, we find such convictions no great ***obstacle*** to a spiritual experience.(p.28)

• We have been trying to get a new attitude, a new relationship with our Creator, and to discover the ***obstacle*** in our path.(p.72)

obstacles

• I, who had thought so well of myself and my abilities, of my capacity to surmount ***obstacles***, was cornered at last.(p.8)

• Suppose we tell you some of the ***obstacles*** a family will meet; suppose we suggest how they may be avoided — even converted to good use for others.(p.123)

• It sounds simple, but there were ***obstacles*** and doubts to overcome.(p.282)

obstinacy

• Besides a seeming inability to accept much on faith, we often found ourselves handicapped by ***obstinacy***, sensitiveness, and unreasoning prejudice.(p.47)

• How it finally broke a Southerner's ***obstinacy*** and destined this salesman to start A.A. at Philadelphia.(p.238)

obstreperous

• An ***obstreperous*** woman in a bar is a nuisance, and they wanted no trouble with the police.(p.410)

obtain

• If there is no Al-Anon listing in your local telephone book, you may ***obtain*** further information on Al-Anon Family Groups by writing to its World Service Office: Box 182, Madison Square Station, New York, NY 10159.(p.121)

• At that time I was not aware of the almost unlimited supply the government made it possible for us doctors to ***obtain***, neither had I any knowledge of the bootlegger who soon appeared on the horizon.(p.175)

• It did help to certain extent, since I got in places where I could not ***obtain*** anything to drink, and so broke the habitual drinking.(p.183)

• The parties waxed more liquid and hilarious as time went on, and eventually I discovered that a little shot of liquor now and then between beers had the tendency to put me in a whacky mood much quicker than having to down several quarts of beer to ***obtain*** the same effect.(p.298)

obtainable

• Then Prohibition came into effect, and the facts that the stuff ***obtainable*** was so horrible and sometimes deadly, and that I had married and had a job which I had to look after, helped me for a period of some three or four years, although I would get drunk every time I could get hold of enough to drink to get started.(p.183)

obtained

• I took a night law course, and ***obtained*** employment as investigator for a surety company.(p.2)

• If we have ***obtained*** permission, have consulted with others, asked God to help and the drastic step is indicated we must not shrink.(p.80)

• Suggestions about these may be ***obtained*** from one's priest, minister, or rabbi.(p.87)

• I was always interested in mechanics and after having about twenty miscellaneous jobs, lasting from one day to two weeks, I ***obtained*** a job as a toolmaker apprentice.(p.211)

• The school then ***obtained*** a job for me in the drafting department of another company.(p.211)

obvious

• Even ***obvious*** intoxication is excused by younger people as something "he's earned the right to do," and they say, "After all, who's he hurting?"(p.330)

• Suddenly, it was ***obvious*** to me: I had a brain tumor and would die, and everyone would be sorry for me.(p.444)

• But it quickly became ***obvious*** that he had this childish notion instead: If he could get me to go to enough meetings while in the hospital, I would continue to go after he let me out.(p.447)

• It was ***obvious*** even to me, in my drunken state, that I wasn't wanted.(p.466)

• If I write with the air of one who has discovered the ***obvious***, which is to say, the eternal truths which have been offered to us since the beginning, forgive my callowness; I had to find these things out for myself.(p.536)

• Still another friend and temporary host received me at four in the morning from the charge of a policeman who had found me "going to bed" in a garage far from the last place I could remember having been, a fashionable bar and restaurant in the theatrical district of New York, to which I had repaired after my date for that evening, a charming lady of the theatre who had refused my company for ***obvious*** reasons.(p.538)

obviously

• ***Obviously*** it had not.(p.11)

• That the man who is making the approach has had the same difficulty, that he ***obviously*** knows what he is talking about, that his whole deportment shouts at the new prospect that he is a man with a real answer, that he has no attitude of Holier Than Thou, nothing whatever except the sincere desire to be helpful; that there are no fees to pay, no axes to grind, no people to please, no lectures to be endured -- these are the conditions we have found most effective.(p.18)

• So we shall describe some of the mental states that precede a relapse into drinking, for ***obviously*** this is the crux of the problem.(p.35)

• ***Obviously***.(p.45)

• ***Obviously***, no rule can be laid down.(p.99)

• But ***obviously*** you cannot transmit something you haven't got.(p.164)

• That had been in the center of New York, on noisy 42nd Street . . . this was ***obviously*** a quiet residential section.(p.223)

• They were earnest and ***obviously*** trying to help me on the road I had chosen.(p.259)

• ***Obviously*** I have overcome fear to a sufficient degree to think in terms of success in business.(p.284)

• Both times, my reaction was that I had had nothing to drink the night before, so ***obviously*** alcohol had nothing to do with it.(p.444)

occasion

• He becomes, on the next ***occasion***, still more demanding or gracious, as the case may be.(p.61)

• Therefore, ask yourself on each ***occasion***, "Have I any good social, business, or personal reason for going to this place?(p.101)

• Do not think of what you will get out of the ***occasion***.(p.102)

• If it is a happy ***occasion***, try to increase the pleasure of those there; if a business ***occasion***, go and attend to your business enthusiastically.(p.102)

• When we were invited out, our husbands sneaked so many drinks that they spoiled the ***occasion***.(p.105)

• We think each family which has been relieved owes something to those who have not, and when the ***occasion*** requires, each member of it should be only too willing to bring former mistakes, no matter how grievous, out of their hiding places.(p.124)

• Eventually, there would be a ball game, or a show, or some sort of special ***occasion*** to celebrate and I would turn up drunk.(p.196)

• I remember one ***occasion*** when I did not drink for three hundred and sixty-four days, but I didn't quite make the year.(p.200)

• To show you the point to which this obsession went, there came an ***occasion*** when I had spent a most delightful week-end, and at nine o'clock on Sunday night I was on my way home, and I thought I would get a drink.(p.204)

• In fact, on one ***occasion***, I was picked up by the police and brought home.(p.211)

• There was more than one ***occasion*** when I got up in the morning with just enough money for coffee and toast and the bus fare to carry me to my first appointment.(p.283)

• On more than one ***occasion*** my wife would threaten to leave me.(p.362)

• On another ***occasion*** I arrived home covered with blood.(p.435)

• On each ***occasion***, I had a convulsion on Sunday morning.(p.444)

• After a while I really did enjoy drinking and what it did to me, and I became dependent upon it for every ***occasion***.(p.464)

• Eventually the day came when I was dependent upon it even when there wasn't any ***occasion***.(p.464)

• On one ***occasion*** when I was serving time in my favorite drying-out place while I was having a session with the psychiatrist, she left my case history on her desk when she was called away from the room.(p.470)

• For instance, the fiftieth wedding anniversary of my wife's parents was the ***occasion*** for a huge family reunion at our home.(p.556)

• At first, just one drink, on ***occasion***.(p.557)

occasional

• There were many failures, but there was an ***occasional*** heartening success.(p.xvii)

• What used to be the hunch or the ***occasional*** inspiration gradually becomes a working part of the mind.(p.87)

• You can all remember that in the first few months after the change, a great many men, who had formerly been used to a few beers every day or an ***occasional*** drink of whiskey, simply quit all alcoholic drinks.(p.232)

• I stayed so sober that I used to keep a quart of medicinal whiskey in my bureau which I used to taper off the ***occasional*** newspaper alcoholics who were sent to see me.(p.253)

• I stayed sober during the trip except for an *occasional* bottle of beer because funds barely met expenses.(p.255)
• Some were drinking heavily and there had been *occasional* serious episodes.(p.315)
• At first it was just that – an *occasional* drink.(p.374)
• Neurotic fears plagued me, and I had *occasional*, uncontrollable tremors.(p.555)

occasionally
• In the early days of our drinking we *occasionally* remained sober for a year or more, becoming serious drinkers again later.(p.34)
• *Occasionally*, they will offer assistance.(p.78)
• *Occasionally* you will have to meet such conditions.(p.97)
• He added that *occasionally* in the night a vague craving arose which would be satisfied by candy.(p.134)
• Couples are *occasionally* dismayed to find that when drinking is stopped the man tends to be impotent.(p.134)
• Drinking *occasionally*, and understanding your own reactions, it is possible for you to become quite sure of many things which, so far as the alcoholic is concerned, are not always so.(p.139)
• *Occasionally*, I would yield to the morning craving, but if I did, it would be only a few hours before I would be quite unfit for work.(p.176)
• I came of good stock, of men and women who drank wine all their lives as a beverage, and while they *occasionally* got drunk at special celebrations, they were up and about their business the next day.(p.231)
• In recent years I have had the happy combination of time and money to travel *occasionally*.(p.285)
• *Occasionally*, it is accorded to a few of us to watch something fine grow from a tiny kernel into something of gigantic goodness.(p.295)
• We went out *occasionally*, and I would take a drink to ease the tensions of daily life.(p.370)
• I disliked being different so, ultimately, I began to join them *occasionally*.(p.374)
• The only other *occasionally* limiting factor was that I might run out of money before the next payday rolled around.(p.398)
• Through going to meetings and listening, and *occasionally* speaking, through doing Twelve Step work, whereby in helping others you are both the teacher and the student, by making many wonderful A.A. friends, I have been taught all the things in life that are worth having.(p.416)
• I go back to my old alma mater *occasionally* to give A.A. talks, and -- just think! -- the warden is my friend.(p.462)
• I had been using paraldehyde more or less like ordinary drink for the last six years though, *occasionally*, I'd bounce back to phenobarbital and things like that.(p.524)
• Even among those who *occasionally* land back in here again, we observe a profound change in personality.(p.572)

occasions
• On each of these *occasions* we worked with him, reviewing carefully what had happened.(p.35)
• His drinking may be constant or it may be heavy only on certain *occasions*.(p.109)
• They spoke with great freedom from embarrassment, which I could never do, and they seemed very much at ease on all *occasions* and appeared very healthy.(p.178)
• I can remember *occasions* when friends recommended me for positions or business opportunities that I wouldn't take because I felt that at some future date I'd get drunk and they would be hurt.(p.198)
• I could discipline myself but along the way there would be festivities and *occasions* when I got drunk.(p.211)
• There had been some *occasions* -- there was an automobile wreck, for instance -- when I had police escort home but not to jail, all of which, instead of doing me a favor, did me harm because I was then full of self-esteem as to the progress I had made both professionally and financially.(p.213)
• However, on a couple of other *occasions*, Clarence seemed to bob up at the last saloon that I would stop at on the way home every day.(p.216)
• Gradually the quantity increased, the *occasions* for a drink came more frequently; a hard day, worries and pressure, bad news, good news – there were more and more reasons for a drink.(p.374)
• I tried the wagon on numerous *occasions* but I always felt unhappy and abused.(p.375)
• This suggestion had been made before on a number of *occasions*, but like all alcoholics I wanted to handle my problem my own way, which really meant I didn't want anything to interfere with my drinking.(p.378)
• In all the twenty-five years of my drinking there were only a few *occasions* when I took a morning drink.(p.432)
• On two *occasions*, over weekends, I decided I would take absolutely nothing.(p.443)
• I felt very sorry for myself and attempted suicide on many *occasions*, making sure there was always somebody within reaching distance to see that I didn't finish the job.(p.478)
• At this point I believe I had only been intoxicated on maybe three or four *occasions*, and certainly whiskey was no problem to me.(p.487)
• We had several fights and on one or two *occasions* I struck her with my fist.(p.491)
• I also got into my first disciplinary trouble caused by drinking, on two separate *occasions*.(p.555)

occupation
• Then I went over again to Germany for four years on an *occupation* job.(p.519)
• We define professionalism as the *occupation* of counseling alcoholics for fees or hire.(p.566)

occupations
• Being mostly business or professional folk, we could not well carry on our *occupations* in such an event.(p.xiii)
• All sections of this country and many of its *occupations* are represented, as well as many political, economic, social, and religious backgrounds.(p.17)
• A much more important demonstration of our principles lies before us in our respective homes, *occupations* and affairs.(p.19)

occupied
• He consented, however, to go the hospital, where he *occupied* the very room recently vacated by the lawyer.(p.159)

occupy
• The horrors of increasing hangover sickness to *occupy* the entire day; nausea, dry heaves, the rocking bed, the nightmare-filled mind.(p.408)

occupying
• When the war was over, we had about a year in Germany, *occupying* the place.(p.518)

occur
• If these thoughts *occur*, they are hazy and readily supplanted with the old threadbare idea that this time we shall handle ourselves like other people.(p.24)
• Well, just that did happen and more, for what I had learned of alcoholism did not *occur* to me at all.(p.42)
• It did not *occur* to me that marriage might be a job, too.(p.402)
• Today I think of life in terms of happiness, contentment, freedom from fear and despair, sane thinking, ability to face problems as they *occur*, the opportunity to help other alcoholics and to be decent.(p.430)

occurred
• On the other hand – and strange as this may seem to those who do not understand -- once a psychic change has *occurred*, the very same person who seemed doomed, who had so many problems he despaired of ever solving them, suddenly finds himself easily able to control his desire for alcohol, the only effort necessary being that required to follow a few simple rules.(p.xxvii)
• It never *occurred* to him that perhaps he could not do so, in spite of character and standing.(p.39)
• It then *occurred* to me that after one was all smelled up with beer nobody could tell what had been drunk, so I began to fortify my beer with straight alcohol.(p.178)
• I never left the church, but I was a fringe member, and the thought simply never *occurred* to me that through the exercise of what I had I might find the answer to my problem, simply because I wouldn't admit that I had a problem.(p.214)
• In my own experience I was so jubilant at finding myself sober, and I had so many things to catch up on, that a month went by before the thought even *occurred* to me.(p.219)
• Then *occurred* the event that saved me.(p.235)
• The same thing *occurred* in medical school.(p.345)
• Up to this time it just hadn't *occurred* to me to drink.(p.402)
• It had never *occurred* to me before that I could live simply and be independent of my family.(p.409)
• Never in my wildest moments had it *occurred* to me that I might like to be an alcoholic.(p.439)
• The thought of stopping drinking just never *occurred* to me.(p.522)

occurrence
• This was a regular *occurrence* for a little while.(p.196)

occurrences
• To me these *occurrences* are phenomena.(p.27)
• So we think that unless some good and useful purpose is to be served, past *occurrences* should not be discussed.(p.125)
• Among us, these are rare *occurrences*.(p.125)
• Cleaning up old scrapes, helping to settle family differences, explaining the disinherited son to his irate parents, lending money and securing jobs for each other, when justified -- these are everyday *occurrences*.(p.161)

occurring
• Exceptions to cases such as yours have been *occurring* since early times.(p.27)
• But they were *occurring* with alarming frequency.(p.434)

occurs
• We believe, and so suggested a few years ago, that the action of alcohol on these chronic alcoholics is a manifestation of an allergy; that the phenomenon of craving is limited to this class and never *occurs* in the average temperate drinker.(p.xxvi)

October
• Abruptly in *October* 1929 hell broke loose on the New York stock exchange.(p.4)
• During this vacation, in the months of September and *October*, I decided to go on the water wagon.(p.343)
• I got drunk one night in *October*, went to sleep in the rain and woke up with pneumonia.(p.490)
• It is the last day of the following *October*, a dark, rainy morning.(p.502)
• On *October* 28th, I was sent to Sing Sing with a minimum of thirty-three and a half years to serve out of that thirty-five.(p.509)

odd
• The circumstances under which I reached these people were very *odd* because I was led there through things that I said when I couldn't even remember speaking.(p.202)
• I managed to maintain myself with *odd* jobs, did ten weeks in a social rescue institution, and at length wound up in a second-hand bookstore in an adjacent town as manager.(p.257)

oddly
• *Oddly* enough, he is often difficult to deal with.(p.110)
• *Oddly* enough, the big shot who fired me from this company was one of the first men I met when I later joined the New York A.A. Group.(p.242)
• *Oddly* enough, the circumstances and surroundings were pleasant.(p.285)
• *Oddly* enough, the dentist who started A.A. in Amarillo, Tex., benevolently arranged my admission to dental college.(p.419)

odds
• I was always at *odds* with the entire world, not to say the universe.(p.400)

off
• We had to unify our Fellowship or pass *off* the scene.(p.xix)
• We gave up our positions and *off* we roared on a motorcycle, the sidecar stuffed with tent, blankets, a change of clothes, and three huge volumes of a financial reference service.(p.2)
• The curve of my declining moral and bodily health fell *off* like a ski-jump.(p.7)
• Then came the insidious insanity of that first drink, and on Armistice Day 1935, I was *off* again.(p.8)
• "Lay *off* the hard stuff."(p.20)
• He may start *off* as a moderate drinker; he may or may not become a continuous hard drinker; but at some stage of his drinking career he begins to lose all control of his liquor consumption, once he starts to drink.(p.21)
• Perhaps he goes to a doctor who gives him morphine or some sedative with which to taper *off*.(p.22)
• If you draw this fallacious reasoning to the attention of an alcoholic, he will laugh it *off*, or become irritated and refuse to talk.(p.23)
• If anyone who is showing inability to control his drinking can do the right-about-face and drink like a gentleman, our hats are *off* to him.(p.31)
• Here are some of the methods we have tried: Drinking beer only, limiting the number of drinks, never drinking alone, never drinking in the morning, drinking only at home, never having it in the house, never drinking during business hours, drinking only at parties, switching from scotch to brandy, drinking only

natural wines, agreeing to resign if ever drunk on the job, taking a trip, not taking a trip, swearing *off* forever (with and without a solemn oath), taking more physical exercise, reading inspirational books, going to health farms and sanitariums, accepting voluntary commitment to asylums -- we could increase the list ad infinitum.(p.31)

• But here is a man who at fifty-five years found he was just where he had left *off* at thirty.(p.33)

• On through the years this conduct continues, accompanied by his continual promises to be careful or to keep *off* the streets altogether.(p.38)

• My business came *off* well, I was pleased and knew my partners would be too.(p.41)

• Not only had I been *off* guard, I had made no fight whatever against the first drink.(p.41)

• The show doesn't come *off* very well.(p.61)

• For when harboring such feelings we shut ourselves *off* from the sunlight of the Spirit.(p.66)

• It's so easy to get way *off* the track.(p.68)

• We hope you are convinced now that God can remove whatever self-will has blocked you *off* from Him.(p.71)

• We are there to sweep *off* our side of the street realizing that nothing worth while can be accomplished until we do so, never trying to tell him what he should do.(p.77)

• We have not even sworn *off*.(p.85)

• You should not be offended if he wants to call it *off*, for he has helped you more than you have helped him.(p.94)

• Nothing will help the man who is *off* on a spiritual tangent so much as the wife who adopts a sane spiritual program, making a better practical use of it.(p.130)

• I pointed out that I had had nothing to drink whatever for three years, and this in the face of difficulties that would have made nine out of ten men drink their heads *off*.(p.138)

• If he feels free to discuss his problems with you, if he knows you understand and will not be upset by anything he wishes to say, he will probably be *off* to a fast start.(p.144)

• Can you charge this *off* as you would a bad account and start fresh with him?(p.145)

• From a business standpoint, his trip came *off* badly.(p.153)

• Goes *off* his head completely when he's drinking.(p.156)

• That sure did take a load *off* of my mind.(p.188)

• And this, as I said, certainly gave me a lot of confidence, seemed to take a lot of the burden *off* me.(p.190)

• He tossed *off* half of his martini; I tossed *off* half of mine and it nearly blew the top of my head *off*.(p.195)

• But I watched him, and he tossed *off* the rest of his, so I tossed *off* the rest of mine.(p.195)

• I would put *off* doing anything that I could until the next day and, consequently, everything would pile up and then there would be the blackout.(p.197)

• I optioned a piece of land just *off* East Market Street to put up a three-hundred suite apartment.(p.198)

• And we stood there for twenty minutes, telling each other how much better we were, how much better we looked, how much better *off* we were financially, mentally, physically, morally, and in every way, shape and manner.(p.201)

• And I continued to drink, on and *off* then, until every dollar I had in the world was gone again and I was right back living at my sister's, getting my cigarettes by calling her grocer and telling him to put in a couple of cartons with her order, exactly as I had before I started to work at Max's.(p.202)

• I think the longest drunk I was ever on was eleven days, but usually only two days with a complete blackout for a day, and then backing *off* by drinking as long as I could get anything.(p.203)

• He took *off* his hat and his overcoat, and he said, "You don't look very good.(p.207)

• I found in the fall of 1939, that I was not mentally impaired, so far as trial work was concerned, and thereafter took up where I had left *off* when I was about forty-five years old.(p.220)

• My divorce coincided with my father's bankruptcy, and I went to work, casting *off* all allegiances and responsibilities to any other than myself.(p.225)

• He said something about God or a Higher Power, but I brushed that *off* -- that was for the birds, not for me.(p.239)

• At thirteen I was packed *off* to a very fine Protestant boarding school in Virginia where I stayed four years, graduating without any special achievements.(p.240)

• I was startled to learn he had only been *off* the booze a month or so himself when he brought me the message!(p.245)

• There was one meeting a week at Bill's home in Brooklyn, and we all took turns there spouting *off* about how we had changed our lives overnight, how many drunks we had saved and straightened out, and last, but not least, how God had touched each of us personally on the shoulder.(p.246)

• Peddling *off* my polish samples for expenses, I crawled back to New York a few days later in a very chastened frame of mind.(p.248)

• With nothing but a liberal arts education, very definitely estranged from my family and already married, soon after graduation from college I became a bookmaker's clerk on the British racing circuits, far better *off* financially than the average professional man.(p.251)

• I stayed so sober that I used to keep a quart of medicinal whiskey in my bureau which I used to taper *off* the occasional newspaper alcoholics who were sent to see me.(p.253)

• He knew too well that didn't mean a thing, just as I knew in my heart that it would be only a question of time -- a few days, a week, or even a month, it was inevitable -- till I would be *off* on another bender.(p.257)

• I remember one instance when he took *off* and went down to Cincinnati and was gone a week on a drunk.(p.262)

• If I'd had a gun I'd have shot the horns right *off* the thing, because it made me raving mad.(p.265)

• I sipped the drink *off* the bar because I couldn't hold it in my hand, but I was still a lady, believe it or not, and I was deeply ashamed.(p.266)

• I paced the floor with a bath towel around my shoulders, the perspiration running *off* me.(p.268)

• In the spring of 1939, Bill stopped *off* in Akron on his way to Detroit on business.(p.281)

• A doctor tipped me *off* to my first prospect.(p.282)

• I landed him and shipped him by train to Akron, with a pint of whiskey in his pocket to keep him from wanting to get *off* the train in Toledo!(p.282)

• Then when we got back to the apartment, he was willing to wait two or three days until I got my health back to be paid *off* for the liquor and fare.(p.289)

• The day before I was due to go back to Chicago, a Wednesday and Dr. Bob's afternoon *off*, he had me down to the office and we spent three or four hours formally going through the Six-Step program as it was at that time.(p.291)

• My wife became pregnant and the doctor recommended the use of port or ale . . . so . . . I bought a six gallon crock and a few bottles, listened to advice from amateur brewmeisters, and was *off* on my beer manufacturing career on a small scale (for the time being).(p.297)

• As a result, I would fall *off* in a drunken stupor every night.(p.299)

• How many times I swore *off* in the morning and got drunk before sunset I don't know.(p.300)

• From a physical standpoint, I gained sixteen pounds in the first two months I was *off* liquor.(p.303)

• And then, in the spring of 1939, a very remarkable book was rolled *off* a New York press with the title "Alcoholics Anonymous."(p.307)

• While I was in basic, I got high *off* booze almost every night.(p.317)

• He turned me in to the company commander, but I got *off* the hook, and that was all that mattered.(p.317)

• Somehow, I made it through basic and then laid *off* the booze for about three months, because I was in school at night.(p.317)

• If I could lay *off* it, that meant I didn't have to worry about a drinking problem, I thought.(p.317)

• An alcoholic can't lay *off* the booze – right?(p.317)

• It would be a little thing that I'd think was wrong, and *off* I'd go, drinking.(p.324)

• I used to make excuses to try and get George *off* the wagon.(p.325)

• No jail booking, drunk-driving citation, barroom fight, or even a tumble *off* a barstool.(p.327)

• I was aware of symptoms of impending dependence, and I told myself I had gotten out of the rat race just in time to head *off* any booze problem.(p.327)

• Whatever it was, it brushed all the heavy burdens *off* my back.(p.334)

• After that I sat for a week, a body in a chair, a mind *off* in space.(p.338)

• And when I took that first drink, I was *off* on the usual merry-go-round.(p.339)

• And as that thought came to me, it was as though someone had reached down and taken a heavy overcoat *off* my shoulders, for that was the last one.(p.347)

• So I went to her and said, "There's only one thing I want in my whole life, and I don't want any commendation; I don't want any credit; I don't want anything from you or Janey for the rest of your life except one thing; and that is, the opportunity to do anything you want always, and I would like to start *off* by doing the dishes."(p.351)

• They were neither poor nor wealthy, but far better *off* than the average couple.(p.357)

• I was living in a small room on West 53rd Street right *off* Fifth Avenue, when I met a young lady who eventually was responsible for altering my entire way of living.(p.359)

• With new hope in my heart and new resolutions I set *off* for Vermont.(p.360)

• I had thrown *off* a big lie that had been burdening me down for months.(p.366)

• After his death, my mother soon picked up drinking where Dad left *off*, and in a very short time she died of cirrhosis of the liver.(p.370)

• I would gather up all my soiled clothes, as much as I could cram into a grocery cart, and be *off*.(p.370)

• I couldn't walk, having it in a cast, and the doctor left the cast on three weeks longer than was necessary because he never found me sober enough to take it *off*.(p.390)

• I displayed alcoholic tendencies actually from the age of fourteen, when I started to steal wine from the family jug, siphoning it *off* one drink at a time so it wouldn't be missed, not drinking it immediately, but saving it until about a pint was accumulated, so that I could get drunk.(p.397)

• I'd better taper *off*.(p.408)

• They were awfully good about not cutting me *off*.(p.409)

• In my cups I used to tell them *off*, giving them lengthy advice on how to lead the right life.(p.410)

• Years of drinking and general high jinks had cut her *off* from old friends.(p.414)

• A load weighing a thousand pounds came *off* my back.(p.414)

• I got *off* the so-called wagon, and on the twenty-four hour plan.(p.415)

• They were doing very well – at least a fifth apiece a day, except on dad's days *off* when they did some serious drinking.(p.425)

• I planned to stay home the night before I left, but my folks got so drunk I walked *off* early in the evening and spent the night with my girl, getting very drunk myself.(p.425)

• We were supposed to take *off* at noon, but were delayed until six p.m.(p.428)

• I took more through the day to increase the high, and more to maintain it; when I overshot the mark, I'd take tranquilizers to level *off*.(p.442)

• Still, I couldn't turn my mouth *off*.(p.442)

• By early July, I had tapered *off* alcohol completely, and I got *off* all pills in the ensuing few months.(p.448)

• When the compulsion to drink left, it was relatively easy to stay *off* alcohol.(p.448)

• After I had been around A.A. for seven months, tapering *off* alcohol and pills, not finding the program working very well, I was finally able to say, "Okay, God.(p.448)

• So I'm better *off* if I don't give advice, don't figure I know what's best, and just accept life on life's terms, as it is today -- especially my own life, as it actually is.(p.450)

• I must keep my magic magnifying mind on my acceptance and *off* my expectations, for my serenity is directly proportional to my level of acceptance.(p.452)

• I was not eligible for parole, until -- with God's help, I'm sure – the governor cut five years *off* my sentence.(p.462)

• Now, I have been an alcoholism counselor for over a year and am *off* parole.(p.462)

• The word "alcoholic" does not turn me *off* any more; in fact, it is music to my ears when it applies to me.(p.463)

• Had I tried honestly and sincerely to practice the Twelve Steps I would have seen from my continuous moral inventory that I was getting *off* the beam -- I would have found that there were some active resentments in my life, a terrific amount of self-pity.(p.471)

• If someone had told me last year that I would be excited about gardening this year, I would have said he was *off* his rocker.(p.481)

• I had my own medical practice in Washington at that time, but the practice slackened and the mail order business started to fall *off*.(p.486)

• I went back to my mother's for a few days until things cooled *off*, because the District Attorney had put out a summons for me to come to see him in his office.(p.491)

• The November following, I took a few days *off* after pay day to celebrate my birthday on the 25th of the month.(p.491)

• The Armistice is signed on the 11th and the draft is called *off*.(p.499)
• This time I'm *off* of it for good.(p.502)
• She had looked for me last evening after I left the car and wandered *off* into the night.(p.502)
• Maybe a drink -- I put on my hat and dash *off* in the car.(p.505)
• I get in the car and drive *off*.(p.506)
• There was no time *off* for so-called good behavior, first-timers, or anything else.(p.509)
• I spent about six or seven weeks in Sing Sing, and was finally sent *off* to Dannemora in the Adirondacks.(p.509)
• I rounded up a few more of my friends and *off* we went to the meeting, not for anything we would gain from it as much as to make a burlesque out of it.(p.509)
• I started prowling around with a couple of these A.A. boys, which kept me pretty busy and kept my mind *off* of down town.(p.511)
• Then instead of going out with A.A. again I went out with some of the other crowd, and *off* again I went.(p.511)
• I've stuck pretty close to A.A. ever since then, taken it day by day, not biting *off* more than I can chew.(p.511)
• And so I got to the swearing *off* process.(p.513)
• And I was *off* again.(p.514)
• They were harder to get *off*.(p.514)
• I wasn't the type that could taper *off*.(p.514)
• I had just come *off* a good one, and I went back on to the next one.(p.514)
• It didn't worry me very much, because at that time I could shut *off* for a couple of months without taking a drink or even wanting one, and without feeling that I was giving anything up.(p.518)
• The Abyssinian war broke out just as things were going very badly for me, and I went *off* to Egypt on a job there.(p.519)
• I thought, well, now that I've been put out for drinking, I'll just show them that they were completely wrong, so I went *off* on the biggest bout I had been on up to then, involving about a fortnight's blackout.(p.521)
• I stopped *off* just to have one drink to see if it tasted the same on the way back to London, and that night I was carried back to bed again.(p.522)
• As I say, this specialist put a scare in me for about a fortnight or three weeks, then I started my last bout which went on and *off* for about three months.(p.523)
• But if I came back in the usual state, then I'd have to go *off* for good the next day.(p.523)
• I was down to my shorts, unaware of wrong-doing, before the ambulance got there and hauled me *off* to a hospital from which anxious friends rescued me, later that night.(p.537)
• There were debts totaling nearly ten thousand dollars to be paid *off*.(p.541)
• I stood *off* and took a long look at life and the values I found in it: I saw a paradox, that he who loses his life does indeed find it.(p.542)
• I swore *off* hard liquor and turned to wine.(p.555)
• We cast *off* the burdens of the past and the anxieties of the future, as we begin to live in the present, one day at a time.(p.560)

off-again

• Not understanding the twenty-four hour plan, or not wanting to, I began drinking and was *off-again* on-again, during that first month.(p.414)

offended

• When a person *offended* we said to ourselves, "This is a sick man.(p.67)
• You should not be *offended* if he wants to call it off, for he has helped you more than you have helped him.(p.94)

offender

• Resentment is the "number one" *offender*.(p.64)

offending

• And so on and on, for several weeks, while I grudgingly plowed through some more of the *offending* book, and felt more and more hopeless about myself.(p.227)

offense

• Perhaps we have committed a criminal *offense* which might land us in jail if it were known to the authorities.(p.78)
• Maybe it's only a petty *offense* such as padding the expense account.(p.78)
• Then I committed my last *offense*.(p.460)
• But on the other hand, I was terribly fortunate because that should have been a court martial *offense* and I should have been out on my ear.(p.520)

offer

• More often than not, it is imperative that a man's brain be cleared before he is approached, as he has then a better chance of understanding and accepting what we have to *offer*.(p.xxiv)
• If you ask him why he started on that last bender, the chances are he will *offer* you any one of a hundred alibis.(p.23)
• Many of us said to our Maker, as we understood Him: "God, I *offer* myself to Thee -- to build with me and to do with me as Thou wilt.(p.63)
• Occasionally, they will *offer* assistance.(p.78)
• Make use of what they *offer*.(p.87)
• But you may talk to him about the hopelessness of alcoholism because you *offer* a solution.(p.92)
• *Offer* him friendship and fellowship.(p.95)
• You are sure to find someone desperate enough to accept with eagerness what you *offer*.(p.96)
• If your man accepts your *offer*, it should be pointed out that physical treatment is but a small part of the picture.(p.143)
• By no means do we *offer* it as the last word on this subject, but so far as we are concerned, it has worked with us.(p.144)
• An *offer* of appreciation for not having had a drink for those few months and then and there, without anybody promising me anything or threatening me, I made a solemn vow that never so long as I lived would I take another drink.(p.200)
• So I indulged with my comrades in everything the Far East had to *offer*.(p.231)
• This time he had a suggestion to *offer*.(p.289)
• The only thing I have really to *offer* you is my own story, telling you just what sort of a drunk I was.(p.384)
• An alcoholic cannot accept the news that he's an alcoholic unless there is a meaningful explanation given, and an *offer* of help, such as you get in A.A.(p.406)
• Dr. John F. Stouffer, Chief Psychiatrist, Philadelphia General Hospital, citing his experience with A.A., said: "The alcoholics we get here at Philadelphia General are mostly those who cannot afford private treatment, and A.A. is by far the greatest thing we have been able to *offer* them.(p.572)

offered

• There I humbly *offered* myself to God, as I then understood Him, to do with me as He would.(p.13)
• Had you *offered* yourselves as patients at this hospital, I would not have taken you, if I had been able to avoid it.(p.43)
• He humbly *offered* himself to his Maker -- then he knew.(p.57)
• The family should be *offered* your way of life.(p.97)
• I *offered* them a drink, and they came to the bottom of the stairs and the good woman fainted, just looking at me.(p.205)
• Following graduation I was *offered* a pretty good job which I took.(p.212)
• I resented it of course, and I *offered* Clarence his commission, whatever it might be, if he would please not bother me because I had arrived at the conclusion that he was a solicitor for some alcoholic institute.(p.216)
• Sitting in a Second Avenue bar, accepting drinks from anyone who *offered*, after my small stake was gone; or sitting at home alone, with the inevitable glass in my hand, I would remember, and remembering, I would drink faster, seeking speedy oblivion.(p.225)
• Many friends of my family had emigrated to America, so at twenty-four I decided that the United States *offered* me the opportunity I was never likely to find in my native land.(p.231)
• I re-organized their city sales policy and eighteen months later, when I was thirty, they *offered* me the branch managership.(p.243)
• Bill and Hank had just taken over a small automobile polishing company and they *offered* me a job -- ten dollars a week and keep at Hank's house.(p.246)
• *Offered* the job of advertising manager for an eastern automotive company, I moved to Philadelphia to begin life anew.(p.254)
• Finally, an old business acquaintance of mine, whom I hadn't seen for several years *offered* me a job.(p.301)
• She *offered* me the alternative of going to see him or her leaving me for good and all.(p.301)
• Strangely enough, right through to the end of my twenty-six years in the Army, I was still being *offered* very good and important jobs in spite of the fact that my superiors must have known that I wasn't thoroughly reliable.(p.519)
• If I write with the air of one who has discovered the obvious, which is to say, the eternal truths which have been *offered* to us since the beginning, forgive my callowness; I had to find these things out for myself.(p.536)

offers

• Alcoholics can stop drinking in many places and many ways -- but Alcoholics Anonymous *offers* us a way to stay sober.(p.559)

offhand

• I'd thought of it in an *offhand* way, of course.(p.429)

office

• This brought a rush of 800 frantic inquiries into the little New York *office* which meanwhile had been established.(p.xviii)
• After one of those days of inferno, I wobbled from a hotel bar to a brokerage *office*.(p.4)
• Brown may get my job at the *office*.(p.65)
• It should not matter, however, if someone does throw us out of his *office*.(p.78)
• If there is no Al-Anon listing in your local telephone book, you may obtain further information on Al-Anon Family Groups by writing to its World Service *Office*: Box 182, Madison Square Station, New York, NY 10159.(p.121)
• Wherever men are gathered together in business there will be rivalries and, arising out of these, a certain amount of *office* politics.(p.145)
• When those two years were up, I opened an *office* downtown.(p.174)
• Away from my *office* two or three weeks at a time; horrible days and nights when I would lie on the floor of my home, lying awake and reaching over to get the bottle, taking a drink and going back into oblivion.(p.184)
• Three years later, at twenty-five, I opened and operated their Philadelphia *office* and was earning more than I ever have since.(p.242)
• I think his entry into A.A. was through spending some hours with Dr. Bob at his *office*.(p.267)
• It took five years of A.A. living, and a substantial improvement in my health, before I could take a full-time *office* job where someone else was boss.(p.283)
• This *office* job brought me face to face with a problem which I had sidestepped all my adult life, lack of training.(p.284)
• The day before I was due to go back to Chicago, a Wednesday and Dr. Bob's afternoon off, he had me down to the *office* and we spent three or four hours formally going through the Six-Step program as it was at that time.(p.291)
• In the spring of 1939, the Big Book was printed, and we had two inquiries from the New York *office* because of a fifteen-minute radio talk that was made.(p.294)
• Upon leaving the *office* in the evening, my first stop would be a saloon about a block away.(p.298)
• How I was able to discharge my duties at the *office* during those horrible mornings, I will never be able to explain.(p.299)
• I arrived at the stage where I couldn't quite make it to the *office* some mornings.(p.299)
• While working in an *office*, there was some semblance of restraint, but, oh boy, when I got on the outside with this new company without supervision, did I go to town!(p.300)
• It wasn't necessary to report to the *office* in person every day, and when I did go in, it was just to make an appearance and bounce right out again.(p.300)
• The encouragement received in the early days, especially from the A.A. General Service *Office*, made a tremendous difference to my sobriety.(p.342)
• I was sitting in my *office* one time after I had operated on a woman.(p.350)
• Here I am down at my *office* behind my desk and there she is out at the hospital.(p.350)
• My hours of work were flexible so that returning to the *office* was not always important.(p.376)
• I know that when Frank came home, I said, "I want to try this thing," and he said, "There's a post *office* box to write to in New York."(p.392)
• It was the A.A. General Service *Office* in New York that I wrote to, and that *office* has always meant a lot to me.(p.392)
• (That was the man the A.A. *office* had referred me to.)(p.393)
• At age twenty-one, I enlisted in the Navy for two reasons: (1) to avoid being drafted into the Army, and (2) out of a burst of patriotic fervor inspired by the advent of World War II and as the result of an all-night drinking binge which found me sitting on the doorstep of the Navy recruiting *office* when the chief petty officer arrived to open for business at nine o'clock Monday morning.(p.398)
• I was now with the Paris *office*.(p.405)

• I did not reflect that half the *office* was composed of A.A. members, and that I was as unexciting as any client in any *office*.(p.413)
• I had just begun a dental practice in a beautiful new *office*.(p.418)
• The last time I drank, when I was twenty-nine, I drank for only four days, yet I threatened to kill my children; I beat my wife at home and on the church steps; I mistreated a child in my *office*; and I ran to a hospital for mental illness to avoid jail.(p.418)
• My life there was a nightmare of periodic binges on alcohol and pills, adultery, unhappy hours at the dental *office*, seeing my wife give birth to our second child and have several miscarriages, living in a turbulent household, and making continual attempts to be the respectable dentist, husband, father, and community leader.(p.419)
• I teamed up with a cute little blonde with whom I was working at the *office*, and for about a year we were inseparable.(p.425)
• The boys at the Post *Office* used to bring me my jugs; mail couldn't be opened for inspection at the gate.(p.426)
• Much of my time was spent writing letters, notes, orders, and lists of things for Max, who was also my *office* nurse, to do to keep the world running while I was locked up.(p.445)
• Max still works with me in the *office*, but we have turned our wills and our lives and our work over to the care of God.(p.446)
• As an indication of just how confused and mixed up I was, just as soon as I could I left the *office* and hurried around to tell other patients that I was getting better.(p.470)
• I've never seen him drunk in my life, although he'd take a shot in the morning and usually one in the evening, and so did I; but for the most part he kept his whiskey in his *office*.(p.484)
• At that time the repeal whiskies were back, and I'd go to the store and buy my whiskey and take it to my *office* and put it under the desk, first in one place and then in another, and there soon was an accumulation of empty bottles.(p.488)
• That year, on a Friday night, a man whom I had known for years came to my *office*.(p.488)
• I worked for the Government about a year and still maintained my evening *office* practice when the Government agencies were decentralized.(p.489)
• I went back to my mother's for a few days until things cooled off, because the District Attorney had put out a summons for me to come to see him in his *office*.(p.491)
• But there happened to be a liquor store between the post *office* and the mill, and I stopped to get that one drink.(p.493)
• I, and the books of my division, have been transferred to the head *office*.(p.500)
• They are the custodians of our A.A. Tradition and the receivers of voluntary A.A. contributions by which we maintain our A.A. General Service *Office* at New York.(p.567)
• In such places, A.A. can be located through the local telephone directory, newspaper *office*, or police station, or by contacting local priests or ministers.(p.575)
• The General Service Board of A.A. (the trustees) administers A.A.'s General Service *Office*, A.A. World Services, Inc., and our monthly magazine, the A.A. Grapevine.(p.575)

officer

• Here, for instance, is a typical example: An *officer* of one of the largest banking institutions in America knows I no longer drink.(p.138)
• At three-thirty the next morning, I was in Champlain Street Station, in jail for driving while intoxicated and insulting an *officer*; and the suit of which I was so proud was in such shape that the turnkey had to get me a pair of trousers to go into court in the next morning.(p.201)
• I went downstairs and there was the grizzly old veteran police *officer* in charge of the property desk, and as he gave me the stuff, he asked, "Are you going out in the street that way?"(p.204)
• For this *officer* in the Indian Army, going on the wagon was not enough; attempts at control failed.(p.342)
• In time I became an *officer* and director of one of the largest commercial banks in the country.(p.374)
• At age twenty-one, I enlisted in the Navy for two reasons: (1) to avoid being drafted into the Army, and (2) out of a burst of patriotic fervor inspired by the advent of World War II and as the result of an all-night drinking binge which found me sitting on the doorstep of the Navy recruiting office when the chief petty *officer* arrived to open for business at nine o'clock Monday morning.(p.398)
• Each time I would make a report to the parole *officer* he would ask me, "Have you been to an A.A. meeting yet?"(p.510)
• THE CAREER *OFFICER*(p.517)
• A British *officer*, this Irishman – that is, until brandy "retired" him.(p.517)
• The Commanding *Officer* only spoke to me when he wanted to tell me exactly who I was and what I was and how little I counted in the scheme of things and how glad he would be if I went away.(p.520)
• I think the Commanding *Officer* was rather tired of this particular chicken coming back to roost so often because he very soon wrote in to the medical authorities to tell them that they had to get me into hospital, to be thoroughly examined for drinking.(p.520)
• When the policeman released me to my stupefied and exasperated friend at four in the morning, I went to my traveling bag and groped until I found – well, let the *officer* speak: "Ah," said the policeman, "he's got anuder pair, t'ank God!"(p.538)
• Later, I went to sea, serving as a gunnery *officer* on a destroyer escort and emerging a lieutenant commander.(p.555)

officer's

• India lent itself to drinking then, if you were disposed to drink, because you lived in bungalows; you didn't live all together as you do at home in an *Officer's* Mess.(p.519)

officers

• War fever ran high in the New England town to which we new, young *officers* from Plattsburg were assigned, and we were flattered when the first citizens took us to their homes, making us feel heroic.(p.1)

offices

• *Offices* closed up and workers discharged.(p.500)
• My doctor finally declared he could no longer be responsible for me, and sent me to a psychiatrist who practiced in the same suite of *offices*.(p.558)
• In large cities, groups often maintain local *offices* where alcoholics or their families may arrange for interviews or hospitalization.(p.575)

official

• By the latter part of September 1939, we had a nucleus of six and held our first *official* group meeting.(p.310)

offset

• However, what I had gained materially on the credit side of my ledger, I have since learned was more than *offset* on the debit side by egotism, resentment and dishonesty.(p.356)

often

• More *often* than not, it is imperative that a man's brain be cleared before he is approached, as he has then a better chance of understanding and accepting what we have to offer.(p.xxiv)
• Of course an alcoholic ought to be freed from his physical craving for liquor, and this *often* requires a definite hospital procedure, before psychological measures can be of maximum benefit.(p.xxv)
• Although he gives all that is in him, it *often* is not enough.(p.xxvii)
• They are *often* able, intelligent, friendly people.(p.xxviii)
• When I need a mental uplift, I *often* think of another case brought in by a physician prominent in New York.(p.xxix)
• "Bathtub" gin, two bottles a day, and *often* three, got to be routine.(p.5)
• It relieved me somewhat to learn that in alcoholics the will is amazingly weakened when it comes to combating liquor, though it *often* remains strong in other respects.(p.7)
• I had *often* pondered these things.(p.10)
• At these informal gatherings one may *often* see from 50 to 200 persons.(p.16)
• He is *often* perfectly sensible and well balanced concerning everything except liquor, but in that respect he is incredibly dishonest and selfish.(p.21)
• He *often* possesses special abilities, skills, and aptitudes, and has a promising career ahead of him.(p.21)
• But they *often* suspect they are down for the count.(p.23)
• How *often* have some of us begun to drink in this nonchalant way, and after the third or fourth, pounded on the bar and said to ourselves, "For God's sake, how did I ever get started again?"(p.24)
• Potential female alcoholics *often* turn into the real thing and are gone beyond recall in a few years.(p.33)
• Besides a seeming inability to accept much on faith, we *often* found ourselves handicapped by obstinacy, sensitiveness, and unreasoning prejudice.(p.47)
• And there *often* seems no way of entirely getting rid of self without His aid.(p.62)
• The first thing apparent was that this world and its people were *often* quite wrong.(p.65)
• Counsel with persons is *often* desirable, but we let God be the final judge.(p.69)
• We *often* find such a person quick to see and understand our problem.(p.74)
• The feeling that the drink problem has disappeared will *often* come strongly.(p.75)
• A man so involved *often* feels very remorseful at times, especially if he is married to a loyal and courageous girl who has literally gone through hell for him.(p.81)
• Though there may be justifiable exceptions, and though we wish to lay down no rule of any sort, we have *often* found this the best course to take.(p.81)
• We are *often* surprised how the right answers come after we have tried this for a while.(p.86)
• He *often* says that if he had continued to work on them, he might have deprived many others, who have since recovered, of their chance.(p.96)
• That *often* makes the difference between failure and success.(p.98)
• We *often* need it to carry green recruits through a severe hangover.(p.102)
• Death was *often* near.(p.107)
• He *often* gets entirely out of hand when drinking.(p.109)
• Oddly enough, he is *often* difficult to deal with.(p.110)
• Yet *often* such men had spectacular and powerful recoveries.(p.113)
• *Often* you must carry the burden of avoiding them or keeping them under control.(p.117)
• A man may criticize or laugh at himself and it will affect others favorably, but criticism or ridicule coming from another *often* produces the contrary effect.(p.125)
• They are all disappointed, and *often* let him feel it.(p.126)
• They *often* forget father was beyond human aid.(p.128)
• By force of circumstances, she was *often* obliged to treat father as a sick or wayward child.(p.130)
• Father, coming suddenly to life again, *often* begins to assert himself.(p.131)
• Now about health: A body badly burned by alcohol does not *often* recover overnight nor do twisted thinking and depression vanish in a twinkling.(p.133)
• Their services are *often* indispensable in treating a newcomer and in following his case afterward.(p.133)
• One of the many doctors who had the opportunity of reading this book in manuscript form told us that the use of sweets was *often* helpful, of course depending upon a doctor's advice.(p.133)
• Marvelous results *often* follow such a reunion.(p.134)
• To him the alcoholic has *often* seemed a fool of the first magnitude.(p.137)
• Of course that isn't so, and such people *often* may impose on you.(p.141)
• *Often* this is not so at all.(p.145)
• These juniors are *often* in a difficult position.(p.147)
• They *often* jeopardize their own positions by trying to help serious drinkers who should have been fired long ago, or else given an opportunity to get well.(p.147)
• He need not, and *often* should not show it to his alcoholic prospect.(p.148)
• We believe that managers of large enterprises *often* have little idea how prevalent this problem is.(p.149)
• He entered a political campaign, making speeches, frequenting men's gathering places of all sorts, *often* staying up all night.(p.158)
• Those of us who travel drop in as *often* as we can.(p.162)
• My marriage was happy and, as I have said, I never had any of the reasons, conscious or unconscious, which are *often* given for drinking.(p.182)
• There were times when I got to drinking, and I had been warned by Firestone that they wouldn't stand for this much longer, so, clearly, they were conscious of the fact that I drank too much and too *often*.(p.204)
• In fact, as I look back, I have *often* thought that they probably concluded that they would put up with me for a couple of years, that I couldn't live much longer, and that they would inherit whatever was left of the practice.(p.215)
• I had found friends, understanding friends who *often* knew what I was thinking and feeling better than I knew myself, and didn't allow me to retreat into my prison of loneliness and fear over a fancied slight or hurt.(p.228)
• My wife upbraided me *often* and plenty when she saw that my "periodics" were gradually losing me

what business I could get.(p.233)
• If anything, he had known all of them even better and more *often* than I.(p.239)
• The lesson of his death still remains with me, yet I *often* wonder what would have happened if somebody else had made that first call on me.(p.239)
• In those days we really took each other's inventories firmly and *often*.(p.245)
• Dr. Bob *often* said that it was a record for what he felt was a typical alcoholic.(p.263)
• I *often* think how that could have turned some people away, because there were no other women alcoholics there then.(p.269)
• I called her every night from a local bar, and *often* she was not at home.(p.318)
• But the percentages started tobogganing, and it was *often* a shock to read over some of the pages when sober.(p.331)
• No matter how *often* I had gone into and come out of alcoholic lows during the day, the pattern bounced me out of bed each night about 2:00 a.m., shaking and hurting in the agitation that always follows a drug's sedation.(p.332)
• During the next three years, I tried *often* again to give it up, but failed miserably.(p.343)
• I never drank socially; I drank as *often* and as much as I could.(p.353)
• I went back to my group meetings, but not wholeheartedly, and I *often* skipped them with the excuse that I was too tired.(p.364)
• But I was a careful and cunning alcoholic, and this didn't happen very *often*.(p.399)
• Above all, he noticed that I drank a good deal, *often* got tight in his company and told him naughty stories.(p.403)
• I wanted to die and *often* I would think of ways.(p.411)
• They were kind when they thought about it, but that wasn't *often*.(p.424)
• Yet prisoners *often* can't identify with many A.A. members' drinking stories.(p.458)
• This career girl preferred solitary drinking, the blackout kind, *often* hoping she'd stay that way for keeps.(p.464)
• And I landed right smack back in that sanitarium that I had gone to so *often*.(p.472)
• We lived just a few doors from the First Baptist Church and when they had funerals I remember very *often* asking my mother whether the person was good or bad and whether they were going to heaven or hell.(p.483)
• But I can remember in post graduate days, and during interneship, that very *often* I'd go to a patient's bed and start a process of elimination and then, very *often*, I'd wind up guessing.(p.485)
• Economic conditions had a great deal to do with it, because I've *often* heard my father say that his mother would take one of the old time flour sacks and cut a hole through the bottom and two corners of it and there you'd have a gown.(p.486)
• Of course, when father finally came to Virginia to work his way through school, he resented the southern "cracker," as he *often* called them, so much that he didn't even go back to his mother's funeral.(p.486)
• Very *often* we rode to and from work together, but being separated really galled me deep down.(p.491)
• Even when we were paying that two dollars a night, they *often* paid it for us because our collection was so small.(p.496)
• I wish I were dead, as I have *often* wished before.(p.502)
• I had drunk too *often* and too much.(p.515)
• Even at that he spoke quite *often*.(p.520)
• I think the Commanding Officer was rather tired of this particular chicken coming back to roost so *often* because he very soon wrote in to the medical authorities to tell them that they had to get me into hospital, to be thoroughly examined for drinking.(p.520)
• I don't know when I became an alcoholic, but I do believe I became one because I drank too much too *often*.(p.526)
• The only way existence was possible was through rationalizing every sober moment and drinking myself into complete oblivion as *often* as I could.(p.547)
• Too *often*, I would overdo it and behave badly at the very time I wanted to be at my best!(p.556)
• To those now in its fold, Alcoholics Anonymous has made the difference between misery and sobriety, and *often* the difference between life and death.(p.563)
• Experience has *often* warned us that nothing can so surely destroy our spiritual heritage as futile disputes over property, money, and authority.(p.566)
• The small group may elect its secretary, the large group its rotating committee, and the groups of a large metropolitan area their central or intergroup committee, which *often* employs a full-time secretary.(p.567)
• Quite *often* friends of the newcomer are aware of the difference long before he is himself.(p.569)
• What *often* takes place in a few months could seldom have been accomplished by years of self discipline.(p.569)
• Dr. Harry M. Tiebout, psychiatrist: "As a psychiatrist, I have thought a great deal about the relationship of my specialty to A.A. and I have come to the conclusion that our particular function can very *often* lie in preparing the way for the patient to accept any sort of treatment or outside help.(p.571)
• In this atmosphere the alcoholic *often* overcomes his excessive concentration upon himself.(p.572)
• In large cities, groups *often* maintain local offices where alcoholics or their families may arrange for interviews or hospitalization.(p.575)

often-painful

• After such *often-painful* vigilance (and numerous phony stints of abstinence), retirement naturally created an impulse to live without restraints.(p.328)

oh

• "*Oh* no," said my friend, "this chap is either through with liquor, or he is minus a job.(p.138)
• Hopelessness was written large on the man's face as he replied, "*Oh*, but that's no use.(p.157)
• "*Oh*, some darn thing they've got here in the paper about it."(p.266)
• While working in an office, there was some semblance of restraint, but, *oh* boy, when I got on the outside with this new company without supervision, did I go to town!(p.300)
• I said, "*Oh*, goodness, no!(p.321)
• And she said, "*Oh*, yes.(p.321)
• This girl and her husband are both in A.A., and she said to me, "*Oh*, but you're not the alcoholic; it's your husband."(p.322)
• I nudged George next morning, and I said, "I'm in," and he said, "*Oh*, I knew you'd make it."(p.322)
• Shortly after I was starting to work on the program I realized that I was not a good father; I wasn't a good husband, but, *oh*, I was a good provider.(p.351)
• Like most statistics, it doesn't prove anything -- just satisfies a little curiosity engendered by the wail "*Oh*, those initiation fees" that prompted this investigation.(p.399)
• *Oh*, poor self-centered, sick little me.(p.413)
• I thought, "*Oh* well, these people are just like all the people I've known all my life.(p.472)
• *Oh*, I was beautiful in those days!(p.479)
• "*Oh*," I said, "that's not for me!(p.510)
• *Oh* yes, I get the dry jitters once in a while, but that isn't anything to worry about.(p.516)
• *Oh*, I might drink too much at times – everyone I knew drank.(p.527)

Ohio

• The spark that was to flare into the first A.A. group was struck at Akron, *Ohio*, in June 1935, during a talk between a New York stockbroker and an Akron physician.(p.xv)
• In his prodigy of service, he was well assisted by Sister Ignatia at St. Thomas Hospital in Akron, *Ohio*, one of the greatest friends our Fellowship will ever know.(p.171)
• I was born in Cleveland, *Ohio*, in 1889, the last child of a family of eight children.(p.210)
• Drifting back to *Ohio*, I landed on a small newspaper and later was impressed into the direction of boy-welfare work at the local "Y."(p.253)
• My wife came over from Scotland and we started housekeeping in a large *Ohio* city.(p.254)
• One year we got as far as Bellaire, *Ohio*.(p.264)
• On Wednesday night Jack M. said, "You meet me at the *Ohio* Edison Building, and I will take you to the meeting."(p.269)
• I grew up in a small town outside Akron, *Ohio*, where the life was typical of any average small town.(p.287)
• I was born in Cleveland, *Ohio*, the only child of a prominent dentist, and a very proud mother.(p.357)

oil

• Being certain he wants to stop, you can go to him with this volume as joyfully as though you had struck *oil*.(p.113)
• My next job was in sales promotion for an *oil* company in Mississippi where I promptly became high man and got lots of pats on the back.(p.242)
• After the *oil* job blew up, I went back to Baltimore and mother, my first wife having said a permanent "Goodbye."(p.243)
• In the two succeeding years I held ten different jobs ranging from newspaper copy-desk and rewrite, to traffic director for an *oil* field equipment company.(p.255)
• Looking directly at me was a large *oil* painting of my wife, and her very words seemed to shout at me -- "I am not leaving you because I don't love you; it's because I do love you.(p.363)
• I found I could boost my income by figuring out a lot of cute little tricks that the boss wouldn't be likely to notice – filching money from the Coke machine, short-sticking the customers on *oil*, and selling *oil* I'd drained out of other cars.(p.423)
• "You've got to space your drinks and take plenty of water in between," or "coat the stomach with a little olive *oil*," or "drink anything but those damn martinis."(p.433)
• There, I received several soda crackers and water daily, and before I could have my third-day meal (again the only meal in ten days), I had to drink a glass of castor *oil* or mineral *oil*, depending on the cruelty of the person who was doing the dispensing.(p.459)

oil-field

• As my father climbed the ladder of success in the *oil-field* business, his drinking also climbed.(p.369)

oilman

• Dad's image for me was that of a big Irish *oilman* who came up through the school of hard knocks and so had to be a two-fisted drinker.(p.369)

okay

• I said I was *okay*, but if it would make her feel better I would go "as tired as I was after the strenuous holidays."(p.365)
• I can't say, "I'm powerless over alcohol, but solid alcohol is *okay*."(p.443)
• After I had been around A.A. for seven months, tapering off alcohol and pills, not finding the program working very well, I was finally able to say, "*Okay*, God.(p.448)
• *Okay*, I wanted to be God.(p.535)

Oklahoma

• Then we moved up to *Oklahoma*.(p.386)

old

• My attention was caught by a doggerel on an *old* tombstone:(p.1)
• As I drank, the *old* fierce determination to win came back.(p.4)
• The cheery voice of an *old* school friend asked if he might come over.(p.8)
• Yes, the *old* boy was on fire all right.(p.9)
• That war-time day in *old* Winchester Cathedral came back again.(p.10)
• Despite the living example of my friend there remained in me the vestiges of my *old* prejudice.(p.12)
• It was fortunate, for my *old* business associates remained skeptical for a year and a half, during which I found little work.(p.15)
• Many times I have gone to my *old* hospital in despair.(p.15)
• If these thoughts occur, they are hazy and readily supplanted with the *old* threadbare idea that this time we shall handle ourselves like other people.(p.24)
• My *old* manner of life was by no means a bad one, but I would not exchange its best moments for the worst I have now.(p.43)
• Only thirty years later the conquest of the air was almost an *old* story and airplane travel was in full swing.(p.52)
• Is not our age characterized by the ease with which we discard *old* ideas for new, by the complete readiness with which we throw away the theory or gadget which does not work for something new which does?(p.52)
• For faith in a Power greater than ourselves, and miraculous demonstrations of that power in human lives, are facts as *old* as man himself.(p.55)
• Some of us have tried to hold on to our *old* ideas and the result was nil until we let go absolutely.(p.58)
• If he opened that *old* affair, he was afraid it would destroy the reputation of his partner, disgrace his family and take away his means of livelihood.(p.80)
• If their *old* relationship is to be resumed it must be on a better basis, since the former did not work.(p.99)
• Why sit with a long face in places where there is drinking, sighing about the good *old* days.(p.102)
• For a while they would be their *old* sweet selves, only to dash the new structure of affection to pieces once more.(p.107)
• Many of the *old* problems will still be with you.(p.117)
• You will lose the *old* life to find one much better.(p.120)
• The good *old* days will soon be back, they think.(p.123)

• Though ***old*** buildings will eventually be replaced by finer ones, the new structures will take years to complete.(p.123)
• Then, under one provocation or another, the aggrieved one would unearth the ***old*** affair and angrily cast its ashes about.(p.124)
• The ***old*** pleasures were gone.(p.151)
• He will presently try the ***old*** game again, for he isn't happy about his sobriety.(p.152)
• Again it was the ***old***, insidious insanity -- that first drink.(p.154)
• I guess the ***old*** folks were right after all."(p.159)
• Cleaning up ***old*** scrapes, helping to settle family differences, explaining the disinherited son to his irate parents, lending money and securing jobs for each other, when justified -- these are everyday occurrences.(p.161)
• I drank with moderation at first, but it took me only a relatively short time to drift back into the ***old*** habits which had wound up so disastrously before.(p.175)
• I also made use of ***old*** trunks and chests, the ***old*** can container, and even the ash container.(p.176)
• The first time that I became intoxicated I was eight years ***old***.(p.182)
• Knowing Bob of ***old***, she jokingly replied, "Well, Doctor, I suppose you've already tried it yourself?"(p.188)
• My father died in 1901 when I was eight years ***old*** and I was in the second or third grade at school.(p.193)
• When I was sixteen years ***old***, my mother remarried and I was given the opportunity of going back to school.(p.193)
• We shook hands, and he hung onto my hand for a moment and said, "Tell you what I'll do for ***old*** times sake.(p.201)
• I went downstairs and there was the grizzly ***old*** veteran police officer in charge of the property desk, and as he gave me the stuff, he asked, "Are you going out in the street that way?"(p.204)
• My mother was eighty-nine years ***old*** when she died, and I was a full-blown alcoholic at the time of her death.(p.210)
• I was then about sixteen years ***old***.(p.211)
• I married when I was twenty-eight years ***old***, and started in law school after I was married.(p.212)
• By that time, I had one boy in college, another a senior in high school, and a daughter about twelve years ***old***.(p.215)
• I was forty-nine and a half years ***old*** when I was first approached about the Akron Group.(p.215)
• I found in the fall of 1939, that I was not mentally impaired, so far as trial work was concerned, and thereafter took up where I had left off when I was about forty-five years ***old***.(p.220)
• I was thirty-two years ***old***.(p.224)
• There I sat in the evenings, enjoying with my friends our memories of the "***old*** country," singing the ***old*** songs we all knew, playing simple card games for drinks and consuming great quantities of beer.(p.231)
• It wasn't very long before home-brewing was an institution and men began to search feverishly for ***old*** recipe books on wine-making.(p.232)
• I missed the ***old*** social times, of course, but had no definite craving even for beer.(p.232)
• Before long I had a definite taste for hard liquor, knew nausea and headaches I had never known before, but as in the ***old*** days, I suffered them out.(p.233)
• Here I was, thirty-nine years ***old*** and a complete washout.(p.238)
• I had not asked for help and seriously doubt that I would have, but Fitz, an ***old*** school friend of mine, had persuaded Jackie to call on me.(p.238)
• Jackie told me about a group of fellows in New York, of whom my ***old*** friend Fitz was one, who had the same problem I had, and who by working together to help each other were not now drinking and were happy like himself.(p.239)
• In the eight years before A.A. found me, I had over forty jobs -- selling and travelling -- one thing after another, and the same ***old*** routine.(p.244)
• The same ***old*** routines seemed to be common to us all.(p.246)
• An ***old*** avocation, the collecting of first editions, rare books and Americana, fascinated me between times.(p.255)
• Loading a car with good ***old*** books to sell to collectors, librarians, universities and historical societies, I started out to travel the country.(p.255)
• "Well," I said to dad, when the A.A. people kept coming with these lovely cars and looked so nice, "I suppose the neighbors say, 'Now those ***old*** fools must have up and died, but where's the hearse?'"(p.269)
• All this changed when I was thirty years ***old***.(p.277)
• I was suddenly and uncontrollably seized with the ***old***, paralyzing panic.(p.279)
• During that first year, however, I managed to make both ends meet, and to avoid ever going back to my ***old*** habit pattern of borrowing money when I could not earn it.(p.283)
• I found some wool stockings, some white flannels that had shrunk to my knees, and an ***old*** jacket.(p.288)
• A week later, I had to get an ***old*** friend from Akron to spend two days sobering me up.(p.293)
• Acceptance of things as they are has replaced the ***old*** impatient champing at the bit to conquer the world.(p.295)
• Finally, an ***old*** business acquaintance of mine, whom I hadn't seen for several years offered me a job.(p.301)
• I was thirty-three years ***old*** and my life was spent.(p.304)
• And still by the time I was thirty years ***old*** I was being pushed around with a compulsion to drink that was completely beyond my control.(p.305)
• I was sure I wouldn't belong in an A.A. group -- they were all ***old*** men, I thought, and all skid-row bums.(p.319)
• After having a few drinks, I went to a meeting -- and the people there were not all ***old*** men and definitely not skid-row types!(p.319)
• That was on a hot summer evening, down in the Greenwich Village Group, and there was a little porch out there in the ***old*** meeting place on Sullivan Street, and after the meeting I went out on the steps for some air.(p.321)
• In the ***old*** days I hated to wake up and look back at what last night was like.(p.325)
• While I sought the comforting arms of alcohol, I knew this was a sign of weakness on the part of a longtime-successful ***old*** codger with white hair, the image of dignity.(p.331)
• He'd told a villain, "The trouble is, ***old*** man, you've lived too long."(p.333)
• Before long I was at the luncheon meeting an hour before the others, that ***old*** and familiar trademark of every alcoholic.(p.360)
• Attending his fourth or fifth meeting was an ***old*** friend I had not seen for twenty years.(p.365)
• When I was called upon for a few words I had to tell my friends that I wasn't one year ***old*** in A.A. that evening but only a "nine month baby."(p.366)
• Before too long, my husband (who seemed to prefer his shirts dirty) put his foot down, declaring that our family might have the cleanest clothes in town, but that I hadn't been out of the same ***old*** dirty slacks and blouse for a week.(p.371)
• The servant he turned to was our ***old*** cook, and she liked to drink.(p.385)
• Even when I was ***old*** enough to know better, I dreamed about being as beautiful as Venus, as pure as the Madonna and as brilliant as the President of the United States is supposed to be.(p.400)
• My ***old*** friends showed distress.(p.404)
• Years of drinking and general high jinks had cut her off from ***old*** friends.(p.414)
• I have my A.A. friends, and I have become reacquainted with my ***old*** friends on a new basis.(p.416)
• I was twenty-eight years ***old***.(p.418)
• I neither drank nor smoked until I was nineteen years ***old***.(p.419)
• Awarded a scholarship to a famous ***old*** Eastern college, I began to drink at the end of my freshman year, and by junior year, I had to transfer to an easier state university to keep my grades up.(p.419)
• So we rolled ***old*** newspapers together and made torches to find a good soft pew and get some sleep.(p.424)
• I talked the ***Old*** Man into letting me live in the photo lab instead of the barracks, and for eighteen months nothing interfered with my drinking.(p.426)
• So I'd sit up, watch ***old*** Wallace Beery movies on all-night TV, and drink.(p.441)
• And life keeps getting simpler and easier as we try to reverse my ***old*** idea, by taking care of the internal environment via the Twelve Steps, and letting the external environment take care of itself.)(p.446)
• What else can I do except what I have always done in the past? -- act as my ***old*** self and return to prison.(p.458)
• We reverted to the ***old*** way of life we knew -- a life full of anger, vindictiveness, resentment, fear, dependence, denial, self-will, irresponsibility.(p.459)
• All Twelve Steps of A.A. are designed to kill the ***old*** self (deflate the ***old*** ego) and build a new, free self.(p.459)
• I was forty-four years ***old***; my life had been wasted.(p.461)
• I nearly reverted to my ***old***, incorrigible self -- had trouble with a couple of other prisoners, was planning an escape.(p.461)
• I go back to my ***old*** alma mater occasionally to give A.A. talks, and -- just think! -- the warden is my friend.(p.462)
• I haven't seen my son since he was three and a half years ***old***.(p.463)
• My daughter was one and a half years ***old*** when I last saw her.(p.463)
• I will be fifty years ***old*** next month, haven't seen my son or daughter yet, nor my daughter's two children, my grandchildren; but I am grateful.(p.463)
• I started drinking socially and at parties and proms when I was about twenty years ***old***.(p.464)
• I not listen to ***old*** woman.(p.474)
• He ***old***, sick, want to be alone with bottle.(p.476)
• He was ***old***, but now he grow young with new life in A.A. and travel all time.(p.476)
• Mother was of the ***old*** school and figured that anyone I associated with should be of the proper type.(p.484)
• Economic conditions had a great deal to do with it, because I've often heard my father say that his mother would take one of the ***old*** time flour sacks and cut a hole through the bottom and two corners of it and there you'd have a gown.(p.486)
• Both he and ***old*** Maud are glad to get home.(p.497)
• Good ***old*** John!(p.498)
• Good ***old*** John Barleycorn!(p.499)
• Good ***old*** Charlie!(p.500)
• The same ***old*** problems and worries surround me.(p.505)
• I was immediately arrested, arraigned in Homicide Court, held without bail, and remanded to the ***old*** Tombs Prison to await trial.(p.508)
• After I had made my third report, I stepped down town, met some of the ***old*** crowd, and of course you know the answer.(p.510)
• I don't miss any of the ***old*** crowd nor do I miss any of their parties.(p.511)
• The ***old*** pattern reasserted itself, but it was no longer once every six months.(p.514)
• I went back to the ***old*** family doctor who had helped me the first time I had the D.T.'s.(p.515)
• But somehow or other, with my ***old*** alcoholic brain, sitting there in that chair, I kept saying to myself, "I wonder if it'll work?(p.515)
• Everybody I had known in the ***old*** days had gone.(p.522)
• There was the father one lost respect for at the age of eleven, because the father broke his solemn word in a circumstance where you, eleven years ***old***, had assumed guilt when you were innocent; but the father would not believe you, no matter what; and to ease his suffering you "confessed" and were "forgiven," only -- months later -- to have your "guilt" brought up -- only he and you knew what he was talking bout -- brought up in front of the stern grandmother.(p.533)
• I have been appointed to the faculty of my ***old*** school, to teach in my new field.(p.541)
• At fifty-four, I have had come true for me the ***old*** wish, "If only I could live my life over, knowing what I know."(p.543)
• I am an only child, and when I was seven years ***old*** my parents separated very abruptly.(p.544)
• I was married and divorced again before I was twenty-three years ***old***, this time to a prominent band leader -- a man that many women wanted.(p.546)
• It was against my mother and it was twenty-five years ***old***.(p.551)

old-drunks

• Hidden ***old-drunks*** can pass out on their beds and snooze unreproached, under the guise of taking those vital retirement-age naps.(p.330)

old-time

• I feel that one of the things that I still have to guard against is that I used to be set in my way about what I considered the ***old-time*** A.A.(p.272)

old-timers

• We ***old-timers*** who get scattered and separated and then witness the construction of services to get in more people and to make this thing function, we think that A.A. has changed, but the root of it hasn't.(p.272)

older

• I was sixteen when we were married and he was seven years ***older***.(p.262)
• I looked much ***older*** than I was, I was always large, and I went back to work in this job.(p.262)
• We are ***older*** in A.A., and we're ***older*** in years.(p.273)
• The three of us did not feel up to the job, and after a few meetings we convinced the prospects that they

too should go to Akron where they could see an *older* group in action.(p.295)
- Age and the law were still against me, but laws were not as strictly enforced in those days as they are now, and I discovered that as long as I had the green blood, there was always a way to get alcohol, either from a nondiscriminatory bartender or from an *older* friend who would be glad to purchase the joy juice for the privilege of sharing it.(p.397)
- In the first year there were episodes such as kicking Priscilla in the shins, getting the lock changed on the desk in the A.A. Club, because I, as secretary, didn't want the Intergroup secretary "interfering," and taking an *older* woman member out to lunch for the express purpose of informing her that she was "a phony."(p.416)
- I tried to mimic the talk, ideas, moods and even the drinking the *older* men.(p.423)
- But the *older* members in A.A. told me, "easy does it."(p.471)
- "Well," said the *older* boy, "do you?"(p.498)
- Lots of the *older* people had taken to drinking quite a good deal more during the war, but the younger generation was, I think, about the same.(p.518)
- I also began visiting bars after work, with my *older* associates.(p.555)
- The American Psychiatric Association requested, in 1949, that a paper be prepared by one of the *older* members of Alcoholics Anonymous to be read at the Association's annual meeting of that year.(p.572)

oldest
- I say this after many years' experience as Medical Director of one of the *oldest* hospitals in the country treating alcoholic and drug addiction.(p.xxv)
- I was the *oldest* of three children, and my father was an alcoholic.(p.193)
- My *oldest* child sometimes sat in on the meetings.(p.220)
- I was the *oldest* in a family of seven, and my father was an alcoholic.(p.261)
- Our *oldest* daughter got married; they were living at our house.(p.263)
- *Oldest* of thirteen children.(p.474)

oldsters
- So *oldsters* are advised to develop interest, find hobbies.(p.330)

oldtimer
- When I had been in A.A. only a short while, an *oldtimer* told me something that has affected my life ever since.(p.554)

olive
- He ate his *olive* and I ate mine.(p.195)
- I didn't even like the *olive*.(p.195)
- "You've got to space your drinks and take plenty of water in between," or "coat the stomach with a little *olive* oil," or "drink anything but those damn martinis."(p.433)

Omaha
- My migrations extended for over a year as far west as *Omaha*.(p.253)
- We got to *Omaha*, from my home in Chicago.(p.424)

omega
- Instead of regarding ourselves as intelligent agents, spearheads of God's ever advancing Creation, we agnostics and atheists chose to believe that our human intelligence was the last word, the alpha and the *omega*, the beginning and end of all.(p.49)

ominous
- *Ominous* warning -- which I failed to heed.(p.1)

omit
- When writing or speaking publicly about alcoholism, we urge each of our Fellowship to *omit* his personal name, designating himself instead as "a member of Alcoholics Anonymous."(p.xiii)

omitted
- Carefully reading the first five proposals we ask if we have *omitted* anything, for we are building an arch through which we shall walk a free man at last.(p.75)
- I have *omitted* details of transgressions that I made when drunk for several reasons.(p.301)

omnipotence
- Avoid then, the deliberate manufacture of misery, but if trouble comes, cheerfully capitalize it as an opportunity to demonstrate His *omnipotence*.(p.133)

on-again
- Not understanding the twenty-four hour plan, or not wanting to, I began drinking and was off-again *on-again*, during that first month.(p.414)

on-the-job
- I was intolerant of people who drank, particularly those who drank to an extent that interfered with *on-the-job* performance.(p.374)

once
- Of alcoholics who came to A.A. and really tried, 50% got sober at *once* and remained that way; 25% sobered up after some relapses, and among the remainder, those who stayed on with A.A. showed improvement.(p.xx)
- Many years ago one of the leading contributors to this book came under our care in this hospital and while here he acquired some ideas which he put into practical application at *once*.(p.xxv)
- These allergic types can never safely use alcohol in any form at all; and *once* having formed the habit and found they cannot break it, *once* having lost their self-confidence, their reliance upon things human, their problems pile up on them and become astonishingly difficult to solve.(p.xxvi)
- They are restless, irritable and discontented, unless they can again experience the sense of ease and comfort which comes at *once* by taking a few drinks -- drinks which they see others taking with impunity.(p.xxvi)
- On the other hand – and strange as this may seem to those who do not understand – *once* a psychic change has occurred, the very same person who seemed doomed, who had so many problems he despaired of ever solving them, suddenly finds himself easily able to control his desire for alcohol, the only effort necessary being that required to follow a few simple rules.(p.xxvii)
- They took a drink a day or so prior to the date, and then the phenomenon of craving at *once* became paramount to all other interests so that the important appointment was not met.(p.xxvii)
- I had had some success at speculation, so we had a little money, but we *once* worked on a farm for a month to avoid drawing on our small capital.(p.3)
- We went at *once* to the country, my wife to applaud while I started out to overtake Walter Hagen.(p.3)
- But it was not, for the frightful day came when I drank *once* more.(p.7)
- We of ALCOHOLICS ANONYMOUS, know thousands of men and women who were *once* just as hopeless as Bill.(p.17)
- He may start off as a moderate drinker; he may or may not become a continuous hard drinker; but at some stage of his drinking career he begins to lose all control of his liquor consumption, *once* he starts to drink.(p.21)
- We are not sure why, *once* a certain point is reached, little can be done for him.(p.22)
- We are equally positive that *once* he takes any alcohol whatever into his system, something happens, both in the bodily and mental sense, which makes it virtually impossible for him to stop.(p.22)
- *Once* in a while he may tell the truth.(p.23)
- *Once* this malady has a real hold, they are a baffled lot.(p.23)
- Here and there, *once* in a while, alcoholics have had what are called vital spiritual experiences.(p.27)
- Ideas, emotions, and attitudes which were *once* the guiding forces of the lives of these men are suddenly cast to one side, and a completely new set of conceptions and motives begin to dominate them.(p.27)
- Many who *once* were in this class are now among our members.(p.28)
- Try it more than *once*.(p.31)
- *Once* he started, he had no control whatever.(p.32)
- We have seen the truth demonstrated again and again: "*Once* an alcoholic, always an alcoholic."(p.33)
- I remember I felt irritated that I had to be a salesman for a concern I *once* owned.(p.36)
- *Once* more: The alcoholic at certain times has no effective mental defense against the first drink.(p.43)
- *Once* confused and baffled by the seeming futility of existence they show the underlying reasons why they were making heavy going of life.(p.50)
- This was only a beginning, though if honestly and humbly made, an effect, sometimes a very great one, was felt at *once*.(p.63)
- Though our decision was a vital and crucial step, it could have little permanent effect unless at *once* followed by a strenuous effort to face, and to be rid of, the things in ourselves which had been blocking us.(p.64)
- Some of us *once* had great self-confidence, but it didn't fully solve the fear problem, or any other.(p.68)
- At *once*, we commence to outgrow fear.(p.68)
- *Once* we have taken this step, withholding nothing, we are delighted.(p.75)
- When these crop up, we ask God at *once* to remove them.(p.84)
- Have we kept something to ourselves which should be discussed with another person at *once*?(p.86)
- If he is alcoholic, he will understand you at *once*.(p.92)
- Tell him you *once* felt as he does, but you doubt whether you would have made much progress had you not taken action.(p.94)
- Sometimes a new man is anxious to proceed at *once*, and you may be tempted to let him do so.(p.95)
- Do not be discouraged if your prospect does not respond at *once*.(p.96)
- A kindly act *once* in a while isn't enough.(p.97)
- Some of us veered from extreme to extreme, ever hoping that one day our loved ones would be themselves *once* more.(p.105)
- For a while they would be their old sweet selves, only to dash the new structure of affection to pieces *once* more.(p.107)
- But when he gets over the spree, he begins to think *once* more how he can drink moderately next time.(p.109)
- Though *once* like number two he became worse.(p.109)
- Sooner or later, you are likely to find him reading the book *once* more.(p.113)
- He may not share your enthusiasm, but he is practically sure to read the book and he may go for the program at *once*.(p.113)
- But all problems will not be solved at *once*.(p.117)
- It is the most natural thing in the world, *once* his liquor problem is solved, to feel that he will now measure up to that cherished vision.(p.118)
- Your husband will see at *once* that he must redouble his spiritual activities if he expects to survive.(p.120)
- Henry Ford *once* made a wise remark to the effect that experience is the thing of supreme value in life.(p.124)
- They should be thankful he is sober and able to be of this world *once* more.(p.127)
- He may not see at *once* that he has barely scratched a limitless lode which will pay dividends only if he mines it for the rest of his life and insists on giving away the entire product.(p.129)
- We cannot subscribe to the belief that this life is a vale of tears, though it *once* was just that for many of us.(p.133)
- You may need to encourage him to play *once* in a while.(p.146)
- In case he does stumble, even *once*, you will have to decide whether to let him go.(p.147)
- There was an insistent yearning to enjoy life as we *once* did and a heartbreaking obsession that some new miracle of control would enable us to do it.(p.151)
- It may seem incredible that these men are to become happy, respected, and useful *once* more.(p.153)
- Understand he was *once* a well-known lawyer in town, but just now we've got him strapped down tight."(p.156)
- I was *once*, but I'm a nobody now.(p.157)
- Never *once* in my life have I had a headache, which fact leads me to believe that I was an alcoholic almost from the start.(p.172)
- I used to get terribly upset when I saw my friends drink and knew I could not, but I schooled myself to believe that though I *once* had the same privilege, I had abused it so frightfully that it was withdrawn.(p.181)
- They said, "Let's forget about those other things, that is, trying to eliminate them all at *once*, and concentrate on the drink."(p.190)
- It took me a year, or a year and a half to get to feeling physically well, and it was rather tough, but I soon found folks whose friendship I had *once* had, and I found, after I had been sober for quite some little time, that these people began to act like they had in previous years, before I had gotten so bad, so that I didn't pay too awful much attention to financial gains.(p.190)
- Blackout drinking at *once*.(p.195)
- One of the things that came up repeatedly in the stories they told me was that *once* they had accepted the program, they never had a desire to take a drink.(p.219)
- I believe that my *once* over-weening self-will has finally found its proper place, for I can say many times daily, "Thy will be done, not mine" . . . and mean it.(p.229)
- The visits from these men impressed me at *once*.(p.235)
- I refused to join any fraternity, as I wanted to be a free lance, and that year my drinking was confined to one-night stands, *once* or twice a week.(p.241)
- *Once* I found out.(p.244)

• *Once* again, there was the challenge of a tough job, but this time I was determined to follow through.(p.248)
• One evening, the book, after checking up, was very definitely in the red for plenty through a piece of studied carelessness on my part, and my boss, very shrewd and able, fired me with a parting statement to the effect that *once* was enough.(p.251)
• I visited my family just *once* in that time.(p.255)
• He introduced himself and began to tell me about a bunch of some sixty former drinkers and drunkards who met *once* a week, and he invited me to go with him to the next meeting.(p.257)
• The doctor who came to see me almost at *once* did not assail me with any new doctrines; he made sure that I had a need and that I wanted to have that need filled, and little by little I learned how my need could be met.(p.258)
• Out of this maelstrom just two coherent thoughts came to the surface; one, a drink would mean homelessness and death; two, I could no longer relieve the pressure of fear by starting home, as was *once* my habitual solution to this problem, because I no longer had a home.(p.279)
• What about those fears which *once* paralyzed me to the point of my becoming a semi-hermit?(p.284)
• Some of the things which used to stop me in my tracks from fear still make me nervous in the anticipation of their doing, but *once* I kick myself into doing them nervousness disappears and I enjoy myself.(p.285)
• I am very apt to get into quite an uproar for a day or two before starting, but I do start, and *once* started, I have a swell time.(p.285)
• Only *once* did I suffer from a nearly overpowering compulsion to take a drink.(p.285)
• *Once* dad came all the way to Florida to sober me up, after a hotel manager called him and said that if he wanted to see me alive he better get there fast.(p.288)
• He said he had finally learned that drinking was a fatal illness made up of an allergy plus an obsession, and *once* the drinking had passed from habit to obsession, we were completely hopeless, and could look forward only to spending the balance of our lives in mental institutions or to death.(p.290)
• Immediately on her return we began to have formal meetings *once* a week, in the autumn of 1939, and we have continued to do this and to expand ever since.(p.295)
• Where derision, contempt and pity were *once* shown me, I now enjoy the respect of many people.(p.296)
• Where *once* I had casual acquaintances, all of whom were fair weather friends, I now have a host of friends who accept me for what I am.(p.296)
• Finally this company also became involved and I was *once* more looking for a job.(p.300)
• I have self confidence and assurance that cannot be confused with the cockiness I *once* possessed.(p.303)
• The next three years saw me in sanitariums, *once* in a ten day coma, from which I very nearly did not recover, in and out of hospitals or confined at home with day and night nurses.(p.306)
• Perhaps I could find freedom and peace and be able *once* again to call my soul my own.(p.309)
• Letting go of everything at *once* was both painful and terrifying.(p.311)
• *Once* I did have a slip – tried drinking again – but the A.A.'s tell me not to worry about yesterday, because nobody can change it, and not to worry about tomorrow, because it hasn't come yet.(p.320)
• And I was able to go on the wagon for long periods of time – *once* for four years, to cure an ulcer.(p.328)
• I surrendered *once* to the bottle, and I couldn't do these things.(p.340)
• I have been of a very religious outlook all my life, but that made no difference *once* John Barleycorn got the better of me.(p.343)
• And I knew this: *Once* an alcoholic, always an alcoholic.(p.344)
• As someone in A.A. said to me *once* upon a time, there is nothing worse than a confused psychiatrist.(p.347)
• *Once* again I asked my girl to marry me and join me in this new venture.(p.359)
• *Once* again I was back in the big time operations, and along with them, big shot complexes.(p.361)
• Help which you *once* continually rejected, suggestions *once* turned aside are finally accepted in desperation.(p.377)
• We moved *once* more, to Houston; my husband thought maybe a change of environment would help and I'd be all right.(p.389)
• I was really trying, *once* more, to escape from myself.(p.405)
• My tweed suit, *once* a very good one, was shapeless and baggy with bare places worn in the elbows from leaning on the bar.(p.411)
• *Once*, in a strange gin mill, I stole a bottle from behind the bar.(p.411)
• *Once*, when I called my analyst, and told her I was contemplating death, she came over and tried to get me into a sanitarium.(p.411)
• She was attractive; she was like the friends I had *once* had.(p.414)
• I am a young alcoholic with a drug problem, a doctor, the husband of an alcoholic, the son of an alcoholic, and a man *once* diagnosed as a violent manic-depressive.(p.421)
• *Once* in a while I stayed home for a night, to see how my folks were doing.(p.425)
• I seldom left the base any more except *once* in a while when I felt the need of talking to some girl.(p.427)
• *Once* or twice, during my early drinking, I carried it over into the second day, and only *once*, that I can remember, did it continue into the third.(p.432)
• Never *once* had my mother even hinted at the idea that, when I grew up, I might like to be president of A.A.(p.439)
• (That dog hasn't wet my pants *once* since I joined A.A., and neither have I!)(p.440)
• There is really nothing to dressing with chains and shackles on, *once* you learn the technique of pulling inside-out pants through the shackles.(p.460)
• My pattern of drinking at that time had reached the point where *once* I really started, I would retire to my bed and drink myself into oblivion.(p.466)
• This time I didn't put up any fight because I knew why they were there and where I was going, the psychopathic ward of the City Hospital, where I had been *once* before.(p.468)
• But more important, I would have found that *once* again I was sitting in the driver's seat – I was running the show.(p.471)
• The Higher Power to whom I had turned, and who had sustained me, had *once* again been thrust into the background, while my emotions were running my life and, as always, my emotions ran me to the bottle.(p.472)
• I *once* hear people say only Indians crazy when drunk.(p.477)
• *Once*, I phoned my brother-in-law and told him I was going to take a handful of pills (in fact, I already had) and I would slash my wrists if he didn't come over to stop me.(p.479)
• "*Once* in a while," I lied.(p.498)
• I drink and go to bed; I take a few the next morning and go see my mother *once* more.(p.501)
• A former employer of mine said to me a little over ten years ago, "Pat, you seem to be one of those unfortunate people who at least *once* every six months must go out and roll in the gutter."(p.513)
• The old pattern reasserted itself, but it was no longer *once* every six months.(p.514)
• Oh yes, I get the dry jitters *once* in a while, but that isn't anything to worry about.(p.516)
• *Once* I started drinking, I didn't care that the rent wasn't paid, or that there was no food in the house, or that my boys needed shoes.(p.527)
• *Once* this was in front of the Paramount Theatre in Times Square.(p.537)
• *Once*, or even twice, such incidents might be amusing.(p.538)
• For by now I had been exposed *once* to A.A., but I had treated it as a vaudeville and had taken friends to meetings so that they too could enjoy the fascination of the naked revelation of suffering and recovery.(p.539)
• In the nearby little town there was a plumber who *once* had tried to get an A.A. group going.(p.541)
• Fear of rejection and its ensuing pain were not to be risked, and I turned away from myself *once* more for the answer, this time to the drinks I had always refused before, and in alcohol I found a false courage.(p.546)
• Like most other alcoholics I have known, I did quit drinking at various times – *once* for ten months on my own and during other interludes when I was hospitalized.(p.554)
• My company advanced me rapidly, *once* my reliability was established again.(p.559)
• I have learned to deal with disappointments and problems that *once* would have sent me right to the bottle.(p.559)
• Though it was not our intention to create such an impression, many alcoholics have nevertheless concluded that in order to recover they must acquire an immediate and overwhelming "God-consciousness" followed at *once* by a vast change in feeling and outlook.(p.569)

one

• "Bill's Story," "Doctor Bob's Nightmare," and *one* other personal history from the first edition were retained intact; three were edited and *one* of these was retitled; new versions of two stories were written with new titles; thirty completely new stories were added; and the story section was divided into three parts, under the same headings that are used now.(p.xi)
• If you have a drinking problem, we hope that you may pause in reading *one* of the forty-four personal stories and think: "Yes, that happened to me"; or, more important, "Yes, I've felt like that"; or most important, "Yes, I believe this program can work for me, too."(p.xii)
• We, of Alcoholics Anonymous, are more than *one* hundred men and women who have recovered from a seemingly hopeless state of mind and body.(p.xiii)
• This seemed to prove that *one* alcoholic could affect another as no nonalcoholic could.(p.xvi)
• It also indicated that strenuous work, *one* alcoholic with another, was vital to permanent recovery.(p.xvii)
• Their very first case, a desperate *one*, recovered immediately and became A.A. number three.(p.xvii)
• When the broker returned to New York in the fall of 1935, the first A.A. group had actually been formed, though no *one* realized it at the time.(p.xvii)
• Today the remarkable unity of A.A. is *one* of the greatest assets that our Society has.(p.xix)
• Yet it is our great hope that all those who have as yet found no answer may begin to find *one* in the pages of this book and will presently join us on the highroad to a new freedom.(p.xxi)
• The Twelve Steps that summarize the program may be called los Doce Pasos in *one* country, los Douze Etapes in another, but they trace exactly the same path to recovery that was blazed by the earliest members of Alcoholics Anonymous.(p.xxii)
• Each day, somewhere in the world, recovery begins when *one* alcoholic talks with another alcoholic, sharing experience, strength, and hope.(p.xxii)
• This man and over *one* hundred others appear to have recovered.(p.xxiii)
• I say this after many years' experience as Medical Director of *one* of the oldest hospitals in the country treating alcoholic and drug addiction.(p.xxv)
• Many years ago *one* of the leading contributors to this book came under our care in this hospital and while here he acquired some ideas which he put into practical application at once.(p.xxv)
• The unselfishness of these men as we have come to know them, the entire absence of profit motive, and their community spirit, is indeed inspiring to *one* who has labored long and wearily in this alcoholic field.(p.xxv)
• To them, their alcoholic life seems the only normal *one*.(p.xxvi)
• *One* feels that something more than human power is needed to produce the essential psychic change.(p.xxvii)
• All these, and many others, have *one* symptom in common: they cannot start drinking without developing the phenomenon of craving.(p.xxviii)
• Perhaps I can best answer this by relating *one* of my experiences.(p.xxix)
• About *one* year prior to this experience a man was brought in to be treated for chronic alcoholism.(p.xxix)
• He had lost everything worthwhile in life and was only living, *one* might say, to drink.(p.xxix)
• *One* year later he called to see me, and I experienced a very strange sensation.(p.xxix)
• Following his physical rehabilitation, he had a talk with me in which he frankly stated he thought the treatment a waste of effort, unless I could assure him, which no *one* ever had, that in the future he would have the "will power" to resist the impulse to drink.(p.xxix)
• I see him now and then and he is as fine a specimen of manhood as *one* could wish to meet.(p.xxx)
• At *one* of the finals I was too drunk to think or write.(p.2)
• Out of this alloy of drink and speculation, I commenced to forge the weapon that *one* day would turn in its flight like a boomerang and all but cut me to ribbons.(p.2)
• I acquired the impeccable coat of tan *one* sees upon the well-to-do.(p.4)
• After *one* of those days of inferno, I wobbled from a hotel bar to a brokerage office.(p.4)
• Mercifully, no *one* could guess that I was to have no real employment for five years, or hardly draw a sober breath.(p.4)
• I saw I could not take so much as *one* drink.(p.5)

• *One* day I walked into a cafe to telephone.(p.6)
• In *one* western city and its environs there are *one* thousand of us and our families.(p.15)
• At these informal gatherings *one* may often see from 50 to 200 persons.(p.16)
• *One* poor chap committed suicide in my home.(p.16)
• The feeling of having shared in a common peril is *one* element in the powerful cement which binds us.(p.17)
• The tremendous fact for every *one* of us is that we have discovered a common solution.(p.17)
• If a person has cancer all are sorry for him and no *one* is angry or hurt.(p.18)
• He may be *one* of the finest fellows in the world.(p.21)
• If he can afford it, he may have liquor concealed all over his house to be certain no *one* gets his entire supply away from him to throw down the waterpipe.(p.22)
• If hundreds of experiences have shown him that *one* drink means another debacle with all its attendant suffering and humiliation, why is it he takes that *one* drink?(p.22)
• If you ask him why he started on that last bender, the chances are he will offer you any *one* of a hundred alibis.(p.23)
• There is a complete failure of the kind of defense that keeps *one* from putting his hand on a hot stove.(p.24)
• We were in a position where life was becoming impossible, and if we had passed into the region from which there is no return through human aid we had but two alternatives: *One* was to go on to the bitter end, blotting out the consciousness of our intolerable situation as best we could; and the other, to accept spiritual help.(p.25)
• For years he had floundered from *one* sanitarium to another.(p.26)
• I have never seen *one* single case recover, where that state of mind existed to the extent that it does in you."(p.27)
• Ideas, emotions, and attitudes which were once the guiding forces of the lives of these men are suddenly cast to *one* side, and a completely new set of conceptions and motives begin to dominate them.(p.27)
• We have no desire to convince anyone that there is only *one* way by which faith can be acquired.(p.28)
• This should be an entirely personal affair which each *one* decides for himself in the light of past associations, or his present choice.(p.28)
• We hope no *one* will consider these self-revealing accounts in bad taste.(p.29)
• Our hope is that many alcoholic men and women, desperately in need, will see these pages, and we believe that it is only by fully disclosing ourselves and our problems that they will be persuaded to say, "Yes, I am *one* of them too; I must have this thing."(p.29)
• Science may *one* day accomplish this, but it hasn't done so yet.(p.31)
• Here is *one*.(p.32)
• We doubt if many of them can do it, because none will really want to stop, and hardly *one* of them, because of the peculiar mental twist already acquired, will find he can win out.(p.33)
• To be gravely affected, *one* does not necessarily have to drink a long time nor take the quantities some of us have.(p.33)
• If anyone questions whether he has entered this dangerous area, let him try leaving liquor alone for *one* year.(p.34)
• How then shall we help our readers determine, to their own satisfaction, whether they are *one* of us?(p.34)
• Then I decided to drive into the country and see *one* of my prospects for a car.(p.36)
• Thus started *one* more journey to the asylum for Jim.(p.36)
• To us it is not far-fetched, for this kind of thinking has been characteristic of every single *one* of us.(p.37)
• *One* day we were told that he was back in the hospital.(p.40)
• *One* day I went to Washington to present some accounting evidence to a government bureau.(p.40)
• When I returned to the hotel it struck me a highball would be fine before going to bed, so I stepped into the bar and had *one*.(p.41)
• They had said that though I did raise a defense, it would *one* day give way before some trivial reason for having a drink.(p.42)
• My old manner of life was by no means a bad *one*, but I would not exchange its best moments for the worst I have now.(p.43)
• *One* of these men, staff member of a world-renowned hospital, recently made this statement to some of us: "What you say about the general hopelessness of the average alcoholic's plight is, in my opinion, correct.(p.43)
• To *one* who feels he is an atheist or agnostic such an experience seems impossible, but to continue as he is means disaster, especially if he is an alcoholic of the hopeless variety.(p.44)
• We needed to ask ourselves but *one* short question.(p.47)
• Sometimes this was a tedious process; we hope no *one* else will be prejudiced for as long as some of us were.(p.48)
• On *one* proposition, however, these men and women are strikingly agreed.(p.50)
• Every *one* of them has gained access to, and believes in, a Power greater than himself.(p.50)
• When many hundreds of people are able to say that the consciousness of the Presence of God is today the most important fact of their lives, they present a powerful reason why *one* should have faith.(p.51)
• That is *one* of man's magnificent attributes.(p.53)
• So, in *one* way or another, we discovered that faith had been involved all the time!(p.54)
• In *one* form or another we had been living by faith and little else.(p.54)
• *One* night, when confined in a hospital, he was approached by an acholic who had known a spiritual experience.(p.56)
• But there is *One* who has all power -- that *One* is God.(p.59)
• No *one* among us has been able to maintain anything like perfect adherence to these principles.(p.60)
• But it is better to meet God alone than with *one* who might misunderstand.(p.63)
• This was only a beginning, though if honestly and humbly made, an effect, sometimes a very great *one*, was felt at once.(p.63)
• *One* object is to disclose damaged or unsalable goods, to get rid of them promptly and without regret.(p.64)
• Resentment is the "number *one*" offender.(p.64)
• We cannot be helpful to all people, but at least God will show us how to take a kindly and tolerant view of each and every *one*.(p.67)
• *One* set of voices cry that sex is a lust of our lower nature, a base necessity of procreation.(p.68)
• *One* school would allow man no flavor for his fare and the other would have us all on a straight pepper diet.(p.69)
• This is the *one* he likes his fellows to see.(p.73)
• Unwilling to be honest with these sympathetic men, we were honest with no *one* else.(p.73)
• It may be *one* of our own family, but we cannot disclose anything to our wives or our parents which will hurt them and make them unhappy.(p.74)
• Notwithstanding the great necessity for discussing ourselves with someone, it may be *one* is so situated that there is no suitable person available.(p.74)
• Can He now take them all -- every *one*?(p.76)
• Maybe we are divorced, and have remarried but haven't kept up the alimony to number *one*.(p.79)
• This brings to mind a story about *one* of our friends.(p.80)
• His action met widespread approval, and today his is *one* of the most trusted citizens of his town.(p.80)
• It is better, however, that *one* does not needlessly name a person upon whom she can vent jealously.(p.82)
• You can help when no *one* else can.(p.89)
• You should be described to him as *one* of a fellowship who, as part of their own recovery, try to help others and who will be glad to talk to him if he cares to see you.(p.90)
• To spend too much time on any *one* situation is to deny some other alcoholic an opportunity to live and be happy.(p.96)
• *One* of our Fellowship failed entirely with his first half dozen prospects.(p.96)
• In some cases the wife will never come back for *one* reason or another.(p.99)
• We would not even do the cause of temperate drinking any good, for not *one* drinker in a thousand likes to be told anything about alcohol by *one* who hates it.(p.103)
• Some day we hope that Alcoholics Anonymous will help the public to a better realization of the gravity of the alcoholic problem, but we shall be of little use if our attitude is *one* of bitterness or hostility.(p.103)
• Some of us veered from extreme to extreme, ever hoping that *one* day our loved ones would be themselves once more.(p.105)
• We have believed them when no *one* else could or would.(p.105)
• If you are positive he is *one* of this type you may feel you had better leave.(p.108)
• The problem with which you struggle usually falls within *one* of four categories:(p.108)
• *One*: Your husband may be only a heavy drinker.(p.108)
• He has been placed in *one* institution after another.(p.110)
• Let's now go back to husband number *one*.(p.110)
• Your husband may be willing to talk to *one* of them.(p.112)
• The same principles which apply to husband number *one* should be practiced.(p.112)
• His reaction may be *one* of enthusiasm.(p.114)
• Another feeling we are very likely to entertain is *one* of resentment that love and loyalty could not cure our husbands of alcoholism.(p.118)
• You will lose the old life to find *one* much better.(p.120)
• In a weak moment he may take your dislike of his high-stepping friends as *one* of those insanely trivial excuses to drink.(p.120)
• The alcoholic, his wife, his children, his "in-laws," each *one* is likely to have fixed ideas about the family's attitude toward himself or herself.(p.122)
• We find the more *one* member of the family demands that the others concede to him, the more resentful they become.(p.122)
• That is true only if *one* is willing to turn the past to good account.(p.124)
• The alcoholic's past thus becomes the principal asset of the family and frequently it is almost the only *one*!(p.124)
• Then, under *one* provocation or another, the aggrieved *one* would unearth the old affair and angrily cast its ashes about.(p.124)
• Members of a family should watch such matters carefully, for *one* careless, inconsiderate remark has been known to raise the very devil.(p.125)
• At the beginning of recovery a man will take, as a rule, *one* of two directions.(p.125)
• *One* more suggestion: Whether the family has spiritual convictions or not, they may do well to examine the principles by which the alcoholic member is trying to live.(p.130)
• Hardly *one* of our crowd now shows any mark of dissipation.(p.133)
• *One* of the many doctors who had the opportunity of reading this book in manuscript form told us that the use of sweets was often helpful, of course depending upon a doctor's advice.(p.133)
• Here is a case in point: *One* of our friends is a heavy smoker and coffee drinker.(p.135)
• His wife is *one* of those persons who really feels there is something rather sinful about these commodities, so she nagged, and her intolerance finally threw him into a fit of anger.(p.135)
• Among many employers nowadays, we think of *one* member who has spent much of his life in the world of big business.(p.136)
• I was at *one* time assistant manager of a corporation department employing sixty-six hundred men.(p.136)
• *One* day my secretary came in saying that Mr. B---- insisted on speaking with me.(p.136)
• I had warned him several times that he had but *one* more chance.(p.136)
• It was the obituary of *one* of the best salesmen I ever had.(p.137)
• I had been obliged to discharge him for drinking, though he was brilliant, alert, and *one* of the best organizers I have ever known.(p.137)
• Here, for instance, is a typical example: An officer of *one* of the largest banking institutions in America knows I no longer drink.(p.138)
• *One* day he told me about an executive of the same bank who, from his description, was undoubtedly alcoholic.(p.138)
• When the man is presented with this volume it is best that no *one* tell him he must abide by its suggestions.(p.144)
• *One* instance comes to mind in which a malicious individual was always making friendly little jokes about an alcoholic's drinking exploits.(p.145)
• If your organization is a large *one*, your junior executives might be provided with this book.(p.147)
• So, for *one* reason or another, they cover these men, hoping matters will take a turn for the better.(p.147)
• You act like *one*.(p.147)
• There was always *one* more attempt -- and *one* more failure.(p.151)
• Years ago, in 1935, *one* of our number made a journey to a certain western city.(p.153)
• *One* dismal afternoon he paced a hotel lobby wondering how his bill was to be paid.(p.154)
• At *one* end of the room stood a glass covered direc-

tory of local churches.(p.154)
• *One* morning he took the bull by the horns and set out to tell those he feared what his trouble had been.(p.156)
• *One* day they called up the head nurse of a local hospital.(p.156)
• But *one* of the friends said, "Put him in a private room.(p.157)
• Said *one* of the visitors, "We're giving you a treatment for alcoholism."(p.157)
• So *one* more was added to the Fellowship.(p.159)
• In addition to these casual get-togethers, it became customary to set apart *one* night a week for a meeting to be attended by anyone or everyone interested in a spiritual way of life.(p.159)
• *One* man and his wife placed their large home at the disposal of this strangely assorted crowd.(p.160)
• They had seen miracles, and *one* was to come to them.(p.161)
• No *one* is too discredited or has sunk too low to be welcomed cordially – if he means business.(p.161)
• Being wrecked in the same vessel, being restored and united under *one* God, with hearts and minds attuned to the welfare of others, the things which matter so much to some people no longer signify much to them.(p.161)
• In *one* of these there is a well-known hospital for the treatment of alcoholic and drug addiction.(p.161)
• Six years ago *one* of our number was a patient there.(p.162)
• Every few days this doctor suggests our approach to *one* of his patients.(p.162)
• There are the same fast friendships, there is the same helpfulness to *one* another as you find among our western friends.(p.162)
• And so can you, though you be but *one* man with this book in your hand.(p.162)
• In his prodigy of service, he was well assisted by Sister Ignatia at St. Thomas Hospital in Akron, Ohio, *one* of the greatest friends our Fellowship will ever know.(p.171)
• No beer or liquor was sold in the neighborhood, except at the State liquor agency where perhaps *one* might procure a pint if he could convince the agent that he really needed it.(p.171)
• After high school came four years in *one* of the best colleges in the country where drinking seemed to be a major extra-curricular activity.(p.172)
• My next move was to take up the study of medicine, entering *one* of the largest universities in the county.(p.173)
• On account of my enormous capacity for beer, I was elected to membership in *one* of the drinking societies, and soon became *one* of the leading spirits.(p.173)
• By this time I was beginning to pay very dearly physically and, in hope of relief, voluntarily incarcerated myself at least a dozen times in *one* of the local sanitariums.(p.174)
• *One* was the fear of not sleeping, and the other was the fear of running out of liquor.(p.175)
• I would sometimes hide out in *one* of the clubs of which I was a member, and had the habit at times of registering at a hotel under a fictitious name.(p.176)
• It then occurred to me that after *one* was all smelled up with beer nobody could tell what had been drunk, so I began to fortify my beer with straight alcohol.(p.178)
• About this time a lady called up my wife *one* Saturday afternoon, saying she wanted me to come over that evening to meet a friend of hers who might help me.(p.179)
• He came and got me home and to bed, gave me a few drinks that night, and *one* bottle of beer the next morning.(p.179)
• It never fails, if you go about it with *one* half the zeal you have been in the habit of showing when you were getting another drink.(p.181)
• *One* of five children, I was born on a Kentucky farm in Carlyle County.(p.182)
• My parents were well-to-do people and their marriage was a happy *one*.(p.182)
• My case is rather unusual in *one* respect.(p.182)
• I remember that my father kept whiskey around the house for medical purposes and entertainment, and I would drink from this when no *one* was about and then water it to keep my parents from knowing I was drinking.(p.183)
• *One* of the fellows, I think it was Doc, said, "Well, you want to quit?"(p.187)
• Would this *one* do?(p.188)
• I was at *one* time a deacon in the church and I still believe in God.(p.189)
• A.A.'s Number *One* Group dates from that very day.(p.189)
• Then they said, "There is *one* other thing.(p.190)
• I know there was even more, something that I hadn't got, and I remember *one* day, a week or two after I had come out of the hospital, Bill was over to my house talking to my wife and me.(p.191)
• *One* of the earliest memories that I have is of a bottle sitting on his desk with a skull and crossbones and marked "Poison."(p.193)
• I can also remember that he was a salesman and a very good *one*.(p.193)
• They looked at *one* another queerly and, finally, *one* of them allowed he'd have a beer and they all followed him, each of them saying he'd have a beer too.(p.194)
• I didn't even know what a martini looked like, but I had heard a man down the bar order *one*.(p.194)
• I felt having gotten married, I was an adult and *one* of the first things I did was to buy two cases of whiskey with no idea of drinking it.(p.196)
• At the end of this selling of lots, just prior to World War I, I got into the crude rubber business, and six months later there was only *one* broker and myself left in Akron.(p.197)
• So in spite of anything that I might do, I prospered, being *one* of only two brokers in the rubber center of the world.(p.197)
• *One* hundred for unmarried women at *one* end, *one* hundred for men at the other, and *one* hundred for married couples in the middle.(p.198)
• I remember *one* occasion when I did not drink for three hundred and sixty-four days, but I didn't quite make the year.(p.200)
• Another time, I had gone around to Max R. trying to get a job driving *one* of his trucks.(p.200)
• I told him that I had not had a drink for ninety days and that I had come to the conclusion that I was *one* of those individuals who couldn't drink.(p.200)
• I'll buy you *one* drink, and if you suggest a second *one*, I'll poke you right in the nose."(p.201)
• I could take *one* drink and get right back on the wagon.(p.202)
• Nobody would know it, so I agreed to have the *one* drink.(p.202)
• After drinking *one* glass of beer at the end of my work period for about five days, I thought I'd better find out whether I really had the stuff licked.(p.203)
• So I didn't have a beer *one* night, and as I drove home I was breaking my arm patting myself on the back because I had proved I could lick liquor.(p.203)
• So having licked it, there was no reason why I shouldn't have a drink, and I stopped in before I got home and had *one*.(p.203)
• Then I got into the habit of having beers, and decided that a drink of whiskey was not any worse; so I would get the *one* drink of whiskey but, on second thought, I decided that as long as I was only going to have *one*, I might as well make it a double-header.(p.203)
• So I had *one* double-header every night for about two or three weeks.(p.203)
• They called a doctor and it happened that they called *one* I knew.(p.205)
• When I had been in the hospital ten days, Sister Ignatia, who has played such a part in the development of A.A. in this area, stuck her head in the door *one* morning and announced, looking at me quizzically, that they might be able to make something human out of my face after all.(p.205)
• *One* morning, after I had been on a binge for a couple of days, I awoke to find my brother and Doctor Bob in my room talking to me about not drinking.(p.206)
• Not *one* experience registered with me.(p.208)
• I remember well *one* fellow, Joe, walking nearly three miles through slush, wet and snow to come to the hospital to see a man that he had never seen before in his life, and that impressed me very much.(p.208)
• The very simple program they advised me to follow was that I should ask to know God's will for me for that *one* day, and then, to the best of my ability, to follow that, and at night to express my gratefulness to God for the things that had happened to me during the day.(p.208)
• In fact, on *one* occasion, I was picked up by the police and brought home.(p.211)
• I was always interested in mechanics and after having about twenty miscellaneous jobs, lasting from *one* day to two weeks, I obtained a job as a toolmaker apprentice.(p.211)
• Not far from where I lived they built a new technical high school and *one* of the teachers sold me on the idea that I needed a little mechanical drawing if I were going to be a good toolmaker.(p.211)
• By that time, I had *one* boy in college, another a senior in high school, and a daughter about twelve years old.(p.215)
• My wife didn't tell me this, but *one* Sunday afternoon when Mary was trying to get the cobwebs out of my mind, Clarence and his sister-in-law, the hairdresser, called at the house.(p.216)
• *One* evening I had gone out after dinner to take on a couple of double-headers and stayed a little later than usual, and when I came home Clarence was sitting on the davenport with Bill W.(p.216)
• I do not recollect the specific conversation that went on but I believe I did challenge Bill to tell me something about A.A. and I do recall *one* other thing: I wanted to know what this was that worked so many wonders, and hanging over the mantel was a picture of Gethsemane and Bill pointed to it and said, "There it is," which didn't make much sense to me.(p.216)
• I had had no hospitalization up to this time because I would not call doctors when I was getting over a bad *one*.(p.217)
• In fact, the last three years of my drinking was a routine of barbiturates in the morning, so that I could stop shaking enough to shave, and then alcohol beginning about four-thirty or five o'clock, with a struggle not to take a drink at noon or during the day, because I had the idea that if I took *one* drink, I would smell as though I had had a pint.(p.217)
• There was *one* experience with Doc which made a terrific impression upon me.(p.218)
• He then pulled up his chair with *one* of his knees touching mine and said, "Will you pray with me for your success?"(p.218)
• *One* of the things that came up repeatedly in the stories they told me was that once they had accepted the program, they never had a desire to take a drink.(p.219)
• He pointed out to me that probably it was more of a moral or spiritual illness than it was a physical *one*.(p.219)
• Somewhere in *one* of the conversations, I mentioned that I was contemplating forming a new firm.(p.220)
• It must have been a long time since I had my last drink -- but I didn't dare ask this stranger for *one*.(p.223)
• It had been *one* o'clock when I last remember looking.(p.223)
• In fact I had been in very good shape at *one* o'clock -- feeling no pain.(p.223)
• He wasn't a drinking man, he didn't know what it was to need a drink, nor what a drink could do for *one* in a pinch.(p.227)
• I was an intellectual and I needed an intellectual answer, not an emotional *one*.(p.227)
• I wanted to learn to stand on my own feet, not to change *one* prop for another, and an intangible and dubious *one* at that.(p.227)
• At that time I could go into any saloon, have *one* or two beers, walk out and forget about it.(p.231)
• Certainly, at that time I was *one* of those who "can take it or leave it alone."(p.231)
• I had all the usual experiences of the alcoholic, for I was certainly *one* by this time.(p.233)
• The third man who came to see me had been *one* of the greatest business-getters his company had ever employed.(p.235)
• After a couple of days in dollar hotels and *one* night in the pokey, I finally landed on my mother's doorstep -- shaking apart, with several days' beard and, of course, broke as usual.(p.238)
• Jackie told me about a group of fellows in New York, of whom my old friend Fitz was *one*, who had the same problem I had, and who by working together to help each other were not now drinking and were happy like himself.(p.239)
• My sponsor, Jackie, was *one* of these.(p.239)
• There were four of us children, and although both of my brothers later became alcoholic – *one* died of alcoholism -- my sister has never taken a drink in her life.(p.240)
• So it is clear that I never had any fun out of drinking – I would be the soberest-seeming *one* in the crowd and all of a sudden I would be the drunkest.(p.241)
• I am *one* of the lads who came out of the service with a lower rank than when I went in.(p.241)
• With the war over, and back in Baltimore with the folks, there were several small jobs for three years and then I went to work soliciting as *one* of the first ten employees of a new national finance company.(p.242)
• Oddly enough, the big shot who fired me from this company was *one* of the first men I met when I later joined the New York A.A. Group.(p.242)

• The man who was going to take over *one* of their biggest branches come Monday?(p.243)
• No *one* in that company saw me again – ten days later I wired my resignation.(p.243)
• Routine jobs bored me, but I would take on the toughest *one* I could find, work day and night until I had it under control; then it would become tedious and I'd lose all interest in it.(p.243)
• In the eight years before A.A. found me, I had over forty jobs – selling and travelling – *one* thing after another, and the same old routine.(p.244)
• Then broke again, hiding out in cheap hotels all over the country, *one* night jail stands here and there, and always that horrible feeling "What's the use -- nothing is worth while."(p.244)
• I had repaired to *one* of these *one* morning with my jug and when I left late in the afternoon, I picked up a newspaper on the way home.(p.244)
• Imagine my surprise when I read in a page *one* "box" that I had been taken from the theater unconscious around noon that day, removed by ambulance to a hospital and stomach-pumped and then released.(p.244)
• They had also been periodic big shots who had goofed out repeatedly at the wrong time, and they also knew how to split *one* paper match into three separate matches.(p.245)
• They, too, had taken a train to *one* town and had wakened hundreds of miles in the opposite direction, never knowing how they got there.(p.246)
• We would follow *one* man's ideas for a while, decide he was wrong and switch to another's method.(p.246)
• There was *one* meeting a week at Bill's home in Brooklyn, and we all took turns there spouting off about how we had changed our lives overnight, how many drunks we had saved and straightened out, and last, but not least, how God had touched each of us personally on the shoulder.(p.246)
• Yet we all had *one* really sincere purpose in our hearts and that was not to drink.(p.246)
• They did not seem to be getting an answer, for here I was staying sober and selling lots of auto polish, on which they were making *one* thousand per cent profit.(p.247)
• We ordered sandwiches and *one* man said, "Three beers."(p.247)
• So I drank all three beers, *one* after the other, said "I'll be seeing you, boys," and went around the corner for a bottle.(p.247)
• Around this time our big A.A. book was being written and it all became much simpler; we had a definite formula which some sixty of us agreed was the middle course for all alcoholics who wanted sobriety, and that formula has not been changed *one* iota down through the years.(p.248)
• I have served on only *one* committee in the past nine years, for I feel that I had my chance the first few years and that newer members should fill the jobs.(p.250)
• We now live in the West and are very fortunate in our area A.A.; it is good, simple and friendly, and our *one* desire is to stay in A.A. and not on it.(p.250)
• *One* evening, the book, after checking up, was very definitely in the red for plenty through a piece of studied carelessness on my part, and my boss, very shrewd and able, fired me with a parting statement to the effect that once was enough.(p.251)
• Again I spent my bankroll, by no means as thick as the *one* I had when I first saw the skyline of Gotham.(p.252)
• That job began a series of brief working spells, each *one* ending in a "drunk" and the urge to travel.(p.253)
• Always, in between, there were intervals of being broke, riding freights and hitch-hiking interminable distances from *one* big town to another in three states.(p.255)
• I had been drinking heavily from *one* state of semicoma to another and it was several days before I got "defogged," but subconsciously I was in earnest about wanting to quit liquor forever.(p.258)
• But in those days I had no *one* to whom I might take my troubles.(p.260)
• I know that *one* of the outfits I had was a skirt and a very funny looking blouse that my mother had picked up at a rummage sale.(p.261)
• When I came to my aunt, she knew that I had had an unhappy childhood, and she said, "Now, Ethel, you're welcome to have boy friends in our home, but there are two boys in this town that I don't want you to date, and *one* of them comes from a very fine family, *one* of the best.(p.262)
• I remember *one* instance when he took off and went down to Cincinnati and was gone a week on a drunk.(p.262)
• I had never taken *one*.(p.263)
• Our other daughter was in her last year of high school, and *one* night the new son-in-law and my husband went out to a prize fight.(p.263)
• *One* year we got as far as Bellaire, Ohio.(p.264)
• *One* Sunday afternoon, the only time I ever got picked up for drunken driving, I got picked up in Bellaire.(p.264)
• He took his *one* hundred and seventeen dollars and let us go, and we proceeded.(p.264)
• *One* morning after a terrific drinking bout, I was in a little bar near our house, and I shook so that I was very much ashamed, because I was getting the shakes worse and worse.(p.266)
• Time went on and the drinking got worse and worse, and I was in another barroom, down the road the other way, a small *one*, and I took my glass – that morning I'd been able to lift it from the bar -- and I said to the woman behind the bar, "I wish I might never take another drop of that stuff.(p.266)
• Finally, *one* morning, I got up and got in the car and cried all the way down to the M.'s – the people who owned the bar – and told her I was licked and wanted help.(p.267)
• He gave my husband *one* and me *one* about ten-thirty on the eighth day of May in 1941.(p.267)
• *One* of our gifts from the family was a very lovely Bible, but we'd let the bulldog chew it because we weren't too interested in it.(p.268)
• And I realize that there was *one* salvation for me.(p.272)
• I sat down on the side of *one* of their beds, and I started to weep, and I couldn't stop, and I was so startled, and I apologized again and again for it.(p.272)
• I feel that *one* of the things that I still have to guard against is that I used to be set in my way about what I considered the old-time A.A.(p.272)
• I hadn't been in too long when *one* of the men's wives called me *one* Sunday and told me she didn't think I had any part of the program.(p.273)
• In the end I had two problems instead of *one*: Fear and alcohol.(p.275)
• A complete checkup at *one* of the best hospitals revealed nothing.(p.276)
• From this job and the next *one* with another printer I was courteously dismissed.(p.277)
• Liquor had become a crutch on the *one* hand and a means of retreat from life on the other.(p.277)
• When the day of their return was almost upon me, and suicide was the only answer I had been able to think of, I went into Ralph's room *one* evening and told him the truth.(p.278)
• Out of this maelstrom just two coherent thoughts came to the surface; *one*, a drink would mean homelessness and death; two, I could no longer relieve the pressure of fear by starting home, as was once my habitual solution to this problem, because I no longer had a home.(p.279)
• Finally, and I shall never know how much later it was, *one* clear thought came to me: Try prayer.(p.280)
• Having no *one* else to turn to, I was willing to give Him a chance, although with considerable doubt.(p.280)
• It is, however, only the first of a series of miracles which have followed *one* after another as a result of my trying to apply to my daily life the principles embodies in our Twelve Steps.(p.280)
• But – supposing that just *one* man died because I had, for selfish reasons, kept my mouth shut?(p.282)
• There was more than *one* occasion when I got up in the morning with just enough money for coffee and toast and the bus fare to carry me to my first appointment.(p.283)
• I, carried away with the desire to serve A.A., gave what was probably *one* of the first radio broadcasts about A.A., living through a case of mike fright and feeling like a million dollars when it was all over.(p.283)
• I lived through a week of the fidgets because I had agreed to address a group of alcoholic inmates in *one* of our state mental hospitals.(p.283)
• Seven years of work in this field brought an opportunity to affiliate myself actively with *one* of my clients, a fellow A.A.(p.284)
• With God's help I am able, for *one* day at a time, to carry business responsibilities which, not many years ago, I would not have dreamed of assuming.(p.284)
• Instead, I quickly substituted *one* or another vivid scene from the nightmare of my later drinking.(p.286)
• Twenty-odd years ago I made a mess out of my *one* and only marriage.(p.286)
• Here was something requiring a greater willingness to assume responsibility, and take a larger degree of cooperation and "give and take" than even business requires of *one*.(p.286)
• So six months ago I acquired a ready made family consisting of *one* charming wife, four grown children to whom I am devoted, and three grandchildren.(p.286)
• *One* time my wife decided to try this too.(p.288)
• By *one* a.m. I was desperate.(p.288)
• In this small group, during the Depression, there was no *one* who was not hard up.(p.291)
• Every evening we would meet at the home of *one* of the members and have coffee and doughnuts and spend a social evening.(p.291)
• *One* of them was that I would try to get a group started in Chicago; the second was that I would have to return to Akron to attend meetings at least every two months until I did get a group started in Chicago; third, I decided I must place this program above everything else, even my family, because if I did not maintain my sobriety I would lose my family anyway.(p.292)
• That was my lesson, that *one* could not take the moral inventory and then file it away; that the alcoholic has to continue to take inventory every day if he expects to get well and stay well.(p.293)
• In the summer of 1938, almost a year from the time I made my original contact with Akron, the man for whom I was working and who knew about the program, approached me and asked if I could do anything about *one* of his salesmen who was drinking very heavily.(p.294)
• So I suggested that he take a trip to Akron for a couple of weeks, which he did, living with *one* of the A.A. families there.(p.294)
• A few months later *one* of the men who had been in touch with the group in Akron came to Chicago to live, and then there were three of us who continued to have informal meetings quite regularly.(p.294)
• Neither *one* of the two was interested for himself, *one* being a mother who wanted to do something for her son.(p.294)
• An originator of Cleveland's Group No. 3, this *one* fought Prohibition in vain.(p.297)
• At that time, I was living out of town, so I moved back to the home town and made a connection in a responsible position with *one* of the larger companies in the finance business.(p.298)
• If I were alone I would stop at four or five of them, but only *one* or two in the event I had my mistrusting wife with me.(p.299)
• *One* is that I don't remember too many of them, as I was *one* of those drunks who could be on his feet and attend a meeting or a party, engage in a conversation with people and do things that any nearly normal person would do, and the next day not remember a thing about where I was, what I did, whom I saw, or how I got home.(p.301)
• After holding good positions, making better than an average income for over ten years, I was in debt, had no clothes to speak of, no money, no friends, and no *one* any longer tolerating me but my wife.(p.301)
• He mentioned lies and deceptions in the course of his story in the presence of the *one* person in the world I wouldn't want to know such things.(p.302)
• I began making the rounds of the doctors in the hope that *one* of them might find some cure for my accumulating ailments, preferably something that could be removed surgically.(p.305)
• But how does *one* get a prescription for a miracle?(p.306)
• For about *one* year, prior to this time, there was *one* doctor who had continued to struggle with me.(p.306)
• Fortunately for me, my doctor was *one* of the enlightened.(p.307)
• However, due to financial difficulties the whole printing was, for a while, held up and the book received no publicity, nor, of course, was it available in the stores, even if *one* knew it existed.(p.307)
• Some of us struggle with these people because we know that they are really very sick, but we also know that short of some miracle, we are not going to help them except temporarily, and that they will inevitably get worse and worse until *one* of two things happens.(p.308)
• And we wonder how much further this man could go if his alcoholic problem could be removed and he could throw *one* hundred per cent of his abilities into action.(p.308)
• Not only were they at peace with themselves, but they were getting a kick out of life such as *one* seldom encounters, except in the very young.(p.310)
• Keeping *one* foot in front of the other is essential for maintaining our arrestment.(p.311)
• And, as the years go by, working together, sharing our experiences with *one* another, and also sharing a mutual trust, understanding and love – without strings, without obligation – we acquire relationships that are unique and priceless.(p.312)
• *One* morning when I was feeling really bad, I was

put on K.P. and the head cook wanted me to go out and scrub the garbage cans.(p.317)
• I halfway washed them, and he told me to do them again, and I did, and he yelled at me to do them again, and I picked up *one* of the cans and threw it at him and told him to do them himself.(p.317)
• No *one* seemed to care if I made it or not.(p.319)
• I heard voices when no *one* was around, and I saw things that weren't there.(p.319)
• Then *one* day, whammo!(p.319)
• I found out that the people in all A.A. groups were as nice as the people in the first *one*.(p.320)
• In the doorway stood a lovely young girl who said, "Are you *one* of us souses, too?"(p.321)
• I said, "Eileen, are you *one* of those people?"(p.321)
• If we were invited to a formal party and I knew they were only going to have *one* or two drinks, I wouldn't have any.(p.323)
• I was being very cagey, because I knew that if I did take *one* or two, I might want to take five or six or seven or eight.(p.323)
• No *one* else would have stayed with me.(p.323)
• Sometimes I would lie on the bathroom floor, deathly sick, praying I would die, and praying to God as I always had prayed to Him when I was drinking: "Dear God, get me out of this *one* and I'll never do it again."(p.324)
• He used to wonder, when he'd spot *one* of my bottles around the house, just how he could have overlooked that particular bottle.(p.325)
• And "Think" -- that *one* important word means so much to me.(p.325)
• I try to live our program as it has been outlined to me, *one* day at a time.(p.325)
• There was *one* girl especially, and I'd watch her from my window every morning, leaving faithfully to go to the hospital in the neighborhood.(p.326)
• I said to her *one* day when I met her on the street, "What sort of volunteer work do you do?"(p.326)
• We need them so badly even if you can only give *one* day, or perhaps two days?"(p.326)
• I was afraid to set even *one* day.(p.326)
• Then, *one* night, my whole pattern for drinking was set.(p.328)
• He may even read in a newspaper that *one* out of every seven drinkers will become alcoholic, but he rarely is told that it holds true for all ages -- or that the tolerance to alcohol (and other drugs) decreases steadily, year after year, in the bodies of all persons.(p.330)
• There's only *one* answer -- liquid comfort.(p.331)
• *One* night, I hit the jackpot.(p.332)
• I would take a gulp, then warn the jug not to try to entice, lure, or seduce me into having more than *one* "medicinal" jolt.(p.332)
• *One* night, I was struck with the memory of a line Alan Ladd used in "Shane," a movie that I'd worked on.(p.333)
• Out of those forty years as a movie press agent came *one* blessing that granted me a blind faith in the program.(p.334)
• At *one* time, the admission that I was and am an alcoholic meant shame, defeat, and failure to me.(p.335)
• We all have them, and I thought a little brandy or a little wine now and then could certainly hurt no *one*.(p.336)
• But from *one* or two drinks of an afternoon or evening, my intake mounted, and mounted fast.(p.336)
• I couldn't go to *one* wine store and look the man honestly in the face and buy a bottle, as I used to do when I had parties and entertained and did normal drinking.(p.336)
• I wanted him to be sure that I wasn't the *one* who was going to drink the whole bottle.(p.336)
• I became *one* of the most active women in the community, what with P.T.A., other community organizations and drives.(p.339)
• No *one* likes to admit that they're a drunk, that they can't control this thing.(p.340)
• Easy does it, first things first, *one* day at a time.(p.340)
• I heard *one* very ill woman say that she didn't believe in the surrender part of the A.A. program.(p.340)
• That life for me is lived *one* day at a time, letting the problems of the future rest with the future.(p.340)
• I returned to my home in Lucknow, India, at the end of November last year from a vacation in *one* of the most famous beauty spots in our country, a mountain resort 6,800 feet up, with a wonderful lake.(p.342)
• On the second, I knew -- as I know now -- that if I remained away from the first drink, then I had not to worry about the hundredth *one*.(p.344)
• And then *one* ill-defined day, *one* day that I can't recall, I stepped across the line that alcoholics know so well, and from that day on drinking was miserable.(p.346)
• *One* said, "Don't feel that you are a martyr because you stopped drinking," and this hit me between the eyes.(p.346)
• The second *one* said, "Don't feel that you stop drinking for anyone other than yourself," and this hit me between the eyes.(p.346)
• The thought came to me -- This is the last *one*!(p.347)
• And as that thought came to me, it was as though someone had reached down and taken a heavy overcoat off my shoulders, for that was the last *one*.(p.347)
• At *one* end of the table sat our community butcher.(p.347)
• At the other side of the table sat *one* of the carpenters in our community, and at the further end of the table sat the man who ran the bakery, while on *one* side sat my friend who was a mechanic.(p.347)
• I recall, as I walked into that meeting, saying to myself, "Here I am, a fellow of the American College of Surgeons, a Fellow of the International College of Surgeons, a diplomate of *one* of the great specialty boards in these United States, a member of the American Psychiatric Society, and I have to go to the butcher, the baker and the carpenter to help make a man out of me!"(p.347)
• And so *one* gets to thinking to oneself, "Who is this God?(p.350)
• I was sitting in my office *one* time after I had operated on a woman.(p.350)
• So I went to her and said, "There's only *one* thing I want in my whole life, and I don't want any commendation; I don't want any credit; I don't want anything from you or Janey for the rest of your life except *one* thing; and that is, the opportunity to do anything you want always, and I would like to start off by doing the dishes."(p.351)
• My parents' car had a strong attraction to fences, and *one* night I blacked out and drove the car down a bank, ramming the steel fence around someone's backyard.(p.353)
• We did, and spent a month boozing it up, popping pills, and smoking marijuana; taking shelter where we could, which included a veterinary hospital *one* night; accepting meals from anyone; actually begging; stealing anything we were in need of, which was about everything.(p.354)
• I had no *one* in the world to talk to.(p.355)
• And the only *one* who can take it away from me is me -- by taking that first drink.(p.355)
• I have always considered myself *one* of the lucky members of our fraternity.(p.356)
• All of which could turn out but *one* thing -- a very popular, but spoiled, brat.(p.357)
• I had run away from school to join the army in World War I, but missed it by *one* day since the Armistice was signed the very day I landed in Atlanta to sign up with Uncle Sam.(p.357)
• High living, a great many fair weather friends, the 1929 stock market crash, and a couple of years of Depression, soon relieved me *one* by *one* of my worldly goods including my wife.(p.358)
• In this I was greatly aided and abetted by *one* John Barleycorn.(p.358)
• It was strictly a *one* man operation and I knew I had to tend to my knitting to make a go of it.(p.360)
• *One* of the things I needed badly was business for the station.(p.360)
• I graduated there from a five o'clock alcoholic to a noon-day *one*.(p.361)
• By hook or crook I usually managed to sober up before I reached home, but always "terribly tired" from a "hard day's work," and just having to have *one* or two before dinner.(p.361)
• On more than *one* occasion my wife would threaten to leave me.(p.362)
• *One* Saturday noon I staggered home with every intention of showing her.(p.362)
• We had some people in, and I was making drinks in the kitchen, when I suddenly decided to hoist the bottle for a quick *one*.(p.365)
• *One* night at the dinner table my wife said that tonight was my first birthday in A.A., and that the group would have the usual ice cream and cake for the "*one* year man."(p.365)
• For the next couple of hours a terrible battle went on between the good gremlins and the bad ones, *one* faction urging me to tell the truth, the other telling me to sit tight and say nothing.(p.366)
• When I was called upon for a few words I had to tell my friends that I wasn't *one* year old in A.A. that evening but only a "nine month baby."(p.366)
• I repeat, I am *one* of the fortunate members of A.A. -- a lucky guy who is very grateful.(p.368)
• I had no qualms, because I felt the source of a drinking problem was all in how weak *one* was, and I wasn't like my dad (I thought).(p.370)
• Then my father fell down a flight of stairs on *one* of his lost weekends, at the peak of his career, and died.(p.370)
• Near the Laundromat, I would buy *one* bottle of pop and a few bottles of beer or wine, and go into the rest room, empty the pop bottle, refill it with the booze, and proceed to do my laundering.(p.370)
• *One* night, a few weeks after joining the Fellowship, much to my surprise and delight I saw a familiar but no longer frowning face.(p.371)
• During three years in A.A., I haven't lost so much as *one* shirt.(p.372)
• It shows nothing or no *one* to blame for alcoholism.(p.373)
• In time I became an officer and director of *one* of the largest commercial banks in the country.(p.374)
• The only *one* we are fooling is ourselves.(p.376)
• Whenever we went out she appeared to go out of her way to keep me from having more than *one* drink.(p.376)
• What alcoholic can be satisfied with *one* drink?(p.377)
• After every cocktail party or dinner party she would say she couldn't understand how I could get in such a drunken stupor on *one* drink.(p.377)
• She of course didn't realize how cunning an alcoholic can be and the lengths to which he will go in finding ways to satisfy the compulsion for more and more drinks after having had the first *one*.(p.377)
• The following spring she left me *one* day without giving me any idea of where she had gone, hoping this would bring me to my senses.(p.377)
• This didn't say we had to be in jail, ten, fifty, or *one* hundred times.(p.379)
• There may be many reasons which bring *one* to A.A. for the first time, but the lasting *one* must be to want sobriety and the A.A. way of living for oneself.(p.379)
• The why is not important; the fact is that *one* drink will set up a reaction in our system which requires more; that *one* drink was too much and *one* hundred drinks were not enough.(p.380)
• No *one* individual can carry all the burdens of the world.(p.382)
• I think that no *one* comes to A.A. until he's tried everything else.(p.384)
• So finally, he said to me *one* morning, "Esther, why do you do this?"(p.386)
• So the doctor let me go home on *one* condition.(p.387)
• I cooperated with that man *one* hundred per cent!(p.388)
• The only time my dog would have anything to do with me was when I had a hangover, and when I was so sick he was the only *one* who would have anything to do with me at all.(p.390)
• *One* afternoon, the year after moving to Houston, I got as drunk as a skunk, and while I do not walk very straight sober, you should see me when I'm drunk!(p.390)
• Frank was out of town, and I remember that he'd gotten in this *one* night and found me drunk.(p.391)
• There was no *one* I could call.(p.392)
• So I wrote this letter in very shaky handwriting, and in just *one* week came back a letter with A.A. literature from New York.(p.392)
• I had learned an awful lot about myself in that *one* little article.(p.393)
• It was *one* of the worst I ever had.(p.393)
• It was the first time in my life that I could not get a lift out of what I was drinking; and so *one* Friday night, at five minutes to six, I had half a water glass of warm gin, and that is when I first asked God to help me.(p.393)
• It has changed not simply *one* department of my life -- it has changed my whole life.(p.394)
• However, a rough estimate of *one* alcoholic's initiation fee seemed possible.(p.396)
• After all, upon coming out of a week-long or ten-day drunk, it was hard enough to figure up just how much that *one* drunk cost, let alone trying to calculate the cost of approximately twenty-five years of active alcoholism.(p.396)
• I displayed alcoholic tendencies actually from the age of fourteen, when I started to steal wine from the family jug, siphoning it off *one* drink at a time so it wouldn't be missed, not drinking it immediately, but saving it until about a pint was accumulated, so that I could get drunk.(p.397)
• Even at that age, I had learned that *one* drink was not enough.(p.397)

• This eliminated *one* of the limiting factors, the financial.(p.397)
• Saying these sprees were limited to *one* a week (they were not), and saying that the average spree was ten of these drinks (sometimes more, sometimes less), we come up with the first boring statistic: two-fifty per week out of twelve dollars.(p.397)
• Now my drinking was limited by only *one* factor, the enforced periods of dryness caused by lengthy tours at sea.(p.398)
• But now, with His help and grace, this child of His has paid his initiation fee for good, as long as he remembers to stay away from that first drink (the *one* that does all the damage) *one* day at a time.(p.399)
• Even the critics kidded me about this *one*.(p.405)
• Tasting the best of burgundy at a famous restaurant *one* night, landed me passed out on a park bench in the public square.(p.405)
• Bruised, and deadly ashamed, I told no *one*.(p.406)
• I had already been to *one* analyst at home.(p.406)
• This went in *one* ear and out the other.(p.406)
• Other girls whom I had known all my life asked for *one* weak scotch after dinner.(p.406)
• I was accepting help with *one* hand and pushing it away with the other.(p.407)
• This *one* was a dandy.(p.407)
• *One* day soon, the analyses would reveal why I drank and how to stop.(p.408)
• This new analyst was a woman doctor, *one* of the best in the country.(p.409)
• Finally my new friends told me, *one* by *one*, that I could not come around any more.(p.410)
• There was *one* Village bar in particular for which I formed an obsession.(p.410)
• For three generations, my family had had a charge account in *one* of the big New York hotels.(p.410)
• My tweed suit, once a very good *one*, was shapeless and baggy with bare places worn in the elbows from leaning on the bar.(p.411)
• I was not fit to be on the loose, and there was no *one* to commit me.(p.412)
• My analyst was *one* of the first to learn of A.A. and to make subsequent use of it in her work.(p.412)
• He said to me, gently and simply, "Do you think that you are *one* of us?"(p.413)
• Never in my entire life had anyone asked me "Are you *one* of us?"(p.413)
• In those days there was only *one* big meeting a week in New York.(p.414)
• Priscilla, an A.A. who, like Marty, has become *one* of my greatest friends, decided that I was a stubborn case.(p.414)
• On the train going back, Anne's *one* idea was to get to the nearest bar.(p.415)
• Except for *one* short slip, during the first eight months, which was an angry "the world can't do this to me" reaction to a personal tragedy in my life, I have been sober for twelve years.(p.416)
• No *one* could have told me then that I had not earned all my success, nor could anyone have told me that I was an alcoholic and a drug addict.(p.418)
• I am *one* of the growing number of A.A. members who are second-generation.(p.419)
• No *one* could live such an irresponsible, immature life as I had without consequences.(p.420)
• At *one* end of the bed, near the foot, was a printed card, and beneath that was a charted graph.(p.422)
• School was getting to be *one* big bore.(p.423)
• *One* night I was sitting in the lab alone with a fifth and a case of beer listening to dreamy Hawaiian music on the radio.(p.427)
• All I'd wanted was *one* more drink.(p.428)
• I owe no *one* -- except A.A.(p.431)
• *One*, the side I turned to myself and the world, was respectable -- even, in some ways, distinguished.(p.432)
• The binge had been just "*one* of those things."(p.433)
• *One* night I barely made my downtown club; if I'd had to go another fifty feet I'd have collapsed in the gutter.(p.435)
• My personality was stretched almost to splitting in the effort; schizophrenia stared me in the face, and *one* night I was in a suicidal despair.(p.435)
• *One* night my son, when he was only sixteen, was suddenly and tragically killed.(p.437)
• I remember very well saying, "There's only *one* person in the world whose guts I hate worse than yours, and those're my own."(p.440)
• I had sent her to four consecutive psychiatrists, and not *one* of them had gotten me sober.(p.440)
• I remember, *one* time, even the dog had a psychiatric diagnosis.(p.440)
• But then, when that steel door slammed shut, and she was the *one* that went home, I was amazed.(p.440)
• After going to school all day, working in the family drugstore all evening, and then studying until *one* or two in the morning, I would not be able to sleep soundly, with everything I had been studying going round in my head.(p.440)
• I remember finding myself in the middle of the night in the doctors' parking lot at the hospital with *one* foot in the car and *one* foot on the ground, not knowing which was the lead foot; finding myself hanging up the telephone -- then realizing I had gotten out of bed, answered the phone, turned on the light, and carried on a conversation with a patient.(p.441)
• If it was *one* minute before five, I'd drink myself back to sleep.(p.441)
• If it was *one* minute after, I'd stay up and act like a martyr all day.(p.441)
• It became progressively harder to get up in the morning, until *one* day I asked myself what I would do for a patient who felt this rotten.(p.441)
• Following an injection I would have to keep *one* hand busy scratching my constantly itching nose and would also have sudden uncontrollable urges to vomit.(p.442)
• *One* night, I had to put myself back to sleep three times, and then I finally decided to give it up.(p.443)
• That's when that steel door slammed shut, and Max was the *one* who went home.(p.444)
• *One* has to be pretty sick to do that, and perhaps *one* has to be even sicker to come back every day for a new list, as she did.(p.446)
• *One* day as I sat there in the hospital, my psychiatrist walked up behind me and asked, "How'd you like to talk to the man from A.A.?"(p.446)
• I wanted to talk about my many big problems; drinking seemed a small *one*.(p.447)
• And I knew that giving up "*one* drink for *one* day" wouldn't really do any good.(p.448)
• Then, *one* day in A.A., I was told that I had the lenses in my glasses backwards; "the courage to change" in the Serenity Prayer meant, not that I should change my marriage, but rather that I should change myself and learn to accept my spouse as she was.(p.451)
• However, *one* thing I am certain of: Inmates in prison who attend A.A. have their chances of remaining free greatly enhanced -- this is a proved fact.(p.458)
• Each ten-day period in the dark hole, I was fed bread and water daily, with *one* full meal on the third day only.(p.459)
• I was *one* of those bad cons nobody can reach.(p.460)
• Three weeks after an armed robbery in which *one* person received a superficial flesh wound (I could have killed someone!), I was apprehended.(p.460)
• While I was taking inventory in the cold-storage locker *one* Sunday, a wooden sign bolted to the inside door stopped me in my tracks.(p.461)
• I suddenly remembered *one* of my first A.A. meetings, where I heard, "If you are an alcoholic and if you continue to drink, the end is death or insanity."(p.461)
• *One* would have to understand the correctional machinery to see what a miracle this really was.(p.462)
• My daughter was *one* and a half years old when I last saw her.(p.463)
• I don't mean that I went to bed *one* night a normal drinker, and awoke the next morning an alcoholic.(p.464)
• The doctor, apparently realizing that *one* thing that I certainly needed was sleep, left a bottle of sleeping pills there and in my drunken state I took them all, instead of the *one* or two he had prescribed.(p.465)
• Then I remember him coming into my room *one* night with a friend, and telling me to get dressed -- we were going away.(p.466)
• The trip back was completed in *one* of those dead, awful silences.(p.467)
• It was the *one* redeeming act of that Christmas.(p.467)
• Also, after that first visit I learned I could refuse to sign myself in unless they gave me a glass of whiskey in *one* hand and a glass of paraldehyde in the other.(p.468)
• On *one* occasion when I was serving time in my favorite drying-out place while I was having a session with the psychiatrist, she left my case history on her desk when she was called away from the room.(p.470)
• In other words, the kindest doctor in the whole world, and I had *one* such, couldn't help me because I always felt, "You can't know about me -- you can't possibly know -- you don't even drink!"(p.471)
• And so for three months this *one* woman was my A.A.(p.472)
• I went to meetings, I spent a lot of time at the clubroom, but it was all centered in this *one* woman.(p.472)
• And when she broke a luncheon date with me *one* Saturday, after I had been in A.A. for about three months, I said, "I'll show her!(p.472)
• I remember particularly *one* sentence that seemed to say, "This is for you."(p.473)
• You can help where no *one* else can."(p.473)
• The poorest person has no less and the wealthiest has no more -- each of us has but *one* day.(p.473)
• We all *one* as Great Spirit walks through A.A. like sun walks through day.(p.474)
• Met father (Tall Man) at fork in road -- *one* way to reservation, other way to State of Maine.(p.475)
• I hear men say, "*One* day not drink.(p.476)
• Just *one* day."(p.476)
• At *one* time, I was using twenty caps a day; I nearly died half a dozen times on the street.(p.480)
• We are told to practice the Twelve Steps and Twelve Traditions to the best of our ability every day, *one* day at a time.(p.481)
• It is suggested that we do not try to do a lifetime of repairs in *one* day.(p.481)
• I've never seen him drunk in my life, although he'd take a shot in the morning and usually *one* in the evening, and so did I; but for the most part he kept his whiskey in his office.(p.484)
• Economic conditions had a great deal to do with it, because I've often heard my father say that his mother would take *one* of the old time flour sacks and cut a hole through the bottom and two corners of it and there you'd have a gown.(p.486)
• To get rid of me *one* evening, she decided to go to the movies, she and another friend.(p.487)
• At that time the repeal whiskies were back, and I'd go to the store and buy my whiskey and take it to my office and put it under the desk, first in *one* place and then in another, and there soon was an accumulation of empty bottles.(p.488)
• He got me *one*.(p.489)
• My wife received me graciously, although she was living in a *one* room with kitchen affair.(p.490)
• I got drunk *one* night in October, went to sleep in the rain and woke up with pneumonia.(p.490)
• We had several fights and on *one* or two occasions I struck her with my fist.(p.491)
• The *one* thing I can remember now was that Vi was on the corner of 8th and L, and I remember vividly that she had an envelope in her hand.(p.492)
• But there happened to be a liquor store between the post office and the mill, and I stopped to get that *one* drink.(p.493)
• Finally, I broke the last *one* hundred dollar bill the Saturday before I left.(p.493)
• I got out of that bill *one* pair of shoes, and the rest of that money was blown.(p.493)
• I'd been home about a week or ten days when *one* of my friends asked if I could repair *one* of his electrical outlets.(p.493)
• She asked me *one* other thing.(p.494)
• When he left I walked with him to the streetcar line, which was just about a half a block, but there were two liquor stores, *one* on each corner from my home.(p.495)
• But, finally, we got *one* or two to come in and stick and from there, of course, we started to grow.(p.495)
• My last exam and an easy *one*.(p.499)
• I concentrate on *one* of the questions.(p.499)
• *One* more foolish idea.(p.502)
• *One* man comes back, closing the door behind him.(p.503)
• I told him that I believe in electricity and other forces of nature, but as for a God, if there is *one*, He has never done anything for me.(p.503)
• *One* girl suggests that I phone her.(p.505)
• Get into the lives of other people, is *one* thing the fellows in New York had said.(p.505)
• During the course of that drinking, I had shot and killed *one* person and almost completed the job on a second *one*.(p.508)
• An ailment developed in *one* of my eyes, and I was transferred back to Sing Sing and operated upon.(p.509)
• *One* evening I decided to go because two of those friends were to speak.(p.509)
• Those poor stiffs probably went to a doctor and were told that if they quit they'd live three weeks and if they didn't they'd die in *one*."(p.510)
• She was the *one* who really helped me to make a go of that twenty years and nine months in prison.(p.511)
• A former employer of mine said to me a little over ten years ago, "Pat, you seem to be *one* of those unfor-

tunate people who at least once every six months must go out and roll in the gutter."(p.513)
• But at the end of nine months we went to a party *one* night, and I took the first drink.(p.514)
• No *one* had ever told me it was the first drink that did the damage.(p.514)
• My last binge followed the previous *one* by two weeks.(p.514)
• I had just come off a good *one*, and I went back on to the next *one*.(p.514)
• *One* morning I didn't wake up until after four o'clock.(p.515)
• Each *one* has its own place.(p.516)
• I belonged to *one* of the Irish families who, more or less traditionally, sent their boys to the British armies.(p.517)
• I was *one* of the star singers in the choir and *one* of the leading violins in the orchestra.(p.517)
• At first, like everybody else, I could keep control when I drank, but if I did start to drink, even in those days, I was always *one* of the last to leave the party.(p.518)
• It didn't worry me very much, because at that time I could shut off for a couple of months without taking a drink or even wanting *one*, and without feeling that I was giving anything up.(p.518)
• I got a job by myself which suited me down to the ground, because there was nobody really to interfere with what I did, *one* way or the other, and I usually had my nerves in good trim when anybody was coming around to inspect.(p.519)
• The gradual result was that I was drifting into making drinking *one* of the more important parts of my life.(p.519)
• Then I was sent out to India and from then on drinking just increased and increased, and I started having two or three day spells instead of just the ordinary concentrated *one* day.(p.519)
• I was up to international standards in *one* particular game, and that again covered quite a lot of my sins.(p.519)
• I went to a dinner he gave *one* night, rather drunk.(p.520)
• I stopped off just to have *one* drink to see if it tasted the same on the way back to London, and that night I was carried back to bed again.(p.522)
• It has made me understand that I must be *one* of my world, that I cannot exist in any happiness as a rebel by myself.(p.524)
• I don't know when I became an alcoholic, but I do believe I became *one* because I drank too much too often.(p.526)
• I was not able to hold a job – no *one* wants a drunk around.(p.526)
• On *one* of these trips, the judge must have thought I was worth saving, for instead of sending me to jail, he sent me to A.A. for *one* month.(p.526)
• That was *one* of the worst things that could have happened to an alcoholic woman.(p.527)
• If it was daylight, I would go down alleys to make sure no *one* saw me.(p.527)
• My father was and still is a minister, and I was afraid that I might run into him, or that someone might tell him where I was, and I could still remember what he had done to me when I got drunk *one* Christmas when I was very young.(p.527)
• But then *one* good doctor told me there was nothing wrong with me except drinking too much.(p.528)
• *One* morning, I woke up with a thousand dollars.(p.528)
• I don't know if it's force of habit or something else that keeps them in *one* place, but I do know that in A.A. there is much work to do, and none of us can do standing still.(p.529)
• I just want to say that you don't have to be afraid, because no *one* at any A.A. meeting will bite you.(p.529)
• I have not seen a black face but mine since I've been here, and if I didn't look in the mirror, I wouldn't know that I was black, because these people treat me as *one* of them, which I am.(p.530)
• We all have the same sickness, and in helping *one* another, we are able to stay sober.(p.530)
• That was *one* aspect of it, and a true *one*.(p.532)
• There was the father *one* lost respect for at the age of eleven, because the father broke his solemn word in a circumstance where you, eleven years old, had assumed guilt when you were innocent; but the father could not believe you, no matter what; and to ease his suffering you "confessed" and were "forgiven," only – months later – to have your "guilt" brought up only he and you knew what he was talking bout -- brought up in front of the stern grandmother.(p.533)
• I want to be *one* of His children, a member of the human race.(p.535)
• If I write with the air of *one* who has discovered the obvious, which is to say, the eternal truths which have been offered to us since the beginning, forgive my callowness; I had to find these things out for myself.(p.536)
• I'd visit *one* bar after another, having *one* martini in each, and in each hoping to find someone interesting to talk to.(p.536)
• This question so insulted the emotions that clearly there was only *one* thing to do, go and get drunk again, and put that enquiring mind in its proper place, which was oblivion.(p.537)
• *One* by *one*, the understanding friends dropped away.(p.538)
• I wandered, craving peace, from *one* spot to another of youthful happy memory, and loathed the man I had become.(p.539)
• Back to the big city, for another year of precarious living, paid for largely by *one* or two friends I still had not milked dry or worn to exhaustion with demands on their bounty.(p.540)
• I had even borrowed money from her, over her protest: "Bob, please don't ask me to lend you money -- you're the only *one* who hasn't."(p.540)
• I have seen that there is only *one* law, the law of love, and there are only two sins; the first is to interfere with the growth of another human being, and the second is to interfere with one's own growth.(p.542)
• The mental twists that led up to my drinking began many years before I ever took a drink for I am *one* of those whose history proves conclusively that my drinking was "a symptom of a deeper trouble."(p.544)
• I grew up believing that *one* had to be totally self-sufficient, for *one* never dared to depend on another human being.(p.545)
• This caused the rather cryptic comment from *one* of my A.A. friends, when I told my story after coming into the program, that I had always been a cinch for the program, for I had always been interested in mankind, but that I was just taking them *one* man at a time.(p.548)
• I've heard it said many times in A.A., "There is just *one* good drunk in every alcoholic's life, and that's the *one* that brings us into A.A.," and I believe it.(p.549)
• I attended my first A.A. meeting eight years ago, and it is with deep gratitude that I'm able to say I've not had a drink since that time, and that I take no sedation or narcotics, for this program is to me *one* of complete sobriety and I no longer need to escape reality.(p.549)
• *One* of the truly great things A.A. has taught me is that reality too has two sides; I had only known the grim side before the program, but now I had a chance to learn about the pleasant side as well.(p.550)
• But *one* was so outstanding that I like to pass it on whenever I can in the hope that it will help someone else as it has me.(p.551)
• All but *one* "responded to the treatment" suggested in the Steps immediately, but this *one* posed a problem.(p.551)
• I had fed it, fanned it and nurtured it as *one* might a delicate child, and it had become as much a part of me as my breathing.(p.551)
• *One* morning, however, I realized I had to get rid of it, for my reprieve was running out, and if I didn't get rid of it I was going to get drunk – and I didn't want to get drunk any more.(p.552)
• During the day a friend of mine brought me some magazines to take to a hospital group I was interested in, and I looked through them and a "banner" across the front of *one* featured an article by a prominent clergyman in which I caught the word "resentment."(p.552)
• At first, just *one* drink, on occasion.(p.557)
• My employer gave me *one* warning, then another.(p.558)
• In the next half-year, I experienced two more esophageal hemorrhages, miraculously surviving each *one* by a hair.(p.558)
• As our children grew up, I was able to be a father to them when they most needed *one*.(p.559)
• We cast off the burdens of the past and the anxieties of the future, as we begin to live in the present, *one* day at a time.(p.560)
• *One* -- Our common welfare should come first; personal recovery depends upon A.A. unity.(p.564)
• Two – For our group purpose there is but *one* ultimate authority – a loving God as He may express Himself in our group conscience.(p.564)
• Five – Each group has but *one* primary purpose -- to carry its message to the alcoholic who still suffers.(p.564)
• 2. -- For our group purpose there is but *one* ultimate authority -- a loving God as He may express Himself in our group conscience.(p.565)
• 5. – Each Alcoholics Anonymous group ought to be a spiritual entity having but *one* primary purpose -- that of carrying its message to the alcoholic who still suffers.(p.565)
• An A.A. group can bind itself to no *one*.(p.566)
• The Alcoholics Anonymous groups oppose no *one*.(p.567)
• We find that no *one* need have difficulty with the spirituality of the program.(p.570)
• The American Psychiatric Association requested, in 1949, that a paper be prepared by *one* of the older members of Alcoholics Anonymous to be read at the Association's annual meeting of that year.(p.572)
• Historians may *one* day recognize Alcoholics Anonymous to have been a great venture in social pioneering which forged a new instrument for social action; a new therapy based on the kinship of common suffering; *one* having a vast potential for the myriad other ills of mankind."(p.573)

one-fourth

• Women now make up more than *one-fourth* of the membership; among newer members, the proportion is nearly one-third.(p.xxii)

one-half

• Unlike most of our crowd, I did not get over my craving for liquor much during the first two and *one-half* years of abstinence.(p.181)

one-night

• I refused to join any fraternity, as I wanted to be a free lance, and that year my drinking was confined to *one-night* stands, once or twice a week.(p.241)
• I stayed sober for four years except for a *one-night* carousal in Chicago.(p.253)
• My binges were *one-night* stands only.(p.432)

one-nighter

• After a particularly ugly *one-nighter*, my wife suggested I try it, and I agreed.(p.434)

one-nighters

• My daily alcoholic consumption remained about the same through all this, with perhaps a slight increase, and my binges remained *one-nighters*.(p.434)

one-third

• Women now make up more than one-fourth of the membership; among newer members, the proportion is nearly *one-third*.(p.xxii)

one-way

• Our design for living is not a *one-way* street.(p.81)
• Cops now sick of me, so they buy me *one-way* ticket to Canada.(p.475)

one's

• Each might pray about it, having the other *one's* happiness uppermost in mind.(p.82)
• Unless *one's* family expresses a desire to live upon spiritual principles we think we ought not to urge them.(p.83)
• Suggestions about these may be obtained from *one's* priest, minister, or rabbi.(p.87)
• But what a difference there is between going through hell without a power greater than *one's* self, and with it!(p.437)
• Intake of alcohol changes *one's* personality -- even the healthy personality.(p.458)
• I have seen that there is only one law, the law of love, and there are only two sins; the first is to interfere with the growth of another human being, and the second is to interfere with *one's* own growth.(p.542)
• Dr. Foster Kennedy, neurologist: "This organization of Alcoholics Anonymous calls on two of the greatest reservoirs of power known to man, religion and that instinct for association with *one's* fellows . . . the 'herd instinct.'(p.571)

ones

• We are like men who have lost their legs; they never grow new *ones*.(p.30)
• Some of us veered from extreme to extreme, ever hoping that one day our loved *ones* would be themselves once more.(p.105)
• The alarming physical and mental symptoms, the deepening pall of remorse, depression and inferiority that settled down on our loved *ones* -- these things terrified and distracted us.(p.106)
• You and your husband will find that you can dispose of serious problems easier than you can the trivial *ones*.(p.118)
• Though old buildings will eventually be replaced by finer *ones*, the new structures will take years to complete.(p.123)
• Your man has probably been trying to conceal a number of scrapes, perhaps pretty messy *ones*.(p.140)
• They will approach still other sick *ones* and fellowships of Alcoholics Anonymous may spring up in each city and hamlet, havens for those who must find a way out.(p.153)

• Eagerly he pointed to us saying, "These are the fellows I told you about; they are the *ones* who understand."(p.189)
• They had a hunch that there must be an answer for these apparently hopeless *ones*, somewhere.(p.307)
• Most of these fortunate *ones* have had little or no acquaintance with delirium, with hospitals, asylums, and jails.(p.315)
• For the next couple of hours a terrible battle went on between the good gremlins and the bad *ones*, one faction urging me to tell the truth, the other telling me to sit tight and say nothing.(p.366)
• I would have three quick strong *ones* in order to endure the evening.(p.407)
• He himself took me to many of them, including the *ones* out of town.(p.416)
• After all, it was self (you, me) that stood in our own way, that ran the show and ran ourselves into bankruptcy, that hurt the *ones* we loved.(p.459)
• Aside from being a common drunk, I had a very serious pill affliction and all the garbage that goes with it -- lying, stealing, cheating anybody and everybody, conning the people I could, and staying clear of the *ones* I couldn't.(p.478)
• In those years I was in jail nine times, in an alcoholic ward, overnight, twice; and I was fired from three jobs, two of them very good *ones*.(p.536)
• All of my family and loved *ones*, all of my friends, are nearer and dearer to me than ever before and I have literally dozens of new friends who say they cannot believe that a short eight years ago I was ready for the scrap heap.(p.541)
• Harm is done by sick people, as I was sick, and doing dreadful harm to myself and to my loved *ones*.(p.542)
• I was immersed in self-pity and resentment, and the only people who would support this attitude or who I felt understood me at all were the people I met in bars and the *ones* who drank as I did.(p.547)

oneself

• "Complete abandon";"Half measures availed us nothing";"Thoroughly follow our path"; "Completely give *oneself* to this simple program" -- rang in my swelled head.(p.349)
• And so one gets to thinking to *oneself*, "Who is this God?(p.350)
• There may be many reasons which bring one to A.A. for the first time, but the lasting one must be to want sobriety and the A.A. way of living for *oneself*.(p.379)

ongoing

• Most of us did not stay out of prison long enough to run the alcoholic gamut -- to develop the *ongoing* kind of alcoholism or alcoholic drinking you hear about in A.A. talks.(p.458)

only

• The *only* requirement for membership is an honest desire to stop drinking.(p.xiv)
• Many of our friends encourage us by saying that this is but a beginning, *only* the augury of a much larger future ahead.(p.xv)
• Prior to his journey to Akron, the broker had worked hard with many alcoholics on the theory that *only* an alcoholic could help an alcoholic, but he had succeeded *only* in keeping sober himself.(p.xvi)
• Without such support, A.A. could have made *only* the slowest progress.(p.xx)
• So far, upon the total problem of several million actual and potential alcoholics in the world, we have made *only* a scratch.(p.xx)
• Surveys of groups in the United States and Canada indicate that A.A. is reaching out, not *only* to more and more people, but to a wider and wider range.(p.xxii)
• To them, their alcoholic life seems the *only* normal one.(p.xxvi)
• On the other hand -- and strange as this may seem to those who do not understand -- once a psychic change has occurred, the very same person who seemed doomed, who had so many problems he despaired of ever solving them, suddenly finds himself easily able to control his desire for alcohol, the *only* effort necessary being that required to follow a few simple rules.(p.xxvii)
• The *only* relief we have to suggest is entire abstinence.(p.xxviii)
• He had lost everything worthwhile in life and was *only* living, one might say, to drink.(p.xxix)
• His alcoholic problem was so complex, and his depression so great, that we felt his *only* hope would be through what we then called "moral psychology," and we doubted if even that would have any effect.(p.xxix)
• Unmindful of his welfare, I thought *only* of recapturing the spirit of other days.(p.9)
• It was *only* a matter of being willing to believe in a Power greater than myself.(p.12)
• I was to sit quietly when in doubt, asking *only* for direction and strength to meet my problems as He would have me.(p.13)
• Then *only* might I expect to receive.(p.13)
• *Only* to have that thought supplanted by "Well, I'll stop with the sixth drink."(p.24)
• We have no desire to convince anyone that there is *only* one way by which faith can be acquired.(p.28)
• Our hope is that many alcoholic men and women, desperately in need, will see these pages, and we believe that it is *only* by fully disclosing ourselves and our problems that they will be persuaded to say, "Yes, I am one of them too; I must have this thing."(p.29)
• Here are some of the methods we have tried: Drinking beer *only*, limiting the number of drinks, never drinking alone, never drinking in the morning, drinking *only* at home, never having it in the house, never drinking during business hours, drinking *only* at parties, switching from scotch to brandy, drinking *only* natural wines, agreeing to resign if ever drunk on the job, taking a trip, not taking a trip, swearing off forever (with and without a solemn oath), taking more physical exercise, reading inspirational books, going to health farms and sanitariums, accepting voluntary commitment to asylums -- we could increase the list ad infinitum.(p.31)
• Several of our crowd, men of thirty or less, had been drinking *only* a few years, but they found themselves as helpless as those who had been drinking twenty years.(p.33)
• Yet all reasons for not drinking were easily pushed aside in favor of the foolish idea that he could take whiskey if *only* he mixed it with milk!(p.36)
• I felt I had every right to be self-confident, that it would be *only* a matter of exercising my will power and keeping on guard.(p.40)
• Not *only* had I been off guard, I had made no fight whatever against the first drink.(p.41)
• Though I had been *only* a nominal churchman, their proposals were not, intellectually, hard to swallow.(p.42)
• He had felt *only* the first nip of the wringer.(p.43)
• If that be the case, you may be suffering from an illness which *only* a spiritual experience will conquer.(p.44)
• I'm sure it would work if I could *only* believe as he believes.(p.47)
• *Only* thirty years later the conquest of the air was almost an old story and airplane travel was in full swing.(p.52)
• They said God made these things possible, and we *only* smiled.(p.55)
• In the last analysis it is *only* there that He may be found.(p.55)
• We can *only* clear the ground a bit.(p.55)
• 11.Sought through prayer and meditation to improve our conscious contact with God as we understood Him, praying *only* for knowledge of His will for us and the power to carry that out.(p.59)
• If his arrangements would *only* stay put, if *only* people would do as he wished, the show would be great.(p.60)
• Is he not a victim of the delusion that he can wrest satisfaction and happiness out of this world if he *only* manages well?(p.61)
• He is like the retired business man who lolls in the Florida sunshine in the winter complaining of the sad state of the nation; the minister who sighs over the sins of the twentieth century; politicians and reformers who are sure all would be Utopia if the rest of the world would *only* behave; the outlaw safe cracker who thinks society has wronged him; and the alcoholic who has lost all and is locked up.(p.61)
• This was *only* a beginning, though if honestly and humbly made, an effect, sometimes a very great one, was felt at once.(p.63)
• From it stem all forms of spiritual disease, for we have been not *only* mentally and physically ill, we have been spiritually sick.(p.64)
• As in war, the victor *only* seemed to win.(p.66)
• It is plain that a life which includes deep resentment leads *only* to futility and unhappiness.(p.66)
• But this is *only* a half-truth.(p.70)
• They *only* thought they had lost their egoism and fear; they *only* thought they had humbled themselves.(p.73)
• If that is so, this step may be postponed, *only* however, if we hold ourselves in complete readiness to go through with it at the first opportunity.(p.74)
• Maybe it's *only* a petty offense such as padding the expense account.(p.78)
• Sometimes we hear an alcoholic say that the *only* thing he needs to do is to keep sober.(p.82)
• We ask especially for freedom from self-will, and are careful to make no request for ourselves *only*.(p.87)
• They will be *only* too glad to assist you.(p.89)
• To be helpful is our *only* aim.(p.89)
• We are dealing *only* with general principles common to most denominations.(p.94)
• Make it plain he is under no obligation to you, that you hope *only* that he will try to help other alcoholics when he escapes his own difficulties.(p.94)
• If he is not interested in your solution, if he expects you to act *only* as a banker for his financial difficulties or a nurse for his sprees, you may have to drop him until he changes his mind.(p.95)
• Permit that and you *only* harm him.(p.96)
• The *only* condition is that he trust in God and clean house.(p.98)
• His *only* chance for sobriety would be some place like the Greenland Ice Cap, and even there an Eskimo might turn up with a bottle of scotch and ruin everything!(p.101)
• Bottles were *only* a symbol.(p.103)
• Our friends have counseled chucking the men and we have done so with finality, *only* to be back in a little while hoping, always hoping.(p.105)
• For a while they would be their old sweet selves, *only* to dash the new structure of affection to pieces once more.(p.107)
• Of course, there is such a thing as incompatibility, but in nearly every instance the alcoholic *only* seems to be unloving and inconsiderate; it is usually because he is warped and sickened that he says and does these appalling things.(p.108)
• One: Your husband may be *only* a heavy drinker.(p.108)
• His drinking may be constant or it may be heavy *only* on certain occasions.(p.109)
• Say you do not want to be a wet blanket; that you *only* want him to take care of his health.(p.112)
• Talk about his condition or this book *only* when he raises the issue.(p.113)
• Seed has started to sprout in a new soil, but growth has *only* begun.(p.117)
• The foregoing pages (though addressed *only* to wives) indicate the problems such people may face.(p.121)
• The family may be possessed by the idea that future happiness can be based *only* upon forgetfulness of the past.(p.123)
• That is true *only* if one is willing to turn the past to good account.(p.124)
• The alcoholic's past thus becomes the principal asset of the family and frequently it is almost the *only* one!(p.124)
• We think each family which has been relieved owes something to those who have not, and when the occasion requires, each member of it should be *only* too willing to bring former mistakes, no matter how grievous, out of their hiding places.(p.124)
• It is of little use to argue and *only* makes the impasse worse.(p.126)
• He may not see at once that he has barely scratched a limitless lode which will pay dividends *only* if he mines it for the rest of his life and insists on giving away the entire product.(p.129)
• We intend the foregoing as a helpful suggestion *only*.(p.132)
• Some of us had this experience, *only* to enjoy, in a few months, a finer intimacy than ever.(p.134)
• In *only* a few instances has there been lack of patience and tolerance.(p.137)
• The *only* answer I could make was that if the man followed the usual pattern, he would go on a bigger bust than ever.(p.138)
• Can you discard the feeling that you are dealing *only* with habit, with stubbornness, or a weak will?(p.140)
• He wants to quit drinking and you want to help him, even if it be *only* a matter of good business.(p.141)
• *Only* a few knew of it at first but, within a short time, it was billboarded throughout the entire company.(p.145)
• Why, he argued, should he lose the remainder of his business, *only* to bring still more suffering to his family by foolishly admitting his plight to people from whom he made his livelihood?(p.155)
• He lost the race by *only* a narrow margin.(p.158)
• Under *only* slightly different conditions, the same thing is taking place in many eastern cities.(p.161)
• To duplicate, with such backing, what we have accomplished is *only* a matter of willingness, patience and labor.(p.163)
• This was *only* a few days ago at this writing.(p.163)
• Our book is meant to be suggestive *only*.(p.164)

• We realize we know *only* a little.(p.164)
• Unfortunately for me, I was the *only* child, which perhaps engendered the selfishness which played such an important part in bringing on my alcoholism.(p.172)
• I lost *only* a half day's work during these three years.(p.173)
• I drank with moderation at first, but it took me *only* a relatively short time to drift back into the old habits which had wound up so disastrously before.(p.175)
• Occasionally, I would yield to the morning craving, but if I did, it would be *only* a few hours before I would be quite unfit for work.(p.176)
• All the other people that had talked to me wanted to help me, and my pride prevented me from listening to them, and caused *only* resentment on my part, but I felt as if I would be a real stinker if I did not listen to a couple of fellows for a short time, if that would cure them.(p.185)
• At the end of this selling of lots, just prior to World War I, I got into the crude rubber business, and six months later there was *only* one broker and myself left in Akron.(p.197)
• So in spite of anything that I might do, I prospered, being one of *only* two brokers in the rubber center of the world.(p.197)
• Near success, *only* near.(p.197)
• I figured the *only* difference between me and a millionaire was that I hadn't the strength, or that he got the breaks and I didn't.(p.197)
• I can well remember over a long period of years when I thought I was the *only* person in the world who knew that sooner or later I was going to get drunk.(p.198)
• At the end of about four months, I not *only* had good looking clothes --and I might say that at the time I first talked to Max I didn't have a suit of clothes I could bend over in real sudden; now I had six suits of clothes.(p.200)
• Then I got into the habit of having beers, and decided that a drink of whiskey was not any worse; so I would get the one drink of whiskey but, on second thought, I decided that as long as I was *only* going to have one, I might as well make it a double-header.(p.203)
• I think the longest drunk I was ever on was eleven days, but usually *only* two days with a complete blackout for a day, and then backing off by drinking as long as I could get anything.(p.203)
• My *only* thought that day was getting a drink, and how to get rid of those clowns was my big problem.(p.206)
• There were *only* seven or eight people in the group before me and they all visited me during my period in the hospital.(p.208)
• After two or three years of effort along this line, I reached the point of actual despair that I ever would be able to drink *only* a harmless amount each day.(p.215)
• My children had lost respect for me and, in fact, it was *only* after three or four years of sobriety that any of them ever said anything to me to indicate that I had recouped even a little of their respect.(p.215)
• She knew that at that time any suggestion she made about my drinking would *only* build up a barrier, a consideration for which I am ever grateful.(p.216)
• I still had enough practice to earn a good living if I would *only* work, so I resolved that in January of 1940 I would launch a patent law firm of my own.(p.220)
• I'd *only* had two with her, but I'd managed four in the fifteen minutes I'd waited for her, and of course I'd had the usual uncounted swigs from the bottle as I painfully got up and did my slow spasmodic dressing.(p.223)
• My husband was an alcoholic -- I had *only* contempt for those without my own amazing capacity -- the outcome was inevitable.(p.225)
• For me, work was *only* a different means to the same end, to be able to do exactly what I wanted to do.(p.225)
• I wasn't the *only* person in the world who felt and behaved like this!(p.227)
• My "periodics" became more frequent until I reached the point where I wanted to devote all my time to drinking, working as little as possible, and then *only* when the necessity of my family demanded it.(p.234)
• My customers lost confidence in me to the point where I retained what business I had *only* because I was a well-trained and reputedly fine craftsman.(p.234)
• Mother would take me in *only* if I would stay locked in a small storeroom and give her my clothes and shoes.(p.238)
• The *only* salesman invited to talk at the convention?(p.243)
• I was startled to learn he had *only* been off the booze a month or so himself when he brought me the message!(p.245)
• At the time, I thought them just a swell pair of screwballs, for they were not *only* going to save all the drunks in the world but also all the so-called normal people!(p.245)
• For a long time the *only* Higher Power I could concede was the power of the group, but this was far more than I had ever recognized before, and it was at least a beginning.(p.248)
• I don't think the boys were completely convinced of my personality change, for they fought shy of including my story in the book, so my *only* contribution to their literary efforts was my firm conviction, being still a theological rebel, that the word God should be qualified with the phrase "as we understand him" -- for that was the *only* way I could accept spirituality.(p.248)
• In June, 1945, with another member, I made my first -- and *only* -- Twelfth Step call on a female alcoholic and a year later I married her.(p.249)
• In conclusion, I can *only* say that whatever growth or understanding has come to me, I have no wish to graduate.(p.249)
• I have served on *only* one committee in the past nine years, for I feel that I had my chance the first few years and that newer members should fill the jobs.(p.250)
• Slight casualties, complicated however by a long and serious illness, were my *only* mishaps.(p.253)
• Federal Theatre in Texas gave me an administrative job which I held for a year, *only* because I worked hard and productively when I worked, and because my very tolerant chief ascribed my frequent lapses to a bohemian temperament.(p.256)
• I found my friend was there for alcoholism and now he was insisting that he had found the *only* cure.(p.257)
• He knew too well that didn't mean a thing, just as I knew in my heart that it would be *only* a question of time -- a few days, a week, or even a month, it was inevitable -- till I would be off on another bender.(p.257)
• All sorts were represented and their relation of experiences and how they had found the *only* remedy, added to their human existence as sober men, laid the foundation of a very necessary faith.(p.258)
• One Sunday afternoon, the *only* time I ever got picked up for drunken driving, I got picked up in Bellaire.(p.264)
• I drove these three or four miles down the road *only* to find that Jack was out.(p.267)
• That was the *only* part I was interested in.(p.269)
• It's *only* natural that we don't have the capacity to change, but we ought not to criticize those who have, There's another thing I would stress.(p.273)
• Probably *only* a few readers of this story will be able, from personal experiences of their own, to understand the exhilaration and sense of accomplishment which I felt after finishing this seemingly simple assignment.(p.276)
• When the day of their return was almost upon me, and suicide was the *only* answer I had been able to think of, I went into Ralph's room one evening and told him the truth.(p.278)
• The *only* stipulation they made was this: I had to make the decision myself.(p.278)
• It is, however, *only* the first of a series of miracles which have followed one after another as a result of my trying to apply to my daily life the principles embodies in our Twelve Steps.(p.280)
• After six months of sobriety I saw the picture in a different light: Detroit was the place I had to return to, not *only* because I must face the mess I had made there, but because it was there that I could be of the most service to A.A.(p.281)
• The most accurate answer I can give you is this: Fear has never again ruled my life since that day in September, 1938, when I found that a Power greater than myself could not *only* restore me to sanity but could keep me both sober and sane.(p.285)
• *Only* once did I suffer from a nearly overpowering compulsion to take a drink.(p.285)
• Twenty-odd years ago I made a mess out of my one and *only* marriage.(p.286)
• However, I must have felt, deep down inside myself, that living the selfish life of a bachelor was *only* half living.(p.286)
• So I told dad that I would lick it on my own, that I would drink nothing for a month and after that *only* beer.(p.289)
• He said he had finally learned that drinking was a fatal illness made up of an allergy plus an obsession, and once the drinking had passed from habit to obsession, we were completely hopeless, and could look forward *only* to spending the balance of our lives in mental institutions or to death.(p.290)
• Then and then *only*, after a thorough indoctrination by eight or nine individuals, was I allowed to attend my first meeting.(p.291)
• That was my *only* slip.(p.294)
• Doctors told me before I stopped that I had *only* three years at the outside to live.(p.295)
• Somehow or other, I must have misunderstood the doctor's instructions, for I not *only* made the beer for my wife, I also drank it for her.(p.297)
• If I were alone I would stop at four or five of them, but *only* one or two in the event I had my mistrusting wife with me.(p.299)
• However, he explained to me that he had been just such a rummy as I, *only* for a much longer period of time.(p.302)
• I tried them mixed, unmixed, drinking *only* when gay, *only* when depressed.(p.305)
• Certainly now, anyone would have agreed that *only* a miracle could prevent my final breakdown.(p.306)
• With the alcoholic, they could *only* give temporary relief and in the last stages not even that.(p.307)
• Not *only* were they at peace with themselves, but they were getting a kick out of life such as one seldom encounters, except in the very young.(p.310)
• This, plus mounting emotional disturbances, convinced them that compulsive alcoholism already had them; that complete ruin would be *only* a question of time.(p.315)
• When I came home again, the *only* thing I had left to love was the bottle.(p.318)
• The *only* way I knew to do it was to drink right along with him.(p.322)
• If we were invited to a formal party and I knew they were *only* going to have one or two drinks, I wouldn't have any.(p.323)
• I should have lost my husband, and I think that *only* the fact that he was an alcoholic too kept us together.(p.323)
• We have *only* been in A.A. a few years, but now we're trying to make up for lost time.(p.325)
• Now I feel so very grateful not *only* for my sobriety, which I try to maintain day by day, but I'm grateful also for the ability to help other people.(p.326)
• We need them so badly even if you can *only* give one day, or perhaps two days?"(p.326)
• *Only* death could wipe out that security.(p.329)
• There's *only* one answer -- liquid comfort.(p.331)
• Death seemed the *only* way out.(p.333)
• I told her that I was an alcoholic, victim of a disease, that there was no cure, *only* arrestment through total abstinence.(p.333)
• It was the *only* hope I had.(p.334)
• Because it was *only* through feeling defeat and feeling failure, the inability to cope with my life and with alcohol, that I was able to surrender and accept the fact that I had this disease, and that I had to learn to live again without alcohol.(p.335)
• The *only* incentive that I had, toward the end, for getting dressed in the morning was to get out and get supplies to help me get my day started.(p.336)
• But the *only* thing that got started was my drinking.(p.336)
• If I could *only* stop thinking, I wouldn't drink.(p.337)
• If I could *only* stop drinking, maybe I wouldn't think.(p.337)
• But I *only* succeeded in fighting it.(p.338)
• I succeeded in this attempt for approximately fifteen months with *only* a couple of slips.(p.343)
• I am not even there, and if I was there the *only* thing I could do would be to give her moral support, and yet he thanks me for curing his wife."(p.350)
• So I went to her and said, "There's *only* one thing I want in my whole life, and I don't want any commendation; I don't want any credit; I don't want anything from you or Janey for the rest of your life except one thing; and that is, the opportunity to do anything you want always, and I would like to start off by doing the dishes."(p.351)
• It *only* became another excuse to drink.(p.354)
• Without hesitation, I did the *only* logical thing -- ran away from home.(p.354)
• And with this came the *only* real freedom, the freedom of truth.(p.355)
• My sponsor used to say to me, "If I could *only* paint you a picture of how beautiful life can be without booze . . ."(p.355)
• And the *only* one who can take it away from me is me -- by taking that first drink.(p.355)
• I was born in Cleveland, Ohio, the *only* child of a prominent dentist, and a very proud mother.(p.357)

• It was the first of many such experiences that became the *only* cause of harsh words, tears and heartaches in an otherwise truly beautiful marriage.(p.361)
• I had not *only* let my wife down but also a lot of other wonderful people who had helped me.(p.364)
• When I was called upon for a few words I had to tell my friends that I wasn't one year old in A.A. that evening but *only* a "nine month baby."(p.366)
• My mother was a lovely, sweet woman, whose *only* weakness was my father.(p.369)
• A few months after that, I was released and left the world of insanity, *only* to return to the world of alcoholic insanity.(p.370)
• The *only* drawback was, I always knew how I arrived there, but somehow, between the rest room, the rinse, and the fluff-dry, I never knew when or how I got home.(p.370)
• I saw at last that I had the same disease my father had, *only* I was being given a chance to live, not die.(p.371)
• The *only* one we are fooling is ourselves.(p.376)
• I *only* know that it does -- if you desire it with your whole heart and without reservation.(p.384)
• The *only* thing I have really to offer you is my own story, telling you just what sort of a drunk I was.(p.384)
• For some reason I can't remember, it finally dawned on me that I had a problem, and yet nobody was very critical about it except my family, and that was *only* because I decided, after seven years of marriage, that I would divorce my husband.(p.386)
• It *only* took a month to get a divorce in Texas.(p.386)
• But they kept me there -- I was supposed to stay a month, but they *only* kept me there seventeen days.(p.387)
• Because of this state of confusion and frustration I had hysterics on the seventeenth day for the first and *only* time in my life.(p.387)
• I know now that I asked questions and told him what I wanted to learn, but I told him *only* what I wanted to believe about myself.(p.388)
• Frank had to go to New York, but because I had a dog, we had a duplex, and I thought -- if *only* we had a house!(p.388)
• The *only* thing that I could do would be to call the doctor to help sober me up.(p.389)
• The *only* time my dog would have anything to do with me was when I had a hangover, and when I was so sick he was the *only* one who would have anything to do with me at all.(p.390)
• I *only* know that it first reached me through that Saturday Evening Post article.(p.392)
• I know that I must work at it as long as I live; I know that it is *only* by working at it that I can stay sober and have a happy life.(p.394)
• Now my drinking was limited by *only* one factor, the enforced periods of dryness caused by lengthy tours at sea.(p.398)
• The *only* other occasionally limiting factor was that I might run out of money before the next payday rolled around.(p.398)
• *Only* God as we understand Him can calculate these.(p.399)
• It was the *only* real home she knew.(p.402)
• I *only* saw that I had not become Mrs. Shakespeare.(p.403)
• Drink *only* beer or wine.(p.408)
• In those days there was *only* one big meeting a week in New York.(p.414)
• The *only* thing that bothered me was a queasy feeling I had in the pit of my stomach.(p.418)
• The last time I drank, when I was twenty-nine, I drank for *only* four days, yet I threatened to kill my children; I beat my wife at home and on the church steps; I mistreated a child in my office; and I ran to a hospital for mental illness to avoid jail.(p.418)
• *Only* A.A. kept me from running away.(p.420)
• I smoked as much, tried to drink as much, and do everything they did, *only* more so.(p.423)
• I was *only* twenty now, but I was a man.(p.427)
• He even went to bat for me before the court martial that inevitably followed and, as a result, I drew *only* thirty days -- fifteen in solitary.(p.428)
• Mom has said the *only* requisite to start is willingness.(p.430)
• *Only* show me how."(p.430)
• In all the twenty-five years of my drinking there were *only* a few occasions when I took a morning drink.(p.432)
• My binges were one-night stands *only*.(p.432)
• Once or twice, during my early drinking, I carried it over into the second day, and *only* once, that I can remember, did it continue into the third.(p.432)
• I can *only* list a few of its elements.(p.435)
• I'd had absolute faith in science, and *only* in science.(p.435)
• *Only* through being beaten down by my own misery would I ever have accepted the term "alcoholic" as applied to myself.(p.436)
• One night my son, when he was *only* sixteen, was suddenly and tragically killed.(p.437)
• Not *only* did I not think that being an alcoholic was a good idea, I didn't even feel that I had all that much of a drinking problem!(p.439)
• I remember very well saying, "There's *only* one person in the world whose guts I hate worse than yours, and those're my own."(p.440)
• She cried a bit and went to bed; that was the *only* answer to problems that she had left.(p.440)
• I always took it because I had the symptom that *only* that pill would relieve.(p.443)
• Today, I find I can't work my A.A. program while taking pills, nor may I even have them around for dire emergencies *only*.(p.443)
• (I am pleased to state, however, that I had gone to *only* a very few A.A. meetings before I was able to make a really beautiful pair of moccasins -- and half a wallet.(p.445)
• I really felt sorry for him; the *only* thing in life he had to brag about was the fact that he was an alcoholic.(p.446)
• We sat in the back and talked *only* to each other.(p.447)
• Each ten-day period in the dark hole, I was fed bread and water daily, with one full meal on the third day *only*.(p.459)
• There, I received several soda crackers and water daily, and before I could have my third-day meal (again the *only* meal in ten days), I had to drink a glass of castor oil or mineral oil, depending on the cruelty of the person who was doing the dispensing.(p.459)
• Fortunately, I received *only* fifteen-twenty years, and I went back to my alma mater (where I had spent so much time in the hole).(p.461)
• When I had served *only* eighteen months of my sentence, this ex-incorrigible was placed in honor grade.(p.461)
• Besides, I can *only* live today.(p.463)
• This is difficult, but it is the *only* way it has worked for me.(p.463)
• In fact it has been *only* within the last fifteen years that I changed from a fairly normal, controlled drinker into an alcoholic.(p.464)
• From that time on, fear was with me because I realized that not *only* would I not remember what happened to me while I was drinking, but apparently I couldn't control what happened.(p.465)
• *Only* a few days before Christmas I went to the dentist for a periodic checkup.(p.465)
• And then I went back home to live with my parents, and the merry-go-round started again -- *only* this time I didn't have to worry about waking up behind bars in a psychiatric ward.(p.468)
• Even the Jack Alexander Saturday Evening Post article hadn't been written, and there was *only* a tiny group of people in Washington.(p.469)
• *Only* they had been scratched out and over them was written, "Chronic Alcoholic."(p.470)
• During these seven years a thing called the Twenty-four Hour Program --a gadget I used to think was *only* a snare to trap the newcomer -- has come to mean much to me, not *only* as regards my drinking but in the whole pattern of my life.(p.473)
• Remember *only* first two drinks.(p.475)
• I once hear people say *only* Indians crazy when drunk.(p.477)
• This was the *only* period when I didn't drink, but that was hardly any consolation.(p.480)
• He has also taught me that I must help myself first; *only* then may I be able to help others.(p.481)
• *Only* God is.(p.482)
• The *only* time that I have ever seen my mother take anything alcoholic was around Christmas time, when she would drink some eggnog or light wine.(p.484)
• A man wasn't actually mistreated, though if he was he could *only* resent it.(p.485)
• At this point I believe I had *only* been intoxicated on maybe three or four occasions, and certainly whiskey was no problem to me.(p.487)
• A very good friend of mine who owned a drug store across the street from us, came by *only* about two hours later and said that he had seen Vi down town.(p.487)
• Thinking *only* of two or three dollars to buy some whiskey, I did the job and that's how I met Ella G., who was responsible for my coming into A.A.(p.493)
• And, not *only* that, but they gave us financial help.(p.496)
• She had been warned numerous times, not *only* by her family but by my own mother, that I was a hopeless drunk, that there wasn't anything anybody could do with me, that I'd never stop, and that eventually I'd break her heart.(p.513)
• But this proved *only* a temporary setback.(p.517)
• The Commanding Officer *only* spoke to me when he wanted to tell me exactly who I was and what I was and how little I counted in the scheme of things and how glad he would be if I went away.(p.520)
• My *only* hope was to try and get through what was left of life as best I could, but I could never visualize doing that without drinking.(p.522)
• This was the *only* time in my life that I'd ever known my mother to be almost pitiless, but she couldn't be blamed for that.(p.523)
• Because I had been drunk, the judge gave me *only* a twelve-year sentence in prison.(p.528)
• By the grace of God, I *only* served three years.(p.528)
• The *only* thing that bothers me is that there are *only* about five Negroes in A.A. in my city.(p.529)
• I, a man of steel, with very high ideals, well brought up, an honor student and the recipient of scholarships and prizes, a boy wonder in business -- I, Bob, the author of this essay, looked and saw that the universe was beneath my contempt, and that to remove myself from it was the *only* thing of dignity a man could do.(p.531)
• There was the father one lost respect for at the age of eleven, because the father broke his solemn word in a circumstance where you, eleven years old, had assumed guilt when you were innocent; but the father would not believe you, no matter what; and to ease his suffering you "confessed" and were "forgiven," *only* -- months later -- to have your "guilt" brought up -- *only* he and you knew what he was talking bout -- brought up in front of the stern grandmother.(p.533)
• *Only*, having found them, I threw them away, and ordered another extra dry martini.(p.533)
• Which is *only* another way of saying, I had to be right all the time, and *only* God can be that.(p.535)
• My personal definition, which I submit as applying *only* to myself (although everyone is welcome to it who wants it), includes every waking activity of the human being; to have a creative attitude towards things is a more exact meaning, to live and to deal with other human beings creatively, which to me means seeing the God in them, and respecting and worshipping this God.(p.535)
• This question so insulted the emotions that clearly there was *only* one thing to do, go and get drunk again, and put that enquiring mind in its proper place, which was oblivion.(p.537)
• I bear a few scars on my face from these fights, which I always lost, because the "stick" existed *only* in my mind.(p.537)
• But not for long; now, for five Friday nights in a row, I went to jail, picked up sodden with beer (which I always disliked, but which was the *only* drink available); in jail five consecutive Friday nights in the town where I had grown up, where I had been an honor student in high school, where a kindly uncle, bailing me out, said, "Bob, our family just doesn't do this sort of thing."(p.539)
• I had even borrowed money from her, over her protest: "Bob, please don't ask me to lend you money -- you're the *only* one who hasn't."(p.540)
• I had no money -- well, maybe a dime -- and *only* the clothes I stood in.(p.540)
• I have seen that there is *only* one law, the law of love, and there are *only* two sins; the first is to interfere with the growth of another human being, and the second is to interfere with one's own growth.(p.542)
• I don't care too much about personal fame or glory, and I want *only* enough money to enable me to do the work I feel I can perhaps do best.(p.542)
• At fifty-four, I have had come true for me the old wish, "If *only* I could live my life over, knowing what I know."(p.543)
• I am an *only* child, and when I was seven years old my parents separated very abruptly.(p.544)
• I thought that life was a pretty simple thing; you simply made a plan for your life, based upon what you wanted, and then you needed *only* the courage to go after it.(p.545)
• The *only* kind of security I knew anything about at that time was material security and I decided that all these intruders would vanish immediately if I *only* had a lot of money.(p.545)
• The *only* thing this changed, however, was my surroundings, and it was soon apparent that I could have the same uncomfortable emotions with an unlimited checking account that I could on a

working girl's salary.(p.545)
• The ***only*** importance in all of this lies in the fact that at twenty-three I was just as sick as I was at thirty three, when I came into A.A., but at that time I apparently had no place to go because I had no drinking problem.(p.546)
• It seems ***only*** fitting that when I did finally fall in love it was with an alcoholic, and for the next ten years I progressed as rapidly as is humanly possible into what I believed to be hopeless alcoholism.(p.547)
• I was immersed in self-pity and resentment, and the ***only*** people who would support this attitude or who I felt understood me at all were the people I met in bars and the ones who drank as I did.(p.547)
• The ***only*** way existence was possible was through rationalizing every sober moment and drinking myself into complete oblivion as often as I could.(p.547)
• The ***only*** reality I was able to face had been forced upon me by its very repetition – I had to drink; and I didn't know there was anything in the world that could be done about it.(p.548)
• I was the ***only*** person I'd ever known personally who had ever been in jail, and I guess it is most significant that the second time was less humiliating that the first had been.(p.549)
• One of the truly great things A.A. has taught me is that reality too has two sides; I had ***only*** known the grim side before the program, but now I had a chance to learn about the pleasant side as well.(p.550)
• The A.A. members who sponsored me told me in the beginning that I would not ***only*** find a way to live without having a drink, but that I would find a way to live without wanting to drink, if I would do these simple things.(p.550)
• I had ***only*** to reflect on the contrast between the plans I made so many years ago for my life with what really happened to know I couldn't manage my life drunk or sober.(p.550)
• For the ***only*** problems I have now are those I create when I break out in a rash of self-will.(p.551)
• Even when you don't really want it for them, and your prayers are ***only*** words and you don't mean it, go ahead and do it anyway.(p.552)
• As another great man says, "The ***only*** real freedom a human being can ever know is doing what you ought to do because you want to do it."(p.553)
• When I had been in A.A. ***only*** a short while, an oldtimer told me something that has affected my life ever since.(p.554)
• I was raised in Kansas, the ***only*** child of loving parents who just drank socially.(p.554)
• Three -- The ***only*** requirement for A.A. membership is a desire to stop drinking.(p.564)
• He can ***only*** be defeated by an attitude of intolerance or belligerent denial.(p.570)

onslaught
• In an attempt to get over that feeling, there was a quick ***onslaught*** of a greater number of drinks, and then all was lost.(p.346)

onto
• I used to put eight or twelve ounce bottles of alcohol in a fur lined glove and toss it ***onto*** the back airing porch when winter days got dark enough.(p.176)
• We shook hands, and he hung ***onto*** my hand for a moment and said, "Tell you what I'll do for old times sake.(p.201)
• They suffered from my conduct without saying anything, but the reason for this was I still managed to hang ***onto*** a very substantial practice.(p.215)
• But for some reason – she just didn't know why -- she just had to hold ***onto*** that clipping, with its thin hope.(p.367)
• My eyes opened ***onto*** a hazy world.(p.422)
• At Great Lakes Boot Camp I latched ***onto*** a soft billet.(p.425)
• I tumble out of bed ***onto*** my knees.(p.504)
• I found myself being lifted ***onto*** a stretcher and whisked away in an ambulance to a strange hospital.(p.558)

open
• Again I swayed dizzily before an ***open*** window, or the medicine cabinet where there was poison, cursing myself for a weakling.(p.6)
• It is ***open,*** we believe, to all men.(p.46)
• Faced with alcoholic destruction, we soon became as ***open*** minded on spiritual matters as we tried to be on other questions.(p.48)
• Why lay ourselves ***open*** to being branded fanatics or religious bores?(p.77)
• If our manner is calm, frank, and ***open,*** we will be gratified with the result.(p.78)
• And as I fumed helplessly and planned to get good and drunk and show them, my eye caught a sentence in the book lying ***open*** on my bed: "We cannot live with anger."(p.228)
• Had he come two or three days later I think I would have thrown him out, but he hit when I was ***open*** for anything.(p.239)
• I welcomed him with ***open*** arms.(p.263)
• As time went on, I found that it was customary to ***open*** a few bottles whenever visitors dropped in.(p.297)
• I screamed on the telephone for my mother to get up there; something was going to happen; I didn't know what, but if she didn't get there quick, I'd split wide ***open.***(p.338)
• I went to closed meetings and ***open*** meetings.(p.340)
• Why don't you go home and get the Big Book and ***open*** it at page fifty-eight and see what it says?"(p.349)
• I had no trouble making the right decision when I saw my wife ***open*** her purse at the meeting that night and deposit a cute little angel in the middle of my birthday cake.(p.366)
• The Twelve Steps, which to me are a spiritual way of living, soon meant honest thinking, not wishful thinking, ***open*** mindedness, a willingness to try and a faith to accept.(p.381)
• At age twenty-one, I enlisted in the Navy for two reasons: (1) to avoid being drafted into the Army, and (2) out of a burst of patriotic fervor inspired by the advent of World War II and as the result of an all-night drinking binge which found me sitting on the doorstep of the Navy recruiting office when the chief petty officer arrived to ***open*** for business at nine o'clock Monday morning.(p.398)
• He asked me if I had any spiritual belief, and when I said No, he suggested that I keep an ***open*** mind.(p.413)
• I came to A.A. simply because there were no other doors of help ***open*** to me in my hometown.(p.420)
• We broke ***open*** a window and got inside.(p.424)
• I don't know why I didn't fall out of the ***open*** cockpit of some of those planes I flew in while taking aerial pictures.(p.426)
• We do this by going to many A.A. meetings with an ***open*** mind and a desire to live the good-feeling life without chemicals -- liquid or otherwise.(p.459)
• You hit the street about ten minutes to eight, and you walk around the block, God knows how many times, waiting for that joint to ***open.***(p.514)
• It was their ***open*** night meeting, but of course I thought they were all alcoholics; I couldn't imagine why anybody else would want to go there, and my first reaction was, well, I've come to something that's not for me.(p.524)
• If you give us a try, you will see that we are really human beings, and we will welcome you with ***open*** arms and hearts.(p.529)
• A.A. led me gently from this fantasizing to embrace reality with ***open*** arms.(p.561)
• Willingness, honesty and ***open*** mindedness are the essentials of recovery.(p.570)

open-mindedness
• They said if you want to know how this program works, take the first word of your question – the H is for honesty, the O is for ***open-mindedness*** and the W is for willingness; these our Book calls the essentials of recovery.(p.550)

opened
• The door ***opened*** and he stood there, fresh-skinned and glowing.(p.9)
• If he ***opened*** that old affair, he was afraid it would destroy the reputation of his partner, disgrace his family and take away his means of livelihood.(p.80)
• Time after time, this apparent calamity has been a boon to us, for it ***opened*** up a path which led to the discovery of God.(p.116)
• Another time, as I ***opened*** a letter which lay on my desk, a newspaper clipping fell out.(p.136)
• Down the lobby a door ***opened*** into an attractive bar.(p.154)
• When those two years were up, I ***opened*** an office downtown.(p.174)
• Three years later, at twenty-five, I ***opened*** and operated their Philadelphia office and was earning more than I ever have since.(p.242)
• They ***opened*** with a little prayer, and I thought it was very fine that we stood, all of us together, and closed with the Lord's Prayer.(p.270)
• Whole new vistas were ***opened*** and life began to take on color and interest.(p.311)
• I entered the house, ***opened*** a new bottle of whiskey and sat down to drink myself into the right frame of mind to get in my car, start the motor and close the garage door behind me.(p.363)
• That night she too had new hope because I had made sure she would know what I was doing about my drinking by packing every bit of A.A. literature I could put my hands on right on top so she couldn't help but see it when she ***opened*** my bag.(p.364)
• I had just raised the bottle to my lips when my wife ***opened*** the door and froze me completely in my tracks with "Happy New Year, dear."(p.365)
• My eyes ***opened*** onto a hazy world.(p.422)
• I ***opened*** my eyes again and a shadow fell across the bed.(p.422)
• The boys at the Post Office used to bring me my jugs; mail couldn't be ***opened*** for inspection at the gate.(p.426)
• When my mother ***opened*** the door, I almost fell in on my face.(p.510)
• But when she began a prison sentence, a door ***opened.***(p.526)

opening
• I was ***opening*** up these lots that I spoke of.(p.195)
• With these new and enlightening doors ***opening*** up to me, I was able to make the eventual decision to stop drinking, a day at a time -- because I, too, was an alcoholic.(p.355)
• I didn't realize I would find so much more, but a new and different outlook on life started ***opening*** up almost immediately.(p.383)

openly
• Of course he would have dinner, and then I could drink ***openly*** with him.(p.9)
• Lying on the divan, "getting in the mood" to write, I cried ***openly*** or inwardly, as I listened to sad songs.(p.332)
• But when we come into A.A., we can face our problem honestly and ***openly.***(p.340)

operated
• Three years later, at twenty-five, I opened and ***operated*** their Philadelphia office and was earning more than I ever have since.(p.242)
• I was sitting in my office one time after I had ***operated*** on a woman.(p.350)
• An ailment developed in one of my eyes, and I was transferred back to Sing Sing and ***operated*** upon.(p.509)

operation
• It was a long four or five hour ***operation,*** a large surgical procedure, and she was on her ninth or tenth post-operative day.(p.350)
• It was strictly a one man ***operation*** and I knew I had to tend to my knitting to make a go of it.(p.360)

operations
• Once again I was back in the big time ***operations,*** and along with them, big shot complexes.(p.361)

operative
• If a sufficiently strong reason – ill health, falling in love, change of environment, or the warning of a doctor -- becomes ***operative,*** this man can also stop or moderate, although he may find it difficult and troublesome and may even need medical attention.(p.21)

operator
• My wife traveled with me, but with a baby coming I decided to settle in a large city where I got a job with a commission agent which is a polite term for a handbook ***operator.***(p.251)

opined
• How hurt I was when editors bounced back my ideas quickly and my best friends ***opined*** that my output needed a lot of rewriting.(p.331)

opinion
• The section called "The Doctor's ***Opinion***" has been kept intact, just as it was originally written in 1939 by the late Dr. William D. Silkworth, our Society's great medical benefactor.(p.xi)
• THE DOCTOR'S ***OPINION***(p.xxiii)
• As laymen, our ***opinion*** as to its soundness may, of course, mean little.(p.xxiv)
• Much has been written pro and con, but among physicians, the general ***opinion*** seems to be that most chronic alcoholics are doomed.(p.xxviii)
• Doubtless you are curious to discover how and why, in the face of expert ***opinion*** to the contrary, we have recovered from a hopeless condition of mind and body.(p.20)
• That was a great physician's ***opinion.***(p.26)
• One of these men, staff member of a world-renowned hospital, recently made this statement to some of us: "What you say about the general hopelessness of the average alcoholic's plight is, in my ***opinion,*** correct.(p.43)
• Small wonder many in the medical profession have a low ***opinion*** of alcoholics and their chance for recovery!(p.73)
• We do not mean that you have to agree with your husband whenever there is an honest difference of ***opinion.***(p.117)

• We, who have collectively seen a great deal of business life, at least from the alcoholic angle, had to smile at this gentleman's sincere ***opinion***.(p.149)
• "Who is convinced against his will is of the same ***opinion*** still."(p.193)
• To the new man I would also like to say that this program is not for sissies for, in my humble ***opinion***, it takes a man to make the grade.(p.367)
• If I were asked what in my ***opinion*** was the most important factor in being successful in this program, besides following the Twelve Steps, I would say Honesty.(p.367)
• The next day, Max called the neurologist and told him about the Mayo psychiatrist's ***opinion***.(p.445)
• I wish we did not have to have jails; I wish everyone could be in A.A., and if everyone were there would be no need for jails, in my ***opinion***.(p.542)
• They suggested that I study the A.A. book and try to take the Twelve Steps according to the explanation in the Book, for it was their ***opinion*** that the application of these principles in our daily lives will get us sober and keep us sober.(p.550)
• Ten – Alcoholics Anonymous has no ***opinion*** on outside issues; hence the A.A. name ought never be drawn into public controversy.(p.564)
• 10. – No A.A. group or member should ever, in such a way as to implicate A.A., express any ***opinion*** on outside controversial issues – particularly those of politics, alcohol reform, or sectarian religion.(p.567)

opinions

• Most of us sense that real tolerance of other people's shortcomings and viewpoints and a respect for their ***opinions*** are attitudes which make us more useful to others.(p.19)
• ***Opinions*** vary considerably as to why the alcoholic reacts differently from normal people.(p.22)
• Here we find human ***opinions*** running to extremes - - absurd extremes, perhaps.(p.68)
• Whether you are a hard drinker, a moderated drinker or a teetotaler, you may have some pretty strong ***opinions***, perhaps prejudices.(p.139)
• My ***opinions*** were quoted in Time and Newsweek with pictures, and I addressed the public by radio and television.(p.435)

opportunities

• I thought of what liquor had done to me, the ***opportunities*** that I had discarded, the abilities that had been given me and how I had wasted them, and I finally came to the conclusion, that if I didn't want to quit, I certainly ought to want to, and that I was willing to do anything in the world to stop drinking.(p.186)
• I can remember occasions when friends recommended me for positions or business ***opportunities*** that I wouldn't take because I felt that at some future date I'd get drunk and they would be hurt.(p.198)
• Despite great ***opportunities***, alcohol nearly ended her life.(p.222)
• The ambition to succeed was instilled in me by my Scandinavian parents who came to this country where ***opportunities*** were so great.(p.373)

opportunity

• Then I got a promising business ***opportunity***.(p.5)
• Many could recover if they had the ***opportunity*** we have enjoyed.(p.19)
• If that is so, this step may be postponed, only however, if we hold ourselves in complete readiness to go through with it at the first ***opportunity***.(p.74)
• We may kill a future ***opportunity*** to carry a beneficial message.(p.77)
• You may spoil a later ***opportunity***.(p.90)
• To spend too much time on any one situation is to deny some other alcoholic an ***opportunity*** to live and be happy.(p.96)
• Avoid then, the deliberate manufacture of misery, but if trouble comes, cheerfully capitalize it as an ***opportunity*** to demonstrate His omnipotence.(p.133)
• One of the many doctors who had the ***opportunity*** of reading this book in manuscript form told us that the use of sweets was often helpful, of course depending upon a doctor's advice.(p.133)
• This seemed to me like an ***opportunity*** to be helpful, so I spent two hours talking about alcoholism, the malady, and described the symptoms and results as well as I could.(p.138)
• Why not at least afford him an ***opportunity*** to hear my story?(p.138)
• They often jeopardize their own positions by trying to help serious drinkers who should have been fired long ago, or else given an ***opportunity*** to get well.(p.147)
• When a few men in this city have found themselves, and have discovered the joy of helping others to face life again, there will be no stopping until everyone in that town has had his ***opportunity*** to recover – if he can and will.(p.163)
• When I was sixteen years old, my mother remarried and I was given the ***opportunity*** of going back to school.(p.193)
• Many friends of my family had emigrated to America, so at twenty-four I decided that the United States offered me the ***opportunity*** I was never likely to find in my native land.(p.231)
• In the Army, I became a periodic alcoholic – the periods always coming whenever I could make the ***opportunity***.(p.241)
• What an ***opportunity*** I shot to pieces there!(p.242)
• At our weekly meeting I was a menace to serenity those first few months, for I took every ***opportunity*** to lambaste the "spiritual angle" as we called it, or anything else that had any tinge of theology.(p.246)
• We can share in the laughter and tears of our many friends, and most important, we can share our A.A. way of life and are given a daily ***opportunity*** to help others.(p.249)
• Long before I had any real ***opportunity*** to give, I had to learn the equally important lesson of receiving graciously.(p.281)
• I remained with them for three weeks, using part of the time in making many amends, which I had had no earlier ***opportunity*** of making.(p.281)
• Seven years of work in this field brought an ***opportunity*** to affiliate myself actively with one of my clients, a fellow A.A.(p.284)
• Instead of wanting to escape some perplexing problem, we experience a thrill of challenge in the ***opportunity*** it affords for another application of A.A. techniques, and we find ourselves tackling it with surprising vigor.(p.311)
• So I went to her and said, "There's only one thing I want in my whole life, and I don't want any commendation; I don't want any credit; I don't want anything from you or Janey for the rest of your life except one thing; and that is, the ***opportunity*** to do anything you want always, and I would like to start off by doing the dishes."(p.351)
• In January 1938, I had the ***opportunity*** to go to northern Vermont to manage a small daytime radio station that was up against it financially, and was about to fold its antenna.(p.359)
• The challenge intrigued me; also it was another ***opportunity*** to run away from myself and the "fast life of the big city."(p.359)
• At this time, however, she had an ***opportunity*** to go to Salt Lake City on a new project for the government, but she did promise me that if I would curtail my drinking and buckle down to hard work she would give serious consideration to my latest proposal and maybe join me at a later date when I got settled.(p.359)
• In 1940 another good ***opportunity*** came up and we moved to Pittsburgh where I was to manage two radio stations under the same ownership.(p.361)
• Slowly, my life seemed to unfold before me, shedding insights on childhood resentments, jealousies, and fears that had mushroomed in adulthood, and also on the self-pity that I had wallowed in at every ***opportunity***.(p.371)
• They told me to go to meetings, and I still do at every available ***opportunity***, whether I am at home or in some other city.(p.381)
• Today I think of life in terms of happiness, contentment, freedom from fear and despair, sane thinking, ability to face problems as they occur, the ***opportunity*** to help other alcoholics and to be decent.(p.430)
• A.A. has given me serenity of purpose, the ***opportunity*** to be of service to God and to the people about me, and I am serene in the infallibility of these principles that provide the fulfillment of my purpose.(p.551)
• I suspect that if it is wisely handled – and it seems to be in wise and prudent hands – there are doors of ***opportunity*** ahead of this project that may surpass our capacities to imagine."(p.574)

oppose

• We are not allied with any particular faith, sect or denomination, nor do we ***oppose*** anyone.(p.xiv)
• The Alcoholics Anonymous groups ***oppose*** no one.(p.567)

opposed

• This was no fault of my father or mother, as they were both very much ***opposed*** to drinking.(p.182)
• Then I went on my first week-long bender of solitary drinking, locked up in a hotel room, because my family ***opposed*** my coming marriage.(p.464)

opposite

• On our grudge list we set ***opposite*** each name our injuries.(p.65)
• Successful readjustment means the ***opposite***.(p.122)
• The ***opposite*** may happen should the family condemn and criticize.(p.129)
• They, too, had taken a train to one town and had wakened hundreds of miles in the ***opposite*** direction, never knowing how they got there.(p.246)
• Honesty is the easiest word for me to understand because it is the exact ***opposite*** of what I've been doing all my life.(p.482)
• About then too, I realized that my point of view on the ***opposite*** sex wasn't entirely like that of most of the boys I knew.(p.484)

optimism

• But, as it was with drinking, this project will be entered into with enthusiasm and ***optimism*** – and probably wind up the same way, depressed.(p.396)
• I depended on ***optimism*** and ambition to live in society; when I began to tire, I had to depend on chemicals instead to keep going.(p.420)

option

• The exercise of an ***option*** brought in more money, leaving us with a profit of several thousand dollars for that year.(p.3)
• At that particular stage, I lost interest in it, sold the ***option*** for $5,000 and forgot the whole deal.(p.198)

optional

• The wording was, of course, quite ***optional*** so long as we expressed the idea, voicing it without reservation.(p.63)

optioned

• I ***optioned*** a piece of land just off East Market Street to put up a three-hundred suite apartment.(p.198)

oral

• That's the stuff used when the ***oral*** surgeon puts the needle in your vein and says, "Count to ten," and before you get to two, you're asleep.(p.442)

orchestra

• I was one of the star singers in the choir and one of the leading violins in the ***orchestra***.(p.517)

orchid

• You didn't carry a little ***orchid*** up the aisle in those days; you carried a great big bouquet, like a funeral spray, and you didn't have your picture taken until just before you went to the church.(p.385)

ordained

• Though we have no religious connection, we may still do well to talk with someone ***ordained*** by an established religion.(p.74)

ordeal

• In most cases, the alcoholic survived this ***ordeal*** without relapse, but not always.(p.125)
• Evenings at home were an ***ordeal***.(p.299)

order

• He suddenly realized that in ***order*** to save himself he must carry his message to another alcoholic.(p.xvi)
• Belief in the power of God, plus enough willingness, honesty and humility to establish and maintain the new ***order*** of things, were the essential requirements.(p.13)
• Many of us exclaimed, "What an ***order***!(p.60)
• At the moment we are trying to put our lives in ***order***.(p.77)
• She went to court and got an ***order*** for his arrest.(p.79)
• The answers will come, if your own house is in ***order***.(p.164)
• My phobia for sleeplessness demanded that I get drunk every night, but in ***order*** to get more liquor for the next night, I had to stay sober during the day, at least up to four o'clock.(p.177)
• I didn't even know what a martini looked like, but I had heard a man down the bar ***order*** one.(p.194)
• And I continued to drink, on and off then, until every dollar I had in the world was gone again and I was right back living at my sister's, getting my cigarettes by calling her grocer and telling him to put in a couple of cartons with her ***order***, exactly as I had before I started to work at Max's.(p.202)
• He walked to the hospital to save bus fare and did it gladly in ***order*** to be helpful to an individual he had never even seen.(p.208)
• I'd been sitting comfortably in a restaurant with Rita, drinking my sixth martini and hoping the waiter would forget about the lunch ***order*** -- at least long enough for me to have a couple more.(p.223)
• In the spring of 1917, in ***order*** to beat being fired from school, I became "patriotic" and joined the Army.(p.241)
• The next steps were bottle hiding, and excuses for trips in ***order*** to drink without restraint.(p.375)
• I lived in New Orleans where, at that time, cocktail parties, dances and night spots were almost the ***order*** of the day -- or rather the night.(p.384)

• Drunkalogues and statistics can be boring, but it is necessary to delve a little into each in ***order*** to come up with some kind of rough estimate.(p.396)

• I would have three quick strong ones in ***order*** to endure the evening.(p.407)

• I had begun to drink in the early years of pharmacy school, in ***order*** to get to sleep.(p.440)

• In the garage, I would put the needle in my vein and then try to figure out exactly how much medication to inject to overcome the pep pills while adding to the sleeping pills while ignoring the tranquilizers, in ***order*** to get just enough to be able to pull out the needle, jerk the tourniquet, throw it in the car, slam the car door shut, run down the hall, and fall in bed before I fell asleep.(p.442)

• Giving up alcohol alone was not enough for me; I've had to give up all mood-and mind-affecting chemicals in ***order*** to stay sober and comfortable.(p.443)

• The people of A.A. had something that looked much better than what I had, but I was afraid to let go of what I had in ***order*** to try something new; there was a certain sense of security in the familiar.(p.448)

• Father, through the years, had built up a very good mail ***order*** business because, at that time, there wasn't too much money in medicine.(p.485)

• I had my own medical practice in Washington at that time, but the practice slackened and the mail ***order*** business started to fall off.(p.486)

• Am I willing to be honest with myself about myself and tell someone about myself, and am I willing to think of other people, of their needs instead of myself, in ***order*** to get rid of the drink problem?(p.503)

• Instead of drinking in fancy bars and clubs, I had to carry a bottle of vodka in my briefcase, duck into public toilets, and gulp from the bottle, trembling, in ***order*** to keep from falling apart.(p.557)

• Though it was not our intention to create such an impression, many alcoholics have nevertheless concluded that in ***order*** to recover they must acquire an immediate and overwhelming "God-consciousness" followed at once by a vast change in feeling and outlook.(p.569)

ordered

• I sat down at a table and ***ordered*** a sandwich and a glass of milk.(p.36)

• I ***ordered*** another sandwich and decided to have another glass of milk.(p.36)

• I ***ordered*** a whiskey and poured it into the milk.(p.36)

• The experiment went so well that I ***ordered*** another whiskey and poured it into more milk.(p.36)

• I ***ordered*** a cocktail and my meal.(p.41)

• Then I ***ordered*** another cocktail.(p.41)

• After prescribing medicines, Dr. Bob ***ordered***, "Put him in a private room.(p.188)

• I ***ordered*** a martini, extra dry.(p.194)

• We ***ordered*** sandwiches and one man said, "Three beers."(p.247)

• Then it was my turn -- I ***ordered*** "Three beers," but this time it was different, I had a cash investment of thirty cents and, on a ten dollar a week salary, that's a big thing.(p.247)

• I was given every advantage in a well ***ordered*** home.(p.304)

• Only, having found them, I threw them away, and ***ordered*** another extra dry martini.(p.533)

• To wear expensive clothes, to have bartenders know what to serve me before I ***ordered***, to be recognized by headwaiters and shown to the best table, to play gin rummy for high stakes with the insouciance of a riverboat gambler -- these were the enduring values in life, I thought.(p.556)

orders

• I got ***orders*** to go to Vietnam, and I spent most of the year over there either drunk or sick with a hangover.(p.317)

• I got ***orders*** to go to Germany, and everyone in Germany was against me.(p.318)

• Much of my time was spent writing letters, notes, ***orders***, and lists of things for Max, who was also my office nurse, to do to keep the world running while I was locked up.(p.445)

• I visit a friend who is awaiting ***orders***.(p.499)

ordinary

• Many types do not respond to the ***ordinary*** psychological approach.(p.xxvii)

• For the type of alcoholic who is able and willing to get well, little charity, in the ***ordinary*** sense of the word, is needed or wanted.(p.97)

• That includes bars, nightclubs, dances, receptions, weddings, even plain ***ordinary*** whoopee parties.(p.101)

• This is a condition which, in ***ordinary*** life, would produce untold grief; there might be scandalous gossip, laughter at the expense of other people, and a tendency to take advantage of intimate information.(p.125)

• But at least he will understand the problem and will no longer be misled by ***ordinary*** promises.(p.148)

• My job was to make out the guard schedules and thus I was exempt from ***ordinary*** recruit training activities.(p.425)

• When I came home to ***ordinary*** garrison life in England, I found that I was drinking rather more than most people of my age.(p.518)

• Then I was sent out to India and from then on drinking just increased and increased, and I started having two or three day spells instead of just the ***ordinary*** concentrated one day.(p.519)

• I had been using paraldehyde more or less like ***ordinary*** drink for the last six years though, occasionally, I'd bounce back to phenobarbital and things like that.(p.524)

• I thought that if these kind of ***ordinary*** people can do it, a man of my brains ought to find it much more easy, and I joined.(p.524)

organ

• Finally, he was drinking to keep away those little men, and those strange voices, and the ***organ*** music that came out of the walls.(p.512)

• I was drinking to keep away the shakes, drinking to keep away those little men and those strange voices and the ***organ*** music that comes out of the walls.(p.514)

organically

• I heard for the first time an expression which I was to grow to loathe: "There is nothing ***organically*** wrong."(p.276)

organization

• We are not an ***organization*** in the conventional sense of the word.(p.xiii)

• There was to be the least possible ***organization***, even in our service centers.(p.xix)

• Alcoholics Anonymous is not a religious ***organization***.(p.xx)

• A look at the alcoholic in your ***organization*** is many times illuminating.(p.139)

• If your ***organization*** is a large one, your junior executives might be provided with this book.(p.147)

• You might let them know you have no quarrel with the alcoholics of your ***organization***.(p.147)

• Alcoholism may be causing your ***organization*** considerable damage in its waste of time, men and reputation.(p.148)

• He might be shocked if he knew how much alcoholism is costing his ***organization*** a year.(p.149)

• Even if you feel your ***organization*** has no alcoholic problem, it might pay to take another look down the line.(p.149)

• It was finally decided to undertake the ***organization*** of a Cleveland group and toward the end of May, 1939, the first meeting was held in Cleveland in my home.(p.219)

• I'd go into an ***organization***, and it wasn't long before I was on the committee, then I was chairman of the committee; and if I was in a group, I'd soon be treasurer or secretary of the group.(p.339)

• We have here in this community an ***organization*** which helps people, and this ***organization*** is known as Alcoholics Anonymous.(p.348)

• However, I've heard of an ***organization*** called Alcoholics Anonymous that has had some success with people like you.(p.436)

• "That's a devil of a way to run an ***organization***," I thought, and I reported Frank to the psychiatrist, who didn't seem perturbed; he just got someone else to take me on Fridays.(p.447)

• 9. -- Each A.A. group needs the least possible ***organization***.(p.567)

• Dr. Foster Kennedy, neurologist: "This ***organization*** of Alcoholics Anonymous calls on two of the greatest reservoirs of power known to man, religion and that instinct for association with one's fellows . . . the 'herd instinct.'(p.571)

organizations

• I became one of the most active women in the community, what with P.T.A., other community ***organizations*** and drives.(p.339)

organized

• We, who have traveled this dubious path, beg you to lay aside prejudice, even against ***organized*** religion.(p.49)

• Tuesday I started in the morning, getting well ***organized*** by noon.(p.179)

• Nine -- A.A., as such, ought never be ***organized***; but we may create service boards or committees directly responsible to those they serve.(p.564)

organizers

• I had been obliged to discharge him for drinking, though he was brilliant, alert, and one of the best ***organizers*** I have ever known.(p.137)

original

• Since the ***original*** Foreword to this book was written in 1939, a wholesale miracle has taken place.(p.xv)

• About half our ***original*** fellowship were of exactly that type.(p.44)

• He brought in many of our ***original*** members, yet he himself could not make it and died of alcoholism.(p.239)

• A few months after I made my ***original*** trip to Akron I was feeling pretty cocky, and I didn't think my wife was treating me with proper respect, now that I was an outstanding citizen.(p.293)

• In the summer of 1938, almost a year from the time I made my ***original*** contact with Akron, the man for whom I was working and who knew about the program, approached me and asked if I could do anything about one of his salesmen who was drinking very heavily.(p.294)

• This is a condensed version of the ***original*** "long form" A.A. Traditions as first printed in 1946.(p.563)

originally

• The section called "The Doctor's Opinion" has been kept intact, just as it was ***originally*** written in 1939 by the late Dr. William D. Silkworth, our Society's great medical benefactor.(p.xi)

• This duty together with my weekly meetings with my fellow alcoholics, and my daily renewal of the contract I ***originally*** made with God, have kept me sober when nothing else ever did.(p.237)

originated

• Few people really are, for that means blind faith in the strange proposition that this universe ***originated*** in a cipher and aimlessly rushes nowhere.(p.10)

• Had this power ***originated*** in him?(p.11)

• Were our contentions true, it would follow that life ***originated*** out of nothing, and proceeds nowhere.(p.49)

originator

• An ***originator*** of Cleveland's Group No. 3, this one fought Prohibition in vain.(p.297)

• This physician, the ***originator*** of A.A.'s first black group, but badly caught in the toils, tells of his release and of how freedom came as he worked among his own people.(p.483)

orthodox

• My new friends made fun of God and all the ***orthodox*** beliefs.(p.408)

ostracized

• During all this time we became more or less ***ostracized*** by our friends.(p.177)

OTC

• I had been to ***OTC*** the previous summer so I went into the Army as a sergeant, but I came out a private, and you really have to be unusual to do that.(p.241)

other's

• People have wars and kill each other; they struggle and cut each ***other's*** throats for success and what does anyone get out of it?(p.244)

• In those days we really took each ***other's*** inventories firmly and often.(p.245)

• We had meetings at each ***other's*** homes and, of course, that was a grand place for people to get together out there; they seemed to think so too.(p.270)

others

• Though he could not accept all the tenets of the Oxford Groups, he was convinced of the need for moral inventory, confession of personality defects, restitution to those harmed, helpfulness to ***others***, and the necessity of belief in and dependence upon God.(p.xvi)

• Another reason for the wide acceptance of A.A. was the ministration of friends -- friends in medicine, religion, and the press, together with innumerable ***others*** who became our able and persistent advocates.(p.xx)

• As part of his rehabilitation he commenced to present his conceptions to other alcoholics, impressing upon them that they must do likewise with still ***others***.(p.xxiii)

• This man and over one hundred ***others*** appear to have recovered.(p.xxiii)

• They are restless, irritable and discontented, unless they can again experience the sense of ease and comfort which comes at once by taking a few drinks -- drinks which they see ***others*** taking with impunity.(p.xxvi)

• All these, and many ***others***, have one symptom in common: they cannot start drinking without developing the phenomenon of craving.(p.xxviii)

• Never was I to pray for myself, except as my requests bore on my usefulness to ***others***.(p.13)
• They in turn might work with ***others***.(p.14)
• Particularly was it imperative to work with ***others*** as he had worked with me.(p.14)
• For if an alcoholic failed to perfect and enlarge his spiritual life through work and self-sacrifice for ***others***, he could not survive the certain trials and low spots ahead.(p.14)
• Most of us sense that real tolerance of other people's shortcomings and viewpoints and a respect for their opinions are attitudes which make us more useful to ***others***.(p.19)
• Our very lives, as ex-problem drinkers, depend upon our constant thought of ***others*** and how we may help meet their needs.(p.20)
• But we saw that it really worked in ***others***, and we had come to believe in the hopelessness and futility of life as we had been living it.(p.25)
• To ***others***, the word "God" brought up a particular idea of Him with which someone had tried to impress them during childhood.(p.45)
• ***Others*** came near putting Galileo to death for his astronomical heresies.(p.51)
• When we saw ***others*** solve their problems by a simple reliance upon the Spirit of the Universe, we had to stop doubting the power of God.(p.52)
• When ***others*** showed us that "God-sufficiency" worked with them, we began to feel like those who had insisted the Wrights would never fly.(p.52)
• 9.Made direct amends to such people wherever possible, except when to do so would injure them or ***others***.(p.59)
• To conclude that ***others*** were wrong was as far as most of us ever got.(p.66)
• In that state, the wrong-doing of ***others***, fancied or real, had power to actually kill.(p.66)
• Putting out of our minds the wrongs ***others*** had done, we resolutely looked for our own mistakes.(p.67)
• We realize that some people are as fanatical about sex as ***others*** are loose.(p.70)
• If we are not sorry, and our conduct continues to harm ***others***, we are quite sure to drink.(p.70)
• If sex is very troublesome, we throw ourselves the harder into helping ***others***.(p.70)
• The rule is we must be hard on ourself, but always considerate of ***others***.(p.74)
• Therefore, we are not to be the hasty and foolish martyr who would needlessly sacrifice ***others*** to save himself from the alcoholic pit.(p.79)
• If we have obtained permission, have consulted with ***others***, asked God to help and the drastic step is indicated we must not shrink.(p.80)
• The alcoholic is like a tornado roaring his way through the lives of ***others***.(p.82)
• No matter how far down the scale we have gone, we will see how our experience can benefit ***others***.(p.84)
• Love and tolerance of ***others*** is our code.(p.84)
• Or were we thinking of what we could do for ***others***, of what we could pack into the stream of life?(p.86)
• But we must be careful not to drift into worry, remorse or morbid reflection, for that would diminish our usefulness to ***others***.(p.86)
• We may ask for ourselves, however, if ***others*** will be helped.(p.87)
• WORKING WITH ***OTHERS***(p.89)
• You can secure their confidence when ***others*** fail.(p.89)
• To watch people recover, to see them help ***others***, to watch loneliness vanish, to see a fellowship grow up about you, to have a host of friends – this is an experience you must not miss.(p.89)
• You should be described to him as one of a fellowship who, as part of their own recovery, try to help ***others*** and who will be glad to talk to him if he cares to see you.(p.90)
• He often says that if he had continued to work on them, he might have deprived many ***others***, who have since recovered, of their chance.(p.96)
• Helping ***others*** is the foundation stone of your recovery.(p.97)
• We have seen ***others*** slip when the family came back too soon.(p.100)
• Your job now is to be at the place where you may be of maximum helpfulness to ***others***, so never hesitate to go anywhere if you can be helpful.(p.102)
• But for every man who drinks ***others*** are involved -- the wife who trembles in fear of the next debauch; the mother and father who see their son wasting away.(p.104)
• Both of you will awaken to a new sense of responsibility for ***others***.(p.119)
• Though it is entirely separate from Alcoholics Anonymous, it uses the general principles of the A.A. program as a guide for husbands, wives, relatives, friends, and ***others*** close to alcoholics.(p.121)
• We find the more one member of the family demands that the ***others*** concede to him, the more resentful they become.(p.122)
• Suppose we tell you some of the obstacles a family will meet; suppose we suggest how they may be avoided – even converted to good use for ***others***.(p.123)
• Showing ***others*** who suffer how we were given help is the very thing which makes life seem so worth while to us now.(p.124)
• Cling to the thought that, in God's hands, the dark past is the greatest possession you have -- the key to life and happiness for ***others***.(p.124)
• A man may criticize or laugh at himself and it will affect ***others*** favorably, but criticism or ridicule coming from another often produces the contrary effect.(p.125)
• As each member of a resentful family begins to see his short comings and admits them to the ***others***, he lays a basis for helpful discussion.(p.127)
• But those of us who have tried to shoulder the entire burden and trouble of ***others*** find we are soon overcome by them.(p.132)
• We have recovered, and have been given the power to help ***others***.(p.132)
• The ***others*** must be convinced of his new status beyond the shadow of a doubt.(p.135)
• In some cases it will, and in ***others*** it may not.(p.144)
• Then you will know what it means to give of yourself that ***others*** may survive and rediscover life.(p.153)
• In the chapter "Working With ***Others***" you gathered an idea of how we approach and aid ***others*** to health.(p.153)
• So, you see, there were three alcoholics in that town, who now felt they had to give to ***others*** what they had found, or be sunk.(p.158)
• After several failures to find ***others***, a fourth turned up.(p.158)
• It was transcended by the happiness they found in giving themselves for ***others***.(p.159)
• Being wrecked in the same vessel, being restored and united under one God, with hearts and minds attuned to the welfare of ***others***, the things which matter so much to some people no longer signify much to them.(p.161)
• Arrangements were also made with the chief psychiatrist of a large public hospital to select still ***others*** from the stream of misery which flows through that institution.(p.163)
• When a few men in this city have found themselves, and have discovered the joy of helping ***others*** to face life again, there will be no stopping until everyone in that town has had his opportunity to recover -- if he can and will.(p.163)
• See to it that your relationship with Him is right, and great events will come to pass for you and countless ***others***.(p.164)
• The question which might naturally come into your mind would be: "What did the man do or say that was different from what ***others*** had done or said?"(p.180)
• I spend a great deal of time passing on what I learned to ***others*** who want and need it badly.(p.180)
• He kept the faith; therefore, he and countless ***others*** found a new life.(p.182)
• I noticed that the ***others*** seemed to have such a release, a happiness, a something that I thought a person ought to have.(p.191)
• The next day, ***others*** from the group came in to see me.(p.208)
• Rules were made for ***others***, but not for me.(p.210)
• So far, so good -- all according to plan, like thousands of ***others***.(p.225)
• I get my greatest thrill of accomplishment from the knowledge that I have played a part in the new happiness achieved by countless ***others*** like myself.(p.229)
• Searching where I have been at fault, it is not hard to discover and get right again, for I have proven to myself and to many ***others*** who know me that God can keep a man sober if he will let Him.(p.237)
• When the ***others*** saw my altered attitude they took me back in, but for me they had to make it tough; if they hadn't I don't think I ever would have stuck it out.(p.248)
• We can share in the laughter and tears of our many friends, and most important, we can share our A.A. way of life and are given a daily opportunity to help ***others***.(p.249)
• Today I have Someone who will always hear me; I have a warm fellowship among men who understand my problems; I have tasks to do and am glad to do them, to see ***others*** who are alcoholics and to help them in any way I can to become sober men.(p.260)
• Above all, I have gained the greatest thing accorded to any man, the love and understanding of a gracious God, who has lifted me from the alcoholic scrap-heap to a position of trust where I have been able to reap the rich rewards that come from showing a little love for ***others*** and from serving them as I can.(p.296)
• I definitely liked it, everything about it, the taste, the effects; and I realize now that a drink did something for me or to me that was different from the way it affected ***others***.(p.305)
• ***Others*** may idle in a retrogressive groove without too much danger, but retrogression can spell death for us.(p.311)
• And, unlike many ***others***, I never took a drink in the morning.(p.323)
• It becomes vital, also, that ***others*** not know of our defeats, nor suspect our loss of confidence.(p.331)
• I suppose ***others*** would say, "This is group psychotherapy."(p.352)
• Well, now I'm living it and trying to paint it for ***others***.(p.355)
• Before long I was at the luncheon meeting an hour before the ***others***, that old and familiar trademark of every alcoholic.(p.360)
• I can't bear to be here when you lose the respect of ***others***, and above all -- when you lose your own self respect."(p.362)
• I can't bear to be here when you lose the respect of ***others***, and above all when you lose your own self respect."(p.363)
• But success brought increased social activities and I realized that many of my friends enjoyed a social drink with no apparent harm to themselves or ***others***.(p.374)
• "First Things First": solving our immediate problems before we try to solve all the ***others*** and get muddled in our thinking and doing.(p.382)
• There are so many to whom I feel deeply grateful; to my husband (and best critic), whose generous love, compassion and understanding have helped me along the way; to those before me in A.A. who inspired the first article I read, and the friend who sent that article to Frank; to Ruth for her personal note, and the first A.A. to talk to me; to my Bishop, whose loving and believing spirit inspired me; and to all the members of the Houston Group who were so patient, kind and helpful – and to countless ***others***.(p.393)
• It pays daily in more harmonious relations with my fellow men, in ever clearer insight into the true meaning of life, and in the answering love and gratitude wherever and whenever I have been the instrument of God's will in the lives of ***others***.(p.394)
• (I can't know how much ***others*** of our Fellowship have paid financially and, even more important, mentally and physically.)(p.396)
• ***Others*** have come back, ***others*** I have lost.(p.404)
• She, more than the ***others***, showed me what ailed me basically, why I was immature and insecure.(p.409)
• Through going to meetings and listening, and occasionally speaking, through doing Twelve Step work, whereby in helping ***others*** you are both the teacher and the student, by making many wonderful A.A. friends, I have been taught all the things in life that are worth having.(p.416)
• Prior to our marriage, when she was a shy, scrawny adolescent, I was able to see things in her that ***others*** couldn't necessarily see – things like beauty, charm, gaiety, a gift for being easy to talk to, a sense of humor, and many other fine qualities.(p.450)
• ***Others*** wanted to die.(p.455)
• You may wonder why, since I was having all this trouble, and was having to seek the assistance of ***others***, A.A. hadn't come into the picture.(p.469)
• We can have this new way of life – learning to live with our sickness and to be happy and content -- if we are willing to change our way of thinking and be honest, first with ourselves, then with ***others***.(p.480)
• He has also taught me that I must help myself first; only then may I be able to help ***others***.(p.481)
• But I knew at that point that I couldn't stop and I knew that I was a danger to myself and to ***others***.(p.489)
• It was Charlie and three or four ***others***.(p.495)
• I can hold a lot now, more than the ***others***.(p.499)
• But it takes ***others*** to keep me there.(p.500)
• Then he asks me if I am willing to right all the wrongs I have ever done to anyone, no matter how wrong I thought the ***others*** were.(p.503)
• I begin to see I am not the person I had thought myself, that I had judged myself by comparing myself to ***others***, and always to my own advantage.(p.504)
• Soon I have ***others*** who are alcoholics and some

who have other problems.(p.506)
• I had a rough lot, but I don't worry about that, after hearing the stories of many ***others***.(p.511)
• It has taught me that I can best keep my sobriety by sharing it out with ***others***; that I must bring that sobriety to ***others*** who need it, in my own interest.(p.524)
• There were several ***others***.(p.532)
• To create: Everyone does it, some at the instinct level, ***others*** in the arts.(p.535)
• And with ***others***.(p.561)
• They help ***others*** with similar problems . . .(p.572)
• The Episcopal magazine, The Living Church, observes editorially: "The basis of the technique of Alcoholics Anonymous is the truly Christian principle that a man cannot help himself except by helping ***others***.(p.574)

others'
• Everyone knows about the ***others'*** alcoholic troubles.(p.125)
• As non-denominational people, we cannot make up ***others'*** minds for them.(p.132)

otherwise
• Very earnestly we ask the press also, to observe this request, for ***otherwise*** we shall be greatly handicapped.(p.xiii)
• It explains many things for which we cannot ***otherwise*** account.(p.xxiv)
• If your husband is ***otherwise*** a normal individual, your chances are good at this stage.(p.113)
• It was the first of many such experiences that became the only cause of harsh words, tears and heartaches in an ***otherwise*** truly beautiful marriage.(p.361)
• ***Otherwise*** I got nothing out of it.(p.401)
• And the folks said A.A. was for people who wanted to quit, ***otherwise*** it wouldn't work.(p.429)
• We do this by going to many A.A. meetings with an open mind and a desire to live the good-feeling life without chemicals – liquid or ***otherwise***.(p.459)
• But we may employ alcoholics where they are going to perform those services for which we might ***otherwise*** have to engage nonalcoholics.(p.566)

ought
• It was decided that all members ***ought*** to be anonymous at the level of press, radio, TV and films.(p.xix)
• Of course an alcoholic ***ought*** to be freed from his physical craving for liquor, and this often requires a definite hospital procedure, before psychological measures can be of maximum benefit.(p.xxv)
• He is the fellow who goes to bed so intoxicated he ***ought*** to sleep the clock around.(p.21)
• Sometimes we think fear ***ought*** to be classed with stealing.(p.67)
• We thought he ***ought*** to be willing to do that if necessary, but if he were in jail he could provide nothing for either family.(p.79)
• We feel we ***ought*** to say to her that we have no right to involve another person.(p.81)
• We ***ought*** to sit down with the family and frankly analyze the past as we now see it, being very careful not to criticize them.(p.83)
• Unless one's family expresses a desire to live upon spiritual principles we think we ***ought*** not to urge them.(p.83)
• You will thus get a better idea of how you ***ought*** to proceed.(p.91)
• We feel that each family, in the light of their own circumstances, ***ought*** to decide for themselves.(p.103)
• You think he ***ought*** to know the subject better, as everyone should have a clear understanding of the risk he takes if he drinks too much.(p.112)
• You, as well as your husband, ***ought*** to think of what you can put into life instead of how much you can take out.(p.120)
• The head of the house ***ought*** to remember that he is mainly to blame for what befell his home.(p.127)
• We have come to believe He would like us to keep our heads in the clouds with Him, but that our feet ***ought*** to be firmly planted on earth.(p.130)
• At the very beginning, the couple ***ought*** to frankly face the fact that each will have to yield here and there if the family is going to play an effective part in the new life.(p.131)
• His present views ***ought*** to prove exceptionally useful to business men everywhere.(p.136)
• But if you cannot or will not stop drinking, I think you ***ought*** to resign."(p.148)
• "God ***ought*** to be able to do anything."(p.158)
• I thought of what liquor had done to me, the opportunities that I had discarded, the abilities that had been given me and how I had wasted them, and I finally came to the conclusion, that if I didn't want to quit, I certainly ***ought*** to want to, and that I was willing to do anything in the world to stop drinking.(p.186)
• I noticed that the others seemed to have such a release, a happiness, a something that I thought a person ***ought*** to have.(p.191)
• It's only natural that we don't have the capacity to change, but we ***ought*** not to criticize those who have, There's another thing I would stress.(p.273)
• Well, I wasn't sure I did, and it was awful foggy, and I wept and asked her what she thought I ***ought*** to do about it.(p.273)
• He might have handed me fifty dollars and said that I ***ought*** to pull myself together and make a new start.(p.278)
• So I located a house, and I thought we ***ought*** to move into it immediately, but Frank was horrified, because he never knew what was going to happen to me.(p.388)
• The people there insisted on putting me in a ward, when Max and I both knew I ***ought*** to have a private room.(p.445)
• I can tell her she ***ought*** not to think a certain way, but I certainly can't take away her right to feel however she does feel.(p.451)
• I thought that if these kind of ordinary people can do it, a man of my brains ***ought*** to find it much more easy, and I joined.(p.524)
• And having sung that phrase, I'd chuckle with amusement, turning into irony turning into self-contempt turning into self-pity, at the sad fate of Bob, that wonderful, poor little motherless boy who was so smart in school and who grew up to accept responsibility so early and so fast and who staggered under his burdens without a whimper until the time came when he thought he was too good for this world and so he ***ought*** to be out of it.(p.532)
• As another great man says, "The only real freedom a human being can ever know is doing what you ***ought*** to do because you want to do it."(p.553)
• Six -- An A.A. group ***ought*** never endorse, finance or lend the A.A. name to any related facility or outside enterprise, lest problems of money, property and prestige divert us from our primary purpose.(p.564)
• Seven – Every A.A. group ***ought*** to be fully self-supporting, declining outside contributions.(p.564)
• Nine – A.A., as such, ***ought*** never be organized; but we may create service boards or committees directly responsible to those they serve.(p.564)
• Ten – Alcoholics Anonymous has no opinion on outside issues; hence the A.A. name ***ought*** never be drawn into public controversy.(p.564)
• 3. -- Our membership ***ought*** to include all who suffer from alcoholism.(p.565)
• Nor ***ought*** A.A. membership ever depend upon money or conformity.(p.565)
• But when its plans concern the welfare of neighboring groups also, those groups ***ought*** to be consulted.(p.565)
• 5. – Each Alcoholics Anonymous group ***ought*** to be a spiritual entity having but one primary purpose -- that of carrying its message to the alcoholic who still suffers.(p.565)
• Secondary aids to A.A., such as clubs or hospitals which require much property or administration, ***ought*** to be incorporated and so set apart that, if necessary, they can be freely discarded by the groups.(p.566)
• Hence such facilities ***ought*** not to use the A.A. name.(p.566)
• But hospitals, as well as other places of recuperation, ***ought*** to be well outside A.A. – and medically supervised.(p.566)
• While an A.A. group may cooperate with anyone, such cooperation ***ought*** never go so far as affiliation or endorsement, actual or implied.(p.566)
• 7. – The A.A. groups themselves ***ought*** to be fully supported by the voluntary contributions of their own members.(p.566)
• We think A.A. ***ought*** to avoid sensational advertising.(p.567)
• Our names and pictures as A.A. members ***ought*** not be broadcast, filmed, or publicly printed.(p.567)

ounce
• "Suddenly the thought crossed my mind that if I were to put an ***ounce*** of whiskey in my milk it couldn't hurt me on a full stomach.(p.36)
• Like a gaunt prospector, belt drawn in over the last ***ounce*** of food, our pick struck gold.(p.128)
• I used to put eight or twelve ***ounce*** bottles of alcohol in a fur lined glove and toss it onto the back airing porch when winter days got dark enough.(p.176)
• I used also to put it up in four ***ounce*** bottles and stick several in my stocking tops.(p.177)

ounces
• I had taken five and a half ***ounces*** of paraldehyde.(p.207)

our
• Because this book has become the basic text for ***our*** Society and has helped such large numbers of alcoholic men and women to recover, there exists a sentiment against any radical changes being made in it.(p.xi)
• The section called "The Doctor's Opinion" has been kept intact, just as it was originally written in 1939 by the late Dr. William D. Silkworth, ***our*** Society's great medical benefactor.(p.xi)
• We think this account of ***our*** experiences will help everyone to better understand the alcoholic.(p.xiii)
• And besides, we are sure that ***our*** way of living has its advantages for all.(p.xiii)
• Being mostly business or professional folk, we could not well carry on ***our*** occupations in such an event.(p.xiii)
• We would like it understood that ***our*** alcoholic work is an avocation.(p.xiii)
• When writing or speaking publicly about alcoholism, we urge each of ***our*** Fellowship to omit his personal name, designating himself instead as "a member of Alcoholics Anonymous."(p.xiii)
• ***Our*** earliest printing voiced the hope "that every alcoholic who journeys will find the Fellowship of Alcoholics Anonymous at his destination.(p.xv)
• Sixteen years have elapsed between ***our*** first printing of this book and the presentation in 1955 of ***our*** second edition.(p.xv)
• Many of ***our*** friends encourage us by saying that this is but a beginning, only the augury of a much larger future ahead.(p.xv)
• He had also been greatly helped by the late Dr. William D. Silkworth, a New York specialist in alcoholism who is now accounted no less than a medical saint by A.A. members, and whose story of the early days of ***our*** Society appears in the next pages.(p.xvi)
• ***Our*** Society then entered a fearsome and exciting adolescent period.(p.xviii)
• We had to unify ***our*** Fellowship or pass off the scene.(p.xix)
• It was thought that no alcoholic man or woman could be excluded from ***our*** Society; that ***our*** leaders might serve but never govern; that each group was to be autonomous and there was to be no professional class of therapy.(p.xix)
• There were to be no fees or dues; ***our*** expenses were to be met by ***our*** own voluntary contributions.(p.xix)
• There was to be the least possible organization, even in ***our*** service centers.(p.xix)
• ***Our*** public relations were to be based upon attraction rather than promotion.(p.xix)
• Though none of these principles had the force of rules or laws, they had become so widely accepted by 1950 that they were confirmed by ***our*** first International Conference held at Cleveland.(p.xix)
• Today the remarkable unity of A.A. is one of the greatest assets that ***our*** Society has.(p.xix)
• While the internal difficulties of ***our*** adolescent period were being ironed out, public acceptance of A.A. grew by leaps and bounds.(p.xix)
• Another reason for the wide acceptance of A.A. was the ministration of friends -- friends in medicine, religion, and the press, together with innumerable others who became ***our*** able and persistent advocates.(p.xx)
• At present, ***our*** membership is increasing at the rate of about seven per cent a year.(p.xx)
• Yet it is ***our*** great hope that all those who have as yet found no answer may begin to find one in the pages of this book and will presently join us on the highroad to a new freedom.(p.xxi)
• Convincing testimony must surely come from the medical men who have had experience with the sufferings of ***our*** members and have witnessed ***our*** return to health.(p.xxiii)
• The physician who at ***our*** request, gave us this letter, has been kind enough to enlarge upon his views in another statement which follows.(p.xxiv)
• It did not satisfy us to be told that we could not control ***our*** drinking just because we were maladjusted to life, that we were in full flight from reality, or were outright mental defectives.(p.xxiv)
• But we are sure that ***our*** bodies were sickened as well.(p.xxiv)
• In ***our*** belief, any picture of the alcoholic which leaves out this physical factor is incomplete.(p.xxiv)
• As laymen, ***our*** opinion as to its soundness may, of course, mean little.(p.xxiv)
• Though we work out ***our*** solution on the spiritual as well as an altruistic plane, we favor hospitalization for the alcoholic who is very jittery or befogged.(p.xxiv)
• We doctors have realized for a long time that some form of moral psychology was of urgent importance to alcoholics, but its application presented difficulties

beyond ***our*** conception.(p.xxv)
• What with ***our*** ultra-modern standards, ***our*** scientific approach to everything, we are perhaps not well equipped to apply the powers of good that lie outside ***our*** synthetic knowledge.(p.xxv)
• Many years ago one of the leading contributors to this book came under ***our*** care in this hospital and while here he acquired some ideas which he put into practical application at once.(p.xxv)
• We gave up ***our*** positions and off we roared on a motorcycle, the sidecar stuffed with tent, blankets, a change of clothes, and three huge volumes of a financial reference service.(p.2)
• ***Our*** friends thought a lunacy commission should be appointed.(p.3)
• I had had some success at speculation, so we had a little money, but we once worked on a farm for a month to avoid drawing on ***our*** small capital.(p.3)
• There were many unhappy scenes in ***our*** sumptuous apartment.(p.3)
• By the following spring we were living in ***our*** accustomed style.(p.4)
• I wondered whether I dared hide a full bottle of gin near the head of ***our*** bed.(p.8)
• In one western city and its environs there are one thousand of us and ***our*** families.(p.15)
• ***Our*** struggles with them are variously strenuous, comic and tragic.(p.16)
• He could not, or would not, see ***our*** way of life.(p.16)
• I suppose some would be shocked at ***our*** seeming worldliness and levity.(p.16)
• Each day my friend's simple talk in ***our*** kitchen multiplies itself in a widening circle of peace on earth and good will to men.(p.16)
• Unlike the feelings of the ship's passengers, however, ***our*** joy in escape from disaster does not subside as we go ***our*** individual ways.(p.17)
• We feel that elimination of ***our*** drinking is but a beginning.(p.19)
• A much more important demonstration of ***our*** principles lies before us in ***our*** respective homes, occupations and affairs.(p.19)
• All of us spend much of ***our*** spare time in the sort of effort which we are going to describe.(p.19)
• We shall bring to the task ***our*** combined experience and knowledge.(p.19)
• We shall do ***our*** utmost to achieve that ideal.(p.19)
• ***Our*** very lives, as ex-problem drinkers, depend upon ***our*** constant thought of others and how we may help meet their needs.(p.20)
• This is by no means a comprehensive picture of the true alcoholic, as ***our*** behavior patterns vary.(p.22)
• These observations would be academic and pointless if ***our*** friend never took the first drink, thereby setting the terrible cycle in motion.(p.23)
• ***Our*** so-called will power becomes practically nonexistent.(p.24)
• We are unable, at certain times, to bring into ***our*** consciousness with sufficient force the memory of the suffering and humiliation of even a week or a month ago.(p.24)
• Almost none of us liked the self-searching, the leveling of ***our*** pride, the confession of shortcomings which the process requires for its successful consummation.(p.25)
• When, therefore, we were approached by those in whom the problem had been solved, there was nothing left for us but to pick up the simple kit of spiritual tools laid at ***our*** feet.(p.25)
• The great fact is just this, and nothing less: That we have had deep and effective spiritual experiences which have revolutionized ***our*** whole attitude toward life, toward ***our*** fellows and toward God's universe.(p.25)
• The central fact of ***our*** lives today is the absolute certainty that ***our*** Creator has entered into ***our*** hearts and lives in a way which is indeed miraculous.(p.25)
• We were in a position where life was becoming impossible, and if we had passed into the region from which there is no return through human aid we had but two alternatives: One was to go on to the bitter end, blotting out the consciousness of ***our*** intolerable situation as best we could; and the other, to accept spiritual help.(p.25)
• Some of ***our*** alcoholic readers may think they can do without spiritual help.(p.27)
• Let us tell you the rest of the conversation ***our*** friend had with his doctor.(p.27)
• ***Our*** friend felt as though the gates of hell had closed on him with a clang.(p.27)
• Upon hearing this, ***our*** friend was somewhat relieved, for he reflected that after all, he was a good church member.(p.27)
• Here was the terrible dilemma in which ***our*** friend found himself when he had the extraordinary experience which as we have already told you, made him a free man.(p.28)
• We, in ***our*** turn, sought the same escape with all the desperation of drowning men.(p.28)
• If what we have learned and felt and seen means anything at all, it means that all of us, whatever ***our*** race, creed, or color are the children of a living Creator with whom we may form a relationship upon simple and understandable terms as soon as we are willing and honest enough to try.(p.28)
• We think it no concern of ours what religious bodies ***our*** members identify themselves with as individuals.(p.28)
• Many who once were in this class are now among ***our*** members.(p.28)
• These give a fair cross section of ***our*** membership and a clear-cut idea of what has actually happened in their lives.(p.29)
• ***Our*** hope is that many alcoholic men and women, desperately in need, will see these pages, and we believe that it is only by fully disclosing ourselves and ***our*** problems that they will be persuaded to say, "Yes, I am one of them too; I must have this thing."(p.29)
• Therefore, it is not surprising that ***our*** drinking careers have been characterized by countless vain attempts to prove we could drink like other people.(p.30)
• We learned that we had to fully concede to ***our*** innermost selves that we were alcoholics.(p.30)
• We alcoholics are men and women who have lost the ability to control ***our*** drinking.(p.30)
• We are convinced to a man that alcoholics of ***our*** type are in the grip of a progressive illness.(p.30)
• Neither does there appear to be any kind of treatment which will make alcoholics of ***our*** kind like other men.(p.30)
• If anyone who is showing inability to control his drinking can do the right-about-face and drink like a gentleman, ***our*** hats are off to him.(p.31)
• Though there is no way of proving it, we believe that early in ***our*** drinking careers most of us could have stopped drinking.(p.32)
• Several of ***our*** crowd, men of thirty or less, had been drinking only a few years, but they found themselves as helpless as those who had been drinking twenty years.(p.33)
• As we look back, we feel we had gone on drinking many years beyond the point where we could quit on ***our*** will power.(p.34)
• In the early days of ***our*** drinking we occasionally remained sober for a year or more, becoming serious drinkers again later.(p.34)
• How then shall we help ***our*** readers determine, to their own satisfaction, whether they are one of us?(p.34)
• ***Our*** first example is a friend we shall call Jim.(p.35)
• But there was always the curious mental phenomenon that parallel with ***our*** sound reasoning there inevitably ran some insanely trivial excuse for taking the first drink.(p.37)
• ***Our*** sound reasoning failed to hold us in check.(p.37)
• But even in this type of beginning we are obliged to admit that ***our*** justification for a spree was insanely insufficient in the light of what always happened.(p.37)
• ***Our*** behavior is as absurd and incomprehensible with respect to the first drink as that of an individual with a passion, say, for jay-walking.(p.37)
• You may think ***our*** illustration is too ridiculous.(p.38)
• This is a point we wish to emphasize and re-emphasize, to smash home upon ***our*** alcoholic readers as it has been revealed to us out of bitter experience.(p.39)
• Many doctors and psychiatrists agree with ***our*** conclusions.(p.43)
• About half ***our*** original fellowship were of exactly that type.(p.44)
• ***Our*** experience shows that you need not be disconcerted.(p.44)
• We could wish to be moral, we could wish to be philosophically comforted, in fact, we could will these things with all ***our*** might, but the needed power wasn't there.(p.45)
• ***Our*** human resources, as marshalled by the will were not sufficient; they failed utterly.(p.45)
• Lack of power, that was ***our*** dilemma.(p.45)
• Many times we talk to a new man and watch his hope rise as we discuss his alcoholic problems and explain ***our*** fellowship.(p.45)
• But his face falls when we speak of spiritual matters, especially when we mention God, for we have re-opened a subject which ***our*** man thought he had neatly evaded or entirely ignored.(p.45)
• Much to ***our*** relief, we discovered we did not need to consider another's conception of God.(p.46)
• ***Our*** own conception, however inadequate, was sufficient to make the approach and to effect a contact with Him.(p.46)
• At the start, this was all we needed to commence spiritual growth, to effect ***our*** first conscious relation with God as we understood Him.(p.47)
• So we used ***our*** own conception, however limited it was.(p.47)
• When, however, the perfectly logical assumption is suggested that underneath the material world and life as we see it, there is an All Powerful, Guiding, Creative Intelligence, right there ***our*** perverse streak comes to the surface and we laboriously set out to convince ourselves it isn't so.(p.49)
• Were ***our*** contentions true, it would follow that life originated out of nothing, and proceeds nowhere.(p.49)
• Instead of regarding ourselves as intelligent agents, spearheads of God's ever advancing Creation, we agnostics and atheists chose to believe that ***our*** human intelligence was the last word, the alpha and the omega, the beginning and end of all.(p.49)
• In ***our*** personal stories you will find a wide variation in the way each teller approaches and conceives of the Power which is greater than himself.(p.50)
• Experience has taught us that these are matters about which, for ***our*** purpose, we need not be worried.(p.50)
• But in most fields ***our*** generation has witnessed complete liberation of ***our*** thinking.(p.52)
• Is not ***our*** age characterized by the ease with which we discard old ideas for new, by the complete readiness with which we throw away the theory or gadget which does not work for something new which does?(p.52)
• We had to ask ourselves why we shouldn't apply to ***our*** human problems this same readiness to change ***our*** point of view.(p.52)
• We were having trouble with personal relationships, we couldn't control ***our*** emotional natures, we were a prey to misery and depression, we couldn't make a living, we had a feeling of uselessness, we were full of fear, we were unhappy, we couldn't seem to be of real help to other people – was not a basic solution of these bedevilments more important than whether we should see newsreels of lunar flight?(p.52)
• ***Our*** ideas did not work.(p.52)
• We agnostics and atheists were sticking to the idea that self-sufficiency would solve ***our*** problems.(p.52)
• It is not by chance we were given the power to reason, to examine the evidence of ***our*** senses, and to draw conclusions.(p.53)
• Hence we are at pains to tell why we think ***our*** present faith is reasonable, why we think it more sane and logical to believe than not to believe, why we say ***our*** former thinking was soft and mushy when we threw up ***our*** hands in doubt and said, "We don't know."(p.53)
• What was ***our*** choice to be?(p.53)
• Perhaps we had been leaning too heavily on Reason that last mile and we did not like to lose ***our*** support.(p.53)
• For did we not believe in ***our*** own reasoning?(p.53)
• Did we not have confidence in ***our*** ability to think?(p.54)
• Were not these things the tissue out of which ***our*** lives were constructed?(p.54)
• Did not these feelings, after all, determine the course of ***our*** existence?(p.54)
• Neither is reason, as most of us use it, entirely dependable, though it emanate from ***our*** best minds.(p.54)
• We finally saw that faith in some kind of God was a part of ***our*** make-up, just as much as the feeling we have for a friend.(p.55)
• If ***our*** testimony helps sweep away prejudice, enables you to think honestly, encourages you to search diligently within yourself, then, if you wish, you can join us on the Broad Highway.(p.55)
• ***Our*** friend was a minister's son.(p.56)
• ***Our*** friend's gorge rose as he bitterly cried out: "If there is a God, He certainly hasn't done anything for me!"(p.56)
• Thus was ***our*** friend's cornerstone fixed in place.(p.56)
• Even so has God restored us all to ***our*** right minds.(p.57)
• Rarely have we seen a person fail who has thoroughly followed ***our*** path.(p.58)
• ***Our*** stories disclose in a general way what we used to be like, what happened, and what we are like now.(p.58)
• With all the earnestness at ***our*** command, we beg of

you to be fearless and thorough from the very start.(p.58)
• Some of us have tried to hold on to ***our*** old ideas and the result was nil until we let go absolutely.(p.58)
• 1.We admitted we were powerless over alcohol -- that ***our*** lives had become unmanageable.(p.59)
• 3.Made a decision to turn ***our*** will and ***our*** lives over to the care of God as we understood Him.(p.59)
• 5.Admitted to God, to ourselves, and to another human being the exact nature of ***our*** wrongs.(p.59)
• 7.Humbly asked Him to remove ***our*** shortcomings.(p.59)
• 11.Sought through prayer and meditation to improve ***our*** conscious contact with God as we understood Him, praying only for knowledge of His will for us and the power to carry that out.(p.59)
• 12.Having had a spiritual awakening as the result of these steps, we tried to carry this message to alcoholics, and to practice these principles in all ***our*** affairs.(p.60)
• ***Our*** description of the alcoholic, the chapter to the agnostic, and ***our*** personal adventures before and after make clear three pertinent ideas:(p.60)
• (a) That we were alcoholic and could not manage ***our*** own lives.(p.60)
• (b) That probably no human power could have relieved ***our*** alcoholism.(p.60)
• Being convinced, we were at Step Three, which is that we decided to turn ***our*** will and ***our*** life over to God as we understood Him.(p.60)
• On that basis we are almost always in collision with something or somebody, even though ***our*** motives are good.(p.60)
• In trying to make these arrangements ***our*** actor may sometimes be quite virtuous.(p.61)
• ***Our*** actor is self-centered -- ego-centric, as people like to call it nowadays.(p.61)
• Whatever ***our*** protestations, are not most of us concerned with ourselves, ***our*** resentments, or ***our*** self-pity?(p.62)
• That, we think, is the root of ***our*** troubles.(p.62)
• Driven by a hundred forms of fear, self-delusion, self-seeking, and self-pity, we step on the toes of ***our*** fellows and they retaliate.(p.62)
• So ***our*** troubles, we think, are basically of ***our*** own making.(p.62)
• Neither could we reduce ***our*** self-centeredness much by wishing or trying on ***our*** own power.(p.62)
• Next, we decided that hereafter in this drama of life, God was going to be ***our*** Director.(p.62)
• Established on such a footing we became less and less interested in ourselves, ***our*** little plans and designs.(p.63)
• As we felt new power flow in, as we enjoyed peace of mind, as we discovered we could face life successfully, as we became conscious of His presence, we began to lose ***our*** fear of today, tomorrow or the hereafter.(p.63)
• Many of us said to ***our*** Maker, as we understood Him: "God, I offer myself to Thee -- to build with me and to do with me as Thou wilt.(p.63)
• We found it very desirable to take this spiritual step with an understanding person, such as ***our*** wife, best friend or spiritual adviser.(p.63)
• Though ***our*** decision was a vital and crucial step, it could have little permanent effect unless at once followed by a strenuous effort to face, and to be rid of, the things in ourselves which had been blocking us.(p.64)
• ***Our*** liquor was but a symptom.(p.64)
• We did exactly the same thing with ***our*** lives.(p.64)
• First, we searched out the flaws in ***our*** make-up which caused ***our*** failure.(p.64)
• In most cases it was found that ***our*** self-esteem, ***our*** pocketbooks, ***our*** ambitions, ***our*** personal relationships (including sex) were hurt or threatened.(p.64)
• On ***our*** grudge list we set opposite each name ***our*** injuries.(p.65)
• Was it ***our*** self-esteem, ***our*** security, ***our*** ambitions, ***our*** personal, or sex relations, which had been interfered with?(p.65)
• We went back through ***our*** lives.(p.65)
• But the more we fought and tried to have ***our*** own way, the worse matters got.(p.66)
• ***Our*** moments of triumph were short-lived.(p.66)
• This was ***our*** course: We realized that the people who wronged us were perhaps spiritually sick.(p.66)
• If we do, we destroy ***our*** chance of being helpful.(p.67)
• Referring to ***our*** list again.(p.67)
• Putting out of ***our*** minds the wrongs others had done, we resolutely looked for ***our*** own mistakes.(p.67)
• Though a situation had not been entirely ***our*** fault, we tried to disregard the other person involved entirely.(p.67)
• When we saw ***our*** faults we listed them.(p.67)
• We admitted ***our*** wrongs honestly and were willing to set these matters straight.(p.67)
• This short word somehow touches about every aspect of ***our*** lives.(p.67)
• It was an evil and corroding thread; the fabric of ***our*** existence was shot through with it.(p.67)
• We reviewed ***our*** fears thoroughly.(p.68)
• We trust infinite God rather than ***our*** finite selves.(p.68)
• We never apologize to anyone for depending upon ***our*** Creator.(p.68)
• We ask Him to remove ***our*** fear and direct ***our*** attention to what He would have us be.(p.68)
• One set of voices cry that sex is a lust of ***our*** lower nature, a base necessity of procreation.(p.68)
• We reviewed ***our*** own conduct over the years past.(p.69)
• In this way we tried to shape a sane and sound ideal for ***our*** future sex life.(p.69)
• We asked God to mold ***our*** ideals and help us to live up to them.(p.69)
• We remembered always that ***our*** sex powers were God-given and therefore good, neither to be used lightly or selfishly nor to be despised and loathed.(p.69)
• Whatever ***our*** ideal turns out to be, we must be willing to grow toward it.(p.69)
• God alone can judge ***our*** sex situation.(p.69)
• It depends on us and on ***our*** motives.(p.70)
• If we are sorry for what we have done, and have the honest desire to let God take us to better things, we believe we will be forgiven and will have learned ***our*** lesson.(p.70)
• If we are not sorry, and ***our*** conduct continues to harm others, we are quite sure to drink.(p.70)
• These are facts out of ***our*** experience.(p.70)
• If we have been thorough about ***our*** personal inventory, we have written down a lot.(p.70)
• We have listed and analyzed ***our*** resentments.(p.70)
• We have begun to learn tolerance, patience and good will toward all men, even ***our*** enemies, for we look on them as sick people.(p.70)
• We have listed the people we have hurt by ***our*** conduct, and are willing to straighten out the past if we can.(p.70)
• Having made ***our*** personal inventory, what shall we do about it?(p.72)
• We have been trying to get a new attitude, a new relationship with ***our*** Creator, and to discover the obstacle in ***our*** path.(p.72)
• We have admitted certain defects; we have ascertained in a rough way what the trouble is; we have put ***our*** finger on the weak items in ***our*** personal inventory.(p.72)
• This requires action on ***our*** part, which, when completed, will mean that we have admitted to God, to ourselves, and to another human being the exact nature of ***our*** defects.(p.72)
• This is perhaps difficult -- especially discussing ***our*** defects with another person.(p.72)
• We often find such a person quick to see and understand ***our*** problem.(p.74)
• If we cannot or would rather not do this, we search ***our*** acquaintance for a close-mouthed, understanding friend.(p.74)
• Perhaps ***our*** doctor or psychologist will be the person.(p.74)
• It may be one of ***our*** own family, but we cannot disclose anything to ***our*** wives or ***our*** parents which will hurt them and make them unhappy.(p.74)
• We have no right to save ***our*** own skin at another person's expense.(p.74)
• Such parts of ***our*** story we tell to someone who will understand, yet be unaffected.(p.74)
• It is important that he be able to keep a confidence; that he fully understand and approve what we are driving at; that he will not try to change ***our*** plan.(p.74)
• When we decide who is to hear ***our*** story, we waste no time.(p.75)
• We explain to ***our*** partner what we are about to do and why we have to do it.(p.75)
• Most people approached in this way will be glad to help; they will be honored by ***our*** confidence.(p.75)
• We pocket ***our*** pride and go to it, illuminating every twist of character, every dark cranny of the past.(p.75)
• ***Our*** fears fall from us.(p.75)
• We begin to feel the nearness of ***our*** Creator.(p.75)
• We thank God from the bottom of ***our*** heart that we know Him better.(p.75)
• Taking this book down from ***our*** shelf we turn to the page which contains the twelve steps.(p.75)
• Is ***our*** work solid so far?(p.75)
• If we can answer to ***our*** satisfaction, we then look at Step Six.(p.76)
• Now we go out to ***our*** fellows and repair the damage done in the past.(p.76)
• We attempt to sweep away the debris which has accumulated out of ***our*** effort to live on self-will and run the show ourselves.(p.76)
• To some people we need not, and probably should not emphasize the spiritual feature on ***our*** first approach.(p.76)
• At the moment we are trying to put ***our*** lives in order.(p.77)
• ***Our*** real purpose is to fit ourselves to be of maximum service to God and the people about us.(p.77)
• It is seldom wise to approach an individual, who still smarts from ***our*** injustice to him, and announce that we have gone religious.(p.77)
• But ***our*** man is sure to be impressed with a sincere desire to set right the wrong.(p.77)
• He is going to be more interested in a demonstration of good will than in ***our*** talk of spiritual discoveries.(p.77)
• When it will serve any good purpose, we are willing to announce ***our*** convictions with tact and common sense.(p.77)
• It may be he has done us more harm than we have done him and, though we may have acquired a better attitude toward him, we are still not too keen about admitting ***our*** faults.(p.77)
• Nevertheless, with a person we dislike, we take the bit in ***our*** teeth.(p.77)
• We go to him in a helpful and forgiving spirit, confessing ***our*** former ill feeling and expressing ***our*** regret.(p.77)
• Simply we tell him that we will never get over drinking until we have done ***our*** utmost to straighten out the past.(p.77)
• We are there to sweep off ***our*** side of the street realizing that nothing worth while can be accomplished until we do so, never trying to tell him what he should do.(p.77)
• We stick to ***our*** own.(p.78)
• If ***our*** manner is calm, frank, and open, we will be gratified with the result.(p.78)
• ***Our*** former enemies sometimes praise what we are doing and wish us well.(p.78)
• We have made ***our*** demonstration, done ***our*** part.(p.78)
• We do not dodge ***our*** creditors.(p.78)
• Telling them what we are trying to do, we make no bones about ***our*** drinking; they usually know it anyway, whether we think so or not.(p.78)
• Nor are we afraid of disclosing ***our*** alcoholism on the theory it may cause financial harm.(p.78)
• ***Our*** drinking has made us slow to pay.(p.78)
• We must lose ***our*** fear of creditors no matter how far we have to go, for we are liable to drink if we are afraid to face them.(p.78)
• We may be short in ***our*** accounts and unable to make good.(p.78)
• We have already admitted this in confidence to another person, but we are sure we would be imprisoned or lose ***our*** job if it were known.(p.78)
• She is indignant about it, and has a warrant out for ***our*** arrest.(p.79)
• We may lose ***our*** position or reputation or face jail, but we are willing.(p.79)
• He had commenced ***our*** way of life, had secured a position, and was getting his head above water.(p.79)
• This brings to mind a story about one of ***our*** friends.(p.80)
• If we are sure ***our*** wife does not know, should we tell her?(p.81)
• Undoubtedly we should admit ***our*** fault.(p.81)
• ***Our*** design for living is not a one-way street.(p.81)
• Their defects may be glaring, but the chances are that ***our*** own actions are partly responsible.(p.83)
• So we clean house with the family, asking each morning in meditation that ***our*** Creator show us the way of patience, tolerance, kindliness and love.(p.83)
• ***Our*** behavior will convince them more than ***our*** words.(p.83)
• As God's people we stand on ***our*** feet; we don't crawl before anyone.(p.83)
• If we are painstaking about this phase of ***our*** development, we will be amazed before we are half way through.(p.83)
• No matter how far down the scale we have gone, we will see how ***our*** experience can benefit others.(p.84)

• We will lose interest in selfish things and gain interest in ***our*** fellows.(p.84)
• ***Our*** whole attitude and outlook upon life will change.(p.84)
• ***Our*** next function is to grow in understanding and effectiveness.(p.84)
• It should continue for ***our*** lifetime.(p.84)
• Then we resolutely turn ***our*** thoughts to someone we can help.(p.84)
• Love and tolerance of others is ***our*** code.(p.84)
• We will see that ***our*** new attitude toward liquor has been given us without any thought or effort on ***our*** part.(p.85)
• That is ***our*** experience.(p.85)
• It is easy to let up on the spiritual program of action and rest on ***our*** laurels.(p.85)
• What we really have is a daily reprieve contingent on the maintenance of ***our*** spiritual condition.(p.85)
• Every day is a day when we must carry the vision of God's will into all of ***our*** activities.(p.85)
• We can exercise ***our*** will power along this line all we wish.(p.85)
• When we retire at night, we constructively review ***our*** day.(p.86)
• But we must be careful not to drift into worry, remorse or morbid reflection, for that would diminish ***our*** usefulness to others.(p.86)
• After making ***our*** review we ask God's forgiveness and inquire what corrective measures should be taken.(p.86)
• We consider ***our*** plans for the day.(p.86)
• Before we begin, we ask God to direct ***our*** thinking, especially asking that it be divorced from self-pity, dishonest or self-seeking motives.(p.86)
• Under these conditions we can employ ***our*** mental faculties with assurance, for after all God gave us brains to use.(p.86)
• ***Our*** thought-life will be placed on a much higher plane when ***our*** thinking is cleared of wrong motives.(p.86)
• In thinking about ***our*** day we may face indecision.(p.86)
• Nevertheless, we find that ***our*** thinking will as time passes, be more and more on the plane of inspiration.(p.87)
• We usually conclude the period of meditation with a prayer that we be shown all through the day what ***our*** next step is to be, that we be given whatever we need to take care of such problems.(p.87)
• We are careful never to pray for ***our*** own selfish ends.(p.87)
• If circumstances warrant, we ask ***our*** wives or friends to join us in morning meditation.(p.87)
• This is ***our*** twelfth suggestion: Carry this message to other alcoholics!(p.89)
• Frequent contact with newcomers and with each other is the bright spot of ***our*** lives.(p.89)
• To be helpful is ***our*** only aim.(p.89)
• One of ***our*** Fellowship failed entirely with his first half dozen prospects.(p.96)
• We seldom allow an alcoholic to live in ***our*** homes for long at a time.(p.97)
• The minute we put ***our*** work on a service plane, the alcoholic commences to rely upon ***our*** assistance rather than upon God.(p.98)
• People have said we must not go where liquor is served; we must not have it in ***our*** homes; we must shun friends who drink; we must avoid moving pictures which show drinking scenes; we must not go into bars; ***our*** friends must hide their bottles if we go to their houses; we mustn't think or be reminded about alcohol at all.(p.100)
• ***Our*** experience shows that this is not necessarily so.(p.101)
• In ***our*** belief any scheme of combating alcoholism which proposes to shield the sick man from temptation is doomed to failure.(p.101)
• So ***our*** rule is not to avoid a place where there is drinking, if we have a legitimate reason for being there.(p.101)
• Many of us keep liquor in ***our*** homes.(p.102)
• Some of us still serve it to ***our*** friends provided they are not alcoholic.(p.102)
• Some day we hope that Alcoholics Anonymous will help the public to a better realization of the gravity of the alcoholic problem, but we shall be of little use if ***our*** attitude is one of bitterness or hostility.(p.103)
• After all, ***our*** problems were of ***our*** own making.(p.103)
• With few exceptions, ***our*** book thus far has spoken of men.(p.104)
• ***Our*** activities in behalf of women who drink are on the increase.(p.104)
• There is every evidence that women regain their health as readily as men if they try ***our*** suggestions.(p.104)
• Some of us veered from extreme to extreme, ever hoping that one day ***our*** loved ones would be themselves once more.(p.105)
• ***Our*** loyalty and the desire that ***our*** husbands hold up their heads and be like other men have begotten all sorts of predicaments.(p.105)
• We have told innumerable lies to protect ***our*** pride and ***our*** husbands' reputations.(p.105)
• ***Our*** homes have been battle-grounds many an evening.(p.105)
• ***Our*** friends have counseled chucking the men and we have done so with finality, only to be back in a little while hoping, always hoping.(p.105)
• ***Our*** men have sworn great solemn oaths that they were through drinking forever.(p.105)
• We seldom had friends at ***our*** homes, never knowing how or when the men of the house would appear.(p.105)
• When we were invited out, ***our*** husbands sneaked so many drinks that they spoiled the occasion.(p.105)
• How heartbreaking was this discovery; how cruel to be told they understood ***our*** men as we did not!(p.106)
• The bill collectors, the sheriffs, the angry taxi drivers, the policemen, the bums, the pals, and even the ladies they sometimes brought home – ***our*** husbands thought we were so inhospitable.(p.106)
• We have tried to hold the love of ***our*** children for their father.(p.106)
• The unexpected result was that ***our*** husbands seemed to like it.(p.106)
• Then we were severely criticized by ***our*** husband's parents for desertion.(p.106)
• We finally sought employment ourselves as destitution faced us and ***our*** families.(p.106)
• The alarming physical and mental symptoms, the deepening pall of remorse, depression and inferiority that settled down on ***our*** loved ones – these things terrified and distracted us.(p.106)
• Today most of ***our*** men are better husbands and fathers than ever before.(p.108)
• Many of ***our*** husbands were just as far gone.(p.110)
• ***Our*** next thought is that you should never tell him what he must do about his drinking.(p.111)
• Avoid urging him to follow ***our*** program.(p.113)
• If he is already committed to an institution, but can convince you and your doctor that he means business, give him a chance to try ***our*** method, unless the doctor thinks his mental condition too abnormal or dangerous.(p.114)
• As ***our*** husbands began to apply spiritual principles in their lives, we began to see the desirability of doing so too.(p.116)
• We thought, on the whole, we were pretty good women, capable of being nicer if ***our*** husbands stopped drinking.(p.116)
• Now we try to put spiritual principles to work in every department of ***our*** lives.(p.116)
• When we do that, we find it solves ***our*** problems too; the ensuing lack of fear, worry and hurt feelings is a wonderful thing.(p.116)
• We urge you to try ***our*** program, for nothing will be so helpful to your husband as the radically changed attitude toward him which God will show you how to have.(p.117)
• We women carry with us a picture of the ideal man, the sort of chap we would like ***our*** husbands to be.(p.118)
• Another feeling we are very likely to entertain is one of resentment that love and loyalty could not cure ***our*** husbands of alcoholism.(p.118)
• Though it is infinitely better that he have no relapse at all, as has been true with many of ***our*** men, it is by no means a bad thing in some cases.(p.120)
• ***Our*** women folk have suggested certain attitudes a wife may take with the husband who is recovering.(p.122)
• We grow by ***our*** willingness to face and rectify errors and convert them into assets.(p.124)
• We find it better when possible, to stick to ***our*** own stories.(p.125)
• Like a gaunt prospector, belt drawn in over the last ounce of food, ***our*** pick struck gold.(p.128)
• Joy at ***our*** release from a lifetime of frustration knew no bounds.(p.128)
• This dream world has been replaced by a great sense of purpose, accompanied by a growing consciousness of the power of God in ***our*** lives.(p.130)
• We have come to believe He would like us to keep ***our*** heads in the clouds with Him, but that ***our*** feet ought to be firmly planted on earth.(p.130)
• That is where ***our*** fellow travelers are, and that is where ***our*** work must be done.(p.130)
• He may bring new hope and new courage to many a priest, minister, or rabbi, who gives his all to minister to ***our*** troubled world.(p.132)
• If newcomers could see no joy or fun in ***our*** existence, they wouldn't want it.(p.132)
• We try not to indulge in cynicism over the state of the nations, nor do we carry the world's troubles on ***our*** shoulders.(p.132)
• For his sake, we do recount and almost relive the horrors of ***our*** past.(p.132)
• But it is clear that we made ***our*** own misery.(p.133)
• But we have seen remarkable transformations in ***our*** bodies.(p.133)
• Hardly one of ***our*** crowd now shows any mark of dissipation.(p.133)
• Here is a case in point: One of ***our*** friends is a heavy smoker and coffee drinker.(p.135)
• Of course ***our*** friend was wrong -- dead wrong.(p.135)
• Why not bring him into contact with some of ***our*** alcoholic crowd?(p.138)
• As ***our*** work spreads and ***our*** numbers increase, we hope your employees may be put in personal contact with some of us.(p.144)
• In fact, he may say almost anything if he has accepted ***our*** solution which, as you know, demands rigorous honesty.(p.145)
• But sometimes ***our*** drinking will be used politically.(p.145)
• Your junior executive may not agree with the contents of ***our*** book.(p.148)
• We hope ***our*** suggestions will help you plug up this sometimes serious leak.(p.148)
• But the policy of this company is not to interfere with the habits of ***our*** employees.(p.148)
• What ***our*** friend, the vice president, had in mind was the habitual or whoopee drinker.(p.149)
• We know ***our*** friend is like a boy whistling in the dark to keep up his spirits.(p.152)
• Should you wish them above all else, and be willing to make use of ***our*** experience, we are sure they will come.(p.153)
• ***Our*** own recovery proves that!(p.153)
• ***Our*** hope is that when this chip of a book is launched on the world tide of alcoholism, defeated drinkers will seize upon it, to follow its suggestions.(p.153)
• Years ago, in 1935, one of ***our*** number made a journey to a certain western city.(p.153)
• When ***our*** friend related his experience, the man agreed that no amount of will power he might muster could stop his drinking for long.(p.155)
• Being intrigued, however, he invited ***our*** friend to his home.(p.155)
• All this time ***our*** friend of the hotel lobby incident remained in that town.(p.159)
• Six years ago one of ***our*** number was a patient there.(p.162)
• Every few days this doctor suggests ***our*** approach to one of his patients.(p.162)
• Understanding ***our*** work, he can do this with an eye to selecting those who are willing and able to recover on a spiritual basis.(p.162)
• There are the same fast friendships, there is the same helpfulness to one another as you find among ***our*** western friends.(p.162)
• Little clusters of twos and threes and fives of us have sprung up in other communities, through contact with ***our*** two larger centers.(p.162)
• So he inquired, what did ***our*** friend have on the ball?(p.163)
• ***Our*** friend proceeded to tell him.(p.163)
• So ***our*** fellow worker will soon have friends galore.(p.163)
• Some of them may sink and perhaps never get up, but if ***our*** experience is a criterion, more than half of those approached will become fellows of Alcoholics Anonymous.(p.163)
• ***Our*** book is meant to be suggestive only.(p.164)
• The birth of ***our*** Society dates from his first day of permanent sobriety, June 10, 1935.(p.171)
• In his prodigy of service, he was well assisted by Sister Ignatia at St. Thomas Hospital in Akron, Ohio, one of the greatest friends ***our*** Fellowship will ever know.(p.171)
• During all this time we became more or less ostracized by ***our*** friends.(p.177)
• Unlike most of ***our*** crowd, I did not get over my craving for liquor much during the first two and one-half years of abstinence.(p.181)
• This continued until I enrolled in ***our*** state university and, at the end of four years, I realized that

I was a drunk.(p.183)
• Before very long we began to relate some incidents of ***our*** drinking and, naturally, pretty soon, I realized both of them knew what they were talking about because you can see things and smell things when you're drunk, that you can't other times, and, if I had thought they didn't know what they were talking about, I wouldn't have been willing to talk to them at all.(p.185)
• It's none of ***our*** business about your drinking.(p.186)
• Before ***our*** visit was over, Bill suddenly turned to his wife and said, "Go fetch my clothes, dear.(p.189)
• Early member, she spread the word among women in ***our*** pioneering period.(p.222)
• They were undoubtedly the alcoholics of ***our*** village.(p.230)
• There I sat in the evenings, enjoying with my friends ***our*** memories of the "old country," singing the old songs we all knew, playing simple card games for drinks and consuming great quantities of beer.(p.231)
• But I hardly tasted anything for two years and started in business for myself, founding a mattress factory which is today an important industrial enterprise in ***our*** city.(p.232)
• Little more of ***our*** talk stayed in my memory, but I do know I slept the rest of that night while before I had never known what a real night's sleep was.(p.239)
• This was my introduction to this "understanding fellowship" although it was to be more than a year later before ***our*** Society was to bear the name, Alcoholics Anonymous.(p.239)
• All of us in A.A. know the tremendous happiness that is in ***our*** sobriety, but there are also tragedies.(p.239)
• He brought in many of ***our*** original members, yet he himself could not make it and died of alcoholism.(p.239)
• Father was a very well-integrated person, and while mother was highstrung and a bit selfish and demanding, ***our*** home life was reasonably harmonious.(p.240)
• We checked into the home of Hank, the man who had fired me eleven years before in Mississippi, and there I met Bill, ***our*** founder.(p.245)
• There was one meeting a week at Bill's home in Brooklyn, and we all took turns there spouting off about how we had changed ***our*** lives overnight, how many drunks we had saved and straightened out, and last, but not least, how God had touched each of us personally on the shoulder.(p.246)
• Yet we all had one really sincere purpose in ***our*** hearts and that was not to drink.(p.246)
• At ***our*** weekly meeting I was a menace to serenity those first few months, for I took every opportunity to lambaste the "spiritual angle" as we called it, or anything else that had any tinge of theology.(p.246)
• Around this time ***our*** big A.A. book was being written and it all became much simpler; we had a definite formula which some sixty of us agreed was the middle course for all alcoholics who wanted sobriety, and that formula has not been changed one iota down through the years.(p.248)
• After the book appeared we all became very busy in ***our*** efforts to save all and sundry, but I was still actually on the fringes of A.A.(p.248)
• We can share in the laughter and tears of ***our*** many friends, and most important, we can share ***our*** A.A. way of life and are given a daily opportunity to help others.(p.249)
• They are far more alert and progressive than we floundering fathers were, and the future of ***our*** fellowship is in their hands.(p.250)
• We now live in the West and are very fortunate in ***our*** area A.A.; it is good, simple and friendly, and ***our*** one desire is to stay in A.A. and not on it.(p.250)
• ***Our*** pet slogan is "Easy Does It."(p.250)
• When I came to my aunt, she knew that I had had an unhappy childhood, and she said, "Now, Ethel, you're welcome to have boy friends in ***our*** home, but there are two boys in this town that I don't want you to date, and one of them comes from a very fine family, one of the best.(p.262)
• ***Our*** oldest daughter got married; they were living at ***our*** house.(p.263)
• ***Our*** other daughter was in her last year of high school, and one night the new son-in-law and my husband went out to a prize fight.(p.263)
• It would stop out in front of ***our*** house, and I still believe those people sent it!(p.265)
• One morning after a terrific drinking bout, I was in a little bar near ***our*** house, and I shook so that I was very much ashamed, because I was getting the shakes worse and worse.(p.266)
• That was ***our*** last drink of anything alcoholic.(p.267)
• One of ***our*** gifts from the family was a very lovely Bible, but we'd let the bulldog chew it because we weren't too interested in it.(p.268)
• I always feel that ***our*** God Consciousness was a steady growth after we became associated with A.A.(p.270)
• I give a great deal of credit to Doc and Anne for changing ***our*** life.(p.270)
• They spent at least an evening a week in ***our*** home out there for weeks and weeks.(p.270)
• I told ***our*** family doctor, an understanding man who gave hours of his time trying to help me, about this experience.(p.276)
• When I reached a point directly back of ***our*** house, where I could have cut through a friend's garden, I was almost overpowered by the desire to get home, but I made the whole journey.(p.276)
• ***Our*** marriage lasted four years.(p.277)
• It is, however, only the first of a series of miracles which have followed one after another as a result of my trying to apply to my daily life the principles embodies in ***our*** Twelve Steps.(p.280)
• I lived through a week of the fidgets because I had agreed to address a group of alcoholic inmates in one of ***our*** state mental hospitals.(p.283)
• We are both depending upon God and ***our*** use of the A.A. program to help us make a success of this joint undertaking.(p.286)
• After finding every bottle that I had hidden around the apartment, she took away my pants, my shoes, my money and my keys, threw them under the bed in the back bedroom and slip-locked ***our*** door.(p.288)
• He said he had finally learned that drinking was a fatal illness made up of an allergy plus an obsession, and once the drinking had passed from habit to obsession, we were completely hopeless, and could look forward only to spending the balance of ***our*** lives in mental institutions or to death.(p.290)
• ***Our*** home is always full of friends and visitors.(p.303)
• By the latter part of September 1939, we had a nucleus of six and held ***our*** first official group meeting.(p.310)
• Keeping one foot in front of the other is essential for maintaining ***our*** arrestment.(p.311)
• A complete change takes place in ***our*** approach to life.(p.311)
• And, as the years go by, working together, sharing ***our*** experiences with one another, and also sharing a mutual trust, understanding and love – without strings, without obligation – we acquire relationships that are unique and priceless.(p.312)
• As my son, ***our*** second child, came along, and as he became school age and was away at school most of the time, something happened.(p.323)
• It's surprising, how we think we fool everybody in ***our*** drinking.(p.324)
• I try to live ***our*** program as it has been outlined to me, one day at a time.(p.325)
• No more snoops or big shots breathing down ***our*** necks.(p.329)
• No monkeys on ***our*** backs.(p.329)
• We're free at last to do ***our*** thing, to live uninhibited lives, to drink when and how and where we wish, when we want to and when we need to.(p.329)
• We even can be rebels for the first time in ***our*** lives.(p.329)
• It becomes vital, also, that others not know of ***our*** defeats, nor suspect ***our*** loss of confidence.(p.331)
• He did not know it was A.A., and it was useless to tell him, for he doesn't have ***our*** disease.(p.334)
• But when we come into A.A., we can face ***our*** problem honestly and openly.(p.340)
• I returned to my home in Lucknow, India, at the end of November last year from a vacation in one of the most famous beauty spots in ***our*** country, a mountain resort 6,800 feet up, with a wonderful lake.(p.342)
• At one end of the table sat ***our*** community butcher.(p.347)
• At the other side of the table sat one of the carpenters in ***our*** community, and at the further end of the table sat the man who ran the bakery, while on one side sat my friend who was a mechanic.(p.347)
• I got the Big Book and I read it, and this is what it said: "Rarely have we seen a person fail who has thoroughly followed ***our*** path."(p.349)
• "Complete abandon"; "Half measures availed us nothing"; "Thoroughly follow ***our*** path"; "Completely give oneself to this simple program" – rang in my swelled head.(p.349)
• The Third Step said: "Made a decision to turn ***our*** will and ***our*** lives over to the care of God as we understood Him."(p.350)
• They have contributed fantastic amounts of time and work to ***our*** problem, but they aren't able, it seems, to arrest either your alcoholism or mine.(p.352)
• And the psychiatrist has had thousands of couches, and has put you and me on them many, many times, but he hasn't helped us very much, though he has tried hard; and we owe the clergy and the doctor and the psychiatrist a deep debt of gratitude, but they haven't helped ***our*** alcoholism, except in a rare few instances.(p.352)
• I have always considered myself one of the lucky members of ***our*** fraternity.(p.356)
• It was to be short lived, for on the day before Christmas I completely disillusioned my wife and ruined ***our*** first Christmas by coming home from the Rotary lunch dead drunk.(p.361)
• A few hours later I came out of a complete stupor in ***our*** living room with a flash of sanity.(p.363)
• I stayed on in Florida for three weeks, enjoying ***our*** reunion, a new found health and a deeper love than I had ever experienced before.(p.364)
• We attended meetings together, and mutually enjoyed ***our*** new found friends.(p.364)
• When ***our*** meeting night came around the next evening, I went -- "for her sake" I told her.(p.365)
• You'll read and hear a great deal about the spiritual part of ***our*** program.(p.366)
• Before too long, my husband (who seemed to prefer his shirts dirty) put his foot down, declaring that ***our*** family might have the cleanest clothes in town, but that I hadn't been out of the same old dirty slacks and blouse for a week.(p.371)
• We soon resumed ***our*** marriage, even moved away from the street of sad memories and found a new home.(p.371)
• We rationalize and excuse ***our*** conduct beyond all reason.(p.376)
• We had always encouraged ***our*** children to bring their friends home at any time, but after a few experiences with a drunken father they eliminated home as a place to entertain friends.(p.376)
• Finally ***our*** invitations became fewer and fewer as friends had more experience with my drinking pattern.(p.377)
• "We admitted we were powerless over alcohol -- that ***our*** lives had become unmanageable."(p.379)
• Somehow ***our*** bodies had reached the point where we could no longer absorb alcohol in ***our*** systems.(p.380)
• The why is not important; the fact is that one drink will set up a reaction in ***our*** system which requires more; that one drink was too much and one hundred drinks were not enough.(p.380)
• To most of us, making amends will take the rest of ***our*** lives, but we can start immediately.(p.381)
• Just being sober will be making amends to many we have hurt by ***our*** drunken actions.(p.381)
• Making amends is sometimes doing what we are capable of doing but failed to do because of alcohol; carrying out community responsibilities such as Community Funds, Red Cross, educational and religious activities in proportion to ***our*** abilities and energy.(p.381)
• "First Things First": solving ***our*** immediate problems before we try to solve all the others and get muddled in ***our*** thinking and doing.(p.382)
• Doing ***our*** best, living each day to the fullest is the art of living.(p.382)
• These thoughts become part of ***our*** daily lives.(p.382)
• The servant he turned to was ***our*** old cook, and she liked to drink.(p.385)
• The church was just three blocks from ***our*** home.(p.385)
• There was a doctor in ***our*** church congregation who was interested in my case, and he thought it was a vitamin deficiency.(p.389)
• Dr. Bob said, "Love and service keep us dry," and Bill said, "Always we must remember that ***our*** first duty is face-to-face help for the alcoholic who still suffers."(p.395)
• (I can't know how much others of ***our*** Fellowship have paid financially and, even more important, mentally and physically.)(p.396)
• He got half custody of ***our*** child, but later kept her during most of the school terms.(p.402)
• I saw him recently and he told me that he had always felt guilty, because, after ***our*** separation, I had become a serious alcoholic.(p.403)
• On ***our*** honeymoon in Egypt, he cuffed me around quite a bit, and subsequently hit me some more.(p.405)
• We were to go up to ***our*** A.A. farm in Kent, and I spent the evening before riding herd on Anne.(p.415)
• I had accomplished all the right things that ***our*** society expected, and I had no real peace of mind nor gratitude.(p.418)
• My life there was a nightmare of periodic binges on

alcohol and pills, adultery, unhappy hours at the dental office, seeing my wife give birth to *our* second child and have several miscarriages, living in a turbulent household, and making continual attempts to be the respectable dentist, husband, father, and community leader.(p.419)

- I came to understand the intricate processes of projection, by which we cast into *our* adult world the images of the horrors of *our* childhood.(p.434)
- And that was how Max and I and *our* two daughters spent Christmas Day, eight years ago.(p.444)
- He arranged for me to see a local psychiatrist, who quickly decided I should be in the mental-health unit of *our* local hospital.(p.445)
- Max still works with me in the office, but we have turned *our* wills and *our* lives and *our* work over to the care of God.(p.446)
- Prior to *our* marriage, when she was a shy, scrawny adolescent, I was able to see things in her that others couldn't necessarily see – things like beauty, charm, gaiety, a gift for being easy to talk to, a sense of humor, and many other fine qualities.(p.450)
- We used to argue about *our* differing ideas, but we can't argue about *our* feelings.(p.451)
- But with the first drink, *our* good intentions dissolved; *our* personalities changed.(p.458)
- And we found ourselves back in prison, where *our* personalities became even more warped.(p.459)
- After all, it was self (you, me) that stood in *our* own way, that ran the show and ran ourselves into bankruptcy, that hurt the ones we loved.(p.459)
- We were on *our* way to New York where he planned to leave me with my sister.(p.466)
- What we do with it is *our* own business; how we use it is up to us individually.(p.473)
- *Our* language has few words to say many things.(p.474)
- If *our* hair is half-bleached (with dark roots), poker-straight, and not combed, this adds to *our* beauty.(p.479)
- Some of us always remember *our* big mouths when it comes to a drink, but somewhere along the line, we seem to have forgotten about taking care of *our* teeth.(p.479)
- *Our* shoes are not better than the average hobo's, and if we are fortunate enough to have a pair of stockings on, nobody notices the runs in them, because of *our* dazzling beauty and *our* dirty feet.(p.479)
- (We don't have much time for bathing in *our* crowded schedule.)(p.479)
- A couple of years later, we lost *our* elder brother in a house fire, because of pills and booze.(p.480)
- We can have this new way of life – learning to live with *our* sickness and to be happy and content -- if we are willing to change *our* way of thinking and be honest, first with ourselves, then with others.(p.480)
- We are told to practice the Twelve Steps and Twelve Traditions to the best of *our* ability every day, one day at a time.(p.481)
- He has taught me that, in *our* new life, I am the most important person of all.(p.481)
- We are aware of the nice things around us, things we never noticed before in *our* drunken stupor.(p.481)
- We weren't even permitted to play cards in *our* home, but father would give us just a little toddy with whiskey and sugar and warm water now and then.(p.484)
- My mother resented it so that the first Christmas after *our* marriage, she didn't even invite us to dinner.(p.485)
- After *our* first child came my parents both became allies, but in later days, after I became an alcoholic, they both turned against me.(p.485)
- I continued to work and continued to go to lunch with Vi, and none of *our* acquaintances on the job knew that we had separated.(p.491)
- At that time we had *our* meetings on Friday nights.(p.495)
- I haven't mentioned it, but Charlie, my sponsor, was white, and when we got *our* group started we got help from other white groups in Washington.(p.495)
- Even when we were paying that two dollars a night, they often paid it for us because *our* collection was so small.(p.496)
- *OUR* SOUTHERN FRIEND(p.497)
- My wife's parents come to *our* assistance.(p.501)
- I learn that when we act upon the highest conception of honesty which is given us, *our* sense of honesty becomes more acute.(p.507)
- When we first come into A.A., many of us are confused because as a general rule we're at the end of *our* respective ropes, and we don't know what to do.(p.512)
- Sometimes we are told in A.A. not to try and learn the reasons for *our* drinking.(p.533)
- But not for long; now, for five Friday nights in a row, I went to jail, picked up sodden with beer (which I always disliked, but which was the only drink available); in jail five consecutive Friday nights in the town where I had grown up, where I had been an honor student in high school, where a kindly uncle, bailing me out, said, "Bob, *our* family just doesn't do this sort of thing."(p.539)
- During this time, *our* country was at war.(p.547)
- My husband eventually returned, but it was not long until we realized we could not continue *our* marriage.(p.547)
- They said if you want to know how this program works, take the first word of your question – the H is for honesty, the O is for open-mindedness and the W is for willingness; these *our* Book calls the essentials of recovery.(p.550)
- They suggested that I study the A.A. book and try to take the Twelve Steps according to the explanation in the Book, for it was their opinion that the application of these principles in *our* daily lives will get us sober and keep us sober.(p.550)
- I believe this, and I believe too that it is equally impossible to practice these principles to the best of *our* ability, a day at a time, and still drink, for I don't think the two things are compatible.(p.550)
- "A.A. does not teach us how to handle *our* drinking," he said.(p.554)
- *Our* courtship was mainly in bars and night spots when my ship was in New York.(p.555)
- On *our* honeymoon, we had iced champagne by the bedside day and night.(p.555)
- For instance, the fiftieth wedding anniversary of my wife's parents was the occasion for a huge family reunion at *our* home.(p.556)
- As *our* children grew up, I was able to be a father to them when they most needed one.(p.559)
- By learning -- through practicing the Twelve Steps and through sharing at meetings – how to cope with the problems that we looked to booze to solve, back in *our* drinking days.(p.560)
- Similarly, we rid ourselves of guilt and remorse as we "clean out the garbage" from *our* minds through the Fourth and Fifth Steps of *our* recovery program.(p.560)
- We are taught to differentiate between *our* wants (which are never satisfied) and *our* needs (which are always provided for).(p.560)
- We are granted "the serenity to accept the things we cannot change" -- and thus lose *our* quickness to anger and *our* sensitivity to criticism.(p.560)
- The "12 Traditions" of Alcoholics Anonymous are, we A.A.'s believe, the best answers that *our* experience has yet given to those ever urgent questions, "How can A.A. best function?" and, "How can A.A. best stay whole and so survive?"(p.563)
- One – *Our* common welfare should come first; personal recovery depends upon A.A. unity.(p.564)
- Two -- For *our* group purpose there is but one ultimate authority – a loving God as He may express Himself in *our* group conscience.(p.564)
- *Our* leaders are but trusted servants; they do not govern.(p.564)
- Six – An A.A. group ought never endorse, finance or lend the A.A. name to any related facility or outside enterprise, lest problems of money, property and prestige divert us from *our* primary purpose.(p.564)
- Eight – Alcoholics Anonymous should remain forever nonprofessional, but *our* service centers may employ special workers.(p.564)
- Eleven – *Our* public relations policy is based on attraction rather than promotion; we need always maintain personal anonymity at the level of press, radio and films.(p.564)
- Twelve – Anonymity is the spiritual foundation of all *our* Traditions, ever reminding us to place principles before personalities.(p.564)
- *Our* A.A. experience has taught us that:(p.565)
- Hence *our* common welfare comes first.(p.565)
- 2. -- For *our* group purpose there is but one ultimate authority -- a loving God as He may express Himself in *our* group conscience.(p.565)
- 3. – *Our* membership ought to include all who suffer from alcoholism.(p.565)
- On such issues *our* common welfare is paramount.(p.565)
- 6. – Problems of money, property, and authority may easily divert us from *our* primary spiritual aim.(p.565)
- Experience has often warned us that nothing can so surely destroy *our* spiritual heritage as futile disputes over property, money, and authority.(p.566)
- But *our* usual A.A. "12th Step" work is never to be paid for.(p.567)
- The trustees of the General Service Board are, in effect, *our* A.A. General Service Committee.(p.567)
- They are the custodians of *our* A.A. Tradition and the receivers of voluntary A.A. contributions by which we maintain *our* A.A. General Service Office at New York.(p.567)
- They are authorized by the groups to handle *our* over-all public relations and they guarantee the integrity of *our* principal newspaper, the A.A. Grapevine.(p.567)
- 11. – *Our* relations with the general public should be characterized by personal anonymity.(p.567)
- *Our* names and pictures as A.A. members ought not be broadcast, filmed, or publicly printed.(p.567)
- *Our* public relations should be guided by the principle of attraction rather than promotion.(p.567)
- We feel it better to let *our* friends recommend us.(p.567)
- This to the end that *our* great blessings may never spoil us; that we shall forever live in thankful contemplation of Him who presides over us all.(p.568)
- Yet it is true that *our* first printing gave many readers the impression that these personality changes, or religious experiences, must be in the nature of sudden and spectacular upheavals.(p.569)
- Though it was not *our* intention to create such an impression, many alcoholics have nevertheless concluded that in order to recover they must acquire an immediate and overwhelming "God-consciousness" followed at once by a vast change in feeling and outlook.(p.569)
- Among *our* rapidly growing membership of thousands of alcoholics such transformations, though frequent, are by no means the rule.(p.569)
- Most of *our* experiences are what the psychologist William James calls the "educational variety" because they develop slowly over a period of time.(p.569)
- With few exceptions *our* members find that they have tapped an unsuspected inner resource which they presently identify with their own conception of a Power greater than themselves.(p.569)
- *Our* more religious members call it "God-consciousness."(p.570)
- Most emphatically we wish to say that any alcoholic capable of honestly facing his problems in the light of *our* experience can recover, provided he does not close his mind to all spiritual concepts.(p.570)
- I think *our* profession must take appreciative cognizance of this great therapeutic weapon.(p.571)
- Any therapeutic or philosophic procedure which can prove a recovery rate of 50% to 60% must merit *our* consideration."(p.571)
- Dr. Harry M. Tiebout, psychiatrist: "As a psychiatrist, I have thought a great deal about the relationship of my specialty to A.A. and I have come to the conclusion that *our* particular function can very often lie in preparing the way for the patient to accept any sort of treatment or outside help.(p.571)
- There is something spiritual about an art museum or a symphony, and the Catholic Church approves of *our* use of them.(p.574)
- I suspect that if it is wisely handled – and it seems to be in wise and prudent hands – there are doors of opportunity ahead of this project that may surpass *our* capacities to imagine."(p.574)
- The General Service Board of A.A. (the trustees) administers A.A.'s General Service Office, A.A. World Services, Inc., and *our* monthly magazine, the A.A. Grapevine.(p.575)

ours

- We see that these expressions refer to people whose reactions are very different from *ours*.(p.20)
- We think it no concern of *ours* what religious bodies our members identify themselves with as individuals.(p.28)
- That may be true of certain nonalcoholic people who, though drinking foolishly and heavily at the present time, are able to stop or moderate, because their brains and bodies have not been damaged as *ours* were.(p.39)
- This world of *ours* has made more material progress in the last century than in all the millenniums which went before.(p.51)
- The inventory was *ours*, not the other man's.(p.67)
- We are greatly indebted to the doctor in attendance there, for he, although it might prejudice his own work, has told us of his belief in *ours*.(p.162)
- At times, when I noticed other families, I felt something was very wrong with *ours*.(p.369)
- To me, A.A. is within the reach of every alcoholic, because it can be achieved in any walk of life and because the achievement is not *ours* but God's.(p.395)

ourself

- The rule is we must be hard on *ourself*, but always considerate of others.(p.74)

ourselves

• My wife and I abandoned *ourselves* with enthusiasm to the idea of helping other alcoholics to a solution of their problems.(p.15)
• If these thoughts occur, they are hazy and readily supplanted with the old threadbare idea that this time we shall handle *ourselves* like other people.(p.24)
• How often have some of us begun to drink in this nonchalant way, and after the third or fourth, pounded on the bar and said to *ourselves*, "For God's sake, how did I ever get started again?"(p.24)
• He has commenced to accomplish those things for us which we could never do by *ourselves*.(p.25)
• Our hope is that many alcoholic men and women, desperately in need, will see these pages, and we believe that it is only by fully disclosing *ourselves* and our problems that they will be persuaded to say, "Yes, I am one of them too; I must have this thing."(p.29)
• Next day we would ask *ourselves*, in all earnestness and sincerity, how it could have happened.(p.37)
• In some circumstances we have gone out deliberately to get drunk, feeling *ourselves* justified by nervousness, anger, worry, depression, jealousy or the like.(p.37)
• We admit we have some of these symptoms, but we have not gone to the extremes you fellows did, nor are we likely to, for we understand *ourselves* so well after what you have told us that such things cannot happen again.(p.38)
• We had to find a power by which we could live and it had to be a Power greater than *ourselves*.(p.45)
• We were bothered with the thought that faith and dependence upon a Power beyond *ourselves* was somewhat weak, even cowardly.(p.45)
• Yet, in other moments, we found *ourselves* thinking, when enchanted by a starlit night, "Who, then, made all this?"(p.46)
• We found that as soon as we were able to lay aside prejudice and express even a willingness to believe in a Power greater than *ourselves*, we commenced to get results, even though it was impossible for any of us to fully define or comprehend that Power, which is God.(p.46)
• Afterward, we found *ourselves* accepting many things which then seemed entirely out of reach.(p.47)
• We needed to ask *ourselves* but one short question.(p.47)
• Besides a seeming inability to accept much on faith, we often found *ourselves* handicapped by obstinacy, sensitiveness, and unreasoning prejudice.(p.47)
• When, however, the perfectly logical assumption is suggested that underneath the material world and life as we see it, there is an All Powerful, Guiding, Creative Intelligence, right there our perverse streak comes to the surface and we laboriously set out to convince *ourselves* it isn't so.(p.49)
• Instead of regarding *ourselves* as intelligent agents, spearheads of God's ever advancing Creation, we agnostics and atheists chose to believe that our human intelligence was the last word, the alpha and the omega, the beginning and end of all.(p.49)
• We used to amuse *ourselves* by cynically dissecting spiritual beliefs and practices when we might have observed that many spiritually-minded persons of all races, colors, and creeds were demonstrating a degree of stability, happiness and usefulness which we should have sought *ourselves*.(p.49)
• We talked of intolerance, while we were intolerant *ourselves*.(p.50)
• We asked *ourselves* this: Are not some of us just as biased and unreasonable about the realm of the material?(p.51)
• We had to ask *ourselves* why we shouldn't apply to our human problems this same readiness to change our point of view.(p.52)
• Had we not variously worshipped people, sentiment, things, money, and *ourselves*?(p.54)
• We had seen spiritual release, but liked to tell *ourselves* it wasn't true.(p.55)
• Actually we were fooling *ourselves*, for deep down in every man, woman, and child, is the fundamental idea of God.(p.55)
• For faith in a Power greater than *ourselves*, and miraculous demonstrations of that power in human lives, are facts as old as man himself.(p.55)
• 2.Came to believe that a Power greater than *ourselves* could restore us to sanity.(p.59)
• 4.Made a searching and fearless moral inventory of *ourselves*.(p.59)
• 5.Admitted to God, to *ourselves*, and to another human being the exact nature of our wrongs.(p.59)
• Whatever our protestations, are not most of us concerned with *ourselves*, our resentments, or our self-pity?(p.62)
• They arise out of *ourselves*, and the alcoholic is an extreme example of self-will run riot, though he usually doesn't think so.(p.62)
• Established on such a footing we became less and less interested in *ourselves*, our little plans and designs.(p.63)
• We thought well before taking this step making sure we were ready; that we could at last abandon *ourselves* utterly to Him.(p.63)
• Though our decision was a vital and crucial step, it could have little permanent effect unless at once followed by a strenuous effort to face, and to be rid of, the things in *ourselves* which had been blocking us.(p.64)
• We asked *ourselves* why we were angry.(p.64)
• Sometimes it was remorse and then we were sore at *ourselves*.(p.66)
• For when harboring such feelings we shut *ourselves* off from the sunlight of the Spirit.(p.66)
• Though we did not like their symptoms and the way these disturbed us, they, like *ourselves*, were sick too.(p.67)
• When a person offended we said to *ourselves*, "This is a sick man.(p.67)
• But did not we, *ourselves*, set the ball rolling?(p.67)
• We asked *ourselves* why we had them.(p.68)
• If sex is very troublesome, we throw *ourselves* the harder into helping others.(p.70)
• This takes us out of *ourselves*.(p.70)
• In this book you read again and again that faith did for us what we could not do for *ourselves*.(p.70)
• This requires action on our part, which, when completed, will mean that we have admitted to God, to *ourselves*, and to another human being the exact nature of our defects.(p.72)
• We think we have done well enough in admitting these things to *ourselves*.(p.72)
• We will be more reconciled to discussing *ourselves* with another person when we see good reasons why we should do so.(p.72)
• Notwithstanding the great necessity for discussing *ourselves* with someone, it may be one is so situated that there is no suitable person available.(p.74)
• If that is so, this step may be postponed, only however, if we hold *ourselves* in complete readiness to go through with it at the first opportunity.(p.74)
• We subjected *ourselves* to a drastic self-appraisal.(p.76)
• We attempt to sweep away the debris which has accumulated out of our effort to live on self-will and run the show *ourselves*.(p.76)
• Our real purpose is to fit *ourselves* to be of maximum service to God and the people about us.(p.77)
• Why lay *ourselves* open to being branded fanatics or religious bores?(p.77)
• Reminding *ourselves* that we have decided to go to any length to find a spiritual experience we ask that we be given strength and direction to do the right thing, no matter what the personal consequences may be.(p.79)
• We don't worry about them if we can honestly say to *ourselves* that we would right them if we could.(p.83)
• We will suddenly realize that God is doing for us what we could not do for *ourselves*.(p.84)
• Have we kept something to *ourselves* which should be discussed with another person at once?(p.86)
• Were we thinking of *ourselves* most of the time?(p.86)
• We ask especially for freedom from self-will, and are careful to make no request for *ourselves* only.(p.87)
• We may ask for *ourselves*, however, if others will be helped.(p.87)
• We constantly remind *ourselves* we are no longer running the show, humbly saying to *ourselves* many times each day "Thy will be done."(p.87)
• We do not tire so easily, for we are not burning up energy foolishly as we did when we were trying to arrange life to suit *ourselves*.(p.88)
• When we look back, we realize that the things which came to us when we put *ourselves* in God's hands were better than anything we could have planned.(p.100)
• In desperation, we have even got tight *ourselves* -- the drunk to end all drunks.(p.106)
• We finally sought employment *ourselves* as destitution faced us and our families.(p.106)
• As we say among *ourselves*, "He wants to want to stop."(p.109)
• We have enjoyed such evenings *ourselves*; we had a good time.(p.110)
• If that is so we are sorry, for we *ourselves* don't always care for people who lecture us.(p.121)
• Where we used to run from responsibility, we find *ourselves* accepting it with gratitude that we can successfully shoulder it.(p.311)
• Instead of wanting to escape some perplexing problem, we experience a thrill of challenge in the opportunity it affords for another application of A.A. techniques, and we find *ourselves* tackling it with surprising vigor.(p.311)
• What can He do for us that we can't do for *ourselves*?"(p.350)
• The only one we are fooling is *ourselves*.(p.376)
• Eventually, the psychiatrist discharged me from the hospital, and Max and I began going to meetings *ourselves*.(p.447)
• When we deal in feelings, we tend to come to know *ourselves* and each other much better.(p.451)
• And we found *ourselves* back in prison, where our personalities became even more warped.(p.459)
• After all, it was self (you, me) that stood in our own way, that ran the show and ran *ourselves* into bankruptcy, that hurt the ones we loved.(p.459)
• You see how much work some of us have to do on *ourselves* when we finally come into A.A.!(p.480)
• We can have this new way of life -- learning to live with our sickness and to be happy and content -- if we are willing to change our way of thinking and be honest, first with *ourselves*, then with others.(p.480)
• I choose to believe that the Power greater than *ourselves* we ask for help, wrapped my shivering body in loving warmth and strength which has never left me.(p.541)
• Similarly, we rid *ourselves* of guilt and remorse as we "clean out the garbage" from our minds through the Fourth and Fifth Steps of our recovery program.(p.560)
• There is never need to praise *ourselves*.(p.567)
• Most of us think this awareness of a Power greater than *ourselves* is the essence of spiritual experience.(p.570)

Oursler

• In the fall of 1939, Fulton *Oursler*, then editor of Liberty, printed a piece in his magazine, called "Alcoholics and God."(p.xviii)

out-grow

• We do not, cannot, *out-grow* this plan.(p.311)

outburst

• Then, in days, weeks, or months, a fresh *outburst*.(p.105)

outcome

• The usual *outcome* was that people continued to wrong us and we stayed sore.(p.66)
• He saw that he had to place the *outcome* in God's hands or he would soon start drinking again, and all would be lost anyhow.(p.80)
• My husband was an alcoholic -- I had only contempt for those without my own amazing capacity -- the *outcome* was inevitable.(p.225)

outdo

• The times in which I grew up (the Prohibition era immortalized by Scott Fitzgerald and John Held Jr.) had taught me to be gay with the gayest; my own inner urges led me to *outdo* them all.(p.225)

outer

• To the *outer* world he presents his stage character.(p.73)

outfit

• Right away, I saw it was the same *outfit* this other guy told me about, and then again hope died.(p.267)
• I think the thing that galled me was that just after Easter I had drawn my salary for two weeks' work and had decided that I was going to send some money to Vi; and above all else I was going to send my baby daughter an Easter *outfit*.(p.493)
• Of course the kid never got the Easter *outfit*.(p.493)
• I clung to the *outfit* for the balance of my time, and finally I was released, after having spent twenty years and nine months behind bars.(p.510)

outfits

• I know that one of the *outfits* I had was a skirt and a very funny looking blouse that my mother had picked up at a rummage sale.(p.261)

outgrow

• At once, we commence to *outgrow* fear.(p.68)
• It takes some of us a long time to *outgrow* that serious handicap.(p.125)

outlaw

• He is like the retired business man who lolls in the Florida sunshine in the winter complaining of the sad state of the nation; the minister who sighs over the sins of the twentieth century; politicians and reformers who are sure all would be Utopia if the rest of the world would only behave; the *outlaw* safe cracker who thinks society has wronged him; and the alcoholic who has lost all and is locked up.(p.61)

outlet

• I went to this friend's shop to repair his electrical *outlet* and I noticed this lady.(p.493)

outlets

• I'd been home about a week or ten days when one of my friends asked if I could repair one of his electrical *outlets*.(p.493)

outline

• *Outline* the program of action, explaining how you made a self-appraisal, how you straightened out your past and why you are now endeavoring to be helpful to him.(p.94)

outlined

• He accepted the plan *outlined* in this book.(p.xxix)

• "Then they *outlined* the spiritual answer and program of action which a hundred of them had followed successfully.(p.42)

• So we let God discipline us in the simple way we have just *outlined*.(p.88)

• After being in the hospital for several days, a plan of living was *outlined* to me.(p.302)

• I try to live our program as it has been *outlined* to me, one day at a time.(p.325)

outlines

• The *outlines* and the promise of the New Land had brought lustre to tired eyes and fresh courage to flagging spirits.(p.53)

outlook

• He uses his gifts to build up a bright *outlook* for his family and himself, and then pulls the structure down on his head by a senseless series of sprees.(p.21)

• Our whole attitude and *outlook* upon life will change.(p.84)

• Here was a man with essentially the same *outlook* on life, except that he had done something about it.(p.290)

• I have been of a very religious *outlook* all my life, but that made no difference once John Barleycorn got the better of me.(p.343)

• Mentally, the fears and tensions, the complete change in attitude and *outlook*, bewildered me.(p.378)

• I didn't realize I would find so much more, but a new and different *outlook* on life started opening up almost immediately.(p.383)

• Though it was not our intention to create such an impression, many alcoholics have nevertheless concluded that in order to recover they must acquire an immediate and overwhelming "God-consciousness" followed at once by a vast change in feeling and *outlook*.(p.569)

output

• How hurt I was when editors bounced back my ideas quickly and my best friends opined that my *output* needed a lot of rewriting.(p.331)

outrageous

• Now it was semi-blackouts every night, *outrageous* behavior, passing out in some friend's Village studio or not knowing how I got home.(p.407)

outright

• It did not satisfy us to be told that we could not control our drinking just because we were maladjusted to life, that we were in full flight from reality, or were *outright* mental defectives.(p.xxiv)

outset

• Assume on the other hand that father has, at the *outset*, a stirring spiritual experience.(p.128)

outside

• What with our ultra-modern standards, our scientific approach to everything, we are perhaps not well equipped to apply the powers of good that lie *outside* our synthetic knowledge.(p.xxv)

• The classification of alcoholics seems most difficult, and in much detail is *outside* the scope of this book.(p.xxviii)

• Much moved, I wandered *outside*.(p.1)

• In some cases it may be better to let someone *outside* of the family present the book.(p.113)

• Drinking isolates most homes from the *outside* world.(p.131)

• This problem was soon solved, however, as I began to take my bottle along with me and hide it in the bathroom or in the shrubbery *outside*.(p.184)

• If I could, that was wonderful, that was just fine, and they would very much appreciate a person who had that kind of power, but they were looking for a man that knew he had a problem, and knew that he couldn't handle it himself and needed *outside* help.(p.186)

• When I was eighteen, at the end of high school, the high school team had a banquet at a well-known roadhouse *outside* of Akron.(p.194)

• I kept myself so busy that *outside* of some school and group parties, I didn't go overboard on drinking very much between the ages of twenty-five and thirty.(p.213)

• My experience in the hospital I considered to be terrific because Dr. Bob told me very quickly that medicine would have very little to do with it, *outside* of trying to restore my appetite for food.(p.217)

• I grew up in a small town *outside* Akron, Ohio, where the life was typical of any average small town.(p.287)

• Doctors told me before I stopped that I had only three years at the *outside* to live.(p.295)

• While working in an office, there was some semblance of restraint, but, oh boy, when I got on the *outside* with this new company without supervision, did I go to town!(p.300)

• People didn't behave this way *outside* of an asylum.(p.306)

• I said to my husband, "I'm going to try, every free moment that I have, to get interested in something *outside*, get myself over this rut I'm in."(p.338)

• All my life, it seemed, was spent on the *outside* looking in.(p.353)

• Too many *outside* activities to do much studying.(p.357)

• She said she felt too horrible inside to be pretty on the *outside*.(p.415)

• We heard some yells *outside*.(p.424)

• Of course, an inmate must begin living the A.A. way "inside," if he is to stand a chance "*outside*."(p.458)

• After twenty years in prison for murder, he knew A.A. was the spot for him . . . if he wanted to stay on the *outside*.(p.508)

• However, before the meeting got started, a group from the *outside* came in unexpectedly.(p.509)

• Most of my attendance there was when people would come in from the *outside*.(p.510)

• It wasn't anything strange to me, and I knew if I wanted to stay on the *outside*, that would be the spot for me.(p.510)

• I had rejected A.A. on the *outside*, but now it came to me in prison.(p.528)

• I realize now that this phase of my development had been arrested by my obsession with self, and my egocentricity had reached such proportions that adjustment to anything *outside* my personal control was impossible for me.(p.547)

• I went on the wagon, with no *outside* help and with no real difficulty -- except that I didn't enjoy life without drinking.(p.557)

• Six – An A.A. group ought never endorse, finance or lend the A.A. name to any related facility or *outside* enterprise, lest problems of money, property and prestige divert us from our primary purpose.(p.564)

• Seven – Every A.A. group ought to be fully self-supporting, declining *outside* contributions.(p.564)

• Ten – Alcoholics Anonymous has no opinion on *outside* issues; hence the A.A. name ought never be drawn into public controversy.(p.564)

• But hospitals, as well as other places of recuperation, ought to be well *outside* A.A. – and medically supervised.(p.566)

• We think that each group should soon achieve this ideal; that any public solicitation of funds using the name of Alcoholics Anonymous is highly dangerous, whether by groups, clubs, hospitals, or other *outside* agencies; that acceptance of large gifts from any source, or of contributions carrying any obligation whatever, is unwise.(p.566)

• 10. – No A.A. group or member should ever, in such a way as to implicate A.A., express any opinion on *outside* controversial issues – particularly those of politics, alcohol reform, or sectarian religion.(p.567)

• Dr. Harry M. Tiebout, psychiatrist: "As a psychiatrist, I have thought a great deal about the relationship of my specialty to A.A. and I have come to the conclusion that our particular function can very often lie in preparing the way for the patient to accept any sort of treatment or *outside* help.(p.571)

outsider

• No *outsider* can appraise such an intimate situation.(p.82)

• To go into a gathering of people was the sort of thing that all my life, from the time I left my private world of books and dreams to meet the real world of people and parties and jobs, had left me feeling an uncomfortable *outsider*, needing the warming stimulus of drinks to join in.(p.228)

outsiders

• The family may feel they hold a mortgage on dad, so big that no equity should be left for *outsiders*.(p.131)

• *Outsiders* are sometimes shocked when we burst into merriment over a seemingly tragic experience out of the past.(p.132)

• *Outsiders* became interested.(p.160)

outstanding

• A few months after I made my original trip to Akron I was feeling pretty cocky, and I didn't think my wife was treating me with proper respect, now that I was an *outstanding* citizen.(p.293)

• But one was so *outstanding* that I like to pass it on whenever I can in the hope that it will help someone else as it has me.(p.551)

outward

• It is being constantly revealed, as mankind studies the material world, that *outward* appearances are not inward reality at all.(p.48)

• My *outward* professional life looked fine, on the surface.(p.435)

outwardly

• All I had left was an iron determination to live my own life in spite of the alien world -- and here I was, an inwardly frightened, *outwardly* defiant woman, who desperately needed a prop to keep going.(p.226)

• And yet my ability to lie *outwardly* and to kid myself inwardly grew with every drink I took.(p.556)

over

• Nine of the stories in Part II ("They Stopped in Time") are carried *over* from the second edition; eight new stories have been added.(p.xii)

• All changes made *over* the years in the Big Book (A.A. members' fond nickname for this volume) have had the same purpose: to represent the current membership of Alcoholics Anonymous more accurately, and thereby to reach more alcoholics.(p.xii)

• Would there be quarrels *over* membership, leadership and money?(p.xviii)

• By March 1976, when this edition went to the printer, the total worldwide membership of Alcoholics Anonymous was conservatively estimated at more than 1,000,000, with almost 28,000 groups meeting in *over* 90 countries.(p.xxii)

• This man and *over* one hundred others appear to have recovered.(p.xxiii)

• This is repeated *over* and *over*, and unless this person can experience an entire psychic change there is very little hope of his recovery.(p.xxvii)

• From a trembling, despairing nervous wreck, had emerged a man brimming *over* with self-reliance and contentment.(p.xxix)

• In time we sailed for "*Over* There."(p.1)

• I failed to persuade my broker friends to send me out looking *over* factories and managements, but my wife and I decided to go anyway.(p.2)

• The house was taken *over* by the mortgage holder, my mother-in-law died, and my wife and father-in-law became ill.(p.5)

• She would soon have to give me *over* to the undertaker or the asylum.(p.7)

• But that was *over* now.(p.8)

• The cheery voice of an old school friend asked if he might come *over*.(p.8)

• I could almost hear the sound of the preacher's voice as I sat, on still Sundays, way *over* there on the hillside; there was that proffered temperance pledge I never signed; my grandfather's good natured contempt of some church folk and their doings; his insistence that the spheres really had their music; but his denial of the preacher's right to tell him how he must listen; his fearlessness as he spoke of these things just before he died; these recollections welled up from the past.(p.10)

• I must turn in all things the Father of Light who presides *over* us all.(p.14)

• If your are an alcoholic who wants to get *over* it, you may already be asking -- "What do I have to do?"(p.20)

• If he can afford it, he may have liquor concealed all *over* his house to be certain no one gets his entire supply away from him to throw down the waterpipe.(p.22)

• Then comes the day when he simply cannot make it and gets drunk all *over* again.(p.22)

• Yet he had no control whatever *over* alcohol.(p.26)

• There is no friction among us *over* such matters.(p.28)

• *Over* any considerable period we get worse, never better.(p.30)

• Step *over* to the nearest barroom and try some controlled drinking.(p.31)

• "As soon as I regained my ability to think, I went carefully *over* that evening in Washington.(p.41)

• They show how the change came *over* them.(p.51)

• Some of us had already walked far *over* the Bridge

of Reason toward the desired shore of faith.(p.53)
• It poured *over* and through him with the certainty and majesty of a great tide at flood.(p.56)
• 1.We admitted we were powerless *over* alcohol -- that our lives had become unmanageable.(p.59)
• 3.Made a decision to turn our will and our lives *over* to the care of God as we understood Him.(p.59)
• Being convinced, we were at Step Three, which is that we decided to turn our will and our life *over* to God as we understood Him.(p.60)
• He is like the retired business man who lolls in the Florida sunshine in the winter complaining of the sad state of the nation; the minister who sighs *over* the sins of the twentieth century; politicians and reformers who are sure all would be Utopia if the rest of the world would only behave; the outlaw safe cracker who thinks society has wronged him; and the alcoholic who has lost all and is locked up.(p.61)
• Take away my difficulties, that victory *over* them may bear witness to those I would help of Thy Power, Thy Love, and Thy Way of life.(p.63)
• We reviewed our own conduct *over* the years past.(p.69)
• Remember it was agreed at the beginning we would go to any lengths for victory *over* alcohol.(p.76)
• As we look *over* the list of business acquaintances and friends we have hurt, we may feel diffident about going to some of them on a spiritual basis.(p.76)
• Simply we tell him that we will never get *over* drinking until we have done our utmost to straighten out the past.(p.77)
• It's water *over* the dam.(p.78)
• Give him a chance to think it *over.*(p.95)
• You should point out that his defects of character are not going to disappear *over* night.(p.100)
• An alcoholic of this temperament may be quick to use this chapter as a club *over* your head.(p.108)
• But when he gets *over* the spree, he begins to think once more how he can drink moderately next time.(p.109)
• His friends feel closer *over* a highball.(p.110)
• But after his next binge, ask him if he would really like to get *over* drinking for good.(p.112)
• Some men cannot or will not get *over* alcoholism.(p.114)
• If your husband is a drinker, you probably worry *over* what other people are thinking and you hate to meet your friends.(p.114)
• At such moments we forget that alcoholism is an illness *over* which we could not possibly have had any power.(p.118)
• If you are satisfied he really wants to get *over* drinking, you need not be alarmed.(p.120)
• Husbands and wives have sometimes been obliged to separate for a time until new perspective, new victory *over* hurt pride could be rewon.(p.125)
• They want him to make a fuss *over* them.(p.126)
• Sometimes he explodes *over* a trifle.(p.126)
• We know there are difficult wives and families, but the man who is getting *over* alcoholism must remember he did much to make them so.(p.127)
• Like a gaunt prospector, belt drawn in *over* the last ounce of food, our pick struck gold.(p.128)
• We try not to indulge in cynicism *over* the state of the nations, nor do we carry the world's troubles on our shoulders.(p.132)
• Outsiders are sometimes shocked when we burst into merriment *over* a seemingly tragic experience out of the past.(p.132)
• Still another experience: A woman's voice came faintly *over* long distance from Virginia.(p.137)
• When drinking, or getting *over* a bout, an alcoholic, sometimes the model of honesty when normal, will do incredible things.(p.140)
• For most alcoholics who are drinking, or who are just getting *over* a spree, a certain amount of physical treatment is desirable, even imperative.(p.142)
• To get *over* drinking will require a transformation of thought and attitude.(p.143)
• The firm wants to help you get *over* it, and if you are interested, there is a way out.(p.147)
• He remarked: "I'm mighty glad you fellows got *over* your drinking.(p.148)
• *Over* and *over*, he would say: "That's me.(p.157)
• He had been thinking it *over.*(p.158)
• Many a man, yet dazed from his hospital experience, has stepped *over* the threshold of that home into freedom.(p.160)
• If my wife was planning to go out in the afternoon, I would get a large supply of liquor and smuggle it home and hide it in the coal bin, the clothes chute, *over* door jambs, *over* beams in the cellar and in cracks in the cellar tile.(p.176)
• About this time a lady called up my wife one Saturday afternoon, saying she wanted me to come *over* that evening to meet a friend of hers who might help me.(p.179)
• Wishing to be polite, though I felt very badly, I said, "Let's make the call," and extracted from my wife a promise that we would not stay *over* fifteen minutes.(p.179)
• These good people notified my wife, who sent my newly made friend *over* to get me.(p.179)
• Unlike most of our crowd, I did not get *over* my craving for liquor much during the first two and one-half years of abstinence.(p.181)
• I would reach *over* and get this and take a shot and in a few moments get up and take another, shave and eat my breakfast, slip a half pint of liquor in my hip pocket, and go on to school.(p.183)
• Away from my office two or three weeks at a time; horrible days and nights when I would lie on the floor of my home, lying awake and reaching *over* to get the bottle, taking a drink and going back into oblivion.(p.184)
• I looked up and there were two great big fellows *over* six foot tall, very likable looking.(p.185)
• They left this with me to think *over,* and I lay there on that hospital bed and went back *over* and reviewed my life.(p.186)
• So, after reviewing these things and realizing what liquor had cost me, I went to this Higher Power which, to me was God, without any reservation, and admitted that I was completely powerless *over* alcohol, and that I was willing to do anything in the world to get rid of the problem.(p.187)
• In fact, I admitted that from now on I was willing to let God take *over*, instead of me.(p.187)
• *Over* and *over* he said this to himself.(p.189)
• At length peace stole *over* him and he slept.(p.189)
• Before our visit was *over,* Bill suddenly turned to his wife and said, "Go fetch my clothes, dear.(p.189)
• It was in the next two or three days after I had first met Doc and Bill, that I finally came to a decision to turn my will *over* to God and to go along with this program the best that I could.(p.189)
• Of course, we had talked *over* quite a number of the failings that I had and made a sort of an inventory, which wasn't too difficult, because I had an awful lot of things wrong that were very apparent to me, because I knew all about them.(p.190)
• I know there was even more, something that I hadn't got, and I remember one day, a week or two after I had come out of the hospital, Bill was *over* to my house talking to my wife and me.(p.191)
• I went *over* and bought a jug of hard cider and a gallon of wine that I gave these fellows to drink.(p.195)
• During the day, looking *over* the contracts and money in my pocket, I found that I had sold six lots that I couldn't even remember, and didn't even know the people I had sold them to.(p.196)
• I was a very young married man, having his whiskey in the cupboard *over* the sink, and when I helped my wife with the dishes at night I would take a cup of tea and spike it with whiskey.(p.196)
• I can well remember *over* a long period of years when I thought I was the only person in the world who knew that sooner or later I was going to get drunk.(p.198)
• At the end of about four months, I not only had good looking clothes --and I might say that at the time I first talked to Max I didn't have a suit of clothes I could bend *over* in real sudden; now I had six suits of clothes.(p.200)
• I knew I could quit because he had quit; he hadn't had a drink for *over* a year.(p.208)
• In the fall of the graduating year, I became involved in some litigation *over* the ownership of inventions and patents.(p.212)
• I do not recollect the specific conversation that went on but I believe I did challenge Bill to tell me something about A.A. and I do recall one other thing: I wanted to know what this was that worked so many wonders, and hanging *over* the mantel was a picture of Gethsemane and Bill pointed to it and said, "There it is," which didn't make much sense to me.(p.216)
• Bill bought me a drink or two on the way, and Dorothy S. came with us, and the three of us went *over* to the City Hospital.(p.217)
• I had had no hospitalization up to this time because I would not call doctors when I was getting *over* a bad one.(p.217)
• I had been going on like that for *over* a year.(p.224)
• I had found friends, understanding friends who often knew what I was thinking and feeling better than I knew myself, and didn't allow me to retreat into my prison of loneliness and fear *over* a fancied slight or hurt.(p.228)
• Talking things *over* with them, great floods of enlightenment showed me myself as I really was and I was like them.(p.229)
• I have something to contribute to humanity, since I am peculiarly qualified, as a fellow-sufferer, to give aid and comfort to those who have stumbled and fallen *over* this business of meeting life.(p.229)
• I had them hidden away in the house and all *over* my shop in careful concealment.(p.233)
• In four or five days I would be hunting all *over* the place, at home and in my workshop, for the bottles I had destroyed, cursing myself for being a fool.(p.234)
• Instead he told me that some of them wanted to talk to me and would be *over* to see me.(p.235)
• That is the way Jackie found me, lying on a cot in my skivvies, with hot and cold sweats, pounding heart and that awful itchy scratchiness all *over.*(p.238)
• I like to think I was fairly normal before alcohol took *over.*(p.240)
• There I was, unshaven, clothes torn and dirty with no recollection of wandering all *over* France but, of course, a hero to the local French.(p.242)
• With the war *over,* and back in Baltimore with the folks, there were several small jobs for three years and then I went to work soliciting as one of the first ten employees of a new national finance company.(p.242)
• This company now does a volume of *over* three billion dollars annually.(p.242)
• Then I turned two company cars *over* in a short time and Bingo -- fired again.(p.242)
• The man who was going to take *over* one of their biggest branches come Monday?(p.243)
• In the eight years before A.A. found me, I had *over* forty jobs -- selling and travelling -- one thing after another, and the same old routine.(p.244)
• Then broke again, hiding out in cheap hotels all *over* the country, one night jail stands here and there, and always that horrible feeling "What's the use -- nothing is worth while."(p.244)
• Bill and Hank had just taken *over* a small automobile polishing company and they offered me a job -- ten dollars a week and keep at Hank's house.(p.246)
• My migrations extended for *over* a year as far west as Omaha.(p.253)
• Curious about it, feeling I was missing something, absolutely without any illusions about the aftermath, with no pronounced feeling of patriotism, I joined up with a Canadian regiment, serving a little *over* two years.(p.253)
• My wife came *over* from Scotland and we started housekeeping in a large Ohio city.(p.254)
• A friend who knew I would soon be broke mounted guard *over* me when I left my job of writing the histories of Texas cities and put me aboard a bus for the town I had left almost five years before.(p.256)
• Instead, *over* coffee cups, this man and his wife told me what had been done for them.(p.259)
• I began to read the Bible daily and to go *over* a simple devotional exercise as a way to begin each day.(p.259)
• They called the Mayor in so we wouldn't have to stay in there *over* the holiday.(p.264)
• I'd hear them on the phone having prayer meetings and so forth, that sort of talk *over* the phone, and it completely burnt me up.(p.265)
• Mrs. M. said she would send Jack *over* as quick as he came in.(p.267)
• His wife was cussing him, raving at him, "I just brought him *over* to show you what kind of a guy he is!(p.271)
• In the spiritual strength I had found, because of A.A., I felt that I had made a complete surrender, that I had really turned my life *over* that summer.(p.271)
• She talked to me and laughed about it and got me all *over* it.(p.273)
• Visits from friends which lasted *over* fifteen minutes exhausted me.(p.275)
• The next day he turned me *over* to a couple who, although neither was an alcoholic, knew Dr. Bob and were willing to drive me to Akron where they would turn me *over* to his care.(p.278)
• So I was driven to Akron the very next day by these Good Samaritans, and turned *over* to Dr. Bob and the then tiny Akron Group.(p.279)
• Please let me turn it *over* to you."(p.280)
• It is well *over* sixteen years since I came back to life.(p.280)
• It would be impossible for me to pass *over* this year without mentioning my love for, and my indebtedness to these two wonderful people who are no longer with us.(p.280)
• I, carried away with the desire to serve A.A., gave what was probably one of the first radio broadcasts about A.A., living through a case of mike fright and

feeling like a million dollars when it was all *over*.(p.283)
• We went *over* these at great length and then he finally asked me if I wanted these defects of character removed.(p.292)
• The doctor, a young man, immediately took fire with the idea, and while he did not convince the son, he turned *over* two prospects who were anxious for the program.(p.294)
• In the meantime, another doctor in Evanston became convinced that the program had possibilities, and turned *over* a woman to us to do something about.(p.295)
• And *over* my A.A. years I have made many real, honest, sincere friendships that I shall always cherish.(p.296)
• After holding good positions, making better than an average income for *over* ten years, I was in debt, had no clothes to speak of, no money, no friends, and no one any longer tolerating me but my wife.(p.301)
• Nevertheless, there were a few doctors who saw alcoholism as a disease and felt that the alcoholic was a victim of something *over* which he had no control.(p.307)
• Nothing in their lives took precedence *over* their response to a call for help from some alcoholic in need.(p.310)
• I got orders to go to Vietnam, and I spent most of the year *over* there either drunk or sick with a hangover.(p.317)
• They passed me *over* for promotion twice.(p.318)
• I had bottles hidden all *over* the apartment.(p.324)
• But the percentages started tobogganing, and it was often a shock to read *over* some of the pages when sober.(p.331)
• When alcohol took me *over*, my bar was my kitchen, my living room, my bedroom, the back bathroom, and the two hampers.(p.335)
• I had to give him a story and ask him the same question *over* and *over* again, "Well, now, how many will that bottle serve?"(p.336)
• I said to my husband, "I'm going to try, every free moment that I have, to get interested in something outside, get myself *over* this rut I'm in."(p.338)
• Since I gave my will *over* to A.A., whatever A.A. has wanted of me I've tried to do to the best of my ability.(p.340)
• At Christmastime next year, I convinced my wife that I had alcohol under control and that I would do controlled drinking *over* Christmas and the New Year.(p.343)
• When a few drinks made me feel good before I went *over* that line, those same drinks now made me wretched.(p.346)
• In an attempt to get *over* that feeling, there was a quick onslaught of a greater number of drinks, and then all was lost.(p.346)
• And he said, "Earle, why don't you come on *over* and let me talk to you for a minute."(p.348)
• The Third Step said: "Made a decision to turn our will and our lives *over* to the care of God as we understood Him."(p.350)
• We've got to turn the whole business *over* to some joker we can't even see!(p.350)
• Here he is powerless, unmanageable, in the grip of something bigger than he is, and he's got to turn the whole business *over* to someone else!(p.350)
• Who is this fellow we are supposed to turn everything *over* to?(p.350)
• As these words are written at fifty-three years of age, with *over* nine years of A.A. behind me, with all its wonderful teachings, I haven't the slightest doubt about being an alcoholic.(p.356)
• While I was in Florida trying to convince my wife with all the A.A. literature that she should come back to me, she went *over* to her desk and picked up a clipping she had taken from the St. Petersburg Times about A.A.(p.366)
• "We admitted we were powerless *over* alcohol -- that our lives had become unmanageable."(p.379)
• It did say, "admitted I was powerless *over* alcohol; that my life had become unmanageable."(p.379)
• Most certainly I was powerless *over* alcohol, and for me, my life had become unmanageable.(p.379)
• *Over* a period of time he has built up self pity, resentments toward anyone or anything that interferes with his drinking.(p.380)
• I was an extremely sensitive person and so self-conscious that I hurt all *over*.(p.385)
• By the time all this was *over*, I was really in a terrific state, and my father taking in things said, "Miss Esther is about to faint.(p.385)
• I got right into the car and they drove me *over*, and just as soon as I got to the church they started the wedding.(p.385)
• I wanted to do it all *over* again.(p.386)
• I was so happy *over* getting home that I changed overnight, but not enough.(p.387)
• They phoned my husband that I was in jail and in such terrible shape that they didn't know what I would do to myself; and they realized that jail was no place for me, but that he was to wait a while before he got me, because at the time they called him to come *over* for me I was beating a tin cup against the wall.(p.390)
• A retired Navy man looks back *over* twenty years of drinking, to add up his A.A. "initiation fee."(p.396)
• After a few more estimates as to income and expenditures for booze *over* a few sample years, taken at random, I conclude that this twenty per cent stayed fairly constant.(p.398)
• For an estimate of salary from the twenty-one a month to start with, to *over* $400 per month upon my retirement after twenty years in the Navy, I believe that an average income of $2,000 a year *over* this period is low, but as I stated earlier, an underestimate is best.(p.399)
• Incalculable are the intangible initiation fees that A.A. members have paid: the sick, sick hangovers, the remorse, guilt, broken homes, jails, and institutions, and the mental anguish in general that has been generated *over* the years.(p.399)
• I, who did not know how to give love, was head *over* heels "in love."(p.403)
• I came to and found a man leaning *over* me.(p.405)
• I also thought that I must have power *over* myself.(p.408)
• I told myself that I had power *over* this thing.(p.408)
• I did not know that I had no power *over* alcohol, that I, alone and unaided, could not stop; that I was on a downgrade, tearing along at full speed with all my brakes gone, and that the end would be a total smash-up, death or insanity.(p.408)
• Once, when I called my analyst, and told her I was contemplating death, she came *over* and tried to get me into a sanitarium.(p.411)
• I said it *over* and *over*, boring my fellow barflies.(p.412)
• GROWING UP ALL *OVER* AGAIN(p.418)
• Most important, A.A. has enabled me to go back and start growing up all *over* again in all areas of my life.(p.420)
• My dad, who was a newspaper man and had some connections, had meantime put a stop on me, and I guess that report went all *over* the country.(p.424)
• It looked as if the war would be *over* any day, but I had to go anyhow.(p.425)
• And when this six month school was *over* I applied for duty in Hawaii and pulled it.(p.426)
• I spent the time in a nearby tavern, was loaded on the ship, went to sleep before take-off, and the next thing I knew someone was shaking me and telling me we were *over* San Diego.(p.428)
• Once or twice, during my early drinking, I carried it *over* into the second day, and only once, that I can remember, did it continue into the third.(p.432)
• Even on my rare (at first) binge nights it never ran much *over* a quart.(p.433)
• "The nervous tension had piled up and just had to spill *over*."(p.433)
• It started out as a good marriage, but it deteriorated *over* the years as she progressed through the various stages of qualifying for Al-Anon.(p.439)
• I can't say, "I'm powerless *over* alcohol, but solid alcohol is okay."(p.443)
• On two occasions, *over* weekends, I decided I would take absolutely nothing.(p.443)
• So I sat down with me and went *over* the facts behind the convulsions: personality changes, daily headaches, sense of impending doom, sense of impending insanity.(p.444)
• We got on the plane and immediately had a big fight *over* whether I'd drink the free booze.(p.444)
• Max still works with me in the office, but we have turned our wills and our lives and our work *over* to the care of God.(p.446)
• *Over* the years, as I thought about Max, her good qualities grew and grew, and we married, and all these qualities became more and more apparent to me, and we were happier and happier.(p.450)
• Eventually, I had to redo each of the Twelve Steps specifically with Max in mind, from the First, saying, "I am powerless *over* alcohol, and my homelife is unmanageable by me," to the Twelfth, in which I tried to think of her as a sick Al-Anon and treat her with the love I would give a sick A.A. newcomer.(p.452)
• The alcoholic suffers death many times *over*.(p.457)
• Now, I have been an alcoholism counselor for *over* a year and am off parole.(p.462)
• Three weeks ago, my phone rang, and a voice I hadn't heard in *over* twenty-three years spoke.(p.462)
• Having passed *over* the border line, the next five years were filled with fear, failure and frustration.(p.465)
• All afternoon I sat there and drank and played Bing Crosby's recording of "Silent Night" *over* and *over* again on the juke box.(p.467)
• Only they had been scratched out and *over* them was written, "Chronic Alcoholic."(p.470)
• That was *over* seven years ago, and thank God and A.A., I haven't had a drink since.(p.473)
• God must watch *over* me.(p.475)
• Start group on reservation and carry message, help start other groups all *over* Maritimes and New England.(p.476)
• Once, I phoned my brother-in-law and told him I was going to take a handful of pills (in fact, I already had) and I would slash my wrists if he didn't come *over* to stop me.(p.479)
• So she went to court and talked it *over* with the judge.(p.491)
• Father is an Episcopal minister and his work takes him *over* long drives on bad roads.(p.497)
• A mellow glow stole *over* me.(p.498)
• What a wonderful power he has *over* the mind!(p.499)
• The day is *over* and business has been not so good.(p.500)
• The game is *over* and the other three leave.(p.502)
• "Then all of your troubles are *over*," says the man and leaves the room.(p.503)
• Suddenly I feel a wave of utter hopelessness sweep *over* me.(p.504)
• I fix up a little apartment *over* the garage with books and drinking water.(p.506)
• After the meeting was *over* and we had returned to the cell block again, I was asked how I was impressed.(p.510)
• She asked me, was I going to do this to her all *over* again?(p.510)
• I'm grateful because that Higher Power led me to A.A. a little *over* three years ago, when I needed it very badly.(p.512)
• A former employer of mine said to me a little *over* ten years ago, "Pat, you seem to be one of those unfortunate people who at least once every six months must go out and roll in the gutter."(p.513)
• We talked for a while, and then he sent me down to the Alanon House *over* on the west side, and there I had my introduction to A.A.(p.515)
• A.A.'s Twelve Steps may confuse you when you read them *over*.(p.516)
• Before I step out and do anything, I stop and check it *over* first, and then let my conscience be my guide.(p.516)
• But I pointed out to him that as I was the first British boy who had been to the school, it wouldn't be a very good advertisement for him, so I got *over* that all right.(p.518)
• The term was nearly *over* and we parted on fairly friendly terms.(p.518)
• When the war was *over*, we had about a year in Germany, occupying the place.(p.518)
• Then I went *over* again to Germany for four years on an occupation job.(p.519)
• However, I kept that job in Egypt and Palestine for about two years, and then I changed *over* to the other battalion in my regiment.(p.520)
• I couldn't wait until the meeting was *over* to get a drink.(p.526)
• I would wake to find myself in some beat-up rooming house, where roaches were crawling *over* everything.(p.527)
• That was the day, that was the decision, I know now, when I crossed *over* the line and became an active alcoholic.(p.531)
• But I wanted a cosmos, a universe all my own which I had created and where I reigned as chief top reigner and ruler *over* everyone else.(p.535)
• For always, *over* and above everything else, was the awfulness of the lack of meaning in life.(p.535)
• Need I add that such was the case because I had no money to provide a roof *over* my head?(p.538)
• The helpful family finally said, *over* long distance, that there would be no more money and that I could not come home.(p.538)
• I had even borrowed money from her, *over* her protest: "Bob, please don't ask me to lend you money -- you're the only one who hasn't."(p.540)
• I went *over* and met him, and we two started the group up again.(p.541)
• At fifty-four, I have had come true for me the old wish, "If only I could live my life *over*, knowing what I know."(p.543)

• I had no problem admitting I was powerless *over* alcohol, and I certainly agreed that my life had become unmanageable.(p.550)

• *Over* the next two years, I sickened rapidly.(p.557)

• Angry bruises appeared mysteriously all *over* my body.(p.558)

• Experience has often warned us that nothing can so surely destroy our spiritual heritage as futile disputes *over* property, money, and authority.(p.566)

• This to the end that our great blessings may never spoil us; that we shall forever live in thankful contemplation of Him who presides *over* us all.(p.568)

• Most of our experiences are what the psychologist William James calls the "educational variety" because they develop slowly *over* a period of time.(p.569)

• Dr. W.W. Bauer, broadcasting under the auspices of The American Medical Association in 1946, *over* the NBC network, said, in part: "Alcoholics Anonymous are no crusaders; not a temperance society.(p.572)

over-achiever

• By the time I reached high school, I was an *over-achiever*.(p.555)

over-all

• They are authorized by the groups to handle our *over-all* public relations and they guarantee the integrity of our principal newspaper, the A.A. Grapevine.(p.567)

over-anxious

• But urge them not to be *over-anxious*, for that might spoil matters.(p.91)

over-concentration

• But he must see the danger of *over-concentration* on financial success.(p.127)

over-indulged

• Alcohol is so sexually stimulating to some men that they have *over-indulged*.(p.134)

• There was no doubt he *over-indulged*.(p.135)

over-powering

• Dr. Bob dwelt at length on how prayer had given him release, time and time again, from the nearly *over-powering* compulsion to take a drink.(p.279)

over-remorseful

• They are *over-remorseful* and make many resolutions, but never a decision.(p.xxviii)

over-train

• I would follow certain drinking schedules or diets faithfully for a few days, and then somewhere along the line would *over-train* and upset the applecart.(p.361)

over-weening

• I believe that my once *over-weening* self-will has finally found its proper place, for I can say many times daily, "Thy will be done, not mine" . . . and mean it.(p.229)

• There was the *over-weening* ambition to be the world's greatest author, when -- at thirty-nine -- I had nothing of importance to say to the world.(p.534)

overbearing

• Unreasonable -- Unjust -- *Overbearing*(p.65)

overboard

• I kept myself so busy that outside of some school and group parties, I didn't go *overboard* on drinking very much between the ages of twenty-five and thirty.(p.213)

overcast

• When the *overcast* lifted, the stars were there as before.(p.400)

overcoat

• He took off his hat and his *overcoat*, and he said, "You don't look very good.(p.207)

• And as that thought came to me, it was as though someone had reached down and taken a heavy *overcoat* off my shoulders, for that was the last one.(p.347)

overcome

• These men were not drinking to escape; they were drinking to *overcome* a craving beyond their mental control.(p.xxviii)

• There is scarcely any form of trouble and misery which has not been *overcome* among us.(p.15)

• Those of us who live in large cities are *overcome* by the reflection that close by hundreds are dropping into oblivion every day.(p.19)

• If a mere code of morals or a better philosophy of life were sufficient to *overcome* alcoholism, many of us would have recovered long ago.(p.44)

• When the spiritual malady is *overcome*, we straighten out mentally and physically.(p.64)

• The best reason first: If we skip this vital step, we may not *overcome* drinking.(p.72)

• We want to leave you with the feeling that no situation is too difficult and no unhappiness too great to be *overcome*.(p.104)

• A better way of life will emerge when they are *overcome*.(p.117)

• But those of us who have tried to shoulder the entire burden and trouble of others find we are soon *overcome* by them.(p.132)

• In a few sentences he made God seem personal to me, explained Him as a being who was interested in me, the alcoholic, and that all I needed to do was to be willing to follow His way; that as long as I followed it I would be able to *overcome* my desire for liquor.(p.236)

• It sounds simple, but there were obstacles and doubts to *overcome*.(p.282)

• Obviously I have *overcome* fear to a sufficient degree to think in terms of success in business.(p.284)

• I feel that there is no situation too difficult, none too desperate, no unhappiness too great to be *overcome* in this great fellowship -- Alcoholics Anonymous.(p.395)

• In the garage, I would put the needle in my vein and then try to figure out exactly how much medication to inject to *overcome* the pep pills while adding to the sleeping pills while ignoring the tranquilizers, in order to get just enough to be able to pull out the needle, jerk the tourniquet, throw it in the car, slam the car door shut, run down the hall, and fall in bed before I fell asleep.(p.442)

overcomes

• In this atmosphere the alcoholic often *overcomes* his excessive concentration upon himself.(p.572)

overdo

• Being somewhat weakened, and faced with physical and mental readjustment to a life which knows no alcohol, he may *overdo*.(p.146)

• Too often, I would *overdo* it and behave badly at the very time I wanted to be at my best!(p.556)

overdoing

• He admitted he was *overdoing* these things, but frankly said that he was not ready to stop.(p.135)

overdose

• He attended church school, where he became rebellious at what he thought an *overdose* of religious education.(p.56)

overdue

• God, they believe, almost owes this recompense on a long *overdue* account.(p.123)

overhauling

• Many of us needed an *overhauling* there.(p.68)

overindulge

• I had suppressed tendencies to *overindulge* and thus reveal my "moral weakness," because false pride was so dominant.(p.327)

overlook

• You are willing to *overlook* his past performances.(p.141)

overlooked

• He used to wonder, when he'd spot one of my bottles around the house, just how he could have *overlooked* that particular bottle.(p.325)

overnight

• This is not an *overnight* matter.(p.84)

• *Overnight*, as it were, he is a different man.(p.128)

• Now about health: A body badly burned by alcohol does not often recover *overnight* nor do twisted thinking and depression vanish in a twinkling.(p.133)

• There was one meeting a week at Bill's home in Brooklyn, and we all took turns there spouting off about how we had changed our lives *overnight*, how many drunks we had saved and straightened out, and last, but not least, how God had touched each of us personally on the shoulder.(p.246)

• I was so happy over getting home that I changed *overnight*, but not enough.(p.387)

• The personality rehabilitation did not come *overnight*.(p.416)

• In those years I was in jail nine times, in an alcoholic ward, *overnight*, twice; and I was fired from three jobs, two of them very good ones.(p.536)

overpowered

• When I reached a point directly back of our house, where I could have cut through a friend's garden, I was almost *overpowered* by the desire to get home, but I made the whole journey.(p.276)

overpowering

• We have heard of few instances where people, who showed definite signs of alcoholism, were able to stop for a long period because of an *overpowering* desire to do so.(p.32)

• Only once did I suffer from a nearly *overpowering* compulsion to take a drink.(p.285)

• I would hang on to sobriety for short intervals, but always there would come the tide of an *overpowering* necessity to drink and, as I was engulfed in it, I felt such a sense of panic that I really believed I would die if I didn't get that drink inside.(p.306)

overseas

• From a Canadian reservation to *overseas* bars to New England lockups, an Indian traveled a long trail that finally led him home to A.A.(p.474)

• Went *overseas* on beer.(p.475)

• My husband was soon in uniform and among the first to go *overseas*.(p.547)

oversensitive

• I had always been *oversensitive* to criticism and was acutely so now.(p.556)

overshot

• I took more through the day to increase the high, and more to maintain it; when I *overshot* the mark, I'd take tranquilizers to level off.(p.442)

overtake

• We went at once to the country, my wife to applaud while I started out to *overtake* Walter Hagen.(p.3)

overtook

• When sleep *overtook* me, my practice was to undress and go to bed, wherever.(p.537)

overwhelmed

• I had been *overwhelmed*.(p.8)

• In a few seconds he was *overwhelmed* by a conviction of the Presence of God.(p.56)

overwhelming

• It is important that we remain anonymous because we are too few, at present to handle the *overwhelming* number of personal appeals which may result from this publication.(p.xiii)

• Though it was not our intention to create such an impression, many alcoholics have nevertheless concluded that in order to recover they must acquire an immediate and *overwhelming* "God-consciousness" followed at once by a vast change in feeling and outlook.(p.569)

overwork

• The strain of *overwork* led me to the bottle again.(p.254)

owe

• Most alcoholics *owe* money.(p.78)

• Do we *owe* an apology?(p.86)

• I *owe* everything to A.A.(p.344)

• And the psychiatrist has had thousands of couches, and has put you and me on them many, many times, but he hasn't helped us very much, though he has tried hard; and we *owe* the clergy and the doctor and the psychiatrist a deep debt of gratitude, but they haven't helped our alcoholism, except in a rare few instances.(p.352)

• I *owe* no one -- except A.A.(p.431)

• I *owe* everything to A.A. and God.(p.463)

• The following day, Saturday, he came back and said, "Jim, I *owe* you for that prescription last night.(p.488)

owed

• This man's wife had been suffering for a couple of months and when he came in he *owed* me a little bill.(p.488)

owes

• Your husband knows he *owes* you more than sobriety.(p.118)

• God, they believe, almost *owes* this recompense on a long overdue account.(p.123)

• We think each family which has been relieved *owes* something to those who have not, and when the occasion requires, each member of it should be only too willing to bring former mistakes, no matter how grievous, out of their hiding places.(p.124)

• Having been neglected and misused in the past, they think father *owes* them more than they are getting.(p.126)

• If he *owes* you money you may wish to make terms.(p.145)

owl

• I've prayed to God on hangover mornings and sworn that I'd never touch another drop but by nine o'clock I'd be boiled as an *owl*."(p.158)

own

• The fledgling society, which had been nameless, now began to be called Alcoholics Anonymous, from the title of its *own* book.(p.xvii)

• There were to be no fees or dues; our expenses were to be met by our *own* voluntary contributions.(p.xix)

• Faced with this problem, if a doctor is honest with

himself, he must sometimes feel his *own* inadequacy.(p.xxvii)
• The patient had made his *own* diagnosis, and deciding his situation hopeless, had hidden in a deserted barn determined to die.(p.xxix)
• He said, "Why don't you choose your *own* conception of God?"(p.12)
• Each individual, in the personal stories, describes in his *own* language and from his *own* point of view the way he established his relationship with God.(p.29)
• Young people may be encouraged by this man's experience to think that they can stop, as he did, on their *own* will power.(p.33)
• How then shall we help our readers determine, to their *own* satisfaction, whether they are one of us?(p.34)
• They cited cases out of their *own* experience by the dozen.(p.42)
• Our *own* conception, however inadequate, was sufficient to make the approach and to effect a contact with Him.(p.46)
• When, therefore, we speak to you of God, we mean your *own* conception of God.(p.47)
• So we used our *own* conception, however limited it was.(p.47)
• For did we not believe in our *own* reasoning?(p.53)
• (a) That we were alcoholic and could not manage our *own* lives.(p.60)
• Each person is like an actor who wants to run the whole show; is forever trying to arrange the lights, the ballet, the scenery and the rest of the players in his *own* way.(p.60)
• So our troubles, we think, are basically of our *own* making.(p.62)
• Neither could we reduce our self-centeredness much by wishing or trying on our *own* power.(p.62)
• But the more we fought and tried to have our *own* way, the worse matters got.(p.66)
• Putting out of our minds the wrongs others had done, we resolutely looked for our *own* mistakes.(p.67)
• We reviewed our *own* conduct over the years past.(p.69)
• It may be one of our *own* family, but we cannot disclose anything to our wives or our parents which will hurt them and make them unhappy.(p.74)
• We have no right to save our *own* skin at another person's expense.(p.74)
• We stick to our *own*.(p.78)
• Sometimes the man we are calling upon admits his *own* fault, so feuds of years' standing melt away in an hour.(p.78)
• He thus used his *own* wrong-doing as a means of destroying the reputation of another.(p.80)
• Their defects may be glaring, but the chances are that our *own* actions are partly responsible.(p.83)
• We are careful never to pray for our *own* selfish ends.(p.87)
• Ministers and doctors are competent and you can learn much from them if you wish, but it happens that because of your *own* drinking experience you can be uniquely useful to other alcoholics.(p.89)
• You should be described to him as one of a fellowship who, as part of their *own* recovery, try to help others and who will be glad to talk to him if he cares to see you.(p.90)
• He will match your mental inconsistencies with some of his *own*.(p.92)
• Show him, from your *own* experience, how the queer mental condition surrounding that first drink prevents normal functioning of the will power.(p.92)
• Let him draw his *own* conclusion.(p.92)
• If his *own* doctor is willing to tell him that he is alcoholic, so much the better.(p.92)
• Don't raise such issues, no matter what your *own* convictions are.(p.93)
• But he will be curious to learn why his *own* convictions have not worked and why yours seem to work so well.(p.93)
• It is important for him to realize that your attempt to pass this on to him plays a vital part in your *own* recovery.(p.94)
• Make it plain he is under no obligation to you, that you hope only that he will try to help other alcoholics when he escapes his *own* difficulties.(p.94)
• Suggest how important it is that he place the welfare of other people ahead of his *own*.(p.94)
• If he thinks he can do the job in some other way, or prefers some other spiritual approach, encourage him to follow his *own* conscience.(p.95)
• He should concentrate on his *own* spiritual demonstration.(p.98)
• Little by little the family may see their *own* defects and admit them.(p.99)
• If you have been successful in solving your *own* domestic problems, tell the newcomer's family how that was accomplished.(p.100)
• We feel that each family, in the light of their *own* circumstances, ought to decide for themselves.(p.103)
• After all, our problems were of our *own* making.(p.103)
• He probably has several alcoholics among his *own* acquaintances.(p.112)
• You avoid the subject of drinking, even with your *own* parents.(p.114)
• If you both show a willingness to remedy your *own* defects, there will be little need to criticize each other.(p.118)
• The fact is that he should work with other people to maintain his *own* sobriety.(p.119)
• We find it better when possible, to stick to our *own* stories.(p.125)
• He is not likely to get far in any direction if he fails to show unselfishness and love under his *own* roof.(p.127)
• Thus mother, through no fault of her *own*, became accustomed to wearing the family trousers.(p.131)
• Each individual should consult his *own* conscience.(p.132)
• But it is clear that we made our *own* misery.(p.133)
• In time they will see that he is a new man and in their *own* way they will let him know it.(p.134)
• Because of the employee's special ability, or of his *own* strong personal attachment to him, the employer has sometimes kept such a man at work long beyond a reasonable period.(p.137)
• If you desire to help it might be well to disregard your *own* drinking, or lack of it.(p.139)
• Drinking occasionally, and understanding your *own* reactions, it is possible for you to become quite sure of many things which, so far as the alcoholic is concerned, are not always so.(p.139)
• I know, in my *own* particular case, that nothing my company could have done would have stopped me for, so long as I was able to hold my position, I could not possibly realize how serious my situation was.(p.141)
• The matter of physical treatment should, of course, be referred to your *own* doctor.(p.143)
• They often jeopardize their *own* positions by trying to help serious drinkers who should have been fired long ago, or else given an opportunity to get well.(p.147)
• Today I *own* a little company.(p.149)
• You are going to meet these new friends in your *own* community.(p.152)
• Our *own* recovery proves that!(p.153)
• Many a distracted wife has visited this house to find loving and understanding companionship among women who knew her problem, to hear from the lips of their husbands what had happened to them, to be advised how her *own* wayward mate might be hospitalized and approached when next he stumbled.(p.160)
• He succumbed to that gay crowd inside, who laughed at their *own* misfortunes and understood his.(p.160)
• Impressed by those who visited him at the hospital, he capitulated entirely when, later, in an upper room of this house, he heard the story of some man whose experience closely tallied with his *own*.(p.160)
• We are greatly indebted to the doctor in attendance there, for he, although it might prejudice his *own* work, has told us of his belief in ours.(p.162)
• The answers will come, if your *own* house is in order.(p.164)
• Each of the seven times that I had left this hospital in the last six months, I had come out fully determined in my *own* mind that I would not get drunk again -- for at least six or eight months.(p.184)
• The next thing they wanted to know was if I thought I could quit of my *own* accord, without any help, if I could just walk out of the hospital and never take another drink.(p.186)
• I always built up in my *own* mind the great things that I was going to do, and in fact I accomplished about fifty percent of them and then lost interest.(p.193)
• Of course, it was always my aim to have my *own* way without being caught.(p.210)
• The law school experience was not inspired by a desire to follow patent law, which has been my profession since: I went to law school primarily to learn the law of contracts following my *own* experience with litigation.(p.212)
• A year later, after I completed the course in contracts, I quit the law school, and undertook some engineering work for a patent law firm on behalf of clients who were in difficulties and who desired to keep their troubles from their *own* engineering department.(p.212)
• In 1924, I had acquired enough clients of my *own* so that the firm made me a junior partner.(p.213)
• I realized that I had a problem, although my realization was not very deep because my *own* conceit wouldn't admit that I had any personality problems.(p.214)
• That was an experience that I have never forgotten, and many times in my *own* work with A.A. newcomers I feel kind of guilty because I haven't done the same thing.(p.219)
• In my *own* experience I was so jubilant at finding myself sober, and I had so many things to catch up on, that a month went by before the thought even occurred to me.(p.219)
• I still had enough practice to earn a good living if I would only work, so I resolved that in January of 1940 I would launch a patent law firm of my *own*.(p.220)
• I believe though that it helped my family tremendously to have the A.A. meetings every week in my *own* home.(p.220)
• From far away, as if in a delirium, I heard my *own* voice -- calling someone "Dorothy," talking of dress shops, of jobs . . . the words came clearer . . . this sound of my *own* voice frightened me as it came closer . . . and suddenly, there I was, talking of I knew not what, to someone I'd never seen before this very moment.(p.222)
• I'd waked up in strange rooms before, fully dressed on a bed or a couch; I'd waked up in my *own* room, in or on my *own* bed, not knowing what hour or day it was, afraid to ask . . . but this was different.(p.222)
• The times in which I grew up (the Prohibition era immortalized by Scott Fitzgerald and John Held Jr.) had taught me to be gay with the gayest; my *own* inner urges led me to outdo them all.(p.225)
• But then the story became my *own*.(p.225)
• My husband was an alcoholic -- I had only contempt for those without my *own* amazing capacity -- the outcome was inevitable.(p.225)
• I had my *own* business, successful enough for me to indulge most of my desires.(p.225)
• All I had left was an iron determination to live my *own* life in spite of the alien world -- and here I was, an inwardly frightened, outwardly defiant woman, who desperately needed a prop to keep going.(p.226)
• I wanted to learn to stand on my *own* feet, not to change one prop for another, and an intangible and dubious one at that.(p.227)
• I went trembling into a house in Brooklyn filled with strangers . . . and I found I had come home at last, to my *own* kind.(p.228)
• He had already imbued them with his *own* spirit until they were ready and willing at all times to go where sent, and as a doctor he well knew that this mission and duty would strengthen them as it later helped me.(p.235)
• His *own* business was practically gone, he told me, when he discovered the answer.(p.236)
• My loneliness was worse than it had ever been before, for now even my *own* kind had turned against me.(p.247)
• I had been too self-sufficient to write a moral inventory, but I discovered in pointing out to the new man his wrong attitudes and actions that I was really taking my *own* inventory, and that if I expected him to change I would have to work on myself too.(p.249)
• I had some financial success through no ability of my *own* and, when jobless and almost wiped out in 1930, I began to trade and sell my collection; much of the proceeds went to keep my apartment stocked with liquor and almost every night saw me helpless to bed.(p.255)
• No conviction was necessary to establish my status as a miserable failure at managing my *own* life.(p.259)
• She said to me, "You know, he used to *own* the Merry-Go-Round.(p.267)
• Probably only a few readers of this story will be able, from personal experiences of their *own*, to understand the exhilaration and sense of accomplishment which I felt after finishing this seemingly simple assignment.(p.276)
• My parents died, both in the same year, leaving me, a sheltered and somewhat immature man, on my *own*.(p.277)
• It was simple, they said, and went on to explain to me in their *own* language the program of recovery and daily living which we know today as the Twelve Steps of A.A.(p.279)
• He it was who convinced me, because his *own* conviction was so real, that a Power greater than myself could help me in the crises of life, and that the means of communicating with this Power was simple prayer.(p.279)
• I had tried to be the center of my *own* little world,

whereas God was the center of a vast universe of which I was perhaps an essential, but a very tiny, part.(p.280)
- When I finally returned to Detroit to find work and to learn to stand on my *own* feet, the ball was already rolling, however slowly.(p.282)
- Within a year of my return to Detroit, A.A. was a definitely established little group of about a dozen members and I too was established in a modest but steady job handling an independent dry-cleaning route of my *own*.(p.283)
- I was my *own* boss.(p.283)
- By the time we reached the bar, he was willing to buy me a quart with his *own* money.(p.288)
- So I told dad that I would lick it on my *own*, that I would drink nothing for a month and after that only beer.(p.289)
- But I have a fortune in friendships, courage, self assurance and honest appraisal of my *own* abilities.(p.296)
- Strangely enough, I became acquainted with the "hilarious life" just at the time in my *own* life when I was beginning really to settle down to a common-sense, sane domesticity.(p.297)
- This was drinking in sheer desperation, alone and locked behind my *own* door.(p.306)
- He asked me to read the book "Alcoholics Anonymous," and then he wanted me to talk with a man who was experiencing success with his *own* arrestment.(p.308)
- Perhaps I could find freedom and peace and be able once again to call my soul my *own*.(p.309)
- The important thing I lost was my *own* self-respect.(p.323)
- Every breadwinner, whether trying to impress a boss or to hold customers in his *own* business, is fettered by people-pleasing.(p.329)
- I tried every gimmick that there was to get some peace of mind, but it was not until I was brought to my alcoholic knees, when I was brought to a group in my *own* community with the butcher, the baker, the carpenter and the mechanic, who were able to give me the Twelve Steps, that I was finally given some semblance of an answer to the last half of the First Step.(p.349)
- Well, I don't know who He is, but I've got my *own* idea.(p.350)
- I can't bear to be here when you lose the respect of others, and above all -- when you lose your *own* self respect."(p.362)
- I can't bear to be here when you lose the respect of others, and above all when you lose your *own* self respect."(p.363)
- This suggestion had been made before on a number of occasions, but like all alcoholics I wanted to handle my problem my *own* way, which really meant I didn't want anything to interfere with my drinking.(p.378)
- I was told that I must want sobriety for my *own* sake and I am convinced this is true.(p.379)
- The only thing I have really to offer you is my *own* story, telling you just what sort of a drunk I was.(p.384)
- I believe the first time I ever realized what alcohol would do for me was at my *own* wedding.(p.385)
- It was nothing to my *own* inner distress, my self-reproach, and my self-loathing, for was I not bearing out all the horrible things I had always suspected of myself?(p.404)
- In the course of drunken arguments, I found my *own* views and sense of responsibility as a citizen.(p.410)
- If I had not become an active alcoholic and joined A.A., I might never have found my *own* identity or become a part of anything.(p.417)
- "I've got to stop if I want to live," I told myself, and if I don't want to break my parents' hearts and maybe jeopardize their *own* carefully built up and hard-fought-for sobriety.(p.429)
- Only through being beaten down by my *own* misery would I ever have accepted the term "alcoholic" as applied to myself.(p.436)
- My new wife and I don't *own* any property to speak of, and the flashy successes of another day are no longer mine.(p.438)
- I remember very well saying, "There's only one person in the world whose guts I hate worse than yours, and those're my *own*."(p.440)
- Now I *own* perhaps the most costly pair of moccasins anyone has ever seen, and they help me remember where I've been.)(p.445)
- My reaction was that I'd already helped all the patients on the ward, and I still had plenty of problems of my *own* without trying to help some drunk from A.A.(p.446)
- So I'm better off if I don't give advice, don't figure I know what's best, and just accept life on life's terms, as it is today -- especially my *own* life, as it actually is.(p.450)
- On the contrary, the hardest place to work this program has been in my *own* home, with my *own* children and, finally, with Max.(p.451)
- After all, it was self (you, me) that stood in our *own* way, that ran the show and ran ourselves into bankruptcy, that hurt the ones we loved.(p.459)
- But the difference lay in the fact that the A.A.'s knew from their *own* bitter experience.(p.471)
- She realized that, and the way I felt, and so for my *own* good she gradually began to pull away.(p.472)
- What we do with it is our *own* business; how we use it is up to us individually.(p.473)
- I feel that I have been restored to health and sanity these past years not through my *own* efforts nor as a result of anything I may have done, but because I've come to believe -- to really believe -- that alone I can do nothing.(p.473)
- That my *own* innate selfishness and stubbornness are the evils which, if left unguarded, can drive me to alcohol.(p.473)
- This physician, the originator of A.A.'s first black group, but badly caught in the toils, tells of his release and of how freedom came as he worked among his *own* people.(p.483)
- I had my *own* medical practice in Washington at that time, but the practice slackened and the mail order business started to fall off.(p.486)
- I have troubles of my *own*."(p.494)
- I begin to see I am not the person I had thought myself, that I had judged myself by comparing myself to others, and always to my *own* advantage.(p.504)
- I am learning that I cannot have my *own* way as I used to.(p.505)
- After hearing the first speaker I could tell myself that my *own* lot was rather mild.(p.509)
- She had been warned numerous times, not only by her family but by my *own* mother, that I was a hopeless drunk, that there wasn't anything anybody could do with me, that I'd never stop, and that eventually I'd break her heart.(p.513)
- Each one has its *own* place.(p.516)
- But as soon as I got out on my *own* in France, I started drinking.(p.518)
- In my *own* generation I stuck out, I can see that now, as being a very much heavier drinker than the average man.(p.518)
- I went to hospitals, I went to retreats and doctors, and finally my mother asked me to go and see a specialist of her *own* choosing.(p.522)
- It has taught me that I can best keep my sobriety by sharing it out with others; that I must bring that sobriety to others who need it, in my *own* interest.(p.524)
- For you learned that he had been guilty of the thing he had accused you of, and his guilt had brought suffering to his entire family; and he thought he saw his young son beginning his *own* tragic pattern.(p.533)
- But I wanted a cosmos, a universe all my *own* which I had created and where I reigned as chief top reigner and ruler over everyone else.(p.535)
- Still, I had had funds sufficient to get plastered because that, of course, was more important than paying my *own* way.(p.538)
- I have had the joy of seeing many a human being, down and out, learn to stand straight again, and to proceed under his *own* power to happiness in life.(p.541)
- I have seen that there is only one law, the law of love, and there are only two sins; the first is to interfere with the growth of another human being, and the second is to interfere with one's *own* growth.(p.542)
- Like most other alcoholics I have known, I did quit drinking at various times -- once for ten months on my *own* and during other interludes when I was hospitalized.(p.554)
- Above all, I was suffering inner pain because my performance and my accomplishments in life failed to live up to my *own* expectations of myself.(p.557)
- 4. -- With respect to its *own* affairs, each A.A group should be responsible to no other authority than its *own* conscience.(p.565)
- 7. -- The A.A. groups themselves ought to be fully supported by the voluntary contributions of their *own* members.(p.566)
- With few exceptions our members find that they have tapped an unsuspected inner resource which they presently identify with their *own* conception of a Power greater than themselves.(p.569)
- Dr. G. Kirby Collier, psychiatrist: "I have felt that A.A. is a group unto themselves and their best results can be had under their *own* guidance, as a result of their philosophy.(p.571)

owned

- I remember I felt irritated that I had to be a salesman for a concern I once ***owned***.(p.36)
- This went from bad to worse until Sophomore spring when, after a prolonged period of drinking, I made up my mind that I could not complete my course, so I packed my grip and went South to spend a month on a large farm ***owned*** by a friend of mine.(p.173)
- Finally, one morning, I got up and got in the car and cried all the way down to the M.'s -- the people who ***owned*** the bar -- and told her I was licked and wanted help.(p.267)
- They ***owned*** this joint, she ran it, and he sold for a brewery.(p.267)
- The apartment was charming; the shelves were full of books, many of which I myself ***owned***.(p.413)
- A very good friend of mine who ***owned*** a drug store across the street from us, came by only about two hours later and said that he had seen Vi down town.(p.487)
- I knew I wasn't capable of keeping the bulk of the money myself, so I gave it to a white fellow who ***owned*** the bar which I frequented.(p.493)

owner

- If the ***owner*** of the business is to be successful, he cannot fool himself about values.(p.64)
- (Jack was the ***owner*** of the place.(p.266)
- I was father, husband, taxpayer, home ***owner***.(p.432)

owners

- It was also my job to entertain the ***owners*** of these stations when they came East on business -- or the pretense of business.(p.359)

ownership

- In the fall of the graduating year, I became involved in some litigation over the ***ownership*** of inventions and patents.(p.212)
- In 1940 another good opportunity came up and we moved to Pittsburgh where I was to manage two radio stations under the same ***ownership***.(p.361)

Oxford

- Six months earlier, the broker had been relieved of his drink obsession by a sudden spiritual experience, following a meeting with an alcoholic friend who had been in contact with the ***Oxford*** Groups of that day.(p.xv)
- Though he could not accept all the tenets of the ***Oxford*** Groups, he was convinced of the need for moral inventory, confession of personality defects, restitution to those harmed, helpfulness to others, and the necessity of belief in and dependence upon God.(p.xvi)
- That is, it was sort of a mixed bunch of ***Oxford*** Groupers, who were interested in the alcoholic problem, and of alcoholics themselves.(p.218)

Pp

pace
• I couldn't stand the ***pace.***(p.254)

paced
• One dismal afternoon he ***paced*** a hotel lobby wondering how his bill was to be paid.(p.154)
• I ***paced*** the floor with a bath towel around my shoulders, the perspiration running off me.(p.268)
• I ***paced*** back and forth in the apartment with the cold sweats.(p.338)
• I waited all the rest of that day and ***paced*** the floor all that night.(p.467)

pacifist
• I don't know whether she was a ***pacifist*** or whether she just thought that in the event of another war it would have some bearing on my joining up.(p.484)

pacify
• I got to the place where I'd look forward to the week-end's drinking and ***pacify*** myself by saying that the week-ends were mine, that it didn't interfere with my family or with my business if I drank on the week-ends.(p.488)

pack
• Or were we thinking of what we could do for others, of what we could ***pack*** into the stream of life?(p.86)
• ***Pack*** my clothes and put me on train.(p.475)
• I ***pack*** my bag and leave.(p.505)
• I was to ***pack*** and go and get out of their lives for good.(p.523)
• Just as I was wondering what on earth I could do -- I was too drunk even to ***pack*** a handkerchief -- the memory of an A.A. write-up that I had seen in the Evening Mail flashed across my mind -- and I thought to myself, this is something I haven't tried yet.(p.523)

packed
• This went from bad to worse until Sophomore spring when, after a prolonged period of drinking, I made up my mind that I could not complete my course, so I ***packed*** my grip and went South to spend a month on a large farm owned by a friend of mine.(p.173)
• At thirteen I was ***packed*** off to a very fine Protestant boarding school in Virginia where I stayed four years, graduating without any special achievements.(p.240)
• After another of my "never again episodes" she ***packed*** up and left for her parents' home in Florida.(p.362)
• A year later, while we were on a vacation trip she ***packed*** up to go home because of my excessive drinking, and I talked her out of it with the promise I would go on the wagon for at least a year.(p.377)
• I'd ***packed*** more drinking into seven years than many a heavy drinker does in a lifetime.(p.429)
• My husband helped me into the house, ***packed*** himself a bag, and gave me some money.(p.467)

packet
• I wanted to roam again and through relatives got a supercargo job on an Australian ***packet*** which allowed me to visit my people in Australia where I was born.(p.252)

packing
• That night she too had new hope because I had made sure she would know what I was doing about my drinking by ***packing*** every bit of A.A. literature I could put my hands on right on top so she couldn't help but see it when she opened my bag.(p.364)

padded
• He may, for example, reveal that he has ***padded*** his expense account or that he has planned to take your best customers away from you.(p.145)

padding
• Threatens to fire me for drinking and ***padding*** my expense account.(p.65)
• Maybe it's only a petty offense such as ***padding*** the expense account.(p.78)

padlock
• The first impulse will be to bury these skeletons in a dark closet and ***padlock*** the door.(p.123)

pagan
• My education had been pretty much ***pagan*** -- science.(p.221)
• I had never known him to be anything but a good healthy ***pagan*** with a propensity for getting into liquor jams and scrapes.(p.257)

paganistic
• What philosophy I had was thoroughly ***paganistic*** -- all my life was devoted to a search for pleasure.(p.256)

page
• This was the substance of A.A.'s Twelve Traditions, which are stated in full on ***page*** 564 of this book.(p.xix)
• Taking this book down from our shelf we turn to the ***page*** which contains the twelve steps.(p.75)
• Unhappy drinkers who read this ***page*** will understand!(p.151)
• Imagine my surprise when I read in a ***page*** one "box" that I had been taken from the theater unconscious around noon that day, removed by ambulance to a hospital and stomach-pumped and then released.(p.244)
• Why don't you go home and get the Big Book and open it at ***page*** fifty-eight and see what it says?"(p.349)
• I took two or three drinks so my eyes could focus, and I could see that horrible picture of the awful drunk on the first ***page;*** he couldn't get the drink to his mouth, he had a towel around his hand and he needed a shave.(p.391)
• I read the book and God leapt at me from every ***page.***(p.412)
• On the next ***page,*** A.A.'s "12 Traditions" are seen in their so-called "short form," the form in general use today.(p.563)

pages
• For them, we hope these ***pages*** will prove so convincing that no further authentication will be necessary.(p.xiii)
• He had also been greatly helped by the late Dr. William D. Silkworth, a New York specialist in alcoholism who is now accounted no less than a medical saint by A.A. members, and whose story of the early days of our Society appears in the next ***pages.***(p.xvi)
• Yet it is our great hope that all those who have as yet found no answer may begin to find one in the ***pages*** of this book and will presently join us on the highroad to a new freedom.(p.xxi)
• There was, therefore, a sense of real satisfaction when I was asked to contribute a few words on a subject which is covered in such masterly detail in these ***pages.***(p.xxv)
• Our hope is that many alcoholic men and women, desperately in need, will see these ***pages,*** and we believe that it is only by fully disclosing ourselves and our problems that they will be persuaded to say, "Yes, I am one of them too; I must have this thing."(p.29)
• The foregoing ***pages*** (though addressed only to wives) indicate the problems such people may face.(p.121)
• But the percentages started tobogganing, and it was often a shock to read over some of the ***pages*** when sober.(p.331)

paid
• Simple, but not easy; a price had to be ***paid.***(p.14)
• Because of resentment and drinking, he had not ***paid*** alimony to his first wife.(p.79)
• One dismal afternoon he paced a hotel lobby wondering how his bill was to be ***paid.***(p.154)
• As far as I know that was the first time I had ever ***paid*** any attention to that word.(p.187)
• She ***paid*** me in cash.(p.196)
• Then when we got back to the apartment, he was willing to wait two or three days until I got my health back to be ***paid*** off for the liquor and fare.(p.289)
• A few times at meetings, I have heard this statement: "Members of A.A. have ***paid*** the highest initiation fee of any club members in the world."(p.396)
• (I can't know how much others of our Fellowship have ***paid*** financially and, even more important, mentally and physically.)(p.396)
• Incalculable are the intangible initiation fees that A.A. members have ***paid:*** the sick, sick hangovers, the remorse, guilt, broken homes, jails, and institutions, and the mental anguish in general that has been generated over the years.(p.399)
• But now, with His help and grace, this child of His has ***paid*** his initiation fee for good, as long as he remembers to stay away from that first drink (the one that does all the damage) one day at a time.(p.399)
• I still think dad ***paid*** him something to let me go.(p.424)
• I ***paid*** nine hundred dollars for a second hand car on my return.(p.429)
• Mind you, I had absolutely nothing to show for that eighteen years, except a beat-up car that I hadn't even ***paid*** for, but I was doing all right.(p.478)
• Even when we were paying that two dollars a night, they often ***paid*** it for us because our collection was so small.(p.496)
• Once I started drinking, I didn't care that the rent wasn't ***paid,*** or that there was no food in the house, or that my boys needed shoes.(p.527)
• Back to the big city, for another year of precarious living, ***paid*** for largely by one or two friends I still had not milked dry or worn to exhaustion with demands on their bounty.(p.540)
• It ***paid*** for a ten-day binge which was the end of my drinking days.(p.540)
• There were debts totaling nearly ten thousand dollars to be ***paid*** off.(p.541)
• They are almost ***paid;*** the end is in sight.(p.541)
• But our usual A.A. "12th Step" work is never to be ***paid*** for.(p.567)

pain
• In fact I had been in very good shape at one o'clock -- feeling no ***pain.***(p.223)
• It no longer gave me pleasure -- it merely dulled the ***pain*** -- but I had to have it.(p.226)
• Formerly, in the acute mental and physical ***pain*** during the remorseful periods succeeding each drunk, I found my recollection of the misery I had gone through a bolsterer of resolution and afterward, perhaps, a deterrent for a time.(p.260)
• I lay across the bed on my stomach with nothing but ***pain*** and sickness.(p.267)
• In all honesty though, I was skeptical, but I wanted so definitely to quit drinking that I would have welcomed any sort of physical torture or ***pain*** to accomplish the result.(p.302)
• First, through mutual ***pain*** and despair, and later through mutual objectives and new-found faith and hope.(p.312)
• Next morning I was sworn in, feeling no ***pain.***(p.425)
• But for some time, it was difficult to keep from taking a pill when I had an appropriate symptom, such as a cough, ***pain,*** anxiety, insomnia, a muscle spasm, or an upset stomach.(p.448)
• Fear of rejection and its ensuing ***pain*** were not to be risked, and I turned away from myself once more for the answer, this time to the drinks I had always refused before, and in alcohol I found a false courage.(p.546)
• Above all, I was suffering inner ***pain*** because my performance and my accomplishments in life failed to live up to my own expectations of myself.(p.557)
• I had to anesthetize that ***pain*** with alcohol.(p.557)

painful
• But what we have related is based upon experience, some of it ***painful.***(p.121)
• This ***painful*** past may be of infinite value to other families still struggling with their problem.(p.124)
• After many ***painful*** discussions, they finally gave me my credits and I migrated to another of the leading universities of the country and entered as a Junior that fall.(p.173)
• But, of course," he continued, "eventually the alcoholic loses all of his capacities as his disease gets progressively worse, and this is a tragedy that is ***painful*** to watch; the disintegration of a sound mind and body."(p.308)
• Letting go of everything at once was both ***painful*** and terrifying.(p.311)
• But it began to be an awfully ***painful*** answer as hangovers, blackouts, trouble, and remorse set in.(p.353)
• Then I was transferred to the honor-grade unit, where I spent the most ***painful*** year of my life.(p.462)
• It is ***painful*** to grow, and without the help of my "civilian" A.A. companion, big Gene, I might not have survived that critical year of adjustment.(p.462)
• When I got home my mouth was very ***painful,*** so I got an ice-bag and went to bed.(p.466)

painfully
• Yet in ancient times material progress was ***painfully*** slow.(p.51)
• He had to ***painfully*** admit that and mend his spiritual fences.(p.135)
• ***Painfully*** aware of being somehow abnormal, the man did not fully realize what it meant to be alcoholic.(p.155)
• I'd only had two with her, but I'd managed four in the fifteen minutes I'd waited for her, and of course

I'd had the usual uncounted swigs from the bottle as I ***painfully*** got up and did my slow spasmodic dressing.(p.223)
• I ***painfully*** awakened each time, mentally, physically, and spiritually sick.(p.457)

pains
• Hence we are at ***pains*** to tell why we think our present faith is reasonable, why we think it more sane and logical to believe than not to believe, why we say our former thinking was soft and mushy when we threw up our hands in doubt and said, "We don't know."(p.53)
• A few of us have had these growing ***pains*** and they hurt a great deal.(p.124)

painstaking
• If we are ***painstaking*** about this phase of our development, we will be amazed before we are half way through.(p.83)

painstakingly
• Each inquiry was ***painstakingly*** answered; pamphlets and books were sent out.(p.xviii)

paint
• So, on that Saturday before Labor Day, I got drunk and set the house on fire – so we didn't have to ***paint*** it.(p.265)
• My sponsor used to say to me, "If I could only ***paint*** you a picture of how beautiful life can be without booze . . ."(p.355)
• Well, now I'm living it and trying to ***paint*** it for others.(p.355)

painting
• Of course, this year we decided on staying home and being sensible, doing a little drinking, and ***painting*** the house.(p.265)
• Looking directly at me was a large oil ***painting*** of my wife, and her very words seemed to shout at me -- "I am not leaving you because I don't love you; it's because I do love you.(p.363)

pair
• At three-thirty the next morning, I was in Champlain Street Station, in jail for driving while intoxicated and insulting an officer; and the suit of which I was so proud was in such shape that the turnkey had to get me a ***pair*** of trousers to go into court in the next morning.(p.201)
• At the time, I thought them just a swell ***pair*** of screwballs, for they were not only going to save all the drunks in the world but also all the so-called normal people!(p.245)
• He had taken up light work, and he had a safety valve and a ***pair*** of spurs and the clothes on his back, and that was all.(p.263)
• I had turned eighteen during the trip, and I despondently returned home by jet (on Daddy's bankbook) to a ***pair*** of miserable, hurt parents.(p.354)
• (I am pleased to state, however, that I had gone to only a very few A.A. meetings before I was able to make a really beautiful ***pair*** of moccasins -- and half a wallet.(p.445)
• Now I own perhaps the most costly ***pair*** of moccasins anyone has ever seen, and they help me remember where I've been.)(p.445)
• It's as though A.A. had given me a new ***pair*** of glasses.(p.450)
• A.A. has given me a new ***pair*** of glasses.(p.451)
• Our shoes are not better than the average hobo's, and if we are fortunate enough to have a ***pair*** of stockings on, nobody notices the runs in them, because of our dazzling beauty and our dirty feet.(p.479)
• I got out of that bill one ***pair*** of shoes, and the rest of that money was blown.(p.493)
• The war leaves me with a ***pair*** of blankets, a toilet kit, a sweater knit by my sister, and a still greater inferiority.(p.499)
• When the policeman released me to my stupefied and exasperated friend at four in the morning, I went to my traveling bag and groped until I found – well, let the officer speak: "Ah," said the policeman, "he's got anuder ***pair***, t'ank God!"(p.538)

pal
• He was my ***pal***, all right.(p.498)

palace
• I am no longer interested in living in a ***palace***, because ***palace*** living was not the answer for me.(p.416)

Palestine
• However, I kept that job in Egypt and ***Palestine*** for about two years, and then I changed over to the other battalion in my regiment.(p.520)

pall
• The alarming physical and mental symptoms, the deepening ***pall*** of remorse, depression and inferiority that settled down on our loved ones -- these things terrified and distracted us.(p.106)

Palm Springs
• Many retirees embrace alcoholism while secluded in motor trailers, rest homes, leisure-world bungalows, mountain cabins, or beach cottages, or even in penthouses, on yachts, and inside ***Palm Springs*** cabanas.(p.329)

palms
• Pearl Harbor was a breeze of nine months, a gay Hawaiian paradise, drinking under the ***palms***, listening to the surf beat on the shore, a bottle of whiskey near at hand.(p.426)

pals
• The bill collectors, the sheriffs, the angry taxi drivers, the policemen, the bums, the ***pals***, and even the ladies they sometimes brought home – our husbands thought we were so inhospitable.(p.106)
• I was too busy devising excuses to be out with drinking ***pals***.(p.376)

pamphlet
• This friend gave me a ***pamphlet***, and I took it home and had my wife read it to me.(p.346)
• (This address is now available in ***pamphlet*** form at nominal cost through most A.A. groups or from Box 459, Grand Central Station, New York, NY 10163, under the title "Three Talks to Medical Societies by Bill W." – formerly called "Bill on Alcoholism" and earlier "Alcoholism the Illness.")(p.572)

pamphlets
• Each inquiry was painstakingly answered; ***pamphlets*** and books were sent out.(p.xviii)
• The big A.A. book had not been written and there was no literature except various religious ***pamphlets***.(p.291)
• The satisfaction I got from giving him a little of what I had read in those ***pamphlets*** far surpassed any feeling that I had ever had before in helping patients.(p.347)

panacea
• Without this proof the expectant purchaser would be forced to depart empty handed with none of what I later came to believe was the great ***panacea*** for all human ills.(p.171)

pandemonium
• In the midst of such ***pandemonium*** they may have rushed out threatening to live with the other woman forever.(p.106)

panels
• They struck the children, kicked out door ***panels***, smashed treasured crockery, and ripped the keys out of pianos.(p.106)

panic
• I was suddenly and uncontrollably seized with the old, paralyzing ***panic***.(p.279)
• ***Panic***, confusion and chaos were supreme.(p.279)
• I would hang on to sobriety for short intervals, but always there would come the tide of an overpowering necessity to drink and, as I was engulfed in it, I felt such a sense of ***panic*** that I really believed I would die if I didn't get that drink inside.(p.306)
• Heartsickness, shame, and fear, fear bordering on ***panic***, and no complete escape any longer except in oblivion.(p.306)

pans
• In the next two years I washed more ***pans*** and peeled more potatoes than any other doughboy.(p.241)

pant-leg
• This worked nicely until my wife and I went to see Wallace Beery in "Tugboat Annie," after which the ***pant-leg*** and stocking racket were out!(p.177)

pants
• They went into a huddle and dad explained that he simply took my ***pants***, shoes and money away, so that I could get no liquor and had to sober up.(p.288)
• After finding every bottle that I had hidden around the apartment, she took away my ***pants***, my shoes, my money and my keys, threw them under the bed in the back bedroom and slip-locked our door.(p.288)
• (That dog hasn't wet my ***pants*** once since I joined A.A., and neither have I!)(p.440)
• There is really nothing to dressing with chains and shackles on, once you learn the technique of pulling inside-out ***pants*** through the shackles.(p.460)

panty-waist
• When he left, I realized from his story that as a drinker I was just a ***panty-waist***.(p.208)

paper
• My judgment and ideas were followed by many to the tune of ***paper*** millions.(p.3)
• A morning ***paper*** told me the market had gone to hell again.(p.6)
• In dealing with resentments, we set them on ***paper***.(p.64)
• We put them on ***paper***, even though we had no resentment in connection with them.(p.68)
• We got this all down on ***paper*** and looked at it.(p.69)
• They had also been periodic big shots who had goofed out repeatedly at the wrong time, and they also knew how to split one ***paper*** match into three separate matches.(p.245)
• Russ read a piece in the ***paper***, and he kind of snickered, and said, "See here, where John D. has found something to keep him from drinking!"(p.265)
• "Oh, some darn thing they've got here in the ***paper*** about it."(p.266)
• It is impossible to put on ***paper*** all the benefits I have derived . . . physical, mental, domestic, spiritual, and monetary.(p.302)
• She said she cut this clipping from the ***paper*** at about ten on the same night, and at the same time as I called A.A. in Pittsburgh -- some 1300 miles away.(p.367)
• The other pupils kept books, pencils, ***paper***, gym equipment and such stuff in their lockers.(p.423)
• Following are excerpts from the comments of doctors present at the annual meeting of the Medical Society of the State of New York where a ***paper*** on A.A. was read:(p.571)
• The American Psychiatric Association requested, in 1949, that a ***paper*** be prepared by one of the older members of Alcoholics Anonymous to be read at the Association's annual meeting of that year.(p.572)
• This was done, and the ***paper*** was printed in the American Journal of Psychiatry for November, 1949.(p.572)

papers
• The ***papers*** reported men jumping to death from the towers of High Finance.(p.4)
• I looked so terrible in the court that the judge suggested that I get a continuance and let me sign all the ***papers*** to go to a hospital and to a doctor.(p.204)
• I'd lost my car again, pawned my wallet and all identification ***papers*** for a bottle, and gotten home somehow.(p.429)

paracounselors
• Shortly thereafter, I was selected, with eight other inmates out of the 10,000 in the state's prisons at that time, to attend a school designed to take former "management problems" like me and convert them into ***paracounselors***.(p.462)

parade
• I'd get downstairs to the gin mill, get enough in to hold me until eight o'clock in the morning, then I'd go out to join that "misery ***parade***" that so many of us know so well.(p.514)

paradise
• Pearl Harbor was a breeze of nine months, a gay Hawaiian ***paradise***, drinking under the palms, listening to the surf beat on the shore, a bottle of whiskey near at hand.(p.426)

paradox
• I stood off and took a long look at life and the values I found in it: I saw a ***paradox***, that he who loses his life does indeed find it.(p.542)

paradoxically
• ***Paradoxically***, it is the way of strength.(p.68)

paragraph
• But, from the very first ***paragraph*** on, something happened to me.(p.392)

paraldehyde
• I had taken five and a half ounces of ***paraldehyde***.(p.207)
• Also, after that first visit I learned I could refuse to sign myself in unless they gave me a glass of whiskey in one hand and a glass of ***paraldehyde*** in the other.(p.468)
• I was taking Benzedrine and ***paraldehyde*** quite impartially during the day then, and by the time I arrived at my first A.A. meeting, I was pretty drunk and certainly doped up to the eyes and completely jittery.(p.523)
• I had been using ***paraldehyde*** more or less like ordinary drink for the last six years though, occasionally, I'd bounce back to phenobarbital and things like that.(p.524)

parallel
• But there was always the curious mental phenomenon that ***parallel*** with our sound reasoning there inevitably ran some insanely trivial excuse for taking the first drink.(p.37)

paralyzed

• What about those fears which once ***paralyzed*** me to the point of my becoming a semi-hermit?(p.284)

paralyzing

• There is another ***paralyzing*** fear.(p.116)

• Fear froze me in my tracks, but the instant I turned back toward home this ***paralyzing*** fear left me.(p.276)

• I was suddenly and uncontrollably seized with the old, ***paralyzing*** panic.(p.279)

paramount

• The subject presented in this book seems to me to be of ***paramount*** importance to those afflicted with alcoholic addiction.(p.xxv)

• They took a drink a day or so prior to the date, and then the phenomenon of craving at once became ***paramount*** to all other interests so that the important appointment was not met.(p.xxvii)

• Once this was in front of the ***Paramount*** Theatre in Times Square.(p.537)

• On such issues our common welfare is ***paramount.***(p.565)

pardon

• But we have a baby who, if you'll ***pardon*** a little post-alcoholic sentimentality, is right out of Heaven.(p.438)

pardoned

• The next day, they called me in for an examination, and the doctor wouldn't let me continue working and ***pardoned*** me from the plant for ten days because he said my eye had been injured.(p.205)

parent

• I loved them, I think, as much as any ***parent.***(p.199)

parental

• This had the effect of making me resolve that when I was free from ***parental*** domination, I would never again darken the doors of a church.(p.172)

• I was very much interested in athletics, and because of this and ***parental*** influence, I didn't drink or smoke in either grade or high school.(p.287)

• I wasn't burdened with ***parental*** guidance and I didn't want any.(p.424)

parents

• We went to live with my wife's ***parents.***(p.4)

• It brings misunderstanding, fierce resentment, financial insecurity, disgusted friends and employers, warped lives of blameless children, sad wives and ***parents*** -- anyone can increase the list.(p.18)

• Strangely enough, wives, ***parents*** and intimate friends usually find us even more unapproachable than do the psychiatrist and the doctor.(p.18)

• It may be one of our own family, but we cannot disclose anything to our wives or our ***parents*** which will hurt them and make them unhappy.(p.74)

• But he is yet a long way from making good to the wife or ***parents*** whom for years he has so shockingly treated.(p.82)

• Then we were severely criticized by our husband's ***parents*** for desertion.(p.106)

• You avoid the subject of drinking, even with your own ***parents.***(p.114)

• He proved to be a devil-may-care young fellow whose ***parents*** could not make out whether he wanted to stop drinking or not.(p.158)

• Cleaning up old scrapes, helping to settle family differences, explaining the disinherited son to his irate ***parents,*** lending money and securing jobs for each other, when justified -- these are everyday occurrences.(p.161)

• My ***parents*** were well-to-do people and their marriage was a happy one.(p.182)

• I remember that my father kept whiskey around the house for medical purposes and entertainment, and I would drink from this when no one was about and then water it to keep my ***parents*** from knowing I was drinking.(p.183)

• My ***parents*** were hard working people.(p.210)

• My ***parents*** had some vague idea of making a priest out of me and for some years I attended the Franciscan school at Basle, Switzerland, just across the border, about six miles from my home.(p.230)

• My family lived in very prosperous circumstances, and while both my ***parents*** drank, sometimes too much, neither was an alcoholic.(p.240)

• My ***parents*** died, both in the same year, leaving me, a sheltered and somewhat immature man, on my own.(p.277)

• After I left school, I went to work in Akron, living at home with my ***parents.***(p.287)

• I couldn't have chosen more loving and conscientious ***parents.***(p.304)

• I had turned eighteen during the trip, and I despondently returned home by jet (on Daddy's bankbook) to a pair of miserable, hurt ***parents.***(p.354)

• The ambition to succeed was instilled in me by my Scandinavian ***parents*** who came to this country where opportunities were so great.(p.373)

• So did my ***parents.***(p.424)

• I headed home for the most wonderful experience of all time -- meeting my "new" ***parents*** -- mom and dad looked different than I had pictured them.(p.428)

• Or maybe I'd come home wild drunk, singing and raving about what a fine place home was and what grand ***parents*** I had since they joined A.A.(p.428)

• I have kind and sympathetic ***parents.***(p.431)

• My ***parents*** were due for the holidays that day, and she didn't want them to find their drunken daughter there.(p.467)

• And then I went back home to live with my ***parents,*** and the merry-go-round started again – only this time I didn't have to worry about waking up behind bars in a psychiatric ward.(p.468)

• After our first child came my ***parents*** both became allies, but in later days, after I became an alcoholic, they both turned against me.(p.485)

• My wife's ***parents*** come to our assistance.(p.501)

• I am an only child, and when I was seven years old my ***parents*** separated very abruptly.(p.544)

• In time I concluded that the reason I was hurt was because I loved my ***parents,*** and I concluded too that if I never allowed myself to love anybody or anything I could never be hurt again.(p.545)

• My reaction to this was identical in many respects to my reaction to my ***parents*** leaving me when I was seven.(p.547)

• I was raised in Kansas, the only child of loving ***parents*** who just drank socially.(p.554)

• For instance, the fiftieth wedding anniversary of my wife's ***parents*** was the occasion for a huge family reunion at our home.(p.556)

parents'

• My ***parents'*** car had a strong attraction to fences, and one night I blacked out and drove the car down a bank, ramming the steel fence around someone's backyard.(p.353)

• After another of my "never again episodes" she packed up and left for her ***parents'*** home in Florida.(p.362)

• I told the doctor my ***parents'*** drinking history and blamed them.(p.428)

• "I've got to stop if I want to live," I told myself, and if I don't want to break my ***parents'*** hearts and maybe jeopardize their own carefully built up and hard-fought-for sobriety.(p.429)

Paris

• I was now with the ***Paris*** office.(p.405)

• I stayed with them until I got drunk and had a row with the ***Paris*** editor.(p.405)

• An American doctor in ***Paris*** said I had an enlarged liver.(p.406)

parishioners

• His ***parishioners*** are limited in number, but his friends are many, for to him race, creed, or social position makes no difference.(p.497)

park

• Tasting the best of burgundy at a famous restaurant one night, landed me passed out on a ***park*** bench in the public square.(p.405)

parking

• I remember finding myself in the middle of the night in the doctors' ***parking*** lot at the hospital with one foot in the car and one foot on the ground, not knowing which was the lead foot; finding myself hanging up the telephone – then realizing I had gotten out of bed, answered the phone, turned on the light, and carried on a conversation with a patient.(p.441)

parlors

• The other kids would light out for the hamburger huts or ice cream ***parlors,*** the pizza joints or bowling alleys, after football games and dances.(p.423)

parole

• I was not eligible for ***parole,*** until – with God's help, I'm sure – the governor cut five years off my sentence.(p.462)

• Now, I have been an alcoholism counselor for over a year and am off ***parole.***(p.462)

• Each time I would make a report to the ***parole*** officer he would ask me, "Have you been to an A.A. meeting yet?"(p.510)

paroled

• After nine months of training, all the rest of my class was ***paroled*** and I went to work in the Department of Corrections.(p.462)

• I was ***paroled*** when I had served less than three years.(p.462)

part

• In this third edition, ***Part*** I ("Pioneers of A.A.") stands unchanged.(p.xii)

• Nine of the stories in ***Part*** II ("They Stopped in Time") are carried over from the second edition; eight new stories have been added.(p.xii)

• In ***Part*** III ("They Lost Nearly All"), eight stories have been retained; five are new.(p.xii)

• As ***part*** of his rehabilitation he commenced to present his conceptions to other alcoholics, impressing upon them that they must do likewise with still others.(p.xxiii)

• If any feel that as psychiatrists directing a hospital for alcoholics we appear somewhat sentimental, let them stand with us a while on the firing line, see the tragedies, the despairing wives, the little children; let the solving of these problems become a ***part*** of their daily work, and even of their sleeping moments, and the most cynical will not wonder that we have accepted and encouraged this movement.(p.xxvi)

• I was ***part*** of life at last, and in the midst of the excitement I discovered liquor.(p.1)

• That was the last honest manual labor on my ***part*** for many a day.(p.3)

• Drink was taking an important and exhilarating ***part*** in my life.(p.3)

• We commenced to make many fast friends and a fellowship has grown up among us of which it is a wonderful thing to feel a ***part.***(p.15)

• Some drinkers have excuses with which they are satisfied ***part*** of the time.(p.23)

• We finally saw that faith in some kind of God was a ***part*** of our make-up, just as much as the feeling we have for a friend.(p.55)

• This requires action on our ***part,*** which, when completed, will mean that we have admitted to God, to ourselves, and to another human being the exact nature of our defects.(p.72)

• We have made our demonstration, done our ***part.***(p.78)

• We will see that our new attitude toward liquor has been given us without any thought or effort on our ***part.***(p.85)

• What used to be the hunch or the occasional inspiration gradually becomes a working ***part*** of the mind.(p.87)

• You should be described to him as one of a fellowship who, as ***part*** of their own recovery, try to help others and who will be glad to talk to him if he cares to see you.(p.90)

• It is important for him to realize that your attempt to pass this on to him plays a vital ***part*** in your own recovery.(p.94)

• These work-outs should be regarded as ***part*** of your education, for thus you will be learning to live.(p.117)

• The slightest disposition on your ***part*** to guide his appointments or his affairs so he will not be tempted will be noticed.(p.120)

• Alateen, for teen-aged children of alcoholics, is a ***part*** of Al-Anon.(p.121)

• At the very beginning, the couple ought to frankly face the fact that each will have to yield here and there if the family is going to play an effective ***part*** in the new life.(p.131)

• When this happens, they can be invited to join in morning meditation and then they can take ***part*** in the daily discussion without rancor or bias.(p.134)

• To me, this incident illustrates lack of understanding as to what really ails the alcoholic, and lack of knowledge as to what ***part*** employers might profitably take in salvaging their sick employees.(p.139)

• If your man accepts your offer, it should be pointed out that physical treatment is but a small ***part*** of the picture.(p.143)

• ***Part*** I(p.167)

• ***Part*** II(p.167)

• ***Part*** III(p.167)

• ***Part*** I(p.169)

• Unfortunately for me, I was the only child, which perhaps engendered the selfishness which played such an important ***part*** in bringing on my alcoholism.(p.172)

• I left the university in the latter ***part*** of my senior year and enlisted in the army.(p.183)

• Then she told me that these two drunks she had been talking to had a plan whereby they thought they could quit drinking, and ***part*** of that plan was that they tell it to another drunk.(p.185)

• All the other people that had talked to me wanted to help me, and my pride prevented me from listening to them, and caused only resentment on my ***part,*** but I felt as if I would be a real stinker if I did not listen to a couple of fellows for a short time, if that would cure them.(p.185)

• *Part* of that program is that we take it to someone else, that needs it and wants it.(p.186)
• I lost money, and then just fooled away a large *part* of that profit.(p.194)
• When they got through the day's work, *part* was left which I proceeded to drink.(p.196)
• But I didn't do a thing about giving them any *part* of the seven bucks I had in my pocket.(p.197)
• During the latter *part* of the Christian Science experience I had gotten a job and was working at Firestone.(p.203)
• I had a broken nose, a fractured cheekbone, and was black from the lower *part* of my face up into my hair.(p.204)
• When I had been in the hospital ten days, Sister Ignatia, who has played such a *part* in the development of A.A. in this area, stuck her head in the door one morning and announced, looking at me quizzically, that they might be able to make something human out of my face after all.(p.205)
• Naturally, I wanted no *part* of any meetings.(p.205)
• But me, I wanted no *part* of it!(p.206)
• The people in the group hadn't been around that day; *part* of my family was in Florida and the rest of them weren't speaking to me, so I spent a very lonesome day and by evening I was feeling very sorry for myself.(p.207)
• I get my greatest thrill of accomplishment from the knowledge that I have played a *part* in the new happiness achieved by countless others like myself.(p.229)
• Military service was compulsory and I did my stretch with the class of my age, goose-stepping in German barracks and taking *part* in the Boxer Rebellion in China, my first time at any great distance from home.(p.230)
• And, because as I have discovered since, it is *part* of the "treatment" that these men be sent to see and talk with alcoholics who want to quit, he kept them busy.(p.235)
• As *part* of this promotion, they sent me to their national convention in Atlantic City to tell the big wheels how I'd done it.(p.243)
• When I started to tell the boys how we did it in New York and all about the spiritual *part* of the program, I found they would not believe me unless I was practicing what I preached.(p.249)
• One evening, the book, after checking up, was very definitely in the red for plenty through a piece of studied carelessness on my *part*, and my boss, very shrewd and able, fired me with a parting statement to the effect that once was enough.(p.251)
• No, I was all interested in this *part* that told you how to do it.(p.269)
• That was the only *part* I was interested in.(p.269)
• I hadn't been in too long when one of the men's wives called me one Sunday and told me she didn't think I had any *part* of the program.(p.273)
• She said she didn't know, but that I sure showed plain enough I didn't have any *part* of it.(p.273)
• I was crying, and I said, "Alice says she knows I don't have any *part* of the program."(p.273)
• I had tried to be the center of my own little world, whereas God was the center of a vast universe of which I was perhaps an essential, but a very tiny, *part*.(p.280)
• They made me feel as if I were a *part* of their family, and so did their children.(p.281)
• I remained with them for three weeks, using *part* of the time in making many amends, which I had had no earlier opportunity of making.(p.281)
• Then I started traveling, with the United States and Canada as my territory, and with so much freedom and with an unlimited expense account, I was soon drinking every night and kidding myself that it was all *part* of the job.(p.287)
• This latest *part* of my life has had a purpose, not in great things accomplished but in daily living.(p.295)
• I have stopped tilting at windmills, and instead have tried to accomplish the little daily tasks, unimportant in themselves, but tasks that are an integral *part* of living fully.(p.295)
• I didn't dare hope I might find for myself all that these people had found, but if I could acquire some small *part* of their intriguing quality of living – and sobriety – that would be enough.(p.310)
• By the latter *part* of September 1939, we had a nucleus of six and held our first official group meeting.(p.310)
• *PART* II(p.313)
• While I sought the comforting arms of alcohol, I knew this was a sign of weakness on the *part* of a longtime-successful old codger with white hair, the image of dignity.(p.331)
• I knew that alcohol and I had to *part*.(p.338)
• I heard one very ill woman say that she didn't believe in the surrender *part* of the A.A. program.(p.340)
• You'll read and hear a great deal about the spiritual *part* of our program.(p.366)
• I haven't written anything about that *part* of my story, but I believe in a Greater Power which I call God and I ask for His wisdom and guidance daily.(p.366)
• Rehearsals then became a *part* of the pattern, stopping at bars on the way to or from the place where drinks were to be served.(p.375)
• I was living in constant fear that I would get caught while driving a car, so I used taxis *part* of the time.(p.375)
• Dishonest thinking, prejudice, ego, antagonism toward anyone and everyone who dares to cross him, vanity and a critical attitude are character defects that gradually creep in and become a *part* of his life.(p.380)
• These thoughts become *part* of our daily lives.(p.382)
• But I did not feel a *part* of my family or a *part* of the set-up.(p.401)
• I am a *part* of A.A. which is a way of life.(p.417)
• If I had not become an active alcoholic and joined A.A., I might never have found my own identity or become a *part* of anything.(p.417)
• Then came my tour in the U.S. Navy, *part* of it being two years in the Philippines.(p.419)
• *PART* III(p.453)
• It was in Washington, D.C. that this transition took place, and that the really bad *part* of alcoholism began happening.(p.465)
• And so, in those following years, whenever A.A. was mentioned I would have no *part* of it.(p.469)
• It is no problem to me now, but this is not good management on my *part* -- just plain good luck.(p.480)
• To tell you a small *part* of what my mother's life must have been like: Three of her kids were in jail that year – two sons and a daughter.(p.480)
• I've never seen him drunk in my life, although he'd take a shot in the morning and usually one in the evening, and so did I; but for the most *part* he kept his whiskey in his office.(p.484)
• I do not fix anyone, but I am getting *part* of a tremendous education and I have made some new friends.(p.506)
• In *part*, it was a feeling of intense shame at having to leave the Army during the war, but mostly it was resentment that this kind of thing should happen to me for, strange as it may seem, up to then I still thought I could control drinking.(p.521)
• I was intensely unhappy the whole time, but I didn't seem to be able to do anything about it, and the worst *part* to me was the realization that all this was going to happen again and again until I died.(p.522)
• Even those don't take *part* in A.A. functions as I would like to see them do.(p.529)
• And, as a child is a *part* of his father, so do I now want to be a *part* of God.(p.535)
• I had fed it, fanned it and nurtured it as one might a delicate child, and it had become as much a *part* of me as my breathing.(p.551)
• It had provided me with excuses for my lack of education, my marital failures, personal failures, inadequacy, and of course, my alcoholism and, though I really thought I had been willing to *part* with it, now I knew I was reluctant to let it go.(p.552)
• Immediately, it was *part* of the pattern and *part* of the problem.(p.556)
• 1. – Each member of Alcoholics Anonymous is but a small *part* of a great whole.(p.565)
• Dr. W.W. Bauer, broadcasting under the auspices of The American Medical Association in 1946, over the NBC network, said, in *part*: "Alcoholics Anonymous are no crusaders; not a temperance society.(p.572)
• The citation reads in *part* as follows:(p.573)

part-time
• I got an easy, *part-time* job selling printing for a small neighborhood printer.(p.276)
• All this while, I wondered whether I could do laundry for the neighbors as a *part-time* job.(p.371)
• I was raised like the majority of American boys, coming from a family of modest circumstances, attending public schools, having the social life of a small midwestern town, with *part-time* work and some athletics.(p.373)

parted
• With ministers, and world's religions, I *parted* right there.(p.10)
• The term was nearly over and we *parted* on fairly friendly terms.(p.518)

partially
• He had but *partially* recovered from a gastric hemorrhage and seemed to be a case of pathological mental deterioration.(p.xxix)
• *Partially* so, anyway.(p.263)

participate
• When working with a man and his family, you should take care not to *participate* in their quarrels.(p.100)

participation
• There is something spiritual about A.A. too, and Catholic *participation* in it almost invariably results in poor Catholics becoming better Catholics."(p.574)

particular
• We are not allied with any *particular* faith, sect or denomination, nor do we oppose anyone.(p.xiv)
• Neither does A.A. take any *particular* medical point of view, though we cooperate widely with the men of medicine as well as with the men of religion.(p.xx)
• I had been out of town before during this *particular* dry spell, so there was nothing new about that.(p.41)
• To others, the word "God" brought up a *particular* idea of Him with which someone had tried to impress them during childhood.(p.45)
• Perhaps we rejected this *particular* conception because it seemed inadequate.(p.45)
• Whether we agree with a *particular* approach or conception seems to make little difference.(p.50)
• We represent no *particular* faith or denomination.(p.93)
• I know, in my own *particular* case, that nothing my company could have done would have stopped me for, so long as I was able to hold my position, I could not possibly realize how serious my situation was.(p.141)
• At that *particular* time, the boys put me on a shutter and took me out to the shed, and I lay in the car while they enjoyed their banquet.(p.195)
• At that *particular* stage, I lost interest in it, sold the option for $5,000 and forgot the whole deal.(p.198)
• I have never shown any *particular* talents nor have I had any really frustrating ambitions.(p.240)
• I learned early in my A.A. life that I could not afford to fondle such thoughts, as you might fondle a pet, because this *particular* pet could grow into a monster.(p.285)
• He advised me to enter the *particular* hospital with which he was connected and I readily agreed.(p.302)
• He used to wonder, when he'd spot one of my bottles around the house, just how he could have overlooked that *particular* bottle.(p.325)
• My story happens to be a *particular* kind of woman's story; the story of the woman who drinks at home.(p.335)
• But during a period of *particular* stress and strain about thirteen years ago, I resorted to alcohol in my home, alone, as a means of temporary release, as a means of getting a little extra sleep.(p.335)
• There was one Village bar in *particular* for which I formed an obsession.(p.410)
• Then I went South, because they told me that the *particular* county I was going to in North Carolina was a dry county.(p.489)
• I was up to international standards in one *particular* game, and that again covered quite a lot of my sins.(p.519)
• I think the Commanding Officer was rather tired of this *particular* chicken coming back to roost so often because he very soon wrote in to the medical authorities to tell them that they had to get me into hospital, to be thoroughly examined for drinking.(p.520)
• Dr. Harry M. Tiebout, psychiatrist: "As a psychiatrist, I have thought a great deal about the relationship of my specialty to A.A. and I have come to the conclusion that our *particular* function can very often lie in preparing the way for the patient to accept any sort of treatment or outside help.(p.571)

particularly
• We shall be interested to hear from those who are getting results from this book, *particularly* from those who have commenced work with other alcoholics.(p.xiv)
• *Particularly* was it imperative to work with others as he had worked with me.(p.14)
• He has a positive genius for getting tight at exactly the wrong moment, *particularly* when some important decision must be made or engagement kept.(p.21)
• This is *particularly* true of women.(p.33)
• He trembled as he went about, for this might mean ruin, *particularly* to a person in his line of business.(p.156)
• Coming up to final exams I went on a *particularly* strenuous spree.(p.174)

• I was deprived of many of the things that we feel are important in life, such as education ***particularly***, because of my father's drinking.(p.261)
• I had bad nervous headaches, ***particularly*** at the base of my neck.(p.277)
• After a ***particularly*** bad Christmas and New Year's holiday, dad picked me up again early in January, 1937, to go through the usual sobering up routine.(p.289)
• The second way in which, perhaps, I differ from some other alcoholics is this; many alcoholics state that they didn't ***particularly*** like the taste of alcohol, but that they liked the effect.(p.345)
• I didn't ***particularly*** like it, but I loved the effects, and managed for the next twenty-five years to drink anything and everything, either handed to me or purchased, at the slightest excuse.(p.357)
• I was intolerant of people who drank, ***particularly*** those who drank to an extent that interfered with on-the-job performance.(p.374)
• Never having enough, always craving more, the obsession for alcohol gradually dominated all my activities, ***particularly*** while travelling.(p.375)
• After a ***particularly*** ugly one-nighter, my wife suggested I try it, and I agreed.(p.434)
• I didn't like being on the nut ward, and I ***particularly*** didn't like being forced to ice cookies on Christmas Eve.(p.444)
• I didn't like it ***particularly*** at first, but I did like the effect I got from it.(p.464)
• I remember ***particularly*** one sentence that seemed to say, "This is for you."(p.473)
• 10. – No A.A. group or member should ever, in such a way as to implicate A.A., express any opinion on outside controversial issues – ***particularly*** those of politics, alcohol reform, or sectarian religion.(p.567)

particulars

• She may insist on knowing all the ***particulars***.(p.81)

parties

• Here are some of the methods we have tried: Drinking beer only, limiting the number of drinks, never drinking alone, never drinking in the morning, drinking only at home, never having it in the house, never drinking during business hours, drinking only at ***parties***, switching from scotch to brandy, drinking only natural wines, agreeing to resign if ever drunk on the job, taking a trip, not taking a trip, swearing off forever (with and without a solemn oath), taking more physical exercise, reading inspirational books, going to health farms and sanitariums, accepting voluntary commitment to asylums -- we could increase the list ad infinitum.(p.31)
• When the time for living together has come, it will be apparent to both ***parties***.(p.99)
• That includes bars, nightclubs, dances, receptions, weddings, even plain ordinary whoopee ***parties***.(p.101)
• Perhaps you both like ***parties*** which would be dull without liquor.(p.110)
• I kept myself so busy that outside of some school and group ***parties***, I didn't go overboard on drinking very much between the ages of twenty-five and thirty.(p.213)
• To go into a gathering of people was the sort of thing that all my life, from the time I left my private world of books and dreams to meet the real world of people and ***parties*** and jobs, had left me feeling an uncomfortable outsider, needing the warming stimulus of drinks to join in.(p.228)
• Washington, D.C. and news-gathering agency work followed, along with many ***parties***.(p.254)
• During my first year out of college I had endless dates, and went to countless dances, balls and dinner ***parties***.(p.275)
• I joined their Saturday night ***parties*** and enjoyed myself too.(p.277)
• We were having card ***parties*** with limburger and beer quite regularly.(p.297)
• The ***parties*** waxed more liquid and hilarious as time went on, and eventually I discovered that a little shot of liquor now and then between beers had the tendency to put me in a whacky mood much quicker than having to down several quarts of beer to obtain the same effect.(p.298)
• I got along fairly well with my party drinking for quite some time, but eventually I began to visit beer joints in between ***parties***.(p.298)
• I didn't care to go visiting unless the ***parties*** we might visit had plenty of liquor on hand and I could get drunk.(p.301)
• I couldn't go to one wine store and look the man honestly in the face and buy a bottle, as I used to do when I had ***parties*** and entertained and did normal drinking.(p.336)
• I lived in New Orleans where, at that time, cocktail ***parties***, dances and night spots were almost the order of the day -- or rather the night.(p.384)
• Men danced with me at ***parties***.(p.402)
• Fear, love of dentistry, and an imitation of my father's periodic drinking pattern took me through dental college soberly, except for the few ***parties*** and vacations in those four years.(p.419)
• Beaches, ***parties***, dances, movies – everything.(p.425)
• I started drinking socially and at ***parties*** and proms when I was about twenty years old.(p.464)
• I don't miss any of the old crowd nor do I miss any of their ***parties***.(p.511)
• I also began to drink at fraternity ***parties*** and beer busts.(p.555)

parting

• One evening, the book, after checking up, was very definitely in the red for plenty through a piece of studied carelessness on my part, and my boss, very shrewd and able, fired me with a ***parting*** statement to the effect that once was enough.(p.251)
• Her ***parting*** words were "I am not leaving you because I don't love you; it's because I do love you.(p.362)

partly

• I knew the man by name, and ***partly*** recognized his features, but there all resemblance ended.(p.xxix)
• Their defects may be glaring, but the chances are that our own actions are ***partly*** responsible.(p.83)

partner

• Fred is ***partner*** in a well known accounting firm.(p.39)
• We explain to our ***partner*** what we are about to do and why we have to do it.(p.75)
• If he opened that old affair, he was afraid it would destroy the reputation of his ***partner***, disgrace his family and take away his means of livelihood.(p.80)
• After consulting with his wife and ***partner*** he came to the conclusion that it was better to take those risks than to stand before his Creator guilty of such ruinous slander.(p.80)
• In 1924, I had acquired enough clients of my own so that the firm made me a junior ***partner***.(p.213)
• On hearing that, these people induced me to make the move immediately and join them as a senior ***partner***, which I did.(p.220)
• While there I was called to the hospital in my home town to see a former ***partner*** who had insisted that I visit him.(p.257)

partners

• My business came off well, I was pleased and knew my ***partners*** would be too.(p.41)
• I had two ***partners***.(p.215)
• Professionally, after I was sober for a month or so I realized that I should school myself to dissolve the partnership I was in because I felt that I would never regain the respect of my ***partners*** no matter how long I was sober, and that I would be at a disadvantage.(p.220)

partnership

• My drinking career began about four years after I had moved up into ***partnership*** and had joined certain clubs, societies and so fourth, and during which period we had Prohibition.(p.213)
• Professionally, after I was sober for a month or so I realized that I should school myself to dissolve the ***partnership*** I was in because I felt that I would never regain the respect of my partners no matter how long I was sober, and that I would be at a disadvantage.(p.220)

parts

• "Bill's Story," "Doctor Bob's Nightmare," and one other personal history from the first edition were retained intact; three were edited and one of these was retitled; new versions of two stories were written with new titles; thirty completely new stories were added; and the story section was divided into three ***parts***, under the same headings that are used now.(p.xi)
• For myself, I had adopted those ***parts*** which seemed convenient and not too difficult; the rest I disregarded.(p.11)
• Such ***parts*** of our story we tell to someone who will understand, yet be unaffected.(p.74)
• In foreign ***parts*** many a soldier who has been abstemious at home learns to use new and potent drinks.(p.230)
• I, who had never made a speech in my life and who would have been frightened sick at the prospect, stood up in front of Rotary groups in different ***parts*** of the city and talked about Alcoholics Anonymous.(p.283)
• The gradual result was that I was drifting into making drinking one of the more important ***parts*** of my life.(p.519)

party

• He was rescued by a searching ***party***, and, in desperate condition, brought to me.(p.xxix)
• After your man has gone along without drinking for a few months, you may be able to make use of his services with other employees who are giving you the alcoholic run-around -- provided, of course, they are willing to have a third ***party*** in the picture.(p.146)
• There was a very religious family that lived down the road from us, and we were on the same ***party*** line.(p.265)
• I got along fairly well with my ***party*** drinking for quite some time, but eventually I began to visit beer joints in between parties.(p.298)
• A night or so a week in a joint, and a ***party*** or so a week at home or with friends, along with a little lone drinking, soon had me preparing for the existence of a top flight drunkard.(p.298)
• One is that I don't remember too many of them, as I was one of those drunks who could be on his feet and attend a meeting or a ***party***, engage in a conversation with people and do things that any nearly normal person would do, and the next day not remember a thing about where I was, what I did, whom I saw, or how I got home.(p.301)
• It wasn't long before any ***party*** without drinks was a dud for me.(p.305)
• If we were invited to a formal ***party*** and I knew they were only going to have one or two drinks, I wouldn't have any.(p.323)
• I was assigned to keep media guests happy at a Halloween ***party*** given by a major star in his plush home.(p.328)
• After every cocktail ***party*** or dinner ***party*** she would say she couldn't understand how I could get in such a drunken stupor on one drink.(p.377)
• That first night I blacked out at a large dinner ***party***.(p.404)
• At a large ***party*** in Geneva, with people from many countries represented, the kind of ***party*** that is "protocol" in the extreme, I swayed, laughed hysterically, made naughty remarks in an unhushed voice, and was finally led from the scene.(p.406)
• By this time I had ceased to be the life of the ***party***.(p.410)
• But at the end of nine months we went to a ***party*** one night, and I took the first drink.(p.514)
• At first, like everybody else, I could keep control when I drank, but if I did start to drink, even in those days, I was always one of the last to leave the ***party***.(p.518)
• When I was faced with a special challenge or social event – such as an important business presentation or a dinner ***party*** -- I had to fortify myself with a couple of belts.(p.556)

pass

• We had to unify our Fellowship or ***pass*** off the scene.(p.xix)
• After they have succumbed to the desire again, as so many do, and the phenomenon of craving develops, they ***pass*** through the well-known stages of a spree, emerging remorseful, with a firm resolution not to drink again.(p.xxvii)
• He had come to ***pass*** his experience along to me -- if I cared to have it.(p.9)
• It is important for him to realize that your attempt to ***pass*** this on to him plays a vital part in your own recovery.(p.94)
• These things will come to ***pass*** naturally and in good time provided, however, the alcoholic continues to demonstrate that he can be sober, considerate, and helpful, regardless of what anyone says or does.(p.99)
• See to it that your relationship with Him is right, and great events will come to ***pass*** for you and countless others.(p.164)
• 3.Because in so doing I am paying my debt to the man who took time to ***pass*** it on to me.(p.181)
• And I remembered the creeping horror of the interminable night, in which I slept for short spells and woke up dripping with cold sweat and shaken with utter despair, to drink hastily from my bottle and mercifully ***pass*** out again, "You're mad, you're mad, you're mad!" pounded through my brain with each returning ray of consciousness, and I drowned the refrain with drink.(p.224)
• It would be impossible for me to ***pass*** over this year without mentioning my love for, and my indebtedness to these two wonderful people who are no longer with us.(p.280)
• I spent several days with him, but I did not feel adequate to ***pass*** the program on to him alone.(p.294)
• They daily ***pass*** into oblivion, alone or with mates.(p.329)
• Hidden old-drunks can ***pass*** out on their beds and

snooze unreproached, under the guise of taking those vital retirement-age naps.(p.330)
• Then I'd get a *pass* to Honolulu.(p.427)
• This A.A. friend took me into his home when he had me out on *pass*.(p.462)
• I am examined for the draft and *pass* the physical test.(p.499)
• But one was so outstanding that I like to *pass* it on whenever I can in the hope that it will help someone else as it has me.(p.551)

passed
• But great numbers of these -- about two out of three -- began to return as time *passed*.(p.xx)
• A long time has *passed* with no return to alcohol.(p.xxix)
• Some time *passed*, and confidence began to be replaced by cock-sureness.(p.5)
• We were in a position where life was becoming impossible, and if we had *passed* into the region from which there is no return through human aid we had but two alternatives: One was to go on to the bitter end, blotting out the consciousness of our intolerable situation as best we could; and the other, to accept spiritual help.(p.25)
• Most good ideas are simple, and this concept was the keystone of the new and triumphant arch through which we *passed* to freedom.(p.62)
• You have *passed* happy evenings together chatting and drinking before your fire.(p.110)
• Seeing much of each other, scarce an evening *passed* that someone's home did not shelter a little gathering of men and women, happy in their release, and constantly thinking how they might present their discovery to some newcomer.(p.159)
• All have now *passed* away from natural causes, having maintained complete sobriety.(p.169)
• My whole life seemed to be centered around doing what I wanted to do, without regard for the rights, wishes, or privileges of anyone else; a state of mind which became more and more predominant as the years *passed*.(p.172)
• After much argument they allowed me to return and take my exams, all of which I *passed* creditably.(p.173)
• I *passed* in at least three absolutely blank books.(p.174)
• It was the day before Mother's Day and I had come home plastered, carrying a big potted plant which I set down on the table and forthwith went upstairs and *passed* out.(p.179)
• As I write nearly four years have *passed*.(p.180)
• On the return trip, after two or three loads, I *passed* out and had to be carried to the house.(p.183)
• In fifteen seconds or less, the feeling *passed*.(p.285)
• He said he had finally learned that drinking was a fatal illness made up of an allergy plus an obsession, and once the drinking had *passed* from habit to obsession, we were completely hopeless, and could look forward only to spending the balance of our lives in mental institutions or to death.(p.290)
• On the way home numerous places must be *passed*.(p.299)
• This worldly lady helped to develop A.A. in Chicago and thus *passed* her keys to many.(p.304)
• They *passed* me over for promotion twice.(p.318)
• I usually *passed* out when I hit the bed.(p.319)
• Frank, my husband, would come home day after day and find me *passed* out.(p.386)
• Or he would leave on a trip and by the time he came home, I'd be *passed* out.(p.386)
• A patrol car *passed*.(p.390)
• Tasting the best of burgundy at a famous restaurant one night, landed me *passed* out on a park bench in the public square.(p.405)
• I *passed* out frequently in my home, alone.(p.406)
• Having *passed* over the border line, the next five years were filled with fear, failure and frustration.(p.465)
• I put Charlie on the car and when I left him I *passed* both of those liquor stores without even thinking about them.(p.495)
• He finally *passed* away, and the fear of him left me.(p.508)
• But after I *passed* through the gates I took a change of heart and mind.(p.510)
• He had a shot of brandy against the cold and *passed* me the bottle.(p.541)

passengers
• We are like the *passengers* of a great liner the moment after rescue from shipwreck when camaraderie, joyousness and democracy pervade the vessel from steerage to Captain's table.(p.17)
• Unlike the feelings of the ship's *passengers*, however, our joy in escape from disaster does not subside as we go our individual ways.(p.17)

passes
• I was to know happiness, peace, and usefulness, in a way of life that is incredibly more wonderful as time *passes*.(p.8)
• At a certain point in the drinking of every alcoholic, he *passes* into a state where the most powerful desire to stop drinking is of absolutely no avail.(p.24)
• Nevertheless, we find that our thinking will as time *passes*, be more and more on the plane of inspiration.(p.87)
• It *passes* away.(p.516)

passing
• *Passing* all understanding is the patience mothers and wives have had with alcoholics.(p.82)
• With the *passing* of the Eighteenth Amendment I felt quite safe.(p.175)
• I spend a great deal of time *passing* on what I learned to others who want and need it badly.(p.180)
• This experience sent me to law school where I went at night and which course I completed in less than three years, taking the highest state bar examinations and *passing* them.(p.212)
• Now it was semi-blackouts every night, outrageous behavior, *passing* out in some friend's Village studio or not knowing how I got home.(p.407)
• I thought, "Aha, he's *passing* the buck.(p.413)
• A busload of basketball players had been *passing* and saw the flames.(p.424)
• I would embarrass everyone by coming in drunk or *passing* out.(p.526)

passion
• Our behavior is as absurd and incomprehensible with respect to the first drink as that of an individual with a *passion*, say, for jay-walking.(p.37)
• You will be most successful with alcoholics if you do not exhibit any *passion* for crusade or reform.(p.95)

password
• I'll get you the *password*, and I can find out where they meet because I know a guy that belongs.(p.266)

past
• I could almost hear the sound of the preacher's voice as I sat, on still Sundays, way over there on the hillside; there was that proffered temperance pledge I never signed; my grandfather's good natured contempt of some church folk and their doings; his insistence that the spheres really had their music; but his denial of the preacher's right to tell him how he must listen; his fearlessness as he spoke of these things just before he died; these recollections welled up from the *past*.(p.10)
• Never mind the musty *past*; here sat a miracle directly across the kitchen table.(p.11)
• This should be an entirely personal affair which each one decides for himself in the light of *past* associations, or his present choice.(p.28)
• Sometimes they hurt us, seemingly without provocation, but we invariably find that at some time in the *past* we have made decisions based on self which later placed us in a position to be hurt.(p.62)
• We reviewed our own conduct over the years *past*.(p.69)
• We have listed the people we have hurt by our conduct, and are willing to straighten out the *past* if we can.(p.70)
• We pocket our pride and go to it, illuminating every twist of character, every dark cranny of the *past*.(p.75)
• Now we go out to our fellows and repair the damage done in the *past*.(p.76)
• Simply we tell him that we will never get over drinking until we have done our utmost to straighten out the *past*.(p.77)
• We ought to sit down with the family and frankly analyze the *past* as we now see it, being very careful not to criticize them.(p.83)
• We will not regret the *past* nor wish to shut the door on it.(p.83)
• We vigorously commenced this way of living as we cleaned up the *past*.(p.84)
• Outline the program of action, explaining how you made a self-appraisal, how you straightened out your *past* and why you are now endeavoring to be helpful to him.(p.94)
• Now and then the family will be plagued by spectres from the *past*, for the drinking career of almost every alcoholic has been marked by escapades, funny, humiliating, shameful or tragic.(p.123)
• The family may be possessed by the idea that future happiness can be based only upon forgetfulness of the *past*.(p.123)
• That is true only if one is willing to turn the *past* to good account.(p.124)
• The alcoholic's *past* thus becomes the principal asset of the family and frequently it is almost the only one!(p.124)
• This painful *past* may be of infinite value to other families still struggling with their problem.(p.124)
• Cling to the thought that, in God's hands, the dark *past* is the greatest possession you have -- the key to life and happiness for others.(p.124)
• It is possible to dig up *past* misdeeds so they become a blight, a veritable plague.(p.124)
• So we think that unless some good and useful purpose is to be served, *past* occurrences should not be discussed.(p.125)
• Having been neglected and misused in the *past*, they think father owes them more than they are getting.(p.126)
• If he means to right his *past* wrongs, why all this concern for everyone in the world but his family?(p.128)
• For his sake, we do recount and almost relive the horrors of our *past*.(p.132)
• Outsiders are sometimes shocked when we burst into merriment over a seemingly tragic experience out of the *past*.(p.132)
• If you concede that your employee is ill, can he be forgiven for what he has done in the *past*?(p.140)
• Can his *past* absurdities be forgotten?(p.140)
• You are willing to overlook his *past* performances.(p.141)
• If you take it, your *past* will be forgotten and the fact that you went away for treatment will not be mentioned.(p.147)
• Never could we recapture the great moments of the *past*.(p.151)
• Clear away the wreckage of your *past*.(p.164)
• Whether you quit six days, months, or years, if you go out and take a drink or two you'll end up in this hospital tied down, just like you have been in these *past* six months.(p.187)
• Somehow I got out of there and walked five blocks *past* brownstone houses.(p.223)
• It was hard to reconcile this ghastly present with the simple facts of the *past*.(p.225)
• I have served on only one committee in the *past* nine years, for I feel that I had my chance the first few years and that newer members should fill the jobs.(p.250)
• In the long ago *past* I used to start at the top as president or treasurer and end up with the sheriff breathing down my neck.(p.284)
• From a monetary standpoint . . . in the *past* few years, I have reduced my reckless debts to almost nothing, and have had money to get along on comfortably.(p.303)
• A lot of lost dreams, empty futures, and crazy things of the *past* went through my mind.(p.333)
• A.A. made it possible for me to face the consequences of my *past* actions.(p.420)
• I quit, when I was just *past* sixteen.(p.424)
• My *past* had slipped before me in a twinkling.(p.427)
• What else can I do except what I have always done in the *past*? -- act as my old self and return to prison.(p.458)
• I didn't know I was an alcoholic and (like most men in prison today) could not relate alcohol to any of my *past* troubles.(p.460)
• I feel that I have been restored to health and sanity these *past* years not through my own efforts nor as a result of anything I may have done, but because I've come to believe -- to really believe -- that alone I can do nothing.(p.473)
• I know I will be grateful for a chance to make amends to everybody I have hurt in the *past*.(p.482)
• For me, it was a little different because I couldn't help thinking about the *past*, and I saw the future more or less mirrored in the *past*.(p.513)
• I stumbled agonizedly *past* the theatre where in years gone by a great star had played my play.(p.540)
• By this time I was such a *past* master at kidding myself that I had convinced myself I had sat out a war and waited for this man to come home and, as my resentment and self-pity grew, so did my alcoholic problem.(p.548)
• We cast off the burdens of the *past* and the anxieties of the future, as we begin to live in the present, one day at a time.(p.560)

pasture
• Boredom was no worry to me when I went out to *pasture*.(p.330)

pat
• As long as things were tough and the job a chal-

lenge I could always manage to hold on pretty well, but as soon as I learned the combination, got the puzzle under control and the boss to ***pat*** me on the back, I was gone again.(p.243)

Pat

• A former employer of mine said to me a little over ten years ago, "***Pat,*** you seem to be one of those unfortunate people who at least once every six months must go out and roll in the gutter."(p.513)

• He just looked at me and said, "***Pat,*** for you there isn't any cure."(p.515)

patent

• The law school experience was not inspired by a desire to follow ***patent*** law, which has been my profession since: I went to law school primarily to learn the law of contracts following my own experience with litigation.(p.212)

• A year later, after I completed the course in contracts, I quit the law school, and undertook some engineering work for a ***patent*** law firm on behalf of clients who were in difficulties and who desired to keep their troubles from their own engineering department.(p.212)

• This work consumed a period of about two-thirds of a year, and worked out successfully so I decided to follow ***patent*** law.(p.212)

• By the time I had completed law school I had picked up some experience in ***patent*** law, for I remained with the ***patent*** law firm and worked too in Washington where they found that I was a capable infringement investigator.(p.213)

• I still had enough practice to earn a good living if I would only work, so I resolved that in January of 1940 I would launch a ***patent*** law firm of my own.(p.220)

• Shortly after I came to this conclusion, I was importuned by another well-known ***patent*** law firm to help them out on some trial work because their trial man had had a heart attack and had been forbidden to go into the courtroom.(p.220)

• That age of the flapper and the "It" girl, speakeasies and the hip flask, the boyish bob and the drugstore cowboy, John Held Jr. and F. Scott Fitzgerald, all generously sprinkled with a ***patent*** pseudo-sophistication.(p.304)

patents

• In the fall of the graduating year, I became involved in some litigation over the ownership of inventions and ***patents.***(p.212)

path

• The Twelve Steps that summarize the program may be called los Doce Pasos in one country, los Douze Etapes in another, but they trace exactly the same ***path*** to recovery that was blazed by the earliest members of Alcoholics Anonymous.(p.xxii)

• I have seen hundreds of families set their feet in the ***path*** that really goes somewhere; have seen the most impossible domestic situations righted; feuds and bitterness of all sorts wiped out.(p.15)

• We, who have traveled this dubious ***path,*** beg you to lay aside prejudice, even against organized religion.(p.49)

• Rarely have we seen a person fail who has thoroughly followed our ***path.***(p.58)

• We have been trying to get a new attitude, a new relationship with our Creator, and to discover the obstacle in our ***path.***(p.72)

• Both you and the new man must walk day by day in the ***path*** of spiritual progress.(p.100)

• Time after time, this apparent calamity has been a boon to us, for it opened up a ***path*** which led to the discovery of God.(p.116)

• I got the Big Book and I read it, and this is what it said: "Rarely have we seen a person fail who has thoroughly followed our ***path.***"(p.349)

• "Complete abandon"; "Half measures availed us nothing"; "Thoroughly follow our ***path***"; "Completely give oneself to this simple program" – rang in my swelled head.(p.349)

pathetic

• The children are sometimes dominated by a ***pathetic*** hardness and cynicism.(p.134)

pathological

• He had but partially recovered from a gastric hemorrhage and seemed to be a case of ***pathological*** mental deterioration.(p.xxix)

pathologically

• I don't think I actually started to drink ***pathologically*** until approximately 1935.(p.487)

patience

• We asked God to help us show them the same tolerance, pity, and ***patience*** that we would cheerfully grant a sick friend.(p.67)

• We have begun to learn tolerance, ***patience*** and good will toward all men, even our enemies, for we look on them as sick people.(p.70)

• Passing all understanding is the ***patience*** mothers and wives have had with alcoholics.(p.82)

• So we clean house with the family, asking each morning in meditation that our Creator show us the way of ***patience,*** tolerance, kindliness and love.(p.83)

• We realize some men are thoroughly bad-intentioned, that no amount of ***patience*** will make any difference.(p.108)

• ***Patience*** and good temper are most necessary.(p.111)

• Your husband may come to appreciate your reasonableness and ***patience.***(p.111)

• ***Patience,*** tolerance, understanding and love are the watchwords.(p.118)

• In only a few instances has there been lack of ***patience*** and tolerance.(p.137)

• To duplicate, with such backing, what we have accomplished is only a matter of willingness, ***patience*** and labor.(p.163)

• At long last I am doing the kind of work I have always wanted to do, but never had the ***patience*** and emotional stability to train myself for.(p.284)

• They meant ***patience,*** tolerance and humility, and above all the belief that a Power greater than myself could help.(p.381)

patient

• In late 1934 I attended a ***patient*** who, though he had been a competent businessman of good earning capacity, was an alcoholic of a type I had come to regard as hopeless.(p.xxiii)

• The ***patient*** had made his own diagnosis, and deciding his situation hopeless, had hidden in a deserted barn determined to die.(p.xxix)

• He may be kind, considerate, ***patient,*** generous; even modest and self-sacrificing.(p.61)

• They should be ***patient,*** realizing they are dealing with a sick person.(p.90)

• We have prayed, we have begged, we have been ***patient.***(p.105)

• This may take ***patient*** waiting, but it will be worth it.(p.112)

• Be ***patient.***(p.118)

• We suggest you draw the book to the attention of the doctor who is to attend your ***patient*** during treatment.(p.144)

• If the book is read the moment the ***patient*** is able, while acutely depressed, realization of his condition may come to him.(p.144)

• We hope the doctor will tell the ***patient*** the truth about his condition, whatever that happens to be.(p.144)

• Six years ago one of our number was a ***patient*** there.(p.162)

• (That condition was a distinct handicap to me in trying to vindicate myself with the not so ***patient*** wife.)(p.301)

• Few doctors will tell a hopeless ***patient*** that there is no answer for him or for her.(p.307)

• (My addiction bloomed within a small apartment I shared with my wife, a heart ***patient.***)(p.329)

• These words may be difficult for you to understand now, but be ***patient*** and you'll know what I mean.(p.367)

• There are so many to whom I feel deeply grateful; to my husband (and best critic), whose generous love, compassion and understanding have helped me along the way; to those before me in A.A. who inspired the first article I read, and the friend who sent that article to Frank; to Ruth for her personal note, and the first A.A. to talk to me; to my Bishop, whose loving and believing spirit inspired me; and to all the members of the Houston Group who were so ***patient,*** kind and helpful – and to countless others.(p.393)

• She was endlessly ***patient*** as we looked together for an answer.(p.409)

• I remember finding myself in the middle of the night in the doctors' parking lot at the hospital with one foot in the car and one foot on the ground, not knowing which was the lead foot; finding myself hanging up the telephone – then realizing I had gotten out of bed, answered the phone, turned on the light, and carried on a conversation with a ***patient.***(p.441)

• It became progressively harder to get up in the morning, until one day I asked myself what I would do for a ***patient*** who felt this rotten.(p.441)

• Dr. Harry M. Tiebout, psychiatrist: "As a psychiatrist, I have thought a great deal about the relationship of my specialty to A.A. and I have come to the conclusion that our particular function can very often lie in preparing the way for the ***patient*** to accept any sort of treatment or outside help.(p.571)

patient's

• But I can remember in post graduate days, and during interneship, that very often I'd go to a ***patient's*** bed and start a process of elimination and then, very often, I'd wind up guessing.(p.485)

• I now conceive the psychiatrist's job to be the task of breaking down the ***patient's*** inner resistance so that which is inside him will flower, as under the activity of the A.A. program."(p.571)

patiently

• As animals on a treadmill, we have ***patiently*** and wearily climbed, falling back in exhaustion after each futile effort to reach solid ground.(p.107)

patients

• Later, he requested the privilege of being allowed to tell his story to other ***patients*** here and with some misgiving, we consented.(p.xxv)

• Had you offered yourselves as ***patients*** at this hospital, I would not have taken you, if I had been able to avoid it.(p.43)

• Doctors are rightly loath to tell alcoholic ***patients*** the whole story unless it will serve some good purpose.(p.92)

• Every few days this doctor suggests our approach to one of his ***patients.***(p.162)

• Many of us, former ***patients,*** go there to help.(p.162)

• And with such good effect that the doctor agreed to a test among his ***patients*** and certain other alcoholics from a clinic which he attends.(p.163)

• During the subsequent fifteen years I had sense enough never to go to the hospital if I had been drinking, and very seldom did I receive ***patients.***(p.176)

• He had tried everything from having me attend daily mass at six a.m. to performing the most menial labor for his charity ***patients.***(p.306)

• Doctors were advised to attend ***patients*** who could be benefited by medicine.(p.307)

• Every doctor gets his quota of alcoholic ***patients.***(p.308)

• Shortly after I returned to Chicago, my doctor, encouraged by the results of my contact with A.A., sent us two more of his alcoholic ***patients.***(p.310)

• The satisfaction I got from giving him a little of what I had read in those pamphlets far surpassed any feeling that I had ever had before in helping ***patients.***(p.347)

• All I do in a very simple way, is to help Him cure my ***patients.***(p.351)

• My reaction was that I'd already helped all the ***patients*** on the ward, and I still had plenty of problems of my own without trying to help some drunk from A.A.(p.446)

• As an indication of just how confused and mixed up I was, just as soon as I could I left the office and hurried around to tell other ***patients*** that I was getting better.(p.470)

patients'

• It was a waste of the doctors' time and the ***patients'*** money.(p.307)

patriotic

• In the spring of 1917, in order to beat being fired from school, I became "***patriotic***" and joined the Army.(p.241)

• At age twenty-one, I enlisted in the Navy for two reasons: (1) to avoid being drafted into the Army, and (2) out of a burst of ***patriotic*** fervor inspired by the advent of World War II and as the result of an all-night drinking binge which found me sitting on the doorstep of the Navy recruiting office when the chief petty officer arrived to open for business at nine o'clock Monday morning.(p.398)

patriotism

• At the time, I called it ***patriotism.***(p.183)

• Curious about it, feeling I was missing something, absolutely without any illusions about the aftermath, with no pronounced feeling of ***patriotism,*** I joined up with a Canadian regiment, serving a little over two years.(p.253)

patrol

• A ***patrol*** car passed.(p.390)

• I was escorted back to San Diego next morning -- by the Shore ***Patrol,*** but I was discharged on schedule.(p.428)

patronize

• However, as there happened to be several saloons within that distance, I didn't find it necessary to ***patronize*** the same place each evening.(p.298)

patrons

• From the top of the heap in a few years he had skidded to becoming a shuffling customer, still entering the better barrooms but welcomed by neither mine host nor his ***patrons.***(p.236)

pats

• My next job was in sales promotion for an oil company in Mississippi where I promptly became high man and got lots of ***pats*** on the back.(p.242)

pattern

• The only answer I could make was that if the man followed the usual ***pattern***, he would go on a bigger bust than ever.(p.138)

• That was the reverse of my former ***pattern*** of fearing to go to work because I might drink!(p.199)

• He had known something of my drinking ***pattern***, and he asked me what I was doing about it.(p.200)

• Then I started drinking again, with possibly a little more restraint, periods a little bit longer than they had been before, but substantially the same ***pattern***.(p.203)

• Although, during this period I was not addicted to any ***pattern*** of alcohol consumption, when I did drink the drinking was pretty wild.(p.212)

• The first definite indications of an alcoholic ***pattern*** began to arise when I would go to New York on business and disappear, and wind up in Philadelphia or Boston for two or three day periods.(p.213)

• Forty came and went and then the resolution was advanced to forty-one, forty-two, and so on in the usual ***pattern***.(p.214)

• This ***pattern*** deepened and became worse.(p.214)

• I did six years of newspaper advertising, and trade journal work with many, many drunks of drab and dreary hue woven into the ***pattern*** of my life.(p.254)

• My ***pattern*** of drinking became very different from theirs.(p.277)

• During that first year, however, I managed to make both ends meet, and to avoid ever going back to my old habit ***pattern*** of borrowing money when I could not earn it.(p.283)

• Then, one night, my whole ***pattern*** for drinking was set.(p.328)

• No matter how often I had gone into and come out of alcoholic lows during the day, the ***pattern*** bounced me out of bed each night about 2:00 a.m., shaking and hurting in the agitation that always follows a drug's sedation.(p.332)

• Rehearsals then became a part of the ***pattern***, stopping at bars on the way to or from the place where drinks were to be served.(p.375)

• Finally our invitations became fewer and fewer as friends had more experience with my drinking ***pattern***.(p.377)

• But I did not fit into this ***pattern*** either.(p.402)

• I was an alcoholic, with a recognizable behavior ***pattern***.(p.414)

• Fear, love of dentistry, and an imitation of my father's periodic drinking ***pattern*** took me through dental college soberly, except for the few parties and vacations in those four years.(p.419)

• My ***pattern*** of drinking at that time had reached the point where once I really started, I would retire to my bed and drink myself into oblivion.(p.466)

• During these seven years a thing called the Twenty-four Hour Program —a gadget I used to think was only a snare to trap the newcomer -- has come to mean much to me, not only as regards my drinking but in the whole ***pattern*** of my life.(p.473)

• That was the usual ***pattern***.(p.491)

• My drinking ***pattern*** isn't very different from the average you find in A.A.(p.512)

• So that ***pattern*** continued until I went into the Army.(p.513)

• The old ***pattern*** reasserted itself, but it was no longer once every six months.(p.514)

• For you learned that he had been guilty of the thing he had accused you of, and his guilt had brought suffering to his entire family; and he thought he saw his young son beginning his own tragic ***pattern***.(p.533)

• A ***pattern*** established itself.(p.536)

• What is much more important to me, A.A. has taught me that through this simple program I may experience a change in this reaction ***pattern*** that will indeed allow me to "match calamity with serenity."(p.544)

• The ***pattern*** was set.(p.555)

• Immediately, it was part of the ***pattern*** and part of the problem.(p.556)

patterns

• This is by no means a comprehensive picture of the true alcoholic, as our behavior ***patterns*** vary.(p.22)

patting

• So I didn't have a beer one night, and as I drove home I was breaking my arm ***patting*** myself on the back because I had proved I could lick liquor.(p.203)

Paul

• I still expected a plea for clemency, but these words came through the receiver: "I just wanted to tell you ***Paul*** jumped from a hotel window in Hartford last Saturday.(p.136)

• So ***Paul*** was dispatched and brought back a pint.(p.206)

• And I said, "Well, what about ***Paul***, have you got him all dried up?"(p.207)

• He said ***Paul*** would have to answer for himself.(p.207)

• So ***Paul*** repeated substantially what Dr. Bob had said.(p.207)

• ***Paul*** measured the medicine out, but he figured that with my track record that little bit wouldn't be enough, so he doubled it and added a few drops more and then gave it to me.(p.207)

• On Sunday when I came to, it was a bad, wet, snowy day in February, 1937, and ***Paul*** and Doc and a lot of other fellows were in Cleveland on business.(p.207)

• ***Paul*** S. had just called me, and I remember he stressed reading the Big Book.(p.269)

pause

• If you have a drinking problem, we hope that you may ***pause*** in reading one of the forty-four personal stories and think: "Yes, that happened to me"; or, more important, "Yes, I've felt like that"; or most important, "Yes, I believe this program can work for me, too."(p.xii)

• As we go through the day we ***pause***, when agitated or doubtful, and ask for the right thought or action.(p.87)

• When resentful thoughts come, try to ***pause*** and count your blessings.(p.119)

paused

• But I can remember, in my teens, that there were a few characters who caused the village heads to nod pityingly and sometimes in anger as they ***paused*** to say, "That sot, Henri" and "Ce pauvre Jules," who drank too much.(p.230)

pauvre

• But I can remember, in my teens, that there were a few characters who caused the village heads to nod pityingly and sometimes in anger as they paused to say, "That sot, Henri" and "Ce ***pauvre*** Jules," who drank too much.(p.230)

pawned

• I'd lost my car again, ***pawned*** my wallet and all identification papers for a bottle, and gotten home somehow.(p.429)

pawnshop

• After a while, I found that the psycho ward was a good place to hide when I had taken something stolen to the ***pawnshop***.(p.528)

pay

• Sometimes a small deal would net a few hundred dollars, and I would ***pay*** my bills at the bars and delicatessens.(p.5)

• That the man who is making the approach has had the same difficulty, that he obviously knows what he is talking about, that his whole deportment shouts at the new prospect that he is a man with a real answer, that he has no attitude of Holier Than Thou, nothing whatever except the sincere desire to be helpful; that there are no fees to ***pay***, no axes to grind, no people to please, no lectures to be endured -- these are the conditions we have found most effective.(p.18)

• Our drinking has made us slow to ***pay***.(p.78)

• We might ***pay*** for this presumption in all sorts of absurd actions and ideas.(p.87)

• But we must try to repair the damage immediately lest we ***pay*** the penalty by a spree.(p.99)

• An armored car could not have brought the ***pay*** envelopes home.(p.105)

• Especially when he has before him a way to stop his drinking and abuse if he really wants to ***pay*** the price.(p.108)

• He may not see at once that he has barely scratched a limitless lode which will ***pay*** dividends only if he mines it for the rest of his life and insists on giving away the entire product.(p.129)

• Your understanding treatment of their cases will ***pay*** dividends.(p.141)

• If you propose such a procedure to him, it may be necessary to advance the cost of treatment, but we believe it should be made plain that any expense will later be deducted from his ***pay***.(p.143)

• Even if you feel your organization has no alcoholic problem, it might ***pay*** to take another look down the line.(p.149)

• By this time I was beginning to ***pay*** very dearly physically and, in hope of relief, voluntarily incarcerated myself at least a dozen times in one of the local sanitariums.(p.174)

• She also told me that I could not ***pay*** them even if I wanted to and had the money, which I did not.(p.185)

• It took me a year, or a year and a half to get to feeling physically well, and it was rather tough, but I soon found folks whose friendship I had once had, and I found, after I had been sober for quite some little time, that these people began to act like they had in previous years, before I had gotten so bad, so that I didn't ***pay*** too awful much attention to financial gains.(p.190)

• I couldn't afford to be found with those people, but I said I would certainly ***pay*** his dues if it would keep him from drinking.(p.205)

• I'd work like mad for three or four weeks without a single drink, save my money, ***pay*** a few bills and then "reward" myself with alcohol.(p.244)

• Quebec, Toronto, Buffalo, and finally Pittsburgh, were the scenes of man-sized drunks until I had gone through my readjusted discharge ***pay***, a fair sum.(p.253)

• In those days my system was always to drink up my last ***pay*** check and believe that necessity would bring the next job.(p.256)

• If he thinks he needs to go to the hospital, I'll ***pay*** for him."(p.271)

• She said, "He's not going to the hospital, whether you ***pay*** for it or I ***pay*** for it, he's not going!"(p.271)

• It doesn't ***pay*** to be seen in the same place at the same hour every day.(p.299)

• And then I'd say, "God, don't ***pay*** any attention to me.(p.324)

• My first ***pay*** was ten dollars, ***pay*** for recruits at that time being twenty-one dollars per month.(p.398)

• I didn't ***pay*** you."(p.488)

• I thought, "I know you didn't ***pay*** me, because you didn't get a prescription."(p.488)

• The November following, I took a few days off after ***pay*** day to celebrate my birthday on the 25th of the month.(p.491)

• I got very little out of the two hundred, that I drew on that ***pay*** day.(p.493)

• In any case, I made myself believe that, so I just drifted about, existing on my retired ***pay***, drinking, and living at home.(p.522)

• I don't remember any of them getting put out in the winter because they didn't ***pay*** their rent.(p.527)

• (There was a time, for about three months, when I bought a ten-dollar wrist watch every ***pay*** day – that is every two weeks.(p.532)

• If the listener were drunk enough, the lecture might go on through several martinis, which I was glad to ***pay*** for.(p.537)

payday

• Now on a new job I was always thinking about ***payday*** and how much liquor I could buy and the pleasure I could have.(p.255)

• Two weeks later found me being sworn in, and the first ***payday*** in the Navy made me realize I had found a home.(p.398)

• The only other occasionally limiting factor was that I might run out of money before the next ***payday*** rolled around.(p.398)

paying

• During these years, I drank as much as my purse permitted, still without ***paying*** too great a penalty, although I was beginning to have morning jitters at times.(p.173)

• 3.Because in so doing I am ***paying*** my debt to the man who took time to pass it on to me.(p.181)

• By this time I was married and was ***paying*** for a home.(p.232)

• He wants to go to the hospital, and I'm not ***paying*** for the hospital again!"(p.271)

• Even when we were ***paying*** that two dollars a night, they often paid it for us because our collection was so small.(p.496)

• Still, I had had funds sufficient to get plastered because that, of course, was more important than ***paying*** my own way.(p.538)

payment

• After the trial, I got big-hearted again and felt that I should do something in ***payment*** for Vi's kindness to me; so I left Washington and went to Seattle to work.(p.492)

payroll

• But the firm became violently ill with my drunkenness and their course of treatment was to remove their ulcer, in the form of me, from the ***payroll***, amid much fanfare and very personal and slighting remarks and insinuations.(p.300)

pays

• It is a way of life that ***pays*** as it goes, every step of the way, in compensations that have been wonderfully rich and rewarding.(p.394)

• It ***pays*** daily in more harmonious relations with my fellow men, in ever clearer insight into the true meaning of life, and in the answering love and gratitude wherever and whenever I have been the instrument of God's will in the lives of others.(p.394)

peace

• I was to know happiness, ***peace***, and usefulness, in a way of life that is incredibly more wonderful as time passes.(p.8)

• There was a sense of victory, followed by such a ***peace*** and serenity as I had never known.(p.14)

• Each day my friend's simple talk in our kitchen multiplies itself in a widening circle of ***peace*** on earth and good will to men.(p.16)

• In the face of collapse and despair, in the face of the total failure of their human resources, they found that a new power, ***peace***, happiness, and sense of direction flowed into them.(p.50)

• As we felt new power flow in, as we enjoyed ***peace*** of mind, as we discovered we could face life successfully, as we became conscious of His presence, we began to lose our fear of today, tomorrow or the hereafter.(p.63)

• We can be alone at perfect ***peace*** and ease.(p.75)

• We will comprehend the word serenity and we will know ***peace***.(p.83)

• At length ***peace*** stole over him and he slept.(p.189)

• Immediately a great feeling of ***peace*** descended upon me, intermingled with a feeling of being suffused with a quiet strength.(p.280)

• They had that certain something that seemed to glow, a ***peace*** and a serenity combined with happiness.(p.290)

• I can actually take my problems to Him and He gives me comfort, ***peace***, and happiness.(p.303)

• Perhaps I could find freedom and ***peace*** and be able once again to call my soul my own.(p.309)

• I saw in these people a quality of ***peace*** and serenity that I knew I must have for myself.(p.310)

• Not only were they at ***peace*** with themselves, but they were getting a kick out of life such as one seldom encounters, except in the very young.(p.310)

• I have had my share of problems, heartaches and disappointments, because that is life, but also I have known a great deal of joy, and a ***peace*** that is the handmaiden of an inner freedom, I have a wealth of friends and, with my A.A. friends, an unusual quality of fellowship.(p.312)

• And when all of life is a substitute for drink, there's no happiness, no ***peace***.(p.339)

• I tried every gimmick that there was to get some ***peace*** of mind, but it was not until I was brought to my alcoholic knees, when I was brought to a group in my own community with the butcher, the baker, the carpenter and the mechanic, who were able to give me the Twelve Steps, that I was finally given some semblance of an answer to the last half of the First Step.(p.349)

• I gave them everything, except the greatest thing in the world, and that is ***peace*** of mind.(p.351)

• I had accomplished all the right things that our society expected, and I had no real ***peace*** of mind nor gratitude.(p.418)

• Today, I feel I have used up my right to chemical ***peace*** of mind.(p.448)

• I know ***peace***.(p.477)

• Walk with me up Twelve Steps of A.A. to ***peace***."(p.477)

• But slowly a great ***peace*** comes to me.(p.504)

• I tell them of the ***peace***, and that I believe in God.(p.505)

• I wandered, craving ***peace***, from one spot to another of youthful happy memory, and loathed the man I had become.(p.539)

• A.A. has taught me that I will have ***peace*** of mind in exact proportion to the ***peace*** of mind I bring into the lives of other people, and it has taught me the true meaning of the admonition "happy are ye who know these things and do them."(p.551)

• For, at last, I was at ***peace*** with myself.(p.561)

peaceful

• Tall Man die five years ago, a sober, ***peaceful***, happy man.(p.476)

peak

• As a matter of fact, when I came into Alcoholics Anonymous I was close to being at the ***peak*** of my career.(p.356)

• Then my father fell down a flight of stairs on one of his lost weekends, at the ***peak*** of his career, and died.(p.370)

Pearl Harbor

• ***Pearl Harbor*** was a breeze of nine months, a gay Hawaiian paradise, drinking under the palms, listening to the surf beat on the shore, a bottle of whiskey near at hand.(p.426)

peculiar

• We doubt if many of them can do it, because none will really want to stop, and hardly one of them, because of the ***peculiar*** mental twist already acquired, will find he can win out.(p.33)

• He had a very ***peculiar*** look on his face, and he said, "He's coming."(p.263)

• A ***peculiar*** thing happened in 1940.(p.488)

peculiarly

• I have something to contribute to humanity, since I am ***peculiarly*** qualified, as a fellow-sufferer, to give aid and comfort to those who have stumbled and fallen over this business of meeting life.(p.229)

peddling

• ***Peddling*** off my polish samples for expenses, I crawled back to New York a few days later in a very chastened frame of mind.(p.248)

pedestal

• Perhaps they created the impression that he is to be wrapped in cotton wool and placed on a ***pedestal***.(p.122)

• She gave me such hope and inspiration that I set her right up on a ***pedestal***.(p.472)

peeled

• In the next two years I washed more pans and ***peeled*** more potatoes than any other doughboy.(p.241)

pen

• My ***pen*** moves rapidly.(p.499)

penalty

• But we must try to repair the damage immediately lest we pay the ***penalty*** by a spree.(p.99)

• During these years, I drank as much as my purse permitted, still without paying too great a ***penalty***, although I was beginning to have morning jitters at times.(p.173)

pencil

• When I went in to write the examinations, my hand trembled so I could not hold a ***pencil***.(p.174)

pencils

• The other pupils kept books, ***pencils***, paper, gym equipment and such stuff in their lockers.(p.423)

penetrated

• Psychiatry might have helped, but psychiatrists had not ***penetrated*** the middle west.(p.276)

penitentiaries

• I served time in four ***penitentiaries*** and several prison camps, including a maximum-security camp.(p.457)

penknife

• What actually happened was that I had taken a ***penknife*** and stabbed Vi three times with it.(p.492)

penniless

• I ended up, homeless, jobless, ***penniless*** and rudderless, as the problem guest of a close friend whose family was out of town.(p.278)

Pennsylvania

• My business reputation had reached from Vermont to ***Pennsylvania***, but, thank goodness, my drinking reputation had not.(p.361)

• I was there about three weeks, and then I got restless and started to tramp across the country, here and there, until I finally wound up in ***Pennsylvania***, in a steel mill.(p.492)

penny

• I remember telling them too that it was going to be awfully tough, because I did some other things, smoked cigarettes and played ***penny*** ante poker, sometimes bet on the horse races and they said, "Don't you think you're having more trouble with this drinking than with anything else at the present time?(p.190)

penology

• I do not want to digress into the dynamics of ***penology***.(p.458)

Pensacola

• I applied for photo school at ***Pensacola*** Air Base and made it.(p.426)

• While I was at ***Pensacola*** my dad became dangerously ill and almost died of pneumonia plus a heart attack.(p.426)

pension

• Until I took Social Security and a ***pension*** at the age of sixty-eight, after forty years in motion-picture-studio public relations, I had successfully hidden even any hints of approaching alcoholism.(p.327)

pensioned

• Safely ***pensioned***, with no job to protect, at last he could drink as he pleased.(p.327)

penthouses

• Many retirees embrace alcoholism while secluded in motor trailers, rest homes, leisure-world bungalows, mountain cabins, or beach cottages, or even in ***penthouses***, on yachts, and inside Palm Springs cabanas.(p.329)

pentothal

• However, for a period of time I was injecting ***Pentothal*** intravenously to put myself to sleep.(p.442)

people

• News of this got on the world wires; inquiries poured in again and many ***people*** went to the bookstores to get the book "Alcoholics Anonymous."(p.xviii)

• Surveys of groups in the United States and Canada indicate that A.A. is reaching out, not only to more and more ***people***, but to a wider and wider range.(p.xxii)

• The message which can interest and hold these alcoholic ***people*** must have depth and weight.(p.xxvi)

• They are often able, intelligent, friendly ***people***.(p.xxviii)

• This phenomenon, as we have suggested, may be the manifestation of an allergy which differentiates these ***people***, and sets them apart as a distinct entity.(p.xxviii)

• I forgot the strong warnings and the prejudices of my ***people*** concerning drink.(p.1)

• Many ***people*** lost money -- but some became very rich.(p.2)

• I had developed a theory that most ***people*** lost money in stocks through ignorance of markets.(p.2)

• ***People*** feared for my sanity.(p.7)

• Few ***people*** really are, for that means blind faith in the strange proposition that this universe originated in a cipher and aimlessly rushes nowhere.(p.10)

• It began to look as though religious ***people*** were right after all.(p.11)

• We made a list of ***people*** I had hurt or toward whom I felt resentment.(p.13)

• We are ***people*** who normally would not mix.(p.17)

• That the man who is making the approach has had the same difficulty, that he obviously knows what he is talking about, that his whole deportment shouts at the new prospect that he is a man with a real answer, that he has no attitude of Holier Than Thou, nothing whatever except the sincere desire to be helpful; that there are no fees to pay, no axes to grind, no ***people*** to please, no lectures to be endured -- these are the conditions we have found most effective.(p.18)

• How many times ***people*** have said to us: "I can take it or leave it alone.(p.20)

• We see that these expressions refer to ***people*** whose reactions are very different from ours.(p.20)

• Opinions vary considerably as to why the alcoholic reacts differently from normal ***people***.(p.22)

• If these thoughts occur, they are hazy and readily supplanted with the old threadbare idea that this time we shall handle ourselves like other ***people***.(p.24)

• Therefore, it is not surprising that our drinking careers have been characterized by countless vain attempts to prove we could drink like other ***people***.(p.30)

• The delusion that we are like other ***people***, or presently may be, has to be smashed.(p.30)

• Heaven knows, we have tried hard enough and long enough to drink like other ***people***!(p.31)

• We have heard of few instances where ***people***, who showed definite signs of alcoholism, were able to stop for a long period because of an overpowering desire to do so.(p.32)

• Young ***people*** may be encouraged by this man's experience to think that they can stop, as he did, on their own will power.(p.33)

• We, who are familiar with the symptoms, see large numbers of potential alcoholics among young ***people*** everywhere.(p.33)

• That may be true of certain nonalcoholic ***people*** who, though drinking foolishly and heavily at the present time, are able to stop or moderate, because their brains and bodies have not been damaged as ours were.(p.39)

• I had never been able to understand ***people*** who said that a problem had them hopelessly defeated.(p.42)

• ***People*** like you are too heartbreaking.(p.43)

• When ***people*** presented us with spiritual approaches, how frequently did we all say, "I wish I had what that man has.(p.47)

• ***People*** of faith have a logical idea of what life is all about.(p.49)

• Instead, we looked at the human defects of these ***people***, and sometimes used their shortcomings as a basis of wholesale condemnation.(p.50)

• When many hundreds of ***people*** are able to say that

the consciousness of the Presence of God is today the most important fact of their lives, they present a powerful reason why one should have faith.(p.51)

• Had not ***people*** said God had reserved this privilege to the birds?(p.51)

• We were having trouble with personal relationships, we couldn't control our emotional natures, we were a prey to misery and depression, we couldn't make a living, we had a feeling of uselessness, we were full of fear, we were unhappy, we couldn't seem to be of real help to other ***people*** -- was not a basic solution of these bedevilments more important than whether we should see newsreels of lunar flight?(p.52)

• Had we not variously worshipped ***people***, sentiment, things, money, and ourselves?(p.54)

• What about ***people*** who proved that man could never fly?(p.55)

• Yet we had been seeing another kind of flight, a spiritual liberation from this world, ***people*** who rose above their problems.(p.55)

• But later, alone in his room, he asked himself this question: "Is it possible that all the religious ***people*** I have known are wrong?"(p.56)

• Those who do not recover are ***people*** who cannot or will not completely give themselves to this simple program, usually men and women who are constitutionally incapable of being honest with themselves.(p.58)

• 9.Made direct amends to such ***people*** wherever possible, except when to do so would injure them or others.(p.59)

• Most ***people*** try to live by self-propulsion.(p.60)

• If his arrangements would only stay put, if only ***people*** would do as he wished, the show would be great.(p.60)

• Admitting he may be somewhat at fault, he is sure that other ***people*** are more to blame.(p.61)

• Our actor is self-centered — ego-centric, as ***people*** like to call it nowadays.(p.61)

• We listed ***people***, institutions or principles with whom we were angry.(p.64)

• The first thing apparent was that this world and its ***people*** were often quite wrong.(p.65)

• The usual outcome was that ***people*** continued to wrong us and we stayed sore.(p.66)

• We began to see that the world and its ***people*** really dominated us.(p.66)

• This was our course: We realized that the ***people*** who wronged us were perhaps spiritually sick.(p.66)

• We wouldn't treat sick ***people*** that way.(p.67)

• We cannot be helpful to all ***people***, but at least God will show us how to take a kindly and tolerant view of each and every one.(p.67)

• We realize that some ***people*** are as fanatical about sex as others are loose.(p.70)

• Some ***people*** tell us so.(p.70)

• We have begun to learn tolerance, patience and good will toward all men, even our enemies, for we look on them as sick ***people***.(p.70)

• We have listed the ***people*** we have hurt by our conduct, and are willing to straighten out the past if we can.(p.70)

• More than most ***people***, the alcoholic leads a double life.(p.73)

• Of course, we sometimes encounter ***people*** who do not understand alcoholics.(p.74)

• Most ***people*** approached in this way will be glad to help; they will be honored by our confidence.(p.75)

• To some ***people*** we need not, and probably should not emphasize the spiritual feature on our first approach.(p.76)

• Our real purpose is to fit ourselves to be of maximum service to God and the ***people*** about us.(p.77)

• Arranging the best deal we can we let these ***people*** know we are sorry.(p.78)

• Usually, however, other ***people*** are involved.(p.79)

• Before taking drastic action which might implicate other ***people*** we secure their consent.(p.80)

• We doubt if, in this respect, alcoholics are fundamentally much worse than other ***people***.(p.81)

• Some ***people*** cannot be seen — we send them an honest letter.(p.83)

• As God's ***people*** we stand on our feet; we don't crawl before anyone.(p.83)

• Fear of ***people*** and of economic insecurity will leave us.(p.84)

• Be quick to see where religious ***people*** are right.(p.87)

• To watch ***people*** recover, to see them help others, to watch loneliness vanish, to see a fellowship grow up about you, to have a host of friends — this is an experience you must not miss.(p.89)

• Suggest how important it is that he place the welfare of other ***people*** ahead of his own.(p.94)

• He may rebel at the thought of a drastic housecleaning which requires discussion with other ***people***.(p.94)

• Some of us have taken very hard knocks to learn this truth: Job or no job — wife or no wife -- we simply do not stop drinking so long as we place dependence upon other ***people*** ahead of dependence on God.(p.98)

• The most incompatible ***people*** discover they have a basis upon which they can meet.(p.99)

• Remind the prospect that his recovery is not dependent upon ***people***.(p.99)

• ***People*** have said we must not go where liquor is served; we must not have it in our homes; we must shun friends who drink; we must avoid moving pictures which show drinking scenes; we must not go into bars; our friends must hide their bottles if we go to their houses; we mustn't think or be reminded about alcohol at all.(p.100)

• If you do this thoroughly, few ***people*** will ask you to drink.(p.102)

• This world is full of ***people*** like him.(p.109)

• He is worried at times, and is becoming aware that he cannot drink like other ***people***.(p.109)

• He admits he cannot drink like other ***people***, but does not see why.(p.110)

• If your husband is a drinker, you probably worry over what other ***people*** are thinking and you hate to meet your friends.(p.114)

• When you have carefully explained to such ***people*** that he is a sick person, you will have created a new atmosphere.(p.115)

• Your desire to protect him should not cause you to lie to ***people*** when they have a right to know where he is and what he is doing.(p.115)

• Still another difficulty is that you may become jealous of the attention he bestows on other ***people***, especially alcoholics.(p.119)

• The fact is that he should work with other ***people*** to maintain his own sobriety.(p.119)

• If that is so we are sorry, for we ourselves don't always care for ***people*** who lecture us.(p.121)

• The foregoing pages (though addressed only to wives) indicate the problems such ***people*** may face.(p.121)

• This is a condition which, in ordinary life, would produce untold grief; there might be scandalous gossip, laughter at the expense of other ***people***, and a tendency to take advantage of intimate information.(p.125)

• We alcoholics are sensitive ***people***.(p.125)

• Alcoholics who have derided religious ***people*** will be helped by such contacts.(p.131)

• Being possessed of a spiritual experience, the alcoholic will find he has much in common with these ***people***, though he may differ with them on many matters.(p.131)

• As non-denominational ***people***, we cannot make up others' minds for them.(p.132)

• Of course that isn't so, and such ***people*** often may impose on you.(p.141)

• Sometimes we alcoholics have an idea that ***people*** are trying to pull us down.(p.145)

• As a class, alcoholics are energetic ***people***.(p.146)

• Of course, this chapter refers to alcoholics, sick ***people***, deranged men.(p.149)

• As to them, his policy is undoubtedly sound, but he did not distinguish between such ***people*** and the alcoholic.(p.149)

• The less ***people*** tolerated us, the more we withdrew from society, from life itself.(p.151)

• But am I to be consigned to a life where I shall be stupid, boring and glum, like some righteous ***people*** I see?(p.152)

• "Where am I to find these ***people***?"(p.152)

• Near you, alcoholics are dying helplessly like ***people*** in a sinking ship.(p.152)

• Why, he argued, should he lose the remainder of his business, only to bring still more suffering to his family by foolishly admitting his plight to ***people*** from whom he made his livelihood?(p.155)

• Stepping into his car, he made the rounds of ***people*** he had hurt.(p.156)

• They were deeply religious ***people***, much shocked by their son's refusal to have anything to do with the church.(p.158)

• Aside from fellowship and sociability, the prime object was to provide a time and place where new ***people*** might bring their problems.(p.160)

• The very practical approach to his problems, the absence of intolerance of any kind, the informality, the genuine democracy, the uncanny understanding which these ***people*** had were irresistible.(p.160)

• Being wrecked in the same vessel, being restored and united under one God, with hearts and minds attuned to the welfare of others, the things which matter so much to some ***people*** no longer signify much to them.(p.161)

• We could not be invited out because I would surely get tight and my wife dared not invite ***people*** in for the same reason.(p.177)

• About the time of the beer experiment I was thrown in with a crowd of ***people*** who attracted me because of their seeming poise, health, and happiness.(p.178)

• These good ***people*** notified my wife, who sent my newly made friend over to get me.(p.179)

• My parents were well-to-do ***people*** and their marriage was a happy one.(p.182)

• All the other ***people*** that had talked to me wanted to help me, and my pride prevented me from listening to them, and caused only resentment on my part, but I felt as if I would be a real stinker if I did not listen to a couple of fellows for a short time, if that would cure them.(p.185)

• I said, "Yes, Doc, I would like to quit, at least for five, six, or eight months, until I get things straightened up, and begin to get the respect of my wife and some other ***people*** back, and get my finances fixed up and so on."(p.187)

• It took me a year, or a year and a half to get to feeling physically well, and it was rather tough, but I soon found folks whose friendship I had once had, and I found, after I had been sober for quite some little time, that these ***people*** began to act like they had in previous years, before I had gotten so bad, so that I didn't pay too awful much attention to financial gains.(p.190)

• Bill looked across at my wife, and said to her, "Henrietta, the Lord has been so wonderful to me, curing me of this terrible disease, that I just want to keep talking about it and telling ***people***."(p.191)

• Bill was very, very grateful that he had been released from this terrible thing and he had given God the credit for having done it, and he's so grateful about it he wants to tell other ***people*** about it.(p.191)

• That sentence, "The Lord has been so wonderful to me, curing me of this terrible disease, that I just want to keep telling ***people*** about it," has been sort of a golden text for the A.A. program and for me.(p.191)

• Of course, as time went on, and I began to get my health back and began to be so I didn't have to hide from ***people*** all the time, it's just been wonderful.(p.192)

• I meet the ***people*** that I like to talk to.(p.192)

• I'm so grateful for both the program and the ***people*** in it that I still want to go, and then probably the most wonderful thing that I learned from the program -- I've seen this in the 'A.A. Grapevine' a lot of times, and I've had ***people*** say it to me personally, and I've heard ***people*** get up in meetings and make the same statement: The statement is, "I came into A.A. solely for the purpose of sobriety, but it has been through A.A. that I have found God."(p.192)

• During the day, looking over the contracts and money in my pocket, I found that I had sold six lots that I couldn't even remember, and didn't even know the ***people*** I had sold them to.(p.196)

• I had to look in the telephone book later to find out who these ***people*** were.(p.196)

• Anyhow, I recognized the fact that I couldn't drink like normal ***people***, but I tried hard and kept on trying for twenty-two years.(p.196)

• I made a point of knowing important ***people***.(p.197)

• I didn't want to jeopardize the lives of innocent ***people*** by driving an automobile while intoxicated, but I did.(p.199)

• My big job was to keep other ***people*** from finding it out.(p.199)

• The circumstances under which I reached these ***people*** were very odd because I was led there through things that I said when I couldn't even remember speaking.(p.202)

• Pretty soon, I wasn't going at all, and was avoiding those ***people*** who had been so kind to me.(p.203)

• Shortly after that, my brother, who had then become associated with a group of ***people*** and had stopped drinking, urged me to attend meetings with him.(p.205)

• I explained to my sister that some of the ***people*** he was meeting with had been in hospitals.(p.205)

• I couldn't afford to be found with those ***people***, but I said I would certainly pay his dues if it would keep him from drinking.(p.205)

• I got two drinks, each of them a quarter of that pint, in me, and was talking along with these ***people***, but I felt that sooner or later they were going to have me cornered because they were smarter than I was and the drink was beginning to take effect; but as I reached for the third drink Bob said, "Listen, Buster, you promised to take some medicine if we got you a drink.(p.206)

• The *people* in the group hadn't been around that day; part of my family was in Florida and the rest of them weren't speaking to me, so I spent a very lonesome day and by evening I was feeling very sorry for myself.(p.207)
• There were only seven or eight *people* in the group before me and they all visited me during my period in the hospital.(p.208)
• My parents were hard working *people*.(p.210)
• We went to Akron for about six weeks and we did a lot of visiting among the *people* in Akron.(p.219)
• At that meeting, there were a number of Akron *people* and all the Cleveland *people*.(p.219)
• On hearing that, these *people* induced me to make the move immediately and join them as a senior partner, which I did.(p.220)
• I realized that there wasn't anything I could say to place myself in a more favorable light with my children, that it was going to be a matter of time; for I also understood the intolerance of young *people* towards deficiencies in their elders.(p.220)
• I met all the *people* I wanted to meet; I saw all the places I wanted to see; I did all the things I wanted to do -- and I was increasingly miserable.(p.225)
• I wanted to live, not in a desert, but in a normal world; and my idea of a normal world was among *people* who drank -- teetotallers were not included.(p.227)
• And I was sure that I couldn't be with *people* who drank, without drinking.(p.227)
• In that I was correct: I couldn't be comfortable with any kind of *people* without drinking.(p.227)
• To go into a gathering of *people* was the sort of thing that all my life, from the time I left my private world of books and dreams to meet the real world of *people* and parties and jobs, had left me feeling an uncomfortable outsider, needing the warming stimulus of drinks to join in.(p.228)
• *People* have wars and kill each other; they struggle and cut each other's throats for success and what does anyone get out of it?(p.244)
• At the time, I thought them just a swell pair of screwballs, for they were not only going to save all the drunks in the world but also all the so-called normal *people*!(p.245)
• I wanted to roam again and through relatives got a supercargo job on an Australian packet which allowed me to visit my *people* in Australia where I was born.(p.252)
• I look back and remember these things because they made me very unhappy, and added to my feeling of inferiority at never being the same as other *people*.(p.261)
• It would stop out in front of our house, and I still believe those *people* sent it!(p.265)
• Finally, one morning, I got up and got in the car and cried all the way down to the M.'s -- the *people* who owned the bar -- and told her I was licked and wanted help.(p.267)
• He brought many *people* into A.A. through his barroom.)(p.267)
• I thought when *people* did what we did that they just locked them up.(p.267)
• I could never go and make up to all the *people* I've done wrong to."(p.269)
• "Well," I said to dad, when the A.A. *people* kept coming with these lovely cars and looked so nice, "I suppose the neighbors say, 'Now those old fools must have up and died, but where's the hearse?'"(p.269)
• I often think how that could have turned some *people* away, because there were no other women alcoholics there then.(p.269)
• I'd like to say here how important it was to us then that we do all the little things that *people* said were important, because later when Russ was so sick that I had to hold him up, they had a meeting out at the house.(p.270)
• We had meetings at each other's homes and, of course, that was a grand place for *people* to get together out there; they seemed to think so too.(p.270)
• At that time they didn't let us know that *people* ever had trouble.(p.271)
• We old-timers who get scattered and separated and then witness the construction of services to get in more *people* and to make this thing function, we think that A.A. has changed, but the root of it hasn't.(p.272)
• I think it's awfully hard on *people*, especially if they're new *people*, to hear these long drawn out talks.(p.273)
• It would be impossible for me to pass over this year without mentioning my love for, and my indebtedness to these two wonderful *people* who are no longer with us.(p.280)
• Sometimes during that year I rebelled inwardly at what seemed like lost time, and at having to be a burden to these good *people* whose means were limited.(p.281)
• So I spent much of my time calling on the *people* who I felt would logically come in contact with alcoholic cases, doctors, ministers, lawyers and the personnel men in industry.(p.281)
• He laid great stress on the progression of his attitude toward life and *people*, and most of his attitudes had been very similar to mine.(p.290)
• I had thought that I was completely different from other *people*, that I was beginning to become a little balmy, even to the point of withdrawing more and more from society and wanting to be alone with my bottle.(p.290)
• He was happy, getting a kick out of life and *people*, and beginning to get his medical practice back again.(p.290)
• I spent a great deal of time with Dr. Bob, whenever he had the time to spare, and in the homes of two or three other *people*, trying to see how the family lived the program.(p.291)
• Where derision, contempt and pity were once shown me, I now enjoy the respect of many *people*.(p.296)
• Handling customers, dealers, insurance *people*, dictation, telephoning, directing new employees, answering to superiors, and all the rest of it.(p.299)
• One is that I don't remember too many of them, as I was one of those drunks who could be on his feet and attend a meeting or a party, engage in a conversation with *people* and do things that any nearly normal person would do, and the next day not remember a thing about where I was, what I did, whom I saw, or how I got home.(p.301)
• I studied art; I desperately endeavored to create an interest in many things, in a new place among new *people*.(p.305)
• *People* didn't behave this way outside of an asylum.(p.306)
• But somehow my good doctor heard of this book and also he learned a little about the *people* responsible for its publication.(p.307)
• But this day my doctor gave it to me straight and said, "*People* like you are pretty well known to the medical profession.(p.307)
• Some of us struggle with these *people* because we know that they are really very sick, but we also know that short of some miracle, we are not going to help them except temporarily, and that they will inevitably get worse and worse until one of two things happens.(p.308)
• Then he told me there was a handful of *people* in Akron and New York who had worked out a technique for arresting their alcoholism.(p.308)
• By this time, with the doctor's explanation, the revelations contained in the book, and the hope-inspiring interview with Mr. T., I was ready and willing to go into the interior of the African jungles, if that was what it took, for me to find what these *people* had.(p.309)
• I saw in these *people* a quality of peace and serenity that I knew I must have for myself.(p.310)
• Extraordinary *people*!(p.310)
• I didn't dare hope I might find for myself all that these *people* had found, but if I could acquire some small part of their intriguing quality of living -- and sobriety -- that would be enough.(p.310)
• For, to these *people*, I am truly related.(p.312)
• After having a few drinks, I went to a meeting -- and the *people* there were not all old men and definitely not skid-row types!(p.319)
• I found out that the *people* in all A.A. groups were as nice as the *people* in the first one.(p.320)
• I said, "Eileen, are you one of those *people*?"(p.321)
• I couldn't face *people*.(p.323)
• Now I feel so very grateful not only for my sobriety, which I try to maintain day by day, but I'm grateful also for the ability to help other *people*.(p.326)
• Even obvious intoxication is excused by younger *people* as something "he's earned the right to do," and they say, "After all, who's he hurting?"(p.330)
• I began to have to have supplies on hand for the *people* who "might come in."(p.336)
• And of course a half empty bottle wasn't worth keeping, so I finished it up and naturally had to get more in right away for the *people* who "might come in unexpectedly."(p.336)
• I had to hide, as a great many *people* in A.A. have had to do.(p.336)
• The *people* who would have come to help me were just the *people* I would have nothing to do with.(p.338)
• There were five *people* present, including myself.(p.347)
• We have here in this community an organization which helps *people*, and this organization is known as Alcoholics Anonymous.(p.348)
• We are great *people*.(p.350)
• Here were *people* who had thought and felt as I had.(p.355)
• These *people* were my friends, and I felt their sincere interest in me.(p.355)
• I had not only let my wife down but also a lot of other wonderful *people* who had helped me.(p.364)
• We had some *people* in, and I was making drinks in the kitchen, when I suddenly decided to hoist the bottle for a quick one.(p.365)
• I went to many meetings and met many beautiful *people*.(p.371)
• I was intolerant of *people* who drank, particularly those who drank to an extent that interfered with on-the-job performance.(p.374)
• I will never know all the *people* I hurt, all the friends I abused, the humiliation of my family, the worry of my business associates, or how far reaching it was.(p.376)
• I continue to be surprised by the *people* I meet who say, "You haven't had a drink for a long time, have you?"(p.376)
• I don't know what I expected, but I most certainly didn't visualize a group of *people* talking about their drinking problems, making light of their personal tragedies and at the same time enjoying themselves.(p.378)
• What could be more reasonable than that some *people*, including myself, were allergic to alcohol?(p.380)
• A "spiritual experience" to me meant attending meetings, seeing a group of *people*, all there for the purpose of helping each other; hearing the Twelve Steps and the Twelve Traditions read at a meeting, and hearing the Lord's Prayer, which in an A.A. meeting has such great meaning -- "Thy will be done, not mine."(p.381)
• I could not identify myself with the *people* with whom I found myself and there was no understanding, and I can't stand confinement anyhow.(p.387)
• He always thought that maybe I was safer in a building where there were other *people*.(p.388)
• He even had the *people* come out, and tell me what kind of room I was going to have, and that he could come and see me, and that the dog could come and see me.(p.389)
• I realized that there were other *people* in this world who behaved and acted as I did, and that I was a sick person, that I was suffering from an actual disease.(p.392)
• I was out of step with life, with my family, with *people* in general.(p.400)
• Like most sick *people* before me, I was implacably selfish, and chronically self-centered.(p.401)
• The *people* I knew rode hard, and some of them drank hard.(p.404)
• At a large party in Geneva, with *people* from many countries represented, the kind of party that is "protocol" in the extreme, I swayed, laughed hysterically, made naughty remarks in an unhushed voice, and was finally led from the scene.(p.406)
• I had a tiny trust fund, and I moved into a small apartment where I learned to cook, keep house, and do the things that normal *people* do.(p.409)
• "These *people* all had your problem," she told me.(p.412)
• All the *people* involved in these flare-ups took it with remarkable grace, have teased me about it since, and have become good friends of mine.(p.416)
• And the folks said A.A. was for *people* who wanted to quit, otherwise it wouldn't work.(p.429)
• I attended meetings, I talked to my folks, I talked to younger *people* they had gotten in contact with to sponsor me.(p.430)
• How exciting to learn the inward mysteries that govern the behavior of *people*, how wonderful to know, at last, all about myself!(p.434)
• However, I've heard of an organization called Alcoholics Anonymous that has had some success with *people* like you.(p.436)
• Here was power to live to the end of any given day, power to have the courage to face the next day, power to have friends, power to help *people*, power to be sane, power to stay sober.(p.436)
• The *people* there insisted on putting me in a ward, when Max and I both knew I ought to have a private room.(p.445)
• The *people* of A.A. had something that looked much better than what I had, but I was afraid to let go of what I had in order to try something new; there was a certain sense of security in the familiar.(p.448)
• It is true that I -- of all *people*, strange as it may seem, and even though I didn't give my permission -- really, really am an alcoholic of sorts.(p.448)
• The higher my expectations of Max and other

people are, the lower is my serenity.(p.452)
• Through A.A., many receive the needed change and awakening just by trying to live by A.A. principles and associating with A.A. ***people***.(p.459)
• (God works through ***people***.)(p.462)
• God bless all you ***people*** in A.A. and especially you fellows in prison.(p.463)
• Even the Jack Alexander Saturday Evening Post article hadn't been written, and there was only a tiny group of ***people*** in Washington.(p.469)
• I thought, "Oh well, these ***people*** are just like all the ***people*** I've known all my life.(p.472)
• I once hear ***people*** say only Indians crazy when drunk.(p.477)
• Aside from being a common drunk, I had a very serious pill affliction and all the garbage that goes with it -- lying, stealing, cheating anybody and everybody, conning the ***people*** I could, and staying clear of the ones I couldn't.(p.478)
• I ran out of ***people***!(p.478)
• Then getting and staying honest with other ***people*** will come automatically.(p.482)
• This physician, the originator of A.A.'s first black group, but badly caught in the toils, tells of his release and of how freedom came as he worked among his own ***people***.(p.483)
• I don't know whether it was right or wrong, but at least I know that ***people*** weren't thinking the same.(p.484)
• All my troubles arose when I was thrown socially among groups of ***people***.(p.486)
• Am I willing to be honest with myself about myself and tell someone about myself, and am I willing to think of other ***people***, of their needs instead of myself, in order to get rid of the drink problem?(p.503)
• Can all the worth while ***people*** I have known be wrong about God?(p.503)
• I have never seen ***people*** that joyous before.(p.504)
• Get into the lives of other ***people***, is one thing the fellows in New York had said.(p.505)
• ***People*** annoy me.(p.506)
• Most of my attendance there was when ***people*** would come in from the outside.(p.510)
• It's no bed of roses, but somehow or other I've been able to make it, through the kindness of ***people*** in A.A.(p.511)
• I think I am very lucky that there are ***people*** like A.A.'s and an A.A. program to hang on to and carry me through.(p.511)
• Yes, we find it rather confusing, but as we get around and get to know ***people*** in the group, they lead the way and all we have to do is to follow.(p.512)
• A former employer of mine said to me a little over ten years ago, "Pat, you seem to be one of those unfortunate ***people*** who at least once every six months must go out and roll in the gutter."(p.513)
• It was a revelation to me to find that there were such ***people*** as those I found in Alcoholics Anonymous.(p.515)
• I took the advice of ***people*** I had heard at meetings, the ***people*** in the group.(p.516)
• But the more meetings you attend, the more ***people*** you meet at these meetings, the clearer the Steps become.(p.516)
• I was going to be sent to the Indian Civil Service, which, in those days, meant that ***people*** thought you had a certain amount of brains.(p.517)
• When I came home to ordinary garrison life in England, I found that I was drinking rather more than most ***people*** of my age.(p.518)
• Lots of the older ***people*** had taken to drinking quite a good deal more during the war, but the younger generation was, I think, about the same.(p.518)
• I stayed there just long enough to work up a real good resentment against the doctor in charge, who I didn't think was doing anything at all except collecting fees, and I left there fully determined that I'd never put myself in the power of medical ***people*** again.(p.521)
• When I arrived at The Country Shop, which was a restaurant where they met in Dublin, I found about thirty-five or forty ***people*** in the room.(p.524)
• ***People*** seemed to be carefully dressed, too happy, too normal.(p.524)
• But I did understand this eventually, that these ***people*** had been through a lot of drinking experience just as I had, and had managed to make a job of it.(p.524)
• I thought that if these kind of ordinary ***people*** can do it, a man of my brains ought to find it much more easy, and I joined.(p.524)
• I am talking about A.A. ***people***, who have gone through some of the same things that you might be going through now.(p.529)
• I'm writing this during an A.A. convention, where I have spent the weekend with nothing but white ***people***.(p.529)
• I have not seen a black face but mine since I've been here, and if I didn't look in the mirror, I wouldn't know that I was black, because these ***people*** treat me as one of them, which I am.(p.530)
• I have published a book covering certain aspects of this field which has been well-reviewed and which is helping other ***people***.(p.541)
• Harm is done by sick ***people***, as I was sick, and doing dreadful harm to myself and to my loved ones.(p.542)
• I looked around me at ***people*** who seemed happy and tried to analyze their happiness, and it seemed to me that without exception these ***people*** had something or somebody they loved very much.(p.546)
• I was immersed in self-pity and resentment, and the only ***people*** who would support this attitude or who I felt understood me at all were the ***people*** I met in bars and the ones who drank as I did.(p.547)
• The ***people*** who came knew immediately I was in no condition to absorb anything of the program, and I was put in a sanitarium to be defogged so that I could make a sober decision about this for myself.(p.549)
• Society can do anything it chooses to do with me when I am drunk and I can't lift a finger to stop it, for I forfeit my rights through the simple expedient of becoming a menace to myself and to the ***people*** around me.(p.549)
• A.A. has given me serenity of purpose, the opportunity to be of service to God and to the ***people*** about me, and I am serene in the infallibility of these principles that provide the fulfillment of my purpose.(p.551)
• A.A. has taught me that I will have peace of mind in exact proportion to the peace of mind I bring into the lives of other ***people***, and it has taught me the true meaning of the admonition "happy are ye who know these things and do them."(p.551)
• Much later, when I had progressed to full-blown alcoholism, ***people*** told me I should quit.(p.554)
• I have learned how to relate to ***people***; before A.A., I could never do that comfortably without alcohol.(p.559)
• Their management should be the sole responsibility of those ***people*** who financially support them.(p.566)

people-pleaser

• Away down deep, I was motivated into dishonest behavior because I was a ***people-pleaser***.(p.328)
• A ***people-pleaser*** beaten down?(p.331)

people-pleasing

• I believe that the release from ***people-pleasing*** restrictions gives retirees more motivation to drink than boredom does.(p.329)
• Every breadwinner, whether trying to impress a boss or to hold customers in his own business, is fettered by ***people-pleasing***.(p.329)

people's

• Most of us sense that real tolerance of other ***people's*** shortcomings and viewpoints and a respect for their opinions are attitudes which make us more useful to others.(p.19)
• In a sick ***people's*** place, myself among the sickest.(p.410)

pep

• I simply did not have the ***pep*** to do hard, "cold-turkey" selling.(p.277)
• The answer came right back: I'd give him something to ***pep*** him up.(p.441)
• So I immediately started taking and shooting ***pep*** pills.(p.442)
• The ***pep*** pills affected my hearing at times: I couldn't listen fast enough to hear what I was saying.(p.442)
• In the garage, I would put the needle in my vein and then try to figure out exactly how much medication to inject to overcome the ***pep*** pills while adding to the sleeping pills while ignoring the tranquilizers, in order to get just enough to be able to pull out the needle, jerk the tourniquet, throw it in the car, slam the car door shut, run down the hall, and fall in bed before I fell asleep.(p.442)
• I never in my life took a tranquilizer, sedative, or ***pep*** pill because I was a pillhead.(p.443)

pepper

• One school would allow man no flavor for his fare and the other would have us all on a straight ***pepper*** diet.(p.69)

per

• At present, our membership is increasing at the rate of about seven ***per*** cent a year.(p.xx)
• He had lived there but a few weeks when he found that the place probably contained more alcoholics ***per*** square mile than any city in the country.(p.163)
• My efficiency as a professional man was probably reduced to twenty-five ***per*** cent of what it should have been.(p.215)
• They did not seem to be getting an answer, for here I was staying sober and selling lots of auto polish, on which they were making one thousand ***per*** cent profit.(p.247)
• I know now that sixty ***per*** cent of the time I drank alone without benefit of customers.(p.287)
• "We watch the alcoholic performing in a position of responsibility and we know that because he is drinking heavily and daily he has cut his capacities by fifty ***per*** cent, and still he seems able to do a satisfactory job.(p.308)
• And we wonder how much further this man could go if his alcoholic problem could be removed and he could throw one hundred ***per*** cent of his abilities into action.(p.308)
• I cooperated with that man one hundred ***per*** cent!(p.388)
• Saying these sprees were limited to one a week (they were not), and saying that the average spree was ten of these drinks (sometimes more, sometimes less), we come up with the first boring statistic: two-fifty ***per*** week out of twelve dollars.(p.397)
• To keep it in round figures, let's say twenty ***per*** cent of my income went for giggle gurgles.(p.397)
• After a few more estimates as to income and expenditures for booze over a few sample years, taken at random, I conclude that this twenty ***per*** cent stayed fairly constant.(p.398)
• My first pay was ten dollars, pay for recruits at that time being twenty-one dollars ***per*** month.(p.398)
• For an estimate of salary from the twenty-one a month to start with, to over $400 ***per*** month upon my retirement after twenty years in the Navy, I believe that an average income of $2,000 a year over this period is low, but as I stated earlier, an underestimate is best.(p.399)
• $2,000 a year for twenty-five years is $50,000, twenty ***per*** cent of which is $10,000.(p.399)

perceive

• He will ***perceive*** that his spiritual growth is lopsided, that for an average man like himself, a spiritual life which does not include his family obligations may not be so perfect after all.(p.129)
• Some of these were hard to believe, but it did not require a giant brain to ***perceive*** that they had something I could use.(p.279)

percent

• Seven ***percent*** of the A.A.'s surveyed are less than 30 years of age -- among them, many in their teens.(p.xxii)
• I always built up in my own mind the great things that I was going to do, and in fact I accomplished about fifty ***percent*** of them and then lost interest.(p.193)
• So I believe that twenty ***percent*** is a very conservative estimate of the amount of income I blew.(p.399)

percentage

• But we think that if you persevere, the ***percentage*** of successes will gratify you.(p.144)

percentages

• But the ***percentages*** started tobogganing, and it was often a shock to read over some of the pages when sober.(p.331)

percodan

• I never got much effect out of codeine and ***Percodan*** and the tranquilizers.(p.442)

perfect

• For if an alcoholic failed to ***perfect*** and enlarge his spiritual life through work and self-sacrifice for others, he could not survive the certain trials and low spots ahead.(p.14)
• It was the end of a ***perfect*** day, not a cloud on the horizon.(p.41)
• Everybody nowadays, believes in scores of assumptions for which there is good evidence, but no ***perfect*** visual proof.(p.48)
• No one among us has been able to maintain anything like ***perfect*** adherence to these principles.(p.60)
• We can be alone at ***perfect*** peace and ease.(p.75)
• He will perceive that his spiritual growth is lopsided, that for an average man like himself, a spiritual life which does not include his family obligations may not be so ***perfect*** after all.(p.129)
• "I'll Never Smile Again" -- how ***perfect***.(p.332)
• My personality, from the time I can remember anything, was the ***perfect*** set-up for an alcoholic career.(p.400)
• But I will never be totally honest -- that would make me ***perfect***, and none of us can claim to be ***perfect***.(p.482)

• I thought that all women should be ***perfect***.(p.487)
• She maintains a ***perfect*** calm.(p.507)

perfection
• We claim spiritual progress rather than spiritual ***perfection***.(p.60)
• And I was always glad to point it out, because I knew you wanted ***perfection***, just as I did.(p.449)

perfectionists
• We "instant ***perfectionists***" also are hypersensitive, alas.(p.331)

perfectly
• He is often ***perfectly*** sensible and well balanced concerning everything except liquor, but in that respect he is incredibly dishonest and selfish.(p.21)
• When, however, the ***perfectly*** logical assumption is suggested that underneath the material world and life as we see it, there is an All Powerful, Guiding, Creative Intelligence, right there our perverse streak comes to the surface and we laboriously set out to convince ourselves it isn't so.(p.49)
• He said he was ***perfectly*** willing to go to jail if she insisted.(p.79)
• On the third day the lawyer gave his life to the care and direction of his Creator, and said he was ***perfectly*** willing to do anything necessary.(p.158)
• This time I seemed to be already awake, sitting upright in a big easy chair, in the middle of an animated conversation with a ***perfectly*** strange young woman, who didn't appear to think it strange.(p.222)
• In fact his language was ***perfectly*** suited to my understanding.(p.235)
• That was ***perfectly*** logical.(p.236)
• I was in a ***perfectly*** happy frame of mind.(p.285)
• I took that bottle of medicine and gave it to a very good friend of mine who was a pharmacist and had it analyzed, and the bottle was ***perfectly*** all right.(p.489)

perform
• But we may employ alcoholics where they are going to ***perform*** those services for which we might otherwise have to engage nonalcoholics.(p.566)

performance
• Far from expecting praise for their deeds, they claimed the ***performance*** a privilege and insisted that they invariably received more than they gave.(p.310)
• It wasn't long before I quit caring how I looked or what my job ***performance*** was.(p.318)
• I was intolerant of people who drank, particularly those who drank to an extent that interfered with on-the-job ***performance***.(p.374)
• Above all, I was suffering inner pain because my ***performance*** and my accomplishments in life failed to live up to my own expectations of myself.(p.557)
• Of course, the more I drank, the more unrealistic my expectations became and the poorer my ***performance***, and the gap widened.(p.557)

performances
• You are willing to overlook his past ***performances***.(p.141)

performed
• Being all powerful, He provided what we needed, if we kept close to Him and ***performed*** His work well.(p.63)
• There was the necessity for sticking to a job I hated, a dull, repetitive job ***performed*** in association with other men I had nothing in common with . . . ***performed*** for years on end, because the money was needed at home.(p.532)

performing
• He had tried everything from having me attend daily mass at six a.m. to ***performing*** the most menial labor for his charity patients.(p.306)
• "We watch the alcoholic ***performing*** in a position of responsibility and we know that because he is drinking heavily and daily he has cut his capacities by fifty per cent, and still he seems able to do a satisfactory job.(p.308)

perhaps
• What with our ultra-modern standards, our scientific approach to everything, we are ***perhaps*** not well equipped to apply the powers of good that lie outside our synthetic knowledge.(p.xxv)
• There is the manic-depressive type, who is, ***perhaps***, the least understood by his friends, and about whom a whole chapter could be written.(p.xxviii)
• ***Perhaps*** I can best answer this by relating one of my experiences.(p.xxix)
• I earnestly advise every alcoholic to read this book through, and though ***perhaps*** he came to scoff, he may remain to pray.(p.xxx)
• ***Perhaps*** they were right.(p.3)
• My weary and despairing wife was informed that it would all end with heart failure during delirium tremens, or I would develop a wet brain, ***perhaps*** within a year.(p.7)
• ***Perhaps*** I could help some of them.(p.14)
• ***Perhaps*** he goes to a doctor who gives him morphine or some sedative with which to taper off.(p.22)
• ***Perhaps*** there never will be a full answer to these questions.(p.22)
• Or ***perhaps*** he doesn't think at all.(p.24)
• The experiment of quitting for a period of time will be helpful, but we think we can render an even greater service to alcoholic sufferers and ***perhaps*** to the medical fraternity.(p.34)
• It never occurred to him that ***perhaps*** he could not do so, in spite of character and standing.(p.39)
• ***Perhaps*** it is going to be that way with you.(p.44)
• ***Perhaps*** we rejected this particular conception because it seemed inadequate.(p.45)
• ***Perhaps*** we had been leaning too heavily on Reason that last mile and we did not like to lose our support.(p.53)
• This was our course: We realized that the people who wronged us were ***perhaps*** spiritually sick.(p.66)
• ***Perhaps*** there is a better way -- we think so.(p.68)
• Here we find human opinions running to extremes -- absurd extremes, ***perhaps***.(p.68)
• This is ***perhaps*** difficult -- especially discussing our defects with another person.(p.72)
• ***Perhaps*** our doctor or psychologist will be the person.(p.74)
• ***Perhaps*** we have committed a criminal offense which might land us in jail if it were known to the authorities.(p.78)
• ***Perhaps*** we are mixed up with women in a fashion we wouldn't care to have advertised.(p.80)
• ***Perhaps*** he is having a secret and exciting affair with "the girl who understands."(p.81)
• ***Perhaps*** there are some cases where the utmost frankness is demanded.(p.82)
• Had this not been so, many of us would have no homes today, would ***perhaps*** be dead.(p.82)
• ***Perhaps*** you are not acquainted with any drinkers who want to recover.(p.89)
• ***Perhaps*** your story will help him see where he has failed to practice the very precepts he knows so well.(p.93)
• If your talk has been sane, quiet and full of human understanding, you have ***perhaps*** made a friend.(p.94)
• ***Perhaps*** you will want to take the man into your home for a few days.(p.96)
• After they have seen tangible results, the family will ***perhaps*** want to go along.(p.99)
• As wives of Alcoholics Anonymous, we would like you to feel that we understand as ***perhaps*** few can.(p.104)
• ***Perhaps*** at this point we got a divorce and took the children home to father and mother.(p.106)
• ***Perhaps*** your husband has been living in that strange world of alcoholism where everything is distorted and exaggerated.(p.108)
• ***Perhaps*** he spends too much money for liquor.(p.109)
• ***Perhaps*** he can still tend to business fairly well.(p.109)
• ***Perhaps*** he has had delirium tremens.(p.110)
• ***Perhaps*** you enjoy drinking with him yourself when he doesn't go too far.(p.110)
• ***Perhaps*** you both like parties which would be dull without liquor.(p.110)
• Tell him you have been worried, though ***perhaps*** needlessly.(p.112)
• Then ***perhaps*** he will be interested enough to continue.(p.113)
• ***Perhaps*** you have a husband who is at large, but who should be committed.(p.114)
• ***Perhaps*** your husband will make a fair start on the new basis, but just as things are going beautifully he dismays you by coming home drunk.(p.120)
• ***Perhaps*** they created the impression that he is to be wrapped in cotton wool and placed on a pedestal.(p.122)
• ***Perhaps*** he will never have much money again.(p.123)
• Whether you are a hard drinker, a moderated drinker or a teetotaler, you may have some pretty strong opinions, ***perhaps*** prejudices.(p.139)
• Your man has probably been trying to conceal a number of scrapes, ***perhaps*** pretty messy ones.(p.140)
• ***Perhaps*** you have such a man in mind.(p.141)
• Say that you believe he is a gravely ill person, with this qualification -- being ***perhaps*** fatally ill, does he want to get well?(p.142)
• ***Perhaps*** you are not quite in sympathy with the approach we suggest.(p.144)
• ***Perhaps*** this is a typical attitude.(p.149)
• ***Perhaps*** the best way of treating you to a glimpse of your future will be to describe the growth of the fellowship among us.(p.153)
• ***Perhaps*** he could handle, say, three drinks — no more!(p.154)
• Some of them may sink and ***perhaps*** never get up, but if our experience is a criterion, more than half of those approached will become fellows of Alcoholics Anonymous.(p.163)
• No beer or liquor was sold in the neighborhood, except at the State liquor agency where ***perhaps*** one might procure a pint if he could convince the agent that he really needed it.(p.171)
• Unfortunately for me, I was the only child, which ***perhaps*** engendered the selfishness which played such an important part in bringing on my alcoholism.(p.172)
• I seemed to be able to snap back the next morning better than most of my fellow drinkers, who were cursed (or ***perhaps*** blessed) with a great deal of morning-after nausea.(p.172)
• Formerly, in the acute mental and physical pain during the remorseful periods succeeding each drunk, I found my recollection of the misery I had gone through a bolsterer of resolution and afterward, ***perhaps***, a deterrent for a time.(p.260)
• I had tried to be the center of my own little world, whereas God was the center of a vast universe of which I was ***perhaps*** an essential, but a very tiny, part.(p.280)
• As I look back on that first evening I realize that I began to hope, then, for the first time; and I felt that if he could regain these things, ***perhaps*** it would be possible for me too.(p.290)
• The meeting consisted of ***perhaps*** eight or nine alcoholics and seven or eight wives.(p.291)
• I suggested to her that she should see the son's minister or doctor, and that ***perhaps*** he would recommend the A.A. program.(p.294)
• ***Perhaps*** I could find freedom and peace and be able once again to call my soul my own.(p.309)
• I never thought I could be useful to anyone except my husband and my children and ***perhaps*** a few friends.(p.326)
• We need them so badly even if you can only give one day, or ***perhaps*** two days?"(p.326)
• The second way in which, ***perhaps***, I differ from some other alcoholics is this; many alcoholics state that they didn't particularly like the taste of alcohol, but that they liked the effect.(p.345)
• Many times have I heard the above expressions since I have been in A.A., and many times I have had to reply "Definitely I am an alcoholic, and while it may be hard for you to believe, it is not hard for me, for I have learned many things about alcohol and myself that would, ***perhaps***, be difficult for you to understand."(p.356)
• ***Perhaps*** it was He who sent my analyst to a psychiatrist's meeting at which Bill spoke.(p.412)
• My daily alcoholic consumption remained about the same through all this, with ***perhaps*** a slight increase, and my binges remained one-nighters.(p.434)
• ***Perhaps*** the single flicker of decency that shone through the fog of my drinking days was a clumsy affection for my two children, a boy and a girl.(p.437)
• Now I own ***perhaps*** the most costly pair of moccasins anyone has ever seen, and they help me remember where I've been.)(p.445)
• One has to be pretty sick to do that, and ***perhaps*** one has to be even sicker to come back every day for a new list, as she did.(p.446)
• ***Perhaps*** the best thing of all for me is to remember that my serenity is inversely proportional to my expectations.(p.452)
• I figured that ***perhaps*** if I went ahead with that marriage, which I was sure was right for me, that would be the answer to my drinking problem.(p.465)
• In my screwed up mind I kept thinking I could have gone to A.A. way back there in 1940, and ***perhaps*** saved my marriage and home.(p.469)
• ***Perhaps*** a better way of saying it is that, on that day, with that decision, I no longer fought drinking as an escape.(p.531)
• Since, ***perhaps***, suicide was a bit too drastic (actually, I was afraid), dry martinis were chosen as the slow, pleasant, private, gradual instrument of self-destruction.(p.531)
• ***Perhaps***, without realizing it, I was.)(p.532)
• I don't care too much about personal fame or glory, and I want only enough money to enable me to do the work I feel I can ***perhaps*** do best.(p.542)

peril
• The feeling of having shared in a common ***peril*** is one element in the powerful cement

which binds us.(p.17)

period

• The flying-blind *period* ended and A.A. entered a new phase of its pioneering time.(p.xvii)

• Our Society then entered a fearsome and exciting adolescent *period*.(p.xviii)

• While the internal difficulties of our adolescent *period* were being ironed out, public acceptance of A.A. grew by leaps and bounds.(p.xix)

• I have had many men who had, for example, worked a *period* of months on some problem or business deal which was to be settled on a certain date, favorable to them.(p.xxvii)

• There is the type who always believes that after being entirely free from alcohol for a *period* of time he can take a drink without danger.(p.xxviii)

• Over any considerable *period* we get worse, never better.(p.30)

• We have heard of few instances where people, who showed definite signs of alcoholism, were able to stop for a long *period* because of an overpowering desire to do so.(p.32)

• Then he fell victim to a belief which practically every alcoholic has – that his long *period* of sobriety and self-discipline had qualified him to drink as other men.(p.32)

• Commencing to drink after a *period* of sobriety, we are in a short time as bad as ever.(p.33)

• Though you may be able to stop for a considerable *period*, you may yet be a potential alcoholic.(p.34)

• The experiment of quitting for a *period* of time will be helpful, but we think we can render an even greater service to alcoholic sufferers and perhaps to the medical fraternity.(p.34)

• We now see that when we began to drink deliberately, instead of casually, there was little serious or effective thought during the *period* of premeditation of what the terrific consequences might be.(p.37)

• Yes, there is a long *period* of reconstruction ahead.(p.83)

• We usually conclude the *period* of meditation with a prayer that we be shown all through the day what our next step is to be, that we be given whatever we need to take care of such problems.(p.87)

• Show them that he has entered upon a *period* of growth.(p.100)

• Because of the employee's special ability, or of his own strong personal attachment to him, the employer has sometimes kept such a man at work long beyond a reasonable *period*.(p.137)

• This went from bad to worse until Sophomore spring when, after a prolonged *period* of drinking, I made up my mind that I could not complete my course, so I packed my grip and went South to spend a month on a large farm owned by a friend of mine.(p.173)

• Then Prohibition came into effect, and the facts that the stuff obtainable was so horrible and sometimes deadly, and that I had married and had a job which I had to look after, helped me for a *period* of some three or four years, although I would get drunk every time I could get hold of enough to drink to get started.(p.183)

• About that *period*, too, came increasing procrastination and the avoidance of responsibilities.(p.197)

• I can well remember over a long *period* of years when I thought I was the only person in the world who knew that sooner or later I was going to get drunk.(p.198)

• After drinking one glass of beer at the end of my work *period* for about five days, I thought I'd better find out whether I really had the stuff licked.(p.203)

• So I was barred from the plant for ten days, and during that ten day *period* I was drunk twice, showing how little control these restraints had on me.(p.205)

• There were only seven or eight people in the group before me and they all visited me during my *period* in the hospital.(p.208)

• Although, during this *period* I was not addicted to any pattern of alcohol consumption, when I did drink the drinking was pretty wild.(p.212)

• This work consumed a *period* of about two-thirds of a year, and worked out successfully so I decided to follow patent law.(p.212)

• My drinking career began about four years after I had moved up into partnership and had joined certain clubs, societies and so fourth, and during which *period* we had Prohibition.(p.213)

• When I was about forty-seven, after indulging in all kinds of self-deception to control my drinking, I arrived at a *period* when I felt convinced I had to have so much alcohol every day and that the real problem was to control how much.(p.214)

• Early member, she spread the word among women in our pioneering *period*.(p.222)

• It was a *period* of binges coming closer and closer together and being of longer duration.(p.288)

• However, he explained to me that he had been just such a rummy as I, only for a much longer *period* of time.(p.302)

• But during a *period* of particular stress and strain about thirteen years ago, I resorted to alcohol in my home, alone, as a means of temporary release, as a means of getting a little extra sleep.(p.335)

• Over a *period* of time he has built up self pity, resentments toward anyone or anything that interferes with his drinking.(p.380)

• For an estimate of salary from the twenty-one a month to start with, to over $400 per month upon my retirement after twenty years in the Navy, I believe that an average income of $2,000 a year over this *period* is low, but as I stated earlier, an underestimate is best.(p.399)

• During this *period* I married again.(p.405)

• A return to the United States proved effective as a geographical cure, and a *period* of sobriety ensued, with the help of the church.(p.419)

• However, for a *period* of time I was injecting Pentothal intravenously to put myself to sleep.(p.442)

• Each ten-day *period* in the dark hole, I was fed bread and water daily, with one full meal on the third day only.(p.459)

• This was the only *period* when I didn't drink, but that was hardly any consolation.(p.480)

• In that short *period* he built within me something that I had long since lost, which was hope.(p.495)

• They tell me that I killed a man during that *period*, but I can't remember anything.(p.528)

• I went to jail for the second time during this *period* for being drunk in an automobile.(p.549)

• Most of our experiences are what the psychologist William James calls the "educational variety" because they develop slowly over a *period* of time.(p.569)

periodic

• I was a *periodic*.(p.197)

• I became a *periodic* drinker.(p.233)

• In the Army, I became a *periodic* alcoholic – the periods always coming whenever I could make the opportunity.(p.241)

• They had also been *periodic* big shots who had goofed out repeatedly at the wrong time, and they also knew how to split one paper match into three separate matches.(p.245)

• Fear, love of dentistry, and an imitation of my father's *periodic* drinking pattern took me through dental college soberly, except for the few parties and vacations in those four years.(p.419)

• My life there was a nightmare of *periodic* binges on alcohol and pills, adultery, unhappy hours at the dental office, seeing my wife give birth to our second child and have several miscarriages, living in a turbulent household, and making continual attempts to be the respectable dentist, husband, father, and community leader.(p.419)

• Only a few days before Christmas I went to the dentist for a *periodic* checkup.(p.465)

• There at the top of the folder was my name, age and address, and underneath were the words, "*Periodic* Drinker."(p.470)

• I had been promoted from a *periodic* drinker to a chronic alcoholic!(p.470)

periodics

• My wife upbraided me often and plenty when she saw that my "*periodics*" were gradually losing me what business I could get.(p.233)

• My "*periodics*" became more frequent until I reached the point where I wanted to devote all my time to drinking, working as little as possible, and then only when the necessity of my family demanded it.(p.234)

periods

• Nevertheless, I still thought I could control the situation, and there were *periods* of sobriety which renewed my wife's hope.(p.5)

• If they sense these things, they will not take so seriously his *periods* of crankiness, depression, or apathy, which will disappear when there is tolerance, love, and spiritual understanding.(p.127)

• The *periods* of sobriety attained by these thirteen A.A.'s range from fifteen to forty-six years.(p.169)

• Then I started drinking again, with possibly a little more restraint, *periods* a little bit longer than they had been before, but substantially the same pattern.(p.203)

• The first definite indications of an alcoholic pattern began to arise when I would go to New York on business and disappear, and wind up in Philadelphia or Boston for two or three day *periods*.(p.213)

• These *periods* became more frequent and I resolved that when I became forty, which was very shortly, I was going on the wagon.(p.213)

• For there were of course *periods* of clear realization of what I had become, attended by memories of what I had been, what I had expected to be.(p.224)

• Unlike many other Catholics who frequently take pledges for definite *periods* -- a year, two years or for good, I never had any desire to "take a pledge" before the priest.(p.234)

• In the Army, I became a periodic alcoholic -- the *periods* always coming whenever I could make the opportunity.(p.241)

• Every encouragement was given me with frequent salary increases, but the sober times between "*periods*" became shorter.(p.254)

• Formerly, in the acute mental and physical pain during the remorseful *periods* succeeding each drunk, I found my recollection of the misery I had gone through a bolsterer of resolution and afterward, perhaps, a deterrent for a time.(p.260)

• Three more months of being up and around the house for brief *periods* and in bed the rest of the time.(p.275)

• This gave me the freedom to do A.A. work, and to rest for *periods* of two or three days when I became too exhausted to carry on.(p.283)

• And I was able to go on the wagon for long *periods* of time – once for four years, to cure an ulcer.(p.328)

• Now my drinking was limited by only one factor, the enforced *periods* of dryness caused by lengthy tours at sea.(p.398)

perish

• Faith has to work twenty-four hours a day in and through us, or we *perish*.(p.16)

permanent

• It also indicated that strenuous work, one alcoholic with another, was vital to *permanent* recovery.(p.xvii)

• Following the elimination of alcohol, there was found to be no *permanent* brain injury.(p.xxix)

• Though our decision was a vital and crucial step, it could have little *permanent* effect unless at once followed by a strenuous effort to face, and to be rid of, the things in ourselves which had been blocking us.(p.64)

• They bear witness that release from alcoholism can really be *permanent*.(p.169)

• The birth of our Society dates from his first day of *permanent* sobriety, June 10, 1935.(p.171)

• After the oil job blew up, I went back to Baltimore and mother, my first wife having said a *permanent* "Goodbye."(p.243)

• Therefore, no society of men and women ever had more urgent need for continuous effectiveness and *permanent* unity.(p.563)

permanently

• It has never been, by any treatment with which we are familiar, *permanently* eradicated.(p.xxviii)

• When this sort of thinking is fully established in an individual with alcoholic tendencies, he has probably placed himself beyond human aid, and unless locked up, may die or go *permanently* insane.(p.24)

• Either they die of acute alcoholism or they develop wet brains and have to be put away *permanently*."(p.308)

• Shackles were *permanently* affixed to my ankles.(p.460)

permission

• If we have obtained *permission*, have consulted with others, asked God to help and the drastic step is indicated we must not shrink.(p.80)

• So I filled the cellar full, with the *permission* of my good wife.(p.177)

• It is true that I -- of all people, strange as it may seem, and even though I didn't give my *permission* -- really, really am an alcoholic of sorts.(p.448)

permit

• To the precise extent that we *permit* these, do we squander the hours that might have been worth while.(p.66)

• *Permit* that and you only harm him.(p.96)

• It will *permit* the rehabilitation of good men.(p.148)

permitted

• Golf *permitted* drinking every day and every night.(p.3)

• During these years, I drank as much as my purse *permitted*, still without paying too great a penalty, although I was beginning to have morning jitters at times.(p.173)

• I knew everyone would buy a few bottles, or cases, of liquor as their exchequers *permitted*, and that it would soon be gone.(p.175)

• Since the radio station was getting on its feet, it didn't require so many nights of evening work, and that *permitted* leisure time for drinking.(p.360)

• We weren't even *permitted* to play cards in our home, but father would give us just a little toddy with whiskey and sugar and warm water now and then.(p.484)
• So, finally, I went to the YMCA and they graciously *permitted* us to use a room at two dollars a night.(p.495)

peroxide
• I remembered filling the *peroxide* bottle in my medicine chest with gin, in case my sister found the bottle I hid under the mattress.(p.224)

perpetually
• I very early came to see that there had to be a continual renewal for that simple deal with God; that I had *perpetually* to keep the bargain.(p.237)

perplexing
• Instead of wanting to escape some *perplexing* problem, we experience a thrill of challenge in the opportunity it affords for another application of A.A. techniques, and we find ourselves tackling it with surprising vigor.(p.311)

persevere
• But we think that if you *persevere*, the percentage of successes will gratify you.(p.144)

persevered
• Having *persevered* with the rest of the program, they wondered why they fell.(p.73)

persist
• If you *persist*, remarkable things will happen.(p.100)
• I had to *persist* in my attempts to get straightened out enough to be able to use the drinks I needed, without their turning on me.(p.227)

persisted
• If *persisted* in for a few months, the effect on a man's family is sure to be great.(p.99)

persistence
• The *persistence* of this illusion is astonishing.(p.30)
• By *persistence* and salesmanship I managed to see more and more of my new friend, and because of her sympathetic nature she tolerated my company.(p.359)

persistent
• Another reason for the wide acceptance of A.A. was the ministration of friends -- friends in medicine, religion, and the press, together with innumerable others who became our able and *persistent* advocates.(p.xx)

persists
• If the family *persists* in criticism, this fallacy may take a still greater hold on father.(p.129)
• There should be no hesitancy in consulting a doctor or psychologist if the condition *persists*.(p.134)

person
• Many do not comprehend that the alcoholic is a very sick *person*.(p.xiii)
• This is repeated over and over, and unless this *person* can experience an entire psychic change there is very little hope of his recovery.(p.xxvii)
• On the other hand -- and strange as this may seem to those who do not understand -- once a psychic change has occurred, the very same *person* who seemed doomed, who had so many problems he despaired of ever solving them, suddenly finds himself easily able to control his desire for alcohol, the only effort necessary being that required to follow a few simple rules.(p.xxvii)
• If a *person* has cancer all are sorry for him and no one is angry or hurt.(p.18)
• No *person* likes to think he is bodily and mentally different from his fellows.(p.30)
• Whether such a *person* can quit upon a nonspiritual basis depends upon the extent to which he has already lost the power to choose whether he will drink or not.(p.34)
• Though not a religious *person*, I have profound respect for the spiritual approach in such cases as yours.(p.43)
• Rarely have we seen a *person* fail who has thoroughly followed our path.(p.58)
• Each *person* is like an actor who wants to run the whole show; is forever trying to arrange the lights, the ballet, the scenery and the rest of the players in his own way.(p.60)
• We found it very desirable to take this spiritual step with an understanding *person*, such as our wife, best friend or spiritual adviser.(p.63)
• When a *person* offended we said to ourselves, "This is a sick man.(p.67)
• Though a situation had not been entirely our fault, we tried to disregard the other *person* involved entirely.(p.67)
• This is perhaps difficult -- especially discussing our defects with another *person*.(p.72)
• We will be more reconciled to discussing ourselves with another *person* when we see good reasons why we should do so.(p.72)
• Rightly and naturally, we think well before we choose the *person* or persons with whom to take this intimate and confidential step.(p.74)
• We often find such a *person* quick to see and understand our problem.(p.74)
• Perhaps our doctor or psychologist will be the *person*.(p.74)
• Notwithstanding the great necessity for discussing ourselves with someone, it may be one is so situated that there is no suitable *person* available.(p.74)
• We say this because we are very anxious that we talk to the right *person*.(p.74)
• Nevertheless, with a *person* we dislike, we take the bit in our teeth.(p.77)
• Under no condition do we criticize such a *person* or argue.(p.77)
• We have already admitted this in confidence to another *person*, but we are sure we would be imprisoned or lose our job if it were known.(p.78)
• We feel we ought to say to her that we have no right to involve another *person*.(p.81)
• It is better, however, that one does not needlessly name a *person* upon whom she can vent jealously.(p.82)
• Have we kept something to ourselves which should be discussed with another *person* at once?(p.86)
• They should be patient, realizing they are dealing with a sick *person*.(p.90)
• If there is any indication that he wants to stop, have a good talk with the *person* most interested in him -- usually his wife.(p.90)
• If he says yes, then his attention should be drawn to you as a *person* who has recovered.(p.90)
• When dealing with such a *person*, you had better use everyday language to describe spiritual principles.(p.93)
• If you leave such a *person* alone, he may soon become convinced that he cannot recover by himself.(p.96)
• But urge upon a man's family that he has been a very sick *person* and should be treated accordingly.(p.100)
• To a *person* who has had experience with an alcoholic, this may seem like tempting Providence, but it isn't.(p.101)
• If you are with a *person* who wants to eat in a bar, by all means go along.(p.102)
• He is just another very sick, unreasonable *person*.(p.108)
• We think this *person* is in danger.(p.109)
• When you have carefully explained to such people that he is a sick *person*, you will have created a new atmosphere.(p.115)
• We wives found that, like everybody else, we were afflicted with pride, self-pity, vanity and all the things which go to make up the self-centered *person*; and we were not above selfishness or dishonesty.(p.116)
• Another principle we observe carefully is that we do not relate intimate experiences of another *person* unless we are sure he would approve.(p.125)
• Dad may feel that for years his drinking has placed him on the wrong side of every argument, but now he has become a superior *person* with God on his side.(p.129)
• And but for the intervention of an understanding *person*, I might have followed in their footsteps.(p.137)
• Say that you believe he is a gravely ill *person*, with this qualification -- being perhaps fatally ill, does he want to get well?(p.142)
• He trembled as he went about, for this might mean ruin, particularly to a *person* in his line of business.(p.156)
• If I could, that was wonderful, that was just fine, and they would very much appreciate a *person* who had that kind of power, but they were looking for a man that knew he had a problem, and knew that he couldn't handle it himself and needed outside help.(p.186)
• I noticed that the others seemed to have such a release, a happiness, a something that I thought a *person* ought to have.(p.191)
• I feel that is about the most wonderful thing that a *person* can do.(p.192)
• I can well remember over a long period of years when I thought I was the only *person* in the world who knew that sooner or later I was going to get drunk.(p.198)
• I wasn't the only *person* in the world who felt and behaved like this!(p.227)
• I wasn't mad or vicious -- I was a sick *person*.(p.227)
• Father was a very well-integrated *person*, and while mother was highstrung and a bit selfish and demanding, our home life was reasonably harmonious.(p.240)
• On my ride to the nearest bar, I sold the driver on how misunderstood I was by my wife and what an unreasonable *person* she was.(p.288)
• It wasn't necessary to report to the office in *person* every day, and when I did go in, it was just to make an appearance and bounce right out again.(p.300)
• I learned that a *person* just can't find a job hanging in a dive or barroom all day and all night, as jobs don't seem to turn up in those places.(p.300)
• One is that I don't remember too many of them, as I was one of those drunks who could be on his feet and attend a meeting or a party, engage in a conversation with people and do things that any nearly normal *person* would do, and the next day not remember a thing about where I was, what I did, whom I saw, or how I got home.(p.301)
• He mentioned lies and deceptions in the course of his story in the presence of the one *person* in the world I wouldn't want to know such things.(p.302)
• I don't know what sort of *person* I was expecting, but I was very agreeably surprised to find Mr. T. a poised, intelligent, well groomed and mannered gentleman.(p.309)
• I couldn't look them straight in the eyes, although I was always a self-possessed brazen sort of *person*.(p.323)
• I vowed that never again would any important *person* whom I wished to please and impress ever see me drunk.(p.328)
• But I was always the unexpected *person* who had to finish the bottle.(p.336)
• The very *person* who stood with me through it all and has been my greatest help was the *person* that I turned against, my husband.(p.338)
• I became a Jekyll-and-Hyde *person*.(p.339)
• I got the Big Book and I read it, and this is what it said: "Rarely have we seen a *person* fail who has thoroughly followed our path."(p.349)
• And the most important *person* to be honest with is Yourself.(p.368)
• How can a *person* with a fine family, an attractive home, an excellent position and high standing in an important city become an alcoholic?(p.373)
• Cunning, baffling, powerful -- the gradual creeping up of the frequency and quantity of alcohol, and what it does to a *person* is apparent to everyone but the *person* involved.(p.375)
• The last two years of my drinking my entire personality changed to a cynical, intolerant and arrogant *person* completely different from my normal self.(p.376)
• I liked the description of the alcoholic as a *person* who had found that alcohol is interfering with his social or business life.(p.380)
• As I grow in A.A., I realize that a *person* with as much self-will as I had, as hard a head and as diseased an ego, had to try everything that I could think of, butting my head against every stone wall before I was ready to come in.(p.384)
• I was an extremely sensitive *person* and so self-conscious that I hurt all over.(p.385)
• I realized that there were other people in this world who behaved and acted as I did, and that I was a sick *person*, that I was suffering from an actual disease.(p.392)
• With ten years of A.A. behind me, I was able to tell him that I'd have been alcoholic, no matter what; that I had been a sick *person*, unfit for marriage.(p.403)
• A normal *person*, hit with adversity, can go on a drinking spree and then snap out of it.(p.404)
• I remember very well saying, "There's only one *person* in the world whose guts I hate worse than yours, and those're my own."(p.440)
• When I am disturbed, it is because I find some *person*, place, thing, or situation -- some fact of my life -- unacceptable to me, and I can find no serenity until I accept that *person*, place, thing, or situation as being exactly the way it is supposed to be at this moment.(p.449)
• I was always able to see the flaw in every *person*, every situation.(p.449)
• There, I received several soda crackers and water daily, and before I could have my third-day meal (again the only meal in ten days), I had to drink a glass of castor oil or mineral oil, depending on the cruelty of the *person* who was doing the dispensing.(p.459)
• Three weeks after an armed robbery in which one *person* received a superficial flesh wound (I could have killed someone!), I was apprehended.(p.460)
• I am still arrogant, egocentric, self-righteous, with no humility, even phony at times, but I'm trying to be a better *person* and help my fellowman.(p.463)

• And she was a charming, delightful, lovely ***person***.(p.472)
• The poorest ***person*** has no less and the wealthiest has no more – each of us has but one day.(p.473)
• He has taught me that, in our new life, I am the most important ***person*** of all.(p.481)
• We lived just a few doors from the First Baptist Church and when they had funerals I remember very often asking my mother whether the ***person*** was good or bad and whether they were going to heaven or hell.(p.483)
• I'm sure my ideas as to what life should be like were quite different from that of the average ***person*** with whom I associated.(p.483)
• On the other hand, I believe that I've always been medically inclined, though I have never been able to see medicine quite as the average ***person*** sees it.(p.485)
• Around eight or nine o'clock there came two big detectives and a policeman to arrest me for assault; and I was the most amazed ***person*** in the world when they said I had assaulted someone, and especially that I had assaulted my wife.(p.492)
• But as he continued to talk, I realized that this was the first time I had met a ***person*** who had the same problems I did and who, I sincerely believe, understood me as an individual.(p.494)
• The drive was long and cold but he was thankful for the hot bricks which some thoughtful ***person*** had given him for his feet.(p.497)
• I begin to see I am not the ***person*** I had thought myself, that I had judged myself by comparing myself to others, and always to my own advantage.(p.504)
• During the course of that drinking, I had shot and killed one ***person*** and almost completed the job on a second one.(p.508)
• I always blamed my drinking on being poor, or on anything other than the truth – that I liked what booze did for me, that when I had a drink I was as big and had as much as the next ***person***.(p.526)
• I remember the day when I decided to drink myself to death quietly, without bothering anyone, because I was tired of having been a dependable, trustworthy ***person*** for about thirty-nine years without having received what I thought was a proper reward for my virtue.(p.531)
• After nearly eight years of sobriety in A.A., I still can set down such thoughts, "against my instinct and training," showing that I still consider myself a "special" ***person***, entitled to special privileges.(p.536)
• The less you think of yourself the more of a ***person*** you become.(p.542)
• I was the only ***person*** I'd ever known personally who had ever been in jail, and I guess it is most significant that the second time was less humiliating that the first had been.(p.549)
• It's been true in my case, nor could I quarrel with "restore us to sanity," for my actions drunk or sober, before A.A., were not those of a sane ***person***.(p.550)
• He said, in effect: "If you have a resentment you want to be free of, if you will pray for the ***person*** or the thing that you resent, you will be free.(p.552)

person's

• We have no right to save our own skin at another ***person's*** expense.(p.74)

personal

• But the chief change was in the section of ***personal*** stories, which was expanded to reflect the Fellowship's growth.(p.xi)
• "Bill's Story," "Doctor Bob's Nightmare," and one other ***personal*** history from the first edition were retained intact; three were edited and one of these was retitled; new versions of two stories were written with new titles; thirty completely new stories were added; and the story section was divided into three parts, under the same headings that are used now.(p.xi)
• If you have a drinking problem, we hope that you may pause in reading one of the forty-four ***personal*** stories and think: "Yes, that happened to me"; or, more important, "Yes, I've felt like that"; or most important, "Yes, I believe this program can work for me, too."(p.xii)
• It is important that we remain anonymous because we are too few, at present to handle the overwhelming number of ***personal*** appeals which may result from this publication.(p.xiii)
• When writing or speaking publicly about alcoholism, we urge each of our Fellowship to omit his ***personal*** name, designating himself instead as "a member of Alcoholics Anonymous."(p.xiii)
• By ***personal*** religious affiliation, we include Catholics, Protestants, Jews, Hindus, and a sprinkling of Moslems and Buddhists.(p.xx)
• In spite of the great increase in the size and the span of this Fellowship, at its core it remains simple and ***personal***.(p.xxii)
• When they talked of a God ***personal*** to me, who was love, superhuman strength and direction, I became irritated and my mind snapped shut against such a theory.(p.10)
• When the thought was expressed that there might be a God ***personal*** to me this feeling was intensified.(p.12)
• This should be an entirely ***personal*** affair which each one decides for himself in the light of past associations, or his present choice.(p.28)
• These are followed by forty-three ***personal*** experiences.(p.29)
• Each individual, in the ***personal*** stories, describes in his own language and from his own point of view the way he established his relationship with God.(p.29)
• I reasoned I was not so far advanced as most of you fellows, that I had been usually successful in licking my other ***personal*** problems, and that I would therefore be successful where you men failed.(p.40)
• In our ***personal*** stories you will find a wide variation in the way each teller approaches and conceives of the Power which is greater than himself.(p.50)
• We were having trouble with ***personal*** relationships, we couldn't control our emotional natures, we were a prey to misery and depression, we couldn't make a living, we had a feeling of uselessness, we were full of fear, we were unhappy, we couldn't seem to be of real help to other people – was not a basic solution of these bedevilments more important than whether we should see newsreels of lunar flight?(p.52)
• 10.Continued to take ***personal*** inventory and when we were wrong promptly admitted it.(p.59)
• Our description of the alcoholic, the chapter to the agnostic, and our ***personal*** adventures before and after make clear three pertinent ideas:(p.60)
• Next we launched out on a course of vigorous action, the first step of which is a ***personal*** housecleaning, which many of us had never attempted.(p.63)
• Therefore, we started upon a ***personal*** inventory.(p.64)
• In most cases it was found that our self-esteem, our pocketbooks, our ambitions, our ***personal*** relationships (including sex) were hurt or threatened.(p.64)
• Was it our self-esteem, our security, our ambitions, our ***personal***, or sex relations, which had been interfered with?(p.65)
• ***Personal*** relationship.(p.65)
• ***Personal*** sex relations.(p.65)
• If we have been thorough about our ***personal*** inventory, we have written down a lot.(p.70)
• Having made our ***personal*** inventory, what shall we do about it?(p.72)
• We have admitted certain defects; we have ascertained in a rough way what the trouble is; we have put our finger on the weak items in our ***personal*** inventory.(p.72)
• Reminding ourselves that we have decided to go to any length to find a spiritual experience we ask that we be given strength and direction to do the right thing, no matter what the ***personal*** consequences may be.(p.79)
• This thought brings us to Step Ten, which suggests we continue to take ***personal*** inventory and continue to set right any new mistakes as we go along.(p.84)
• Keep his attention focussed mainly on your ***personal*** experience.(p.92)
• Therefore, ask yourself on each occasion, "Have I any good social, business, or ***personal*** reason for going to this place?(p.101)
• Because of the employee's special ability, or of his own strong ***personal*** attachment to him, the employer has sometimes kept such a man at work long beyond a reasonable period.(p.137)
• While on the subject of confidence, can you adopt the attitude that so far as you are concerned this will be a strictly ***personal*** matter, that his alcoholic derelictions, the treatment about to be undertaken, will never be discussed without his consent?(p.143)
• As our work spreads and our numbers increase, we hope your employees may be put in ***personal*** contact with some of us.(p.144)
• *PERSONAL* STORIES(p.165)
• Beginning with the story of "Dr. Bob," a co-founder of A.A., there are here presented three groups of ***personal*** histories.(p.165)
• It isn't always so sudden with everyone, but I ran into a ***personal*** crisis which filled me with a raging and righteous anger.(p.228)
• In a few sentences he made God seem ***personal*** to me, explained Him as a being who was interested in me, the alcoholic, and that all I needed to do was to be willing to follow His way; that as long as I followed it I would be able to overcome my desire for liquor.(p.236)
• We talked, too, about ***personal*** morals.(p.236)
• Probably only a few readers of this story will be able, from ***personal*** experiences of their own, to understand the exhilaration and sense of accomplishment which I felt after finishing this seemingly simple assignment.(p.276)
• But the firm became violently ill with my drunkenness and their course of treatment was to remove their ulcer, in the form of me, from the payroll, amid much fanfare and very ***personal*** and slighting remarks and insinuations.(p.300)
• I cared nothing about my ***personal*** appearance.(p.337)
• Resenting anyone and everyone who might interfere with my ***personal*** plans and ways of doing things, I was full of self pity, especially for any interference with my drinking.(p.376)
• I don't know what I expected, but I most certainly didn't visualize a group of people talking about their drinking problems, making light of their ***personal*** tragedies and at the same time enjoying themselves.(p.378)
• That ***personal*** touch did help me too.(p.393)
• There are so many to whom I feel deeply grateful; to my husband (and best critic), whose generous love, compassion and understanding have helped me along the way; to those before me in A.A. who inspired the first article I read, and the friend who sent that article to Frank; to Ruth for her ***personal*** note, and the first A.A. to talk to me; to my Bishop, whose loving and believing spirit inspired me; and to all the members of the Houston Group who were so patient, kind and helpful -- and to countless others.(p.393)
• Except for one short slip, during the first eight months, which was an angry "the world can't do this to me" reaction to a ***personal*** tragedy in my life, I have been sober for twelve years.(p.416)
• My ***personal*** definition, which I submit as applying only to myself (although everyone is welcome to it who wants it), includes every waking activity of the human being; to have a creative attitude towards things is a more exact meaning, to live and to deal with other human beings creatively, which to me means seeing the God in them, and respecting and worshipping this God.(p.535)
• I don't care too much about ***personal*** fame or glory, and I want only enough money to enable me to do the work I feel I can perhaps do best.(p.542)
• Had I been able to explain to a psychiatrist the feeling of futility, loneliness and lack of purpose that had come with my deep sense of ***personal*** failure at this second divorce, I seriously doubt that the good doctor could have convinced me that my basic problem was a spiritual hunger, but A.A. has shown me this was the truth.(p.546)
• I realize now that this phase of my development had been arrested by my obsession with self, and my egocentricity had reached such proportions that adjustment to anything outside my ***personal*** control was impossible for me.(p.547)
• It had provided me with excuses for my lack of education, my marital failures, ***personal*** failures, inadequacy, and of course, my alcoholism and, though I really thought I had been willing to part with it, now I knew I was reluctant to let it go.(p.552)
• One -- Our common welfare should come first; ***personal*** recovery depends upon A.A. unity.(p.564)
• Eleven -- Our public relations policy is based on attraction rather than promotion; we need always maintain ***personal*** anonymity at the level of press, radio and films.(p.564)
• 11. -- Our relations with the general public should be characterized by ***personal*** anonymity.(p.567)

personalities

• But with the first drink, our good intentions dissolved; our ***personalities*** changed.(p.458)
• And we found ourselves back in prison, where our ***personalities*** became even more warped.(p.459)
• Twelve -- Anonymity is the spiritual foundation of all our Traditions, ever reminding us to place principles before ***personalities***.(p.564)
• It reminds us that we are to place principles before ***personalities***; that we are actually to practice a genuine humility.(p.568)

personality

• Though he could not accept all the tenets of the Oxford Groups, he was convinced of the need for moral inventory, confession of ***personality*** defects, restitution to those harmed, helpfulness to others, and the necessity of belief in and dependence upon God.(p.xvi)
• He has so attractive a ***personality*** that he makes friends with everyone.(p.39)
• As I look back, all the brothers developed ***personality*** problems.(p.210)

• I apparently was willing to subdue these ***personality*** disturbances in a tremendous drive to succeed.(p.211)
• I realized that I had a problem, although my realization was not very deep because my own conceit wouldn't admit that I had any ***personality*** problems.(p.214)
• I don't think the boys were completely convinced of my ***personality*** change, for they fought shy of including my story in the book, so my only contribution to their literary efforts was my firm conviction, being still a theological rebel, that the word God should be qualified with the phrase "as we understand him" -- for that was the only way I could accept spirituality.(p.248)
• Then I found that as I gave in to this spiritual or ***personality*** change I was getting a little more serenity.(p.249)
• At the moral inventory, he brought up some of my bad ***personality*** traits or character defects, such as selfishness, conceit, jealousy, carelessness, intolerance, ill-temper, sarcasm and resentments.(p.292)
• The last two years of my drinking my entire ***personality*** changed to a cynical, intolerant and arrogant person completely different from my normal self.(p.376)
• My ***personality***, from the time I can remember anything, was the perfect set-up for an alcoholic career.(p.400)
• The ***personality*** rehabilitation did not come overnight.(p.416)
• My ***personality*** was stretched almost to splitting in the effort; schizophrenia stared me in the face, and one night I was in a suicidal despair.(p.435)
• So I sat down with me and went over the facts behind the convulsions: ***personality*** changes, daily headaches, sense of impending doom, sense of impending insanity.(p.444)
• Intake of alcohol changes one's ***personality*** -- even the healthy ***personality***.(p.458)
• If my ***personality*** is inadequate, antisocial, or full of kinks and I alter it with alcohol or any chemical, bingo!(p.458)
• Sobriety and a plan for living that produces a ***personality*** change and a spiritual awakening are imperative.(p.459)
• The terms "spiritual experience" and "spiritual awakening" are used many times in this book which, upon careful reading, shows that the ***personality*** change sufficient to bring about recovery from alcoholism has manifested itself among us in many different forms.(p.569)
• Yet it is true that our first printing gave many readers the impression that these ***personality*** changes, or religious experiences, must be in the nature of sudden and spectacular upheavals.(p.569)
• Even among those who occasionally land back in here again, we observe a profound change in ***personality***.(p.572)

personally

• I ***personally*** know scores of cases who were of the type with whom other methods had failed completely.(p.xxiii)
• I'm so grateful for both the program and the people in it that I still want to go, and then probably the most wonderful thing that I learned from the program -- I've seen this in the 'A.A. Grapevine' a lot of times, and I've had people say it to me ***personally***, and I've heard people get up in meetings and make the same statement: The statement is, "I came into A.A. solely for the purpose of sobriety, but it has been through A.A. that I have found God."(p.192)
• There was one meeting a week at Bill's home in Brooklyn, and we all took turns there spouting off about how we had changed our lives overnight, how many drunks we had saved and straightened out, and last, but not least, how God had touched each of us ***personally*** on the shoulder.(p.246)
• The ensuing nine years were the Depression years, both nationally and ***personally***.(p.277)
• I was the only person I'd ever known ***personally*** who had ever been in jail, and I guess it is most significant that the second time was less humiliating that the first had been.(p.549)

personnel

• So I spent much of my time calling on the people who I felt would logically come in contact with alcoholic cases, doctors, ministers, lawyers and the ***personnel*** men in industry.(p.281)

persons

• Alcohol being no respecter of ***persons***, we are an accurate cross section of America, and in distant lands, the same democratic evening-up process is now going on.(p.xx)
• At these informal gatherings one may often see from 50 to 200 ***persons***.(p.16)
• We used to amuse ourselves by cynically dissecting spiritual beliefs and practices when we might have observed that many spiritually-minded ***persons*** of all races, colors, and creeds were demonstrating a degree of stability, happiness and usefulness which we should have sought ourselves.(p.49)
• 8.Made a list of all ***persons*** we had harmed, and became willing to make amends to them all.(p.59)
• Counsel with ***persons*** is often desirable, but we let God be the final judge.(p.69)
• Rightly and naturally, we think well before we choose the person or ***persons*** with whom to take this intimate and confidential step.(p.74)
• We have a list of all ***persons*** we have harmed and to whom we are willing to make amends.(p.76)
• There could be no love in such ***persons***, we thought.(p.107)
• Do not hesitate to take your health problems to such ***persons***.(p.133)
• His wife is one of those ***persons*** who really feels there is something rather sinful about these commodities, so she nagged, and her intolerance finally threw him into a fit of anger.(p.135)
• This doctor had imparted his knowledge to just a few other men at that time -- not more than four or five -- they now number more than seventy ***persons***.(p.235)
• My wife made several attempts to get me to stop and I had the usual visits from ***persons*** who would always ask me "Why?" -- as if I knew!(p.254)
• In five years a good many ***persons*** had forgotten that I had been somewhat notorious.(p.256)
• But I had never been a flippant, wise-cracking sneerer at the few ***persons*** I had met who had impressed me as Christian men and women, or at any institution whose sincerity of purpose I could see.(p.259)
• Dr. Bob then led me through the restitution step, in which I made a list of all of the ***persons*** I had harmed, and worked out ways and means of slowly making restitution.(p.292)
• He may even read in a newspaper that one out of every seven drinkers will become alcoholic, but he rarely is told that it holds true for all ages -- or that the tolerance to alcohol (and other drugs) decreases steadily, year after year, in the bodies of all ***persons***.(p.330)

perspective

• I began to wonder, for such an appalling lack of ***perspective*** seemed near being just that.(p.5)
• Husbands and wives have sometimes been obliged to separate for a time until new ***perspective***, new victory over hurt pride could be rewon.(p.125)
• The scales had dropped from my eyes and I could see life in its proper ***perspective***.(p.280)

perspiration

• I paced the floor with a bath towel around my shoulders, the ***perspiration*** running off me.(p.268)

persuade

• I failed to ***persuade*** my broker friends to send me out looking over factories and managements, but my wife and I decided to go anyway.(p.2)
• Highly competent psychiatrists who have dealt with us have found it sometimes impossible to ***persuade*** an alcoholic to discuss his situation without reserve.(p.18)
• If he does not want to stop drinking, don't waste time trying to ***persuade*** him.(p.90)

persuaded

• Our hope is that many alcoholic men and women, desperately in need, will see these pages, and we believe that it is only by fully disclosing ourselves and our problems that they will be ***persuaded*** to say, "Yes, I am one of them too; I must have this thing."(p.29)
• I had not asked for help and seriously doubt that I would have, but Fitz, an old school friend of mine, had ***persuaded*** Jackie to call on me.(p.238)
• It was the late Dr. Tiebout, then, who ***persuaded*** me to seek help through A.A.(p.559)

persuader

• In this respect alcohol was a great ***persuader***.(p.48)

persuading

• In a matter of fact way he told how two men had appeared in court, ***persuading*** the judge to suspend his commitment.(p.9)

pertaining

• I was still bitter because I felt that drink had completely ruined my childhood and my married life, and I hated everything ***pertaining*** to it.(p.262)
• I used to think I was cowardly because when things came out ***pertaining*** to the program that troubled me, I said to her many times, "Annie, am I being a coward because I lay those things away on the shelf and skip it?"(p.273)

pertinent

• Our description of the alcoholic, the chapter to the agnostic, and our personal adventures before and after make clear three ***pertinent*** ideas:(p.60)

perturbed

• "That's a devil of a way to run an organization," I thought, and I reported Frank to the psychiatrist, who didn't seem ***perturbed***; he just got someone else to take me on Fridays.(p.447)

pervade

• We are like the passengers of a great liner the moment after rescue from shipwreck when camaraderie, joyousness and democracy ***pervade*** the vessel from steerage to Captain's table.(p.17)

perverse

• When, however, the perfectly logical assumption is suggested that underneath the material world and life as we see it, there is an All Powerful, Guiding, Creative Intelligence, right there our ***perverse*** streak comes to the surface and we laboriously set out to convince ourselves it isn't so.(p.49)

pet

• Our ***pet*** slogan is "Easy Does It."(p.250)
• I learned early in my A.A. life that I could not afford to fondle such thoughts, as you might fondle a ***pet***, because this particular ***pet*** could grow into a monster.(p.285)

petty

• Maybe it's only a ***petty*** offense such as padding the expense account.(p.78)
• Social distinctions, ***petty*** rivalries and jealousies -- these are laughed out of countenance.(p.161)
• At age twenty-one, I enlisted in the Navy for two reasons: (1) to avoid being drafted into the Army, and (2) out of a burst of patriotic fervor inspired by the advent of World War II and as the result of an all-night drinking binge which found me sitting on the doorstep of the Navy recruiting office when the chief ***petty*** officer arrived to open for business at nine o'clock Monday morning.(p.398)

pew

• So we rolled old newspapers together and made torches to find a good soft ***pew*** and get some sleep.(p.424)
• My torch blazed madly and the ***pew*** caught fire.(p.424)

pharmacist

• As a physician and ***pharmacist*** who had grown up in a drugstore-home, I had a pill for every ill, and I was sick a lot.(p.443)
• I took that bottle of medicine and gave it to a very good friend of mine who was a ***pharmacist*** and had it analyzed, and the bottle was perfectly all right.(p.489)

pharmacy

• I had begun to drink in the early years of ***pharmacy*** school, in order to get to sleep.(p.440)
• And as I went through ***pharmacy*** school, graduate school, medical school, internship, residency, and specialty training and, finally, went into practice, my drinking kept increasing.(p.441)

phase

• The flying-blind period ended and A.A. entered a new ***phase*** of its pioneering time.(p.xvii)
• If we are painstaking about this ***phase*** of our development, we will be amazed before we are half way through.(p.83)
• After a while, turn the talk to some ***phase*** of drinking.(p.91)
• If the family will appreciate that dad's current behavior is but a ***phase*** of his development, all will be well.(p.129)
• This ***phase*** was right down my alley; I had my master's degree in the art of making "whoopee."(p.359)
• I realize now that this ***phase*** of my development had been arrested by my obsession with self, and my egocentricity had reached such proportions that adjustment to anything outside my personal control was impossible for me.(p.547)

phenobarbital

• I had been using paraldehyde more or less like ordinary drink for the last six years though, occasionally, I'd bounce back to ***phenobarbital*** and things like that.(p.524)

phenomena

• To me these occurrences are ***phenomena***.(p.27)

phenomenon

• We believe, and so suggested a few years ago, that the action of alcohol on these chronic alcoholics is a manifestation of an allergy; that the ***phenomenon*** of craving is limited to this class and never occurs in the average temperate drinker.(p.xxvi)

• After they have succumbed to the desire again, as so many do, and the ***phenomenon*** of craving develops, they pass through the well-known stages of a spree, emerging remorseful, with a firm resolution not to drink again.(p.xxvii)
• They took a drink a day or so prior to the date, and then the ***phenomenon*** of craving at once became paramount to all other interests so that the important appointment was not met.(p.xxvii)
• There are many situations which arise out of the ***phenomenon*** of craving which cause men to make the supreme sacrifice rather than continue to fight.(p.xxviii)
• All these, and many others, have one symptom in common: they cannot start drinking without developing the ***phenomenon*** of craving.(p.xxviii)
• This ***phenomenon***, as we have suggested, may be the manifestation of an allergy which differentiates these people, and sets them apart as a distinct entity.(p.xxviii)
• But there was always the curious mental ***phenomenon*** that parallel with our sound reasoning there inevitably ran some insanely trivial excuse for taking the first drink.(p.37)

Philadelphia
• The first definite indications of an alcoholic pattern began to arise when I would go to New York on business and disappear, and wind up in ***Philadelphia*** or Boston for two or three day periods.(p.213)
• How it finally broke a Southerner's obstinacy and destined this salesman to start A.A. at ***Philadelphia***.(p.238)
• Three years later, at twenty-five, I opened and operated their ***Philadelphia*** office and was earning more than I ever have since.(p.242)
• Then I got a very good position in ***Philadelphia*** and quickly found I would need a few fellow alcoholics around me if I was to stay sober.(p.249)
• Offered the job of advertising manager for an eastern automotive company, I moved to ***Philadelphia*** to begin life anew.(p.254)
• Dr. John F. Stouffer, Chief Psychiatrist, ***Philadelphia*** General Hospital, citing his experience with A.A., said: "The alcoholics we get here at ***Philadelphia*** General are mostly those who cannot afford private treatment, and A.A. is by far the greatest thing we have been able to offer them.(p.572)

Philander
• I finished high school here in an American-sponsored Methodist public school, know as ***Philander*** Smith College.(p.342)

Philippines
• Then came my tour in the U.S. Navy, part of it being two years in the ***Philippines***.(p.419)

Philistine
• If he were still sober, chances are that very quickly I put him down as a ***Philistine*** with no appreciation of literary genius; and then I went on to another bar to find a new victim.(p.537)

philosophic
• We had long talks when I would still her foreboding by telling her that men of genius conceived their best projects when drunk; that the most majestic constructions of ***philosophic*** thought were so derived.(p.2)
• Any therapeutic or ***philosophic*** procedure which can prove a recovery rate of 50% to 60% must merit our consideration."(p.571)

philosophical
• Many of us had moral and ***philosophical*** convictions galore, but we could not live up to them even though we would have liked to.(p.62)

philosophically
• We could wish to be moral, we could wish to be ***philosophically*** comforted, in fact, we could will these things with all our might, but the needed power wasn't there.(p.45)

philosophies
• But we found that such codes and ***philosophies*** did not save us, no matter how much we tried.(p.45)

philosophy
• They sound like the ***philosophy*** of the man who, having a headache, beats himself on the head with a hammer so that he can't feel the ache.(p.23)
• If a mere code of morals or a better ***philosophy*** of life were sufficient to overcome alcoholism, many of us would have recovered long ago.(p.44)
• What ***philosophy*** I had was thoroughly paganistic -- all my life was devoted to a search for pleasure.(p.256)
• I stayed in Akron two or three weeks on my initial trip trying to absorb as much of the program and ***philosophy*** as possible.(p.291)
• ***Philosophy***, faith, a sense of humor (they could laugh at themselves), clear-cut objectives, appreciation -- and most especially appreciation and sympathetic understanding for their fellow man.(p.310)
• In learning to practice these steps in my daily living I began to acquire faith and a ***philosophy*** to live by.(p.311)
• For me, A.A. is a synthesis of all the ***philosophy*** I've ever read, all of the positive, good ***philosophy***, all of it based on love.(p.542)
• It was impossible for me to say at this point, "Maybe there is something wrong with my ***philosophy***," and I certainly couldn't say, "Maybe there is something wrong with me."(p.545)
• Dr. G. Kirby Collier, psychiatrist: "I have felt that A.A. is a group unto themselves and their best results can be had under their own guidance, as a result of their ***philosophy***.(p.571)

phobia
• My ***phobia*** for sleeplessness demanded that I get drunk every night, but in order to get more liquor for the next night, I had to stay sober during the day, at least up to four o'clock.(p.177)

phobias
• During the next few years, I developed two distinct ***phobias***.(p.175)
• We all had hundreds of character traits, of fears and ***phobias***, likes and dislikes, in common.(p.229)

Phoenix
• For the next five years, I was in and out of A.A. in Los Angeles, ***Phoenix***, and San Francisco.(p.460)

phone
• My secretary returned to say that it was not Mr. B---- on the ***phone***; it was Mr. B-----'s brother, and he wished to give me a message.(p.136)
• He would ***phone*** a clergyman.(p.154)
• I'd hear them on the ***phone*** having prayer meetings and so forth, that sort of talk over the ***phone***, and it completely burnt me up.(p.265)
• I got so that I hid quite a bit of the time, wouldn't answer the ***phone***, and stayed by myself as much as I could.(p.324)
• I had read and heard a little about A.A. and so, groping for the ***phone*** book, I found the A.A. number and with hope in my heart eagerly telephoned.(p.363)
• I remember finding myself in the middle of the night in the doctors' parking lot at the hospital with one foot in the car and one foot on the ground, not knowing which was the lead foot; finding myself hanging up the telephone -- then realizing I had gotten out of bed, answered the ***phone***, turned on the light, and carried on a conversation with a patient.(p.441)
• Three weeks ago, my ***phone*** rang, and a voice I hadn't heard in over twenty-three years spoke.(p.462)
• Get sponsor and ***phone*** numbers.(p.477)
• One girl suggests that I ***phone*** her.(p.505)
• A man calls me on the ***phone***.(p.506)

phoned
• She was doing fine, she was up and around, and that day her husband ***phoned*** me and said, "Doctor, thanks very much for curing my wife," and I thanked him for his felicitations, and he hung up.(p.350)
• They ***phoned*** my husband that I was in jail and in such terrible shape that they didn't know what I would do to myself; and they realized that jail was no place for me, but that he was to wait a while before he got me, because at the time they called him to come over for me I was beating a tin cup against the wall.(p.390)
• However, I had ***phoned*** New York from the farm, appealing for help, and there in the station to meet us were two A.A.'s, John and Bud.(p.415)
• Once, I ***phoned*** my brother-in-law and told him I was going to take a handful of pills (in fact, I already had) and I would slash my wrists if he didn't come over to stop me.(p.479)

phony
• After such often-painful vigilance (and numerous ***phony*** stints of abstinence), retirement naturally created an impulse to live without restraints.(p.328)
• In the first year there were episodes such as kicking Priscilla in the shins, getting the lock changed on the desk in the A.A. Club, because I, as secretary, didn't want the Intergroup secretary "interfering," and taking an older woman member out to lunch for the express purpose of informing her that she was "a ***phony***."(p.416)
• It hinted to me that everything was ***phony***.(p.418)
• I am still arrogant, egocentric, self-righteous, with no humility, even ***phony*** at times, but I'm trying to be a better person and help my fellowman.(p.463)

photo
• I liked it and soon moved into the ***photo*** department which was what I wanted to do.(p.425)
• I applied for ***photo*** school at Pensacola Air Base and made it.(p.426)
• I talked the Old Man into letting me live in the ***photo*** lab instead of the barracks, and for eighteen months nothing interfered with my drinking.(p.426)

photographer
• "Ace crime ***photographer***," that's me.(p.425)

phrase
• I don't think the boys were completely convinced of my personality change, for they fought shy of including my story in the book, so my only contribution to their literary efforts was my firm conviction, being still a theological rebel, that the word God should be qualified with the ***phrase*** "as we understand him" -- for that was the only way I could accept spirituality.(p.248)
• No, it can best be explained in a little ***phrase*** I coined and sang to myself: "What happened to Bob?(p.532)
• And having sung that ***phrase***, I'd chuckle with amusement, turning into irony turning into self-contempt turning into self-pity, at the sad fate of Bob, that wonderful, poor little motherless boy who was so smart in school and who grew up to accept responsibility so early and so fast and who staggered under his burdens without a whimper until the time came when he thought he was too good for this world and so he ought to be out of it.(p.532)

phrases
• There are many short ***phrases*** and expressions in A.A. which make sound sense.(p.382)
• I used all those well-known ***phrases***.(p.408)

physical
• In our belief, any picture of the alcoholic which leaves out this ***physical*** factor is incomplete.(p.xxiv)
• Of course an alcoholic ought to be freed from his ***physical*** craving for liquor, and this often requires a definite hospital procedure, before psychological measures can be of maximum benefit.(p.xxv)
• Following his ***physical*** rehabilitation, he had a talk with me in which he frankly stated he thought the treatment a waste of effort, unless I could assure him, which no one ever had, that in the future he would have the "will power" to resist the impulse to drink.(p.xxix)
• Then came the night when the ***physical*** and mental torture was so hellish I feared I would burst through my window, sash and all.(p.6)
• My bother-in-law is a physician, and through his kindness and that of my mother I was placed in a nationally-known hospital for the mental and ***physical*** rehabilitation of alcoholics.(p.7)
• His ***physical*** and mental condition were unusually good.(p.26)
• Here are some of the methods we have tried: Drinking beer only, limiting the number of drinks, never drinking alone, never drinking in the morning, drinking only at home, never having it in the house, never drinking during business hours, drinking only at parties, switching from scotch to brandy, drinking only natural wines, agreeing to resign if ever drunk on the job, taking a trip, not taking a trip, swearing off forever (with and without a solemn oath), taking more ***physical*** exercise, reading inspirational books, going to health farms and sanitariums, accepting voluntary commitment to asylums -- we could increase the list ad infinitum.(p.31)
• Here was the threat of commitment, the loss of family and position, to say nothing of that intense mental and ***physical*** suffering which drinking always caused him.(p.36)
• Then came the hospital with unbearable mental and ***physical*** suffering.(p.41)
• Post-war disillusionment, ever more serious alcoholism, impending mental and ***physical*** collapse, brought him to the point of self-destruction.(p.56)
• The family may object to this, but unless he is in a dangerous ***physical*** condition, it is better to risk it.(p.90)
• The alarming ***physical*** and mental symptoms, the deepening pall of remorse, depression and inferiority that settled down on our loved ones -- these things terrified and distracted us.(p.106)
• For most alcoholics who are drinking, or who are just getting over a spree, a certain amount of ***physical*** treatment is desirable, even imperative.(p.142)
• The matter of ***physical*** treatment should, of course, be referred to your own doctor.(p.143)
• Your man will fare better if placed in such ***physical*** condition that he can think straight and no longer craves liquor.(p.143)
• If your man accepts your offer, it should be pointed

out that *physical* treatment is but a small part of the picture.(p.143)
• Being somewhat weakened, and faced with *physical* and mental readjustment to a life which knows no alcohol, he may overdo.(p.146)
• I did it more and more, and had lots of fun without much grief, either *physical* or financial.(p.172)
• He pointed out to me that probably it was more of a moral or spiritual illness than it was a *physical* one.(p.219)
• My *physical* health was badly shaken, but I began to pick up.(p.220)
• Formerly, in the acute mental and *physical* pain during the remorseful periods succeeding each drunk, I found my recollection of the misery I had gone through a bolsterer of resolution and afterward, perhaps, a deterrent for a time.(p.260)
• However, it finally caught up with me, and when it did, I was a mental, *physical,* and nervous wreck.(p.299)
• In all honesty though, I was skeptical, but I wanted so definitely to quit drinking that I would have welcomed any sort of *physical* torture or pain to accomplish the result.(p.302)
• It is impossible to put on paper all the benefits I have derived . . . *physical,* mental, domestic, spiritual, and monetary.(p.302)
• From a *physical* standpoint, I gained sixteen pounds in the first two months I was off liquor.(p.303)
• The *physical* skid row in any city is miserable.(p.345)
• I think I had the *physical* allergy right away.(p.402)
• He now said that we had a *physical* allergy combined with a mental obsession, and he explained this so that I saw for the first time how this could be.(p.413)
• With more *physical* courage than I had possessed, she had twice tried to take her life.(p.414)
• I had never had the *physical* courage to shake it out before.(p.415)
• Or, "My *physical* plant had got a little run down and the stuff rushed right to my head."(p.433)
• Loneliness, great *physical* and mental agony – these were the common lot.(p.455)
• I have come to believe that my illness is spiritual as well as *physical* and mental, and I know that for help in the spiritual sphere I have to turn to a Higher Power.(p.473)
• About this time an incident took place in grade school that I have never forgotten because it made me realize that I was actually a *physical* coward.(p.484)
• I am examined for the draft and pass the *physical* test.(p.499)
• There was the *physical* aspect; to be the youngest and the runt of the brood of children, to have to wear glasses very early and so to be teased, to be bookish and bored in school because the captain of the football team could not translate Virgil and yet was the school god while you, you, you little shrimp, were the school egghead, junior size and an early model.(p.533)
• This self-insurance has resulted in the restoration of *physical,* mental and spiritual health and self-respect to hundreds of men and women who would be hopelessly down and out without its unique but effective therapy."(p.574)

physically

• He may have the habit badly enough to gradually impair him *physically* and mentally.(p.20)
• *Physically,* I felt fine.(p.41)
• From it stem all forms of spiritual disease, for we have been not only mentally and *physically* ill, we have been spiritually sick.(p.64)
• When the spiritual malady is overcome, we straighten out mentally and *physically*.(p.64)
• It may be slowing him up mentally and *physically,* but he does not see it.(p.109)
• You can see that he is mentally and *physically* sick.(p.141)
• Still *physically* weak, and sober but a few months, he saw that his predicament was dangerous.(p.154)
• By this time I was beginning to pay very dearly *physically* and, in hope of relief, voluntarily incarcerated myself at least a dozen times in one of the local sanitariums.(p.174)
• Naturally, for quite a time, I wasn't too well *physically,* either.(p.190)
• It took me a year, or a year and a half to get to feeling *physically* well, and it was rather tough, but I soon found folks whose friendship I had once had, and I found, after I had been sober for quite some little time, that these people began to act like they had in previous years, before I had gotten so bad, so that I didn't pay too awful much attention to financial gains.(p.190)
• And we stood there for twenty minutes, telling each other how much better we were, how much better we looked, how much better off we were financially, mentally, *physically,* morally, and in every way, shape and manner.(p.201)
• When I look back on that last horrible year of constant drinking I wonder how I survived it either *physically* or mentally.(p.224)
• I myself could see deterioration in my work from being *physically* and mentally affected by liquor, although I had not yet reached the point where all I wanted was more to drink.(p.254)
• I felt better mentally and *physically*.(p.320)
• *Physically* I couldn't take it any more.(p.378)
• (I can't know how much others of our Fellowship have paid financially and, even more important, mentally and *physically*.)(p.396)
• I painfully awakened each time, mentally, *physically,* and spiritually sick.(p.457)
• No clothes, no money, no home, no real friends to speak of, mentally and *physically* pooped, but I was doing all right!(p.478)
• There was the sense of being "misunderstood," when as a matter of fact by my middle twenties I was quite popular, although I hadn't grown much bigger *physically*.(p.534)
• Apparently I'd grown *physically* at the customary rate of speed, and I had acquired an average amount of intellectual training in the intervening years, but there had been no emotional maturity at all.(p.547)

physician

• The spark that was to flare into the first A.A. group was struck at Akron, Ohio, in June 1935, during a talk between a New York stockbroker and an Akron *physician*.(p.xv)
• That alcoholic turned out to be the Akron *physician*.(p.xvi)
• This *physician* had repeatedly tried spiritual means to resolve his alcoholic dilemma but had failed.(p.xvi)
• But when the broker gave him Dr. Silkworth's description of alcoholism and its hopelessness, the *physician* began to pursue the spiritual remedy for his malady with a willingness he had never before been able to muster.(p.xvi)
• A well-known doctor, chief *physician* at a nationally prominent hospital specializing in alcoholic and drug addiction, gave Alcoholics Anonymous this letter:(p.xxiii)
• The *physician* who at our request, gave us this letter, has been kind enough to enlarge upon his views in another statement which follows.(p.xxiv)
• When I need a mental uplift, I often think of another case brought in by a *physician* prominent in New York.(p.xxix)
• My bother-in-law is a *physician,* and through his kindness and that of my mother I was placed in a nationally-known hospital for the mental and physical rehabilitation of alcoholics.(p.7)
• Then he had gone to Europe, placing himself in the care of a celebrated *physician* (the psychiatrist, Dr. Jung) who prescribed for him.(p.26)
• My early life was spent in Baltimore where my father was a *physician* and a grain merchant.(p.240)
• *PHYSICIAN,* HEAL THYSELF!(p.345)
• I am a *physician,* licensed to practice in a western state.(p.345)
• I couldn't practice medicine without the Great *Physician*.(p.351)
• The *physician* wasn't hooked, he thought – he just prescribed drugs medically indicated for his many ailments.(p.439)
• As a *physician* and pharmacist who had grown up in a drugstore-home, I had a pill for every ill, and I was sick a lot.(p.443)
• This *physician,* the originator of A.A.'s first black group, but badly caught in the toils, tells of his release and of how freedom came as he worked among his own people.(p.483)
• My father, a Negro, was a country *physician*.(p.483)

physician's

• That was a great *physician's* opinion.(p.26)

physicians

• Though the aggregate of recoveries resulting from psychiatric effort is considerable, we *physicians* must admit we have made little impression upon the problem as a whole.(p.xxvii)
• Much has been written pro and con, but among *physicians,* the general opinion seems to be that most chronic alcoholics are doomed.(p.xxviii)
• *Physicians* who are familiar with alcoholism agree there is no such thing as making a normal drinker out of an alcoholic.(p.31)
• Since Dr. Silkworth's first endorsement of Alcoholics Anonymous, medical societies and *physicians* throughout the world have set their approval upon us.(p.571)

piano

• I remember being dragged, drink in hand, from beneath the grand *piano,* where I had hidden, to be locked in my room in disgrace.(p.557)

pianos

• They struck the children, kicked out door panels, smashed treasured crockery, and ripped the keys out of *pianos*.(p.106)

pick

• When, therefore, we were approached by those in whom the problem had been solved, there was nothing left for us but to *pick* up the simple kit of spiritual tools laid at our feet.(p.25)
• Like a gaunt prospector, belt drawn in over the last ounce of food, our *pick* struck gold.(p.128)
• I came to Cleveland with the deeds to these lots and to *pick* up my money.(p.196)
• I would have to return to New York and *pick* up my bills and bags.(p.213)
• My physical health was badly shaken, but I began to *pick* up.(p.220)
• That same year, my wife became fed up with my drinking around the house and called my dad in Akron to come and *pick* me up.(p.288)
• Several months later dad was back in Chicago to *pick* me up again, but this time my attitude was entirely different.(p.289)
• I *pick* up a book and try to read, but I cannot concentrate.(p.503)

picked

• And besides, there were scattered alcoholics who had *picked* up the basic ideas in Akron or New York and were trying to form A.A. groups in other cities.(p.xvii)
• He knew all the answers, and certainly not because he had *picked* them up in his reading.(p.180)
• I was *picked* up at two-thirty that morning with my car smashed up by a street-car because I had run into a big concrete safety zone, and the street-car had run into me, and they took me out through the roof -- there's where I lost the suit.(p.202)
• In fact, on one occasion, I was *picked* up by the police and brought home.(p.211)
• By the time I had completed law school I had *picked* up some experience in patent law, for I remained with the patent law firm and worked too in Washington where they found that I was a capable infringement investigator.(p.213)
• I had repaired to one of these one morning with my jug and when I left late in the afternoon, I *picked* up a newspaper on the way home.(p.244)
• As soon as I could get up and walk I started to drink again and kept it up until my friend of the hospital, who, in his first try at the new way of life had stubbed his toe in Chicago but had come back to the town to take counsel and make a new start, *picked* me up and got me into a hospital.(p.258)
• I know that one of the outfits I had was a skirt and a very funny looking blouse that my mother had *picked* up at a rummage sale.(p.261)
• One Sunday afternoon, the only time I ever got *picked* up for drunken driving, I got *picked* up in Bellaire.(p.264)
• I wasn't nearly in the condition I had been in many times to be *picked* up.(p.264)
• After a particularly bad Christmas and New Year's holiday, dad *picked* me up again early in January, 1937, to go through the usual sobering up routine.(p.289)
• I halfway washed them, and he told me to do them again, and I did, and he yelled at me to do them again, and I *picked* up one of the cans and threw it at him and told him to do them himself.(p.317)
• Next, I was sent to Arizona, where my drinking *picked* up some more, and I started having blackouts, and I was thrown in jail for speeding and drunken driving.(p.318)
• While I was in Florida trying to convince my wife with all the A.A. literature that she should come back to me, she went over to her desk and *picked* up a clipping she had taken from the St. Petersburg Times about A.A.(p.366)
• After his death, my mother soon *picked* up drinking where Dad left off, and in a very short time she died of cirrhosis of the liver.(p.370)
• Then there was wartime service to interrupt my plans, and an education to be *picked* up after the war.(p.373)
• When he *picked* me up, I must have gotten sassy and told him that he couldn't do that, so he took my dog home and took me to jail!(p.390)
• The cops had *picked* her up, and she told them she had bought it from me.(p.528)

• But not for long; now, for five Friday nights in a row, I went to jail, ***picked*** up sodden with beer (which I always disliked, but which was the only drink available); in jail five consecutive Friday nights in the town where I had grown up, where I had been an honor student in high school, where a kindly uncle, bailing me out, said, "Bob, our family just doesn't do this sort of thing."(p.539)

picking

• For some reason, we alcoholics seem to have the gift of ***picking*** out the world's finest women.(p.178)

• Sergeants, doctors, girl friends -- everybody seemed to be ***picking*** on him.(p.317)

• They were all ***picking*** on me.(p.319)

picnics

• We had big ***picnics*** out at the house with A.A.(p.270)

picture

• Then Jack Alexander wrote a feature article in the Saturday Evening Post and placed such a compelling ***picture*** of A.A. before the general public that alcoholics in need of help really deluged us.(p.xviii)

• In our belief, any ***picture*** of the alcoholic which leaves out this physical factor is incomplete.(p.xxiv)

• This is by no means a comprehensive ***picture*** of the true alcoholic, as our behavior patterns vary.(p.22)

• This ***picture*** may not be as dark as it looks.(p.110)

• We women carry with us a ***picture*** of the ideal man, the sort of chap we would like our husbands to be.(p.118)

• If your man accepts your offer, it should be pointed out that physical treatment is but a small part of the ***picture***.(p.143)

• After your man has gone along without drinking for a few months, you may be able to make use of his services with other employees who are giving you the alcoholic run-around — provided, of course, they are willing to have a third party in the ***picture***.(p.146)

• He cannot ***picture*** life without alcohol.(p.152)

• I do not recollect the specific conversation that went on but I believe I did challenge Bill to tell me something about A.A. and I do recall one other thing: I wanted to know what this was that worked so many wonders, and hanging over the mantel was a ***picture*** of Gethsemane and Bill pointed to it and said, "There it is," which didn't make much sense to me.(p.216)

• As the treatment progressed I began to get a ***picture*** of myself, of the temperament that had caused me so much trouble.(p.226)

• After six months of sobriety I saw the ***picture*** in a different light: Detroit was the place I had to return to, not only because I must face the mess I had made there, but because it was there that I could be of the most service to A.A.(p.281)

• This ***picture*** is still vivid.(p.292)

• Now the ***picture*** has changed completely.(p.325)

• And unless I had some rosy ***picture*** of what was going to happen that day, I wouldn't even feel like getting up in the morning at all.(p.325)

• I'd been on the board of governors of the Academy of Motion ***Picture*** Arts and Sciences for six years.(p.328)

• Can you ***picture*** two girls hitchhiking their way to Las Vegas from Washington State?(p.354)

• My sponsor used to say to me, "If I could only paint you a ***picture*** of how beautiful life can be without booze . . ."(p.355)

• I wanted so badly to see the ***picture*** as it was in her mind.(p.355)

• You didn't carry a little orchid up the aisle in those days; you carried a great big bouquet, like a funeral spray, and you didn't have your ***picture*** taken until just before you went to the church.(p.385)

• I took two or three drinks so my eyes could focus, and I could see that horrible ***picture*** of the awful drunk on the first page; he couldn't get the drink to his mouth, he had a towel around his hand and he needed a shave.(p.391)

• You may wonder why, since I was having all this trouble, and was having to seek the assistance of others, A.A. hadn't come into the ***picture***.(p.469)

• On the other hand, I got quite a different ***picture*** farther south.(p.486)

pictured

• I headed home for the most wonderful experience of all time — meeting my "new" parents — mom and dad looked different than I had ***pictured*** them.(p.428)

pictures

• People have said we must not go where liquor is served; we must not have it in our homes; we must shun friends who drink; we must avoid moving ***pictures*** which show drinking scenes; we must not go into bars; our friends must hide their bottles if we go to their houses; we mustn't think or be reminded about alcohol at all.(p.100)

• As self-conscious as I was, I had to pose for those ***pictures***, holding this huge bouquet.(p.385)

• I don't know why I didn't fall out of the open cockpit of some of those planes I flew in while taking aerial ***pictures***.(p.426)

• My opinions were quoted in Time and Newsweek with ***pictures***, and I addressed the public by radio and television.(p.435)

• Our names and ***pictures*** as A.A. members ought not be broadcast, filmed, or publicly printed.(p.567)

piddling

• I worked when I could — ***piddling*** jobs I thought them.(p.540)

piece

• In the fall of 1939, Fulton Oursler, then editor of Liberty, printed a ***piece*** in his magazine, called "Alcoholics and God."(p.xviii)

• I had bought a ***piece*** of ground in Cuyahoga Falls and cut it into lots and had a profit of approximately $40,000 and that was a lot of money in those days.(p.194)

• I optioned a ***piece*** of land just off East Market Street to put up a three-hundred suite apartment.(p.198)

• One evening, the book, after checking up, was very definitely in the red for plenty through a ***piece*** of studied carelessness on my part, and my boss, very shrewd and able, fired me with a parting statement to the effect that once was enough.(p.251)

• Russ read a ***piece*** in the paper, and he kind of snickered, and said, "See here, where John D. has found something to keep him from drinking!"(p.265)

• So he got me a cup of coffee, and a ***piece*** of cake, and sat me down and said, "Why, there's nothing wrong with you.(p.348)

piecemakers

• Making my way to Pittsburgh, I met other former friends and got a job in a large factory where ***piecemakers*** were making good money.(p.252)

pieces

• Though a robust man at retirement, he went to ***pieces*** quickly and was dead within four years.(p.33)

• For a while they would be their old sweet selves, only to dash the new structure of affection to ***pieces*** once more.(p.107)

• Without you he would have gone to ***pieces*** long ago.(p.119)

• What an opportunity I shot to ***pieces*** there!(p.242)

• Somehow, I managed to read ***pieces*** on alcoholism.(p.332)

• I do recall lying on a cold cement floor and shredding into little bits several ***pieces*** of stolen identification cards, and washing my face in the toilet bowl trying to sober up, and screaming hysterically while clinging to bars too high to see out of, and cursing everyone that came near me.(p.354)

pier

• Coming out of a pub near the Cunard ***pier*** I saw the Lusitania standing out in the middle of the Mersey.(p.252)

pig

• I put on thirty pounds of weight in about two months, looked like a ***pig***, and was uncomfortable from shortness of breath.(p.177)

pile

• These allergic types can never safely use alcohol in any form at all; and once having formed the habit and found they cannot break it, once having lost their self-confidence, their reliance upon things human, their problems ***pile*** up on them and become astonishingly difficult to solve.(p.xxvi)

• I would put off doing anything that I could until the next day and, consequently, everything would ***pile*** up and then there would be the blackout.(p.197)

• Slowly a ***pile*** of pineapples started to build up on the table.(p.427)

• I crawl under a ***pile*** of blankets and blow out the candle.(p.497)

• I come to on a ***pile*** of hay in a barn.(p.502)

piled

• They ***piled*** on me heaps of evidence to the effect that an alcoholic mentality, such as I had exhibited in Washington, was a hopeless condition.(p.42)

• "The nervous tension had ***piled*** up and just had to spill over."(p.433)

pill

• I never in my life took a tranquilizer, sedative, or pep ***pill*** because I was a pillhead.(p.443)

• I always took it because I had the symptom that only that ***pill*** would relieve.(p.443)

• Therefore, every ***pill*** was medically indicated at the time it was taken.(p.443)

• For me, pills don't produce the desire to swallow a ***pill***; they produce the symptoms that require that the ***pill*** be taken for relief.(p.443)

• As a physician and pharmacist who had grown up in a drugstore-home, I had a ***pill*** for every ill, and I was sick a lot.(p.443)

• I can't say, "Thy will be done," and take a ***pill***.(p.443)

• Max accepted responsibility for me after I had promised never to drink again, never to take another ***pill***, never to swear again, and never to talk to girls again.(p.444)

• But for some time, it was difficult to keep from taking a ***pill*** when I had an appropriate symptom, such as a cough, pain, anxiety, insomnia, a muscle spasm, or an upset stomach.(p.448)

• Aside from being a common drunk, I had a very serious ***pill*** affliction and all the garbage that goes with it -- lying, stealing, cheating anybody and everybody, conning the people I could, and staying clear of the ones I couldn't.(p.478)

pilled-up

• Any time I tried to kill myself, I was either drunk or ***pilled-up*** or both — usually the last.(p.479)

pillhead

• I never in my life took a tranquilizer, sedative, or pep pill because I was a ***pillhead***.(p.443)

pills

• We did, and spent a month boozing it up, popping ***pills***, and smoking marijuana; taking shelter where we could, which included a veterinary hospital one night; accepting meals from anyone; actually begging; stealing anything we were in need of, which was about everything.(p.354)

• Defeated by alcohol and ***pills***, he found the way to a new life.(p.418)

• My life there was a nightmare of periodic binges on alcohol and ***pills***, adultery, unhappy hours at the dental office, seeing my wife give birth to our second child and have several miscarriages, living in a turbulent household, and making continual attempts to be the respectable dentist, husband, father, and community leader.(p.419)

• So I immediately started taking and shooting pep ***pills***.(p.442)

• The pep ***pills*** affected my hearing at times: I couldn't listen fast enough to hear what I was saying.(p.442)

• In the garage, I would put the needle in my vein and then try to figure out exactly how much medication to inject to overcome the pep ***pills*** while adding to the sleeping ***pills*** while ignoring the tranquilizers, in order to get just enough to be able to pull out the needle, jerk the tourniquet, throw it in the car, slam the car door shut, run down the hall, and fall in bed before I fell asleep.(p.442)

• In the end, I had to do the same with alcohol and all ***pills***.(p.443)

• If they were around, I always found a need for them -- especially the ***pills***.(p.443)

• For me, ***pills*** don't produce the desire to swallow a pill; they produce the symptoms that require that the pill be taken for relief.(p.443)

• Today, I find I can't work my A.A. program while taking ***pills***, nor may I even have them around for dire emergencies only.(p.443)

• I can't say, "God could restore me to sanity, but until He does, I'll control myself -- with ***pills***."(p.443)

• I had already given up all the narcotics, most of the ***pills***, and some of the alcohol when I first came to A.A.(p.448)

• By early July, I had tapered off alcohol completely, and I got off all ***pills*** in the ensuing few months.(p.448)

• After I had been around A.A. for seven months, tapering off alcohol and ***pills***, not finding the program working very well, I was finally able to say, "Okay, God.(p.448)

• The doctor, apparently realizing that one thing that I certainly needed was sleep, left a bottle of sleeping ***pills*** there and in my drunken state I took them all, instead of the one or two he had prescribed.(p.465)

• Once, I phoned my brother-in-law and told him I was going to take a handful of ***pills*** (in fact, I already had) and I would slash my wrists if he didn't come over to stop me.(p.479)

• When I got out of there, I lasted about fifteen minutes at home, before I headed for the drugstore and more ***pills***, and then the bar.(p.479)

• A couple of years later, we lost our elder brother in a house fire, because of ***pills*** and booze.(p.480)

pilot

• I was club-man, athlete, artist, musician, author, editor, aircraft ***pilot*** and world traveller.(p.432)

pin

• I realized that I was trying to ***pin*** everything on an individual – not the book or the group or the Higher Power, or anything else.(p.472)

pinch

• He wasn't a drinking man, he didn't know what it was to need a drink, nor what a drink could do for one in a ***pinch***.(p.227)

pine

• To go north into the empty ***pine*** country and shoot myself, or to go south in the faint hope that a bunch of strangers might help me with my drinking problem.(p.278)

pineapple

• I swung, I swore, I started throwing beer cans at the advancing hordes of ***pineapple*** faces.(p.427)

pineapples

• Slowly a pile of ***pineapples*** started to build up on the table.(p.427)

• I was knocked to the floor, swinging madly at the faces on those ***pineapples***.(p.427)

• Again I went into a mild form of D.T.'s, but with no ***pineapples*** this time.(p.429)

pink

• And the first thing you know I was lifted right out of the A.A. group, and I floated higher, and higher, and even higher, until I was way up on a ***pink*** cloud which is known as ***Pink*** Seven, and I felt miserable again.(p.348)

pint

• No beer or liquor was sold in the neighborhood, except at the State liquor agency where perhaps one might procure a ***pint*** if he could convince the agent that he really needed it.(p.171)

• I would reach over and get this and take a shot and in a few moments get up and take another, shave and eat my breakfast, slip a half ***pint*** of liquor in my hip pocket, and go on to school.(p.183)

• So Paul was dispatched and brought back a ***pint***.(p.206)

• I got two drinks, each of them a quarter of that ***pint***, in me, and was talking along with these people, but I felt that sooner or later they were going to have me cornered because they were smarter than I was and the drink was beginning to take effect; but as I reached for the third drink Bob said, "Listen, Buster, you promised to take some medicine if we got you a drink.(p.206)

• I said, "In that case, there's no use of wasting this," and I got the last of that ***pint***.(p.207)

• In fact, the last three years of my drinking was a routine of barbiturates in the morning, so that I could stop shaking enough to shave, and then alcohol beginning about four-thirty or five o'clock, with a struggle not to take a drink at noon or during the day, because I had the idea that if I took one drink, I would smell as though I had had a ***pint***.(p.217)

• I landed him and shipped him by train to Akron, with a ***pint*** of whiskey in his pocket to keep him from wanting to get off the train in Toledo!(p.282)

• So I went down to him quite a few times a month and had him shoot me full of the stuff; and then I went across the street to a little drug store to take a glass of beer or two beers, and then stopped at the liquor store to get myself a ***pint*** and go home.(p.389)

• Monday morning I was feeling just like a million dollars – all I needed was half a ***pint***!(p.393)

• So I got a half ***pint*** and at midnight that night, I called the number I had been given, but the man who had started the group was in the hospital so I didn't know what to do.(p.393)

• I displayed alcoholic tendencies actually from the age of fourteen, when I started to steal wine from the family jug, siphoning it off one drink at a time so it wouldn't be missed, not drinking it immediately, but saving it until about a ***pint*** was accumulated, so that I could get drunk.(p.397)

• Evening cocktails were as standard as morning coffee, and I suppose my average daily consumption ran a little more or less than a ***pint***.(p.433)

pints

• With a great deal of determination, I would throw out full ***pints*** -- pour them out and smash the bottles -- firmly resolved never to take another drink of the stuff.(p.234)

• He and mom smuggled in a couple of ***pints*** to me.(p.425)

pioneer

• ***Pioneer*** member of Akron's Group No. 1, the first A.A. group in the world.(p.182)

• A ***pioneer*** woman member of A.A.'s first Group.(p.261)

• ***Pioneer*** A.A., minister's son, and southern farmer, he asked, "Who am I to say there is no God?"(p.497)

pioneering

• The flying-blind period ended and A.A. entered a new phase of its ***pioneering*** time.(p.xvii)

• Early member, she spread the word among women in our ***pioneering*** period.(p.222)

• Historians may one day recognize Alcoholics Anonymous to have been a great venture in social ***pioneering*** which forged a new instrument for social action; a new therapy based on the kinship of common suffering; one having a vast potential for the myriad other ills of mankind."(p.573)

pioneers

• In this third edition, Part I ("***Pioneers*** of A.A.") stands unchanged.(p.xii)

• ***PIONEERS*** OF A.A.(p.167)

• ***PIONEERS*** OF A.A.(p.169)

• All of these, then, are the ***pioneers*** of A.A.(p.169)

pious

• I could just hear their sweet, ***pious*** talk.(p.412)

pit

• Therefore, we are not to be the hasty and foolish martyr who would needlessly sacrifice others to save himself from the alcoholic ***pit***.(p.79)

• Down in the ***pit*** of his depression, new hope had somehow been born.(p.189)

• The only thing that bothered me was a queasy feeling I had in the ***pit*** of my stomach.(p.418)

pitcher

• And I said, "Well, they brought a ***pitcher*** of coffee, and a sandwich wrapped up for me."(p.264)

pitiful

• All of us felt at times that we were regaining control, but such intervals – usually brief – were inevitably followed by still less control, which led in time to ***pitiful*** and incomprehensible demoralization.(p.30)

pitiless

• This was the only time in my life that I'd ever known my mother to be almost ***pitiless***, but she couldn't be blamed for that.(p.523)

Pittsburgh

• Making my way to ***Pittsburgh***, I met other former friends and got a job in a large factory where piecemakers were making good money.(p.252)

• I quit the factory and got a job on a small newspaper, going from that to a ***Pittsburgh*** daily, long ago defunct.(p.252)

• Quebec, Toronto, Buffalo, and finally ***Pittsburgh***, were the scenes of man-sized drunks until I had gone through my readjusted discharge pay, a fair sum.(p.253)

• I again became a reporter on a ***Pittsburgh*** daily.(p.254)

• In 1940 another good opportunity came up and we moved to ***Pittsburgh*** where I was to manage two radio stations under the same ownership.(p.361)

• We came back to ***Pittsburgh*** as happy as a bride and groom.(p.364)

• It was the first she had heard or read about it and she said she had considered sending it to me or trying to have someone in ***Pittsburgh*** send it to me so I wouldn't know where it came from.(p.366)

• She said she cut this clipping from the paper at about ten on the same night, and at the same time as I called A.A. in ***Pittsburgh*** -- some 1300 miles away.(p.367)

pity

• We asked God to help us show them the same tolerance, ***pity***, and patience that we would cheerfully grant a sick friend.(p.67)

• Somebody must have taken ***pity*** on you and gone out and got it for you."(p.264)

• Where derision, contempt and ***pity*** were once shown me, I now enjoy the respect of many people.(p.296)

• Resenting anyone and everyone who might interfere with my personal plans and ways of doing things, I was full of self ***pity***, especially for any interference with my drinking.(p.376)

• Over a period of time he has built up self ***pity***, resentments toward anyone or anything that interferes with his drinking.(p.380)

• It has shown me, through the tragic stories of so many other alcoholics, the utter futility of self ***pity***.(p.525)

• "***Pity*** me the heart that is slow to learn What the quick mind sees at every turn."(p.534)

pityingly

• But I can remember, in my teens, that there were a few characters who caused the village heads to nod ***pityingly*** and sometimes in anger as they paused to say, "That sot, Henri" and "Ce pauvre Jules," who drank too much.(p.230)

pizza

• The other kids would light out for the hamburger huts or ice cream parlors, the ***pizza*** joints or bowling alleys, after football games and dances.(p.423)

placard

• I checked into my hotel room and then noticed a ***placard*** tucked under the glass on the bureau stating "There will be positively NO drinking at this convention" signed by the president of the company.(p.243)

placate

• I went on the wagon more to ***placate*** my wife than anything else.(p.344)

place

• Since the original Foreword to this book was written in 1939, a wholesale miracle has taken ***place***.(p.xv)

• It was now time, the struggling groups thought, to ***place*** their message and unique experience before the world.(p.xvii)

• My talent for leadership, I imagined, would ***place*** me at the head of vast enterprises which I would manage with the utmost assurance.(p.1)

• An all night ***place*** supplied me with a dozen glasses of ale.(p.6)

• I have seen men come out of asylums and resume a vital ***place*** in the lives of their families and communities.(p.15)

• In the doctor's judgment he was utterly hopeless; he could never regain his position in society and he would have to ***place*** himself under lock and key or hire a bodyguard if he expected to live long.(p.26)

• On the way I felt hungry so I stopped at a roadside ***place*** where they have a bar.(p.36)

• I also had the notion that I might find a customer for a car at this ***place***, which was familiar for I had been going to it for years.(p.36)

• I now remembered what my alcoholic friends had told me, how they prophesied that if I had an alcoholic mind, the time and ***place*** would come – I would drink again.(p.41)

• Thus was our friend's cornerstone fixed in ***place***.(p.56)

• Returning home we find a ***place*** where we can be quiet for an hour carefully reviewing what we have done.(p.75)

• Are the stones properly in ***place***?(p.75)

• He saw that he had to ***place*** the outcome in God's hands or he would soon start drinking again, and all would be lost anyhow.(p.80)

• You need this information to put yourself in his ***place***, to see how you would like him to approach you if the tables were turned.(p.90)

• You might ***place*** this book where he can see it in the interval.(p.90)

• Suggest how important it is that he ***place*** the welfare of other people ahead of his own.(p.94)

• Some of us have taken very hard knocks to learn this truth: Job or no job – wife or no wife -- we simply do not stop drinking so long as we ***place*** dependence upon other people ahead of dependence on God.(p.98)

• His only chance for sobriety would be some ***place*** like the Greenland Ice Cap, and even there an Eskimo might turn up with a bottle of scotch and ruin everything!(p.101)

• So our rule is not to avoid a ***place*** where there is drinking, if we have a legitimate reason for being there.(p.101)

• Therefore, ask yourself on each occasion, "Have I any good social, business, or personal reason for going to this ***place***?(p.101)

• At proper time and ***place*** explain to all your friends why alcohol disagrees with you.(p.102)

• Your job now is to be at the ***place*** where you may be of maximum helpfulness to others, so never hesitate to go anywhere if you can be helpful.(p.102)

• Attempt instead, to put yourself in his ***place***.(p.111)

• If a repetition is to be prevented, ***place*** the problem, along with everything else, in God's hands.(p.120)

• Although financial recovery is on the way for many of us, we found we could not ***place*** money first.(p.127)

• When we see a man sinking into the mire that is alcoholism, we give him first aid and ***place*** what we have at his disposal.(p.132)

• We all had to ***place*** recovery above everything, for without recovery we would have lost both home and business.(p.143)

• He will be at the jumping-off ***place***.(p.152)

• If you live in a large ***place***, there are hundreds.(p.152)

• Bitterly discouraged, he found himself in a strange ***place***, discredited and almost broke.(p.154)

• They were willing, by day or night, to ***place*** a new

man in the hospital and visit him afterward.(p.159)
• Aside from fellowship and sociability, the prime object was to provide a time and *place* where new people might bring their problems.(p.160)
• The expression on the faces of the women, that indefinable something in the eyes of the men, the stimulating and electric atmosphere of the *place*, conspired to let him know that here was haven at last.(p.160)
• Being a large *place*, we think that some day its Fellowship will number many hundreds.(p.161)
• Under only slightly different conditions, the same thing is taking *place* in many eastern cities.(p.161)
• He had lived there but a few weeks when he found that the *place* probably contained more alcoholics per square mile than any city in the country.(p.163)
• I have already done it, and I am willing to do it again here in the presence of you or I am willing to say it any *place*, anywhere in the world from now on and not be ashamed of it."(p.190)
• We went into a bootleg joint and I don't remember leaving that *place*.(p.202)
• Yet I wound up at this *place*.(p.202)
• I realized that there wasn't anything I could say to *place* myself in a more favorable light with my children, that it was going to be a matter of time; for I also understood the intolerance of young people towards deficiencies in their elders.(p.220)
• I moved from group to group -- then from *place* to *place* -- and went on drinking.(p.226)
• I believe that my once over-weening self-will has finally found its proper *place*, for I can say many times daily, "Thy will be done, not mine" . . . and mean it.(p.229)
• In four or five days I would be hunting all over the *place*, at home and in my workshop, for the bottles I had destroyed, cursing myself for being a fool.(p.234)
• So I began to pray; to *place* my problems in God's hands.(p.237)
• January 8, 1938 -- that was my D-Day; the *place*, Washington, D.C.(p.238)
• (Jack was the owner of the *place*.(p.266)
• We had meetings at each other's homes and, of course, that was a grand *place* for people to get together out there; they seemed to think so too.(p.270)
• After six months of sobriety I saw the picture in a different light: Detroit was the *place* I had to return to, not only because I must face the mess I had made there, but because it was there that I could be of the most service to A.A.(p.281)
• There was a glass of sherry at my *place*.(p.285)
• One of them was that I would try to get a group started in Chicago; the second was that I would have to return to Akron to attend meetings at least every two months until I did get a group started in Chicago; third, I decided I must *place* this program above everything else, even my family, because if I did not maintain my sobriety I would lose my family anyway.(p.292)
• However, as there happened to be several saloons within that distance, I didn't find it necessary to patronize the same *place* each evening.(p.298)
• It doesn't pay to be seen in the same *place* at the same hour every day.(p.299)
• The general procedure was to take four or five shots in the first *place* I stopped at.(p.299)
• I studied art; I desperately endeavored to create an interest in many things, in a new *place* among new people.(p.305)
• Alone in the relative safety of my home because I knew I dare not risk the danger of blacking out in some public *place* or at the wheel of a car.(p.306)
• A complete change takes *place* in our approach to life.(p.311)
• That was on a hot summer evening, down in the Greenwich Village Group, and there was a little porch out there in the old meeting *place* on Sullivan Street, and after the meeting I went out on the steps for some air.(p.321)
• My home at that time was a *place* to mill around in.(p.337)
• To me, taking a bath was just being in a *place* with a bottle where I could drink in privacy.(p.337)
• The *place* is Naini Tal, in the foothills of the mighty Himalaya Mountains, and it has some very significant memories for me.(p.342)
• My sister-in-law took me to a *place* she had heard about that helps women like me.(p.371)
• Rehearsals then became a part of the pattern, stopping at bars on the way to or from the *place* where drinks were to be served.(p.375)
• We had always encouraged our children to bring their friends home at any time, but after a few experiences with a drunken father they eliminated home as a *place* to entertain friends.(p.376)
• Scared that my dress wasn't going to fit right, that the church wasn't going to be filled, that I'd fall flat on my face walking up the aisle; in fact, I was afraid I wasn't going to be a prima donna in the *place* where I should be.(p.385)
• I knew this, and right away I got furious and would not even talk to the doctor in the *place*.(p.387)
• A duplex apartment isn't any *place* to raise a dog.(p.388)
• Then he said I couldn't possibly move on the first of February because I couldn't stay in that *place* by myself.(p.388)
• They phoned my husband that I was in jail and in such terrible shape that they didn't know what I would do to myself; and they realized that jail was no *place* for me, but that he was to wait a while before he got me, because at the time they called him to come over for me I was beating a tin cup against the wall.(p.390)
• So when he came for me, as he walked down the stairs, I could see him through the bars, and he was signing for me; I looked at him and said, "Don't you sign anything in this *place*!"(p.391)
• A house in Virginia, during the fox hunting season; a little chalet in Switzerland during the summer or a *place* on Long Island -- each house complete with cooks, butlers and maids.(p.403)
• In a sick people's *place*, myself among the sickest.(p.410)
• The *place* -- Hawaii.(p.422)
• Or maybe I'd come home wild drunk, singing and raving about what a fine *place* home was and what grand parents I had since they joined A.A.(p.428)
• My drinking took *place* after work hours.(p.441)
• The Mayo Clinic seemed like a good *place* to have my diagnosis confirmed.(p.444)
• I never could quite get the knack of it and kept asking myself, "What's a nice guy like me doing in a *place* like this?"(p.445)
• When I am disturbed, it is because I find some person, *place*, thing, or situation -- some fact of my life -- unacceptable to me, and I can find no serenity until I accept that person, *place*, thing, or situation as being exactly the way it is supposed to be at this moment.(p.449)
• On the contrary, the hardest *place* to work this program has been in my own home, with my own children and, finally, with Max.(p.451)
• And when I *place* more value on my serenity and sobriety than on anything else, I can maintain them at a higher level -- at least for the time being.(p.452)
• It was in Washington, D.C. that this transition took *place*, and that the really bad part of alcoholism began happening.(p.465)
• After the first two or three days you were allowed the run of the *place* and it was a lot of fun.(p.468)
• On one occasion when I was serving time in my favorite drying-out *place* while I was having a session with the psychiatrist, she left my case history on her desk when she was called away from the room.(p.470)
• At every *place*, I find A.A. group first.(p.476)
• About this time an incident took *place* in grade school that I have never forgotten because it made me realize that I was actually a physical coward.(p.484)
• In the first *place*, she had been married before; I was her second husband.(p.485)
• About that time I had lost practically all my property except the *place* we were living in.(p.487)
• At that time the repeal whiskies were back, and I'd go to the store and buy my whiskey and take it to my office and put it under the desk, first in one *place* and then in another, and there soon was an accumulation of empty bottles.(p.488)
• I got to the *place* where I'd look forward to the week-end's drinking and pacify myself by saying that the week-ends were mine, that it didn't interfere with my family or with my business if I drank on the week-ends.(p.488)
• Then Charlie or someone in the group suggested that we try to get a *place* in a church or hall to hold meetings.(p.495)
• I want to sell the *place* and move away.(p.506)
• I remained there for about ten months, and then I was sent to a *place* called Wallkill, a so-called rehabilitation center.(p.509)
• Each one has its own *place*.(p.516)
• When I came back, I told the priest, the Chaplain of the *place*, exactly what I thought of him and he didn't like it.(p.517)
• When the war was over, we had about a year in Germany, occupying the *place*.(p.518)
• Then a change in management took *place* in the regiment and the new O.C. didn't like me very much and I didn't like him, and he started to lie in wait for me.(p.519)
• Then it got to the *place* I couldn't drink without getting in jail.(p.526)
• I hated that judge for sending me to a *place* with all those drunks.(p.527)
• After a while, I found that the psycho ward was a good *place* to hide when I had taken something stolen to the pawnshop.(p.528)
• Now I had gotten to the *place* where I would wake up with black eyes and not know where I got them, or wake up with a lot of money and not know where I got it.(p.528)
• I don't know if it's force of habit or something else that keeps them in one *place*, but I do know that in A.A. there is much work to do, and none of us can do it standing still.(p.529)
• This question so insulted the emotions that clearly there was only one thing to do, go and get drunk again, and put that enquiring mind in its proper *place*, which was oblivion.(p.537)
• Still another friend and temporary host received me at four in the morning from the charge of a policeman who had found me "going to bed" in a garage far from the last *place* I could remember having been, a fashionable bar and restaurant in the theatrical district of New York, to which I had repaired after my date for that evening, a charming lady of the theatre who had refused my company for obvious reasons.(p.538)
• I had nothing to put in the *place* of alcohol, of the forgetfulness, of the oblivion, which alcohol provides.(p.539)
• The only importance in all of this lies in the fact that at twenty-three I was just as sick as I was at thirty three, when I came into A.A., but at that time I apparently had no *place* to go because I had no drinking problem.(p.546)
• So I had no *place* to go.(p.546)
• To do that, I had come to A.A. to learn how to handle sobriety -- which is what I could not handle in the first *place*.(p.554)
• In each new *place*, I was the new kid -- a skinny, shy kid -- to be tested and beaten up.(p.555)
• Twelve -- Anonymity is the spiritual foundation of all our Traditions, ever reminding us to *place* principles before personalities.(p.564)
• It reminds us that we are to *place* principles before personalities; that we are actually to practice a genuine humility.(p.568)
• What often takes *place* in a few months could seldom have been accomplished by years of self discipline.(p.569)

placed

• Then Jack Alexander wrote a feature article in the Saturday Evening Post and *placed* such a compelling picture of A.A. before the general public that alcoholics in need of help really deluged us.(p.xviii)
• My bother-in-law is a physician, and through his kindness and that of my mother I was *placed* in a nationally-known hospital for the mental and physical rehabilitation of alcoholics.(p.7)
• I *placed* myself unreservedly under His care and direction.(p.13)
• When this sort of thinking is fully established in an individual with alcoholic tendencies, he has probably *placed* himself beyond human aid, and unless locked up, may die or go permanently insane.(p.24)
• Sometimes they hurt us, seemingly without provocation, but we invariably find that at some time in the past we have made decisions based on self which later *placed* us in a position to be hurt.(p.62)
• We *placed* them before us in black and white.(p.67)
• We feel as though we had been *placed* in a position of neutrality -- safe and protected.(p.85)
• Our thought-life will be *placed* on a much higher plane when our thinking is cleared of wrong motives.(p.86)
• He has been *placed* in one institution after another.(p.110)
• Perhaps they created the impression that he is to be wrapped in cotton wool and *placed* on a pedestal.(p.122)
• Dad may feel that for years his drinking has *placed* him on the wrong side of every argument, but now he has become a superior person with God on his side.(p.129)
• Even when he wanted to assert himself he could not, for his drinking *placed* him constantly in the wrong.(p.130)
• After two weeks of drinking, he had *placed* his toe on the trigger of a loaded shotgun -- the barrel in his mouth.(p.137)
• Your man will fare better if *placed* in such physical condition that he can think straight and no longer craves liquor.(p.143)
• One man and his wife *placed* their large home at the disposal of this strangely assorted crowd.(p.160)

• When I had served only eighteen months of my sentence, this ex-incorrigible was ***placed*** in honor grade.(p.461)

places

• There was loud talk in the jazz ***places*** uptown.(p.3)
• I became an unwelcome hanger-on at brokerage ***places***.(p.5)
• Ask any woman who has sent her husband to distant ***places*** on the theory he would escape the alcohol problem.(p.101)
• Or am I expecting to steal a little vicarious pleasure from the atmosphere of such ***places***?"(p.101)
• Why sit with a long face in ***places*** where there is drinking, sighing about the good old days.(p.102)
• Ask him what you should do if he ***places*** you in such a position again.(p.116)
• We think each family which has been relieved owes something to those who have not, and when the occasion requires, each member of it should be only too willing to bring former mistakes, no matter how grievous, out of their hiding ***places***.(p.124)
• Some of us sought out sordid ***places***, hoping to find understanding companionship and approval.(p.151)
• He entered a political campaign, making speeches, frequenting men's gathering ***places*** of all sorts, often staying up all night.(p.158)
• It did help to certain extent, since I got in ***places*** where I could not obtain anything to drink, and so broke the habitual drinking.(p.183)
• I met all the people I wanted to meet; I saw all the ***places*** I wanted to see; I did all the things I wanted to do -- and I was increasingly miserable.(p.225)
• (This is very useful knowledge in ***places*** where matches are prohibited.)(p.245)
• On the way home numerous ***places*** must be passed.(p.299)
• I learned that a person just can't find a job hanging in a dive or barroom all day and all night, as jobs don't seem to turn up in those ***places***.(p.300)
• Even some of the saloon-keepers, where I had spent so much time and money, requested that I stay away from their ***places***.(p.301)
• I myself didn't know all the ***places*** I had them hidden.(p.325)
• I tried to hide my drinking by going ***places*** where I was unlikely to see anyone I knew.(p.375)
• My tweed suit, once a very good one, was shapeless and baggy with bare ***places*** worn in the elbows from leaning on the bar.(p.411)
• After nine days of tests at Mayo, I was put in the locked ward – of all ***places***!(p.444)
• I do think that some of the Negroes here – and other ***places***, too – are afraid to go to other meetings.(p.529)
• Alcoholics can stop drinking in many ***places*** and many ways – but Alcoholics Anonymous offers us a way to stay sober.(p.559)
• But hospitals, as well as other ***places*** of recuperation, ought to be well outside A.A. – and medically supervised.(p.566)
• In such ***places***, A.A. can be located through the local telephone directory, newspaper office, or police station, or by contacting local priests or ministers.(p.575)

placing

• Then he had gone to Europe, ***placing*** himself in the care of a celebrated physician (the psychiatrist, Dr. Jung) who prescribed for him.(p.26)
• Though some of his manifestations are alarming and disagreeable, we think dad will be on a firmer foundation than the man who is ***placing*** business or professional success ahead of spiritual development.(p.129)

plague

• Argument and fault-finding are to be avoided like the ***plague***.(p.98)
• It is possible to dig up past misdeeds so they become a blight, a veritable ***plague***.(p.124)

plagued

• I was not too well at the time, and was ***plagued*** by waves of self-pity and resentment.(p.15)
• Now and then the family will be ***plagued*** by spectres from the past, for the drinking career of almost every alcoholic has been marked by escapades, funny, humiliating, shameful or tragic.(p.123)
• Neurotic fears ***plagued*** me, and I had occasional, uncontrollable tremors.(p.555)

plain

• Whatever the precise definition of the word may be, we call this ***plain*** insanity.(p.37)
• But I cannot accept as surely true the many articles of faith which are so ***plain*** to him."(p.47)
• It is ***plain*** that a life which includes deep resentment leads only to futility and unhappiness.(p.66)
• Make it ***plain*** he is under no obligation to you, that you hope only that he will try to help other alcoholics when he escapes his own difficulties.(p.94)
• That includes bars, nightclubs, dances, receptions, weddings, even ***plain*** ordinary whoopee parties.(p.101)
• If you propose such a procedure to him, it may be necessary to advance the cost of treatment, but we believe it should be made ***plain*** that any expense will later be deducted from his pay.(p.143)
• She said she didn't know, but that I sure showed ***plain*** enough I didn't have any part of it.(p.273)
• It is no problem to me now, but this is not good management on my part -- just ***plain*** good luck.(p.480)

plainly

• I have my brilliant moments yet, but whenever the boys catch me at it they tell me so very ***plainly***.(p.512)

plaintively

• But the saddest, and thus the most consoling, drifted through from the country-music station – stories of broken hearts, wasted lives, lost loves, sung ***plaintively***.(p.332)

plan

• We of Alcoholics Anonymous believe that the reader will be interested in the medical estimate of the ***plan*** of recovery described in this book.(p.xxiii)
• He accepted the ***plan*** outlined in this book.(p.xxix)
• It is important that he be able to keep a confidence; that he fully understand and approve what we are driving at; that he will not try to change our ***plan***.(p.74)
• Then she told me that these two drunks she had been talking to had a ***plan*** whereby they thought they could quit drinking, and part of that ***plan*** was that they tell it to another drunk.(p.185)
• So far, so good – all according to ***plan***, like thousands of others.(p.225)
• He went on talking and told me that he had found the ***plan*** has a basis of love, and the practice of Christ's injunction, "Love thy neighbor as thyself."(p.236)
• After being in the hospital for several days, a ***plan*** of living was outlined to me.(p.302)
• A very simple ***plan*** that I still find much joy and happiness in following.(p.302)
• A.A. is not a ***plan*** for recovery that can be finished and done with.(p.311)
• We do not, cannot, out-grow this ***plan***.(p.311)
• Not understanding the twenty-four hour ***plan***, or not wanting to, I began drinking and was off-again on-again, during that first month.(p.414)
• I got off the so-called wagon, and on the twenty-four hour ***plan***.(p.415)
• And also, on the twenty-four hour ***plan***, it taught me how to live.(p.416)
• Sobriety and a ***plan*** for living that produces a personality change and a spiritual awakening are imperative.(p.459)
• They cooked up a ***plan*** whereby she didn't have to be molested by me if she didn't want to be.(p.491)
• I thought that life was a pretty simple thing; you simply made a ***plan*** for your life, based upon what you wanted, and then you needed only the courage to go after it.(p.545)
• The A.A. ***plan*** is described by the members themselves as 'self-insurance.'(p.574)

plane

• Though we work out our solution on the spiritual as well as an altruistic ***plane***, we favor hospitalization for the alcoholic who is very jittery or befogged.(p.xxiv)
• Our thought-life will be placed on a much higher ***plane*** when our thinking is cleared of wrong motives.(p.86)
• Nevertheless, we find that our thinking will as time passes, be more and more on the ***plane*** of inspiration.(p.87)
• The minute we put our work on a service ***plane***, the alcoholic commences to rely upon our assistance rather than upon God.(p.98)
• We have elsewhere remarked how much better life is when lived on a spiritual ***plane***.(p.116)
• We got on the ***plane*** and immediately had a big fight over whether I'd drink the free booze.(p.444)

planes

• I don't know why I didn't fall out of the open cockpit of some of those ***planes*** I flew in while taking aerial pictures.(p.426)

planned

• When we look back, we realize that the things which came to us when we put ourselves in God's hands were better than anything we could have ***planned***.(p.100)
• He may, for example, reveal that he has padded his expense account or that he has ***planned*** to take your best customers away from you.(p.145)
• And as I fumed helplessly and ***planned*** to get good and drunk and show them, my eye caught a sentence in the book lying open on my bed: "We cannot live with anger."(p.228)
• I ***planned*** to stay home the night before I left, but my folks got so drunk I walked off early in the evening and spent the night with my girl, getting very drunk myself.(p.425)
• We were on our way to New York where he ***planned*** to leave me with my sister.(p.466)

planning

• If we are ***planning*** to stop drinking, there must be no reservation of any kind, nor any lurking notion that someday we will be immune to alcohol.(p.33)
• If my wife was ***planning*** to go out in the afternoon, I would get a large supply of liquor and smuggle it home and hide it in the coal bin, the clothes chute, over door jambs, over beams in the cellar and in cracks in the cellar tile.(p.176)
• I can well remember sitting with seven dollars in my pocket, ***planning*** on giving my family a hundred or two hundred dollars, when I made it next year.(p.197)
• I could work a deal up to where all I had to do was to go ahead with it; all the ***planning*** had been done, all the financing had been done, but then I'd say "Nuts to it!" and walk away.(p.197)
• Drink ***planning*** became more important than any other plans.(p.375)
• I nearly reverted to my old, incorrigible self – had trouble with a couple of other prisoners, was ***planning*** an escape.(p.461)

plans

• He ***plans*** various ways of drinking.(p.xxviii)
• Established on such a footing we became less and less interested in ourselves, our little ***plans*** and designs.(p.63)
• We consider our ***plans*** for the day.(p.86)
• Mother made all the ***plans*** and gave the directions.(p.131)
• Then there was wartime service to interrupt my ***plans***, and an education to be picked up after the war.(p.373)
• Drink planning became more important than any other ***plans***.(p.375)
• Resenting anyone and everyone who might interfere with my personal ***plans*** and ways of doing things, I was full of self pity, especially for any interference with my drinking.(p.376)
• I had only to reflect on the contrast between the ***plans*** I made so many years ago for my life with what really happened to know I couldn't manage my life drunk or sober.(p.550)
• But when its ***plans*** concern the welfare of neighboring groups also, those groups ought to be consulted.(p.565)

plant

• It was the day before Mother's Day and I had come home plastered, carrying a big potted ***plant*** which I set down on the table and forthwith went upstairs and passed out.(p.179)
• The next day, they called me in for an examination, and the doctor wouldn't let me continue working and pardoned me from the ***plant*** for ten days because he said my eye had been injured.(p.205)
• So I was barred from the ***plant*** for ten days, and during that ten day period I was drunk twice, showing how little control these restraints had on me.(p.205)
• Or, "My physical ***plant*** had got a little run down and the stuff rushed right to my head."(p.433)

planted

• The seed has been ***planted*** in his mind.(p.113)
• We have come to believe He would like us to keep our heads in the clouds with Him, but that our feet ought to be firmly ***planted*** on earth.(p.130)
• He ***planted*** many seeds, and it will be many moons before another rises to walk in his shoes."(p.476)
• I ***planted*** my first flower garden this year and am actually excited to see the results.(p.481)

plastered

• It was the day before Mother's Day and I had come home ***plastered***, carrying a big potted plant which I set down on the table and forthwith went upstairs and passed out.(p.179)
• I stayed in the barracks all day, "making out guard schedules," and getting mildly ***plastered*** from the jug under my desk.(p.426)
• Still, I had had funds sufficient to get ***plastered*** because that, of course, was more important than paying my own way.(p.538)

platoon
• I was sent to a psychiatrist, for they didn't think it was normal for me to want to kill my ***platoon*** sergeant or to attempt suicide twice.(p.318)

Plattsburg
• War fever ran high in the New England town to which we new, young officers from ***Plattsburg*** were assigned, and we were flattered when the first citizens took us to their homes, making us feel heroic.(p.1)

plausibility
• Sometimes these excuses have a certain ***plausibility***, but none of them really makes sense in the light of the havoc an alcoholic's drinking bout creates.(p.23)

play
• Still the ***play*** does not suit him.(p.61)
• We are in the world to ***play*** the role He assigns.(p.68)
• Is it not because each wants to ***play*** the lead?(p.122)
• At the very beginning, the couple ought to frankly face the fact that each will have to yield here and there if the family is going to ***play*** an effective part in the new life.(p.131)
• Everybody knows that those in bad health, and those who seldom ***play***, do not laugh much.(p.132)
• So let each family ***play*** together or separately, as much as their circumstances warrant.(p.132)
• The employer cannot ***play*** favorites, but he can always defend a man from needless provocation and unfair criticism.(p.146)
• They work hard and they ***play*** hard.(p.146)
• You may need to encourage him to ***play*** once in a while.(p.146)
• They'd sit out there and ***play*** hymns and I'd be lying in there with a terrific hangover.(p.265)
• I was accused of it many times when I went to ***play*** bridge in the afternoon, but I really never did take a morning drink.(p.323)
• A friend of mine, a golf nut, rushed out on retirement to ***play*** every day.(p.330)
• My wonderful wife did everything to ***play*** along with me.(p.361)
• We weren't even permitted to ***play*** cards in our home, but father would give us just a little toddy with whiskey and sugar and warm water now and then.(p.484)
• Four alcoholics ***play*** bridge in a smoke-filled room.(p.502)
• I begin to ***play*** God.(p.506)
• Things weren't going as I thought they should, for my greater enjoyment, comfort and fame; therefore, if the universe wouldn't ***play*** my way, I wouldn't ***play*** at all.(p.531)
• I stumbled agonizedly past the theatre where in years gone by a great star had played my ***play***.(p.540)
• I still want to write a fine ***play*** and to get it on.(p.542)
• To wear expensive clothes, to have bartenders know what to serve me before I ordered, to be recognized by headwaiters and shown to the best table, to ***play*** gin rummy for high stakes with the insouciance of a riverboat gambler -- these were the enduring values in life, I thought.(p.556)

played
• Unfortunately for me, I was the only child, which perhaps engendered the selfishness which ***played*** such an important part in bringing on my alcoholism.(p.172)
• I remember telling them too that it was going to be awfully tough, because I did some other things, smoked cigarettes and ***played*** penny ante poker, sometimes bet on the horse races and they said, "Don't you think you're having more trouble with this drinking than with anything else at the present time?(p.190)
• When I had been in the hospital ten days, Sister Ignatia, who has ***played*** such a part in the development of A.A. in this area, stuck her head in the door one morning and announced, looking at me quizzically, that they might be able to make something human out of my face after all.(p.205)
• I get my greatest thrill of accomplishment from the knowledge that I have ***played*** a part in the new happiness achieved by countless others like myself.(p.229)
• We had ***played*** this game before.(p.238)
• All afternoon I sat there and drank and ***played*** Bing Crosby's recording of "Silent Night" over and over again on the juke box.(p.467)
• I had ***played*** all that out long ago.(p.523)
• I stumbled agonizedly past the theatre where in years gone by a great star had ***played*** my play.(p.540)
• In my mind's eye, I ***played*** and replayed scenes in which I was plucked magically from the bar where I stood nursing a drink, and was instantly exalted to some position of power and prestige.(p.560)

players
• Each person is like an actor who wants to run the whole show; is forever trying to arrange the lights, the ballet, the scenery and the rest of the ***players*** in his own way.(p.60)
• Is it not evident to all the rest of the ***players*** that these are the things he wants?(p.61)
• A busload of basketball ***players*** had been passing and saw the flames.(p.424)
• Shakespeare said, "All the world's a stage, all the men and women merely ***players***."(p.449)

playing
• First of all, we had to quit ***playing*** God.(p.62)
• There I sat in the evenings, enjoying with my friends our memories of the "old country," singing the old songs we all knew, ***playing*** simple card games for drinks and consuming great quantities of beer.(p.231)
• Eventually, of course, what with all the hilarity that could be provoked with a few gallons of beer, there seemed to be no need of bridge or poker ***playing*** for entertainment.(p.297)
• During recess we were ***playing*** basketball and I had accidentally tripped a fellow just a little larger than I was.(p.484)
• I began sneaking drinks when ***playing*** bartender for guests.(p.556)

plays
• It is important for him to realize that your attempt to pass this on to him ***plays*** a vital part in your own recovery.(p.94)

playwright
• An ambitious ***playwright***, he let his brains get so far ahead of his emotions that he collapsed into suicidal drinking.(p.531)

plea
• I still expected a ***plea*** for clemency, but these words came through the receiver: "I just wanted to tell you Paul jumped from a hotel window in Hartford last Saturday.(p.136)
• I heard a lovely voice, and a sympathetic ear listened to my ***plea***.(p.363)

plead
• Neither should the family hysterically ***plead*** with him to do anything, nor should they tell him much about you.(p.90)

pleaded
• I thanked him, ***pleaded*** business engagements and promised I'd go with him at some future date.(p.257)

pleasant
• These are not ***pleasant*** companions.(p.104)
• This happy combination of ***pleasant*** work and alcohol lasted for five years.(p.277)
• Oddly enough, the circumstances and surroundings were ***pleasant***.(p.285)
• Such thinking usually began with thoughts of the ***pleasant*** drinking of my youth.(p.285)
• Living just for today is a ***pleasant*** adventure.(p.383)
• A drink never gave me a normal, ***pleasant*** glow.(p.402)
• Bill was tall, grey haired, with the kind of asymmetrical good looks and ***pleasant*** easy manner that inspire confidence in the shaken and afraid.(p.413)
• That type of drinking is not ***pleasant***.(p.514)
• Since, perhaps, suicide was a bit too drastic (actually, I was afraid), dry martinis were chosen as the slow, ***pleasant***, private, gradual instrument of self-destruction.(p.531)
• One of the truly great things A.A. has taught me is that reality too has two sides; I had only known the grim side before the program, but now I had a chance to learn about the ***pleasant*** side as well.(p.550)

pleasantly
• The family will be affected also, ***pleasantly*** at first, as they feel their money troubles are about to be solved, then not so ***pleasantly*** as they find themselves neglected.(p.126)
• She was chatting on, ***pleasantly*** and comfortably.(p.222)

please
• That the man who is making the approach has had the same difficulty, that he obviously knows what he is talking about, that his whole deportment shouts at the new prospect that he is a man with a real answer, that he has no attitude of Holier Than Thou, nothing whatever except the sincere desire to be helpful; that there are no fees to pay, no axes to grind, no people to ***please***, no lectures to be endured -- these are the conditions we have found most effective.(p.18)
• Nothing would ***please*** us so much as to write a book which would contain no basis for contention or argument.(p.19)
• And I then and there said a prayer, if you ***please***.(p.200)
• I resented it of course, and I offered Clarence his commission, whatever it might be, if he would ***please*** not bother me because I had arrived at the conclusion that he was a solicitor for some alcoholic institute.(p.216)
• ***Please*** let me turn it over to you."(p.280)
• I vowed that never again would any important person whom I wished to ***please*** and impress ever see me drunk.(p.328)
• So ***please*** accept these humble calculations as, if anything, an underestimation.(p.396)
• So ***please*** bear in mind, and I would like to emphasize, that this is a very rough estimate.(p.399)
• When you've been in a jam you've said, 'God, ***please*** do this or that,' and if it turned out your way that was the last of it, and if it didn't you've said 'There isn't any God' or 'He doesn't do anything for me.'(p.504)
• I had even borrowed money from her, over her protest: "Bob, ***please*** don't ask me to lend you money -- you're the only one who hasn't."(p.540)
• ***Please*** do not think it ended so simply and so easily.(p.541)
• The children kept me sober for darn near three weeks, and then I went on (***please*** God) my last drunk.(p.549)

pleased
• My business came off well, I was ***pleased*** and knew my partners would be too.(p.41)
• Everybody, including himself, would be ***pleased***.(p.61)
• I wanted to do nothing except what it ***pleased*** me to do when I wanted to do it.(p.256)
• Russ used to be very much ***pleased*** because he'd say, "I think Dr. Bob thoroughly enjoys coming out here.(p.271)
• Safely pensioned, with no job to protect, at last he could drink as he ***pleased***.(p.327)
• I did as I ***pleased*** most of the time.(p.424)
• (I am ***pleased*** to state, however, that I had gone to only a very few A.A. meetings before I was able to make a really beautiful pair of moccasins -- and half a wallet.(p.445)
• The fear of the loss of Vi and the feeling that, though she had the right to do as she ***pleased***, she should have told me the truth about it, upset me.(p.487)
• What struck me most was that they all seemed to be quite ***pleased*** with having made a job of it and having stopped drinking.(p.524)

pleasurable
• Needless to say, this was not ***pleasurable*** drinking.(p.306)
• In time, I found myself looking forward to each new day with ***pleasurable*** anticipation.(p.311)

pleasure
• Or am I expecting to steal a little vicarious ***pleasure*** from the atmosphere of such places?"(p.101)
• If it is a happy occasion, try to increase the ***pleasure*** of those there; if a business occasion, go and attend to your business enthusiastically.(p.102)
• If he does not argue about religion, he will make new friends and is sure to find new avenues of usefulness and ***pleasure***.(p.132)
• 2.It is a ***pleasure***.(p.181)
• I had no ***pleasure*** out of the drinking at all.(p.195)
• Headstrong and willful, I rushed from ***pleasure*** to ***pleasure***, and found the returns diminishing to the vanishing point.(p.226)
• It no longer gave me ***pleasure*** -- it merely dulled the pain -- but I had to have it.(p.226)
• Now on a new job I was always thinking about payday and how much liquor I could buy and the ***pleasure*** I could have.(p.255)
• What philosophy I had was thoroughly paganistic -- all my life was devoted to a search for ***pleasure***.(p.256)
• I experienced some of the ***pleasure*** of social drinking when I was sixteen.(p.305)
• I find an inner ***pleasure*** in simple things.(p.383)
• The remorse would turn inside out, and become anticipatory ***pleasure***.(p.408)

pleasures
• It may mean the loss of many nights' sleep, great interference with your ***pleasures***, interruptions to your business.(p.97)
• The old ***pleasures*** were gone.(p.151)

pledge
• I could almost hear the sound of the preacher's

voice as I sat, on still Sundays, way over there on the hillside; there was that proffered temperance ***pledge*** I never signed; my grandfather's good natured contempt of some church folk and their doings; his insistence that the spheres really had their music; but his denial of the preacher's right to tell him how he must listen; his fearlessness as he spoke of these things just before he died; these recollections welled up from the past.(p.10)
• Unlike many other Catholics who frequently take pledges for definite periods – a year, two years or for good, I never had any desire to "take a ***pledge***" before the priest.(p.234)

pledges
• Unlike many other Catholics who frequently take ***pledges*** for definite periods – a year, two years or for good, I never had any desire to "take a pledge" before the priest.(p.234)
• Take many ***pledges***, but break them.(p.475)

plenty
• He had ***plenty*** of money left and thought I had better go to Canada.(p.4)
• Many of us felt that we had ***plenty*** of character.(p.34)
• I remember having several more that night and ***plenty*** the next morning.(p.41)
• If we have no such complication, there is ***plenty*** we should do at home.(p.82)
• ***Plenty*** of difficulties presented themselves.(p.156)
• It wasn't very long until I had developed a pretty good brew with uniformity and ***plenty*** of authority.(p.232)
• My wife upbraided me often and ***plenty*** when she saw that my "periodics" were gradually losing me what business I could get.(p.233)
• One evening, the book, after checking up, was very definitely in the red for ***plenty*** through a piece of studied carelessness on my part, and my boss, very shrewd and able, fired me with a parting statement to the effect that once was enough.(p.251)
• I didn't care to go visiting unless the parties we might visit had ***plenty*** of liquor on hand and I could get drunk.(p.301)
• I guess there are ***plenty*** of other graduates of this treatment around.(p.389)
• My father had a title; there was ***plenty*** of means in the family.(p.401)
• "You've got to space your drinks and take ***plenty*** of water in between," or "coat the stomach with a little olive oil," or "drink anything but those damn martinis."(p.433)
• My reaction was that I'd already helped all the patients on the ward, and I still had ***plenty*** of problems of my own without trying to help some drunk from A.A.(p.446)

plight
• One of these men, staff member of a world-renowned hospital, recently made this statement to some of us: "What you say about the general hopelessness of the average alcoholic's ***plight*** is, in my opinion, correct.(p.43)
• Why, he argued, should he lose the remainder of his business, only to bring still more suffering to his family by foolishly admitting his ***plight*** to people from whom he made his livelihood?(p.155)
• I began to sleep, to relax, to accept my ***plight***.(p.461)

plowed
• And so on and on, for several weeks, while I grudgingly ***plowed*** through some more of the offending book, and felt more and more hopeless about myself.(p.227)

plucked
• In my mind's eye, I played and replayed scenes in which I was ***plucked*** magically from the bar where I stood nursing a drink, and was instantly exalted to some position of power and prestige.(p.560)

plug
• We hope our suggestions will help you ***plug*** up this sometimes serious leak.(p.148)

plumber
• In the nearby little town there was a ***plumber*** who once had tried to get an A.A. group going.(p.541)

plunge
• Now I was to ***plunge*** into the dark, joining that endless procession of sots who had gone on before.(p.8)
• He may either ***plunge*** into a frantic attempt to get on his feet in business, or he may be so enthralled by his new life that he talks or thinks of little else.(p.125)

plus
• Belief in the power of God, ***plus*** enough willingness, honesty and humility to establish and maintain the new order of things, were the essential requirements.(p.13)
• He was positive that his humiliating experience, ***plus*** the knowledge he had acquired, would keep him sober the rest of his life.(p.40)
• You are betting, of course, that your changed attitude ***plus*** the contents of this book will turn the trick.(p.144)
• He said he had finally learned that drinking was a fatal illness made up of an allergy ***plus*** an obsession, and once the drinking had passed from habit to obsession, we were completely hopeless, and could look forward only to spending the balance of our lives in mental institutions or to death.(p.290)
• This, ***plus*** mounting emotional disturbances, convinced them that compulsive alcoholism already had them; that complete ruin would be only a question of time.(p.315)
• And I still felt it was a weakness – ***plus***, in her case, adverse circumstances.(p.370)
• While I was at Pensacola my dad became dangerously ill and almost died of pneumonia ***plus*** a heart attack.(p.426)

pluses
• I had been far too busy building, protecting, and maintaining an image of respectability and all the other business ***pluses***.(p.327)

plush
• I was assigned to keep media guests happy at a Halloween party given by a major star in his ***plush*** home.(p.328)
• There was a red ***plush*** carpet to welcome me, but even so it wasn't easy.(p.430)

pneumonia
• Treat him, when you can, as though he had ***pneumonia***.(p.108)
• While I was at Pensacola my dad became dangerously ill and almost died of ***pneumonia*** plus a heart attack.(p.426)
• I got drunk one night in October, went to sleep in the rain and woke up with ***pneumonia***.(p.490)
• True, I have recently recovered from ***pneumonia*** and have an alibi, but my friends are in the war or going, and I am not.(p.499)

pocket
• We ***pocket*** our pride and go to it, illuminating every twist of character, every dark cranny of the past.(p.75)
• I would reach over and get this and take a shot and in a few moments get up and take another, shave and eat my breakfast, slip a half pint of liquor in my hip ***pocket***, and go on to school.(p.183)
• During the day, looking over the contracts and money in my ***pocket***, I found that I had sold six lots that I couldn't even remember, and didn't even know the people I had sold them to.(p.196)
• I can well remember sitting with seven dollars in my ***pocket***, planning on giving my family a hundred or two hundred dollars, when I made it next year.(p.197)
• But I didn't do a thing about giving them any part of the seven bucks I had in my ***pocket***.(p.197)
• I had lost a hundred dollars I had in my ***pocket***, and lost a wristwatch too.(p.202)
• I thought he had it is his ***pocket***, so I said, "You got some?"(p.208)
• I landed him and shipped him by train to Akron, with a pint of whiskey in his ***pocket*** to keep him from wanting to get off the train in Toledo!(p.282)
• I had to put up a three hundred dollar bond because he was carrying the same summons around in his ***pocket*** for me.(p.491)
• I guess I had five or ten dollars in my ***pocket***.(p.491)

pocketbooks
• In most cases it was found that our self-esteem, our ***pocketbooks***, our ambitions, our personal relationships (including sex) were hurt or threatened.(p.64)

pockets
• Sometimes I would bring it in my ***pockets***, but they were inspected, and that became too risky.(p.176)

poetry
• I read sad ***poetry***, cried, drank red wine, wrote sad ***poetry***, and drank some more.(p.405)

point
• Neither does A.A. take any particular medical ***point*** of view, though we cooperate widely with the men of medicine as well as with the men of religion.(p.xx)
• Stocks were at the low ***point*** of 1932, and I had somehow formed a group to buy.(p.5)
• I saw that growth could start from that ***point***.(p.12)
• We are not sure why, once a certain ***point*** is reached, little can be done for him.(p.22)
• At a certain ***point*** in the drinking of every alcoholic, he passes into a state where the most powerful desire to stop drinking is of absolutely no avail.(p.24)
• Each individual, in the personal stories, describes in his own language and from his own ***point*** of view the way he established his relationship with God.(p.29)
• As we look back, we feel we had gone on drinking many years beyond the ***point*** where we could quit on our will power.(p.34)
• Friends who have reasoned with him after a spree which has brought him to the ***point*** of divorce or bankruptcy are mystified when he walks directly into a saloon.(p.35)
• Up to this ***point*** you would label him as a foolish chap having queer ideas of fun.(p.37)
• This is a ***point*** we wish to emphasize and re-emphasize, to smash home upon our alcoholic readers as it has been revealed to us out of bitter experience.(p.39)
• Simply because it is impossible to explain what we see, feel, direct, and use, without a reasonable assumption as a starting ***point***.(p.48)
• We had to ask ourselves why we shouldn't apply to our human problems this same readiness to change our ***point*** of view.(p.52)
• Arrived at this ***point***, we were squarely confronted with the question of faith.(p.53)
• Post-war disillusionment, ever more serious alcoholism, impending mental and physical collapse, brought him to the ***point*** of self-destruction.(p.56)
• We stood at the turning ***point***.(p.59)
• The ***point*** is, that we are willing to grow along spiritual lines.(p.60)
• But ***point*** out that we alcoholics have much in common and that you would like, in any case, to be friendly.(p.95)
• You should ***point*** out that his defects of character are not going to disappear over night.(p.100)
• Perhaps at this ***point*** we got a divorce and took the children home to father and mother.(p.106)
• He may have come to the ***point*** where he desperately wants to stop but cannot.(p.110)
• Your husband will be the first to say it was your devotion and care which brought him to the ***point*** where he could have a spiritual experience.(p.118)
• It will do little good if you ***point*** that out and urge more attention for yourself.(p.119)
• From that ***point*** on, progress will be rapid.(p.134)
• Here is a case in ***point***: One of our friends is a heavy smoker and coffee drinker.(p.135)
• A firm attitude at this ***point*** has helped many of us.(p.142)
• At this ***point***, it might be well to explain alcoholism, the illness.(p.142)
• Their cost of production is figured to a fine decimal ***point***.(p.149)
• You will want to know more of how to proceed from that ***point***.(p.153)
• I was self conscious and ill at ease most of the time, my health was at the breaking ***point***, and I was thoroughly miserable.(p.178)
• (At this ***point***, the Editors intrude just long enough to supplement Bill D.'s account, that of the man on the bed, with that of Bill W., the man who sat by the side of the bed.)(p.188)
• I made a ***point*** of knowing important people.(p.197)
• When rubber reached a certain low ***point***, they would draw on the rubber out of the pool and buy.(p.198)
• To show you the ***point*** to which this obsession went, there came an occasion when I had spent a most delightful week-end, and at nine o'clock on Sunday night I was on my way home, and I thought I would get a drink.(p.204)
• My practice had advanced to the ***point*** where it could stand a lot of abuse and it got it.(p.214)
• After two or three years of effort along this line, I reached the ***point*** of actual despair that I ever would be able to drink only a harmless amount each day.(p.215)
• It took three-quarters of an hour and two changes to get there – back to my starting ***point***.(p.223)
• Headstrong and willful, I rushed from pleasure to pleasure, and found the returns diminishing to the vanishing ***point***.(p.226)
• That was the ***point*** at which my doctor gave me the book "Alcoholics Anonymous" to read.(p.227)
• My "periodics" became more frequent until I reached the ***point*** where I wanted to devote all my time to drinking, working as little as possible, and then only when the necessity of my family demanded it.(p.234)
• My customers lost confidence in me to the ***point*** where I retained what business I had only because I was a well-trained and reputedly fine craftsman.(p.234)
• I really had a chance to see myself from a non-drinking ***point*** of view.(p.245)

• I myself could see deterioration in my work from being physically and mentally affected by liquor, although I had not yet reached the ***point*** where all I wanted was more to drink.(p.254)
• When I reached a ***point*** directly back of our house, where I could have cut through a friend's garden, I was almost overpowered by the desire to get home, but I made the whole journey.(p.276)
• What about those fears which once paralyzed me to the ***point*** of my becoming a semi-hermit?(p.284)
• I do feel, though, that the fact that I finally grew up to a ***point*** where I could even tackle such a job is the apex of the story of a man who spent eighteen years running away from life.(p.286)
• I had thought that I was completely different from other people, that I was beginning to become a little balmy, even to the ***point*** of withdrawing more and more from society and wanting to be alone with my bottle.(p.290)
• From that ***point*** on, I secured crocks of ten gallon capacity and really took quite an active interest in the manufacture of home brew.(p.297)
• Up to this ***point*** I had spent six years in the business and had enjoyed the reputation of being very successful.(p.298)
• Things eventually came to the ***point*** where I had no friends.(p.301)
• That was the turning ***point*** of my life.(p.302)
• That call marked the turning ***point*** in my life.(p.307)
• But there came a ***point*** when I could no longer live with it.(p.337)
• It was at that ***point*** that I reached surrender.(p.340)
• We stood at the turning ***point***."(p.349)
• I had my first drink when I was fifteen and my alcoholic potential had ripened me to the ***point*** of necessary escapism.(p.353)
• When it became noticeable to the ***point*** of comment, I devised ways of sneaking drinks on the side.(p.375)
• Some crisis brings you to a ***point*** of making a decision to do something about your drinking problem.(p.377)
• Somehow our bodies had reached the ***point*** where we could no longer absorb alcohol in our systems.(p.380)
• Eighteen will be used as the starting ***point***, because my drinking before was limited by age, the law, and money.(p.397)
• And I was always glad to ***point*** it out, because I knew you wanted perfection, just as I did.(p.449)
• My pattern of drinking at that time had reached the ***point*** where once I really started, I would retire to my bed and drink myself into oblivion.(p.466)
• There were doctors and psychiatrists there who tried to help me, but at that ***point*** I wasn't having help from anyone.(p.468)
• At that ***point*** everyone decided something drastic had to be done.(p.469)
• Another thing that mother drilled into me was a very Puritanical ***point*** of view as to sex relations and as to motherhood and womanhood.(p.483)
• About then too, I realized that my ***point*** of view on the opposite sex wasn't entirely like that of most of the boys I knew.(p.484)
• At this ***point*** I believe I had only been intoxicated on maybe three or four occasions, and certainly whiskey was no problem to me.(p.487)
• From that ***point*** on, it's just the average drinker's story.(p.488)
• But I knew at that ***point*** that I couldn't stop and I knew that I was a danger to myself and to others.(p.489)
• At this ***point***, I was no longer the wise boy.(p.515)
• It was impossible for me to say at this ***point***, "Maybe there is something wrong with my philosophy," and I certainly couldn't say, "Maybe there is something wrong with me."(p.545)
• In my prayers that morning I asked God to ***point*** out to me some way to be free of this resentment.(p.552)
• Edward Dowling, S.J., of the Queen's Work staff says, "Alcoholics Anonymous is natural; it is natural at the ***point*** where nature comes closest to the supernatural, namely in humiliations and in consequent humility.(p.574)
• Speaking at a dinner given by John D. Rockefeller Jr. to introduce Alcoholics Anonymous to some of his friends, Dr. Harry Emerson Fosdick remarked: "I think that psychologically speaking there is a ***point*** of advantage in the approach that is being made in this movement that cannot be duplicated.(p.574)

point-blank
• But my friend sat before me, and he made the ***point-blank*** declaration that God had done for him what he could not do for himself.(p.11)
• So he returned to this doctor, whom he admired, and asked him ***point-blank*** why he could not recover.(p.26)

pointed
• Why was it, when these dangers were ***pointed*** out that they agreed, and then got drunk again immediately?(p.107)
• I ***pointed*** out that I had had nothing to drink whatever for three years, and this in the face of difficulties that would have made nine out of ten men drink their heads off.(p.138)
• If your man accepts your offer, it should be ***pointed*** out that physical treatment is but a small part of the picture.(p.143)
• Eagerly he ***pointed*** to us saying, "These are the fellows I told you about; they are the ones who understand."(p.189)
• I do not recollect the specific conversation that went on but I believe I did challenge Bill to tell me something about A.A. and I do recall one other thing: I wanted to know what this was that worked so many wonders, and hanging over the mantel was a picture of Gethsemane and Bill ***pointed*** to it and said, "There it is," which didn't make much sense to me.(p.216)
• He ***pointed*** out to me that probably it was more of a moral or spiritual illness than it was a physical one.(p.219)
• Need I say that in a very short time I was walking along a prairie highway with arm extended and thumb ***pointed***?(p.255)
• I was an honor graduate in high school, and I was a "good boy" to whom mothers ***pointed*** when their sons went astray.(p.419)
• Every defect I ***pointed*** out to her became greater and greater.(p.450)
• But I ***pointed*** out to him that as I was the first British boy who had been to the school, it wouldn't be a very good advertisement for him, so I got over that all right.(p.518)

pointing
• They criticize, ***pointing*** out how he is falling down on his spiritual program.(p.126)
• I had been too self-sufficient to write a moral inventory, but I discovered in ***pointing*** out to the new man his wrong attitudes and actions that I was really taking my own inventory, and that if I expected him to change I would have to work on myself too.(p.249)

pointless
• These observations would be academic and ***pointless*** if our friend never took the first drink, thereby setting the terrible cycle in motion.(p.23)

points
• Before going into a detailed discussion, it may be well to summarize some ***points*** as we see them.(p.20)
• We could not prove life in the sense that you can prove a straight line is the shortest distance between two ***points***, yet, there it was.(p.54)
• We believe a man should be thoroughly probed on these ***points***.(p.142)
• I would rather talk about the good things A.A. has taught me; I feel that hitting on just a few sordid ***points*** should be sufficient to let those of you in institutions know where I came from.(p.459)

poise
• About the time of the beer experiment I was thrown in with a crowd of people who attracted me because of their seeming ***poise***, health, and happiness.(p.178)

poised
• I don't know what sort of person I was expecting, but I was very agreeably surprised to find Mr. T. a ***poised***, intelligent, well groomed and mannered gentleman.(p.309)

poison
• Again I swayed dizzily before an open window, or the medicine cabinet where there was ***poison***, cursing myself for a weakling.(p.6)
• They may be the dubious luxury of normal men, but for alcoholics these things are ***poison***.(p.66)
• One of the earliest memories that I have is of a bottle sitting on his desk with a skull and crossbones and marked "***Poison***."(p.193)

poisoning
• The man in the bed was told of the acute ***poisoning*** from which he suffered, how it deteriorates the body of an alcoholic and warps his mind.(p.157)

poke
• I'll buy you one drink, and if you suggest a second one, I'll ***poke*** you right in the nose."(p.201)

poker
• I remember telling them too that it was going to be awfully tough, because I did some other things, smoked cigarettes and played penny ante ***poker***, sometimes bet on the horse races and they said, "Don't you think you're having more trouble with this drinking than with anything else at the present time?(p.190)
• The first year in college I just got by in my studies, and that year I majored in ***poker*** and drinking.(p.241)
• Eventually, of course, what with all the hilarity that could be provoked with a few gallons of beer, there seemed to be no need of bridge or ***poker*** playing for entertainment.(p.297)

poker-straight
• If our hair is half-bleached (with dark roots), ***poker-straight***, and not combed, this adds to our beauty.(p.479)

pokey
• After a couple of days in dollar hotels and one night in the ***pokey***, I finally landed on my mother's doorstep -- shaking apart, with several days' beard and, of course, broke as usual.(p.238)

police
• It may mean sharing your money and your home, counseling frantic wives and relatives, innumerable trips to ***police*** courts, sanitariums, hospitals, jails and asylums.(p.97)
• Another time you may have to send for the ***police*** or an ambulance.(p.97)
• I went downstairs and there was the grizzly old veteran ***police*** officer in charge of the property desk, and as he gave me the stuff, he asked, "Are you going out in the street that way?"(p.204)
• In fact, on one occasion, I was picked up by the ***police*** and brought home.(p.211)
• There had been some occasions -- there was an automobile wreck, for instance -- when I had ***police*** escort home but not to jail, all of which, instead of doing me a favor, did me harm because I was then full of self-esteem as to the progress I had made both professionally and financially.(p.213)
• An obstreperous woman in a bar is a nuisance, and they wanted no trouble with the ***police***.(p.410)
• Luckily a friend was with me, who dragged me out, screaming and cursing, while the bartender threatened to call the ***police***.(p.411)
• Within a month, the ***police***, the hospital authorities, several kind strangers, most of my friends, all of my close relatives, and a few adepts at rolling a drunk and removing his wrist watch and wallet had been involved.(p.532)
• In such places, A.A. can be located through the local telephone directory, newspaper office, or ***police*** station, or by contacting local priests or ministers.(p.575)

policeman
• A ***policeman*** came to the door and asked for James S., but there wasn't any James S. there.(p.491)
• Within about ten days I got locked up for being drunk and this same ***policeman*** was in the station house as I was being booked.(p.491)
• Around eight or nine o'clock there came two big detectives and a ***policeman*** to arrest me for assault; and I was the most amazed person in the world when they said I had assaulted someone, and especially that I had assaulted my wife.(p.492)
• Still another friend and temporary host received me at four in the morning from the charge of a ***policeman*** who had found me "going to bed" in a garage far from the last place I could remember having been, a fashionable bar and restaurant in the theatrical district of New York, to which I had repaired after my date for that evening, a charming lady of the theatre who had refused my company for obvious reasons.(p.538)
• When the ***policeman*** released me to my stupefied and exasperated friend at four in the morning, I went to my traveling bag and groped until I found -- well, let the officer speak: "Ah," said the ***policeman***, "he's got anuder pair, t'ank God!"(p.538)
• Thank you, Mr. ***Policeman***, wherever you are now.(p.538)

policemen
• The bill collectors, the sheriffs, the angry taxi drivers, the ***policemen***, the bums, the pals, and even the ladies they sometimes brought home -- our husbands thought we were so inhospitable.(p.106)
• The next recollection I have is of my husband coming into my room (later found out it was on New Year's Eve) accompanied by two ***policemen***.(p.468)

policy
• But the ***policy*** of this company is not to interfere with the habits of our employees.(p.148)
• As to them, his ***policy*** is undoubtedly sound, but he did not distinguish between such people and the alcoholic.(p.149)
• I re-organized their city sales ***policy*** and eighteen months later, when I was thirty, they offered me the

branch managership.(p.243)
• Eleven -- Our public relations *policy* is based on attraction rather than promotion; we need always maintain personal anonymity at the level of press, radio and films.(p.564)

polish
• They did not seem to be getting an answer, for here I was staying sober and selling lots of auto *polish*, on which they were making one thousand per cent profit.(p.247)
• So I rocked along my merry independent way until June, when I went out selling auto *polish* in New England.(p.247)
• Peddling off my *polish* samples for expenses, I crawled back to New York a few days later in a very chastened frame of mind.(p.248)

polishing
• Bill and Hank had just taken over a small automobile *polishing* company and they offered me a job -- ten dollars a week and keep at Hank's house.(p.246)

polite
• Wishing to be *polite*, though I felt very badly, I said, "Let's make the call," and extracted from my wife a promise that we would not stay over fifteen minutes.(p.179)
• My wife traveled with me, but with a baby coming I decided to settle in a large city where I got a job with a commission agent which is a *polite* term for a handbook operator.(p.251)
• When I told them six weeks, they were *polite* and said that they would contact me in case they had anyone with an alcoholic problem.(p.293)
• A fanatic, I thought to myself, but I was *polite*.(p.503)

politely
• After several months of acquaintance I asked her to marry me, but was *politely* refused.(p.359)

political
• All sections of this country and many of its occupations are represented, as well as many *political*, economic, social, and religious backgrounds.(p.17)
• He entered a *political* campaign, making speeches, frequenting men's gathering places of all sorts, often staying up all night.(p.158)
• They were bright and well read, they held various *political* views.(p.410)

politically
• But sometimes our drinking will be used *politically*.(p.145)

politicians
• He is like the retired business man who lolls in the Florida sunshine in the winter complaining of the sad state of the nation; the minister who sighs over the sins of the twentieth century; *politicians* and reformers who are sure all would be Utopia if the rest of the world would only behave; the outlaw safe cracker who thinks society has wronged him; and the alcoholic who has lost all and is locked up.(p.61)

politics
• Wherever men are gathered together in business there will be rivalries and, arising out of these, a certain amount of office *politics*.(p.145)
• 10. -- No A.A. group or member should ever, in such a way as to implicate A.A., express any opinion on outside controversial issues -- particularly those of *politics*, alcohol reform, or sectarian religion.(p.567)

pollens
• The allergy I could understand because I am allergic to certain *pollens*.(p.380)

pomp
• It may be obscured by calamity, by *pomp*, by worship of other things, but in some form or other it is there.(p.55)

pondered
• I had often *pondered* these things.(p.10)

pondering
• While *pondering* the answer he felt as though he lived in hell.(p.56)

pool
• In the basement were to be dry-cleaning facilities, a barbershop, a *pool* room, a grocery shop and everything.(p.198)
• Another time, I had a rubber *pool* project.(p.198)
• My idea was to have all the companies *pool* their funds and buy rubber when rubber was cheap and then put it in a *pool*.(p.198)
• When rubber reached a certain low point, they would draw on the rubber out of the *pool* and buy.(p.198)
• This was in Virginia, where I had rented a house with stables and a swimming *pool*, and the fall fox hunting had begun.(p.404)

pooped
• No clothes, no money, no home, no real friends to speak of, mentally and physically *pooped*, but I was doing all right!(p.478)

poor
• I thought of my *poor* wife.(p.8)
• One *poor* chap committed suicide in my home.(p.16)
• High and low, rich and *poor*, these are future fellows of Alcoholics Anonymous.(p.152)
• I can remember telling the *poor* little soul that I could probably quit drinking if I wasn't married to her, and told her that, after all, I didn't like restraint!(p.199)
• I didn't like having to come home at a certain time; I didn't like this, I didn't like that, and I think the *poor* girl actually divorced me to help me stop drinking!(p.199)
• I come from a very *poor* family in material things, with a fine Christian mother, but with no religious background.(p.261)
• *Poor* health and a complete lack of money necessitated my remaining with Dr. Bob and Anne for very close to a year.(p.280)
• And he, *poor* dear, didn't know what was going on.(p.325)
• But I couldn't help thinking, "You *poor* guy.(p.334)
• They were neither *poor* nor wealthy, but far better off than the average couple.(p.357)
• I put my *poor* mother and father through agonies but, finally, I couldn't stand living with them and having them watch everything I did.(p.386)
• I also wrote another novel, all about Scott Fitzgerald's *poor*, misbegotten, unloved, tipsy little debutante.(p.405)
• My *poor* child could not know this.(p.409)
• Oh, *poor* self-centered, sick little me.(p.413)
• Alcoholism had respected nobody, neither rich nor *poor*, learned nor unlettered.(p.455)
• We are so beautiful that it is never too much trouble to get some *poor* stranger to buy us a drink.(p.479)
• Those *poor* stiffs probably went to a doctor and were told that if they quit they'd live three weeks and if they didn't they'd die in one."(p.510)
• *Poor*, black, totally ruled by alcohol, she felt shut away from any life worth living.(p.526)
• I always blamed my drinking on being *poor*, or on anything other than the truth -- that I liked what booze did for me, that when I had a drink I was as big and had as much as the next person.(p.526)
• I am hoping that writing this may bring some *poor*, mixed-up soul into the program.(p.530)
• And having sung that phrase, I'd chuckle with amusement, turning into irony turning into self-contempt turning into self-pity, at the sad fate of Bob, that wonderful, *poor* little motherless boy who was so smart in school and who grew up to accept responsibility so early and so fast and who staggered under his burdens without a whimper until the time came when he thought he was too good for this world and so he ought to be out of it.(p.532)
• *Poor* Bob!(p.532)
• There is something spiritual about A.A. too, and Catholic participation in it almost invariably results in *poor* Catholics becoming better Catholics."(p.574)

poorer
• Of course, the more I drank, the more unrealistic my expectations became and the *poorer* my performance, and the gap widened.(p.557)

poorest
• The *poorest* person has no less and the wealthiest has no more -- each of us has but one day.(p.473)

poorly
• I was in a large, dark, rather *poorly* furnished room -- the living room of a basement flat.(p.222)
• Just an unstable woman, undisciplined, *poorly* adjusted and filled with nameless fears.(p.305)

pop
• Near the Laundromat, I would buy one bottle of *pop* and a few bottles of beer or wine, and go into the rest room, empty the *pop* bottle, refill it with the booze, and proceed to do my laundering.(p.370)

popped
• I had been on the wagon when I came to A.A. and this sobriety-tension eventually *popped*.(p.414)

popping
• We did, and spent a month boozing it up, *popping* pills, and smoking marijuana; taking shelter where we could, which included a veterinary hospital one night; accepting meals from anyone; actually begging; stealing anything we were in need of, which was about everything.(p.354)

popular
• All of which could turn out but one thing -- a very *popular*, but spoiled, brat.(p.357)
• There was the sense of being "misunderstood," when as a matter of fact by my middle twenties I was quite *popular*, although I hadn't grown much bigger physically.(p.534)
• I know there are some alcoholics who seem terribly, terribly grown-up, but I think that they are trying to make themselves think they are grown-up, and the strain of their effort is what is causing them to drink -- a sense of inadequacy, a childish vanity to be the most *popular*, the most sought after, the mostest of the most.(p.535)
• And all this, of course, is, in the *popular* modern jargon, "compensation" for immaturity.(p.535)

porch
• I used to put eight or twelve ounce bottles of alcohol in a fur lined glove and toss it onto the back airing *porch* when winter days got dark enough.(p.176)
• That was on a hot summer evening, down in the Greenwich Village Group, and there was a little *porch* out there in the old meeting place on Sullivan Street, and after the meeting I went out on the steps for some air.(p.321)

port
• My wife became pregnant and the doctor recommended the use of *port* or ale . . . so . . . I bought a six gallon crock and a few bottles, listened to advice from amateur brewmeisters, and was off on my beer manufacturing career on a small scale (for the time being).(p.297)

portion
• Therefore, the first *portion* of this volume, describing the A.A. recovery program, has been left untouched in the course of revisions made for both the second and the third editions.(p.xi)

portrayed
• Seated at the typewriter, I faked deep thinking or *portrayed* creativity by key-tapping.(p.332)

pose
• As self-conscious as I was, I had to *pose* for those pictures, holding this huge bouquet.(p.385)

posed
• All but one "responded to the treatment" suggested in the Steps immediately, but this one *posed* a problem.(p.551)

position
• At the end of it, my reports to Wall street procured me a *position* there and the use of a large expense account.(p.3)
• We were in a *position* where life was becoming impossible, and if we had passed into the region from which there is no return through human aid we had but two alternatives: One was to go on to the bitter end, blotting out the consciousness of our intolerable situation as best we could; and the other, to accept spiritual help.(p.25)
• In the doctor's judgment he was utterly hopeless; he could never regain his *position* in society and he would have to place himself under lock and key or hire a bodyguard if he expected to live long.(p.26)
• Here was the threat of commitment, the loss of family and *position*, to say nothing of that intense mental and physical suffering which drinking always caused him.(p.36)
• Sometimes they hurt us, seemingly without provocation, but we invariably find that at some time in the past we have made decisions based on self which later placed us in a *position* to be hurt.(p.62)
• When we sincerely took such a *position*, all sorts of remarkable things followed.(p.63)
• We may lose our *position* or reputation or face jail, but we are willing.(p.79)
• He had commenced our way of life, had secured a *position*, and was getting his head above water.(p.79)
• We feel as though we had been placed in a *position* of neutrality -- safe and protected.(p.85)
• His friends have slipped away, his home is a near-wreck and he cannot hold a *position*.(p.110)
• Ask him what you should do if he places you in such a *position* again.(p.116)
• You may be afraid your husband will lose his *position*; you are thinking of the disgrace and hard times which will befall you and the children.(p.116)
• My downfall cost the business community unknown thousands of dollars, for it takes real money to train a man for an executive *position*.(p.137)
• I know, in my own particular case, that nothing my company could have done would have stopped me for, so long as I was able to hold my *position*, I could not possibly realize how serious

my situation was.(p.141)
• An alcoholic who has recovered, but holds a relatively unimportant job, can talk to a man with a better ***position.***(p.146)
• These juniors are often in a difficult ***position.***(p.147)
• He will be able to take a ***position*** with such a man which is eminently fair and square.(p.148)
• Then I got a very good ***position*** in Philadelphia and quickly found I would need a few fellow alcoholics around me if I was to stay sober.(p.249)
• Above all, I have gained the greatest thing accorded to any man, the love and understanding of a gracious God, who has lifted me from the alcoholic scrap-heap to a ***position*** of trust where I have been able to reap the rich rewards that come from showing a little love for others and from serving them as I can.(p.296)
• At that time, I was living out of town, so I moved back to the home town and made a connection in a responsible ***position*** with one of the larger companies in the finance business.(p.298)
• After being fired, I lined up with a new finance company that was just starting in business, and took the ***position*** of business promotion man, contacting automobile dealers.(p.300)
• "We watch the alcoholic performing in a ***position*** of responsibility and we know that because he is drinking heavily and daily he has cut his capacities by fifty per cent, and still he seems able to do a satisfactory job.(p.308)
• How can a person with a fine family, an attractive home, an excellent ***position*** and high standing in an important city become an alcoholic?(p.373)
• His parishioners are limited in number, but his friends are many, for to him race, creed, or social ***position*** makes no difference.(p.497)
• In my mind's eye, I played and replayed scenes in which I was plucked magically from the bar where I stood nursing a drink, and was instantly exalted to some ***position*** of power and prestige.(p.560)

positions

• We gave up our ***positions*** and off we roared on a motorcycle, the sidecar stuffed with tent, blankets, a change of clothes, and three huge volumes of a financial reference service.(p.2)
• ***Positions*** were always in jeopardy or gone.(p.105)
• They often jeopardize their own ***positions*** by trying to help serious drinkers who should have been fired long ago, or else given an opportunity to get well.(p.147)
• I can remember occasions when friends recommended me for ***positions*** or business opportunities that I wouldn't take because I felt that at some future date I'd get drunk and they would be hurt.(p.198)
• After holding good ***positions,*** making better than an average income for over ten years, I was in debt, had no clothes to speak of, no money, no friends, and no one any longer tolerating me but my wife.(p.301)

positive

• He has a ***positive*** genius for getting tight at exactly the wrong moment, particularly when some important decision must be made or engagement kept.(p.21)
• We are equally ***positive*** that once he takes any alcohol whatever into his system, something happens, both in the bodily and mental sense, which makes it virtually impossible for him to stop.(p.22)
• He was ***positive*** that his humiliating experience, plus the knowledge he had acquired, would keep him sober the rest of his life.(p.40)
• If you are ***positive*** he is one of this type you may feel you had better leave.(p.108)
• He is ***positive*** he can handle his liquor, that it does him no harm, that drinking is necessary in his business.(p.109)
• He admits this is true, but is ***positive*** that he will do better.(p.109)
• Showing all the courage and ingenuity that I had not used in a ***positive*** way, I covered my tracks and hid from my family so successfully that they did not find me for months.(p.401)
• For me, A.A. is a synthesis of all the philosophy I've ever read, all of the ***positive,*** good philosophy, all of it based on love.(p.542)

positively

• I checked into my hotel room and then noticed a placard tucked under the glass on the bureau stating "There will be ***positively*** NO drinking at this convention" signed by the president of the company.(p.243)

possess

• He said the alcoholic seemed to ***possess*** a native acuteness and usually excelled in his field, regardless of environmental or educational advantages.(p.308)

possessed

• As soon as we admitted the possible existence of a Creative Intelligence, a Spirit of the Universe underlying the totality of things, we began to be ***possessed*** of a new sense of power and direction, provided we took other simple steps.(p.46)
• The family may be ***possessed*** by the idea that future happiness can be based only upon forgetfulness of the past.(p.123)
• Being ***possessed*** of a spiritual experience, the alcoholic will find he has much in common with these people, though he may differ with them on many matters.(p.131)
• I have self confidence and assurance that cannot be confused with the cockiness I once ***possessed.***(p.303)
• With more physical courage than I had ***possessed,*** she had twice tried to take her life.(p.414)

possesses

• He often ***possesses*** special abilities, skills, and aptitudes, and has a promising career ahead of him.(p.21)
• What is this power that A.A. ***possesses?***(p.352)
• Anger ***possesses*** me, anger such as I have never felt before.(p.505)

possession

• Cling to the thought that, in God's hands, the dark past is the greatest ***possession*** you have – the key to life and happiness for others.(p.124)
• I read, studied, and meditated on every bit of A.A. literature in my ***possession.***(p.344)
• But to do so, I had to get all the stuff out of the house and out of my ***possession.***(p.443)

possessions

• All told, promising beginnings have been made in some 50 foreign countries and U.S. ***possessions.***(p.xv)

possessive

• She was very ***possessive*** with us children.(p.483)

possibilities

• These facts appear to be of extreme medical importance; because of the extraordinary ***possibilities*** of rapid growth inherent in this group they may mark a new epoch in the annals of alcoholism.(p.xxiii)
• In the meantime, another doctor in Evanston became convinced that the program had ***possibilities,*** and turned over a woman to us to do something about.(p.295)

possible

• There was to be the least ***possible*** organization, even in our service centers.(p.xix)
• In the course of his third treatment he acquired certain ideas concerning a ***possible*** means of recovery.(p.xxiii)
• Let him tell you about it: "I was much impressed with what you fellows said about alcoholism, and I frankly did not believe it would be ***possible*** for me to drink again.(p.40)
• As soon as we admitted the ***possible*** existence of a Creative Intelligence, a Spirit of the Universe underlying the totality of things, we began to be possessed of a new sense of power and direction, provided we took other simple steps.(p.46)
• They said God made these things ***possible,*** and we only smiled.(p.55)
• But later, alone in his room, he asked himself this question: "Is it ***possible*** that all the religious people I have known are wrong?"(p.56)
• 9.Made direct amends to such people wherever ***possible,*** except when to do so would injure them or others.(p.59)
• God makes that ***possible.***(p.62)
• When ***possible,*** avoid meeting a man through his family.(p.91)
• See your man alone, if ***possible.***(p.91)
• You will be making it ***possible*** for him to be insincere.(p.96)
• It is ***possible*** to have a full and useful life, though your husband continues to drink.(p.111)
• Whenever ***possible,*** let your husband explain.(p.115)
• It is ***possible*** to dig up past misdeeds so they become a blight, a veritable plague.(p.124)
• We find it better when ***possible,*** to stick to our own stories.(p.125)
• Drinking occasionally, and understanding your own reactions, it is ***possible*** for you to become quite sure of many things which, so far as the alcoholic is concerned, are not always so.(p.139)
• If ***possible*** express a lack of hard feeling toward him.(p.142)
• Though you are providing him with the best ***possible*** medical attention, he should understand that he must undergo a change of heart.(p.143)
• At that time I was not aware of the almost unlimited supply the government made it ***possible*** for us doctors to obtain, neither had I any knowledge of the bootlegger who soon appeared on the horizon.(p.175)
• It was really a horrible nightmare, this earning money, getting liquor, smuggling it home, getting drunk, morning jitters, taking large doses of sedatives to make it ***possible*** for me to earn more money, and so on ad nauseam.(p.177)
• 4.Because every time I do it I take out a little more insurance for myself against a ***possible*** slip.(p.181)
• I went back to law school, and doubled up on the courses because I was then approaching thirty years of age and I wanted to get through as quickly as ***possible.***(p.212)
• That was the beginning of a new life, a fuller life, a happier life than I had ever known or believed ***possible.***(p.228)
• There was a concrete program, designed to secure the greatest ***possible*** inner security for us long-time escapists.(p.229)
• My "periodics" became more frequent until I reached the point where I wanted to devote all my time to drinking, working as little as ***possible,*** and then only when the necessity of my family demanded it.(p.234)
• As I look back on that first evening I realize that I began to hope, then, for the first time; and I felt that if he could regain these things, perhaps it would be ***possible*** for me too.(p.290)
• I stayed in Akron two or three weeks on my initial trip trying to absorb as much of the program and philosophy as ***possible.***(p.291)
• Every reasonable desire was ***possible*** of attainment for me.(p.304)
• I was desperately in earnest to follow through and understand what was expected of me as a member of A.A. and to take each Step of the Twelve as rapidly as ***possible.***(p.382)
• However, a rough estimate of one alcoholic's initiation fee seemed ***possible.***(p.396)
• A.A. made it ***possible*** for me to face the consequences of my past actions.(p.420)
• I wanted to get as far away from home as ***possible.***(p.426)
• So I attended as many meetings as ***possible.***(p.516)
• It seems only fitting that when I did finally fall in love it was with an alcoholic, and for the next ten years I progressed as rapidly as is humanly ***possible*** into what I believed to be hopeless alcoholism.(p.547)
• The only way existence was ***possible*** was through rationalizing every sober moment and drinking myself into complete oblivion as often as I could.(p.547)
• The amount of will power exercised to control my drinking during working hours, diverted into a constructive channel, would have made me President, and the thing that made the will power ***possible*** was the knowledge that as soon as my day was finished I could drink myself into oblivion.(p.548)
• Because the "long form" is more explicit and of ***possible*** historic value, it is also reproduced.(p.563)
• 9. -- Each A.A. group needs the least ***possible*** organization.(p.567)

possibly

• He felt that he had done a wrong he could not ***possibly*** make right.(p.80)
• How could he ***possibly*** make a public statement exonerating his rival?(p.80)
• If he sticks to the ideas that he can still control his drinking, tell him that ***possibly*** he can – if he is not too alcoholic.(p.92)
• Go along with your husband if you ***possibly*** can.(p.117)
• At such moments we forget that alcoholism is an illness over which we could not ***possibly*** have had any power.(p.118)
• You should join in his efforts as much as you ***possibly*** can.(p.119)
• I know, in my own particular case, that nothing my company could have done would have stopped me for, so long as I was able to hold my position, I could not ***possibly*** realize how serious my situation was.(p.141)
• Everything in the world a man could ***possibly*** want, and I was driving from Akron to Cleveland, having just been to the bank and discovered that I had approximately $5,000.(p.200)
• Then I started drinking again, with ***possibly*** a little more restraint, periods a little bit longer than they had been before, but substantially the same pattern.(p.203)
• I had always been a good Catholic, ***possibly*** not so devoted as I should have been, but fairly regular in my attendance at services.(p.234)
• I remember sometime, it was ***possibly*** six months after we had been going steadily to King School, that we were coming home from a meeting and saw a car along the way, and a fellow in back drinking a bottle of beer.(p.271)

• It ran something like this: If I go around shouting from the rooftops about my alcoholism, it might very ***possibly*** prevent me from getting a good job.(p.282)
• I could not ***possibly*** be that bad.(p.289)
• Then he said I couldn't ***possibly*** move on the first of February because I couldn't stay in that place by myself.(p.388)
• Up to my early thirties, when my drinking had become a major problem, I lived in large houses, with servants and all the luxuries that I could ***possibly*** ask for.(p.401)
• How could such a man ***possibly*** be called an alcoholic?(p.433)
• Whatever the root of my unhappiness might turn out to be, I thought, it could not ***possibly*** be booze.(p.433)
• In other words, the kindest doctor in the whole world, and I had one such, couldn't help me because I always felt, "You can't know about me – you can't ***possibly*** know – you don't even drink!"(p.471)
• I think, with him it ***possibly*** was a gift – intuitive diagnosis.(p.485)
• I worked in the steel mill for ***possibly*** two months, and then I became disgusted with myself and decided to go back home.(p.492)
• She asked me if I would try to be sober if I ***possibly*** could.(p.494)
• Indeed, without their aid we couldn't ***possibly*** have gone on.(p.496)
• When I remark that I have been in jail nine times, and in an alcoholic ward twice, they think I'm kidding, or ***possibly*** dramatizing for the sake of a good yarn.(p.542)

post
• Then Jack Alexander wrote a feature article in the Saturday Evening ***Post*** and placed such a compelling picture of A.A. before the general public that alcoholics in need of help really deluged us.(p.xviii)
• Jack brought the Saturday ***Post*** with Jack Alexander's story.(p.268)
• From my ***post***, I'd go spend weekends with her.(p.318)
• I think I actually read more contempt than was really there because just a week before someone had sent him the Saturday Evening ***Post*** article on A.A., and there was some glimmer of hope in it for him.(p.391)
• I only know that it first reached me through that Saturday Evening ***Post*** article.(p.392)
• I know that when Frank came home, I said, "I want to try this thing," and he said, "There's a ***post*** office box to write to in New York."(p.392)
• The boys at the ***Post*** Office used to bring me my jugs; mail couldn't be opened for inspection at the gate.(p.426)
• Even the Jack Alexander Saturday Evening ***Post*** article hadn't been written, and there was only a tiny group of people in Washington.(p.469)
• But I can remember in ***post*** graduate days, and during interneship, that very often I'd go to a patient's bed and start a process of elimination and then, very often, I'd wind up guessing.(p.485)
• But there happened to be a liquor store between the ***post*** office and the mill, and I stopped to get that one drink.(p.493)

post-alcoholic
• But we have a baby who, if you'll pardon a little ***post-alcoholic*** sentimentality, is right out of Heaven.(p.438)

post-operative
• It was a long four or five hour operation, a large surgical procedure, and she was on her ninth or tenth ***post-operative*** day.(p.350)

post-war
• ***Post-war*** disillusionment, ever more serious alcoholism, impending mental and physical collapse, brought him to the point of self-destruction.(p.56)
• I was a product of the ***post-war*** prohibition era of the roaring '20's.(p.304)

posted
• Of course I kept her ***posted*** on how well the station was doing and wrote convincing letters of how well I was doing with the liquor problem.(p.360)

postpone
• When we became alcoholics, crushed by a self-imposed crisis we could not ***postpone*** or evade, we had to fearlessly face the proposition that either God is everything or else He is nothing.(p.53)
• But we must not use this as a mere excuse to ***postpone***.(p.75)

postponed
• If that is so, this step may be ***postponed***, only however, if we hold ourselves in complete readiness to go through with it at the first opportunity.(p.74)

postponement
• And there may be a valid reason for ***postponement*** in some cases.(p.83)

pot
• A good soldier is ne'er forgot Whether he dieth by musket Or by ***pot***."(p.1)

pot-belly
• At age forty, I developed a large lump in my ***pot-belly***, and I feared it was a tumor.(p.557)

potatoes
• In the next two years I washed more pans and peeled more ***potatoes*** than any other doughboy.(p.241)
• I would rather have stayed in jail except I didn't like bologna and cold ***potatoes*** for breakfast.(p.425)

potent
• In foreign parts many a soldier who has been abstemious at home learns to use new and ***potent*** drinks.(p.230)
• I don't mean that in any sense as a derogatory statement about psychotherapy; it's a great tool, not too ***potent***, but a great tool.(p.349)

potential
• So far, upon the total problem of several million actual and ***potential*** alcoholics in the world, we have made only a scratch.(p.xx)
• ***Potential*** alcoholic that I was, I nearly failed my law course.(p.2)
• ***Potential*** female alcoholics often turn into the real thing and are gone beyond recall in a few years.(p.33)
• We, who are familiar with the symptoms, see large numbers of ***potential*** alcoholics among young people everywhere.(p.33)
• Though you may be able to stop for a considerable period, you may yet be a ***potential*** alcoholic.(p.34)
• But the actual or ***potential*** alcoholic, with hardly an exception, will be absolutely unable to stop drinking on the basis of self-knowledge.(p.39)
• That company may harbor many actual or ***potential*** alcoholics.(p.149)
• They saw that they had become actual or ***potential*** alcoholics, even though no serious harm had yet been done.(p.315)
• Retirement rids the ***potential*** alcoholic of many shackles.(p.329)
• I had my first drink when I was fifteen and my alcoholic ***potential*** had ripened me to the point of necessary escapism.(p.353)
• Historians may one day recognize Alcoholics Anonymous to have been a great venture in social pioneering which forged a new instrument for social action; a new therapy based on the kinship of common suffering; one having a vast ***potential*** for the myriad other ills of mankind."(p.573)

Potomac
• Did not Professor Langley's flying machine go to the bottom of the ***Potomac*** River?(p.51)

potted
• It was the day before Mother's Day and I had come home plastered, carrying a big ***potted*** plant which I set down on the table and forthwith went upstairs and passed out.(p.179)

pounded
• How often have some of us begun to drink in this nonchalant way, and after the third or fourth, ***pounded*** on the bar and said to ourselves, "For God's sake, how did I ever get started again?"(p.24)
• And I remembered the creeping horror of the interminable night, in which I slept for short spells and woke up dripping with cold sweat and shaken with utter despair, to drink hastily from my bottle and mercifully pass out again, "You're mad, you're mad, you're mad!" ***pounded*** through my brain with each returning ray of consciousness, and I drowned the refrain with drink.(p.224)

pounding
• That is the way Jackie found me, lying on a cot in my skivvies, with hot and cold sweats, ***pounding*** heart and that awful itchy scratchiness all over.(p.238)

pounds
• I could eat little or nothing when drinking, and I was forty ***pounds*** under weight.(p.7)
• I put on thirty ***pounds*** of weight in about two months, looked like a pig, and was uncomfortable from shortness of breath.(p.177)
• In fact, after six months of living on food instead of on whiskey, I gained about thirty ***pounds***.(p.220)
• From a physical standpoint, I gained sixteen ***pounds*** in the first two months I was off liquor.(p.303)
• A load weighing a thousand ***pounds*** came off my back.(p.414)
• Ten days of this treatment the first time knocked me from 200 ***pounds*** to 130, and I seldom stayed out of the hole long enough to gain back my weight.(p.460)
• And we usually have some kind of grimy sweater that we think we look sexy in, even if we weigh ninety-five ***pounds*** soaking wet and are not wearing a bra.(p.479)

pour
• So it doesn't behoove me to squawk about it for, after all, nobody ever had to throw me down and ***pour*** liquor down my throat.(p.181)
• With a great deal of determination, I would throw out full pints – ***pour*** them out and smash the bottles -- firmly resolved never to take another drink of the stuff.(p.234)
• I ***pour*** out half a tumbler of grain alcohol and fill it with ginger ale.(p.499)
• I ***pour*** drinks down my throat.(p.501)

poured
• News of this got on the world wires; inquiries ***poured*** in again and many people went to the bookstores to get the book "Alcoholics Anonymous."(p.xviii)
• I ordered a whiskey and ***poured*** it into the milk.(p.36)
• The experiment went so well that I ordered another whiskey and ***poured*** it into more milk.(p.36)
• It ***poured*** over and through him with the certainty and majesty of a great tide at flood.(p.56)
• The last day of my drinking career, I drank twenty-two of them between ten and twelve a.m. and I shall never know how many more followed them until I was ***poured*** into bed that night.(p.298)
• Dad got out a jug for me and ***poured*** welcome home drinks.(p.428)
• He ***poured*** out two drinks.(p.498)

pouring
• I tried to control her drinking by ***pouring*** her whiskey down the sink before I'd leave for the night, to get drunker myself.(p.426)

powder
• I remember starting to city school, coming from a country school, and wanting so very, very much to be like the other girls and trying flour on my face for ***powder*** because I wasn't able to have any real ***powder***.(p.261)

power
• Would there be strivings for ***power*** and prestige?(p.xviii)
• They believe in themselves, and still more in the ***Power*** which pulls chronic alcoholics back from the gates of death.(p.xxv)
• In nearly all cases, their ideals must be grounded in a ***power*** greater than themselves, if they are to re-create their lives.(p.xxvi)
• One feels that something more than human ***power*** is needed to produce the essential psychic change.(p.xxvii)
• Following his physical rehabilitation, he had a talk with me in which he frankly stated he thought the treatment a waste of effort, unless I could assure him, which no one ever had, that in the future he would have the "will ***power***" to resist the impulse to drink.(p.xxix)
• I had always believed in a ***Power*** greater than myself.(p.10)
• Judging from what I had seen in Europe and since, the ***power*** of God in human affairs was negligible, the Brotherhood of Man a grim jest.(p.11)
• Had this ***power*** originated in him?(p.11)
• There had been no more ***power*** in him than there was in me at the minute; and this was none at all.(p.11)
• It was only a matter of being willing to believe in a ***Power*** greater than myself.(p.12)
• Belief in the ***power*** of God, plus enough willingness, honesty and humility to establish and maintain the new order of things, were the essential requirements.(p.13)
• We are growing in numbers and ***power***.(p.16)
• "His will ***power*** must be weak."(p.20)
• What has become of the common sense and will ***power*** that he still sometimes displays with respect to other matters?(p.22)
• In a vague way their families and friends sense that these drinkers are abnormal, but everybody hopefully awaits the day when the sufferer will rouse himself from his lethargy and assert his ***power*** of will.(p.23)
• The fact is that most alcoholics, for reasons yet obscure, have lost the ***power*** of choice in drink.(p.24)
• Our so-called will ***power*** becomes practically nonexistent.(p.24)
• Young people may be encouraged by this man's ex-

perience to think that they can stop, as he did, on their own will ***power***.(p.33)
• As we look back, we feel we had gone on drinking many years beyond the point where we could quit on our will ***power***.(p.34)
• Whether such a person can quit upon a nonspiritual basis depends upon the extent to which he has already lost the ***power*** to choose whether he will drink or not.(p.34)
• I felt I had every right to be self-confident, that it would be only a matter of exercising my will ***power*** and keeping on guard.(p.40)
• I saw that will ***power*** and self-knowledge would not help in those strange mental blank spots.(p.42)
• His defense must come from a Higher ***Power***.(p.43)
• We could wish to be moral, we could wish to be philosophically comforted, in fact, we could will these things with all our might, but the needed ***power*** wasn't there.(p.45)
• Lack of ***power***, that was our dilemma.(p.45)
• We had to find a ***power*** by which we could live and it had to be a ***Power*** greater than ourselves.(p.45)
• But where and how were we to find this ***Power***?(p.45)
• Its main object is to enable you to find a ***Power*** greater than yourself which will solve your problem.(p.45)
• We were bothered with the thought that faith and dependence upon a ***Power*** beyond ourselves was somewhat weak, even cowardly.(p.45)
• We found that as soon as we were able to lay aside prejudice and express even a willingness to believe in a ***Power*** greater than ourselves, we commenced to get results, even though it was impossible for any of us to fully define or comprehend that ***Power***, which is God.(p.46)
• As soon as we admitted the possible existence of a Creative Intelligence, a Spirit of the Universe underlying the totality of things, we began to be possessed of a new sense of ***power*** and direction, provided we took other simple steps.(p.46)
• "Do I now believe, or am I even willing to believe, that there is a ***Power*** greater than myself?"(p.47)
• The reader may still ask why he should believe in a ***Power*** greater than himself.(p.48)
• In our personal stories you will find a wide variation in the way each teller approaches and conceives of the ***Power*** which is greater than himself.(p.50)
• Every one of them has gained access to, and believes in, a ***Power*** greater than himself.(p.50)
• This ***Power*** has in each case accomplished the miraculous, the humanly impossible.(p.50)
• They flatly declare that since they have come to believe in a ***Power*** greater than themselves, to take a certain attitude toward that ***Power***, and to do certain simple things, there has been a revolutionary change in their way of living and thinking.(p.50)
• In the face of collapse and despair, in the face of the total failure of their human resources, they found that a new ***power***, peace, happiness, and sense of direction flowed into them.(p.50)
• When we saw others solve their problems by a simple reliance upon the Spirit of the Universe, we had to stop doubting the ***power*** of God.(p.52)
• It is not by chance we were given the ***power*** to reason, to examine the evidence of our senses, and to draw conclusions.(p.53)
• For faith in a ***Power*** greater than ourselves, and miraculous demonstrations of that ***power*** in human lives, are facts as old as man himself.(p.55)
• He stood in the Presence of Infinite ***Power*** and Love.(p.56)
• But there is One who has all ***power*** -- that One is God.(p.59)
• 2.Came to believe that a ***Power*** greater than ourselves could restore us to sanity.(p.59)
• 11.Sought through prayer and meditation to improve our conscious contact with God as we understood Him, praying only for knowledge of His will for us and the ***power*** to carry that out.(p.59)
• (b) That probably no human ***power*** could have relieved our alcoholism.(p.60)
• Neither could we reduce our self-centeredness much by wishing or trying on our own ***power***.(p.62)
• As we felt new ***power*** flow in, as we enjoyed peace of mind, as we discovered we could face life successfully, as we became conscious of His presence, we began to lose our fear of today, tomorrow or the hereafter.(p.63)
• Take away my difficulties, that victory over them may bear witness to those I would help of Thy ***Power***, Thy Love, and Thy Way of life.(p.63)
• In that state, the wrong-doing of others, fancied or real, had ***power*** to actually kill.(p.66)
• We can exercise our will ***power*** along this line all we wish.(p.85)
• Much has already been said about receiving strength, inspiration, and direction from Him who has all knowledge and ***power***.(p.85)
• Show him, from your own experience, how the queer mental condition surrounding that first drink prevents normal functioning of the will ***power***.(p.92)
• The main thing is that he be willing to believe in a ***Power*** greater than himself and that he live by spiritual principles.(p.93)
• Follow the dictates of a Higher ***Power*** and you will presently live in a new and wonderful world, no matter what your present circumstances!(p.100)
• What had become of their judgment, their common sense, their will ***power***?(p.107)
• Show him you have confidence in his ***power*** to stop or moderate.(p.112)
• The ***power*** of God goes deep!(p.114)
• If your husband is trying to live on a spiritual basis, he will also be doing everything in his ***power*** to avoid disagreement or contention.(p.118)
• At such moments we forget that alcoholism is an illness over which we could not possibly have had any ***power***.(p.118)
• This dream world has been replaced by a great sense of purpose, accompanied by a growing consciousness of the ***power*** of God in our lives.(p.130)
• We have recovered, and have been given the ***power*** to help others.(p.132)
• If he has your will ***power*** and guts, he will make the grade."(p.138)
• When our friend related his experience, the man agreed that no amount of will ***power*** he might muster could stop his drinking for long.(p.155)
• He has helped other men recover, and is a ***power*** in the church from which he was long absent.(p.158)
• Many of us have felt, for the first time, the Presence and ***Power*** of God within its walls.(p.162)
• You forget that you have just now tapped a source of ***power*** much greater than yourself.(p.163)
• If I could, that was wonderful, that was just fine, and they would very much appreciate a person who had that kind of ***power***, but they were looking for a man that knew he had a problem, and knew that he couldn't handle it himself and needed outside help.(p.186)
• The next question, they wanted to know was if I believed in a Higher ***Power***.(p.186)
• The next thing they wanted to know was would I be willing to go to this Higher ***Power*** and ask for help, calmly and without any reservations.(p.186)
• So, after reviewing these things and realizing what liquor had cost me, I went to this Higher ***Power*** which, to me was God, without any reservation, and admitted that I was completely powerless over alcohol, and that I was willing to do anything in the world to get rid of the problem.(p.187)
• I wasn't afraid that the program wouldn't work, but I still was doubtful whether I would be able to hang on to the program, but I did come to the conclusion that I was willing to put everything I had into it, with God's ***power***, and that I wanted to do just that.(p.189)
• Then I remember when the boys came back, that I told them, "I have gone to this Higher ***Power*** and I have told Him that I am willing to put His world first, above everything.(p.190)
• He said something about God or a Higher ***Power***, but I brushed that off – that was for the birds, not for me.(p.239)
• My brilliant agnosticism vanished, and I saw for the first time that those who really believed, or at least honestly tried to find a ***Power*** greater than themselves, were much more composed and contented than I had ever been, and they seemed to have a degree of happiness which I had never known.(p.247)
• For a long time the only Higher ***Power*** I could concede was the ***power*** of the group, but this was far more than I had ever recognized before, and it was at least a beginning.(p.248)
• He it was who convinced me, because his own conviction was so real, that a ***Power*** greater than myself could help me in the crises of life, and that the means of communicating with this ***Power*** was simple prayer.(p.279)
• The most accurate answer I can give you is this: Fear has never again ruled my life since that day in September, 1938, when I found that a ***Power*** greater than myself could not only restore me to sanity but could keep me both sober and sane.(p.285)
• But he found that there was a Higher ***Power*** which had more faith in him than he had in himself.(p.287)
• 2.Dependence and guidance from a Higher ***Power***.(p.292)
• I was without ***power*** to change the course my life had taken.(p.304)
• I had been brought up to believe in God, but I know that until I found this A.A. program, I had never found or known faith in the reality of God, the reality of His ***power*** that is now with me in everything I do.(p.341)
• What is this ***power*** that A.A. possesses?(p.352)
• This curative ***power***?(p.352)
• I haven't written anything about that part of my story, but I believe in a Greater ***Power*** which I call God and I ask for His wisdom and guidance daily.(p.366)
• In meeting me casually, I don't think my strong belief in "The Man Upstairs" shows, but I have no other explanation for the many good things that have happened to me since I have been in A.A. -- they came to me from a Greater ***Power***.(p.367)
• They meant patience, tolerance and humility, and above all the belief that a ***Power*** greater than myself could help.(p.381)
• That ***Power*** I chose to call God.(p.381)
• I also thought that I must have ***power*** over myself.(p.408)
• I told myself that I had ***power*** over this thing.(p.408)
• I did not know that I had no ***power*** over alcohol, that I, alone and unaided, could not stop; that I was on a downgrade, tearing along at full speed with all my brakes gone, and that the end would be a total smash-up, death or insanity.(p.408)
• "Knowledge is ***power***," I'd always been taught.(p.435)
• Now I had to face up to the fact that knowledge of this sort, applied to my individual case, was not ***power***.(p.435)
• And I knew that somewhere along the line I'd lost the ***power*** to stop drinking.(p.436)
• Here was – ***power***!(p.436)
• Here was ***power*** to live to the end of any given day, ***power*** to have the courage to face the next day, ***power*** to have friends, ***power*** to help people, ***power*** to be sane, ***power*** to stay sober.(p.436)
• Moreover, I am deeply convinced that so long as I continue to strive, in my bumbling way, toward the principles I first encountered in the earlier chapters of this book, this remarkable ***power*** will continue to flow through me.(p.437)
• What is this ***power***?(p.437)
• With my A.A. friends, all I can say is that it's a ***power*** greater than myself.(p.437)
• But what a difference there is between going through hell without a ***power*** greater than one's self, and with it!(p.437)
• The Higher ***Power*** was on deck to see me through, sober.(p.437)
• With their help I also saw that certainly, because of some of the things I had done during the years, I was bordering on insanity, and so, facing the record, I tried to believe that a ***Power*** greater than I could and would restore me to sanity.(p.471)
• The Higher ***Power*** to whom I had turned, and who had sustained me, had once again been thrust into the background, while my emotions were running my life and, as always, my emotions ran me to the bottle.(p.472)
• I realized that I was trying to pin everything on an individual – not the book or the group or the Higher ***Power***, or anything else.(p.472)
• I have come to believe that my illness is spiritual as well as physical and mental, and I know that for help in the spiritual sphere I have to turn to a Higher ***Power***.(p.473)
• What a wonderful ***power*** he has over the mind!(p.499)
• Then he asks me if I believe in a ***power*** greater than myself, whether I call that ***power*** God, Allah, Confucius, Prime Cause, Divine Mind, or any other name.(p.503)
• I'm grateful because that Higher ***Power*** led me to A.A. a little over three years ago, when I needed it very badly.(p.512)
• It's like the fellow who came in A.A., and his sponsor said to him, "Listen, buddy, do you believe in a Higher ***Power***?"(p.512)
• I stayed there just long enough to work up a real good resentment against the doctor in charge, who I didn't think was doing anything at all except collecting fees, and I left there fully determined that I'd never put myself in the ***power*** of medical people again.(p.521)
• Today, I thank my Higher ***Power*** for giving me another chance at life and A.A. and being able to try and help some other alcoholic.(p.529)
• I choose to believe that the ***Power*** greater than ourselves we ask for help, wrapped my shivering body in loving warmth and strength which has never left me.(p.541)

• I have had the joy of seeing many a human being, down and out, learn to stand straight again, and to proceed under his own *power* to happiness in life.(p.541)
• I hope I have been able to impart to you, the reader, at least a bit of what I know; the joy of living, the irresistible *power* of divine love and its healing strength, and the fact that we, as sentient beings, have the knowledge to choose between good and evil, and, choosing good, are made happy.(p.543)
• The amount of will *power* exercised to control my drinking during working hours, diverted into a constructive channel, would have made me President, and the thing that made the will *power* possible was the knowledge that as soon as my day was finished I could drink myself into oblivion.(p.548)
• In my mind's eye, I played and replayed scenes in which I was plucked magically from the bar where I stood nursing a drink, and was instantly exalted to some position of *power* and prestige.(p.560)
• With few exceptions our members find that they have tapped an unsuspected inner resource which they presently identify with their own conception of a *Power* greater than themselves.(p.569)
• Most of us think this awareness of a *Power* greater than ourselves is the essence of spiritual experience.(p.570)
• Dr. Foster Kennedy, neurologist: "This organization of Alcoholics Anonymous calls on two of the greatest reservoirs of *power* known to man, religion and that instinct for association with one's fellows . . . the 'herd instinct.'(p.571)
• Learning to depend upon a higher *power* and absorb himself in his work with other alcoholics, he remains sober day by day.(p.572)

powerful

• The feeling of having shared in a common peril is one element in the *powerful* cement which binds us.(p.17)
• At a certain point in the drinking of every alcoholic, he passes into a state where the most *powerful* desire to stop drinking is of absolutely no avail.(p.24)
• What seemed at first a flimsy reed, has proved to be the loving and *powerful* hand of God.(p.28)
• This case contains a *powerful* lesson.(p.33)
• When, however, the perfectly logical assumption is suggested that underneath the material world and life as we see it, there is an All *Powerful*, Guiding, Creative Intelligence, right there our perverse streak comes to the surface and we laboriously set out to convince ourselves it isn't so.(p.49)
• When many hundreds of people are able to say that the consciousness of the Presence of God is today the most important fact of their lives, they present a *powerful* reason why one should have faith.(p.51)
• Remember that we deal with alcohol – cunning, baffling, *powerful*!(p.58)
• Being all *powerful*, He provided what we needed, if we kept close to Him and performed His work well.(p.63)
• Yet often such men had spectacular and *powerful* recoveries.(p.113)
• We have found nothing incompatible between a *powerful* spiritual experience and a life of sane and happy usefulness.(p.130)
• We are convinced that a spiritual mode of living is a most *powerful* health restorative.(p.133)
• They had visioned the Great Reality – their loving and All *Powerful* Creator.(p.161)
• Cunning, baffling, *powerful* – the gradual creeping up of the frequency and quantity of alcohol, and what it does to a person is apparent to everyone but the person involved.(p.375)
• I knew my wife didn't because I had been sincere in all my promises to her as well as to my mother and to my close friends, but the urge to take that drink was more *powerful* than anything else.(p.494)

powerless

• 1.We admitted we were *powerless* over alcohol -- that our lives had become unmanageable.(p.59)
• So, after reviewing these things and realizing what liquor had cost me, I went to this Higher Power which, to me was God, without any reservation, and admitted that I was completely *powerless* over alcohol, and that I was willing to do anything in the world to get rid of the problem.(p.187)
• Here he is *powerless*, unmanageable, in the grip of something bigger than he is, and he's got to turn the whole business over to someone else!(p.350)
• "We admitted we were *powerless* over alcohol -- that our lives had become unmanageable."(p.379)
• It did say, "admitted I was *powerless* over alcohol; that my life had become unmanageable."(p.379)
• Most certainly I was *powerless* over alcohol, and for me, my life had become unmanageable.(p.379)
• I can't say, "I'm *powerless* over alcohol, but solid alcohol is okay."(p.443)
• Eventually, I had to redo each of the Twelve Steps specifically with Max in mind, from the First, saying, "I am *powerless* over alcohol, and my homelife is unmanageable by me," to the Twelfth, in which I tried to think of her as a sick Al-Anon and treat her with the love I would give a sick A.A. newcomer.(p.452)
• I had no problem admitting I was *powerless* over alcohol, and I certainly agreed that my life had become unmanageable.(p.550)

powers

• What with our ultra-modern standards, our scientific approach to everything, we are perhaps not well equipped to apply the *powers* of good that lie outside our synthetic knowledge.(p.xxv)
• We remembered always that our sex *powers* were God-given and therefore good, neither to be used lightly or selfishly nor to be despised and loathed.(p.69)
• This was such a new thought that I got all sorts of books on Higher *Powers*, and I put a Bible by my bedside, and I put a Bible in my car.(p.348)

practical

• Many years ago one of the leading contributors to this book came under our care in this hospital and while here he acquired some ideas which he put into *practical* application at once.(p.xxv)
• They had told of a simple religious idea and a *practical* program of action.(p.9)
• The *practical* individual of today is a stickler for facts and results.(p.48)
• *Practical* experience shows that nothing will so much insure immunity from drinking as intensive work with other alcoholics.(p.89)
• Having had the experience yourself, you can give him much *practical* advice.(p.96)
• Nothing will help the man who is off on a spiritual tangent so much as the wife who adopts a sane spiritual program, making a better *practical* use of it.(p.130)
• The *practical* answer is that since these things have happened among us, they can happen with you.(p.153)
• The very *practical* approach to his problems, the absence of intolerance of any kind, the informality, the genuine democracy, the uncanny understanding which these people had were irresistible.(p.160)

practically

• This tragic situation has already arrived in *practically* every case long before it is suspected.(p.24)
• Our so-called will power becomes *practically* non-existent.(p.24)
• Then he fell victim to a belief which *practically* every alcoholic has – that his long period of sobriety and self-discipline had qualified him to drink as other men.(p.32)
• He may not share your enthusiasm, but he is *practically* sure to read the book and he may go for the program at once.(p.113)
• Of course, by this time, my business was *practically* non-existent.(p.190)
• I was born in Europe, in Alsace to be exact, shortly after it had become German, and *practically* grew up with the "good Rhine wine" of song and story.(p.230)
• I came directly to a growing industrial city in the middle west, where I have lived *practically* ever since.(p.231)
• His own business was *practically* gone, he told me, when he discovered the answer.(p.236)
• "I'm doing a job I like and it's quiet where I live, *practically* no temptations.(p.257)
• When he returned, we had *practically* daily meetings from that time on.(p.294)
• About that time I had lost *practically* all my property except the place we were living in.(p.487)
• Clergymen of *practically* every denomination have given A.A. their blessing.(p.574)

practice

• 12.Having had a spiritual awakening as the result of these steps, we tried to carry this message to alcoholics, and to *practice* these principles in all our affairs.(p.60)
• In actual *practice*, we usually find a solitary self-appraisal insufficient.(p.72)
• Perhaps your story will help him see where he has failed to *practice* the very precepts he knows so well.(p.93)
• Should they accept and *practice* spiritual principles, there is a much better chance that the head of the family will recover.(p.97)
• Many of us have noticed a tendency to eat sweets and have found this *practice* beneficial.(p.134)
• This *practice* enables us to lend a hand, at the same time avoiding certain alluring distractions of the road, about which any traveling man can inform you.(p.162)
• I stayed about town a couple of months more and then returned to resume my *practice*.(p.175)
• My *practice* had advanced to the point where it could stand a lot of abuse and it got it.(p.214)
• They suffered from my conduct without saying anything, but the reason for this was I still managed to hang onto a very substantial *practice*.(p.215)
• In fact, as I look back, I have often thought that they probably concluded that they would put up with me for a couple of years, that I couldn't live much longer, and that they would inherit whatever was left of the *practice*.(p.215)
• I still had enough *practice* to earn a good living if I would only work, so I resolved that in January of 1940 I would launch a patent law firm of my own.(p.220)
• The feeling of impending disaster that had haunted me for years began to dissolve as I put into *practice* more and more of the Twelve Steps.(p.229)
• He went on talking and told me that he had found the plan has a basis of love, and the *practice* of Christ's injunction, "Love thy neighbor as thyself."(p.236)
• And I began putting into *practice* what I was learning every day.(p.237)
• He was happy, getting a kick out of life and people, and beginning to get his medical *practice* back again.(p.290)
• In learning to *practice* these steps in my daily living I began to acquire faith and a philosophy to live by.(p.311)
• I am a physician, licensed to *practice* in a western state.(p.345)
• (I belong to the American Psychiatric Society, but I don't *practice* psychiatry as such.(p.347)
• I couldn't *practice* medicine without the Great Physician.(p.351)
• I had just begun a dental *practice* in a beautiful new office.(p.418)
• In less than two years, I lost my *practice*, my home, my wife, and my children.(p.418)
• When I went back to my hometown to go into private *practice*, I experienced another brief lull in my addiction to alcohol and drugs.(p.420)
• After I came to A.A., I was divorced by my wife; I lost my *practice*; I was legally restrained from seeing my children; I went broke; and the dental society threatened me with the loss of my license.(p.420)
• A.A. has given me a new wife, a beautiful stepdaughter, a new *practice*, a new home, and a new relationship with my four children.(p.420)
• And as I went through pharmacy school, graduate school, medical school, internship, residency, and specialty training and, finally, went into *practice*, my drinking kept increasing.(p.441)
• For the leveling-off process, I just loved intravenous Demerol, but I found it hard to *practice* good medicine while shooting morphine.(p.442)
• Had I tried honestly and sincerely to *practice* the Twelve Steps I would have seen from my continuous moral inventory that I was getting off the beam -- I would have found that there were some active resentments in my life, a terrific amount of self-pity.(p.471)
• We are told to *practice* the Twelve Steps and Twelve Traditions to the best of our ability every day, one day at a time.(p.481)
• I had my own medical *practice* in Washington at that time, but the *practice* slackened and the mail order business started to fall off.(p.486)
• My *practice* at that juncture was just barely getting us a living.(p.488)
• I worked for the Government about a year and still maintained my evening office *practice* when the Government agencies were decentralized.(p.489)
• When sleep overtook me, my *practice* was to undress and go to bed, wherever.(p.537)
• I believe this, and I believe too that it is equally impossible to *practice* these principles to the best of our ability, a day at a time, and still drink, for I don't think the two things are compatible.(p.550)
• It reminds us that we are to place principles before personalities; that we are actually to *practice* a genuine humility.(p.568)

practiced

• The same principles which apply to husband number one should be *practiced*.(p.112)
• My doctor finally declared he could no longer be responsible for me, and sent me to a psychiatrist who *practiced* in the same suite of offices.(p.558)

practices

• We used to amuse ourselves by cynically dissecting spiritual beliefs and *practices* when we might have observed that many spiritually-minded persons of all races, colors, and creeds were demonstrating a degree of stability, happiness and usefulness which we should have sought ourselves.(p.49)

practicing

• They can hardly fail to approve these simple principles, though the head of the house still fails somewhat in ***practicing*** them.(p.130)

• When I started to tell the boys how we did it in New York and all about the spiritual part of the program, I found they would not believe me unless I was ***practicing*** what I preached.(p.249)

• There are many things worse than dying, but is there any death worse than the progressive, self-induced, slow suicide of the ***practicing*** alcoholic?(p.457)

• It was here that I realized for the first time that as a ***practicing*** alcoholic I had no rights.(p.549)

• By learning – through ***practicing*** the Twelve Steps and through sharing at meetings – how to cope with the problems that we looked to booze to solve, back in our drinking days.(p.560)

practised

• She tried reasoning with me, endeavored to work out various drinking schedules, in fact all the tricks were ***practised*** faithfully for a short time somewhere along my shaky road to unhappiness.(p.361)

practitioner

• Under the skilled guidance of an expert ***practitioner*** I wallowed in the world's individual and collective mental agony.(p.434)

practitioners

• God has abundantly supplied this world with fine doctors, psychologists, and ***practitioners*** of various kinds.(p.133)

prairie

• Need I say that in a very short time I was walking along a ***prairie*** highway with arm extended and thumb pointed?(p.255)

praise

• Our former enemies sometimes ***praise*** what we are doing and wish us well.(p.78)

• Let them ***praise*** his progress.(p.127)

• Far from expecting ***praise*** for their deeds, they claimed the performance a privilege and insisted that they invariably received more than they gave.(p.310)

• There is never need to ***praise*** ourselves.(p.567)

praised

• During this time, I had been threatened, beaten, kissed, ***praised*** and damned alternately by relatives, family, friends and strangers, but of course it all went for naught.(p.300)

pray

• I earnestly advise every alcoholic to read this book through, and though perhaps he came to scoff, he may remain to ***pray***.(p.xxx)

• Never was I to ***pray*** for myself, except as my requests bore on my usefulness to others.(p.13)

• To sum up about sex: We earnestly ***pray*** for the right ideal, for guidance in each questionable situation, for sanity, and for the strength to do the right thing.(p.70)

• I ***pray*** that you now remove from me every single defect of character which stands in the way of my usefulness to you and my fellows.(p.76)

• Each might ***pray*** about it, having the other one's happiness uppermost in mind.(p.82)

• We are careful never to ***pray*** for our own selfish ends.(p.87)

• He then pulled up his chair with one of his knees touching mine and said, "Will you ***pray*** with me for your success?"(p.218)

• So I began to ***pray***; to place my problems in God's hands.(p.237)

• I try to ***pray***.(p.506)

• I learned to ***pray*** honestly.(p.516)

• I ask the forgiveness of the reader; and from now on I shall try to write with the humility I honestly ***pray*** for.)(p.536)

• He said, in effect: "If you have a resentment you want to be free of, if you will ***pray*** for the person or the thing that you resent, you will be free.(p.552)

prayed

• We have ***prayed***, we have begged, we have been patient.(p.105)

• I've ***prayed*** to God on hangover mornings and sworn that I'd never touch another drop but by nine o'clock I'd be boiled as an owl."(p.158)

• It was not known to me as a group, but I later learned that my wife had known about it for nine months and had ***prayed*** constantly that I would stumble into Akron some way or another.(p.215)

• For the last two years of my drinking I ***prayed*** on every drunk that I wouldn't wake up again.(p.245)

• When I said yes, we both knelt at his desk and ***prayed***, each of us asking to have these defects taken away.(p.292)

• Sometimes I would lie on the bathroom floor, deathly sick, praying I would die, and praying to God as I always had ***prayed*** to Him when I was drinking: "Dear God, get me out of this one and I'll never do it again."(p.324)

• After my very first drink – a tiny glass of sherry my father gave me to celebrate the New Year when I was thirteen -- I went up to bed, dizzy with exhilaration and excitement, and I ***prayed*** I wouldn't drink any more!(p.554)

prayer

• 11.Sought through ***prayer*** and meditation to improve our conscious contact with God as we understood Him, praying only for knowledge of His will for us and the power to carry that out.(p.59)

• Step Eleven suggests ***prayer*** and meditation.(p.85)

• We shouldn't be shy on this matter of ***prayer***.(p.85)

• We usually conclude the period of meditation with a ***prayer*** that we be shown all through the day what our next step is to be, that we be given whatever we need to take care of such problems.(p.87)

• From childhood through high school I was more or less forced to go to church, Sunday School and evening service, Monday night Christian Endeavor and sometimes to Wednesday evening ***prayer*** meeting.(p.172)

• And I then and there said a ***prayer***, if you please.(p.200)

• And he then said a beautiful ***prayer***.(p.219)

• Much later I discovered the elders held many ***prayer*** meetings hoping to find a way to give me the heave-ho, but at the same time stay tolerant and spiritual.(p.247)

• I'd hear them on the phone having ***prayer*** meetings and so forth, that sort of talk over the phone, and it completely burnt me up.(p.265)

• They opened with a little ***prayer***, and I thought it was very fine that we stood, all of us together, and closed with the Lord's ***Prayer***.(p.270)

• When we closed the meeting with the Lord's ***Prayer***, Russ said, "Mother, help me stand."(p.270)

• Dr. Bob dwelt at length on how ***prayer*** had given him release, time and time again, from the nearly over-powering compulsion to take a drink.(p.279)

• He it was who convinced me, because his own conviction was so real, that a Power greater than myself could help me in the crises of life, and that the means of communicating with this Power was simple ***prayer***.(p.279)

• Here was a tall, rugged, highly educated Yankee talking in a matter of course way about God and ***prayer***.(p.279)

• Finally, and I shall never know how much later it was, one clear thought came to me: Try ***prayer***.(p.280)

• The ***prayer*** I said was simple.(p.280)

• The meeting lasted an hour and closed with the Lord's ***Prayer***.(p.291)

• A "spiritual experience" to me meant attending meetings, seeing a group of people, all there for the purpose of helping each other; hearing the Twelve Steps and the Twelve Traditions read at a meeting, and hearing the Lord's ***Prayer***, which in an A.A. meeting has such great meaning – "Thy will be done, not mine."(p.381)

• Then, one day in A.A., I was told that I had the lenses in my glasses backwards; "the courage to change" in the Serenity ***Prayer*** meant, not that I should change my marriage, but rather that I should change myself and learn to accept my spouse as she was.(p.451)

• It was the Serenity ***Prayer***!(p.461)

• Yes, I knew what the Serenity ***Prayer*** was -- A.A. had taught me.(p.461)

• During the twenty-four hours after running into the Serenity ***Prayer***, I think I took the first three Steps for the first time.(p.461)

• "How does ***prayer*** fit into this thing?"(p.504)

• If you will ask in ***prayer*** for everything you want for yourself to be given to them, you will be free.(p.552)

prayers

• If not members of religious bodies, we sometimes select and memorize a few set ***prayers*** which emphasize the principles we have been discussing.(p.87)

• Where preaching and ***prayers*** had touched me very little, I immediately desired further knowledge of these men.(p.235)

• In my ***prayers*** that morning I asked God to point out to me some way to be free of this resentment.(p.552)

• Even when you don't really want it for them, and your ***prayers*** are only words and you don't mean it, go ahead and do it anyway.(p.552)

praying

• 11.Sought through prayer and meditation to improve our conscious contact with God as we understood Him, ***praying*** only for knowledge of His will for us and the power to carry that out.(p.59)

• Sometimes I would lie on the bathroom floor, deathly sick, ***praying*** I would die, and ***praying*** to God as I always had prayed to Him when I was drinking: "Dear God, get me out of this one and I'll never do it again."(p.324)

• "Well," he answers, "You've probably tried ***praying*** like I have.(p.504)

preached

• When I started to tell the boys how we did it in New York and all about the spiritual part of the program, I found they would not believe me unless I was practicing what I ***preached***.(p.249)

preacher

• He didn't talk like a ***preacher*** at all.(p.235)

preacher's

• I could almost hear the sound of the ***preacher's*** voice as I sat, on still Sundays, way over there on the hillside; there was that proffered temperance pledge I never signed; my grandfather's good natured contempt of some church folk and their doings; his insistence that the spheres really had their music; but his denial of the ***preacher's*** right to tell him how he must listen; his fearlessness as he spoke of these things just before he died; these recollections welled up from the past.(p.10)

preachers

• I have stood listening to street-corner ***preachers*** tell how they beat the game.(p.256)

preaching

• Besides, my gin would last longer than his ***preaching***.(p.9)

• Where ***preaching*** and prayers had touched me very little, I immediately desired further knowledge of these men.(p.235)

precarious

• Back to the big city, for another year of ***precarious*** living, paid for largely by one or two friends I still had not milked dry or worn to exhaustion with demands on their bounty.(p.540)

precede

• So we shall describe some of the mental states that ***precede*** a relapse into drinking, for obviously this is the crux of the problem.(p.35)

preceded

• For us, material well-being always followed spiritual progress; it never ***preceded***.(p.127)

• I was warmly welcomed by friends of my youth who had ***preceded*** me.(p.231)

precedence

• Nothing in their lives took ***precedence*** over their response to a call for help from some alcoholic in need.(p.310)

precedes

• I rather appreciated your ideas about the subtle insanity which ***precedes*** the first drink, but I was confident it could not happen to me after what I had learned.(p.40)

preceding

• In the ***preceding*** chapters you have learned something of alcoholism.(p.44)

• This brings us to the Fifth Step in the program of recovery mentioned in the ***preceding*** chapter.(p.72)

• There was much talk about the mental state ***preceding*** the first drink.(p.157)

• But I remembered the years of agony ***preceding*** the binge, I remembered the years I had thrown away.(p.540)

precepts

• Perhaps your story will help him see where he has failed to practice the very ***precepts*** he knows so well.(p.93)

precipitated

• A big event of any kind ***precipitated*** heavy drinking.(p.197)

precipitates

• This immediately ***precipitates*** us into a seething caldron of debate.(p.xxviii)

precise

• How could there be so much of ***precise*** and immutable law and no intelligence?(p.10)

• Whatever the ***precise*** definition of the word may be, we call this plain insanity.(p.37)

• These tiny bodies are governed by ***precise*** laws, and these laws hold true throughout the material world.(p.49)

• To the ***precise*** extent that we permit these, do we squander the hours that might have been worth while.(p.66)

precisely

• To show other alcoholics ***precisely*** how we have recovered is the main purpose of this book.(p.xiii)

• It was ***precisely*** a year before I spoke at an A.A. meeting.(p.447)

predicament

• Explain that many are doomed who never realize their ***predicament.***(p.92)

• Still physically weak, and sober but a few months, he saw that his ***predicament*** was dangerous.(p.154)

predicaments

• Our loyalty and the desire that our husbands hold up their heads and be like other men have begotten all sorts of ***predicaments.***(p.105)

predicted

• As might have been ***predicted,*** my teetering tower of worldly success collapsed.(p.437)

predisposed

• When I look back, I can't see anything that would have ***predisposed*** me towards being either a neurotic or a drunk.(p.517)

predominant

• My whole life seemed to be centered around doing what I wanted to do, without regard for the rights, wishes, or privileges of anyone else; a state of mind which became more and more ***predominant*** as the years passed.(p.172)

preface

• ***PREFACE***(p.xi)

prefer

• A new life has been given us or, if you ***prefer,*** "a design for living" that really works.(p.28)

• Before too long, my husband (who seemed to ***prefer*** his shirts dirty) put his foot down, declaring that our family might have the cleanest clothes in town, but that I hadn't been out of the same old dirty slacks and blouse for a week.(p.371)

preferable

• He will be less likely to drink again, and anything is ***preferable*** to that.(p.130)

preferably

• I began making the rounds of the doctors in the hope that one of them might find some cure for my accumulating ailments, ***preferably*** something that could be removed surgically.(p.305)

preferred

• This career girl ***preferred*** solitary drinking, the black-out kind, often hoping she'd stay that way for keeps.(p.464)

• For clubs, A.A. managers are usually ***preferred.***(p.566)

prefers

• If he thinks he can do the job in some other way, or ***prefers*** some other spiritual approach, encourage him to follow his own conscience.(p.95)

• Let him know you are available if he wishes to make a decision and tell his story, but do not insist upon it if he ***prefers*** to consult someone else.(p.96)

pregnant

• My wife became ***pregnant*** and the doctor recommended the use of port or ale . . . so . . . I bought a six gallon crock and a few bottles, listened to advice from amateur brewmeisters, and was off on my beer manufacturing career on a small scale (for the time being).(p.297)

prejudice

• Despite the living example of my friend there remained in me the vestiges of my old ***prejudice.***(p.12)

• Scales of pride and ***prejudice*** fell from my eyes.(p.12)

• We have shared his honest doubt and ***prejudice.***(p.45)

• We found that as soon as we were able to lay aside ***prejudice*** and express even a willingness to believe in a Power greater than ourselves, we commenced to get results, even though it was impossible for any of us to fully define or comprehend that Power, which is God.(p.46)

• Do not let any ***prejudice*** you may have against spiritual terms deter you from honestly asking yourself what they mean to you.(p.47)

• Besides a seeming inability to accept much on faith, we often found ourselves handicapped by obstinacy, sensitiveness, and unreasoning ***prejudice.***(p.47)

• We, who have traveled this dubious path, beg you to lay aside ***prejudice,*** even against organized religion.(p.49)

• If our testimony helps sweep away ***prejudice,*** enables you to think honestly, encourages you to search diligently within yourself, then, if you wish, you can join us on the Broad Highway.(p.55)

• We might ***prejudice*** them.(p.77)

• Unfortunately a lot of ***prejudice*** exists.(p.89)

• There is no use arousing any ***prejudice*** he may have against certain theological terms and conceptions about which he may already be confused.(p.93)

• We are greatly indebted to the doctor in attendance there, for he, although it might ***prejudice*** his own work, has told us of his belief in ours.(p.162)

• Dishonest thinking, ***prejudice,*** ego, antagonism toward anyone and everyone who dares to cross him, vanity and a critical attitude are character defects that gradually creep in and become a part of his life.(p.380)

• The fact that A.A. is a spiritual program didn't scare me or raise any ***prejudice*** in my mind.(p.383)

• I couldn't afford the luxury of ***prejudice.***(p.383)

prejudiced

• Sometimes this was a tedious process; we hope no one else will be ***prejudiced*** for as long as some of us were.(p.48)

prejudices

• I forgot the strong warnings and the ***prejudices*** of my people concerning drink.(p.1)

• Whether you are a hard drinker, a moderated drinker or a teetotaler, you may have some pretty strong opinions, perhaps ***prejudices.***(p.139)

premature

• We heard by wireless on the 5th that the Armistice would be signed the next day (this was a ***premature*** report) so I had a couple of cognacs to celebrate; then I hopped a truck and went AWOL.(p.242)

premeditated

• It is ***premeditated.***(p.506)

premeditation

• We now see that when we began to drink deliberately, instead of casually, there was little serious or effective thought during the period of ***premeditation*** of what the terrific consequences might be.(p.37)

preoccupied

• Dad may be tired at night and ***preoccupied*** by day.(p.126)

prepared

• We were ***prepared*** to look at it from an entirely different angle.(p.66)

• We have a written inventory and we are ***prepared*** for a long talk.(p.75)

• He has read this volume and says he is ***prepared*** to go through with the Twelve Steps of the program of recovery.(p.96)

• Many mornings I have gone to classes, and even though fully ***prepared,*** would turn and walk back to the fraternity house because of my jitters, not daring to enter the classroom for fear of making a scene should I be called on for recitation.(p.173)

• In fact, I never lost my faith, since I had been ***prepared*** by some conversations toward the end of my sojourn in the hospital with Dr. Bob, conversations pretty much along spiritual lines.(p.218)

• The American Psychiatric Association requested, in 1949, that a paper be ***prepared*** by one of the older members of Alcoholics Anonymous to be read at the Association's annual meeting of that year.(p.572)

preparing

• A night or so a week in a joint, and a party or so a week at home or with friends, along with a little lone drinking, soon had me ***preparing*** for the existence of a top flight drunkard.(p.298)

• Dr. Harry M. Tiebout, psychiatrist: "As a psychiatrist, I have thought a great deal about the relationship of my specialty to A.A. and I have come to the conclusion that our particular function can very often lie in ***preparing*** the way for the patient to accept any sort of treatment or outside help.(p.571)

preposterous

• Some of the contemporaries of Columbus thought a round earth ***preposterous.***(p.51)

prescribed

• Then he had gone to Europe, placing himself in the care of a celebrated physician (the psychiatrist, Dr. Jung) who ***prescribed*** for him.(p.26)

• Most of them ***prescribed*** sedatives and advised rest and moderation.(p.305)

• The doctor ***prescribed*** brandy for the boy to help him through the night when he coughed, a teaspoon of brandy.(p.338)

• The physician wasn't hooked, he thought -- he just ***prescribed*** drugs medically indicated for his many ailments.(p.439)

• The doctor, apparently realizing that one thing that I certainly needed was sleep, left a bottle of sleeping pills there and in my drunken state I took them all, instead of the one or two he had ***prescribed.***(p.465)

prescribing

• After ***prescribing*** medicines, Dr. Bob ordered, "Put him in a private room.(p.188)

prescription

• But how does one get a ***prescription*** for a miracle?(p.306)

• I filled a ***prescription*** for him.(p.488)

• The following day, Saturday, he came back and said, "Jim, I owe you for that ***prescription*** last night.(p.488)

• I thought, "I know you didn't pay me, because you didn't get a ***prescription.***"(p.488)

• You know the ***prescription*** that you gave me for my wife last night."(p.488)

• The next morning I carried another ***prescription*** to this man's house and exchanged it for the bottle his wife had.(p.489)

presence

• But soon the sense of His ***presence*** had been blotted out by worldly clamors, mostly those within myself.(p.12)

• When many hundreds of people are able to say that the consciousness of the ***Presence*** of God is today the most important fact of their lives, they present a powerful reason why one should have faith.(p.51)

• In a few seconds he was overwhelmed by a conviction of the ***Presence*** of God.(p.56)

• He stood in the ***Presence*** of Infinite Power and Love.(p.56)

• As we felt new power flow in, as we enjoyed peace of mind, as we discovered we could face life successfully, as we became conscious of His ***presence,*** we began to lose our fear of today, tomorrow or the hereafter.(p.63)

• Many of us have felt, for the first time, the ***Presence*** and Power of God within its walls.(p.162)

• But they were much disgusted and told me they would attempt to struggle along without my ***presence.***(p.173)

• I have already done it, and I am willing to do it again here in the ***presence*** of you or I am willing to say it any place, anywhere in the world from now on and not be ashamed of it."(p.190)

• He mentioned lies and deceptions in the course of his story in the ***presence*** of the one person in the world I wouldn't want to know such things.(p.302)

• I left this home town, then, after I had made a public spectacle of myself in the ***presence*** of a revered teacher whose favorite pupil I had been.(p.539)

present

• It is important that we remain anonymous because we are too few, at ***present*** to handle the overwhelming number of personal appeals which may result from this publication.(p.xiii)

• At ***present,*** our membership is increasing at the rate of about seven per cent a year.(p.xx)

• As part of his rehabilitation he commenced to ***present*** his conceptions to other alcoholics, impressing upon them that they must do likewise with still others.(p.xxiii)

• How then shall we ***present*** that which has been so freely given us?(p.19)

• This should be an entirely personal affair which each one decides for himself in the light of past associations, or his ***present*** choice.(p.28)

• That may be true of certain nonalcoholic people who, though drinking foolishly and heavily at the ***present*** time, are able to stop or moderate, because their brains and bodies have not been damaged as ours were.(p.39)

• One day I went to Washington to ***present*** some accounting evidence to a government bureau.(p.40)

• When many hundreds of people are able to say that the consciousness of the Presence of God is today the most important fact of their lives, they ***present*** a powerful reason why one should have faith.(p.51)

• Even in the ***present*** century, American newspapers were afraid to print an account of the Wright brothers' first successful flight at Kitty Hawk.(p.51)

• Hence we are at pains to tell why we think our ***present*** faith is reasonable, why we think it more sane and logical to believe than not to believe, why we say our former thinking was soft and mushy when we threw up our hands in doubt and said, "We don't know."(p.53)

• Follow the dictates of a Higher Power and you will presently live in a new and wonderful world, no matter what your ***present*** circumstances!(p.100)

• In some cases it may be better to let someone outside of the family *present* the book.(p.113)
• His *present* views ought to prove exceptionally useful to business men everywhere.(p.136)
• Seeing much of each other, scarce an evening passed that someone's home did not shelter a little gathering of men and women, happy in their release, and constantly thinking how they might *present* their discovery to some newcomer.(p.159)
• From surrounding towns, families drive long distances to be *present*.(p.161)
• I remember telling them too that it was going to be awfully tough, because I did some other things, smoked cigarettes and played penny ante poker, sometimes bet on the horse races and they said, "Don't you think you're having more trouble with this drinking than with anything else at the *present* time?(p.190)
• It was hard to reconcile this ghastly *present* with the simple facts of the past.(p.225)
• I was greeted warmly, honestly, and with a true ring of sincerity by everyone *present*.(p.259)
• There were five people *present*, including myself.(p.347)
• I wore a man's raincoat, turned inside out, a *present* from a friend, for now my funds were low.(p.411)
• I'd gladly do it anonymously, as I have done this brief account of my struggle with alcohol -- merely to *present* certain ideas for the consideration of the reader.(p.542)
• Through my efforts to get down to "causes and conditions," I stand convinced that my emotional illness has been *present* from my earliest recollection.(p.544)
• We cast off the burdens of the past and the anxieties of the future, as we begin to live in the *present*, one day at a time.(p.560)
• Following are excerpts from the comments of doctors *present* at the annual meeting of the Medical Society of the State of New York where a paper on A.A. was read:(p.571)

presentation
• Sixteen years have elapsed between our first printing of this book and the *presentation* in 1955 of our second edition.(p.xv)
• When I was faced with a special challenge or social event -- such as an important business *presentation* or a dinner party -- I had to fortify myself with a couple of belts.(p.556)

presented
• The subject *presented* in this book seems to me to be of paramount importance to those afflicted with alcoholic addiction.(p.xxv)
• We doctors have realized for a long time that some form of moral psychology was of urgent importance to alcoholics, but its application *presented* difficulties beyond our conception.(p.xxv)
• When people *presented* us with spiritual approaches, how frequently did we all say, "I wish I had what that man has.(p.47)
• Had they fired me first, and had they then taken steps to see that I was *presented* with the solution contained in this book, I might have returned to them six months later, a well man.(p.141)
• When the man is *presented* with this volume it is best that no one tell him he must abide by its suggestions.(p.144)
• Plenty of difficulties *presented* themselves.(p.156)
• Beginning with the story of "Dr. Bob," a co-founder of A.A., there are here *presented* three groups of personal histories.(p.165)
• (I am looking at it now in my bedroom -- a copy that was *presented* to me a couple of years ago by the A.A. group in that same prison.)(p.461)

presently
• Yet it is our great hope that all those who have as yet found no answer may begin to find one in the pages of this book and will *presently* join us on the highroad to a new freedom.(p.xxi)
• The delusion that we are like other people, or *presently* may be, has to be smashed.(p.30)
• *Presently* he is hit again and this time has a fractured skull.(p.38)
• Follow the dictates of a Higher Power and you will *presently* live in a new and wonderful world, no matter what your present circumstances!(p.100)
• *Presently* the man did slip and was fired.(p.139)
• He will *presently* try the old game again, for he isn't happy about his sobriety.(p.152)
• His call to the clergyman led him *presently* to a certain resident of the town, who, though formerly able and respected, was then nearing the nadir of alcoholic despair.(p.155)
• With few exceptions our members find that they have tapped an unsuspected inner resource which they *presently* identify with their own conception of a Power greater than themselves.(p.569)

presents
• To the outer world he *presents* his stage character.(p.73)
• His case *presents* additional questions which we shall try to answer for you.(p.110)
• If this *presents* difficulty, re-reading chapters two and three, where the alcoholic sickness is discussed at length might be worth while.(p.140)
• "The American Public Health Association *presents* a Lasker Group Award for 1951 to Alcoholics Anonymous in recognition of its unique and highly successful approach to that age-old public health and social problem, alcoholism . . .(p.573)

president
• The other day an approach was made to the vice *president* of a large industrial concern.(p.148)
• What our friend, the vice *president*, had in mind was the habitual or whoopee drinker.(p.149)
• I checked into my hotel room and then noticed a placard tucked under the glass on the bureau stating "There will be positively NO drinking at this convention" signed by the *president* of the company.(p.243)
• In the long ago past I used to start at the top as *president* or treasurer and end up with the sheriff breathing down my neck.(p.284)
• My guild had elected me *president* twice and later given me a "man of the year" award.(p.328)
• I was *president* of my grammar school student body.(p.345)
• I was *president* of all my classes in high school and in my last year I was *president* of that student body.(p.345)
• I was *president* of each class in the University, and *president* of that student body.(p.345)
• Even when I was old enough to know better, I dreamed about being as beautiful as Venus, as pure as the Madonna and as brilliant as the *President* of the United States is supposed to be.(p.400)
• I had been elected *president* of a civic club.(p.418)
• Never once had my mother even hinted at the idea that, when I grew up, I might like to be *president* of A.A.(p.439)
• The amount of will power exercised to control my drinking during working hours, diverted into a constructive channel, would have made me *President*, and the thing that made the will power possible was the knowledge that as soon as my day was finished I could drink myself into oblivion.(p.548)

presides
• I must turn in all things the Father of Light who *presides* over us all.(p.14)
• This to the end that our great blessings may never spoil us; that we shall forever live in thankful contemplation of Him who *presides* over us all.(p.568)

press
• Very earnestly we ask the *press* also, to observe this request, for otherwise we shall be greatly handicapped.(p.xiii)
• It was decided that all members ought to be anonymous at the level of *press*, radio, TV and films.(p.xix)
• Another reason for the wide acceptance of A.A. was the ministration of friends -- friends in medicine, religion, and the *press*, together with innumerable others who became our able and persistent advocates.(p.xx)
• And then, in the spring of 1939, a very remarkable book was rolled off a New York *press* with the title "Alcoholics Anonymous."(p.307)
• Out of those forty years as a movie *press* agent came one blessing that granted me a blind faith in the program.(p.334)
• Eleven -- Our public relations policy is based on attraction rather than promotion; we need always maintain personal anonymity at the level of *press*, radio and films.(p.564)

pressed
• If *pressed* further, all I can do is follow the psalmist who said it long, long before me: "Be still, and know that I am God."(p.437)

pressing
• Neither did I have any *pressing* problems or worries.(p.41)
• If you and your husband find a solution for the *pressing* problem of drink you are, of course, going to be very happy.(p.117)

pressure
• The joy of living we really have, even under *pressure* and difficulty.(p.15)
• Under these conditions your prospect will see he is under no *pressure*.(p.91)
• Make it clear that he is not under *pressure*, that he needn't see you again if he doesn't want to.(p.94)
• I well remember the shock I received when a prominent doctor in Chicago told me of cases where *pressure* of the spinal fluid actually ruptured the brain.(p.140)
• Out of this maelstrom just two coherent thoughts came to the surface; one, a drink would mean homelessness and death; two, I could no longer relieve the *pressure* of fear by starting home, as was once my habitual solution to this problem, because I no longer had a home.(p.279)
• Now, no longer under *pressure*, I could safely guard against loss of control.(p.327)
• Gradually the quantity increased, the occasions for a drink came more frequently; a hard day, worries and *pressure*, bad news, good news -- there were more and more reasons for a drink.(p.374)

pressures
• No more business *pressures*.(p.329)
• But it did not take long for the *pressures* of living to bring out my immaturity and my insecurity.(p.420)
• These things were all *pressures*.(p.533)
• The *pressures* had started long ago.(p.533)

prestige
• Would there be strivings for power and *prestige*?(p.xviii)
• In my mind's eye, I played and replayed scenes in which I was plucked magically from the bar where I stood nursing a drink, and was instantly exalted to some position of power and *prestige*.(p.560)
• Six -- An A.A. group ought never endorse, finance or lend the A.A. name to any related facility or outside enterprise, lest problems of money, property and *prestige* divert us from our primary purpose.(p.564)

presumption
• We might pay for this *presumption* in all sorts of absurd actions and ideas.(p.87)

pretend
• I no longer had to *pretend*.(p.531)

pretense
• I had long since given up any *pretense* of the "social" cocktail hour.(p.306)
• I could hide my alcoholic stupor behind *pretense*.(p.332)
• It was also my job to entertain the owners of these stations when they came East on business -- or the *pretense* of business.(p.359)

pretty
• But the program of action, though entirely sensible, was *pretty* drastic.(p.42)
• Most alcoholics have to be *pretty* badly mangled before they really commence to solve their problems.(p.43)
• We thought, on the whole, we were *pretty* good women, capable of being nicer if our husbands stopped drinking.(p.116)
• Whether you are a hard drinker, a moderated drinker or a teetotaler, you may have some *pretty* strong opinions, perhaps prejudices.(p.139)
• Your man has probably been trying to conceal a number of scrapes, perhaps *pretty* messy ones.(p.140)
• Before very long we began to relate some incidents of our drinking and, naturally, *pretty* soon, I realized both of them knew what they were talking about because you can see things and smell things when you're drunk, that you can't other times, and, if I had thought they didn't know what they were talking about, I wouldn't have been willing to talk to them at all.(p.185)
• *Pretty* soon, I wasn't going at all, and was avoiding those people who had been so kind to me.(p.203)
• It was getting *pretty* dark and I hadn't turned on any lights, when some big fellow stepped inside the door and flipped on the light switch.(p.207)
• Although, during this period I was not addicted to any pattern of alcohol consumption, when I did drink the drinking was *pretty* wild.(p.212)
• Following graduation I was offered a *pretty* good job which I took.(p.212)
• In fact, I never lost my faith, since I had been prepared by some conversations toward the end of my sojourn in the hospital with Dr. Bob, conversations *pretty* much along spiritual lines.(p.218)
• That was skeptically received by me when I first heard it, but after some twenty-eight or thirty fellows had come to see me, and *pretty* nearly all of them had said the same thing, I began to believe it.(p.219)
• Doc dwelt on the idea that this was an illness, but Doc was *pretty* frank with me.(p.219)
• My education had been *pretty* much pagan -- science.(p.221)
• And the contrast was *pretty* shattering.(p.225)
• It wasn't very long until I had developed a *pretty* good brew with uniformity and plenty

of authority.(p.232)
• For a long time I kept on trying, in a *pretty* dumb way at first, I know, but very earnestly.(p.237)
• I was never homesick and was always *pretty* self-sufficient.(p.240)
• As long as things were tough and the job a challenge I could always manage to hold on *pretty* well, but as soon as I learned the combination, got the puzzle under control and the boss to pat me on the back, I was gone again.(p.243)
• I'm *pretty* near afraid of Labor Day yet.(p.264)
• By living alone you can *pretty* much eliminate grief from you life, but you also eliminate joy.(p.286)
• A few months after I made my original trip to Akron I was feeling *pretty* cocky, and I didn't think my wife was treating me with proper respect, now that I was an outstanding citizen.(p.293)
• But this day my doctor gave it to me straight and said, "People like you are *pretty* well known to the medical profession.(p.307)
• The same as before, I stayed drunk *pretty* much of the time.(p.318)
• It was a *pretty* blurry night.(p.353)
• It was a terrible blow at the time and I thought he was *pretty* much of a heel, but of course it was the finest thing he could have done for me under the circumstances.(p.357)
• Furthermore, I knew that I was looked upon as a city slicker from New York, and I had to be *pretty* cautious among small town, conservative Yankees.(p.360)
• New programing was beginning to build an audience, but sponsors were *pretty* scarce.(p.360)
• Life was *pretty* miserable.(p.388)
• My mother's heartbreak, or the unpleasant publicity I had caused did not bother my *pretty* head.(p.401)
• She said she felt too horrible inside to be *pretty* on the outside.(p.415)
• One has to be *pretty* sick to do that, and perhaps one has to be even sicker to come back every day for a new list, as she did.(p.446)
• The rest of that week is *pretty* hazy.(p.466)
• Men are supposed to be tough and rugged to start with, but if a woman becomes that way, it is *pretty* hard to get back the niceties of womanhood.(p.480)
• I borrowed five hundred dollars from the bank and three hundred from the loan shop, and I drank that up *pretty* fast.(p.490)
• He had gone through the windshields of cars a couple of times and was *pretty* well banged up.(p.510)
• I started prowling around with a couple of these A.A. boys, which kept me *pretty* busy and kept my mind off of down town.(p.511)
• I went along *pretty* well for the next ten months.(p.511)
• I've stuck *pretty* close to A.A. ever since then, taken it day by day, not biting off more than I can chew.(p.511)
• It wasn't *pretty*.(p.513)
• I was taking Benzedrine and paraldehyde quite impartially during the day then, and by the time I arrived at my first A.A. meeting, I was *pretty* drunk and certainly doped up to the eyes and completely jittery.(p.523)
• Actually, of course, I wanted someone to listen to me, because when I had a few martinis inside, I became the great author I longed to be; and the right listener was in for some *pretty* highflown theories of literature and of genius.(p.536)
• I thought that life was a *pretty* simple thing; you simply made a plan for your life, based upon what you wanted, and then you needed only the courage to go after it.(p.545)

prevails
• The atmosphere of "eat, drink, and be merry" *prevails* and I absorb it.(p.499)

prevalent
• We believe that managers of large enterprises often have little idea how *prevalent* this problem is.(p.149)

prevent
• It ran something like this: If I go around shouting from the rooftops about my alcoholism, it might very possibly *prevent* me from getting a good job.(p.282)
• Certainly now, anyone would have agreed that only a miracle could *prevent* my final breakdown.(p.306)

prevented
• If a repetition is to be *prevented*, place the problem, along with everything else, in God's hands.(p.120)
• All the other people that had talked to me wanted to help me, and my pride *prevented* me from listening to them, and caused only resentment on my part, but I felt as if I would be a real stinker if I did not listen to a couple of fellows for a short time, if that would cure them.(p.185)

prevents
• Show him, from your own experience, how the queer mental condition surrounding that first drink *prevents* normal functioning of the will power.(p.92)

previous
• It took me a year, or a year and a half to get to feeling physically well, and it was rather tough, but I soon found folks whose friendship I had once had, and I found, after I had been sober for quite some little time, that these people began to act like they had in *previous* years, before I had gotten so bad, so that I didn't pay too awful much attention to financial gains.(p.190)
• I had been to OTC the *previous* summer so I went into the Army as a sergeant, but I came out a private, and you really have to be unusual to do that.(p.241)
• I had worked the *previous* summer on a New York fashion magazine, a job I really enjoyed.(p.405)
• My last binge followed the *previous* one by two weeks.(p.514)

previously
• There I took up the business of drinking with much greater earnestness than I had *previously* shown.(p.173)

prey
• We were having trouble with personal relationships, we couldn't control our emotional natures, we were a *prey* to misery and depression, we couldn't make a living, we had a feeling of uselessness, we were full of fear, we were unhappy, we couldn't seem to be of real help to other people -- was not a basic solution of these bedevilments more important than whether we should see newsreels of lunar flight?(p.52)

price
• Simple, but not easy; a *price* had to be paid.(p.14)
• Especially when he has before him a way to stop his drinking and abuse if he really wants to pay the *price*.(p.108)
• A spiritual experience, he conceded, was absolutely necessary, but the *price* seemed high upon the basis suggested.(p.155)
• Everyone had my number and wouldn't hire me at any *price*.(p.301)
• At this time, the *price* of booze in the bars was fifteen cents a shot and ten cents a beer.(p.397)
• As income increased, the *price* of liquor increased proportionately.(p.398)
• I did not resort to semi-prostitution for the *price* of a drink.(p.412)

priceless
• And, as the years go by, working together, sharing our experiences with one another, and also sharing a mutual trust, understanding and love -- without strings, without obligation -- we acquire relationships that are unique and *priceless*.(p.312)

pricked
• My analyst *pricked* up her ears.(p.412)

prickling
• No *prickling* consciences to needle us with guilt feelings.(p.329)

pride
• It was a devastating blow to my *pride*.(p.7)
• Scales of *pride* and prejudice fell from my eyes.(p.12)
• Almost none of us liked the self-searching, the leveling of our *pride*, the confession of shortcomings which the process requires for its successful consummation.(p.25)
• *Pride*.(p.65)
• We pocket our *pride* and go to it, illuminating every twist of character, every dark cranny of the past.(p.75)
• We have had long rendezvous with hurt *pride*, frustration, self-pity, misunderstanding and fear.(p.104)
• We have told innumerable lies to protect our *pride* and our husbands' reputations.(p.105)
• We wives found that, like everybody else, we were afflicted with *pride*, self-pity, vanity and all the things which go to make up the self-centered person; and we were not above selfishness or dishonesty.(p.116)
• Husbands and wives have sometimes been obliged to separate for a time until new perspective, new victory over hurt *pride* could be rewon.(p.125)
• If you think you are an atheist, an agnostic, a skeptic, or have any other form of intellectual *pride* which keeps you from accepting what is in this book, I feel sorry for you.(p.181)
• All the other people that had talked to me wanted to help me, and my *pride* prevented me from listening to them, and caused only resentment on my part, but I felt as if I would be a real stinker if I did not listen to a couple of fellows for a short time, if that would cure them.(p.185)
• They seemed to be happy in their fashion, they and their little groups of supporters, but always *pride* of intellect stopped me from seeking what they evidently had.(p.256)
• I had suppressed tendencies to overindulge and thus reveal my "moral weakness," because false *pride* was so dominant.(p.327)
• I am filled with hurt *pride* and self-pity.(p.501)
• But as the years go by, the stretch becomes unbearable; and the man with the grown-up brain and the childish emotions -- vanity, self-interest, false *pride*, jealousy, longing for social approval, to name few -- becomes a prime candidate for alcohol.(p.534)

priest
• Suggestions about these may be obtained from one's *priest*, minister, or rabbi.(p.87)
• He may bring new hope and new courage to many a *priest*, minister, or rabbi, who gives his all to minister to our troubled world.(p.132)
• My parents had some vague idea of making a *priest* out of me and for some years I attended the Franciscan school at Basle, Switzerland, just across the border, about six miles from my home.(p.230)
• Unfortunately, I had no desire to consult my *priest* about my drinking.(p.234)
• Unlike many other Catholics who frequently take pledges for definite periods -- a year, two years or for good, I never had any desire to "take a pledge" before the *priest*.(p.234)
• When I came back, I told the *priest*, the Chaplain of the place, exactly what I thought of him and he didn't like it.(p.517)
• It was no use talking of putting myself into a home, a hospital, or of going to see a doctor again, or of going to see a *priest* or anyone else.(p.523)

priests
• You can easily find some by asking a few doctors, ministers, *priests* or hospitals.(p.89)
• Here was a book that said I could do something that all these doctors and *priests* and ministers and psychiatrists that I'd been going to for years couldn't do!(p.473)
• In such places, A.A. can be located through the local telephone directory, newspaper office, or police station, or by contacting local *priests* or ministers.(p.575)

prim
• He said, "This is my story" -- real *prim*.(p.268)

prima donna
• Scared that my dress wasn't going to fit right, that the church wasn't going to be filled, that I'd fall flat on my face walking up the aisle; in fact, I was afraid I wasn't going to be a *prima donna* in the place where I should be.(p.385)

primarily
• I went to five grade schools, *primarily* because I was expelled for my conduct, but I eventually graduated from the eighth grade.(p.211)
• The law school experience was not inspired by a desire to follow patent law, which has been my profession since: I went to law school *primarily* to learn the law of contracts following my own experience with litigation.(p.212)
• It was then that I began to hate myself, and drank *primarily* to ease my conscience and forget.(p.354)

primary
• I could not see why I couldn't drink like a gentleman, and that was my *primary* ambition -- until I landed in A.A.(p.214)
• Five -- Each group has but one *primary* purpose -- to carry its message to the alcoholic who still suffers.(p.564)
• Six -- An A.A. group ought never endorse, finance or lend the A.A. name to any related facility or outside enterprise, lest problems of money, property and prestige divert us from our *primary* purpose.(p.564)
• 5. -- Each Alcoholics Anonymous group ought to be a spiritual entity having but one *primary* purpose -- that of carrying its message to the alcoholic who still suffers.(p.565)
• 6. -- Problems of money, property, and authority may easily divert us from our *primary* spiritual aim.(p.565)

prime
• Aside from fellowship and sociability, the *prime* object was to provide a time and place where new people might bring their problems.(p.160)
• I walked up that aisle just like Mae West in her *prime*.(p.385)
• Then he asks me if I believe in a power greater than myself, whether I call that power God, Allah, Confucius, *Prime* Cause, Divine Mind, or any other name.(p.503)

• But as the years go by, the stretch becomes unbearable; and the man with the grown-up brain and the childish emotions – vanity, self-interest, false pride, jealousy, longing for social approval, to name few -- becomes a ***prime*** candidate for alcohol.(p.534)

primitive

• The farm, in those days, was ***primitive***.(p.415)

prince

• I also wanted to be the queen of society, with a glittering salon, the bride of a dream ***prince*** and the mother of a happy brood.(p.400)
• He was the dream ***prince***, the answer.(p.403)

principal

• For this there were two ***principal*** reasons: the large numbers of recoveries, and reunited homes.(p.xx)
• He is the ***Principal***; we are His agents.(p.62)
• The alcoholic's past thus becomes the ***principal*** asset of the family and frequently it is almost the only one!(p.124)
• The ***principal*** had no alternative but to expel me.(p.424)
• They are authorized by the groups to handle our over-all public relations and they guarantee the integrity of our ***principal*** newspaper, the A.A. Grapevine.(p.567)

principle

• The first ***principle*** of success is that you should never be angry.(p.111)
• The same ***principle*** applies in dealing with the children.(p.115)
• Another ***principle*** we observe carefully is that we do not relate intimate experiences of another person unless we are sure he would approve.(p.125)
• Giving, rather than getting, will become the guiding ***principle***.(p.128)
• At that time the group in New York was composed of about twelve men who were working on the ***principle*** of every drunk for himself; we had no real formula and no name.(p.246)
• Our public relations should be guided by the ***principle*** of attraction rather than promotion.(p.567)
• 12. – And finally, we of Alcoholics Anonymous believe that the ***principle*** of anonymity has immense spiritual significance.(p.567)
• "There is a ***principle*** which is a bar against all information, which is proof against all arguments and which cannot fail to keep a man in everlasting ignorance -- that ***principle*** is contempt prior to investigation."(p.570)
• The Episcopal magazine, The Living Church, observes editorially: "The basis of the technique of Alcoholics Anonymous is the truly Christian ***principle*** that a man cannot help himself except by helping others.(p.574)

principles

• As we discovered the ***principles*** by which the individual alcoholic could live, so we had to evolve ***principles*** by which the A.A. groups and A.A. as a whole could survive and function effectively.(p.xix)
• Though none of these ***principles*** had the force of rules or laws, they had become so widely accepted by 1950 that they were confirmed by our first International Conference held at Cleveland.(p.xix)
• The basic ***principles*** of the A.A. program, it appears, hold good for individuals with many different life-styles, just as the program has brought recovery to those of many different nationalities.(p.xxii)
• My friend had emphasized the absolute necessity of demonstrating these ***principles*** in all my affairs.(p.14)
• A much more important demonstration of our ***principles*** lies before us in our respective homes, occupations and affairs.(p.19)
• "Quite as important was the discovery that spiritual ***principles*** would solve all my problems.(p.42)
• That was great news to us, for we had assumed we could not make use of spiritual ***principles*** unless we accepted many things on faith which seemed difficult to believe.(p.47)
• 12.Having had a spiritual awakening as the result of these steps, we tried to carry this message to alcoholics, and to practice these ***principles*** in all our affairs.(p.60)
• No one among us has been able to maintain anything like perfect adherence to these ***principles***.(p.60)
• The ***principles*** we have set down are guides to progress.(p.60)
• We listed people, institutions or ***principles*** with whom we were angry.(p.64)
• Although these reparations take innumerable forms, there are some general ***principles*** which we find guiding.(p.79)
• Unless one's family expresses a desire to live upon spiritual ***principles*** we think we ought not to urge them.(p.83)
• If not members of religious bodies, we sometimes select and memorize a few set prayers which emphasize the ***principles*** we have been discussing.(p.87)
• The main thing is that he be willing to believe in a Power greater than himself and that he live by spiritual ***principles***.(p.93)
• When dealing with such a person, you had better use everyday language to describe spiritual ***principles***.(p.93)
• We are dealing only with general ***principles*** common to most denominations.(p.94)
• Should they accept and practice spiritual ***principles***, there is a much better chance that the head of the family will recover.(p.97)
• When your prospect has made such reparation as he can to his family, and has thoroughly explained to them the new ***principles*** by which he is living, he should proceed to put those ***principles*** into action at home.(p.98)
• If you act upon these ***principles***, your husband may stop or moderate.(p.112)
• The same ***principles*** which apply to husband number one should be practiced.(p.112)
• As our husbands began to apply spiritual ***principles*** in their lives, we began to see the desirability of doing so too.(p.116)
• Now we try to put spiritual ***principles*** to work in every department of our lives.(p.116)
• Though it is entirely separate from Alcoholics Anonymous, it uses the general ***principles*** of the A.A. program as a guide for husbands, wives, relatives, friends, and others close to alcoholics.(p.121)
• One more suggestion: Whether the family has spiritual convictions or not, they may do well to examine the ***principles*** by which the alcoholic member is trying to live.(p.130)
• They can hardly fail to approve these simple ***principles***, though the head of the house still fails somewhat in practicing them.(p.130)
• Without much ado, he accepted the ***principles*** and procedure that had helped us.(p.139)
• The use of spiritual ***principles*** in such cases was not so well understood as it is now.(p.156)
• It is, however, only the first of a series of miracles which have followed one after another as a result of my trying to apply to my daily life the ***principles*** embodies in our Twelve Steps.(p.280)
• It is a way of life, and the challenge contained in its ***principles*** is great enough to keep any human being striving for as long as he lives.(p.311)
• Moreover, I am deeply convinced that so long as I continue to strive, in my bumbling way, toward the ***principles*** I first encountered in the earlier chapters of this book, this remarkable power will continue to flow through me.(p.437)
• Through A.A., many receive the needed change and awakening just by trying to live by A.A. ***principles*** and associating with A.A. people.(p.459)
• They suggested that I study the A.A. book and try to take the Twelve Steps according to the explanation in the Book, for it was their opinion that the application of these ***principles*** in our daily lives will get us sober and keep us sober.(p.550)
• I believe this, and I believe too that it is equally impossible to practice these ***principles*** to the best of our ability, a day at a time, and still drink, for I don't think the two things are compatible.(p.550)
• A.A. has given me serenity of purpose, the opportunity to be of service to God and to the people about me, and I am serene in the infallibility of these ***principles*** that provide the fulfillment of my purpose.(p.551)
• Twelve – Anonymity is the spiritual foundation of all our Traditions, ever reminding us to place ***principles*** before personalities.(p.564)
• It reminds us that we are to place ***principles*** before personalities; that we are actually to practice a genuine humility.(p.568)

print

• Even in the present century, American newspapers were afraid to ***print*** an account of the Wright brothers' first successful flight at Kitty Hawk.(p.51)
• I had a little Testament, which was very small ***print***.(p.268)
• When you have a hangover and can't even sit still, try to read small ***print***!(p.268)

printed

• In the fall of 1939, Fulton Oursler, then editor of Liberty, ***printed*** a piece in his magazine, called "Alcoholics and God."(p.xviii)
• In the spring of 1939, the Big Book was ***printed***, and we had two inquiries from the New York office because of a fifteen-minute radio talk that was made.(p.294)
• At one end of the bed, near the foot, was a ***printed*** card, and beneath that was a charted graph.(p.422)
• This is a condensed version of the original "long form" A.A. Traditions as first ***printed*** in 1946.(p.563)
• Our names and pictures as A.A. members ought not be broadcast, filmed, or publicly ***printed***.(p.567)
• This was done, and the paper was ***printed*** in the American Journal of Psychiatry for November, 1949.(p.572)

printer

• By March 1976, when this edition went to the ***printer***, the total worldwide membership of Alcoholics Anonymous was conservatively estimated at more than 1,000,000, with almost 28,000 groups meeting in over 90 countries.(p.xxii)
• I got an easy, part-time job selling printing for a small neighborhood ***printer***.(p.276)
• A year later I was able to buy a Model T roadster and take a better job with a downtown ***printer***.(p.276)
• From this job and the next one with another ***printer*** I was courteously dismissed.(p.277)

printing

• This is the Foreword as it appeared in the first ***printing*** of the first edition in 1939(p.xiii)
• Our earliest ***printing*** voiced the hope "that every alcoholic who journeys will find the Fellowship of Alcoholics Anonymous at his destination.(p.xv)
• Sixteen years have elapsed between our first ***printing*** of this book and the presentation in 1955 of our second edition.(p.xv)
• I got an easy, part-time job selling ***printing*** for a small neighborhood printer.(p.276)
• However, due to financial difficulties the whole ***printing*** was, for a while, held up and the book received no publicity, nor, of course, was it available in the stores, even if one knew it existed.(p.307)
• Yet it is true that our first ***printing*** gave many readers the impression that these personality changes, or religious experiences, must be in the nature of sudden and spectacular upheavals.(p.569)

prior

• ***Prior*** to his journey to Akron, the broker had worked hard with many alcoholics on the theory that only an alcoholic could help an alcoholic, but he had succeeded only in keeping sober himself.(p.xvi)
• They took a drink a day or so ***prior*** to the date, and then the phenomenon of craving at once became paramount to all other interests so that the important appointment was not met.(p.xxvii)
• About one year ***prior*** to this experience a man was brought in to be treated for chronic alcoholism.(p.xxix)
• At the end of this selling of lots, just ***prior*** to World War I, I got into the crude rubber business, and six months later there was only one broker and myself left in Akron.(p.197)
• I still have my job, and just ***prior*** to the writing of this narrative, I received an advancement.(p.303)
• For about one year, ***prior*** to this time, there was one doctor who had continued to struggle with me.(p.306)
• ***Prior*** to our marriage, when she was a shy, scrawny adolescent, I was able to see things in her that others couldn't necessarily see – things like beauty, charm, gaiety, a gift for being easy to talk to, a sense of humor, and many other fine qualities.(p.450)
• My father had treated him many years ***prior*** to this.(p.488)
• I had a habit of getting up just ***prior*** to the closing time of the saloons, about two or three o'clock in the morning.(p.514)
• "There is a principle which is a bar against all information, which is proof against all arguments and which cannot fail to keep a man in everlasting ignorance -- that principle is contempt ***prior*** to investigation."(p.570)

Priscilla

• ***Priscilla***, an A.A. who, like Marty, has become one of my greatest friends, decided that I was a stubborn case.(p.414)
• Since they could do nothing with Anne either, ***Priscilla*** suggested that I go and look after Anne.(p.414)
• In the first year there were episodes such as kicking ***Priscilla*** in the shins, getting the lock changed on the desk in the A.A. Club, because I, as secretary, didn't want the Intergroup secretary "interfering," and taking an older woman member out to lunch for the express purpose of informing her that she was "a phony."(p.416)

prison

• That armor had turned into ***prison*** walls, locking me in loneliness – and fear.(p.226)
• I had found friends, understanding friends who often knew what I was thinking and feeling better than I knew myself, and didn't allow me to retreat into my ***prison*** of loneliness and fear over a fancied

slight or hurt.(p.228)
• First, we all hear at A.A. meetings about those who have lost everything, those who have been in jail, those who have been in *prison*, those who have lost their families, those who have lost their income.(p.345)
• The worst of *prison* treatment couldn't break this tough con.(p.457)
• I served twelve years in *prison*, never suspecting that without alcohol I would not have been in *prison* at all.(p.457)
• Had it not been for A.A. in *prison*. . . I'll never know, but my educated guess is that I would not be alive today.(p.457)
• I served time in four penitentiaries and several *prison* camps, including a maximum-security camp.(p.457)
• However, one thing I am certain of: Inmates in *prison* who attend A.A. have their chances of remaining free greatly enhanced – this is a proved fact.(p.458)
• What else can I do except what I have always done in the past? -- act as my old self and return to *prison*.(p.458)
• It is estimated that two-thirds of the men in *prison* were under the influence of alcohol and/or drugs when they committed their offenses.(p.458)
• Most of us did not stay out of *prison* long enough to run the alcoholic gamut -- to develop the ongoing kind of alcoholism or alcoholic drinking you hear about in A.A. talks.(p.458)
• We always, or nearly always, had good intentions when we were released from *prison*.(p.458)
• And we found ourselves back in *prison*, where our personalities became even more warped.(p.459)
• In a *prison* in my native state, I spent eleven months in solitary confinement, bouncing in and out of the "hole" (a bare concrete-and-steel cubicle) about five times during those eleven months.(p.459)
• I thought that was bad until I hit the hole at a *prison* camp; it was just wide enough and long enough to lie down in.(p.459)
• They were having a large A.A. meeting in the *prison* auditorium.(p.460)
• I didn't know I was an alcoholic and (like most men in *prison* today) could not relate alcohol to any of my past troubles.(p.460)
• Four years later, I was taken to my first A.A. meeting out of *prison*, in Los Angeles.(p.460)
• However, I still would not attend A.A. in *prison*.(p.461)
• (I am looking at it now in my bedroom – a copy that was presented to me a couple of years ago by the A.A. group in that same *prison*.)(p.461)
• I started going to A.A. in *prison* at the group's next meeting.(p.461)
• I count my sobriety date from the day I began going to A.A. in *prison*, not from the date of my last drink.(p.462)
• God bless all you people in A.A. and especially you fellows in *prison*.(p.463)
• After twenty years in *prison* for murder, he knew A.A. was the spot for him . . . if he wanted to stay on the outside.(p.508)
• I was immediately arrested, arraigned in Homicide Court, held without bail, and remanded to the old Tombs *Prison* to await trial.(p.508)
• She was the one who really helped me to make a go of that twenty years and nine months in *prison*.(p.511)
• But when she began a *prison* sentence, a door opened.(p.526)
• Because I had been drunk, the judge gave me only a twelve-year sentence in *prison*.(p.528)
• I had rejected A.A. on the outside, but now it came to me in *prison*.(p.528)
• Since I have been in A.A., I have more friends than I ever had in my life – friends who care about me and my welfare, friends who don't care that I am black and that I have been in *prison*.(p.529)

prisoner
• THE *PRISONER* FREED(p.508)

prisoners
• Yet *prisoners* often can't identify with many A.A. members' drinking stories.(p.458)
• I nearly reverted to my old, incorrigible self -- had trouble with a couple of other *prisoners*, was planning an escape.(p.461)

prisons
• Shortly thereafter, I was selected, with eight other inmates out of the 10,000 in the state's *prisons* at that time, to attend a school designed to take former "management problems" like me and convert them into paracounselors.(p.462)

privacy
• To me, taking a bath was just being in a place with a bottle where I could drink in *privacy*.(p.337)

private
• But one of the friends said, "Put him in a *private* room.(p.157)
• "Who are you fellows, and why this *private* room?(p.157)
• After prescribing medicines, Dr. Bob ordered, "Put him in a *private* room.(p.188)
• To go into a gathering of people was the sort of thing that all my life, from the time I left my *private* world of books and dreams to meet the real world of people and parties and jobs, had left me feeling an uncomfortable outsider, needing the warming stimulus of drinks to join in.(p.228)
• I had been to OTC the previous summer so I went into the Army as a sergeant, but I came out a *private*, and you really have to be unusual to do that.(p.241)
• I had every advantage a child could have, *private* schools (several of them), dancing schools, two colleges, coon skin coats, automobiles, a listing in the social register and all the rest.(p.357)
• I had never been inside of an insane asylum and I really thought I was going to a *private* hospital.(p.387)
• When I went back to my hometown to go into *private* practice, I experienced another brief lull in my addiction to alcohol and drugs.(p.420)
• The people there insisted on putting me in a ward, when Max and I both knew I ought to have a *private* room.(p.445)
• And I got my *private* room.(p.445)
• Instead, I started going to a nice *private* sanitarium which, after the first visit, turned out to be more like a country club than anything else.(p.468)
• We had no whiskey in the house, other than my father's *private* stock.(p.484)
• But as long as you did your work and didn't disgrace yourself, you were socially acceptable and nobody really intruded on your *private* life very much.(p.518)
• Since, perhaps, suicide was a bit too drastic (actually, I was afraid), dry martinis were chosen as the slow, pleasant, *private*, gradual instrument of self-destruction.(p.531)
• I wasn't afraid of anything or anybody after I learned about drinking, for it seemed right from the beginning that with liquor I could always retire to my little *private* world where nobody could get at me to hurt me.(p.547)
• Dr. John F. Stouffer, Chief Psychiatrist, Philadelphia General Hospital, citing his experience with A.A., said: "The alcoholics we get here at Philadelphia General are mostly those who cannot afford *private* treatment, and A.A. is by far the greatest thing we have been able to offer them.(p.572)

privately
• It was my ex-wife, and she said my twenty-seven-year-old son, who has completed his Marine Corps training and graduated from college, wanted to see me *privately*, was getting married in three months, and wanted me at the wedding.(p.462)
• I call my wife into a room where we can talk *privately*.(p.506)

privilege
• Later, he requested the *privilege* of being allowed to tell his story to other patients here and with some misgiving, we consented.(p.xxv)
• Had not people said God had reserved this *privilege* to the birds?(p.51)
• Next time you and he have a heated discussion, no matter what the subject, it should be the *privilege* of either to smile and say, "This is getting serious.(p.118)
• I used to get terribly upset when I saw my friends drink and knew I could not, but I schooled myself to believe that though I once had the same *privilege*, I had abused it so frightfully that it was withdrawn.(p.181)
• Such has been my *privilege*, both nationally and in my home city.(p.295)
• Far from expecting praise for their deeds, they claimed the performance a *privilege* and insisted that they invariably received more than they gave.(p.310)
• Age and the law were still against me, but laws were not as strictly enforced in those days as they are now, and I discovered that as long as I had the green blood, there was always a way to get alcohol, either from a nondiscriminatory bartender or from an older friend who would be glad to purchase the joy juice for the *privilege* of sharing it.(p.397)

privileges
• My whole life seemed to be centered around doing what I wanted to do, without regard for the rights, wishes, or *privileges* of anyone else; a state of mind which became more and more predominant as the years passed.(p.172)
• We're not up here trying to take any of your rights or *privileges* away from you, but we have a program whereby we think we can stay sober.(p.186)
• After nearly eight years of sobriety in A.A., I still can set down such thoughts, "against my instinct and training," showing that I still consider myself a "special" person, entitled to special *privileges*.(p.536)

prize
• In the *prize* ring, this would be called leading with the chin.(p.77)
• Our other daughter was in her last year of high school, and one night the new son-in-law and my husband went out to a *prize* fight.(p.263)

prizes
• I, a man of steel, with very high ideals, well brought up, an honor student and the recipient of scholarships and *prizes*, a boy wonder in business – I, Bob, the author of this essay, looked and saw that the universe was beneath my contempt, and that to remove myself from it was the only thing of dignity a man could do.(p.531)

pro
• Much has been written *pro* and con, but among physicians, the general opinion seems to be that most chronic alcoholics are doomed.(p.xxviii)

probability
• In all *probability*, we shall never be able to touch more than a fair fraction of the alcohol problem in all its ramifications.(p.xxi)

probable
• Being still inexperienced and having just made conscious contact with God, it is not *probable* that we are going to be inspired at all times.(p.87)

probably
• When this sort of thinking is fully established in an individual with alcoholic tendencies, he has *probably* placed himself beyond human aid, and unless locked up, may die or go permanently insane.(p.24)
• (b) That *probably* no human power could have relieved our alcoholism.(p.60)
• *Probably* there are still some misgivings.(p.76)
• To some people we need not, and *probably* should not emphasize the spiritual feature on our first approach.(p.76)
• Admit that he *probably* knows more about it than you do, but call to his attention the fact that however deep his faith and knowledge, he could not have applied it or he would not drink.(p.93)
• He would *probably* be insulted if he were called an alcoholic.(p.109)
• He *probably* has several alcoholics among his own acquaintances.(p.112)
• If he does not, you will *probably* not have long to wait.(p.113)
• If your husband is a drinker, you *probably* worry over what other people are thinking and you hate to meet your friends.(p.114)
• It is *probably* true that you and your husband have been living too much alone, for drinking many times isolates the wife of an alcoholic.(p.119)
• Therefore, you *probably* need fresh interests and a great cause to live for as much as your husband.(p.119)
• Your man has *probably* been trying to conceal a number of scrapes, perhaps pretty messy ones.(p.140)
• If he feels free to discuss his problems with you, if he knows you understand and will not be upset by anything he wishes to say, he will *probably* be off to a fast start.(p.144)
• He had lived there but a few weeks when he found that the place *probably* contained more alcoholics per square mile than any city in the country.(p.163)
• I think I must have been thoroughly scared by what had happened, or by the doctor, or *probably* both, so that I did not touch a drink again until the country went dry.(p.175)
• It was bad news for us, and it will *probably* be bad news for you.(p.187)
• I said, "Yes," reluctantly, "I *probably* will."(p.190)
• I'm so grateful for both the program and the people in it that I still want to go, and then *probably* the most wonderful thing that I learned from the program -- I've seen this in the 'A.A. Grapevine' a lot of times, and I've had people say it to me personally, and I've heard people get up in meetings and make the same statement: The statement is, "I came into A.A. solely for the purpose of sobriety, but it has been through A.A. that I have found God."(p.192)
• I think it was *probably* more than a year before I had anything more to do with liquor.(p.195)
• I can remember telling the poor little soul that I

could ***probably*** quit drinking if I wasn't married to her, and told her that, after all, I didn't like restraint!(p.199)
• My efficiency as a professional man was ***probably*** reduced to twenty-five per cent of what it should have been.(p.215)
• They ***probably*** felt that it was useless, that surely I had enough intelligence to know what I was doing.(p.215)
• In fact, as I look back, I have often thought that they ***probably*** concluded that they would put up with me for a couple of years, that I couldn't live much longer, and that they would inherit whatever was left of the practice.(p.215)
• Had anyone undertaken to explain to me what the A.A. movement was, what its real function was, I ***probably*** would have been set back several years and I doubt if I would have survived at all.(p.216)
• He pointed out to me that ***probably*** it was more of a moral or spiritual illness than it was a physical one.(p.219)
• However, here I ***probably*** took my first step towards my coming alcoholism by developing a terrific aversion to all churches and established religions.(p.240)
• ***Probably*** only a few readers of this story will be able, from personal experiences of their own, to understand the exhilaration and sense of accomplishment which I felt after finishing this seemingly simple assignment.(p.276)
• While there, two or three more "cash customers" (as Dr. Bob used to call them – ***probably*** because they had so little cash) were shipped in to us from Detroit.(p.282)
• I, carried away with the desire to serve A.A., gave what was ***probably*** one of the first radio broadcasts about A.A., living through a case of mike fright and feeling like a million dollars when it was all over.(p.283)
• She's a good-natured soul and said, "I wouldn't worry about it; ***probably*** something will happen."(p.346)
• But, as it was with drinking, this project will be entered into with enthusiasm and optimism – and ***probably*** wind up the same way, depressed.(p.396)
• In the back of my mind, I ***probably*** thought, "They won't take me as drunk as I am."(p.398)
• "Well," he answers, "You've ***probably*** tried praying like I have.(p.504)
• Those poor stiffs ***probably*** went to a doctor and were told that if they quit they'd live three weeks and if they didn't they'd die in one."(p.510)
• The medical profession would ***probably*** tell me I was conditioned for alcoholism by the things that happened to me in my childhood.(p.544)
• He happened to be, by the grace of God, Dr. Harry Tiebout, the psychiatrist who ***probably*** knew more about alcoholism than any other in the world.(p.559)

probation

• I lost my driver's license, was made a ward of the court, and was put on ***probation*** (not to mention the fact that I might have killed three friends and myself).(p.354)
• Providentially, this was a Monday might when the Dublin Group met in those days, and my family agreed that if A.A. could do anything for me at all, that I'd be allowed to stay on at home on ***probation***.(p.523)

probed

• We believe a man should be thoroughly ***probed*** on these points.(p.142)

problem

• If you have a drinking ***problem***, we hope that you may pause in reading one of the forty-four personal stories and think: "Yes, that happened to me"; or, more important, "Yes, I've felt like that"; or most important, "Yes, I believe this program can work for me, too."(p.xii)
• So far, upon the total ***problem*** of several million actual and potential alcoholics in the world, we have made only a scratch.(p.xx)
• In all probability, we shall never be able to touch more than a fair fraction of the alcohol ***problem*** in all its ramifications.(p.xxi)
• Faced with this ***problem***, if a doctor is honest with himself, he must sometimes feel his own inadequacy.(p.xxvii)
• Though the aggregate of recoveries resulting from psychiatric effort is considerable, we physicians must admit we have made little impression upon the ***problem*** as a whole.(p.xxvii)
• I do not hold with those who believe that alcoholism is entirely a ***problem*** of mental control.(p.xxvii)
• I have had many men who had, for example, worked a period of months on some ***problem*** or business deal which was to be settled on a certain date, favorable to them.(p.xxvii)
• His alcoholic ***problem*** was so complex, and his depression so great, that we felt his only hope would be through what we then called "moral psychology," and we doubted if even that would have any effect.(p.xxix)
• They have solved the drink ***problem***.(p.17)
• If we keep on the way we are going there is little doubt that much good will result, but the surface of the ***problem*** would hardly be scratched.(p.19)
• We have concluded to publish an anonymous volume setting forth the ***problem*** as we see it.(p.19)
• This should suggest a useful program for anyone concerned with a drinking ***problem***.(p.19)
• Therefore, the main ***problem*** of the alcoholic centers in his mind, rather than in his body.(p.23)
• When, therefore, we were approached by those in whom the ***problem*** had been solved, there was nothing left for us but to pick up the simple kit of spiritual tools laid at our feet.(p.25)
• Every means of solving his ***problem*** which money could buy was at his disposal.(p.32)
• So we shall describe some of the mental states that precede a relapse into drinking, for obviously this is the crux of the ***problem***.(p.35)
• Fred would not believe himself an alcoholic, much less accept a spiritual remedy for his ***problem***.(p.39)
• I had never been able to understand people who said that a ***problem*** had them hopelessly defeated.(p.42)
• Its main object is to enable you to find a Power greater than yourself which will solve your ***problem***.(p.45)
• His alcoholic ***problem*** was taken away.(p.56)
• Some of us once had great self-confidence, but it didn't fully solve the fear ***problem***, or any other.(p.68)
• In other words, we treat sex as we would any other ***problem***.(p.69)
• We often find such a person quick to see and understand our ***problem***.(p.74)
• The feeling that the drink ***problem*** has disappeared will often come strongly.(p.75)
• Good generalship may decide that the ***problem*** be attacked on the flank rather than risk a face-to-face combat.(p.82)
• Instead, the ***problem*** has been removed.(p.85)
• Now, the domestic ***problem***: There may be divorce, separation, or just strained relations.(p.98)
• Ask any woman who has sent her husband to distant places on the theory he would escape the alcohol ***problem***.(p.101)
• Some day we hope that Alcoholics Anonymous will help the public to a better realization of the gravity of the alcoholic ***problem***, but we shall be of little use if our attitude is one of bitterness or hostility.(p.103)
• Among us are wives, relatives and friends whose ***problem*** has been solved, as well as some who have not yet found a happy solution.(p.104)
• The ***problem*** with which you struggle usually falls within one of four categories:(p.108)
• This may lay the groundwork for a friendly talk about his alcoholic ***problem***.(p.111)
• Then that terrible tension which grips the home of every ***problem*** drinker will be lessened.(p.115)
• If you and your husband find a solution for the pressing ***problem*** of drink you are, of course, going to be very happy.(p.117)
• It is the most natural thing in the world, once his liquor ***problem*** is solved, to feel that he will now measure up to that cherished vision.(p.118)
• After all, your family is reunited, alcohol is no longer a ***problem*** and you and your husband are working together toward an undreamed-of future.(p.119)
• God has either removed your husband's liquor ***problem*** or He has not.(p.120)
• If a repetition is to be prevented, place the ***problem***, along with everything else, in God's hands.(p.120)
• This painful past may be of infinite value to other families still struggling with their ***problem***.(p.124)
• We think it dangerous if he rushes headlong at his economic ***problem***.(p.126)
• To you, liquor is no real ***problem***.(p.139)
• To return to the subject matter of this book: It contains full suggestions by which the employee may solve his ***problem***.(p.143)
• But at least he will understand the ***problem*** and will no longer be misled by ordinary promises.(p.148)
• I don't see how you can be of any help to us for, as you see, we don't have any alcoholic ***problem***."(p.148)
• We believe that managers of large enterprises often have little idea how prevalent this ***problem*** is.(p.149)
• Even if you feel your organization has no alcoholic ***problem***, it might pay to take another look down the line.(p.149)
• Many a distracted wife has visited this house to find loving and understanding companionship among women who knew her ***problem***, to hear from the lips of their husbands what had happened to them, to be advised how her own wayward mate might be hospitalized and approached when next he stumbled.(p.160)
• My wife became deeply interested and it was her interest that sustained mine, though I at no time sensed that it might be an answer to my liquor ***problem***.(p.178)
• This ***problem*** was soon solved, however, as I began to take my bottle along with me and hide it in the bathroom or in the shrubbery outside.(p.184)
• If I could, that was wonderful, that was just fine, and they would very much appreciate a person who had that kind of power, but they were looking for a man that knew he had a ***problem***, and knew that he couldn't handle it himself and needed outside help.(p.186)
• So, after reviewing these things and realizing what liquor had cost me, I went to this Higher Power which, to me was God, without any reservation, and admitted that I was completely powerless over alcohol, and that I was willing to do anything in the world to get rid of the ***problem***.(p.187)
• It had long since become a serious ***problem***.(p.197)
• My only thought that day was getting a drink, and how to get rid of those clowns was my big ***problem***.(p.206)
• I realized that I had a ***problem***, although my realization was not very deep because my own conceit wouldn't admit that I had any personality problems.(p.214)
• I never left the church, but I was a fringe member, and the thought simply never occurred to me that through the exercise of what I had I might find the answer to my ***problem***, simply because I wouldn't admit that I had a ***problem***.(p.214)
• When I was about forty-seven, after indulging in all kinds of self-deception to control my drinking, I arrived at a period when I felt convinced I had to have so much alcohol every day and that the real ***problem*** was to control how much.(p.214)
• That is, it was sort of a mixed bunch of Oxford Groupers, who were interested in the alcoholic ***problem***, and of alcoholics themselves.(p.218)
• Every man has his ***problem*** of this kind, but we didn't discuss it very much.(p.236)
• Jackie told me about a group of fellows in New York, of whom my old friend Fitz was one, who had the same ***problem*** I had, and who by working together to help each other were not now drinking and were happy like himself.(p.239)
• If, on Sunday, I could be there, trying to think of something that would help her with this ***problem***, then we must have something that could work.(p.272)
• I ended up, homeless, jobless, penniless and rudderless, as the ***problem*** guest of a close friend whose family was out of town.(p.278)
• To go north into the empty pine country and shoot myself, or to go south in the faint hope that a bunch of strangers might help me with my drinking ***problem***.(p.278)
• Out of this maelstrom just two coherent thoughts came to the surface; one, a drink would mean homelessness and death; two, I could no longer relieve the pressure of fear by starting home, as was once my habitual solution to this ***problem***, because I no longer had a home.(p.279)
• It went something like this: "God, for eighteen years I have been unable to handle this ***problem***.(p.280)
• This office job brought me face to face with a ***problem*** which I had sidestepped all my adult life, lack of training.(p.284)
• He waited until I was completely sober and the day before I was to head back for Chicago, he told me of a small group of men in Akron who apparently had the same ***problem*** that I had but were doing something about it.(p.289)
• When I told them six weeks, they were polite and said that they would contact me in case they had anyone with an alcoholic ***problem***.(p.293)
• At twenty-five I had developed an alcoholic ***problem***.(p.305)
• And we wonder how much further this man could go if his alcoholic ***problem*** could be removed and he could throw one hundred per cent of his abilities into action.(p.308)
• Instead of wanting to escape some perplexing ***problem***, we experience a thrill of challenge in the opportunity it affords for another application of A.A. techniques, and we find ourselves tackling it with surprising vigor.(p.311)
• They realized that repeated lack of drinking control,

when they really wanted control, was the fatal symptom that spelled ***problem*** drinking.(p.315)
• If I could lay off it, that meant I didn't have to worry about a drinking ***problem***, I thought.(p.317)
• I thought my ***problem*** was that I had been married to a drunk for twenty-seven years.(p.321)
• I was aware of symptoms of impending dependence, and I told myself I had gotten out of the rat race just in time to head off any booze ***problem***.(p.327)
• The fellowship I found in A.A. enabled me to face my ***problem*** honestly and squarely.(p.340)
• But when we come into A.A., we can face our ***problem*** honestly and openly.(p.340)
• So I went to my wife and asked her, wasn't there something that she and I could do to somehow get together, and she turned on her heel and looked me squarely in the eye, and said, "You don't care anything about my ***problem***," and I could have smacked her, but I said to myself, "Grab on to your serenity!"(p.351)
• They have contributed fantastic amounts of time and work to our ***problem***, but they aren't able, it seems, to arrest either your alcoholism or mine.(p.352)
• Of course I kept her posted on how well the station was doing and wrote convincing letters of how well I was doing with the liquor ***problem***.(p.360)
• Sure enough in a couple of hours two men were at my door and for the first time I heard some facts about liquor and my ***problem*** that sounded sensible to me.(p.363)
• I had no qualms, because I felt the source of a drinking ***problem*** was all in how weak one was, and I wasn't like my dad (I thought).(p.370)
• Some crisis brings you to a point of making a decision to do something about your drinking ***problem***.(p.377)
• This suggestion had been made before on a number of occasions, but like all alcoholics I wanted to handle my ***problem*** my own way, which really meant I didn't want anything to interfere with my drinking.(p.378)
• The baffling ***problem*** of getting drunk when I had every intention of staying sober was simplified.(p.379)
• For some reason I can't remember, it finally dawned on me that I had a ***problem***, and yet nobody was very critical about it except my family, and that was only because I decided, after seven years of marriage, that I would divorce my husband.(p.386)
• I could see no reason why they should have any relationship to this ***problem*** of getting drunk every now and then.(p.388)
• My alcoholic ***problem*** began long before I drank.(p.400)
• Up to my early thirties, when my drinking had become a major ***problem***, I lived in large houses, with servants and all the luxuries that I could possibly ask for.(p.401)
• "These people all had your ***problem***," she told me.(p.412)
• Anybody who had my ***problem*** was beneath contempt!(p.412)
• He did not take out a folder and say, "What is the nature of your ***problem***?"(p.413)
• I am a young alcoholic with a drug ***problem***, a doctor, the husband of an alcoholic, the son of an alcoholic, and a man once diagnosed as a violent manic-depressive.(p.421)
• I had a drinking ***problem*** on my hands even at that time.(p.424)
• I'd acquired a new girl, a lovely girl who knew of my ***problem*** and had tried to help me.(p.430)
• I have a lovely wife who understands my ***problem*** and helps me with it.(p.431)
• Not only did I not think that being an alcoholic was a good idea, I didn't even feel that I had all that much of a drinking ***problem***!(p.439)
• With a ***problem*** like that, I couldn't go back to sleep.(p.441)
• At last, acceptance proved to be the key to my drinking ***problem***.(p.448)
• When I stopped living in the ***problem*** and began living in the answer, the ***problem*** went away.(p.449)
• If I focus on a ***problem***, the ***problem*** increases; if I focus on the answer, the answer increases.(p.451)
• I figured that perhaps if I went ahead with that marriage, which I was sure was right for me, that would be the answer to my drinking ***problem***.(p.465)
• I join Canadian Army, but could not run away from ***problem***.(p.474)
• It is no ***problem*** to me now, but this is not good management on my part -- just plain good luck.(p.480)
• At this point I believe I had only been intoxicated on maybe three or four occasions, and certainly whiskey was no ***problem*** to me.(p.487)
• I had found this new "something," and I wanted to give it to everyone who had a ***problem***.(p.496)
• Am I willing to be honest with myself about myself and tell someone about myself, and am I willing to think of other people, of their needs instead of myself, in order to get rid of the drink ***problem***?(p.503)
• The only importance in all of this lies in the fact that at twenty-three I was just as sick as I was at thirty three, when I came into A.A., but at that time I apparently had no place to go because I had no drinking ***problem***.(p.546)
• Had I been able to explain to a psychiatrist the feeling of futility, loneliness and lack of purpose that had come with my deep sense of personal failure at this second divorce, I seriously doubt that the good doctor could have convinced me that my basic ***problem*** was a spiritual hunger, but A.A. has shown me this was the truth.(p.546)
• By this time I was such a past master at kidding myself that I had convinced myself I had sat out a war and waited for this man to come home and, as my resentment and self-pity grew, so did my alcoholic ***problem***.(p.548)
• About this time, I met a man who had three motherless children and it seemed that might be a solution to my ***problem***.(p.548)
• I had no ***problem*** admitting I was powerless over alcohol, and I certainly agreed that my life had become unmanageable.(p.550)
• All but one "responded to the treatment" suggested in the Steps immediately, but this one posed a ***problem***.(p.551)
• Immediately, it was part of the pattern and part of the ***problem***.(p.556)
• "The American Public Health Association presents a Lasker Group Award for 1951 to Alcoholics Anonymous in recognition of its unique and highly successful approach to that age-old public health and social ***problem***, alcoholism . . .(p.573)

problems

• Soon A.A. was beset by these very ***problems*** on every side and in every group.(p.xix)
• These allergic types can never safely use alcohol in any form at all; and once having formed the habit and found they cannot break it, once having lost their self-confidence, their reliance upon things human, their ***problems*** pile up on them and become astonishingly difficult to solve.(p.xxvi)
• If any feel that as psychiatrists directing a hospital for alcoholics we appear somewhat sentimental, let them stand with us a while on the firing line, see the tragedies, the despairing wives, the little children; let the solving of these ***problems*** become a part of their daily work, and even of their sleeping moments, and the most cynical will not wonder that we have accepted and encouraged this movement.(p.xxvi)
• On the other hand -- and strange as this may seem to those who do not understand -- once a psychic change has occurred, the very same person who seemed doomed, who had so many ***problems*** he despaired of ever solving them, suddenly finds himself easily able to control his desire for alcohol, the only effort necessary being that required to follow a few simple rules.(p.xxvii)
• My schoolmate visited me, and I fully acquainted him with my ***problems*** and deficiencies.(p.13)
• I was to sit quietly when in doubt, asking only for direction and strength to meet my ***problems*** as He would have me.(p.13)
• My friend promised when these things were done I would enter upon a new relationship with my Creator; that I would have the elements of a way of living which answered all my ***problems***.(p.13)
• My wife and I abandoned ourselves with enthusiasm to the idea of helping other alcoholics to a solution of their ***problems***.(p.15)
• He seemed quite rational and well-balanced with respect to other ***problems***.(p.26)
• Our hope is that many alcoholic men and women, desperately in need, will see these pages, and we believe that it is only by fully disclosing ourselves and our ***problems*** that they will be persuaded to say, "Yes, I am one of them too; I must have this thing."(p.29)
• I reasoned I was not so far advanced as most of you fellows, that I had been usually successful in licking my other personal ***problems***, and that I would therefore be successful where you men failed.(p.40)
• Neither did I have any pressing ***problems*** or worries.(p.41)
• "Quite as important was the discovery that spiritual principles would solve all my ***problems***.(p.42)
• Most alcoholics have to be pretty badly mangled before they really commence to solve their ***problems***.(p.43)
• Many times we talk to a new man and watch his hope rise as we discuss his alcoholic ***problems*** and explain our fellowship.(p.45)
• We had to ask ourselves why we shouldn't apply to our human ***problems*** this same readiness to change our point of view.(p.52)
• When we saw others solve their ***problems*** by a simple reliance upon the Spirit of the Universe, we had to stop doubting the power of God.(p.52)
• We agnostics and atheists were sticking to the idea that self-sufficiency would solve our ***problems***.(p.52)
• Yet we had been seeing another kind of flight, a spiritual liberation from this world, people who rose above their ***problems***.(p.55)
• We all have sex ***problems***.(p.69)
• We usually conclude the period of meditation with a prayer that we be shown all through the day what our next step is to be, that we be given whatever we need to take care of such ***problems***.(p.87)
• Get an idea of his behavior, his ***problems***, his background, the seriousness of his condition, and his religious leanings.(p.90)
• If you have been successful in solving your own domestic ***problems***, tell the newcomer's family how that was accomplished.(p.100)
• After all, our ***problems*** were of our own making.(p.103)
• If God can solve the age-old riddle of alcoholism, He can solve your ***problems*** too.(p.116)
• When we do that, we find it solves our ***problems*** too; the ensuing lack of fear, worry and hurt feelings is a wonderful thing.(p.116)
• But all ***problems*** will not be solved at once.(p.117)
• Many of the old ***problems*** will still be with you.(p.117)
• You and your husband will find that you can dispose of serious ***problems*** easier than you can the trivial ones.(p.118)
• The foregoing pages (though addressed only to wives) indicate the ***problems*** such people may face.(p.121)
• In either case certain family ***problems*** will arise.(p.126)
• The ***problems*** of the community might engage attention.(p.131)
• Do not hesitate to take your health ***problems*** to such persons.(p.133)
• If he feels free to discuss his ***problems*** with you, if he knows you understand and will not be upset by anything he wishes to say, he will probably be off to a fast start.(p.144)
• He saw that he would have to face his ***problems*** squarely that God might give him mastery.(p.155)
• Aside from fellowship and sociability, the prime object was to provide a time and place where new people might bring their ***problems***.(p.160)
• The very practical approach to his ***problems***, the absence of intolerance of any kind, the informality, the genuine democracy, the uncanny understanding which these people had were irresistible.(p.160)
• As I look back, all the brothers developed personality ***problems***.(p.210)
• I realized that I had a problem, although my realization was not very deep because my own conceit wouldn't admit that I had any personality ***problems***.(p.214)
• The successful demonstration I had made of my life ***problems*** in other respects convinced me that some day I was going to be able to drink like a gentleman.(p.214)
• So I began to pray; to place my ***problems*** in God's hands.(p.237)
• Today I have Someone who will always hear me; I have a warm fellowship among men who understand my ***problems***; I have tasks to do and am glad to do them, to see others who are alcoholics and to help them in any way I can to become sober men.(p.260)
• In the end I had two ***problems*** instead of one: Fear and alcohol.(p.275)
• Too many economic and social ***problems*** would beset me there.(p.281)
• I can actually take my ***problems*** to Him and He gives me comfort, peace, and happiness.(p.303)
• I have had my share of ***problems***, heartaches and disappointments, because that is life, but also I have known a great deal of joy, and a peace that is the handmaiden of an inner freedom, I have a wealth of friends and, with my A.A. friends, an unusual quality of fellowship.(p.312)
• I had ***problems***.(p.336)
• I had ***problems***.(p.338)
• Surrender to me has meant the ability to run my home, to face my responsibilities as they should be faced, to take life as it comes to me day by day, and work my ***problems*** out.(p.340)
• That life for me is lived one day at a time, letting the ***problems*** of the future rest with the future.(p.340)
• I had been unhappy, lonely, and scared for so long

that the discovery of liquor seemed to be the answer to all my ***problems***.(p.353)
• I've had more ***problems*** but, thank God, I have had the teachings of A.A. with which to face them.(p.367)
• I don't know what I expected, but I most certainly didn't visualize a group of people talking about their drinking ***problems***, making light of their personal tragedies and at the same time enjoying themselves.(p.378)
• "First Things First": solving our immediate ***problems*** before we try to solve all the others and get muddled in our thinking and doing.(p.382)
• Everyone has ***problems***.(p.382)
• It solved their ***problems*** and they started living a sane life again.(p.427)
• Today I think of life in terms of happiness, contentment, freedom from fear and despair, sane thinking, ability to face ***problems*** as they occur, the opportunity to help other alcoholics and to be decent.(p.430)
• Of course, I had ***problems***, all sort of ***problems***.(p.439)
• "If you had my ***problems***, you'd drink, too" was my feeling.(p.439)
• My major ***problems*** were marital.(p.439)
• She cried a bit and went to bed; that was the only answer to ***problems*** that she had left.(p.440)
• My reaction was that I'd already helped all the patients on the ward, and I still had plenty of ***problems*** of my own without trying to help some drunk from A.A.(p.446)
• I wanted to talk about my many big ***problems***; drinking seemed a small one.(p.447)
• To this day, I am amazed at how many of my ***problems*** -- most of which had nothing to do with drinking, I believed -- have become manageable or have simply disappeared since I quit drinking.(p.448)
• And acceptance is the answer to all my ***problems*** today.(p.449)
• Acceptance has been the answer to my marital ***problems***.(p.450)
• Shortly thereafter, I was selected, with eight other inmates out of the 10,000 in the state's prisons at that time, to attend a school designed to take former "management ***problems***" like me and convert them into paracounselors.(p.462)
• But as he continued to talk, I realized that this was the first time I had met a person who had the same ***problems*** I did and who, I sincerely believe, understood me as an individual.(p.494)
• The same old ***problems*** and worries surround me.(p.505)
• Soon I have others who are alcoholics and some who have other ***problems***.(p.506)
• For the only ***problems*** I have now are those I create when I break out in a rash of self-will.(p.551)
• I have learned to deal with disappointments and ***problems*** that once would have sent me right to the bottle.(p.559)
• By learning -- through practicing the Twelve Steps and through sharing at meetings -- how to cope with the ***problems*** that we looked to booze to solve, back in our drinking days.(p.560)
• Six -- An A.A. group ought never endorse, finance or lend the A.A. name to any related facility or outside enterprise, lest ***problems*** of money, property and prestige divert us from our primary purpose.(p.564)
• 6. -- ***Problems*** of money, property, and authority may easily divert us from our primary spiritual aim.(p.565)
• Most emphatically we wish to say that any alcoholic capable of honestly facing his ***problems*** in the light of our experience can recover, provided he does not close his mind to all spiritual concepts.(p.570)
• They help others with similar ***problems*** . . .(p.572)
• This headquarters will give the location of the nearest family group and will if you wish, correspond with you about your special ***problems***.(p.575)

procedure

• Of course an alcoholic ought to be freed from his physical craving for liquor, and this often requires a definite hospital ***procedure***, before psychological measures can be of maximum benefit.(p.xxv)
• Without much ado, he accepted the principles and ***procedure*** that had helped us.(p.139)
• If you propose such a ***procedure*** to him, it may be necessary to advance the cost of treatment, but we believe it should be made plain that any expense will later be deducted from his pay.(p.143)
• I remembered going through what my sister assured me was my nightly ***procedure*** of trying to find Willie Seabrook's name in the telephone book.(p.224)
• The general ***procedure*** was to take four or five shots in the first place I stopped at.(p.299)
• It was a long four or five hour operation, a large surgical ***procedure***, and she was on her ninth or tenth post-operative day.(p.350)
• Any therapeutic or philosophic ***procedure*** which can prove a recovery rate of 50% to 60% must merit our consideration."(p.571)

proceed

• You will thus get a better idea of how you ought to ***proceed***.(p.91)
• Sometimes a new man is anxious to ***proceed*** at once, and you may be tempted to let him do so.(p.95)
• When your prospect has made such reparation as he can to his family, and has thoroughly explained to them the new principles by which he is living, he should ***proceed*** to put those principles into action at home.(p.98)
• You will want to know more of how to ***proceed*** from that point.(p.153)
• Near the Laundromat, I would buy one bottle of pop and a few bottles of beer or wine, and go into the rest room, empty the pop bottle, refill it with the booze, and ***proceed*** to do my laundering.(p.370)
• I have had the joy of seeing many a human being, down and out, learn to stand straight again, and to ***proceed*** under his own power to happiness in life.(p.541)

proceeded

• Our friend ***proceeded*** to tell him.(p.163)
• I got tight that night, stayed sober Monday till after the dinner and then ***proceeded*** to get tight again.(p.179)
• When they got through the day's work, part was left which I ***proceeded*** to drink.(p.196)
• I ***proceeded*** to take up the drawing and advanced rapidly in it.(p.211)
• I was introduced to them and Clarence ***proceeded*** to put on his Twelve Step work.(p.216)
• He took his one hundred and seventeen dollars and let us go, and we ***proceeded***.(p.264)
• I spent five and a half years in psychoanalysis and ***proceeded*** to become a drunk.(p.349)

proceeding

• The ***proceeding*** was shot through with much hard feeling and controversy.(p.154)

proceeds

• Were our contentions true, it would follow that life originated out of nothing, and ***proceeds*** nowhere.(p.49)
• In this connection, can you remain undisturbed if the man ***proceeds*** to tell you shocking things?(p.145)
• I had some financial success through no ability of my own and, when jobless and almost wiped out in 1930, I began to trade and sell my collection; much of the ***proceeds*** went to keep my apartment stocked with liquor and almost every night saw me helpless to bed.(p.255)

process

• The mushrooming ***process*** was in full swing.(p.xviii)
• Alcohol being no respecter of persons, we are an accurate cross section of America, and in distant lands, the same democratic evening-up ***process*** is now going on.(p.xx)
• Almost none of us liked the self-searching, the leveling of our pride, the confession of shortcomings which the ***process*** requires for its successful consummation.(p.25)
• This ***process*** snuffed out the last flicker of conviction that I could do the job myself.(p.42)
• But the moment I made up my mind to go through with the ***process***, I had the curious feeling that my alcoholic condition was relieved, as in fact it proved to be.(p.42)
• Sometimes this was a tedious ***process***; we hope no one else will be prejudiced for as long as some of us were.(p.48)
• Taking a commercial inventory is a fact-finding and a fact-facing ***process***.(p.64)
• This involves a ***process*** of deflation.(p.122)
• This change had been a long, slow ***process*** for me, but through these latter years the dividends have been tremendous.(p.249)
• The next two years were simply a long drawn out ***process*** of less and less work and more and more whiskey.(p.278)
• For the leveling-off ***process***, I just loved intravenous Demerol, but I found it hard to practice good medicine while shooting morphine.(p.442)
• But I can remember in post graduate days, and during interneship, that very often I'd go to a patient's bed and start a ***process*** of elimination and then, very often, I'd wind up guessing.(p.485)
• And so I got to the swearing off ***process***.(p.513)

processes

• I came to understand the intricate ***processes*** of projection, by which we cast into our adult world the images of the horrors of our childhood.(p.434)

procession

• Now I was to plunge into the dark, joining that endless ***procession*** of sots who had gone on before.(p.8)

proclaimed

• We worked in five below zero weather, fixing on an elm tree a wrought iron device which modestly ***proclaimed*** that he was indeed a country doctor.(p.540)

procrastination

• About that period, too, came increasing ***procrastination*** and the avoidance of responsibilities.(p.197)

procreation

• One set of voices cry that sex is a lust of our lower nature, a base necessity of ***procreation***.(p.68)

procure

• No beer or liquor was sold in the neighborhood, except at the State liquor agency where perhaps one might ***procure*** a pint if he could convince the agent that he really needed it.(p.171)

procured

• At the end of it, my reports to Wall street ***procured*** me a position there and the use of a large expense account.(p.3)

prodded

• He should not be pushed or ***prodded*** by you, his wife, or his friends.(p.95)

Prodigal

• But I can remember the urge of the ***Prodigal*** Son to return to his Father.(p.260)

prodigious

• Then I went on a ***prodigious*** bender, and that chance vanished.(p.5)

prodigy

• In his ***prodigy*** of service, he was well assisted by Sister Ignatia at St. Thomas Hospital in Akron, Ohio, one of the greatest friends our Fellowship will ever know.(p.171)

produce

• One feels that something more than human power is needed to ***produce*** the essential psychic change.(p.xxvii)
• In fact, I have been trying to ***produce*** some such emotional rearrangement within you.(p.27)
• This is a condition which, in ordinary life, would ***produce*** untold grief; there might be scandalous gossip, laughter at the expense of other people, and a tendency to take advantage of intimate information.(p.125)
• There are two alcoholic employees, who ***produce*** as much as five normal salesmen.(p.149)
• Or: If I'm really a genius, I must ***produce*** a great work, to show why I act like a genius.(p.408)
• For me, pills don't ***produce*** the desire to swallow a pill; they ***produce*** the symptoms that require that the pill be taken for relief.(p.443)

produced

• Men and women drink essentially because they like the effect ***produced*** by alcohol.(p.xxvi)

producer

• Is he not, even in his best moments, a ***producer*** of confusion rather than harmony?(p.61)

produces

• A man may criticize or laugh at himself and it will affect others favorably, but criticism or ridicule coming from another often ***produces*** the contrary effect.(p.125)
• Sobriety and a plan for living that ***produces*** a personality change and a spiritual awakening are imperative.(p.459)
• The idea behind it is that, having taken the treatment, your system is so "conditioned" that the mere sight or smell or taste of alcohol ***produces*** a violent reaction, and you become ill.(p.469)

product

• He may not see at once that he has barely scratched a limitless lode which will pay dividends only if he mines it for the rest of his life and insists on giving away the entire ***product***.(p.129)
• I was a ***product*** of the post-war prohibition era of the roaring '20's.(p.304)

production

• Their cost of ***production*** is figured to a fine decimal point.(p.149)

productive

• Each day seems to be so much more ***productive*** and satisfying.(p.383)

productively

• Federal Theatre in Texas gave me an administrative

job which I held for a year, only because I worked hard and *productively* when I worked, and because my very tolerant chief ascribed my frequent lapses to a bohemian temperament.(p.256)

profession
• Small wonder many in the medical *profession* have a low opinion of alcoholics and their chance for recovery!(p.73)
• The law school experience was not inspired by a desire to follow patent law, which has been my *profession* since: I went to law school primarily to learn the law of contracts following my own experience with litigation.(p.212)
• But this day my doctor gave it to me straight and said, "People like you are pretty well known to the medical *profession*.(p.307)
• I'd worked hard to be tops in my *profession*.(p.328)
• I had worked so long in a *profession* where fakery, deceit, and untruths are tools of trade that I instantly recognized honesty when I heard it, from the mouths of A.A. members.(p.334)
• I eventually became a schoolmaster, but gave up that *profession* to join the Indian Army.(p.342)
• I achieved recognized and national standing in my *profession*, as well as becoming a director in many important institutions having to do with the civic life of a large city.(p.374)
• Many times in the intervening years I have thanked God for that man, a man who had the courage to admit failure, a man who had the humility to confess that all the hard-won learning of his *profession* could not turn up the answer.(p.436)
• The medical *profession* would probably tell me I was conditioned for alcoholism by the things that happened to me in my childhood.(p.544)
• I think our *profession* must take appreciative cognizance of this great therapeutic weapon.(p.571)

professional
• Being mostly business or *professional* folk, we could not well carry on our occupations in such an event.(p.xiii)
• It was thought that no alcoholic man or woman could be excluded from our Society; that our leaders might serve but never govern; that each group was to be autonomous and there was to be no *professional* class of therapy.(p.xix)
• Business and *professional* men have regained their standing.(p.15)
• Though some of his manifestations are alarming and disagreeable, we think dad will be on a firmer foundation than the man who is placing business or *professional* success ahead of spiritual development.(p.129)
• My father was a *professional* man of recognized ability and both my father and mother were most active in church affairs.(p.171)
• My efficiency as a *professional* man was probably reduced to twenty-five per cent of what it should have been.(p.215)
• With nothing but a liberal arts education, very definitely estranged from my family and already married, soon after graduation from college I became a bookmaker's clerk on the British racing circuits, far better off financially than the average *professional* man.(p.251)
• There were business men, *professional* men, and factory workers.(p.258)
• My outward *professional* life looked fine, on the surface.(p.435)

professionalism
• We define *professionalism* as the occupation of counseling alcoholics for fees or hire.(p.566)

professionally
• There had been some occasions -- there was an automobile wreck, for instance -- when I had police escort home but not to jail, all of which, instead of doing me a favor, did me harm because I was then full of self-esteem as to the progress I had made both *professionally* and financially.(p.213)
• *Professionally*, after I was sober for a month or so I realized that I should school myself to dissolve the partnership I was in because I felt that I would never regain the respect of my partners no matter how long I was sober, and that I would be at a disadvantage.(p.220)

professor
• Did not *Professor* Langley's flying machine go to the bottom of the Potomac River?(p.51)

proffered
• I could almost hear the sound of the preacher's voice as I sat, on still Sundays, way over there on the hillside; there was that *proffered* temperance pledge I never signed; my grandfather's good natured contempt of some church folk and their doings; his insistence that the spheres really had their music; but his denial of the preacher's right to tell him how he must listen; his fearlessness as he spoke of these things just before he died; these recollections welled up from the past.(p.10)

profit
• The unselfishness of these men as we have come to know them, the entire absence of *profit* motive, and their community spirit, is indeed inspiring to one who has labored long and wearily in this alcoholic field.(p.xxv)
• The exercise of an option brought in more money, leaving us with a *profit* of several thousand dollars for that year.(p.3)
• I sensed they had something I did not have, from which I might readily *profit*.(p.178)
• I had bought a piece of ground in Cuyahoga Falls and cut it into lots and had a *profit* of approximately $40,000 and that was a lot of money in those days.(p.194)
• With that *profit*, I built a number of houses, but then I neglected them.(p.194)
• I lost money, and then just fooled away a large part of that *profit*.(p.194)
• They did not seem to be getting an answer, for here I was staying sober and selling lots of auto polish, on which they were making one thousand per cent *profit*.(p.247)

profited
• And again these were things that I really *profited* by after I sobered up.(p.409)

profitably
• To me, this incident illustrates lack of understanding as to what really ails the alcoholic, and lack of knowledge as to what part employers might *profitably* take in salvaging their sick employees.(p.139)

profits
• I was to share generously in the *profits*.(p.5)

profound
• God comes to most men gradually, but His impact on me was sudden and *profound*.(p.14)
• Above all, he believed he had acquired such a *profound* knowledge of the inner workings of his mind and its hidden springs that relapse was unthinkable.(p.26)
• Though not a religious person, I have *profound* respect for the spiritual approach in such cases as yours.(p.43)
• There will be other *profound* changes in the household.(p.130)
• He finally realizes that he has undergone a *profound* alteration in his reaction to life; that such a change could hardly have been brought about by himself alone.(p.569)
• Even among those who occasionally land back in here again, we observe a *profound* change in personality.(p.572)

program
• Therefore, the first portion of this volume, describing the A.A. recovery *program*, has been left untouched in the course of revisions made for both the second and the third editions.(p.xi)
• If you have a drinking problem, we hope that you may pause in reading one of the forty-four personal stories and think: "Yes, that happened to me"; or, more important, "Yes, I've felt like that"; or most important, "Yes, I believe this *program* can work for me, too."(p.xii)
• Other thousands came to a few A.A. meetings and at first decided they didn't want the *program*.(p.xx)
• The basic principles of the A.A. *program*, it appears, hold good for individuals with many different lifestyles, just as the *program* has brought recovery to those of many different nationalities.(p.xxii)
• The Twelve Steps that summarize the *program* may be called los Doce Pasos in one country, los Douze Etapes in another, but they trace exactly the same path to recovery that was blazed by the earliest members of Alcoholics Anonymous.(p.xxii)
• They had told of a simple religious idea and a practical *program* of action.(p.9)
• This should suggest a useful *program* for anyone concerned with a drinking problem.(p.19)
• "Then they outlined the spiritual answer and *program* of action which a hundred of them had followed successfully.(p.42)
• But the *program* of action, though entirely sensible, was pretty drastic.(p.42)
• Those who do not recover are people who cannot or will not completely give themselves to this simple *program*, usually men and women who are constitutionally incapable of being honest with themselves.(p.58)
• Here are the steps we took, which are suggested as a *program* of recovery:(p.59)
• This brings us to the Fifth Step in the *program* of recovery mentioned in the preceding chapter.(p.72)
• Having persevered with the rest of the *program*, they wondered why they fell.(p.73)
• It is easy to let up on the spiritual *program* of action and rest on our laurels.(p.85)
• Outline the *program* of action, explaining how you made a self-appraisal, how you straightened out your past and why you are now endeavoring to be helpful to him.(p.94)
• Your candidate may give reasons why he need not follow all of the *program*.(p.94)
• He has read this volume and says he is prepared to go through with the Twelve Steps of the *program* of recovery.(p.96)
• Let the alcoholic continue his *program* day by day.(p.99)
• Avoid urging him to follow our *program*.(p.113)
• He may not share your enthusiasm, but he is practically sure to read the book and he may go for the *program* at once.(p.113)
• We urge you to try our *program*, for nothing will be so helpful to your husband as the radically changed attitude toward him which God will show you how to have.(p.117)
• Though it is entirely separate from Alcoholics Anonymous, it uses the general principles of the A.A. *program* as a guide for husbands, wives, relatives, friends, and others close to alcoholics.(p.121)
• They criticize, pointing out how he is falling down on his spiritual *program*.(p.126)
• Nothing will help the man who is off on a spiritual tangent so much as the wife who adopts a sane spiritual *program*, making a better practical use of it.(p.130)
• If he is conscientiously following the *program* of recovery he can go anywhere your business may call him.(p.147)
• They came in and began to give me instruction in the *program* which later became known as Alcoholics Anonymous.(p.185)
• We're not up here trying to take any of your rights or privileges away from you, but we have a *program* whereby we think we can stay sober.(p.186)
• Part of that *program* is that we take it to someone else, that needs it and wants it.(p.186)
• It was in the next two or three days after I had first met Doc and Bill, that I finally came to a decision to turn my will over to God and to go along with this *program* the best that I could.(p.189)
• I wasn't afraid that the *program* wouldn't work, but I still was doubtful whether I would be able to hang on to the *program*, but I did come to the conclusion that I was willing to put everything I had into it, with God's power, and that I wanted to do just that.(p.189)
• You should go out and take this *program* to somebody else that needs it and wants it."(p.190)
• I really wanted the *program* and I wanted to go along with it.(p.191)
• That sentence, "The Lord has been so wonderful to me, curing me of this terrible disease, that I just want to keep telling people about it," has been sort of a golden text for the A.A. *program* and for me.(p.191)
• I'm so grateful for both the *program* and the people in it that I still want to go, and then probably the most wonderful thing that I learned from the *program* -- I've seen this in the 'A.A. Grapevine' a lot of times, and I've had people say it to me personally, and I've heard people get up in meetings and make the same statement: The statement is, "I came into A.A. solely for the purpose of sobriety, but it has been through A.A. that I have found God."(p.192)
• The very simple *program* they advised me to follow was that I should ask to know God's will for me for that one day, and then, to the best of my ability, to follow that, and at night to express my gratefulness to God for the things that had happened to me during the day.(p.208)
• Dr. Bob did not lay out the whole *program*.(p.218)
• The afternoon that I was to leave the hospital, he came in to see me and asked me if I were willing to attempt to follow the *program*.(p.218)
• One of the things that came up repeatedly in the stories they told me was that once they had accepted the *program*, they never had a desire to take a drink.(p.219)
• There was a concrete *program*, designed to secure the greatest possible inner security for us long-time escapists.(p.229)
• When I started to tell the boys how we did it in New York and all about the spiritual part of the *program*, I found they would not believe me unless I was practicing what I preached.(p.249)
• And that woman told me long after that was the surest proof to her that this *program* could work.(p.272)

• I hadn't been in too long when one of the men's wives called me one Sunday and told me she didn't think I had any part of the ***program.***(p.273)
• I was crying, and I said, "Alice says she knows I don't have any part of the ***program.***"(p.273)
• I used to think I was cowardly because when things came out pertaining to the ***program*** that troubled me, I said to her many times, "Annie, am I being a coward because I lay those things away on the shelf and skip it?"(p.273)
• It was simple, they said, and went on to explain to me in their own language the ***program*** of recovery and daily living which we know today as the Twelve Steps of A.A.(p.279)
• The A.A. ***program*** showed me the way to come down to earth, start from the bottom and work up.(p.284)
• We are both depending upon God and our use of the A.A. ***program*** to help us make a success of this joint undertaking.(p.286)
• In the next two or three days the balance of this handful of men contacted me, encouraged me, and told me how they were trying to live this ***program*** of recovery and the fun they were having doing it.(p.291)
• The ***program*** was carried on entirely by word of mouth.(p.291)
• I stayed in Akron two or three weeks on my initial trip trying to absorb as much of the ***program*** and philosophy as possible.(p.291)
• I spent a great deal of time with Dr. Bob, whenever he had the time to spare, and in the homes of two or three other people, trying to see how the family lived the ***program.***(p.291)
• The day before I was due to go back to Chicago, a Wednesday and Dr. Bob's afternoon off, he had me down to the office and we spent three or four hours formally going through the Six-Step ***program*** as it was at that time.(p.291)
• One of them was that I would try to get a group started in Chicago; the second was that I would have to return to Akron to attend meetings at least every two months until I did get a group started in Chicago; third, I decided I must place this ***program*** above everything else, even my family, because if I did not maintain my sobriety I would lose my family anyway.(p.292)
• In the summer of 1938, almost a year from the time I made my original contact with Akron, the man for whom I was working and who knew about the ***program,*** approached me and asked if I could do anything about one of his salesmen who was drinking very heavily.(p.294)
• I spent several days with him, but I did not feel adequate to pass the ***program*** on to him alone.(p.294)
• I suggested to her that she should see the son's minister or doctor, and that perhaps he would recommend the A.A. ***program.***(p.294)
• The doctor, a young man, immediately took fire with the idea, and while he did not convince the son, he turned over two prospects who were anxious for the ***program.***(p.294)
• In the meantime, another doctor in Evanston became convinced that the ***program*** had possibilities, and turned over a woman to us to do something about.(p.295)
• This and the ***program*** of recovery embodied in the Twelve Steps.(p.311)
• As arrested alcoholics, we must have a ***program*** for living that allows for limitless expansion.(p.311)
• I try to live our ***program*** as it has been outlined to me, one day at a time.(p.325)
• That fear, of course, necessitated a ***program*** of hidden alcoholism.(p.331)
• Out of those forty years as a movie press agent came one blessing that granted me a blind faith in the ***program.***(p.334)
• I heard one very ill woman say that she didn't believe in the surrender part of the A.A. ***program.***(p.340)
• I had been brought up to believe in God, but I know that until I found this A.A. ***program,*** I had never found or known faith in the reality of God, the reality of His power that is now with me in everything I do.(p.341)
• I have never attended an A.A. meeting, so it is essentially the literature that has kept me on the A.A. ***program.***(p.342)
• He had come back, however, and he was on this ***program.***(p.346)
• And I gave him some idea of what you do, and so I made my first Twelfth Step call before I ever came into the ***program.***(p.347)
• I have been on this ***program*** for three months and I feel terrible."(p.348)
• "Complete abandon"; "Half measures availed us nothing"; "Thoroughly follow our path"; "Completely give oneself to this simple ***program***" – rang in my swelled head.(p.349)
• Shortly after I was starting to work on the ***program*** I realized that I was not a good father; I wasn't a good husband, but, oh, I was a good provider.(p.351)
• You'll read and hear a great deal about the spiritual part of our ***program.***(p.366)
• To the new man I would also like to say that this ***program*** is not for sissies for, in my humble opinion, it takes a man to make the grade.(p.367)
• If I were asked what in my opinion was the most important factor in being successful in this ***program,*** besides following the Twelve Steps, I would say Honesty.(p.367)
• From the start I liked everything about the A.A. ***program.***(p.380)
• A willingness to do whatever I was told to do simplified the ***program*** for me.(p.381)
• The fact that A.A. is a spiritual ***program*** didn't scare me or raise any prejudice in my mind.(p.383)
• Today, I find I can't work my A.A. ***program*** while taking pills, nor may I even have them around for dire emergencies only.(p.443)
• After I had been around A.A. for seven months, tapering off alcohol and pills, not finding the ***program*** working very well, I was finally able to say, "Okay, God.(p.448)
• On the contrary, the hardest place to work this ***program*** has been in my own home, with my own children and, finally, with Max.(p.451)
• During these seven years a thing called the Twenty-four Hour ***Program*** --a gadget I used to think was only a snare to trap the newcomer -- has come to mean much to me, not only as regards my drinking but in the whole pattern of my life.(p.473)
• To me, ***program*** is spiritual.(p.477)
• There is no cure for alcoholism, but it can be arrested in the ***program*** of A.A.(p.480)
• I don't believe this ***program*** would work for me if I didn't get honest with myself about everything.(p.482)
• When I had heard about it, it meant nothing but just two letters to me, but some friends of mine in the institution were very active in the ***program*** and really believed in it.(p.509)
• I don't know anyone in the ***program.***"(p.510)
• I think I am very lucky that there are people like A.A.'s and an A.A. ***program*** to hang on to and carry me through.(p.511)
• Because, thank God, since I came into this ***program*** I haven't had any trouble.(p.516)
• In this ***program*** there aren't any half way measures.(p.516)
• I am hoping that writing this may bring some poor, mixed-up soul into the ***program.***(p.530)
• It's time to stop finding excuses for drinking and getting into trouble, because now there is a way out, and if you want what we have, try coming around and giving the ***program*** a chance.(p.530)
• What is much more important to me, A.A. has taught me that through this simple ***program*** I may experience a change in this reaction pattern that will indeed allow me to "match calamity with serenity."(p.544)
• This caused the rather cryptic comment from one of my A.A. friends, when I told my story after coming into the ***program,*** that I had always been a cinch for the ***program,*** for I had always been interested in mankind, but that I was just taking them one man at a time.(p.548)
• The people who came knew immediately I was in no condition to absorb anything of the ***program,*** and I was put in a sanitarium to be defogged so that I could make a sober decision about this for myself.(p.549)
• I attended my first A.A. meeting eight years ago, and it is with deep gratitude that I'm able to say I've not had a drink since that time, and that I take no sedation or narcotics, for this ***program*** is to me one of complete sobriety and I no longer need to escape reality.(p.549)
• One of the truly great things A.A. has taught me is that reality too has two sides; I had only known the grim side before the ***program,*** but now I had a chance to learn about the pleasant side as well.(p.550)
• They said if you want to know how this ***program*** works, take the first word of your question – the H is for honesty, the O is for open-mindedness and the W is for willingness; these our Book calls the essentials of recovery.(p.550)
• I've had many spiritual experiences since I've been in the ***program,*** many that I didn't recognize right away, for I'm slow to learn and they take many guises.(p.551)
• While there, I read the Big Book and the Grapevine and began the slow road back to health and sanity through the recovery ***program*** of A.A.(p.559)
• Similarly, we rid ourselves of guilt and remorse as we "clean out the garbage" from our minds through the Fourth and Fifth Steps of our recovery ***program.***(p.560)
• We find that no one need have difficulty with the spirituality of the ***program.***(p.570)
• I now conceive the psychiatrist's job to be the task of breaking down the patient's inner resistance so that which is inside him will flower, as under the activity of the A.A. ***program.***"(p.571)

program-oriented

• For my seventh A.A. birthday, my ***program-oriented,*** Al-Anon wife had my moccasins bronzed.(p.445)

programing

• New ***programing*** was beginning to build an audience, but sponsors were pretty scarce.(p.360)

progress

• Without such support, A.A. could have made only the slowest ***progress.***(p.xx)
• This world of ours has made more material ***progress*** in the last century than in all the millenniums which went before.(p.51)
• Yet in ancient times material ***progress*** was painfully slow.(p.51)
• The principles we have set down are guides to ***progress.***(p.60)
• We claim spiritual ***progress*** rather than spiritual perfection.(p.60)
• Rarely do we fail to make satisfactory ***progress.***(p.78)
• Tell him you once felt as he does, but you doubt whether you would have made much ***progress*** had you not taken action.(p.94)
• Both you and the new man must walk day by day in the path of spiritual ***progress.***(p.100)
• Let them praise his ***progress.***(p.127)
• For us, material well-being always followed spiritual ***progress;*** it never preceded.(p.127)
• From that point on, ***progress*** will be rapid.(p.134)
• There had been some occasions -- there was an automobile wreck, for instance -- when I had police escort home but not to jail, all of which, instead of doing me a favor, did me harm because I was then full of self-esteem as to the ***progress*** I had made both professionally and financially.(p.213)
• Many things happened; business trials, little worries, and feelings of general despondency came near driving me to the bottle, but I made ***progress.***(p.237)
• He is my best teacher; without him, I am sure I would never have made the ***progress*** I have.(p.481)

progressed

• As the treatment ***progressed*** I began to get a picture of myself, of the temperament that had caused me so much trouble.(p.226)
• It started out as a good marriage, but it deteriorated over the years as she ***progressed*** through the various stages of qualifying for Al-Anon.(p.439)
• As I ***progressed*** and gained in capacity, I had blackouts.(p.512)
• It seems only fitting that when I did finally fall in love it was with an alcoholic, and for the next ten years I ***progressed*** as rapidly as is humanly possible into what I believed to be hopeless alcoholism.(p.547)
• Much later, when I had ***progressed*** to full-blown alcoholism, people told me I should quit.(p.554)

progressing

• I have to tell myself, "Other things are ***progressing*** and A.A. must too."(p.272)

progression

• He laid great stress on the ***progression*** of his attitude toward life and people, and most of his attitudes had been very similar to mine.(p.290)

progressive

• We are convinced to a man that alcoholics of our type are in the grip of a ***progressive*** illness.(p.30)
• They are far more alert and ***progressive*** than we floundering fathers were, and the future of our fellowship is in their hands.(p.250)
• There are many things worse than dying, but is there any death worse than the ***progressive,*** self-induced, slow suicide of the practicing alcoholic?(p.457)

progressively

• As time went on my drinking became ***progressively*** worse.(p.184)
• But, of course," he continued, "eventually the alcoholic loses all of his capacities as his disease gets ***progressively*** worse, and this is a tragedy that is painful to watch; the disintegration of a sound mind and body."(p.308)
• They had been drinking for many years and were getting ***progressively*** worse.(p.424)

• It became ***progressively*** harder to get up in the morning, until one day I asked myself what I would do for a patient who felt this rotten.(p.441)
• It has gotten ***progressively*** easier.(p.448)

prohibited
• (This is very useful knowledge in places where matches are ***prohibited.***)(p.245)

prohibition
• Then ***Prohibition*** came into effect, and the facts that the stuff obtainable was so horrible and sometimes deadly, and that I had married and had a job which I had to look after, helped me for a period of some three or four years, although I would get drunk every time I could get hold of enough to drink to get started.(p.183)
• My drinking career began about four years after I had moved up into partnership and had joined certain clubs, societies and so fourth, and during which period we had ***Prohibition.***(p.213)
• All during ***Prohibition,*** every alcoholic felt that he made the best hooch, regardless of how bad it was.(p.213)
• The times in which I grew up (the ***Prohibition*** era immortalized by Scott Fitzgerald and John Held Jr.) had taught me to be gay with the gayest; my own inner urges led me to outdo them all.(p.225)
• ***Prohibition*** came.(p.232)
• We saw very early that ***Prohibition*** wasn't going to work.(p.232)
• An originator of Cleveland's Group No. 3, this one fought ***Prohibition*** in vain.(p.297)
• I was a product of the post-war ***prohibition*** era of the roaring '20's.(p.304)
• ***Prohibition*** came along, and with it my first taste of moonshine.(p.357)
• This was at the height of the Depression and the end of ***Prohibition.***(p.358)

project
• Another time, I had a rubber pool ***project.***(p.198)
• At this time, however, she had an opportunity to go to Salt Lake City on a new ***project*** for the government, but she did promise me that if I would curtail my drinking and buckle down to hard work she would give serious consideration to my latest proposal and maybe join me at a later date when I got settled.(p.359)
• But, as it was with drinking, this ***project*** will be entered into with enthusiasm and optimism -- and probably wind up the same way, depressed.(p.396)
• I suspect that if it is wisely handled – and it seems to be in wise and prudent hands – there are doors of opportunity ahead of this ***project*** that may surpass our capacities to imagine."(p.574)

projection
• I came to understand the intricate processes of ***projection,*** by which we cast into our adult world the images of the horrors of our childhood.(p.434)

projects
• We had long talks when I would still her foreboding by telling her that men of genius conceived their best ***projects*** when drunk; that the most majestic constructions of philosophic thought were so derived.(p.2)

prolonged
• This went from bad to worse until Sophomore spring when, after a ***prolonged*** period of drinking, I made up my mind that I could not complete my course, so I packed my grip and went South to spend a month on a large farm owned by a friend of mine.(p.173)
• When I entered a sanitarium for ***prolonged*** and intensive psychiatric treatment, I was convinced that I was having a serious mental breakdown.(p.226)

prominent
• A well-known doctor, chief physician at a nationally ***prominent*** hospital specializing in alcoholic and drug addiction, gave Alcoholics Anonymous this letter:(p.xxiii)
• When I need a mental uplift, I often think of another case brought in by a physician ***prominent*** in New York.(p.xxix)
• I well remember the shock I received when a ***prominent*** doctor in Chicago told me of cases where pressure of the spinal fluid actually ruptured the brain.(p.140)
• He got in touch with a ***prominent*** psychiatrist who had undertaken certain responsibilities for the mental health of the community.(p.163)
• I was born in Cleveland, Ohio, the only child of a ***prominent*** dentist, and a very proud mother.(p.357)
• I was married and divorced again before I was twenty-three years old, this time to a ***prominent*** band leader -- a man that many women wanted.(p.546)
• During the day a friend of mine brought me some magazines to take to a hospital group I was interested in, and I looked through them and a "banner" across the front of one featured an article by a ***prominent*** clergyman in which I caught the word "resentment."(p.552)

promise
• The outlines and the ***promise*** of the New Land had brought lustre to tired eyes and fresh courage to flagging spirits.(p.53)
• I used to ***promise*** my wife, my friends, and my children that I would drink no more – promises which seldom kept me sober even through the day, though I was very sincere when I made them.(p.177)
• Wishing to be polite, though I felt very badly, I said, "Let's make the call," and extracted from my wife a ***promise*** that we would not stay over fifteen minutes.(p.179)
• So I was driving to Cleveland when I made this solemn ***promise*** never to drink again.(p.201)
• I would ***promise*** to have jobs done and never do them.(p.234)
• As I look back on the events of two months, I can clearly see that I had been circling around, half-afraid of encountering the remedy for my situation, half wanting it, deferring fulfillment of my ***promise*** to get in touch with the doctor I had heard about.(p.258)
• At this time, however, she had an opportunity to go to Salt Lake City on a new project for the government, but she did ***promise*** me that if I would curtail my drinking and buckle down to hard work she would give serious consideration to my latest proposal and maybe join me at a later date when I got settled.(p.359)
• Time after time I would beg forgiveness on bended knees, with tears rolling down my cheeks, and ***promise*** I would never again drink too much.(p.362)
• A year later, while we were on a vacation trip she packed up to go home because of my excessive drinking, and I talked her out of it with the ***promise*** I would go on the wagon for at least a year.(p.377)
• The early ***promise*** of the "boy wonder" faded, and my career began to drift.(p.556)

promised
• My friend ***promised*** when these things were done I would enter upon a new relationship with my Creator; that I would have the elements of a way of living which answered all my problems.(p.13)
• But my friends usually found me and I would go home if they ***promised*** that I should not be scolded.(p.176)
• At that time, as I remember, he had ***promised*** never to take another drink.(p.193)
• They asked me if I would take some medicine, and I ***promised*** that I would if they got me a drink.(p.206)
• I got two drinks, each of them a quarter of that pint, in me, and was talking along with these people, but I felt that sooner or later they were going to have me cornered because they were smarter than I was and the drink was beginning to take effect; but as I reached for the third drink Bob said, "Listen, Buster, you ***promised*** to take some medicine if we got you a drink.(p.206)
• I arrived drunk, but I ***promised*** my wife I would keep sober, and I knew I could get work if I did.(p.256)
• I thanked him, pleaded business engagements and ***promised*** I'd go with him at some future date.(p.257)
• It explained so much I had not understood about myself and, best of all, it ***promised*** recovery if I would do a few simple things and be willing to have the desire to drink removed.(p.309)
• I ***promised*** my two sponsors that I would attend their meeting the next Tuesday evening.(p.363)
• It was a shock of course, but I ***promised*** to stop and she returned.(p.377)
• I ***promised,*** but within two months, I began again.(p.377)
• Again I ***promised*** to do something about it.(p.377)
• Max accepted responsibility for me after I had ***promised*** never to drink again, never to take another pill, never to swear again, and never to talk to girls again.(p.444)
• I ***promised*** that I was going to do the right thing.(p.490)
• I ***promised*** on the grave of a beloved sister that I would stop drinking.(p.539)

promises
• Before then, I had written lots of sweet ***promises,*** but my wife happily observed that this time I meant business.(p.5)
• On through the years this conduct continues, accompanied by his continual ***promises*** to be careful or to keep off the streets altogether.(p.38)
• Are these extravagant ***promises?***(p.84)
• But at least he will understand the problem and will no longer be misled by ordinary ***promises.***(p.148)
• I used to promise my wife, my friends, and my children that I would drink no more – ***promises*** which seldom kept me sober even through the day, though I was very sincere when I made them.(p.177)
• With the big companies, and with the amount of money we could have gotten and the ***promises*** I had, it could have been done.(p.198)
• How could I continually break my ***promises?***(p.362)
• I made ***promises*** to myself, my family and friends – and broke them.(p.375)
• Broken ***promises,*** humiliation, hopelessness, worry, anxiety – but still not enough.(p.377)
• They build you up with a lot of false hopes and ***promises,*** and rush you around here and there and then, all of a sudden, it's gone."(p.472)
• I knew my wife didn't because I had been sincere in all my ***promises*** to her as well as to my mother and to my close friends, but the urge to take that drink was more powerful than anything else.(p.494)

promising
• All told, ***promising*** beginnings have been made in some 50 foreign countries and U.S. possessions.(p.xv)
• Then I got a ***promising*** business opportunity.(p.5)
• He often possesses special abilities, skills, and aptitudes, and has a ***promising*** career ahead of him.(p.21)
• His income is good, he has a fine home, is happily married and the father of ***promising*** children of college age.(p.39)
• Here was a prospect all right but, by the description, none too ***promising.***(p.156)
• An offer of appreciation for not having had a drink for those few months and then and there, without anybody ***promising*** me anything or threatening me, I made a solemn vow that never so long as I lived would I take another drink.(p.200)

promote
• Use your energies to ***promote*** a better understanding all around.(p.115)

promoted
• *PROMOTED* TO CHRONIC(p.464)
• I had been ***promoted*** from a periodic drinker to a chronic alcoholic!(p.470)

promotion
• Our public relations were to be based upon attraction rather than ***promotion.***(p.xix)
• My next job was in sales ***promotion*** for an oil company in Mississippi where I promptly became high man and got lots of pats on the back.(p.242)
• As part of this ***promotion,*** they sent me to their national convention in Atlantic City to tell the big wheels how I'd done it.(p.243)
• After being fired, I lined up with a new finance company that was just starting in business, and took the position of business ***promotion*** man, contacting automobile dealers.(p.300)
• They passed me over for ***promotion*** twice.(p.318)
• Eleven -- Our public relations policy is based on attraction rather than ***promotion;*** we need always maintain personal anonymity at the level of press, radio and films.(p.564)
• Our public relations should be guided by the principle of attraction rather than ***promotion.***(p.567)

promotions
• Until I was thirteen I attended public schools, with regular ***promotions*** and average grades.(p.240)

prompt
• If you cannot find A.A. in your locality, a letter addressed to Alcoholics Anonymous, Box 459, Grand Central Station, New York, NY 10163, U.S.A., will receive a ***prompt*** reply from this world center, referring you to the nearest A.A. group.(p.575)

prompted
• Like most statistics, it doesn't prove anything -- just satisfies a little curiosity engendered by the wail "Oh, those initiation fees" that ***prompted*** this investigation.(p.399)

promptly
• A second small group had ***promptly*** taken shape at New York.(p.xvii)
• 10.Continued to take personal inventory and when we were wrong ***promptly*** admitted it.(p.59)
• One object is to disclose damaged or unsalable goods, to get rid of them ***promptly*** and without regret.(p.64)
• My next job was in sales promotion for an oil company in Mississippi where I ***promptly*** became high man and got lots of pats on the back.(p.242)
• I made arrangements to enter the hospital three days later and ***promptly*** went out and got stiff for three days.(p.302)

proms
• I started drinking socially and at parties and *proms* when I was about twenty years old.(p.464)

prone
• I was *prone* to do everything on a big scale.(p.197)

pronounce
• We do not like to *pronounce* any individual as alcoholic, but you can quickly diagnose yourself.(p.31)

pronounced
• Doctors had *pronounced* him incurable.(p.11)
• Curious about it, feeling I was missing something, absolutely without any illusions about the aftermath, with no *pronounced* feeling of patriotism, I joined up with a Canadian regiment, serving a little over two years.(p.253)
• The doctor *pronounced* it a badly enlarged liver and said I had to quit drinking.(p.557)

proof
• Everybody nowadays, believes in scores of assumptions for which there is good evidence, but no perfect visual *proof*.(p.48)
• And does not science demonstrate that visual *proof* is the weakest *proof*?(p.48)
• Without this *proof* the expectant purchaser would be forced to depart empty handed with none of what I later came to believe was the great panacea for all human ills.(p.171)
• And that woman told me long after that was the surest *proof* to her that this program could work.(p.272)
• For myself, I have an absolute *proof* of the existence of God.(p.350)
• This to me is the *proof* of the existence of a Somethingness greater than I am.(p.351)
• "There is a principle which is a bar against all information, which is *proof* against all arguments and which cannot fail to keep a man in everlasting ignorance – that principle is contempt prior to investigation."(p.570)

prop
• All I had left was an iron determination to live my own life in spite of the alien world -- and here I was, an inwardly frightened, outwardly defiant woman, who desperately needed a *prop* to keep going.(p.226)
• Alcohol was that *prop*, and I didn't see how I could live without it.(p.226)
• I wanted to learn to stand on my own feet, not to change one *prop* for another, and an intangible and dubious one at that.(p.227)

propelled
• A little more than fifteen years ago, through a long and calamitous series of shattering experiences, I found myself being helplessly *propelled* toward total destruction.(p.304)

propensity
• I had never known him to be anything but a good healthy pagan with a *propensity* for getting into liquor jams and scrapes.(p.257)

proper
• It is the *proper* use of the will.(p.85)
• It works, if we have the *proper* attitude and work at it.(p.86)
• At *proper* time and place explain to all your friends why alcohol disagrees with you.(p.102)
• I believe that my once over-weening self-will has finally found its *proper* place, for I can say many times daily, "Thy will be done, not mine" . . . and mean it.(p.229)
• The scales had dropped from my eyes and I could see life in its *proper* perspective.(p.280)
• A few months after I made my original trip to Akron I was feeling pretty cocky, and I didn't think my wife was treating me with *proper* respect, now that I was an outstanding citizen.(p.293)
• I still had a wife and family, a home and a car, my driver's license, and a *proper* amount of insurance.(p.327)
• There, I could be a *proper* mother and wife while drinking up a storm.(p.369)
• Mother was of the old school and figured that anyone I associated with should be of the *proper* type.(p.484)
• I remember the day when I decided to drink myself to death quietly, without bothering anyone, because I was tired of having been a dependable, trustworthy person for about thirty-nine years without having received what I thought was a *proper* reward for my virtue.(p.531)
• This question so insulted the emotions that clearly there was only one thing to do, go and get drunk again, and put that enquiring mind in its *proper* place, which was oblivion.(p.537)

properly
• But the ex-problem drinker who has found this solution, who is *properly* armed with facts about himself, can generally win the entire confidence of another alcoholic in a few hours.(p.18)
• Those of us belonging to a religious denomination which requires confession must, and of course, will want to go to the *properly* appointed authority whose duty it is to receive it.(p.74)
• Are the stones *properly* in place?(p.75)
• It was here I came to know *properly* what alcohol was.(p.343)

property
• I went downstairs and there was the grizzly old veteran police officer in charge of the *property* desk, and as he gave me the stuff, he asked, "Are you going out in the street that way?"(p.204)
• I switched into real estate brokerage and *property* management work.(p.277)
• My alcoholic wife took up someone else, divorced me, and took with her all my remaining *property*.(p.437)
• My new wife and I don't own any *property* to speak of, and the flashy successes of another day are no longer mine.(p.438)
• Dad, due to having spent most of his time in a small Virginia town, didn't have any too much money, and the money he had saved and the *property* he had acquired were in Washington.(p.486)
• About that time I had lost practically all my *property* except the place we were living in.(p.487)
• Six – An A.A. group ought never endorse, finance or lend the A.A. name to any related facility or outside enterprise, lest problems of money, *property* and prestige divert us from our primary purpose.(p.564)
• 6. – Problems of money, *property*, and authority may easily divert us from our primary spiritual aim.(p.565)
• We think, therefore, that any considerable *property* of genuine use to A.A. should be separately incorporated and managed, thus dividing the material from the spiritual.(p.565)
• Secondary aids to A.A., such as clubs or hospitals which require much *property* or administration, ought to be incorporated and so set apart that, if necessary, they can be freely discarded by the groups.(p.566)
• Experience has often warned us that nothing can so surely destroy our spiritual heritage as futile disputes over *property*, money, and authority.(p.566)

prophesied
• I now remembered what my alcoholic friends had told me, how they *prophesied* that if I had an alcoholic mind, the time and place would come – I would drink again.(p.41)

proportion
• Women now make up more than one-fourth of the membership; among newer members, the *proportion* is nearly one-third.(p.xxii)
• How can such a lack of *proportion*, of the ability to think straight, be called anything else?(p.37)
• Making amends is sometimes doing what we are capable of doing but failed to do because of alcohol; carrying out community responsibilities such as Community Funds, Red Cross, educational and religious activities in *proportion* to our abilities and energy.(p.381)
• A.A. has taught me that I will have peace of mind in exact *proportion* to the peace of mind I bring into the lives of other people, and it has taught me the true meaning of the admonition "happy are ye who know these things and do them."(p.551)

proportional
• Perhaps the best thing of all for me is to remember that my serenity is inversely *proportional* to my expectations.(p.452)
• I must keep my magic magnifying mind on my acceptance and off my expectations, for my serenity is directly *proportional* to my level of acceptance.(p.452)

proportionately
• As income increased, the price of liquor increased *proportionately*.(p.398)

proportions
• My drinking assumed more serious *proportions*, continuing all day and almost every night.(p.3)
• Hangovers began to assume monstrous *proportions* and the morning drink became an urgent necessity.(p.226)
• I realize now that this phase of my development had been arrested by my obsession with self, and my egocentricity had reached such *proportions* that adjustment to anything outside my personal control was impossible for me.(p.547)

proposal
• Show any longshoreman a Sunday supplement describing a *proposal* to explore the moon by means of a rocket and he will say, "I bet they do it -- maybe not so long either."(p.52)
• We agnostically inclined would not feel satisfied with a *proposal* which does not lend itself to reasonable approach and interpretation.(p.53)
• At this time, however, she had an opportunity to go to Salt Lake City on a new project for the government, but she did promise me that if I would curtail my drinking and buckle down to hard work she would give serious consideration to my latest *proposal* and maybe join me at a later date when I got settled.(p.359)

proposals
• These were revolutionary and drastic *proposals*, but the moment I fully accepted them, the effect was electric.(p.14)
• Though I had been only a nominal churchman, their *proposals* were not, intellectually, hard to swallow.(p.42)
• Carefully reading the first five *proposals* we ask if we have omitted anything, for we are building an arch through which we shall walk a free man at last.(p.75)

propose
• If you *propose* such a procedure to him, it may be necessary to advance the cost of treatment, but we believe it should be made plain that any expense will later be deducted from his pay.(p.143)

proposes
• In our belief any scheme of combating alcoholism which *proposes* to shield the sick man from temptation is doomed to failure.(p.101)

proposition
• Few people really are, for that means blind faith in the strange *proposition* that this universe originated in a cipher and aimlessly rushes nowhere.(p.10)
• On one *proposition*, however, these men and women are strikingly agreed.(p.50)
• When we became alcoholics, crushed by a self-imposed crisis we could not postpone or evade, we had to fearlessly face the *proposition* that either God is everything or else He is nothing.(p.53)

propositions
• I had to concede both *propositions*.(p.42)

prosaic
• The *prosaic* steel girder is a mass of electrons whirling around each other at incredible speed.(p.48)

prospect
• That the man who is making the approach has had the same difficulty, that he obviously knows what he is talking about, that his whole deportment shouts at the new *prospect* that he is a man with a real answer, that he has no attitude of Holier Than Thou, nothing whatever except the sincere desire to be helpful; that there are no fees to pay, no axes to grind, no people to please, no lectures to be endured – these are the conditions we have found most effective.(p.18)
• When you discover a *prospect* for Alcoholics Anonymous, find out all you can about him.(p.90)
• Under these conditions your *prospect* will see he is under no pressure.(p.91)
• Your *prospect* may belong to a religious denomination.(p.93)
• Do not be discouraged if your *prospect* does not respond at once.(p.96)
• When your *prospect* has made such reparation as he can to his family, and has thoroughly explained to them the new principles by which he is living, he should proceed to put those principles into action at home.(p.98)
• Remind the *prospect* that his recovery is not dependent upon people.(p.99)
• He need not, and often should not show it to his alcoholic *prospect*.(p.148)
• They explained their need and inquired if she had a first class alcoholic *prospect*.(p.156)
• Here was a *prospect* all right but, by the description, none too promising.(p.156)
• Next day found the *prospect* more receptive.(p.158)
• A doctor tipped me off to my first *prospect*.(p.282)
• I, who had never made a speech in my life and who would have been frightened sick at the *prospect*, stood up in front of Rotary groups in different parts of the city and talked about Alcoholics Anonymous.(p.283)

prospective
• Businessmen, traveling out of existing groups, were referred to these *prospective* newcomers.(p.xviii)

prospector
• Like a gaunt *prospector,* belt drawn in over the last ounce of food, our pick struck gold.(p.128)

prospects
• Then I decided to drive into the country and see one of my *prospects* for a car.(p.36)
• One of our Fellowship failed entirely with his first half dozen *prospects.*(p.96)
• I was married at the age of nineteen to a grand girl and had good business *prospects.*(p.194)
• I wanted "ripe" *prospects* and I didn't feel that I would get very far chasing individual drunks in and out of bars.(p.281)
• The doctor, a young man, immediately took fire with the idea, and while he did not convince the son, he turned over two *prospects* who were anxious for the program.(p.294)
• The three of us did not feel up to the job, and after a few meetings we convinced the *prospects* that they too should go to Akron where they could see an older group in action.(p.295)

prospered
• So in spite of anything that I might do, I *prospered,* being one of only two brokers in the rubber center of the world.(p.197)

prosperity
• The rubber *prosperity* went on for about six years -- 1916 to 1922.(p.197)
• Ask for their health, their *prosperity,* their happiness, and you will be free.(p.552)

prosperous
• I had run into him, and he looked real *prosperous;* his face and eyes looked clear and he started to compliment me on my good front and how well I looked, and I said, "I haven't had a drink for nine months."(p.201)
• My family lived in very *prosperous* circumstances, and while both my parents drank, sometimes too much, neither was an alcoholic.(p.240)

protect
• We have told innumerable lies to *protect* our pride and our husbands' reputations.(p.105)
• Your desire to *protect* him should not cause you to lie to people when they have a right to know where he is and what he is doing.(p.115)
• The employer can many times *protect* the victim from this kind of talk.(p.145)
• Safely pensioned, with no job to *protect,* at last he could drink as he pleased.(p.327)
• She did all she could to help this situation and to *protect* my child.(p.409)
• Let group spirit of love and understanding *protect* you.(p.477)

protected
• We feel as though we had been placed in a position of neutrality – safe and *protected.*(p.85)
• Naturally, in spite of my good intentions, in spite of my *protected* life behind sanitarium walls, I several times got drunk, and was astounded . . . and badly shaken.(p.227)

protecting
• I had been far too busy building, *protecting,* and maintaining an image of respectability and all the other business pluses.(p.327)

protection
• We asked His *protection* and care with complete abandon.(p.59)
• Unless they actually need *protection* from their father, it is best not to take sides in any argument he has with them while drinking.(p.115)
• And the last sentence was "We asked His *protection* and care with complete abandon."(p.349)

protective
• My inability to accept the harsh realities of life had resulted in a disillusioned cynic, clothed in *protective* armor against the world's misunderstanding.(p.226)

protege
• Even though your *protege* may not have entirely admitted his condition, he has become very curious to know how you got well.(p.92)

protest
• I had even borrowed money from her, over her *protest:* "Bob, please don't ask me to lend you money -- you're the only one who hasn't."(p.540)

Protestant
• (My mother and father were Catholics and I had been baptized, but at the end of my instructions for Confirmation I had not gone to church, and then when my mother remarried, she married a *Protestant* and the whole religious angle was forgotten.(p.201)
• At thirteen I was packed off to a very fine *Protestant* boarding school in Virginia where I stayed four years, graduating without any special achievements.(p.240)

Protestants
• By personal religious affiliation, we include Catholics, *Protestants,* Jews, Hindus, and a sprinkling of Moslems and Buddhists.(p.xx)

protested
• When I *protested,* his lawyer, my lawyer, and my third and last analyst had a conference.(p.409)

protocol
• At a large party in Geneva, with people from many countries represented, the kind of party that is "*protocol*" in the extreme, I swayed, laughed hysterically, made naughty remarks in an unhushed voice, and was finally led from the scene.(p.406)

proud
• At three-thirty the next morning, I was in Champlain Street Station, in jail for driving while intoxicated and insulting an officer; and the suit of which I was so *proud* was in such shape that the turnkey had to get me a pair of trousers to go into court in the next morning.(p.201)
• She took me by the hand and introduced me to the girl that I'm very *proud* to call my sponsor.(p.321)
• I was born in Cleveland, Ohio, the only child of a prominent dentist, and a very *proud* mother.(p.357)
• All I can remember about the Roaring Twenties is that I drank a great deal, thought I was having a grand time, managed to get to Europe for a few weeks, was very *proud* of the dozens of speak-easy cards entitling me to an entree in the better joints between Cleveland and New York, took on a wife, and built a home in a fashionable suburb of Cleveland.(p.358)
• *Proud* of my little station and of my new bride I settled down to a happy married life.(p.361)
• I had a family to be *proud* of, actively sharing in the responsibilities of good citizenship.(p.374)
• I *proud* to be son of Tall Man, American Indian, and member of A.A. for many moons.(p.474)
• She must have been real *proud* of us, I'm sure.(p.480)
• My *proud* southern blood would have boiled if anyone had named me such a despicable thing.(p.532)

prove
• For them, we hope these pages will *prove* so convincing that no further authentication will be necessary.(p.xiii)
• This seemed to *prove* that one alcoholic could affect another as no nonalcoholic could.(p.xvi)
• I'd *prove* to the world I was important.(p.2)
• Therefore, it is not surprising that our drinking careers have been characterized by countless vain attempts to *prove* we could drink like other people.(p.30)
• By every form of self-deception and experimentation, they will try to *prove* themselves exceptions to the rule, therefore nonalcoholic.(p.31)
• We could not *prove* life in the sense that you can *prove* a straight line is the shortest distance between two points, yet, there it was.(p.54)
• Maybe it will *prove* a blessing!(p.116)
• His present views ought to *prove* exceptionally useful to business men everywhere.(p.136)
• Firing such an individual may *prove* a blessing to him.(p.141)
• I was going to *prove* to her that liquor wasn't necessary in my life, and above all that I still loved her more than anything else in the world and that I wanted her back.(p.362)
• Like most statistics, it doesn't *prove* anything -- just satisfies a little curiosity engendered by the wail "Oh, those initiation fees" that prompted this investigation.(p.399)
• To be sure, I learned many fascinating things, and many things that were to *prove* helpful later.(p.434)
• They *prove* to almost anyone's satisfaction that it's never too late to try Alcoholics Anonymous.(p.455)
• Any therapeutic or philosophic procedure which can *prove* a recovery rate of 50% to 60% must merit our consideration."(p.571)

proved
• What seemed at first a flimsy reed, has *proved* to be the loving and powerful hand of God.(p.28)
• But the moment I made up my mind to go through with the process, I had the curious feeling that my alcoholic condition was relieved, as in fact it *proved* to be.(p.42)
• Was it not true that the best mathematical minds had *proved* man could never fly?(p.51)
• What about people who *proved* that man could never fly?(p.55)
• He *proved* to be a devil-may-care young fellow whose parents could not make out whether he wanted to stop drinking or not.(p.158)
• The doctor *proved* to be able and exceedingly anxious to adopt any workable method of handling the situation.(p.163)
• This I did, and *proved* myself satisfactory to the faculty, both in deportment and scholastically.(p.174)
• So I didn't have a beer one night, and as I drove home I was breaking my arm patting myself on the back because I had *proved* I could lick liquor.(p.203)
• I had *proved* that liquor was not my master.(p.203)
• A return to the United States *proved* effective as a geographical cure, and a period of sobriety ensued, with the help of the church.(p.419)
• And I'd *proved* I couldn't handle it, time and again.(p.429)
• At last, acceptance *proved* to be the key to my drinking problem.(p.448)
• However, one thing I am certain of: Inmates in prison who attend A.A. have their chances of remaining free greatly enhanced -- this is a *proved* fact.(p.458)
• But this *proved* only a temporary setback.(p.517)

proven
• It has been repeatedly *proven* among us that upon this simple cornerstone a wonderfully effective spiritual structure can be built.(p.47)
• Searching where I have been at fault, it is not hard to discover and get right again, for I have *proven* to myself and to many others who know me that God can keep a man sober if he will let Him.(p.237)

proves
• Our own recovery *proves* that!(p.153)
• This *proves* I don't know what's good for me.(p.450)
• The mental twists that led up to my drinking began many years before I ever took a drink for I am one of those whose history *proves* conclusively that my drinking was "a symptom of a deeper trouble."(p.544)

provide
• Except in a few rare cases, neither he nor any other human being can *provide* such a defense.(p.43)
• We thought he ought to be willing to do that if necessary, but if he were in jail he could *provide* nothing for either family.(p.79)
• Yet we do go to great extremes to *provide* each other with these very things, when such action is warranted.(p.98)
• Aside from fellowship and sociability, the prime object was to *provide* a time and place where new people might bring their problems.(p.160)
• He would invariably reply, "When you are right and the time is right, Providence will *provide.*(p.293)
• Need I add that such was the case because I had no money to *provide* a roof over my head?(p.538)
• A.A. has given me serenity of purpose, the opportunity to be of service to God and to the people about me, and I am serene in the infallibility of these principles that *provide* the fulfillment of my purpose.(p.551)

provided
• He can go anywhere on this earth where other free men may go without disaster, *provided* he remains willing to maintain a certain simple attitude.(p.26)
• As soon as we admitted the possible existence of a Creative Intelligence, a Spirit of the Universe underlying the totality of things, we began to be possessed of a new sense of power and direction, *provided* we took other simple steps.(p.46)
• Nevertheless, the twentieth century readily accepts theories of all kinds, *provided* they are firmly grounded in fact.(p.48)
• Being all powerful, He *provided* what we needed, if we kept close to Him and performed His work well.(p.63)
• We must be willing to make amends where we have done harm, *provided* that we do not bring about still more harm in so doing.(p.69)
• He can choose any conception he likes, *provided* it makes sense to him.(p.93)
• These things will come to pass naturally and in good time *provided,* however, the alcoholic continues to demonstrate that he can be sober, considerate, and helpful, regardless of what anyone says or does.(p.99)
• Some of us still serve it to our friends *provided* they are not alcoholic.(p.102)
• After your man has gone along without drinking for a few months, you may be able to make use of his services with other employees who are giving you the alcoholic run-around -- *provided,* of course, they are willing to have a third party in the picture.(p.146)
• If your organization is a large one, your junior executives might be *provided* with this book.(p.147)
• Why should this happen to me – hadn't I *provided* a good home – wasn't I making a good living – didn't

I just get a substantial raise that had put me in the upper bracket class?(p.362)

• It had *provided* me with excuses for my lack of education, my marital failures, personal failures, inadequacy, and of course, my alcoholism and, though I really thought I had been willing to part with it, now I knew I was reluctant to let it go.(p.552)

• We are taught to differentiate between our wants (which are never satisfied) and our needs (which are always *provided* for).(p.560)

• Any two or three alcoholics gathered together for sobriety may call themselves an A.A. group, *provided* that, as a group, they have no other affiliation.(p.565)

• Most emphatically we wish to say that any alcoholic capable of honestly facing his problems in the light of our experience can recover, *provided* he does not close his mind to all spiritual concepts.(p.570)

Providence

• To a person who has had experience with an alcoholic, this may seem like tempting *Providence*, but it isn't.(p.101)

• He would invariably reply, "When you are right and the time is right, *Providence* will provide.(p.293)

• But *Providence* had other ideas.(p.464)

providentially

• *Providentially*, this was a Monday might when the Dublin Group met in those days, and my family agreed that if A.A. could do anything for me at all, that I'd be allowed to stay on at home on probation.(p.523)

provider

• Shortly after I was starting to work on the program I realized that I was not a good father; I wasn't a good husband, but, oh, I was a good *provider*.(p.351)

provides

• I had nothing to put in the place of alcohol, of the forgetfulness, of the oblivion, which alcohol *provides*.(p.539)

providing

• Though you are *providing* him with the best possible medical attention, he should understand that he must undergo a change of heart.(p.143)

provinces

• Groups are to be found in each of the United States and all of the *provinces* of Canada.(p.xv)

proving

• Though there is no way of *proving* it, we believe that early in our drinking careers most of us could have stopped drinking.(p.32)

• I was caught in a cycle of alcohol and sedation that was *proving* inescapable and consciousness had become intolerable.(p.304)

• When I did make it home in 1920, I re-entered school and caught up with my class in a few short months – I actually did a year's work in three months, *proving* much to the disgust of my dad that I could do it when I wanted to.(p.358)

provocation

• Sometimes they hurt us, seemingly without *provocation*, but we invariably find that at some time in the past we have made decisions based on self which later placed us in a position to be hurt.(p.62)

• Then, under one *provocation* or another, the aggrieved one would unearth the old affair and angrily cast its ashes about.(p.124)

• The employer cannot play favorites, but he can always defend a man from needless *provocation* and unfair criticism.(p.146)

• That was enough *provocation* to fight but I didn't fight, and I realized after recess why I didn't.(p.484)

provoked

• Eventually, of course, what with all the hilarity that could be *provoked* with a few gallons of beer, there seemed to be no need of bridge or poker playing for entertainment.(p.297)

prowling

• I started *prowling* around with a couple of these A.A. boys, which kept me pretty busy and kept my mind off of down town.(p.511)

prudent

• Then too, we view with much concern those A.A. treasuries which continue, beyond *prudent* reserves, to accumulate funds for no stated A.A. purpose.(p.566)

• I suspect that if it is wisely handled – and it seems to be in wise and *prudent* hands – there are doors of opportunity ahead of this project that may surpass our capacities to imagine."(p.574)

psalmist

• If pressed further, all I can do is follow the *psalmist* who said it long, long before me: "Be still, and know that I am God."(p.437)

pseudo-sophistication

• That age of the flapper and the "It" girl, speakeasies and the hip flask, the boyish bob and the drugstore cowboy, John Held Jr. and F. Scott Fitzgerald, all generously sprinkled with a patent *pseudo-sophistication*.(p.304)

psychiatric

• Though the aggregate of recoveries resulting from *psychiatric* effort is considerable, we physicians must admit we have made little impression upon the problem as a whole.(p.xxvii)

• Of necessity there will have to be discussion of matters medical, *psychiatric*, social, and religious.(p.19)

• When I entered a sanitarium for prolonged and intensive *psychiatric* treatment, I was convinced that I was having a serious mental breakdown.(p.226)

• (I belong to the American *Psychiatric* Society, but I don't practice psychiatry as such.(p.347)

• I recall, as I walked into that meeting, saying to myself, "Here I am, a fellow of the American College of Surgeons, a Fellow of the International College of Surgeons, a diplomate of one of the great specialty boards in these United States, a member of the American *Psychiatric* Society, and I have to go to the butcher, the baker and the carpenter to help make a man out of me!"(p.347)

• To cut a long story short, I spent seven years and ten thousand dollars on my *psychiatric* adventure, and emerged in worse condition than ever.(p.434)

• I remember, one time, even the dog had a *psychiatric* diagnosis.(p.440)

• And then I went back home to live with my parents, and the merry-go-round started again – only this time I didn't have to worry about waking up behind bars in a *psychiatric* ward.(p.468)

• But I would always wake up in the *psychiatric* ward to begin another long treatment.(p.528)

• The American *Psychiatric* Association requested, in 1949, that a paper be prepared by one of the older members of Alcoholics Anonymous to be read at the Association's annual meeting of that year.(p.572)

psychiatrist

• Strangely enough, wives, parents and intimate friends usually find us even more unapproachable than do the *psychiatrist* and the doctor.(p.18)

• Then he had gone to Europe, placing himself in the care of a celebrated physician (the *psychiatrist*, Dr. Jung) who prescribed for him.(p.26)

• A good doctor or *psychiatrist* can tell you whether these complications are serious.(p.114)

• Try to remember that though God has wrought miracles among us, we should never belittle a good doctor or *psychiatrist*.(p.133)

• He got in touch with a prominent *psychiatrist* who had undertaken certain responsibilities for the mental health of the community.(p.163)

• Arrangements were also made with the chief *psychiatrist* of a large public hospital to select still others from the stream of misery which flows through that institution.(p.163)

• I was sent to a *psychiatrist*, for they didn't think it was normal for me to want to kill my platoon sergeant or to attempt suicide twice.(p.318)

• *Psychiatrist* and surgeon, he had lost his way until he realized that God, not he, was the Great Healer.(p.345)

• I was introduced as a *psychiatrist*.(p.347)

• As someone in A.A. said to me once upon a time, there is nothing worse than a confused *psychiatrist*.(p.347)

• And the *psychiatrist* has had thousands of couches, and has put you and me on them many, many times, but he hasn't helped us very much, though he has tried hard; and we owe the clergy and the doctor and the *psychiatrist* a deep debt of gratitude, but they haven't helped our alcoholism, except in a rare few instances.(p.352)

• I suppose the *psychiatrist* might say, "This is benevolent interpersonal relations.(p.352)

• I tried psychiatry, but of course I gave the *psychiatrist* no co-operation.(p.375)

• I had been reading a lot about psychiatry and I thought, "Maybe if I talk to a *psychiatrist* he can find out what is happening, and then I can drink like a lady."(p.387)

• Frank said, "If you'd like to talk to a *psychiatrist*, I'll see a doctor and find out who to go to here."(p.387)

• You tell that dumb cat-and-dog doctor he's not a Beverly Hills *psychiatrist*.(p.440)

• He arranged for me to see a local *psychiatrist*, who quickly decided I should be in the mental-health unit of our local hospital.(p.445)

• One day as I sat there in the hospital, my *psychiatrist* walked up behind me and asked, "How'd you like to talk to the man from A.A.?"(p.446)

• The *psychiatrist*, who had generally been ignoring me, now became quite interested; every day, he would ask me all kinds of questions about the A.A. meetings.(p.446)

• "That's a devil of a way to run an organization," I thought, and I reported Frank to the *psychiatrist*, who didn't seem perturbed; he just got someone else to take me on Fridays.(p.447)

• Eventually, the *psychiatrist* discharged me from the hospital, and Max and I began going to meetings ourselves.(p.447)

• On one occasion when I was serving time in my favorite drying-out place while I was having a session with the *psychiatrist*, she left my case history on her desk when she was called away from the room.(p.470)

• I had a long talk with a *psychiatrist*, but nothing came of that, and I had also, just about that time, talked with a minister for whom I had a great deal of respect.(p.489)

• The closest I came to a *psychiatrist* during that time was an interne who came to take blood tests.(p.492)

• Had I been able to explain to a *psychiatrist* the feeling of futility, loneliness and lack of purpose that had come with my deep sense of personal failure at this second divorce, I seriously doubt that the good doctor could have convinced me that my basic problem was a spiritual hunger, but A.A. has shown me this was the truth.(p.546)

• My doctor finally declared he could no longer be responsible for me, and sent me to a *psychiatrist* who practiced in the same suite of offices.(p.558)

• He happened to be, by the grace of God, Dr. Harry Tiebout, the *psychiatrist* who probably knew more about alcoholism than any other in the world.(p.559)

• Dr. G. Kirby Collier, *psychiatrist*: "I have felt that A.A. is a group unto themselves and their best results can be had under their own guidance, as a result of their philosophy.(p.571)

• Dr. Harry M. Tiebout, *psychiatrist*: "As a *psychiatrist*, I have thought a great deal about the relationship of my specialty to A.A. and I have come to the conclusion that our particular function can very often lie in preparing the way for the patient to accept any sort of treatment or outside help.(p.571)

• Dr. John F. Stouffer, Chief *Psychiatrist*, Philadelphia General Hospital, citing his experience with A.A., said: "The alcoholics we get here at Philadelphia General are mostly those who cannot afford private treatment, and A.A. is by far the greatest thing we have been able to offer them.(p.572)

psychiatrist's

• Perhaps it was He who sent my analyst to a *psychiatrist's* meeting at which Bill spoke.(p.412)

• The next day, Max called the neurologist and told him about the Mayo *psychiatrist's* opinion.(p.445)

• But, by the look on the *psychiatrist's* face, I could tell that it would really make him happy if I agreed.(p.446)

• I now conceive the *psychiatrist's* job to be the task of breaking down the patient's inner resistance so that which is inside him will flower, as under the activity of the A.A. program."(p.571)

psychiatrists

• If any feel that as *psychiatrists* directing a hospital for alcoholics we appear somewhat sentimental, let them stand with us a while on the firing line, see the tragedies, the despairing wives, the little children; let the solving of these problems become a part of their daily work, and even of their sleeping moments, and the most cynical will not wonder that we have accepted and encouraged this movement.(p.xxvi)

• Highly competent *psychiatrists* who have dealt with us have found it sometimes impossible to persuade an alcoholic to discuss his situation without reserve.(p.18)

• He had consulted the best known American *psychiatrists*.(p.26)

• Many doctors and *psychiatrists* agree with our conclusions.(p.43)

• Psychiatry might have helped, but *psychiatrists* had not penetrated the middle west.(p.276)

• I had sent her to four consecutive *psychiatrists*, and not one of them had gotten me sober.(p.440)

• I also sent my kids to *psychiatrists*.(p.440)

• There were doctors and *psychiatrists* there who tried to help me, but at that point I wasn't having help from anyone.(p.468)

• Here was a book that said I could do something that all these doctors and priests and ministers and *psychiatrists* that I'd been going to for years couldn't do!(p.473)

psychiatry

• *Psychiatry* might have helped, but psychiatrists had not penetrated the middle west.(p.276)

• (I belong to the American Psychiatric Society, but I don't practice *psychiatry* as such.(p.347)
• I tried *psychiatry*, but of course I gave the psychiatrist no co-operation.(p.375)
• I had been reading a lot about *psychiatry* and I thought, "Maybe if I talk to a psychiatrist he can find out what is happening, and then I can drink like a lady."(p.387)
• In those days, *psychiatry* and A.A. had not gotten together as they have since.(p.412)
• I tried the church and *psychiatry* and finally came to A.A.(p.418)
• This was done, and the paper was printed in the American Journal of *Psychiatry* for November, 1949.(p.572)

psychic
• This is repeated over and over, and unless this person can experience an entire *psychic* change there is very little hope of his recovery.(p.xxvii)
• On the other hand – and strange as this may seem to those who do not understand – once a *psychic* change has occurred, the very same person who seemed doomed, who had so many problems he despaired of ever solving them, suddenly finds himself easily able to control his desire for alcohol, the only effort necessary being that required to follow a few simple rules.(p.xxvii)
• One feels that something more than human power is needed to produce the essential *psychic* change.(p.xxvii)

psycho
• So, when it ended up at a *psycho* ward, I wasn't all that surprised.(p.440)
• The same doctor who had sent me to the *psycho* had asked my husband, "Why don't you send her to this Alcoholics Anonymous?"(p.469)
• In all the sanitariums and *psycho* wards I had never met a single woman who said she was an alcoholic.(p.471)
• After a while, I found that the *psycho* ward was a good place to hide when I had taken something stolen to the pawnshop.(p.528)
• I didn't want that, so I stopped going to the *psycho* ward.(p.528)

psychoanalysis
• Years earlier, I had gone into *psychoanalysis* to get relief.(p.349)
• I spent five and a half years in *psychoanalysis* and proceeded to become a drunk.(p.349)
• A friend had found help in *psychoanalysis*.(p.434)

psychoanalysts
• It took me three *psychoanalysts* and several years in A.A. to really get this through my head.(p.401)

psychological
• Of course an alcoholic ought to be freed from his physical craving for liquor, and this often requires a definite hospital procedure, before *psychological* measures can be of maximum benefit.(p.xxv)
• Many types do not respond to the ordinary *psychological* approach.(p.xxvii)

psychologically
• Speaking at a dinner given by John D. Rockefeller Jr. to introduce Alcoholics Anonymous to some of his friends, Dr. Harry Emerson Fosdick remarked: "I think that *psychologically* speaking there is a point of advantage in the approach that is being made in this movement that cannot be duplicated.(p.574)

psychologist
• The distinguished American *psychologist*, William James, in his book "Varieties of Religious Experience," indicates a multitude of ways in which men have discovered God.(p.28)
• Perhaps our doctor or *psychologist* will be the person.(p.74)
• There should be no hesitancy in consulting a doctor or *psychologist* if the condition persists.(p.134)
• Most of our experiences are what the *psychologist* William James calls the "educational variety" because they develop slowly over a period of time.(p.569)

psychologists
• *Psychologists* are inclined to agree with us.(p.73)
• God has abundantly supplied this world with fine doctors, *psychologists*, and practitioners of various kinds.(p.133)

psychology
• We doctors have realized for a long time that some form of moral *psychology* was of urgent importance to alcoholics, but its application presented difficulties beyond our conception.(p.xxv)
• His alcoholic problem was so complex, and his depression so great, that we felt his only hope would be through what we then called "moral *psychology*," and we doubted if even that would have any effect.(p.xxix)

psychopathic
• This time I didn't put up any fight because I knew why they were there and where I was going, the *psychopathic* ward of the City Hospital, where I had been once before.(p.468)

psychopaths
• There are, of course, the *psychopaths* who are emotionally unstable.(p.xxviii)

psychosis
• So it drove me deeper into the *psychosis* or neurosis that I had, and that I hated deep down in my heart.(p.388)

psychosomatic
• I suppose the doctor might say, "This is *psychosomatic* medicine."(p.352)

psychotherapy
• I don't mean that in any sense as a derogatory statement about *psychotherapy*; it's a great tool, not too potent, but a great tool.(p.349)
• I suppose others would say, "This is group *psychotherapy*."(p.352)

pub
• Coming out of a *pub* near the Cunard pier I saw the Lusitania standing out in the middle of the Mersey.(p.252)

public
• Then Jack Alexander wrote a feature article in the Saturday Evening Post and placed such a compelling picture of A.A. before the general *public* that alcoholics in need of help really deluged us.(p.xviii)
• Our *public* relations were to be based upon attraction rather than promotion.(p.xix)
• And in no circumstances should we give endorsements, make alliances, or enter *public* controversies.(p.xix)
• While the internal difficulties of our adolescent period were being ironed out, *public* acceptance of A.A. grew by leaps and bounds.(p.xix)
• How could he possibly make a *public* statement exonerating his rival?(p.80)
• Some day we hope that Alcoholics Anonymous will help the *public* to a better realization of the gravity of the alcoholic problem, but we shall be of little use if our attitude is one of bitterness or hostility.(p.103)
• Arrangements were also made with the chief psychiatrist of a large *public* hospital to select still others from the stream of misery which flows through that institution.(p.163)
• I went to both Catholic and *public* schools.(p.214)
• Until I was thirteen I attended *public* schools, with regular promotions and average grades.(p.240)
• Alone in the relative safety of my home because I knew I dare not risk the danger of blacking out in some *public* place or at the wheel of a car.(p.306)
• Until I took Social Security and a pension at the age of sixty-eight, after forty years in motion-picture-studio *public* relations, I had successfully hidden even any hints of approaching alcoholism.(p.327)
• So long as a retiree woos his bottle at home, he stays out of *public* trouble.(p.330)
• I finished high school here in an American-sponsored Methodist *public* school, know as Philander Smith College.(p.342)
• I was raised like the majority of American boys, coming from a family of modest circumstances, attending *public* schools, having the social life of a small midwestern town, with part-time work and some athletics.(p.373)
• The book was published, but the reading *public* said -- So what?(p.403)
• Tasting the best of burgundy at a famous restaurant one night, landed me passed out on a park bench in the *public* square.(p.405)
• My opinions were quoted in Time and Newsweek with pictures, and I addressed the *public* by radio and television.(p.435)
• I went to a very good *public* school run by Jesuits.(p.517)
• I left this home town, then, after I had made a *public* spectacle of myself in the presence of a revered teacher whose favorite pupil I had been.(p.539)
• Instead of drinking in fancy bars and clubs, I had to carry a bottle of vodka in my briefcase, duck into *public* toilets, and gulp from the bottle, trembling, in order to keep from falling apart.(p.557)
• Ten – Alcoholics Anonymous has no opinion on outside issues; hence the A.A. name ought never be drawn into *public* controversy.(p.564)
• Eleven – Our *public* relations policy is based on attraction rather than promotion; we need always maintain personal anonymity at the level of press, radio and films.(p.564)
• We think that each group should soon achieve this ideal; that any *public* solicitation of funds using the name of Alcoholics Anonymous is highly dangerous, whether by groups, clubs, hospitals, or other outside agencies; that acceptance of large gifts from any source, or of contributions carrying any obligation whatever, is unwise.(p.566)
• They are authorized by the groups to handle our over-all *public* relations and they guarantee the integrity of our principal newspaper, the A.A. Grapevine.(p.567)
• 11. – Our relations with the general *public* should be characterized by personal anonymity.(p.567)
• Our *public* relations should be guided by the principle of attraction rather than promotion.(p.567)
• "The American *Public* Health Association presents a Lasker Group Award for 1951 to Alcoholics Anonymous in recognition of its unique and highly successful approach to that age-old *public* health and social problem, alcoholism . . .(p.573)

publication
• It is important that we remain anonymous because we are too few, at present to handle the overwhelming number of personal appeals which may result from this *publication*.(p.xiii)
• This determination bore fruit in the spring of 1939 by the *publication* of this volume.(p.xvii)
• But somehow my good doctor heard of this book and also he learned a little about the people responsible for its *publication*.(p.307)
• I landed a good job with a company *publication* and was moonlighting on other magazines.(p.555)

publications
• He'll never read in his "sweetness and light" senior-citizen *publications* anything but the joys of lolling in the rocking chair, angling on the riverbank, or bowling on the green.(p.330)
• I was active and did well, however, in school *publications*, dramatics (which came in handy during my drinking career), and Greek letter societies.(p.357)

publicist
• All the joys of retirement lay ahead for this movie *publicist*.(p.327)
• Not long ago, I was lunching with another retired *publicist*.(p.334)

publicity
• I applied for a *publicity* job and got it.(p.254)
• Returning to the town I had left three months before, I became editor of a monthly magazine, soon had additional *publicity* and advertising accounts and the money rolled in.(p.254)
• However, due to financial difficulties the whole printing was, for a while, held up and the book received no *publicity*, nor, of course, was it available in the stores, even if one knew it existed.(p.307)
• A square from ultra-dry Kansas, I did not taste grog until I had finished college, done a stint on newspapers, married, become a father, and been in studio *publicity* two years.(p.328)
• My mother's heartbreak, or the unpleasant *publicity* I had caused did not bother my pretty head.(p.401)
• At that time there hadn't been any *publicity* such as we have now.(p.469)

publicly
• When writing or speaking *publicly* about alcoholism, we urge each of our Fellowship to omit his personal name, designating himself instead as "a member of Alcoholics Anonymous."(p.xiii)
• Our names and pictures as A.A. members ought not be broadcast, filmed, or *publicly* printed.(p.567)

publish
• We have concluded to *publish* an anonymous volume setting forth the problem as we see it.(p.19)

published
• The second edition, *published* in 1955, reached a total of more than 1,150,000 copies.(p.xi)
• Since this book was first *published*, A.A. has released thousands of alcoholics from asylums and hospitals of every kind.(p.114)
• The book was *published*, but the reading public said – So what?(p.403)
• I have *published* a book covering certain aspects of this field which has been well-reviewed and which is helping other people.(p.541)

publishing
• I was now head of a *publishing* venture in which nearly a million dollars had been invested.(p.435)

pubs
• I moved in a gay crowd in the various "*pubs*" and sporting clubs.(p.251)

pudding
• My Quaker mother-in-law, bless her heart, used to

set the Christmas ***pudding*** ablaze with lumps of sugar dipped in rubbing alcohol.(p.402)

puffs

• He took a couple of ***puffs*** of a cigarette and I took a couple of ***puffs*** of my cigarette.(p.195)

pull

• Sometimes we alcoholics have an idea that people are trying to ***pull*** us down.(p.145)

• They roll on the floor and holler, and ***pull*** their hair."(p.266)

• He might have handed me fifty dollars and said that I ought to ***pull*** myself together and make a new start.(p.278)

• I had a tough ***pull*** back to normal good health.(p.310)

• I would ***pull*** out early, and go to the hunt breakfast and the flowing bowl of milk-punch.(p.404)

• In the garage, I would put the needle in my vein and then try to figure out exactly how much medication to inject to overcome the pep pills while adding to the sleeping pills while ignoring the tranquilizers, in order to get just enough to be able to ***pull*** out the needle, jerk the tourniquet, throw it in the car, slam the car door shut, run down the hall, and fall in bed before I fell asleep.(p.442)

• Nothing could ***pull*** me out of the abyss but more alcohol.(p.457)

• Later on, it took alcohol fortified with other drugs to ***pull*** me up.(p.457)

• She realized that, and the way I felt, and so for my own good she gradually began to ***pull*** away.(p.472)

pulled

• He then ***pulled*** up his chair with one of his knees touching mine and said, "Will you pray with me for your success?"(p.218)

• But my dad ***pulled*** some strings and got in to see me after three weeks.(p.425)

• And when this six month school was over I applied for duty in Hawaii and ***pulled*** it.(p.426)

• We ***pulled*** up in front of my sister's house just as dawn broke.(p.466)

pulling

• But the head of the house has spent years in ***pulling*** down the structures of business, romance, friendship, health -- these things are now ruined or damaged.(p.123)

• There is really nothing to dressing with chains and shackles on, once you learn the technique of ***pulling*** inside-out pants through the shackles.(p.460)

pulls

• They believe in themselves, and still more in the Power which ***pulls*** chronic alcoholics back from the gates of death.(p.xxv)

• He uses his gifts to build up a bright outlook for his family and himself, and then ***pulls*** the structure down on his head by a senseless series of sprees.(p.21)

pumped

• There was the love affair which was ridiculous -- "imagine that midget being able to fall in love!" -- and my head knew it while my heart ***pumped*** real, genuine anguish, for it hurt like hell, and since it was first love, things have never been quite the same.(p.534)

pumping

• I got a job after school ***pumping*** gas and worked until ten or eleven at night.(p.423)

punch

• Gone are time cards to ***punch***, alarm clocks to obey, nosey rumor-mongers and talebearers to evade.(p.329)

pupil

• I left this home town, then, after I had made a public spectacle of myself in the presence of a revered teacher whose favorite ***pupil*** I had been.(p.539)

pupils

• The other ***pupils*** kept books, pencils, paper, gym equipment and such stuff in their lockers.(p.423)

purchase

• The details of the long road back to something resembling normal living -- the first short streetcar ride, the ***purchase*** of a used bike which enabled me to widen the narrow horizon of life, the first trip downtown – I will not dwell on.(p.276)

• Age and the law were still against me, but laws were not as strictly enforced in those days as they are now, and I discovered that as long as I had the green blood, there was always a way to get alcohol, either from a nondiscriminatory bartender or from an older friend who would be glad to ***purchase*** the joy juice for the privilege of sharing it.(p.397)

purchased

• I didn't particularly like it, but I loved the effects, and managed for the next twenty-five years to drink anything and everything, either handed to me or ***purchased***, at the slightest excuse.(p.357)

• My father had ***purchased*** a restaurant, which he felt would take up some of my spare time, and that's how I met Vi.(p.487)

purchaser

• Without this proof the expectant ***purchaser*** would be forced to depart empty handed with none of what I later came to believe was the great panacea for all human ills.(p.171)

pure

• How much did these feelings, these loves, these worships, have to do with ***pure*** reason?(p.54)

• Were nothing left but ***pure*** reason, it wouldn't be life.(p.54)

• You can never know the ***pure*** joy of recovering within the Fellowship of Alcoholics Anonymous."(p.334)

• Even when I was old enough to know better, I dreamed about being as beautiful as Venus, as ***pure*** as the Madonna and as brilliant as the President of the United States is supposed to be.(p.400)

Puritanical

• Another thing that mother drilled into me was a very ***Puritanical*** point of view as to sex relations and as to motherhood and womanhood.(p.483)

purpose

• All changes made over the years in the Big Book (A.A. members' fond nickname for this volume) have had the same ***purpose***: to represent the current membership of Alcoholics Anonymous more accurately, and thereby to reach more alcoholics.(p.xii)

• To show other alcoholics precisely how we have recovered is the main ***purpose*** of this book.(p.xiii)

• Despite contrary indications, I had little doubt that a mighty ***purpose*** and rhythm underlay all.(p.10)

• It is the ***purpose*** of this book to answer such questions specifically.(p.20)

• We have learned that whatever the human frailties of various faiths may be, those faiths have given ***purpose*** and direction to millions.(p.49)

• Experience has taught us that these are matters about which, for our ***purpose***, we need not be worried.(p.50)

• Our real ***purpose*** is to fit ourselves to be of maximum service to God and the people about us.(p.77)

• When it will serve any good ***purpose***, we are willing to announce our convictions with tact and common sense.(p.77)

• Doctors are rightly loath to tell alcoholic patients the whole story unless it will serve some good ***purpose***.(p.92)

• So we think that unless some good and useful ***purpose*** is to be served, past occurrences should not be discussed.(p.125)

• This dream world has been replaced by a great sense of ***purpose***, accompanied by a growing consciousness of the power of God in our lives.(p.130)

• I'm so grateful for both the program and the people in it that I still want to go, and then probably the most wonderful thing that I learned from the program -- I've seen this in the 'A.A. Grapevine' a lot of times, and I've had people say it to me personally, and I've heard people get up in meetings and make the same statement: The statement is, "I came into A.A. solely for the ***purpose*** of sobriety, but it has been through A.A. that I have found God."(p.192)

• Yet we all had one really sincere ***purpose*** in our hearts and that was not to drink.(p.246)

• But I had never been a flippant, wise-cracking sneerer at the few persons I had met who had impressed me as Christian men and women, or at any institution whose sincerity of ***purpose*** I could see.(p.259)

• This latest part of my life has had a ***purpose***, not in great things accomplished but in daily living.(p.295)

• Alcohol failed to serve the ***purpose***.(p.346)

• A "spiritual experience" to me meant attending meetings, seeing a group of people, all there for the ***purpose*** of helping each other; hearing the Twelve Steps and the Twelve Traditions read at a meeting, and hearing the Lord's Prayer, which in an A.A. meeting has such great meaning – "Thy will be done, not mine."(p.381)

• When I joined A.A. I did so for the sole ***purpose*** of getting sober and staying sober.(p.383)

• In the first year there were episodes such as kicking Priscilla in the shins, getting the lock changed on the desk in the A.A. Club, because I, as secretary, didn't want the Intergroup secretary "interfering," and taking an older woman member out to lunch for the express ***purpose*** of informing her that she was "a phony."(p.416)

• Now, for me, and to my satisfaction, I know the ***purpose*** of life: The ***purpose*** of life is to create and the byproduct is happiness.(p.535)

• Had I been able to explain to a psychiatrist the feeling of futility, loneliness and lack of ***purpose*** that had come with my deep sense of personal failure at this second divorce, I seriously doubt that the good doctor could have convinced me that my basic problem was a spiritual hunger, but A.A. has shown me this was the truth.(p.546)

• A.A. has given me serenity of ***purpose***, the opportunity to be of service to God and to the people about me, and I am serene in the infallibility of these principles that provide the fulfillment of my ***purpose***.(p.551)

• Two – For our group ***purpose*** there is but one ultimate authority – a loving God as He may express Himself in our group conscience.(p.564)

• Five – Each group has but one primary ***purpose*** -- to carry its message to the alcoholic who still suffers.(p.564)

• Six – An A.A. group ought never endorse, finance or lend the A.A. name to any related facility or outside enterprise, lest problems of money, property and prestige divert us from our primary ***purpose***.(p.564)

• 2. -- For our group ***purpose*** there is but one ultimate authority -- a loving God as He may express Himself in our group conscience.(p.565)

• 5. – Each Alcoholics Anonymous group ought to be a spiritual entity having but one primary ***purpose*** -- that of carrying its message to the alcoholic who still suffers.(p.565)

• Then too, we view with much concern those A.A. treasuries which continue, beyond prudent reserves, to accumulate funds for no stated A.A. ***purpose***.(p.566)

purposefulness

• Here, while in a hospital bed, men with clear eyes, happy faces, and a look of assurance and ***purposefulness*** about them, came to see me and told me their stories.(p.279)

purposes

• I remember that my father kept whiskey around the house for medical ***purposes*** and entertainment, and I would drink from this when no one was about and then water it to keep my parents from knowing I was drinking.(p.183)

• Took down notes for reference ***purposes***.(p.344)

purse

• Sometimes I stole from my wife's slender ***purse*** when the morning terror and madness were on me.(p.6)

• During these years, I drank as much as my ***purse*** permitted, still without paying too great a penalty, although I was beginning to have morning jitters at times.(p.173)

• I had no trouble making the right decision when I saw my wife open her ***purse*** at the meeting that night and deposit a cute little angel in the middle of my birthday cake.(p.366)

pursue

• But when the broker gave him Dr. Silkworth's description of alcoholism and its hopelessness, the physician began to ***pursue*** the spiritual remedy for his malady with a willingness he had never before been able to muster.(p.xvi)

• Many ***pursue*** it into the gates of insanity or death.(p.30)

• Upon graduation, I ventured to New York to ***pursue*** my writing career.(p.555)

pursued

• The town was well supplied with churches and schools in which I ***pursued*** my early educational activities.(p.171)

• So I enrolled at the university for night courses in religion, and I ***pursued*** those courses for a year.(p.221)

pushed

• Someone had ***pushed*** a drink my way, and I had taken it.(p.5)

• I ***pushed*** a drink across the table.(p.9)

• Yet all reasons for not drinking were easily ***pushed*** aside in favor of the foolish idea that he could take whiskey if only he mixed it with milk!(p.36)

• He should not be ***pushed*** or prodded by you, his wife, or his friends.(p.95)

• And still by the time I was thirty years old I was being ***pushed*** around with a compulsion to drink that was completely beyond my control.(p.305)

• Just three years of drinking ***pushed*** a shy, lonely young girl to the depth of depression.(p.353)

• A young veteran tells how a few rough experiences ***pushed*** him into A.A. – and how he was therefore spared years of suffering.(p.422)

pushes

• As fast as he can, he ***pushes*** these memories far

inside himself.(p.73)

pushing

• I was accepting help with one hand and *pushing* it away with the other.(p.407)

• It never entered my head that I would have been *pushing* up the daisies if he had decided not to come.(p.479)

put

• Many years ago one of the leading contributors to this book came under our care in this hospital and while here he acquired some ideas which he *put* into practical application at once.(p.xxv)

• "Suddenly the thought crossed my mind that if I were to *put* an ounce of whiskey in my milk it couldn't hurt me on a full stomach.(p.36)

• As a celebrated American statesman *put* it, "Let's look at the record."(p.50)

• If his arrangements would only stay *put*, if only people would do as he wished, the show would be great.(p.60)

• Wants house *put* in her name.(p.65)

• We *put* them on paper, even though we had no resentment in connection with them.(p.68)

• We have admitted certain defects; we have ascertained in a rough way what the trouble is; we have *put* our finger on the weak items in our personal inventory.(p.72)

• Have we skimped on the cement *put* into the foundation?(p.75)

• At the moment we are trying to *put* our lives in order.(p.77)

• You need this information to *put* yourself in his place, to see how you would like him to approach you if the tables were turned.(p.90)

• The minute we *put* our work on a service plane, the alcoholic commences to rely upon our assistance rather than upon God.(p.98)

• When your prospect has made such reparation as he can to his family, and has thoroughly explained to them the new principles by which he is living, he should proceed to *put* those principles into action at home.(p.98)

• When we look back, we realize that the things which came to us when we *put* ourselves in God's hands were better than anything we could have planned.(p.100)

• Maybe you have already been obliged to *put* him away.(p.110)

• Attempt instead, to *put* yourself in his place.(p.111)

• Now we try to *put* spiritual principles to work in every department of our lives.(p.116)

• The faith and sincerity of both you and your husband will be *put* to the test.(p.117)

• You, as well as your husband, ought to think of what you can *put* into life instead of how much you can take out.(p.120)

• As our work spreads and our numbers increase, we hope your employees may be *put* in personal contact with some of us.(p.144)

• You *put* me on the spot every time you get drunk.(p.147)

• But one of the friends said, "*Put* him in a private room.(p.157)

• That afternoon he *put* on his clothes and walked from the hospital a free man.(p.158)

• After a bit, he said, "The way you fellows *put* this spiritual stuff makes sense.(p.159)

• I used to *put* eight or twelve ounce bottles of alcohol in a fur lined glove and toss it onto the back airing porch when winter days got dark enough.(p.176)

• I used also to *put* it up in four ounce bottles and stick several in my stocking tops.(p.177)

• I *put* on thirty pounds of weight in about two months, looked like a pig, and was uncomfortable from shortness of breath.(p.177)

• On June 26, 1935, I came to in the hospital and to say I was discouraged is to *put* it mildly.(p.184)

• After prescribing medicines, Dr. Bob ordered, "*Put* him in a private room.(p.188)

• I wasn't afraid that the program wouldn't work, but I still was doubtful whether I would be able to hang on to the program, but I did come to the conclusion that I was willing to *put* everything I had into it, with God's power, and that I wanted to do just that.(p.189)

• Then I remember when the boys came back, that I told them, "I have gone to this Higher Power and I have told Him that I am willing to *put* His world first, above everything.(p.190)

• I wouldn't *put* sufficient time on them.(p.194)

• At that particular time, the boys *put* me on a shutter and took me out to the shed, and I lay in the car while they enjoyed their banquet.(p.195)

• I would *put* off doing anything that I could until the next day and, consequently, everything would pile up and then there would be the blackout.(p.197)

• I optioned a piece of land just off East Market Street to *put* up a three-hundred suite apartment.(p.198)

• My idea was to have all the companies pool their funds and buy rubber when rubber was cheap and then *put* it in a pool.(p.198)

• And I continued to drink, on and off then, until every dollar I had in the world was gone again and I was right back living at my sister's, getting my cigarettes by calling her grocer and telling him to *put* in a couple of cartons with her order, exactly as I had before I started to work at Max's.(p.202)

• In fact, as I look back, I have often thought that they probably concluded that they would *put* up with me for a couple of years, that I couldn't live much longer, and that they would inherit whatever was left of the practice.(p.215)

• I was introduced to them and Clarence proceeded to *put* on his Twelve Step work.(p.216)

• The interne came along with a glassful of bleached lightning that *put* me away for about fifteen hours.(p.217)

• The feeling of impending disaster that had haunted me for years began to dissolve as I *put* into practice more and more of the Twelve Steps.(p.229)

• We were all set to *put* DuPont out of business.(p.246)

• A friend who knew I would soon be broke mounted guard over me when I left my job of writing the histories of Texas cities and *put* me aboard a bus for the town I had left almost five years before.(p.256)

• He said, "Let's *put* the Big Book away again, and when you read it again, turn to the back and read some of the stories.(p.269)

• Instead, he got dressed, took me out, bought me three or four double shots and *put* me to bed.(p.278)

• The parties waxed more liquid and hilarious as time went on, and eventually I discovered that a little shot of liquor now and then between beers had the tendency to *put* me in a whacky mood much quicker than having to down several quarts of beer to obtain the same effect.(p.298)

• It is impossible to *put* on paper all the benefits I have derived . . . physical, mental, domestic, spiritual, and monetary.(p.302)

• And all the while my fear fed a growing conviction that before long it would be necessary for me to be *put* away in some institution.(p.306)

• Either they die of acute alcoholism or they develop wet brains and have to be *put* away permanently."(p.308)

• He *put* me at ease with his first few words.(p.309)

• One morning when I was feeling really bad, I was *put* on K.P. and the head cook wanted me to go out and scrub the garbage cans.(p.317)

• She said "Suppose I *put* your name down as a volunteer.(p.326)

• Toward five o'clock, helter-skelter, I'd get everything *put* away and try to get supper on the table, and after supper I'd finish the job up and knock myself out.(p.337)

• This was such a new thought that I got all sorts of books on Higher Powers, and I *put* a Bible by my bedside, and I *put* a Bible in my car.(p.348)

• And I *put* a Bible in my locker at the hospital.(p.348)

• And I *put* a Bible in my desk.(p.348)

• And I *put* a Big Book by my night stand, and I *put* a "Twelve Steps and Twelve Tradition" in my locker at the hospital, and I got books by Emmet Fox, and I got books by God-knows-who, and I got to reading all these things.(p.348)

• Yes, I *put* in those stitches.(p.350)

• And the psychiatrist has had thousands of couches, and has *put* you and me on them many, many times, but he hasn't helped us very much, though he has tried hard; and we owe the clergy and the doctor and the psychiatrist a deep debt of gratitude, but they haven't helped our alcoholism, except in a rare few instances.(p.352)

• I lost my driver's license, was made a ward of the court, and was *put* on probation (not to mention the fact that I might have killed three friends and myself).(p.354)

• Why should this happen to me – hadn't I provided a good home – wasn't I making a good living – didn't I just get a substantial raise that had *put* me in the upper bracket class?(p.362)

• They told me their stories, which were much more rugged than mine -- yet what they said made sense, and the way they *put* it was easy for me to understand, with an understanding I had never had before.(p.363)

• That night she too had new hope because I had made sure she would know what I was doing about my drinking by packing every bit of A.A. literature I could *put* my hands on right on top so she couldn't help but see it when she opened my bag.(p.364)

• Before too long, my husband (who seemed to prefer his shirts dirty) *put* his foot down, declaring that our family might have the cleanest clothes in town, but that I hadn't been out of the same old dirty slacks and blouse for a week.(p.371)

• I *put* my poor mother and father through agonies but, finally, I couldn't stand living with them and having them watch everything I did.(p.386)

• I wish I could tell you all that A.A. has done for me, all that I think and feel about A.A., but it's something that I have experienced and have never been able to *put* into words.(p.394)

• Sometimes they'd *put* it on the mantel, and forget it.(p.407)

• Her father, quite rightly, wanted to *put* her in a school.(p.409)

• The strange A.A. *put* me at ease.(p.413)

• In A.A., I have had to be torn down and then *put* back together differently.(p.420)

• My dad, who was a newspaper man and had some connections, had meantime *put* a stop on me, and I guess that report went all over the country.(p.424)

• We were identified and I was *put* on a train for Chicago.(p.424)

• Science could take my mind apart expertly, but it couldn't seem to *put* it together again.(p.435)

• However, for a period of time I was injecting Pentothal intravenously to *put* myself to sleep.(p.442)

• In the garage, I would *put* the needle in my vein and then try to figure out exactly how much medication to inject to overcome the pep pills while adding to the sleeping pills while ignoring the tranquilizers, in order to get just enough to be able to pull out the needle, jerk the tourniquet, throw it in the car, slam the car door shut, run down the hall, and fall in bed before I fell asleep.(p.442)

• One night, I had to *put* myself back to sleep three times, and then I finally decided to give it up.(p.443)

• After nine days of tests at Mayo, I was *put* in the locked ward – of all places!(p.444)

• I was taken out of the house and *put* bodily into a waiting car with nothing on but a robe and gown.(p.466)

• This time I didn't *put* up any fight because I knew why they were there and where I was going, the psychopathic ward of the City Hospital, where I had been once before.(p.468)

• Pack my clothes and *put* me on train.(p.475)

• This sober Indian say to sick, red-eyed alcoholic who want good medicine: "*Put* cork in bottle.(p.477)

• At that time the repeal whiskies were back, and I'd go to the store and buy my whiskey and take it to my office and *put* it under the desk, first in one place and then in another, and there soon was an accumulation of empty bottles.(p.488)

• I went back to my mother's for a few days until things cooled off, because the District Attorney had *put* out a summons for me to come to see him in his office.(p.491)

• I had to *put* up a three hundred dollar bond because he was carrying the same summons around in his pocket for me.(p.491)

• So I *put* forth some effort that day to try to stay sober if I could, though my sobriety was just a daze.(p.494)

• I *put* Charlie on the car and when I left him I passed both of those liquor stores without even thinking about them.(p.495)

• A little drink will *put* me on my feet.(p.500)

• Maybe a drink – I *put* on my hat and dash off in the car.(p.505)

• About three months after that, my record reached home and I got a letter telling me I was retired from the Army, they *put* it very kindly, on medical grounds.(p.521)

• But I knew that they knew what the medical grounds were, and that they had *put* a big black mark against my name.(p.521)

• I thought, well, now that I've been *put* out for drinking, I'll just show them that they were completely wrong, so I went off on the biggest bout I had been on up to then, involving about a fortnight's blackout.(p.521)

• I *put* myself into a home.(p.521)

• I stayed there just long enough to work up a real good resentment against the doctor in charge, who I didn't think was doing anything at all except collecting fees, and I left there fully determined that I'd never *put* myself in the power of medical people again.(p.521)

• That *put* a scare in me for about a fortnight.(p.522)

• As I say, this specialist *put* a scare in me for about a fortnight or three weeks, then I started my last bout which went on and off for about three months.(p.523)

• I don't remember any of them getting ***put*** out in the winter because they didn't pay their rent.(p.527)
• I would wait for the mailman each month, like any good mother, but as soon as he handed me my check, I ***put*** on my best dress and went looking for my alcoholic friend.(p.527)
• If he were still sober, chances are that very quickly I ***put*** him down as a Philistine with no appreciation of literary genius; and then I went on to another bar to find a new victim.(p.537)
• This question so insulted the emotions that clearly there was only one thing to do, go and get drunk again, and ***put*** that enquiring mind in its proper place, which was oblivion.(p.537)
• I had nothing to ***put*** in the place of alcohol, of the forgetfulness, of the oblivion, which alcohol provides.(p.539)
• The people who came knew immediately I was in no condition to absorb anything of the program, and I was ***put*** in a sanitarium to be defogged so that I could make a sober decision about this for myself.(p.549)

puts

• That's the stuff used when the oral surgeon ***puts*** the needle in your vein and says, "Count to ten," and before you get to two, you're asleep.(p.442)
• She ***puts*** me to bed and gives me a hypodermic.(p.501)

putting

• There is a complete failure of the kind of defense that keeps one from ***putting*** his hand on a hot stove.(p.24)
• Others came near ***putting*** Galileo to death for his astronomical heresies.(p.51)
• ***Putting*** out of our minds the wrongs others had done, we resolutely looked for our own mistakes.(p.67)
• And I began ***putting*** into practice what I was learning every day.(p.237)
• The reply came, ***putting*** me in touch by mail with my sponsor in New Delhi.(p.343)
• The people there insisted on ***putting*** me in a ward, when Max and I both knew I ought to have a private room.(p.445)
• It was no use talking of ***putting*** myself into a home, a hospital, or of going to see a doctor again, or of going to see a priest or anyone else.(p.523)

puzzle

• As long as things were tough and the job a challenge I could always manage to hold on pretty well, but as soon as I learned the combination, got the ***puzzle*** under control and the boss to pat me on the back, I was gone again.(p.243)

puzzled

• In two months he was in a hospital, ***puzzled*** and humiliated.(p.32)

puzzling

• Here is the fellow who has been ***puzzling*** you, especially in his lack of control.(p.21)
• The explanation that alcoholism was a disease of a two fold nature, an allergy of the body and an obsession of the mind, cleared up a number of ***puzzling*** questions for me.(p.380)

Qq

quack
• I could see he wasn't a *quack* or a fanatic.(p.413)

Quaker
• His were good, simple *Quaker* folk who accepted me with love.(p.402)
• My *Quaker* mother-in-law, bless her heart, used to set the Christmas pudding ablaze with lumps of sugar dipped in rubbing alcohol.(p.402)

qualification
• You will note that we made an important *qualification*.(p.101)
• Say that you believe he is a gravely ill person, with this *qualification* – being perhaps fatally ill, does he want to get well?(p.142)

qualified
• Then he fell victim to a belief which practically every alcoholic has – that his long period of sobriety and self-discipline had *qualified* him to drink as other men.(p.32)
• I have something to contribute to humanity, since I am peculiarly *qualified*, as a fellow-sufferer, to give aid and comfort to those who have stumbled and fallen over this business of meeting life.(p.229)
• I don't think the boys were completely convinced of my personality change, for they fought shy of including my story in the book, so my only contribution to their literary efforts was my firm conviction, being still a theological rebel, that the word God should be *qualified* with the phrase "as we understand him" – for that was the only way I could accept spirituality.(p.248)

qualifying
• It started out as a good marriage, but it deteriorated over the years as she progressed through the various stages of *qualifying* for Al-Anon.(p.439)

qualities
• If he had these *qualities* and did not drink would he be worth retaining?(p.140)
• Prior to our marriage, when she was a shy, scrawny adolescent, I was able to see things in her that others couldn't necessarily see – things like beauty, charm, gaiety, a gift for being easy to talk to, a sense of humor, and many other fine *qualities*.(p.450)
• Over the years, as I thought about Max, her good *qualities* grew and grew, and we married, and all these *qualities* became more and more apparent to me, and we were happier and happier.(p.450)
• I can again focus on my wife's good *qualities* and watch them grow and grow and grow.(p.451)

quality
• I was terribly impressed by this meeting and the *quality* of happiness these men displayed, despite their lack of material means.(p.291)
• I saw in these people a *quality* of peace and serenity that I knew I must have for myself.(p.310)
• I didn't dare hope I might find for myself all that these people had found, but if I could acquire some small part of their intriguing *quality* of living – and sobriety – that would be enough.(p.310)
• I have had my share of problems, heartaches and disappointments, because that is life, but also I have known a great deal of joy, and a peace that is the handmaiden of an inner freedom, I have a wealth of friends and, with my A.A. friends, an unusual *quality* of fellowship.(p.312)

qualms
• I had no *qualms*, because I felt the source of a drinking problem was all in how weak one was, and I wasn't like my dad (I thought).(p.370)

quantities
• To be gravely affected, one does not necessarily have to drink a long time nor take the *quantities* some of us have.(p.33)
• There I sat in the evenings, enjoying with my friends our memories of the "old country," singing the old songs we all knew, playing simple card games for drinks and consuming great *quantities* of beer.(p.231)
• Why did I want increasingly greater *quantities* of alcohol?(p.374)
• Suddenly, I began vomiting and losing rectally great *quantities* of blood.(p.558)

quantity
• Gradually the *quantity* increased, the occasions for a drink came more frequently; a hard day, worries and pressure, bad news, good news – there were more and more reasons for a drink.(p.374)
• Cunning, baffling, powerful -- the gradual creeping up of the frequency and *quantity* of alcohol, and what it does to a person is apparent to everyone but the person involved.(p.375)

quarrel
• You might let them know you have no *quarrel* with the alcoholics of your organization.(p.147)
• The differences between my father and my sisters, who were school teachers, made an excellent environment for the type of child I was – that is, slick and cute enough to take advantage of any adult *quarrel*.(p.210)
• I had a drunken *quarrel* with my family, denounced them, and left them forever.(p.409)
• It's been true in my case, nor could I *quarrel* with "restore us to sanity," for my actions drunk or sober, before A.A., were not those of a sane person.(p.550)

quarrels
• Would there be *quarrels* over membership, leadership and money?(p.xviii)
• When working with a man and his family, you should take care not to participate in their *quarrels*.(p.100)
• She was a woman devoted to her family and loyal to her husband, but *quarrels* did not make a happy environment for her.(p.210)
• I remember vaguely violent *quarrels* with my husband, his finding my liquor supply time and time again and throwing it out.(p.466)

quart
• After three years of this, I wound up in the local hospital where they attempted to help me, but I would get my friends to smuggle me a *quart*, or I would steal the alcohol about the building, so that I got rapidly worse.(p.175)
• We drove to a store in North Hill and I sent him in with what money I had to get a *quart*.(p.204)
• He brought the *quart* out and I took a good swig.(p.205)
• My daily consumption of wine was about a *quart*, but that was common where I lived.(p.230)
• I stayed so sober that I used to keep a *quart* of medicinal whiskey in my bureau which I used to taper off the occasional newspaper alcoholics who were sent to see me.(p.253)
• By the time we reached the bar, he was willing to buy me a *quart* with his own money.(p.288)
• Wasn't I drinking more than a *quart* every day?(p.427)
• Even on my rare (at first) binge nights it never ran much over a *quart*.(p.433)

quarter
• I got two drinks, each of them a *quarter* of that pint, in me, and was talking along with these people, but I felt that sooner or later they were going to have me cornered because they were smarter than I was and the drink was beginning to take effect; but as I reached for the third drink Bob said, "Listen, Buster, you promised to take some medicine if we got you a drink.(p.206)
• I would at least have asked for a *quarter*!(p.289)
• I was in the fourth *quarter* of my senior year at high school, and my mother was quite sick in the hospital.(p.354)

quarterback
• So did the waterboy on the high school football team attempt to revenge himself on the big brother who was the star *quarterback*; for I was the waterboy and my brother was the star *quarterback*, innocent of everything except the fact that he was a star *quarterback*.(p.537)

quarters
• I was, of course, soon on the carpet and the upshot was that I had to go back for two more *quarters* and remain absolutely dry, if I wished to graduate.(p.174)

quarts
• I drank all the scotch they had on the train and bought several *quarts* on my way to the hotel.(p.179)
• The parties waxed more liquid and hilarious as time went on, and eventually I discovered that a little shot of liquor now and then between beers had the tendency to put me in a whacky mood much quicker than having to down several *quarts* of beer to obtain the same effect.(p.298)

queasy
• Inside, I went right on being a mass of unlovely self-pity, *queasy* anxiety and sickening self-debasement.(p.400)
• The only thing that bothered me was a *queasy* feeling I had in the pit of my stomach.(p.418)

Quebec
• *Quebec*, Toronto, Buffalo, and finally Pittsburgh, were the scenes of man-sized drunks until I had gone through my readjusted discharge pay, a fair sum.(p.253)

queen
• I also wanted to be the *queen* of society, with a glittering salon, the bride of a dream prince and the mother of a happy brood.(p.400)
• Yes, I, the *queen* of them all!(p.411)
• I know I do not have to be "*queen* of them all" to salve a frightened ego.(p.416)

queen's
• Edward Dowling, S.J., of the *Queen's* Work staff says, "Alcoholics Anonymous is natural; it is natural at the point where nature comes closest to the supernatural, namely in humiliations and in consequent humility.(p.574)

queer
• Up to this point you would label him as a foolish chap having *queer* ideas of fun.(p.37)
• Show him, from your own experience, how the *queer* mental condition surrounding that first drink prevents normal functioning of the will power.(p.92)

queerly
• They looked at one another *queerly* and, finally, one of them allowed he'd have a beer and they all followed him, each of them saying he'd have a beer too.(p.194)

queried
• "Come, what's all this about?" I *queried*.(p.9)
• "Do you know why you're in here?" he *queried*.(p.423)

question
• For those who are unable to drink moderately the *question* is how to stop altogether.(p.34)
• We needed to ask ourselves but one short *question*.(p.47)
• Leaving aside the drink *question*, they tell why living was so unsatisfactory.(p.51)
• Arrived at this point, we were squarely confronted with the *question* of faith.(p.53)
• But later, alone in his room, he asked himself this *question*: "Is it possible that all the religious people I have known are wrong?"(p.56)
• But above all, we tried to be sensible on this *question*.(p.68)
• The *question* of how to approach the man we hated will arise.(p.77)
• Let him ask you that *question*, if he will.(p.93)
• Maybe you have disturbed him about the *question* of alcoholism.(p.94)
• It is not the matter of giving that is in *question*, but when and how to give.(p.98)
• We never argue this *question*.(p.102)
• The *question* which might naturally come into your mind would be: "What did the man do or say that was different from what others had done or said?"(p.180)
• The next *question*, they wanted to know was if I believed in a Higher Power.(p.186)
• The next *question* they asked was, "You can quit twenty-four hours can't you?"(p.188)
• The age-old *question* in A.A. is which came first, the neurosis or the alcoholism.(p.240)
• He knew too well that didn't mean a thing, just as I knew in my heart that it would be only a *question* of time -- a few days, a week, or even a month, it was inevitable – till I would be off on another bender.(p.257)
• The seventeen who now tell their experiences answer that *question*.(p.315)
• This, plus mounting emotional disturbances, convinced them that compulsive alcoholism already had them; that complete ruin would be only a *question* of time.(p.315)
• I had to give him a story and ask him the same *question* over and over again, "Well, now, how many will that bottle serve?"(p.336)
• I asked this *question* weekly for the next couple of years.(p.359)
• I began, here and now, to fear the answer to the *question* -- what is the matter with me?(p.406)
• "I must ask you a *question*," I say to the man.(p.504)
• Does that answer your *question*?"(p.504)

• Sobering up, the mind that was ahead of the emotions would impel the *question*: What have you written or done to be the great man?(p.537)
• This *question* so insulted the emotions that clearly there was only one thing to do, go and get drunk again, and put that enquiring mind in its proper place, which was oblivion.(p.537)
• They said if you want to know how this program works, take the first word of your *question* -- the H is for honesty, the O is for open-mindedness and the W is for willingness; these our Book calls the essentials of recovery.(p.550)

questionable
• To sum up about sex: We earnestly pray for the right ideal, for guidance in each *questionable* situation, for sanity, and for the strength to do the right thing.(p.70)
• At the Laundromat, I was undisturbed by barflies with *questionable* and unwanted intentions.(p.369)

questionnaire
• Now comes the *questionnaire*."(p.413)

questions
• It is the purpose of this book to answer such *questions* specifically.(p.20)
• Perhaps there never will be a full answer to these *questions*.(p.22)
• If anyone *questions* whether he has entered this dangerous area, let him try leaving liquor alone for one year.(p.34)
• Faced with alcoholic destruction, we soon became as open minded on spiritual matters as we tried to be on other *questions*.(p.48)
• They are *questions* for each individual to settle for himself.(p.50)
• If you answer these *questions* satisfactorily, you need have no apprehension.(p.102)
• These are some of the *questions* which race through the mind of every woman who has an alcoholic husband.(p.108)
• His case presents additional *questions* which we shall try to answer for you.(p.110)
• I then began asking a lot of *questions* of both my brother and Dr. Bob about how this thing worked, and I suppose I was becoming more glassy-eyed all the while, for eventually I said to Bob, "You're all dried up.(p.206)
• My first meeting gave me a great deal of hope and lots of willing ears for my tale of woe and for my *questions*.(p.364)
• The explanation that alcoholism was a disease of a two fold nature, an allergy of the body and an obsession of the mind, cleared up a number of puzzling *questions* for me.(p.380)
• I know now that I asked *questions* and told him what I wanted to learn, but I told him only what I wanted to believe about myself.(p.388)
• The *questions* he asked me that I didn't answer honestly, I thought were none of his business.(p.388)
• I, who had feared *questions*, now began trying to interrupt and tell my story.(p.414)
• The psychiatrist, who had generally been ignoring me, now became quite interested; every day, he would ask me all kinds of *questions* about the A.A. meetings.(p.446)
• I gaze at the board with its *questions*.(p.499)
• I concentrate on one of the *questions*.(p.499)
• The "12 Traditions" of Alcoholics Anonymous are, we A.A.'s believe, the best answers that our experience has yet given to those ever urgent *questions*, "How can A.A. best function?" and, "How can A.A. best stay whole and so survive?"(p.563)

quick
• We often find such a person *quick* to see and understand our problem.(p.74)
• Be *quick* to see where religious people are right.(p.87)
• An alcoholic of this temperament may be *quick* to use this chapter as a club over your head.(p.108)
• He thought all alcoholics should constantly have chocolate available for its *quick* energy value at times of fatigue.(p.133)
• Mrs. M. said she would send Jack over as *quick* as he came in.(p.267)
• I screamed on the telephone for my mother to get up there; something was going to happen; I didn't know what, but if she didn't get there *quick*, I'd split wide open.(p.338)
• In an attempt to get over that feeling, there was a *quick* onslaught of a greater number of drinks, and then all was lost.(p.346)
• We had some people in, and I was making drinks in the kitchen, when I suddenly decided to hoist the bottle for a *quick* one.(p.365)
• I would have three *quick* strong ones in order to endure the evening.(p.407)
• So I jump *quick* from First Step to Twelfth Step to help my brother, living with me.(p.476)
• "Pity me the heart that is slow to learn What the *quick* mind sees at every turn."(p.534)

quicker
• The parties waxed more liquid and hilarious as time went on, and eventually I discovered that a little shot of liquor now and then between beers had the tendency to put me in a whacky mood much *quicker* than having to down several quarts of beer to obtain the same effect.(p.298)

quickly
• We do not like to pronounce any individual as alcoholic, but you can *quickly* diagnose yourself.(p.31)
• Though a robust man at retirement, he went to pieces *quickly* and was dead within four years.(p.33)
• They are being fulfilled among us -- sometimes *quickly*, sometimes slowly.(p.84)
• We discuss them with someone immediately and make amends *quickly* if we have harmed anyone.(p.84)
• In the midst of an understanding and sympathetic family, these vagaries of dad's spiritual infancy will *quickly* disappear.(p.129)
• I went back to law school, and doubled up on the courses because I was then approaching thirty years of age and I wanted to get through as *quickly* as possible.(p.212)
• My experience in the hospital I considered to be terrific because Dr. Bob told me very *quickly* that medicine would have very little to do with it, outside of trying to restore my appetite for food.(p.217)
• Then I got a very good position in Philadelphia and *quickly* found I would need a few fellow alcoholics around me if I was to stay sober.(p.249)
• Instead, I *quickly* substituted one or another vivid scene from the nightmare of my later drinking.(p.286)
• How hurt I was when editors bounced back my ideas *quickly* and my best friends opined that my output needed a lot of rewriting.(p.331)
• He arranged for me to see a local psychiatrist, who *quickly* decided I should be in the mental-health unit of our local hospital.(p.445)
• But it *quickly* became obvious that he had this childish notion instead: If he could get me to go to enough meetings while in the hospital, I would continue to go after he let me out.(p.447)
• If he were still sober, chances are that very *quickly* I put him down as a Philistine with no appreciation of literary genius; and then I went on to another bar to find a new victim.(p.537)

quickness
• We are granted "the serenity to accept the things we cannot change" -- and thus lose our *quickness* to anger and our sensitivity to criticism.(p.560)

quicksand
• *Quicksand* stretched around me in all directions.(p.8)

quiet
• As matters grow worse, he begins to use a combination of high-powered sedative and liquor to *quiet* his nerves so he can go to work.(p.22)
• Returning home we find a place where we can be *quiet* for an hour carefully reviewing what we have done.(p.75)
• If your talk has been sane, *quiet* and full of human understanding, you have perhaps made a friend.(p.94)
• Most of the time therefore, I did not take the morning drink which I craved so badly, but instead would fill up on large doses of sedatives to *quiet* the jitters, which distressed me terribly.(p.176)
• That had been in the center of New York, on noisy 42nd Street . . . this was obviously a *quiet* residential section.(p.223)
• "I'm doing a job I like and it's *quiet* where I live, practically no temptations.(p.257)
• He can relax and it's *quiet*."(p.271)
• Immediately a great feeling of peace descended upon me, intermingled with a feeling of being suffused with a *quiet* strength.(p.280)
• I certainly wasn't my shy, *quiet* self that night -- as I was informed the next morning.(p.353)
• Finally they stopped and bought me a bottle; they knew so well that would keep me *quiet*.(p.466)
• I am *quiet* again.(p.505)

quieted
• He was very nervous in the morning after these bouts and *quieted* himself with more liquor.(p.32)

quieter
• I was never a hilarious drunk; the more I drank the *quieter* I got, and the drunker I got the harder I fought to stay sober.(p.241)

quietly
• I was to sit *quietly* when in doubt, asking only for direction and strength to meet my problems as He would have me.(p.13)
• After the sermon, he *quietly* got up and made an explanation.(p.80)
• While you need not discuss your husband at length, you can *quietly* let your friends know the nature of his illness.(p.115)
• I tell her *quietly* what I intend to do.(p.507)
• I remember the day when I decided to drink myself to death *quietly*, without bothering anyone, because I was tired of having been a dependable, trustworthy person for about thirty-nine years without having received what I thought was a proper reward for my virtue.(p.531)
• "Bob," he asked *quietly*, "do you want to live or die?"(p.540)
• When I awoke in the middle of the night with shakes and sweats and fears, I would hear my wife weeping *quietly* in bed beside me.(p.558)

quiets
• It *quiets* the imperious urge, when to yield would mean heartache.(p.70)

quit
• "Why don't you drink like a gentleman or *quit*?"(p.20)
• As we look back, we feel we had gone on drinking many years beyond the point where we could *quit* on our will power.(p.34)
• Whether such a person can *quit* upon a nonspiritual basis depends upon the extent to which he has already lost the power to choose whether he will drink or not.(p.34)
• He made up his mind to *quit* drinking altogether.(p.39)
• First of all, we had to *quit* playing God.(p.62)
• Then let his family or a friend ask him if he wants to *quit* for good and if he would go to any extreme to do so.(p.90)
• If he is not communicative, give him a sketch of your drinking career up to the time you *quit*.(p.91)
• He wants to *quit* drinking and you want to help him, even if it be only a matter of good business.(p.141)
• You ask, because many alcoholics, being warped and drugged, do not want to *quit*.(p.142)
• But if you really and truly want to *quit* drinking liquor for good and all, and sincerely feel that you must have some help, we know that we have an answer for you.(p.181)
• She said, "You are going to *quit*."(p.185)
• Then she told me that these two drunks she had been talking to had a plan whereby they thought they could *quit* drinking, and part of that plan was that they tell it to another drunk.(p.185)
• They said to me, "Do you want to *quit* drinking?(p.186)
• The next thing they wanted to know was if I thought I could *quit* of my own accord, without any help, if I could just walk out of the hospital and never take another drink.(p.186)
• I thought of what liquor had done to me, the opportunities that I had discarded, the abilities that had been given me and how I had wasted them, and I finally came to the conclusion, that if I didn't want to *quit*, I certainly ought to want to, and that I was willing to do anything in the world to stop drinking.(p.186)
• One of the fellows, I think it was Doc, said, "Well, you want to *quit*?"(p.187)
• I said, "Yes, Doc, I would like to *quit*, at least for five, six, or eight months, until I get things straightened up, and begin to get the respect of my wife and some other people back, and get my finances fixed up and so on."(p.187)
• Whether you *quit* six days, months, or years, if you go out and take a drink or two you'll end up in this hospital tied down, just like you have been in these past six months.(p.187)
• The next question they asked was, "You can *quit* twenty-four hours can't you?"(p.188)
• I immediately *quit* school and went to work, and from that time until I was high school age there was never a return to school.(p.193)
• I can remember telling the poor little soul that I could probably *quit* drinking if I wasn't married to her, and told her that, after all, I didn't like restraint!(p.199)
• I can remember well thinking that I would *quit*

drinking, really go to work hard, apply myself eight hours a day, five days a week, make a lot of money, and then I could start drinking again.(p.199)
• Now I attempted to ***quit***.(p.199)
• I ***quit*** drinking immediately.(p.202)
• I knew I could ***quit*** because he had ***quit***; he hadn't had a drink for over a year.(p.208)
• A year later, after I completed the course in contracts, I ***quit*** the law school, and undertook some engineering work for a patent law firm on behalf of clients who were in difficulties and who desired to keep their troubles from their own engineering department.(p.212)
• Having regard for the law of the land, I resigned myself to the will of the national legislators and ***quit*** drinking altogether, not because I had found it harmful, but because I couldn't get what I was accustomed to drink.(p.232)
• You can all remember that in the first few months after the change, a great many men, who had formerly been used to a few beers every day or an occasional drink of whiskey, simply ***quit*** all alcoholic drinks.(p.232)
• Sometimes, after sobering up after a bout of several weeks, I would righteously resolve to ***quit***.(p.233)
• And yet, realizing at last that liquor really had me, I wanted to ***quit***.(p.234)
• He had no desire to know anything, except whether I was definite about my desire to ***quit*** drinking.(p.235)
• And, because as I have discovered since, it is part of the "treatment" that these men be sent to see and talk with alcoholics who want to ***quit***, he kept them busy.(p.235)
• I ***quit*** the factory and got a job on a small newspaper, going from that to a Pittsburgh daily, long ago defunct.(p.252)
• Successive Monday morning hangovers, which despite mid-week resolutions to do better, came with unfailing regularity, eventually caused me to ***quit*** my job.(p.254)
• I had been drinking heavily from one state of semi-coma to another and it was several days before I got "defogged," but subconsciously I was in earnest about wanting to ***quit*** liquor forever.(p.258)
• There was a man watching, and I turned to him and said with a defiant air I carried with me all the time, "If I don't ***quit*** this I'm going to have to join that alcoholic business they're talking about."(p.266)
• He used to drink, and then he found something that started up in Akron that helped him ***quit*** drinking."(p.267)
• His road lay clear before me, and I'd better ***quit*** rationalizing myself into any detours.(p.282)
• In all honesty though, I was skeptical, but I wanted so definitely to ***quit*** drinking that I would have welcomed any sort of physical torture or pain to accomplish the result.(p.302)
• Since I didn't do well in school, I ***quit*** and joined the Army at age seventeen.(p.317)
• It wasn't long before I ***quit*** caring how I looked or what my job performance was.(p.318)
• I realized I couldn't ***quit***.(p.319)
• I decided to ***quit*** drinking.(p.333)
• I ***quit***, when I was just past sixteen.(p.424)
• And the folks said A.A. was for people who wanted to ***quit***, otherwise it wouldn't work.(p.429)
• That doctor in the Navy hospital told me I wouldn't live five years if I didn't ***quit***.(p.429)
• I wasn't able to ***quit*** chemicals as long as they were in the house.(p.443)
• To this day, I am amazed at how many of my problems -- most of which had nothing to do with drinking, I believed -- have become manageable or have simply disappeared since I ***quit*** drinking.(p.448)
• Those poor stiffs probably went to a doctor and were told that if they ***quit*** they'd live three weeks and if they didn't they'd die in one."(p.510)
• I guess I always knew that the way to handle my drinking was to ***quit***.(p.554)
• Much later, when I had progressed to full-blown alcoholism, people told me I should ***quit***.(p.554)
• Like most other alcoholics I have known, I did ***quit*** drinking at various times -- once for ten months on my own and during other interludes when I was hospitalized.(p.554)
• The doctor pronounced it a badly enlarged liver and said I had to ***quit*** drinking.(p.557)

quite

• In this statement he confirms what we who have suffered alcoholic torture must believe — that the body of the alcoholic is ***quite*** as abnormal as his mind.(p.xxiv)
• He seemed ***quite*** rational and well-balanced with respect to other problems.(p.26)
• This time he was ***quite*** shaky.(p.40)
• "***Quite*** as important was the discovery that spiritual principles would solve all my problems.(p.42)
• But somehow, we couldn't ***quite*** step ashore.(p.53)
• In trying to make these arrangements our actor may sometimes be ***quite*** virtuous.(p.61)
• The wording was, of course, ***quite*** optional so long as we expressed the idea, voicing it without reservation.(p.63)
• The first thing apparent was that this world and its people were often ***quite*** wrong.(p.65)
• If we are not sorry, and our conduct continues to harm others, we are ***quite*** sure to drink.(p.70)
• But what we have said applies ***quite*** as much to women.(p.104)
• You can be ***quite*** hopeful of a situation like this.(p.110)
• You would suppose that men in the fourth classification would be ***quite*** hopeless, but that is not so.(p.113)
• Drinking occasionally, and understanding your own reactions, it is possible for you to become ***quite*** sure of many things which, so far as the alcoholic is concerned, are not always so.(p.139)
• Perhaps you are not ***quite*** in sympathy with the approach we suggest.(p.144)
• With the passing of the Eighteenth Amendment I felt ***quite*** safe.(p.175)
• Occasionally, I would yield to the morning craving, but if I did, it would be only a few hours before I would be ***quite*** unfit for work.(p.176)
• Of course, we had talked over ***quite*** a number of the failings that I had and made a sort of an inventory, which wasn't too difficult, because I had an awful lot of things wrong that were very apparent to me, because I knew all about them.(p.190)
• Naturally, for ***quite*** a time, I wasn't too well physically, either.(p.190)
• It took me a year, or a year and a half to get to feeling physically well, and it was rather tough, but I soon found folks whose friendship I had once had, and I found, after I had been sober for ***quite*** some little time, that these people began to act like they had in previous years, before I had gotten so bad, so that I didn't pay too awful much attention to financial gains.(p.190)
• I ***quite*** naturally came to the conclusion that I must be insane.(p.199)
• I remember one occasion when I did not drink for three hundred and sixty-four days, but I didn't ***quite*** make the year.(p.200)
• Then he started to talk to me about his drinking experiences, what his drinking had cost him, how much he had drunk and where, things like that, and I remember I was ***quite*** bored because I had never seen the guy before and had no interest at all in what, where and when he drank.(p.208)
• She had a hairdresser who used to tell her about a brother-in-law who had been ***quite*** a drinker and about some doctor in Akron who had straightened him out.(p.216)
• My wife and family stood by me for ten weeks and then, ***quite*** justifiably, ejected me.(p.257)
• These vacations became ***quite*** something, and he always had two weeks vacation the first two weeks of every September.(p.264)
• During my first few months in Akron I was ***quite*** sure that I never wanted to see my home town again.(p.281)
• I am very apt to get into ***quite*** an uproar for a day or two before starting, but I do start, and once started, I have a swell time.(p.285)
• A few months later one of the men who had been in touch with the group in Akron came to Chicago to live, and then there were three of us who continued to have informal meetings ***quite*** regularly.(p.294)
• From that point on, I secured crocks of ten gallon capacity and really took ***quite*** an active interest in the manufacture of home brew.(p.297)
• We were having card parties with limburger and beer ***quite*** regularly.(p.297)
• I got along fairly well with my party drinking for ***quite*** some time, but eventually I began to visit beer joints in between parties.(p.298)
• I arrived at the stage where I couldn't ***quite*** make it to the office some mornings.(p.299)
• I was strong and healthy and ***quite*** athletic.(p.305)
• Usually, the next morning I would be ***quite*** sick.(p.317)
• We had a small child, and I loved her dearly, so that held me back ***quite*** a bit in my drinking career.(p.322)
• I got so that I hid ***quite*** a bit of the time, wouldn't answer the phone, and stayed by myself as much as I could.(p.324)
• I was in the fourth quarter of my senior year at high school, and my mother was ***quite*** sick in the hospital.(p.354)
• My first spiritual experience in A.A. came ***quite*** early to me.(p.366)
• So I went down to him ***quite*** a few times a month and had him shoot me full of the stuff; and then I went across the street to a little drug store to take a glass of beer or two beers, and then stopped at the liquor store to get myself a pint and go home.(p.389)
• On our honeymoon in Egypt, he cuffed me around ***quite*** a bit, and subsequently hit me some more.(p.405)
• Her father, ***quite*** rightly, wanted to put her in a school.(p.409)
• I now had ***quite*** a nest egg.(p.409)
• I have achieved the inner confidence to write ***quite*** unlike Shakespeare, and I have sold a good deal of what I've written.(p.416)
• I was drinking ***quite*** a bit of whiskey now.(p.425)
• Barleycorn's wringer squeezed this author — but he escaped ***quite*** whole.(p.432)
• I was, so far as anybody could tell, ***quite*** a lad.(p.432)
• I never could ***quite*** get the knack of it and kept asking myself, "What's a nice guy like me doing in a place like this?"(p.445)
• The psychiatrist, who had generally been ignoring me, now became ***quite*** interested; every day, he would ask me all kinds of questions about the A.A. meetings.(p.446)
• It made me feel ***quite*** grown-up and mature, and I think another added attraction was the fact that so far as my family was concerned, it was forbidden, and it had a special attraction for that reason.(p.464)
• I thought I would be ***quite*** happy and never would I drink too much again.(p.465)
• I'm sure my ideas as to what life should be like were ***quite*** different from that of the average person with whom I associated.(p.483)
• I had ***quite*** a heartache about her then because she wasn't the type of girl that my mother wanted me to marry.(p.485)
• On the other hand, I believe that I've always been medically inclined, though I have never been able to see medicine ***quite*** as the average person sees it.(p.485)
• On the other hand, I got ***quite*** a different picture farther south.(p.486)
• Lots of the older people had taken to drinking ***quite*** a good deal more during the war, but the younger generation was, I think, about the same.(p.518)
• I was up to international standards in one particular game, and that again covered ***quite*** a lot of my sins.(p.519)
• He didn't have to lie in wait very long, but fortunately by that time, I had acquired friends upstairs and they covered me for ***quite*** a time.(p.519)
• They weren't ***quite*** so up-to-date on my history and I got away with them for about four years with them.(p.520)
• Even at that he spoke ***quite*** often.(p.520)
• I talked to him for ***quite*** a long time and at the end, he said, "Well, you're not ***quite*** mad enough to be shut up for good yet, but you soon will be if you live long enough."(p.522)
• I was taking Benzedrine and paraldehyde ***quite*** impartially during the day then, and by the time I arrived at my first A.A. meeting, I was pretty drunk and certainly doped up to the eyes and completely jittery.(p.523)
• What struck me most was that they all seemed to be ***quite*** pleased with having made a job of it and having stopped drinking.(p.524)
• There was the love affair which was ridiculous -- "imagine that midget being able to fall in love!" -- and my head knew it while my heart pumped real, genuine anguish, for it hurt like hell, and since it was first love, things have never been ***quite*** the same.(p.534)
• There was the sense of being "misunderstood," when as a matter of fact by my middle twenties I was ***quite*** popular, although I hadn't grown much bigger physically.(p.534)
• ***Quite*** often friends of the newcomer are aware of the difference long before he is himself.(p.569)

quits

• A week after my decision to join A.A., she called it ***quits***.(p.430)

quitting

• The experiment of ***quitting*** for a period of time will be helpful, but we think we can render an even greater service to alcoholic sufferers and perhaps to the medical fraternity.(p.34)
• When I got the fog out of my brain, I decided that ***quitting*** school was very foolish and that I had better return and continue my work.(p.173)
• I went into the high school grades, but having missed all the intermediate grades, I didn't get along

too well, so I developed the habit of going back to school just long enough for the football season and then ***quitting***.(p.193)

• When I came into A.A., I had no intention of ***quitting*** drinking -- I figured I was doing all right.(p.478)

quizzically

• When I had been in the hospital ten days, Sister Ignatia, who has played such a part in the development of A.A. in this area, stuck her head in the door one morning and announced, looking at me ***quizzically***, that they might be able to make something human out of my face after all.(p.205)

• He looked at me ***quizzically***.(p.257)

quota

• Every doctor gets his ***quota*** of alcoholic patients.(p.308)

quoted

• My opinions were ***quoted*** in Time and Newsweek with pictures, and I addressed the public by radio and television.(p.435)

Rr

rabbi
• Suggestions about these may be obtained from one's priest, minister, or *rabbi*.(p.87)
• He may bring new hope and new courage to many a priest, minister, or *rabbi*, who gives his all to minister to our troubled world.(p.132)

race
• If what we have learned and felt and seen means anything at all, it means that all of us, whatever our *race*, creed, or color are the children of a living Creator with whom we may form a relationship upon simple and understandable terms as soon as we are willing and honest enough to try.(p.28)
• Then we have the voices who cry for sex and more sex; who bewail the institution of marriage; who think that most of the troubles of the *race* are traceable to sex causes.(p.69)
• These are some of the questions which *race* through the mind of every woman who has an alcoholic husband.(p.108)
• He lost the *race* by only a narrow margin.(p.158)
• An active member of A.A. since 1939, I feel myself a useful member of the human *race* at last.(p.229)
• I was aware of symptoms of impending dependence, and I told myself I had gotten out of the rat *race* just in time to head off any booze problem.(p.327)
• His parishioners are limited in number, but his friends are many, for to him *race*, creed, or social position makes no difference.(p.497)
• I want to be one of His children, a member of the human *race*.(p.535)

raced
• My brain *raced* uncontrollably and there was a terrible sense of impending calamity.(p.6)

races
• But the day he comes out he *races* in front of a fire engine, which breaks his back.(p.38)
• We used to amuse ourselves by cynically dissecting spiritual beliefs and practices when we might have observed that many spiritually-minded persons of all *races*, colors, and creeds were demonstrating a degree of stability, happiness and usefulness which we should have sought ourselves.(p.49)
• I remember telling them too that it was going to be awfully tough, because I did some other things, smoked cigarettes and played penny ante poker, sometimes bet on the horse *races* and they said, "Don't you think you're having more trouble with this drinking than with anything else at the present time?(p.190)

racial
• I don't think I suffered too much as far as the *racial* situation was concerned because I was born into it and knew nothing other than that.(p.485)

racing
• With nothing but a liberal arts education, very definitely estranged from my family and already married, soon after graduation from college I became a bookmaker's clerk on the British *racing* circuits, far better off financially than the average professional man.(p.251)

racket
• Then he added, "He sure didn't do much for me when I was trying to fight this booze *racket* alone."(p.158)
• This worked nicely until my wife and I went to see Wallace Beery in "Tugboat Annie," after which the pant-leg and stocking *racket* were out!(p.177)
• The movie *racket* had kept me too long from writing those novels, articles, short stories, and scripts on which I had copious notes.(p.330)

radical
• Because this book has become the basic text for our Society and has helped such large numbers of alcoholic men and women to recover, there exists a sentiment against any *radical* changes being made in it.(p.xi)

radically
• We urge you to try our program, for nothing will be so helpful to your husband as the *radically* changed attitude toward him which God will show you how to have.(p.117)
• Being on a *radically* different basis of life, he will never take advantage of the situation.(p.146)

radio
• It was decided that all members ought to be anonymous at the level of press, *radio*, TV and films.(p.xix)
• I, carried away with the desire to serve A.A., gave what was probably one of the first *radio* broadcasts about A.A., living through a case of mike fright and feeling like a million dollars when it was all over.(p.283)
• In the spring of 1939, the Big Book was printed, and we had two inquiries from the New York office because of a fifteen-minute *radio* talk that was made.(p.294)
• The *radio* was my good friend.(p.332)
• RUM, *RADIO* AND REBELLION(p.356)
• I was working for a Chicago firm that represented several large *radio* stations.(p.358)
• In January 1938, I had the opportunity to go to northern Vermont to manage a small daytime *radio* station that was up against it financially, and was about to fold its antenna.(p.359)
• Since the *radio* station was getting on its feet, it didn't require so many nights of evening work, and that permitted leisure time for drinking.(p.360)
• In 1940 another good opportunity came up and we moved to Pittsburgh where I was to manage two *radio* stations under the same ownership.(p.361)
• One night I was sitting in the lab alone with a fifth and a case of beer listening to dreamy Hawaiian music on the *radio*.(p.427)
• My opinions were quoted in Time and Newsweek with pictures, and I addressed the public by *radio* and television.(p.435)
• Eleven -- Our public relations policy is based on attraction rather than promotion; we need always maintain personal anonymity at the level of press, *radio* and films.(p.564)

rage
• It fills the alcoholic with *rage*.(p.350)

raging
• It isn't always so sudden with everyone, but I ran into a personal crisis which filled me with a *raging* and righteous anger.(p.228)

railroad
• My father was a *railroad* man and a Civil War veteran.(p.210)
• I took the last to buy my *railroad* ticket.(p.493)

railway
• The next three years I spent in Boston, Chicago, and Montreal in the employ of a large manufacturing concern, selling *railway* supplies, gas engines of all sorts, and many other items of heavy hardware.(p.172)

rain
• I got drunk one night in October, went to sleep in the *rain* and woke up with pneumonia.(p.490)

raincoat
• I wore a man's *raincoat*, turned inside out, a present from a friend, for now my funds were low.(p.411)

raining
• Then, I started to miss meetings because it was *raining* or snowing or something else.(p.203)

rainstorm
• Forced to detrain from an empty gondola on the other side of Chicago by a terrific *rainstorm* which drenched me to the skin, I hit the first factory building I saw for a job.(p.253)

rainy
• It is the last day of the following October, a dark, *rainy* morning.(p.502)

raise
• They had said that though I did *raise* a defense, it would one day give way before some trivial reason for having a drink.(p.42)
• Don't *raise* such issues, no matter what your own convictions are.(p.93)
• Members of a family should watch such matters carefully, for one careless, inconsiderate remark has been known to *raise* the very devil.(p.125)
• Why should this happen to me – hadn't I provided a good home – wasn't I making a good living – didn't I just get a substantial *raise* that had put me in the upper bracket class?(p.362)
• The fact that A.A. is a spiritual program didn't scare me or *raise* any prejudice in my mind.(p.383)
• A duplex apartment isn't any place to *raise* a dog.(p.388)

raised
• Then he had, in effect, been *raised* from the dead, suddenly taken from the scrap heap to a level of life better than the best he had ever known!(p.11)
• They never *raised* the issue.(p.215)
• But I don't believe now that it was with any deep feeling of resentment that I said to him, "The children are *raised*, and if this is the way you want it, this is the way we'll have it.(p.263)
• I had just *raised* the bottle to my lips when my wife opened the door and froze me completely in my tracks with "Happy New Year, dear."(p.365)
• I was *raised* like the majority of American boys, coming from a family of modest circumstances, attending public schools, having the social life of a small midwestern town, with part-time work and some athletics.(p.373)
• The bartender, a tough Irishman, came around and "gave me the elbow," which means that he *raised* his elbow and smacked me in the face.(p.411)
• So I *raised* enough fuss that they finally agreed to let me sign out, against medical advice.(p.444)
• I was *raised* in Kansas, the only child of loving parents who just drank socially.(p.554)

raises
• Talk about his condition or this book only when he *raises* the issue.(p.113)

Ralph's
• When the day of their return was almost upon me, and suicide was the only answer I had been able to think of, I went into *Ralph's* room one evening and told him the truth.(p.278)

ramifications
• In all probability, we shall never be able to touch more than a fair fraction of the alcohol problem in all its *ramifications*.(p.xxi)

ramming
• My parents' car had a strong attraction to fences, and one night I blacked out and drove the car down a bank, *ramming* the steel fence around someone's backyard.(p.353)

ran
• War fever *ran* high in the New England town to which we new, young officers from Plattsburg were assigned, and we were flattered when the first citizens took us to their homes, making us feel heroic.(p.1)
• But there was always the curious mental phenomenon that parallel with our sound reasoning there inevitably *ran* some insanely trivial excuse for taking the first drink.(p.37)
• Consequently, my labor bills *ran* up.(p.194)
• It isn't always so sudden with everyone, but I *ran* into a personal crisis which filled me with a raging and righteous anger.(p.228)
• I soon *ran* through my stake.(p.251)
• They owned this joint, she *ran* it, and he sold for a brewery.(p.267)
• It *ran* something like this: If I go around shouting from the rooftops about my alcoholism, it might very possibly prevent me from getting a good job.(p.282)
• How I *ran* my home, I don't know.(p.337)
• At the other side of the table sat one of the carpenters in our community, and at the further end of the table sat the man who *ran* the bakery, while on one side sat my friend who was a mechanic.(p.347)
• Without hesitation, I did the only logical thing – *ran* away from home.(p.354)
• As usual, I *ran* out of money, and, as usual, I wired my father for funds to come home.(p.357)
• Emma *ran* out to the kitchen and came back with a water glass full of bourbon and made me drink it down.(p.385)
• At eighteen I *ran* away from home.(p.401)
• The last time I drank, when I was twenty-nine, I drank for only four days, yet I threatened to kill my children; I beat my wife at home and on the church steps; I mistreated a child in my office; and I *ran* to a hospital for mental illness to avoid jail.(p.418)
• I *ran* away for the second time, with another lad.(p.424)
• Evening cocktails were as standard as morning coffee, and I suppose my average daily consumption *ran* a little more or less than a pint.(p.433)
• Even on my rare (at first) binge nights it never *ran* much over a quart.(p.433)
• My alcoholic associates fired me, took control, and *ran* the enterprise into bankruptcy.(p.437)
• After all, it was self (you, me) that stood in our own way, that *ran* the show and *ran* ourselves into bankruptcy, that hurt the ones we loved.(p.459)

• The Higher Power to whom I had turned, and who had sustained me, had once again been thrust into the background, while my emotions were running my life and, as always, my emotions ***ran*** me to the bottle.(p.472)
• I ***ran*** out of people!(p.478)

ranch
• I might go out West on a ***ranch*** where I couldn't get anything to drink.(p.502)

rancor
• Even though your husband becomes unbearable and you have to leave him temporarily, you should, if you can, go without ***rancor***.(p.111)
• When this happens, they can be invited to join in morning meditation and then they can take part in the daily discussion without ***rancor*** or bias.(p.134)

random
• Selecting a church at ***random*** from the directory, he stepped into a booth and lifted the receiver.(p.155)
• After a few more estimates as to income and expenditures for booze over a few sample years, taken at ***random***, I conclude that this twenty per cent stayed fairly constant.(p.398)

rang
• The word "thoroughly" ***rang*** a bell.(p.349)
• "Complete abandon"; "Half measures availed us nothing"; "Thoroughly follow our path"; "Completely give oneself to this simple program" – ***rang*** in my swelled head.(p.349)
• Three weeks ago, my phone ***rang***, and a voice I hadn't heard in over twenty-three years spoke.(p.462)
• It was around noon, a day or two later, when the telephone ***rang*** and it was Ella.(p.494)

range
• Surveys of groups in the United States and Canada indicate that A.A. is reaching out, not only to more and more people, but to a wider and wider ***range***.(p.xxii)
• The periods of sobriety attained by these thirteen A.A.'s ***range*** from fifteen to forty-six years.(p.169)

ranging
• In the two succeeding years I held ten different jobs ***ranging*** from newspaper copy-desk and rewrite, to traffic director for an oil field equipment company.(p.255)

rank
• I am one of the lads who came out of the service with a lower ***rank*** than when I went in.(p.241)

rant
• But bless his heart, let him ***rant***!(p.9)

ranting
• But he did no ***ranting***.(p.9)
• The doctor said I'd been brought into the hospital like a madman, crying, raving, ***ranting***, swearing, completely in the throes of delirium tremens.(p.427)

rapid
• These facts appear to be of extreme medical importance; because of the extraordinary possibilities of ***rapid*** growth inherent in this group they may mark a new epoch in the annals of alcoholism.(p.xxiii)
• To his consternation, he found himself drunk half a dozen times in ***rapid*** succession.(p.35)
• From that point on, progress will be ***rapid***.(p.134)

rapidly
• This has become the basis of a ***rapidly*** growing fellowship of these men and their families.(p.xxiii)
• She sees she was wrong to make a burning issue out of such a matter when his more serious ailments were being ***rapidly*** cured.(p.135)
• After three years of this, I wound up in the local hospital where they attempted to help me, but I would get my friends to smuggle me a quart, or I would steal the alcohol about the building, so that I got ***rapidly*** worse.(p.175)
• I proceeded to take up the drawing and advanced ***rapidly*** in it.(p.211)
• Crises were emerging ***rapidly***.(p.333)
• I was desperately in earnest to follow through and understand what was expected of me as a member of A.A. and to take each Step of the Twelve as ***rapidly*** as possible.(p.382)
• My pen moves ***rapidly***.(p.499)
• It seems only fitting that when I did finally fall in love it was with an alcoholic, and for the next ten years I progressed as ***rapidly*** as humanly possible into what I believed to be hopeless alcoholism.(p.547)
• Over the next two years, I sickened ***rapidly***.(p.557)
• My company advanced me ***rapidly***, once my reliability was established again.(p.559)
• Among our ***rapidly*** growing membership of thousands of alcoholics such transformations, though frequent, are by no means the rule.(p.569)

rare
• Except in a few ***rare*** cases, neither he nor any other human being can provide such a defense.(p.43)
• Among us, these are ***rare*** occurrences.(p.125)
• An old avocation, the collecting of first editions, ***rare*** books and Americana, fascinated me between times.(p.255)
• And the psychiatrist has had thousands of couches, and has put you and me on them many, many times, but he hasn't helped us very much, though he has tried hard; and we owe the clergy and the doctor and the psychiatrist a deep debt of gratitude, but they haven't helped our alcoholism, except in a ***rare*** few instances.(p.352)
• With ***rare*** foresight he realized it could become a tornado.(p.373)
• Even on my ***rare*** (at first) binge nights it never ran much over a quart.(p.433)

rarely
• ***Rarely*** have we seen a person fail who has thoroughly followed our path.(p.58)
• ***Rarely*** do we fail to make satisfactory progress.(p.78)
• Very ***rarely*** do I miss the meetings of my neighborhood A.A. group, and my average has never been less than two meetings a week.(p.249)
• He may even read in a newspaper that one out of every seven drinkers will become alcoholic, but he ***rarely*** is told that it holds true for all ages – or that the tolerance to alcohol (and other drugs) decreases steadily, year after year, in the bodies of all persons.(p.330)
• I got the Big Book and I read it, and this is what it said: "***Rarely*** have we seen a person fail who has thoroughly followed our path."(p.349)
• I ***rarely*** remembered getting home.(p.410)

rash
• For the only problems I have now are those I create when I break out in a ***rash*** of self-will.(p.551)

rat
• I was aware of symptoms of impending dependence, and I told myself I had gotten out of the ***rat*** race just in time to head off any booze problem.(p.327)

rate
• At present, our membership is increasing at the ***rate*** of about seven per cent a year.(p.xx)
• At any ***rate*** the last great step toward a well rounded life still lay ahead of me.(p.286)
• Apparently I'd grown physically at the customary ***rate*** of speed, and I had acquired an average amount of intellectual training in the intervening years, but there had been no emotional maturity at all.(p.547)
• Any therapeutic or philosophic procedure which can prove a recovery ***rate*** of 50% to 60% must merit our consideration."(p.571)

rated
• I'm ***rated*** as a modestly successful man.(p.296)

rather
• Our public relations were to be based upon attraction ***rather*** than promotion.(p.xix)
• There are many situations which arise out of the phenomenon of craving which cause men to make the supreme sacrifice ***rather*** than continue to fight.(p.xxviii)
• It went into certain securities, then cheap and ***rather*** unpopular.(p.2)
• Therefore, the main problem of the alcoholic centers in his mind, ***rather*** than in his body.(p.23)
• I ***rather*** appreciated your ideas about the subtle insanity which precedes the first drink, but I was confident it could not happen to me after what I had learned.(p.40)
• ***Rather*** vain of us, wasn't it?(p.49)
• We claim spiritual progress ***rather*** than spiritual perfection.(p.60)
• Is he not, even in his best moments, a producer of confusion ***rather*** than harmony?(p.61)
• We trust infinite God ***rather*** than our finite selves.(p.68)
• If we cannot or would ***rather*** not do this, we search our acquaintance for a close-mouthed, understanding friend.(p.74)
• Good generalship may decide that the problem be attacked on the flank ***rather*** than risk a face-to-face combat.(p.82)
• You may be aiding in his destruction ***rather*** than his recovery.(p.97)
• The minute we put our work on a service plane, the alcoholic commences to rely upon our assistance ***rather*** than upon God.(p.98)
• Let him see that you want to be helpful ***rather*** than critical.(p.111)
• If you cooperate, ***rather*** than complain, you will find that his excess enthusiasm will tone down.(p.119)
• Is he not unconsciously trying to see what he can take from the family life ***rather*** than give?(p.122)
• But the wise family will admire him for what he is trying to be, ***rather*** than for what he is trying to get.(p.123)
• Giving, ***rather*** than getting, will become the guiding principle.(p.128)
• His wife is one of those persons who really feels there is something ***rather*** sinful about these commodities, so she nagged, and her intolerance finally threw him into a fit of anger.(p.135)
• After all, are you not looking for results ***rather*** than methods?(p.144)
• My case is ***rather*** unusual in one respect.(p.182)
• Each day I would try to find out what His will was, and try to follow that, ***rather*** than trying to get Him to always agree that the things I thought of myself were the things best for me.(p.187)
• It took me a year, or a year and a half to get to feeling physically well, and it was ***rather*** tough, but I soon found folks whose friendship I had once had, and I found, after I had been sober for quite some little time, that these people began to act like they had in previous years, before I had gotten so bad, so that I didn't pay too awful much attention to financial gains.(p.190)
• I avoided them ***rather*** than explain why they weren't seeing me.(p.203)
• I was in a large, dark, ***rather*** poorly furnished room – the living room of a basement flat.(p.222)
• I listened to him, ***rather*** tolerantly.(p.257)
• I lived in New Orleans where, at that time, cocktail parties, dances and night spots were almost the order of the day – or ***rather*** the night.(p.384)
• I would ***rather*** have stayed in jail except I didn't like bologna and cold potatoes for breakfast.(p.425)
• It was as if I had, ***rather*** than a Midas touch which turned everything to gold, a magnifying mind that magnified whatever it focused on.(p.450)
• Then, one day in A.A., I was told that I had the lenses in my glasses backwards; "the courage to change" in the Serenity Prayer meant, not that I should change my marriage, but ***rather*** that I should change myself and learn to accept my spouse as she was.(p.451)
• But when I try to see what I can add to the meeting, ***rather*** than what I can get out of it, and when I focus my mind on what's good about it, ***rather*** than what's wrong with it, the meeting keeps getting better and better.(p.451)
• Today, Max and I try to communicate what we feel, ***rather*** than what we think.(p.451)
• ***Rather***, I do whatever is in front of me to be done, and I leave the results up to Him; however it turns out, that's God's will for me.(p.452)
• I would ***rather*** talk about the good things A.A. has taught me; I feel that hitting on just a few sordid points should be sufficient to let those of you in institutions know where I came from.(p.459)
• A.A. didn't teach me I was an alcoholic; ***rather*** it taught me that because I was an alcoholic my life had become unmanageable.(p.470)
• When I had known her years before she was ***rather*** slender, but at this time she weighed as much as she does now, which is up around in the two hundreds or very close to it.(p.493)
• After hearing the first speaker I could tell myself that my own lot was ***rather*** mild.(p.509)
• Yes, we find it ***rather*** confusing, but as we get around and get to know people in the group, they lead the way and all we have to do is to follow.(p.512)
• I started drinking ***rather*** early, at the age of sixteen.(p.512)
• At first they were ***rather*** amusing, but a little later on they became serious.(p.513)
• When I came home to ordinary garrison life in England, I found that I was drinking ***rather*** more than most people of may age.(p.518)
• I went to a dinner he gave one night, ***rather*** drunk.(p.520)
• I think the Commanding Officer was ***rather*** tired of this particular chicken coming back to roost so often because he very soon wrote in to the medical authorities to tell them that they had to get me into hospital, to be thoroughly examined for drinking.(p.520)
• They sent me up with an attendant, and the attendant and I both arrived at the Egyptian Hospital ***rather*** the worse for wear.(p.521)
• ***Rather***, I embraced it – I must in honesty admit it -- with a great sense of relief.(p.531)
• This caused the ***rather*** cryptic comment from one of

my A.A. friends, when I told my story after coming into the program, that I had always been a cinch for the program, for I had always been interested in mankind, but that I was just taking them one man at a time.(p.548)
- Eleven -- Our public relations policy is based on attraction ***rather*** than promotion; we need always maintain personal anonymity at the level of press, radio and films.(p.564)
- Our public relations should be guided by the principle of attraction ***rather*** than promotion.(p.567)

rational
- He seemed quite ***rational*** and well-balanced with respect to other problems.(p.26)

rationalization
- I've been benefited from a dictionary definition I found that reads: "***rationalization*** is giving a socially acceptable reason for socially unacceptable behavior, and socially unacceptable behavior is a form of insanity."(p.551)

rationalize
- I was able to ***rationalize*** it anyway.(p.198)
- We ***rationalize*** and excuse our conduct beyond all reason.(p.376)

rationalizing
- His road lay clear before me, and I'd better quit ***rationalizing*** myself into any detours.(p.282)
- The only way existence was possible was through ***rationalizing*** every sober moment and drinking myself into complete oblivion as often as I could.(p.547)

rationed
- The short tours could be taken care of by sneaking enough whiskey aboard ship so that it could be ***rationed*** out until another supply could be laid in.(p.398)

Ravenna
- I got a job in the woolen mills in ***Ravenna*** -- very hard work.(p.262)

raving
- If I'd had a gun I'd have shot the horns right off the thing, because it made me ***raving*** mad.(p.265)
- His wife was cussing him, ***raving*** at him, "I just brought him over to show you what kind of a guy he is!(p.271)
- The doctor said I'd been brought into the hospital like a madman, crying, ***raving***, ranting, swearing, completely in the throes of delirium tremens.(p.427)
- Or maybe I'd come home wild drunk, singing and ***raving*** about what a fine place home was and what grand parents I had since they joined A.A.(p.428)

ray
- And I remembered the creeping horror of the interminable night, in which I slept for short spells and woke up dripping with cold sweat and shaken with utter despair, to drink hastily from my bottle and mercifully pass out again, "You're mad, you're mad, you're mad!" pounded through my brain with each returning ***ray*** of consciousness, and I drowned the refrain with drink.(p.224)

re-assembled
- His family was ***re-assembled***, and he began to work as a salesman for the business he had lost through drinking.(p.35)

re-create
- In nearly all cases, their ideals must be grounded in a power greater than themselves, if they are to ***re-create*** their lives.(p.xxvi)

re-emphasize
- This is a point we wish to emphasize and ***re-emphasize***, to smash home upon our alcoholic readers as it has been revealed to us out of bitter experience.(p.39)

re-entered
- When I did make it home in 1920, I ***re-entered*** school and caught up with my class in a few short months -- I actually did a year's work in three months, proving much to the disgust of my dad that I could do it when I wanted to.(p.358)

re-establish
- The alcoholic may find it hard to ***re-establish*** friendly relations with his children.(p.134)

re-opened
- But his face falls when we speak of spiritual matters, especially when we mention God, for we have ***re-opened*** a subject which our man thought he had neatly evaded or entirely ignored.(p.45)

re-organized
- I ***re-organized*** their city sales policy and eighteen months later, when I was thirty, they offered me the branch managership.(p.243)

re-read
- I attended my weekly meetings with regularity, ***re-read*** the Big Book, attended other group meetings, gave leads when asked to and did some Twelve Step work whenever I was called upon to do so.(p.365)

re-reading
- If this presents difficulty, ***re-reading*** chapters two and three, where the alcoholic sickness is discussed at length might be worth while.(p.140)

reach
- All changes made over the years in the Big Book (A.A. members' fond nickname for this volume) have had the same purpose: to represent the current membership of Alcoholics Anonymous more accurately, and thereby to ***reach*** more alcoholics.(p.xii)
- Afterward, we found ourselves accepting many things which then seemed entirely out of ***reach***.(p.47)
- As animals on a treadmill, we have patiently and wearily climbed, falling back in exhaustion after each futile effort to ***reach*** solid ground.(p.107)
- I would ***reach*** over and get this and take a shot and in a few moments get up and take another, shave and eat my breakfast, slip a half pint of liquor in my hip pocket, and go on to school.(p.183)
- I was seized with an almost uncontrollable desire to ***reach*** out for it.(p.285)
- There is no more "aloneness," with that awful ache, so deep in the heart of every alcoholic that nothing, before, could ever ***reach*** it.(p.312)
- To me, A.A. is within the ***reach*** of every alcoholic, because it can be achieved in any walk of life and because the achievement is not ours but God's.(p.395)
- I was one of those bad cons nobody can ***reach***.(p.460)
- I wonder if it will ***reach*** her neck.(p.497)
- I ***reach*** for the bottle which I just got from George, the elevator boy.(p.500)

reached
- The second edition, published in 1955, ***reached*** a total of more than 1,150,000 copies.(p.xi)
- The membership had then ***reached*** about 100 men and women.(p.xvii)
- Until such an understanding is ***reached***, little or nothing can be accomplished.(p.18)
- We are not sure why, once a certain point is ***reached***, little can be done for him.(p.22)
- When I ***reached*** school, I discovered the faculty had other ideas on the subject.(p.173)
- When rubber ***reached*** a certain low point, they would draw on the rubber out of the pool and buy.(p.198)
- The circumstances under which I ***reached*** these people were very odd because I was led there through things that I said when I couldn't even remember speaking.(p.202)
- I got two drinks, each of them a quarter of that pint, in me, and was talking along with these people, but I felt that sooner or later they were going to have me cornered because they were smarter than I was and the drink was beginning to take effect; but as I ***reached*** for the third drink Bob said, "Listen, Buster, you promised to take some medicine if we got you a drink.(p.206)
- After two or three years of effort along this line, I ***reached*** the point of actual despair that I ever would be able to drink only a harmless amount each day.(p.215)
- I was doing very well with that and general upholstering work, and there was every indication that I would be financially independent by the time I ***reached*** middle age.(p.232)
- My "periodics" became more frequent until I ***reached*** the point where I wanted to devote all my time to drinking, working as little as possible, and then only when the necessity of my family demanded it.(p.234)
- I myself could see deterioration in my work from being physically and mentally affected by liquor, although I had not yet ***reached*** the point where all I wanted was more to drink.(p.254)
- When I ***reached*** a point directly back of our house, where I could have cut through a friend's garden, I was almost overpowered by the desire to get home, but I made the whole journey.(p.276)
- By the time we ***reached*** the bar, he was willing to buy me a quart with his own money.(p.288)
- Among today's incoming A.A. members, many have never ***reached*** the advanced stages of alcoholism, though, given time, all might have.(p.315)
- Many women who have ***reached*** the stage that I had ***reached*** in my drinking have lost husbands, children, homes, everything they hold dear.(p.323)
- I ***reached*** a stage where I couldn't go into my apartment without a drink.(p.324)
- It was at that point that I ***reached*** surrender.(p.340)
- And as that thought came to me, it was as though someone had ***reached*** down and taken a heavy overcoat off my shoulders, for that was the last one.(p.347)
- My business reputation had ***reached*** from Vermont to Pennsylvania, but, thank goodness, my drinking reputation had not.(p.361)
- By hook or crook I usually managed to sober up before I ***reached*** home, but always "terribly tired" from a "hard day's work," and just having to have one or two before dinner.(p.361)
- However, my low had been ***reached***.(p.378)
- Somehow our bodies had ***reached*** the point where we could no longer absorb alcohol in our systems.(p.380)
- I only know that it first ***reached*** me through that Saturday Evening Post article.(p.392)
- Until I ***reached*** A.A. my life was a shambles; I was a mess, and I made everybody near and dear to me miserable.(p.400)
- When he ***reached*** for me, I rose and smote him.(p.405)
- Something in the book had ***reached*** me after all.(p.412)
- A "good boy" ***reached*** adulthood and success without achieving maturity or fulfillment.(p.418)
- My pattern of drinking at that time had ***reached*** the point where once I really started, I would retire to my bed and drink myself into oblivion.(p.466)
- She has ***reached*** the end of her rope.(p.502)
- I began drinking as a kid, shortly after I ***reached*** my fourteenth birthday.(p.508)
- About three months after that, my record ***reached*** home and I got a letter telling me I was retired from the Army, they put it very kindly, on medical grounds.(p.521)
- I suppose I had ***reached*** my spiritual gutter that night, but I have never had what you could call a real urge to drink again.(p.524)
- I realize now that this phase of my development had been arrested by my obsession with self, and my egocentricity had ***reached*** such proportions that adjustment to anything outside my personal control was impossible for me.(p.547)
- But I did, when I ***reached*** college age.(p.554)
- By the time I ***reached*** high school, I was an overachiever.(p.555)
- A.A. can, of course, mean just as much to uncounted alcoholics not yet ***reached***.(p.563)

reaches
- I had been in the remote ***reaches*** of Brooklyn.(p.224)

reaching
- Surveys of groups in the United States and Canada indicate that A.A. is ***reaching*** out, not only to more and more people, but to a wider and wider range.(p.xxii)
- Away from my office two or three weeks at a time; horrible days and nights when I would lie on the floor of my home, lying awake and ***reaching*** over to get the bottle, taking a drink and going back into oblivion.(p.184)
- I will never know all the people I hurt, all the friends I abused, the humiliation of my family, the worry of my business associates, or how far ***reaching*** it was.(p.376)
- And as her disease was ***reaching*** the terminal stages, she was screaming, "You hate me!(p.439)
- I felt very sorry for myself and attempted suicide on many occasions, making sure there was always somebody within ***reaching*** distance to see that I didn't finish the job.(p.478)

reacquainted
- I have my A.A. friends, and I have become ***reacquainted*** with my old friends on a new basis.(p.416)

react
- We ***react*** sanely and normally, and we will find that this has happened automatically.(p.84)
- That is how we ***react*** so long as we keep in fit spiritual condition.(p.85)
- When father takes this tack, the family may ***react*** unfavorably.(p.128)
- I seemed to ***react*** by developing a streak of varying meanness, which would cause me to do things to create excitement and to get attention.(p.211)
- My life was always act and ***react***.(p.325)
- I never did ***react*** normally to any emotional situation.(p.544)

reacted
- And I am sure they would be right as far as they go, but A.A. has taught me I am the result of the way I ***reacted*** to what happened to me as a child.(p.544)

reaction
- His *reaction* may be one of enthusiasm.(p.114)
- My *reaction* to those meetings was good.(p.218)
- The why is not important; the fact is that one drink will set up a *reaction* in our system which requires more; that one drink was too much and one hundred drinks were not enough.(p.380)
- Except for one short slip, during the first eight months, which was an angry "the world can't do this to me" *reaction* to a personal tragedy in my life, I have been sober for twelve years.(p.416)
- Both times, my *reaction* was that I had had nothing to drink the night before, so obviously alcohol had nothing to do with it.(p.444)
- My *reaction* was that I'd already helped all the patients on the ward, and I still had plenty of problems of my own without trying to help some drunk from A.A.(p.446)
- The idea behind it is that, having taken the treatment, your system is so "conditioned" that the mere sight or smell or taste of alcohol produces a violent *reaction*, and you become ill.(p.469)
- It was their open night meeting, but of course I thought they were all alcoholics; I couldn't imagine why anybody else would want to go there, and my first *reaction* was, well, I've come to something that's not for me.(p.524)
- What is much more important to me, A.A. has taught me that through this simple program I may experience a change in this *reaction* pattern that will indeed allow me to "match calamity with serenity."(p.544)
- My *reaction* to this was identical in many respects to my *reaction* to my parents leaving me when I was seven.(p.547)
- He finally realizes that he has undergone a profound alteration in his *reaction* to life; that such a change could hardly have been brought about by himself alone.(p.569)

reactions
- We see that these expressions refer to people whose *reactions* are very different from ours.(p.20)
- Drinking occasionally, and understanding your own *reactions*, it is possible for you to become quite sure of many things which, so far as the alcoholic is concerned, are not always so.(p.139)
- My fright was real enough, but it didn't account for these violent *reactions*.(p.222)

reacts
- Opinions vary considerably as to why the alcoholic *reacts* differently from normal people.(p.22)
- We know that while the alcoholic keeps away from drink, as he may do for months or years, he *reacts* much like other men.(p.22)

read
- I earnestly advise every alcoholic to *read* this book through, and though perhaps he came to scoff, he may remain to pray.(p.xxx)
- We *read* wordy books and indulge in windy arguments, thinking we believe this universe needs no God to explain it.(p.49)
- In this book you will *read* the experience of a man who thought he was an atheist.(p.55)
- In this book you *read* again and again that faith did for us what we could not do for ourselves.(p.70)
- If he is sincerely interested and wants to see you again, ask him to *read* this book in the interval.(p.95)
- He has *read* this volume and says he is prepared to go through with the Twelve Steps of the program of recovery.(p.96)
- When a discussion does arise, you might suggest he *read* this book or at least the chapter on alcoholism.(p.111)
- Tell him some of the interesting stories you have *read*.(p.112)
- He may not share your enthusiasm, but he is practically sure to *read* the book and he may go for the program at once.(p.113)
- In any event, try to have your husband *read* this book.(p.114)
- If the book is *read* the moment the patient is able, while acutely depressed, realization of his condition may come to him.(p.144)
- Unhappy drinkers who *read* this page will understand!(p.151)
- I *read* everything I could find, and talked to everyone who I thought knew anything about it.(p.178)
- It must be remembered that I had *read* a great deal and talked to everyone who knew, or thought they knew anything about the subject of alcoholism.(p.180)
- That was the point at which my doctor gave me the book "Alcoholics Anonymous" to *read*.(p.227)
- Imagine my surprise when I *read* in a page one "box" that I had been taken from the theater unconscious around noon that day, removed by ambulance to a hospital and stomach-pumped and then released.(p.244)
- I began to *read* the Bible daily and to go over a simple devotional exercise as a way to begin each day.(p.259)
- Russ *read* a piece in the paper, and he kind of snickered, and said, "See here, where John D. has found something to keep him from drinking!"(p.265)
- But right then the hope died that had been in my heart when we *read* about John D.(p.266)
- He said, "*Read* this."(p.268)
- When you have a hangover and can't even sit still, try to *read* small print!(p.268)
- Russ said, "Mother, if this tells us how to do it, you'll have to *read* it."(p.268)
- He said, "Let's put the Big Book away again, and when you *read* it again, turn to the back and *read* some of the stories.(p.269)
- Have you *read* those?"(p.269)
- He asked me to *read* the book "Alcoholics Anonymous," and then he wanted me to talk with a man who was experiencing success with his own arrestment.(p.308)
- He'll never *read* in his "sweetness and light" senior-citizen publications anything but the joys of lolling in the rocking chair, angling on the riverbank, or bowling on the green.(p.330)
- He may even *read* in a newspaper that one out of every seven drinkers will become alcoholic, but he rarely is told that it holds true for all ages -- or that the tolerance to alcohol (and other drugs) decreases steadily, year after year, in the bodies of all persons.(p.330)
- But the percentages started tobogganing, and it was often a shock to *read* over some of the pages when sober.(p.331)
- Somehow, I managed to *read* pieces on alcoholism.(p.332)
- Following this, I had a short vacation, during which time I *read* as much literature as my sponsor could send me.(p.343)
- I have *read* systematically since then, and A.A. literature has kept me sober.(p.343)
- I *read*, studied, and meditated on every bit of A.A. literature in my possession.(p.344)
- This friend gave me a pamphlet, and I took it home and had my wife *read* it to me.(p.346)
- After my wife had *read* this to me, I said to her, as I had said many times in desperation, "I have got to do something."(p.346)
- The satisfaction I got from giving him a little of what I had *read* in those pamphlets far surpassed any feeling that I had ever had before in helping patients.(p.347)
- I got the Big Book and I *read* it, and this is what it said: "Rarely have we seen a person fail who has thoroughly followed our path."(p.349)
- I had *read* and heard a little about A.A. and so, groping for the phone book, I found the A.A. number and with hope in my heart eagerly telephoned.(p.363)
- You'll *read* and hear a great deal about the spiritual part of our program.(p.366)
- It was the first she had heard or *read* about it and she said she had considered sending it to me or trying to have someone in Pittsburgh send it to me so I wouldn't know where it came from.(p.366)
- Study the A.A. book -- don't just *read* it.(p.381)
- A "spiritual experience" to me meant attending meetings, seeing a group of people, all there for the purpose of helping each other; hearing the Twelve Steps and the Twelve Traditions *read* at a meeting, and hearing the Lord's Prayer, which in an A.A. meeting has such great meaning -- "Thy will be done, not mine."(p.381)
- I think I actually *read* more contempt than was really there because just a week before someone had sent him the Saturday Evening Post article on A.A., and there was some glimmer of hope in it for him.(p.391)
- The next morning he came into my room and said, "Esther, I'm not going to lecture you any more, but I want you to *read* this article.(p.391)
- There are so many to whom I feel deeply grateful; to my husband (and best critic), whose generous love, compassion and understanding have helped me along the way; to those before me in A.A. who inspired the first article I *read*, and the friend who sent that article to Frank; to Ruth for her personal note, and the first A.A. to talk to me; to my Bishop, whose loving and believing spirit inspired me; and to all the members of the Houston Group who were so patient, kind and helpful -- and to countless others.(p.393)
- It's the last thing I ever heard him say, and I think there are some of us who, at times, try to *read* extra messages and complexities into the Steps.(p.395)
- I *read* sad poetry, cried, drank red wine, wrote sad poetry, and drank some more.(p.405)
- They were bright and well *read*, they held various political views.(p.410)
- She *read* this book that you are reading now.(p.412)
- She asked me to *read* it.(p.412)
- I *read* the book and God leapt at me from every page.(p.412)
- It *read* something like this: "Faith without works is dead.(p.473)
- I pick up a book and try to *read*, but I cannot concentrate.(p.503)
- I try to *read*.(p.506)
- Then I shall lock myself in and *read*.(p.506)
- And as I *read*, I shall take little drinks at long intervals.(p.506)
- It was a revelation when I *read* that First Step.(p.515)
- A.A.'s Twelve Steps may confuse you when you *read* them over.(p.516)
- For me, A.A. is a synthesis of all the philosophy I've ever *read*, all of the positive, good philosophy, all of it based on love.(p.542)
- I *read* self-help books.(p.555)
- While there, I *read* the Big Book and the Grapevine and began the slow road back to health and sanity through the recovery program of A.A.(p.559)
- Following are excerpts from the comments of doctors present at the annual meeting of the Medical Society of the State of New York where a paper on A.A. was *read*:(p.571)
- The American Psychiatric Association requested, in 1949, that a paper be prepared by one of the older members of Alcoholics Anonymous to be *read* at the Association's annual meeting of that year.(p.572)

reader
- We of Alcoholics Anonymous believe that the *reader* will be interested in the medical estimate of the plan of recovery described in this book.(p.xxiii)
- We are assuming, of course, that the *reader* desires to stop.(p.34)
- The *reader* may still ask why he should believe in a Power greater than himself.(p.48)
- I ask the forgiveness of the *reader*; and from now on I shall try to write with the humility I honestly pray for.)(p.536)
- I'd gladly do it anonymously, as I have done this brief account of my struggle with alcohol -- merely to present certain ideas for the consideration of the *reader*.(p.542)
- I hope I have been able to impart to you, the *reader*, at least a bit of what I know; the joy of living, the irresistible power of divine love and its healing strength, and the fact that we, as sentient beings, have the knowledge to choose between good and evil, and, choosing good, are made happy.(p.543)

readers
- Some of our alcoholic *readers* may think they can do without spiritual help.(p.27)
- How then shall we help our *readers* determine, to their own satisfaction, whether they are one of us?(p.34)
- This is a point we wish to emphasize and re-emphasize, to smash home upon our alcoholic *readers* as it has been revealed to us out of bitter experience.(p.39)
- So I started to investigate Science through some friends of mine who were *Readers* in the church.(p.202)
- Probably only a few *readers* of this story will be able, from personal experiences of their own, to understand the exhilaration and sense of accomplishment which I felt after finishing this seemingly simple assignment.(p.276)
- Yet it is true that our first printing gave many *readers* the impression that these personality changes, or religious experiences, must be in the nature of sudden and spectacular upheavals.(p.569)

readily
- If these thoughts occur, they are hazy and *readily* supplanted with the old threadbare idea that this time we shall handle ourselves like other people.(p.24)
- Nevertheless, the twentieth century *readily* accepts theories of all kinds, provided they are firmly grounded in fact.(p.48)
- There is every evidence that women regain their health as *readily* as men if they try our suggestions.(p.104)
- I sensed they had something I did not have, from which I might *readily* profit.(p.178)
- Well . . . I had a job, and I really wanted desperately to stop drinking, but couldn't, so I *readily* agreed to visit the doctor she recommended.(p.301)
- He advised me to enter the particular hospital with

which he was connected and I *readily* agreed.(p.302)

readiness

• Is not our age characterized by the ease with which we discard old ideas for new, by the complete *readiness* with which we throw away the theory or gadget which does not work for something new which does?(p.52)

• We had to ask ourselves why we shouldn't apply to our human problems this same *readiness* to change our point of view.(p.52)

• If that is so, this step may be postponed, only however, if we hold ourselves in complete *readiness* to go through with it at the first opportunity.(p.74)

reading

• If you have a drinking problem, we hope that you may pause in *reading* one of the forty-four personal stories and think: "Yes, that happened to me"; or, more important, "Yes, I've felt like that"; or most important, "Yes, I believe this program can work for me, too."(p.xii)

• Here are some of the methods we have tried: Drinking beer only, limiting the number of drinks, never drinking alone, never drinking in the morning, drinking only at home, never having it in the house, never drinking during business hours, drinking only at parties, switching from scotch to brandy, drinking only natural wines, agreeing to resign if ever drunk on the job, taking a trip, not taking a trip, swearing off forever (with and without a solemn oath), taking more physical exercise, *reading* inspirational books, going to health farms and sanitariums, accepting voluntary commitment to asylums -- we could increase the list ad infinitum.(p.31)

• Carefully *reading* the first five proposals we ask if we have omitted anything, for we are building an arch through which we shall walk a free man at last.(p.75)

• Sooner or later, you are likely to find him *reading* the book once more.(p.113)

• One of the many doctors who had the opportunity of *reading* this book in manuscript form told us that the use of sweets was often helpful, of course depending upon a doctor's advice.(p.133)

• After *reading* this book, a junior executive can go to such a man and say approximately this, "Look here, Ed.(p.147)

• He knew all the answers, and certainly not because he had picked them up in his *reading*.(p.180)

• Paul S. had just called me, and I remember he stressed *reading* the Big Book.(p.269)

• I was *reading* it for all that was in it, and I said to Russ, "We can't do this.(p.269)

• And we went down through the valley, and I remembered *reading* about the Ku Klux Klan and how they burnt crosses, and I thought, "God alone knows what we are getting into this time!"(p.269)

• He sent to New York for a copy, and after *reading* it he tucked it under his arm and called on me.(p.307)

• I stayed up all night *reading* that book.(p.309)

• And I put a Big Book by my night stand, and I put a "Twelve Steps and Twelve Tradition" in my locker at the hospital, and I got books by Emmet Fox, and I got books by God-knows-who, and I got to *reading* all these things.(p.348)

• I had been *reading* a lot about psychiatry and I thought, "Maybe if I talk to a psychiatrist he can find out what is happening, and then I can drink like a lady."(p.387)

• The book was published, but the *reading* public said – So what?(p.403)

• She read this book that you are *reading* now.(p.412)

• I knew from my general *reading* that alcoholism was irreversible and fatal.(p.436)

• He is *reading*.(p.504)

• The terms "spiritual experience" and "spiritual awakening" are used many times in this book which, upon careful *reading*, shows that the personality change sufficient to bring about recovery from alcoholism has manifested itself among us in many different forms.(p.569)

readings

• At this school we had Bible *readings* before each meal, and church services four times on Sunday, and I became so rebellious at this that I swore I would never join or go to any church except for weddings or funerals.(p.240)

readjusted

• Quebec, Toronto, Buffalo, and finally Pittsburgh, were the scenes of man-sized drunks until I had gone through my *readjusted* discharge pay, a fair sum.(p.253)

readjustment

• Successful *readjustment* means the opposite.(p.122)

• Being somewhat weakened, and faced with physical and mental *readjustment* to a life which knows no alcohol, he may overdo.(p.146)

reads

• I've been benefited from a dictionary definition I found that *reads*: "rationalization is giving a socially acceptable reason for socially unacceptable behavior, and socially unacceptable behavior is a form of insanity."(p.551)

• The citation *reads* in part as follows:(p.573)

ready

• Why this *ready* acceptance?(p.48)

• If you have decided you want what we have and are willing to go to any length to get it – then you are *ready* to take certain steps.(p.58)

• 6.Were entirely *ready* to have God remove all these defects of character.(p.59)

• We thought well before taking this step making sure we were *ready*; that we could at last abandon ourselves utterly to Him.(p.63)

• Are we now *ready* to let God remove from us all the things which we have admitted are objectionable?(p.76)

• When *ready*, we say something like this: "My Creator, I am now willing that you should have all of me, good and bad.(p.76)

• He admitted he was overdoing these things, but frankly said that he was not *ready* to stop.(p.135)

• I'm *ready* to do business.(p.159)

• They knew what to do about those black abysses that yawned *ready* to swallow me when I felt depressed, or nervous.(p.229)

• Beer was too bulky and it couldn't be kept in a jug under the counter *ready* to be dumped when John Law came around.(p.233)

• He had already imbued them with his own spirit until they were *ready* and willing at all times to go where sent, and as a doctor he well knew that this mission and duty would strengthen them as it later helped me.(p.235)

• And he further said that God could not accept me as a sincere follower of His Divine Law unless I was *ready* to be thoroughly honest about it.(p.236)

• I was seeking something and I was *ready* to learn.(p.258)

• So six months ago I acquired a *ready* made family consisting of one charming wife, four grown children to whom I am devoted, and three grandchildren.(p.286)

• By this time, with the doctor's explanation, the revelations contained in the book, and the hope-inspiring interview with Mr. T., I was *ready* and willing to go into the interior of the African jungles, if that was what it took, for me to find what these people had.(p.309)

• As I grow in A.A., I realize that a person with as much self-will as I had, as hard a head and as diseased an ego, had to try everything that I could think of, butting my head against every stone wall before I was *ready* to come in.(p.384)

• I was just as drunk as I could be, getting *ready* to take an afternoon walk.(p.390)

• I must be *ready* and willing should I never see them.(p.463)

• I rebelled against this, because just about the time that I was getting *ready* to leave high school, a revelation came to me about God and it made things very complicated for me.(p.489)

• All of my family and loved ones, all of my friends, are nearer and dearer to me than ever before and I have literally dozens of new friends who say they cannot believe that a short eight years ago I was *ready* for the scrap heap.(p.541)

real

• There was, therefore, a sense of *real* satisfaction when I was asked to contribute a few words on a subject which is covered in such masterly detail in these pages.(p.xxv)

• There had been no *real* infidelity, for loyalty to my wife, helped at times by extreme drunkenness, kept me out of those scrapes.(p.3)

• Mercifully, no one could guess that I was to have no *real* employment for five years, or hardly draw a sober breath.(p.4)

• The *real* significance of my experience in the Cathedral burst upon me.(p.12)

• He knows that they are *real*.(p.14)

• That the man who is making the approach has had the same difficulty, that he obviously knows what he is talking about, that his whole deportment shouts at the new prospect that he is a man with a *real* answer, that he has no attitude of Holier Than Thou, nothing whatever except the sincere desire to be helpful; that there are no fees to pay, no axes to grind, no people to please, no lectures to be endured -- these are the conditions we have found most effective.(p.18)

• Most of us sense that *real* tolerance of other people's shortcomings and viewpoints and a respect for their opinions are attitudes which make us more useful to others.(p.19)

• But what about the *real* alcoholic?(p.21)

• He is a *real* Dr. Jekyll and Mr. Hyde.(p.21)

• Once this malady has a *real* hold, they are a baffled lot.(p.23)

• The tragic truth is that if the man be a *real* alcoholic, the happy day may not arrive.(p.23)

• Most of us have been unwilling to admit we were *real* alcoholics.(p.30)

• We know that no *real* alcoholic ever recovers control.(p.30)

• Despite all we can say, many who are *real* alcoholics are not going to believe they are in that class.(p.31)

• Potential female alcoholics often turn into the *real* thing and are gone beyond recall in a few years.(p.33)

• If he is a *real* alcoholic and very far advanced, there is scant chance of success.(p.34)

• He agreed he was a *real* alcoholic and in a serious condition.(p.35)

• We were having trouble with personal relationships, we couldn't control our emotional natures, we were a prey to misery and depression, we couldn't make a living, we had a feeling of uselessness, we were full of fear, we were unhappy, we couldn't seem to be of *real* help to other people – was not a basic solution of these bedevilments more important than whether we should see newsreels of lunar flight?(p.52)

• In that state, the wrong-doing of others, fancied or *real*, had power to actually kill.(p.66)

• Our *real* purpose is to fit ourselves to be of maximum service to God and the people about us.(p.77)

• If you are satisfied that he is a *real* alcoholic, begin to dwell on the hopeless feature of the malady.(p.92)

• These are the earmarks of a *real* alcoholic.(p.109)

• We find it a *real* mistake to dampen his enthusiasm for alcoholic work.(p.119)

• My downfall cost the business community unknown thousands of dollars, for it takes *real* money to train a man for an executive position.(p.137)

• To you, liquor is no *real* problem.(p.139)

• If he wants to stop, he should be afforded a *real* chance.(p.148)

• There is a *real* interest, both humanitarian and business, in the well-being of employees.(p.149)

• God will determine that, so you must remember that your *real* reliance is always upon Him.(p.164)

• All the other people that had talked to me wanted to help me, and my pride prevented me from listening to them, and caused only resentment on my part, but I felt as if I would be a *real* stinker if I did not listen to a couple of fellows for a short time, if that would cure them.(p.185)

• That certainly was *real* disheartening news, at the time.(p.188)

• At the end of about four months, I not only had good looking clothes –and I might say that at the time I first talked to Max I didn't have a suit of clothes I could bend over in *real* sudden; now I had six suits of clothes.(p.200)

• I had run into him, and he looked *real* prosperous; his face and eyes looked clear and he started to compliment me on my good front and how well I looked, and I said, "I haven't had a drink for nine months."(p.201)

• When I was about forty-seven, after indulging in all kinds of self-deception to control my drinking, I arrived at a period when I felt convinced I had to have so much alcohol every day and that the *real* problem was to control how much.(p.214)

• Had anyone undertaken to explain to me what the A.A. movement was, what its *real* function was, I probably would have been set back several years and I doubt if I would have survived at all.(p.216)

• In summing up, I can say that A.A. had made me, I hope, a *real* Catholic.(p.221)

• My fright was *real* enough, but it didn't account for these violent reactions.(p.222)

• To go into a gathering of people was the sort of thing that all my life, from the time I left my private world of books and dreams to meet the *real* world of people and parties and jobs, had left me feeling an uncomfortable outsider, needing the warming stimulus of drinks to join in.(p.228)

• This last *real* merry-go-round had started the day before Christmas and I had really accomplished a lot in those fourteen days.(p.238)

• Little more of our talk stayed in my memory, but I do know I slept the rest of that night while before I had never known what a *real* night's sleep was.(p.239)

• It was November 11th and bells were ringing and whistles blowing for the *real* Armistice.(p.242)

• At that time the group in New York was composed of about twelve men who were working on the principle of every drunk for himself; we had no ***real*** formula and no name.(p.246)
• I remember starting to city school, coming from a country school, and wanting so very, very much to be like the other girls and trying flour on my face for powder because I wasn't able to have any ***real*** powder.(p.261)
• He said, "This is my story" -- ***real*** prim.(p.268)
• I switched into ***real*** estate brokerage and property management work.(p.277)
• He it was who convinced me, because his own conviction was so ***real***, that a Power greater than myself could help me in the crises of life, and that the means of communicating with this Power was simple prayer.(p.279)
• Long before I had any ***real*** opportunity to give, I had to learn the equally important lesson of receiving graciously.(p.281)
• And over my A.A. years I have made many ***real***, honest, sincere friendships that I shall always cherish.(p.296)
• But I met a ***real*** wonderful girl I'll call Jean.(p.318)
• ***Real*** soon.(p.333)
• And with this came the only ***real*** freedom, the freedom of truth.(p.355)
• It was the only ***real*** home she knew.(p.402)
• I experienced my first ***real*** guilt and shame.(p.404)
• I had accomplished all the right things that our society expected, and I had no ***real*** peace of mind nor gratitude.(p.418)
• I graduated with honors, but could not feel any ***real*** responsibility as a father or a husband.(p.419)
• My growing inward unhappiness was a very ***real*** thing, however, and I knew that something would have to be done about it.(p.434)
• Then I found the solution: At the end of study time, I would drink two beers, jump in bed, sleep ***real*** fast, and wake up smart.(p.440)
• No clothes, no money, no home, no ***real*** friends to speak of, mentally and physically pooped, but I was doing all right!(p.478)
• She must have been ***real*** proud of us, I'm sure.(p.480)
• He has so much understanding, a ***real*** asset in sharing sobriety.(p.481)
• This was the ***real*** thing!(p.498)
• He is a ***real*** friend but I do not appreciate him.(p.501)
• I stayed there just long enough to work up a ***real*** good resentment against the doctor in charge, who I didn't think was doing anything at all except collecting fees, and I left there fully determined that I'd never put myself in the power of medical people again.(p.521)
• I suppose I had reached my spiritual gutter that night, but I have never had what you could call a ***real*** urge to drink again.(p.524)
• It continues to try to teach me the ***real*** charity, the charity that gives time and good will and service, and not just money.(p.525)
• There was the love affair which was ridiculous -- "imagine that midget being able to fall in love!" -- and my head knew it while my heart pumped ***real***, genuine anguish, for it hurt like hell, and since it was first love, things have never been quite the same.(p.534)
• As another great man says, "The only ***real*** freedom a human being can ever know is doing what you ought to do because you want to do it."(p.553)
• I went on the wagon, with no outside help and with no ***real*** difficulty -- except that I didn't enjoy life without drinking.(p.557)
• They derive no ***real*** authority from their titles; they do not govern.(p.567)

realities

• These are the ***realities*** for us.(p.130)
• My inability to accept the harsh ***realities*** of life had resulted in a disillusioned cynic, clothed in protective armor against the world's misunderstanding.(p.226)
• Neither of these circumstances was very helpful to my type since I had not learned to face ***realities***.(p.358)

reality

• It did not satisfy us to be told that we could not control our drinking just because we were maladjusted to life, that we were in full flight from ***reality***, or were outright mental defectives.(p.xxiv)
• In ***reality*** that was the beginning of my last debauch.(p.8)
• It is being constantly revealed, as mankind studies the material world, that outward appearances are not inward ***reality*** at all.(p.48)
• We missed the ***reality*** and beauty of the forest because we were diverted by the ugliness of some of its trees.(p.50)
• We found the Great ***Reality*** deep down within us.(p.55)
• They had visioned the Great ***Reality*** -- their loving and All Powerful Creator.(p.161)
• I had been brought up to believe in God, but I know that until I found this A.A. program, I had never found or known faith in the ***reality*** of God, the ***reality*** of His power that is now with me in everything I do.(p.341)
• I could not face the boy and youth I was in the ***reality*** of the contemptible man I had become.(p.540)
• The only ***reality*** I was able to face had been forced upon me by its very repetition -- I had to drink; and I didn't know there was anything in the world that could be done about it.(p.548)
• I attended my first A.A. meeting eight years ago, and it is with deep gratitude that I'm able to say I've not had a drink since that time, and that I take no sedation or narcotics, for this program is to me one of complete sobriety and I no longer need to escape ***reality***.(p.549)
• One of the truly great things A.A. has taught me is that ***reality*** too has two sides; I had only known the grim side before the program, but now I had a chance to learn about the pleasant side as well.(p.550)
• Above all, we reject fantasizing and accept ***reality***.(p.560)
• A.A. led me gently from this fantasizing to embrace ***reality*** with open arms.(p.561)

realization

• Some day we hope that Alcoholics Anonymous will help the public to a better ***realization*** of the gravity of the alcoholic problem, but we shall be of little use if our attitude is one of bitterness or hostility.(p.103)
• If the book is read the moment the patient is able, while acutely depressed, ***realization*** of his condition may come to him.(p.144)
• I realized that I had a problem, although my ***realization*** was not very deep because my own conceit wouldn't admit that I had any personality problems.(p.214)
• For there were of course periods of clear ***realization*** of what I had become, attended by memories of what I had been, what I had expected to be.(p.224)
• At first it was a shock to realize I was an alcoholic, but the ***realization*** that there was hope made it easier.(p.379)
• It was such a feeling of relief that I wanted to know more about it and with that, I think for the first time, came the ***realization*** that there was something horribly, horribly wrong with me.(p.392)
• The ***realization*** came to me that I had to stop drinking, that I had to find a way.(p.515)
• I was intensely unhappy the whole time, but I didn't seem to be able to do anything about it, and the worst part to me was the ***realization*** that all this was going to happen again and again until I died.(p.522)
• It has brought me back to a ***realization*** of my Maker and my duties to Him.(p.525)

realize

• How true this is, few ***realize***.(p.23)
• We ***realize*** that some people are as fanatical about sex as others are loose.(p.70)
• He should ***realize*** that we are engaged upon a life-and-death errand.(p.75)
• We will suddenly ***realize*** that God is doing for us what we could not do for ourselves.(p.84)
• Explain that many are doomed who never ***realize*** their predicament.(p.92)
• It is important for him to ***realize*** that your attempt to pass this on to him plays a vital part in your own recovery.(p.94)
• When we look back, we ***realize*** that the things which came to us when we put ourselves in God's hands were better than anything we could have planned.(p.100)
• We ***realize*** some men are thoroughly bad-intentioned, that no amount of patience will make any difference.(p.108)
• We ***realize*** that we have been giving you much direction and advice.(p.121)
• Let families ***realize***, as they start their journey, that all will not be fair weather.(p.122)
• The family must ***realize*** that dad, though marvelously improved, is still convalescing.(p.127)
• I know, in my own particular case, that nothing my company could have done would have stopped me for, so long as I was able to hold my position, I could not possibly ***realize*** how serious my situation was.(p.141)
• Painfully aware of being somehow abnormal, the man did not fully ***realize*** what it meant to be alcoholic.(p.155)
• We ***realize*** we know only a little.(p.164)
• I don't remember much of what he said, but I did ***realize*** that here was another guy exactly like me; he had been in the same laughing academies and the same jails, known the same loss of jobs, same frustrations, same boredom and the same loneliness.(p.239)
• I didn't ***realize*** how I still felt about him.(p.263)
• And I ***realize*** that there was one salvation for me.(p.272)
• As I look back on that first evening I ***realize*** that I began to hope, then, for the first time; and I felt that if he could regain these things, perhaps it would be possible for me too.(p.290)
• I definitely liked it, everything about it, the taste, the effects; and I ***realize*** now that a drink did something for me or to me that was different from the way it affected others.(p.305)
• Of course, more than anything else I had let myself down, but I didn't ***realize*** how much then -- as I do now.(p.364)
• To wake up at home, not knowing how I got there, and to ***realize*** I had driven my car, became torture.(p.375)
• She of course didn't ***realize*** how cunning an alcoholic can be and the lengths to which he will go in finding ways to satisfy the compulsion for more and more drinks after having had the first one.(p.377)
• At first it was a shock to ***realize*** I was an alcoholic, but the realization that there was hope made it easier.(p.379)
• It took me some time to ***realize*** that the Twelve Steps of A.A. were designed to help correct these defects of character and so help remove the obsession to drink.(p.380)
• I didn't ***realize*** I would find so much more, but a new and different outlook on life started opening up almost immediately.(p.383)
• As I grow in A.A., I ***realize*** that a person with as much self-will as I had, as hard a head and as diseased an ego, had to try everything that I could think of, butting my head against every stone wall before I was ready to come in.(p.384)
• Two weeks later found me being sworn in, and the first payday in the Navy made me ***realize*** I had found a home.(p.398)
• Finally, she asked, "Do you ***realize*** he's on the staff of this hospital?"(p.445)
• I hadn't been drinking much about that time, for I had begun to ***realize*** that there was something abnormal about my drinking, although as yet, I didn't ***realize*** that it was so out of control.(p.465)
• I ***realize*** that all I'm guaranteed in life is today.(p.473)
• I ***realize*** that now.(p.483)
• About this time an incident took place in grade school that I have never forgotten because it made me ***realize*** that I was actually a physical coward.(p.484)
• I ***realize*** now that this phase of my development had been arrested by my obsession with self, and my egocentricity had reached such proportions that adjustment to anything outside my personal control was impossible for me.(p.547)
• My desire to be honest with myself made it necessary for me to ***realize*** that my thinking was irrational.(p.550)
• Do it every day for two weeks and you will find you have come to mean it and to want it for them, and you will ***realize*** that where you used to feel bitterness and resentment and hatred, you now feel compassionate understanding and love."(p.552)
• I have come to ***realize*** that the name of the game is not so much to stop drinking as to stay sober.(p.559)

realized

• He suddenly ***realized*** that in order to save himself he must carry his message to another alcoholic.(p.xvi)
• When the broker returned to New York in the fall of 1935, the first A.A. group had actually been formed, though no one ***realized*** it at the time.(p.xvii)
• We doctors have ***realized*** for a long time that some form of moral psychology was of urgent importance to alcoholics, but its application presented difficulties beyond our conception.(p.xxv)
• The doctor intimated strongly that he might be worse than he ***realized***.(p.39)
• This was our course: We ***realized*** that the people who wronged us were perhaps spiritually sick.(p.66)
• We have told small tots that father was sick, which was much nearer the truth than we ***realized***.(p.106)
• This continued until I enrolled in our state university and, at the end of four years, I ***realized*** that I was a drunk.(p.183)
• Later, I ***realized*** that I was running from alcohol.(p.183)
• Before very long we began to relate some incidents

of our drinking and, naturally, pretty soon, I ***realized*** both of them knew what they were talking about because you can see things and smell things when you're drunk, that you can't other times, and, if I had thought they didn't know what they were talking about, I wouldn't have been willing to talk to them at all.(p.185)
• And then we both ***realized*** we should go.(p.201)
• When he left, I ***realized*** from his story that as a drinker I was just a panty-waist.(p.208)
• I ***realized*** that I had a problem, although my realization was not very deep because my own conceit wouldn't admit that I had any personality problems.(p.214)
• Professionally, after I was sober for a month or so I ***realized*** that I should school myself to dissolve the partnership I was in because I felt that I would never regain the respect of my partners no matter how long I was sober, and that I would be at a disadvantage.(p.220)
• I ***realized*** that there wasn't anything I could say to place myself in a more favorable light with my children, that it was going to be a matter of time; for I also understood the intolerance of young people towards deficiencies in their elders.(p.220)
• In any case I must get out of here before I let slip my abysmal ignorance of how I came to be here, and she ***realized*** that I was stark, staring mad.(p.223)
• They ***realized*** that repeated lack of drinking control, when they really wanted control, was the fatal symptom that spelled problem drinking.(p.315)
• They ***realized*** that in the end alcoholism could be a mortal as cancer; certainly no sane man would wait for a malignant growth to become fatal before seeking help.(p.315)
• I ***realized*** I couldn't quit.(p.319)
• I thought I was losing my mind when I ***realized*** that I couldn't stop drinking.(p.324)
• She ***realized*** what she was becoming.(p.335)
• I should have ***realized*** that alcohol was getting hold of me when I started to become secretive in my drinking.(p.336)
• Psychiatrist and surgeon, he had lost his way until he ***realized*** that God, not he, was the Great Healer.(p.345)
• Shortly after I was starting to work on the program I ***realized*** that I was not a good father; I wasn't a good husband, but, oh, I was a good provider.(p.351)
• With rare foresight he ***realized*** it could become a tornado.(p.373)
• But success brought increased social activities and I ***realized*** that many of my friends enjoyed a social drink with no apparent harm to themselves or others.(p.374)
• I ***realized*** I had been going down and down.(p.378)
• I believe the first time I ever ***realized*** what alcohol would do for me was at my own wedding.(p.385)
• They phoned my husband that I was in jail and in such terrible shape that they didn't know what I would do to myself; and they ***realized*** that jail was no place for me, but that he was to wait a while before he got me, because at the time they called him to come over for me I was beating a tin cup against the wall.(p.390)
• I ***realized*** that there were other people in this world who behaved and acted as I did, and that I was a sick person, that I was suffering from an actual disease.(p.392)
• Slowly I ***realized*** I was in bed and that the objects were my feet, encased in a harness affair.(p.422)
• Very shortly, I ***realized*** that had been a mistake -- when this big clown came bounding into the room, almost shouting, "My name is Frank, and I'm an alcoholic, ha-ha-ha!"(p.446)
• From that time on, fear was with me because I ***realized*** that not only would I not remember what happened to me while I was drinking, but apparently I couldn't control what happened.(p.465)
• She ***realized*** that, and the way I felt, and so for my own good she gradually began to pull away.(p.472)
• While I was there I ***realized*** that I had missed something.(p.472)
• I ***realized*** that I was trying to pin everything on an individual – not the book or the group or the Higher Power, or anything else.(p.472)
• That was enough provocation to fight but I didn't fight, and I ***realized*** after recess why I didn't.(p.484)
• About then too, I ***realized*** that my point of view on the opposite sex wasn't entirely like that of most of the boys I knew.(p.484)
• But as he continued to talk, I ***realized*** that this was the first time I had met a person who had the same problems I did and who, I sincerely believe, understood me as an individual.(p.494)
• That morning was the first time I really ***realized*** where I'd got to in my life.(p.523)
• My husband eventually returned, but it was not long until we ***realized*** we could not continue our marriage.(p.547)
• It was here that I ***realized*** for the first time that as a practicing alcoholic I had no rights.(p.549)
• One morning, however, I ***realized*** I had to get rid of it, for my reprieve was running out, and if I didn't get rid of it I was going to get drunk – and I didn't want to get drunk any more.(p.552)

realizes

• He finally ***realizes*** that he has undergone a profound alteration in his reaction to life; that such a change could hardly have been brought about by himself alone.(p.569)

realizing

• We are there to sweep off our side of the street ***realizing*** that nothing worth while can be accomplished until we do so, never trying to tell him what he should do.(p.77)
• They should be patient, ***realizing*** they are dealing with a sick person.(p.90)
• So, after reviewing these things and ***realizing*** what liquor had cost me, I went to this Higher Power which, to me was God, without any reservation, and admitted that I was completely powerless over alcohol, and that I was willing to do anything in the world to get rid of the problem.(p.187)
• And yet, ***realizing*** at last that liquor really had me, I wanted to quit.(p.234)
• I went on, ***realizing*** what I was becoming, hating myself for it, bitter, blaming life, blaming everything else but the fact that I should turn about and do something about my drinking.(p.337)
• I remember finding myself in the middle of the night in the doctors' parking lot at the hospital with one foot in the car and one foot on the ground, not knowing which was the lead foot; finding myself hanging up the telephone – then ***realizing*** I had gotten out of bed, answered the phone, turned on the light, and carried on a conversation with a patient.(p.441)
• The doctor, apparently ***realizing*** that one thing that I certainly needed was sleep, left a bottle of sleeping pills there and in my drunken state I took them all, instead of the one or two he had prescribed.(p.465)
• Perhaps, without ***realizing*** it, I was.)(p.532)

really

• Then Jack Alexander wrote a feature article in the Saturday Evening Post and placed such a compelling picture of A.A. before the general public that alcoholics in need of help ***really*** deluged us.(p.xviii)
• Of alcoholics who came to A.A. and ***really*** tried, 50% got sober at once and remained that way; 25% sobered up after some relapses, and among the remainder, those who stayed on with A.A. showed improvement.(p.xx)
• I could almost hear the sound of the preacher's voice as I sat, on still Sundays, way over there on the hillside; there was that proffered temperance pledge I never signed; my grandfather's good natured contempt of some church folk and their doings; his insistence that the spheres ***really*** had their music; but his denial of the preacher's right to tell him how he must listen; his fearlessness as he spoke of these things just before he died; these recollections welled up from the past.(p.10)
• Few people ***really*** are, for that means blind faith in the strange proposition that this universe originated in a cipher and aimlessly rushes nowhere.(p.10)
• The joy of living we ***really*** have, even under pressure and difficulty.(p.15)
• I have seen hundreds of families set their feet in the path that ***really*** goes somewhere; have seen the most impossible domestic situations righted; feuds and bitterness of all sorts wiped out.(p.15)
• Sometimes these excuses have a certain plausibility, but none of them ***really*** makes sense in the light of the havoc an alcoholic's drinking bout creates.(p.23)
• But in their hearts they ***really*** do not know why they do it.(p.23)
• But we saw that it ***really*** worked in others, and we had come to believe in the hopelessness and futility of life as we had been living it.(p.25)
• A new life has been given us or, if you prefer, "a design for living" that ***really*** works.(p.28)
• We doubt if many of them can do it, because none will ***really*** want to stop, and hardly one of them, because of the peculiar mental twist already acquired, will find he can win out.(p.33)
• They grinned, which I didn't like so much, and then asked me if I thought myself alcoholic and if I were ***really*** licked this time.(p.42)
• Most alcoholics have to be pretty badly mangled before they ***really*** commence to solve their problems.(p.43)
• Is he not ***really*** a self-seeker even when trying to be kind?(p.61)
• We began to see that the world and its people ***really*** dominated us.(p.66)
• What we ***really*** have is a daily reprieve contingent on the maintenance of our spiritual condition.(p.85)
• It works – it ***really*** does.(p.88)
• You can see that he ***really*** does love you with his better self.(p.108)
• Especially when he has before him a way to stop his drinking and abuse if he ***really*** wants to pay the price.(p.108)
• But after his next binge, ask him if he would ***really*** like to get over drinking for good.(p.112)
• Sometimes he will be so interested that he becomes ***really*** neglectful.(p.119)
• If you are satisfied he ***really*** wants to get over drinking, you need not be alarmed.(p.120)
• His wife is one of those persons who ***really*** feels there is something rather sinful about these commodities, so she nagged, and her intolerance finally threw him into a fit of anger.(p.135)
• To me, this incident illustrates lack of understanding as to what ***really*** ails the alcoholic, and lack of knowledge as to what part employers might profitably take in salvaging their sick employees.(p.139)
• If he says yes, does he ***really*** mean it, or down inside does he think he is fooling you, and that after rest and treatment he will be able to get away with a few drinks now and then?(p.142)
• They bear witness that release from alcoholism can ***really*** be permanent.(p.169)
• No beer or liquor was sold in the neighborhood, except at the State liquor agency where perhaps one might procure a pint if he could convince the agent that he ***really*** needed it.(p.171)
• It was ***really*** a horrible nightmare, this earning money, getting liquor, smuggling it home, getting drunk, morning jitters, taking large doses of sedatives to make it possible for me to earn more money, and so on ad nauseam.(p.177)
• But if you ***really*** and truly want to quit drinking liquor for good and all, and sincerely feel that you must have some help, we know that we have an answer for you.(p.181)
• I ***really*** wanted the program and I wanted to go along with it.(p.191)
• Akron was ***really*** on the boom in those days, 1919-1920; expansion was terrific.(p.198)
• I worked along until I had ***really*** big names in rubber on a tentative contract, and then I neglected to go through with it.(p.198)
• I can remember well thinking that I would quit drinking, ***really*** go to work hard, apply myself eight hours a day, five days a week, make a lot of money, and then I could start drinking again.(p.199)
• After drinking one glass of beer at the end of my work period for about five days, I thought I'd better find out whether I ***really*** had the stuff licked.(p.203)
• Talking things over with them, great floods of enlightenment showed me myself as I ***really*** was and I was like them.(p.229)
• And yet, realizing at last that liquor ***really*** had me, I wanted to quit.(p.234)
• This last real merry-go-round had started the day before Christmas and I had ***really*** accomplished a lot in those fourteen days.(p.238)
• That night for the first time in my life I ***really*** let down my hair and admitted my general loneliness.(p.239)
• I have never shown any particular talents nor have I had any ***really*** frustrating ambitions.(p.240)
• At seventeen I entered the University, ***really*** to satisfy my father who wanted me to study medicine there as he had.(p.241)
• I had been to OTC the previous summer so I went into the Army as a sergeant, but I came out a private, and you ***really*** have to be unusual to do that.(p.241)
• I ***really*** had a chance to see myself from a non-drinking point of view.(p.245)
• In those days we ***really*** took each other's inventories firmly and often.(p.245)
• Yet we all had one ***really*** sincere purpose in our hearts and that was not to drink.(p.246)
• This was when I ***really*** took my first good look at myself.(p.247)
• This time it ***really*** hurt, more than any hangover ever had.(p.247)
• My brilliant agnosticism vanished, and I saw for the first time that those who ***really*** believed, or at least honestly tried to find a Power greater than themselves, were much more composed and contented than I had ever been, and they seemed to have a degree of happiness which I had never known.(p.247)

• I had been too self-sufficient to write a moral inventory, but I discovered in pointing out to the new man his wrong attitudes and actions that I was ***really*** taking my own inventory, and that if I expected him to change I would have to work on myself too.(p.249)
• Discharged in 1919, I ***really*** made up for my dry spell.(p.253)
• I ***really*** wasn't very high.(p.264)
• She said, "Do you ***really*** mean that?"(p.266)
• This is based, ***really***, on the Sermon on the Mount.(p.268)
• In the spiritual strength I had found, because of A.A., I felt that I had made a complete surrender, that I had ***really*** turned my life over that summer.(p.271)
• Strangely enough, I became acquainted with the "hilarious life" just at the time in my own life when I was beginning ***really*** to settle down to a common-sense, sane domesticity.(p.297)
• From that point on, I secured crocks of ten gallon capacity and ***really*** took quite an active interest in the manufacture of home brew.(p.297)
• I was on the toboggan and ***really*** making time.(p.300)
• I ***really*** worked for several weeks, and having had a fairly wide acquaintance with the dealer trade, it was not difficult for me to line up enough of them to give me a very substantial volume of business with a minimum of effort.(p.300)
• Well . . . I had a job, and I ***really*** wanted desperately to stop drinking, but couldn't, so I readily agreed to visit the doctor she recommended.(p.301)
• My wife accompanied me on my visit and the doctor ***really*** told me some things that in my state of jitters nearly knocked me out of the chair.(p.302)
• I eat three good meals a day now, and ***really*** enjoy them.(p.303)
• From a domestic standpoint, we ***really*** have a home now.(p.303)
• I would hang on to sobriety for short intervals, but always there would come the tide of an overpowering necessity to drink and, as I was engulfed in it, I felt such a sense of panic that I ***really*** believed I would die if I didn't get that drink inside.(p.306)
• Some of us struggle with these people because we know that they are ***really*** very sick, but we also know that short of some miracle, we are not going to help them except temporarily, and that they will inevitably get worse and worse until one of two things happens.(p.308)
• They realized that repeated lack of drinking control, when they ***really*** wanted control, was the fatal symptom that spelled problem drinking.(p.315)
• One morning when I was feeling ***really*** bad, I was put on K.P. and the head cook wanted me to go out and scrub the garbage cans.(p.317)
• I ***really*** started drinking with a bang.(p.323)
• I was accused of it many times when I went to play bridge in the afternoon, but I ***really*** never did take a morning drink.(p.323)
• It ***really*** wasn't living.(p.326)
• Hiding behind a newspaper, magazine, or book, I ***really*** saw nothing, but simulated deep interest.(p.332)
• I was sure those who needed a bit of the hair of the dog ***really*** were alcoholics.(p.332)
• None of this ***really*** impressed me.(p.354)
• And deep in my heart I ***really*** meant what I said because I loved her more than anything else in the world, yes — even more than liquor.(p.362)
• She told me not to bother going "for her sake"; she told me in a nice way that it didn't make any difference to her -- and that ***really*** scared me -- so I went.(p.365)
• It was frightening that drink was being substituted for more and more of the things I ***really*** enjoyed doing.(p.374)
• That is where we are ***really*** fooled.(p.376)
• This suggestion had been made before on a number of occasions, but like all alcoholics I wanted to handle my problem my own way, which ***really*** meant I didn't want anything to interfere with my drinking.(p.378)
• However, after I heard a few stories of jails, sanitariums, broken homes and skid row, I wondered if I ***really*** was an alcoholic.(p.378)
• The only thing I have ***really*** to offer you is my own story, telling you just what sort of a drunk I was.(p.384)
• By the time all this was over, I was ***really*** in a terrific state, and my father taking in things said, "Miss Esther is about to faint.(p.385)
• It was ***really*** medicinal that night, that whiskey, and it was a medication after that.(p.386)
• I ***really*** started drinking then.(p.386)
• I had never been inside of an insane asylum and I ***really*** thought I was going to a private hospital.(p.387)
• I think I actually read more contempt than was ***really*** there because just a week before someone had sent him the Saturday Evening Post article on A.A., and there was some glimmer of hope in it for him.(p.391)
• Up to that time, I was so completely baffled by my behavior that I had never ***really*** stopped to think at all.(p.392)
• They sent me the regular letter they send to everybody else, but along with it, Ruth Hock, the nonalcoholic secretary, wrote a longhand note because she could see from the letter that I ***really*** needed help badly.(p.392)
• It took me three psychoanalysts and several years in A.A. to ***really*** get this through my head.(p.401)
• But at this time, I began gravitating toward the ***really*** hard drinkers, hanging around with them more and more.(p.404)
• I was ***really*** trying, once more, to escape from myself.(p.405)
• I had worked the previous summer on a New York fashion magazine, a job I ***really*** enjoyed.(p.405)
• Or: If I'm ***really*** a genius, I must produce a great work, to show why I act like a genius.(p.408)
• I was ***really*** scolding my mortal enemy, the inner me.(p.408)
• And again these were things that I ***really*** profited by after I sobered up.(p.409)
• I was ***really*** scared.(p.415)
• I thought it was my duty to keep her from drinking, not knowing that if the other fellow is ***really*** determined to drink there is nothing you can do about it.(p.415)
• Nor were those impossible dreams I used to have the things I ***really*** wanted.(p.416)
• Because A.A. ***really*** works for me!(p.421)
• They ***really*** needed it.(p.427)
• After a month it seemed unlikely that it ever ***really*** happened.(p.433)
• (I am pleased to state, however, that I had gone to only a very few A.A. meetings before I was able to make a ***really*** beautiful pair of moccasins — and half a wallet.(p.445)
• But, by the look on the psychiatrist's face, I could tell that it would ***really*** make him happy if I agreed.(p.446)
• I ***really*** felt sorry for him; the only thing in life he had to brag about was the fact that he was an alcoholic.(p.446)
• And I knew that giving up "one drink for one day" wouldn't ***really*** do any good.(p.448)
• It is true that I -- of all people, strange as it may seem, and even though I didn't give my permission -- ***really, really*** am an alcoholic of sorts.(p.448)
• I have to discard my "rights," as well as my expectations, by asking myself, "How important is it, ***really***?(p.452)
• There is ***really*** nothing to dressing with chains and shackles on, once you learn the technique of pulling inside-out pants through the shackles.(p.460)
• One would have to understand the correctional machinery to see what a miracle this ***really*** was.(p.462)
• After a while I ***really*** did enjoy drinking and what it did to me, and I became dependent upon it for every occasion.(p.464)
• It was in Washington, D.C. that this transition took place, and that the ***really*** bad part of alcoholism began happening.(p.465)
• My pattern of drinking at that time had reached the point where once I ***really*** started, I would retire to my bed and drink myself into oblivion.(p.466)
• On the way I tried, and I mean ***really*** tried, to throw myself out of the car.(p.466)
• So the doctor said, "I ***really*** don't know too much about it, but they tell me it is a bunch of drunks who get together . . ."(p.469)
• I feel that I have been restored to health and sanity these past years not through my own efforts nor as a result of anything I may have done, but because I've come to believe -- to ***really*** believe — that alone I can do nothing.(p.473)
• Some drunken women ***really*** are, you know.(p.479)
• This ***really*** makes for an attractive woman!(p.479)
• I ***really*** do believe it is much harder for a woman to gain back her self-respect than it is for a man.(p.480)
• He also cares; he ***really*** cares.(p.481)
• That's the first time I was ever ***really*** drunk in my life.(p.487)
• Very often we rode to and from work together, but being separated ***really*** galled me deep down.(p.491)
• I rolled along with the mob this way, that way and the other way, but in those years nothing ***really*** bad happened to me.(p.508)
• When I had heard about it, it meant nothing but just two letters to me, but some friends of mine in the institution were very active in the program and ***really*** believed in it.(p.509)
• That ***really*** stopped me for a little bit.(p.510)
• She was the one who ***really*** helped me to make a go of that twenty years and nine months in prison.(p.511)
• Of course I ***really*** didn't have to worry on that score, because I wasn't the type that got half drunk.(p.515)
• Up to that time, drinking didn't ***really*** mean anything to me at all.(p.518)
• But as long as you did your work and didn't disgrace yourself, you were socially acceptable and nobody ***really*** intruded on your private life very much.(p.518)
• I got a job by myself which suited me down to the ground, because there was nobody ***really*** to interfere with what I did, one way or the other, and I usually had my nerves in good trim when anybody was coming around to inspect.(p.519)
• Then Hitler's war broke out, and again, I was given a ***really*** important job on the Suez Canal, dealing with military shipping.(p.520)
• That morning was the first time I ***really*** realized where I'd got to in my life.(p.523)
• She ***really*** meant business this time.(p.523)
• It was there that I ***really*** found out what A.A. was.(p.528)
• If you give us a try, you will see that we are ***really*** human beings, and we will welcome you with open arms and hearts.(p.529)
• The truth is, I did not know how to stop it, nor did I want to, ***really***.(p.539)
• Without alcohol, I would be ***really*** alone.(p.539)
• I had only to reflect on the contrast between the plans I made so many years ago for my life with what ***really*** happened to know I couldn't manage my life drunk or sober.(p.550)
• It had provided me with excuses for my lack of education, my marital failures, personal failures, inadequacy, and of course, my alcoholism and, though I ***really*** thought I had been willing to part with it, now I knew I was reluctant to let it go.(p.552)
• Even when you don't ***really*** want it for them, and your prayers are only words and you don't mean it, go ahead and do it anyway.(p.552)
• This great experience that released me from the bondage of hatred and replaced it with love is ***really*** just another affirmation of the truth I know: I get everything I need in Alcoholics Anonymous — everything I need I get — and when I get what I need I invariably find that it was just what I wanted all the time.(p.553)

realm

• To us, the ***Realm*** of Spirit is broad, roomy, all inclusive; never exclusive or forbidding to those who earnestly seek.(p.46)
• In the ***realm*** of the material, men's minds were fettered by superstition, tradition, and all sorts of fixed ideas.(p.51)
• We asked ourselves this: Are not some of us just as biased and unreasonable about the ***realm*** of the material?(p.51)
• As we became subjects of King Alcohol, shivering denizens of his mad ***realm***, the chilling vapor that is loneliness settled down.(p.151)

reap

• Above all, I have gained the greatest thing accorded to any man, the love and understanding of a gracious God, who has lifted me from the alcoholic scrap-heap to a position of trust where I have been able to ***reap*** the rich rewards that come from showing a little love for others and from serving them as I can.(p.296)

reaped

• I, who had dreamed these sick dreams, now ***reaped*** the nightmare.(p.411)

rear

• I went out to a restaurant, found a booth way back in the ***rear***, and started drinking.(p.467)

rearrangement

• In fact, I have been trying to produce some such emotional ***rearrangement*** within you.(p.27)

rearrangements

• They appear to be in the nature of huge emotional displacements and ***rearrangements***.(p.27)

reason

• Another ***reason*** for the wide acceptance of A.A. was the ministration of friends -- friends in medicine, religion, and the press, together with innumerable others who became our able and persistent advocates.(p.xx)
• Moderate drinkers have little trouble in giving up li-

quor entirely if they have good *reason* for it.(p.20)
• If a sufficiently strong *reason* -- ill health, falling in love, change of environment, or the warning of a doctor – becomes operative, this man can also stop or moderate, although he may find it difficult and troublesome and may even need medical attention.(p.21)
• They had said that though I did raise a defense, it would one day give way before some trivial *reason* for having a drink.(p.42)
• We have no *reason* to doubt it.(p.49)
• When many hundreds of people are able to say that the consciousness of the Presence of God is today the most important fact of their lives, they present a powerful *reason* why one should have faith.(p.51)
• Almost everyone knows the *reason.*(p.51)
• It is not by chance we were given the power to *reason*, to examine the evidence of our senses, and to draw conclusions.(p.53)
• Some of us had already walked far over the Bridge of *Reason* toward the desired shore of faith.(p.53)
• We were grateful that *Reason* had brought us so far.(p.53)
• Perhaps we had been leaning too heavily on *Reason* that last mile and we did not like to lose our support.(p.53)
• Yes, we had been faithful, abjectly faithful to the God of *Reason.*(p.54)
• How much did these feelings, these loves, these worships, have to do with pure *reason?*(p.54)
• Were nothing left but pure *reason,* it wouldn't be life.(p.54)
• Hence, we saw that *reason* isn't everything.(p.54)
• Neither is *reason,* as most of us use it, entirely dependable, though it emanate from our best minds.(p.54)
• The best *reason* first: If we skip this vital step, we may not overcome drinking.(p.72)
• We think the *reason* is that they never completed their housecleaning.(p.73)
• And there may be a valid *reason* for postponement in some cases.(p.83)
• Though an alcoholic does not respond, there is no *reason* why you should neglect his family.(p.97)
• In some cases the wife will never come back for one *reason* or another.(p.99)
• So our rule is not to avoid a place where there is drinking, if we have a legitimate *reason* for being there.(p.101)
• Therefore, ask yourself on each occasion, "Have I any good social, business, or personal *reason* for going to this place?(p.101)
• Unless the *reason* is understood, there may be an emotional upset.(p.134)
• If your decision is yes, whether the *reason* be humanitarian or business or both, then the following suggestions may be helpful.(p.140)
• So, for one *reason* or another, they cover these men, hoping matters will take a turn for the better.(p.147)
• He will have no further *reason* for covering up an alcoholic employee.(p.148)
• We could not be invited out because I would surely get tight and my wife dared not invite people in for the same *reason.*(p.177)
• For some *reason,* we alcoholics seem to have the gift of picking out the world's finest women.(p.178)
• Another *reason* I go is that I'm still grateful for the good years that I've had.(p.192)
• I had no more *reason* to drink those martinis than a jackrabbit.(p.195)
• So having licked it, there was no *reason* why I shouldn't have a drink, and I stopped in before I got home and had one.(p.203)
• They suffered from my conduct without saying anything, but the *reason* for this was I still managed to hang onto a very substantial practice.(p.215)
• But for some *reason* -- she just didn't know why -- she just had to hold onto that clipping, with its thin hope.(p.367)
• I had nowhere else to go, and I knew something was terribly wrong, and the *reason* had to lie within myself.(p.371)
• We rationalize and excuse our conduct beyond all *reason.*(p.376)
• For some *reason* I can't remember, it finally dawned on me that I had a problem, and yet nobody was very critical about it except my family, and that was only because I decided, after seven years of marriage, that I would divorce my husband.(p.386)
• I could see no *reason* why they should have any relationship to this problem of getting drunk every now and then.(p.388)
• There was no material or external *reason* for this.(p.400)
• So, for no better *reason* than to make him happy, I agreed.(p.446)
• So, for no better *reason* than to fool him, I asked Frank to take me to a meeting every night.(p.447)
• It made me feel quite grown-up and mature, and I think another added attraction was the fact that so far as my family was concerned, it was forbidden, and it had a special attraction for that *reason.*(p.464)
• They were always there because of a nervous breakdown, or for a "rest cure" -- any *reason* except because of drinking.(p.471)
• For that *reason,* I believe, I married at a much younger age than I would have, had it not been for my home training.(p.485)
• But such is my nature that I must know the *reason* for things and I didn't stop until I had satisfied myself about the reasons for my drinking.(p.533)
• For a little while, I was the great man I wanted to be, and thought myself entitled to be just by *reason* of being.(p.537)
• I wonder if ever there has been a sillier *reason* for getting drunk all the time.(p.537)
• The *reason,* as I learned later, was that I had not worked for A.A.(p.539)
• In time I concluded that the *reason* I was hurt was because I loved my parents, and I concluded too that if I never allowed myself to love anybody or anything I could never be hurt again.(p.545)
• I've been benefited from a dictionary definition I found that reads: "rationalization is giving a socially acceptable *reason* for socially unacceptable behavior, and socially unacceptable behavior is a form of insanity."(p.551)

reasonable

• Simply because it is impossible to explain what we see, feel, direct, and use, without a *reasonable* assumption as a starting point.(p.48)
• Actually, we used to have no *reasonable* conception whatever.(p.49)
• We agnostically inclined would not feel satisfied with a proposal which does not lend itself to *reasonable* approach and interpretation.(p.53)
• Hence we are at pains to tell why we think our present faith is *reasonable,* why we think it more sane and logical to believe than not to believe, why we say our former thinking was soft and mushy when we threw up our hands in doubt and said, "We don't know."(p.53)
• Because of the employee's special ability, or of his own strong personal attachment to him, the employer has sometimes kept such a man at work long beyond a *reasonable* period.(p.137)
• A *reasonable* amount of latitude will be helpful.(p.146)
• Every *reasonable* desire was possible of attainment for me.(p.304)
• What could be more *reasonable* than that some people, including myself, were allergic to alcohol?(p.380)

reasonableness

• It finally beat us into a state of *reasonableness.*(p.48)
• Your husband may come to appreciate your *reasonableness* and patience.(p.111)

reasonably

• Some, but not all of us, think it has its advantages when *reasonably* used.(p.110)
• Father was a very well-integrated person, and while mother was highstrung and a bit selfish and demanding, our home life was *reasonably* harmonious.(p.240)

reasoned

• Friends who have *reasoned* with him after a spree which has brought him to the point of divorce or bankruptcy are mystified when he walks directly into a saloon.(p.35)
• I *reasoned* I was not so far advanced as most of you fellows, that I had been usually successful in licking my other personal problems, and that I would therefore be successful where you men failed.(p.40)
• Taking that as a foundation, he *reasoned* that if a man followed that rule he could not be selfish.(p.236)
• But I had my health back and besides, I *reasoned,* they were much worse than I would ever be.(p.289)

reasoning

• If you draw this fallacious *reasoning* to the attention of an alcoholic, he will laugh it off, or become irritated and refuse to talk.(p.23)
• But there was always the curious mental phenomenon that parallel with our sound *reasoning* there inevitably ran some insanely trivial excuse for taking the first drink.(p.37)
• Our sound *reasoning* failed to hold us in check.(p.37)
• For did we not believe in our own *reasoning?*(p.53)
• She tried *reasoning* with me, endeavored to work out various drinking schedules, in fact all the tricks were practised faithfully for a short time somewhere along my shaky road to unhappiness.(p.361)

reasons

• For this there were two principal *reasons*: the large numbers of recoveries, and reunited homes.(p.xx)
• I discovered many more *reasons* later on.(p.2)
• The fact is that most alcoholics, for *reasons* yet obscure, have lost the power of choice in drink.(p.24)
• Yet all *reasons* for not drinking were easily pushed aside in favor of the foolish idea that he could take whiskey if only he mixed it with milk!(p.36)
• We think there are good *reasons.*(p.48)
• Once confused and baffled by the seeming futility of existence they show the underlying *reasons* why they were making heavy going of life.(p.50)
• We will be more reconciled to discussing ourselves with another person when we see good *reasons* why we should do so.(p.72)
• Your candidate may give *reasons* why he need not follow all of the program.(p.94)
• I do it for four *reasons:*(p.180)
• My marriage was happy and, as I have said, I never had any of the *reasons,* conscious or unconscious, which are often given for drinking.(p.182)
• But – supposing that just one man died because I had, for selfish *reasons,* kept my mouth shut?(p.282)
• I never enjoyed any meal, but I ate my lunch at noon for two *reasons;* first, to help me get out of the fog of the night before and, second, to furnish some measure of nourishment.(p.299)
• I have omitted details of transgressions that I made when drunk for several *reasons.*(p.301)
• My broken home and broken heart fanned my smoldering self-pity into a fair-sized bonfire and this kept me well supplied with *reasons* for having another drink, and then another.(p.305)
• If *reasons* for covering up are strong enough, secrets can be hidden from the world.(p.327)
• I had all kinds of *reasons* for my drinking.(p.338)
• I have had many more *reasons* to drink since I have been in A.A. than I had in all the years of my drinking.(p.367)
• Gradually the quantity increased, the occasions for a drink came more frequently; a hard day, worries and pressure, bad news, good news – there were more and more *reasons* for a drink.(p.374)
• There may be many *reasons* which bring one to A.A. for the first time, but the lasting one must be to want sobriety and the A.A. way of living for oneself.(p.379)
• At age twenty-one, I enlisted in the Navy for two *reasons*: (1) to avoid being drafted into the Army, and (2) out of a burst of patriotic fervor inspired by the advent of World War II and as the result of an all-night drinking binge which found me sitting on the doorstep of the Navy recruiting office when the chief petty officer arrived to open for business at nine o'clock Monday morning.(p.398)
• I could tell him a lot of *reasons* why I am here in an alky ward at the age of twenty.(p.423)
• "Two *reasons,*" he said.(p.436)
• Sometimes we are told in A.A. not to try and learn the *reasons* for our drinking.(p.533)
• But such is my nature that I must know the reason for things and I didn't stop until I had satisfied myself about the *reasons* for my drinking.(p.533)
• For to have accepted the *reasons* and to have acted on them would have been too great a blow to my ego, which was as great, in reverse, as my body was small.(p.534)
• That couplet contains most of my *reasons* for drinking.(p.534)
• Still another friend and temporary host received me at four in the morning from the charge of a policeman who had found me "going to bed" in a garage far from the last place I could remember having been, a fashionable bar and restaurant in the theatrical district of New York, to which I had repaired after my date for that evening, a charming lady of the theatre who had refused my company for obvious *reasons.*(p.538)

reasserted

• The old pattern *reasserted* itself, but it was no longer once every six months.(p.514)

reassure

• Let us make haste to *reassure* you.(p.46)

reassured

• I vaguely sensed I was not being any too smart, but felt *reassured* as I was taking the whiskey on a full stomach.(p.36)
• Let us be *reassured.*(p.76)

rebel

• He may *rebel* at the thought of a drastic housecleaning which requires discussion with other people.(p.94)

• I don't think the boys were completely convinced of my personality change, for they fought shy of including my story in the book, so my only contribution to their literary efforts was my firm conviction, being still a theological *rebel*, that the word God should be qualified with the phrase "as we understand him" -- for that was the only way I could accept spirituality.(p.248)
• It has made me understand that I must be one of my world, that I cannot exist in any happiness as a *rebel* by myself.(p.524)

rebelled
• Sometimes during that year I *rebelled* inwardly at what seemed like lost time, and at having to be a burden to these good people whose means were limited.(p.281)
• I *rebelled* against this, because just about the time that I was getting ready to leave high school, a revelation came to me about God and it made things very complicated for me.(p.489)
• I *rebelled*, and from that time on I don't think I attended church more than a dozen times.(p.489)

rebellion
• Military service was compulsory and I did my stretch with the class of my age, goose-stepping in German barracks and taking part in the Boxer *Rebellion* in China, my first time at any great distance from home.(p.230)
• RUM, RADIO AND *REBELLION*(p.356)

rebellious
• He attended church school, where he became *rebellious* at what he thought an overdose of religious education.(p.56)
• At this school we had Bible readings before each meal, and church services four times on Sunday, and I became so *rebellious* at this that I swore I would never join or go to any church except for weddings or funerals.(p.240)

rebels
• We even can be *rebels* for the first time in our lives.(p.329)

reborn
• We were *reborn*.(p.63)
• Then A.A. showed her the beauty of normal living, in a whole family *reborn*.(p.478)

recall
• Potential female alcoholics often turn into the real thing and are gone beyond *recall* in a few years.(p.33)
• The general moral standard was, as I *recall* it, far above the average.(p.171)
• I do not recollect the specific conversation that went on but I believe I did challenge Bill to tell me something about A.A. and I do *recall* one other thing: I wanted to know what this was that worked so many wonders, and hanging over the mantel was a picture of Gethsemane and Bill pointed to it and said, "There it is," which didn't make much sense to me.(p.216)
• And then one ill-defined day, one day that I can't *recall*, I stepped across the line that alcoholics know so well, and from that day on drinking was miserable.(p.346)
• I *recall*, as I walked into that meeting, saying to myself, "Here I am, a fellow of the American College of Surgeons, a Fellow of the International College of Surgeons, a diplomate of one of the great specialty boards in these United States, a member of the American Psychiatric Society, and I have to go to the butcher, the baker and the carpenter to help make a man out of me!"(p.347)
• I do *recall* lying on a cold cement floor and shredding into little bits several pieces of stolen identification cards, and washing my face in the toilet bowl trying to sober up, and screaming hysterically while clinging to bars too high to see out of, and cursing everyone that came near me.(p.354)
• You will *recall* that I said the time that I got the idea out of a clear sky to call A.A. on a certain night was at about ten.(p.366)
• I couldn't *recall*.(p.422)

recalled
• Yet I recently *recalled* that each morning I used to talk to the bottle when I took it down from the closet.(p.332)

recapture
• Never could we *recapture* the great moments of the past.(p.151)

recapturing
• Unmindful of his welfare, I thought only of *recapturing* the spirit of other days.(p.9)

receded
• Each time I told her she was a nothing, she *receded* a little more into nowhere.(p.450)

receipt
• While drinking, he accepted a sum of money from a bitterly-hated business rival, giving him no *receipt* for it.(p.80)

receive
• Then only might I expect to *receive*.(p.13)
• Those of us belonging to a religious denomination which requires confession must, and of course, will want to go to the properly appointed authority whose duty it is to *receive* it.(p.74)
• It is not to be expected that an alcoholic employee will *receive* a disproportionate amount of time and attention.(p.149)
• During the subsequent fifteen years I had sense enough never to go to the hospital if I had been drinking, and very seldom did I *receive* patients.(p.176)
• However, this isn't as rough as it sounds, as we do become grateful for the necessity that makes us toe the line, for we find that we are more than compensated for a consistent effort by the countless dividends we *receive*.(p.311)
• Through A.A., many *receive* the needed change and awakening just by trying to live by A.A. principles and associating with A.A. people.(p.459)
• If you cannot find A.A. in your locality, a letter addressed to Alcoholics Anonymous, Box 459, Grand Central Station, New York, NY 10163, U.S.A., will *receive* a prompt reply from this world center, referring you to the nearest A.A. group.(p.575)

received
• He subsequently denied having *received* the money and used the incident as a basis for discrediting the man.(p.80)
• I well remember the shock I *received* when a prominent doctor in Chicago told me of cases where pressure of the spinal fluid actually ruptured the brain.(p.140)
• He found himself surprisingly well *received*, and learned that many knew of his drinking.(p.156)
• That was skeptically *received* by me when I first heard it, but after some twenty-eight or thirty fellows had come to see me, and pretty nearly all of them had said the same thing, I began to believe it.(p.219)
• I still have my job, and just prior to the writing of this narrative, I *received* an advancement.(p.303)
• However, due to financial difficulties the whole printing was, for a while, held up and the book *received* no publicity, nor, of course, was it available in the stores, even if one knew it existed.(p.307)
• The next day I *received* a visit from Mr. T., a recovered alcoholic.(p.309)
• Far from expecting praise for their deeds, they claimed the performance a privilege and insisted that they invariably *received* more than they gave.(p.310)
• The encouragement *received* in the early days, especially from the A.A. General Service Office, made a tremendous difference to my sobriety.(p.342)
• There, I *received* several soda crackers and water daily, and before I could have my third-day meal (again the only meal in ten days), I had to drink a glass of castor oil or mineral oil, depending on the cruelty of the person who was doing the dispensing.(p.459)
• Three weeks after an armed robbery in which one person *received* a superficial flesh wound (I could have killed someone!), I was apprehended.(p.460)
• Fortunately, I *received* only fifteen-twenty years, and I went back to my alma mater (where I had spent so much time in the hole).(p.461)
• My wife *received* me graciously, although she was living in a one room with kitchen affair.(p.490)
• For that crime I *received* a minimum of twenty years and a maximum of natural life.(p.508)
• I *received* an additional fifteen years for that, making a minimum of thirty-five years and a maximum of natural life.(p.509)
• I remember the day when I decided to drink myself to death quietly, without bothering anyone, because I was tired of having been a dependable, trustworthy person for about thirty-nine years without having *received* what I thought was a proper reward for my virtue.(p.531)
• Still another friend and temporary host *received* me at four in the morning from the charge of a policeman who had found me "going to bed" in a garage far from the last place I could remember having been, a fashionable bar and restaurant in the theatrical district of New York, to which I had repaired after my date for that evening, a charming lady of the theatre who had refused my company for obvious reasons.(p.538)

receiver
• I still expected a plea for clemency, but these words came through the *receiver*: "I just wanted to tell you Paul jumped from a hotel window in Hartford last Saturday.(p.136)
• Selecting a church at random from the directory, he stepped into a booth and lifted the *receiver*.(p.155)

receivers
• They are the custodians of our A.A. Tradition and the *receivers* of voluntary A.A. contributions by which we maintain our A.A. General Service Office at New York.(p.567)

receiving
• Much has already been said about *receiving* strength, inspiration, and direction from Him who has all knowledge and power.(p.85)
• Straightway, Bob called Akron's City Hospital and asked for the nurse on the *receiving* ward.(p.188)
• Long before I had any real opportunity to give, I had to learn the equally important lesson of *receiving* graciously.(p.281)

recent
• In *recent* years I have had the happy combination of time and money to travel occasionally.(p.285)

recently
• One of these men, staff member of a world-renowned hospital, *recently* made this statement to some of us: "What you say about the general hopelessness of the average alcoholic's plight is, in my opinion, correct.(p.43)
• He consented, however, to go the hospital, where he occupied the very room *recently* vacated by the lawyer.(p.159)
• Yet I *recently* recalled that each morning I used to talk to the bottle when I took it down from the closet.(p.332)
• I saw him *recently* and he told me that he had always felt guilty, because, after our separation, I had become a serious alcoholic.(p.403)
• My mother had been *recently* converted and, actually, had become a religious fanatic.(p.483)
• True, I have *recently* recovered from pneumonia and have an alibi, but my friends are in the war or going, and I am not.(p.499)

receptions
• That includes bars, nightclubs, dances, *receptions*, weddings, even plain ordinary whoopee parties.(p.101)

receptive
• He may be more *receptive* when depressed.(p.91)
• Next day found the prospect more *receptive*.(p.158)

recess
• During *recess* we were playing basketball and I had accidentally tripped a fellow just a little larger than I was.(p.484)
• That was enough provocation to fight but I didn't fight, and I realized after *recess* why I didn't.(p.484)

recharged
• On my trips back to Akron to get my spirits *recharged* and to work with other alcoholics, I would ask Dr. Bob about this delay and wonder just what was wrong with me.(p.293)

recipe
• It wasn't very long before home-brewing was an institution and men began to search feverishly for old *recipe* books on wine-making.(p.232)

recipient
• I, a man of steel, with very high ideals, well brought up, an honor student and the *recipient* of scholarships and prizes, a boy wonder in business -- I, Bob, the author of this essay, looked and saw that the universe was beneath my contempt, and that to remove myself from it was the only thing of dignity a man could do.(p.531)

recitation
• Many mornings I have gone to classes, and even though fully prepared, would turn and walk back to the fraternity house because of my jitters, not daring to enter the classroom for fear of making a scene should I be called on for *recitation*.(p.173)

reckless
• From a monetary standpoint . . . in the past few years, I have reduced my *reckless* debts to almost nothing, and have had money to get along on comfortably.(p.303)

recluse
• When your husband is bad, you become a trembling *recluse*, wishing the telephone had never been invented.(p.115)

recognition
• They are not ideas of resignation but of the *recognition* of certain basic facts of living.(p.382)
• "The American Public Health Association presents a Lasker Group Award for 1951 to Alcoholics Anonymous in *recognition* of its unique and highly success-

ful approach to that age-old public health and social problem, alcoholism . . .(p.573)

recognizable

• I was an alcoholic, with a ***recognizable*** behavior pattern.(p.414)

recognize

• It was the first blackout I had to ***recognize*** as a blackout.(p.489)

• I've had many spiritual experiences since I've been in the program, many that I didn't ***recognize*** right away, for I'm slow to learn and they take many guises.(p.551)

• You would hardly ***recognize*** them."(p.572)

• Historians may one day ***recognize*** Alcoholics Anonymous to have been a great venture in social pioneering which forged a new instrument for social action; a new therapy based on the kinship of common suffering; one having a vast potential for the myriad other ills of mankind."(p.573)

recognized

• I knew the man by name, and partly ***recognized*** his features, but there all resemblance ended.(p.xxix)

• My father was a professional man of ***recognized*** ability and both my father and mother were most active in church affairs.(p.171)

• There was always a tremendous drive and ambition to become a great guy, because I think I ***recognized*** inwardly that I didn't have any special talents.(p.194)

• Anyhow, I ***recognized*** the fact that I couldn't drink like normal people, but I tried hard and kept on trying for twenty-two years.(p.196)

• For a long time the only Higher Power I could concede was the power of the group, but this was far more than I had ever ***recognized*** before, and it was at least a beginning.(p.248)

• I had worked so long in a profession where fakery, deceit, and untruths are tools of trade that I instantly ***recognized*** honesty when I heard it, from the mouths of A.A. members.(p.334)

• I achieved ***recognized*** and national standing in my profession, as well as becoming a director in many important institutions having to do with the civic life of a large city.(p.374)

• I had not ***recognized*** her, but as soon as she said who she was I remembered her right away.(p.493)

• To wear expensive clothes, to have bartenders know what to serve me before I ordered, to be ***recognized*** by headwaiters and shown to the best table, to play gin rummy for high stakes with the insouciance of a riverboat gambler — these were the enduring values in life, I thought.(p.556)

recognizing

• She gave no sign of ***recognizing*** anything wrong, but what had I been doing for those lost five hours?(p.223)

recoil

• If tempted, we ***recoil*** from it as from a hot flame.(p.84)

recollect

• I do not ***recollect*** the specific conversation that went on but I believe I did challenge Bill to tell me something about A.A. and I do recall one other thing: I wanted to know what this was that worked so many wonders, and hanging over the mantel was a picture of Gethsemane and Bill pointed to it and said, "There it is," which didn't make much sense to me.(p.216)

recollection

• I have a shadowy ***recollection*** of being in an airplane bound for New York, and of finding a friendly taxicab driver at the landing field instead of my wife.(p.41)

• There I was, unshaven, clothes torn and dirty with no ***recollection*** of wandering all over France but, of course, a hero to the local French.(p.242)

• Evidently I had gone right back to the movie with a bottle, stayed there several hours and started home with no ***recollection*** of what had happened.(p.244)

• Formerly, in the acute mental and physical pain during the remorseful periods succeeding each drunk, I found my ***recollection*** of the misery I had gone through a bolsterer of resolution and afterward, perhaps, a deterrent for a time.(p.260)

• To the best of my ***recollection*** I was completely free from any abnormal fears.(p.275)

• The next ***recollection*** I have is of my husband coming into my room (later found out it was on New Year's Eve) accompanied by two policemen.(p.468)

• Through my efforts to get down to "causes and conditions," I stand convinced that my emotional illness has been present from my earliest ***recollection.***(p.544)

recollections

• I could almost hear the sound of the preacher's voice as I sat, on still Sundays, way over there on the hillside; there was that proffered temperance pledge I never signed; my grandfather's good natured contempt of some church folk and their doings; his insistence that the spheres really had their music; but his denial of the preacher's right to tell him how he must listen; his fearlessness as he spoke of these things just before he died; these ***recollections*** welled up from the past.(p.10)

recommend

• I suggested to her that she should see the son's minister or doctor, and that perhaps he would ***recommend*** the A.A. program.(p.294)

• We feel it better to let our friends ***recommend*** us.(p.567)

recommendation

• We make this ***recommendation*** with some confidence.(p.114)

recommendations

• Some of the ***recommendations*** of A.A.'s early medical and religious friends will be found further on in this book.(p.xx)

recommended

• I can remember occasions when friends ***recommended*** me for positions or business opportunities that I wouldn't take because I felt that at some future date I'd get drunk and they would be hurt.(p.198)

• My wife became pregnant and the doctor ***recommended*** the use of port or ale . . . so . . . I bought a six gallon crock and a few bottles, listened to advice from amateur brewmeisters, and was off on my beer manufacturing career on a small scale (for the time being).(p.297)

• Well . . . I had a job, and I really wanted desperately to stop drinking, but couldn't, so I readily agreed to visit the doctor she ***recommended.***(p.301)

• She begs me to go to a hospital for alcoholics which has been ***recommended.***(p.502)

recompense

• God, they believe, almost owes this ***recompense*** on a long overdue account.(p.123)

• I spent most of my time trying to get back these friendships, and to make some ***recompense*** towards my wife, whom I had hurt a lot.(p.191)

recompensed

• Such special services may be well ***recompensed.***(p.566)

reconcile

• It was hard to ***reconcile*** this ghastly present with the simple facts of the past.(p.225)

reconciled

• We will be more ***reconciled*** to discussing ourselves with another person when we see good reasons why we should do so.(p.72)

reconciliation

• The miracle of ***reconciliation*** was at hand.(p.124)

• Anyhow, on the 24th, after drinking all day on the 23rd, I must have decided I wanted to see my wife and have some kind of ***reconciliation*** or at least talk with her.(p.491)

reconstruct

• When I try to ***reconstruct*** what my life was like "before," I see a coin with two faces.(p.432)

reconstruction

• Yes, there is a long period of ***reconstruction*** ahead.(p.83)

record

• He had a commendable World War ***record.***(p.35)

• As a celebrated American statesman put it, "Let's look at the ***record.***"(p.50)

• Yet, as my ***record*** shows, I did become an extremely serious case.(p.182)

• Paul measured the medicine out, but he figured that with my track ***record*** that little bit wouldn't be enough, so he doubled it and added a few drops more and then gave it to me.(p.207)

• Dr. Bob often said that it was a ***record*** for what he felt was a typical alcoholic.(p.263)

• We had that ***record.***(p.270)

• Let's look at the ***record.***"(p.322)

• With their help I also saw that certainly, because of some of the things I had done during the years, I was bordering on insanity, and so, facing the ***record,*** I tried to believe that a Power greater than I could and would restore me to sanity.(p.471)

• About three months after that, my ***record*** reached home and I got a letter telling me I was retired from the Army, they put it very kindly, on medical grounds.(p.521)

recording

• All afternoon I sat there and drank and played Bing Crosby's ***recording*** of "Silent Night" over and over again on the juke box.(p.467)

records

• The two years I spent there, I was incorrigible, and the ***records*** bear this out.(p.458)

recount

• For his sake, we do ***recount*** and almost relive the horrors of our past.(p.132)

recounts

• This man ***recounts*** that he tumbled out of bed to his knees.(p.56)

recouped

• My children had lost respect for me and, in fact, it was only after three or four years of sobriety that any of them ever said anything to me to indicate that I had ***recouped*** even a little of their respect.(p.215)

recourse

• He had not developed this art and had no ***recourse*** but his fists.(p.405)

recover

• Because this book has become the basic text for our Society and has helped such large numbers of alcoholic men and women to ***recover,*** there exists a sentiment against any radical changes being made in it.(p.xi)

• The market would ***recover,*** but I wouldn't.(p.6)

• Many could ***recover*** if they had the opportunity we have enjoyed.(p.19)

• So he returned to this doctor, whom he admired, and asked him point-blank why he could not ***recover.***(p.26)

• I have never seen one single case ***recover,*** where that state of mind existed to the extent that it does in you."(p.27)

• We first saw Fred about a year ago in a hospital where he had gone to ***recover*** from a bad case of jitters.(p.39)

• Those who do not ***recover*** are people who cannot or will not completely give themselves to this simple program, usually men and women who are constitutionally incapable of being honest with themselves.(p.58)

• There are those, too, who suffer from grave emotional and mental disorders, but many of them do ***recover*** if they have the capacity to be honest.(p.58)

• To watch people ***recover,*** to see them help others, to watch loneliness vanish, to see a fellowship grow up about you, to have a host of friends — this is an experience you must not miss.(p.89)

• Perhaps you are not acquainted with any drinkers who want to ***recover.***(p.89)

• But insist that if he is severely afflicted, there may be little chance he can ***recover*** by himself.(p.92)

• If you leave such a person alone, he may soon become convinced that he cannot ***recover*** by himself.(p.96)

• Should they accept and practice spiritual principles, there is a much better chance that the head of the family will ***recover.***(p.97)

• Let no alcoholic say he cannot ***recover*** unless he has his family back.(p.99)

• He is striving to ***recover*** fortune and reputation and feels he is doing very well.(p.126)

• Now about health: A body badly burned by alcohol does not often ***recover*** overnight nor do twisted thinking and depression vanish in a twinkling.(p.133)

• Whether the family goes on a spiritual basis or not, the alcoholic member has to if he would ***recover.***(p.135)

• After satisfying yourself that your man wants to ***recover*** and that he will go to any extreme to do so, you may suggest a definite course of action.(p.142)

• Can you have every confidence in his ability to ***recover?***(p.143)

• If he is, and is still trying to ***recover,*** he will tell you about it even if it means the loss of his job.(p.146)

• He has helped other men ***recover,*** and is a power in the church from which he was long absent.(p.158)

• Understanding our work, he can do this with an eye to selecting those who are willing and able to ***recover*** on a spiritual basis.(p.162)

• When a few men in this city have found themselves, and have discovered the joy of helping others to face life again, there will be no stopping until everyone in that town has had his opportunity to ***recover*** — if he can and will.(p.163)

• The next afternoon and evening, two other men visited me and each told me his story and the things that they were doing to try to ***recover*** from this tragic illness.(p.290)

• The next three years saw me in sanitariums, once in a ten day coma, from which I very nearly did not ***recover,*** in and out of hospitals or confined at home with day and night nurses.(p.306)

- Hence we may refuse none who wish to *recover*.(p.565)
- Though it was not our intention to create such an impression, many alcoholics have nevertheless concluded that in order to *recover* they must acquire an immediate and overwhelming "God-consciousness" followed at once by a vast change in feeling and outlook.(p.569)
- Most emphatically we wish to say that any alcoholic capable of honestly facing his problems in the light of our experience can *recover*, provided he does not close his mind to all spiritual concepts.(p.570)

recovered

- We, of Alcoholics Anonymous, are more than one hundred men and women who have *recovered* from a seemingly hopeless state of mind and body.(p.xiii)
- To show other alcoholics precisely how we have *recovered* is the main purpose of this book.(p.xiii)
- In that brief space, Alcoholics Anonymous has mushroomed into nearly 6,000 groups whose membership is far above 150,000 *recovered* alcoholics.(p.xv)
- Their very first case, a desperate one, *recovered* immediately and became A.A. number three.(p.xvii)
- This man and over one hundred others appear to have *recovered*.(p.xxiii)
- He had but partially *recovered* from a gastric hemorrhage and seemed to be a case of pathological mental deterioration.(p.xxix)
- Nearly all have *recovered*.(p.17)
- Doubtless you are curious to discover how and why, in the face of expert opinion to the contrary, we have *recovered* from a hopeless condition of mind and body.(p.20)
- Further on, clear-cut directions are given showing how we *recovered*.(p.29)
- If a mere code of morals or a better philosophy of life were sufficient to overcome alcoholism, many of us would have *recovered* long ago.(p.44)
- If he says yes, then his attention should be drawn to you as a person who has *recovered*.(p.90)
- He often says that if he had continued to work on them, he might have deprived many others, who have since *recovered*, of their chance.(p.96)
- He knows that thousands of men, much like himself, have *recovered*.(p.113)
- We have *recovered*, and have been given the power to help others.(p.132)
- We, who have *recovered* from serious drinking, are miracles of mental health.(p.133)
- An alcoholic who has *recovered*, but holds a relatively unimportant job, can talk to a man with a better position.(p.146)
- How Forty-Three Alcoholics *Recovered* From Their Malady(p.165)
- The next day I received a visit from Mr. T., a *recovered* alcoholic.(p.309)
- He had been dry for two and a half years and had been maintaining his contact with a group of *recovered* alcoholics in Akron.(p.309)
- So I went to Akron, and also to Cleveland, and I met more *recovered* alcoholics.(p.310)
- True, I have recently *recovered* from pneumonia and have an alibi, but my friends are in the war or going, and I am not.(p.499)
- I thought I had *recovered*.(p.539)
- So, when my liver had *recovered* after ten months, I resumed drinking.(p.557)

recoveries

- For this there were two principal reasons: the large numbers of *recoveries*, and reunited homes.(p.xx)
- Though the aggregate of *recoveries* resulting from psychiatric effort is considerable, we physicians must admit we have made little impression upon the problem as a whole.(p.xxvii)
- Yet often such men had spectacular and powerful *recoveries*.(p.113)

recovering

- Our women folk have suggested certain attitudes a wife may take with the husband who is *recovering*.(p.122)
- You can never know the pure joy of *recovering* within the Fellowship of Alcoholics Anonymous."(p.334)

recovers

- We know that no real alcoholic ever *recovers* control.(p.30)
- The right kind of man, the kind who *recovers*, will not want this sort of thing.(p.149)

recovery

- Therefore, the first portion of this volume, describing the A.A. *recovery* program, has been left untouched in the course of revisions made for both the second and the third editions.(p.xi)
- It also indicated that strenuous work, one alcoholic with another, was vital to permanent *recovery*.(p.xvii)
- By the end of 1939, it was estimated that 800 alcoholics were on their way to *recovery*.(p.xviii)
- The basic principles of the A.A. program, it appears, hold good for individuals with many different life-styles, just as the program has brought *recovery* to those of many different nationalities.(p.xxii)
- The Twelve Steps that summarize the program may be called los Doce Pasos in one country, los Douze Etapes in another, but they trace exactly the same path to *recovery* that was blazed by the earliest members of Alcoholics Anonymous.(p.xxii)
- Each day, somewhere in the world, *recovery* begins when one alcoholic talks with another alcoholic, sharing experience, strength, and hope.(p.xxii)
- We of Alcoholics Anonymous believe that the reader will be interested in the medical estimate of the plan of *recovery* described in this book.(p.xxiii)
- In the course of his third treatment he acquired certain ideas concerning a possible means of *recovery*.(p.xxiii)
- This is repeated over and over, and unless this person can experience an entire psychic change there is very little hope of his *recovery*.(p.xxvii)
- This is the first step in *recovery*.(p.30)
- In some instances there has been brief *recovery*, followed always by a still worse relapse.(p.31)
- Here are the steps we took, which are suggested as a program of *recovery*:(p.59)
- This brings us to the Fifth Step in the program of *recovery* mentioned in the preceding chapter.(p.72)
- Small wonder many in the medical profession have a low opinion of alcoholics and their chance for *recovery*!(p.73)
- You should be described to him as one of a fellowship who, as part of their own *recovery*, try to help others and who will be glad to talk to him if he cares to see you.(p.90)
- It is important for him to realize that your attempt to pass this on to him plays a vital part in your own *recovery*.(p.94)
- He has read this volume and says he is prepared to go through with the Twelve Steps of the program of *recovery*.(p.96)
- You may be aiding in his destruction rather than his *recovery*.(p.97)
- Helping others is the foundation stone of your *recovery*.(p.97)
- The man should be sure of his *recovery*.(p.99)
- Remind the prospect that his *recovery* is not dependent upon people.(p.99)
- Wait until repeated stumbling convinces him he must act, for the more you hurry him the longer his *recovery* may be delayed.(p.113)
- The slightest sign of fear or intolerance may lessen your husband's chance of *recovery*.(p.120)
- At the beginning of *recovery* a man will take, as a rule, one of two directions.(p.125)
- Although financial *recovery* is on the way for many of us, we found we could not place money first.(p.127)
- He is undoubtedly on the road to *recovery*.(p.139)
- We all had to place *recovery* above everything, for without *recovery* we would have lost both home and business.(p.143)
- Naturally this sort of thing decreased the man's chance of *recovery*.(p.145)
- If he is conscientiously following the program of *recovery* he can go anywhere your business may call him.(p.147)
- Our own *recovery* proves that!(p.153)
- It was simple, they said, and went on to explain to me in their own language the program of *recovery* and daily living which we know today as the Twelve Steps of A.A.(p.279)
- In the next two or three days the balance of this handful of men contacted me, encouraged me, and told me how they were trying to live this program of *recovery* and the fun they were having doing it.(p.291)
- It explained so much I had not understood about myself and, best of all, it promised *recovery* if I would do a few simple things and be willing to have the desire to drink removed.(p.309)
- This and the program of *recovery* embodied in the Twelve Steps.(p.311)
- A.A. is not a plan for *recovery* that can be finished and done with.(p.311)
- There are steps of *recovery*, of maintenance.(p.516)
- For by now I had been exposed once to A.A., but I had treated it as a vaudeville and had taken friends to meetings so that they too could enjoy the fascination of the naked revelation of suffering and *recovery*.(p.539)
- They said if you want to know how this program works, take the first word of your question – the H is for honesty, the O is for open-mindedness and the W is for willingness; these our Book calls the essentials of *recovery*.(p.550)
- While there, I read the Big Book and the Grapevine and began the slow road back to health and sanity through the *recovery* program of A.A.(p.559)
- Similarly, we rid ourselves of guilt and remorse as we "clean out the garbage" from our minds through the Fourth and Fifth Steps of our *recovery* program.(p.560)
- One – Our common welfare should come first; personal *recovery* depends upon A.A. unity.(p.564)
- The terms "spiritual experience" and "spiritual awakening" are used many times in this book which, upon careful reading, shows that the personality change sufficient to bring about *recovery* from alcoholism has manifested itself among us in many different forms.(p.569)
- Willingness, honesty and open mindedness are the essentials of *recovery*.(p.570)
- Any therapeutic or philosophic procedure which can prove a *recovery* rate of 50% to 60% must merit our consideration."(p.571)

recreational

- They have *recreational* facilities.(p.149)

recruit

- My job was to make out the guard schedules and thus I was exempt from ordinary *recruit* training activities.(p.425)

recruiting

- At age twenty-one, I enlisted in the Navy for two reasons: (1) to avoid being drafted into the Army, and (2) out of a burst of patriotic fervor inspired by the advent of World War II and as the result of an all-night drinking binge which found me sitting on the doorstep of the Navy *recruiting* office when the chief petty officer arrived to open for business at nine o'clock Monday morning.(p.398)

recruits

- We often need it to carry green *recruits* through a severe hangover.(p.102)
- My first pay was ten dollars, pay for *recruits* at that time being twenty-one dollars per month.(p.398)

rectally

- Suddenly, I began vomiting and losing *rectally* great quantities of blood.(p.558)

rectify

- We grow by our willingness to face and *rectify* errors and convert them into assets.(p.124)

recuperation

- But hospitals, as well as other places of *recuperation*, ought to be well outside A.A. – and medically supervised.(p.566)

red

- One evening, the book, after checking up, was very definitely in the *red* for plenty through a piece of studied carelessness on my part, and my boss, very shrewd and able, fired me with a parting statement to the effect that once was enough.(p.251)
- I sat up in the big *red* chair, suddenly thinking, "My God, with my kind of lousy luck, I might not die soon!(p.333)
- By the time I figured out what had happened, I saw two flashing *red* lights atop squad cars, sedately coming around the corner.(p.353)
- Making amends is sometimes doing what we are capable of doing but failed to do because of alcohol; carrying out community responsibilities such as Community Funds, *Red* Cross, educational and religious activities in proportion to our abilities and energy.(p.381)
- I read sad poetry, cried, drank *red* wine, wrote sad poetry, and drank some more.(p.405)
- There was a *red* plush carpet to welcome me, but even so it wasn't easy.(p.430)
- (Two large *red* A's stand out in my memory.)(p.460)

red-eyed

- This sober Indian say to sick, *red-eyed* alcoholic who want good medicine: "Put cork in bottle.(p.477)

red-leather

- Not wishing to disturb my wife, I slumped in a big *red-leather* chair and suffered.(p.332)

redeeming

- It was the one *redeeming* act of that Christmas.(p.467)

rediscover

- Then you will know what it means to give of yourself that others may survive and *rediscover* life.(p.153)

redo
• Eventually, I had to *redo* each of the Twelve Steps specifically with Max in mind, from the First, saying, "I am powerless over alcohol, and my homelife is unmanageable by me," to the Twelfth, in which I tried to think of her as a sick Al-Anon and treat her with the love I would give a sick A.A. newcomer.(p.452)

redouble
• Your husband will see at once that he must *redouble* his spiritual activities if he expects to survive.(p.120)

reduce
• Neither could we *reduce* our self-centeredness much by wishing or trying on our own power.(p.62)

reduced
• My efficiency as a professional man was probably *reduced* to twenty-five per cent of what it should have been.(p.215)
• I was eased out of the business I had founded and was *reduced* to doing general upholstery in a small shop at the back of my house.(p.233)
• From a monetary standpoint . . . in the past few years, I have *reduced* my reckless debts to almost nothing, and have had money to get along on comfortably.(p.303)
• She'd been *reduced* to that.(p.490)
• However, as time went on laws were enacted that *reduced* the sentence.(p.509)

reed
• What seemed at first a flimsy *reed*, has proved to be the loving and powerful hand of God.(p.28)

reenlisted
• Finally, I *reenlisted* to go back to Nam.(p.318)

refer
• We see that these expressions *refer* to people whose reactions are very different from ours.(p.20)
• Don't, at this stage, *refer* to this book, unless he has seen it and wishes to discuss it.(p.92)

reference
• We gave up our positions and off we roared on a motorcycle, the sidecar stuffed with tent, blankets, a change of clothes, and three huge volumes of a financial *reference* service.(p.2)
• Many of us have been so touchy that even casual *reference* to spiritual things made us bristle with antagonism.(p.48)
• Took down notes for *reference* purposes.(p.344)

referred
• Businessmen, traveling out of existing groups, were *referred* to these prospective newcomers.(p.xviii)
• The matter of physical treatment should, of course, be *referred* to your own doctor.(p.143)
• (That was the man the A.A. office had *referred* me to.)(p.393)

referring
• *Referring* to our list again.(p.67)
• If you cannot find A.A. in your locality, a letter addressed to Alcoholics Anonymous, Box 459, Grand Central Station, New York, NY 10163, U.S.A., will receive a prompt reply from this world center, *referring* you to the nearest A.A. group.(p.575)

refers
• Of course, this chapter *refers* to alcoholics, sick people, deranged men.(p.149)

refill
• And then we went up the side of a hill where we have a little barbecue area to make the fire for the barbecue, and on the way up, I thought to myself – I'll go back down to the kitchen and *refill* this drink.(p.347)
• Near the Laundromat, I would buy one bottle of pop and a few bottles of beer or wine, and go into the rest room, empty the pop bottle, *refill* it with the booze, and proceed to do my laundering.(p.370)

reflect
• But the chief change was in the section of personal stories, which was expanded to *reflect* the Fellowship's growth.(p.xi)
• I did not *reflect* that half the office was composed of A.A. members, and that I was as unexciting as any client in any office.(p.413)
• I had only to *reflect* on the contrast between the plans I made so many years ago for my life with what really happened to know I couldn't manage my life drunk or sober.(p.550)

reflected
• With a certain satisfaction I *reflected* there was enough gin concealed about the house to carry me through that night and the next day.(p.8)
• Upon hearing this, our friend was somewhat relieved, for he *reflected* that after all, he was a good church member.(p.27)
• We have sometimes *reflected* more than Jim did upon the consequences.(p.37)
• Show him these things in yourself and they will be *reflected* back to you from him.(p.118)

reflection
• Those of us who live in large cities are overcome by the *reflection* that close by hundreds are dropping into oblivion every day.(p.19)
• But we must be careful not to drift into worry, remorse or morbid *reflection*, for that would diminish our usefulness to others.(p.86)

reflex
• They held consultations and discussions, and finally decided to give me the "Conditioned *Reflex*" treatment.(p.469)

reform
• You will be most successful with alcoholics if you do not exhibit any passion for crusade or *reform*.(p.95)
• Nobody was going to *reform* me!(p.412)
• I was going to *reform* myself!(p.412)
• 10. – No A.A. group or member should ever, in such a way as to implicate A.A., express any opinion on outside controversial issues – particularly those of politics, alcohol *reform*, or sectarian religion.(p.567)

reformer
• Don't start out as an evangelist or *reformer*.(p.89)
• Marty came in, looking clean, neat, well-dressed and, like Bill, she was neither a bloated wreck nor a *reformer*.(p.413)

reformers
• He is like the retired business man who lolls in the Florida sunshine in the winter complaining of the sad state of the nation; the minister who sighs over the sins of the twentieth century; politicians and *reformers* who are sure all would be Utopia if the rest of the world would only behave; the outlaw safe cracker who thinks society has wronged him; and the alcoholic who has lost all and is locked up.(p.61)
• So this was a group of *reformers*!(p.412)

reforming
• Do not set your heart on *reforming* your husband.(p.111)

refrain
• And I remembered the creeping horror of the interminable night, in which I slept for short spells and woke up dripping with cold sweat and shaken with utter despair, to drink hastily from my bottle and mercifully pass out again, "You're mad, you're mad, you're mad!" pounded through my brain with each returning ray of consciousness, and I drowned the *refrain* with drink.(p.224)

refreshing
• Meetings are both relaxing and *refreshing* to me after a hard day.(p.381)

refuge
• Also, I believed I was the image of all domestic virtues, secluded in my washday (any day) *refuge*.(p.369)
• When I was criticized or reprimanded, the bottle was my *refuge* and comfort.(p.556)

refusal
• They were deeply religious people, much shocked by their son's *refusal* to have anything to do with the church.(p.158)

refuse
• If you draw this fallacious reasoning to the attention of an alcoholic, he will laugh it off, or become irritated and *refuse* to talk.(p.23)
• So I would *refuse* to drink.(p.184)
• It was I who had to tell the bank, after a certain time, to *refuse* all further deposits.(p.409)
• Also, after that first visit I learned I could *refuse* to sign myself in unless they gave me a glass of whiskey in one hand and a glass of paraldehyde in the other.(p.468)
• Hence we may *refuse* none who wish to recover.(p.565)

refused
• He *refused* it.(p.9)
• I *refused* to join any fraternity, as I wanted to be a free lance, and that year my drinking was confined to one-night stands, once or twice a week.(p.241)
• After several months of acquaintance I asked her to marry me, but was politely *refused*.(p.359)
• Frightened and shamed, I *refused*, and sobered up temporarily.(p.411)
• I tried to wash a little, but Anne *refused* to wash at all.(p.415)
• Still another friend and temporary host received me at four in the morning from the charge of a policeman who had found me "going to bed" in a garage far from the last place I could remember having been, a fashionable bar and restaurant in the theatrical district of New York, to which I had repaired after my date for that evening, a charming lady of the theatre who had *refused* my company for obvious reasons.(p.538)
• Repeated year on end, they are horrible -- frightening and degrading, a chronicle of tragedy which may be greater because the individual undergoing the tragedy, myself, knew what was happening, and yet *refused* to do anything to stop it.(p.538)
• I say, "*refused* to do anything to stop it."(p.539)
• Fear of rejection and its ensuing pain were not to be risked, and I turned away from myself once more for the answer, this time to the drinks I had always *refused* before, and in alcohol I found a false courage.(p.546)

refusing
• I had no trouble *refusing* drinks, and began to wonder if I had not been making too hard work of a simple matter.(p.40)

regain
• He wished above all things to *regain* self-control.(p.26)
• In the doctor's judgment he was utterly hopeless; he could never *regain* his position in society and he would have to place himself under lock and key or hire a bodyguard if he expected to live long.(p.26)
• There is every evidence that women *regain* their health as readily as men if they try our suggestions.(p.104)
• Professionally, after I was sober for a month or so I realized that I should school myself to dissolve the partnership I was in because I felt that I would never *regain* the respect of my partners no matter how long I was sober, and that I would be at a disadvantage.(p.220)
• As I look back on that first evening I realize that I began to hope, then, for the first time; and I felt that if he could *regain* these things, perhaps it would be possible for me too.(p.290)

regained
• Business and professional men have *regained* their standing.(p.15)
• "As soon as I *regained* my ability to think, I went carefully over that evening in Washington.(p.41)
• My health is good and I have *regained* my self-respect and the respect of my colleagues.(p.180)
• I *regained* consciousness on Sunday.(p.207)

regaining
• All of us felt at times that we were *regaining* control, but such intervals -- usually brief -- were inevitably followed by still less control, which led in time to pitiful and incomprehensible demoralization.(p.30)
• *Regaining* my health, I became an avid jogger, sailor, and skier.(p.559)

regard
• In late 1934 I attended a patient who, though he had been a competent businessman of good earning capacity, was an alcoholic of a type I had come to *regard* as hopeless.(p.xxiii)
• Should it happen again, *regard* it in a different light.(p.116)
• My whole life seemed to be centered around doing what I wanted to do, without *regard* for the rights, wishes, or privileges of anyone else; a state of mind which became more and more predominant as the years passed.(p.172)
• Of far more importance was the fact that he was the first living human with whom I had ever talked, who knew what he was talking about in *regard* to alcoholism from actual experience.(p.180)
• Having *regard* for the law of the land, I resigned myself to the will of the national legislators and quit drinking altogether, not because I had found it harmful, but because I couldn't get what I was accustomed to drink.(p.232)

regarded
• These work-outs should be *regarded* as part of your education, for thus you will be learning to live.(p.117)
• Everybody did, in the set which I *regarded* as the apex of civilization.(p.433)
• *Regarded* as something of a "boy wonder," I began to see myself that way.(p.555)

regarding
• Instead of *regarding* ourselves as intelligent agents, spearheads of God's ever advancing Creation, we agnostics and atheists chose to believe that our human intelligence was the last word, the alpha and the omega, the beginning and end of all.(p.49)

regardless
• Burn the idea into the consciousness of every man that he can get well *regardless* of anyone.(p.98)
• These things will come to pass naturally and in good time provided, however, the alcoholic continues

to demonstrate that he can be sober, considerate, and helpful, ***regardless*** of what anyone says or does.(p.99)
• All during Prohibition, every alcoholic felt that he made the best hooch, ***regardless*** of how bad it was.(p.213)
• He said the alcoholic seemed to possess a native acuteness and usually excelled in his field, ***regardless*** of environmental or educational advantages.(p.308)

regards
• Meanwhile, I was getting worse, both as ***regards*** my inward misery and my drinking.(p.434)
• During these seven years a thing called the Twenty-four Hour Program —a gadget I used to think was only a snare to trap the newcomer -- has come to mean much to me, not only as ***regards*** my drinking but in the whole pattern of my life.(p.473)

regiment
• Curious about it, feeling I was missing something, absolutely without any illusions about the aftermath, with no pronounced feeling of patriotism, I joined up with a Canadian ***regiment***, serving a little over two years.(p.253)
• Then a change in management took place in the ***regiment*** and the new O.C. didn't like me very much and I didn't like him, and he started to lie in wait for me.(p.519)
• However, I kept that job in Egypt and Palestine for about two years, and then I changed over to the other battalion in my ***regiment***.(p.520)
• I buttonholed him after dinner and gave him a few tips on how to run his colony better and the result of that was about a fortnight or so later I was shipped back to my ***regiment***.(p.520)
• I had three or four very uncomfortable months with my ***regiment*** then on the Suez Canal.(p.520)
• At the end of that time, they shipped me back to my ***regiment*** again.(p.520)

region
• We were in a position where life was becoming impossible, and if we had passed into the ***region*** from which there is no return through human aid we had but two alternatives: One was to go on to the bitter end, blotting out the consciousness of our intolerable situation as best we could; and the other, to accept spiritual help.(p.25)

regional
• And no group, ***regional*** committee, or individual should ever take any action that might greatly affect A.A. as a whole without conferring with the trustees of the General Service Board.(p.565)

register
• I had every advantage a child could have, private schools (several of them), dancing schools, two colleges, coon skin coats, automobiles, a listing in the social ***register*** and all the rest.(p.357)

registered
• Not one experience ***registered*** with me.(p.208)
• I don't think that I was conscious of what had happened to me, but I think that it ***registered*** subconsciously.(p.386)

registering
• I would sometimes hide out in one of the clubs of which I was a member, and had the habit at times of ***registering*** at a hotel under a fictitious name.(p.176)

regret
• One object is to disclose damaged or unsalable goods, to get rid of them promptly and without ***regret***.(p.64)
• We go to him in a helpful and forgiving spirit, confessing our former ill feeling and expressing our ***regret***.(p.77)
• We will not ***regret*** the past nor wish to shut the door on it.(p.83)

regrets
• I don't have any ***regrets***.(p.511)

regular
• A business which takes no ***regular*** inventory usually goes broke.(p.64)
• This was a ***regular*** occurrence for a little while.(p.196)
• I had always been a good Catholic, possibly not so devoted as I should have been, but fairly ***regular*** in my attendance at services.(p.234)
• Until I was thirteen I attended public schools, with ***regular*** promotions and average grades.(p.240)
• The ***regular*** flow of all the literature, which I keep meticulously and which, of course, I study, has been wonderful.(p.342)
• They sent me the ***regular*** letter they send to everybody else, but along with it, Ruth Hock, the nonalcoholic secretary, wrote a longhand note because she could see from the letter that I really needed help badly.(p.392)

regularity
• Successive Monday morning hangovers, which despite mid-week resolutions to do better, came with unfailing ***regularity***, eventually caused me to quit my job.(p.254)
• I attended my weekly meetings with ***regularity***, reread the Big Book, attended other group meetings, gave leads when asked to and did some Twelve Step work whenever I was called upon to do so.(p.365)

regularly
• I went to town ***regularly*** and even made a little money.(p.7)
• A few months later one of the men who had been in touch with the group in Akron came to Chicago to live, and then there were three of us who continued to have informal meetings quite ***regularly***.(p.294)
• We were having card parties with limburger and beer quite ***regularly***.(p.297)
• He went into the religious side and told me that I didn't attend church as ***regularly*** as I should, and that he felt, more or less, that this was responsible for my trouble.(p.489)

regulate
• He tried to ***regulate*** his drinking for a while, making several trips to the hospital meantime.(p.32)

rehabilitation
• As part of his ***rehabilitation*** he commenced to present his conceptions to other alcoholics, impressing upon them that they must do likewise with still others.(p.xxiii)
• We feel, after many years of experience, that we have found nothing which has contributed more to the ***rehabilitation*** of these men than the altruistic movement now growing up among them.(p.xxvi)
• Following his physical ***rehabilitation***, he had a talk with me in which he frankly stated he thought the treatment a waste of effort, unless I could assure him, which no one ever had, that in the future he would have the "will power" to resist the impulse to drink.(p.xxix)
• My bother-in-law is a physician, and through his kindness and that of my mother I was placed in a nationally-known hospital for the mental and physical ***rehabilitation*** of alcoholics.(p.7)
• It will permit the ***rehabilitation*** of good men.(p.148)
• I still couldn't make it through the nights without drinking, so I went back into the hospital, this time to a ***rehabilitation*** center.(p.320)
• The personality ***rehabilitation*** did not come overnight.(p.416)
• I remained there for about ten months, and then I was sent to a place called Wallkill, a so-called ***rehabilitation*** center.(p.509)

rehearsals
• ***Rehearsals*** then became a part of the pattern, stopping at bars on the way to or from the place where drinks were to be served.(p.375)

reigned
• But I wanted a cosmos, a universe all my own which I had created and where I ***reigned*** as chief top reigner and ruler over everyone else.(p.535)

reigner
• But I wanted a cosmos, a universe all my own which I had created and where I reigned as chief top ***reigner*** and ruler over everyone else.(p.535)

reinvestigated
• Matters got worse all the time until finally they got so bad that I was ***reinvestigated*** by the Government.(p.490)

reject
• Above all, we ***reject*** fantasizing and accept reality.(p.560)

rejected
• Perhaps we ***rejected*** this particular conception because it seemed inadequate.(p.45)
• Help which you once continually ***rejected***, suggestions once turned aside are finally accepted in desperation.(p.377)
• I had ***rejected*** A.A. on the outside, but now it came to me in prison.(p.528)

rejection
• With that ***rejection*** we imagined we had abandoned the God idea entirely.(p.45)
• What alcoholic can live with ***rejection***?(p.331)
• Fear of ***rejection*** and its ensuing pain were not to be risked, and I turned away from myself once more for the answer, this time to the drinks I had always refused before, and in alcohol I found a false courage.(p.546)

rejections
• I imagined getting even for hurts and ***rejections***.(p.560)

relapse
• Above all, he believed he had acquired such a profound knowledge of the inner workings of his mind and its hidden springs that ***relapse*** was unthinkable.(p.26)
• In some instances there has been brief recovery, followed always by a still worse ***relapse***.(p.31)
• So we shall describe some of the mental states that precede a ***relapse*** into drinking, for obviously this is the crux of the problem.(p.35)
• Though it is infinitely better that he have no ***relapse*** at all, as has been true with many of our men, it is by no means a bad thing in some cases.(p.120)
• In most cases, the alcoholic survived this ordeal without ***relapse***, but not always.(p.125)
• Today, hundreds of additional A.A. members can be found who have had no ***relapse*** for more than thirty years.(p.169)

relapses
• Of alcoholics who came to A.A. and really tried, 50% got sober at once and remained that way; 25% sobered up after some ***relapses***, and among the remainder, those who stayed on with A.A. showed improvement.(p.xx)

relate
• Another principle we observe carefully is that we do not ***relate*** intimate experiences of another person unless we are sure he would approve.(p.125)
• I will not take space to ***relate*** all my hospital or sanitarium experiences.(p.177)
• Before very long we began to ***relate*** some incidents of our drinking and, naturally, pretty soon, I realized both of them knew what they were talking about because you can see things and smell things when you're drunk, that you can't other times, and, if I had thought they didn't know what they were talking about, I wouldn't have been willing to talk to them at all.(p.185)
• I didn't know I was an alcoholic and (like most men in prison today) could not ***relate*** alcohol to any of my past troubles.(p.460)
• I have learned how to ***relate*** to people; before A.A., I could never do that comfortably without alcohol.(p.559)

related
• But what we have ***related*** is based upon experience, some of it painful.(p.121)
• When our friend ***related*** his experience, the man agreed that no amount of will power he might muster could stop his drinking for long.(p.155)
• Bill then ***related*** how he had lain awake nearly all night.(p.189)
• For, to these people, I am truly ***related***.(p.312)
• Six – An A.A. group ought never endorse, finance or lend the A.A. name to any ***related*** facility or outside enterprise, lest problems of money, property and prestige divert us from our primary purpose.(p.564)

relating
• Perhaps I can best answer this by ***relating*** one of my experiences.(p.xxix)

relation
• At the start, this was all we needed to commence spiritual growth, to effect our first conscious ***relation*** with God as we understood Him.(p.47)
• We subjected each ***relation*** to this test -- was it selfish or not?(p.69)
• All sorts were represented and their ***relation*** of experiences and how they had found the only remedy, added to their human existence as sober men, laid the foundation of a very necessary faith.(p.258)

relations
• Our public ***relations*** were to be based upon attraction rather than promotion.(p.xix)
• Was it our self-esteem, our security, our ambitions, our personal, or sex ***relations***, which had been interfered with?(p.65)
• Sex ***relations***.(p.65)
• Sex ***relations***.(p.65)
• Personal sex ***relations***.(p.65)
• But drinking does complicate sex ***relations*** in the home.(p.81)
• Now, the domestic problem: There may be divorce, separation, or just strained ***relations***.(p.98)
• Be determined that your husband's drinking is not going to spoil your ***relations*** with your children or your friends.(p.111)
• A word about sex ***relations***.(p.134)
• The alcoholic may find it hard to re-establish friendly ***relations*** with his children.(p.134)

• Until I took Social Security and a pension at the age of sixty-eight, after forty years in motion-picture-studio public *relations*, I had successfully hidden even any hints of approaching alcoholism.(p.327)
• I suppose the psychiatrist might say, "This is benevolent interpersonal *relations*.(p.352)
• It pays daily in more harmonious *relations* with my fellow men, in ever clearer insight into the true meaning of life, and in the answering love and gratitude wherever and whenever I have been the instrument of God's will in the lives of others.(p.394)
• Another thing that mother drilled into me was a very Puritanical point of view as to sex *relations* and as to motherhood and womanhood.(p.483)
• Eleven – Our public *relations* policy is based on attraction rather than promotion; we need always maintain personal anonymity at the level of press, radio and films.(p.564)
• They are authorized by the groups to handle our over-all public *relations* and they guarantee the integrity of our principal newspaper, the A.A. Grapevine.(p.567)
• 11. -- Our *relations* with the general public should be characterized by personal anonymity.(p.567)
• Our public *relations* should be guided by the principle of attraction rather than promotion.(p.567)

relationship

• My friend promised when these things were done I would enter upon a new *relationship* with my Creator; that I would have the elements of a way of living which answered all my problems.(p.13)
• If what we have learned and felt and seen means anything at all, it means that all of us, whatever our race, creed, or color are the children of a living Creator with whom we may form a *relationship* upon simple and understandable terms as soon as we are willing and honest enough to try.(p.28)
• Each individual, in the personal stories, describes in his own language and from his own point of view the way he established his *relationship* with God.(p.29)
• Personal *relationship*.(p.65)
• We have been trying to get a new attitude, a new *relationship* with our Creator, and to discover the obstacle in our path.(p.72)
• If their old *relationship* is to be resumed it must be on a better basis, since the former did not work.(p.99)
• It is dependent upon his *relationship* with God.(p.100)
• See to it that your *relationship* with Him is right, and great events will come to pass for you and countless others.(p.164)
• I could see no reason why they should have any *relationship* to this problem of getting drunk every now and then.(p.388)
• A.A. has given me a new wife, a beautiful stepdaughter, a new practice, a new home, and a new *relationship* with my four children.(p.420)
• It hasn't been easy to work out this *relationship* with Max.(p.451)
• Acceptance is the key to my *relationship* with God today.(p.452)
• The *relationship* between my wife and me was restored to a love and happiness that we had not known even before my alcoholism became acute.(p.559)
• Dr. Harry M. Tiebout, psychiatrist: "As a psychiatrist, I have thought a great deal about the *relationship* of my specialty to A.A. and I have come to the conclusion that our particular function can very often lie in preparing the way for the patient to accept any sort of treatment or outside help.(p.571)

relationships

• We were having trouble with personal *relationships*, we couldn't control our emotional natures, we were a prey to misery and depression, we couldn't make a living, we had a feeling of uselessness, we were full of fear, we were unhappy, we couldn't seem to be of real help to other people – was not a basic solution of these bedevilments more important than whether we should see newsreels of lunar flight?(p.52)
• In most cases it was found that our self-esteem, our pocketbooks, our ambitions, our personal *relationships* (including sex) were hurt or threatened.(p.64)
• Sweet *relationships* are dead.(p.82)
• And, as the years go by, working together, sharing our experiences with one another, and also sharing a mutual trust, understanding and love – without strings, without obligation – we acquire *relationships* that are unique and priceless.(p.312)

relative

• Alone in the *relative* safety of my home because I knew I dare not risk the danger of blacking out in some public place or at the wheel of a car.(p.306)
• Should you be the *relative* or friend of an alcoholic who shows no immediate interest in A.A., it is suggested that you write the Al-Anon Family Groups, Inc., Box 182, Madison Square Station, New York, NY 10159, U.S.A.(p.575)

relatively

• An alcoholic who has recovered, but holds a *relatively* unimportant job, can talk to a man with a better position.(p.146)
• I drank with moderation at first, but it took me only a *relatively* short time to drift back into the old habits which had wound up so disastrously before.(p.175)
• My work is on a much deeper and more significant level than it ever was before, and I am today a fairly creative, *relatively* sane human being.(p.438)
• When the compulsion to drink left, it was *relatively* easy to stay off alcohol.(p.448)

relatives

• It may mean sharing your money and your home, counseling frantic wives and *relatives*, innumerable trips to police courts, sanitariums, hospitals, jails and asylums.(p.97)
• Among us are wives, *relatives* and friends whose problem has been solved, as well as some who have not yet found a happy solution.(p.104)
• Though it is entirely separate from Alcoholics Anonymous, it uses the general principles of the A.A. program as a guide for husbands, wives, *relatives*, friends, and others close to alcoholics.(p.121)
• I wanted to roam again and through *relatives* got a supercargo job on an Australian packet which allowed me to visit my people in Australia where I was born.(p.252)
• During this time, I had been threatened, beaten, kissed, praised and damned alternately by *relatives*, family, friends and strangers, but of course it all went for naught.(p.300)
• I couldn't do it among my *relatives*, I couldn't do it among my friends.(p.340)
• My wife and new baby are fortunately staying with *relatives*.(p.500)
• Within a month, the police, the hospital authorities, several kind strangers, most of my friends, all of my close *relatives*, and a few adepts at rolling a drunk and removing his wrist watch and wallet had been involved.(p.532)

relax

• We *relax* and take it easy.(p.86)
• He can *relax* and it's quiet."(p.271)
• I had to sleep, I had to clear my mind and free it from worry, and I had to *relax*.(p.336)
• *Relax* a little.(p.382)
• I began to sleep, to *relax*, to accept my plight.(p.461)

relaxation

• What I needed was a change, mental *relaxation*, getting out and doing something.(p.338)

relaxed

• Yet he was happy, *relaxed*, confident and laughing.(p.239)

relaxing

• Meetings are both *relaxing* and refreshing to me after a hard day.(p.381)

release

• We had seen spiritual *release*, but liked to tell ourselves it wasn't true.(p.55)
• Joy at our *release* from a lifetime of frustration knew no bounds.(p.128)
• It means *release* from care, boredom and worry.(p.151)
• There you will find *release* from care, boredom and worry.(p.152)
• In there he would find companionship and *release*.(p.154)
• Seeing much of each other, scarce an evening passed that someone's home did not shelter a little gathering of men and women, happy in their *release*, and constantly thinking how they might present their discovery to some newcomer.(p.159)
• They bear witness that *release* from alcoholism can really be permanent.(p.169)
• As soon as I had done that I did feel a great *release*.(p.189)
• I noticed that the others seemed to have such a *release*, a happiness, a something that I thought a person ought to have.(p.191)
• We were eating lunch, and I was listening and trying to find out why they had this *release* that they seemed to have.(p.191)
• I had a genuine *release* right from the start.(p.219)
• Dr. Bob dwelt at length on how prayer had given him *release*, time and time again, from the nearly overpowering compulsion to take a drink.(p.279)
• I believe that the *release* from people-pleasing restrictions gives retirees more motivation to drink than boredom does.(p.329)
• But during a period of particular stress and strain about thirteen years ago, I resorted to alcohol in my home, alone, as a means of temporary *release*, as a means of getting a little extra sleep.(p.335)
• This physician, the originator of A.A.'s first black group, but badly caught in the toils, tells of his *release* and of how freedom came as he worked among his own people.(p.483)

released

• Since this book was first published, A.A. has *released* thousands of alcoholics from asylums and hospitals of every kind.(p.114)
• Bill was very, very grateful that he had been *released* from this terrible thing and he had given God the credit for having done it, and he's so grateful about it he wants to tell other people about it.(p.191)
• He was *released*, relieved from his alcoholism and was happy and contented because of it.(p.208)
• Imagine my surprise when I read in a page one "box" that I had been taken from the theater unconscious around noon that day, removed by ambulance to a hospital and stomach-pumped and then *released*.(p.244)
• When I was *released* from the hospital, I went back to my unit, and nothing had changed.(p.319)
• A few months after that, I was *released* and left the world of insanity, only to return to the world of alcoholic insanity.(p.370)
• I was *released* in a week, a week of hell with no drinks.(p.428)
• We always, or nearly always, had good intentions when we were *released* from prison.(p.458)
• I clung to the outfit for the balance of my time, and finally I was *released*, after having spent twenty years and nine months behind bars.(p.510)
• When the policeman *released* me to my stupefied and exasperated friend at four in the morning, I went to my traveling bag and groped until I found – well, let the officer speak: "Ah," said the policeman, "he's got anuder pair, t'ank God!"(p.538)
• This great experience that *released* me from the bondage of hatred and replaced it with love is really just another affirmation of the truth I know: I get everything I need in Alcoholics Anonymous – everything I need I get – and when I get what I need I invariably find that it was just what I wanted all the time.(p.553)

relegated

• But he noticed that I was not a good mother to my child, that I *relegated* her to nurses when she was with me.(p.403)

reliability

• My company advanced me rapidly, once my *reliability* was established again.(p.559)

reliable

• Strangely enough, right through to the end of my twenty-six years in the Army, I was still being offered very good and important jobs in spite of the fact that my superiors must have known that I wasn't thoroughly *reliable*.(p.519)

reliance

• These allergic types can never safely use alcohol in any form at all; and once having formed the habit and found they cannot break it, once having lost their self-confidence, their *reliance* upon things human, their problems pile up on them and become astonishingly difficult to solve.(p.xxvi)
• When we saw others solve their problems by a simple *reliance* upon the Spirit of the Universe, we had to stop doubting the power of God.(p.52)
• God will determine that, so you must remember that your real *reliance* is always upon Him.(p.164)

relied

• It had been so many years since I had not *relied* on some artificial crutch, either alcohol or sedatives.(p.310)

relief

• The only *relief* we have to suggest is entire abstinence.(p.xxviii)
• Much to our *relief*, we discovered we did not need to consider another's conception of God.(p.46)
• By this time I was beginning to pay very dearly physically and, in hope of *relief*, voluntarily incarcerated myself at least a dozen times in one of the local sanitariums.(p.174)
• With the alcoholic, they could only give temporary *relief* and in the last stages not even that.(p.307)
• Years earlier, I had gone into psychoanalysis to get *relief*.(p.349)
• What a wonderful new feeling, what a wonderful *relief*!(p.366)
• The time for decision had arrived, and it was a *relief*

to say "Yes" when my family said they would call Alcoholics Anonymous for me.(p.378)
• A ***relief,*** even though I dreaded it, feeling that this was the end of everything.(p.378)
• It was a great ***relief*** to know I didn't have to drink any more.(p.379)
• It was such a feeling of ***relief*** that I wanted to know more about it and with that, I think for the first time, came the realization that there was something horribly, horribly wrong with me.(p.392)
• For me, pills don't produce the desire to swallow a pill; they produce the symptoms that require that the pill be taken for ***relief.***(p.443)
• Rather, I embraced it – I must in honesty admit it -- with a great sense of ***relief.***(p.531)

relieve

• ***Relieve*** me of the bondage of self, that I may better do Thy will.(p.63)
• Out of this maelstrom just two coherent thoughts came to the surface; one, a drink would mean homelessness and death; two, I could no longer ***relieve*** the pressure of fear by starting home, as was once my habitual solution to this problem, because I no longer had a home.(p.279)
• I always took it because I had the symptom that only that pill would ***relieve.***(p.443)

relieved

• Six months earlier, the broker had been ***relieved*** of his drink obsession by a sudden spiritual experience, following a meeting with an alcoholic friend who had been in contact with the Oxford Groups of that day.(p.xv)
• It ***relieved*** me somewhat to learn that in alcoholics the will is amazingly weakened when it comes to combating liquor, though it often remains strong in other respects.(p.7)
• Upon hearing this, our friend was somewhat ***relieved,*** for he reflected that after all, he was a good church member.(p.27)
• But the moment I made up my mind to go through with the process, I had the curious feeling that my alcoholic condition was ***relieved,*** as in fact it proved to be.(p.42)
• (b) That probably no human power could have ***relieved*** our alcoholism.(p.60)
• Every new alcoholic looks for this spirit among us and is immensely ***relieved*** when he finds we are not witch-burners.(p.103)
• We think each family which has been ***relieved*** owes something to those who have not, and when the occasion requires, each member of it should be only too willing to bring former mistakes, no matter how grievous, out of their hiding places.(p.124)
• It is a most wonderful blessing to be ***relieved*** of the terrible curse with which I was afflicted.(p.180)
• He was released, ***relieved*** from his alcoholism and was happy and contented because of it.(p.208)
• As he talked I gathered vaguely, (because he was a faltering beginner then, just as I am now) that to be ***relieved*** of alcoholism I would have to be different.(p.257)
• Almost simultaneously, I discovered that cocktails in the late afternoon and highballs in the evening ***relieved*** the many tensions of the day.(p.277)
• Liquor ***relieved*** these.(p.277)
• High living, a great many fair weather friends, the 1929 stock market crash, and a couple of years of Depression, soon ***relieved*** me one by one of my worldly goods including my wife.(p.358)

relieving

• They experienced a few distressing failures, but in those cases they made an effort to bring the man's family into a spiritual way of living, thus ***relieving*** much worry and suffering.(p.159)

religion

• Another reason for the wide acceptance of A.A. was the ministration of friends -- friends in medicine, ***religion,*** and the press, together with innumerable others who became our able and persistent advocates.(p.xx)
• Neither does A.A. take any particular medical point of view, though we cooperate widely with the men of medicine as well as with the men of ***religion.***(p.xx)
• Simply, but smilingly, he said, "I've got ***religion.***"(p.9)
• So that was it -- last summer an alcoholic crackpot; now, I suspected, a little cracked about ***religion.***(p.9)
• We, who have traveled this dubious path, beg you to lay aside prejudice, even against organized ***religion.***(p.49)
• Though we have no religious connection, we may still do well to talk with someone ordained by an established ***religion.***(p.74)
• Let him see that you are not there to instruct him in ***religion.***(p.93)
• If he does not argue about ***religion,*** he will make new friends and is sure to find new avenues of usefulness and pleasure.(p.132)
• You don't have to sell me ***religion,*** either.(p.188)
• So I had never had any lasting contact with any kind of ***religion.***)(p.201)
• Insofar as ***religion*** was concerned, I had a Catholic training in my youth.(p.214)
• So I enrolled at the university for night courses in ***religion,*** and I pursued those courses for a year.(p.221)
• I couldn't stomach ***religion,*** and I didn't like the mention of God or any of the other capital letters.(p.227)
• This wasn't "***religion***" – this was freedom!(p.228)
• Sniffing at emotional ***religion,*** I walked away.(p.256)
• I don't think that there was anything said about ***religion.***(p.268)
• I hear about A.A., but think it ***religion.***(p.475)
• I have a ***religion.***(p.475)
• I turned to ***religion*** with fervor.(p.555)
• 10. – No A.A. group or member should ever, in such a way as to implicate A.A., express any opinion on outside controversial issues – particularly those of politics, alcohol reform, or sectarian ***religion.***(p.567)
• Dr. Foster Kennedy, neurologist: "This organization of Alcoholics Anonymous calls on two of the greatest reservoirs of power known to man, ***religion*** and that instinct for association with one's fellows . . . the 'herd instinct.'(p.571)

religions

• With ministers, and world's ***religions,*** I parted right there.(p.10)
• I honestly doubted whether, on balance, the ***religions*** of mankind had done any good.(p.11)
• However, here I probably took my first step towards my coming alcoholism by developing a terrific aversion to all churches and established ***religions.***(p.240)

religious

• Inquiry by scientific, medical, and ***religious*** societies will be welcomed.(p.xiv)
• Some of the recommendations of A.A.'s early medical and ***religious*** friends will be found further on in this book.(p.xx)
• Alcoholics Anonymous is not a ***religious*** organization.(p.xx)
• By personal ***religious*** affiliation, we include Catholics, Protestants, Jews, Hindus, and a sprinkling of Moslems and Buddhists.(p.xx)
• They had told of a simple ***religious*** idea and a practical program of action.(p.9)
• The wars which had been fought, the burnings and chicanery that ***religious*** dispute had facilitated, made me sick.(p.11)
• It began to look as though ***religious*** people were right after all.(p.11)
• All sections of this country and many of its occupations are represented, as well as many political, economic, social, and ***religious*** backgrounds.(p.17)
• Of necessity there will have to be discussion of matters medical, psychiatric, social, and ***religious.***(p.19)
• This hope, however, was destroyed by the doctor's telling him that while his ***religious*** convictions were very good, in his case they did not spell the necessary vital spiritual experience.(p.27)
• The distinguished American psychologist, William James, in his book "Varieties of ***Religious*** Experience," indicates a multitude of ways in which men have discovered God.(p.28)
• Those having ***religious*** affiliations will find here nothing disturbing to their beliefs or ceremonies.(p.28)
• We think it no concern of ours what ***religious*** bodies our members identify themselves with as individuals.(p.28)
• Not all of us join ***religious*** bodies, but most of us favor such memberships.(p.28)
• Though not a ***religious*** person, I have profound respect for the spiritual approach in such cases as yours.(p.43)
• He attended church school, where he became rebellious at what he thought an overdose of ***religious*** education.(p.56)
• But later, alone in his room, he asked himself this question: "Is it possible that all the ***religious*** people I have known are wrong?"(p.56)
• Those of us belonging to a ***religious*** denomination which requires confession must, and of course, will want to go to the properly appointed authority whose duty it is to receive it.(p.74)
• Though we have no ***religious*** connection, we may still do well to talk with someone ordained by an established religion.(p.74)
• It is seldom wise to approach an individual, who still smarts from our injustice to him, and announce that we have gone ***religious.***(p.77)
• Why lay ourselves open to being branded fanatics or ***religious*** bores?(p.77)
• If we belong to a ***religious*** denomination which requires a definite morning devotion, we attend to that also.(p.87)
• If not members of ***religious*** bodies, we sometimes select and memorize a few set prayers which emphasize the principles we have been discussing.(p.87)
• Be quick to see where ***religious*** people are right.(p.87)
• Get an idea of his behavior, his problems, his background, the seriousness of his condition, and his ***religious*** leanings.(p.90)
• Your prospect may belong to a ***religious*** denomination.(p.93)
• His ***religious*** education and training may be far superior to yours.(p.93)
• He becomes a ***religious*** enthusiast.(p.128)
• He may tell mother, who has been ***religious*** all her life, that she doesn't know what it's all about, and that she had better get his brand of spirituality while there is yet time.(p.128)
• Though the family has no ***religious*** connections, they may wish to make contact with or take membership in a ***religious*** body.(p.131)
• Alcoholics who have derided ***religious*** people will be helped by such contacts.(p.131)
• They were deeply ***religious*** people, much shocked by their son's refusal to have anything to do with the church.(p.158)
• (My mother and father were Catholics and I had been baptized, but at the end of my instructions for Confirmation I had not gone to church, and then when my mother remarried, she married a Protestant and the whole ***religious*** angle was forgotten.(p.201)
• I come from a very poor family in material things, with a fine Christian mother, but with no ***religious*** background.(p.261)
• There was a very ***religious*** family that lived down the road from us, and we were on the same party line.(p.265)
• The big A.A. book had not been written and there was no literature except various ***religious*** pamphlets.(p.291)
• Dr. Bob always emphasized the ***religious*** angle very strongly, and I think it helped.(p.292)
• I have been of a very ***religious*** outlook all my life, but that made no difference once John Barleycorn got the better of me.(p.343)
• Making amends is sometimes doing what we are capable of doing but failed to do because of alcohol; carrying out community responsibilities such as Community Funds, Red Cross, educational and ***religious*** activities in proportion to our abilities and energy.(p.381)
• I was born in a little town in Virginia in an average ***religious*** home.(p.483)
• My mother had been recently converted and, actually, had become a ***religious*** fanatic.(p.483)
• He went into the ***religious*** side and told me that I didn't attend church as regularly as I should, and that he felt, more or less, that this was responsible for my trouble.(p.489)
• V. The ***Religious*** View on A.A.(p.563)
• Yet it is true that our first printing gave many readers the impression that these personality changes, or ***religious*** experiences, must be in the nature of sudden and spectacular upheavals.(p.569)
• Our more ***religious*** members call it "God-consciousness."(p.570)
• THE ***RELIGIOUS*** VIEW ON A.A.(p.574)

relinquished

• I approached several ministers and all of them thought it was a very good idea, but they never ***relinquished*** any space.(p.495)

relish

• Eventually I would arrive home for a late supper for which, of course, I had absolutely no ***relish.***(p.299)

relive

• For his sake, we do recount and almost ***relive*** the horrors of our past.(p.132)

reluctance

• At the same time you will feel no ***reluctance*** to rid yourself of those who cannot or will not stop.(p.148)

reluctant

• It had provided me with excuses for my lack of education, my marital failures, personal failures, inadequacy, and of course, my alcoholism and, though I really thought I had been willing to part with it, now I knew I was ***reluctant*** to let it go.(p.552)

reluctantly

• I said, "Yes," ***reluctantly,*** "I probably will."(p.190)

rely

• You may ***rely*** absolutely on anything they say about themselves.(p.xxiv)

• Just to the extent that we do as we think He would have us, and humbly ***rely*** on Him, does He enable us to match calamity with serenity.(p.68)

• We come to ***rely*** upon it.(p.87)

• The minute we put our work on a service plane, the alcoholic commences to ***rely*** upon our assistance rather than upon God.(p.98)

• I knew that I had a helper that I could ***rely*** upon, who wouldn't fail me.(p.189)

relying

• For we are now on a different basis; the basis of trusting and ***relying*** upon God.(p.68)

remain

• It is important that we ***remain*** anonymous because we are too few, at present to handle the overwhelming number of personal appeals which may result from this publication.(p.xiii)

• I earnestly advise every alcoholic to read this book through, and though perhaps he came to scoff, he may ***remain*** to pray.(p.xxx)

• Sometimes it is to the best interests of all concerned that a couple ***remain*** apart.(p.99)

• In this connection, can you ***remain*** undisturbed if the man proceeds to tell you shocking things?(p.145)

• Though they knew they must help other alcoholics if they would ***remain*** sober, that motive became secondary.(p.159)

• I was, of course, soon on the carpet and the upshot was that I had to go back for two more quarters and ***remain*** absolutely dry, if I wished to graduate.(p.174)

• The sisters seemed to ***remain*** unaffected.(p.211)

• So I always say that as long as I remember January 8th that is how long I will ***remain*** sober.(p.240)

• In describing his suffering, his fears, his many years of groping for some answer to that which always seemed to ***remain*** unanswerable, he could have been describing me, and nothing short of experience and knowledge could have afforded him that much insight!(p.309)

• Some even ***remain*** agnostics.)(p.417)

• Eight -- Alcoholics Anonymous should ***remain*** forever nonprofessional, but our service centers may employ special workers.(p.564)

• 8. – Alcoholics Anonymous should ***remain*** forever nonprofessional.(p.566)

remainder

• Of alcoholics who came to A.A. and really tried, 50% got sober at once and remained that way; 25% sobered up after some relapses, and among the ***remainder,*** those who stayed on with A.A. showed improvement.(p.xx)

• Why, he argued, should he lose the ***remainder*** of his business, only to bring still more suffering to his family by foolishly admitting his plight to people from whom he made his livelihood?(p.155)

remained

• Of alcoholics who came to A.A. and really tried, 50% got sober at once and ***remained*** that way; 25% sobered up after some relapses, and among the remainder, those who stayed on with A.A. showed improvement.(p.xx)

• Despite the living example of my friend there ***remained*** in me the vestiges of my old prejudice.(p.12)

• It was fortunate, for my old business associates ***remained*** skeptical for a year and a half, during which I found little work.(p.15)

• An exceptional man, he ***remained*** bone dry for twenty-five years and retired at the age of fifty-five, after a successful and happy business career.(p.32)

• Most of us have believed that if we ***remained*** sober for a long stretch, we could thereafter drink normally.(p.33)

• In the early days of our drinking we occasionally ***remained*** sober for a year or more, becoming serious drinkers again later.(p.34)

• All this time our friend of the hotel lobby incident ***remained*** in that town.(p.159)

• By the time I had completed law school I had picked up some experience in patent law, for I ***remained*** with the patent law firm and worked too in Washington where they found that I was a capable infringement investigator.(p.213)

• I ***remained*** with them for three weeks, using part of the time in making many amends, which I had had no earlier opportunity of making.(p.281)

• On the second, I knew -- as I know now -- that if I ***remained*** away from the first drink, then I had not to worry about the hundredth one.(p.344)

• My daily alcoholic consumption ***remained*** about the same through all this, with perhaps a slight increase, and my binges ***remained*** one-nighters.(p.434)

• I ***remained*** there for about ten months, and then I was sent to a place called Wallkill, a so-called rehabilitation center.(p.509)

remaining

• Poor health and a complete lack of money necessitated my ***remaining*** with Dr. Bob and Anne for very close to a year.(p.280)

• My alcoholic wife took up someone else, divorced me, and took with her all my ***remaining*** property.(p.437)

• However, one thing I am certain of: Inmates in prison who attend A.A. have their chances of ***remaining*** free greatly enhanced – this is a proved fact.(p.458)

• What a revelation of ego and arrogance still ***remaining*** in me – as if anyone, instinct and training apart, likes to be in jail or in an alcoholic ward or fired from his job.(p.536)

remains

• In spite of the great increase in the size and the span of this Fellowship, at its core it ***remains*** simple and personal.(p.xxii)

• It relieved me somewhat to learn that in alcoholics the will is amazingly weakened when it comes to combating liquor, though it often ***remains*** strong in other respects.(p.7)

• He can go anywhere on this earth where other free men may go without disaster, provided he ***remains*** willing to maintain a certain simple attitude.(p.26)

• The lesson of his death still ***remains*** with me, yet I often wonder what would have happened if somebody else had made that first call on me.(p.239)

• Learning to depend upon a higher power and absorb himself in his work with other alcoholics, he ***remains*** sober day by day.(p.572)

remanded

• I was immediately arrested, arraigned in Homicide Court, held without bail, and ***remanded*** to the old Tombs Prison to await trial.(p.508)

remark

• Henry Ford once made a wise ***remark*** to the effect that experience is the thing of supreme value in life.(p.124)

• Members of a family should watch such matters carefully, for one careless, inconsiderate ***remark*** has been known to raise the very devil.(p.125)

• When I ***remark*** that I have been in jail nine times, and in an alcoholic ward twice, they think I'm kidding, or possibly dramatizing for the sake of a good yarn.(p.542)

remarkable

• Today the ***remarkable*** unity of A.A. is one of the greatest assets that our Society has.(p.xix)

• When we sincerely took such a position, all sorts of ***remarkable*** things followed.(p.63)

• If you persist, ***remarkable*** things will happen.(p.100)

• But we have seen ***remarkable*** transformations in our bodies.(p.133)

• And then, in the spring of 1939, a very ***remarkable*** book was rolled off a New York press with the title "Alcoholics Anonymous."(p.307)

• All the people involved in these flare-ups took it with ***remarkable*** grace, have teased me about it since, and have become good friends of mine.(p.416)

• Moreover, I am deeply convinced that so long as I continue to strive, in my bumbling way, toward the principles I first encountered in the earlier chapters of this book, this ***remarkable*** power will continue to flow through me.(p.437)

remarkably

• ***Remarkably*** enough, I was a very abstemious soldier.(p.253)

remarked

• To his wife, he ***remarked,*** "Don't see anything the matter here, Ma.(p.82)

• We have elsewhere ***remarked*** how much better life is when lived on a spiritual plane.(p.116)

• He ***remarked:*** "I'm mighty glad you fellows got over your drinking.(p.148)

• Speaking at a dinner given by John D. Rockefeller Jr. to introduce Alcoholics Anonymous to some of his friends, Dr. Harry Emerson Fosdick ***remarked:*** "I think that psychologically speaking there is a point of advantage in the approach that is being made in this movement that cannot be duplicated.(p.574)

remarks

• But the firm became violently ill with my drunkenness and their course of treatment was to remove their ulcer, in the form of me, from the payroll, amid much fanfare and very personal and slighting ***remarks*** and insinuations.(p.300)

• At a large party in Geneva, with people from many countries represented, the kind of party that is "protocol" in the extreme, I swayed, laughed hysterically, made naughty ***remarks*** in an unhushed voice, and was finally led from the scene.(p.406)

remarried

• Maybe we are divorced, and have ***remarried*** but haven't kept up the alimony to number one.(p.79)

• A man we know had ***remarried.***(p.79)

• When I was sixteen years old, my mother ***remarried*** and I was given the opportunity of going back to school.(p.193)

• (My mother and father were Catholics and I had been baptized, but at the end of my instructions for Confirmation I had not gone to church, and then when my mother ***remarried,*** she married a Protestant and the whole religious angle was forgotten.(p.201)

• I had no feeling of security, and I knew that I had done a very stupid thing, so I went back to Texas and ***remarried*** my ex-husband.(p.386)

remedy

• But when the broker gave him Dr. Silkworth's description of alcoholism and its hopelessness, the physician began to pursue the spiritual ***remedy*** for his malady with a willingness he had never before been able to muster.(p.xvi)

• These men may well have a ***remedy*** for thousands of such situations.(p.xxiv)

• We have tried every imaginable ***remedy.***(p.31)

• Fred would not believe himself an alcoholic, much less accept a spiritual ***remedy*** for his problem.(p.39)

• If you think he will be shy of a spiritual ***remedy,*** ask him to look at the chapter on alcoholism.(p.112)

• If you both show a willingness to ***remedy*** your own defects, there will be little need to criticize each other.(p.118)

• Some employers have tried every known ***remedy.***(p.137)

• That won't hurt him a bit, even though he does not go for this ***remedy.***(p.144)

• I had never heard of the ***remedy*** expressed in just this language.(p.236)

• My thoughts sometimes turned to the idea that there must be a ***remedy.***(p.256)

• As I look back on the events of two months, I can clearly see that I had been circling around, half-afraid of encountering the ***remedy*** for my situation, half wanting it, deferring fulfillment of my promise to get in touch with the doctor I had heard about.(p.258)

• All sorts were represented and their relation of experiences and how they had found the only ***remedy,*** added to their human existence as sober men, laid the foundation of a very necessary faith.(p.258)

remember

• It was years since I could ***remember*** his coming to New York in that condition.(p.9)

• I ***remember*** I felt irritated that I had to be a salesman for a concern I once owned.(p.36)

• I ***remember*** having several more that night and plenty the next morning.(p.41)

• ***Remember*** that we deal with alcohol -- cunning, baffling, powerful!(p.58)

• ***Remember*** it was agreed at the beginning we would go to any lengths for victory over alcohol.(p.76)

• We must ***remember*** that ten or twenty years of drunkenness would make a skeptic out of anyone.(p.83)

• ***Remember*** they are very ill.(p.89)

• Ask them to ***remember,*** when they are impatient, the blessed fact of his sobriety.(p.100)

• When he angers you, ***remember*** that he is very ill.(p.108)

• They ***remember*** when father was romantic, thoughtful and successful.(p.123)

• Let them ***remember*** that his drinking wrought all kinds of damage that may take long to repair.(p.127)

• The head of the house ought to ***remember*** that he is mainly to blame for what befell his home.(p.127)

• We know there are difficult wives and families, but the man who is getting over alcoholism must ***remember*** he did much to make them so.(p.127)

• Try to ***remember*** that though God has wrought miracles among us, we should never belittle a good doctor or psychiatrist.(p.133)

• I well ***remember*** the shock I received when a prominent doctor in Chicago told me of cases where pressure of the spinal fluid actually ruptured the brain.(p.140)

• God will determine that, so you must ***remember*** that your real reliance is always upon Him.(p.164)

• I ***remember*** nothing from then on until I woke up at a friend's house, in a town near home.(p.179)

• I *remember* that my father kept whiskey around the house for medical purposes and entertainment, and I would drink from this when no one was about and then water it to keep my parents from knowing I was drinking.(p.183)

• Then I *remember* when the boys came back, that I told them, "I have gone to this Higher Power and I have told Him that I am willing to put His world first, above everything.(p.190)

• I *remember* telling them too that it was going to be awfully tough, because I did some other things, smoked cigarettes and played penny ante poker, sometimes bet on the horse races and they said, "Don't you think you're having more trouble with this drinking than with anything else at the present time?(p.190)

• I know there was even more, something that I hadn't got, and I *remember* one day, a week or two after I had come out of the hospital, Bill was over to my house talking to my wife and me.(p.191)

• At that time, as I *remember*, he had promised never to take another drink.(p.193)

• I can also *remember* that he was a salesman and a very good one.(p.193)

• At a comparatively early age, I can *remember* being jealous of my brother.(p.194)

• During the day, looking over the contracts and money in my pocket, I found that I had sold six lots that I couldn't even *remember*, and didn't even know the people I had sold them to.(p.196)

• I didn't *remember* anything that had happened.(p.196)

• I can well *remember* sitting with seven dollars in my pocket, planning on giving my family a hundred or two hundred dollars, when I made it next year.(p.197)

• I can well *remember* over a long period of years when I thought I was the only person in the world who knew that sooner or later I was going to get drunk.(p.198)

• I can *remember* occasions when friends recommended me for positions or business opportunities that I wouldn't take because I felt that at some future date I'd get drunk and they would be hurt.(p.198)

• I can *remember* telling the poor little soul that I could probably quit drinking if I wasn't married to her, and told her that, after all, I didn't like restraint!(p.199)

• I can *remember* well thinking that I would quit drinking, really go to work hard, apply myself eight hours a day, five days a week, make a lot of money, and then I could start drinking again.(p.199)

• I *remember* one occasion when I did not drink for three hundred and sixty-four days, but I didn't quite make the year.(p.200)

• We went into a bootleg joint and I don't *remember* leaving that place.(p.202)

• The circumstances under which I reached these people were very odd because I was led there through things that I said when I couldn't even *remember* speaking.(p.202)

• I told somebody that I was going down to get Christian Science and they took me down, but I don't *remember* saying that.(p.202)

• Then he started to talk to me about his drinking experiences, what his drinking had cost him, how much he had drunk and where, things like that, and I *remember* I was quite bored because I had never seen the guy before and had no interest at all in what, where and when he drank.(p.208)

• I *remember* well one fellow, Joe, walking nearly three miles through slush, wet and snow to come to the hospital to see a man that he had never seen before in his life, and that impressed me very much.(p.208)

• I can *remember* that in my childhood, he was ill at ease with the children because he attempted to assert an army discipline that had been ground into him during his three and a half years of army service.(p.210)

• It had been one o'clock when I last *remember* looking.(p.223)

• I *remember* looking longingly at the window as an easier solution, and shuddering at the memory of that other window, three years before, and the six agonizing months in a London hospital ward.(p.224)

• Sitting in a Second Avenue bar, accepting drinks from anyone who offered, after my small stake was gone; or sitting at home alone, with the inevitable glass in my hand, I would *remember*, and remembering, I would drink faster, seeking speedy oblivion.(p.225)

• But I can *remember*, in my teens, that there were a few characters who caused the village heads to nod pityingly and sometimes in anger as they paused to say, "That sot, Henri" and "Ce pauvre Jules," who drank too much.(p.230)

• You can all *remember* that in the first few months after the change, a great many men, who had formerly been used to a few beers every day or an occasional drink of whiskey, simply quit all alcoholic drinks.(p.232)

• I don't *remember* much of what he said, but I did realize that here was another guy exactly like me; he had been in the same laughing academies and the same jails, known the same loss of jobs, same frustrations, same boredom and the same loneliness.(p.239)

• So I always say that as long as I *remember* January 8th that is how long I will remain sober.(p.240)

• That is where I had my first drink and I still *remember* it, for every "first" drink afterwards did exactly the same trick -- I could feel it go right through every bit of my body and down to my very toes.(p.241)

• And I still say that as long as I *remember* that January 8th in Washington, that is how long, by the grace of God as I understand Him, I will retain a happy sobriety.(p.250)

• But I can *remember* the urge of the Prodigal Son to return to his Father.(p.260)

• I *remember* starting to city school, coming from a country school, and wanting so very, very much to be like the other girls and trying flour on my face for powder because I wasn't able to have any real powder.(p.261)

• I *remember* feeling that they were all making fun of me.(p.261)

• I look back and *remember* these things because they made me very unhappy, and added to my feeling of inferiority at never being the same as other people.(p.261)

• I *remember* one instance when he took off and went down to Cincinnati and was gone a week on a drunk.(p.262)

• Paul S. had just called me, and I *remember* he stressed reading the Big Book.(p.269)

• I *remember* sometime, it was possibly six months after we had been going steadily to King School, that we were coming home from a meeting and saw a car along the way, and a fellow in back drinking a bottle of beer.(p.271)

• I don't ever *remember* that I was bored myself when we first came in, and they came out to the house and talked to us about these things.(p.273)

• I didn't think I was going to get drunk right then, but I *remember* how comforting it was when I called Anne and told her.(p.273)

• I well *remember* a session I had with myself soon after I returned.(p.282)

• I can still *remember* very distinctly getting into Akron at eleven p.m. and routing this same Howard out of bed to do something about me.(p.290)

• I cannot *remember* just when I became the victim of insomnia, but I do know that the last year and a half I never went to bed sober a single night.(p.299)

• One is that I don't *remember* too many of them, as I was one of those drunks who could be on his feet and attend a meeting or a party, engage in a conversation with people and do things that any nearly normal person would do, and the next day not *remember* a thing about where I was, what I did, whom I saw, or how I got home.(p.301)

• I couldn't *remember* what had been said five minutes ago.(p.319)

• All I can *remember* about the Roaring Twenties is that I drank a great deal, thought I was having a grand time, managed to get to Europe for a few weeks, was very proud of the dozens of speak-easy cards entitling me to an entree in the better joints between Cleveland and New York, took on a wife, and built a home in a fashionable suburb of Cleveland.(p.358)

• I can't *remember* a dinner at home that we didn't have white wine or claret on the table.(p.384)

• For some reason I can't *remember*, it finally dawned on me that I had a problem, and yet nobody was very critical about it except my family, and that was only because I decided, after seven years of marriage, that I would divorce my husband.(p.386)

• But Frank turned around and looked at me and said, "Esther, *remember* you're in jail and not at home."(p.391)

• Frank was out of town, and I *remember* that he'd gotten in this one night and found me drunk.(p.391)

• Dr. Bob said, "Love and service keep us dry," and Bill said, "Always we must *remember* that our first duty is face-to-face help for the alcoholic who still suffers."(p.395)

• My personality, from the time I can *remember* anything, was the perfect set-up for an alcoholic career.(p.400)

• Once or twice, during my early drinking, I carried it over into the second day, and only once, that I can *remember*, did it continue into the third.(p.432)

• I *remember* very well saying, "There's only one person in the world whose guts I hate worse than yours, and those're my own."(p.440)

• I *remember*, one time, even the dog had a psychiatric diagnosis.(p.440)

• I *remember* finding myself in the middle of the night in the doctors' parking lot at the hospital with one foot in the car and one foot on the ground, not knowing which was the lead foot; finding myself hanging up the telephone – then realizing I had gotten out of bed, answered the phone, turned on the light, and carried on a conversation with a patient.(p.441)

• Now I own perhaps the most costly pair of moccasins anyone has ever seen, and they help me *remember* where I've been.)(p.445)

• Perhaps the best thing of all for me is to *remember* that my serenity is inversely proportional to my expectations.(p.452)

• When I *remember* this, I can see I've never had it so good.(p.452)

• The first time I *remember* seeing or hearing of A.A. was twenty years ago.(p.460)

• *Remember*, now you have a choice.(p.463)

• From that time on, fear was with me because I realized that not only would I not *remember* what happened to me while I was drinking, but apparently I couldn't control what happened.(p.465)

• I *remember* vaguely violent quarrels with my husband, his finding my liquor supply time and time again and throwing it out.(p.466)

• Then I *remember* him coming into my room one night with a friend, and telling me to get dressed – we were going away.(p.466)

• I *remember* particularly one sentence that seemed to say, "This is for you."(p.473)

• *Remember* only first two drinks.(p.475)

• By grace of God I stop, think two things: This would kill good mother and father; then *remember* boys talk about Indian fellow who been sober three years.(p.475)

• Some of us always *remember* our big mouths when it comes to a drink, but somewhere along the line, we seem to have forgotten about taking care of our teeth.(p.479)

• It is so beautiful to get up in the morning not being hung-over and being able to *remember* where we were the night before.(p.481)

• I *remember* in my early youth my mother dressed me just as she did my two sisters, and I wore curls until I was six years of age.(p.483)

• We lived just a few doors from the First Baptist Church and when they had funerals I *remember* very often asking my mother whether the person was good or bad and whether they were going to heaven or hell.(p.483)

• I *remember* in my first year in high school, that mother suggested that I do not join the cadet unit.(p.484)

• But I can *remember* in post graduate days, and during interneship, that very often I'd go to a patient's bed and start a process of elimination and then, very often, I'd wind up guessing.(p.485)

• I'd go into my home with a bottle, and I *remember* clearly how I would look around to see if Vi was watching.(p.487)

• I can *remember* her watching.(p.487)

• Fear gripped me then, because I could *remember* nothing about it.(p.489)

• I don't *remember* whether I went by streetcar, whether I walked or went in a taxicab.(p.492)

• The one thing I can *remember* now was that Vi was on the corner of 8th and L, and I *remember* vividly that she had an envelope in her hand.(p.492)

• I *remember* talking to her, but what happened after that I don't know.(p.492)

• Can't *remember* the answer to the first.(p.499)

• I don't seem to *remember* anything.(p.499)

• I *remember* the day I came back to New York.(p.513)

• Having made that bargain, I immediately began to feel I'd been trapped into it and I went out and had some drinks – four glasses of gin, I *remember*.(p.523)

• But I don't *remember* that any of them ever went to sleep in joints and woke up with no shoes on in the winter, or fell out of chairs.(p.527)

• I don't *remember* any of them getting put out in the winter because they didn't pay their rent.(p.527)

• My father was and still is a minister, and I was afraid that I might run into him, or that someone might tell him where I was, and I could still *remember* what he had done to me when I got drunk one Christmas when I was very young.(p.527)

• I was trying to *remember* where it came from, when two of the biggest cops I ever saw walked in and took me to jail.(p.528)

• They tell me that I killed a man during that period, but I can't *remember* anything.(p.528)
• I *remember* the day when I decided to drink myself to death quietly, without bothering anyone, because I was tired of having been a dependable, trustworthy person for about thirty-nine years without having received what I thought was a proper reward for my virtue.(p.531)
• Still another friend and temporary host received me at four in the morning from the charge of a policeman who had found me "going to bed" in a garage far from the last place I could *remember* having been, a fashionable bar and restaurant in the theatrical district of New York, to which I had repaired after my date for that evening, a charming lady of the theatre who had refused my company for obvious reasons.(p.538)
• I did not *remember* much of the ten-day binge.(p.540)
• I *remember* how horrible jails are, how dreadful a thing it is to be behind steel bars.(p.542)
• My grandparents were strangers to me and I *remember* being lonely, and terrified and hurt.(p.545)
• I *remember* being dragged, drink in hand, from beneath the grand piano, where I had hidden, to be locked in my room in disgrace.(p.557)

remembered

• I now *remembered* what my alcoholic friends had told me, how they prophesied that if I had an alcoholic mind, the time and place would come – I would drink again.(p.41)
• We *remembered* always that our sex powers were God-given and therefore good, neither to be used lightly or selfishly nor to be despised and loathed.(p.69)
• It must be *remembered* that I had read a great deal and talked to everyone who knew, or thought they knew anything about the subject of alcoholism.(p.180)
• That night I got very drunk, which was usual, but I *remembered* everything, which was very unusual.(p.224)
• I *remembered* going through what my sister assured me was my nightly procedure of trying to find Willie Seabrook's name in the telephone book.(p.224)
• I *remembered* my loud resolution to find him and ask him to help me get into that "Asylum" he had written about.(p.224)
• I *remembered* asserting that I was going to do something about this, that I couldn't go on . . .(p.224)
• I *remembered* filling the peroxide bottle in my medicine chest with gin, in case my sister found the bottle I hid under the mattress.(p.224)
• And I *remembered* the creeping horror of the interminable night, in which I slept for short spells and woke up dripping with cold sweat and shaken with utter despair, to drink hastily from my bottle and mercifully pass out again, "You're mad, you're mad, you're mad!" pounded through my brain with each returning ray of consciousness, and I drowned the refrain with drink.(p.224)
• And we went down through the valley, and I *remembered* reading about the Ku Klux Klan and how they burnt crosses, and I thought, "God alone knows what we are getting into this time!"(p.269)
• But I *remembered* that every night after dinner my wife would get up and do the dishes.(p.351)
• But somewhere during that time, I *remembered* going back on the bunk and crying my eyes out.(p.390)
• I rarely *remembered* getting home.(p.410)
• I *remembered* having had a little drink of whiskey with a can of warm beer as a chaser.(p.422)
• I *remembered* back to high school when I was fifteen.(p.423)
• I suddenly *remembered* one of my first A.A. meetings, where I heard, "If you are an alcoholic and if you continue to drink, the end is death or insanity."(p.461)
• I had not recognized her, but as soon as she said who she was I *remembered* her right away.(p.493)
• But I *remembered* the years of agony preceding the binge, I *remembered* the years I had thrown away.(p.540)

remembering

• Sitting in a Second Avenue bar, accepting drinks from anyone who offered, after my small stake was gone; or sitting at home alone, with the inevitable glass in my hand, I would remember, and *remembering*, I would drink faster, seeking speedy oblivion.(p.225)
• To this day I can't hear that song without *remembering* that awful Christmas.(p.468)
• Since it was wartime, I explained to the somewhat startled shopkeeper that I had many friends in the service whom I was *remembering* with a watch.(p.532)

remembers

• Coming to his senses, he is revolted at certain episodes he vaguely *remembers*.(p.73)
• But now, with His help and grace, this child of His has paid his initiation fee for good, as long as he *remembers* to stay away from that first drink (the one that does all the damage) one day at a time.(p.399)

remind

• We constantly *remind* ourselves we are no longer running the show, humbly saying to ourselves many times each day "Thy will be done."(p.87)
• *Remind* the prospect that his recovery is not dependent upon people.(p.99)
• But don't *remind* him of this after he has been drinking, for he may be angry.(p.113)
• You need not *remind* him of his spiritual deficiency -- he will know of it.(p.120)

reminded

• People have said we must not go where liquor is served; we must not have it in our homes; we must shun friends who drink; we must avoid moving pictures which show drinking scenes; we must not go into bars; our friends must hide their bottles if we go to their houses; we mustn't think or be *reminded* about alcohol at all.(p.100)
• My alcoholism-prone mind, however, *reminded* me that all great authors had needed a stimulus to build up inspiration and inventiveness before each day's work.(p.331)

reminding

• *Reminding* ourselves that we have decided to go to any length to find a spiritual experience we ask that we be given strength and direction to do the right thing, no matter what the personal consequences may be.(p.79)
• Twelve – Anonymity is the spiritual foundation of all our Traditions, ever *reminding* us to place principles before personalities.(p.564)

reminds

• It *reminds* us that we are to place principles before personalities; that we are actually to practice a genuine humility.(p.568)

remonstrances

• The *remonstrances* of my friends terminated in a row and I became a lone wolf.(p.3)

remorse

• The *remorse*, horror and hopelessness of the next morning are unforgettable.(p.6)
• Sometimes it was *remorse* and then we were sore at ourselves.(p.66)
• But we must be careful not to drift into worry, *remorse* or morbid reflection, for that would diminish our usefulness to others.(p.86)
• The alarming physical and mental symptoms, the deepening pall of *remorse*, depression and inferiority that settled down on our loved ones -- these things terrified and distracted us.(p.106)
• But it began to be an awfully painful answer as hangovers, blackouts, trouble, and *remorse* set in.(p.353)
• I began hitting the bottle again, and with it self-pity, resentment, loneliness and *remorse* set in deeply.(p.362)
• Hangovers and *remorse* were always with me.(p.375)
• Incalculable are the intangible initiation fees that A.A. members have paid: the sick, sick hangovers, the *remorse*, guilt, broken homes, jails, and institutions, and the mental anguish in general that has been generated over the years.(p.399)
• In the morning, because I was young and healthy, my *remorse* was worse than my hangover.(p.404)
• They woke up with hangovers, but with no *remorse*.(p.407)
• The *remorse* would turn inside out, and become anticipatory pleasure.(p.408)
• Next day *remorse* would be on me like a tiger.(p.432)
• After a day or two of grovelling *remorse* I'd come up with an explanation.(p.433)
• Then I would go home full of *remorse*, and wonder what I was going to do until I got my next check.(p.527)
• It became more and more necessary to escape from myself, for my *remorse* and shame and humiliation when I was sober were almost unbearable.(p.547)
• Similarly, we rid ourselves of guilt and *remorse* as we "clean out the garbage" from our minds through the Fourth and Fifth Steps of our recovery program.(p.560)

remorseful

• After they have succumbed to the desire again, as so many do, and the phenomenon of craving develops, they pass through the well-known stages of a spree, emerging *remorseful*, with a firm resolution not to drink again.(p.xxvii)
• A man so involved often feels very *remorseful* at times, especially if he is married to a loyal and courageous girl who has literally gone through hell for him.(p.81)
• A *remorseful* mumbling that we are sorry won't fill the bill at all.(p.83)
• He is *remorseful* after serious drinking bouts and tells you he wants to stop.(p.109)
• Formerly, in the acute mental and physical pain during the *remorseful* periods succeeding each drunk, I found my recollection of the misery I had gone through a bolsterer of resolution and afterward, perhaps, a deterrent for a time.(p.260)

remote

• I had been in the *remote* reaches of Brooklyn.(p.224)
• Inside, though, I was scared to death, for I knew that the time was coming (and it couldn't be too *remote*) when I would be unable to hold that job.(p.548)

remove

• 6.Were entirely ready to have God *remove* all these defects of character.(p.59)
• 7.Humbly asked Him to *remove* our shortcomings.(p.59)
• We ask Him to *remove* our fear and direct our attention to what He would have us be.(p.68)
• We hope you are convinced now that God can *remove* whatever self-will has blocked you off from Him.(p.71)
• Are we now ready to let God *remove* from us all the things which we have admitted are objectionable?(p.76)
• I pray that you now *remove* from me every single defect of character which stands in the way of my usefulness to you and my fellows.(p.76)
• When these crop up, we ask God at once to *remove* them.(p.84)
• But the firm became violently ill with my drunkenness and their course of treatment was to *remove* their ulcer, in the form of me, from the payroll, amid much fanfare and very personal and slighting remarks and insinuations.(p.300)
• It took me some time to realize that the Twelve Steps of A.A. were designed to help correct these defects of character and so help *remove* the obsession to drink.(p.380)
• I, a man of steel, with very high ideals, well brought up, an honor student and the recipient of scholarships and prizes, a boy wonder in business -- I, Bob, the author of this essay, looked and saw that the universe was beneath my contempt, and that to *remove* myself from it was the only thing of dignity a man could do.(p.531)
• It became second nature for me to *remove* myself from anything or anybody I found myself growing fond of.(p.545)

removed

• Instead, the problem has been *removed*.(p.85)
• God has either *removed* your husband's liquor problem or He has not.(p.120)
• Imagine my surprise when I read in a page one "box" that I had been taken from the theater unconscious around noon that day, *removed* by ambulance to a hospital and stomach-pumped and then released.(p.244)
• We went over these at great length and then he finally asked me if I wanted these defects of character *removed*.(p.292)
• I began making the rounds of the doctors in the hope that one of them might find some cure for my accumulating ailments, preferably something that could be *removed* surgically.(p.305)
• And we wonder how much further this man could go if his alcoholic problem could be *removed* and he could throw one hundred per cent of his abilities into action.(p.308)
• It explained so much I had not understood about myself and, best of all, it promised recovery if I would do a few simple things and be willing to have the desire to drink *removed*.(p.309)

removing

• Within a month, the police, the hospital authorities, several kind strangers, most of my friends, all of my close relatives, and a few adepts at rolling a drunk and *removing* his wrist watch and wallet had been involved.(p.532)

render

• The experiment of quitting for a period of time will be helpful, but we think we can *render* an even greater service to alcoholic sufferers and perhaps to the medical fraternity.(p.34)

rendered

• I was never drunk on the job, never missed a day's work, was seldom *rendered* totally ineffective by a hangover and kept my liquor expenses well within my adequate budget.(p.433)

rendezvous
• We have had long ***rendezvous*** with hurt pride, frustration, self-pity, misunderstanding and fear.(p.104)

renewal
• I very early came to see that there had to be a continual ***renewal*** for that simple deal with God; that I had perpetually to keep the bargain.(p.237)
• This duty together with my weekly meetings with my fellow alcoholics, and my daily ***renewal*** of the contract I originally made with God, have kept me sober when nothing else ever did.(p.237)

renewed
• Nevertheless, I still thought I could control the situation, and there were periods of sobriety which ***renewed*** my wife's hope.(p.5)

renewing
• ***Renewing*** my resolve, I tried again.(p.5)
• During my visit there, ***renewing*** acquaintance with former friends, I soon spent most of my money.(p.252)

renews
• When he ***renews*** interest in such things, a feeling of jealousy may arise.(p.131)

rent
• I got behind in my ***rent***, but never in my drinking.(p.358)
• I don't remember any of them getting put out in the winter because they didn't pay their ***rent***.(p.527)
• Once I started drinking, I didn't care that the ***rent*** wasn't paid, or that there was no food in the house, or that my boys needed shoes.(p.527)

rented
• This was in Virginia, where I had ***rented*** a house with stables and a swimming pool, and the fall fox hunting had begun.(p.404)
• I ***rented*** a beautiful apartment on the banks of the Seine in the winter, and a chalet in Switzerland in the summer.(p.405)

renting
• He saw that I was unsettled, living away from my family and ***renting*** houses here and there.(p.403)

reorganized
• I saw that my friend was much more than inwardly ***reorganized***.(p.11)
• Every company in the country, except Firestone, was ***reorganized*** at that time.(p.197)

repair
• Now we go out to our fellows and ***repair*** the damage done in the past.(p.76)
• But we must try to ***repair*** the damage immediately lest we pay the penalty by a spree.(p.99)
• Let them remember that his drinking wrought all kinds of damage that may take long to ***repair***.(p.127)
• I'd been home about a week or ten days when one of my friends asked if I could ***repair*** one of his electrical outlets.(p.493)
• I went to this friend's shop to ***repair*** his electrical outlet and I noticed this lady.(p.493)

repaired
• As we shall see, he now means a great deal to his community, and the major liabilities of thirty years of hard drinking have been ***repaired*** in four.(p.156)
• I had ***repaired*** to one of these one morning with my jug and when I left late in the afternoon, I picked up a newspaper on the way home.(p.244)
• Still another friend and temporary host received me at four in the morning from the charge of a policeman who had found me "going to bed" in a garage far from the last place I could remember having been, a fashionable bar and restaurant in the theatrical district of New York, to which I had ***repaired*** after my date for that evening, a charming lady of the theatre who had refused my company for obvious reasons.(p.538)

repairs
• It is suggested that we do not try to do a lifetime of ***repairs*** in one day.(p.481)

reparation
• When your prospect has made such ***reparation*** as he can to his family, and has thoroughly explained to them the new principles by which he is living, he should proceed to put those principles into action at home.(p.98)

reparations
• Although these ***reparations*** take innumerable forms, there are some general principles which we find guiding.(p.79)

repeal
• At that time the ***repeal*** whiskies were back, and I'd go to the store and buy my whiskey and take it to my office and put it under the desk, first in one place and then in another, and there soon was an accumulation of empty bottles.(p.488)

repeat
• I ***repeat***, I am one of the fortunate members of A.A. -- a lucky guy who is very grateful.(p.368)

repeated
• This is ***repeated*** over and over, and unless this person can experience an entire psychic change there is very little hope of his recovery.(p.xxvii)
• We are sorry for what we have done and, God willing, it shall not be ***repeated***.(p.81)
• Wait until ***repeated*** stumbling convinces him he must act, for the more you hurry him the longer his recovery may be delayed.(p.113)
• So Paul ***repeated*** substantially what Dr. Bob had said.(p.207)
• They realized that ***repeated*** lack of drinking control, when they really wanted control, was the fatal symptom that spelled problem drinking.(p.315)
• ***Repeated*** year on end, they are horrible -- frightening and degrading, a chronicle of tragedy which may be greater because the individual undergoing the tragedy, myself, knew what was happening, and yet refused to do anything to stop it.(p.538)

repeatedly
• This physician had ***repeatedly*** tried spiritual means to resolve his alcoholic dilemma but had failed.(p.xvi)
• It has been ***repeatedly*** proven among us that upon this simple cornerstone a wonderfully effective spiritual structure can be built.(p.47)
• One of the things that came up ***repeatedly*** in the stories they told me was that once they had accepted the program, they never had a desire to take a drink.(p.219)
• They had also been periodic big shots who had goofed out ***repeatedly*** at the wrong time, and they also knew how to split one paper match into three separate matches.(p.245)

repeats
• What sort of thinking dominates an alcoholic who ***repeats*** time after time the desperate experiment of the first drink?(p.35)

repel
• A spirit of intolerance might ***repel*** alcoholics whose lives could have been saved, had it not been for such stupidity.(p.103)

repetition
• If a ***repetition*** is to be prevented, place the problem, along with everything else, in God's hands.(p.120)
• The only reality I was able to face had been forced upon me by its very ***repetition*** -- I had to drink; and I didn't know there was anything in the world that could be done about it.(p.548)

replaced
• Some time passed, and confidence began to be ***replaced*** by cock-sureness.(p.5)
• Though old buildings will eventually be ***replaced*** by finer ones, the new structures will take years to complete.(p.123)
• This dream world has been ***replaced*** by a great sense of purpose, accompanied by a growing consciousness of the power of God in our lives.(p.130)
• Courage to face each day has ***replaced*** the fears and uncertainties of earlier years.(p.295)
• Acceptance of things as they are has ***replaced*** the old impatient champing at the bit to conquer the world.(p.295)
• This great experience that released me from the bondage of hatred and ***replaced*** it with love is really just another affirmation of the truth I know: I get everything I need in Alcoholics Anonymous – everything I need I get – and when I get what I need I invariably find that it was just what I wanted all the time.(p.553)

replayed
• In my mind's eye, I played and ***replayed*** scenes in which I was plucked magically from the bar where I stood nursing a drink, and was instantly exalted to some position of power and prestige.(p.560)

replenish
• And then my waiting until I was sure he was asleep, and stealing money from him to ***replenish*** the supply.(p.466)

replied
• "Yes," ***replied*** the doctor, "there is.(p.27)
• She ***replied***, "Yes, we've got a corker.(p.156)
• Hopelessness was written large on the man's face as he ***replied***, "Oh, but that's no use.(p.157)
• Knowing Bob of old, she jokingly ***replied***, "Well, Doctor, I suppose you've already tried it yourself?"(p.188)
• "Sure I would," ***replied*** Bill, "Maybe it won't do any good, but I'd like to see you both, anyhow.(p.189)
• I had ***replied***, "Uncle, give the judge ten dollars, or I'll have to work it out on the county road."(p.539)

reply
• Asked why they commenced to drink again, they would ***reply*** with some silly excuse, or none.(p.107)
• He would invariably ***reply***, "When you are right and the time is right, Providence will provide.(p.293)
• The ***reply*** came, putting me in touch by mail with my sponsor in New Delhi.(p.343)
• Many times have I heard the above expressions since I have been in A.A., and many times I have had to ***reply*** "Definitely I am an alcoholic, and while it may be hard for you to believe, it is not hard for me, for I have learned many things about alcohol and myself that would, perhaps, be difficult for you to understand."(p.356)
• I didn't ***reply***.(p.422)
• I'd ***reply*** and some of my letters they saved.(p.427)
• He makes no ***reply***, and hardly seems to see me.(p.501)
• "I know it," I ***reply***.(p.503)
• "I'll do anything," I ***reply***.(p.503)
• "Yes," I ***reply***.(p.504)
• If you cannot find A.A. in your locality, a letter addressed to Alcoholics Anonymous, Box 459, Grand Central Station, New York, NY 10163, U.S.A., will receive a prompt ***reply*** from this world center, referring you to the nearest A.A. group.(p.575)

report
• We heard by wireless on the 5th that the Armistice would be signed the next day (this was a premature ***report***) so I had a couple of cognacs to celebrate; then I hopped a truck and went AWOL.(p.242)
• It wasn't necessary to ***report*** to the office in person every day, and when I did go in, it was just to make an appearance and bounce right out again.(p.300)
• My dad, who was a newspaper man and had some connections, had meantime put a stop on me, and I guess that ***report*** went all over the country.(p.424)
• Each time I would make a ***report*** to the parole officer he would ask me, "Have you been to an A.A. meeting yet?"(p.510)
• After I had made my third ***report***, I stepped down town, met some of the old crowd, and of course you know the answer.(p.510)

reported
• The papers ***reported*** men jumping to death from the towers of High Finance.(p.4)
• "That's a devil of a way to run an organization," I thought, and I ***reported*** Frank to the psychiatrist, who didn't seem perturbed; he just got someone else to take me on Fridays.(p.447)
• He ***reported*** to the Headmaster and the Headmaster was going to expel me.(p.517)

reporter
• I again became a ***reporter*** on a Pittsburgh daily.(p.254)

reports
• At the end of it, my ***reports*** to Wall street procured me a position there and the use of a large expense account.(p.3)

represent
• All changes made over the years in the Big Book (A.A. members' fond nickname for this volume) have had the same purpose: to ***represent*** the current membership of Alcoholics Anonymous more accurately, and thereby to reach more alcoholics.(p.xii)
• We ***represent*** no particular faith or denomination.(p.93)

representatives
• All such ***representatives*** are to be guided in the spirit of service, for true leaders in A.A. are but trusted and experienced servants of the whole.(p.567)

represented
• All sections of this country and many of its occupations are ***represented***, as well as many political, economic, social, and religious backgrounds.(p.17)
• All sorts were ***represented*** and their relation of experiences and how they had found the only remedy, added to their human existence as sober men, laid the foundation of a very necessary faith.(p.258)
• I was working for a Chicago firm that ***represented*** several large radio stations.(p.358)
• At a large party in Geneva, with people from many countries ***represented***, the kind of party that is "protocol" in the extreme, I swayed, laughed hysterically, made naughty remarks in an unhushed voice, and

was finally led from the scene.(p.406)

represents
• This *represents* another great change for me.(p.284)

reprieve
• What we really have is a daily *reprieve* contingent on the maintenance of our spiritual condition.(p.85)
• One morning, however, I realized I had to get rid of it, for my *reprieve* was running out, and if I didn't get rid of it I was going to get drunk – and I didn't want to get drunk any more.(p.552)

reprimanded
• When I was criticized or *reprimanded,* the bottle was my refuge and comfort.(p.556)

reproached
• Father knows he is to blame; it may take him many seasons of hard work to be restored financially, but he shouldn't be *reproached.*(p.123)

reproduce
• It is impossible for me to *reproduce* my despair.(p.435)

reproduced
• Because the "long form" is more explicit and of possible historic value, it is also *reproduced.*(p.563)

reproved
• He may take small interest in the children and may show irritation when *reproved* for his delinquencies.(p.126)

repugnantly
• The word "insanity" came through clearly – and *repugnantly.*(p.332)

repulsive
• It was *repulsive* to me from every standpoint.(p.195)

reputation
• He wants to enjoy a certain *reputation,* but knows in his heart he doesn't deserve it.(p.73)
• We may lose our position or *reputation* or face jail, but we are willing.(p.79)
• He thus used his own wrong-doing as a means of destroying the *reputation* of another.(p.80)
• If he opened that old affair, he was afraid it would destroy the *reputation* of his partner, disgrace his family and take away his means of livelihood.(p.80)
• He is striving to recover fortune and *reputation* and feels he is doing very well.(p.126)
• Alcoholism may be causing your organization considerable damage in its waste of time, men and *reputation.*(p.148)
• Up to this point I had spent six years in the business and had enjoyed the *reputation* of being very successful.(p.298)
• My business *reputation* had reached from Vermont to Pennsylvania, but, thank goodness, my drinking *reputation* had not.(p.361)

reputations
• We have told innumerable lies to protect our pride and our husbands' *reputations.*(p.105)

repute
• How can they rise out of such misery, bad *repute* and hopelessness?(p.153)

reputedly
• My customers lost confidence in me to the point where I retained what business I had only because I was a well-trained and *reputedly* fine craftsman.(p.234)

request
• Very earnestly we ask the press also, to observe this *request,* for otherwise we shall be greatly handicapped.(p.xiii)
• The physician who at our *request,* gave us this letter, has been kind enough to enlarge upon his views in another statement which follows.(p.xxiv)
• We ask especially for freedom from self-will, and are careful to make no *request* for ourselves only.(p.87)

requested
• Later, he *requested* the privilege of being allowed to tell his story to other patients here and with some misgiving, we consented.(p.xxv)
• Even some of the saloon-keepers, where I had spent so much time and money, *requested* that I stay away from their places.(p.301)
• The American Psychiatric Association *requested,* in 1949, that a paper be prepared by one of the older members of Alcoholics Anonymous to be read at the Association's annual meeting of that year.(p.572)

requests
• Never was I to pray for myself, except as my *requests* bore on my usefulness to others.(p.13)

require
• To get over drinking will *require* a transformation of thought and attitude.(p.143)
• Indeed, I was beginning to see that I would *require* implicit faith, like a small child, if I was going to get anywhere.(p.259)
• Some of these were hard to believe, but it did not *require* a giant brain to perceive that they had something I could use.(p.279)
• Since the radio station was getting on its feet, it didn't *require* so many nights of evening work, and that permitted leisure time for drinking.(p.360)
• For me, pills don't produce the desire to swallow a pill; they produce the symptoms that *require* that the pill be taken for relief.(p.443)
• Secondary aids to A.A., such as clubs or hospitals which *require* much property or administration, ought to be incorporated and so set apart that, if necessary, they can be freely discarded by the groups.(p.566)

required
• On the other hand – and strange as this may seem to those who do not understand -- once a psychic change has occurred, the very same person who seemed doomed, who had so many problems he despaired of ever solving them, suddenly finds himself easily able to control his desire for alcohol, the only effort necessary being that *required* to follow a few simple rules.(p.xxvii)
• A tumbler full of gin followed by half a dozen bottles of beer would be *required* if I were to eat any breakfast.(p.5)
• Nothing more was *required* of me to make my beginning.(p.12)
• We went through two years of deadlock *required* by the English divorce laws.(p.405)

requirement
• The only *requirement* for membership is an honest desire to stop drinking.(p.xiv)
• The first *requirement* is that we be convinced that any life run on self-will can hardly be a success.(p.60)
• Three -- The only *requirement* for A.A. membership is a desire to stop drinking.(p.564)

requirements
• Belief in the power of God, plus enough willingness, honesty and humility to establish and maintain the new order of things, were the essential *requirements.*(p.13)
• This happened soon after they wholeheartedly met a few simple *requirements.*(p.50)

requires
• Of course an alcoholic ought to be freed from his physical craving for liquor, and this often *requires* a definite hospital procedure, before psychological measures can be of maximum benefit.(p.xxv)
• Almost none of us liked the self-searching, the leveling of our pride, the confession of shortcomings which the process *requires* for its successful consummation.(p.25)
• This *requires* action on our part, which, when completed, will mean that we have admitted to God, to ourselves, and to another human being the exact nature of our defects.(p.72)
• Those of us belonging to a religious denomination which *requires* confession must, and of course, will want to go to the properly appointed authority whose duty it is to receive it.(p.74)
• If we belong to a religious denomination which *requires* a definite morning devotion, we attend to that also.(p.87)
• He may rebel at the thought of a drastic housecleaning which *requires* discussion with other people.(p.94)
• We think each family which has been relieved owes something to those who have not, and when the occasion *requires,* each member of it should be only too willing to bring former mistakes, no matter how grievous, out of their hiding places.(p.124)
• Here was something requiring a greater willingness to assume responsibility, and take a larger degree of cooperation and "give and take" than even business *requires* of one.(p.286)
• The unwillingness to admit failure *requires* even further friendly intake.(p.331)
• The why is not important; the fact is that one drink will set up a reaction in our system which *requires* more; that one drink was too much and one hundred drinks were not enough.(p.380)

requiring
• Here was something *requiring* a greater willingness to assume responsibility, and take a larger degree of cooperation and "give and take" than even business requires of one.(p.286)

requisite
• Mom has said the only *requisite* to start is willingness.(p.430)

rescue
• We are like the passengers of a great liner the moment after *rescue* from shipwreck when camaraderie, joyousness and democracy pervade the vessel from steerage to Captains's table.(p.17)
• I managed to maintain myself with odd jobs, did ten weeks in a social *rescue* institution, and at length wound up in a second-hand bookstore in an adjacent town as manager.(p.257)

rescued
• He was *rescued* by a searching party, and, in desperate condition, brought to me.(p.xxix)
• I was down to my shorts, unaware of wrong-doing, before the ambulance got there and hauled me off to a hospital from which anxious friends *rescued* me, later that night.(p.537)

research
• The spirit of modern scientific inquiry, *research* and invention was almost unknown.(p.51)
• This same company spends millions for *research* every year.(p.149)
• This good and gentle man, a brilliant *research* doctor, got nowhere with me fast.(p.407)

resemblance
• I knew the man by name, and partly recognized his features, but there all *resemblance* ended.(p.xxix)

resembles
• His disposition while drinking *resembles* his normal nature but little.(p.21)

resembling
• The details of the long road back to something *resembling* normal living – the first short streetcar ride, the purchase of a used bike which enabled me to widen the narrow horizon of life, the first trip downtown – I will not dwell on.(p.276)

resent
• A man wasn't actually mistreated, though if he was he could only *resent it.*(p.485)
• He said, in effect: "If you have a resentment you want to be free of, if you will pray for the person or the thing that you *resent,* you will be free.(p.552)

resented
• I *resented* this very much, until she informed me that they were a couple of drunks just as I was.(p.184)
• I *resented* it of course, and I offered Clarence his commission, whatever it might be, if he would please not bother me because I had arrived at the conclusion that he was a solicitor for some alcoholic institute.(p.216)
• I *resented* the fact that Frank had done this to me, and I just didn't know what was going on.(p.388)
• But Frank was frightened to death to give it to me, because I *resented* everything he said and did.(p.391)
• I *resented* this, but I did nothing constructive about it.(p.402)
• My mother *resented* it so that the first Christmas after our marriage, she didn't even invite us to dinner.(p.485)
• Of course, when father finally came to Virginia to work his way through school, he *resented* the southern "cracker," as he often called them, so much that he didn't even go back to his mother's funeral.(p.486)

resentful
• I'm *resentful* at:(p.65)
• After a few years with an alcoholic, a wife gets worn out, *resentful* and uncommunicative.(p.81)
• Were we *resentful,* selfish, dishonest or afraid?(p.86)
• But be careful not to be *resentful* about the last time he did so.(p.116)
• Just be careful not to disagree in a *resentful* or critical spirit.(p.117)
• When *resentful* thoughts come, try to pause and count your blessings.(p.119)
• We find the more one member of the family demands that the others concede to him, the more *resentful* they become.(p.122)
• As each member of a *resentful* family begins to see his short comings and admits them to the others, he lays a basis for helpful discussion.(p.127)
• These family talks will be constructive if they can be carried on without heated argument, self-pity, self-justification or *resentful* criticism.(p.127)
• And I wasn't *resentful* toward her, either.(p.270)

resenting
• *Resenting* anyone and everyone who might interfere with my personal plans and ways of doing things, I was full of self pity, especially for any interference with my drinking.(p.376)

resentment

- We made a list of people I had hurt or toward whom I felt ***resentment***.(p.13)
- I was not too well at the time, and was plagued by waves of self-pity and ***resentment***.(p.15)
- It brings misunderstanding, fierce ***resentment***, financial insecurity, disgusted friends and employers, warped lives of blameless children, sad wives and parents -- anyone can increase the list.(p.18)
- ***Resentment*** is the "number one" offender.(p.64)
- It is plain that a life which includes deep ***resentment*** leads only to futility and unhappiness.(p.66)
- But with the alcoholic, whose hope is the maintenance and growth of a spiritual experience, this business of ***resentment*** is infinitely grave.(p.66)
- We put them on paper, even though we had no ***resentment*** in connection with them.(p.68)
- Because of ***resentment*** and drinking, he had not paid alimony to his first wife.(p.79)
- Continue to watch for selfishness, dishonesty, ***resentment***, and fear.(p.84)
- You should warn against arousing ***resentment*** or jealousy.(p.100)
- We have been driven to maudlin sympathy, to bitter ***resentment***.(p.104)
- Never forget that ***resentment*** is a deadly hazard to an alcoholic.(p.117)
- Another feeling we are very likely to entertain is one of ***resentment*** that love and loyalty could not cure our husbands of alcoholism.(p.118)
- ***Resentment*** grows.(p.126)
- The greatest enemies of us alcoholics are ***resentment***, jealousy, envy, frustration, and fear.(p.145)
- All the other people that had talked to me wanted to help me, and my pride prevented me from listening to them, and caused only ***resentment*** on my part, but I felt as if I would be a real stinker if I did not listen to a couple of fellows for a short time, if that would cure them.(p.185)
- But I don't believe now that it was with any deep feeling of ***resentment*** that I said to him, "The children are raised, and if this is the way you want it, this is the way we'll have it.(p.263)
- However, what I had gained materially on the credit side of my ledger, I have since learned was more than offset on the debit side by egotism, ***resentment*** and dishonesty.(p.356)
- I began hitting the bottle again, and with it self-pity, ***resentment***, loneliness and remorse set in deeply.(p.362)
- We reverted to the old way of life we knew -- a life full of anger, vindictiveness, ***resentment***, fear, dependence, denial, self-will, irresponsibility.(p.459)
- In part, it was a feeling of intense shame at having to leave the Army during the war, but mostly it was ***resentment*** that this kind of thing should happen to me for, strange as it may seem, up to then I still thought I could control drinking.(p.521)
- I stayed there just long enough to work up a real good ***resentment*** against the doctor in charge, who I didn't think was doing anything at all except collecting fees, and I left there fully determined that I'd never put myself in the power of medical people again.(p.521)
- I was immersed in self-pity and ***resentment***, and the only people who would support this attitude or who I felt understood me at all were the people I met in bars and the ones who drank as I did.(p.547)
- By this time I was such a past master at kidding myself that I had convinced myself I had sat out a war and waited for this man to come home and, as my ***resentment*** and self-pity grew, so did my alcoholic problem.(p.548)
- As I said earlier, self-pity and ***resentment*** were my constant companions and my inventory began to look like a thirty-three year diary, for I seemed to have a ***resentment*** against everybody I had ever known.(p.551)
- In my prayers that morning I asked God to point out to me some way to be free of this ***resentment***.(p.552)
- During the day a friend of mine brought me some magazines to take to a hospital group I was interested in, and I looked through them and a "banner" across the front of one featured an article by a prominent clergyman in which I caught the word "***resentment***."(p.552)
- He said, in effect: "If you have a ***resentment*** you want to be free of, if you will pray for the person or the thing that you resent, you will be free.(p.552)
- Do it every day for two weeks and you will find you have come to mean it and to want it for them, and you will realize that where you used to feel bitterness and ***resentment*** and hatred, you now feel compassionate understanding and love."(p.552)
- Bewilderment, fear, and ***resentment*** moved into my life.(p.556)

resentments

- Whatever our protestations, are not most of us concerned with ourselves, our ***resentments***, or our self-pity?(p.62)
- In dealing with ***resentments***, we set them on paper.(p.64)
- We saw that these ***resentments*** must be mastered, but how?(p.66)
- We have listed and analyzed our ***resentments***.(p.70)
- Some of the snags you will encounter are irritation, hurt feeling and ***resentments***.(p.117)
- I had no ***resentments*** against individuals -- the whole world was all wrong.(p.244)
- At the moral inventory, he brought up some of my bad personality traits or character defects, such as selfishness, conceit, jealousy, carelessness, intolerance, ill-temper, sarcasm and ***resentments***.(p.292)
- I can't afford ***resentments*** against anyone, because they are the build-up of another drunk.(p.325)
- Slowly, my life seemed to unfold before me, shedding insights on childhood ***resentments***, jealousies, and fears that had mushroomed in adulthood, and also on the self-pity that I had wallowed in at every opportunity.(p.371)
- It was at this stage of my life that ***resentments*** came in.(p.376)
- Over a period of time he has built up self pity, ***resentments*** toward anyone or anything that interferes with his drinking.(p.380)
- Had I tried honestly and sincerely to practice the Twelve Steps I would have seen from my continuous moral inventory that I was getting off the beam -- I would have found that there were some active ***resentments*** in my life, a terrific amount of self-pity.(p.471)
- I don't have any ***resentments***.(p.511)
- But I came out of the Army just as big a drunk as when I went in, if not worse, because now I had a lot more ***resentments***.(p.513)
- For example, we are told in A.A. that we cannot afford ***resentments*** and self-pity, so we learn to avoid these festering mental attitudes.(p.560)

reservation

- If we are planning to stop drinking, there must be no ***reservation*** of any kind, nor any lurking notion that someday we will be immune to alcohol.(p.33)
- The wording was, of course, quite optional so long as we expressed the idea, voicing it without ***reservation***.(p.63)
- So, after reviewing these things and realizing what liquor had cost me, I went to this Higher Power which, to me was God, without any ***reservation***, and admitted that I was completely powerless over alcohol, and that I was willing to do anything in the world to get rid of the problem.(p.187)
- I only know that it does -- if you desire it with your whole heart and without ***reservation***.(p.384)
- From a Canadian ***reservation*** to overseas bars to New England lockups, an Indian traveled a long trail that finally led him home to A.A.(p.474)
- I was born a Maliseet Indian on ***reservation*** in Canada.(p.474)
- Was altar boy at church on ***reservation***.(p.474)
- Met father (Tall Man) at fork in road -- one way to ***reservation***, other way to State of Maine.(p.475)
- Start group on ***reservation*** and carry message, help start other groups all over Maritimes and New England.(p.476)

reservations

- The next thing they wanted to know was would I be willing to go to this Higher Power and ask for help, calmly and without any ***reservations***.(p.186)

reserve

- Highly competent psychiatrists who have dealt with us have found it sometimes impossible to persuade an alcoholic to discuss his situation without ***reserve***.(p.18)

reserved

- Had not people said God had ***reserved*** this privilege to the birds?(p.51)

reserves

- Then too, we view with much concern those A.A. treasuries which continue, beyond prudent ***reserves***, to accumulate funds for no stated A.A. purpose.(p.566)

reservoirs

- Dr. Foster Kennedy, neurologist: "This organization of Alcoholics Anonymous calls on two of the greatest ***reservoirs*** of power known to man, religion and that instinct for association with one's fellows . . . the 'herd instinct.'(p.571)

residency

- And as I went through pharmacy school, graduate school, medical school, internship, ***residency***, and specialty training and, finally, went into practice, my drinking kept increasing.(p.441)

resident

- His call to the clergyman led him presently to a certain ***resident*** of the town, who, though formerly able and respected, was then nearing the nadir of alcoholic despair.(p.155)

residential

- That had been in the center of New York, on noisy 42nd Street . . . this was obviously a quiet ***residential*** section.(p.223)

resign

- Here are some of the methods we have tried: Drinking beer only, limiting the number of drinks, never drinking alone, never drinking in the morning, drinking only at home, never having it in the house, never drinking during business hours, drinking only at parties, switching from scotch to brandy, drinking only natural wines, agreeing to ***resign*** if ever drunk on the job, taking a trip, not taking a trip, swearing off forever (with and without a solemn oath), taking more physical exercise, reading inspirational books, going to health farms and sanitariums, accepting voluntary commitment to asylums -- we could increase the list ad infinitum.(p.31)
- But if you cannot or will not stop drinking, I think you ought to ***resign***."(p.148)

resignation

- No one in that company saw me again -- ten days later I wired my ***resignation***.(p.243)
- They are not ideas of ***resignation*** but of the recognition of certain basic facts of living.(p.382)

resigned

- Everyone became ***resigned*** to the certainty that I would have to be shut up somewhere, or would stumble along to a miserable end.(p.8)
- Having regard for the law of the land, I ***resigned*** myself to the will of the national legislators and quit drinking altogether, not because I had found it harmful, but because I couldn't get what I was accustomed to drink.(p.232)

resist

- Following his physical rehabilitation, he had a talk with me in which he frankly stated he thought the treatment a waste of effort, unless I could assure him, which no one ever had, that in the future he would have the "will power" to ***resist*** the impulse to drink.(p.xxix)
- As I go along I seem to get strength daily to be able to ***resist*** more easily.(p.237)

resistance

- I now conceive the psychiatrist's job to be the task of breaking down the patient's inner ***resistance*** so that which is inside him will flower, as under the activity of the A.A. program."(p.571)

resisted

- I could go for such conceptions as Creative Intelligence, Universal Mind or Spirit of Nature but I ***resisted*** the thought of a Czar of the Heavens, however loving His sway might be.(p.12)
- Though some of us ***resisted***, we found no great difficulty in casting aside such feelings.(p.48)

resolutely

- Putting out of our minds the wrongs others had done, we ***resolutely*** looked for our own mistakes.(p.67)
- Then we ***resolutely*** turn our thoughts to someone we can help.(p.84)

resolution

- After they have succumbed to the desire again, as so many do, and the phenomenon of craving develops, they pass through the well-known stages of a spree, emerging remorseful, with a firm ***resolution*** not to drink again.(p.xxvii)
- This ***resolution*** I kept steadfastly for the next forty years, except when circumstances made it seem unwise to absent myself.(p.172)
- Forty came and went and then the ***resolution*** was advanced to forty-one, forty-two, and so on in the usual pattern.(p.214)
- I remembered my loud ***resolution*** to find him and ask him to help me get into that "Asylum" he had written about.(p.224)
- Formerly, in the acute mental and physical pain during the remorseful periods succeeding each drunk, I found my recollection of the misery I had gone through a bolsterer of ***resolution*** and afterward, perhaps, a deterrent for a time.(p.260)

resolutions

- They are over-remorseful and make many *resolutions*, but never a decision.(p.xxviii)
- Some will be drunk the day after making their *resolutions*; most of them within a few weeks.(p.34)
- Successive Monday morning hangovers, which despite mid-week *resolutions* to do better, came with unfailing regularity, eventually caused me to quit my job.(p.254)
- Enduring all the hangover hells that every alcoholic experiences, I made the usual *resolutions*.(p.256)
- With new hope in my heart and new *resolutions* I set off for Vermont.(p.360)

resolve

- This physician had repeatedly tried spiritual means to *resolve* his alcoholic dilemma but had failed.(p.xvi)
- Where had been my high *resolve*?(p.5)
- Renewing my *resolve*, I tried again.(p.5)
- This had the effect of making me *resolve* that when I was free from parental domination, I would never again darken the doors of a church.(p.172)
- Sometimes, after sobering up after a bout of several weeks, I would righteously *resolve* to quit.(p.233)

resolved

- These periods became more frequent and I *resolved* that when I became forty, which was very shortly, I was going on the wagon.(p.213)
- I still had enough practice to earn a good living if I would only work, so I *resolved* that in January of 1940 I would launch a patent law firm of my own.(p.220)
- I *resolved* that if I were going to continue with the Catholic Church, I was going to know the roots of the doctrine, since those roots had caused me some confusion.(p.221)
- With a great deal of determination, I would throw out full pints – pour them out and smash the bottles -- firmly *resolved* never to take another drink of the stuff.(p.234)

resolves

- And just as we were being convinced of their heartlessness, they would surprise us with fresh *resolves* and new attentions.(p.107)

resort

- I had the best schools, summer camps, *resort* vacations and travel.(p.304)
- I returned to my home in Lucknow, India, at the end of November last year from a vacation in one of the most famous beauty spots in our country, a mountain *resort* 6,800 feet up, with a wonderful lake.(p.342)
- Eight years ago, my wife and I decided to spend a vacation in Naini Tal, the mountain *resort*.(p.343)
- I did not *resort* to semi-prostitution for the price of a drink.(p.412)

resorted

- But during a period of particular stress and strain about thirteen years ago, I *resorted* to alcohol in my home, alone, as a means of temporary release, as a means of getting a little extra sleep.(p.335)

resorts

- Most of us have entered the final stage with its commitment to health *resorts*, sanitariums, hospitals, and jails.(p.107)

resource

- With few exceptions our members find that they have tapped an unsuspected inner *resource* which they presently identify with their own conception of a Power greater than themselves.(p.569)

resources

- Our human *resources*, as marshalled by the will were not sufficient; they failed utterly.(p.45)
- In the face of collapse and despair, in the face of the total failure of their human *resources*, they found that a new power, peace, happiness, and sense of direction flowed into them.(p.50)
- They shared their homes, their slender *resources*, and gladly devoted their spare hours to fellow-sufferers.(p.159)

respect

- Then there are types entirely normal in every *respect* except in the effect alcohol has upon them.(p.xxviii)
- Most of us sense that real tolerance of other people's shortcomings and viewpoints and a *respect* for their opinions are attitudes which make us more useful to others.(p.19)
- He is often perfectly sensible and well balanced concerning everything except liquor, but in that *respect* he is incredibly dishonest and selfish.(p.21)
- What has become of the common sense and will power that he still sometimes displays with *respect* to other matters?(p.22)
- He seemed quite rational and well-balanced with *respect* to other problems.(p.26)
- Our behavior is as absurd and incomprehensible with *respect* to the first drink as that of an individual with a passion, say, for jay-walking.(p.37)
- Though not a religious person, I have profound *respect* for the spiritual approach in such cases as yours.(p.43)
- In this *respect* alcohol was a great persuader.(p.48)
- We doubt if, in this *respect*, alcoholics are fundamentally much worse than other people.(p.81)
- My health is good and I have regained my self-respect and the *respect* of my colleagues.(p.180)
- My case is rather unusual in one *respect*.(p.182)
- I said, "Yes, Doc, I would like to quit, at least for five, six, or eight months, until I get things straightened up, and begin to get the *respect* of my wife and some other people back, and get my finances fixed up and so on."(p.187)
- My children had lost *respect* for me and, in fact, it was only after three or four years of sobriety that any of them ever said anything to me to indicate that I had recouped even a little of their *respect*.(p.215)
- Professionally, after I was sober for a month or so I realized that I should school myself to dissolve the partnership I was in because I felt that I would never regain the *respect* of my partners no matter how long I was sober, and that I would be at a disadvantage.(p.220)
- When I drank, I hid it from my folks out of *respect* for their feelings.(p.287)
- He said they were sober, happy and had their self-respect back as well as the *respect* of their neighbors.(p.289)
- A few months after I made my original trip to Akron I was feeling pretty cocky, and I didn't think my wife was treating me with proper *respect*, now that I was an outstanding citizen.(p.293)
- Where derision, contempt and pity were once shown me, I now enjoy the *respect* of many people.(p.296)
- I can't bear to be here when you lose the *respect* of others, and above all – when you lose your own self *respect*."(p.362)
- I can't bear to be here when you lose the *respect* of others, and above all when you lose your own self *respect*."(p.363)
- I had a long talk with a psychiatrist, but nothing came of that, and I had also, just about that time, talked with a minister for whom I had a great deal of *respect*.(p.489)
- Since I've been home, I have been able to gain the *respect* of my two sons again.(p.529)
- There was the father one lost *respect* for at the age of eleven, because the father broke his solemn word in a circumstance where you, eleven years old, had assumed guilt when you were innocent; but the father would not believe you, no matter what; and to ease his suffering you "confessed" and were "forgiven," only – months later – to have your "guilt" brought up – only he and you knew what he was talking bout -- brought up in front of the stern grandmother.(p.533)
- 4. -- With *respect* to its own affairs, each A.A group should be responsible to no other authority than its own conscience.(p.565)
- Universal *respect* is the key to their usefulness.(p.567)

respectability

- I had been far too busy building, protecting, and maintaining an image of *respectability* and all the other business pluses.(p.327)
- There would be times when the life of *respectability* and achievement seemed insufferably dull -- I had to break out.(p.432)
- I'd claw my way back to "*respectability*" and stay there – until the inevitable next time.(p.432)
- With all this, it was becoming increasingly hard to maintain my front of distinction and *respectability* to the world.(p.435)

respectable

- I was suffering from an actual disease that had a name and symptoms like diabetes or cancer or TB -- and a disease was *respectable*, not a moral stigma!(p.227)
- My life there was a nightmare of periodic binges on alcohol and pills, adultery, unhappy hours at the dental office, seeing my wife give birth to our second child and have several miscarriages, living in a turbulent household, and making continual attempts to be the *respectable* dentist, husband, father, and community leader.(p.419)
- One, the side I turned to myself and the world, was *respectable* -- even, in some ways, distinguished.(p.432)

respected

- Each is interested in having his or her wishes *respected*.(p.122)
- It may seem incredible that these men are to become happy, *respected*, and useful once more.(p.153)
- His call to the clergyman led him presently to a certain resident of the town, who, though formerly able and *respected*, was then nearing the nadir of alcoholic despair.(p.155)
- He too, has become a *respected* and useful member of his community.(p.158)
- Why am I alive, free, a *respected* member of my community?(p.421)
- Alcoholism had *respected* nobody, neither rich nor poor, learned nor unlettered.(p.455)

respecter

- Alcohol being no *respecter* of persons, we are an accurate cross section of America, and in distant lands, the same democratic evening-up process is now going on.(p.xx)
- He further explained that alcohol was no *respecter* of sex or background, but that most of the alcoholics he had encountered had better than average minds and abilities.(p.308)
- As I later found out through Alcoholics Anonymous, alcohol is no *respecter* of economic status, social and business standing or intelligence.(p.373)

respecting

- My personal definition, which I submit as applying only to myself (although everyone is welcome to it who wants it), includes every waking activity of the human being; to have a creative attitude towards things is a more exact meaning, to live and to deal with other human beings creatively, which to me means seeing the God in them, and *respecting* and worshipping this God.(p.535)

respective

- A much more important demonstration of our principles lies before us in our *respective* homes, occupations and affairs.(p.19)
- When we first come into A.A., many of us are confused because as a general rule we're at the end of our *respective* ropes, and we don't know what to do.(p.512)

respects

- It relieved me somewhat to learn that in alcoholics the will is amazingly weakened when it comes to combating liquor, though it often remains strong in other *respects*.(p.7)
- However intelligent we may have been in other *respects*, where alcohol has been involved, we have been strangely insane.(p.38)
- Though his family be at fault in many *respects*, he should not be concerned about that.(p.98)
- The successful demonstration I had made of my life problems in other *respects* convinced me that some day I was going to be able to drink like a gentleman.(p.214)
- I see where I have been wrong in some *respects*.(p.505)
- My reaction to this was identical in many *respects* to my reaction to my parents leaving me when I was seven.(p.547)

respond

- Many types do not *respond* to the ordinary psychological approach.(p.xxvii)
- Do not be discouraged if your prospect does not *respond* at once.(p.96)
- Though an alcoholic does not *respond*, there is no reason why you should neglect his family.(p.97)

responded

- All but one "*responded* to the treatment" suggested in the Steps immediately, but this one posed a problem.(p.551)

response

- Nothing in their lives took precedence over their *response* to a call for help from some alcoholic in need.(p.310)

responsibilities

- Never avoid these *responsibilities*, but be sure you are doing the right thing if you assume them.(p.97)
- She met these *responsibilities* gallantly.(p.130)
- Nearly every modern employer feels a moral responsibility for the well-being of his help, and he tries to meet these *responsibilities*.(p.137)
- But what about his *responsibilities* -- his family and the men who would die because they would not know how to get well, ah -- yes, those other alcoholics?(p.154)
- He got in touch with a prominent psychiatrist who had undertaken certain *responsibilities* for the mental health of the community.(p.163)
- About that period, too, came increasing procrastination and the avoidance of *responsibilities*.(p.197)

• My divorce coincided with my father's bankruptcy, and I went to work, casting off all allegiances and ***responsibilities*** to any other than myself.(p.225)
• With God's help I am able, for one day at a time, to carry business ***responsibilities*** which, not many years ago, I would not have dreamed of assuming.(p.284)
• Surrender to me has meant the ability to run my home, to face my ***responsibilities*** as they should be faced, to take life as it comes to me day by day, and work my problems out.(p.340)
• I had a family to be proud of, actively sharing in the ***responsibilities*** of good citizenship.(p.374)
• My ***responsibilities*** had been a restraining influence.(p.379)
• Making amends is sometimes doing what we are capable of doing but failed to do because of alcohol; carrying out community ***responsibilities*** such as Community Funds, Red Cross, educational and religious activities in proportion to our abilities and energy.(p.381)
• But I thought it was because my ***responsibilities*** were increasing.(p.441)
• "If you had my ***responsibilities***, if you needed the sleep like I do, you'd drink too."(p.441)

responsibility

• Both of you will awaken to a new sense of ***responsibility*** for others.(p.119)
• Nearly every modern employer feels a moral ***responsibility*** for the well-being of his help, and he tries to meet these responsibilities.(p.137)
• Here was something requiring a greater willingness to assume ***responsibility***, and take a larger degree of cooperation and "give and take" than even business requires of one.(p.286)
• "We watch the alcoholic performing in a position of ***responsibility*** and we know that because he is drinking heavily and daily he has cut his capacities by fifty per cent, and still he seems able to do a satisfactory job.(p.308)
• Where we used to run from ***responsibility***, we find ourselves accepting it with gratitude that we can successfully shoulder it.(p.311)
• ***Responsibility*** again.(p.402)
• In the course of drunken arguments, I found my own views and sense of ***responsibility*** as a citizen.(p.410)
• I graduated with honors, but could not feel any real ***responsibility*** as a father or a husband.(p.419)
• Max accepted ***responsibility*** for me after I had promised never to drink again, never to take another pill, never to swear again, and never to talk to girls again.(p.444)
• There go my good intentions, fear of consequences, will to care, ***responsibility*** for my behavior.(p.458)
• And having sung that phrase, I'd chuckle with amusement, turning into irony turning into self-contempt turning into self-pity, at the sad fate of Bob, that wonderful, poor little motherless boy who was so smart in school and who grew up to accept ***responsibility*** so early and so fast and who staggered under his burdens without a whimper until the time came when he thought he was too good for this world and so he ought to be out of it.(p.532)
• It seemed logical to me that if I married this man and took the ***responsibility*** for these children that they would keep me sober.(p.548)
• With deep shame came the knowledge too that I had lived with no sense of social obligation nor had I known the meaning of moral ***responsibility*** to my fellow men.(p.549)
• Their management should be the sole ***responsibility*** of those people who financially support them.(p.566)

responsible

• Their defects may be glaring, but the chances are that our own actions are partly ***responsible***.(p.83)
• It is better for him to feel fully ***responsible***.(p.143)
• At that time, I was living out of town, so I moved back to the home town and made a connection in a ***responsible*** position with one of the larger companies in the finance business.(p.298)
• But somehow my good doctor heard of this book and also he learned a little about the people ***responsible*** for its publication.(p.307)
• I was living in a small room on West 53rd Street right off Fifth Avenue, when I met a young lady who eventually was ***responsible*** for altering my entire way of living.(p.359)
• He went into the religious side and told me that I didn't attend church as regularly as I should, and that he felt, more or less, that this was ***responsible*** for my trouble.(p.489)
• Thinking only of two or three dollars to buy some whiskey, I did the job and that's how I met Ella G., who was ***responsible*** for my coming into A.A.(p.493)
• There was nothing in my school life that I can look back on which was ***responsible*** for anything that happened afterwards.(p.517)
• My doctor finally declared he could no longer be ***responsible*** for me, and sent me to a psychiatrist who practiced in the same suite of offices.(p.558)
• Nine – A.A., as such, ought never be organized; but we may create service boards or committees directly ***responsible*** to those they serve.(p.564)
• 4. – With respect to its own affairs, each A.A group should be ***responsible*** to no other authority than its own conscience.(p.565)

rest

• For myself, I had adopted those parts which seemed convenient and not too difficult; the ***rest*** I disregarded.(p.11)
• Let us tell you the ***rest*** of the conversation our friend had with his doctor.(p.27)
• Far from admitting he was an alcoholic, he told himself he came to the hospital to ***rest*** his nerves.(p.39)
• He was positive that his humiliating experience, plus the knowledge he had acquired, would keep him sober the ***rest*** of his life.(p.40)
• Each person is like an actor who wants to run the whole show; is forever trying to arrange the lights, the ballet, the scenery and the ***rest*** of the players in his own way.(p.60)
• Is it not evident to all the ***rest*** of the players that these are the things he wants?(p.61)
• He is like the retired business man who lolls in the Florida sunshine in the winter complaining of the sad state of the nation; the minister who sighs over the sins of the twentieth century; politicians and reformers who are sure all would be Utopia if the ***rest*** of the world would only behave; the outlaw safe cracker who thinks society has wronged him; and the alcoholic who has lost all and is locked up.(p.61)
• Having persevered with the ***rest*** of the program, they wondered why they fell.(p.73)
• It is easy to let up on the spiritual program of action and ***rest*** on our laurels.(p.85)
• He may not see at once that he has barely scratched a limitless lode which will pay dividends only if he mines it for the ***rest*** of his life and insists on giving away the entire product.(p.129)
• If he says yes, does he really mean it, or down inside does he think he is fooling you, and that after ***rest*** and treatment he will be able to get away with a few drinks now and then?(p.142)
• But I watched him, and he tossed off the ***rest*** of his, so I tossed off the ***rest*** of mine.(p.195)
• The people in the group hadn't been around that day; part of my family was in Florida and the ***rest*** of them weren't speaking to me, so I spent a very lonesome day and by evening I was feeling very sorry for myself.(p.207)
• Little more of our talk stayed in my memory, but I do know I slept the ***rest*** of that night while before I had never known what a real night's sleep was.(p.239)
• They did not show me to my room and wish me a good night's ***rest***.(p.259)
• I feared that I wasn't dressed like the ***rest***.(p.261)
• Three more months of being up and around the house for brief periods and in bed the ***rest*** of the time.(p.275)
• The ***rest*** of my time was devoted to A.A. spadework.(p.281)
• Those three weeks left me completely exhausted and I had to return to Akron for three more months of ***rest***.(p.282)
• This gave me the freedom to do A.A. work, and to ***rest*** for periods of two or three days when I became too exhausted to carry on.(p.283)
• Handling customers, dealers, insurance people, dictation, telephoning, directing new employees, answering to superiors, and all the ***rest*** of it.(p.299)
• Most of them prescribed sedatives and advised ***rest*** and moderation.(p.305)
• Many retirees embrace alcoholism while secluded in motor trailers, ***rest*** homes, leisure-world bungalows, mountain cabins, or beach cottages, or even in penthouses, on yachts, and inside Palm Springs cabanas.(p.329)
• That life for me is lived one day at a time, letting the problems of the future ***rest*** with the future.(p.340)
• The Great Boss has given me diagnostic and surgical talent, and He has loaned it to me to use for the ***rest*** of my life.(p.350)
• So I went to her and said, "There's only one thing I want in my whole life, and I don't want any commendation; I don't want any credit; I don't want anything from you or Janey for the ***rest*** of your life except one thing; and that is, the opportunity to do anything you want always, and I would like to start off by doing the dishes."(p.351)
• I had every advantage a child could have, private schools (several of them), dancing schools, two colleges, coon skin coats, automobiles, a listing in the social register and all the ***rest***.(p.357)
• Near the Laundromat, I would buy one bottle of pop and a few bottles of beer or wine, and go into the ***rest*** room, empty the pop bottle, refill it with the booze, and proceed to do my laundering.(p.370)
• The only drawback was, I always knew how I arrived there, but somehow, between the ***rest*** room, the rinse, and the fluff-dry, I never knew when or how I got home.(p.370)
• To most of us, making amends will take the ***rest*** of our lives, but we can start immediately.(p.381)
• After nine months of training, all the ***rest*** of my class was paroled and I went to work in the Department of Corrections.(p.462)
• The ***rest*** of that week is pretty hazy.(p.466)
• I waited all the ***rest*** of that day and paced the floor all that night.(p.467)
• They were always there because of a nervous breakdown, or for a "***rest*** cure" – any reason except because of drinking.(p.471)
• I got out of that bill one pair of shoes, and the ***rest*** of that money was blown.(p.493)
• I have my ups and downs the same as the ***rest***.(p.511)

restaurant

• I'd been sitting comfortably in a ***restaurant*** with Rita, drinking my sixth martini and hoping the waiter would forget about the lunch order – at least long enough for me to have a couple more.(p.223)
• Tasting the best of burgundy at a famous ***restaurant*** one night, landed me passed out on a park bench in the public square.(p.405)
• I went out to a ***restaurant***, found a booth way back in the rear, and started drinking.(p.467)
• My father had purchased a ***restaurant***, which he felt would take up some of my spare time, and that's how I met Vi.(p.487)
• When I arrived at The Country Shop, which was a ***restaurant*** where they met in Dublin, I found about thirty-five or forty people in the room.(p.524)
• Still another friend and temporary host received me at four in the morning from the charge of a policeman who had found me "going to bed" in a garage far from the last place I could remember having been, a fashionable bar and ***restaurant*** in the theatrical district of New York, to which I had repaired after my date for that evening, a charming lady of the theatre who had refused my company for obvious reasons.(p.538)

restitution

• Though he could not accept all the tenets of the Oxford Groups, he was convinced of the need for moral inventory, confession of personality defects, ***restitution*** to those harmed, helpfulness to others, and the necessity of belief in and dependence upon God.(p.xvi)
• Dr. Bob then led me through the ***restitution*** step, in which I made a list of all of the persons I had harmed, and worked out ways and means of slowly making ***restitution***.(p.292)

restless

• They are ***restless***, irritable and discontented, unless they can again experience the sense of ease and comfort which comes at once by taking a few drinks -- drinks which they see others taking with impunity.(p.xxvi)
• I was there about three weeks, and then I got ***restless*** and started to tramp across the country, here and there, until I finally wound up in Pennsylvania, in a steel mill.(p.492)

restlessness

• In my late teens I became aware of emotions I'd not counted on; ***restlessness***, anxiety, fear and insecurity.(p.545)

restoration

• This self-insurance has resulted in the ***restoration*** of physical, mental and spiritual health and self-respect to hundreds of men and women who would be hopelessly down and out without its unique but effective therapy."(p.574)

restorative

• We are convinced that a spiritual mode of living is a most powerful health ***restorative***.(p.133)

restore

• 2.Came to believe that a Power greater than ourselves could ***restore*** us to sanity.(p.59)
• My experience in the hospital I considered to be terrific because Dr. Bob told me very quickly that medicine would have very little to do with it, outside of trying to ***restore*** my appetite for food.(p.217)
• The most accurate answer I can give you is this:

Fear has never again ruled my life since that day in September, 1938, when I found that a Power greater than myself could not only *restore* me to sanity but could keep me both sober and sane.(p.285)

• I can't say, "God could *restore* me to sanity, but until He does, I'll control myself – with pills."(p.443)

• With their help I also saw that certainly, because of some of the things I had done during the years, I was bordering on insanity, and so, facing the record, I tried to believe that a Power greater than I could and would *restore* me to sanity.(p.471)

• It's been true in my case, nor could I quarrel with "*restore* us to sanity," for my actions drunk or sober, before A.A., were not those of a sane person.(p.550)

restored

• God had *restored* his sanity.(p.57)

• Even so has God *restored* us all to our right minds.(p.57)

• Father knows he is to blame; it may take him many seasons of hard work to be *restored* financially, but he shouldn't be reproached.(p.123)

• Being wrecked in the same vessel, being *restored* and united under one God, with hearts and minds attuned to the welfare of others, the things which matter so much to some people no longer signify much to them.(p.161)

• I feel that I have been *restored* to health and sanity these past years not through my own efforts nor as a result of anything I may have done, but because I've come to believe -- to really believe – that alone I can do nothing.(p.473)

• The relationship between my wife and me was *restored* to a love and happiness that we had not known even before my alcoholism became acute.(p.559)

restrained

• After I came to A.A., I was divorced by my wife; I lost my practice; I was legally *restrained* from seeing my children; I went broke; and the dental society threatened me with the loss of my license.(p.420)

restraining

• Home life was again a *restraining* influence.(p.287)

• My responsibilities had been a *restraining* influence.(p.379)

• Tragedies during those years that were caused by my drinking, such as the breaking up of my marriage, the death of my child, other things -- had little *restraining* effect.(p.465)

restraint

• I can remember telling the poor little soul that I could probably quit drinking if I wasn't married to her, and told her that, after all, I didn't like *restraint*!(p.199)

• Naturally, what little *restraint* I had exercised before was gone now, and my drinking became worse.(p.199)

• Then I started drinking again, with possibly a little more *restraint*, periods a little bit longer than they had been before, but substantially the same pattern.(p.203)

• While working in an office, there was some semblance of *restraint*, but, oh boy, when I got on the outside with this new company without supervision, did I go to town!(p.300)

• The next steps were bottle hiding, and excuses for trips in order to drink without *restraint*.(p.375)

restraints

• So I was barred from the plant for ten days, and during that ten day period I was drunk twice, showing how little control these *restraints* had on me.(p.205)

• After such often-painful vigilance (and numerous phony stints of abstinence), retirement naturally created an impulse to live without *restraints*.(p.328)

• The doctor motioned to the corpsman to undo my straitjacket and leg *restraints*.(p.422)

restricted

• The second year my drinking was more or less *restricted* to week-ends, but I was nearly kicked out for scholastic failure.(p.241)

restrictions

• I believe that the release from people-pleasing *restrictions* gives retirees more motivation to drink than boredom does.(p.329)

result

• It is important that we remain anonymous because we are too few, at present to handle the overwhelming number of personal appeals which may *result* from this publication.(p.xiii)

• I found a job; then lost it as the *result* of a brawl with a taxi driver.(p.4)

• That was two months ago and the *result* was self-evident.(p.9)

• If we keep on the way we are going there is little doubt that much good will *result*, but the surface of the problem would hardly be scratched.(p.19)

• Some of us have tried to hold on to our old ideas and the *result* was nil until we let go absolutely.(p.58)

• 12.Having had a spiritual awakening as the *result* of these steps, we tried to carry this message to alcoholics, and to practice these principles in all our affairs.(p.60)

• If our manner is calm, frank, and open, we will be gratified with the *result*.(p.78)

• The unexpected *result* was that our husbands seemed to like it.(p.106)

• You, as a business man, want to know the necessities before considering the *result*.(p.140)

• Of course, the *result* was very bad, and that ended the beer experiment.(p.178)

• I cannot say, however, that I acquired any craving for hard liquor as a *result*.(p.231)

• It is, however, only the first of a series of miracles which have followed one after another as a *result* of my trying to apply to my daily life the principles embodies in our Twelve Steps.(p.280)

• The inevitable *result* of this discovery was that I soon learned that beer made a very good chaser for whiskey.(p.298)

• As a *result*, I would fall off in a drunken stupor every night.(p.299)

• In all honesty though, I was skeptical, but I wanted so definitely to quit drinking that I would have welcomed any sort of physical torture or pain to accomplish the *result*.(p.302)

• It finally got such a hold on me that I was completely at my wits' end, not knowing what the *result* would be.(p.343)

• The *result* was as usual.(p.343)

• At age twenty-one, I enlisted in the Navy for two reasons: (1) to avoid being drafted into the Army, and (2) out of a burst of patriotic fervor inspired by the advent of World War II and as the *result* of an all-night drinking binge which found me sitting on the doorstep of the Navy recruiting office when the chief petty officer arrived to open for business at nine o'clock Monday morning.(p.398)

• He even went to bat for me before the court martial that inevitably followed and, as a *result*, I drew only thirty days – fifteen in solitary.(p.428)

• As a *result*, he couldn't figure out why I had the convulsions, and he decided to send me to the Mayo Clinic.(p.444)

• It helped me a great deal to become convinced that alcoholism was a disease, not a moral issue; that I had been drinking as a *result* of a compulsion, even though I had not been aware of the compulsion at the time; and that sobriety was not a matter of will-power.(p.448)

• I feel that I have been restored to health and sanity these past years not through my own efforts nor as a *result* of anything I may have done, but because I've come to believe -- to really believe – that alone I can do nothing.(p.473)

• He had been in and out of Matteawan and many other mental institutions as a *result* of his drinking.(p.509)

• The gradual *result* was that I was drifting into making drinking one of the more important parts of my life.(p.519)

• I buttonholed him after dinner and gave him a few tips on how to run his colony better and the *result* of that was about a fortnight or so later I was shipped back to my regiment.(p.520)

• Young when she joined, this A.A. believes her serious drinking was the *result* of even deeper defects.(p.544)

• And I am sure they would be right as far as they go, but A.A. has taught me I am the *result* of the way I reacted to what happened to me as a child.(p.544)

• Dr. G. Kirby Collier, psychiatrist: "I have felt that A.A. is a group unto themselves and their best results can be had under their own guidance, as a *result* of their philosophy.(p.571)

resulted

• My inability to accept the harsh realities of life had *resulted* in a disillusioned cynic, clothed in protective armor against the world's misunderstanding.(p.226)

• My spiritual awakening in A.A. finally *resulted* in my joining a church some years ago.(p.417)

• This self-insurance has *resulted* in the restoration of physical, mental and spiritual health and self-respect to hundreds of men and women who would be hopelessly down and out without its unique but effective therapy."(p.574)

resulting

• Though the aggregate of recoveries *resulting* from psychiatric effort is considerable, we physicians must admit we have made little impression upon the problem as a whole.(p.xxvii)

results

• We shall be interested to hear from those who are getting *results* from this book, particularly from those who have commenced work with other alcoholics.(p.xiv)

• We found that as soon as we were able to lay aside prejudice and express even a willingness to believe in a Power greater than ourselves, we commenced to get *results*, even though it was impossible for any of us to fully define or comprehend that Power, which is God.(p.46)

• The practical individual of today is a stickler for facts and *results*.(p.48)

• In many homes this is a difficult thing to do, but it must be done if any *results* are to be expected.(p.98)

• After they have seen tangible *results*, the family will perhaps want to go along.(p.99)

• Marvelous *results* often follow such a reunion.(p.134)

• This seemed to me like an opportunity to be helpful, so I spent two hours talking about alcoholism, the malady, and described the symptoms and *results* as well as I could.(p.138)

• After all, are you not looking for *results* rather than methods?(p.144)

• Shortly after I returned to Chicago, my doctor, encouraged by the *results* of my contact with A.A., sent us two more of his alcoholic patients.(p.310)

• Living with fear and tension inevitably *results* in wanting to ease that tension, which alcohol seems to do temporarily.(p.380)

• Rather, I do whatever is in front of me to be done, and I leave the *results* up to Him; however it turns out, that's God's will for me.(p.452)

• I planted my first flower garden this year and am actually excited to see the *results*.(p.481)

• Dr. G. Kirby Collier, psychiatrist: "I have felt that A.A. is a group unto themselves and their best *results* can be had under their own guidance, as a result of their philosophy.(p.571)

• There is something spiritual about A.A. too, and Catholic participation in it almost invariably *results* in poor Catholics becoming better Catholics."(p.574)

resume

• I have seen men come out of asylums and *resume* a vital place in the lives of their families and communities.(p.15)

• I stayed about town a couple of months more and then returned to *resume* my practice.(p.175)

resumed

• If their old relationship is to be *resumed* it must be on a better basis, since the former did not work.(p.99)

• We soon *resumed* our marriage, even moved away from the street of sad memories and found a new home.(p.371)

• So, when my liver had recovered after ten months, I *resumed* drinking.(p.557)

retain

• And I still say that as long as I remember that January 8th in Washington, that is how long, by the grace of God as I understand Him, I will *retain* a happy sobriety.(p.250)

retained

• "Bill's Story," "Doctor Bob's Nightmare," and one other personal history from the first edition were *retained* intact; three were edited and one of these was retitled; new versions of two stories were written with new titles; thirty completely new stories were added; and the story section was divided into three parts, under the same headings that are used now.(p.xi)

• In Part III ("They Lost Nearly All"), eight stories have been *retained*; five are new.(p.xii)

• My customers lost confidence in me to the point where I *retained* what business I had only because I was a well-trained and reputedly fine craftsman.(p.234)

retaining

• If he had these qualities and did not drink would he be worth *retaining*?(p.140)

retaliate

• And do not his actions make each of them wish to *retaliate*, snatching all they can get out of the show?(p.61)

• Driven by a hundred forms of fear, self-delusion, self-seeking, and self-pity, we step on the toes of our fellows and they *retaliate*.(p.62)

retaliation

• We avoid *retaliation* or argument.(p.67)

retaliatory

• We have had *retaliatory* love affairs with other men.(p.105)

retarded
• My wife was in the Junior League, and I was on the board of directors of the local center for the mentally *retarded*.(p.418)
retire
• When we *retire* at night, we constructively review our day.(p.86)
• My pattern of drinking at that time had reached the point where once I really started, I would *retire* to my bed and drink myself into oblivion.(p.466)
• I wasn't afraid of anything or anybody after I learned about drinking, for it seemed right from the beginning that with liquor I could always *retire* to my little private world where nobody could get at me to hurt me.(p.547)
retired
• He made up his mind that until he had been successful in business and had *retired*, he would not touch another drop.(p.32)
• An exceptional man, he remained bone dry for twenty-five years and *retired* at the age of fifty-five, after a successful and happy business career.(p.32)
• He is like the *retired* business man who lolls in the Florida sunshine in the winter complaining of the sad state of the nation; the minister who sighs over the sins of the twentieth century; politicians and reformers who are sure all would be Utopia if the rest of the world would only behave; the outlaw safe cracker who thinks society has wronged him; and the alcoholic who has lost all and is locked up.(p.61)
• But – I also stayed up week nights after they had *retired* and drank myself into bed.(p.277)
• After it was closed we all *retired* to the kitchen and had coffee and doughnuts and more discussion until the small hours of the morning.(p.291)
• When I *retired*, I said I'd never be bored.(p.334)
• Not long ago, I was lunching with another *retired* publicist.(p.334)
• A *retired* Navy man looks back over twenty years of drinking, to add up his A.A. "initiation fee."(p.396)
• A British officer, this Irishman – that is, until brandy "*retired*" him.(p.517)
• About three months after that, my record reached home and I got a letter telling me I was *retired* from the Army, they put it very kindly, on medical grounds.(p.521)
• In any case, I made myself believe that, so I just drifted about, existing on my *retired* pay, drinking, and living at home.(p.522)
retiree
• So long as a *retiree* woos his bottle at home, he stays out of public trouble.(p.330)
• Boredom sets up every *retiree* for two chief dangers: obesity and alcoholism.(p.330)
retirees
• I believe that the release from people-pleasing restrictions gives *retirees* more motivation to drink than boredom does.(p.329)
• Many *retirees* embrace alcoholism while secluded in motor trailers, rest homes, leisure-world bungalows, mountain cabins, or beach cottages, or even in penthouses, on yachts, and inside Palm Springs cabanas.(p.329)
retirement
• Though a robust man at *retirement*, he went to pieces quickly and was dead within four years.(p.33)
• All the joys of *retirement* lay ahead for this movie publicist.(p.327)
• After such often-painful vigilance (and numerous phony stints of abstinence), *retirement* naturally created an impulse to live without restraints.(p.328)
• Now, with the arrival at *retirement*, it was gone.(p.329)
• *Retirement* rids the potential alcoholic of many shackles.(p.329)
• Nobody could take away my *retirement* income.(p.329)
• And *retirement* is a time for thinking, not of death, but of living – at long last.(p.329)
• A friend of mine, a golf nut, rushed out on *retirement* to play every day.(p.330)
• How full it has kept my *retirement* years -- the five I've lived since the first two lost in traveling a rocky road to hell, before I made a U-turn.(p.334)
• For an estimate of salary from the twenty-one a month to start with, to over $400 per month upon my *retirement* after twenty years in the Navy, I believe that an average income of $2,000 a year over this period is low, but as I stated earlier, an underestimate is best.(p.399)
retirement-age
• Hidden old-drunks can pass out on their beds and snooze unreproached, under the guise of taking those vital *retirement-age* naps.(p.330)
retitled
• "Bill's Story," "Doctor Bob's Nightmare," and one other personal history from the first edition were retained intact; three were edited and one of these was *retitled*; new versions of two stories were written with new titles; thirty completely new stories were added; and the story section was divided into three parts, under the same headings that are used now.(p.xi)
retreat
• Instead of treating the family as he should, he may *retreat* further into himself and feel he has spiritual justification for so doing.(p.129)
• I had found friends, understanding friends who often knew what I was thinking and feeling better than I knew myself, and didn't allow me to *retreat* into my prison of loneliness and fear over a fancied slight or hurt.(p.228)
• Liquor had become a crutch on the one hand and a means of *retreat* from life on the other.(p.277)
• It was my "secret garden" -- bluntly, it was my *retreat* from life, and I didn't want to give it up.(p.534)
retreats
• I went to hospitals, I went to *retreats* and doctors, and finally my mother asked me to go and see a specialist of her own choosing.(p.522)
retrogression
• Others may idle in a retrogressive groove without too much danger, but *retrogression* can spell death for us.(p.311)
retrogressive
• Others may idle in a *retrogressive* groove without too much danger, but retrogression can spell death for us.(p.311)
return
• But great numbers of these -- about two out of three – began to *return* as time passed.(p.xx)
• Convincing testimony must surely come from the medical men who have had experience with the sufferings of our members and have witnessed our *return* to health.(p.xxiii)
• A long time has passed with no *return* to alcohol.(p.xxix)
• We were in a position where life was becoming impossible, and if we had passed into the region from which there is no *return* through human aid we had but two alternatives: One was to go on to the bitter end, blotting out the consciousness of our intolerable situation as best we could; and the other, to accept spiritual help.(p.25)
• The family of an alcoholic longs for the *return* of happiness and security.(p.123)
• It might be well to have a long chat with him on his *return*.(p.143)
• To *return* to the subject matter of this book: It contains full suggestions by which the employee may solve his problem.(p.143)
• On your employee's *return*, talk with him.(p.144)
• When I got the fog out of my brain, I decided that quitting school was very foolish and that I had better *return* and continue my work.(p.173)
• After much argument they allowed me to *return* and take my exams, all of which I passed creditably.(p.173)
• I soon discovered that a couple of drinks would alleviate my gastric distress, at least for a few hours at a time, so it was not at all difficult for me to *return* to my former excessive indulgence.(p.174)
• On the *return* trip, after two or three loads, I passed out and had to be carried to the house.(p.183)
• I immediately quit school and went to work, and from that time until I was high school age there was never a *return* to school.(p.193)
• I would have to *return* to New York and pick up my bills and bags.(p.213)
• But I can remember the urge of the Prodigal Son to *return* to his Father.(p.260)
• When the day of their *return* was almost upon me, and suicide was the only answer I had been able to think of, I went into Ralph's room one evening and told him the truth.(p.278)
• After six months of sobriety I saw the picture in a different light: Detroit was the place I had to *return* to, not only because I must face the mess I had made there, but because it was there that I could be of the most service to A.A.(p.281)
• Those three weeks left me completely exhausted and I had to *return* to Akron for three more months of rest.(p.282)
• Within a year of my *return* to Detroit, A.A. was a definitely established little group of about a dozen members and I too was established in a modest but steady job handling an independent dry-cleaning route of my own.(p.283)
• One of them was that I would try to get a group started in Chicago; the second was that I would have to *return* to Akron to attend meetings at least every two months until I did get a group started in Chicago; third, I decided I must place this program above everything else, even my family, because if I did not maintain my sobriety I would lose my family anyway.(p.292)
• Immediately on her *return* we began to have formal meetings once a week, in the autumn of 1939, and we have continued to do this and to expand ever since.(p.295)
• That ache is gone and never need *return* again.(p.312)
• In *return* for a bottle and a hangover, we have been given the Keys of the Kingdom.(p.312)
• A few months after that, I was released and left the world of insanity, only to *return* to the world of alcoholic insanity.(p.370)
• Two years before I joined A.A. my wife took a long trip during which she wrote me she just couldn't *return* unless I did something about my drinking.(p.377)
• A *return* to the United States proved effective as a geographical cure, and a period of sobriety ensued, with the help of the church.(p.419)
• I paid nine hundred dollars for a second hand car on my *return*.(p.429)
• What else can I do except what I have always done in the past? – act as my old self and *return* to prison.(p.458)
• Finally, I threw away all my books and decided never to *return* to A.A.(p.460)
• I *return* to the hotel where I am staying and get gin from the bellboy.(p.501)
• I *return* to bed.(p.504)
• I *return* home and say I am sorry for my wrong.(p.505)
• But I have not seen yet that I should do some constructive acts of love without expecting any *return*.(p.505)
returned
• When the broker *returned* to New York in the fall of 1935, the first A.A. group had actually been formed, though no one realized it at the time.(p.xvii)
• After a time I *returned* to the hospital.(p.7)
• So he *returned* to this doctor, whom he admired, and asked him point-blank why he could not recover.(p.26)
• When I *returned* to the hotel it struck me a highball would be fine before going to bed, so I stepped into the bar and had one.(p.41)
• Save for a few brief moments of temptation the thought of drink has never *returned*; and at such times a great revulsion has risen up in him.(p.57)
• For by this time sanity will have *returned*.(p.84)
• We have seen men get well whose families have not *returned* at all.(p.100)
• The majority have never *returned*.(p.114)
• My secretary *returned* to say that it was not Mr. B—– on the phone; it was Mr. B—–'s brother, and he wished to give me a message.(p.136)
• He has just *returned* from a three-months leave of absence, has taken a cure, looks fine, and to clinch the matter, the board of directors told him this was his last chance."(p.138)
• Had they fired me first, and had they then taken steps to see that I was presented with the solution contained in this book, I might have *returned* to them six months later, a well man.(p.141)
• His sanity *returned* and he thanked God.(p.154)
• He now *returned* home, leaving behind his first acquaintance, the lawyer and the devil-may-care chap.(p.159)
• I stayed about town a couple of months more and then *returned* to resume my practice.(p.175)
• Following a big drunk on that sheet, where I was doing leg-work and rewrite, a feeling of nostalgia made me buy a ticket for Liverpool and I *returned* to Britain.(p.252)
• We spent two days there together before he *returned* to New York.(p.281)
• When I finally *returned* to Detroit to find work and to learn to stand on my own feet, the ball was already rolling, however slowly.(p.282)
• I well remember a session I had with myself soon after I *returned*.(p.282)
• When he *returned*, we had practically daily meetings from that time on.(p.294)
• Shortly after I *returned* to Chicago, my doctor, encouraged by the results of my contact with A.A., sent us two more of his alcoholic patients.(p.310)
• My memory slowly *returned*.(p.320)

- I *returned* to my home in Lucknow, India, at the end of November last year from a vacation in one of the most famous beauty spots in our country, a mountain resort 6,800 feet up, with a wonderful lake.(p.342)
- I had turned eighteen during the trip, and I despondently *returned* home by jet (on Daddy's bankbook) to a pair of miserable, hurt parents.(p.354)
- Then I became careless and *returned* sometimes when I shouldn't have.(p.376)
- It was a shock of course, but I promised to stop and she *returned*.(p.377)
- I *returned* from Europe a while after that encounter, and I never went back.(p.406)
- I *returned* the book to my analyst and shook my head.(p.412)
- Gradually consciousness *returned* enough to let me know I was in a hospital.(p.422)
- After the meeting was over and we had *returned* to the cell block again, I was asked how I was impressed.(p.510)
- My husband eventually *returned*, but it was not long until we realized we could not continue our marriage.(p.547)

returning
- I felt like Napoleon *returning* from Elba.(p.4)
- *Returning* home we find a place where we can be quiet for an hour carefully reviewing what we have done.(p.75)
- And I remembered the creeping horror of the interminable night, in which I slept for short spells and woke up dripping with cold sweat and shaken with utter despair, to drink hastily from my bottle and mercifully pass out again, "You're mad, you're mad, you're mad!" pounded through my brain with each *returning* ray of consciousness, and I drowned the refrain with drink.(p.224)
- *Returning* to the town I had left three months before, I became editor of a monthly magazine, soon had additional publicity and advertising accounts and the money rolled in.(p.254)
- My hours of work were flexible so that *returning* to the office was not always important.(p.376)
- In a few days an attorney called on me and explained that something would have to be done as she couldn't face *returning* to me as I was.(p.377)

returns
- The insanity of alcohol *returns* and we drink again.(p.66)
- Headstrong and willful, I rushed from pleasure to pleasure, and found the *returns* diminishing to the vanishing point.(p.226)

reunion
- Marvelous results often follow such a *reunion*.(p.134)
- I stayed on in Florida for three weeks, enjoying our *reunion*, a new found health and a deeper love than I had ever experienced before.(p.364)
- For instance, the fiftieth wedding anniversary of my wife's parents was the occasion for a huge family *reunion* at our home.(p.556)

reunited
- For this there were two principal reasons: the large numbers of recoveries, and *reunited* homes.(p.xx)
- After all, your family is *reunited*, alcohol is no longer a problem and you and your husband are working together toward an undreamed-of future.(p.119)

reveal
- He may, for example, *reveal* that he has padded his expense account or that he has planned to take your best customers away from you.(p.145)
- I had suppressed tendencies to overindulge and thus *reveal* my "moral weakness," because false pride was so dominant.(p.327)
- One day soon, the analyses would *reveal* why I drank and how to stop.(p.408)

revealed
- This is a point we wish to emphasize and re-emphasize, to smash home upon our alcoholic readers as it has been *revealed* to us out of bitter experience.(p.39)
- It is being constantly *revealed*, as mankind studies the material world, that outward appearances are not inward reality at all.(p.48)
- A complete checkup at one of the best hospitals *revealed* nothing.(p.276)

revelation
- To this man, the *revelation* was sudden.(p.57)
- The first chapters were a *revelation* to me.(p.227)
- It has brought about a *revelation* of self, the discovery of an inner being, an awareness of God.(p.355)
- I rebelled against this, because just about the time that I was getting ready to leave high school, a *revelation* came to me about God and it made things very complicated for me.(p.489)
- It was a *revelation* to me to find that there were such people as those I found in Alcoholics Anonymous.(p.515)
- It was a *revelation* when I read that First Step.(p.515)
- What a *revelation* of ego and arrogance still remaining in me – as if anyone, instinct and training apart, likes to be in jail or in an alcoholic ward or fired from his job.(p.536)
- For by now I had been exposed once to A.A., but I had treated it as a vaudeville and had taken friends to meetings so that they too could enjoy the fascination of the naked *revelation* of suffering and recovery.(p.539)

revelations
- By this time, with the doctor's explanation, the *revelations* contained in the book, and the hope-inspiring interview with Mr. T., I was ready and willing to go into the interior of the African jungles, if that was what it took, for me to find what these people had.(p.309)

revenge
- So did the waterboy on the high school football team attempt to *revenge* himself on the big brother who was the star quarterback; for I was the waterboy and my brother was the star quarterback, innocent of everything except the fact that he was a star quarterback.(p.537)

revered
- I left this home town, then, after I had made a public spectacle of myself in the presence of a *revered* teacher whose favorite pupil I had been.(p.539)

reverse
- You may have the *reverse* situation on your hands.(p.114)
- That was the *reverse* of my former pattern of fearing to go to work because I might drink!(p.199)
- And life keeps getting simpler and easier as we try to *reverse* my old idea, by taking care of the internal environment via the Twelve Steps, and letting the external environment take care of itself.)(p.446)
- For to have accepted the reasons and to have acted on them would have been too great a blow to my ego, which was as great, in *reverse*, as my body was small.(p.534)

revert
- Were I to *revert* to drinking, even now, I wouldn't give anything for these four years in A.A.(p.430)

reverted
- We *reverted* to the old way of life we knew -- a life full of anger, vindictiveness, resentment, fear, dependence, denial, self-will, irresponsibility.(p.459)
- I nearly *reverted* to my old, incorrigible self – had trouble with a couple of other prisoners, was planning an escape.(p.461)

review
- When we retire at night, we constructively *review* our day.(p.86)
- After making our *review* we ask God's forgiveness and inquire what corrective measures should be taken.(p.86)

reviewed
- Dr. Harry Emerson Fosdick, the noted clergyman, *reviewed* it with approval.(p.xvii)
- We *reviewed* our fears thoroughly.(p.68)
- We *reviewed* our own conduct over the years past.(p.69)
- They left this with me to think over, and I lay there on that hospital bed and went back over and *reviewed* my life.(p.186)

reviewing
- On each of these occasions we worked with him, *reviewing* carefully what had happened.(p.35)
- Returning home we find a place where we can be quiet for an hour carefully *reviewing* what we have done.(p.75)
- So, after *reviewing* these things and realizing what liquor had cost me, I went to this Higher Power which, to me was God, without any reservation, and admitted that I was completely powerless over alcohol, and that I was willing to do anything in the world to get rid of the problem.(p.187)

revised
- My ideas about miracles were drastically *revised* right then.(p.11)

revisions
- Therefore, the first portion of this volume, describing the A.A. recovery program, has been left untouched in the course of *revisions* made for both the second and the third editions.(p.xi)

revive
- If this kind of approach does not catch your husband's interest, it may be best to drop the subject, but after a friendly talk your husband will usually *revive* the topic himself.(p.112)

revolted
- Coming to his senses, he is *revolted* at certain episodes he vaguely remembers.(p.73)

revolutionary
- These were *revolutionary* and drastic proposals, but the moment I fully accepted them, the effect was electric.(p.14)
- They flatly declare that since they have come to believe in a Power greater than themselves, to take a certain attitude toward that Power, and to do certain simple things, there has been a *revolutionary* change in their way of living and thinking.(p.50)
- In the first few chapters a number of sudden *revolutionary* changes are described.(p.569)

revolutionized
- The great fact is just this, and nothing less: That we have had deep and effective spiritual experiences which have *revolutionized* our whole attitude toward life, toward our fellows and toward God's universe.(p.25)

revulsion
- Save for a few brief moments of temptation the thought of drink has never returned; and at such times a great *revulsion* has risen up in him.(p.57)
- Afterward, his *revulsion* will be terrible.(p.141)

reward
- I could never be bothered with the follow-through and would invariably *reward* myself for my efforts with that "first" drink.(p.243)
- I'd work like mad for three or four weeks without a single drink, save my money, pay a few bills and then "*reward*" myself with alcohol.(p.244)
- There was the same *reward* -- exhilaration at a mission accomplished.(p.283)
- I remember the day when I decided to drink myself to death quietly, without bothering anyone, because I was tired of having been a dependable, trustworthy person for about thirty-nine years without having received what I thought was a proper *reward* for my virtue.(p.531)

rewarding
- It is a way of life that pays as it goes, every step of the way, in compensations that have been wonderfully rich and *rewarding*.(p.394)

rewards
- Above all, I have gained the greatest thing accorded to any man, the love and understanding of a gracious God, who has lifted me from the alcoholic scrap-heap to a position of trust where I have been able to reap the rich *rewards* that come from showing a little love for others and from serving them as I can.(p.296)
- In all these ways I've experienced, in ever growing measure and beyond all expectations and *rewards*, a joy which I had never before imagined.(p.395)

rewon
- Husbands and wives have sometimes been obliged to separate for a time until new perspective, new victory over hurt pride could be *rewon*.(p.125)

rewrite
- Following a big drunk on that sheet, where I was doing leg-work and *rewrite*, a feeling of nostalgia made me buy a ticket for Liverpool and I returned to Britain.(p.252)
- In the two succeeding years I held ten different jobs ranging from newspaper copy-desk and *rewrite*, to traffic director for an oil field equipment company.(p.255)

rewriting
- How hurt I was when editors bounced back my ideas quickly and my best friends opined that my output needed a lot of *rewriting*.(p.331)

Rhine
- I was born in Europe, in Alsace to be exact, shortly after it had become German, and practically grew up with the "good *Rhine* wine" of song and story.(p.230)

rhythm
- Despite contrary indications, I had little doubt that a mighty purpose and *rhythm* underlay all.(p.10)

ribald
- Ribaldry was the substance of the conversation, and I set out to be the funniest and most *ribald* of them all.(p.407)

ribaldry
- *Ribaldry* was the substance of the conversation, and I set out to be the funniest and most ribald of them all.(p.407)

ribbons
• Out of this alloy of drink and speculation, I commenced to forge the weapon that one day would turn in its flight like a boomerang and all but cut me to *ribbons*.(p.2)

rich
• Many people lost money -- but some became very *rich*.(p.2)
• High and low, *rich* and poor, these are future fellows of Alcoholics Anonymous.(p.152)
• Above all, I have gained the greatest thing accorded to any man, the love and understanding of a gracious God, who has lifted me from the alcoholic scrap-heap to a position of trust where I have been able to reap the *rich* rewards that come from showing a little love for others and from serving them as I can.(p.296)
• The last fifteen years of my life have been *rich* and meaningful.(p.312)
• It is a way of life that pays as it goes, every step of the way, in compensations that have been wonderfully *rich* and rewarding.(p.394)
• Alcoholism had respected nobody, neither *rich* nor poor, learned nor unlettered.(p.455)

richer
• My work with other alcoholics has led me, day by day, into ever wider and *richer* experiences.(p.394)

rid
• Above everything, we alcoholics must be *rid* of this selfishness.(p.62)
• And there often seems no way of entirely getting *rid* of self without His aid.(p.62)
• Though our decision was a vital and crucial step, it could have little permanent effect unless at once followed by a strenuous effort to face, and to be *rid* of, the things in ourselves which had been blocking us.(p.64)
• One object is to disclose damaged or unsalable goods, to get *rid* of them promptly and without regret.(p.64)
• At the same time you will feel no reluctance to *rid* yourself of those who cannot or will not stop.(p.148)
• So, after reviewing these things and realizing what liquor had cost me, I went to this Higher Power which, to me was God, without any reservation, and admitted that I was completely powerless over alcohol, and that I was willing to do anything in the world to get *rid* of the problem.(p.187)
• Don't you believe you are going to have all you can do to get *rid* of that?"(p.190)
• My only thought that day was getting a drink, and how to get *rid* of those clowns was my big problem.(p.206)
• (Actually, he does it solely to get *rid* of us.)(p.480)
• At that time I started school and that's how I got *rid* of the curls.(p.483)
• To get *rid* of me one evening, she decided to go to the movies, she and another friend.(p.487)
• Am I willing to be honest with myself about myself and tell someone about myself, and am I willing to think of other people, of their needs instead of myself, in order to get *rid* of the drink problem?(p.503)
• It rings in my head; I can't get *rid* of it.(p.504)
• One morning, however, I realized I had to get *rid* of it, for my reprieve was running out, and if I didn't get *rid* of it I was going to get drunk -- and I didn't want to get drunk any more.(p.552)
• Similarly, we *rid* ourselves of guilt and remorse as we "clean out the garbage" from our minds through the Fourth and Fifth Steps of our recovery program.(p.560)

riddle
• We cannot answer the *riddle*.(p.22)
• If God can solve the age-old *riddle* of alcoholism, He can solve your problems too.(p.116)

ride
• A couple of hired hands were cleaning out the barn on the farm and I would *ride* to and fro on the sled, and while they were loading I would drink hard cider out of a barrel in the barn.(p.183)
• He'd always say, "Take me for a *ride*, Ma."(p.264)
• The details of the long road back to something resembling normal living -- the first short streetcar *ride*, the purchase of a used bike which enabled me to widen the narrow horizon of life, the first trip downtown -- I will not dwell on.(p.276)
• On my *ride* to the nearest bar, I sold the driver on how misunderstood I was by my wife and what an unreasonable person she was.(p.288)

ridicule
• Finally, he can no longer work, his wife gets a divorce and he is held up to *ridicule*.(p.38)
• A man may criticize or laugh at himself and it will affect others favorably, but criticism or *ridicule* coming from another often produces the contrary effect.(p.125)

ridiculous
• You may think our illustration is too *ridiculous*.(p.38)
• There was the love affair which was *ridiculous* -- "imagine that midget being able to fall in love!" -- and my head knew it while my heart pumped real, genuine anguish, for it hurt like hell, and since it was first love, things have never been quite the same.(p.534)

riding
• I got my first introduction to "*riding* the rods and making a blind."(p.252)
• Always, in between, there were intervals of being broke, *riding* freights and hitch-hiking interminable distances from one big town to another in three states.(p.255)
• We were to go up to our A.A. farm in Kent, and I spent the evening before *riding* herd on Anne.(p.415)

rids
• Retirement *rids* the potential alcoholic of many shackles.(p.329)

right
• Perhaps they were *right*.(p.3)
• Yes, the old boy was on fire all *right*.(p.9)
• I could almost hear the sound of the preacher's voice as I sat, on still Sundays, way over there on the hillside; there was that proffered temperance pledge I never signed; my grandfather's good natured contempt of some church folk and their doings; his insistence that the spheres really had their music; but his denial of the preacher's *right* to tell him how he must listen; his fearlessness as he spoke of these things just before he died; these recollections welled up from the past.(p.10)
• With ministers, and world's religions, I parted *right* there.(p.10)
• It began to look as though religious people were *right* after all.(p.11)
• My ideas about miracles were drastically revised *right* then.(p.11)
• I was to *right* all such matters to the utmost of my ability.(p.13)
• We have it with us *right* here and now.(p.16)
• I felt I had every *right* to be self-confident, that it would be only a matter of exercising my will power and keeping on guard.(p.40)
• When, however, the perfectly logical assumption is suggested that underneath the material world and life as we see it, there is an All Powerful, Guiding, Creative Intelligence, *right* there our perverse streak comes to the surface and we laboriously set out to convince ourselves it isn't so.(p.49)
• Even so has God restored us all to our *right* minds.(p.57)
• He begins to think life doesn't treat him *right*.(p.61)
• They think we do not have enough of it, or that it isn't the *right* kind.(p.69)
• The *right* answer will come, if we want it.(p.69)
• To sum up about sex: We earnestly pray for the *right* ideal, for guidance in each questionable situation, for sanity, and for the strength to do the *right* thing.(p.70)
• They took inventory all *right*, but hung on to some of the worst items in stock.(p.73)
• We have no *right* to save our own skin at another person's expense.(p.74)
• We say this because we are very anxious that we talk to the *right* person.(p.74)
• But our man is sure to be impressed with a sincere desire to set *right* the wrong.(p.77)
• Reminding ourselves that we have decided to go to any length to find a spiritual experience we ask that we be given strength and direction to do the *right* thing, no matter what the personal consequences may be.(p.79)
• He felt that he had done a wrong he could not possibly make *right*.(p.80)
• What *right* had he to involve those dependent upon him?(p.80)
• We feel we ought to say to her that we have no *right* to involve another person.(p.81)
• More than that we cannot do; we have no *right* to go further.(p.81)
• There may be some wrongs we can never fully *right*.(p.83)
• We don't worry about them if we can honestly say to ourselves that we would *right* them if we could.(p.83)
• This thought brings us to Step Ten, which suggests we continue to take personal inventory and continue to set *right* any new mistakes as we go along.(p.84)
• We are often surprised how the *right* answers come after we have tried this for a while.(p.86)
• Be quick to see where religious people are *right*.(p.87)
• As we go through the day we pause, when agitated or doubtful, and ask for the *right* thought or action.(p.87)
• Never avoid these responsibilities, but be sure you are doing the *right* thing if you assume them.(p.97)
• In this way you can set them on the *right* track without becoming critical of them.(p.100)
• Is it *right* to let him ruin your life and the lives of your children?(p.108)
• Your desire to protect him should not cause you to lie to people when they have a *right* to know where he is and what he is doing.(p.115)
• If not, it had better be found out *right* away.(p.120)
• Then you and your husband can get *right* down to fundamentals.(p.120)
• If he means to *right* his past wrongs, why all this concern for everyone in the world but his family?(p.128)
• It boils *right* down to this: No man should be fired just because he is alcoholic.(p.148)
• The *right* kind of man, the kind who recovers, will not want this sort of thing.(p.149)
• Here was a prospect all *right* but, by the description, none too promising.(p.156)
• You fellows know your stuff all *right*, but I don't see what good it'll do.(p.157)
• "Maybe you're *right*," he said.(p.158)
• I guess the old folks were *right* after all."(p.159)
• See to it that your relationship with Him is *right*, and great events will come to pass for you and countless others.(p.164)
• *Right* then I determined that never so long as I lived would I have anything more to do with martinis.(p.195)
• (I might say *right* here that never in my life did I ever intend to get drunk.(p.196)
• I'll buy you one drink, and if you suggest a second one, I'll poke you *right* in the nose."(p.201)
• I could take one drink and get *right* back on the wagon.(p.202)
• And I continued to drink, on and off then, until every dollar I had in the world was gone again and I was *right* back living at my sister's, getting my cigarettes by calling her grocer and telling him to put in a couple of cartons with her order, exactly as I had before I started to work at Max's.(p.202)
• I said, "All *right*, call me a cab," as though I was talking to a bell boy.(p.204)
• I had a genuine release *right* from the start.(p.219)
• I knew what they were all *right* -- a drink would fix them.(p.223)
• Searching where I have been at fault, it is not hard to discover and get *right* again, for I have proven to myself and to many others who know me that God can keep a man sober if he will let Him.(p.237)
• That is where I had my first drink and I still remember it, for every "first" drink afterwards did exactly the same trick -- I could feel it go *right* through every bit of my body and down to my very toes.(p.241)
• I was the fair-haired boy all *right*, but two years later I was blacklisted as an irresponsible drunk.(p.242)
• Evidently I had gone *right* back to the movie with a bottle, stayed there several hours and started home with no recollection of what had happened.(p.244)
• I knew they needed to straighten out their thinking and habits, but I was all *right*, I just drank too much.(p.246)
• Just give me a good front and a couple of bucks and I'd be *right* back in the big time.(p.246)
• I tried to contact the boys in New York, but telegrams bounced *right* back and when I finally got Hank on the telephone he fired me *right* then.(p.247)
• My fellow-workers were mostly good Saturday night drinkers and I was *right* with them.(p.252)
• If I'd had a gun I'd have shot the horns *right* off the thing, because it made me raving mad.(p.265)
• But *right* then the hope died that had been in my heart when we read about John D.(p.266)
• *Right* away, I saw it was the same outfit this other guy told me about, and then again hope died.(p.267)
• He talked about his wife taking his little boy away from him because of his drinking, and how he got back together with them through A.A., and we began feeling grateful *right* then that all these things hadn't been taken from us.(p.270)
• I didn't think I was going to get drunk *right* then, but I remember how comforting it was when I called Anne and told her.(p.273)
• He would invariably reply, "When you are *right* and the time is *right*, Providence will provide.(p.293)

• It wasn't necessary to report to the office in person every day, and when I did go in, it was just to make an appearance and bounce ***right*** out again.(p.300)
• An alcoholic can't lay off the booze – ***right***?(p.317)
• I started my drinking nearly thirty years ago – ***right*** after I was married.(p.322)
• The only way I knew to do it was to drink ***right*** along with him.(p.322)
• Even obvious intoxication is excused by younger people as something "he's earned the ***right*** to do," and they say, "After all, who's he hurting?"(p.330)
• And of course a half empty bottle wasn't worth keeping, so I finished it up and naturally had to get more in ***right*** away for the people who "might come in unexpectedly."(p.336)
• I figured I'd be all ***right*** if I could find something I liked to do.(p.339)
• And the first thing you know I was lifted ***right*** out of the A.A. group, and I floated higher, and higher, and even higher, until I was way up on a pink cloud which is known as Pink Seven, and I felt miserable again.(p.348)
• I don't feel ***right***.(p.348)
• You've been doing all ***right***."(p.348)
• This phase was ***right*** down my alley; I had my master's degree in the art of making "whoopee."(p.359)
• I was living in a small room on West 53rd Street ***right*** off Fifth Avenue, when I met a young lady who eventually was responsible for altering my entire way of living.(p.359)
• I entered the house, opened a new bottle of whiskey and sat down to drink myself into the ***right*** frame of mind to get in my car, start the motor and close the garage door behind me.(p.363)
• That night she too had new hope because I had made sure she would know what I was doing about my drinking by packing every bit of A.A. literature I could put my hands on ***right*** on top so she couldn't help but see it when she opened my bag.(p.364)
• I got through the holidays all ***right*** until New Year's Day.(p.365)
• Later I told her I had not taken the drink and that I was all ***right***.(p.365)
• I had no trouble making the ***right*** decision when I saw my wife open her purse at the meeting that night and deposit a cute little angel in the middle of my birthday cake.(p.366)
• I knew he was ***right***, except for that last statement.(p.371)
• That's ***right***!(p.372)
• Scared that my dress wasn't going to fit ***right***, that the church wasn't going to be filled, that I'd fall flat on my face walking up the aisle; in fact, I was afraid I wasn't going to be a prima donna in the place where I should be.(p.385)
• I got ***right*** into the car and they drove me over, and just as soon as I got to the church they started the wedding.(p.385)
• As I started down the aisle, that bourbon went ***right*** through me.(p.385)
• I knew this, and ***right*** away I got furious and would not even talk to the doctor in the place.(p.387)
• We moved once more, to Houston; my husband thought maybe a change of environment would help and I'd be all ***right***.(p.389)
• Inside, I went ***right*** on being a mass of unlovely self-pity, queasy anxiety and sickening self-debasement.(p.400)
• I think I had the physical allergy ***right*** away.(p.402)
• So I did the ***right*** thing in the wrong way.(p.409)
• In my cups I used to tell them off, giving them lengthy advice on how to lead the ***right*** life.(p.410)
• I had accomplished all the ***right*** things that our society expected, and I had no real peace of mind nor gratitude.(p.418)
• Or, "My physical plant had got a little run down and the stuff rushed ***right*** to my head."(p.433)
• Weeks would go by without further trouble, and I'd be assured I'd at last hit on the ***right*** formula.(p.433)
• I had to admit to myself that he was ***right***.(p.436)
• But we have a baby who, if you'll pardon a little post-alcoholic sentimentality, is ***right*** out of Heaven.(p.438)
• The answer came ***right*** back: I'd give him something to pep him up.(p.441)
• It was hard to judge the ***right*** amount.(p.443)
• ***Right*** from the start, I felt that they weren't doing anything for me, but they sure were helping Max.(p.447)
• Today, I feel I have used up my ***right*** to chemical peace of mind.(p.448)
• And it's all ***right*** with me.(p.449)
• A.A. and acceptance have taught me that there is a bit of good in the worst of us and a bit of bad in the best of us; that we are all children of God and we each have a ***right*** to be here.(p.449)
• I can tell her she ought not to think a certain way, but I certainly can't take away her ***right*** to feel however she does feel.(p.451)
• I figured that perhaps if I went ahead with that marriage, which I was sure was ***right*** for me, that would be the answer to my drinking problem.(p.465)
• What's the sense in trying to do the ***right*** thing?"(p.467)
• She gave me such hope and inspiration that I set her ***right*** up on a pedestal.(p.472)
• And I landed ***right*** smack back in that sanitarium that I had gone to so often.(p.472)
• No drunk hopeless if he want to follow guide along ***right*** trail.(p.477)
• When I came into A.A., I had no intention of quitting drinking – I figured I was doing all ***right***.(p.478)
• Mind you, I had absolutely nothing to show for that eighteen years, except a beat-up car that I hadn't even paid for, but I was doing all ***right***.(p.478)
• No clothes, no money, no home, no real friends to speak of, mentally and physically pooped, but I was doing all ***right***!(p.478)
• Knowing that he was sober, I timed it just ***right***, so I could do the slashing just before he hit the steps.(p.479)
• I don't know whether it was ***right*** or wrong, but at least I know that people weren't thinking the same.(p.484)
• The fear of the loss of Vi and the feeling that, though she had the ***right*** to do as she pleased, she should have told me the truth about it, upset me.(p.487)
• I took that bottle of medicine and gave it to a very good friend of mine who was a pharmacist and had it analyzed, and the bottle was perfectly all ***right***.(p.489)
• I promised that I was going to do the ***right*** thing.(p.490)
• I had not recognized her, but as soon as she said who she was I remembered her ***right*** away.(p.493)
• She never mentioned anything about my whiskey drinking because if she had I would have told her, "No" ***right*** then.(p.494)
• He was my pal, all ***right***.(p.498)
• Then he asks me if I am willing to ***right*** all the wrongs I have ever done to anyone, no matter how wrong I thought the others were.(p.503)
• Is that ***right***?"(p.504)
• Nothing seems to be working out ***right***.(p.505)
• Nothing is ***right***.(p.506)
• But I pointed out to him that as I was the first British boy who had been to the school, it wouldn't be a very good advertisement for him, so I got over that all ***right***.(p.518)
• Strangely enough, ***right*** through to the end of my twenty-six years in the Army, I was still being offered very good and important jobs in spite of the fact that my superiors must have known that I wasn't thoroughly reliable.(p.519)
• I got out on bail ***right*** away, but when I went to trial, the judge gave me thirty days.(p.528)
• Which is only another way of saying, I had to be ***right*** all the time, and only God can be that.(p.535)
• Actually, of course, I wanted someone to listen to me, because when I had a few martinis inside, I became the great author I longed to be; and the ***right*** listener was in for some pretty highflown theories of literature and of genius.(p.536)
• And I am sure they would be ***right*** as far as they go, but A.A. has taught me I am the result of the way I reacted to what happened to me as a child.(p.544)
• I wasn't afraid of anything or anybody after I learned about drinking, for it seemed ***right*** from the beginning that with liquor I could always retire to my little private world where nobody could get at me to hurt me.(p.547)
• I've had many spiritual experiences since I've been in the program, many that I didn't recognize ***right*** away, for I'm slow to learn and they take many guises.(p.551)
• It wasn't strong enough, so I added a shot of vodka - - and was ***right*** back to worse trouble than before.(p.556)
• I have learned to deal with disappointments and problems that once would have sent me ***right*** to the bottle.(p.559)

right-about-face
• If anyone who is showing inability to control his drinking can do the ***right-about-face*** and drink like a gentleman, our hats are off to him.(p.31)

righted
• I have seen hundreds of families set their feet in the path that really goes somewhere; have seen the most impossible domestic situations ***righted***; feuds and bitterness of all sorts wiped out.(p.15)

righteous
• But am I to be consigned to a life where I shall be stupid, boring and glum, like some ***righteous*** people I see?(p.152)
• It isn't always so sudden with everyone, but I ran into a personal crisis which filled me with a raging and ***righteous*** anger.(p.228)

righteously
• Sometimes, after sobering up after a bout of several weeks, I would ***righteously*** resolve to quit.(p.233)

rightly
• I ***rightly*** imagined that they would some day have a great rise.(p.2)
• ***Rightly*** and naturally, we think well before we choose the person or persons with whom to take this intimate and confidential step.(p.74)
• Doctors are ***rightly*** loath to tell alcoholic patients the whole story unless it will serve some good purpose.(p.92)
• Her father, quite ***rightly***, wanted to put her in a school.(p.409)

rights
• My whole life seemed to be centered around doing what I wanted to do, without regard for the ***rights***, wishes, or privileges of anyone else; a state of mind which became more and more predominant as the years passed.(p.172)
• We're not up here trying to take any of your ***rights*** or privileges away from you, but we have a program whereby we think we can stay sober.(p.186)
• But then my "***rights***" try to move in, and they, too, can force my serenity level down.(p.452)
• I have to discard my "***rights***," as well as my expectations, by asking myself, "How important is it, really?(p.452)
• It was here that I realized for the first time that as a practicing alcoholic I had no ***rights***.(p.549)
• Society can do anything it chooses to do with me when I am drunk and I can't lift a finger to stop it, for I forfeit my ***rights*** through the simple expedient of becoming a menace to myself and to the people around me.(p.549)

rigorous
• They are naturally incapable of grasping and developing a manner of living which demands ***rigorous*** honesty.(p.58)
• In fact, he may say almost anything if he has accepted our solution which, as you know, demands ***rigorous*** honesty.(p.145)

ring
• In the prize ***ring***, this would be called leading with the chin.(p.77)
• I was greeted warmly, honestly, and with a true ***ring*** of sincerity by everyone present.(p.259)

ringing
• It was November 11th and bells were ***ringing*** and whistles blowing for the real Armistice.(p.242)

rings
• If there is something in my story that ***rings*** a bell with you, then do something – now!(p.368)
• It ***rings*** in my head; I can't get rid of it.(p.504)

rinse
• The only drawback was, I always knew how I arrived there, but somehow, between the rest room, the ***rinse***, and the fluff-dry, I never knew when or how I got home.(p.370)

riot
• They arise out of ourselves, and the alcoholic is an extreme example of self-will run ***riot***, though he usually doesn't think so.(p.62)

ripe
• I wanted "***ripe***" prospects and I didn't feel that I would get very far chasing individual drunks in and out of bars.(p.281)

ripened
• I had my first drink when I was fifteen and my alcoholic potential had ***ripened*** me to the point of necessary escapism.(p.353)

ripped
• They struck the children, kicked out door panels, smashed treasured crockery, and ***ripped*** the keys out of pianos.(p.106)

rise
• I rightly imagined that they would some day have a great ***rise***.(p.2)
• Many times we talk to a new man and watch his hope ***rise*** as we discuss his alcoholic problems and ex-

plain our fellowship.(p.45)
• How can they *rise* out of such misery, bad repute and hopelessness?(p.153)
• Many, we are sure, will *rise* to their feet and march on.(p.153)
• I can watch my serenity level *rise* when I discard my expectations.(p.452)

risen
• Save for a few brief moments of temptation the thought of drink has never returned; and at such times a great revulsion has *risen* up in him.(p.57)

rises
• He planted many seeds, and it will be many moons before another *rises* to walk in his shoes."(p.476)

rising
• Family confidence in dad is *rising* high.(p.123)
• Even when you understand the malady better, you may feel this feeling *rising*.(p.139)
• The wind is *rising* and howls around the house.(p.497)

risk
• Good generalship may decide that the problem be attacked on the flank rather than *risk* a face-to-face combat.(p.82)
• The family may object to this, but unless he is in a dangerous physical condition, it is better to *risk* it.(p.90)
• You think he ought to know the subject better, as everyone should have a clear understanding of the *risk* he takes if he drinks too much.(p.112)
• Alone in the relative safety of my home because I knew I dare not *risk* the danger of blacking out in some public place or at the wheel of a car.(p.306)

risked
• Fear of rejection and its ensuing pain were not to be *risked*, and I turned away from myself once more for the answer, this time to the drinks I had always refused before, and in alcohol I found a false courage.(p.546)

risks
• After consulting with his wife and partner he came to the conclusion that it was better to take those *risks* than to stand before his Creator guilty of such ruinous slander.(p.80)
• Now, she no longer *risks* losing her home, her self-respect, or her laundry.(p.369)

risky
• Sometimes I would bring it in my pockets, but they were inspected, and that became too *risky*.(p.176)

Rita
• I'd been sitting comfortably in a restaurant with *Rita*, drinking my sixth martini and hoping the waiter would forget about the lunch order -- at least long enough for me to have a couple more.(p.223)

rival
• While drinking, he accepted a sum of money from a bitterly-hated business *rival*, giving him no receipt for it.(p.80)
• In fact, his *rival* was ruined.(p.80)
• How could he possibly make a public statement exonerating his *rival*?(p.80)

rivalries
• Wherever men are gathered together in business there will be *rivalries* and, arising out of these, a certain amount of office politics.(p.145)
• Social distinctions, petty *rivalries* and jealousies -- these are laughed out of countenance.(p.161)

river
• Did not Professor Langley's flying machine go to the bottom of the Potomac *River*?(p.51)

riverbank
• He'll never read in his "sweetness and light" senior-citizen publications anything but the joys of lolling in the rocking chair, angling on the *riverbank*, or bowling on the green.(p.330)

riverboat
• To wear expensive clothes, to have bartenders know what to serve me before I ordered, to be recognized by headwaiters and shown to the best table, to play gin rummy for high stakes with the insouciance of a *riverboat* gambler -- these were the enduring values in life, I thought.(p.556)

roaches
• I would wake to find myself in some beat-up rooming house, where *roaches* were crawling over everything.(p.527)

road
• We have traveled a rocky *road*, there is no mistake about that.(p.104)
• If such women adopt a spiritual way of life their *road* will be smoother.(p.114)
• He is undoubtedly on the *road* to recovery.(p.139)
• This practice enables us to lend a hand, at the same time avoiding certain alluring distractions of the *road*, about which any traveling man can inform you.(p.162)
• We shall be with you in the Fellowship of the Spirit, and you will surely meet some of us as you trudge the *Road* of Happy Destiny.(p.164)
• After the tire job came the thirties, the Depression and the down hill *road*.(p.244)
• They were earnest and obviously trying to help me on the *road* I had chosen.(p.259)
• There was a very religious family that lived down the *road* from us, and we were on the same party line.(p.265)
• Time went on and the drinking got worse and worse, and I was in another barroom, down the *road* the other way, a small one, and I took my glass -- that morning I'd been able to lift it from the bar -- and I said to the woman behind the bar, "I wish I might never take another drop of that stuff.(p.266)
• I drove these three or four miles down the *road* only to find that Jack was out.(p.267)
• The details of the long *road* back to something resembling normal living -- the first short streetcar ride, the purchase of a used bike which enabled me to widen the narrow horizon of life, the first trip downtown -- I will not dwell on.(p.276)
• His *road* lay clear before me, and I'd better quit rationalizing myself into any detours.(p.282)
• How full it has kept my retirement years -- the five I've lived since the first two lost in traveling a rocky *road* to hell, before I made a U-turn.(p.334)
• I said, "I can't find my middle *road* in life.(p.340)
• She tried reasoning with me, endeavored to work out various drinking schedules, in fact all the tricks were practised faithfully for a short time somewhere along my shaky *road* to unhappiness.(p.361)
• Met father (Tall Man) at fork in *road* -- one way to reservation, other way to State of Maine.(p.475)
• I had replied, "Uncle, give the judge ten dollars, or I'll have to work it out on the county *road*."(p.539)
• While there, I read the Big Book and the Grapevine and began the slow *road* back to health and sanity through the recovery program of A.A.(p.559)

roadhouse
• When I was eighteen, at the end of high school, the high school team had a banquet at a well-known *roadhouse* outside of Akron.(p.194)

roads
• Father is an Episcopal minister and his work takes him over long drives on bad *roads*.(p.497)

roadside
• On the way I felt hungry so I stopped at a *roadside* place where they have a bar.(p.36)

roadster
• A year later I was able to buy a Model T *roadster* and take a better job with a downtown printer.(p.276)

roam
• I wanted to *roam* again and through relatives got a supercargo job on an Australian packet which allowed me to visit my people in Australia where I was born.(p.252)

roar
• In my mind's eye I saw Broadway again and Tom Sharkey's bar; the *roar* of the subway was in my ears.(p.252)

roared
• We gave up our positions and off we *roared* on a motorcycle, the sidecar stuffed with tent, blankets, a change of clothes, and three huge volumes of a financial reference service.(p.2)

roaring
• The alcoholic is like a tornado *roaring* his way through the lives of others.(p.82)
• Some time later, and just as he thought he was getting control of his liquor situation, he went on a *roaring* bender.(p.155)
• I was a product of the post-war prohibition era of the *roaring* '20's.(p.304)
• All I can remember about the *Roaring* Twenties is that I drank a great deal, thought I was having a grand time, managed to get to Europe for a few weeks, was very proud of the dozens of speak-easy cards entitling me to an entree in the better joints between Cleveland and New York, took on a wife, and built a home in a fashionable suburb of Cleveland.(p.358)

robbed
• I never *robbed* my family of anything.(p.351)

robbery
• Three weeks after an armed *robbery* in which one person received a superficial flesh wound (I could have killed someone!), I was apprehended.(p.460)

robe
• I was taken out of the house and put bodily into a waiting car with nothing on but a *robe* and gown.(p.466)

robust
• Though a *robust* man at retirement, he went to pieces quickly and was dead within four years.(p.33)

rock
• But when I cracked my leg with a sixteen-pound sledgehammer in the *rock* hole, I was fighting the system, using my body.(p.458)

rocked
• So I *rocked* along my merry independent way until June, when I went out selling auto polish in New England.(p.247)

Rockefeller
• In the spring of 1940, John D. *Rockefeller*, Jr. gave a dinner for many of his friends to which he invited A.A. members to tell their stories.(p.xviii)
• Speaking at a dinner given by John D. *Rockefeller* Jr. to introduce Alcoholics Anonymous to some of his friends, Dr. Harry Emerson Fosdick remarked: "I think that psychologically speaking there is a point of advantage in the approach that is being made in this movement that cannot be duplicated.(p.574)

rocker
• If someone had told me last year that I would be excited about gardening this year, I would have said he was off his *rocker*.(p.481)

rocket
• Show any longshoreman a Sunday supplement describing a proposal to explore the moon by means of a *rocket* and he will say, "I bet they do it -- maybe not so long either."(p.52)

rocketed
• We have found much of heaven and we have been *rocketed* into a fourth dimension of existence of which we had not even dreamed.(p.25)

rocking
• He'll never read in his "sweetness and light" senior-citizen publications anything but the joys of lolling in the *rocking* chair, angling on the riverbank, or bowling on the green.(p.330)
• The horrors of increasing hangover sickness to occupy the entire day; nausea, dry heaves, the *rocking* bed, the nightmare-filled mind.(p.408)

rocks
• This combination soon landed me on the *rocks*.(p.7)

rocky
• We have traveled a *rocky* road, there is no mistake about that.(p.104)
• How full it has kept my retirement years -- the five I've lived since the first two lost in traveling a *rocky* road to hell, before I made a U-turn.(p.334)

rode
• The people I knew *rode* hard, and some of them drank hard.(p.404)
• Very often we *rode* to and from work together, but being separated really galled me deep down.(p.491)

rods
• I got my first introduction to "riding the *rods* and making a blind."(p.252)

role
• We are in the world to play the *role* He assigns.(p.68)
• The best boarding schools and a finishing school in Europe had fitted me for the conventional *role* of debutante and young matron.(p.225)

roll
• They *roll* on the floor and holler, and pull their hair."(p.266)
• A former employer of mine said to me a little over ten years ago, "Pat, you seem to be one of those unfortunate people who at least once every six months must go out and *roll* in the gutter."(p.513)

rolled
• Returning to the town I had left three months before, I became editor of a monthly magazine, soon had additional publicity and advertising accounts and the money *rolled* in.(p.254)
• The next time vacation time *rolled* around that was a bitter lesson to us.(p.265)
• And then, in the spring of 1939, a very remarkable book was *rolled* off a New York press with the title "Alcoholics Anonymous."(p.307)

• The only other occasionally limiting factor was that I might run out of money before the next payday *rolled* around.(p.398)
• So we *rolled* old newspapers together and made torches to find a good soft pew and get some sleep.(p.424)
• I *rolled* along with the mob this way, that way and the other way, but in those years nothing really bad happened to me.(p.508)
• This time, whoever had *rolled* me had taken my glasses as well (they were gold).(p.538)

rolling

• But did not we, ourselves, set the ball *rolling*?(p.67)
• When I finally returned to Detroit to find work and to learn to stand on my own feet, the ball was already *rolling*, however slowly.(p.282)
• Time after time I would beg forgiveness on bended knees, with tears *rolling* down my cheeks, and promise I would never again drink too much.(p.362)
• This I would do by going completely "bohemian" for a night, getting drunk and *rolling* home with the dawn.(p.432)
• Within a month, the police, the hospital authorities, several kind strangers, most of my friends, all of my close relatives, and a few adepts at *rolling* a drunk and removing his wrist watch and wallet had been involved.(p.532)

romance

• But the head of the house has spent years in pulling down the structures of business, *romance*, friendship, health -- these things are now ruined or damaged.(p.123)

romantic

• They remember when father was *romantic*, thoughtful and successful.(p.123)

roof

• He is not likely to get far in any direction if he fails to show unselfishness and love under his own *roof*.(p.127)
• I was picked up at two-thirty that morning with my car smashed up by a street-car because I had run into a big concrete safety zone, and the street-car had run into me, and they took me out through the *roof* -- there's where I lost the suit.(p.202)
• Need I add that such was the case because I had no money to provide a *roof* over my head?(p.538)

rooftops

• It ran something like this: If I go around shouting from the *rooftops* about my alcoholism, it might very possibly prevent me from getting a good job.(p.282)

room

• As I crossed the threshold of the dining *room*, the thought came to mind that it would be nice to have a couple of cocktails with dinner.(p.41)
• But later, alone in his *room*, he asked himself this question: "Is it possible that all the religious people I have known are wrong?"(p.56)
• At one end of the *room* stood a glass covered directory of local churches.(p.154)
• But one of the friends said, "Put him in a private *room*.(p.157)
• "Who are you fellows, and why this private *room*?(p.157)
• He consented, however, to go the hospital, where he occupied the very *room* recently vacated by the lawyer.(p.159)
• Impressed by those who visited him at the hospital, he capitulated entirely when, later, in an upper *room* of this house, he heard the story of some man whose experience closely tallied with his own.(p.160)
• I drank all I dared in the bar, and then went to my *room* to finish the job.(p.179)
• Between classes I would run down to the wash *room*, take enough to steady my nerves and then go on to the next class.(p.183)
• I was moved into another *room* that morning and there was my wife.(p.184)
• After prescribing medicines, Dr. Bob ordered, "Put him in a private *room*.(p.188)
• We boys drove out in somebody's car and went to the bar on the way do the dining *room* and I, in an effort to impress the other boys that I was city-bred, having lived in Scranton and Cleveland, asked them if they didn't want a drink.(p.194)
• In the basement were to be dry-cleaning facilities, a barbershop, a pool *room*, a grocery shop and everything.(p.198)
• One morning, after I had been on a binge for a couple of days, I awoke to find my brother and Doctor Bob in my *room* talking to me about not drinking.(p.206)
• The next morning, my wife came into my *room* and wakened me and said, "That man is downstairs and he said you said you'd go to Akron."(p.217)
• Bill left me at the elevator and said, "Your *room* is so and so," and I didn't see him again for six months.(p.217)
• I'd waked up in strange rooms before, fully dressed on a bed or a couch; I'd waked up in my own *room*, in or on my own bed, not knowing what hour or day it was, afraid to ask . . . but this was different.(p.222)
• I was in a large, dark, rather poorly furnished *room* -- the living *room* of a basement flat.(p.222)
• I checked into my hotel *room* and then noticed a placard tucked under the glass on the bureau stating "There will be positively NO drinking at this convention" signed by the president of the company.(p.243)
• They did not show me to my *room* and wish me a good night's rest.(p.259)
• There were two women in the St. Thomas Hospital at that time in a *room*.(p.272)
• When the day of their return was almost upon me, and suicide was the only answer I had been able to think of, I went into Ralph's *room* one evening and told him the truth.(p.278)
• I shut myself in my *room*, which began to go around in circles.(p.279)
• This first meeting was held in the living *room* of a home and was led by Bill D., the first man that Bill W. and Dr. Bob had worked with successfully.(p.291)
• When alcohol took me over, my bar was my kitchen, my living *room*, my bedroom, the back bathroom, and the two hampers.(p.335)
• I wandered from *room* to *room*, thinking, drinking, drinking, thinking.(p.337)
• I was living in a small *room* on West 53rd Street right off Fifth Avenue, when I met a young lady who eventually was responsible for altering my entire way of living.(p.359)
• A few hours later I came out of a complete stupor in our living *room* with a flash of sanity.(p.363)
• Near the Laundromat, I would buy one bottle of pop and a few bottles of beer or wine, and go into the rest *room*, empty the pop bottle, refill it with the booze, and proceed to do my laundering.(p.370)
• The only drawback was, I always knew how I arrived there, but somehow, between the rest *room*, the rinse, and the fluff-dry, I never knew when or how I got home.(p.370)
• I woke up in this bare *room* with nothing around me but bars; they wouldn't let me smoke and treated me, well, like I was nuts.(p.387)
• He even had the people come out, and tell me what kind of *room* I was going to have, and that he could come and see me, and that the dog could come and see me.(p.389)
• I wanted a cigarette and *room* service, which I didn't get.(p.390)
• The next morning he came into my *room* and said, "Esther, I'm not going to lecture you any more, but I want you to read this article.(p.391)
• But my board, *room*, and clothing were free, and I could spend the whole ten bucks on booze.(p.398)
• I looked about the *room*.(p.422)
• After my last binge I came home and smashed my dining *room* furniture to splinters, kicked out six windows and two balustrades.(p.435)
• The people there insisted on putting me in a ward, when Max and I both knew I ought to have a private *room*.(p.445)
• And I got my private *room*.(p.445)
• Very shortly, I realized that had been a mistake -- when this big clown came bounding into the *room*, almost shouting, "My name is Frank, and I'm an alcoholic, ha-ha-ha!"(p.446)
• When I didn't have anything else to do -- a dull evening at home -- I'd sneak a few drinks upstairs in my *room*, and that began to be a habit.(p.464)
• Then I went on my first week-long bender of solitary drinking, locked up in a hotel *room*, because my family opposed my coming marriage.(p.464)
• (I think my first feeling of fear came with my first week's solitary drinking, locked up in that hotel *room*.(p.465)
• Then I remember him coming into my *room* one night with a friend, and telling me to get dressed -- we were going away.(p.466)
• The next recollection I have is of my husband coming into my *room* (later found out it was on New Year's Eve) accompanied by two policemen.(p.468)
• On one occasion when I was serving time in my favorite drying-out place while I was having a session with the psychiatrist, she left my case history on her desk when she was called away from the *room*.(p.470)
• Last time I drink, I go to *room*.(p.475)
• My wife received me graciously, although she was living in a one *room* with kitchen affair.(p.490)
• So, finally, I went to the YMCA and they graciously permitted us to use a *room* at two dollars a night.(p.495)
• I climb to my *room* in the attic.(p.497)
• I am in another fellow's *room* at college.(p.497)
• A haze filled the *room*.(p.498)
• I leave the *room*, which the honor system allows.(p.499)
• I go to my *room*.(p.499)
• I must get out of the *room* or I shall jump out of the window.(p.501)
• My wife is in the living *room*.(p.502)
• Four alcoholics play bridge in a smoke-filled *room*.(p.502)
• "Then all of your troubles are over," says the man and leaves the *room*.(p.503)
• I get out of bed and go to the man's *room*.(p.504)
• I call my wife into a *room* where we can talk privately.(p.506)
• When I arrived at The Country Shop, which was a restaurant where they met in Dublin, I found about thirty-five or forty people in the *room*.(p.524)
• I remember being dragged, drink in hand, from beneath the grand piano, where I had hidden, to be locked in my *room* in disgrace.(p.557)

roomed

• At night, I woke up and the folks with whom I *roomed* were home by then.(p.205)

rooming

• But it took six more months of work and disappointments before a group of three men got together in my *rooming* house bedroom for their first A.A. meeting.(p.282)
• She was studying fashion design, was living in the same *rooming* house, and was from my home town of Cleveland.(p.359)
• I would wake to find myself in some beat-up *rooming* house, where roaches were crawling over everything.(p.527)

rooms

• I'd waked up in strange *rooms* before, fully dressed on a bed or a couch; I'd waked up in my own room, in or on my own bed, not knowing what hour or day it was, afraid to ask . . . but this was different.(p.222)

roomy

• To us, the Realm of Spirit is broad, *roomy*, all inclusive; never exclusive or forbidding to those who earnestly seek.(p.46)

roost

• I think the Commanding Officer was rather tired of this particular chicken coming back to *roost* so often because he very soon wrote in to the medical authorities to tell them that they had to get me into hospital, to be thoroughly examined for drinking.(p.520)

root

• I ruthlessly faced my sins and became willing to have my new-found Friend take them away, *root* and branch.(p.13)
• That, we think, is the *root* of our troubles.(p.62)
• We old-timers who get scattered and separated and then witness the construction of services to get in more people and to make this thing function, we think that A.A. has changed, but the *root* of it hasn't.(p.272)
• Whatever the *root* of my unhappiness might turn out to be, I thought, it could not possibly be booze.(p.433)

roots

• His *roots* grasped a new soil.(p.12)
• I resolved that if I were going to continue with the Catholic Church, I was going to know the *roots* of the doctrine, since those *roots* had caused me some confusion.(p.221)
• If our hair is half-bleached (with dark *roots*), poker-straight, and not combed, this adds to our beauty.(p.479)

rope

• She has reached the end of her *rope*.(p.502)
• I was at the end of my *rope*.(p.515)

ropes

• When we first come into A.A., many of us are confused because as a general rule we're at the end of our respective *ropes*, and we don't know what to do.(p.512)

rose

• As the whisky *rose* to my head I told myself I would manage better next time, but I might as well get good and drunk then.(p.6)
• Childhood memories *rose* before me.(p.10)
• Yet we had been seeing another kind of flight, a spiritual liberation from this world, people who *rose* above their problems.(p.55)

• Our friend's gorge ***rose*** as he bitterly cried out: "If there is a God, He certainly hasn't done anything for me!"(p.56)
• Some of them ***rose*** out of ignorance of alcoholism.(p.107)
• When he reached for me, I ***rose*** and smote him.(p.405)

roses
• It's no bed of ***roses***, but somehow or other I've been able to make it, through the kindness of people in A.A.(p.511)

rosy
• And unless I had some ***rosy*** picture of what was going to happen that day, I wouldn't even feel like getting up in the morning at all.(p.325)
• When I landed of course I hit a gin mill, and with three or four good shots under my belt the world began to go into that ***rosy*** glow.(p.513)

Rotary
• I, who had never made a speech in my life and who would have been frightened sick at the prospect, stood up in front of ***Rotary*** groups in different parts of the city and talked about Alcoholics Anonymous.(p.283)
• I got around this by joining the local ***Rotary*** Club, and through this association with the business men of the community my little station began to grow.(p.360)
• It started when I joined a few of the men for cocktails before the noonday ***Rotary*** luncheon.(p.360)
• It was to be short lived, for on the day before Christmas I completely disillusioned my wife and ruined our first Christmas by coming home from the ***Rotary*** lunch dead drunk.(p.361)

rotating
• ***Rotating*** leadership is the best.(p.567)
• The small group may elect its secretary, the large group its ***rotating*** committee, and the groups of a large metropolitan area their central or intergroup committee, which often employs a full-time secretary.(p.567)

rotten
• It became progressively harder to get up in the morning, until one day I asked myself what I would do for a patient who felt this ***rotten***.(p.441)

rouge
• My four years of abstinence had something to do with it, but soldiering is a tough enough game for a sober man, and I had no yen for full-pack slogging through mud with a cognac or vin ***rouge*** hangover.(p.253)

rough
• It is a design for living that works in ***rough*** going.(p.15)
• We have admitted certain defects; we have ascertained in a ***rough*** way what the trouble is; we have put our finger on the weak items in our personal inventory.(p.72)
• She tells how A.A. works when the going is ***rough***.(p.261)
• However, this isn't as ***rough*** as it sounds, as we do become grateful for the necessity that makes us toe the line, for we find that we are more than compensated for a consistent effort by the countless dividends we receive.(p.311)
• However, a ***rough*** estimate of one alcoholic's initiation fee seemed possible.(p.396)
• Drunkalogues and statistics can be boring, but it is necessary to delve a little into each in order to come up with some kind of ***rough*** estimate.(p.396)
• It is bound to be ***rough***, because who can say exactly how much of that green blood – commonly known as money -- was dissipated on dissipation?(p.396)
• So please bear in mind, and I would like to emphasize, that this is a very ***rough*** estimate.(p.399)
• A young veteran tells how a few ***rough*** experiences pushed him into A.A. – and how he was therefore spared years of suffering.(p.422)
• I had a ***rough*** lot, but I don't worry about that, after hearing the stories of many others.(p.511)

roughly
• But this description should identify him ***roughly***.(p.22)

round
• Some of the contemporaries of Columbus thought a ***round*** earth preposterous.(p.51)
• Maybe the doctor has been called in, and the weary ***round*** of sanitariums and hospitals has begun.(p.110)
• My thoughts went ***round*** and ***round*** with "What's it all about anyhow?(p.244)
• To keep it in ***round*** figures, let's say twenty per cent of my income went for giggle gurgles.(p.397)
• After going to school all day, working in the family drugstore all evening, and then studying until one or two in the morning, I would not be able to sleep soundly, with everything I had been studying going ***round*** in my head.(p.440)

rounded
• At any rate the last great step toward a well ***rounded*** life still lay ahead of me.(p.286)
• I ***rounded*** up a few more of my friends and off we went to the meeting, not for anything we would gain from it as much as to make a burlesque out of it.(p.509)

rounds
• Stepping into his car, he made the ***rounds*** of people he had hurt.(p.156)
• I even began to go the ***rounds*** of churches.(p.255)
• I began making the ***rounds*** of the doctors in the hope that one of them might find some cure for my accumulating ailments, preferably something that could be removed surgically.(p.305)
• When my thirty days were up, I started back on my ***rounds***.(p.528)

rouse
• In a vague way their families and friends sense that these drinkers are abnormal, but everybody hopefully awaits the day when the sufferer will ***rouse*** himself from his lethargy and assert his power of will.(p.23)

roused
• I was black and blue, with my lips all swollen, when they ***roused*** us to go into court in the morning.(p.204)

route
• As we left, and they were escorting us across the bridge into Wheeling, I, with great dignity and sarcasm, told them if their wives were ever visiting in Akron, and they, too, were looking for their ***route*** sign as I was, that I hoped I could extend to them the hospitality that had been shown to me in Bellaire.(p.264)
• Within a year of my return to Detroit, A.A. was a definitely established little group of about a dozen members and I too was established in a modest but steady job handling an independent dry-cleaning ***route*** of my own.(p.283)

routine
• "Bathtub" gin, two bottles a day, and often three, got to be ***routine***.(p.5)
• This ***routine*** went on with few interruptions for seventeen years.(p.177)
• In fact, the last three years of my drinking was a ***routine*** of barbiturates in the morning, so that I could stop shaking enough to shave, and then alcohol beginning about four-thirty or five o'clock, with a struggle not to take a drink at noon or during the day, because I had the idea that if I took one drink, I would smell as though I had had a pint.(p.217)
• ***Routine*** jobs bored me, but I would take on the toughest one I could find, work day and night until I had it under control; then it would become tedious and I'd lose all interest in it.(p.243)
• In the eight years before A.A. found me, I had over forty jobs -- selling and travelling -- one thing after another, and the same old ***routine***.(p.244)
• After a particularly bad Christmas and New Year's holiday, dad picked me up again early in January, 1937, to go through the usual sobering up ***routine***.(p.289)
• This ***routine*** was short lived too.(p.362)
• The cocktail hour became a daily ***routine***.(p.374)
• At this stage, I began a daily mental ***routine***.(p.408)

routines
• The same old ***routines*** seemed to be common to us all.(p.246)

routing
• I can still remember very distinctly getting into Akron at eleven p.m. and ***routing*** this same Howard out of bed to do something about me.(p.290)

row
• The remonstrances of my friends terminated in a ***row*** and I became a lone wolf.(p.3)
• I never was on skid ***row***.(p.345)
• Mine was the skid ***row*** of success.(p.345)
• The physical skid ***row*** in any city is miserable.(p.345)
• The skid ***row*** of success is just as miserable.(p.345)
• However, after I heard a few stories of jails, sanitariums, broken homes and skid ***row***, I wondered if I really was an alcoholic.(p.378)
• It didn't say I had to finally live on skid ***row*** and drink bay rum, canned heat or lemon extract.(p.379)
• I stayed with them until I got drunk and had a ***row*** with the Paris editor.(p.405)
• But my attempts at community service ended in a drunken and abusive ***row*** with a fellow volunteer.(p.410)
• But not for long; now, for five Friday nights in a ***row***, I went to jail, picked up sodden with beer (which I always disliked, but which was the only drink available); in jail five consecutive Friday nights in the town where I had grown up, where I had been an honor student in high school, where a kindly uncle, bailing me out, said, "Bob, our family just doesn't do this sort of thing."(p.539)
• I knew it didn't make any difference where I started, the inevitable end would be skid ***row***.(p.548)

rowed
• We never ***rowed*** or fought.(p.264)

rubber
• At the end of this selling of lots, just prior to World War I, I got into the crude ***rubber*** business, and six months later there was only one broker and myself left in Akron.(p.197)
• So in spite of anything that I might do, I prospered, being one of only two brokers in the ***rubber*** center of the world.(p.197)
• The ***rubber*** prosperity went on for about six years -- 1916 to 1922.(p.197)
• Another time, I had a ***rubber*** pool project.(p.198)
• My idea was to have all the companies pool their funds and buy ***rubber*** when ***rubber*** was cheap and then put it in a pool.(p.198)
• When ***rubber*** reached a certain low point, they would draw on the ***rubber*** out of the pool and buy.(p.198)
• I worked along until I had really big names in ***rubber*** on a tentative contract, and then I neglected to go through with it.(p.198)

rubbing
• My Quaker mother-in-law, bless her heart, used to set the Christmas pudding ablaze with lumps of sugar dipped in ***rubbing*** alcohol.(p.402)

rudderless
• I ended up, homeless, jobless, penniless and ***rudderless***, as the problem guest of a close friend whose family was out of town.(p.278)

rugged
• Here was a tall, ***rugged***, highly educated Yankee talking in a matter of course way about God and prayer.(p.279)
• They told me their stories, which were much more ***rugged*** than mine – yet what they said made sense, and the way they put it was easy for me to understand, with an understanding I had never had before.(p.363)
• When I hear the more ***rugged*** stories of alcoholics who became sicker than I did with this affliction, I humbly thank God for showing me "the handwriting on the wall."(p.367)
• Men are supposed to be tough and ***rugged*** to start with, but if a woman becomes that way, it is pretty hard to get back the niceties of womanhood.(p.480)

ruin
• His only chance for sobriety would be some place like the Greenland Ice Cap, and even there an Eskimo might turn up with a bottle of scotch and ***ruin*** everything!(p.101)
• Why could they not see that drink meant ***ruin*** to them?(p.107)
• Is it right to let him ***ruin*** your life and the lives of your children?(p.108)
• He trembled as he went about, for this might mean ***ruin***, particularly to a person in his line of business.(p.156)
• This, plus mounting emotional disturbances, convinced them that compulsive alcoholism already had them; that complete ***ruin*** would be only a question of time.(p.315)

ruined
• In fact, his rival was ***ruined***.(p.80)
• He is like the farmer who came up out of his cyclone cellar to find his home ***ruined***.(p.82)
• He by no means ***ruined*** everything.(p.109)
• But the head of the house has spent years in pulling down the structures of business, romance, friendship, health -- these things are now ***ruined*** or damaged.(p.123)
• I was still bitter because I felt that drink had completely ***ruined*** my childhood and my married life, and I hated everything pertaining to it.(p.262)
• It was to be short lived, for on the day before Christmas I completely disillusioned my wife and ***ruined*** our first Christmas by coming home from the Rotary lunch dead drunk.(p.361)
• The final decision came when my daughter, following a drunk which ***ruined*** my wife's birthday, said, "It's Alcoholics Anonymous -- or else!"(p.378)

ruinous

• After consulting with his wife and partner he came to the conclusion that it was better to take those risks than to stand before his Creator guilty of such *ruinous* slander.(p.80)

rule

• By every form of self-deception and experimentation, they will try to prove themselves exceptions to the *rule*, therefore nonalcoholic.(p.31)

• The *rule* is we must be hard on ourself, but always considerate of others.(p.74)

• Though there may be justifiable exceptions, and though we wish to lay down no *rule* of any sort, we have often found this the best course to take.(p.81)

• Here no specific *rule* can be given.(p.90)

• Obviously, no *rule* can be laid down.(p.99)

• So our *rule* is not to avoid a place where there is drinking, if we have a legitimate reason for being there.(p.101)

• Live and let live is the *rule*.(p.118)

• At the beginning of recovery a man will take, as a *rule*, one of two directions.(p.125)

• Now, this house will hardly accommodate its weekly visitors, for they number sixty or eighty as a *rule*.(p.161)

• Taking that as a foundation, he reasoned that if a man followed that *rule* he could not be selfish.(p.236)

• When we first come into A.A., many of us are confused because as a general *rule* we're at the end of our respective ropes, and we don't know what to do.(p.512)

• Among our rapidly growing membership of thousands of alcoholics such transformations, though frequent, are by no means the *rule*.(p.569)

ruled

• The most accurate answer I can give you is this: Fear has never again *ruled* my life since that day in September, 1938, when I found that a Power greater than myself could not only restore me to sanity but could keep me both sober and sane.(p.285)

• Poor, black, totally *ruled* by alcohol, she felt shut away from any life worth living.(p.526)

ruler

• But I wanted a cosmos, a universe all my own which I had created and where I reigned as chief top reigner and *ruler* over everyone else.(p.535)

rules

• Though none of these principles had the force of *rules* or laws, they had become so widely accepted by 1950 that they were confirmed by our first International Conference held at Cleveland.(p.xix)

• On the other hand – and strange as this may seem to those who do not understand -- once a psychic change has occurred, the very same person who seemed doomed, who had so many problems he despaired of ever solving them, suddenly finds himself easily able to control his desire for alcohol, the only effort necessary being that required to follow a few simple *rules*.(p.xxvii)

• *Rules* were made for others, but not for me.(p.210)

ruling

• I needed alcohol from that night on, and it in turn used me, *ruling* my life for three years.(p.353)

rum

• *RUM*, RADIO AND REBELLION(p.356)

• It didn't say I had to finally live on skid row and drink bay *rum*, canned heat or lemon extract.(p.379)

rummy

• However, he explained to me that he had been just such a *rummy* as I, only for a much longer period of time.(p.302)

• I'm a *rummy*.(p.423)

• To wear expensive clothes, to have bartenders know what to serve me before I ordered, to be recognized by headwaiters and shown to the best table, to play gin *rummy* for high stakes with the insouciance of a riverboat gambler – these were the enduring values in life, I thought.(p.556)

rumor

• *Rumor* had it that he had been committed for alcoholic insanity.(p.9)

rumor-mongers

• Gone are time cards to punch, alarm clocks to obey, nosey *rumor-mongers* and talebearers to evade.(p.329)

run

• I hardly dared cross the street, lest I collapse and be *run* down by an early morning truck, for it was scarcely daylight.(p.6)

• The first requirement is that we be convinced that any life *run* on self-will can hardly be a success.(p.60)

• Each person is like an actor who wants to *run* the whole show; is forever trying to arrange the lights, the ballet, the scenery and the rest of the players in his own way.(p.60)

• They arise out of ourselves, and the alcoholic is an extreme example of self-will *run* riot, though he usually doesn't think so.(p.62)

• We attempt to sweep away the debris which has accumulated out of our effort to live on self-will and *run* the show ourselves.(p.76)

• We have *run* away.(p.105)

• They *run* to extremes.(p.125)

• He will appreciate knowing you are not bothering your head about him, that you are not suspicious nor are you trying to *run* his life so he will be shielded from temptation to drink.(p.146)

• Not being a man of means, I knew that if I did not stay sober enough to earn money, I would *run* out of liquor.(p.175)

• So, at the time Dr. Bob and Bill came along I had about *run* out my strength.(p.182)

• Between classes I would *run* down to the wash room, take enough to steady my nerves and then go on to the next class.(p.183)

• I had *run* into a man I always drank with.(p.201)

• I had *run* into him, and he looked real prosperous; his face and eyes looked clear and he started to compliment me on my good front and how well I looked, and I said, "I haven't had a drink for nine months."(p.201)

• I was picked up at two-thirty that morning with my car smashed up by a street-car because I had *run* into a big concrete safety zone, and the street-car had *run* into me, and they took me out through the roof -- there's where I lost the suit.(p.202)

• He spent eighteen years in running away; and then found he didn't have to *run*.(p.275)

• Where we used to *run* from responsibility, we find ourselves accepting it with gratitude that we can successfully shoulder it.(p.311)

• Surrender to me has meant the ability to *run* my home, to face my responsibilities as they should be faced, to take life as it comes to me day by day, and work my problems out.(p.340)

• I had *run* away from school to join the army in World War I, but missed it by one day since the Armistice was signed the very day I landed in Atlanta to sign up with Uncle Sam.(p.357)

• Like all alcoholics endeavoring to *run* away from themselves and their environment, I decided to go to New York.(p.358)

• The challenge intrigued me; also it was another opportunity to *run* away from myself and the "fast life of the big city."(p.359)

• The only other occasionally limiting factor was that I might *run* out of money before the next payday rolled around.(p.398)

• Or, "My physical plant had got a little *run* down and the stuff rushed right to my head."(p.433)

• In the garage, I would put the needle in my vein and then try to figure out exactly how much medication to inject to overcome the pep pills while adding to the sleeping pills while ignoring the tranquilizers, in order to get just enough to be able to pull out the needle, jerk the tourniquet, throw it in the car, slam the car door shut, *run* down the hall, and fall in bed before I fell asleep.(p.442)

• "That's a devil of a way to *run* an organization," I thought, and I reported Frank to the psychiatrist, who didn't seem perturbed; he just got someone else to take me on Fridays.(p.447)

• Most of us did not stay out of prison long enough to *run* the alcoholic gamut -- to develop the ongoing kind of alcoholism or alcoholic drinking you hear about in A.A. talks.(p.458)

• After the first two or three days you were allowed the *run* of the place and it was a lot of fun.(p.468)

• I join Canadian Army, but could not *run* away from problem.(p.474)

• When counties *run* out, I move to Connecticut.(p.475)

• We must learn to walk before we can *run*.(p.516)

• I went to a very good public school *run* by Jesuits.(p.517)

• I buttonholed him after dinner and gave him a few tips on how to *run* his colony better and the result of that was about a fortnight or so later I was shipped back to my regiment.(p.520)

• My father was and still is a minister, and I was afraid that I might *run* into him, or that someone might tell him where I was, and I could still remember what he had done to me when I got drunk one Christmas when I was very young.(p.527)

run-around

• After your man has gone along without drinking for a few months, you may be able to make use of his services with other employees who are giving you the alcoholic *run-around* -- provided, of course, they are willing to have a third party in the picture.(p.146)

running

• Here we find human opinions *running* to extremes -- absurd extremes, perhaps.(p.68)

• We constantly remind ourselves we are no longer *running* the show, humbly saying to ourselves many times each day "Thy will be done."(p.87)

• One was the fear of not sleeping, and the other was the fear of *running* out of liquor.(p.175)

• Later, I realized that I was *running* from alcohol.(p.183)

• I paced the floor with a bath towel around my shoulders, the perspiration *running* off me.(p.268)

• He spent eighteen years in *running* away; and then found he didn't have to run.(p.275)

• I have faced life instead of *running* away from it.(p.285)

• I do feel, though, that the fact that I finally grew up to a point where I could even tackle such a job is the apex of the story of a man who spent eighteen years *running* away from life.(p.286)

• It was all about Scott Fitzgerald's little lost debutante, abused, misunderstood and *running* wild.(p.402)

• It combined *running* away from my world, and drinking all I wanted to.(p.407)

• Most of the time I was covered with bruises from "*running* into doors."(p.411)

• Only A.A. kept me from *running* away.(p.420)

• Much of my time was spent writing letters, notes, orders, and lists of things for Max, who was also my office nurse, to do to keep the world *running* while I was locked up.(p.445)

• During the twenty-four hours after *running* into the Serenity Prayer, I think I took the first three Steps for the first time.(p.461)

• But more important, I would have found that once again I was sitting in the driver's seat – I was *running* the show.(p.471)

• The Higher Power to whom I had turned, and who had sustained me, had once again been thrust into the background, while my emotions were *running* my life and, as always, my emotions ran me to the bottle.(p.472)

• One morning, however, I realized I had to get rid of it, for my reprieve was *running* out, and if I didn't get rid of it I was going to get drunk – and I didn't want to get drunk any more.(p.552)

runs

• Our shoes are not better than the average hobo's, and if we are fortunate enough to have a pair of stockings on, nobody notices the *runs* in them, because of our dazzling beauty and our dirty feet.(p.479)

runt

• There was the physical aspect; to be the youngest and the *runt* of the brood of children, to have to wear glasses very early and so to be teased, to be bookish and bored in school because the captain of the football team could not translate Virgil and yet was the school god while you, you, you little shrimp, were the school egghead, junior size and an early model.(p.533)

ruptured

• I well remember the shock I received when a prominent doctor in Chicago told me of cases where pressure of the spinal fluid actually *ruptured* the brain.(p.140)

rush

• This brought a *rush* of 800 frantic inquiries into the little New York office which meanwhile had been established.(p.xviii)

• I didn't know whether I had told him to *rush* to the hospital and I'd meet him there, or to take two aspirin and call me in the morning.(p.441)

• They build you up with a lot of false hopes and promises, and *rush* you around here and there and then, all of a sudden, it's gone."(p.472)

rushed

• If he has trouble later, he is likely to say you *rushed* him.(p.95)

• In the midst of such pandemonium they may have *rushed* out threatening to live with the other woman forever.(p.106)

• Headstrong and willful, I *rushed* from pleasure to pleasure, and found the returns diminishing to the vanishing point.(p.226)

• A friend of mine, a golf nut, *rushed* out on retirement to play every day.(p.330)

• Or, "My physical plant had got a little run down and the stuff *rushed* right to my head."(p.433)

rushes

• Few people really are, for that means blind faith in

the strange proposition that this universe originated in a cipher and aimlessly ***rushes*** nowhere.(p.10)
• We think it dangerous if he ***rushes*** headlong at his economic problem.(p.126)

Russ

• I could do something for their ***Russ***.(p.262)
• And ***Russ*** didn't tell me he'd stop drinking, and he certainly didn't stop.(p.262)
• ***Russ*** read a piece in the paper, and he kind of snickered, and said, "See here, where John D. has found something to keep him from drinking!"(p.265)
• ***Russ*** said, "Mother, if this tells us how to do it, you'll have to read it."(p.268)
• I was reading it for all that was in it, and I said to ***Russ***, "We can't do this.(p.269)
• I'd like to say here how important it was to us then that we do all the little things that people said were important, because later when ***Russ*** was so sick that I had to hold him up, they had a meeting out at the house.(p.270)
• When we closed the meeting with the Lord's Prayer, ***Russ*** said, "Mother, help me stand."(p.270)
• ***Russ*** used to be very much pleased because he'd say, "I think Dr. Bob thoroughly enjoys coming out here.(p.271)
• And ***Russ*** said, "I would have sworn that was Jack M."(p.271)
• The next morning his wife came dragging him in before ***Russ*** went to work, while I was getting breakfast.(p.271)
• We wept and ***Russ*** didn't go to work.(p.271)
• ***Russ*** said, "Don't do another thing today but help him.(p.271)
• I thought I had done that until ***Russ***' second collapse, and the doctor told me very candidly that he wasn't long for this world.(p.271)
• ***Russ*** lived a year longer than they expected him to live, and in that year he was in bed for at least six months.(p.272)
• (***Russ*** was buried on Friday, and on Sunday afternoon Hilda S. had invited me there to dinner Sunday night, and I didn't think I could do it.(p.272)

rut

• I said to my husband, "I'm going to try, every free moment that I have, to get interested in something outside, get myself over this ***rut*** I'm in."(p.338)

Ruth

• They sent me the regular letter they send to everybody else, but along with it, ***Ruth*** Hock, the nonalcoholic secretary, wrote a longhand note because she could see from the letter that I really needed help badly.(p.392)
• There are so many to whom I feel deeply grateful; to my husband (and best critic), whose generous love, compassion and understanding have helped me along the way; to those before me in A.A. who inspired the first article I read, and the friend who sent that article to Frank; to ***Ruth*** for her personal note, and the first A.A. to talk to me; to my Bishop, whose loving and believing spirit inspired me; and to all the members of the Houston Group who were so patient, kind and helpful -- and to countless others.(p.393)

ruthless

• Approached in this way, the most ***ruthless*** creditor will sometimes surprise us.(p.78)

ruthlessly

• I ***ruthlessly*** faced my sins and became willing to have my new-found Friend take them away, root and branch.(p.13)

Ss

sacks
- Economic conditions had a great deal to do with it, because I've often heard my father say that his mother would take one of the old time flour *sacks* and cut a hole through the bottom and two corners of it and there you'd have a gown.(p.486)

sacred
- The *sacred* word was broken and you never trusted your father again, and avoided him.(p.533)

sacrifice
- There are many situations which arise out of the phenomenon of craving which cause men to make the supreme *sacrifice* rather than continue to fight.(p.xxviii)
- Therefore, we are not to be the hasty and foolish martyr who would needlessly *sacrifice* others to save himself from the alcoholic pit.(p.79)
- To be vital, faith must be accompanied by self *sacrifice* and unselfish, constructive action.(p.93)

sad
- It brings misunderstanding, fierce resentment, financial insecurity, disgusted friends and employers, warped lives of blameless children, *sad* wives and parents – anyone can increase the list.(p.18)
- He is like the retired business man who lolls in the Florida sunshine in the winter complaining of the *sad* state of the nation; the minister who sighs over the sins of the twentieth century; politicians and reformers who are sure all would be Utopia if the rest of the world would only behave; the outlaw safe cracker who thinks society has wronged him; and the alcoholic who has lost all and is locked up.(p.61)
- Lying on the divan, "getting in the mood" to write, I cried openly or inwardly, as I listened to *sad* songs.(p.332)
- We soon resumed our marriage, even moved away from the street of *sad* memories and found a new home.(p.371)
- I read *sad* poetry, cried, drank red wine, wrote *sad* poetry, and drank some more.(p.405)
- And having sung that phrase, I'd chuckle with amusement, turning into irony turning into self-contempt turning into self-pity, at the *sad* fate of Bob, that wonderful, poor little motherless boy who was so smart in school and who grew up to accept responsibility so early and so fast and who staggered under his burdens without a whimper until the time came when he thought he was too good for this world and so he ought to be out of it.(p.532)

sadder
- Looking *sadder* than ever, he wearily ventured, "Well this is wonderful for you fellows, but it can't be for me.(p.188)

saddest
- But the *saddest*, and thus the most consoling, drifted through from the country-music station – stories of broken hearts, wasted lives, lost loves, sung plaintively.(p.332)

saddles
- Many of them carried a flask and sandwich case, strapped to their *saddles* so they could stay out all day.(p.404)

safe
- He is like the retired business man who lolls in the Florida sunshine in the winter complaining of the sad state of the nation; the minister who sighs over the sins of the twentieth century; politicians and reformers who are sure all would be Utopia if the rest of the world would only behave; the outlaw *safe* cracker who thinks society has wronged him; and the alcoholic who has lost all and is locked up.(p.61)
- We feel as though we had been placed in a position of neutrality – *safe* and protected.(p.85)
- With the passing of the Eighteenth Amendment I felt quite *safe*.(p.175)
- When beer first came back, I thought that I was *safe*.(p.177)
- In other words, I was always *safe* from the discipline of my father, and having developed along that line, I had considerable difficulty in school.(p.210)
- The hospital had seemed so *safe*.(p.279)
- But I am *safe* and warm.(p.497)

safely
- These allergic types can never *safely* use alcohol in any form at all; and once having formed the habit and found they cannot break it, once having lost their self-confidence, their reliance upon things human, their problems pile up on them and become astonishingly difficult to solve.(p.xxvi)
- This newsman covered life from top to bottom; but he ended up, *safely* enough, in the middle.(p.251)
- *Safely* pensioned, with no job to protect, at last he could drink as he pleased.(p.327)
- Now, no longer under pressure, I could *safely* guard against loss of control.(p.327)

safer
- He always thought that maybe I was *safer* in a building where there were other people.(p.388)

safety
- I was picked up at two-thirty that morning with my car smashed up by a street-car because I had run into a big concrete *safety* zone, and the street-car had run into me, and they took me out through the roof -- there's where I lost the suit.(p.202)
- He had taken up light work, and he had a *safety* valve and a pair of spurs and the clothes on his back, and that was all.(p.263)
- Alone in the relative *safety* of my home because I knew I dare not risk the danger of blacking out in some public place or at the wheel of a car.(p.306)

sail
- She had just come in and was scheduled to *sail* in two days.(p.252)

sailed
- In time we *sailed* for "Over There."(p.1)
- With a good stake I *sailed* for New York.(p.251)

sailor
- Regaining my health, I became an avid jogger, *sailor*, and skier.(p.559)

sailors
- Her idea of fun on a bender was to hit *sailors* and insult cops.(p.414)

saint
- He had also been greatly helped by the late Dr. William D. Silkworth, a New York specialist in alcoholism who is now accounted no less than a medical *saint* by A.A. members, and whose story of the early days of our Society appears in the next pages.(p.xvi)
- Guess I'll never be a *saint*, but whatever I am, I want to be sober and in A.A.(p.463)

saints
- We are not *saints*.(p.60)

sake
- "She's such a sweet girl, I should think he'd stop for her *sake*."(p.20)
- How often have some of us begun to drink in this nonchalant way, and after the third or fourth, pounded on the bar and said to ourselves, "For God's *sake*, how did I ever get started again?"(p.24)
- For his *sake*, we do recount and almost relive the horrors of our past.(p.132)
- We shook hands, and he hung onto my hand for a moment and said, "Tell you what I'll do for old times *sake*.(p.201)
- I said, "Well, I stood it to keep the home together, and for the children's *sake*."(p.322)
- She left, and I sat down and crossed my hands, and looked up and said, "For God's *sake*, help me."(p.351)
- When our meeting night came around the next evening, I went -- "for her *sake*" I told her.(p.365)
- She told me not to bother going "for her *sake*"; she told me in a nice way that it didn't make any difference to her – and that really scared me – so I went.(p.365)
- I was told that I must want sobriety for my own *sake* and I am convinced this is true.(p.379)
- When a big, healthy-looking young fellow stood up there and said, "I'm a success today if I don't drink today," I thought, "Man, I've got a thousand things to do today before I can brag about not taking a drink, for God's *sake*!"(p.447)
- I was trying for her *sake*.(p.514)
- When I remark that I have been in jail nine times, and in an alcoholic ward twice, they think I'm kidding, or possibly dramatizing for the *sake* of a good yarn.(p.542)

salary
- Then it was my turn – I ordered "Three beers," but this time it was different, I had a cash investment of thirty cents and, on a ten dollar a week *salary*, that's a big thing.(p.247)
- Every encouragement was given me with frequent *salary* increases, but the sober times between "periods" became shorter.(p.254)
- For an estimate of *salary* from the twenty-one a month to start with, to over $400 per month upon my retirement after twenty years in the Navy, I believe that an average income of $2,000 a year over this period is low, but as I stated earlier, an underestimate is best.(p.399)
- I think the thing that galled me was that just after Easter I had drawn my *salary* for two weeks' work and had decided that I was going to send some money to Vi; and above all else I was going to send my baby daughter an Easter outfit.(p.493)
- My *salary* has been cut.(p.500)
- The only thing this changed, however, was my surroundings, and it was soon apparent that I could have the same uncomfortable emotions with an unlimited checking account that I could on a working girl's *salary*.(p.545)

sale
- I know that one of the outfits I had was a skirt and a very funny looking blouse that my mother had picked up at a rummage *sale*.(p.261)
- No *sale* -- no lunch.(p.283)

sales
- I was moved in as *Sales* Manager and had four men working under me.(p.200)
- My next job was in *sales* promotion for an oil company in Mississippi where I promptly became high man and got lots of pats on the back.(p.242)
- Then came a *sales* job with a national tire company.(p.243)
- I re-organized their city *sales* policy and eighteen months later, when I was thirty, they offered me the branch managership.(p.243)

salesman
- He is a good *salesman*.(p.35)
- His family was re-assembled, and he began to work as a *salesman* for the business he had lost through drinking.(p.35)
- I remember I felt irritated that I had to be a *salesman* for a concern I once owned.(p.36)
- I can also remember that he was a *salesman* and a very good one.(p.193)
- How it finally broke a Southerner's obstinacy and destined this *salesman* to start A.A. at Philadelphia.(p.238)
- The only *salesman* invited to talk at the convention?(p.243)
- We complement each other beautifully, as he is a born *salesman* and my taste is for finance and management.(p.284)
- I was a good *salesman*.(p.289)
- I am a traveling *salesman*.(p.500)

salesmanship
- By persistence and *salesmanship* I managed to see more and more of my new friend, and because of her sympathetic nature she tolerated my company.(p.359)
- My *salesmanship* was still good, for in the fall of 1938 she called me from Salt Lake and finally agreed to take me on for better or for worse.(p.360)

salesmen
- It was the obituary of one of the best *salesmen* I ever had.(p.137)
- There are two alcoholic employees, who produce as much as five normal *salesmen*.(p.149)
- Some of us are *salesmen* and go about.(p.162)
- In the summer of 1938, almost a year from the time I made my original contact with Akron, the man for whom I was working and who knew about the program, approached me and asked if I could do anything about one of his *salesmen* who was drinking very heavily.(p.294)

sally
- As ex-problem drinkers, we smile at such a *sally*.(p.151)

salon
- I also wanted to be the queen of society, with a glittering *salon*, the bride of a dream prince and the mother of a happy brood.(p.400)

saloon
- Friends who have reasoned with him after a spree which has brought him to the point of divorce or bankruptcy are mystified when he walks directly into a *saloon*.(p.35)
- However, on a couple of other occasions, Clarence

seemed to bob up at the last *saloon* that I would stop at on the way home every day.(p.216)
• At that time I could go into any *saloon,* have one or two beers, walk out and forget about it.(p.231)
• Upon leaving the office in the evening, my first stop would be a *saloon* about a block away.(p.298)

saloon-keepers
• Even some of the *saloon-keepers,* where I had spent so much time and money, requested that I stay away from their places.(p.301)

saloons
• For weeks after my arrival I was feted and entertained in the already large colony of Alsatians in the city, and among the Germans in their *saloons* and clubs.(p.231)
• However, as there happened to be several *saloons* within that distance, I didn't find it necessary to patronize the same place each evening.(p.298)
• I went to *saloons* where I could get drinks.(p.423)
• I had a habit of getting up just prior to the closing time of the *saloons,* about two or three o'clock in the morning.(p.514)

Salt Lake
• At this time, however, she had an opportunity to go to *Salt Lake* City on a new project for the government, but she did promise me that if I would curtail my drinking and buckle down to hard work she would give serious consideration to my latest proposal and maybe join me at a later date when I got settled.(p.359)
• My salesmanship was still good, for in the fall of 1938 she called me from *Salt Lake* and finally agreed to take me on for better or for worse.(p.360)

Salt Lake City
• At this time, however, she had an opportunity to go to *Salt Lake City* on a new project for the government, but she did promise me that if I would curtail my drinking and buckle down to hard work she would give serious consideration to my latest proposal and maybe join me at a later date when I got settled.(p.359)

salvaging
• To me, this incident illustrates lack of understanding as to what really ails the alcoholic, and lack of knowledge as to what part employers might profitably take in *salvaging* their sick employees.(p.139)
• Is he worth *salvaging*?(p.140)

salvation
• There is another meaning for the Hebrew word that in the King James version of the Bible is translated "*salvation.*"(p.228)
• I had found my *salvation*.(p.228)
• And I realize that there was one *salvation* for me.(p.272)
• I felt like a gangster's moll about to be interviewed by the *Salvation* Army.(p.413)

salve
• I know I do not have to be "queen of them all" to *salve* a frightened ego.(p.416)

Sam
• I had run away from school to join the army in World War I, but missed it by one day since the Armistice was signed the very day I landed in Atlanta to sign up with Uncle *Sam*.(p.357)

Samaritan
• You have to act the Good *Samaritan* every day, if need be.(p.97)
• He talked me into taking the *Samaritan* Treatment.(p.389)
• So I took the *Samaritan* Treatment.(p.389)

Samaritans
• So I was driven to Akron the very next day by these Good *Samaritans,* and turned over to Dr. Bob and the then tiny Akron Group.(p.279)

same
• "Bill's Story," "Doctor Bob's Nightmare," and one other personal history from the first edition were retained intact; three were edited and one of these was retitled; new versions of two stories were written with new titles; thirty completely new stories were added; and the story section was divided into three parts, under the *same* headings that are used now.(p.xi)
• All changes made over the years in the Big Book (A.A. members' fond nickname for this volume) have had the *same* purpose: to represent the current membership of Alcoholics Anonymous more accurately, and thereby to reach more alcoholics.(p.xii)
• Alcohol being no respecter of persons, we are an accurate cross section of America, and in distant lands, the *same* democratic evening-up process is now going on.(p.xx)
• The Twelve Steps that summarize the program may be called los Doce Pasos in one country, los Douze Etapes in another, but they trace exactly the *same* path to recovery that was blazed by the earliest members of Alcoholics Anonymous.(p.xxii)
• On the other hand – and strange as this may seem to those who do not understand -- once a psychic change has occurred, the very *same* person who seemed doomed, who had so many problems he despaired of ever solving them, suddenly finds himself easily able to control his desire for alcohol, the only effort necessary being that required to follow a few simple rules.(p.xxvii)
• I have since talked with scores of men who felt the *same* way.(p.12)
• That the man who is making the approach has had the *same* difficulty, that he obviously knows what he is talking about, that his whole deportment shouts at the new prospect that he is a man with a real answer, that he has no attitude of Holier Than Thou, nothing whatever except the sincere desire to be helpful; that there are no fees to pay, no axes to grind, no people to please, no lectures to be endured -- these are the conditions we have found most effective.(p.18)
• We, in our turn, sought the *same* escape with all the desperation of drowning men.(p.28)
• We had to ask ourselves why we shouldn't apply to our human problems this *same* readiness to change our point of view.(p.52)
• We did exactly the *same* thing with our lives.(p.64)
• We asked God to help us show them the *same* tolerance, pity, and patience that we would cheerfully grant a sick friend.(p.67)
• The *same* principles which apply to husband number one should be practiced.(p.112)
• The *same* principle applies in dealing with the children.(p.115)
• One day he told me about an executive of the *same* bank who, from his description, was undoubtedly alcoholic.(p.138)
• Should he have the *same* consideration as other ailing employees?(p.140)
• At the *same* time you will feel no reluctance to rid yourself of those who cannot or will not stop.(p.148)
• This *same* company spends millions for research every year.(p.149)
• Being wrecked in the *same* vessel, being restored and united under one God, with hearts and minds attuned to the welfare of others, the things which matter so much to some people no longer signify much to them.(p.161)
• Under only slightly different conditions, the *same* thing is taking place in many eastern cities.(p.161)
• There are the *same* fast friendships, there is the *same* helpfulness to one another as you find among our western friends.(p.162)
• This practice enables us to lend a hand, at the *same* time avoiding certain alluring distractions of the road, about which any traveling man can inform you.(p.162)
• I was between Scylla and Charybdis now, because if I did not drink my stomach tortured me, and if I did, my nerves did the *same* thing.(p.175)
• We could not be invited out because I would surely get tight and my wife dared not invite people in for the *same* reason.(p.177)
• I used to get terribly upset when I saw my friends drink and knew I could not, but I schooled myself to believe that though I once had the *same* privilege, I had abused it so frightfully that it was withdrawn.(p.181)
• I'm so grateful for both the program and the people in it that I still want to go, and then probably the most wonderful thing that I learned from the program -- I've seen this in the 'A.A. Grapevine' a lot of times, and I've had people say it to me personally, and I've heard people get up in meetings and make the *same* statement: The statement is, "I came into A.A. solely for the purpose of sobriety, but it has been through A.A. that I have found God."(p.192)
• "Who is convinced against his will is of the *same* opinion still."(p.193)
• I kept watching the man down the bar to see what he did with a contraption like that, and he just smelled of his drink and set it down again, so I did the *same*.(p.195)
• Then I started drinking again, with possibly a little more restraint, periods a little bit longer than they had been before, but substantially the *same* pattern.(p.203)
• That was an experience that I have never forgotten, and many times in my own work with A.A. newcomers I feel kind of guilty because I haven't done the *same* thing.(p.219)
• That was skeptically received by me when I first heard it, but after some twenty-eight or thirty fellows had come to see me, and pretty nearly all of them had said the *same* thing, I began to believe it.(p.219)
• For me, work was only a different means to the *same* end, to be able to do exactly what I wanted to do.(p.225)
• Many of these *same* things had happened to me many times before, but this time they had all descended together.(p.238)
• I don't remember much of what he said, but I did realize that here was another guy exactly like me; he had been in the *same* laughing academies and the *same* jails, known the *same* loss of jobs, *same* frustrations, *same* boredom and the *same* loneliness.(p.239)
• Jackie told me about a group of fellows in New York, of whom my old friend Fitz was one, who had the *same* problem I had, and who by working together to help each other were not now drinking and were happy like himself.(p.239)
• That is where I had my first drink and I still remember it, for every "first" drink afterwards did exactly the *same* trick -- I could feel it go right through every bit of my body and down to my very toes.(p.241)
• In the eight years before A.A. found me, I had over forty jobs -- selling and travelling -- one thing after another, and the *same* old routine.(p.244)
• The *same* old routines seemed to be common to us all.(p.246)
• Much later I discovered the elders held many prayer meetings hoping to find a way to give me the heave-ho, but at the *same* time stay tolerant and spiritual.(p.247)
• I look back and remember these things because they made me very unhappy, and added to my feeling of inferiority at never being the *same* as other people.(p.261)
• We drank with exactly the *same* accord that we finally accepted A.A.(p.265)
• There was a very religious family that lived down the road from us, and we were on the *same* party line.(p.265)
• Right away, I saw it was the *same* outfit this other guy told me about, and then again hope died.(p.267)
• My parents died, both in the *same* year, leaving me, a sheltered and somewhat immature man, on my own.(p.277)
• There was the *same* reward – exhilaration at a mission accomplished.(p.283)
• That *same* year, my wife became fed up with my drinking around the house and called my dad in Akron to come and pick me up.(p.288)
• He waited until I was completely sober and the day before I was to head back for Chicago, he told me of a small group of men in Akron who apparently had the *same* problem that I had but were doing something about it.(p.289)
• I can still remember very distinctly getting into Akron at eleven p.m. and routing this *same* Howard out of bed to do something about me.(p.290)
• Here was a man with essentially the *same* outlook on life, except that he had done something about it.(p.290)
• Their answer was always the *same*: If they should need it at any time they would surely get in touch with me.(p.293)
• The parties waxed more liquid and hilarious as time went on, and eventually I discovered that a little shot of liquor now and then between beers had the tendency to put me in a whacky mood much quicker than having to down several quarts of beer to obtain the *same* effect.(p.298)
• However, as there happened to be several saloons within that distance, I didn't find it necessary to patronize the *same* place each evening.(p.298)
• It doesn't pay to be seen in the *same* place at the *same* hour every day.(p.299)
• The *same* as before, I stayed drunk pretty much of the time.(p.318)
• You know I'll do it tomorrow, the very *same* thing."(p.325)
• I had to give him a story and ask him the *same* question over and over again, "Well, now, how many will that bottle serve?"(p.336)
• The *same* thing occurred in medical school.(p.345)
• When a few drinks made me feel good before I went over that line, those *same* drinks now made me wretched.(p.346)
• But I made my admission just the *same*.(p.350)
• She was studying fashion design, was living in the *same* rooming house, and was from my home town of Cleveland.(p.359)
• In 1940 another good opportunity came up and we moved to Pittsburgh where I was to manage two radio stations under the *same* ownership.(p.361)
• In September of this *same* year I went to New York alone.(p.364)

• She said she cut this clipping from the paper at about ten on the *same* night, and at the *same* time as I called A.A. in Pittsburgh -- some 1300 miles away.(p.367)
• Before too long, my husband (who seemed to prefer his shirts dirty) put his foot down, declaring that our family might have the cleanest clothes in town, but that I hadn't been out of the *same* old dirty slacks and blouse for a week.(p.371)
• I saw at last that I had the *same* disease my father had, only I was being given a chance to live, not die.(p.371)
• I don't know what I expected, but I most certainly didn't visualize a group of people talking about their drinking problems, making light of their personal tragedies and at the *same* time enjoying themselves.(p.378)
• But, as it was with drinking, this project will be entered into with enthusiasm and optimism -- and probably wind up the *same* way, depressed.(p.396)
• Three years later I was discharged in the *same* way.(p.425)
• My daily alcoholic consumption remained about the *same* through all this, with perhaps a slight increase, and my binges remained one-nighters.(p.434)
• In the end, I had to do the *same* with alcohol and all pills.(p.443)
• I can do the *same* thing with an A.A. meeting.(p.451)
• All found themselves headed for the *same* destruction, and it seemed they could to nothing whatever to stop it.(p.455)
• *Same* thing when I let lye and water eat away at four of my toes and my foot for five hours.(p.458)
• (I am looking at it now in my bedroom – a copy that was presented to me a couple of years ago by the A.A. group in that *same* prison.)(p.461)
• The *same* doctor who had sent me to the psycho had asked my husband, "Why don't you send her to this Alcoholics Anonymous?"(p.469)
• (I've met some of these *same* women since in A.A.)(p.471)
• Then I know we walk *same* trail.(p.476)
• Find *same* A.A., *same* Spirit.(p.476)
• I don't know whether it was right or wrong, but at least I know that people weren't thinking the *same*.(p.484)
• We were now both working in the *same* agency.(p.490)
• Within about ten days I got locked up for being drunk and this *same* policeman was in the station house as I was being booked.(p.491)
• I had to put up a three hundred dollar bond because he was carrying the *same* summons around in his pocket for me.(p.491)
• But as he continued to talk, I realized that this was the first time I had met a person who had the *same* problems I did and who, I sincerely believe, understood me as an individual.(p.494)
• The *same* old problems and worries surround me.(p.505)
• I have my ups and downs the *same* as the rest.(p.511)
• Lots of the older people had taken to drinking quite a good deal more during the war, but the younger generation was, I think, about the *same*.(p.518)
• I stopped off just to have one drink to see if it tasted the *same* on the way back to London, and that night I was carried back to bed again.(p.522)
• I am talking about A.A. people, who have gone through some of the *same* things that you might be going through now.(p.529)
• We all have the *same* sickness, and in helping one another, we are able to stay sober.(p.530)
• There was the love affair which was ridiculous -- "imagine that midget being able to fall in love!" -- and my head knew it while my heart pumped real, genuine anguish, for it hurt like hell, and since it was first love, things have never been quite the *same*.(p.534)
• The only thing this changed, however, was my surroundings, and it was soon apparent that I could have the *same* uncomfortable emotions with an unlimited checking account that I could on a working girl's salary.(p.545)
• My doctor finally declared he could no longer be responsible for me, and sent me to a psychiatrist who practiced in the *same* suite of offices.(p.558)

sample
• After a few more estimates as to income and expenditures for booze over a few *sample* years, taken at random, I conclude that this twenty per cent stayed fairly constant.(p.398)

sampled
• I very early *sampled* the effects of alcohol.(p.211)

samples
• Peddling off my polish *samples* for expenses, I crawled back to New York a few days later in a very chastened frame of mind.(p.248)

San Antonio
• When it was closed through Washington edict I began with Federal Writers in *San Antonio*.(p.256)

San Diego
• I spent the time in a nearby tavern, was loaded on the ship, went to sleep before take-off, and the next thing I knew someone was shaking me and telling me we were over *San Diego*.(p.428)
• I was escorted back to *San Diego* next morning -- by the Shore Patrol, but I was discharged on schedule.(p.428)

San Francisco
• For the next five years, I was in and out of A.A. in Los Angeles, Phoenix, and *San Francisco*.(p.460)

sand
• Have we tried to make mortar without *sand*?(p.75)

Sandhurst
• I had two years at Dublin University, and then in 1916, I got a nomination for *Sandhurst*, the British Military College.(p.518)

sandwich
• I just thought I would get a *sandwich*.(p.36)
• I sat down at a table and ordered a *sandwich* and a glass of milk.(p.36)
• I ordered another *sandwich* and decided to have another glass of milk.(p.36)
• And I said, "Well, they brought a pitcher of coffee, and a *sandwich* wrapped up for me."(p.264)
• Many of them carried a flask and *sandwich* case, strapped to their saddles so they could stay out all day.(p.404)

sandwiches
• We ordered *sandwiches* and one man said, "Three beers."(p.247)

sane
• For a moment I was alarmed, and called my friend, the doctor, to ask if I were still *sane*.(p.14)
• Hence we are at pains to tell why we think our present faith is reasonable, why we think it more *sane* and logical to believe than not to believe, why we say our former thinking was soft and mushy when we threw up our hands in doubt and said, "We don't know."(p.53)
• In this way we tried to shape a *sane* and sound ideal for our future sex life.(p.69)
• If your talk has been *sane*, quiet and full of human understanding, you have perhaps made a friend.(p.94)
• We have found nothing incompatible between a powerful spiritual experience and a life of *sane* and happy usefulness.(p.130)
• Nothing will help the man who is off on a spiritual tangent so much as the wife who adopts a *sane* spiritual program, making a better practical use of it.(p.130)
• The most accurate answer I can give you is this: Fear has never again ruled my life since that day in September, 1938, when I found that a Power greater than myself could not only restore me to sanity but could keep me both sober and *sane*.(p.285)
• Strangely enough, I became acquainted with the "hilarious life" just at the time in my own life when I was beginning really to settle down to a common-sense, *sane* domesticity.(p.297)
• They realized that in the end alcoholism could be a mortal as cancer; certainly no *sane* man would wait for a malignant growth to become fatal before seeking help.(p.315)
• It solved their problems and they started living a *sane* life again.(p.427)
• Today I think of life in terms of happiness, contentment, freedom from fear and despair, *sane* thinking, ability to face problems as they occur, the opportunity to help other alcoholics and to be decent.(p.430)
• Here was power to live to the end of any given day, power to have the courage to face the next day, power to have friends, power to help people, power to be *sane*, power to stay sober.(p.436)
• My work is on a much deeper and more significant level than it ever was before, and I am today a fairly creative, relatively *sane* human being.(p.438)
• It's been true in my case, nor could I quarrel with "restore us to sanity," for my actions drunk or sober, before A.A., were not those of a *sane* person.(p.550)

sanely
• We react *sanely* and normally, and we will find that this has happened automatically.(p.84)

sang
• The grand fellow who at my call made me a hail-fellow-well-met, who gave me such a fine voice, as we *sang* "Hail, hail, the gang's all here," and "Sweet Adeline," who gave me freedom from fear and feelings of inferiority.(p.498)
• No, it can best be explained in a little phrase I coined and *sang* to myself: "What happened to Bob?(p.532)

sanitarium
• For years he had floundered from one *sanitarium* to another.(p.26)
• I will not take space to relate all my hospital or *sanitarium* experiences.(p.177)
• When I entered a *sanitarium* for prolonged and intensive psychiatric treatment, I was convinced that I was having a serious mental breakdown.(p.226)
• Naturally, in spite of my good intentions, in spite of my protected life behind *sanitarium* walls, I several times got drunk, and was astounded . . . and badly shaken.(p.227)
• I went to the *sanitarium* where this chap was incarcerated and found to my surprise that he was interested.(p.294)
• I didn't get into a *sanitarium* either.(p.411)
• Once, when I called my analyst, and told her I was contemplating death, she came over and tried to get me into a *sanitarium*.(p.411)
• The *sanitarium* should have happened.(p.412)
• Instead, I started going to a nice private *sanitarium* which, after the first visit, turned out to be more like a country club than anything else.(p.468)
• My visits to that *sanitarium* went on for nearly three years, until in March of 1944, my father died and I was too drunk to attend his funeral.(p.469)
• And I landed right smack back in that *sanitarium* that I had gone to so often.(p.472)
• The people who came knew immediately I was in no condition to absorb anything of the program, and I was put in a *sanitarium* to be defogged so that I could make a sober decision about this for myself.(p.549)

sanitariums
• Then he begins to appear at hospitals and *sanitariums*.(p.22)
• Here are some of the methods we have tried: Drinking beer only, limiting the number of drinks, never drinking alone, never drinking in the morning, drinking only at home, never having it in the house, never drinking during business hours, drinking only at parties, switching from scotch to brandy, drinking only natural wines, agreeing to resign if ever drunk on the job, taking a trip, not taking a trip, swearing off forever (with and without a solemn oath), taking more physical exercise, reading inspirational books, going to health farms and *sanitariums*, accepting voluntary commitment to asylums -- we could increase the list ad infinitum.(p.31)
• It may mean sharing your money and your home, counseling frantic wives and relatives, innumerable trips to police courts, *sanitariums*, hospitals, jails and asylums.(p.97)
• Most of us have entered the final stage with its commitment to health resorts, *sanitariums*, hospitals, and jails.(p.107)
• Maybe the doctor has been called in, and the weary round of *sanitariums* and hospitals has begun.(p.110)
• By this time I was beginning to pay very dearly physically and, in hope of relief, voluntarily incarcerated myself at least a dozen times in one of the local *sanitariums*.(p.174)
• The next three years saw me in *sanitariums*, once in a ten day coma, from which I very nearly did not recover, in and out of hospitals or confined at home with day and night nurses.(p.306)
• However, after I heard a few stories of jails, *sanitariums*, broken homes and skid row, I wondered if I really was an alcoholic.(p.378)
• She had been in *sanitariums*.(p.414)
• Many tried everything – hospitals, special treatments, *sanitariums*, asylums, and jails.(p.455)
• In all the *sanitariums* and psycho wards I had never met a single woman who said she was an alcoholic.(p.471)

sanity
• People feared for my *sanity*.(p.7)
• God had restored his *sanity*.(p.57)
• 2.Came to believe that a Power greater than ourselves could restore us to *sanity*.(p.59)
• To sum up about sex: We earnestly pray for the right ideal, for guidance in each questionable situation, for *sanity*, and for the strength to do the right thing.(p.70)
• For by this time *sanity* will have returned.(p.84)
• His *sanity* returned and he thanked God.(p.154)

• The most accurate answer I can give you is this: Fear has never again ruled my life since that day in September, 1938, when I found that a Power greater than myself could not only restore me to *sanity* but could keep me both sober and sane.(p.285)
• A few hours later I came out of a complete stupor in our living room with a flash of *sanity*.(p.363)
• I can't say, "God could restore me to *sanity*, but until He does, I'll control myself – with pills."(p.443)
• With their help I also saw that certainly, because of some of the things I had done during the years, I was bordering on insanity, and so, facing the record, I tried to believe that a Power greater than I could and would restore me to *sanity*.(p.471)
• I feel that I have been restored to health and *sanity* these past years not through my own efforts nor as a result of anything I may have done, but because I've come to believe -- to really believe – that alone I can do nothing.(p.473)
• He was drinking to hold on to his job, to hold on to his wife, to hold on to his *sanity*.(p.512)
• I was drinking to try to hold on to a job, to try and hold on to my home, to try to hold on to my wife, to try to hold on to my *sanity*.(p.514)
• It's been true in my case, nor could I quarrel with "restore us to *sanity*," for my actions drunk or sober, before A.A., were not those of a sane person.(p.550)
• While there, I read the Big Book and the Grapevine and began the slow road back to health and *sanity* through the recovery program of A.A.(p.559)

sank

• I *sank* into total despair.(p.461)

sarcasm

• As we left, and they were escorting us across the bridge into Wheeling, I, with great dignity and *sarcasm*, told them if their wives were ever visiting in Akron, and they, too, were looking for their route sign as I was, that I hoped I could extend to them the hospitality that had been shown to me in Bellaire.(p.264)
• At the moral inventory, he brought up some of my bad personality traits or character defects, such as selfishness, conceit, jealousy, carelessness, intolerance, ill-temper, *sarcasm* and resentments.(p.292)

sarcastic

• And another thing, it's a wonder they didn't throw us back in because I could become very dignified and *sarcastic*.(p.264)

sash

• Then came the night when the physical and mental torture was so hellish I feared I would burst through my window, *sash* and all.(p.6)

sassy

• When he picked me up, I must have gotten *sassy* and told him that he couldn't do that, so he took my dog home and took me to jail!(p.390)

sat

• Near the end of that bleak November, I *sat* drinking in my kitchen.(p.8)
• I could almost hear the sound of the preacher's voice as I *sat*, on still Sundays, way over there on the hillside; there was that proffered temperance pledge I never signed; my grandfather's good natured contempt of some church folk and their doings; his insistence that the spheres really had their music; but his denial of the preacher's right to tell him how he must listen; his fearlessness as he spoke of these things just before he died; these recollections welled up from the past.(p.10)
• But my friend *sat* before me, and he made the point-blank declaration that God had done for him what he could not do for himself.(p.11)
• Never mind the musty past; here *sat* a miracle directly across the kitchen table.(p.11)
• I *sat* down at a table and ordered a sandwich and a glass of milk.(p.36)
• (At this point, the Editors intrude just long enough to supplement Bill D.'s account, that of the man on the bed, with that of Bill W., the man who *sat* by the side of the bed.)(p.188)
• My oldest child sometimes *sat* in on the meetings.(p.220)
• There I *sat* in the evenings, enjoying with my friends our memories of the "old country," singing the old songs we all knew, playing simple card games for drinks and consuming great quantities of beer.(p.231)
• An attorney *sat* at the side of the bed where I was lying, and he *sat* on the edge of his chair and looked as innocent as a baby.(p.268)
• I *sat* down on the side of one of their beds, and I started to weep, and I couldn't stop, and I was so startled, and I apologized again and again for it.(p.272)
• I *sat* and listened and heard the first speaker say, "I'm an alcoholic."(p.319)
• I *sat* up in the big red chair, suddenly thinking, "My God, with my kind of lousy luck, I might not die soon!(p.333)
• Hauling her to the divan, I *sat* with her and began to talk, frantically but clearly – and making sense.(p.333)
• After that I *sat* for a week, a body in a chair, a mind off in space.(p.338)
• At one end of the table *sat* our community butcher.(p.347)
• At the other side of the table *sat* one of the carpenters in our community, and at the further end of the table *sat* the man who ran the bakery, while on one side *sat* my friend who was a mechanic.(p.347)
• So he got me a cup of coffee, and a piece of cake, and *sat* me down and said, "Why, there's nothing wrong with you.(p.348)
• She left, and I *sat* down and crossed my hands, and looked up and said, "For God's sake, help me."(p.351)
• I entered the house, opened a new bottle of whiskey and *sat* down to drink myself into the right frame of mind to get in my car, start the motor and close the garage door behind me.(p.363)
• The doctor *sat* down beside the bed and asked me how I felt.(p.423)
• So I *sat* down with me and went over the facts behind the convulsions: personality changes, daily headaches, sense of impending doom, sense of impending insanity.(p.444)
• One day as I *sat* there in the hospital, my psychiatrist walked up behind me and asked, "How'd you like to talk to the man from A.A.?"(p.446)
• We *sat* in the back and talked only to each other.(p.447)
• All afternoon I *sat* there and drank and played Bing Crosby's recording of "Silent Night" over and over again on the juke box.(p.467)
• Because as I *sat* on that bed, I knew that I was in a terrible spot and didn't know how to get out of it.(p.515)
• By this time I was such a past master at kidding myself that I had convinced myself I had *sat* out a war and waited for this man to come home and, as my resentment and self-pity grew, so did my alcoholic problem.(p.548)

satisfaction

• There was, therefore, a sense of real *satisfaction* when I was asked to contribute a few words on a subject which is covered in such masterly detail in these pages.(p.xxv)
• With a certain *satisfaction* I reflected there was enough gin concealed about the house to carry me through that night and the next day.(p.8)
• How then shall we help our readers determine, to their own *satisfaction*, whether they are one of us?(p.34)
• Is he not a victim of the delusion that he can wrest *satisfaction* and happiness out of this world if he only manages well?(p.61)
• If we can answer to our *satisfaction*, we then look at Step Six.(p.76)
• The *satisfaction* I got from giving him a little of what I had read in those pamphlets far surpassed any feeling that I had ever had before in helping patients.(p.347)
• They prove to almost anyone's *satisfaction* that it's never too late to try Alcoholics Anonymous.(p.455)
• Now, for me, and to my *satisfaction*, I know the purpose of life: The purpose of life is to create and the by-product is happiness.(p.535)

satisfactorily

• If you answer these questions *satisfactorily*, you need have no apprehension.(p.102)

satisfactory

• More baffling still, he could give himself no *satisfactory* explanation for his fall.(p.26)
• Rarely do we fail to make *satisfactory* progress.(p.78)
• The most *satisfactory* years of your existence lie ahead.(p.152)
• This I did, and proved myself *satisfactory* to the faculty, both in deportment and scholastically.(p.174)
• However, after two or three trials, I found this was not *satisfactory* because they did not serve enough to satisfy me.(p.184)
• "We watch the alcoholic performing in a position of responsibility and we know that because he is drinking heavily and daily he has cut his capacities by fifty per cent, and still he seems able to do a *satisfactory* job.(p.308)
• I had never had a child and this had been a *satisfactory* excuse many times for my drinking.(p.548)

satisfied

• Some drinkers have excuses with which they are *satisfied* part of the time.(p.23)
• We agnostically inclined would not feel *satisfied* with a proposal which does not lend itself to reasonable approach and interpretation.(p.53)
• If you are *satisfied* that he is a real alcoholic, begin to dwell on the hopeless feature of the malady.(p.92)
• If you are *satisfied* he really wants to get over drinking, you need not be alarmed.(p.120)
• He added that occasionally in the night a vague craving arose which would be *satisfied* by candy.(p.134)
• Be *satisfied* he is not deceiving himself or you.(p.142)
• As soon as I had *satisfied* that, what I earned as an upholsterer went for liquor.(p.234)
• What alcoholic can be *satisfied* with one drink?(p.377)
• But such is my nature that I must know the reason for things and I didn't stop until I had *satisfied* myself about the reasons for my drinking.(p.533)
• We are taught to differentiate between our wants (which are never *satisfied*) and our needs (which are always provided for).(p.560)

satisfies

• Like most statistics, it doesn't prove anything -- just *satisfies* a little curiosity engendered by the wail "Oh, those initiation fees" that prompted this investigation.(p.399)

satisfy

• It did not *satisfy* us to be told that we could not control our drinking just because we were maladjusted to life, that we were in full flight from reality, or were outright mental defectives.(p.xxiv)
• However, after two or three trials, I found this was not satisfactory because they did not serve enough to *satisfy* me.(p.184)
• At seventeen I entered the University, really to *satisfy* my father who wanted me to study medicine there as he had.(p.241)
• She of course didn't realize how cunning an alcoholic can be and the lengths to which he will go in finding ways to *satisfy* the compulsion for more and more drinks after having had the first one.(p.377)

satisfying

• I have since been brought into a way of living infinitely more *satisfying* and, I hope, more useful than the life I lived before.(p.42)
• After *satisfying* yourself that your man wants to recover and that he will go to any extreme to do so, you may suggest a definite course of action.(p.142)
• I would like to sketch for you the highlights of these sixteen years of a slow but steady and *satisfying* upward climb.(p.280)
• Each day seems to be so much more productive and *satisfying*.(p.383)

Saturday

• Then Jack Alexander wrote a feature article in the *Saturday* Evening Post and placed such a compelling picture of A.A. before the general public that alcoholics in need of help really deluged us.(p.xviii)
• I still expected a plea for clemency, but these words came through the receiver: "I just wanted to tell you Paul jumped from a hotel window in Hartford last *Saturday*.(p.136)
• About this time a lady called up my wife one *Saturday* afternoon, saying she wanted me to come over that evening to meet a friend of hers who might help me.(p.179)
• After a very good week, two of my customers took me to lunch on *Saturday*.(p.247)
• My fellow-workers were mostly good *Saturday* night drinkers and I was right with them.(p.252)
• We always started out on the *Saturday* before Labor Day.(p.264)
• So, on that *Saturday* before Labor Day, I got drunk and set the house on fire -- so we didn't have to paint it.(p.265)
• Jack brought the *Saturday* Post with Jack Alexander's story.(p.268)
• These men all drank on *Saturday* nights, and enjoyed themselves.(p.277)
• I joined their *Saturday* night parties and enjoyed myself too.(p.277)
• How will I feel next *Saturday* morning?(p.326)
• One *Saturday* noon I staggered home with every intention of showing her.(p.362)
• I think I actually read more contempt than was really there because just a week before someone had sent him the *Saturday* Evening Post article on A.A., and there was some glimmer of hope in it for him.(p.391)
• I only know that it first reached me through that *Saturday* Evening Post article.(p.392)

• I wrote on ***Saturday***.(p.392)
• That was on ***Saturday*** and my husband was leaving town Sunday night.(p.393)
• Even the Jack Alexander ***Saturday*** Evening Post article hadn't been written, and there was only a tiny group of people in Washington.(p.469)
• And when she broke a luncheon date with me one ***Saturday***, after I had been in A.A. for about three months, I said, "I'll show her!(p.472)
• The following day, ***Saturday***, he came back and said, "Jim, I owe you for that prescription last night.(p.488)
• Finally, I broke the last one hundred dollar bill the ***Saturday*** before I left.(p.493)
• It is ten o'clock of a ***Saturday*** night.(p.500)

Saturdays

• I have no assistance and am working nights, ***Saturdays*** and Sundays.(p.500)

sausage

• Father says grace, which delays my attack on the buckwheat cakes and ***sausage***.(p.497)

savagely

• I learned what a devastating effect it can have on a child to coddle him and build him up, and then turn and beat him ***savagely***, as had happened to me.(p.434)

save

• He suddenly realized that in order to ***save*** himself he must carry his message to another alcoholic.(p.xvi)
• This sometimes nearly drove me back to drink, but I soon found that when all other measures failed, work with another alcoholic would ***save*** the day.(p.15)
• But we found that such codes and philosophies did not ***save*** us, no matter how much we tried.(p.45)
• ***Save*** for a few brief moments of temptation the thought of drink has never returned; and at such times a great revulsion has risen up in him.(p.57)
• God ***save*** me from being angry.(p.67)
• We have no right to ***save*** our own skin at another person's expense.(p.74)
• Therefore, we are not to be the hasty and foolish martyr who would needlessly sacrifice others to ***save*** himself from the alcoholic pit.(p.79)
• We know these suggestions are sometimes difficult to follow, but you will ***save*** many a heartbreak if you can succeed in observing them.(p.111)
• You cannot see why it should be to anyone else, ***save*** the spineless and stupid.(p.139)
• He walked to the hospital to ***save*** bus fare and did it gladly in order to be helpful to an individual he had never even seen.(p.208)
• I'd work like mad for three or four weeks without a single drink, ***save*** my money, pay a few bills and then "reward" myself with alcohol.(p.244)
• At the time, I thought them just a swell pair of screwballs, for they were not only going to ***save*** all the drunks in the world but also all the so-called normal people!(p.245)
• After the book appeared we all became very busy in our efforts to ***save*** all and sundry, but I was still actually on the fringes of A.A.(p.248)
• Here I found an ingredient that had been lacking in any other effort I had made to ***save*** myself.(p.436)
• I just gathered up this and that alcoholic, because, in the back of my mind, I wanted to ***save*** all the world.(p.496)
• We didn't ***save*** the world, but we did manage to help some individuals.(p.496)

saved

• Living modestly, my wife and I ***saved*** $1,000.(p.2)
• A spirit of intolerance might repel alcoholics whose lives could have been ***saved***, had it not been for such stupidity.(p.103)
• They have a new attitude, and they have been ***saved*** from a living death.(p.150)
• Then occurred the event that ***saved*** me.(p.235)
• There was one meeting a week at Bill's home in Brooklyn, and we all took turns there spouting off about how we had changed our lives overnight, how many drunks we had ***saved*** and straightened out, and last, but not least, how God had touched each of us personally on the shoulder.(p.246)
• Therefore, these seventeen A.A.'s, and hundreds of thousands like them, have been ***saved*** years of infinite suffering.(p.315)
• I had ***saved*** my allowance.(p.409)
• But the money I had ***saved*** up went for cases of liquor.(p.409)
• I'd reply and some of my letters they ***saved***.(p.427)
• In my screwed up mind I kept thinking I could have gone to A.A. way back there in 1940, and perhaps ***saved*** my marriage and home.(p.469)
• Dad, due to having spent most of his time in a small Virginia town, didn't have any too much money, and the money he had ***saved*** and the property he had acquired were in Washington.(p.486)
• They ***saved*** us endless time and lost motion.(p.496)
• A case of measles ***saved*** me from being kicked out during my Sophomore year.(p.499)

saving

• So, after hearing some more of my story, he turned around and said to Doc -- I don't think he knew I heard him, but I did -- he said, "Well, I believe he's worth ***saving*** and working on."(p.185)
• I displayed alcoholic tendencies actually from the age of fourteen, when I started to steal wine from the family jug, siphoning it off one drink at a time so it wouldn't be missed, not drinking it immediately, but ***saving*** it until about a pint was accumulated, so that I could get drunk.(p.397)
• On one of these trips, the judge must have thought I was worth ***saving***, for instead of sending me to jail, he sent me to A.A. for one month.(p.526)

saw

• I ***saw*** I could not take so much as one drink.(p.5)
• I ***saw*** that my friend was much more than inwardly reorganized.(p.11)
• I ***saw*** that growth could start from that point.(p.12)
• Upon a foundation of complete willingness I might build what I ***saw*** in my friend.(p.12)
• At long last I ***saw***, I felt, I believed.(p.12)
• But we ***saw*** that it really worked in others, and we had come to believe in the hopelessness and futility of life as we had been living it.(p.25)
• He was ambitious to succeed in business, but ***saw*** that he would get nowhere if he drank at all.(p.32)
• We first ***saw*** Fred about a year ago in a hospital where he had gone to recover from a bad case of jitters.(p.39)
• I ***saw*** that will power and self-knowledge would not help in those strange mental blank spots.(p.42)
• When we ***saw*** others solve their problems by a simple reliance upon the Spirit of the Universe, we had to stop doubting the power of God.(p.52)
• Little or nothing, we ***saw*** at last.(p.54)
• Hence, we ***saw*** that reason isn't everything.(p.54)
• We finally ***saw*** that faith in some kind of God was a part of our make-up, just as much as the feeling we have for a friend.(p.55)
• We ***saw*** that these resentments must be mastered, but how?(p.66)
• When we ***saw*** our faults we listed them.(p.67)
• He ***saw*** that he had to place the outcome in God's hands or he would soon start drinking again, and all would be lost anyhow.(p.80)
• I wanted to throw up my hands in discouragement, for I ***saw*** that I had failed to help my banker friend understand.(p.138)
• Still physically weak, and sober but a few months, he ***saw*** that his predicament was dangerous.(p.154)
• He had a desperate desire to stop, but ***saw*** no way out, for he had earnestly tried many avenues of escape.(p.155)
• He ***saw*** that he would have to face his problems squarely that God might give him mastery.(p.155)
• Both ***saw*** that they must keep spiritually active.(p.156)
• His wife came, scarcely daring to be hopeful, though she thought she ***saw*** something different about her husband already.(p.158)
• I used to get terribly upset when I ***saw*** my friends drink and knew I could not, but I schooled myself to believe that though I once had the same privilege, I had abused it so frightfully that it was withdrawn.(p.181)
• Nineteen years ago last summer, Dr. Bob and I ***saw*** him (Bill D.) for the first time.(p.188)
• I met all the people I wanted to meet; I ***saw*** all the places I wanted to see; I did all the things I wanted to do -- and I was increasingly miserable.(p.225)
• We ***saw*** very early that Prohibition wasn't going to work.(p.232)
• My wife upbraided me often and plenty when she ***saw*** that my "periodics" were gradually losing me what business I could get.(p.233)
• He had also gone all the way through the wringer and had been dry two years when I ***saw*** him again.(p.243)
• No one in that company ***saw*** me again -- ten days later I wired my resignation.(p.243)
• I never ***saw*** either of them again.(p.247)
• My brilliant agnosticism vanished, and I ***saw*** for the first time that those who really believed, or at least honestly tried to find a Power greater than themselves, were much more composed and contented than I had ever been, and they seemed to have a degree of happiness which I had never known.(p.247)
• When the others ***saw*** my altered attitude they took me back in, but for me they had to make it tough; if they hadn't I don't think I ever would have stuck it out.(p.248)
• Coming out of a pub near the Cunard pier I ***saw*** the Lusitania standing out in the middle of the Mersey.(p.252)
• In my mind's eye I ***saw*** Broadway again and Tom Sharkey's bar; the roar of the subway was in my ears.(p.252)
• Again I spent my bankroll, by no means as thick as the one I had when I first ***saw*** the skyline of Gotham.(p.252)
• Forced to detrain from an empty gondola on the other side of Chicago by a terrific rainstorm which drenched me to the skin, I hit the first factory building I ***saw*** for a job.(p.253)
• I had some financial success through no ability of my own and, when jobless and almost wiped out in 1930, I began to trade and sell my collection; much of the proceeds went to keep my apartment stocked with liquor and almost every night ***saw*** me helpless to bed.(p.255)
• We were together all the time, but this night I got up and ***saw*** it was late.(p.263)
• We were the most congenial drinkers you ever ***saw***.(p.264)
• Right away, I ***saw*** it was the same outfit this other guy told me about, and then again hope died.(p.267)
• I remember sometime, it was possibly six months after we had been going steadily to King School, that we were coming home from a meeting and ***saw*** a car along the way, and a fellow in back drinking a bottle of beer.(p.271)
• After six months of sobriety I ***saw*** the picture in a different light: Detroit was the place I had to return to, not only because I must face the mess I had made there, but because it was there that I could be of the most service to A.A.(p.281)
• One is that I don't remember too many of them, as I was one of those drunks who could be on his feet and attend a meeting or a party, engage in a conversation with people and do things that any nearly normal person would do, and the next day not remember a thing about where I was, what I did, whom I ***saw***, or how I got home.(p.301)
• The next three years ***saw*** me in sanitariums, once in a ten day coma, from which I very nearly did not recover, in and out of hospitals or confined at home with day and night nurses.(p.306)
• Nevertheless, there were a few doctors who ***saw*** alcoholism as a disease and felt that the alcoholic was a victim of something over which he had no control.(p.307)
• I ***saw*** in these people a quality of peace and serenity that I knew I must have for myself.(p.310)
• They ***saw*** that they had become actual or potential alcoholics, even though no serious harm had yet been done.(p.315)
• I heard voices when no one was around, and I ***saw*** things that weren't there.(p.319)
• Hiding behind a newspaper, magazine, or book, I really ***saw*** nothing, but simulated deep interest.(p.332)
• My husband, my children ***saw*** the other side of me.(p.339)
• Then I ***saw*** an A.A. advertisement in a newspaper, and I wrote to the address it gave.(p.343)
• By the time I figured out what had happened, I ***saw*** two flashing red lights atop squad cars, sedately coming around the corner.(p.353)
• I had no trouble making the right decision when I ***saw*** my wife open her purse at the meeting that night and deposit a cute little angel in the middle of my birthday cake.(p.366)
• (In fact, every time I ***saw*** him he had a frown on his face.)(p.370)
• I ***saw*** at last that I had the same disease my father had, only I was being given a chance to live, not die.(p.371)
• One night, a few weeks after joining the Fellowship, much to my surprise and delight I ***saw*** a familiar but no longer frowning face.(p.371)
• A titled lady, she still ***saw*** her world darkening.(p.400)
• When I was a baby, my mother brought me to America, and I never again ***saw*** my father.(p.401)
• I only ***saw*** that I had not become Mrs. Shakespeare.(p.403)
• He ***saw*** that I was unsettled, living away from my family and renting houses here and there.(p.403)
• I ***saw*** him recently and he told me that he had always felt guilty, because, after our separation, I had become a serious alcoholic.(p.403)
• I ***saw*** that my Village friends, all of whom had

small jobs, were living happily on about a tenth of my sinecure.(p.409)
• They got so they moved their barstools when they *saw* me coming.(p.411)
• He now said that we had a physical allergy combined with a mental obsession, and he explained this so that I *saw* for the first time how this could be.(p.413)
• A busload of basketball players had been passing and *saw* the flames.(p.424)
• My daughter was one and a half years old when I last *saw* her.(p.463)
• But by listening and talking to these A.A.'s – talking to them as I had never talked to anyone in my whole life, I *saw* that it was my life that was unmanageable – not just my drinking.(p.471)
• With their help I also *saw* that certainly, because of some of the things I had done during the years, I was bordering on insanity, and so, facing the record, I tried to believe that a Power greater than I could and would restore me to sanity.(p.471)
• When they *saw* me coming, they locked up the silverware and everything else of value.(p.478)
• For me, it was a little different because I couldn't help thinking about the past, and I *saw* the future more or less mirrored in the past.(p.513)
• If it was daylight, I would go down alleys to make sure no one *saw* me.(p.527)
• I was trying to remember where it came from, when two of the biggest cops I ever *saw* walked in and took me to jail.(p.528)
• I, a man of steel, with very high ideals, well brought up, an honor student and the recipient of scholarships and prizes, a boy wonder in business -- I, Bob, the author of this essay, looked and *saw* that the universe was beneath my contempt, and that to remove myself from it was the only thing of dignity a man could do.(p.531)
• For you learned that he had been guilty of the thing he had accused you of, and his guilt had brought suffering to his entire family; and he thought he *saw* his young son beginning his own tragic pattern.(p.533)
• I stood off and took a long look at life and the values I found in it: I *saw* a paradox, that he who loses his life does indeed find it.(p.542)

sawdust

• I literally hit the *sawdust.*(p.411)

say

• You may rely absolutely on anything they *say* about themselves.(p.xxiv)
• But as ex-problem drinkers, we can *say* that his explanation makes good sense.(p.xxiv)
• I *say* this after many years' experience as Medical Director of one of the oldest hospitals in the country treating alcoholic and drug addiction.(p.xxv)
• He had lost everything worthwhile in life and was only living, one might *say*, to drink.(p.xxix)
• And the truth, strange to *say*, is usually that he has no more idea why he took that first drink than you have.(p.23)
• The alcoholic may *say* to himself in the most casual way, "It won't burn me this time, so here's how!"(p.24)
• Our hope is that many alcoholic men and women, desperately in need, will see these pages, and we believe that it is only by fully disclosing ourselves and our problems that they will be persuaded to *say*, "Yes, I am one of them too; I must have this thing."(p.29)
• Despite all we can *say*, many who are real alcoholics are not going to believe they are in that class.(p.31)
• Here was the threat of commitment, the loss of family and position, to *say* nothing of that intense mental and physical suffering which drinking always caused him.(p.36)
• Our behavior is as absurd and incomprehensible with respect to the first drink as that of an individual with a passion, *say*, for jay-walking.(p.37)
• One of these men, staff member of a world-renowned hospital, recently made this statement to some of us: "What you *say* about the general hopelessness of the average alcoholic's plight is, in my opinion, correct.(p.43)
• As soon as a man can *say* that he does believe, or is willing to believe, we emphatically assure him that he is on his way.(p.47)
• When people presented us with spiritual approaches, how frequently did we all *say*, "I wish I had what that man has.(p.47)
• When many hundreds of people are able to *say* that the consciousness of the Presence of God is today the most important fact of their lives, they present a powerful reason why one should have faith.(p.51)
• Show any longshoreman a Sunday supplement describing a proposal to explore the moon by means of a rocket and he will *say*, "I bet they do it – maybe not so long either."(p.52)
• Hence we are at pains to tell why we think our present faith is reasonable, why we think it more sane and logical to believe than not to believe, why we *say* our former thinking was soft and mushy when we threw up our hands in doubt and said, "We don't know."(p.53)
• It was impossible to *say* we had no capacity for faith, or love, or worship.(p.54)
• Could we still *say* the whole thing was nothing but a mass of electrons, created out of nothing, meaning nothing, whirling on to a destiny of nothingness?(p.54)
• "Who are you to *say* there is no God?"(p.56)
• We *say* this because we are very anxious that we talk to the right person.(p.74)
• When ready, we *say* something like this: "My Creator, I am now willing that you should have all of me, good and bad.(p.76)
• In fairness we must *say* that she may understand, but what are we going to do about a thing like that?(p.81)
• We feel we ought to *say* to her that we have no right to involve another person.(p.81)
• Sometimes we hear an alcoholic *say* that the only thing he needs to do is to keep sober.(p.82)
• We don't worry about them if we can honestly *say* to ourselves that we would right them if we could.(p.83)
• But *say* nothing, for the moment, of how that was accomplished.(p.91)
• If he has trouble later, he is likely to *say* you rushed him.(p.95)
• Your wife may sometimes *say* she is neglected.(p.97)
• Let no alcoholic *say* he cannot recover unless he has his family back.(p.99)
• What they *say* will apply to nearly everyone bound by ties of blood or affections to an alcoholic.(p.104)
• As we *say* among ourselves, "He wants to want to stop."(p.109)
• *Say* you do not want to be a wet blanket; that you only want him to take care of his health.(p.112)
• Next time you and he have a heated discussion, no matter what the subject, it should be the privilege of either to smile and *say*, "This is getting serious.(p.118)
• Your husband will be the first to *say* it was your devotion and care which brought him to the point where he could have a spiritual experience.(p.118)
• So to you out there -- who may soon be with us -- we *say* "Good luck and God bless you!"(p.121)
• He may demand that the family find God in a hurry, or exhibit amazing indifference to them and *say* he is above worldly considerations.(p.128)
• Dad is not so spiritual after all, they *say*.(p.128)
• I told her to *say* that I was not interested.(p.136)
• My secretary returned to *say* that it was not Mr. B---on the phone; it was Mr. B-----'s brother, and he wished to give me a message.(p.136)
• This is not to *say* that all alcoholics are honest and upright when not drinking.(p.141)
• You might *say* you appreciated his abilities, would like to keep him, but cannot if he continues to drink.(p.141)
• *Say* that you believe he is a gravely ill person, with this qualification – being perhaps fatally ill, does he want to get well?(p.142)
• If he feels free to discuss his problems with you, if he knows you understand and will not be upset by anything he wishes to *say*, he will probably be off to a fast start.(p.144)
• In fact, he may *say* almost anything if he has accepted our solution which, as you know, demands rigorous honesty.(p.145)
• After reading this book, a junior executive can go to such a man and *say* approximately this, "Look here, Ed.(p.147)
• You *say*, "Yes, I'm willing.(p.152)
• Perhaps he could handle, *say*, three drinks – no more!(p.154)
• Over and over, he would *say*: "That's me.(p.157)
• Still you may *say*: "But I will not have the benefit of contact with you who write this book."(p.164)
• The question which might naturally come into your mind would be: "What did the man do or *say* that was different from what others had done or said?"(p.180)
• But this was a man who had experienced many years of frightful drinking, who had had most all the drunkard's experiences known to man, but who had been cured by the very means I had been trying to employ, that is to *say* the spiritual approach.(p.180)
• On June 26, 1935, I came to in the hospital and to *say* I was discouraged is to put it mildly.(p.184)
• I have already done it, and I am willing to do it again here in the presence of you or I am willing to *say* it any place, anywhere in the world from now on and not be ashamed of it."(p.190)
• I'm so grateful for both the program and the people in it that I still want to go, and then probably the most wonderful thing that I learned from the program -- I've seen this in the 'A.A. Grapevine' a lot of times, and I've had people *say* it to me personally, and I've heard people get up in meetings and make the same statement: The statement is, "I came into A.A. solely for the purpose of sobriety, but it has been through A.A. that I have found God."(p.192)
• (I might *say* right here that never in my life did I ever intend to get drunk.(p.196)
• I could work a deal up to where all I had to do was to go ahead with it; all the planning had been done, all the financing had been done, but then I'd *say* "Nuts to it!" and walk away.(p.197)
• At the end of about four months, I not only had good looking clothes --and I might *say* that at the time I first talked to Max I didn't have a suit of clothes I could bend over in real sudden; now I had six suits of clothes.(p.200)
• I said, "Did I *say* that?"(p.217)
• She said, "Well, he wouldn't be here if you didn't *say* so."(p.217)
• I realized that there wasn't anything I could *say* to place myself in a more favorable light with my children, that it was going to be a matter of time; for I also understood the intolerance of young people towards deficiencies in their elders.(p.220)
• In summing up, I can *say* that A.A. had made me, I hope, a real Catholic.(p.221)
• I believe that my once over-weening self-will has finally found its proper place, for I can *say* many times daily, "Thy will be done, not mine" . . . and mean it.(p.229)
• But I can remember, in my teens, that there were a few characters who caused the village heads to nod pityingly and sometimes in anger as they paused to *say*, "That sot, Henri" and "Ce pauvre Jules," who drank too much.(p.230)
• I cannot *say*, however, that I acquired any craving for hard liquor as a result.(p.231)
• "Best in the business, when he's sober," my customers would *say*, and I still had a following who would give me work though they deplored my habits, because they knew the job would be well done when they eventually got it.(p.234)
• So I always *say* that as long as I remember January 8th that is how long I will remain sober.(p.240)
• In conclusion, I can only *say* that whatever growth or understanding has come to me, I have no wish to graduate.(p.249)
• And I still *say* that as long as I remember that January 8th in Washington, that is how long, by the grace of God as I understand Him, I will retain a happy sobriety.(p.250)
• Lots of times, vain-gloriously, I used to take the bottle out, look at it and *say*, "I've got you licked."(p.253)
• Need I *say* that in a very short time I was walking along a prairie highway with arm extended and thumb pointed?(p.255)
• I cannot *say* that my taste for liquor has entirely disappeared.(p.259)
• Neither can I honestly *say* that I have forgotten the "fleshpots of Egypt."(p.259)
• He'd always *say*, "Take me for a ride, Ma."(p.264)
• I thought, "No matter how crazy they are I'll do anything they *say* to do."(p.267)
• "Well," I said to dad, when the A.A. people kept coming with these lovely cars and looked so nice, "I suppose the neighbors *say*, 'Now those old fools must have up and died, but where's the hearse?'"(p.269)
• I'd like to *say* here how important it was to us then that we do all the little things that people said were important, because later when Russ was so sick that I had to hold him up, they had a meeting out at the house.(p.270)
• Sometimes saying very little, but letting us *say*.(p.271)
• Russ used to be very much pleased because he'd *say*, "I think Dr. Bob thoroughly enjoys coming out here.(p.271)
• Before the end finally came, I had, I guess made the surrender because I finally had been able to *say* that I would not mind too much.(p.272)
• Before I stop -- I always was a great talker -- I want to *say* that nobody will ever know how I miss Annie's advice about things.(p.273)
• It is undoubtedly too soon for me to *say* how much of a success I shall be as a husband in time to come.(p.286)

• Needless to *say*, it was a year or more before they did contact me.(p.293)
• Needless to *say*, this was not pleasurable drinking.(p.306)
• I sat and listened and heard the first speaker *say*, "I'm an alcoholic."(p.319)
• Live twenty-four hours at a time, they *say*.(p.320)
• Fortunately, I didn't *say* a word to George on the way home.(p.322)
• And then I'd *say*, "God, don't pay any attention to me.(p.324)
• Even obvious intoxication is excused by younger people as something "he's earned the right to do," and they *say*, "After all, who's he hurting?"(p.330)
• I heard one very ill woman *say* that she didn't believe in the surrender part of the A.A. program.(p.340)
• But then he said, "Let me *say* something to you.(p.348)
• And then it went on to *say*: "Half measures availed us nothing.(p.349)
• And then I scratched my head and said to myself, "What a fantastic thing for a man to *say*, that I cured his wife.(p.350)
• I suppose the doctor might *say*, "This is psychosomatic medicine."(p.352)
• I suppose the psychiatrist might *say*, "This is benevolent interpersonal relations.(p.352)
• I suppose others would *say*, "This is group psychotherapy."(p.352)
• My sponsor used to *say* to me, "If I could only paint you a picture of how beautiful life can be without booze . . ."(p.355)
• I didn't *say* a word to anyone about my lapse.(p.364)
• For the next couple of hours a terrible battle went on between the good gremlins and the bad ones, one faction urging me to tell the truth, the other telling me to sit tight and *say* nothing.(p.366)
• To the new man I would also like to *say* that this program is not for sissies for, in my humble opinion, it takes a man to make the grade.(p.367)
• If I were asked what in my opinion was the most important factor in being successful in this program, besides following the Twelve Steps, I would *say* Honesty.(p.367)
• I continue to be surprised by the people I meet who *say*, "You haven't had a drink for a long time, have you?"(p.376)
• After every cocktail party or dinner party she would *say* she couldn't understand how I could get in such a drunken stupor on one drink.(p.377)
• The time for decision had arrived, and it was a relief to *say* "Yes" when my family said they would call Alcoholics Anonymous for me.(p.378)
• This didn't *say* we had to be in jail, ten, fifty, or one hundred times.(p.379)
• It didn't *say* I had to lose my family.(p.379)
• It didn't *say* I had to finally live on skid row and drink bay rum, canned heat or lemon extract.(p.379)
• It did *say*, "admitted I was powerless over alcohol; that my life had become unmanageable."(p.379)
• It's the last thing I ever heard him *say*, and I think there are some of us who, at times, try to read extra messages and complexities into the Steps.(p.395)
• It is bound to be rough, because who can *say* exactly how much of that green blood -- commonly known as money -- was dissipated on dissipation?(p.396)
• To keep it in round figures, let's *say* twenty per cent of my income went for giggle gurgles.(p.397)
• I was always at odds with the entire world, not to *say* the universe.(p.400)
• In my cups I began to *say*, "I can't stop."(p.412)
• He did not take out a folder and *say*, "What is the nature of your problem?"(p.413)
• With my A.A. friends, all I can *say* is that it's a power greater than myself.(p.437)
• At first, she would *say*, "You don't love me.(p.439)
• Later, she would *say*, "You don't like me.(p.439)
• I can't *say*, "Thy will be done," and take a pill.(p.443)
• I can't *say*, "I'm powerless over alcohol, but solid alcohol is okay."(p.443)
• I can't *say*, "God could restore me to sanity, but until He does, I'll control myself -- with pills."(p.443)
• After I had been around A.A. for seven months, tapering off alcohol and pills, not finding the program working very well, I was finally able to *say*, "Okay, God.(p.448)
• I remember particularly one sentence that seemed to *say*, "This is for you."(p.473)
• Our language has few words to *say* many things.(p.474)
• Judge *say* I go to jail next time.(p.475)
• Cops *say* for me to call them, they get me out.(p.475)
• He *say* he take me to A.A. meeting.(p.476)
• My sponsor *say* men who talk speak truth.(p.476)
• I hear men *say*, "One day not drink.(p.476)
• They *say* call friend before I buy drink.(p.476)
• Maine newsletter (Boomerang) *say*: "With tireless devotion and humility, this venerable Indian gentleman traveled thousands of miles humbly pleading for sobriety.(p.476)
• I *say*, "Just let it happen."(p.477)
• This sober Indian *say* to sick, red-eyed alcoholic who want good medicine: "Put cork in bottle.(p.477)
• To Indians, I *say*: "Don't be afraid to join A.A.(p.477)
• I once hear people *say* only Indians crazy when drunk.(p.477)
• Economic conditions had a great deal to do with it, because I've often heard my father *say* that his mother would take one of the old time flour sacks and cut a hole through the bottom and two corners of it and there you'd have a gown.(p.486)
• There came a time when she spoke to me about it, and I would *say* that I had a bad cold or that I wasn't feeling well.(p.487)
• She continued to watch me, although she didn't *say* anything.(p.493)
• She didn't *say* anything about A.A. or getting me a sponsor at that time, but she did ask about Vi, and I told her Vi was working and how she could locate her.(p.494)
• I asked her just what this deal was, but she wouldn't *say*.(p.494)
• I guess I felt, and he sensed it, that I wanted him to hurry up and *say* what he had to *say* and get out.(p.494)
• Pioneer A.A., minister's son, and southern farmer, he asked, "Who am I to *say* there is no God?"(p.497)
• I didn't like it, but I would not *say* so.(p.498)
• I *say* I will go.(p.502)
• "Don't *say* anything," I *say* to her.(p.502)
• "Who are you to *say* there is no God?"(p.504)
• "I must ask you a question," I *say* to the man.(p.504)
• "The thing I do is to *say* 'God here I am and here are all my troubles.(p.504)
• I know not what I *say*.(p.504)
• I return home and *say* I am sorry for my wrong.(p.505)
• I'd *say*, "No, I don't know where they're at or when they meet.(p.510)
• I should *say* there was less drinking in the Army than I thought at that time.(p.518)
• As I *say*, this specialist put a scare in me for about a fortnight or three weeks, then I started my last bout which went on and off for about three months.(p.523)
• I just want to *say* that you don't have to be afraid, because no one at any A.A. meeting will bite you.(p.529)
• There was the over-weening ambition to be the world's greatest author, when -- at thirty-nine -- I had nothing of importance to *say* to the world.(p.534)
• If I write with the air of one who has discovered the obvious, which is to *say*, the eternal truths which have been offered to us since the beginning, forgive my callowness; I had to find these things out for myself.(p.536)
• I *say*, "refused to do anything to stop it."(p.539)
• All of my family and loved ones, all of my friends, are nearer and dearer to me than ever before and I have literally dozens of new friends who *say* they cannot believe that a short eight years ago I was ready for the scrap heap.(p.541)
• It was impossible for me to *say* at this point, "Maybe there is something wrong with my philosophy," and I certainly couldn't *say*, "Maybe there is something wrong with me."(p.545)
• I attended my first A.A. meeting eight years ago, and it is with deep gratitude that I'm able to *say* I've not had a drink since that time, and that I take no sedation or narcotics, for this program is to me one of complete sobriety and I no longer need to escape reality.(p.549)
• Most emphatically we wish to *say* that any alcoholic capable of honestly facing his problems in the light of our experience can recover, provided he does not close his mind to all spiritual concepts.(p.570)

saying

• Many of our friends encourage us by *saying* that this is but a beginning, only the augury of a much larger future ahead.(p.xv)
• Finally he shook his head *saying*, "Something has happened to you I don't understand.(p.14)
• We constantly remind ourselves we are no longer running the show, humbly *saying* to ourselves many times each day "Thy will be done."(p.87)
• Without *saying* so, they may cordially hate him for what he has done to them and to their mother.(p.134)
• One day my secretary came in *saying* that Mr. B---- insisted on speaking with me.(p.136)
• He left us a note *saying* you were the best boss he ever had, and that you were not to blame in any way."(p.136)
• When his wife next calls *saying* he is sick, you might jump to the conclusion he is drunk.(p.146)
• You are *saying* to yourself: "I'm jittery and alone.(p.163)
• About this time a lady called up my wife one Saturday afternoon, *saying* she wanted me to come over that evening to meet a friend of hers who might help me.(p.179)
• Eagerly he pointed to us *saying*, "These are the fellows I told you about; they are the ones who understand."(p.189)
• They looked at one another queerly and, finally, one of them allowed he'd have a beer and they all followed him, each of them *saying* he'd have a beer too.(p.194)
• I told somebody that I was going down to get Christian Science and they took me down, but I don't remember *saying* that.(p.202)
• They suffered from my conduct without *saying* anything, but the reason for this was I still managed to hang onto a very substantial practice.(p.215)
• What was I *saying* . . .(p.222)
• *Saying* goodbye to my wife and baby, I was treading Manhattan's streets in a little more than a week.(p.252)
• Sometimes *saying* very little, but letting us say.(p.271)
• They described what had happened when they went out and tried drinking again, and I knew they were sincere in *saying* that it could happen to me.(p.334)
• I recall, as I walked into that meeting, *saying* to myself, "Here I am, a fellow of the American College of Surgeons, a Fellow of the International College of Surgeons, a diplomate of one of the great specialty boards in these United States, a member of the American Psychiatric Society, and I have to go to the butcher, the baker and the carpenter to help make a man out of me!"(p.347)
• *Saying* these sprees were limited to one a week (they were not), and *saying* that the average spree was ten of these drinks (sometimes more, sometimes less), we come up with the first boring statistic: two-fifty per week out of twelve dollars.(p.397)
• After talking with him for a time I heard myself *saying*, "Doc, I think I'm an alcoholic."(p.436)
• I remember very well *saying*, "There's only one person in the world whose guts I hate worse than yours, and those're my own."(p.440)
• The pep pills affected my hearing at times: I couldn't listen fast enough to hear what I was *saying*.(p.442)
• I'd think, "I wonder why I'm *saying* that again -- I've already said it three times."(p.442)
• I am *saying* that I know better than God.(p.449)
• Eventually, I had to redo each of the Twelve Steps specifically with Max in mind, from the First, *saying*, "I am powerless over alcohol, and my homelife is unmanageable by me," to the Twelfth, in which I tried to think of her as a sick Al-Anon and treat her with the love I would give a sick A.A. newcomer.(p.452)
• I got to the place where I'd look forward to the week-end's drinking and pacify myself by *saying* that the week-ends were mine, that it didn't interfere with my family or with my business if I drank on the week-ends.(p.488)
• "I went out of here nine days ago *saying* that I was going to be honest, and I wasn't," he answers.(p.503)
• But somehow or other, with my old alcoholic brain, sitting there in that chair, I kept *saying* to myself, "I wonder if it'll work?(p.515)
• Perhaps a better way of *saying* it is that, on that day, with that decision, I no longer fought drinking as an escape.(p.531)
• Which is only another way of *saying*, I had to be right all the time, and only God can be that.(p.535)

says

• We feel a man is unthinking when he *says* that sobriety is enough.(p.82)
• If he *says* yes, then his attention should be drawn to you as a person who has recovered.(p.90)
• He often *says* that if he had continued to work on them, he might have deprived many others, who have since recovered, of their chance.(p.96)
• He has read this volume and *says* he is prepared to go through with the Twelve Steps of the

program of recovery.(p.96)
• These things will come to pass naturally and in good time provided, however, the alcoholic continues to demonstrate that he can be sober, considerate, and helpful, regardless of what anyone *says* or does.(p.99)
• Of course, there is such a thing as incompatibility, but in nearly every instance the alcoholic only seems to be unloving and inconsiderate; it is usually because he is warped and sickened that he *says* and does these appalling things.(p.108)
• Try not to condemn your alcoholic husband no matter what he *says* or does.(p.108)
• If he *says* yes, does he really mean it, or down inside does he think he is fooling you, and that after rest and treatment he will be able to get away with a few drinks now and then?(p.142)
• Now and then a serious drinker, being dry at the moment *says*, "I don't miss it at all.(p.151)
• *Says* Bill W.:(p.188)
• I was crying, and I said, "Alice *says* she knows I don't have any part of the program."(p.273)
• Why don't you go home and get the Big Book and open it at page fifty-eight and see what it *says*?"(p.349)
• That's the stuff used when the oral surgeon puts the needle in your vein and *says*, "Count to ten," and before you get to two, you're asleep.(p.442)
• Each with the other as a witness, we took the Third Step out loud – just as it *says* in the Big Book.(p.446)
• Father *says* grace, which delays my attack on the buckwheat cakes and sausage.(p.497)
• He never *says* an unkind word.(p.501)
• "Well, you're not," *says* the man.(p.503)
• "Then all of your troubles are over," *says* the man and leaves the room.(p.503)
• She *says* nothing.(p.507)
• As another great man *says*, "The only real freedom a human being can ever know is doing what you ought to do because you want to do it."(p.553)
• Edward Dowling, S.J., of the Queen's Work staff *says*, "Alcoholics Anonymous is natural; it is natural at the point where nature comes closest to the supernatural, namely in humiliations and in consequent humility.(p.574)

scale
• No matter how far down the *scale* we have gone, we will see how our experience can benefit others.(p.84)
• I was prone to do everything on a big *scale*.(p.197)
• My wife became pregnant and the doctor recommended the use of port or ale . . . so . . . I bought a six gallon crock and a few bottles, listened to advice from amateur brewmeisters, and was off on my beer manufacturing career on a small *scale* (for the time being).(p.297)

scales
• *Scales* of pride and prejudice fell from my eyes.(p.12)
• The *scales* had dropped from my eyes and I could see life in its proper perspective.(p.280)

scandalous
• This is a condition which, in ordinary life, would produce untold grief; there might be *scandalous* gossip, laughter at the expense of other people, and a tendency to take advantage of intimate information.(p.125)

Scandinavian
• A.A. has flourishing communities in the British Isles, the *Scandinavian* countries, South Africa, South America, Mexico, Alaska, Australia and Hawaii.(p.xv)
• The ambition to succeed was instilled in me by my *Scandinavian* parents who came to this country where opportunities were so great.(p.373)

scant
• If he is a real alcoholic and very far advanced, there is *scant* chance of success.(p.34)

scarce
• Seeing much of each other, *scarce* an evening passed that someone's home did not shelter a little gathering of men and women, happy in their release, and constantly thinking how they might present their discovery to some newcomer.(p.159)
• The Depression was still on and jobs were *scarce*.(p.282)
• New programing was beginning to build an audience, but sponsors were pretty *scarce*.(p.360)

scarcely
• I hardly dared cross the street, lest I collapse and be run down by an early morning truck, for it was *scarcely* daylight.(p.6)
• There is *scarcely* any form of trouble and misery which has not been overcome among us.(p.15)
• He can *scarcely* square the account in his lifetime.(p.127)
• And we, who have imposed on the best of employers, can *scarcely* blame them if they have been short with us.(p.138)
• His wife came, *scarcely* daring to be hopeful, though she thought she saw something different about her husband already.(p.158)

scare
• The fact that A.A. is a spiritual program didn't *scare* me or raise any prejudice in my mind.(p.383)
• That put a *scare* in me for about a fortnight.(p.522)
• As I say, this specialist put a *scare* in me for about a fortnight or three weeks, then I started my last bout which went on and off for about three months.(p.523)

scared
• I think I must have been thoroughly *scared* by what had happened, or by the doctor, or probably both, so that I did not touch a drink again until the country went dry.(p.175)
• My case is so terrible that I'm *scared* to go out of this hospital at all.(p.188)
• In fact I was *scared* to talk to him about it, for I feared the kind of talk he would give me.(p.234)
• I was *scared* to death to call a doctor.(p.267)
• I became a drunk anyway, but I was *scared* to death to take that morning drink.(p.323)
• When I found this impossible, I became *scared* for the first time.(p.333)
• I had been unhappy, lonely, and *scared* for so long that the discovery of liquor seemed to be the answer to all my problems.(p.353)
• I was *scared* -- would she leave me again?(p.365)
• She told me not to bother going "for her sake"; she told me in a nice way that it didn't make any difference to her – and that really *scared* me – so I went.(p.365)
• But I couldn't enjoy anything; I was *scared* to death.(p.385)
• *Scared* that my dress wasn't going to fit right, that the church wasn't going to be filled, that I'd fall flat on my face walking up the aisle; in fact, I was afraid I wasn't going to be a prima donna in the place where I should be.(p.385)
• I was as defiant as anybody could be because I was *scared*.(p.391)
• I was so busy keeping her out of trouble, and so *scared* she'd swing on me, that I had my last two drinks that night.(p.415)
• I was really *scared*.(p.415)
• Well, I'm willing, if it will curb this awful desire to drink, this fear of not having a drink, this feeling of always being alone, *scared*, deserted, sick.(p.430)
• Had first drink in young teens, but was *scared* of my father.(p.474)
• Inside, though, I was *scared* to death, for I knew that the time was coming (and it couldn't be too remote) when I would be unable to hold that job.(p.548)

scars
• I bear a few *scars* on my face from these fights, which I always lost, because the "stick" existed only in my mind.(p.537)

scattered
• And besides, there were *scattered* alcoholics who had picked up the basic ideas in Akron or New York and were trying to form A.A. groups in other cities.(p.xvii)
• We old-timers who get *scattered* and separated and then witness the construction of services to get in more people and to make this thing function, we think that A.A. has changed, but the root of it hasn't.(p.272)

scene
• We had to unify our Fellowship or pass off the *scene*.(p.xix)
• Many mornings I have gone to classes, and even though fully prepared, would turn and walk back to the fraternity house because of my jitters, not daring to enter the classroom for fear of making a *scene* should I be called on for recitation.(p.173)
• Instead, I quickly substituted one or another vivid *scene* from the nightmare of my later drinking.(p.286)
• At a large party in Geneva, with people from many countries represented, the kind of party that is "protocol" in the extreme, I swayed, laughed hysterically, made naughty remarks in an unhushed voice, and was finally led from the *scene*.(p.406)

scenery
• Each person is like an actor who wants to run the whole show; is forever trying to arrange the lights, the ballet, the *scenery* and the rest of the players in his own way.(p.60)

scenes
• There were many unhappy *scenes* in our sumptuous apartment.(p.3)
• People have said we must not go where liquor is served; we must not have it in our homes; we must shun friends who drink; we must avoid moving pictures which show drinking *scenes*; we must not go into bars; our friends must hide their bottles if we go to their houses; we mustn't think or be reminded about alcohol at all.(p.100)
• Quebec, Toronto, Buffalo, and finally Pittsburgh, were the *scenes* of man-sized drunks until I had gone through my readjusted discharge pay, a fair sum.(p.253)
• In my mind's eye, I played and replayed *scenes* in which I was plucked magically from the bar where I stood nursing a drink, and was instantly exalted to some position of power and prestige.(p.560)

schedule
• I was escorted back to San Diego next morning -- by the Shore Patrol, but I was discharged on *schedule*.(p.428)
• (We don't have much time for bathing in our crowded *schedule*.)(p.479)

scheduled
• She had just come in and was *scheduled* to sail in two days.(p.252)

schedules
• She tried reasoning with me, endeavored to work out various drinking *schedules*, in fact all the tricks were practised faithfully for a short time somewhere along my shaky road to unhappiness.(p.361)
• I would follow certain drinking *schedules* or diets faithfully for a few days, and then somewhere along the line would over-train and upset the applecart.(p.361)
• My job was to make out the guard *schedules* and thus I was exempt from ordinary recruit training activities.(p.425)
• I stayed in the barracks all day, "making out guard *schedules*," and getting mildly plastered from the jug under my desk.(p.426)

scheme
• In our belief any *scheme* of combating alcoholism which proposes to shield the sick man from temptation is doomed to failure.(p.101)
• The Commanding Officer only spoke to me when he wanted to tell me exactly who I was and what I was and how little I counted in the *scheme* of things and how glad he would be if I went away.(p.520)

schisms
• Would there be *schisms* which would split A.A. apart?(p.xix)

schizophrenia
• My personality was stretched almost to splitting in the effort; *schizophrenia* stared me in the face, and one night I was in a suicidal despair.(p.435)

scholarship
• Awarded a *scholarship* to a famous old Eastern college, I began to drink at the end of my freshman year, and by junior year, I had to transfer to an easier state university to keep my grades up.(p.419)

scholarships
• I, a man of steel, with very high ideals, well brought up, an honor student and the recipient of *scholarships* and prizes, a boy wonder in business – I, Bob, the author of this essay, looked and saw that the universe was beneath my contempt, and that to remove myself from it was the only thing of dignity a man could do.(p.531)

scholastic
• The second year my drinking was more or less restricted to week-ends, but I was nearly kicked out for *scholastic* failure.(p.241)
• I didn't give a whoop about anything *scholastic*.(p.423)

scholastically
• This I did, and proved myself satisfactory to the faculty, both in deportment and *scholastically*.(p.174)

school
• The cheery voice of an old *school* friend asked if he might come over.(p.8)
• He attended church *school*, where he became rebellious at what he thought an overdose of religious education.(p.56)
• One *school* would allow man no flavor for his fare and the other would have us all on a straight pepper diet.(p.69)
• From childhood through high *school* I was more or less forced to go to church, Sunday *School* and evening service, Monday night Christian Endeavor and sometimes to Wednesday evening

prayer meeting.(p.172)
• After high *school* came four years in one of the best colleges in the country where drinking seemed to be a major extra-curricular activity.(p.172)
• When I got the fog out of my brain, I decided that quitting *school* was very foolish and that I had better return and continue my work.(p.173)
• When I reached *school*, I discovered the faculty had other ideas on the subject.(p.173)
• My wife, a Kentucky girl, came with me to Akron where I completed my course in law at the Akron Law *School*.(p.182)
• I would reach over and get this and take a shot and in a few moments get up and take another, shave and eat my breakfast, slip a half pint of liquor in my hip pocket, and go on to *school*.(p.183)
• My father died in 1901 when I was eight years old and I was in the second or third grade at *school*.(p.193)
• I immediately quit *school* and went to work, and from that time until I was high *school* age there was never a return to *school*.(p.193)
• When I was sixteen years old, my mother remarried and I was given the opportunity of going back to *school*.(p.193)
• I went into the high *school* grades, but having missed all the intermediate grades, I didn't get along too well, so I developed the habit of going back to *school* just long enough for the football season and then quitting.(p.193)
• When I was eighteen, at the end of high *school*, the high *school* team had a banquet at a well-known road-house outside of Akron.(p.194)
• The differences between my father and my sisters, who were *school* teachers, made an excellent environment for the type of child I was – that is, slick and cute enough to take advantage of any adult quarrel.(p.210)
• In other words, I was always safe from the discipline of my father, and having developed along that line, I had considerable difficulty in *school*.(p.210)
• I didn't go to high *school*.(p.211)
• Not far from where I lived they built a new technical high *school* and one of the teachers sold me on the idea that I needed a little mechanical drawing if I were going to be a good toolmaker.(p.211)
• The *school* then obtained a job for me in the drafting department of another company.(p.211)
• I did not have a high *school* education so I went to night *school* to take the full high *school* course, which I finished in two years and nine months.(p.211)
• I then entered Case *School* and worked while I went to *school* and finished there.(p.212)
• This experience sent me to law *school* where I went at night and which course I completed in less than three years, taking the highest state bar examinations and passing them.(p.212)
• The law *school* experience was not inspired by a desire to follow patent law, which has been my profession since: I went to law *school* primarily to learn the law of contracts following my own experience with litigation.(p.212)
• A year later, after I completed the course in contracts, I quit the law *school*, and undertook some engineering work for a patent law firm on behalf of clients who were in difficulties and who desired to keep their troubles from their own engineering department.(p.212)
• I went back to law *school*, and doubled up on the courses because I was then approaching thirty years of age and I wanted to get through as quickly as possible.(p.212)
• I married when I was twenty-eight years old, and started in law *school* after I was married.(p.212)
• I kept myself so busy that outside of some *school* and group parties, I didn't go overboard on drinking very much between the ages of twenty-five and thirty.(p.213)
• By the time I had completed law *school* I had picked up some experience in patent law, for I remained with the patent law firm and worked too in Washington where they found that I was a capable infringement investigator.(p.213)
• By that time, I had one boy in college, another a senior in high *school*, and a daughter about twelve years old.(p.215)
• Professionally, after I was sober for a month or so I realized that I should *school* myself to dissolve the partnership I was in because I felt that I would never regain the respect of my partners no matter how long I was sober, and that I would be at a disadvantage.(p.220)
• The best boarding schools and a finishing *school* in Europe had fitted me for the conventional role of debutante and young matron.(p.225)
• My parents had some vague idea of making a priest out of me and for some years I attended the Franciscan *school* at Basle, Switzerland, just across the border, about six miles from my home.(p.230)
• I had not asked for help and seriously doubt that I would have, but Fitz, an old *school* friend of mine, had persuaded Jackie to call on me.(p.238)
• At thirteen I was packed off to a very fine Protestant boarding *school* in Virginia where I stayed four years, graduating without any special achievements.(p.240)
• At this *school* we had Bible readings before each meal, and church services four times on Sunday, and I became so rebellious at this that I swore I would never join or go to any church except for weddings or funerals.(p.240)
• In the spring of 1917, in order to beat being fired from *school*, I became "patriotic" and joined the Army.(p.241)
• I remember starting to city *school*, coming from a country *school*, and wanting so very, very much to be like the other girls and trying flour on my face for powder because I wasn't able to have any real powder.(p.261)
• Our other daughter was in her last year of high *school*, and one night the new son-in-law and my husband went out to a prize fight.(p.263)
• So we came to King *School*.(p.269)
• We had never missed a Wednesday night at King *School* for a year.(p.270)
• I remember sometime, it was possibly six months after we had been going steadily to King *School*, that we were coming home from a meeting and saw a car along the way, and a fellow in back drinking a bottle of beer.(p.271)
• Vacations from *school* and from work, spelled "travel" to me – and I travelled with gusto.(p.275)
• I enrolled in a correspondence *school* which taught nothing but accounting.(p.284)
• With this specialized training, and a liberal business education in the *school* of hard knocks, I was able to set up shop some two years later as an independent accountant.(p.284)
• I was very much interested in athletics, and because of this and parental influence, I didn't drink or smoke in either grade or high *school*.(p.287)
• After I left *school*, I went to work in Akron, living at home with my parents.(p.287)
• Since I didn't do well in *school*, I quit and joined the Army at age seventeen.(p.317)
• Somehow, I made it through basic and then laid off the booze for about three months, because I was in *school* at night.(p.317)
• It turned out that she had been in high *school* with my daughter.(p.321)
• As my son, our second child, came along, and as he became *school* age and was away at *school* most of the time, something happened.(p.323)
• So when the children were in *school* from nine to three, I started up a nice little business and was fairly successful in it.(p.339)
• I finished high *school* here in an American-sponsored Methodist public *school*, know as Philander Smith College.(p.342)
• Everything that I touched from grammar *school* on was successful.(p.345)
• I was president of my grammar *school* student body.(p.345)
• I was president of all my classes in high *school* and in my last year I was president of that student body.(p.345)
• The same thing occurred in medical *school*.(p.345)
• I was in the fourth quarter of my senior year at high *school*, and my mother was quite sick in the hospital.(p.354)
• I was active and did well, however, in *school* publications, dramatics (which came in handy during my drinking career), and Greek letter societies.(p.357)
• I had run away from *school* to join the army in World War I, but missed it by one day since the Armistice was signed the very day I landed in Atlanta to sign up with Uncle Sam.(p.357)
• When I did make it home in 1920, I re-entered *school* and caught up with my class in a few short months – I actually did a year's work in three months, proving much to the disgust of my dad that I could do it when I wanted to.(p.358)
• Dad's image for me was that of a big Irish oilman who came up through the *school* of hard knocks and so had to be a two-fisted drinker.(p.369)
• I did work of all kinds after *school* and during vacations, trying to find that which would appeal most as a goal for a life work.(p.373)
• He got half custody of our child, but later kept her during most of the *school* terms.(p.402)
• Her father, quite rightly, wanted to put her in a *school*.(p.409)
• She was duly sent to *school*, away from me.(p.409)
• I was an honor graduate in high *school*, and I was a "good boy" to whom mothers pointed when their sons went astray.(p.419)
• I remembered back to high *school* when I was fifteen.(p.423)
• I got a job after *school* pumping gas and worked until ten or eleven at night.(p.423)
• *School* was getting to be one big bore.(p.423)
• I applied for photo *school* at Pensacola Air Base and made it.(p.426)
• And when this six month *school* was over I applied for duty in Hawaii and pulled it.(p.426)
• I had begun to drink in the early years of pharmacy *school*, in order to get to sleep.(p.440)
• After going to *school* all day, working in the family drugstore all evening, and then studying until one or two in the morning, I would not be able to sleep soundly, with everything I had been studying going round in my head.(p.440)
• And as I went through pharmacy *school*, graduate *school*, medical *school*, internship, residency, and specialty training and, finally, went into practice, my drinking kept increasing.(p.441)
• Had I gone to *school* all those years just to sit and make leather belts?(p.445)
• Shortly thereafter, I was selected, with eight other inmates out of the 10,000 in the state's prisons at that time, to attend a *school* designed to take former "management problems" like me and convert them into paracounselors.(p.462)
• At that time I started *school* and that's how I got rid of the curls.(p.483)
• About this time an incident took place in grade *school* that I have never forgotten because it made me realize that I was actually a physical coward.(p.484)
• Mother was of the old *school* and figured that anyone I associated with should be of the proper type.(p.484)
• I remember in my first year in high *school*, that mother suggested that I do not join the cadet unit.(p.484)
• Of course, when father finally came to Virginia to work his way through *school*, he resented the southern "cracker," as he often called them, so much that he didn't even go back to his mother's funeral.(p.486)
• I went to elementary and high *school* in Washington, D.C. and then to Howard University.(p.486)
• I never had too much trouble in *school*.(p.486)
• As far as *school* was concerned, I made fair grades throughout.(p.486)
• I rebelled against this, because just about the time that I was getting ready to leave high *school*, a revelation came to me about God and it made things very complicated for me.(p.489)
• I become a teacher in a boys' *school*.(p.500)
• I went to a very good public *school* run by Jesuits.(p.517)
• There was nothing in my *school* life that I can look back on which was responsible for anything that happened afterwards.(p.517)
• Then I had a year in Germany at *school* -- that was, incidentally, when I got drunk for the first time.(p.517)
• But I pointed out to him that as I was the first British boy who had been to the *school*, it wouldn't be a very good advertisement for him, so I got over that all right.(p.518)
• And having sung that phrase, I'd chuckle with amusement, turning into irony turning into self-contempt turning into self-pity, at the sad fate of Bob, that wonderful, poor little motherless boy who was so smart in *school* and who grew up to accept responsibility so early and so fast and who staggered under his burdens without a whimper until the time came when he thought he was too good for this world and so he ought to be out of it.(p.532)
• There was the physical aspect; to be the youngest and the runt of the brood of children, to have to wear glasses very early and so to be teased, to be bookish and bored in *school* because the captain of the football team could not translate Virgil and yet was the *school* god while you, you, you little shrimp, were the *school* egghead, junior size and an early model.(p.533)
• So did the waterboy on the high *school* football team attempt to revenge himself on the big brother who was the star quarterback; for I was the waterboy and my brother was the star quarterback, innocent of everything except the fact that he was a star quarterback.(p.537)
• But not for long; now, for five Friday nights in a row, I went to jail, picked up sodden with beer (which I always disliked, but which was the only drink available); in jail five consecutive Friday nights in the town where I had grown up, where I had been an honor student in high *school*, where a kindly uncle, bailing me

out, said, "Bob, our family just doesn't do this sort of thing."(p.539)
• I have been appointed to the faculty of my old *school*, to teach in my new field.(p.541)
• In fact, I changed schools every year until high *school.*(p.555)
• By the time I reached high *school*, I was an over-achiever.(p.555)

schooled
• I used to get terribly upset when I saw my friends drink and knew I could not, but I *schooled* myself to believe that though I once had the same privilege, I had abused it so frightfully that it was with-drawn.(p.181)

schooling
• Soon, it became apparent that my *schooling* was interfering with my drinking.(p.354)

schoolmaster
• I eventually became a *schoolmaster*, but gave up that profession to join the Indian Army.(p.342)

schoolmate
• My *schoolmate* visited me, and I fully acquainted him with my problems and deficiencies.(p.13)

schools
• The town was well supplied with churches and *schools* in which I pursued my early educational activities.(p.171)
• I went to five grade *schools*, primarily because I was expelled for my conduct, but I eventually graduated from the eighth grade.(p.211)
• I went to both Catholic and public *schools.*(p.214)
• The best boarding *schools* and a finishing school in Europe had fitted me for the conventional role of debutante and young matron.(p.225)
• Until I was thirteen I attended public *schools*, with regular promotions and average grades.(p.240)
• I had the best *schools*, summer camps, resort vacations and travel.(p.304)
• I had every advantage a child could have, private *schools* (several of them), dancing *schools*, two colleges, coon skin coats, automobiles, a listing in the social register and all the rest.(p.357)
• In the various *schools* I attended, it was always a case of just getting by.(p.357)
• I was raised like the majority of American boys, coming from a family of modest circumstances, attending public *schools*, having the social life of a small midwestern town, with part-time work and some athletics.(p.373)
• I drank my way through *schools* and always got honors.(p.441)
• In fact, I changed *schools* every year until high school.(p.555)

science
• *Science* may one day accomplish this, but it hasn't done so yet.(p.31)
• And does not *science* demonstrate that visual proof is the weakest proof?(p.48)
• *Science* tells us so.(p.49)
• In 1932, some friends of mine advised me that I might try Christian *Science*, which had done a lot for some of their friends.(p.202)
• So I started to investigate *Science* through some friends of mine who were Readers in the church.(p.202)
• I told somebody that I was going down to get Christian *Science* and they took me down, but I don't remember saying that.(p.202)
• This Christian *Science* experience with a sobriety of fifteen months was in 1932.(p.203)
• During the latter part of the Christian *Science* experience I had gotten a job and was working at Firestone.(p.203)
• My education had been pretty much pagan -- *science.*(p.221)
• Educated child of the scientific age that I was, I had complete faith in the *science* of the mind.(p.434)
• I'd had absolute faith in *science*, and only in *science.*(p.435)
• *Science* could take my mind apart expertly, but it couldn't seem to put it together again.(p.435)

sciences
• I'd been on the board of governors of the Academy of Motion Picture Arts and *Sciences* for six years.(p.328)

scientific
• Inquiry by *scientific*, medical, and religious societies will be welcomed.(p.xiv)
• What with our ultra-modern standards, our *scientific* approach to everything, we are perhaps not well equipped to apply the powers of good that lie outside our synthetic knowledge.(p.xxv)
• The spirit of modern *scientific* inquiry, research and invention was almost unknown.(p.51)
• Educated child of the *scientific* age that I was, I had complete faith in the science of the mind.(p.434)

scoff
• I earnestly advise every alcoholic to read this book through, and though perhaps he came to *scoff*, he may remain to pray.(p.xxx)
• Scoffers could *scoff* and be damned.(p.3)

scoffers
• *Scoffers* could scoff and be damned.(p.3)

scold
• I became a menace, the fish-wife, the common *scold.*(p.410)

scolded
• But my friends usually found me and I would go home if they promised that I should not be *scolded.*(p.176)

scolding
• She was also the victim of my *scolding* and incessant nagging.(p.408)
• I was really *scolding* my mortal enemy, the inner me.(p.408)

scope
• The classification of alcoholics seems most difficult, and in much detail is outside the *scope* of this book.(p.xxviii)
• This widened the *scope* of my activities.(p.276)

score
• Of course I really didn't have to worry on that *score*, because I wasn't the type that got half drunk.(p.515)

scores
• I personally know *scores* of cases who were of the type with whom other methods had failed completely.(p.xxiii)
• I have since talked with *scores* of men who felt the same way.(p.12)
• Everybody nowadays, believes in *scores* of assumptions for which there is good evidence, but no perfect visual proof.(p.48)
• Then, in this eastern city, there are informal meetings such as we have described to you, where you may now see *scores* of members.(p.162)

scorn
• I was unwilling to bare my secrets to those who might display *scorn.*(p.331)

scotch
• Here are some of the methods we have tried: Drinking beer only, limiting the number of drinks, never drinking alone, never drinking in the morning, drinking only at home, never having it in the house, never drinking during business hours, drinking only at parties, switching from *scotch* to brandy, drinking only natural wines, agreeing to resign if ever drunk on the job, taking a trip, not taking a trip, swearing off forever (with and without a solemn oath), taking more physical exercise, reading inspirational books, going to health farms and sanitariums, accepting voluntary commitment to asylums -- we could increase the list ad infinitum.(p.31)
• His only chance for sobriety would be some place like the Greenland Ice Cap, and even there an Eskimo might turn up with a bottle of *scotch* and ruin everything!(p.101)
• I drank all the *scotch* they had on the train and bought several quarts on my way to the hotel.(p.179)
• I graduated from shots and beer chasers to *Scotch* and sodas.(p.398)
• Other girls whom I had known all my life asked for one weak *scotch* after dinner.(p.406)
• When we got home, I got a bottle of *Scotch* and went to bed.(p.445)

Scotland
• My wife came over from *Scotland* and we started housekeeping in a large Ohio city.(p.254)

Scott
• The times in which I grew up (the Prohibition era immortalized by *Scott* Fitzgerald and John Held Jr.) had taught me to be gay with the gayest; my own inner urges led me to outdo them all.(p.225)
• That age of the flapper and the "It" girl, speakeasies and the hip flask, the boyish bob and the drugstore cowboy, John Held Jr. and F. *Scott* Fitzgerald, all generously sprinkled with a patent pseudo-sophistication.(p.304)
• It was all about *Scott* Fitzgerald's little lost debutante, abused, misunderstood and running wild.(p.402)
• I also wrote another novel, all about *Scott* Fitzgerald's poor, misbegotten, unloved, tipsy little debutante.(p.405)

Scranton
• We boys drove out in somebody's car and went to the bar on the way do the dining room and I, in an effort to impress the other boys that I was city-bred, having lived in *Scranton* and Cleveland, asked them if they didn't want a drink.(p.194)

scrap
• Then he had, in effect, been raised from the dead, suddenly taken from the *scrap* heap to a level of life better than the best he had ever known!(p.11)
• All of my family and loved ones, all of my friends, are nearer and dearer to me than ever before and I have literally dozens of new friends who say they cannot believe that a short eight years ago I was ready for the *scrap* heap.(p.541)

scrap-heap
• Above all, I have gained the greatest thing accorded to any man, the love and understanding of a gracious God, who has lifted me from the alcoholic *scrap-heap* to a position of trust where I have been able to reap the rich rewards that come from showing a little love for others and from serving them as I can.(p.296)

scrape
• Unless he took some drinks, he might not have the courage to *scrape* an acquaintance and would have a lonely week-end.(p.154)

scrapes
• There had been no real infidelity, for loyalty to my wife, helped at times by extreme drunkenness, kept me out of those *scrapes.*(p.3)
• Your man has probably been trying to conceal a number of *scrapes*, perhaps pretty messy ones.(p.140)
• But these *scrapes* can generally be charged, no matter how bad, to the abnormal action of alcohol on his mind.(p.140)
• Cleaning up old *scrapes*, helping to settle family differences, explaining the disinherited son to his irate parents, lending money and securing jobs for each other, when justified -- these are everyday occurrences.(p.161)
• I had never known him to be anything but a good healthy pagan with a propensity for getting into liquor jams and *scrapes.*(p.257)
• But he's in all sorts of *scrapes* because he drinks too much."(p.262)
• I lied like a trooper to get out of many *scrapes.*(p.324)

scraping
• We should be sensible, tactful, considerate and humble without being servile or *scraping.*(p.83)

scratch
• So far, upon the total problem of several million actual and potential alcoholics in the world, we have made only a *scratch.*(p.xx)

scratched
• If we keep on the way we are going there is little doubt that much good will result, but the surface of the problem would hardly be *scratched.*(p.19)
• He may not see at once that he has barely *scratched* a limitless lode which will pay dividends only if he mines it for the rest of his life and insists on giving away the entire product.(p.129)
• And then I *scratched* my head and said to myself, "What a fantastic thing for a man to say, that I cured his wife.(p.350)
• Only they had been *scratched* out and over them was written, "Chronic Alcoholic."(p.470)

scratchiness
• That is the way Jackie found me, lying on a cot in my skivvies, with hot and cold sweats, pounding heart and that awful itchy *scratchiness* all over.(p.238)

scratching
• Following an injection I would have to keep one hand busy *scratching* my constantly itching nose and would also have sudden uncontrollable urges to vomit.(p.442)

scrawny
• Prior to our marriage, when she was a shy, *scrawny* adolescent, I was able to see things in her that others couldn't necessarily see -- things like beauty, charm, gaiety, a gift for being easy to talk to, a sense of humor, and many other fine qualities.(p.450)

screamed
• I *screamed* on the telephone for my mother to get up there; something was going to happen; I didn't know what, but if she didn't get there quick, I'd split wide open.(p.338)

screaming
• Sometimes there were *screaming* delirium and insanity.(p.107)

• I do recall lying on a cold cement floor and shredding into little bits several pieces of stolen identification cards, and washing my face in the toilet bowl trying to sober up, and *screaming* hysterically while clinging to bars too high to see out of, and cursing everyone that came near me.(p.354)
• Luckily a friend was with me, who dragged me out, *screaming* and cursing, while the bartender threatened to call the police.(p.411)
• And as her disease was reaching the terminal stages, she was *screaming*, "You hate me!(p.439)

screwball
• He said, "Sister, if you think you're a *screwball* now, all you have to do is join up with that.(p.266)

screwballs
• At the time, I thought them just a swell pair of *screwballs*, for they were not only going to save all the drunks in the world but also all the so-called normal people!(p.245)

screwed
• I know that I was terribly *screwed* up inside, but I came out much worse.(p.387)
• In my *screwed* up mind I kept thinking I could have gone to A.A. way back there in 1940, and perhaps saved my marriage and home.(p.469)

screwy
• My mind was too *screwy* to be able to understand much of what was being said.(p.524)

scripts
• The movie racket had kept me too long from writing those novels, articles, short stories, and *scripts* on which I had copious notes.(p.330)

scrub
• One morning when I was feeling really bad, I was put on K.P. and the head cook wanted me to go out and *scrub* the garbage cans.(p.317)

Scylla
• I was between *Scylla* and Charybdis now, because if I did not drink my stomach tortured me, and if I did, my nerves did the same thing.(p.175)

sea
• And then, with a better motive, had we not worshipfully beheld the sunset, the *sea*, or a flower?(p.54)
• Now my drinking was limited by only one factor, the enforced periods of dryness caused by lengthy tours at *sea*.(p.398)
• Later, I went to *sea*, serving as a gunnery officer on a destroyer escort and emerging a lieutenant commander.(p.555)

Seabrook's
• I remembered going through what my sister assured me was my nightly procedure of trying to find Willie *Seabrook's* name in the telephone book.(p.224)

search
• Sometimes we had to *search* fearlessly, but He was there.(p.55)
• If our testimony helps sweep away prejudice, enables you to think honestly, encourages you to *search* diligently within yourself, then, if you wish, you can join us on the Broad Highway.(p.55)
• If we cannot or would rather not do this, we *search* our acquaintance for a close-mouthed, understanding friend.(p.74)
• *Search* out another alcoholic and try again.(p.96)
• It wasn't very long before home-brewing was an institution and men began to *search* feverishly for old recipe books on wine-making.(p.232)
• What philosophy I had was thoroughly paganistic -- all my life was devoted to a *search* for pleasure.(p.256)
• I tried to encourage a *search* for some new goal.(p.334)

searched
• First, we *searched* out the flaws in our make-up which caused our failure.(p.64)

searches
• Yet early next morning he *searches* madly for the bottle he misplaced the night before.(p.21)

searching
• He was rescued by a *searching* party, and, in desperate condition, brought to me.(p.xxix)
• 4.Made a *searching* and fearless moral inventory of ourselves.(p.59)
• *Searching* where I have been at fault, it is not hard to discover and get right again, for I have proven to myself and to many others who know me that God can keep a man sober if he will let Him.(p.237)
• Here was the understanding I'd been *searching* for all my life.(p.355)

season
• I went into the high school grades, but having missed all the intermediate grades, I didn't get along too well, so I developed the habit of going back to school just long enough for the football *season* and then quitting.(p.193)
• A house in Virginia, during the fox hunting *season*; a little chalet in Switzerland during the summer or a place on Long Island – each house complete with cooks, butlers and maids.(p.403)

seasons
• Father knows he is to blame; it may take him many *seasons* of hard work to be restored financially, but he shouldn't be reproached.(p.123)

seat
• But more important, I would have found that once again I was sitting in the driver's *seat* -- I was running the show.(p.471)
• I talk to the stranger in the *seat* beside me.(p.505)

seated
• *Seated* at the typewriter, I faked deep thinking or portrayed creativity by key-tapping.(p.332)

Seattle
• After the trial, I got big-hearted again and felt that I should do something in payment for Vi's kindness to me; so I left Washington and went to *Seattle* to work.(p.492)

secluded
• Many retirees embrace alcoholism while *secluded* in motor trailers, rest homes, leisure-world bungalows, mountain cabins, or beach cottages, or even in penthouses, on yachts, and inside Palm Springs cabanas.(p.329)
• Also, I believed I was the image of all domestic virtues, *secluded* in my washday (any day) refuge.(p.369)

second
• The *second* edition, published in 1955, reached a total of more than 1,150,000 copies.(p.xi)
• Therefore, the first portion of this volume, describing the A.A. recovery program, has been left untouched in the course of revisions made for both the *second* and the third editions.(p.xi)
• The *second* edition added the appendices, the Twelve Traditions, and the directions for getting in touch with A.A.(p.xi)
• Nine of the stories in Part II ("They Stopped in Time") are carried over from the *second* edition; eight new stories have been added.(p.xii)
• FOREWORD TO *SECOND* EDITION(p.xv)
• Sixteen years have elapsed between our first printing of this book and the presentation in 1955 of our *second* edition.(p.xv)
• A *second* small group had promptly taken shape at New York.(p.xvii)
• Suppose now you are making your *second* visit to a man.(p.96)
• My father died in 1901 when I was eight years old and I was in the *second* or third grade at school.(p.193)
• I had contracted for half of it, at least verbally, and the contractors were taking half of the *second* mortgage bond.(p.198)
• I'll buy you one drink, and if you suggest a *second* one, I'll poke you right in the nose."(p.201)
• Then I got into the habit of having beers, and decided that a drink of whiskey was not any worse; so I would get the one drink of whiskey but, on *second* thought, I decided that as long as I was only going to have one, I might as well make it a double-header.(p.203)
• Sitting in a *Second* Avenue bar, accepting drinks from anyone who offered, after my small stake was gone; or sitting at home alone, with the inevitable glass in my hand, I would remember, and remembering, I would drink faster, seeking speedy oblivion.(p.225)
• The *second* year my drinking was more or less restricted to week-ends, but I was nearly kicked out for scholastic failure.(p.241)
• Three months before I met Jackie I had made my *second* feeble try at suicide.(p.245)
• I thought I had done that until Russ' *second* collapse, and the doctor told me very candidly that he wasn't long for this world.(p.271)
• One of them was that I would try to get a group started in Chicago; the *second* was that I would have to return to Akron to attend meetings at least every two months until I did get a group started in Chicago; third, I decided I must place this program above everything else, even my family, because if I did not maintain my sobriety I would lose my family anyway.(p.292)
• I never enjoyed any meal, but I ate my lunch at noon for two reasons; first, to help me get out of the fog of the night before and, *second*, to furnish some measure of nourishment.(p.299)
• I could no longer gage my capacity and it might be the *second* or the tenth drink that would erase my consciousness.(p.306)
• And when my husband found A.A., I came to the *second* meeting with him.(p.321)
• As my son, our *second* child, came along, and as he became school age and was away at school most of the time, something happened.(p.323)
• For the *second* time, I was licked.(p.340)
• But this *second* time, I found I couldn't live normally without it, and I was licked worse than ever.(p.340)
• On the *second*, I knew -- as I know now -- that if I remained away from the first drink, then I had not to worry about the hundredth one.(p.344)
• The *second* way in which, perhaps, I differ from some other alcoholics is this; many alcoholics state that they didn't particularly like the taste of alcohol, but that they liked the effect.(p.345)
• The *second* one said, "Don't feel that you stop drinking for anyone other than yourself," and this hit me between the eyes.(p.346)
• I was well into the *second* fifth by this time.(p.347)
• In my *second* year in A.A. we were transferred to Dallas.(p.394)
• My life there was a nightmare of periodic binges on alcohol and pills, adultery, unhappy hours at the dental office, seeing my wife give birth to our *second* child and have several miscarriages, living in a turbulent household, and making continual attempts to be the respectable dentist, husband, father, and community leader.(p.419)
• My *second* wife is a young A.A. member, too, and what a terrific adventure this is for us!(p.420)
• UNTO THE *SECOND* GENERATION(p.422)
• I ran away for the *second* time, with another lad.(p.424)
• I paid nine hundred dollars for a *second* hand car on my return.(p.429)
• But as I came out of this *second* bout with D.T.'s I knew I was licked.(p.429)
• Once or twice, during my early drinking, I carried it over into the *second* day, and only once, that I can remember, did it continue into the third.(p.432)
• *Second*, you wouldn't have believed me even if I had told you."(p.436)
• Time went by very, very slowly on my *second* nut ward.(p.445)
• In the first place, she had been married before; I was her *second* husband.(p.485)
• I'll try the *second*.(p.499)
• During the course of that drinking, I had shot and killed one person and almost completed the job on a *second* one.(p.508)
• However, a verdict was brought in of murder in the *second* degree.(p.508)
• In the meantime I had been indicted for the *second* crime, attempted murder.(p.508)
• It was my *second* arrival in New York.(p.513)
• I have seen that there is only one law, the law of love, and there are only two sins; the first is to interfere with the growth of another human being, and the *second* is to interfere with one's own growth.(p.542)
• It became *second* nature for me to remove myself from anything or anybody I found myself growing fond of.(p.545)
• Had I been able to explain to a psychiatrist the feeling of futility, loneliness and lack of purpose that had come with my deep sense of personal failure at this *second* divorce, I seriously doubt that the good doctor could have convinced me that my basic problem was a spiritual hunger, but A.A. has shown me this was the truth.(p.546)
• I went to jail for the *second* time during this period for being drunk in an automobile.(p.549)
• I was the only person I'd ever known personally who had ever been in jail, and I guess it is most significant that the *second* time was less humiliating that the first had been.(p.549)

second-generation
• I am one of the growing number of A.A. members who are *second-generation*.(p.419)

second-hand
• I managed to maintain myself with odd jobs, did ten weeks in a social rescue institution, and at length wound up in a *second-hand* bookstore in an adjacent town as manager.(p.257)

secondary
• Though they knew they must help other alcoholics if they would remain sober, that motive became *secondary*.(p.159)

• The fact that I can work again and earn my living, is important, but *secondary*.(p.229)
• *Secondary* aids to A.A., such as clubs or hospitals which require much property or administration, ought to be incorporated and so set apart that, if necessary, they can be freely discarded by the groups.(p.566)

seconds
• In a few *seconds* he was overwhelmed by a conviction of the Presence of God.(p.56)
• In fifteen *seconds* or less, the feeling passed.(p.285)

secret
• Perhaps he is having a *secret* and exciting affair with "the girl who understands."(p.81)
• This *secret* drinker favored the local Laundromat as a watering hole.(p.369)
• I woke up filled with *secret* guilt and shame.(p.407)
• It was my "*secret* garden" – bluntly, it was my retreat from life, and I didn't want to give it up.(p.534)
• I never was a "*secret*" drinker, and I never kept a bottle at home.(p.536)

secretary
• One day my *secretary* came in saying that Mr. B—— insisted on speaking with me.(p.136)
• My *secretary* returned to say that it was not Mr. B— -on the phone; it was Mr. B——'s brother, and he wished to give me a message.(p.136)
• I'd go into an organization, and it wasn't long before I was on the committee, then I was chairman of the committee; and if I was in a group, I'd soon be treasurer or *secretary* of the group.(p.339)
• They sent me the regular letter they send to everybody else, but along with it, Ruth Hock, the nonalcoholic *secretary*, wrote a longhand note because she could see from the letter that I really needed help badly.(p.392)
• In the first year there were episodes such as kicking Priscilla in the shins, getting the lock changed on the desk in the A.A. Club, because I, as *secretary*, didn't want the Intergroup *secretary* "interfering," and taking an older woman member out to lunch for the express purpose of informing her that she was "a phony."(p.416)
• The small group may elect its *secretary*, the large group its rotating committee, and the groups of a large metropolitan area their central or intergroup committee, which often employs a full-time *secretary*.(p.567)

secretive
• I should have realized that alcohol was getting hold of me when I started to become *secretive* in my drinking.(p.336)

secretly
• What I had *secretly* believed myself to be all along, this I had become.(p.411)

secrets
• If reasons for covering up are strong enough, *secrets* can be hidden from the world.(p.327)
• I was unwilling to bare my *secrets* to those who might display scorn.(p.331)

sect
• We are not allied with any particular faith, *sect* or denomination, nor do we oppose anyone.(p.xiv)

sectarian
• 10. – No A.A. group or member should ever, in such a way as to implicate A.A., express any opinion on outside controversial issues – particularly those of politics, alcohol reform, or *sectarian* religion.(p.567)

section
• The *section* called "The Doctor's Opinion" has been kept intact, just as it was originally written in 1939 by the late Dr. William D. Silkworth, our Society's great medical benefactor.(p.xi)
• But the chief change was in the *section* of personal stories, which was expanded to reflect the Fellowship's growth.(p.xi)
• "Bill's Story," "Doctor Bob's Nightmare," and one other personal history from the first edition were retained intact; three were edited and one of these was retitled; new versions of two stories were written with new titles; thirty completely new stories were added; and the story *section* was divided into three parts, under the same headings that are used now.(p.xi)
• Alcohol being no respecter of persons, we are an accurate cross *section* of America, and in distant lands, the same democratic evening-up process is now going on.(p.xx)
• These give a fair cross *section* of our membership and a clear-cut idea of what has actually happened in their lives.(p.29)
• That had been in the center of New York, on noisy 42nd Street . . . this was obviously a quiet residential *section*.(p.223)
• My job was to collect bets and betting-slips in the business *section*, a lucrative spot.(p.251)

sections
• All *sections* of this country and many of its occupations are represented, as well as many political, economic, social, and religious backgrounds.(p.17)

secure
• Before taking drastic action which might implicate other people we *secure* their consent.(p.80)
• You can *secure* their confidence when others fail.(p.89)
• I conducted myself so creditably that I was able to *secure* a much coveted internship in a western city, where I spent two years.(p.174)
• There was a concrete program, designed to *secure* the greatest possible inner security for us long-time escapists.(p.229)
• I thought this would give me ego-strength, make me feel wanted and *secure*, and alleviate my fears, but again nothing changed inside me.(p.546)

secured
• He had commenced our way of life, had *secured* a position, and was getting his head above water.(p.79)
• From that point on, I *secured* crocks of ten gallon capacity and really took quite an active interest in the manufacture of home brew.(p.297)
• Vi had *secured* work in Washington.(p.490)

securing
• Cleaning up old scrapes, helping to settle family differences, explaining the disinherited son to his irate parents, lending money and *securing* jobs for each other, when justified -- these are everyday occurrences.(p.161)

securities
• It went into certain *securities*, then cheap and rather unpopular.(p.2)

security
• Was it our self-esteem, our *security*, our ambitions, our personal, or sex relations, which had been interfered with?(p.65)
• *Security*.(p.65)
• *Security*.(p.65)
• *Security* (fear).(p.65)
• There was never financial *security*.(p.105)
• The family of an alcoholic longs for the return of happiness and *security*.(p.123)
• There was a concrete program, designed to secure the greatest possible inner *security* for us long-time escapists.(p.229)
• Until I took Social *Security* and a pension at the age of sixty-eight, after forty years in motion-picture-studio public relations, I had successfully hidden even any hints of approaching alcoholism.(p.327)
• I was keenly aware that my all-important *security*, which I had been constantly afraid of losing for four decades, no longer was endangered.(p.329)
• Only death could wipe out that *security*.(p.329)
• But for him, financial *security* or even affluence can be a tragedy.(p.330)
• I had no feeling of *security*, and I knew that I had done a very stupid thing, so I went back to Texas and remarried my ex-husband.(p.386)
• Even then I knew in my heart that I was unfit for the very things I wanted most, a happy marriage, *security*, a home and love.(p.403)
• The people of A.A. had something that looked much better than what I had, but I was afraid to let go of what I had in order to try something new; there was a certain sense of *security* in the familiar.(p.448)
• The only kind of *security* I knew anything about at that time was material *security* and I decided that all these intruders would vanish immediately if I only had a lot of money.(p.545)

sedately
• By the time I figured out what had happened, I saw two flashing red lights atop squad cars, *sedately* coming around the corner.(p.353)

sedation
• I was caught in a cycle of alcohol and *sedation* that was proving inescapable and consciousness had become intolerable.(p.304)
• No matter how often I had gone into and come out of alcoholic lows during the day, the pattern bounced me out of bed each night about 2:00 a.m., shaking and hurting in the agitation that always follows a drug's *sedation*.(p.332)
• I attended my first A.A. meeting eight years ago, and it is with deep gratitude that I'm able to say I've not had a drink since that time, and that I take no *sedation* or narcotics, for this program is to me one of complete sobriety and I no longer need to escape reality.(p.549)

sedative
• A doctor came with a heavy *sedative*.(p.6)
• Next day found me drinking both gin and *sedative*.(p.7)
• As matters grow worse, he begins to use a combination of high-powered *sedative* and liquor to quiet his nerves so he can go to work.(p.22)
• Perhaps he goes to a doctor who gives him morphine or some *sedative* with which to taper off.(p.22)
• I never in my life took a tranquilizer, *sedative*, or pep pill because I was a pillhead.(p.443)

sedatives
• Sometimes you will have to call a doctor and administer *sedatives* under his direction.(p.97)
• Most of the time therefore, I did not take the morning drink which I craved so badly, but instead would fill up on large doses of *sedatives* to quiet the jitters, which distressed me terribly.(p.176)
• It was really a horrible nightmare, this earning money, getting liquor, smuggling it home, getting drunk, morning jitters, taking large doses of *sedatives* to make it possible for me to earn more money, and so on ad nauseam.(p.177)
• Most of them prescribed *sedatives* and advised rest and moderation.(p.305)
• It had been so many years since I had not relied on some artificial crutch, either alcohol or *sedatives*.(p.310)
• The folks called a doctor and he knocked me out with *sedatives*.(p.429)

seduce
• I would take a gulp, then warn the jug not to try to entice, lure, or *seduce* me into having more than one "medicinal" jolt.(p.332)

seduction
• I always succumbed to its *seduction*.(p.332)

see
• If any feel that as psychiatrists directing a hospital for alcoholics we appear somewhat sentimental, let them stand with us a while on the firing line, *see* the tragedies, the despairing wives, the little children; let the solving of these problems become a part of their daily work, and even of their sleeping moments, and the most cynical will not wonder that we have accepted and encouraged this movement.(p.xxvi)
• They are restless, irritable and discontented, unless they can again experience the sense of ease and comfort which comes at once by taking a few drinks -- drinks which they *see* others taking with impunity.(p.xxvi)
• One year later he called to *see* me, and I experienced a very strange sensation.(p.xxix)
• I *see* him now and then and he is as fine a specimen of manhood as one could wish to meet.(p.xxx)
• At these informal gatherings one may often *see* from 50 to 200 persons.(p.16)
• He could not, or would not, *see* our way of life.(p.16)
• We have concluded to publish an anonymous volume setting forth the problem as we *see* it.(p.19)
• Before going into a detailed discussion, it may be well to summarize some points as we *see* them.(p.20)
• We *see* that these expressions refer to people whose reactions are very different from ours.(p.20)
• Our hope is that many alcoholic men and women, desperately in need, will *see* these pages, and we believe that it is only by fully disclosing ourselves and our problems that they will be persuaded to say, "Yes, I am one of them too; I must have this thing."(p.29)
• We, who are familiar with the symptoms, *see* large numbers of potential alcoholics among young people everywhere.(p.33)
• But try and get them to *see* it!(p.34)
• He is an intelligent man, normal so far as we can *see*, except for a nervous disposition.(p.35)
• Then I decided to drive into the country and *see* one of my prospects for a car.(p.36)
• We now *see* that when we began to drink deliberately, instead of casually, there was little serious or effective thought during the period of premeditation of what the terrific consequences might be.(p.37)
• He soon indicated he was anxious to *see* us.(p.40)
• "Two of the members of Alcoholics Anonymous came to *see* me.(p.42)
• Simply because it is impossible to explain what we *see*, feel, direct, and use, without a reasonable assumption as a starting point.(p.48)
• When, however, the perfectly logical assumption is suggested that underneath the material world and life as we *see* it, there is an All Powerful, Guiding, Creative Intelligence, right there our perverse streak comes to the surface and we laboriously set out to

convince ourselves it isn't so.(p.49)
- We were having trouble with personal relationships, we couldn't control our emotional natures, we were a prey to misery and depression, we couldn't make a living, we had a feeling of uselessness, we were full of fear, we were unhappy, we couldn't seem to be of real help to other people -- was not a basic solution of these bedevilments more important than whether we should *see* newsreels of lunar flight?(p.52)
- We began to *see* that the world and its people really dominated us.(p.66)
- They *see* its significance everywhere.(p.69)
- We have commenced to *see* their terrible destructiveness.(p.70)
- We will be more reconciled to discussing ourselves with another person when we *see* good reasons why we should do so.(p.72)
- This is the one he likes his fellows to *see.*(p.73)
- He hopes they will never *see* the light of day.(p.73)
- We often find such a person quick to *see* and understand our problem.(p.74)
- To his wife, he remarked, "Don't *see* anything the matter here, Ma.(p.82)
- We ought to sit down with the family and frankly analyze the past as we now *see* it, being very careful not to criticize them.(p.83)
- No matter how far down the scale we have gone, we will *see* how our experience can benefit others.(p.84)
- We will *see* that our new attitude toward liquor has been given us without any thought or effort on our part.(p.85)
- You can easily *see* why.(p.87)
- Be quick to *see* where religious people are right.(p.87)
- To watch people recover, to *see* them help others, to watch loneliness vanish, to *see* a fellowship grow up about you, to have a host of friends -- this is an experience you must not miss.(p.89)
- You need this information to put yourself in his place, to *see* how you would like him to approach you if the tables were turned.(p.90)
- You should be described to him as one of a fellowship who, as part of their own recovery, try to help others and who will be glad to talk to him if he cares to *see* you.(p.90)
- If he does not want to *see* you, never force yourself upon him.(p.90)
- You might place this book where he can *see* it in the interval.(p.90)
- Under these conditions your prospect will *see* he is under no pressure.(p.91)
- *See* your man alone, if possible.(p.91)
- Let him *see* that you are not there to instruct him in religion.(p.93)
- Perhaps your story will help him *see* where he has failed to practice the very precepts he knows so well.(p.93)
- Make it clear that he is not under pressure, that he needn't *see* you again if he doesn't want to.(p.94)
- If he is sincerely interested and wants to *see* you again, ask him to read this book in the interval.(p.95)
- Little by little the family may *see* their own defects and admit them.(p.99)
- But for every man who drinks others are involved -- the wife who trembles in fear of the next debauch; the mother and father who *see* their son wasting away.(p.104)
- Why could they not *see* that drink meant ruin to them?(p.107)
- You can *see* that he really does love you with his better self.(p.108)
- It may be slowing him up mentally and physically, but he does not *see* it.(p.109)
- He admits he cannot drink like other people, but does not *see* why.(p.110)
- Let him *see* that you want to be helpful rather than critical.(p.111)
- Cheerfully *see* him through more sprees.(p.113)
- As our husbands began to apply spiritual principles in their lives, we began to *see* the desirability of doing so too.(p.116)
- Your husband will *see* at once that he must redouble his spiritual activities if he expects to survive.(p.120)
- Is he not unconsciously trying to *see* what he can take from the family life rather than give?(p.122)
- But he must *see* the danger of over-concentration on financial success.(p.127)
- As each member of a resentful family begins to *see* his short comings and admits them to the others, he lays a basis for helpful discussion.(p.127)
- Little by little, mother and children will *see* they ask too much, and father will *see* he gives too little.(p.127)
- They may not *see* why their love and devotion did not straighten him out.(p.128)
- He may not *see* at once that he has barely scratched a limitless lode which will pay dividends only if he mines it for the rest of his life and insists on giving away the entire product.(p.129)
- If the family cooperates, dad will soon *see* that he is suffering from a distortion of values.(p.129)
- If newcomers could *see* no joy or fun in our existence, they wouldn't want it.(p.132)
- When we *see* a man sinking into the mire that is alcoholism, we give him first aid and place what we have at his disposal.(p.132)
- In time they will *see* that he is a new man and in their own way they will let him know it.(p.134)
- You cannot *see* why it should be to anyone else, save the spineless and stupid.(p.139)
- Had they fired me first, and had they then taken steps to *see* that I was presented with the solution contained in this book, I might have returned to them six months later, a well man.(p.141)
- You can *see* that he is mentally and physically sick.(p.141)
- I don't *see* how you can be of any help to us for, as you *see*, we don't have any alcoholic problem."(p.148)
- But am I to be consigned to a life where I shall be stupid, boring and glum, like some righteous people I *see*?(p.152)
- He could *see* the gay crowd inside.(p.154)
- As we shall *see*, he now means a great deal to his community, and the major liabilities of thirty years of hard drinking have been repaired in four.(p.156)
- You fellows know your stuff all right, but I don't *see* what good it'll do.(p.157)
- Said the future Fellow Anonymous: "Damn little to laugh about that I can *see*."(p.157)
- So, you *see*, there were three alcoholics in that town, who now felt they had to give to others what they had found, or be sunk.(p.158)
- Then, in this eastern city, there are informal meetings such as we have described to you, where you may now *see* scores of members.(p.162)
- *See* to it that your relationship with Him is right, and great events will come to pass for you and countless others.(p.164)
- This worked nicely until my wife and I went to *see* Wallace Beery in "Tugboat Annie," after which the pant-leg and stocking racket were out!(p.177)
- Before very long we began to relate some incidents of our drinking and, naturally, pretty soon, I realized both of them knew what they were talking about because you can *see* things and smell things when you're drunk, that you can't other times, and, if I had thought they didn't know what they were talking about, I wouldn't have been willing to talk to them at all.(p.185)
- Wouldn't you like to *see* us again?"(p.189)
- "Sure I would," replied Bill, "Maybe it won't do any good, but I'd like to *see* you both, anyhow.(p.189)
- I kept watching the man down the bar to *see* what he did with a contraption like that, and he just smelled of his drink and set it down again, so I did the same.(p.195)
- The next day, others from the group came in to *see* me.(p.208)
- I remember well one fellow, Joe, walking nearly three miles through slush, wet and snow to come to the hospital to *see* a man that he had never seen before in his life, and that impressed me very much.(p.208)
- I could not *see* why I couldn't drink like a gentleman, and that was my primary ambition -- until I landed in A.A.(p.214)
- As far as my home was concerned, I did not *see* then, though of course I can *see* now, that it was anything but a happy situation for my wife.(p.215)
- Bill left me at the elevator and said, "Your room is so and so," and I didn't *see* him again for six months.(p.217)
- He told me that there were some other fellows that had tried this with success, and if I cared to *see* any of them he'd have them come in to *see* me.(p.218)
- I believe every member of the Akron Group did come to *see* me, which impressed me terrifically, not so much because of the stories they told, but because they would take the time to come and talk to me without even knowing who I was.(p.218)
- The afternoon that I was to leave the hospital, he came in to *see* me and asked me if I were willing to attempt to follow the program.(p.218)
- That was skeptically received by me when I first heard it, but after some twenty-eight or thirty fellows had come to *see* me, and pretty nearly all of them had said the same thing, I began to believe it.(p.219)
- I met all the people I wanted to meet; I saw all the places I wanted to *see*; I did all the things I wanted to do -- and I was increasingly miserable.(p.225)
- Alcohol was that prop, and I didn't *see* how I could live without it.(p.226)
- I went to a meeting to *see* for myself this group of freaks or bums who had done this thing.(p.228)
- An alcoholic who was a doctor came to *see* me.(p.235)
- Instead he told me that some of them wanted to talk to me and would be over to *see* me.(p.235)
- And, because as I have discovered since, it is part of the "treatment" that these men be sent to *see* and talk with alcoholics who want to quit, he kept them busy.(p.235)
- I could *see* they were sober.(p.235)
- The third man who came to *see* me had been one of the greatest business-getters his company had ever employed.(p.235)
- I could *see* that.(p.236)
- I very early came to *see* that there had to be a continual renewal for that simple deal with God; that I had perpetually to keep the bargain.(p.237)
- I really had a chance to *see* myself from a non-drinking point of view.(p.245)
- I stayed so sober that I used to keep a quart of medicinal whiskey in my bureau which I used to taper off the occasional newspaper alcoholics who were sent to *see* me.(p.253)
- I myself could *see* deterioration in my work from being physically and mentally affected by liquor, although I had not yet reached the point where all I wanted was more to drink.(p.254)
- While there I was called to the hospital in my home town to *see* a former partner who had insisted that I visit him.(p.257)
- As I look back on the events of two months, I can clearly *see* that I had been circling around, half-afraid of encountering the remedy for my situation, half wanting it, deferring fulfillment of my promise to get in touch with the doctor I had heard about.(p.258)
- The doctor who came to *see* me almost at once did not assail me with any new doctrines; he made sure that I had a need and that I wanted to have that need filled, and little by little I learned how my need could be met.(p.258)
- Indeed, I was beginning to *see* that I would require implicit faith, like a small child, if I was going to get anywhere.(p.259)
- But I had never been a flippant, wise-cracking sneerer at the few persons I had met who had impressed me as Christian men and women, or at any institution whose sincerity of purpose I could *see.*(p.259)
- Today I have Someone who will always hear me; I have a warm fellowship among men who understand my problems; I have tasks to do and am glad to do them, to *see* others who are alcoholics and to help them in any way I can to become sober men.(p.260)
- I didn't *see* him for a year, or even hear from him.(p.262)
- I had gone to an attorney to *see* about getting a divorce during that year.(p.263)
- Russ read a piece in the paper, and he kind of snickered, and said, "*See* here, where John D. has found something to keep him from drinking!"(p.265)
- I'm going in to *see* him, and *see* what can be done."(p.267)
- And I'd try, but I couldn't even *see* the letters.(p.268)
- Here, while in a hospital bed, men with clear eyes, happy faces, and a look of assurance and purposefulness about them, came to *see* me and told me their stories.(p.279)
- The scales had dropped from my eyes and I could *see* life in its proper perspective.(p.280)
- During my first few months in Akron I was quite sure that I never wanted to *see* my home town again.(p.281)
- Once dad came all the way to Florida to sober me up, after a hotel manager called him and said that if he wanted to *see* me alive he better get there fast.(p.288)
- I spent a great deal of time with Dr. Bob, whenever he had the time to spare, and in the homes of two or three other people, trying to *see* how the family lived the program.(p.291)
- I suggested to her that she should *see* the son's minister or doctor, and that perhaps he would recommend the A.A. program.(p.294)
- The three of us did not feel up to the job, and after a few meetings we convinced the prospects that they too should go to Akron where they could *see* an older group in action.(p.295)
- She offered me the alternative of going to *see* him or her leaving me for good and all.(p.301)
- I had never seen him before, and at the time hoped I would never *see* him again.(p.302)

• My wife is glad to *see* me come in.(p.303)
• They sum it up like this: "We didn't wait to hit bottom because, thank God, we could *see* the bottom.(p.315)
• Karen didn't want to *see* me any more, and neither did two other girls I'd been going out with.(p.318)
• I vowed that never again would any important person whom I wished to please and impress ever *see* me drunk.(p.328)
• On the last day I was drinking I went up to *see* a friend who had had a good deal of trouble with alcohol, and whose wife had left him a number of times.(p.346)
• In my stupid way I went up to *see* him with the idea in the back of my mind that I would investigate Alcoholics Anonymous from a medical standpoint.(p.346)
• Why don't you go home and get the Big Book and open it at page fifty-eight and *see* what it says?"(p.349)
• We've got to turn the whole business over to some joker we can't even *see*!(p.350)
• I could hardly *see* at all, and my memory kept eluding me.(p.353)
• I do recall lying on a cold cement floor and shredding into little bits several pieces of stolen identification cards, and washing my face in the toilet bowl trying to sober up, and screaming hysterically while clinging to bars too high to *see* out of, and cursing everyone that came near me.(p.354)
• I wanted so badly to *see* the picture as it was in her mind.(p.355)
• By persistence and salesmanship I managed to *see* more and more of my new friend, and because of her sympathetic nature she tolerated my company.(p.359)
• After a few meetings I decided to drive to Florida unannounced to *see* my wife and tell her about my new found friends and association.(p.364)
• That night she too had new hope because I had made sure she would know what I was doing about my drinking by packing every bit of A.A. literature I could put my hands on right on top so she couldn't help but *see* it when she opened my bag.(p.364)
• I tried to hide my drinking by going places where I was unlikely to *see* anyone I knew.(p.375)
• It was important to me to *see* what alcohol had done to me and would continue to do if I didn't have help.(p.379)
• Frank said, "If you'd like to talk to a psychiatrist, I'll *see* a doctor and find out who to go to here."(p.387)
• I could *see* no reason why they should have any relationship to this problem of getting drunk every now and then.(p.388)
• He even had the people come out, and tell me what kind of room I was going to have, and that he could come and *see* me, and that the dog could come and *see* me.(p.389)
• One afternoon, the year after moving to Houston, I got as drunk as a skunk, and while I do not walk very straight sober, you should *see* me when I'm drunk!(p.390)
• So when he came for me, as he walked down the stairs, I could *see* him through the bars, and he was signing for me; I looked at him and said, "Don't you sign anything in this place!"(p.391)
• I took two or three drinks so my eyes could focus, and I could *see* that horrible picture of the awful drunk on the first page; he couldn't get the drink to his mouth, he had a towel around his hand and he needed a shave.(p.391)
• They sent me the regular letter they send to everybody else, but along with it, Ruth Hock, the nonalcoholic secretary, wrote a longhand note because she could *see* from the letter that I really needed help badly.(p.392)
• He said, "Wait until I get back and I will go with you to *see* this man."(p.393)
• The letter from A.A. had said this man would *see* me – there weren't any women.(p.393)
• I did not *see* that the book dripped with self-pity.(p.403)
• "Why don't you just go down and *see* Mr. W.?" she asked.(p.412)
• "*See* what you think."(p.412)
• I could *see* he wasn't a quack or a fanatic.(p.413)
• I did not want to go and *see* her, but I went.(p.413)
• We started to light matches to *see*, but the draft blew them out.(p.424)
• Once in a while I stayed home for a night, to *see* how my folks were doing.(p.425)
• But my dad pulled some strings and got in to *see* me after three weeks.(p.425)
• Sometimes I'd make it home and go to sleep at the wheel of my car, for all the neighbors to *see* next morning as they left for work.(p.429)
• When I try to reconstruct what my life was like "before," I *see* a coin with two faces.(p.432)
• The Higher Power was on deck to *see* me through, sober.(p.437)
• I think He's on hand to *see* my son through, too.(p.437)
• I think He's on hand to *see* all of us through whatever may come to us.(p.437)
• He arranged for me to *see* a local psychiatrist, who quickly decided I should be in the mental-health unit of our local hospital.(p.445)
• I was always able to *see* the flaw in every person, every situation.(p.449)
• Prior to our marriage, when she was a shy, scrawny adolescent, I was able to *see* things in her that others couldn't necessarily *see* -- things like beauty, charm, gaiety, a gift for being easy to talk to, a sense of humor, and many other fine qualities.(p.450)
• But then, as I drank more and more, the alcohol seemed to affect my vision: Instead of continuing to *see* what was good about my wife, I began to *see* her defects.(p.450)
• But when I try to *see* what I can add to the meeting, rather than what I can get out of it, and when I focus my mind on what's good about it, rather than what's wrong with it, the meeting keeps getting better and better.(p.451)
• When I remember this, I can *see* I've never had it so good.(p.452)
• You *see*, I am a five-time loser, which means five felony convictions (not including the cases beaten).(p.457)
• One would have to understand the correctional machinery to *see* what a miracle this really was.(p.462)
• It was my ex-wife, and she said my twenty-seven-year-old son, who has completed his Marine Corps training and graduated from college, wanted to *see* me privately, was getting married in three months, and wanted me at the wedding.(p.462)
• I thank God I am to *see* him this month.(p.463)
• At the wedding, I hope I will also get to *see* my daughter and their mother.(p.463)
• I must be ready and willing should I never *see* them.(p.463)
• He said he was finally and completely through -- that he never wanted to *see* me again.(p.467)
• He said he'd *see*.(p.467)
• Tall Man was blind, but soon he *see*.(p.476)
• Tall Man now *see* Great Spirit in Big Group in sky.(p.476)
• I felt very sorry for myself and attempted suicide on many occasions, making sure there was always somebody within reaching distance to *see* that I didn't finish the job.(p.478)
• You *see* how much work some of us have to do on ourselves when we finally come into A.A.!(p.480)
• I planted my first flower garden this year and am actually excited to *see* the results.(p.481)
• On the other hand, I believe that I've always been medically inclined, though I have never been able to *see* medicine quite as the average person sees it.(p.485)
• I do surgery because that's something that you can *see*; it's more tangible.(p.485)
• I'd go into my home with a bottle, and I remember clearly how I would look around to *see* if Vi was watching.(p.487)
• I went back to my mother's for a few days until things cooled off, because the District Attorney had put out a summons for me to come to *see* him in his office.(p.491)
• Anyhow, on the 24th, after drinking all day on the 23rd, I must have decided I wanted to *see* my wife and have some kind of reconciliation or at least talk with her.(p.491)
• She said, "He has something of interest, if you will *see* him."(p.494)
• "Let your light so shine before men that they may *see* your good works –."(p.497)
• It's great to *see* him.(p.500)
• He makes no reply, and hardly seems to *see* me.(p.501)
• I *see* her about to go.(p.501)
• I drink and go to bed; I take a few the next morning and go *see* my mother once more.(p.501)
• I am at the hospital to *see* my wife.(p.501)
• But she is not glad to *see* me.(p.502)
• I begin to *see* I am not the person I had thought myself, that I had judged myself by comparing myself to others, and always to my own advantage.(p.504)
• I go to *see* a man I had been asked to visit and tell him my story.(p.505)
• I *see* where I have been wrong in some respects.(p.505)
• I cannot *see* the cause of this temptation now.(p.507)
• When I look back, I can't *see* anything that would have predisposed me towards being either a neurotic or a drunk.(p.517)
• In my own generation I stuck out, I can *see* that now, as being a very much heavier drinker than the average man.(p.518)
• I stopped off just to have one drink to *see* if it tasted the same on the way back to London, and that night I was carried back to bed again.(p.522)
• I went to hospitals, I went to retreats and doctors, and finally my mother asked me to go and *see* a specialist of her own choosing.(p.522)
• I couldn't *see* that there was any way out of it, and I got absolutely despairing.(p.522)
• It was no use talking of putting myself into a home, a hospital, or of going to *see* a doctor again, or of going to *see* a priest or anyone else.(p.523)
• Even those don't take part in A.A. functions as I would like to *see* them do.(p.529)
• If you give us a try, you will *see* that we are really human beings, and we will welcome you with open arms and hearts.(p.529)
• Regarded as something of a "boy wonder," I began to *see* myself that way.(p.555)
• We alcoholics *see* that we must work together and hang together, else most of us will finally die alone.(p.563)

seed

• The *seed* has been planted in his mind.(p.113)
• *Seed* has started to sprout in a new soil, but growth has only begun.(p.117)

seeds

• But in the light of the new understanding that I have found in A.A., I have been able to interpret that defeat, and that failure, and that shame, as *seeds* of victory.(p.335)
• He planted many *seeds*, and it will be many moons before another rises to walk in his shoes."(p.476)

seeing

• Yet we had been *seeing* another kind of flight, a spiritual liberation from this world, people who rose above their problems.(p.55)
• More and more we became interested in *seeing* what we could contribute to life.(p.63)
• *Seeing* is believing to most families who have lived with a drinker.(p.135)
• *Seeing* this, and meaning to be helpful, his wife commenced to admonish him about it.(p.135)
• *Seeing* your attempt to understand and help, some men will try to take advantage of your kindness.(p.141)
• *Seeing* much of each other, scarce an evening passed that someone's home did not shelter a little gathering of men and women, happy in their release, and constantly thinking how they might present their discovery to some newcomer.(p.159)
• I avoided them rather than explain why they weren't *seeing* me.(p.203)
• So I drank all three beers, one after the other, said "I'll be *seeing* you, boys," and went around the corner for a bottle.(p.247)
• *Seeing* this danger, they came to A.A.(p.315)
• A "spiritual experience" to me meant attending meetings, *seeing* a group of people, all there for the purpose of helping each other; hearing the Twelve Steps and the Twelve Traditions read at a meeting, and hearing the Lord's Prayer, which in an A.A. meeting has such great meaning – "Thy will be done, not mine."(p.381)
• My life there was a nightmare of periodic binges on alcohol and pills, adultery, unhappy hours at the dental office, *seeing* my wife give birth to our second child and have several miscarriages, living in a turbulent household, and making continual attempts to be the respectable dentist, husband, father, and community leader.(p.419)
• After I came to A.A., I was divorced by my wife; I lost my practice; I was legally restrained from *seeing* my children; I went broke; and the dental society threatened me with the loss of my license.(p.420)
• The first time I remember *seeing* or hearing of A.A. was twenty years ago.(p.460)
• Forgive me – I cannot write further about this latest turn of events, anticipating *seeing* the family I deserted so long ago.(p.463)
• Finally, I got so lowdown, I was ashamed of my friends' *seeing* me, so I went to the worst joints I could find.(p.527)
• My personal definition, which I submit as applying only to myself (although everyone is welcome to it who wants it), includes every waking activity of the human being; to have a creative attitude towards things is a more exact meaning, to live and to deal

with other human beings creatively, which to me means ***seeing*** the God in them, and respecting and worshipping this God.(p.535)
• I have had the joy of ***seeing*** many a human being, down and out, learn to stand straight again, and to proceed under his own power to happiness in life.(p.541)

seek
• We meet frequently so that newcomers may find the fellowship they ***seek***.(p.15)
• We found that God does not make too hard terms with those who ***seek*** Him.(p.46)
• To us, the Realm of Spirit is broad, roomy, all inclusive; never exclusive or forbidding to those who earnestly ***seek***.(p.46)
• He may ***seek*** someone else to console him -- not always another man.(p.111)
• He said he was through and would ***seek*** a divorce.(p.371)
• You may wonder why, since I was having all this trouble, and was having to ***seek*** the assistance of others, A.A. hadn't come into the picture.(p.469)
• It was the late Dr. Tiebout, then, who persuaded me to ***seek*** help through A.A.(p.559)

seeking
• Sitting in a Second Avenue bar, accepting drinks from anyone who offered, after my small stake was gone; or sitting at home alone, with the inevitable glass in my hand, I would remember, and remembering, I would drink faster, ***seeking*** speedy oblivion.(p.225)
• They seemed to be happy in their fashion, they and their little groups of supporters, but always pride of intellect stopped me from ***seeking*** what they evidently had.(p.256)
• I was ***seeking*** something and I was ready to learn.(p.258)
• They realized that in the end alcoholism could be a mortal as cancer; certainly no sane man would wait for a malignant growth to become fatal before ***seeking*** help.(p.315)

seem
• On the other hand -- and strange as this may ***seem*** to those who do not understand -- once a psychic change has occurred, the very same person who seemed doomed, who had so many problems he despaired of ever solving them, suddenly finds himself easily able to control his desire for alcohol, the only effort necessary being that required to follow a few simple rules.(p.xxvii)
• That didn't ***seem*** to bother me so I tried another."(p.36)
• We were having trouble with personal relationships, we couldn't control our emotional natures, we were a prey to misery and depression, we couldn't make a living, we had a feeling of uselessness, we were full of fear, we were unhappy, we couldn't ***seem*** to be of real help to other people -- was not a basic solution of these bedevilments more important than whether we should see newsreels of lunar flight?(p.52)
• They are not at fault; they ***seem*** to have been born that way.(p.58)
• But he will be curious to learn why his own convictions have not worked and why yours ***seem*** to work so well.(p.93)
• This may ***seem*** inconsistent, but we think it is not.(p.98)
• To a person who has had experience with an alcoholic, this may ***seem*** like tempting Providence, but it isn't.(p.101)
• Showing others who suffer how we were given help is the very thing which makes life ***seem*** so worth while to us now.(p.124)
• If not irritable, he may ***seem*** dull and boring, not gay and affectionate as the family would like him to be.(p.126)
• They cannot ***seem*** to forgive and forget.(p.134)
• This may ***seem*** severe, but it is usually the best course.(p.142)
• It may ***seem*** incredible that these men are to become happy, respected, and useful once more.(p.153)
• This resolution I kept steadfastly for the next forty years, except when circumstances made it ***seem*** unwise to absent myself.(p.172)
• For some reason, we alcoholics ***seem*** to have the gift of picking out the world's finest women.(p.178)
• Bill didn't ***seem*** too impressed.(p.188)
• My life was fairly well crowded and I didn't ***seem*** to need any stimulants to keep me going.(p.213)
• In a few sentences he made God ***seem*** personal to me, explained Him as a being who was interested in me, the alcoholic, and that all I needed to do was to be willing to follow His way; that as long as I followed it I would be able to overcome my desire for liquor.(p.236)
• As I go along I ***seem*** to get strength daily to be able to resist more easily.(p.237)
• They did not ***seem*** to be getting an answer, for here I was staying sober and selling lots of auto polish, on which they were making one thousand per cent profit.(p.247)
• Jack didn't ***seem*** to have too much of the spiritual understanding.(p.268)
• These last eighteen years have been the happiest of my life, trite though that statement may ***seem***.(p.295)
• I learned that a person just can't find a job hanging in a dive or barroom all day and all night, as jobs don't ***seem*** to turn up in those places.(p.300)
• They did not ***seem*** ashamed to be with us, these strangers.(p.415)
• Science could take my mind apart expertly, but it couldn't ***seem*** to put it together again.(p.435)
• "That's a devil of a way to run an organization," I thought, and I reported Frank to the psychiatrist, who didn't ***seem*** perturbed; he just got someone else to take me on Fridays.(p.447)
• It is true that I -- of all people, strange as it may ***seem***, and even though I didn't give my permission -- really, really am an alcoholic of sorts.(p.448)
• And there didn't ***seem*** to be anything to do about it.)(p.465)
• Some of us always remember our big mouths when it comes to a drink, but somewhere along the line, we ***seem*** to have forgotten about taking care of our teeth.(p.479)
• He didn't ***seem*** too much at ease in the beginning.(p.494)
• I don't ***seem*** to remember anything.(p.499)
• I don't ***seem*** to be able to keep my mind on what I am doing.(p.499)
• I ***seem*** to get no sympathy for my illness and have no appreciation of the love behind the gift.(p.501)
• A former employer of mine said to me a little over ten years ago, "Pat, you ***seem*** to be one of those unfortunate people who at least once every six months must go out and roll in the gutter."(p.513)
• In part, it was a feeling of intense shame at having to leave the Army during the war, but mostly it was resentment that this kind of thing should happen to me for, strange as it may ***seem***, up to then I still thought I could control drinking.(p.521)
• I was intensely unhappy the whole time, but I didn't ***seem*** to be able to do anything about it, and the worst part to me was the realization that all this was going to happen again and again until I died.(p.522)
• I know there are some alcoholics who ***seem*** terribly, terribly grown-up, but I think that they are trying to make themselves think they are grown-up, and the strain of their effort is what is causing them to drink -- a sense of inadequacy, a childish vanity to be the most popular, the most sought after, the mostest of the most.(p.535)

seemed
• This ***seemed*** to prove that one alcoholic could affect another as no nonalcoholic could.(p.xvi)
• On the other hand -- and strange as this may seem to those who do not understand -- once a psychic change has occurred, the very same person who ***seemed*** doomed, who had so many problems he despaired of ever solving them, suddenly finds himself easily able to control his desire for alcohol, the only effort necessary being that required to follow a few simple rules.(p.xxvii)
• He had but partially recovered from a gastric hemorrhage and ***seemed*** to be a case of pathological mental deterioration.(p.xxix)
• I began to wonder, for such an appalling lack of perspective ***seemed*** near being just that.(p.5)
• This was the finish, the curtain, it ***seemed*** to me.(p.7)
• For myself, I had adopted those parts which ***seemed*** convenient and not too difficult; the rest I disregarded.(p.11)
• If there was a Devil, he ***seemed*** the Boss Universal, and he certainly had me.(p.11)
• My friend suggested what then ***seemed*** a novel idea.(p.12)
• Treatment ***seemed*** wise, for I showed signs of delirium tremens.(p.13)
• He ***seemed*** quite rational and well-balanced with respect to other problems.(p.26)
• What ***seemed*** at first a flimsy reed, has proved to be the loving and powerful hand of God.(p.28)
• Perhaps we rejected this particular conception because it ***seemed*** inadequate.(p.45)
• Afterward, we found ourselves accepting many things which then ***seemed*** entirely out of reach.(p.47)
• That was great news to us, for we had assumed we could not make use of spiritual principles unless we accepted many things on faith which ***seemed*** difficult to believe.(p.47)
• The electrons themselves ***seemed*** more intelligent than that.(p.54)
• As in war, the victor only ***seemed*** to win.(p.66)
• The unexpected result was that our husbands ***seemed*** to like it.(p.106)
• sometimes they were so inaccessible that it ***seemed*** as though a great wall had been built around them.(p.107)
• Defeat ***seemed*** certain.(p.113)
• We may have ***seemed*** to lecture.(p.121)
• To him the alcoholic has often ***seemed*** a fool of the first magnitude.(p.137)
• This ***seemed*** to me like an opportunity to be helpful, so I spent two hours talking about alcoholism, the malady, and described the symptoms and results as well as I could.(p.138)
• Had he been successful in his enterprise, he would have been set on his feet financially which at the time, ***seemed*** vitally important.(p.153)
• A spiritual experience, he conceded, was absolutely necessary, but the price ***seemed*** high upon the basis suggested.(p.155)
• He suffered horribly from his sprees, but it ***seemed*** as if nothing could be done for him.(p.159)
• They knew they had a host of new friends; it ***seemed*** they had known these strangers always.(p.161)
• After high school came four years in one of the best colleges in the country where drinking ***seemed*** to be a major extra-curricular activity.(p.172)
• Almost everyone ***seemed*** to do it.(p.172)
• I ***seemed*** to be able to snap back the next morning better than most of my fellow drinkers, who were cursed (or perhaps blessed) with a great deal of morning-after nausea.(p.172)
• My whole life ***seemed*** to be centered around doing what I wanted to do, without regard for the rights, wishes, or privileges of anyone else; a state of mind which became more and more predominant as the years passed.(p.172)
• They spoke with great freedom from embarrassment, which I could never do, and they ***seemed*** very much at ease on all occasions and appeared very healthy.(p.178)
• More than these attributes, they ***seemed*** to be happy.(p.178)
• And this, as I said, certainly gave me a lot of confidence, ***seemed*** to take a lot of the burden off me.(p.190)
• I noticed that the others ***seemed*** to have such a release, a happiness, a something that I thought a person ought to have.(p.191)
• We were eating lunch, and I was listening and trying to find out why they had this release that they ***seemed*** to have.(p.191)
• The sisters ***seemed*** to remain unaffected.(p.211)
• I ***seemed*** to react by developing a streak of varying meanness, which would cause me to do things to create excitement and to get attention.(p.211)
• However, on a couple of other occasions, Clarence ***seemed*** to bob up at the last saloon that I would stop at on the way home every day.(p.216)
• This time I ***seemed*** to be already awake, sitting upright in a big easy chair, in the middle of an animated conversation with a perfectly strange young woman, who didn't appear to think it strange.(p.222)
• But each drink after the "first" ***seemed*** to become less effective and after three or four they all ***seemed*** like water.(p.241)
• The same old routines ***seemed*** to be common to us all.(p.246)
• My brilliant agnosticism vanished, and I saw for the first time that those who really believed, or at least honestly tried to find a Power greater than themselves, were much more composed and contented than I had ever been, and they ***seemed*** to have a degree of happiness which I had never known.(p.247)
• They ***seemed*** to be happy in their fashion, they and their little groups of supporters, but always pride of intellect stopped me from seeking what they evidently had.(p.256)
• We had meetings at each other's homes and, of course, that was a grand place for people to get together out there; they ***seemed*** to think so too.(p.270)
• The hospital had ***seemed*** so safe.(p.279)
• Sometimes during that year I rebelled inwardly at what ***seemed*** like lost time, and at having to be a burden to these good people whose means were limited.(p.281)
• I had to adapt to new associations and associates, and it ***seemed*** to be the smart thing to drink and smoke.(p.287)
• They had that certain something that ***seemed*** to

glow, a peace and a serenity combined with happiness.(p.290)
• Eventually, of course, what with all the hilarity that could be provoked with a few gallons of beer, there *seemed* to be no need of bridge or poker playing for entertainment.(p.297)
• He said the alcoholic *seemed* to possess a native acuteness and usually excelled in his field, regardless of environmental or educational advantages.(p.308)
• In describing his suffering, his fears, his many years of groping for some answer to that which always *seemed* to remain unanswerable, he could have been describing me, and nothing short of experience and knowledge could have afforded him that much insight!(p.309)
• They *seemed* to have all the ingredients for successful living.(p.310)
• Sergeants, doctors, girl friends – everybody *seemed* to be picking on him.(p.317)
• No one *seemed* to care if I made it or not.(p.319)
• Even so, every time I drank, I *seemed* to get in trouble.(p.322)
• Death *seemed* the only way out.(p.333)
• All my life, it *seemed*, was spent on the outside looking in.(p.353)
• I had been unhappy, lonely, and scared for so long that the discovery of liquor *seemed* to be the answer to all my problems.(p.353)
• Looking directly at me was a large oil painting of my wife, and her very words *seemed* to shout at me -- "I am not leaving you because I don't love you; it's because I do love you.(p.363)
• It left us dazed, because he had *seemed* so indestructible.(p.370)
• Before too long, my husband (who *seemed* to prefer his shirts dirty) put his foot down, declaring that our family might have the cleanest clothes in town, but that I hadn't been out of the same old dirty slacks and blouse for a week.(p.371)
• Slowly, my life *seemed* to unfold before me, shedding insights on childhood resentments, jealousies, and fears that had mushroomed in adulthood, and also on the self-pity that I had wallowed in at every opportunity.(p.371)
• It *seemed* to me my wife was becoming more intolerant and narrow minded all the time.(p.376)
• However, a rough estimate of one alcoholic's initiation fee *seemed* possible.(p.396)
• There would be times when the life of respectability and achievement *seemed* insufferably dull – I had to break out.(p.432)
• After a month it *seemed* unlikely that it ever really happened.(p.433)
• Indeed, it *seemed* that I cared too much.(p.440)
• Instant blackout was what it was, and it *seemed* delightful.(p.442)
• It *seemed* to me I needed a consultation first.(p.444)
• The Mayo Clinic *seemed* like a good place to have my diagnosis confirmed.(p.444)
• It *seemed* that all they talked about at meetings was drinking, drinking, drinking.(p.447)
• I wanted to talk about my many big problems; drinking *seemed* a small one.(p.447)
• But then, as I drank more and more, the alcohol *seemed* to affect my vision: Instead of continuing to see what was good about my wife, I began to see her defects.(p.450)
• All found themselves headed for the same destruction, and it *seemed* they could to nothing whatever to stop it.(p.455)
• It *seemed* to me that those A.A.'s to whom I talked knew all about me.(p.470)
• The other of the Twelve Steps of Alcoholics Anonymous *seemed* insurmountable to me at first.(p.471)
• I remember particularly one sentence that *seemed* to say, "This is for you."(p.473)
• I lasted at that for four months chiefly on alcohol, because I never *seemed* to find any time to eat.(p.520)
• I had no work to do and I was at an age where it *seemed* too late to start anything new.(p.522)
• People *seemed* to be carefully dressed, too happy, too normal.(p.524)
• What struck me most was that they all *seemed* to be quite pleased with having made a job of it and having stopped drinking.(p.524)
• The solution *seemed* very simple.(p.545)
• Or so it *seemed* to me.(p.546)
• I looked around me at people who *seemed* happy and tried to analyze their happiness, and it *seemed* to me that without exception these people had something or somebody they loved very much.(p.546)
• I wasn't afraid of anything or anybody after I learned about drinking, for it *seemed* right from the beginning that with liquor I could always retire to my little private world where nobody could get at me to hurt me.(p.547)
• About this time, I met a man who had three motherless children and it *seemed* that might be a solution to my problem.(p.548)
• It *seemed* logical to me that if I married this man and took the responsibility for these children that they would keep me sober.(p.548)
• As I said earlier, self-pity and resentment were my constant companions and my inventory began to look like a thirty-three year diary, for I *seemed* to have a resentment against everybody I had ever known.(p.551)

seeming

• I suppose some would be shocked at our *seeming* worldliness and levity.(p.16)
• Besides a *seeming* inability to accept much on faith, we often found ourselves handicapped by obstinacy, sensitiveness, and unreasoning prejudice.(p.47)
• Once confused and baffled by the *seeming* futility of existence they show the underlying reasons why they were making heavy going of life.(p.50)
• About the time of the beer experiment I was thrown in with a crowd of people who attracted me because of their *seeming* poise, health, and happiness.(p.178)

seemingly

• We, of Alcoholics Anonymous, are more than one hundred men and women who have recovered from a *seemingly* hopeless state of mind and body.(p.xiii)
• *Seemingly* he could not drink even if he would.(p.57)
• Sometimes they hurt us, *seemingly* without provocation, but we invariably find that at some time in the past we have made decisions based on self which later placed us in a position to be hurt.(p.62)
• Outsiders are sometimes shocked when we burst into merriment over a *seemingly* tragic experience out of the past.(p.132)
• You may be at a loss to understand how such a *seemingly* above-board chap could be so involved.(p.140)
• I had, *seemingly*, just a natural affinity for grog.(p.182)
• Probably only a few readers of this story will be able, from personal experiences of their own, to understand the exhilaration and sense of accomplishment which I felt after finishing this *seemingly* simple assignment.(p.276)

seems

• The subject presented in this book *seems* to me to be of paramount importance to those afflicted with alcoholic addiction.(p.xxv)
• To them, their alcoholic life *seems* the only normal one.(p.xxvi)
• The classification of alcoholics *seems* most difficult, and in much detail is outside the scope of this book.(p.xxviii)
• Much has been written pro and con, but among physicians, the general opinion *seems* to be that most chronic alcoholics are doomed.(p.xxviii)
• To one who feels he is an atheist or agnostic such an experience *seems* impossible, but to continue as he is means disaster, especially if he is an alcoholic of the hopeless variety.(p.44)
• Whether we agree with a particular approach or conception *seems* to make little difference.(p.50)
• And there often *seems* no way of entirely getting rid of self without His aid.(p.62)
• It *seems* to cause more trouble.(p.68)
• Go or stay away, whichever *seems* best.(p.102)
• Of course, there is such a thing as incompatibility, but in nearly every instance the alcoholic only *seems* to be unloving and inconsiderate; it is usually because he is warped and sickened that he says and does these appalling things.(p.108)
• "We watch the alcoholic performing in a position of responsibility and we know that because he is drinking heavily and daily he has cut his capacities by fifty per cent, and still he *seems* able to do a satisfactory job.(p.308)
• They have contributed fantastic amounts of time and work to our problem, but they aren't able, it *seems*, to arrest either your alcoholism or mine.(p.352)
• Living with fear and tension inevitably results in wanting to ease that tension, which alcohol *seems* to do temporarily.(p.380)
• Each day *seems* to be so much more productive and satisfying.(p.383)
• It *seems* I should have learned to love my wife and family first; the newcomer to A.A., last.(p.451)
• He makes no reply, and hardly *seems* to see me.(p.501)
• Nothing *seems* to be working out right.(p.505)
• The family *seems* to think of nothing but spending.(p.506)
• As I write these words, it *seems* incredible that these things should have happened to me, for they are, truly, against all my instincts and training.(p.536)
• It *seems* only fitting that when I did finally fall in love it was with an alcoholic, and for the next ten years I progressed as rapidly as is humanly possible into what I believed to be hopeless alcoholism.(p.547)
• I suspect that if it is wisely handled – and it *seems* to be in wise and prudent hands – there are doors of opportunity ahead of this project that may surpass our capacities to imagine."(p.574)

seen

• Judging from what I had *seen* in Europe and since, the power of God in human affairs was negligible, the Brotherhood of Man a grim jest.(p.11)
• I have *seen* hundreds of families set their feet in the path that really goes somewhere; have *seen* the most impossible domestic situations righted; feuds and bitterness of all sorts wiped out.(p.15)
• I have *seen* men come out of asylums and resume a vital place in the lives of their families and communities.(p.15)
• I have never *seen* one single case recover, where that state of mind existed to the extent that it does in you."(p.27)
• If what we have learned and felt and *seen* means anything at all, it means that all of us, whatever our race, creed, or color are the children of a living Creator with whom we may form a relationship upon simple and understandable terms as soon as we are willing and honest enough to try.(p.28)
• We have *seen* the truth demonstrated again and again: "Once an alcoholic, always an alcoholic."(p.33)
• We had *seen* spiritual release, but liked to tell ourselves it wasn't true.(p.55)
• Rarely have we *seen* a person fail who has thoroughly followed our path.(p.58)
• Some people cannot be *seen* -- we send them an honest letter.(p.83)
• Don't, at this stage, refer to this book, unless he has *seen* it and wishes to discuss it.(p.92)
• After they have *seen* tangible results, the family will perhaps want to go along.(p.99)
• We have *seen* men get well whose families have not returned at all.(p.100)
• We have *seen* others slip when the family came back too soon.(p.100)
• Those of us who have spent much time in the world of spiritual make-believe have eventually *seen* the childishness of it.(p.130)
• But we have *seen* remarkable transformations in our bodies.(p.133)
• We, who have collectively *seen* a great deal of business life, at least from the alcoholic angle, had to smile at this gentleman's sincere opinion.(p.149)
• They had *seen* miracles, and one was to come to them.(p.161)
• I'm so grateful for both the program and the people in it that I still want to go, and then probably the most wonderful thing that I learned from the program -- I've *seen* this in the 'A.A. Grapevine' a lot of times, and I've had people say it to me personally, and I've heard people get up in meetings and make the same statement: The statement is, "I came into A.A. solely for the purpose of sobriety, but it has been through A.A. that I have found God."(p.192)
• I'll never forget, he never even hesitated and I had never *seen* him before in my life.(p.207)
• Then he started to talk to me about his drinking experiences, what his drinking had cost him, how much he had drunk and where, things like that, and I remember I was quite bored because I had never *seen* the guy before and had no interest at all in what, where and when he drank.(p.208)
• I remember well one fellow, Joe, walking nearly three miles through slush, wet and snow to come to the hospital to see a man that he had never *seen* before in his life, and that impressed me very much.(p.208)
• He walked to the hospital to save bus fare and did it gladly in order to be helpful to an individual he had never even *seen*.(p.208)
• From far away, as if in a delirium, I heard my own voice – calling someone "Dorothy," talking of dress shops, of jobs . . . the words came clearer . . . this sound of my own voice frightened me as it came closer . . . and suddenly, there I was, talking of I knew not what, to someone I'd never *seen* before this very moment.(p.222)
• Why, even a year ago, I had *seen* Howard, an ex-doctor, mooching a dime for a drink.(p.289)
• It doesn't pay to be *seen* in the same place at the same hour every day.(p.299)
• Finally, an old business acquaintance of mine, whom I hadn't *seen* for several years offered

me a job.(p.301)
• I had never *seen* him before, and at the time hoped I would never see him again.(p.302)
• I got the Big Book and I read it, and this is what it said: "Rarely have we *seen* a person fail who has thoroughly followed our path."(p.349)
• "Sure, I've *seen* you tight several times, but you're no alcoholic!"(p.356)
• Attending his fourth or fifth meeting was an old friend I had not *seen* for twenty years.(p.365)
• In fact I was afraid to try it for fear that I would wind up like many examples I had *seen* of excessive drinking in the Army.(p.374)
• The cop must have *seen* the condition that I was in because he decided to take me home.(p.390)
• Now I own perhaps the most costly pair of moccasins anyone has ever *seen*, and they help me remember where I've been.)(p.445)
• I haven't *seen* my son since he was three and a half years old.(p.463)
• I will be fifty years old next month, haven't *seen* my son or daughter yet, nor my daughter's two children, my grandchildren; but I am grateful.(p.463)
• Had I tried honestly and sincerely to practice the Twelve Steps I would have *seen* from my continuous moral inventory that I was getting off the beam -- I would have found that there were some active resentments in my life, a terrific amount of self-pity.(p.471)
• I've never *seen* him drunk in my life, although he'd take a shot in the morning and usually one in the evening, and so did I; but for the most part he kept his whiskey in his office.(p.484)
• The only time that I have ever *seen* my mother take anything alcoholic was around Christmas time, when she would drink some eggnog or light wine.(p.484)
• A very good friend of mine who owned a drug store across the street from us, came by only about two hours later and said that he had *seen* Vi down town.(p.487)
• I hunt for my nickel to drop in the plate so that mine will be *seen*.(p.497)
• I had never had a drink, but I had *seen* enough merriment in the boys who were drinking to be interested.(p.498)
• I have never *seen* people that joyous before.(p.504)
• But I have not *seen* yet that I should do some constructive acts of love without expecting any return.(p.505)
• Just as I was wondering what on earth I could do -- I was too drunk even to pack a handkerchief -- the memory of an A.A. write-up that I had *seen* in the Evening Mail flashed across my mind -- and I thought to myself, this is something I haven't tried yet.(p.523)
• I have not *seen* a black face but mine since I've been here, and if I didn't look in the mirror, I wouldn't know that I was black, because these people treat me as one of them, which I am.(p.530)
• I have *seen* that there is only one law, the law of love, and there are only two sins; the first is to interfere with the growth of another human being, and the second is to interfere with one's own growth.(p.542)
• On the next page, A.A.'s "12 Traditions" are *seen* in their so-called "short form," the form in general use today.(p.563)

sees
• I acquired the impeccable coat of tan one *sees* upon the well-to-do.(p.4)
• The good doctor now *sees* many men who have such experiences.(p.14)
• When he *sees* you know all about the drinking game, commence to describe yourself as an alcoholic.(p.91)
• She *sees* she was wrong to make a burning issue out of such a matter when his more serious ailments were being rapidly cured.(p.135)
• He knows the alcoholic as the employer *sees* him.(p.136)
• On the other hand, I believe that I've always been medically inclined, though I have never been able to see medicine quite as the average person *sees* it.(p.485)
• "Pity me the heart that is slow to learn What the quick mind *sees* at every turn."(p.534)

seesaw
• We lived a kind of *seesaw* existence in the early days.(p.369)

seething
• This immediately precipitates us into a *seething* caldron of debate.(p.xxviii)
• The great boom of the late twenties was *seething* and swelling.(p.3)

Seine
• I rented a beautiful apartment on the banks of the *Seine* in the winter, and a chalet in Switzerland in the summer.(p.405)

seize
• Our hope is that when this chip of a book is launched on the world tide of alcoholism, defeated drinkers will *seize* upon it, to follow its suggestions.(p.153)

seized
• I was suddenly and uncontrollably *seized* with the old, paralyzing panic.(p.279)
• I was *seized* with an almost uncontrollable desire to reach out for it.(p.285)

seizes
• A great fear *seizes* me.(p.505)

seldom
• Frothy emotional appeal *seldom* suffices.(p.xxvi)
• He is *seldom* mildly intoxicated.(p.21)
• We have *seldom* told them the whole truth nor have we followed their advice.(p.73)
• It is *seldom* wise to approach an individual, who still smarts from our injustice to him, and announce that we have gone religious.(p.77)
• We will *seldom* be interested in liquor.(p.84)
• We *seldom* allow an alcoholic to live in our homes for long at a time.(p.97)
• We *seldom* had friends at our homes, never knowing how or when the men of the house would appear.(p.105)
• Everybody knows that those in bad health, and those who *seldom* play, do not laugh much.(p.132)
• In competent hands, this *seldom* takes long nor is it very expensive.(p.143)
• During the subsequent fifteen years I had sense enough never to go to the hospital if I had been drinking, and very *seldom* did I receive patients.(p.176)
• I used to promise my wife, my friends, and my children that I would drink no more -- promises which *seldom* kept me sober even through the day, though I was very sincere when I made them.(p.177)
• "Blanks" were more frequent, and I *seldom* knew how I'd got home.(p.226)
• Not only were they at peace with themselves, but they were getting a kick out of life such as one *seldom* encounters, except in the very young.(p.310)
• *Seldom* had any of these lost either health, business, family, or friends.(p.315)
• He *seldom* is a disgrace.(p.330)
• I *seldom* left the base any more except once in a while when I felt the need of talking to some girl.(p.427)
• I was never drunk on the job, never missed a day's work, was *seldom* rendered totally ineffective by a hangover and kept my liquor expenses well within my adequate budget.(p.433)
• Ten days of this treatment the first time knocked me from 200 pounds to 130, and I *seldom* stayed out of the hole long enough to gain back my weight.(p.460)
• What often takes place in a few months could *seldom* have been accomplished by years of self discipline.(p.569)

select
• If not members of religious bodies, we sometimes *select* and memorize a few set prayers which emphasize the principles we have been discussing.(p.87)
• Arrangements were also made with the chief psychiatrist of a large public hospital to *select* still others from the stream of misery which flows through that institution.(p.163)

selected
• While waiting to depart I was *selected* -- by giving a CPO five dollars -- to be bartender in the Navy Chief's Club.(p.426)
• Shortly thereafter, I was *selected*, with eight other inmates out of the 10,000 in the state's prisons at that time, to attend a school designed to take former "management problems" like me and convert them into paracounselors.(p.462)
• Brandishing my "motto," which was "A little man with a stick is equal to a big man," sometimes I varied the literary lecture by a fight with a big man, *selected* solely because he was big and I was little.(p.537)

selecting
• *Selecting* a church at random from the directory, he stepped into a booth and lifted the receiver.(p.155)
• Understanding our work, he can do this with an eye to *selecting* those who are willing and able to recover on a spiritual basis.(p.162)

self
• Sometimes they hurt us, seemingly without provocation, but we invariably find that at some time in the past we have made decisions based on *self* which later placed us in a position to be hurt.(p.62)
• And there often seems no way of entirely getting rid of *self* without His aid.(p.62)
• Relieve me of the bondage of *self*, that I may better do Thy will.(p.63)
• Being convinced that *self*, manifested in various ways, was what had defeated us, we considered its common manifestations.(p.64)
• To be vital, faith must be accompanied by *self* sacrifice and unselfish, constructive action.(p.93)
• You can see that he really does love you with his better *self*.(p.108)
• I was *self* conscious and ill at ease most of the time, my health was at the breaking point, and I was thoroughly miserable.(p.178)
• But I have a fortune in friendships, courage, *self* assurance and honest appraisal of my own abilities.(p.296)
• I have *self* confidence and assurance that cannot be confused with the cockiness I once possessed.(p.303)
• I certainly wasn't my shy, quiet *self* that night -- as I was informed the next morning.(p.353)
• It has brought about a revelation of *self*, the discovery of an inner being, an awareness of God.(p.355)
• I can't bear to be here when you lose the respect of others, and above all -- when you lose your own *self* respect."(p.362)
• I can't bear to be here when you lose the respect of others, and above all when you lose your own *self* respect."(p.363)
• The last two years of my drinking my entire personality changed to a cynical, intolerant and arrogant person completely different from my normal *self*.(p.376)
• Resenting anyone and everyone who might interfere with my personal plans and ways of doing things, I was full of *self* pity, especially for any interference with my drinking.(p.376)
• Over a period of time he has built up *self* pity, resentments toward anyone or anything that interferes with his drinking.(p.380)
• But what a difference there is between going through hell without a power greater than one's *self*, and with it!(p.437)
• What else can I do except what I have always done in the past? -- act as my old *self* and return to prison.(p.458)
• Through A.A., we can experience freedom from *self*.(p.459)
• After all, it was *self* (you, me) that stood in our own way, that ran the show and ran ourselves into bankruptcy, that hurt the ones we loved.(p.459)
• All Twelve Steps of A.A. are designed to kill the old *self* (deflate the old ego) and build a new, free *self*.(p.459)
• I nearly reverted to my old, incorrigible *self* -- had trouble with a couple of other prisoners, was planning an escape.(p.461)
• It has shown me, through the tragic stories of so many other alcoholics, the utter futility of *self* pity.(p.525)
• I realize now that this phase of my development had been arrested by my obsession with *self*, and my egocentricity had reached such proportions that adjustment to anything outside my personal control was impossible for me.(p.547)
• What often takes place in a few months could seldom have been accomplished by years of *self* discipline.(p.569)

self-analysis
• And if I had been able to turn to the church at that time I'm sure they could not have convinced me my sickness was within myself, nor could they have shown me the need for *self-analysis* that A.A. has shown me is vital if I am to survive.(p.546)

self-appraisal
• In actual practice, we usually find a solitary *self-appraisal* insufficient.(p.72)
• We subjected ourselves to a drastic *self-appraisal*.(p.76)
• Outline the program of action, explaining how you made a *self-appraisal*, how you straightened out your past and why you are now endeavoring to be helpful to him.(p.94)

self-centered
• Our actor is *self-centered* -- ego-centric, as people like to call it nowadays.(p.61)
• We wives found that, like everybody else, we were afflicted with pride, self-pity, vanity and all the things which go to make up the *self-centered* person; and we were not above selfishness or dishonesty.(p.116)
• We think that such a view is *self-centered* and in direct conflict with the new way of living.(p.124)
• Like most sick people before me, I was implacably selfish, and chronically *self-centered*.(p.401)
• Oh, poor *self-centered*, sick little me.(p.413)

self-centeredness
• It meant destruction of ***self-centeredness.***(p.14)
• Selfishness -- ***self-centeredness!***(p.62)
• Neither could we reduce our ***self-centeredness*** much by wishing or trying on our own power.(p.62)

self-confidence
• These allergic types can never safely use alcohol in any form at all; and once having formed the habit and found they cannot break it, once having lost their ***self-confidence,*** their reliance upon things human, their problems pile up on them and become astonishingly difficult to solve.(p.xxvi)
• Some of us once had great ***self-confidence,*** but it didn't fully solve the fear problem, or any other.(p.68)

self-confident
• I felt I had every right to be ***self-confident,*** that it would be only a matter of exercising my will power and keeping on guard.(p.40)

self-conscious
• You will no longer be ***self-conscious*** or feel that you must apologize as though your husband were a weak character.(p.115)
• I was an extremely sensitive person and so ***self-conscious*** that I hurt all over.(p.385)
• As ***self-conscious*** as I was, I had to pose for those pictures, holding this huge bouquet.(p.385)

self-consciousness
• Your new courage, good nature and lack of ***self-consciousness*** will do wonders for you socially.(p.115)

self-contempt
• And having sung that phrase, I'd chuckle with amusement, turning into irony turning into ***self-contempt*** turning into self-pity, at the sad fate of Bob, that wonderful, poor little motherless boy who was so smart in school and who grew up to accept responsibility so early and so fast and who staggered under his burdens without a whimper until the time came when he thought he was too good for this world and so he ought to be out of it.(p.532)

self-control
• He wished above all things to regain ***self-control.***(p.26)
• I must use self-will, ***self-control.***(p.408)

self-debasement
• Inside, I went right on being a mass of unlovely self-pity, queasy anxiety and sickening ***self-debasement.***(p.400)

self-deception
• By every form of ***self-deception*** and experimentation, they will try to prove themselves exceptions to the rule, therefore nonalcoholic.(p.31)
• When I was about forty-seven, after indulging in all kinds of ***self-deception*** to control my drinking, I arrived at a period when I felt convinced I had to have so much alcohol every day and that the real problem was to control how much.(p.214)

self-delusion
• Driven by a hundred forms of fear, ***self-delusion,*** self-seeking, and self-pity, we step on the toes of our fellows and they retaliate.(p.62)

self-destruction
• Post-war disillusionment, ever more serious alcoholism, impending mental and physical collapse, brought him to the point of ***self-destruction.***(p.56)
• Since, perhaps, suicide was a bit too drastic (actually, I was afraid), dry martinis were chosen as the slow, pleasant, private, gradual instrument of ***self-destruction.***(p.531)

self-discipline
• Then he fell victim to a belief which practically every alcoholic has -- that his long period of sobriety and ***self-discipline*** had qualified him to drink as other men.(p.32)

self-esteem
• In most cases it was found that our ***self-esteem,*** our pocketbooks, our ambitions, our personal relationships (including sex) were hurt or threatened.(p.64)
• Was it our ***self-esteem,*** our security, our ambitions, our personal, or sex relations, which had been interfered with?(p.65)
• ***Self-esteem*** (fear).(p.65)
• ***Self-esteem*** (fear).(p.65)
• ***Self-esteem*** (fear).(p.65)
• ***Self-esteem*** (fear).(p.65)
• ***Self-esteem*** (fear).(p.65)
• There had been some occasions -- there was an automobile wreck, for instance -- when I had police escort home but not to jail, all of which, instead of doing me a favor, did me harm because I was then full of ***self-esteem*** as to the progress I had made both professionally and financially.(p.213)

self-evident
• That was two months ago and the result was ***self-evident.***(p.9)

self-help
• I read ***self-help*** books.(p.555)

self-imposed
• When we became alcoholics, crushed by a ***self-imposed*** crisis we could not postpone or evade, we had to fearlessly face the proposition that either God is everything or else He is nothing.(p.53)

self-induced
• There are many things worse than dying, but is there any death worse than the progressive, ***self-induced,*** slow suicide of the practicing alcoholic?(p.457)

self-insurance
• The A.A. plan is described by the members themselves as ***'self-insurance.'***(p.574)
• This ***self-insurance*** has resulted in the restoration of physical, mental and spiritual health and self-respect to hundreds of men and women who would be hopelessly down and out without its unique but effective therapy."(p.574)

self-interest
• The bartenders took care of me, not out of brotherly love, but through enlightened ***self-interest.***(p.410)
• But as the years go by, the stretch becomes unbearable; and the man with the grown-up brain and the childish emotions -- vanity, ***self-interest,*** false pride, jealousy, longing for social approval, to name few -- becomes a prime candidate for alcohol.(p.534)

self-justification
• These family talks will be constructive if they can be carried on without heated argument, self-pity, ***self-justification*** or resentful criticism.(p.127)

self-knowledge
• Surely this was the answer -- ***self-knowledge.***(p.7)
• But the actual or potential alcoholic, with hardly an exception, will be absolutely unable to stop drinking on the basis of ***self-knowledge.***(p.39)
• ***Self-knowledge*** would fix it.(p.40)
• I saw that will power and ***self-knowledge*** would not help in those strange mental blank spots.(p.42)

self-loathing
• It was nothing to my own inner distress, my self-reproach, and my ***self-loathing,*** for was I not bearing out all the horrible things I had always suspected of myself?(p.404)

self-pity
• No words can tell of the loneliness and despair I found in that bitter morass of ***self-pity.***(p.8)
• I was not too well at the time, and was plagued by waves of ***self-pity*** and resentment.(p.15)
• Whatever our protestations, are not most of us concerned with ourselves, our resentments, or our ***self-pity?***(p.62)
• Driven by a hundred forms of fear, self-delusion, self-seeking, and ***self-pity,*** we step on the toes of our fellows and they retaliate.(p.62)
• That feeling of uselessness and ***self-pity*** will disappear.(p.84)
• Before we begin, we ask God to direct our thinking, especially asking that it be divorced from ***self-pity,*** dishonest or self-seeking motives.(p.86)
• We are then in much less danger of excitement, fear, anger, worry, ***self-pity,*** or foolish decisions.(p.88)
• We have had long rendezvous with hurt pride, frustration, ***self-pity,*** misunderstanding and fear.(p.104)
• If, on the other hand, they took nothing, their ***self-pity*** made them killjoys.(p.105)
• We wives found that, like everybody else, we were afflicted with pride, ***self-pity,*** vanity and all the things which go to make up the self-centered person; and we were not above selfishness or dishonesty.(p.116)
• These family talks will be constructive if they can be carried on without heated argument, ***self-pity,*** self-justification or resentful criticism.(p.127)
• It was no momentary emotionalism born of ***self-pity*** in a maudlin condition.(p.258)
• My broken home and broken heart fanned my smoldering ***self-pity*** into a fair-sized bonfire and this kept me well supplied with reasons for having another drink, and then another.(p.305)
• How devastating, too, are the subsequent feelings of inadequacy and ***self-pity.***(p.331)
• Two nights later, ***self-pity*** went even further.(p.333)
• I began hitting the bottle again, and with it ***self-pity,*** resentment, loneliness and remorse set in deeply.(p.362)
• Slowly, my life seemed to unfold before me, shedding insights on childhood resentments, jealousies, and fears that had mushroomed in adulthood, and also on the ***self-pity*** that I had wallowed in at every opportunity.(p.371)
• Inside, I went right on being a mass of unlovely ***self-pity,*** queasy anxiety and sickening self-debasement.(p.400)
• I did not see that the book dripped with ***self-pity.***(p.403)
• Had I tried honestly and sincerely to practice the Twelve Steps I would have seen from my continuous moral inventory that I was getting off the beam -- I would have found that there were some active resentments in my life, a terrific amount of ***self-pity.***(p.471)
• I am filled with hurt pride and ***self-pity.***(p.501)
• And having sung that phrase, I'd chuckle with amusement, turning into irony turning into self-contempt turning into ***self-pity,*** at the sad fate of Bob, that wonderful, poor little motherless boy who was so smart in school and who grew up to accept responsibility so early and so fast and who staggered under his burdens without a whimper until the time came when he thought he was too good for this world and so he ought to be out of it.(p.532)
• I was immersed in ***self-pity*** and resentment, and the only people who would support this attitude or who I felt understood me at all were the people I met in bars and the ones who drank as I did.(p.547)
• By this time I was such a past master at kidding myself that I had convinced myself I had sat out a war and waited for this man to come home and, as my resentment and ***self-pity*** grew, so did my alcoholic problem.(p.548)
• As I said earlier, ***self-pity*** and resentment were my constant companions and my inventory began to look like a thirty-three year diary, for I seemed to have a resentment against everybody I had ever known.(p.551)
• For example, we are told in A.A. that we cannot afford resentments and ***self-pity,*** so we learn to avoid these festering mental attitudes.(p.560)

self-pitying
• He becomes angry, indignant, ***self-pitying.***(p.61)

self-possessed
• I couldn't look them straight in the eyes, although I was always a ***self-possessed*** brazen sort of person.(p.323)

self-propulsion
• Most people try to live by ***self-propulsion.***(p.60)

self-punishing
• For, after those daily ***self-punishing*** sessions with myself, after the vows to stop, I would change entirely as evening came on.(p.408)

self-reliance
• From a trembling, despairing nervous wreck, had emerged a man brimming over with ***self-reliance*** and contentment.(p.xxix)
• Wasn't it because ***self-reliance*** failed us?(p.68)
• ***Self-reliance*** was good as far as it went, but it didn't go far enough.(p.68)

self-reproach
• It was nothing to my own inner distress, my ***self-reproach,*** and my self-loathing, for was I not bearing out all the horrible things I had always suspected of myself?(p.404)

self-respect
• My health is good and I have regained my ***self-respect*** and the respect of my colleagues.(p.180)
• He said they were sober, happy and had their ***self-respect*** back as well as the respect of their neighbors.(p.289)
• The important thing I lost was my own ***self-respect.***(p.323)
• Now, she no longer risks losing her home, her ***self-respect,*** or her laundry.(p.369)
• I really do believe it is much harder for a woman to gain back her ***self-respect*** than it is for a man.(p.480)
• This self-insurance has resulted in the restoration of physical, mental and spiritual health and ***self-respect*** to hundreds of men and women who would be hopelessly down and out without its unique but effective therapy."(p.574)

self-revealing
• We hope no one will consider these ***self-revealing*** accounts in bad taste.(p.29)

self-righteous
• I am still arrogant, egocentric, ***self-righteous,*** with no humility, even phony at times, but I'm trying to be a better person and help my fellowman.(p.463)

self-sacrifice
• For if an alcoholic failed to perfect and enlarge his spiritual life through work and ***self-sacrifice*** for others, he could not survive the certain trials and low spots ahead.(p.14)

self-sacrificing

• He may be kind, considerate, patient, generous; even modest and *self-sacrificing*.(p.61)

• We have been unselfish and *self-sacrificing*.(p.105)

self-searching

• Almost none of us liked the *self-searching*, the leveling of our pride, the confession of shortcomings which the process requires for its successful consummation.(p.25)

self-seeker

• Is he not really a *self-seeker* even when trying to be kind?(p.61)

self-seeking

• Driven by a hundred forms of fear, self-delusion, *self-seeking*, and self-pity, we step on the toes of our fellows and they retaliate.(p.62)

• Where had we been selfish, dishonest, *self-seeking* and frightened?(p.67)

• *Self-seeking* will slip away.(p.84)

• Before we begin, we ask God to direct our thinking, especially asking that it be divorced from self-pity, dishonest or *self-seeking* motives.(p.86)

self-sufficient

• I was never homesick and was always pretty *self-sufficient*.(p.240)

• I had been too *self-sufficient* to write a moral inventory, but I discovered in pointing out to the new man his wrong attitudes and actions that I was really taking my own inventory, and that if I expected him to change I would have to work on myself too.(p.249)

• I grew up believing that one had to be totally *self-sufficient*, for one never dared to depend on another human being.(p.545)

self-sufficiency

• We agnostics and atheists were sticking to the idea that *self-sufficiency* would solve our problems.(p.52)

self-supporting

• Seven – Every A.A. group ought to be fully *self-supporting*, declining outside contributions.(p.564)

self-will

• The first requirement is that we be convinced that any life run on *self-will* can hardly be a success.(p.60)

• They arise out of ourselves, and the alcoholic is an extreme example of *self-will* run riot, though he usually doesn't think so.(p.62)

• We hope you are convinced now that God can remove whatever *self-will* has blocked you off from Him.(p.71)

• We attempt to sweep away the debris which has accumulated out of our effort to live on *self-will* and run the show ourselves.(p.76)

• We ask especially for freedom from *self-will*, and are careful to make no request for ourselves only.(p.87)

• I believe that my once over-weening *self-will* has finally found its proper place, for I can say many times daily, "Thy will be done, not mine" . . . and mean it.(p.229)

• As I grow in A.A., I realize that a person with as much *self-will* as I had, as hard a head and as diseased an ego, had to try everything that I could think of, butting my head against every stone wall before I was ready to come in.(p.384)

• I must use *self-will*, self-control.(p.408)

• We reverted to the old way of life we knew -- a life full of anger, vindictiveness, resentment, fear, dependence, denial, *self-will*, irresponsibility.(p.459)

• For the only problems I have now are those I create when I break out in a rash of *self-will*.(p.551)

selfish

• Best of all, I met a kind doctor who explained that though certainly *selfish* and foolish, I had been seriously ill, bodily and mentally.(p.7)

• He is often perfectly sensible and well balanced concerning everything except liquor, but in that respect he is incredibly dishonest and *selfish*.(p.21)

• On the other hand, he may be mean, egotistical, *selfish* and dishonest.(p.61)

• Where had we been *selfish*, dishonest, self-seeking and frightened?(p.67)

• Where had we been *selfish*, dishonest, or inconsiderate?(p.69)

• We subjected each relation to this test – was it *selfish* or not?(p.69)

• *Selfish* and inconsiderate habits have kept the home in turmoil.(p.82)

• We will lose interest in *selfish* things and gain interest in our fellows.(p.84)

• Were we resentful, *selfish*, dishonest or afraid?(p.86)

• We are careful never to pray for our own *selfish* ends.(p.87)

• Taking that as a foundation, he reasoned that if a man followed that rule he could not be *selfish*.(p.236)

• Father was a very well-integrated person, and while mother was highstrung and a bit *selfish* and demanding, our home life was reasonably harmonious.(p.240)

• But – supposing that just one man died because I had, for *selfish* reasons, kept my mouth shut?(p.282)

• However, I must have felt, deep down inside myself, that living the *selfish* life of a bachelor was only half living.(p.286)

• I am trying now, each day, to make up for all those *selfish*, thoughtless, foolish things I did in my drinking days.(p.326)

• Like most sick people before me, I was implacably *selfish*, and chronically self-centered.(p.401)

selfishly

• We remembered always that our sex powers were God-given and therefore good, neither to be used lightly or *selfishly* nor to be despised and loathed.(p.69)

selfishness

• *Selfishness* – self-centeredness!(p.62)

• Above everything, we alcoholics must be rid of this *selfishness*.(p.62)

• Continue to watch for *selfishness*, dishonesty, resentment, and fear.(p.84)

• We wives found that, like everybody else, we were afflicted with pride, self-pity, vanity and all the things which go to make up the self-centered person; and we were not above *selfishness* or dishonesty.(p.116)

• Unfortunately for me, I was the only child, which perhaps engendered the *selfishness* which played such an important part in bringing on my alcoholism.(p.172)

• At the moral inventory, he brought up some of my bad personality traits or character defects, such as *selfishness*, conceit, jealousy, carelessness, intolerance, ill-temper, sarcasm and resentments.(p.292)

• That my own innate *selfishness* and stubbornness are the evils which, if left unguarded, can drive me to alcohol.(p.473)

sell

• You don't have to *sell* me religion, either.(p.188)

• I had a crew of men working there and I wanted them to work Sunday afternoons so that I could *sell* lots on Sunday.(p.195)

• I had some financial success through no ability of my own and, when jobless and almost wiped out in 1930, I began to trade and *sell* my collection; much of the proceeds went to keep my apartment stocked with liquor and almost every night saw me helpless to bed.(p.255)

• Loading a car with good old books to *sell* to collectors, librarians, universities and historical societies, I started out to travel the country.(p.255)

• It was my job to *sell* time on these stations to advertising agencies in New York.(p.359)

• I want to write better and *sell* more.(p.417)

• I want to *sell* the place and move away.(p.506)

selling

• The next three years I spent in Boston, Chicago, and Montreal in the employ of a large manufacturing concern, *selling* railway supplies, gas engines of all sorts, and many other items of heavy hardware.(p.172)

• At the end of this *selling* of lots, just prior to World War I, I got into the crude rubber business, and six months later there was only one broker and myself left in Akron.(p.197)

• On that statement and the fact that I had been sober for ninety days, he gave me a job *selling* lots in an allotment he had.(p.200)

• In the eight years before A.A. found me, I had over forty jobs – *selling* and travelling – one thing after another, and the same old routine.(p.244)

• They did not seem to be getting an answer, for here I was staying sober and *selling* lots of auto polish, on which they were making one thousand per cent profit.(p.247)

• So I rocked along my merry independent way until June, when I went out *selling* auto polish in New England.(p.247)

• I got an easy, part-time job *selling* printing for a small neighborhood printer.(p.276)

• I simply did not have the pep to do hard, "cold-turkey" *selling*.(p.277)

• So I created a job for myself *selling* women's hosiery and men's made-to-order shirts.(p.282)

• I found I could boost my income by figuring out a lot of cute little tricks that the boss wouldn't be likely to notice – filching money from the Coke machine, short-sticking the customers on oil, and *selling* oil I'd drained out of other cars.(p.423)

• I have had experience in *selling*, collecting, and accounting, and am on my way up the ladder.(p.500)

selves

• We learned that we had to fully concede to our innermost *selves* that we were alcoholics.(p.30)

• We trust infinite God rather than our finite *selves*.(p.68)

• For a while they would be their old sweet *selves*, only to dash the new structure of affection to pieces once more.(p.107)

semblance

• While working in an office, there was some *semblance* of restraint, but, oh boy, when I got on the outside with this new company without supervision, did I go to town!(p.300)

• I tried every gimmick that there was to get some peace of mind, but it was not until I was brought to my alcoholic knees, when I was brought to a group in my own community with the butcher, the baker, the carpenter and the mechanic, who were able to give me the Twelve Steps, that I was finally given some *semblance* of an answer to the last half of the First Step.(p.349)

semi-blackouts

• Now it was *semi-blackouts* every night, outrageous behavior, passing out in some friend's Village studio or not knowing how I got home.(p.407)

semi-coma

• I had been drinking heavily from one state of *semi-coma* to another and it was several days before I got "defogged," but subconsciously I was in earnest about wanting to quit liquor forever.(p.258)

semi-hermit

• What about those fears which once paralyzed me to the point of my becoming a *semi-hermit*?(p.284)

semi-prostitution

• I did not resort to *semi-prostitution* for the price of a drink.(p.412)

send

• I failed to persuade my broker friends to *send* me out looking over factories and managements, but my wife and I decided to go anyway.(p.2)

• Some people cannot be seen -- we *send* them an honest letter.(p.83)

• Another time you may have to *send* for the police or an ambulance.(p.97)

• There my drinking became so much worse that the boys in the fraternity house where I lived felt forced to *send* for my father, who made a long journey in the vain endeavor to get me straightened around.(p.174)

• Finally my father had to *send* a doctor out from my home town who managed to get me back there in some way, and I was in bed about two months before I could venture out of the house.(p.175)

• Mrs. M. said she would *send* Jack over as quick as he came in.(p.267)

• Then I would *send* an excuse of illness.(p.299)

• Following this, I had a short vacation, during which time I read as much literature as my sponsor could *send* me.(p.343)

• It was the first she had heard or read about it and she said she had considered sending it to me or trying to have someone in Pittsburgh *send* it to me so I wouldn't know where it came from.(p.366)

• Every time I got drunk, my husband would *send* me to a nursing home.(p.388)

• He hesitated to *send* me back to that hospital.(p.388)

• They sent me the regular letter they *send* to everybody else, but along with it, Ruth Hock, the nonalcoholic secretary, wrote a longhand note because she could see from the letter that I really needed help badly.(p.392)

• I suspect that those bartenders would wait until I shot my wad, then call a cab and *send* me home.(p.410)

• As a result, he couldn't figure out why I had the convulsions, and he decided to *send* me to the Mayo Clinic.(p.444)

• The same doctor who had sent me to the psycho had asked my husband, "Why don't you *send* her to this Alcoholics Anonymous?"(p.469)

• I think the thing that galled me was that just after Easter I had drawn my salary for two weeks' work and had decided that I was going to *send* some money to Vi; and above all else I was going to *send* my baby daughter an Easter outfit.(p.493)

• He said if I came back again, they would *send* me to the state hospital.(p.528)

sending

• It was the first she had heard or read about it and she said she had considered *sending* it to me or trying to have someone in Pittsburgh send it to me so I wouldn't know where it came from.(p.366)

• At first, I wondered whether he was alcoholic himself, and was *sending* me to find out about A.A.(p.446)

• On one of these trips, the judge must have thought I was worth saving, for instead of *sending* me to jail, he sent me to A.A. for one month.(p.526)
• I hated that judge for *sending* me to a place with all those drunks.(p.527)

senior

• I left the university in the latter part of my *senior* year and enlisted in the army.(p.183)
• By that time, I had one boy in college, another a *senior* in high school, and a daughter about twelve years old.(p.215)
• On hearing that, these people induced me to make the move immediately and join them as a *senior* partner, which I did.(p.220)
• Through studied sneaky-drinking, I'd become a *senior* citizen without having lost a day's work because of booze.(p.327)
• I belong to more medical societies and honor societies than men ten to twenty years my *senior*.(p.345)
• I was in the fourth quarter of my *senior* year at high school, and my mother was quite sick in the hospital.(p.354)
• Final exams of my *Senior* year and I may somehow graduate.(p.499)

senior-citizen

• Happy, happy *senior-citizen* existence!(p.329)
• He'll never read in his "sweetness and light" *senior-citizen* publications anything but the joys of lolling in the rocking chair, angling on the riverbank, or bowling on the green.(p.330)

sensation

• The *sensation* is so elusive that, while they admit it is injurious, they cannot after a time differentiate the true from the false.(p.xxvi)
• One year later he called to see me, and I experienced a very strange *sensation*.(p.xxix)

sensational

• We think A.A. ought to avoid *sensational* advertising.(p.567)

sense

• We are not an organization in the conventional *sense* of the word.(p.xiii)
• But as ex-problem drinkers, we can say that his explanation makes good *sense*.(p.xxiv)
• There was, therefore, a *sense* of real satisfaction when I was asked to contribute a few words on a subject which is covered in such masterly detail in these pages.(p.xxv)
• They are restless, irritable and discontented, unless they can again experience the *sense* of ease and comfort which comes at once by taking a few drinks -- drinks which they see others taking with impunity.(p.xxvi)
• My brain raced uncontrollably and there was a terrible *sense* of impending calamity.(p.6)
• But soon the *sense* of His presence had been blotted out by worldly clamors, mostly those within myself.(p.12)
• Common *sense* would thus become uncommon *sense*.(p.13)
• There was a *sense* of victory, followed by such a peace and serenity as I had never known.(p.14)
• Most of us *sense* that real tolerance of other people's shortcomings and viewpoints and a respect for their opinions are attitudes which make us more useful to others.(p.19)
• What has become of the common *sense* and will power that he still sometimes displays with respect to other matters?(p.22)
• We are equally positive that once he takes any alcohol whatever into his system, something happens, both in the bodily and mental *sense*, which makes it virtually impossible for him to stop.(p.22)
• Sometimes these excuses have a certain plausibility, but none of them really makes *sense* in the light of the havoc an alcoholic's drinking bout creates.(p.23)
• In a vague way their families and friends *sense* that these drinkers are abnormal, but everybody hopefully awaits the day when the sufferer will rouse himself from his lethargy and assert his power of will.(p.23)
• A certain American business man had ability, good *sense*, and high character.(p.26)
• As soon as we admitted the possible existence of a Creative Intelligence, a Spirit of the Universe underlying the totality of things, we began to be possessed of a new *sense* of power and direction, provided we took other simple steps.(p.46)
• In the face of collapse and despair, in the face of the total failure of their human resources, they found that a new power, peace, happiness, and *sense* of direction flowed into them.(p.50)
• We could not prove life in the *sense* that you can prove a straight line is the shortest distance between two points, yet, there it was.(p.54)
• But they had not learned enough of humility, fearlessness and honesty, in the *sense* we find it necessary, until they told someone else all their life story.(p.73)
• When it will serve any good purpose, we are willing to announce our convictions with tact and common *sense*.(p.77)
• It may be that both will decide that the way of good *sense* and loving kindness is to let by-gones be bygones.(p.82)
• If we have carefully followed directions, we have begun to *sense* the flow of His Spirit into us.(p.85)
• We have begun to develop this vital sixth *sense*.(p.85)
• He can choose any conception he likes, provided it makes *sense* to him.(p.93)
• For the type of alcoholic who is able and willing to get well, little charity, in the ordinary *sense* of the word, is needed or wanted.(p.97)
• What had become of their judgment, their common *sense*, their will power?(p.107)
• Both of you will awaken to a new *sense* of responsibility for others.(p.119)
• If they *sense* these things, they will not take so seriously his periods of crankiness, depression, or apathy, which will disappear when there is tolerance, love, and spiritual understanding.(p.127)
• This dream world has been replaced by a great *sense* of purpose, accompanied by a growing consciousness of the power of God in our lives.(p.130)
• After a bit, he said, "The way you fellows put this spiritual stuff makes *sense*.(p.159)
• During the subsequent fifteen years I had *sense* enough never to go to the hospital if I had been drinking, and very seldom did I receive patients.(p.176)
• I do not recollect the specific conversation that went on but I believe I did challenge Bill to tell me something about A.A. and I do recall one other thing: I wanted to know what this was that worked so many wonders, and hanging over the mantel was a picture of Gethsemane and Bill pointed to it and said, "There it is," which didn't make much *sense* to me.(p.216)
• I felt that his family were accepting me because it was good *sense*.(p.262)
• And Jim G. had such a wonderful *sense* of humor, and when he came I was in tears, and I told him, "I want to do this, but I can't.(p.269)
• Probably only a few readers of this story will be able, from personal experiences of their own, to understand the exhilaration and *sense* of accomplishment which I felt after finishing this seemingly simple assignment.(p.276)
• I would hang on to sobriety for short intervals, but always there would come the tide of an overpowering necessity to drink and, as I was engulfed in it, I felt such a *sense* of panic that I really believed I would die if I didn't get that drink inside.(p.306)
• Philosophy, faith, a *sense* of humor (they could laugh at themselves), clear-cut objectives, appreciation – and most especially appreciation and sympathetic understanding for their fellow man.(p.310)
• Now there is a *sense* of belonging, of being wanted and needed and loved.(p.312)
• Hauling her to the divan, I sat with her and began to talk, frantically but clearly – and making *sense*.(p.333)
• I don't mean that in any *sense* as a derogatory statement about psychotherapy; it's a great tool, not too potent, but a great tool.(p.349)
• They told me their stories, which were much more rugged than mine – yet what they said made *sense*, and the way they put it was easy for me to understand, with an understanding I had never had before.(p.363)
• It was worrying my wife a little, but she had the good *sense* not to take me to task about it or goad me into going.(p.364)
• There are many short phrases and expressions in A.A. which make sound *sense*.(p.382)
• I learned a whole new *sense* of values.(p.409)
• In the course of drunken arguments, I found my own views and *sense* of responsibility as a citizen.(p.410)
• In a *sense*, I had taken the first step.(p.412)
• Never had I felt a *sense* of belonging.(p.413)
• So I sat down with me and went over the facts behind the convulsions: personality changes, daily headaches, *sense* of impending doom, *sense* of impending insanity.(p.444)
• The people of A.A. had something that looked much better than what I had, but I was afraid to let go of what I had in order to try something new; there was a certain *sense* of security in the familiar.(p.448)
• Prior to our marriage, when she was a shy, scrawny adolescent, I was able to see things in her that others couldn't necessarily see – things like beauty, charm, gaiety, a gift for being easy to talk to, a *sense* of humor, and many other fine qualities.(p.450)
• What's the *sense* in trying to do the right thing?"(p.467)
• Being an alcoholic, slick, and having some good *sense* left, I survived the investigation.(p.490)
• It doesn't make *sense*.(p.504)
• I learn that when we act upon the highest conception of honesty which is given us, our *sense* of honesty becomes more acute.(p.507)
• Rather, I embraced it – I must in honesty admit it -- with a great *sense* of relief.(p.531)
• There was the *sense* of being "misunderstood," when as a matter of fact by my middle twenties I was quite popular, although I hadn't grown much bigger physically.(p.534)
• I know there are some alcoholics who seem terribly, terribly grown-up, but I think that they are trying to make themselves think they are grown-up, and the strain of their effort is what is causing them to drink -- a *sense* of inadequacy, a childish vanity to be the most popular, the most sought after, the mostest of the most.(p.535)
• Had I been able to explain to a psychiatrist the feeling of futility, loneliness and lack of purpose that had come with my deep *sense* of personal failure at this second divorce, I seriously doubt that the good doctor could have convinced me that my basic problem was a spiritual hunger, but A.A. has shown me this was the truth.(p.546)
• With deep shame came the knowledge too that I had lived with no *sense* of social obligation nor had I known the meaning of moral responsibility to my fellow men.(p.549)

sensed

• I vaguely *sensed* I was not being any too smart, but felt reassured as I was taking the whiskey on a full stomach.(p.36)
• Sometimes we *sensed* dimly that we were dealing with sick men.(p.107)
• I *sensed* they had something I did not have, from which I might readily profit.(p.178)
• My wife became deeply interested and it was her interest that sustained mine, though I at no time *sensed* that it might be an answer to my liquor problem.(p.178)
• I guess I felt, and he *sensed* it, that I wanted him to hurry up and say what he had to say and get out.(p.494)

senseless

• He uses his gifts to build up a bright outlook for his family and himself, and then pulls the structure down on his head by a *senseless* series of sprees.(p.21)

senses

• It is not by chance we were given the power to reason, to examine the evidence of our *senses*, and to draw conclusions.(p.53)
• Coming to his *senses*, he is revolted at certain episodes he vaguely remembers.(p.73)
• The following spring she left me one day without giving me any idea of where she had gone, hoping this would bring me to my *senses*.(p.377)

sensible

• He is often perfectly *sensible* and well balanced concerning everything except liquor, but in that respect he is incredibly dishonest and selfish.(p.21)
• But the program of action, though entirely *sensible*, was pretty drastic.(p.42)
• But above all, we tried to be *sensible* on this question.(p.68)
• We should be *sensible*, tactful, considerate and humble without being servile or scraping.(p.83)
• We think we are *sensible* when we urge that you stop this waste and give your worthwhile man a chance.(p.148)
• Of course, this year we decided on staying home and being *sensible*, doing a little drinking, and painting the house.(p.265)
• Sure enough in a couple of hours two men were at my door and for the first time I heard some facts about liquor and my problem that sounded *sensible* to me.(p.363)

sensitive

• We alcoholics are *sensitive* people.(p.125)
• I was an extremely *sensitive* person and so self-conscious that I hurt all over.(p.385)
• Of course I had the *sensitive*, hurt feelings of the a[l]coholic.(p.472)

sensitiveness

• Besides a seeming inability to accept muc[h]
we often found ourselves handicapped b[y]

sensitiveness, and unreasoning prejudice.(p.47)

sensitivity

• We are granted "the serenity to accept the things we cannot change" -- and thus lose our quickness to anger and our ***sensitivity*** to criticism.(p.560)

sent

• Each inquiry was painstakingly answered; pamphlets and books were ***sent*** out.(p.xviii)

• He did, and also ***sent*** a small amount of money.(p.79)

• Ask any woman who has ***sent*** her husband to distant places on the theory he would escape the alcohol problem.(p.101)

• In another case, an alcoholic was ***sent*** to a hospital for treatment.(p.145)

• These good people notified my wife, who ***sent*** my newly made friend over to get me.(p.179)

• We drove to a store in North Hill and I ***sent*** him in with what money I had to get a quart.(p.204)

• He came in and took a look at me and ***sent*** me to the hospital.(p.205)

• This experience ***sent*** me to law school where I went at night and which course I completed in less than three years, taking the highest state bar examinations and passing them.(p.212)

• And, because as I have discovered since, it is part of the "treatment" that these men be ***sent*** to see and talk with alcoholics who want to quit, he kept them busy.(p.235)

• He had already imbued them with his own spirit until they were ready and willing at all times to go where ***sent***, and as a doctor he well knew that this mission and duty would strengthen them as it later helped me.(p.235)

• It wasn't very long until my doctor friend ***sent*** me to tell another alcoholic what my experience had been.(p.237)

• As part of this promotion, they ***sent*** me to their national convention in Atlantic City to tell the big wheels how I'd done it.(p.243)

• I stayed so sober that I used to keep a quart of medicinal whiskey in my bureau which I used to taper off the occasional newspaper alcoholics who were ***sent*** to see me.(p.253)

• It would stop out in front of our house, and I still believe those people ***sent*** it!(p.265)

• He ***sent*** to New York for a copy, and after reading it he tucked it under his arm and called on me.(p.307)

• Shortly after I returned to Chicago, my doctor, encouraged by the results of my contact with A.A., ***sent*** us two more of his alcoholic patients.(p.310)

• Next, I was ***sent*** to Arizona, where my drinking picked up some more, and I started having blackouts, and I was thrown in jail for speeding and drunken driving.(p.318)

• I was ***sent*** to a psychiatrist, for they didn't think it was normal for me to want to kill my platoon sergeant or to attempt suicide twice.(p.318)

• This man faced the last ditch when his wife's voice from 1,300 miles away ***sent*** him to A.A.(p.356)

• I think I actually read more contempt than was really there because just a week before someone had ***sent*** him the Saturday Evening Post article on A.A., and there was some glimmer of hope in it for him.(p.391)

• They ***sent*** me the regular letter they send to everybody else, but along with it, Ruth Hock, the nonalcoholic secretary, wrote a longhand note because she could see from the letter that I really needed help badly.(p.392)

• There are so many to whom I feel deeply grateful; to my husband (and best critic), whose generous love, compassion and understanding have helped me along the way; to those before me in A.A. who inspired the first article I read, and the friend who ***sent*** that article to Frank; to Ruth for her personal note, and the first A.A. to talk to me; to my Bishop, whose loving and believing spirit inspired me; and to all the members of the Houston Group who were so patient, kind and helpful -- and to countless others.(p.393)

• My first analyst said, "You are becoming more and more of an alcoholic," and ***sent*** me to another analyst.(p.407)

• She was duly ***sent*** to school, away from me.(p.409)

• Perhaps it was He who ***sent*** my analyst to a psychiatrist's meeting at which Bill spoke.(p.412)

• I had ***sent*** her to four consecutive psychiatrists, and not one of them had gotten me sober.(p.440)

• I also ***sent*** my kids to psychiatrists.(p.440)

• The hotel management, knowing that something was wrong, ***sent*** for a doctor.(p.465)

• The same doctor who had ***sent*** me to the psycho ad asked my husband, "Why don't you send her to s Alcoholics Anonymous?"(p.469)

• On October 28th, I was ***sent*** to Sing Sing with a minimum of thirty-three and a half years to serve out of that thirty-five.(p.509)

• I spent about six or seven weeks in Sing Sing, and was finally ***sent*** off to Dannemora in the Adirondacks.(p.509)

• I remained there for about ten months, and then I was ***sent*** to a place called Wallkill, a so-called rehabilitation center.(p.509)

• We talked for a while, and then he ***sent*** me down to the Alanon House over on the west side, and there I had my introduction to A.A.(p.515)

• I belonged to one of the Irish families who, more or less traditionally, ***sent*** their boys to the British armies.(p.517)

• I was going to be ***sent*** to the Indian Civil Service, which, in those days, meant that people thought you had a certain amount of brains.(p.517)

• Then I was ***sent*** out to India and from then on drinking just increased and increased, and I started having two or three day spells instead of just the ordinary concentrated one day.(p.519)

• They kept me in hospital for two months, and then they ***sent*** me up to Egypt, a three days journey.(p.521)

• They ***sent*** me up with an attendant, and the attendant and I both arrived at the Egyptian Hospital rather the worse for wear.(p.521)

• On one of these trips, the judge must have thought I was worth saving, for instead of sending me to jail, he ***sent*** me to A.A. for one month.(p.526)

• My doctor finally declared he could no longer be responsible for me, and ***sent*** me to a psychiatrist who practiced in the same suite of offices.(p.558)

• I have learned to deal with disappointments and problems that once would have ***sent*** me right to the bottle.(p.559)

sentence

• That ***sentence***, "The Lord has been so wonderful to me, curing me of this terrible disease, that I just want to keep telling people about it," has been sort of a golden text for the A.A. program and for me.(p.191)

• And as I fumed helplessly and planned to get good and drunk and show them, my eye caught a ***sentence*** in the book lying open on my bed: "We cannot live with anger."(p.228)

• And the last ***sentence*** was "We asked His protection and care with complete abandon."(p.349)

• When I had served only eighteen months of my ***sentence***, this ex-incorrigible was placed in honor grade.(p.461)

• I was not eligible for parole, until -- with God's help, I'm sure -- the governor cut five years off my ***sentence***.(p.462)

• I remember particularly one ***sentence*** that seemed to say, "This is for you."(p.473)

• However, as time went on laws were enacted that reduced the ***sentence***.(p.509)

• But when she began a prison ***sentence***, a door opened.(p.526)

• Because I had been drunk, the judge gave me only a twelve-year ***sentence*** in prison.(p.528)

• I started to cross out that last ***sentence***, but decided to let it stand.(p.536)

sentences

• In a few ***sentences*** he made God seem personal to me, explained Him as a being who was interested in me, the alcoholic, and that all I needed to do was to be willing to follow His way; that as long as I followed it I would be able to overcome my desire for liquor.(p.236)

• There were two ***sentences*** in it that struck me.(p.346)

sentient

• I hope I have been able to impart to you, the reader, at least a bit of what I know; the joy of living, the irresistible power of divine love and its healing strength, and the fact that we, as ***sentient*** beings, have the knowledge to choose between good and evil, and, choosing good, are made happy.(p.543)

sentiment

• Because this book has become the basic text for our Society and has helped such large numbers of alcoholic men and women to recover, there exists a ***sentiment*** against any radical changes being made in it.(p.xi)

• Had we not variously worshipped people, ***sentiment***, things, money, and ourselves?(p.54)

sentimental

• If any feel that as psychiatrists directing a hospital for alcoholics we appear somewhat ***sentimental***, let them stand with us a while on the firing line, see the tragedies, the despairing wives, the little children; let the solving of these problems become a part of their daily work, and even of their sleeping moments, and the most cynical will not wonder that we have accepted and encouraged this movement.(p.xxvi)

sentimentality

• But we have a baby who, if you'll pardon a little post-alcoholic ***sentimentality***, is right out of Heaven.(p.438)

separate

• Though it is entirely ***separate*** from Alcoholics Anonymous, it uses the general principles of the A.A. program as a guide for husbands, wives, relatives, friends, and others close to alcoholics.(p.121)

• Husbands and wives have sometimes been obliged to ***separate*** for a time until new perspective, new victory over hurt pride could be rewon.(p.125)

• They had also been periodic big shots who had goofed out repeatedly at the wrong time, and they also knew how to split one paper match into three ***separate*** matches.(p.245)

• I also got into my first disciplinary trouble caused by drinking, on two ***separate*** occasions.(p.555)

separated

• At the hospital I was ***separated*** from alcohol for the last time.(p.13)

• We old-timers who get scattered and ***separated*** and then witness the construction of services to get in more people and to make this thing function, we think that A.A. has changed, but the root of it hasn't.(p.272)

• Here, also, I had good friends, but I became more and more ***separated*** from them.(p.406)

• So I went down to talk to the District Attorney, and the arrangement was made that I would go home to stay with my mother, and that meant Vi and I were ***separated***.(p.491)

• I continued to work and continued to go to lunch with Vi, and none of our acquaintances on the job knew that we had ***separated***.(p.491)

• Very often we rode to and from work together, but being ***separated*** really galled me deep down.(p.491)

• I am an only child, and when I was seven years old my parents ***separated*** very abruptly.(p.544)

separately

• But out of this frightening and at first disrupting experience the conviction grew that A.A.'s had to hang together or die ***separately***.(p.xix)

• So let each family play together or ***separately***, as much as their circumstances warrant.(p.132)

• We think, therefore, that any considerable property of genuine use to A.A. should be ***separately*** incorporated and managed, thus dividing the material from the spiritual.(p.565)

separation

• Now, the domestic problem: There may be divorce, ***separation***, or just strained relations.(p.98)

• If there be divorce or ***separation***, there should be no undue haste for the couple to get together.(p.99)

• I saw him recently and he told me that he had always felt guilty, because, after our ***separation***, I had become a serious alcoholic.(p.403)

September

• These vacations became quite something, and he always had two weeks vacation the first two weeks of every ***September***.(p.264)

• The most accurate answer I can give you is this: Fear has never again ruled my life since that day in ***September***, 1938, when I found that a Power greater than myself could not only restore me to sanity but could keep me both sober and sane.(p.285)

• By the latter part of ***September*** 1939, we had a nucleus of six and held our first official group meeting.(p.310)

• During this vacation, in the months of ***September*** and October, I decided to go on the water wagon.(p.343)

• In ***September*** of this same year I went to New York alone.(p.364)

serene

• A.A. has given me serenity of purpose, the opportunity to be of service to God and to the people about me, and I am ***serene*** in the infallibility of these principles that provide the fulfillment of my purpose.(p.551)

serenity

• There was a sense of victory, followed by such a peace and ***serenity*** as I had never known.(p.14)

• Just to the extent that we do as we think He would have us, and humbly rely on Him, does He enable us to match calamity with ***serenity***.(p.68)

• We will comprehend the word ***serenity*** and we will know peace.(p.83)

• At our weekly meeting I was a menace to ***serenity*** those first few months, for I took every opportunity to lambaste the "spiritual angle" as we called it, or anything else that had any tinge of theology.(p.246)

• Then I found that as I gave in to this spiritual or personality change I was getting a little more *serenity*.(p.249)
• They had that certain something that seemed to glow, a peace and a *serenity* combined with happiness.(p.290)
• I saw in these people a quality of peace and *serenity* that I knew I must have for myself.(p.310)
• So I went to my wife and asked her, wasn't there something that she and I could do to somehow get together, and she turned on her heel and looked me squarely in the eye, and said, "You don't care anything about my problem," and I could have smacked her, but I said to myself, "Grab on to your *serenity*!"(p.351)
• "Grant us the *serenity* to accept the things we cannot change, courage to change the things we can, and the wisdom to know the difference."(p.382)
• When I am disturbed, it is because I find some person, place, thing, or situation -- some fact of my life -- unacceptable to me, and I can find no *serenity* until I accept that person, place, thing, or situation as being exactly the way it is supposed to be at this moment.(p.449)
• Then, one day in A.A., I was told that I had the lenses in my glasses backwards; "the courage to change" in the *Serenity* Prayer meant, not that I should change my marriage, but rather that I should change myself and learn to accept my spouse as she was.(p.451)
• Perhaps the best thing of all for me is to remember that my *serenity* is inversely proportional to my expectations.(p.452)
• The higher my expectations of Max and other people are, the lower is my *serenity*.(p.452)
• I can watch my *serenity* level rise when I discard my expectations.(p.452)
• But then my "rights" try to move in, and they, too, can force my *serenity* level down.(p.452)
• How important is it compared to my *serenity*, my emotional sobriety?"(p.452)
• And when I place more value on my *serenity* and sobriety than on anything else, I can maintain them at a higher level -- at least for the time being.(p.452)
• I must keep my magic magnifying mind on my acceptance and off my expectations, for my *serenity* is directly proportional to my level of acceptance.(p.452)
• It was the *Serenity* Prayer!(p.461)
• Yes, I knew what the *Serenity* Prayer was -- A.A. had taught me.(p.461)
• During the twenty-four hours after running into the *Serenity* Prayer, I think I took the first three Steps for the first time.(p.461)
• What is much more important to me, A.A. has taught me that through this simple program I may experience a change in this reaction pattern that will indeed allow me to "match calamity with *serenity*."(p.544)
• A.A. has given me *serenity* of purpose, the opportunity to be of service to God and to the people about me, and I am serene in the infallibility of these principles that provide the fulfillment of my purpose.(p.551)
• We are granted "the *serenity* to accept the things we cannot change" -- and thus lose our quickness to anger and our sensitivity to criticism.(p.560)

sergeant
• I had been to OTC the previous summer so I went into the Army as a *sergeant*, but I came out a private, and you really have to be unusual to do that.(p.241)
• I was sent to a psychiatrist, for they didn't think it was normal for me to want to kill my platoon *sergeant* or to attempt suicide twice.(p.318)
• The third time, after almost five years as an S.P. 4, I finally made *sergeant*.(p.318)
• I talked to the first *sergeant* and the battalion commander, and they got me in contact with an A.A. member.(p.319)

sergeants
• *Sergeants*, doctors, girl friends -- everybody seemed to be picking on him.(p.317)

series
• He uses his gifts to build up a bright outlook for his family and himself, and then pulls the structure down on his head by a senseless *series* of sprees.(p.21)
• That job began a *series* of brief working spells, each one ending in a "drunk" and the urge to travel.(p.253)
• This was the beginning of an unending *series* of such experiences.(p.276)
• It is, however, only the first of a *series* of miracles which have followed one after another as a result of my trying to apply to my daily life the principles embodies in our Twelve Steps.(p.280)
• A little more than fifteen years ago, through a long and calamitous *series* of shattering experiences, I found myself being helplessly propelled toward total destruction.(p.304)

serious
• My drinking assumed more *serious* proportions, continuing all day and almost every night.(p.3)
• In the early days of our drinking we occasionally remained sober for a year or more, becoming *serious* drinkers again later.(p.34)
• He agreed he was a real alcoholic and in a *serious* condition.(p.35)
• I had a few words with the boss, but nothing *serious*.(p.36)
• We now see that when we began to drink deliberately, instead of casually, there was little *serious* or effective thought during the period of premeditation of what the terrific consequences might be.(p.37)
• Post-war disillusionment, ever more *serious* alcoholism, impending mental and physical collapse, brought him to the point of self-destruction.(p.56)
• If he is in a *serious* mood dwell on the trouble liquor has caused you, being careful not to moralize or lecture.(p.91)
• It is not good for him, and it sometimes creates *serious* complications in a family.(p.97)
• He is remorseful after *serious* drinking bouts and tells you he wants to stop.(p.109)
• Meanwhile you might try to help the wife of another *serious* drinker.(p.112)
• A good doctor or psychiatrist can tell you whether these complications are *serious*.(p.114)
• You and your husband will find that you can dispose of *serious* problems easier than you can the trivial ones.(p.118)
• Next time you and he have a heated discussion, no matter what the subject, it should be the privilege of either to smile and say, "This is getting *serious*.(p.118)
• It takes some of us a long time to outgrow that *serious* handicap.(p.125)
• We have been speaking to you of *serious*, sometimes tragic things.(p.132)
• We, who have recovered from *serious* drinking, are miracles of mental health.(p.133)
• She sees she was wrong to make a burning issue out of such a matter when his more *serious* ailments were being rapidly cured.(p.135)
• He simply could not believe that his brother-executive suffered from a *serious* illness.(p.138)
• I know, in my own particular case, that nothing my company could have done would have stopped me for, so long as I was able to hold my position, I could not possibly realize how *serious* my situation was.(p.141)
• They often jeopardize their own positions by trying to help *serious* drinkers who should have been fired long ago, or else given an opportunity to get well.(p.147)
• We hope our suggestions will help you plug up this sometimes *serious* leak.(p.148)
• Now and then a *serious* drinker, being dry at the moment says, "I don't miss it at all.(p.151)
• Yet, as my record shows, I did become an extremely *serious* case.(p.182)
• It had long since become a *serious* problem.(p.197)
• When I entered a sanitarium for prolonged and intensive psychiatric treatment, I was convinced that I was having a *serious* mental breakdown.(p.226)
• Slight casualties, complicated however by a long and *serious* illness, were my only mishaps.(p.253)
• It was therefore not extraordinary that I should shy away from any *serious* thought of marriage for a great many years after joining A.A.(p.286)
• Some were drinking heavily and there had been occasional *serious* episodes.(p.315)
• They saw that they had become actual or potential alcoholics, even though no *serious* harm had yet been done.(p.315)
• At this time, however, she had an opportunity to go to Salt Lake City on a new project for the government, but she did promise me that if I would curtail my drinking and buckle down to hard work she would give *serious* consideration to my latest proposal and maybe join me at a later date when I got settled.(p.359)
• I saw him recently and he told me that he had always felt guilty, because, after our separation, I had become a *serious* alcoholic.(p.403)
• Was my mental state more *serious* than he said?(p.406)
• They were doing very well -- at least a fifth apiece a day, except on dad's days off when they did some *serious* drinking.(p.425)
• Aside from being a common drunk, I had a very *serious* pill affliction and all the garbage that goes with it -- lying, stealing, cheating anybody and everybody, conning the people I could, and staying clear of the ones I couldn't.(p.478)
• At first they were rather amusing, but a little later on they became *serious*.(p.513)
• My *serious* drinking covered about seven years.(p.536)
• Young when she joined, this A.A. believes her *serious* drinking was the result of even deeper defects.(p.544)

seriously
• Best of all, I met a kind doctor who explained that though certainly selfish and foolish, I had been *seriously* ill, bodily and mentally.(p.7)
• If you are as *seriously* alcoholic as we were, we believe there is no middle-of-the-road solution.(p.25)
• If they sense these things, they will not take so *seriously* his periods of crankiness, depression, or apathy, which will disappear when there is tolerance, love, and spiritual understanding.(p.127)
• I had not asked for help and *seriously* doubt that I would have, but Fitz, an old school friend of mine, had persuaded Jackie to call on me.(p.238)
• I started to take A.A. *seriously*, and A.A. gave me a new way of life.(p.320)
• Before I started to drink *seriously*, I tried a couple of other escapes.(p.401)
• Had I been able to explain to a psychiatrist the feeling of futility, loneliness and lack of purpose that had come with my deep sense of personal failure at this second divorce, I *seriously* doubt that the good doctor could have convinced me that my basic problem was a spiritual hunger, but A.A. has shown me this was the truth.(p.546)

seriousness
• Get an idea of his behavior, his problems, his background, the *seriousness* of his condition, and his religious leanings.(p.90)

sermon
• After the *sermon*, he quietly got up and made an explanation.(p.80)
• This is based, really, on the *Sermon* on the Mount.(p.268)
• I didn't know anything about the *Sermon* on the Mount.(p.268)
• Father is delivering his *sermon*.(p.497)

servant
• The *servant* he turned to was our old cook, and she liked to drink.(p.385)

servants
• Up to my early thirties, when my drinking had become a major problem, I lived in large houses, with *servants* and all the luxuries that I could possibly ask for.(p.401)
• Our leaders are but trusted *servants*; they do not govern.(p.564)
• All such representatives are to be guided in the spirit of service, for true leaders in A.A. are but trusted and experienced *servants* of the whole.(p.567)

serve
• It was thought that no alcoholic man or woman could be excluded from our Society; that our leaders might *serve* but never govern; that each group was to be autonomous and there was to be no professional class of therapy.(p.xix)
• When it will *serve* any good purpose, we are willing to announce our convictions with tact and common sense.(p.77)
• "How can I best *serve* Thee -- Thy will (not mine) be done."(p.85)
• Doctors are rightly loath to tell alcoholic patients the whole story unless it will *serve* some good purpose.(p.92)
• Some of us still *serve* it to our friends provided they are not alcoholic.(p.102)
• But some of us think we should not *serve* liquor to anyone.(p.102)
• My wife and I belonged to some bridge clubs and they began to make wine and *serve* it.(p.184)
• However, after two or three trials, I found this was not satisfactory because they did not *serve* enough to satisfy me.(p.184)
• I, carried away with the desire to *serve* A.A., gave what was probably one of the first radio broadcasts about A.A., living through a case of mike fright and feeling like a million dollars when it was all over.(p.283)
• I had to give him a story and ask him the same question over and over again, "Well, now, how many will that bottle *serve*?"(p.336)
• Alcohol failed to *serve* the purpose.(p.346)
• Soon found wet canteens *serve* drinks to Indians in uniform.(p.474)

• On October 28th, I was sent to Sing Sing with a minimum of thirty-three and a half years to *serve* out of that thirty-five.(p.509)
• To wear expensive clothes, to have bartenders know what to *serve* me before I ordered, to be recognized by headwaiters and shown to the best table, to play gin rummy for high stakes with the insouciance of a riverboat gambler – these were the enduring values in life, I thought.(p.556)
• Nine – A.A., as such, ought never be organized; but we may create service boards or committees directly responsible to those they *serve*.(p.564)

served

• People have said we must not go where liquor is *served*; we must not have it in our homes; we must shun friends who drink; we must avoid moving pictures which show drinking scenes; we must not go into bars; our friends must hide their bottles if we go to their houses; we mustn't think or be reminded about alcohol at all.(p.100)
• So we think that unless some good and useful purpose is to be *served*, past occurrences should not be discussed.(p.125)
• I have *served* on only one committee in the past nine years, for I feel that I had my chance the first few years and that newer members should fill the jobs.(p.250)
• Rehearsals then became a part of the pattern, stopping at bars on the way to or from the place where drinks were to be *served*.(p.375)
• I *served* twelve years in prison, never suspecting that without alcohol I would not have been in prison at all.(p.457)
• I *served* time in four penitentiaries and several prison camps, including a maximum-security camp.(p.457)
• When I had *served* only eighteen months of my sentence, this ex-incorrigible was placed in honor grade.(p.461)
• I was paroled when I had *served* less than three years.(p.462)
• In fact, sometimes they *served* as good excuses to drink more, to forget.(p.465)
• By the grace of God, I only *served* three years.(p.528)

service

• There was to be the least possible organization, even in our *service* centers.(p.xix)
• We gave up our positions and off we roared on a motorcycle, the sidecar stuffed with tent, blankets, a change of clothes, and three huge volumes of a financial reference *service*.(p.2)
• The experiment of quitting for a period of time will be helpful, but we think we can render an even greater *service* to alcoholic sufferers and perhaps to the medical fraternity.(p.34)
• Our real purpose is to fit ourselves to be of maximum *service* to God and the people about us.(p.77)
• The minute we put our work on a *service* plane, the alcoholic commences to rely upon our assistance rather than upon God.(p.98)
• If there is no Al-Anon listing in your local telephone book, you may obtain further information on Al-Anon Family Groups by writing to its World *Service* Office: Box 182, Madison Square Station, New York, NY 10159.(p.121)
• In his prodigy of *service*, he was well assisted by Sister Ignatia at St. Thomas Hospital in Akron, Ohio, one of the greatest friends our Fellowship will ever know.(p.171)
• From childhood through high school I was more or less forced to go to church, Sunday School and evening *service*, Monday night Christian Endeavor and sometimes to Wednesday evening prayer meeting.(p.172)
• I can remember that in my childhood, he was ill at ease with the children because he attempted to assert an army discipline that had been ground into him during his three and a half years of army *service*.(p.210)
• Military *service* was compulsory and I did my stretch with the class of my age, goose-stepping in German barracks and taking part in the Boxer Rebellion in China, my first time at any great distance from home.(p.230)
• I am one of the lads who came out of the *service* with a lower rank than when I went in.(p.241)
• The example which they and Bill W., whose visits to Akron were fairly frequent, set me of *service* to their fellow men imbued me with a great desire to emulate them.(p.281)
• After six months of sobriety I saw the picture in a different light: Detroit was the place I had to return to, not only because I must face the mess I had made there, but because it was there that I could be of the most *service* to A.A.(p.281)
• The encouragement received in the early days, especially from the A.A. General *Service* Office, made a tremendous difference to my sobriety.(p.342)
• Then there was wartime *service* to interrupt my plans, and an education to be picked up after the war.(p.373)
• As I said before, I don't like to be fenced in, and with those bars you don't get hotel *service*.(p.390)
• I wanted a cigarette and room *service*, which I didn't get.(p.390)
• It was the A.A. General *Service* Office in New York that I wrote to, and that office has always meant a lot to me.(p.392)
• Dr. Bob said, "Love and *service* keep us dry," and Bill said, "Always we must remember that our first duty is face-to-face help for the alcoholic who still suffers."(p.395)
• But my attempts at community *service* ended in a drunken and abusive row with a fellow volunteer.(p.410)
• I had a very good friend who was in the Government *service*, and I went to him about a job.(p.489)
• She also was in the government *service*.(p.490)
• Three attempts to enlist in the *service*, and three failures because of being skinny.(p.499)
• Never in the *service*!(p.499)
• Like many of us who went into the *service*, I thought it would be a cure-all, a new life.(p.513)
• I was going to be sent to the Indian Civil *Service*, which, in those days, meant that people thought you had a certain amount of brains.(p.517)
• It continues to try to teach me the real charity, the charity that gives time and good will and *service*, and not just money.(p.525)
• Since it was wartime, I explained to the somewhat startled shopkeeper that I had many friends in the *service* whom I was remembering with a watch.(p.532)
• A.A. has given me serenity of purpose, the opportunity to be of *service* to God and to the people about me, and I am serene in the infallibility of these principles that provide the fulfillment of my purpose.(p.551)
• In the last year of my navy *service*, I was married to a lovely, lively girl, who enjoyed drinking.(p.555)
• At that very time, he was a nonalcoholic trustee on the General *Service* Board of Alcoholics Anonymous!(p.559)
• Eight – Alcoholics Anonymous should remain forever nonprofessional, but our *service* centers may employ special workers.(p.564)
• Nine – A.A., as such, ought never be organized; but we may create *service* boards or committees directly responsible to those they serve.(p.564)
• And no group, regional committee, or individual should ever take any action that might greatly affect A.A. as a whole without conferring with the trustees of the General *Service* Board.(p.565)
• The trustees of the General *Service* Board are, in effect, our A.A. General *Service* Committee.(p.567)
• They are the custodians of our A.A. Tradition and the receivers of voluntary A.A. contributions by which we maintain our A.A. General *Service* Office at New York.(p.567)
• All such representatives are to be guided in the spirit of *service*, for true leaders in A.A. are but trusted and experienced servants of the whole.(p.567)
• At New York, U.S.A., Alcoholics Anonymous maintains its international *service* center.(p.575)
• The General *Service* Board of A.A. (the trustees) administers A.A.'s General *Service* Office, A.A. World Services, Inc., and our monthly magazine, the A.A. Grapevine.(p.575)

services

• Their *services* are often indispensable in treating a newcomer and in following his case afterward.(p.133)
• After your man has gone along without drinking for a few months, you may be able to make use of his *services* with other employees who are giving you the alcoholic run-around -- provided, of course, they are willing to have a third party in the picture.(p.146)
• To 1950, the year of his death, he carried the A.A. message to more than 5,000 alcoholic men and women, and to all these he gave his medical *services* without thought of charge.(p.171)
• I had always been a good Catholic, possibly not so devoted as I should have been, but fairly regular in my attendance at *services*.(p.234)
• At this school we had Bible readings before each meal, and church *services* four times on Sunday, and I became so rebellious at this that I swore I would never join or go to any church except for weddings or funerals.(p.240)
• We old-timers who get scattered and separated and then witness the construction of *services* to get in more people and to make this thing function, we think that A.A. has changed, but the root of it hasn't.(p.272)
• But we may employ alcoholics where they are going to perform those *services* for which we might otherwise have to engage nonalcoholics.(p.566)
• Such special *services* may be well recompensed.(p.566)
• The General Service Board of A.A. (the trustees) administers A.A.'s General Service Office, A.A. World *Services*, Inc., and our monthly magazine, the A.A. Grapevine.(p.575)

servile

• We should be sensible, tactful, considerate and humble without being *servile* or scraping.(p.83)

serving

• Curious about it, feeling I was missing something, absolutely without any illusions about the aftermath, with no pronounced feeling of patriotism, I joined up with a Canadian regiment, *serving* a little over two years.(p.253)
• Above all, I have gained the greatest thing accorded to any man, the love and understanding of a gracious God, who has lifted me from the alcoholic scrap-heap to a position of trust where I have been able to reap the rich rewards that come from showing a little love for others and from *serving* them as I can.(p.296)
• He was *serving* time on his fifth felony conviction when a miracle happened.(p.457)
• On one occasion when I was *serving* time in my favorite drying-out place while I was having a session with the psychiatrist, she left my case history on her desk when she was called away from the room.(p.470)
• Later, I went to sea, *serving* as a gunnery officer on a destroyer escort and emerging a lieutenant commander.(p.555)

session

• I well remember a *session* I had with myself soon after I returned.(p.282)
• On one occasion when I was serving time in my favorite drying-out place while I was having a *session* with the psychiatrist, she left my case history on her desk when she was called away from the room.(p.470)

sessions

• For, after those daily self-punishing *sessions* with myself, after the vows to stop, I would change entirely as evening came on.(p.408)

set

• Hence the two men *set* to work almost frantically upon alcoholics arriving in the ward of the Akron City Hospital.(p.xvii)
• On talking to a man there, I would be amazingly lifted up and *set* on my feet.(p.15)
• I have seen hundreds of families *set* their feet in the path that really goes somewhere; have seen the most impossible domestic situations righted; feuds and bitterness of all sorts wiped out.(p.15)
• Ideas, emotions, and attitudes which were once the guiding forces of the lives of these men are suddenly cast to one side, and a completely new *set* of conceptions and motives begin to dominate them.(p.27)
• When, however, the perfectly logical assumption is suggested that underneath the material world and life as we see it, there is an All Powerful, Guiding, Creative Intelligence, right there our perverse streak comes to the surface and we laboriously *set* out to convince ourselves it isn't so.(p.49)
• The principles we have *set* down are guides to progress.(p.60)
• In dealing with resentments, we *set* them on paper.(p.64)
• On our grudge list we *set* opposite each name our injuries.(p.65)
• We admitted our wrongs honestly and were willing to *set* these matters straight.(p.67)
• It *set* in motion trains of circumstances which brought us misfortune we felt we didn't deserve.(p.67)
• But did not we, ourselves, *set* the ball rolling?(p.67)
• One *set* of voices cry that sex is a lust of our lower nature, a base necessity of procreation.(p.68)
• But our man is sure to be impressed with a sincere desire to *set* right the wrong.(p.77)
• This thought brings us to Step Ten, which suggests we continue to take personal inventory and continue to *set* right any new mistakes as we go along.(p.84)
• If not members of religious bodies, we sometimes select and memorize a few *set* prayers which emphasize the principles we have been discussing.(p.87)
• In this way you can *set* them on the right track without becoming critical of them.(p.100)
• Do not *set* your heart on reforming your husband.(p.111)
• Had he been successful in his enterprise, he would have been *set* on his feet financially which at the time, seemed vitally important.(p.153)

• One morning he took the bull by the horns and ***set*** out to tell those he feared what his trouble had been.(p.156)
• In addition to these casual get-togethers, it became customary to ***set*** apart one night a week for a meeting to be attended by anyone or everyone interested in a spiritual way of life.(p.159)
• It was the day before Mother's Day and I had come home plastered, carrying a big potted plant which I ***set*** down on the table and forthwith went upstairs and passed out.(p.179)
• I kept watching the man down the bar to see what he did with a contraption like that, and he just smelled of his drink and ***set*** it down again, so I did the same.(p.195)
• I drove towards Cleveland wondering why I found myself in such a changed ***set*** of conditions as compared with those of six months before.(p.200)
• Had anyone undertaken to explain to me what the A.A. movement was, what its real function was, I probably would have been ***set*** back several years and I doubt if I would have survived at all.(p.216)
• We were all ***set*** to put DuPont out of business.(p.246)
• So, on that Saturday before Labor Day, I got drunk and ***set*** the house on fire -- so we didn't have to paint it.(p.265)
• I feel that one of the things that I still have to guard against is that I used to be ***set*** in my way about what I considered the old-time A.A.(p.272)
• The example which they and Bill W., whose visits to Akron were fairly frequent, ***set*** me of service to their fellow men imbued me with a great desire to emulate them.(p.281)
• With this specialized training, and a liberal business education in the school of hard knocks, I was able to ***set*** up shop some two years later as an independent accountant.(p.284)
• I was at a beautifully ***set*** dinner table.(p.285)
• So I ***set*** out to get drunk deliberately, just to teach her what she was missing.(p.293)
• I was afraid to ***set*** even one day.(p.326)
• Then, one night, my whole pattern for drinking was ***set***.(p.328)
• But it began to be an awfully painful answer as hangovers, blackouts, trouble, and remorse ***set*** in.(p.353)
• With new hope in my heart and new resolutions I ***set*** off for Vermont.(p.360)
• I began hitting the bottle again, and with it self-pity, resentment, loneliness and remorse ***set*** in deeply.(p.362)
• The why is not important; the fact is that one drink will ***set*** up a reaction in our system which requires more; that one drink was too much and one hundred drinks were not enough.(p.380)
• My Quaker mother-in-law, bless her heart, used to ***set*** the Christmas pudding ablaze with lumps of sugar dipped in rubbing alcohol.(p.402)
• Ribaldry was the substance of the conversation, and I ***set*** out to be the funniest and most ribald of them all.(p.407)
• Everybody did, in the ***set*** which I regarded as the apex of civilization.(p.433)
• And Frank did ***set*** me up for a meeting every night except Friday, when he thought he might have a date with his girl friend.(p.447)
• On the day ***set*** for the extractions, on my way to the dentist's I felt a little nervous, so I had a couple of drinks, and after the teeth were out I was very nervous, so I had a few more.(p.466)
• She gave me such hope and inspiration that I ***set*** her right up on a pedestal.(p.472)
• He said he never wanted to ***set*** foot in the deep south again and he didn't.(p.486)
• After nearly eight years of sobriety in A.A., I still can ***set*** down such thoughts, "against my instinct and training," showing that I still consider myself a "special" person, entitled to special privileges.(p.536)
• I ***set*** it down and made myself a cup of coffee.(p.541)
• She here tells how she was ***set*** free.(p.544)
• With cold calculation I ***set*** about to marry a fortune, and I did.(p.545)
• The pattern was ***set***.(p.555)
• Secondary aids to A.A., such as clubs or hospitals which require much property or administration, ought to be incorporated and so ***set*** apart that, if necessary, they can be freely discarded by the groups.(p.566)
• Since Dr. Silkworth's first endorsement of Alcoholics Anonymous, medical societies and physicians throughout the world have ***set*** their approval upon us.(p.571)

set-up

• My personality, from the time I can remember anything, was the perfect ***set-up*** for an alcoholic career.(p.400)
• But I did not feel a part of my family or a part of the ***set-up***.(p.401)
• This was an ideal ***set-up***.(p.426)

setback

• But this proved only a temporary ***setback***.(p.517)

sets

• This phenomenon, as we have suggested, may be the manifestation of an allergy which differentiates these people, and ***sets*** them apart as a distinct entity.(p.xxviii)
• Boredom ***sets*** up every retiree for two chief dangers: obesity and alcoholism.(p.330)

setting

• We have concluded to publish an anonymous volume ***setting*** forth the problem as we see it.(p.19)
• These observations would be academic and pointless if our friend never took the first drink, thereby ***setting*** the terrible cycle in motion.(p.23)
• Twenty-two years later, Doctor Bob told me that what I had done was like turning a switch and ***setting*** up a demand for more alcohol in my system.(p.195)

settle

• They are questions for each individual to ***settle*** for himself.(p.50)
• Cleaning up old scrapes, helping to ***settle*** family differences, explaining the disinherited son to his irate parents, lending money and securing jobs for each other, when justified -- these are everyday occurrences.(p.161)
• My wife traveled with me, but with a baby coming I decided to ***settle*** in a large city where I got a job with a commission agent which is a polite term for a handbook operator.(p.251)
• Strangely enough, I became acquainted with the "hilarious life" just at the time in my own life when I was beginning really to ***settle*** down to a common-sense, sane domesticity.(p.297)

settled

• I have had many men who had, for example, worked a period of months on some problem or business deal which was to be ***settled*** on a certain date, favorable to them.(p.xxvii)
• Then a mental fog ***settled*** down.(p.6)
• The story of how you and your wife ***settled*** your difficulties is worth any amount of criticism.(p.100)
• The alarming physical and mental symptoms, the deepening pall of remorse, depression and inferiority that ***settled*** down on our loved ones -- these things terrified and distracted us.(p.106)
• As we became subjects of King Alcohol, shivering denizens of his mad realm, the chilling vapor that is loneliness ***settled*** down.(p.151)
• When I got back to Germany I ***settled*** down to finish my apprenticeship, drinking the wine of the country as usual.(p.231)
• At this time, however, she had an opportunity to go to Salt Lake City on a new project for the government, but she did promise me that if I would curtail my drinking and buckle down to hard work she would give serious consideration to my latest proposal and maybe join me at a later date when I got ***settled***.(p.359)
• Proud of my little station and of my new bride I ***settled*** down to a happy married life.(p.361)
• All of them have since ***settled*** down to jobs and good marriages.(p.407)

seven

• At present, our membership is increasing at the rate of about ***seven*** per cent a year.(p.xx)
• ***Seven*** percent of the A.A.'s surveyed are less than 30 years of age -- among them, many in their teens.(p.xxii)
• We have then completed Step ***Seven***.(p.76)
• A year and six months later these three had succeeded with ***seven*** more.(p.159)
• I was born in a small New England village of about ***seven*** thousand souls.(p.171)
• Each of the ***seven*** times that I had left this hospital in the last six months, I had come out fully determined in my own mind that I would not get drunk again -- for at least six or eight months.(p.184)
• I can well remember sitting with ***seven*** dollars in my pocket, planning on giving my family a hundred or two hundred dollars, when I made it next year.(p.197)
• But I didn't do a thing about giving them any part of the ***seven*** bucks I had in my pocket.(p.197)
• There were only ***seven*** or eight people in the group before me and they all visited me during my period in the hospital.(p.208)
• Jackie arrived about ***seven*** in the evening and talked until three a.m.(p.239)
• I was the oldest in a family of ***seven***, and my father was an alcoholic.(p.261)
• I was sixteen when we were married and he was ***seven*** years older.(p.262)
• That was ***seven*** or eight years after we were married.(p.262)
• ***Seven*** years of work in this field brought an opportunity to affiliate myself actively with one of my clients, a fellow A.A.(p.284)
• The meeting consisted of perhaps eight or nine alcoholics and ***seven*** or eight wives.(p.291)
• I was being very cagey, because I knew that if I did take one or two, I might want to take five or six or ***seven*** or eight.(p.323)
• He may even read in a newspaper that one out of every ***seven*** drinkers will become alcoholic, but he rarely is told that it holds true for all ages -- or that the tolerance to alcohol (and other drugs) decreases steadily, year after year, in the bodies of all persons.(p.330)
• And the first thing you know I was lifted right out of the A.A. group, and I floated higher, and higher, and even higher, until I was way up on a pink cloud which is known as Pink ***Seven***, and I felt miserable again.(p.348)
• For some reason I can't remember, it finally dawned on me that I had a problem, and yet nobody was very critical about it except my family, and that was only because I decided, after ***seven*** years of marriage, that I would divorce my husband.(p.386)
• I'd packed more drinking into ***seven*** years than many a heavy drinker does in a lifetime.(p.429)
• To cut a long story short, I spent ***seven*** years and ten thousand dollars on my psychiatric adventure, and emerged in worse condition than ever.(p.434)
• In ***seven*** years the intervals between them decreased from eight months to ten days!(p.434)
• That was ***seven*** years ago -- and many A.A. meetings ago -- and I haven't had a drink during those ***seven*** years.(p.437)
• I wore those moccasins every night for the next ***seven*** years, until they wore out.(p.445)
• Finally after ***seven*** months, I decided to try it.(p.448)
• After I had been around A.A. for ***seven*** months, tapering off alcohol and pills, not finding the program working very well, I was finally able to say, "Okay, God.(p.448)
• That was over ***seven*** years ago, and thank God and A.A., I haven't had a drink since.(p.473)
• During these ***seven*** years a thing called the Twenty-four Hour Program --a gadget I used to think was only a snare to trap the newcomer -- has come to mean much to me, not only as regards my drinking but in the whole pattern of my life.(p.473)
• About ***seven*** that evening my sponsor walked in, Charlie G.(p.494)
• I spent about six or ***seven*** weeks in Sing Sing, and was finally sent off to Dannemora in the Adirondacks.(p.509)
• My serious drinking covered about ***seven*** years.(p.536)
• I am an only child, and when I was ***seven*** years old my parents separated very abruptly.(p.544)
• My reaction to this was identical in many respects to my reaction to my parents leaving me when I was ***seven***.(p.547)
• ***Seven*** -- Every A.A. group ought to be fully self-supporting, declining outside contributions.(p.564)

seventeen

• ***Seventeen*** stories may help you decide whether you are alcoholic; also, whether A.A. is for you.(p.167)
• This routine went on with few interruptions for ***seventeen*** years.(p.177)
• At ***seventeen*** I entered the University, really to satisfy my father who wanted me to study medicine there as he had.(p.241)
• He took his one hundred and ***seventeen*** dollars and let us go, and we proceeded.(p.264)
• The ***seventeen*** who now tell their experiences answer that question.(p.315)
• Therefore, these ***seventeen*** A.A.'s, and hundreds of thousands like them, have been saved years of infinite suffering.(p.315)
• Since I didn't do well in school, I quit and joined the Army at age ***seventeen***.(p.317)
• But they kept me there -- I was supposed to stay a month, but they only kept me there ***seventeen*** days.(p.387)
• I spent my last ***seventeen*** months in Wallkill, and it was there that I first got my introduction to A.A.(p.509)

seventeenth
- Because of this state of confusion and frustration I had hysterics on the ***seventeenth*** day for the first and only time in my life.(p.387)

seventh
- For my ***seventh*** A.A. birthday, my program-oriented, Al-Anon wife had my moccasins bronzed.(p.445)

seventieth
- It was a month beyond my ***seventieth*** birthday.(p.333)

seventy
- This doctor had imparted his knowledge to just a few other men at that time -- not more than four or five -- they now number more than ***seventy*** persons.(p.235)
- Two years later, a month beyond age ***seventy***, I was crying for help from A.A.(p.327)

several
- So far, upon the total problem of ***several*** million actual and potential alcoholics in the world, we have made only a scratch.(p.xx)
- The exercise of an option brought in more money, leaving us with a profit of ***several*** thousand dollars for that year.(p.3)
- My friends had dropped ***several*** million since ten o'clock -- so what?(p.4)
- He tried to regulate his drinking for a while, making ***several*** trips to the hospital meantime.(p.32)
- ***Several*** of our crowd, men of thirty or less, had been drinking only a few years, but they found themselves as helpless as those who had been drinking twenty years.(p.33)
- Luck then deserts him and he is slightly injured ***several*** times in succession.(p.38)
- I remember having ***several*** more that night and plenty the next morning.(p.41)
- The driver escorted me about for ***several*** days.(p.41)
- It meant I would have to throw ***several*** lifelong conceptions out of the window.(p.42)
- He probably has ***several*** alcoholics among his own acquaintances.(p.112)
- Or you may already have had it ***several*** times.(p.116)
- I had warned him ***several*** times that he had but one more chance.(p.136)
- We think this method of approach will accomplish ***several*** things.(p.148)
- Suppose now that through you ***several*** families have adopted this way of life.(p.153)
- After ***several*** failures to find others, a fourth turned up.(p.158)
- I used also to put it up in four ounce bottles and stick ***several*** in my stocking tops.(p.177)
- This dry spell lasted for about three weeks; then I went to Atlantic City to attend ***several*** days' meeting of a national society of which I was a member.(p.179)
- I drank all the scotch they had on the train and bought ***several*** quarts on my way to the hotel.(p.179)
- As a draftsman, I worked for ***several*** large companies and gained a variety of experience.(p.211)
- Had anyone undertaken to explain to me what the A.A. movement was, what its real function was, I probably would have been set back ***several*** years and I doubt if I would have survived at all.(p.216)
- I had attended ***several*** of these meetings before I discovered that all those who were there were not alcoholics.(p.218)
- Naturally, in spite of my good intentions, in spite of my protected life behind sanitarium walls, I ***several*** times got drunk, and was astounded . . . and badly shaken.(p.227)
- And so on and on, for ***several*** weeks, while I grudgingly plowed through some more of the offending book, and felt more and more hopeless about myself.(p.227)
- Sometimes, after sobering up after a bout of ***several*** weeks, I would righteously resolve to quit.(p.233)
- After a couple of days in dollar hotels and one night in the pokey, I finally landed on my mother's doorstep -- shaking apart, with ***several*** days' beard and, of course, broke as usual.(p.238)
- With the war over, and back in Baltimore with the folks, there were ***several*** small jobs for three years and then I went to work soliciting as one of the first ten employees of a new national finance company.(p.242)
- Evidently I had gone right back to the movie with a bottle, stayed there ***several*** hours and started home with no recollection of what had happened.(p.244)
- My wife made ***several*** attempts to get me to stop and I had the usual visits from persons who would always ask me "Why?" -- as if I knew!(p.254)
- I had been drinking heavily from one state of semi-coma to another and it was ***several*** days before I got "defogged," but subconsciously I was in earnest about wanting to quit liquor forever.(p.258)
- I confined drinking to weekends, and drank normally in college and for ***several*** years thereafter.(p.287)
- ***Several*** months later dad was back in Chicago to pick me up again, but this time my attitude was entirely different.(p.289)
- I made ***several*** decisions at that time.(p.292)
- I spent ***several*** days with him, but I did not feel adequate to pass the program on to him alone.(p.294)
- The parties waxed more liquid and hilarious as time went on, and eventually I discovered that a little shot of liquor now and then between beers had the tendency to put me in a whacky mood much quicker than having to down ***several*** quarts of beer to obtain the same effect.(p.298)
- However, as there happened to be ***several*** saloons within that distance, I didn't find it necessary to patronize the same place each evening.(p.298)
- I really worked for ***several*** weeks, and having had a fairly wide acquaintance with the dealer trade, it was not difficult for me to line up enough of them to give me a very substantial volume of business with a minimum of effort.(p.300)
- I have omitted details of transgressions that I made when drunk for ***several*** reasons.(p.301)
- Finally, an old business acquaintance of mine, whom I hadn't seen for ***several*** years offered me a job.(p.301)
- After being in the hospital for ***several*** days, a plan of living was outlined to me.(p.302)
- I do recall lying on a cold cement floor and shredding into little bits ***several*** pieces of stolen identification cards, and washing my face in the toilet bowl trying to sober up, and screaming hysterically while clinging to bars too high to see out of, and cursing everyone that came near me.(p.354)
- "Sure, I've seen you tight ***several*** times, but you're no alcoholic!"(p.356)
- I had every advantage a child could have, private schools (***several*** of them), dancing schools, two colleges, coon skin coats, automobiles, a listing in the social register and all the rest.(p.357)
- I was working for a Chicago firm that represented ***several*** large radio stations.(p.358)
- After ***several*** months of acquaintance I asked her to marry me, but was politely refused.(p.359)
- It took me three psychoanalysts and ***several*** years in A.A. to really get this through my head.(p.401)
- I went to ***several*** Village bars, and drank cokes or tea.(p.414)
- My life there was a nightmare of periodic binges on alcohol and pills, adultery, unhappy hours at the dental office, seeing my wife give birth to our second child and have ***several*** miscarriages, living in a turbulent household, and making continual attempts to be the respectable dentist, husband, father, and community leader.(p.419)
- I served time in four penitentiaries and ***several*** prison camps, including a maximum-security camp.(p.457)
- There, I received ***several*** soda crackers and water daily, and before I could have my third-day meal (again the only meal in ten days), I had to drink a glass of castor oil or mineral oil, depending on the cruelty of the person who was doing the dispensing.(p.459)
- I had been in ***several*** hospitals for alcoholism.(p.460)
- We had ***several*** fights and on one or two occasions I struck her with my fist.(p.491)
- He came back ***several*** times.(p.491)
- I approached ***several*** ministers and all of them thought it was a very good idea, but they never relinquished any space.(p.495)
- Within a month, the police, the hospital authorities, ***several*** kind strangers, most of my friends, all of my close relatives, and a few adepts at rolling a drunk and removing his wrist watch and wallet had been involved.(p.532)
- There were ***several*** others.(p.532)
- If the listener were drunk enough, the lecture might go on through ***several*** martinis, which I was glad to pay for.(p.537)

severe
- We often need it to carry green recruits through a ***severe*** hangover.(p.102)
- This may seem ***severe***, but it is usually the best course.(p.142)
- These things were carried out in moments of less ***severe*** hangover or short stretches on the wagon.(p.409)
- I had ***severe*** nosebleeds.(p.558)

severely
- But insist that if he is ***severely*** afflicted, there may be little chance he can recover by himself.(p.92)
- Then we were ***severely*** criticized by our husband's parents for desertion.(p.106)

sex
- In most cases it was found that our self-esteem, our pocketbooks, our ambitions, our personal relationships (including ***sex***) were hurt or threatened.(p.64)
- Was it our self-esteem, our security, our ambitions, our personal, or ***sex*** relations, which had been interfered with?(p.65)
- ***Sex*** relations.(p.65)
- ***Sex*** relations.(p.65)
- Personal ***sex*** relations.(p.65)
- Now about ***sex***.(p.68)
- One set of voices cry that ***sex*** is a lust of our lower nature, a base necessity of procreation.(p.68)
- Then we have the voices who cry for ***sex*** and more ***sex***; who bewail the institution of marriage; who think that most of the troubles of the race are traceable to ***sex*** causes.(p.69)
- We do not want to be the arbiter of anyone's ***sex*** conduct.(p.69)
- We all have ***sex*** problems.(p.69)
- In this way we tried to shape a sane and sound ideal for our future ***sex*** life.(p.69)
- We remembered always that our ***sex*** powers were God-given and therefore good, neither to be used lightly or selfishly nor to be despised and loathed.(p.69)
- In other words, we treat ***sex*** as we would any other problem.(p.69)
- God alone can judge our ***sex*** situation.(p.69)
- We realize that some people are as fanatical about ***sex*** as others are loose.(p.70)
- To sum up about ***sex***: We earnestly pray for the right ideal, for guidance in each questionable situation, for sanity, and for the strength to do the right thing.(p.70)
- If ***sex*** is very troublesome, we throw ourselves the harder into helping others.(p.70)
- But drinking does complicate ***sex*** relations in the home.(p.81)
- A word about ***sex*** relations.(p.134)
- He further explained that alcohol was no respecter of ***sex*** or background, but that most of the alcoholics he had encountered had better than average minds and abilities.(p.308)
- Another thing that mother drilled into me was a very Puritanical point of view as to ***sex*** relations and as to motherhood and womanhood.(p.483)
- About then too, I realized that my point of view on the opposite ***sex*** wasn't entirely like that of most of the boys I knew.(p.484)

sexually
- Alcohol is so ***sexually*** stimulating to some men that they have over-indulged.(p.134)

sexy
- And we usually have some kind of grimy sweater that we think we look ***sexy*** in, even if we weigh ninety-five pounds soaking wet and are not wearing a bra.(p.479)

shackled
- During the first six months of 1935, I was hospitalized eight times for intoxication and ***shackled*** to the bed two or three days before I even knew where I was.(p.184)

shackles
- Retirement rids the potential alcoholic of many ***shackles***.(p.329)
- ***Shackles*** were permanently affixed to my ankles.(p.460)
- There is really nothing to dressing with chains and ***shackles*** on, once you learn the technique of pulling inside-out pants through the ***shackles***.(p.460)

shadow
- It melted the icy intellectual mountain in whose ***shadow*** I had lived and shivered many years.(p.12)
- The others must be convinced of his new status beyond the ***shadow*** of a doubt.(p.135)
- I opened my eyes again and a ***shadow*** fell across the bed.(p.422)

shadowy
- I have a ***shadowy*** recollection of being in an airplane bound for New York, and of finding a friendly taxicab driver at the landing field instead of my wife.(p.41)

shake
- Doctors may ***shake*** their heads and advise you to have him committed.(p.110)

• Of an evening, you can go on a mild bender, get up in the morning, ***shake*** your head and go to business.(p.139)
• I had never had the physical courage to ***shake*** it out before.(p.415)

shaken
• No later vicissitude has ***shaken*** it.(p.56)
• My physical health was badly ***shaken***, but I began to pick up.(p.220)
• And I remembered the creeping horror of the interminable night, in which I slept for short spells and woke up dripping with cold sweat and ***shaken*** with utter despair, to drink hastily from my bottle and mercifully pass out again, "You're mad, you're mad, you're mad!" pounded through my brain with each returning ray of consciousness, and I drowned the refrain with drink.(p.224)
• Naturally, in spite of my good intentions, in spite of my protected life behind sanitarium walls, I several times got drunk, and was astounded . . . and badly ***shaken***.(p.227)
• Bill was tall, grey haired, with the kind of asymmetrical good looks and pleasant easy manner that inspire confidence in the ***shaken*** and afraid.(p.413)

shakes
• The ***shakes*** grew worse and I looked at my watch -- six o'clock.(p.223)
• One morning after a terrific drinking bout, I was in a little bar near our house, and I shook so that I was very much ashamed, because I was getting the ***shakes*** worse and worse.(p.266)
• I was drinking to keep away the ***shakes***, drinking to keep away those little men and those strange voices and the organ music that comes out of the walls.(p.514)
• When I awoke in the middle of the night with ***shakes*** and sweats and fears, I would hear my wife weeping quietly in bed beside me.(p.558)

Shakespeare
• I had writing ambitions, and nothing would do but that I'd write like ***Shakespeare***.(p.400)
• I only saw that I had not become Mrs. ***Shakespeare***.(p.403)
• The glittering society belle, the modern ***Shakespeare***, the happy wife, the loving and beloved.(p.411)
• I have achieved the inner confidence to write quite unlike ***Shakespeare***, and I have sold a good deal of what I've written.(p.416)
• ***Shakespeare*** said, "All the world's a stage, all the men and women merely players."(p.449)

shaking
• This went on endlessly, and I began to waken very early in the morning ***shaking*** violently.(p.5)
• In fact, the last three years of my drinking was a routine of barbiturates in the morning, so that I could stop ***shaking*** enough to shave, and then alcohol beginning about four-thirty or five o'clock, with a struggle not to take a drink at noon or during the day, because I had the idea that if I took one drink, I would smell as though I had had a pint.(p.217)
• Cold chills started chasing up and down my spine; my teeth were chattering; my hands were ***shaking*** so I tucked them under me to keep them from flying away.(p.222)
• After a couple of days in dollar hotels and one night in the pokey, I finally landed on my mother's doorstep -- ***shaking*** apart, with several days' beard and, of course, broke as usual.(p.238)
• No matter how often I had gone into and come out of alcoholic lows during the day, the pattern bounced me out of bed each night about 2:00 a.m., ***shaking*** and hurting in the agitation that always follows a drug's sedation.(p.332)
• I was ***shaking*** so, I asked my husband to write the letter for me, but he said no.(p.392)
• I spent the time in a nearby tavern, was loaded on the ship, went to sleep before take-off, and the next thing I knew someone was ***shaking*** me and telling me we were over San Diego.(p.428)

shaky
• This time he was quite ***shaky***.(p.40)
• But if you are ***shaky***, you had better work with another alcoholic instead!(p.102)
• She tried reasoning with me, endeavored to work out various drinking schedules, in fact all the tricks were practised faithfully for a short time somewhere along my ***shaky*** road to unhappiness.(p.361)
• So I wrote this letter in very ***shaky*** handwriting, and in just one week came back a letter with A.A. literature from New York.(p.392)

shall
• Very earnestly we ask the press also, to observe this request, for otherwise we ***shall*** be greatly handicapped.(p.xiii)
• We ***shall*** be interested to hear from those who are getting results from this book, particularly from those who have commenced work with other alcoholics.(p.xiv)
• In all probability, we ***shall*** never be able to touch more than a fair fraction of the alcohol problem in all its ramifications.(p.xxi)
• How then ***shall*** we present that which has been so freely given us?(p.19)
• We ***shall*** bring to the task our combined experience and knowledge.(p.19)
• We ***shall*** do our utmost to achieve that ideal.(p.19)
• We ***shall*** tell you what we have done.(p.20)
• If these thoughts occur, they are hazy and readily supplanted with the old threadbare idea that this time we ***shall*** handle ourselves like other people.(p.24)
• How then ***shall*** we help our readers determine, to their own satisfaction, whether they are one of us?(p.34)
• So we ***shall*** describe some of the mental states that precede a relapse into drinking, for obviously this is the crux of the problem.(p.35)
• Our first example is a friend we ***shall*** call Jim.(p.35)
• Having made our personal inventory, what ***shall*** we do about it?(p.72)
• Carefully reading the first five proposals we ask if we have omitted anything, for we are building an arch through which we ***shall*** walk a free man at last.(p.75)
• We are sorry for what we have done and, God willing, it ***shall*** not be repeated.(p.81)
• Some day we hope that Alcoholics Anonymous will help the public to a better realization of the gravity of the alcoholic problem, but we ***shall*** be of little use if our attitude is one of bitterness or hostility.(p.103)
• His case presents additional questions which we ***shall*** try to answer for you.(p.110)
• But am I to be consigned to a life where I ***shall*** be stupid, boring and glum, like some righteous people I see?(p.152)
• As we ***shall*** see, he now means a great deal to his community, and the major liabilities of thirty years of hard drinking have been repaired in four.(p.156)
• We ***shall*** be with you in the Fellowship of the Spirit, and you will surely meet some of us as you trudge the Road of Happy Destiny.(p.164)
• That I ***shall*** never forget.(p.208)
• They told Annabelle to take me under her wing, and I ***shall*** never forget how she sort of curled up her nose and said, "They tell me you drink too."(p.269)
• Finally, and I ***shall*** never know how much later it was, one clear thought came to me: Try prayer.(p.280)
• It is undoubtedly too soon for me to say how much of a success I ***shall*** be as a husband in time to come.(p.286)
• And over my A.A. years I have made many real, honest, sincere friendships that I ***shall*** always cherish.(p.296)
• The last day of my drinking career, I drank twenty-two of them between ten and twelve a.m. and I ***shall*** never know how many more followed them until I was poured into bed that night.(p.298)
• Why he bothered with me as long as he did I ***shall*** never know, for he knew there was no answer for me in medicine and he, like all doctors of his day, had been taught that the alcoholic was incurable and should be ignored.(p.307)
• I must get out of the room or I ***shall*** jump out of the window.(p.501)
• I ***shall*** learn this after some more explosions.(p.506)
• I ***shall*** not drink until I get back to the apartment.(p.506)
• Then I ***shall*** lock myself in and read.(p.506)
• And as I read, I ***shall*** take little drinks at long intervals.(p.506)
• I ***shall*** get myself "mellow" and stay that way.(p.506)
• I learn that honesty is truth, and that truth ***shall*** make us free!(p.507)
• I ask the forgiveness of the reader; and from now on I ***shall*** try to write with the humility I honestly pray for.)(p.536)
• This to the end that our great blessings may never spoil us; that we ***shall*** forever live in thankful contemplation of Him who presides over us all.(p.568)
• If we do not do so, we ***shall*** stand convicted of emotional sterility and of having lost the faith that moves mountains, without which medicine can do little."(p.571)

shambles
• Until I reached A.A. my life was a ***shambles***; I was a mess, and I made everybody near and dear to me miserable.(p.400)
• As the sober days grew into sober months and then into sober years, a new and beautiful life began to emerge from the ***shambles*** of my former existence.(p.559)

shame
• Heartsickness, ***shame***, and fear, fear bordering on panic, and no complete escape any longer except in oblivion.(p.306)
• At one time, the admission that I was and am an alcoholic meant ***shame***, defeat, and failure to me.(p.335)
• But in the light of the new understanding that I have found in A.A., I have been able to interpret that defeat, and that failure, and that ***shame***, as seeds of victory.(p.335)
• I have told you some of the funny things, but not much of the ***shame*** and degradation.(p.390)
• I experienced my first real guilt and ***shame***.(p.404)
• I woke up filled with secret guilt and ***shame***.(p.407)
• In part, it was a feeling of intense ***shame*** at having to leave the Army during the war, but mostly it was resentment that this kind of thing should happen to me for, strange as it may seem, up to then I still thought I could control drinking.(p.521)
• It became more and more necessary to escape from myself, for my remorse and ***shame*** and humiliation when I was sober were almost unbearable.(p.547)
• With deep ***shame*** came the knowledge too that I had lived with no sense of social obligation nor had I known the meaning of moral responsibility to my fellow men.(p.549)

shamed
• Frightened and ***shamed***, I refused, and sobered up temporarily.(p.411)

shameful
• Now and then the family will be plagued by spectres from the past, for the drinking career of almost every alcoholic has been marked by escapades, funny, humiliating, ***shameful*** or tragic.(p.123)

Shane
• One night, I was struck with the memory of a line Alan Ladd used in "***Shane***," a movie that I'd worked on.(p.333)

shape
• Some are just now taking ***shape*** in Asia.(p.xv)
• A second small group had promptly taken ***shape*** at New York.(p.xvii)
• In this way we tried to ***shape*** a sane and sound ideal for our future sex life.(p.69)
• At three-thirty the next morning, I was in Champlain Street Station, in jail for driving while intoxicated and insulting an officer; and the suit of which I was so proud was in such ***shape*** that the turnkey had to get me a pair of trousers to go into court in the next morning.(p.201)
• And we stood there for twenty minutes, telling each other how much better we were, how much better we looked, how much better off we were financially, mentally, physically, morally, and in every way, ***shape*** and manner.(p.201)
• In fact I had been in very good ***shape*** at one o'clock -- feeling no pain.(p.223)
• They phoned my husband that I was in jail and in such terrible ***shape*** that they didn't know what I would do to myself; and they realized that jail was no place for me, but that he was to wait a while before he got me, because at the time they called him to come over for me I was beating a tin cup against the wall.(p.390)
• The man is in bad mental ***shape*** certainly.(p.503)
• Finances are in bad ***shape***.(p.506)
• Despite my wife's entreaties to take it easy that day, I arrived home in bad ***shape***.(p.557)

shapeless
• My tweed suit, once a very good one, was ***shapeless*** and baggy with bare places worn in the elbows from leaning on the bar.(p.411)

share
• I was to ***share*** generously in the profits.(p.5)
• He may not ***share*** your enthusiasm, but he is practically sure to read the book and he may go for the program at once.(p.113)
• We can ***share*** in the laughter and tears of our many friends, and most important, we can ***share*** our A.A. way of life and are given a daily opportunity to help others.(p.249)
• I have had my ***share*** of problems, heartaches and disappointments, because that is life, but also I have known a great deal of joy, and a peace that is the handmaiden of an inner freedom, I have a wealth of friends and, with my A.A. friends, an unusual quality of fellowship.(p.312)

shared
• The feeling of having ***shared*** in a common peril is one element in the powerful cement which

binds us.(p.17)
• We have ***shared*** his honest doubt and prejudice.(p.45)
• They ***shared*** their homes, their slender resources, and gladly devoted their spare hours to fellow-sufferers.(p.159)
• (My addiction bloomed within a small apartment I ***shared*** with my wife, a heart patient.)(p.329)

sharing
• Each day, somewhere in the world, recovery begins when one alcoholic talks with another alcoholic, ***sharing*** experience, strength, and hope.(p.xxii)
• It may mean ***sharing*** your money and your home, counseling frantic wives and relatives, innumerable trips to police courts, sanitariums, hospitals, jails and asylums.(p.97)
• And, as the years go by, working together, ***sharing*** our experiences with one another, and also ***sharing*** a mutual trust, understanding and love – without strings, without obligation – we acquire relationships that are unique and priceless.(p.312)
• I had a family to be proud of, actively ***sharing*** in the responsibilities of good citizenship.(p.374)
• Age and the law were still against me, but laws were not as strictly enforced in those days as they are now, and I discovered that as long as I had the green blood, there was always a way to get alcohol, either from a nondiscriminatory bartender or from an older friend who would be glad to purchase the joy juice for the privilege of ***sharing*** it.(p.397)
• He has so much understanding, a real asset in ***sharing*** sobriety.(p.481)
• It has taught me that I can best keep my sobriety by ***sharing*** it out with others; that I must bring that sobriety to others who need it, in my own interest.(p.524)
• By learning -- through practicing the Twelve Steps and through ***sharing*** at meetings -- how to cope with the problems that we looked to booze to solve, back in our drinking days.(p.560)

Sharkey's
• Tom ***Sharkey's*** brawling bar on 14th Street and the famous wine-room at the back were headquarters for me.(p.251)
• In my mind's eye I saw Broadway again and Tom ***Sharkey's*** bar; the roar of the subway was in my ears.(p.252)

sharp
• My aunt had ***sharp*** words for me about drinking.(p.474)

shattering
• And the contrast was pretty ***shattering***.(p.225)
• I underwent a ***shattering*** nervous breakdown.(p.275)
• A little more than fifteen years ago, through a long and calamitous series of ***shattering*** experiences, I found myself being helplessly propelled toward total destruction.(p.304)
• Most had taken ***shattering*** losses on nearly every front of life.(p.455)

shave
• I would reach over and get this and take a shot and in a few moments get up and take another, ***shave*** and eat my breakfast, slip a half pint of liquor in my hip pocket, and go on to school.(p.183)
• In fact, the last three years of my drinking was a routine of barbiturates in the morning, so that I could stop shaking enough to ***shave***, and then alcohol beginning about four-thirty or five o'clock, with a struggle not to take a drink at noon or during the day, because I had the idea that if I took one drink, I would smell as though I had had a pint.(p.217)
• I took two or three drinks so my eyes could focus, and I could see that horrible picture of the awful drunk on the first page; he couldn't get the drink to his mouth, he had a towel around his hand and he needed a ***shave***.(p.391)

Shaw
• Alas for us men toward whom ***Shaw*** hurled his cry, "Must a Christ be crucified in every generation for the benefit of those who have no imagination?"(p.536)

shed
• At that particular time, the boys put me on a shutter and took me out to the ***shed***, and I lay in the car while they enjoyed their banquet.(p.195)

shedding
• Slowly, my life seemed to unfold before me, ***shedding*** insights on childhood resentments, jealousies, and fears that had mushroomed in adulthood, and also on the self-pity that I had wallowed in at every opportunity.(p.371)

sheer
• This was drinking in ***sheer*** desperation, alone and locked behind my own door.(p.306)
• There was a bar, and what I tasted spelled ***sheer*** heaven.(p.328)
• Out of ***sheer*** despair, she called for help.(p.353)

sheet
• Following a big drunk on that ***sheet***, where I was doing leg-work and rewrite, a feeling of nostalgia made me buy a ticket for Liverpool and I returned to Britain.(p.252)

shelf
• Taking this book down from our ***shelf*** we turn to the page which contains the twelve steps.(p.75)
• I used to think I was cowardly because when things came out pertaining to the program that troubled me, I said to her many times, "Annie, am I being a coward because I lay those things away on the ***shelf*** and skip it?"(p.273)

shelter
• Be certain he will be welcomed by your family, and that he is not trying to impose upon you for money, connections, or ***shelter***.(p.96)
• The men who cry for money and ***shelter*** before conquering alcohol, are on the wrong track.(p.98)
• Seeing much of each other, scarce an evening passed that someone's home did not ***shelter*** a little gathering of men and women, happy in their release, and constantly thinking how they might present their discovery to some newcomer.(p.159)
• We did, and spent a month boozing it up, popping pills, and smoking marijuana; taking ***shelter*** where we could, which included a veterinary hospital one night; accepting meals from anyone; actually begging; stealing anything we were in need of, which was about everything.(p.354)

sheltered
• My parents died, both in the same year, leaving me, a ***sheltered*** and somewhat immature man, on my own.(p.277)

shelves
• The apartment was charming; the ***shelves*** were full of books, many of which I myself owned.(p.413)

sheriff
• In the long ago past I used to start at the top as president or treasurer and end up with the ***sheriff*** breathing down my neck.(p.284)
• They summoned the fire department and the ***sheriff***.(p.424)
• The ***sheriff*** bade us goodbye very happily.(p.424)

sheriffs
• The bill collectors, the ***sheriffs***, the angry taxi drivers, the policemen, the bums, the pals, and even the ladies they sometimes brought home – our husbands thought we were so inhospitable.(p.106)

sherry
• There was a glass of ***sherry*** at my place.(p.285)
• In fact, I couldn't have told you the difference between ***sherry*** and brandy.(p.518)
• After my very first drink – a tiny glass of ***sherry*** my father gave me to celebrate the New Year when I was thirteen -- I went up to bed, dizzy with exhilaration and excitement, and I prayed I wouldn't drink any more!(p.554)

shield
• In our belief any scheme of combating alcoholism which proposes to ***shield*** the sick man from temptation is doomed to failure.(p.101)
• If the alcoholic tries to ***shield*** himself he may succeed for a time, but he usually winds up with a bigger explosion than ever.(p.101)
• We never, never try to arrange a man's life so as to ***shield*** him from temptation.(p.120)

shielded
• He will appreciate knowing you are not bothering your head about him, that you are not suspicious nor are you trying to run his life so he will be ***shielded*** from temptation to drink.(p.146)

shifted
• I blinked slowly as I ***shifted*** my gaze to my arms.(p.422)

shine
• "Let your light so ***shine*** before men that they may see your good works –."(p.497)

shins
• In the first year there were episodes such as kicking Priscilla in the ***shins***, getting the lock changed on the desk in the A.A. Club, because I, as secretary, didn't want the Intergroup secretary "interfering," and taking an older woman member out to lunch for the express purpose of informing her that she was "a phony."(p.416)

ship
• Near you, alcoholics are dying helplessly like people in a sinking ***ship***.(p.152)
• The short tours could be taken care of by sneaking enough whiskey aboard ***ship*** so that it could be rationed out until another supply could be laid in.(p.398)
• I was supposed to come home on a troop ***ship***, but I talked the base commander into flying me home.(p.428)
• I spent the time in a nearby tavern, was loaded on the ***ship***, went to sleep before take-off, and the next thing I knew someone was shaking me and telling me we were over San Diego.(p.428)
• Our courtship was mainly in bars and night spots when my ***ship*** was in New York.(p.555)

ship's
• Unlike the feelings of the ***ship's*** passengers, however, our joy in escape from disaster does not subside as we go our individual ways.(p.17)

shipped
• Men who had liquor ***shipped*** in from Boston or New York by express were looked upon with great distrust and disfavor by most of the good townspeople.(p.171)
• I landed him and ***shipped*** him by train to Akron, with a pint of whiskey in his pocket to keep him from wanting to get off the train in Toledo!(p.282)
• While there, two or three more "cash customers" (as Dr. Bob used to call them -- probably because they had so little cash) were ***shipped*** in to us from Detroit.(p.282)
• I buttonholed him after dinner and gave him a few tips on how to run his colony better and the result of that was about a fortnight or so later I was ***shipped*** back to my regiment.(p.520)
• At the end of that time, they ***shipped*** me back to my regiment again.(p.520)
• I was there for another couple of months and then, after a few more adventures in the East, I was ***shipped*** home.(p.521)

shipping
• Then Hitler's war broke out, and again, I was given a really important job on the Suez Canal, dealing with military ***shipping***.(p.520)

shipwreck
• We are like the passengers of a great liner the moment after rescue from ***shipwreck*** when camaraderie, joyousness and democracy pervade the vessel from steerage to Captain's table.(p.17)

shirt
• I had white trousers on, white shoes and a white ***shirt*** that was streaked with blood.(p.204)
• During three years in A.A., I haven't lost so much as one ***shirt***.(p.372)

shirts
• So I created a job for myself selling women's hosiery and men's made-to-order ***shirts***.(p.282)
• I lost a lot of ***shirts*** that way, and sometimes I was minus a whole wash.(p.371)
• Before too long, my husband (who seemed to prefer his ***shirts*** dirty) put his foot down, declaring that our family might have the cleanest clothes in town, but that I hadn't been out of the same old dirty slacks and blouse for a week.(p.371)

shiver
• With a ***shiver***, he turned away and walked down the lobby to the church directory.(p.154)

shivered
• It melted the icy intellectual mountain in whose shadow I had lived and ***shivered*** many years.(p.12)

shivering
• As we became subjects of King Alcohol, ***shivering*** denizens of his mad realm, the chilling vapor that is loneliness settled down.(p.151)
• I choose to believe that the Power greater than ourselves we ask for help, wrapped my ***shivering*** body in loving warmth and strength which has never left me.(p.541)

shock
• I well remember the ***shock*** I received when a prominent doctor in Chicago told me of cases where pressure of the spinal fluid actually ruptured the brain.(p.140)
• But the percentages started tobogganing, and it was often a ***shock*** to read over some of the pages when sober.(p.331)
• It was a ***shock*** of course, but I promised to stop and she returned.(p.377)
• At first it was a ***shock*** to realize I was an alcoholic, but the realization that there was hope made it easier.(p.379)
• It is a ***shock***.(p.504)

shocked

- I was ***shocked***, but interested.(p.10)
- I suppose some would be ***shocked*** at our seeming worldliness and levity.(p.16)
- Outsiders are sometimes ***shocked*** when we burst into merriment over a seemingly tragic experience out of the past.(p.132)
- He might be ***shocked*** if he knew how much alcoholism is costing his organization a year.(p.149)
- They were deeply religious people, much ***shocked*** by their son's refusal to have anything to do with the church.(p.158)
- I was kind of ***shocked*** about anybody talking about themselves the way he did, and my impression was that the guy was a little "touched."(p.216)

shocking

- In this connection, can you remain undisturbed if the man proceeds to tell you ***shocking*** things?(p.145)

shockingly

- But he is yet a long way from making good to the wife or parents whom for years he has so ***shockingly*** treated.(p.82)

shoes

- I had white trousers on, white ***shoes*** and a white shirt that was streaked with blood.(p.204)
- Mother would take me in only if I would stay locked in a small storeroom and give her my clothes and ***shoes***.(p.238)
- They went into a huddle and dad explained that he simply took my pants, ***shoes*** and money away, so that I could get no liquor and had to sober up.(p.288)
- After finding every bottle that I had hidden around the apartment, she took away my pants, my ***shoes***, my money and my keys, threw them under the bed in the back bedroom and slip-locked our door.(p.288)
- He planted many seeds, and it will be many moons before another rises to walk in his ***shoes***."(p.476)
- Our ***shoes*** are not better than the average hobo's, and if we are fortunate enough to have a pair of stockings on, nobody notices the runs in them, because of our dazzling beauty and our dirty feet.(p.479)
- I got out of that bill one pair of ***shoes***, and the rest of that money was blown.(p.493)
- But I don't remember that any of them ever went to sleep in joints and woke up with no ***shoes*** on in the winter, or fell out of chairs.(p.527)
- Once I started drinking, I didn't care that the rent wasn't paid, or that there was no food in the house, or that my boys needed ***shoes***.(p.527)

shone

- Perhaps the single flicker of decency that ***shone*** through the fog of my drinking days was a clumsy affection for my two children, a boy and a girl.(p.437)

shook

- Finally he ***shook*** his head saying, "Something has happened to you I don't understand.(p.14)
- We ***shook*** hands, and he hung onto my hand for a moment and said, "Tell you what I'll do for old times sake.(p.201)
- One morning after a terrific drinking bout, I was in a little bar near our house, and I ***shook*** so that I was very much ashamed, because I was getting the shakes worse and worse.(p.266)
- I returned the book to my analyst and ***shook*** my head.(p.412)

shoot

- To go north into the empty pine country and ***shoot*** myself, or to go south in the faint hope that a bunch of strangers might help me with my drinking problem.(p.278)
- So I went down to him quite a few times a month and had him ***shoot*** me full of the stuff; and then I went across the street to a little drug store to take a glass of beer or two beers, and then stopped at the liquor store to get myself a pint and go home.(p.389)

shooting

- So I immediately started taking and ***shooting*** pep pills.(p.442)
- For the leveling-off process, I just loved intravenous Demerol, but I found it hard to practice good medicine while ***shooting*** morphine.(p.442)

shop

- In the basement were to be dry-cleaning facilities, a barbershop, a pool room, a grocery ***shop*** and everything.(p.198)
- I was eased out of the business I had founded and was reduced to doing general upholstery in a small ***shop*** at the back of my house.(p.233)
- I had them hidden away in the house and all over my ***shop*** in careful concealment.(p.233)
- My last venture, a book ***shop***, was hastened to closed doors by my steady intoxication.(p.255)
- Some days later, after he had been discharged, a stranger came into my ***shop*** in the nearby town.(p.257)
- With this specialized training, and a liberal business education in the school of hard knocks, I was able to set up ***shop*** some two years later as an independent accountant.(p.284)
- I borrowed five hundred dollars from the bank and three hundred from the loan ***shop***, and I drank that up pretty fast.(p.490)
- I went to this friend's ***shop*** to repair his electrical outlet and I noticed this lady.(p.493)
- When I arrived at The Country ***Shop***, which was a restaurant where they met in Dublin, I found about thirty-five or forty people in the room.(p.524)

shopkeeper

- Since it was wartime, I explained to the somewhat startled ***shopkeeper*** that I had many friends in the service whom I was remembering with a watch.(p.532)

shops

- From far away, as if in a delirium, I heard my own voice — calling someone "Dorothy," talking of dress ***shops***, of jobs . . . the words came clearer . . . this sound of my own voice frightened me as it came closer . . . and suddenly, there I was, talking of I knew not what, to someone I'd never seen before this very moment.(p.222)

shore

- Some of us had already walked far over the Bridge of Reason toward the desired ***shore*** of faith.(p.53)
- He had stepped from bridge to ***shore***.(p.56)
- Pearl Harbor was a breeze of nine months, a gay Hawaiian paradise, drinking under the palms, listening to the surf beat on the ***shore***, a bottle of whiskey near at hand.(p.426)
- I was escorted back to San Diego next morning -- by the ***Shore*** Patrol, but I was discharged on schedule.(p.428)

short

- Nevertheless, he was drunk in a ***short*** time.(p.26)
- Commencing to drink after a period of sobriety, we are in a ***short*** time as bad as ever.(p.33)
- We needed to ask ourselves but one ***short*** question.(p.47)
- This ***short*** word somehow touches about every aspect of our lives.(p.67)
- Suppose we fall ***short*** of the chosen ideal and stumble?(p.70)
- We may be ***short*** in our accounts and unable to make good.(p.78)
- Today's life is measured against that of other years and, when it falls ***short***, the family may be unhappy.(p.123)
- As each member of a resentful family begins to see his ***short*** comings and admits them to the others, he lays a basis for helpful discussion.(p.127)
- And we, who have imposed on the best of employers, can scarcely blame them if they have been ***short*** with us.(p.138)
- Only a few knew of it at first but, within a ***short*** time, it was billboarded throughout the entire company.(p.145)
- I drank with moderation at first, but it took me only a relatively ***short*** time to drift back into the old habits which had wound up so disastrously before.(p.175)
- All the other people that had talked to me wanted to help me, and my pride prevented me from listening to them, and caused only resentment on my part, but I felt as if I would be a real stinker if I did not listen to a couple of fellows for a ***short*** time, if that would cure them.(p.185)
- And I remembered the creeping horror of the interminable night, in which I slept for ***short*** spells and woke up dripping with cold sweat and shaken with utter despair, to drink hastily from my bottle and mercifully pass out again, "You're mad, you're mad, you're mad!" pounded through my brain with each returning ray of consciousness, and I drowned the refrain with drink.(p.224)
- Then I turned two company cars over in a ***short*** time and Bingo -- fired again.(p.242)
- Need I say that in a very ***short*** time I was walking along a prairie highway with arm extended and thumb pointed?(p.255)
- The details of the long road back to something resembling normal living — the first ***short*** streetcar ride, the purchase of a used bike which enabled me to widen the narrow horizon of life, the first trip downtown — I will not dwell on.(p.276)
- HE SOLD HIMSELF ***SHORT***(p.287)
- I would hang on to sobriety for ***short*** intervals, but always there would come the tide of an overpowering necessity to drink and, as I was engulfed in it, I felt such a sense of panic that I really believed I would die if I didn't get that drink inside.(p.306)
- Some of us struggle with these people because we know that they are really very sick, but we also know that ***short*** of some miracle, we are not going to help them except temporarily, and that they will inevitably get worse and worse until one of two things happens.(p.308)
- In describing his suffering, his fears, his many years of groping for some answer to that which always seemed to remain unanswerable, he could have been describing me, and nothing ***short*** of experience and knowledge could have afforded him that much insight!(p.309)
- The movie racket had kept me too long from writing those novels, articles, ***short*** stories, and scripts on which I had copious notes.(p.330)
- In a ***short*** time, it became uncontrolled drinking.(p.343)
- Following this, I had a ***short*** vacation, during which time I read as much literature as my sponsor could send me.(p.343)
- When I did make it home in 1920, I re-entered school and caught up with my class in a few ***short*** months — I actually did a year's work in three months, proving much to the disgust of my dad that I could do it when I wanted to.(p.358)
- It was to be ***short*** lived, for on the day before Christmas I completely disillusioned my wife and ruined our first Christmas by coming home from the Rotary lunch dead drunk.(p.361)
- She tried reasoning with me, endeavored to work out various drinking schedules, in fact all the tricks were practised faithfully for a ***short*** time somewhere along my shaky road to unhappiness.(p.361)
- This routine was ***short*** lived too.(p.362)
- After his death, my mother soon picked up drinking where Dad left off, and in a very ***short*** time she died of cirrhosis of the liver.(p.370)
- ***Short*** dry spells ended in heavy drinking.(p.375)
- There are many ***short*** phrases and expressions in A.A. which make sound sense.(p.382)
- The ***short*** tours could be taken care of by sneaking enough whiskey aboard ship so that it could be rationed out until another supply could be laid in.(p.398)
- I wrote and sold some ***short*** stories.(p.409)
- These things were carried out in moments of less severe hangover or ***short*** stretches on the wagon.(p.409)
- This was how I had looked and acted a few ***short*** weeks ago.(p.415)
- Except for one ***short*** slip, during the first eight months, which was an angry "the world can't do this to me" reaction to a personal tragedy in my life, I have been sober for twelve years.(p.416)
- To cut a long story ***short***, I spent seven years and ten thousand dollars on my psychiatric adventure, and emerged in worse condition than ever.(p.434)
- In that ***short*** period he built within me something that I had long since lost, which was hope.(p.495)
- The war was on and it was a fairly ***short*** course, about eight months.(p.518)
- I wish I knew a ***short*** cut to maturity.(p.535)
- All of my family and loved ones, all of my friends, are nearer and dearer to me than ever before and I have literally dozens of new friends who say they cannot believe that a ***short*** eight years ago I was ready for the scrap heap.(p.541)
- When I had been in A.A. only a ***short*** while, an oldtimer told me something that has affected my life ever since.(p.554)
- On the next page, A.A.'s "12 Traditions" are seen in their so-called "***short*** form," the form in general use today.(p.563)

short-acting

- Eventually, I was taking forty-five milligrams of the long-acting Benzedrine and forty-five of the ***short-acting*** just to get out of bed in the morning.(p.442)

short-lived

- Our moments of triumph were ***short-lived***.(p.66)

short-sticking

- I found I could boost my income by figuring out a lot of cute little tricks that the boss wouldn't be likely to notice — filching money from the Coke machine, ***short-sticking*** the customers on oil, and selling oil I'd drained out of other cars.(p.423)

shortcomings

- Most of us sense that real tolerance of other people's ***shortcomings*** and viewpoints and a respect for their opinions are attitudes which make us more useful to others.(p.19)
- Almost none of us liked the self-searching, the leveling of our pride, the confession of ***shortcomings*** which the process requires for its successful consummation.(p.25)

• Instead, we looked at the human defects of these people, and sometimes used their ***shortcomings*** as a basis of wholesale condemnation.(p.50)

• 7.Humbly asked Him to remove our ***shortcomings***.(p.59)

shortcuts

• There will be alluring ***shortcuts*** and by-paths down which they may wander and lose their way.(p.123)

shorter

• I had a couple of ***shorter*** talks with this man afterward, and stopped drinking abruptly.(p.179)

• Every encouragement was given me with frequent salary increases, but the sober times between "periods" became ***shorter***.(p.254)

• The longer the drinking continued, the ***shorter*** the time the alcohol would keep me asleep; I would have to drink myself back to sleep again and again throughout the night.(p.441)

• The intervals grew ***shorter***.(p.514)

shortest

• We could not prove life in the sense that you can prove a straight line is the ***shortest*** distance between two points, yet, there it was.(p.54)

shortly

• ***Shortly*** afterward I came home drunk.(p.5)

• ***Shortly*** after that, my brother, who had then become associated with a group of people and had stopped drinking, urged me to attend meetings with him.(p.205)

• These periods became more frequent and I resolved that when I became forty, which was very ***shortly***, I was going on the wagon.(p.213)

• ***Shortly*** after I came to this conclusion, I was importuned by another well-known patent law firm to help them out on some trial work because their trial man had had a heart attack and had been forbidden to go into the courtroom.(p.220)

• I was born in Europe, in Alsace to be exact, ***shortly*** after it had become German, and practically grew up with the "good Rhine wine" of song and story.(p.230)

• ***Shortly*** thereafter, aided by the Depression, I found that I had a great deal of spare time and that a little drink in the morning helped.(p.287)

• ***Shortly*** after I returned to Chicago, my doctor, encouraged by the results of my contact with A.A., sent us two more of his alcoholic patients.(p.310)

• ***Shortly*** after I was starting to work on the program I realized that I was not a good father; I wasn't a good husband, but, oh, I was a good provider.(p.351)

• I was told that someone would call on me ***shortly***, to sit tight and not take another drink.(p.363)

• Very ***shortly***, I realized that had been a mistake -- when this big clown came bounding into the room, almost shouting, "My name is Frank, and I'm an alcoholic, ha-ha-ha!"(p.446)

• ***Shortly*** thereafter, I was selected, with eight other inmates out of the 10,000 in the state's prisons at that time, to attend a school designed to take former "management problems" like me and convert them into paracounselors.(p.462)

• I began drinking as a kid, ***shortly*** after I reached my fourteenth birthday.(p.508)

shortness

• I put on thirty pounds of weight in about two months, looked like a pig, and was uncomfortable from ***shortness*** of breath.(p.177)

shorts

• I was down to my ***shorts***, unaware of wrong-doing, before the ambulance got there and hauled me off to a hospital from which anxious friends rescued me, later that night.(p.537)

shot

• By March 1941, the membership had ***shot*** up to 2,000.(p.xviii)

• It was an evil and corroding thread; the fabric of our existence was ***shot*** through with it.(p.67)

• We think the business fabric is ***shot*** through with a situation which might be helped by better understanding all around.(p.137)

• The proceeding was ***shot*** through with much hard feeling and controversy.(p.154)

• I would reach over and get this and take a ***shot*** and in a few moments get up and take another, shave and eat my breakfast, slip a half pint of liquor in my hip pocket, and go on to school.(p.183)

• What an opportunity I ***shot*** to pieces there!(p.242)

• Oddly enough, the big ***shot*** who fired me from this company was one of the first men I met when I later joined the New York A.A. Group.(p.242)

• The Big ***Shot***?(p.243)

• If I'd had a gun I'd have ***shot*** the horns right off the thing, because it made me raving mad.(p.265)

• The parties waxed more liquid and hilarious as time went on, and eventually I discovered that a little ***shot*** of liquor now and then between beers had the tendency to put me in a whacky mood much quicker than having to down several quarts of beer to obtain the same effect.(p.298)

• By this time, my chances of getting lined up in my chosen business were ***shot***.(p.301)

• That, of course, was a ***shot*** of booze.(p.331)

• Once again I was back in the big time operations, and along with them, big ***shot*** complexes.(p.361)

• At this time, the price of booze in the bars was fifteen cents a ***shot*** and ten cents a beer.(p.397)

• I suspect that those bartenders would wait until I ***shot*** my wad, then call a cab and send me home.(p.410)

• I've never seen him drunk in my life, although he'd take a ***shot*** in the morning and usually one in the evening, and so did I; but for the most part he kept his whiskey in his office.(p.484)

• During the course of that drinking, I had ***shot*** and killed one person and almost completed the job on a second one.(p.508)

• He had a ***shot*** of brandy against the cold and passed me the bottle.(p.541)

• It wasn't strong enough, so I added a ***shot*** of vodka - - and was right back to worse trouble than before.(p.556)

shotgun

• After two weeks of drinking, he had placed his toe on the trigger of a loaded ***shotgun*** -- the barrel in his mouth.(p.137)

shots

• They had also been periodic big ***shots*** who had goofed out repeatedly at the wrong time, and they also knew how to split one paper match into three separate matches.(p.245)

• Instead, he got dressed, took me out, bought me three or four double ***shots*** and put me to bed.(p.278)

• The general procedure was to take four or five ***shots*** in the first place I stopped at.(p.299)

• No more snoops or big ***shots*** breathing down our necks.(p.329)

• I found out fast that the cheapest way to get drunk was on ***shots*** with beer chasers at two bits a crack.(p.397)

• I graduated from ***shots*** and beer chasers to Scotch and sodas.(p.398)

• When I landed of course I hit a gin mill, and with three or four good ***shots*** under my belt the world began to go into that rosy glow.(p.513)

should

• We ***should*** like to be helpful to such cases.(p.xiv)

• And in no circumstances ***should*** we give endorsements, make alliances, or enter public controversies.(p.xix)

• Our friends thought a lunacy commission ***should*** be appointed.(p.3)

• This ***should*** suggest a useful program for anyone concerned with a drinking problem.(p.19)

• "She's such a sweet girl, I ***should*** think he'd stop for her sake."(p.20)

• But this description ***should*** identify him roughly.(p.22)

• This ***should*** be an entirely personal affair which each one decides for himself in the light of past associations, or his present choice.(p.28)

• The reader may still ask why he ***should*** believe in a Power greater than himself.(p.48)

• We used to amuse ourselves by cynically dissecting spiritual beliefs and practices when we might have observed that many spiritually-minded persons of all races, colors, and creeds were demonstrating a degree of stability, happiness and usefulness which we ***should*** have sought ourselves.(p.49)

• When many hundreds of people are able to say that the consciousness of the Presence of God is today the most important fact of their lives, they present a powerful reason why one ***should*** have faith.(p.51)

• We were having trouble with personal relationships, we couldn't control our emotional natures, we were a prey to misery and depression, we couldn't make a living, we had a feeling of uselessness, we were full of fear, we were unhappy, we couldn't seem to be of real help to other people -- was not a basic solution of these bedevilments more important than whether we ***should*** see newsreels of lunar flight?(p.52)

• His story is so interesting that some of it ***should*** be told now.(p.55)

• Where were we at fault, what ***should*** we have done instead?(p.69)

• In meditation, we ask God what we ***should*** do about each specific matter.(p.69)

• We will be more reconciled to discussing ourselves with another person when we see good reasons why we ***should*** do so.(p.72)

• He ***should*** realize that we are engaged upon a life-and-death errand.(p.75)

• When ready, we say something like this: "My Creator, I am now willing that you ***should*** have all of me, good and bad.(p.76)

• To some people we need not, and probably ***should*** not emphasize the spiritual feature on our first approach.(p.76)

• We are there to sweep off our side of the street realizing that nothing worth while can be accomplished until we do so, never trying to tell him what he ***should*** do.(p.77)

• It ***should*** not matter, however, if someone does throw us out of his office.(p.78)

• If we are sure our wife does not know, ***should*** we tell her?(p.81)

• If she knows in a general way that we have been wild, ***should*** we tell her in detail?(p.81)

• Undoubtedly we ***should*** admit our fault.(p.81)

• If we have no such complication, there is plenty we ***should*** do at home.(p.82)

• We ***should*** not talk incessantly to them about spiritual matters.(p.83)

• We ***should*** be sensible, tactful, considerate and humble without being servile or scraping.(p.83)

• It ***should*** continue for our lifetime.(p.84)

• Have we kept something to ourselves which ***should*** be discussed with another person at once?(p.86)

• After making our review we ask God's forgiveness and inquire what corrective measures ***should*** be taken.(p.86)

• They ***should*** be patient, realizing they are dealing with a sick person.(p.90)

• If he says yes, then his attention ***should*** be drawn to you as a person who has recovered.(p.90)

• You ***should*** be described to him as one of a fellowship who, as part of their own recovery, try to help others and who will be glad to talk to him if he cares to see you.(p.90)

• Neither ***should*** the family hysterically plead with him to do anything, nor ***should*** they tell him much about you.(p.90)

• They ***should*** wait for the end of his next drinking bout.(p.90)

• Usually the family ***should*** not try to tell your story.(p.91)

• If your man needs hospitalization, he ***should*** have it, but not forcibly unless he is violent.(p.91)

• You ***should*** not be offended if he wants to call it off, for he has helped you more than you have helped him.(p.94)

• He ***should*** not be pushed or prodded by you, his wife, or his friends.(p.95)

• But you ***should*** not deprive your family or creditors of money they ***should*** have.(p.96)

• Though an alcoholic does not respond, there is no reason why you ***should*** neglect his family.(p.97)

• You ***should*** continue to be friendly to them.(p.97)

• The family ***should*** be offered your way of life.(p.97)

• ***Should*** they accept and practice spiritual principles, there is a much better chance that the head of the family will recover.(p.97)

• When your prospect has made such reparation as he can to his family, and has thoroughly explained to them the new principles by which he is living, he ***should*** proceed to put those principles into action at home.(p.98)

• Though his family be at fault in many respects, he ***should*** not be concerned about that.(p.98)

• He ***should*** concentrate on his own spiritual demonstration.(p.98)

• If there be divorce or separation, there ***should*** be no undue haste for the couple to get together.(p.99)

• The man ***should*** be sure of his recovery.(p.99)

• The wife ***should*** fully understand his new way of life.(p.99)

• When working with a man and his family, you ***should*** take care not to participate in their quarrels.(p.100)

• But urge upon a man's family that he has been a very sick person and ***should*** be treated accordingly.(p.100)

• You ***should*** warn against arousing resentment or jealousy.(p.100)

• You ***should*** point out that his defects of character are not going to disappear over night.(p.100)

• You ***should*** not hesitate to visit the most sordid spot on earth on such an errand.(p.102)

• But some of us think we ***should*** not serve liquor to anyone.(p.102)

• The first principle of success is that you ***should***

never be angry.(p.111)
• Even though your husband becomes unbearable and you have to leave him temporarily, you ***should***, if you can, go without rancor.(p.111)
• Our next thought is that you ***should*** never tell him what he must do about his drinking.(p.111)
• You think he ought to know the subject better, as everyone ***should*** have a clear understanding of the risk he takes if he drinks too much.(p.112)
• The same principles which apply to husband number one ***should*** be practiced.(p.112)
• Again, you ***should*** not crowd him.(p.113)
• Perhaps you have a husband who is at large, but who ***should*** be committed.(p.114)
• When they become too dangerous, we think the kind thing is to lock them up, but of course a good doctor ***should*** always be consulted.(p.114)
• Your desire to protect him ***should*** not cause you to lie to people when they have a right to know where he is and what he is doing.(p.115)
• Ask him what you ***should*** do if he places you in such a position again.(p.116)
• ***Should*** it happen again, regard it in a different light.(p.116)
• This is as it ***should*** be.(p.117)
• These work-outs ***should*** be regarded as part of your education, for thus you will be learning to live.(p.117)
• Next time you and he have a heated discussion, no matter what the subject, it ***should*** be the privilege of either to smile and say, "This is getting serious.(p.118)
• You feel he ***should*** now be yours.(p.119)
• The fact is that he ***should*** work with other people to maintain his own sobriety.(p.119)
• You ***should*** join in his efforts as much as you possibly can.(p.119)
• All members of the family ***should*** meet upon the common ground of tolerance, understanding and love.(p.122)
• We think each family which has been relieved owes something to those who have not, and when the occasion requires, each member of it ***should*** be only too willing to bring former mistakes, no matter how grievous, out of their hiding places.(p.124)
• So we think that unless some good and useful purpose is to be served, past occurrences ***should*** not be discussed.(p.125)
• Members of a family ***should*** watch such matters carefully, for one careless, inconsiderate remark has been known to raise the very devil.(p.125)
• They ***should*** be thankful he is sober and able to be of this world once more.(p.127)
• The opposite may happen ***should*** the family condemn and criticize.(p.129)
• Instead of treating the family as he ***should***, he may retreat further into himself and feel he has spiritual justification for so doing.(p.129)
• Though the family does not fully agree with dad's spiritual activities, they ***should*** let him have his head.(p.129)
• The family may feel they hold a mortgage on dad, so big that no equity ***should*** be left for outsiders.(p.131)
• Father will necessarily spend much time with other alcoholics, but this activity ***should*** be balanced.(p.131)
• Each individual ***should*** consult his own conscience.(p.132)
• Try to remember that though God has wrought miracles among us, we ***should*** never belittle a good doctor or psychiatrist.(p.133)
• He thought all alcoholics ***should*** constantly have chocolate available for its quick energy value at times of fatigue.(p.133)
• There ***should*** be no hesitancy in consulting a doctor or psychologist if the condition persists.(p.134)
• You cannot see why it ***should*** be to anyone else, save the spineless and stupid.(p.139)
• ***Should*** he have the same consideration as other ailing employees?(p.140)
• We believe a man ***should*** be thoroughly probed on these points.(p.142)
• He ***should*** understand that emphatically.(p.142)
• The matter of physical treatment ***should***, of course, be referred to your own doctor.(p.143)
• If you propose such a procedure to him, it may be necessary to advance the cost of treatment, but we believe it ***should*** be made plain that any expense will later be deducted from his pay.(p.143)
• If your man accepts your offer, it ***should*** be pointed out that physical treatment is but a small part of the picture.(p.143)
• Though you are providing him with the best possible medical attention, he ***should*** understand that he must undergo a change of heart.(p.143)
• Your man ***should*** be on his mettle to make good.(p.146)
• If you are sure he doesn't mean business, there is no doubt you ***should*** discharge him.(p.147)
• But you ***should*** feel under no obligation to keep him on, for your obligation has been well discharged already.(p.147)
• They often jeopardize their own positions by trying to help serious drinkers who ***should*** have been fired long ago, or else given an opportunity to get well.(p.147)
• He need not, and often ***should*** not show it to his alcoholic prospect.(p.148)
• It boils right down to this: No man ***should*** be fired just because he is alcoholic.(p.148)
• If he wants to stop, he ***should*** be afforded a real chance.(p.148)
• If he cannot or does not want to stop, he ***should*** be discharged.(p.148)
• He ***should*** not be made a favorite.(p.149)
• ***Should*** you wish them above all else, and be willing to make use of our experience, we are sure they will come.(p.153)
• Why, he argued, ***should*** he lose the remainder of his business, only to bring still more suffering to his family by foolishly admitting his plight to people from whom he made his livelihood?(p.155)
• Many mornings I have gone to classes, and even though fully prepared, would turn and walk back to the fraternity house because of my jitters, not daring to enter the classroom for fear of making a scene ***should*** I be called on for recitation.(p.173)
• Therefore it would make no great difference, even if I ***should*** do some drinking.(p.175)
• But my friends usually found me and I would go home if they promised that I ***should*** not be scolded.(p.176)
• For the benefit of those experimentally inclined, I ***should*** mention the so-called beer experiment.(p.177)
• Why they ***should*** be subjected to the tortures we inflict upon them, I cannot explain.(p.178)
• You ***should*** go out and take this program to somebody else that needs it and wants it."(p.190)
• And then we both realized we ***should*** go.(p.201)
• So they decided that I ***should*** have a doctor.(p.205)
• A few minutes later, Dr. Bob left, leaving with my brother some medicine I ***should*** get.(p.207)
• The very simple program they advised me to follow was that I ***should*** ask to know God's will for me for that one day, and then, to the best of my ability, to follow that, and at night to express my gratefulness to God for the things that had happened to me during the day.(p.208)
• My efficiency as a professional man was probably reduced to twenty-five per cent of what it ***should*** have been.(p.215)
• Professionally, after I was sober for a month or so I realized that I ***should*** school myself to dissolve the partnership I was in because I felt that I would never regain the respect of my partners no matter how long I was sober, and that I would be at a disadvantage.(p.220)
• No doubt I had been an exile too long – I ***should*** go home to America.(p.226)
• When my doctor told me I ***should*** never touch a drink again, I couldn't afford to believe him.(p.226)
• I had always been a good Catholic, possibly not so devoted as I ***should*** have been, but fairly regular in my attendance at services.(p.234)
• I don't think the boys were completely convinced of my personality change, for they fought shy of including my story in the book, so my only contribution to their literary efforts was my firm conviction, being still a theological rebel, that the word God ***should*** be qualified with the phrase "as we understand him" -- for that was the only way I could accept spirituality.(p.248)
• I have served on only one committee in the past nine years, for I feel that I had my chance the first few years and that newer members ***should*** fill the jobs.(p.250)
• I had none of these things that children ***should*** have to make them happy.(p.261)
• I felt it certainly must be very depressing to her that I ***should*** sit there by her bedside and cry.(p.272)
• If it isn't anything that's going to help you or anybody else, why ***should*** you become involved in it, and get all disturbed about it?"(p.273)
• It was therefore not extraordinary that I ***should*** shy away from any serious thought of marriage for a great many years after joining A.A.(p.286)
• Their answer was always the same: If they ***should*** need it at any time they would surely get in touch with me.(p.293)
• I suggested to her that she ***should*** see the son's minister or doctor, and that perhaps he would recommend the A.A. program.(p.294)
• The three of us did not feel up to the job, and after a few meetings we convinced the prospects that they too ***should*** go to Akron where they could see an older group in action.(p.295)
• Why he bothered with me as long as he did I shall never know, for he knew there was no answer for me in medicine and he, like all doctors of his day, had been taught that the alcoholic was incurable and ***should*** be ignored.(p.307)
• I ***should*** have lost my husband, and I think that only the fact that he was an alcoholic too kept us together.(p.323)
• I ***should*** have realized that alcohol was getting hold of me when I started to become secretive in my drinking.(p.336)
• I needed it, and I knew I was drinking too much, but I wasn't conscious of the fact that I ***should*** stop.(p.336)
• I went on, realizing what I was becoming, hating myself for it, bitter, blaming life, blaming everything else but the fact that I ***should*** turn about and do something about my drinking.(p.337)
• Surrender to me has meant the ability to run my home, to face my responsibilities as they ***should*** be faced, to take life as it comes to me day by day, and work my problems out.(p.340)
• Why ***should*** this happen to me – hadn't I provided a good home – wasn't I making a good living -- didn't I just get a substantial raise that had put me in the upper bracket class?(p.362)
• While I was in Florida trying to convince my wife with all the A.A. literature that she ***should*** come back to me, she went over to her desk and picked up a clipping she had taken from the St. Petersburg Times about A.A.(p.366)
• I had had no brushes with the law, though I ***should*** have had many.(p.379)
• The A.A. way of life is the way we always ***should*** have tried to live.(p.382)
• Scared that my dress wasn't going to fit right, that the church wasn't going to be filled, that I'd fall flat on my face walking up the aisle; in fact, I was afraid I wasn't going to be a prima donna in the place where I ***should*** be.(p.385)
• I could see no reason why they ***should*** have any relationship to this problem of getting drunk every now and then.(p.388)
• One afternoon, the year after moving to Houston, I got as drunk as a skunk, and while I do not walk very straight sober, you ***should*** see me when I'm drunk!(p.390)
• The sanitarium ***should*** have happened.(p.412)
• And ***should*** I have more bad times, I know that I'll never again have to go through them alone.(p.438)
• He arranged for me to see a local psychiatrist, who quickly decided I ***should*** be in the mental-health unit of our local hospital.(p.445)
• Then, one day in A.A., I was told that I had the lenses in my glasses backwards; "the courage to change" in the Serenity Prayer meant, not that I ***should*** change my marriage, but rather that I ***should*** change myself and learn to accept my spouse as she was.(p.451)
• It seems I ***should*** have learned to love my wife and family first; the newcomer to A.A., last.(p.451)
• I would rather talk about the good things A.A. has taught me; I feel that hitting on just a few sordid points ***should*** be sufficient to let those of you in institutions know where I came from.(p.459)
• I must be ready and willing ***should*** I never see them.(p.463)
• I'm sure my ideas as to what life ***should*** be like were quite different from that of the average person with whom I associated.(p.483)
• Mother was of the old school and figured that anyone I associated with ***should*** be of the proper type.(p.484)
• She got a medical certificate so that I ***should*** not have to join it.(p.484)
• The fear of the loss of Vi and the feeling that, though she had the right to do as she pleased, she ***should*** have told me the truth about it, upset me.(p.487)
• I thought that all women ***should*** be perfect.(p.487)
• Something ***should*** have told me then that things were haywire.(p.487)
• He went into the religious side and told me that I didn't attend church as regularly as I ***should***, and that he felt, more or less, that this was responsible for my trouble.(p.489)
• Vi was very kind and explained to the jury that I was basically a fine fellow and a good husband, but that I drank too much and that she thought I had lost my mind and felt that I ***should*** be committed to an asylum.(p.492)

• After the trial, I got big-hearted again and felt that I ***should*** do something in payment for Vi's kindness to me; so I left Washington and went to Seattle to work.(p.492)

• But I have not seen yet that I ***should*** do some constructive acts of love without expecting any return.(p.505)

• I ***should*** say there was less drinking in the Army than I thought at that time.(p.518)

• But on the other hand, I was terribly fortunate because that ***should*** have been a court martial offense and I ***should*** have been out on my ear.(p.520)

• In part, it was a feeling of intense shame at having to leave the Army during the war, but mostly it was resentment that this kind of thing ***should*** happen to me for, strange as it may seem, up to then I still thought I could control drinking.(p.521)

• I would never admit that I was drinking too much, or spending money that I ***should*** have used to buy food for my two little boys.(p.526)

• Things weren't going as I thought they ***should***, for my greater enjoyment, comfort and fame; therefore, if the universe wouldn't play my way, I wouldn't play at all.(p.531)

• As I write these words, it seems incredible that these things ***should*** have happened to me, for they are, truly, against all my instincts and training.(p.536)

• Much later, when I had progressed to full-blown alcoholism, people told me I ***should*** quit.(p.554)

• One -- Our common welfare ***should*** come first; personal recovery depends upon A.A. unity.(p.564)

• Four -- Each group ***should*** be autonomous except in matters affecting other groups or A.A. as a whole.(p.564)

• Eight -- Alcoholics Anonymous ***should*** remain forever nonprofessional, but our service centers may employ special workers.(p.564)

• 4. -- With respect to its own affairs, each A.A group ***should*** be responsible to no other authority than its own conscience.(p.565)

• And no group, regional committee, or individual ***should*** ever take any action that might greatly affect A.A. as a whole without conferring with the trustees of the General Service Board.(p.565)

• We think, therefore, that any considerable property of genuine use to A.A. ***should*** be separately incorporated and managed, thus dividing the material from the spiritual.(p.565)

• An A.A. group, as such, ***should*** never go into business.(p.566)

• Their management ***should*** be the sole responsibility of those people who financially support them.(p.566)

• We think that each group ***should*** soon achieve this ideal; that any public solicitation of funds using the name of Alcoholics Anonymous is highly dangerous, whether by groups, clubs, hospitals, or other outside agencies; that acceptance of large gifts from any source, or of contributions carrying any obligation whatever, is unwise.(p.566)

• 8. -- Alcoholics Anonymous ***should*** remain forever nonprofessional.(p.566)

• 10. -- No A.A. group or member ***should*** ever, in such a way as to implicate A.A., express any opinion on outside controversial issues -- particularly those of politics, alcohol reform, or sectarian religion.(p.567)

• 11. -- Our relations with the general public ***should*** be characterized by personal anonymity.(p.567)

• Our public relations ***should*** be guided by the principle of attraction rather than promotion.(p.567)

• ***Should*** you be the relative or friend of an alcoholic who shows no immediate interest in A.A., it is suggested that you write the Al-Anon Family Groups, Inc., Box 182, Madison Square Station, New York, NY 10159, U.S.A.(p.575)

shoulder

• But those of us who have tried to ***shoulder*** the entire burden and trouble of others find we are soon overcome by them.(p.132)

• You will be bound to them with new and wonderful ties, for you will escape disaster together and you will commence ***shoulder*** to ***shoulder*** your common journey.(p.152)

• There was one meeting a week at Bill's home in Brooklyn, and we all took turns there spouting off about how we had changed our lives overnight, how many drunks we had saved and straightened out, and last, but not least, how God had touched each of us personally on the ***shoulder***.(p.246)

• Where we used to run from responsibility, we find ourselves accepting it with gratitude that we can successfully ***shoulder*** it.(p.311)

shoulders

• We try not to indulge in cynicism over the state of the nations, nor do we carry the world's troubles on our ***shoulders***.(p.132)

• I paced the floor with a bath towel around my ***shoulders***, the perspiration running off me.(p.268)

• And as that thought came to me, it was as though someone had reached down and taken a heavy overcoat off my ***shoulders***, for that was the last one.(p.347)

• There were gold bars on his ***shoulders***.(p.422)

• He was in his late fifties, and all that he had undertaken fell upon my ***shoulders*** at his death in 1928.(p.486)

shouldn't

• We had to ask ourselves why we ***shouldn't*** apply to our human problems this same readiness to change our point of view.(p.52)

• We ***shouldn't*** be shy on this matter of prayer.(p.85)

• Father knows he is to blame; it may take him many seasons of hard work to be restored financially, but he ***shouldn't*** be reproached.(p.123)

• But why ***shouldn't*** we laugh?(p.132)

• So having licked it, there was no reason why I ***shouldn't*** have a drink, and I stopped in before I got home and had one.(p.203)

• Then I became careless and returned sometimes when I ***shouldn't*** have.(p.376)

• He said that because of my drinking, he ***shouldn't*** leave, but that he had to go to New York for two weeks.(p.388)

• ***Shouldn't*** have drunk so much or so fast.(p.498)

• And it had gone underground now, because everyone knew I ***shouldn't*** be drinking.(p.557)

shout

• Looking directly at me was a large oil painting of my wife, and her very words seemed to ***shout*** at me -- "I am not leaving you because I don't love you; it's because I do love you.(p.363)

shouted

• He ***shouted*** great tidings.(p.11)

shouting

• It ran something like this: If I go around ***shouting*** from the rooftops about my alcoholism, it might very possibly prevent me from getting a good job.(p.282)

• Very shortly, I realized that had been a mistake -- when this big clown came bounding into the room, almost ***shouting***, "My name is Frank, and I'm an alcoholic, ha-ha-ha!"(p.446)

shouts

• That the man who is making the approach has had the same difficulty, that he obviously knows what he is talking about, that his whole deportment ***shouts*** at the new prospect that he is a man with a real answer, that he has no attitude of Holier Than Thou, nothing whatever except the sincere desire to be helpful; that there are no fees to pay, no axes to grind, no people to please, no lectures to be endured -- these are the conditions we have found most effective.(p.18)

show

• To ***show*** other alcoholics precisely how we have recovered is the main purpose of this book.(p.xiii)

• Once confused and baffled by the seeming futility of existence they ***show*** the underlying reasons why they were making heavy going of life.(p.50)

• They ***show*** how the change came over them.(p.51)

• ***Show*** any longshoreman a Sunday supplement describing a proposal to explore the moon by means of a rocket and he will say, "I bet they do it -- maybe not so long either."(p.52)

• Each person is like an actor who wants to run the whole ***show***; is forever trying to arrange the lights, the ballet, the scenery and the rest of the players in his own way.(p.60)

• If his arrangements would only stay put, if only people would do as he wished, the ***show*** would be great.(p.60)

• The ***show*** doesn't come off very well.(p.61)

• And do not his actions make each of them wish to retaliate, snatching all they can get out of the ***show***?(p.61)

• We asked God to help us ***show*** them the same tolerance, pity, and patience that we would cheerfully grant a sick friend.(p.67)

• We cannot be helpful to all people, but at least God will ***show*** us how to take a kindly and tolerant view of each and every one.(p.67)

• We attempt to sweep away the debris which has accumulated out of our effort to live on self-will and run the ***show*** ourselves.(p.76)

• So we clean house with the family, asking each morning in meditation that our Creator ***show*** us the way of patience, tolerance, kindliness and love.(p.83)

• We constantly remind ourselves we are no longer running the ***show***, humbly saying to ourselves many times each day "Thy will be done."(p.87)

• ***Show*** him the mental twist which leads to the first drink of a spree.(p.92)

• ***Show*** him, from your own experience, how the queer mental condition surrounding that first drink prevents normal functioning of the will power.(p.92)

• ***Show*** him how they worked with you.(p.95)

• ***Show*** them that he has entered upon a period of growth.(p.100)

• People have said we must not go where liquor is served; we must not have it in our homes; we must shun friends who drink; we must avoid moving pictures which ***show*** drinking scenes; we must not go into bars; our friends must hide their bottles if we go to their houses; we mustn't think or be reminded about alcohol at all.(p.100)

• We are careful never to ***show*** intolerance or hatred of drinking as an institution.(p.103)

• ***Show*** him you have confidence in his power to stop or moderate.(p.112)

• ***Show*** him your copy of this book and tell him what you have found out about alcoholism.(p.112)

• ***Show*** him that as alcoholics, the writers of the book understand.(p.112)

• We urge you to try our program, for nothing will be so helpful to your husband as the radically changed attitude toward him which God will ***show*** you how to have.(p.117)

• ***Show*** him these things in yourself and they will be reflected back to you from him.(p.118)

• If you both ***show*** a willingness to remedy your own defects, there will be little need to criticize each other.(p.118)

• Is not each trying to arrange the family ***show*** to his liking?(p.122)

• He may take small interest in the children and may ***show*** irritation when reproved for his delinquencies.(p.126)

• They expect him to give them the nice times they used to have before he drank so much, and to ***show*** his contrition for what they suffered.(p.126)

• He is not likely to get far in any direction if he fails to ***show*** unselfishness and love under his own roof.(p.127)

• He need not, and often should not ***show*** it to his alcoholic prospect.(p.148)

• He will ***show*** you how to create the fellowship you crave.(p.164)

• Eventually, there would be a ball game, or a ***show***, or some sort of special occasion to celebrate and I would turn up drunk.(p.196)

• To ***show*** you the point to which this obsession went, there came an occasion when I had spent a most delightful week-end, and at nine o'clock on Sunday night I was on my way home, and I thought I would get a drink.(p.204)

• And as I fumed helplessly and planned to get good and drunk and ***show*** them, my eye caught a sentence in the book lying open on my bed: "We cannot live with anger."(p.228)

• I was free, and I didn't have to drink to "***show*** them."(p.228)

• I'd ***show*** 'em who was boss!(p.243)

• They did not ***show*** me to my room and wish me a good night's rest.(p.259)

• His wife was cussing him, raving at him, "I just brought him over to ***show*** you what kind of a guy he is!(p.271)

• Everyone was against me -- I'd ***show*** them I didn't need them.(p.318)

• I'd ***show*** them -- I'd get drunker!(p.319)

• I was "too important" to ***show*** any indication of being a drunk.(p.328)

• Or: If I'm really a genius, I must produce a great work, to ***show*** why I act like a genius.(p.408)

• Only ***show*** me how."(p.430)

• After all, it was self (you, me) that stood in our own way, that ran the ***show*** and ran ourselves into bankruptcy, that hurt the ones we loved.(p.459)

• But more important, I would have found that once again I was sitting in the driver's seat -- I was running the ***show***.(p.471)

• And when she broke a luncheon date with me one Saturday, after I had been in A.A. for about three months, I said, "I'll ***show*** her!(p.472)

• Mind you, I had absolutely nothing to ***show*** for that eighteen years, except a beat-up car that I hadn't even paid for, but I was doing all right.(p.478)

• I thought, well, now that I've been put out for drinking, I'll just ***show*** them that they were completely wrong, so I went off on the biggest bout I had been on up to then, involving about a fortnight's blackout.(p.521)

showed

• Of alcoholics who came to A.A. and really tried, 50% got sober at once and remained that way; 25% sobered up after some relapses, and among the remain-

der, those who stayed on with A.A. *showed* improvement.(p.xx)
• Treatment seemed wise, for I *showed* signs of delirium tremens.(p.13)
• We have heard of few instances where people, who *showed* definite signs of alcoholism, were able to stop for a long period because of an overpowering desire to do so.(p.32)
• When others *showed* us that "God-sufficiency" worked with them, we began to feel like those who had insisted the Wrights would never fly.(p.52)
• Talking things over with them, great floods of enlightenment *showed* me myself as I really was and I was like them.(p.229)
• She said she didn't know, but that I sure *showed* plain enough I didn't have any part of it.(p.273)
• The A.A. program *showed* me the way to come down to earth, start from the bottom and work up.(p.284)
• A.A.'s Twelve Steps *showed* me the way to sobriety if I wanted it.(p.320)
• My old friends *showed* distress.(p.404)
• She, more than the others, *showed* me what ailed me basically, why I was immature and insecure.(p.409)
• X-rays *showed* that a couple of teeth had to come out.(p.465)
• Well, you know who I *showed.*(p.472)
• I *showed* myself.(p.472)
• Then A.A. *showed* her the beauty of normal living, in a whole family reborn.(p.478)

showing

• Further on, clear-cut directions are given *showing* how we recovered.(p.29)
• If anyone who is *showing* inability to control his drinking can do the right-about-face and drink like a gentleman, our hats are off to him.(p.31)
• Two: Your husband is *showing* lack of control, for he is unable to stay on the water wagon even when he wants to.(p.109)
• *Showing* others who suffer how we were given help is the very thing which makes life seem so worth while to us now.(p.124)
• It never fails, if you go about it with one half the zeal you have been in the habit of *showing* when you were getting another drink.(p.181)
• So I was barred from the plant for ten days, and during that ten day period I was drunk twice, *showing* how little control these restraints had on me.(p.205)
• Above all, I have gained the greatest thing accorded to any man, the love and understanding of a gracious God, who has lifted me from the alcoholic scrap-heap to a position of trust where I have been able to reap the rich rewards that come from *showing* a little love for others and from serving them as I can.(p.296)
• One Saturday noon I staggered home with every intention of *showing* her.(p.362)
• When I hear the more rugged stories of alcoholics who became sicker than I did with this affliction, I humbly thank God for *showing* me "the handwriting on the wall."(p.367)
• *Showing* all the courage and ingenuity that I had not used in a positive way, I covered my tracks and hid from my family so successfully that they did not find me for months.(p.401)
• After nearly eight years of sobriety in A.A., I still can set down such thoughts, "against my instinct and training," *showing* that I still consider myself a "special" person, entitled to special privileges.(p.536)

shown

• If hundreds of experiences have *shown* him that one drink means another debacle with all its attendant suffering and humiliation, why is it he takes that one drink?(p.22)
• We usually conclude the period of meditation with a prayer that we be *shown* all through the day what our next step is to be, that we be given whatever we need to take care of such problems.(p.87)
• We have *shown* how we got out from under.(p.152)
• There I took up the business of drinking with much greater earnestness than I had previously *shown.*(p.173)
• HE HAD TO BE *SHOWN*(p.193)
• I have never *shown* any particular talents nor have I had any really frustrating ambitions.(p.240)
• As we left, and they were escorting us across the bridge into Wheeling, I, with great dignity and sarcasm, told them if their wives were ever visiting in Akron, and they, too, were looking for their route sign as I was, that I hoped I could extend to them the hospitality that had been *shown* to me in Bellaire.(p.264)
• I had been brought up to believe this, and I had *shown* during my 'teens considerable enterprise and imagination about earning money.(p.275)
• Where derision, contempt and pity were once *shown* me, I now enjoy the respect of many people.(p.296)
• But A.A. has *shown* me that I can help other alcoholics.(p.326)
• It has *shown* me, through the tragic stories of so many other alcoholics, the utter futility of self pity.(p.525)
• Had I been able to explain to a psychiatrist the feeling of futility, loneliness and lack of purpose that had come with my deep sense of personal failure at this second divorce, I seriously doubt that the good doctor could have convinced me that my basic problem was a spiritual hunger, but A.A. has *shown* me this was the truth.(p.546)
• And if I had been able to turn to the church at that time I'm sure they could not have convinced me my sickness was within myself, nor could they have *shown* me the need for self-analysis that A.A. has *shown* me is vital if I am to survive.(p.546)
• To wear expensive clothes, to have bartenders know what to serve me before I ordered, to be recognized by headwaiters and *shown* to the best table, to play gin rummy for high stakes with the insouciance of a riverboat gambler -- these were the enduring values in life, I thought.(p.556)

shows

• Our experience *shows* that you need not be disconcerted.(p.44)
• Practical experience *shows* that nothing will so much insure immunity from drinking as intensive work with other alcoholics.(p.89)
• If he *shows* interest, lend him your copy of this book.(p.94)
• Our experience *shows* that this is not necessarily so.(p.101)
• Experience *shows* that such an attitude is not helpful to anyone.(p.103)
• Hardly one of our crowd now *shows* any mark of dissipation.(p.133)
• This group of thirteen stories *shows* that sobriety in A.A. can be lasting.(p.167)
• Yet, as my record *shows,* I did become an extremely serious case.(p.182)
• In meeting me casually, I don't think my strong belief in "The Man Upstairs" *shows,* but I have no other explanation for the many good things that have happened to me since I have been in A.A. -- they came to me from a Greater Power.(p.367)
• It *shows* nothing or no one to blame for alcoholism.(p.373)
• The terms "spiritual experience" and "spiritual awakening" are used many times in this book which, upon careful reading, *shows* that the personality change sufficient to bring about recovery from alcoholism has manifested itself among us in many different forms.(p.569)
• Should you be the relative or friend of an alcoholic who *shows* no immediate interest in A.A., it is suggested that you write the Al-Anon Family Groups, Inc., Box 182, Madison Square Station, New York, NY 10159, U.S.A.(p.575)

shredding

• I do recall lying on a cold cement floor and *shredding* into little bits several pieces of stolen identification cards, and washing my face in the toilet bowl trying to sober up, and screaming hysterically while clinging to bars too high to see out of, and cursing everyone that came near me.(p.354)

shrewd

• One evening, the book, after checking up, was very definitely in the red for plenty through a piece of studied carelessness on my part, and my boss, very *shrewd* and able, fired me with a parting statement to the effect that once was enough.(p.251)

shrieks

• They said I was so funny, and told me, with *shrieks* of laughter, what I'd done the night before.(p.407)

shrimp

• There was the physical aspect; to be the youngest and the runt of the brood of children, to have to wear glasses very early and so to be teased, to be bookish and bored in school because the captain of the football team could not translate Virgil and yet was the school god while you, you, you little *shrimp,* were the school egghead, junior size and an early model.(p.533)

shrink

• We must not *shrink* at anything.(p.79)
• If we have obtained permission, have consulted with others, asked God to help and the drastic step is indicated we must not *shrink.*(p.80)

shrouded

• My childhood was *shrouded* in the fumes of alcohol.(p.369)

shrubbery

• This problem was soon solved, however, as I began to take my bottle along with me and hide it in the bathroom or in the *shrubbery* outside.(p.184)

shrunk

• I found some wool stockings, some white flannels that had *shrunk* to my knees, and an old jacket.(p.288)

shucks

• *Shucks!*(p.497)

shuddering

• I remember looking longingly at the window as an easier solution, and *shuddering* at the memory of that other window, three years before, and the six agonizing months in a London hospital ward.(p.224)

shuffling

• From the top of the heap in a few years he had skidded to becoming a *shuffling* customer, still entering the better barrooms but welcomed by neither mine host nor his patrons.(p.236)

shun

• People have said we must not go where liquor is served; we must not have it in our homes; we must *shun* friends who drink; we must avoid moving pictures which show drinking scenes; we must not go into bars; our friends must hide their bottles if we go to their houses; we mustn't think or be reminded about alcohol at all.(p.100)

shut

• Everyone became resigned to the certainty that I would have to be *shut* up somewhere, or would stumble along to a miserable end.(p.8)
• When they talked of a God personal to me, who was love, superhuman strength and direction, I became irritated and my mind snapped *shut* against such a theory.(p.10)
• For when harboring such feelings we *shut* ourselves off from the sunlight of the Spirit.(p.66)
• We will not regret the past nor wish to *shut* the door on it.(p.83)
• I *shut* myself in my room, which began to go around in circles.(p.279)
• But -- supposing that just one man died because I had, for selfish reasons, kept my mouth *shut?*(p.282)
• I *shut* my eyes and asked for help.(p.285)
• But then, when that steel door slammed *shut,* and she was the one that went home, I was amazed.(p.440)
• In the garage, I would put the needle in my vein and then try to figure out exactly how much medication to inject to overcome the pep pills while adding to the sleeping pills while ignoring the tranquilizers, in order to get just enough to be able to pull out the needle, jerk the tourniquet, throw it in the car, slam the car door *shut,* run down the hall, and fall in bed before I fell asleep.(p.442)
• That's when that steel door slammed *shut,* and Max was the one who went home.(p.444)
• It didn't worry me very much, because at that time I could *shut* off for a couple of months without taking a drink or even wanting one, and without feeling that I was giving anything up.(p.518)
• I talked to him for quite a long time and at the end, he said, "Well, you're not quite mad enough to be *shut* up for good yet, but you soon will be if you live long enough."(p.522)
• Poor, black, totally ruled by alcohol, she felt *shut* away from any life worth living.(p.526)

shutoff

• Instead, I had a 5:00 a.m. *shutoff* time.(p.441)

shuts

• He *shuts* himself up in an asylum, hoping to mend his ways.(p.38)

shutter

• At that particular time, the boys put me on a *shutter* and took me out to the shed, and I lay in the car while they enjoyed their banquet.(p.195)

shy

• We shouldn't be *shy* on this matter of prayer.(p.85)
• If you think he will be *shy* of a spiritual remedy, ask him to look at the chapter on alcoholism.(p.112)
• I had been hypersensitive, *shy,* idealistic.(p.226)
• I don't think the boys were completely convinced of my personality change, for they fought *shy* of including my story in the book, so my only contribution to their literary efforts was my firm conviction, being still a theological rebel, that the word God should be qualified with the phrase "as we understand him" -- for that was the only way I could accept spirituality.(p.248)
• It was therefore not extraordinary that I should *shy* away from any serious thought of marriage for a great many years after joining A.A.(p.286)

• Just three years of drinking pushed a ***shy***, lonely young girl to the depth of depression.(p.353)
• I certainly wasn't my ***shy***, quiet self that night – as I was informed the next morning.(p.353)
• What had happened to the ***shy***, lonely, churchgoing wallflower?(p.355)
• Prior to our marriage, when she was a ***shy***, scrawny adolescent, I was able to see things in her that others couldn't necessarily see – things like beauty, charm, gaiety, a gift for being easy to talk to, a sense of humor, and many other fine qualities.(p.450)
• In each new place, I was the new kid -- a skinny, ***shy*** kid – to be tested and beaten up.(p.555)

shying
• We don't use this as an excuse for ***shying*** away from the subject of God.(p.77)

shyness
• I lost my ***shyness***.(p.402)

sick
• Many do not comprehend that the alcoholic is a very ***sick*** person.(p.xiii)
• The wars which had been fought, the burnings and chicanery that religious dispute had facilitated, made me ***sick***.(p.11)
• From it stem all forms of spiritual disease, for we have been not only mentally and physically ill, we have been spiritually ***sick***.(p.64)
• This was our course: We realized that the people who wronged us were perhaps spiritually ***sick***.(p.66)
• Though we did not like their symptoms and the way these disturbed us, they, like ourselves, were ***sick*** too.(p.67)
• We asked God to help us show them the same tolerance, pity, and patience that we would cheerfully grant a ***sick*** friend.(p.67)
• When a person offended we said to ourselves, "This is a ***sick*** man.(p.67)
• We wouldn't treat ***sick*** people that way.(p.67)
• We have begun to learn tolerance, patience and good will toward all men, even our enemies, for we look on them as ***sick*** people.(p.70)
• They should be patient, realizing they are dealing with a ***sick*** person.(p.90)
• Tell him how baffled you were, how you finally learned that you were ***sick***.(p.92)
• But urge upon a man's family that he has been a very ***sick*** person and should be treated accordingly.(p.100)
• In our belief any scheme of combating alcoholism which proposes to shield the ***sick*** man from temptation is doomed to failure.(p.101)
• We have told small tots that father was ***sick***, which was much nearer the truth than we realized.(p.106)
• Sometimes we sensed dimly that we were dealing with ***sick*** men.(p.107)
• He is just another very ***sick***, unreasonable person.(p.108)
• When you have carefully explained to such people that he is a ***sick*** person, you will have created a new atmosphere.(p.115)
• Frequently, you have felt obliged to tell your husband's employer and his friends that he was ***sick***, when as a matter of fact he was tight.(p.115)
• By force of circumstances, she was often obliged to treat father as a ***sick*** or wayward child.(p.130)
• To me, this incident illustrates lack of understanding as to what really ails the alcoholic, and lack of knowledge as to what part employers might profitably take in salvaging their ***sick*** employees.(p.139)
• You can see that he is mentally and physically ***sick***.(p.141)
• When his wife next calls saying he is ***sick***, you might jump to the conclusion he is drunk.(p.146)
• If you are an alcoholic, you are a mighty ***sick*** man.(p.147)
• Of course, this chapter refers to alcoholics, ***sick*** people, deranged men.(p.149)
• They will approach still other ***sick*** ones and fellowships of Alcoholics Anonymous may spring up in each city and hamlet, havens for those who must find a way out.(p.153)
• "Yes, that's me," said the ***sick*** man, "the very image.(p.157)
• Ask Him in your morning meditation what you can do each day for the man who is still ***sick***.(p.164)
• Morning after morning I would awake ***sick*** and with terrible jitters, but there was always a flask of liquor sitting on the table beside my bed.(p.183)
• I wasn't mad or vicious – I was a ***sick*** person.(p.227)
• The mental state of the ***sick*** alcoholic is beyond description.(p.244)
• I'd like to say here how important it was to us then that we do all the little things that people said were important, because later when Russ was so ***sick*** that I had to hold him up, they had a meeting out at the house.(p.270)
• I, who had never made a speech in my life and who would have been frightened ***sick*** at the prospect, stood up in front of Rotary groups in different parts of the city and talked about Alcoholics Anonymous.(p.283)
• Some of us struggle with these people because we know that they are really very ***sick***, but we also know that short of some miracle, we are not going to help them except temporarily, and that they will inevitably get worse and worse until one of two things happens.(p.308)
• Usually, the next morning I would be quite ***sick***.(p.317)
• I got orders to go to Vietnam, and I spent most of the year over there either drunk or ***sick*** with a hangover.(p.317)
• I was deathly ***sick*** every time I took a drink.(p.322)
• Sometimes I would lie on the bathroom floor, deathly ***sick***, praying I would die, and praying to God as I always had prayed to Him when I was drinking: "Dear God, get me out of this one and I'll never do it again."(p.324)
• I was in the fourth quarter of my senior year at high school, and my mother was quite ***sick*** in the hospital.(p.354)
• The only time my dog would have anything to do with me was when I had a hangover, and when I was so ***sick*** he was the only one who would have anything to do with me at all.(p.390)
• I realized that there were other people in this world who behaved and acted as I did, and that I was a ***sick*** person, that I was suffering from an actual disease.(p.392)
• (It was the beer and cheap whiskey that was making me so ***sick***.(p.398)
• Incalculable are the intangible initiation fees that A.A. members have paid: the ***sick***, ***sick*** hangovers, the remorse, guilt, broken homes, jails, and institutions, and the mental anguish in general that has been generated over the years.(p.399)
• Like most ***sick*** people before me, I was implacably selfish, and chronically self-centered.(p.401)
• With ten years of A.A. behind me, I was able to tell him that I'd have been alcoholic, no matter what; that I had been a ***sick*** person, unfit for marriage.(p.403)
• I was the center of attention, just what my ***sick*** ego craved.(p.407)
• In a ***sick*** people's place, myself among the sickest.(p.410)
• I, who had dreamed these ***sick*** dreams, now reaped the nightmare.(p.411)
• Oh, poor self-centered, ***sick*** little me.(p.413)
• Well, I'm willing, if it will curb this awful desire to drink, this fear of not having a drink, this feeling of always being alone, scared, deserted, ***sick***.(p.430)
• As a physician and pharmacist who had grown up in a drugstore-home, I had a pill for every ill, and I was ***sick*** a lot.(p.443)
• One has to be pretty ***sick*** to do that, and perhaps one has to be even sicker to come back every day for a new list, as she did.(p.446)
• Eventually, I had to redo each of the Twelve Steps specifically with Max in mind, from the First, saying, "I am powerless over alcohol, and my homelife is unmanageable by me," to the Twelfth, in which I tried to think of her as a ***sick*** Al-Anon and treat her with the love I would give a ***sick*** A.A. newcomer.(p.452)
• I painfully awakened each time, mentally, physically, and spiritually ***sick***.(p.457)
• I woke up in jail, ***sick***, withdrawing from alcohol and speed, already a four-time loser, and now with a fifth felony charge against me.(p.460)
• Cops now ***sick*** of me, so they buy me one-way ticket to Canada.(p.475)
• He old, ***sick***, want to be alone with bottle.(p.476)
• This sober Indian say to ***sick***, red-eyed alcoholic who want good medicine: "Put cork in bottle.(p.477)
• How ***sick*** I felt.(p.498)
• I have left my wife at home, ***sick***, and I have been unkind to her in leaving.(p.505)
• Harm is done by ***sick*** people, as I was ***sick***, and doing dreadful harm to myself and to my loved ones.(p.542)
• The only importance in all of this lies in the fact that at twenty-three I was just as ***sick*** as I was at thirty three, when I came into A.A., but at that time I apparently had no place to go because I had no drinking problem.(p.546)
• I got ***sick*** of the sweetness and turned to ale.(p.556)

sickened
• But we are sure that our bodies were ***sickened*** as well.(p.xxiv)
• Of course, there is such a thing as incompatibility, but in nearly every instance the alcoholic only seems to be unloving and inconsiderate; it is usually because he is warped and ***sickened*** that he says and does these appalling things.(p.108)
• Over the next two years, I ***sickened*** rapidly.(p.557)

sickening
• Inside, I went right on being a mass of unlovely self-pity, queasy anxiety and ***sickening*** self-debasement.(p.400)

sicker
• When I hear the more rugged stories of alcoholics who became ***sicker*** than I did with this affliction, I humbly thank God for showing me "the handwriting on the wall."(p.367)
• The harder I worked with Max, the ***sicker*** she got.(p.440)
• One has to be pretty sick to do that, and perhaps one has to be even ***sicker*** to come back every day for a new list, as she did.(p.446)
• Instead, I had gotten ***sicker***.(p.539)

sickest
• In a sick people's place, myself among the ***sickest***.(p.410)

sickness
• An illness of this sort – and we have come to believe it an illness –involves those about us in a way no other human ***sickness*** can.(p.18)
• If this presents difficulty, re-reading chapters two and three, where the alcoholic ***sickness*** is discussed at length might be worth while.(p.140)
• I lay across the bed on my stomach with nothing but pain and ***sickness***.(p.267)
• The horrors of increasing hangover ***sickness*** to occupy the entire day; nausea, dry heaves, the rocking bed, the nightmare-filled mind.(p.408)
• We can have this new way of life – learning to live with our ***sickness*** and to be happy and content – if we are willing to change our way of thinking and be honest, first with ourselves, then with others.(p.480)
• We all have the same ***sickness***, and in helping one another, we are able to stay sober.(p.530)
• And if I had been able to turn to the church at that time I'm sure they could not have convinced me my ***sickness*** was within myself, nor could they have shown me the need for self-analysis that A.A. has shown me is vital if I am to survive.(p.546)

side
• Soon A.A. was beset by these very problems on every ***side*** and in every group.(p.xix)
• Ideas, emotions, and attitudes which were once the guiding forces of the lives of these men are suddenly cast to one ***side***, and a completely new set of conceptions and motives begin to dominate them.(p.27)
• We never gave the spiritual ***side*** of life a fair hearing.(p.50)
• We are there to sweep off our ***side*** of the street realizing that nothing worth while can be accomplished until we do so, never trying to tell him what he should do.(p.77)
• Both father and the family are mistaken, though each ***side*** may have some justification.(p.126)
• Dad may feel that for years his drinking has placed him on the wrong ***side*** of every argument, but now he has become a superior person with God on his ***side***.(p.129)
• (At this point, the Editors intrude just long enough to supplement Bill D.'s account, that of the man on the bed, with that of Bill W., the man who sat by the ***side*** of the bed.)(p.188)
• Forced to detrain from an empty gondola on the other ***side*** of Chicago by a terrific rainstorm which drenched me to the skin, I hit the first factory building I saw for a job.(p.253)
• I'm sure his family felt that it was a marriage that -- well, I was a girl from the wrong ***side*** of the tracks -- definitely!(p.262)
• An attorney sat at the ***side*** of the bed where I was lying, and he sat on the edge of his chair and looked as innocent as a baby.(p.268)
• I sat down on the ***side*** of one of their beds, and I started to weep, and I couldn't stop, and I was so startled, and I apologized again and again for it.(p.272)
• My husband, my children saw the other ***side*** of me.(p.339)
• And then we went up the ***side*** of a hill where we have a little barbecue area to make the fire for the barbecue, and on the way up, I thought to myself – I'll go back down to the kitchen and refill this drink.(p.347)
• At the other ***side*** of the table sat one of the carpenters in our community, and at the further end of the table sat the man who ran the bakery, while on one ***side*** sat my friend who was a mechanic.(p.347)
• However, what I had gained materially on the

credit ***side*** of my ledger, I have since learned was more than offset on the debit ***side*** by egotism, resentment and dishonesty.(p.356)
• When it became noticeable to the point of comment, I devised ways of sneaking drinks on the ***side***.(p.375)
• My family, on my mother's ***side***, was brilliant, gifted and charming.(p.401)
• I talked out of the ***side*** of my mouth, as they did.(p.423)
• I was transferred to Kaneohe Bay, across the hump to the windward ***side*** of Oahu, to the aviation base.(p.426)
• One, the ***side*** I turned to myself and the world, was respectable -- even, in some ways, distinguished.(p.432)
• The other ***side*** of the coin was sinister, baffling.(p.432)
• He went into the religious ***side*** and told me that I didn't attend church as regularly as I should, and that he felt, more or less, that this was responsible for my trouble.(p.489)
• It was a thorn in my ***side***, because I knew it was the truth, and I hated to hear the truth, especially about myself.(p.513)
• We talked for a while, and then he sent me down to the Alanon House over on the west ***side***, and there I had my introduction to A.A.(p.515)
• One of the truly great things A.A. has taught me is that reality too has two sides; I had only known the grim ***side*** before the program, but now I had a chance to learn about the pleasant ***side*** as well.(p.550)

sidecar
• We gave up our positions and off we roared on a motorcycle, the ***sidecar*** stuffed with tent, blankets, a change of clothes, and three huge volumes of a financial reference service.(p.2)

sides
• Unless they actually need protection from their father, it is best not to take ***sides*** in any argument he has with them while drinking.(p.115)
• When we went to bed my ***sides*** ached, and I said to my husband, "I thought I would never laugh again, but I have laughed."(p.269)
• One of the truly great things A.A. has taught me is that reality too has two ***sides***; I had only known the grim side before the program, but now I had a chance to learn about the pleasant side as well.(p.550)

sidestepped
• This office job brought me face to face with a problem which I had ***sidestepped*** all my adult life, lack of training.(p.284)

sighing
• Why sit with a long face in places where there is drinking, ***sighing*** about the good old days.(p.102)

sighs
• He is like the retired business man who lolls in the Florida sunshine in the winter complaining of the sad state of the nation; the minister who ***sighs*** over the sins of the twentieth century; politicians and reformers who are sure all would be Utopia if the rest of the world would only behave; the outlaw safe cracker who thinks society has wronged him; and the alcoholic who has lost all and is locked up.(p.61)

sight
• Keep it always in ***sight*** that we are dealing with that most terrible human emotion -- jealousy.(p.82)
• There wasn't a bar in ***sight***, but I found the subway station.(p.223)
• The idea behind it is that, having taken the treatment, your system is so "conditioned" that the mere ***sight*** or smell or taste of alcohol produces a violent reaction, and you become ill.(p.469)
• But the end is in ***sight***.(p.499)
• They are almost paid; the end is in ***sight***.(p.541)

sign
• The slightest ***sign*** of fear or intolerance may lessen your husband's chance of recovery.(p.120)
• I looked so terrible in the court that the judge suggested that I get a continuance and let me ***sign*** all the papers to go to a hospital and to a doctor.(p.204)
• She gave no ***sign*** of recognizing anything wrong, but what had I been doing for those lost five hours?(p.223)
• As we left, and they were escorting us across the bridge into Wheeling, I, with great dignity and sarcasm, told them if their wives were ever visiting in Akron, and they, too, were looking for their route ***sign*** as I was, that I hoped I could extend to them the hospitality that had been shown to me in Bellaire.(p.264)
• While I sought the comforting arms of alcohol, I knew this was a ***sign*** of weakness on the part of a longtime-successful old codger with white hair, the image of dignity.(p.331)
• I had run away from school to join the army in World War I, but missed it by one day since the Armistice was signed the very day I landed in Atlanta to ***sign*** up with Uncle Sam.(p.357)
• So when he came for me, as he walked down the stairs, I could see him through the bars, and he was signing for me; I looked at him and said, "Don't you ***sign*** anything in this place!"(p.391)
• So I raised enough fuss that they finally agreed to let me ***sign*** out, against medical advice.(p.444)
• While I was taking inventory in the cold-storage locker one Sunday, a wooden ***sign*** bolted to the inside door stopped me in my tracks.(p.461)
• Then in a couple of hours, when there was still no word from my husband and no ***sign*** of him, I had the feeling we alcoholics all know.(p.467)
• Also, after that first visit I learned I could refuse to ***sign*** myself in unless they gave me a glass of whiskey in one hand and a glass of paraldehyde in the other.(p.468)

signed
• I could almost hear the sound of the preacher's voice as I sat, on still Sundays, way over there on the hillside; there was that proffered temperance pledge I never ***signed***; my grandfather's good natured contempt of some church folk and their doings; his insistence that the spheres really had their music; but his denial of the preacher's right to tell him how he must listen; his fearlessness as he spoke of these things just before he died; these recollections welled up from the past.(p.10)
• We heard by wireless on the 5th that the Armistice would be ***signed*** the next day (this was a premature report) so I had a couple of cognacs to celebrate; then I hopped a truck and went AWOL.(p.242)
• I checked into my hotel room and then noticed a placard tucked under the glass on the bureau stating "There will be positively NO drinking at this convention" ***signed*** by the president of the company.(p.243)
• I had run away from school to join the army in World War I, but missed it by one day since the Armistice was ***signed*** the very day I landed in Atlanta to sign up with Uncle Sam.(p.357)
• The Armistice is ***signed*** on the 11th and the draft is called off.(p.499)

significance
• The real ***significance*** of my experience in the Cathedral burst upon me.(p.12)
• They see its ***significance*** everywhere.(p.69)
• 12. -- And finally, we of Alcoholics Anonymous believe that the principle of anonymity has immense spiritual ***significance***.(p.567)

significant
• The place is Naini Tal, in the foothills of the mighty Himalaya Mountains, and it has some very ***significant*** memories for me.(p.342)
• My work is on a much deeper and more ***significant*** level than it ever was before, and I am today a fairly creative, relatively sane human being.(p.438)
• I was the only person I'd ever known personally who had ever been in jail, and I guess it is most ***significant*** that the second time was less humiliating that the first had been.(p.549)

signify
• Being wrecked in the same vessel, being restored and united under one God, with hearts and minds attuned to the welfare of others, the things which matter so much to some people no longer ***signify*** much to them.(p.161)

signing
• So when he came for me, as he walked down the stairs, I could see him through the bars, and he was ***signing*** for me; I looked at him and said, "Don't you sign anything in this place!"(p.391)

signs
• Treatment seemed wise, for I showed ***signs*** of delirium tremens.(p.13)
• We have heard of few instances where people, who showed definite ***signs*** of alcoholism, were able to stop for a long period because of an overpowering desire to do so.(p.32)

silences
• The trip back was completed in one of those dead, awful ***silences***.(p.467)

silent
• All afternoon I sat there and drank and played Bing Crosby's recording of "***Silent*** Night" over and over again on the juke box.(p.467)

Silkworth
• The section called "The Doctor's Opinion" has been kept intact, just as it was originally written in 1939 by the late Dr. William D. ***Silkworth***, our Society's great medical benefactor.(p.xi)
• He had also been greatly helped by the late Dr. William D. ***Silkworth***, a New York specialist in alcoholism who is now accounted no less than a medical saint by A.A. members, and whose story of the early days of our Society appears in the next pages.(p.xvi)
• Very truly yours, William D. ***Silkworth***, M.D.(p.xxiv)
• William D. ***Silkworth***, M.D.(p.xxx)

Silkworth's
• But when the broker gave him Dr. ***Silkworth's*** description of alcoholism and its hopelessness, the physician began to pursue the spiritual remedy for his malady with a willingness he had never before been able to muster.(p.xvi)
• Since Dr. ***Silkworth's*** first endorsement of Alcoholics Anonymous, medical societies and physicians throughout the world have set their approval upon us.(p.571)

sillier
• I wonder if ever there has been a ***sillier*** reason for getting drunk all the time.(p.537)

silly
• Asked why they commenced to drink again, they would reply with some ***silly*** excuse, or none.(p.107)
• But it was a ***silly*** idea that we were too good to need God.(p.116)
• And then a ***silly***, simple thought came to me.(p.351)

silverware
• When they saw me coming, they locked up the ***silverware*** and everything else of value.(p.478)

similar
• He laid great stress on the progression of his attitude toward life and people, and most of his attitudes had been very ***similar*** to mine.(p.290)
• They help others with ***similar*** problems . . .(p.572)

similarly
• ***Similarly***, we rid ourselves of guilt and remorse as we "clean out the garbage" from our minds through the Fourth and Fifth Steps of our recovery program.(p.560)

simple
• In spite of the great increase in the size and the span of this Fellowship, at its core it remains ***simple*** and personal.(p.xxii)
• On the other hand -- and strange as this may seem to those who do not understand -- once a psychic change has occurred, the very same person who seemed doomed, who had so many problems he despaired of ever solving them, suddenly finds himself easily able to control his desire for alcohol, the only effort necessary being that required to follow a few ***simple*** rules.(p.xxvii)
• They had told of a ***simple*** religious idea and a practical program of action.(p.9)
• ***Simple***, but not easy; a price had to be paid.(p.14)
• Each day my friend's ***simple*** talk in our kitchen multiplies itself in a widening circle of peace on earth and good will to men.(p.16)
• When, therefore, we were approached by those in whom the problem had been solved, there was nothing left for us but to pick up the ***simple*** kit of spiritual tools laid at our feet.(p.25)
• He can go anywhere on this earth where other free men may go without disaster, provided he remains willing to maintain a certain ***simple*** attitude.(p.26)
• If what we have learned and felt and seen means anything at all, it means that all of us, whatever our race, creed, or color are the children of a living Creator with whom we may form a relationship upon ***simple*** and understandable terms as soon as we are willing and honest enough to try.(p.28)
• I had no trouble refusing drinks, and began to wonder if I had not been making too hard work of a ***simple*** matter.(p.40)
• As soon as we admitted the possible existence of a Creative Intelligence, a Spirit of the Universe underlying the totality of things, we began to be possessed of a new sense of power and direction, provided we took other ***simple*** steps.(p.46)
• It has been repeatedly proven among us that upon this ***simple*** cornerstone a wonderfully effective spiritual structure can be built.(p.47)
• They flatly declare that since they have come to believe in a Power greater than themselves, to take a certain attitude toward that Power, and to do certain ***simple*** things, there has been a revolutionary change in their way of living and thinking.(p.50)
• This happened soon after they wholeheartedly met a few ***simple*** requirements.(p.50)
• When we saw others solve their problems by a ***simple*** reliance upon the Spirit of the Universe, we had to stop doubting the power of God.(p.52)

• Yet its elements are ***simple***.(p.57)
• Those who do not recover are people who cannot or will not completely give themselves to this ***simple*** program, usually men and women who are constitutionally incapable of being honest with themselves.(p.58)
• Most good ideas are ***simple***, and this concept was the keystone of the new and triumphant arch through which we passed to freedom.(p.62)
• So we let God discipline us in the ***simple*** way we have just outlined.(p.88)
• They can hardly fail to approve these ***simple*** principles, though the head of the house still fails somewhat in practicing them.(p.130)
• The very ***simple*** program they advised me to follow was that I should ask to know God's will for me for that one day, and then, to the best of my ability, to follow that, and at night to express my gratefulness to God for the things that had happened to me during the day.(p.208)
• It was hard to reconcile this ghastly present with the ***simple*** facts of the past.(p.225)
• There I sat in the evenings, enjoying with my friends our memories of the "old country," singing the old songs we all knew, playing ***simple*** card games for drinks and consuming great quantities of beer.(p.231)
• I very early came to see that there had to be a continual renewal for that ***simple*** deal with God; that I had perpetually to keep the bargain.(p.237)
• We now live in the West and are very fortunate in our area A.A.; it is good, ***simple*** and friendly, and our one desire is to stay in A.A. and not on it.(p.250)
• I began to read the Bible daily and to go over a ***simple*** devotional exercise as a way to begin each day.(p.259)
• Probably only a few readers of this story will be able, from personal experiences of their own, to understand the exhilaration and sense of accomplishment which I felt after finishing this seemingly ***simple*** assignment.(p.276)
• It was ***simple***, they said, and went on to explain to me in their own language the program of recovery and daily living which we know today as the Twelve Steps of A.A.(p.279)
• He it was who convinced me, because his own conviction was so real, that a Power greater than myself could help me in the crises of life, and that the means of communicating with this Power was ***simple*** prayer.(p.279)
• The prayer I said was ***simple***.(p.280)
• It sounds ***simple***, but there were obstacles and doubts to overcome.(p.282)
• A very ***simple*** plan that I still find much joy and happiness in following.(p.302)
• It explained so much I had not understood about myself and, best of all, it promised recovery if I would do a few ***simple*** things and be willing to have the desire to drink removed.(p.309)
• She told me; it was ***simple***; I could have done it very easily.(p.326)
• In so ***simple*** a manner did my morning drinking begin.(p.331)
• "Complete abandon"; "Half measures availed us nothing"; "Thoroughly follow our path"; "Completely give oneself to this ***simple*** program" -- rang in my swelled head.(p.349)
• All I do in a very ***simple*** way, is to help Him cure my patients.(p.351)
• And then a silly, ***simple*** thought came to me.(p.351)
• I find an inner pleasure in ***simple*** things.(p.383)
• Dr. Bob tells about keeping it ***simple*** and not to louse it up.(p.395)
• The statement fascinates me because of its ***simple*** verity.(p.396)
• Some ***simple*** mathematics and more statistics:(p.399)
• His were good, ***simple*** Quaker folk who accepted me with love.(p.402)
• It wasn't that ***simple***.(p.464)
• I keep it ***simple***; go to many meetings; carry message to those who listen.(p.476)
• It was very, very ***simple***.(p.515)
• What is much more important to me, A.A. has taught me that through this ***simple*** program I may experience a change in this reaction pattern that will indeed allow me to "match calamity with serenity."(p.544)
• I thought that life was a pretty ***simple*** thing; you simply made a plan for your life, based upon what you wanted, and then you needed only the courage to go after it.(p.545)
• The solution seemed very ***simple***.(p.545)
• Society can do anything it chooses to do with me when I am drunk and I can't lift a finger to stop it, for I forfeit my rights through the ***simple*** expedient of becoming a menace to myself and to the people around me.(p.549)
• The A.A. members who sponsored me told me in the beginning that I would not only find a way to live without having a drink, but that I would find a way to live without wanting to drink, if I would do these ***simple*** things.(p.550)

simpler

• So it was comforting to learn that we could commence at a ***simpler*** level.(p.47)
• Around this time our big A.A. book was being written and it all became much ***simpler***; we had a definite formula which some sixty of us agreed was the middle course for all alcoholics who wanted sobriety, and that formula has not been changed one iota down through the years.(p.248)
• It has made life a thousand times easier and ***simpler*** than did the endless compromises and conflicts by which I lived before.(p.394)
• And life keeps getting ***simpler*** and easier as we try to reverse my old idea, by taking care of the internal environment via the Twelve Steps, and letting the external environment take care of itself.)(p.446)

simplified

• The baffling problem of getting drunk when I had every intention of staying sober was ***simplified***.(p.379)
• A willingness to do whatever I was told to do ***simplified*** the program for me.(p.381)

simply

• We ***simply*** wish to be helpful to those who are afflicted.(p.xiv)
• I ***simply*** didn't know.(p.5)
• ***Simply***, but smilingly, he said, "I've got religion."(p.9)
• I ***simply*** had to believe in a Spirit of the Universe, who knew neither time nor limitation.(p.10)
• Then comes the day when he ***simply*** cannot make it and gets drunk all over again.(p.22)
• ***Simply*** because it is impossible to explain what we see, feel, direct, and use, without a reasonable assumption as a starting point.(p.48)
• ***Simply*** we tell him that we will never get over drinking until we have done our utmost to straighten out the past.(p.77)
• Never talk down to an alcoholic from any moral or spiritual hilltop; ***simply*** lay out the kit of spiritual tools for his inspection.(p.95)
• Some of us have taken very hard knocks to learn this truth: Job or no job -- wife or no wife -- we ***simply*** do not stop drinking so long as we place dependence upon other people ahead of dependence on God.(p.98)
• He ***simply*** could not believe that his brother-executive suffered from a serious illness.(p.138)
• Whenever a situation arose that fast talk wouldn't explain away, I ***simply*** withdrew.(p.214)
• I never left the church, but I was a fringe member, and the thought ***simply*** never occurred to me that through the exercise of what I had I might find the answer to my problem, ***simply*** because I wouldn't admit that I had a problem.(p.214)
• You can all remember that in the first few months after the change, a great many men, who had formerly been used to a few beers every day or an occasional drink of whiskey, ***simply*** quit all alcoholic drinks.(p.232)
• Gradually, however, I'd suffer so much that I ***simply*** had to have the morning-after drink.(p.233)
• I ***simply*** did not have the pep to do hard, "cold-turkey" selling.(p.277)
• The next two years were ***simply*** a long drawn out process of less and less work and more and more whiskey.(p.278)
• They went into a huddle and dad explained that he ***simply*** took my pants, shoes and money away, so that I could get no liquor and had to sober up.(p.288)
• I thought it was wonderful, ***simply*** marvelous, for him.(p.321)
• The answer came to me very ***simply*** in the first step of the Twelve Steps of A.A.(p.379)
• It has changed not ***simply*** one department of my life -- it has changed my whole life.(p.394)
• I tried to compensate with impossible dreams and ambitions, which were ***simply*** early forms of escape.(p.400)
• It had never occurred to me before that I could live ***simply*** and be independent of my family.(p.409)
• He said to me, gently and ***simply***, "Do you think that you are one of us?"(p.413)
• I came to A.A. ***simply*** because there were no other doors of help open to me in my hometown.(p.420)
• To this day, I am amazed at how many of my problems -- most of which had nothing to do with drinking, I believed -- have become manageable or have ***simply*** disappeared since I quit drinking.(p.448)
• Please do not think it ended so ***simply*** and so easily.(p.541)
• ***Simply***, yes it did end; for I had changed my mind about alcohol, and it stayed changed.(p.541)
• My mother went to a nearby city to go to work, and my father, being an alcoholic, ***simply*** went.(p.544)
• I thought that life was a pretty simple thing; you ***simply*** made a plan for your life, based upon what you wanted, and then you needed only the courage to go after it.(p.545)

simulated

• Hiding behind a newspaper, magazine, or book, I really saw nothing, but ***simulated*** deep interest.(p.332)

simultaneously

• Almost ***simultaneously***, I discovered that cocktails in the late afternoon and highballs in the evening relieved the many tensions of the day.(p.277)

since

• ***Since*** the original Foreword to this book was written in 1939, a wholesale miracle has taken place.(p.xv)
• My friends had dropped several million ***since*** ten o'clock -- so what?(p.4)
• It was years ***since*** I could remember his coming to New York in that condition.(p.9)
• Judging from what I had seen in Europe and ***since***, the power of God in human affairs was negligible, the Brotherhood of Man a grim jest.(p.11)
• I have ***since*** talked with scores of men who felt the same way.(p.12)
• And so it had been ever ***since***.(p.13)
• I have not had a drink ***since***.(p.13)
• Exceptions to cases such as yours have been occurring ***since*** early times.(p.27)
• I have ***since*** been brought into a way of living infinitely more satisfying and, I hope, more useful than the life I lived before.(p.42)
• They flatly declare that ***since*** they have come to believe in a Power greater than themselves, to take a certain attitude toward that Power, and to do certain simple things, there has been a revolutionary change in their way of living and thinking.(p.50)
• Of course she did not, and the whole situation has long ***since*** been adjusted.(p.79)
• He often says that if he had continued to work on them, he might have deprived many others, who have ***since*** recovered, of their chance.(p.96)
• If their old relationship is to be resumed it must be on a better basis, ***since*** the former did not work.(p.99)
• ***Since*** this book was first published, A.A. has released thousands of alcoholics from asylums and hospitals of every kind.(p.114)
• ***Since*** the home has suffered more than anything else, it is well that a man exert himself there.(p.127)
• The practical answer is that ***since*** these things have happened among us, they can happen with you.(p.153)
• He has not had a drink ***since***.(p.156)
• This couple has ***since*** become so fascinated that they have dedicated their home to the work.(p.160)
• It did help to certain extent, ***since*** I got in places where I could not obtain anything to drink, and so broke the habitual drinking.(p.183)
• It had long ***since*** become a serious problem.(p.197)
• Long ***since*** I had come to believe I was insane because I did so many things I didn't want to do.(p.199)
• The law school experience was not inspired by a desire to follow patent law, which has been my profession ***since***: I went to law school primarily to learn the law of contracts following my own experience with litigation.(p.212)
• In fact, I never lost my faith, ***since*** I had been prepared by some conversations toward the end of my sojourn in the hospital with Dr. Bob, conversations pretty much along spiritual lines.(p.218)
• I resolved that if I were going to continue with the Catholic Church, I was going to know the roots of the doctrine, ***since*** those roots had caused me some confusion.(p.221)
• It must have been a long time ***since*** I had my last drink -- but I didn't dare ask this stranger for one.(p.223)
• An active member of A.A. ***since*** 1939, I feel myself a useful member of the human race at last.(p.229)
• I have something to contribute to humanity, ***since*** I am peculiarly qualified, as a fellow-sufferer, to give aid and comfort to those who have stumbled and fallen over this business of meeting life.(p.229)
• I came directly to a growing industrial city in the middle west, where I have lived practically ever ***since***.(p.231)
• And, because as I have discovered ***since***, it is part of the "treatment" that these men be sent to see and talk with alcoholics who want to quit, he kept them busy.(p.235)

• Back at camp, all was forgiven because it was the End, but in the light of what I have *since* learned I know I was a confirmed alcoholic at nineteen.(p.242)
• Three years later, at twenty-five, I opened and operated their Philadelphia office and was earning more than I ever have *since*.(p.242)
• It was also an ending, for never *since* June 16th, 1938, have I had to walk alone.(p.248)
• I had never, *since* the believing days of childhood, been able to conceive an authority directing the universe.(p.259)
• And I was glad, and I have been ever *since*, that I said that.(p.270)
• It is well over sixteen years *since* I came back to life.(p.280)
• I have never had a drink *since*.(p.280)
• The most accurate answer I can give you is this: Fear has never again ruled my life *since* that day in September, 1938, when I found that a Power greater than myself could not only restore me to sanity but could keep me both sober and sane.(p.285)
• Immediately on her return we began to have formal meetings once a week, in the autumn of 1939, and we have continued to do this and to expand ever *since*.(p.295)
• I had long *since* given up any pretense of the "social" cocktail hour.(p.306)
• It had been so many years *since* I had not relied on some artificial crutch, either alcohol or sedatives.(p.310)
• *Since* I didn't do well in school, I quit and joined the Army at age seventeen.(p.317)
• *Since* I started out eager for early-day efforts, that meant guzzling before noon.(p.331)
• And I have not had a drink *since* that night.(p.334)
• How full it has kept my retirement years -- the five I've lived *since* the first two lost in traveling a rocky road to hell, before I made a U-turn.(p.334)
• *Since* I gave my will over to A.A., whatever A.A. has wanted of me I've tried to do to the best of my ability.(p.340)
• This was my first long vacation of sixty days *since* I had joined the army.(p.343)
• I have read systematically *since* then, and A.A. literature has kept me sober.(p.343)
• Many times have I heard the above expressions *since* I have been in A.A., and many times I have had to reply "Definitely I am an alcoholic, and while it may be hard for you to believe, it is not hard for me, for I have learned many things about alcohol and myself that would, perhaps, be difficult for you to understand."(p.356)
• However, what I had gained materially on the credit side of my ledger, I have *since* learned was more than offset on the debit side by egotism, resentment and dishonesty.(p.356)
• I had run away from school to join the army in World War I, but missed it by one day *since* the Armistice was signed the very day I landed in Atlanta to sign up with Uncle Sam.(p.357)
• Neither of these circumstances was very helpful to my type *since* I had not learned to face realities.(p.358)
• *Since* the radio station was getting on its feet, it didn't require so many nights of evening work, and that permitted leisure time for drinking.(p.360)
• I have had many more reasons to drink *since* I have been in A.A. than I had in all the years of my drinking.(p.367)
• In meeting me casually, I don't think my strong belief in "The Man Upstairs" shows, but I have no other explanation for the many good things that have happened to me *since* I have been in A.A. – they came to me from a Greater Power.(p.367)
• It was fun at first, *since* I never had indulged before.(p.370)
• He has *since* become famous and distinguished, an asset to his country.(p.403)
• All of them have *since* settled down to jobs and good marriages.(p.407)
• In those days, psychiatry and A.A. had not gotten together as they have *since*.(p.412)
• *Since* they could do nothing with Anne either, Priscilla suggested that I go and look after Anne.(p.414)
• All the people involved in these flare-ups took it with remarkable grace, have teased me about it *since*, and have become good friends of mine.(p.416)
• Or maybe I'd come home wild drunk, singing and raving about what a fine place home was and what grand parents I had *since* they joined A.A.(p.428)
• I'm twenty-six now and I haven't had a drink *since* I made my decision.(p.430)
• (That dog hasn't wet my pants once *since* I joined A.A., and neither have I!)(p.440)
• To this day, I am amazed at how many of my problems -- most of which had nothing to do with drinking, I believed -- have become manageable or have simply disappeared *since* I quit drinking.(p.448)
• I haven't seen my son *since* he was three and a half years old.(p.463)
• Things went from bad to worse, and *since* I had finally and completely failed at the job of being a wife and a mother, my marriage ended.(p.468)
• You may wonder why, *since* I was having all this trouble, and was having to seek the assistance of others, A.A. hadn't come into the picture.(p.469)
• (I've met some of these same women *since* in A.A.)(p.471)
• That was over seven years ago, and thank God and A.A., I haven't had a drink *since*.(p.473)
• Have not take drink *since*.(p.476)
• Have not drink *since*.(p.476)
• *Since* then, I have never been back to heroin.(p.480)
• In that short period he built within me something that I had long *since* lost, which was hope.(p.495)
• I've stuck pretty close to A.A. ever *since* then, taken it day by day, not biting off more than I can chew.(p.511)
• Because, thank God, *since* I came into this program I haven't had any trouble.(p.516)
• *Since* I joined on that April night, A.A. has done more for me than just stop me from drinking; it has brought me back to life again.(p.524)
• *Since* I have been in A.A., I have more friends than I ever had in my life – friends who care about me and my welfare, friends who don't care that I am black and that I have been in prison.(p.529)
• *Since* I've been home, I have been able to gain the respect of my two sons again.(p.529)
• I have not seen a black face but mine *since* I've been here, and if I didn't look in the mirror, I wouldn't know that I was black, because these people treat me as one of them, which I am.(p.530)
• *Since*, perhaps, suicide was a bit too drastic (actually, I was afraid), dry martinis were chosen as the slow, pleasant, private, gradual instrument of self-destruction.(p.531)
• *Since* it was wartime, I explained to the somewhat startled shopkeeper that I had many friends in the service whom I was remembering with a watch.(p.532)
• There was the love affair which was ridiculous -- "imagine that midget being able to fall in love!" -- and my head knew it while my heart pumped real, genuine anguish, for it hurt like hell, and *since* it was first love, things have never been quite the same.(p.534)
• If I write with the air of one who has discovered the obvious, which is to say, the eternal truths which have been offered to us *since* the beginning, forgive my callowness; I had to find these things out for myself.(p.536)
• I fled, finally, after having been fired from my job by a boss who wept a little (*since* I had worked hard) as he gave notice for me to clear out.(p.539)
• On another small borrowed sum, I went up into the country to the home of a doctor I had known *since* boyhood.(p.540)
• I have not had a drink of anything alcoholic *since* that ten-day binge.(p.541)
• I attended my first A.A. meeting eight years ago, and it is with deep gratitude that I'm able to say I've not had a drink *since* that time, and that I take no sedation or narcotics, for this program is to me one of complete sobriety and I no longer need to escape reality.(p.549)
• I've had many spiritual experiences *since* I've been in the program, many that I didn't recognize right away, for I'm slow to learn and they take many guises.(p.551)
• It worked for me then, and it has worked for me many times *since*, and it will work for me every time I am willing to work it.(p.552)
• When I had been in A.A. only a short while, an oldtimer told me something that has affected my life ever *since*.(p.554)
• *Since* Dr. Silkworth's first endorsement of Alcoholics Anonymous, medical societies and physicians throughout the world have set their approval upon us.(p.571)

sincere

• Men have cried out to me in *sincere* and despairing appeal: "Doctor, I cannot go on like this!(p.xxvii)
• That the man who is making the approach has had the same difficulty, that he obviously knows what he is talking about, that his whole deportment shouts at the new prospect that he is a man with a real answer, that he has no attitude of Holier Than Thou, nothing whatever except the *sincere* desire to be helpful; that there are no fees to pay, no axes to grind, no people to please, no lectures to be endured -- these are the conditions we have found most effective.(p.18)
• But our man is sure to be impressed with a *sincere* desire to set right the wrong.(p.77)
• We, who have collectively seen a great deal of business life, at least from the alcoholic angle, had to smile at this gentleman's *sincere* opinion.(p.149)
• I used to promise my wife, my friends, and my children that I would drink no more – promises which seldom kept me sober even through the day, though I was very *sincere* when I made them.(p.177)
• And he further said that God could not accept me as a *sincere* follower of His Divine Law unless I was ready to be thoroughly honest about it.(p.236)
• Yet we all had one really *sincere* purpose in our hearts and that was not to drink.(p.246)
• And over my A.A. years I have made many real, honest, *sincere* friendships that I shall always cherish.(p.296)
• If I had been *sincere* in what I thought I wanted more than anything else in life – a sober husband and a happy, contented home – I would have gone on the wagon with him.(p.324)
• They described what had happened when they went out and tried drinking again, and I knew they were *sincere* in saying that it could happen to me.(p.334)
• These people were my friends, and I felt their *sincere* interest in me.(p.355)
• I knew my wife didn't because I had been *sincere* in all my promises to her as well as to my mother and to my close friends, but the urge to take that drink was more powerful than anything else.(p.494)

sincerely

• When we *sincerely* took such a position, all sorts of remarkable things followed.(p.63)
• If he is *sincerely* interested and wants to see you again, ask him to read this book in the interval.(p.95)
• But if you really and truly want to quit drinking liquor for good and all, and *sincerely* feel that you must have some help, we know that we have an answer for you.(p.181)
• Had I tried honestly and *sincerely* to practice the Twelve Steps I would have seen from my continuous moral inventory that I was getting off the beam -- I would have found that there were some active resentments in my life, a terrific amount of self-pity.(p.471)
• But as he continued to talk, I realized that this was the first time I had met a person who had the same problems I did and who, I *sincerely* believe, understood me as an individual.(p.494)
• It was the first time that I had asked for help *sincerely* and honestly.(p.515)

sincerity

• Next day we would ask ourselves, in all earnestness and *sincerity*, how it could have happened.(p.37)
• The faith and *sincerity* of both you and your husband will be put to the test.(p.117)
• I told him with all the *sincerity* at my command that I did.(p.235)
• I was greeted warmly, honestly, and with a true ring of *sincerity* by everyone present.(p.259)
• But I had never been a flippant, wise-cracking sneerer at the few persons I had met who had impressed me as Christian men and women, or at any institution whose *sincerity* of purpose I could see.(p.259)
• Truth and *sincerity* do not come easily to me.(p.420)

sinecure

• I saw that my Village friends, all of whom had small jobs, were living happily on about a tenth of my *sinecure*.(p.409)

sinful

• His wife is one of those persons who really feels there is something rather *sinful* about these commodities, so she nagged, and her intolerance finally threw him into a fit of anger.(p.135)

sing

• On October 28th, I was sent to *Sing Sing* with a minimum of thirty-three and a half years to serve out of that thirty-five.(p.509)
• I spent about six or seven weeks in *Sing Sing*, and was finally sent off to Dannemora in the Adirondacks.(p.509)
• An ailment developed in one of my eyes, and I was transferred back to *Sing Sing* and operated upon.(p.509)

singers

• I was one of the star *singers* in the choir and one of the leading violins in the orchestra.(p.517)

singing

• Fond of *singing*, I joined a German *singing* society which had good club headquarters.(p.231)
• There I sat in the evenings, enjoying with my friends our memories of the "old country," *singing* the

old songs we all knew, playing simple card games for drinks and consuming great quantities of beer.(p.231)
• Or maybe I'd come home wild drunk, ***singing*** and raving about what a fine place home was and what grand parents I had since they joined A.A.(p.428)

single
• I have never seen one ***single*** case recover, where that state of mind existed to the extent that it does in you."(p.27)
• To us it is not far-fetched, for this kind of thinking has been characteristic of every ***single*** one of us.(p.37)
• I pray that you now remove from me every ***single*** defect of character which stands in the way of my usefulness to you and my fellows.(p.76)
• I'd work like mad for three or four weeks without a ***single*** drink, save my money, pay a few bills and then "reward" myself with alcohol.(p.244)
• My wife, a sister member in A.A., had been a widow nine years and I had been ***single*** eighteen years.(p.286)
• From a ***single*** member in the Chicago area, commuting to Akron, we now exceed six thousand.(p.295)
• I cannot remember just when I became the victim of insomnia, but I do know that the last year and a half I never went to bed sober a ***single*** night.(p.299)
• Perhaps the ***single*** flicker of decency that shone through the fog of my drinking days was a clumsy affection for my two children, a boy and a girl.(p.437)
• From that moment on, I have not had a ***single*** compulsion to drink.(p.449)
• In all the sanitariums and psycho wards I had never met a ***single*** woman who said she was an alcoholic.(p.471)

singly
• ***Singly*** and in groups of two or three, they came to visit me.(p.258)

sinister
• The other side of the coin was ***sinister***, baffling.(p.432)

sink
• Some of them may ***sink*** and perhaps never get up, but if our experience is a criterion, more than half of those approached will become fellows of Alcoholics Anonymous.(p.163)
• I was a very young married man, having his whiskey in the cupboard over the ***sink***, and when I helped my wife with the dishes at night I would take a cup of tea and spike it with whiskey.(p.196)
• I tried to control her drinking by pouring her whiskey down the ***sink*** before I'd leave for the night, to get drunker myself.(p.426)

sinking
• When we see a man ***sinking*** into the mire that is alcoholism, we give him first aid and place what we have at his disposal.(p.132)
• Near you, alcoholics are dying helplessly like people in a ***sinking*** ship.(p.152)

sins
• I ruthlessly faced my ***sins*** and became willing to have my new-found Friend take them away, root and branch.(p.13)
• He is like the retired business man who lolls in the Florida sunshine in the winter complaining of the sad state of the nation; the minister who sighs over the ***sins*** of the twentieth century; politicians and reformers who are sure all would be Utopia if the rest of the world would only behave; the outlaw safe cracker who thinks society has wronged him; and the alcoholic who has lost all and is locked up.(p.61)
• I was up to international standards in one particular game, and that again covered quite a lot of my ***sins***.(p.519)
• I have seen that there is only one law, the law of love, and there are only two ***sins***; the first is to interfere with the growth of another human being, and the second is to interfere with one's own growth.(p.542)

siphoning
• I displayed alcoholic tendencies actually from the age of fourteen, when I started to steal wine from the family jug, ***siphoning*** it off one drink at a time so it wouldn't be missed, not drinking it immediately, but saving it until about a pint was accumulated, so that I could get drunk.(p.397)

sipped
• I ***sipped*** the drink off the bar because I couldn't hold it in my hand, but I was still a lady, believe it or not, and I was deeply ashamed.(p.266)

sissies
• To the new man I would also like to say that this program is not for ***sissies*** for, in my humble opinion, it takes a man to make the grade.(p.367)

sissy
• And I thought, "I bet he's a ***sissy***.(p.268)
• I could not let him think I was a ***sissy***.(p.498)

sister
• In his prodigy of service, he was well assisted by ***Sister*** Ignatia at St. Thomas Hospital in Akron, Ohio, one of the greatest friends our Fellowship will ever know.(p.171)
• When I had been in the hospital ten days, ***Sister*** Ignatia, who has played such a part in the development of A.A. in this area, stuck her head in the door one morning and announced, looking at me quizzically, that they might be able to make something human out of my face after all.(p.205)
• I explained to my ***sister*** that some of the people he was meeting with had been in hospitals.(p.205)
• I remembered going through what my ***sister*** assured me was my nightly procedure of trying to find Willie Seabrook's name in the telephone book.(p.224)
• I remembered filling the peroxide bottle in my medicine chest with gin, in case my ***sister*** found the bottle I hid under the mattress.(p.224)
• There were four of us children, and although both of my brothers later became alcoholic – one died of alcoholism – my ***sister*** has never taken a drink in her life.(p.240)
• He said, "***Sister***, if you think you're a screwball now, all you have to do is join up with that.(p.266)
• My wife, a ***sister*** member in A.A., had been a widow nine years and I had been single eighteen years.(p.286)
• We always had cordials after dinner and I know my ***sister*** and my brother and I loved creme de menthe.(p.384)
• We were on our way to New York where he planned to leave me with my ***sister***.(p.466)
• There was a long discussion between my husband, my ***sister*** and her husband.(p.466)
• The war leaves me with a pair of blankets, a toilet kit, a sweater knit by my ***sister***, and a still greater inferiority.(p.499)
• I promised on the grave of a beloved ***sister*** that I would stop drinking.(p.539)

sister-in-law
• My wife didn't tell me this, but one Sunday afternoon when Mary was trying to get the cobwebs out of my mind, Clarence and his ***sister-in-law***, the hairdresser, called at the house.(p.216)
• My ***sister-in-law*** took me to a place she had heard about that helps women like me.(p.371)

sister's
• And I continued to drink, on and off then, until every dollar I had in the world was gone again and I was right back living at my ***sister's***, getting my cigarettes by calling her grocer and telling him to put in a couple of cartons with her order, exactly as I had before I started to work at Max's.(p.202)
• We pulled up in front of my ***sister's*** house just as dawn broke.(p.466)

sisters
• The differences between my father and my ***sisters***, who were school teachers, made an excellent environment for the type of child I was – that is, slick and cute enough to take advantage of any adult quarrel.(p.210)
• I had four brothers and three ***sisters***.(p.210)
• The ***sisters*** seemed to remain unaffected.(p.211)
• I remember in my early youth my mother dressed me just as she did my two ***sisters***, and I wore curls until I was six years of age.(p.483)

sit
• I was to ***sit*** quietly when in doubt, asking only for direction and strength to meet my problems as He would have me.(p.13)
• We ought to ***sit*** down with the family and frankly analyze the past as we now see it, being very careful not to criticize them.(p.83)
• Why ***sit*** with a long face in places where there is drinking, sighing about the good old days.(p.102)
• Of course he couldn't drink, but why not ***sit*** hopefully at a table, a bottle of ginger ale before him?(p.154)
• I had no desire whatever to ***sit*** down at a table and stay a whole morning or afternoon drinking.(p.231)
• I let mine ***sit***.(p.247)
• I let that ***sit***, too.(p.247)
• They'd ***sit*** out there and play hymns and I'd be lying in there with a terrific hangover.(p.265)
• When you have a hangover and can't even ***sit*** still, try to read small print!(p.268)
• I felt it certainly must be very depressing to her that I should ***sit*** there by her bedside and cry.(p.272)
• I was told that someone would call on me shortly, to ***sit*** tight and not take another drink.(p.363)
• For the next couple of hours a terrible battle went on between the good gremlins and the bad ones, one faction urging me to tell the truth, the other telling me to ***sit*** tight and say nothing.(p.366)
• I cannot ***sit*** by and watch you destroy yourself."(p.391)
• Why did I have to have at least three cocktails to ***sit*** through dinner?(p.406)
• So I'd ***sit*** up, watch old Wallace Beery movies on all-night TV, and drink.(p.441)
• Had I gone to school all those years just to ***sit*** and make leather belts?(p.445)
• I never just ***sit*** and do nothing while waiting for Him to tell me what to do.(p.452)
• Her father comes to ***sit*** with me.(p.501)

sitting
• Morning after morning I would awake sick and with terrible jitters, but there was always a flask of liquor ***sitting*** on the table beside my bed.(p.183)
• One of the earliest memories that I have is of a bottle ***sitting*** on his desk with a skull and crossbones and marked "Poison."(p.193)
• I can well remember ***sitting*** with seven dollars in my pocket, planning on giving my family a hundred or two hundred dollars, when I made it next year.(p.197)
• One evening I had gone out after dinner to take on a couple of double-headers and stayed a little later than usual, and when I came home Clarence was ***sitting*** on the davenport with Bill W.(p.216)
• This time I seemed to be already awake, ***sitting*** upright in a big easy chair, in the middle of an animated conversation with a perfectly strange young woman, who didn't appear to think it strange.(p.222)
• I'd been ***sitting*** comfortably in a restaurant with Rita, drinking my sixth martini and hoping the waiter would forget about the lunch order – at least long enough for me to have a couple more.(p.223)
• ***Sitting*** in a Second Avenue bar, accepting drinks from anyone who offered, after my small stake was gone; or ***sitting*** at home alone, with the inevitable glass in my hand, I would remember, and remembering, I would drink faster, seeking speedy oblivion.(p.225)
• I was ***sitting*** in my office one time after I had operated on a woman.(p.350)
• At age twenty-one, I enlisted in the Navy for two reasons: (1) to avoid being drafted into the Army, and (2) out of a burst of patriotic fervor inspired by the advent of World War II and as the result of an all-night drinking binge which found me ***sitting*** on the doorstep of the Navy recruiting office when the chief petty officer arrived to open for business at nine o'clock Monday morning.(p.398)
• One night I was ***sitting*** in the lab alone with a fifth and a case of beer listening to dreamy Hawaiian music on the radio.(p.427)
• The doctor was still ***sitting*** beside my bed.(p.427)
• But more important, I would have found that once again I was ***sitting*** in the driver's seat – I was running the show.(p.471)
• But somehow or other, with my old alcoholic brain, ***sitting*** there in that chair, I kept saying to myself, "I wonder if it'll work?(p.515)

situated
• A few are fortunate enough to be so ***situated*** that they can give nearly all their time to the work.(p.19)
• Notwithstanding the great necessity for discussing ourselves with someone, it may be one is so ***situated*** that there is no suitable person available.(p.74)

situation
• The patient had made his own diagnosis, and deciding his ***situation*** hopeless, had hidden in a deserted barn determined to die.(p.xxix)
• Nevertheless, I still thought I could control the ***situation***, and there were periods of sobriety which renewed my wife's hope.(p.5)
• Highly competent psychiatrists who have dealt with us have found it sometimes impossible to persuade an alcoholic to discuss his ***situation*** without reserve.(p.18)
• This tragic ***situation*** has already arrived in practically every case long before it is suspected.(p.24)
• We were in a position where life was becoming impossible, and if we had passed into the region from which there is no return through human aid we had but two alternatives: One was to go on to the bitter end, blotting out the consciousness of our intolerable ***situation*** as best we could; and the other, to accept spiritual help.(p.25)
• Though a ***situation*** had not been entirely our fault, we tried to disregard the other person involved entirely.(p.67)

- God alone can judge our sex ***situation***.(p.69)
- To sum up about sex: We earnestly pray for the right ideal, for guidance in each questionable ***situation***, for sanity, and for the strength to do the right thing.(p.70)
- Of course she did not, and the whole ***situation*** has long since been adjusted.(p.79)
- Whatever the ***situation***, we usually have to do something about it.(p.81)
- No outsider can appraise such an intimate ***situation***.(p.82)
- To spend too much time on any one ***situation*** is to deny some other alcoholic an opportunity to live and be happy.(p.96)
- We want to leave you with the feeling that no ***situation*** is too difficult and no unhappiness too great to be overcome.(p.104)
- You can be quite hopeful of a ***situation*** like this.(p.110)
- You may have the reverse ***situation*** on your hands.(p.114)
- We think the business fabric is shot through with a ***situation*** which might be helped by better understanding all around.(p.137)
- I know, in my own particular case, that nothing my company could have done would have stopped me for, so long as I was able to hold my position, I could not possibly realize how serious my ***situation*** was.(p.141)
- If he speaks of his home ***situation***, you can undoubtedly make helpful suggestions.(p.145)
- Being on a radically different basis of life, he will never take advantage of the ***situation***.(p.146)
- It was the usual ***situation***: home in jeopardy, wife ill, children distracted, bills in arrears and standing damaged.(p.155)
- Some time later, and just as he thought he was getting control of his liquor ***situation***, he went on a roaring bender.(p.155)
- The doctor proved to be able and exceedingly anxious to adopt any workable method of handling the ***situation***.(p.163)
- In the meantime, the domestic ***situation*** was not getting along too well.(p.199)
- Whenever a ***situation*** arose that fast talk wouldn't explain away, I simply withdrew.(p.214)
- As far as my home was concerned, I did not see then, though of course I can see now, that it was anything but a happy ***situation*** for my wife.(p.215)
- As I look back on the events of two months, I can clearly see that I had been circling around, half-afraid of encountering the remedy for my ***situation***, half wanting it, deferring fulfillment of my promise to get in touch with the doctor I had heard about.(p.258)
- I feel that there is no ***situation*** too difficult, none too desperate, no unhappiness too great to be overcome in this great fellowship -- Alcoholics Anonymous.(p.395)
- She did all she could to help this ***situation*** and to protect my child.(p.409)
- When I am disturbed, it is because I find some person, place, thing, or ***situation*** -- some fact of my life -- unacceptable to me, and I can find no serenity until I accept that person, place, thing, or ***situation*** as being exactly the way it is supposed to be at this moment.(p.449)
- I was always able to see the flaw in every person, every ***situation***.(p.449)
- I don't think I suffered too much as far as the racial ***situation*** was concerned because I was born into it and knew nothing other than that.(p.485)
- I never did react normally to any emotional ***situation***.(p.544)

situations

- These men may well have a remedy for thousands of such ***situations***.(p.xxiv)
- There are many ***situations*** which arise out of the phenomenon of craving which cause men to make the supreme sacrifice rather than continue to fight.(p.xxviii)
- I have seen hundreds of families set their feet in the path that really goes somewhere; have seen the most impossible domestic ***situations*** righted; feuds and bitterness of all sorts wiped out.(p.15)
- We will intuitively know how to handle ***situations*** which used to baffle us.(p.84)
- For example, we know of ***situations*** in which the alcoholic or his wife have had love affairs.(p.124)
- As long as it eased ***situations*** socially, it helped just fine, but somewhere along the line, it backfired.(p.386)

six

- ***Six*** months earlier, the broker had been relieved of his drink obsession by a sudden spiritual experience, following a meeting with an alcoholic friend who had been in contact with the Oxford Groups of that day.(p.xv)
- If we can answer to our satisfaction, we then look at Step ***Six***.(p.76)
- I had discharged him for drinking ***six*** weeks before.(p.137)
- Had they fired me first, and had they then taken steps to see that I was presented with the solution contained in this book, I might have returned to them ***six*** months later, a well man.(p.141)
- After all, had he not been sober ***six*** months now?(p.154)
- But he's a grand chap when he's sober, though he's been in here eight times in the last ***six*** months.(p.156)
- A year and ***six*** months later these three had succeeded with seven more.(p.159)
- ***Six*** years ago one of our number was a patient there.(p.162)
- During the first ***six*** months of 1935, I was hospitalized eight times for intoxication and shackled to the bed two or three days before I even knew where I was.(p.184)
- Each of the seven times that I had left this hospital in the last ***six*** months, I had come out fully determined in my own mind that I would not get drunk again -- for at least ***six*** or eight months.(p.184)
- I looked up and there were two great big fellows over ***six*** foot tall, very likable looking.(p.185)
- I said, "Yes, Doc, I would like to quit, at least for five, ***six***, or eight months, until I get things straightened up, and begin to get the respect of my wife and some other people back, and get my finances fixed up and so on."(p.187)
- Whether you quit ***six*** days, months, or years, if you go out and take a drink or two you'll end up in this hospital tied down, just like you have been in these past ***six*** months.(p.187)
- I was not more that ***six*** at that time.(p.193)
- During the day, looking over the contracts and money in my pocket, I found that I had sold ***six*** lots that I couldn't even remember, and didn't even know the people I had sold them to.(p.196)
- This was ***six*** or eight months after the last drinking episode.(p.196)
- At the end of this selling of lots, just prior to World War I, I got into the crude rubber business, and ***six*** months later there was only one broker and myself left in Akron.(p.197)
- The rubber prosperity went on for about ***six*** years -- 1916 to 1922.(p.197)
- At the end of about four months, I not only had good looking clothes --and I might say that at the time I first talked to Max I didn't have a suit of clothes I could bend over in real sudden; now I had ***six*** suits of clothes.(p.200)
- I drove towards Cleveland wondering why I found myself in such a changed set of conditions as compared with those of ***six*** months before.(p.200)
- My sobriety continued for another ***six*** months.(p.203)
- Bill left me at the elevator and said, "Your room is so and so," and I didn't see him again for ***six*** months.(p.217)
- We went to Akron for about ***six*** weeks and we did a lot of visiting among the people in Akron.(p.219)
- In fact, after ***six*** months of living on food instead of on whiskey, I gained about thirty pounds.(p.220)
- The shakes grew worse and I looked at my watch -- ***six*** o'clock.(p.223)
- I remember looking longingly at the window as an easier solution, and shuddering at the memory of that other window, three years before, and the ***six*** agonizing months in a London hospital ward.(p.224)
- My parents had some vague idea of making a priest out of me and for some years I attended the Franciscan school at Basle, Switzerland, just across the border, about ***six*** miles from my home.(p.230)
- I did ***six*** years of newspaper advertising, and trade journal work with many, many drunks of drab and dreary hue woven into the pattern of my life.(p.254)
- I remember sometime, it was possibly ***six*** months after we had been going steadily to King School, that we were coming home from a meeting and saw a car along the way, and a fellow in back drinking a bottle of beer.(p.271)
- Russ lived a year longer than they expected him to live, and in that year he was in bed for at least ***six*** months.(p.272)
- By the time I was twenty-one I had ***six*** years of life in foreign countries, spoke three languages fluently, and had attended college for two years.(p.275)
- After ***six*** months of sobriety I saw the picture in a different light: Detroit was the place I had to return to, not only because I must face the mess I had made there, but because it was there that I could be of the most service to A.A.(p.281)
- But it took ***six*** more months of work and disappointments before a group of three men got together in my rooming house bedroom for their first A.A. meeting.(p.282)
- So ***six*** months ago I acquired a ready made family consisting of one charming wife, four grown children to whom I am devoted, and three grandchildren.(p.286)
- The ***six*** steps were:(p.292)
- When I told them ***six*** weeks, they were polite and said that they would contact me in case they had anyone with an alcoholic problem.(p.293)
- From a single member in the Chicago area, commuting to Akron, we now exceed ***six*** thousand.(p.295)
- My wife became pregnant and the doctor recommended the use of port or ale . . . so . . . I bought a ***six*** gallon crock and a few bottles, listened to advice from amateur brewmeisters, and was off on my beer manufacturing career on a small scale (for the time being).(p.297)
- Up to this point I had spent ***six*** years in the business and had enjoyed the reputation of being very successful.(p.298)
- He had tried everything from having me attend daily mass at ***six*** a.m. to performing the most menial labor for his charity patients.(p.306)
- By the latter part of September 1939, we had a nucleus of ***six*** and held our first official group meeting.(p.310)
- I was being very cagey, because I knew that if I did take one or two, I might want to take five or ***six*** or seven or eight.(p.323)
- I'd been on the board of governors of the Academy of Motion Picture Arts and Sciences for ***six*** years.(p.328)
- He and I had a large family -- ***six*** children, to be exact.(p.370)
- In ***six*** years of worry, I hadn't learned anything.(p.387)
- It was the first time in my life that I could not get a lift out of what I was drinking; and so one Friday night, at five minutes to ***six***, I had half a water glass of warm gin, and that is when I first asked God to help me.(p.393)
- Five or ***six*** drinks and I was terrific.(p.402)
- And when this ***six*** month school was over I applied for duty in Hawaii and pulled it.(p.426)
- We were supposed to take off at noon, but were delayed until ***six*** p.m.(p.428)
- After my last binge I came home and smashed my dining room furniture to splinters, kicked out ***six*** windows and two balustrades.(p.435)
- After ***six*** months, we move to Bridgeport, Conn.(p.476)
- Finally, I was arrested and got ***six*** months for drugs.(p.480)
- I remember in my early youth my mother dressed me just as she did my two sisters, and I wore curls until I was ***six*** years of age.(p.483)
- I was about ***six*** then.(p.483)
- I'd known her five or ***six*** months.(p.487)
- Nevertheless, I stayed sober there about ***six*** months, because I knew that Vi was to come later and bring the children.(p.490)
- I worked at that alone for ***six*** months.(p.496)
- I spent about ***six*** or seven weeks in Sing Sing, and was finally sent off to Dannemora in the Adirondacks.(p.509)
- A former employer of mine said to me a little over ten years ago, "Pat, you seem to be one of those unfortunate people who at least once every ***six*** months must go out and roll in the gutter."(p.513)
- The old pattern reasserted itself, but it was no longer once every ***six*** months.(p.514)
- Then I had about ***six*** months on a small island in command of the troops there.(p.520)
- That went on for about ***six*** years.(p.522)
- Finally, my mother came and said she had kept me at home for ***six*** years because she thought she could help me, but that now she had come to the conclusion that I wasn't even worth trying to help.(p.523)
- I had been using paraldehyde more or less like ordinary drink for the last ***six*** years though, occasionally, I'd bounce back to phenobarbital and things like that.(p.524)
- ***Six*** -- An A.A. group ought never endorse, finance or lend the A.A. name to any related facility or outside enterprise, lest problems of money, property and prestige divert us from our primary purpose.(p.564)

six-step

- The day before I was due to go back to Chicago, a Wednesday and Dr. Bob's afternoon off, he had me down to the office and we spent three or four hours formally going through the ***Six-Step*** program as it was at that time.(p.291)

sixteen
- The first edition appeared in April 1939, and in the following ***sixteen*** years, more than 300,000 copies went into circulation.(p.xi)
- ***Sixteen*** years have elapsed between our first printing of this book and the presentation in 1955 of our second edition.(p.xv)
- You may have to curb his desire to work ***sixteen*** hours a day.(p.146)
- When I was ***sixteen*** years old, my mother remarried and I was given the opportunity of going back to school.(p.193)
- I was then about ***sixteen*** years old.(p.211)
- At the age of ***sixteen***, I was invited to spend the summer with an aunt and I, very delightedly, accepted the invitation.(p.261)
- I was ***sixteen*** when we were married and he was seven years older.(p.262)
- I have thanked God many times in the last ***sixteen*** years that that was just what he did not do!(p.278)
- It is well over ***sixteen*** years since I came back to life.(p.280)
- I would like to sketch for you the highlights of these ***sixteen*** years of a slow but steady and satisfying upward climb.(p.280)
- Never in ***sixteen*** years have I dodged anything because I was afraid of it.(p.285)
- From a physical standpoint, I gained ***sixteen*** pounds in the first two months I was off liquor.(p.303)
- I experienced some of the pleasure of social drinking when I was ***sixteen***.(p.305)
- I didn't graduate to the hard stuff until I was ***sixteen***.(p.423)
- I quit, when I was just past ***sixteen***.(p.424)
- One night my son, when he was only ***sixteen***, was suddenly and tragically killed.(p.437)
- I started drinking rather early, at the age of ***sixteen***.(p.512)

sixteen-pound
- But when I cracked my leg with a ***sixteen-pound*** sledgehammer in the rock hole, I was fighting the system, using my body.(p.458)

sixth
- Only to have that thought supplanted by "Well, I'll stop with the ***sixth*** drink."(p.24)
- We have begun to develop this vital ***sixth*** sense.(p.85)
- I'd been sitting comfortably in a restaurant with Rita, drinking my ***sixth*** martini and hoping the waiter would forget about the lunch order – at least long enough for me to have a couple more.(p.223)

sixty
- Now, this house will hardly accommodate its weekly visitors, for they number ***sixty*** or eighty as a rule.(p.161)
- Around this time our big A.A. book was being written and it all became much simpler; we had a definite formula which some ***sixty*** of us agreed was the middle course for all alcoholics who wanted sobriety, and that formula has not been changed one iota down through the years.(p.248)
- He introduced himself and began to tell me about a bunch of some ***sixty*** former drinkers and drunkards who met once a week, and he invited me to go with him to the next meeting.(p.257)
- I know now that ***sixty*** per cent of the time I drank alone without benefit of customers.(p.287)
- This was my first long vacation of ***sixty*** days since I had joined the army.(p.343)
- I was drunk for ***sixty*** days around the clock and it was my intention, literally, to drink myself to death.(p.549)

sixty-eight
- Until I took Social Security and a pension at the age of ***sixty-eight***, after forty years in motion-picture-studio public relations, I had successfully hidden even any hints of approaching alcoholism.(p.327)

sixty-four
- I remember one occasion when I did not drink for three hundred and ***sixty-four*** days, but I didn't quite make the year.(p.200)

sixty-six
- I was at one time assistant manager of a corporation department employing ***sixty-six*** hundred men.(p.136)

size
- In spite of the great increase in the ***size*** and the span of this Fellowship, at its core it remains simple and personal.(p.xxii)
- There was the physical aspect; to be the youngest and the runt of the brood of children, to have to wear glasses very early and so to be teased, to be bookish and bored in school because the captain of the football team could not translate Virgil and yet was the school god while you, you, you little shrimp, were the school egghead, junior ***size*** and an early model.(p.533)

skate
- I was always able to ***skate*** along the fringe of big money.(p.197)

skeletons
- The first impulse will be to bury these ***skeletons*** in a dark closet and padlock the door.(p.123)
- We families of Alcoholics Anonymous keep few ***skeletons*** in the closet.(p.125)

skeptic
- We must remember that ten or twenty years of drunkenness would make a ***skeptic*** out of anyone.(p.83)
- If you think you are an atheist, an agnostic, a ***skeptic***, or have any other form of intellectual pride which keeps you from accepting what is in this book, I feel sorry for you.(p.181)

skeptical
- It was fortunate, for my old business associates remained ***skeptical*** for a year and a half, during which I found little work.(p.15)
- Though experience had made him ***skeptical***, he finished his treatment with unusual confidence.(p.26)
- In all honesty though, I was ***skeptical***, but I wanted so definitely to quit drinking that I would have welcomed any sort of physical torture or pain to accomplish the result.(p.302)

skeptically
- That was ***skeptically*** received by me when I first heard it, but after some twenty-eight or thirty fellows had come to see me, and pretty nearly all of them had said the same thing, I began to believe it.(p.219)

skepticism
- The local banker watched me whirl fat checks in and out of his till with amused ***skepticism***.(p.4)
- We looked upon this world of warring individuals, warring theological systems, and inexplicable calamity, with deep ***skepticism***.(p.46)

sketch
- If he is not communicative, give him a ***sketch*** of your drinking career up to the time you quit.(p.91)
- I would like to ***sketch*** for you the highlights of these sixteen years of a slow but steady and satisfying upward climb.(p.280)

ski
- Anne and I went up in ***ski*** clothes and fur coats, and it was so cold we slept in them.(p.415)
- We, who were dirty, bedraggled and in ***ski*** clothes.(p.415)

ski-jump
- The curve of my declining moral and bodily health fell off like a ***ski-jump***.(p.7)

skid
- I never was on ***skid*** row.(p.345)
- Mine was the ***skid*** row of success.(p.345)
- The physical ***skid*** row in any city is miserable.(p.345)
- The ***skid*** row of success is just as miserable.(p.345)
- However, after I heard a few stories of jails, sanitariums, broken homes and ***skid*** row, I wondered if I really was an alcoholic.(p.378)
- It didn't say I had to finally live on ***skid*** row and drink bay rum, canned heat or lemon extract.(p.379)
- I knew it didn't make any difference where I started, the inevitable end would be ***skid*** row.(p.548)

skid-row
- I was sure I wouldn't belong in an A.A. group -- they were all old men, I thought, and all ***skid-row*** bums.(p.319)
- After having a few drinks, I went to a meeting -- and the people there were not all old men and definitely not ***skid-row*** types!(p.319)
- Unlike his ***skid-row*** brother, he isn't heckled for sleeping in alleys or doorways.(p.330)

skidded
- From the top of the heap in a few years he had ***skidded*** to becoming a shuffling customer, still entering the better barrooms but welcomed by neither mine host nor his patrons.(p.236)

skids
- I knew I was hitting the ***skids***, but what of it?(p.427)
- Cotton struck the ***skids*** and collections went cold.(p.500)

skier
- Regaining my health, I became an avid jogger, sailor, and ***skier***.(p.559)

skilled
- My tongue had become increasingly ***skilled*** at venomous home truths.(p.405)
- Under the ***skilled*** guidance of an expert practitioner I wallowed in the world's individual and collective mental agony.(p.434)

skills
- He often possesses special abilities, ***skills***, and aptitudes, and has a promising career ahead of him.(p.21)

skimped
- Have we ***skimped*** on the cement put into the foundation?(p.75)

skin
- We have no right to save our own ***skin*** at another person's expense.(p.74)
- Forced to detrain from an empty gondola on the other side of Chicago by a terrific rainstorm which drenched me to the ***skin***, I hit the first factory building I saw for a job.(p.253)
- I had every advantage a child could have, private schools (several of them), dancing schools, two colleges, coon ***skin*** coats, automobiles, a listing in the social register and all the rest.(p.357)

skinny
- Why, I wasn't even ashamed of my ***skinny*** legs!(p.498)
- Three attempts to enlist in the service, and three failures because of being ***skinny***.(p.499)
- In each new place, I was the new kid – a ***skinny***, shy kid – to be tested and beaten up.(p.555)

skip
- The best reason first: If we ***skip*** this vital step, we may not overcome drinking.(p.72)
- I used to think I was cowardly because when things came out pertaining to the program that troubled me, I said to her many times, "Annie, am I being a coward because I lay those things away on the shelf and ***skip*** it?"(p.273)

skipped
- I went back to my group meetings, but not wholeheartedly, and I often ***skipped*** them with the excuse that I was too tired.(p.364)

skipping
- He gets a thrill out of ***skipping*** in front of fast-moving vehicles.(p.37)
- I was ***skipping*** classes about two days a week and doing no book work whatever.(p.423)

skirt
- I know that one of the outfits I had was a ***skirt*** and a very funny looking blouse that my mother had picked up at a rummage sale.(p.261)

skivvies
- That is the way Jackie found me, lying on a cot in my ***skivvies***, with hot and cold sweats, pounding heart and that awful itchy scratchiness all over.(p.238)

skull
- Presently he is hit again and this time has a fractured ***skull***.(p.38)
- One of the earliest memories that I have is of a bottle sitting on his desk with a ***skull*** and crossbones and marked "Poison."(p.193)

skunk
- One afternoon, the year after moving to Houston, I got as drunk as a ***skunk***, and while I do not walk very straight sober, you should see me when I'm drunk!(p.390)

sky
- My writing career was described in the couplet "Alcohol gave me wings to fly,/ And then it took away the ***sky***."(p.331)
- You will recall that I said the time that I got the idea out of a clear ***sky*** to call A.A. on a certain night was at about ten.(p.366)
- Alcohol was a looming cloud in this banker's bright ***sky***.(p.373)
- Tall Man now see Great Spirit in Big Group in ***sky***.(p.476)

skyline
- Again I spent my bankroll, by no means as thick as the one I had when I first saw the ***skyline*** of Gotham.(p.252)

slackened
- I had my own medical practice in Washington at that time, but the practice ***slackened*** and the mail order business started to fall off.(p.486)

slacks
- Before too long, my husband (who seemed to prefer his shirts dirty) put his foot down, declaring that our

family might have the cleanest clothes in town, but that I hadn't been out of the same old dirty ***slacks*** and blouse for a week.(p.371)
• I got into ***slacks*** and out I went, weaving with the dog.(p.390)
• Then, of course, there are always the wrinkled ***slacks,*** which have been slept in and are so dirty, they could walk away by themselves.(p.479)

slam
• In the garage, I would put the needle in my vein and then try to figure out exactly how much medication to inject to overcome the pep pills while adding to the sleeping pills while ignoring the tranquilizers, in order to get just enough to be able to pull out the needle, jerk the tourniquet, throw it in the car, ***slam*** the car door shut, run down the hall, and fall in bed before I fell asleep.(p.442)

slammed
• But then, when that steel door ***slammed*** shut, and she was the one that went home, I was amazed.(p.440)
• That's when that steel door ***slammed*** shut, and Max was the one who went home.(p.444)

slander
• After consulting with his wife and partner he came to the conclusion that it was better to take those risks than to stand before his Creator guilty of such ruinous ***slander.***(p.80)

slash
• Once, I phoned my brother-in-law and told him I was going to take a handful of pills (in fact, I already had) and I would ***slash*** my wrists if he didn't come over to stop me.(p.479)

slashing
• Knowing that he was sober, I timed it just right, so I could do the ***slashing*** just before he hit the steps.(p.479)

sled
• A couple of hired hands were cleaning out the barn on the farm and I would ride to and fro on the ***sled,*** and while they were loading I would drink hard cider out of a barrel in the barn.(p.183)

sledgehammer
• But when I cracked my leg with a sixteen-pound ***sledgehammer*** in the rock hole, I was fighting the system, using my body.(p.458)

sleep
• He is the fellow who goes to bed so intoxicated he ought to ***sleep*** the clock around.(p.21)
• It may mean the loss of many nights' ***sleep,*** great interference with your pleasures, interruptions to your business.(p.97)
• Little more of our talk stayed in my memory, but I do know I slept the rest of that night while before I had never known what a real night's ***sleep*** was.(p.239)
• Many alcoholics have learned they can bring their bottle to a cheap movie theater and drink, ***sleep,*** wake up and drink again in the darkness.(p.244)
• I couldn't ***sleep.***(p.299)
• I ***sleep*** like a baby, and never give a thought to such a thing as insomnia.(p.303)
• But that night I tried to go to ***sleep.***(p.322)
• I'd just take a couple or three barbiturates to get back to ***sleep*** -- eating my alcohol.(p.333)
• But during a period of particular stress and strain about thirteen years ago, I resorted to alcohol in my home, alone, as a means of temporary release, as a means of getting a little extra ***sleep.***(p.335)
• I had to ***sleep,*** I had to clear my mind and free it from worry, and I had to relax.(p.336)
• Cold sweats, jumpy nerves and lack of ***sleep*** were becoming intolerable.(p.378)
• So we rolled old newspapers together and made torches to find a good soft pew and get some ***sleep.***(p.424)
• I spent the time in a nearby tavern, was loaded on the ship, went to ***sleep*** before take-off, and the next thing I knew someone was shaking me and telling me we were over San Diego.(p.428)
• Sometimes I'd make it home and go to ***sleep*** at the wheel of my car, for all the neighbors to see next morning as they left for work.(p.429)
• I had begun to drink in the early years of pharmacy school, in order to get to ***sleep.***(p.440)
• After going to school all day, working in the family drugstore all evening, and then studying until one or two in the morning, I would not be able to ***sleep*** soundly, with everything I had been studying going round in my head.(p.440)
• Then I found the solution: At the end of study time, I would drink two beers, jump in bed, ***sleep*** real fast, and wake up smart.(p.440)
• "If you had my responsibilities, if you needed the ***sleep*** like I do, you'd drink too."(p.441)
• With a problem like that, I couldn't go back to ***sleep.***(p.441)
• The longer the drinking continued, the shorter the time the alcohol would keep me asleep; I would have to drink myself back to ***sleep*** again and again throughout the night.(p.441)
• If it was one minute before five, I'd drink myself back to ***sleep.***(p.441)
• However, for a period of time I was injecting Pentothal intravenously to put myself to ***sleep.***(p.442)
• One night, I had to put myself back to ***sleep*** three times, and then I finally decided to give it up.(p.443)
• I began to ***sleep,*** to relax, to accept my plight.(p.461)
• The doctor, apparently realizing that one thing that I certainly needed was ***sleep,*** left a bottle of sleeping pills there and in my drunken state I took them all, instead of the one or two he had prescribed.(p.465)
• I got drunk one night in October, went to ***sleep*** in the rain and woke up with pneumonia.(p.490)
• I fall into a dreamless ***sleep.***(p.497)
• I cannot ***sleep.***(p.501)
• But I cannot ***sleep.***(p.503)
• I crawl back into bed and ***sleep*** like a child.(p.504)
• But I don't remember that any of them ever went to ***sleep*** in joints and woke up with no shoes on in the winter, or fell out of chairs.(p.527)
• Depending on the stage of drunkenness, eventually I either fought or went to ***sleep.***(p.537)
• When ***sleep*** overtook me, my practice was to undress and go to bed, wherever.(p.537)

sleeping
• If any feel that as psychiatrists directing a hospital for alcoholics we appear somewhat sentimental, let them stand with us a while on the firing line, see the tragedies, the despairing wives, the little children; let the solving of these problems become a part of their daily work, and even of their ***sleeping*** moments, and the most cynical will not wonder that we have accepted and encouraged this movement.(p.xxvi)
• One was the fear of not ***sleeping,*** and the other was the fear of running out of liquor.(p.175)
• Unlike his skid-row brother, he isn't heckled for ***sleeping*** in alleys or doorways.(p.330)
• In the garage, I would put the needle in my vein and then try to figure out exactly how much medication to inject to overcome the pep pills while adding to the ***sleeping*** pills while ignoring the tranquilizers, in order to get just enough to be able to pull out the needle, jerk the tourniquet, throw it in the car, slam the car door shut, run down the hall, and fall in bed before I fell asleep.(p.442)
• The doctor, apparently realizing that one thing that I certainly needed was sleep, left a bottle of ***sleeping*** pills there and in my drunken state I took them all, instead of the one or two he had prescribed.(p.465)

sleeplessness
• My phobia for ***sleeplessness*** demanded that I get drunk every night, but in order to get more liquor for the next night, I had to stay sober during the day, at least up to four o'clock.(p.177)

slender
• Sometimes I stole from my wife's ***slender*** purse when the morning terror and madness were on me.(p.6)
• They shared their homes, their ***slender*** resources, and gladly devoted their spare hours to fellow-sufferers.(p.159)
• When I had known her years before she was rather ***slender,*** but at this time she weighed as much as she does now, which is up around in the two hundreds or very close to it.(p.493)

slept
• At length peace stole over him and he ***slept.***(p.189)
• I drank some more and ***slept*** through the day.(p.205)
• And I remembered the creeping horror of the interminable night, in which I ***slept*** for short spells and woke up dripping with cold sweat and shaken with utter despair, to drink hastily from my bottle and mercifully pass out again, "You're mad, you're mad, you're mad!" pounded through my brain with each returning ray of consciousness, and I drowned the refrain with drink.(p.224)
• Little more of our talk stayed in my memory, but I do know I ***slept*** the rest of that night while before I had never known what a real night's sleep was.(p.239)
• I lay down on the bed and ***slept*** like a child.(p.280)
• Anne and I went up in ski clothes and fur coats, and it was so cold we ***slept*** in them.(p.415)
• Then, of course, there are always the wrinkled slacks, which have been ***slept*** in and are so dirty, they could walk away by themselves.(p.479)

slick
• The differences between my father and my sisters, who were school teachers, made an excellent environment for the type of child I was – that is, ***slick*** and cute enough to take advantage of any adult quarrel.(p.210)
• Being an alcoholic, ***slick,*** and having some good sense left, I survived the investigation.(p.490)

slicker
• Furthermore, I knew that I was looked upon as a city ***slicker*** from New York, and I had to be pretty cautious among small town, conservative Yankees.(p.360)

slide
• Now I ***slide*** down mountain fast.(p.475)

slight
• I had found friends, understanding friends who often knew what I was thinking and feeling better than I knew myself, and didn't allow me to retreat into my prison of loneliness and fear over a fancied ***slight*** or hurt.(p.228)
• ***Slight*** casualties, complicated however by a long and serious illness, were my only mishaps.(p.253)
• My daily alcoholic consumption remained about the same through all this, with perhaps a ***slight*** increase, and my binges remained one-nighters.(p.434)

slightest
• The ***slightest*** sign of fear or intolerance may lessen your husband's chance of recovery.(p.120)
• The ***slightest*** disposition on your part to guide his appointments or his affairs so he will not be tempted will be noticed.(p.120)
• As these words are written at fifty-three years of age, with over nine years of A.A. behind me, with all its wonderful teachings, I haven't the ***slightest*** doubt about being an alcoholic.(p.356)
• I didn't particularly like it, but I loved the effects, and managed for the next twenty-five years to drink anything and everything, either handed to me or purchased, at the ***slightest*** excuse.(p.357)
• From that instant to this, nearly eight years later, I have not had the ***slightest*** urge to drink.(p.541)

slighting
• But the firm became violently ill with my drunkenness and their course of treatment was to remove their ulcer, in the form of me, from the payroll, amid much fanfare and very personal and ***slighting*** remarks and insinuations.(p.300)

slightly
• Luck then deserts him and he is ***slightly*** injured several times in succession.(p.38)
• Under only ***slightly*** different conditions, the same thing is taking place in many eastern cities.(p.161)

slinging
• After all, I had been working for eighteen years, ***slinging*** hash, and I was managing.(p.478)

slip
• Self-seeking will ***slip*** away.(p.84)
• We have seen others ***slip*** when the family came back too soon.(p.100)
• Presently the man did ***slip*** and was fired.(p.139)
• 4.Because every time I do it I take out a little more insurance for myself against a possible ***slip.***(p.181)
• I would reach over and get this and take a shot and in a few moments get up and take another, shave and eat my breakfast, ***slip*** a half pint of liquor in my hip pocket, and go on to school.(p.183)
• In any case I must get out of here before I let ***slip*** my abysmal ignorance of how I came to be here, and she realized that I was stark, staring mad.(p.223)
• That was my only ***slip.***(p.294)
• Once I did have a ***slip*** -- tried drinking again – but the A.A.'s tell me not to worry about yesterday, because nobody can change it, and not to worry about tomorrow, because it hasn't come yet.(p.320)
• Three years and three months of sobriety, without a ***slip,*** has meant a lot to me, my wife, and my family.(p.342)
• Except for one short ***slip,*** during the first eight months, which was an angry "the world can't do this to me" reaction to a personal tragedy in my life, I have been sober for twelve years.(p.416)

slip-locked
• After finding every bottle that I had hidden around the apartment, she took away my pants, my shoes, my money and my keys, threw them under the bed in the back bedroom and ***slip-locked*** our door.(p.288)

slipped
• His friends have ***slipped*** away, his home is a near-wreck and he cannot hold a position.(p.110)

• My past had ***slipped*** before me in a twinkling.(p.427)

slippers

• Out came his carpet ***slippers*** and a bottle.(p.32)

slips

• I mean ***slips***.(p.271)
• I succeeded in this attempt for approximately fifteen months with only a couple of ***slips***.(p.343)

slogan

• Our pet ***slogan*** is "Easy Does It."(p.250)

slogans

• That's why we have these ***slogans***.(p.516)

slogging

• My four years of abstinence had something to do with it, but soldiering is a tough enough game for a sober man, and I had no yen for full-pack ***slogging*** through mud with a cognac or vin rouge hangover.(p.253)

slow

• Yet in ancient times material progress was painfully ***slow***.(p.51)
• Our drinking has made us ***slow*** to pay.(p.78)
• I'd only had two with her, but I'd managed four in the fifteen minutes I'd waited for her, and of course I'd had the usual uncounted swigs from the bottle as I painfully got up and did my ***slow*** spasmodic dressing.(p.223)
• That went on for two more months before I landed in a hospital and started my ***slow*** fight back to normalcy.(p.224)
• This change had been a long, ***slow*** process for me, but through these latter years the dividends have been tremendous.(p.249)
• I would like to sketch for you the highlights of these sixteen years of a ***slow*** but steady and satisfying upward climb.(p.280)
• There are many things worse than dying, but is there any death worse than the progressive, self-induced, ***slow*** suicide of the practicing alcoholic?(p.457)
• I use that "Easy Does It" every day, to ***slow*** me down a little.(p.516)
• Since, perhaps, suicide was a bit too drastic (actually, I was afraid), dry martinis were chosen as the ***slow***, pleasant, private, gradual instrument of self-destruction.(p.531)
• "Pity me the heart that is ***slow*** to learn What the quick mind sees at every turn."(p.534)
• I've had many spiritual experiences since I've been in the program, many that I didn't recognize right away, for I'm ***slow*** to learn and they take many guises.(p.551)
• While there, I read the Big Book and the Grapevine and began the ***slow*** road back to health and sanity through the recovery program of A.A.(p.559)

slowest

• Without such support, A.A. could have made only the ***slowest*** progress.(p.xx)

slowing

• It may be ***slowing*** him up mentally and physically, but he does not see it.(p.109)

slowly

• Some of us grow into it more ***slowly***.(p.57)
• They are being fulfilled among us -- sometimes quickly, sometimes ***slowly***.(p.84)
• When I finally returned to Detroit to find work and to learn to stand on my own feet, the ball was already rolling, however ***slowly***.(p.282)
• Dr. Bob then led me through the restitution step, in which I made a list of all of the persons I had harmed, and worked out ways and means of ***slowly*** making restitution.(p.292)
• My memory ***slowly*** returned.(p.320)
• ***Slowly***, my life seemed to unfold before me, shedding insights on childhood resentments, jealousies, and fears that had mushroomed in adulthood, and also on the self-pity that I had wallowed in at every opportunity.(p.371)
• ***Slowly*** I realized I was in bed and that the objects were my feet, encased in a harness affair.(p.422)
• I blinked ***slowly*** as I shifted my gaze to my arms.(p.422)
• ***Slowly*** a pile of pineapples started to build up on the table.(p.427)
• Time went by very, very ***slowly*** on my second nut ward.(p.445)
• But ***slowly*** a great peace comes to me.(p.504)
• Most of our experiences are what the psychologist William James calls the "educational variety" because they develop ***slowly*** over a period of time.(p.569)

slumped

• Not wishing to disturb my wife, I ***slumped*** in a big red-leather chair and suffered.(p.332)

slush

• I remember well one fellow, Joe, walking nearly three miles through ***slush***, wet and snow to come to the hospital to see a man that he had never seen before in his life, and that impressed me very much.(p.208)

sly

• ***Sly*** and crafty, I thought now I'll find out what they think of me here, what they "have on" me, what I've said coming in here drunk.(p.470)

slyly

• In this way he was ***slyly*** carrying tales.(p.145)

smack

• And I landed right ***smack*** back in that sanitarium that I had gone to so often.(p.472)

smacked

• So I went to my wife and asked her, wasn't there something that she and I could do to somehow get together, and she turned on her heel and looked me squarely in the eye, and said, "You don't care anything about my problem," and I could have ***smacked*** her, but I said to myself, "Grab on to your serenity!"(p.351)
• The bartender, a tough Irishman, came around and "gave me the elbow," which means that he raised his elbow and ***smacked*** me in the face.(p.411)

small

• A second ***small*** group had promptly taken shape at New York.(p.xvii)
• "Here lies a Hampshire Grenadier Who caught his death Drinking cold ***small*** beer.(p.1)
• I had had some success at speculation, so we had a little money, but we once worked on a farm for a month to avoid drawing on our ***small*** capital.(p.3)
• Sometimes a ***small*** deal would net a few hundred dollars, and I would pay my bills at the bars and delicatessens.(p.5)
• ***Small*** wonder many in the medical profession have a low opinion of alcoholics and their chance for recovery!(p.73)
• He did, and also sent a ***small*** amount of money.(p.79)
• We have told ***small*** tots that father was sick, which was much nearer the truth than we realized.(p.106)
• He may take ***small*** interest in the children and may show irritation when reproved for his delinquencies.(p.126)
• If your man accepts your offer, it should be pointed out that physical treatment is but a ***small*** part of the picture.(p.143)
• I was born in a ***small*** New England village of about seven thousand souls.(p.171)
• Sitting in a Second Avenue bar, accepting drinks from anyone who offered, after my ***small*** stake was gone; or sitting at home alone, with the inevitable glass in my hand, I would remember, and remembering, I would drink faster, seeking speedy oblivion.(p.225)
• I was eased out of the business I had founded and was reduced to doing general upholstery in a ***small*** shop at the back of my house.(p.233)
• Mother would take me in only if I would stay locked in a ***small*** storeroom and give her my clothes and shoes.(p.238)
• With the war over, and back in Baltimore with the folks, there were several ***small*** jobs for three years and then I went to work soliciting as one of the first ten employees of a new national finance company.(p.242)
• Bill and Hank had just taken over a ***small*** automobile polishing company and they offered me a job -- ten dollars a week and keep at Hank's house.(p.246)
• I quit the factory and got a job on a ***small*** newspaper, going from that to a Pittsburgh daily, long ago defunct.(p.252)
• Drifting back to Ohio, I landed on a ***small*** newspaper and later was impressed into the direction of boy-welfare work at the local "Y."(p.253)
• Indeed, I was beginning to see that I would require implicit faith, like a ***small*** child, if I was going to get anywhere.(p.259)
• It was a ***small*** town -- Liberty, Indiana.(p.262)
• Time went on and the drinking got worse and worse, and I was in another barroom, down the road the other way, a ***small*** one, and I took my glass -- that morning I'd been able to lift it from the bar -- and I said to the woman behind the bar, "I wish I might never take another drop of that stuff.(p.266)
• I had a little Testament, which was very ***small*** print.(p.268)
• When you have a hangover and can't even sit still, try to read ***small*** print!(p.268)
• I got an easy, part-time job selling printing for a ***small*** neighborhood printer.(p.276)
• I grew up in a ***small*** town outside Akron, Ohio, where the life was typical of any average ***small*** town.(p.287)
• He waited until I was completely sober and the day before I was to head back for Chicago, he told me of a ***small*** group of men in Akron who apparently had the same problem that I had but were doing something about it.(p.289)
• After it was closed we all retired to the kitchen and had coffee and doughnuts and more discussion until the ***small*** hours of the morning.(p.291)
• In this ***small*** group, during the Depression, there was no one who was not hard up.(p.291)
• My wife became pregnant and the doctor recommended the use of port or ale . . . so . . . I bought a six gallon crock and a few bottles, listened to advice from amateur brewmeisters, and was off on my beer manufacturing career on a ***small*** scale (for the time being).(p.297)
• I didn't dare hope I might find for myself all that these people had found, but if I could acquire some ***small*** part of their intriguing quality of living -- and sobriety -- that would be enough.(p.310)
• We had a ***small*** child, and I loved her dearly, so that held me back quite a bit in my drinking career.(p.322)
• (My addiction bloomed within a ***small*** apartment I shared with my wife, a heart patient.)(p.329)
• I was living in a ***small*** room on West 53rd Street right off Fifth Avenue, when I met a young lady who eventually was responsible for altering my entire way of living.(p.359)
• In January 1938, I had the opportunity to go to northern Vermont to manage a ***small*** daytime radio station that was up against it financially, and was about to fold its antenna.(p.359)
• Furthermore, I knew that I was looked upon as a city slicker from New York, and I had to be pretty cautious among ***small*** town, conservative Yankees.(p.360)
• I was raised like the majority of American boys, coming from a family of modest circumstances, attending public schools, having the social life of a ***small*** midwestern town, with part-time work and some athletics.(p.373)
• Instead it was like a tap on the head with a ***small*** mallet.(p.402)
• I saw that my Village friends, all of whom had ***small*** jobs, were living happily on about a tenth of my sinecure.(p.409)
• I had a tiny trust fund, and I moved into a ***small*** apartment where I learned to cook, keep house, and do the things that normal people do.(p.409)
• We spotted a church in a ***small*** town.(p.424)
• I wanted to talk about my many big problems; drinking seemed a ***small*** one.(p.447)
• I go with him to first meeting, in ***small*** town in Maine.(p.476)
• To tell you a ***small*** part of what my mother's life must have been like: Three of her kids were in jail that year -- two sons and a daughter.(p.480)
• Dad, due to having spent most of his time in a ***small*** Virginia town, didn't have any too much money, and the money he had saved and the property he had acquired were in Washington.(p.486)
• Even when we were paying that two dollars a night, they often paid it for us because our collection was so ***small***.(p.496)
• Then I had about six months on a ***small*** island in command of the troops there.(p.520)
• For to have accepted the reasons and to have acted on them would have been too great a blow to my ego, which was as great, in reverse, as my body was ***small***.(p.534)
• On another ***small*** borrowed sum, I went up into the country to the home of a doctor I had known since boyhood.(p.540)
• 1. -- Each member of Alcoholics Anonymous is but a ***small*** part of a great whole.(p.565)
• The ***small*** group may elect its secretary, the large group its rotating committee, and the groups of a large metropolitan area their central or intergroup committee, which often employs a full-time secretary.(p.567)

smart

• I vaguely sensed I was not being any too ***smart***, but felt reassured as I was taking the whiskey on a full stomach.(p.36)
• I had to adapt to new associations and associates, and it seemed to be the ***smart*** thing to drink and smoke.(p.287)
• Marty was ***smart***.(p.414)
• Then I found the solution: At the end of study time, I would drink two beers, jump in bed, sleep real fast, and wake up ***smart***.(p.440)

• And having sung that phrase, I'd chuckle with amusement, turning into irony turning into self-contempt turning into self-pity, at the sad fate of Bob, that wonderful, poor little motherless boy who was so ***smart*** in school and who grew up to accept responsibility so early and so fast and who staggered under his burdens without a whimper until the time came when he thought he was too good for this world and so he ought to be out of it.(p.532)

smarter

• I got two drinks, each of them a quarter of that pint, in me, and was talking along with these people, but I felt that sooner or later they were going to have me cornered because they were ***smarter*** than I was and the drink was beginning to take effect; but as I reached for the third drink Bob said, "Listen, Buster, you promised to take some medicine if we got you a drink.(p.206)

smartest

• That was the ***smartest*** man I'd met in months.(p.208)

smarts

• It is seldom wise to approach an individual, who still ***smarts*** from our injustice to him, and announce that we have gone religious.(p.77)

smash

• This is a point we wish to emphasize and re-emphasize, to ***smash*** home upon our alcoholic readers as it has been revealed to us out of bitter experience.(p.39)

• A drunk may ***smash*** the furniture in your home, or burn a mattress.(p.97)

• With a great deal of determination, I would throw out full pints -- pour them out and ***smash*** the bottles -- firmly resolved never to take another drink of the stuff.(p.234)

smash-up

• I did not know that I had no power over alcohol, that I, alone and unaided, could not stop; that I was on a downgrade, tearing along at full speed with all my brakes gone, and that the end would be a total ***smash-up***, death or insanity.(p.408)

smashed

• The delusion that we are like other people, or presently may be, has to be ***smashed***.(p.30)

• They struck the children, kicked out door panels, ***smashed*** treasured crockery, and ripped the keys out of pianos.(p.106)

• I was picked up at two-thirty that morning with my car ***smashed*** up by a street-car because I had run into a big concrete safety zone, and the street-car had run into me, and they took me out through the roof -- there's where I lost the suit.(p.202)

• Nobody but me got ***smashed***.(p.328)

• I'd deliberately ***smashed*** a window.(p.435)

• After my last binge I came home and ***smashed*** my dining room furniture to splinters, kicked out six windows and two balustrades.(p.435)

• He took the basketball and ***smashed*** me in the face with it.(p.484)

smashups

• I spent eighteen hundred dollars fixing up that car in the first year I was home, after four bad ***smash-ups***.(p.429)

smell

• Before very long we began to relate some incidents of our drinking and, naturally, pretty soon, I realized both of them knew what they were talking about because you can see things and ***smell*** things when you're drunk, that you can't other times, and, if I had thought they didn't know what they were talking about, I wouldn't have been willing to talk to them at all.(p.185)

• In fact, the last three years of my drinking was a routine of barbiturates in the morning, so that I could stop shaking enough to shave, and then alcohol beginning about four-thirty or five o'clock, with a struggle not to take a drink at noon or during the day, because I had the idea that if I took one drink, I would ***smell*** as though I had had a pint.(p.217)

• The idea behind it is that, having taken the treatment, your system is so "conditioned" that the mere sight or ***smell*** or taste of alcohol produces a violent reaction, and you become ill.(p.469)

smelled

• It then occurred to me that after one was all ***smelled*** up with beer nobody could tell what had been drunk, so I began to fortify my beer with straight alcohol.(p.178)

• I kept watching the man down the bar to see what he did with a contraption like that, and he just ***smelled*** of his drink and set it down again, so I did the same.(p.195)

• I thought if they ***smelled*** whiskey on my breath, they would lock me up, and I couldn't live without my bottle.(p.526)

smile

• Next time you and he have a heated discussion, no matter what the subject, it should be the privilege of either to ***smile*** and say, "This is getting serious.(p.118)

• We, who have collectively seen a great deal of business life, at least from the alcoholic angle, had to ***smile*** at this gentleman's sincere opinion.(p.149)

• As ex-problem drinkers, we ***smile*** at such a sally.(p.151)

• "I'll Never ***Smile*** Again" -- how perfect.(p.332)

smiled

• They said God made these things possible, and we only ***smiled***.(p.55)

smilingly

• Simply, but ***smilingly***, he said, "I've got religion."(p.9)

Smith

• I finished high school here in an American-sponsored Methodist public school, know as Philander ***Smith*** College.(p.342)

smoke

• I was very much interested in athletics, and because of this and parental influence, I didn't drink or ***smoke*** in either grade or high school.(p.287)

• I had to adapt to new associations and associates, and it seemed to be the smart thing to drink and ***smoke***.(p.287)

• I woke up in this bare room with nothing around me but bars; they wouldn't let me ***smoke*** and treated me, well, like I was nuts.(p.387)

• The more I focus my mind on its defects -- late start, long drunkalogues, cigarette ***smoke*** -- the worse the meeting becomes.(p.451)

smoke-filled

• Four alcoholics play bridge in a ***smoke-filled*** room.(p.502)

smoked

• I remember telling them too that it was going to be awfully tough, because I did some other things, ***smoked*** cigarettes and played penny ante poker, sometimes bet on the horse races and they said, "Don't you think you're having more trouble with this drinking than with anything else at the present time?(p.190)

• I neither drank nor ***smoked*** until I was nineteen years old.(p.419)

• I ***smoked*** as much, tried to drink as much, and do everything they did, only more so.(p.423)

smoker

• Here is a case in point: One of our friends is a heavy ***smoker*** and coffee drinker.(p.135)

smokes

• Though he is now a most effective member of Alcoholics Anonymous, he still ***smokes*** and drinks coffee, but neither his wife or anyone else stands in judgment.(p.135)

smoking

• We did, and spent a month boozing it up, popping pills, and ***smoking*** marijuana; taking shelter where we could, which included a veterinary hospital one night; accepting meals from anyone; actually begging; stealing anything we were in need of, which was about everything.(p.354)

smoldering

• My broken home and broken heart fanned my ***smoldering*** self-pity into a fair-sized bonfire and this kept me well supplied with reasons for having another drink, and then another.(p.305)

smoother

• If such women adopt a spiritual way of life their road will be ***smoother***.(p.114)

smote

• When he reached for me, I rose and ***smote*** him.(p.405)

smuggle

• After three years of this, I wound up in the local hospital where they attempted to help me, but I would get my friends to ***smuggle*** me a quart, or I would steal the alcohol about the building, so that I got rapidly worse.(p.175)

• If my wife was planning to go out in the afternoon, I would get a large supply of liquor and ***smuggle*** it home and hide it in the coal bin, the clothes chute, over door jambs, over beams in the cellar and in cracks in the cellar tile.(p.176)

smuggled

• He and mom ***smuggled*** in a couple of pints to me.(p.425)

smuggling

• This would lessen my chances of ***smuggling*** some home that evening, which in turn would mean a night of futile tossing around in bed followed by a morning of unbearable jitters.(p.176)

• It was really a horrible nightmare, this earning money, getting liquor, ***smuggling*** it home, getting drunk, morning jitters, taking large doses of sedatives to make it possible for me to earn more money, and so on ad nauseam.(p.177)

• Each time, I went back to drinking – even ***smuggling*** a bottle of vodka into the hospital as soon as the blood transfusions had ceased.(p.558)

snag

• But then I hit a ***snag***.(p.227)

snags

• Some of the ***snags*** you will encounter are irritation, hurt feeling and resentments.(p.117)

snap

• I seemed to be able to ***snap*** back the next morning better than most of my fellow drinkers, who were cursed (or perhaps blessed) with a great deal of morning-after nausea.(p.172)

• A normal person, hit with adversity, can go on a drinking spree and then ***snap*** out of it.(p.404)

snapped

• When they talked of a God personal to me, who was love, superhuman strength and direction, I became irritated and my mind ***snapped*** shut against such a theory.(p.10)

snare

• During these seven years a thing called the Twenty-four Hour Program –a gadget I used to think was only a ***snare*** to trap the newcomer -- has come to mean much to me, not only as regards my drinking but in the whole pattern of my life.(p.473)

snatching

• And do not his actions make each of them wish to retaliate, ***snatching*** all they can get out of the show?(p.61)

sneak

• When I didn't have anything else to do – a dull evening at home -- I'd ***sneak*** a few drinks upstairs in my room, and that began to be a habit.(p.464)

• I ***sneak*** downstairs and get a bottle of whiskey from the cellaret.(p.501)

sneaked

• When we were invited out, our husbands ***sneaked*** so many drinks that they spoiled the occasion.(p.105)

sneaking

• And ***sneaking*** my drinks.(p.324)

• When it became noticeable to the point of comment, I devised ways of ***sneaking*** drinks on the side.(p.375)

• The short tours could be taken care of by ***sneaking*** enough whiskey aboard ship so that it could be rationed out until another supply could be laid in.(p.398)

• I began ***sneaking*** drinks when playing bartender for guests.(p.556)

sneaky-drinking

• Through studied ***sneaky-drinking***, I'd become a senior citizen without having lost a day's work because of booze.(p.327)

sneerer

• But I had never been a flippant, wise-cracking ***sneerer*** at the few persons I had met who had impressed me as Christian men and women, or at any institution whose sincerity of purpose I could see.(p.259)

snickered

• Russ read a piece in the paper, and he kind of ***snickered***, and said, "See here, where John D. has found something to keep him from drinking!"(p.265)

sniffing

• ***Sniffing*** at emotional religion, I walked away.(p.256)

snoops

• No more ***snoops*** or big shots breathing down our necks.(p.329)

snooze

• Hidden old-drunks can pass out on their beds and ***snooze*** unreproached, under the guise of taking those vital retirement-age naps.(p.330)

snorts

• I could get through an evening with just a couple of ***snorts***.(p.196)

snow

• The checking account melted like ***snow*** in June.(p.106)

• I remember well one fellow, Joe, walking nearly three miles through slush, wet and ***snow*** to come to the hospital to see a man that he had never seen before in his life, and that impressed me very much.(p.208)
• It was February with ***snow*** and ice on the ground and I had a four blocks walk to the nearest cab stand, but I made it.(p.288)

snowballed
• I said that she told me she was going to the movies, and I became foolishly disturbed about it and, as things ***snowballed***, I decided to go out and get drunk.(p.487)

snowing
• Then, I started to miss meetings because it was raining or ***snowing*** or something else.(p.203)

snowy
• On Sunday when I came to, it was a bad, wet, ***snowy*** day in February, 1937, and Paul and Doc and a lot of other fellows were in Cleveland on business.(p.207)

snubbed
• She's a nut – she ***snubbed*** me.(p.65)

snuffed
• This process ***snuffed*** out the last flicker of conviction that I could do the job myself.(p.42)

so-called
• Under the ***so-called*** belladonna treatment my brain cleared.(p.7)
• Our ***so-called*** will power becomes practically nonexistent.(p.24)
• For the benefit of those experimentally inclined, I should mention the ***so-called*** beer experiment.(p.177)
• At the time, I thought them just a swell pair of screwballs, for they were not only going to save all the drunks in the world but also all the ***so-called*** normal people!(p.245)
• The next day I went back to Chicago and started a vigorous campaign among my ***so-called*** friends or drinking companions.(p.293)
• I got off the ***so-called*** wagon, and on the twenty-four hour plan.(p.415)
• There was no time off for ***so-called*** good behavior, first-timers, or anything else.(p.509)
• I remained there for about ten months, and then I was sent to a place called Wallkill, a ***so-called*** rehabilitation center.(p.509)
• On the next page, A.A.'s "12 Traditions" are seen in their ***so-called*** "short form," the form in general use today.(p.563)
• These ***so-called*** intergroup associations are found under the listing "A.A." or "Alcoholics Anonymous" in telephone directories.(p.575)

soaking
• And we usually have some kind of grimy sweater that we think we look sexy in, even if we weigh ninety-five pounds ***soaking*** wet and are not wearing a bra.(p.479)

soap
• No ***soap*** there.(p.499)

sober
• Prior to his journey to Akron, the broker had worked hard with many alcoholics on the theory that only an alcoholic could help an alcoholic, but he had succeeded only in keeping ***sober*** himself.(p.xvi)
• Of alcoholics who came to A.A. and really tried, 50% got ***sober*** at once and remained that way; 25% sobered up after some relapses, and among the remainder, those who stayed on with A.A. showed improvement.(p.xx)
• Mercifully, no one could guess that I was to have no real employment for five years, or hardly draw a ***sober*** breath.(p.4)
• He was ***sober***.(p.9)
• Most of us have believed that if we remained ***sober*** for a long stretch, we could thereafter drink normally.(p.33)
• In the early days of our drinking we occasionally remained ***sober*** for a year or more, becoming serious drinkers again later.(p.34)
• I had eaten there many times during the months I was ***sober***.(p.36)
• He was positive that his humiliating experience, plus the knowledge he had acquired, would keep him ***sober*** the rest of his life.(p.40)
• Sometimes we hear an alcoholic say that the only thing he needs to do is to keep ***sober***.(p.82)
• Certainly he must keep ***sober***, for there will be no home if he doesn't.(p.82)
• These things will come to pass naturally and in good time provided, however, the alcoholic continues to demonstrate that he can be ***sober***, considerate, and helpful, regardless of what anyone says or does.(p.99)
• Discuss this with him when he is ***sober*** and in good spirits.(p.115)
• They should be thankful he is ***sober*** and able to be of this world once more.(p.127)
• When ***sober***, father usually obeyed.(p.131)
• When ***sober***, does he not work hard and have a knack of getting things done?(p.139)
• Still physically weak, and ***sober*** but a few months, he saw that his predicament was dangerous.(p.154)
• After all, had he not been ***sober*** six months now?(p.154)
• But he's a grand chap when he's ***sober***, though he's been in here eight times in the last six months.(p.156)
• Though they knew they must help other alcoholics if they would remain ***sober***, that motive became secondary.(p.159)
• Not being a man of means, I knew that if I did not stay ***sober*** enough to earn money, I would run out of liquor.(p.175)
• My phobia for sleeplessness demanded that I get drunk every night, but in order to get more liquor for the next night, I had to stay ***sober*** during the day, at least up to four o'clock.(p.177)
• I used to promise my wife, my friends, and my children that I would drink no more – promises which seldom kept me ***sober*** even through the day, though I was very sincere when I made them.(p.177)
• I got tight that night, stayed ***sober*** Monday till after the dinner and then proceeded to get tight again.(p.179)
• This was going to help them to stay ***sober***.(p.185)
• We're not up here trying to take any of your rights or privileges away from you, but we have a program whereby we think we can stay ***sober***.(p.186)
• Two days before this, Dr. Bob had said to me, "If you and I are going to stay ***sober***, we had better get busy."(p.188)
• It took me a year, or a year and a half to get to feeling physically well, and it was rather tough, but I soon found folks whose friendship I had once had, and I found, after I had been ***sober*** for quite some little time, that these people began to act like they had in previous years, before I had gotten so bad, so that I didn't pay too awful much attention to financial gains.(p.190)
• On that statement and the fact that I had been ***sober*** for ninety days, he gave me a job selling lots in an allotment he had.(p.200)
• In my own experience I was so jubilant at finding myself ***sober***, and I had so many things to catch up on, that a month went by before the thought even occurred to me.(p.219)
• There were, at that time, in the neighborhood of twelve or thirteen Cleveland members who had been ***sober*** anywhere from a year and a half to a couple of months.(p.219)
• Professionally, after I was ***sober*** for a month or so I realized that I should school myself to dissolve the partnership I was in because I felt that I would never regain the respect of my partners no matter how long I was ***sober***, and that I would be at a disadvantage.(p.220)
• "Best in the business, when he's ***sober***," my customers would say, and I still had a following who would give me work though they deplored my habits, because they knew the job would be well done when they eventually got it.(p.234)
• I could see they were ***sober***.(p.235)
• This duty together with my weekly meetings with my fellow alcoholics, and my daily renewal of the contract I originally made with God, have kept me ***sober*** when nothing else ever did.(p.237)
• I have been ***sober*** for many years now.(p.237)
• Searching where I have been at fault, it is not hard to discover and get right again, for I have proven to myself and to many others who know me that God can keep a man ***sober*** if he will let Him.(p.237)
• So I always say that as long as I remember January 8th that is how long I will remain ***sober***.(p.240)
• I was never a hilarious drunk; the more I drank the quieter I got, and the drunker I got the harder I fought to stay ***sober***.(p.241)
• But we were staying ***sober*** as long as we kept and talked together.(p.246)
• They did not seem to be getting an answer, for here I was staying ***sober*** and selling lots of auto polish, on which they were making one thousand per cent profit.(p.247)
• I had completely forgotten the January 8th when I found the fellowship, and I spent the next four days wandering around New England half drunk, by which I mean I couldn't get drunk and I couldn't get ***sober***.(p.247)
• Then I got a very good position in Philadelphia and quickly found I would need a few fellow alcoholics around me if I was to stay ***sober***.(p.249)
• She has been ***sober*** all the way through and for me that has been good.(p.249)
• I stayed ***sober*** for four years except for a one-night carousal in Chicago.(p.253)
• I stayed so ***sober*** that I used to keep a quart of medicinal whiskey in my bureau which I used to taper off the occasional newspaper alcoholics who were sent to see me.(p.253)
• My four years of abstinence had something to do with it, but soldiering is a tough enough game for a ***sober*** man, and I had no yen for full-pack slogging through mud with a cognac or vin rouge hangover.(p.253)
• Every encouragement was given me with frequent salary increases, but the ***sober*** times between "periods" became shorter.(p.254)
• I stayed ***sober*** during the trip except for an occasional bottle of beer because funds barely met expenses.(p.255)
• I arrived drunk, but I promised my wife I would keep ***sober***, and I knew I could get work if I did.(p.256)
• Of course I didn't keep ***sober***.(p.257)
• All sorts were represented and their relation of experiences and how they had found the only remedy, added to their human existence as ***sober*** men, laid the foundation of a very necessary faith.(p.258)
• The big thing was that these men were all ***sober*** and evidently had something I didn't have.(p.259)
• Today I have Someone who will always hear me; I have a warm fellowship among men who understand my problems; I have tasks to do and am glad to do them, to see others who are alcoholics and to help them in any way I can to become ***sober*** men.(p.260)
• Jack had been ***sober*** about a year and a half.(p.271)
• I ate up every bit of it, because I wanted to find out how to stay ***sober***.(p.273)
• The most accurate answer I can give you is this: Fear has never again ruled my life since that day in September, 1938, when I found that a Power greater than myself could not only restore me to sanity but could keep me both ***sober*** and sane.(p.285)
• This was the beginning of five years of bounding back and forth between my home in Chicago and Akron to ***sober*** up.(p.288)
• Once dad came all the way to Florida to ***sober*** me up, after a hotel manager called him and said that if he wanted to see me alive he better get there fast.(p.288)
• My wife could not understand why I would ***sober*** up for dad but not for her.(p.288)
• They went into a huddle and dad explained that he simply took my pants, shoes and money away, so that I could get no liquor and had to ***sober*** up.(p.288)
• He waited until I was completely ***sober*** and the day before I was to head back for Chicago, he told me of a small group of men in Akron who apparently had the same problem that I had but were doing something about it.(p.289)
• He said they were ***sober***, happy and had their self-respect back as well as the respect of their neighbors.(p.289)
• I went to a minister and a doctor that I still knew and they, in turn, asked me how long I had been ***sober***.(p.293)
• I cannot remember just when I became the victim of insomnia, but I do know that the last year and a half I never went to bed ***sober*** a single night.(p.299)
• I also found out that all they wanted was to help me get ***sober*** and to stay ***sober*** themselves.(p.320)
• I'm ***sober*** today.(p.320)
• If I had been sincere in what I thought I wanted more than anything else in life – a ***sober*** husband and a happy, contented home – I would have gone on the wagon with him.(p.324)
• But the percentages started tobogganing, and it was often a shock to read over some of the pages when ***sober***.(p.331)
• I have read systematically since then, and A.A. literature has kept me ***sober***.(p.343)
• You've been ***sober*** for three months, been working hard.(p.348)
• "Well," he said, "you've been ***sober***, but you've been floating way up on a cloud somewhere.(p.349)
• I do recall lying on a cold cement floor and shredding into little bits several pieces of stolen identification cards, and washing my face in the toilet bowl trying to ***sober*** up, and screaming hysterically while clinging to bars too high to see out of, and cursing everyone that came near me.(p.354)
• By hook or crook I usually managed to ***sober*** up before I reached home, but always "terribly tired" from a "hard day's work," and just having to have one or two

before dinner.(p.361)
• The baffling problem of getting drunk when I had every intention of staying ***sober*** was simplified.(p.379)
• Just being ***sober*** will be making amends to many we have hurt by our drunken actions.(p.381)
• When I joined A.A. I did so for the sole purpose of getting ***sober*** and staying ***sober***.(p.383)
• I know that if I do daily what I have done for these last thirteen and a half years, I will stay ***sober***.(p.384)
• There are no easy ways to ***sober*** up, but that's the most excruciating.(p.389)
• You know those vitamins just don't keep you ***sober***!(p.389)
• The only thing that I could do would be to call the doctor to help ***sober*** me up.(p.389)
• I couldn't walk, having it in a cast, and the doctor left the cast on three weeks longer than was necessary because he never found me ***sober*** enough to take it off.(p.390)
• One afternoon, the year after moving to Houston, I got as drunk as a skunk, and while I do not walk very straight ***sober***, you should see me when I'm drunk!(p.390)
• So he waited another week or two and I don't think I stayed ***sober*** hardly at all.(p.391)
• So Frank left town, and by Monday morning I had been ***sober*** for that whole week.(p.393)
• I know that I must work at it as long as I live; I know that it is only by working at it that I can stay ***sober*** and have a happy life.(p.394)
• Drunk or ***sober***, I was hectic, unpredictable, irresponsible.(p.406)
• But I was not able to make use of this knowledge until after I became ***sober***.(p.409)
• But my life, even ***sober***, was all askew and so were my emotions.(p.414)
• They were a couple of normal, ***sober***, attractive men.(p.415)
• Except for one short slip, during the first eight months, which was an angry "the world can't do this to me" reaction to a personal tragedy in my life, I have been ***sober*** for twelve years.(p.416)
• My friendships are meaningful, loving and interesting because I am ***sober***.(p.416)
• My gratitude to A.A. grows deeper each day I am ***sober***.(p.420)
• And somehow or other I stayed ***sober***.(p.430)
• When I woke up ***sober***, my handiwork confronted me.(p.435)
• Here was power to live to the end of any given day, power to have the courage to face the next day, power to have friends, power to help people, power to be sane, power to stay ***sober***.(p.436)
• The Higher Power was on deck to see me through, ***sober***.(p.437)
• I had sent her to four consecutive psychiatrists, and not one of them had gotten me ***sober***.(p.440)
• Giving up alcohol alone was not enough for me; I've had to give up all mood-and mind-affecting chemicals in order to stay ***sober*** and comfortable.(p.443)
• I interpreted "***sober***" as meaning "drinking but not being drunk."(p.447)
• (Today, there is absolutely nothing in the world more important to me than my keeping this alcoholic ***sober***; not taking a drink is by far the most important thing I do each day.)(p.447)
• Until I could accept my alcoholism, I could not stay ***sober***; unless I accept life completely on life's terms, I cannot be happy.(p.449)
• Now ***sober*** for years, they tell us how they got well.(p.455)
• Being dry is not being ***sober***.(p.462)
• Guess I'll never be a saint, but whatever I am, I want to be ***sober*** and in A.A.(p.463)
• He said he didn't care what I did with the money, but there was going to be no more until I was completely ***sober***.(p.467)
• I was frightened -- terribly frightened, and in about three days I was ***sober***.(p.467)
• On the day before Christmas I telephoned him and told him I was ***sober*** and asked him to come home.(p.467)
• By grace of God I stop, think two things: This would kill good mother and father; then remember boys talk about Indian fellow who been ***sober*** three years.(p.475)
• He stay ***sober***.(p.476)
• Tall Man die five years ago, a ***sober***, peaceful, happy man.(p.476)
• This ***sober*** Indian say to sick, red-eyed alcoholic who want good medicine: "Put cork in bottle.(p.477)
• Knowing that he was ***sober***, I timed it just right, so I could do the slashing just before he hit the steps.(p.479)
• Nevertheless, I stayed ***sober*** there about six months, because I knew that Vi was to come later and bring the children.(p.490)
• She asked me if I would try to be ***sober*** if I possibly could.(p.494)
• So I put forth some effort that day to try to stay ***sober*** if I could, though my sobriety was just a daze.(p.494)
• We were married, and during the first nine months of that marriage I was ***sober***.(p.514)
• All they care about is that I am a human being and that I want to stay ***sober***.(p.529)
• We all have the same sickness, and in helping one another, we are able to stay ***sober***.(p.530)
• If he were still ***sober***, chances are that very quickly I put him down as a Philistine with no appreciation of literary genius; and then I went on to another bar to find a new victim.(p.537)
• It became more and more necessary to escape from myself, for my remorse and shame and humiliation when I was ***sober*** were almost unbearable.(p.547)
• The only way existence was possible was through rationalizing every ***sober*** moment and drinking myself into complete oblivion as often as I could.(p.547)
• It seemed logical to me that if I married this man and took the responsibility for these children that they would keep me ***sober***.(p.548)
• The children kept me ***sober*** for darn near three weeks, and then I went on (please God) my last drunk.(p.549)
• The people who came knew immediately I was in no condition to absorb anything of the program, and I was put in a sanitarium to be defogged so that I could make a ***sober*** decision about this for myself.(p.549)
• They suggested that I study the A.A. book and try to take the Twelve Steps according to the explanation in the Book, for it was their opinion that the application of these principles in our daily lives will get us ***sober*** and keep us ***sober***.(p.550)
• I had only to reflect on the contrast between the plans I made so many years ago for my life with what really happened to know I couldn't manage my life drunk or ***sober***.(p.550)
• It's been true in my case, nor could I quarrel with "restore us to sanity," for my actions drunk or ***sober***, before A.A., were not those of a sane person.(p.550)
• As the ***sober*** days grew into ***sober*** months and then into ***sober*** years, a new and beautiful life began to emerge from the shambles of my former existence.(p.559)
• I have come to realize that the name of the game is not so much to stop drinking as to stay ***sober***.(p.559)
• Alcoholics can stop drinking in many places and many ways – but Alcoholics Anonymous offers us a way to stay ***sober***.(p.559)
• Learning to depend upon a higher power and absorb himself in his work with other alcoholics, he remains ***sober*** day by day.(p.572)

sobered

• He ***sobered***, never to drink again up to the moment of his death in 1950.(p.xvi)
• Of alcoholics who came to A.A. and really tried, 50% got sober at once and remained that way; 25% ***sobered*** up after some relapses, and among the remainder, those who stayed on with A.A. showed improvement.(p.xx)
• Fear ***sobered*** me for a bit.(p.8)
• I'd been dry three weeks, had the wrinkles out and had ***sobered*** up my sponsor all by myself!(p.246)
• And again these were things that I really profited by after I ***sobered*** up.(p.409)
• Frightened and shamed, I refused, and ***sobered*** up temporarily.(p.411)

soberest-seeming

• So it is clear that I never had any fun out of drinking – I would be the ***soberest-seeming*** one in the crowd and all of a sudden I would be the drunkest.(p.241)

sobering

• Sometimes, after ***sobering*** up after a bout of several weeks, I would righteously resolve to quit.(p.233)
• After a particularly bad Christmas and New Year's holiday, dad picked me up again early in January, 1937, to go through the usual ***sobering*** up routine.(p.289)
• A week later, I had to get an old friend from Akron to spend two days ***sobering*** me up.(p.293)
• This easy method of ***sobering*** up would last at least three days.(p.468)
• ***Sobering*** up, the mind that was ahead of the emotions would impel the question: What have you written or done to be the great man?(p.537)

soberly

• Fear, love of dentistry, and an imitation of my father's periodic drinking pattern took me through dental college ***soberly***, except for the few parties and vacations in those four years.(p.419)

sobriety

• By late 1937, the number of members having substantial ***sobriety*** time behind them was sufficient to convince the membership that a new light had entered the dark world of the alcoholic.(p.xvii)
• Nevertheless, I still thought I could control the situation, and there were periods of ***sobriety*** which renewed my wife's hope.(p.5)
• Then he fell victim to a belief which practically every alcoholic has -- that his long period of ***sobriety*** and self-discipline had qualified him to drink as other men.(p.32)
• Commencing to drink after a period of ***sobriety***, we are in a short time as bad as ever.(p.33)
• We feel a man is unthinking when he says that ***sobriety*** is enough.(p.82)
• Ask them to remember, when they are impatient, the blessed fact of his ***sobriety***.(p.100)
• His only chance for ***sobriety*** would be some place like the Greenland Ice Cap, and even there an Eskimo might turn up with a bottle of scotch and ruin everything!(p.101)
• Your husband knows he owes you more than ***sobriety***.(p.118)
• The fact is that he should work with other people to maintain his own ***sobriety***.(p.119)
• As soon as his ***sobriety*** begins to be taken as a matter of course, the family may look at their strange new dad with apprehension, then with irritation.(p.128)
• During those first days of convalescence, this will do more to insure his ***sobriety*** than anything else.(p.129)
• This work is necessary to maintain his ***sobriety***.(p.146)
• He will presently try the old game again, for he isn't happy about his ***sobriety***.(p.152)
• This group of thirteen stories shows that ***sobriety*** in A.A. can be lasting.(p.167)
• All have now passed away from natural causes, having maintained complete ***sobriety***.(p.169)
• The periods of ***sobriety*** attained by these thirteen A.A.'s range from fifteen to forty-six years.(p.169)
• The birth of our Society dates from his first day of permanent ***sobriety***, June 10, 1935.(p.171)
• I'm so grateful for both the program and the people in it that I still want to go, and then probably the most wonderful thing that I learned from the program -- I've seen this in the 'A.A. Grapevine' a lot of times, and I've had people say it to me personally, and I've heard people get up in meetings and make the same statement: The statement is, "I came into A.A. solely for the purpose of ***sobriety***, but it has been through A.A. that I have found God."(p.192)
• But more important, I lost my ***sobriety***.(p.202)
• My ***sobriety*** continued for another six months.(p.203)
• This Christian Science experience with a ***sobriety*** of fifteen months was in 1932.(p.203)
• My children had lost respect for me and, in fact, it was only after three or four years of ***sobriety*** that any of them ever said anything to me to indicate that I had recouped even a little of their respect.(p.215)
• All of us in A.A. know the tremendous happiness that is in our ***sobriety***, but there are also tragedies.(p.239)
• Around this time our big A.A. book was being written and it all became much simpler; we had a definite formula which some sixty of us agreed was the middle course for all alcoholics who wanted ***sobriety***, and that formula has not been changed one iota down through the years.(p.248)
• And I still say that as long as I remember that January 8th in Washington, that is how long, by the grace of God as I understand Him, I will retain a happy ***sobriety***.(p.250)
• I think that was the last vacation before ***sobriety***.(p.265)
• After six months of ***sobriety*** I saw the picture in a different light: Detroit was the place I had to return to, not only because I must face the mess I had made there, but because it was there that I could be of the most service to A.A.(p.281)
• One of them was that I would try to get a group started in Chicago; the second was that I would have to return to Akron to attend meetings at least every two months until I did get a group started in Chicago; third, I decided I must place this program above everything else, even my family, because if I did not maintain my ***sobriety*** I would lose my family anyway.(p.292)

• If I did not maintain my ***sobriety,*** I would not have a job.(p.293)

• If I did not maintain my ***sobriety,*** I would have no friends left.(p.293)

• I would hang on to ***sobriety*** for short intervals, but always there would come the tide of an overpowering necessity to drink and, as I was engulfed in it, I felt such a sense of panic that I really believed I would die if I didn't get that drink inside.(p.306)

• I didn't dare hope I might find for myself all that these people had found, but if I could acquire some small part of their intriguing quality of living -- and ***sobriety*** -- that would be enough.(p.310)

• A.A.'s Twelve Steps showed me the way to ***sobriety*** if I wanted it.(p.320)

• Now I feel so very grateful not only for my ***sobriety,*** which I try to maintain day by day, but I'm grateful also for the ability to help other people.(p.326)

• Three years and three months of ***sobriety,*** without a slip, has meant a lot to me, my wife, and my family.(p.342)

• The encouragement received in the early days, especially from the A.A. General Service Office, made a tremendous difference to my ***sobriety.***(p.342)

• He was full of his new found life of happiness and ***sobriety.***(p.365)

• I was told that I must want ***sobriety*** for my own sake and I am convinced this is true.(p.379)

• There may be many reasons which bring one to A.A. for the first time, but the lasting one must be to want ***sobriety*** and the A.A. way of living for oneself.(p.379)

• To me this meant telling my associates that I had joined Alcoholics Anonymous; that I didn't know what was expected of me by A.A., but that whatever it was, it was the most important thing in life for me; that ***sobriety*** meant more to me than anything in this world.(p.382)

• Above all, I am grateful to A.A. for my ***sobriety,*** which means so much to my family, friends and business associates, because God and A.A. were able to do for me something I was unable to do for myself.(p.383)

• A return to the United States proved effective as a geographical cure, and a period of ***sobriety*** ensued, with the help of the church.(p.419)

• "I've got to stop if I want to live," I told myself, and if I don't want to break my parents' hearts and maybe jeopardize their own carefully built up and hard-fought-for ***sobriety.***(p.429)

• The most terrible blow of my life befell me after I'd found ***sobriety*** through A.A.(p.437)

• It helped me a great deal to become convinced that alcoholism was a disease, not a moral issue; that I had been drinking as a result of a compulsion, even though I had not been aware of the compulsion at the time; and that ***sobriety*** was not a matter of will-power.(p.448)

• How important is it compared to my serenity, my emotional ***sobriety?***"(p.452)

• And when I place more value on my serenity and ***sobriety*** than on anything else, I can maintain them at a higher level -- at least for the time being.(p.452)

• ***Sobriety*** and a plan for living that produces a personality change and a spiritual awakening are imperative.(p.459)

• I count my ***sobriety*** date from the day I began going to A.A. in prison, not from the date of my last drink.(p.462)

• In the light of subsequent events it became evident that I took their advice far too literally, for, after some months of happy ***sobriety*** I drank again.(p.471)

• Maine newsletter (Boomerang) say: "With tireless devotion and humility, this venerable Indian gentleman traveled thousands of miles humbly pleading for ***sobriety.***(p.476)

• He has so much understanding, a real asset in sharing ***sobriety.***(p.481)

• For me, my ***sobriety*** comes before his or even before my feeling for him.(p.481)

• So I put forth some effort that day to try to stay sober if I could, though my ***sobriety*** was just a daze.(p.494)

• The days have grown into a little better than four years of ***sobriety.***(p.511)

• God has been good to me both in my drinking and in my ***sobriety.***(p.516)

• It has taught me that I can best keep my ***sobriety*** by sharing it out with others; that I must bring that ***sobriety*** to others who need it, in my own interest.(p.524)

• After nearly eight years of ***sobriety*** in A.A., I still can set down such thoughts, "against my instinct and training," showing that I still consider myself a "special" person, entitled to special privileges.(p.536)

• I attended my first A.A. meeting eight years ago, and it is with deep gratitude that I'm able to say I've not had a drink since that time, and that I take no sedation or narcotics, for this program is to me one of complete ***sobriety*** and I no longer need to escape reality.(p.549)

• A.A. TAUGHT HIM TO HANDLE *SOBRIETY*(p.554)

• "God willing, we . . . may never again have to deal with drinking, but we have to deal with ***sobriety*** every day."(p.554)

• "It teaches us how to handle ***sobriety.***"(p.554)

• To do that, I had come to A.A. to learn how to handle ***sobriety*** -- which is what I could not handle in the first place.(p.554)

• But above all, it taught me how to handle ***sobriety.***(p.559)

• God willing, we members of A.A. may never again have to deal with drinking, but we have to deal with ***sobriety*** every day.(p.560)

• To those now in its fold, Alcoholics Anonymous has made the difference between misery and ***sobriety,*** and often the difference between life and death.(p.563)

• Any two or three alcoholics gathered together for ***sobriety*** may call themselves an A.A. group, provided that, as a group, they have no other affiliation.(p.565)

• If there is none nearby, you will be invited to carry on a correspondence which will do much to insure your ***sobriety*** no matter how isolated you are.(p.575)

sobriety-tension

• I had been on the wagon when I came to A.A. and this ***sobriety-tension*** eventually popped.(p.414)

sociability

• Aside from fellowship and ***sociability,*** the prime object was to provide a time and place where new people might bring their problems.(p.160)

social

• All sections of this country and many of its occupations are represented, as well as many political, economic, ***social,*** and religious backgrounds.(p.17)

• Of necessity there will have to be discussion of matters medical, psychiatric, ***social,*** and religious.(p.19)

• Therefore, ask yourself on each occasion, "Have I any good ***social,*** business, or personal reason for going to this place?(p.101)

• Now you are getting back into the ***social*** life of this world.(p.102)

• We could make few ***social*** engagements.(p.105)

• We know all about liquor as a ***social*** lubricant.(p.110)

• ***Social*** distinctions, petty rivalries and jealousies -- these are laughed out of countenance.(p.161)

• I missed the old ***social*** times, of course, but had no definite craving even for beer.(p.232)

• I managed to maintain myself with odd jobs, did ten weeks in a ***social*** rescue institution, and at length wound up in a second-hand bookstore in an adjacent town as manager.(p.257)

• Too many economic and ***social*** problems would beset me there.(p.281)

• But what about my ***social*** life?(p.284)

• Every evening we would meet at the home of one of the members and have coffee and doughnuts and spend a ***social*** evening.(p.291)

• That being the case, it didn't take me long to figure out that my meager manufacturing facilities were entirely inadequate to the manufacture of beer for ***social*** and domestic consumption.(p.297)

• I experienced some of the pleasure of ***social*** drinking when I was sixteen.(p.305)

• I had long since given up any pretense of the "***social***" cocktail hour.(p.306)

• I noticed that I was avoiding all my ***social*** friends except for my bridge.(p.324)

• Until I took ***Social*** Security and a pension at the age of sixty-eight, after forty years in motion-picture-studio public relations, I had successfully hidden even any hints of approaching alcoholism.(p.327)

• I felt disgraced and humiliated -- a man who couldn't hold booze -- a ***social*** disaster.(p.328)

• I was never a very heavy ***social*** drinker.(p.335)

• I had every advantage a child could have, private schools (several of them), dancing schools, two colleges, coon skin coats, automobiles, a listing in the ***social*** register and all the rest.(p.357)

• As I later found out through Alcoholics Anonymous, alcohol is no respecter of economic status, ***social*** and business standing or intelligence.(p.373)

• I was raised like the majority of American boys, coming from a family of modest circumstances, attending public schools, having the ***social*** life of a small midwestern town, with part-time work and some athletics.(p.373)

• The drive to get ahead, to succeed, kept me too busy for many years to have any great experience with ***social*** life.(p.374)

• But success brought increased ***social*** activities and I realized that many of my friends enjoyed a ***social*** drink with no apparent harm to themselves or others.(p.374)

• I liked the description of the alcoholic as a person who had found that alcohol is interfering with his ***social*** or business life.(p.380)

• But now I was a young divorcee, leading a Washington ***social*** life.(p.402)

• My new friends had a ***social*** conscience.(p.410)

• His parishioners are limited in number, but his friends are many, for to him race, creed, or ***social*** position makes no difference.(p.497)

• I didn't stick at ***social*** drinking very long.(p.512)

• But as the years go by, the stretch becomes unbearable; and the man with the grown-up brain and the childish emotions -- vanity, self-interest, false pride, jealousy, longing for ***social*** approval, to name few -- becomes a prime candidate for alcohol.(p.534)

• With deep shame came the knowledge too that I had lived with no sense of ***social*** obligation nor had I known the meaning of moral responsibility to my fellow men.(p.549)

• When I was faced with a special challenge or ***social*** event -- such as an important business presentation or a dinner party -- I had to fortify myself with a couple of belts.(p.556)

• "The American Public Health Association presents a Lasker Group Award for 1951 to Alcoholics Anonymous in recognition of its unique and highly successful approach to that age-old public health and ***social*** problem, alcoholism . . .(p.573)

• In emphasizing alcoholism as an illness, the ***social*** stigma associated with this condition is being blotted out . . .(p.573)

• Historians may one day recognize Alcoholics Anonymous to have been a great venture in ***social*** pioneering which forged a new instrument for ***social*** action; a new therapy based on the kinship of common suffering; one having a vast potential for the myriad other ills of mankind."(p.573)

socially

• Your new courage, good nature and lack of self-consciousness will do wonders for you ***socially.***(p.115)

• I never drank ***socially;*** I drank as often and as much as I could.(p.353)

• I came from a family where alcohol was ***socially*** acceptable.(p.384)

• As long as it eased situations ***socially,*** it helped just fine, but somewhere along the line, it backfired.(p.386)

• I started drinking ***socially*** and at parties and proms when I was about twenty years old.(p.464)

• All my troubles arose when I was thrown ***socially*** among groups of people.(p.486)

• But as long as you did your work and didn't disgrace yourself, you were ***socially*** acceptable and nobody really intruded on your private life very much.(p.518)

• I've been benefited from a dictionary definition I found that reads: "rationalization is giving a ***socially*** acceptable reason for ***socially*** unacceptable behavior, and ***socially*** unacceptable behavior is a form of insanity."(p.551)

• I was raised in Kansas, the only child of loving parents who just drank ***socially.***(p.554)

societies

• Inquiry by scientific, medical, and religious ***societies*** will be welcomed.(p.xiv)

• On account of my enormous capacity for beer, I was elected to membership in one of the drinking ***societies,*** and soon became one of the leading spirits.(p.173)

• My drinking career began about four years after I had moved up into partnership and had joined certain clubs, ***societies*** and so fourth, and during which period we had Prohibition.(p.213)

• Loading a car with good old books to sell to collectors, librarians, universities and historical ***societies,*** I started out to travel the country.(p.255)

• I belong to more medical ***societies*** and honor ***societies*** than men ten to twenty years my senior.(p.345)

• I was active and did well, however, in school publications, dramatics (which came in handy during my drinking career), and Greek letter ***societies.***(p.357)

• I had no trouble at all in being elected to the two drinking ***societies*** at my college.(p.357)

• Since Dr. Silkworth's first endorsement of Alcoholics Anonymous, medical ***societies*** and physicians throughout the world have set their approval upon us.(p.571)

• (This address is now available in pamphlet form at nominal cost through most A.A. groups or from Box 459, Grand Central Station, New York, NY 10163, under the title "Three Talks to Medical *Societies* by Bill W." – formerly called "Bill on Alcoholism" and earlier "Alcoholism the Illness.")(p.572)

society

• Because this book has become the basic text for our *Society* and has helped such large numbers of alcoholic men and women to recover, there exists a sentiment against any radical changes being made in it.(p.xi)

• He had also been greatly helped by the late Dr. William D. Silkworth, a New York specialist in alcoholism who is now accounted no less than a medical saint by A.A. members, and whose story of the early days of our *Society* appears in the next pages.(p.xvi)

• The fledgling *society*, which had been nameless, now began to be called Alcoholics Anonymous, from the title of its own book.(p.xvii)

• Our *Society* then entered a fearsome and exciting adolescent period.(p.xviii)

• It was thought that no alcoholic man or woman could be excluded from our *Society*; that our leaders might serve but never govern; that each group was to be autonomous and there was to be no professional class of therapy.(p.xix)

• Today the remarkable unity of A.A. is one of the greatest assets that our *Society* has.(p.xix)

• *Society* was about to lock him up.(p.11)

• In the doctor's judgment he was utterly hopeless; he could never regain his position in *society* and he would have to place himself under lock and key or hire a bodyguard if he expected to live long.(p.26)

• He is like the retired business man who lolls in the Florida sunshine in the winter complaining of the sad state of the nation; the minister who sighs over the sins of the twentieth century; politicians and reformers who are sure all would be Utopia if the rest of the world would only behave; the outlaw safe cracker who thinks *society* has wronged him; and the alcoholic who has lost all and is locked up.(p.61)

• The less people tolerated us, the more we withdrew from *society*, from life itself.(p.151)

• The birth of our *Society* dates from his first day of permanent sobriety, June 10, 1935.(p.171)

• This dry spell lasted for about three weeks; then I went to Atlantic City to attend several days' meeting of a national *society* of which I was a member.(p.179)

• Fond of singing, I joined a German singing *society* which had good club headquarters.(p.231)

• This was my introduction to this "understanding fellowship" although it was to be more than a year later before our *Society* was to bear the name, Alcoholics Anonymous.(p.239)

• I had thought that I was completely different from other people, that I was beginning to become a little balmy, even to the point of withdrawing more and more from *society* and wanting to be alone with my bottle.(p.290)

• (I belong to the American Psychiatric *Society*, but I don't practice psychiatry as such.(p.347)

• I recall, as I walked into that meeting, saying to myself, "Here I am, a fellow of the American College of Surgeons, a Fellow of the International College of Surgeons, a diplomate of one of the great specialty boards in these United States, a member of the American Psychiatric *Society*, and I have to go to the butcher, the baker and the carpenter to help make a man out of me!"(p.347)

• I also wanted to be the queen of *society*, with a glittering salon, the bride of a dream prince and the mother of a happy brood.(p.400)

• The glittering *society* belle, the modern Shakespeare, the happy wife, the loving and beloved.(p.411)

• I had accomplished all the right things that our *society* expected, and I had no real peace of mind nor gratitude.(p.418)

• I depended on optimism and ambition to live in *society*; when I began to tire, I had to depend on chemicals instead to keep going.(p.420)

• After I came to A.A., I was divorced by my wife; I lost my practice; I was legally restrained from seeing my children; I went broke; and the dental *society* threatened me with the loss of my license.(p.420)

• Also, I was insane at times -- according to *society*'s yardstick.(p.458)

• *Society* can do anything it chooses to do with me when I am drunk and I can't lift a finger to stop it, for I forfeit my rights through the simple expedient of becoming a menace to myself and to the people around me.(p.549)

• Therefore, no *society* of men and women ever had more urgent need for continuous effectiveness and permanent unity.(p.563)

• Following are excerpts from the comments of doctors present at the annual meeting of the Medical *Society* of the State of New York where a paper on A.A. was read:(p.571)

• Dr. W.W. Bauer, broadcasting under the auspices of The American Medical Association in 1946, over the NBC network, said, in part: "Alcoholics Anonymous are no crusaders; not a temperance *society*.(p.572)

society's

• The section called "The Doctor's Opinion" has been kept intact, just as it was originally written in 1939 by the late Dr. William D. Silkworth, our *Society's* great medical benefactor.(p.xi)

sociologists

• I believe the *sociologists* would call it "upper middle class."(p.275)

soda

• There, I received several *soda* crackers and water daily, and before I could have my third-day meal (again the only meal in ten days), I had to drink a glass of castor oil or mineral oil, depending on the cruelty of the person who was doing the dispensing.(p.459)

sodas

• I graduated from shots and beer chasers to Scotch and *sodas*.(p.398)

sodden

• But not for long; now, for five Friday nights in a row, I went to jail, picked up *sodden* with beer (which I always disliked, but which was the only drink available); in jail five consecutive Friday nights in the town where I had grown up, where I had been an honor student in high school, where a kindly uncle, bailing me out, said, "Bob, our family just doesn't do this sort of thing."(p.539)

soft

• Hence we are at pains to tell why we think our present faith is reasonable, why we think it more sane and logical to believe than not to believe, why we say our former thinking was *soft* and mushy when we threw up our hands in doubt and said, "We don't know."(p.53)

• So we rolled old newspapers together and made torches to find a good *soft* pew and get some sleep.(p.424)

• At Great Lakes Boot Camp I latched onto a *soft* billet.(p.425)

softer

• We thought we could find an easier, *softer* way.(p.58)

• I was trying to find an easier, *softer* way.(p.378)

soil

• His roots grasped a new *soil*.(p.12)

• Seed has started to sprout in a new *soil*, but growth has only begun.(p.117)

soiled

• I would gather up all my *soiled* clothes, as much as I could cram into a grocery cart, and be off.(p.370)

sojourn

• In fact, I never lost my faith, since I had been prepared by some conversations toward the end of my *sojourn* in the hospital with Dr. Bob, conversations pretty much along spiritual lines.(p.218)

solace

• Three months later, he hated the game and found *solace* in the bottle.(p.330)

sold

• However, he did become "*sold*" on the ideas contained in this book.(p.xxx)

• No beer or liquor was *sold* in the neighborhood, except at the State liquor agency where perhaps one might procure a pint if he could convince the agent that he really needed it.(p.171)

• During the day, looking over the contracts and money in my pocket, I found that I had *sold* six lots that I couldn't even remember, and didn't even know the people I had *sold* them to.(p.196)

• I *sold* three lots to an elderly lady in Cleveland.(p.196)

• At that particular stage, I lost interest in it, *sold* the option for $5,000 and forgot the whole deal.(p.198)

• Not far from where I lived they built a new technical high school and one of the teachers *sold* me on the idea that I needed a little mechanical drawing if I were going to be a good toolmaker.(p.211)

• The "speaks" usually *sold* whiskey.(p.233)

• They owned this joint, she ran it, and he *sold* for a brewery.(p.267)

• HE *SOLD* HIMSELF SHORT(p.287)

• On my ride to the nearest bar, I *sold* the driver on how misunderstood I was by my wife and what an unreasonable person she was.(p.288)

• That *sold* us on Alcoholics Anonymous."(p.315)

• I did some things I liked, and even *sold* some.(p.331)

• I went out to the West Coast, waited on table, washed dishes and *sold* newspaper subscriptions.(p.401)

• I wrote and *sold* some short stories.(p.409)

• Having heard Bill speak, she was instantly *sold*.(p.412)

• I was *sold*, intellectually.(p.414)

• I have achieved the inner confidence to write quite unlike Shakespeare, and I have *sold* a good deal of what I've written.(p.416)

• I was always able to get a boyfriend who had a drinking joint or *sold* whiskey, but it didn't last long.(p.526)

• Later, I found out that I went into stores and stole clothes, then *sold* them.(p.528)

• It came out that I had *sold* a woman a fur coat.(p.528)

• I *sold* my first article to a national magazine while still an undergraduate.(p.555)

soldier

• A good *soldier* is ne'er forgot Whether he dieth by musket Or by pot."(p.1)

• In foreign parts many a *soldier* who has been abstemious at home learns to use new and potent drinks.(p.230)

• Remarkably enough, I was a very abstemious *soldier*.(p.253)

soldiering

• My four years of abstinence had something to do with it, but *soldiering* is a tough enough game for a sober man, and I had no yen for full-pack slogging through mud with a cognac or vin rouge hangover.(p.253)

sole

• None of us makes a *sole* vocation of this work, nor do we think its effectiveness would be increased if we did.(p.19)

• When I joined A.A. I did so for the *sole* purpose of getting sober and staying sober.(p.383)

• Their management should be the *sole* responsibility of those people who financially support them.(p.566)

solely

• I'm so grateful for both the program and the people in it that I still want to go, and then probably the most wonderful thing that I learned from the program -- I've seen this in the 'A.A. Grapevine' a lot of times, and I've had people say it to me personally, and I've heard people get up in meetings and make the same statement: The statement is, "I came into A.A. *solely* for the purpose of sobriety, but it has been through A.A. that I have found God."(p.192)

• (Actually, he does it *solely* to get rid of us.)(p.480)

• Brandishing my "motto," which was "A little man with a stick is equal to a big man," sometimes I varied the literary lecture by a fight with a big man, selected *solely* because he was big and I was little.(p.537)

solemn

• Here are some of the methods we have tried: Drinking beer only, limiting the number of drinks, never drinking alone, never drinking in the morning, drinking only at home, never having it in the house, never drinking during business hours, drinking only at parties, switching from scotch to brandy, drinking only natural wines, agreeing to resign if ever drunk on the job, taking a trip, not taking a trip, swearing off forever (with and without a *solemn* oath), taking more physical exercise, reading inspirational books, going to health farms and sanitariums, accepting voluntary commitment to asylums -- we could increase the list ad infinitum.(p.31)

• Our men have sworn great *solemn* oaths that they were through drinking forever.(p.105)

• An offer of appreciation for not having had a drink for those few months and then and there, without anybody promising me anything or threatening me, I made a *solemn* vow that never so long as I lived would I take another drink.(p.200)

• So I was driving to Cleveland when I made this *solemn* promise never to drink again.(p.201)

• There was the father one lost respect for at the age of eleven, because the father broke his *solemn* word in a circumstance where you, eleven years old, had assumed guilt when you were innocent; but the father would not believe you, no matter what; and to ease his suffering you "confessed" and were "forgiven," only – months later – to have your "guilt" brought up – only he and you knew what he was talking bout – brought up in front of the stern grandmother.(p.533)

solicitation

• We think that each group should soon achieve this ideal; that any public *solicitation* of funds using the name of Alcoholics Anonymous is highly dangerous, whether by groups, clubs, hospitals, or other outside agencies; that acceptance of large gifts from any source, or of contributions carrying any obligation whatever, is unwise.(p.566)

soliciting

• With the war over, and back in Baltimore with the folks, there were several small jobs for three years and then I went to work ***soliciting*** as one of the first ten employees of a new national finance company.(p.242)

solicitor

• I resented it of course, and I offered Clarence his commission, whatever it might be, if he would please not bother me because I had arrived at the conclusion that he was a ***solicitor*** for some alcoholic institute.(p.216)

solid

• Is our work ***solid*** so far?(p.75)

• But be sure you are on ***solid*** spiritual ground before you start and that your motive in going is thoroughly good.(p.102)

• As animals on a treadmill, we have patiently and wearily climbed, falling back in exhaustion after each futile effort to reach ***solid*** ground.(p.107)

• I can't say, "I'm powerless over alcohol, but ***solid*** alcohol is okay."(p.443)

solitary

• In actual practice, we usually find a ***solitary*** self-appraisal insufficient.(p.72)

• I was becoming a ***solitary*** drinker, but I didn't care.(p.426)

• He even went to bat for me before the court martial that inevitably followed and, as a result, I drew only thirty days -- fifteen in ***solitary***.(p.428)

• In a prison in my native state, I spent eleven months in ***solitary*** confinement, bouncing in and out of the "hole" (a bare concrete-and-steel cubicle) about five times during those eleven months.(p.459)

• This career girl preferred ***solitary*** drinking, the blackout kind, often hoping she'd stay that way for keeps.(p.464)

• Then I went on my first week-long bender of ***solitary*** drinking, locked up in a hotel room, because my family opposed my coming marriage.(p.464)

• (I think my first feeling of fear came with my first week's ***solitary*** drinking, locked up in that hotel room.(p.465)

solution

• Though we work out our ***solution*** on the spiritual as well as an altruistic plane, we favor hospitalization for the alcoholic who is very jittery or befogged.(p.xxiv)

• What is the ***solution***?(p.xxix)

• My wife and I abandoned ourselves with enthusiasm to the idea of helping other alcoholics to a ***solution*** of their problems.(p.15)

• THERE IS A ***SOLUTION***(p.17)

• The tremendous fact for every one of us is that we have discovered a common ***solution***.(p.17)

• But the ex-problem drinker who has found this ***solution***, who is properly armed with facts about himself, can generally win the entire confidence of another alcoholic in a few hours.(p.18)

• There is a ***solution***.(p.25)

• If you are as seriously alcoholic as we were, we believe there is no middle-of-the-road ***solution***.(p.25)

• For most cases, there is virtually no other ***solution***."(p.43)

• We were having trouble with personal relationships, we couldn't control our emotional natures, we were a prey to misery and depression, we couldn't make a living, we had a feeling of uselessness, we were full of fear, we were unhappy, we couldn't seem to be of real help to other people -- was not a basic ***solution*** of these bedevilments more important than whether we should see newsreels of lunar flight?(p.52)

• Let the doctor, if he will, tell him he has something in the way of a ***solution***.(p.91)

• But you may talk to him about the hopelessness of alcoholism because you offer a ***solution***.(p.92)

• If he is not interested in your ***solution***, if he expects you to act only as a banker for his financial difficulties or a nurse for his sprees, you may have to drop him until he changes his mind.(p.95)

• Among us are wives, relatives and friends whose problem has been solved, as well as some who have not yet found a happy ***solution***.(p.104)

• If you and your husband find a ***solution*** for the pressing problem of drink you are, of course, going to be very happy.(p.117)

• Had they fired me first, and had they then taken steps to see that I was presented with the ***solution*** contained in this book, I might have returned to them six months later, a well man.(p.141)

• In fact, he may say almost anything if he has accepted our ***solution*** which, as you know, demands rigorous honesty.(p.145)

• I remember looking longingly at the window as an easier ***solution***, and shuddering at the memory of that other window, three years before, and the six agonizing months in a London hospital ward.(p.224)

• Out of this maelstrom just two coherent thoughts came to the surface; one, a drink would mean homelessness and death; two, I could no longer relieve the pressure of fear by starting home, as was once my habitual ***solution*** to this problem, because I no longer had a home.(p.279)

• Then I found the ***solution***: At the end of study time, I would drink two beers, jump in bed, sleep real fast, and wake up smart.(p.440)

• The ***solution*** seemed very simple.(p.545)

• About this time, I met a man who had three motherless children and it seemed that might be a ***solution*** to my problem.(p.548)

• When I encountered disappointments or frustrations -- as I did more and more frequently -- my ***solution*** was to drink.(p.556)

solve

• These allergic types can never safely use alcohol in any form at all; and once having formed the habit and found they cannot break it, once having lost their self-confidence, their reliance upon things human, their problems pile up on them and become astonishingly difficult to ***solve***.(p.xxvi)

• "Quite as important was the discovery that spiritual principles would ***solve*** all my problems.(p.42)

• Most alcoholics have to be pretty badly mangled before they really commence to ***solve*** their problems.(p.43)

• Its main object is to enable you to find a Power greater than yourself which will ***solve*** your problem.(p.45)

• When we saw others ***solve*** their problems by a simple reliance upon the Spirit of the Universe, we had to stop doubting the power of God.(p.52)

• We agnostics and atheists were sticking to the idea that self-sufficiency would ***solve*** our problems.(p.52)

• Some of us once had great self-confidence, but it didn't fully ***solve*** the fear problem, or any other.(p.68)

• If God can ***solve*** the age-old riddle of alcoholism, He can ***solve*** your problems too.(p.116)

• To return to the subject matter of this book: It contains full suggestions by which the employee may ***solve*** his problem.(p.143)

• When the time comes to ***solve*** them, God will give me strength for that day.(p.341)

• "First Things First": solving our immediate problems before we try to ***solve*** all the others and get muddled in our thinking and doing.(p.382)

• Getting drunk won't ***solve*** them.(p.382)

• By learning -- through practicing the Twelve Steps and through sharing at meetings -- how to cope with the problems that we looked to booze to ***solve***, back in our drinking days.(p.560)

solved

• They have ***solved*** the drink problem.(p.17)

• When, therefore, we were approached by those in whom the problem had been ***solved***, there was nothing left for us but to pick up the simple kit of spiritual tools laid at our feet.(p.25)

• Among us are wives, relatives and friends whose problem has been ***solved***, as well as some who have not yet found a happy solution.(p.104)

• But all problems will not be ***solved*** at once.(p.117)

• It is the most natural thing in the world, once his liquor problem is ***solved***, to feel that he will now measure up to that cherished vision.(p.118)

• The family will be affected also, pleasantly at first, as they feel their money troubles are about to be ***solved***, then not so pleasantly as they find themselves neglected.(p.126)

• This problem was soon ***solved***, however, as I began to take my bottle along with me and hide it in the bathroom or in the shrubbery outside.(p.184)

• It ***solved*** their problems and they started living a sane life again.(p.427)

solves

• When we do that, we find it ***solves*** our problems too; the ensuing lack of fear, worry and hurt feelings is a wonderful thing.(p.116)

solving

• If any feel that as psychiatrists directing a hospital for alcoholics we appear somewhat sentimental, let them stand with us a while on the firing line, see the tragedies, the despairing wives, the little children; let the ***solving*** of these problems become a part of their daily work, and even of their sleeping moments, and the most cynical will not wonder that we have accepted and encouraged this movement.(p.xxvi)

• On the other hand -- and strange as this may seem to those who do not understand -- once a psychic change has occurred, the very same person who seemed doomed, who had so many problems he despaired of ever ***solving*** them, suddenly finds himself easily able to control his desire for alcohol, the only effort necessary being that required to follow a few simple rules.(p.xxvii)

• Every means of ***solving*** his problem which money could buy was at his disposal.(p.32)

• If you have been successful in ***solving*** your own domestic problems, tell the newcomer's family how that was accomplished.(p.100)

• "First Things First": ***solving*** our immediate problems before we try to solve all the others and get muddled in our thinking and doing.(p.382)

somebody

• Who of us had not loved something or ***somebody***?(p.54)

• On that basis we are almost always in collision with something or ***somebody***, even though our motives are good.(p.60)

• We must be entirely honest with ***somebody*** if we expect to live long or happily in this world.(p.73)

• You fellows are ***somebody***.(p.157)

• You should go out and take this program to ***somebody*** else that needs it and wants it."(p.190)

• I told ***somebody*** that I was going down to get Christian Science and they took me down, but I don't remember saying that.(p.202)

• Like most immigrants I wanted to be ***somebody*** and have something and I was very happy and contented as I felt success crown my efforts.(p.232)

• The lesson of his death still remains with me, yet I often wonder what would have happened if ***somebody*** else had made that first call on me.(p.239)

• ***Somebody*** must have taken pity on you and gone out and got it for you."(p.264)

• I felt very sorry for myself and attempted suicide on many occasions, making sure there was always ***somebody*** within reaching distance to see that I didn't finish the job.(p.478)

• If something does come along that sort of upsets me, instead of walking in and throwing a buck at the barman and asking for a drink, I walk into a telephone booth, drop a dime in the box, and call ***somebody*** who was so kind as to give me his name and telephone number to meet such an emergency.(p.511)

• I looked around me at people who seemed happy and tried to analyze their happiness, and it seemed to me that without exception these people had something or ***somebody*** they loved very much.(p.546)

somebody's

• We boys drove out in ***somebody's*** car and went to the bar on the way do the dining room and I, in an effort to impress the other boys that I was city-bred, having lived in Scranton and Cleveland, asked them if they didn't want a drink.(p.194)

someday

• There is the obsession that somehow, ***someday***, they will beat the game.(p.23)

• The idea that somehow, ***someday*** he will control and enjoy his drinking is the great obsession of every abnormal drinker.(p.30)

• If we are planning to stop drinking, there must be no reservation of any kind, nor any lurking notion that ***someday*** we will be immune to alcohol.(p.33)

somehow

• Stocks were at the low point of 1932, and I had ***somehow*** formed a group to buy.(p.5)

• ***Somehow*** I managed to drag my mattress to a lower floor, lest I suddenly leap.(p.6)

• There is the obsession that ***somehow***, someday, they will beat the game.(p.23)

• The idea that ***somehow***, someday he will control and enjoy his drinking is the great obsession of every abnormal drinker.(p.30)

• But ***somehow***, we couldn't quite step ashore.(p.53)

• This short word ***somehow*** touches about every aspect of our lives.(p.67)

• Painfully aware of being ***somehow*** abnormal, the man did not fully realize what it meant to be alcoholic.(p.155)

• Down in the pit of his depression, new hope had ***somehow*** been born.(p.189)

• ***Somehow*** I got out of there and walked five blocks past brownstone houses.(p.223)

• I knew ***somehow*** that it meant more than just going to church and living a moral life.(p.236)

• ***Somehow*** I had always managed to avoid D.T.'s.(p.238)

• ***Somehow*** or other, I must have misunderstood the doctor's instructions, for I not only made the beer for my wife, I also drank it for her.(p.297)

• But *somehow* my good doctor heard of this book and also he learned a little about the people responsible for its publication.(p.307)
• *Somehow*, I made it through basic and then laid off the booze for about three months, because I was in school at night.(p.317)
• *Somehow*, I managed to read pieces on alcoholism.(p.332)
• But I had to get back to that first drink *somehow*.(p.339)
• So I went to my wife and asked her, wasn't there something that she and I could do to *somehow* get together, and she turned on her heel and looked me squarely in the eye, and said, "You don't care anything about my problem," and I could have smacked her, but I said to myself, "Grab on to your serenity!"(p.351)
• The only drawback was, I always knew how I arrived there, but *somehow*, between the rest room, the rinse, and the fluff-dry, I never knew when or how I got home.(p.370)
• *Somehow* our bodies had reached the point where we could no longer absorb alcohol in our systems.(p.380)
• I'd lost my car again, pawned my wallet and all identification papers for a bottle, and gotten home *somehow*.(p.429)
• And *somehow* or other I stayed sober.(p.430)
• Final exams of my Senior year and I may *somehow* graduate.(p.499)
• It's no bed of roses, but *somehow* or other I've been able to make it, through the kindness of people in A.A.(p.511)
• *Somehow* or other I was coming face to face with myself, and I didn't like it.(p.513)
• But *somehow* or other, with my old alcoholic brain, sitting there in that chair, I kept saying to myself, "I wonder if it'll work?(p.515)

someone

• *Someone* had pushed a drink my way, and I had taken it.(p.5)
• To others, the word "God" brought up a particular idea of Him with which *someone* had tried to impress them during childhood.(p.45)
• But they had not learned enough of humility, fearlessness and honesty, in the sense we find it necessary, until they told *someone* else all their life story.(p.73)
• He trembles to think *someone* might have observed him.(p.73)
• Though we have no religious connection, we may still do well to talk with *someone* ordained by an established religion.(p.74)
• Such parts of our story we tell to *someone* who will understand, yet be unaffected.(p.74)
• Notwithstanding the great necessity for discussing ourselves with *someone*, it may be one is so situated that there is no suitable person available.(p.74)
• It should not matter, however, if *someone* does throw us out of his office.(p.78)
• We discuss them with *someone* immediately and make amends quickly if we have harmed anyone.(p.84)
• Then we resolutely turn our thoughts to *someone* we can help.(p.84)
• You are sure to find *someone* desperate enough to accept with eagerness what you offer.(p.96)
• Let him know you are available if he wishes to make a decision and tell his story, but do not insist upon it if he prefers to consult *someone* else.(p.96)
• He may seek *someone* else to console him -- not always another man.(p.111)
• In some cases it may be better to let *someone* outside of the family present the book.(p.113)
• He wanted so much to talk with *someone*, but whom?(p.154)
• Part of that program is that we take it to *someone* else, that needs it and wants it.(p.186)
• Now, if you don't want it, we'll not take up your time, and we'll be going and looking for *someone* else."(p.186)
• From far away, as if in a delirium, I heard my own voice – calling *someone* "Dorothy," talking of dress shops, of jobs . . . the words came clearer . . . this sound of my own voice frightened me as it came closer . . . and suddenly, there I was, talking of I knew not what, to *someone* I'd never seen before this very moment.(p.222)
• Today I have *Someone* who will always hear me; I have a warm fellowship among men who understand my problems; I have tasks to do and am glad to do them, to see others who are alcoholics and to help them in any way I can to become sober men.(p.260)
• It took five years of A.A. living, and a substantial improvement in my health, before I could take a full-time office job where *someone* else was boss.(p.283)
• They would travel miles and stay up all night with *someone* they had never laid eyes on before and think nothing of it.(p.310)
• And as that thought came to me, it was as though *someone* had reached down and taken a heavy overcoat off my shoulders, for that was the last one.(p.347)
• As *someone* in A.A. said to me once upon a time, there is nothing worse than a confused psychiatrist.(p.347)
• Here he is powerless, unmanageable, in the grip of something bigger than he is, and he's got to turn the whole business over to *someone* else!(p.350)
• I was told that *someone* would call on me shortly, to sit tight and not take another drink.(p.363)
• It was the first she had heard or read about it and she said she had considered sending it to me or trying to have *someone* in Pittsburgh send it to me so I wouldn't know where it came from.(p.366)
• I think I actually read more contempt than was really there because just a week before *someone* had sent him the Saturday Evening Post article on A.A., and there was some glimmer of hope in it for him.(p.391)
• I drank alone or with *someone*, anyone who would stay and drink with me.(p.406)
• I spent the time in a nearby tavern, was loaded on the ship, went to sleep before take-off, and the next thing I knew *someone* was shaking me and telling me we were over San Diego.(p.428)
• My alcoholic wife took up *someone* else, divorced me, and took with her all my remaining property.(p.437)
• "That's a devil of a way to run an organization," I thought, and I reported Frank to the psychiatrist, who didn't seem perturbed; he just got *someone* else to take me on Fridays.(p.447)
• Three weeks after an armed robbery in which one person received a superficial flesh wound (I could have killed *someone*!), I was apprehended.(p.460)
• If *someone* had told me last year that I would be excited about gardening this year, I would have said he was off his rocker.(p.481)
• *Someone* had taken it from me.(p.491)
• Around eight or nine o'clock there came two big detectives and a policeman to arrest me for assault; and I was the most amazed person in the world when they said I had assaulted *someone*, and especially that I had assaulted my wife.(p.492)
• She asked me if I would let *someone* come up and talk to me concerning a business deal.(p.494)
• Then Charlie or *someone* in the group suggested that we try to get a place in a church or hall to hold meetings.(p.495)
• Am I willing to be honest with myself about myself and tell *someone* about myself, and am I willing to think of other people, of their needs instead of myself, in order to get rid of the drink problem?(p.503)
• I knew it, and I turned for help to *someone* upon whom I had turned my back for many years.(p.515)
• *Someone* told me, "When you drank, you didn't get half drunk.(p.516)
• My father was and still is a minister, and I was afraid that I might run into him, or that *someone* might tell him where I was, and I could still remember what he had done to me when I got drunk one Christmas when I was very young.(p.527)
• I'd visit one bar after another, having one martini in each, and in each hoping to find *someone* interesting to talk to.(p.536)
• Actually, of course, I wanted *someone* to listen to me, because when I had a few martinis inside, I became the great author I longed to be; and the right listener was in for some pretty highflown theories of literature and of genius.(p.536)
• But one was so outstanding that I like to pass it on whenever I can in the hope that it will help *someone* else as it has me.(p.551)

someone's

• Seeing much of each other, scarce an evening passed that *someone's* home did not shelter a little gathering of men and women, happy in their release, and constantly thinking how they might present their discovery to some newcomer.(p.159)
• My parents' car had a strong attraction to fences, and one night I blacked out and drove the car down a bank, ramming the steel fence around *someone's* backyard.(p.353)

something

• One feels that *something* more than human power is needed to produce the essential psychic change.(p.xxvii)
• There was *something* about his eyes.(p.9)
• Here was *something* at work in a human heart which had done the impossible.(p.11)
• Finally he shook his head saying, "*Something* has happened to you I don't understand.(p.14)
• We are equally positive that once he takes any alcohol whatever into his system, *something* happens, both in the bodily and mental sense, which makes it virtually impossible for him to stop.(p.22)
• In the preceding chapters you have learned *something* of alcoholism.(p.44)
• But cheer up, *something* like half of us thought we were atheists or agnostics.(p.44)
• Is not our age characterized by the ease with which we discard old ideas for new, by the complete readiness with which we throw away the theory or gadget which does not work for *something* new which does?(p.52)
• Who of us had not loved *something* or somebody?(p.54)
• On that basis we are almost always in collision with *something* or somebody, even though our motives are good.(p.60)
• If we still cling to *something* we will not let go, we ask God to help us be willing.(p.76)
• When ready, we say *something* like this: "My Creator, I am now willing that you should have all of me, good and bad.(p.76)
• He commences to look around in the night clubs, or their equivalent, for *something* besides liquor.(p.81)
• Whatever the situation, we usually have to do *something* about it.(p.81)
• Have we kept *something* to ourselves which should be discussed with another person at once?(p.86)
• Let the doctor, if he will, tell him he has *something* in the way of a solution.(p.91)
• An alcoholic who cannot meet them, still has an alcoholic mind; there is *something* the matter with his spiritual status.(p.101)
• We think each family which has been relieved owes *something* to those who have not, and when the occasion requires, each member of it should be only too willing to bring former mistakes, no matter how grievous, out of their hiding places.(p.124)
• Father feels he has struck *something* better than gold.(p.129)
• His wife is one of those persons who really feels there is *something* rather sinful about these commodities, so she nagged, and her intolerance finally threw him into a fit of anger.(p.135)
• Suppose an approach is made *something* like this:(p.141)
• He may wish to do a lot for other alcoholics and *something* of the sort may come up during business hours.(p.146)
• I have been learning *something* about alcoholism.(p.147)
• Life will mean *something* at last.(p.152)
• His wife came, scarcely daring to be hopeful, though she thought she saw *something* different about her husband already.(p.158)
• These men had found *something* brand new in life.(p.159)
• The expression on the faces of the women, that indefinable *something* in the eyes of the men, the stimulating and electric atmosphere of the place, conspired to let him know that here was haven at last.(p.160)
• But obviously you cannot transmit *something* you haven't got.(p.164)
• I sensed they had *something* I did not have, from which I might readily profit.(p.178)
• I learned that it was *something* of a spiritual nature, which did not appeal to me very much, but I thought it could do no harm.(p.178)
• I was willing to admit to myself that I had hit bottom, that I had gotten hold of *something* that I didn't know how to handle by myself.(p.187)
• I noticed that the others seemed to have such a release, a happiness, a *something* that I thought a person ought to have.(p.191)
• I know there was even more, *something* that I hadn't got, and I remember one day, a week or two after I had come out of the hospital, Bill was over to my house talking to my wife and me.(p.191)
• He had known *something* of my drinking pattern, and he asked me what I was doing about it.(p.200)
• Then, I started to miss meetings because it was raining or snowing or *something* else.(p.203)
• When I had been in the hospital ten days, Sister Ignatia, who has played such a part in the development of A.A. in this area, stuck her head in the door one morning and announced, looking at me quizzically, that they might be able to make *something* human out of my face after all.(p.205)
• I do not recollect the specific conversation that went on but I believe I did challenge Bill to tell me *something* about A.A. and I do recall one other thing: I wanted to know what this was that worked so many

wonders, and hanging over the mantel was a picture of Gethsemane and Bill pointed to it and said, "There it is," which didn't make much sense to me.(p.216)

• I remembered asserting that I was going to do ***something*** about this, that I couldn't go on . . .(p.224)

• And, accepting, I felt a new inner comfort, and the willingness and strength to do ***something*** about the traits I couldn't live with.(p.229)

• I have ***something*** to contribute to humanity, since I am peculiarly qualified, as a fellow-sufferer, to give aid and comfort to those who have stumbled and fallen over this business of meeting life.(p.229)

• Like most immigrants I wanted to be somebody and have ***something*** and I was very happy and contented as I felt success crown my efforts.(p.232)

• I knew the stuff I was making was a lot stronger than I had been used to, but I never suspected that steady drinking of it might develop a taste for ***something*** even stronger still.(p.233)

• But I have never thought of that as ***something*** to do and then forget about.(p.237)

• He said ***something*** about God or a Higher Power, but I brushed that off – that was for the birds, not for me.(p.239)

• Curious about it, feeling I was missing ***something***, absolutely without any illusions about the aftermath, with no pronounced feeling of patriotism, I joined up with a Canadian regiment, serving a little over two years.(p.253)

• My four years of abstinence had ***something*** to do with it, but soldiering is a tough enough game for a sober man, and I had no yen for full-pack slogging through mud with a cognac or vin rouge hang-over.(p.253)

• I was seeking ***something*** and I was ready to learn.(p.258)

• The big thing was that these men were all sober and evidently had ***something*** I didn't have.(p.259)

• I could do ***something*** for their Russ.(p.262)

• These vacations became quite ***something***, and he always had two weeks vacation the first two weeks of every September.(p.264)

• Russ read a piece in the paper, and he kind of snickered, and said, "See here, where John D. has found ***something*** to keep him from drinking!"(p.265)

• He used to drink, and then he found ***something*** that started up in Akron that helped him quit drinking."(p.267)

• Do ***something*** for him!(p.271)

• If, on Sunday, I could be there, trying to think of ***something*** that would help her with this problem, then we must have ***something*** that could work.(p.272)

• I would get in the biggest dither about ***something***.(p.273)

• The details of the long road back to ***something*** resembling normal living -- the first short streetcar ride, the purchase of a used bike which enabled me to widen the narrow horizon of life, the first trip downtown – I will not dwell on.(p.276)

• Some of these were hard to believe, but it did not require a giant brain to perceive that they had ***something*** I could use.(p.279)

• It went ***something*** like this: "God, for eighteen years I have been unable to handle this problem.(p.280)

• It ran ***something*** like this: If I go around shouting from the rooftops about my alcoholism, it might very possibly prevent me from getting a good job.(p.282)

• This time I did ***something*** about it.(p.284)

• Here was ***something*** requiring a greater willingness to assume responsibility, and take a larger degree of cooperation and "give and take" than even business requires of one.(p.286)

• She asked him to do ***something*** about me because she couldn't.(p.288)

• He waited until I was completely sober and the day before I was to head back for Chicago, he told me of a small group of men in Akron who apparently had the same problem that I had but were doing ***something*** about it.(p.289)

• I can still remember very distinctly getting into Akron at eleven p.m. and routing this same Howard out of bed to do ***something*** about me.(p.290)

• Here was a man with essentially the same outlook on life, except that he had done ***something*** about it.(p.290)

• They had that certain ***something*** that seemed to glow, a peace and a serenity combined with happiness.(p.290)

• He had been wanting to do ***something*** about his drinking for a long time, but did not know how.(p.294)

• Neither one of the two was interested for himself, one being a mother who wanted to do ***something*** for her son.(p.294)

• In the meantime, another doctor in Evanston became convinced that the program had possibilities, and turned over a woman to us to do ***something*** about.(p.295)

• Occasionally, it is accorded to a few of us to watch ***something*** fine grow from a tiny kernel into ***something*** of gigantic goodness.(p.295)

• Then I learned ***something*** else.(p.300)

• I definitely liked it, everything about it, the taste, the effects; and I realize now that a drink did ***something*** for me or to me that was different from the way it affected others.(p.305)

• I began making the rounds of the doctors in the hope that one of them might find some cure for my accumulating ailments, preferably ***something*** that could be removed surgically.(p.305)

• Nevertheless, there were a few doctors who saw alcoholism as a disease and felt that the alcoholic was a victim of ***something*** over which he had no control.(p.307)

• All of them were so nice to me that I figured I must be careful – they were bound to want ***something***, being that nice.(p.319)

• As my son, our second child, came along, and as he became school age and was away at school most of the time, ***something*** happened.(p.323)

• I did try, for a day or two, but ***something*** always would come up that would throw me.(p.324)

• Even obvious intoxication is excused by younger people as ***something*** "he's earned the right to do," and they say, "After all, who's he hurting?"(p.330)

• I went on, realizing what I was becoming, hating myself for it, bitter, blaming life, blaming everything else but the fact that I should turn about and do ***something*** about my drinking.(p.337)

• I screamed on the telephone for my mother to get up there; ***something*** was going to happen; I didn't know what, but if she didn't get there quick, I'd split wide open.(p.338)

• What I needed was a change, mental relaxation, getting out and doing ***something***.(p.338)

• I said to my husband, "I'm going to try, every free moment that I have, to get interested in ***something*** outside, get myself over this rut I'm in."(p.338)

• If I didn't have a drink, I had to do ***something***.(p.339)

• I figured I'd be all right if I could find ***something*** I liked to do.(p.339)

• After my wife had read this to me, I said to her, as I had said many times in desperation, "I have got to do ***something***."(p.346)

• She's a good-natured soul and said, "I wouldn't worry about it; probably ***something*** will happen."(p.346)

• And just then ***something*** did happen.(p.347)

• ***Something*** else happened to me.(p.348)

• But then he said, "Let me say ***something*** to you.(p.348)

• So, after taking the first half of the First Step, and very gingerly admitting myself to Alcoholics Anonymous, ***something*** happened.(p.349)

• Here he is powerless, unmanageable, in the grip of ***something*** bigger than he is, and he's got to turn the whole business over to someone else!(p.350)

• So I went to my wife and asked her, wasn't there ***something*** that she and I could do to somehow get together, and she turned on her heel and looked me squarely in the eye, and said, "You don't care anything about my problem," and I could have smacked her, but I said to myself, "Grab on to your serenity!"(p.351)

• It had happened to me and I had to do ***something*** about it.(p.363)

• I had done ***something*** terrible!(p.364)

• In other words, I began contributing, and so, naturally, I began to get ***something*** more.(p.365)

• If there is ***something*** in my story that rings a bell with you, then do ***something*** – now!(p.368)

• At times, when I noticed other families, I felt ***something*** was very wrong with ours.(p.369)

• I had nowhere else to go, and I knew ***something*** was terribly wrong, and the reason had to lie within myself.(p.371)

• "Keep busy; always have ***something*** constructive to do."(p.373)

• Two years before I joined A.A. my wife took a long trip during which she wrote me she just couldn't return unless I did ***something*** about my drinking.(p.377)

• In a few days an attorney called on me and explained that ***something*** would have to be done as she couldn't face returning to me as I was.(p.377)

• Again I promised to do ***something*** about it.(p.377)

• Some crisis brings you to a point of making a decision to do ***something*** about your drinking problem.(p.377)

• Above all, I am grateful to A.A. for my sobriety, which means so much to my family, friends and business associates, because God and A.A. were able to do for me ***something*** I was unable to do for myself.(p.383)

• Get her ***something*** to drink."(p.385)

• ***Something*** went haywire and I got to depend on it so I could do nothing without it.(p.386)

• My husband couldn't tell whether I wanted to do ***something*** about my drinking.(p.391)

• There was ***something*** else that I could try -- A.A.(p.391)

• But, from the very first paragraph on, ***something*** happened to me.(p.392)

• It was such a feeling of relief that I wanted to know more about it and with that, I think for the first time, came the realization that there was ***something*** horribly, horribly wrong with me.(p.392)

• This was ***something*** I had to do all by myself.(p.392)

• I wish I could tell you all that A.A. has done for me, all that I think and feel about A.A., but it's ***something*** that I have experienced and have never been able to put into words.(p.394)

• Then I was able to do ***something*** about me.(p.409)

• ***Something*** in the book had reached me after all.(p.412)

• Then ***something*** happened.(p.422)

• I still think dad paid him ***something*** to let me go.(p.424)

• My growing inward unhappiness was a very real thing, however, and I knew that ***something*** would have to be done about it.(p.434)

• The answer came right back: I'd give him ***something*** to pep him up.(p.441)

• The people of A.A. had ***something*** that looked much better than what I had, but I was afraid to let go of what I had in order to try ***something*** new; there was a certain sense of security in the familiar.(p.448)

• The hotel management, knowing that ***something*** was wrong, sent for a doctor.(p.465)

• I hadn't been drinking much about that time, for I had begun to realize that there was ***something*** abnormal about my drinking, although as yet, I didn't realize that it was so out of control.(p.465)

• At that point everyone decided ***something*** drastic had to be done.(p.469)

• While I was there I realized that I had missed ***something***.(p.472)

• It read ***something*** like this: "Faith without works is dead.(p.473)

• Here was a book that said I could do ***something*** that all these doctors and priests and ministers and psychiatrists that I'd been going to for years couldn't do!(p.473)

• I wasted twenty years of my life, and there is nothing I can do about that, but there is ***something*** I can do about now.(p.480)

• I do surgery because that's ***something*** that you can see; it's more tangible.(p.485)

• ***Something*** should have told me then that things were haywire.(p.487)

• Then I said to my wife, "***Something*** has to be done."(p.489)

• ***Something*** happened.(p.490)

• After the trial, I got big-hearted again and felt that I should do ***something*** in payment for Vi's kindness to me; so I left Washington and went to Seattle to work.(p.492)

• She said, "He has ***something*** of interest, if you will see him."(p.494)

• After Charlie had talked a while, I knew that this man had ***something***.(p.495)

• In that short period he built within me ***something*** that I had long since lost, which was hope.(p.495)

• I had found this new "***something***," and I wanted to give it to everyone who had a problem.(p.496)

• "I am going to do ***something***."(p.502)

• If ***something*** does come along that sort of upsets me, instead of walking in and throwing a buck at the barman and asking for a drink, I walk into a telephone booth, drop a dime in the box, and call somebody who was so kind as to give me his name and telephone number to meet such an emergency.(p.511)

• Just as I was wondering what on earth I could do -- I was too drunk even to pack a handkerchief – the memory of an A.A. write-up that I had seen in the Evening Mail flashed across my mind -- and I thought to myself, this is ***something*** I haven't tried yet.(p.523)

• It was their open night meeting, but of course I thought they were all alcoholics; I couldn't imagine why anybody else would want to go there, and my first reaction was, well, I've come to ***something*** that's not for me.(p.524)

• After a while, I found that the psycho ward was a

good place to hide when I had taken *something* stolen to the pawnshop.(p.528)
• I don't know if it's force of habit or *something* else that keeps them in one place, but I do know that in A.A. there is much work to do, and none of us can do it standing still.(p.529)
• It was impossible for me to say at this point, "Maybe there is *something* wrong with my philosophy," and I certainly couldn't say, "Maybe there is *something* wrong with me."(p.545)
• I looked around me at people who seemed happy and tried to analyze their happiness, and it seemed to me that without exception these people had *something* or somebody they loved very much.(p.546)
• When I had been in A.A. only a short while, an oldtimer told me *something* that has affected my life ever since.(p.554)
• Regarded as *something* of a "boy wonder," I began to see myself that way.(p.555)
• There is *something* spiritual about an art museum or a symphony, and the Catholic Church approves of our use of them.(p.574)
• There is *something* spiritual about A.A. too, and Catholic participation in it almost invariably results in poor Catholics becoming better Catholics."(p.574)

something's

• When we begin to do things like that with alcohol, *something's* gone wrong.(p.336)

somethingness

• This to me is the proof of the existence of a *Somethingness* greater than I am.(p.351)

sometime

• I remember *sometime*, it was possibly six months after we had been going steadily to King School, that we were coming home from a meeting and saw a car along the way, and a fellow in back drinking a bottle of beer.(p.271)
• I was afraid that *sometime* I would get half drunk and go through with it.(p.515)

sometimes

• Faced with this problem, if a doctor is honest with himself, he must *sometimes* feel his own inadequacy.(p.xxvii)
• *Sometimes* a small deal would net a few hundred dollars, and I would pay my bills at the bars and delicatessens.(p.5)
• *Sometimes* I stole from my wife's slender purse when the morning terror and madness were on me.(p.6)
• This *sometimes* nearly drove me back to drink, but I soon found that when all other measures failed, work with another alcoholic would save the day.(p.15)
• Highly competent psychiatrists who have dealt with us have found it *sometimes* impossible to persuade an alcoholic to discuss his situation without reserve.(p.18)
• What has become of the common sense and will power that he still *sometimes* displays with respect to other matters?(p.22)
• *Sometimes* these excuses have a certain plausibility, but none of them really makes sense in the light of the havoc an alcoholic's drinking bout creates.(p.23)
• We have *sometimes* reflected more than Jim did upon the consequences.(p.37)
• *Sometimes* this was a tedious process; we hope no one else will be prejudiced for as long as some of us were.(p.48)
• Instead, we looked at the human defects of these people, and *sometimes* used their shortcomings as a basis of wholesale condemnation.(p.50)
• *Sometimes* we had to search fearlessly, but He was there.(p.55)
• In trying to make these arrangements our actor may *sometimes* be quite virtuous.(p.61)
• *Sometimes* they hurt us, seemingly without provocation, but we invariably find that at some time in the past we have made decisions based on self which later placed us in a position to be hurt.(p.62)
• This was only a beginning, though if honestly and humbly made, an effect, *sometimes* a very great one, was felt at once.(p.63)
• *Sometimes* it was remorse and then we were sore at ourselves.(p.66)
• *Sometimes* we think fear ought to be classed with stealing.(p.67)
• Of course, we *sometimes* encounter people who do not understand alcoholics.(p.74)
• *Sometimes* the man we are calling upon admits his own fault, so feuds of years' standing melt away in an hour.(p.78)
• Our former enemies *sometimes* praise what we are doing and wish us well.(p.78)
• Approached in this way, the most ruthless creditor will *sometimes* surprise us.(p.78)
• *Sometimes* we hear an alcoholic say that the only thing he needs to do is to keep sober.(p.82)
• They are being fulfilled among us — *sometimes* quickly, *sometimes* slowly.(p.84)
• If not members of religious bodies, we *sometimes* select and memorize a few set prayers which emphasize the principles we have been discussing.(p.87)
• *Sometimes* it is wise to wait till he goes on a binge.(p.90)
• *Sometimes* a new man is anxious to proceed at once, and you may be tempted to let him do so.(p.95)
• This is *sometimes* a mistake.(p.95)
• Your wife may *sometimes* say she is neglected.(p.97)
• *Sometimes* you will have to call a doctor and administer sedatives under his direction.(p.97)
• It is not good for him, and it *sometimes* creates serious complications in a family.(p.97)
• *Sometimes* it is to the best interests of all concerned that a couple remain apart.(p.99)
• *Sometimes* there were other women.(p.106)
• The bill collectors, the sheriffs, the angry taxi drivers, the policemen, the bums, the pals, and even the ladies they *sometimes* brought home — our husbands thought we were so inhospitable.(p.106)
• *Sometimes* there were screaming delirium and insanity.(p.107)
• *Sometimes* we sensed dimly that we were dealing with sick men.(p.107)
• *sometimes* they were so inaccessible that it seemed as though a great wall had been built around them.(p.107)
• *Sometimes* he is a source of embarrassment to you and his friends.(p.109)
• He *sometimes* drinks in the morning and through the day also, to hold his nervousness in check.(p.109)
• *Sometimes* he drinks on the way home from the hospital.(p.110)
• We know these suggestions are *sometimes* difficult to follow, but you will save many a heartbreak if you can succeed in observing them.(p.111)
• *Sometimes* there are cases where alcoholism is complicated by other disorders.(p.114)
• But *sometimes* you must start life anew.(p.114)
• Your husband will *sometimes* be unreasonable and you will want to criticize.(p.117)
• *Sometimes* he will be so interested that he becomes really neglectful.(p.119)
• *Sometimes* they demand that dad bring them back instantly!(p.123)
• Husbands and wives have *sometimes* been obliged to separate for a time until new perspective, new victory over hurt pride could be rewon.(p.125)
• *Sometimes* mother and children don't think so.(p.126)
• *Sometimes* he explodes over a trifle.(p.126)
• We have been speaking to you of serious, *sometimes* tragic things.(p.132)
• Outsiders are *sometimes* shocked when we burst into merriment over a seemingly tragic experience out of the past.(p.132)
• The children are *sometimes* dominated by a pathetic hardness and cynicism.(p.134)
• Because of the employee's special ability, or of his own strong personal attachment to him, the employer has *sometimes* kept such a man at work long beyond a reasonable period.(p.137)
• When drinking, or getting over a bout, an alcoholic, *sometimes* the model of honesty when normal, will do incredible things.(p.140)
• *Sometimes* we alcoholics have an idea that people are trying to pull us down.(p.145)
• But *sometimes* our drinking will be used politically.(p.145)
• We hope our suggestions will help you plug up this *sometimes* serious leak.(p.148)
• From childhood through high school I was more or less forced to go to church, Sunday School and evening service, Monday night Christian Endeavor and *sometimes* to Wednesday evening prayer meeting.(p.172)
• I would *sometimes* hide out in one of the clubs of which I was a member, and had the habit at times of registering at a hotel under a fictitious name.(p.176)
• *Sometimes* I would bring it in my pockets, but they were inspected, and that became too risky.(p.176)
• Then Prohibition came into effect, and the facts that the stuff obtainable was so horrible and *sometimes* deadly, and that I had married and had a job which I had to look after, helped me for a period of some three or four years, although I would get drunk every time I could get hold of enough to drink to get started.(p.183)
• I remember telling them too that it was going to be awfully tough, because I did some other things, smoked cigarettes and played penny ante poker, *sometimes* bet on the horse races and they said, "Don't you think you're having more trouble with this drinking than with anything else at the present time?(p.190)
• My oldest child *sometimes* sat in on the meetings.(p.220)
• But I can remember, in my teens, that there were a few characters who caused the village heads to nod pityingly and *sometimes* in anger as they paused to say, "That sot, Henri" and "Ce pauvre Jules," who drank too much.(p.230)
• *Sometimes*, after sobering up after a bout of several weeks, I would righteously resolve to quit.(p.233)
• My family lived in very prosperous circumstances, and while both my parents drank, *sometimes* too much, neither was an alcoholic.(p.240)
• My thoughts *sometimes* turned to the idea that there must be a remedy.(p.256)
• So, *sometimes* we'd end up in Charleston, West Virginia, or here or there, drinking all along the way.(p.264)
• *Sometimes* saying very little, but letting us say.(p.271)
• *Sometimes* during that year I rebelled inwardly at what seemed like lost time, and at having to be a burden to these good people whose means were limited.(p.281)
• But with many, drinking had been little more than a *sometimes* uncontrollable nuisance.(p.315)
• *Sometimes* I would lie on the bathroom floor, deathly sick, praying I would die, and praying to God as I always had prayed to Him when I was drinking: "Dear God, get me out of this one and I'll never do it again."(p.324)
• I lost a lot of shirts that way, and *sometimes* I was minus a whole wash.(p.371)
• Then I became careless and returned *sometimes* when I shouldn't have.(p.376)
• Making amends is *sometimes* doing what we are capable of doing but failed to do because of alcohol; carrying out community responsibilities such as Community Funds, Red Cross, educational and religious activities in proportion to our abilities and energy.(p.381)
• Saying these sprees were limited to one a week (they were not), and saying that the average spree was ten of these drinks (*sometimes* more, *sometimes* less), we come up with the first boring statistic: two-fifty per week out of twelve dollars.(p.397)
• *Sometimes* they'd put it on the mantel, and forget it.(p.407)
• *Sometimes* I'd make it home and go to sleep at the wheel of my car, for all the neighbors to see next morning as they left for work.(p.429)
• In fact, *sometimes* they served as good excuses to drink more, to forget.(p.465)
• I *sometimes* gave it to my mother and then I'd go back and hound her for it.(p.491)
• *Sometimes* we are told in A.A. not to try and learn the reasons for our drinking.(p.533)
• Brandishing my "motto," which was "A little man with a stick is equal to a big man," *sometimes* I varied the literary lecture by a fight with a big man, selected solely because he was big and I was little.(p.537)
• *Sometimes* I have to ask first for the willingness, but it too always comes.(p.552)

somewhat

• If any feel that as psychiatrists directing a hospital for alcoholics we appear *somewhat* sentimental, let them stand with us a while on the firing line, see the tragedies, the despairing wives, the little children; let the solving of these problems become a part of their daily work, and even of their sleeping moments, and the most cynical will not wonder that we have accepted and encouraged this movement.(p.xxvi)
• It relieved me *somewhat* to learn that in alcoholics the will is amazingly weakened when it comes to combating liquor, though it often remains strong in other respects.(p.7)
• Upon hearing this, our friend was *somewhat* relieved, for he reflected that after all, he was a good church member.(p.27)
• We were bothered with the thought that faith and dependence upon a Power beyond ourselves was *somewhat* weak, even cowardly.(p.45)
• Admitting he may be *somewhat* at fault, he is sure that other people are more to blame.(p.61)
• His business may suffer *somewhat*.(p.109)
• They can hardly fail to approve these simple principles, though the head of the house still fails *somewhat* in practicing them.(p.130)
• Being *somewhat* weakened, and faced with physical and mental readjustment to a life which knows no

alcohol, he may overdo.(p.146)
- I had accepted Catholicism ***somewhat*** as an inheritance.(p.220)
- In five years a good many persons had forgotten that I had been ***somewhat*** notorious.(p.256)
- My parents died, both in the same year, leaving me, a sheltered and ***somewhat*** immature man, on my own.(p.277)
- ***Somewhat*** faded, she nevertheless bloomed afresh.(p.384)
- Since it was wartime, I explained to the ***somewhat*** startled shopkeeper that I had many friends in the service whom I was remembering with a watch.(p.532)

somewhere

- Each day, ***somewhere*** in the world, recovery begins when one alcoholic talks with another alcoholic, sharing experience, strength, and hope.(p.xxii)
- Everyone became resigned to the certainty that I would have to be shut up ***somewhere,*** or would stumble along to a miserable end.(p.8)
- I have seen hundreds of families set their feet in the path that really goes ***somewhere;*** have seen the most impossible domestic situations righted; feuds and bitterness of all sorts wiped out.(p.15)
- That was growth, but if we wished to grow we had to begin ***somewhere.***(p.47)
- ***Somewhere*** in one of the conversations, I mentioned that I was contemplating forming a new firm.(p.220)
- I would make a fresh start ***somewhere*** else.(p.281)
- They had a hunch that there must be an answer for these apparently hopeless ones, ***somewhere.***(p.307)
- She told me her name, and I said, "I know you from ***somewhere.***"(p.321)
- "Well," he said, "you've been sober, but you've been floating way up on a cloud ***somewhere.***(p.349)
- She tried reasoning with me, endeavored to work out various drinking schedules, in fact all the tricks were practised faithfully for a short time ***somewhere*** along my shaky road to unhappiness.(p.361)
- I would follow certain drinking schedules or diets faithfully for a few days, and then ***somewhere*** along the line would over-train and upset the applecart.(p.361)
- As long as it eased situations socially, it helped just fine, but ***somewhere*** along the line, it backfired.(p.386)
- But ***somewhere*** during that time, I remembered going back on the bunk and crying my eyes out.(p.390)
- And I knew that ***somewhere*** along the line I'd lost the power to stop drinking.(p.436)
- Some of us always remember our big mouths when it comes to a drink, but ***somewhere*** along the line, we seem to have forgotten about taking care of our teeth.(p.479)

son

- Our friend was a minister's ***son.***(p.56)
- But for every man who drinks others are involved -- the wife who trembles in fear of the next debauch; the mother and father who see their ***son*** wasting away.(p.104)
- Cleaning up old scrapes, helping to settle family differences, explaining the disinherited ***son*** to his irate parents, lending money and securing jobs for each other, when justified -- these are everyday occurrences.(p.161)
- But I can remember the urge of the Prodigal ***Son*** to return to his Father.(p.260)
- Neither one of the two was interested for himself, one being a mother who wanted to do something for her ***son.***(p.294)
- The doctor, a young man, immediately took fire with the idea, and while he did not convince the ***son,*** he turned over two prospects who were anxious for the program.(p.294)
- My ***son*** had absolutely no use for me.(p.301)
- As my ***son,*** our second child, came along, and as he became school age and was away at school most of the time, something happened.(p.323)
- And that came after a three-weeks' illness of my ***son.***(p.338)
- I am a young alcoholic with a drug problem, a doctor, the husband of an alcoholic, the ***son*** of an alcoholic, and a man once diagnosed as a violent manic-depressive.(p.421)
- One night my ***son,*** when he was only sixteen, was suddenly and tragically killed.(p.437)
- I think He's on hand to see my ***son*** through, too.(p.437)
- It was my ex-wife, and she said my twenty-seven-year-old ***son,*** who has completed his Marine Corps training and graduated from college, wanted to see me privately, was getting married in three months, and wanted me at the wedding.(p.462)
- I haven't seen my ***son*** since he was three and a half years old.(p.463)
- I will be fifty years old next month, haven't seen my ***son*** or daughter yet, nor my daughter's two children, my grandchildren; but I am grateful.(p.463)
- I proud to be ***son*** of Tall Man, American Indian, and member of A.A. for many moons.(p.474)
- Year later, I go to Canada to carry message to Tall Man, but he not listen to ***son.***(p.476)
- Pioneer A.A., minister's ***son,*** and southern farmer, he asked, "Who am I to say there is no God?"(p.497)
- For you learned that he had been guilty of the thing he had accused you of, and his guilt had brought suffering to his entire family; and he thought he saw his young ***son*** beginning his own tragic pattern.(p.533)

son-in-law

- Our other daughter was in her last year of high school, and one night the new ***son-in-law*** and my husband went out to a prize fight.(p.263)
- I heard my ***son-in-law*** coming upstairs, and I asked him where dad was.(p.263)

son's

- They were deeply religious people, much shocked by their ***son's*** refusal to have anything to do with the church.(p.158)
- I suggested to her that she should see the ***son's*** minister or doctor, and that perhaps he would recommend the A.A. program.(p.294)
- I knew nothing about alcoholism or the D.T.'s, but when I woke up on this last morning of my ***son's*** illness, I taped the keyhole on my door because "everyone was out there."(p.338)

song

- I was born in Europe, in Alsace to be exact, shortly after it had become German, and practically grew up with the "good Rhine wine" of ***song*** and story.(p.230)
- To this day I can't hear that ***song*** without remembering that awful Christmas.(p.468)

songs

- There I sat in the evenings, enjoying with my friends our memories of the "old country," singing the old ***songs*** we all knew, playing simple card games for drinks and consuming great quantities of beer.(p.231)
- Lying on the divan, "getting in the mood" to write, I cried openly or inwardly, as I listened to sad ***songs.***(p.332)

sons

- I was an honor graduate in high school, and I was a "good boy" to whom mothers pointed when their ***sons*** went astray.(p.419)
- To tell you a small part of what my mother's life must have been like: Three of her kids were in jail that year – two ***sons*** and a daughter.(p.480)
- But to me, whiskey meant more than a home for my ***sons.***(p.527)
- Since I've been home, I have been able to gain the respect of my two ***sons*** again.(p.529)

soon

- ***Soon*** A.A. was beset by these very problems on every side and in every group.(p.xix)
- This combination ***soon*** landed me on the rocks.(p.7)
- She would ***soon*** have to give me over to the undertaker or the asylum.(p.7)
- I was ***soon*** to be catapulted into what I like to call the fourth dimension of existence.(p.8)
- But ***soon*** the sense of His presence had been blotted out by worldly clamors, mostly those within myself.(p.12)
- This sometimes nearly drove me back to drink, but I ***soon*** found that when all other measures failed, work with another alcoholic would save the day.(p.15)
- If what we have learned and felt and seen means anything at all, it means that all of us, whatever our race, creed, or color are the children of a living Creator with whom we may form a relationship upon simple and understandable terms as ***soon*** as we are willing and honest enough to try.(p.28)
- He ***soon*** indicated he was anxious to see us.(p.40)
- "As ***soon*** as I regained my ability to think, I went carefully over that evening in Washington.(p.41)
- There was a feeling of awe and wonder, but it was fleeting and ***soon*** lost.(p.46)
- We found that as ***soon*** as we were able to lay aside prejudice and express even a willingness to believe in a Power greater than ourselves, we commenced to get results, even though it was impossible for any of us to fully define or comprehend that Power, which is God.(p.46)
- As ***soon*** as we admitted the possible existence of a Creative Intelligence, a Spirit of the Universe underlying the totality of things, we began to be possessed of a new sense of power and direction, provided we took other simple steps.(p.46)
- As ***soon*** as a man can say that he does believe, or is willing to believe, we emphatically assure him that he is on his way.(p.47)
- Faced with alcoholic destruction, we ***soon*** became as open minded on spiritual matters as we tried to be on other questions.(p.48)
- This happened ***soon*** after they wholeheartedly met a few simple requirements.(p.50)
- He saw that he had to place the outcome in God's hands or he would ***soon*** start drinking again, and all would be lost anyhow.(p.80)
- You will ***soon*** have your friend admitting he has many, if not all, of the traits of the alcoholic.(p.92)
- If you leave such a person alone, he may ***soon*** become convinced that he cannot recover by himself.(p.96)
- We have seen others slip when the family came back too ***soon.***(p.100)
- So to you out there – who may ***soon*** be with us -- we say "Good luck and God bless you!"(p.121)
- The good old days will ***soon*** be back, they think.(p.123)
- As ***soon*** as his sobriety begins to be taken as a matter of course, the family may look at their strange new dad with apprehension, then with irritation.(p.128)
- If the family cooperates, dad will ***soon*** see that he is suffering from a distortion of values.(p.129)
- But those of us who have tried to shoulder the entire burden and trouble of others find we are ***soon*** overcome by them.(p.132)
- So our fellow worker will ***soon*** have friends galore.(p.163)
- On account of my enormous capacity for beer, I was elected to membership in one of the drinking societies, and ***soon*** became one of the leading spirits.(p.173)
- I was, of course, ***soon*** on the carpet and the upshot was that I had to go back for two more quarters and remain absolutely dry, if I wished to graduate.(p.174)
- I ***soon*** discovered that a couple of drinks would alleviate my gastric distress, at least for a few hours at a time, so it was not at all difficult for me to return to my former excessive indulgence.(p.174)
- I knew everyone would buy a few bottles, or cases, of liquor as their exchequers permitted, and that it would ***soon*** be gone.(p.175)
- At that time I was not aware of the almost unlimited supply the government made it possible for us doctors to obtain, neither had I any knowledge of the bootlegger who ***soon*** appeared on the horizon.(p.175)
- This problem was ***soon*** solved, however, as I began to take my bottle along with me and hide it in the bathroom or in the shrubbery outside.(p.184)
- Before very long we began to relate some incidents of our drinking and, naturally, pretty ***soon,*** I realized both of them knew what they were talking about because you can see things and smell things when you're drunk, that you can't other times, and, if I had thought they didn't know what they were talking about, I wouldn't have been willing to talk to them at all.(p.185)
- We'll be down as ***soon*** as he clears up."(p.188)
- As ***soon*** as I had done that I did feel a great release.(p.189)
- It took me a year, or a year and a half to get to feeling physically well, and it was rather tough, but I ***soon*** found folks whose friendship I had once had, and I found, after I had been sober for quite some little time, that these people began to act like they had in previous years, before I had gotten so bad, so that I didn't pay too awful much attention to financial gains.(p.190)
- Pretty ***soon,*** I wasn't going at all, and was avoiding those people who had been so kind to me.(p.203)
- As ***soon*** as I had satisfied that, what I earned as an upholsterer went for liquor.(p.234)
- As long as things were tough and the job a challenge I could always manage to hold on pretty well, but as ***soon*** as I learned the combination, got the puzzle under control and the boss to pat me on the back, I was gone again.(p.243)
- With nothing but a liberal arts education, very definitely estranged from my family and already married, ***soon*** after graduation from college I became a bookmaker's clerk on the British racing circuits, far better off financially than the average professional man.(p.251)
- I ***soon*** ran through my stake.(p.251)
- During my visit there, renewing acquaintance with former friends, I ***soon*** spent most of my money.(p.252)
- I was ***soon*** back in Liverpool.(p.252)
- I was ***soon*** broke, this time without trainfare to go anywhere.(p.252)
- Returning to the town I had left three months before, I became editor of a monthly magazine, ***soon*** had additional publicity and advertising accounts and the money rolled in.(p.254)

• A friend who knew I would *soon* be broke mounted guard over me when I left my job of writing the histories of Texas cities and put me aboard a bus for the town I had left almost five years before.(p.256)

• As *soon* as I could get up and walk I started to drink again and kept it up until my friend of the hospital, who, in his first try at the new way of life had stubbed his toe in Chicago but had come back to the town to take counsel and make a new start, picked me up and got me into a hospital.(p.258)

• I well remember a session I had with myself *soon* after I returned.(p.282)

• It is undoubtedly too *soon* for me to say how much of a success I shall be as a husband in time to come.(p.286)

• Then I started traveling, with the United States and Canada as my territory, and with so much freedom and with an unlimited expense account, I was *soon* drinking every night and kidding myself that it was all part of the job.(p.287)

• The inevitable result of this discovery was that I *soon* learned that beer made a very good chaser for whiskey.(p.298)

• A night or so a week in a joint, and a party or so a week at home or with friends, along with a little lone drinking, *soon* had me preparing for the existence of a top flight drunkard.(p.298)

• I *soon* was to ask myself, "What living?"(p.329)

• Real *soon*.(p.333)

• I sat up in the big red chair, suddenly thinking, "My God, with my kind of lousy luck, I might not die *soon*!(p.333)

• I'd go into an organization, and it wasn't long before I was on the committee, then I was chairman of the committee; and if I was in a group, I'd *soon* be treasurer or secretary of the group.(p.339)

• *Soon*, it became apparent that my schooling was interfering with my drinking.(p.354)

• High living, a great many fair weather friends, the 1929 stock market crash, and a couple of years of Depression, *soon* relieved me one by one of my worldly goods including my wife.(p.358)

• *Soon* I was to discover the answer.(p.362)

• After his death, my mother *soon* picked up drinking where Dad left off, and in a very short time she died of cirrhosis of the liver.(p.370)

• Very *soon* after I lost Mother, my five-year-old little girl was killed by a neighbor's car.(p.370)

• We *soon* resumed our marriage, even moved away from the street of sad memories and found a new home.(p.371)

• The Twelve Steps, which to me are a spiritual way of living, *soon* meant honest thinking, not wishful thinking, open mindedness, a willingness to try and a faith to accept.(p.381)

• A spiritual awakening *soon* came to mean trying each day to be a little more thoughtful, more considerate, a little more courteous to those with whom I came in contact.(p.381)

• I got right into the car and they drove me over, and just as *soon* as I got to the church they started the wedding.(p.385)

• He finally decided that he did not love me enough, and *soon* he told me so and said he was engaged to another girl.(p.403)

• One day *soon*, the analyses would reveal why I drank and how to stop.(p.408)

• I liked it and *soon* moved into the photo department which was what I wanted to do.(p.425)

• But I was *soon* drinking as heavily as I had been.(p.428)

• As an indication of just how confused and mixed up I was, just as *soon* as I could I left the office and hurried around to tell other patients that I was getting better.(p.470)

• *Soon* found wet canteens serve drinks to Indians in uniform.(p.474)

• *Soon* change to hard stuff.(p.475)

• *Soon* I drink beer.(p.475)

• Tall Man was blind, but *soon* he see.(p.476)

• At that time the repeal whiskies were back, and I'd go to the store and buy my whiskey and take it to my office and put it under the desk, first in one place and then in another, and there *soon* was an accumulation of empty bottles.(p.488)

• But the week-ends stretched on into Mondays and the time *soon* came when I drank every day.(p.488)

• I had not recognized her, but as *soon* as she said who she was I remembered her right away.(p.493)

• *Soon* supper is on the table.(p.497)

• If I don't get started *soon*, I won't have time to finish.(p.499)

• *Soon* I have others who are alcoholics and some who have other problems.(p.506)

• But as *soon* as I got out on my own in France, I started drinking.(p.518)

• I think the Commanding Officer was rather tired of this particular chicken coming back to roost so often because he very *soon* wrote in to the medical authorities to tell them that they had to get me into hospital, to be thoroughly examined for drinking.(p.520)

• I talked to him for quite a long time and at the end, he said, "Well, you're not quite mad enough to be shut up for good yet, but you *soon* will be if you live long enough."(p.522)

• I would wait for the mailman each month, like any good mother, but as *soon* as he handed me my check, I put on my best dress and went looking for my alcoholic friend.(p.527)

• I think I am dreaming and will *soon* wake up.(p.529)

• The only thing this changed, however, was my surroundings, and it was *soon* apparent that I could have the same uncomfortable emotions with an unlimited checking account that I could on a working girl's salary.(p.545)

• My husband was *soon* in uniform and among the first to go overseas.(p.547)

• The amount of will power exercised to control my drinking during working hours, diverted into a constructive channel, would have made me President, and the thing that made the will power possible was the knowledge that as *soon* as my day was finished I could drink myself into oblivion.(p.548)

• As *soon* as I had made a few friends and had begun to feel accepted, we moved again.(p.555)

• *Soon* my drinking was as bad as ever -- all day long every day.(p.557)

• Each time, I went back to drinking – even smuggling a bottle of vodka into the hospital as *soon* as the blood transfusions had ceased.(p.558)

• We think that each group should *soon* achieve this ideal; that any public solicitation of funds using the name of Alcoholics Anonymous is highly dangerous, whether by groups, clubs, hospitals, or other outside agencies; that acceptance of large gifts from any source, or of contributions carrying any obligation whatever, is unwise.(p.566)

sooner

• *Sooner* or later, you are likely to find him reading the book once more.(p.113)

• If you are sure your man does not want to stop, he may as well be discharged, the *sooner* the better.(p.141)

• I can well remember over a long period of years when I thought I was the only person in the world who knew that *sooner* or later I was going to get drunk.(p.198)

• I got two drinks, each of them a quarter of that pint, in me, and was talking along with these people, but I felt that *sooner* or later they were going to have me cornered because they were smarter than I was and the drink was beginning to take effect; but as I reached for the third drink Bob said, "Listen, Buster, you promised to take some medicine if we got you a drink.(p.206)

• I had decided I was no good – never would be any good, and the *sooner* I could drink myself out of this life, the better.(p.468)

sophomore

• This went from bad to worse until *Sophomore* spring when, after a prolonged period of drinking, I made up my mind that I could not complete my course, so I packed my grip and went South to spend a month on a large farm owned by a friend of mine.(p.173)

• A case of measles saved me from being kicked out during my *Sophomore* year.(p.499)

sordid

• You should not hesitate to visit the most *sordid* spot on earth on such an errand.(p.102)

• Some of us sought out *sordid* places, hoping to find understanding companionship and approval.(p.151)

• I would rather talk about the good things A.A. has taught me; I feel that hitting on just a few *sordid* points should be sufficient to let those of you in institutions know where I came from.(p.459)

sore

• So we were *sore*.(p.65)

• The usual outcome was that people continued to wrong us and we stayed *sore*.(p.66)

• Sometimes it was remorse and then we were *sore* at ourselves.(p.66)

sorrows

• So I took my bottle and went and drowned my *sorrows*.(p.318)

• The more I thought like this the more I drank to submerge my *sorrows*.(p.362)

sorry

• If a person has cancer all are *sorry* for him and no one is angry or hurt.(p.18)

• If we are *sorry* for what we have done, and have the honest desire to let God take us to better things, we believe we will be forgiven and will have learned our lesson.(p.70)

• If we are not *sorry*, and our conduct continues to harm others, we are quite sure to drink.(p.70)

• Arranging the best deal we can we let these people know we are *sorry*.(p.78)

• The husband begins to feel lonely, *sorry* for himself.(p.81)

• We are *sorry* for what we have done and, God willing, it shall not be repeated.(p.81)

• A remorseful mumbling that we are *sorry* won't fill the bill at all.(p.83)

• I'm *sorry* I got disturbed.(p.118)

• If that is so we are *sorry*, for we ourselves don't always care for people who lecture us.(p.121)

• If you think you are an atheist, an agnostic, a skeptic, or have any other form of intellectual pride which keeps you from accepting what is in this book, I feel *sorry* for you.(p.181)

• The people in the group hadn't been around that day; part of my family was in Florida and the rest of them weren't speaking to me, so I spent a very lonesome day and by evening I was feeling very *sorry* for myself.(p.207)

• Then everyone would be *sorry* for me.(p.333)

• I feel so *sorry* for you.(p.334)

• I would end it all, and then, by George, she'd be *sorry*!(p.363)

• Mom and I drank every waking moment because we felt so *sorry* for dad.(p.426)

• Suddenly, it was obvious to me: I had a brain tumor and would die, and everyone would be *sorry* for me.(p.444)

• I really felt *sorry* for him; the only thing in life he had to brag about was the fact that he was an alcoholic.(p.446)

• *Sorry* for mistakes.(p.474)

• I think they *sorry* they tell me this.(p.475)

• I felt very *sorry* for myself and attempted suicide on many occasions, making sure there was always somebody within reaching distance to see that I didn't finish the job.(p.478)

• I return home and say I am *sorry* for my wrong.(p.505)

sort

• An illness of this *sort* -- and we have come to believe it an illness --involves those about us in a way no other human sickness can.(p.18)

• All of us spend much of our spare time in the *sort* of effort which we are going to describe.(p.19)

• When this *sort* of thinking is fully established in an individual with alcoholic tendencies, he has probably placed himself beyond human aid, and unless locked up, may die or go permanently insane.(p.24)

• What *sort* of thinking dominates an alcoholic who repeats time after time the desperate experiment of the first drink?(p.35)

• This *sort* of thinking had to be abandoned.(p.48)

• What was that but a *sort* of faith?(p.54)

• Most of us have done that *sort* of thing.(p.78)

• Though there may be justifiable exceptions, and though we wish to lay down no rule of any *sort*, we have often found this the best course to take.(p.81)

• We women carry with us a picture of the ideal man, the *sort* of chap we would like our husbands to be.(p.118)

• This *sort* of thing can be avoided.(p.126)

• Naturally this *sort* of thing decreased the man's chance of recovery.(p.145)

• He may wish to do a lot for other alcoholics and something of the *sort* may come up during business hours.(p.146)

• The right kind of man, the kind who recovers, will not want this *sort* of thing.(p.149)

• Of course, we had talked over quite a number of the failings that I had and made a *sort* of an inventory, which wasn't too difficult, because I had an awful lot of things wrong that were very apparent to me, because I knew all about them.(p.190)

• That sentence, "The Lord has been so wonderful to me, curing me of this terrible disease, that I just want to keep telling people about it," has been *sort* of a golden text for the A.A. program and for me.(p.191)

• Eventually, there would be a ball game, or a show, or some *sort* of special occasion to celebrate and I would turn up drunk.(p.196)

• That is, it was *sort* of a mixed bunch of Oxford Groupers, who were interested in the alcoholic prob-

lem, and of alcoholics themselves.(p.218)
• To go into a gathering of people was the *sort* of thing that all my life, from the time I left my private world of books and dreams to meet the real world of people and parties and jobs, had left me feeling an uncomfortable outsider, needing the warming stimulus of drinks to join in.(p.228)
• I'd hear them on the phone having prayer meetings and so forth, that *sort* of talk over the phone, and it completely burnt me up.(p.265)
• They told Annabelle to take me under her wing, and I shall never forget how she *sort* of curled up her nose and said, "They tell me you drink too."(p.269)
• In all honesty though, I was skeptical, but I wanted so definitely to quit drinking that I would have welcomed any *sort* of physical torture or pain to accomplish the result.(p.302)
• I don't know what *sort* of person I was expecting, but I was very agreeably surprised to find Mr. T. a poised, intelligent, well groomed and mannered gentleman.(p.309)
• I couldn't look them straight in the eyes, although I was always a self-possessed brazen *sort* of person.(p.323)
• I said to her one day when I met her on the street, "What *sort* of volunteer work do you do?"(p.326)
• The only thing I have really to offer you is my own story, telling you just what *sort* of a drunk I was.(p.384)
• They also were held in some *sort* of strap arrangement.(p.422)
• Now I had to face up to the fact that knowledge of this *sort*, applied to my individual case, was not power.(p.435)
• Of course, I had problems, all *sort* of problems.(p.439)
• If something does come along that *sort* of upsets me, instead of walking in and throwing a buck at the barman and asking for a drink, I walk into a telephone booth, drop a dime in the box, and call somebody who was so kind as to give me his name and telephone number to meet such an emergency.(p.511)
• Was I the disloyal *sort* who would turn his back on this, my last and truest friend?(p.539)
• But not for long; now, for five Friday nights in a row, I went to jail, picked up sodden with beer (which I always disliked, but which was the only drink available); in jail five consecutive Friday nights in the town where I had grown up, where I had been an honor student in high school, where a kindly uncle, bailing me out, said, "Bob, our family just doesn't do this *sort* of thing."(p.539)
• Dr. Harry M. Tiebout, psychiatrist: "As a psychiatrist, I have thought a great deal about the relationship of my specialty to A.A. and I have come to the conclusion that our particular function can very often lie in preparing the way for the patient to accept any *sort* of treatment or outside help.(p.571)

sorts
• I have seen hundreds of families set their feet in the path that really goes somewhere; have seen the most impossible domestic situations righted; feuds and bitterness of all *sorts* wiped out.(p.15)
• In the realm of the material, men's minds were fettered by superstition, tradition, and all *sorts* of fixed ideas.(p.51)
• When we sincerely took such a position, all *sorts* of remarkable things followed.(p.63)
• We might pay for this presumption in all *sorts* of absurd actions and ideas.(p.87)
• Assuming we are spiritually fit, we can do all *sorts* of things alcoholics are not supposed to do.(p.100)
• Our loyalty and the desire that our husbands hold up their heads and be like other men have begotten all *sorts* of predicaments.(p.105)
• He entered a political campaign, making speeches, frequenting men's gathering places of all *sorts*, often staying up all night.(p.158)
• The next three years I spent in Boston, Chicago, and Montreal in the employ of a large manufacturing concern, selling railway supplies, gas engines of all *sorts*, and many other items of heavy hardware.(p.172)
• All *sorts* were represented and their relation of experiences and how they had found the only remedy, added to their human existence as sober men, laid the foundation of a very necessary faith.(p.258)
• We moved in from the country at the age when girls want all *sorts* of nice things.(p.261)
• But he's in all *sorts* of scrapes because he drinks too much."(p.262)
• This was such a new thought that I got all *sorts* of books on Higher Powers, and I put a Bible by my bedside, and I put a Bible in my car.(p.348)
• It is true that I -- of all people, strange as it may seem, and even though I didn't give my permission -- really, really am an alcoholic of *sorts*.(p.448)

SOS
• However, I made an *SOS* call to the New York Group, whom I hadn't met yet, and they suggested we both come there.(p.245)

sot
• But I can remember, in my teens, that there were a few characters who caused the village heads to nod pityingly and sometimes in anger as they paused to say, "That *sot*, Henri" and "Ce pauvre Jules," who drank too much.(p.230)

sots
• Now I was to plunge into the dark, joining that endless procession of *sots* who had gone on before.(p.8)

sought
• There were flights from city to country and back, as my wife and I *sought* escape.(p.6)
• We, in our turn, *sought* the same escape with all the desperation of drowning men.(p.28)
• We used to amuse ourselves by cynically dissecting spiritual beliefs and practices when we might have observed that many spiritually-minded persons of all races, colors, and creeds were demonstrating a degree of stability, happiness and usefulness which we should have *sought* ourselves.(p.49)
• But He has come to all who have honestly *sought* Him.(p.57)
• (c) That God could and would if He were *sought*.(p.60)
• We have *sought* sympathy.(p.105)
• We finally *sought* employment ourselves as destitution faced us and our families.(p.106)
• Some of us *sought* out sordid places, hoping to find understanding companionship and approval.(p.151)
• While I *sought* the comforting arms of alcohol, I knew this was a sign of weakness on the part of a longtime-successful old codger with white hair, the image of dignity.(p.331)
• After this incident in 1940, I *sought* some other means of livelihood.(p.489)
• I know there are some alcoholics who seem terribly, terribly grown-up, but I think that they are trying to make themselves think they are grown-up, and the strain of their effort is what is causing them to drink -- a sense of inadequacy, a childish vanity to be the most popular, the most *sought* after, the mostest of the most.(p.535)

soul
• I can remember telling the poor little *soul* that I could probably quit drinking if I wasn't married to her, and told her that, after all, I didn't like restraint!(p.199)
• Perhaps I could find freedom and peace and be able once again to call my *soul* my own.(p.309)
• I thought, now here's a nice sympathetic *soul*!(p.322)
• She's a good-natured *soul* and said, "I wouldn't worry about it; probably something will happen."(p.346)
• I had never told a *soul* about my lapse in New York.(p.366)
• I wanted to try A.A. with my whole heart and *soul*.(p.393)
• I thought I was the captain of my *soul*.(p.408)
• I am hoping that writing this may bring some poor, mixed-up *soul* into the program.(p.530)

souls
• I was born in a small New England village of about seven thousand *souls*.(p.171)

sound
• I could almost hear the *sound* of the preacher's voice as I sat, on still Sundays, way over there on the hillside; there was that proffered temperance pledge I never signed; my grandfather's good natured contempt of some church folk and their doings; his insistence that the spheres really had their music; but his denial of the preacher's right to tell him how he must listen; his fearlessness as he spoke of these things just before he died; these recollections welled up from the past.(p.10)
• They *sound* like the philosophy of the man who, having a headache, beats himself on the head with a hammer so that he can't feel the ache.(p.23)
• But there was always the curious mental phenomenon that parallel with our *sound* reasoning there inevitably ran some insanely trivial excuse for taking the first drink.(p.37)
• Our *sound* reasoning failed to hold us in check.(p.37)
• In this way we tried to shape a sane and *sound* ideal for our future sex life.(p.69)
• Most of them give freely of themselves, that their fellows may enjoy *sound* minds and bodies.(p.133)
• As to them, his policy is undoubtedly *sound*, but he did not distinguish between such people and the alcoholic.(p.149)
• From far away, as if in a delirium, I heard my own voice – calling someone "Dorothy," talking of dress shops, of jobs . . . the words came clearer . . . this *sound* of my own voice frightened me as it came closer . . . and suddenly, there I was, talking of I knew not what, to someone I'd never seen before this very moment.(p.222)
• They used a *sound* truck some.(p.265)
• But, of course," he continued, "eventually the alcoholic loses all of his capacities as his disease gets progressively worse, and this is a tragedy that is painful to watch; the disintegration of a *sound* mind and body."(p.308)
• There are many short phrases and expressions in A.A. which make *sound* sense.(p.382)
• This *sound* easy, so will try.(p.476)

sounded
• Sure enough in a couple of hours two men were at my door and for the first time I heard some facts about liquor and my problem that *sounded* sensible to me.(p.363)

soundly
• After going to school all day, working in the family drugstore all evening, and then studying until one or two in the morning, I would not be able to sleep *soundly*, with everything I had been studying going round in my head.(p.440)

soundness
• As laymen, our opinion as to its *soundness* may, of course, mean little.(p.xxiv)

sounds
• It *sounds* simple, but there were obstacles and doubts to overcome.(p.282)
• However, this isn't as rough as it *sounds*, as we do become grateful for the necessity that makes us toe the line, for we find that we are more than compensated for a consistent effort by the countless dividends we receive.(p.311)

source
• Sometimes he is a *source* of embarrassment to you and his friends.(p.109)
• You forget that you have just now tapped a *source* of power much greater than yourself.(p.163)
• I had no qualms, because I felt the *source* of a drinking problem was all in how weak one was, and I wasn't like my dad (I thought).(p.370)
• We think that each group should soon achieve this ideal; that any public solicitation of funds using the name of Alcoholics Anonymous is highly dangerous, whether by groups, clubs, hospitals, or other outside agencies; that acceptance of large gifts from any *source*, or of contributions carrying any obligation whatever, is unwise.(p.566)

souses
• In the doorway stood a lovely young girl who said, "Are you one of us *souses*, too?"(p.321)

south
• A.A. has flourishing communities in the British Isles, the Scandinavian countries, *South* Africa, *South* America, Mexico, Alaska, Australia and Hawaii.(p.xv)
• This went from bad to worse until Sophomore spring when, after a prolonged period of drinking, I made up my mind that I could not complete my course, so I packed my grip and went *South* to spend a month on a large farm owned by a friend of mine.(p.173)
• To go north into the empty pine country and shoot myself, or to go *south* in the faint hope that a bunch of strangers might help me with my drinking problem.(p.278)
• A FLOWER OF THE *SOUTH*(p.384)
• My father had come out of the *South* and had suffered a great deal down there.(p.485)
• On the other hand, I got quite a different picture farther *south*.(p.486)
• He said he never wanted to set foot in the deep *south* again and he didn't.(p.486)
• Then I went *South*, because they told me that the particular county I was going to in North Carolina was a dry county.(p.489)

South Africa
• A.A. has flourishing communities in the British Isles, the Scandinavian countries, *South Africa*, South America, Mexico, Alaska, Australia and Hawaii.(p.xv)

South America
• A.A. has flourishing communities in the British Isles, the Scandinavian countries, South Africa, *South America*, Mexico, Alaska, Australia and Hawaii.(p.xv)

southern
• Of course, when father finally came to Virginia to work his way through school, he resented the *southern* "cracker," as he often called them, so much that he didn't even go back to his mother's funeral.(p.486)
• OUR *SOUTHERN* FRIEND(p.497)
• Pioneer A.A., minister's son, and *southern* farmer, he asked, "Who am I to say there is no God?"(p.497)
• My proud *southern* blood would have boiled if anyone had named me such a despicable thing.(p.532)

southerner's
• How it finally broke a *Southerner's* obstinacy and destined this salesman to start A.A. at Philadelphia.(p.238)

sowing
• I had met a bunch of gay young Bohemians who lived in the Village, and were *sowing* their wild oats.(p.407)

space
• In that brief *space*, Alcoholics Anonymous has mushroomed into nearly 6,000 groups whose membership is far above 150,000 recovered alcoholics.(p.xv)
• I will not take *space* to relate all my hospital or sanitarium experiences.(p.177)
• After that I sat for a week, a body in a chair, a mind off in *space*.(p.338)
• "You've got to *space* your drinks and take plenty of water in between," or "coat the stomach with a little olive oil," or "drink anything but those damn martinis."(p.433)
• I approached several ministers and all of them thought it was a very good idea, but they never relinquished any *space*.(p.495)

spaced
• My drinking was never the *spaced* doses of the careful tippler; it was always gluttonous.(p.254)
• Then the drinks came more frequently, but carefully *spaced* out.(p.557)

spacing
• I tried the beer diet, the wine diet, timing, measuring, and *spacing* of drinks.(p.305)

span
• In spite of the great increase in the size and the *span* of this Fellowship, at its core it remains simple and personal.(p.xxii)

spaniel
• Anyhow, after Christmas my husband gave me a cocker *spaniel* who is, I think, just as notorious in A.A. as I am.(p.388)

spare
• All of us spend much of our *spare* time in the sort of effort which we are going to describe.(p.19)
• They shared their homes, their slender resources, and gladly devoted their *spare* hours to fellow-sufferers.(p.159)
• My family would have nothing to do with me, in fact couldn't because I couldn't *spare* any of my money, which I needed for drink, to support them.(p.255)
• Shortly thereafter, aided by the Depression, I found that I had a great deal of *spare* time and that a little drink in the morning helped.(p.287)
• I spent a great deal of time with Dr. Bob, whenever he had the time to *spare*, and in the homes of two or three other people, trying to see how the family lived the program.(p.291)
• My father had purchased a restaurant, which he felt would take up some of my *spare* time, and that's how I met Vi.(p.487)

spared
• A young veteran tells how a few rough experiences pushed him into A.A. – and how he was therefore *spared* years of suffering.(p.422)

spark
• The *spark* that was to flare into the first A.A. group was struck at Akron, Ohio, in June 1935, during a talk between a New York stockbroker and an Akron physician.(p.xv)

sparkle
• They had color in their faces, *sparkle* in their eyes and love in their hearts.(p.428)

spasm
• But for some time, it was difficult to keep from taking a pill when I had an appropriate symptom, such as a cough, pain, anxiety, insomnia, a muscle *spasm*, or an upset stomach.(p.448)

spasmodic
• I'd only had two with her, but I'd managed four in the fifteen minutes I'd waited for her, and of course I'd had the usual uncounted swigs from the bottle as I painfully got up and did my slow *spasmodic* dressing.(p.223)

speak
• But his face falls when we *speak* of spiritual matters, especially when we mention God, for we have reopened a subject which our man thought he had neatly evaded or entirely ignored.(p.45)
• When, therefore, we *speak* to you of God, we mean your own conception of God.(p.47)
• Tell him enough about your drinking habits, symptoms, and experiences to encourage him to *speak* of himself.(p.91)
• Continue to *speak* of alcoholism as an illness, a fatal malady.(p.92)
• Not long afterward he had called me from Hartford on two successive days, so drunk he could hardly *speak*.(p.136)
• After holding good positions, making better than an average income for over ten years, I was in debt, had no clothes to *speak* of, no money, no friends, and no one any longer tolerating me but my wife.(p.301)
• Having heard Bill *speak*, she was instantly sold.(p.412)
• My new wife and I don't own any property to *speak* of, and the flashy successes of another day are no longer mine.(p.438)
• My sponsor say men who talk *speak* truth.(p.476)
• When he *speak* from heart, big men cry.(p.476)
• No clothes, no money, no home, no real friends to *speak* of, mentally and physically pooped, but I was doing all right!(p.478)
• One evening I decided to go because two of those friends were to *speak*.(p.509)
• When the policeman released me to my stupefied and exasperated friend at four in the morning, I went to my traveling bag and groped until I found – well, let the officer *speak*: "Ah," said the policeman, "he's got anuder pair, t'ank God!"(p.538)

speak-easy
• All I can remember about the Roaring Twenties is that I drank a great deal, thought I was having a grand time, managed to get to Europe for a few weeks, was very proud of the dozens of *speak-easy* cards entitling me to an entree in the better joints between Cleveland and New York, took on a wife, and built a home in a fashionable suburb of Cleveland.(p.358)

speakeasies
• That age of the flapper and the "It" girl, *speakeasies* and the hip flask, the boyish bob and the drugstore cowboy, John Held Jr. and F. Scott Fitzgerald, all generously sprinkled with a patent pseudo-sophistication.(p.304)

speakeasy
• I was doing well in business, and in going around town I was frequently invited to have a drink in a *speakeasy*.(p.233)
• More and more I formed the habit of doing some of my business in the *speakeasy*, and after a time I did not need that as an excuse.(p.233)

speaker
• I sat and listened and heard the first *speaker* say, "I'm an alcoholic."(p.319)
• After hearing the first *speaker* I could tell myself that my own lot was rather mild.(p.509)

speaking
• When writing or *speaking* publicly about alcoholism, we urge each of our Fellowship to omit his personal name, designating himself instead as "a member of Alcoholics Anonymous."(p.xiii)
• We have been *speaking* to you of serious, sometimes tragic things.(p.132)
• One day my secretary came in saying that Mr. B—— insisted on *speaking* with me.(p.136)
• The circumstances under which I reached these people were very odd because I was led there through things that I said when I couldn't even remember *speaking*.(p.202)
• The people in the group hadn't been around that day; part of my family was in Florida and the rest of them weren't *speaking* to me, so I spent a very lonesome day and by evening I was feeling very sorry for myself.(p.207)
• Abruptly I stopped *speaking*.(p.222)
• Through going to meetings and listening, and occasionally *speaking*, through doing Twelve Step work, whereby in helping others you are both the teacher and the student, by making many wonderful A.A. friends, I have been taught all the things in life that are worth having.(p.416)
• When I am through *speaking*, the whole idea has become absurd.(p.507)
• *Speaking* at a dinner given by John D. Rockefeller Jr. to introduce Alcoholics Anonymous to some of his friends, Dr. Harry Emerson Fosdick remarked: "I think that psychologically *speaking* there is a point of advantage in the approach that is being made in this movement that cannot be duplicated.(p.574)

speaks
• Fred's story *speaks* for itself.(p.43)
• If he *speaks* of his home situation, you can undoubtedly make helpful suggestions.(p.145)
• The "*speaks*" usually sold whiskey.(p.233)

spearheads
• Instead of regarding ourselves as intelligent agents, *spearheads* of God's ever advancing Creation, we agnostics and atheists chose to believe that our human intelligence was the last word, the alpha and the omega, the beginning and end of all.(p.49)

special
• I fancied myself a leader, for had not the men of my battery given me a *special* token of appreciation?(p.1)
• He often possesses *special* abilities, skills, and aptitudes, and has a promising career ahead of him.(p.21)
• Because of the employee's *special* ability, or of his own strong personal attachment to him, the employer has sometimes kept such a man at work long beyond a reasonable period.(p.137)
• There was always a tremendous drive and ambition to become a great guy, because I think I recognized inwardly that I didn't have any *special* talents.(p.194)
• Eventually, there would be a ball game, or a show, or some sort of *special* occasion to celebrate and I would turn up drunk.(p.196)
• I came of good stock, of men and women who drank wine all their lives as a beverage, and while they occasionally got drunk at *special* celebrations, they were up and about their business the next day.(p.231)
• At thirteen I was packed off to a very fine Protestant boarding school in Virginia where I stayed four years, graduating without any *special* achievements.(p.240)
• Many tried everything – hospitals, *special* treatments, sanitariums, asylums, and jails.(p.455)
• It made me feel quite grown-up and mature, and I think another added attraction was the fact that so far as my family was concerned, it was forbidden, and it had a *special* attraction for that reason.(p.464)
• After nearly eight years of sobriety in A.A., I still can set down such thoughts, "against my instinct and training," showing that I still consider myself a "*special*" person, entitled to *special* privileges.(p.536)
• When I was faced with a *special* challenge or social event – such as an important business presentation or a dinner party – I had to fortify myself with a couple of belts.(p.556)
• Eight – Alcoholics Anonymous should remain forever nonprofessional, but our service centers may employ *special* workers.(p.564)
• Such *special* services may be well recompensed.(p.566)
• This headquarters will give the location of the nearest family group and will if you wish, correspond with you about your *special* problems.(p.575)

specialist
• He had also been greatly helped by the late Dr. William D. Silkworth, a New York *specialist* in alcoholism who is now accounted no less than a medical saint by A.A. members, and whose story of the early days of our Society appears in the next pages.(p.xvi)
• I became a *specialist* in making elderberry blossom wine.(p.213)
• I went to hospitals, I went to retreats and doctors, and finally my mother asked me to go and see a *specialist* of her own choosing.(p.522)
• As I say, this *specialist* put a scare in me for about a fortnight or three weeks, then I started my last bout which went on and off for about three months.(p.523)

specialized
• I have *specialized* in the treatment of alcoholism for many years.(p.xxiii)
• With this *specialized* training, and a liberal business education in the school of hard knocks, I was able to set up shop some two years later as an independent accountant.(p.284)

specializing
• A well-known doctor, chief physician at a nationally prominent hospital *specializing* in alcoholic and drug addiction, gave Alcoholics Anonymous this letter:(p.xxiii)

specialty
• I recall, as I walked into that meeting, saying to myself, "Here I am, a fellow of the American College of Surgeons, a Fellow of the International College of Sur-

geons, a diplomate of one of the great *specialty* boards in these United States, a member of the American Psychiatric Society, and I have to go to the butcher, the baker and the carpenter to help make a man out of me!"(p.347)
• And as I went through pharmacy school, graduate school, medical school, internship, residency, and *specialty* training and, finally, went into practice, my drinking kept increasing.(p.441)
• Dr. Harry M. Tiebout, psychiatrist: "As a psychiatrist, I have thought a great deal about the relationship of my *specialty* to A.A. and I have come to the conclusion that our particular function can very often lie in preparing the way for the patient to accept any sort of treatment or outside help.(p.571)

specific
• In meditation, we ask God what we should do about each *specific* matter.(p.69)
• Here no *specific* rule can be given.(p.90)
• I do not recollect the *specific* conversation that went on but I believe I did challenge Bill to tell me something about A.A. and I do recall one other thing: I wanted to know what this was that worked so many wonders, and hanging over the mantel was a picture of Gethsemane and Bill pointed to it and said, "There it is," which didn't make much sense to me.(p.216)

specifically
• It is the purpose of this book to answer such questions *specifically*.(p.20)
• Eventually, I had to redo each of the Twelve Steps *specifically* with Max in mind, from the First, saying, "I am powerless over alcohol, and my homelife is unmanageable by me," to the Twelfth, in which I tried to think of her as a sick Al-Anon and treat her with the love I would give a sick A.A. newcomer.(p.452)

specimen
• I see him now and then and he is as fine a *specimen* of manhood as one could wish to meet.(p.xxx)

speck
• Starting from a *speck* on the domestic horizon, great thunderclouds of dispute may gather.(p.117)

spectacle
• I left this home town, then, after I had made a public *spectacle* of myself in the presence of a revered teacher whose favorite pupil I had been.(p.539)

spectacular
• Yet often such men had *spectacular* and powerful recoveries.(p.113)
• Yet it is true that our first printing gave many readers the impression that these personality changes, or religious experiences, must be in the nature of sudden and *spectacular* upheavals.(p.569)

spectres
• Now and then the family will be plagued by *spectres* from the past, for the drinking career of almost every alcoholic has been marked by escapades, funny, humiliating, shameful or tragic.(p.123)

speculation
• Out of this alloy of drink and *speculation*, I commenced to forge the weapon that one day would turn in its flight like a boomerang and all but cut me to ribbons.(p.2)
• I had had some success at *speculation*, so we had a little money, but we once worked on a farm for a month to avoid drawing on our small capital.(p.3)

speech
• I, who had never made a *speech* in my life and who would have been frightened sick at the prospect, stood up in front of Rotary groups in different parts of the city and talked about Alcoholics Anonymous.(p.283)

speeches
• He entered a political campaign, making *speeches*, frequenting men's gathering places of all sorts, often staying up all night.(p.158)
• Then I joined the Navy and was commissioned as an ensign to write *speeches* for admirals.(p.555)

speed
• The prosaic steel girder is a mass of electrons whirling around each other at incredible *speed*.(p.48)
• I did not know that I had no power over alcohol, that I, alone and unaided, could not stop; that I was on a downgrade, tearing along at full *speed* with all my brakes gone, and that the end would be a total smash-up, death or insanity.(p.408)
• I woke up in jail, sick, withdrawing from alcohol and *speed*, already a four-time loser, and now with a fifth felony charge against me.(p.460)
• Apparently I'd grown physically at the customary rate of *speed*, and I had acquired an average amount of intellectual training in the intervening years, but there had been no emotional maturity at all.(p.547)

speeding
• Next, I was sent to Arizona, where my drinking picked up some more, and I started having blackouts, and I was thrown in jail for *speeding* and drunken driving.(p.318)

speedy
• Sitting in a Second Avenue bar, accepting drinks from anyone who offered, after my small stake was gone; or sitting at home alone, with the inevitable glass in my hand, I would remember, and remembering, I would drink faster, seeking *speedy* oblivion.(p.225)

spell
• This hope, however, was destroyed by the doctor's telling him that while his religious convictions were very good, in his case they did not *spell* the necessary vital spiritual experience.(p.27)
• I had been out of town before during this particular dry *spell*, so there was nothing new about that.(p.41)
• This dry *spell* lasted for about three weeks; then I went to Atlantic City to attend several days' meeting of a national society of which I was a member.(p.179)
• Discharged in 1919, I really made up for my dry *spell*.(p.253)
• Others may idle in a retrogressive groove without too much danger, but retrogression can *spell* death for us.(p.311)
• Love has no words to *spell* or lines to start and stop.(p.474)

spelled
• Vacations from school and from work, *spelled* "travel" to me — and I travelled with gusto.(p.275)
• They realized that repeated lack of drinking control, when they really wanted control, was the fatal symptom that *spelled* problem drinking.(p.315)
• There was a bar, and what I tasted *spelled* sheer heaven.(p.328)
• At that time life to me was *spelled* "w-h-i-s-k-e-y."(p.430)

spells
• And I remembered the creeping horror of the interminable night, in which I slept for short *spells* and woke up dripping with cold sweat and shaken with utter despair, to drink hastily from my bottle and mercifully pass out again, "You're mad, you're mad, you're mad!" pounded through my brain with each returning ray of consciousness, and I drowned the refrain with drink.(p.224)
• That job began a series of brief working *spells*, each one ending in a "drunk" and the urge to travel.(p.253)
• Short dry *spells* ended in heavy drinking.(p.375)
• Then I was sent out to India and from then on drinking just increased and increased, and I started having two or three day *spells* instead of just the ordinary concentrated one day.(p.519)

Spencer
• -HERBERT *SPENCER*(p.570)

spend
• All of us *spend* much of our spare time in the sort of effort which we are going to describe.(p.19)
• To *spend* too much time on any one situation is to deny some other alcoholic an opportunity to live and be happy.(p.96)
• Father will necessarily *spend* much time with other alcoholics, but this activity should be balanced.(p.131)
• This went from bad to worse until Sophomore spring when, after a prolonged period of drinking, I made up my mind that I could not complete my course, so I packed my grip and went South to *spend* a month on a large farm owned by a friend of mine.(p.173)
• I *spend* a great deal of time passing on what I learned to others who want and need it badly.(p.180)
• At the age of sixteen, I was invited to *spend* the summer with an aunt and I, very delightedly, accepted the invitation.(p.261)
• Every evening we would meet at the home of one of the members and have coffee and doughnuts and *spend* a social evening.(p.291)
• A week later, I had to get an old friend from Akron to *spend* two days sobering me up.(p.293)
• From my post, I'd go *spend* weekends with her.(p.318)
• Eight years ago, my wife and I decided to *spend* a vacation in Naini Tal, the mountain resort.(p.343)
• That way, I could *spend* most of my time at the Laundromat!(p.371)
• But my board, room, and clothing were free, and I could *spend* the whole ten bucks on booze.(p.398)

spending
• I think his entry into A.A. was through *spending* some hours with Dr. Bob at his office.(p.267)
• He said he had finally learned that drinking was a fatal illness made up of an allergy plus an obsession, and once the drinking had passed from habit to obsession, we were completely hopeless, and could look forward only to *spending* the balance of our lives in mental institutions or to death.(p.290)
• The family seems to think of nothing but *spending*.(p.506)
• I would never admit that I was drinking too much, or *spending* money that I should have used to buy food for my two little boys.(p.526)

spends
• Perhaps he *spends* too much money for liquor.(p.109)
• You have been starving for his companionship, yet he *spends* long hours helping other men and their families.(p.119)
• This same company *spends* millions for research every year.(p.149)

spent
• Everyone *spent* in thousands and chattered in millions.(p.3)
• We have *spent* thousands of dollars for examinations.(p.73)
• But the head of the house has *spent* years in pulling down the structures of business, romance, friendship, health -- these things are now ruined or damaged.(p.123)
• Those of us who have *spent* much time in the world of spiritual make-believe have eventually seen the childishness of it.(p.130)
• Among many employers nowadays, we think of one member who has *spent* much of his life in the world of big business.(p.136)
• This seemed to me like an opportunity to be helpful, so I *spent* two hours talking about alcoholism, the malady, and described the symptoms and results as well as I could.(p.138)
• I have enjoyed every moment *spent* in getting them straightened out.(p.150)
• The next three years I *spent* in Boston, Chicago, and Montreal in the employ of a large manufacturing concern, selling railway supplies, gas engines of all sorts, and many other items of heavy hardware.(p.172)
• I conducted myself so creditably that I was able to secure a much coveted internship in a western city, where I *spent* two years.(p.174)
• I *spent* most of my time trying to get back these friendships, and to make some recompense towards my wife, whom I had hurt a lot.(p.191)
• To show you the point to which this obsession went, there came an occasion when I had *spent* a most delightful week-end, and at nine o'clock on Sunday night I was on my way home, and I thought I would get a drink.(p.204)
• The people in the group hadn't been around that day; part of my family was in Florida and the rest of them weren't speaking to me, so I *spent* a very lonesome day and by evening I was feeling very sorry for myself.(p.207)
• My early life was *spent* in Baltimore where my father was a physician and a grain merchant.(p.240)
• I had completely forgotten the January 8th when I found the fellowship, and I *spent* the next four days wandering around New England half drunk, by which I mean I couldn't get drunk and I couldn't get sober.(p.247)
• During my visit there, renewing acquaintance with former friends, I soon *spent* most of my money.(p.252)
• Again I *spent* my bankroll, by no means as thick as the one I had when I first saw the skyline of Gotham.(p.252)
• They *spent* at least an evening a week in our home out there for weeks and weeks.(p.270)
• He *spent* eighteen years in running away; and then found he didn't have to run.(p.275)
• We *spent* two days there together before he returned to New York.(p.281)
• So I *spent* much of my time calling on the people who I felt would logically come in contact with alcoholic cases, doctors, ministers, lawyers and the personnel men in industry.(p.281)
• I do feel, though, that the fact that I finally grew up to a point where I could even tackle such a job is the apex of the story of a man who *spent* eighteen years running away from life.(p.286)
• He *spent* two hours with me that night telling me his story.(p.290)
• I *spent* a great deal of time with Dr. Bob, whenever he had the time to spare, and in the homes of two or three other people, trying to see how the family lived the program.(p.291)
• The day before I was due to go back to Chicago, a Wednesday and Dr. Bob's afternoon off, he had me down to the office and we *spent* three or four hours

formally going through the Six-Step program as it was at that time.(p.291)
• I *spent* several days with him, but I did not feel adequate to pass the program on to him alone.(p.294)
• Up to this point I had *spent* six years in the business and had enjoyed the reputation of being very successful.(p.298)
• I became convinced of that because I *spent* most of my time there and nary a job turned up.(p.300)
• Even some of the saloon-keepers, where I had *spent* so much time and money, requested that I stay away from their places.(p.301)
• I was thirty-three years old and my life was *spent*.(p.304)
• I got orders to go to Vietnam, and I *spent* most of the year over there either drunk or sick with a hang-over.(p.317)
• I *spent* five and a half years in psychoanalysis and proceeded to become a drunk.(p.349)
• All my life, it seemed, was *spent* on the outside looking in.(p.353)
• We did, and *spent* a month boozing it up, popping pills, and smoking marijuana; taking shelter where we could, which included a veterinary hospital one night; accepting meals from anyone; actually begging; stealing anything we were in need of, which was about everything.(p.354)
• It is also stated that we will never be able to figure out how much we have *spent* on alcohol.(p.396)
• So I *spent* twenty years in the Navy.(p.398)
• We were to go up to our A.A. farm in Kent, and I *spent* the evening before riding herd on Anne.(p.415)
• I *spent* the next three days in a cell.(p.424)
• I planned to stay home the night before I left, but my folks got so drunk I walked off early in the evening and *spent* the night with my girl, getting very drunk myself.(p.425)
• I *spent* the time in a nearby tavern, was loaded on the ship, went to sleep before take-off, and the next thing I knew someone was shaking me and telling me we were over San Diego.(p.428)
• I *spent* eighteen hundred dollars fixing up that car in the first year I was home, after four bad smash-ups.(p.429)
• To cut a long story short, I *spent* seven years and ten thousand dollars on my psychiatric adventure, and emerged in worse condition than ever.(p.434)
• And that was how Max and I and our two daughters *spent* Christmas Day, eight years ago.(p.444)
• Much of my time was *spent* writing letters, notes, orders, and lists of things for Max, who was also my office nurse, to do to keep the world running while I was locked up.(p.445)
• The two years I *spent* there, I was incorrigible, and the records bear this out.(p.458)
• In a prison in my native state, I *spent* eleven months in solitary confinement, bouncing in and out of the "hole" (a bare concrete-and-steel cubicle) about five times during those eleven months.(p.459)
• Fortunately, I received only fifteen-twenty years, and I went back to my alma mater (where I had *spent* so much time in the hole).(p.461)
• Then I was transferred to the honor-grade unit, where I *spent* the most painful year of my life.(p.462)
• The last Christmas I *spent* in Washington, fourteen years ago, comes to mind.(p.465)
• I went to meetings, I *spent* a lot of time at the clubroom, but it was all centered in this one woman.(p.472)
• Dad, due to having *spent* most of his time in a small Virginia town, didn't have any too much money, and the money he had saved and the property he had acquired were in Washington.(p.486)
• I *spent* about six or seven weeks in Sing Sing, and was finally sent off to Dannemora in the Adirondacks.(p.509)
• I have *spent* eighteen years in that institution.(p.509)
• I *spent* my last seventeen months in Wallkill, and it was there that I first got my introduction to A.A.(p.509)
• I clung to the outfit for the balance of my time, and finally I was released, after having *spent* twenty years and nine months behind bars.(p.510)
• I'm writing this during an A.A. convention, where I have *spent* the weekend with nothing but white people.(p.529)

sphere

• I have come to believe that my illness is spiritual as well as physical and mental, and I know that for help in the spiritual *sphere* I have to turn to a Higher Power.(p.473)

spheres

• I could almost hear the sound of the preacher's voice as I sat, on still Sundays, way over there on the hillside; there was that proffered temperance pledge I never signed; my grandfather's good natured contempt of some church folk and their doings; his insistence that the *spheres* really had their music; but his denial of the preacher's right to tell him how he must listen; his fearlessness as he spoke of these things just before he died; these recollections welled up from the past.(p.10)

spike

• I was a very young married man, having his whiskey in the cupboard over the sink, and when I helped my wife with the dishes at night I would take a cup of tea and *spike* it with whiskey.(p.196)

spill

• I stayed drunk from Monday until Friday, and I call that my *spill* into A.A.(p.393)
• "The nervous tension had piled up and just had to *spill* over."(p.433)

spinal

• I well remember the shock I received when a prominent doctor in Chicago told me of cases where pressure of the *spinal* fluid actually ruptured the brain.(p.140)

spine

• Cold chills started chasing up and down my *spine*; my teeth were chattering; my hands were shaking so I tucked them under me to keep them from flying away.(p.222)

spineless

• You cannot see why it should be to anyone else, save the *spineless* and stupid.(p.139)

spiral

• The birth of a baby boy did nothing toward staying the downward *spiral*.(p.278)

spirit

• The unselfishness of these men as we have come to know them, the entire absence of profit motive, and their community *spirit*, is indeed inspiring to one who has labored long and wearily in this alcoholic field.(p.xxv)
• Unmindful of his welfare, I thought only of recapturing the *spirit* of other days.(p.9)
• I simply had to believe in a *Spirit* of the Universe, who knew neither time nor limitation.(p.10)
• I could go for such conceptions as Creative Intelligence, Universal Mind or *Spirit* of Nature but I resisted the thought of a Czar of the Heavens, however loving His sway might be.(p.12)
• As soon as we admitted the possible existence of a Creative Intelligence, a *Spirit* of the Universe underlying the totality of things, we began to be possessed of a new sense of power and direction, provided we took other simple steps.(p.46)
• To us, the Realm of *Spirit* is broad, roomy, all inclusive; never exclusive or forbidding to those who earnestly seek.(p.46)
• The *spirit* of modern scientific inquiry, research and invention was almost unknown.(p.51)
• When we saw others solve their problems by a simple reliance upon the *Spirit* of the Universe, we had to stop doubting the power of God.(p.52)
• For when harboring such feelings we shut ourselves off from the sunlight of the *Spirit*.(p.66)
• We feel we are on the Broad Highway, walking hand in hand with the *Spirit* of the Universe.(p.75)
• We go to him in a helpful and forgiving *spirit*, confessing our former ill feeling and expressing our regret.(p.77)
• We have entered the world of the *Spirit*.(p.84)
• If we have carefully followed directions, we have begun to sense the flow of His *Spirit* into us.(p.85)
• This means a new attitude and *spirit* all around.(p.99)
• Every new alcoholic looks for this *spirit* among us and is immensely relieved when he finds we are not witch-burners.(p.103)
• A *spirit* of intolerance might repel alcoholics whose lives could have been saved, had it not been for such stupidity.(p.103)
• Just be careful not to disagree in a resentful or critical *spirit*.(p.117)
• We do talk about each other a great deal, but we almost invariably temper such talk by a *spirit* of love and tolerance.(p.125)
• We shall be with you in the Fellowship of the *Spirit*, and you will surely meet some of us as you trudge the Road of Happy Destiny.(p.164)
• That's about the *spirit* in which I went to Akron.(p.217)
• He had already imbued them with his own *spirit* until they were ready and willing at all times to go where sent, and as a doctor he well knew that this mission and duty would strengthen them as it later helped me.(p.235)
• There are so many to whom I feel deeply grateful; to my husband (and best critic), whose generous love, compassion and understanding have helped me along the way; to those before me in A.A. who inspired the first article I read, and the friend who sent that article to Frank; to Ruth for her personal note, and the first A.A. to talk to me; to my Bishop, whose loving and believing *spirit* inspired me; and to all the members of the Houston Group who were so patient, kind and helpful -- and to countless others.(p.393)
• We all one as Great *Spirit* walks through A.A. like sun walks through day.(p.474)
• Find same A.A., same *Spirit*.(p.476)
• Tall Man now see Great *Spirit* in Big Group in sky.(p.476)
• I feel Great *Spirit* at all meetings and when talk to A.A. friends.(p.477)
• Let group *spirit* of love and understanding protect you.(p.477)
• All such representatives are to be guided in the *spirit* of service, for true leaders in A.A. are but trusted and experienced servants of the whole.(p.567)

spirits

• The outlines and the promise of the New Land had brought lustre to tired eyes and fresh courage to flagging *spirits*.(p.53)
• Discuss this with him when he is sober and in good *spirits*.(p.115)
• We know our friend is like a boy whistling in the dark to keep up his *spirits*.(p.152)
• On account of my enormous capacity for beer, I was elected to membership in one of the drinking societies, and soon became one of the leading *spirits*.(p.173)
• On my trips back to Akron to get my *spirits* recharged and to work with other alcoholics, I would ask Dr. Bob about this delay and wonder just what was wrong with me.(p.293)
• His enthusiasm and keen interest in A.A. fired my *spirits* again.(p.365)

spiritual

• Six months earlier, the broker had been relieved of his drink obsession by a sudden *spiritual* experience, following a meeting with an alcoholic friend who had been in contact with the Oxford Groups of that day.(p.xv)
• This physician had repeatedly tried *spiritual* means to resolve his alcoholic dilemma but had failed.(p.xvi)
• But when the broker gave him Dr. Silkworth's description of alcoholism and its hopelessness, the physician began to pursue the *spiritual* remedy for his malady with a willingness he had never before been able to muster.(p.xvi)
• Though we work out our solution on the *spiritual* as well as an altruistic plane, we favor hospitalization for the alcoholic who is very jittery or befogged.(p.xxiv)
• For if an alcoholic failed to perfect and enlarge his *spiritual* life through work and self-sacrifice for others, he could not survive the certain trials and low spots ahead.(p.14)
• When, therefore, we were approached by those in whom the problem had been solved, there was nothing left for us but to pick up the simple kit of *spiritual* tools laid at our feet.(p.25)
• The great fact is just this, and nothing less: That we have had deep and effective *spiritual* experiences which have revolutionized our whole attitude toward life, toward our fellows and toward God's universe.(p.25)
• We were in a position where life was becoming impossible, and if we had passed into the region from which there is no return through human aid we had but two alternatives: One was to go on to the bitter end, blotting out the consciousness of our intolerable situation as best we could; and the other, to accept *spiritual* help.(p.25)
• Some of our alcoholic readers may think they can do without *spiritual* help.(p.27)
• Here and there, once in a while, alcoholics have had what are called vital *spiritual* experiences.(p.27)
• This hope, however, was destroyed by the doctor's telling him that while his religious convictions were very good, in his case they did not spell the necessary vital *spiritual* experience.(p.27)
• Surprisingly enough, we find such convictions no great obstacle to a *spiritual* experience.(p.28)
• All went well for a time, but he failed to enlarge his *spiritual* life.(p.35)
• Fred would not believe himself an alcoholic, much less accept a *spiritual* remedy for his problem.(p.39)
• "Then they outlined the *spiritual* answer and program of action which a hundred of them had followed successfully.(p.42)

• "Quite as important was the discovery that *spiritual* principles would solve all my problems.(p.42)
• Though not a religious person, I have profound respect for the *spiritual* approach in such cases as yours.(p.43)
• If that be the case, you may be suffering from an illness which only a *spiritual* experience will conquer.(p.44)
• To be doomed to an alcoholic death or to live on a *spiritual* basis are not always easy alternatives to face.(p.44)
• But after a while we had to face the fact that we must find a *spiritual* basis of life – or else.(p.44)
• That means we have written a book which we believe to be *spiritual* as well as moral.(p.45)
• But his face falls when we speak of *spiritual* matters, especially when we mention God, for we have reopened a subject which our man thought he had neatly evaded or entirely ignored.(p.45)
• This applies, too, to other *spiritual* expressions which you find in this book.(p.47)
• Do not let any prejudice you may have against *spiritual* terms deter you from honestly asking yourself what they mean to you.(p.47)
• At the start, this was all we needed to commence *spiritual* growth, to effect our first conscious relation with God as we understood Him.(p.47)
• It has been repeatedly proven among us that upon this simple cornerstone a wonderfully effective *spiritual* structure can be built.(p.47)
• That was great news to us, for we had assumed we could not make use of *spiritual* principles unless we accepted many things on faith which seemed difficult to believe.(p.47)
• When people presented us with *spiritual* approaches, how frequently did we all say, "I wish I had what that man has.(p.47)
• Many of us have been so touchy that even casual reference to *spiritual* things made us bristle with antagonism.(p.48)
• Faced with alcoholic destruction, we soon became as open minded on *spiritual* matters as we tried to be on other questions.(p.48)
• We used to amuse ourselves by cynically dissecting *spiritual* beliefs and practices when we might have observed that many spiritually-minded persons of all races, colors, and creeds were demonstrating a degree of stability, happiness and usefulness which we should have sought ourselves.(p.49)
• We never gave the *spiritual* side of life a fair hearing.(p.50)
• Yet we had been seeing another kind of flight, a *spiritual* liberation from this world, people who rose above their problems.(p.55)
• We had seen *spiritual* release, but liked to tell ourselves it wasn't true.(p.55)
• One night, when confined in a hospital, he was approached by an acholic who had known a *spiritual* experience.(p.56)
• 12.Having had a *spiritual* awakening as the result of these steps, we tried to carry this message to alcoholics, and to practice these principles in all our affairs.(p.60)
• The point is, that we are willing to grow along *spiritual* lines.(p.60)
• We claim *spiritual* progress rather than *spiritual* perfection.(p.60)
• We found it very desirable to take this *spiritual* step with an understanding person, such as our wife, best friend or *spiritual* adviser.(p.63)
• From it stem all forms of *spiritual* disease, for we have been not only mentally and physically ill, we have been spiritually sick.(p.64)
• When the *spiritual* malady is overcome, we straighten out mentally and physically.(p.64)
• But with the alcoholic, whose hope is the maintenance and growth of a *spiritual* experience, this business of resentment is infinitely grave.(p.66)
• We may have had certain *spiritual* beliefs, but now we begin to have a *spiritual* experience.(p.75)
• As we look over the list of business acquaintances and friends we have hurt, we may feel diffident about going to some of them on a *spiritual* basis.(p.76)
• To some people we need not, and probably should not emphasize the *spiritual* feature on our first approach.(p.76)
• He is going to be more interested in a demonstration of good will than in our talk of *spiritual* discoveries.(p.77)
• Reminding ourselves that we have decided to go to any length to find a *spiritual* experience we ask that we be given strength and direction to do the right thing, no matter what the personal consequences may be.(p.79)
• The *spiritual* life is not a theory.(p.83)
• Unless one's family expresses a desire to live upon *spiritual* principles we think we ought not to urge them.(p.83)
• We should not talk incessantly to them about *spiritual* matters.(p.83)
• That is how we react so long as we keep in fit *spiritual* condition.(p.85)
• It is easy to let up on the *spiritual* program of action and rest on our laurels.(p.85)
• What we really have is a daily reprieve contingent on the maintenance of our *spiritual* condition.(p.85)
• Stress the *spiritual* feature freely.(p.93)
• The main thing is that he be willing to believe in a Power greater than himself and that he live by *spiritual* principles.(p.93)
• When dealing with such a person, you had better use everyday language to describe *spiritual* principles.(p.93)
• Never talk down to an alcoholic from any moral or *spiritual* hilltop; simply lay out the kit of *spiritual* tools for his inspection.(p.95)
• If he thinks he can do the job in some other way, or prefers some other *spiritual* approach, encourage him to follow his own conscience.(p.95)
• Should they accept and practice *spiritual* principles, there is a much better chance that the head of the family will recover.(p.97)
• He should concentrate on his own *spiritual* demonstration.(p.98)
• Both you and the new man must walk day by day in the path of *spiritual* progress.(p.100)
• An alcoholic who cannot meet them, still has an alcoholic mind; there is something the matter with his *spiritual* status.(p.101)
• But be sure you are on solid *spiritual* ground before you start and that your motive in going is thoroughly good.(p.102)
• If you think he will be shy of a *spiritual* remedy, ask him to look at the chapter on alcoholism.(p.112)
• If such women adopt a *spiritual* way of life their road will be smoother.(p.114)
• We have elsewhere remarked how much better life is when lived on a *spiritual* plane.(p.116)
• As our husbands began to apply *spiritual* principles in their lives, we began to see the desirability of doing so too.(p.116)
• Now we try to put *spiritual* principles to work in every department of our lives.(p.116)
• If your husband is trying to live on a *spiritual* basis, he will also be doing everything in his power to avoid disagreement or contention.(p.118)
• Your husband will be the first to say it was your devotion and care which brought him to the point where he could have a *spiritual* experience.(p.118)
• Your husband will see at once that he must redouble his *spiritual* activities if he expects to survive.(p.120)
• You need not remind him of his *spiritual* deficiency – he will know of it.(p.120)
• In the first flush of *spiritual* experience they forgave each other and drew closer together.(p.124)
• They criticize, pointing out how he is falling down on his *spiritual* program.(p.126)
• If they sense these things, they will not take so seriously his periods of crankiness, depression, or apathy, which will disappear when there is tolerance, love, and *spiritual* understanding.(p.127)
• For us, material well-being always followed *spiritual* progress; it never preceded.(p.127)
• Assume on the other hand that father has, at the outset, a stirring *spiritual* experience.(p.128)
• There is talk about *spiritual* matters morning, noon and night.(p.128)
• Dad is not so *spiritual* after all, they say.(p.128)
• We have indulged in *spiritual* intoxication.(p.128)
• He will perceive that his *spiritual* growth is lopsided, that for an average man like himself, a *spiritual* life which does not include his family obligations may not be so perfect after all.(p.129)
• In the midst of an understanding and sympathetic family, these vagaries of dad's *spiritual* infancy will quickly disappear.(p.129)
• Instead of treating the family as he should, he may retreat further into himself and feel he has *spiritual* justification for so doing.(p.129)
• Though the family does not fully agree with dad's *spiritual* activities, they should let him have his head.(p.129)
• Though some of his manifestations are alarming and disagreeable, we think dad will be on a firmer foundation than the man who is placing business or professional success ahead of *spiritual* development.(p.129)
• Those of us who have spent much time in the world of *spiritual* make-believe have eventually seen the childishness of it.(p.130)
• We have found nothing incompatible between a powerful *spiritual* experience and a life of sane and happy usefulness.(p.130)
• One more suggestion: Whether the family has *spiritual* convictions or not, they may do well to examine the principles by which the alcoholic member is trying to live.(p.130)
• Nothing will help the man who is off on a *spiritual* tangent so much as the wife who adopts a sane *spiritual* program, making a better practical use of it.(p.130)
• Being possessed of a *spiritual* experience, the alcoholic will find he has much in common with these people, though he may differ with them on many matters.(p.131)
• We are convinced that a *spiritual* mode of living is a most powerful health restorative.(p.133)
• Whether the family goes on a *spiritual* basis or not, the alcoholic member has to if he would recover.(p.135)
• He had to painfully admit that and mend his *spiritual* fences.(p.135)
• A *spiritual* experience, he conceded, was absolutely necessary, but the price seemed high upon the basis suggested.(p.155)
• The use of *spiritual* principles in such cases was not so well understood as it is now.(p.156)
• The two friends spoke of their *spiritual* experience and told him about the course of action they carried out.(p.157)
• He had begun to have a *spiritual* experience.(p.158)
• After a bit, he said, "The way you fellows put this *spiritual* stuff makes sense.(p.159)
• They experienced a few distressing failures, but in those cases they made an effort to bring the man's family into a *spiritual* way of living, thus relieving much worry and suffering.(p.159)
• In addition to these casual get-togethers, it became customary to set apart one night a week for a meeting to be attended by anyone or everyone interested in a *spiritual* way of life.(p.159)
• Understanding our work, he can do this with an eye to selecting those who are willing and able to recover on a *spiritual* basis.(p.162)
• I learned that it was something of a *spiritual* nature, which did not appeal to me very much, but I thought it could do no harm.(p.178)
• But this was a man who had experienced many years of frightful drinking, who had had most all the drunkard's experiences known to man, but who had been cured by the very means I had been trying to employ, that is to say the *spiritual* approach.(p.180)
• In fact, I never lost my faith, since I had been prepared by some conversations toward the end of my sojourn in the hospital with Dr. Bob, conversations pretty much along *spiritual* lines.(p.218)
• He pointed out to me that probably it was more of a moral or *spiritual* illness than it was a physical one.(p.219)
• At our weekly meeting I was a menace to serenity those first few months, for I took every opportunity to lambaste the "*spiritual* angle" as we called it, or anything else that had any tinge of theology.(p.246)
• Much later I discovered the elders held many prayer meetings hoping to find a way to give me the heave-ho, but at the same time stay tolerant and *spiritual*.(p.247)
• When I started to tell the boys how we did it in New York and all about the *spiritual* part of the program, I found they would not believe me unless I was practicing what I preached.(p.249)
• Then I found that as I gave in to this *spiritual* or personality change I was getting a little more serenity.(p.249)
• Jack didn't seem to have too much of the *spiritual* understanding.(p.268)
• In the *spiritual* strength I had found, because of A.A., I felt that I had made a complete surrender, that I had really turned my life over that summer.(p.271)
• It is impossible to put on paper all the benefits I have derived . . . physical, mental, domestic, *spiritual*, and monetary.(p.302)
• I can think clearly and am helped much in my thinking and judgment by my *spiritual* development which grows daily.(p.303)
• *Spiritual* experience?(p.334)
• You'll read and hear a great deal about the *spiritual* part of our program.(p.366)
• My first *spiritual* experience in A.A. came quite early to me.(p.366)
• The Twelve Steps, which to me are a *spiritual* way of living, soon meant honest thinking, not wishful thinking, open mindedness, a willingness to try and a

faith to accept.(p.381)

• A "*spiritual* experience" to me meant attending meetings, seeing a group of people, all there for the purpose of helping each other; hearing the Twelve Steps and the Twelve Traditions read at a meeting, and hearing the Lord's Prayer, which in an A.A. meeting has such great meaning – "Thy will be done, not mine."(p.381)

• A *spiritual* awakening soon came to mean trying each day to be a little more thoughtful, more considerate, a little more courteous to those with whom I came in contact.(p.381)

• The fact that A.A. is a *spiritual* program didn't scare me or raise any prejudice in my mind.(p.383)

• He asked me if I had any *spiritual* belief, and when I said No, he suggested that I keep an open mind.(p.413)

• My *spiritual* awakening in A.A. finally resulted in my joining a church some years ago.(p.417)

• Sobriety and a plan for living that produces a personality change and a *spiritual* awakening are imperative.(p.459)

• I have come to believe that my illness is *spiritual* as well as physical and mental, and I know that for help in the *spiritual* sphere I have to turn to a Higher Power.(p.473)

• To me, program is *spiritual*.(p.477)

• I suppose I had reached my *spiritual* gutter that night, but I have never had what you could call a real urge to drink again.(p.524)

• Had I been able to explain to a psychiatrist the feeling of futility, loneliness and lack of purpose that had come with my deep sense of personal failure at this second divorce, I seriously doubt that the good doctor could have convinced me that my basic problem was a *spiritual* hunger, but A.A. has shown me this was the truth.(p.546)

• I've had many *spiritual* experiences since I've been in the program, many that I didn't recognize right away, for I'm slow to learn and they take many guises.(p.551)

• II. *Spiritual* Experience(p.563)

• Twelve -- Anonymity is the *spiritual* foundation of all our Traditions, ever reminding us to place principles before personalities.(p.564)

• 5. – Each Alcoholics Anonymous group ought to be a *spiritual* entity having but one primary purpose -- that of carrying its message to the alcoholic who still suffers.(p.565)

• 6. – Problems of money, property, and authority may easily divert us from our primary *spiritual* aim.(p.565)

• We think, therefore, that any considerable property of genuine use to A.A. should be separately incorporated and managed, thus dividing the material from the *spiritual*.(p.565)

• Experience has often warned us that nothing can so surely destroy our *spiritual* heritage as futile disputes over property, money, and authority.(p.566)

• 12. – And finally, we of Alcoholics Anonymous believe that the principle of anonymity has immense *spiritual* significance.(p.567)

• *SPIRITUAL* EXPERIENCE(p.569)

• The terms "*spiritual* experience" and "*spiritual* awakening" are used many times in this book which, upon careful reading, shows that the personality change sufficient to bring about recovery from alcoholism has manifested itself among us in many different forms.(p.569)

• Most of us think this awareness of a Power greater than ourselves is the essence of *spiritual* experience.(p.570)

• Most emphatically we wish to say that any alcoholic capable of honestly facing his problems in the light of our experience can recover, provided he does not close his mind to all *spiritual* concepts.(p.570)

• There is something *spiritual* about an art museum or a symphony, and the Catholic Church approves of our use of them.(p.574)

• There is something *spiritual* about A.A. too, and Catholic participation in it almost invariably results in poor Catholics becoming better Catholics."(p.574)

• This self-insurance has resulted in the restoration of physical, mental and *spiritual* health and self-respect to hundreds of men and women who would be hopelessly down and out without its unique but effective therapy."(p.574)

spirituality

• We can laugh at those who think *spirituality* the way of weakness.(p.68)

• He may tell mother, who has been religious all her life, that she doesn't know what it's all about, and that she had better get his brand of *spirituality* while there is yet time.(p.128)

• I don't think the boys were completely convinced of my personality change, for they fought shy of including my story in the book, so my only contribution to their literary efforts was my firm conviction, being still a theological rebel, that the word God should be qualified with the phrase "as we understand him" -- for that was the only way I could accept *spirituality*.(p.248)

• We find that no one need have difficulty with the *spirituality* of the program.(p.570)

spiritually

• From it stem all forms of spiritual disease, for we have been not only mentally and physically ill, we have been *spiritually* sick.(p.64)

• This was our course: We realized that the people who wronged us were perhaps *spiritually* sick.(p.66)

• Assuming we are *spiritually* fit, we can do all sorts of things alcoholics are not supposed to do.(p.100)

• Both saw that they must keep *spiritually* active.(p.156)

• *Spiritually* . . . I found a Friend who never lets me down and is ever eager to help.(p.303)

• I have been helped morally, *spiritually*, mentally and materially through A.A.(p.430)

• I painfully awakened each time, mentally, physically, and *spiritually* sick.(p.457)

spiritually-minded

• We used to amuse ourselves by cynically dissecting spiritual beliefs and practices when we might have observed that many *spiritually-minded* persons of all races, colors, and creeds were demonstrating a degree of stability, happiness and usefulness which we should have sought ourselves.(p.49)

spite

• In *spite* of the great increase in the size and the span of this Fellowship, at its core it remains simple and personal.(p.xxii)

• He enjoys himself for a few years in *spite* of friendly warnings.(p.37)

• It never occurred to him that perhaps he could not do so, in *spite* of character and standing.(p.39)

• In *spite* of your new-found happiness, there will be ups and downs.(p.117)

• So in *spite* of anything that I might do, I prospered, being one of only two brokers in the rubber center of the world.(p.197)

• All I had left was an iron determination to live my own life in *spite* of the alien world -- and here I was, an inwardly frightened, outwardly defiant woman, who desperately needed a prop to keep going.(p.226)

• Naturally, in *spite* of my good intentions, in *spite* of my protected life behind sanitarium walls, I several times got drunk, and was astounded . . . and badly shaken.(p.227)

• My drinking habits increased in *spite* of my struggle for control.(p.305)

• Thank God that in *spite* of my heavy drinking my mind was clear enough to make a decision then and there.(p.363)

• In *spite* of knowing that my drunkenness was a symptom of the things that were wrong with me, and that I could never drink again, I thought I couldn't yet give it up, although I was going to try.(p.393)

• Strangely enough, right through to the end of my twenty-six years in the Army, I was still being offered very good and important jobs in *spite* of the fact that my superiors must have known that I wasn't thoroughly reliable.(p.519)

splendid

• The story he told is most instructive, for here was a chap absolutely convinced he had to stop drinking, who had no excuse for drinking, who exhibited *splendid* judgment and determination in all his other concerns, yet was flat on his back nevertheless.(p.40)

• We built up a *splendid* life.(p.263)

splinters

• After my last binge I came home and smashed my dining room furniture to *splinters*, kicked out six windows and two balustrades.(p.435)

split

• Would there be schisms which would *split* A.A. apart?(p.xix)

• They had also been periodic big shots who had goofed out repeatedly at the wrong time, and they also knew how to *split* one paper match into three separate matches.(p.245)

• I screamed on the telephone for my mother to get up there; something was going to happen; I didn't know what, but if she didn't get there quick, I'd *split* wide open.(p.338)

splitting

• My personality was stretched almost to *splitting* in the effort; schizophrenia stared me in the face, and one night I was in a suicidal despair.(p.435)

spoil

• You may *spoil* a later opportunity.(p.90)

• But urge them not to be over-anxious, for that might *spoil* matters.(p.91)

• You may *spoil* your chance of being helpful if you do.(p.100)

• Be determined that your husband's drinking is not going to *spoil* your relations with your children or your friends.(p.111)

• This to the end that our great blessings may never *spoil* us; that we shall forever live in thankful contemplation of Him who presides over us all.(p.568)

spoiled

• When we were invited out, our husbands sneaked so many drinks that they *spoiled* the occasion.(p.105)

• All of which could turn out but one thing – a very popular, but *spoiled*, brat.(p.357)

• I was nothing more than a *spoiled*, indulged, and talented brat.(p.418)

spoke

• I could almost hear the sound of the preacher's voice as I sat, on still Sundays, way over there on the hillside; there was that proffered temperance pledge I never signed; my grandfather's good natured contempt of some church folk and their doings; his insistence that the spheres really had their music; but his denial of the preacher's right to tell him how he must listen; his fearlessness as he *spoke* of these things just before he died; these recollections welled up from the past.(p.10)

• The two friends *spoke* of their spiritual experience and told him about the course of action they carried out.(p.157)

• They *spoke* with great freedom from embarrassment, which I could never do, and they seemed very much at ease on all occasions and appeared very healthy.(p.178)

• I was opening up these lots that I *spoke* of.(p.195)

• By the time I was twenty-one I had six years of life in foreign countries, *spoke* three languages fluently, and had attended college for two years.(p.275)

• Perhaps it was He who sent my analyst to a psychiatrist's meeting at which Bill *spoke*.(p.412)

• It was precisely a year before I *spoke* at an A.A. meeting.(p.447)

• Three weeks ago, my phone rang, and a voice I hadn't heard in over twenty-three years *spoke*.(p.462)

• There came a time when she *spoke* to me about it, and I would say that I had a bad cold or that I wasn't feeling well.(p.487)

• The Commanding Officer only *spoke* to me when he wanted to tell me exactly who I was and what I was and how little I counted in the scheme of things and how glad he would be if I went away.(p.520)

• Even at that he *spoke* quite often.(p.520)

spoken

• With few exceptions, our book thus far has *spoken* of men.(p.104)

• Father had never directly *spoken* to me about drinking but he never drank any, so far as I knew.(p.498)

sponsor

• My *sponsor*, Jackie, was one of these.(p.239)

• After being dry two weeks and sticking close to Jackie, all of a sudden I found I had become the *sponsor* of my *sponsor*, for he was suddenly taken drunk.(p.245)

• I'd been dry three weeks, had the wrinkles out and had sobered up my *sponsor* all by myself!(p.246)

• She took me by the hand and introduced me to the girl that I'm very proud to call my *sponsor*.(p.321)

• The reply came, putting me in touch by mail with my *sponsor* in New Delhi.(p.343)

• Following this, I had a short vacation, during which time I read as much literature as my *sponsor* could send me.(p.343)

• My *sponsor* used to say to me, "If I could only paint you a picture of how beautiful life can be without booze . . ."(p.355)

• I attended meetings, I talked to my folks, I talked to younger people they had gotten in contact with to *sponsor* me.(p.430)

• When I first came into A.A., the woman who was my *sponsor* was the first woman I had ever met who admitted that she was an alcoholic.(p.472)

• My *sponsor* say men who talk speak truth.(p.476)

• Get *sponsor* and phone numbers.(p.477)

• She didn't say anything about A.A. or getting me a *sponsor* at that time, but she did ask about Vi, and I told her Vi was working and how she could locate her.(p.494)

• About seven that evening my *sponsor* walked in, Charlie G.(p.494)

• I haven't mentioned it, but Charlie, my *sponsor*,

was white, and when we got our group started we got help from other white groups in Washington.(p.495)
• It's like the fellow who came in A.A., and his *sponsor* said to him, "Listen, buddy, do you believe in a Higher Power?"(p.512)
• I acquired a *sponsor* and began attending meetings, but continued to drink.(p.559)

sponsored
• The A.A. members who *sponsored* me told me in the beginning that I would not only find a way to live without having a drink, but that I would find a way to live without wanting to drink, if I would do these simple things.(p.550)

sponsors
• New programing was beginning to build an audience, but *sponsors* were pretty scarce.(p.360)
• I promised my two *sponsors* that I would attend their meeting the next Tuesday evening.(p.363)

sponsorship
• It was very impressive and I wish that every A.A. could have the benefit of this type of *sponsorship* today.(p.292)

sporting
• I moved in a gay crowd in the various "pubs" and *sporting* clubs.(p.251)

sports
• Father may have laid aside for years all normal activities — clubs, civic duties, *sports*.(p.131)
• In *sports* I made the track and tennis teams; I got along well with the other boys and had a fairly large circle of acquaintances but no intimate friends.(p.240)

spot
• Frequent contact with newcomers and with each other is the bright *spot* of our lives.(p.89)
• You should not hesitate to visit the most sordid *spot* on earth on such an errand.(p.102)
• He and his family can be a bright *spot* in such congregations.(p.132)
• You put me on the *spot* every time you get drunk.(p.147)
• My job was to collect bets and betting-slips in the business section, a lucrative *spot*.(p.251)
• He used to wonder, when he'd *spot* one of my bottles around the house, just how he could have overlooked that particular bottle.(p.325)
• Now I was on the *spot*.(p.366)
• In my drinking days, I found the ideal *spot* for the alcoholic housewife: the neighborhood Laundromat.(p.369)
• After twenty years in prison for murder, he knew A.A. was the *spot* for him . . . if he wanted to stay on the outside.(p.508)
• It wasn't anything strange to me, and I knew if I wanted to stay on the outside, that would be the *spot* for me.(p.510)
• Because as I sat on that bed, I knew that I was in a terrible *spot* and didn't know how to get out of it.(p.515)
• I wandered, craving peace, from one *spot* to another of youthful happy memory, and loathed the man I had become.(p.539)

spots
• For if an alcoholic failed to perfect and enlarge his spiritual life through work and self-sacrifice for others, he could not survive the certain trials and low *spots* ahead.(p.14)
• I saw that will power and self-knowledge would not help in those strange mental blank *spots*.(p.42)
• I returned to my home in Lucknow, India, at the end of November last year from a vacation in one of the most famous beauty *spots* in our country, a mountain resort 6,800 feet up, with a wonderful lake.(p.342)
• Looking back, it is surprising to me now that I managed to keep working and have enough money to squander at the various *spots* in the big city.(p.358)
• I lived in New Orleans where, at that time, cocktail parties, dances and night *spots* were almost the order of the day -- or rather the night.(p.384)
• Our courtship was mainly in bars and night *spots* when my ship was in New York.(p.555)

spotted
• We *spotted* a church in a small town.(p.424)

spouse
• Then, one day in A.A., I was told that I had the lenses in my glasses backwards; "the courage to change" in the Serenity Prayer meant, not that I should change my marriage, but rather that I should change myself and learn to accept my *spouse* as she was.(p.451)

spout
• But, of course, this all went up the *spout* with my increased drinking.(p.182)

spouting
• There was one meeting a week at Bill's home in Brooklyn, and we all took turns there *spouting* off about how we had changed our lives overnight, how many drunks we had saved and straightened out, and last, but not least, how God had touched each of us personally on the shoulder.(p.246)

spray
• You didn't carry a little orchid up the aisle in those days; you carried a great big bouquet, like a funeral *spray*, and you didn't have your picture taken until just before you went to the church.(p.385)

spread
• Early member, she *spread* the word among women in our pioneering period.(p.222)
• From a mere handful in Akron we have *spread* throughout the world.(p.295)

spreads
• As our work *spreads* and our numbers increase, we hope your employees may be put in personal contact with some of us.(p.144)

spree
• After they have succumbed to the desire again, as so many do, and the phenomenon of craving develops, they pass through the well-known stages of a *spree*, emerging remorseful, with a firm resolution not to drink again.(p.xxvii)
• A man of thirty was doing a great deal of *spree* drinking.(p.32)
• Friends who have reasoned with him after a *spree* which has brought him to the point of divorce or bankruptcy are mystified when he walks directly into a saloon.(p.35)
• But even in this type of beginning we are obliged to admit that our justification for a *spree* was insanely insufficient in the light of what always happened.(p.37)
• Wait for the end of the *spree*, or at least for a lucid interval.(p.90)
• Show him the mental twist which leads to the first drink of a *spree*.(p.92)
• But we must try to repair the damage immediately lest we pay the penalty by a *spree*.(p.99)
• But when he gets over the *spree*, he begins to think once more how he can drink moderately next time.(p.109)
• For most alcoholics who are drinking, or who are just getting over a *spree*, a certain amount of physical treatment is desirable, even imperative.(p.142)
• For him, this was the *spree* that ended all sprees.(p.155)
• Coming up to final exams I went on a particularly strenuous *spree*.(p.174)
• My first drinking *spree* was on corn liquor and I was allergic to it, believe me.(p.322)
• Saying these sprees were limited to one a week (they were not), and saying that the average *spree* was ten of these drinks (sometimes more, sometimes less), we come up with the first boring statistic: two-fifty per week out of twelve dollars.(p.397)
• A normal person, hit with adversity, can go on a drinking *spree* and then snap out of it.(p.404)

sprees
• He uses his gifts to build up a bright outlook for his family and himself, and then pulls the structure down on his head by a senseless series of *sprees*.(p.21)
• The inconsistency is made worse by the things he does on his *sprees*.(p.73)
• If he is not interested in your solution, if he expects you to act only as a banker for his financial difficulties or a nurse for his *sprees*, you may have to drop him until he changes his mind.(p.95)
• We began to ask medical advice as the *sprees* got closer together.(p.106)
• Cheerfully see him through more *sprees*.(p.113)
• For him, this was the spree that ended all *sprees*.(p.155)
• He suffered horribly from his *sprees*, but it seemed as if nothing could be done for him.(p.159)
• Saying these *sprees* were limited to one a week (they were not), and saying that the average spree was ten of these drinks (sometimes more, sometimes less), we come up with the first boring statistic: two-fifty per week out of twelve dollars.(p.397)

spring
• This determination bore fruit in the *spring* of 1939 by the publication of this volume.(p.xvii)
• In the *spring* of 1940, John D. Rockefeller, Jr. gave a dinner for many of his friends to which he invited A.A. members to tell their stories.(p.xviii)
• By the following *spring* we were living in our accustomed style.(p.4)
• They will approach still other sick ones and fellowships of Alcoholics Anonymous may *spring* up in each city and hamlet, havens for those who must find a way out.(p.153)
• This went from bad to worse until Sophomore *spring* when, after a prolonged period of drinking, I made up my mind that I could not complete my course, so I packed my grip and went South to spend a month on a large farm owned by a friend of mine.(p.173)
• In the *spring* of 1917, in order to beat being fired from school, I became "patriotic" and joined the Army.(p.241)
• *Spring* came.(p.276)
• In the *spring* of 1939, Bill stopped off in Akron on his way to Detroit on business.(p.281)
• In the *spring* of 1939, the Big Book was printed, and we had two inquiries from the New York office because of a fifteen-minute radio talk that was made.(p.294)
• And then, in the *spring* of 1939, a very remarkable book was rolled off a New York press with the title "Alcoholics Anonymous."(p.307)
• In the very early *spring* of 1944, my frustrated wife couldn't take it any longer.(p.362)
• The following *spring* she left me one day without giving me any idea of where she had gone, hoping this would bring me to my senses.(p.377)

springs
• Above all, he believed he had acquired such a profound knowledge of the inner workings of his mind and its hidden *springs* that relapse was unthinkable.(p.26)
• Many retirees embrace alcoholism while secluded in motor trailers, rest homes, leisure-world bungalows, mountain cabins, or beach cottages, or even in penthouses, on yachts, and inside Palm *Springs* cabanas.(p.329)

sprinkled
• That age of the flapper and the "It" girl, speakeasies and the hip flask, the boyish bob and the drugstore cowboy, John Held Jr. and F. Scott Fitzgerald, all generously *sprinkled* with a patent pseudo-sophistication.(p.304)

sprinkling
• By personal religious affiliation, we include Catholics, Protestants, Jews, Hindus, and a *sprinkling* of Moslems and Buddhists.(p.xx)

sprout
• Seed has started to *sprout* in a new soil, but growth has only begun.(p.117)

sprung
• Already," continues the early text, "twos and threes and fives of us have *sprung* up in other communities."(p.xv)
• Barriers which have *sprung* up between you and your friends will disappear with the growth of sympathetic understanding.(p.115)
• Little clusters of twos and threes and fives of us have *sprung* up in other communities, through contact with our two larger centers.(p.162)

spurs
• He had taken up light work, and he had a safety valve and a pair of *spurs* and the clothes on his back, and that was all.(p.263)

squad
• By the time I figured out what had happened, I saw two flashing red lights atop *squad* cars, sedately coming around the corner.(p.353)

squander
• To the precise extent that we permit these, do we *squander* the hours that might have been worth while.(p.66)
• Looking back, it is surprising to me now that I managed to keep working and have enough money to *squander* at the various spots in the big city.(p.358)

square
• If there is no Al-Anon listing in your local telephone book, you may obtain further information on Al-Anon Family Groups by writing to its World Service Office: Box 182, Madison *Square* Station, New York, NY 10159.(p.121)
• He can scarcely *square* the account in his lifetime.(p.127)
• He will be able to take a position with such a man which is eminently fair and *square*.(p.148)
• He had lived there but a few weeks when he found that the place probably contained more alcoholics per *square* mile than any city in the country.(p.163)
• A *square* from ultra-dry Kansas, I did not taste grog until I had finished college, done a stint on newspapers, married, become a father, and been in studio publicity two years.(p.328)

• Tasting the best of burgundy at a famous restaurant one night, landed me passed out on a park bench in the public *square.*(p.405)

• Once this was in front of the Paramount Theatre in Times *Square.*(p.537)

• Should you be the relative or friend of an alcoholic who shows no immediate interest in A.A., it is suggested that you write the Al-Anon Family Groups, Inc., Box 182, Madison *Square* Station, New York, NY 10159, U.S.A.(p.575)

squarely

• Arrived at this point, we were *squarely* confronted with the question of faith.(p.53)

• He saw that he would have to face his problems *squarely* that God might give him mastery.(p.155)

• The fellowship I found in A.A. enabled me to face my problem honestly and *squarely.*(p.340)

• So I went to my wife and asked her, wasn't there something that she and I could do to somehow get together, and she turned on her heel and looked me *squarely* in the eye, and said, "You don't care anything about my problem," and I could have smacked her, but I said to myself, "Grab on to your serenity!"(p.351)

squawk

• So it doesn't behoove me to *squawk* about it for, after all, nobody ever had to throw me down and pour liquor down my throat.(p.181)

squeezed

• Barleycorn's wringer *squeezed* this author – but he escaped quite whole.(p.432)

squirt

• I didn't feel I could lie in bed and *squirt* the stuff in my veins while my kids and wife stood around watching me, so I kept the drug in my bag and the bag in the car and the car in the garage.(p.442)

St. Helena

• No *St. Helena* for me!(p.4)

St. Petersburg

• While I was in Florida trying to convince my wife with all the A.A. literature that she should come back to me, she went over to her desk and picked up a clipping she had taken from the *St. Petersburg* Times about A.A.(p.366)

St. Thomas

• In his prodigy of service, he was well assisted by Sister Ignatia at *St. Thomas* Hospital in Akron, Ohio, one of the greatest friends our Fellowship will ever know.(p.171)

• There were two women in the *St. Thomas* Hospital at that time in a room.(p.272)

• I knew Doc and Anne were going to be there, and all of them thought it would be good for me, but the first thing I did was to go to *St. Thomas* and try to talk to those women.)(p.272)

St. Vincent

• In my twenties, I found Edna *St. Vincent* Millay's verse:(p.534)

stabbed

• What actually happened was that I had taken a penknife and *stabbed* Vi three times with it.(p.492)

stability

• We used to amuse ourselves by cynically dissecting spiritual beliefs and practices when we might have observed that many spiritually-minded persons of all races, colors, and creeds were demonstrating a degree of *stability,* happiness and usefulness which we should have sought ourselves.(p.49)

• At long last I am doing the kind of work I have always wanted to do, but never had the patience and emotional *stability* to train myself for.(p.284)

• After all, I hadn't started to drink early in life, so I had some *stability* and maturity to guide me for a while.(p.379)

stable

• To all appearance he is a *stable,* well balanced individual.(p.39)

• I wander to a *stable* and drink five bottles of beer.(p.502)

stables

• This was in Virginia, where I had rented a house with *stables* and a swimming pool, and the fall fox hunting had begun.(p.404)

staff

• One of these men, *staff* member of a world-renowned hospital, recently made this statement to some of us: "What you say about the general hopelessness of the average alcoholic's plight is, in my opinion, correct.(p.43)

• In those days, I was doing a *staff* appointment in the army headquarters in New Delhi.(p.343)

• Finally, she asked, "Do you realize he's on the *staff* of this hospital?"(p.445)

• Edward Dowling, S.J., of the Queen's Work *staff* says, "Alcoholics Anonymous is natural; it is natural at the point where nature comes closest to the supernatural, namely in humiliations and in consequent humility.(p.574)

stage

• He may start off as a moderate drinker; he may or may not become a continuous hard drinker; but at some *stage* of his drinking career he begins to lose all control of his liquor consumption, once he starts to drink.(p.21)

• To the outer world he presents his *stage* character.(p.73)

• Don't, at this *stage,* refer to this book, unless he has seen it and wishes to discuss it.(p.92)

• Most of us have entered the final *stage* with its commitment to health resorts, sanitariums, hospitals, and jails.(p.107)

• If your husband is otherwise a normal individual, your chances are good at this *stage.*(p.113)

• At that particular *stage,* I lost interest in it, sold the option for $5,000 and forgot the whole deal.(p.198)

• I arrived at the *stage* where I couldn't quite make it to the office some mornings.(p.299)

• Many women who have reached the *stage* that I had reached in my drinking have lost husbands, children, homes, everything they hold dear.(p.323)

• I reached a *stage* where I couldn't go into my apartment without a drink.(p.324)

• It was at this *stage* of my life that resentments came in.(p.376)

• At this *stage,* I began a daily mental routine.(p.408)

• Shakespeare said, "All the world's a *stage,* all the men and women merely players."(p.449)

• Depending on the *stage* of drunkenness, eventually I either fought or went to sleep.(p.537)

stages

• After they have succumbed to the desire again, as so many do, and the phenomenon of craving develops, they pass through the well-known *stages* of a spree, emerging remorseful, with a firm resolution not to drink again.(p.xxvii)

• With the alcoholic, they could only give temporary relief and in the last *stages* not even that.(p.307)

• Among today's incoming A.A. members, many have never reached the advanced *stages* of alcoholism, though, given time, all might have.(p.315)

• It started out as a good marriage, but it deteriorated over the years as she progressed through the various *stages* of qualifying for Al-Anon.(p.439)

• And as her disease was reaching the terminal *stages,* she was screaming, "You hate me!(p.439)

staggered

• One Saturday noon I *staggered* home with every intention of showing her.(p.362)

• I *staggered* to the bathroom.(p.498)

• I *staggered* home next morning.(p.510)

• And having sung that phrase, I'd chuckle with amusement, turning into irony turning into self-contempt turning into self-pity, at the sad fate of Bob, that wonderful, poor little motherless boy who was so smart in school and who grew up to accept responsibility so early and so fast and who *staggered* under his burdens without a whimper until the time came when he thought he was too good for this world and so he ought to be out of it.(p.532)

stairs

• I offered them a drink, and they came to the bottom of the *stairs* and the good woman fainted, just looking at me.(p.205)

• He was coming, on his hands and knees, up the *stairs.*(p.263)

• Then my father fell down a flight of *stairs* on one of his lost weekends, at the peak of his career, and died.(p.370)

• So when he came for me, as he walked down the *stairs,* I could see him through the bars, and he was signing for me; I looked at him and said, "Don't you sign anything in this place!"(p.391)

stake

• Sitting in a Second Avenue bar, accepting drinks from anyone who offered, after my small *stake* was gone; or sitting at home alone, with the inevitable glass in my hand, I would remember, and remembering, I would drink faster, seeking speedy oblivion.(p.225)

• With a good *stake* I sailed for New York.(p.251)

• I soon ran through my *stake.*(p.251)

stakes

• To wear expensive clothes, to have bartenders know what to serve me before I ordered, to be recognized by headwaiters and shown to the best table, to play gin rummy for high *stakes* with the insouciance of a riverboat gambler -- these were the enduring values in life, I thought.(p.556)

stand

• If any feel that as psychiatrists directing a hospital for alcoholics we appear somewhat sentimental, let them *stand* with us a while on the firing line, see the tragedies, the despairing wives, the little children; let the solving of these problems become a part of their daily work, and even of their sleeping moments, and the most cynical will not wonder that we have accepted and encouraged this movement.(p.xxvi)

• After consulting with his wife and partner he came to the conclusion that it was better to take those risks than to *stand* before his Creator guilty of such ruinous slander.(p.80)

• As God's people we *stand* on our feet; we don't crawl before anyone.(p.83)

• Drinkers will not *stand* for it.(p.103)

• There were times when I got to drinking, and I had been warned by Firestone that they wouldn't *stand* for this much longer, so, clearly, they were conscious of the fact that I drank too much and too often.(p.204)

• My practice had advanced to the point where it could *stand* a lot of abuse and it got it.(p.214)

• I wanted to learn to *stand* on my own feet, not to change one prop for another, and an intangible and dubious one at that.(p.227)

• I couldn't *stand* the pace.(p.254)

• When we closed the meeting with the Lord's Prayer, Russ said, "Mother, help me *stand.*"(p.270)

• When I finally returned to Detroit to find work and to learn to *stand* on my own feet, the ball was already rolling, however slowly.(p.282)

• It was February with snow and ice on the ground and I had a four blocks walk to the nearest cab *stand,* but I made it.(p.288)

• If I live to be a hundred, it will always *stand* out in my mind.(p.292)

• Other days, I had to miss work because I was still too drunk to *stand* up.(p.318)

• How did you ever *stand* it?"(p.322)

• And I put a Big Book by my night *stand,* and I put a "Twelve Steps and Twelve Tradition" in my locker at the hospital, and I got books by Emmet Fox, and I got books by God-knows-who, and I got to reading all these things.(p.348)

• I put my poor mother and father through agonies but, finally, I couldn't *stand* living with them and having them watch everything I did.(p.386)

• I could not identify myself with the people with whom I found myself and there was no understanding, and I can't *stand* confinement anyhow.(p.387)

• Of course, an inmate must begin living the A.A. way "inside," if he is to *stand* a chance "outside."(p.458)

• (Two large red A's *stand* out in my memory.)(p.460)

• I cannot *stand* it.(p.501)

• I will not *stand* for it.(p.505)

• I started to cross out that last sentence, but decided to let it *stand.*(p.536)

• I have had the joy of seeing many a human being, down and out, learn to *stand* straight again, and to proceed under his own power to happiness in life.(p.541)

• Through my efforts to get down to "causes and conditions," I *stand* convinced that my emotional illness has been present from my earliest recollection.(p.544)

• If we do not do so, we shall *stand* convicted of emotional sterility and of having lost the faith that moves mountains, without which medicine can do little."(p.571)

standard

• Of course, we all fall much below this *standard* many times.(p.99)

• The general moral *standard* was, as I recall it, far above the average.(p.171)

• I certainly was, as far as my living *standard* was concerned.(p.356)

• Evening cocktails were as *standard* as morning coffee, and I suppose my average daily consumption ran a little more or less than a pint.(p.433)

standards

• What with our ultra-modern *standards,* our scientific approach to everything, we are perhaps not well equipped to apply the powers of good that lie outside our synthetic knowledge.(p.xxv)

• I was up to international *standards* in one particular game, and that again covered quite a lot of my sins.(p.519)

standing

• Business and professional men have regained

their *standing*.(p.15)
• It never occurred to him that perhaps he could not do so, in spite of character and *standing*.(p.39)
• Sometimes the man we are calling upon admits his own fault, so feuds of years' *standing* melt away in an hour.(p.78)
• It was the usual situation: home in jeopardy, wife ill, children distracted, bills in arrears and *standing* damaged.(p.155)
• Coming out of a pub near the Cunard pier I saw the Lusitania *standing* out in the middle of the Mersey.(p.252)
• How can a person with a fine family, an attractive home, an excellent position and high *standing* in an important city become an alcoholic?(p.373)
• As I later found out through Alcoholics Anonymous, alcohol is no respecter of economic status, social and business *standing* or intelligence.(p.373)
• I achieved recognized and national *standing* in my profession, as well as becoming a director in many important institutions having to do with the civic life of a large city.(p.374)
• My financial *standing* had not been impaired.(p.379)
• *Standing* there was a gray haired man – tall, trim and in uniform.(p.422)
• I don't know if it's force of habit or something else that keeps them in one place, but I do know that in A.A. there is much work to do, and none of us can do it *standing* still.(p.529)

standpoint

• From a business *standpoint*, his trip came off badly.(p.153)
• It was repulsive to me from every *standpoint*.(p.195)
• From a physical *standpoint*, I gained sixteen pounds in the first two months I was off liquor.(p.303)
• From a domestic *standpoint*, we really have a home now.(p.303)
• From a monetary *standpoint* . . . in the past few years, I have reduced my reckless debts to almost nothing, and have had money to get along on comfortably.(p.303)
• In my stupid way I went up to see him with the idea in the back of my mind that I would investigate Alcoholics Anonymous from a medical *standpoint*.(p.346)

stands

• In this third edition, Part I ("Pioneers of A.A.") *stands* unchanged.(p.xii)
• I pray that you now remove from me every single defect of character which *stands* in the way of my usefulness to you and my fellows.(p.76)
• Though he is now a most effective member of Alcoholics Anonymous, he still smokes and drinks coffee, but neither his wife or anyone else *stands* in judgment.(p.135)
• I refused to join any fraternity, as I wanted to be a free lance, and that year my drinking was confined to one-night *stands*, once or twice a week.(p.241)
• Then broke again, hiding out in cheap hotels all over the country, one night jail *stands* here and there, and always that horrible feeling "What's the use -- nothing is worth while."(p.244)
• My binges were one-night *stands* only.(p.432)

star

• I was assigned to keep media guests happy at a Halloween party given by a major *star* in his plush home.(p.328)
• I was one of the *star* singers in the choir and one of the leading violins in the orchestra.(p.517)
• So did the waterboy on the high school football team attempt to revenge himself on the big brother who was the *star* quarterback; for I was the waterboy and my brother was the *star* quarterback, innocent of everything except the fact that he was a *star* quarterback.(p.537)
• I stumbled agonizedly past the theatre where in years gone by a great *star* had played my play.(p.540)

stare

• They would all *stare* at me and whisper!(p.413)

stared

• Two days later, a future fellow of Alcoholics Anonymous *stared* glassily at the strangers beside his bed.(p.157)
• My personality was stretched almost to splitting in the effort; schizophrenia *stared* me in the face, and one night I was in a suicidal despair.(p.435)

staring

• I was *staring* at an inch of the tape which bore the inscription XYZ-32.(p.4)
• In any case I must get out of here before I let slip my abysmal ignorance of how I came to be here, and she realized that I was stark, *staring* mad.(p.223)

stark

• These *stark* and ugly facts have been confirmed by legions of alcoholics throughout history.(p.24)
• In any case I must get out of here before I let slip my abysmal ignorance of how I came to be here, and she realized that I was *stark*, staring mad.(p.223)

starlit

• Yet, in other moments, we found ourselves thinking, when enchanted by a *starlit* night, "Who, then, made all this?"(p.46)

starry-eyed

• He had that *starry-eyed* look.(p.9)

stars

• *STARS* DON'T FALL(p.400)
• When the overcast lifted, the *stars* were there as before.(p.400)

start

• The broker had gone to Akron on a business venture which had collapsed, leaving him greatly in fear that he might *start* drinking again.(p.xvi)
• All these, and many others, have one symptom in common: they cannot *start* drinking without developing the phenomenon of craving.(p.xxviii)
• I saw that growth could *start* from that point.(p.12)
• He may *start* off as a moderate drinker; he may or may not become a continuous hard drinker; but at some stage of his drinking career he begins to lose all control of his liquor consumption, once he starts to drink.(p.21)
• At the *start*, this was all we needed to commence spiritual growth, to effect our first conscious relation with God as we understood Him.(p.47)
• With all the earnestness at our command, we beg of you to be fearless and thorough from the very *start*.(p.58)
• He saw that he had to place the outcome in God's hands or he would soon *start* drinking again, and all would be lost anyhow.(p.80)
• Don't *start* out as an evangelist or reformer.(p.89)
• But be sure you are on solid spiritual ground before you *start* and that your motive in going is thoroughly good.(p.102)
• Don't *start* to withdraw again just because your friends drink liquor.(p.102)
• But sometimes you must *start* life anew.(p.114)
• Perhaps your husband will make a fair *start* on the new basis, but just as things are going beautifully he dismays you by coming home drunk.(p.120)
• Let families realize, as they *start* their journey, that all will not be fair weather.(p.122)
• If he feels free to discuss his problems with you, if he knows you understand and will not be upset by anything he wishes to say, he will probably be off to a fast *start*.(p.144)
• Can you charge this off as you would a bad account and *start* fresh with him?(p.145)
• Never once in my life have I had a headache, which fact leads me to believe that I was an alcoholic almost from the *start*.(p.172)
• Every time I'd *start* thinking about drinking, I would think of the long, dry years ahead without having a drink; but this idea of twenty-four hours, that it was up to me from then on, was a lot of help.(p.188)
• I can remember well thinking that I would quit drinking, really go to work hard, apply myself eight hours a day, five days a week, make a lot of money, and then I could *start* drinking again.(p.199)
• I had a genuine release right from the *start*.(p.219)
• How it finally broke a Southerner's obstinacy and destined this salesman to *start* A.A. at Philadelphia.(p.238)
• As soon as I could get up and walk I started to drink again and kept it up until my friend of the hospital, who, in his first try at the new way of life had stubbed his toe in Chicago but had come back to the town to take counsel and make a new *start*, picked me up and got me into a hospital.(p.258)
• We'd *start* out on the craziest trips.(p.264)
• Jack said, "Now you *start* and go to these meetings, and then you'll find out all about it."(p.268)
• He might have handed me fifty dollars and said that I ought to pull myself together and make a new *start*.(p.278)
• I would make a fresh *start* somewhere else.(p.281)
• The A.A. program showed me the way to come down to earth, *start* from the bottom and work up.(p.284)
• In the long ago past I used to *start* at the top as president or treasurer and end up with the sheriff breathing down my neck.(p.284)
• I am very apt to get into quite an uproar for a day or two before starting, but I do *start*, and once started, I have a swell time.(p.285)
• This would get me feeling fit, and then I would *start* for home and fireside, thirteen miles away.(p.299)
• I would not *start* that.(p.333)
• So I went to her and said, "There's only one thing I want in my whole life, and I don't want any commendation; I don't want any credit; I don't want anything from you or Janey for the rest of your life except one thing; and that is, the opportunity to do anything you want always, and I would like to *start* off by doing the dishes."(p.351)
• I entered the house, opened a new bottle of whiskey and sat down to drink myself into the right frame of mind to get in my car, *start* the motor and close the garage door behind me.(p.363)
• My drinking did not *start* until after I was thirty-five, and a fairly successful career had been established.(p.374)
• From the *start* I liked everything about the A.A. program.(p.380)
• To most of us, making amends will take the rest of our lives, but we can *start* immediately.(p.381)
• She still had her husband, her home, and a chance to help *start* A.A. in Texas.(p.384)
• For an estimate of salary from the twenty-one a month to *start* with, to over $400 per month upon my retirement after twenty years in the Navy, I believe that an average income of $2,000 a year over this period is low, but as I stated earlier, an underestimate is best.(p.399)
• But whereas my horse was always equipped with a flask, I merely endured the fox hunting so I could *start* drinking at lunch time.(p.404)
• Most important, A.A. has enabled me to go back and *start* growing up all over again in all areas of my life.(p.420)
• Mom has said the only requisite to *start* is willingness.(p.430)
• Right from the *start*, I felt that they weren't doing anything for me, but they sure were helping Max.(p.447)
• The more I focus my mind on its defects – late *start*, long drunkalogues, cigarette smoke – the worse the meeting becomes.(p.451)
• Love has no words to spell or lines to *start* and stop.(p.474)
• *Start* group on reservation and carry message, help *start* other groups all over Maritimes and New England.(p.476)
• Men are supposed to be tough and rugged to *start* with, but if a woman becomes that way, it is pretty hard to get back the niceties of womanhood.(p.480)
• But I can remember in post graduate days, and during interneship, that very often I'd go to a patient's bed and *start* a process of elimination and then, very often, I'd wind up guessing.(p.485)
• I *start* to clean up the debris.(p.502)
• At first, like everybody else, I could keep control when I drank, but if I did *start* to drink, even in those days, I was always one of the last to leave the party.(p.518)
• I had no work to do and I was at an age where it seemed too late to *start* anything new.(p.522)

started

• New groups *started* up and it was found, to the astonishment of everyone, that A.A.'s message could be transmitted in the mail as well as by word of mouth.(p.xviii)
• We went at once to the country, my wife to applaud while I *started* out to overtake Walter Hagen.(p.3)
• If you ask him why he *started* on that last bender, the chances are he will offer you any one of a hundred alibis.(p.23)
• How often have some of us begun to drink in this nonchalant way, and after the third or fourth, pounded on the bar and said to ourselves, "For God's sake, how did I ever get *started* again?"(p.24)
• Once he *started*, he had no control whatever.(p.32)
• Thus *started* one more journey to the asylum for Jim.(p.36)
• Therefore, we *started* upon a personal inventory.(p.64)
• Seed has *started* to sprout in a new soil, but growth has only begun.(p.117)
• Tuesday I *started* in the morning, getting well organized by noon.(p.179)
• Then Prohibition came into effect, and the facts that the stuff obtainable was so horrible and sometimes deadly, and that I had married and had a job which I had to look after, helped me for a period of some three or four years, although I would get drunk every time I could get hold of enough to drink to get *started*.(p.183)
• I had run into him, and he looked real prosperous; his face and eyes looked clear and he *started* to com-

pliment me on my good front and how well I looked, and I said, "I haven't had a drink for nine months."(p.201)
• And I continued to drink, on and off then, until every dollar I had in the world was gone again and I was right back living at my sister's, getting my cigarettes by calling her grocer and telling him to put in a couple of cartons with her order, exactly as I had before I *started* to work at Max's.(p.202)
• So I *started* to investigate Science through some friends of mine who were Readers in the church.(p.202)
• Then, I *started* to miss meetings because it was raining or snowing or something else.(p.203)
• Then I *started* drinking again, with possibly a little more restraint, periods a little bit longer than they had been before, but substantially the same pattern.(p.203)
• Then he *started* to talk to me about his drinking experiences, what his drinking had cost him, how much he had drunk and where, things like that, and I remember I was quite bored because I had never seen the guy before and had no interest at all in what, where and when he drank.(p.208)
• I married when I was twenty-eight years old, and *started* in law school after I was married.(p.212)
• Cold chills *started* chasing up and down my spine; my teeth were chattering; my hands were shaking so I tucked them under me to keep them from flying away.(p.222)
• That went on for two more months before I landed in a hospital and *started* my slow fight back to normalcy.(p.224)
• But I hardly tasted anything for two years and *started* in business for myself, founding a mattress factory which is today an important industrial enterprise in our city.(p.232)
• This last real merry-go-round had *started* the day before Christmas and I had really accomplished a lot in those fourteen days.(p.238)
• Evidently I had gone right back to the movie with a bottle, stayed there several hours and *started* home with no recollection of what had happened.(p.244)
• When I *started* to tell the boys how we did it in New York and all about the spiritual part of the program, I found they would not believe me unless I was practicing what I preached.(p.249)
• My wife came over from Scotland and we *started* housekeeping in a large Ohio city.(p.254)
• Loading a car with good old books to sell to collectors, librarians, universities and historical societies, I *started* out to travel the country.(p.255)
• As soon as I could get up and walk I *started* to drink again and kept it up until my friend of the hospital, who, in his first try at the new way of life had stubbed his toe in Chicago but had come back to the town to take counsel and make a new start, picked me up and got me into a hospital.(p.258)
• That's when I *started* drinking.(p.264)
• We always *started* out on the Saturday before Labor Day.(p.264)
• He used to drink, and then he found something that *started* up in Akron that helped him quit drinking."(p.267)
• Men from A.A. *started* coming out to the house the next day.(p.268)
• I sat down on the side of one of their beds, and I *started* to weep, and I couldn't stop, and I was so startled, and I apologized again and again for it.(p.272)
• So he *started* A.A. in Detroit.(p.275)
• I am very apt to get into quite an uproar for a day or two before starting, but I do start, and once *started*, I have a swell time.(p.285)
• Then I *started* traveling, with the United States and Canada as my territory, and with so much freedom and with an unlimited expense account, I was soon drinking every night and kidding myself that it was all part of the job.(p.287)
• One of them was that I would try to get a group *started* in Chicago; the second was that I would have to return to Akron to attend meetings at least every two months until I did get a group *started* in Chicago; third, I decided I must place this program above everything else, even my family, because if I did not maintain my sobriety I would lose my family anyway.(p.292)
• The next day I went back to Chicago and *started* a vigorous campaign among my so-called friends or drinking companions.(p.293)
• Three years after I *started* on my drinking career, I lost my first job.(p.298)
• He told me that eventually he hoped such a group would develop in the Chicago area, but that so far this had not been *started*.(p.309)
• I *started* drinking about age thirteen.(p.317)
• Next, I was sent to Arizona, where my drinking picked up some more, and I *started* having blackouts, and I was thrown in jail for speeding and drunken driving.(p.318)
• I began taking drinks in the morning to get *started*.(p.318)
• I *started* to take A.A. seriously, and A.A. gave me a new way of life.(p.320)
• I *started* my drinking nearly thirty years ago – right after I was married.(p.322)
• I really *started* drinking with a bang.(p.323)
• I'd get so fed up with drinking all alone and bearing the burden of guilt all by myself, that I'd egg him on to drink, to get *started* again.(p.325)
• And then I'd fight with him because he had *started*!(p.325)
• My drinking career *started* late.(p.328)
• Since I *started* out eager for early-day efforts, that meant guzzling before noon.(p.331)
• But the percentages *started* tobogganing, and it was often a shock to read over some of the pages when sober.(p.331)
• I don't believe, when I *started*, that I even had in mind the thought that I was drinking.(p.336)
• The only incentive that I had, toward the end, for getting dressed in the morning was to get out and get supplies to help me get my day *started*.(p.336)
• But the only thing that got *started* was my drinking.(p.336)
• I should have realized that alcohol was getting hold of me when I *started* to become secretive in my drinking.(p.336)
• So when the children were in school from nine to three, I *started* up a nice little business and was fairly successful in it.(p.339)
• It *started* when I joined a few of the men for cocktails before the noonday Rotary luncheon.(p.360)
• After that came marriage, getting *started* in business, and a family.(p.373)
• After all, I hadn't *started* to drink early in life, so I had some stability and maturity to guide me for a while.(p.379)
• I didn't realize I would find so much more, but a new and different outlook on life *started* opening up almost immediately.(p.383)
• I got right into the car and they drove me over, and just as soon as I got to the church they *started* the wedding.(p.385)
• As I *started* down the aisle, that bourbon went right through me.(p.385)
• I really *started* drinking then.(p.386)
• So I got a half pint and at midnight that night, I called the number I had been given, but the man who had *started* the group was in the hospital so I didn't know what to do.(p.393)
• I displayed alcoholic tendencies actually from the age of fourteen, when I *started* to steal wine from the family jug, siphoning it off one drink at a time so it wouldn't be missed, not drinking it immediately, but saving it until about a pint was accumulated, so that I could get drunk.(p.397)
• Before I *started* to drink seriously, I tried a couple of other escapes.(p.401)
• This was where I *started* my first drinking lessons.(p.402)
• Oddly enough, the dentist who *started* A.A. in Amarillo, Tex., benevolently arranged my admission to dental college.(p.419)
• We *started* to light matches to see, but the draft blew them out.(p.424)
• It solved their problems and they *started* living a sane life again.(p.427)
• Slowly a pile of pineapples *started* to build up on the table.(p.427)
• I swung, I swore, I *started* throwing beer cans at the advancing hordes of pineapple faces.(p.427)
• It *started* out as a good marriage, but it deteriorated over the years as she progressed through the various stages of qualifying for Al-Anon.(p.439)
• So I immediately *started* taking and shooting pep pills.(p.442)
• I *started* going to A.A. in prison at the group's next meeting.(p.461)
• I *started* drinking socially and at parties and proms when I was about twenty years old.(p.464)
• My pattern of drinking at that time had reached the point where once I really *started*, I would retire to my bed and drink myself into oblivion.(p.466)
• So we turned around and *started* back to Washington.(p.467)
• I went out to a restaurant, found a booth way back in the rear, and *started* drinking.(p.467)
• And then I went back home to live with my parents, and the merry-go-round *started* again -- only this time I didn't have to worry about waking up behind bars in a psychiatric ward.(p.468)
• Instead, I *started* going to a nice private sanitarium which, after the first visit, turned out to be more like a country club than anything else.(p.468)
• At that time I *started* school and that's how I got rid of the curls.(p.483)
• This was around 1935, and it was about this time that I actually *started* drinking.(p.486)
• I had my own medical practice in Washington at that time, but the practice slackened and the mail order business *started* to fall off.(p.486)
• But when things became crucial, everything *started* going haywire and I *started* going haywire with them.(p.486)
• I don't think I actually *started* to drink pathologically until approximately 1935.(p.487)
• I think that was basically the thing that *started* me drinking in 1935.(p.487)
• I *started* drinking alone then.(p.487)
• I *started* inquiring where I could get a drink and, of course, I found that it wasn't hard.(p.490)
• I was there about three weeks, and then I got restless and *started* to tramp across the country, here and there, until I finally wound up in Pennsylvania, in a steel mill.(p.492)
• Anyhow, he *started* talking about himself.(p.494)
• He *started* telling me how much trouble he had, and I said to myself, "I wonder why this guy is telling me all his troubles.(p.494)
• But, finally, we got one or two to come in and stick and from there, of course, we *started* to grow.(p.495)
• I haven't mentioned it, but Charlie, my sponsor, was white, and when we got our group *started* we got help from other white groups in Washington.(p.495)
• If I don't get *started* soon, I won't have time to finish.(p.499)
• It *started* July 23.(p.508)
• However, before the meeting got *started*, a group from the outside came in unexpectedly.(p.509)
• I *started* prowling around with a couple of these A.A. boys, which kept me pretty busy and kept my mind off of down town.(p.511)
• I *started* drinking rather early, at the age of sixteen.(p.512)
• But as soon as I got out on my own in France, I *started* drinking.(p.518)
• Then I was sent out to India and from then on drinking just increased and increased, and I *started* having two or three day spells instead of just the ordinary concentrated one day.(p.519)
• Then a change in management took place in the regiment and the new O.C. didn't like me very much and I didn't like him, and he *started* to lie in wait for me.(p.519)
• As I say, this specialist put a scare in me for about a fortnight or three weeks, then I *started* my last bout which went on and off for about three months.(p.523)
• Once I *started* drinking, I didn't care that the rent wasn't paid, or that there was no food in the house, or that my boys needed shoes.(p.527)
• When my thirty days were up, I *started* back on my rounds.(p.528)
• The pressures had *started* long ago.(p.533)
• I *started* to cross out that last sentence, but decided to let it stand.(p.536)
• I went over and met him, and we two *started* the group up again.(p.541)
• I knew it didn't make any difference where I *started*, the inevitable end would be skid row.(p.548)

starting

• Simply because it is impossible to explain what we see, feel, direct, and use, without a reasonable assumption as a *starting* point.(p.48)
• *Starting* from a speck on the domestic horizon, great thunderclouds of dispute may gather.(p.117)
• It took three-quarters of an hour and two changes to get there – back to my *starting* point.(p.223)
• I remember *starting* to city school, coming from a country school, and wanting so very, very much to be like the other girls and trying flour on my face for powder because I wasn't able to have any real powder.(p.261)
• Out of this maelstrom just two coherent thoughts came to the surface; one, a drink would mean homelessness and death; two, I could no longer relieve the pressure of fear by *starting* home, as was once my habitual solution to this problem, because I no longer had a home.(p.279)
• I am very apt to get into quite an uproar for a day or two before *starting*, but I do start, and once started, I have a swell time.(p.285)
• After being fired, I lined up with a new finance company that was just *starting* in business, and took the

position of business promotion man, contacting automobile dealers.(p.300)
• Shortly after I was *starting* to work on the program I realized that I was not a good father; I wasn't a good husband, but, oh, I was a good provider.(p.351)
• Eighteen will be used as the *starting* point, because my drinking before was limited by age, the law, and money.(p.397)

startled

• He *startled* me by informing me that he was an alcoholic, that he had found a way which so far enabled him to live without taking a drink, and that the main idea was to find a way how not to take that first drink.(p.218)
• I was *startled* to learn he had only been off the booze a month or so himself when he brought me the message!(p.245)
• I sat down on the side of one of their beds, and I started to weep, and I couldn't stop, and I was so *startled*, and I apologized again and again for it.(p.272)
• Since it was wartime, I explained to the somewhat *startled* shopkeeper that I had many friends in the service whom I was remembering with a watch.(p.532)

starts

• He may start off as a moderate drinker; he may or may not become a continuous hard drinker; but at some stage of his drinking career he begins to lose all control of his liquor consumption, once he *starts* to drink.(p.21)

starving

• You have been *starving* for his companionship, yet he spends long hours helping other men and their families.(p.119)

state

• We, of Alcoholics Anonymous, are more than one hundred men and women who have recovered from a seemingly hopeless *state* of mind and body.(p.xiii)
• At a certain point in the drinking of every alcoholic, he passes into a *state* where the most powerful desire to stop drinking is of absolutely no avail.(p.24)
• I have never seen one single case recover, where that *state* of mind existed to the extent that it does in you."(p.27)
• It finally beat us into a *state* of reasonableness.(p.48)
• What a *state* of mental goose-flesh that used to bring on!(p.54)
• He is like the retired business man who lolls in the Florida sunshine in the winter complaining of the sad *state* of the nation; the minister who sighs over the sins of the twentieth century; politicians and reformers who are sure all would be Utopia if the rest of the world would only behave; the outlaw safe cracker who thinks society has wronged him; and the alcoholic who has lost all and is locked up.(p.61)
• In that *state*, the wrong-doing of others, fancied or real, had power to actually kill.(p.66)
• We try not to indulge in cynicism over the *state* of the nations, nor do we carry the world's troubles on our shoulders.(p.132)
• *State* that you know about his drinking, and that it must stop.(p.141)
• There was much talk about the mental *state* preceding the first drink.(p.157)
• No beer or liquor was sold in the neighborhood, except at the *State* liquor agency where perhaps one might procure a pint if he could convince the agent that he really needed it.(p.171)
• My whole life seemed to be centered around doing what I wanted to do, without regard for the rights, wishes, or privileges of anyone else; a *state* of mind which became more and more predominant as the years passed.(p.172)
• This continued until I enrolled in our *state* university and, at the end of four years, I realized that I was a drunk.(p.183)
• This experience sent me to law school where I went at night and which course I completed in less than three years, taking the highest *state* bar examinations and passing them.(p.212)
• The mental *state* of the sick alcoholic is beyond description.(p.244)
• I had been drinking heavily from one *state* of semicoma to another and it was several days before I got "defogged," but subconsciously I was in earnest about wanting to quit liquor forever.(p.258)
• I lived through a week of the fidgets because I had agreed to address a group of alcoholic inmates in one of our *state* mental hospitals.(p.283)
• My wife accompanied me on my visit and the doctor really told me some things that in my *state* of jitters nearly knocked me out of the chair.(p.302)
• I am a physician, licensed to practice in a western *state*.(p.345)
• The second way in which, perhaps, I differ from some other alcoholics is this; many alcoholics *state* that they didn't particularly like the taste of alcohol, but that they liked the effect.(p.345)
• Can you picture two girls hitchhiking their way to Las Vegas from Washington *State*?(p.354)
• Within a few months, I was admitted to a *state* hospital for the mentally ill.(p.370)
• By the time all this was over, I was really in a terrific *state*, and my father taking in things said, "Miss Esther is about to faint.(p.385)
• Because of this *state* of confusion and frustration I had hysterics on the seventeenth day for the first and only time in my life.(p.387)
• Was my mental *state* more serious than he said?(p.406)
• Awarded a scholarship to a famous old Eastern college, I began to drink at the end of my freshman year, and by junior year, I had to transfer to an easier *state* university to keep my grades up.(p.419)
• (I am pleased to *state*, however, that I had gone to only a very few A.A. meetings before I was able to make a really beautiful pair of moccasins – and half a wallet.(p.445)
• In a prison in my native *state*, I spent eleven months in solitary confinement, bouncing in and out of the "hole" (a bare concrete-and-steel cubicle) about five times during those eleven months.(p.459)
• I left California and came back to my native *state*.(p.460)
• The doctor, apparently realizing that one thing that I certainly needed was sleep, left a bottle of sleeping pills there and in my drunken *state* I took them all, instead of the one or two he had prescribed.(p.465)
• It was obvious even to me, in my drunken *state*, that I wasn't wanted.(p.466)
• Met father (Tall Man) at fork in road – one way to reservation, other way to *State* of Maine.(p.475)
• The *State* was different, but I wasn't .(p.490)
• Her brother had been a drinker and had died in a *State* Hospital for the insane.(p.498)
• But if I came back in the usual *state*, then I'd have to go off for good the next day.(p.523)
• He said if I came back again, they would send me to the *state* hospital.(p.528)
• To my way of thinking, that is a definition of alcoholism; a *state* of being in which the emotions have failed to grow to the stature of the intellect.(p.535)
• Following are excerpts from the comments of doctors present at the annual meeting of the Medical Society of the *State* of New York where a paper on A.A. was read:(p.571)

state-wide

• It is going strong still, these eight years later, and some of its members have been of great influence for good in *state-wide* A.A. work.(p.541)

state's

• Shortly thereafter, I was selected, with eight other inmates out of the 10,000 in the *state's* prisons at that time, to attend a school designed to take former "management problems" like me and convert them into paracounselors.(p.462)

stated

• This was the substance of A.A.'s Twelve Traditions, which are *stated* in full on page 564 of this book.(p.xix)
• Following his physical rehabilitation, he had a talk with me in which he frankly *stated* he thought the treatment a waste of effort, unless I could assure him, which no one ever had, that in the future he would have the "will power" to resist the impulse to drink.(p.xxix)
• It is also *stated* that we will never be able to figure out how much we have spent on alcohol.(p.396)
• For an estimate of salary from the twenty-one a month to start with, to over $400 per month upon my retirement after twenty years in the Navy, I believe that an average income of $2,000 a year over this period is low, but as I *stated* earlier, an underestimate is best.(p.399)
• Then too, we view with much concern those A.A. treasuries which continue, beyond prudent reserves, to accumulate funds for no *stated* A.A. purpose.(p.566)

statement

• The physician who at our request, gave us this letter, has been kind enough to enlarge upon his views in another *statement* which follows.(p.xxiv)
• In this *statement* he confirms what we who have suffered alcoholic torture must believe – that the body of the alcoholic is quite as abnormal as his mind.(p.xxiv)
• That *statement* hit me hard.(p.12)
• One of these men, staff member of a world-renowned hospital, recently made this *statement* to some of us: "What you say about the general hopelessness of the average alcoholic's plight is, in my opinion, correct.(p.43)
• How could he possibly make a public *statement* exonerating his rival?(p.80)
• I'm so grateful for both the program and the people in it that I still want to go, and then probably the most wonderful thing that I learned from the program – I've seen this in the 'A.A. Grapevine' a lot of times, and I've had people say it to me personally, and I've heard people get up in meetings and make the same *statement*: The *statement* is, "I came into A.A. solely for the purpose of sobriety, but it has been through A.A. that I have found God."(p.192)
• On that *statement* and the fact that I had been sober for ninety days, he gave me a job selling lots in an allotment he had.(p.200)
• One evening, the book, after checking up, was very definitely in the red for plenty through a piece of studied carelessness on my part, and my boss, very shrewd and able, fired me with a parting *statement* to the effect that once was enough.(p.251)
• These last eighteen years have been the happiest of my life, trite though that *statement* may seem.(p.295)
• I don't mean that in any sense as a derogatory *statement* about psychotherapy; it's a great tool, not too potent, but a great tool.(p.349)
• I knew he was right, except for that last *statement*.(p.371)
• A few times at meetings, I have heard this *statement*: "Members of A.A. have paid the highest initiation fee of any club members in the world."(p.396)
• The *statement* fascinates me because of its simple verity.(p.396)

states

• Groups are to be found in each of the United *States* and all of the provinces of Canada.(p.xv)
• Surveys of groups in the United *States* and Canada indicate that A.A. is reaching out, not only to more and more people, but to a wider and wider range.(p.xxii)
• We covered the whole eastern United *States* in a year.(p.3)
• So we shall describe some of the mental *states* that precede a relapse into drinking, for obviously this is the crux of the problem.(p.35)
• Many friends of my family had emigrated to America, so at twenty-four I decided that the United *States* offered me the opportunity I was never likely to find in my native land.(p.231)
• Always, in between, there were intervals of being broke, riding freights and hitch-hiking interminable distances from one big town to another in three *states*.(p.255)
• Then I started traveling, with the United *States* and Canada as my territory, and with so much freedom and with an unlimited expense account, I was soon drinking every night and kidding myself that it was all part of the job.(p.287)
• I recall, as I walked into that meeting, saying to myself, "Here I am, a fellow of the American College of Surgeons, a Fellow of the International College of Surgeons, a diplomate of one of the great specialty boards in these United *States*, a member of the American Psychiatric Society, and I have to go to the butcher, the baker and the carpenter to help make a man out of me!"(p.347)
• Even when I was old enough to know better, I dreamed about being as beautiful as Venus, as pure as the Madonna and as brilliant as the President of the United *States* is supposed to be.(p.400)
• A return to the United *States* proved effective as a geographical cure, and a period of sobriety ensued, with the help of the church.(p.419)
• In the United *States* and Canada, most towns and cities have A.A. groups.(p.575)

statesman

• As a celebrated American *statesman* put it, "Let's look at the record."(p.50)

stating

• I checked into my hotel room and then noticed a placard tucked under the glass on the bureau *stating* "There will be positively NO drinking at this convention" signed by the president of the company.(p.243)

station

• If there is no Al-Anon listing in your local telephone book, you may obtain further information on Al-Anon Family Groups by writing to its World Service Office: Box 182, Madison Square *Station*, New York, NY 10159.(p.121)
• At three-thirty the next morning, I was in Champlain Street *Station*, in jail for driving while intoxicated and insulting an officer; and the suit of which I was so proud was in such shape that the turnkey had to get me a pair of trousers to go into court in the next morning.(p.201)

• There wasn't a bar in sight, but I found the subway ***station.***(p.223)
• But the saddest, and thus the most consoling, drifted through from the country-music ***station*** -- stories of broken hearts, wasted lives, lost loves, sung plaintively.(p.332)
• In January 1938, I had the opportunity to go to northern Vermont to manage a small daytime radio ***station*** that was up against it financially, and was about to fold its antenna.(p.359)
• One of the things I needed badly was business for the ***station.***(p.360)
• I got around this by joining the local Rotary Club, and through this association with the business men of the community my little ***station*** began to grow.(p.360)
• Since the radio ***station*** was getting on its feet, it didn't require so many nights of evening work, and that permitted leisure time for drinking.(p.360)
• Of course I kept her posted on how well the ***station*** was doing and wrote convincing letters of how well I was doing with the liquor problem.(p.360)
• Proud of my little ***station*** and of my new bride I settled down to a happy married life.(p.361)
• However, I had phoned New York from the farm, appealing for help, and there in the ***station*** to meet us were two A.A.'s, John and Bud.(p.415)
• Within about ten days I got locked up for being drunk and this same policeman was in the ***station*** house as I was being booked.(p.491)
• I was taken to the ***station*** house and locked up.(p.492)
• (This address is now available in pamphlet form at nominal cost through most A.A. groups or from Box 459, Grand Central ***Station,*** New York, NY 10163, under the title "Three Talks to Medical Societies by Bill W." – formerly called "Bill on Alcoholism" and earlier "Alcoholism the Illness.")(p.572)
• In such places, A.A. can be located through the local telephone directory, newspaper office, or police ***station,*** or by contacting local priests or ministers.(p.575)
• If you cannot find A.A. in your locality, a letter addressed to Alcoholics Anonymous, Box 459, Grand Central ***Station,*** New York, NY 10163, U.S.A., will receive a prompt reply from this world center, referring you to the nearest A.A. group.(p.575)
• Should you be the relative or friend of an alcoholic who shows no immediate interest in A.A., it is suggested that you write the Al-Anon Family Groups, Inc., Box 182, Madison Square ***Station,*** New York, NY 10159, U.S.A.(p.575)

stations

• I was working for a Chicago firm that represented several large radio ***stations.***(p.358)
• It was my job to sell time on these ***stations*** to advertising agencies in New York.(p.359)
• It was also my job to entertain the owners of these ***stations*** when they came East on business – or the pretense of business.(p.359)
• In 1940 another good opportunity came up and we moved to Pittsburgh where I was to manage two radio ***stations*** under the same ownership.(p.361)

statistic

• Saying these sprees were limited to one a week (they were not), and saying that the average spree was ten of these drinks (sometimes more, sometimes less), we come up with the first boring ***statistic:*** two-fifty per week out of twelve dollars.(p.397)

statistics

• Drunkalogues and ***statistics*** can be boring, but it is necessary to delve a little into each in order to come up with some kind of rough estimate.(p.396)
• Some simple mathematics and more ***statistics:***(p.399)
• Like most ***statistics,*** it doesn't prove anything -- just satisfies a little curiosity engendered by the wail "Oh, those initiation fees" that prompted this investigation.(p.399)
• All the ***statistics*** are against me.(p.420)

stature

• To my way of thinking, that is a definition of alcoholism; a state of being in which the emotions have failed to grow to the ***stature*** of the intellect.(p.535)

status

• An alcoholic who cannot meet them, still has an alcoholic mind; there is something the matter with his spiritual ***status.***(p.101)
• The others must be convinced of his new ***status*** beyond the shadow of a doubt.(p.135)
• No conviction was necessary to establish my ***status*** as a miserable failure at managing my own life.(p.259)
• As I later found out through Alcoholics Anonymous, alcohol is no respecter of economic ***status,*** social and business standing or intelligence.(p.373)

stay

• Why can't he ***stay*** on the water wagon?(p.22)
• We think few, to whom this book will appeal, can ***stay*** dry anything like a year.(p.34)
• If his arrangements would only ***stay*** put, if only people would do as he wished, the show would be great.(p.60)
• We want to ***stay*** out of this controversy.(p.69)
• If you do ***stay,*** let him steer the conversation in any direction he likes.(p.95)
• Go or ***stay*** away, whichever seems best.(p.102)
• Two: Your husband is showing lack of control, for he is unable to ***stay*** on the water wagon even when he wants to.(p.109)
• Instead of developing new channels of activity for themselves, mother and children demand that he ***stay*** home and make up the deficiency.(p.131)
• Not being a man of means, I knew that if I did not ***stay*** sober enough to earn money, I would run out of liquor.(p.175)
• My phobia for sleeplessness demanded that I get drunk every night, but in order to get more liquor for the next night, I had to ***stay*** sober during the day, at least up to four o'clock.(p.177)
• Wishing to be polite, though I felt very badly, I said, "Let's make the call," and extracted from my wife a promise that we would not ***stay*** over fifteen minutes.(p.179)
• This was going to help them to ***stay*** sober.(p.185)
• We're not up here trying to take any of your rights or privileges away from you, but we have a program whereby we think we can ***stay*** sober.(p.186)
• Two days before this, Dr. Bob had said to me, "If you and I are going to ***stay*** sober, we had better get busy."(p.188)
• I said, "I'm certainly not going to ***stay*** in here!"(p.204)
• I had no desire whatever to sit down at a table and ***stay*** a whole morning or afternoon drinking.(p.231)
• Mother would take me in only if I would ***stay*** locked in a small storeroom and give her my clothes and shoes.(p.238)
• I was never a hilarious drunk; the more I drank the quieter I got, and the drunker I got the harder I fought to ***stay*** sober.(p.241)
• During that first week-end I decided to ***stay*** in New York and take all they gave out with, except the "God stuff."(p.246)
• Much later I discovered the elders held many prayer meetings hoping to find a way to give me the heave-ho, but at the same time ***stay*** tolerant and spiritual.(p.247)
• Then I got a very good position in Philadelphia and quickly found I would need a few fellow alcoholics around me if I was to ***stay*** sober.(p.249)
• We now live in the West and are very fortunate in our area A.A.; it is good, simple and friendly, and our one desire is to ***stay*** in A.A. and not on it.(p.250)
• But I didn't ***stay*** long.(p.252)
• They called the Mayor in so we wouldn't have to ***stay*** in there over the holiday.(p.264)
• I ate up every bit of it, because I wanted to find out how to ***stay*** sober.(p.273)
• When I got out of the hospital, I was invited to ***stay*** with Dr. Bob and his dear wife, Anne.(p.279)
• Friends invited me to ***stay*** on for as long as I cared to.(p.281)
• That was my lesson, that one could not take the moral inventory and then file it away; that the alcoholic has to continue to take inventory every day if he expects to get well and ***stay*** well.(p.293)
• Even some of the saloon-keepers, where I had spent so much time and money, requested that I ***stay*** away from their places.(p.301)
• They would travel miles and ***stay*** up all night with someone they had never laid eyes on before and think nothing of it.(p.310)
• I also found out that all they wanted was to help me get sober and to ***stay*** sober themselves.(p.320)
• I did ***stay*** fairly good for a few years.(p.323)
• He answered by wiring that I could ***stay*** there until I earned enough to get home.(p.357)
• I know that if I do daily what I have done for these last thirteen and a half years, I will ***stay*** sober.(p.384)
• But they kept me there – I was supposed to ***stay*** a month, but they only kept me there seventeen days.(p.387)
• He asked if I would cooperate with him after I went home, and if I would have a trained nurse ***stay*** with me for at least two weeks.(p.387)
• Then he said I couldn't possibly move on the first of February because I couldn't ***stay*** in that place by myself.(p.388)
• He said, "If your father will come out and ***stay*** with you, you can have the house."(p.389)
• So I called my father and he said, "Yes," he'd come out and ***stay*** with me for that time.(p.389)
• I know that I must work at it as long as I live; I know that it is only by working at it that I can ***stay*** sober and have a happy life.(p.394)
• But now, with His help and grace, this child of His has paid his initiation fee for good, as long as he remembers to ***stay*** away from that first drink (the one that does all the damage) one day at a time.(p.399)
• But when this happened to me, I declared to friends that I would get drunk, dead drunk that very night, and ***stay*** drunk for a month.(p.403)
• Many of them carried a flask and sandwich case, strapped to their saddles so they could ***stay*** out all day.(p.404)
• I drank alone or with someone, anyone who would ***stay*** and drink with me.(p.406)
• I, who could never ***stay*** on the wagon for more than a week.(p.416)
• I planned to ***stay*** home the night before I left, but my folks got so drunk I walked off early in the evening and spent the night with my girl, getting very drunk myself.(p.425)
• I'd claw my way back to "respectability" and ***stay*** there – until the inevitable next time.(p.432)
• Here was power to live to the end of any given day, power to have the courage to face the next day, power to have friends, power to help people, power to be sane, power to ***stay*** sober.(p.436)
• If it was one minute after, I'd ***stay*** up and act like a martyr all day.(p.441)
• Giving up alcohol alone was not enough for me; I've had to give up all mood-and mind-affecting chemicals in order to ***stay*** sober and comfortable.(p.443)
• When the compulsion to drink left, it was relatively easy to ***stay*** off alcohol.(p.448)
• Until I could accept my alcoholism, I could not ***stay*** sober; unless I accept life completely on life's terms, I cannot be happy.(p.449)
• Most of us did not ***stay*** out of prison long enough to run the alcoholic gamut -- to develop the ongoing kind of alcoholism or alcoholic drinking you hear about in A.A. talks.(p.458)
• This career girl preferred solitary drinking, the blackout kind, often hoping she'd ***stay*** that way for keeps.(p.464)
• I ***stay*** with him at aunt's house in Maine.(p.474)
• I ***stay*** on wagon for while, but miserable.(p.475)
• He ***stay*** sober.(p.476)
• So I went down to talk to the District Attorney, and the arrangement was made that I would go home to ***stay*** with my mother, and that meant Vi and I were separated.(p.491)
• So I put forth some effort that day to try to ***stay*** sober if I could, though my sobriety was just a daze.(p.494)
• I ***stay*** with understanding friends.(p.505)
• I shall get myself "mellow" and ***stay*** that way.(p.506)
• After twenty years in prison for murder, he knew A.A. was the spot for him . . . if he wanted to ***stay*** on the outside.(p.508)
• It wasn't anything strange to me, and I knew if I wanted to ***stay*** on the outside, that would be the spot for me.(p.510)
• Providentially, this was a Monday might when the Dublin Group met in those days, and my family agreed that if A.A. could do anything for me at all, that I'd be allowed to ***stay*** on at home on probation.(p.523)
• I would ***stay*** out until my money was gone.(p.527)
• All they care about is that I am a human being and that I want to ***stay*** sober.(p.529)
• We all have the same sickness, and in helping one another, we are able to ***stay*** sober.(p.530)
• It's no great trick to stop drinking; the trick is to ***stay*** stopped.(p.554)
• I have come to realize that the name of the game is not so much to stop drinking as to ***stay*** sober.(p.559)
• Alcoholics can stop drinking in many places and many ways – but Alcoholics Anonymous offers us a way to ***stay*** sober.(p.559)
• The "12 Traditions" of Alcoholics Anonymous are, we A.A.'s believe, the best answers that our experience has yet given to those ever urgent questions, "How can A.A. best function?" and, "How can A.A. best ***stay*** whole and so survive?"(p.563)

stayed

• Of alcoholics who came to A.A. and really tried, 50% got sober at once and remained that way; 25% sobered up after some relapses, and among the remainder, those who ***stayed*** on with

A.A. showed improvement.(p.xx)
• This time we ***stayed*** broke.(p.4)
• The usual outcome was that people continued to wrong us and we ***stayed*** sore.(p.66)
• We ***stayed*** on and on.(p.106)
• I ***stayed*** about town a couple of months more and then returned to resume my practice.(p.175)
• I got tight that night, ***stayed*** sober Monday till after the dinner and then proceeded to get tight again.(p.179)
• One evening I had gone out after dinner to take on a couple of double-headers and ***stayed*** a little later than usual, and when I came home Clarence was sitting on the davenport with Bill W.(p.216)
• Little more of our talk ***stayed*** in my memory, but I do know I slept the rest of that night while before I had never known what a real night's sleep was.(p.239)
• At thirteen I was packed off to a very fine Protestant boarding school in Virginia where I ***stayed*** four years, graduating without any special achievements.(p.240)
• Evidently I had gone right back to the movie with a bottle, ***stayed*** there several hours and started home with no recollection of what had happened.(p.244)
• I ***stayed*** sober for four years except for a one-night carousal in Chicago.(p.253)
• I ***stayed*** so sober that I used to keep a quart of medicinal whiskey in my bureau which I used to taper off the occasional newspaper alcoholics who were sent to see me.(p.253)
• I ***stayed*** sober during the trip except for an occasional bottle of beer because funds barely met expenses.(p.255)
• He ***stayed*** "dry" for thirteen years!(p.263)
• So I ***stayed*** awake.(p.268)
• But – I also ***stayed*** up week nights after they had retired and drank myself into bed.(p.277)
• When she finally took the baby and left, I locked myself in the house and ***stayed*** drunk for a month.(p.278)
• I ***stayed*** in Akron two or three weeks on my initial trip trying to absorb as much of the program and philosophy as possible.(p.291)
• That discovery so intrigued me, that I ***stayed*** on that diet almost entirely for the balance of my extensive drinking life.(p.298)
• I ***stayed*** up all night reading that book.(p.309)
• The same as before, I ***stayed*** drunk pretty much of the time.(p.318)
• No one else would have ***stayed*** with me.(p.323)
• I got so that I hid quite a bit of the time, wouldn't answer the phone, and ***stayed*** by myself as much as I could.(p.324)
• I ***stayed*** on in Florida for three weeks, enjoying our reunion, a new found health and a deeper love than I had ever experienced before.(p.364)
• So he waited another week or two and I don't think I ***stayed*** sober hardly at all.(p.391)
• I ***stayed*** drunk from Monday until Friday, and I call that my spill into A.A.(p.393)
• After a few more estimates as to income and expenditures for booze over a few sample years, taken at random, I conclude that this twenty per cent ***stayed*** fairly constant.(p.398)
• But I got drunk that night and ***stayed*** drunk, getting increasingly worse until I found A.A. ten years later.(p.404)
• I ***stayed*** with them until I got drunk and had a row with the Paris editor.(p.405)
• I would rather have ***stayed*** in jail except I didn't like bologna and cold potatoes for breakfast.(p.425)
• Once in a while I ***stayed*** home for a night, to see how my folks were doing.(p.425)
• I ***stayed*** in the barracks all day, "making out guard schedules," and getting mildly plastered from the jug under my desk.(p.426)
• And somehow or other I ***stayed*** sober.(p.430)
• Ten days of this treatment the first time knocked me from 200 pounds to 130, and I seldom ***stayed*** out of the hole long enough to gain back my weight.(p.460)
• Nevertheless, I ***stayed*** sober there about six months, because I knew that Vi was to come later and bring the children.(p.490)
• I ***stayed*** there just long enough to work up a real good resentment against the doctor in charge, who I didn't think was doing anything at all except collecting fees, and I left there fully determined that I'd never put myself in the power of medical people again.(p.521)
• Simply, yes it did end; for I had changed my mind about alcohol, and it ***stayed*** changed.(p.541)

staying

• He has begun to try, with or without your cooperation, various means of moderating or ***staying*** dry.(p.109)
• He entered a political campaign, making speeches, frequenting men's gathering places of all sorts, often ***staying*** up all night.(p.158)
• But we were ***staying*** sober as long as we kept and talked together.(p.246)
• They did not seem to be getting an answer, for here I was ***staying*** sober and selling lots of auto polish, on which they were making one thousand per cent profit.(p.247)
• Of course, this year we decided on ***staying*** home and being sensible, doing a little drinking, and painting the house.(p.265)
• The birth of a baby boy did nothing toward ***staying*** the downward spiral.(p.278)
• The baffling problem of getting drunk when I had every intention of ***staying*** sober was simplified.(p.379)
• When I joined A.A. I did so for the sole purpose of getting sober and ***staying*** sober.(p.383)
• Aside from being a common drunk, I had a very serious pill affliction and all the garbage that goes with it -- lying, stealing, cheating anybody and everybody, conning the people I could, and ***staying*** clear of the ones I couldn't.(p.478)
• Then getting and ***staying*** honest with other people will come automatically.(p.482)
• My wife and new baby are fortunately ***staying*** with relatives.(p.500)
• We are ***staying*** with my wife's father.(p.501)
• I return to the hotel where I am ***staying*** and get gin from the bellboy.(p.501)

stays

• So long as a retiree woos his bottle at home, he ***stays*** out of public trouble.(p.330)
• Her father ***stays*** with her.(p.502)

steadfastly

• This resolution I kept ***steadfastly*** for the next forty years, except when circumstances made it seem unwise to absent myself.(p.172)

steadily

• I remember sometime, it was possibly six months after we had been going ***steadily*** to King School, that we were coming home from a meeting and saw a car along the way, and a fellow in back drinking a bottle of beer.(p.271)
• He may even read in a newspaper that one out of every seven drinkers will become alcoholic, but he rarely is told that it holds true for all ages -- or that the tolerance to alcohol (and other drugs) decreases ***steadily***, year after year, in the bodies of all persons.(p.330)
• I drink ***steadily***, I come to at three in the morning.(p.501)

steady

• Between classes I would run down to the wash room, take enough to ***steady*** my nerves and then go on to the next class.(p.183)
• I knew the stuff I was making was a lot stronger than I had been used to, but I never suspected that ***steady*** drinking of it might develop a taste for something even stronger still.(p.233)
• My last venture, a book shop, was hastened to closed doors by my ***steady*** intoxication.(p.255)
• I always feel that our God Consciousness was a ***steady*** growth after we became associated with A.A.(p.270)
• I would like to sketch for you the highlights of these sixteen years of a slow but ***steady*** and satisfying upward climb.(p.280)
• Within a year of my return to Detroit, A.A. was a definitely established little group of about a dozen members and I too was established in a modest but ***steady*** job handling an independent dry-cleaning route of my own.(p.283)
• At eighteen, I got my first ***steady*** job.(p.397)
• Yet I am fairly ***steady*** when I go to bed.(p.500)

steal

• Or am I expecting to ***steal*** a little vicarious pleasure from the atmosphere of such places?"(p.101)
• After three years of this, I wound up in the local hospital where they attempted to help me, but I would get my friends to smuggle me a quart, or I would ***steal*** the alcohol about the building, so that I got rapidly worse.(p.175)
• I displayed alcoholic tendencies actually from the age of fourteen, when I started to ***steal*** wine from the family jug, siphoning it off one drink at a time so it wouldn't be missed, not drinking it immediately, but saving it until about a pint was accumulated, so that I could get drunk.(p.397)

stealing

• Sometimes we think fear ought to be classed with ***stealing***.(p.67)
• We did, and spent a month boozing it up, popping pills, and smoking marijuana; taking shelter where we could, which included a veterinary hospital one night; accepting meals from anyone; actually begging; ***stealing*** anything we were in need of, which was about everything.(p.354)
• And then my waiting until I was sure he was asleep, and ***stealing*** money from him to replenish the supply.(p.466)
• Aside from being a common drunk, I had a very serious pill affliction and all the garbage that goes with it – lying, ***stealing***, cheating anybody and everybody, conning the people I could, and staying clear of the ones I couldn't.(p.478)

steel

• The prosaic ***steel*** girder is a mass of electrons whirling around each other at incredible speed.(p.48)
• My parents' car had a strong attraction to fences, and one night I blacked out and drove the car down a bank, ramming the ***steel*** fence around someone's backyard.(p.353)
• But then, when that ***steel*** door slammed shut, and she was the one that went home, I was amazed.(p.440)
• That's when that ***steel*** door slammed shut, and Max was the one who went home.(p.444)
• I was there about three weeks, and then I got restless and started to tramp across the country, here and there, until I finally wound up in Pennsylvania, in a ***steel*** mill.(p.492)
• I worked in the ***steel*** mill for possibly two months, and then I became disgusted with myself and decided to go back home.(p.492)
• I, a man of ***steel***, with very high ideals, well brought up, an honor student and the recipient of scholarships and prizes, a boy wonder in business -- I, Bob, the author of this essay, looked and saw that the universe was beneath my contempt, and that to remove myself from it was the only thing of dignity a man could do.(p.531)
• I remember how horrible jails are, how dreadful a thing it is to be behind ***steel*** bars.(p.542)

steer

• If you do stay, let him ***steer*** the conversation in any direction he likes.(p.95)

steerage

• We are like the passengers of a great liner the moment after rescue from shipwreck when camaraderie, joyousness and democracy pervade the vessel from ***steerage*** to Captain's table.(p.17)

stem

• From it ***stem*** all forms of spiritual disease, for we have been not only mentally and physically ill, we have been spiritually sick.(p.64)

step

• This is the first ***step*** in recovery.(p.30)
• ***Step*** over to the nearest barroom and try some controlled drinking.(p.31)
• But somehow, we couldn't quite ***step*** ashore.(p.53)
• Being convinced, we were at ***Step*** Three, which is that we decided to turn our will and our life over to God as we understood Him.(p.60)
• Driven by a hundred forms of fear, self-delusion, self-seeking, and self-pity, we ***step*** on the toes of our fellows and they retaliate.(p.62)
• We are now at ***Step*** Three.(p.63)
• We thought well before taking this ***step*** making sure we were ready; that we could at last abandon ourselves utterly to Him.(p.63)
• We found it very desirable to take this spiritual ***step*** with an understanding person, such as our wife, best friend or spiritual adviser.(p.63)
• Next we launched out on a course of vigorous action, the first ***step*** of which is a personal housecleaning, which many of us had never attempted.(p.63)
• Though our decision was a vital and crucial ***step***, it could have little permanent effect unless at once followed by a strenuous effort to face, and to be rid of, the things in ourselves which had been blocking us.(p.64)
• This was ***Step*** Four.(p.64)
• This brings us to the Fifth ***Step*** in the program of recovery mentioned in the preceding chapter.(p.72)
• The best reason first: If we skip this vital ***step***, we may not overcome drinking.(p.72)
• Rightly and naturally, we think well before we choose the person or persons with whom to take this intimate and confidential ***step***.(p.74)
• If that is so, this ***step*** may be postponed, only however, if we hold ourselves in complete readiness to go through with it at the first opportunity.(p.74)
• Once we have taken this ***step***, withholding nothing, we are delighted.(p.75)
• If we can answer to our satisfaction, we then look at ***Step*** Six.(p.76)
• We have then completed ***Step*** Seven.(p.76)

• If we have obtained permission, have consulted with others, asked God to help and the drastic *step* is indicated we must not shrink.(p.80)
• This thought brings us to *Step* Ten, which suggests we continue to take personal inventory and continue to set right any new mistakes as we go along.(p.84)
• *Step* Eleven suggests prayer and meditation.(p.85)
• We usually conclude the period of meditation with a prayer that we be shown all through the day what our next *step* is to be, that we be given whatever we need to take care of such problems.(p.87)
• The next chapter is entirely devoted to *Step* Twelve.(p.88)
• Cessation of drinking is but the first *step* away from a highly strained, abnormal condition.(p.122)
• Will he take every necessary *step*, submit to anything to get well, to stop drinking forever?(p.142)
• I was introduced to them and Clarence proceeded to put on his Twelve *Step* work.(p.216)
• However, here I probably took my first *step* towards my coming alcoholism by developing a terrific aversion to all churches and established religions.(p.240)
• In June, 1945, with another member, I made my first – and only -- Twelfth *Step* call on a female alcoholic and a year later I married her.(p.249)
• Here by itself was a great *step* forward.(p.283)
• At any rate the last great *step* toward a well rounded life still lay ahead of me.(p.286)
• Dr. Bob then led me through the restitution *step*, in which I made a list of all of the persons I had harmed, and worked out ways and means of slowly making restitution.(p.292)
• And I gave him some idea of what you do, and so I made my first Twelfth *Step* call before I ever came into the program.(p.347)
• I tried every gimmick that there was to get some peace of mind, but it was not until I was brought to my alcoholic knees, when I was brought to a group in my own community with the butcher, the baker, the carpenter and the mechanic, who were able to give me the Twelve Steps, that I was finally given some semblance of an answer to the last half of the First *Step*.(p.349)
• So, after taking the first half of the First *Step*, and very gingerly admitting myself to Alcoholics Anonymous, something happened.(p.349)
• The Third *Step* said: "Made a decision to turn our will and our lives over to the care of God as we understood Him."(p.350)
• I attended my weekly meetings with regularity, reread the Big Book, attended other group meetings, gave leads when asked to and did some Twelve *Step* work whenever I was called upon to do so.(p.365)
• The answer came to me very simply in the first *step* of the Twelve Steps of A.A.(p.379)
• I was desperately in earnest to follow through and understand what was expected of me as a member of A.A. and to take each *Step* of the Twelve as rapidly as possible.(p.382)
• However, I threw myself into Twelve *Step* work, and what I feared would be a calamity turned out to be the most blessed of blessings.(p.394)
• It is a way of life that pays as it goes, every *step* of the way, in compensations that have been wonderfully rich and rewarding.(p.394)
• I was out of *step* with life, with my family, with people in general.(p.400)
• In a sense, I had taken the first *step*.(p.412)
• Through going to meetings and listening, and occasionally speaking, through doing Twelve *Step* work, whereby in helping others you are both the teacher and the student, by making many wonderful A.A. friends, I have been taught all the things in life that are worth having.(p.416)
• I consider that I was taking the Eleventh *Step* when I joined this church.(p.417)
• Each with the other as a witness, we took the Third *Step* out loud – just as it says in the Big Book.(p.446)
• So I jump quick from First *Step* to Twelfth *Step* to help my brother, living with me.(p.476)
• They taught us a great deal about Twelve *Step* work too.(p.496)
• It was a revelation when I read that First *Step*.(p.515)
• Before I *step* out and do anything, I stop and check it over first, and then let my conscience be my guide.(p.516)
• But our usual A.A. "12th *Step*" work is never to be paid for.(p.567)

stepdaughter

• A.A. has given me a new wife, a beautiful *stepdaughter*, a new practice, a new home, and a new relationship with my four children.(p.420)

stepped

• Trembling, I *stepped* from the hospital a broken man.(p.8)
• When I returned to the hotel it struck me a highball would be fine before going to bed, so I *stepped* into the bar and had one.(p.41)
• He had *stepped* from bridge to shore.(p.56)
• Selecting a church at random from the directory, he *stepped* into a booth and lifted the receiver.(p.155)
• Many a man, yet dazed from his hospital experience, has *stepped* over the threshold of that home into freedom.(p.160)
• It was getting pretty dark and I hadn't turned on any lights, when some big fellow *stepped* inside the door and flipped on the light switch.(p.207)
• And then one ill-defined day, one day that I can't recall, I *stepped* across the line that alcoholics know so well, and from that day on drinking was miserable.(p.346)
• After I had made my third report, I *stepped* down town, met some of the old crowd, and of course you know the answer.(p.510)

stepping

• *Stepping* into his car, he made the rounds of people he had hurt.(p.156)

steps

• The Twelve *Steps* that summarize the program may be called los Doce Pasos in one country, los Douze Etapes in another, but they trace exactly the same path to recovery that was blazed by the earliest members of Alcoholics Anonymous.(p.xxii)
• As soon as we admitted the possible existence of a Creative Intelligence, a Spirit of the Universe underlying the totality of things, we began to be possessed of a new sense of power and direction, provided we took other simple *steps*.(p.46)
• If you have decided you want what we have and are willing to go to any length to get it – then you are ready to take certain *steps*.(p.58)
• Here are the *steps* we took, which are suggested as a program of recovery:(p.59)
• 12.Having had a spiritual awakening as the result of these *steps*, we tried to carry this message to alcoholics, and to practice these principles in all our affairs.(p.60)
• Taking this book down from our shelf we turn to the page which contains the twelve *steps*.(p.75)
• Let's look at *Steps* Eight and Nine.(p.76)
• He has read this volume and says he is prepared to go through with the Twelve *Steps* of the program of recovery.(p.96)
• Had they fired me first, and had they then taken *steps* to see that I was presented with the solution contained in this book, I might have returned to them six months later, a well man.(p.141)
• My bootlegger had hidden alcohol at the back *steps* where I could get it at my convenience.(p.176)
• The feeling of impending disaster that had haunted me for years began to dissolve as I put into practice more and more of the Twelve *Steps*.(p.229)
• It was simple, they said, and went on to explain to me in their own language the program of recovery and daily living which we know today as the Twelve *Steps* of A.A.(p.279)
• It is, however, only the first of a series of miracles which have followed one after another as a result of my trying to apply to my daily life the principles embodies in our Twelve *Steps*.(p.280)
• It would be wonderful were I able to tell you that my confidence in God and my application of the Twelve *Steps* to my daily living have utterly banished fear.(p.284)
• The six *steps* were:(p.292)
• Dr. Bob led me through all of these *steps*.(p.292)
• This and the program of recovery embodied in the Twelve *Steps*.(p.311)
• In learning to practice these *steps* in my daily living I began to acquire faith and a philosophy to live by.(p.311)
• A.A.'s Twelve *Steps* showed me the way to sobriety if I wanted it.(p.320)
• That was on a hot summer evening, down in the Greenwich Village Group, and there was a little porch out there in the old meeting place on Sullivan Street, and after the meeting I went out on the *steps* for some air.(p.321)
• And I put a Big Book by my night stand, and I put a "Twelve *Steps* and Twelve Tradition" in my locker at the hospital, and I got books by Emmet Fox, and I got books by God-knows-who, and I got to reading all these things.(p.348)
• I tried every gimmick that there was to get some peace of mind, but it was not until I was brought to my alcoholic knees, when I was brought to a group in my own community with the butcher, the baker, the carpenter and the mechanic, who were able to give me the Twelve *Steps*, that I was finally given some semblance of an answer to the last half of the First Step.(p.349)
• If I were asked what in my opinion was the most important factor in being successful in this program, besides following the Twelve *Steps*, I would say Honesty.(p.367)
• The next *steps* were bottle hiding, and excuses for trips in order to drink without restraint.(p.375)
• The answer came to me very simply in the first step of the Twelve *Steps* of A.A.(p.379)
• It took me some time to realize that the Twelve *Steps* of A.A. were designed to help correct these defects of character and so help remove the obsession to drink.(p.380)
• The Twelve *Steps*, which to me are a spiritual way of living, soon meant honest thinking, not wishful thinking, open mindedness, a willingness to try and a faith to accept.(p.381)
• A "spiritual experience" to me meant attending meetings, seeing a group of people, all there for the purpose of helping each other; hearing the Twelve *Steps* and the Twelve Traditions read at a meeting, and hearing the Lord's Prayer, which in an A.A. meeting has such great meaning – "Thy will be done, not mine."(p.381)
• It's the last thing I ever heard him say, and I think there are some of us who, at times, try to read extra messages and complexities into the *Steps*.(p.395)
• The last time I drank, when I was twenty-nine, I drank for only four days, yet I threatened to kill my children; I beat my wife at home and on the church *steps*; I mistreated a child in my office; and I ran to a hospital for mental illness to avoid jail.(p.418)
• My experience has been active: three meetings a week, many tapes, many A.A. conferences, much work on the Twelve *Steps*, and much work with other alcoholics and their families.(p.420)
• And life keeps getting simpler and easier as we try to reverse my old idea, by taking care of the internal environment via the Twelve *Steps*, and letting the external environment take care of itself.)(p.446)
• Eventually, I had to redo each of the Twelve *Steps* specifically with Max in mind, from the First, saying, "I am powerless over alcohol, and my homelife is unmanageable by me," to the Twelfth, in which I tried to think of her as a sick Al-Anon and treat her with the love I would give a sick A.A. newcomer.(p.452)
• All Twelve *Steps* of A.A. are designed to kill the old self (deflate the old ego) and build a new, free self.(p.459)
• During the twenty-four hours after running into the Serenity Prayer, I think I took the first three *Steps* for the first time.(p.461)
• The other of the Twelve *Steps* of Alcoholics Anonymous seemed insurmountable to me at first.(p.471)
• Had I tried honestly and sincerely to practice the Twelve *Steps* I would have seen from my continuous moral inventory that I was getting off the beam -- I would have found that there were some active resentments in my life, a terrific amount of self-pity.(p.471)
• Walk with me up Twelve *Steps* of A.A. to peace."(p.477)
• Knowing that he was sober, I timed it just right, so I could do the slashing just before he hit the *steps*.(p.479)
• We are told to practice the Twelve *Steps* and Twelve Traditions to the best of our ability every day, one day at a time.(p.481)
• There are *steps* of recovery, of maintenance.(p.516)
• A.A.'s Twelve *Steps* may confuse you when you read them over.(p.516)
• But the more meetings you attend, the more people you meet at these meetings, the clearer the *Steps* become.(p.516)
• They suggested that I study the A.A. book and try to take the Twelve *Steps* according to the explanation in the Book, for it was their opinion that the application of these principles in our daily lives will get us sober and keep us sober.(p.550)
• All but one "responded to the treatment" suggested in the *Steps* immediately, but this one posed a problem.(p.551)
• By learning – through practicing the Twelve *Steps* and through sharing at meetings – how to cope with the problems that we looked to booze to solve, back in our drinking days.(p.560)
• Similarly, we rid ourselves of guilt and remorse as we "clean out the garbage" from our minds through the Fourth and Fifth *Steps* of our recovery program.(p.560)

sterility

• If we do not do so, we shall stand convicted of emotional *sterility* and of having lost the faith that moves mountains, without which medicine can do little."(p.571)

stern

• There was the father one lost respect for at the age of eleven, because the father broke his solemn word in a circumstance where you, eleven years old, had assumed guilt when you were innocent; but the father would not believe you, no matter what; and to ease his suffering you "confessed" and were "forgiven," only -- months later -- to have your "guilt" brought up -- only he and you knew what he was talking bout -- brought up in front of the ***stern*** grandmother.(p.533)

stick

• We ***stick*** to our own.(p.78)

• We find it better when possible, to ***stick*** to our own stories.(p.125)

• I used also to put it up in four ounce bottles and ***stick*** several in my stocking tops.(p.177)

• If I could ***stick*** to Him and listen, I would make it.(p.190)

• Some college friends got me jobs when I finally had to go to work, but I didn't ***stick*** to them.(p.251)

• But, finally, we got one or two to come in and ***stick*** and from there, of course, we started to grow.(p.495)

• I didn't ***stick*** at social drinking very long.(p.512)

• Brandishing my "motto," which was "A little man with a ***stick*** is equal to a big man," sometimes I varied the literary lecture by a fight with a big man, selected solely because he was big and I was little.(p.537)

• I bear a few scars on my face from these fights, which I always lost, because the "***stick***" existed only in my mind.(p.537)

sticking

• We agnostics and atheists were ***sticking*** to the idea that self-sufficiency would solve our problems.(p.52)

• After being dry two weeks and ***sticking*** close to Jackie, all of a sudden I found I had become the sponsor of my sponsor, for he was suddenly taken drunk.(p.245)

• There was the necessity for ***sticking*** to a job I hated, a dull, repetitive job performed in association with other men I had nothing in common with . . . performed for years on end, because the money was needed at home.(p.532)

stickler

• The practical individual of today is a ***stickler*** for facts and results.(p.48)

sticks

• If he ***sticks*** to the ideas that he can still control his drinking, tell him that possibly he can -- if he is not too alcoholic.(p.92)

stiff

• I made arrangements to enter the hospital three days later and promptly went out and got ***stiff*** for three days.(p.302)

stiffs

• Those poor ***stiffs*** probably went to a doctor and were told that if they quit they'd live three weeks and if they didn't they'd die in one."(p.510)

stigma

• I was suffering from an actual disease that had a name and symptoms like diabetes or cancer or TB -- and a disease was respectable, not a moral ***stigma***!(p.227)

• In emphasizing alcoholism as an illness, the social ***stigma*** associated with this condition is being blotted out . . .(p.573)

still

• As part of his rehabilitation he commenced to present his conceptions to other alcoholics, impressing upon them that they must do likewise with ***still*** others.(p.xxiii)

• They believe in themselves, and ***still*** more in the Power which pulls chronic alcoholics back from the gates of death.(p.xxv)

• We had long talks when I would ***still*** her forebodings by telling her that men of genius conceived their best projects when drunk; that the most majestic constructions of philosophic thought were so derived.(p.2)

• The ticker ***still*** clattered.(p.4)

• Nevertheless, I ***still*** thought I could control the situation, and there were periods of sobriety which renewed my wife's hope.(p.5)

• I could almost hear the sound of the preacher's voice as I sat, on ***still*** Sundays, way over there on the hillside; there was that proffered temperance pledge I never signed; my grandfather's good natured contempt of some church folk and their doings; his insistence that the spheres really had their music; but his denial of the preacher's right to tell him how he must listen; his fearlessness as he spoke of these things just before he died; these recollections welled up from the past.(p.10)

• The word God ***still*** aroused a certain antipathy.(p.12)

• For a moment I was alarmed, and called my friend, the doctor, to ask if I were ***still*** sane.(p.14)

• What has become of the common sense and will power that he ***still*** sometimes displays with respect to other matters?(p.22)

• More baffling ***still***, he could give himself no satisfactory explanation for his fall.(p.26)

• But this man ***still*** lives, and is a free man.(p.26)

• All of us felt at times that we were regaining control, but such intervals -- usually brief -- were inevitably followed by ***still*** less control, which led in time to pitiful and incomprehensible demoralization.(p.30)

• In some instances there has been brief recovery, followed always by a ***still*** worse relapse.(p.31)

• ***Still*** no thought of drinking.(p.36)

• The reader may ***still*** ask why he should believe in a Power greater than himself.(p.48)

• We ***still*** like it.(p.53)

• Could we ***still*** say the whole thing was nothing but a mass of electrons, created out of nothing, meaning nothing, whirling on to a destiny of nothingness?(p.54)

• He becomes, on the next occasion, ***still*** more demanding or gracious, as the case may be.(p.61)

• ***Still*** the play does not suit him.(p.61)

• We must be willing to make amends where we have done harm, provided that we do not bring about ***still*** more harm in so doing.(p.69)

• Though we have no religious connection, we may ***still*** do well to talk with someone ordained by an established religion.(p.74)

• If we ***still*** cling to something we will not let go, we ask God to help us be willing.(p.76)

• Probably there are ***still*** some misgivings.(p.76)

• It is seldom wise to approach an individual, who ***still*** smarts from our injustice to him, and announce that we have gone religious.(p.77)

• It may be he has done us more harm than we have done him and, though we may have acquired a better attitude toward him, we are ***still*** not too keen about admitting our faults.(p.77)

• Being ***still*** inexperienced and having just made conscious contact with God, it is not probable that we are going to be inspired at all times.(p.87)

• Call on him while he is ***still*** jittery.(p.91)

• If he sticks to the ideas that he can ***still*** control his drinking, tell him that possibly he can -- if he is not too alcoholic.(p.92)

• An alcoholic who cannot meet them, ***still*** has an alcoholic mind; there is something the matter with his spiritual status.(p.101)

• Some of us ***still*** serve it to our friends provided they are not alcoholic.(p.102)

• Perhaps he can ***still*** tend to business fairly well.(p.109)

• Many of the old problems will ***still*** be with you.(p.117)

• ***Still*** another difficulty is that you may become jealous of the attention he bestows on other people, especially alcoholics.(p.119)

• Cheer him up and ask him how you can be ***still*** more helpful.(p.120)

• This painful past may be of infinite value to other families ***still*** struggling with their problem.(p.124)

• He becomes ***still*** less communicative.(p.126)

• The family must realize that dad, though marvelously improved, is ***still*** convalescing.(p.127)

• If the family persists in criticism, this fallacy may take a ***still*** greater hold on father.(p.129)

• They can hardly fail to approve these simple principles, though the head of the house ***still*** fails somewhat in practicing them.(p.130)

• Though he is now a most effective member of Alcoholics Anonymous, he ***still*** smokes and drinks coffee, but neither his wife or anyone else stands in judgment.(p.135)

• I ***still*** expected a plea for clemency, but these words came through the receiver: "I just wanted to tell you Paul jumped from a hotel window in Hartford last Saturday.(p.136)

• ***Still*** another experience: A woman's voice came faintly over long distance from Virginia.(p.137)

• She wanted to know if her husband's company insurance was ***still*** in force.(p.137)

• If he temporizes and ***still*** thinks he can ever drink again, even beer, he might as well be discharged after the next bender which, if an alcoholic, he is almost certain to have.(p.142)

• If he is, and is ***still*** trying to recover, he will tell you about it even if it means the loss of his job.(p.146)

• The age of miracles is ***still*** with us.(p.153)

• They will approach ***still*** other sick ones and fellowships of Alcoholics Anonymous may spring up in each city and hamlet, havens for those who must find a way out.(p.153)

• ***Still*** physically weak, and sober but a few months, he saw that his predicament was dangerous.(p.154)

• Music and gay chatter ***still*** floated to him from the bar.(p.154)

• Why, he argued, should he lose the remainder of his business, only to bring ***still*** more suffering to his family by foolishly admitting his plight to people from whom he made his livelihood?(p.155)

• Arrangements were also made with the chief psychiatrist of a large public hospital to select ***still*** others from the stream of misery which flows through that institution.(p.163)

• ***Still*** you may say: "But I will not have the benefit of contact with you who write this book."(p.164)

• Ask Him in your morning meditation what you can do each day for the man who is ***still*** sick.(p.164)

• During these years, I drank as much as my purse permitted, ***still*** without paying too great a penalty, although I was beginning to have morning jitters at times.(p.173)

• I gave the matter much time and study for the next two and a half years, but ***still*** got tight every night nevertheless.(p.178)

• If you ***still*** think you are strong enough to beat the game alone, that is your affair.(p.181)

• I was at one time a deacon in the church and I ***still*** believe in God.(p.189)

• I wasn't afraid that the program wouldn't work, but I ***still*** was doubtful whether I would be able to hang on to the program, but I did come to the conclusion that I was willing to put everything I had into it, with God's power, and that I wanted to do just that.(p.189)

• I ***still*** go to meetings, because I like to go.(p.192)

• Another reason I go is that I'm ***still*** grateful for the good years that I've had.(p.192)

• I'm so grateful for both the program and the people in it that I ***still*** want to go, and then probably the most wonderful thing that I learned from the program -- I've seen this in the 'A.A. Grapevine' a lot of times, and I've had people say it to me personally, and I've heard people get up in meetings and make the same statement: The statement is, "I came into A.A. solely for the purpose of sobriety, but it has been through A.A. that I have found God."(p.192)

• "Who is convinced against his will is of the same opinion ***still***."(p.193)

• When I left the hospital I tried this for a day and it worked, for a week and it worked, and for a month, and it worked -- and then for a year and it ***still*** worked.(p.209)

• They suffered from my conduct without saying anything, but the reason for this was I ***still*** managed to hang onto a very substantial practice.(p.215)

• I ***still*** had enough practice to earn a good living if I would only work, so I resolved that in January of 1940 I would launch a patent law firm of my own.(p.220)

• I knew the stuff I was making was a lot stronger than I had been used to, but I never suspected that steady drinking of it might develop a taste for something even stronger ***still***.(p.233)

• "Best in the business, when he's sober," my customers would say, and I ***still*** had a following who would give me work though they deplored my habits, because they knew the job would be well done when they eventually got it.(p.234)

• From the top of the heap in a few years he had skidded to becoming a shuffling customer, ***still*** entering the better barrooms but welcomed by neither mine host nor his patrons.(p.236)

• The lesson of his death ***still*** remains with me, yet I often wonder what would have happened if somebody else had made that first call on me.(p.239)

• That is where I had my first drink and I ***still*** remember it, for every "first" drink afterwards did exactly the same trick -- I could feel it go right through every bit of my body and down to my very toes.(p.241)

• I don't think the boys were completely convinced of my personality change, for they fought shy of including my story in the book, so my only contribution to their literary efforts was my firm conviction, being ***still*** a theological rebel, that the word God should be qualified with the phrase "as we understand him" -- for that was the only way I could accept spirituality.(p.248)

• After the book appeared we all became very busy in our efforts to save all and sundry, but I was ***still*** actually on the fringes of A.A.(p.248)

• And I ***still*** say that as long as I remember that January 8th in Washington, that is how long, by the grace of God as I understand Him, I will retain a happy sobriety.(p.250)

• I was ***still*** bitter because I felt that drink had completely ruined my childhood and my married life, and I hated everything pertaining to it.(p.262)
• At the end of a year, the children got a card from their father, which I ***still*** have and cherish.(p.262)
• He said, "Tell Mommy I ***still*** love her."(p.263)
• I didn't realize how I ***still*** felt about him.(p.263)
• As many times as he would tell me that, I ***still*** believed him.(p.263)
• It would stop out in front of our house, and I ***still*** believe those people sent it!(p.265)
• I sipped the drink off the bar because I couldn't hold it in my hand, but I was ***still*** a lady, believe it or not, and I was deeply ashamed.(p.266)
• When you have a hangover and can't even sit ***still***, try to read small print!(p.268)
• I feel that one of the things that I ***still*** have to guard against is that I used to be set in my way about what I considered the old-time A.A.(p.272)
• The Depression was ***still*** on and jobs were scarce.(p.282)
• My health was ***still*** uncertain.(p.282)
• Some of the things which used to stop me in my tracks from fear ***still*** make me nervous in the anticipation of their doing, but once I kick myself into doing them nervousness disappears and I enjoy myself.(p.285)
• At any rate the last great step toward a well rounded life ***still*** lay ahead of me.(p.286)
• I can ***still*** remember very distinctly getting into Akron at eleven p.m. and routing this same Howard out of bed to do something about me.(p.290)
• This picture is ***still*** vivid.(p.292)
• I went to a minister and a doctor that I ***still*** knew and they, in turn, asked me how long I had been sober.(p.293)
• A very simple plan that I ***still*** find much joy and happiness in following.(p.302)
• I ***still*** have my job, and just prior to the writing of this narrative, I received an advancement.(p.303)
• And ***still*** by the time I was thirty years old I was being pushed around with a compulsion to drink that was completely beyond my control.(p.305)
• "We watch the alcoholic performing in a position of responsibility and we know that because he is drinking heavily and daily he has cut his capacities by fifty per cent, and ***still*** he seems able to do a satisfactory job.(p.308)
• Other days, I had to miss work because I was ***still*** too drunk to stand up.(p.318)
• I ***still*** couldn't make it through the nights without drinking, so I went back into the hospital, this time to a rehabilitation center.(p.320)
• Then I went to another meeting, and I ***still*** thought it was wonderful --for him, but not for me.(p.321)
• I was ***still*** woozy from the night before.(p.323)
• I ***still*** had a wife and family, a home and a car, my driver's license, and a proper amount of insurance.(p.327)
• I ***still*** had to drink; I ***still*** needed that drink.(p.339)
• It is ***still*** there.(p.348)
• My salesmanship was ***still*** good, for in the fall of 1938 she called me from Salt Lake and finally agreed to take me on for better or for worse.(p.360)
• I was going to prove to her that liquor wasn't necessary in my life, and above all that I ***still*** loved her more than anything else in the world and that I wanted her back.(p.362)
• Sure I ***still*** loved her, but hang it all, she was unreasonable!(p.362)
• And I ***still*** felt it was a weakness – plus, in her case, adverse circumstances.(p.370)
• I ***still*** wash clothes, lots of them, but I no longer lose them at the Laundromat.(p.372)
• Broken promises, humiliation, hopelessness, worry, anxiety – but ***still*** not enough.(p.377)
• They told me to go to meetings, and I ***still*** do at every available opportunity, whether I am at home or in some other city.(p.381)
• They said "Get active," so I helped whenever I could, and I ***still*** do.(p.381)
• She ***still*** had her husband, her home, and a chance to help start A.A. in Texas.(p.384)
• Dr. Bob said, "Love and service keep us dry," and Bill said, "Always we must remember that our first duty is face-to-face help for the alcoholic who ***still*** suffers."(p.395)
• Age and the law were ***still*** against me, but laws were not as strictly enforced in those days as they are now, and I discovered that as long as I had the green blood, there was always a way to get alcohol, either from a nondiscriminatory bartender or from an older friend who would be glad to purchase the joy juice for the privilege of sharing it.(p.397)
• A titled lady, she ***still*** saw her world darkening.(p.400)
• I was ***still*** untrained for any work but washing dishes and waiting on table.(p.401)
• I could not live on that tiny trust fund and ***still*** drink all I wanted to.(p.411)
• I ***still*** think dad paid him something to let me go.(p.424)
• The doctor was ***still*** sitting beside my bed.(p.427)
• If pressed further, all I can do is follow the psalmist who said it long, long before me: "Be ***still***, and know that I am God."(p.437)
• ***Still***, I couldn't turn my mouth off.(p.442)
• Max ***still*** works with me in the office, but we have turned our wills and our lives and our work over to the care of God.(p.446)
• My reaction was that I'd already helped all the patients on the ward, and I ***still*** had plenty of problems of my own without trying to help some drunk from A.A.(p.446)
• Of course, I was ***still*** drinking at the time.(p.447)
• ***Still*** later, even alcohol and chemicals together could not lift me.(p.457)
• However, I ***still*** would not attend A.A. in prison.(p.461)
• I am ***still*** arrogant, egocentric, self-righteous, with no humility, even phony at times, but I'm trying to be a better person and help my fellowman.(p.463)
• The next day the ice-bag and I were ***still*** in bed -- but we had a bottle too!(p.466)
• Then in a couple of hours, when there was ***still*** no word from my husband and no sign of him, I had the feeling we alcoholics all know.(p.467)
• I worked for the Government about a year and ***still*** maintained my evening office practice when the Government agencies were decentralized.(p.489)
• After he'd talked half an hour, I ***still*** wanted him to hurry up and get out so I could go and get some whiskey before the liquor store closed.(p.494)
• The war leaves me with a pair of blankets, a toilet kit, a sweater knit by my sister, and a ***still*** greater inferiority.(p.499)
• That was ***still*** to come.(p.508)
• She's ***still*** alive today at the age of eighty-two.(p.511)
• I was ***still*** very fit and good at games.(p.519)
• I was ***still*** very good at games.(p.519)
• Strangely enough, right through to the end of my twenty-six years in the Army, I was ***still*** being offered very good and important jobs in spite of the fact that my superiors must have known that I wasn't thoroughly reliable.(p.519)
• In part, it was a feeling of intense shame at having to leave the Army during the war, but mostly it was resentment that this kind of thing should happen to me for, strange as it may seem, up to then I ***still*** thought I could control drinking.(p.521)
• My father was and ***still*** is a minister, and I was afraid that I might run into him, or that someone might tell him where I was, and I could ***still*** remember what he had done to me when I got drunk one Christmas when I was very young.(p.527)
• I don't know if it's force of habit or something else that keeps them in one place, but I do know that in A.A. there is much work to do, and none of us can do it standing ***still***.(p.529)
• I ***still*** do.(p.535)
• What a revelation of ego and arrogance ***still*** remaining in me – as if anyone, instinct and training apart, likes to be in jail or in an alcoholic ward or fired from his job.(p.536)
• After nearly eight years of sobriety in A.A., I ***still*** can set down such thoughts, "against my instinct and training," showing that I ***still*** consider myself a "special" person, entitled to special privileges.(p.536)
• If he were ***still*** sober, chances are that very quickly I put him down as a Philistine with no appreciation of literary genius; and then I went on to another bar to find a new victim.(p.537)
• ***Still*** another friend and temporary host received me at four in the morning from the charge of a policeman who had found me "going to bed" in a garage far from the last place I could remember having been, a fashionable bar and restaurant in the theatrical district of New York, to which I had repaired after my date for that evening, a charming lady of the theatre who had refused my company for obvious reasons.(p.538)
• ***Still***, I had had funds sufficient to get plastered because that, of course, was more important than paying my own way.(p.538)
• Back to the big city, for another year of precarious living, paid for largely by one or two friends I ***still*** had not milked dry or worn to exhaustion with demands on their bounty.(p.540)
• It is going strong ***still***, these eight years later, and some of its members have been of great influence for good in state-wide A.A. work.(p.541)
• I ***still*** want to write a fine play and to get it on.(p.542)
• I believe this, and I believe too that it is equally impossible to practice these principles to the best of our ability, a day at a time, and ***still*** drink, for I don't think the two things are compatible.(p.550)
• I sold my first article to a national magazine while ***still*** an undergraduate.(p.555)
• Although my ambition ***still*** flickered, it now took the form of fantasizing.(p.556)
• So the need to drink grew ***still*** greater.(p.557)
• But my thinking was ***still*** confused, and I was ***still*** unable to deal with the challenges of everyday living without help.(p.558)
• Five – Each group has but one primary purpose -- to carry its message to the alcoholic who ***still*** suffers.(p.564)
• 5. – Each Alcoholics Anonymous group ought to be a spiritual entity having but one primary purpose -- that of carrying its message to the alcoholic who ***still*** suffers.(p.565)

stilled

• My writhing nerves were ***stilled*** at last.(p.6)

stimulants

• My life was fairly well crowded and I didn't seem to need any ***stimulants*** to keep me going.(p.213)

stimulating

• Alcohol is so sexually ***stimulating*** to some men that they have over-indulged.(p.134)
• The expression on the faces of the women, that indefinable something in the eyes of the men, the ***stimulating*** and electric atmosphere of the place, conspired to let him know that here was haven at last.(p.160)

stimulus

• To go into a gathering of people was the sort of thing that all my life, from the time I left my private world of books and dreams to meet the real world of people and parties and jobs, had left me feeling an uncomfortable outsider, needing the warming ***stimulus*** of drinks to join in.(p.228)
• My alcoholism-prone mind, however, reminded me that all great authors had needed a ***stimulus*** to build up inspiration and inventiveness before each day's work.(p.331)

stinker

• All the other people that had talked to me wanted to help me, and my pride prevented me from listening to them, and caused only resentment on my part, but I felt as if I would be a real ***stinker*** if I did not listen to a couple of fellows for a short time, if that would cure them.(p.185)

stint

• A square from ultra-dry Kansas, I did not taste grog until I had finished college, done a ***stint*** on newspapers, married, become a father, and been in studio publicity two years.(p.328)

stints

• After such often-painful vigilance (and numerous phony ***stints*** of abstinence), retirement naturally created an impulse to live without restraints.(p.328)

stipulation

• The only ***stipulation*** they made was this: I had to make the decision myself.(p.278)

stirred

• He gets ***stirred*** up about their troubles, but not at all about yours.(p.119)

stirring

• Assume on the other hand that father has, at the outset, a ***stirring*** spiritual experience.(p.128)

stirs

• It ***stirs*** his imagination.(p.110)

stitches

• Yes, I put in those ***stitches***.(p.350)

stock

• Abruptly in October 1929 hell broke loose on the New York ***stock*** exchange.(p.4)
• We took ***stock*** honestly.(p.64)
• They took inventory all right, but hung on to some of the worst items in ***stock***.(p.73)
• I came of good ***stock***, of men and women who drank wine all their lives as a beverage, and while they occasionally got drunk at special celebrations, they were up and about their business the next day.(p.231)
• My ***stock*** of material goods isn't great.(p.296)
• High living, a great many fair weather friends, the 1929 ***stock*** market crash, and a couple of years of Depression, soon relieved me one by one of my worldly

goods including my wife.(p.358)
• We had no whiskey in the house, other than my father's private *stock*.(p.484)

stock-in-trade
• It is an effort to discover the truth about the *stock-in-trade*.(p.64)

stockbroker
• The spark that was to flare into the first A.A. group was struck at Akron, Ohio, in June 1935, during a talk between a New York *stockbroker* and an Akron physician.(p.xv)

stocked
• I had some financial success through no ability of my own and, when jobless and almost wiped out in 1930, I began to trade and sell my collection; much of the proceeds went to keep my apartment *stocked* with liquor and almost every night saw me helpless to bed.(p.255)

stocking
• I used also to put it up in four ounce bottles and stick several in my *stocking* tops.(p.177)
• This worked nicely until my wife and I went to see Wallace Beery in "Tugboat Annie," after which the pant-leg and *stocking* racket were out!(p.177)

stockings
• I found some wool *stockings*, some white flannels that had shrunk to my knees, and an old jacket.(p.288)
• Our shoes are not better than the average hobo's, and if we are fortunate enough to have a pair of *stockings* on, nobody notices the runs in them, because of our dazzling beauty and our dirty feet.(p.479)

stocks
• I had developed a theory that most people lost money in *stocks* through ignorance of markets.(p.2)
• *Stocks* were at the low point of 1932, and I had somehow formed a group to buy.(p.5)

stole
• Sometimes I *stole* from my wife's slender purse when the morning terror and madness were on me.(p.6)
• At length peace *stole* over him and he slept.(p.189)
• Once, in a strange gin mill, I *stole* a bottle from behind the bar.(p.411)
• A mellow glow *stole* over me.(p.498)
• Later, I found out that I went into stores and *stole* clothes, then sold them.(p.528)

stolen
• They may be jealous of a God who has *stolen* dad's affections.(p.128)
• I do recall lying on a cold cement floor and shredding into little bits several pieces of *stolen* identification cards, and washing my face in the toilet bowl trying to sober up, and screaming hysterically while clinging to bars too high to see out of, and cursing everyone that came near me.(p.354)
• After a while, I found that the psycho ward was a good place to hide when I had taken something *stolen* to the pawnshop.(p.528)

stomach
• "Suddenly the thought crossed my mind that if I were to put an ounce of whiskey in my milk it couldn't hurt me on a full *stomach*.(p.36)
• I vaguely sensed I was not being any too smart, but felt reassured as I was taking the whiskey on a full *stomach*.(p.36)
• I had some money, all the time in the world, and considerable *stomach* trouble.(p.174)
• I was between Scylla and Charybdis now, because if I did not drink my *stomach* tortured me, and if I did, my nerves did the same thing.(p.175)
• I couldn't *stomach* religion, and I didn't like the mention of God or any of the other capital letters.(p.227)
• I lay across the bed on my *stomach* with nothing but pain and sickness.(p.267)
• The only thing that bothered me was a queasy feeling I had in the pit of my *stomach*.(p.418)
• "You've got to space your drinks and take plenty of water in between," or "coat the *stomach* with a little olive oil," or "drink anything but those damn martinis."(p.433)
• But for some time, it was difficult to keep from taking a pill when I had an appropriate symptom, such as a cough, pain, anxiety, insomnia, a muscle spasm, or an upset *stomach*.(p.448)
• Then I had my first bad *stomach* hemorrhage.(p.490)

stomach-pumped
• Imagine my surprise when I read in a page one "box" that I had been taken from the theater unconscious around noon that day, removed by ambulance to a hospital and *stomach-pumped* and then released.(p.244)

stone
• Helping others is the foundation *stone* of your recovery.(p.97)
• As I grow in A.A., I realize that a person with as much self-will as I had, as hard a head and as diseased an ego, had to try everything that I could think of, butting my head against every *stone* wall before I was ready to come in.(p.384)
• I learn more of that foundation *stone* of character, which is honesty.(p.507)

stones
• Are the *stones* properly in place?(p.75)

stood
• The door opened and he *stood* there, fresh-skinned and glowing.(p.9)
• I *stood* in the sunlight at last.(p.12)
• Without knowing it, had we not been brought to where we *stood* by a certain kind of faith?(p.53)
• He *stood* in the Presence of Infinite Power and Love.(p.56)
• We *stood* at the turning point.(p.59)
• At one end of the room *stood* a glass covered directory of local churches.(p.154)
• And we *stood* there for twenty minutes, telling each other how much better we were, how much better we looked, how much better off we were financially, mentally, physically, morally, and in every way, shape and manner.(p.201)
• I have *stood* listening to street-corner preachers tell how they beat the game.(p.256)
• My wife and family *stood* by me for ten weeks and then, quite justifiably, ejected me.(p.257)
• They opened with a little prayer, and I thought it was very fine that we *stood*, all of us together, and closed with the Lord's Prayer.(p.270)
• I, who had never made a speech in my life and who would have been frightened sick at the prospect, *stood* up in front of Rotary groups in different parts of the city and talked about Alcoholics Anonymous.(p.283)
• In the doorway *stood* a lovely young girl who said, "Are you one of us souses, too?"(p.321)
• I said, "Well, I *stood* it to keep the home together, and for the children's sake."(p.322)
• The very person who *stood* with me through it all and has been my greatest help was the person that I turned against, my husband.(p.338)
• We *stood* at the turning point."(p.349)
• A few *stood* by me, at least in their hearts, throughout the whole of my drinking career.(p.404)
• A corpsman *stood* beside him.(p.422)
• I didn't feel I could lie in bed and squirt the stuff in my veins while my kids and wife *stood* around watching me, so I kept the drug in my bag and the bag in the car and the car in the garage.(p.442)
• When a big, healthy-looking young fellow *stood* up there and said, "I'm a success today if I don't drink today," I thought, "Man, I've got a thousand things to do today before I can brag about not taking a drink, for God's sake!"(p.447)
• After all, it was self (you, me) that *stood* in our own way, that ran the show and ran ourselves into bankruptcy, that hurt the ones we loved.(p.459)
• I had no money – well, maybe a dime – and only the clothes I *stood* in.(p.540)
• I *stood* off and took a long look at life and the values I found in it: I saw a paradox, that he who loses his life does indeed find it.(p.542)
• In my mind's eye, I played and replayed scenes in which I was plucked magically from the bar where I *stood* nursing a drink, and was instantly exalted to some position of power and prestige.(p.560)

stop
• The only requirement for membership is an honest desire to *stop* drinking.(p.xiv)
• I must *stop*, but I cannot!(p.xxvii)
• My incredible behavior in the face of a desperate desire to *stop* was explained.(p.7)
• "He could *stop* if he wanted to."(p.20)
• "She's such a sweet girl, I should think he'd *stop* for her sake."(p.20)
• If a sufficiently strong reason – ill health, falling in love, change of environment, or the warning of a doctor – becomes operative, this man can also *stop* or moderate, although he may find it difficult and troublesome and may even need medical attention.(p.21)
• We are equally positive that once he takes any alcohol whatever into his system, something happens, both in the bodily and mental sense, which makes it virtually impossible for him to *stop*.(p.22)
• At a certain point in the drinking of every alcoholic, he passes into a state where the most powerful desire to *stop* drinking is of absolutely no avail.(p.24)
• Only to have that thought supplanted by "Well, I'll *stop* with the sixth drink."(p.24)
• So many want to *stop* but cannot.(p.25)
• Try to drink and *stop* abruptly.(p.31)
• But the difficulty is that few alcoholics have enough desire to *stop* while there is yet time.(p.32)
• We have heard of few instances where people, who showed definite signs of alcoholism, were able to *stop* for a long period because of an overpowering desire to do so.(p.32)
• Then, gathering all his forces, he attempted to *stop* altogether and found he could not.(p.32)
• If we are planning to *stop* drinking, there must be no reservation of any kind, nor any lurking notion that someday we will be immune to alcohol.(p.33)
• Young people may be encouraged by this man's experience to think that they can *stop*, as he did, on their own will power.(p.33)
• We doubt if many of them can do it, because none will really want to *stop*, and hardly one of them, because of the peculiar mental twist already acquired, will find he can win out.(p.33)
• Certain drinkers, who would be greatly insulted if called alcoholics, are astonished at their inability to *stop*.(p.33)
• Though you may be able to *stop* for a considerable period, you may yet be a potential alcoholic.(p.34)
• For those who are unable to drink moderately the question is how to *stop* altogether.(p.34)
• We are assuming, of course, that the reader desires to *stop*.(p.34)
• He tells you he has decided to *stop* jay-walking for good, but in a few weeks he breaks both legs.(p.38)
• That may be true of certain nonalcoholic people who, though drinking foolishly and heavily at the present time, are able to *stop* or moderate, because their brains and bodies have not been damaged as ours were.(p.39)
• But the actual or potential alcoholic, with hardly an exception, will be absolutely unable to *stop* drinking on the basis of self-knowledge.(p.39)
• The story he told is most instructive, for here was a chap absolutely convinced he had to *stop* drinking, who had no excuse for drinking, who exhibited splendid judgment and determination in all his other concerns, yet was flat on his back nevertheless.(p.40)
• When we saw others solve their problems by a simple reliance upon the Spirit of the Universe, we had to *stop* doubting the power of God.(p.52)
• If he does not want to *stop* drinking, don't waste time trying to persuade him.(p.90)
• If there is any indication that he wants to *stop*, have a good talk with the person most interested in him -- usually his wife.(p.90)
• Give him an account of the struggles you made to *stop*.(p.92)
• Some of us have taken very hard knocks to learn this truth: Job or no job – wife or no wife -- we simply do not *stop* drinking so long as we place dependence upon other people ahead of dependence on God.(p.98)
• Especially when he has before him a way to *stop* his drinking and abuse if he really wants to pay the price.(p.108)
• Some will moderate or *stop* altogether, and some will not.(p.109)
• He is remorseful after serious drinking bouts and tells you he wants to *stop*.(p.109)
• As we say among ourselves, "He wants to want to *stop*."(p.109)
• He may have come to the point where he desperately wants to *stop* but cannot.(p.110)
• Show him you have confidence in his power to *stop* or moderate.(p.112)
• If you act upon these principles, your husband may *stop* or moderate.(p.112)
• Being certain he wants to *stop*, you can go to him with this volume as joyfully as though you had struck oil.(p.113)
• Some men have been so impaired by alcohol that they cannot *stop*.(p.114)
• It may convince your husband he wants to *stop* drinking forever.(p.116)
• And now you know that he can *stop* if he will!(p.116)
• He admitted he was overdoing these things, but frankly said that he was not ready to *stop*.(p.135)
• If you are sure your man does not want to *stop*, he may as well be discharged, the sooner the better.(p.141)
• But there are many men who want to *stop*, and with them you can go far.(p.141)
• State that you know about his drinking, and that it must *stop*.(p.141)

• Will he take every necessary step, submit to anything to get well, to ***stop*** drinking forever?(p.142)
• Do you want to ***stop*** drinking or not?(p.147)
• But if you cannot or will not ***stop*** drinking, I think you ought to resign."(p.148)
• If he wants to ***stop***, he should be afforded a real chance.(p.148)
• If he cannot or does not want to ***stop***, he should be discharged.(p.148)
• At the same time you will feel no reluctance to rid yourself of those who cannot or will not ***stop***.(p.148)
• We think we are sensible when we urge that you ***stop*** this waste and give your worthwhile man a chance.(p.148)
• He had a desperate desire to ***stop***, but saw no way out, for he had earnestly tried many avenues of escape.(p.155)
• When our friend related his experience, the man agreed that no amount of will power he might muster could ***stop*** his drinking for long.(p.155)
• From what you tell me, I know more than ever I can't ***stop***."(p.157)
• He proved to be a devil-may-care young fellow whose parents could not make out whether he wanted to ***stop*** drinking or not.(p.158)
• I thought of what liquor had done to me, the opportunities that I had discarded, the abilities that had been given me and how I had wasted them, and I finally came to the conclusion, that if I didn't want to quit, I certainly ought to want to, and that I was willing to do anything in the world to ***stop*** drinking.(p.186)
• I didn't like having to come home at a certain time; I didn't like this, I didn't like that, and I think the poor girl actually divorced me to help me ***stop*** drinking!(p.199)
• However, on a couple of other occasions, Clarence seemed to bob up at the last saloon that I would ***stop*** at on the way home every day.(p.216)
• In fact, the last three years of my drinking was a routine of barbiturates in the morning, so that I could ***stop*** shaking enough to shave, and then alcohol beginning about four-thirty or five o'clock, with a struggle not to take a drink at noon or during the day, because I had the idea that if I took one drink, I would smell as though I had had a pint.(p.217)
• It didn't ***stop*** there.(p.229)
• My wife made several attempts to get me to ***stop*** and I had the usual visits from persons who would always ask me "Why?" – as if I knew!(p.254)
• And Russ didn't tell me he'd ***stop*** drinking, and he certainly didn't ***stop***.(p.262)
• It would ***stop*** out in front of our house, and I still believe those people sent it!(p.265)
• I sat down on the side of one of their beds, and I started to weep, and I couldn't ***stop***, and I was so startled, and I apologized again and again for it.(p.272)
• Before I ***stop*** -- I always was a great talker – I want to say that nobody will ever know how I miss Annie's advice about things.(p.273)
• Some of the things which used to ***stop*** me in my tracks from fear still make me nervous in the anticipation of their doing, but once I kick myself into doing them nervousness disappears and I enjoy myself.(p.285)
• Upon leaving the office in the evening, my first ***stop*** would be a saloon about a block away.(p.298)
• If I were alone I would ***stop*** at four or five of them, but only one or two in the event I had my mistrusting wife with me.(p.299)
• Well . . . I had a job, and I really wanted desperately to ***stop*** drinking, but couldn't, so I readily agreed to visit the doctor she recommended.(p.301)
• I couldn't ***stop*** drinking.(p.306)
• "It can't be my drinking," I thought, "because I can ***stop*** any time I want to.(p.318)
• I thought I was losing my mind when I realized that I couldn't ***stop*** drinking.(p.324)
• I needed it, and I knew I was drinking too much, but I wasn't conscious of the fact that I should ***stop***.(p.336)
• If I could only ***stop*** thinking, I wouldn't drink.(p.337)
• If I could only ***stop*** drinking, maybe I wouldn't think.(p.337)
• The second one said, "Don't feel that you ***stop*** drinking for anyone other than yourself," and this hit me between the eyes.(p.346)
• Naturally, this experience didn't ***stop*** me.(p.354)
• With these new and enlightening doors opening up to me, I was able to make the eventual decision to ***stop*** drinking, a day at a time -- because I, too, was an alcoholic.(p.355)
• It was a shock of course, but I promised to ***stop*** and she returned.(p.377)
• Couldn't I ***stop***, after a few?(p.404)
• One day soon, the analyses would reveal why I drank and how to ***stop***.(p.408)
• I did not know that I had no power over alcohol, that I, alone and unaided, could not ***stop***; that I was on a downgrade, tearing along at full speed with all my brakes gone, and that the end would be a total smash-up, death or insanity.(p.408)
• For, after those daily self-punishing sessions with myself, after the vows to ***stop***, I would change entirely as evening came on.(p.408)
• A.A. had to ***stop*** my drinking first.(p.409)
• In my cups I began to say, "I can't ***stop***."(p.412)
• My dad, who was a newspaper man and had some connections, had meantime put a ***stop*** on me, and I guess that report went all over the country.(p.424)
• But I didn't want to ***stop*** drinking – not at twenty-two.(p.429)
• "I've got to ***stop*** if I want to live," I told myself, and if I don't want to break my parents' hearts and maybe jeopardize their own carefully built up and hard-fought-for sobriety.(p.429)
• And I knew that somewhere along the line I'd lost the power to ***stop*** drinking.(p.436)
• All found themselves headed for the same destruction, and it seemed they could to nothing whatever to ***stop*** it.(p.455)
• Did that ***stop*** my drinking?(p.468)
• Love has no words to spell or lines to start and ***stop***.(p.474)
• I want to ***stop*** this bad life, but where to turn?(p.475)
• By grace of God I ***stop***, think two things: This would kill good mother and father; then remember boys talk about Indian fellow who been sober three years.(p.475)
• Once, I phoned my brother-in-law and told him I was going to take a handful of pills (in fact, I already had) and I would slash my wrists if he didn't come over to ***stop*** me.(p.479)
• But I knew at that point that I couldn't ***stop*** and I knew that I was a danger to myself and to others.(p.489)
• Nevertheless, we continued to work together and I continued to drink, but I guess, deep down within her heart as well as within mine, we both knew I couldn't ***stop*** drinking.(p.490)
• Vi thought I didn't want to ***stop***.(p.490)
• I have fought hard to ***stop*** drinking.(p.502)
• I tell my wife I cannot ***stop*** drinking.(p.502)
• She had been warned numerous times, not only by her family but by my own mother, that I was a hopeless drunk, that there wasn't anything anybody could do with me, that I'd never ***stop***, and that eventually I'd break her heart.(p.513)
• I had to ***stop*** cold.(p.514)
• The realization came to me that I had to ***stop*** drinking, that I had to find a way.(p.515)
• Before I step out and do anything, I ***stop*** and check it over first, and then let my conscience be my guide.(p.516)
• Since I joined on that April night, A.A. has done more for me than just ***stop*** me from drinking; it has brought me back to life again.(p.524)
• It's time to ***stop*** finding excuses for drinking and getting into trouble, because now there is a way out, and if you want what we have, try coming around and giving the program a chance.(p.530)
• But such is my nature that I must know the reason for things and I didn't ***stop*** until I had satisfied myself about the reasons for my drinking.(p.533)
• Repeated year on end, they are horrible -- frightening and degrading, a chronicle of tragedy which may be greater because the individual undergoing the tragedy, myself, knew what was happening, and yet refused to do anything to ***stop*** it.(p.538)
• I say, "refused to do anything to ***stop*** it."(p.539)
• The truth is, I did not know how to ***stop*** it, nor did I want to, really.(p.539)
• I promised on the grave of a beloved sister that I would ***stop*** drinking.(p.539)
• I wanted to ***stop***.(p.539)
• Society can do anything it chooses to do with me when I am drunk and I can't lift a finger to ***stop*** it, for I forfeit my rights through the simple expedient of becoming a menace to myself and to the people around me.(p.549)
• It's no great trick to ***stop*** drinking; the trick is to stay stopped.(p.554)
• I have come to realize that the name of the game is not so much to ***stop*** drinking as to stay sober.(p.559)
• Alcoholics can ***stop*** drinking in many places and many ways – but Alcoholics Anonymous offers us a way to stay sober.(p.559)
• Three – The only requirement for A.A. membership is a desire to ***stop*** drinking.(p.564)

stopped

• Nine of the stories in Part II ("They ***Stopped*** in Time") are carried over from the second edition; eight new stories have been added.(p.xii)
• This had to be ***stopped***.(p.5)
• Though there is no way of proving it, we believe that early in our drinking careers most of us could have ***stopped*** drinking.(p.32)
• On the way I felt hungry so I ***stopped*** at a roadside place where they have a bar.(p.36)
• Ain't it grand the wind ***stopped*** blowin'?"(p.82)
• Besides, we have ***stopped*** fighting anybody or anything.(p.103)
• We thought, on the whole, we were pretty good women, capable of being nicer if our husbands ***stopped*** drinking.(p.116)
• Couples are occasionally dismayed to find that when drinking is ***stopped*** the man tends to be impotent.(p.134)
• I know, in my own particular case, that nothing my company could have done would have ***stopped*** me for, so long as I was able to hold my position, I could not possibly realize how serious my situation was.(p.141)
• THEY *STOPPED* IN TIME(p.167)
• I had a couple of shorter talks with this man afterward, and ***stopped*** drinking abruptly.(p.179)
• So having licked it, there was no reason why I shouldn't have a drink, and I ***stopped*** in before I got home and had one.(p.203)
• Shortly after that, my brother, who had then become associated with a group of people and had ***stopped*** drinking, urged me to attend meetings with him.(p.205)
• Abruptly I ***stopped*** speaking.(p.222)
• They seemed to be happy in their fashion, they and their little groups of supporters, but always pride of intellect ***stopped*** me from seeking what they evidently had.(p.256)
• In the spring of 1939, Bill ***stopped*** off in Akron on his way to Detroit on business.(p.281)
• Doctors told me before I ***stopped*** that I had only three years at the outside to live.(p.295)
• I have ***stopped*** tilting at windmills, and instead have tried to accomplish the little daily tasks, unimportant in themselves, but tasks that are an integral part of living fully.(p.295)
• The general procedure was to take four or five shots in the first place I ***stopped*** at.(p.299)
• THEY *STOPPED* IN TIME(p.315)
• I never ***stopped*** to think.(p.325)
• One said, "Don't feel that you are a martyr because you ***stopped*** drinking," and this hit me between the eyes.(p.346)
• So I went down to him quite a few times a month and had him shoot me full of the stuff; and then I went across the street to a little drug store to take a glass of beer or two beers, and then ***stopped*** at the liquor store to get myself a pint and go home.(p.389)
• Up to that time, I was so completely baffled by my behavior that I had never really ***stopped*** to think at all.(p.392)
• I ***stopped*** at the cashier's any hour of the night on the way to the bar and cashed a check.(p.410)
• When I ***stopped*** living in the problem and began living in the answer, the problem went away.(p.449)
• While I was taking inventory in the cold-storage locker one Sunday, a wooden sign bolted to the inside door ***stopped*** me in my tracks.(p.461)
• Finally they ***stopped*** and bought me a bottle; they knew so well that would keep me quiet.(p.466)
• But there happened to be a liquor store between the post office and the mill, and I ***stopped*** to get that one drink.(p.493)
• That really ***stopped*** me for a little bit.(p.510)
• I ***stopped*** off just to have one drink to see if it tasted the same on the way back to London, and that night I was carried back to bed again.(p.522)
• What struck me most was that they all seemed to be quite pleased with having made a job of it and having ***stopped*** drinking.(p.524)
• I didn't want that, so I ***stopped*** going to the psycho ward.(p.528)
• It's no great trick to stop drinking; the trick is to stay ***stopped***.(p.554)

stopping

• When a few men in this city have found themselves, and have discovered the joy of helping others to face life again, there will be no ***stopping*** until everyone in that town has had his opportunity to recover -- if he can and will.(p.163)

• Rehearsals then became a part of the pattern, ***stopping*** at bars on the way to or from the place where drinks were to be served.(p.375)
• The thought of ***stopping*** drinking just never occurred to me.(p.522)

store

• My wife began to work in a department ***store***, coming home exhausted to find me drunk.(p.4)
• He did call me a cab and when I got into the cab, I said, "Drive me to a liquor ***store***."(p.204)
• We drove to a ***store*** in North Hill and I sent him in with what money I had to get a quart.(p.204)
• I couldn't go to one wine ***store*** and look the man honestly in the face and buy a bottle, as I used to do when I had parties and entertained and did normal drinking.(p.336)
• A lucky break, at least some will call it lucky, was in ***store*** for me at my group that night.(p.365)
• So I went down to him quite a few times a month and had him shoot me full of the stuff; and then I went across the street to a little drug ***store*** to take a glass of beer or two beers, and then stopped at the liquor ***store*** to get myself a pint and go home.(p.389)
• A very good friend of mine who owned a drug ***store*** across the street from us, came by only about two hours later and said that he had seen Vi down town.(p.487)
• At that time the repeal whiskies were back, and I'd go to the ***store*** and buy my whiskey and take it to my office and put it under the desk, first in one place and then in another, and there soon was an accumulation of empty bottles.(p.488)
• But there happened to be a liquor ***store*** between the post office and the mill, and I stopped to get that one drink.(p.493)
• After he'd talked half an hour, I still wanted him to hurry up and get out so I could go and get some whiskey before the liquor ***store*** closed.(p.494)

storeroom

• Mother would take me in only if I would stay locked in a small ***storeroom*** and give her my clothes and shoes.(p.238)

stores

• However, due to financial difficulties the whole printing was, for a while, held up and the book received no publicity, nor, of course, was it available in the ***stores***, even if one knew it existed.(p.307)
• When he left I walked with him to the streetcar line, which was just about a half a block, but there were two liquor ***stores***, one on each corner from my home.(p.495)
• I put Charlie on the car and when I left him I passed both of those liquor ***stores*** without even thinking about them.(p.495)
• Later, I found out that I went into ***stores*** and stole clothes, then sold them.(p.528)

stories

• But the chief change was in the section of personal ***stories***, which was expanded to reflect the Fellowship's growth.(p.xi)
• "Bill's Story," "Doctor Bob's Nightmare," and one other personal history from the first edition were retained intact; three were edited and one of these was retitled; new versions of two ***stories*** were written with new titles; thirty completely new ***stories*** were added; and the story section was divided into three parts, under the same headings that are used now.(p.xi)
• Nine of the ***stories*** in Part II ("They Stopped in Time") are carried over from the second edition; eight new ***stories*** have been added.(p.xii)
• In Part III ("They Lost Nearly All"), eight ***stories*** have been retained; five are new.(p.xii)
• If you have a drinking problem, we hope that you may pause in reading one of the forty-four personal ***stories*** and think: "Yes, that happened to me"; or, more important, "Yes, I've felt like that"; or most important, "Yes, I believe this program can work for me, too."(p.xii)
• In the spring of 1940, John D. Rockefeller, Jr. gave a dinner for many of his friends to which he invited A.A. members to tell their ***stories***.(p.xviii)
• Each individual, in the personal ***stories***, describes in his own language and from his own point of view the way he established his relationship with God.(p.29)
• As to two of you men, whose ***stories*** I have heard, there is no doubt in my mind that you were 100% hopeless, apart from divine help.(p.43)
• In our personal ***stories*** you will find a wide variation in the way each teller approaches and conceives of the Power which is greater than himself.(p.50)
• Our ***stories*** disclose in a general way what we used to be like, what happened, and what we are like now.(p.58)
• If his mood is light, tell him humorous ***stories*** of your escapades.(p.91)
• Tell him some of the interesting ***stories*** you have read.(p.112)
• We find it better when possible, to stick to our own ***stories***.(p.125)
• PERSONAL ***STORIES***(p.165)
• This group of thirteen ***stories*** shows that sobriety in A.A. can be lasting.(p.167)
• Seventeen ***stories*** may help you decide whether you are alcoholic; also, whether A.A. is for you.(p.167)
• Dr. Bob and the twelve men and women who here tell their ***stories*** were among the early members of A.A.'s first groups.(p.169)
• I believe every member of the Akron Group did come to see me, which impressed me terrifically, not so much because of the ***stories*** they told, but because they would take the time to come and talk to me without even knowing who I was.(p.218)
• One of the things that came up repeatedly in the ***stories*** they told me was that once they had accepted the program, they never had a desire to take a drink.(p.219)
• He said, "Let's put the Big Book away again, and when you read it again, turn to the back and read some of the ***stories***.(p.269)
• Here, while in a hospital bed, men with clear eyes, happy faces, and a look of assurance and purposefulness about them, came to see me and told me their ***stories***.(p.279)
• But after hearing their ***stories***, I knew that I was, and I admitted it.(p.320)
• The movie racket had kept me too long from writing those novels, articles, short ***stories***, and scripts on which I had copious notes.(p.330)
• But the saddest, and thus the most consoling, drifted through from the country-music station -- ***stories*** of broken hearts, wasted lives, lost loves, sung plaintively.(p.332)
• They told me their ***stories***, which were much more rugged than mine -- yet what they said made sense, and the way they put it was easy for me to understand, with an understanding I had never had before.(p.363)
• When I hear the more rugged ***stories*** of alcoholics who became sicker than I did with this affliction, I humbly thank God for showing me "the handwriting on the wall."(p.367)
• However, after I heard a few ***stories*** of jails, sanitariums, broken homes and skid row, I wondered if I really was an alcoholic.(p.378)
• Above all, he noticed that I drank a good deal, often got tight in his company and told him naughty ***stories***.(p.403)
• He did not like naughty ***stories***, so I made them naughtier.(p.403)
• I wrote and sold some short ***stories***.(p.409)
• The thirteen ***stories*** in this group tell of alcoholism at its miserable worst.(p.455)
• Yet prisoners often can't identify with many A.A. members' drinking ***stories***.(p.458)
• I had a rough lot, but I don't worry about that, after hearing the ***stories*** of many others.(p.511)
• It has shown me, through the tragic ***stories*** of so many other alcoholics, the utter futility of self pity.(p.525)

storm

• There, I could be a proper mother and wife while drinking up a ***storm***.(p.369)

story

• "Bill's ***Story***," "Doctor Bob's Nightmare," and one other personal history from the first edition were retained intact; three were edited and one of these was retitled; new versions of two stories were written with new titles; thirty completely new stories were added; and the ***story*** section was divided into three parts, under the same headings that are used now.(p.xi)
• He had also been greatly helped by the late Dr. William D. Silkworth, a New York specialist in alcoholism who is now accounted no less than a medical saint by A.A. members, and whose ***story*** of the early days of our Society appears in the next pages.(p.xvi)
• Later, he requested the privilege of being allowed to tell his ***story*** to other patients here and with some misgiving, we consented.(p.xxv)
• BILL'S ***STORY***(p.1)
• This is his ***story***: "I came to work on Tuesday morning.(p.36)
• The ***story*** he told is most instructive, for here was a chap absolutely convinced he had to stop drinking, who had no excuse for drinking, who exhibited splendid judgment and determination in all his other concerns, yet was flat on his back nevertheless.(p.40)
• Fred's ***story*** speaks for itself.(p.43)
• Only thirty years later the conquest of the air was almost an old ***story*** and airplane travel was in full swing.(p.52)
• His ***story*** is so interesting that some of it should be told now.(p.55)
• But they had not learned enough of humility, fearlessness and honesty, in the sense we find it necessary, until they told someone else all their life ***story***.(p.73)
• Such parts of our ***story*** we tell to someone who will understand, yet be unaffected.(p.74)
• When we decide who is to hear our ***story***, we waste no time.(p.75)
• This brings to mind a ***story*** about one of our friends.(p.80)
• Usually the family should not try to tell your ***story***.(p.91)
• Doctors are rightly loath to tell alcoholic patients the whole ***story*** unless it will serve some good purpose.(p.92)
• Perhaps your ***story*** will help him see where he has failed to practice the very precepts he knows so well.(p.93)
• Let him know you are available if he wishes to make a decision and tell his ***story***, but do not insist upon it if he prefers to consult someone else.(p.96)
• The ***story*** of how you and your wife settled your difficulties is worth any amount of criticism.(p.100)
• Why not at least afford him an opportunity to hear my ***story***?(p.138)
• Impressed by those who visited him at the hospital, he capitulated entirely when, later, in an upper room of this house, he heard the ***story*** of some man whose experience closely tallied with his own.(p.160)
• Beginning with the ***story*** of "Dr. Bob," a co-founder of A.A., there are here presented three groups of personal histories.(p.165)
• So, after hearing some more of my ***story***, he turned around and said to Doc -- I don't think he knew I heard him, but I did -- he said, "Well, I believe he's worth saving and working on."(p.185)
• (Bill D. now continues his ***story***.)(p.189)
• When he left, I realized from his ***story*** that as a drinker I was just a panty-waist.(p.208)
• So the ***story*** of my introduction into A.A. begins with the activities of my wife.(p.216)
• But then the ***story*** became my own.(p.225)
• I was born in Europe, in Alsace to be exact, shortly after it had become German, and practically grew up with the "good Rhine wine" of song and ***story***.(p.230)
• I don't think the boys were completely convinced of my personality change, for they fought shy of including my ***story*** in the book, so my only contribution to their literary efforts was my firm conviction, being still a theological rebel, that the word God should be qualified with the phrase "as we understand him" -- for that was the only way I could accept spirituality.(p.248)
• The ***story*** of Alcoholics Anonymous fascinated me.(p.258)
• He said, "This is my ***story***" -- real prim.(p.268)
• But he told a ***story*** of drinking that was amazing to me.(p.268)
• Jack brought the Saturday Post with Jack Alexander's ***story***.(p.268)
• That's my ***story***.(p.274)
• Probably only a few readers of this ***story*** will be able, from personal experiences of their own, to understand the exhilaration and sense of accomplishment which I felt after finishing this seemingly simple assignment.(p.276)
• I do feel, though, that the fact that I finally grew up to a point where I could even tackle such a job is the apex of the ***story*** of a man who spent eighteen years running away from life.(p.286)
• He spent two hours with me that night telling me his ***story***.(p.290)
• I thought at times that he was telling my ***story***!(p.290)
• The next afternoon and evening, two other men visited me and each told me his ***story*** and the things that they were doing to try to recover from this tragic illness.(p.290)
• He mentioned lies and deceptions in the course of his ***story*** in the presence of the one person in the world I wouldn't want to know such things.(p.302)
• However, as he unfolded his ***story*** for me, I could not help but believe him.(p.309)
• It was my line, the ***story*** of my life.(p.333)
• My ***story*** happens to be a particular kind of woman's ***story***; the ***story*** of the woman who drinks at home.(p.335)
• I had to give him a ***story*** and ask him the same question over and over again, "Well, now, how many will

that bottle serve?"(p.336)

• I could end my *story* here, but for the new man I would like to add a few words.(p.366)

• I haven't written anything about that part of my *story*, but I believe in a Greater Power which I call God and I ask for His wisdom and guidance daily.(p.366)

• If there is something in my *story* that rings a bell with you, then do something -- now!(p.368)

• The *story* is not very different from that of thousands of other young men in my generation.(p.373)

• The only thing I have really to offer you is my own *story*, telling you just what sort of a drunk I was.(p.384)

• I, who had feared questions, now began trying to interrupt and tell my *story*.(p.414)

• In ending my *story* I like to think about this.(p.417)

• To cut a long *story* short, I spent seven years and ten thousand dollars on my psychiatric adventure, and emerged in worse condition than ever.(p.434)

• My *story* has a happy ending, but not of the conventional kind.(p.437)

• This first *story* I ever write.(p.474)

• JIM'S *STORY*(p.483)

• From that point on, it's just the average drinker's *story*.(p.488)

• That's my *story* of what A.A. has done for me.(p.496)

• I go to see a man I had been asked to visit and tell him my *story*.(p.505)

• This caused the rather cryptic comment from one of my A.A. friends, when I told my *story* after coming into the program, that I had always been a cinch for the program, for I had always been interested in mankind, but that I was just taking them one man at a time.(p.548)

Stouffer

• Dr. John F. *Stouffer*, Chief Psychiatrist, Philadelphia General Hospital, citing his experience with A.A., said: "The alcoholics we get here at Philadelphia General are mostly those who cannot afford private treatment, and A.A. is by far the greatest thing we have been able to offer them.(p.572)

stove

• There is a complete failure of the kind of defense that keeps one from putting his hand on a hot *stove*.(p.24)

straggle

• Each in his turn may be footsore and may *straggle*.(p.122)

straight

• He looked *straight* at me.(p.9)

• How can such a lack of proportion, of the ability to think *straight*, be called anything else?(p.37)

• We could not prove life in the sense that you can prove a *straight* line is the shortest distance between two points, yet, there it was.(p.54)

• We admitted our wrongs honestly and were willing to set these matters *straight*.(p.67)

• One school would allow man no flavor for his fare and the other would have us all on a *straight* pepper diet.(p.69)

• Your man will fare better if placed in such physical condition that he can think *straight* and no longer craves liquor.(p.143)

• It then occurred to me that after one was all smelled up with beer nobody could tell what had been drunk, so I began to fortify my beer with *straight* alcohol.(p.178)

• But this day my doctor gave it to me *straight* and said, "People like you are pretty well known to the medical profession.(p.307)

• I couldn't think *straight* any more.(p.319)

• I couldn't look them *straight* in the eyes, although I was always a self-possessed brazen sort of person.(p.323)

• One afternoon, the year after moving to Houston, I got as drunk as a skunk, and while I do not walk very *straight* sober, you should see me when I'm drunk!(p.390)

• I would drink all night in bars, come home about five a.m., down a good big glass of whiskey *straight*, and tumble into bed.(p.428)

• I have had the joy of seeing many a human being, down and out, learn to stand *straight* again, and to proceed under his own power to happiness in life.(p.541)

straighten

• When the spiritual malady is overcome, we *straighten* out mentally and physically.(p.64)

• We have listed the people we have hurt by our conduct, and are willing to *straighten* out the past if we can.(p.70)

• Simply we tell him that we will never get over drinking until we have done our utmost to *straighten* out the past.(p.77)

• They may not see why their love and devotion did not *straighten* him out.(p.128)

• I was going to *straighten* up.(p.234)

• All they talked of that first week-end was God, and how they were going to *straighten* out Jackie's and my life.(p.245)

• I knew they needed to *straighten* out their thinking and habits, but I was all right, I just drank too much.(p.246)

straightened

• Outline the program of action, explaining how you made a self-appraisal, how you *straightened* out your past and why you are now endeavoring to be helpful to him.(p.94)

• I have enjoyed every moment spent in getting them *straightened* out.(p.150)

• There my drinking became so much worse that the boys in the fraternity house where I lived felt forced to send for my father, who made a long journey in the vain endeavor to get me *straightened* around.(p.174)

• I said, "Yes, Doc, I would like to quit, at least for five, six, or eight months, until I get things *straightened* up, and begin to get the respect of my wife and some other people back, and get my finances fixed up and so on."(p.187)

• She had a hairdresser who used to tell her about a brother-in-law who had been quite a drinker and about some doctor in Akron who had *straightened* him out.(p.216)

• I had to persist in my attempts to get *straightened* out enough to be able to use the drinks I needed, without their turning on me.(p.227)

• There was one meeting a week at Bill's home in Brooklyn, and we all took turns there spouting off about how we had changed our lives overnight, how many drunks we had saved and *straightened* out, and last, but not least, how God had touched each of us personally on the shoulder.(p.246)

straightway

• *Straightway*, Bob called Akron's City Hospital and asked for the nurse on the receiving ward.(p.188)

strain

• The *strain* of overwork led me to the bottle again.(p.254)

• But during a period of particular stress and *strain* about thirteen years ago, I resorted to alcohol in my home, alone, as a means of temporary release, as a means of getting a little extra sleep.(p.335)

• I know there are some alcoholics who seem terribly, terribly grown-up, but I think that they are trying to make themselves think they are grown-up, and the *strain* of their effort is what is causing them to drink -- a sense of inadequacy, a childish vanity to be the most popular, the most sought after, the mostest of the most.(p.535)

strained

• Now, the domestic problem: There may be divorce, separation, or just *strained* relations.(p.98)

• Cessation of drinking is but the first step away from a highly *strained*, abnormal condition.(p.122)

straining

• He is *straining* every nerve to make up for lost time.(p.126)

straitjacket

• The doctor motioned to the corpsman to undo my *straitjacket* and leg restraints.(p.422)

strange

• On the other hand -- and *strange* as this may seem to those who do not understand -- once a psychic change has occurred, the very same person who seemed doomed, who had so many problems he despaired of ever solving them, suddenly finds himself easily able to control his desire for alcohol, the only effort necessary being that required to follow a few simple rules.(p.xxvii)

• One year later he called to see me, and I experienced a very *strange* sensation.(p.xxix)

• Few people really are, for that means blind faith in the *strange* proposition that this universe originated in a cipher and aimlessly rushes nowhere.(p.10)

• And the truth, *strange* to say, is usually that he has no more idea why he took that first drink than you have.(p.23)

• I saw that will power and self-knowledge would not help in those *strange* mental blank spots.(p.42)

• Perhaps your husband has been living in that *strange* world of alcoholism where everything is distorted and exaggerated.(p.108)

• As soon as his sobriety begins to be taken as a matter of course, the family may look at their *strange* new dad with apprehension, then with irritation.(p.128)

• Bitterly discouraged, he found himself in a *strange* place, discredited and almost broke.(p.154)

• I'd waked up in *strange* rooms before, fully dressed on a bed or a couch; I'd waked up in my own room, in or on my own bed, not knowing what hour or day it was, afraid to ask . . . but this was different.(p.222)

• This time I seemed to be already awake, sitting upright in a big easy chair, in the middle of an animated conversation with a perfectly *strange* young woman, who didn't appear to think it *strange*.(p.222)

• Now I was in a *strange* house, in a *strange* city, and fear gripped me.(p.279)

• Once, in a *strange* gin mill, I stole a bottle from behind the bar.(p.411)

• But now a *strange* thing happened.(p.412)

• The *strange* A.A. put me at ease.(p.413)

• Against my better judgment, I went to a meeting with him that night, and a *strange* thing began to happen.(p.446)

• It is true that I -- of all people, *strange* as it may seem, and even though I didn't give my permission -- really, really am an alcoholic of sorts.(p.448)

• It wasn't anything *strange* to me, and I knew if I wanted to stay on the outside, that would be the spot for me.(p.510)

• Finally, he was drinking to keep away those little men, and those *strange* voices, and the organ music that came out of the walls.(p.512)

• I was drinking to keep away the shakes, drinking to keep away those little men and those *strange* voices and the organ music that comes out of the walls.(p.514)

• In part, it was a feeling of intense shame at having to leave the Army during the war, but mostly it was resentment that this kind of thing should happen to me for, *strange* as it may seem, up to then I still thought I could control drinking.(p.521)

• I found myself being lifted onto a stretcher and whisked away in an ambulance to a *strange* hospital.(p.558)

strangely

• *Strangely* enough, wives, parents and intimate friends usually find us even more unapproachable than do the psychiatrist and the doctor.(p.18)

• However intelligent we may have been in other respects, where alcohol has been involved, we have been *strangely* insane.(p.38)

• No wonder an alcoholic is *strangely* irrational.(p.140)

• One man and his wife placed their large home at the disposal of this *strangely* assorted crowd.(p.160)

• *Strangely* enough, I became acquainted with the "hilarious life" just at the time in my own life when I was beginning really to settle down to a common-sense, sane domesticity.(p.297)

• *Strangely* enough, right through to the end of my twenty-six years in the Army, I was still being offered very good and important jobs in spite of the fact that my superiors must have known that I wasn't thoroughly reliable.(p.519)

stranger

• To me he was a *stranger*, and so he left me.(p.xxix)

• It must have been a long time since I had my last drink -- but I didn't dare ask this *stranger* for one.(p.223)

• Some days later, after he had been discharged, a *stranger* came into my shop in the nearby town.(p.257)

• We are so beautiful that it is never too much trouble to get some poor *stranger* to buy us a drink.(p.479)

• I talk to the *stranger* in the seat beside me.(p.505)

strangers

• When drinking, they were *strangers*.(p.107)

• Your house is filled with *strangers*.(p.119)

• Two days later, a future fellow of Alcoholics Anonymous stared glassily at the *strangers* beside his bed.(p.157)

• They knew they had a host of new friends; it seemed they had known these *strangers* always.(p.161)

• I went trembling into a house in Brooklyn filled with *strangers* . . . and I found I had come home at last, to my own kind.(p.228)

• To go north into the empty pine country and shoot myself, or to go south in the faint hope that a bunch of *strangers* might help me with my drinking problem.(p.278)

• During this time, I had been threatened, beaten, kissed, praised and damned alternately by relatives, family, friends and *strangers*, but of course it all went for naught.(p.300)

• They did not seem ashamed to be with us, these *strangers*.(p.415)

• Within a month, the police, the hospital authorities, several kind ***strangers***, most of my friends, all of my close relatives, and a few adepts at rolling a drunk and removing his wrist watch and wallet had been involved.(p.532)
• My grandparents were ***strangers*** to me and I remember being lonely, and terrified and hurt.(p.545)

strap
• They also were held in some sort of ***strap*** arrangement.(p.422)

strapped
• Understand he was once a well-known lawyer in town, but just now we've got him ***strapped*** down tight."(p.156)
• Had blacked the eyes of two nurses, and now they had him ***strapped*** down tight.(p.188)
• Many of them carried a flask and sandwich case, ***strapped*** to their saddles so they could stay out all day.(p.404)

straw
• Well, suicide was a last ***straw*** matter, and I had not drawn the last ***straw*** yet.(p.278)

streak
• When, however, the perfectly logical assumption is suggested that underneath the material world and life as we see it, there is an All Powerful, Guiding, Creative Intelligence, right there our perverse ***streak*** comes to the surface and we laboriously set out to convince ourselves it isn't so.(p.49)
• I seemed to react by developing a ***streak*** of varying meanness, which would cause me to do things to create excitement and to get attention.(p.211)

streaked
• I had white trousers on, white shoes and a white shirt that was ***streaked*** with blood.(p.204)

stream
• Or were we thinking of what we could do for others, of what we could pack into the ***stream*** of life?(p.86)
• Arrangements were also made with the chief psychiatrist of a large public hospital to select still others from the ***stream*** of misery which flows through that institution.(p.163)

streamed
• The walls crumpled – and the light ***streamed*** in.(p.228)

street
• My work took me about Wall ***street*** and little by little I became interested in the market.(p.2)
• The inviting maelstrom of Wall ***Street*** had me in its grip.(p.2)
• At the end of it, my reports to Wall ***street*** procured me a position there and the use of a large expense account.(p.3)
• I hardly dared cross the ***street***, lest I collapse and be run down by an early morning truck, for it was scarcely daylight.(p.6)
• We are there to sweep off our side of the ***street*** realizing that nothing worth while can be accomplished until we do so, never trying to tell him what he should do.(p.77)
• Our design for living is not a one-way ***street***.(p.81)
• He wouldn't give me any money for the groceries, but he did take me across the ***street*** and buy me a bag of candy, which I later took back and traded for a loaf of bread.(p.193)
• I optioned a piece of land just off East Market ***Street*** to put up a three-hundred suite apartment.(p.198)
• At three-thirty the next morning, I was in Champlain ***Street*** Station, in jail for driving while intoxicated and insulting an officer; and the suit of which I was so proud was in such shape that the turnkey had to get me a pair of trousers to go into court in the next morning.(p.201)
• I went downstairs and there was the grizzly old veteran police officer in charge of the property desk, and as he gave me the stuff, he asked, "Are you going out in the ***street*** that way?"(p.204)
• That had been in the center of New York, on noisy 42nd ***Street*** . . . this was obviously a quiet residential section.(p.223)
• Tom Sharkey's brawling bar on 14th ***Street*** and the famous wine-room at the back were headquarters for me.(p.251)
• I also talked A.A. to every friend who would listen, at lunch, at dinner, on ***street*** corners.(p.282)
• That was on a hot summer evening, down in the Greenwich Village Group, and there was a little porch out there in the old meeting place on Sullivan ***Street***, and after the meeting I went out on the steps for some air.(p.321)
• I said to her one day when I met her on the ***street***, "What sort of volunteer work do you do?"(p.326)
• I was living in a small room on West 53rd ***Street*** right off Fifth Avenue, when I met a young lady who eventually was responsible for altering my entire way of living.(p.359)
• We soon resumed our marriage, even moved away from the ***street*** of sad memories and found a new home.(p.371)
• So I went down to him quite a few times a month and had him shoot me full of the stuff; and then I went across the ***street*** to a little drug store to take a glass of beer or two beers, and then stopped at the liquor store to get myself a pint and go home.(p.389)
• I would walk up and down under the 59th ***Street*** bridge, trying to get up the nerve to go up there and jump.(p.411)
• In those days the A.A. Foundation was down in the Wall ***Street*** district of New York.(p.413)
• At one time, I was using twenty caps a day; I nearly died half a dozen times on the ***street***.(p.480)
• A very good friend of mine who owned a drug store across the ***street*** from us, came by only about two hours later and said that he had seen Vi down town.(p.487)
• I had an advantage in having an idea of what A.A. was about before coming out on the ***street***.(p.510)
• You hit the ***street*** about ten minutes to eight, and you walk around the block, God knows how many times, waiting for that joint to open.(p.514)
• Things got so bad, I was afraid to go on the ***street***, so I turned to Mothers' Aid.(p.527)

street-car
• I was picked up at two-thirty that morning with my car smashed up by a ***street-car*** because I had run into a big concrete safety zone, and the ***street-car*** had run into me, and they took me out through the roof -- there's where I lost the suit.(p.202)

street-corner
• I have stood listening to ***street-corner*** preachers tell how they beat the game.(p.256)

streetcar
• The details of the long road back to something resembling normal living – the first short ***streetcar*** ride, the purchase of a used bike which enabled me to widen the narrow horizon of life, the first trip downtown – I will not dwell on.(p.276)
• I don't remember whether I went by ***streetcar***, whether I walked or went in a taxicab.(p.492)
• When he left I walked with him to the ***streetcar*** line, which was just about a half a block, but there were two liquor stores, one on each corner from my home.(p.495)

streetcars
• During the first three months I carried on all these activities without a car, depending entirely on buses and ***streetcars*** -- I, who had always to have a car at my immediate command.(p.283)

streets
• On through the years this conduct continues, accompanied by his continual promises to be careful or to keep off the ***streets*** altogether.(p.38)
• Saying goodbye to my wife and baby, I was treading Manhattan's ***streets*** in a little more than a week.(p.252)
• "There are men on the ***streets*** of New York today who were worse than you, and they don't drink any more."(p.503)

strength
• Each day, somewhere in the world, recovery begins when one alcoholic talks with another alcoholic, sharing experience, ***strength***, and hope.(p.xxii)
• When they talked of a God personal to me, who was love, superhuman ***strength*** and direction, I became irritated and my mind snapped shut against such a theory.(p.10)
• I was to sit quietly when in doubt, asking only for direction and ***strength*** to meet my problems as He would have me.(p.13)
• Paradoxically, it is the way of ***strength***.(p.68)
• To sum up about sex: We earnestly pray for the right ideal, for guidance in each questionable situation, for sanity, and for the ***strength*** to do the right thing.(p.70)
• Grant me ***strength***, as I go out from here, to do your bidding.(p.76)
• Reminding ourselves that we have decided to go to any length to find a spiritual experience we ask that we be given ***strength*** and direction to do the right thing, no matter what the personal consequences may be.(p.79)
• Much has already been said about receiving ***strength***, inspiration, and direction from Him who has all knowledge and power.(p.85)
• So, at the time Dr. Bob and Bill came along I had about run out my ***strength***.(p.182)
• I figured the only difference between me and a millionaire was that I hadn't the ***strength***, or that he got the breaks and I didn't.(p.197)
• And, accepting, I felt a new inner comfort, and the willingness and ***strength*** to do something about the traits I couldn't live with.(p.229)
• As I go along I seem to get ***strength*** daily to be able to resist more easily.(p.237)
• In the spiritual ***strength*** I had found, because of A.A., I felt that I had made a complete surrender, that I had really turned my life over that summer.(p.271)
• Immediately a great feeling of peace descended upon me, intermingled with a feeling of being suffused with a quiet ***strength***.(p.280)
• When the time comes to solve them, God will give me ***strength*** for that day.(p.341)
• ***Strength*** has come from weakness.(p.507)
• I choose to believe that the Power greater than ourselves we ask for help, wrapped my shivering body in loving warmth and ***strength*** which has never left me.(p.541)
• I hope I have been able to impart to you, the reader, at least a bit of what I know; the joy of living, the irresistible power of divine love and its healing ***strength***, and the fact that we, as sentient beings, have the knowledge to choose between good and evil, and, choosing good, are made happy.(p.543)

strengthen
• He had already imbued them with his own spirit until they were ready and willing at all times to go where sent, and as a doctor he well knew that this mission and duty would ***strengthen*** them as it later helped me.(p.235)

strenuous
• It also indicated that ***strenuous*** work, one alcoholic with another, was vital to permanent recovery.(p.xvii)
• Our struggles with them are variously ***strenuous***, comic and tragic.(p.16)
• Though our decision was a vital and crucial step, it could have little permanent effect unless at once followed by a ***strenuous*** effort to face, and to be rid of, the things in ourselves which had been blocking us.(p.64)
• Coming up to final exams I went on a particularly ***strenuous*** spree.(p.174)
• I said I was okay, but if it would make her feel better I would go "as tired as I was after the ***strenuous*** holidays."(p.365)

strenuously
• Because it affected me so ***strenuously***, they felt that hospitalization was indicated and I awoke in a hospital.(p.207)

stress
• ***Stress*** the spiritual feature freely.(p.93)
• It's only natural that we don't have the capacity to change, but we ought not to criticize those who have, There's another thing I would ***stress***.(p.273)
• He laid great ***stress*** on the progression of his attitude toward life and people, and most of his attitudes had been very similar to mine.(p.290)
• But during a period of particular ***stress*** and strain about thirteen years ago, I resorted to alcohol in my home, alone, as a means of temporary release, as a means of getting a little extra sleep.(p.335)

stressed
• Paul S. had just called me, and I remember he ***stressed*** reading the Big Book.(p.269)

stretch
• Most of us have believed that if we remained sober for a long ***stretch***, we could thereafter drink normally.(p.33)
• Military service was compulsory and I did my ***stretch*** with the class of my age, goose-stepping in German barracks and taking part in the Boxer Rebellion in China, my first time at any great distance from home.(p.230)
• But as the years go by, the ***stretch*** becomes unbearable; and the man with the grown-up brain and the childish emotions – vanity, self-interest, false pride, jealousy, longing for social approval, to name few -- becomes a prime candidate for alcohol.(p.534)

stretched
• Quicksand ***stretched*** around me in all directions.(p.8)
• Friendly hands had ***stretched*** out in welcome.(p.53)
• My personality was ***stretched*** almost to splitting in the effort; schizophrenia stared me in the face, and one night I was in a suicidal despair.(p.435)
• But the week-ends ***stretched*** on into Mondays and the time soon came when I drank every day.(p.488)

stretcher
• I found myself being lifted onto a ***stretcher*** and

whisked away in an ambulance to a strange hospital.(p.558)

stretches

• These things were carried out in moments of less severe hangover or short *stretches* on the wagon.(p.409)

stricken

• We have been terror *stricken*.(p.105)

• He and his wife would leave elated by the thought of what they could now do for some *stricken* acquaintance and his family.(p.160)

strictly

• While on the subject of confidence, can you adopt the attitude that so far as you are concerned this will be a *strictly* personal matter, that his alcoholic derelictions, the treatment about to be undertaken, will never be discussed without his consent?(p.143)

• It was *strictly* a one man operation and I knew I had to tend to my knitting to make a go of it.(p.360)

• Age and the law were still against me, but laws were not as *strictly* enforced in those days as they are now, and I discovered that as long as I had the green blood, there was always a way to get alcohol, either from a nondiscriminatory bartender or from an older friend who would be glad to purchase the joy juice for the privilege of sharing it.(p.397)

• At fifteen I was *strictly* a beer drinker.(p.423)

strikes

• We hope it *strikes* home to thousands like him.(p.43)

• Halfway down the driveway a thought *strikes* me.(p.506)

strikingly

• On one proposition, however, these men and women are *strikingly* agreed.(p.50)

strings

• And, as the years go by, working together, sharing our experiences with one another, and also sharing a mutual trust, understanding and love — without *strings*, without obligation — we acquire relationships that are unique and priceless.(p.312)

• But my dad pulled some *strings* and got in to see me after three weeks.(p.425)

stripes

• I wore *stripes* and chains.(p.460)

strive

• Moreover, I am deeply convinced that so long as I continue to *strive*, in my bumbling way, toward the principles I first encountered in the earlier chapters of this book, this remarkable power will continue to flow through me.(p.437)

striving

• He is *striving* to recover fortune and reputation and feels he is doing very well.(p.126)

• It is a way of life, and the challenge contained in its principles is great enough to keep any human being *striving* for as long as he lives.(p.311)

strivings

• Would there be *strivings* for power and prestige?(p.xviii)

strong

• I forgot the *strong* warnings and the prejudices of my people concerning drink.(p.1)

• It relieved me somewhat to learn that in alcoholics the will is amazingly weakened when it comes to combating liquor, though it often remains *strong* in other respects.(p.7)

• If a sufficiently *strong* reason — ill health, falling in love, change of environment, or the warning of a doctor — becomes operative, this man can also stop or moderate, although he may find it difficult and troublesome and may even need medical attention.(p.21)

• It's *strong* language -- but isn't it true?(p.38)

• Because of the employee's special ability, or of his own *strong* personal attachment to him, the employer has sometimes kept such a man at work long beyond a reasonable period.(p.137)

• Whether you are a hard drinker, a moderated drinker or a teetotaler, you may have some pretty *strong* opinions, perhaps prejudices.(p.139)

• He interrupted: "I used to be *strong* for the church, but that won't fix it.(p.157)

• If you still think you are *strong* enough to beat the game alone, that is your affair.(p.181)

• I was *strong* and healthy and quite athletic.(p.305)

• If reasons for covering up are *strong* enough, secrets can be hidden from the world.(p.327)

• My parents' car had a *strong* attraction to fences, and one night I blacked out and drove the car down a bank, ramming the steel fence around someone's backyard.(p.353)

• In meeting me casually, I don't think my *strong* belief in "The Man Upstairs" shows, but I have no other explanation for the many good things that have happened to me since I have been in A.A. -- they came to me from a Greater Power.(p.367)

• They were ambitious, successful, *strong* and famous.(p.401)

• I would have three quick *strong* ones in order to endure the evening.(p.407)

• Now, I am big and weak, but Anne was bigger than I and *strong*.(p.414)

• Words of truth and love are *strong* medicine.(p.476)

• It is going *strong* still, these eight years later, and some of its members have been of great influence for good in state-wide A.A. work.(p.541)

• It wasn't *strong* enough, so I added a shot of vodka -- and was right back to worse trouble than before.(p.556)

stronger

• I knew the stuff I was making was a lot *stronger* than I had been used to, but I never suspected that steady drinking of it might develop a taste for something even *stronger* still.(p.233)

strongly

• The doctor intimated *strongly* that he might be worse than he realized.(p.39)

• The feeling that the drink problem has disappeared will often come *strongly*.(p.75)

• Dr. Bob always emphasized the religious angle very *strongly*, and I think it helped.(p.292)

struck

• The spark that was to flare into the first A.A. group was *struck* at Akron, Ohio, in June 1935, during a talk between a New York stockbroker and an Akron physician.(p.xv)

• When I returned to the hotel it *struck* me a highball would be fine before going to bed, so I stepped into the bar and had one.(p.41)

• We have *struck* out viciously.(p.105)

• They *struck* the children, kicked out door panels, smashed treasured crockery, and ripped the keys out of pianos.(p.106)

• Being certain he wants to stop, you can go to him with this volume as joyfully as though you had *struck* oil.(p.113)

• Like a gaunt prospector, belt drawn in over the last ounce of food, our pick *struck* gold.(p.128)

• Father feels he has *struck* something better than gold.(p.129)

• One night, I was *struck* with the memory of a line Alan Ladd used in "Shane," a movie that I'd worked on.(p.333)

• There were two sentences in it that *struck* me.(p.346)

• We had several fights and on one or two occasions I *struck* her with my fist.(p.491)

• Cotton *struck* the skids and collections went cold.(p.500)

• What *struck* me most was that they all seemed to be quite pleased with having made a job of it and having stopped drinking.(p.524)

structure

• He uses his gifts to build up a bright outlook for his family and himself, and then pulls the *structure* down on his head by a senseless series of sprees.(p.21)

• It has been repeatedly proven among us that upon this simple cornerstone a wonderfully effective spiritual *structure* can be built.(p.47)

• For a while they would be their old sweet selves, only to dash the new *structure* of affection to pieces once more.(p.107)

• It was a fantastic *structure*, built on a crumbling foundation.(p.435)

structures

• But the head of the house has spent years in pulling down the *structures* of business, romance, friendship, health -- these things are now ruined or damaged.(p.123)

• Though old buildings will eventually be replaced by finer ones, the new *structures* will take years to complete.(p.123)

struggle

• We don't *struggle*.(p.86)

• The problem with which you *struggle* usually falls within one of four categories:(p.108)

• But they were much disgusted and told me they would attempt to *struggle* along without my presence.(p.173)

• In fact, the last three years of my drinking was a routine of barbiturates in the morning, so that I could stop shaking enough to shave, and then alcohol beginning about four-thirty or five o'clock, with a *struggle* not to take a drink at noon or during the day, because I had the idea that if I took one drink, I would smell as though I had had a pint.(p.217)

• People have wars and kill each other; they *struggle* and cut each other's throats for success and what does anyone get out of it?(p.244)

• My drinking habits increased in spite of my *struggle* for control.(p.305)

• For about one year, prior to this time, there was one doctor who had continued to *struggle* with me.(p.306)

• Some of us *struggle* with these people because we know that they are really very sick, but we also know that short of some miracle, we are not going to help them except temporarily, and that they will inevitably get worse and worse until one of two things happens.(p.308)

• I was giving up the *struggle*.(p.531)

• I'd gladly do it anonymously, as I have done this brief account of my *struggle* with alcohol -- merely to present certain ideas for the consideration of the reader.(p.542)

struggled

• We do not like the thought that the contents of a book or the work of another alcoholic has accomplished in a few weeks that for which we *struggled* for years.(p.118)

• I fought and *struggled*, but to no avail.(p.466)

struggles

• Our *struggles* with them are variously strenuous, comic and tragic.(p.16)

• Give him an account of the *struggles* you made to stop.(p.92)

struggling

• It was now time, the *struggling* groups thought, to place their message and unique experience before the world.(p.xvii)

• This painful past may be of infinite value to other families still *struggling* with their problem.(p.124)

stubbed

• As soon as I could get up and walk I started to drink again and kept it up until my friend of the hospital, who, in his first try at the new way of life had *stubbed* his toe in Chicago but had come back to the town to take counsel and make a new start, picked me up and got me into a hospital.(p.258)

stubborn

• Priscilla, an A.A. who, like Marty, has become one of my greatest friends, decided that I was a *stubborn* case.(p.414)

stubbornness

• Can you discard the feeling that you are dealing only with habit, with *stubbornness*, or a weak will?(p.140)

• That my own innate selfishness and *stubbornness* are the evils which, if left unguarded, can drive me to alcohol.(p.473)

stuck

• When I had been in the hospital ten days, Sister Ignatia, who has played such a part in the development of A.A. in this area, *stuck* her head in the door one morning and announced, looking at me quizzically, that they might be able to make something human out of my face after all.(p.205)

• When the others saw my altered attitude they took me back in, but for me they had to make it tough; if they hadn't I don't think I ever would have *stuck* it out.(p.248)

• They came, many of them, and *stuck* by us and told us how to hold meetings.(p.495)

• I've *stuck* pretty close to A.A. ever since then, taken it day by day, not biting off more than I can chew.(p.511)

• That *stuck* with me for a long time.(p.513)

• In my own generation I *stuck* out, I can see that now, as being a very much heavier drinker than the average man.(p.518)

student

• I was president of my grammar school *student* body.(p.345)

• I was president of all my classes in high school and in my last year I was president of that *student* body.(p.345)

• I was president of each class in the University, and president of that *student* body.(p.345)

• Through going to meetings and listening, and occasionally speaking, through doing Twelve Step work, whereby in helping others you are both the teacher and the *student*, by making many wonderful A.A. friends, I have been taught all the things in life that are worth having.(p.416)

• I, a man of steel, with very high ideals, well brought up, an honor *student* and the recipient of scholarships and prizes, a boy wonder in business -- I, Bob, the author of this essay, looked and saw that the universe was beneath my contempt, and that to remove myself

from it was the only thing of dignity a man could do.(p.531)
• But not for long; now, for five Friday nights in a row, I went to jail, picked up sodden with beer (which I always disliked, but which was the only drink available); in jail five consecutive Friday nights in the town where I had grown up, where I had been an honor ***student*** in high school, where a kindly uncle, bailing me out, said, "Bob, our family just doesn't do this sort of thing."(p.539)
• An honor ***student*** in college, I became editor of the yearbook.(p.555)

students
• ***Students*** of ancient history tell us that the intellect of men in those days was equal to the best of today.(p.51)

studied
• I ***studied*** economics and business as well as law.(p.2)
• One evening, the book, after checking up, was very definitely in the red for plenty through a piece of ***studied*** carelessness on my part, and my boss, very shrewd and able, fired me with a parting statement to the effect that once was enough.(p.251)
• I ***studied*** art; I desperately endeavored to create an interest in many things, in a new place among new people.(p.305)
• Through ***studied*** sneaky-drinking, I'd become a senior citizen without having lost a day's work because of booze.(p.327)
• I read, ***studied***, and meditated on every bit of A.A. literature in my possession.(p.344)
• ***Studied*** the Big Book again.(p.344)
• So I concentrated and ***studied*** the book during that time, and I liked a lot of the things it said in there.(p.472)

studies
• It is being constantly revealed, as mankind ***studies*** the material world, that outward appearances are not inward reality at all.(p.48)
• The first year in college I just got by in my ***studies***, and that year I majored in poker and drinking.(p.241)
• She was intent on her ***studies***, and kept her distance.(p.359)

studio
• A square from ultra-dry Kansas, I did not taste grog until I had finished college, done a stint on newspapers, married, become a father, and been in ***studio*** publicity two years.(p.328)
• Now it was semi-blackouts every night, outrageous behavior, passing out in some friend's Village ***studio*** or not knowing how I got home.(p.407)

study
• My next move was to take up the ***study*** of medicine, entering one of the largest universities in the county.(p.173)
• I gave the matter much time and ***study*** for the next two and a half years, but still got tight every night nevertheless.(p.178)
• At seventeen I entered the University, really to satisfy my father who wanted me to ***study*** medicine there as he had.(p.241)
• The regular flow of all the literature, which I keep meticulously and which, of course, I ***study***, has been wonderful.(p.342)
• ***Study*** the A.A. book – don't just read it.(p.381)
• Then I found the solution: At the end of ***study*** time, I would drink two beers, jump in bed, sleep real fast, and wake up smart.(p.440)
• They suggested that I ***study*** the A.A. book and try to take the Twelve Steps according to the explanation in the Book, for it was their opinion that the application of these principles in our daily lives will get us sober and keep us sober.(p.550)

studying
• My visitor well knew, that as I tried to follow God I would get to ***studying*** these things out for myself.(p.236)
• Too many outside activities to do much ***studying***.(p.357)
• She was ***studying*** fashion design, was living in the same rooming house, and was from my home town of Cleveland.(p.359)
• After going to school all day, working in the family drugstore all evening, and then ***studying*** until one or two in the morning, I would not be able to sleep soundly, with everything I had been ***studying*** going round in my head.(p.440)

stuff
• "Lay off the hard ***stuff***."(p.20)
• Logic is great ***stuff***.(p.53)
• You fellows know your ***stuff*** all right, but I don't see what good it'll do.(p.157)
• After a bit, he said, "The way you fellows put this spiritual ***stuff*** makes sense.(p.159)
• Then Prohibition came into effect, and the facts that the ***stuff*** obtainable was so horrible and sometimes deadly, and that I had married and had a job which I had to look after, helped me for a period of some three or four years, although I would get drunk every time I could get hold of enough to drink to get started.(p.183)
• After drinking one glass of beer at the end of my work period for about five days, I thought I'd better find out whether I really had the ***stuff*** licked.(p.203)
• I went downstairs and there was the grizzly old veteran police officer in charge of the property desk, and as he gave me the ***stuff***, he asked, "Are you going out in the street that way?"(p.204)
• I early decided that the wine of America was very inferior ***stuff*** and took up beer instead.(p.231)
• I knew the ***stuff*** I was making was a lot stronger than I had been used to, but I never suspected that steady drinking of it might develop a taste for something even stronger still.(p.233)
• With a great deal of determination, I would throw out full pints – pour them out and smash the bottles -- firmly resolved never to take another drink of the ***stuff***.(p.234)
• During that first week-end I decided to stay in New York and take all they gave out with, except the "God ***stuff***."(p.246)
• Time went on and the drinking got worse and worse, and I was in another barroom, down the road the other way, a small one, and I took my glass – that morning I'd been able to lift it from the bar -- and I said to the woman behind the bar, "I wish I might never take another drop of that ***stuff***.(p.266)
• I agreed it was great ***stuff*** -- for those who needed it.(p.332)
• So I went down to him quite a few times a month and had him shoot me full of the ***stuff***; and then I went across the street to a little drug store to take a glass of beer or two beers, and then stopped at the liquor store to get myself a pint and go home.(p.389)
• The other pupils kept books, pencils, paper, gym equipment and such ***stuff*** in their lockers.(p.423)
• I didn't graduate to the hard ***stuff*** until I was sixteen.(p.423)
• Or, "My physical plant had got a little run down and the ***stuff*** rushed right to my head."(p.433)
• That's the ***stuff*** used when the oral surgeon puts the needle in your vein and says, "Count to ten," and before you get to two, you're asleep.(p.442)
• I didn't feel I could lie in bed and squirt the ***stuff*** in my veins while my kids and wife stood around watching me, so I kept the drug in my bag and the bag in the car and the car in the garage.(p.442)
• But to do so, I had to get all the ***stuff*** out of the house and out of my possession.(p.443)
• He had bottle of hard ***stuff***.(p.474)
• Soon change to hard ***stuff***.(p.475)
• Then hard ***stuff***.(p.475)

stuffed
• We gave up our positions and off we roared on a motorcycle, the sidecar ***stuffed*** with tent, blankets, a change of clothes, and three huge volumes of a financial reference service.(p.2)

stumble
• Everyone became resigned to the certainty that I would have to be shut up somewhere, or would ***stumble*** along to a miserable end.(p.8)
• Suppose we fall short of the chosen ideal and ***stumble***?(p.70)
• In case he does ***stumble***, even once, you will have to decide whether to let him go.(p.147)
• It was not known to me as a group, but I later learned that my wife had known about it for nine months and had prayed constantly that I would ***stumble*** into Akron some way or another.(p.215)

stumbled
• Many a distracted wife has visited this house to find loving and understanding companionship among women who knew her problem, to hear from the lips of their husbands what had happened to them, to be advised how her own wayward mate might be hospitalized and approached when next he ***stumbled***.(p.160)
• I have something to contribute to humanity, since I am peculiarly qualified, as a fellow-sufferer, to give aid and comfort to those who have ***stumbled*** and fallen over this business of meeting life.(p.229)
• I ***stumbled*** agonizedly past the theatre where in years gone by a great star had played my play.(p.540)

stumbling
• Wait until repeated ***stumbling*** convinces him he must act, for the more you hurry him the longer his recovery may be delayed.(p.113)

stupefied
• When the policeman released me to my ***stupefied*** and exasperated friend at four in the morning, I went to my traveling bag and groped until I found -- well, let the officer speak: "Ah," said the policeman, "he's got anuder pair, t'ank God!"(p.538)

stupid
• You cannot see why it should be to anyone else, save the spineless and ***stupid***.(p.139)
• When dealing with an alcoholic, there may be a natural annoyance that a man could be so weak, ***stupid*** and irresponsible.(p.139)
• But am I to be consigned to a life where I shall be ***stupid***, boring and glum, like some righteous people I see?(p.152)
• In my ***stupid*** way I went up to see him with the idea in the back of my mind that I would investigate Alcoholics Anonymous from a medical standpoint.(p.346)
• I had no feeling of security, and I knew that I had done a very ***stupid*** thing, so I went back to Texas and remarried my ex-husband.(p.386)
• I would be half asleep and half awake, and in the morning, I would be both tired and ***stupid***.(p.440)
• Although we enjoyed the laughter in the early days, I heard a lot of things that I thought were ***stupid***.(p.447)

stupidity
• A spirit of intolerance might repel alcoholics whose lives could have been saved, had it not been for such ***stupidity***.(p.103)

stupor
• Haunting me through each day's ***stupor*** -- and there were eighteen or nineteen such days in this man's home -- was the thought: "Where do I go when his family comes home?"(p.278)
• As a result, I would fall off in a drunken ***stupor*** every night.(p.299)
• I could hide my alcoholic ***stupor*** behind pretense.(p.332)
• A few hours later I came out of a complete ***stupor*** in our living room with a flash of sanity.(p.363)
• After every cocktail party or dinner party she would say she couldn't understand how I could get in such a drunken ***stupor*** on one drink.(p.377)
• We are aware of the nice things around us, things we never noticed before in our drunken ***stupor***.(p.481)

style
• By the following spring we were living in our accustomed ***style***.(p.4)
• I went into the Navy in fine ***style***.(p.425)

subconsciously
• I had been drinking heavily from one state of semicoma to another and it was several days before I got "defogged," but ***subconsciously*** I was in earnest about wanting to quit liquor forever.(p.258)
• I don't think that I was conscious of what had happened to me, but I think that it registered ***subconsciously***.(p.386)

subdue
• I apparently was willing to ***subdue*** these personality disturbances in a tremendous drive to succeed.(p.211)

subject
• The ***subject*** presented in this book seems to me to be of paramount importance to those afflicted with alcoholic addiction.(p.xxv)
• There was, therefore, a sense of real satisfaction when I was asked to contribute a few words on a ***subject*** which is covered in such masterly detail in these pages.(p.xxv)
• But his face falls when we speak of spiritual matters, especially when we mention God, for we have reopened a ***subject*** which our man thought he had neatly evaded or entirely ignored.(p.45)
• We don't use this as an excuse for shying away from the ***subject*** of God.(p.77)
• Try to have him bring up the ***subject*** himself.(p.111)
• You think he ought to know the ***subject*** better, as everyone should have a clear understanding of the risk he takes if he drinks too much.(p.112)
• If this kind of approach does not catch your husband's interest, it may be best to drop the ***subject***, but after a friendly talk your husband will usually revive the topic himself.(p.112)
• You avoid the ***subject*** of drinking, even with your own parents.(p.114)
• Next time you and he have a heated discussion, no matter what the ***subject***, it should be the privilege of either to smile and say, "This is getting serious.(p.118)
• While on the ***subject*** of confidence, can you adopt the attitude that so far as you are concerned this will be a strictly personal matter, that his alcoholic

derelictions, the treatment about to be undertaken, will never be discussed without his consent?(p.143)
• To return to the *subject* matter of this book: It contains full suggestions by which the employee may solve his problem.(p.143)
• By no means do we offer it as the last word on this *subject*, but so far as we are concerned, it has worked with us.(p.144)
• When I reached school, I discovered the faculty had other ideas on the *subject*.(p.173)
• It must be remembered that I had read a great deal and talked to everyone who knew, or thought they knew anything about the *subject* of alcoholism.(p.180)
• He gave me information about the *subject* of alcoholism which was undoubtedly helpful.(p.180)
• If there was a lecture on the *subject* within a hundred miles of Akron, I attended.(p.202)

subjected
• We *subjected* each relation to this test -- was it selfish or not?(p.69)
• We *subjected* ourselves to a drastic self-appraisal.(p.76)
• Why they should be *subjected* to the tortures we inflict upon them, I cannot explain.(p.178)

subjects
• As we became *subjects* of King Alcohol, shivering denizens of his mad realm, the chilling vapor that is loneliness settled down.(p.151)

sublime
• Here was love, applause, war; moments *sublime* with intervals hilarious.(p.1)

submerge
• The more I thought like this the more I drank to *submerge* my sorrows.(p.362)

submit
• Will he take every necessary step, *submit* to anything to get well, to stop drinking forever?(p.142)
• My personal definition, which I *submit* as applying only to myself (although everyone is welcome to it who wants it), includes every waking activity of the human being; to have a creative attitude towards things is a more exact meaning, to live and to deal with other human beings creatively, which to me means seeing the God in them, and respecting and worshipping this God.(p.535)

subscribe
• We cannot *subscribe* to the belief that this life is a vale of tears, though it once was just that for many of us.(p.133)

subscriptions
• I went out to the West Coast, waited on table, washed dishes and sold newspaper *subscriptions*.(p.401)

subsequent
• During the *subsequent* fifteen years I had sense enough never to go to the hospital if I had been drinking, and very seldom did I receive patients.(p.176)
• How devastating, too, are the *subsequent* feelings of inadequacy and self-pity.(p.331)
• My analyst was one of the first to learn of A.A. and to make *subsequent* use of it in her work.(p.412)
• In the light of *subsequent* events it became evident that I took their advice far too literally, for, after some months of happy sobriety I drank again.(p.471)

subsequently
• He *subsequently* denied having received the money and used the incident as a basis for discrediting the man.(p.80)
• On our honeymoon in Egypt, he cuffed me around quite a bit, and *subsequently* hit me some more.(p.405)

subside
• Unlike the feelings of the ship's passengers, however, our joy in escape from disaster does not *subside* as we go our individual ways.(p.17)

subsidiary
• I am working hard on the books of a *subsidiary* company of a large corporation.(p.500)

substance
• This was the *substance* of A.A.'s Twelve Traditions, which are stated in full on page 564 of this book.(p.xix)
• Ribaldry was the *substance* of the conversation, and I set out to be the funniest and most ribald of them all.(p.407)

substantial
• By late 1937, the number of members having *substantial* sobriety time behind them was sufficient to convince the membership that a new light had entered the dark world of the alcoholic.(p.xvii)
• They suffered from my conduct without saying anything, but the reason for this was I still managed to hang onto a very *substantial* practice.(p.215)
• It took five years of A.A. living, and a *substantial* improvement in my health, before I could take a full-time office job where someone else was boss.(p.283)
• I really worked for several weeks, and having had a fairly wide acquaintance with the dealer trade, it was not difficult for me to line up enough of them to give me a very *substantial* volume of business with a minimum of effort.(p.300)
• Why should this happen to me – hadn't I provided a good home – wasn't I making a good living -- didn't I just get a *substantial* raise that had put me in the upper bracket class?(p.362)

substantially
• Then I started drinking again, with possibly a little more restraint, periods a little bit longer than they had been before, but *substantially* the same pattern.(p.203)
• So Paul repeated *substantially* what Dr. Bob had said.(p.207)

substitute
• Have you a sufficient *substitute*?"(p.152)
• Yes, there is a *substitute* and it is vastly more than that.(p.152)
• Because I found that everything I turned to became a *substitute* for drink.(p.339)
• And when all of life is a *substitute* for drink, there's no happiness, no peace.(p.339)

substituted
• We, who have been through the wringer, have to admit if we *substituted* alcoholism for jay-walking, the illustration would fit us exactly.(p.38)
• Instead, I quickly *substituted* one or another vivid scene from the nightmare of my later drinking.(p.286)
• It was frightening that drink was being *substituted* for more and more of the things I really enjoyed doing.(p.374)

subtle
• I rather appreciated your ideas about the *subtle* insanity which precedes the first drink, but I was confident it could not happen to me after what I had learned.(p.40)
• We are headed for trouble if we do, for alcohol is a *subtle* foe.(p.85)

suburb
• Before my drinking had cut me down completely, I achieved a considerable measure of success, having been a City Councilman for five years and a financial director of Kenmore, a *suburb* later taken into the city itself.(p.182)
• All I can remember about the Roaring Twenties is that I drank a great deal, thought I was having a grand time, managed to get to Europe for a few weeks, was very proud of the dozens of speak-easy cards entitling me to an entree in the better joints between Cleveland and New York, took on a wife, and built a home in a fashionable *suburb* of Cleveland.(p.358)

subway
• There wasn't a bar in sight, but I found the *subway* station.(p.223)
• In my mind's eye I saw Broadway again and Tom Sharkey's bar; the roar of the *subway* was in my ears.(p.252)

succeed
• He was ambitious to *succeed* in business, but saw that he would get nowhere if he drank at all.(p.32)
• If the alcoholic tries to shield himself he may *succeed* for a time, but he usually winds up with a bigger explosion than ever.(p.101)
• We know these suggestions are sometimes difficult to follow, but you will save many a heartbreak if you can *succeed* in observing them.(p.111)
• Thus you may *succeed* in interesting him in alcoholism.(p.112)
• I apparently was willing to subdue these personality disturbances in a tremendous drive to *succeed*.(p.211)
• I was voted the man most likely to *succeed*.(p.345)
• The ambition to *succeed* was instilled in me by my Scandinavian parents who came to this country where opportunities were so great.(p.373)
• The drive to get ahead, to *succeed*, kept me too busy for many years to have any great experience with social life.(p.374)

succeeded
• Prior to his journey to Akron, the broker had worked hard with many alcoholics on the theory that only an alcoholic could help an alcoholic, but he had *succeeded* only in keeping sober himself.(p.xvi)
• A year and six months later these three had *succeeded* with seven more.(p.159)
• I had no trouble there because I had never actually ceased to believe in God, and had tried lots of times to get help but hadn't *succeeded*.(p.186)
• But I only *succeeded* in fighting it.(p.338)
• I *succeeded* in this attempt for approximately fifteen months with only a couple of slips.(p.343)
• Naturally, I *succeeded* in nothing.(p.400)

succeeding
• In the two *succeeding* years I held ten different jobs ranging from newspaper copy-desk and rewrite, to traffic director for an oil field equipment company.(p.255)
• Formerly, in the acute mental and physical pain during the remorseful periods *succeeding* each drunk, I found my recollection of the misery I had gone through a bolsterer of resolution and afterward, perhaps, a deterrent for a time.(p.260)

success
• There were many failures, but there was an occasional heartening *success*.(p.xvii)
• The drive for *success* was on.(p.2)
• I had had some *success* at speculation, so we had a little money, but we once worked on a farm for a month to avoid drawing on our small capital.(p.3)
• If he is a real alcoholic and very far advanced, there is scant chance of *success*.(p.34)
• The first requirement is that we be convinced that any life run on self-will can hardly be a *success*.(p.60)
• That often makes the difference between failure and *success*.(p.98)
• The first principle of *success* is that you should never be angry.(p.111)
• But he must see the danger of over-concentration on financial *success*.(p.127)
• Though some of his manifestations are alarming and disagreeable, we think dad will be on a firmer foundation than the man who is placing business or professional *success* ahead of spiritual development.(p.129)
• Before my drinking had cut me down completely, I achieved a considerable measure of *success*, having been a City Councilman for five years and a financial director of Kenmore, a suburb later taken into the city itself.(p.182)
• Near *success*, only near.(p.197)
• He told me that there were some other fellows that had tried this with *success*, and if I cared to see any of them he'd have them come in to see me.(p.218)
• He then pulled up his chair with one of his knees touching mine and said, "Will you pray with me for your *success*?"(p.218)
• Like most immigrants I wanted to be somebody and have something and I was very happy and contented as I felt *success* crown my efforts.(p.232)
• People have wars and kill each other; they struggle and cut each other's throats for *success* and what does anyone get out of it?(p.244)
• I had some financial *success* through no ability of my own and, when jobless and almost wiped out in 1930, I began to trade and sell my collection; much of the proceeds went to keep my apartment stocked with liquor and almost every night saw me helpless to bed.(p.255)
• I entered the business world with every confidence that *success* lay ahead of me.(p.275)
• Obviously I have overcome fear to a sufficient degree to think in terms of *success* in business.(p.284)
• We are both depending upon God and our use of the A.A. program to help us make a *success* of this joint undertaking.(p.286)
• It is undoubtedly too soon for me to say how much of a *success* I shall be as a husband in time to come.(p.286)
• I would make a feeble attempt at eating supper, but I never met with any howling *success*.(p.299)
• He asked me to read the book "Alcoholics Anonymous," and then he wanted me to talk with a man who was experiencing *success* with his own arrestment.(p.308)
• Mine was the skid row of *success*.(p.345)
• The skid row of *success* is just as miserable.(p.345)
• As my father climbed the ladder of *success* in the oil-field business, his drinking also climbed.(p.369)
• But *success* brought increased social activities and I realized that many of my friends enjoyed a social drink with no apparent harm to themselves or others.(p.374)
• A "good boy" reached adulthood and *success* without achieving maturity or fulfillment.(p.418)
• No one could have told me then that I had not earned all my *success*, nor could anyone have told me that I was an alcoholic and a drug addict.(p.418)
• However, I've heard of an organization called Alcoholics Anonymous that has had some *success*

with people like you.(p.436)
• As might have been predicted, my teetering tower of worldly *success* collapsed.(p.437)
• When a big, healthy-looking young fellow stood up there and said, "I'm a *success* today if I don't drink today," I thought, "Man, I've got a thousand things to do today before I can brag about not taking a drink, for God's sake!"(p.447)
• But I am to learn later that it began with my desire for material *success* becoming greater than my interest in the welfare of my fellow man.(p.507)
• It has taught me that *success* and failure are never final, and that neither count for very much in the final assessment of any man who has done his best.(p.525)

successes
• But we think that if you persevere, the percentage of *successes* will gratify you.(p.144)
• My new wife and I don't own any property to speak of, and the flashy *successes* of another day are no longer mine.(p.438)

successful
• Almost none of us liked the self-searching, the leveling of our pride, the confession of shortcomings which the process requires for its *successful* consummation.(p.25)
• With many individuals the methods which I employed are *successful*, but I have never been *successful* with an alcoholic of your description."(p.27)
• He made up his mind that until he had been *successful* in business and had retired, he would not touch another drop.(p.32)
• An exceptional man, he remained bone dry for twenty-five years and retired at the age of fifty-five, after a *successful* and happy business career.(p.32)
• If ever there was a *successful* business man, it is Fred.(p.39)
• I reasoned I was not so far advanced as most of you fellows, that I had been usually *successful* in licking my other personal problems, and that I would therefore be *successful* where you men failed.(p.40)
• Even in the present century, American newspapers were afraid to print an account of the Wright brothers' first *successful* flight at Kitty Hawk.(p.51)
• If the owner of the business is to be *successful*, he cannot fool himself about values.(p.64)
• You will be most *successful* with alcoholics if you do not exhibit any passion for crusade or reform.(p.95)
• If you have been *successful* in solving your own domestic problems, tell the newcomer's family how that was accomplished.(p.100)
• *Successful* readjustment means the opposite.(p.122)
• They remember when father was romantic, thoughtful and *successful*.(p.123)
• Had he been *successful* in his enterprise, he would have been set on his feet financially which at the time, seemed vitally important.(p.153)
• The *successful* demonstration I had made of my life problems in other respects convinced me that some day I was going to be able to drink like a gentleman.(p.214)
• I had my own business, *successful* enough for me to indulge most of my desires.(p.225)
• *Successful* home-brewers among my friends began to invite me to their homes.(p.232)
• Haven't I been *successful*, haven't I accomplished extraordinary things in business?(p.245)
• I'm rated as a modestly *successful* man.(p.296)
• Up to this point I had spent six years in the business and had enjoyed the reputation of being very *successful*.(p.298)
• Just at this time my wife heard of a doctor in another city who had been very *successful* with drunks.(p.301)
• They seemed to have all the ingredients for *successful* living.(p.310)
• So when the children were in school from nine to three, I started up a nice little business and was fairly *successful* in it.(p.339)
• Everything that I touched from grammar school on was *successful*.(p.345)
• If I were asked what in my opinion was the most important factor in being *successful* in this program, besides following the Twelve Steps, I would say Honesty.(p.367)
• My drinking did not start until after I was thirty-five, and a fairly *successful* career had been established.(p.374)
• They were ambitious, *successful*, strong and famous.(p.401)
• They make no guarantees and are not always *successful*.(p.436)
• "The American Public Health Association presents a Lasker Group Award for 1951 to Alcoholics Anonymous in recognition of its unique and highly *successful* approach to that age-old public health and social problem, alcoholism . . .(p.573)

successfully
• The test that it faced was this: Could these large numbers of erstwhile erratic alcoholics *successfully* meet and work together?(p.xviii)
• "Then they outlined the spiritual answer and program of action which a hundred of them had followed *successfully*.(p.42)
• As we felt new power flow in, as we enjoyed peace of mind, as we discovered we could face life *successfully*, as we became conscious of His presence, we began to lose our fear of today, tomorrow or the hereafter.(p.63)
• This work consumed a period of about two-thirds of a year, and worked out *successfully* so I decided to follow patent law.(p.212)
• This first meeting was held in the living room of a home and was led by Bill D., the first man that Bill W. and Dr. Bob had worked with *successfully*.(p.291)
• Where we used to run from responsibility, we find ourselves accepting it with gratitude that we can *successfully* shoulder it.(p.311)
• Until I took Social Security and a pension at the age of sixty-eight, after forty years in motion-picture-studio public relations, I had *successfully* hidden even any hints of approaching alcoholism.(p.327)
• Showing all the courage and ingenuity that I had not used in a positive way, I covered my tracks and hid from my family so *successfully* that they did not find me for months.(p.401)

succession
• To his consternation, he found himself drunk half a dozen times in rapid *succession*.(p.35)
• Luck then deserts him and he is slightly injured several times in *succession*.(p.38)
• In *succession* came "What Made Milwaukee Famous Made a Loser Out of Me" and "I'm Drinking My Christmas Dinner All Alone."(p.332)

successive
• Not long afterward he had called me from Hartford on two *successive* days, so drunk he could hardly speak.(p.136)
• *Successive* Monday morning hangovers, which despite mid-week resolutions to do better, came with unfailing regularity, eventually caused me to quit my job.(p.254)

succumbed
• After they have *succumbed* to the desire again, as so many do, and the phenomenon of craving develops, they pass through the well-known stages of a spree, emerging remorseful, with a firm resolution not to drink again.(p.xxvii)
• He *succumbed* to that gay crowd inside, who laughed at their own misfortunes and understood his.(p.160)
• I always *succumbed* to its seduction.(p.332)

such
• Because this book has become the basic text for our Society and has helped *such* large numbers of alcoholic men and women to recover, there exists a sentiment against any radical changes being made in it.(p.xi)
• Being mostly business or professional folk, we could not well carry on our occupations in *such* an event.(p.xiii)
• We should like to be helpful to *such* cases.(p.xiv)
• Then Jack Alexander wrote a feature article in the Saturday Evening Post and placed *such* a compelling picture of A.A. before the general public that alcoholics in need of help really deluged us.(p.xviii)
• Without *such* support, A.A. could have made only the slowest progress.(p.xx)
• These men may well have a remedy for thousands of *such* situations.(p.xxiv)
• There was, therefore, a sense of real satisfaction when I was asked to contribute a few words on a subject which is covered in *such* masterly detail in these pages.(p.xxv)
• It was fun to carom around the exclusive course which had inspired *such* awe in me as a lad.(p.4)
• I began to wonder, for *such* an appalling lack of perspective seemed near being just that.(p.5)
• When they talked of a God personal to me, who was love, superhuman strength and direction, I became irritated and my mind snapped shut against *such* a theory.(p.10)
• I could go for *such* conceptions as Creative Intelligence, Universal Mind or Spirit of Nature but I resisted the thought of a Czar of the Heavens, however loving His sway might be.(p.12)
• I was to right all *such* matters to the utmost of my ability.(p.13)
• There was a sense of victory, followed by *such* a peace and serenity as I had never known.(p.14)
• The good doctor now sees many men who have *such* experiences.(p.14)
• Until *such* an understanding is reached, little or nothing can be accomplished.(p.18)
• After *such* an approach many take up their beds and walk again.(p.19)
• It is the purpose of this book to answer *such* questions specifically.(p.20)
• "She's *such* a sweet girl, I should think he'd stop for her sake."(p.20)
• Above all, he believed he had acquired *such* a profound knowledge of the inner workings of his mind and its hidden springs that relapse was unthinkable.(p.26)
• Exceptions to cases *such* as yours have been occurring since early times.(p.27)
• In fact, I have been trying to produce some *such* emotional rearrangement within you.(p.27)
• There is no friction among us over *such* matters.(p.28)
• Not all of us join religious bodies, but most of us favor *such* memberships.(p.28)
• Surprisingly enough, we find *such* convictions no great obstacle to a spiritual experience.(p.28)
• All of us felt at times that we were regaining control, but *such* intervals – usually brief – were inevitably followed by still less control, which led in time to pitiful and incomprehensible demoralization.(p.30)
• Physicians who are familiar with alcoholism agree there is no *such* thing as making a normal drinker out of an alcoholic.(p.31)
• Whether *such* a person can quit upon a nonspiritual basis depends upon the extent to which he has already lost the power to choose whether he will drink or not.(p.34)
• How can *such* a lack of proportion, of the ability to think straight, be called anything else?(p.37)
• *Such* a man would be crazy, wouldn't he?(p.38)
• We admit we have some of these symptoms, but we have not gone to the extremes you fellows did, nor are we likely to, for we understand ourselves so well after what you have told us that *such* things cannot happen again.(p.38)
• They piled on me heaps of evidence to the effect that an alcoholic mentality, *such* as I had exhibited in Washington, was a hopeless condition.(p.42)
• Though not a religious person, I have profound respect for the spiritual approach in *such* cases as yours.(p.43)
• Except in a few rare cases, neither he nor any other human being can provide *such* a defense.(p.43)
• To one who feels he is an atheist or agnostic *such* an experience seems impossible, but to continue as he is means disaster, especially if he is an alcoholic of the hopeless variety.(p.44)
• But we found that *such* codes and philosophies did not save us, no matter how much we tried.(p.45)
• Though some of us resisted, we found no great difficulty in casting aside *such* feelings.(p.48)
• Save for a few brief moments of temptation the thought of drink has never returned; and at *such* times a great revulsion has risen up in him.(p.57)
• There are *such* unfortunates.(p.58)
• 9.Made direct amends to *such* people wherever possible, except when to do so would injure them or others.(p.59)
• When we sincerely took *such* a position, all sorts of remarkable things followed.(p.63)
• Established on *such* a footing we became less and less interested in ourselves, our little plans and designs.(p.63)
• We found it very desirable to take this spiritual step with an understanding person, *such* as our wife, best friend or spiritual adviser.(p.63)
• For when harboring *such* feelings we shut ourselves off from the sunlight of the Spirit.(p.66)
• We often find *such* a person quick to see and understand our problem.(p.74)
• *Such* parts of our story we tell to someone who will understand, yet be unaffected.(p.74)
• Under no condition do we criticize *such* a person or argue.(p.77)
• Maybe it's only a petty offense *such* as padding the expense account.(p.78)
• After consulting with his wife and partner he came to the conclusion that it was better to take those risks than to stand before his Creator guilty of *such* ruinous slander.(p.80)
• No outsider can appraise *such* an intimate situation.(p.82)
• If we have no *such* complication, there is plenty we should do at home.(p.82)
• We usually conclude the period of meditation with

a prayer that we be shown all through the day what our next step is to be, that we be given whatever we need to take care of ***such*** problems.(p.87)
• When dealing with ***such*** a person, you had better use everyday language to describe spiritual principles.(p.93)
• Don't raise ***such*** issues, no matter what your own convictions are.(p.93)
• Do not contradict ***such*** views.(p.94)
• If you leave ***such*** a person alone, he may soon become convinced that he cannot recover by himself.(p.96)
• Occasionally you will have to meet ***such*** conditions.(p.97)
• Yet we do go to great extremes to provide each other with these very things, when ***such*** action is warranted.(p.98)
• When your prospect has made ***such*** reparation as he can to his family, and has thoroughly explained to them the new principles by which he is living, he should proceed to put those principles into action at home.(p.98)
• Or am I expecting to steal a little vicarious pleasure from the atmosphere of ***such*** places?"(p.101)
• You should not hesitate to visit the most sordid spot on earth on ***such*** an errand.(p.102)
• Experience shows that ***such*** an attitude is not helpful to anyone.(p.103)
• A spirit of intolerance might repel alcoholics whose lives could have been saved, had it not been for ***such*** stupidity.(p.103)
• In the midst of ***such*** pandemonium they may have rushed out threatening to live with the other woman forever.(p.106)
• There could be no love in ***such*** persons, we thought.(p.107)
• Of course, there is ***such*** a thing as incompatibility, but in nearly every instance the alcoholic only seems to be unloving and inconsiderate; it is usually because he is warped and sickened that he says and does these appalling things.(p.108)
• We have enjoyed ***such*** evenings ourselves; we had a good time.(p.110)
• Be sure you are not critical during ***such*** a discussion.(p.111)
• Yet often ***such*** men had spectacular and powerful recoveries.(p.113)
• The wives and children of ***such*** men suffer horribly, but not more than the men themselves.(p.114)
• If ***such*** women adopt a spiritual way of life their road will be smoother.(p.114)
• When you have carefully explained to ***such*** people that he is a sick person, you will have created a new atmosphere.(p.115)
• Ask him what you should do if he places you in ***such*** a position again.(p.116)
• At ***such*** moments we forget that alcoholism is an illness over which we could not possibly have had any power.(p.118)
• The foregoing pages (though addressed only to wives) indicate the problems ***such*** people may face.(p.121)
• We think that ***such*** a view is self-centered and in direct conflict with the new way of living.(p.124)
• We do talk about each other a great deal, but we almost invariably temper ***such*** talk by a spirit of love and tolerance.(p.125)
• Members of a family should watch ***such*** matters carefully, for one careless, inconsiderate remark has been known to raise the very devil.(p.125)
• Beginning with ***such*** complaints, a barrier arises.(p.126)
• When he renews interest in ***such*** things, a feeling of jealousy may arise.(p.131)
• Alcoholics who have derided religious people will be helped by ***such*** contacts.(p.131)
• He and his family can be a bright spot in ***such*** congregations.(p.132)
• Do not hesitate to take your health problems to ***such*** persons.(p.133)
• Marvelous results often follow ***such*** a reunion.(p.134)
• She sees she was wrong to make a burning issue out of ***such*** a matter when his more serious ailments were being rapidly cured.(p.135)
• Because of the employee's special ability, or of his own strong personal attachment to him, the employer has sometimes kept ***such*** a man at work long beyond a reasonable period.(p.137)
• Who wouldn't be, with ***such*** a fevered brain?(p.140)
• You may be at a loss to understand how ***such*** a seemingly above-board chap could be so involved.(p.140)
• Of course that isn't so, and ***such*** people often may impose on you.(p.141)
• Firing ***such*** an individual may prove a blessing to him.(p.141)
• Perhaps you have ***such*** a man in mind.(p.141)
• Your man will fare better if placed in ***such*** physical condition that he can think straight and no longer craves liquor.(p.143)
• If you propose ***such*** a procedure to him, it may be necessary to advance the cost of treatment, but we believe it should be made plain that any expense will later be deducted from his pay.(p.143)
• With this kind of employee ***such*** an attitude will command undying loyalty.(p.145)
• After reading this book, a junior executive can go to ***such*** a man and say approximately this, "Look here, Ed.(p.147)
• He will be able to take a position with ***such*** a man which is eminently fair and square.(p.148)
• As to them, his policy is undoubtedly sound, but he did not distinguish between ***such*** people and the alcoholic.(p.149)
• As ex-problem drinkers, we smile at ***such*** a sally.(p.151)
• Then he will know loneliness ***such*** as few do.(p.152)
• How can they rise out of ***such*** misery, bad repute and hopelessness?(p.153)
• There must be many ***such*** in this town.(p.154)
• The use of spiritual principles in ***such*** cases was not so well understood as it is now.(p.156)
• Then, in this eastern city, there are informal meetings ***such*** as we have described to you, where you may now see scores of members.(p.162)
• To duplicate, with ***such*** backing, what we have accomplished is only a matter of willingness, patience and labor.(p.163)
• And with ***such*** good effect that the doctor agreed to a test among his patients and certain other alcoholics from a clinic which he attends.(p.163)
• Unfortunately for me, I was the only child, which perhaps engendered the selfishness which played ***such*** an important part in bringing on my alcoholism.(p.172)
• I noticed that the others seemed to have ***such*** a release, a happiness, a something that I thought a person ought to have.(p.191)
• I drove towards Cleveland wondering why I found myself in ***such*** a changed set of conditions as compared with those of six months before.(p.200)
• At three-thirty the next morning, I was in Champlain Street Station, in jail for driving while intoxicated and insulting an officer; and the suit of which I was so proud was in ***such*** shape that the turnkey had to get me a pair of trousers to go into court in the next morning.(p.201)
• When I had been in the hospital ten days, Sister Ignatia, who has played ***such*** a part in the development of A.A. in this area, stuck her head in the door one morning and announced, looking at me quizzically, that they might be able to make something human out of my face after all.(p.205)
• I didn't have any need of ***such*** an association!(p.206)
• I did not know there was ***such*** a thing as group activity until I left the hospital.(p.218)
• I was deprived of many of the things that we feel are important in life, ***such*** as education particularly, because of my father's drinking.(p.261)
• And Jim G. had ***such*** a wonderful sense of humor, and when he came I was in tears, and I told him, "I want to do this, but I can't.(p.269)
• This was the beginning of an unending series of ***such*** experiences.(p.276)
• Haunting me through each day's stupor -- and there were eighteen or nineteen ***such*** days in this man's home -- was the thought: "Where do I go when his family comes home?"(p.278)
• He was a man of considerable means and he might have done what many men would have done in ***such*** a case.(p.278)
• ***Such*** thinking usually began with thoughts of the pleasant drinking of my youth.(p.285)
• I learned early in my A.A. life that I could not afford to fondle ***such*** thoughts, as you might fondle a pet, because this particular pet could grow into a monster.(p.285)
• The adjustments in ***such*** a case are difficult and take time, but we both feel that they are certainly worth it.(p.286)
• I do feel, though, that the fact that I finally grew up to a point where I could even tackle ***such*** a job is the apex of the story of a man who spent eighteen years running away from life.(p.286)
• At the moral inventory, he brought up some of my bad personality traits or character defects, ***such*** as selfishness, conceit, jealousy, carelessness, intolerance, ill-temper, sarcasm and resentments.(p.292)
• ***Such*** has been my privilege, both nationally and in my home city.(p.295)
• He mentioned lies and deceptions in the course of his story in the presence of the one person in the world I wouldn't want to know ***such*** things.(p.302)
• However, he explained to me that he had been just ***such*** a rummy as I, only for a much longer period of time.(p.302)
• I sleep like a baby, and never give a thought to ***such*** a thing as insomnia.(p.303)
• I would hang on to sobriety for short intervals, but always there would come the tide of an overpowering necessity to drink and, as I was engulfed in it, I felt ***such*** a sense of panic that I really believed I would die if I didn't get that drink inside.(p.306)
• He told me that eventually he hoped ***such*** a group would develop in the Chicago area, but that so far this had not been started.(p.309)
• Not only were they at peace with themselves, but they were getting a kick out of life ***such*** as one seldom encounters, except in the very young.(p.310)
• But I was in ***such*** deep trouble that I decided to try A.A. anyhow.(p.319)
• After ***such*** often-painful vigilance (and numerous phony stints of abstinence), retirement naturally created an impulse to live without restraints.(p.328)
• It finally got ***such*** a hold on me that I was completely at my wits' end, not knowing what the result would be.(p.343)
• (I belong to the American Psychiatric Society, but I don't practice psychiatry as ***such***.(p.347)
• This was ***such*** a new thought that I got all sorts of books on Higher Powers, and I put a Bible by my bedside, and I put a Bible in my car.(p.348)
• It was the first of many ***such*** experiences that became the only cause of harsh words, tears and heartaches in an otherwise truly beautiful marriage.(p.361)
• After every cocktail party or dinner party she would say she couldn't understand how I could get in ***such*** a drunken stupor on one drink.(p.377)
• A "spiritual experience" to me meant attending meetings, seeing a group of people, all there for the purpose of helping each other; hearing the Twelve Steps and the Twelve Traditions read at a meeting, and hearing the Lord's Prayer, which in an A.A. meeting has ***such*** great meaning -- "Thy will be done, not mine."(p.381)
• Making amends is sometimes doing what we are capable of doing but failed to do because of alcohol; carrying out community responsibilities ***such*** as Community Funds, Red Cross, educational and religious activities in proportion to our abilities and energy.(p.381)
• They phoned my husband that I was in jail and in ***such*** terrible shape that they didn't know what I would do to myself; and they realized that jail was no place for me, but that he was to wait a while before he got me, because at the time they called him to come over for me I was beating a tin cup against the wall.(p.390)
• It was ***such*** a feeling of relief that I wanted to know more about it and with that, I think for the first time, came the realization that there was something horribly, horribly wrong with me.(p.392)
• An alcoholic cannot accept the news that he's an alcoholic unless there is a meaningful explanation given, and an offer of help, ***such*** as you get in A.A.(p.406)
• In the first year there were episodes ***such*** as kicking Priscilla in the shins, getting the lock changed on the desk in the A.A. Club, because I, as secretary, didn't want the Intergroup secretary "interfering," and taking an older woman member out to lunch for the express purpose of informing her that she was "a phony."(p.416)
• No one could live ***such*** an irresponsible, immature life as I had without consequences.(p.420)
• The other pupils kept books, pencils, paper, gym equipment and ***such*** stuff in their lockers.(p.423)
• How could ***such*** a man possibly be called an alcoholic?(p.433)
• But for some time, it was difficult to keep from taking a pill when I had an appropriate symptom, ***such*** as a cough, pain, anxiety, insomnia, a muscle spasm, or an upset stomach.(p.448)
• Alcohol wrings the guts out of life, eats into the brain in ***such*** a way as to make the alcoholic blind to the truth.(p.457)
• Tragedies during those years that were caused by my drinking, ***such*** as the breaking up of my marriage, the death of my child, other things -- had little restraining effect.(p.465)
• At that time there hadn't been any publicity ***such*** as we have now.(p.469)
• In other words, the kindest doctor in the whole world, and I had one ***such***, couldn't help me because I

always felt, "You can't know about me -- you can't possibly know -- you don't even drink!"(p.471)

• She gave me *such* hope and inspiration that I set her right up on a pedestal.(p.472)

• The grand fellow who at my call made me a hail-fellow-well-met, who gave me *such* a fine voice, as we sang "Hail, hail, the gang's all here," and "Sweet Adeline," who gave me freedom from fear and feelings of inferiority.(p.498)

• Anger possesses me, anger *such* as I have never felt before.(p.505)

• If something does come along that sort of upsets me, instead of walking in and throwing a buck at the barman and asking for a drink, I walk into a telephone booth, drop a dime in the box, and call somebody who was so kind as to give me his name and telephone number to meet *such* an emergency.(p.511)

• It was a revelation to me to find that there were *such* people as those I found in Alcoholics Anonymous.(p.515)

• My proud southern blood would have boiled if anyone had named me *such* a despicable thing.(p.532)

• But *such* is my nature that I must know the reason for things and I didn't stop until I had satisfied myself about the reasons for my drinking.(p.533)

• After nearly eight years of sobriety in A.A., I still can set down *such* thoughts, "against my instinct and training," showing that I still consider myself a "special" person, entitled to special privileges.(p.536)

• Need I add that *such* was the case because I had no money to provide a roof over my head?(p.538)

• Once, or even twice, *such* incidents might be amusing.(p.538)

• I realize now that this phase of my development had been arrested by my obsession with self, and my egocentricity had reached *such* proportions that adjustment to anything outside my personal control was impossible for me.(p.547)

• By this time I was *such* a past master at kidding myself that I had convinced myself I had sat out a war and waited for this man to come home and, as my resentment and self-pity grew, so did my alcoholic problem.(p.548)

• When I was faced with a special challenge or social event -- *such* as an important business presentation or a dinner party -- I had to fortify myself with a couple of belts.(p.556)

• Nine -- A.A., as *such*, ought never be organized; but we may create service boards or committees directly responsible to those they serve.(p.564)

• On *such* issues our common welfare is paramount.(p.565)

• An A.A. group, as *such*, should never go into business.(p.566)

• Secondary aids to A.A., *such* as clubs or hospitals which require much property or administration, ought to be incorporated and so set apart that, if necessary, they can be freely discarded by the groups.(p.566)

• Hence *such* facilities ought not to use the A.A. name.(p.566)

• While an A.A. group may cooperate with anyone, *such* cooperation ought never go so far as affiliation or endorsement, actual or implied.(p.566)

• *Such* special services may be well recompensed.(p.566)

• All *such* representatives are to be guided in the spirit of service, for true leaders in A.A. are but trusted and experienced servants of the whole.(p.567)

• 10. -- No A.A. group or member should ever, in *such* a way as to implicate A.A., express any opinion on outside controversial issues -- particularly those of politics, alcohol reform, or sectarian religion.(p.567)

• Concerning *such* matters they can express no views whatever.(p.567)

• Though it was not our intention to create *such* an impression, many alcoholics have nevertheless concluded that in order to recover they must acquire an immediate and overwhelming "God-consciousness" followed at once by a vast change in feeling and outlook.(p.569)

• Among our rapidly growing membership of thousands of alcoholics *such* transformations, though frequent, are by no means the rule.(p.569)

• He finally realizes that he has undergone a profound alteration in his reaction to life; that *such* a change could hardly have been brought about by himself alone.(p.569)

• In *such* places, A.A. can be located through the local telephone directory, newspaper office, or police station, or by contacting local priests or ministers.(p.575)

Sudan

• I was down in the *Sudan* by this time.(p.521)

sudden

• Six months earlier, the broker had been relieved of his drink obsession by a *sudden* spiritual experience, following a meeting with an alcoholic friend who had been in contact with the Oxford Groups of that day.(p.xv)

• God comes to most men gradually, but His impact on me was *sudden* and profound.(p.14)

• To this man, the revelation was *sudden*.(p.57)

• All of a *sudden* I found myself guzzling.(p.195)

• At the end of about four months, I not only had good looking clothes --and I might say that at the time I first talked to Max I didn't have a suit of clothes I could bend over in real *sudden*; now I had six suits of clothes.(p.200)

• It isn't always so *sudden* with everyone, but I ran into a personal crisis which filled me with a raging and righteous anger.(p.228)

• So it is clear that I never had any fun out of drinking -- I would be the soberest-seeming one in the crowd and all of a *sudden* I would be the drunkest.(p.241)

• After being dry two weeks and sticking close to Jackie, all of a *sudden* I found I had become the sponsor of my sponsor, for he was suddenly taken drunk.(p.245)

• In telling newcomers how to change their lives and attitudes, all of a *sudden* I found I was doing a little changing myself.(p.249)

• Following an injection I would have to keep one hand busy scratching my constantly itching nose and would also have *sudden* uncontrollable urges to vomit.(p.442)

• They build you up with a lot of false hopes and promises, and rush you around here and there and then, all of a *sudden*, it's gone."(p.472)

• Yet it is true that our first printing gave many readers the impression that these personality changes, or religious experiences, must be in the nature of *sudden* and spectacular upheavals.(p.569)

• In the first few chapters a number of *sudden* revolutionary changes are described.(p.569)

suddenly

• He *suddenly* realized that in order to save himself he must carry his message to another alcoholic.(p.xvi)

• On the other hand -- and strange as this may seem to those who do not understand -- once a psychic change has occurred, the very same person who seemed doomed, who had so many problems he despaired of ever solving them, *suddenly* finds himself easily able to control his desire for alcohol, the only effort necessary being that required to follow a few simple rules.(p.xxvii)

• Somehow I managed to drag my mattress to a lower floor, lest I *suddenly* leap.(p.6)

• Then he had, in effect, been raised from the dead, *suddenly* taken from the scrap heap to a level of life better than the best he had ever known!(p.11)

• Ideas, emotions, and attitudes which were once the guiding forces of the lives of these men are *suddenly* cast to one side, and a completely new set of conceptions and motives begin to dominate them.(p.27)

• "*Suddenly* the thought crossed my mind that if I were to put an ounce of whiskey in my milk it couldn't hurt me on a full stomach.(p.36)

• We will *suddenly* realize that God is doing for us what we could not do for ourselves.(p.84)

• Father, coming *suddenly* to life again, often begins to assert himself.(p.131)

• Before our visit was over, Bill *suddenly* turned to his wife and said, "Go fetch my clothes, dear.(p.189)

• From far away, as if in a delirium, I heard my own voice -- calling someone "Dorothy," talking of dress shops, of jobs . . . the words came clearer . . . this sound of my own voice frightened me as it came closer . . . and *suddenly*, there I was, talking of I knew not what, to someone I'd never seen before this very moment.(p.222)

• *Suddenly* I could accept myself, faults and all, as I was -- for weren't we all like that?(p.229)

• After being dry two weeks and sticking close to Jackie, all of a sudden I found I had become the sponsor of my sponsor, for he was *suddenly* taken drunk.(p.245)

• *Suddenly* all this changed.(p.275)

• I was *suddenly* and uncontrollably seized with the old, paralyzing panic.(p.279)

• I sat up in the big red chair, *suddenly* thinking, "My God, with my kind of lousy luck, I might not die soon!(p.333)

• We had some people in, and I was making drinks in the kitchen, when I *suddenly* decided to hoist the bottle for a quick one.(p.365)

• So I got drunker and drunker, and then, *suddenly*, I woke up in the booby-hatch.(p.387)

• One night my son, when he was only sixteen, was *suddenly* and tragically killed.(p.437)

• *Suddenly*, it was obvious to me: I had a brain tumor and would die, and everyone would be sorry for me.(p.444)

• I *suddenly* remembered one of my first A.A. meetings, where I heard, "If you are an alcoholic and if you continue to drink, the end is death or insanity."(p.461)

• *Suddenly* I feel hopeless, unable to go on.(p.502)

• *Suddenly* a thought comes.(p.503)

• *Suddenly* I feel a wave of utter hopelessness sweep over me.(p.504)

• *Suddenly*, I began vomiting and losing rectally great quantities of blood.(p.558)

sue

• I was going to *sue* the city for what they did to me.(p.391)

Suez

• I had three or four very uncomfortable months with my regiment then on the *Suez* Canal.(p.520)

• Then Hitler's war broke out, and again, I was given a really important job on the *Suez* Canal, dealing with military shipping.(p.520)

suffer

• This is the great news this book carries to those who *suffer* from alcoholism.(p.17)

• There are those, too, who *suffer* from grave emotional and mental disorders, but many of them do recover if they have the capacity to be honest.(p.58)

• His business may *suffer* somewhat.(p.109)

• The wives and children of such men *suffer* horribly, but not more than the men themselves.(p.114)

• Showing others who *suffer* how we were given help is the very thing which makes life seem so worth while to us now.(p.124)

• WOMEN *SUFFER* TOO(p.222)

• Gradually, however, I'd *suffer* so much that I simply had to have the morning-after drink.(p.233)

• Only once did I *suffer* from a nearly overpowering compulsion to take a drink.(p.285)

• 3. -- Our membership ought to include all who *suffer* from alcoholism.(p.565)

suffered

• In this statement he confirms what we who have *suffered* alcoholic torture must believe -- that the body of the alcoholic is quite as abnormal as his mind.(p.xxiv)

• They expect him to give them the nice times they used to have before he drank so much, and to show his contrition for what they *suffered*.(p.126)

• Since the home has *suffered* more than anything else, it is well that a man exert himself there.(p.127)

• He simply could not believe that his brother-executive *suffered* from a serious illness.(p.138)

• The man in the bed was told of the acute poisoning from which he *suffered*, how it deteriorates the body of an alcoholic and warps his mind.(p.157)

• He *suffered* horribly from his sprees, but it seemed as if nothing could be done for him.(p.159)

• They *suffered* from my conduct without saying anything, but the reason for this was I still managed to hang onto a very substantial practice.(p.215)

• Before long I had a definite taste for hard liquor, knew nausea and headaches I had never known before, but as in the old days, I *suffered* them out.(p.233)

• Not wishing to disturb my wife, I slumped in a big red-leather chair and *suffered*.(p.332)

• And it was my home that *suffered*.(p.339)

• I was very fortunate indeed not to have *suffered* any brain damage.(p.480)

• My father had come out of the South and had *suffered* a great deal down there.(p.485)

• I don't think I *suffered* too much as far as the racial situation was concerned because I was born into it and knew nothing other than that.(p.485)

• I *suffered* frequent blackouts.(p.558)

sufferer

• In a vague way their families and friends sense that these drinkers are abnormal, but everybody hopefully awaits the day when the *sufferer* will rouse himself from his lethargy and assert his power of will.(p.23)

sufferer's

• It engulfs all whose lives touch the *sufferer's*.(p.18)

sufferers

• The experiment of quitting for a period of time will be helpful, but we think we can render an even greater service to alcoholic *sufferers* and perhaps to the medical fraternity.(p.34)

suffering

• If hundreds of experiences have shown him that one drink means another debacle with all its attendant *suffering* and humiliation, why is it he takes that one drink?(p.22)

• We are unable, at certain times, to bring into our consciousness with sufficient force the memory of the

suffering and humiliation of even a week or a month ago.(p.24)
• Here was the threat of commitment, the loss of family and position, to say nothing of that intense mental and physical ***suffering*** which drinking always caused him.(p.36)
• Then came the hospital with unbearable mental and physical ***suffering***.(p.41)
• If that be the case, you may be ***suffering*** from an illness which only a spiritual experience will conquer.(p.44)
• If the family cooperates, dad will soon see that he is ***suffering*** from a distortion of values.(p.129)
• Why, he argued, should he lose the remainder of his business, only to bring still more ***suffering*** to his family by foolishly admitting his plight to people from whom he made his livelihood?(p.155)
• They experienced a few distressing failures, but in those cases they made an effort to bring the man's family into a spiritual way of living, thus relieving much worry and ***suffering***.(p.159)
• I was ***suffering*** from an actual disease that had a name and symptoms like diabetes or cancer or TB -- and a disease was respectable, not a moral stigma!(p.227)
• In describing his ***suffering***, his fears, his many years of groping for some answer to that which always seemed to remain unanswerable, he could have been describing me, and nothing short of experience and knowledge could have afforded him that much insight!(p.309)
• Therefore, these seventeen A.A.'s, and hundreds of thousands like them, have been saved years of infinite ***suffering***.(p.315)
• I realized that there were other people in this world who behaved and acted as I did, and that I was a sick person, that I was ***suffering*** from an actual disease.(p.392)
• A young veteran tells how a few rough experiences pushed him into A.A. – and how he was therefore spared years of ***suffering***.(p.422)
• This man's wife had been ***suffering*** for a couple of months and when he came in he owed me a little bill.(p.488)
• There was the father one lost respect for at the age of eleven, because the father broke his solemn word in a circumstance where you, eleven years old, had assumed guilt when you were innocent; but the father would not believe you, no matter what; and to ease his ***suffering*** you "confessed" and were "forgiven," only – months later – to have your "guilt" brought up – only he and you knew what he was talking bout -- brought up in front of the stern grandmother.(p.533)
• For you learned that he had been guilty of the thing he had accused you of, and his guilt had brought ***suffering*** to his entire family; and he thought he saw his young son beginning his own tragic pattern.(p.533)
• For by now I had been exposed once to A.A., but I had treated it as a vaudeville and had taken friends to meetings so that they too could enjoy the fascination of the naked revelation of ***suffering*** and recovery.(p.539)
• Above all, I was ***suffering*** inner pain because my performance and my accomplishments in life failed to live up to my own expectations of myself.(p.557)
• Historians may one day recognize Alcoholics Anonymous to have been a great venture in social pioneering which forged a new instrument for social action; a new therapy based on the kinship of common ***suffering***; one having a vast potential for the myriad other ills of mankind."(p.573)

sufferings
• Convincing testimony must surely come from the medical men who have had experience with the ***sufferings*** of our members and have witnessed our return to health.(p.xxiii)

suffers
• If a man drinks so much that his job ***suffers***, we fire him.(p.148)
• Dr. Bob said, "Love and service keep us dry," and Bill said, "Always we must remember that our first duty is face-to-face help for the alcoholic who still ***suffers***."(p.395)
• The alcoholic ***suffers*** death many times over.(p.457)
• Five – Each group has but one primary purpose -- to carry its message to the alcoholic who still ***suffers***.(p.564)
• 5. – Each Alcoholics Anonymous group ought to be a spiritual entity having but one primary purpose -- that of carrying its message to the alcoholic who still ***suffers***.(p.565)

suffice
• He wanted to give me the very best and he thought that nothing but being a doctor would ***suffice***.(p.485)

suffices
• Frothy emotional appeal seldom ***suffices***.(p.xxvi)

sufficient
• By late 1937, the number of members having substantial sobriety time behind them was ***sufficient*** to convince the membership that a new light had entered the dark world of the alcoholic.(p.xvii)
• We are unable, at certain times, to bring into our consciousness with ***sufficient*** force the memory of the suffering and humiliation of even a week or a month ago.(p.24)
• If a mere code of morals or a better philosophy of life were ***sufficient*** to overcome alcoholism, many of us would have recovered long ago.(p.44)
• Our human resources, as marshalled by the will were not ***sufficient***; they failed utterly.(p.45)
• Our own conception, however inadequate, was ***sufficient*** to make the approach and to effect a contact with Him.(p.46)
• Have you a ***sufficient*** substitute?"(p.152)
• I wouldn't put ***sufficient*** time on them.(p.194)
• Obviously I have overcome fear to a ***sufficient*** degree to think in terms of success in business.(p.284)
• I would rather talk about the good things A.A. has taught me; I feel that hitting on just a few sordid points should be ***sufficient*** to let those of you in institutions know where I came from.(p.459)
• Still, I had had funds ***sufficient*** to get plastered because that, of course, was more important than paying my own way.(p.538)
• The terms "spiritual experience" and "spiritual awakening" are used many times in this book which, upon careful reading, shows that the personality change ***sufficient*** to bring about recovery from alcoholism has manifested itself among us in many different forms.(p.569)

sufficiently
• If a ***sufficiently*** strong reason -- ill health, falling in love, change of environment, or the warning of a doctor – becomes operative, this man can also stop or moderate, although he may find it difficult and troublesome and may even need medical attention.(p.21)
• Being intensely interested in the work, I changed my conduct ***sufficiently*** to master the job.(p.211)

suffused
• Immediately a great feeling of peace descended upon me, intermingled with a feeling of being ***suffused*** with a quiet strength.(p.280)

sugar
• So I was used to it, but I didn't know what the effect of alcohol was because I always had wine, usually with dinner, but always with a lot of ice and about two tablespoons of ***sugar*** in it.(p.385)
• My Quaker mother-in-law, bless her heart, used to set the Christmas pudding ablaze with lumps of ***sugar*** dipped in rubbing alcohol.(p.402)
• We weren't even permitted to play cards in our home, but father would give us just a little toddy with whiskey and ***sugar*** and warm water now and then.(p.484)

suggest
• The only relief we have to ***suggest*** is entire abstinence.(p.xxviii)
• This should ***suggest*** a useful program for anyone concerned with a drinking problem.(p.19)
• When your man is better, the doctor might ***suggest*** a visit from you.(p.91)
• We ***suggest*** you do this as we have done it in the chapter on alcoholism.(p.92)
• ***Suggest*** how important it is that he place the welfare of other people ahead of his own.(p.94)
• When a discussion does arise, you might ***suggest*** he read this book or at least the chapter on alcoholism.(p.111)
• You might ***suggest*** that you both take an interest in them.(p.112)
• If he is lukewarm or thinks he is not an alcoholic, we ***suggest*** you leave him alone.(p.113)
• We ***suggest*** that you direct some of your thought to the wives of his new alcoholic friends.(p.119)
• Suppose we tell you some of the obstacles a family will meet; suppose we ***suggest*** how they may be avoided – even converted to good use for others.(p.123)
• After satisfying yourself that your man wants to recover and that he will go to any extreme to do so, you may ***suggest*** a definite course of action.(p.142)
• Perhaps you are not quite in sympathy with the approach we ***suggest***.(p.144)
• We ***suggest*** you draw the book to the attention of the doctor who is to attend your patient during treatment.(p.144)
• I'll buy you one drink, and if you ***suggest*** a second one, I'll poke you right in the nose."(p.201)

suggested
• We believe, and so ***suggested*** a few years ago, that the action of alcohol on these chronic alcoholics is a manifestation of an allergy; that the phenomenon of craving is limited to this class and never occurs in the average temperate drinker.(p.xxvi)
• This phenomenon, as we have ***suggested***, may be the manifestation of an allergy which differentiates these people, and sets them apart as a distinct entity.(p.xxviii)
• My intellectual heroes, the chemists the astronomers, even the evolutionists, ***suggested*** vast laws and forces at work.(p.10)
• My friend ***suggested*** what then seemed a novel idea.(p.12)
• When, however, the perfectly logical assumption is ***suggested*** that underneath the material world and life as we see it, there is an All Powerful, Guiding, Creative Intelligence, right there our perverse streak comes to the surface and we laboriously set out to convince ourselves it isn't so.(p.49)
• Here are the steps we took, which are ***suggested*** as a program of recovery:(p.59)
• We ***suggested*** he write his first wife admitting his faults and asking forgiveness.(p.79)
• Our women folk have ***suggested*** certain attitudes a wife may take with the husband who is recovering.(p.122)
• A spiritual experience, he conceded, was absolutely necessary, but the price seemed high upon the basis ***suggested***.(p.155)
• I looked so terrible in the court that the judge ***suggested*** that I get a continuance and let me sign all the papers to go to a hospital and to a doctor.(p.204)
• When my friends ***suggested*** that I was drinking too much – they were no longer my friends.(p.226)
• However, I made an SOS call to the New York Group, whom I hadn't met yet, and they ***suggested*** we both come there.(p.245)
• He mentioned two of them that I had known through the years and ***suggested*** that I talk with them.(p.289)
• So I ***suggested*** that he take a trip to Akron for a couple of weeks, which he did, living with one of the A.A. families there.(p.294)
• I ***suggested*** to her that she should see the son's minister or doctor, and that perhaps he would recommend the A.A. program.(p.294)
• He asked me if I had any spiritual belief, and when I said No, he ***suggested*** that I keep an open mind.(p.413)
• Since they could do nothing with Anne either, Priscilla ***suggested*** that I go and look after Anne.(p.414)
• After a particularly ugly one-nighter, my wife ***suggested*** I try it, and I agreed.(p.434)
• It is ***suggested*** that we do not try to do a lifetime of repairs in one day.(p.481)
• I remember in my first year in high school, that mother ***suggested*** that I do not join the cadet unit.(p.484)
• Then Charlie or someone in the group ***suggested*** that we try to get a place in a church or hall to hold meetings.(p.495)
• Finally, in desperation, my family appealed to a doctor for advice and he ***suggested*** A.A.(p.549)
• They ***suggested*** that I study the A.A. book and try to take the Twelve Steps according to the explanation in the Book, for it was their opinion that the application of these principles in our daily lives will get us sober and keep us sober.(p.550)
• All but one "responded to the treatment" ***suggested*** in the Steps immediately, but this one posed a problem.(p.551)
• Should you be the relative or friend of an alcoholic who shows no immediate interest in A.A., it is ***suggested*** that you write the Al-Anon Family Groups, Inc., Box 182, Madison Square Station, New York, NY 10159, U.S.A.(p.575)

suggestion
• This is our twelfth ***suggestion***: Carry this message to other alcoholics!(p.89)
• One more ***suggestion***: Whether the family has spiritual convictions or not, they may do well to examine the principles by which the alcoholic member is trying to live.(p.130)
• We intend the foregoing as a helpful ***suggestion*** only.(p.132)
• That was at my ***suggestion***.(p.199)
• She knew that at that time any ***suggestion*** she made about my drinking would only build up a barrier, a consideration for which I am ever grateful.(p.216)
• I jumped at the ***suggestion*** that I accompany him.(p.281)

• This time he had a *suggestion* to offer.(p.289)
• This *suggestion* had been made before on a number of occasions, but like all alcoholics I wanted to handle my problem my own way, which really meant I didn't want anything to interfere with my drinking.(p.378)

suggestions
• Yet, we believe we can make some definite and valuable *suggestions*.(p.86)
• *Suggestions* about these may be obtained from one's priest, minister, or rabbi.(p.87)
• He will be more likely to follow your *suggestions*.(p.94)
• There is every evidence that women regain their health as readily as men if they try our *suggestions*.(p.104)
• We know these *suggestions* are sometimes difficult to follow, but you will save many a heartbreak if you can succeed in observing them.(p.111)
• If your decision is yes, whether the reason be humanitarian or business or both, then the following *suggestions* may be helpful.(p.140)
• To return to the subject matter of this book: It contains full *suggestions* by which the employee may solve his problem.(p.143)
• When the man is presented with this volume it is best that no one tell him he must abide by its *suggestions*.(p.144)
• If he speaks of his home situation, you can undoubtedly make helpful *suggestions*.(p.145)
• We hope our *suggestions* will help you plug up this sometimes serious leak.(p.148)
• Our hope is that when this chip of a book is launched on the world tide of alcoholism, defeated drinkers will seize upon it, to follow its *suggestions*.(p.153)
• Help which you once continually rejected, *suggestions* once turned aside are finally accepted in desperation.(p.377)

suggestive
• Our book is meant to be *suggestive* only.(p.164)

suggests
• This thought brings us to Step Ten, which *suggests* we continue to take personal inventory and continue to set right any new mistakes as we go along.(p.84)
• Step Eleven *suggests* prayer and meditation.(p.85)
• Every few days this doctor *suggests* our approach to one of his patients.(p.162)
• One girl *suggests* that I phone her.(p.505)

suicidal
• My personality was stretched almost to splitting in the effort; schizophrenia stared me in the face, and one night I was in a *suicidal* despair.(p.435)
• An ambitious playwright, he let his brains get so far ahead of his emotions that he collapsed into *suicidal* drinking.(p.531)

suicide
• One poor chap committed *suicide* in my home.(p.16)
• Business failure, insanity, fatal illness, *suicide* -- these calamities in his immediate family embittered and depressed him.(p.56)
• Three months before I met Jackie I had made my second feeble try at *suicide*.(p.245)
• When the day of their return was almost upon me, and *suicide* was the only answer I had been able to think of, I went into Ralph's room one evening and told him the truth.(p.278)
• Well, *suicide* was a last straw matter, and I had not drawn the last straw yet.(p.278)
• I was sent to a psychiatrist, for they didn't think it was normal for me to want to kill my platoon sergeant or to attempt *suicide* twice.(p.318)
• With increasing guilt and never-ending depression, I was too weak to continue this day-by-day *suicide*.(p.355)
• There are many things worse than dying, but is there any death worse than the progressive, self-induced, slow *suicide* of the practicing alcoholic?(p.457)
• I felt very sorry for myself and attempted *suicide* on many occasions, making sure there was always somebody within reaching distance to see that I didn't finish the job.(p.478)
• I felt that I didn't have anything to live for, so I tried *suicide* many times.(p.528)
• Since, perhaps, *suicide* was a bit too drastic (actually, I was afraid), dry martinis were chosen as the slow, pleasant, private, gradual instrument of self-destruction.(p.531)

suit
• Still the play does not *suit* him.(p.61)
• We do not tire so easily, for we are not burning up energy foolishly as we did when we were trying to arrange life to *suit* ourselves.(p.88)
• But his venture wound up in a law *suit* and bogged down completely.(p.154)
• At the end of about four months, I not only had good looking clothes —and I might say that at the time I first talked to Max I didn't have a *suit* of clothes I could bend over in real sudden; now I had six suits of clothes.(p.200)
• At three-thirty the next morning, I was in Champlain Street Station, in jail for driving while intoxicated and insulting an officer; and the *suit* of which I was so proud was in such shape that the turnkey had to get me a pair of trousers to go into court in the next morning.(p.201)
• I was picked up at two-thirty that morning with my car smashed up by a street-car because I had run into a big concrete safety zone, and the street-car had run into me, and they took me out through the roof -- there's where I lost the *suit*.(p.202)
• My tweed *suit*, once a very good one, was shapeless and baggy with bare places worn in the elbows from leaning on the bar.(p.411)

suitable
• Notwithstanding the great necessity for discussing ourselves with someone, it may be one is so situated that there is no *suitable* person available.(p.74)

suite
• I optioned a piece of land just off East Market Street to put up a three-hundred *suite* apartment.(p.198)
• My doctor finally declared he could no longer be responsible for me, and sent me to a psychiatrist who practiced in the same *suite* of offices.(p.558)

suited
• In fact his language was perfectly *suited* to my understanding.(p.235)
• I got a job by myself which *suited* me down to the ground, because there was nobody really to interfere with what I did, one way or the other, and I usually had my nerves in good trim when anybody was coming around to inspect.(p.519)

suits
• At the end of about four months, I not only had good looking clothes —and I might say that at the time I first talked to Max I didn't have a suit of clothes I could bend over in real sudden; now I had six *suits* of clothes.(p.200)

Sullivan
• That was on a hot summer evening, down in the Greenwich Village Group, and there was a little porch out there in the old meeting place on *Sullivan* Street, and after the meeting I went out on the steps for some air.(p.321)

sum
• To *sum* up about sex: We earnestly pray for the right ideal, for guidance in each questionable situation, for sanity, and for the strength to do the right thing.(p.70)
• While drinking, he accepted a *sum* of money from a bitterly-hated business rival, giving him no receipt for it.(p.80)
• Quebec, Toronto, Buffalo, and finally Pittsburgh, were the scenes of man-sized drunks until I had gone through my readjusted discharge pay, a fair *sum*.(p.253)
• They *sum* it up like this: "We didn't wait to hit bottom because, thank God, we could see the bottom.(p.315)
• On another small borrowed *sum*, I went up into the country to the home of a doctor I had known since boyhood.(p.540)

summa cum laude
• I was graduated "*summa cum laude*" in the eyes of the drinking fraternity, but not in the eyes of the Dean.(p.172)

summarize
• The Twelve Steps that *summarize* the program may be called los Doce Pasos in one country, los Douze Etapes in another, but they trace exactly the same path to recovery that was blazed by the earliest members of Alcoholics Anonymous.(p.xxii)
• Before going into a detailed discussion, it may be well to *summarize* some points as we see them.(p.20)

summer
• This work at Akron continued through the *summer* of 1935.(p.xvii)
• So that was it -- last *summer* an alcoholic crackpot; now, I suspected, a little cracked about religion.(p.9)
• Nineteen years ago last *summer*, Dr. Bob and I saw him (Bill D.) for the first time.(p.188)
• I had been to OTC the previous *summer* so I went into the Army as a sergeant, but I came out a private, and you really have to be unusual to do that.(p.241)
• At the age of sixteen, I was invited to spend the *summer* with an aunt and I, very delightedly, accepted the invitation.(p.261)
• In the spiritual strength I had found, because of A.A., I felt that I had made a complete surrender, that I had really turned my life over that *summer*.(p.271)
• In the *summer* of 1938, almost a year from the time I made my original contact with Akron, the man for whom I was working and who knew about the program, approached me and asked if I could do anything about one of his salesmen who was drinking very heavily.(p.294)
• I had the best schools, *summer* camps, resort vacations and travel.(p.304)
• That was on a hot *summer* evening, down in the Greenwich Village Group, and there was a little porch out there in the old meeting place on Sullivan Street, and after the meeting I went out on the steps for some air.(p.321)
• A house in Virginia, during the fox hunting season; a little chalet in Switzerland during the *summer* or a place on Long Island -- each house complete with cooks, butlers and maids.(p.403)
• I rented a beautiful apartment on the banks of the Seine in the winter, and a chalet in Switzerland in the *summer*.(p.405)
• I had worked the previous *summer* on a New York fashion magazine, a job I really enjoyed.(p.405)

summing
• In *summing* up, I can say that A.A. had made me, I hope, a real Catholic.(p.221)

summoned
• They *summoned* the fire department and the sheriff.(p.424)

summons
• I went back to my mother's for a few days until things cooled off, because the District Attorney had put out a *summons* for me to come to see him in his office.(p.491)
• I had to put up a three hundred dollar bond because he was carrying the same *summons* around in his pocket for me.(p.491)

sumptuous
• There were many unhappy scenes in our *sumptuous* apartment.(p.3)

sun
• We all one as Great Spirit walks through A.A. like *sun* walks through day.(p.474)

Sunday
• Show any longshoreman a *Sunday* supplement describing a proposal to explore the moon by means of a rocket and he will say, "I bet they do it -- maybe not so long either."(p.52)
• From childhood through high school I was more or less forced to go to church, *Sunday* School and evening service, Monday night Christian Endeavor and sometimes to Wednesday evening prayer meeting.(p.172)
• This was on *Sunday*.(p.179)
• I had a crew of men working there and I wanted them to work *Sunday* afternoons so that I could sell lots on *Sunday*.(p.195)
• I attended their meetings every *Sunday* and Wednesday for about nine months.(p.202)
• To show you the point to which this obsession went, there came an occasion when I had spent a most delightful week-end, and at nine o'clock on *Sunday* night I was on my way home, and I thought I would get a drink.(p.204)
• I regained consciousness on *Sunday*.(p.207)
• On *Sunday* when I came to, it was a bad, wet, snowy day in February, 1937, and Paul and Doc and a lot of other fellows were in Cleveland on business.(p.207)
• My wife didn't tell me this, but one *Sunday* afternoon when Mary was trying to get the cobwebs out of my mind, Clarence and his sister-in-law, the hairdresser, called at the house.(p.216)
• At this school we had Bible readings before each meal, and church services four times on *Sunday*, and I became so rebellious at this that I swore I would never join or go to any church except for weddings or funerals.(p.240)
• One *Sunday* afternoon, the only time I ever got picked up for drunken driving, I got picked up in Bellaire.(p.264)
• (Russ was buried on Friday, and on *Sunday* afternoon Hilda S. had invited me there to dinner *Sunday* night, and I didn't think I could do it.(p.272)
• If, on *Sunday*, I could be there, trying to think of something that would help her with this problem, then we must have something that could work.(p.272)
• I hadn't been in too long when one of the men's wives called me one *Sunday* and told me she didn't

think I had any part of the program.(p.273)
• That was on Saturday and my husband was leaving town ***Sunday*** night.(p.393)
• On each occasion, I had a convulsion on ***Sunday*** morning.(p.444)
• While I was taking inventory in the cold-storage locker one ***Sunday***, a wooden sign bolted to the inside door stopped me in my tracks.(p.461)
• I went to church on Easter ***Sunday*** with my husband, and it didn't hurt at all.(p.482)
• The following ***Sunday*** we met at Ella G.'s.(p.495)

Sunday-school
• I was a deacon and a ***Sunday-school*** teacher.(p.418)

Sundays
• I could almost hear the sound of the preacher's voice as I sat, on still ***Sundays***, way over there on the hillside; there was that proffered temperance pledge I never signed; my grandfather's good natured contempt of some church folk and their doings; his insistence that the spheres really had their music; but his denial of the preacher's right to tell him how he must listen; his fearlessness as he spoke of these things just before he died; these recollections welled up from the past.(p.10)
• I have no assistance and am working nights, Saturdays and ***Sundays***.(p.500)

sundry
• After the book appeared we all became very busy in our efforts to save all and ***sundry***, but I was still actually on the fringes of A.A.(p.248)

sung
• But the saddest, and thus the most consoling, drifted through from the country-music station — stories of broken hearts, wasted lives, lost loves, ***sung*** plaintively.(p.332)
• And having ***sung*** that phrase, I'd chuckle with amusement, turning into irony turning into self-contempt turning into self-pity, at the sad fate of Bob, that wonderful, poor little motherless boy who was so smart in school and who grew up to accept responsibility so early and so fast and who staggered under his burdens without a whimper until the time came when he thought he was too good for this world and so he ought to be out of it.(p.532)

sunk
• So, you see, there were three alcoholics in that town, who now felt they had to give to others what they had found, or be ***sunk***.(p.158)
• No one is too discredited or has ***sunk*** too low to be welcomed cordially — if he means business.(p.161)

sunlight
• I stood in the ***sunlight*** at last.(p.12)
• For when harboring such feelings we shut ourselves off from the ***sunlight*** of the Spirit.(p.66)

sunset
• And then, with a better motive, had we not worshipfully beheld the ***sunset***, the sea, or a flower?(p.54)
• How many times I swore off in the morning and got drunk before ***sunset*** I don't know.(p.300)

sunshine
• He is like the retired business man who lolls in the Florida ***sunshine*** in the winter complaining of the sad state of the nation; the minister who sighs over the sins of the twentieth century; politicians and reformers who are sure all would be Utopia if the rest of the world would only behave; the outlaw safe cracker who thinks society has wronged him; and the alcoholic who has lost all and is locked up.(p.61)

supercargo
• I wanted to roam again and through relatives got a ***supercargo*** job on an Australian packet which allowed me to visit my people in Australia where I was born.(p.252)

superficial
• Three weeks after an armed robbery in which one person received a ***superficial*** flesh wound (I could have killed someone!), I was apprehended.(p.460)

superhuman
• When they talked of a God personal to me, who was love, ***superhuman*** strength and direction, I became irritated and my mind snapped shut against such a theory.(p.10)

superintendent
• I go to the hospital, where I have made friends with the night ***superintendent***.(p.501)

superior
• His religious education and training may be far ***superior*** to yours.(p.93)
• Dad may feel that for years his drinking has placed him on the wrong side of every argument, but now he has become a ***superior*** person with God on his side.(p.129)
• I had never even been told by a ***superior*** that maybe I was drinking too much.(p.327)

superiors
• Handling customers, dealers, insurance people, dictation, telephoning, directing new employees, answering to ***superiors***, and all the rest of it.(p.299)
• Strangely enough, right through to the end of my twenty-six years in the Army, I was still being offered very good and important jobs in spite of the fact that my ***superiors*** must have known that I wasn't thoroughly reliable.(p.519)

supernatural
• Edward Dowling, S.J., of the Queen's Work staff says, "Alcoholics Anonymous is natural; it is natural at the point where nature comes closest to the ***supernatural***, namely in humiliations and in consequent humility.(p.574)

superstition
• In the realm of the material, men's minds were fettered by ***superstition***, tradition, and all sorts of fixed ideas.(p.51)

supervised
• But hospitals, as well as other places of recuperation, ought to be well outside A.A. — and medically ***supervised***.(p.566)

supervision
• While working in an office, there was some semblance of restraint, but, oh boy, when I got on the outside with this new company without ***supervision***, did I go to town!(p.300)

supper
• Eventually I would arrive home for a late ***supper*** for which, of course, I had absolutely no relish.(p.299)
• I would make a feeble attempt at eating ***supper***, but I never met with any howling success.(p.299)
• Toward five o'clock, helter-skelter, I'd get everything put away and try to get ***supper*** on the table, and after ***supper*** I'd finish the job up and knock myself out.(p.337)
• Soon ***supper*** is on the table.(p.497)

supplanted
• If these thoughts occur, they are hazy and readily ***supplanted*** with the old threadbare idea that this time we shall handle ourselves like other people.(p.24)
• Only to have that thought ***supplanted*** by "Well, I'll stop with the sixth drink."(p.24)

supplement
• Show any longshoreman a Sunday ***supplement*** describing a proposal to explore the moon by means of a rocket and he will say, "I bet they do it -- maybe not so long either."(p.52)
• (At this point, the Editors intrude just long enough to ***supplement*** Bill D.'s account, that of the man on the bed, with that of Bill W., the man who sat by the side of the bed.)(p.188)

supplied
• An all night place ***supplied*** me with a dozen glasses of ale.(p.6)
• God has abundantly ***supplied*** this world with fine doctors, psychologists, and practitioners of various kinds.(p.133)
• The town was well ***supplied*** with churches and schools in which I pursued my early educational activities.(p.171)
• My broken home and broken heart fanned my smoldering self-pity into a fair-sized bonfire and this kept me well ***supplied*** with reasons for having another drink, and then another.(p.305)

supplies
• The next three years I spent in Boston, Chicago, and Montreal in the employ of a large manufacturing concern, selling railway ***supplies***, gas engines of all sorts, and many other items of heavy hardware.(p.172)
• The only incentive that I had, toward the end, for getting dressed in the morning was to get out and get ***supplies*** to help me get my day started.(p.336)
• I began to have to have ***supplies*** on hand for the people who "might come in."(p.336)

supply
• If he can afford it, he may have liquor concealed all over his house to be certain no one gets his entire ***supply*** away from him to throw down the waterpipe.(p.22)
• At that time I was not aware of the almost unlimited ***supply*** the government made it possible for us doctors to obtain, neither had I any knowledge of the bootlegger who soon appeared on the horizon.(p.175)
• If my wife was planning to go out in the afternoon, I would get a large ***supply*** of liquor and smuggle it home and hide it in the coal bin, the clothes chute, over door jambs, over beams in the cellar and in cracks in the cellar tile.(p.176)
• The short tours could be taken care of by sneaking enough whiskey aboard ship so that it could be rationed out until another ***supply*** could be laid in.(p.398)
• I remember vaguely violent quarrels with my husband, his finding my liquor ***supply*** time and time again and throwing it out.(p.466)
• And then my waiting until I was sure he was asleep, and stealing money from him to replenish the ***supply***.(p.466)

support
• Without such ***support***, A.A. could have made only the slowest progress.(p.xx)
• Perhaps we had been leaning too heavily on Reason that last mile and we did not like to lose our ***support***.(p.53)
• My family would have nothing to do with me, in fact couldn't because I couldn't spare any of my money, which I needed for drink, to ***support*** them.(p.255)
• I am not even there, and if I was there the only thing I could do would be to give her moral ***support***, and yet he thanks me for curing his wife."(p.350)
• I have a family to ***support*** and have no time to be looking for another job.(p.500)
• I was immersed in self-pity and resentment, and the only people who would ***support*** this attitude or who I felt understood me at all were the people I met in bars and the ones who drank as I did.(p.547)
• Their management should be the sole responsibility of those people who financially ***support*** them.(p.566)

supported
• 7. — The A.A. groups themselves ought to be fully ***supported*** by the voluntary contributions of their own members.(p.566)

supporters
• They seemed to be happy in their fashion, they and their little groups of ***supporters***, but always pride of intellect stopped me from seeking what they evidently had.(p.256)

supporting
• I was ***supporting*** myself through all this education by being a toolmaker and a draftsman.(p.212)

suppose
• I ***suppose*** some would be shocked at our seeming worldliness and levity.(p.16)
• ***Suppose*** we fall short of the chosen ideal and stumble?(p.70)
• ***Suppose*** now you are making your second visit to a man.(p.96)
• ***Suppose***, however, that your husband fits the description of number two.(p.112)
• You would ***suppose*** that men in the fourth classification would be quite hopeless, but that is not so.(p.113)
• ***Suppose*** we tell you some of the obstacles a family will meet; ***suppose*** we suggest how they may be avoided — even converted to good use for others.(p.123)
• ***Suppose*** an approach is made something like this:(p.141)
• ***Suppose*** now that through you several families have adopted this way of life.(p.153)
• Knowing Bob of old, she jokingly replied, "Well, Doctor, I ***suppose*** you've already tried it yourself?"(p.188)
• I then began asking a lot of questions of both my brother and Dr. Bob about how this thing worked, and I ***suppose*** I was becoming more glassy-eyed all the while, for eventually I said to Bob, "You're all dried up.(p.206)
• I said, "How do you ***suppose***?(p.208)
• "Well," I said to dad, when the A.A. people kept coming with these lovely cars and looked so nice, "I ***suppose*** the neighbors say, 'Now those old fools must have up and died, but where's the hearse?'"(p.269)
• She said "***Suppose*** I put your name down as a volunteer.(p.326)
• I ***suppose*** the doctor might say, "This is psychosomatic medicine."(p.352)
• I ***suppose*** the psychiatrist might say, "This is benevolent interpersonal relations.(p.352)
• I ***suppose*** others would say, "This is group psychotherapy."(p.352)
• Evening cocktails were as standard as morning coffee, and I ***suppose*** my average daily consumption ran a little more or less than a pint.(p.433)
• I ***suppose*** I had reached my spiritual gutter that night, but I have never had what you could call a real urge to drink again.(p.524)
• But I said humbly, "I ***suppose*** I want to live."(p.540)

supposed

• Assuming we are spiritually fit, we can do all sorts of things alcoholics are not ***supposed*** to do.(p.100)

• I was ***supposed*** to be doing God's will, not mine.(p.282)

• Who is this fellow we are ***supposed*** to turn everything over to?(p.350)

• But they kept me there – I was ***supposed*** to stay a month, but they only kept me there seventeen days.(p.387)

• Even when I was old enough to know better, I dreamed about being as beautiful as Venus, as pure as the Madonna and as brilliant as the President of the United States is ***supposed*** to be.(p.400)

• During this time, you are ***supposed*** to behave yourself, but I took a little wine-tasting tour through France, all by my lone, with car and chauffeur.(p.405)

• I was ***supposed*** to come home on a troop ship, but I talked the base commander into flying me home.(p.428)

• We were ***supposed*** to take off at noon, but were delayed until six p.m.(p.428)

• When I am disturbed, it is because I find some person, place, thing, or situation – some fact of my life -- unacceptable to me, and I can find no serenity until I accept that person, place, thing, or situation as being exactly the way it is ***supposed*** to be at this moment.(p.449)

• Men are ***supposed*** to be tough and rugged to start with, but if a woman becomes that way, it is pretty hard to get back the niceties of womanhood.(p.480)

supposing

• But – ***supposing*** that just one man died because I had, for selfish reasons, kept my mouth shut?(p.282)

suppressed

• I had ***suppressed*** tendencies to overindulge and thus reveal my "moral weakness," because false pride was so dominant.(p.327)

supreme

• There are many situations which arise out of the phenomenon of craving which cause men to make the ***supreme*** sacrifice rather than continue to fight.(p.xxviii)

• How could a ***Supreme*** Being have anything to do with it all?(p.46)

• And who could comprehend a ***Supreme*** Being anyhow?(p.46)

• Henry Ford once made a wise remark to the effect that experience is the thing of ***supreme*** value in life.(p.124)

• I had never doubted the existence of the ***Supreme*** Being, but now I began to absent myself from my church where I had formerly been a member of the choir.(p.234)

• Panic, confusion and chaos were ***supreme***.(p.279)

sure

• And besides, we are ***sure*** that our way of living has its advantages for all.(p.xiii)

• But we are ***sure*** that our bodies were sickened as well.(p.xxiv)

• We are not ***sure*** why, once a certain point is reached, little can be done for him.(p.22)

• I'm ***sure*** it would work if I could only believe as he believes.(p.47)

• The consciousness of your belief is ***sure*** to come to you.(p.55)

• Admitting he may be somewhat at fault, he is ***sure*** that other people are more to blame.(p.61)

• He is like the retired business man who lolls in the Florida sunshine in the winter complaining of the sad state of the nation; the minister who sighs over the sins of the twentieth century; politicians and reformers who are ***sure*** all would be Utopia if the rest of the world would only behave; the outlaw safe cracker who thinks society has wronged him; and the alcoholic who has lost all and is locked up.(p.61)

• We thought well before taking this step making ***sure*** we were ready; that we could at last abandon ourselves utterly to Him.(p.63)

• If we are not sorry, and our conduct continues to harm others, we are quite ***sure*** to drink.(p.70)

• But our man is ***sure*** to be impressed with a sincere desire to set right the wrong.(p.77)

• We have already admitted this in confidence to another person, but we are ***sure*** we would be imprisoned or lose our job if it were known.(p.78)

• If we are ***sure*** our wife does not know, should we tell her?(p.81)

• You are ***sure*** to find someone desperate enough to accept with eagerness what you offer.(p.96)

• But be ***sure*** you use discretion.(p.96)

• Never avoid these responsibilities, but be ***sure*** you are doing the right thing if you assume them.(p.97)

• If persisted in for a few months, the effect on a man's family is ***sure*** to be great.(p.99)

• The man should be ***sure*** of his recovery.(p.99)

• But be ***sure*** you are on solid spiritual ground before you start and that your motive in going is thoroughly good.(p.102)

• Be ***sure*** you are not critical during such a discussion.(p.111)

• He may not share your enthusiasm, but he is practically ***sure*** to read the book and he may go for the program at once.(p.113)

• A doctor said to us, "Years of living with an alcoholic is almost ***sure*** to make any wife or child neurotic.(p.122)

• Another principle we observe carefully is that we do not relate intimate experiences of another person unless we are ***sure*** he would approve.(p.125)

• If he does not argue about religion, he will make new friends and is ***sure*** to find new avenues of usefulness and pleasure.(p.132)

• We are ***sure*** God wants us to be happy, joyous, and free.(p.133)

• But I'm ***sure*** this man is done drinking.(p.138)

• Drinking occasionally, and understanding your own reactions, it is possible for you to become quite ***sure*** of many things which, so far as the alcoholic is concerned, are not always so.(p.139)

• If you are ***sure*** your man does not want to stop, he may as well be discharged, the sooner the better.(p.141)

• Meanwhile, we are ***sure*** a great deal can be accomplished by the use of the book alone.(p.144)

• If you are ***sure*** he doesn't mean business, there is no doubt you should discharge him.(p.147)

• If, on the contrary, you are ***sure*** he is doing his utmost, you may wish to give him another chance.(p.147)

• Should you wish them above all else, and be willing to make use of our experience, we are ***sure*** they will come.(p.153)

• Many, we are ***sure***, will rise to their feet and march on.(p.153)

• Then he added, "He ***sure*** didn't do much for me when I was trying to fight this booze racket alone."(p.158)

• We cannot be ***sure***.(p.164)

• I said, "***Sure***, yes, anybody can do that, for twenty-four hours."(p.188)

• That ***sure*** did take a load off of my mind.(p.188)

• "***Sure*** I would," replied Bill, "Maybe it won't do any good, but I'd like to see you both, anyhow.(p.189)

• Now he was ***sure***.(p.189)

• And I was ***sure*** that I couldn't be with people who drank, without drinking.(p.227)

• The doctor who came to see me almost at once did not assail me with any new doctrines; he made ***sure*** that I had a need and that I wanted to have that need filled, and little by little I learned how my need could be met.(p.258)

• I'm ***sure*** his family felt that it was a marriage that -- well, I was a girl from the wrong side of the tracks -- definitely!(p.262)

• And I said, "Why ***sure***, that's what I'm here for."(p.270)

• Well, I wasn't ***sure*** I did, and it was awful foggy, and I wept and asked her what she thought I ought to do about it.(p.273)

• She said she didn't know, but that I ***sure*** showed plain enough I didn't have any part of it.(p.273)

• During my first few months in Akron I was quite ***sure*** that I never wanted to see my home town again.(p.281)

• He talked about himself, but I was ***sure*** it was about me.(p.302)

• To be ***sure***, this had been a dizzy and confused interval, but most everyone else I knew had emerged from it with both feet on the ground and a fair amount of adult maturity.(p.304)

• I was ***sure*** I wouldn't belong in an A.A. group -- they were all old men, I thought, and all skid-row bums.(p.319)

• I could never be ***sure*** I'd have a clear head and hands that were willing to do some work.(p.326)

• I was ***sure*** those who needed a bit of the hair of the dog really were alcoholics.(p.332)

• I wanted him to be ***sure*** that I wasn't the one who was going to drink the whole bottle.(p.336)

• "***Sure***, I've seen you tight several times, but you're no alcoholic!"(p.356)

• I ***sure*** had been working awfully hard of late.(p.360)

• ***Sure*** I still loved her, but hang it all, she was unreasonable!(p.362)

• ***Sure*** enough in a couple of hours two men were at my door and for the first time I heard some facts about liquor and my problem that sounded sensible to me.(p.363)

• That night she too had new hope because I had made ***sure*** she would know what I was doing about my drinking by packing every bit of A.A. literature I could put my hands on right on top so she couldn't help but see it when she opened my bag.(p.364)

• It would be a ***sure*** cure and also an adventure.(p.434)

• To be ***sure***, I learned many fascinating things, and many things that were to prove helpful later.(p.434)

• "First, I couldn't be ***sure***.(p.436)

• Right from the start, I felt that they weren't doing anything for me, but they ***sure*** were helping Max.(p.447)

• For years, I was ***sure*** the worst thing that could happen to a nice guy like me would be that I would turn out to be an alcoholic.(p.449)

• I was not eligible for parole, until -- with God's help, I'm ***sure*** -- the governor cut five years off my sentence.(p.462)

• I figured that perhaps if I went ahead with that marriage, which I was ***sure*** was right for me, that would be the answer to my drinking problem.(p.465)

• And then my waiting until I was ***sure*** he was asleep, and stealing money from him to replenish the supply.(p.466)

• I felt very sorry for myself and attempted suicide on many occasions, making ***sure*** there was always somebody within reaching distance to see that I didn't finish the job.(p.478)

• She must have been real proud of us, I'm ***sure***.(p.480)

• He is my best teacher; without him, I am ***sure*** I would never have made the progress I have.(p.481)

• I'm ***sure*** my ideas as to what life should be like were quite different from that of the average person with whom I associated.(p.483)

• ***Sure***, I'd have another.(p.498)

• If it was daylight, I would go down alleys to make ***sure*** no one saw me.(p.527)

• And I am ***sure*** they would be right as far as they go, but A.A. has taught me I am the result of the way I reacted to what happened to me as a child.(p.544)

• And if I had been able to turn to the church at that time I'm ***sure*** they could not have convinced me my sickness was within myself, nor could they have shown me the need for self-analysis that A.A. has shown me is vital if I am to survive.(p.546)

• I didn't have the courage to love; I was not even ***sure*** I had the capacity.(p.546)

surely

• Upon therapy for the alcoholic himself, we ***surely*** have no monopoly.(p.xxi)

• Convincing testimony must ***surely*** come from the medical men who have had experience with the sufferings of our members and have witnessed our return to health.(p.xxiii)

• ***Surely*** this was the answer – self-knowledge.(p.7)

• If he did not work, he would ***surely*** drink again, and if he drank, he would ***surely*** die.(p.15)

• But I cannot accept as ***surely*** true the many articles of faith which are so plain to him."(p.47)

• We shall be with you in the Fellowship of the Spirit, and you will ***surely*** meet some of us as you trudge the Road of Happy Destiny.(p.164)

• We could not be invited out because I would ***surely*** get tight and my wife dared not invite people in for the same reason.(p.177)

• They probably felt that it was useless, that ***surely*** I had enough intelligence to know what I was doing.(p.215)

• Their answer was always the same: If they should need it at any time they would ***surely*** get in touch with me.(p.293)

• A.A. must continue to live or most of us will ***surely*** die.(p.565)

• Experience has often warned us that nothing can so ***surely*** destroy our spiritual heritage as futile disputes over property, money, and authority.(p.566)

surest

• And that woman told me long after that was the ***surest*** proof to her that this program could work.(p.272)

surety

• I took a night law course, and obtained employment as investigator for a ***surety*** company.(p.2)

surf

• Pearl Harbor was a breeze of nine months, a gay Hawaiian paradise, drinking under the palms, listening to the ***surf*** beat on the shore, a bottle of whiskey near at hand.(p.426)

surface

• If we keep on the way we are going there is little doubt that much good will result, but the ***surface*** of

the problem would hardly be scratched.(p.19)
• When, however, the perfectly logical assumption is suggested that underneath the material world and life as we see it, there is an All Powerful, Guiding, Creative Intelligence, right there our perverse streak comes to the ***surface*** and we laboriously set out to convince ourselves it isn't so.(p.49)
• Out of this maelstrom just two coherent thoughts came to the ***surface;*** one, a drink would mean homelessness and death; two, I could no longer relieve the pressure of fear by starting home, as was once my habitual solution to this problem, because I no longer had a home.(p.279)
• My outward professional life looked fine, on the ***surface.***(p.435)

surgeon
• Psychiatrist and ***surgeon,*** he had lost his way until he realized that God, not he, was the Great Healer.(p.345)
• I am a ***surgeon.***)(p.347)
• That's the stuff used when the oral ***surgeon*** puts the needle in your vein and says, "Count to ten," and before you get to two, you're asleep.(p.442)

surgeons
• I recall, as I walked into that meeting, saying to myself, "Here I am, a fellow of the American College of ***Surgeons,*** a Fellow of the International College of ***Surgeons,*** a diplomate of one of the great specialty boards in these United States, a member of the American Psychiatric Society, and I have to go to the butcher, the baker and the carpenter to help make a man out of me!"(p.347)

surgery
• I do ***surgery*** because that's something that you can see; it's more tangible.(p.485)

surgical
• It was a long four or five hour operation, a large ***surgical*** procedure, and she was on her ninth or tenth post-operative day.(p.350)
• The Great Boss has given me diagnostic and ***surgical*** talent, and He has loaned it to me to use for the rest of my life.(p.350)

surgically
• I began making the rounds of the doctors in the hope that one of them might find some cure for my accumulating ailments, preferably something that could be removed ***surgically.***(p.305)

surmount
• I, who had thought so well of myself and my abilities, of my capacity to ***surmount*** obstacles, was cornered at last.(p.8)

surpass
• I suspect that if it is wisely handled – and it seems to be in wise and prudent hands – there are doors of opportunity ahead of this project that may ***surpass*** our capacities to imagine."(p.574)

surpassed
• The satisfaction I got from giving him a little of what I had read in those pamphlets far ***surpassed*** any feeling that I had ever had before in helping patients.(p.347)

surplus
• A twenty-three million dollar ***surplus*** wiped out.(p.500)

surprise
• Approached in this way, the most ruthless creditor will sometimes ***surprise*** us.(p.78)
• And just as we were being convinced of their heartlessness, they would ***surprise*** us with fresh resolves and new attentions.(p.107)
• And to my ***surprise,*** my drinking grew worse.(p.226)
• Imagine my ***surprise*** when I read in a page one "box" that I had been taken from the theater unconscious around noon that day, removed by ambulance to a hospital and stomach-pumped and then released.(p.244)
• I went to the sanitarium where this chap was incarcerated and found to my ***surprise*** that he was interested.(p.294)
• I was certainly a complete ***surprise*** when I arrived at her family's home, but because I arrived on the wings of a tropical hurricane there wasn't much she could do but let me in.(p.364)
• One night, a few weeks after joining the Fellowship, much to my ***surprise*** and delight I saw a familiar but no longer frowning face.(p.371)
• The ***surprise*** to me is the fact that I didn't know that they knew my drinking had gotten out of control.(p.376)
• Imagine my ***surprise*** when I came to, in Europe, and discovered I had brought myself along!(p.405)

surprised
• We are often ***surprised*** how the right answers come after we have tried this for a while.(p.86)
• I don't know what sort of person I was expecting, but I was very agreeably ***surprised*** to find Mr. T. a poised, intelligent, well groomed and mannered gentleman.(p.309)
• They ***surprised*** me.(p.333)
• I continue to be ***surprised*** by the people I meet who say, "You haven't had a drink for a long time, have you?"(p.376)
• So, when it ended up at a psycho ward, I wasn't all that ***surprised.***(p.440)

surprising
• Therefore, it is not ***surprising*** that our drinking careers have been characterized by countless vain attempts to prove we could drink like other people.(p.30)
• Instead of wanting to escape some perplexing problem, we experience a thrill of challenge in the opportunity it affords for another application of A.A. techniques, and we find ourselves tackling it with ***surprising*** vigor.(p.311)
• It's ***surprising,*** how we think we fool everybody in our drinking.(p.324)
• Looking back, it is ***surprising*** to me now that I managed to keep working and have enough money to squander at the various spots in the big city.(p.358)

surprisingly
• ***Surprisingly*** enough, we find such convictions no great obstacle to a spiritual experience.(p.28)
• He found himself ***surprisingly*** well received, and learned that many knew of his drinking.(p.156)
• "Yes," he said, ***surprisingly,*** "you are."(p.436)

surrender
• In the spiritual strength I had found, because of A.A., I felt that I had made a complete ***surrender,*** that I had really turned my life over that summer.(p.271)
• I knew then that I hadn't made a complete ***surrender,*** because I tried to bargain with the God I had found, and I said, "Anything but that!(p.271)
• Before the end finally came, I had, I guess made the ***surrender*** because I finally had been able to say that I would not mind too much.(p.272)
• Because it was only through feeling defeat and feeling failure, the inability to cope with my life and with alcohol, that I was able to ***surrender*** and accept the fact that I had this disease, and that I had to learn to live again without alcohol.(p.335)
• It was at that point that I reached ***surrender.***(p.340)
• I heard one very ill woman say that she didn't believe in the ***surrender*** part of the A.A. program.(p.340)
• ***Surrender*** to me has meant the ability to run my home, to face my responsibilities as they should be faced, to take life as it comes to me day by day, and work my problems out.(p.340)
• That's what ***surrender*** has meant to me.(p.340)

surrendered
• I ***surrendered*** once to the bottle, and I couldn't do these things.(p.340)
• I ***surrendered*** totally.(p.461)

surround
• The same old problems and worries ***surround*** me.(p.505)

surrounding
• Show him, from your own experience, how the queer mental condition ***surrounding*** that first drink prevents normal functioning of the will power.(p.92)
• From ***surrounding*** towns, families drive long distances to be present.(p.161)

surroundings
• Oddly enough, the circumstances and ***surroundings*** were pleasant.(p.285)
• The only thing this changed, however, was my ***surroundings,*** and it was soon apparent that I could have the same uncomfortable emotions with an unlimited checking account that I could on a working girl's salary.(p.545)

surrounds
• Gloom ***surrounds*** me.(p.506)

surveyed
• Seven percent of the A.A.'s ***surveyed*** are less than 30 years of age -- among them, many in their teens.(p.xxii)

surveys
• ***Surveys*** of groups in the United States and Canada indicate that A.A. is reaching out, not only to more and more people, but to a wider and wider range.(p.xxii)

survive
• As we discovered the principles by which the individual alcoholic could live, so we had to evolve principles by which the A.A. groups and A.A. as a whole could ***survive*** and function effectively.(p.xix)
• For if an alcoholic failed to perfect and enlarge his spiritual life through work and self-sacrifice for others, he could not ***survive*** the certain trials and low spots ahead.(p.14)
• Your husband will see at once that he must redouble his spiritual activities if he expects to ***survive.***(p.120)
• Then you will know what it means to give of yourself that others may ***survive*** and rediscover life.(p.153)
• And if I had been able to turn to the church at that time I'm sure they could not have convinced me my sickness was within myself, nor could they have shown me the need for self-analysis that A.A. has shown me is vital if I am to ***survive.***(p.546)
• The "12 Traditions" of Alcoholics Anonymous are, we A.A.'s believe, the best answers that our experience has yet given to those ever urgent questions, "How can A.A. best function?" and, "How can A.A. best stay whole and so ***survive?***"(p.563)

survived
• In most cases, the alcoholic ***survived*** this ordeal without relapse, but not always.(p.125)
• Had anyone undertaken to explain to me what the A.A. movement was, what its real function was, I probably would have been set back several years and I doubt if I would have ***survived*** at all.(p.216)
• When I look back on that last horrible year of constant drinking I wonder how I ***survived*** it either physically or mentally.(p.224)
• It is painful to grow, and without the help of my "civilian" A.A. companion, big Gene, I might not have ***survived*** that critical year of adjustment.(p.462)
• Being an alcoholic, slick, and having some good sense left, I ***survived*** the investigation.(p.490)
• He ***survived*** to become a mainstay of A.A. in Eire.(p.517)

surviving
• In the next half-year, I experienced two more esophageal hemorrhages, miraculously ***surviving*** each one by a hair.(p.558)

survivors
• We ***survivors*** are all in A.A. now, and my mother is in Al-Anon.(p.480)

suspect
• But they often ***suspect*** they are down for the count.(p.23)
• They ***suspect*** father is a bit balmy!(p.128)
• It becomes vital, also, that others not know of our defeats, nor ***suspect*** our loss of confidence.(p.331)
• I ***suspect*** that those bartenders would wait until I shot my wad, then call a cab and send me home.(p.410)
• I ***suspect*** that if it is wisely handled – and it seems to be in wise and prudent hands – there are doors of opportunity ahead of this project that may surpass our capacities to imagine."(p.574)

suspected
• So that was it -- last summer an alcoholic crackpot; now, I ***suspected,*** a little cracked about religion.(p.9)
• This tragic situation has already arrived in practically every case long before it is ***suspected.***(p.24)
• I knew the stuff I was making was a lot stronger than I had been used to, but I never ***suspected*** that steady drinking of it might develop a taste for something even stronger still.(p.233)
• It was nothing to my own inner distress, my self-reproach, and my self-loathing, for was I not bearing out all the horrible things I had always ***suspected*** of myself?(p.404)

suspecting
• I served twelve years in prison, never ***suspecting*** that without alcohol I would not have been in prison at all.(p.457)

suspend
• In a matter of fact way he told how two men had appeared in court, persuading the judge to ***suspend*** his commitment.(p.9)

suspicion
• Did we unjustifiably arouse jealousy, ***suspicion*** or bitterness?(p.69)
• Long experience with alcoholic excuses naturally arouses ***suspicion.***(p.146)

suspicious
• He will appreciate knowing you are not bothering your head about him, that you are not ***suspicious*** nor are you trying to run his life so he will be shielded from temptation to drink.(p.146)

sustained
• My wife became deeply interested and it was her in-

terest that ***sustained*** mine, though I at no time sensed that it might be an answer to my liquor problem.(p.178)
• The Higher Power to whom I had turned, and who had ***sustained*** me, had once again been thrust into the background, while my emotions were running my life and, as always, my emotions ran me to the bottle.(p.472)

swallow
• They made me ***swallow*** hard.(p.10)
• Though I had been only a nominal churchman, their proposals were not, intellectually, hard to ***swallow***.(p.42)
• They knew what to do about those black abysses that yawned ready to ***swallow*** me when I felt depressed, or nervous.(p.229)
• For me, pills don't produce the desire to ***swallow*** a pill; they produce the symptoms that require that the pill be taken for relief.(p.443)

swallowed
• That being so you have ***swallowed*** and digested some big chunks of truth about yourself.(p.71)

sway
• I could go for such conceptions as Creative Intelligence, Universal Mind or Spirit of Nature but I resisted the thought of a Czar of the Heavens, however loving His ***sway*** might be.(p.12)

swayed
• Again I ***swayed*** dizzily before an open window, or the medicine cabinet where there was poison, cursing myself for a weakling.(p.6)
• At a large party in Geneva, with people from many countries represented, the kind of party that is "protocol" in the extreme, I ***swayed***, laughed hysterically, made naughty remarks in an unhushed voice, and was finally led from the scene.(p.406)

swear
• Max accepted responsibility for me after I had promised never to drink again, never to take another pill, never to ***swear*** again, and never to talk to girls again.(p.444)

swearing
• Here are some of the methods we have tried: Drinking beer only, limiting the number of drinks, never drinking alone, never drinking in the morning, drinking only at home, never having it in the house, never drinking during business hours, drinking only at parties, switching from scotch to brandy, drinking only natural wines, agreeing to resign if ever drunk on the job, taking a trip, not taking a trip, ***swearing*** off forever (with and without a solemn oath), taking more physical exercise, reading inspirational books, going to health farms and sanitariums, accepting voluntary commitment to asylums -- we could increase the list ad infinitum.(p.31)
• The doctor said I'd been brought into the hospital like a madman, crying, raving, ranting, ***swearing***, completely in the throes of delirium tremens.(p.427)
• And so I got to the ***swearing*** off process.(p.513)

sweat
• And I remembered the creeping horror of the interminable night, in which I slept for short spells and woke up dripping with cold ***sweat*** and shaken with utter despair, to drink hastily from my bottle and mercifully pass out again, "You're mad, you're mad, you're mad!" pounded through my brain with each returning ray of consciousness, and I drowned the refrain with drink.(p.224)
• I'd wake up covered with ***sweat***.(p.319)

sweater
• And we usually have some kind of grimy ***sweater*** that we think we look sexy in, even if we weigh ninety-five pounds soaking wet and are not wearing a bra.(p.479)
• The war leaves me with a pair of blankets, a toilet kit, a ***sweater*** knit by my sister, and a still greater inferiority.(p.499)

sweats
• That is the way Jackie found me, lying on a cot in my skivvies, with hot and cold ***sweats***, pounding heart and that awful itchy scratchiness all over.(p.238)
• I paced back and forth in the apartment with the cold ***sweats***.(p.338)
• Cold ***sweats***, jumpy nerves and lack of sleep were becoming intolerable.(p.378)
• When I awoke in the middle of the night with shakes and ***sweats*** and fears, I would hear my wife weeping quietly in bed beside me.(p.558)

sweep
• If our testimony helps ***sweep*** away prejudice, enables you to think honestly, encourages you to search diligently within yourself, then, if you wish, you can join us on the Broad Highway.(p.55)
• We attempt to ***sweep*** away the debris which has accumulated out of our effort to live on self-will and run the show ourselves.(p.76)
• We are there to ***sweep*** off our side of the street realizing that nothing worth while can be accomplished until we do so, never trying to tell him what he should do.(p.77)
• Suddenly I feel a wave of utter hopelessness ***sweep*** over me.(p.504)

sweet
• Before then, I had written lots of ***sweet*** promises, but my wife happily observed that this time I meant business.(p.5)
• "She's such a ***sweet*** girl, I should think he'd stop for her sake."(p.20)
• ***Sweet*** relationships are dead.(p.82)
• For a while they would be their old ***sweet*** selves, only to dash the new structure of affection to pieces once more.(p.107)
• My mother was a lovely, ***sweet*** woman, whose only weakness was my father.(p.369)
• I could just hear their ***sweet***, pious talk.(p.412)
• The grand fellow who at my call made me a hail-fellow-well-met, who gave me such a fine voice, as we sang "Hail, hail, the gang's all here," and "***Sweet*** Adeline," who gave me freedom from fear and feelings of inferiority.(p.498)

sweetness
• He'll never read in his "***sweetness*** and light" senior-citizen publications anything but the joys of lolling in the rocking chair, angling on the riverbank, or bowling on the green.(p.330)
• I got sick of the ***sweetness*** and turned to ale.(p.556)

sweets
• One of the many doctors who had the opportunity of reading this book in manuscript form told us that the use of ***sweets*** was often helpful, of course depending upon a doctor's advice.(p.133)
• Many of us have noticed a tendency to eat ***sweets*** and have found this practice beneficial.(p.134)

swell
• At the time, I thought them just a ***swell*** pair of screwballs, for they were not only going to save all the drunks in the world but also all the so-called normal people!(p.245)
• I am very apt to get into quite an uproar for a day or two before starting, but I do start, and once started, I have a ***swell*** time.(p.285)

swelled
• "Complete abandon"; "Half measures availed us nothing"; "Thoroughly follow our path"; "Completely give oneself to this simple program" -- rang in my ***swelled*** head.(p.349)

swelling
• The great boom of the late twenties was seething and ***swelling***.(p.3)

swept
• The barriers he had built through the years were ***swept*** away.(p.56)

swig
• He brought the quart out and I took a good ***swig***.(p.205)

swigs
• I'd only had two with her, but I'd managed four in the fifteen minutes I'd waited for her, and of course I'd had the usual uncounted ***swigs*** from the bottle as I painfully got up and did my slow spasmodic dressing.(p.223)

swimming
• This was in Virginia, where I had rented a house with stables and a ***swimming*** pool, and the fall fox hunting had begun.(p.404)

swing
• The mushrooming process was in full ***swing***.(p.xviii)
• Only thirty years later the conquest of the air was almost an old story and airplane travel was in full ***swing***.(p.52)
• I was so busy keeping her out of trouble, and so scared she'd ***swing*** on me, that I had my last two drinks that night.(p.415)

swinging
• I was knocked to the floor, ***swinging*** madly at the faces on those pineapples.(p.427)

switch
• Twenty-two years later, Doctor Bob told me that what I had done was like turning a ***switch*** and setting up a demand for more alcohol in my system.(p.195)
• It was getting pretty dark and I hadn't turned on any lights, when some big fellow stepped inside the door and flipped on the light ***switch***.(p.207)
• We would follow one man's ideas for a while, decide he was wrong and ***switch*** to another's method.(p.246)
• Well, of course that was all I needed -- to ***switch*** from wine to brandy for three weeks.(p.338)

switched
• I ***switched*** into real estate brokerage and property management work.(p.277)
• I ***switched*** to beer.(p.339)

switching
• Here are some of the methods we have tried: Drinking beer only, limiting the number of drinks, never drinking alone, never drinking in the morning, drinking only at home, never having it in the house, never drinking during business hours, drinking only at parties, ***switching*** from scotch to brandy, drinking only natural wines, agreeing to resign if ever drunk on the job, taking a trip, not taking a trip, swearing off forever (with and without a solemn oath), taking more physical exercise, reading inspirational books, going to health farms and sanitariums, accepting voluntary commitment to asylums -- we could increase the list ad infinitum.(p.31)

Switzerland
• My parents had some vague idea of making a priest out of me and for some years I attended the Franciscan school at Basle, ***Switzerland***, just across the border, about six miles from my home.(p.230)
• A house in Virginia, during the fox hunting season; a little chalet in ***Switzerland*** during the summer or a place on Long Island -- each house complete with cooks, butlers and maids.(p.403)
• I rented a beautiful apartment on the banks of the Seine in the winter, and a chalet in ***Switzerland*** in the summer.(p.405)

swollen
• I was black and blue, with my lips all ***swollen***, when they roused us to go into court in the morning.(p.204)

swore
• At this school we had Bible readings before each meal, and church services four times on Sunday, and I became so rebellious at this that I ***swore*** I would never join or go to any church except for weddings or funerals.(p.240)
• How many times I ***swore*** off in the morning and got drunk before sunset I don't know.(p.300)
• I swung, I ***swore***, I started throwing beer cans at the advancing hordes of pineapple faces.(p.427)
• I ***swore*** off hard liquor and turned to wine.(p.555)

sworn
• We have not even ***sworn*** off.(p.85)
• Our men have ***sworn*** great solemn oaths that they were through drinking forever.(p.105)
• I've prayed to God on hangover mornings and ***sworn*** that I'd never touch another drop but by nine o'clock I'd be boiled as an owl."(p.158)
• And Russ said, "I would have ***sworn*** that was Jack M."(p.271)
• Two weeks later found me being ***sworn*** in, and the first payday in the Navy made me realize I had found a home.(p.398)
• Next morning I was ***sworn*** in, feeling no pain.(p.425)

swung
• I ***swung***, I swore, I started throwing beer cans at the advancing hordes of pineapple faces.(p.427)

symbol
• Bottles were only a ***symbol***.(p.103)

sympathetic
• Unwilling to be honest with these ***sympathetic*** men, we were honest with no one else.(p.73)
• Barriers which have sprung up between you and your friends will disappear with the growth of ***sympathetic*** understanding.(p.115)
• In the midst of an understanding and ***sympathetic*** family, these vagaries of dad's spiritual infancy will quickly disappear.(p.129)
• Philosophy, faith, a sense of humor (they could laugh at themselves), clear-cut objectives, appreciation -- and most especially appreciation and ***sympathetic*** understanding for their fellow man.(p.310)
• I thought, now here's a nice ***sympathetic*** soul!(p.322)
• By persistence and salesmanship I managed to see more and more of my new friend, and because of her ***sympathetic*** nature she tolerated my company.(p.359)
• I heard a lovely voice, and a ***sympathetic*** ear listened to my plea.(p.363)
• I have kind and ***sympathetic*** parents.(p.431)

sympathy
• We have been driven to maudlin ***sympathy***, to bitter resentment.(p.104)

• We have sought ***sympathy***.(p.105)

• Perhaps you are not quite in ***sympathy*** with the approach we suggest.(p.144)

• I seem to get no ***sympathy*** for my illness and have no appreciation of the love behind the gift.(p.501)

symphony

• There is something spiritual about an art museum or a ***symphony***, and the Catholic Church approves of our use of them.(p.574)

symptom

• All these, and many others, have one ***symptom*** in common: they cannot start drinking without developing the phenomenon of craving.(p.xxviii)

• Our liquor was but a ***symptom***.(p.64)

• They realized that repeated lack of drinking control, when they really wanted control, was the fatal ***symptom*** that spelled problem drinking.(p.315)

• In spite of knowing that my drunkenness was a ***symptom*** of the things that were wrong with me, and that I could never drink again, I thought I couldn't yet give it up, although I was going to try.(p.393)

• I always took it because I had the ***symptom*** that only that pill would relieve.(p.443)

• But for some time, it was difficult to keep from taking a pill when I had an appropriate ***symptom***, such as a cough, pain, anxiety, insomnia, a muscle spasm, or an upset stomach.(p.448)

• The mental twists that led up to my drinking began many years before I ever took a drink for I am one of those whose history proves conclusively that my drinking was "a ***symptom*** of a deeper trouble."(p.544)

symptoms

• We, who are familiar with the ***symptoms***, see large numbers of potential alcoholics among young people everywhere.(p.33)

• We admit we have some of these ***symptoms***, but we have not gone to the extremes you fellows did, nor are we likely to, for we understand ourselves so well after what you have told us that such things cannot happen again.(p.38)

• He was interested and conceded that he had some of the ***symptoms***, but he was a long way from admitting that he could do nothing about it himself.(p.40)

• Though we did not like their ***symptoms*** and the way these disturbed us, they, like ourselves, were sick too.(p.67)

• Tell him enough about your drinking habits, ***symptoms***, and experiences to encourage him to speak of himself.(p.91)

• The alarming physical and mental ***symptoms***, the deepening pall of remorse, depression and inferiority that settled down on our loved ones -- these things terrified and distracted us.(p.106)

• This seemed to me like an opportunity to be helpful, so I spent two hours talking about alcoholism, the malady, and described the ***symptoms*** and results as well as I could.(p.138)

• I was suffering from an actual disease that had a name and ***symptoms*** like diabetes or cancer or TB -- and a disease was respectable, not a moral stigma!(p.227)

• I was aware of ***symptoms*** of impending dependence, and I told myself I had gotten out of the rat race just in time to head off any booze problem.(p.327)

• It had a name and ***symptoms***, just like diabetes or T.B.(p.392)

• For me, pills don't produce the desire to swallow a pill; they produce the ***symptoms*** that require that the pill be taken for relief.(p.443)

synthetic

• What with our ultra-modern standards, our scientific approach to everything, we are perhaps not well equipped to apply the powers of good that lie outside our ***synthetic*** knowledge.(p.xxv)

system

• We are equally positive that once he takes any alcohol whatever into his ***system***, something happens, both in the bodily and mental sense, which makes it virtually impossible for him to stop.(p.22)

• Twenty-two years later, Doctor Bob told me that what I had done was like turning a switch and setting up a demand for more alcohol in my ***system***.(p.195)

• In those days my ***system*** was always to drink up my last pay check and believe that necessity would bring the next job.(p.256)

• The why is not important; the fact is that one drink will set up a reaction in our ***system*** which requires more; that one drink was too much and one hundred drinks were not enough.(p.380)

• But when I cracked my leg with a sixteen-pound sledgehammer in the rock hole, I was fighting the ***system***, using my body.(p.458)

• The idea behind it is that, having taken the treatment, your ***system*** is so "conditioned" that the mere sight or smell or taste of alcohol produces a violent reaction, and you become ill.(p.469)

• I leave the room, which the honor ***system*** allows.(p.499)

systematically

• I have read ***systematically*** since then, and A.A. literature has kept me sober.(p.343)

systems

• We looked upon this world of warring individuals, warring theological ***systems***, and inexplicable calamity, with deep skepticism.(p.46)

• Somehow our bodies had reached the point where we could no longer absorb alcohol in our ***systems***.(p.380)

Tt

table
• I pushed a drink across the ***table***.(p.9)
• Never mind the musty past; here sat a miracle directly across the kitchen ***table***.(p.11)
• We are like the passengers of a great liner the moment after rescue from shipwreck when camaraderie, joyousness and democracy pervade the vessel from steerage to Captain's ***table***.(p.17)
• I sat down at a ***table*** and ordered a sandwich and a glass of milk.(p.36)
• Of course he couldn't drink, but why not sit hopefully at a ***table***, a bottle of ginger ale before him?(p.154)
• It was the day before Mother's Day and I had come home plastered, carrying a big potted plant which I set down on the ***table*** and forthwith went upstairs and passed out.(p.179)
• Morning after morning I would awake sick and with terrible jitters, but there was always a flask of liquor sitting on the ***table*** beside my bed.(p.183)
• I had no desire whatever to sit down at a ***table*** and stay a whole morning or afternoon drinking.(p.231)
• I noticed a Bible on his ***table*** and it amazed me.(p.257)
• I was at a beautifully set dinner ***table***.(p.285)
• Toward five o'clock, helter-skelter, I'd get everything put away and try to get supper on the ***table***, and after supper I'd finish the job up and knock myself out.(p.337)
• At one end of the ***table*** sat our community butcher.(p.347)
• At the other side of the ***table*** sat one of the carpenters in our community, and at the further end of the ***table*** sat the man who ran the bakery, while on one side sat my friend who was a mechanic.(p.347)
• One night at the dinner ***table*** my wife said that tonight was my first birthday in A.A., and that the group would have the usual ice cream and cake for the "one year man."(p.365)
• I can't remember a dinner at home that we didn't have white wine or claret on the ***table***.(p.384)
• I went out to the West Coast, waited on ***table***, washed dishes and sold newspaper subscriptions.(p.401)
• I was still untrained for any work but washing dishes and waiting on ***table***.(p.401)
• Slowly a pile of pineapples started to build up on the ***table***.(p.427)
• Two of them leaped from the ***table*** and crashed into my head.(p.427)
• Soon supper is on the ***table***.(p.497)
• To wear expensive clothes, to have bartenders know what to serve me before I ordered, to be recognized by headwaiters and shown to the best ***table***, to play gin rummy for high stakes with the insouciance of a riverboat gambler – these were the enduring values in life, I thought.(p.556)

tables
• You need this information to put yourself in his place, to see how you would like him to approach you if the ***tables*** were turned.(p.90)

tablespoons
• So I was used to it, but I didn't know what the effect of alcohol was because I always had wine, usually with dinner, but always with a lot of ice and about two ***tablespoons*** of sugar in it.(p.385)

tack
• When father takes this ***tack***, the family may react unfavorably.(p.128)

tackle
• I do feel, though, that the fact that I finally grew up to a point where I could even ***tackle*** such a job is the apex of the story of a man who spent eighteen years running away from life.(p.286)

tact
• When it will serve any good purpose, we are willing to announce our convictions with ***tact*** and common sense.(p.77)

tactful
• We should be sensible, ***tactful***, considerate and humble without being servile or scraping.(p.83)

take
• Neither does A.A. ***take*** any particular medical point of view, though we cooperate widely with the men of medicine as well as with the men of religion.(p.xx)
• There is the type of man who is unwilling to admit that he cannot ***take*** a drink.(p.xxviii)
• There is the type who always believes that after being entirely free from alcohol for a period of time he can ***take*** a drink without danger.(p.xxviii)
• I saw I could not ***take*** so much as one drink.(p.5)
• I ruthlessly faced my sins and became willing to have my new-found Friend ***take*** them away, root and branch.(p.13)
• After such an approach many ***take*** up their beds and walk again.(p.19)
• How many times people have said to us: "I can ***take*** it or leave it alone.(p.20)
• They can ***take*** it or leave it alone.(p.20)
• It will not ***take*** long for you to decide if you are honest with yourself about it.(p.32)
• To be gravely affected, one does not necessarily have to drink a long time nor ***take*** the quantities some of us have.(p.33)
• Yet all reasons for not drinking were easily pushed aside in favor of the foolish idea that he could ***take*** whiskey if only he mixed it with milk!(p.36)
• Let us ***take*** another illustration.(p.39)
• After dinner I decided to ***take*** a walk.(p.41)
• They flatly declare that since they have come to believe in a Power greater than themselves, to ***take*** a certain attitude toward that Power, and to do certain simple things, there has been a revolutionary change in their way of living and thinking.(p.50)
• If you have decided you want what we have and are willing to go to any length to get it – then you are ready to ***take*** certain steps.(p.58)
• 10.Continued to ***take*** personal inventory and when we were wrong promptly admitted it.(p.59)
• ***Take*** away my difficulties, that victory over them may bear witness to those I would help of Thy Power, Thy Love, and Thy Way of life.(p.63)
• We found it very desirable to ***take*** this spiritual step with an understanding person, such as our wife, best friend or spiritual adviser.(p.63)
• We cannot be helpful to all people, but at least God will show us how to ***take*** a kindly and tolerant view of each and every one.(p.67)
• If we are sorry for what we have done, and have the honest desire to let God ***take*** us to better things, we believe we will be forgiven and will have learned our lesson.(p.70)
• Rightly and naturally, we think well before we choose the person or persons with whom to ***take*** this intimate and confidential step.(p.74)
• Can He now ***take*** them all -- every one?(p.76)
• Nevertheless, with a person we dislike, we ***take*** the bit in our teeth.(p.77)
• Although these reparations ***take*** innumerable forms, there are some general principles which we find guiding.(p.79)
• If he opened that old affair, he was afraid it would destroy the reputation of his partner, disgrace his family and ***take*** away his means of livelihood.(p.80)
• After consulting with his wife and partner he came to the conclusion that it was better to ***take*** those risks than to stand before his Creator guilty of such ruinous slander.(p.80)
• Though there may be justifiable exceptions, and though we wish to lay down no rule of any sort, we have often found this the best course to ***take***.(p.81)
• We must ***take*** the lead.(p.83)
• This thought brings us to Step Ten, which suggests we continue to ***take*** personal inventory and continue to set right any new mistakes as we go along.(p.84)
• We may not be able to determine which course to ***take***.(p.86)
• We relax and ***take*** it easy.(p.86)
• We usually conclude the period of meditation with a prayer that we be shown all through the day what our next step is to be, that we be given whatever we need to ***take*** care of such problems.(p.87)
• Life will ***take*** on new meaning.(p.89)
• Perhaps you will want to ***take*** the man into your home for a few days.(p.96)
• When working with a man and his family, you should ***take*** care not to participate in their quarrels.(p.100)
• Say you do not want to be a wet blanket; that you only want him to ***take*** care of his health.(p.112)
• You might suggest that you both ***take*** an interest in them.(p.112)
• This may ***take*** patient waiting, but it will be worth it.(p.112)
• Unless they actually need protection from their father, it is best not to ***take*** sides in any argument he has with them while drinking.(p.115)
• You, as well as your husband, ought to think of what you can put into life instead of how much you can ***take*** out.(p.120)
• In a weak moment he may ***take*** your dislike of his high-stepping friends as one of those insanely trivial excuses to drink.(p.120)
• Our women folk have suggested certain attitudes a wife may ***take*** with the husband who is recovering.(p.122)
• Is he not unconsciously trying to see what he can ***take*** from the family life rather than give?(p.122)
• It will ***take*** time to clear away the wreck.(p.123)
• Though old buildings will eventually be replaced by finer ones, the new structures will ***take*** years to complete.(p.123)
• Father knows he is to blame; it may ***take*** him many seasons of hard work to be restored financially, but he shouldn't be reproached.(p.123)
• This is a condition which, in ordinary life, would produce untold grief; there might be scandalous gossip, laughter at the expense of other people, and a tendency to ***take*** advantage of intimate information.(p.125)
• At the beginning of recovery a man will ***take***, as a rule, one of two directions.(p.125)
• He may ***take*** small interest in the children and may show irritation when reproved for his delinquencies.(p.126)
• Let them remember that his drinking wrought all kinds of damage that may ***take*** long to repair.(p.127)
• If they sense these things, they will not ***take*** so seriously his periods of crankiness, depression, or apathy, which will disappear when there is tolerance, love, and spiritual understanding.(p.127)
• What about his talk that God will ***take*** care of them?(p.128)
• If the family persists in criticism, this fallacy may ***take*** a still greater hold on father.(p.129)
• Though the family has no religious connections, they may wish to make contact with or ***take*** membership in a religious body.(p.131)
• Do not hesitate to ***take*** your health problems to such persons.(p.133)
• When this happens, they can be invited to join in morning meditation and then they can ***take*** part in the daily discussion without rancor or bias.(p.134)
• To me, this incident illustrates lack of understanding as to what really ails the alcoholic, and lack of knowledge as to what part employers might profitably ***take*** in salvaging their sick employees.(p.139)
• As a moderate drinker, you can ***take*** your liquor or leave it alone.(p.139)
• Seeing your attempt to understand and help, some men will try to ***take*** advantage of your kindness.(p.141)
• Will he ***take*** every necessary step, submit to anything to get well, to stop drinking forever?(p.142)
• He may, for example, reveal that he has padded his expense account or that he has planned to ***take*** your best customers away from you.(p.145)
• Being on a radically different basis of life, he will never ***take*** advantage of the situation.(p.146)
• So, for one reason or another, they cover these men, hoping matters will ***take*** a turn for the better.(p.147)
• If you ***take*** it, your past will be forgotten and the fact that you went away for treatment will not be mentioned.(p.147)
• He will be able to ***take*** a position with such a man which is eminently fair and square.(p.148)
• Even if you feel your organization has no alcoholic problem, it might pay to ***take*** another look down the line.(p.149)
• Inwardly he would give anything to ***take*** half a dozen drinks and get away with them.(p.152)
• My next move was to ***take*** up the study of medicine, entering one of the largest universities in the county.(p.173)
• After much argument they allowed me to return and ***take*** my exams, all of which I passed creditably.(p.173)
• Most of the time therefore, I did not ***take*** the morning drink which I craved so badly, but instead would fill up on large doses of sedatives to quiet the jitters, which distressed me terribly.(p.176)

• I will not ***take*** space to relate all my hospital or sanitarium experiences.(p.177)
• 4.Because every time I do it I ***take*** out a little more insurance for myself against a possible slip.(p.181)
• I would reach over and get this and ***take*** a shot and in a few moments get up and ***take*** another, shave and eat my breakfast, slip a half pint of liquor in my hip pocket, and go on to school.(p.183)
• Between classes I would run down to the wash room, ***take*** enough to steady my nerves and then go on to the next class.(p.183)
• This problem was soon solved, however, as I began to ***take*** my bottle along with me and hide it in the bathroom or in the shrubbery outside.(p.184)
• We're not up here trying to ***take*** any of your rights or privileges away from you, but we have a program whereby we think we can stay sober.(p.186)
• Part of that program is that we ***take*** it to someone else, that needs it and wants it.(p.186)
• Now, if you don't want it, we'll not ***take*** up your time, and we'll be going and looking for someone else."(p.186)
• The next thing they wanted to know was if I thought I could quit of my own accord, without any help, if I could just walk out of the hospital and never ***take*** another drink.(p.186)
• In fact, I admitted that from now on I was willing to let God ***take*** over, instead of me.(p.187)
• Whether you quit six days, months, or years, if you go out and ***take*** a drink or two you'll end up in this hospital tied down, just like you have been in these past six months.(p.187)
• That sure did ***take*** a load off of my mind.(p.188)
• And this, as I said, certainly gave me a lot of confidence, seemed to ***take*** a lot of the burden off me.(p.190)
• You should go out and ***take*** this program to somebody else that needs it and wants it."(p.190)
• At that time, as I remember, he had promised never to ***take*** another drink.(p.193)
• He wouldn't give me any money for the groceries, but he did ***take*** me across the street and buy me a bag of candy, which I later took back and traded for a loaf of bread.(p.193)
• I was a very young married man, having his whiskey in the cupboard over the sink, and when I helped my wife with the dishes at night I would ***take*** a cup of tea and spike it with whiskey.(p.196)
• I can remember occasions when friends recommended me for positions or business opportunities that I wouldn't ***take*** because I felt that at some future date I'd get drunk and they would be hurt.(p.198)
• So, knowing that, I had determined that so long as I lived I would never ***take*** another drink.(p.200)
• An offer of appreciation for not having had a drink for those few months and then and there, without anybody promising me anything or threatening me, I made a solemn vow that never so long as I lived would I ***take*** another drink.(p.200)
• I could ***take*** one drink and get right back on the wagon.(p.202)
• He said, "Well, why don't you ***take*** a cab?"(p.204)
• They asked me if I would ***take*** some medicine, and I promised that I would if they got me a drink.(p.206)
• I got two drinks, each of them a quarter of that pint, in me, and was talking along with these people, but I felt that sooner or later they were going to have me cornered because they were smarter than I was and the drink was beginning to ***take*** effect; but as I reached for the third drink Bob said, "Listen, Buster, you promised to ***take*** some medicine if we got you a drink.(p.206)
• I told him I'd ***take*** the medicine and I would ***take*** it, but I hadn't told him when, and thereupon I got away with the third drink.(p.206)
• He said, "So long as I'm thinking as I'm thinking now, and so long as I'm doing the things I'm doing now, I don't believe I'll ever ***take*** another drink."(p.206)
• The differences between my father and my sisters, who were school teachers, made an excellent environment for the type of child I was – that is, slick and cute enough to ***take*** advantage of any adult quarrel.(p.210)
• I proceeded to ***take*** up the drawing and advanced rapidly in it.(p.211)
• I did not have a high school education so I went to night school to ***take*** the full high school course, which I finished in two years and nine months.(p.211)
• One evening I had gone out after dinner to ***take*** on a couple of double-headers and stayed a little later than usual, and when I came home Clarence was sitting on the davenport with Bill W.(p.216)
• In fact, the last three years of my drinking was a routine of barbiturates in the morning, so that I could stop shaking enough to shave, and then alcohol beginning about four-thirty or five o'clock, with a struggle not to ***take*** a drink at noon or during the day, because I had the idea that if I took one drink, I would smell as though I had had a pint.(p.217)
• He startled me by informing me that he was an alcoholic, that he had found a way which so far enabled him to live without taking a drink, and that the main idea was to find a way how not to ***take*** that first drink.(p.218)
• I believe every member of the Akron Group did come to see me, which impressed me terrifically, not so much because of the stories they told, but because they would ***take*** the time to come and talk to me without even knowing who I was.(p.218)
• One of the things that came up repeatedly in the stories they told me was that once they had accepted the program, they never had a desire to ***take*** a drink.(p.219)
• I've never had a desire to ***take*** a drink.(p.219)
• Certainly, at that time I was one of those who "can ***take*** it or leave it alone."(p.231)
• With a great deal of determination, I would throw out full pints – pour them out and smash the bottles -- firmly resolved never to ***take*** another drink of the stuff.(p.234)
• Unlike many other Catholics who frequently ***take*** pledges for definite periods – a year, two years or for good, I never had any desire to "***take*** a pledge" before the priest.(p.234)
• Mother would ***take*** me in only if I would stay locked in a small storeroom and give her my clothes and shoes.(p.238)
• It doesn't ***take*** long.(p.242)
• The man who was going to ***take*** over one of their biggest branches come Monday?(p.243)
• Routine jobs bored me, but I would ***take*** on the toughest one I could find, work day and night until I had it under control; then it would become tedious and I'd lose all interest in it.(p.243)
• During that first week-end I decided to stay in New York and ***take*** all they gave out with, except the "God stuff."(p.246)
• Lots of times, vain-gloriously, I used to ***take*** the bottle out, look at it and say, "I've got you licked."(p.253)
• As soon as I could get up and walk I started to drink again and kept it up until my friend of the hospital, who, in his first try at the new way of life had stubbed his toe in Chicago but had come back to the town to ***take*** counsel and make a new start, picked me up and got me into a hospital.(p.258)
• But in those days I had no one to whom I might ***take*** my troubles.(p.260)
• At the end of these thirteen years I never dreamed that he'd ever ***take*** another drink.(p.263)
• He'd always say, "***Take*** me for a ride, Ma."(p.264)
• Time went on and the drinking got worse and worse, and I was in another barroom, down the road the other way, a small one, and I took my glass – that morning I'd been able to lift it from the bar -- and I said to the woman behind the bar, "I wish I might never ***take*** another drop of that stuff.(p.266)
• On Wednesday night Jack M. said, "You meet me at the Ohio Edison Building, and I will ***take*** you to the meeting."(p.269)
• They told Annabelle to ***take*** me under her wing, and I shall never forget how she sort of curled up her nose and said, "They tell me you drink too."(p.269)
• A year later I was able to buy a Model T roadster and ***take*** a better job with a downtown printer.(p.276)
• Dr. Bob dwelt at length on how prayer had given him release, time and time again, from the nearly over-powering compulsion to ***take*** a drink.(p.279)
• It took five years of A.A. living, and a substantial improvement in my health, before I could ***take*** a full-time office job where someone else was boss.(p.283)
• Only once did I suffer from a nearly overpowering compulsion to ***take*** a drink.(p.285)
• Here was something requiring a greater willingness to assume responsibility, and ***take*** a larger degree of cooperation and "give and ***take***" than even business requires of one.(p.286)
• The adjustments in such a case are difficult and ***take*** time, but we both feel that they are certainly worth it.(p.286)
• This consisted of walking the floor for three or four days and nights until I could ***take*** nourishment.(p.289)
• That was my lesson, that one could not ***take*** the moral inventory and then file it away; that the alcoholic has to continue to ***take*** inventory every day if he expects to get well and stay well.(p.293)
• So I suggested that he ***take*** a trip to Akron for a couple of weeks, which he did, living with one of the A.A. families there.(p.294)
• That being the case, it didn't ***take*** me long to figure out that my meager manufacturing facilities were entirely inadequate to the manufacture of beer for social and domestic consumption.(p.297)
• The general procedure was to ***take*** four or five shots in the first place I stopped at.(p.299)
• I can actually ***take*** my problems to Him and He gives me comfort, peace, and happiness.(p.303)
• By now I wanted to die, but had lost the courage even to ***take*** my life.(p.306)
• Whole new vistas were opened and life began to ***take*** on color and interest.(p.311)
• We got along fine for about two weeks, until she told me where to go and to ***take*** my damn bottle with me.(p.318)
• I started to ***take*** A.A. seriously, and A.A. gave me a new way of life.(p.320)
• And she would never, never ***take*** that morning drink!(p.321)
• I was being very cagey, because I knew that if I did ***take*** one or two, I might want to ***take*** five or six or seven or eight.(p.323)
• I needed a drink, but I was afraid to ***take*** a morning drink, because I didn't want to be a drunk.(p.323)
• I became a drunk anyway, but I was scared to death to ***take*** that morning drink.(p.323)
• I was accused of it many times when I went to play bridge in the afternoon, but I really never did ***take*** a morning drink.(p.323)
• Nobody could ***take*** away my retirement income.(p.329)
• I would ***take*** a gulp, then warn the jug not to try to entice, lure, or seduce me into having more than one "medicinal" jolt.(p.332)
• I'd just ***take*** a couple or three barbiturates to get back to sleep -- eating my alcohol.(p.333)
• Surrender to me has meant the ability to run my home, to face my responsibilities as they should be faced, to ***take*** life as it comes to me day by day, and work my problems out.(p.340)
• Every day became that much harder to live through, and I began to ***take*** a look at myself.(p.354)
• And the only one who can ***take*** it away from me is me – by taking that first drink.(p.355)
• My salesmanship was still good, for in the fall of 1938 she called me from Salt Lake and finally agreed to ***take*** me on for better or for worse.(p.360)
• It didn't ***take*** long for me to fall in with a fast crowd who had their lunch in the men's bar of a leading hotel.(p.361)
• In the very early spring of 1944, my frustrated wife couldn't ***take*** it any longer.(p.362)
• I was told that someone would call on me shortly, to sit tight and not ***take*** another drink.(p.363)
• It was worrying my wife a little, but she had the good sense not to ***take*** me to task about it or goad me into going.(p.364)
• I didn't ***take*** the drink.(p.365)
• We went out occasionally, and I would ***take*** a drink to ease the tensions of daily life.(p.370)
• Physically I couldn't ***take*** it any more.(p.378)
• To most of us, making amends will ***take*** the rest of our lives, but we can start immediately.(p.381)
• I was desperately in earnest to follow through and understand what was expected of me as a member of A.A. and to ***take*** each Step of the Twelve as rapidly as possible.(p.382)
• Frank found the doctor, but the doctor didn't want to ***take*** an alcoholic.(p.387)
• So I went down to him quite a few times a month and had him shoot me full of the stuff; and then I went across the street to a little drug store to ***take*** a glass of beer or two beers, and then stopped at the liquor store to get myself a pint and go home.(p.389)
• I couldn't walk, having it in a cast, and the doctor left the cast on three weeks longer than was necessary because he never found me sober enough to ***take*** it off.(p.390)
• I was just as drunk as I could be, getting ready to ***take*** an afternoon walk.(p.390)
• The cop must have seen the condition that I was in because he decided to ***take*** me home.(p.390)
• In the back of my mind, I probably thought, "They won't ***take*** me as drunk as I am."(p.398)
• He did not ***take*** out a folder and say, "What is the nature of your problem?"(p.413)
• With more physical courage than I had possessed, she had twice tried to ***take*** her life.(p.414)
• But it did not ***take*** long for the pressures of living to bring out my immaturity and my insecurity.(p.420)
• We were supposed to ***take*** off at noon, but were delayed until six p.m.(p.428)
• "You've got to space your drinks and ***take*** plenty of water in between," or "coat the stomach with a little

olive oil," or "drink anything but those damn martinis."(p.433)
• Science could ***take*** my mind apart expertly, but it couldn't seem to put it together again.(p.435)
• I didn't know whether I had told him to rush to the hospital and I'd meet him there, or to ***take*** two aspirin and call me in the morning.(p.441)
• I took more through the day to increase the high, and more to maintain it; when I overshot the mark, I'd ***take*** tranquilizers to level off.(p.442)
• I can't say, "Thy will be done," and ***take*** a pill.(p.443)
• On two occasions, over weekends, I decided I would ***take*** absolutely nothing.(p.443)
• Max accepted responsibility for me after I had promised never to drink again, never to ***take*** another pill, never to swear again, and never to talk to girls again.(p.444)
• And life keeps getting simpler and easier as we try to reverse my old idea, by taking care of the internal environment via the Twelve Steps, and letting the external environment ***take*** care of itself.)(p.446)
• So, for no better reason than to fool him, I asked Frank to ***take*** me to a meeting every night.(p.447)
• "That's a devil of a way to run an organization," I thought, and I reported Frank to the psychiatrist, who didn't seem perturbed; he just got someone else to ***take*** me on Fridays.(p.447)
• I can tell her she ought not to think a certain way, but I certainly can't ***take*** away her right to feel however she does feel.(p.451)
• Shortly thereafter, I was selected, with eight other inmates out of the 10,000 in the state's prisons at that time, to attend a school designed to ***take*** former "management problems" like me and convert them into paracounselors.(p.462)
• I ***take*** credit for nothing.(p.463)
• ***Take*** many pledges, but break them.(p.475)
• He say he ***take*** me to A.A. meeting.(p.476)
• Have not ***take*** drink since.(p.476)
• Two years later, my brother ***take*** Tall Man to first A.A. meeting.(p.476)
• ***Take*** my hand.(p.477)
• Once, I phoned my brother-in-law and told him I was going to ***take*** a handful of pills (in fact, I already had) and I would slash my wrists if he didn't come over to stop me.(p.479)
• I've never seen him drunk in my life, although he'd ***take*** a shot in the morning and usually one in the evening, and so did I; but for the most part he kept his whiskey in his office.(p.484)
• The only time that I have ever seen my mother ***take*** anything alcoholic was around Christmas time, when she would drink some eggnog or light wine.(p.484)
• Economic conditions had a great deal to do with it, because I've often heard my father say that his mother would ***take*** one of the old time flour sacks and cut a hole through the bottom and two corners of it and there you'd have a gown.(p.486)
• My father had purchased a restaurant, which he felt would ***take*** up some of my spare time, and that's how I met Vi.(p.487)
• At that time the repeal whiskies were back, and I'd go to the store and buy my whiskey and ***take*** it to my office and put it under the desk, first in one place and then in another, and there soon was an accumulation of empty bottles.(p.488)
• The closest I came to a psychiatrist during that time was an interne who came to ***take*** blood tests.(p.492)
• I knew my wife didn't because I had been sincere in all my promises to her as well as to my mother and to my close friends, but the urge to ***take*** that drink was more powerful than anything else.(p.494)
• "Freshman," said he to me, "do you ever ***take*** a drink?"(p.497)
• I drink and go to bed; I ***take*** a few the next morning and go see my mother once more.(p.501)
• I'll just ***take*** a few beers now and then.(p.502)
• You ***take*** me, and all my troubles, and do anything you want with me.'(p.504)
• Will I ***take*** a young fellow who has been drinking for two weeks to live with me?(p.506)
• And as I read, I shall ***take*** little drinks at long intervals.(p.506)
• I'm fortunate because I live in an era when A.A. is available, and I'm able to ***take*** advantage of it.(p.512)
• So I don't just ***take*** the inventory at night -- I ***take*** it continually throughout the day.(p.516)
• Even those don't ***take*** part in A.A. functions as I would like to see them do.(p.529)
• There was the economic fear which made me too timid to ***take*** any action which might improve my circumstances.(p.534)
• I attended my first A.A. meeting eight years ago, and it is with deep gratitude that I'm able to say I've not had a drink since that time, and that I ***take*** no sedation or narcotics, for this program is to me one of complete sobriety and I no longer need to escape reality.(p.549)
• They said if you want to know how this program works, ***take*** the first word of your question -- the H is for honesty, the O is for open-mindedness and the W is for willingness; these our Book calls the essentials of recovery.(p.550)
• They suggested that I study the A.A. book and try to ***take*** the Twelve Steps according to the explanation in the Book, for it was their opinion that the application of these principles in our daily lives will get us sober and keep us sober.(p.550)
• I've had many spiritual experiences since I've been in the program, many that I didn't recognize right away, for I'm slow to learn and they ***take*** many guises.(p.551)
• During the day a friend of mine brought me some magazines to ***take*** to a hospital group I was interested in, and I looked through them and a "banner" across the front of one featured an article by a prominent clergyman in which I caught the word "resentment."(p.552)
• Despite my wife's entreaties to ***take*** it easy that day, I arrived home in bad shape.(p.557)
• And no group, regional committee, or individual should ever ***take*** any action that might greatly affect A.A. as a whole without conferring with the trustees of the General Service Board.(p.565)
• I think our profession must ***take*** appreciative cognizance of this great therapeutic weapon.(p.571)

take-off

• I spent the time in a nearby tavern, was loaded on the ship, went to sleep before ***take-off***, and the next thing I knew someone was shaking me and telling me we were over San Diego.(p.428)

taken

• Since the original Foreword to this book was written in 1939, a wholesale miracle has ***taken*** place.(p.xv)
• A second small group had promptly ***taken*** shape at New York.(p.xvii)
• The house was ***taken*** over by the mortgage holder, my mother-in-law died, and my wife and father-in-law became ill.(p.5)
• Someone had pushed a drink my way, and I had ***taken*** it.(p.5)
• Then he had, in effect, been raised from the dead, suddenly ***taken*** from the scrap heap to a level of life better than the best he had ever known!(p.11)
• Had you offered yourselves as patients at this hospital, I would not have ***taken*** you, if I had been able to avoid it.(p.43)
• His alcoholic problem was ***taken*** away.(p.56)
• Once we have ***taken*** this step, withholding nothing, we are delighted.(p.75)
• After making our review we ask God's forgiveness and inquire what corrective measures should be ***taken***.(p.86)
• Tell him you once felt as he does, but you doubt whether you would have made much progress had you not ***taken*** action.(p.94)
• Some of us have ***taken*** very hard knocks to learn this truth: Job or no job -- wife or no wife -- we simply do not stop drinking so long as we place dependence upon other people ahead of dependence on God.(p.98)
• As soon as his sobriety begins to be ***taken*** as a matter of course, the family may look at their strange new dad with apprehension, then with irritation.(p.128)
• He has just returned from a three-months leave of absence, has ***taken*** a cure, looks fine, and to clinch the matter, the board of directors told him this was his last chance."(p.138)
• Had they fired me first, and had they then ***taken*** steps to see that I was presented with the solution contained in this book, I might have returned to them six months later, a well man.(p.141)
• Before my drinking had cut me down completely, I achieved a considerable measure of success, having been a City Councilman for five years and a financial director of Kenmore, a suburb later ***taken*** into the city itself.(p.182)
• And I hadn't been drunk because I hadn't ***taken*** a drink.(p.200)
• I was arrested and ***taken*** to jail where I was beaten up by two or three fellows who were already in there and whom I tried to boss.(p.204)
• Now we got you the drink, but you haven't ***taken*** the medicine."(p.206)
• I had ***taken*** five and a half ounces of paraldehyde.(p.207)
• There were four of us children, and although both of my brothers later became alcoholic -- one died of alcoholism -- my sister has never ***taken*** a drink in her life.(p.240)
• Imagine my surprise when I read in a page one "box" that I had been ***taken*** from the theater unconscious around noon that day, removed by ambulance to a hospital and stomach-pumped and then released.(p.244)
• After being dry two weeks and sticking close to Jackie, all of a sudden I found I had become the sponsor of my sponsor, for he was suddenly ***taken*** drunk.(p.245)
• They, too, had ***taken*** a train to one town and had wakened hundreds of miles in the opposite direction, never knowing how they got there.(p.246)
• Bill and Hank had just ***taken*** over a small automobile polishing company and they offered me a job -- ten dollars a week and keep at Hank's house.(p.246)
• That night I was ***taken*** home by a former alcoholic and his wife.(p.259)
• He had ***taken*** up light work, and he had a safety valve and a pair of spurs and the clothes on his back, and that was all.(p.263)
• I had never ***taken*** one.(p.263)
• Somebody must have ***taken*** pity on you and gone out and got it for you."(p.264)
• He talked about his wife taking his little boy away from him because of his drinking, and how he got back together with them through A.A., and we began feeling grateful right then that all these things hadn't been ***taken*** from us.(p.270)
• We were in A.A. three and a half years when he was ***taken*** from me.(p.270)
• When I said yes, we both knelt at his desk and prayed, each of us asking to have these defects ***taken*** away.(p.292)
• I was without power to change the course my life had ***taken***.(p.304)
• And as that thought came to me, it was as though someone had reached down and ***taken*** a heavy overcoat off my shoulders, for that was the last one.(p.347)
• Later I told her I had not ***taken*** the drink and that I was all right.(p.365)
• While I was in Florida trying to convince my wife with all the A.A. literature that she should come back to me, she went over to her desk and picked up a clipping she had ***taken*** from the St. Petersburg Times about A.A.(p.366)
• You didn't carry a little orchid up the aisle in those days; you carried a great big bouquet, like a funeral spray, and you didn't have your picture ***taken*** until just before you went to the church.(p.385)
• After a few more estimates as to income and expenditures for booze over a few sample years, ***taken*** at random, I conclude that this twenty per cent stayed fairly constant.(p.398)
• The short tours could be ***taken*** care of by sneaking enough whiskey aboard ship so that it could be rationed out until another supply could be laid in.(p.398)
• In a sense, I had ***taken*** the first step.(p.412)
• In fact, I was ***taken*** to A.A. by a woman whom my father had ***taken*** to A.A. thirteen years earlier.(p.419)
• Therefore, every pill was medically indicated at the time it was ***taken***.(p.443)
• For me, pills don't produce the desire to swallow a pill; they produce the symptoms that require that the pill be ***taken*** for relief.(p.443)
• Most had ***taken*** shattering losses on nearly every front of life.(p.455)
• Four years later, I was ***taken*** to my first A.A. meeting out of prison, in Los Angeles.(p.460)
• I was ***taken*** out of the house and put bodily into a waiting car with nothing on but a robe and gown.(p.466)
• The idea behind it is that, having ***taken*** the treatment, your system is so "conditioned" that the mere sight or smell or taste of alcohol produces a violent reaction, and you become ill.(p.469)
• Someone had ***taken*** it from me.(p.491)
• What actually happened was that I had ***taken*** a penknife and stabbed Vi three times with it.(p.492)
• I was ***taken*** to the station house and locked up.(p.492)
• The fear and the insane idea are ***taken*** away.(p.505)
• I've stuck pretty close to A.A. ever since then, ***taken*** it day by day, not biting off more than I can chew.(p.511)
• Lots of the older people had ***taken*** to drinking quite a good deal more during the war, but the younger generation was, I think, about the same.(p.518)
• After a while, I found that the psycho ward was a good place to hide when I had ***taken*** something stolen to the pawnshop.(p.528)
• I have been home for a year, and have not ***taken*** a drink in four years.(p.529)

• This time, whoever had rolled me had ***taken*** my glasses as well (they were gold).(p.538)
• For by now I had been exposed once to A.A., but I had treated it as a vaudeville and had ***taken*** friends to meetings so that they too could enjoy the fascination of the naked revelation of suffering and recovery.(p.539)
• With no explanation at all, I was ***taken*** from my home in Florida to my grandparents' home in the middle west.(p.544)

takes

• Now I had what it ***takes***!(p.6)
• If hundreds of experiences have shown him that one drink means another debacle with all its attendant suffering and humiliation, why is it he ***takes*** that one drink?(p.22)
• We are equally positive that once he ***takes*** any alcohol whatever into his system, something happens, both in the bodily and mental sense, which makes it virtually impossible for him to stop.(p.22)
• A business which ***takes*** no regular inventory usually goes broke.(p.64)
• This ***takes*** us out of ourselves.(p.70)
• You think he ought to know the subject better, as everyone should have a clear understanding of the risk he ***takes*** if he drinks too much.(p.112)
• It ***takes*** some of us a long time to outgrow that serious handicap.(p.125)
• When father ***takes*** this tack, the family may react unfavorably.(p.128)
• My downfall cost the business community unknown thousands of dollars, for it ***takes*** real money to train a man for an executive position.(p.137)
• In competent hands, this seldom ***takes*** long nor is it very expensive.(p.143)
• A complete change ***takes*** place in our approach to life.(p.311)
• To the new man I would also like to say that this program is not for sissies for, in my humble opinion, it ***takes*** a man to make the grade.(p.367)
• Father is an Episcopal minister and his work ***takes*** him over long drives on bad roads.(p.497)
• But it ***takes*** others to keep me there.(p.500)
• What often ***takes*** place in a few months could seldom have been accomplished by years of self discipline.(p.569)

taking

• Some are just now ***taking*** shape in Asia.(p.xv)
• They are restless, irritable and discontented, unless they can again experience the sense of ease and comfort which comes at once by ***taking*** a few drinks -- drinks which they see others ***taking*** with impunity.(p.xxvi)
• Drink was ***taking*** an important and exhilarating part in my life.(p.3)
• The almost certain consequences that follow ***taking*** even a glass of beer do not crowd into the mind to deter us.(p.24)
• Here are some of the methods we have tried: Drinking beer only, limiting the number of drinks, never drinking alone, never drinking in the morning, drinking only at home, never having it in the house, never drinking during business hours, drinking only at parties, switching from scotch to brandy, drinking only natural wines, agreeing to resign if ever drunk on the job, ***taking*** a trip, not ***taking*** a trip, swearing off forever (with and without a solemn oath), ***taking*** more physical exercise, reading inspirational books, going to health farms and sanitariums, accepting voluntary commitment to asylums -- we could increase the list ad infinitum.(p.31)
• I vaguely sensed I was not being any too smart, but felt reassured as I was ***taking*** the whiskey on a full stomach.(p.36)
• But there was always the curious mental phenomenon that parallel with our sound reasoning there inevitably ran some insanely trivial excuse for ***taking*** the first drink.(p.37)
• We thought well before ***taking*** this step making sure we were ready; that we could at last abandon ourselves utterly to Him.(p.63)
• ***Taking*** a commercial inventory is a fact-finding and a fact-facing process.(p.64)
• ***Taking*** this book down from our shelf we turn to the page which contains the twelve steps.(p.75)
• Before ***taking*** drastic action which might implicate other people we secure their consent.(p.80)
• Under only slightly different conditions, the same thing is ***taking*** place in many eastern cities.(p.161)
• It was really a horrible nightmare, this earning money, getting liquor, smuggling it home, getting drunk, morning jitters, ***taking*** large doses of sedatives to make it possible for me to earn more money, and so on ad nauseam.(p.177)
• Away from my office two or three weeks at a time; horrible days and nights when I would lie on the floor of my home, lying awake and reaching over to get the bottle, ***taking*** a drink and going back into oblivion.(p.184)
• I had contracted for half of it, at least verbally, and the contractors were ***taking*** half of the second mortgage bond.(p.198)
• This experience sent me to law school where I went at night and which course I completed in less than three years, ***taking*** the highest state bar examinations and passing them.(p.212)
• He startled me by informing me that he was an alcoholic, that he had found a way which so far enabled him to live without ***taking*** a drink, and that the main idea was to find a way how not to take that first drink.(p.218)
• Military service was compulsory and I did my stretch with the class of my age, goose-stepping in German barracks and ***taking*** part in the Boxer Rebellion in China, my first time at any great distance from home.(p.230)
• ***Taking*** that as a foundation, he reasoned that if a man followed that rule he could not be selfish.(p.236)
• I had been too self-sufficient to write a moral inventory, but I discovered in pointing out to the new man his wrong attitudes and actions that I was really ***taking*** my own inventory, and that if I expected him to change I would have to work on myself too.(p.249)
• He talked about his wife ***taking*** his little boy away from him because of his drinking, and how he got back together with them through A.A., and we began feeling grateful right then that all these things hadn't been taken from us.(p.270)
• There have also been numerous times when I have thought about ***taking*** a drink.(p.285)
• I began ***taking*** drinks in the morning to get started.(p.318)
• Hidden old-drunks can pass out on their beds and snooze unreproached, under the guise of ***taking*** those vital retirement-age naps.(p.330)
• To me, ***taking*** a bath was just being in a place with a bottle where I could drink in privacy.(p.337)
• So, after ***taking*** the first half of the First Step, and very gingerly admitting myself to Alcoholics Anonymous, something happened.(p.349)
• We did, and spent a month boozing it up, popping pills, and smoking marijuana; ***taking*** shelter where we could, which included a veterinary hospital one night; accepting meals from anyone; actually begging; stealing anything we were in need of, which was about everything.(p.354)
• And the only one who can take it away from me is me -- by ***taking*** that first drink.(p.355)
• By the time all this was over, I was really in a terrific state, and my father ***taking*** in things said, "Miss Esther is about to faint.(p.385)
• He talked me into ***taking*** the Samaritan Treatment.(p.389)
• They were ***taking*** the trouble to try and help.(p.415)
• In the first year there were episodes such as kicking Priscilla in the shins, getting the lock changed on the desk in the A.A. Club, because I, as secretary, didn't want the Intergroup secretary "interfering," and ***taking*** an older woman member out to lunch for the express purpose of informing her that she was "a phony."(p.416)
• I consider that I was ***taking*** the Eleventh Step when I joined this church.(p.417)
• I don't know why I didn't fall out of the open cockpit of some of those planes I flew in while ***taking*** aerial pictures.(p.426)
• Or, "I got to talking and forgot how many I was ***taking*** and it hit me."(p.433)
• So I immediately started ***taking*** and shooting pep pills.(p.442)
• Eventually, I was ***taking*** forty-five milligrams of the long-acting Benzedrine and forty-five of the short-acting just to get out of bed in the morning.(p.442)
• Today, I find I can't work my A.A. program while ***taking*** pills, nor may I even have them around for dire emergencies only.(p.443)
• And life keeps getting simpler and easier as we try to reverse my old idea, by ***taking*** care of the internal environment via the Twelve Steps, and letting the external environment take care of itself.)(p.446)
• When a big, healthy-looking young fellow stood up there and said, "I'm a success today if I don't drink today," I thought, "Man, I've got a thousand things to do today before I can brag about not ***taking*** a drink, for God's sake!"(p.447)
• (Today, there is absolutely nothing in the world more important to me than my keeping this alcoholic sober; not ***taking*** a drink is by far the most important thing I do each day.)(p.447)
• But for some time, it was difficult to keep from ***taking*** a pill when I had an appropriate symptom, such as a cough, pain, anxiety, insomnia, a muscle spasm, or an upset stomach.(p.448)
• While I was ***taking*** inventory in the cold-storage locker one Sunday, a wooden sign bolted to the inside door stopped me in my tracks.(p.461)
• Some of us always remember our big mouths when it comes to a drink, but somewhere along the line, we seem to have forgotten about ***taking*** care of our teeth.(p.479)
• Vi was ***taking*** care of me and I was devoting all my time to the building of that group.(p.496)
• It didn't worry me very much, because at that time I could shut off for a couple of months without ***taking*** a drink or even wanting one, and without feeling that I was giving anything up.(p.518)
• I was ***taking*** Benzedrine and paraldehyde quite impartially during the day then, and by the time I arrived at my first A.A. meeting, I was pretty drunk and certainly doped up to the eyes and completely jittery.(p.523)
• This caused the rather cryptic comment from one of my A.A. friends, when I told my story after coming into the program, that I had always been a cinch for the program, for I had always been interested in mankind, but that I was just ***taking*** them one man at a time.(p.548)

tale

• My first meeting gave me a great deal of hope and lots of willing ears for my ***tale*** of woe and for my questions.(p.364)

talebearers

• Gone are time cards to punch, alarm clocks to obey, nosey rumor-mongers and ***talebearers*** to evade.(p.329)

talent

• My ***talent*** for leadership, I imagined, would place me at the head of vast enterprises which I would manage with the utmost assurance.(p.1)
• The Great Boss has given me diagnostic and surgical ***talent***, and He has loaned it to me to use for the rest of my life.(p.350)

talented

• I was nothing more than a spoiled, indulged, and ***talented*** brat.(p.418)

talents

• There was always a tremendous drive and ambition to become a great guy, because I think I recognized inwardly that I didn't have any special ***talents***.(p.194)
• I have never shown any particular ***talents*** nor have I had any really frustrating ambitions.(p.240)

tales

• Can he talk frankly with you so long as he does not bear business ***tales*** or criticize his associates?(p.145)
• In this way he was slyly carrying ***tales***.(p.145)
• Those who believe their drinking to be hopeless may again find hope in these thirteen impressive ***tales***.(p.167)

talk

• The spark that was to flare into the first A.A. group was struck at Akron, Ohio, in June 1935, during a ***talk*** between a New York stockbroker and an Akron physician.(p.xv)
• Following his physical rehabilitation, he had a ***talk*** with me in which he frankly stated he thought the treatment a waste of effort, unless I could assure him, which no one ever had, that in the future he would have the "will power" to resist the impulse to drink.(p.xxix)
• There was loud ***talk*** in the jazz places uptown.(p.3)
• Each day my friend's simple ***talk*** in our kitchen multiplies itself in a widening circle of peace on earth and good will to men.(p.16)
• If you draw this fallacious reasoning to the attention of an alcoholic, he will laugh it off, or become irritated and refuse to ***talk***.(p.23)
• And it means, of course, that we are going to ***talk*** about God.(p.45)
• Many times we ***talk*** to a new man and watch his hope rise as we discuss his alcoholic problems and explain our fellowship.(p.45)
• Though we have no religious connection, we may still do well to ***talk*** with someone ordained by an established religion.(p.74)
• We say this because we are very anxious that we ***talk*** to the right person.(p.74)
• We have a written inventory and we are prepared for a long ***talk***.(p.75)
• He is going to be more interested in a demonstration of good will than in our ***talk*** of spiritual discoveries.(p.77)
• We should not ***talk*** incessantly to them about spiritual matters.(p.83)

• If there is any indication that he wants to stop, have a good ***talk*** with the person most interested in him -- usually his wife.(p.90)
• You should be described to him as one of a fellowship who, as part of their own recovery, try to help others and who will be glad to ***talk*** to him if he cares to see you.(p.90)
• After a while, turn the ***talk*** to some phase of drinking.(p.91)
• If he wishes to ***talk***, let him do so.(p.91)
• ***Talk*** about the conditions of body and mind which accompany it.(p.92)
• But you may ***talk*** to him about the hopelessness of alcoholism because you offer a solution.(p.92)
• If your ***talk*** has been sane, quiet and full of human understanding, you have perhaps made a friend.(p.94)
• Unless your friend wants to ***talk*** further about himself, do not wear out your welcome.(p.95)
• Never ***talk*** down to an alcoholic from any moral or spiritual hilltop; simply lay out the kit of spiritual tools for his inspection.(p.95)
• This may lay the groundwork for a friendly ***talk*** about his alcoholic problem.(p.111)
• Your husband may be willing to ***talk*** to one of them.(p.112)
• If this kind of approach does not catch your husband's interest, it may be best to drop the subject, but after a friendly ***talk*** your husband will usually revive the topic himself.(p.112)
• ***Talk*** about his condition or this book only when he raises the issue.(p.113)
• Let's ***talk*** about it later."(p.118)
• We do ***talk*** about each other a great deal, but we almost invariably temper such ***talk*** by a spirit of love and tolerance.(p.125)
• There is ***talk*** about spiritual matters morning, noon and night.(p.128)
• What about his ***talk*** that God will take care of them?(p.128)
• On your employee's return, ***talk*** with him.(p.144)
• Can he ***talk*** frankly with you so long as he does not bear business tales or criticize his associates?(p.145)
• The employer can many times protect the victim from this kind of ***talk***.(p.145)
• An alcoholic who has recovered, but holds a relatively unimportant job, can ***talk*** to a man with a better position.(p.146)
• He wanted so much to ***talk*** with someone, but whom?(p.154)
• There was much ***talk*** about the mental state preceding the first drink.(p.157)
• Before very long we began to relate some incidents of our drinking and, naturally, pretty soon, I realized both of them knew what they were talking about because you can see things and smell things when you're drunk, that you can't other times, and, if I had thought they didn't know what they were talking about, I wouldn't have been willing to ***talk*** to them at all.(p.185)
• After a while, Bill said, "Well, now, you've been talking a good long time, let me ***talk*** a minute or two."(p.185)
• Their ***talk*** and action had instilled me with a certain amount of confidence, although I was not too absolutely certain.(p.189)
• I meet the people that I like to ***talk*** to.(p.192)
• Then he started to ***talk*** to me about his drinking experiences, what his drinking had cost him, how much he had drunk and where, things like that, and I remember I was quite bored because I had never seen the guy before and had no interest at all in what, where and when he drank.(p.208)
• Whenever a situation arose that fast ***talk*** wouldn't explain away, I simply withdrew.(p.214)
• I believe every member of the Akron Group did come to see me, which impressed me terrifically, not so much because of the stories they told, but because they would take the time to come and ***talk*** to me without even knowing who I was.(p.218)
• In fact I was scared to ***talk*** to him about it, for I feared the kind of ***talk*** he would give me.(p.234)
• He didn't ***talk*** like a preacher at all.(p.235)
• Instead he told me that some of them wanted to ***talk*** to me and would be over to see me.(p.235)
• And, because as I have discovered since, it is part of the "treatment" that these men be sent to see and ***talk*** with alcoholics who want to quit, he kept them busy.(p.235)
• Little more of our ***talk*** stayed in my memory, but I do know I slept the rest of that night while before I had never known what a real night's sleep was.(p.239)
• The only salesman invited to ***talk*** at the convention?(p.243)
• They will never know how much their ***talk*** with me helped.(p.259)
• I'd hear them on the phone having prayer meetings and so forth, that sort of ***talk*** over the phone, and it completely burnt me up.(p.265)
• She said, "Well, you better ***talk*** to Jack."(p.266)
• I knew Doc and Anne were going to be there, and all of them thought it would be good for me, but the first thing I did was to go to St. Thomas and try to ***talk*** to those women.)(p.272)
• He mentioned two of them that I had known through the years and suggested that I ***talk*** with them.(p.289)
• In the spring of 1939, the Big Book was printed, and we had two inquiries from the New York office because of a fifteen-minute radio ***talk*** that was made.(p.294)
• This is no idle ***talk***.(p.302)
• He asked me to read the book "Alcoholics Anonymous," and then he wanted me to ***talk*** with a man who was experiencing success with his own arrestment.(p.308)
• The doctor asked about my drinking, but I wouldn't ***talk*** to him.(p.319)
• Yet I recently recalled that each morning I used to ***talk*** to the bottle when I took it down from the closet.(p.332)
• Hauling her to the divan, I sat with her and began to ***talk***, frantically but clearly – and making sense.(p.333)
• And he said, "Earle, why don't you come on over and let me ***talk*** to you for a minute."(p.348)
• I had no one in the world to ***talk*** to.(p.355)
• They would ***talk*** about it.(p.386)
• I had been reading a lot about psychiatry and I thought, "Maybe if I ***talk*** to a psychiatrist he can find out what is happening, and then I can drink like a lady."(p.387)
• Frank said, "If you'd like to ***talk*** to a psychiatrist, I'll see a doctor and find out who to go to here."(p.387)
• I knew this, and right away I got furious and would not even ***talk*** to the doctor in the place.(p.387)
• There are so many to whom I feel deeply grateful; to my husband (and best critic), whose generous love, compassion and understanding have helped me along the way; to those before me in A.A. who inspired the first article I read, and the friend who sent that article to Frank; to Ruth for her personal note, and the first A.A. to ***talk*** to me; to my Bishop, whose loving and believing spirit inspired me; and to all the members of the Houston Group who were so patient, kind and helpful -- and to countless others.(p.393)
• I could just hear their sweet, pious ***talk***.(p.412)
• I tried to mimic the ***talk***, ideas, moods and even the drinking the older men.(p.423)
• Max accepted responsibility for me after I had promised never to drink again, never to take another pill, never to swear again, and never to ***talk*** to girls again.(p.444)
• But by God, I wouldn't ***talk*** or eat, either!(p.444)
• One day as I sat there in the hospital, my psychiatrist walked up behind me and asked, "How'd you like to ***talk*** to the man from A.A.?"(p.446)
• I wanted to ***talk*** about my many big problems; drinking seemed a small one.(p.447)
• Prior to our marriage, when she was a shy, scrawny adolescent, I was able to see things in her that others couldn't necessarily see – things like beauty, charm, gaiety, a gift for being easy to ***talk*** to, a sense of humor, and many other fine qualities.(p.450)
• I would rather ***talk*** about the good things A.A. has taught me; I feel that hitting on just a few sordid points should be sufficient to let those of you in institutions know where I came from.(p.459)
• But to another woman, the first woman I met in A.A., I could ***talk***.(p.471)
• By grace of God I stop, think two things: This would kill good mother and father; then remember boys ***talk*** about Indian fellow who been sober three years.(p.475)
• We ***talk*** long time.(p.475)
• My sponsor say men who ***talk*** speak truth.(p.476)
• ***Talk*** and meeting make me feel good.(p.476)
• I feel Great Spirit at all meetings and when ***talk*** to A.A. friends.(p.477)
• I had a long ***talk*** with a psychiatrist, but nothing came of that, and I had also, just about that time, talked with a minister for whom I had a great deal of respect.(p.489)
• So I went down to ***talk*** to the District Attorney, and the arrangement was made that I would go home to stay with my mother, and that meant Vi and I were separated.(p.491)
• Anyhow, on the 24th, after drinking all day on the 23rd, I must have decided I wanted to see my wife and have some kind of reconciliation or at least ***talk*** with her.(p.491)
• She asked me if I would let someone come up and ***talk*** to me concerning a business deal.(p.494)
• He continued to ***talk*** and I to listen.(p.494)
• But as he continued to ***talk***, I realized that this was the first time I had met a person who had the same problems I did and who, I sincerely believe, understood me as an individual.(p.494)
• We ***talk***.(p.505)
• I ***talk*** to the stranger in the seat beside me.(p.505)
• I call my wife into a room where we can ***talk*** privately.(p.506)
• We ***talk*** of other things.(p.507)
• I'd visit one bar after another, having one martini in each, and in each hoping to find someone interesting to ***talk*** to.(p.536)

talked

• I ***talked*** with him for some time, but was not able to bring myself to feel that I had known him before.(p.xxix)
• He ***talked*** for hours.(p.10)
• When they ***talked*** of a God personal to me, who was love, superhuman strength and direction, I became irritated and my mind snapped shut against such a theory.(p.10)
• I have since ***talked*** with scores of men who felt the same way.(p.12)
• He listened in wonder as I ***talked***.(p.14)
• We ***talked*** of intolerance, while we were intolerant ourselves.(p.50)
• Though you have ***talked*** with the family, leave them out of the first discussion.(p.91)
• I read everything I could find, and ***talked*** to everyone who I thought knew anything about it.(p.178)
• It must be remembered that I had read a great deal and ***talked*** to everyone who knew, or thought they knew anything about the subject of alcoholism.(p.180)
• Of far more importance was the fact that he was the first living human with whom I had ever ***talked***, who knew what he was talking about in regard to alcoholism from actual experience.(p.180)
• In other words, he ***talked*** my language.(p.180)
• All the other people that had ***talked*** to me wanted to help me, and my pride prevented me from listening to them, and caused only resentment on my part, but I felt as if I would be a real stinker if I did not listen to a couple of fellows for a short time, if that would cure them.(p.185)
• Of course, we had ***talked*** over quite a number of the failings that I had and made a sort of an inventory, which wasn't too difficult, because I had an awful lot of things wrong that were very apparent to me, because I knew all about them.(p.190)
• At the end of about four months, I not only had good looking clothes –and I might say that at the time I first ***talked*** to Max I didn't have a suit of clothes I could bend over in real sudden; now I had six suits of clothes.(p.200)
• We ***talked***, too, about personal morals.(p.236)
• Jackie arrived about seven in the evening and ***talked*** until three a.m.(p.239)
• All they ***talked*** of that first week-end was God, and how they were going to straighten out Jackie's and my life.(p.245)
• But we were staying sober as long as we kept and ***talked*** together.(p.246)
• As he ***talked*** I gathered vaguely, (because he was a faltering beginner then, just as I am now) that to be relieved of alcoholism I would have to be different.(p.257)
• We ***talked*** about it afterwards, and we felt that there might be some time we'd need it.(p.266)
• He ***talked*** about his wife taking his little boy away from him because of his drinking, and how he got back together with them through A.A., and we began feeling grateful right then that all these things hadn't been taken from us.(p.270)
• We were so mad at her because she ***talked*** to him that way.(p.271)
• I don't ever remember that I was bored myself when we first came in, and they came out to the house and ***talked*** to us about these things.(p.273)
• She ***talked*** to me and laughed about it and got me all over it.(p.273)
• I know I've ***talked*** too long, but I always do.(p.274)
• I also ***talked*** A.A. to every friend who would listen, at lunch, at dinner, on street corners.(p.282)
• I, who had never made a speech in my life and who would have been frightened sick at the prospect, stood up in front of Rotary groups in different parts of the city and ***talked*** about Alcoholics Anonymous.(p.283)
• He ***talked*** about himself, but I was sure it was about me.(p.302)

• I ***talked*** to the first sergeant and the battalion commander, and they got me in contact with an A.A. member.(p.319)

• A year later, while we were on a vacation trip she packed up to go home because of my excessive drinking, and I ***talked*** her out of it with the promise I would go on the wagon for at least a year.(p.377)

• He ***talked*** me into taking the Samaritan Treatment.(p.389)

• I ***talked*** out of the side of my mouth, as they did.(p.423)

• I ***talked*** the Old Man into letting me live in the photo lab instead of the barracks, and for eighteen months nothing interfered with my drinking.(p.426)

• I was supposed to come home on a troop ship, but I ***talked*** the base commander into flying me home.(p.428)

• I attended meetings, I ***talked*** to my folks, I ***talked*** to younger people they had gotten in contact with to sponsor me.(p.430)

• We sat in the back and ***talked*** only to each other.(p.447)

• It seemed that all they ***talked*** about at meetings was drinking, drinking, drinking.(p.447)

• I almost broke down and cried when I ***talked*** with them but I didn't.(p.467)

• It seemed to me that those A.A.'s to whom I ***talked*** knew all about me.(p.470)

• But by listening and talking to these A.A.'s – talking to them as I had never ***talked*** to anyone in my whole life, I saw that it was my life that was unmanageable – not just my drinking.(p.471)

• I had a long talk with a psychiatrist, but nothing came of that, and I had also, just about that time, ***talked*** with a minister for whom I had a great deal of respect.(p.489)

• So she went to court and ***talked*** it over with the judge.(p.491)

• After he'd ***talked*** half an hour, I still wanted him to hurry up and get out so I could go and get some whiskey before the liquor store closed.(p.494)

• After Charlie had ***talked*** a while, I knew that this man had something.(p.495)

• We ***talked*** for a while, and then he sent me down to the Alanon House over on the west side, and there I had my introduction to A.A.(p.515)

• I ***talked*** to him for quite a long time and at the end, he said, "Well, you're not quite mad enough to be shut up for good yet, but you soon will be if you live long enough."(p.522)

talker

• Before I stop -- I always was a great ***talker*** – I want to say that nobody will ever know how I miss Annie's advice about things.(p.273)

talking

• On ***talking*** to a man there, I would be amazingly lifted up and set on my feet.(p.15)

• That the man who is making the approach has had the same difficulty, that he obviously knows what he is ***talking*** about, that his whole deportment shouts at the new prospect that he is a man with a real answer, that he has no attitude of Holier Than Thou, nothing whatever except the sincere desire to be helpful; that there are no fees to pay, no axes to grind, no people to please, no lectures to be endured -- these are the conditions we have found most effective.(p.18)

• You draw more and more into yourself and you think everyone is ***talking*** about conditions at your home.(p.114)

• This seemed to me like an opportunity to be helpful, so I spent two hours ***talking*** about alcoholism, the malady, and described the symptoms and results as well as I could.(p.138)

• Of far more importance was the fact that he was the first living human with whom I had ever talked, who knew what he was ***talking*** about in regard to alcoholism from actual experience.(p.180)

• She told me that she had been ***talking*** to a couple of fellows about drinking.(p.184)

• Then she told me that these two drunks she had been ***talking*** to had a plan whereby they thought they could quit drinking, and part of that plan was that they tell it to another drunk.(p.185)

• Before very long we began to relate some incidents of our drinking and, naturally, pretty soon, I realized both of them knew what they were ***talking*** about because you can see things and smell things when you're drunk, that you can't other times, and, if I had thought they didn't know what they were ***talking*** about, I wouldn't have been willing to talk to them at all.(p.185)

• After a while, Bill said, "Well, now, you've been ***talking*** a good long time, let me talk a minute or two."(p.185)

• They said, "That's what we're ***talking*** about.(p.188)

• You certainly know what you are ***talking*** about."(p.189)

• I know there was even more, something that I hadn't got, and I remember one day, a week or two after I had come out of the hospital, Bill was over to my house ***talking*** to my wife and me.(p.191)

• Bill looked across at my wife, and said to her, "Henrietta, the Lord has been so wonderful to me, curing me of this terrible disease, that I just want to keep ***talking*** about it and telling people."(p.191)

• I said, "All right, call me a cab," as though I was ***talking*** to a bell boy.(p.204)

• One morning, after I had been on a binge for a couple of days, I awoke to find my brother and Doctor Bob in my room ***talking*** to me about not drinking.(p.206)

• I got two drinks, each of them a quarter of that pint, in me, and was ***talking*** along with these people, but I felt that sooner or later they were going to have me cornered because they were smarter than I was and the drink was beginning to take effect; but as I reached for the third drink Bob said, "Listen, Buster, you promised to take some medicine if we got you a drink.(p.206)

• I was kind of shocked about anybody ***talking*** about themselves the way he did, and my impression was that the guy was a little "touched."(p.216)

• From far away, as if in a delirium, I heard my own voice – calling someone "Dorothy," ***talking*** of dress shops, of jobs . . . the words came clearer . . . this sound of my own voice frightened me as it came closer . . . and suddenly, there I was, ***talking*** of I knew not what, to someone I'd never seen before this very moment.(p.222)

• ***Talking*** things over with them, great floods of enlightenment showed me myself as I really was and I was like them.(p.229)

• He went on ***talking*** and told me that he had found the plan has a basis of love, and the practice of Christ's injunction, "Love thy neighbor as thyself."(p.236)

• There was a man watching, and I turned to him and said with a defiant air I carried with me all the time, "If I don't quit this I'm going to have to join that alcoholic business they're ***talking*** about."(p.266)

• Here was a tall, rugged, highly educated Yankee ***talking*** in a matter of course way about God and prayer.(p.279)

• I don't know what I expected, but I most certainly didn't visualize a group of people ***talking*** about their drinking problems, making light of their personal tragedies and at the same time enjoying themselves.(p.378)

• I seldom left the base any more except once in a while when I felt the need of ***talking*** to some girl.(p.427)

• Or, "I got to ***talking*** and forgot how many I was taking and it hit me."(p.433)

• After ***talking*** with him for a time I heard myself saying, "Doc, I think I'm an alcoholic."(p.436)

• I'm ***talking*** about the good things that have happened.(p.463)

• But by listening and ***talking*** to these A.A.'s – ***talking*** to them as I had never talked to anyone in my whole life, I saw that it was my life that was unmanageable – not just my drinking.(p.471)

• I remember ***talking*** to her, but what happened after that I don't know.(p.492)

• Anyhow, he started ***talking*** about himself.(p.494)

• It was no use ***talking*** of putting myself into a home, a hospital, or of going to see a doctor again, or of going to see a priest or anyone else.(p.523)

• I am ***talking*** about A.A. people, who have gone through some of the same things that you might be going through now.(p.529)

• There was the father one lost respect for at the age of eleven, because the father broke his solemn word in a circumstance where you, eleven years old, had assumed guilt when you were innocent; but the father would not believe you, no matter what; and to ease his suffering you "confessed" and were "forgiven," only – months later – to have your "guilt" brought up – only he and you knew what he was ***talking*** bout -- brought up in front of the stern grandmother.(p.533)

talks

• Each day, somewhere in the world, recovery begins when one alcoholic ***talks*** with another alcoholic, sharing experience, strength, and hope.(p.xxii)

• We had long ***talks*** when I would still her foreboding by telling her that men of genius conceived their best projects when drunk; that the most majestic constructions of philosophic thought were so derived.(p.2)

• He may either plunge into a frantic attempt to get on his feet in business, or he may be so enthralled by his new life that he ***talks*** or thinks of little else.(p.125)

• These family ***talks*** will be constructive if they can be carried on without heated argument, self-pity, self-justification or resentful criticism.(p.127)

• I had a couple of shorter ***talks*** with this man afterward, and stopped drinking abruptly.(p.179)

• I think it's awfully hard on people, especially if they're new people, to hear these long drawn out ***talks***.(p.273)

• Most of us did not stay out of prison long enough to run the alcoholic gamut -- to develop the ongoing kind of alcoholism or alcoholic drinking you hear about in A.A. ***talks***.(p.458)

• I go back to my old alma mater occasionally to give A.A. ***talks***, and -- just think! -- the warden is my friend.(p.462)

• (This address is now available in pamphlet form at nominal cost through most A.A. groups or from Box 459, Grand Central Station, New York, NY 10163, under the title "Three ***Talks*** to Medical Societies by Bill W." -- formerly called "Bill on Alcoholism" and earlier "Alcoholism the Illness.")(p.572)

tall

• I looked up and there were two great big fellows over six foot ***tall***, very likable looking.(p.185)

• Here was a ***tall***, rugged, highly educated Yankee talking in a matter of course way about God and prayer.(p.279)

• Bill was ***tall***, grey haired, with the kind of asymmetrical good looks and pleasant easy manner that inspire confidence in the shaken and afraid.(p.413)

• Standing there was a gray haired man – ***tall***, trim and in uniform.(p.422)

• I proud to be son of ***Tall*** Man, American Indian, and member of A.A. for many moons.(p.474)

• Met father (***Tall*** Man) at fork in road -- one way to reservation, other way to State of Maine.(p.475)

• Year later, I go to Canada to carry message to ***Tall*** Man, but he not listen to son.(p.476)

• Two years later, my brother take ***Tall*** Man to first A.A. meeting.(p.476)

• ***Tall*** Man was blind, but soon he see.(p.476)

• ***Tall*** Man die five years ago, a sober, peaceful, happy man.(p.476)

• ***Tall*** Man now see Great Spirit in Big Group in sky.(p.476)

tallied

• Impressed by those who visited him at the hospital, he capitulated entirely when, later, in an upper room of this house, he heard the story of some man whose experience closely ***tallied*** with his own.(p.160)

tan

• I acquired the impeccable coat of ***tan*** one sees upon the well-to-do.(p.4)

tangent

• Nothing will help the man who is off on a spiritual ***tangent*** so much as the wife who adopts a sane spiritual program, making a better practical use of it.(p.130)

tangible

• After they have seen ***tangible*** results, the family will perhaps want to go along.(p.99)

• I do surgery because that's something that you can see; it's more ***tangible***.(p.485)

t'ank

• When the policeman released me to my stupefied and exasperated friend at four in the morning, I went to my traveling bag and groped until I found – well, let the officer speak: "Ah," said the policeman, "he's got anuder pair, ***t'ank*** God!"(p.538)

tank

• The water ***tank*** on the toilet I never used, because that looked too easy.(p.176)

tap

• Instead it was like a ***tap*** on the head with a small mallet.(p.402)

tape

• I was staring at an inch of the ***tape*** which bore the inscription XYZ-32.(p.4)

taped

• I knew nothing about alcoholism or the D.T.'s, but when I woke up on this last morning of my son's illness, I ***taped*** the keyhole on my door because "everyone was out there."(p.338)

taper

• Perhaps he goes to a doctor who gives him morphine or some sedative with which to ***taper*** off.(p.22)

• I stayed so sober that I used to keep a quart of medicinal whiskey in my bureau which I used to ***taper*** off the occasional newspaper alcoholics who were sent to see me.(p.253)

• I'd better ***taper*** off.(p.408)

• I wasn't the type that could *taper* off.(p.514)

tapered

• By early July, I had *tapered* off alcohol completely, and I got off all pills in the ensuing few months.(p.448)

tapering

• After I had been around A.A. for seven months, *tapering* off alcohol and pills, not finding the program working very well, I was finally able to say, "Okay, God.(p.448)

tapes

• My experience has been active: three meetings a week, many *tapes*, many A.A. conferences, much work on the Twelve Steps, and much work with other alcoholics and their families.(p.420)

tapped

• You forget that you have just now *tapped* a source of power much greater than yourself.(p.163)

• With few exceptions our members find that they have *tapped* an unsuspected inner resource which they presently identify with their own conception of a Power greater than themselves.(p.569)

task

• We shall bring to the *task* our combined experience and knowledge.(p.19)

• It was worrying my wife a little, but she had the good sense not to take me to *task* about it or goad me into going.(p.364)

• I now conceive the psychiatrist's job to be the *task* of breaking down the patient's inner resistance so that which is inside him will flower, as under the activity of the A.A. program."(p.571)

tasks

• Today I have Someone who will always hear me; I have a warm fellowship among men who understand my problems; I have *tasks* to do and am glad to do them, to see others who are alcoholics and to help them in any way I can to become sober men.(p.260)

• I have stopped tilting at windmills, and instead have tried to accomplish the little daily *tasks*, unimportant in themselves, but *tasks* that are an integral part of living fully.(p.295)

taste

• We hope no one will consider these self-revealing accounts in bad *taste*.(p.29)

• I knew the stuff I was making was a lot stronger than I had been used to, but I never suspected that steady drinking of it might develop a *taste* for something even stronger still.(p.233)

• Before long I had a definite *taste* for hard liquor, knew nausea and headaches I had never known before, but as in the old days, I suffered them out.(p.233)

• I cannot say that my *taste* for liquor has entirely disappeared.(p.259)

• We complement each other beautifully, as he is a born salesman and my *taste* is for finance and management.(p.284)

• I definitely liked it, everything about it, the *taste*, the effects; and I realize now that a drink did something for me or to me that was different from the way it affected others.(p.305)

• A square from ultra-dry Kansas, I did not *taste* grog until I had finished college, done a stint on newspapers, married, become a father, and been in studio publicity two years.(p.328)

• The second way in which, perhaps, I differ from some other alcoholics is this; many alcoholics state that they didn't particularly like the *taste* of alcohol, but that they liked the effect.(p.345)

• I used to like to get it on my fingers so I could lick them and get another *taste*.(p.346)

• Prohibition came along, and with it my first *taste* of moonshine.(p.357)

• The idea behind it is that, having taken the treatment, your system is so "conditioned" that the mere sight or smell or *taste* of alcohol produces a violent reaction, and you become ill.(p.469)

tasted

• But I hardly *tasted* anything for two years and started in business for myself, founding a mattress factory which is today an important industrial enterprise in our city.(p.232)

• There was a bar, and what I *tasted* spelled sheer heaven.(p.328)

• I stopped off just to have one drink to see if it *tasted* the same on the way back to London, and that night I was carried back to bed again.(p.522)

tasting

• *Tasting* the best of burgundy at a famous restaurant one night, landed me passed out on a park bench in the public square.(p.405)

taught

• Experience has *taught* us that these are matters about which, for our purpose, we need not be worried.(p.50)

• The times in which I grew up (the Prohibition era immortalized by Scott Fitzgerald and John Held Jr.) had *taught* me to be gay with the gayest; my own inner urges led me to outdo them all.(p.225)

• My church *taught* that.(p.236)

• I enrolled in a correspondence school which *taught* nothing but accounting.(p.284)

• It *taught* me a valuable lesson.(p.294)

• Why he bothered with me as long as he did I shall never know, for he knew there was no answer for me in medicine and he, like all doctors of his day, had been *taught* that the alcoholic was incurable and should be ignored.(p.307)

• It has *taught* me so many things.(p.325)

• A.A. *taught* me how not to drink.(p.416)

• And also, on the twenty-four hour plan, it *taught* me how to live.(p.416)

• Through going to meetings and listening, and occasionally speaking, through doing Twelve Step work, whereby in helping others you are both the teacher and the student, by making many wonderful A.A. friends, I have been *taught* all the things in life that are worth having.(p.416)

• "Knowledge is power," I'd always been *taught*.(p.435)

• A.A. and acceptance have *taught* me that there is a bit of good in the worst of us and a bit of bad in the best of us; that we are all children of God and we each have a right to be here.(p.449)

• I would rather talk about the good things A.A. has *taught* me; I feel that hitting on just a few sordid points should be sufficient to let those of you in institutions know where I came from.(p.459)

• Yes, I knew what the Serenity Prayer was – A.A. had *taught* me.(p.461)

• A.A. didn't teach me I was an alcoholic; rather it *taught* me that because I was an alcoholic my life had become unmanageable.(p.470)

• He has *taught* me that, in our new life, I am the most important person of all.(p.481)

• He has also *taught* me that I must help myself first; only then may I be able to help others.(p.481)

• They *taught* us a great deal about Twelve Step work too.(p.496)

• It has *taught* me that I can best keep my sobriety by sharing it out with others; that I must bring that sobriety to others who need it, in my own interest.(p.524)

• It has *taught* me that success and failure are never final, and that neither count for very much in the final assessment of any man who has done his best.(p.525)

• And I am sure they would be right as far as they go, but A.A. has *taught* me I am the result of the way I reacted to what happened to me as a child.(p.544)

• What is much more important to me, A.A. has *taught* me that through this simple program I may experience a change in this reaction pattern that will indeed allow me to "match calamity with serenity."(p.544)

• One of the truly great things A.A. has *taught* me is that reality too has two sides; I had only known the grim side before the program, but now I had a chance to learn about the pleasant side as well.(p.550)

• A.A. *taught* me that willingness to believe was enough for a beginning.(p.550)

• A.A. has *taught* me that I will have peace of mind in exact proportion to the peace of mind I bring into the lives of other people, and it has *taught* me the true meaning of the admonition "happy are ye who know these things and do them."(p.551)

• A.A. *TAUGHT* HIM TO HANDLE SOBRIETY(p.554)

• But above all, it *taught* me how to handle sobriety.(p.559)

• We are *taught* to differentiate between our wants (which are never satisfied) and our needs (which are always provided for).(p.560)

• Our A.A. experience has *taught* us that:(p.565)

tavern

• I spent the time in a nearby *tavern*, was loaded on the ship, went to sleep before take-off, and the next thing I knew someone was shaking me and telling me we were over San Diego.(p.428)

taverns

• That night we drink beer at *taverns*.(p.474)

tax-free

• I accepted a big *tax-free* income from the family, but I didn't like it when they told me how to live.(p.405)

taxi

• I found a job; then lost it as the result of a brawl with a *taxi* driver.(p.4)

• The bill collectors, the sheriffs, the angry *taxi* drivers, the policemen, the bums, the pals, and even the ladies they sometimes brought home – our husbands thought we were so inhospitable.(p.106)

• When I got home I had to give him a check for the *taxi* fare.(p.205)

taxicab

• I have a shadowy recollection of being in an airplane bound for New York, and of finding a friendly *taxicab* driver at the landing field instead of my wife.(p.41)

• I don't remember whether I went by streetcar, whether I walked or went in a *taxicab*.(p.492)

taxis

• I was living in constant fear that I would get caught while driving a car, so I used *taxis* part of the time.(p.375)

taxpayer

• I was father, husband, *taxpayer*, home owner.(p.432)

TB

• I was suffering from an actual disease that had a name and symptoms like diabetes or cancer or *TB* -- and a disease was respectable, not a moral stigma!(p.227)

tea

• I was a very young married man, having his whiskey in the cupboard over the sink, and when I helped my wife with the dishes at night I would take a cup of *tea* and spike it with whiskey.(p.196)

• I went to several Village bars, and drank cokes or *tea*.(p.414)

teach

• So I set out to get drunk deliberately, just to *teach* her what she was missing.(p.293)

• A.A. didn't *teach* me I was an alcoholic; rather it taught me that because I was an alcoholic my life had become unmanageable.(p.470)

• It continues to try to *teach* me the real charity, the charity that gives time and good will and service, and not just money.(p.525)

• I have been appointed to the faculty of my old school, to *teach* in my new field.(p.541)

• "A.A. does not *teach* us how to handle our drinking," he said.(p.554)

teacher

• Through going to meetings and listening, and occasionally speaking, through doing Twelve Step work, whereby in helping others you are both the *teacher* and the student, by making many wonderful A.A. friends, I have been taught all the things in life that are worth having.(p.416)

• I was a deacon and a Sunday-school *teacher*.(p.418)

• He is my best *teacher*; without him, I am sure I would never have made the progress I have.(p.481)

• I become a *teacher* in a boys' school.(p.500)

• I left this home town, then, after I had made a public spectacle of myself in the presence of a revered *teacher* whose favorite pupil I had been.(p.539)

teachers

• The differences between my father and my sisters, who were school *teachers*, made an excellent environment for the type of child I was – that is, slick and cute enough to take advantage of any adult quarrel.(p.210)

• Not far from where I lived they built a new technical high school and one of the *teachers* sold me on the idea that I needed a little mechanical drawing if I were going to be a good toolmaker.(p.211)

teaches

• "It *teaches* us how to handle sobriety."(p.554)

teaching

• His moral *teaching* – most excellent.(p.11)

teachings

• As these words are written at fifty-three years of age, with over nine years of A.A. behind me, with all its wonderful *teachings*, I haven't the slightest doubt about being an alcoholic.(p.356)

• I've had more problems but, thank God, I have had the *teachings* of A.A. with which to face them.(p.367)

team

• When I was eighteen, at the end of high school, the high school *team* had a banquet at a well-known roadhouse outside of Akron.(p.194)

• There was the physical aspect; to be the youngest and the runt of the brood of children, to have to wear glasses very early and so to be teased, to be bookish and bored in school because the captain of the football *team* could not translate Virgil and yet was the school god while you, you, you little shrimp, were the school egghead, junior size and an early model.(p.533)

• So did the waterboy on the high school football ***team*** attempt to revenge himself on the big brother who was the star quarterback; for I was the waterboy and my brother was the star quarterback, innocent of everything except the fact that he was a star quarterback.(p.537)

teamed

• I ***teamed*** up with a cute little blonde with whom I was working at the office, and for about a year we were inseparable.(p.425)

teams

• In sports I made the track and tennis ***teams;*** I got along well with the other boys and had a fairly large circle of acquaintances but no intimate friends.(p.240)

tearing

• I did not know that I had no power over alcohol, that I, alone and unaided, could not stop; that I was on a downgrade, ***tearing*** along at full speed with all my brakes gone, and that the end would be a total smash-up, death or insanity.(p.408)

tears

• We cannot subscribe to the belief that this life is a vale of ***tears,*** though it once was just that for many of us.(p.133)

• We can share in the laughter and ***tears*** of our many friends, and most important, we can share our A.A. way of life and are given a daily opportunity to help others.(p.249)

• And Jim G. had such a wonderful sense of humor, and when he came I was in ***tears,*** and I told him, "I want to do this, but I can't.(p.269)

• He was close to ***tears*** in describing his boredom without an activity.(p.334)

• It was the first of many such experiences that became the only cause of harsh words, ***tears*** and heartaches in an otherwise truly beautiful marriage.(p.361)

• Time after time I would beg forgiveness on bended knees, with ***tears*** rolling down my cheeks, and promise I would never again drink too much.(p.362)

• A lot of the boys had ***tears*** in their eyes, they were so happy to be home.(p.513)

teased

• All the people involved in these flare-ups took it with remarkable grace, have ***teased*** me about it since, and have become good friends of mine.(p.416)

• There was the physical aspect; to be the youngest and the runt of the brood of children, to have to wear glasses very early and so to be ***teased,*** to be bookish and bored in school because the captain of the football team could not translate Virgil and yet was the school god while you, you, you little shrimp, were the school egghead, junior size and an early model.(p.533)

teaspoon

• The doctor prescribed brandy for the boy to help him through the night when he coughed, a ***teaspoon*** of brandy.(p.338)

technical

• Not far from where I lived they built a new ***technical*** high school and one of the teachers sold me on the idea that I needed a little mechanical drawing if I were going to be a good toolmaker.(p.211)

• After I was on the drafting board about two years I decided I wanted a ***technical*** education.(p.211)

technique

• I was now forming an entirely new drinking ***technique.***(p.233)

• Then he told me there was a handful of people in Akron and New York who had worked out a ***technique*** for arresting their alcoholism.(p.308)

• There is really nothing to dressing with chains and shackles on, once you learn the ***technique*** of pulling inside-out pants through the shackles.(p.460)

• The Episcopal magazine, The Living Church, observes editorially: "The basis of the ***technique*** of Alcoholics Anonymous is the truly Christian principle that a man cannot help himself except by helping others.(p.574)

techniques

• Instead of wanting to escape some perplexing problem, we experience a thrill of challenge in the opportunity it affords for another application of A.A. ***techniques,*** and we find ourselves tackling it with surprising vigor.(p.311)

tedious

• Sometimes this was a ***tedious*** process; we hope no one else will be prejudiced for as long as some of us were.(p.48)

• Routine jobs bored me, but I would take on the toughest one I could find, work day and night until I had it under control; then it would become ***tedious*** and I'd lose all interest in it.(p.243)

teen-aged

• Alateen, for ***teen-aged*** children of alcoholics, is a part of Al-Anon.(p.121)

teen-ager's

• A ***TEEN-AGER'S*** DECISION(p.353)

teens

• Seven percent of the A.A.'s surveyed are less than 30 years of age -- among them, many in their ***teens.***(p.xxii)

• But I can remember, in my ***teens,*** that there were a few characters who caused the village heads to nod pityingly and sometimes in anger as they paused to say, "That sot, Henri" and "Ce pauvre Jules," who drank too much.(p.230)

• Had first drink in young ***teens,*** but was scared of my father.(p.474)

• In my late ***teens*** I became aware of emotions I'd not counted on; restlessness, anxiety, fear and insecurity.(p.545)

'teens

• I had been brought up to believe this, and I had shown during my ***'teens*** considerable enterprise and imagination about earning money.(p.275)

teetering

• As might have been predicted, my ***teetering*** tower of worldly success collapsed.(p.437)

teeth

• Nevertheless, with a person we dislike, we take the bit in our ***teeth.***(p.77)

• Cold chills started chasing up and down my spine; my ***teeth*** were chattering; my hands were shaking so I tucked them under me to keep them from flying away.(p.222)

• I walked away from that girl grinding my ***teeth*** and cursing under my breath.(p.322)

• I fell down and knocked out my front ***teeth.***(p.390)

• X-rays showed that a couple of ***teeth*** had to come out.(p.465)

• On the day set for the extractions, on my way to the dentist's I felt a little nervous, so I had a couple of drinks, and after the ***teeth*** were out I was very nervous, so I had a few more.(p.466)

• Some of us always remember our big mouths when it comes to a drink, but somewhere along the line, we seem to have forgotten about taking care of our ***teeth.***(p.479)

teetotaler

• Whether you are a hard drinker, a moderated drinker or a ***teetotaler,*** you may have some pretty strong opinions, perhaps prejudices.(p.139)

teetotallers

• I wanted to live, not in a desert, but in a normal world; and my idea of a normal world was among people who drank -- ***teetotallers*** were not included.(p.227)

telegram

• Their ***telegram*** was kind and nice.(p.401)

telegrams

• I tried to contact the boys in New York, but ***telegrams*** bounced right back and when I finally got Hank on the telephone he fired me right then.(p.247)

telephone

• One day I walked into a cafe to ***telephone.***(p.6)

• My musing was interrupted by the ***telephone.***(p.8)

• Your ***telephone*** may jangle at any time of the day or night.(p.97)

• When your husband is bad, you become a trembling recluse, wishing the ***telephone*** had never been invented.(p.115)

• If there is no Al-Anon listing in your local ***telephone*** book, you may obtain further information on Al-Anon Family Groups by writing to its World Service Office: Box 182, Madison Square Station, New York, NY 10159.(p.121)

• I had to look in the ***telephone*** book later to find out who these people were.(p.196)

• I remembered going through what my sister assured me was my nightly procedure of trying to find Willie Seabrook's name in the ***telephone*** book.(p.224)

• I tried to contact the boys in New York, but telegrams bounced right back and when I finally got Hank on the ***telephone*** he fired me right then.(p.247)

• I screamed on the ***telephone*** for my mother to get up there; something was going to happen; I didn't know what, but if she didn't get there quick, I'd split wide open.(p.338)

• I remember finding myself in the middle of the night in the doctors' parking lot at the hospital with one foot in the car and one foot on the ground, not knowing which was the lead foot; finding myself hanging up the ***telephone*** -- then realizing I had gotten out of bed, answered the phone, turned on the light, and carried on a conversation with a patient.(p.441)

• It was around noon, a day or two later, when the ***telephone*** rang and it was Ella.(p.494)

• If something does come along that sort of upsets me, instead of walking in and throwing a buck at the barman and asking for a drink, I walk into a ***telephone*** booth, drop a dime in the box, and call somebody who was so kind as to give me his name and ***telephone*** number to meet such an emergency.(p.511)

• In such places, A.A. can be located through the local ***telephone*** directory, newspaper office, or police station, or by contacting local priests or ministers.(p.575)

• These so-called intergroup associations are found under the listing "A.A." or "Alcoholics Anonymous" in ***telephone*** directories.(p.575)

telephoned

• Next morning I ***telephoned*** a friend in Montreal.(p.4)

• I had read and heard a little about A.A. and so, groping for the phone book, I found the A.A. number and with hope in my heart eagerly ***telephoned.***(p.363)

• On the day before Christmas I ***telephoned*** him and told him I was sober and asked him to come home.(p.467)

telephoning

• Handling customers, dealers, insurance people, dictation, ***telephoning,*** directing new employees, answering to superiors, and all the rest of it.(p.299)

television

• My opinions were quoted in Time and Newsweek with pictures, and I addressed the public by radio and ***television.***(p.435)

tell

• In the spring of 1940, John D. Rockefeller, Jr. gave a dinner for many of his friends to which he invited A.A. members to ***tell*** their stories.(p.xviii)

• Later, he requested the privilege of being allowed to ***tell*** his story to other patients here and with some misgiving, we consented.(p.xxv)

• They did not need to ***tell*** me.(p.7)

• No words can ***tell*** of the loneliness and despair I found in that bitter morass of self-pity.(p.8)

• I could almost hear the sound of the preacher's voice as I sat, on still Sundays, way over there on the hillside; there was that proffered temperance pledge I never signed; my grandfather's good natured contempt of some church folk and their doings; his insistence that the spheres really had their music; but his denial of the preacher's right to ***tell*** him how he must listen; his fearlessness as he spoke of these things just before he died; these recollections welled up from the past.(p.10)

• We shall ***tell*** you what we have done.(p.20)

• Once in a while he may ***tell*** the truth.(p.23)

• He begged the doctor to ***tell*** him the whole truth, and he got it.(p.26)

• Let us ***tell*** you the rest of the conversation our friend had with his doctor.(p.27)

• We asked him to ***tell*** us exactly how it happened.(p.36)

• Some of you are thinking: "Yes, what you ***tell*** us is true, but it doesn't fully apply.(p.38)

• Let him ***tell*** you about it: "I was much impressed with what you fellows said about alcoholism, and I frankly did not believe it would be possible for me to drink again.(p.40)

• Leaving aside the drink question, they ***tell*** why living was so unsatisfactory.(p.51)

• Students of ancient history ***tell*** us that the intellect of men in those days was equal to the best of today.(p.51)

• Hence we are at pains to ***tell*** why we think our present faith is reasonable, why we think it more sane and logical to believe than not to believe, why we say our former thinking was soft and mushy when we threw up our hands in doubt and said, "We don't know."(p.53)

• We had seen spiritual release, but liked to ***tell*** ourselves it wasn't true.(p.55)

• Some people ***tell*** us so.(p.70)

• Such parts of our story we ***tell*** to someone who will understand, yet be unaffected.(p.74)

• Simply we ***tell*** him that we will never get over drinking until we have done our utmost to straighten out the past.(p.77)

• We are there to sweep off our side of the street realizing that nothing worth while can be accomplished until we do so, never trying to ***tell*** him what he should do.(p.77)

• If we are sure our wife does not know, should we ***tell*** her?(p.81)

• If she knows in a general way that we have been

wild, should we ***tell*** her in detail?(p.81)
• Neither should the family hysterically plead with him to do anything, nor should they ***tell*** him much about you.(p.90)
• Usually the family should not try to ***tell*** your story.(p.91)
• Let the doctor, if he will, ***tell*** him he has something in the way of a solution.(p.91)
• ***Tell*** him enough about your drinking habits, symptoms, and experiences to encourage him to speak of himself.(p.91)
• If his mood is light, ***tell*** him humorous stories of your escapades.(p.91)
• Get him to ***tell*** some of his.(p.91)
• ***Tell*** him how baffled you were, how you finally learned that you were sick.(p.92)
• If he sticks to the ideas that he can still control his drinking, ***tell*** him that possibly he can -- if he is not too alcoholic.(p.92)
• Doctors are rightly loath to ***tell*** alcoholic patients the whole story unless it will serve some good purpose.(p.92)
• If his own doctor is willing to ***tell*** him that he is alcoholic, so much the better.(p.92)
• ***Tell*** him exactly what happened to you.(p.93)
• ***Tell*** him you once felt as he does, but you doubt whether you would have made much progress had you not taken action.(p.94)
• On your first visit ***tell*** him about the Fellowship of Alcoholics Anonymous.(p.94)
• ***Tell*** him that if he wants to get well you will do anything to help.(p.95)
• Let him know you are available if he wishes to make a decision and ***tell*** his story, but do not insist upon it if he prefers to consult someone else.(p.96)
• If you have been successful in solving your own domestic problems, ***tell*** the newcomer's family how that was accomplished.(p.100)
• Our next thought is that you should never ***tell*** him what he must do about his drinking.(p.111)
• He will ***tell*** you he is misunderstood.(p.111)
• ***Tell*** him you have been worried, though perhaps needlessly.(p.112)
• Show him your copy of this book and ***tell*** him what you have found out about alcoholism.(p.112)
• ***Tell*** him some of the interesting stories you have read.(p.112)
• A good doctor or psychiatrist can ***tell*** you whether these complications are serious.(p.114)
• You do not know what to ***tell*** the children.(p.115)
• Frequently, you have felt obliged to ***tell*** your husband's employer and his friends that he was sick, when as a matter of fact he was tight.(p.115)
• Suppose we ***tell*** you some of the obstacles a family will meet; suppose we suggest how they may be avoided -- even converted to good use for others.(p.123)
• He may ***tell*** mother, who has been religious all her life, that she doesn't know what it's all about, and that she had better get his brand of spirituality while there is yet time.(p.128)
• But let him ***tell*** you:(p.136)
• I still expected a plea for clemency, but these words came through the receiver: "I just wanted to ***tell*** you Paul jumped from a hotel window in Hartford last Saturday.(p.136)
• We hope the doctor will ***tell*** the patient the truth about his condition, whatever that happens to be.(p.144)
• When the man is presented with this volume it is best that no one ***tell*** him he must abide by its suggestions.(p.144)
• In this connection, can you remain undisturbed if the man proceeds to ***tell*** you shocking things?(p.145)
• If he is, and is still trying to recover, he will ***tell*** you about it even if it means the loss of his job.(p.146)
• One morning he took the bull by the horns and set out to ***tell*** those he feared what his trouble had been.(p.156)
• From what you ***tell*** me, I know more than ever I can't stop."(p.157)
• Our friend proceeded to ***tell*** him.(p.163)
• Dr. Bob and the twelve men and women who here ***tell*** their stories were among the early members of A.A.'s first groups.(p.169)
• It then occurred to me that after one was all smelled up with beer nobody could ***tell*** what had been drunk, so I began to fortify my beer with straight alcohol.(p.178)
• I thought to myself, "Well, she is going to ***tell*** me this is the end," and I certainly couldn't blame her and did not intend to try to justify myself.(p.184)
• That wasn't so bad, to ***tell*** it to another drunk.(p.185)
• Then she told me that these two drunks she had been talking to had a plan whereby they thought they could quit drinking, and part of that plan was that they ***tell*** it to another drunk.(p.185)
• Bill was very, very grateful that he had been released from this terrible thing and he had given God the credit for having done it, and he's so grateful about it he wants to ***tell*** other people about it.(p.191)
• We shook hands, and he hung onto my hand for a moment and said, "***Tell*** you what I'll do for old times sake.(p.201)
• The man turned out to be Bill D., a very early member of A.A., and I couldn't ***tell*** you a word of what he said.(p.208)
• She had a hairdresser who used to ***tell*** her about a brother-in-law who had been quite a drinker and about some doctor in Akron who had straightened him out.(p.216)
• My wife didn't ***tell*** me this, but one Sunday afternoon when Mary was trying to get the cobwebs out of my mind, Clarence and his sister-in-law, the hairdresser, called at the house.(p.216)
• I do not recollect the specific conversation that went on but I believe I did challenge Bill to ***tell*** me something about A.A. and I do recall one other thing: I wanted to know what this was that worked so many wonders, and hanging over the mantel was a picture of Gethsemane and Bill pointed to it and said, "There it is," which didn't make much sense to me.(p.216)
• It wasn't very long until my doctor friend sent me to ***tell*** another alcoholic what my experience had been.(p.237)
• As part of this promotion, they sent me to their national convention in Atlantic City to ***tell*** the big wheels how I'd done it.(p.243)
• When I started to ***tell*** the boys how we did it in New York and all about the spiritual part of the program, I found they would not believe me unless I was practicing what I preached.(p.249)
• I have stood listening to street-corner preachers ***tell*** how they beat the game.(p.256)
• He introduced himself and began to ***tell*** me about a bunch of some sixty former drinkers and drunkards who met once a week, and he invited me to go with him to the next meeting.(p.257)
• And Russ didn't ***tell*** me he'd stop drinking, and he certainly didn't stop.(p.262)
• He said, "***Tell*** Mommy I still love her."(p.263)
• As many times as he would ***tell*** me that, I still believed him.(p.263)
• He said, "I think this will ***tell*** you more.(p.268)
• I didn't know what they were going to do because he didn't ***tell*** us much.(p.269)
• They told Annabelle to take me under her wing, and I shall never forget how she sort of curled up her nose and said, "They ***tell*** me you drink too."(p.269)
• I have to ***tell*** myself, "Other things are progressing and A.A. must too."(p.272)
• And, anyhow, if I went on for ten or a hundred times as long I couldn't even begin to ***tell*** you all that A.A. has meant to me.(p.274)
• Do I have to ***tell*** you who gained the most out of all this?(p.283)
• It would be wonderful were I able to ***tell*** you that my confidence in God and my application of the Twelve Steps to my daily living have utterly banished fear.(p.284)
• I could not wait to ***tell*** him that I wanted help, that if these men in Akron had anything I wanted it, and would do anything to get it.(p.289)
• Few doctors will ***tell*** a hopeless patient that there is no answer for him or for her.(p.307)
• This man could ***tell*** me more.(p.308)
• The seventeen who now ***tell*** their experiences answer that question.(p.315)
• Once I did have a slip -- tried drinking again -- but the A.A.'s ***tell*** me not to worry about yesterday, because nobody can change it, and not to worry about tomorrow, because it hasn't come yet.(p.320)
• He did not know it was A.A., and it was useless to ***tell*** him, for he doesn't have our disease.(p.334)
• After a few meetings I decided to drive to Florida unannounced to see my wife and ***tell*** her about my new found friends and association.(p.364)
• For the next couple of hours a terrible battle went on between the good gremlins and the bad ones, one faction urging me to ***tell*** the truth, the other telling me to sit tight and say nothing.(p.366)
• When I was called upon for a few words I had to ***tell*** my friends that I wasn't one year old in A.A. that evening but only a "nine month baby."(p.366)
• I wish I could ***tell*** you how and why A.A. works, but I don't know.(p.384)
• He even had the people come out, and ***tell*** me what kind of room I was going to have, and that he could come and see me, and that the dog could come and see me.(p.389)
• My husband couldn't ***tell*** whether I wanted to do something about my drinking.(p.391)
• I wish I could ***tell*** you all that A.A. has done for me, all that I think and feel about A.A., but it's something that I have experienced and have never been able to put into words.(p.394)
• With ten years of A.A. behind me, I was able to ***tell*** him that I'd have been alcoholic, no matter what; that I had been a sick person, unfit for marriage.(p.403)
• I could not ***tell*** them.(p.406)
• I must drink less, I would ***tell*** myself.(p.408)
• It was I who had to ***tell*** the bank, after a certain time, to refuse all further deposits.(p.409)
• In my cups I used to ***tell*** them off, giving them lengthy advice on how to lead the right life.(p.410)
• I, who had feared questions, now began trying to interrupt and ***tell*** my story.(p.414)
• I could ***tell*** him a lot of reasons why I am here in an alky ward at the age of twenty.(p.423)
• I was, so far as anybody could ***tell***, quite a lad.(p.432)
• You ***tell*** that dumb cat-and-dog doctor he's not a Beverly Hills psychiatrist.(p.440)
• The neurologist in charge of my case didn't think to ask me whether I drank, and I didn't think to ***tell*** him.(p.444)
• But, by the look on the psychiatrist's face, I could ***tell*** that it would really make him happy if I agreed.(p.446)
• I can ***tell*** her she ought not to think a certain way, but I certainly can't take away her right to feel however she does feel.(p.451)
• I never just sit and do nothing while waiting for Him to ***tell*** me what to do.(p.452)
• The thirteen stories in this group ***tell*** of alcoholism at its miserable worst.(p.455)
• Now sober for years, they ***tell*** us how they got well.(p.455)
• So the doctor said, "I really don't know too much about it, but they ***tell*** me it is a bunch of drunks who get together . . ."(p.469)
• As an indication of just how confused and mixed up I was, just as soon as I could I left the office and hurried around to ***tell*** other patients that I was getting better.(p.470)
• I think they sorry they ***tell*** me this.(p.475)
• ***Tell*** him I want to get away from bottle and misery.(p.475)
• To ***tell*** you a small part of what my mother's life must have been like: Three of her kids were in jail that year -- two sons and a daughter.(p.480)
• I can't begin to ***tell*** you of all the benefits I have derived from this new way of living.(p.481)
• I ***tell*** my wife I cannot stop drinking.(p.502)
• Am I willing to be honest with myself about myself and ***tell*** someone about myself, and am I willing to think of other people, of their needs instead of myself, in order to get rid of the drink problem?(p.503)
• I ***tell*** them of the peace, and that I believe in God.(p.505)
• I go to see a man I had been asked to visit and ***tell*** him my story.(p.505)
• I'll ***tell*** my wife what I am going to do.(p.506)
• I ***tell*** her quietly what I intend to do.(p.507)
• After hearing the first speaker I could ***tell*** myself that my own lot was rather mild.(p.509)
• I couldn't ***tell*** you how I got there.(p.510)
• I have my brilliant moments yet, but whenever the boys catch me at it they ***tell*** me so very plainly.(p.512)
• The Commanding Officer only spoke to me when he wanted to ***tell*** me exactly who I was and what I was and how little I counted in the scheme of things and how glad he would be if I went away.(p.520)
• I think the Commanding Officer was rather tired of this particular chicken coming back to roost so often because he very soon wrote in to the medical authorities to ***tell*** them that they had to get me into hospital, to be thoroughly examined for drinking.(p.520)
• My father was and still is a minister, and I was afraid that I might run into him, or that someone might ***tell*** him where I was, and I could still remember what he had done to me when I got drunk one Christmas when I was very young.(p.527)
• I thought if the cops did come to the hospital, the doctors would ***tell*** them I was crazy and didn't know what I was doing.(p.528)
• They ***tell*** me that I killed a man during that period, but I can't remember anything.(p.528)
• The medical profession would probably ***tell*** me I was conditioned for alcoholism by the things that happened to me in my childhood.(p.544)

teller

• In our personal stories you will find a wide variation in the way each ***teller*** approaches and conceives of the Power which is greater than himself.(p.50)

telling

• We had long talks when I would still her foreboding by ***telling*** her that men of genius conceived their best projects when drunk; that the most majestic constructions of philosophic thought were so derived.(p.2)

• This hope, however, was destroyed by the doctor's ***telling*** him that while his religious convictions were very good, in his case they did not spell the necessary vital spiritual experience.(p.27)

• ***Telling*** them what we are trying to do, we make no bones about our drinking; they usually know it anyway, whether we think so or not.(p.78)

• I remember ***telling*** them too that it was going to be awfully tough, because I did some other things, smoked cigarettes and played penny ante poker, sometimes bet on the horse races and they said, "Don't you think you're having more trouble with this drinking than with anything else at the present time?(p.190)

• Bill looked across at my wife, and said to her, "Henrietta, the Lord has been so wonderful to me, curing me of this terrible disease, that I just want to keep talking about it and ***telling*** people."(p.191)

• That sentence, "The Lord has been so wonderful to me, curing me of this terrible disease, that I just want to keep ***telling*** people about it," has been sort of a golden text for the A.A. program and for me.(p.191)

• I can remember ***telling*** the poor little soul that I could probably quit drinking if I wasn't married to her, and told her that, after all, I didn't like restraint!(p.199)

• And we stood there for twenty minutes, ***telling*** each other how much better we were, how much better we looked, how much better off we were financially, mentally, physically, morally, and in every way, shape and manner.(p.201)

• And I continued to drink, on and off then, until every dollar I had in the world was gone again and I was right back living at my sister's, getting my cigarettes by calling her grocer and ***telling*** him to put in a couple of cartons with her order, exactly as I had before I started to work at Max's.(p.202)

• In ***telling*** newcomers how to change their lives and attitudes, all of a sudden I found I was doing a little changing myself.(p.249)

• He spent two hours with me that night ***telling*** me his story.(p.290)

• I thought at times that he was ***telling*** my story!(p.290)

• For the next couple of hours a terrible battle went on between the good gremlins and the bad ones, one faction urging me to tell the truth, the other ***telling*** me to sit tight and say nothing.(p.366)

• To me this meant ***telling*** my associates that I had joined Alcoholics Anonymous; that I didn't know what was expected of me by A.A., but that whatever it was, it was the most important thing in life for me; that sobriety meant more to me than anything in this world.(p.382)

• The only thing I have really to offer you is my own story, ***telling*** you just what sort of a drunk I was.(p.384)

• Meanwhile the letters from home were ***telling*** about how much my folks wanted to make up to me for some of the things I'd missed.(p.427)

• I spent the time in a nearby tavern, was loaded on the ship, went to sleep before take-off, and the next thing I knew someone was shaking me and ***telling*** me we were over San Diego.(p.428)

• Then I remember him coming into my room one night with a friend, and ***telling*** me to get dressed -- we were going away.(p.466)

• He started ***telling*** me how much trouble he had, and I said to myself, "I wonder why this guy is ***telling*** me all his troubles.(p.494)

• About three months after that, my record reached home and I got a letter ***telling*** me I was retired from the Army, they put it very kindly, on medical grounds.(p.521)

tells

• He ***tells*** you he has decided to stop jay-walking for good, but in a few weeks he breaks both legs.(p.38)

• Science ***tells*** us so.(p.49)

• He is remorseful after serious drinking bouts and ***tells*** you he wants to stop.(p.109)

• She ***tells*** how A.A. works when the going is rough.(p.261)

• Russ said, "Mother, if this ***tells*** us how to do it, you'll have to read it."(p.268)

• Dr. Bob ***tells*** about keeping it simple and not to louse it up.(p.395)

• A young veteran ***tells*** how a few rough experiences pushed him into A.A. – and how he was therefore spared years of suffering.(p.422)

• This physician, the originator of A.A.'s first black group, but badly caught in the toils, ***tells*** of his release and of how freedom came as he worked among his own people.(p.483)

• She here ***tells*** how she was set free.(p.544)

temper

• Patience and good ***temper*** are most necessary.(p.111)

• We do talk about each other a great deal, but we almost invariably ***temper*** such talk by a spirit of love and tolerance.(p.125)

temperament

• Yes, we of agnostic ***temperament*** have had these thoughts and experiences.(p.46)

• An alcoholic of this ***temperament*** may be quick to use this chapter as a club over your head.(p.108)

• As the treatment progressed I began to get a picture of myself, of the ***temperament*** that had caused me so much trouble.(p.226)

• Federal Theatre in Texas gave me an administrative job which I held for a year, only because I worked hard and productively when I worked, and because my very tolerant chief ascribed my frequent lapses to a bohemian ***temperament***.(p.256)

temperance

• I could almost hear the sound of the preacher's voice as I sat, on still Sundays, way over there on the hillside; there was that proffered ***temperance*** pledge I never signed; my grandfather's good natured contempt of some church folk and their doings; his insistence that the spheres really had their music; but his denial of the preacher's right to tell him how he must listen; his fearlessness as he spoke of these things just before he died; these recollections welled up from the past.(p.10)

• Dr. W.W. Bauer, broadcasting under the auspices of The American Medical Association in 1946, over the NBC network, said, in part: "Alcoholics Anonymous are no crusaders; not a ***temperance*** society.(p.572)

temperate

• We believe, and so suggested a few years ago, that the action of alcohol on these chronic alcoholics is a manifestation of an allergy; that the phenomenon of craving is limited to this class and never occurs in the average ***temperate*** drinker.(p.xxvi)

• We would not even do the cause of ***temperate*** drinking any good, for not one drinker in a thousand likes to be told anything about alcohol by one who hates it.(p.103)

temporarily

• Even though your husband becomes unbearable and you have to leave him ***temporarily***, you should, if you can, go without rancor.(p.111)

• Some of us struggle with these people because we know that they are really very sick, but we also know that short of some miracle, we are not going to help them except ***temporarily***, and that they will inevitably get worse and worse until one of two things happens.(p.308)

• Living with fear and tension inevitably results in wanting to ease that tension, which alcohol seems to do ***temporarily***.(p.380)

• Frightened and shamed, I refused, and sobered up ***temporarily***.(p.411)

• ***Temporarily***, but not for long.(p.468)

temporary

• Nearly always, these antics indicate nothing more than ***temporary*** conditions.(p.141)

• With the alcoholic, they could only give ***temporary*** relief and in the last stages not even that.(p.307)

• But during a period of particular stress and strain about thirteen years ago, I resorted to alcohol in my home, alone, as a means of ***temporary*** release, as a means of getting a little extra sleep.(p.335)

• But this proved only a ***temporary*** setback.(p.517)

• Still another friend and ***temporary*** host received me at four in the morning from the charge of a policeman who had found me "going to bed" in a garage far from the last place I could remember having been, a fashionable bar and restaurant in the theatrical district of New York, to which I had repaired after my date for that evening, a charming lady of the theatre who had refused my company for obvious reasons.(p.538)

• I mentioned that this friend was my ***temporary*** host.(p.538)

temporizes

• If he ***temporizes*** and still thinks he can ever drink again, even beer, he might as well be discharged after the next bender which, if an alcoholic, he is almost certain to have.(p.142)

temptation

• Save for a few brief moments of ***temptation*** the thought of drink has never returned; and at such times a great revulsion has risen up in him.(p.57)

• We are not fighting it, neither are we avoiding ***temptation***.(p.85)

• In our belief any scheme of combating alcoholism which proposes to shield the sick man from ***temptation*** is doomed to failure.(p.101)

• We never, never try to arrange a man's life so as to shield him from ***temptation***.(p.120)

• He will appreciate knowing you are not bothering your head about him, that you are not suspicious nor are you trying to run his life so he will be shielded from ***temptation*** to drink.(p.146)

• I cannot see the cause of this ***temptation*** now.(p.507)

temptations

• "I'm doing a job I like and it's quiet where I live, practically no ***temptations***.(p.257)

tempted

• If ***tempted***, we recoil from it as from a hot flame.(p.84)

• Sometimes a new man is anxious to proceed at once, and you may be ***tempted*** to let him do so.(p.95)

• The slightest disposition on your part to guide his appointments or his affairs so he will not be ***tempted*** will be noticed.(p.120)

tempting

• To a person who has had experience with an alcoholic, this may seem like ***tempting*** Providence, but it isn't.(p.101)

ten

• My friends had dropped several million since ***ten*** o'clock -- so what?(p.4)

• In nine cases out of ***ten*** the unexpected happens.(p.78)

• We must remember that ***ten*** or twenty years of drunkenness would make a skeptic out of anyone.(p.83)

• This thought brings us to Step ***Ten***, which suggests we continue to take personal inventory and continue to set right any new mistakes as we go along.(p.84)

• I pointed out that I had had nothing to drink whatever for three years, and this in the face of difficulties that would have made nine out of ***ten*** men drink their heads off.(p.138)

• When I had been in the hospital ***ten*** days, Sister Ignatia, who has played such a part in the development of A.A. in this area, stuck her head in the door one morning and announced, looking at me quizzically, that they might be able to make something human out of my face after all.(p.205)

• The next day, they called me in for an examination, and the doctor wouldn't let me continue working and pardoned me from the plant for ***ten*** days because he said my eye had been injured.(p.205)

• So I was barred from the plant for ***ten*** days, and during that ***ten*** day period I was drunk twice, showing how little control these restraints had on me.(p.205)

• For the next ***ten*** years I did just that.(p.225)

• With the war over, and back in Baltimore with the folks, there were several small jobs for three years and then I went to work soliciting as one of the first ***ten*** employees of a new national finance company.(p.242)

• No one in that company saw me again – ***ten*** days later I wired my resignation.(p.243)

• Bill and Hank had just taken over a small automobile polishing company and they offered me a job -- ***ten*** dollars a week and keep at Hank's house.(p.246)

• Then it was my turn – I ordered "Three beers," but this time it was different, I had a cash investment of thirty cents and, on a ***ten*** dollar a week salary, that's a big thing.(p.247)

• In the two succeeding years I held ***ten*** different jobs ranging from newspaper copy-desk and rewrite, to traffic director for an oil field equipment company.(p.255)

• My wife and family stood by me for ***ten*** weeks and then, quite justifiably, ejected me.(p.257)

• I managed to maintain myself with odd jobs, did ***ten*** weeks in a social rescue institution, and at length wound up in a second-hand bookstore in an adjacent town as manager.(p.257)

• And, anyhow, if I went on for ***ten*** or a hundred times as long I couldn't even begin to tell you all that A.A. has meant to me.(p.274)

• From that point on, I secured crocks of ***ten*** gallon capacity and really took quite an active interest in the manufacture of home brew.(p.297)

• The last day of my drinking career, I drank twenty-two of them between *ten* and twelve a.m. and I shall never know how many more followed them until I was poured into bed that night.(p.298)
• After holding good positions, making better than an average income for over *ten* years, I was in debt, had no clothes to speak of, no money, no friends, and no one any longer tolerating me but my wife.(p.301)
• The next three years saw me in sanitariums, once in a *ten* day coma, from which I very nearly did not recover, in and out of hospitals or confined at home with day and night nurses.(p.306)
• I could go on living and hurting *ten* years longer, or more."(p.333)
• I belong to more medical societies and honor societies than men *ten* to twenty years my senior.(p.345)
• This was about *ten* p.m., and the time here is important.(p.363)
• You will recall that I said the time that I got the idea out of a clear sky to call A.A. on a certain night was at about *ten*.(p.366)
• She said she cut this clipping from the paper at about *ten* on the same night, and at the same time as I called A.A. in Pittsburgh -- some 1300 miles away.(p.367)
• This didn't say we had to be in jail, *ten*, fifty, or one hundred times.(p.379)
• At this time, the price of booze in the bars was fifteen cents a shot and *ten* cents a beer.(p.397)
• Saying these sprees were limited to one a week (they were not), and saying that the average spree was *ten* of these drinks (sometimes more, sometimes less), we come up with the first boring statistic: two-fifty per week out of twelve dollars.(p.397)
• My first pay was *ten* dollars, pay for recruits at that time being twenty-one dollars per month.(p.398)
• But my board, room, and clothing were free, and I could spend the whole *ten* bucks on booze.(p.398)
• With *ten* years of A.A. behind me, I was able to tell him that I'd have been alcoholic, no matter what; that I had been a sick person, unfit for marriage.(p.403)
• But I got drunk that night and stayed drunk, getting increasingly worse until I found A.A. *ten* years later.(p.404)
• I got a job after school pumping gas and worked until *ten* or eleven at night.(p.423)
• To cut a long story short, I spent seven years and *ten* thousand dollars on my psychiatric adventure, and emerged in worse condition than ever.(p.434)
• In seven years the intervals between them decreased from eight months to *ten* days!(p.434)
• That's the stuff used when the oral surgeon puts the needle in your vein and says, "Count to *ten*," and before you get to two, you're asleep.(p.442)
• There, I received several soda crackers and water daily, and before I could have my third-day meal (again the only meal in *ten* days), I had to drink a glass of castor oil or mineral oil, depending on the cruelty of the person who was doing the dispensing.(p.459)
• *Ten* days of this treatment the first time knocked me from 200 pounds to 130, and I seldom stayed out of the hole long enough to gain back my weight.(p.460)
• Within about *ten* days I got locked up for being drunk and this same policeman was in the station house as I was being booked.(p.491)
• I guess I had five or *ten* dollars in my pocket.(p.491)
• I'd been home about a week or *ten* days when one of my friends asked if I could repair one of his electrical outlets.(p.493)
• It is *ten* o'clock of a Saturday night.(p.500)
• I remained there for about *ten* months, and then I was sent to a place called Wallkill, a so-called rehabilitation center.(p.509)
• I went along pretty well for the next *ten* months.(p.511)
• A former employer of mine said to me a little over *ten* years ago, "Pat, you seem to be one of those unfortunate people who at least once every six months must go out and roll in the gutter."(p.513)
• You hit the street about *ten* minutes to eight, and you walk around the block, God knows how many times, waiting for that joint to open.(p.514)
• I had replied, "Uncle, give the judge *ten* dollars, or I'll have to work it out on the county road."(p.539)
• There were debts totaling nearly *ten* thousand dollars to be paid off.(p.541)
• It seems only fitting that when I did finally fall in love it was with an alcoholic, and for the next *ten* years I progressed as rapidly as is humanly possible into what I believed to be hopeless alcoholism.(p.547)
• Like most other alcoholics I have known, I did quit drinking at various times -- once for *ten* months on my own and during other interludes when I was hospitalized.(p.554)
• So, when my liver had recovered after *ten* months, I resumed drinking.(p.557)
• *Ten* -- Alcoholics Anonymous has no opinion on outside issues; hence the A.A. name ought never be drawn into public controversy.(p.564)

ten-day
• After all, upon coming out of a week-long or *ten-day* drunk, it was hard enough to figure up just how much that one drunk cost, let alone trying to calculate the cost of approximately twenty-five years of active alcoholism.(p.396)
• Each *ten-day* period in the dark hole, I was fed bread and water daily, with one full meal on the third day only.(p.459)
• It paid for a *ten-day* binge which was the end of my drinking days.(p.540)
• I did not remember much of the *ten-day* binge.(p.540)
• I have not had a drink of anything alcoholic since that *ten-day* binge.(p.541)

ten-dollar
• (There was a time, for about three months, when I bought a *ten-dollar* wrist watch every pay day -- that is every two weeks.(p.532)

ten-thirty
• He gave my husband one and me one about *ten-thirty* on the eighth day of May in 1941.(p.267)

tend
• Perhaps he can still *tend* to business fairly well.(p.109)
• It was strictly a one man operation and I knew I had to *tend* to my knitting to make a go of it.(p.360)
• When we deal in feelings, we *tend* to come to know ourselves and each other much better.(p.451)

tended
• At night I *tended* bar.(p.426)

tendencies
• When this sort of thinking is fully established in an individual with alcoholic *tendencies*, he has probably placed himself beyond human aid, and unless locked up, may die or go permanently insane.(p.24)
• This means trouble, unless the family watches for these *tendencies* in each other and comes to a friendly agreement about them.(p.131)
• I had suppressed *tendencies* to overindulge and thus reveal my "moral weakness," because false pride was so dominant.(p.327)
• I displayed alcoholic *tendencies* actually from the age of fourteen, when I started to steal wine from the family jug, siphoning it off one drink at a time so it wouldn't be missed, not drinking it immediately, but saving it until about a pint was accumulated, so that I could get drunk.(p.397)

tendency
• This is a condition which, in ordinary life, would produce untold grief; there might be scandalous gossip, laughter at the expense of other people, and a *tendency* to take advantage of intimate information.(p.125)
• Many of us have noticed a *tendency* to eat sweets and have found this practice beneficial.(p.134)
• The parties waxed more liquid and hilarious as time went on, and eventually I discovered that a little shot of liquor now and then between beers had the *tendency* to put me in a whacky mood much quicker than having to down several quarts of beer to obtain the same effect.(p.298)

tender
• At the *tender* age of twenty-three, I got a divorce.(p.402)

tends
• Couples are occasionally dismayed to find that when drinking is stopped the man *tends* to be impotent.(p.134)

tenets
• Though he could not accept all the *tenets* of the Oxford Groups, he was convinced of the need for moral inventory, confession of personality defects, restitution to those harmed, helpfulness to others, and the necessity of belief in and dependence upon God.(p.xvi)

tennis
• In sports I made the track and *tennis* teams; I got along well with the other boys and had a fairly large circle of acquaintances but no intimate friends.(p.240)

tension
• He is under constant fear and *tension* -- that makes for more drinking.(p.73)
• Then that terrible *tension* which grips the home of every problem drinker will be lessened.(p.115)
• Living with fear and *tension* inevitably results in wanting to ease that *tension*, which alcohol seems to do temporarily.(p.380)
• "The nervous *tension* had piled up and just had to spill over."(p.433)

tensions
• Almost simultaneously, I discovered that cocktails in the late afternoon and highballs in the evening relieved the many *tensions* of the day.(p.277)
• We went out occasionally, and I would take a drink to ease the *tensions* of daily life.(p.370)
• Mentally, the fears and *tensions*, the complete change in attitude and outlook, bewildered me.(p.378)

tent
• We gave up our positions and off we roared on a motorcycle, the sidecar stuffed with *tent*, blankets, a change of clothes, and three huge volumes of a financial reference service.(p.2)

tentative
• I worked along until I had really big names in rubber on a *tentative* contract, and then I neglected to go through with it.(p.198)

tenth
• I could no longer gage my capacity and it might be the second or the *tenth* drink that would erase my consciousness.(p.306)
• It was a long four or five hour operation, a large surgical procedure, and she was on her ninth or *tenth* post-operative day.(p.350)
• I saw that my Village friends, all of whom had small jobs, were living happily on about a *tenth* of my sinecure.(p.409)

term
• My wife traveled with me, but with a baby coming I decided to settle in a large city where I got a job with a commission agent which is a polite *term* for a handbook operator.(p.251)
• Only through being beaten down by my own misery would I ever have accepted the *term* "alcoholic" as applied to myself.(p.436)
• The *term* was nearly over and we parted on fairly friendly terms.(p.518)

terminal
• And as her disease was reaching the *terminal* stages, she was screaming, "You hate me!(p.439)

terminated
• The remonstrances of my friends *terminated* in a row and I became a lone wolf.(p.3)

terms
• If what we have learned and felt and seen means anything at all, it means that all of us, whatever our race, creed, or color are the children of a living Creator with whom we may form a relationship upon simple and understandable *terms* as soon as we are willing and honest enough to try.(p.28)
• We found that God does not make too hard *terms* with those who seek Him.(p.46)
• Do not let any prejudice you may have against spiritual *terms* deter you from honestly asking yourself what they mean to you.(p.47)
• There is no use arousing any prejudice he may have against certain theological *terms* and conceptions about which he may already be confused.(p.93)
• If he owes you money you may wish to make *terms*.(p.145)
• I agreed with him and told him in no uncertain *terms* that I never broke my word in my life.(p.206)
• I told my doctor so in no uncertain *terms*.(p.227)
• Obviously I have overcome fear to a sufficient degree to think in *terms* of success in business.(p.284)
• He got half custody of our child, but later kept her during most of the school *terms*.(p.402)
• Today I think of life in *terms* of happiness, contentment, freedom from fear and despair, sane thinking, ability to face problems as they occur, the opportunity to help other alcoholics and to be decent.(p.430)
• Until I could accept my alcoholism, I could not stay sober; unless I accept life completely on life's *terms*, I cannot be happy.(p.449)
• So I'm better off if I don't give advice, don't figure I know what's best, and just accept life on life's *terms*, as it is today -- especially my own life, as it actually is.(p.450)
• The term was nearly over and we parted on fairly friendly *terms*.(p.518)
• The *terms* "spiritual experience" and "spiritual awakening" are used many times in this book which, upon careful reading, shows that the personality change sufficient to bring about recovery from alcoholism has manifested itself among us in many different forms.(p.569)

terrapin
• I learned how to hold a *terrapin* fork.(p.401)

terrible

• My brain raced uncontrollably and there was a ***terrible*** sense of impending calamity.(p.6)
• These observations would be academic and pointless if our friend never took the first drink, thereby setting the ***terrible*** cycle in motion.(p.23)
• Here was the ***terrible*** dilemma in which our friend found himself when he had the extraordinary experience which as we have already told you, made him a free man.(p.28)
• We have commenced to see their ***terrible*** destructiveness.(p.70)
• Keep it always in sight that we are dealing with that most ***terrible*** human emotion – jealousy.(p.82)
• Then that ***terrible*** tension which grips the home of every problem drinker will be lessened.(p.115)
• Afterward, his revulsion will be ***terrible***.(p.141)
• It is a most wonderful blessing to be relieved of the ***terrible*** curse with which I was afflicted.(p.180)
• Morning after morning I would awake sick and with ***terrible*** jitters, but there was always a flask of liquor sitting on the table beside my bed.(p.183)
• My case is so ***terrible*** that I'm scared to go out of this hospital at all.(p.188)
• Bill looked across at my wife, and said to her, "Henrietta, the Lord has been so wonderful to me, curing me of this ***terrible*** disease, that I just want to keep talking about it and telling people."(p.191)
• Bill was very, very grateful that he had been released from this ***terrible*** thing and he had given God the credit for having done it, and he's so grateful about it he wants to tell other people about it.(p.191)
• That sentence, "The Lord has been so wonderful to me, curing me of this ***terrible*** disease, that I just want to keep telling people about it," has been sort of a golden text for the A.A. program and for me.(p.191)
• I looked so ***terrible*** in the court that the judge suggested that I get a continuance and let me sign all the papers to go to a hospital and to a doctor.(p.204)
• I'm feeling ***terrible***."(p.208)
• I might have done ***terrible*** things, and I wouldn't even know it!(p.223)
• I have been on this program for three months and I feel ***terrible***."(p.348)
• It was a ***terrible*** blow at the time and I thought he was pretty much of a heel, but of course it was the finest thing he could have done for me under the circumstances.(p.357)
• I had done something ***terrible***!(p.364)
• For the next couple of hours a ***terrible*** battle went on between the good gremlins and the bad ones, one faction urging me to tell the truth, the other telling me to sit tight and say nothing.(p.366)
• They phoned my husband that I was in jail and in such ***terrible*** shape that they didn't know what I would do to myself; and they realized that jail was no place for me, but that he was to wait a while before he got me, because at the time they called him to come over for me I was beating a tin cup against the wall.(p.390)
• A fellow A.A., called Anne, who had helped me, went on a ***terrible*** bender.(p.414)
• The most ***terrible*** blow of my life befell me after I'd found sobriety through A.A.(p.437)
• Then a ***terrible*** thing happened.(p.478)
• Because as I sat on that bed, I knew that I was in a ***terrible*** spot and didn't know how to get out of it.(p.515)

terribly

• Most of the time therefore, I did not take the morning drink which I craved so badly, but instead would fill up on large doses of sedatives to quiet the jitters, which distressed me ***terribly***.(p.176)
• I used to get ***terribly*** upset when I saw my friends drink and knew I could not, but I schooled myself to believe that though I once had the same privilege, I had abused it so frightfully that it was withdrawn.(p.181)
• I was ***terribly*** impressed by this meeting and the quality of happiness these men displayed, despite their lack of material means.(p.291)
• That frightened me ***terribly***.(p.324)
• By hook or crook I usually managed to sober up before I reached home, but always "***terribly*** tired" from a "hard day's work," and just having to have one or two before dinner.(p.361)
• I had nowhere else to go, and I knew something was ***terribly*** wrong, and the reason had to lie within myself.(p.371)
• I know that I was ***terribly*** screwed up inside, but I came out much worse.(p.387)
• I was frightened – ***terribly*** frightened, and in about three days I was sober.(p.467)
• But on the other hand, I was ***terribly*** fortunate because that should have been a court martial offense and I should have been out on my ear.(p.520)
• I was ***terribly*** afraid that I was actually going mad, if I hadn't gone mad already.(p.522)
• I know there are some alcoholics who seem ***terribly***, ***terribly*** grown-up, but I think that they are trying to make themselves think they are grown-up, and the strain of their effort is what is causing them to drink -- a sense of inadequacy, a childish vanity to be the most popular, the most sought after, the mostest of the most.(p.535)

terrific

• We now see that when we began to drink deliberately, instead of casually, there was little serious or effective thought during the period of premeditation of what the ***terrific*** consequences might be.(p.37)
• Akron was really on the boom in those days, 1919-1920; expansion was ***terrific***.(p.198)
• I became a constant drinker with a ***terrific*** fight to control the amount of my consumption each day.(p.214)
• My experience in the hospital I considered to be ***terrific*** because Dr. Bob told me very quickly that medicine would have very little to do with it, outside of trying to restore my appetite for food.(p.217)
• There was one experience with Doc which made a ***terrific*** impression upon me.(p.218)
• However, here I probably took my first step towards my coming alcoholism by developing a ***terrific*** aversion to all churches and established religions.(p.240)
• Forced to detrain from an empty gondola on the other side of Chicago by a ***terrific*** rainstorm which drenched me to the skin, I hit the first factory building I saw for a job.(p.253)
• They'd sit out there and play hymns and I'd be lying in there with a ***terrific*** hangover.(p.265)
• One morning after a ***terrific*** drinking bout, I was in a little bar near our house, and I shook so that I was very much ashamed, because I was getting the shakes worse and worse.(p.266)
• I got into ***terrific*** trouble with my drinking.(p.322)
• By the time all this was over, I was really in a ***terrific*** state, and my father taking in things said, "Miss Esther is about to faint.(p.385)
• Five or six drinks and I was ***terrific***.(p.402)
• My second wife is a young A.A. member, too, and what a ***terrific*** adventure this is for us!(p.420)
• Had I tried honestly and sincerely to practice the Twelve Steps I would have seen from my continuous moral inventory that I was getting off the beam -- I would have found that there were some active resentments in my life, a ***terrific*** amount of self-pity.(p.471)

terrifically

• I believe every member of the Akron Group did come to see me, which impressed me ***terrifically***, not so much because of the stories they told, but because they would take the time to come and talk to me without even knowing who I was.(p.218)

terrified

• The alarming physical and mental symptoms, the deepening pall of remorse, depression and inferiority that settled down on our loved ones – these things ***terrified*** and distracted us.(p.106)
• ***Terrified***, I looked around.(p.222)
• My grandparents were strangers to me and I remember being lonely, and ***terrified*** and hurt.(p.545)

terrifying

• Letting go of everything at once was both painful and ***terrifying***.(p.311)

territory

• Then I started traveling, with the United States and Canada as my ***territory***, and with so much freedom and with an unlimited expense account, I was soon drinking every night and kidding myself that it was all part of the job.(p.287)
• The Army drinking alone covered a lot of ***territory***.(p.513)

terror

• Sometimes I stole from my wife's slender purse when the morning ***terror*** and madness were on me.(p.6)
• We have been ***terror*** stricken.(p.105)
• Momentarily we did – then would come oblivion and the awful awakening to face the hideous Four Horsemen – ***Terror***, Bewilderment, Frustration, Despair.(p.151)

test

• The ***test*** that it faced was this: Could these large numbers of erstwhile erratic alcoholics successfully meet and work together?(p.xviii)
• I was to ***test*** my thinking by the new God-consciousness within.(p.13)
• We subjected each relation to this ***test*** – was it selfish or not?(p.69)
• The faith and sincerity of both you and your husband will be put to the ***test***.(p.117)
• And with such good effect that the doctor agreed to a ***test*** among his patients and certain other alcoholics from a clinic which he attends.(p.163)
• I am examined for the draft and pass the physical ***test***.(p.499)

Testament

• I had a little ***Testament***, which was very small print.(p.268)

tested

• In each new place, I was the new kid – a skinny, shy kid -- to be ***tested*** and beaten up.(p.555)

testimony

• Convincing ***testimony*** must surely come from the medical men who have had experience with the sufferings of our members and have witnessed our return to health.(p.xxiii)
• If our ***testimony*** helps sweep away prejudice, enables you to think honestly, encourages you to search diligently within yourself, then, if you wish, you can join us on the Broad Highway.(p.55)

tests

• After nine days of ***tests*** at Mayo, I was put in the locked ward – of all places!(p.444)
• The closest I came to a psychiatrist during that time was an interne who came to take blood ***tests***.(p.492)

Tex.

• Oddly enough, the dentist who started A.A. in Amarillo, ***Tex.***, benevolently arranged my admission to dental college.(p.419)

Texas

• When I hit Houston, ***Texas***, I found employment in a large bookstore.(p.255)
• Federal Theatre in ***Texas*** gave me an administrative job which I held for a year, only because I worked hard and productively when I worked, and because my very tolerant chief ascribed my frequent lapses to a bohemian temperament.(p.256)
• A friend who knew I would soon be broke mounted guard over me when I left my job of writing the histories of ***Texas*** cities and put me aboard a bus for the town I had left almost five years before.(p.256)
• She still had her husband, her home, and a chance to help start A.A. in ***Texas***.(p.384)
• It only took a month to get a divorce in ***Texas***.(p.386)
• I had no feeling of security, and I knew that I had done a very stupid thing, so I went back to ***Texas*** and remarried my ex-husband.(p.386)
• That went on for about three years, and then we moved back to ***Texas*** again.(p.386)

text

• Because this book has become the basic ***text*** for our Society and has helped such large numbers of alcoholic men and women to recover, there exists a sentiment against any radical changes being made in it.(p.xi)
• Already," continues the early ***text***, "twos and threes and fives of us have sprung up in other communities."(p.xv)
• That sentence, "The Lord has been so wonderful to me, curing me of this terrible disease, that I just want to keep telling people about it," has been sort of a golden ***text*** for the A.A. program and for me.(p.191)

thank

• We ***thank*** God from the bottom of our heart that we know Him better.(p.75)
• He will work like the devil and ***thank*** you to his dying day.(p.149)
• ***Thank*** God I had no desire for a drink when he died.(p.272)
• For all of these blessings, I ***thank*** Him.(p.303)
• They sum it up like this: "We didn't wait to hit bottom because, ***thank*** God, we could see the bottom.(p.315)
• ***Thank*** God I knew of A.A., so I called.(p.355)
• My business reputation had reached from Vermont to Pennsylvania, but, ***thank*** goodness, my drinking reputation had not.(p.361)
• ***Thank*** God that in spite of my heavy drinking my mind was clear enough to make a decision then and there.(p.363)
• I've had more problems but, ***thank*** God, I have had the teachings of A.A. with which to face them.(p.367)
• And, believe me, I ***thank*** God that I found out about A.A. before I had to beat my brains out – before I had been hospitalized, jailed or lost a job.(p.367)
• When I hear the more rugged stories of alcoholics who became sicker than I did with this affliction, I

humbly *thank* God for showing me "the handwriting on the wall."(p.367)
• *Thank* God for A.A.!(p.452)
• I *thank* God I am to see him this month.(p.463)
• That was over seven years ago, and *thank* God and A.A., I haven't had a drink since.(p.473)
• Because, *thank* God, since I came into this program I haven't had any trouble.(p.516)
• Today, I *thank* my Higher Power for giving me another chance at life and A.A. and being able to try and help some other alcoholic.(p.529)
• *Thank* you, Mr. Policeman, wherever you are now.(p.538)
• *Thank* God that those days are gone.(p.540)

thanked
• His sanity returned and he *thanked* God.(p.154)
• I *thanked* him, pleaded business engagements and promised I'd go with him at some future date.(p.257)
• I have *thanked* God many times in the last sixteen years that that was just what he did not do!(p.278)
• She was doing fine, she was up and around, and that day her husband phoned me and said, "Doctor, thanks very much for curing my wife," and I *thanked* him for his felicitations, and he hung up.(p.350)
• Many times in the intervening years I have *thanked* God for that man, a man who had the courage to admit failure, a man who had the humility to confess that all the hard-won learning of his profession could not turn up the answer.(p.436)

thankful
• They should be *thankful* he is sober and able to be of this world once more.(p.127)
• The drive was long and cold but he was *thankful* for the hot bricks which some thoughtful person had given him for his feet.(p.497)
• This to the end that our great blessings may never spoil us; that we shall forever live in *thankful* contemplation of Him who presides over us all.(p.568)

thanks
• *Thanks* for the information."(p.39)
• She was doing fine, she was up and around, and that day her husband phoned me and said, "Doctor, *thanks* very much for curing my wife," and I thanked him for his felicitations, and he hung up.(p.350)
• I am not even there, and if I was there the only thing I could do would be to give her moral support, and yet he *thanks* me for curing his wife."(p.350)

theater
• Many alcoholics have learned they can bring their bottle to a cheap movie *theater* and drink, sleep, wake up and drink again in the darkness.(p.244)
• Imagine my surprise when I read in a page one "box" that I had been taken from the *theater* unconscious around noon that day, removed by ambulance to a hospital and stomach-pumped and then released.(p.244)

theatre
• Federal *Theatre* in Texas gave me an administrative job which I held for a year, only because I worked hard and productively when I worked, and because my very tolerant chief ascribed my frequent lapses to a bohemian temperament.(p.256)
• Once this was in front of the Paramount *Theatre* in Times Square.(p.537)
• Still another friend and temporary host received me at four in the morning from the charge of a policeman who had found me "going to bed" in a garage far from the last place I could remember having been, a fashionable bar and restaurant in the theatrical district of New York, to which I had repaired after my date for that evening, a charming lady of the *theatre* who had refused my company for obvious reasons.(p.538)
• I stumbled agonizedly past the *theatre* where in years gone by a great star had played my play.(p.540)

theatrical
• Still another friend and temporary host received me at four in the morning from the charge of a policeman who had found me "going to bed" in a garage far from the last place I could remember having been, a fashionable bar and restaurant in the *theatrical* district of New York, to which I had repaired after my date for that evening, a charming lady of the theatre who had refused my company for obvious reasons.(p.538)

thee
• Many of us said to our Maker, as we understood Him: "God, I offer myself to *Thee* -- to build with me and to do with me as Thou wilt.(p.63)
• "How can I best serve *Thee* -- Thy will (not mine) be done."(p.85)

theirs
• My pattern of drinking became very different from *theirs*.(p.277)

themselves
• You may rely absolutely on anything they say about *themselves*.(p.xxiv)
• They believe in *themselves*, and still more in the Power which pulls chronic alcoholics back from the gates of death.(p.xxv)
• In nearly all cases, their ideals must be grounded in a power greater than *themselves*, if they are to re-create their lives.(p.xxvi)
• We think it no concern of ours what religious bodies our members identify *themselves* with as individuals.(p.28)
• By every form of self-deception and experimentation, they will try to prove *themselves* exceptions to the rule, therefore nonalcoholic.(p.31)
• Several of our crowd, men of thirty or less, had been drinking only a few years, but they found *themselves* as helpless as those who had been drinking twenty years.(p.33)
• They flatly declare that since they have come to believe in a Power greater than *themselves*, to take a certain attitude toward that Power, and to do certain simple things, there has been a revolutionary change in their way of living and thinking.(p.50)
• The electrons *themselves* seemed more intelligent than that.(p.54)
• Those who do not recover are people who cannot or will not completely give *themselves* to this simple program, usually men and women who are constitutionally incapable of being honest with *themselves*.(p.58)
• Time after time newcomers have tried to keep to *themselves* certain facts about their lives.(p.72)
• They only thought they had lost their egoism and fear; they only thought they had humbled *themselves*.(p.73)
• We feel that each family, in the light of their own circumstances, ought to decide for *themselves*.(p.103)
• Some of us veered from extreme to extreme, ever hoping that one day our loved ones would be *themselves* once more.(p.105)
• Next day they would be *themselves* again and we would forgive and try to forget.(p.106)
• And even if they did not love their families, how could they be so blind about *themselves*?(p.107)
• The wives and children of such men suffer horribly, but not more than the men *themselves*.(p.114)
• The family will be affected also, pleasantly at first, as they feel their money troubles are about to be solved, then not so pleasantly as they find *themselves* neglected.(p.126)
• Instead of developing new channels of activity for *themselves*, mother and children demand that he stay home and make up the deficiency.(p.131)
• Most of them give freely of *themselves*, that their fellows may enjoy sound minds and bodies.(p.133)
• Plenty of difficulties presented *themselves*.(p.156)
• It was transcended by the happiness they found in giving *themselves* for others.(p.159)
• When a few men in this city have found *themselves*, and have discovered the joy of helping others to face life again, there will be no stopping until everyone in that town has had his opportunity to recover -- if he can and will.(p.163)
• I was kind of shocked about anybody talking about *themselves* the way he did, and my impression was that the guy was a little "touched."(p.216)
• That is, it was sort of a mixed bunch of Oxford Groupers, who were interested in the alcoholic problem, and of alcoholics *themselves*.(p.218)
• My brilliant agnosticism vanished, and I saw for the first time that those who really believed, or at least honestly tried to find a Power greater than *themselves*, were much more composed and contented than I had ever been, and they seemed to have a degree of happiness which I had never known.(p.247)
• These men all drank on Saturday nights, and enjoyed *themselves*.(p.277)
• I have stopped tilting at windmills, and instead have tried to accomplish the little daily tasks, unimportant in *themselves*, but tasks that are an integral part of living fully.(p.295)
• Not only were they at peace with *themselves*, but they were getting a kick out of life such as one seldom encounters, except in the very young.(p.310)
• Philosophy, faith, a sense of humor (they could laugh at *themselves*), clear-cut objectives, appreciation -- and most especially appreciation and sympathetic understanding for their fellow man.(p.310)
• I also found out that all they wanted was to help me get sober and to stay sober *themselves*.(p.320)
• Like all alcoholics endeavoring to run away from *themselves* and their environment, I decided to go to New York.(p.358)
• But success brought increased social activities and I realized that many of my friends enjoyed a social drink with no apparent harm to *themselves* or others.(p.374)
• I don't know what I expected, but I most certainly didn't visualize a group of people talking about their drinking problems, making light of their personal tragedies and at the same time enjoying *themselves*.(p.378)
• All found *themselves* headed for the same destruction, and it seemed they could to nothing whatever to stop it.(p.455)
• Then, of course, there are always the wrinkled slacks, which have been slept in and are so dirty, they could walk away by *themselves*.(p.479)
• I know there are some alcoholics who seem terribly, terribly grown-up, but I think that they are trying to make *themselves* think they are grown-up, and the strain of their effort is what is causing them to drink -- a sense of inadequacy, a childish vanity to be the most popular, the most sought after, the mostest of the most.(p.535)
• Any two or three alcoholics gathered together for sobriety may call *themselves* an A.A. group, provided that, as a group, they have no other affiliation.(p.565)
• 7. -- The A.A. groups *themselves* ought to be fully supported by the voluntary contributions of their own members.(p.566)
• With few exceptions our members find that they have tapped an unsuspected inner resource which they presently identify with their own conception of a Power greater than *themselves*.(p.569)
• Dr. G. Kirby Collier, psychiatrist: "I have felt that A.A. is a group unto *themselves* and their best results can be had under their own guidance, as a result of their philosophy.(p.571)
• The A.A. plan is described by the members *themselves* as 'self-insurance.'(p.574)

theological
• We looked upon this world of warring individuals, warring *theological* systems, and inexplicable calamity, with deep skepticism.(p.46)
• There is no use arousing any prejudice he may have against certain *theological* terms and conceptions about which he may already be confused.(p.93)
• I don't think the boys were completely convinced of my personality change, for they fought shy of including my story in the book, so my only contribution to their literary efforts was my firm conviction, being still a *theological* rebel, that the word God should be qualified with the phrase "as we understand him" -- for that was the only way I could accept spirituality.(p.248)

theology
• At our weekly meeting I was a menace to serenity those first few months, for I took every opportunity to lambaste the "spiritual angle" as we called it, or anything else that had any tinge of *theology*.(p.246)

theories
• Nevertheless, the twentieth century readily accepts *theories* of all kinds, provided they are firmly grounded in fact.(p.48)
• We have numerous *theories*, for example, about electricity.(p.48)
• Actually, of course, I wanted someone to listen to me, because when I had a few martinis inside, I became the great author I longed to be; and the right listener was in for some pretty highflown *theories* of literature and of genius.(p.536)

theorizing
• We are not *theorizing*.(p.70)

theory
• Prior to his journey to Akron, the broker had worked hard with many alcoholics on the *theory* that only an alcoholic could help an alcoholic, but he had succeeded only in keeping sober himself.(p.xvi)
• The doctor's *theory* that we have an allergy to alcohol interests us.(p.xxiv)
• I had developed a *theory* that most people lost money in stocks through ignorance of markets.(p.2)
• When they talked of a God personal to me, who was love, superhuman strength and direction, I became irritated and my mind snapped shut against such a *theory*.(p.10)
• Is not our age characterized by the ease with which we discard old ideas for new, by the complete readiness with which we throw away the *theory* or gadget which does not work for something new which does?(p.52)
• Nor are we afraid of disclosing our alcoholism on the *theory* it may cause financial harm.(p.78)
• The spiritual life is not a *theory*.(p.83)
• Ask any woman who has sent her husband to distant places on the *theory* he would escape the alcohol problem.(p.101)
• I had always known that, in *theory*.(p.236)

therapeutic

• I think our profession must take appreciative cognizance of this great ***therapeutic*** weapon.(p.571)

• Any ***therapeutic*** or philosophic procedure which can prove a recovery rate of 50% to 60% must merit our consideration."(p.571)

therapy

• It was thought that no alcoholic man or woman could be excluded from our Society; that our leaders might serve but never govern; that each group was to be autonomous and there was to be no professional class of ***therapy***.(p.xix)

• Upon ***therapy*** for the alcoholic himself, we surely have no monopoly.(p.xxi)

• Historians may one day recognize Alcoholics Anonymous to have been a great venture in social pioneering which forged a new instrument for social action; a new ***therapy*** based on the kinship of common suffering; one having a vast potential for the myriad other ills of mankind."(p.573)

• This self-insurance has resulted in the restoration of physical, mental and spiritual health and self-respect to hundreds of men and women who would be hopelessly down and out without its unique but effective ***therapy***."(p.574)

thereafter

• Most of us have believed that if we remained sober for a long stretch, we could ***thereafter*** drink normally.(p.33)

• For years ***thereafter*** he was dogged by trouble and frustration.(p.56)

• I found in the fall of 1939, that I was not mentally impaired, so far as trial work was concerned, and ***thereafter*** took up where I had left off when I was about forty-five years old.(p.220)

• I confined drinking to weekends, and drank normally in college and for several years ***thereafter***.(p.287)

• Shortly ***thereafter***, aided by the Depression, I found that I had a great deal of spare time and that a little drink in the morning helped.(p.287)

• Shortly ***thereafter***, I was selected, with eight other inmates out of the 10,000 in the state's prisons at that time, to attend a school designed to take former "management problems" like me and convert them into paracounselors.(p.462)

thereby

• All changes made over the years in the Big Book (A.A. members' fond nickname for this volume) have had the same purpose: to represent the current membership of Alcoholics Anonymous more accurately, and ***thereby*** to reach more alcoholics.(p.xii)

• These observations would be academic and pointless if our friend never took the first drink, ***thereby*** setting the terrible cycle in motion.(p.23)

therefore

• ***Therefore***, the first portion of this volume, describing the A.A. recovery program, has been left untouched in the course of revisions made for both the second and the third editions.(p.xi)

• There was, ***therefore***, a sense of real satisfaction when I was asked to contribute a few words on a subject which is covered in such masterly detail in these pages.(p.xxv)

• ***Therefore***, the main problem of the alcoholic centers in his mind, rather than in his body.(p.23)

• When, ***therefore***, we were approached by those in whom the problem had been solved, there was nothing left for us but to pick up the simple kit of spiritual tools laid at our feet.(p.25)

• ***Therefore***, it is not surprising that our drinking careers have been characterized by countless vain attempts to prove we could drink like other people.(p.30)

• By every form of self-deception and experimentation, they will try to prove themselves exceptions to the rule, ***therefore*** nonalcoholic.(p.31)

• I reasoned I was not so far advanced as most of you fellows, that I had been usually successful in licking my other personal problems, and that I would ***therefore*** be successful where you men failed.(p.40)

• When, ***therefore***, we speak to you of God, we mean your own conception of God.(p.47)

• ***Therefore***, we started upon a personal inventory.(p.64)

• We remembered always that our sex powers were God-given and ***therefore*** good, neither to be used lightly or selfishly nor to be despised and loathed.(p.69)

• ***Therefore***, we are not to be the hasty and foolish martyr who would needlessly sacrifice others to save himself from the alcoholic pit.(p.79)

• ***Therefore***, ask yourself on each occasion, "Have I any good social, business, or personal reason for going to this place?(p.101)

• ***Therefore***, you probably need fresh interests and a great cause to live for as much as your husband.(p.119)

• ***Therefore*** it would make no great difference, even if I should do some drinking.(p.175)

• Most of the time ***therefore***, I did not take the morning drink which I craved so badly, but instead would fill up on large doses of sedatives to quiet the jitters, which distressed me terribly.(p.176)

• He kept the faith; ***therefore***, he and countless others found a new life.(p.182)

• It was ***therefore*** not extraordinary that I should shy away from any serious thought of marriage for a great many years after joining A.A.(p.286)

• ***Therefore***, these seventeen A.A.'s, and hundreds of thousands like them, have been saved years of infinite suffering.(p.315)

• A young veteran tells how a few rough experiences pushed him into A.A. -- and how he was ***therefore*** spared years of suffering.(p.422)

• ***Therefore***, every pill was medically indicated at the time it was taken.(p.443)

• ***Therefore***, it will be the hardest to work on.(p.482)

• Things weren't going as I thought they should, for my greater enjoyment, comfort and fame; ***therefore***, if the universe wouldn't play my way, I wouldn't play at all.(p.531)

• ***Therefore***, no society of men and women ever had more urgent need for continuous effectiveness and permanent unity.(p.563)

• We think, ***therefore***, that any considerable property of genuine use to A.A. should be separately incorporated and managed, thus dividing the material from the spiritual.(p.565)

thereupon

• I told him I'd take the medicine and I would take it, but I hadn't told him when, and ***thereupon*** I got away with the third drink.(p.206)

thick

• Again I spent my bankroll, by no means as ***thick*** as the one I had when I first saw the skyline of Gotham.(p.252)

thickened

• It ***thickened***, ever becoming blacker.(p.151)

thin

• He was on ***thin*** ice.(p.154)

• But for some reason -- she just didn't know why -- she just had to hold onto that clipping, with its ***thin*** hope.(p.367)

thing

• The very ***thing*** -- an oasis!(p.9)

• We commenced to make many fast friends and a fellowship has grown up among us of which it is a wonderful ***thing*** to feel a part.(p.15)

• Our hope is that many alcoholic men and women, desperately in need, will see these pages, and we believe that it is only by fully disclosing ourselves and our problems that they will be persuaded to say, "Yes, I am one of them too; I must have this ***thing***."(p.29)

• Physicians who are familiar with alcoholism agree there is no such ***thing*** as making a normal drinker out of an alcoholic.(p.31)

• Potential female alcoholics often turn into the real ***thing*** and are gone beyond recall in a few years.(p.33)

• Could we still say the whole ***thing*** was nothing but a mass of electrons, created out of nothing, meaning nothing, whirling on to a destiny of nothingness?(p.54)

• We did exactly the same ***thing*** with our lives.(p.64)

• The first ***thing*** apparent was that this world and its people were often quite wrong.(p.65)

• To sum up about sex: We earnestly pray for the right ideal, for guidance in each questionable situation, for sanity, and for the strength to do the right ***thing***.(p.70)

• Most of us have done that sort of ***thing***.(p.78)

• Reminding ourselves that we have decided to go to any length to find a spiritual experience we ask that we be given strength and direction to do the right ***thing***, no matter what the personal consequences may be.(p.79)

• In fairness we must say that she may understand, but what are we going to do about a ***thing*** like that?(p.81)

• Sometimes we hear an alcoholic say that the only ***thing*** he needs to do is to keep sober.(p.82)

• The main ***thing*** is that he be willing to believe in a Power greater than himself and that he live by spiritual principles.(p.93)

• Never avoid these responsibilities, but be sure you are doing the right ***thing*** if you assume them.(p.97)

• In many homes this is a difficult ***thing*** to do, but it must be done if any results are to be expected.(p.98)

• Of course, there is such a ***thing*** as incompatibility, but in nearly every instance the alcoholic only seems to be unloving and inconsiderate; it is usually because he is warped and sickened that he says and does these appalling things.(p.108)

• When they become too dangerous, we think the kind ***thing*** is to lock them up, but of course a good doctor should always be consulted.(p.114)

• When we do that, we find it solves our problems too; the ensuing lack of fear, worry and hurt feelings is a wonderful ***thing***.(p.116)

• It is the most natural ***thing*** in the world, once his liquor problem is solved, to feel that he will now measure up to that cherished vision.(p.118)

• Though it is infinitely better that he have no relapse at all, as has been true with many of our men, it is by no means a bad ***thing*** in some cases.(p.120)

• Henry Ford once made a wise remark to the effect that experience is the ***thing*** of supreme value in life.(p.124)

• Showing others who suffer how we were given help is the very ***thing*** which makes life seem so worth while to us now.(p.124)

• This sort of ***thing*** can be avoided.(p.126)

• Naturally this sort of ***thing*** decreased the man's chance of recovery.(p.145)

• There is another ***thing*** you might wish to do.(p.147)

• The right kind of man, the kind who recovers, will not want this sort of ***thing***.(p.149)

• Under only slightly different conditions, the same ***thing*** is taking place in many eastern cities.(p.161)

• I was between Scylla and Charybdis now, because if I did not drink my stomach tortured me, and if I did, my nerves did the same ***thing***.(p.175)

• The next ***thing*** they wanted to know was if I thought I could quit of my own accord, without any help, if I could just walk out of the hospital and never take another drink.(p.186)

• The next ***thing*** they wanted to know was would I be willing to go to this Higher Power and ask for help, calmly and without any reservations.(p.186)

• Then they said, "There is one other ***thing***.(p.190)

• Bill was very, very grateful that he had been released from this terrible ***thing*** and he had given God the credit for having done it, and he's so grateful about it he wants to tell other people about it.(p.191)

• I'm so grateful for both the program and the people in it that I still want to go, and then probably the most wonderful ***thing*** that I learned from the program -- I've seen this in the 'A.A. Grapevine' a lot of times, and I've had people say it to me personally, and I've heard people get up in meetings and make the same statement: The statement is, "I came into A.A. solely for the purpose of sobriety, but it has been through A.A. that I have found God."(p.192)

• I feel that is about the most wonderful ***thing*** that a person can do.(p.192)

• But I didn't do a ***thing*** about giving them any part of the seven bucks I had in my pocket.(p.197)

• I then began asking a lot of questions of both my brother and Dr. Bob about how this ***thing*** worked, and I suppose I was becoming more glassy-eyed all the while, for eventually I said to Bob, "You're all dried up.(p.206)

• The important ***thing*** was that he was happy.(p.208)

• I do not recollect the specific conversation that went on but I believe I did challenge Bill to tell me something about A.A. and I do recall one other ***thing***: I wanted to know what this was that worked so many wonders, and hanging over the mantel was a picture of Gethsemane and Bill pointed to it and said, "There it is," which didn't make much sense to me.(p.216)

• I did not know there was such a ***thing*** as group activity until I left the hospital.(p.218)

• That was an experience that I have never forgotten, and many times in my own work with A.A. newcomers I feel kind of guilty because I haven't done the same ***thing***.(p.219)

• That was skeptically received by me when I first heard it, but after some twenty-eight or thirty fellows had come to see me, and pretty nearly all of them had said the same ***thing***, I began to believe it.(p.219)

• I went to a meeting to see for myself this group of freaks or bums who had done this ***thing***.(p.228)

• To go into a gathering of people was the sort of ***thing*** that all my life, from the time I left my private world of books and dreams to meet the real world of people and parties and jobs, had left me feeling an uncomfortable outsider, needing the warming stimulus of drinks to join in.(p.228)

• In the eight years before A.A. found me, I had over forty jobs -- selling and travelling -- one ***thing*** after another, and the same old routine.(p.244)

• Then it was my turn -- I ordered "Three beers," but

this time it was different, I had a cash investment of thirty cents and, on a ten dollar a week salary, that's a big *thing*.(p.247)
• He knew too well that didn't mean a *thing*, just as I knew in my heart that it would be only a question of time -- a few days, a week, or even a month, it was inevitable – till I would be off on another bender.(p.257)
• The big *thing* was that these men were all sober and evidently had something I didn't have.(p.259)
• And another *thing*, it's a wonder they didn't throw us back in because I could become very dignified and sarcastic.(p.264)
• If I'd had a gun I'd have shot the horns right off the *thing*, because it made me raving mad.(p.265)
• "Oh, some darn *thing* they've got here in the paper about it."(p.266)
• There was a young fellow who led the meeting and that was a beautiful *thing* to me.(p.270)
• Russ said, "Don't do another *thing* today but help him.(p.271)
• I knew Doc and Anne were going to be there, and all of them thought it would be good for me, but the first *thing* I did was to go to St. Thomas and try to talk to those women.)(p.272)
• We old-timers who get scattered and separated and then witness the construction of services to get in more people and to make this *thing* function, we think that A.A. has changed, but the root of it hasn't.(p.272)
• It's only natural that we don't have the capacity to change, but we ought not to criticize those who have, There's another *thing* I would stress.(p.273)
• Another *thing* that was helpful to me.(p.273)
• I had been in A.A. a year, and the last *thing* in my mind was a drink.(p.285)
• I had to adapt to new associations and associates, and it seemed to be the smart *thing* to drink and smoke.(p.287)
• Above all, I have gained the greatest *thing* accorded to any man, the love and understanding of a gracious God, who has lifted me from the alcoholic scrap-heap to a position of trust where I have been able to reap the rich rewards that come from showing a little love for others and from serving them as I can.(p.296)
• One is that I don't remember too many of them, as I was one of those drunks who could be on his feet and attend a meeting or a party, engage in a conversation with people and do things that any nearly normal person would do, and the next day not remember a *thing* about where I was, what I did, whom I saw, or how I got home.(p.301)
• I sleep like a baby, and never give a thought to such a *thing* as insomnia.(p.303)
• When I came home again, the only *thing* I had left to love was the bottle.(p.318)
• The important *thing* I lost was my own self-respect.(p.323)
• It would be a little *thing* that I'd think was wrong, and off I'd go, drinking.(p.324)
• You know I'll do it tomorrow, the very same *thing*."(p.325)
• I had the time, I certainly had the capability, but I never did a *thing*.(p.326)
• We're free at last to do our *thing*, to live uninhibited lives, to drink when and how and where we wish, when we want to and when we need to.(p.329)
• But the only *thing* that got started was my drinking.(p.336)
• No one likes to admit that they're a drunk, that they can't control this *thing*.(p.340)
• The same *thing* occurred in medical school.(p.345)
• And the first *thing* you know I was lifted right out of the A.A. group, and I floated higher, and higher, and even higher, until I was way up on a pink cloud which is known as Pink Seven, and I felt miserable again.(p.348)
• And then I scratched my head and said to myself, "What a fantastic *thing* for a man to say, that I cured his wife.(p.350)
• I am not even there, and if I was there the only *thing* I could do would be to give her moral support, and yet he thanks me for curing his wife."(p.350)
• I gave them everything, except the greatest *thing* in the world, and that is peace of mind.(p.351)
• So I went to her and said, "There's only one *thing* I want in my whole life, and I don't want any commendation; I don't want any credit; I don't want anything from you or Janey for the rest of your life except one *thing*; and that is, the opportunity to do anything you want always, and I would like to start off by doing the dishes."(p.351)
• Without hesitation, I did the only logical *thing* – ran away from home.(p.354)
• All of which could turn out but one *thing* -- a very popular, but spoiled, brat.(p.357)
• It was a terrible blow at the time and I thought he was pretty much of a heel, but of course it was the finest *thing* he could have done for me under the circumstances.(p.357)
• To me this meant telling my associates that I had joined Alcoholics Anonymous; that I didn't know what was expected of me by A.A., but that whatever it was, it was the most important *thing* in life for me; that sobriety meant more to me than anything in this world.(p.382)
• The only *thing* I have really to offer you is my own story, telling you just what sort of a drunk I was.(p.384)
• I had no feeling of security, and I knew that I had done a very stupid *thing*, so I went back to Texas and remarried my ex-husband.(p.386)
• The only *thing* that I could do would be to call the doctor to help sober me up.(p.389)
• If you will try this *thing*, I'll go along with you.(p.391)
• When he left I thought, what is this crack-pot *thing*?(p.391)
• I know that when Frank came home, I said, "I want to try this *thing*," and he said, "There's a post office box to write to in New York."(p.392)
• It's the last *thing* I ever heard him say, and I think there are some of us who, at times, try to read extra messages and complexities into the Steps.(p.395)
• Now I had done some living but I hadn't learned a *thing*.(p.402)
• I told myself that I had power over this *thing*.(p.408)
• So I did the right *thing* in the wrong way.(p.409)
• But now a strange *thing* happened.(p.412)
• I now said a lucky and wonderful *thing*.(p.412)
• This has been a wonderful *thing* in my life.(p.417)
• The only *thing* that bothered me was a queasy feeling I had in the pit of my stomach.(p.418)
• I spent the time in a nearby tavern, was loaded on the ship, went to sleep before take-off, and the next *thing* I knew someone was shaking me and telling me we were over San Diego.(p.428)
• The insidiousness of alcoholism is an appalling *thing*.(p.432)
• My growing inward unhappiness was a very real *thing*, however, and I knew that something would have to be done about it.(p.434)
• I really felt sorry for him; the only *thing* in life he had to brag about was the fact that he was an alcoholic.(p.446)
• Against my better judgment, I went to a meeting with him that night, and a strange *thing* began to happen.(p.446)
• (Today, there is absolutely nothing in the world more important to me than my keeping this alcoholic sober; not taking a drink is by far the most important *thing* I do each day.)(p.447)
• When I am disturbed, it is because I find some person, place, *thing*, or situation – some fact of my life -- unacceptable to me, and I can find no serenity until I accept that person, place, *thing*, or situation as being exactly the way it is supposed to be at this moment.(p.449)
• For years, I was sure the worst *thing* that could happen to a nice guy like me would be that I would turn out to be an alcoholic.(p.449)
• Today, I find it's the best *thing* that has ever happened to me.(p.450)
• I can do the same *thing* with an A.A. meeting.(p.451)
• Perhaps the best *thing* of all for me is to remember that my serenity is inversely proportional to my expectations.(p.452)
• Same *thing* when I let lye and water eat away at four of my toes and my foot for five hours.(p.458)
• However, one *thing* I am certain of: Inmates in prison who attend A.A. have their chances of remaining free greatly enhanced – this is a proved fact.(p.458)
• The doctor, apparently realizing that one *thing* that I certainly needed was sleep, left a bottle of sleeping pills there and in my drunken state I took them all, instead of the one or two he had prescribed.(p.465)
• What's the sense in trying to do the right *thing*?"(p.467)
• During these seven years a *thing* called the Twenty-four Hour Program –a gadget I used to think was only a snare to trap the newcomer -- has come to mean much to me, not only as regards my drinking but in the whole pattern of my life.(p.473)
• Next *thing* I know, it was next day.(p.474)
• Then a terrible *thing* happened.(p.478)
• Another *thing* that mother drilled into me was a very Puritanical point of view as to sex relations and as to motherhood and womanhood.(p.483)
• It meant that I had to give up a lot of the things that I had been accustomed to and that wasn't the easiest *thing* in the world for me.(p.487)
• I think that was basically the *thing* that started me drinking in 1935.(p.487)
• A peculiar *thing* happened in 1940.(p.488)
• I promised that I was going to do the right *thing*.(p.490)
• The one *thing* I can remember now was that Vi was on the corner of 8th and L, and I remember vividly that she had an envelope in her hand.(p.492)
• I think the *thing* that galled me was that just after Easter I had drawn my salary for two weeks' work and had decided that I was going to send some money to Vi; and above all else I was going to send my baby daughter an Easter outfit.(p.493)
• She asked me one other *thing*.(p.494)
• This was the real *thing*!(p.498)
• "How does prayer fit into this *thing*?"(p.504)
• "The *thing* I do is to say 'God here I am and here are all my troubles.(p.504)
• Get into the lives of other people, is one *thing* the fellows in New York had said.(p.505)
• In part, it was a feeling of intense shame at having to leave the Army during the war, but mostly it was resentment that this kind of *thing* should happen to me for, strange as it may seem, up to then I still thought I could control drinking.(p.521)
• The only *thing* that bothers me is that there are only about five Negroes in A.A. in my city.(p.529)
• I, a man of steel, with very high ideals, well brought up, an honor student and the recipient of scholarships and prizes, a boy wonder in business -- I, Bob, the author of this essay, looked and saw that the universe was beneath my contempt, and that to remove myself from it was the only *thing* of dignity a man could do.(p.531)
• My proud southern blood would have boiled if anyone had named me such a despicable *thing*.(p.532)
• For you learned that he had been guilty of the *thing* he had accused you of, and his guilt had brought suffering to his entire family; and he thought he saw his young son beginning his own tragic pattern.(p.533)
• This question so insulted the emotions that clearly there was only one *thing* to do, go and get drunk again, and put that enquiring mind in its proper place, which was oblivion.(p.537)
• But not for long; now, for five Friday nights in a row, I went to jail, picked up sodden with beer (which I always disliked, but which was the only drink available); in jail five consecutive Friday nights in the town where I had grown up, where I had been an honor student in high school, where a kindly uncle, bailing me out, said, "Bob, our family just doesn't do this sort of *thing*."(p.539)
• I remember how horrible jails are, how dreadful a *thing* it is to be behind steel bars.(p.542)
• I thought that life was a pretty simple *thing*; you simply made a plan for your life, based upon what you wanted, and then you needed only the courage to go after it.(p.545)
• The only *thing* this changed, however, was my surroundings, and it was soon apparent that I could have the same uncomfortable emotions with an unlimited checking account that I could on a working girl's salary.(p.545)
• The amount of will power exercised to control my drinking during working hours, diverted into a constructive channel, would have made me President, and the *thing* that made the will power possible was the knowledge that as soon as my day was finished I could drink myself into oblivion.(p.548)
• He said, in effect: "If you have a resentment you want to be free of, if you will pray for the person or the *thing* that you resent, you will be free.(p.552)
• Dr. John F. Stouffer, Chief Psychiatrist, Philadelphia General Hospital, citing his experience with A.A., said: "The alcoholics we get here at Philadelphia General are mostly those who cannot afford private treatment, and A.A. is by far the greatest *thing* we have been able to offer them.(p.572)

things

• These *things* were true to some extent, in fact, to a considerable extent with some of us.(p.xxiv)
• It explains many *things* for which we cannot otherwise account.(p.xxiv)
• These allergic types can never safely use alcohol in any form at all; and once having formed the habit and found they cannot break it, once having lost their self-confidence, their reliance upon *things* human, their problems pile up on them and become astonishingly difficult to solve.(p.xxvi)
• Gradually *things* got worse.(p.5)
• I could almost hear the sound of the preacher's voice as I sat, on still Sundays, way over there on the

hillside; there was that proffered temperance pledge I never signed; my grandfather's good natured contempt of some church folk and their doings; his insistence that the spheres really had their music; but his denial of the preacher's right to tell him how he must listen; his fearlessness as he spoke of these ***things*** just before he died; these recollections welled up from the past.(p.10)
• I had often pondered these ***things***.(p.10)
• My friend promised when these ***things*** were done I would enter upon a new relationship with my Creator; that I would have the elements of a way of living which answered all my problems.(p.13)
• Belief in the power of God, plus enough willingness, honesty and humility to establish and maintain the new order of ***things***, were the essential requirements.(p.13)
• I must turn in all ***things*** the Father of Light who presides over us all.(p.14)
• But not so with the alcoholic illness, for with it there goes annihilation of all the ***things*** worth while in life.(p.18)
• He does absurd, incredible, tragic ***things*** while drinking.(p.21)
• He has commenced to accomplish those ***things*** for us which we could never do by ourselves.(p.25)
• He wished above all ***things*** to regain self-control.(p.26)
• We admit we have some of these symptoms, but we have not gone to the extremes you fellows did, nor are we likely to, for we understand ourselves so well after what you have told us that such ***things*** cannot happen again.(p.38)
• We could wish to be moral, we could wish to be philosophically comforted, in fact, we could will these ***things*** with all our might, but the needed power wasn't there.(p.45)
• As soon as we admitted the possible existence of a Creative Intelligence, a Spirit of the Universe underlying the totality of ***things***, we began to be possessed of a new sense of power and direction, provided we took other simple steps.(p.46)
• Afterward, we found ourselves accepting many ***things*** which then seemed entirely out of reach.(p.47)
• That was great news to us, for we had assumed we could not make use of spiritual principles unless we accepted many ***things*** on faith which seemed difficult to believe.(p.47)
• Many of us have been so touchy that even casual reference to spiritual ***things*** made us bristle with antagonism.(p.48)
• They flatly declare that since they have come to believe in a Power greater than themselves, to take a certain attitude toward that Power, and to do certain simple ***things***, there has been a revolutionary change in their way of living and thinking.(p.50)
• Had we not variously worshipped people, sentiment, ***things***, money, and ourselves?(p.54)
• Were not these ***things*** the tissue out of which our lives were constructed?(p.54)
• They said God made these ***things*** possible, and we only smiled.(p.55)
• It may be obscured by calamity, by pomp, by worship of other ***things***, but in some form or other it is there.(p.55)
• Is it not evident to all the rest of the players that these are the ***things*** he wants?(p.61)
• When we sincerely took such a position, all sorts of remarkable ***things*** followed.(p.63)
• Though our decision was a vital and crucial step, it could have little permanent effect unless at once followed by a strenuous effort to face, and to be rid of, the ***things*** in ourselves which had been blocking us.(p.64)
• They may be the dubious luxury of normal men, but for alcoholics these ***things*** are poison.(p.66)
• If we are sorry for what we have done, and have the honest desire to let God take us to better ***things***, we believe we will be forgiven and will have learned our lesson.(p.70)
• We think we have done well enough in admitting these ***things*** to ourselves.(p.72)
• The inconsistency is made worse by the ***things*** he does on his sprees.(p.73)
• Are we now ready to let God remove from us all the ***things*** which we have admitted are objectionable?(p.76)
• We will lose interest in selfish ***things*** and gain interest in our fellows.(p.84)
• The family must decide these ***things***.(p.90)
• Yet we do go to great extremes to provide each other with these very ***things***, when such action is warranted.(p.98)
• These ***things*** will come to pass naturally and in good time provided, however, the alcoholic continues to demonstrate that he can be sober, considerate, and helpful, regardless of what anyone says or does.(p.99)
• If you persist, remarkable ***things*** will happen.(p.100)
• When we look back, we realize that the ***things*** which came to us when we put ourselves in God's hands were better than anything we could have planned.(p.100)
• Assuming we are spiritually fit, we can do all sorts of ***things*** alcoholics are not supposed to do.(p.100)
• The alarming physical and mental symptoms, the deepening pall of remorse, depression and inferiority that settled down on our loved ones -- these ***things*** terrified and distracted us.(p.106)
• Of course, there is such a thing as incompatibility, but in nearly every instance the alcoholic only seems to be unloving and inconsiderate; it is usually because he is warped and sickened that he says and does these appalling ***things***.(p.108)
• We wives found that, like everybody else, we were afflicted with pride, self-pity, vanity and all the ***things*** which go to make up the self-centered person; and we were not above selfishness or dishonesty.(p.116)
• Show him these ***things*** in yourself and they will be reflected back to you from him.(p.118)
• Perhaps your husband will make a fair start on the new basis, but just as ***things*** are going beautifully he dismays you by coming home drunk.(p.120)
• We had to learn these ***things*** the hard way.(p.121)
• But the head of the house has spent years in pulling down the structures of business, romance, friendship, health -- these ***things*** are now ruined or damaged.(p.123)
• If they sense these ***things***, they will not take so seriously his periods of crankiness, depression, or apathy, which will disappear when there is tolerance, love, and spiritual understanding.(p.127)
• When he renews interest in such ***things***, a feeling of jealousy may arise.(p.131)
• We have been speaking to you of serious, sometimes tragic ***things***.(p.132)
• He admitted he was overdoing these ***things***, but frankly said that he was not ready to stop.(p.135)
• First ***Things*** First(p.135)
• Drinking occasionally, and understanding your own reactions, it is possible for you to become quite sure of many ***things*** which, so far as the alcoholic is concerned, are not always so.(p.139)
• When sober, does he not work hard and have a knack of getting ***things*** done?(p.139)
• When drinking, or getting over a bout, an alcoholic, sometimes the model of honesty when normal, will do incredible ***things***.(p.140)
• In this connection, can you remain undisturbed if the man proceeds to tell you shocking ***things***?(p.145)
• We think this method of approach will accomplish several ***things***.(p.148)
• The practical answer is that since these ***things*** have happened among us, they can happen with you.(p.153)
• Being wrecked in the same vessel, being restored and united under one God, with hearts and minds attuned to the welfare of others, the ***things*** which matter so much to some people no longer signify much to them.(p.161)
• Before very long we began to relate some incidents of our drinking and, naturally, pretty soon, I realized both of them knew what they were talking about because you can see ***things*** and smell ***things*** when you're drunk, that you can't other times, and, if I had thought they didn't know what they were talking about, I wouldn't have been willing to talk to them at all.(p.185)
• So, after reviewing these ***things*** and realizing what liquor had cost me, I went to this Higher Power which, to me was God, without any reservation, and admitted that I was completely powerless over alcohol, and that I was willing to do anything in the world to get rid of the problem.(p.187)
• Each day I would try to find out what His will was, and try to follow that, rather than trying to get Him to always agree that the ***things*** I thought of myself were the ***things*** best for me.(p.187)
• I said, "Yes, Doc, I would like to quit, at least for five, six, or eight months, until I get ***things*** straightened up, and begin to get the respect of my wife and some other people back, and get my finances fixed up and so on."(p.187)
• I remember telling them too that it was going to be awfully tough, because I did some other ***things***, smoked cigarettes and played penny ante poker, sometimes bet on the horse races and they said, "Don't you think you're having more trouble with this drinking than with anything else at the present time?(p.190)
• They said, "Let's forget about those other ***things***, that is, trying to eliminate them all at once, and concentrate on the drink."(p.190)
• Of course, we had talked over quite a number of the failings that I had and made a sort of an inventory, which wasn't too difficult, because I had an awful lot of ***things*** wrong that were very apparent to me, because I knew all about them.(p.190)
• I always built up in my own mind the great ***things*** that I was going to do, and in fact I accomplished about fifty percent of them and then lost interest.(p.193)
• He did ***things*** much better than I did because he applied himself and learned how to do them, and I never applied myself.(p.194)
• I felt having gotten married, I was an adult and one of the first ***things*** I did was to buy two cases of whiskey with no idea of drinking it.(p.196)
• To my mind, drinking didn't have anything to do with not going through with ***things***.(p.198)
• Long since I had come to believe I was insane because I did so many ***things*** I didn't want to do.(p.199)
• The circumstances under which I reached these people were very odd because I was led there through ***things*** that I said when I couldn't even remember speaking.(p.202)
• He said, "So long as I'm thinking as I'm thinking now, and so long as I'm doing the ***things*** I'm doing now, I don't believe I'll ever take another drink."(p.206)
• Then he started to talk to me about his drinking experiences, what his drinking had cost him, how much he had drunk and where, ***things*** like that, and I remember I was quite bored because I had never seen the guy before and had no interest at all in what, where and when he drank.(p.208)
• The very simple program they advised me to follow was that I should ask to know God's will for me for that one day, and then, to the best of my ability, to follow that, and at night to express my gratefulness to God for the ***things*** that had happened to me during the day.(p.208)
• I seemed to react by developing a streak of varying meanness, which would cause me to do ***things*** to create excitement and to get attention.(p.211)
• I was willful, full of will to do the ***things*** I wanted to do and to get the ***things*** that I wanted to have.(p.214)
• One of the ***things*** that came up repeatedly in the stories they told me was that once they had accepted the program, they never had a desire to take a drink.(p.219)
• In my own experience I was so jubilant at finding myself sober, and I had so many ***things*** to catch up on, that a month went by before the thought even occurred to me.(p.219)
• I might have done terrible ***things***, and I wouldn't even know it!(p.223)
• I met all the people I wanted to meet; I saw all the places I wanted to see; I did all the ***things*** I wanted to do -- and I was increasingly miserable.(p.225)
• Talking ***things*** over with them, great floods of enlightenment showed me myself as I really was and I was like them.(p.229)
• My visitor well knew, that as I tried to follow God I would get to studying these ***things*** out for myself.(p.236)
• Many ***things*** happened; business trials, little worries, and feelings of general despondency came near driving me to the bottle, but I made progress.(p.237)
• Many of these same ***things*** had happened to me many times before, but this time they had all descended together.(p.238)
• As long as ***things*** were tough and the job a challenge I could always manage to hold on pretty well, but as soon as I learned the combination, got the puzzle under control and the boss to pat me on the back, I was gone again.(p.243)
• Haven't I been successful, haven't I accomplished extraordinary ***things*** in business?(p.245)
• I come from a very poor family in material ***things***, with a fine Christian mother, but with no religious background.(p.261)
• I was deprived of many of the ***things*** that we feel are important in life, such as education particularly, because of my father's drinking.(p.261)
• I had none of these ***things*** that children should have to make them happy.(p.261)
• We moved in from the country at the age when girls want all sorts of nice ***things***.(p.261)
• I look back and remember these ***things*** because they made me very unhappy, and added to my feeling of inferiority at never being the same as other people.(p.261)
• But it was so important that we do the ***things*** we were told to do!(p.268)
• He talked about his wife taking his little boy away

from him because of his drinking, and how he got back together with them through A.A., and we began feeling grateful right then that all these *things* hadn't been taken from us.(p.270)

• I'd like to say here how important it was to us then that we do all the little *things* that people said were important, because later when Russ was so sick that I had to hold him up, they had a meeting out at the house.(p.270)

• I feel that one of the *things* that I still have to guard against is that I used to be set in my way about what I considered the old-time A.A.(p.272)

• I have to tell myself, "Other *things* are progressing and A.A. must too."(p.272)

• I don't ever remember that I was bored myself when we first came in, and they came out to the house and talked to us about these *things*.(p.273)

• Before I stop -- I always was a great talker -- I want to say that nobody will ever know how I miss Annie's advice about *things*.(p.273)

• I used to think I was cowardly because when *things* came out pertaining to the program that troubled me, I said to her many times, "Annie, am I being a coward because I lay those *things* away on the shelf and skip it?"(p.273)

• Some of the *things* which used to stop me in my tracks from fear still make me nervous in the anticipation of their doing, but once I kick myself into doing them nervousness disappears and I enjoy myself.(p.285)

• As I look back on that first evening I realize that I began to hope, then, for the first time; and I felt that if he could regain these *things*, perhaps it would be possible for me too.(p.290)

• The next afternoon and evening, two other men visited me and each told me his story and the *things* that they were doing to try to recover from this tragic illness.(p.290)

• This latest part of my life has had a purpose, not in great *things* accomplished but in daily living.(p.295)

• Acceptance of *things* as they are has replaced the old impatient champing at the bit to conquer the world.(p.295)

• One is that I don't remember too many of them, as I was one of those drunks who could be on his feet and attend a meeting or a party, engage in a conversation with people and do *things* that any nearly normal person would do, and the next day not remember a thing about where I was, what I did, whom I saw, or how I got home.(p.301)

• *Things* eventually came to the point where I had no friends.(p.301)

• My wife accompanied me on my visit and the doctor really told me some *things* that in my state of jitters nearly knocked me out of the chair.(p.302)

• He mentioned lies and deceptions in the course of his story in the presence of the one person in the world I wouldn't want to know such *things*.(p.302)

• I studied art; I desperately endeavored to create an interest in many *things*, in a new place among new people.(p.305)

• Some of us struggle with these people because we know that they are really very sick, but we also know that short of some miracle, we are not going to help them except temporarily, and that they will inevitably get worse and worse until one of two *things* happens.(p.308)

• It explained so much I had not understood about myself and, best of all, it promised recovery if I would do a few simple *things* and be willing to have the desire to drink removed.(p.309)

• I heard voices when no one was around, and I saw *things* that weren't there.(p.319)

• It has taught me so many *things*.(p.325)

• I am trying now, each day, to make up for all those selfish, thoughtless, foolish *things* I did in my drinking days.(p.326)

• I did some *things* I liked, and even sold some.(p.331)

• A lot of lost dreams, empty futures, and crazy *things* of the past went through my mind.(p.333)

• When we begin to do *things* like that with alcohol, something's gone wrong.(p.336)

• Easy does it, first *things* first, one day at a time.(p.340)

• I surrendered once to the bottle, and I couldn't do these *things*.(p.340)

• And I put a Big Book by my night stand, and I put a "Twelve Steps and Twelve Tradition" in my locker at the hospital, and I got books by Emmet Fox, and I got books by God-knows-who, and I got to reading all these *things*.(p.348)

• Many times have I heard the above expressions since I have been in A.A., and many times I have had to reply "Definitely I am an alcoholic, and while it may be hard for you to believe, it is not hard for me, for I have learned many *things* about alcohol and myself that would, perhaps, be difficult for you to understand."(p.356)

• One of the *things* I needed badly was business for the station.(p.360)

• In meeting me casually, I don't think my strong belief in "The Man Upstairs" shows, but I have no other explanation for the many good *things* that have happened to me since I have been in A.A. -- they came to me from a Greater Power.(p.367)

• It was frightening that drink was being substituted for more and more of the *things* I really enjoyed doing.(p.374)

• Resenting anyone and everyone who might interfere with my personal plans and ways of doing *things*, I was full of self pity, especially for any interference with my drinking.(p.376)

• "First *Things* First": solving our immediate problems before we try to solve all the others and get muddled in our thinking and doing.(p.382)

• "Grant us the serenity to accept the *things* we cannot change, courage to change the *things* we can, and the wisdom to know the difference."(p.382)

• I find an inner pleasure in simple *things*.(p.383)

• By the time all this was over, I was really in a terrific state, and my father taking in *things* said, "Miss Esther is about to faint.(p.385)

• So Frank went to New York and despite all these *things*, I got drunk.(p.389)

• I have told you some of the funny *things*, but not much of the shame and degradation.(p.390)

• In spite of knowing that my drunkenness was a symptom of the *things* that were wrong with me, and that I could never drink again, I thought I couldn't yet give it up, although I was going to try.(p.393)

• Even then I knew in my heart that I was unfit for the very *things* I wanted most, a happy marriage, security, a home and love.(p.403)

• It was nothing to my own inner distress, my self-reproach, and my self-loathing, for was I not bearing out all the horrible *things* I had always suspected of myself?(p.404)

• *Things* were no better with the family, so I moved to New York.(p.406)

• There were a couple of good *things*.(p.409)

• And again these were *things* that I really profited by after I sobered up.(p.409)

• I had a tiny trust fund, and I moved into a small apartment where I learned to cook, keep house, and do the *things* that normal people do.(p.409)

• These *things* were carried out in moments of less severe hangover or short stretches on the wagon.(p.409)

• But all these *things* could have happened.(p.412)

• All these *things* together brought me into A.A.(p.415)

• Through going to meetings and listening, and occasionally speaking, through doing Twelve Step work, whereby in helping others you are both the teacher and the student, by making many wonderful A.A. friends, I have been taught all the *things* in life that are worth having.(p.416)

• Nor were those impossible dreams I used to have the *things* I really wanted.(p.416)

• I had accomplished all the right *things* that our society expected, and I had no real peace of mind nor gratitude.(p.418)

• Meanwhile the letters from home were telling about how much my folks wanted to make up to me for some of the *things* I'd missed.(p.427)

• The binge had been just "one of those *things*."(p.433)

• To be sure, I learned many fascinating *things*, and many *things* that were to prove helpful later.(p.434)

• There have been some wonderful *things*, too.(p.438)

• They wanted me to make leather belts, of all *things*!(p.445)

• Much of my time was spent writing letters, notes, orders, and lists of *things* for Max, who was also my office nurse, to do to keep the world running while I was locked up.(p.445)

• Although we enjoyed the laughter in the early days, I heard a lot of *things* that I thought were stupid.(p.447)

• When a big, healthy-looking young fellow stood up there and said, "I'm a success today if I don't drink today," I thought, "Man, I've got a thousand *things* to do today before I can brag about not taking a drink, for God's sake!"(p.447)

• Prior to our marriage, when she was a shy, scrawny adolescent, I was able to see *things* in her that others couldn't necessarily see -- *things* like beauty, charm, gaiety, a gift for being easy to talk to, a sense of humor, and many other fine qualities.(p.450)

• There are many *things* worse than dying, but is there any death worse than the progressive, self-induced, slow suicide of the practicing alcoholic?(p.457)

• I would rather talk about the good *things* A.A. has taught me; I feel that hitting on just a few sordid points should be sufficient to let those of you in institutions know where I came from.(p.459)

• I'm talking about the good *things* that have happened.(p.463)

• Tragedies during those years that were caused by my drinking, such as the breaking up of my marriage, the death of my child, other *things* -- had little restraining effect.(p.465)

• *Things* went from bad to worse, and since I had finally and completely failed at the job of being a wife and a mother, my marriage ended.(p.468)

• With their help I also saw that certainly, because of some of the *things* I had done during the years, I was bordering on insanity, and so, facing the record, I tried to believe that a Power greater than I could and would restore me to sanity.(p.471)

• So I concentrated and studied the book during that time, and I liked a lot of the *things* it said in there.(p.472)

• Our language has few words to say many *things*.(p.474)

• By grace of God I stop, think two *things*: This would kill good mother and father; then remember boys talk about Indian fellow who been sober three years.(p.475)

• We are aware of the nice *things* around us, *things* we never noticed before in our drunken stupor.(p.481)

• For the first couple of years it wasn't too bad because the momentum kept *things* going.(p.486)

• But when *things* became crucial, everything started going haywire and I started going haywire with them.(p.486)

• I said that she told me she was going to the movies, and I became foolishly disturbed about it and, as *things* snowballed, I decided to go out and get drunk.(p.487)

• *Things* had just gone from bad to worse.(p.487)

• It meant that I had to give up a lot of the *things* that I had been accustomed to and that wasn't the easiest thing in the world for me.(p.487)

• Something should have told me then that *things* were haywire.(p.487)

• I rebelled against this, because just about the time that I was getting ready to leave high school, a revelation came to me about God and it made *things* very complicated for me.(p.489)

• I went back to my mother's for a few days until *things* cooled off, because the District Attorney had put out a summons for me to come to see him in his office.(p.491)

• Then I find myself thinking about myself, and a few *things* that I had wanted to forget.(p.503)

• I've made a mess of *things* and can't do anything about it.(p.504)

• *Things* are not going so well at home.(p.505)

• We talk of other *things*.(p.507)

• However, she had faith and she had hope (*things* I didn't have).(p.514)

• The Abyssinian war broke out just as *things* were going very badly for me, and I went off to Egypt on a job there.(p.519)

• The Commanding Officer only spoke to me when he wanted to tell me exactly who I was and what I was and how little I counted in the scheme of *things* and how glad he would be if I went away.(p.520)

• *Things* were getting worse and worse.(p.522)

• I had been using paraldehyde more or less like ordinary drink for the last six years though, occasionally, I'd bounce back to phenobarbital and *things* like that.(p.524)

• *Things* got so bad, I was afraid to go on the street, so I turned to Mothers' Aid.(p.527)

• That was one of the worst *things* that could have happened to an alcoholic woman.(p.527)

• So many wonderful *things* have happened to me that at times I can't believe this is me.(p.529)

• I am talking about A.A. people, who have gone through some of the same *things* that you might be going through now.(p.529)

• *Things* weren't going as I thought they should, for my greater enjoyment, comfort and fame; therefore, if the universe wouldn't play my way, I wouldn't play at all.(p.531)

• These *things* were all pressures.(p.533)

• But such is my nature that I must know the reason for *things* and I didn't stop until I had satisfied myself about the reasons for my drinking.(p.533)

• There was the love affair which was ridiculous -- "imagine that midget being able to fall in love!" -- and my head knew it while my heart pumped real, genuine anguish, for it hurt like hell, and since it was first love, *things* have never been quite the same.(p.534)

• My personal definition, which I submit as applying

only to myself (although everyone is welcome to it who wants it), includes every waking activity of the human being; to have a creative attitude towards ***things*** is a more exact meaning, to live and to deal with other human beings creatively, which to me means seeing the God in them, and respecting and worshipping this God.(p.535)
• If I write with the air of one who has discovered the obvious, which is to say, the eternal truths which have been offered to us since the beginning, forgive my callowness; I had to find these ***things*** out for myself.(p.536)
• As I write these words, it seems incredible that these ***things*** should have happened to me, for they are, truly, against all my instincts and training.(p.536)
• The medical profession would probably tell me I was conditioned for alcoholism by the ***things*** that happened to me in my childhood.(p.544)
• One of the truly great ***things*** A.A. has taught me is that reality too has two sides; I had only known the grim side before the program, but now I had a chance to learn about the pleasant side as well.(p.550)
• The A.A. members who sponsored me told me in the beginning that I would not only find a way to live without having a drink, but that I would find a way to live without wanting to drink, if I would do these simple ***things***.(p.550)
• I believe this, and I believe too that it is equally impossible to practice these principles to the best of our ability, a day at a time, and still drink, for I don't think the two ***things*** are compatible.(p.550)
• A.A. has taught me that I will have peace of mind in exact proportion to the peace of mind I bring into the lives of other people, and it has taught me the true meaning of the admonition "happy are ye who know these ***things*** and do them."(p.551)
• All these ***things*** and many, many more, A.A. gave me.(p.559)
• We are granted "the serenity to accept the ***things*** we cannot change" -- and thus lose our quickness to anger and our sensitivity to criticism.(p.560)

think

• If you have a drinking problem, we hope that you may pause in reading one of the forty-four personal stories and ***think***: "Yes, that happened to me"; or, more important, "Yes, I've felt like that"; or most important, "Yes, I believe this program can work for me, too."(p.xii)
• We ***think*** this account of our experiences will help everyone to better understand the alcoholic.(p.xiii)
• When I need a mental uplift, I often ***think*** of another case brought in by a physician prominent in New York.(p.xxix)
• At one of the finals I was too drunk to ***think*** or write.(p.2)
• None of us makes a sole vocation of this work, nor do we ***think*** its effectiveness would be increased if we did.(p.19)
• "She's such a sweet girl, I should ***think*** he'd stop for her sake."(p.20)
• Or perhaps he doesn't ***think*** at all.(p.24)
• Some of our alcoholic readers may ***think*** they can do without spiritual help.(p.27)
• We ***think*** it no concern of ours what religious bodies our members identify themselves with as individuals.(p.28)
• No person likes to ***think*** he is bodily and mentally different from his fellows.(p.30)
• Young people may be encouraged by this man's experience to ***think*** that they can stop, as he did, on their own will power.(p.33)
• We ***think*** few, to whom this book will appeal, can stay dry anything like a year.(p.34)
• The experiment of quitting for a period of time will be helpful, but we ***think*** we can render an even greater service to alcoholic sufferers and perhaps to the medical fraternity.(p.34)
• How can such a lack of proportion, of the ability to ***think*** straight, be called anything else?(p.37)
• You may ***think*** this an extreme case.(p.37)
• You may ***think*** our illustration is too ridiculous.(p.38)
• "As soon as I regained my ability to ***think***, I went carefully over that evening in Washington.(p.41)
• We ***think*** there are good reasons.(p.48)
• Hence we are at pains to tell why we ***think*** our present faith is reasonable, why we ***think*** it more sane and logical to believe than not to believe, why we say our former thinking was soft and mushy when we threw up our hands in doubt and said, "We don't know."(p.53)
• That was natural, but let us ***think*** a little more closely.(p.53)
• Did we not have confidence in our ability to ***think***?(p.54)
• If our testimony helps sweep away prejudice, enables you to ***think*** honestly, encourages you to search diligently within yourself, then, if you wish, you can join us on the Broad Highway.(p.55)
• He begins to ***think*** life doesn't treat him right.(p.61)
• That, we ***think***, is the root of our troubles.(p.62)
• So our troubles, we ***think***, are basically of our own making.(p.62)
• They arise out of ourselves, and the alcoholic is an extreme example of self-will run riot, though he usually doesn't ***think*** so.(p.62)
• Sometimes we ***think*** fear ought to be classed with stealing.(p.67)
• Perhaps there is a better way — we ***think*** so.(p.68)
• Just to the extent that we do as we ***think*** He would have us, and humbly rely on Him, does He enable us to match calamity with serenity.(p.68)
• We can laugh at those who ***think*** spirituality the way of weakness.(p.68)
• Then we have the voices who cry for sex and more sex; who bewail the institution of marriage; who ***think*** that most of the troubles of the race are traceable to sex causes.(p.69)
• They ***think*** we do not have enough of it, or that it isn't the right kind.(p.69)
• We ***think*** of their needs and work for them.(p.70)
• We ***think*** we have done well enough in admitting these things to ourselves.(p.72)
• We ***think*** the reason is that they never completed their housecleaning.(p.73)
• He trembles to ***think*** someone might have observed him.(p.73)
• Rightly and naturally, we ***think*** well before we choose the person or persons with whom to take this intimate and confidential step.(p.74)
• Telling them what we are trying to do, we make no bones about our drinking; they usually know it anyway, whether we ***think*** so or not.(p.78)
• Not always we ***think***.(p.81)
• Unless one's family expresses a desire to live upon spiritual principles we ***think*** we ought not to urge them.(p.83)
• We ***think*** not.(p.84)
• On awakening let us ***think*** about the twenty-four hours ahead.(p.86)
• Give him a chance to ***think*** it over.(p.95)
• This may seem inconsistent, but we ***think*** it is not.(p.98)
• People have said we must not go where liquor is served; we must not have it in our homes; we must shun friends who drink; we must avoid moving pictures which show drinking scenes; we must not go into bars; our friends must hide their bottles if we go to their houses; we mustn't ***think*** or be reminded about alcohol at all.(p.100)
• Do not ***think*** of what you will get out of the occasion.(p.102)
• ***Think*** of what you can bring to it.(p.102)
• But some of us ***think*** we should not serve liquor to anyone.(p.102)
• But when he gets over the spree, he begins to ***think*** once more how he can drink moderately next time.(p.109)
• We ***think*** this person is in danger.(p.109)
• Some, but not all of us, ***think*** it has its advantages when reasonably used.(p.110)
• You ***think*** he ought to know the subject better, as everyone should have a clear understanding of the risk he takes if he drinks too much.(p.112)
• If you ***think*** he will be shy of a spiritual remedy, ask him to look at the chapter on alcoholism.(p.112)
• When they become too dangerous, we ***think*** the kind thing is to lock them up, but of course a good doctor should always be consulted.(p.114)
• You draw more and more into yourself and you ***think*** everyone is talking about conditions at your home.(p.114)
• You, as well as your husband, ought to ***think*** of what you can put into life instead of how much you can take out.(p.120)
• The good old days will soon be back, they ***think***.(p.123)
• We ***think*** that such a view is self-centered and in direct conflict with the new way of living.(p.124)
• We ***think*** each family which has been relieved owes something to those who have not, and when the occasion requires, each member of it should be only too willing to bring former mistakes, no matter how grievous, out of their hiding places.(p.124)
• So we ***think*** that unless some good and useful purpose is to be served, past occurrences should not be discussed.(p.125)
• We ***think*** it dangerous if he rushes headlong at his economic problem.(p.126)
• Sometimes mother and children don't ***think*** so.(p.126)
• Having been neglected and misused in the past, they ***think*** father owes them more than they are getting.(p.126)
• He is not so unbalanced as they might ***think***.(p.128)
• Though some of his manifestations are alarming and disagreeable, we ***think*** dad will be on a firmer foundation than the man who is placing business or professional success ahead of spiritual development.(p.129)
• So we ***think*** cheerfulness and laughter make for usefulness.(p.132)
• Among many employers nowadays, we ***think*** of one member who has spent much of his life in the world of big business.(p.136)
• We ***think*** the business fabric is shot through with a situation which might be helped by better understanding all around.(p.137)
• If he says yes, does he really mean it, or down inside does he ***think*** he is fooling you, and that after rest and treatment he will be able to get away with a few drinks now and then?(p.142)
• Your man will fare better if placed in such physical condition that he can ***think*** straight and no longer craves liquor.(p.143)
• But we ***think*** that if you persevere, the percentage of successes will gratify you.(p.144)
• But if you cannot or will not stop drinking, I ***think*** you ought to resign."(p.148)
• We ***think*** this method of approach will accomplish several things.(p.148)
• We ***think*** we are sensible when we urge that you stop this waste and give your worthwhile man a chance.(p.148)
• Being a large place, we ***think*** that some day its Fellowship will number many hundreds.(p.161)
• I ***think*** I must have been thoroughly scared by what had happened, or by the doctor, or probably both, so that I did not touch a drink again until the country went dry.(p.175)
• If you ***think*** you are an atheist, an agnostic, a skeptic, or have any other form of intellectual pride which keeps you from accepting what is in this book, I feel sorry for you.(p.181)
• If you still ***think*** you are strong enough to beat the game alone, that is your affair.(p.181)
• So, after hearing some more of my story, he turned around and said to Doc -- I don't ***think*** he knew I heard him, but I did — he said, "Well, I believe he's worth saving and working on."(p.185)
• We're not up here trying to take any of your rights or privileges away from you, but we have a program whereby we ***think*** we can stay sober.(p.186)
• They left this with me to ***think*** over, and I lay there on that hospital bed and went back over and reviewed my life.(p.186)
• One of the fellows, I ***think*** it was Doc, said, "Well, you want to quit?"(p.187)
• Every time I'd start thinking about drinking, I would ***think*** of the long, dry years ahead without having a drink; but this idea of twenty-four hours, that it was up to me from then on, was a lot of help.(p.188)
• I remember telling them too that it was going to be awfully tough, because I did some other things, smoked cigarettes and played penny ante poker, sometimes bet on the horse races and they said, "Don't you ***think*** you're having more trouble with this drinking than with anything else at the present time?(p.190)
• I thought, "I ***think*** I have the answer."(p.191)
• There was always a tremendous drive and ambition to become a great guy, because I ***think*** I recognized inwardly that I didn't have any special talents.(p.194)
• I ***think*** it was probably more than a year before I had anything more to do with liquor.(p.195)
• I didn't like having to come home at a certain time; I didn't like this, I didn't like that, and I ***think*** the poor girl actually divorced me to help me stop drinking!(p.199)
• I loved them, I ***think***, as much as any parent.(p.199)
• I ***think*** this was about 1927.(p.199)
• And I ***think*** we calculated, or I did, that there wasn't anybody who knew that I wasn't drinking.(p.202)
• I ***think*** the longest drunk I was ever on was eleven days, but usually only two days with a complete blackout for a day, and then backing off by drinking as long as I could get anything.(p.203)
• This time I seemed to be already awake, sitting upright in a big easy chair, in the middle of an animated conversation with a perfectly strange young woman, who didn't appear to ***think*** it strange.(p.222)
• Had he come two or three days later I ***think*** I would have thrown him out, but he hit when I

was open for anything.(p.239)
• I like to ***think*** I was fairly normal before alcohol took over.(p.240)
• When the others saw my altered attitude they took me back in, but for me they had to make it tough; if they hadn't I don't ***think*** I ever would have stuck it out.(p.248)
• I don't ***think*** the boys were completely convinced of my personality change, for they fought shy of including my story in the book, so my only contribution to their literary efforts was my firm conviction, being still a theological rebel, that the word God should be qualified with the phrase "as we understand him" -- for that was the only way I could accept spirituality.(p.248)
• That to me was the greatest humiliation, to ***think*** that I'd finally landed in jail.(p.264)
• I ***think*** that was the last vacation before sobriety.(p.265)
• He said, "Sister, if you ***think*** you're a screwball now, all you have to do is join up with that.(p.266)
• I don't ***think*** Jack was hospitalized.(p.267)
• I ***think*** his entry into A.A. was through spending some hours with Dr. Bob at his office.(p.267)
• He said, "I ***think*** this will tell you more.(p.268)
• I don't ***think*** that there was anything said about religion.(p.268)
• I often ***think*** how that could have turned some people away, because there were no other women alcoholics there then.(p.269)
• We had meetings at each other's homes and, of course, that was a grand place for people to get together out there; they seemed to ***think*** so too.(p.270)
• Russ used to be very much pleased because he'd say, "I ***think*** Dr. Bob thoroughly enjoys coming out here.(p.271)
• (Russ was buried on Friday, and on Sunday afternoon Hilda S. had invited me there to dinner Sunday night, and I didn't ***think*** I could do it.(p.272)
• If, on Sunday, I could be there, trying to ***think*** of something that would help her with this problem, then we must have something that could work.(p.272)
• We old-timers who get scattered and separated and then witness the construction of services to get in more people and to make this thing function, we ***think*** that A.A. has changed, but the root of it hasn't.(p.272)
• I ***think*** it's awfully hard on people, especially if they're new people, to hear these long drawn out talks.(p.273)
• I hadn't been in too long when one of the men's wives called me one Sunday and told me she didn't ***think*** I had any part of the program.(p.273)
• I didn't ***think*** I was going to get drunk right then, but I remember how comforting it was when I called Anne and told her.(p.273)
• I used to ***think*** I was cowardly because when things came out pertaining to the program that troubled me, I said to her many times, "Annie, am I being a coward because I lay those things away on the shelf and skip it?"(p.273)
• When the day of their return was almost upon me, and suicide was the only answer I had been able to ***think*** of, I went into Ralph's room one evening and told him the truth.(p.278)
• Obviously I have overcome fear to a sufficient degree to ***think*** in terms of success in business.(p.284)
• Dr. Bob always emphasized the religious angle very strongly, and I ***think*** it helped.(p.292)
• A few months after I made my original trip to Akron I was feeling pretty cocky, and I didn't ***think*** my wife was treating me with proper respect, now that I was an outstanding citizen.(p.293)
• I can ***think*** clearly and am helped much in my thinking and judgment by my spiritual development which grows daily.(p.303)
• They would travel miles and stay up all night with someone they had never laid eyes on before and ***think*** nothing of it.(p.310)
• I was sent to a psychiatrist, for they didn't ***think*** it was normal for me to want to kill my platoon sergeant or to attempt suicide twice.(p.318)
• I couldn't ***think*** straight any more.(p.319)
• I didn't ***think*** I was an alcoholic.(p.321)
• I should have lost my husband, and I ***think*** that only the fact that he was an alcoholic too kept us together.(p.323)
• It would be a little thing that I'd ***think*** was wrong, and off I'd go, drinking.(p.324)
• I didn't ***think*** my children knew about it, but I found out they did.(p.324)
• It's surprising, how we ***think*** we fool everybody in our drinking.(p.324)
• And "***Think***" – that one important word means so much to me.(p.325)
• I never stopped to ***think***.(p.325)
• If I could only stop drinking, maybe I wouldn't ***think***.(p.337)
• I said, "What do you ***think*** I've been doing?"(p.349)
• In meeting me casually, I don't ***think*** my strong belief in "The Man Upstairs" shows, but I have no other explanation for the many good things that have happened to me since I have been in A.A. -- they came to me from a Greater Power.(p.367)
• We ***think*** we can drink to excess without anyone knowing it.(p.376)
• I knew that I wanted to try A.A. and if that didn't work, I didn't ***think*** anything would.(p.384)
• I ***think*** that no one comes to A.A. until he's tried everything else.(p.384)
• As I grow in A.A., I realize that a person with as much self-will as I had, as hard a head and as diseased an ego, had to try everything that I could ***think*** of, butting my head against every stone wall before I was ready to come in.(p.384)
• I don't ***think*** that I was conscious of what had happened to me, but I ***think*** that it registered subconsciously.(p.386)
• I ***think*** I disrupted the hospital.(p.388)
• Anyhow, after Christmas my husband gave me a cocker spaniel who is, I ***think***, just as notorious in A.A. as I am.(p.388)
• I ***think*** that is when I hit bottom.(p.391)
• I ***think*** I actually read more contempt than was really there because just a week before someone had sent him the Saturday Evening Post article on A.A., and there was some glimmer of hope in it for him.(p.391)
• So he waited another week or two and I don't ***think*** I stayed sober hardly at all.(p.391)
• It was such a feeling of relief that I wanted to know more about it and with that, I ***think*** for the first time, came the realization that there was something horribly, horribly wrong with me.(p.392)
• Up to that time, I was so completely baffled by my behavior that I had never really stopped to ***think*** at all.(p.392)
• I wish I could tell you all that A.A. has done for me, all that I ***think*** and feel about A.A., but it's something that I have experienced and have never been able to put into words.(p.394)
• It's the last thing I ever heard him say, and I ***think*** there are some of us who, at times, try to read extra messages and complexities into the Steps.(p.395)
• I ***think*** I had the physical allergy right away.(p.402)
• I did not dare to ***think***.(p.406)
• I was afraid to ***think*** why.(p.406)
• I wanted to die and often I would ***think*** of ways.(p.411)
• I ***think*** now that a God, in whom I did not believe, was looking after me.(p.412)
• "See what you ***think***."(p.412)
• He said to me, gently and simply, "Do you ***think*** that you are one of us?"(p.413)
• In ending my story I like to ***think*** about this.(p.417)
• I closed my eyes and tried to ***think***.(p.422)
• I still ***think*** dad paid him something to let me go.(p.424)
• Today I ***think*** of life in terms of happiness, contentment, freedom from fear and despair, sane thinking, ability to face problems as they occur, the opportunity to help other alcoholics and to be decent.(p.430)
• I used to ***think***, "Why live without whiskey?"(p.430)
• After talking with him for a time I heard myself saying, "Doc, I ***think*** I'm an alcoholic."(p.436)
• I ***think*** He's on hand to see my son through, too.(p.437)
• I ***think*** He's on hand to see all of us through whatever may come to us.(p.437)
• Not only did I not ***think*** that being an alcoholic was a good idea, I didn't even feel that I had all that much of a drinking problem!(p.439)
• I'd ***think***, "I wonder why I'm saying that again -- I've already said it three times."(p.442)
• The neurologist in charge of my case didn't ***think*** to ask me whether I drank, and I didn't ***think*** to tell him.(p.444)
• Today, Max and I try to communicate what we feel, rather than what we ***think***.(p.451)
• I can tell her she ought not to ***think*** a certain way, but I certainly can't take away her right to feel however she does feel.(p.451)
• Eventually, I had to redo each of the Twelve Steps specifically with Max in mind, from the First, saying, "I am powerless over alcohol, and my homelife is unmanageable by me," to the Twelfth, in which I tried to ***think*** of her as a sick Al-Anon and treat her with the love I would give a sick A.A. newcomer.(p.452)
• During the twenty-four hours after running into the Serenity Prayer, I ***think*** I took the first three Steps for the first time.(p.461)
• I go back to my old alma mater occasionally to give A.A. talks, and – just ***think***! – the warden is my friend.(p.462)
• It made me feel quite grown-up and mature, and I ***think*** another added attraction was the fact that so far as my family was concerned, it was forbidden, and it had a special attraction for that reason.(p.464)
• (I ***think*** my first feeling of fear came with my first week's solitary drinking, locked up in that hotel room.(p.465)
• Sly and crafty, I thought now I'll find out what they ***think*** of me here, what they "have on" me, what I've said coming in here drunk.(p.470)
• During these seven years a thing called the Twenty-four Hour Program --a gadget I used to ***think*** was only a snare to trap the newcomer -- has come to mean much to me, not only as regards my drinking but in the whole pattern of my life.(p.473)
• Now ***think*** I was alcoholic from first drink.(p.474)
• I ***think*** they sorry they tell me this.(p.475)
• ***Think*** about kill myself.(p.475)
• By grace of God I stop, ***think*** two things: This would kill good mother and father; then remember boys talk about Indian fellow who been sober three years.(p.475)
• I hear about A.A., but ***think*** it religion.(p.475)
• And we usually have some kind of grimy sweater that we ***think*** we look sexy in, even if we weigh ninety-five pounds soaking wet and are not wearing a bra.(p.479)
• I ***think***, with him it possibly was a gift – intuitive diagnosis.(p.485)
• I don't ***think*** I suffered too much as far as the racial situation was concerned because I was born into it and knew nothing other than that.(p.485)
• I don't ***think*** I actually started to drink pathologically until approximately 1935.(p.487)
• I ***think*** that was basically the thing that started me drinking in 1935.(p.487)
• I rebelled, and from that time on I don't ***think*** I attended church more than a dozen times.(p.489)
• I ***think*** whiskey was cheaper there than it was in Washington.(p.490)
• I ***think*** the thing that galled me was that just after Easter I had drawn my salary for two weeks' work and had decided that I was going to send some money to Vi; and above all else I was going to send my baby daughter an Easter outfit.(p.493)
• I could not let him ***think*** I was a sissy.(p.498)
• I can't ***think***.(p.499)
• "You ***think*** you are hopeless, don't you?" he asks.(p.503)
• Am I willing to be honest with myself about myself and tell someone about myself, and am I willing to ***think*** of other people, of their needs instead of myself, in order to get rid of the drink problem?(p.503)
• I ***think*** of my wife.(p.505)
• The family seems to ***think*** of nothing but spending.(p.506)
• I ***think*** I am very lucky that there are people like A.A.'s and an A.A. program to hang on to and carry me through.(p.511)
• I used to ***think*** I was.(p.512)
• Lots of the older people had taken to drinking quite a good deal more during the war, but the younger generation was, I ***think***, about the same.(p.518)
• I ***think*** the Commanding Officer was rather tired of this particular chicken coming back to roost so often because he very soon wrote in to the medical authorities to tell them that they had to get me into hospital, to be thoroughly examined for drinking.(p.520)
• I stayed there just long enough to work up a real good resentment against the doctor in charge, who I didn't ***think*** was doing anything at all except collecting fees, and I left there fully determined that I'd never put myself in the power of medical people again.(p.521)
• I couldn't ***think*** of anything at all to do.(p.523)
• I ***think*** I am dreaming and will soon wake up.(p.529)
• I do ***think*** that some of the Negroes here – and other places, too -- are afraid to go to other meetings.(p.529)
• I know there are some alcoholics who seem terribly, terribly grown-up, but I ***think*** that they are trying to make themselves ***think*** they are grown-up, and the strain of their effort is what is causing them to drink -- a sense of inadequacy, a childish vanity to be the most popular, the most sought after, the mostest of the most.(p.535)
• Please do not ***think*** it ended so simply and so easily.(p.541)

• When I remark that I have been in jail nine times, and in an alcoholic ward twice, they *think* I'm kidding, or possibly dramatizing for the sake of a good yarn.(p.542)
• The less you *think* of yourself the more of a person you become.(p.542)
• I believe this, and I believe too that it is equally impossible to practice these principles to the best of our ability, a day at a time, and still drink, for I don't *think* the two things are compatible.(p.550)
• We *think*, therefore, that any considerable property of genuine use to A.A. should be separately incorporated and managed, thus dividing the material from the spiritual.(p.565)
• We *think* that each group should soon achieve this ideal; that any public solicitation of funds using the name of Alcoholics Anonymous is highly dangerous, whether by groups, clubs, hospitals, or other outside agencies; that acceptance of large gifts from any source, or of contributions carrying any obligation whatever, is unwise.(p.566)
• We *think* A.A. ought to avoid sensational advertising.(p.567)
• Most of us *think* this awareness of a Power greater than ourselves is the essence of spiritual experience.(p.570)
• I *think* our profession must take appreciative cognizance of this great therapeutic weapon.(p.571)
• Speaking at a dinner given by John D. Rockefeller Jr. to introduce Alcoholics Anonymous to some of his friends, Dr. Harry Emerson Fosdick remarked: "I *think* that psychologically speaking there is a point of advantage in the approach that is being made in this movement that cannot be duplicated.(p.574)

thinking

• I was to test my *thinking* by the new God-consciousness within.(p.13)
• When this sort of *thinking* is fully established in an individual with alcoholic tendencies, he has probably placed himself beyond human aid, and unless locked up, may die or go permanently insane.(p.24)
• What sort of *thinking* dominates an alcoholic who repeats time after time the desperate experiment of the first drink?(p.35)
• Of what is he *thinking*?(p.35)
• To us it is not far-fetched, for this kind of *thinking* has been characteristic of every single one of us.(p.37)
• Some of you are *thinking*: "Yes, what you tell us is true, but it doesn't fully apply.(p.38)
• Yet, in other moments, we found ourselves *thinking*, when enchanted by a starlit night, "Who, then, made all this?"(p.46)
• This sort of *thinking* had to be abandoned.(p.48)
• We read wordy books and indulge in windy arguments, *thinking* we believe this universe needs no God to explain it.(p.49)
• They flatly declare that since they have come to believe in a Power greater than themselves, to take a certain attitude toward that Power, and to do certain simple things, there has been a revolutionary change in their way of living and *thinking*.(p.50)
• But in most fields our generation has witnessed complete liberation of our *thinking*.(p.52)
• Hence we are at pains to tell why we think our present faith is reasonable, why we think it more sane and logical to believe than not to believe, why we say our former *thinking* was soft and mushy when we threw up our hands in doubt and said, "We don't know."(p.53)
• We avoid hysterical *thinking* or advice.(p.70)
• Were we *thinking* of ourselves most of the time?(p.86)
• Or were we *thinking* of what we could do for others, of what we could pack into the stream of life?(p.86)
• Before we begin, we ask God to direct our *thinking*, especially asking that it be divorced from self-pity, dishonest or self-seeking motives.(p.86)
• Our thought-life will be placed on a much higher plane when our *thinking* is cleared of wrong motives.(p.86)
• In *thinking* about our day we may face indecision.(p.86)
• Nevertheless, we find that our *thinking* will as time passes, be more and more on the plane of inspiration.(p.87)
• If your husband is a drinker, you probably worry over what other people are *thinking* and you hate to meet your friends.(p.114)
• You may be afraid your husband will lose his position; you are *thinking* of the disgrace and hard times which will befall you and the children.(p.116)
• His ways of *thinking* and doing are the habit of years.(p.118)
• Now about health: A body badly burned by alcohol does not often recover overnight nor do twisted *thinking* and depression vanish in a twinkling.(p.133)
• This may hang on for months, long after their mother has accepted dad's new way of living and *thinking*.(p.134)
• Can it be appreciated that he has been a victim of crooked *thinking*, directly caused by the action of alcohol on his brain?(p.140)
• He had been *thinking* it over.(p.158)
• Seeing much of each other, scarce an evening passed that someone's home did not shelter a little gathering of men and women, happy in their release, and constantly *thinking* how they might present their discovery to some newcomer.(p.159)
• We know what you are *thinking*.(p.163)
• Every time I'd start *thinking* about drinking, I would think of the long, dry years ahead without having a drink; but this idea of twenty-four hours, that it was up to me from then on, was a lot of help.(p.188)
• I can remember well *thinking* that I would quit drinking, really go to work hard, apply myself eight hours a day, five days a week, make a lot of money, and then I could start drinking again.(p.199)
• He said, "So long as I'm *thinking* as I'm *thinking* now, and so long as I'm doing the things I'm doing now, I don't believe I'll ever take another drink."(p.206)
• And then my *thinking* became calculation as to how much longer I had to live, how long the assets would last.(p.215)
• I had found friends, understanding friends who often knew what I was *thinking* and feeling better than I knew myself, and didn't allow me to retreat into my prison of loneliness and fear over a fancied slight or hurt.(p.228)
• I knew they needed to straighten out their *thinking* and habits, but I was all right, I just drank too much.(p.246)
• Now on a new job I was always *thinking* about payday and how much liquor I could buy and the pleasure I could have.(p.255)
• My *thinking* about drinking had undergone a great change.(p.277)
• Such *thinking* usually began with thoughts of the pleasant drinking of my youth.(p.285)
• I can think clearly and am helped much in my *thinking* and judgment by my spiritual development which grows daily.(p.303)
• It has changed my *thinking* entirely, about everything I do.(p.325)
• And retirement is a time for *thinking*, not of death, but of living – at long last.(p.329)
• Seated at the typewriter, I faked deep *thinking* or portrayed creativity by key-tapping.(p.332)
• I sat up in the big red chair, suddenly *thinking*, "My God, with my kind of lousy luck, I might not die soon!(p.333)
• But I couldn't help *thinking*, "You poor guy.(p.334)
• I wandered from room to room, *thinking*, drinking, drinking, *thinking*.(p.337)
• I never knew which came first, the *thinking* or the drinking.(p.337)
• If I could only stop *thinking*, I wouldn't drink.(p.337)
• And so one gets to *thinking* to oneself, "Who is this God?(p.350)
• Dishonest *thinking*, prejudice, ego, antagonism toward anyone and everyone who dares to cross him, vanity and a critical attitude are character defects that gradually creep in and become a part of his life.(p.380)
• The Twelve Steps, which to me are a spiritual way of living, soon meant honest *thinking*, not wishful *thinking*, open mindedness, a willingness to try and a faith to accept.(p.381)
• "First Things First": solving our immediate problems before we try to solve all the others and get muddled in our *thinking* and doing.(p.382)
• Now my whole *thinking* was crazy.(p.408)
• Today I think of life in terms of happiness, contentment, freedom from fear and despair, sane *thinking*, ability to face problems as they occur, the opportunity to help other alcoholics and to be decent.(p.430)
• But it didn't condition this girl's *thinking*.(p.469)
• In my screwed up mind I kept *thinking* I could have gone to A.A. way back there in 1940, and perhaps saved my marriage and home.(p.469)
• We can have this new way of life – learning to live with our sickness and to be happy and content -- if we are willing to change our way of *thinking* and be honest, first with ourselves, then with others.(p.480)
• I don't know whether it was right or wrong, but at least I know that people weren't *thinking* the same.(p.484)
• *Thinking* only of two or three dollars to buy some whiskey, I did the job and that's how I met Ella G., who was responsible for my coming into A.A.(p.493)
• I put Charlie on the car and when I left him I passed both of those liquor stores without even *thinking* about them.(p.495)
• Then I find myself *thinking* about myself, and a few things that I had wanted to forget.(p.503)
• For me, it was a little different because I couldn't help *thinking* about the past, and I saw the future more or less mirrored in the past.(p.513)
• To my way of *thinking*, that is a definition of alcoholism; a state of being in which the emotions have failed to grow to the stature of the intellect.(p.535)
• My desire to be honest with myself made it necessary for me to realize that my *thinking* was irrational.(p.550)
• But my *thinking* was still confused, and I was still unable to deal with the challenges of everyday living without help.(p.558)

thinks

• He is like the retired business man who lolls in the Florida sunshine in the winter complaining of the sad state of the nation; the minister who sighs over the sins of the twentieth century; politicians and reformers who are sure all would be Utopia if the rest of the world would only behave; the outlaw safe cracker who *thinks* society has wronged him; and the alcoholic who has lost all and is locked up.(p.61)
• If he *thinks* he can do the job in some other way, or prefers some other spiritual approach, encourage him to follow his own conscience.(p.95)
• If he is lukewarm or *thinks* he is not an alcoholic, we suggest you leave him alone.(p.113)
• If he is already committed to an institution, but can convince you and your doctor that he means business, give him a chance to try our method, unless the doctor *thinks* his mental condition too abnormal or dangerous.(p.114)
• He may either plunge into a frantic attempt to get on his feet in business, or he may be so enthralled by his new life that he talks or *thinks* of little else.(p.125)
• If he temporizes and still *thinks* he can ever drink again, even beer, he might as well be discharged after the next bender which, if an alcoholic, he is almost certain to have.(p.142)
• Ask him if he *thinks* he has the answer.(p.144)
• If he *thinks* he needs to go to the hospital, I'll pay for him."(p.271)

third

• This is the *third* edition of the book "Alcoholics Anonymous."(p.xi)
• Therefore, the first portion of this volume, describing the A.A. recovery program, has been left untouched in the course of revisions made for both the second and the *third* editions.(p.xi)
• In this *third* edition, Part I ("Pioneers of A.A.") stands unchanged.(p.xii)
• FOREWORD TO THE *THIRD* EDITION(p.xxii)
• In the course of his *third* treatment he acquired certain ideas concerning a possible means of recovery.(p.xxiii)
• How often have some of us begun to drink in this nonchalant way, and after the *third* or fourth, pounded on the bar and said to ourselves, "For God's sake, how did I ever get started again?"(p.24)
• After your man has gone along without drinking for a few months, you may be able to make use of his services with other employees who are giving you the alcoholic run-around – provided, of course, they are willing to have a *third* party in the picture.(p.146)
• On the *third* day the lawyer gave his life to the care and direction of his Creator, and said he was perfectly willing to do anything necessary.(p.158)
• My father died in 1901 when I was eight years old and I was in the second or *third* grade at school.(p.193)
• I got two drinks, each of them a quarter of that pint, in me, and was talking along with these people, but I felt that sooner or later they were going to have me cornered because they were smarter than I was and the drink was beginning to take effect; but as I reached for the *third* drink Bob said, "Listen, Buster, you promised to take some medicine if we got you a drink.(p.206)
• I told him I'd take the medicine and I would take it, but I hadn't told him when, and thereupon I got away with the *third* drink.(p.206)
• The *third* man who came to see me had been one of the greatest business-getters his company had ever employed.(p.235)
• One of them was that I would try to get a group started in Chicago; the second was that I would have to return to Akron to attend meetings at least every two months until I did get a group started in Chicago; *third*, I decided I must place this program above

everything else, even my family, because if I did not maintain my sobriety I would lose my family anyway.(p.292)
• The ***third*** time, after almost five years as an S.P. 4, I finally made sergeant.(p.318)
• The ***Third*** Step said: "Made a decision to turn our will and our lives over to the care of God as we understood Him."(p.350)
• When I protested, his lawyer, my lawyer, and my ***third*** and last analyst had a conference.(p.409)
• Once or twice, during my early drinking, I carried it over into the second day, and only once, that I can remember, did it continue into the ***third***.(p.432)
• Each with the other as a witness, we took the ***Third*** Step out loud – just as it says in the Big Book.(p.446)
• Each ten-day period in the dark hole, I was fed bread and water daily, with one full meal on the ***third*** day only.(p.459)
• After I had made my ***third*** report, I stepped down town, met some of the old crowd, and of course you know the answer.(p.510)

third-day
• There, I received several soda crackers and water daily, and before I could have my ***third-day*** meal (again the only meal in ten days), I had to drink a glass of castor oil or mineral oil, depending on the cruelty of the person who was doing the dispensing.(p.459)

thirsty
• It made me ***thirsty***.(p.447)

thirteen
• The fellowship of Al-Anon Family Groups was formed about ***thirteen*** years after this chapter was written.(p.121)
• This group of ***thirteen*** stories shows that sobriety in A.A. can be lasting.(p.167)
• Those who believe their drinking to be hopeless may again find hope in these ***thirteen*** impressive tales.(p.167)
• The periods of sobriety attained by these ***thirteen*** A.A.'s range from fifteen to forty-six years.(p.169)
• There were, at that time, in the neighborhood of twelve or ***thirteen*** Cleveland members who had been sober anywhere from a year and a half to a couple of months.(p.219)
• Until I was ***thirteen*** I attended public schools, with regular promotions and average grades.(p.240)
• At ***thirteen*** I was packed off to a very fine Protestant boarding school in Virginia where I stayed four years, graduating without any special achievements.(p.240)
• He stayed "dry" for ***thirteen*** years!(p.263)
• At the end of these ***thirteen*** years I never dreamed that he'd ever take another drink.(p.263)
• This would get me feeling fit, and then I would start for home and fireside, ***thirteen*** miles away.(p.299)
• I started drinking about age ***thirteen***.(p.317)
• But during a period of particular stress and strain about ***thirteen*** years ago, I resorted to alcohol in my home, alone, as a means of temporary release, as a means of getting a little extra sleep.(p.335)
• I know that if I do daily what I have done for these last ***thirteen*** and a half years, I will stay sober.(p.384)
• In fact, I was taken to A.A. by a woman whom my father had taken to A.A. ***thirteen*** years earlier.(p.419)
• This went on for ***thirteen*** weeks, the first eight of which I wasn't allowed visitors.(p.425)
• The ***thirteen*** stories in this group tell of alcoholism at its miserable worst.(p.455)
• Oldest of ***thirteen*** children.(p.474)
• After my very first drink – a tiny glass of sherry my father gave me to celebrate the New Year when I was ***thirteen*** -- I went up to bed, dizzy with exhilaration and excitement, and I prayed I wouldn't drink any more!(p.554)

thirties
• After the tire job came the ***thirties***, the Depression and the down hill road.(p.244)
• Up to my early ***thirties***, when my drinking had become a major problem, I lived in large houses, with servants and all the luxuries that I could possibly ask for.(p.401)

thirty
• "Bill's Story," "Doctor Bob's Nightmare," and one other personal history from the first edition were retained intact; three were edited and one of these was retitled; new versions of two stories were written with new titles; ***thirty*** completely new stories were added; and the story section was divided into three parts, under the same headings that are used now.(p.xi)
• A man of ***thirty*** was doing a great deal of spree drinking.(p.32)
• But here is a man who at fifty-five years found he was just where he had left off at ***thirty***.(p.33)
• Several of our crowd, men of ***thirty*** or less, had been drinking only a few years, but they found themselves as helpless as those who had been drinking twenty years.(p.33)
• Only ***thirty*** years later the conquest of the air was almost an old story and airplane travel was in full swing.(p.52)
• As we shall see, he now means a great deal to his community, and the major liabilities of ***thirty*** years of hard drinking have been repaired in four.(p.156)
• A community ***thirty*** miles away has fifteen fellows of Alcoholics Anonymous.(p.161)
• Today, hundreds of additional A.A. members can be found who have had no relapse for more than ***thirty*** years.(p.169)
• I put on ***thirty*** pounds of weight in about two months, looked like a pig, and was uncomfortable from shortness of breath.(p.177)
• I went back to law school, and doubled up on the courses because I was then approaching ***thirty*** years of age and I wanted to get through as quickly as possible.(p.212)
• I kept myself so busy that outside of some school and group parties, I didn't go overboard on drinking very much between the ages of twenty-five and ***thirty***.(p.213)
• That was skeptically received by me when I first heard it, but after some twenty-eight or ***thirty*** fellows had come to see me, and pretty nearly all of them had said the same thing, I began to believe it.(p.219)
• In fact, after six months of living on food instead of on whiskey, I gained about ***thirty*** pounds.(p.220)
• I re-organized their city sales policy and eighteen months later, when I was ***thirty***, they offered me the branch managership.(p.243)
• Then it was my turn – I ordered "Three beers," but this time it was different, I had a cash investment of ***thirty*** cents and, on a ten dollar a week salary, that's a big thing.(p.247)
• By the time I was ***thirty*** I had found that alcohol dissolved fear.(p.275)
• All this changed when I was ***thirty*** years old.(p.277)
• I got down on my knees for the first time in ***thirty*** years.(p.280)
• Between the ages of twenty-five and ***thirty*** I tried everything.(p.305)
• And still by the time I was ***thirty*** years old I was being pushed around with a compulsion to drink that was completely beyond my control.(p.305)
• I started my drinking nearly ***thirty*** years ago – right after I was married.(p.322)
• Within ***thirty*** minutes I knew A.A. was the answer for me.(p.378)
• He even went to bat for me before the court martial that inevitably followed and, as a result, I drew only ***thirty*** days – fifteen in solitary.(p.428)
• My wife and I have been married for some ***thirty*** years now.(p.485)
• The judge said that if she felt that way he would confine me for ***thirty*** days' examination and observation.(p.492)
• I got out on bail right away, but when I went to trial, the judge gave me ***thirty*** days.(p.528)
• When my ***thirty*** days were up, I started back on my rounds.(p.528)
• The only importance in all of this lies in the fact that at twenty-three I was just as sick as I was at ***thirty*** three, when I came into A.A., but at that time I apparently had no place to go because I had no drinking problem.(p.546)

thirty-eight
• I was then about thirty-seven or ***thirty-eight***.(p.213)

thirty-five
• He did no drinking until he was ***thirty-five***.(p.35)
• My drinking did not start until after I was ***thirty-five***, and a fairly successful career had been established.(p.374)
• Max and I have been married now for ***thirty-five*** years.(p.450)
• I received an additional fifteen years for that, making a minimum of ***thirty-five*** years and a maximum of natural life.(p.509)
• On October 28th, I was sent to Sing Sing with a minimum of thirty-three and a half years to serve out of that ***thirty-five***.(p.509)
• When I arrived at The Country Shop, which was a restaurant where they met in Dublin, I found about ***thirty-five*** or forty people in the room.(p.524)
• You were ***thirty-five*** before you understood your father's horrible anguish, and forgave him, and loved him again.(p.533)
• For by ***thirty-five*** I had been drinking for a few years.(p.533)

thirty-nine
• Here I was, ***thirty-nine*** years old and a complete washout.(p.238)
• For eighteen years, from the age of twenty-one to ***thirty-nine***, fear governed my life.(p.275)
• I remember the day when I decided to drink myself to death quietly, without bothering anyone, because I was tired of having been a dependable, trustworthy person for about ***thirty-nine*** years without having received what I thought was a proper reward for my virtue.(p.531)
• There was the over-weening ambition to be the world's greatest author, when -- at ***thirty-nine*** – I had nothing of importance to say to the world.(p.534)

thirty-seven
• I was then about ***thirty-seven*** or thirty-eight.(p.213)

thirty-three
• I was ***thirty-three*** years old and my life was spent.(p.304)
• On October 28th, I was sent to Sing Sing with a minimum of ***thirty-three*** and a half years to serve out of that thirty-five.(p.509)
• As I said earlier, self-pity and resentment were my constant companions and my inventory began to look like a ***thirty-three*** year diary, for I seemed to have a resentment against everybody I had ever known.(p.551)

thirty-two
• I was ***thirty-two*** years old.(p.224)
• I was ***thirty-two***, a babe in Boozeville.(p.328)
• I drank from the age of twelve until I was ***thirty-two***.(p.480)

thorn
• It was a ***thorn*** in my side, because I knew it was the truth, and I hated to hear the truth, especially about myself.(p.513)

thorough
• With all the earnestness at our command, we beg of you to be fearless and ***thorough*** from the very start.(p.58)
• If we have been ***thorough*** about our personal inventory, we have written down a lot.(p.70)
• Then and then only, after a ***thorough*** indoctrination by eight or nine individuals, was I allowed to attend my first meeting.(p.291)

thoroughly
• Rarely have we seen a person fail who has ***thoroughly*** followed our path.(p.58)
• We reviewed our fears ***thoroughly***.(p.68)
• When your prospect has made such reparation as he can to his family, and has ***thoroughly*** explained to them the new principles by which he is living, he should proceed to put those principles into action at home.(p.98)
• But be sure you are on solid spiritual ground before you start and that your motive in going is ***thoroughly*** good.(p.102)
• If you do this ***thoroughly***, few people will ask you to drink.(p.102)
• We realize some men are ***thoroughly*** bad-intentioned, that no amount of patience will make any difference.(p.108)
• We believe a man should be ***thoroughly*** probed on these points.(p.142)
• Whatever the method, its object is to ***thoroughly*** clear mind and body of the effects of alcohol.(p.143)
• I think I must have been ***thoroughly*** scared by what had happened, or by the doctor, or probably both, so that I did not touch a drink again until the country went dry.(p.175)
• I was self conscious and ill at ease most of the time, my health was at the breaking point, and I was ***thoroughly*** miserable.(p.178)
• And he further said that God could not accept me as a sincere follower of His Divine Law unless I was ready to be ***thoroughly*** honest about it.(p.236)
• What philosophy I had was ***thoroughly*** paganistic -- all my life was devoted to a search for pleasure.(p.256)
• Russ used to be very much pleased because he'd say, "I think Dr. Bob ***thoroughly*** enjoys coming out here.(p.271)
• She was ***thoroughly*** disgusted.(p.288)
• I got the Big Book and I read it, and this is what it said: "Rarely have we seen a person fail who has ***thoroughly*** followed our path."(p.349)
• The word "***thoroughly***" rang a bell.(p.349)
• "Complete abandon"; "Half measures availed us nothing"; "***Thoroughly*** follow our path"; "Completely give oneself to this simple program" – rang in my swelled head.(p.349)
• Strangely enough, right through to the end of my twenty-six years in the Army, I was still being offered very good and important jobs in spite of the fact that

my superiors must have known that I wasn't *thoroughly* reliable.(p.519)
• I think the Commanding Officer was rather tired of this particular chicken coming back to roost so often because he very soon wrote in to the medical authorities to tell them that they had to get me into hospital, to be *thoroughly* examined for drinking.(p.520)

thoroughness

• Nothing counted but *thoroughness* and honesty.(p.65)

thou

• That the man who is making the approach has had the same difficulty, that he obviously knows what he is talking about, that his whole deportment shouts at the new prospect that he is a man with a real answer, that he has no attitude of Holier Than *Thou*, nothing whatever except the sincere desire to be helpful; that there are no fees to pay, no axes to grind, no people to please, no lectures to be endured -- these are the conditions we have found most effective.(p.18)
• Many of us said to our Maker, as we understood Him: "God, I offer myself to Thee -- to build with me and to do with me as *Thou* wilt.(p.63)

though

• *Though* he could not accept all the tenets of the Oxford Groups, he was convinced of the need for moral inventory, confession of personality defects, restitution to those harmed, helpfulness to others, and the necessity of belief in and dependence upon God.(p.xvi)
• When the broker returned to New York in the fall of 1935, the first A.A. group had actually been formed, *though* no one realized it at the time.(p.xvii)
• *Though* none of these principles had the force of rules or laws, they had become so widely accepted by 1950 that they were confirmed by our first International Conference held at Cleveland.(p.xix)
• Neither does A.A. take any particular medical point of view, *though* we cooperate widely with the men of medicine as well as with the men of religion.(p.xx)
• In late 1934 I attended a patient who, *though* he had been a competent businessman of good earning capacity, was an alcoholic of a type I had come to regard as hopeless.(p.xxiii)
• *Though* we work out our solution on the spiritual as well as an altruistic plane, we favor hospitalization for the alcoholic who is very jittery or befogged.(p.xxiv)
• *Though* the aggregate of recoveries resulting from psychiatric effort is considerable, we physicians must admit we have made little impression upon the problem as a whole.(p.xxvii)
• I earnestly advise every alcoholic to read this book through, and *though* perhaps he came to scoff, he may remain to pray.(p.xxx)
• *Though* my drinking was not yet continuous, it disturbed my wife.(p.2)
• Best of all, I met a kind doctor who explained that *though* certainly selfish and foolish, I had been seriously ill, bodily and mentally.(p.7)
• It relieved me somewhat to learn that in alcoholics the will is amazingly weakened when it comes to combating liquor, *though* it often remains strong in other respects.(p.7)
• It began to look as *though* religious people were right after all.(p.11)
• I felt lifted up, as *though* the great clean wind of a mountain top blew through and through.(p.14)
• *Though* experience had made him skeptical, he finished his treatment with unusual confidence.(p.26)
• Our friend felt as *though* the gates of hell had closed on him with a clang.(p.27)
• *Though* there is no way of proving it, we believe that early in our drinking careers most of us could have stopped drinking.(p.32)
• *Though* a robust man at retirement, he went to pieces quickly and was dead within four years.(p.33)
• *Though* you may be able to stop for a considerable period, you may yet be a potential alcoholic.(p.34)
• That may be true of certain nonalcoholic people who, *though* drinking foolishly and heavily at the present time, are able to stop or moderate, because their brains and bodies have not been damaged as ours were.(p.39)
• I had commenced to drink as carelessly as *though* the cocktails were ginger ale.(p.41)
• They had said that *though* I did raise a defense, it would one day give way before some trivial reason for having a drink.(p.42)
• *Though* I had been only a nominal churchman, their proposals were not, intellectually, hard to swallow.(p.42)
• But the program of action, *though* entirely sensible, was pretty drastic.(p.42)
• *Though* not a religious person, I have profound respect for the spiritual approach in such cases as yours.(p.43)
• We found that as soon as we were able to lay aside prejudice and express even a willingness to believe in a Power greater than ourselves, we commenced to get results, even *though* it was impossible for any of us to fully define or comprehend that Power, which is God.(p.46)
• *Though* some of us resisted, we found no great difficulty in casting aside such feelings.(p.48)
• Neither is reason, as most of us use it, entirely dependable, *though* it emanate from our best minds.(p.54)
• While pondering the answer he felt as *though* he lived in hell.(p.56)
• On that basis we are almost always in collision with something or somebody, even *though* our motives are good.(p.60)
• They arise out of ourselves, and the alcoholic is an extreme example of self-will run riot, *though* he usually doesn't think so.(p.62)
• Many of us had moral and philosophical convictions galore, but we could not live up to them even *though* we would have liked to.(p.62)
• This was only a beginning, *though* if honestly and humbly made, an effect, sometimes a very great one, was felt at once.(p.63)
• *Though* our decision was a vital and crucial step, it could have little permanent effect unless at once followed by a strenuous effort to face, and to be rid of, the things in ourselves which had been blocking us.(p.64)
• *Though* we did not like their symptoms and the way these disturbed us, they, like ourselves, were sick too.(p.67)
• *Though* a situation had not been entirely our fault, we tried to disregard the other person involved entirely.(p.67)
• We put them on paper, even *though* we had no resentment in connection with them.(p.68)
• *Though* we have no religious connection, we may still do well to talk with someone ordained by an established religion.(p.74)
• It may be he has done us more harm than we have done him and, *though* we may have acquired a better attitude toward him, we are still not too keen about admitting our faults.(p.77)
• *Though* there may be justifiable exceptions, and *though* we wish to lay down no rule of any sort, we have often found this the best course to take.(p.81)
• We feel as *though* we had been placed in a position of neutrality -- safe and protected.(p.85)
• *Though* you have talked with the family, leave them out of the first discussion.(p.91)
• Even *though* your protege may not have entirely admitted his condition, he has become very curious to know how you got well.(p.92)
• *Though* an alcoholic does not respond, there is no reason why you should neglect his family.(p.97)
• And even *though* he continues to drink, the family will find life more bearable.(p.97)
• *Though* his family be at fault in many respects, he should not be concerned about that.(p.98)
• sometimes they were so inaccessible that it seemed as *though* a great wall had been built around them.(p.107)
• Treat him, when you can, as *though* he had pneumonia.(p.108)
• *Though* once like number two he became worse.(p.109)
• Even *though* your husband becomes unbearable and you have to leave him temporarily, you should, if you can, go without rancor.(p.111)
• It is possible to have a full and useful life, *though* your husband continues to drink.(p.111)
• Tell him you have been worried, *though* perhaps needlessly.(p.112)
• Being certain he wants to stop, you can go to him with this volume as joyfully as *though* you had struck oil.(p.113)
• You will no longer be self-conscious or feel that you must apologize as *though* your husband were a weak character.(p.115)
• *Though* it is infinitely better that he have no relapse at all, as has been true with many of our men, it is by no means a bad thing in some cases.(p.120)
• *Though* it is entirely separate from Alcoholics Anonymous, it uses the general principles of the A.A. program as a guide for husbands, wives, relatives, friends, and others close to alcoholics.(p.121)
• The foregoing pages (*though* addressed only to wives) indicate the problems such people may face.(p.121)
• *Though* old buildings will eventually be replaced by finer ones, the new structures will take years to complete.(p.123)
• Both father and the family are mistaken, *though* each side may have some justification.(p.126)
• The family must realize that dad, *though* marvelously improved, is still convalescing.(p.127)
• *Though* the family does not fully agree with dad's spiritual activities, they should let him have his head.(p.129)
• *Though* some of his manifestations are alarming and disagreeable, we think dad will be on a firmer foundation than the man who is placing business or professional success ahead of spiritual development.(p.129)
• They can hardly fail to approve these simple principles, *though* the head of the house still fails somewhat in practicing them.(p.130)
• *Though* the family has no religious connections, they may wish to make contact with or take membership in a religious body.(p.131)
• Being possessed of a spiritual experience, the alcoholic will find he has much in common with these people, *though* he may differ with them on many matters.(p.131)
• We cannot subscribe to the belief that this life is a vale of tears, *though* it once was just that for many of us.(p.133)
• Try to remember that *though* God has wrought miracles among us, we should never belittle a good doctor or psychiatrist.(p.133)
• *Though* he is now a most effective member of Alcoholics Anonymous, he still smokes and drinks coffee, but neither his wife or anyone else stands in judgment.(p.135)
• I had been obliged to discharge him for drinking, *though* he was brilliant, alert, and one of the best organizers I have ever known.(p.137)
• *Though* you are providing him with the best possible medical attention, he should understand that he must undergo a change of heart.(p.143)
• That won't hurt him a bit, even *though* he does not go for this remedy.(p.144)
• His call to the clergyman led him presently to a certain resident of the town, who, *though* formerly able and respected, was then nearing the nadir of alcoholic despair.(p.155)
• But he's a grand chap when he's sober, *though* he's been in here eight times in the last six months.(p.156)
• His wife came, scarcely daring to be hopeful, *though* she thought she saw something different about her husband already.(p.158)
• *Though* they knew they must help other alcoholics if they would remain sober, that motive became secondary.(p.159)
• And so can you, *though* you be but one man with this book in your hand.(p.162)
• Many mornings I have gone to classes, and even *though* fully prepared, would turn and walk back to the fraternity house because of my jitters, not daring to enter the classroom for fear of making a scene should I be called on for recitation.(p.173)
• I used to promise my wife, my friends, and my children that I would drink no more – promises which seldom kept me sober even through the day, *though* I was very sincere when I made them.(p.177)
• My wife became deeply interested and it was her interest that sustained mine, *though* I at no time sensed that it might be an answer to my liquor problem.(p.178)
• Wishing to be polite, *though* I felt very badly, I said, "Let's make the call," and extracted from my wife a promise that we would not stay over fifteen minutes.(p.179)
• I used to get terribly upset when I saw my friends drink and knew I could not, but I schooled myself to believe that *though* I once had the same privilege, I had abused it so frightfully that it was withdrawn.(p.181)
• That was worth a lot even *though* I did not believe it.(p.185)
• I said, "All right, call me a cab," as *though* I was talking to a bell boy.(p.204)
• As far as my home was concerned, I did not see then, *though* of course I can see now, that it was anything but a happy situation for my wife.(p.215)
• In fact, the last three years of my drinking was a routine of barbiturates in the morning, so that I could stop shaking enough to shave, and then alcohol beginning about four-thirty or five o'clock, with a struggle not to take a drink at noon or during the day, because I had the idea that if I took one drink, I would smell as *though* I had had a pint.(p.217)
• I believe *though* that it helped my family tremendously to have the A.A. meetings every week in my own home.(p.220)
• "Best in the business, when he's sober," my customers would say, and I still had a following who

would give me work ***though*** they deplored my habits, because they knew the job would be well done when they eventually got it.(p.234)
• I do feel, ***though***, that the fact that I finally grew up to a point where I could even tackle such a job is the apex of the story of a man who spent eighteen years running away from life.(p.286)
• These last eighteen years have been the happiest of my life, trite ***though*** that statement may seem.(p.295)
• In all honesty ***though***, I was skeptical, but I wanted so definitely to quit drinking that I would have welcomed any sort of physical torture or pain to accomplish the result.(p.302)
• Among today's incoming A.A. members, many have never reached the advanced stages of alcoholism, ***though***, given time, all might have.(p.315)
• They saw that they had become actual or potential alcoholics, even ***though*** no serious harm had yet been done.(p.315)
• On the first, ***though*** on the water wagon, I looked forward to my next drink.(p.344)
• And as that thought came to me, it was as ***though*** someone had reached down and taken a heavy overcoat off my shoulders, for that was the last one.(p.347)
• And the psychiatrist has had thousands of couches, and has put you and me on them many, many times, but he hasn't helped us very much, ***though*** he has tried hard; and we owe the clergy and the doctor and the psychiatrist a deep debt of gratitude, but they haven't helped our alcoholism, except in a rare few instances.(p.352)
• A relief, even ***though*** I dreaded it, feeling that this was the end of everything.(p.378)
• I had had no brushes with the law, ***though*** I should have had many.(p.379)
• I had not yet lost my job or family, even ***though*** both were on the verge of going.(p.379)
• It helped me a great deal to become convinced that alcoholism was a disease, not a moral issue; that I had been drinking as a result of a compulsion, even ***though*** I had not been aware of the compulsion at the time; and that sobriety was not a matter of willpower.(p.448)
• It is true that I -- of all people, strange as it may seem, and even ***though*** I didn't give my permission -- really, really am an alcoholic of sorts.(p.448)
• It's as ***though*** A.A. had given me a new pair of glasses.(p.450)
• On the other hand, I believe that I've always been medically inclined, ***though*** I have never been able to see medicine quite as the average person sees it.(p.485)
• A man wasn't actually mistreated, ***though*** if he was he could only resent it.(p.485)
• The fear of the loss of Vi and the feeling that, ***though*** she had the right to do as she pleased, she should have told me the truth about it, upset me.(p.487)
• So I put forth some effort that day to try to stay sober if I could, ***though*** my sobriety was just a daze.(p.494)
• I had been using paraldehyde more or less like ordinary drink for the last six years ***though***, occasionally, I'd bounce back to phenobarbital and things like that.(p.524)
• I took her money, ***though***; I had to have it.(p.540)
• Inside, ***though***, I was scared to death, for I knew that the time was coming (and it couldn't be too remote) when I would be unable to hold that job.(p.548)
• It had provided me with excuses for my lack of education, my marital failures, personal failures, inadequacy, and of course, my alcoholism and, ***though*** I really thought I had been willing to part with it, now I knew I was reluctant to let it go.(p.552)
• ***Though*** it was not our intention to create such an impression, many alcoholics have nevertheless concluded that in order to recover they must acquire an immediate and overwhelming "God-consciousness" followed at once by a vast change in feeling and outlook.(p.569)
• Among our rapidly growing membership of thousands of alcoholics such transformations, ***though*** frequent, are by no means the rule.(p.569)

thought

• It was now time, the struggling groups ***thought***, to place their message and unique experience before the world.(p.xvii)
• It was ***thought*** that no alcoholic man or woman could be excluded from our Society; that our leaders might serve but never govern; that each group was to be autonomous and there was to be no professional class of therapy.(p.xix)
• Following his physical rehabilitation, he had a talk with me in which he frankly stated he ***thought*** the treatment a waste of effort, unless I could assure him, which no one ever had, that in the future he would have the "will power" to resist the impulse to drink.(p.xxix)
• We had long talks when I would still her foreboding by telling her that men of genius conceived their best projects when drunk; that the most majestic constructions of philosophic ***thought*** were so derived.(p.2)
• Our friends ***thought*** a lunacy commission should be appointed.(p.3)
• He had plenty of money left and ***thought*** I had better go to Canada.(p.4)
• Nevertheless, I still ***thought*** I could control the situation, and there were periods of sobriety which renewed my wife's hope.(p.5)
• I, who had ***thought*** so well of myself and my abilities, of my capacity to surmount obstacles, was cornered at last.(p.8)
• I ***thought*** of my poor wife.(p.8)
• Unmindful of his welfare, I ***thought*** only of recapturing the spirit of other days.(p.9)
• When the ***thought*** was expressed that there might be a God personal to me this feeling was intensified.(p.12)
• I could go for such conceptions as Creative Intelligence, Universal Mind or Spirit of Nature but I resisted the ***thought*** of a Czar of the Heavens, however loving His sway might be.(p.12)
• While I lay in the hospital the ***thought*** came that there were thousands of hopeless alcoholics who might be glad to have what had been so freely given me.(p.14)
• Our very lives, as ex-problem drinkers, depend upon our constant ***thought*** of others and how we may help meet their needs.(p.20)
• Only to have that ***thought*** supplanted by "Well, I'll stop with the sixth drink."(p.24)
• I just ***thought*** I would get a sandwich.(p.36)
• Still no ***thought*** of drinking.(p.36)
• "Suddenly the ***thought*** crossed my mind that if I were to put an ounce of whiskey in my milk it couldn't hurt me on a full stomach.(p.36)
• We now see that when we began to drink deliberately, instead of casually, there was little serious or effective ***thought*** during the period of premeditation of what the terrific consequences might be.(p.37)
• As I crossed the threshold of the dining room, the ***thought*** came to mind that it would be nice to have a couple of cocktails with dinner.(p.41)
• This time I had not ***thought*** of the consequences at all.(p.41)
• They grinned, which I didn't like so much, and then asked me if I ***thought*** myself alcoholic and if I were really licked this time.(p.42)
• But cheer up, something like half of us ***thought*** we were atheists or agnostics.(p.44)
• But his face falls when we speak of spiritual matters, especially when we mention God, for we have reopened a subject which our man ***thought*** he had neatly evaded or entirely ignored.(p.45)
• We were bothered with the ***thought*** that faith and dependence upon a Power beyond ourselves was somewhat weak, even cowardly.(p.45)
• Some of the contemporaries of Columbus ***thought*** a round earth preposterous.(p.51)
• In this book you will read the experience of a man who ***thought*** he was an atheist.(p.55)
• He attended church school, where he became rebellious at what he ***thought*** an overdose of religious education.(p.56)
• Then, like a thunderbolt, a great ***thought*** came.(p.56)
• Save for a few brief moments of temptation the ***thought*** of drink has never returned; and at such times a great revulsion has risen up in him.(p.57)
• We ***thought*** we could find an easier, softer way.(p.58)
• We ***thought*** well before taking this step making sure we were ready; that we could at last abandon ourselves utterly to Him.(p.63)
• Many of us ***thought*** it necessary to go much further.(p.72)
• They only ***thought*** they had lost their egoism and fear; they only ***thought*** they had humbled themselves.(p.73)
• We ***thought*** he ought to be willing to do that if necessary, but if he were in jail he could provide nothing for either family.(p.79)
• This ***thought*** brings us to Step Ten, which suggests we continue to take personal inventory and continue to set right any new mistakes as we go along.(p.84)
• We will see that our new attitude toward liquor has been given us without any ***thought*** or effort on our part.(p.85)
• Here we ask God for inspiration, an intuitive ***thought*** or a decision.(p.86)
• As we go through the day we pause, when agitated or doubtful, and ask for the right ***thought*** or action.(p.87)
• He may rebel at the ***thought*** of a drastic housecleaning which requires discussion with other people.(p.94)
• The bill collectors, the sheriffs, the angry taxi drivers, the policemen, the bums, the pals, and even the ladies they sometimes brought home -- our husbands ***thought*** we were so inhospitable.(p.106)
• There could be no love in such persons, we ***thought***.(p.107)
• Our next ***thought*** is that you should never tell him what he must do about his drinking.(p.111)
• We ***thought***, on the whole, we were pretty good women, capable of being nicer if our husbands stopped drinking.(p.116)
• We do not like the ***thought*** that the contents of a book or the work of another alcoholic has accomplished in a few weeks that for which we struggled for years.(p.118)
• We suggest that you direct some of your ***thought*** to the wives of his new alcoholic friends.(p.119)
• Cling to the ***thought*** that, in God's hands, the dark past is the greatest possession you have -- the key to life and happiness for others.(p.124)
• He ***thought*** all alcoholics should constantly have chocolate available for its quick energy value at times of fatigue.(p.133)
• To get over drinking will require a transformation of ***thought*** and attitude.(p.143)
• Some time later, and just as he ***thought*** he was getting control of his liquor situation, he went on a roaring bender.(p.155)
• His wife came, scarcely daring to be hopeful, though she ***thought*** she saw something different about her husband already.(p.158)
• He and his wife would leave elated by the ***thought*** of what they could now do for some stricken acquaintance and his family.(p.160)
• To 1950, the year of his death, he carried the A.A. message to more than 5,000 alcoholic men and women, and to all these he gave his medical services without ***thought*** of charge.(p.171)
• When beer first came back, I ***thought*** that I was safe.(p.177)
• I learned that it was something of a spiritual nature, which did not appeal to me very much, but I ***thought*** it could do no harm.(p.178)
• I read everything I could find, and talked to everyone who I ***thought*** knew anything about it.(p.178)
• It must be remembered that I had read a great deal and talked to everyone who knew, or ***thought*** they knew anything about the subject of alcoholism.(p.180)
• I ***thought*** to myself, "Well, she is going to tell me this is the end," and I certainly couldn't blame her and did not intend to try to justify myself.(p.184)
• Then she told me that these two drunks she had been talking to had a plan whereby they ***thought*** they could quit drinking, and part of that plan was that they tell it to another drunk.(p.185)
• Before very long we began to relate some incidents of our drinking and, naturally, pretty soon, I realized both of them knew what they were talking about because you can see things and smell things when you're drunk, that you can't other times, and, if I had ***thought*** they didn't know what they were talking about, I wouldn't have been willing to talk to them at all.(p.185)
• The next thing they wanted to know was if I ***thought*** I could quit of my own accord, without any help, if I could just walk out of the hospital and never take another drink.(p.186)
• I ***thought*** of what liquor had done to me, the opportunities that I had discarded, the abilities that had been given me and how I had wasted them, and I finally came to the conclusion, that if I didn't want to quit, I certainly ought to want to, and that I was willing to do anything in the world to stop drinking.(p.186)
• Each day I would try to find out what His will was, and try to follow that, rather than trying to get Him to always agree that the things I ***thought*** of myself were the things best for me.(p.187)
• The ***thought*** flashed through his mind, "If they can do it, I can do it!"(p.189)
• I noticed that the others seemed to have such a release, a happiness, a something that I ***thought*** a person ought to have.(p.191)
• I ***thought***, "I think I have the answer."(p.191)
• So I consciously ***thought***.)(p.196)
• I can well remember over a long period of years when I ***thought*** I was the only person in the world who knew that sooner or later I was going to get drunk.(p.198)
• After drinking one glass of beer at the end of my work period for about five days, I ***thought*** I'd better find out whether I really had the stuff licked.(p.203)

• Then I got into the habit of having beers, and decided that a drink of whiskey was not any worse; so I would get the one drink of whiskey but, on second ***thought***, I decided that as long as I was only going to have one, I might as well make it a double-header.(p.203)
• To show you the point to which this obsession went, there came an occasion when I had spent a most delightful week-end, and at nine o'clock on Sunday night I was on my way home, and I ***thought*** I would get a drink.(p.204)
• My only ***thought*** that day was getting a drink, and how to get rid of those clowns was my big problem.(p.206)
• I ***thought*** he had it is his pocket, so I said, "You got some?"(p.208)
• HE ***THOUGHT*** HE COULD DRINK LIKE A GENTLEMAN(p.210)
• I never left the church, but I was a fringe member, and the ***thought*** simply never occurred to me that through the exercise of what I had I might find the answer to my problem, simply because I wouldn't admit that I had a problem.(p.214)
• In fact, as I look back, I have often ***thought*** that they probably concluded that they would put up with me for a couple of years, that I couldn't live much longer, and that they would inherit whatever was left of the practice.(p.215)
• In my own experience I was so jubilant at finding myself sober, and I had so many things to catch up on, that a month went by before the ***thought*** even occurred to me.(p.219)
• But I have never ***thought*** of that as something to do and then forget about.(p.237)
• At the time, I ***thought*** them just a swell pair of screwballs, for they were not only going to save all the drunks in the world but also all the so-called normal people!(p.245)
• It was a ***thought*** that there might be some hope for us.(p.266)
• I ***thought***, "No matter how crazy they are I'll do anything they say to do."(p.267)
• At two-forty-five that morning I ***thought*** I would die.(p.267)
• I ***thought*** when people did what we did that they just locked them up.(p.267)
• I ***thought***, "That guy never could have been a drunk."(p.268)
• And I ***thought***, "I bet he's a sissy.(p.268)
• When we went to bed my sides ached, and I said to my husband, "I ***thought*** I would never laugh again, but I have laughed."(p.269)
• And we went down through the valley, and I remembered reading about the Ku Klux Klan and how they burnt crosses, and I ***thought***, "God alone knows what we are getting into this time!"(p.269)
• They opened with a little prayer, and I ***thought*** it was very fine that we stood, all of us together, and closed with the Lord's Prayer.(p.270)
• I ***thought*** I had done that until Russ' second collapse, and the doctor told me very candidly that he wasn't long for this world.(p.271)
• I knew Doc and Anne were going to be there, and all of them ***thought*** it would be good for me, but the first thing I did was to go to St. Thomas and try to talk to those women.)(p.272)
• Well, I wasn't sure I did, and it was awful foggy, and I wept and asked her what she ***thought*** I ought to do about it.(p.273)
• Haunting me through each day's stupor -- and there were eighteen or nineteen such days in this man's home -- was the ***thought***: "Where do I go when his family comes home?"(p.278)
• Finally, and I shall never know how much later it was, one clear ***thought*** came to me: Try prayer.(p.280)
• There have also been numerous times when I have ***thought*** about taking a drink.(p.285)
• It was therefore not extraordinary that I should shy away from any serious ***thought*** of marriage for a great many years after joining A.A.(p.286)
• I ***thought*** at times that he was telling my story!(p.290)
• I had ***thought*** that I was completely different from other people, that I was beginning to become a little balmy, even to the point of withdrawing more and more from society and wanting to be alone with my bottle.(p.290)
• I sleep like a baby, and never give a ***thought*** to such a thing as insomnia.(p.303)
• He ***thought*** it would be helpful for me to visit the Akron group and meet many like himself.(p.309)
• If I could lay off it, that meant I didn't have to worry about a drinking problem, I ***thought***.(p.317)
• "It can't be my drinking," I ***thought***, "because I can stop any time I want to.(p.318)
• "I'm not crazy," I ***thought***, "and I can't be an alcoholic -- I'm too young."(p.319)
• I was sure I wouldn't belong in an A.A. group -- they were all old men, I ***thought***, and all skid-row bums.(p.319)
• I ***thought*** my problem was that I had been married to a drunk for twenty-seven years.(p.321)
• I ***thought*** it was wonderful, simply marvelous, for him.(p.321)
• Then I went to another meeting, and I still ***thought*** it was wonderful --for him, but not for me.(p.321)
• I ***thought***, now here's a nice sympathetic soul!(p.322)
• And I ***thought***, "You're some martyr, Jane!(p.322)
• I ***thought*** I was losing my mind when I realized that I couldn't stop drinking.(p.324)
• If I had been sincere in what I ***thought*** I wanted more than anything else in life -- a sober husband and a happy, contented home -- I would have gone on the wagon with him.(p.324)
• I never ***thought*** I could be useful to anyone except my husband and my children and perhaps a few friends.(p.326)
• But then I ***thought***, well, now wait, how will I feel next Tuesday?(p.326)
• We all have them, and I ***thought*** a little brandy or a little wine now and then could certainly hurt no one.(p.336)
• I don't believe, when I started, that I even had in mind the ***thought*** that I was drinking.(p.336)
• I ***thought*** the two would never get together.(p.338)
• I ***thought*** that was my answer.(p.338)
• I ***thought*** I was going out of my mind.(p.339)
• And then we went up the side of a hill where we have a little barbecue area to make the fire for the barbecue, and on the way up, I ***thought*** to myself -- I'll go back down to the kitchen and refill this drink.(p.347)
• The ***thought*** came to me -- This is the last one!(p.347)
• And as that ***thought*** came to me, it was as though someone had reached down and taken a heavy overcoat off my shoulders, for that was the last one.(p.347)
• This was such a new ***thought*** that I got all sorts of books on Higher Powers, and I put a Bible by my bedside, and I put a Bible in my car.(p.348)
• So I ***thought*** to myself, I might just as well be drunk as feel like this.(p.348)
• And then I ***thought*** to myself: "Imagine an alcoholic admitting anything!"(p.349)
• I ***thought*** to myself -- what is curing that woman?(p.350)
• And then a silly, simple ***thought*** came to me.(p.351)
• Here were people who had ***thought*** and felt as I had.(p.355)
• It was a terrible blow at the time and I ***thought*** he was pretty much of a heel, but of course it was the finest thing he could have done for me under the circumstances.(p.357)
• All I can remember about the Roaring Twenties is that I drank a great deal, ***thought*** I was having a grand time, managed to get to Europe for a few weeks, was very proud of the dozens of speak-easy cards entitling me to an entree in the better joints between Cleveland and New York, took on a wife, and built a home in a fashionable suburb of Cleveland.(p.358)
• The more I ***thought*** like this the more I drank to submerge my sorrows.(p.362)
• I ***thought*** this was a good time to experiment with liquor.(p.364)
• However, knowing me, she ***thought*** it was a foolish idea, that I wouldn't be interested.(p.367)
• I ***thought*** he merely had a "weakness."(p.369)
• I had no qualms, because I felt the source of a drinking problem was all in how weak one was, and I wasn't like my dad (I ***thought***).(p.370)
• I had been reading a lot about psychiatry and I ***thought***, "Maybe if I talk to a psychiatrist he can find out what is happening, and then I can drink like a lady."(p.387)
• I had never been inside of an insane asylum and I really ***thought*** I was going to a private hospital.(p.387)
• The questions he asked me that I didn't answer honestly, I ***thought*** were none of his business.(p.388)
• Frank had to go to New York, but because I had a dog, we had a duplex, and I ***thought*** -- if only we had a house!(p.388)
• So I located a house, and I ***thought*** we ought to move into it immediately, but Frank was horrified, because he never knew what was going to happen to me.(p.388)
• He always ***thought*** that maybe I was safer in a building where there were other people.(p.388)
• There was a doctor in our church congregation who was interested in my case, and he ***thought*** it was a vitamin deficiency.(p.389)
• We moved once more, to Houston; my husband ***thought*** maybe a change of environment would help and I'd be all right.(p.389)
• When he left I ***thought***, what is this crack-pot thing?(p.391)
• In spite of knowing that my drunkenness was a symptom of the things that were wrong with me, and that I could never drink again, I ***thought*** I couldn't yet give it up, although I was going to try.(p.393)
• In the back of my mind, I probably ***thought***, "They won't take me as drunk as I am."(p.398)
• I went to Europe to escape them, so I ***thought***.(p.405)
• I also ***thought*** that I must have power over myself.(p.408)
• I was an agnostic, so I ***thought***.(p.408)
• I ***thought*** I was the captain of my soul.(p.408)
• I ***thought***, "Aha, he's passing the buck.(p.413)
• I ***thought*** it was my duty to keep her from drinking, not knowing that if the other fellow is really determined to drink there is nothing you can do about it.(p.415)
• They were kind when they ***thought*** about it, but that wasn't often.(p.424)
• She didn't like it, but I ***thought*** it made a man of me.(p.425)
• I ***thought*** it was fine for them.(p.427)
• I'd heard a lot about A.A. and met a great many A.A.'s during that year at home, but I hadn't ***thought*** of it for myself.(p.429)
• I'd ***thought*** of it in an offhand way, of course.(p.429)
• I ***thought***, "If this is A.A. why not go back to drinking, kill myself with booze in the next three years the doctor had given me, and call it a bad job?"(p.430)
• Whatever the root of my unhappiness might turn out to be, I ***thought***, it could not possibly be booze.(p.433)
• The physician wasn't hooked, he ***thought*** -- he just prescribed drugs medically indicated for his many ailments.(p.439)
• But I ***thought*** it was because my responsibilities were increasing.(p.441)
• And Frank did set me up for a meeting every night except Friday, when he ***thought*** he might have a date with his girl friend.(p.447)
• "That's a devil of a way to run an organization," I ***thought***, and I reported Frank to the psychiatrist, who didn't seem perturbed; he just got someone else to take me on Fridays.(p.447)
• Although we enjoyed the laughter in the early days, I heard a lot of things that I ***thought*** were stupid.(p.447)
• When a big, healthy-looking young fellow stood up there and said, "I'm a success today if I don't drink today," I ***thought***, "Man, I've got a thousand things to do today before I can brag about not taking a drink, for God's sake!"(p.447)
• Over the years, as I ***thought*** about Max, her good qualities grew and grew, and we married, and all these qualities became more and more apparent to me, and we were happier and happier.(p.450)
• I ***thought*** that was bad until I hit the hole at a prison camp; it was just wide enough and long enough to lie down in.(p.459)
• In those days, I trusted no church-goer, and ***thought*** A.A. was for weaklings.(p.460)
• I ***thought*** I would be quite happy and never would I drink too much again.(p.465)
• Sly and crafty, I ***thought*** now I'll find out what they think of me here, what they "have on" me, what I've said coming in here drunk.(p.470)
• I ***thought***, "Oh well, these people are just like all the people I've known all my life.(p.472)
• I don't know whether she was a pacifist or whether she just ***thought*** that in the event of another war it would have some bearing on my joining up.(p.484)
• He wanted to give me the very best and he ***thought*** that nothing but being a doctor would suffice.(p.485)
• I ***thought*** that all women should be perfect.(p.487)
• I ***thought***, "I know you didn't pay me, because you didn't get a prescription."(p.488)
• The ***thought*** came to me that if God, as my mother said, was a vengeful God, he couldn't be a loving God.(p.489)
• I ***thought*** that this would be a big help to me.(p.490)
• Vi ***thought*** I didn't want to stop.(p.490)
• Vi was very kind and explained to the jury that I was basically a fine fellow and a good husband, but that I drank too much and that she ***thought*** I had lost my mind and felt that I should be committed to an asylum.(p.492)

• I approached several ministers and all of them ***thought*** it was a very good idea, but they never relinquished any space.(p.495)
• A fanatic, I ***thought*** to myself, but I was polite.(p.503)
• Then he asks me if I am willing to right all the wrongs I have ever done to anyone, no matter how wrong I ***thought*** the others were.(p.503)
• Suddenly a ***thought*** comes.(p.503)
• I begin to see I am not the person I had ***thought*** myself, that I had judged myself by comparing myself to others, and always to my own advantage.(p.504)
• Then comes a ***thought*** that is like a Voice.(p.504)
• Halfway down the driveway a ***thought*** strikes me.(p.506)
• I also ***thought*** I was a brilliant drunk.(p.512)
• Like many of us who went into the service, I ***thought*** it would be a cure-all, a new life.(p.513)
• That ***thought*** had come to me many, many times.(p.515)
• I was going to be sent to the Indian Civil Service, which, in those days, meant that people ***thought*** you had a certain amount of brains.(p.517)
• When I came back, I told the priest, the Chaplain of the place, exactly what I ***thought*** of him and he didn't like it.(p.517)
• I should say there was less drinking in the Army than I ***thought*** at that time.(p.518)
• In part, it was a feeling of intense shame at having to leave the Army during the war, but mostly it was resentment that this kind of thing should happen to me for, strange as it may seem, up to then I still ***thought*** I could control drinking.(p.521)
• I ***thought,*** well, now that I've been put out for drinking, I'll just show them that they were completely wrong, so I went off on the biggest bout I had been on up to then, involving about a fortnight's blackout.(p.521)
• The ***thought*** of stopping drinking just never occurred to me.(p.522)
• Finally, my mother came and said she had kept me at home for six years because she ***thought*** she could help me, but that now she had come to the conclusion that I wasn't even worth trying to help.(p.523)
• Just as I was wondering what on earth I could do -- I was too drunk even to pack a handkerchief – the memory of an A.A. write-up that I had seen in the Evening Mail flashed across my mind – and I ***thought*** to myself, this is something I haven't tried yet.(p.523)
• It was their open night meeting, but of course I ***thought*** they were all alcoholics; I couldn't imagine why anybody else would want to go there, and my first reaction was, well, I've come to something that's not for me.(p.524)
• I ***thought*** that if these kind of ordinary people can do it, a man of my brains ought to find it much more easy, and I joined.(p.524)
• On one of these trips, the judge must have ***thought*** I was worth saving, for instead of sending me to jail, he sent me to A.A. for one month.(p.526)
• I ***thought*** if they smelled whiskey on my breath, they would lock me up, and I couldn't live without my bottle.(p.526)
• I ***thought*** if the cops did come to the hospital, the doctors would tell them I was crazy and didn't know what I was doing.(p.528)
• I remember the day when I decided to drink myself to death quietly, without bothering anyone, because I was tired of having been a dependable, trustworthy person for about thirty-nine years without having received what I ***thought*** was a proper reward for my virtue.(p.531)
• Things weren't going as I ***thought*** they should, for my greater enjoyment, comfort and fame; therefore, if the universe wouldn't play my way, I wouldn't play at all.(p.531)
• So I ***thought.***(p.532)
• And having sung that phrase, I'd chuckle with amusement, turning into irony turning into self-contempt turning into self-pity, at the sad fate of Bob, that wonderful, poor little motherless boy who was so smart in school and who grew up to accept responsibility so early and so fast and who staggered under his burdens without a whimper until the time came when he ***thought*** he was too good for this world and so he ought to be out of it.(p.532)
• For you learned that he had been guilty of the thing he had accused you of, and his guilt had brought suffering to his entire family; and he ***thought*** he saw his young son beginning his own tragic pattern.(p.533)
• For a little while, I was the great man I wanted to be, and ***thought*** myself entitled to be just by reason of being.(p.537)
• I ***thought*** I had recovered.(p.539)
• I worked when I could – piddling jobs I ***thought*** them.(p.540)
• Hope had died, or so I ***thought.***(p.540)
• I ***thought*** I could never be happy.(p.542)
• I ***thought*** that life was a pretty simple thing; you simply made a plan for your life, based upon what you wanted, and then you needed only the courage to go after it.(p.545)
• I ***thought*** I knew exactly what I wanted out of life and I ***thought*** I knew exactly how to get it.(p.545)
• I ***thought*** this would give me ego-strength, make me feel wanted and secure, and alleviate my fears, but again nothing changed inside me.(p.546)
• It had provided me with excuses for my lack of education, my marital failures, personal failures, inadequacy, and of course, my alcoholism and, though I really ***thought*** I had been willing to part with it, now I knew I was reluctant to let it go.(p.552)
• To wear expensive clothes, to have bartenders know what to serve me before I ordered, to be recognized by headwaiters and shown to the best table, to play gin rummy for high stakes with the insouciance of a riverboat gambler – these were the enduring values in life, I ***thought.***(p.556)
• I ***thought*** I had learned my lesson.(p.558)
• Dr. Harry M. Tiebout, psychiatrist: "As a psychiatrist, I have ***thought*** a great deal about the relationship of my specialty to A.A. and I have come to the conclusion that our particular function can very often lie in preparing the way for the patient to accept any sort of treatment or outside help.(p.571)

thought-life

• Our ***thought-life*** will be placed on a much higher plane when our thinking is cleared of wrong motives.(p.86)

thoughtful

• They remember when father was romantic, ***thoughtful*** and successful.(p.123)
• New acquaintances who know nothing of alcoholism might be made and ***thoughtful*** consideration given their needs.(p.131)
• A spiritual awakening soon came to mean trying each day to be a little more ***thoughtful,*** more considerate, a little more courteous to those with whom I came in contact.(p.381)
• The drive was long and cold but he was thankful for the hot bricks which some ***thoughtful*** person had given him for his feet.(p.497)

thoughtless

• I am trying now, each day, to make up for all those selfish, ***thoughtless,*** foolish things I did in my drinking days.(p.326)

thoughts

• If these ***thoughts*** occur, they are hazy and readily supplanted with the old threadbare idea that this time we shall handle ourselves like other people.(p.24)
• Yes, we of agnostic temperament have had these ***thoughts*** and experiences.(p.46)
• Then we resolutely turn our ***thoughts*** to someone we can help.(p.84)
• These are ***thoughts*** which must go with us constantly.(p.85)
• When resentful ***thoughts*** come, try to pause and count your blessings.(p.119)
• My ***thoughts*** went round and round with "What's it all about anyhow?(p.244)
• My ***thoughts*** sometimes turned to the idea that there must be a remedy.(p.256)
• Out of this maelstrom just two coherent ***thoughts*** came to the surface; one, a drink would mean homelessness and death; two, I could no longer relieve the pressure of fear by starting home, as was once my habitual solution to this problem, because I no longer had a home.(p.279)
• Such thinking usually began with ***thoughts*** of the pleasant drinking of my youth.(p.285)
• I learned early in my A.A. life that I could not afford to fondle such ***thoughts,*** as you might fondle a pet, because this particular pet could grow into a monster.(p.285)
• These ***thoughts*** become part of our daily lives.(p.382)
• The contempt and disgust that was in his face and ***thoughts***!(p.391)
• Call friend in A.A. when bad ***thoughts*** come.(p.477)
• After nearly eight years of sobriety in A.A., I still can set down such ***thoughts,*** "against my instinct and training," showing that I still consider myself a "special" person, entitled to special privileges.(p.536)

thousand

• The exercise of an option brought in more money, leaving us with a profit of several ***thousand*** dollars for that year.(p.3)
• In one western city and its environs there are one ***thousand*** of us and our families.(p.15)
• We would not even do the cause of temperate drinking any good, for not one drinker in a ***thousand*** likes to be told anything about alcohol by one who hates it.(p.103)
• I was born in a small New England village of about seven ***thousand*** souls.(p.171)
• They did not seem to be getting an answer, for here I was staying sober and selling lots of auto polish, on which they were making one ***thousand*** per cent profit.(p.247)
• From a single member in the Chicago area, commuting to Akron, we now exceed six ***thousand.***(p.295)
• I moved a ***thousand*** miles away from home to Chicago and a new environment.(p.305)
• It has made life a ***thousand*** times easier and simpler than did the endless compromises and conflicts by which I lived before.(p.394)
• A load weighing a ***thousand*** pounds came off my back.(p.414)
• To cut a long story short, I spent seven years and ten ***thousand*** dollars on my psychiatric adventure, and emerged in worse condition than ever.(p.434)
• When a big, healthy-looking young fellow stood up there and said, "I'm a success today if I don't drink today," I thought, "Man, I've got a ***thousand*** things to do today before I can brag about not taking a drink, for God's sake!"(p.447)
• One morning, I woke up with a ***thousand*** dollars.(p.528)
• There were debts totaling nearly ten ***thousand*** dollars to be paid off.(p.541)

thousands

• Other ***thousands*** came to a few A.A. meetings and at first decided they didn't want the program.(p.xx)
• These men may well have a remedy for ***thousands*** of such situations.(p.xxiv)
• Everyone spent in ***thousands*** and chattered in millions.(p.3)
• While I lay in the hospital the thought came that there were ***thousands*** of hopeless alcoholics who might be glad to have what had been so freely given me.(p.14)
• We of ALCOHOLICS ANONYMOUS, know ***thousands*** of men and women who were once just as hopeless as Bill.(p.17)
• But for the grace of God, there would have been ***thousands*** more convincing demonstrations.(p.25)
• We hope it strikes home to ***thousands*** like him.(p.43)
• Here are ***thousands*** of men and women, worldly indeed.(p.50)
• We have spent ***thousands*** of dollars for examinations.(p.73)
• He knows that ***thousands*** of men, much like himself, have recovered.(p.113)
• Since this book was first published, A.A. has released ***thousands*** of alcoholics from asylums and hospitals of every kind.(p.114)
• My downfall cost the business community unknown ***thousands*** of dollars, for it takes real money to train a man for an executive position.(p.137)
• So far, so good -- all according to plan, like ***thousands*** of others.(p.225)
• Therefore, these seventeen A.A.'s, and hundreds of ***thousands*** like them, have been saved years of infinite suffering.(p.315)
• And the psychiatrist has had ***thousands*** of couches, and has put you and me on them many, many times, but he hasn't helped us very much, though he has tried hard; and we owe the clergy and the doctor and the psychiatrist a deep debt of gratitude, but they haven't helped our alcoholism, except in a rare few instances.(p.352)
• The story is not very different from that of ***thousands*** of other young men in my generation.(p.373)
• Maine newsletter (Boomerang) say: "With tireless devotion and humility, this venerable Indian gentleman traveled ***thousands*** of miles humbly pleading for sobriety.(p.476)
• Among our rapidly growing membership of ***thousands*** of alcoholics such transformations, though frequent, are by no means the rule.(p.569)

thread

• It was an evil and corroding ***thread;*** the fabric of our existence was shot through with it.(p.67)

threadbare

• If these thoughts occur, they are hazy and readily supplanted with the old ***threadbare*** idea that this time we shall handle ourselves like other people.(p.24)

threat

• Here was the ***threat*** of commitment, the loss of family and position, to say nothing of that intense mental and physical suffering which drinking always caused him.(p.36)

threaten

• On more than one occasion my wife would *threaten* to leave me.(p.362)

threatened

• In most cases it was found that our self-esteem, our pocketbooks, our ambitions, our personal relationships (including sex) were hurt or *threatened*.(p.64)
• During this time, I had been *threatened*, beaten, kissed, praised and damned alternately by relatives, family, friends and strangers, but of course it all went for naught.(p.300)
• Luckily a friend was with me, who dragged me out, screaming and cursing, while the bartender *threatened* to call the police.(p.411)
• The last time I drank, when I was twenty-nine, I drank for only four days, yet I *threatened* to kill my children; I beat my wife at home and on the church steps; I mistreated a child in my office; and I ran to a hospital for mental illness to avoid jail.(p.418)
• After I came to A.A., I was divorced by my wife; I lost my practice; I was legally restrained from seeing my children; I went broke; and the dental society *threatened* me with the loss of my license.(p.420)

threatening

• In the midst of such pandemonium they may have rushed out *threatening* to live with the other woman forever.(p.106)
• An offer of appreciation for not having had a drink for those few months and then and there, without anybody promising me anything or *threatening* me, I made a solemn vow that never so long as I lived would I take another drink.(p.200)

threatens

• *Threatens* to fire me for drinking and padding my expense account.(p.65)

three

• "Bill's Story," "Doctor Bob's Nightmare," and one other personal history from the first edition were retained intact; *three* were edited and one of these was retitled; new versions of two stories were written with new titles; thirty completely new stories were added; and the story section was divided into *three* parts, under the same headings that are used now.(p.xi)
• Their very first case, a desperate one, recovered immediately and became A.A. number *three*.(p.xvii)
• But great numbers of these -- about two out of *three* -- began to return as time passed.(p.xx)
• We gave up our positions and off we roared on a motorcycle, the sidecar stuffed with tent, blankets, a change of clothes, and *three* huge volumes of a financial reference service.(p.2)
• "Bathtub" gin, two bottles a day, and often *three*, got to be routine.(p.5)
• For *three* or four months the goose hung high.(p.7)
• Our description of the alcoholic, the chapter to the agnostic, and our personal adventures before and after make clear *three* pertinent ideas:(p.60)
• Being convinced, we were at Step *Three*, which is that we decided to turn our will and our life over to God as we understood Him.(p.60)
• We are now at Step *Three*.(p.63)
• *Three*: This husband has gone much further than husband number two.(p.109)
• If you have a number *three* husband, you may be in luck.(p.113)
• We have *three* little mottoes which are apropos.(p.135)
• Here were *three* exceptional men lost to this world because I did not understand alcoholism as I do now.(p.137)
• I pointed out that I had had nothing to drink whatever for *three* years, and this in the face of difficulties that would have made nine out of ten men drink their heads off.(p.138)
• If this presents difficulty, re-reading chapters two and *three*, where the alcoholic sickness is discussed at length might be worth while.(p.140)
• Perhaps he could handle, say, *three* drinks -- no more!(p.154)
• The last *three* times, I got drunk on the way home from here.(p.157)
• So, you see, there were *three* alcoholics in that town, who now felt they had to give to others what they had found, or be sunk.(p.158)
• He had *three* visitors.(p.159)
• He was there *three* months.(p.159)
• A year and six months later these *three* had succeeded with seven more.(p.159)
• Beginning with the story of "Dr. Bob," a co-founder of A.A., there are here presented *three* groups of personal histories.(p.165)
• The next *three* years I spent in Boston, Chicago, and Montreal in the employ of a large manufacturing concern, selling railway supplies, gas engines of all sorts, and many other items of heavy hardware.(p.172)
• I lost only a half day's work during these *three* years.(p.173)
• I passed in at least *three* absolutely blank books.(p.174)
• After *three* years of this, I wound up in the local hospital where they attempted to help me, but I would get my friends to smuggle me a quart, or I would steal the alcohol about the building, so that I got rapidly worse.(p.175)
• This dry spell lasted for about *three* weeks; then I went to Atlantic City to attend several days' meeting of a national society of which I was a member.(p.179)
• ALCOHOLIC ANONYMOUS NUMBER *THREE*(p.182)
• On the return trip, after two or *three* loads, I passed out and had to be carried to the house.(p.183)
• Then Prohibition came into effect, and the facts that the stuff obtainable was so horrible and sometimes deadly, and that I had married and had a job which I had to look after, helped me for a period of some *three* or four years, although I would get drunk every time I could get hold of enough to drink to get started.(p.183)
• However, after two or *three* trials, I found this was not satisfactory because they did not serve enough to satisfy me.(p.184)
• Away from my office two or *three* weeks at a time; horrible days and nights when I would lie on the floor of my home, lying awake and reaching over to get the bottle, taking a drink and going back into oblivion.(p.184)
• During the first six months of 1935, I was hospitalized eight times for intoxication and shackled to the bed two or *three* days before I even knew where I was.(p.184)
• It was in the next two or *three* days after I had first met Doc and Bill, that I finally came to a decision to turn my will over to God and to go along with this program the best that I could.(p.189)
• I was the oldest of *three* children, and my father was an alcoholic.(p.193)
• I sold *three* lots to an elderly lady in Cleveland.(p.196)
• I remember one occasion when I did not drink for *three* hundred and sixty-four days, but I didn't quite make the year.(p.200)
• He said, "Well, I haven't had a drink for *three* months."(p.201)
• So I had one double-header every night for about two or *three* weeks.(p.203)
• I was arrested and taken to jail where I was beaten up by two or *three* fellows who were already in there and whom I tried to boss.(p.204)
• *Three* days later I went to work.(p.205)
• I remember well one fellow, Joe, walking nearly *three* miles through slush, wet and snow to come to the hospital to see a man that he had never seen before in his life, and that impressed me very much.(p.208)
• I can remember that in my childhood, he was ill at ease with the children because he attempted to assert an army discipline that had been ground into him during his *three* and a half years of army service.(p.210)
• I had four brothers and *three* sisters.(p.210)
• This experience sent me to law school where I went at night and which course I completed in less than *three* years, taking the highest state bar examinations and passing them.(p.212)
• The first definite indications of an alcoholic pattern began to arise when I would go to New York on business and disappear, and wind up in Philadelphia or Boston for two or *three* day periods.(p.213)
• After two or *three* years of effort along this line, I reached the point of actual despair that I ever would be able to drink only a harmless amount each day.(p.215)
• My children had lost respect for me and, in fact, it was only after *three* or four years of sobriety that any of them ever said anything to me to indicate that I had recouped even a little of their respect.(p.215)
• Bill bought me a drink or two on the way, and Dorothy S. came with us, and the *three* of us went over to the City Hospital.(p.217)
• In fact, the last *three* years of my drinking was a routine of barbiturates in the morning, so that I could stop shaking enough to shave, and then alcohol beginning about four-thirty or five o'clock, with a struggle not to take a drink at noon or during the day, because I had the idea that if I took one drink, I would smell as though I had had a pint.(p.217)
• I remember looking longingly at the window as an easier solution, and shuddering at the memory of that other window, *three* years before, and the six agonizing months in a London hospital ward.(p.224)
• Had he come two or *three* days later I think I would have thrown him out, but he hit when I was open for anything.(p.239)
• Jackie arrived about seven in the evening and talked until *three* a.m.(p.239)
• But each drink after the "first" seemed to become less effective and after *three* or four they all seemed like water.(p.241)
• With the war over, and back in Baltimore with the folks, there were several small jobs for *three* years and then I went to work soliciting as one of the first ten employees of a new national finance company.(p.242)
• This company now does a volume of over *three* billion dollars annually.(p.242)
• *Three* years later, at twenty-five, I opened and operated their Philadelphia office and was earning more than I ever have since.(p.242)
• I'd work like mad for *three* or four weeks without a single drink, save my money, pay a few bills and then "reward" myself with alcohol.(p.244)
• *Three* months before I met Jackie I had made my second feeble try at suicide.(p.245)
• Bill had then been dry *three* years and Hank, two.(p.245)
• They had also been periodic big shots who had goofed out repeatedly at the wrong time, and they also knew how to split one paper match into *three* separate matches.(p.245)
• I'd been dry *three* weeks, had the wrinkles out and had sobered up my sponsor all by myself!(p.246)
• We ordered sandwiches and one man said, "*Three* beers."(p.247)
• After a bit, the other man said "*Three* beers."(p.247)
• Then it was my turn -- I ordered "*Three* beers," but this time it was different, I had a cash investment of thirty cents and, on a ten dollar a week salary, that's a big thing.(p.247)
• So I drank all *three* beers, one after the other, said "I'll be seeing you, boys," and went around the corner for a bottle.(p.247)
• Returning to the town I had left *three* months before, I became editor of a monthly magazine, soon had additional publicity and advertising accounts and the money rolled in.(p.254)
• In *three* months John Barleycorn had me kicked out.(p.254)
• Always, in between, there were intervals of being broke, riding freights and hitch-hiking interminable distances from one big town to another in *three* states.(p.255)
• An accident while drunk laid me low for about *three* weeks.(p.258)
• Singly and in groups of two or *three*, they came to visit me.(p.258)
• I drove these *three* or four miles down the road only to find that Jack was out.(p.267)
• We were in A.A. *three* and a half years when he was taken from me.(p.270)
• By the time I was twenty-one I had six years of life in foreign countries, spoke *three* languages fluently, and had attended college for two years.(p.275)
• *Three* months in bed.(p.275)
• *Three* more months of being up and around the house for brief periods and in bed the rest of the time.(p.275)
• At least *three* of those four years must have been a living hell for my wife, because she had to watch the man she loved disintegrate morally, mentally and financially.(p.277)
• Instead, he got dressed, took me out, bought me *three* or four double shots and put me to bed.(p.278)
• I remained with them for *three* weeks, using part of the time in making many amends, which I had had no earlier opportunity of making.(p.281)
• Those *three* weeks left me completely exhausted and I had to return to Akron for *three* more months of rest.(p.282)
• While there, two or *three* more "cash customers" (as Dr. Bob used to call them -- probably because they had so little cash) were shipped in to us from Detroit.(p.282)
• But it took six more months of work and disappointments before a group of *three* men got together in my rooming house bedroom for their first A.A. meeting.(p.282)
• This gave me the freedom to do A.A. work, and to rest for periods of two or *three* days when I became too exhausted to carry on.(p.283)
• During the first *three* months I carried on all these activities without a car, depending entirely on buses and streetcars -- I, who had always to have a car at

my immediate command.(p.283)
• So six months ago I acquired a ready made family consisting of one charming wife, four grown children to whom I am devoted, and *three* grandchildren.(p.286)
• By 1932, I was going on two or *three* day benders.(p.288)
• Then when we got back to the apartment, he was willing to wait two or *three* days until I got my health back to be paid off for the liquor and fare.(p.289)
• This consisted of walking the floor for *three* or four days and nights until I could take nourishment.(p.289)
• In the next two or *three* days the balance of this handful of men contacted me, encouraged me, and told me how they were trying to live this program of recovery and the fun they were having doing it.(p.291)
• I stayed in Akron two or *three* weeks on my initial trip trying to absorb as much of the program and philosophy as possible.(p.291)
• I spent a great deal of time with Dr. Bob, whenever he had the time to spare, and in the homes of two or *three* other people, trying to see how the family lived the program.(p.291)
• The day before I was due to go back to Chicago, a Wednesday and Dr. Bob's afternoon off, he had me down to the office and we spent *three* or four hours formally going through the Six-Step program as it was at that time.(p.291)
• A few months later one of the men who had been in touch with the group in Akron came to Chicago to live, and then there were *three* of us who continued to have informal meetings quite regularly.(p.294)
• The *three* of us did not feel up to the job, and after a few meetings we convinced the prospects that they too should go to Akron where they could see an older group in action.(p.295)
• Doctors told me before I stopped that I had only *three* years at the outside to live.(p.295)
• *Three* years after I started on my drinking career, I lost my first job.(p.298)
• I made arrangements to enter the hospital *three* days later and promptly went out and got stiff for *three* days.(p.302)
• I eat *three* good meals a day now, and really enjoy them.(p.303)
• The next *three* years saw me in sanitariums, once in a ten day coma, from which I very nearly did not recover, in and out of hospitals or confined at home with day and night nurses.(p.306)
• Somehow, I made it through basic and then laid off the booze for about *three* months, because I was in school at night.(p.317)
• After about *three* months, no more weekends.(p.318)
• *Three* months later, he hated the game and found solace in the bottle.(p.330)
• I'd just take a couple or *three* barbiturates to get back to sleep -- eating my alcohol.(p.333)
• Well, of course that was all I needed -- to switch from wine to brandy for *three* weeks.(p.338)
• So when the children were in school from nine to *three*, I started up a nice little business and was fairly successful in it.(p.339)
• *Three* years and *three* months of sobriety, without a slip, has meant a lot to me, my wife, and my family.(p.342)
• During the next *three* years, I tried often again to give it up, but failed miserably.(p.343)
• I have been on this program for *three* months and I feel terrible."(p.348)
• You've been sober for *three* months, been working hard.(p.348)
• Just *three* years of drinking pushed a shy, lonely young girl to the depth of depression.(p.353)
• I needed alcohol from that night on, and it in turn used me, ruling my life for *three* years.(p.353)
• I lost my driver's license, was made a ward of the court, and was put on probation (not to mention the fact that I might have killed *three* friends and myself).(p.354)
• When I did make it home in 1920, I re-entered school and caught up with my class in a few short months -- I actually did a year's work in *three* months, proving much to the disgust of my dad that I could do it when I wanted to.(p.358)
• I stayed on in Florida for *three* weeks, enjoying our reunion, a new found health and a deeper love than I had ever experienced before.(p.364)
• During *three* years in A.A., I haven't lost so much as one shirt.(p.372)
• The church was just *three* blocks from our home.(p.385)
• That went on for about *three* years, and then we moved back to Texas again.(p.386)
• I took that treatment *three* times and it didn't work -- at least, for me.(p.389)
• I couldn't walk, having it in a cast, and the doctor left the cast on *three* weeks longer than was necessary because he never found me sober enough to take it off.(p.390)
• I took two or *three* drinks so my eyes could focus, and I could see that horrible picture of the awful drunk on the first page; he couldn't get the drink to his mouth, he had a towel around his hand and he needed a shave.(p.391)
• It took me *three* psychoanalysts and several years in A.A. to really get this through my head.(p.401)
• Why did I have to have at least *three* cocktails to sit through dinner?(p.406)
• I would have *three* quick strong ones in order to endure the evening.(p.407)
• For *three* generations, my family had had a charge account in one of the big New York hotels.(p.410)
• I had a lovely wife and *three* children.(p.418)
• My experience has been active: *three* meetings a week, many tapes, many A.A. conferences, much work on the Twelve Steps, and much work with other alcoholics and their families.(p.420)
• I spent the next *three* days in a cell.(p.424)
• *Three* years later I was discharged in the same way.(p.425)
• But my dad pulled some strings and got in to see me after *three* weeks.(p.425)
• *Three* days later I lost my job.(p.430)
• I thought, "If this is A.A. why not go back to drinking, kill myself with booze in the next *three* years the doctor had given me, and call it a bad job?"(p.430)
• After *three* months it was forgotten.(p.434)
• I'd think, "I wonder why I'm saying that again -- I've already said it *three* times."(p.442)
• One night, I had to put myself back to sleep *three* times, and then I finally decided to give it up.(p.443)
• *Three* weeks after an armed robbery in which one person received a superficial flesh wound (I could have killed someone!), I was apprehended.(p.460)
• During the twenty-four hours after running into the Serenity Prayer, I think I took the first *three* Steps for the first time.(p.461)
• I was paroled when I had served less than *three* years.(p.462)
• *Three* weeks ago, my phone rang, and a voice I hadn't heard in over twenty-three years spoke.(p.462)
• It was my ex-wife, and she said my twenty-seven-year-old son, who has completed his Marine Corps training and graduated from college, wanted to see me privately, was getting married in *three* months, and wanted me at the wedding.(p.462)
• I haven't seen my son since he was *three* and a half years old.(p.463)
• I was frightened -- terribly frightened, and in about *three* days I was sober.(p.467)
• After the first two or *three* days you were allowed the run of the place and it was a lot of fun.(p.468)
• This easy method of sobering up would last at least *three* days.(p.468)
• My visits to that sanitarium went on for nearly *three* years, until in March of 1944, my father died and I was too drunk to attend his funeral.(p.469)
• And so for *three* months this one woman was my A.A.(p.472)
• And when she broke a luncheon date with me one Saturday, after I had been in A.A. for about *three* months, I said, "I'll show her!(p.472)
• By grace of God I stop, think two things: This would kill good mother and father; then remember boys talk about Indian fellow who been sober *three* years.(p.475)
• To tell you a small part of what my mother's life must have been like: *Three* of her kids were in jail that year -- two sons and a daughter.(p.480)
• At this point I believe I had only been intoxicated on maybe *three* or four occasions, and certainly whiskey was no problem to me.(p.487)
• I borrowed five hundred dollars from the bank and *three* hundred from the loan shop, and I drank that up pretty fast.(p.490)
• I had to put up a *three* hundred dollar bond because he was carrying the same summons around in his pocket for me.(p.491)
• What actually happened was that I had taken a penknife and stabbed Vi *three* times with it.(p.492)
• I was there about *three* weeks, and then I got restless and started to tramp across the country, here and there, until I finally wound up in Pennsylvania, in a steel mill.(p.492)
• Thinking only of two or *three* dollars to buy some whiskey, I did the job and that's how I met Ella G., who was responsible for my coming into A.A.(p.493)
• It was Charlie and *three* or four others.(p.495)
• We held some two or *three* meetings at Ella's home and from there we held some two or *three* at her mother's home.(p.495)
• *Three* attempts to enlist in the service, and *three* failures because of being skinny.(p.499)
• I drink steadily, I come to at *three* in the morning.(p.501)
• The game is over and the other *three* leave.(p.502)
• Those poor stiffs probably went to a doctor and were told that if they quit they'd live *three* weeks and if they didn't they'd die in one."(p.510)
• I'm grateful because that Higher Power led me to A.A. a little over *three* years ago, when I needed it very badly.(p.512)
• When I landed of course I hit a gin mill, and with *three* or four good shots under my belt the world began to go into that rosy glow.(p.513)
• I had a habit of getting up just prior to the closing time of the saloons, about two or *three* o'clock in the morning.(p.514)
• Then I was sent out to India and from then on drinking just increased and increased, and I started having two or *three* day spells instead of just the ordinary concentrated one day.(p.519)
• I had *three* or four very uncomfortable months with my regiment then on the Suez Canal.(p.520)
• They kept me in hospital for two months, and then they sent me up to Egypt, a *three* days journey.(p.521)
• About *three* months after that, my record reached home and I got a letter telling me I was retired from the Army, they put it very kindly, on medical grounds.(p.521)
• I had two or *three* feelings about that.(p.521)
• As I say, this specialist put a scare in me for about a fortnight or *three* weeks, then I started my last bout which went on and off for about *three* months.(p.523)
• By the grace of God, I only served *three* years.(p.528)
• (There was a time, for about *three* months, when I bought a ten-dollar wrist watch every pay day -- that is every two weeks.(p.532)
• In those years I was in jail nine times, in an alcoholic ward, overnight, twice; and I was fired from *three* jobs, two of them very good ones.(p.536)
• The only importance in all of this lies in the fact that at twenty-three I was just as sick as I was at thirty *three*, when I came into A.A., but at that time I apparently had no place to go because I had no drinking problem.(p.546)
• The last *three* years of my drinking, I drank on my job.(p.548)
• About this time, I met a man who had *three* motherless children and it seemed that might be a solution to my problem.(p.548)
• The children kept me sober for darn near *three* weeks, and then I went on (please God) my last drunk.(p.549)
• *Three* -- The only requirement for A.A. membership is a desire to stop drinking.(p.564)
• Any two or *three* alcoholics gathered together for sobriety may call themselves an A.A. group, provided that, as a group, they have no other affiliation.(p.565)
• (This address is now available in pamphlet form at nominal cost through most A.A. groups or from Box 459, Grand Central Station, New York, NY 10163, under the title "*Three* Talks to Medical Societies by Bill W." -- formerly called "Bill on Alcoholism" and earlier "Alcoholism the Illness.")(p.572)

three-hundred

• I optioned a piece of land just off East Market Street to put up a *three-hundred* suite apartment.(p.198)

three-months

• He has just returned from a *three-months* leave of absence, has taken a cure, looks fine, and to clinch the matter, the board of directors told him this was his last chance."(p.138)

three-quarters

• It took *three-quarters* of an hour and two changes to get there -- back to my starting point.(p.223)

three-thirty

• That was at *three-thirty* in the afternoon.(p.201)
• At *three-thirty* the next morning, I was in Champlain Street Station, in jail for driving while intoxicated and insulting an officer; and the suit of which I was so proud was in such shape that the turnkey had to get me a pair of trousers to go into court in the next morning.(p.201)

three-weeks'

• And that came after a *three-weeks'* illness of my son.(p.338)

three-year

• I had completed a *three-year* tour in the Navy.(p.418)

threes

• Already," continues the early text, "twos and ***threes*** and fives of us have sprung up in other communities."(p.xv)

• Little clusters of twos and ***threes*** and fives of us have sprung up in other communities, through contact with our two larger centers.(p.162)

threshold

• As I crossed the ***threshold*** of the dining room, the thought came to mind that it would be nice to have a couple of cocktails with dinner.(p.41)

• Many a man, yet dazed from his hospital experience, has stepped over the ***threshold*** of that home into freedom.(p.160)

threw

• For the next few years fortune ***threw*** money and applause my way.(p.3)

• Hence we are at pains to tell why we think our present faith is reasonable, why we think it more sane and logical to believe than not to believe, why we say our former thinking was soft and mushy when we ***threw*** up our hands in doubt and said, "We don't know."(p.53)

• His wife is one of those persons who really feels there is something rather sinful about these commodities, so she nagged, and her intolerance finally ***threw*** him into a fit of anger.(p.135)

• They ***threw*** us in the jail.(p.264)

• After finding every bottle that I had hidden around the apartment, she took away my pants, my shoes, my money and my keys, ***threw*** them under the bed in the back bedroom and slip-locked our door.(p.288)

• I halfway washed them, and he told me to do them again, and I did, and he yelled at me to do them again, and I picked up one of the cans and ***threw*** it at him and told him to do them himself.(p.317)

• I ***threw*** up.(p.328)

• However, I ***threw*** myself into Twelve Step work, and what I feared would be a calamity turned out to be the most blessed of blessings.(p.394)

• This combination nearly ***threw*** me.(p.430)

• Finally, I ***threw*** away all my books and decided never to return to A.A.(p.460)

• Only, having found them, I ***threw*** them away, and ordered another extra dry martini.(p.533)

thrill

• He gets a ***thrill*** out of skipping in front of fast-moving vehicles.(p.37)

• I get my greatest ***thrill*** of accomplishment from the knowledge that I have played a part in the new happiness achieved by countless others like myself.(p.229)

• Nothing has ever to this day equalled the ***thrill*** of that first case.(p.282)

• Instead of wanting to escape some perplexing problem, we experience a ***thrill*** of challenge in the opportunity it affords for another application of A.A. techniques, and we find ourselves tackling it with surprising vigor.(p.311)

thrilled

• I loved my father dearly and I adored my dog, and I'd gotten this new house and Frank had just given me a new fur coat and I was ***thrilled*** to death.(p.389)

throat

• So it doesn't behoove me to squawk about it for, after all, nobody ever had to throw me down and pour liquor down my ***throat***.(p.181)

• I pour drinks down my ***throat***.(p.501)

throats

• People have wars and kill each other; they struggle and cut each other's ***throats*** for success and what does anyone get out of it?(p.244)

throes

• The doctor said I'd been brought into the hospital like a madman, crying, raving, ranting, swearing, completely in the ***throes*** of delirium tremens.(p.427)

through

• This work at Akron continued ***through*** the summer of 1935.(p.xvii)

• The cases we have followed ***through*** have been most interesting; in fact, many of them are amazing.(p.xxv)

• After they have succumbed to the desire again, as so many do, and the phenomenon of craving develops, they pass ***through*** the well-known stages of a spree, emerging remorseful, with a firm resolution not to drink again.(p.xxvii)

• His alcoholic problem was so complex, and his depression so great, that we felt his only hope would be ***through*** what we then called "moral psychology," and we doubted if even that would have any effect.(p.xxix)

• I earnestly advise every alcoholic to read this book ***through***, and though perhaps he came to scoff, he may remain to pray.(p.xxx)

• I had developed a theory that most people lost money in stocks ***through*** ignorance of markets.(p.2)

• I was ***through*** forever.(p.5)

• Then came the night when the physical and mental torture was so hellish I feared I would burst ***through*** my window, sash and all.(p.6)

• My bother-in-law is a physician, and ***through*** his kindness and that of my mother I was placed in a nationally-known hospital for the mental and physical rehabilitation of alcoholics.(p.7)

• With a certain satisfaction I reflected there was enough gin concealed about the house to carry me ***through*** that night and the next day.(p.8)

• I felt lifted up, as though the great clean wind of a mountain top blew ***through*** and ***through***.(p.14)

• For if an alcoholic failed to perfect and enlarge his spiritual life ***through*** work and self-sacrifice for others, he could not survive the certain trials and low spots ahead.(p.14)

• Faith has to work twenty-four hours a day in and ***through*** us, or we perish.(p.16)

• We were in a position where life was becoming impossible, and if we had passed into the region from which there is no return ***through*** human aid we had but two alternatives: One was to go on to the bitter end, blotting out the consciousness of our intolerable situation as best we could; and the other, to accept spiritual help.(p.25)

• His family was re-assembled, and he began to work as a salesman for the business he had lost ***through*** drinking.(p.35)

• On ***through*** the years this conduct continues, accompanied by his continual promises to be careful or to keep off the streets altogether.(p.38)

• We, who have been ***through*** the wringer, have to admit if we substituted alcoholism for jay-walking, the illustration would fit us exactly.(p.38)

• We have not lost everything in life ***through*** drinking and we certainly do not intend to.(p.38)

• But the moment I made up my mind to go ***through*** with the process, I had the curious feeling that my alcoholic condition was relieved, as in fact it proved to be.(p.42)

• It poured over and ***through*** him with the certainty and majesty of a great tide at flood.(p.56)

• The barriers he had built ***through*** the years were swept away.(p.56)

• 11.Sought ***through*** prayer and meditation to improve our conscious contact with God as we understood Him, praying only for knowledge of His will for us and the power to carry that out.(p.59)

• I can't go ***through*** with it."(p.60)

• Most good ideas are simple, and this concept was the keystone of the new and triumphant arch ***through*** which we passed to freedom.(p.62)

• We went back ***through*** our lives.(p.65)

• It was an evil and corroding thread; the fabric of our existence was shot ***through*** with it.(p.67)

• Instead we let Him demonstrate, ***through*** us, what He can do.(p.68)

• If that is so, this step may be postponed, only however, if we hold ourselves in complete readiness to go ***through*** with it at the first opportunity.(p.74)

• Carefully reading the first five proposals we ask if we have omitted anything, for we are building an arch ***through*** which we shall walk a free man at last.(p.75)

• A man so involved often feels very remorseful at times, especially if he is married to a loyal and courageous girl who has literally gone ***through*** hell for him.(p.81)

• The alcoholic is like a tornado roaring his way ***through*** the lives of others.(p.82)

• If we are painstaking about this phase of our development, we will be amazed before we are half way ***through***.(p.83)

• We usually conclude the period of meditation with a prayer that we be shown all ***through*** the day what our next step is to be, that we be given whatever we need to take care of such problems.(p.87)

• As we go ***through*** the day we pause, when agitated or doubtful, and ask for the right thought or action.(p.87)

• When possible, avoid meeting a man ***through*** his family.(p.91)

• Approach ***through*** a doctor or an institution is a better bet.(p.91)

• He has read this volume and says he is prepared to go ***through*** with the Twelve Steps of the program of recovery.(p.96)

• We often need it to carry green recruits ***through*** a severe hangover.(p.102)

• Our men have sworn great solemn oaths that they were ***through*** drinking forever.(p.105)

• These are some of the questions which race ***through*** the mind of every woman who has an alcoholic husband.(p.108)

• He sometimes drinks in the morning and ***through*** the day also, to hold his nervousness in check.(p.109)

• Cheerfully see him ***through*** more sprees.(p.113)

• They need the counsel and love of a woman who has gone ***through*** what you have.(p.119)

• Thus mother, ***through*** no fault of her own, became accustomed to wearing the family trousers.(p.131)

• I told him he was ***through*** -- finally and forever.(p.136)

• I still expected a plea for clemency, but these words came ***through*** the receiver: "I just wanted to tell you Paul jumped from a hotel window in Hartford last Saturday.(p.136)

• We think the business fabric is shot ***through*** with a situation which might be helped by better understanding all around.(p.137)

• "Oh no," said my friend, "this chap is either ***through*** with liquor, or he is minus a job.(p.138)

• Suppose now that ***through*** you several families have adopted this way of life.(p.153)

• The proceeding was shot ***through*** with much hard feeling and controversy.(p.154)

• He came ***through*** an acquaintance who had heard the good news.(p.158)

• Little clusters of twos and threes and fives of us have sprung up in other communities, ***through*** contact with our two larger centers.(p.162)

• Arrangements were also made with the chief psychiatrist of a large public hospital to select still others from the stream of misery which flows ***through*** that institution.(p.163)

• From childhood ***through*** high school I was more or less forced to go to church, Sunday School and evening service, Monday night Christian Endeavor and sometimes to Wednesday evening prayer meeting.(p.172)

• I used to promise my wife, my friends, and my children that I would drink no more -- promises which seldom kept me sober even ***through*** the day, though I was very sincere when I made them.(p.177)

• The thought flashed ***through*** his mind, "If they can do it, I can do it!"(p.189)

• I'm so grateful for both the program and the people in it that I still want to go, and then probably the most wonderful thing that I learned from the program -- I've seen this in the 'A.A. Grapevine' a lot of times, and I've had people say it to me personally, and I've heard people get up in meetings and make the same statement: The statement is, "I came into A.A. solely for the purpose of sobriety, but it has been ***through*** A.A. that I have found God."(p.192)

• That continued ***through*** my entire life.(p.193)

• When they got ***through*** the day's work, part was left which I proceeded to drink.(p.196)

• I could get ***through*** an evening with just a couple of snorts.(p.196)

• I worked along until I had really big names in rubber on a tentative contract, and then I neglected to go ***through*** with it.(p.198)

• To my mind, drinking didn't have anything to do with not going ***through*** with things.(p.198)

• I was picked up at two-thirty that morning with my car smashed up by a street-car because I had run into a big concrete safety zone, and the street-car had run into me, and they took me out ***through*** the roof -- there's where I lost the suit.(p.202)

• So I started to investigate Science ***through*** some friends of mine who were Readers in the church.(p.202)

• The circumstances under which I reached these people were very odd because I was led there ***through*** things that I said when I couldn't even remember speaking.(p.202)

• I drank some more and slept ***through*** the day.(p.205)

• I remember well one fellow, Joe, walking nearly three miles ***through*** slush, wet and snow to come to the hospital to see a man that he had never seen before in his life, and that impressed me very much.(p.208)

• I went back to law school, and doubled up on the courses because I was then approaching thirty years of age and I wanted to get ***through*** as quickly as possible.(p.212)

• I was supporting myself ***through*** all this education by being a toolmaker and a draftsman.(p.212)

• I never left the church, but I was a fringe member, and the thought simply never occurred to me that ***through*** the exercise of what I had I might find the answer to my problem, simply because I wouldn't admit that I had a problem.(p.214)

• I remembered going ***through*** what my sister as-

sured me was my nightly procedure of trying to find Willie Seabrook's name in the telephone book.(p.224)
• And I remembered the creeping horror of the interminable night, in which I slept for short spells and woke up dripping with cold sweat and shaken with utter despair, to drink hastily from my bottle and mercifully pass out again, "You're mad, you're mad, you're mad!" pounded ***through*** my brain with each returning ray of consciousness, and I drowned the refrain with drink.(p.224)
• And so on and on, for several weeks, while I grudgingly plowed ***through*** some more of the offending book, and felt more and more hopeless about myself.(p.227)
• That is where I had my first drink and I still remember it, for every "first" drink afterwards did exactly the same trick – I could feel it go right ***through*** every bit of my body and down to my very toes.(p.241)
• He had also gone all the way ***through*** the wringer and had been dry two years when I saw him again.(p.243)
• Once again, there was the challenge of a tough job, but this time I was determined to follow ***through***.(p.248)
• Around this time our big A.A. book was being written and it all became much simpler; we had a definite formula which some sixty of us agreed was the middle course for all alcoholics who wanted sobriety, and that formula has not been changed one iota down ***through*** the years.(p.248)
• This change had been a long, slow process for me, but ***through*** these latter years the dividends have been tremendous.(p.249)
• She has been sober all the way ***through*** and for me that has been good.(p.249)
• One evening, the book, after checking up, was very definitely in the red for plenty ***through*** a piece of studied carelessness on my part, and my boss, very shrewd and able, fired me with a parting statement to the effect that once was enough.(p.251)
• I knew I was ***through*** among the English "bookies."(p.251)
• I soon ran ***through*** my stake.(p.251)
• I wanted to roam again and ***through*** relatives got a supercargo job on an Australian packet which allowed me to visit my people in Australia where I was born.(p.252)
• My four years of abstinence had something to do with it, but soldiering is a tough enough game for a sober man, and I had no yen for full-pack slogging ***through*** mud with a cognac or vin rouge hangover.(p.253)
• Quebec, Toronto, Buffalo, and finally Pittsburgh, were the scenes of man-sized drunks until I had gone ***through*** my readjusted discharge pay, a fair sum.(p.253)
• I had some financial success ***through*** no ability of my own and, when jobless and almost wiped out in 1930, I began to trade and sell my collection; much of the proceeds went to keep my apartment stocked with liquor and almost every night saw me helpless to bed.(p.255)
• When it was closed ***through*** Washington edict I began with Federal Writers in San Antonio.(p.256)
• Formerly, in the acute mental and physical pain during the remorseful periods succeeding each drunk, I found my recollection of the misery I had gone ***through*** a bolsterer of resolution and afterward, perhaps, a deterrent for a time.(p.260)
• I think his entry into A.A. was ***through*** spending some hours with Dr. Bob at his office.(p.267)
• He brought many people into A.A. ***through*** his barroom.)(p.267)
• And we went down ***through*** the valley, and I remembered reading about the Ku Klux Klan and how they burnt crosses, and I thought, "God alone knows what we are getting into this time!"(p.269)
• He talked about his wife taking his little boy away from him because of his drinking, and how he got back together with them ***through*** A.A., and we began feeling grateful right then that all these things hadn't been taken from us.(p.270)
• When I reached a point directly back of our house, where I could have cut ***through*** a friend's garden, I was almost overpowered by the desire to get home, but I made the whole journey.(p.276)
• Haunting me ***through*** each day's stupor -- and there were eighteen or nineteen such days in this man's home -- was the thought: "Where do I go when his family comes home?"(p.278)
• I, carried away with the desire to serve A.A., gave what was probably one of the first radio broadcasts about A.A., living ***through*** a case of mike fright and feeling like a million dollars when it was all over.(p.283)
• I lived ***through*** a week of the fidgets because I had agreed to address a group of alcoholic inmates in one of our state mental hospitals.(p.283)
• After a particularly bad Christmas and New Year's holiday, dad picked me up again early in January, 1937, to go ***through*** the usual sobering up routine.(p.289)
• He mentioned two of them that I had known ***through*** the years and suggested that I talk with them.(p.289)
• The day before I was due to go back to Chicago, a Wednesday and Dr. Bob's afternoon off, he had me down to the office and we spent three or four hours formally going ***through*** the Six-Step program as it was at that time.(p.291)
• Dr. Bob led me ***through*** all of these steps.(p.292)
• Dr. Bob then led me ***through*** the restitution step, in which I made a list of all of the persons I had harmed, and worked out ways and means of slowly making restitution.(p.292)
• A little more than fifteen years ago, ***through*** a long and calamitous series of shattering experiences, I found myself being helplessly propelled toward total destruction.(p.304)
• First, ***through*** mutual pain and despair, and later ***through*** mutual objectives and new-found faith and hope.(p.312)
• Somehow, I made it ***through*** basic and then laid off the booze for about three months, because I was in school at night.(p.317)
• I still couldn't make it ***through*** the nights without drinking, so I went back into the hospital, this time to a rehabilitation center.(p.320)
• As we walked back ***through*** the hall, I, for the first time in my life, said to another human being, "I'm having trouble with my drinking, too."(p.321)
• ***Through*** studied sneaky-drinking, I'd become a senior citizen without having lost a day's work because of booze.(p.327)
• But the saddest, and thus the most consoling, drifted ***through*** from the country-music station – stories of broken hearts, wasted lives, lost loves, sung plaintively.(p.332)
• The word "insanity" came ***through*** clearly -- and repugnantly.(p.332)
• A lot of lost dreams, empty futures, and crazy things of the past went ***through*** my mind.(p.333)
• How that line echoed ***through*** my mind!(p.333)
• I told her that I was an alcoholic, victim of a disease, that there was no cure, only arrestment ***through*** total abstinence.(p.333)
• Because it was only ***through*** feeling defeat and feeling failure, the inability to cope with my life and with alcohol, that I was able to surrender and accept the fact that I had this disease, and that I had to learn to live again without alcohol.(p.335)
• I just wanted to live to a certain age, carry ***through*** with what I felt was my job with the children, and after that – no matter.(p.337)
• The doctor prescribed brandy for the boy to help him ***through*** the night when he coughed, a teaspoon of brandy.(p.338)
• The very person who stood with me ***through*** it all and has been my greatest help was the person that I turned against, my husband.(p.338)
• Every day became that much harder to live ***through***, and I began to take a look at myself.(p.354)
• I'd managed to drink my way ***through*** all my friends.(p.355)
• I got around this by joining the local Rotary Club, and ***through*** this association with the business men of the community my little station began to grow.(p.360)
• I got ***through*** the holidays all right until New Year's Day.(p.365)
• Dad's image for me was that of a big Irish oilman who came up ***through*** the school of hard knocks and so had to be a two-fisted drinker.(p.369)
• He said he was ***through*** and would seek a divorce.(p.371)
• As I later found out ***through*** Alcoholics Anonymous, alcohol is no respecter of economic status, social and business standing or intelligence.(p.373)
• I was desperately in earnest to follow ***through*** and understand what was expected of me as a member of A.A. and to take each Step of the Twelve as rapidly as possible.(p.382)
• As I started down the aisle, that bourbon went right ***through*** me.(p.385)
• I put my poor mother and father ***through*** agonies but, finally, I couldn't stand living with them and having them watch everything I did.(p.386)
• So when he came for me, as he walked down the stairs, I could see him ***through*** the bars, and he was signing for me; I looked at him and said, "Don't you sign anything in this place!"(p.391)
• I only know that it first reached me ***through*** that Saturday Evening Post article.(p.392)
• I had to go ***through*** extreme alcoholism to find my answer.(p.400)
• It took me three psychoanalysts and several years in A.A. to really get this ***through*** my head.(p.401)
• We went ***through*** two years of deadlock required by the English divorce laws.(p.405)
• During this time, you are supposed to behave yourself, but I took a little wine-tasting tour ***through*** France, all by my lone, with car and chauffeur.(p.405)
• Why did I have to have at least three cocktails to sit ***through*** dinner?(p.406)
• The bartenders took care of me, not out of brotherly love, but ***through*** enlightened self-interest.(p.410)
• ***Through*** going to meetings and listening, and occasionally speaking, ***through*** doing Twelve Step work, whereby in helping others you are both the teacher and the student, by making many wonderful A.A. friends, I have been taught all the things in life that are worth having.(p.416)
• Fear, love of dentistry, and an imitation of my father's periodic drinking pattern took me ***through*** dental college soberly, except for the few parties and vacations in those four years.(p.419)
• I have been helped morally, spiritually, mentally and materially ***through*** A.A.(p.430)
• My daily alcoholic consumption remained about the same ***through*** all this, with perhaps a slight increase, and my binges remained one-nighters.(p.434)
• Only ***through*** being beaten down by my own misery would I ever have accepted the term "alcoholic" as applied to myself.(p.436)
• Moreover, I am deeply convinced that so long as I continue to strive, in my bumbling way, toward the principles I first encountered in the earlier chapters of this book, this remarkable power will continue to flow ***through*** me.(p.437)
• I had a lot more hell to go ***through***.(p.437)
• But what a difference there is between going ***through*** hell without a power greater than one's self, and with it!(p.437)
• The most terrible blow of my life befell me after I'd found sobriety ***through*** A.A.(p.437)
• Perhaps the single flicker of decency that shone ***through*** the fog of my drinking days was a clumsy affection for my two children, a boy and a girl.(p.437)
• The Higher Power was on deck to see me ***through***, sober.(p.437)
• I think He's on hand to see my son ***through***, too.(p.437)
• I think He's on hand to see all of us ***through*** whatever may come to us.(p.437)
• And should I have more bad times, I know that I'll never again have to go ***through*** them alone.(p.438)
• It started out as a good marriage, but it deteriorated over the years as she progressed ***through*** the various stages of qualifying for Al-Anon.(p.439)
• I drank my way ***through*** schools and always got honors.(p.441)
• And as I went ***through*** pharmacy school, graduate school, medical school, internship, residency, and specialty training and, finally, went into practice, my drinking kept increasing.(p.441)
• I took more ***through*** the day to increase the high, and more to maintain it; when I overshot the mark, I'd take tranquilizers to level off.(p.442)
• ***Through*** A.A., many receive the needed change and awakening just by trying to live by A.A. principles and associating with A.A. people.(p.459)
• ***Through*** A.A., we can experience freedom from self.(p.459)
• There is really nothing to dressing with chains and shackles on, once you learn the technique of pulling inside-out pants ***through*** the shackles.(p.460)
• (God works ***through*** people.)(p.462)
• He said he was finally and completely ***through*** -- that he never wanted to see me again.(p.467)
• I feel that I have been restored to health and sanity these past years not ***through*** my own efforts nor as a result of anything I may have done, but because I've come to believe -- to really believe – that alone I can do nothing.(p.473)
• We all one as Great Spirit walks ***through*** A.A. like sun walks ***through*** day.(p.474)
• Father, ***through*** the years, had built up a very good mail order business because, at that time, there wasn't too much money in medicine.(p.485)
• Economic conditions had a great deal to do with it, because I've often heard my father say that his mother would take one of the old time flour sacks and cut a hole ***through*** the bottom and two corners of it and there you'd have a gown.(p.486)
• Of course, when father finally came to Virginia to work his way ***through*** school, he resented the southern "cracker," as he often called them, so much that he

didn't even go back to his mother's funeral.(p.486)
• When I am ***through*** speaking, the whole idea has become absurd.(p.507)
• He had gone ***through*** the windshields of cars a couple of times and was pretty well banged up.(p.510)
• But after I passed ***through*** the gates I took a change of heart and mind.(p.510)
• It's no bed of roses, but somehow or other I've been able to make it, ***through*** the kindness of people in A.A.(p.511)
• I think I am very lucky that there are people like A.A.'s and an A.A. program to hang on to and carry me ***through***.(p.511)
• I was afraid that sometime I would get half drunk and go ***through*** with it.(p.515)
• By and large, I got ***through***.(p.519)
• Strangely enough, right ***through*** to the end of my twenty-six years in the Army, I was still being offered very good and important jobs in spite of the fact that my superiors must have known that I wasn't thoroughly reliable.(p.519)
• My only hope was to try and get ***through*** what was left of life as best I could, but I could never visualize doing that without drinking.(p.522)
• But I did understand this eventually, that these people had been ***through*** a lot of drinking experience just as I had, and had managed to make a job of it.(p.524)
• It has shown me, ***through*** the tragic stories of so many other alcoholics, the utter futility of self pity.(p.525)
• I am talking about A.A. people, who have gone ***through*** some of the same things that you might be going ***through*** now.(p.529)
• If the listener were drunk enough, the lecture might go on ***through*** several martinis, which I was glad to pay for.(p.537)
• ***Through*** my efforts to get down to "causes and conditions," I stand convinced that my emotional illness has been present from my earliest recollection.(p.544)
• What is much more important to me, A.A. has taught me that ***through*** this simple program I may experience a change in this reaction pattern that will indeed allow me to "match calamity with serenity."(p.544)
• The only way existence was possible was ***through*** rationalizing every sober moment and drinking myself into complete oblivion as often as I could.(p.547)
• Society can do anything it chooses to do with me when I am drunk and I can't lift a finger to stop it, for I forfeit my rights ***through*** the simple expedient of becoming a menace to myself and to the people around me.(p.549)
• During the day a friend of mine brought me some magazines to take to a hospital group I was interested in, and I looked ***through*** them and a "banner" across the front of one featured an article by a prominent clergyman in which I caught the word "resentment."(p.552)
• It was the late Dr. Tiebout, then, who persuaded me to seek help ***through*** A.A.(p.559)
• While there, I read the Big Book and the Grapevine and began the slow road back to health and sanity ***through*** the recovery program of A.A.(p.559)
• By learning – ***through*** practicing the Twelve Steps and ***through*** sharing at meetings -- how to cope with the problems that we looked to booze to solve, back in our drinking days.(p.560)
• Similarly, we rid ourselves of guilt and remorse as we "clean out the garbage" from our minds ***through*** the Fourth and Fifth Steps of our recovery program.(p.560)
• (This address is now available in pamphlet form at nominal cost ***through*** most A.A. groups or from Box 459, Grand Central Station, New York, NY 10163, under the title "Three Talks to Medical Societies by Bill W." – formerly called "Bill on Alcoholism" and earlier "Alcoholism the Illness.")(p.572)
• In such places, A.A. can be located ***through*** the local telephone directory, newspaper office, or police station, or by contacting local priests or ministers.(p.575)

throughout

• These stark and ugly facts have been confirmed by legions of alcoholics ***throughout*** history.(p.24)
• These tiny bodies are governed by precise laws, and these laws hold true ***throughout*** the material world.(p.49)
• Only a few knew of it at first but, within a short time, it was billboarded ***throughout*** the entire company.(p.145)
• From a mere handful in Akron we have spread ***throughout*** the world.(p.295)
• A few stood by me, at least in their hearts, ***throughout*** the whole of my drinking career.(p.404)
• The longer the drinking continued, the shorter the time the alcohol would keep me asleep; I would have to drink myself back to sleep again and again ***throughout*** the night.(p.441)
• As far as school was concerned, I made fair grades ***throughout***.(p.486)
• So I don't just take the inventory at night – I take it continually ***throughout*** the day.(p.516)
• Since Dr. Silkworth's first endorsement of Alcoholics Anonymous, medical societies and physicians ***throughout*** the world have set their approval upon us.(p.571)

throw

• If he can afford it, he may have liquor concealed all over his house to be certain no one gets his entire supply away from him to ***throw*** down the waterpipe.(p.22)
• It meant I would have to ***throw*** several lifelong conceptions out of the window.(p.42)
• Is not our age characterized by the ease with which we discard old ideas for new, by the complete readiness with which we ***throw*** away the theory or gadget which does not work for something new which does?(p.52)
• If sex is very troublesome, we ***throw*** ourselves the harder into helping others.(p.70)
• It should not matter, however, if someone does ***throw*** us out of his office.(p.78)
• I wanted to ***throw*** up my hands in discouragement, for I saw that I had failed to help my banker friend understand.(p.138)
• So it doesn't behoove me to squawk about it for, after all, nobody ever had to ***throw*** me down and pour liquor down my throat.(p.181)
• With a great deal of determination, I would ***throw*** out full pints – pour them out and smash the bottles -- firmly resolved never to take another drink of the stuff.(p.234)
• And another thing, it's a wonder they didn't ***throw*** us back in because I could become very dignified and sarcastic.(p.264)
• And we wonder how much further this man could go if his alcoholic problem could be removed and he could ***throw*** one hundred per cent of his abilities into action.(p.308)
• I did try, for a day or two, but something always would come up that would ***throw*** me.(p.324)
• In the garage, I would put the needle in my vein and then try to figure out exactly how much medication to inject to overcome the pep pills while adding to the sleeping pills while ignoring the tranquilizers, in order to get just enough to be able to pull out the needle, jerk the tourniquet, ***throw*** it in the car, slam the car door shut, run down the hall, and fall in bed before I fell asleep.(p.442)
• If I failed, they would ***throw*** away the key, and I would never get out again.(p.461)
• On the way I tried, and I mean really tried, to ***throw*** myself out of the car.(p.466)
• I was too weak and exhausted to even try to ***throw*** myself out of the car.(p.467)

throwing

• I swung, I swore, I started ***throwing*** beer cans at the advancing hordes of pineapple faces.(p.427)
• I remember vaguely violent quarrels with my husband, his finding my liquor supply time and time again and ***throwing*** it out.(p.466)
• If something does come along that sort of upsets me, instead of walking in and ***throwing*** a buck at the barman and asking for a drink, I walk into a telephone booth, drop a dime in the box, and call somebody who was so kind as to give me his name and telephone number to meet such an emergency.(p.511)

thrown

• About the time of the beer experiment I was ***thrown*** in with a crowd of people who attracted me because of their seeming poise, health, and happiness.(p.178)
• First, my new wife had walked out, ' ag, baggage and furniture; then the apartment landlord had ***thrown*** me out of the empty apartment and the finish was the loss of another job.(p.238)
• Had he come two or three days later I think I would have ***thrown*** him out, but he hit when I was open for anything.(p.239)
• Next, I was sent to Arizona, where my drinking picked up some more, and I started having blackouts, and I was ***thrown*** in jail for speeding and drunken driving.(p.318)
• I had ***thrown*** off a big lie that had been burdening me down for months.(p.366)
• All my troubles arose when I was ***thrown*** socially among groups of people.(p.486)
• But I remembered the years of agony preceding the binge, I remembered the years I had ***thrown*** away.(p.540)

thrust

• The Higher Power to whom I had turned, and who had sustained me, had once again been ***thrust*** into the background, while my emotions were running my life and, as always, my emotions ran me to the bottle.(p.472)

thumb

• Need I say that in a very short time I was walking along a prairie highway with arm extended and ***thumb*** pointed?(p.255)

thunderbolt

• Then, like a ***thunderbolt***, a great thought came.(p.56)

thunderclouds

• Starting from a speck on the domestic horizon, great ***thunderclouds*** of dispute may gather.(p.117)

Thursday

• This was on ***Thursday***.(p.207)

thus

• ***Thus*** was I convinced that God is concerned with us humans when we want Him enough.(p.12)
• Common sense would ***thus*** become uncommon sense.(p.13)
• ***Thus*** started one more journey to the asylum for Jim.(p.36)
• ***Thus*** was our friend's cornerstone fixed in place.(p.56)
• He ***thus*** used his own wrong-doing as a means of destroying the reputation of another.(p.80)
• You will ***thus*** get a better idea of how you ought to proceed.(p.91)
• With few exceptions, our book ***thus*** far has spoken of men.(p.104)
• ***Thus*** you may succeed in interesting him in alcoholism.(p.112)
• These work-outs should be regarded as part of your education, for ***thus*** you will be learning to live.(p.117)
• The alcoholic's past ***thus*** becomes the principal asset of the family and frequently it is almost the only one!(p.124)
• ***Thus*** mother, through no fault of her own, became accustomed to wearing the family trousers.(p.131)
• ***Thus*** we find the fellowship, and so will you.(p.152)
• They experienced a few distressing failures, but in those cases they made an effort to bring the man's family into a spiritual way of living, ***thus*** relieving much worry and suffering.(p.159)
• ***Thus*** we grow.(p.162)
• ***Thus*** I found myself in the middle of a brand new group.(p.249)
• ***Thus***, A.A. was born in Chicago.(p.287)
• This worldly lady helped to develop A.A. in Chicago and ***thus*** passed her keys to many.(p.304)
• I had suppressed tendencies to overindulge and ***thus*** reveal my "moral weakness," because false pride was so dominant.(p.327)
• But the saddest, and ***thus*** the most consoling, drifted through from the country-music station – stories of broken hearts, wasted lives, lost loves, sung plaintively.(p.332)
• My job was to make out the guard schedules and ***thus*** I was exempt from ordinary recruit training activities.(p.425)
• I'd fooled him ***thus*** far.(p.429)
• We are granted "the serenity to accept the things we cannot change" -- and ***thus*** lose our quickness to anger and our sensitivity to criticism.(p.560)
• We think, therefore, that any considerable property of genuine use to A.A. should be separately incorporated and managed, ***thus*** dividing the material from the spiritual.(p.565)

thy

• Relieve me of the bondage of self, that I may better do ***Thy*** will.(p.63)
• Take away my difficulties, that victory over them may bear witness to those I would help of ***Thy*** Power, ***Thy*** Love, and ***Thy*** Way of life.(p.63)
• May I do ***Thy*** will always!"(p.63)
• ***Thy*** will be done."(p.67)
• "How can I best serve Thee – ***Thy*** will (not mine) be done."(p.85)
• We constantly remind ourselves we are no longer running the show, humbly saying to ourselves many times each day "***Thy*** will be done."(p.87)
• You will learn the full meaning of "Love ***thy*** neighbor as thyself."(p.153)
• I believe that my once over-weening self-will has finally found its proper place, for I can say many times daily, "***Thy*** will be done, not mine" . . . and mean it.(p.229)
• He went on talking and told me that he had found

the plan has a basis of love, and the practice of Christ's injunction, "Love *thy* neighbor as thyself."(p.236)
• A "spiritual experience" to me meant attending meetings, seeing a group of people, all there for the purpose of helping each other; hearing the Twelve Steps and the Twelve Traditions read at a meeting, and hearing the Lord's Prayer, which in an A.A. meeting has such great meaning -- "*Thy* will be done, not mine."(p.381)
• I can't say, "*Thy* will be done," and take a pill.(p.443)

thyself
• You will learn the full meaning of "Love thy neighbor as *thyself*."(p.153)
• He went on talking and told me that he had found the plan has a basis of love, and the practice of Christ's injunction, "Love thy neighbor as *thyself*."(p.236)
• PHYSICIAN, HEAL *THYSELF*!(p.345)

ticker
• The *ticker* still clattered.(p.4)

ticket
• Following a big drunk on that sheet, where I was doing leg-work and rewrite, a feeling of nostalgia made me buy a *ticket* for Liverpool and I returned to Britain.(p.252)
• Cops now sick of me, so they buy me one-way *ticket* to Canada.(p.475)
• I took the last to buy my railroad *ticket*.(p.493)

tide
• It poured over and through him with the certainty and majesty of a great *tide* at flood.(p.56)
• Our hope is that when this chip of a book is launched on the world *tide* of alcoholism, defeated drinkers will seize upon it, to follow its suggestions.(p.153)
• I would hang on to sobriety for short intervals, but always there would come the *tide* of an overpowering necessity to drink and, as I was engulfed in it, I felt such a sense of panic that I really believed I would die if I didn't get that drink inside.(p.306)

tidings
• He shouted great *tidings*.(p.11)

Tiebout
• He happened to be, by the grace of God, Dr. Harry *Tiebout*, the psychiatrist who probably knew more about alcoholism than any other in the world.(p.559)
• It was the late Dr. *Tiebout*, then, who persuaded me to seek help through A.A.(p.559)
• Dr. Harry M. *Tiebout*, psychiatrist: "As a psychiatrist, I have thought a great deal about the relationship of my specialty to A.A. and I have come to the conclusion that our particular function can very often lie in preparing the way for the patient to accept any sort of treatment or outside help.(p.571)

tied
• Whether you quit six days, months, or years, if you go out and take a drink or two you'll end up in this hospital *tied* down, just like you have been in these past six months.(p.187)
• I was a woman, *tied* to my home.(p.338)
• My wife loved to drink, and we *tied* on many a hooter in the name of marital bliss.(p.433)

ties
• What they say will apply to nearly everyone bound by *ties* of blood or affections to an alcoholic.(p.104)
• You will be bound to them with new and wonderful *ties*, for you will escape disaster together and you will commence shoulder to shoulder your common journey.(p.152)

tiger
• Next day remorse would be on me like a *tiger*.(p.432)

tight
• He has a positive genius for getting *tight* at exactly the wrong moment, particularly when some important decision must be made or engagement kept.(p.21)
• In desperation, we have even got *tight* ourselves -- the drunk to end all drunks.(p.106)
• Frequently, you have felt obliged to tell your husband's employer and his friends that he was sick, when as a matter of fact he was *tight*.(p.115)
• Understand he was once a well-known lawyer in town, but just now we've got him strapped down *tight*."(p.156)
• We could not be invited out because I would surely get *tight* and my wife dared not invite people in for the same reason.(p.177)
• I gave the matter much time and study for the next two and a half years, but still got *tight* every night nevertheless.(p.178)
• I got *tight* that night, stayed sober Monday till after the dinner and then proceeded to get *tight* again.(p.179)
• Had blacked the eyes of two nurses, and now they had him strapped down *tight*.(p.188)
• "Sure, I've seen you *tight* several times, but you're no alcoholic!"(p.356)
• I was told that someone would call on me shortly, to sit *tight* and not take another drink.(p.363)
• For the next couple of hours a terrible battle went on between the good gremlins and the bad ones, one faction urging me to tell the truth, the other telling me to sit *tight* and say nothing.(p.366)
• Above all, he noticed that I drank a good deal, often got *tight* in his company and told him naughty stories.(p.403)
• By two-thirty in the afternoon I was always *tight*.(p.404)

Tijuana
• I went to *Tijuana* that night and landed in jail.(p.428)

tile
• If my wife was planning to go out in the afternoon, I would get a large supply of liquor and smuggle it home and hide it in the coal bin, the clothes chute, over door jambs, over beams in the cellar and in cracks in the cellar *tile*.(p.176)

till
• The local banker watched me whirl fat checks in and out of his *till* with amused skepticism.(p.4)
• Sometimes it is wise to wait *till* he goes on a binge.(p.90)
• I got tight that night, stayed sober Monday *till* after the dinner and then proceeded to get tight again.(p.179)
• He knew too well that didn't mean a thing, just as I knew in my heart that it would be only a question of time -- a few days, a week, or even a month, it was inevitable -- *till* I would be off on another bender.(p.257)

tilting
• I have stopped *tilting* at windmills, and instead have tried to accomplish the little daily tasks, unimportant in themselves, but tasks that are an integral part of living fully.(p.295)

time
• Nine of the stories in Part II ("They Stopped in *Time*") are carried over from the second edition; eight new stories have been added.(p.xii)
• When the broker returned to New York in the fall of 1935, the first A.A. group had actually been formed, though no one realized it at the *time*.(p.xvii)
• By late 1937, the number of members having substantial sobriety *time* behind them was sufficient to convince the membership that a new light had entered the dark world of the alcoholic.(p.xvii)
• It was now *time*, the struggling groups thought, to place their message and unique experience before the world.(p.xvii)
• The flying-blind period ended and A.A. entered a new phase of its pioneering *time*.(p.xvii)
• But great numbers of these -- about two out of three -- began to return as *time* passed.(p.xx)
• We doctors have realized for a long *time* that some form of moral psychology was of urgent importance to alcoholics, but its application presented difficulties beyond our conception.(p.xxv)
• The sensation is so elusive that, while they admit it is injurious, they cannot after a *time* differentiate the true from the false.(p.xxvi)
• There is the type who always believes that after being entirely free from alcohol for a period of *time* he can take a drink without danger.(p.xxviii)
• I talked with him for some *time*, but was not able to bring myself to feel that I had known him before.(p.xxix)
• A long *time* has passed with no return to alcohol.(p.xxix)
• In *time* we sailed for "Over There."(p.1)
• By the *time* I had completed the course, I knew the law was not for me.(p.2)
• This *time* we stayed broke.(p.4)
• Before then, I had written lots of sweet promises, but my wife happily observed that this *time* I meant business.(p.5)
• Some *time* passed, and confidence began to be replaced by cock-sureness.(p.5)
• In no *time* I was beating on the bar asking myself how it happened.(p.6)
• As the whisky rose to my head I told myself I would manage better next *time*, but I might as well get good and drunk then.(p.6)
• After a *time* I returned to the hospital.(p.7)
• I was to know happiness, peace, and usefulness, in a way of life that is incredibly more wonderful as *time* passes.(p.8)
• There was that *time* we had chartered an airplane to complete a jag!(p.9)
• I simply had to believe in a Spirit of the Universe, who knew neither *time* nor limitation.(p.10)
• At the hospital I was separated from alcohol for the last *time*.(p.13)
• I admitted for the first *time* that of myself I was nothing; that without Him I was lost.(p.13)
• I was not too well at the *time*, and was plagued by waves of self-pity and resentment.(p.15)
• All of us spend much of our spare *time* in the sort of effort which we are going to describe.(p.19)
• A few are fortunate enough to be so situated that they can give nearly all their *time* to the work.(p.19)
• Now these are commonplace observations on drinkers which we hear all the *time*.(p.20)
• It may cause him to die a few years before his *time*.(p.21)
• Some drinkers have excuses with which they are satisfied part of the *time*.(p.23)
• If these thoughts occur, they are hazy and readily supplanted with the old threadbare idea that this *time* we shall handle ourselves like other people.(p.24)
• The alcoholic may say to himself in the most casual way, "It won't burn me this *time*, so here's how!"(p.24)
• Nevertheless, he was drunk in a short *time*.(p.26)
• All of us felt at times that we were regaining control, but such intervals -- usually brief -- were inevitably followed by still less control, which led in *time* to pitiful and incomprehensible demoralization.(p.30)
• But the difficulty is that few alcoholics have enough desire to stop while there is yet *time*.(p.32)
• Commencing to drink after a period of sobriety, we are in a short *time* as bad as ever.(p.33)
• To be gravely affected, one does not necessarily have to drink a long *time* nor take the quantities some of us have.(p.33)
• The experiment of quitting for a period of *time* will be helpful, but we think we can render an even greater service to alcoholic sufferers and perhaps to the medical fraternity.(p.34)
• What sort of thinking dominates an alcoholic who repeats *time* after *time* the desperate experiment of the first drink?(p.35)
• All went well for a *time*, but he failed to enlarge his spiritual life.(p.35)
• Presently he is hit again and this *time* has a fractured skull.(p.38)
• That may be true of certain nonalcoholic people who, though drinking foolishly and heavily at the present *time*, are able to stop or moderate, because their brains and bodies have not been damaged as ours were.(p.39)
• This *time* he was quite shaky.(p.40)
• "In this frame of mind, I went about my business and for a *time* all was well.(p.40)
• This *time* I had not thought of the consequences at all.(p.41)
• I now remembered what my alcoholic friends had told me, how they prophesied that if I had an alcoholic mind, the *time* and place would come -- I would drink again.(p.41)
• They grinned, which I didn't like so much, and then asked me if I thought myself alcoholic and if I were really licked this *time*.(p.42)
• So, in one way or another, we discovered that faith had been involved all the *time*!(p.54)
• For the first *time*, he lived in conscious companionship with his Creator.(p.56)
• Sometimes they hurt us, seemingly without provocation, but we invariably find that at some *time* in the past we have made decisions based on self which later placed us in a position to be hurt.(p.62)
• *Time* after *time* newcomers have tried to keep to themselves certain facts about their lives.(p.72)
• When we decide who is to hear our story, we waste no *time*.(p.75)
• He attended church for the first *time* in many years.(p.80)
• They will change in *time*.(p.83)
• For by this *time* sanity will have returned.(p.84)
• Were we thinking of ourselves most of the *time*?(p.86)
• Nevertheless, we find that our thinking will as *time* passes, be more and more on the plane of inspiration.(p.87)
• Many of us have wasted a lot of *time* doing that and it doesn't work.(p.87)
• If he does not want to stop drinking, don't waste *time* trying to persuade him.(p.90)
• If he is not communicative, give him a sketch of

your drinking career up to the ***time*** you quit.(p.91)
• We find it a waste of ***time*** to keep chasing a man who cannot or will not work with you.(p.96)
• To spend too much ***time*** on any one situation is to deny some other alcoholic an opportunity to live and be happy.(p.96)
• Your telephone may jangle at any ***time*** of the day or night.(p.97)
• Another ***time*** you may have to send for the police or an ambulance.(p.97)
• We seldom allow an alcoholic to live in our homes for long at a ***time***.(p.97)
• These things will come to pass naturally and in good ***time*** provided, however, the alcoholic continues to demonstrate that he can be sober, considerate, and helpful, regardless of what anyone says or does.(p.99)
• When the ***time*** for living together has come, it will be apparent to both parties.(p.99)
• If the alcoholic tries to shield himself he may succeed for a ***time***, but he usually winds up with a bigger explosion than ever.(p.101)
• At proper ***time*** and place explain to all your friends why alcohol disagrees with you.(p.102)
• But when he gets over the spree, he begins to think once more how he can drink moderately next ***time***.(p.109)
• We have enjoyed such evenings ourselves; we had a good ***time***.(p.110)
• But be careful not to be resentful about the last ***time*** he did so.(p.116)
• ***Time*** after ***time***, this apparent calamity has been a boon to us, for it opened up a path which led to the discovery of God.(p.116)
• Next ***time*** you and he have a heated discussion, no matter what the subject, it should be the privilege of either to smile and say, "This is getting serious.(p.118)
• It will take ***time*** to clear away the wreck.(p.123)
• Husbands and wives have sometimes been obliged to separate for a ***time*** until new perspective, new victory over hurt pride could be rewon.(p.125)
• It takes some of us a long ***time*** to outgrow that serious handicap.(p.125)
• He is straining every nerve to make up for lost ***time***.(p.126)
• He may tell mother, who has been religious all her life, that she doesn't know what it's all about, and that she had better get his brand of spirituality while there is yet ***time***.(p.128)
• For a ***time*** he may try to hug the new treasure to himself.(p.129)
• Those of us who have spent much ***time*** in the world of spiritual make-believe have eventually seen the childishness of it.(p.130)
• Father will necessarily spend much ***time*** with other alcoholics, but this activity should be balanced.(p.131)
• In ***time*** they will see that he is a new man and in their own way they will let him know it.(p.134)
• I was at one ***time*** assistant manager of a corporation department employing sixty-six hundred men.(p.136)
• Another ***time***, as I opened a letter which lay on my desk, a newspaper clipping fell out.(p.136)
• If not, why waste ***time*** with him?(p.142)
• Only a few knew of it at first but, within a short ***time***, it was billboarded throughout the entire company.(p.145)
• You put me on the spot every ***time*** you get drunk.(p.147)
• At the same ***time*** you will feel no reluctance to rid yourself of those who cannot or will not stop.(p.148)
• Alcoholism may be causing your organization considerable damage in its waste of ***time***, men and reputation.(p.148)
• It is not to be expected that an alcoholic employee will receive a disproportionate amount of ***time*** and attention.(p.149)
• Having a better ***time***."(p.151)
• Had he been successful in his enterprise, he would have been set on his feet financially which at the ***time***, seemed vitally important.(p.153)
• Some ***time*** later, and just as he thought he was getting control of his liquor situation, he went on a roaring bender.(p.155)
• All this ***time*** our friend of the hotel lobby incident remained in that town.(p.159)
• Aside from fellowship and sociability, the prime object was to provide a ***time*** and place where new people might bring their problems.(p.160)
• Many of us have felt, for the first ***time***, the Presence and Power of God within its walls.(p.162)
• This practice enables us to lend a hand, at the same ***time*** avoiding certain alluring distractions of the road, about which any traveling man can inform you.(p.162)
• THEY STOPPED IN ***TIME***(p.167)
• I had some money, all the ***time*** in the world, and considerable stomach trouble.(p.174)
• I soon discovered that a couple of drinks would alleviate my gastric distress, at least for a few hours at a ***time***, so it was not at all difficult for me to return to my former excessive indulgence.(p.174)
• By this ***time*** I was beginning to pay very dearly physically and, in hope of relief, voluntarily incarcerated myself at least a dozen times in one of the local sanitariums.(p.174)
• At that ***time*** I was not aware of the almost unlimited supply the government made it possible for us doctors to obtain, neither had I any knowledge of the bootlegger who soon appeared on the horizon.(p.175)
• I drank with moderation at first, but it took me only a relatively short ***time*** to drift back into the old habits which had wound up so disastrously before.(p.175)
• Most of the ***time*** therefore, I did not take the morning drink which I craved so badly, but instead would fill up on large doses of sedatives to quiet the jitters, which distressed me terribly.(p.176)
• During all this ***time*** we became more or less ostracized by our friends.(p.177)
• About the ***time*** of the beer experiment I was thrown in with a crowd of people who attracted me because of their seeming poise, health, and happiness.(p.178)
• I was self conscious and ill at ease most of the ***time***, my health was at the breaking point, and I was thoroughly miserable.(p.178)
• I gave the matter much ***time*** and study for the next two and a half years, but still got tight every night nevertheless.(p.178)
• My wife became deeply interested and it was her interest that sustained mine, though I at no ***time*** sensed that it might be an answer to my liquor problem.(p.178)
• If she had not, I know I would have been dead a long ***time*** ago.(p.178)
• About this ***time*** a lady called up my wife one Saturday afternoon, saying she wanted me to come over that evening to meet a friend of hers who might help me.(p.179)
• I had to wait some ***time*** for the train.(p.179)
• I spend a great deal of ***time*** passing on what I learned to others who want and need it badly.(p.180)
• 3.Because in so doing I am paying my debt to the man who took ***time*** to pass it on to me.(p.181)
• 4.Because every ***time*** I do it I take out a little more insurance for myself against a possible slip.(p.181)
• But at no ***time*** have I been anywhere near yielding.(p.181)
• So, at the ***time*** Dr. Bob and Bill came along I had about run out my strength.(p.182)
• The first ***time*** that I became intoxicated I was eight years old.(p.182)
• At the ***time***, I called it patriotism.(p.183)
• Then Prohibition came into effect, and the facts that the stuff obtainable was so horrible and sometimes deadly, and that I had married and had a job which I had to look after, helped me for a period of some three or four years, although I would get drunk every ***time*** I could get hold of enough to drink to get started.(p.183)
• As ***time*** went on my drinking became progressively worse.(p.184)
• Away from my office two or three weeks at a ***time***; horrible days and nights when I would lie on the floor of my home, lying awake and reaching over to get the bottle, taking a drink and going back into oblivion.(p.184)
• All the other people that had talked to me wanted to help me, and my pride prevented me from listening to them, and caused only resentment on my part, but I felt as if I would be a real stinker if I did not listen to a couple of fellows for a short ***time***, if that would cure them.(p.185)
• There was not much of it at that ***time***.(p.185)
• After a while, Bill said, "Well, now, you've been talking a good long ***time***, let me talk a minute or two."(p.185)
• Now, if you don't want it, we'll not take up your ***time***, and we'll be going and looking for someone else."(p.186)
• As far as I know that was the first ***time*** I had ever paid any attention to that word.(p.187)
• That certainly was real disheartening news, at the ***time***.(p.188)
• Just twenty-four hours at a ***time***."(p.188)
• Every ***time*** I'd start thinking about drinking, I would think of the long, dry years ahead without having a drink; but this idea of twenty-four hours, that it was up to me from then on, was a lot of help.(p.188)
• Nineteen years ago last summer, Dr. Bob and I saw him (Bill D.) for the first ***time***.(p.188)
• I was at one ***time*** a deacon in the church and I still believe in God.(p.189)
• I remember telling them too that it was going to be awfully tough, because I did some other things, smoked cigarettes and played penny ante poker, sometimes bet on the horse races and they said, "Don't you think you're having more trouble with this drinking than with anything else at the present ***time***?(p.190)
• Of course, by this ***time***, my business was practically non-existent.(p.190)
• Naturally, for quite a ***time***, I wasn't too well physically, either.(p.190)
• It took me a year, or a year and a half to get to feeling physically well, and it was rather tough, but I soon found folks whose friendship I had once had, and I found, after I had been sober for quite some little ***time***, that these people began to act like they had in previous years, before I had gotten so bad, so that I didn't pay too awful much attention to financial gains.(p.190)
• I spent most of my ***time*** trying to get back these friendships, and to make some recompense towards my wife, whom I had hurt a lot.(p.191)
• Of course, as ***time*** went on, and I began to get my health back and began to be so I didn't have to hide from people all the ***time***, it's just been wonderful.(p.192)
• At that ***time***, as I remember, he had promised never to take another drink.(p.193)
• I was not more that six at that ***time***.(p.193)
• I immediately quit school and went to work, and from that ***time*** until I was high school age there was never a return to school.(p.193)
• I wouldn't put sufficient ***time*** on them.(p.194)
• At that particular ***time***, the boys put me on a shutter and took me out to the shed, and I lay in the car while they enjoyed their banquet.(p.195)
• That was the first ***time*** I ever drank hard liquor.(p.195)
• Every company in the country, except Firestone, was reorganized at that ***time***.(p.197)
• Another ***time***, I had a rubber pool project.(p.198)
• I didn't like having to come home at a certain ***time***; I didn't like this, I didn't like that, and I think the poor girl actually divorced me to help me stop drinking!(p.199)
• Another ***time***, I had gone around to Max R. trying to get a job driving one of his trucks.(p.200)
• At the end of about four months, I not only had good looking clothes --and I might say that at the ***time*** I first talked to Max I didn't have a suit of clothes I could bend over in real sudden; now I had six suits of clothes.(p.200)
• I had avoided a drink this ***time***.(p.203)
• I didn't drink very long at a ***time***.(p.203)
• My mother was eighty-nine years old when she died, and I was a full-blown alcoholic at the ***time*** of her death.(p.210)
• As a matter of fact, I had two children at the ***time*** I was admitted to the bar.(p.212)
• By the ***time*** I had completed law school I had picked up some experience in patent law, for I remained with the patent law firm and worked too in Washington where they found that I was a capable infringement investigator.(p.213)
• By that ***time***, I had one boy in college, another a senior in high school, and a daughter about twelve years old.(p.215)
• She knew that at that ***time*** any suggestion she made about my drinking would only build up a barrier, a consideration for which I am ever grateful.(p.216)
• I had had no hospitalization up to this ***time*** because I would not call doctors when I was getting over a bad one.(p.217)
• I believe every member of the Akron Group did come to see me, which impressed me terrifically, not so much because of the stories they told, but because they would take the ***time*** to come and talk to me without even knowing who I was.(p.218)
• There were, at that ***time***, in the neighborhood of twelve or thirteen Cleveland members who had been sober anywhere from a year and a half to a couple of months.(p.219)
• I realized that there wasn't anything I could say to place myself in a more favorable light with my children, that it was going to be a matter of ***time***; for I also understood the intolerance of young people towards deficiencies in their elders.(p.220)
• This ***time*** I seemed to be already awake, sitting upright in a big easy chair, in the middle of an animated conversation with a perfectly strange young woman, who didn't appear to think it strange.(p.222)
• It must have been a long ***time*** since I had my last drink -- but I didn't dare ask this stranger for one.(p.223)

• To go into a gathering of people was the sort of thing that all my life, from the ***time*** I left my private world of books and dreams to meet the real world of people and parties and jobs, had left me feeling an uncomfortable outsider, needing the warming stimulus of drinks to join in.(p.228)
• Military service was compulsory and I did my stretch with the class of my age, goose-stepping in German barracks and taking part in the Boxer Rebellion in China, my first ***time*** at any great distance from home.(p.230)
• At that ***time*** I could go into any saloon, have one or two beers, walk out and forget about it.(p.231)
• Certainly, at that ***time*** I was one of those who "can take it or leave it alone."(p.231)
• I was doing very well with that and general upholstering work, and there was every indication that I would be financially independent by the ***time*** I reached middle age.(p.232)
• By this ***time*** I was married and was paying for a home.(p.232)
• More and more I formed the habit of doing some of my business in the speakeasy, and after a ***time*** I did not need that as an excuse.(p.233)
• I had all the usual experiences of the alcoholic, for I was certainly one by this ***time***.(p.233)
• My "periodics" became more frequent until I reached the point where I wanted to devote all my ***time*** to drinking, working as little as possible, and then only when the necessity of my family demanded it.(p.234)
• This doctor had imparted his knowledge to just a few other men at that ***time*** -- not more than four or five -- they now number more than seventy persons.(p.235)
• For a long ***time*** I kept on trying, in a pretty dumb way at first, I know, but very earnestly.(p.237)
• Many of these same things had happened to me many times before, but this ***time*** they had all descended together.(p.238)
• That night for the first ***time*** in my life I really let down my hair and admitted my general loneliness.(p.239)
• Then I turned two company cars over in a short ***time*** and Bingo -- fired again.(p.242)
• At this ***time*** I was holding what drinking I did down to weekends, but I hadn't had a drink at all in a month.(p.243)
• Every ***time*** I blacked out, and that was every ***time*** I drank, there was always that gnawing fear, "What did I do this ***time***?"(p.244)
• At the ***time***, I thought them just a swell pair of screwballs, for they were not only going to save all the drunks in the world but also all the so-called normal people!(p.245)
• They had also been periodic big shots who had goofed out repeatedly at the wrong ***time***, and they also knew how to split one paper match into three separate matches.(p.245)
• Just give me a good front and a couple of bucks and I'd be right back in the big ***time***.(p.246)
• At that ***time*** the group in New York was composed of about twelve men who were working on the principle of every drunk for himself; we had no real formula and no name.(p.246)
• Much later I discovered the elders held many prayer meetings hoping to find a way to give me the heave-ho, but at the same ***time*** stay tolerant and spiritual.(p.247)
• Then it was my turn – I ordered "Three beers," but this ***time*** it was different, I had a cash investment of thirty cents and, on a ten dollar a week salary, that's a big thing.(p.247)
• This ***time*** it really hurt, more than any hangover ever had.(p.247)
• My brilliant agnosticism vanished, and I saw for the first ***time*** that those who really believed, or at least honestly tried to find a Power greater than themselves, were much more composed and contented than I had ever been, and they seemed to have a degree of happiness which I had never known.(p.247)
• Once again, there was the challenge of a tough job, but this ***time*** I was determined to follow through.(p.248)
• For a long ***time*** the only Higher Power I could concede was the power of the group, but this was far more than I had ever recognized before, and it was at least a beginning.(p.248)
• Around this ***time*** our big A.A. book was being written and it all became much simpler; we had a definite formula which some sixty of us agreed was the middle course for all alcoholics who wanted sobriety, and that formula has not been changed one iota down through the years.(p.248)
• I was soon broke, this ***time*** without trainfare to go anywhere.(p.252)
• I visited my family just once in that ***time***.(p.255)
• Need I say that in a very short ***time*** I was walking along a prairie highway with arm extended and thumb pointed?(p.255)
• He knew too well that didn't mean a thing, just as I knew in my heart that it would be only a question of ***time*** -- a few days, a week, or even a month, it was inevitable -- till I would be off on another bender.(p.257)
• The ***time*** came just a week later.(p.258)
• Formerly, in the acute mental and physical pain during the remorseful periods succeeding each drunk, I found my recollection of the misery I had gone through a bolsterer of resolution and afterward, perhaps, a deterrent for a ***time***.(p.260)
• We were together all the ***time***, but this night I got up and saw it was late.(p.263)
• We had the grandest ***time*** ever.(p.264)
• One Sunday afternoon, the only ***time*** I ever got picked up for drunken driving, I got picked up in Bellaire.(p.264)
• The next ***time*** vacation ***time*** rolled around that was a bitter lesson to us.(p.265)
• It was just about this ***time***, in 1940, that we met up with A.A.(p.265)
• We talked about it afterwards, and we felt that there might be some ***time*** we'd need it.(p.266)
• There was a man watching, and I turned to him and said with a defiant air I carried with me all the ***time***, "If I don't quit this I'm going to have to join that alcoholic business they're talking about."(p.266)
• ***Time*** went on and the drinking got worse and worse, and I was in another barroom, down the road the other way, a small one, and I took my glass – that morning I'd been able to lift it from the bar -- and I said to the woman behind the bar, "I wish I might never take another drop of that stuff.(p.266)
• And we went down through the valley, and I remembered reading about the Ku Klux Klan and how they burnt crosses, and I thought, "God alone knows what we are getting into this ***time***!"(p.269)
• At that ***time*** they didn't let us know that people ever had trouble.(p.271)
• There were two women in the St. Thomas Hospital at that ***time*** in a room.(p.272)
• By the ***time*** I was thirty I had found that alcohol dissolved fear.(p.275)
• By the ***time*** I was twenty-one I had six years of life in foreign countries, spoke three languages fluently, and had attended college for two years.(p.275)
• Three more months of being up and around the house for brief periods and in bed the rest of the ***time***.(p.275)
• I heard for the first ***time*** an expression which I was to grow to loathe: "There is nothing organically wrong."(p.276)
• I told our family doctor, an understanding man who gave hours of his ***time*** trying to help me, about this experience.(p.276)
• Dr. Bob dwelt at length on how prayer had given him release, ***time*** and ***time*** again, from the nearly over-powering compulsion to take a drink.(p.279)
• I got down on my knees for the first ***time*** in thirty years.(p.280)
• Sometimes during that year I rebelled inwardly at what seemed like lost ***time***, and at having to be a burden to these good people whose means were limited.(p.281)
• I remained with them for three weeks, using part of the ***time*** in making many amends, which I had had no earlier opportunity of making.(p.281)
• The rest of my ***time*** was devoted to A.A. spadework.(p.281)
• So I spent much of my ***time*** calling on the people who I felt would logically come in contact with alcoholic cases, doctors, ministers, lawyers and the personnel men in industry.(p.281)
• This ***time*** I did something about it.(p.284)
• With God's help I am able, for one day at a ***time***, to carry business responsibilities which, not many years ago, I would not have dreamed of assuming.(p.284)
• In recent years I have had the happy combination of ***time*** and money to travel occasionally.(p.285)
• I am very apt to get into quite an uproar for a day or two before starting, but I do start, and once started, I have a swell ***time***.(p.285)
• The adjustments in such a case are difficult and take ***time***, but we both feel that they are certainly worth it.(p.286)
• It is undoubtedly too soon for me to say how much of a success I shall be as a husband in ***time*** to come.(p.286)
• I know now that sixty per cent of the ***time*** I drank alone without benefit of customers.(p.287)
• Shortly thereafter, aided by the Depression, I found that I had a great deal of spare ***time*** and that a little drink in the morning helped.(p.287)
• One ***time*** my wife decided to try this too.(p.288)
• By the ***time*** we reached the bar, he was willing to buy me a quart with his own money.(p.288)
• This ***time*** he had a suggestion to offer.(p.289)
• Several months later dad was back in Chicago to pick me up again, but this ***time*** my attitude was entirely different.(p.289)
• As I look back on that first evening I realize that I began to hope, then, for the first ***time***; and I felt that if he could regain these things, perhaps it would be possible for me too.(p.290)
• I spent a great deal of ***time*** with Dr. Bob, whenever he had the ***time*** to spare, and in the homes of two or three other people, trying to see how the family lived the program.(p.291)
• The day before I was due to go back to Chicago, a Wednesday and Dr. Bob's afternoon off, he had me down to the office and we spent three or four hours formally going through the Six-Step program as it was at that ***time***.(p.291)
• I made several decisions at that ***time***.(p.292)
• I had few enough at that ***time***.(p.293)
• Their answer was always the same: If they should need it at any ***time*** they would surely get in touch with me.(p.293)
• He would invariably reply, "When you are right and the ***time*** is right, Providence will provide.(p.293)
• In the summer of 1938, almost a year from the ***time*** I made my original contact with Akron, the man for whom I was working and who knew about the program, approached me and asked if I could do anything about one of his salesmen who was drinking very heavily.(p.294)
• He had been wanting to do something about his drinking for a long ***time***, but did not know how.(p.294)
• When he returned, we had practically daily meetings from that ***time*** on.(p.294)
• Strangely enough, I became acquainted with the "hilarious life" just at the ***time*** in my own life when I was beginning really to settle down to a common-sense, sane domesticity.(p.297)
• My wife became pregnant and the doctor recommended the use of port or ale . . . so . . . I bought a six gallon crock and a few bottles, listened to advice from amateur brewmeisters, and was off on my beer manufacturing career on a small scale (for the ***time*** being).(p.297)
• As ***time*** went on, I found that it was customary to open a few bottles whenever visitors dropped in.(p.297)
• The parties waxed more liquid and hilarious as ***time*** went on, and eventually I discovered that a little shot of liquor now and then between beers had the tendency to put me in a whacky mood much quicker than having to down several quarts of beer to obtain the same effect.(p.298)
• I got along fairly well with my party drinking for quite some ***time***, but eventually I began to visit beer joints in between parties.(p.298)
• At that ***time***, I was living out of town, so I moved back to the home town and made a connection in a responsible position with one of the larger companies in the finance business.(p.298)
• During this ***time***, I had been threatened, beaten, kissed, praised and damned alternately by relatives, family, friends and strangers, but of course it all went for naught.(p.300)
• I was on the toboggan and really making ***time***.(p.300)
• Now I was getting drunk all the ***time***.(p.300)
• I became convinced of that because I spent most of my ***time*** there and nary a job turned up.(p.300)
• By this ***time***, my chances of getting lined up in my chosen business were shot.(p.301)
• Even some of the saloon-keepers, where I had spent so much ***time*** and money, requested that I stay away from their places.(p.301)
• I was on that job a month and drunk most of the ***time***.(p.301)
• Just at this ***time*** my wife heard of a doctor in another city who had been very successful with drunks.(p.301)
• I had never seen him before, and at the ***time*** hoped I would never see him again.(p.302)
• However, he explained to me that he had been just such a rummy as I, only for a much longer period of ***time***.(p.302)
• And still by the ***time*** I was thirty years old I was being pushed around with a compulsion to drink that was completely beyond my control.(p.305)
• For about one year, prior to this ***time***, there was one doctor who had continued to struggle with me.(p.306)
• It was a waste of the doctors' ***time*** and the

patients' money.(p.307)
• By this *time*, with the doctor's explanation, the revelations contained in the book, and the hope-inspiring interview with Mr. T., I was ready and willing to go into the interior of the African jungles, if that was what it took, for me to find what these people had.(p.309)
• In *time*, I found myself looking forward to each new day with pleasurable anticipation.(p.311)
• THEY STOPPED IN *TIME*(p.315)
• Among today's incoming A.A. members, many have never reached the advanced stages of alcoholism, though, given *time*, all might have.(p.315)
• This, plus mounting emotional disturbances, convinced them that compulsive alcoholism already had them; that complete ruin would be only a question of *time*.(p.315)
• The same as before, I stayed drunk pretty much of the *time*.(p.318)
• "It can't be my drinking," I thought, "because I can stop any *time* I want to.(p.318)
• The third *time*, after almost five years as an S.P. 4, I finally made sergeant.(p.318)
• I still couldn't make it through the nights without drinking, so I went back into the hospital, this *time* to a rehabilitation center.(p.320)
• After a *time*, my mind began to clear of the fog that had covered it.(p.320)
• Live twenty-four hours at a *time*, they say.(p.320)
• As we walked back through the hall, I, for the first *time* in my life, said to another human being, "I'm having trouble with my drinking, too."(p.321)
• I was deathly sick every *time* I took a drink.(p.322)
• But we had to do a lot of entertaining, my husband liked to have a good *time*; I was very young; and I wanted to have a good *time* too.(p.322)
• Even so, every *time* I drank, I seemed to get in trouble.(p.322)
• As my son, our second child, came along, and as he became school age and was away at school most of the *time*, something happened.(p.323)
• I got so that I hid quite a bit of the *time*, wouldn't answer the phone, and stayed by myself as much as I could.(p.324)
• We have only been in A.A. a few years, but now we're trying to make up for lost *time*.(p.325)
• I try to live our program as it has been outlined to me, one day at a *time*.(p.325)
• Many of my neighbors devoted *time* to volunteer work.(p.326)
• I had the *time*, I certainly had the capability, but I never did a thing.(p.326)
• I was aware of symptoms of impending dependence, and I told myself I had gotten out of the rat race just in *time* to head off any booze problem.(p.327)
• And I was able to go on the wagon for long periods of *time* -- once for four years, to cure an ulcer.(p.328)
• Gone are *time* cards to punch, alarm clocks to obey, nosey rumor-mongers and talebearers to evade.(p.329)
• We even can be rebels for the first *time* in our lives.(p.329)
• And retirement is a *time* for thinking, not of death, but of living -- at long last.(p.329)
• When I found this impossible, I became scared for the first *time*.(p.333)
• At one *time*, the admission that I was and am an alcoholic meant shame, defeat, and failure to me.(p.335)
• My home at that *time* was a place to mill around in.(p.337)
• For the second *time*, I was licked.(p.340)
• The first *time* was when I knew I couldn't live with alcohol.(p.340)
• But this second *time*, I found I couldn't live normally without it, and I was licked worse than ever.(p.340)
• Easy does it, first things first, one day at a *time*.(p.340)
• That life for me is lived one day at a *time*, letting the problems of the future rest with the future.(p.340)
• When the *time* comes to solve them, God will give me strength for that day.(p.341)
• In a short *time*, it became uncontrolled drinking.(p.343)
• Following this, I had a short vacation, during which *time* I read as much literature as my sponsor could send me.(p.343)
• I was well into the second fifth by this *time*.(p.347)
• As someone in A.A. said to me once upon a *time*, there is nothing worse than a confused psychiatrist.(p.347)
• I was sitting in my office one *time* after I had operated on a woman.(p.350)
• They have contributed fantastic amounts of *time* and work to our problem, but they aren't able, it seems, to arrest either your alcoholism or mine.(p.352)
• By the *time* I figured out what had happened, I saw two flashing red lights atop squad cars, sedately coming around the corner.(p.353)
• With these new and enlightening doors opening up to me, I was able to make the eventual decision to stop drinking, a day at a *time* -- because I, too, was an alcoholic.(p.355)
• It was a terrible blow at the *time* and I thought he was pretty much of a heel, but of course it was the finest thing he could have done for me under the circumstances.(p.357)
• All I can remember about the Roaring Twenties is that I drank a great deal, thought I was having a grand *time*, managed to get to Europe for a few weeks, was very proud of the dozens of speak-easy cards entitling me to an entree in the better joints between Cleveland and New York, took on a wife, and built a home in a fashionable suburb of Cleveland.(p.358)
• By this *time* I had become associated with the fast growing and fascinating business of broadcasting.(p.358)
• It was my job to sell *time* on these stations to advertising agencies in New York.(p.359)
• At this *time*, however, she had an opportunity to go to Salt Lake City on a new project for the government, but she did promise me that if I would curtail my drinking and buckle down to hard work she would give serious consideration to my latest proposal and maybe join me at a later date when I got settled.(p.359)
• Since the radio station was getting on its feet, it didn't require so many nights of evening work, and that permitted leisure *time* for drinking.(p.360)
• During this *time* I faithfully was writing my girl in Utah.(p.360)
• Once again I was back in the big *time* operations, and along with them, big shot complexes.(p.361)
• She tried reasoning with me, endeavored to work out various drinking schedules, in fact all the tricks were practised faithfully for a short *time* somewhere along my shaky road to unhappiness.(p.361)
• *Time* after *time* I would beg forgiveness on bended knees, with tears rolling down my cheeks, and promise I would never again drink too much.(p.362)
• This was about ten p.m., and the *time* here is important.(p.363)
• Sure enough in a couple of hours two men were at my door and for the first *time* I heard some facts about liquor and my problem that sounded sensible to me.(p.363)
• I thought this was a good *time* to experiment with liquor.(p.364)
• You will recall that I said the *time* that I got the idea out of a clear sky to call A.A. on a certain night was at about ten.(p.366)
• She said she cut this clipping from the paper at about ten on the same night, and at the same *time* as I called A.A. in Pittsburgh -- some 1300 miles away.(p.367)
• After his death, my mother soon picked up drinking where Dad left off, and in a very short *time* she died of cirrhosis of the liver.(p.370)
• (In fact, every *time* I saw him he had a frown on his face.)(p.370)
• That way, I could spend most of my *time* at the Laundromat!(p.371)
• I would have begrudged the *time* or money for alcohol.(p.374)
• In *time* I became an officer and director of one of the largest commercial banks in the country.(p.374)
• I was living in constant fear that I would get caught while driving a car, so I used taxis part of the *time*.(p.375)
• I continue to be surprised by the people I meet who say, "You haven't had a drink for a long *time*, have you?"(p.376)
• We had always encouraged our children to bring their friends home at any *time*, but after a few experiences with a drunken father they eliminated home as a place to entertain friends.(p.376)
• At the *time* this didn't mean much to me.(p.376)
• It seemed to me my wife was becoming more intolerant and narrow minded all the *time*.(p.376)
• There comes a *time* when you don't want to live and are afraid to die.(p.377)
• The *time* for decision had arrived, and it was a relief to say "Yes" when my family said they would call Alcoholics Anonymous for me.(p.378)
• I don't know what I expected, but I most certainly didn't visualize a group of people talking about their drinking problems, making light of their personal tragedies and at the same *time* enjoying themselves.(p.378)
• There may be many reasons which bring one to A.A. for the first *time*, but the lasting one must be to want sobriety and the A.A. way of living for oneself.(p.379)
• Over a period of *time* he has built up self pity, resentments toward anyone or anything that interferes with his drinking.(p.380)
• It took me some *time* to realize that the Twelve Steps of A.A. were designed to help correct these defects of character and so help remove the obsession to drink.(p.380)
• I lived in New Orleans where, at that *time*, cocktail parties, dances and night spots were almost the order of the day -- or rather the night.(p.384)
• I believe the first *time* I ever realized what alcohol would do for me was at my own wedding.(p.385)
• By the *time* all this was over, I was really in a terrific state, and my father taking in things said, "Miss Esther is about to faint.(p.385)
• I was free, white and twenty-one and I had a *time* for myself.(p.386)
• Or he would leave on a trip and by the *time* he came home, I'd be passed out.(p.386)
• Because of this state of confusion and frustration I had hysterics on the seventeenth day for the first and only *time* in my life.(p.387)
• About this *time*, at Christmas, after being under this doctor's care, we decided that there wasn't anything more to do.(p.388)
• Every *time* I got drunk, my husband would send me to a nursing home.(p.388)
• So I called my father and he said, "Yes," he'd come out and stay with me for that *time*.(p.389)
• The only *time* my dog would have anything to do with me was when I had a hangover, and when I was so sick he was the only one who would have anything to do with me at all.(p.390)
• They phoned my husband that I was in jail and in such terrible shape that they didn't know what I would do to myself; and they realized that jail was no place for me, but that he was to wait a while before he got me, because at the *time* they called him to come over for me I was beating a tin cup against the wall.(p.390)
• But somewhere during that *time*, I remembered going back on the bunk and crying my eyes out.(p.390)
• It was such a feeling of relief that I wanted to know more about it and with that, I think for the first *time*, came the realization that there was something horribly, horribly wrong with me.(p.392)
• Up to that *time*, I was so completely baffled by my behavior that I had never really stopped to think at all.(p.392)
• It was the first *time* in my life that I could not get a lift out of what I was drinking; and so one Friday night, at five minutes to six, I had half a water glass of warm gin, and that is when I first asked God to help me.(p.393)
• The words of Dr. Bob and Bill are with me all the *time*.(p.395)
• I displayed alcoholic tendencies actually from the age of fourteen, when I started to steal wine from the family jug, siphoning it off one drink at a *time* so it wouldn't be missed, not drinking it immediately, but saving it until about a pint was accumulated, so that I could get drunk.(p.397)
• At this *time*, the price of booze in the bars was fifteen cents a shot and ten cents a beer.(p.397)
• My first pay was ten dollars, pay for recruits at that *time* being twenty-one dollars per month.(p.398)
• But now, with His help and grace, this child of His has paid his initiation fee for good, as long as he remembers to stay away from that first drink (the one that does all the damage) one day at a *time*.(p.399)
• My personality, from the *time* I can remember anything, was the perfect set-up for an alcoholic career.(p.400)
• Up to this *time* it just hadn't occurred to me to drink.(p.402)
• But whereas my horse was always equipped with a flask, I merely endured the fox hunting so I could start drinking at lunch *time*.(p.404)
• But at this *time*, I began gravitating toward the really hard drinkers, hanging around with them more and more.(p.404)
• This was an Englishman who, at least at this *time*, drank as much as I did.(p.405)
• During this *time*, you are supposed to behave yourself, but I took a little wine-tasting tour through France, all by my lone, with car and chauffeur.(p.405)
• None of them were alcoholics, but at this *time* they

were drinking as much as I was.(p.407)
• I had already feared insanity for a long *time*.(p.408)
• It was I who had to tell the bank, after a certain *time*, to refuse all further deposits.(p.409)
• By this *time* I had ceased to be the life of the party.(p.410)
• Most of the *time* I was covered with bruises from "running into doors."(p.411)
• He now said that we had a physical allergy combined with a mental obsession, and he explained this so that I saw for the first *time* how this could be.(p.413)
• The last *time* I drank, when I was twenty-nine, I drank for only four days, yet I threatened to kill my children; I beat my wife at home and on the church steps; I mistreated a child in my office; and I ran to a hospital for mental illness to avoid jail.(p.418)
• I had a drinking problem on my hands even at that *time*.(p.424)
• I did as I pleased most of the *time*.(p.424)
• I ran away for the second *time*, with another lad.(p.424)
• About this *time* I got my first crush on a girl.(p.425)
• This was fine, but it was just an extra dividend, for I'd made connections by this *time* and was buying a bottle a day from the cook.(p.426)
• About this *time* my folks found A.A.(p.427)
• I spent the *time* in a nearby tavern, was loaded on the ship, went to sleep before take-off, and the next thing I knew someone was shaking me and telling me we were over San Diego.(p.428)
• I headed home for the most wonderful experience of all *time* -- meeting my "new" parents -- mom and dad looked different than I had pictured them.(p.428)
• Again I went into a mild form of D.T.'s, but with no pineapples this *time*.(p.429)
• And I'd proved I couldn't handle it, *time* and again.(p.429)
• At that *time* life to me was spelled "w-h-i-s-k-e-y."(p.430)
• I was inwardly unhappy most of the *time*.(p.432)
• I'd claw my way back to "respectability" and stay there -- until the inevitable next *time*.(p.432)
• My opinions were quoted in *Time* and Newsweek with pictures, and I addressed the public by radio and television.(p.435)
• After talking with him for a *time* I heard myself saying, "Doc, I think I'm an alcoholic."(p.436)
• I remember, one *time*, even the dog had a psychiatric diagnosis.(p.440)
• All I want to know is, why does that dog wet in my lap every *time* I hold him?"(p.440)
• Then I found the solution: At the end of study *time*, I would drink two beers, jump in bed, sleep real fast, and wake up smart.(p.440)
• The longer the drinking continued, the shorter the *time* the alcohol would keep me asleep; I would have to drink myself back to sleep again and again throughout the night.(p.441)
• Instead, I had a 5:00 a.m. shutoff *time*.(p.441)
• However, for a period of *time* I was injecting Pentothal intravenously to put myself to sleep.(p.442)
• Therefore, every pill was medically indicated at the *time* it was taken.(p.443)
• I happened to be the best diagnostician I knew at the *time*, and certainly I knew my case better than anyone else.(p.444)
• *Time* went by very, very slowly on my second nut ward.(p.445)
• Much of my *time* was spent writing letters, notes, orders, and lists of things for Max, who was also my office nurse, to do to keep the world running while I was locked up.(p.445)
• Of course, I was still drinking at the *time*.(p.447)
• But for some *time*, it was difficult to keep from taking a pill when I had an appropriate symptom, such as a cough, pain, anxiety, insomnia, a muscle spasm, or an upset stomach.(p.448)
• It helped me a great deal to become convinced that alcoholism was a disease, not a moral issue; that I had been drinking as a result of a compulsion, even though I had not been aware of the compulsion at the *time*; and that sobriety was not a matter of willpower.(p.448)
• Each *time* I told her she was a nothing, she receded a little more into nowhere.(p.450)
• And when I place more value on my serenity and sobriety than on anything else, I can maintain them at a higher level -- at least for the *time* being.(p.452)
• He was serving *time* on his fifth felony conviction when a miracle happened.(p.457)
• I painfully awakened each *time*, mentally, physically, and spiritually sick.(p.457)
• I served *time* in four penitentiaries and several prison camps, including a maximum-security camp.(p.457)
• Ten days of this treatment the first *time* knocked me from 200 pounds to 130, and I seldom stayed out of the hole long enough to gain back my weight.(p.460)
• The first *time* I remember seeing or hearing of A.A. was twenty years ago.(p.460)
• Fortunately, I received only fifteen-twenty years, and I went back to my alma mater (where I had spent so much *time* in the hole).(p.461)
• During the twenty-four hours after running into the Serenity Prayer, I think I took the first three Steps for the first *time*.(p.461)
• Shortly thereafter, I was selected, with eight other inmates out of the 10,000 in the state's prisons at that *time*, to attend a school designed to take former "management problems" like me and convert them into paracounselors.(p.462)
• I attempted nearly two years ago to make some amends and contact my children, but it wasn't God's *time* yet.(p.463)
• From that *time* on, fear was with me because I realized that not only would I not remember what happened to me while I was drinking, but apparently I couldn't control what happened.(p.465)
• I hadn't been drinking much about that *time*, for I had begun to realize that there was something abnormal about my drinking, although as yet, I didn't realize that it was so out of control.(p.465)
• My pattern of drinking at that *time* had reached the point where once I really started, I would retire to my bed and drink myself into oblivion.(p.466)
• I remember vaguely violent quarrels with my husband, his finding my liquor supply *time* and *time* again and throwing it out.(p.466)
• This *time* I didn't put up any fight because I knew why they were there and where I was going, the psychopathic ward of the City Hospital, where I had been once before.(p.468)
• And then I went back home to live with my parents, and the merry-go-round started again -- only this *time* I didn't have to worry about waking up behind bars in a psychiatric ward.(p.468)
• At that *time* there hadn't been any publicity such as we have now.(p.469)
• On one occasion when I was serving *time* in my favorite drying-out place while I was having a session with the psychiatrist, she left my case history on her desk when she was called away from the room.(p.470)
• I went to meetings, I spent a lot of *time* at the clubroom, but it was all centered in this one woman.(p.472)
• So I concentrated and studied the book during that *time*, and I liked a lot of the things it said in there.(p.472)
• First *time* I have blackout, but not last.(p.474)
• Judge say I go to jail next *time*.(p.475)
• Last *time* in jail, I have two black eyes.(p.475)
• Last *time* I drink, I go to room.(p.475)
• We talk long *time*.(p.475)
• Miracle happen all *time* in A.A.(p.476)
• He was old, but now he grow young with new life in A.A. and travel all *time*.(p.476)
• Any *time* I tried to kill myself, I was either drunk or pilled-up or both -- usually the last.(p.479)
• (We don't have much *time* for bathing in our crowded schedule.)(p.479)
• At one *time*, I was using twenty caps a day; I nearly died half a dozen times on the street.(p.480)
• We are told to practice the Twelve Steps and Twelve Traditions to the best of our ability every day, one day at a *time*.(p.481)
• At that *time* I started school and that's how I got rid of the curls.(p.483)
• About this *time* an incident took place in grade school that I have never forgotten because it made me realize that I was actually a physical coward.(p.484)
• The only *time* that I have ever seen my mother take anything alcoholic was around Christmas *time*, when she would drink some eggnog or light wine.(p.484)
• Father, through the years, had built up a very good mail order business because, at that *time*, there wasn't too much money in medicine.(p.485)
• Economic conditions had a great deal to do with it, because I've often heard my father say that his mother would take one of the old *time* flour sacks and cut a hole through the bottom and two corners of it and there you'd have a gown.(p.486)
• This was around 1935, and it was about this *time* that I actually started drinking.(p.486)
• I had my own medical practice in Washington at that *time*, but the practice slackened and the mail order business started to fall off.(p.486)
• Dad, due to having spent most of his *time* in a small Virginia town, didn't have any too much money, and the money he had saved and the property he had acquired were in Washington.(p.486)
• My father had purchased a restaurant, which he felt would take up some of my spare *time*, and that's how I met Vi.(p.487)
• That's the first *time* I was ever really drunk in my life.(p.487)
• About that *time* I had lost practically all my property except the place we were living in.(p.487)
• There came a *time* when she spoke to me about it, and I would say that I had a bad cold or that I wasn't feeling well.(p.487)
• At that *time* the repeal whiskies were back, and I'd go to the store and buy my whiskey and take it to my office and put it under the desk, first in one place and then in another, and there soon was an accumulation of empty bottles.(p.488)
• My brother-in-law was living with us at that *time* and I said to Vi, "Maybe the bottles are brother's.(p.488)
• But the week-ends stretched on into Mondays and the *time* soon came when I drank every day.(p.488)
• I had a long talk with a psychiatrist, but nothing came of that, and I had also, just about that *time*, talked with a minister for whom I had a great deal of respect.(p.489)
• I rebelled against this, because just about the *time* that I was getting ready to leave high school, a revelation came to me about God and it made things very complicated for me.(p.489)
• I rebelled, and from that *time* on I don't think I attended church more than a dozen times.(p.489)
• We had two girls and a boy at that *time*.(p.490)
• Matters got worse all the *time* until finally they got so bad that I was reinvestigated by the Government.(p.490)
• The closest I came to a psychiatrist during that *time* was an interne who came to take blood tests.(p.492)
• When I had known her years before she was rather slender, but at this *time* she weighed as much as she does now, which is up around in the two hundreds or very close to it.(p.493)
• She didn't say anything about A.A. or getting me a sponsor at that *time*, but she did ask about Vi, and I told her Vi was working and how she could locate her.(p.494)
• But as he continued to talk, I realized that this was the first *time* I had met a person who had the same problems I did and who, I sincerely believe, understood me as an individual.(p.494)
• At that *time* we had our meetings on Friday nights.(p.495)
• Of course, it wasn't very much of a meeting in the beginning; most of the *time* it was just Vi and myself.(p.495)
• They saved us endless *time* and lost motion.(p.496)
• At this *time* I wasn't working.(p.496)
• Vi was taking care of me and I was devoting all my *time* to the building of that group.(p.496)
• If I don't get started soon, I won't have *time* to finish.(p.499)
• I have a family to support and have no *time* to be looking for another job.(p.500)
• Mother has been dying of cancer for a long *time*.(p.501)
• This *time* I'm off of it for good.(p.502)
• There was no *time* off for so-called good behavior, first-timers, or anything else.(p.509)
• However, as *time* went on laws were enacted that reduced the sentence.(p.509)
• That was my attitude toward A.A. at that *time*.(p.510)
• I clung to the outfit for the balance of my *time*, and finally I was released, after having spent twenty years and nine months behind bars.(p.510)
• Each *time* I would make a report to the parole officer he would ask me, "Have you been to an A.A. meeting yet?"(p.510)
• That stuck with me for a long *time*.(p.513)
• I had a habit of getting up just prior to the closing *time* of the saloons, about two or three o'clock in the morning.(p.514)
• It was the first *time* that I had asked for help sincerely and honestly.(p.515)
• I went back to the old family doctor who had helped me the first *time* I had the D.T.'s.(p.515)
• I have to watch myself all the *time*.(p.516)
• Then I had a year in Germany at school -- that was, incidentally, when I got drunk for the first *time*.(p.517)
• Up to that *time*, drinking didn't really mean anything to me at all.(p.518)
• It didn't worry me very much, because at that *time* I

could shut off for a couple of months without taking a drink or even wanting one, and without feeling that I was giving anything up.(p.518)
• I should say there was less drinking in the Army than I thought at that *time*.(p.518)
• I was alone by myself in that job for a long *time*.(p.519)
• He didn't have to lie in wait very long, but fortunately by that *time*, I had acquired friends upstairs and they covered me for quite a *time*.(p.519)
• I lasted at that for four months chiefly on alcohol, because I never seemed to find any *time* to eat.(p.520)
• At the end of that *time*, they shipped me back to my regiment again.(p.520)
• I was down in the Sudan by this *time*.(p.521)
• I talked to him for quite a long *time* and at the end, he said, "Well, you're not quite mad enough to be shut up for good yet, but you soon will be if you live long enough."(p.522)
• I was intensely unhappy the whole *time*, but I didn't seem to be able to do anything about it, and the worst part to me was the realization that all this was going to happen again and again until I died.(p.522)
• That morning was the first *time* I really realized where I'd got to in my life.(p.523)
• She really meant business this *time*.(p.523)
• This was the only *time* in my life that I'd ever known my mother to be almost pitiless, but she couldn't be blamed for that.(p.523)
• I was taking Benzedrine and paraldehyde quite impartially during the day then, and by the *time* I arrived at my first A.A. meeting, I was pretty drunk and certainly doped up to the eyes and completely jittery.(p.523)
• It continues to try to teach me the real charity, the charity that gives *time* and good will and service, and not just money.(p.525)
• Not least of my debts to A.A. is the knowledge that in that *time* when she wanted me most, I was there -- and that I wasn't drunk.(p.525)
• As *time* went on, I drank more.(p.526)
• In *time*, I began to go out and forget the way back home.(p.527)
• Then the *time* came when I couldn't afford whiskey, so I turned to wine.(p.527)
• It's *time* to stop finding excuses for drinking and getting into trouble, because now there is a way out, and if you want what we have, try coming around and giving the program a chance.(p.530)
• (There was a *time*, for about three months, when I bought a ten-dollar wrist watch every pay day – that is every two weeks.(p.532)
• And having sung that phrase, I'd chuckle with amusement, turning into irony turning into self-contempt turning into self-pity, at the sad fate of Bob, that wonderful, poor little motherless boy who was so smart in school and who grew up to accept responsibility so early and so fast and who staggered under his burdens without a whimper until the *time* came when he thought he was too good for this world and so he ought to be out of it.(p.532)
• For a while, for a long *time*, we can endure the intellect's being ahead of the emotions, which is the import of Millay's couplet.(p.534)
• Which is only another way of saying, I had to be right all the *time*, and only God can be that.(p.535)
• I wonder if ever there has been a sillier reason for getting drunk all the *time*.(p.537)
• This *time*, whoever had rolled me had taken my glasses as well (they were gold).(p.538)
• Maybe it was *time* to die.(p.540)
• In *time* I concluded that the reason I was hurt was because I loved my parents, and I concluded too that if I never allowed myself to love anybody or anything I could never be hurt again.(p.545)
• The only kind of security I knew anything about at that *time* was material security and I decided that all these intruders would vanish immediately if I only had a lot of money.(p.545)
• I was married and divorced again before I was twenty-three years old, this *time* to a prominent band leader -- a man that many women wanted.(p.546)
• The only importance in all of this lies in the fact that at twenty-three I was just as sick as I was at thirty three, when I came into A.A., but at that *time* I apparently had no place to go because I had no drinking problem.(p.546)
• And if I had been able to turn to the church at that *time* I'm sure they could not have convinced me my sickness was within myself, nor could they have shown me the need for self-analysis that A.A. has shown me is vital if I am to survive.(p.546)
• Fear of rejection and its ensuing pain were not to be risked, and I turned away from myself once more for the answer, this *time* to the drinks I had always refused before, and in alcohol I found a false courage.(p.546)
• During this *time*, our country was at war.(p.547)
• By this *time* I was such a past master at kidding myself that I had convinced myself I had sat out a war and waited for this man to come home and, as my resentment and self-pity grew, so did my alcoholic problem.(p.548)
• Inside, though, I was scared to death, for I knew that the *time* was coming (and it couldn't be too remote) when I would be unable to hold that job.(p.548)
• About this *time*, I met a man who had three motherless children and it seemed that might be a solution to my problem.(p.548)
• This caused the rather cryptic comment from one of my A.A. friends, when I told my story after coming into the program, that I had always been a cinch for the program, for I had always been interested in mankind, but that I was just taking them one man at a *time*.(p.548)
• I went to jail for the second *time* during this period for being drunk in an automobile.(p.549)
• I was the only person I'd ever known personally who had ever been in jail, and I guess it is most significant that the second *time* was less humiliating that the first had been.(p.549)
• It was here that I realized for the first *time* that as a practicing alcoholic I had no rights.(p.549)
• I attended my first A.A. meeting eight years ago, and it is with deep gratitude that I'm able to say I've not had a drink since that *time*, and that I take no sedation or narcotics, for this program is to me one of complete sobriety and I no longer need to escape reality.(p.549)
• I believe this, and I believe too that it is equally impossible to practice these principles to the best of our ability, a day at a *time*, and still drink, for I don't think the two things are compatible.(p.550)
• It worked for me then, and it has worked for me many times since, and it will work for me every *time* I am willing to work it.(p.552)
• This great experience that released me from the bondage of hatred and replaced it with love is really just another affirmation of the truth I know: I get everything I need in Alcoholics Anonymous – everything I need I get – and when I get what I need I invariably find that it was just what I wanted all the *time*.(p.553)
• By the *time* I reached high school, I was an over-achiever.(p.555)
• Too often, I would overdo it and behave badly at the very *time* I wanted to be at my best!(p.556)
• Each *time*, I went back to drinking – even smuggling a bottle of vodka into the hospital as soon as the blood transfusions had ceased.(p.558)
• At that very *time*, he was a nonalcoholic trustee on the General Service Board of Alcoholics Anonymous!(p.559)
• We cast off the burdens of the past and the anxieties of the future, as we begin to live in the present, one day at a *time*.(p.560)
• Most of our experiences are what the psychologist William James calls the "educational variety" because they develop slowly over a period of *time*.(p.569)

timed

• Knowing that he was sober, I *timed* it just right, so I could do the slashing just before he hit the steps.(p.479)

times

• There had been no real infidelity, for loyalty to my wife, helped at *times* by extreme drunkenness, kept me out of those scrapes.(p.3)
• Many *times* I have gone to my old hospital in despair.(p.15)
• How many *times* people have said to us: "I can take it or leave it alone.(p.20)
• We are unable, at certain *times*, to bring into our consciousness with sufficient force the memory of the suffering and humiliation of even a week or a month ago.(p.24)
• Exceptions to cases such as yours have been occurring since early *times*.(p.27)
• All of us felt at *times* that we were regaining control, but such intervals – usually brief – were inevitably followed by still less control, which led in time to pitiful and incomprehensible demoralization.(p.30)
• To his consternation, he found himself drunk half a dozen *times* in rapid succession.(p.35)
• I had eaten there many *times* during the months I was sober.(p.36)
• Luck then deserts him and he is slightly injured several *times* in succession.(p.38)
• Once more: The alcoholic at certain *times* has no effective mental defense against the first drink.(p.43)
• Many *times* we talk to a new man and watch his hope rise as we discuss his alcoholic problems and explain our fellowship.(p.45)
• Yet in ancient *times* material progress was painfully slow.(p.51)
• Save for a few brief moments of temptation the thought of drink has never returned; and at such *times* a great revulsion has risen up in him.(p.57)
• A man so involved often feels very remorseful at *times*, especially if he is married to a loyal and courageous girl who has literally gone through hell for him.(p.81)
• Being still inexperienced and having just made conscious contact with God, it is not probable that we are going to be inspired at all *times*.(p.87)
• We constantly remind ourselves we are no longer running the show, humbly saying to ourselves many *times* each day "Thy will be done."(p.87)
• Of course, we all fall much below this standard many *times*.(p.99)
• He is worried at *times*, and is becoming aware that he cannot drink like other people.(p.109)
• You may be afraid your husband will lose his position; you are thinking of the disgrace and hard *times* which will befall you and the children.(p.116)
• Or you may already have had it several *times*.(p.116)
• It is probably true that you and your husband have been living too much alone, for drinking many *times* isolates the wife of an alcoholic.(p.119)
• They expect him to give them the nice *times* they used to have before he drank so much, and to show his contrition for what they suffered.(p.126)
• He thought all alcoholics should constantly have chocolate available for its quick energy value at *times* of fatigue.(p.133)
• I had warned him several *times* that he had but one more chance.(p.136)
• A look at the alcoholic in your organization is many *times* illuminating.(p.139)
• The employer can many *times* protect the victim from this kind of talk.(p.145)
• But he's a grand chap when he's sober, though he's been in here eight *times* in the last six months.(p.156)
• The last three *times*, I got drunk on the way home from here.(p.157)
• During these years, I drank as much as my purse permitted, still without paying too great a penalty, although I was beginning to have morning jitters at *times*.(p.173)
• By this time I was beginning to pay very dearly physically and, in hope of relief, voluntarily incarcerated myself at least a dozen *times* in one of the local sanitariums.(p.174)
• I would sometimes hide out in one of the clubs of which I was a member, and had the habit at *times* of registering at a hotel under a fictitious name.(p.176)
• My home life is ideal and my business is as good as can be expected in these uncertain *times*.(p.180)
• During the first six months of 1935, I was hospitalized eight *times* for intoxication and shackled to the bed two or three days before I even knew where I was.(p.184)
• Each of the seven *times* that I had left this hospital in the last six months, I had come out fully determined in my own mind that I would not get drunk again -- for at least six or eight months.(p.184)
• Before very long we began to relate some incidents of our drinking and, naturally, pretty soon, I realized both of them knew what they were talking about because you can see things and smell things when you're drunk, that you can't other *times*, and, if I had thought they didn't know what they were talking about, I wouldn't have been willing to talk to them at all.(p.185)
• I had no trouble there because I had never actually ceased to believe in God, and I had tried lots of *times* to get help but hadn't succeeded.(p.186)
• I'm so grateful for both the program and the people in it that I still want to go, and then probably the most wonderful thing that I learned from the program -- I've seen this in the 'A.A. Grapevine' a lot of *times*, and I've had people say it to me personally, and I've heard people get up in meetings and make the same statement: The statement is, "I came into A.A. solely for the purpose of sobriety, but it has been through A.A. that I have found God."(p.192)
• We shook hands, and he hung onto my hand for a moment and said, "Tell you what I'll do for old *times* sake.(p.201)
• There were *times* when I got to drinking, and I had been warned by Firestone that they wouldn't stand for this much longer, so, clearly, they were conscious of the fact that I drank too much and too often.(p.204)
• That was an experience that I have never forgotten, and many *times* in my own work with A.A. newcomers I feel kind of guilty because I haven't done the

same thing.(p.219)
• The *times* in which I grew up (the Prohibition era immortalized by Scott Fitzgerald and John Held Jr.) had taught me to be gay with the gayest; my own inner urges led me to outdo them all.(p.225)
• Naturally, in spite of my good intentions, in spite of my protected life behind sanitarium walls, I several *times* got drunk, and was astounded . . . and badly shaken.(p.227)
• I believe that my once over-weening self-will has finally found its proper place, for I can say many *times* daily, "Thy will be done, not mine" . . . and mean it.(p.229)
• I missed the old social *times*, of course, but had no definite craving even for beer.(p.232)
• He had already imbued them with his own spirit until they were ready and willing at all *times* to go where sent, and as a doctor he well knew that this mission and duty would strengthen them as it later helped me.(p.235)
• Many of these same things had happened to me many *times* before, but this time they had all descended together.(p.238)
• At this school we had Bible readings before each meal, and church services four *times* on Sunday, and I became so rebellious at this that I swore I would never join or go to any church except for weddings or funerals.(p.240)
• Lots of *times*, vain-gloriously, I used to take the bottle out, look at it and say, "I've got you licked."(p.253)
• Every encouragement was given me with frequent salary increases, but the sober *times* between "periods" became shorter.(p.254)
• An old avocation, the collecting of first editions, rare books and Americana, fascinated me between *times*.(p.255)
• As many *times* as he would tell me that, I still believed him.(p.263)
• I wasn't nearly in the condition I had been in many *times* to be picked up.(p.264)
• I used to think I was cowardly because when things came out pertaining to the program that troubled me, I said to her many *times*, "Annie, am I being a coward because I lay those things away on the shelf and skip it?"(p.273)
• And, anyhow, if I went on for ten or a hundred *times* as long I couldn't even begin to tell you all that A.A. has meant to me.(p.274)
• I have thanked God many *times* in the last sixteen years that that was just what he did not do!(p.278)
• There have also been numerous *times* when I have thought about taking a drink.(p.285)
• I thought at *times* that he was telling my story!(p.290)
• How many *times* I swore off in the morning and got drunk before sunset I don't know.(p.300)
• I was accused of it many *times* when I went to play bridge in the afternoon, but I really never did take a morning drink.(p.323)
• George tried many *times* to go on the wagon.(p.324)
• On the last day I was drinking I went up to see a friend who had had a good deal of trouble with alcohol, and whose wife had left him a number of *times*.(p.346)
• After my wife had read this to me, I said to her, as I had said many *times* in desperation, "I have got to do something."(p.346)
• And the psychiatrist has had thousands of couches, and has put you and me on them many, many *times*, but he hasn't helped us very much, though he has tried hard; and we owe the clergy and the doctor and the psychiatrist a deep debt of gratitude, but they haven't helped our alcoholism, except in a rare few instances.(p.352)
• "Sure, I've seen you tight several *times*, but you're no alcoholic!"(p.356)
• Many *times* have I heard the above expressions since I have been in A.A., and many *times* I have had to reply "Definitely I am an alcoholic, and while it may be hard for you to believe, it is not hard for me, for I have learned many things about alcohol and myself that would, perhaps, be difficult for you to understand."(p.356)
• While I was in Florida trying to convince my wife with all the A.A. literature that she should come back to me, she went over to her desk and picked up a clipping she had taken from the St. Petersburg *Times* about A.A.(p.366)
• At *times*, when I noticed other families, I felt something was very wrong with ours.(p.369)
• This didn't say we had to be in jail, ten, fifty, or one hundred *times*.(p.379)
• I took that treatment three *times* and it didn't work -- at least, for me.(p.389)
• So I went down to him quite a few *times* a month and had him shoot me full of the stuff; and then I went across the street to a little drug store to take a glass of beer or two beers, and then stopped at the liquor store to get myself a pint and go home.(p.389)
• It has made life a thousand *times* easier and simpler than did the endless compromises and conflicts by which I lived before.(p.394)
• It's the last thing I ever heard him say, and I think there are some of us who, at *times*, try to read extra messages and complexities into the Steps.(p.395)
• A few *times* at meetings, I have heard this statement: "Members of A.A. have paid the highest initiation fee of any club members in the world."(p.396)
• I lost it many *times* and mom and dad would drive me around until I found it.(p.429)
• There would be *times* when the life of respectability and achievement seemed insufferably dull -- I had to break out.(p.432)
• Many *times* in the intervening years I have thanked God for that man, a man who had the courage to admit failure, a man who had the humility to confess that all the hard-won learning of his profession could not turn up the answer.(p.436)
• And should I have more bad *times*, I know that I'll never again have to go through them alone.(p.438)
• The pep pills affected my hearing at *times*: I couldn't listen fast enough to hear what I was saying.(p.442)
• I'd think, "I wonder why I'm saying that again -- I've already said it three *times*."(p.442)
• One night, I had to put myself back to sleep three *times*, and then I finally decided to give it up.(p.443)
• Both *times*, my reaction was that I had had nothing to drink the night before, so obviously alcohol had nothing to do with it.(p.444)
• The girl had explained them to me four *times*, and I was too embarrassed to ask her again.(p.445)
• The alcoholic suffers death many *times* over.(p.457)
• Also, I was insane at *times* -- according to society's yardstick.(p.458)
• In a prison in my native state, I spent eleven months in solitary confinement, bouncing in and out of the "hole" (a bare concrete-and-steel cubicle) about five *times* during those eleven months.(p.459)
• I am still arrogant, egocentric, self-righteous, with no humility, even phony at *times*, but I'm trying to be a better person and help my fellowman.(p.463)
• Next two years, I call them many *times*.(p.475)
• At one time, I was using twenty caps a day; I nearly died half a dozen *times* on the street.(p.480)
• Of course, in my day, *times* had changed; she just hadn't changed with the *times*.(p.484)
• I rebelled, and from that time on I don't think I attended church more than a dozen *times*.(p.489)
• He came back several *times*.(p.491)
• What actually happened was that I had taken a penknife and stabbed Vi three *times* with it.(p.492)
• He had gone through the windshields of cars a couple of *times* and was pretty well banged up.(p.510)
• She had been warned numerous *times*, not only by her family but by my own mother, that I was a hopeless drunk, that there wasn't anything anybody could do with me, that I'd never stop, and that eventually I'd break her heart.(p.513)
• You hit the street about ten minutes to eight, and you walk around the block, God knows how many *times*, waiting for that joint to open.(p.514)
• That thought had come to me many, many *times*.(p.515)
• Oh, I might drink too much at *times* -- everyone I knew drank.(p.527)
• I felt that I didn't have anything to live for, so I tried suicide many *times*.(p.528)
• So many wonderful things have happened to me that at *times* I can't believe this is me.(p.529)
• In those years I was in jail nine *times*, in an alcoholic ward, overnight, twice; and I was fired from three jobs, two of them very good ones.(p.536)
• Once this was in front of the Paramount Theatre in *Times* Square.(p.537)
• When I remark that I have been in jail nine *times*, and in an alcoholic ward twice, they think I'm kidding, or possibly dramatizing for the sake of a good yarn.(p.542)
• I had never had a child and this had been a satisfactory excuse many *times* for my drinking.(p.548)
• I've heard it said many *times* in A.A., "There is just one good drunk in every alcoholic's life, and that's the one that brings us into A.A.," and I believe it.(p.549)
• It worked for me then, and it has worked for me many *times* since, and it will work for me every time I am willing to work it.(p.552)
• Like most other alcoholics I have known, I did quit drinking at various *times* -- once for ten months on my own and during other interludes when I was hospitalized.(p.554)
• The terms "spiritual experience" and "spiritual awakening" are used many *times* in this book which, upon careful reading, shows that the personality change sufficient to bring about recovery from alcoholism has manifested itself among us in many different forms.(p.569)

timid

• There was the economic fear which made me too *timid* to take any action which might improve my circumstances.(p.534)

timing

• I tried the beer diet, the wine diet, *timing*, measuring, and spacing of drinks.(p.305)

tin

• They phoned my husband that I was in jail and in such terrible shape that they didn't know what I would do to myself; and they realized that jail was no place for me, but that he was to wait a while before he got me, because at the time they called him to come over for me I was beating a *tin* cup against the wall.(p.390)

tinge

• At our weekly meeting I was a menace to serenity those first few months, for I took every opportunity to lambaste the "spiritual angle" as we called it, or anything else that had any *tinge* of theology.(p.246)

tinkering

• So I wasn't just *tinkering* around with it -- I had to get in with both feet.(p.480)

tiny

• These *tiny* bodies are governed by precise laws, and these laws hold true throughout the material world.(p.49)
• So I was driven to Akron the very next day by these Good Samaritans, and turned over to Dr. Bob and the then *tiny* Akron Group.(p.279)
• I had tried to be the center of my own little world, whereas God was the center of a vast universe of which I was perhaps an essential, but a very *tiny*, part.(p.280)
• Occasionally, it is accorded to a few of us to watch something fine grow from a *tiny* kernel into something of gigantic goodness.(p.295)
• I had a *tiny* trust fund, and I moved into a small apartment where I learned to cook, keep house, and do the things that normal people do.(p.409)
• I could not live on that *tiny* trust fund and still drink all I wanted to.(p.411)
• Even the Jack Alexander Saturday Evening Post article hadn't been written, and there was only a *tiny* group of people in Washington.(p.469)
• After my very first drink -- a *tiny* glass of sherry my father gave me to celebrate the New Year when I was thirteen -- I went up to bed, dizzy with exhilaration and excitement, and I prayed I wouldn't drink any more!(p.554)

tipped

• A doctor *tipped* me off to my first prospect.(p.282)

tippler

• My drinking was never the spaced doses of the careful *tippler*; it was always gluttonous.(p.254)

tips

• I buttonholed him after dinner and gave him a few *tips* on how to run his colony better and the result of that was about a fortnight or so later I was shipped back to my regiment.(p.520)

tipsy

• I also wrote another novel, all about Scott Fitzgerald's poor, misbegotten, unloved, *tipsy* little debutante.(p.405)

tire

• We do not *tire* so easily, for we are not burning up energy foolishly as we did when we were trying to arrange life to suit ourselves.(p.88)
• Then came a sales job with a national *tire* company.(p.243)
• After the *tire* job came the thirties, the Depression and the down hill road.(p.244)
• I depended on optimism and ambition to live in society; when I began to *tire*, I had to depend on chemicals instead to keep going.(p.420)

tired

• The outlines and the promise of the New Land had brought lustre to *tired* eyes and fresh courage to flagging spirits.(p.53)
• Dad may be *tired* at night and preoccupied by day.(p.126)
• By hook or crook I usually managed to sober up before I reached home, but always "terribly *tired*" from a "hard day's work," and just having to have one or two

before dinner.(p.361)

• I went back to my group meetings, but not wholeheartedly, and I often skipped them with the excuse that I was too ***tired***.(p.364)

• I said I was okay, but if it would make her feel better I would go "as ***tired*** as I was after the strenuous holidays."(p.365)

• I would be half asleep and half awake, and in the morning, I would be both ***tired*** and stupid.(p.440)

• I think the Commanding Officer was rather ***tired*** of this particular chicken coming back to roost so often because he very soon wrote in to the medical authorities to tell them that they had to get me into hospital, to be thoroughly examined for drinking.(p.520)

• I remember the day when I decided to drink myself to death quietly, without bothering anyone, because I was ***tired*** of having been a dependable, trustworthy person for about thirty-nine years without having received what I thought was a proper reward for my virtue.(p.531)

tireless

• Maine newsletter (Boomerang) say: "With ***tireless*** devotion and humility, this venerable Indian gentleman traveled thousands of miles humbly pleading for sobriety.(p.476)

tissue

• Were not these things the ***tissue*** out of which our lives were constructed?(p.54)

tissues

• What healed those ***tissues***, those ***tissues*** that I closed, what healed them?(p.351)

title

• The fledgling society, which had been nameless, now began to be called Alcoholics Anonymous, from the ***title*** of its own book.(p.xvii)

• And then, in the spring of 1939, a very remarkable book was rolled off a New York press with the ***title*** "Alcoholics Anonymous."(p.307)

• My father had a ***title***; there was plenty of means in the family.(p.401)

• (This address is now available in pamphlet form at nominal cost through most A.A. groups or from Box 459, Grand Central Station, New York, NY 10163, under the ***title*** "Three Talks to Medical Societies by Bill W." – formerly called "Bill on Alcoholism" and earlier "Alcoholism the Illness.")(p.572)

titled

• A ***titled*** lady, she still saw her world darkening.(p.400)

titles

• "Bill's Story," "Doctor Bob's Nightmare," and one other personal history from the first edition were retained intact; three were edited and one of these was retitled; new versions of two stories were written with new ***titles***; thirty completely new stories were added; and the story section was divided into three parts, under the same headings that are used now.(p.xi)

• They derive no real authority from their ***titles***; they do not govern.(p.567)

toast

• There was more than one occasion when I got up in the morning with just enough money for coffee and ***toast*** and the bus fare to carry me to my first appointment.(p.283)

toboggan

• I was on the ***toboggan*** and really making time.(p.300)

tobogganing

• But the percentages started ***tobogganing***, and it was often a shock to read over some of the pages when sober.(p.331)

today

• ***Today*** the remarkable unity of A.A. is one of the greatest assets that our Society has.(p.xix)

• The central fact of our lives ***today*** is the absolute certainty that our Creator has entered into our hearts and lives in a way which is indeed miraculous.(p.25)

• The practical individual of ***today*** is a stickler for facts and results.(p.48)

• When many hundreds of people are able to say that the consciousness of the Presence of God is ***today*** the most important fact of their lives, they present a powerful reason why one should have faith.(p.51)

• Students of ancient history tell us that the intellect of men in those days was equal to the best of ***today***.(p.51)

• As we felt new power flow in, as we enjoyed peace of mind, as we discovered we could face life successfully, as we became conscious of His presence, we began to lose our fear of ***today***, tomorrow or the hereafter.(p.63)

• His action met widespread approval, and ***today*** his is one of the most trusted citizens of his town.(p.80)

• Had this not been so, many of us would have no homes ***today***, would perhaps be dead.(p.82)

• ***Today*** most of our men are better husbands and fathers than ever before.(p.108)

• ***Today*** I own a little company.(p.149)

• ***Today***, hundreds of additional A.A. members can be found who have had no relapse for more than thirty years.(p.169)

• But I hardly tasted anything for two years and started in business for myself, founding a mattress factory which is ***today*** an important industrial enterprise in our city.(p.232)

• ***Today*** I have.(p.260)

• ***Today*** I have Someone who will always hear me; I have a warm fellowship among men who understand my problems; I have tasks to do and am glad to do them, to see others who are alcoholics and to help them in any way I can to become sober men.(p.260)

• Russ said, "Don't do another thing ***today*** but help him.(p.271)

• It was simple, they said, and went on to explain to me in their own language the program of recovery and daily living which we know ***today*** as the Twelve Steps of A.A.(p.279)

• It was very impressive and I wish that every A.A. could have the benefit of this type of sponsorship ***today***.(p.292)

• I'm sober ***today***.(p.320)

• I try to live ***today*** so that tomorrow I won't be ashamed when I wake up in the morning.(p.325)

• ***Today***, I'm counting my blessings instead of my troubles.(p.355)

• ***Today*** is the day.(p.382)

• If we do a good job of living ***today***, and if tomorrow comes for us, then the chances are we will do a good job when it arrives – so why worry about it?(p.382)

• Living just for ***today*** is a pleasant adventure.(p.383)

• ***Today***, because of A.A.'s growth during the intervening years, it is of course much bigger than it was then.(p.392)

• ***Today*** I think of life in terms of happiness, contentment, freedom from fear and despair, sane thinking, ability to face problems as they occur, the opportunity to help other alcoholics and to be decent.(p.430)

• ***Today*** I have all that anyone could ask.(p.431)

• My work is on a much deeper and more significant level than it ever was before, and I am ***today*** a fairly creative, relatively sane human being.(p.438)

• (***Today***, we don't have to live like that any more.)(p.440)

• ***Today***, I find I can't work my A.A. program while taking pills, nor may I even have them around for dire emergencies only.(p.443)

• (***Today***, we don't have to live that way.(p.446)

• When a big, healthy-looking young fellow stood up there and said, "I'm a success ***today*** if I don't drink ***today***," I thought, "Man, I've got a thousand things to do ***today*** before I can brag about not taking a drink, for God's sake!"(p.447)

• (***Today***, there is absolutely nothing in the world more important to me than my keeping this alcoholic sober; not taking a drink is by far the most important thing I do each day.)(p.447)

• ***Today***, I feel I have used up my right to chemical peace of mind.(p.448)

• And acceptance is the answer to all my problems ***today***.(p.449)

• ***Today***, I find it's the best thing that has ever happened to me.(p.450)

• So I'm better off if I don't give advice, don't figure I know what's best, and just accept life on life's terms, as it is ***today*** -- especially my own life, as it actually is.(p.450)

• When I focus on what's good ***today***, I have a good day, and when I focus on what's bad, I have a bad day.(p.451)

• ***Today***, Max and I try to communicate what we feel, rather than what we think.(p.451)

• Acceptance is the key to my relationship with God ***today***.(p.452)

• Had it not been for A.A. in prison. . . I'll never know, but my educated guess is that I would not be alive ***today***.(p.457)

• I didn't know I was an alcoholic and (like most men in prison ***today***) could not relate alcohol to any of my past troubles.(p.460)

• Besides, I can only live ***today***.(p.463)

• I realize that all I'm guaranteed in life is ***today***.(p.473)

• "There are men on the streets of New York ***today*** who were worse than you, and they don't drink any more."(p.503)

• She's still alive ***today*** at the age of eighty-two.(p.511)

• ***Today***, I thank my Higher Power for giving me another chance at life and A.A. and being able to try and help some other alcoholic.(p.529)

• On the next page, A.A.'s "12 Traditions" are seen in their so-called "short form," the form in general use ***today***.(p.563)

today's

• ***Today's*** life is measured against that of other years and, when it falls short, the family may be unhappy.(p.123)

• Among ***today's*** incoming A.A. members, many have never reached the advanced stages of alcoholism, though, given time, all might have.(p.315)

toddy

• We weren't even permitted to play cards in our home, but father would give us just a little ***toddy*** with whiskey and sugar and warm water now and then.(p.484)

toe

• After two weeks of drinking, he had placed his ***toe*** on the trigger of a loaded shotgun -- the barrel in his mouth.(p.137)

• As soon as I could get up and walk I started to drink again and kept it up until my friend of the hospital, who, in his first try at the new way of life had stubbed his ***toe*** in Chicago but had come back to the town to take counsel and make a new start, picked me up and got me into a hospital.(p.258)

• However, this isn't as rough as it sounds, as we do become grateful for the necessity that makes us ***toe*** the line, for we find that we are more than compensated for a consistent effort by the countless dividends we receive.(p.311)

• I dropped a two-quart water bottle on my big ***toe***.(p.390)

toed

• In a few weeks I ***toed*** the line.(p.362)

toes

• Driven by a hundred forms of fear, self-delusion, self-seeking, and self-pity, we step on the ***toes*** of our fellows and they retaliate.(p.62)

• That is where I had my first drink and I still remember it, for every "first" drink afterwards did exactly the same trick -- I could feel it go right through every bit of my body and down to my very ***toes***.(p.241)

• Same thing when I let lye and water eat away at four of my ***toes*** and my foot for five hours.(p.458)

together

• The test that it faced was this: Could these large numbers of erstwhile erratic alcoholics successfully meet and work ***together***?(p.xviii)

• But out of this frightening and at first disrupting experience the conviction grew that A.A.'s had to hang ***together*** or die separately.(p.xix)

• Another reason for the wide acceptance of A.A. was the ministration of friends -- friends in medicine, religion, and the press, ***together*** with innumerable others who became our able and persistent advocates.(p.xx)

• But that in itself would never have held us ***together*** as we are now joined.(p.17)

• If there be divorce or separation, there should be no undue haste for the couple to get ***together***.(p.99)

• When the time for living ***together*** has come, it will be apparent to both parties.(p.99)

• We began to ask medical advice as the sprees got closer ***together***.(p.106)

• You have passed happy evenings ***together*** chatting and drinking before your fire.(p.110)

• After all, your family is reunited, alcohol is no longer a problem and you and your husband are working ***together*** toward an undreamed-of future.(p.119)

• In the first flush of spiritual experience they forgave each other and drew closer ***together***.(p.124)

• So let each family play ***together*** or separately, as much as their circumstances warrant.(p.132)

• Wherever men are gathered ***together*** in business there will be rivalries and, arising out of these, a certain amount of office politics.(p.145)

• You will be bound to them with new and wonderful ties, for you will escape disaster ***together*** and you will commence shoulder to shoulder your common journey.(p.152)

• This duty ***together*** with my weekly meetings with my fellow alcoholics, and my daily renewal of the contract I originally made with God, have kept me sober when nothing else ever did.(p.237)

• Many of these same things had happened to me many times before, but this time they had all descended ***together***.(p.238)

• Jackie told me about a group of fellows in New York, of whom my old friend Fitz was one, who had the same problem I had, and who by working *together* to help each other were not now drinking and were happy like himself.(p.239)

• But we were staying sober as long as we kept and talked *together*.(p.246)

• We were *together* all the time, but this night I got up and saw it was late.(p.263)

• He talked about his wife taking his little boy away from him because of his drinking, and how he got back *together* with them through A.A., and we began feeling grateful right then that all these things hadn't been taken from us.(p.270)

• They opened with a little prayer, and I thought it was very fine that we stood, all of us *together*, and closed with the Lord's Prayer.(p.270)

• We had meetings at each other's homes and, of course, that was a grand place for people to get *together* out there; they seemed to think so too.(p.270)

• He might have handed me fifty dollars and said that I ought to pull myself *together* and make a new start.(p.278)

• We spent two days there *together* before he returned to New York.(p.281)

• But it took six more months of work and disappointments before a group of three men got *together* in my rooming house bedroom for their first A.A. meeting.(p.282)

• It was a period of binges coming closer and closer *together* and being of longer duration.(p.288)

• And, as the years go by, working *together*, sharing our experiences with one another, and also sharing a mutual trust, understanding and love – without strings, without obligation – we acquire relationships that are unique and priceless.(p.312)

• I said, "Well, I stood it to keep the home *together*, and for the children's sake."(p.322)

• I should have lost my husband, and I think that only the fact that he was an alcoholic too kept us *together*.(p.323)

• But they were all mixed up *together*, and I was all mixed up inside.(p.337)

• I thought the two would never get *together*.(p.338)

• So I went to my wife and asked her, wasn't there something that she and I could do to somehow get *together*, and she turned on her heel and looked me squarely in the eye, and said, "You don't care anything about my problem," and I could have smacked her, but I said to myself, "Grab on to your serenity!"(p.351)

• We attended meetings *together*, and mutually enjoyed our new found friends.(p.364)

• She was endlessly patient as we looked *together* for an answer.(p.409)

• In those days, psychiatry and A.A. had not gotten *together* as they have since.(p.412)

• All these things *together* brought me into A.A.(p.415)

• In A.A., I have had to be torn down and then put back *together* differently.(p.420)

• So we rolled old newspapers *together* and made torches to find a good soft pew and get some sleep.(p.424)

• Science could take my mind apart expertly, but it couldn't seem to put it *together* again.(p.435)

• Still later, even alcohol and chemicals *together* could not lift me.(p.457)

• So the doctor said, "I really don't know too much about it, but they tell me it is a bunch of drunks who get *together* . . ."(p.469)

• Nevertheless, we continued to work *together* and I continued to drink, but I guess, deep down within her heart as well as within mine, we both knew I couldn't stop drinking.(p.490)

• Very often we rode to and from work *together*, but being separated really galled me deep down.(p.491)

• I must get myself *together*.(p.501)

• India lent itself to drinking then, if you were disposed to drink, because you lived in bungalows; you didn't live all *together* as you do at home in an Officer's Mess.(p.519)

• We alcoholics see that we must work *together* and hang *together*, else most of us will finally die alone.(p.563)

• Any two or three alcoholics gathered *together* for sobriety may call themselves an A.A. group, provided that, as a group, they have no other affiliation.(p.565)

toilet

• The water tank on the *toilet* I never used, because that looked too easy.(p.176)

• I do recall lying on a cold cement floor and shredding into little bits several pieces of stolen identification cards, and washing my face in the *toilet* bowl trying to sober up, and screaming hysterically while clinging to bars too high to see out of, and cursing everyone that came near me.(p.354)

• The war leaves me with a pair of blankets, a *toilet* kit, a sweater knit by my sister, and a still greater inferiority.(p.499)

toilets

• Instead of drinking in fancy bars and clubs, I had to carry a bottle of vodka in my briefcase, duck into public *toilets*, and gulp from the bottle, trembling, in order to keep from falling apart.(p.557)

toils

• This physician, the originator of A.A.'s first black group, but badly caught in the *toils*, tells of his release and of how freedom came as he worked among his own people.(p.483)

token

• I fancied myself a leader, for had not the men of my battery given me a special *token* of appreciation?(p.1)

told

• All *told*, promising beginnings have been made in some 50 foreign countries and U.S. possessions.(p.xv)

• It did not satisfy us to be *told* that we could not control our drinking just because we were maladjusted to life, that we were in full flight from reality, or were outright mental defectives.(p.xxiv)

• As the whisky rose to my head I *told* myself I would manage better next time, but I might as well get good and drunk then.(p.6)

• A morning paper *told* me the market had gone to hell again.(p.6)

• In a matter of fact way he *told* how two men had appeared in court, persuading the judge to suspend his commitment.(p.9)

• They had *told* of a simple religious idea and a practical program of action.(p.9)

• "The doctor *told* him that if he ever drank again it would kill him, but there he is all lit up again."(p.20)

• Here was the terrible dilemma in which our friend found himself when he had the extraordinary experience which as we have already *told* you, made him a free man.(p.28)

• We *told* him what we knew of alcoholism and the answer we had found.(p.35)

• We admit we have some of these symptoms, but we have not gone to the extremes you fellows did, nor are we likely to, for we understand ourselves so well after what you have *told* us that such things cannot happen again.(p.38)

• Far from admitting he was an alcoholic, he *told* himself he came to the hospital to rest his nerves.(p.39)

• We *told* him what we knew about alcoholism.(p.39)

• One day we were *told* that he was back in the hospital.(p.40)

• The story he *told* is most instructive, for here was a chap absolutely convinced he had to stop drinking, who had no excuse for drinking, who exhibited splendid judgment and determination in all his other concerns, yet was flat on his back nevertheless.(p.40)

• I now remembered what my alcoholic friends had *told* me, how they prophesied that if I had an alcoholic mind, the time and place would come – I would drink again.(p.41)

• His story is so interesting that some of it should be *told* now.(p.55)

• *Told* my wife of my mistress.(p.65)

• But they had not learned enough of humility, fearlessness and honesty, in the sense we find it necessary, until they *told* someone else all their life story.(p.73)

• We have seldom *told* them the whole truth nor have we followed their advice.(p.73)

• He *told* her what he would try to do in the future.(p.79)

• We would not even do the cause of temperate drinking any good, for not one drinker in a thousand likes to be *told* anything about alcohol by one who hates it.(p.103)

• We have *told* innumerable lies to protect our pride and our husbands' reputations.(p.105)

• How heartbreaking was this discovery; how cruel to be *told* they understood our men as we did not!(p.106)

• We have *told* small tots that father was sick, which was much nearer the truth than we realized.(p.106)

• One of the many doctors who had the opportunity of reading this book in manuscript form *told* us that the use of sweets was often helpful, of course depending upon a doctor's advice.(p.133)

• I *told* her to say that I was not interested.(p.136)

• I *told* him he was through – finally and forever.(p.136)

• One day he *told* me about an executive of the same bank who, from his description, was undoubtedly alcoholic.(p.138)

• He has just returned from a three-months leave of absence, has taken a cure, looks fine, and to clinch the matter, the board of directors *told* him this was his last chance."(p.138)

• I well remember the shock I received when a prominent doctor in Chicago *told* me of cases where pressure of the spinal fluid actually ruptured the brain.(p.140)

• He *told* how he lived in constant worry about those who might find out about his alcoholism.(p.155)

• For an hour, the two friends *told* him about their drinking experiences.(p.157)

• The man in the bed was *told* of the acute poisoning from which he suffered, how it deteriorates the body of an alcoholic and warps his mind.(p.157)

• The two friends spoke of their spiritual experience and *told* him about the course of action they carried out.(p.157)

• We are greatly indebted to the doctor in attendance there, for he, although it might prejudice his own work, has *told* us of his belief in ours.(p.162)

• But they were much disgusted and *told* me they would attempt to struggle along without my presence.(p.173)

• She *told* me that she had been talking to a couple of fellows about drinking.(p.184)

• Then she *told* me that these two drunks she had been talking to had a plan whereby they thought they could quit drinking, and part of that plan was that they tell it to another drunk.(p.185)

• She also *told* me that I could not pay them even if I wanted to and had the money, which I did not.(p.185)

• So, when they came back, I *told* them.(p.187)

• Eagerly he pointed to us saying, "These are the fellows I *told* you about; they are the ones who understand."(p.189)

• Then I remember when the boys came back, that I *told* them, "I have gone to this Higher Power and I have *told* Him that I am willing to put His world first, above everything.(p.190)

• Twenty-two years later, Doctor Bob *told* me that what I had done was like turning a switch and setting up a demand for more alcohol in my system.(p.195)

• I can remember telling the poor little soul that I could probably quit drinking if I wasn't married to her, and *told* her that, after all, I didn't like restraint!(p.199)

• I *told* him that I had not had a drink for ninety days and that I had come to the conclusion that I was one of those individuals who couldn't drink.(p.200)

• I *told* somebody that I was going down to get Christian Science and they took me down, but I don't remember saying that.(p.202)

• I agreed with him and *told* him in no uncertain terms that I never broke my word in my life.(p.206)

• I *told* him I'd take the medicine and I would take it, but I hadn't *told* him when, and thereupon I got away with the third drink.(p.206)

• My experience in the hospital I considered to be terrific because Dr. Bob *told* me very quickly that medicine would have very little to do with it, outside of trying to restore my appetite for food.(p.217)

• He *told* me that there were some other fellows that had tried this with success, and if I cared to see any of them he'd have them come in to see me.(p.218)

• I believe every member of the Akron Group did come to see me, which impressed me terrifically, not so much because of the stories they *told*, but because they would take the time to come and talk to me without even knowing who I was.(p.218)

• I *told* him that I had no other intention.(p.218)

• One of the things that came up repeatedly in the stories they *told* me was that once they had accepted the program, they never had a desire to take a drink.(p.219)

• When my doctor *told* me I should never touch a drink again, I couldn't afford to believe him.(p.226)

• I *told* my doctor so in no uncertain terms.(p.227)

• I *told* him with all the sincerity at my command that I did.(p.235)

• Instead he *told* me that some of them wanted to talk to me and would be over to see me.(p.235)

• His own business was practically gone, he *told* me, when he discovered the answer.(p.236)

• "You've been trying man's ways and they always fail," he *told* me.(p.236)

• He went on talking and *told* me that he had found the plan has a basis of love, and the practice of Christ's injunction, "Love thy neighbor as thyself."(p.236)

• Jackie *told* me about a group of fellows in New York, of whom my old friend Fitz was one, who had the same problem I had, and who by working together to help each other were not now drinking and

were happy like himself.(p.239)
• I did not need to be ***told*** that my efforts were and would be unavailing if I did not get help.(p.258)
• Instead, over coffee cups, this man and his wife ***told*** me what had been done for them.(p.259)
• He ***told*** me that he would never drink again.(p.263)
• As we left, and they were escorting us across the bridge into Wheeling, I, with great dignity and sarcasm, ***told*** them if their wives were ever visiting in Akron, and they, too, were looking for their route sign as I was, that I hoped I could extend to them the hospitality that had been shown to me in Bellaire.(p.264)
• We always tried to buy him a drink, and he always ***told*** us he had liquor trouble -- couldn't drink.)(p.266)
• Right away, I saw it was the same outfit this other guy ***told*** me about, and then again hope died.(p.267)
• Finally, one morning, I got up and got in the car and cried all the way down to the M.'s – the people who owned the bar – and ***told*** her I was licked and wanted help.(p.267)
• But he ***told*** a story of drinking that was amazing to me.(p.268)
• But it was so important that we do the things we were ***told*** to do!(p.268)
• And Jim G. had such a wonderful sense of humor, and when he came I was in tears, and I ***told*** him, "I want to do this, but I can't.(p.269)
• No, I was all interested in this part that ***told*** you how to do it.(p.269)
• They ***told*** Annabelle to take me under her wing, and I shall never forget how she sort of curled up her nose and said, "They tell me you drink too."(p.269)
• I thought I had done that until Russ' second collapse, and the doctor ***told*** me very candidly that he wasn't long for this world.(p.271)
• And that woman ***told*** me long after that was the surest proof to her that this program could work.(p.272)
• I hadn't been in too long when one of the men's wives called me one Sunday and ***told*** me she didn't think I had any part of the program.(p.273)
• I didn't think I was going to get drunk right then, but I remember how comforting it was when I called Anne and ***told*** her.(p.273)
• I ***told*** our family doctor, an understanding man who gave hours of his time trying to help me, about this experience.(p.276)
• He ***told*** me that it was imperative that I walk around the entire block, cost me what it might in mental agony.(p.276)
• When the day of their return was almost upon me, and suicide was the only answer I had been able to think of, I went into Ralph's room one evening and ***told*** him the truth.(p.278)
• Here, while in a hospital bed, men with clear eyes, happy faces, and a look of assurance and purposefulness about them, came to see me and ***told*** me their stories.(p.279)
• He waited until I was completely sober and the day before I was to head back for Chicago, he ***told*** me of a small group of men in Akron who apparently had the same problem that I had but were doing something about it.(p.289)
• So I ***told*** dad that I would lick it on my own, that I would drink nothing for a month and after that only beer.(p.289)
• The next afternoon and evening, two other men visited me and each ***told*** me his story and the things that they were doing to try to recover from this tragic illness.(p.290)
• In the next two or three days the balance of this handful of men contacted me, encouraged me, and ***told*** me how they were trying to live this program of recovery and the fun they were having doing it.(p.291)
• When I ***told*** them six weeks, they were polite and said that they would contact me in case they had anyone with an alcoholic problem.(p.293)
• Doctors ***told*** me before I stopped that I had only three years at the outside to live.(p.295)
• My wife accompanied me on my visit and the doctor really ***told*** me some things that in my state of jitters nearly knocked me out of the chair.(p.302)
• Until now, I had never been ***told*** that I was an alcoholic.(p.307)
• Then he ***told*** me there was a handful of people in Akron and New York who had worked out a technique for arresting their alcoholism.(p.308)
• He ***told*** me that eventually he hoped such a group would develop in the Chicago area, but that so far this had not been started.(p.309)
• I halfway washed them, and he ***told*** me to do them again, and I did, and he yelled at me to do them again, and I picked up one of the cans and threw it at him and ***told*** him to do them himself.(p.317)
• We got along fine for about two weeks, until she ***told*** me where to go and to take my damn bottle with me.(p.318)
• She ***told*** me her name, and I said, "I know you from somewhere."(p.321)
• She ***told*** me; it was simple; I could have done it very easily.(p.326)
• I had never even been ***told*** by a superior that maybe I was drinking too much.(p.327)
• I was aware of symptoms of impending dependence, and I ***told*** myself I had gotten out of the rat race just in time to head off any booze problem.(p.327)
• He may even read in a newspaper that one out of every seven drinkers will become alcoholic, but he rarely is ***told*** that it holds true for all ages – or that the tolerance to alcohol (and other drugs) decreases steadily, year after year, in the bodies of all persons.(p.330)
• He'd ***told*** a villain, "The trouble is, old man, you've lived too long."(p.333)
• I ***told*** her that I was an alcoholic, victim of a disease, that there was no cure, only arrestment through total abstinence.(p.333)
• I ***told*** her I had to go to A.A.(p.334)
• I called my husband up and ***told*** him to come home.(p.338)
• I was ***told*** that someone would call on me shortly, to sit tight and not take another drink.(p.363)
• They ***told*** me their stories, which were much more rugged than mine -- yet what they said made sense, and the way they put it was easy for me to understand, with an understanding I had never had before.(p.363)
• Later I ***told*** her I had not taken the drink and that I was all right.(p.365)
• When our meeting night came around the next evening, I went – "for her sake" I ***told*** her.(p.365)
• She ***told*** me not to bother going "for her sake"; she ***told*** me in a nice way that it didn't make any difference to her – and that really scared me – so I went.(p.365)
• I had never ***told*** a soul about my lapse in New York.(p.366)
• With that, he ***told*** me to leave, because I was unfit as a mother, a wife, and a laundress.(p.371)
• I was ***told*** that I must want sobriety for my own sake and I am convinced this is true.(p.379)
• A willingness to do whatever I was ***told*** to do simplified the program for me.(p.381)
• They ***told*** me to go to meetings, and I still do at every available opportunity, whether I am at home or in some other city.(p.381)
• I know now that I asked questions and ***told*** him what I wanted to learn, but I ***told*** him only what I wanted to believe about myself.(p.388)
• I have ***told*** you some of the funny things, but not much of the shame and degradation.(p.390)
• When he picked me up, I must have gotten sassy and ***told*** him that he couldn't do that, so he took my dog home and took me to jail!(p.390)
• Above all, he noticed that I drank a good deal, often got tight in his company and ***told*** him naughty stories.(p.403)
• He finally decided that he did not love me enough, and soon he ***told*** me so and said he was engaged to another girl.(p.403)
• I saw him recently and he ***told*** me that he had always felt guilty, because, after our separation, I had become a serious alcoholic.(p.403)
• I accepted a big tax-free income from the family, but I didn't like it when they ***told*** me how to live.(p.405)
• Bruised, and deadly ashamed, I ***told*** no one.(p.406)
• They said I was so funny, and ***told*** me, with shrieks of laughter, what I'd done the night before.(p.407)
• I ***told*** myself that I had power over this thing.(p.408)
• Finally my new friends ***told*** me, one by one, that I could not come around any more.(p.410)
• Once, when I called my analyst, and ***told*** her I was contemplating death, she came over and tried to get me into a sanitarium.(p.411)
• "These people all had your problem," she ***told*** me.(p.412)
• On non-meeting nights I was lonesome, or so I ***told*** myself.(p.414)
• No one could have ***told*** me then that I had not earned all my success, nor could anyone have ***told*** me that I was an alcoholic and a drug addict.(p.418)
• I hadn't ***told*** them about my drinking, but I guess they knew.(p.427)
• I ***told*** the doctor my parents' drinking history and blamed them.(p.428)
• That doctor in the Navy hospital ***told*** me I wouldn't live five years if I didn't quit.(p.429)
• "I've got to stop if I want to live," I ***told*** myself, and if I don't want to break my parents' hearts and maybe jeopardize their own carefully built up and hard-fought-for sobriety.(p.429)
• "I'll do it," I ***told*** myself.(p.430)
• "Then why in God's name haven't you ***told*** me so, during all these years?"(p.436)
• Second, you wouldn't have believed me even if I had ***told*** you."(p.436)
• I didn't know whether I had ***told*** him to rush to the hospital and I'd meet him there, or to take two aspirin and call me in the morning.(p.441)
• The next day, Max called the neurologist and ***told*** him about the Mayo psychiatrist's opinion.(p.445)
• It wasn't until later that he ***told*** me he was an attorney.(p.446)
• Each time I ***told*** her she was a nothing, she receded a little more into nowhere.(p.450)
• Then, one day in A.A., I was ***told*** that I had the lenses in my glasses backwards; "the courage to change" in the Serenity Prayer meant, not that I should change my marriage, but rather that I should change myself and learn to accept my spouse as she was.(p.451)
• On the day before Christmas I telephoned him and ***told*** him I was sober and asked him to come home.(p.467)
• Was it because they ***told*** me in A.A. that I was an alcoholic?(p.470)
• But the older members in A.A. ***told*** me, "easy does it."(p.471)
• Once, I phoned my brother-in-law and ***told*** him I was going to take a handful of pills (in fact, I already had) and I would slash my wrists if he didn't come over to stop me.(p.479)
• We are ***told*** to practice the Twelve Steps and Twelve Traditions to the best of our ability every day, one day at a time.(p.481)
• If someone had ***told*** me last year that I would be excited about gardening this year, I would have said he was off his rocker.(p.481)
• If anyone had ***told*** me I would be enjoying a hockey game with my husband and my brother without being all boozed up, I would not have believed it.(p.481)
• I said that she ***told*** me she was going to the movies, and I became foolishly disturbed about it and, as things snowballed, I decided to go out and get drunk.(p.487)
• The fear of the loss of Vi and the feeling that, though she had the right to do as she pleased, she should have ***told*** me the truth about it, upset me.(p.487)
• Something should have ***told*** me then that things were haywire.(p.487)
• He went into the religious side and ***told*** me that I didn't attend church as regularly as I should, and that he felt, more or less, that this was responsible for my trouble.(p.489)
• Then I went South, because they ***told*** me that the particular county I was going to in North Carolina was a dry county.(p.489)
• Then she ***told*** me who she was.(p.493)
• She didn't say anything about A.A. or getting me a sponsor at that time, but she did ask about Vi, and I ***told*** her Vi was working and how she could locate her.(p.494)
• She never mentioned anything about my whiskey drinking because if she had I would have ***told*** her, "No" right then.(p.494)
• I ***told*** her that I would.(p.494)
• They came, many of them, and stuck by us and ***told*** us how to hold meetings.(p.495)
• The doctor has ***told*** me that if I don't give up inside work, I'll have tuberculosis.(p.500)
• I ***told*** him that I believe in electricity and other forces of nature, but as for a God, if there is one, He has never done anything for me.(p.503)
• Those poor stiffs probably went to a doctor and were ***told*** that if they quit they'd live three weeks and if they didn't they'd die in one."(p.510)
• No one had ever ***told*** me it was the first drink that did the damage.(p.514)
• Someone ***told*** me, "When you drank, you didn't get half drunk.(p.516)
• When I came back, I ***told*** the priest, the Chaplain of the place, exactly what I thought of him and he didn't like it.(p.517)
• In fact, I couldn't have ***told*** you the difference between sherry and brandy.(p.518)
• But then one good doctor ***told*** me there was nothing wrong with me except drinking too much.(p.528)

- The cops had picked her up, and she *told* them she had bought it from me.(p.528)
- Sometimes we are *told* in A.A. not to try and learn the reasons for our drinking.(p.533)
- This caused the rather cryptic comment from one of my A.A. friends, when I *told* my story after coming into the program, that I had always been a cinch for the program, for I had always been interested in mankind, but that I was just taking them one man at a time.(p.548)
- The A.A. members who sponsored me *told* me in the beginning that I would not only find a way to live without having a drink, but that I would find a way to live without wanting to drink, if I would do these simple things.(p.550)
- When I had been in A.A. only a short while, an oldtimer *told* me something that has affected my life ever since.(p.554)
- Much later, when I had progressed to full-blown alcoholism, people *told* me I should quit.(p.554)
- The doctors *told* me that if I ever took another drink, it might be my last.(p.558)
- For example, we are *told* in A.A. that we cannot afford resentments and self-pity, so we learn to avoid these festering mental attitudes.(p.560)

Toledo

- I landed him and shipped him by train to Akron, with a pint of whiskey in his pocket to keep him from wanting to get off the train in *Toledo*!(p.282)

tolerance

- Most of us sense that real *tolerance* of other people's shortcomings and viewpoints and a respect for their opinions are attitudes which make us more useful to others.(p.19)
- We asked God to help us show them the same *tolerance*, pity, and patience that we would cheerfully grant a sick friend.(p.67)
- We have begun to learn *tolerance*, patience and good will toward all men, even our enemies, for we look on them as sick people.(p.70)
- So we clean house with the family, asking each morning in meditation that our Creator show us the way of patience, *tolerance*, kindliness and love.(p.83)
- Love and *tolerance* of others is our code.(p.84)
- Patience, *tolerance*, understanding and love are the watchwords.(p.118)
- All members of the family should meet upon the common ground of *tolerance*, understanding and love.(p.122)
- We do talk about each other a great deal, but we almost invariably temper such talk by a spirit of love and *tolerance*.(p.125)
- If they sense these things, they will not take so seriously his periods of crankiness, depression, or apathy, which will disappear when there is *tolerance*, love, and spiritual understanding.(p.127)
- In only a few instances has there been lack of patience and *tolerance*.(p.137)
- He may even read in a newspaper that one out of every seven drinkers will become alcoholic, but he rarely is told that it holds true for all ages -- or that the *tolerance* to alcohol (and other drugs) decreases steadily, year after year, in the bodies of all persons.(p.330)
- They meant patience, *tolerance* and humility, and above all the belief that a Power greater than myself could help.(p.381)

tolerant

- We cannot be helpful to all people, but at least God will show us how to take a kindly and *tolerant* view of each and every one.(p.67)
- Much later I discovered the elders held many prayer meetings hoping to find a way to give me the heave-ho, but at the same time stay *tolerant* and spiritual.(p.247)
- Federal Theatre in Texas gave me an administrative job which I held for a year, only because I worked hard and productively when I worked, and because my very *tolerant* chief ascribed my frequent lapses to a bohemian temperament.(p.256)
- She was *tolerant* beyond all belief.(p.361)

tolerantly

- I listened to him, rather *tolerantly*.(p.257)

tolerated

- The less people *tolerated* us, the more we withdrew from society, from life itself.(p.151)
- By persistence and salesmanship I managed to see more and more of my new friend, and because of her sympathetic nature she *tolerated* my company.(p.359)

tolerating

- After holding good positions, making better than an average income for over ten years, I was in debt, had no clothes to speak of, no money, no friends, and no one any longer *tolerating* me but my wife.(p.301)

toll

- Later on in life that took its *toll*.(p.483)

Tom

- *Tom* Sharkey's brawling bar on 14th Street and the famous wine-room at the back were headquarters for me.(p.251)
- In my mind's eye I saw Broadway again and *Tom* Sharkey's bar; the roar of the subway was in my ears.(p.252)

tombs

- I was immediately arrested, arraigned in Homicide Court, held without bail, and remanded to the old *Tombs* Prison to await trial.(p.508)

tombstone

- My attention was caught by a doggerel on an old *tombstone*:(p.1)

tomorrow

- *Tomorrow* was another day.(p.4)
- As we felt new power flow in, as we enjoyed peace of mind, as we discovered we could face life successfully, as we became conscious of His presence, we began to lose our fear of today, *tomorrow* or the hereafter.(p.63)
- Then Dr. Bob said, "Well, Bill, maybe you'll feel better *tomorrow*.(p.189)
- Once I did have a slip – tried drinking again – but the A.A.'s tell me not to worry about yesterday, because nobody can change it, and not to worry about *tomorrow*, because it hasn't come yet.(p.320)
- You know I'll do it *tomorrow*, the very same thing."(p.325)
- I try to live today so that *tomorrow* I won't be ashamed when I wake up in the morning.(p.325)
- Yesterday is gone, and we don't know whether we will be here *tomorrow*.(p.382)
- If we do a good job of living today, and if *tomorrow* comes for us, then the chances are we will do a good job when it arrives – so why worry about it?(p.382)
- For me, as for most alcoholics, it was "Eat, drink, and be merry, for *tomorrow* you die."(p.457)

tone

- If you cooperate, rather than complain, you will find that his excess enthusiasm will *tone* down.(p.119)

tongue

- My *tongue* had become increasingly skilled at venomous home truths.(p.405)
- My *tongue* loosened.(p.498)

tonight

- One night at the dinner table my wife said that *tonight* was my first birthday in A.A., and that the group would have the usual ice cream and cake for the "one year man."(p.365)

took

- They *took* a drink a day or so prior to the date, and then the phenomenon of craving at once became paramount to all other interests so that the important appointment was not met.(p.xxvii)
- War fever ran high in the New England town to which we new, young officers from Plattsburg were assigned, and we were flattered when the first citizens *took* us to their homes, making us feel heroic.(p.1)
- I *took* a night law course, and obtained employment as investigator for a surety company.(p.2)
- My work *took* me about Wall street and little by little I became interested in the market.(p.2)
- These observations would be academic and pointless if our friend never *took* the first drink, thereby setting the terrible cycle in motion.(p.23)
- And the truth, strange to say, is usually that he has no more idea why he *took* that first drink than you have.(p.23)
- As soon as we admitted the possible existence of a Creative Intelligence, a Spirit of the Universe underlying the totality of things, we began to be possessed of a new sense of power and direction, provided we *took* other simple steps.(p.46)
- Here are the steps we *took*, which are suggested as a program of recovery:(p.59)
- When we sincerely *took* such a position, all sorts of remarkable things followed.(p.63)
- We *took* stock honestly.(p.64)
- They *took* inventory all right, but hung on to some of the worst items in stock.(p.73)
- We made it when we *took* inventory.(p.76)
- If, on the other hand, they *took* nothing, their self-pity made them killjoys.(p.105)
- Perhaps at this point we got a divorce and *took* the children home to father and mother.(p.106)
- Unless he *took* some drinks, he might not have the courage to scrape an acquaintance and would have a lonely week-end.(p.154)
- One morning he *took* the bull by the horns and set out to tell those he feared what his trouble had been.(p.156)
- There I *took* up the business of drinking with much greater earnestness than I had previously shown.(p.173)
- I drank with moderation at first, but it *took* me only a relatively short time to drift back into the old habits which had wound up so disastrously before.(p.175)
- 3.Because in so doing I am paying my debt to the man who *took* time to pass it on to me.(p.181)
- It *took* me a year, or a year and a half to get to feeling physically well, and it was rather tough, but I soon found folks whose friendship I had once had, and I found, after I had been sober for quite some little time, that these people began to act like they had in previous years, before I had gotten so bad, so that I didn't pay too awful much attention to financial gains.(p.190)
- He wouldn't give me any money for the groceries, but he did take me across the street and buy me a bag of candy, which I later *took* back and traded for a loaf of bread.(p.193)
- He *took* a couple of puffs of a cigarette and I *took* a couple of puffs of my cigarette.(p.195)
- At that particular time, the boys put me on a shutter and *took* me out to the shed, and I lay in the car while they enjoyed their banquet.(p.195)
- I was picked up at two-thirty that morning with my car smashed up by a street-car because I had run into a big concrete safety zone, and the street-car had run into me, and they *took* me out through the roof -- there's where I lost the suit.(p.202)
- I told somebody that I was going down to get Christian Science and they *took* me down, but I don't remember saying that.(p.202)
- He brought the quart out and I *took* a good swig.(p.205)
- He came in and *took* a look at me and sent me to the hospital.(p.205)
- He *took* off his hat and his overcoat, and he said, "You don't look very good.(p.207)
- Following graduation I was offered a pretty good job which I *took*.(p.212)
- In fact, the last three years of my drinking was a routine of barbiturates in the morning, so that I could stop shaking enough to shave, and then alcohol beginning about four-thirty or five o'clock, with a struggle not to take a drink at noon or during the day, because I had the idea that if I *took* one drink, I would smell as though I had had a pint.(p.217)
- I found in the fall of 1939, that I was not mentally impaired, so far as trial work was concerned, and thereafter *took* up where I had left off when I was about forty-five years old.(p.220)
- It *took* three-quarters of an hour and two changes to get there – back to my starting point.(p.223)
- I early decided that the wine of America was very inferior stuff and *took* up beer instead.(p.231)
- I like to think I was fairly normal before alcohol *took* over.(p.240)
- However, here I probably *took* my first step towards my coming alcoholism by developing a terrific aversion to all churches and established religions.(p.240)
- In those days we really *took* each other's inventories firmly and often.(p.245)
- There was one meeting a week at Bill's home in Brooklyn, and we all *took* turns there spouting off about how we had changed our lives overnight, how many drunks we had saved and straightened out, and last, but not least, how God had touched each of us personally on the shoulder.(p.246)
- At our weekly meeting I was a menace to serenity those first few months, for I *took* every opportunity to lambaste the "spiritual angle" as we called it, or anything else that had any tinge of theology.(p.246)
- After a very good week, two of my customers *took* me to lunch on Saturday.(p.247)
- This was when I really *took* my first good look at myself.(p.247)
- When the others saw my altered attitude they *took* me back in, but for me they had to make it tough; if they hadn't I don't think I ever would have stuck it out.(p.248)
- While I went along with all that was done and attended the meetings, I never *took* an active job of leadership until February 1940.(p.249)
- I *took* my last drink in 1937.(p.260)
- I remember one instance when he *took* off and went down to Cincinnati and was gone a week on a drunk.(p.262)
- Finally, it got so bad that I left him and went back home and *took* my two children with me.(p.262)
- He *took* his one hundred and seventeen dollars and

let us go, and we proceeded.(p.264)
• Time went on and the drinking got worse and worse, and I was in another barroom, down the road the other way, a small one, and I *took* my glass -- that morning I'd been able to lift it from the bar -- and I said to the woman behind the bar, "I wish I might never take another drop of that stuff.(p.266)
• When she finally *took* the baby and left, I locked myself in the house and stayed drunk for a month.(p.278)
• Instead, he got dressed, *took* me out, bought me three or four double shots and put me to bed.(p.278)
• But it *took* six more months of work and disappointments before a group of three men got together in my rooming house bedroom for their first A.A. meeting.(p.282)
• It *took* five years of A.A. living, and a substantial improvement in my health, before I could take a full-time office job where someone else was boss.(p.283)
• They went into a huddle and dad explained that he simply *took* my pants, shoes and money away, so that I could get no liquor and had to sober up.(p.288)
• After finding every bottle that I had hidden around the apartment, she *took* away my pants, my shoes, my money and my keys, threw them under the bed in the back bedroom and slip-locked our door.(p.288)
• My wife could not understand the next morning why I was drunker than the night before when she *took* my bottles.(p.289)
• The doctor, a young man, immediately *took* fire with the idea, and while he did not convince the son, he turned over two prospects who were anxious for the program.(p.294)
• From that point on, I secured crocks of ten gallon capacity and really *took* quite an active interest in the manufacture of home brew.(p.297)
• After being fired, I lined up with a new finance company that was just starting in business, and *took* the position of business promotion man, contacting automobile dealers.(p.300)
• By this time, with the doctor's explanation, the revelations contained in the book, and the hope-inspiring interview with Mr. T., I was ready and willing to go into the interior of the African jungles, if that was what it *took*, for me to find what these people had.(p.309)
• Nothing in their lives *took* precedence over their response to a call for help from some alcoholic in need.(p.310)
• It *took* the help, understanding and wonderful companionship that was given so freely to me by my "ex-alkie" friends.(p.311)
• So I *took* my bottle and went and drowned my sorrows.(p.318)
• She *took* me by the hand and introduced me to the girl that I'm very proud to call my sponsor.(p.321)
• I was deathly sick every time I *took* a drink.(p.322)
• And, unlike many others, I never *took* a drink in the morning.(p.323)
• Until I *took* Social Security and a pension at the age of sixty-eight, after forty years in motion-picture-studio public relations, I had successfully hidden even any hints of approaching alcoholism.(p.327)
• My writing career was described in the couplet "Alcohol gave me wings to fly,/And then it *took* away the sky."(p.331)
• Yet I recently recalled that each morning I used to talk to the bottle when I *took* it down from the closet.(p.332)
• When alcohol *took* me over, my bar was my kitchen, my living room, my bedroom, the back bathroom, and the two hampers.(p.335)
• And when I *took* that first drink, I was off on the usual merry-go-round.(p.339)
• And I *took* everything that A.A. had to give me.(p.340)
• *Took* down notes for reference purposes.(p.344)
• This friend gave me a pamphlet, and I *took* it home and had my wife read it to me.(p.346)
• It *took* me a year to make it home.(p.357)
• All I can remember about the Roaring Twenties is that I drank a great deal, thought I was having a grand time, managed to get to Europe for a few weeks, was very proud of the dozens of speak-easy cards entitling me to an entree in the better joints between Cleveland and New York, *took* on a wife, and built a home in a fashionable suburb of Cleveland.(p.358)
• My sister-in-law *took* me to a place she had heard about that helps women like me.(p.371)
• Two years before I joined A.A. my wife *took* a long trip during which she wrote me she just couldn't return unless I did something about my drinking.(p.377)
• It *took* me some time to realize that the Twelve Steps of A.A. were designed to help correct these defects of character and so help remove the obsession to drink.(p.380)
• It only *took* a month to get a divorce in Texas.(p.386)
• So I *took* the Samaritan Treatment.(p.389)
• I *took* that treatment three times and it didn't work -- at least, for me.(p.389)
• When he picked me up, I must have gotten sassy and told him that he couldn't do that, so he *took* my dog home and *took* me to jail!(p.390)
• I *took* two or three drinks so my eyes could focus, and I could see that horrible picture of the awful drunk on the first page; he couldn't get the drink to his mouth, he had a towel around his hand and he needed a shave.(p.391)
• It *took* me three psychoanalysts and several years in A.A. to really get this through my head.(p.401)
• During this time, you are supposed to behave yourself, but I *took* a little wine-tasting tour through France, all by my lone, with car and chauffeur.(p.405)
• I *took* everybody else's inventory.(p.410)
• The bartenders *took* care of me, not out of brotherly love, but through enlightened self-interest.(p.410)
• They *took* Anne and me to dinner.(p.415)
• He himself *took* me to many of them, including the ones out of town.(p.416)
• All the people involved in these flare-ups *took* it with remarkable grace, have teased me about it since, and have become good friends of mine.(p.416)
• Fear, love of dentistry, and an imitation of my father's periodic drinking pattern *took* me through dental college soberly, except for the few parties and vacations in those four years.(p.419)
• I *took* it easy, because they didn't know about me.(p.428)
• In all the twenty-five years of my drinking there were only a few occasions when I *took* a morning drink.(p.432)
• My alcoholic associates fired me, *took* control, and ran the enterprise into bankruptcy.(p.437)
• My alcoholic wife *took* up someone else, divorced me, and *took* with her all my remaining property.(p.437)
• My drinking *took* place after work hours.(p.441)
• I *took* more through the day to increase the high, and more to maintain it; when I overshot the mark, I'd take tranquilizers to level off.(p.442)
• I never in my life *took* a tranquilizer, sedative, or pep pill because I was a pillhead.(p.443)
• I always *took* it because I had the symptom that only that pill would relieve.(p.443)
• Each with the other as a witness, we *took* the Third Step out loud -- just as it says in the Big Book.(p.446)
• Later on, it *took* alcohol fortified with other drugs to pull me up.(p.457)
• During the twenty-four hours after running into the Serenity Prayer, I think I *took* the first three Steps for the first time.(p.461)
• This A.A. friend *took* me into his home when he had me out on pass.(p.462)
• The doctor, apparently realizing that one thing that I certainly needed was sleep, left a bottle of sleeping pills there and in my drunken state I *took* them all, instead of the one or two he had prescribed.(p.465)
• It was in Washington, D.C. that this transition *took* place, and that the really bad part of alcoholism began happening.(p.465)
• And A.A. *took* this wreck of a woman and brought her back to life.(p.470)
• In the light of subsequent events it became evident that I *took* their advice far too literally, for, after some months of happy sobriety I drank again.(p.471)
• Later on in life that *took* its toll.(p.483)
• About this time an incident *took* place in grade school that I have never forgotten because it made me realize that I was actually a physical coward.(p.484)
• He *took* the basketball and smashed me in the face with it.(p.484)
• Vi was the first girl that I ever *took* out.(p.485)
• I *took* that bottle of medicine and gave it to a very good friend of mine who was a pharmacist and had it analyzed, and the bottle was perfectly all right.(p.489)
• The November following, I *took* a few days off after pay day to celebrate my birthday on the 25th of the month.(p.491)
• I *took* the last to buy my railroad ticket.(p.493)
• But after I passed through the gates I *took* a change of heart and mind.(p.510)
• But at the end of nine months we went to a party one night, and I *took* the first drink.(p.514)
• I *took* the advice of people I had heard at meetings, the people in the group.(p.516)
• Then a change in management *took* place in the regiment and the new O.C. didn't like me very much and I didn't like him, and he started to lie in wait for me.(p.519)
• I was trying to remember where it came from, when two of the biggest cops I ever saw walked in and *took* me to jail.(p.528)
• I *took* her money, though; I had to have it.(p.540)
• I stood off and *took* a long look at life and the values I found in it: I saw a paradox, that he who loses his life does indeed find it.(p.542)
• The mental twists that led up to my drinking began many years before I ever *took* a drink for I am one of those whose history proves conclusively that my drinking was "a symptom of a deeper trouble."(p.544)
• It seemed logical to me that if I married this man and *took* the responsibility for these children that they would keep me sober.(p.548)
• Although my ambition still flickered, it now *took* the form of fantasizing.(p.556)
• And yet my ability to lie outwardly and to kid myself inwardly grew with every drink I *took*.(p.556)
• The doctors told me that if I ever *took* another drink, it might be my last.(p.558)

tool

• I don't mean that in any sense as a derogatory statement about psychotherapy; it's a great *tool*, not too potent, but a great *tool*.(p.349)

toolmaker

• I was always interested in mechanics and after having about twenty miscellaneous jobs, lasting from one day to two weeks, I obtained a job as a *toolmaker* apprentice.(p.211)
• Not far from where I lived they built a new technical high school and one of the teachers sold me on the idea that I needed a little mechanical drawing if I were going to be a good *toolmaker*.(p.211)
• I was supporting myself through all this education by being a *toolmaker* and a draftsman.(p.212)

tools

• When, therefore, we were approached by those in whom the problem had been solved, there was nothing left for us but to pick up the simple kit of spiritual *tools* laid at our feet.(p.25)
• Never talk down to an alcoholic from any moral or spiritual hilltop; simply lay out the kit of spiritual *tools* for his inspection.(p.95)
• I had worked so long in a profession where fakery, deceit, and untruths are *tools* of trade that I instantly recognized honesty when I heard it, from the mouths of A.A. members.(p.334)

top

• I felt lifted up, as though the great clean wind of a mountain *top* blew through and through.(p.14)
• He tossed off half of his martini; I tossed off half of mine and it nearly blew the *top* of my head off.(p.195)
• From the *top* of the heap in a few years he had skidded to becoming a shuffling customer, still entering the better barrooms but welcomed by neither mine host nor his patrons.(p.236)
• This newsman covered life from *top* to bottom; but he ended up, safely enough, in the middle.(p.251)
• In the long ago past I used to start at the *top* as president or treasurer and end up with the sheriff breathing down my neck.(p.284)
• A night or so a week in a joint, and a party or so a week at home or with friends, along with a little lone drinking, soon had me preparing for the existence of a *top* flight drunkard.(p.298)
• That night she too had new hope because I had made sure she would know what I was doing about my drinking by packing every bit of A.A. literature I could put my hands on right on *top* so she couldn't help but see it when she opened my bag.(p.364)
• There at the *top* of the folder was my name, age and address, and underneath were the words, "Periodic Drinker."(p.470)
• But I wanted a cosmos, a universe all my own which I had created and where I reigned as chief *top* reigner and ruler over everyone else.(p.535)

topic

• If this kind of approach does not catch your husband's interest, it may be best to drop the subject, but after a friendly talk your husband will usually revive the *topic* himself.(p.112)

tops

• I used also to put it up in four ounce bottles and stick several in my stocking *tops*.(p.177)
• I'd worked hard to be *tops* in my profession.(p.328)

torch

• My *torch* blazed madly and the pew caught fire.(p.424)

torches
• So we rolled old newspapers together and made *torches* to find a good soft pew and get some sleep.(p.424)
torn
• There I was, unshaven, clothes *torn* and dirty with no recollection of wandering all over France but, of course, a hero to the local French.(p.242)
• In A.A., I have had to be *torn* down and then put back together differently.(p.420)
tornado
• The alcoholic is like a *tornado* roaring his way through the lives of others.(p.82)
• With rare foresight he realized it could become a *tornado.*(p.373)
Toronto
• Quebec, *Toronto*, Buffalo, and finally Pittsburgh, were the scenes of man-sized drunks until I had gone through my readjusted discharge pay, a fair sum.(p.253)
torture
• In this statement he confirms what we who have suffered alcoholic *torture* must believe -- that the body of the alcoholic is quite as abnormal as his mind.(p.xxiv)
• Then came the night when the physical and mental *torture* was so hellish I feared I would burst through my window, sash and all.(p.6)
• In all honesty though, I was skeptical, but I wanted so definitely to quit drinking that I would have welcomed any sort of physical *torture* or pain to accomplish the result.(p.302)
• To wake up at home, not knowing how I got there, and to realize I had driven my car, became *torture.*(p.375)
• The indescribable *torture* has me again.(p.501)
tortured
• I was between Scylla and Charybdis now, because if I did not drink my stomach *tortured* me, and if I did, my nerves did the same thing.(p.175)
tortures
• Why they should be subjected to the *tortures* we inflict upon them, I cannot explain.(p.178)
toss
• I used to put eight or twelve ounce bottles of alcohol in a fur lined glove and *toss* it onto the back airing porch when winter days got dark enough.(p.176)
tossed
• He *tossed* off half of his martini; I *tossed* off half of mine and it nearly blew the top of my head off.(p.195)
• But I watched him, and he *tossed* off the rest of his, so I *tossed* off the rest of mine.(p.195)
tossing
• This would lessen my chances of smuggling some home that evening, which in turn would mean a night of futile *tossing* around in bed followed by a morning of unbearable jitters.(p.176)
• I had a mortal fear of going to bed and *tossing* all night.(p.299)
total
• The second edition, published in 1955, reached a *total* of more than 1,150,000 copies.(p.xi)
• So far, upon the *total* problem of several million actual and potential alcoholics in the world, we have made only a scratch.(p.xx)
• By March 1976, when this edition went to the printer, the *total* worldwide membership of Alcoholics Anonymous was conservatively estimated at more than 1,000,000, with almost 28,000 groups meeting in over 90 countries.(p.xxii)
• In the face of collapse and despair, in the face of the *total* failure of their human resources, they found that a new power, peace, happiness, and sense of direction flowed into them.(p.50)
• Those who drink moderately may be more annoyed with an alcoholic than a *total* abstainer would be.(p.139)
• A little more than fifteen years ago, through a long and calamitous series of shattering experiences, I found myself being helplessly propelled toward *total* destruction.(p.304)
• I told her that I was an alcoholic, victim of a disease, that there was no cure, only arrestment through *total* abstinence.(p.333)
• I did not know that I had no power over alcohol, that I, alone and unaided, could not stop; that I was on a downgrade, tearing along at full speed with all my brakes gone, and that the end would be a *total* smash-up, death or insanity.(p.408)
• I sank into *total* despair.(p.461)
• It was a *total* blackout.(p.528)
totaling
• There were debts *totaling* nearly ten thousand dollars to be paid off.(p.541)
totality
• As soon as we admitted the possible existence of a Creative Intelligence, a Spirit of the Universe underlying the *totality* of things, we began to be possessed of a new sense of power and direction, provided we took other simple steps.(p.46)
totally
• I was never drunk on the job, never missed a day's work, was seldom rendered *totally* ineffective by a hangover and kept my liquor expenses well within my adequate budget.(p.433)
• I surrendered *totally.*(p.461)
• But I will never be *totally* honest -- that would make me perfect, and none of us can claim to be perfect.(p.482)
• Poor, black, *totally* ruled by alcohol, she felt shut away from any life worth living.(p.526)
• I grew up believing that one had to be *totally* self-sufficient, for one never dared to depend on another human being.(p.545)
tots
• We have told small *tots* that father was sick, which was much nearer the truth than we realized.(p.106)
tottering
• It was *tottering* and it had to fall.(p.435)
touch
• The second edition added the appendices, the Twelve Traditions, and the directions for getting in *touch* with A.A.(p.xi)
• In all probability, we shall never be able to *touch* more than a fair fraction of the alcohol problem in all its ramifications.(p.xxi)
• It engulfs all whose lives *touch* the sufferer's.(p.18)
• He made up his mind that until he had been successful in business and had retired, he would not *touch* another drop.(p.32)
• I've prayed to God on hangover mornings and sworn that I'd never *touch* another drop but by nine o'clock I'd be boiled as an owl."(p.158)
• He got in *touch* with a prominent psychiatrist who had undertaken certain responsibilities for the mental health of the community.(p.163)
• I think I must have been thoroughly scared by what had happened, or by the doctor, or probably both, so that I did not *touch* a drink again until the country went dry.(p.175)
• When my doctor told me I should never *touch* a drink again, I couldn't afford to believe him.(p.226)
• As I look back on the events of two months, I can clearly see that I had been circling around, half-afraid of encountering the remedy for my situation, half wanting it, deferring fulfillment of my promise to get in *touch* with the doctor I had heard about.(p.258)
• Their answer was always the same: If they should need it at any time they would surely get in *touch* with me.(p.293)
• A few months later one of the men who had been in *touch* with the group in Akron came to Chicago to live, and then there were three of us who continued to have informal meetings quite regularly.(p.294)
• The reply came, putting me in *touch* by mail with my sponsor in New Delhi.(p.343)
• That personal *touch* did help me too.(p.393)
• It was as if I had, rather than a Midas *touch* which turned everything to gold, a magnifying mind that magnified whatever it focused on.(p.450)
• VI. How to Get in *Touch* With A.A.(p.563)
• HOW TO GET IN *TOUCH* WITH A.A.(p.575)
touched
• I was kind of shocked about anybody talking about themselves the way he did, and my impression was that the guy was a little "*touched.*"(p.216)
• Where preaching and prayers had *touched* me very little, I immediately desired further knowledge of these men.(p.235)
• There was one meeting a week at Bill's home in Brooklyn, and we all took turns there spouting off about how we had changed our lives overnight, how many drunks we had saved and straightened out, and last, but not least, how God had *touched* each of us personally on the shoulder.(p.246)
• I was about twenty-five then, and I had never *touched* a drop.(p.262)
• Everything that I *touched* from grammar school on was successful.(p.345)
touches
• This short word somehow *touches* about every aspect of our lives.(p.67)
touching
• He then pulled up his chair with one of his knees *touching* mine and said, "Will you pray with me for your success?"(p.218)
touchy
• Many of us have been so *touchy* that even casual reference to spiritual things made us bristle with antagonism.(p.48)
tough
• I remember telling them too that it was going to be awfully *tough*, because I did some other things, smoked cigarettes and played penny ante poker, sometimes bet on the horse races and they said, "Don't you think you're having more trouble with this drinking than with anything else at the present time?(p.190)
• It took me a year, or a year and a half to get to feeling physically well, and it was rather *tough*, but I soon found folks whose friendship I had once had, and I found, after I had been sober for quite some little time, that these people began to act like they had in previous years, before I had gotten so bad, so that I didn't pay too awful much attention to financial gains.(p.190)
• As long as things were *tough* and the job a challenge I could always manage to hold on pretty well, but as soon as I learned the combination, got the puzzle under control and the boss to pat me on the back, I was gone again.(p.243)
• When the others saw my altered attitude they took me back in, but for me they had to make it *tough*; if they hadn't I don't think I ever would have stuck it out.(p.248)
• Once again, there was the challenge of a *tough* job, but this time I was determined to follow through.(p.248)
• My four years of abstinence had something to do with it, but soldiering is a *tough* enough game for a sober man, and I had no yen for full-pack slogging through mud with a cognac or vin rouge hangover.(p.253)
• I had a *tough* pull back to normal good health.(p.310)
• The bartender, a *tough* Irishman, came around and "gave me the elbow," which means that he raised his elbow and smacked me in the face.(p.411)
• The worst of prison treatment couldn't break this *tough* con.(p.457)
• Men are supposed to be *tough* and rugged to start with, but if a woman becomes that way, it is pretty hard to get back the niceties of womanhood.(p.480)
toughest
• Routine jobs bored me, but I would take on the *toughest* one I could find, work day and night until I had it under control; then it would become tedious and I'd lose all interest in it.(p.243)
tour
• During this time, you are supposed to behave yourself, but I took a little wine-tasting *tour* through France, all by my lone, with car and chauffeur.(p.405)
• I had completed a three-year *tour* in the Navy.(p.418)
• Then came my *tour* in the U.S. Navy, part of it being two years in the Philippines.(p.419)
tourniquet
• In the garage, I would put the needle in my vein and then try to figure out exactly how much medication to inject to overcome the pep pills while adding to the sleeping pills while ignoring the tranquilizers, in order to get just enough to be able to pull out the needle, jerk the *tourniquet*, throw it in the car, slam the car door shut, run down the hall, and fall in bed before I fell asleep.(p.442)
tours
• Now my drinking was limited by only one factor, the enforced periods of dryness caused by lengthy *tours* at sea.(p.398)
• The short *tours* could be taken care of by sneaking enough whiskey aboard ship so that it could be rationed out until another supply could be laid in.(p.398)
toward
• We made a list of people I had hurt or *toward* whom I felt resentment.(p.13)
• The great fact is just this, and nothing less: That we have had deep and effective spiritual experiences which have revolutionized our whole attitude *toward* life, *toward* our fellows and *toward* God's universe.(p.25)
• They flatly declare that since they have come to believe in a Power greater than themselves, to take a certain attitude *toward* that Power, and to do certain simple things, there has been a revolutionary change in their way of living and thinking.(p.50)

• Some of us had already walked far over the Bridge of Reason *toward* the desired shore of faith.(p.53)
• Whatever our ideal turns out to be, we must be willing to grow *toward* it.(p.69)
• We have begun to learn tolerance, patience and good will *toward* all men, even our enemies, for we look on them as sick people.(p.70)
• It may be he has done us more harm than we have done him and, though we may have acquired a better attitude *toward* him, we are still not too keen about admitting our faults.(p.77)
• We will see that our new attitude *toward* liquor has been given us without any thought or effort on our part.(p.85)
• Were we kind and loving *toward* all?(p.86)
• We urge you to try our program, for nothing will be so helpful to your husband as the radically changed attitude *toward* him which God will show you how to have.(p.117)
• After all, your family is reunited, alcohol is no longer a problem and you and your husband are working together *toward* an undreamed-of future.(p.119)
• The alcoholic, his wife, his children, his "in-laws," each one is likely to have fixed ideas about the family's attitude *toward* himself or herself.(p.122)
• If possible express a lack of hard feeling *toward* him.(p.142)
• In fact, I never lost my faith, since I had been prepared by some conversations *toward* the end of my sojourn in the hospital with Dr. Bob, conversations pretty much along spiritual lines.(p.218)
• It was finally decided to undertake the organization of a Cleveland group and *toward* the end of May, 1939, the first meeting was held in Cleveland in my home.(p.219)
• And I wasn't resentful *toward* her, either.(p.270)
• Fear froze me in my tracks, but the instant I turned back *toward* home this paralyzing fear left me.(p.276)
• The birth of a baby boy did nothing *toward* staying the downward spiral.(p.278)
• At any rate the last great step *toward* a well rounded life still lay ahead of me.(p.286)
• He laid great stress on the progression of his attitude *toward* life and people, and most of his attitudes had been very similar to mine.(p.290)
• A little more than fifteen years ago, through a long and calamitous series of shattering experiences, I found myself being helplessly propelled *toward* total destruction.(p.304)
• The only incentive that I had, *toward* the end, for getting dressed in the morning was to get out and get supplies to help me get my day started.(p.336)
• *Toward* five o'clock, helter-skelter, I'd get everything put away and try to get supper on the table, and after supper I'd finish the job up and knock myself out.(p.337)
• Over a period of time he has built up self pity, resentments *toward* anyone or anything that interferes with his drinking.(p.380)
• Dishonest thinking, prejudice, ego, antagonism *toward* anyone and everyone who dares to cross him, vanity and a critical attitude are character defects that gradually creep in and become a part of his life.(p.380)
• But at this time, I began gravitating *toward* the really hard drinkers, hanging around with them more and more.(p.404)
• Moreover, I am deeply convinced that so long as I continue to strive, in my bumbling way, *toward* the principles I first encountered in the earlier chapters of this book, this remarkable power will continue to flow through me.(p.437)
• That was my attitude *toward* A.A. at that time.(p.510)
• Alas for us men *toward* whom Shaw hurled his cry, "Must a Christ be crucified in every generation for the benefit of those who have no imagination?"(p.536)

towards

• Even if he displays a certain amount of neglect and irresponsibility *towards* the family, it is well to let him go as far as he likes in helping other alcoholics.(p.129)
• I spent most of my time trying to get back these friendships, and to make some recompense *towards* my wife, whom I had hurt a lot.(p.191)
• I drove *towards* Cleveland wondering why I found myself in such a changed set of conditions as compared with those of six months before.(p.200)
• I realized that there wasn't anything I could say to place myself in a more favorable light with my children, that it was going to be a matter of time; for I also understood the intolerance of young people *towards* deficiencies in their elders.(p.220)
• However, here I probably took my first step *towards* my coming alcoholism by developing a terrific aversion to all churches and established religions.(p.240)
• I hated myself worse and worse, and as I hated myself I became more defiant *towards* everything and everybody.(p.265)
• When I look back, I can't see anything that would have predisposed me *towards* being either a neurotic or a drunk.(p.517)
• My personal definition, which I submit as applying only to myself (although everyone is welcome to it who wants it), includes every waking activity of the human being; to have a creative attitude *towards* things is a more exact meaning, to live and to deal with other human beings creatively, which to me means seeing the God in them, and respecting and worshipping this God.(p.535)

towel

• I paced the floor with a bath *towel* around my shoulders, the perspiration running off me.(p.268)
• I took two or three drinks so my eyes could focus, and I could see that horrible picture of the awful drunk on the first page; he couldn't get the drink to his mouth, he had a *towel* around his hand and he needed a shave.(p.391)

tower

• As might have been predicted, my teetering *tower* of worldly success collapsed.(p.437)

towers

• The papers reported men jumping to death from the *towers* of High Finance.(p.4)

town

• War fever ran high in the New England *town* to which we new, young officers from Plattsburg were assigned, and we were flattered when the first citizens took us to their homes, making us feel heroic.(p.1)
• I went to *town* regularly and even made a little money.(p.7)
• I had been out of *town* before during this particular dry spell, so there was nothing new about that.(p.41)
• His action met widespread approval, and today his is one of the most trusted citizens of his *town*.(p.80)
• There must be many such in this *town*.(p.154)
• His call to the clergyman led him presently to a certain resident of the *town*, who, though formerly able and respected, was then nearing the nadir of alcoholic despair.(p.155)
• Understand he was once a well-known lawyer in *town*, but just now we've got him strapped down tight."(p.156)
• So, you see, there were three alcoholics in that *town*, who now felt they had to give to others what they had found, or be sunk.(p.158)
• All this time our friend of the hotel lobby incident remained in that *town*.(p.159)
• When a few men in this city have found themselves, and have discovered the joy of helping others to face life again, there will be no stopping until everyone in that *town* has had his opportunity to recover — if he can and will.(p.163)
• The *town* was well supplied with churches and schools in which I pursued my early educational activities.(p.171)
• Finally my father had to send a doctor out from my home *town* who managed to get me back there in some way, and I was in bed about two months before I could venture out of the house.(p.175)
• I stayed about *town* a couple of months more and then returned to resume my practice.(p.175)
• I remember nothing from then on until I woke up at a friend's house, in a *town* near home.(p.179)
• When he was uptown — we were living in the little *town* of Moscow — I went up to try to get some money from him to buy groceries.(p.193)
• I was doing well in business, and in going around *town* I was frequently invited to have a drink in a speakeasy.(p.233)
• They, too, had taken a train to one *town* and had wakened hundreds of miles in the opposite direction, never knowing how they got there.(p.246)
• Returning to the *town* I had left three months before, I became editor of a monthly magazine, soon had additional publicity and advertising accounts and the money rolled in.(p.254)
• Always, in between, there were intervals of being broke, riding freights and hitch-hiking interminable distances from one big *town* to another in three states.(p.255)
• A friend who knew I would soon be broke mounted guard over me when I left my job of writing the histories of Texas cities and put me aboard a bus for the *town* I had left almost five years before.(p.256)
• I managed to maintain myself with odd jobs, did ten weeks in a social rescue institution, and at length wound up in a second-hand bookstore in an adjacent *town* as manager.(p.257)
• While there I was called to the hospital in my home *town* to see a former partner who had insisted that I visit him.(p.257)
• Some days later, after he had been discharged, a stranger came into my shop in the nearby *town*.(p.257)
• As soon as I could get up and walk I started to drink again and kept it up until my friend of the hospital, who, in his first try at the new way of life had stubbed his toe in Chicago but had come back to the *town* to take counsel and make a new start, picked me up and got me into a hospital.(p.258)
• I had missed them myself from the barrooms of the *town*.(p.258)
• It was a small *town* — Liberty, Indiana.(p.262)
• When I came to my aunt, she knew that I had had an unhappy childhood, and she said, "Now, Ethel, you're welcome to have boy friends in our home, but there are two boys in this *town* that I don't want you to date, and one of them comes from a very fine family, one of the best.(p.262)
• Then he came into *town* on the bum.(p.263)
• I ended up, homeless, jobless, penniless and rudderless, as the problem guest of a close friend whose family was out of *town*.(p.278)
• During my first few months in Akron I was quite sure that I never wanted to see my home *town* again.(p.281)
• I grew up in a small *town* outside Akron, Ohio, where the life was typical of any average small *town*.(p.287)
• At that time, I was living out of *town*, so I moved back to the home *town* and made a connection in a responsible position with one of the larger companies in the finance business.(p.298)
• While working in an office, there was some semblance of restraint, but, oh boy, when I got on the outside with this new company without supervision, did I go to *town*!(p.300)
• She was studying fashion design, was living in the same rooming house, and was from my home *town* of Cleveland.(p.359)
• Furthermore, I knew that I was looked upon as a city slicker from New York, and I had to be pretty cautious among small *town*, conservative Yankees.(p.360)
• Before too long, my husband (who seemed to prefer his shirts dirty) put his foot down, declaring that our family might have the cleanest clothes in *town*, but that I hadn't been out of the same old dirty slacks and blouse for a week.(p.371)
• I was raised like the majority of American boys, coming from a family of modest circumstances, attending public schools, having the social life of a small midwestern *town*, with part-time work and some athletics.(p.373)
• Frank was out of *town*, and I remember that he'd gotten in this one night and found me drunk.(p.391)
• That was on Saturday and my husband was leaving *town* Sunday night.(p.393)
• So Frank left *town*, and by Monday morning I had been sober for that whole week.(p.393)
• He himself took me to many of them, including the ones out of *town*.(p.416)
• We headed out of *town* walking -- no money, cold and hungry.(p.424)
• We spotted a church in a small *town*.(p.424)
• I go with him to first meeting, in small *town* in Maine.(p.476)
• I was born in a little *town* in Virginia in an average religious home.(p.483)
• Dad, due to having spent most of his time in a small Virginia *town*, didn't have any too much money, and the money he had saved and the property he had acquired were in Washington.(p.486)
• A very good friend of mine who owned a drug store across the street from us, came by only about two hours later and said that he had seen Vi down *town*.(p.487)
• I am going to *town* to get some liquor and food.(p.506)
• After I had made my third report, I stepped down *town*, met some of the old crowd, and of course you know the answer.(p.510)
• I started prowling around with a couple of these A.A. boys, which kept me pretty busy and kept my mind off of down *town*.(p.511)
• But not for long; now, for five Friday nights in a row, I went to jail, picked up sodden with beer (which I always disliked, but which was the only drink available); in jail five consecutive Friday nights in the *town* where I had grown up, where I had been

an honor student in high school, where a kindly uncle, bailing me out, said, "Bob, our family just doesn't do this sort of thing."(p.539)
• I left this home *town*, then, after I had made a public spectacle of myself in the presence of a revered teacher whose favorite pupil I had been.(p.539)
• In the nearby little *town* there was a plumber who once had tried to get an A.A. group going.(p.541)

towns
• From surrounding *towns*, families drive long distances to be present.(p.161)
• It wasn't long before the bootlegger was an established institution in this, as in other *towns*.(p.233)
• In the United States and Canada, most *towns* and cities have A.A. groups.(p.575)

townspeople
• Men who had liquor shipped in from Boston or New York by express were looked upon with great distrust and disfavor by most of the good *townspeople*.(p.171)

trace
• The Twelve Steps that summarize the program may be called los Doce Pasos in one country, los Douze Etapes in another, but they *trace* exactly the same path to recovery that was blazed by the earliest members of Alcoholics Anonymous.(p.xxii)
• Not a *trace* of fear is in me.(p.507)

traceable
• Then we have the voices who cry for sex and more sex; who bewail the institution of marriage; who think that most of the troubles of the race are *traceable* to sex causes.(p.69)

track
• It's so easy to get way off the *track*.(p.68)
• The men who cry for money and shelter before conquering alcohol, are on the wrong *track*.(p.98)
• In this way you can set them on the right *track* without becoming critical of them.(p.100)
• Paul measured the medicine out, but he figured that with my *track* record that little bit wouldn't be enough, so he doubled it and added a few drops more and then gave it to me.(p.207)
• In sports I made the *track* and tennis teams; I got along well with the other boys and had a fairly large circle of acquaintances but no intimate friends.(p.240)

tracks
• I'm sure his family felt that it was a marriage that -- well, I was a girl from the wrong side of the *tracks* -- definitely!(p.262)
• Fear froze me in my *tracks*, but the instant I turned back toward home this paralyzing fear left me.(p.276)
• Some of the things which used to stop me in my *tracks* from fear still make me nervous in the anticipation of their doing, but once I kick myself into doing them nervousness disappears and I enjoy myself.(p.285)
• I had just raised the bottle to my lips when my wife opened the door and froze me completely in my *tracks* with "Happy New Year, dear."(p.365)
• Showing all the courage and ingenuity that I had not used in a positive way, I covered my *tracks* and hid from my family so successfully that they did not find me for months.(p.401)
• While I was taking inventory in the cold-storage locker one Sunday, a wooden sign bolted to the inside door stopped me in my *tracks*.(p.461)

trade
• I wanted to *trade*.(p.252)
• I did six years of newspaper advertising, and *trade* journal work with many, many drunks of drab and dreary hue woven into the pattern of my life.(p.254)
• I had some financial success through no ability of my own and, when jobless and almost wiped out in 1930, I began to *trade* and sell my collection; much of the proceeds went to keep my apartment stocked with liquor and almost every night saw me helpless to bed.(p.255)
• I really worked for several weeks, and having had a fairly wide acquaintance with the dealer *trade*, it was not difficult for me to line up enough of them to give me a very substantial volume of business with a minimum of effort.(p.300)
• I had worked so long in a profession where fakery, deceit, and untruths are tools of *trade* that I instantly recognized honesty when I heard it, from the mouths of A.A. members.(p.334)
• I wouldn't give it up or *trade* it for anything.(p.355)

traded
• He wouldn't give me any money for the groceries, but he did take me across the street and buy me a bag of candy, which I later took back and *traded* for a loaf of bread.(p.193)

trademark
• Before long I was at the luncheon meeting an hour before the others, that old and familiar *trademark* of every alcoholic.(p.360)

tradition
• In the realm of the material, men's minds were fettered by superstition, *tradition*, and all sorts of fixed ideas.(p.51)
• And I put a Big Book by my night stand, and I put a "Twelve Steps and Twelve *Tradition*" in my locker at the hospital, and I got books by Emmet Fox, and I got books by God-knows-who, and I got to reading all these things.(p.348)
• They are the custodians of our A.A. *Tradition* and the receivers of voluntary A.A. contributions by which we maintain our A.A. General Service Office at New York.(p.567)

traditionally
• I belonged to one of the Irish families who, more or less *traditionally*, sent their boys to the British armies.(p.517)

traditions
• The second edition added the appendices, the Twelve *Traditions*, and the directions for getting in touch with A.A.(p.xi)
• This was the substance of A.A.'s Twelve *Traditions*, which are stated in full on page 564 of this book.(p.xix)
• A "spiritual experience" to me meant attending meetings, seeing a group of people, all there for the purpose of helping each other; hearing the Twelve Steps and the Twelve *Traditions* read at a meeting, and hearing the Lord's Prayer, which in an A.A. meeting has such great meaning – "Thy will be done, not mine."(p.381)
• We are told to practice the Twelve Steps and Twelve *Traditions* to the best of our ability every day, one day at a time.(p.481)
• The "12 *Traditions*" of Alcoholics Anonymous are, we A.A.'s believe, the best answers that our experience has yet given to those ever urgent questions, "How can A.A. best function?" and, "How can A.A. best stay whole and so survive?"(p.563)
• On the next page, A.A.'s "12 *Traditions*" are seen in their so-called "short form," the form in general use today.(p.563)
• This is a condensed version of the original "long form" A.A. *Traditions* as first printed in 1946.(p.563)
• THE TWELVE *TRADITIONS*(p.564)
• Twelve – Anonymity is the spiritual foundation of all our *Traditions*, ever reminding us to place principles before personalities.(p.564)
• THE TWELVE *TRADITIONS* (The Long Form)(p.565)

traffic
• In the two succeeding years I held ten different jobs ranging from newspaper copy-desk and rewrite, to *traffic* director for an oil field equipment company.(p.255)

tragedies
• If any feel that as psychiatrists directing a hospital for alcoholics we appear somewhat sentimental, let them stand with us a while on the firing line, see the *tragedies*, the despairing wives, the little children; let the solving of these problems become a part of their daily work, and even of their sleeping moments, and the most cynical will not wonder that we have accepted and encouraged this movement.(p.xxvi)
• All of us in A.A. know the tremendous happiness that is in our sobriety, but there are also *tragedies*.(p.239)
• I don't know what I expected, but I most certainly didn't visualize a group of people talking about their drinking problems, making light of their personal *tragedies* and at the same time enjoying themselves.(p.378)
• *Tragedies* during those years that were caused by my drinking, such as the breaking up of my marriage, the death of my child, other things – had little restraining effect.(p.465)

tragedy
• But, of course," he continued, "eventually the alcoholic loses all of his capacities as his disease gets progressively worse, and this is a *tragedy* that is painful to watch; the disintegration of a sound mind and body."(p.308)
• But for him, financial security or even affluence can be a *tragedy*.(p.330)
• Except for one short slip, during the first eight months, which was an angry "the world can't do this to me" reaction to a personal *tragedy* in my life, I have been sober for twelve years.(p.416)
• Repeated year on end, they are horrible -- frightening and degrading, a chronicle of *tragedy* which may be greater because the individual undergoing the *tragedy*, myself, knew what was happening, and yet refused to do anything to stop it.(p.538)

tragic
• Our struggles with them are variously strenuous, comic and *tragic*.(p.16)
• He does absurd, incredible, *tragic* things while drinking.(p.21)
• The *tragic* truth is that if the man be a real alcoholic, the happy day may not arrive.(p.23)
• This *tragic* situation has already arrived in practically every case long before it is suspected.(p.24)
• Now and then the family will be plagued by spectres from the past, for the drinking career of almost every alcoholic has been marked by escapades, funny, humiliating, shameful or *tragic*.(p.123)
• We have been speaking to you of serious, sometimes *tragic* things.(p.132)
• Outsiders are sometimes shocked when we burst into merriment over a seemingly *tragic* experience out of the past.(p.132)
• The next afternoon and evening, two other men visited me and each told me his story and the things that they were doing to try to recover from this *tragic* illness.(p.290)
• How I had arrived at this *tragic* impasse I could not have explained to anyone.(p.304)
• It has shown me, through the *tragic* stories of so many other alcoholics, the utter futility of self pity.(p.525)
• For you learned that he had been guilty of the thing he had accused you of, and his guilt had brought suffering to his entire family; and he thought he saw his young son beginning his own *tragic* pattern.(p.533)

tragically
• One night my son, when he was only sixteen, was suddenly and *tragically* killed.(p.437)

trail
• From a Canadian reservation to overseas bars to New England lockups, an Indian traveled a long *trail* that finally led him home to A.A.(p.474)
• Then I know we walk same *trail*.(p.476)
• No drunk hopeless if he want to follow guide along right *trail*.(p.477)

trailers
• Many retirees embrace alcoholism while secluded in motor *trailers*, rest homes, leisure-world bungalows, mountain cabins, or beach cottages, or even in penthouses, on yachts, and inside Palm Springs cabanas.(p.329)

train
• My downfall cost the business community unknown thousands of dollars, for it takes real money to *train* a man for an executive position.(p.137)
• I drank all the scotch they had on the *train* and bought several quarts on my way to the hotel.(p.179)
• I had to wait some time for the *train*.(p.179)
• They, too, had taken a *train* to one town and had wakened hundreds of miles in the opposite direction, never knowing how they got there.(p.246)
• I landed him and shipped him by *train* to Akron, with a pint of whiskey in his pocket to keep him from wanting to get off the *train* in Toledo!(p.282)
• At long last I am doing the kind of work I have always wanted to do, but never had the patience and emotional stability to *train* myself for.(p.284)
• Luck was with me for I made my *train*, but I arrived home the next morning with a new kind of hangover.(p.364)
• On the *train* going back, Anne's one idea was to get to the nearest bar.(p.415)
• We were identified and I was put on a *train* for Chicago.(p.424)
• Pack my clothes and put me on *train*.(p.475)
• I am on a *train* headed for a city.(p.505)

trained
• He asked if I would cooperate with him after I went home, and if I would have a *trained* nurse stay with me for at least two weeks.(p.387)
• I wouldn't go to hospitals because I wanted my dog there, so I had to have a *trained* nurse.(p.390)

trainfare
• I was soon broke, this time without *trainfare* to go anywhere.(p.252)

training
• His religious education and *training* may be far superior to yours.(p.93)
• Insofar as religion was concerned, I had a Catholic *training* in my youth.(p.214)
• This office job brought me face to face with a problem which I had sidestepped all my adult life, lack of *training*.(p.284)

• With this specialized *training*, and a liberal business education in the school of hard knocks, I was able to set up shop some two years later as an independent accountant.(p.284)
• After *training*, I was commissioned as a first lieutenant.(p.342)
• My job was to make out the guard schedules and thus I was exempt from ordinary recruit *training* activities.(p.425)
• And as I went through pharmacy school, graduate school, medical school, internship, residency, and specialty *training* and, finally, went into practice, my drinking kept increasing.(p.441)
• After nine months of *training*, all the rest of my class was paroled and I went to work in the Department of Corrections.(p.462)
• It was my ex-wife, and she said my twenty-seven-year-old son, who has completed his Marine Corps *training* and graduated from college, wanted to see me privately, was getting married in three months, and wanted me at the wedding.(p.462)
• For that reason, I believe, I married at a much younger age than I would have, had it not been for my home *training*.(p.485)
• As I write these words, it seems incredible that these things should have happened to me, for they are, truly, against all my instincts and *training*.(p.536)
• What a revelation of ego and arrogance still remaining in me – as if anyone, instinct and *training* apart, likes to be in jail or in an alcoholic ward or fired from his job.(p.536)
• After nearly eight years of sobriety in A.A., I still can set down such thoughts, "against my instinct and *training*," showing that I still consider myself a "special" person, entitled to special privileges.(p.536)
• Apparently I'd grown physically at the customary rate of speed, and I had acquired an average amount of intellectual *training* in the intervening years, but there had been no emotional maturity at all.(p.547)

trains
• It set in motion *trains* of circumstances which brought us misfortune we felt we didn't deserve.(p.67)

traits
• But, as with most humans, he is more likely to have varied *traits*.(p.61)
• You will soon have your friend admitting he has many, if not all, of the *traits* of the alcoholic.(p.92)
• We all had hundreds of character *traits*, of fears and phobias, likes and dislikes, in common.(p.229)
• And, accepting, I felt a new inner comfort, and the willingness and strength to do something about the *traits* I couldn't live with.(p.229)
• At the moral inventory, he brought up some of my bad personality *traits* or character defects, such as selfishness, conceit, jealousy, carelessness, intolerance, ill-temper, sarcasm and resentments.(p.292)

tramp
• In my early twenties the hardships of hobo life did not discourage me, but I had no wish to become just a *tramp*.(p.253)
• I was there about three weeks, and then I got restless and started to *tramp* across the country, here and there, until I finally wound up in Pennsylvania, in a steel mill.(p.492)

tranquilizer
• I never in my life took a *tranquilizer*, sedative, or pep pill because I was a pillhead.(p.443)

tranquilizers
• I took more through the day to increase the high, and more to maintain it; when I overshot the mark, I'd take *tranquilizers* to level off.(p.442)
• I never got much effect out of codeine and Percodan and the *tranquilizers*.(p.442)
• In the garage, I would put the needle in my vein and then try to figure out exactly how much medication to inject to overcome the pep pills while adding to the sleeping pills while ignoring the *tranquilizers*, in order to get just enough to be able to pull out the needle, jerk the tourniquet, throw it in the car, slam the car door shut, run down the hall, and fall in bed before I fell asleep.(p.442)

transcended
• It was *transcended* by the happiness they found in giving themselves for others.(p.159)

transfer
• Awarded a scholarship to a famous old Eastern college, I began to drink at the end of my freshman year, and by junior year, I had to *transfer* to an easier state university to keep my grades up.(p.419)

transferred
• In my second year in A.A. we were *transferred* to Dallas.(p.394)
• I was *transferred* to Kaneohe Bay, across the hump to the windward side of Oahu, to the aviation base.(p.426)
• Then I was *transferred* to the honor-grade unit, where I spent the most painful year of my life.(p.462)
• I, and the books of my division, have been *transferred* to the head office.(p.500)
• An ailment developed in one of my eyes, and I was *transferred* back to Sing Sing and operated upon.(p.509)

transformation
• To get over drinking will require a *transformation* of thought and attitude.(p.143)

transformations
• But we have seen remarkable *transformations* in our bodies.(p.133)
• Among our rapidly growing membership of thousands of alcoholics such *transformations*, though frequent, are by no means the rule.(p.569)

transfusions
• Each time, I went back to drinking – even smuggling a bottle of vodka into the hospital as soon as the blood *transfusions* had ceased.(p.558)

transgressions
• I have omitted details of *transgressions* that I made when drunk for several reasons.(p.301)

transition
• It was in Washington, D.C. that this *transition* took place, and that the really bad part of alcoholism began happening.(p.465)

translate
• There was the physical aspect; to be the youngest and the runt of the brood of children, to have to wear glasses very early and so to be teased, to be bookish and bored in school because the captain of the football team could not *translate* Virgil and yet was the school god while you, you, you little shrimp, were the school egghead, junior size and an early model.(p.533)

translated
• There is another meaning for the Hebrew word that in the King James version of the Bible is *translated* "salvation."(p.228)

transmit
• But obviously you cannot *transmit* something you haven't got.(p.164)

transmitted
• New groups started up and it was found, to the astonishment of everyone, that A.A.'s message could be *transmitted* in the mail as well as by word of mouth.(p.xviii)

trap
• During these seven years a thing called the Twenty-four Hour Program –a gadget I used to think was only a snare to *trap* the newcomer -- has come to mean much to me, not only as regards my drinking but in the whole pattern of my life.(p.473)

trapped
• I wasn't *trapped*.(p.228)
• I was *trapped*, and for the life of me I did not know how or why this had happened to me.(p.306)
• Having made that bargain, I immediately began to feel I'd been *trapped* into it and I went out and had some drinks – four glasses of gin, I remember.(p.523)

travel
• Only thirty years later the conquest of the air was almost an old story and airplane *travel* was in full swing.(p.52)
• There is a good bit of *travel* between East and West and we foresee a great increase in this helpful interchange.(p.162)
• Those of us who *travel* drop in as often as we can.(p.162)
• Young and able to *travel* with the best of them, I managed to hold my job and keep my end up in the barrooms.(p.252)
• That job began a series of brief working spells, each one ending in a "drunk" and the urge to *travel*.(p.253)
• Loading a car with good old books to sell to collectors, librarians, universities and historical societies, I started out to *travel* the country.(p.255)
• Vacations from school and from work, spelled "*travel*" to me -- and I travelled with gusto.(p.275)
• What about my fear of *travel*?(p.284)
• In recent years I have had the happy combination of time and money to *travel* occasionally.(p.285)
• I had the best schools, summer camps, resort vacations and *travel*.(p.304)
• They would *travel* miles and stay up all night with someone they had never laid eyes on before and think nothing of it.(p.310)
• He was old, but now he grow young with new life in A.A. and *travel* all time.(p.476)
• To find work, I have *travel* much.(p.476)

traveled
• We, who have *traveled* this dubious path, beg you to lay aside prejudice, even against organized religion.(p.49)
• We have *traveled* a rocky road, there is no mistake about that.(p.104)
• My wife *traveled* with me, but with a baby coming I decided to settle in a large city where I got a job with a commission agent which is a polite term for a handbook operator.(p.251)
• From a Canadian reservation to overseas bars to New England lockups, an Indian *traveled* a long trail that finally led him home to A.A.(p.474)
• Maine newsletter (Boomerang) say: "With tireless devotion and humility, this venerable Indian gentleman *traveled* thousands of miles humbly pleading for sobriety.(p.476)

travelers
• That is where our fellow *travelers* are, and that is where our work must be done.(p.130)

traveling
• Businessmen, *traveling* out of existing groups, were referred to these prospective newcomers.(p.xviii)
• This practice enables us to lend a hand, at the same time avoiding certain alluring distractions of the road, about which any *traveling* man can inform you.(p.162)
• Then I started *traveling*, with the United States and Canada as my territory, and with so much freedom and with an unlimited expense account, I was soon drinking every night and kidding myself that it was all part of the job.(p.287)
• How full it has kept my retirement years -- the five I've lived since the first two lost in *traveling* a rocky road to hell, before I made a U-turn.(p.334)
• I am a *traveling* salesman.(p.500)
• When the policeman released me to my stupefied and exasperated friend at four in the morning, I went to my *traveling* bag and groped until I found – well, let the officer speak: "Ah," said the policeman, "he's got anuder pair, t'ank God!"(p.538)

travelled
• Vacations from school and from work, spelled "travel" to me – and I *travelled* with gusto.(p.275)

traveller
• I was club-man, athlete, artist, musician, author, editor, aircraft pilot and world *traveller*.(p.432)

travelling
• In the eight years before A.A. found me, I had over forty jobs – selling and *travelling* -- one thing after another, and the same old routine.(p.244)
• Never having enough, always craving more, the obsession for alcohol gradually dominated all my activities, particularly while *travelling*.(p.375)

treading
• Saying goodbye to my wife and baby, I was *treading* Manhattan's streets in a little more than a week.(p.252)

treadmill
• As animals on a *treadmill*, we have patiently and wearily climbed, falling back in exhaustion after each futile effort to reach solid ground.(p.107)

treasure
• For a time he may try to hug the new *treasure* to himself.(p.129)

treasured
• They struck the children, kicked out door panels, smashed *treasured* crockery, and ripped the keys out of pianos.(p.106)

treasurer
• In the long ago past I used to start at the top as president or *treasurer* and end up with the sheriff breathing down my neck.(p.284)
• I'd go into an organization, and it wasn't long before I was on the committee, then I was chairman of the committee; and if I was in a group, I'd soon be *treasurer* or secretary of the group.(p.339)

treasuries
• Then too, we view with much concern those A.A. *treasuries* which continue, beyond prudent reserves, to accumulate funds for no stated A.A. purpose.(p.566)

treat
• He begins to think life doesn't *treat* him right.(p.61)
• We wouldn't *treat* sick people that way.(p.67)
• In other words, we *treat* sex as we would any other problem.(p.69)
• *Treat* him, when you can, as though he had pneumonia.(p.108)

• By force of circumstances, she was often obliged to ***treat*** father as a sick or wayward child.(p.130)
• Eventually, I had to redo each of the Twelve Steps specifically with Max in mind, from the First, saying, "I am powerless over alcohol, and my homelife is unmanageable by me," to the Twelfth, in which I tried to think of her as a sick Al-Anon and ***treat*** her with the love I would give a sick A.A. newcomer.(p.452)
• I have not seen a black face but mine since I've been here, and if I didn't look in the mirror, I wouldn't know that I was black, because these people ***treat*** me as one of them, which I am.(p.530)

treated

• About one year prior to this experience a man was brought in to be ***treated*** for chronic alcoholism.(p.xxix)
• But he is yet a long way from making good to the wife or parents whom for years he has so shockingly ***treated.***(p.82)
• But urge upon a man's family that he has been a very sick person and should be ***treated*** accordingly.(p.100)
• I woke up in this bare room with nothing around me but bars; they wouldn't let me smoke and ***treated*** me, well, like I was nuts.(p.387)
• The bartenders too, ***treated*** me with contempt.(p.411)
• He and his wife more than accepted me; he listened to all my woes; both of them ***treated*** me as a human being.(p.462)
• My father had ***treated*** him many years prior to this.(p.488)
• For by now I had been exposed once to A.A., but I had ***treated*** it as a vaudeville and had taken friends to meetings so that they too could enjoy the fascination of the naked revelation of suffering and recovery.(p.539)

treating

• I say this after many years' experience as Medical Director of one of the oldest hospitals in the country ***treating*** alcoholic and drug addiction.(p.xxv)
• Instead of ***treating*** the family as he should, he may retreat further into himself and feel he has spiritual justification for so doing.(p.129)
• Their services are often indispensable in ***treating*** a newcomer and in following his case afterward.(p.133)
• Perhaps the best way of ***treating*** you to a glimpse of your future will be to describe the growth of the fellowship among us.(p.153)
• A few months after I made my original trip to Akron I was feeling pretty cocky, and I didn't think my wife was ***treating*** me with proper respect, now that I was an outstanding citizen.(p.293)

treatment

• I have specialized in the ***treatment*** of alcoholism for many years.(p.xxiii)
• In the course of his third ***treatment*** he acquired certain ideas concerning a possible means of recovery.(p.xxiii)
• It has never been, by any ***treatment*** with which we are familiar, permanently eradicated.(p.xxviii)
• Following his physical rehabilitation, he had a talk with me in which he frankly stated he thought the ***treatment*** a waste of effort, unless I could assure him, which no one ever had, that in the future he would have the "will power" to resist the impulse to drink.(p.xxix)
• Under the so-called belladonna ***treatment*** my brain cleared.(p.7)
• ***Treatment*** seemed wise, for I showed signs of delirium tremens.(p.13)
• Though experience had made him skeptical, he finished his ***treatment*** with unusual confidence.(p.26)
• Neither does there appear to be any kind of ***treatment*** which will make alcoholics of our kind like other men.(p.30)
• Your understanding ***treatment*** of their cases will pay dividends.(p.141)
• If he says yes, does he really mean it, or down inside does he think he is fooling you, and that after rest and ***treatment*** he will be able to get away with a few drinks now and then?(p.142)
• For most alcoholics who are drinking, or who are just getting over a spree, a certain amount of physical ***treatment*** is desirable, even imperative.(p.142)
• The matter of physical ***treatment*** should, of course, be referred to your own doctor.(p.143)
• If you propose such a procedure to him, it may be necessary to advance the cost of ***treatment,*** but we believe it should be made plain that any expense will later be deducted from his pay.(p.143)
• If your man accepts your offer, it should be pointed out that physical ***treatment*** is but a small part of the picture.(p.143)
• While on the subject of confidence, can you adopt the attitude that so far as you are concerned this will be a strictly personal matter, that his alcoholic derelictions, the ***treatment*** about to be undertaken, will never be discussed without his consent?(p.143)
• We suggest you draw the book to the attention of the doctor who is to attend your patient during ***treatment.***(p.144)
• In another case, an alcoholic was sent to a hospital for ***treatment.***(p.145)
• If you take it, your past will be forgotten and the fact that you went away for ***treatment*** will not be mentioned.(p.147)
• Said one of the visitors, "We're giving you a ***treatment*** for alcoholism."(p.157)
• In one of these there is a well-known hospital for the ***treatment*** of alcoholic and drug addiction.(p.161)
• When I entered a sanitarium for prolonged and intensive psychiatric ***treatment,*** I was convinced that I was having a serious mental breakdown.(p.226)
• As the ***treatment*** progressed I began to get a picture of myself, of the temperament that had caused me so much trouble.(p.226)
• And, because as I have discovered since, it is part of the "***treatment***" that these men be sent to see and talk with alcoholics who want to quit, he kept them busy.(p.235)
• But the firm became violently ill with my drunkenness and their course of ***treatment*** was to remove their ulcer, in the form of me, from the payroll, amid much fanfare and very personal and slighting remarks and insinuations.(p.300)
• Of course, I had no hint or intimation as to what the ***treatment*** was to consist of.(p.302)
• He talked me into taking the Samaritan ***Treatment.***(p.389)
• So I took the Samaritan ***Treatment.***(p.389)
• I guess there are plenty of other graduates of this ***treatment*** around.(p.389)
• I took that ***treatment*** three times and it didn't work - - at least, for me.(p.389)
• The worst of prison ***treatment*** couldn't break this tough con.(p.457)
• Ten days of this ***treatment*** the first time knocked me from 200 pounds to 130, and I seldom stayed out of the hole long enough to gain back my weight.(p.460)
• They held consultations and discussions, and finally decided to give me the "Conditioned Reflex" ***treatment.***(p.469)
• The idea behind it is that, having taken the ***treatment,*** your system is so "conditioned" that the mere sight or smell or taste of alcohol produces a violent reaction, and you become ill.(p.469)
• But I would always wake up in the psychiatric ward to begin another long ***treatment.***(p.528)
• All but one "responded to the ***treatment***" suggested in the Steps immediately, but this one posed a problem.(p.551)
• Dr. Harry M. Tiebout, psychiatrist: "As a psychiatrist, I have thought a great deal about the relationship of my specialty to A.A. and I have come to the conclusion that our particular function can very often lie in preparing the way for the patient to accept any sort of ***treatment*** or outside help.(p.571)
• Dr. John F. Stouffer, Chief Psychiatrist, Philadelphia General Hospital, citing his experience with A.A., said: "The alcoholics we get here at Philadelphia General are mostly those who cannot afford private ***treatment,*** and A.A. is by far the greatest thing we have been able to offer them.(p.572)

treatments

• Many tried everything – hospitals, special ***treatments,*** sanitariums, asylums, and jails.(p.455)

tree

• We worked in five below zero weather, fixing on an elm ***tree*** a wrought iron device which modestly proclaimed that he was indeed a country doctor.(p.540)

trees

• We missed the reality and beauty of the forest because we were diverted by the ugliness of some of its ***trees.***(p.50)

trembled

• He ***trembled*** as he went about, for this might mean ruin, particularly to a person in his line of business.(p.156)
• When I went in to write the examinations, my hand ***trembled*** so I could not hold a pencil.(p.174)

trembles

• He ***trembles*** to think someone might have observed him.(p.73)
• But for every man who drinks others are involved -- the wife who ***trembles*** in fear of the next debauch; the mother and father who see their son wasting away.(p.104)

trembling

• From a ***trembling,*** despairing nervous wreck, had emerged a man brimming over with self-reliance and contentment.(p.xxix)
• ***Trembling,*** I stepped from the hospital a broken man.(p.8)
• When your husband is bad, you become a ***trembling*** recluse, wishing the telephone had never been invented.(p.115)
• I went ***trembling*** into a house in Brooklyn filled with strangers . . . and I found I had come home at last, to my own kind.(p.228)
• Instead of drinking in fancy bars and clubs, I had to carry a bottle of vodka in my briefcase, duck into public toilets, and gulp from the bottle, ***trembling,*** in order to keep from falling apart.(p.557)

tremendous

• The ***tremendous*** fact for every one of us is that we have discovered a common solution.(p.17)
• There was a ***tremendous*** urge to cease forever.(p.34)
• There was always a ***tremendous*** drive and ambition to become a great guy, because I think I recognized inwardly that I didn't have any special talents.(p.194)
• I apparently was willing to subdue these personality disturbances in a ***tremendous*** drive to succeed.(p.211)
• All of us in A.A. know the ***tremendous*** happiness that is in our sobriety, but there are also tragedies.(p.239)
• This change had been a long, slow process for me, but through these latter years the dividends have been ***tremendous.***(p.249)
• The encouragement received in the early days, especially from the A.A. General Service Office, made a ***tremendous*** difference to my sobriety.(p.342)
• And there a ***tremendous*** hope is born.(p.504)
• I do not fix anyone, but I am getting part of a ***tremendous*** education and I have made some new friends.(p.506)

tremendously

• I believe though that it helped my family ***tremendously*** to have the A.A. meetings every week in my own home.(p.220)

tremens

• My weary and despairing wife was informed that it would all end with heart failure during delirium ***tremens,*** or I would develop a wet brain, perhaps within a year.(p.7)
• Treatment seemed wise, for I showed signs of delirium ***tremens.***(p.13)
• Perhaps he has had delirium ***tremens.***(p.110)
• The doctor said I'd been brought into the hospital like a madman, crying, raving, ranting, swearing, completely in the throes of delirium ***tremens.***(p.427)

tremors

• Neurotic fears plagued me, and I had occasional, uncontrollable ***tremors.***(p.555)

trial

• Shortly after I came to this conclusion, I was importuned by another well-known patent law firm to help them out on some ***trial*** work because their ***trial*** man had had a heart attack and had been forbidden to go into the courtroom.(p.220)
• I found in the fall of 1939, that I was not mentally impaired, so far as ***trial*** work was concerned, and thereafter took up where I had left off when I was about forty-five years old.(p.220)
• After the ***trial,*** I got big-hearted again and felt that I should do something in payment for Vi's kindness to me; so I left Washington and went to Seattle to work.(p.492)
• I was immediately arrested, arraigned in Homicide Court, held without bail, and remanded to the old Tombs Prison to await ***trial.***(p.508)
• The ***trial*** lasted about a week, and whether or not I was going to the death house was anybody's guess.(p.508)
• I got out on bail right away, but when I went to ***trial,*** the judge gave me thirty days.(p.528)

trials

• For if an alcoholic failed to perfect and enlarge his spiritual life through work and self-sacrifice for others, he could not survive the certain ***trials*** and low spots ahead.(p.14)
• However, after two or three ***trials,*** I found this was not satisfactory because they did not serve enough to satisfy me.(p.184)
• Many things happened; business ***trials,*** little worries, and feelings of general despondency came near driving me to the bottle, but I made progress.(p.237)
• When I was nineteen, I married a fine man who had never known an insecure moment in his life, let alone the ***trials*** and tribulations of booze.(p.369)

tribe

• JOIN THE *TRIBE*!(p.474)
• Join the *tribe*!"(p.477)

tribulations

• When I was nineteen, I married a fine man who had never known an insecure moment in his life, let alone the trials and *tribulations* of booze.(p.369)

trick

• You are betting, of course, that your changed attitude plus the contents of this book will turn the *trick*.(p.144)
• That is where I had my first drink and I still remember it, for every "first" drink afterwards did exactly the same *trick* -- I could feel it go right through every bit of my body and down to my very toes.(p.241)
• It's no great *trick* to stop drinking; the *trick* is to stay stopped.(p.554)

tricks

• She tried reasoning with me, endeavored to work out various drinking schedules, in fact all the *tricks* were practised faithfully for a short time somewhere along my shaky road to unhappiness.(p.361)
• I found I could boost my income by figuring out a lot of cute little *tricks* that the boss wouldn't be likely to notice – filching money from the Coke machine, short-sticking the customers on oil, and selling oil I'd drained out of other cars.(p.423)

tried

• This physician had repeatedly *tried* spiritual means to resolve his alcoholic dilemma but had failed.(p.xvi)
• Of alcoholics who came to A.A. and really *tried*, 50% got sober at once and remained that way; 25% sobered up after some relapses, and among the remainder, those who stayed on with A.A. showed improvement.(p.xx)
• Renewing my resolve, I *tried* again.(p.5)
• We have *tried* every imaginable remedy.(p.31)
• Heaven knows, we have *tried* hard enough and long enough to drink like other people!(p.31)
• Here are some of the methods we have *tried*: Drinking beer only, limiting the number of drinks, never drinking alone, never drinking in the morning, drinking only at home, never having it in the house, never drinking during business hours, drinking only at parties, switching from scotch to brandy, drinking only natural wines, agreeing to resign if ever drunk on the job, taking a trip, not taking a trip, swearing off forever (with and without a solemn oath), taking more physical exercise, reading inspirational books, going to health farms and sanitariums, accepting voluntary commitment to asylums -- we could increase the list ad infinitum.(p.31)
• He *tried* to regulate his drinking for a while, making several trips to the hospital meantime.(p.32)
• That didn't seem to bother me so I *tried* another."(p.36)
• At first some of us *tried* to avoid the issue, hoping against hope we were not true alcoholics.(p.44)
• But we found that such codes and philosophies did not save us, no matter how much we *tried*.(p.45)
• To others, the word "God" brought up a particular idea of Him with which someone had *tried* to impress them during childhood.(p.45)
• Faced with alcoholic destruction, we soon became as open minded on spiritual matters as we *tried* to be on other questions.(p.48)
• Some of us have *tried* to hold on to our old ideas and the result was nil until we let go absolutely.(p.58)
• 12.Having had a spiritual awakening as the result of these steps, we *tried* to carry this message to alcoholics, and to practice these principles in all our affairs.(p.60)
• But the more we fought and *tried* to have our own way, the worse matters got.(p.66)
• Though a situation had not been entirely our fault, we *tried* to disregard the other person involved entirely.(p.67)
• But above all, we *tried* to be sensible on this question.(p.68)
• In this way we *tried* to shape a sane and sound ideal for our future sex life.(p.69)
• Time after time newcomers have *tried* to keep to themselves certain facts about their lives.(p.72)
• Have we *tried* to make mortar without sand?(p.75)
• We are often surprised how the right answers come after we have *tried* this for a while.(p.86)
• We have *tried* these methods.(p.101)
• We have *tried* to hold the love of our children for their father.(p.106)
• But those of us who have *tried* to shoulder the entire burden and trouble of others find we are soon overcome by them.(p.132)
• Some employers have *tried* every known remedy.(p.137)
• He had a desperate desire to stop, but saw no way out, for he had earnestly *tried* many avenues of escape.(p.155)
• I had no trouble there because I had never actually ceased to believe in God, and had *tried* lots of times to get help but hadn't succeeded.(p.186)
• Did she have an alcoholic customer on whom it could be *tried*?(p.188)
• Knowing Bob of old, she jokingly replied, "Well, Doctor, I suppose you've already *tried* it yourself?"(p.188)
• Anyhow, I recognized the fact that I couldn't drink like normal people, but I *tried* hard and kept on trying for twenty-two years.(p.196)
• At the end of fifteen months, I *tried* the beer experiment.(p.203)
• I was arrested and taken to jail where I was beaten up by two or three fellows who were already in there and whom I *tried* to boss.(p.204)
• I *tried* to conduct a kangaroo court and hit them with a broomstick.(p.204)
• When I left the hospital I *tried* this for a day and it worked, for a week and it worked, and for a month, and it worked – and then for a year and it still worked.(p.209)
• He told me that there were some other fellows that had *tried* this with success, and if I cared to see any of them he'd have them come in to see me.(p.218)
• I wanted help, and I *tried* to cooperate.(p.226)
• I even got them myself and *tried* them.(p.235)
• My visitor well knew, that as I *tried* to follow God I would get to studying these things out for myself.(p.236)
• I *tried* to contact the boys in New York, but telegrams bounced right back and when I finally got Hank on the telephone he fired me right then.(p.247)
• My brilliant agnosticism vanished, and I saw for the first time that those who really believed, or at least honestly *tried* to find a Power greater than themselves, were much more composed and contented than I had ever been, and they seemed to have a degree of happiness which I had never known.(p.247)
• I *tried* to help myself.(p.255)
• We always *tried* to buy him a drink, and he always told us he had liquor trouble -- couldn't drink.)(p.266)
• I knew then that I hadn't made a complete surrender, because I *tried* to bargain with the God I had found, and I said, "Anything but that!(p.271)
• Half a block from the house, I *tried* to turn the corner.(p.276)
• I had *tried* to be the center of my own little world, whereas God was the center of a vast universe of which I was perhaps an essential, but a very tiny, part.(p.280)
• I have stopped tilting at windmills, and instead have *tried* to accomplish the little daily tasks, unimportant in themselves, but tasks that are an integral part of living fully.(p.295)
• Between the ages of twenty-five and thirty I *tried* everything.(p.305)
• I *tried* the beer diet, the wine diet, timing, measuring, and spacing of drinks.(p.305)
• I *tried* them mixed, unmixed, drinking only when gay, only when depressed.(p.305)
• He had *tried* everything from having me attend daily mass at six a.m. to performing the most menial labor for his charity patients.(p.306)
• Once I did have a slip – *tried* drinking again – but the A.A.'s tell me not to worry about yesterday, because nobody can change it, and not to worry about tomorrow, because it hasn't come yet.(p.320)
• But that night I *tried* to go to sleep.(p.322)
• George *tried* many times to go on the wagon.(p.324)
• They described what had happened when they went out and *tried* drinking again, and I knew they were sincere in saying that it could happen to me.(p.334)
• I *tried* to encourage a search for some new goal.(p.334)
• Since I gave my will over to A.A., whatever A.A. has wanted of me I've *tried* to do to the best of my ability.(p.340)
• During the next three years, I *tried* often again to give it up, but failed miserably.(p.343)
• I *tried* every gimmick that there was to get some peace of mind, but it was not until I was brought to my alcoholic knees, when I was brought to a group in my own community with the butcher, the baker, the carpenter and the mechanic, who were able to give me the Twelve Steps, that I was finally given some semblance of an answer to the last half of the First Step.(p.349)
• And the clergy have *tried* hard to help us, but we haven't been helped.(p.352)
• And the psychiatrist has had thousands of couches, and has put you and me on them many, many times, but he hasn't helped us very much, though he has *tried* hard; and we owe the clergy and the doctor and the psychiatrist a deep debt of gratitude, but they haven't helped our alcoholism, except in a rare few instances.(p.352)
• She *tried* reasoning with me, endeavored to work out various drinking schedules, in fact all the tricks were practised faithfully for a short time somewhere along my shaky road to unhappiness.(p.361)
• I *tried* a few drinks my last night in the city before coming home.(p.364)
• I *tried* to hide my drinking by going places where I was unlikely to see anyone I knew.(p.375)
• I *tried* the wagon on numerous occasions but I always felt unhappy and abused.(p.375)
• I *tried* psychiatry, but of course I gave the psychiatrist no co-operation.(p.375)
• The A.A. way of life is the way we always should have *tried* to live.(p.382)
• I had *tried* my way and had failed.(p.383)
• I think that no one comes to A.A. until he's *tried* everything else.(p.384)
• We had *tried* everything.(p.389)
• I *tried* to compensate with impossible dreams and ambitions, which were simply early forms of escape.(p.400)
• Before I started to drink seriously, I *tried* a couple of other escapes.(p.401)
• I *tried* volunteer activity.(p.410)
• Once, when I called my analyst, and told her I was contemplating death, she came over and *tried* to get me into a sanitarium.(p.411)
• With more physical courage than I had possessed, she had twice *tried* to take her life.(p.414)
• I *tried* to wash a little, but Anne refused to wash at all.(p.415)
• I *tried* the church and psychiatry and finally came to A.A.(p.418)
• I closed my eyes and *tried* to think.(p.422)
• I *tried* to mimic the talk, ideas, moods and even the drinking the older men.(p.423)
• I smoked as much, *tried* to drink as much, and do everything they did, only more so.(p.423)
• I *tried* to control her drinking by pouring her whiskey down the sink before I'd leave for the night, to get drunker myself.(p.426)
• I'd acquired a new girl, a lovely girl who knew of my problem and had *tried* to help me.(p.430)
• Eventually, I had to redo each of the Twelve Steps specifically with Max in mind, from the First, saying, "I am powerless over alcohol, and my homelife is unmanageable by me," to the Twelfth, in which I *tried* to think of her as a sick Al-Anon and treat her with the love I would give a sick A.A. newcomer.(p.452)
• Many *tried* everything -- hospitals, special treatments, sanitariums, asylums, and jails.(p.455)
• So – I *tried* that.(p.465)
• On the way I *tried*, and I mean really *tried*, to throw myself out of the car.(p.466)
• There were doctors and psychiatrists there who *tried* to help me, but at that point I wasn't having help from anyone.(p.468)
• With their help I also saw that certainly, because of some of the things I had done during the years, I was bordering on insanity, and so, facing the record, I *tried* to believe that a Power greater than I could and would restore me to sanity.(p.471)
• Had I *tried* honestly and sincerely to practice the Twelve Steps I would have seen from my continuous moral inventory that I was getting off the beam -- I would have found that there were some active resentments in my life, a terrific amount of self-pity.(p.471)
• Any time I *tried* to kill myself, I was either drunk or pilled-up or both – usually the last.(p.479)
• I would never have *tried*, but mother counts on it so.(p.499)
• "Well," he answers, "You've probably *tried* praying like I have.(p.504)
• Just as I was wondering what on earth I could do -- I was too drunk even to pack a handkerchief – the memory of an A.A. write-up that I had seen in the Evening Mail flashed across my mind -- and I thought to myself, this is something I haven't *tried* yet.(p.523)
• I felt that I didn't have anything to live for, so I *tried* suicide many times.(p.528)
• In the nearby little town there was a plumber who once had *tried* to get an A.A. group going.(p.541)
• I looked around me at people who seemed happy and *tried* to analyze their happiness, and it seemed to me that without exception these people had something or somebody they loved very much.(p.546)

tries
- He ***tries*** every known means to get the jay-walking idea out of his head.(p.38)
- If the alcoholic ***tries*** to shield himself he may succeed for a time, but he usually winds up with a bigger explosion than ever.(p.101)
- Nearly every modern employer feels a moral responsibility for the well-being of his help, and he ***tries*** to meet these responsibilities.(p.137)

trifle
- Sometimes he explodes over a ***trifle***.(p.126)

trigger
- After two weeks of drinking, he had placed his toe on the ***trigger*** of a loaded shotgun – the barrel in his mouth.(p.137)

trim
- Standing there was a gray haired man – tall, ***trim*** and in uniform.(p.422)
- I got a job by myself which suited me down to the ground, because there was nobody really to interfere with what I did, one way or the other, and I usually had my nerves in good ***trim*** when anybody was coming around to inspect.(p.519)

trip
- Here are some of the methods we have tried: Drinking beer only, limiting the number of drinks, never drinking alone, never drinking in the morning, drinking only at home, never having it in the house, never drinking during business hours, drinking only at parties, switching from scotch to brandy, drinking only natural wines, agreeing to resign if ever drunk on the job, taking a ***trip***, not taking a ***trip***, swearing off forever (with and without a solemn oath), taking more physical exercise, reading inspirational books, going to health farms and sanitariums, accepting voluntary commitment to asylums -- we could increase the list ad infinitum.(p.31)
- He knew he faced another ***trip*** to the asylum if he kept on.(p.35)
- From a business standpoint, his ***trip*** came off badly.(p.153)
- On the return ***trip***, after two or three loads, I passed out and had to be carried to the house.(p.183)
- This we did the next day, and what a ***trip***!(p.245)
- I stayed sober during the ***trip*** except for an occasional bottle of beer because funds barely met expenses.(p.255)
- The details of the long road back to something resembling normal living -- the first short streetcar ride, the purchase of a used bike which enabled me to widen the narrow horizon of life, the first ***trip*** downtown – I will not dwell on.(p.276)
- I stayed in Akron two or three weeks on my initial ***trip*** trying to absorb as much of the program and philosophy as possible.(p.291)
- A few months after I made my original ***trip*** to Akron I was feeling pretty cocky, and I didn't think my wife was treating me with proper respect, now that I was an outstanding citizen.(p.293)
- So I suggested that he take a ***trip*** to Akron for a couple of weeks, which he did, living with one of the A.A. families there.(p.294)
- The girl was full of enthusiasm and she made the ***trip*** to Akron too.(p.295)
- I had turned eighteen during the ***trip***, and I despondently returned home by jet (on Daddy's bankbook) to a pair of miserable, hurt parents.(p.354)
- Two years before I joined A.A. my wife took a long ***trip*** during which she wrote me she just couldn't return unless I did something about my drinking.(p.377)
- A year later, while we were on a vacation ***trip*** she packed up to go home because of my excessive drinking, and I talked her out of it with the promise I would go on the wagon for at least a year.(p.377)
- Or he would leave on a ***trip*** and by the time he came home, I'd be passed out.(p.386)
- I don't know how I got here this ***trip***, but it doesn't matter very much.(p.423)
- The ***trip*** back was completed in one of those dead, awful silences.(p.467)

tripped
- During recess we were playing basketball and I had accidentally ***tripped*** a fellow just a little larger than I was.(p.484)

trips
- He tried to regulate his drinking for a while, making several ***trips*** to the hospital meantime.(p.32)
- It may mean sharing your money and your home, counseling frantic wives and relatives, innumerable ***trips*** to police courts, sanitariums, hospitals, jails and asylums.(p.97)
- We'd start out on the craziest ***trips***.(p.264)
- On my ***trips*** back to Akron to get my spirits recharged and to work with other alcoholics, I would ask Dr. Bob about this delay and wonder just what was wrong with me.(p.293)
- The next steps were bottle hiding, and excuses for ***trips*** in order to drink without restraint.(p.375)
- On one of these ***trips***, the judge must have thought I was worth saving, for instead of sending me to jail, he sent me to A.A. for one month.(p.526)

trite
- These last eighteen years have been the happiest of my life, ***trite*** though that statement may seem.(p.295)

triumph
- Our moments of ***triumph*** were short-lived.(p.66)

triumphant
- Most good ideas are simple, and this concept was the keystone of the new and ***triumphant*** arch through which we passed to freedom.(p.62)

trivial
- But there was always the curious mental phenomenon that parallel with our sound reasoning there inevitably ran some insanely ***trivial*** excuse for taking the first drink.(p.37)
- They had said that though I did raise a defense, it would one day give way before some ***trivial*** reason for having a drink.(p.42)
- You and your husband will find that you can dispose of serious problems easier than you can the ***trivial*** ones.(p.118)
- In a weak moment he may take your dislike of his high-stepping friends as one of those insanely ***trivial*** excuses to drink.(p.120)

trolley
- Within a week after leaving the hospital a fast-moving ***trolley*** car breaks his arm.(p.38)

troop
- I was supposed to come home on a ***troop*** ship, but I talked the base commander into flying me home.(p.428)

trooper
- I lied like a ***trooper*** to get out of many scrapes.(p.324)

troops
- Then I had about six months on a small island in command of the ***troops*** there.(p.520)

tropical
- I was certainly a complete surprise when I arrived at her family's home, but because I arrived on the wings of a ***tropical*** hurricane there wasn't much she could do but let me in.(p.364)

trouble
- There is scarcely any form of ***trouble*** and misery which has not been overcome among us.(p.15)
- Moderate drinkers have little ***trouble*** in giving up liquor entirely if they have good reason for it.(p.20)
- I had no ***trouble*** refusing drinks, and began to wonder if I had not been making too hard work of a simple matter.(p.40)
- We were having ***trouble*** with personal relationships, we couldn't control our emotional natures, we were a prey to misery and depression, we couldn't make a living, we had a feeling of uselessness, we were full of fear, we were unhappy, we couldn't seem to be of real help to other people – was not a basic solution of these bedevilments more important than whether we should see newsreels of lunar flight?(p.52)
- For years thereafter he was dogged by ***trouble*** and frustration.(p.56)
- What is his basic ***trouble***?(p.61)
- It seems to cause more ***trouble***.(p.68)
- We have admitted certain defects; we have ascertained in a rough way what the ***trouble*** is; we have put our finger on the weak items in our personal inventory.(p.72)
- That's a common form of ***trouble*** too.(p.79)
- We are headed for ***trouble*** if we do, for alcohol is a subtle foe.(p.85)
- If he is in a serious mood dwell on the ***trouble*** liquor has caused you, being careful not to moralize or lecture.(p.91)
- If he has ***trouble*** later, he is likely to say you rushed him.(p.95)
- This means ***trouble***, unless the family watches for these tendencies in each other and comes to a friendly agreement about them.(p.131)
- But those of us who have tried to shoulder the entire burden and ***trouble*** of others find we are soon overcome by them.(p.132)
- Avoid then, the deliberate manufacture of misery, but if ***trouble*** comes, cheerfully capitalize it as an opportunity to demonstrate His omnipotence.(p.133)
- One morning he took the bull by the horns and set out to tell those he feared what his ***trouble*** had been.(p.156)
- Consequently, I could not get into any ***trouble***.(p.174)
- I had some money, all the time in the world, and considerable stomach ***trouble***.(p.174)
- I had no ***trouble*** there because I had never actually ceased to believe in God, and had tried lots of times to get help but hadn't succeeded.(p.186)
- I remember telling them too that it was going to be awfully tough, because I did some other things, smoked cigarettes and played penny ante poker, sometimes bet on the horse races and they said, "Don't you think you're having more ***trouble*** with this drinking than with anything else at the present time?(p.190)
- As the treatment progressed I began to get a picture of myself, of the temperament that had caused me so much ***trouble***.(p.226)
- We always tried to buy him a drink, and he always told us he had liquor ***trouble*** – couldn't drink.)(p.266)
- At that time they didn't let us know that people ever had ***trouble***.(p.271)
- But I was in such deep ***trouble*** that I decided to try A.A. anyhow.(p.319)
- As we walked back through the hall, I, for the first time in my life, said to another human being, "I'm having ***trouble*** with my drinking, too."(p.321)
- I got into terrific ***trouble*** with my drinking.(p.322)
- Even so, every time I drank, I seemed to get in ***trouble***.(p.322)
- So long as a retiree woos his bottle at home, he stays out of public ***trouble***.(p.330)
- He'd told a villain, "The ***trouble*** is, old man, you've lived too long."(p.333)
- On the last day I was drinking I went up to see a friend who had had a good deal of ***trouble*** with alcohol, and whose wife had left him a number of times.(p.346)
- But it began to be an awfully painful answer as hangovers, blackouts, ***trouble***, and remorse set in.(p.353)
- I had no ***trouble*** at all in being elected to the two drinking societies at my college.(p.357)
- I had no ***trouble*** making the right decision when I saw my wife open her purse at the meeting that night and deposit a cute little angel in the middle of my birthday cake.(p.366)
- An obstreperous woman in a bar is a nuisance, and they wanted no ***trouble*** with the police.(p.410)
- I was so busy keeping her out of ***trouble***, and so scared she'd swing on me, that I had my last two drinks that night.(p.415)
- They were taking the ***trouble*** to try and help.(p.415)
- Always we'd emerge with a new formula for avoiding future ***trouble***.(p.433)
- Weeks would go by without further ***trouble***, and I'd be assured I'd at last hit on the right formula.(p.433)
- I nearly reverted to my old, incorrigible self – had ***trouble*** with a couple of other prisoners, was planning an escape.(p.461)
- You may wonder why, since I was having all this ***trouble***, and was having to seek the assistance of others, A.A. hadn't come into the picture.(p.469)
- Got into no ***trouble***.(p.475)
- We are so beautiful that it is never too much ***trouble*** to get some poor stranger to buy us a drink.(p.479)
- I never had too much ***trouble*** in school.(p.486)
- That was my ***trouble***.(p.487)
- He went into the religious side and told me that I didn't attend church as regularly as I should, and that he felt, more or less, that this was responsible for my ***trouble***.(p.489)
- He started telling me how much ***trouble*** he had, and I said to myself, "I wonder why this guy is telling me all his troubles.(p.494)
- Because, thank God, since I came into this program I haven't had any ***trouble***.(p.516)
- They brought me in and of course, they hadn't very much ***trouble*** in finding that I was alcoholic.(p.521)
- It's time to stop finding excuses for drinking and getting into ***trouble***, because now there is a way out, and if you want what we have, try coming around and giving the program a chance.(p.530)
- The mental twists that led up to my drinking began many years before I ever took a drink for I am one of those whose history proves conclusively that my drinking was "a symptom of a deeper ***trouble***."(p.544)
- I also got into my first disciplinary ***trouble*** caused by drinking, on two separate occasions.(p.555)
- By twenty-nine, I was having ***trouble*** coping with life because of my drinking.(p.555)
- It wasn't strong enough, so I added a shot of

vodka -- and was right back to worse *trouble* than before.(p.556)
• We learn how to level out the emotional wings that got us into *trouble* both when we were up and when we were down.(p.560)

troubled
• He may bring new hope and new courage to many a priest, minister, or rabbi, who gives his all to minister to our *troubled* world.(p.132)
• I used to think I was cowardly because when things came out pertaining to the program that *troubled* me, I said to her many times, "Annie, am I being a coward because I lay those things away on the shelf and skip it?"(p.273)

troublemaker
• I was an agitator, a *troublemaker*, and many men as bitter as I was followed me.(p.458)

troubles
• That, we think, is the root of our *troubles*.(p.62)
• So our *troubles*, we think, are basically of our own making.(p.62)
• Then we have the voices who cry for sex and more sex; who bewail the institution of marriage; who think that most of the *troubles* of the race are traceable to sex causes.(p.69)
• The chances are that we have domestic *troubles*.(p.80)
• He gets stirred up about their *troubles*, but not at all about yours.(p.119)
• Everyone knows about the others' alcoholic *troubles*.(p.125)
• The family will be affected also, pleasantly at first, as they feel their money *troubles* are about to be solved, then not so pleasantly as they find themselves neglected.(p.126)
• We try not to indulge in cynicism over the state of the nations, nor do we carry the world's *troubles* on our shoulders.(p.132)
• A year later, after I completed the course in contracts, I quit the law school, and undertook some engineering work for a patent law firm on behalf of clients who were in difficulties and who desired to keep their *troubles* from their own engineering department.(p.212)
• But in those days I had no one to whom I might take my *troubles*.(p.260)
• Today, I'm counting my blessings instead of my *troubles*.(p.355)
• I didn't know I was an alcoholic and (like most men in prison today) could not relate alcohol to any of my past *troubles*.(p.460)
• All my *troubles* arose when I was thrown socially among groups of people.(p.486)
• He started telling me how much trouble he had, and I said to myself, "I wonder why this guy is telling me all his *troubles*.(p.494)
• I have *troubles* of my own."(p.494)
• "Then all of your *troubles* are over," says the man and leaves the room.(p.503)
• "The thing I do is to say 'God here I am and here are all my *troubles*.(p.504)
• You take me, and all my *troubles*, and do anything you want with me.'(p.504)

troublesome
• If a sufficiently strong reason -- ill health, falling in love, change of environment, or the warning of a doctor -- becomes operative, this man can also stop or moderate, although he may find it difficult and *troublesome* and may even need medical attention.(p.21)
• If sex is very *troublesome*, we throw ourselves the harder into helping others.(p.70)

trousers
• Thus mother, through no fault of her own, became accustomed to wearing the family *trousers*.(p.131)
• At three-thirty the next morning, I was in Champlain Street Station, in jail for driving while intoxicated and insulting an officer; and the suit of which I was so proud was in such shape that the turnkey had to get me a pair of *trousers* to go into court in the next morning.(p.201)
• I had white *trousers* on, white shoes and a white shirt that was streaked with blood.(p.204)

truck
• I hardly dared cross the street, lest I collapse and be run down by an early morning *truck*, for it was scarcely daylight.(p.6)
• We heard by wireless on the 5th that the Armistice would be signed the next day (this was a premature report) so I had a couple of cognacs to celebrate; then I hopped a *truck* and went AWOL.(p.242)
• They used a sound *truck* some.(p.265)

trucks
• Another time, I had gone around to Max R. trying to get a job driving one of his *trucks*.(p.200)

trudge
• We shall be with you in the Fellowship of the Spirit, and you will surely meet some of us as you *trudge* the Road of Happy Destiny.(p.164)

true
• These things were *true* to some extent, in fact, to a considerable extent with some of us.(p.xxiv)
• The sensation is so elusive that, while they admit it is injurious, they cannot after a time differentiate the *true* from the false.(p.xxvi)
• And how appallingly *true* for the alcoholic!(p.14)
• This is by no means a comprehensive picture of the *true* alcoholic, as our behavior patterns vary.(p.22)
• How *true* this is, few realize.(p.23)
• This is particularly *true* of women.(p.33)
• It's strong language -- but isn't it *true*?(p.38)
• Some of you are thinking: "Yes, what you tell us is *true*, but it doesn't fully apply.(p.38)
• That may be *true* of certain nonalcoholic people who, though drinking foolishly and heavily at the present time, are able to stop or moderate, because their brains and bodies have not been damaged as ours were.(p.39)
• At first some of us tried to avoid the issue, hoping against hope we were not *true* alcoholics.(p.44)
• But I cannot accept as surely *true* the many articles of faith which are so plain to him."(p.47)
• These tiny bodies are governed by precise laws, and these laws hold *true* throughout the material world.(p.49)
• Were our contentions *true*, it would follow that life originated out of nothing, and proceeds nowhere.(p.49)
• Was it not *true* that the best mathematical minds had proved man could never fly?(p.51)
• We had seen spiritual release, but liked to tell ourselves it wasn't *true*.(p.55)
• Of those who keep on, a good number will become *true* alcoholics after a while.(p.109)
• He admits this is *true*, but is positive that he will do better.(p.109)
• It is probably *true* that you and your husband have been living too much alone, for drinking many times isolates the wife of an alcoholic.(p.119)
• Though it is infinitely better that he have no relapse at all, as has been *true* with many of our men, it is by no means a bad thing in some cases.(p.120)
• That is *true* only if one is willing to turn the past to good account.(p.124)
• To some extent this is already *true*.(p.162)
• Which of course was *true*.(p.187)
• And it is *true* that there was no great amount of drunkenness.(p.230)
• I was greeted warmly, honestly, and with a *true* ring of sincerity by everyone present.(p.259)
• He may even read in a newspaper that one out of every seven drinkers will become alcoholic, but he rarely is told that it holds *true* for all ages -- or that the tolerance to alcohol (and other drugs) decreases steadily, year after year, in the bodies of all persons.(p.330)
• I was told that I must want sobriety for my own sake and I am convinced this is *true*.(p.379)
• It pays daily in more harmonious relations with my fellow men, in ever clearer insight into the *true* meaning of life, and in the answering love and gratitude wherever and whenever I have been the instrument of God's will in the lives of others.(p.394)
• *True*!(p.396)
• It is *true* that I -- of all people, strange as it may seem, and even though I didn't give my permission -- really, really am an alcoholic of sorts.(p.448)
• It is *true* that the doctors and nurses in the various institutions I attended knew too.(p.470)
• *True*, I have recently recovered from pneumonia and have an alibi, but my friends are in the war or going, and I am not.(p.499)
• It might be *true*.(p.504)
• That was one aspect of it, and a *true* one.(p.532)
• I learned the *true* meaning of bread cast upon the waters.(p.541)
• At fifty-four, I have had come *true* for me the old wish, "If only I could live my life over, knowing what I know."(p.543)
• It's been *true* in my case, nor could I quarrel with "restore us to sanity," for my actions drunk or sober, before A.A., were not those of a sane person.(p.550)
• A.A. has taught me that I will have peace of mind in exact proportion to the peace of mind I bring into the lives of other people, and it has taught me the *true* meaning of the admonition "happy are ye who know these things and do them."(p.551)
• All such representatives are to be guided in the spirit of service, for *true* leaders in A.A. are but trusted and experienced servants of the whole.(p.567)
• Yet it is *true* that our first printing gave many readers the impression that these personality changes, or religious experiences, must be in the nature of sudden and spectacular upheavals.(p.569)

truest
• Was I the disloyal sort who would turn his back on this, my last and *truest* friend?(p.539)

truly
• Very *truly* yours, William D. Silkworth, M.D.(p.xxiv)
• But if you really and *truly* want to quit drinking liquor for good and all, and sincerely feel that you must have some help, we know that we have an answer for you.(p.181)
• For, to these people, I am *truly* related.(p.312)
• It was the first of many such experiences that became the only cause of harsh words, tears and heartaches in an otherwise *truly* beautiful marriage.(p.361)
• A whole new world of happiness and love began to unfold before my eyes, a *truly* new way of living.(p.365)
• As I write these words, it seems incredible that these things should have happened to me, for they are, *truly*, against all my instincts and training.(p.536)
• One of the *truly* great things A.A. has taught me is that reality too has two sides; I had only known the grim side before the program, but now I had a chance to learn about the pleasant side as well.(p.550)
• The Episcopal magazine, The Living Church, observes editorially: "The basis of the technique of Alcoholics Anonymous is the *truly* Christian principle that a man cannot help himself except by helping others.(p.574)

trunks
• I also made use of old *trunks* and chests, the old can container, and even the ash container.(p.176)

trust
• We *trust* infinite God rather than our finite selves.(p.68)
• They *trust* their God.(p.68)
• The only condition is that he *trust* in God and clean house.(p.98)
• Above all, I have gained the greatest thing accorded to any man, the love and understanding of a gracious God, who has lifted me from the alcoholic scrap-heap to a position of *trust* where I have been able to reap the rich rewards that come from showing a little love for others and from serving them as I can.(p.296)
• And, as the years go by, working together, sharing our experiences with one another, and also sharing a mutual *trust*, understanding and love -- without strings, without obligation -- we acquire relationships that are unique and priceless.(p.312)
• I couldn't *trust* them.(p.319)
• We have faith in each other, *trust* in each other, and understanding.(p.325)
• I had a tiny *trust* fund, and I moved into a small apartment where I learned to cook, keep house, and do the things that normal people do.(p.409)
• I could not live on that tiny *trust* fund and still drink all I wanted to.(p.411)

trusted
• His action met widespread approval, and today his is one of the most *trusted* citizens of his town.(p.80)
• Your man may be *trusted*.(p.146)
• In those days, I *trusted* no church-goer, and thought A.A. was for weaklings.(p.460)
• The sacred word was broken and you never *trusted* your father again, and avoided him.(p.533)
• Our leaders are but *trusted* servants; they do not govern.(p.564)
• All such representatives are to be guided in the spirit of service, for true leaders in A.A. are but *trusted* and experienced servants of the whole.(p.567)

trustee
• At that very time, he was a nonalcoholic *trustee* on the General Service Board of Alcoholics Anonymous!(p.559)

trustees
• And no group, regional committee, or individual should ever take any action that might greatly affect A.A. as a whole without conferring with the *trustees* of the General Service Board.(p.565)
• The *trustees* of the General Service Board are, in effect, our A.A. General Service Committee.(p.567)
• The General Service Board of A.A. (the *trustees*) administers A.A.'s General Service Office, A.A. World Services, Inc., and our monthly magazine,

the A.A. Grapevine.(p.575)

trusting

- For we are now on a different basis; the basis of ***trusting*** and relying upon God.(p.68)

trustworthy

- I remember the day when I decided to drink myself to death quietly, without bothering anyone, because I was tired of having been a dependable, ***trustworthy*** person for about thirty-nine years without having received what I thought was a proper reward for my virtue.(p.531)

truth

- Once in a while he may tell the ***truth***.(p.23)
- And the ***truth***, strange to say, is usually that he has no more idea why he took that first drink than you have.(p.23)
- The tragic ***truth*** is that if the man be a real alcoholic, the happy day may not arrive.(p.23)
- He begged the doctor to tell him the whole ***truth***, and he got it.(p.26)
- We have seen the ***truth*** demonstrated again and again: "Once an alcoholic, always an alcoholic."(p.33)
- It is an effort to discover the ***truth*** about the stock-in-trade.(p.64)
- That being so you have swallowed and digested some big chunks of ***truth*** about yourself.(p.71)
- We have seldom told them the whole ***truth*** nor have we followed their advice.(p.73)
- He may be an example of the ***truth*** that faith alone is insufficient.(p.93)
- Some of us have taken very hard knocks to learn this ***truth***: Job or no job -- wife or no wife -- we simply do not stop drinking so long as we place dependence upon other people ahead of dependence on God.(p.98)
- We have told small tots that father was sick, which was much nearer the ***truth*** than we realized.(p.106)
- Whether your employee likes it or not, he will learn the grim ***truth*** about alcoholism.(p.144)
- We hope the doctor will tell the patient the ***truth*** about his condition, whatever that happens to be.(p.144)
- When the day of their return was almost upon me, and suicide was the only answer I had been able to think of, I went into Ralph's room one evening and told him the ***truth***.(p.278)
- But this would not be the ***truth***.(p.285)
- It is the ***truth***.(p.302)
- And with this came the only real freedom, the freedom of ***truth***.(p.355)
- For the next couple of hours a terrible battle went on between the good gremlins and the bad ones, one faction urging me to tell the ***truth***, the other telling me to sit tight and say nothing.(p.366)
- ***Truth*** and sincerity do not come easily to me.(p.420)
- Alcohol wrings the guts out of life, eats into the brain in such a way as to make the alcoholic blind to the ***truth***.(p.457)
- My sponsor say men who talk speak ***truth***.(p.476)
- Words of ***truth*** and love are strong medicine.(p.476)
- The fear of the loss of Vi and the feeling that, though she had the right to do as she pleased, she should have told me the ***truth*** about it, upset me.(p.487)
- I learn that honesty is ***truth***, and that ***truth*** shall make us free!(p.507)
- It was a thorn in my side, because I knew it was the ***truth***, and I hated to hear the ***truth***, especially about myself.(p.513)
- I always blamed my drinking on being poor, or on anything other than the ***truth*** -- that I liked what booze did for me, that when I had a drink I was as big and had as much as the next person.(p.526)
- The ***truth*** is, I did not know how to stop it, nor did I want to, really.(p.539)
- Had I been able to explain to a psychiatrist the feeling of futility, loneliness and lack of purpose that had come with my deep sense of personal failure at this second divorce, I seriously doubt that the good doctor could have convinced me that my basic problem was a spiritual hunger, but A.A. has shown me this was the ***truth***.(p.546)
- This great experience that released me from the bondage of hatred and replaced it with love is really just another affirmation of the ***truth*** I know: I get everything I need in Alcoholics Anonymous -- everything I need I get -- and when I get what I need I invariably find that it was just what I wanted all the time.(p.553)

truths

- My tongue had become increasingly skilled at venomous home ***truths***.(p.405)
- If I write with the air of one who has discovered the obvious, which is to say, the eternal ***truths*** which have been offered to us since the beginning, forgive my callowness; I had to find these things out for myself.(p.536)

try

- "Why don't you ***try*** beer and wine?"(p.20)
- If what we have learned and felt and seen means anything at all, it means that all of us, whatever our race, creed, or color are the children of a living Creator with whom we may form a relationship upon simple and understandable terms as soon as we are willing and honest enough to ***try***.(p.28)
- By every form of self-deception and experimentation, they will ***try*** to prove themselves exceptions to the rule, therefore nonalcoholic.(p.31)
- Step over to the nearest barroom and ***try*** some controlled drinking.(p.31)
- ***Try*** to drink and stop abruptly.(p.31)
- ***Try*** it more than once.(p.31)
- But ***try*** and get them to see it!(p.34)
- If anyone questions whether he has entered this dangerous area, let him ***try*** leaving liquor alone for one year.(p.34)
- Most people ***try*** to live by self-propulsion.(p.60)
- It is important that he be able to keep a confidence; that he fully understand and approve what we are driving at; that he will not ***try*** to change our plan.(p.74)
- He told her what he would ***try*** to do in the future.(p.79)
- You should be described to him as one of a fellowship who, as part of their own recovery, ***try*** to help others and who will be glad to talk to him if he cares to see you.(p.90)
- Usually the family should not ***try*** to tell your story.(p.91)
- Make it plain he is under no obligation to you, that you hope only that he will ***try*** to help other alcoholics when he escapes his own difficulties.(p.94)
- Search out another alcoholic and ***try*** again.(p.96)
- If he is, you might ***try*** to help him about getting a job, or give him a little financial assistance.(p.96)
- But we must ***try*** to repair the damage immediately lest we pay the penalty by a spree.(p.99)
- If it is a happy occasion, ***try*** to increase the pleasure of those there; if a business occasion, go and attend to your business enthusiastically.(p.102)
- There is every evidence that women regain their health as readily as men if they ***try*** our suggestions.(p.104)
- Next day they would be themselves again and we would forgive and ***try*** to forget.(p.106)
- ***Try*** not to condemn your alcoholic husband no matter what he says or does.(p.108)
- He has begun to ***try***, with or without your cooperation, various means of moderating or staying dry.(p.109)
- His case presents additional questions which we shall ***try*** to answer for you.(p.110)
- You may be unable to do so, no matter how hard you ***try***.(p.111)
- ***Try*** to have him bring up the subject himself.(p.111)
- Meanwhile you might ***try*** to help the wife of another serious drinker.(p.112)
- In any event, ***try*** to have your husband read this book.(p.114)
- If he is already committed to an institution, but can convince you and your doctor that he means business, give him a chance to ***try*** our method, unless the doctor thinks his mental condition too abnormal or dangerous.(p.114)
- Now we ***try*** to put spiritual principles to work in every department of our lives.(p.116)
- We urge you to ***try*** our program, for nothing will be so helpful to your husband as the radically changed attitude toward him which God will show you how to have.(p.117)
- When resentful thoughts come, ***try*** to pause and count your blessings.(p.119)
- We never, never ***try*** to arrange a man's life so as to shield him from temptation.(p.120)
- For a time he may ***try*** to hug the new treasure to himself.(p.129)
- We ***try*** not to indulge in cynicism over the state of the nations, nor do we carry the world's troubles on our shoulders.(p.132)
- ***Try*** to remember that though God has wrought miracles among us, we should never belittle a good doctor or psychiatrist.(p.133)
- Seeing your attempt to understand and help, some men will ***try*** to take advantage of your kindness.(p.141)
- He will presently ***try*** the old game again, for he isn't happy about his sobriety.(p.152)
- I thought to myself, "Well, she is going to tell me this is the end," and I certainly couldn't blame her and did not intend to ***try*** to justify myself.(p.184)
- Each day I would ***try*** to find out what His will was, and ***try*** to follow that, rather than trying to get Him to always agree that the things I thought of myself were the things best for me.(p.187)
- When he was uptown -- we were living in the little town of Moscow -- I went up to ***try*** to get some money from him to buy groceries.(p.193)
- In 1932, some friends of mine advised me that I might ***try*** Christian Science, which had done a lot for some of their friends.(p.202)
- I decided that if these fellows could make it I would ***try*** it myself, and so I did.(p.232)
- "You can't win unless you ***try*** God's way."(p.236)
- Well, there I was, willing to ***try*** it, but I didn't know how, except in a vague way.(p.236)
- Three months before I met Jackie I had made my second feeble ***try*** at suicide.(p.245)
- As soon as I could get up and walk I started to drink again and kept it up until my friend of the hospital, who, in his first ***try*** at the new way of life had stubbed his toe in Chicago but had come back to the town to take counsel and make a new start, picked me up and got me into a hospital.(p.258)
- When you have a hangover and can't even sit still, ***try*** to read small print!(p.268)
- And I'd ***try***, but I couldn't even see the letters.(p.268)
- I knew Doc and Anne were going to be there, and all of them thought it would be good for me, but the first thing I did was to go to St. Thomas and ***try*** to talk to those women.)(p.272)
- Finally, and I shall never know how much later it was, one clear thought came to me: ***Try*** prayer.(p.280)
- One time my wife decided to ***try*** this too.(p.288)
- The next afternoon and evening, two other men visited me and each told me his story and the things that they were doing to ***try*** to recover from this tragic illness.(p.290)
- One of them was that I would ***try*** to get a group started in Chicago; the second was that I would have to return to Akron to attend meetings at least every two months until I did get a group started in Chicago; third, I decided I must place this program above everything else, even my family, because if I did not maintain my sobriety I would lose my family anyway.(p.292)
- But I was in such deep trouble that I decided to ***try*** A.A. anyhow.(p.319)
- I did ***try***, for a day or two, but something always would come up that would throw me.(p.324)
- I used to make excuses to ***try*** and get George off the wagon.(p.325)
- I ***try*** to live our program as it has been outlined to me, one day at a time.(p.325)
- I ***try*** to live today so that tomorrow I won't be ashamed when I wake up in the morning.(p.325)
- Now I feel so very grateful not only for my sobriety, which I ***try*** to maintain day by day, but I'm grateful also for the ability to help other people.(p.326)
- I would take a gulp, then warn the jug not to ***try*** to entice, lure, or seduce me into having more than one "medicinal" jolt.(p.332)
- I had forgotten "If I ever I get that bad, I'll ***try*** A.A."(p.333)
- Toward five o'clock, helter-skelter, I'd get everything put away and ***try*** to get supper on the table, and after supper I'd finish the job up and knock myself out.(p.337)
- Nevertheless, I began to ***try*** to live without alcohol.(p.338)
- I said to my husband, "I'm going to ***try***, every free moment that I have, to get interested in something outside, get myself over this rut I'm in."(p.338)
- He said, "Why don't you ***try*** Alcoholics Anonymous?"(p.340)
- I was willing to ***try*** anything.(p.340)
- In fact I was afraid to ***try*** it for fear that I would wind up like many examples I had seen of excessive drinking in the Army.(p.374)
- ***Try*** anything.(p.377)
- The Twelve Steps, which to me are a spiritual way of living, soon meant honest thinking, not wishful thinking, open mindedness, a willingness to ***try*** and a faith to accept.(p.381)
- "First Things First": solving our immediate problems before we ***try*** to solve all the others and get muddled in our thinking and doing.(p.382)
- ***Try*** for inner contentment.(p.382)
- I knew that I wanted to ***try*** A.A. and if that didn't work, I didn't think anything would.(p.384)
- As I grow in A.A., I realize that a person with as

much self-will as I had, as hard a head and as diseased an ego, had to ***try*** everything that I could think of, butting my head against every stone wall before I was ready to come in.(p.384)
• There was nothing else left to ***try***.(p.389)
• There was something else that I could ***try*** -- A.A.(p.391)
• If you will ***try*** this thing, I'll go along with you.(p.391)
• I know that when Frank came home, I said, "I want to ***try*** this thing," and he said, "There's a post office box to write to in New York."(p.392)
• I wanted to ***try*** A.A. with my whole heart and soul.(p.393)
• In spite of knowing that my drunkenness was a symptom of the things that were wrong with me, and that I could never drink again, I thought I couldn't yet give it up, although I was going to ***try***.(p.393)
• It's the last thing I ever heard him say, and I think there are some of us who, at times, ***try*** to read extra messages and complexities into the Steps.(p.395)
• They were taking the trouble to ***try*** and help.(p.415)
• When I ***try*** to reconstruct what my life was like "before," I see a coin with two faces.(p.432)
• After a particularly ugly one-nighter, my wife suggested I ***try*** it, and I agreed.(p.434)
• But if you want to, you're free to ***try*** them.(p.436)
• In the garage, I would put the needle in my vein and then ***try*** to figure out exactly how much medication to inject to overcome the pep pills while adding to the sleeping pills while ignoring the tranquilizers, in order to get just enough to be able to pull out the needle, jerk the tourniquet, throw it in the car, slam the car door shut, run down the hall, and fall in bed before I fell asleep.(p.442)
• And life keeps getting simpler and easier as we ***try*** to reverse my old idea, by taking care of the internal environment via the Twelve Steps, and letting the external environment take care of itself.)(p.446)
• Finally after seven months, I decided to ***try*** it.(p.448)
• The people of A.A. had something that looked much better than what I had, but I was afraid to let go of what I had in order to ***try*** something new; there was a certain sense of security in the familiar.(p.448)
• But when I ***try*** to see what I can add to the meeting, rather than what I can get out of it, and when I focus my mind on what's good about it, rather than what's wrong with it, the meeting keeps getting better and better.(p.451)
• Today, Max and I ***try*** to communicate what we feel, rather than what we think.(p.451)
• But then my "rights" ***try*** to move in, and they, too, can force my serenity level down.(p.452)
• They prove to almost anyone's satisfaction that it's never too late to ***try*** Alcoholics Anonymous.(p.455)
• I didn't even ***try*** to understand.(p.460)
• I was too weak and exhausted to even ***try*** to throw myself out of the car.(p.467)
• Not ***try*** no drinks for Lent or for life.(p.476)
• This sound easy, so will ***try***.(p.476)
• It is suggested that we do not ***try*** to do a lifetime of repairs in one day.(p.481)
• She asked me if I would ***try*** to be sober if I possibly could.(p.494)
• So I put forth some effort that day to ***try*** to stay sober if I could, though my sobriety was just a daze.(p.494)
• Then Charlie or someone in the group suggested that we ***try*** to get a place in a church or hall to hold meetings.(p.495)
• I'll ***try*** the second.(p.499)
• There is no use trying any more, for there is nothing to ***try***.(p.502)
• I pick up a book and ***try*** to read, but I cannot concentrate.(p.503)
• I ***try*** to read.(p.506)
• I ***try*** to pray.(p.506)
• I was drinking to ***try*** to hold on to a job, to ***try*** and hold on to my home, to ***try*** to hold on to my wife, to ***try*** to hold on to my sanity.(p.514)
• So I decided I'd go back and live in Ireland to ***try*** the geography cure.(p.522)
• My only hope was to ***try*** and get through what was left of life as best I could, but I could never visualize doing that without drinking.(p.522)
• It continues to ***try*** to teach me the real charity, the charity that gives time and good will and service, and not just money.(p.525)
• Today, I thank my Higher Power for giving me another chance at life and A.A. and being able to ***try*** and help some other alcoholic.(p.529)
• If you give us a ***try***, you will see that we are really human beings, and we will welcome you with open arms and hearts.(p.529)
• It's time to stop finding excuses for drinking and getting into trouble, because now there is a way out, and if you want what we have, ***try*** coming around and giving the program a chance.(p.530)
• Sometimes we are told in A.A. not to ***try*** and learn the reasons for our drinking.(p.533)
• I ask the forgiveness of the reader; and from now on I shall ***try*** to write with the humility I honestly pray for.)(p.536)
• They suggested that I study the A.A. book and ***try*** to take the Twelve Steps according to the explanation in the Book, for it was their opinion that the application of these principles in our daily lives will get us sober and keep us sober.(p.550)

trying

• And besides, there were scattered alcoholics who had picked up the basic ideas in Akron or New York and were ***trying*** to form A.A. groups in other cities.(p.xvii)
• In fact, I have been ***trying*** to produce some such emotional rearrangement within you.(p.27)
• Each person is like an actor who wants to run the whole show; is forever ***trying*** to arrange the lights, the ballet, the scenery and the rest of the players in his own way.(p.60)
• In ***trying*** to make these arrangements our actor may sometimes be quite virtuous.(p.61)
• Is he not really a self-seeker even when ***trying*** to be kind?(p.61)
• Neither could we reduce our self-centeredness much by wishing or ***trying*** on our own power.(p.62)
• We have been ***trying*** to get a new attitude, a new relationship with our Creator, and to discover the obstacle in our path.(p.72)
• ***Trying*** to avoid this humbling experience, they have turned to easier methods.(p.72)
• At the moment we are ***trying*** to put our lives in order.(p.77)
• We are there to sweep off our side of the street realizing that nothing worth while can be accomplished until we do so, never ***trying*** to tell him what he should do.(p.77)
• Telling them what we are ***trying*** to do, we make no bones about our drinking; they usually know it anyway, whether we think so or not.(p.78)
• We do not tire so easily, for we are not burning up energy foolishly as we did when we were ***trying*** to arrange life to suit ourselves.(p.88)
• If he does not want to stop drinking, don't waste time ***trying*** to persuade him.(p.90)
• Be certain he will be welcomed by your family, and that he is not ***trying*** to impose upon you for money, connections, or shelter.(p.96)
• If your husband is ***trying*** to live on a spiritual basis, he will also be doing everything in his power to avoid disagreement or contention.(p.118)
• Is not each ***trying*** to arrange the family show to his liking?(p.122)
• Is he not unconsciously ***trying*** to see what he can take from the family life rather than give?(p.122)
• But the wise family will admire him for what he is ***trying*** to be, rather than for what he is ***trying*** to get.(p.123)
• One more suggestion: Whether the family has spiritual convictions or not, they may do well to examine the principles by which the alcoholic member is ***trying*** to live.(p.130)
• Your man has probably been ***trying*** to conceal a number of scrapes, perhaps pretty messy ones.(p.140)
• Sometimes we alcoholics have an idea that people are ***trying*** to pull us down.(p.145)
• If he is, and is still ***trying*** to recover, he will tell you about it even if it means the loss of his job.(p.146)
• He will appreciate knowing you are not bothering your head about him, that you are not suspicious nor are you ***trying*** to run his life so he will be shielded from temptation to drink.(p.146)
• They often jeopardize their own positions by ***trying*** to help serious drinkers who should have been fired long ago, or else given an opportunity to get well.(p.147)
• Then he added, "He sure didn't do much for me when I was ***trying*** to fight this booze racket alone."(p.158)
• But this was a man who had experienced many years of frightful drinking, who had had most all the drunkard's experiences known to man, but who had been cured by the very means I had been ***trying*** to employ, that is to say the spiritual approach.(p.180)
• We're not up here ***trying*** to take any of your rights or privileges away from you, but we have a program whereby we think we can stay sober.(p.186)
• Each day I would try to find out what His will was, and try to follow that, rather than ***trying*** to get Him to always agree that the things I thought of myself were the things best for me.(p.187)
• They said, "Let's forget about those other things, that is, ***trying*** to eliminate them all at once, and concentrate on the drink."(p.190)
• I spent most of my time ***trying*** to get back these friendships, and to make some recompense towards my wife, whom I had hurt a lot.(p.191)
• I was ***trying*** to find the answer.(p.191)
• We were eating lunch, and I was listening and ***trying*** to find out why they had this release that they seemed to have.(p.191)
• Anyhow, I recognized the fact that I couldn't drink like normal people, but I tried hard and kept on ***trying*** for twenty-two years.(p.196)
• Another time, I had gone around to Max R. ***trying*** to get a job driving one of his trucks.(p.200)
• My wife didn't tell me this, but one Sunday afternoon when Mary was ***trying*** to get the cobwebs out of my mind, Clarence and his sister-in-law, the hairdresser, called at the house.(p.216)
• My experience in the hospital I considered to be terrific because Dr. Bob told me very quickly that medicine would have very little to do with it, outside of ***trying*** to restore my appetite for food.(p.217)
• I remembered going through what my sister assured me was my nightly procedure of ***trying*** to find Willie Seabrook's name in the telephone book.(p.224)
• "You've been ***trying*** man's ways and they always fail," he told me.(p.236)
• For a long time I kept on ***trying***, in a pretty dumb way at first, I know, but very earnestly.(p.237)
• They were earnest and obviously ***trying*** to help me on the road I had chosen.(p.259)
• I remember starting to city school, coming from a country school, and wanting so very, very much to be like the other girls and ***trying*** flour on my face for powder because I wasn't able to have any real powder.(p.261)
• If, on Sunday, I could be there, ***trying*** to think of something that would help her with this problem, then we must have something that could work.(p.272)
• I told our family doctor, an understanding man who gave hours of his time ***trying*** to help me, about this experience.(p.276)
• It is, however, only the first of a series of miracles which have followed one after another as a result of my ***trying*** to apply to my daily life the principles embodies in our Twelve Steps.(p.280)
• In the next two or three days the balance of this handful of men contacted me, encouraged me, and told me how they were ***trying*** to live this program of recovery and the fun they were having doing it.(p.291)
• I stayed in Akron two or three weeks on my initial trip ***trying*** to absorb as much of the program and philosophy as possible.(p.291)
• I spent a great deal of time with Dr. Bob, whenever he had the time to spare, and in the homes of two or three other people, ***trying*** to see how the family lived the program.(p.291)
• (That condition was a distinct handicap to me in ***trying*** to vindicate myself with the not so patient wife.)(p.301)
• We have only been in A.A. a few years, but now we're ***trying*** to make up for lost time.(p.325)
• I am ***trying*** now, each day, to make up for all those selfish, thoughtless, foolish things I did in my drinking days.(p.326)
• Every breadwinner, whether ***trying*** to impress a boss or to hold customers in his own business, is fettered by people-pleasing.(p.329)
• He knew what I was doing, how I was ***trying***.(p.339)
• I do recall lying on a cold cement floor and shredding into little bits several pieces of stolen identification cards, and washing my face in the toilet bowl ***trying*** to sober up, and screaming hysterically while clinging to bars too high to see out of, and cursing everyone that came near me.(p.354)
• Well, now I'm living it and ***trying*** to paint it for others.(p.355)
• While I was in Florida ***trying*** to convince my wife with all the A.A. literature that she should come back to me, she went over to her desk and picked up a clipping she had taken from the St. Petersburg Times about A.A.(p.366)
• It was the first she had heard or read about it and she said she had considered sending it to me or ***trying*** to have someone in Pittsburgh send it to me so I wouldn't know where it came from.(p.366)
• I did work of all kinds after school and during vacations, ***trying*** to find that which would appeal most as a goal for a life work.(p.373)
• I was ***trying*** to find an easier, softer way.(p.378)
• A spiritual awakening soon came to mean ***trying***

each day to be a little more thoughtful, more considerate, a little more courteous to those with whom I came in contact.(p.381)
• After all, upon coming out of a week-long or ten-day drunk, it was hard enough to figure up just how much that one drunk cost, let alone ***trying*** to calculate the cost of approximately twenty-five years of active alcoholism.(p.396)
• I was really ***trying***, once more, to escape from myself.(p.405)
• I would walk up and down under the 59th Street bridge, ***trying*** to get up the nerve to go up there and jump.(p.411)
• I, who had feared questions, now began ***trying*** to interrupt and tell my story.(p.414)
• I completely forgot myself in ***trying*** vainly to help Anne, whose misery I understood.(p.415)
• My reaction was that I'd already helped all the patients on the ward, and I still had plenty of problems of my own without ***trying*** to help some drunk from A.A.(p.446)
• Some went on ***trying*** to live with alcohol.(p.455)
• Through A.A., many receive the needed change and awakening just by ***trying*** to live by A.A. principles and associating with A.A. people.(p.459)
• I am still arrogant, egocentric, self-righteous, with no humility, even phony at times, but I'm ***trying*** to be a better person and help my fellowman.(p.463)
• What's the sense in ***trying*** to do the right thing?"(p.467)
• I realized that I was ***trying*** to pin everything on an individual – not the book or the group or the Higher Power, or anything else.(p.472)
• There is no use ***trying*** any more, for there is nothing to try.(p.502)
• I was ***trying*** for her sake.(p.514)
• Finally, my mother came and said she had kept me at home for six years because she thought she could help me, but that now she had come to the conclusion that I wasn't even worth ***trying*** to help.(p.523)
• I was ***trying*** to remember where it came from, when two of the biggest cops I ever saw walked in and took me to jail.(p.528)
• I know there are some alcoholics who seem terribly, terribly grown-up, but I think that they are ***trying*** to make themselves think they are grown-up, and the strain of their effort is what is causing them to drink -- a sense of inadequacy, a childish vanity to be the most popular, the most sought after, the mostest of the most.(p.535)
• But I was ***trying*** frantically to control it.(p.557)

tuberculosis
• The doctor has told me that if I don't give up inside work, I'll have ***tuberculosis***.(p.500)

tubes
• I awoke next day with ***tubes*** in both arms.(p.558)

tucked
• Cold chills started chasing up and down my spine; my teeth were chattering; my hands were shaking so I ***tucked*** them under me to keep them from flying away.(p.222)
• I checked into my hotel room and then noticed a placard ***tucked*** under the glass on the bureau stating "There will be positively NO drinking at this convention" signed by the president of the company.(p.243)
• He sent to New York for a copy, and after reading it he ***tucked*** it under his arm and called on me.(p.307)

Tuesday
• This is his story: "I came to work on ***Tuesday*** morning.(p.36)
• ***Tuesday*** I started in the morning, getting well organized by noon.(p.179)
• But then I thought, well, now wait, how will I feel next ***Tuesday***?(p.326)
• I promised my two sponsors that I would attend their meeting the next ***Tuesday*** evening.(p.363)

tugboat
• This worked nicely until my wife and I went to see Wallace Beery in "***Tugboat*** Annie," after which the pant-leg and stocking racket were out!(p.177)

tumble
• No jail booking, drunk-driving citation, barroom fight, or even a ***tumble*** off a barstool.(p.327)
• I would drink all night in bars, come home about five a.m., down a good big glass of whiskey straight, and ***tumble*** into bed.(p.428)
• I ***tumble*** out of bed onto my knees.(p.504)

tumbled
• This man recounts that he ***tumbled*** out of bed to his knees.(p.56)
• (And the church walls haven't ***tumbled*** down yet.)(p.482)

tumbler
• A ***tumbler*** full of gin followed by half a dozen bottles of beer would be required if I were to eat any breakfast.(p.5)
• I pour out half a ***tumbler*** of grain alcohol and fill it with ginger ale.(p.499)

tumor
• Suddenly, it was obvious to me: I had a brain ***tumor*** and would die, and everyone would be sorry for me.(p.444)
• At age forty, I developed a large lump in my pot-belly, and I feared it was a ***tumor***.(p.557)

tune
• My judgment and ideas were followed by many to the ***tune*** of paper millions.(p.3)
• And when I get upset, cross-grained and out of ***tune*** with my fellow man I know that I am out of ***tune*** with God.(p.237)

turbulent
• My life there was a nightmare of periodic binges on alcohol and pills, adultery, unhappy hours at the dental office, seeing my wife give birth to our second child and have several miscarriages, living in a ***turbulent*** household, and making continual attempts to be the respectable dentist, husband, father, and community leader.(p.419)

turmoil
• Selfish and inconsiderate habits have kept the home in ***turmoil***.(p.82)

turn
• Out of this alloy of drink and speculation, I commenced to forge the weapon that one day would ***turn*** in its flight like a boomerang and all but cut me to ribbons.(p.2)
• I must ***turn*** in all things the Father of Light who presides over us all.(p.14)
• They in ***turn*** might work with others.(p.14)
• We, in our ***turn***, sought the same escape with all the desperation of drowning men.(p.28)
• Potential female alcoholics often ***turn*** into the real thing and are gone beyond recall in a few years.(p.33)
• 3.Made a decision to ***turn*** our will and our lives over to the care of God as we understood Him.(p.59)
• Being convinced, we were at Step Three, which is that we decided to ***turn*** our will and our life over to God as we understood Him.(p.60)
• Taking this book down from our shelf we ***turn*** to the page which contains the twelve steps.(p.75)
• Then we resolutely ***turn*** our thoughts to someone we can help.(p.84)
• After a while, ***turn*** the talk to some phase of drinking.(p.91)
• His only chance for sobriety would be some place like the Greenland Ice Cap, and even there an Eskimo might ***turn*** up with a bottle of scotch and ruin everything!(p.101)
• Each in his ***turn*** may be footsore and may straggle.(p.122)
• That is true only if one is willing to ***turn*** the past to good account.(p.124)
• You are betting, of course, that your changed attitude plus the contents of this book will ***turn*** the trick.(p.144)
• So, for one reason or another, they cover these men, hoping matters will take a ***turn*** for the better.(p.147)
• Many mornings I have gone to classes, and even though fully prepared, would ***turn*** and walk back to the fraternity house because of my jitters, not daring to enter the classroom for fear of making a scene should I be called on for recitation.(p.173)
• This would lessen my chances of smuggling some home that evening, which in ***turn*** would mean a night of futile tossing around in bed followed by a morning of unbearable jitters.(p.176)
• It was in the next two or three days after I had first met Doc and Bill, that I finally came to a decision to ***turn*** my will over to God and to go along with this program the best that I could.(p.189)
• Eventually, there would be a ball game, or a show, or some sort of special occasion to celebrate and I would ***turn*** up drunk.(p.196)
• I said, "Look, Bub, if I want those lights on, I'll ***turn*** them on."(p.207)
• Then it was my ***turn*** -- I ordered "Three beers," but this time it was different, I had a cash investment of thirty cents and, on a ten dollar a week salary, that's a big thing.(p.247)
• He said, "Let's put the Big Book away again, and when you read it again, ***turn*** to the back and read some of the stories.(p.269)
• Half a block from the house, I tried to ***turn*** the corner.(p.276)
• The next day he turned me over to a couple who, although neither was an alcoholic, knew Dr. Bob and were willing to drive me to Akron where they would ***turn*** me over to his care.(p.278)
• Having no one else to ***turn*** to, I was willing to give Him a chance, although with considerable doubt.(p.280)
• Please let me ***turn*** it over to you."(p.280)
• I went to a minister and a doctor that I still knew and they, in ***turn***, asked me how long I had been sober.(p.293)
• I learned that a person just can't find a job hanging in a dive or barroom all day and all night, as jobs don't seem to ***turn*** up in those places.(p.300)
• I went on, realizing what I was becoming, hating myself for it, bitter, blaming life, blaming everything else but the fact that I should ***turn*** about and do something about my drinking.(p.337)
• The Third Step said: "Made a decision to ***turn*** our will and our lives over to the care of God as we understood Him."(p.350)
• We've got to ***turn*** the whole business over to some joker we can't even see!(p.350)
• Here he is powerless, unmanageable, in the grip of something bigger than he is, and he's got to ***turn*** the whole business over to someone else!(p.350)
• Who is this fellow we are supposed to ***turn*** everything over to?(p.350)
• I needed alcohol from that night on, and it in ***turn*** used me, ruling my life for three years.(p.353)
• All of which could ***turn*** out but one thing -- a very popular, but spoiled, brat.(p.357)
• I didn't know which way to ***turn***.(p.391)
• He, in ***turn***, kicked me so I fell to the ground.(p.406)
• The remorse would ***turn*** inside out, and become anticipatory pleasure.(p.408)
• Whatever the root of my unhappiness might ***turn*** out to be, I thought, it could not possibly be booze.(p.433)
• I learned what a devastating effect it can have on a child to coddle him and build him up, and then ***turn*** and beat him savagely, as had happened to me.(p.434)
• I crawled back to my analyst, not so much because I had faith in him, but because I had nowhere else to ***turn***.(p.435)
• Many times in the intervening years I have thanked God for that man, a man who had the courage to admit failure, a man who had the humility to confess that all the hard-won learning of his profession could not ***turn*** up the answer.(p.436)
• Still, I couldn't ***turn*** my mouth off.(p.442)
• For years, I was sure the worst thing that could happen to a nice guy like me would be that I would ***turn*** out to be an alcoholic.(p.449)
• Forgive me – I cannot write further about this latest ***turn*** of events, anticipating seeing the family I deserted so long ago.(p.463)
• The word "alcoholic" does not ***turn*** me off any more; in fact, it is music to my ears when it applies to me.(p.463)
• I have come to believe that my illness is spiritual as well as physical and mental, and I know that for help in the spiritual sphere I have to ***turn*** to a Higher Power.(p.473)
• I want to stop this bad life, but where to ***turn***?(p.475)
• I ***turn*** on the light.(p.501)
• I get in bed and ***turn*** out the light.(p.503)
• "Pity me the heart that is slow to learn What the quick mind sees at every ***turn***."(p.534)
• Was I the disloyal sort who would ***turn*** his back on this, my last and truest friend?(p.539)
• And if I had been able to ***turn*** to the church at that time I'm sure they could not have convinced me my sickness was within myself, nor could they have shown me the need for self-analysis that A.A. has shown me is vital if I am to survive.(p.546)

turned
• That alcoholic ***turned*** out to be the Akron physician.(p.xvi)
• I was very lonely and again ***turned*** to alcohol.(p.1)
• We ***turned*** back to the list, for it held the key to the future.(p.66)
• Trying to avoid this humbling experience, they have ***turned*** to easier methods.(p.72)
• You need this information to put yourself in his place, to see how you would like him to approach you if the tables were ***turned***.(p.90)
• With a shiver, he ***turned*** away and walked down the lobby to the church directory.(p.154)
• After several failures to find others, a fourth ***turned*** up.(p.158)
• So, after hearing some more of my story, he ***turned*** around and said to Doc -- I don't think he knew I heard him, but I did – he said, "Well, I believe he's worth saving and working on."(p.185)

• Before our visit was over, Bill suddenly *turned* to his wife and said, "Go fetch my clothes, dear.(p.189)
• It was getting pretty dark and I hadn't *turned* on any lights, when some big fellow stepped inside the door and flipped on the light switch.(p.207)
• The man *turned* out to be Bill D., a very early member of A.A., and I couldn't tell you a word of what he said.(p.208)
• That armor had *turned* into prison walls, locking me in loneliness – and fear.(p.226)
• Then I *turned* two company cars over in a short time and Bingo -- fired again.(p.242)
• My loneliness was worse than it had ever been before, for now even my own kind had *turned* against me.(p.247)
• My thoughts sometimes *turned* to the idea that there must be a remedy.(p.256)
• There was a man watching, and I *turned* to him and said with a defiant air I carried with me all the time, "If I don't quit this I'm going to have to join that alcoholic business they're talking about."(p.266)
• I often think how that could have *turned* some people away, because there were no other women alcoholics there then.(p.269)
• In the spiritual strength I had found, because of A.A., I felt that I had made a complete surrender, that I had really *turned* my life over that summer.(p.271)
• Fear froze me in my tracks, but the instant I *turned* back toward home this paralyzing fear left me.(p.276)
• The next day he *turned* me over to a couple who, although neither was an alcoholic, knew Dr. Bob and were willing to drive me to Akron where they would turn me over to his care.(p.278)
• So I was driven to Akron the very next day by these Good Samaritans, and *turned* over to Dr. Bob and the then tiny Akron Group.(p.279)
• The doctor, a young man, immediately took fire with the idea, and while he did not convince the son, he *turned* over two prospects who were anxious for the program.(p.294)
• In the meantime, another doctor in Evanston became convinced that the program had possibilities, and *turned* over a woman to us to do something about.(p.295)
• I became convinced of that because I spent most of my time there and nary a job *turned* up.(p.300)
• He *turned* me in to the company commander, but I got off the hook, and that was all that mattered.(p.317)
• It *turned* out that she had been in high school with my daughter.(p.321)
• The very person who stood with me through it all and has been my greatest help was the person that I *turned* against, my husband.(p.338)
• I also *turned* against my family, my mother.(p.338)
• Because I found that everything I *turned* to became a substitute for drink.(p.339)
• So I went to my wife and asked her, wasn't there something that she and I could do to somehow get together, and she *turned* on her heel and looked me squarely in the eye, and said, "You don't care anything about my problem," and I could have smacked her, but I said to myself, "Grab on to your serenity!"(p.351)
• I had *turned* eighteen during the trip, and I despondently returned home by jet (on Daddy's bankbook) to a pair of miserable, hurt parents.(p.354)
• Help which you once continually rejected, suggestions once *turned* aside are finally accepted in desperation.(p.377)
• The servant he *turned* to was our old cook, and she liked to drink.(p.385)
• But Frank *turned* around and looked at me and said, "Esther, remember you're in jail and not at home."(p.391)
• However, I threw myself into Twelve Step work, and what I feared would be a calamity *turned* out to be the most blessed of blessings.(p.394)
• It has been a fellowship with God and man that has held good wherever I've *turned* and whatever I've done.(p.394)
• I wore a man's raincoat, *turned* inside out, a present from a friend, for now my funds were low.(p.411)
• One, the side I *turned* to myself and the world, was respectable -- even, in some ways, distinguished.(p.432)
• I remember finding myself in the middle of the night in the doctors' parking lot at the hospital with one foot in the car and one foot on the ground, not knowing which was the lead foot; finding myself hanging up the telephone – then realizing I had gotten out of bed, answered the phone, *turned* on the light, and carried on a conversation with a patient.(p.441)
• Max still works with me in the office, but we have *turned* our wills and our lives and our work over to the care of God.(p.446)
• It was as if I had, rather than a Midas touch which *turned* everything to gold, a magnifying mind that magnified whatever it focused on.(p.450)
• So we *turned* around and started back to Washington.(p.467)
• Instead, I started going to a nice private sanitarium which, after the first visit, *turned* out to be more like a country club than anything else.(p.468)
• The Higher Power to whom I had *turned*, and who had sustained me, had once again been thrust into the background, while my emotions were running my life and, as always, my emotions ran me to the bottle.(p.472)
• After our first child came my parents both became allies, but in later days, after I became an alcoholic, they both *turned* against me.(p.485)
• When you've been in a jam you've said, 'God, please do this or that,' and if it *turned* out your way that was the last of it, and if it didn't you've said 'There isn't any God' or 'He doesn't do anything for me.'(p.504)
• I knew it, and I *turned* for help to someone upon whom I had *turned* my back for many years.(p.515)
• Things got so bad, I was afraid to go on the street, so I *turned* to Mothers' Aid.(p.527)
• Then the time came when I couldn't afford whiskey, so I *turned* to wine.(p.527)
• I had just *turned* forty-six.(p.540)
• Fear of rejection and its ensuing pain were not to be risked, and I *turned* away from myself once more for the answer, this time to the drinks I had always refused before, and in alcohol I found a false courage.(p.546)
• I *turned* to religion with fervor.(p.555)
• I swore off hard liquor and *turned* to wine.(p.555)
• I got sick of the sweetness and *turned* to ale.(p.556)

turning

• We stood at the *turning* point.(p.59)
• Twenty-two years later, Doctor Bob told me that what I had done was like *turning* a switch and setting up a demand for more alcohol in my system.(p.195)
• I had to persist in my attempts to get straightened out enough to be able to use the drinks I needed, without their *turning* on me.(p.227)
• That was the *turning* point of my life.(p.302)
• That call marked the *turning* point in my life.(p.307)
• We stood at the *turning* point."(p.349)
• And having sung that phrase, I'd chuckle with amusement, *turning* into irony *turning* into self-contempt *turning* into self-pity, at the sad fate of Bob, that wonderful, poor little motherless boy who was so smart in school and who grew up to accept responsibility so early and so fast and who staggered under his burdens without a whimper until the time came when he thought he was too good for this world and so he ought to be out of it.(p.532)

turnkey

• At three-thirty the next morning, I was in Champlain Street Station, in jail for driving while intoxicated and insulting an officer; and the suit of which I was so proud was in such shape that the *turnkey* had to get me a pair of trousers to go into court in the next morning.(p.201)

turnpike

• My brother and me find work on *turnpike* in Maine.(p.475)

turns

• Whatever our ideal *turns* out to be, we must be willing to grow toward it.(p.69)
• There was one meeting a week at Bill's home in Brooklyn, and we all took *turns* there spouting off about how we had changed our lives overnight, how many drunks we had saved and straightened out, and last, but not least, how God had touched each of us personally on the shoulder.(p.246)
• Rather, I do whatever is in front of me to be done, and I leave the results up to Him; however it *turns* out, that's God's will for me.(p.452)

TV

• It was decided that all members ought to be anonymous at the level of press, radio, *TV* and films.(p.xix)
• So I'd sit up, watch old Wallace Beery movies on all-night *TV*, and drink.(p.441)

tweed

• My *tweed* suit, once a very good one, was shapeless and baggy with bare places worn in the elbows from leaning on the bar.(p.411)

twelfth

• This is our *twelfth* suggestion: Carry this message to other alcoholics!(p.89)
• In June, 1945, with another member, I made my first – and only – *Twelfth* Step call on a female alcoholic and a year later I married her.(p.249)
• And I gave him some idea of what you do, and so I made my first *Twelfth* Step call before I ever came into the program.(p.347)
• Eventually, I had to redo each of the Twelve Steps specifically with Max in mind, from the First, saying, "I am powerless over alcohol, and my homelife is unmanageable by me," to the *Twelfth*, in which I tried to think of her as a sick Al-Anon and treat her with the love I would give a sick A.A. newcomer.(p.452)
• So I jump quick from First Step to *Twelfth* Step to help my brother, living with me.(p.476)

twelve

• The second edition added the appendices, the *Twelve* Traditions, and the directions for getting in touch with A.A.(p.xi)
• This was the substance of A.A.'s *Twelve* Traditions, which are stated in full on page 564 of this book.(p.xix)
• The *Twelve* Steps that summarize the program may be called los Doce Pasos in one country, los Douze Etapes in another, but they trace exactly the same path to recovery that was blazed by the earliest members of Alcoholics Anonymous.(p.xxii)
• Taking this book down from our shelf we turn to the page which contains the *twelve* steps.(p.75)
• The next chapter is entirely devoted to Step *Twelve*.(p.88)
• He has read this volume and says he is prepared to go through with the *Twelve* Steps of the program of recovery.(p.96)
• Dr. Bob and the *twelve* men and women who here tell their stories were among the early members of A.A.'s first groups.(p.169)
• I used to put eight or *twelve* ounce bottles of alcohol in a fur lined glove and toss it onto the back airing porch when winter days got dark enough.(p.176)
• We had two children, a boy and a girl, and when the boy was about *twelve*, we broke up the marriage.(p.199)
• By that time, I had one boy in college, another a senior in high school, and a daughter about *twelve* years old.(p.215)
• I was introduced to them and Clarence proceeded to put on his *Twelve* Step work.(p.216)
• There were, at that time, in the neighborhood of *twelve* or thirteen Cleveland members who had been sober anywhere from a year and a half to a couple of months.(p.219)
• The feeling of impending disaster that had haunted me for years began to dissolve as I put into practice more and more of the *Twelve* Steps.(p.229)
• At that time the group in New York was composed of about *twelve* men who were working on the principle of every drunk for himself; we had no real formula and no name.(p.246)
• It was simple, they said, and went on to explain to me in their own language the program of recovery and daily living which we know today as the *Twelve* Steps of A.A.(p.279)
• It is, however, only the first of a series of miracles which have followed one after another as a result of my trying to apply to my daily life the principles embodies in our *Twelve* Steps.(p.280)
• It would be wonderful were I able to tell you that my confidence in God and my application of the *Twelve* Steps to my daily living have utterly banished fear.(p.284)
• The last day of my drinking career, I drank twenty-two of them between ten and *twelve* a.m. and I shall never know how many more followed them until I was poured into bed that night.(p.298)
• This and the program of recovery embodied in the *Twelve* Steps.(p.311)
• A.A.'s *Twelve* Steps showed me the way to sobriety if I wanted it.(p.320)
• And I put a Big Book by my night stand, and I put a "*Twelve* Steps and *Twelve* Tradition" in my locker at the hospital, and I got books by Emmet Fox, and I got books by God-knows-who, and I got to reading all these things.(p.348)
• I tried every gimmick that there was to get some peace of mind, but it was not until I was brought to my alcoholic knees, when I was brought to a group in my own community with the butcher, the baker, the carpenter and the mechanic, who were able to give me the *Twelve* Steps, that I was finally given some semblance of an answer to the last half of the First Step.(p.349)
• I attended my weekly meetings with regularity, reread the Big Book, attended other group meetings, gave leads when asked to and did some *Twelve* Step work whenever I was called upon to do so.(p.365)
• If I were asked what in my opinion was the most important factor in being successful in this program, besides following the *Twelve* Steps, I

would say Honesty.(p.367)
• The answer came to me very simply in the first step of the *Twelve* Steps of A.A.(p.379)
• It took me some time to realize that the *Twelve* Steps of A.A. were designed to help correct these defects of character and so help remove the obsession to drink.(p.380)
• The *Twelve* Steps, which to me are a spiritual way of living, soon meant honest thinking, not wishful thinking, open mindedness, a willingness to try and a faith to accept.(p.381)
• A "spiritual experience" to me meant attending meetings, seeing a group of people, all there for the purpose of helping each other; hearing the *Twelve* Steps and the *Twelve* Traditions read at a meeting, and hearing the Lord's Prayer, which in an A.A. meeting has such great meaning – "Thy will be done, not mine."(p.381)
• I was desperately in earnest to follow through and understand what was expected of me as a member of A.A. and to take each Step of the *Twelve* as rapidly as possible.(p.382)
• However, I threw myself into *Twelve* Step work, and what I feared would be a calamity turned out to be the most blessed of blessings.(p.394)
• *Twelve* dollars a week.(p.397)
• Saying these sprees were limited to one a week (they were not), and saying that the average spree was ten of these drinks (sometimes more, sometimes less), we come up with the first boring statistic: two-fifty per week out of *twelve* dollars.(p.397)
• Except for one short slip, during the first eight months, which was an angry "the world can't do this to me" reaction to a personal tragedy in my life, I have been sober for *twelve* years.(p.416)
• Through going to meetings and listening, and occasionally speaking, through doing *Twelve* Step work, whereby in helping others you are both the teacher and the student, by making many wonderful A.A. friends, I have been taught all the things in life that are worth having.(p.416)
• My experience has been active: three meetings a week, many tapes, many A.A. conferences, much work on the *Twelve* Steps, and much work with other alcoholics and their families.(p.420)
• And life keeps getting simpler and easier as we try to reverse my old idea, by taking care of the internal environment via the *Twelve* Steps, and letting the external environment take care of itself.)(p.446)
• Eventually, I had to redo each of the *Twelve* Steps specifically with Max in mind, from the First, saying, "I am powerless over alcohol, and my homelife is unmanageable by me," to the Twelfth, in which I tried to think of her as a sick Al-Anon and treat her with the love I would give a sick A.A. newcomer.(p.452)
• I served *twelve* years in prison, never suspecting that without alcohol I would not have been in prison at all.(p.457)
• All *Twelve* Steps of A.A. are designed to kill the old self (deflate the old ego) and build a new, free self.(p.459)
• The other of the *Twelve* Steps of Alcoholics Anonymous seemed insurmountable to me at first.(p.471)
• Had I tried honestly and sincerely to practice the *Twelve* Steps I would have seen from my continuous moral inventory that I was getting off the beam -- I would have found that there were some active resentments in my life, a terrific amount of self-pity.(p.471)
• Walk with me up *Twelve* Steps of A.A. to peace."(p.477)
• I drank from the age of *twelve* until I was thirty-two.(p.480)
• We are told to practice the *Twelve* Steps and *Twelve* Traditions to the best of our ability every day, one day at a time.(p.481)
• They taught us a great deal about *Twelve* Step work too.(p.496)
• A.A.'s *Twelve* Steps may confuse you when you read them over.(p.516)
• They suggested that I study the A.A. book and try to take the *Twelve* Steps according to the explanation in the Book, for it was their opinion that the application of these principles in our daily lives will get us sober and keep us sober.(p.550)
• By learning – through practicing the *Twelve* Steps and through sharing at meetings – how to cope with the problems that we looked to booze to solve, back in our drinking days.(p.560)
• THE *TWELVE* TRADITIONS(p.564)
• *Twelve* – Anonymity is the spiritual foundation of all our Traditions, ever reminding us to place principles before personalities.(p.564)
• THE *TWELVE* TRADITIONS (The Long Form)(p.565)

twelve-year

• Because I had been drunk, the judge gave me only a *twelve-year* sentence in prison.(p.528)

Twelve Steps

• The *Twelve Steps* that summarize the program may be called los Doce Pasos in one country, los Douze Etapes in another, but they trace exactly the same path to recovery that was blazed by the earliest members of Alcoholics Anonymous.(p.xxii)
• Taking this book down from our shelf we turn to the page which contains the *twelve steps*.(p.75)
• He has read this volume and says he is prepared to go through with the *Twelve Steps* of the program of recovery.(p.96)
• The feeling of impending disaster that had haunted me for years began to dissolve as I put into practice more and more of the *Twelve Steps*.(p.229)
• It was simple, they said, and went on to explain to me in their own language the program of recovery and daily living which we know today as the *Twelve Steps* of A.A.(p.279)
• It is, however, only the first of a series of miracles which have followed one after another as a result of my trying to apply to my daily life the principles embodies in our *Twelve Steps*.(p.280)
• It would be wonderful were I able to tell you that my confidence in God and my application of the *Twelve Steps* to my daily living have utterly banished fear.(p.284)
• This and the program of recovery embodied in the *Twelve Steps*.(p.311)
• A.A.'s *Twelve Steps* showed me the way to sobriety if I wanted it.(p.320)
• And I put a Big Book by my night stand, and I put a "*Twelve Steps* and Twelve Tradition" in my locker at the hospital, and I got books by Emmet Fox, and I got books by God-knows-who, and I got to reading all these things.(p.348)
• I tried every gimmick that there was to get some peace of mind, but it was not until I was brought to my alcoholic knees, when I was brought to a group in my own community with the butcher, the baker, the carpenter and the mechanic, who were able to give me the *Twelve Steps*, that I was finally given some semblance of an answer to the last half of the First Step.(p.349)
• If I were asked what in my opinion was the most important factor in being successful in this program, besides following the *Twelve Steps*, I would say Honesty.(p.367)
• The answer came to me very simply in the first step of the *Twelve Steps* of A.A.(p.379)
• It took me some time to realize that the *Twelve Steps* of A.A. were designed to help correct these defects of character and so help remove the obsession to drink.(p.380)
• The *Twelve Steps*, which to me are a spiritual way of living, soon meant honest thinking, not wishful thinking, open mindedness, a willingness to try and a faith to accept.(p.381)
• A "spiritual experience" to me meant attending meetings, seeing a group of people, all there for the purpose of helping each other; hearing the *Twelve Steps* and the Twelve Traditions read at a meeting, and hearing the Lord's Prayer, which in an A.A. meeting has such great meaning – "Thy will be done, not mine."(p.381)
• My experience has been active: three meetings a week, many tapes, many A.A. conferences, much work on the *Twelve Steps*, and much work with other alcoholics and their families.(p.420)
• And life keeps getting simpler and easier as we try to reverse my old idea, by taking care of the internal environment via the *Twelve Steps*, and letting the external environment take care of itself.)(p.446)
• Eventually, I had to redo each of the *Twelve Steps* specifically with Max in mind, from the First, saying, "I am powerless over alcohol, and my homelife is unmanageable by me," to the Twelfth, in which I tried to think of her as a sick Al-Anon and treat her with the love I would give a sick A.A. newcomer.(p.452)
• All *Twelve Steps* of A.A. are designed to kill the old self (deflate the old ego) and build a new, free self.(p.459)
• The other of the *Twelve Steps* of Alcoholics Anonymous seemed insurmountable to me at first.(p.471)
• Had I tried honestly and sincerely to practice the *Twelve Steps* I would have seen from my continuous moral inventory that I was getting off the beam -- I would have found that there were some active resentments in my life, a terrific amount of self-pity.(p.471)
• Walk with me up *Twelve Steps* of A.A. to peace."(p.477)
• We are told to practice the *Twelve Steps* and Twelve Traditions to the best of our ability every day, one day at a time.(p.481)
• A.A.'s *Twelve Steps* may confuse you when you read them over.(p.516)
• They suggested that I study the A.A. book and try to take the *Twelve Steps* according to the explanation in the Book, for it was their opinion that the application of these principles in our daily lives will get us sober and keep us sober.(p.550)
• By learning – through practicing the *Twelve Steps* and through sharing at meetings – how to cope with the problems that we looked to booze to solve, back in our drinking days.(p.560)

Twelve Traditions

• The second edition added the appendices, the *Twelve Traditions*, and the directions for getting in touch with A.A.(p.xi)
• This was the substance of A.A.'s *Twelve Traditions*, which are stated in full on page 564 of this book.(p.xix)
• A "spiritual experience" to me meant attending meetings, seeing a group of people, all there for the purpose of helping each other; hearing the Twelve Steps and the *Twelve Traditions* read at a meeting, and hearing the Lord's Prayer, which in an A.A. meeting has such great meaning – "Thy will be done, not mine."(p.381)
• We are told to practice the Twelve Steps and *Twelve Traditions* to the best of our ability every day, one day at a time.(p.481)
• THE *TWELVE TRADITIONS*(p.564)
• THE *TWELVE TRADITIONS* (The Long Form)(p.565)

twenties

• The great boom of the late *twenties* was seething and swelling.(p.3)
• It fell apart in the *twenties*.(p.197)
• In my early *twenties* the hardships of hobo life did not discourage me, but I had no wish to become just a tramp.(p.253)
• All I can remember about the Roaring *Twenties* is that I drank a great deal, thought I was having a grand time, managed to get to Europe for a few weeks, was very proud of the dozens of speak-easy cards entitling me to an entree in the better joints between Cleveland and New York, took on a wife, and built a home in a fashionable suburb of Cleveland.(p.358)
• In my *twenties*, I found Edna St. Vincent Millay's verse:(p.534)
• There was the sense of being "misunderstood," when as a matter of fact by my middle *twenties* I was quite popular, although I hadn't grown much bigger physically.(p.534)

twentieth

• Nevertheless, the *twentieth* century readily accepts theories of all kinds, provided they are firmly grounded in fact.(p.48)
• He is like the retired business man who lolls in the Florida sunshine in the winter complaining of the sad state of the nation; the minister who sighs over the sins of the *twentieth* century; politicians and reformers who are sure all would be Utopia if the rest of the world would only behave; the outlaw safe cracker who thinks society has wronged him; and the alcoholic who has lost all and is locked up.(p.61)

twenty

• Several of our crowd, men of thirty or less, had been drinking only a few years, but they found themselves as helpless as those who had been drinking *twenty* years.(p.33)
• We must remember that ten or *twenty* years of drunkenness would make a skeptic out of anyone.(p.83)
• And we stood there for *twenty* minutes, telling each other how much better we were, how much better we looked, how much better off we were financially, mentally, physically, morally, and in every way, shape and manner.(p.201)
• I was always interested in mechanics and after having about *twenty* miscellaneous jobs, lasting from one day to two weeks, I obtained a job as a toolmaker apprentice.(p.211)
• A low ebb in the family fortunes necessitated my going to work when I was *twenty*.(p.275)
• I was married at *twenty*, had two children and was divorced at twenty-three.(p.305)
• I belong to more medical societies and honor societies than men ten to *twenty* years my senior.(p.345)
• Attending his fourth or fifth meeting was an old friend I had not seen for *twenty* years.(p.365)
• A retired Navy man looks back over *twenty* years of drinking, to add up his A.A. "initiation fee."(p.396)
• To keep it in round figures, let's say *twenty* per cent of my income went for giggle gurgles.(p.397)
• After a few more estimates as to income and expenditures for booze over a few sample years, taken at

random, I conclude that this *twenty* per cent stayed fairly constant.(p.398)

• So I spent *twenty* years in the Navy.(p.398)

• So I believe that *twenty* percent is a very conservative estimate of the amount of income I blew.(p.399)

• For an estimate of salary from the twenty-one a month to start with, to over $400 per month upon my retirement after *twenty* years in the Navy, I believe that an average income of $2,000 a year over this period is low, but as I stated earlier, an underestimate is best.(p.399)

• $2,000 a year for twenty-five years is $50,000, *twenty* per cent of which is $10,000.(p.399)

• I could tell him a lot of reasons why I am here in an alky ward at the age of *twenty*.(p.423)

• I got emergency leave for *twenty* days.(p.426)

• I was only *twenty* now, but I was a man.(p.427)

• The first time I remember seeing or hearing of A.A. was *twenty* years ago.(p.460)

• I started drinking socially and at parties and proms when I was about *twenty* years old.(p.464)

• I wasted *twenty* years of my life, and there is nothing I can do about that, but there is something I can do about now.(p.480)

• At one time, I was using *twenty* caps a day; I nearly died half a dozen times on the street.(p.480)

• After *twenty* years in prison for murder, he knew A.A. was the spot for him . . . if he wanted to stay on the outside.(p.508)

• For that crime I received a minimum of *twenty* years and a maximum of natural life.(p.508)

• I clung to the outfit for the balance of my time, and finally I was released, after having spent *twenty* years and nine months behind bars.(p.510)

• She was the one who really helped me to make a go of that *twenty* years and nine months in prison.(p.511)

twenty-eight

• I married when I was *twenty-eight* years old, and started in law school after I was married.(p.212)

• That was skeptically received by me when I first heard it, but after some *twenty-eight* or thirty fellows had come to see me, and pretty nearly all of them had said the same thing, I began to believe it.(p.219)

• I was *twenty-eight* years old.(p.418)

• Max and I had been married for *twenty-eight* years when I ended up in A.A.(p.439)

twenty-five

• An exceptional man, he remained bone dry for *twenty-five* years and retired at the age of fifty-five, after a successful and happy business career.(p.32)

• I kept myself so busy that outside of some school and group parties, I didn't go overboard on drinking very much between the ages of *twenty-five* and thirty.(p.213)

• My efficiency as a professional man was probably reduced to *twenty-five* per cent of what it should have been.(p.215)

• Three years later, at *twenty-five*, I opened and operated their Philadelphia office and was earning more than I ever have since.(p.242)

• I was about *twenty-five* then, and I had never touched a drop.(p.262)

• At *twenty-five* I had developed an alcoholic problem.(p.305)

• Between the ages of *twenty-five* and thirty I tried everything.(p.305)

• I didn't particularly like it, but I loved the effects, and managed for the next *twenty-five* years to drink anything and everything, either handed to me or purchased, at the slightest excuse.(p.357)

• After all, upon coming out of a week-long or ten-day drunk, it was hard enough to figure up just how much that one drunk cost, let alone trying to calculate the cost of approximately *twenty-five* years of active alcoholism.(p.396)

• *Twenty-five* years of drinking!(p.397)

• $2,000 a year for *twenty-five* years is $50,000, twenty per cent of which is $10,000.(p.399)

• In all the *twenty-five* years of my drinking there were only a few occasions when I took a morning drink.(p.432)

• It was against my mother and it was *twenty-five* years old.(p.551)

twenty-four

• Faith has to work *twenty-four* hours a day in and through us, or we perish.(p.16)

• On awakening let us think about the *twenty-four* hours ahead.(p.86)

• The next question they asked was, "You can quit *twenty-four* hours can't you?"(p.188)

• I said, "Sure, yes, anybody can do that, for *twenty-four* hours."(p.188)

• Just *twenty-four* hours at a time."(p.188)

• Every time I'd start thinking about drinking, I would think of the long, dry years ahead without having a drink; but this idea of *twenty-four* hours, that it was up to me from then on, was a lot of help.(p.188)

• Many friends of my family had emigrated to America, so at *twenty-four* I decided that the United States offered me the opportunity I was never likely to find in my native land.(p.231)

• Live *twenty-four* hours at a time, they say.(p.320)

• "*Twenty-four* hours a day."(p.382)

• Not understanding the *twenty-four* hour plan, or not wanting to, I began drinking and was off-again on-again, during that first month.(p.414)

• I got off the so-called wagon, and on the *twenty-four* hour plan.(p.415)

• And also, on the *twenty-four* hour plan, it taught me how to live.(p.416)

• During the *twenty-four* hours after running into the Serenity Prayer, I think I took the first three Steps for the first time.(p.461)

• During these seven years a thing called the *Twenty-four* Hour Program --a gadget I used to think was only a snare to trap the newcomer -- has come to mean much to me, not only as regards my drinking but in the whole pattern of my life.(p.473)

twenty-four-year-old

• I am a *twenty-four-year-old* alcoholic.(p.317)

• Like I said, I'm a *twenty-four-year-old* alcoholic -- and I'm happy.(p.320)

twenty-nine

• The last time I drank, when I was *twenty-nine*, I drank for only four days, yet I threatened to kill my children; I beat my wife at home and on the church steps; I mistreated a child in my office; and I ran to a hospital for mental illness to avoid jail.(p.418)

• By *twenty-nine*, I was having trouble coping with life because of my drinking.(p.555)

twenty-odd

• *Twenty-odd* years ago I made a mess out of my one and only marriage.(p.286)

twenty-one

• For eighteen years, from the age of *twenty-one* to thirty-nine, fear governed my life.(p.275)

• By the time I was *twenty-one* I had six years of life in foreign countries, spoke three languages fluently, and had attended college for two years.(p.275)

• I was free, white and *twenty-one* and I had a time for myself.(p.386)

• At age *twenty-one*, I enlisted in the Navy for two reasons: (1) to avoid being drafted into the Army, and (2) out of a burst of patriotic fervor inspired by the advent of World War II and as the result of an all-night drinking binge which found me sitting on the doorstep of the Navy recruiting office when the chief petty officer arrived to open for business at nine o'clock Monday morning.(p.398)

• My first pay was ten dollars, pay for recruits at that time being *twenty-one* dollars per month.(p.398)

• For an estimate of salary from the *twenty-one* a month to start with, to over $400 per month upon my retirement after twenty years in the Navy, I believe that an average income of $2,000 a year over this period is low, but as I stated earlier, an underestimate is best.(p.399)

• When I was *twenty-one*, my cousin come home from U.S. Army on leave.(p.474)

twenty-seven

• This continued until I was *twenty-seven*.(p.287)

• I thought my problem was that I had been married to a drunk for *twenty-seven* years.(p.321)

• I said, "*Twenty-seven* years."(p.322)

• She said, "*Twenty-seven* years to an alcoholic!(p.322)

• *Twenty-seven* years of confusion is what my early married life was.(p.325)

twenty-seven-year-old

• It was my ex-wife, and she said my *twenty-seven-year-old* son, who has completed his Marine Corps training and graduated from college, wanted to see me privately, was getting married in three months, and wanted me at the wedding.(p.462)

twenty-six

• I'm *twenty-six* now and I haven't had a drink since I made my decision.(p.430)

• Strangely enough, right through to the end of my *twenty-six* years in the Army, I was still being offered very good and important jobs in spite of the fact that my superiors must have known that I wasn't thoroughly reliable.(p.519)

twenty-three

• I was married at twenty, had two children and was divorced at *twenty-three*.(p.305)

• At the tender age of *twenty-three*, I got a divorce.(p.402)

• Three weeks ago, my phone rang, and a voice I hadn't heard in over *twenty-three* years spoke.(p.462)

• A *twenty-three* million dollar surplus wiped out.(p.500)

• I was married and divorced again before I was *twenty-three* years old, this time to a prominent band leader -- a man that many women wanted.(p.546)

• The only importance in all of this lies in the fact that at *twenty-three* I was just as sick as I was at thirty three, when I came into A.A., but at that time I apparently had no place to go because I had no drinking problem.(p.546)

twenty-two

• *Twenty-two*, and a veteran of foreign wars, I went home at last.(p.1)

• *Twenty-two* years later, Doctor Bob told me that what I had done was like turning a switch and setting up a demand for more alcohol in my system.(p.195)

• Anyhow, I recognized the fact that I couldn't drink like normal people, but I tried hard and kept on trying for *twenty-two* years.(p.196)

• The last day of my drinking career, I drank *twenty-two* of them between ten and twelve a.m. and I shall never know how many more followed them until I was poured into bed that night.(p.298)

• But I didn't want to stop drinking — not at *twenty-two*.(p.429)

• I joined A.A. at *twenty-two*.(p.430)

• By age *twenty-two*, I was a daily drinker.(p.555)

twice

• So I was barred from the plant for ten days, and during that ten day period I was drunk *twice*, showing how little control these restraints had on me.(p.205)

• I refused to join any fraternity, as I wanted to be a free lance, and that year my drinking was confined to one-night stands, once or *twice* a week.(p.241)

• I was sent to a psychiatrist, for they didn't think it was normal for me to want to kill my platoon sergeant or to attempt suicide *twice*.(p.318)

• They passed me over for promotion *twice*.(p.318)

• I went to A.A. meetings *twice* a week.(p.320)

• My guild had elected me president *twice* and later given me a "man of the year" award.(p.328)

• With more physical courage than I had possessed, she had *twice* tried to take her life.(p.414)

• Once or *twice*, during my early drinking, I carried it over into the second day, and only once, that I can remember, did it continue into the third.(p.432)

• In those years I was in jail nine times, in an alcoholic ward, overnight, *twice*; and I was fired from three jobs, two of them very good ones.(p.536)

• Once, or even *twice*, such incidents might be amusing.(p.538)

• When I remark that I have been in jail nine times, and in an alcoholic ward *twice*, they think I'm kidding, or possibly dramatizing for the sake of a good yarn.(p.542)

twinkling

• Now about health: A body badly burned by alcohol does not often recover overnight nor do twisted thinking and depression vanish in a *twinkling*.(p.133)

• My past had slipped before me in a *twinkling*.(p.427)

twist

• We doubt if many of them can do it, because none will really want to stop, and hardly one of them, because of the peculiar mental *twist* already acquired, will find he can win out.(p.33)

• We pocket our pride and go to it, illuminating every *twist* of character, every dark cranny of the past.(p.75)

• Show him the mental *twist* which leads to the first drink of a spree.(p.92)

twisted

• Now about health: A body badly burned by alcohol does not often recover overnight nor do *twisted* thinking and depression vanish in a twinkling.(p.133)

twists

• The mental *twists* that led up to my drinking began many years before I ever took a drink for I am one of those whose history proves conclusively that my drinking was "a symptom of a deeper trouble."(p.544)

two

• "Bill's Story," "Doctor Bob's Nightmare," and one other personal history from the first edition were retained intact; three were edited and one of these was retitled; new versions of *two* stories were written with new titles; thirty completely new stories were added; and the story section was divided into three

parts, under the same headings that are used now.(p.xi)
• Hence the *two* men set to work almost frantically upon alcoholics arriving in the ward of the Akron City Hospital.(p.xvii)
• For this there were *two* principal reasons: the large numbers of recoveries, and reunited homes.(p.xx)
• But great numbers of these – about *two* out of three – began to return as time passed.(p.xx)
• "Bathtub" gin, *two* bottles a day, and often three, got to be routine.(p.5)
• So *two* bottles, and – oblivion.(p.6)
• The mind and body are marvelous mechanisms, for mine endured this agony *two* more years.(p.6)
• In a matter of fact way he told how *two* men had appeared in court, persuading the judge to suspend his commitment.(p.9)
• That was *two* months ago and the result was self-evident.(p.9)
• We were in a position where life was becoming impossible, and if we had passed into the region from which there is no return through human aid we had but *two* alternatives: One was to go on to the bitter end, blotting out the consciousness of our intolerable situation as best we could; and the other, to accept spiritual help.(p.25)
• In *two* months he was in a hospital, puzzled and humiliated.(p.32)
• "*Two* of the members of Alcoholics Anonymous came to see me.(p.42)
• As to *two* of you men, whose stories I have heard, there is no doubt in my mind that you were 100% hopeless, apart from divine help.(p.43)
• We could not prove life in the sense that you can prove a straight line is the shortest distance between *two* points, yet, there it was.(p.54)
• *Two*: Your husband is showing lack of control, for he is unable to stay on the water wagon even when he wants to.(p.109)
• Three: This husband has gone much further than husband number *two*.(p.109)
• Though once like number *two* he became worse.(p.109)
• Suppose, however, that your husband fits the description of number *two*.(p.112)
• At the beginning of recovery a man will take, as a rule, one of *two* directions.(p.125)
• Not long afterward he had called me from Hartford on *two* successive days, so drunk he could hardly speak.(p.136)
• After *two* weeks of drinking, he had placed his toe on the trigger of a loaded shotgun -- the barrel in his mouth.(p.137)
• This seemed to me like an opportunity to be helpful, so I spent *two* hours talking about alcoholism, the malady, and described the symptoms and results as well as I could.(p.138)
• If this presents difficulty, re-reading chapters *two* and three, where the alcoholic sickness is discussed at length might be worth while.(p.140)
• There are *two* alcoholic employees, who produce as much as five normal salesmen.(p.149)
• But life was not easy for the *two* friends.(p.156)
• *Two* days later, a future fellow of Alcoholics Anonymous stared glassily at the strangers beside his bed.(p.157)
• For an hour, the *two* friends told him about their drinking experiences.(p.157)
• The *two* friends spoke of their spiritual experience and told him about the course of action they carried out.(p.157)
• Little clusters of twos and threes and fives of us have sprung up in other communities, through contact with our *two* larger centers.(p.162)
• I was, of course, soon on the carpet and the upshot was that I had to go back for *two* more quarters and remain absolutely dry, if I wished to graduate.(p.174)
• I conducted myself so creditably that I was able to secure a much coveted internship in a western city, where I spent *two* years.(p.174)
• During these *two* years I was kept so busy that I hardly left the hospital at all.(p.174)
• When those *two* years were up, I opened an office downtown.(p.174)
• Finally my father had to send a doctor out from my home town who managed to get me back there in some way, and I was in bed about *two* months before I could venture out of the house.(p.175)
• During the next few years, I developed *two* distinct phobias.(p.175)
• I put on thirty pounds of weight in about *two* months, looked like a pig, and was uncomfortable from shortness of breath.(p.177)
• I gave the matter much time and study for the next *two* and a half years, but still got tight every night nevertheless.(p.178)
• Unlike most of our crowd, I did not get over my craving for liquor much during the first *two* and one-half years of abstinence.(p.181)
• On the return trip, after *two* or three loads, I passed out and had to be carried to the house.(p.183)
• However, after *two* or three trials, I found this was not satisfactory because they did not serve enough to satisfy me.(p.184)
• Away from my office *two* or three weeks at a time; horrible days and nights when I would lie on the floor of my home, lying awake and reaching over to get the bottle, taking a drink and going back into oblivion.(p.184)
• During the first six months of 1935, I was hospitalized eight times for intoxication and shackled to the bed *two* or three days before I even knew where I was.(p.184)
• Then she told me that these *two* drunks she had been talking to had a plan whereby they thought they could quit drinking, and part of that plan was that they tell it to another drunk.(p.185)
• I looked up and there were *two* great big fellows over six foot tall, very likable looking.(p.185)
• (I knew afterwards that the *two* who came in were Bill W. and Doctor Bob.)(p.185)
• After a while, Bill said, "Well, now, you've been talking a good long time, let me talk a minute or *two*."(p.185)
• Whether you quit six days, months, or years, if you go out and take a drink or *two* you'll end up in this hospital tied down, just like you have been in these past six months.(p.187)
• And they said, "No, you have a disease, and it doesn't make any difference how long you do without it, after a drink or *two* you'll end up just like you are now."(p.187)
• *Two* days before this, Dr. Bob had said to me, "If you and I are going to stay sober, we had better get busy."(p.188)
• Had blacked the eyes of *two* nurses, and now they had him strapped down tight.(p.188)
• It was in the next *two* or three days after I had first met Doc and Bill, that I finally came to a decision to turn my will over to God and to go along with this program the best that I could.(p.189)
• I know there was even more, something that I hadn't got, and I remember one day, a week or *two* after I had come out of the hospital, Bill was over to my house talking to my wife and me.(p.191)
• I felt having gotten married, I was an adult and one of the first things I did was to buy *two* cases of whiskey with no idea of drinking it.(p.196)
• So in spite of anything that I might do, I prospered, being one of only *two* brokers in the rubber center of the world.(p.197)
• I can well remember sitting with seven dollars in my pocket, planning on giving my family a hundred or *two* hundred dollars, when I made it next year.(p.197)
• We had *two* children, a boy and a girl, and when the boy was about twelve, we broke up the marriage.(p.199)
• So I had one double-header every night for about *two* or three weeks.(p.203)
• I think the longest drunk I was ever on was eleven days, but usually only *two* days with a complete blackout for a day, and then backing off by drinking as long as I could get anything.(p.203)
• I was arrested and taken to jail where I was beaten up by *two* or three fellows who were already in there and whom I tried to boss.(p.204)
• I got *two* drinks, each of them a quarter of that pint, in me, and was talking along with these people, but I felt that sooner or later they were going to have me cornered because they were smarter than I was and the drink was beginning to take effect; but as I reached for the third drink Bob said, "Listen, Buster, you promised to take some medicine if we got you a drink.(p.206)
• I was always interested in mechanics and after having about twenty miscellaneous jobs, lasting from one day to *two* weeks, I obtained a job as a toolmaker apprentice.(p.211)
• After I was on the drafting board about *two* years I decided I wanted a technical education.(p.211)
• I did not have a high school education so I went to night school to take the full high school course, which I finished in *two* years and nine months.(p.211)
• As a matter of fact, I had *two* children at the time I was admitted to the bar.(p.212)
• The first definite indications of an alcoholic pattern began to arise when I would go to New York on business and disappear, and wind up in Philadelphia or Boston for *two* or three day periods.(p.213)
• After *two* or three years of effort along this line, I reached the point of actual despair that I ever would be able to drink only a harmless amount each day.(p.215)
• I had *two* partners.(p.215)
• Bill bought me a drink or *two* on the way, and Dorothy S. came with us, and the three of us went over to the City Hospital.(p.217)
• I'd only had *two* with her, but I'd managed four in the fifteen minutes I'd waited for her, and of course I'd had the usual uncounted swigs from the bottle as I painfully got up and did my slow spasmodic dressing.(p.223)
• It took three-quarters of an hour and *two* changes to get there -- back to my starting point.(p.223)
• That went on for *two* more months before I landed in a hospital and started my slow fight back to normalcy.(p.224)
• At that time I could go into any saloon, have one or *two* beers, walk out and forget about it.(p.231)
• But I hardly tasted anything for *two* years and started in business for myself, founding a mattress factory which is today an important industrial enterprise in our city.(p.232)
• Unlike many other Catholics who frequently take pledges for definite periods – a year, *two* years or for good, I never had any desire to "take a pledge" before the priest.(p.234)
• Had he come *two* or three days later I think I would have thrown him out, but he hit when I was open for anything.(p.239)
• In the next *two* years I washed more pans and peeled more potatoes than any other dough-boy.(p.241)
• I was the fair-haired boy all right, but *two* years later I was blacklisted as an irresponsible drunk.(p.242)
• Then I turned *two* company cars over in a short time and Bingo -- fired again.(p.242)
• He had also gone all the way through the wringer and had been dry *two* years when I saw him again.(p.243)
• For the last *two* years of my drinking I prayed on every drunk that I wouldn't wake up again.(p.245)
• After being dry *two* weeks and sticking close to Jackie, all of a sudden I found I had become the sponsor of my sponsor, for he was suddenly taken drunk.(p.245)
• Bill had then been dry three years and Hank, *two*.(p.245)
• After a very good week, *two* of my customers took me to lunch on Saturday.(p.247)
• Very rarely do I miss the meetings of my neighborhood A.A. group, and my average has never been less than *two* meetings a week.(p.249)
• She had just come in and was scheduled to sail in *two* days.(p.252)
• Curious about it, feeling I was missing something, absolutely without any illusions about the aftermath, with no pronounced feeling of patriotism, I joined up with a Canadian regiment, serving a little over *two* years.(p.253)
• In the *two* succeeding years I held ten different jobs ranging from newspaper copy-desk and rewrite, to traffic director for an oil field equipment company.(p.255)
• As I look back on the events of *two* months, I can clearly see that I had been circling around, half-afraid of encountering the remedy for my situation, half wanting it, deferring fulfillment of my promise to get in touch with the doctor I had heard about.(p.258)
• Singly and in groups of *two* or three, they came to visit me.(p.258)
• When I came to my aunt, she knew that I had had an unhappy childhood, and she said, "Now, Ethel, you're welcome to have boy friends in our home, but there are *two* boys in this town that I don't want you to date, and one of them comes from a very fine family, one of the best.(p.262)
• We had *two* daughters.(p.262)
• Finally, it got so bad that I left him and went back home and took my *two* children with me.(p.262)
• These vacations became quite something, and he always had *two* weeks vacation the first *two* weeks of every September.(p.264)
• He came with *two* cans of beer.(p.267)
• There were *two* women in the St. Thomas Hospital at that time in a room.(p.272)
• In the end I had *two* problems instead of one: Fear and alcohol.(p.275)
• By the time I was twenty-one I had six years of life in foreign countries, spoke three languages fluently, and had attended college for *two* years.(p.275)
• The next *two* years were simply a long drawn out process of less and less work and more and

more whiskey.(p.278)

• Out of this maelstrom just *two* coherent thoughts came to the surface; one, a drink would mean homelessness and death; *two*, I could no longer relieve the pressure of fear by starting home, as was once my habitual solution to this problem, because I no longer had a home.(p.279)

• It would be impossible for me to pass over this year without mentioning my love for, and my indebtedness to these *two* wonderful people who are no longer with us.(p.280)

• We spent *two* days there together before he returned to New York.(p.281)

• While there, *two* or three more "cash customers" (as Dr. Bob used to call them -- probably because they had so little cash) were shipped in to us from Detroit.(p.282)

• This gave me the freedom to do A.A. work, and to rest for periods of *two* or three days when I became too exhausted to carry on.(p.283)

• With this specialized training, and a liberal business education in the school of hard knocks, I was able to set up shop some *two* years later as an independent accountant.(p.284)

• I am very apt to get into quite an uproar for a day or *two* before starting, but I do start, and once started, I have a swell time.(p.285)

• By 1932, I was going on *two* or three day benders.(p.288)

• Then when we got back to the apartment, he was willing to wait *two* or three days until I got my health back to be paid off for the liquor and fare.(p.289)

• He mentioned *two* of them that I had known through the years and suggested that I talk with them.(p.289)

• He spent *two* hours with me that night telling me his story.(p.290)

• The next afternoon and evening, *two* other men visited me and each told me his story and the things that they were doing to try to recover from this tragic illness.(p.290)

• In the next *two* or three days the balance of this handful of men contacted me, encouraged me, and told me how they were trying to live this program of recovery and the fun they were having doing it.(p.291)

• I stayed in Akron *two* or three weeks on my initial trip trying to absorb as much of the program and philosophy as possible.(p.291)

• I spent a great deal of time with Dr. Bob, whenever he had the time to spare, and in the homes of *two* or three other people, trying to see how the family lived the program.(p.291)

• One of them was that I would try to get a group started in Chicago; the second was that I would have to return to Akron to attend meetings at least every *two* months until I did get a group started in Chicago; third, I decided I must place this program above everything else, even my family, because if I did not maintain my sobriety I would lose my family anyway.(p.292)

• A week later, I had to get an old friend from Akron to spend *two* days sobering me up.(p.293)

• In the spring of 1939, the Big Book was printed, and we had *two* inquiries from the New York office because of a fifteen-minute radio talk that was made.(p.294)

• Neither one of the *two* was interested for himself, one being a mother who wanted to do something for her son.(p.294)

• The doctor, a young man, immediately took fire with the idea, and while he did not convince the son, he turned over *two* prospects who were anxious for the program.(p.294)

• If I were alone I would stop at four or five of them, but only one or *two* in the event I had my mistrusting wife with me.(p.299)

• I never enjoyed any meal, but I ate my lunch at noon for *two* reasons; first, to help me get out of the fog of the night before and, second, to furnish some measure of nourishment.(p.299)

• From a physical standpoint, I gained sixteen pounds in the first *two* months I was off liquor.(p.303)

• I was married at twenty, had *two* children and was divorced at twenty-three.(p.305)

• Some of us struggle with these people because we know that they are really very sick, but we also know that short of some miracle, we are not going to help them except temporarily, and that they will inevitably get worse and worse until one of *two* things happens.(p.308)

• He had been dry for *two* and a half years and had been maintaining his contact with a group of recovered alcoholics in Akron.(p.309)

• Shortly after I returned to Chicago, my doctor, encouraged by the results of my contact with A.A., sent us *two* more of his alcoholic patients.(p.310)

• We got along fine for about *two* weeks, until she told me where to go and to take my damn bottle with me.(p.318)

• Karen didn't want to see me any more, and neither did *two* other girls I'd been going out with.(p.318)

• If we were invited to a formal party and I knew they were only going to have one or *two* drinks, I wouldn't have any.(p.323)

• I was being very cagey, because I knew that if I did take one or *two*, I might want to take five or six or seven or eight.(p.323)

• I did try, for a day or *two*, but something always would come up that would throw me.(p.324)

• We need them so badly even if you can only give one day, or perhaps *two* days?"(p.326)

• *Two* years later, a month beyond age seventy, I was crying for help from A.A.(p.327)

• A square from ultra-dry Kansas, I did not taste grog until I had finished college, done a stint on newspapers, married, become a father, and been in studio publicity *two* years.(p.328)

• Boredom sets up every retiree for *two* chief dangers: obesity and alcoholism.(p.330)

• *Two* nights later, self-pity went even further.(p.333)

• I did go to A.A., *two* days later, walking in alone.(p.334)

• How full it has kept my retirement years -- the five I've lived since the first *two* lost in traveling a rocky road to hell, before I made a U-turn.(p.334)

• I had *two* babies.(p.335)

• When alcohol took me over, my bar was my kitchen, my living room, my bedroom, the back bathroom, and the *two* hampers.(p.335)

• But from one or *two* drinks of an afternoon or evening, my intake mounted, and mounted fast.(p.336)

• I thought the *two* would never get together.(p.338)

• The difference between the *two* vacations was this:(p.344)

• In *two* ways I may be a little different from other alcoholics.(p.345)

• There were *two* sentences in it that struck me.(p.346)

• About *two* days later I was called by a friend of mine from Nevada City -- he's a brother of my wife's closest friend.(p.347)

• By the time I figured out what had happened, I saw *two* flashing red lights atop squad cars, sedately coming around the corner.(p.353)

• Can you picture *two* girls hitchhiking their way to Las Vegas from Washington State?(p.354)

• I had every advantage a child could have, private schools (several of them), dancing schools, *two* colleges, coon skin coats, automobiles, a listing in the social register and all the rest.(p.357)

• I had no trouble at all in being elected to the *two* drinking societies at my college.(p.357)

• In 1940 another good opportunity came up and we moved to Pittsburgh where I was to manage *two* radio stations under the same ownership.(p.361)

• By hook or crook I usually managed to sober up before I reached home, but always "terribly tired" from a "hard day's work," and just having to have one or *two* before dinner.(p.361)

• Sure enough in a couple of hours *two* men were at my door and for the first time I heard some facts about liquor and my problem that sounded sensible to me.(p.363)

• I promised my *two* sponsors that I would attend their meeting the next Tuesday evening.(p.363)

• It now became necessary to have noon drinks; at first just *two*, then gradually more.(p.375)

• The last *two* years of my drinking my entire personality changed to a cynical, intolerant and arrogant person completely different from my normal self.(p.376)

• *Two* years before I joined A.A. my wife took a long trip during which she wrote me she just couldn't return unless I did something about my drinking.(p.377)

• I promised, but within *two* months, I began again.(p.377)

• The explanation that alcoholism was a disease of a *two* fold nature, an allergy of the body and an obsession of the mind, cleared up a number of puzzling questions for me.(p.380)

• So I was used to it, but I didn't know what the effect of alcohol was because I always had wine, usually with dinner, but always with a lot of ice and about *two* tablespoons of sugar in it.(p.385)

• He asked if I would cooperate with him after I went home, and if I would have a trained nurse stay with me for at least *two* weeks.(p.387)

• He said that because of my drinking, he shouldn't leave, but that he had to go to New York for *two* weeks.(p.388)

• So I went down to him quite a few times a month and had him shoot me full of the stuff; and then I went across the street to a little drug store to take a glass of beer or *two* beers, and then stopped at the liquor store to get myself a pint and go home.(p.389)

• So he waited another week or *two* and I don't think I stayed sober hardly at all.(p.391)

• I took *two* or three drinks so my eyes could focus, and I could see that horrible picture of the awful drunk on the first page; he couldn't get the drink to his mouth, he had a towel around his hand and he needed a shave.(p.391)

• I found out fast that the cheapest way to get drunk was on shots with beer chasers at *two* bits a crack.(p.397)

• At age twenty-one, I enlisted in the Navy for *two* reasons: (1) to avoid being drafted into the Army, and (2) out of a burst of patriotic fervor inspired by the advent of World War II and as the result of an all-night drinking binge which found me sitting on the doorstep of the Navy recruiting office when the chief petty officer arrived to open for business at nine o'clock Monday morning.(p.398)

• *Two* weeks later found me being sworn in, and the first payday in the Navy made me realize I had found a home.(p.398)

• We went through *two* years of deadlock required by the English divorce laws.(p.405)

• In the morning I would wake up with a dollar or *two*.(p.410)

• I was so busy keeping her out of trouble, and so scared she'd swing on me, that I had my last *two* drinks that night.(p.415)

• However, I had phoned New York from the farm, appealing for help, and there in the station to meet us were *two* A.A.'s, John and Bud.(p.415)

• In less than *two* years, I lost my practice, my home, my wife, and my children.(p.418)

• Then came my tour in the U.S. Navy, part of it being *two* years in the Philippines.(p.419)

• *Two* fuzzy objects came into focus.(p.422)

• I couldn't focus enough to make out the chart, but the card contained *two* words -- "ACUTE ALCOHOLISM."(p.422)

• I was skipping classes about *two* days a week and doing no book work whatever.(p.423)

• *Two* of them leaped from the table and crashed into my head.(p.427)

• *Two* months later I was discharged.(p.428)

• I have *two* wonderful little boys.(p.431)

• When I try to reconstruct what my life was like "before," I see a coin with *two* faces.(p.432)

• After a day or *two* of grovelling remorse I'd come up with an explanation.(p.433)

• After my last binge I came home and smashed my dining room furniture to splinters, kicked out six windows and *two* balustrades.(p.435)

• "*Two* reasons," he said.(p.436)

• Perhaps the single flicker of decency that shone through the fog of my drinking days was a clumsy affection for my *two* children, a boy and a girl.(p.437)

• After going to school all day, working in the family drugstore all evening, and then studying until one or *two* in the morning, I would not be able to sleep soundly, with everything I had been studying going round in my head.(p.440)

• Then I found the solution: At the end of study time, I would drink *two* beers, jump in bed, sleep real fast, and wake up smart.(p.440)

• I didn't know whether I had told him to rush to the hospital and I'd meet him there, or to take *two* aspirin and call me in the morning.(p.441)

• That's the stuff used when the oral surgeon puts the needle in your vein and says, "Count to ten," and before you get to *two*, you're asleep.(p.442)

• On *two* occasions, over weekends, I decided I would take absolutely nothing.(p.443)

• And that was how Max and I and our *two* daughters spent Christmas Day, eight years ago.(p.444)

• The *two* years I spent there, I was incorrigible, and the records bear this out.(p.458)

• (*Two* large red A's stand out in my memory.)(p.460)

• I attempted nearly *two* years ago to make some amends and contact my children, but it wasn't God's time yet.(p.463)

• I will be fifty years old next month, haven't seen my son or daughter yet, nor my daughter's *two* children, my grandchildren; but I am grateful.(p.463)

• The doctor, apparently realizing that one thing that I certainly needed was sleep, left a bottle of sleeping pills there and in my drunken state I took them all, instead of the one or *two* he had prescribed.(p.465)

• The next recollection I have is of my husband coming into my room (later found out it was on New Year's Eve) accompanied by *two* policemen.(p.468)
• After the first *two* or three days you were allowed the run of the place and it was a lot of fun.(p.468)
• Then many blackouts for next *two* years.(p.475)
• Remember only first *two* drinks.(p.475)
• Next *two* years, I call them many times.(p.475)
• Last time in jail, I have *two* black eyes.(p.475)
• By grace of God I stop, think *two* things: This would kill good mother and father; then remember boys talk about Indian fellow who been sober three years.(p.475)
• *Two* weeks later, he come to A.A. meeting.(p.476)
• *Two* years later, my brother take Tall Man to first A.A. meeting.(p.476)
• For *two* years, I was also addicted to heroin.(p.480)
• To tell you a small part of what my mother's life must have been like: Three of her kids were in jail that year -- *two* sons and a daughter.(p.480)
• I remember in my early youth my mother dressed me just as she did my *two* sisters, and I wore curls until I was six years of age.(p.483)
• Economic conditions had a great deal to do with it, because I've often heard my father say that his mother would take one of the old time flour sacks and cut a hole through the bottom and *two* corners of it and there you'd have a gown.(p.486)
• A very good friend of mine who owned a drug store across the street from us, came by only about *two* hours later and said that he had seen Vi down town.(p.487)
• That went on for maybe *two* months, and then she got after me again about drinking.(p.488)
• We had *two* girls and a boy at that time.(p.490)
• We had several fights and on one or *two* occasions I struck her with my fist.(p.491)
• Around eight or nine o'clock there came *two* big detectives and a policeman to arrest me for assault; and I was the most amazed person in the world when they said I had assaulted someone, and especially that I had assaulted my wife.(p.492)
• I worked in the steel mill for possibly *two* months, and then I became disgusted with myself and decided to go back home.(p.492)
• I think the thing that galled me was that just after Easter I had drawn my salary for *two* weeks' work and had decided that I was going to send some money to Vi; and above all else I was going to send my baby daughter an Easter outfit.(p.493)
• I got very little out of the *two* hundred, that I drew on that pay day.(p.493)
• Thinking only of *two* or three dollars to buy some whiskey, I did the job and that's how I met Ella G., who was responsible for my coming into A.A.(p.493)
• When I had known her years before she was rather slender, but at this time she weighed as much as she does now, which is up around in the *two* hundreds or very close to it.(p.493)
• It was around noon, a day or *two* later, when the telephone rang and it was Ella.(p.494)
• When he left I walked with him to the streetcar line, which was just about a half a block, but there were *two* liquor stores, one on each corner from my home.(p.495)
• We held some *two* or three meetings at Ella's home and from there we held some *two* or three at her mother's home.(p.495)
• So, finally, I went to the YMCA and they graciously permitted us to use a room at *two* dollars a night.(p.495)
• But, finally, we got one or *two* to come in and stick and from there, of course, we started to grow.(p.495)
• Even when we were paying that *two* dollars a night, they often paid it for us because our collection was so small.(p.496)
• He poured out *two* drinks.(p.498)
• Then *two* bulbs appeared.(p.498)
• Will I take a young fellow who has been drinking for *two* weeks to live with me?(p.506)
• When I had heard about it, it meant nothing but just *two* letters to me, but some friends of mine in the institution were very active in the program and really believed in it.(p.509)
• One evening I decided to go because *two* of those friends were to speak.(p.509)
• However, my *two* friends kept coaxing and cajoling to get me back again.(p.510)
• My last binge followed the previous one by *two* weeks.(p.514)
• I had a habit of getting up just prior to the closing time of the saloons, about *two* or three o'clock in the morning.(p.514)
• I had *two* years at Dublin University, and then in 1916, I got a nomination for Sandhurst, the British Military College.(p.518)
• Then I was sent out to India and from then on drinking just increased and increased, and I started having *two* or three day spells instead of just the ordinary concentrated one day.(p.519)
• We had a minor campaign or *two* and that helped distract attention from my drinking.(p.519)
• However, I kept that job in Egypt and Palestine for about *two* years, and then I changed over to the other battalion in my regiment.(p.520)
• They kept me in hospital for *two* months, and then they sent me up to Egypt, a three days journey.(p.521)
• I had *two* or three feelings about that.(p.521)
• My mother lived on for five years after I joined A.A., the last *two* in complete blindness.(p.525)
• I would never admit that I was drinking too much, or spending money that I should have used to buy food for my *two* little boys.(p.526)
• I was trying to remember where it came from, when *two* of the biggest cops I ever saw walked in and took me to jail.(p.528)
• Since I've been home, I have been able to gain the respect of my *two* sons again.(p.529)
• (There was a time, for about three months, when I bought a ten-dollar wrist watch every pay day -- that is every *two* weeks.(p.532)
• In those years I was in jail nine times, in an alcoholic ward, overnight, twice; and I was fired from three jobs, *two* of them very good ones.(p.536)
• Back to the big city, for another year of precarious living, paid for largely by one or *two* friends I still had not milked dry or worn to exhaustion with demands on their bounty.(p.540)
• I went over and met him, and we *two* started the group up again.(p.541)
• I have seen that there is only one law, the law of love, and there are only *two* sins; the first is to interfere with the growth of another human being, and the second is to interfere with one's own growth.(p.542)
• One of the truly great things A.A. has taught me is that reality too has *two* sides; I had only known the grim side before the program, but now I had a chance to learn about the pleasant side as well.(p.550)
• I believe this, and I believe too that it is equally impossible to practice these principles to the best of our ability, a day at a time, and still drink, for I don't think the *two* things are compatible.(p.550)
• Do it every day for *two* weeks and you will find you have come to mean it and to want it for them, and you will realize that where you used to feel bitterness and resentment and hatred, you now feel compassionate understanding and love."(p.552)
• I also got into my first disciplinary trouble caused by drinking, on *two* separate occasions.(p.555)
• Over the next *two* years, I sickened rapidly.(p.557)
• Within *two* months, I was drinking again.(p.558)
• In the next half-year, I experienced *two* more esophageal hemorrhages, miraculously surviving each one by a hair.(p.558)
• *Two* -- For our group purpose there is but one ultimate authority -- a loving God as He may express Himself in our group conscience.(p.564)
• Any *two* or three alcoholics gathered together for sobriety may call themselves an A.A. group, provided that, as a group, they have no other affiliation.(p.565)
• Dr. Foster Kennedy, neurologist: "This organization of Alcoholics Anonymous calls on *two* of the greatest reservoirs of power known to man, religion and that instinct for association with one's fellows . . . the 'herd instinct.'(p.571)

two-fifty

• Saying these sprees were limited to one a week (they were not), and saying that the average spree was ten of these drinks (sometimes more, sometimes less), we come up with the first boring statistic: *two-fifty* per week out of twelve dollars.(p.397)

two-fisted

• Some of them I had known for years, good *two-fisted* drinkers who had disappeared from their former haunts.(p.258)
• Dad's image for me was that of a big Irish oilman who came up through the school of hard knocks and so had to be a *two-fisted* drinker.(p.369)

two-forty-five

• At *two-forty-five* that morning I thought I would die.(p.267)

two-quart

• I dropped a *two-quart* water bottle on my big toe.(p.390)

two-thirds

• This work consumed a period of about *two-thirds* of a year, and worked out successfully so I decided to follow patent law.(p.212)
• It is estimated that *two-thirds* of the men in prison were under the influence of alcohol and/or drugs when they committed their offenses.(p.458)

two-thirty

• I was picked up at *two-thirty* that morning with my car smashed up by a street-car because I had run into a big concrete safety zone, and the street-car had run into me, and they took me out through the roof -- there's where I lost the suit.(p.202)
• By *two-thirty* in the afternoon I was always tight.(p.404)

twos

• Already," continues the early text, "*twos* and threes and fives of us have sprung up in other communities."(p.xv)
• Little clusters of *twos* and threes and fives of us have sprung up in other communities, through contact with our two larger centers.(p.162)

type

• In late 1934 I attended a patient who, though he had been a competent businessman of good earning capacity, was an alcoholic of a *type* I had come to regard as hopeless.(p.xxiii)
• I personally know scores of cases who were of the *type* with whom other methods had failed completely.(p.xxiii)
• We are all familiar with this *type*.(p.xxviii)
• There is the *type* of man who is unwilling to admit that he cannot take a drink.(p.xxviii)
• There is the *type* who always believes that after being entirely free from alcohol for a period of time he can take a drink without danger.(p.xxviii)
• There is the manic-depressive *type*, who is, perhaps, the least understood by his friends, and about whom a whole chapter could be written.(p.xxviii)
• Then we have a certain *type* of hard drinker.(p.20)
• We are convinced to a man that alcoholics of our *type* are in the grip of a progressive illness.(p.30)
• But even in this *type* of beginning we are obliged to admit that our justification for a spree was insanely insufficient in the light of what always happened.(p.37)
• About half our original fellowship were of exactly that *type*.(p.44)
• For the *type* of alcoholic who is able and willing to get well, little charity, in the ordinary sense of the word, is needed or wanted.(p.97)
• If you are positive he is one of this *type* you may feel you had better leave.(p.108)
• The differences between my father and my sisters, who were school teachers, made an excellent environment for the *type* of child I was -- that is, slick and cute enough to take advantage of any adult quarrel.(p.210)
• It was very impressive and I wish that every A.A. could have the benefit of this *type* of sponsorship today.(p.292)
• Neither of these circumstances was very helpful to my *type* since I had not learned to face realities.(p.358)
• Mother was of the old school and figured that anyone I associated with should be of the proper *type*.(p.484)
• I had quite a heartache about her then because she wasn't the *type* of girl that my mother wanted me to marry.(p.485)
• I wasn't the *type* that could taper off.(p.514)
• That *type* of drinking is not pleasant.(p.514)
• Of course I really didn't have to worry on that score, because I wasn't the *type* that got half drunk.(p.515)

types

• These allergic *types* can never safely use alcohol in any form at all; and once having formed the habit and found they cannot break it, once having lost their self-confidence, their reliance upon things human, their problems pile up on them and become astonishingly difficult to solve.(p.xxvi)
• Many *types* do not respond to the ordinary psychological approach.(p.xxvii)
• Then there are *types* entirely normal in every respect except in the effect alcohol has upon them.(p.xxviii)
• After having a few drinks, I went to a meeting -- and the people there were not all old men and definitely not skid-row *types*!(p.319)

typewriter

• Creativity at the *typewriter* would keep me busy and alert, I said.(p.331)
• Seated at the *typewriter*, I faked deep thinking or portrayed creativity by key-tapping.(p.332)

typical

• Here, for instance, is a *typical* example: An officer of one of the largest banking institutions in America knows I no longer drink.(p.138)

- Perhaps this is a ***typical*** attitude.(p.149)
- Dr. Bob often said that it was a record for what he felt was a ***typical*** alcoholic.(p.263)
- I grew up in a small town outside Akron, Ohio, where the life was ***typical*** of any average small town.(p.287)

Uu

U.S.

- All told, promising beginnings have been made in some 50 foreign countries and ***U.S.*** possessions.(p.xv)
- Then came my tour in the ***U.S.*** Navy, part of it being two years in the Philippines.(p.419)
- I'm in the ***U.S.*** Navy.(p.422)
- When I was twenty-one, my cousin come home from ***U.S.*** Army on leave.(p.474)

U.S.A.

- At New York, ***U.S.A.***, Alcoholics Anonymous maintains its international service center.(p.575)
- If you cannot find A.A. in your locality, a letter addressed to Alcoholics Anonymous, Box 459, Grand Central Station, New York, NY 10163, ***U.S.A.***, will receive a prompt reply from this world center, referring you to the nearest A.A. group.(p.575)
- Should you be the relative or friend of an alcoholic who shows no immediate interest in A.A., it is suggested that you write the Al-Anon Family Groups, Inc., Box 182, Madison Square Station, New York, NY 10159, ***U.S.A.***(p.575)

U-turn

- How full it has kept my retirement years -- the five I've lived since the first two lost in traveling a rocky road to hell, before I made a ***U-turn***.(p.334)

uglier

- And they were growing ***uglier***.(p.435)

ugliness

- We missed the reality and beauty of the forest because we were diverted by the ***ugliness*** of some of its trees.(p.50)

ugly

- These stark and ***ugly*** facts have been confirmed by legions of alcoholics throughout history.(p.24)
- Don't deal with him when he is very drunk, unless he is ***ugly*** and the family needs your help.(p.90)
- After a particularly ***ugly*** one-nighter, my wife suggested I try it, and I agreed.(p.434)

ulcer

- But the firm became violently ill with my drunkenness and their course of treatment was to remove their ***ulcer***, in the form of me, from the payroll, amid much fanfare and very personal and slighting remarks and insinuations.(p.300)
- And I was able to go on the wagon for long periods of time – once for four years, to cure an ***ulcer***.(p.328)

ultimate

- Two – For our group purpose there is but one ***ultimate*** authority – a loving God as He may express Himself in our group conscience.(p.564)
- 2. – For our group purpose there is but one ***ultimate*** authority – a loving God as He may express Himself in our group conscience.(p.565)

ultimately

- Of course, the latter ***ultimately*** killed the former, but of this, more anon.(p.277)
- I disliked being different so, ***ultimately***, I began to join them occasionally.(p.374)

ultra-dry

- A square from ***ultra-dry*** Kansas, I did not taste grog until I had finished college, done a stint on newspapers, married, become a father, and been in studio publicity two years.(p.328)

ultra-modern

- What with our ***ultra-modern*** standards, our scientific approach to everything, we are perhaps not well equipped to apply the powers of good that lie outside our synthetic knowledge.(p.xxv)

unabated

- This kind of waste goes on ***unabated***.(p.137)

unable

- We are ***unable***, at certain times, to bring into our consciousness with sufficient force the memory of the suffering and humiliation of even a week or a month ago.(p.24)
- For those who are ***unable*** to drink moderately the question is how to stop altogether.(p.34)
- But the actual or potential alcoholic, with hardly an exception, will be absolutely ***unable*** to stop drinking on the basis of self-knowledge.(p.39)
- We may be short in our accounts and ***unable*** to make good.(p.78)
- Two: Your husband is showing lack of control, for he is ***unable*** to stay on the water wagon even when he wants to.(p.109)
- You may be ***unable*** to do so, no matter how hard you try.(p.111)
- He is ***unable*** to focus on anything else.(p.128)
- Some day he will be ***unable*** to imagine life either with alcohol or without it.(p.152)
- It went something like this: "God, for eighteen years I have been ***unable*** to handle this problem.(p.280)
- Above all, I am grateful to A.A. for my sobriety, which means so much to my family, friends and business associates, because God and A.A. were able to do for me something I was ***unable*** to do for myself.(p.383)
- Suddenly I feel hopeless, ***unable*** to go on.(p.502)
- Inside, though, I was scared to death, for I knew that the time was coming (and it couldn't be too remote) when I would be ***unable*** to hold that job.(p.548)
- But my thinking was still confused, and I was still ***unable*** to deal with the challenges of everyday living without help.(p.558)

unacceptable

- When I am disturbed, it is because I find some person, place, thing, or situation -- some fact of my life -- ***unacceptable*** to me, and I can find no serenity until I accept that person, place, thing, or situation as being exactly the way it is supposed to be at this moment.(p.449)
- I've been benefited from a dictionary definition I found that reads: "rationalization is giving a socially acceptable reason for socially ***unacceptable*** behavior, and socially ***unacceptable*** behavior is a form of insanity."(p.551)

unaffected

- Such parts of our story we tell to someone who will understand, yet be ***unaffected***.(p.74)
- The sisters seemed to remain ***unaffected***.(p.211)

unafraid

- We know women who are ***unafraid***, even happy under these conditions.(p.111)

unaided

- I did not know that I had no power over alcohol, that I, alone and ***unaided***, could not stop; that I was on a downgrade, tearing along at full speed with all my brakes gone, and that the end would be a total smash-up, death or insanity.(p.408)

unannounced

- After a few meetings I decided to drive to Florida ***unannounced*** to see my wife and tell her about my new found friends and association.(p.364)

unanswerable

- In describing his suffering, his fears, his many years of groping for some answer to that which always seemed to remain ***unanswerable***, he could have been describing me, and nothing short of experience and knowledge could have afforded him that much insight!(p.309)

unapproachable

- Strangely enough, wives, parents and intimate friends usually find us even more ***unapproachable*** than do the psychiatrist and the doctor.(p.18)

unavailing

- I did not need to be told that my efforts were and would be ***unavailing*** if I did not get help.(p.258)

unaware

- I was down to my shorts, ***unaware*** of wrong-doing, before the ambulance got there and hauled me off to a hospital from which anxious friends rescued me, later that night.(p.537)

unbalanced

- He is not so ***unbalanced*** as they might think.(p.128)

unbearable

- Then came the hospital with ***unbearable*** mental and physical suffering.(p.41)
- Even though your husband becomes ***unbearable*** and you have to leave him temporarily, you should, if you can, go without rancor.(p.111)
- This would lessen my chances of smuggling some home that evening, which in turn would mean a night of futile tossing around in bed followed by a morning of ***unbearable*** jitters.(p.176)
- I had never been very happy, but now it was ***unbearable***.(p.355)
- But as the years go by, the stretch becomes ***unbearable***; and the man with the grown-up brain and the childish emotions – vanity, self-interest, false pride, jealousy, longing for social approval, to name few – becomes a prime candidate for alcohol.(p.534)
- It became more and more necessary to escape from myself, for my remorse and shame and humiliation when I was sober were almost ***unbearable***.(p.547)

uncanny

- The very practical approach to his problems, the absence of intolerance of any kind, the informality, the genuine democracy, the ***uncanny*** understanding which these people had were irresistible.(p.160)

uncertain

- My home life is ideal and my business is as good as can be expected in these ***uncertain*** times.(p.180)
- I agreed with him and told him in no ***uncertain*** terms that I never broke my word in my life.(p.206)
- I told my doctor so in no ***uncertain*** terms.(p.227)
- My health was still ***uncertain***.(p.282)

uncertainties

- Courage to face each day has replaced the fears and ***uncertainties*** of earlier years.(p.295)
- The drinker's mind is full of ***uncertainties*** and insecurities.(p.331)

unchanged

- In this third edition, Part I ("Pioneers of A.A.") stands ***unchanged***.(p.xii)

uncle

- I had run away from school to join the army in World War I, but missed it by one day since the Armistice was signed the very day I landed in Atlanta to sign up with ***Uncle*** Sam.(p.357)
- But not for long; now, for five Friday nights in a row, I went to jail, picked up sodden with beer (which I always disliked, but which was the only drink available); in jail five consecutive Friday nights in the town where I had grown up, where I had been an honor student in high school, where a kindly ***uncle***, bailing me out, said, "Bob, our family just doesn't do this sort of thing."(p.539)
- I had replied, "***Uncle***, give the judge ten dollars, or I'll have to work it out on the county road."(p.539)

uncomfortable

- I put on thirty pounds of weight in about two months, looked like a pig, and was ***uncomfortable*** from shortness of breath.(p.177)
- To go into a gathering of people was the sort of thing that all my life, from the time I left my private world of books and dreams to meet the real world of people and parties and jobs, had left me feeling an ***uncomfortable*** outsider, needing the warming stimulus of drinks to join in.(p.228)
- I had three or four very ***uncomfortable*** months with my regiment then on the Suez Canal.(p.520)
- The only thing this changed, however, was my surroundings, and it was soon apparent that I could have the same ***uncomfortable*** emotions with an unlimited checking account that I could on a working girl's salary.(p.545)

uncommon

- Common sense would thus become ***uncommon*** sense.(p.13)

uncommunicative

- After a few years with an alcoholic, a wife gets worn out, resentful and ***uncommunicative***.(p.81)

unconscious

- My marriage was happy and, as I have said, I never had any of the reasons, conscious or ***unconscious***, which are often given for drinking.(p.182)
- I immediately became ***unconscious***.(p.207)
- Imagine my surprise when I read in a page one "box" that I had been taken from the theater ***unconscious*** around noon that day, removed by ambulance to a hospital and stomach-pumped and then released.(p.244)

unconsciously

- Is he not ***unconsciously*** trying to see what he can take from the family life rather than give?(p.122)

uncontrollable

- I was seized with an almost ***uncontrollable*** desire to reach out for it.(p.285)
- But with many, drinking had been little more than a sometimes ***uncontrollable*** nuisance.(p.315)
- Following an injection I would have to keep one hand busy scratching my constantly itching nose and would also have sudden ***uncontrollable*** urges to vomit.(p.442)
- Neurotic fears plagued me, and I had occasional, ***uncontrollable*** tremors.(p.555)

uncontrollably
• My brain raced *uncontrollably* and there was a terrible sense of impending calamity.(p.6)
• I was suddenly and *uncontrollably* seized with the old, paralyzing panic.(p.279)

uncontrolled
• In a short time, it became *uncontrolled* drinking.(p.343)

uncounted
• I'd only had two with her, but I'd managed four in the fifteen minutes I'd waited for her, and of course I'd had the usual *uncounted* swigs from the bottle as I painfully got up and did my slow spasmodic dressing.(p.223)
• A.A. can, of course, mean just as much to *uncounted* alcoholics not yet reached.(p.563)

under
• "Bill's Story," "Doctor Bob's Nightmare," and one other personal history from the first edition were retained intact; three were edited and one of these was retitled; new versions of two stories were written with new titles; thirty completely new stories were added; and the story section was divided into three parts, *under* the same headings that are used now.(p.xi)
• Many years ago one of the leading contributors to this book came *under* our care in this hospital and while here he acquired some ideas which he put into practical application at once.(p.xxv)
• I could eat little or nothing when drinking, and I was forty pounds *under* weight.(p.7)
• *Under* the so-called belladonna treatment my brain cleared.(p.7)
• I placed myself unreservedly *under* His care and direction.(p.13)
• The joy of living we really have, even *under* pressure and difficulty.(p.15)
• In the doctor's judgment he was utterly hopeless; he could never regain his position in society and he would have to place himself *under* lock and key or hire a bodyguard if he expected to live long.(p.26)
• He is *under* constant fear and tension -- that makes for more drinking.(p.73)
• *Under* no condition do we criticize such a person or argue.(p.77)
• *Under* these conditions we can employ our mental faculties with assurance, for after all God gave us brains to use.(p.86)
• *Under* these conditions your prospect will see he is *under* no pressure.(p.91)
• Make it plain he is *under* no obligation to you, that you hope only that he will try to help other alcoholics when he escapes his own difficulties.(p.94)
• Make it clear that he is not *under* pressure, that he needn't see you again if he doesn't want to.(p.94)
• Sometimes you will have to call a doctor and administer sedatives *under* his direction.(p.97)
• *Under* these conditions we naturally made mistakes.(p.107)
• We know women who are unafraid, even happy *under* these conditions.(p.111)
• Often you must carry the burden of avoiding them or keeping them *under* control.(p.117)
• Then, *under* one provocation or another, the aggrieved one would unearth the old affair and angrily cast its ashes about.(p.124)
• He is not likely to get far in any direction if he fails to show unselfishness and love *under* his own roof.(p.127)
• But you should feel *under* no obligation to keep him on, for your obligation has been well discharged already.(p.147)
• Men *under* them are frequently their friends.(p.147)
• We have shown how we got out from *under*.(p.152)
• Being wrecked in the same vessel, being restored and united *under* one God, with hearts and minds attuned to the welfare of others, the things which matter so much to some people no longer signify much to them.(p.161)
• *Under* only slightly different conditions, the same thing is taking place in many eastern cities.(p.161)
• I would sometimes hide out in one of the clubs of which I was a member, and had the habit at times of registering at a hotel *under* a fictitious name.(p.176)
• I was moved in as Sales Manager and had four men working *under* me.(p.200)
• The circumstances *under* which I reached these people were very odd because I was led there through things that I said when I couldn't even remember speaking.(p.202)
• Cold chills started chasing up and down my spine; my teeth were chattering; my hands were shaking so I tucked them *under* me to keep them from flying away.(p.222)
• I remembered filling the peroxide bottle in my medicine chest with gin, in case my sister found the bottle I hid *under* the mattress.(p.224)
• Beer was too bulky and it couldn't be kept in a jug *under* the counter ready to be dumped when John Law came around.(p.233)
• I checked into my hotel room and then noticed a placard tucked *under* the glass on the bureau stating "There will be positively NO drinking at this convention" signed by the president of the company.(p.243)
• As long as things were tough and the job a challenge I could always manage to hold on pretty well, but as soon as I learned the combination, got the puzzle *under* control and the boss to pat me on the back, I was gone again.(p.243)
• Routine jobs bored me, but I would take on the toughest one I could find, work day and night until I had it *under* control; then it would become tedious and I'd lose all interest in it.(p.243)
• They told Annabelle to take me *under* her wing, and I shall never forget how she sort of curled up her nose and said, "They tell me you drink too."(p.269)
• After finding every bottle that I had hidden around the apartment, she took away my pants, my shoes, my money and my keys, threw them *under* the bed in the back bedroom and slip-locked our door.(p.288)
• He sent to New York for a copy, and after reading it he tucked it *under* his arm and called on me.(p.307)
• I walked away from that girl grinding my teeth and cursing *under* my breath.(p.322)
• Now, no longer *under* pressure, I could safely guard against loss of control.(p.327)
• Hidden old-drunks can pass out on their beds and snooze unreproached, *under* the guise of taking those vital retirement-age naps.(p.330)
• At Christmastime next year, I convinced my wife that I had alcohol *under* control and that I would do controlled drinking over Christmas and the New Year.(p.343)
• It was a terrible blow at the time and I thought he was pretty much of a heel, but of course it was the finest thing he could have done for me *under* the circumstances.(p.357)
• In 1940 another good opportunity came up and we moved to Pittsburgh where I was to manage two radio stations *under* the same ownership.(p.361)
• About this time, at Christmas, after being *under* this doctor's care, we decided that there wasn't anything more to do.(p.388)
• I would walk up and down *under* the 59th Street bridge, trying to get up the nerve to go up there and jump.(p.411)
• I stayed in the barracks all day, "making out guard schedules," and getting mildly plastered from the jug *under* my desk.(p.426)
• Pearl Harbor was a breeze of nine months, a gay Hawaiian paradise, drinking *under* the palms, listening to the surf beat on the shore, a bottle of whiskey near at hand.(p.426)
• *Under* the skilled guidance of an expert practitioner I wallowed in the world's individual and collective mental agony.(p.434)
• It is estimated that two-thirds of the men in prison were *under* the influence of alcohol and/or drugs when they committed their offenses.(p.458)
• At that time the repeal whiskies were back, and I'd go to the store and buy my whiskey and take it to my office and put it *under* the desk, first in one place and then in another, and there soon was an accumulation of empty bottles.(p.488)
• I crawl *under* a pile of blankets and blow out the candle.(p.497)
• My father was alive, and I had to do as he wanted, so I drank *under* cover.(p.508)
• When I landed of course I hit a gin mill, and with three or four good shots *under* my belt the world began to go into that rosy glow.(p.513)
• And having sung that phrase, I'd chuckle with amusement, turning into irony turning into self-contempt turning into self-pity, at the sad fate of Bob, that wonderful, poor little motherless boy who was so smart in school and who grew up to accept responsibility so early and so fast and who staggered *under* his burdens without a whimper until the time came when he thought he was too good for this world and so he ought to be out of it.(p.532)
• I have had the joy of seeing many a human being, down and out, learn to stand straight again, and to proceed *under* his own power to happiness in life.(p.541)
• Dr. G. Kirby Collier, psychiatrist: "I have felt that A.A. is a group unto themselves and their best results can be had *under* their own guidance, as a result of their philosophy.(p.571)
• I now conceive the psychiatrist's job to be the task of breaking down the patient's inner resistance so that which is inside him will flower, as *under* the activity of the A.A. program."(p.571)
• Dr. W.W. Bauer, broadcasting *under* the auspices of The American Medical Association in 1946, over the NBC network, said, in part: "Alcoholics Anonymous are no crusaders; not a temperance society.(p.572)
• (This address is now available in pamphlet form at nominal cost through most A.A. groups or from Box 459, Grand Central Station, New York, NY 10163, *under* the title "Three Talks to Medical Societies by Bill W." -- formerly called "Bill on Alcoholism" and earlier "Alcoholism the Illness.")(p.572)
• These so-called intergroup associations are found *under* the listing "A.A." or "Alcoholics Anonymous" in telephone directories.(p.575)

underestimate
• For an estimate of salary from the twenty-one a month to start with, to over $400 per month upon my retirement after twenty years in the Navy, I believe that an average income of $2,000 a year over this period is low, but as I stated earlier, an *underestimate* is best.(p.399)

underestimation
• So please accept these humble calculations as, if anything, an *underestimation*.(p.396)

undergo
• Though you are providing him with the best possible medical attention, he should understand that he must *undergo* a change of heart.(p.143)

undergoing
• Repeated year on end, they are horrible -- frightening and degrading, a chronicle of tragedy which may be greater because the individual *undergoing* the tragedy, myself, knew what was happening, and yet refused to do anything to stop it.(p.538)

undergone
• My thinking about drinking had *undergone* a great change.(p.277)
• He finally realizes that he has *undergone* a profound alteration in his reaction to life; that such a change could hardly have been brought about by himself alone.(p.569)

undergraduate
• I sold my first article to a national magazine while still an *undergraduate*.(p.555)

underground
• And it had gone *underground* now, because everyone knew I shouldn't be drinking.(p.557)

underlay
• Despite contrary indications, I had little doubt that a mighty purpose and rhythm *underlay* all.(p.10)

underlying
• As soon as we admitted the possible existence of a Creative Intelligence, a Spirit of the Universe *underlying* the totality of things, we began to be possessed of a new sense of power and direction, provided we took other simple steps.(p.46)
• Once confused and baffled by the seeming futility of existence they show the *underlying* reasons why they were making heavy going of life.(p.50)

underneath
• But just *underneath* there is deadly earnestness.(p.16)
• When, however, the perfectly logical assumption is suggested that *underneath* the material world and life as we see it, there is an All Powerful, Guiding, Creative Intelligence, right there our perverse streak comes to the surface and we laboriously set out to convince ourselves it isn't so.(p.49)
• *Underneath*, I knew this was all wrong.(p.407)
• There at the top of the folder was my name, age and address, and *underneath* were the words, "Periodic Drinker."(p.470)

understand
• We think this account of our experiences will help everyone to better *understand* the alcoholic.(p.xiii)
• On the other hand -- and strange as this may seem to those who do not *understand* -- once a psychic change has occurred, the very same person who seemed doomed, who had so many problems he despaired of ever solving them, suddenly finds himself easily able to control his desire for alcohol, the only effort necessary being that required to follow a few simple rules.(p.xxvii)
• Finally he shook his head saying, "Something has happened to you I don't *understand*.(p.14)
• In the following chapter, there appears an explanation of alcoholism, as we *understand* it, then a chapter addressed to the agnostic.(p.28)
• We admit we have some of these symptoms, but we have not gone to the extremes you fellows did, nor

are we likely to, for we ***understand*** ourselves so well after what you have told us that such things cannot happen again.(p.38)
• I had never been able to ***understand*** people who said that a problem had them hopelessly defeated.(p.42)
• We often find such a person quick to see and ***understand*** our problem.(p.74)
• Of course, we sometimes encounter people who do not ***understand*** alcoholics.(p.74)
• Such parts of our story we tell to someone who will ***understand***, yet be unaffected.(p.74)
• It is important that he be able to keep a confidence; that he fully ***understand*** and approve what we are driving at; that he will not try to change our plan.(p.74)
• In fairness we must say that she may ***understand***, but what are we going to do about a thing like that?(p.81)
• If he is alcoholic, he will ***understand*** you at once.(p.92)
• The wife should fully ***understand*** his new way of life.(p.99)
• As wives of Alcoholics Anonymous, we would like you to feel that we ***understand*** as perhaps few can.(p.104)
• Show him that as alcoholics, the writers of the book ***understand***.(p.112)
• That is why we are anxious that you ***understand***, and that you avoid these unnecessary difficulties.(p.121)
• Here were three exceptional men lost to this world because I did not ***understand*** alcoholism as I do now.(p.137)
• I wanted to throw up my hands in discouragement, for I saw that I had failed to help my banker friend ***understand***.(p.138)
• Even when you ***understand*** the malady better, you may feel this feeling rising.(p.139)
• Normal drinkers are not so affected, nor can they ***understand*** the aberrations of the alcoholic.(p.140)
• You may be at a loss to ***understand*** how such a seemingly above-board chap could be so involved.(p.140)
• Seeing your attempt to ***understand*** and help, some men will try to take advantage of your kindness.(p.141)
• He should ***understand*** that emphatically.(p.142)
• Though you are providing him with the best possible medical attention, he should ***understand*** that he must undergo a change of heart.(p.143)
• If he feels free to discuss his problems with you, if he knows you ***understand*** and will not be upset by anything he wishes to say, he will probably be off to a fast start.(p.144)
• But at least he will ***understand*** the problem and will no longer be misled by ordinary promises.(p.148)
• Unhappy drinkers who read this page will ***understand***!(p.151)
• ***Understand*** he was once a well-known lawyer in town, but just now we've got him strapped down tight."(p.156)
• I can't ***understand*** it."(p.157)
• Abandon yourself to God as you ***understand*** God.(p.164)
• Eagerly he pointed to us saying, "These are the fellows I told you about; they are the ones who ***understand***."(p.189)
• Besides, how could he ***understand***?(p.227)
• I don't think the boys were completely convinced of my personality change, for they fought shy of including my story in the book, so my only contribution to their literary efforts was my firm conviction, being still a theological rebel, that the word God should be qualified with the phrase "as we ***understand*** him" -- for that was the only way I could accept spirituality.(p.248)
• And I still say that as long as I remember that January 8th in Washington, that is how long, by the grace of God as I ***understand*** Him, I will retain a happy sobriety.(p.250)
• Gradually I began to ***understand***.(p.259)
• Today I have Someone who will always hear me; I have a warm fellowship among men who ***understand*** my problems; I have tasks to do and am glad to do them, to see others who are alcoholics and to help them in any way I can to become sober men.(p.260)
• Probably only a few readers of this story will be able, from personal experiences of their own, to ***understand*** the exhilaration and sense of accomplishment which I felt after finishing this seemingly simple assignment.(p.276)
• My wife could not ***understand*** why I would sober up for dad but not for her.(p.288)
• My wife could not ***understand*** the next morning why I was drunker than the night before when she took my bottles.(p.289)
• Many times have I heard the above expressions since I have been in A.A., and many times I have had to reply "Definitely I am an alcoholic, and while it may be hard for you to believe, it is not hard for me, for I have learned many things about alcohol and myself that would, perhaps, be difficult for you to ***understand***."(p.356)
• Even I couldn't ***understand*** it, because I did love her so.(p.362)
• They told me their stories, which were much more rugged than mine -- yet what they said made sense, and the way they put it was easy for me to ***understand***, with an understanding I had never had before.(p.363)
• These words may be difficult for you to ***understand*** now, but be patient and you'll know what I mean.(p.367)
• After every cocktail party or dinner party she would say she couldn't ***understand*** how I could get in such a drunken stupor on one drink.(p.377)
• The allergy I could ***understand*** because I am allergic to certain pollens.(p.380)
• The obsession of the mind was a little harder to ***understand*** and yet everyone has obsessions of various kinds.(p.380)
• I was desperately in earnest to follow through and ***understand*** what was expected of me as a member of A.A. and to take each Step of the Twelve as rapidly as possible.(p.382)
• Only God as we ***understand*** Him can calculate these.(p.399)
• I came to ***understand*** the intricate processes of projection, by which we cast into our adult world the images of the horrors of our childhood.(p.434)
• Besides, I couldn't ***understand*** the instructions.(p.445)
• I didn't even try to ***understand***.(p.460)
• One would have to ***understand*** the correctional machinery to see what a miracle this really was.(p.462)
• Honesty is the easiest word for me to ***understand*** because it is the exact opposite of what I've been doing all my life.(p.482)
• Those that ***understand*** me are far away.(p.505)
• I cannot ***understand***.(p.506)
• I couldn't ***understand*** myself.(p.522)
• My mind was too screwy to be able to ***understand*** much of what was being said.(p.524)
• But I did ***understand*** this eventually, that these people had been through a lot of drinking experience just as I had, and had managed to make a job of it.(p.524)
• It has made me ***understand*** that I must be one of my world, that I cannot exist in any happiness as a rebel by myself.(p.524)

understandable

• If what we have learned and felt and seen means anything at all, it means that all of us, whatever our race, creed, or color are the children of a living Creator with whom we may form a relationship upon simple and ***understandable*** terms as soon as we are willing and honest enough to try.(p.28)
• Well, this is ***understandable***.(p.458)

understandably

• My friends were ***understandably*** hurt and angry.(p.406)

understanding

• More often than not, it is imperative that a man's brain be cleared before he is approached, as he has then a better chance of ***understanding*** and accepting what we have to offer.(p.xxiv)
• ***Understanding*** myself now, I fared forth in high hope.(p.7)
• But there exists among us a fellowship, a friendliness, and an ***understanding*** which is indescribably wonderful.(p.17)
• Until such an ***understanding*** is reached, little or nothing can be accomplished.(p.18)
• We found it very desirable to take this spiritual step with an ***understanding*** person, such as our wife, best friend or spiritual adviser.(p.63)
• If we cannot or would rather not do this, we search our acquaintance for a close-mouthed, ***understanding*** friend.(p.74)
• Passing all ***understanding*** is the patience mothers and wives have had with alcoholics.(p.82)
• Our next function is to grow in ***understanding*** and effectiveness.(p.84)
• If your talk has been sane, quiet and full of human ***understanding***, you have perhaps made a friend.(p.94)
• You think he ought to know the subject better, as everyone should have a clear ***understanding*** of the risk he takes if he drinks too much.(p.112)
• Barriers which have sprung up between you and your friends will disappear with the growth of sympathetic ***understanding***.(p.115)
• Use your energies to promote a better ***understanding*** all around.(p.115)
• Patience, tolerance, ***understanding*** and love are the watchwords.(p.118)
• All members of the family should meet upon the common ground of tolerance, ***understanding*** and love.(p.122)
• If they sense these things, they will not take so seriously his periods of crankiness, depression, or apathy, which will disappear when there is tolerance, love, and spiritual ***understanding***.(p.127)
• In the midst of an ***understanding*** and sympathetic family, these vagaries of dad's spiritual infancy will quickly disappear.(p.129)
• And but for the intervention of an ***understanding*** person, I might have followed in their footsteps.(p.137)
• We think the business fabric is shot through with a situation which might be helped by better ***understanding*** all around.(p.137)
• To me, this incident illustrates lack of ***understanding*** as to what really ails the alcoholic, and lack of knowledge as to what part employers might profitably take in salvaging their sick employees.(p.139)
• Drinking occasionally, and ***understanding*** your own reactions, it is possible for you to become quite sure of many things which, so far as the alcoholic is concerned, are not always so.(p.139)
• Your ***understanding*** treatment of their cases will pay dividends.(p.141)
• Some of us sought out sordid places, hoping to find ***understanding*** companionship and approval.(p.151)
• Many a distracted wife has visited this house to find loving and ***understanding*** companionship among women who knew her problem, to hear from the lips of their husbands what had happened to them, to be advised how her own wayward mate might be hospitalized and approached when next he stumbled.(p.160)
• The very practical approach to his problems, the absence of intolerance of any kind, the informality, the genuine democracy, the uncanny ***understanding*** which these people had were irresistible.(p.160)
• ***Understanding*** our work, he can do this with an eye to selecting those who are willing and able to recover on a spiritual basis.(p.162)
• I had found friends, ***understanding*** friends who often knew what I was thinking and feeling better than I knew myself, and didn't allow me to retreat into my prison of loneliness and fear over a fancied slight or hurt.(p.228)
• In fact his language was perfectly suited to my ***understanding***.(p.235)
• This was my introduction to this "***understanding*** fellowship" although it was to be more than a year later before our Society was to bear the name, Alcoholics Anonymous.(p.239)
• In conclusion, I can only say that whatever growth or ***understanding*** has come to me, I have no wish to graduate.(p.249)
• Jack didn't seem to have too much of the spiritual ***understanding***.(p.268)
• I told our family doctor, an ***understanding*** man who gave hours of his time trying to help me, about this experience.(p.276)
• Above all, I have gained the greatest thing accorded to any man, the love and ***understanding*** of a gracious God, who has lifted me from the alcoholic scrap-heap to a position of trust where I have been able to reap the rich rewards that come from showing a little love for others and from serving them as I can.(p.296)
• Philosophy, faith, a sense of humor (they could laugh at themselves), clear-cut objectives, appreciation -- and most especially appreciation and sympathetic ***understanding*** for their fellow man.(p.310)
• It took the help, ***understanding*** and wonderful companionship that was given so freely to me by my "ex-alkie" friends.(p.311)
• And, as the years go by, working together, sharing our experiences with one another, and also sharing a mutual trust, ***understanding*** and love -- without strings, without obligation -- we acquire relationships that are unique and priceless.(p.312)
• We have faith in each other, trust in each other, and ***understanding***.(p.325)
• But in the light of the new ***understanding*** that I have found in A.A., I have been able to interpret that defeat, and that failure, and that shame, as seeds of victory.(p.335)
• Here was the ***understanding*** I'd been searching for all my life.(p.355)
• They told me their stories, which were much more rugged than mine -- yet what they said made sense,

and the way they put it was easy for me to understand, with an ***understanding*** I had never had before.(p.363)
• I could not identify myself with the people with whom I found myself and there was no ***understanding***, and I can't stand confinement anyhow.(p.387)
• There are so many to whom I feel deeply grateful; to my husband (and best critic), whose generous love, compassion and ***understanding*** have helped me along the way; to those before me in A.A. who inspired the first article I read, and the friend who sent that article to Frank; to Ruth for her personal note, and the first A.A. to talk to me; to my Bishop, whose loving and believing spirit inspired me; and to all the members of the Houston Group who were so patient, kind and helpful -- and to countless others.(p.393)
• Not ***understanding*** the twenty-four hour plan, or not wanting to, I began drinking and was off-again on-again, during that first month.(p.414)
• Let group spirit of love and ***understanding*** protect you.(p.477)
• He has so much ***understanding***, a real asset in sharing sobriety.(p.481)
• I stay with ***understanding*** friends.(p.505)
• When you come in here, you find the ***understanding*** that you need.(p.516)
• One by one, the ***understanding*** friends dropped away.(p.538)
• Do it every day for two weeks and you will find you have come to mean it and to want it for them, and you will realize that where you used to feel bitterness and resentment and hatred, you now feel compassionate ***understanding*** and love."(p.552)

understands
• Perhaps he is having a secret and exciting affair with "the girl who ***understands***."(p.81)
• I have a lovely wife who ***understands*** my problem and helps me with it.(p.431)

understood
• We would like it ***understood*** that our alcoholic work is an avocation.(p.xiii)
• There is the manic-depressive type, who is, perhaps, the least ***understood*** by his friends, and about whom a whole chapter could be written.(p.xxviii)
• There I humbly offered myself to God, as I then ***understood*** Him, to do with me as He would.(p.13)
• At the start, this was all we needed to commence spiritual growth, to effect our first conscious relation with God as we ***understood*** Him.(p.47)
• 3.Made a decision to turn our will and our lives over to the care of God as we ***understood*** Him.(p.59)
• 11.Sought through prayer and meditation to improve our conscious contact with God as we ***understood*** Him, praying only for knowledge of His will for us and the power to carry that out.(p.59)
• Being convinced, we were at Step Three, which is that we decided to turn our will and our life over to God as we ***understood*** Him.(p.60)
• Many of us said to our Maker, as we ***understood*** Him: "God, I offer myself to Thee -- to build with me and to do with me as Thou wilt.(p.63)
• How heartbreaking was this discovery; how cruel to be told they ***understood*** our men as we did not!(p.106)
• Had we fully ***understood*** the nature of the alcoholic illness, we might have behaved differently.(p.107)
• Unless the reason is ***understood***, there may be an emotional upset.(p.134)
• That he has not always done so for the alcoholic is easily ***understood***.(p.137)
• The use of spiritual principles in such cases was not so well ***understood*** as it is now.(p.156)
• He succumbed to that gay crowd inside, who laughed at their own misfortunes and ***understood*** his.(p.160)
• I realized that there wasn't anything I could say to place myself in a more favorable light with my children, that it was going to be a matter of time; for I also ***understood*** the intolerance of young people towards deficiencies in their elders.(p.220)
• It explained so much I had not ***understood*** about myself and, best of all, it promised recovery if I would do a few simple things and be willing to have the desire to drink removed.(p.309)
• The Third Step said: "Made a decision to turn our will and our lives over to the care of God as we ***understood*** Him."(p.350)
• This I ***understood***.(p.415)
• I completely forgot myself in trying vainly to help Anne, whose misery I ***understood***.(p.415)
• I felt very lonely and hurt, because nobody ***understood*** me.(p.478)
• But as he continued to talk, I realized that this was the first time I had met a person who had the same problems I did and who, I sincerely believe, ***understood*** me as an individual.(p.494)
• You were thirty-five before you ***understood*** your father's horrible anguish, and forgave him, and loved him again.(p.533)
• I was immersed in self-pity and resentment, and the only people who would support this attitude or who I felt ***understood*** me at all were the people I met in bars and the ones who drank as I did.(p.547)

undertake
• It was finally decided to ***undertake*** the organization of a Cleveland group and toward the end of May, 1939, the first meeting was held in Cleveland in my home.(p.219)
• Indeed, I was always well on my way before I would ***undertake*** to go visiting at all.(p.301)

undertaken
• While on the subject of confidence, can you adopt the attitude that so far as you are concerned this will be a strictly personal matter, that his alcoholic derelictions, the treatment about to be ***undertaken***, will never be discussed without his consent?(p.143)
• He got in touch with a prominent psychiatrist who had ***undertaken*** certain responsibilities for the mental health of the community.(p.163)
• Had anyone ***undertaken*** to explain to me what the A.A. movement was, what its real function was, I probably would have been set back several years and I doubt if I would have survived at all.(p.216)
• He was in his late fifties, and all that he had ***undertaken*** fell upon my shoulders at his death in 1928.(p.486)

undertaker
• She would soon have to give me over to the ***undertaker*** or the asylum.(p.7)

undertaking
• We are both depending upon God and our use of the A.A. program to help us make a success of this joint ***undertaking***.(p.286)

undertook
• A year later, after I completed the course in contracts, I quit the law school, and ***undertook*** some engineering work for a patent law firm on behalf of clients who were in difficulties and who desired to keep their troubles from their own engineering department.(p.212)

underweight
• ***Underweight***!(p.499)

underwent
• I ***underwent*** a shattering nervous breakdown.(p.275)

undisciplined
• We alcoholics are ***undisciplined***.(p.88)
• Just an unstable woman, ***undisciplined***, poorly adjusted and filled with nameless fears.(p.305)
• I was, when drunk, just as ***undisciplined*** and erratic as ever.(p.410)

undisturbed
• In this connection, can you remain ***undisturbed*** if the man proceeds to tell you shocking things?(p.145)
• At the Laundromat, I was ***undisturbed*** by barflies with questionable and unwanted intentions.(p.369)

undo
• The doctor motioned to the corpsman to ***undo*** my straitjacket and leg restraints.(p.422)

undoubtedly
• ***Undoubtedly*** we should admit our fault.(p.81)
• One day he told me about an executive of the same bank who, from his description, was ***undoubtedly*** alcoholic.(p.138)
• He is ***undoubtedly*** on the road to recovery.(p.139)
• If he speaks of his home situation, you can ***undoubtedly*** make helpful suggestions.(p.145)
• As to them, his policy is ***undoubtedly*** sound, but he did not distinguish between such people and the alcoholic.(p.149)
• He gave me information about the subject of alcoholism which was ***undoubtedly*** helpful.(p.180)
• They were ***undoubtedly*** the alcoholics of our village.(p.230)
• It is ***undoubtedly*** too soon for me to say how much of a success I shall be as a husband in time to come.(p.286)
• Alcoholics being the argumentative lot that we are, the A.A. membership will ***undoubtedly*** come up with a few who will dispute these figures.(p.399)

undreamed-of
• After all, your family is reunited, alcohol is no longer a problem and you and your husband are working together toward an ***undreamed-of*** future.(p.119)

undress
• When sleep overtook me, my practice was to ***undress*** and go to bed, wherever.(p.537)

undue
• If there be divorce or separation, there should be no ***undue*** haste for the couple to get together.(p.99)

undying
• With this kind of employee such an attitude will command ***undying*** loyalty.(p.145)

unearth
• Then, under one provocation or another, the aggrieved one would ***unearth*** the old affair and angrily cast its ashes about.(p.124)

uneasy
• I get ***uneasy***.(p.499)

unending
• This was the beginning of an ***unending*** series of such experiences.(p.276)

unexciting
• I did not reflect that half the office was composed of A.A. members, and that I was as ***unexciting*** as any client in any office.(p.413)

unexpected
• In nine cases out of ten the ***unexpected*** happens.(p.78)
• The ***unexpected*** result was that our husbands seemed to like it.(p.106)
• But I was always the ***unexpected*** person who had to finish the bottle.(p.336)

unexpectedly
• And of course a half empty bottle wasn't worth keeping, so I finished it up and naturally had to get more in right away for the people who "might come in ***unexpectedly***."(p.336)
• However, before the meeting got started, a group from the outside came in ***unexpectedly***.(p.509)

unfailing
• Successive Monday morning hangovers, which despite mid-week resolutions to do better, came with ***unfailing*** regularity, eventually caused me to quit my job.(p.254)

unfair
• The employer cannot play favorites, but he can always defend a man from needless provocation and ***unfair*** criticism.(p.146)

unfamiliar
• The name on it was ***unfamiliar*** and I had to ask the way to Grand Central.(p.223)

unfavorably
• When father takes this tack, the family may react ***unfavorably***.(p.128)

unfit
• Occasionally, I would yield to the morning craving, but if I did, it would be only a few hours before I would be quite ***unfit*** for work.(p.176)
• With that, he told me to leave, because I was ***unfit*** as a mother, a wife, and a laundress.(p.371)
• With ten years of A.A. behind me, I was able to tell him that I'd have been alcoholic, no matter what; that I had been a sick person, ***unfit*** for marriage.(p.403)
• Even then I knew in my heart that I was ***unfit*** for the very things I wanted most, a happy marriage, security, a home and love.(p.403)

unfold
• A whole new world of happiness and love began to ***unfold*** before my eyes, a truly new way of living.(p.365)
• Slowly, my life seemed to ***unfold*** before me, shedding insights on childhood resentments, jealousies, and fears that had mushroomed in adulthood, and also on the self-pity that I had wallowed in at every opportunity.(p.371)

unfolded
• However, as he ***unfolded*** his story for me, I could not help but believe him.(p.309)

unforgettable
• The remorse, horror and hopelessness of the next morning are ***unforgettable***.(p.6)

unfortunate
• A former employer of mine said to me a little over ten years ago, "Pat, you seem to be one of those ***unfortunate*** people who at least once every six months must go out and roll in the gutter."(p.513)

unfortunately
• ***Unfortunately*** a lot of prejudice exists.(p.89)
• ***Unfortunately*** for me, I was the only child, which perhaps engendered the selfishness which played such an important part in bringing on

my alcoholism.(p.172)
• ***Unfortunately,*** I had no desire to consult my priest about my drinking.(p.234)

unfortunates
• There are such ***unfortunates.***(p.58)

unguarded
• That my own innate selfishness and stubbornness are the evils which, if left ***unguarded,*** can drive me to alcohol.(p.473)

unhappiness
• It is plain that a life which includes deep resentment leads only to futility and ***unhappiness.***(p.66)
• We want to leave you with the feeling that no situation is too difficult and no ***unhappiness*** too great to be overcome.(p.104)
• This makes for discord and ***unhappiness.***(p.122)
• There were no childhood episodes of ***unhappiness*** to account for my alcoholism.(p.182)
• She tried reasoning with me, endeavored to work out various drinking schedules, in fact all the tricks were practised faithfully for a short time somewhere along my shaky road to ***unhappiness.***(p.361)
• I was unhappy myself and I had brought ***unhappiness*** to all who cared for me.(p.378)
• I feel that there is no situation too difficult, none too desperate, no ***unhappiness*** too great to be overcome in this great fellowship -- Alcoholics Anonymous.(p.395)
• Whatever the root of my ***unhappiness*** might turn out to be, I thought, it could not possibly be booze.(p.433)
• My growing inward ***unhappiness*** was a very real thing, however, and I knew that something would have to be done about it.(p.434)
• It was not difficult to convince myself that my ***unhappiness*** was the fault of the man I had married, and I divorced him at the end of a year.(p.545)

unhappy
• There were many ***unhappy*** scenes in our sumptuous apartment.(p.3)
• We were having trouble with personal relationships, we couldn't control our emotional natures, we were a prey to misery and depression, we couldn't make a living, we had a feeling of uselessness, we were full of fear, we were ***unhappy,*** we couldn't seem to be of real help to other people – was not a basic solution of these bedevilments more important than whether we should see newsreels of lunar flight?(p.52)
• It may be one of our own family, but we cannot disclose anything to our wives or our parents which will hurt them and make them ***unhappy.***(p.74)
• Today's life is measured against that of other years and, when it falls short, the family may be ***unhappy.***(p.123)
• ***Unhappy*** drinkers who read this page will understand!(p.151)
• I was bitterly ***unhappy.***(p.226)
• I look back and remember these things because they made me very ***unhappy,*** and added to my feeling of inferiority at never being the same as other people.(p.261)
• When I came to my aunt, she knew that I had had an ***unhappy*** childhood, and she said, "Now, Ethel, you're welcome to have boy friends in our home, but there are two boys in this town that I don't want you to date, and one of them comes from a very fine family, one of the best.(p.262)
• I had been ***unhappy,*** lonely, and scared for so long that the discovery of liquor seemed to be the answer to all my problems.(p.353)
• I tried the wagon on numerous occasions but I always felt ***unhappy*** and abused.(p.375)
• I was ***unhappy*** myself and I had brought unhappiness to all who cared for me.(p.378)
• My life there was a nightmare of periodic binges on alcohol and pills, adultery, ***unhappy*** hours at the dental office, seeing my wife give birth to our second child and have several miscarriages, living in a turbulent household, and making continual attempts to be the respectable dentist, husband, father, and community leader.(p.419)
• I was inwardly ***unhappy*** most of the time.(p.432)
• My wife is extremely ***unhappy.***(p.501)
• I am blue and ***unhappy.***(p.505)
• I am very ***unhappy.***(p.505)
• I was intensely ***unhappy*** the whole time, but I didn't seem to be able to do anything about it, and the worst part to me was the realization that all this was going to happen again and again until I died.(p.522)

unharmed
• Keep on the firing line of life with these motives and God will keep you ***unharmed.***(p.102)

unhushed
• At a large party in Geneva, with people from many countries represented, the kind of party that is "protocol" in the extreme, I swayed, laughed hysterically, made naughty remarks in an ***unhushed*** voice, and was finally led from the scene.(p.406)

uniform
• Standing there was a gray haired man – tall, trim and in ***uniform.***(p.422)
• Soon found wet canteens serve drinks to Indians in ***uniform.***(p.474)
• My husband was soon in ***uniform*** and among the first to go overseas.(p.547)

uniformity
• It wasn't very long until I had developed a pretty good brew with ***uniformity*** and plenty of authority.(p.232)

unify
• We had to ***unify*** our Fellowship or pass off the scene.(p.xix)

unimportant
• An alcoholic who has recovered, but holds a relatively ***unimportant*** job, can talk to a man with a better position.(p.146)
• I have stopped tilting at windmills, and instead have tried to accomplish the little daily tasks, ***unimportant*** in themselves, but tasks that are an integral part of living fully.(p.295)

uninhibited
• We're free at last to do our thing, to live ***uninhibited*** lives, to drink when and how and where we wish, when we want to and when we need to.(p.329)

unique
• It was now time, the struggling groups thought, to place their message and ***unique*** experience before the world.(p.xvii)
• And, as the years go by, working together, sharing our experiences with one another, and also sharing a mutual trust, understanding and love – without strings, without obligation – we acquire relationships that are ***unique*** and priceless.(p.312)
• "The American Public Health Association presents a Lasker Group Award for 1951 to Alcoholics Anonymous in recognition of its ***unique*** and highly successful approach to that age-old public health and social problem, alcoholism . . .(p.573)
• This self-insurance has resulted in the restoration of physical, mental and spiritual health and self-respect to hundreds of men and women who would be hopelessly down and out without its ***unique*** but effective therapy."(p.574)

uniquely
• Ministers and doctors are competent and you can learn much from them if you wish, but it happens that because of your own drinking experience you can be ***uniquely*** useful to other alcoholics.(p.89)

unit
• When I was released from the hospital, I went back to my ***unit,*** and nothing had changed.(p.319)
• He arranged for me to see a local psychiatrist, who quickly decided I should be in the mental-health ***unit*** of our local hospital.(p.445)
• Then I was transferred to the honor-grade ***unit,*** where I spent the most painful year of my life.(p.462)
• I remember in my first year in high school, that mother suggested that I do not join the cadet ***unit.***(p.484)

united
• Groups are to be found in each of the ***United*** States and all of the provinces of Canada.(p.xv)
• Surveys of groups in the ***United*** States and Canada indicate that A.A. is reaching out, not only to more and more people, but to a wider and wider range.(p.xxii)
• We covered the whole eastern ***United*** States in a year.(p.3)
• Being wrecked in the same vessel, being restored and ***united*** under one God, with hearts and minds attuned to the welfare of others, the things which matter so much to some people no longer signify much to them.(p.161)
• Many friends of my family had emigrated to America, so at twenty-four I decided that the ***United*** States offered me the opportunity I was never likely to find in my native land.(p.231)
• Then I started traveling, with the ***United*** States and Canada as my territory, and with so much freedom and with an unlimited expense account, I was soon drinking every night and kidding myself that it was all part of the job.(p.287)
• I recall, as I walked into that meeting, saying to myself, "Here I am, a fellow of the American College of Surgeons, a Fellow of the International College of Surgeons, a diplomate of one of the great specialty boards in these ***United*** States, a member of the American Psychiatric Society, and I have to go to the butcher, the baker and the carpenter to help make a man out of me!"(p.347)
• Even when I was old enough to know better, I dreamed about being as beautiful as Venus, as pure as the Madonna and as brilliant as the President of the ***United*** States is supposed to be.(p.400)
• A return to the ***United*** States proved effective as a geographical cure, and a period of sobriety ensued, with the help of the church.(p.419)
• In the ***United*** States and Canada, most towns and cities have A.A. groups.(p.575)

United States
• Groups are to be found in each of the ***United States*** and all of the provinces of Canada.(p.xv)
• Surveys of groups in the ***United States*** and Canada indicate that A.A. is reaching out, not only to more and more people, but to a wider and wider range.(p.xxii)
• We covered the whole eastern ***United States*** in a year.(p.3)
• Many friends of my family had emigrated to America, so at twenty-four I decided that the ***United States*** offered me the opportunity I was never likely to find in my native land.(p.231)
• Then I started traveling, with the ***United States*** and Canada as my territory, and with so much freedom and with an unlimited expense account, I was soon drinking every night and kidding myself that it was all part of the job.(p.287)
• I recall, as I walked into that meeting, saying to myself, "Here I am, a fellow of the American College of Surgeons, a Fellow of the International College of Surgeons, a diplomate of one of the great specialty boards in these ***United States,*** a member of the American Psychiatric Society, and I have to go to the butcher, the baker and the carpenter to help make a man out of me!"(p.347)
• Even when I was old enough to know better, I dreamed about being as beautiful as Venus, as pure as the Madonna and as brilliant as the President of the ***United States*** is supposed to be.(p.400)
• A return to the ***United States*** proved effective as a geographical cure, and a period of sobriety ensued, with the help of the church.(p.419)
• In the ***United States*** and Canada, most towns and cities have A.A. groups.(p.575)

unity
• Today the remarkable ***unity*** of A.A. is one of the greatest assets that our Society has.(p.xix)
• Therefore, no society of men and women ever had more urgent need for continuous effectiveness and permanent ***unity.***(p.563)
• One – Our common welfare should come first; personal recovery depends upon A.A. ***unity.***(p.564)

universal
• If there was a Devil, he seemed the Boss ***Universal,*** and he certainly had me.(p.11)
• I could go for such conceptions as Creative Intelligence, ***Universal*** Mind or Spirit of Nature but I resisted the thought of a Czar of the Heavens, however loving His sway might be.(p.12)
• ***Universal*** respect is the key to their usefulness.(p.567)

universe
• Few people really are, for that means blind faith in the strange proposition that this ***universe*** originated in a cipher and aimlessly rushes nowhere.(p.10)
• I simply had to believe in a Spirit of the ***Universe,*** who knew neither time nor limitation.(p.10)
• The great fact is just this, and nothing less: That we have had deep and effective spiritual experiences which have revolutionized our whole attitude toward life, toward our fellows and toward God's ***universe.***(p.25)
• As soon as we admitted the possible existence of a Creative Intelligence, a Spirit of the ***Universe*** underlying the totality of things, we began to be possessed of a new sense of power and direction, provided we took other simple steps.(p.46)
• We read wordy books and indulge in windy arguments, thinking we believe this ***universe*** needs no God to explain it.(p.49)
• When we saw others solve their problems by a simple reliance upon the Spirit of the ***Universe,*** we had to stop doubting the power of God.(p.52)
• We feel we are on the Broad Highway, walking hand in hand with the Spirit of the ***Universe.***(p.75)
• I had never, since the believing days of childhood, been able to conceive an authority directing the ***universe.***(p.259)
• I had tried to be the center of my own little world,

whereas God was the center of a vast ***universe*** of which I was perhaps an essential, but a very tiny, part.(p.280)

• I was always at odds with the entire world, not to say the ***universe***.(p.400)

• Things weren't going as I thought they should, for my greater enjoyment, comfort and fame; therefore, if the ***universe*** wouldn't play my way, I wouldn't play at all.(p.531)

• I, a man of steel, with very high ideals, well brought up, an honor student and the recipient of scholarships and prizes, a boy wonder in business -- I, Bob, the author of this essay, looked and saw that the ***universe*** was beneath my contempt, and that to remove myself from it was the only thing of dignity a man could do.(p.531)

• But I wanted a cosmos, a ***universe*** all my own which I had created and where I reigned as chief top reigner and ruler over everyone else.(p.535)

universities

• My next move was to take up the study of medicine, entering one of the largest ***universities*** in the county.(p.173)

• After many painful discussions, they finally gave me my credits and I migrated to another of the leading ***universities*** of the country and entered as a Junior that fall.(p.173)

• Loading a car with good old books to sell to collectors, librarians, ***universities*** and historical societies, I started out to travel the country.(p.255)

university

• This continued until I enrolled in our state ***university*** and, at the end of four years, I realized that I was a drunk.(p.183)

• I left the ***university*** in the latter part of my senior year and enlisted in the army.(p.183)

• So I enrolled at the ***university*** for night courses in religion, and I pursued those courses for a year.(p.221)

• At seventeen I entered the ***University***, really to satisfy my father who wanted me to study medicine there as he had.(p.241)

• I was president of each class in the ***University***, and president of that student body.(p.345)

• Awarded a scholarship to a famous old Eastern college, I began to drink at the end of my freshman year, and by junior year, I had to transfer to an easier state ***university*** to keep my grades up.(p.419)

• I went to elementary and high school in Washington, D.C. and then to Howard ***University***.(p.486)

• I had two years at Dublin ***University***, and then in 1916, I got a nomination for Sandhurst, the British Military College.(p.518)

unjust

• Unreasonable -- ***Unjust*** -- Overbearing(p.65)

unjustifiably

• Did we ***unjustifiably*** arouse jealousy, suspicion or bitterness?(p.69)

unkempt

• I was fat, bloated, dirty and ***unkempt***.(p.411)

unkind

• He never says an ***unkind*** word.(p.501)

• I have left my wife at home, sick, and I have been ***unkind*** to her in leaving.(p.505)

unknown

• The spirit of modern scientific inquiry, research and invention was almost ***unknown***.(p.51)

• My downfall cost the business community ***unknown*** thousands of dollars, for it takes real money to train a man for an executive position.(p.137)

unless

• They are restless, irritable and discontented, ***unless*** they can again experience the sense of ease and comfort which comes at once by taking a few drinks -- drinks which they see others taking with impunity.(p.xxvi)

• This is repeated over and over, and ***unless*** this person can experience an entire psychic change there is very little hope of his recovery.(p.xxvii)

• Following his physical rehabilitation, he had a talk with me in which he frankly stated he thought the treatment a waste of effort, ***unless*** I could assure him, which no one ever had, that in the future he would have the "will power" to resist the impulse to drink.(p.xxix)

• When this sort of thinking is fully established in an individual with alcoholic tendencies, he has probably placed himself beyond human aid, and ***unless*** locked up, may die or go permanently insane.(p.24)

• That was great news to us, for we had assumed we could not make use of spiritual principles ***unless*** we accepted many things on faith which seemed difficult to believe.(p.47)

• Though our decision was a vital and crucial step, it could have little permanent effect ***unless*** at once followed by a strenuous effort to face, and to be rid of, the things in ourselves which had been blocking us.(p.64)

• ***Unless*** one's family expresses a desire to live upon spiritual principles we think we ought not to urge them.(p.83)

• The family may object to this, but ***unless*** he is in a dangerous physical condition, it is better to risk it.(p.90)

• Don't deal with him when he is very drunk, ***unless*** he is ugly and the family needs your help.(p.90)

• If your man needs hospitalization, he should have it, but not forcibly ***unless*** he is violent.(p.91)

• Don't, at this stage, refer to this book, ***unless*** he has seen it and wishes to discuss it.(p.92)

• Doctors are rightly loath to tell alcoholic patients the whole story ***unless*** it will serve some good purpose.(p.92)

• ***Unless*** your friend wants to talk further about himself, do not wear out your welcome.(p.95)

• Let no alcoholic say he cannot recover ***unless*** he has his family back.(p.99)

• If he is already committed to an institution, but can convince you and your doctor that he means business, give him a chance to try our method, ***unless*** the doctor thinks his mental condition too abnormal or dangerous.(p.114)

• ***Unless*** they actually need protection from their father, it is best not to take sides in any argument he has with them while drinking.(p.115)

• So we think that ***unless*** some good and useful purpose is to be served, past occurrences should not be discussed.(p.125)

• Another principle we observe carefully is that we do not relate intimate experiences of another person ***unless*** we are sure he would approve.(p.125)

• This means trouble, ***unless*** the family watches for these tendencies in each other and comes to a friendly agreement about them.(p.131)

• ***Unless*** the reason is understood, there may be an emotional upset.(p.134)

• ***Unless*** he took some drinks, he might not have the courage to scrape an acquaintance and would have a lonely week-end.(p.154)

• "You can't win ***unless*** you try God's way."(p.236)

• And he further said that God could not accept me as a sincere follower of His Divine Law ***unless*** I was ready to be thoroughly honest about it.(p.236)

• When I started to tell the boys how we did it in New York and all about the spiritual part of the program, I found they would not believe me ***unless*** I was practicing what I preached.(p.249)

• I could not expect to keep what I had gained ***unless*** I gave it away.(p.282)

• I didn't care to go visiting ***unless*** the parties we might visit had plenty of liquor on hand and I could get drunk.(p.301)

• I couldn't keep up with any of my other friends, and I wouldn't go to anyone's house ***unless*** I knew they drank as heavily as I did.(p.324)

• And ***unless*** I had some rosy picture of what was going to happen that day, I wouldn't even feel like getting up in the morning at all.(p.325)

• Although I did drink, it always was with caution -- ***unless*** I was alone.(p.328)

• Two years before I joined A.A. my wife took a long trip during which she wrote me she just couldn't return ***unless*** I did something about my drinking.(p.377)

• An alcoholic cannot accept the news that he's an alcoholic ***unless*** there is a meaningful explanation given, and an offer of help, such as you get in A.A.(p.406)

• Until I could accept my alcoholism, I could not stay sober; ***unless*** I accept life completely on life's terms, I cannot be happy.(p.449)

• Also, after that first visit I learned I could refuse to sign myself in ***unless*** they gave me a glass of whiskey in one hand and a glass of paraldehyde in the other.(p.468)

unlettered

• Alcoholism had respected nobody, neither rich nor poor, learned nor ***unlettered***.(p.455)

unlike

• ***Unlike*** the feelings of the ship's passengers, however, our joy in escape from disaster does not subside as we go our individual ways.(p.17)

• ***Unlike*** most of our crowd, I did not get over my craving for liquor much during the first two and one-half years of abstinence.(p.181)

• ***Unlike*** many other Catholics who frequently take pledges for definite periods -- a year, two years or for good, I never had any desire to "take a pledge" before the priest.(p.234)

• And, ***unlike*** many others, I never took a drink in the morning.(p.323)

• ***Unlike*** his skid-row brother, he isn't heckled for sleeping in alleys or doorways.(p.330)

• ***Unlike*** the drinking driver, he avoids facing judges.(p.330)

• I have achieved the inner confidence to write quite ***unlike*** Shakespeare, and I have sold a good deal of what I've written.(p.416)

unlikely

• I tried to hide my drinking by going places where I was ***unlikely*** to see anyone I knew.(p.375)

• After a month it seemed ***unlikely*** that it ever really happened.(p.433)

unlimited

• At that time I was not aware of the almost ***unlimited*** supply the government made it possible for us doctors to obtain, neither had I any knowledge of the bootlegger who soon appeared on the horizon.(p.175)

• Then I started traveling, with the United States and Canada as my territory, and with so much freedom and with an ***unlimited*** expense account, I was soon drinking every night and kidding myself that it was all part of the job.(p.287)

• The only thing this changed, however, was my surroundings, and it was soon apparent that I could have the same uncomfortable emotions with an ***unlimited*** checking account that I could on a working girl's salary.(p.545)

unloved

• I also wrote another novel, all about Scott Fitzgerald's poor, misbegotten, ***unloved***, tipsy little debutante.(p.405)

unlovely

• An alcoholic in his cups is an ***unlovely*** creature.(p.16)

• Inside, I went right on being a mass of ***unlovely*** self-pity, queasy anxiety and sickening self-debasement.(p.400)

unloving

• Of course, there is such a thing as incompatibility, but in nearly every instance the alcoholic only seems to be ***unloving*** and inconsiderate; it is usually because he is warped and sickened that he says and does these appalling things.(p.108)

unmanageable

• 1.We admitted we were powerless over alcohol -- that our lives had become ***unmanageable***.(p.59)

• Here he is powerless, ***unmanageable***, in the grip of something bigger than he is, and he's got to turn the whole business over to someone else!(p.350)

• "We admitted we were powerless over alcohol -- that our lives had become ***unmanageable***."(p.379)

• It did say, "admitted I was powerless over alcohol; that my life had become ***unmanageable***."(p.379)

• Most certainly I was powerless over alcohol, and for me, my life had become ***unmanageable***.(p.379)

• Eventually, I had to redo each of the Twelve Steps specifically with Max in mind, from the First, saying, "I am powerless over alcohol, and my homelife is ***unmanageable*** by me," to the Twelfth, in which I tried to think of her as a sick Al-Anon and treat her with the love I would give a sick A.A. newcomer.(p.452)

• A.A. didn't teach me I was an alcoholic; rather it taught me that because I was an alcoholic my life had become ***unmanageable***.(p.470)

• But by listening and talking to these A.A.'s -- talking to them as I had never talked to anyone in my whole life, I saw that it was my life that was ***unmanageable*** -- not just my drinking.(p.471)

• My life had become ***unmanageable*** due to the excessive use of alcohol.(p.515)

• I had no problem admitting I was powerless over alcohol, and I certainly agreed that my life had become ***unmanageable***.(p.550)

unmarried

• One hundred for ***unmarried*** women at one end, one hundred for men at the other, and one hundred for married couples in the middle.(p.198)

unmentioned

• But his life was ***unmentioned***, so far as I was concerned.(p.498)

unmindful

• ***Unmindful*** of his welfare, I thought only of recapturing the spirit of other days.(p.9)

unmixed

• I tried them mixed, ***unmixed***, drinking only when gay, only when depressed.(p.305)

unmoved

• And when he died, you were ***unmoved***.(p.533)

unnecessary
• We find that most of this embarrassment is ***unnecessary***.(p.115)
• That is why we are anxious that you understand, and that you avoid these ***unnecessary*** difficulties.(p.121)

unpleasant
• My mother's heartbreak, or the ***unpleasant*** publicity I had caused did not bother my pretty head.(p.401)

unpopular
• It went into certain securities, then cheap and rather ***unpopular***.(p.2)

unpredictable
• Drunk or sober, I was hectic, ***unpredictable***, irresponsible.(p.406)

unrealistic
• Of course, the more I drank, the more ***unrealistic*** my expectations became and the poorer my performance, and the gap widened.(p.557)

unreasonable
• We asked ourselves this: Are not some of us just as biased and ***unreasonable*** about the realm of the material?(p.51)
• ***Unreasonable*** -- Unjust -- Overbearing(p.65)
• He is just another very sick, ***unreasonable*** person.(p.108)
• Your husband will sometimes be ***unreasonable*** and you will want to criticize.(p.117)
• On my ride to the nearest bar, I sold the driver on how misunderstood I was by my wife and what an ***unreasonable*** person she was.(p.288)
• Sure I still loved her, but hang it all, she was ***unreasonable***!(p.362)

unreasoning
• Besides a seeming inability to accept much on faith, we often found ourselves handicapped by obstinacy, sensitiveness, and ***unreasoning*** prejudice.(p.47)

unreproached
• Hidden old-drunks can pass out on their beds and snooze ***unreproached***, under the guise of taking those vital retirement-age naps.(p.330)

unreservedly
• I placed myself ***unreservedly*** under His care and direction.(p.13)

unsalable
• One object is to disclose damaged or ***unsalable*** goods, to get rid of them promptly and without regret.(p.64)

unsatisfactory
• Leaving aside the drink question, they tell why living was so ***unsatisfactory***.(p.51)

unselfish
• To be vital, faith must be accompanied by self sacrifice and ***unselfish***, constructive action.(p.93)
• We have been ***unselfish*** and self-sacrificing.(p.105)

unselfishness
• The ***unselfishness*** of these men as we have come to know them, the entire absence of profit motive, and their community spirit, is indeed inspiring to one who has labored long and wearily in this alcoholic field.(p.xxv)
• He is not likely to get far in any direction if he fails to show ***unselfishness*** and love under his own roof.(p.127)

unsettled
• He saw that I was ***unsettled***, living away from my family and renting houses here and there.(p.403)

unshaven
• There I was, ***unshaven***, clothes torn and dirty with no recollection of wandering all over France but, of course, a hero to the local French.(p.242)

unstable
• There are, of course, the psychopaths who are emotionally ***unstable***.(p.xxviii)
• Just an ***unstable*** woman, undisciplined, poorly adjusted and filled with nameless fears.(p.305)

unsuccessful
• Doctors have been notoriously ***unsuccessful*** in helping alcoholics.(p.352)

unsuspected
• With few exceptions our members find that they have tapped an ***unsuspected*** inner resource which they presently identify with their own conception of a Power greater than themselves.(p.569)

unthinkable
• Above all, he believed he had acquired such a profound knowledge of the inner workings of his mind and its hidden springs that relapse was ***unthinkable***.(p.26)

unthinking
• We feel a man is ***unthinking*** when he says that sobriety is enough.(p.82)
• How could men who loved their wives and children be so ***unthinking***, so callous, so cruel?(p.107)

until
• ***Until*** such an understanding is reached, little or nothing can be accomplished.(p.18)
• He made up his mind that ***until*** he had been successful in business and had retired, he would not touch another drop.(p.32)
• He did no drinking ***until*** he was thirty-five.(p.35)
• Some of us have tried to hold on to our old ideas and the result was nil ***until*** we let go absolutely.(p.58)
• But they had not learned enough of humility, fearlessness and honesty, in the sense we find it necessary, ***until*** they told someone else all their life story.(p.73)
• If we haven't the will to do this, we ask ***until*** it comes.(p.76)
• Simply we tell him that we will never get over drinking ***until*** we have done our utmost to straighten out the past.(p.77)
• We are there to sweep off our side of the street realizing that nothing worth while can be accomplished ***until*** we do so, never trying to tell him what he should do.(p.77)
• If he is not interested in your solution, if he expects you to act only as a banker for his financial difficulties or a nurse for his sprees, you may have to drop him ***until*** he changes his mind.(p.95)
• He clamors for this or that, claiming he cannot master alcohol ***until*** his material needs are cared for.(p.98)
• Wait ***until*** repeated stumbling convinces him he must act, for the more you hurry him the longer his recovery may be delayed.(p.113)
• Husbands and wives have sometimes been obliged to separate for a time ***until*** new perspective, new victory over hurt pride could be rewon.(p.125)
• When a few men in this city have found themselves, and have discovered the joy of helping others to face life again, there will be no stopping ***until*** everyone in that town has had his opportunity to recover -- if he can and will.(p.163)
• May God bless you and keep you -- ***until*** then.(p.164)
• This went from bad to worse ***until*** Sophomore spring when, after a prolonged period of drinking, I made up my mind that I could not complete my course, so I packed my grip and went South to spend a month on a large farm owned by a friend of mine.(p.173)
• I think I must have been thoroughly scared by what had happened, or by the doctor, or probably both, so that I did not touch a drink again ***until*** the country went dry.(p.175)
• This worked nicely ***until*** my wife and I went to see Wallace Beery in "Tugboat Annie," after which the pant-leg and stocking racket were out!(p.177)
• I remember nothing from then on ***until*** I woke up at a friend's house, in a town near home.(p.179)
• This continued ***until*** I enrolled in our state university and, at the end of four years, I realized that I was a drunk.(p.183)
• I resented this very much, ***until*** she informed me that they were a couple of drunks just as I was.(p.184)
• I said, "Yes, Doc, I would like to quit, at least for five, six, or eight months, ***until*** I get things straightened up, and begin to get the respect of my wife and some other people back, and get my finances fixed up and so on."(p.187)
• I immediately quit school and went to work, and from that time ***until*** I was high school age there was never a return to school.(p.193)
• I would put off doing anything that I could ***until*** the next day and, consequently, everything would pile up and then there would be the blackout.(p.197)
• I worked along ***until*** I had really big names in rubber on a tentative contract, and then I neglected to go through with it.(p.198)
• And I continued to drink, on and off then, ***until*** every dollar I had in the world was gone again and I was right back living at my sister's, getting my cigarettes by calling her grocer and telling him to put in a couple of cartons with her order, exactly as I had before I started to work at Max's.(p.202)
• I could not see why I couldn't drink like a gentleman, and that was my primary ambition -- ***until*** I landed in A.A.(p.214)
• I did not know there was such a thing as group activity ***until*** I left the hospital.(p.218)
• It wasn't very long ***until*** I had developed a pretty good brew with uniformity and plenty of authority.(p.232)
• My "periodics" became more frequent ***until*** I reached the point where I wanted to devote all my time to drinking, working as little as possible, and then only when the necessity of my family demanded it.(p.234)
• He had already imbued them with his own spirit ***until*** they were ready and willing at all times to go where sent, and as a doctor he well knew that this mission and duty would strengthen them as it later helped me.(p.235)
• It wasn't very long ***until*** my doctor friend sent me to tell another alcoholic what my experience had been.(p.237)
• Jackie arrived about seven in the evening and talked ***until*** three a.m.(p.239)
• ***Until*** I was thirteen I attended public schools, with regular promotions and average grades.(p.240)
• Routine jobs bored me, but I would take on the toughest one I could find, work day and night ***until*** I had it under control; then it would become tedious and I'd lose all interest in it.(p.243)
• So I rocked along my merry independent way ***until*** June, when I went out selling auto polish in New England.(p.247)
• While I went along with all that was done and attended the meetings, I never took an active job of leadership ***until*** February 1940.(p.249)
• Quebec, Toronto, Buffalo, and finally Pittsburgh, were the scenes of man-sized drunks ***until*** I had gone through my readjusted discharge pay, a fair sum.(p.253)
• As soon as I could get up and walk I started to drink again and kept it up ***until*** my friend of the hospital, who, in his first try at the new way of life had stubbed his toe in Chicago but had come back to the town to take counsel and make a new start, picked me up and got me into a hospital.(p.258)
• I thought I had done that ***until*** Russ' second collapse, and the doctor told me very candidly that he wasn't long for this world.(p.271)
• This continued ***until*** I was twenty-seven.(p.287)
• Then when we got back to the apartment, he was willing to wait two or three days ***until*** I got my health back to be paid off for the liquor and fare.(p.289)
• This consisted of walking the floor for three or four days and nights ***until*** I could take nourishment.(p.289)
• He waited ***until*** I was completely sober and the day before I was to head back for Chicago, he told me of a small group of men in Akron who apparently had the same problem that I had but were doing something about it.(p.289)
• After it was closed we all retired to the kitchen and had coffee and doughnuts and more discussion ***until*** the small hours of the morning.(p.291)
• One of them was that I would try to get a group started in Chicago; the second was that I would have to return to Akron to attend meetings at least every two months ***until*** I did get a group started in Chicago; third, I decided I must place this program above everything else, even my family, because if I did not maintain my sobriety I would lose my family anyway.(p.292)
• The last day of my drinking career, I drank twenty-two of them between ten and twelve a.m. and I shall never know how many more followed them ***until*** I was poured into bed that night.(p.298)
• ***Until*** now, I had never been told that I was an alcoholic.(p.307)
• Some of us struggle with these people because we know that they are really very sick, but we also know that short of some miracle, we are not going to help them except temporarily, and that they will inevitably get worse and worse ***until*** one of two things happens.(p.308)
• We got along fine for about two weeks, ***until*** she told me where to go and to take my damn bottle with me.(p.318)
• ***Until*** I took Social Security and a pension at the age of sixty-eight, after forty years in motion-picture-studio public relations, I had successfully hidden even any hints of approaching alcoholism.(p.327)
• A square from ultra-dry Kansas, I did not taste grog ***until*** I had finished college, done a stint on newspapers, married, become a father, and been in studio publicity two years.(p.328)
• I had been brought up to believe in God, but I know that ***until*** I found this A.A. program, I had never found or known faith in the reality of God, the reality of His power that is now with me in everything I do.(p.341)
• Psychiatrist and surgeon, he had lost his way ***until*** he realized that God, not he, was the Great Healer.(p.345)
• And the first thing you know I was lifted right out of the A.A. group, and I floated higher, and higher, and even higher, ***until*** I was way up on a pink cloud

which is known as Pink Seven, and I felt miserable again.(p.348)

• I tried every gimmick that there was to get some peace of mind, but it was not ***until*** I was brought to my alcoholic knees, when I was brought to a group in my own community with the butcher, the baker, the carpenter and the mechanic, who were able to give me the Twelve Steps, that I was finally given some semblance of an answer to the last half of the First Step.(p.349)

• He answered by wiring that I could stay there ***until*** I earned enough to get home.(p.357)

• I got through the holidays all right ***until*** New Year's Day.(p.365)

• My drinking did not start ***until*** after I was thirty-five, and a fairly successful career had been established.(p.374)

• I think that no one comes to A.A. ***until*** he's tried everything else.(p.384)

• You didn't carry a little orchid up the aisle in those days; you carried a great big bouquet, like a funeral spray, and you didn't have your picture taken ***until*** just before you went to the church.(p.385)

• He said, "Wait ***until*** I get back and I will go with you to see this man."(p.393)

• I stayed drunk from Monday ***until*** Friday, and I call that my spill into A.A.(p.393)

• I displayed alcoholic tendencies actually from the age of fourteen, when I started to steal wine from the family jug, siphoning it off one drink at a time so it wouldn't be missed, not drinking it immediately, but saving it ***until*** about a pint was accumulated, so that I could get drunk.(p.397)

• The short tours could be taken care of by sneaking enough whiskey aboard ship so that it could be rationed out ***until*** another supply could be laid in.(p.398)

• ***Until*** I reached A.A. my life was a shambles; I was a mess, and I made everybody near and dear to me miserable.(p.400)

• But I got drunk that night and stayed drunk, getting increasingly worse ***until*** I found A.A. ten years later.(p.404)

• I stayed with them ***until*** I got drunk and had a row with the Paris editor.(p.405)

• But I was not able to make use of this knowledge ***until*** after I became sober.(p.409)

• I suspect that those bartenders would wait ***until*** I shot my wad, then call a cab and send me home.(p.410)

• I neither drank nor smoked ***until*** I was nineteen years old.(p.419)

• I didn't graduate to the hard stuff ***until*** I was sixteen.(p.423)

• I got a job after school pumping gas and worked ***until*** ten or eleven at night.(p.423)

• We were supposed to take off at noon, but were delayed ***until*** six p.m.(p.428)

• I lost it many times and mom and dad would drive me around ***until*** I found it.(p.429)

• I'd claw my way back to "respectability" and stay there – ***until*** the inevitable next time.(p.432)

• It wasn't ***until*** just lately that, in your case, I could draw it.(p.436)

• After going to school all day, working in the family drugstore all evening, and then studying ***until*** one or two in the morning, I would not be able to sleep soundly, with everything I had been studying going round in my head.(p.440)

• It became progressively harder to get up in the morning, ***until*** one day I asked myself what I would do for a patient who felt this rotten.(p.441)

• I can't say, "God could restore me to sanity, but ***until*** He does, I'll control myself -- with pills."(p.443)

• I wore those moccasins every night for the next seven years, ***until*** they wore out.(p.445)

• It wasn't ***until*** later that he told me he was an attorney.(p.446)

• When I am disturbed, it is because I find some person, place, thing, or situation – some fact of my life -- unacceptable to me, and I can find no serenity ***until*** I accept that person, place, thing, or situation as being exactly the way it is supposed to be at this moment.(p.449)

• ***Until*** I could accept my alcoholism, I could not stay sober; unless I accept life completely on life's terms, I cannot be happy.(p.449)

• I thought that was bad ***until*** I hit the hole at a prison camp; it was just wide enough and long enough to lie down in.(p.459)

• I was not eligible for parole, ***until*** -- with God's help, I'm sure – the governor cut five years off my sentence.(p.462)

• And then my waiting ***until*** I was sure he was asleep, and stealing money from him to replenish the supply.(p.466)

• He said he didn't care what I did with the money, but there was going to be no more ***until*** I was completely sober.(p.467)

• My visits to that sanitarium went on for nearly three years, ***until*** in March of 1944, my father died and I was too drunk to attend his funeral.(p.469)

• I drank from the age of twelve ***until*** I was thirty-two.(p.480)

• I remember in my early youth my mother dressed me just as she did my two sisters, and I wore curls ***until*** I was six years of age.(p.483)

• I don't think I actually started to drink pathologically ***until*** approximately 1935.(p.487)

• Matters got worse all the time ***until*** finally they got so bad that I was reinvestigated by the Government.(p.490)

• I went back to my mother's for a few days ***until*** things cooled off, because the District Attorney had put out a summons for me to come to see him in his office.(p.491)

• I was there about three weeks, and then I got restless and started to tramp across the country, here and there, ***until*** I finally wound up in Pennsylvania, in a steel mill.(p.492)

• I shall not drink ***until*** I get back to the apartment.(p.506)

• So that pattern continued ***until*** I went into the Army.(p.513)

• I'd get downstairs to the gin mill, get enough in to hold me ***until*** eight o'clock in the morning, then I'd go out to join that "misery parade" that so many of us know so well.(p.514)

• One morning I didn't wake up ***until*** after four o'clock.(p.515)

• A British officer, this Irishman – that is, ***until*** brandy "retired" him.(p.517)

• I was intensely unhappy the whole time, but I didn't seem to be able to do anything about it, and the worst part to me was the realization that all this was going to happen again and again ***until*** I died.(p.522)

• I couldn't wait ***until*** the meeting was over to get a drink.(p.526)

• I would stay out ***until*** my money was gone.(p.527)

• Then I would go home full of remorse, and wonder what I was going to do ***until*** I got my next check.(p.527)

• And having sung that phrase, I'd chuckle with amusement, turning into irony turning into self-contempt turning into self-pity, at the sad fate of Bob, that wonderful, poor little motherless boy who was so smart in school and who grew up to accept responsibility so early and so fast and who staggered under his burdens without a whimper ***until*** the time came when he thought he was too good for this world and so he ought to be out of it.(p.532)

• But such is my nature that I must know the reason for things and I didn't stop ***until*** I had satisfied myself about the reasons for my drinking.(p.533)

• When the policeman released me to my stupefied and exasperated friend at four in the morning, I went to my traveling bag and groped ***until*** I found – well, let the officer speak: "Ah," said the policeman, "he's got anuder pair, t'ank God!"(p.538)

• My husband eventually returned, but it was not long ***until*** we realized we could not continue our marriage.(p.547)

• In fact, I changed schools every year ***until*** high school.(p.555)

unto

• ***UNTO*** THE SECOND GENERATION(p.422)

• Dr. G. Kirby Collier, psychiatrist: "I have felt that A.A. is a group ***unto*** themselves and their best results can be had under their own guidance, as a result of their philosophy.(p.571)

untold

• This is a condition which, in ordinary life, would produce ***untold*** grief; there might be scandalous gossip, laughter at the expense of other people, and a tendency to take advantage of intimate information.(p.125)

untouched

• Therefore, the first portion of this volume, describing the A.A. recovery program, has been left ***untouched*** in the course of revisions made for both the second and the third editions.(p.xi)

untrained

• I was still ***untrained*** for any work but washing dishes and waiting on table.(p.401)

untruths

• I had worked so long in a profession where fakery, deceit, and ***untruths*** are tools of trade that I instantly recognized honesty when I heard it, from the mouths of A.A. members.(p.334)

unusual

• Though experience had made him skeptical, he finished his treatment with ***unusual*** confidence.(p.26)

• My case is rather ***unusual*** in one respect.(p.182)

• That is not ***unusual***.(p.215)

• That night I got very drunk, which was usual, but I remembered everything, which was very ***unusual***.(p.224)

• I had been to OTC the previous summer so I went into the Army as a sergeant, but I came out a private, and you really have to be ***unusual*** to do that.(p.241)

• I have had my share of problems, heartaches and disappointments, because that is life, but also I have known a great deal of joy, and a peace that is the handmaiden of an inner freedom, I have a wealth of friends and, with my A.A. friends, an ***unusual*** quality of fellowship.(p.312)

unusually

• His physical and mental condition were ***unusually*** good.(p.26)

unwanted

• At the Laundromat, I was undisturbed by barflies with questionable and ***unwanted*** intentions.(p.369)

unwelcome

• I became an ***unwelcome*** hanger-on at brokerage places.(p.5)

unwilling

• There is the type of man who is ***unwilling*** to admit that he cannot take a drink.(p.xxviii)

• Most of us have been ***unwilling*** to admit we were real alcoholics.(p.30)

• ***Unwilling*** to be honest with these sympathetic men, we were honest with no one else.(p.73)

• I was ***unwilling*** to bare my secrets to those who might display scorn.(p.331)

unwillingness

• The ***unwillingness*** to admit failure requires even further friendly intake.(p.331)

unwise

• This resolution I kept steadfastly for the next forty years, except when circumstances made it seem ***unwise*** to absent myself.(p.172)

• We think that each group should soon achieve this ideal; that any public solicitation of funds using the name of Alcoholics Anonymous is highly dangerous, whether by groups, clubs, hospitals, or other outside agencies; that acceptance of large gifts from any source, or of contributions carrying any obligation whatever, is ***unwise***.(p.566)

up-to-date

• They weren't quite so ***up-to-date*** on my history and I got away with about four years with them.(p.520)

upbraided

• My wife ***upbraided*** me often and plenty when she saw that my "periodics" were gradually losing me what business I could get.(p.233)

upbringing

• I had a very happy ***upbringing*** at home.(p.517)

upheavals

• Yet it is true that our first printing gave many readers the impression that these personality changes, or religious experiences, must be in the nature of sudden and spectacular ***upheavals***.(p.569)

uphold

• The need to ***uphold*** a facade had been irksome.(p.328)

upholsterer

• As soon as I had satisfied that, what I earned as an ***upholsterer*** went for liquor.(p.234)

upholstering

• Very early I became apprenticed to harness-making and acquired considerable knowledge of ***upholstering***.(p.230)

• I was doing very well with that and general ***upholstering*** work, and there was every indication that I would be financially independent by the time I reached middle age.(p.232)

upholstery

• I was eased out of the business I had founded and was reduced to doing general ***upholstery*** in a small shop at the back of my house.(p.233)

uplift

• When I need a mental ***uplift***, I often think of another case brought in by a physician prominent in New York.(p.xxix)

upon

• Though he could not accept all the tenets of the Oxford Groups, he was convinced of the need for moral inventory, confession of personality defects, restitu-

tion to those harmed, helpfulness to others, and the necessity of belief in and dependence *upon* God.(p.xvi)
• Hence the two men set to work almost frantically *upon* alcoholics arriving in the ward of the Akron City Hospital.(p.xvii)
• Our public relations were to be based *upon* attraction rather than promotion.(p.xix)
• So far, *upon* the total problem of several million actual and potential alcoholics in the world, we have made only a scratch.(p.xx)
• *Upon* therapy for the alcoholic himself, we surely have no monopoly.(p.xxi)
• As part of his rehabilitation he commenced to present his conceptions to other alcoholics, impressing *upon* them that they must do likewise with still others.(p.xxiii)
• The physician who at our request, gave us this letter, has been kind enough to enlarge *upon* his views in another statement which follows.(p.xxiv)
• These allergic types can never safely use alcohol in any form at all; and once having formed the habit and found they cannot break it, once having lost their self-confidence, their reliance *upon* things human, their problems pile up on them and become astonishingly difficult to solve.(p.xxvi)
• Though the aggregate of recoveries resulting from psychiatric effort is considerable, we physicians must admit we have made little impression *upon* the problem as a whole.(p.xxvii)
• Then there are types entirely normal in every respect except in the effect alcohol has *upon* them.(p.xxviii)
• I acquired the impeccable coat of tan one sees *upon* the well-to-do.(p.4)
• *Upon* a foundation of complete willingness I might build what I saw in my friend.(p.12)
• The real significance of my experience in the Cathedral burst *upon* me.(p.12)
• My friend promised when these things were done I would enter *upon* a new relationship with my Creator; that I would have the elements of a way of living which answered all my problems.(p.13)
• We have a way out on which we can absolutely agree, and *upon* which we can join in brotherly and harmonious action.(p.17)
• Our very lives, as ex-problem drinkers, depend *upon* our constant thought of others and how we may help meet their needs.(p.20)
• *Upon* hearing this, our friend was somewhat relieved, for he reflected that after all, he was a good church member.(p.27)
• If what we have learned and felt and seen means anything at all, it means that all of us, whatever our race, creed, or color are the children of a living Creator with whom we may form a relationship *upon* simple and understandable terms as soon as we are willing and honest enough to try.(p.28)
• Whether such a person can quit *upon* a nonspiritual basis depends *upon* the extent to which he has already lost the power to choose whether he will drink or not.(p.34)
• We have sometimes reflected more than Jim did *upon* the consequences.(p.37)
• This is a point we wish to emphasize and re-emphasize, to smash home *upon* our alcoholic readers as it has been revealed to us out of bitter experience.(p.39)
• We were bothered with the thought that faith and dependence *upon* a Power beyond ourselves was somewhat weak, even cowardly.(p.45)
• We looked *upon* this world of warring individuals, warring theological systems, and inexplicable calamity, with deep skepticism.(p.46)
• It has been repeatedly proven among us that *upon* this simple cornerstone a wonderfully effective spiritual structure can be built.(p.47)
• When we saw others solve their problems by a simple reliance *upon* the Spirit of the Universe, we had to stop doubting the power of God.(p.52)
• Therefore, we started *upon* a personal inventory.(p.64)
• For we are now on a different basis; the basis of trusting and relying *upon* God.(p.68)
• We never apologize to anyone for depending *upon* our Creator.(p.68)
• He should realize that we are engaged *upon* a life-and-death errand.(p.75)
• Sometimes the man we are calling *upon* admits his own fault, so feuds of years' standing melt away in an hour.(p.78)
• What right had he to involve those dependent *upon* him?(p.80)
• It is better, however, that one does not needlessly name a person *upon* whom she can vent jealously.(p.82)
• Unless one's family expresses a desire to live *upon* spiritual principles we think we ought not to urge them.(p.83)
• Our whole attitude and outlook *upon* life will change.(p.84)
• We come to rely *upon* it.(p.87)
• If he does not want to see you, never force yourself *upon* him.(p.90)
• Let him know you are available if he wishes to make a decision and tell his story, but do not insist *upon* it if he prefers to consult someone else.(p.96)
• Be certain he will be welcomed by your family, and that he is not trying to impose *upon* you for money, connections, or shelter.(p.96)
• The minute we put our work on a service plane, the alcoholic commences to rely *upon* our assistance rather than *upon* God.(p.98)
• Some of us have taken very hard knocks to learn this truth: Job or no job -- wife or no wife -- we simply do not stop drinking so long as we place dependence *upon* other people ahead of dependence on God.(p.98)
• The most incompatible people discover they have a basis *upon* which they can meet.(p.99)
• Remind the prospect that his recovery is not dependent *upon* people.(p.99)
• It is dependent *upon* his relationship with God.(p.100)
• But urge *upon* a man's family that he has been a very sick person and should be treated accordingly.(p.100)
• Show them that he has entered *upon* a period of growth.(p.100)
• If you act *upon* these principles, your husband may stop or moderate.(p.112)
• But what we have related is based *upon* experience, some of it painful.(p.121)
• All members of the family should meet *upon* the common ground of tolerance, understanding and love.(p.122)
• The family may be possessed by the idea that future happiness can be based only *upon* forgetfulness of the past.(p.123)
• One of the many doctors who had the opportunity of reading this book in manuscript form told us that the use of sweets was often helpful, of course depending *upon* a doctor's advice.(p.133)
• Our hope is that when this chip of a book is launched on the world tide of alcoholism, defeated drinkers will seize *upon* it, to follow its suggestions.(p.153)
• A spiritual experience, he conceded, was absolutely necessary, but the price seemed high *upon* the basis suggested.(p.155)
• God will determine that, so you must remember that your real reliance is always *upon* Him.(p.164)
• Men who had liquor shipped in from Boston or New York by express were looked *upon* with great distrust and disfavor by most of the good townspeople.(p.171)
• Why they should be subjected to the tortures we inflict *upon* them, I cannot explain.(p.178)
• I knew that I had a helper that I could rely *upon*, who wouldn't fail me.(p.189)
• There was one experience with Doc which made a terrific impression *upon* me.(p.218)
• When the day of their return was almost *upon* me, and suicide was the only answer I had been able to think of, I went into Ralph's room one evening and told him the truth.(p.278)
• Immediately a great feeling of peace descended *upon* me, intermingled with a feeling of being suffused with a quiet strength.(p.280)
• We are both depending *upon* God and our use of the A.A. program to help us make a success of this joint undertaking.(p.286)
• *Upon* leaving the office in the evening, my first stop would be a saloon about a block away.(p.298)
• As someone in A.A. said to me once *upon* a time, there is nothing worse than a confused psychiatrist.(p.347)
• Furthermore, I knew that I was looked *upon* as a city slicker from New York, and I had to be pretty cautious among small town, conservative Yankees.(p.360)
• I attended my weekly meetings with regularity, re-read the Big Book, attended other group meetings, gave leads when asked to and did some Twelve Step work whenever I was called *upon* to do so.(p.365)
• When I was called *upon* for a few words I had to tell my friends that I wasn't one year old in A.A. that evening but only a "nine month baby."(p.366)
• I couldn't drink at home, because my husband frowned *upon* this.(p.370)
• After all, *upon* coming out of a week-long or ten-day drunk, it was hard enough to figure up just how much that one drunk cost, let alone trying to calculate the cost of approximately twenty-five years of active alcoholism.(p.396)
• For an estimate of salary from the twenty-one a month to start with, to over $400 per month *upon* my retirement after twenty years in the Navy, I believe that an average income of $2,000 a year over this period is low, but as I stated earlier, an underestimate is best.(p.399)
• After a while I really did enjoy drinking and what it did to me, and I became dependent *upon* it for every occasion.(p.464)
• Eventually the day came when I was dependent *upon* it even when there wasn't any occasion.(p.464)
• He was in his late fifties, and all that he had undertaken fell *upon* my shoulders at his death in 1928.(p.486)
• I learn that when we act *upon* the highest conception of honesty which is given us, our sense of honesty becomes more acute.(p.507)
• An ailment developed in one of my eyes, and I was transferred back to Sing Sing and operated *upon*.(p.509)
• I knew it, and I turned for help to someone *upon* whom I had turned my back for many years.(p.515)
• I learned the true meaning of bread cast *upon* the waters.(p.541)
• I thought that life was a pretty simple thing; you simply made a plan for your life, based *upon* what you wanted, and then you needed only the courage to go after it.(p.545)
• The only reality I was able to face had been forced *upon* me by its very repetition – I had to drink; and I didn't know there was anything in the world that could be done about it.(p.548)
• *Upon* graduation, I ventured to New York to pursue my writing career.(p.555)
• One – Our common welfare should come first; personal recovery depends *upon* A.A. unity.(p.564)
• Nor ought A.A. membership ever depend *upon* money or conformity.(p.565)
• The terms "spiritual experience" and "spiritual awakening" are used many times in this book which, *upon* careful reading, shows that the personality change sufficient to bring about recovery from alcoholism has manifested itself among us in many different forms.(p.569)
• Since Dr. Silkworth's first endorsement of Alcoholics Anonymous, medical societies and physicians throughout the world have set their approval *upon* us.(p.571)
• In this atmosphere the alcoholic often overcomes his excessive concentration *upon* himself.(p.572)
• Learning to depend *upon* a higher power and absorb himself in his work with other alcoholics, he remains sober day by day.(p.572)

upper

• Impressed by those who visited him at the hospital, he capitulated entirely when, later, in an *upper* room of this house, he heard the story of some man whose experience closely tallied with his own.(p.160)
• I believe the sociologists would call it "*upper* middle class."(p.275)
• There was an *upper* cupboard full of empties.(p.333)
• Why should this happen to me – hadn't I provided a good home – wasn't I making a good living – didn't I just get a substantial raise that had put me in the *upper* bracket class?(p.362)

uppermost

• Each might pray about it, having the other one's happiness *uppermost* in mind.(p.82)

upright

• This is not to say that all alcoholics are honest and *upright* when not drinking.(p.141)
• This time I seemed to be already awake, sitting *upright* in a big easy chair, in the middle of an animated conversation with a perfectly strange young woman, who didn't appear to think it strange.(p.222)

uproar

• I am very apt to get into quite an *uproar* for a day or two before starting, but I do start, and once started, I have a swell time.(p.285)

uprooted

• Affections have been *uprooted*.(p.82)

ups

• In spite of your new-found happiness, there will be *ups* and downs.(p.117)
• Life, including some *ups* and downs, is a lot of fun.(p.417)
• I have my *ups* and downs the same as the rest.(p.511)

upset

• Unless the reason is understood, there may be an emotional *upset*.(p.134)

• If he feels free to discuss his problems with you, if he knows you understand and will not be ***upset*** by anything he wishes to say, he will probably be off to a fast start.(p.144)

• I used to get terribly ***upset*** when I saw my friends drink and knew I could not, but I schooled myself to believe that though I once had the same privilege, I had abused it so frightfully that it was withdrawn.(p.181)

• And when I get ***upset***, cross-grained and out of tune with my fellow man I know that I am out of tune with God.(p.237)

• I would follow certain drinking schedules or diets faithfully for a few days, and then somewhere along the line would over-train and ***upset*** the applecart.(p.361)

• But for some time, it was difficult to keep from taking a pill when I had an appropriate symptom, such as a cough, pain, anxiety, insomnia, a muscle spasm, or an ***upset*** stomach.(p.448)

• The fear of the loss of Vi and the feeling that, though she had the right to do as she pleased, she should have told me the truth about it, ***upset*** me.(p.487)

upsets

• If something does come along that sort of ***upsets*** me, instead of walking in and throwing a buck at the barman and asking for a drink, I walk into a telephone booth, drop a dime in the box, and call somebody who was so kind as to give me his name and telephone number to meet such an emergency.(p.511)

upshot

• I was, of course, soon on the carpet and the ***upshot*** was that I had to go back for two more quarters and remain absolutely dry, if I wished to graduate.(p.174)

upstairs

• It was the day before Mother's Day and I had come home plastered, carrying a big potted plant which I set down on the table and forthwith went ***upstairs*** and passed out.(p.179)

• I heard my son-in-law coming ***upstairs***, and I asked him where dad was.(p.263)

• In meeting me casually, I don't think my strong belief in "The Man ***Upstairs***" shows, but I have no other explanation for the many good things that have happened to me since I have been in A.A. -- they came to me from a Greater Power.(p.367)

• When I didn't have anything else to do – a dull evening at home -- I'd sneak a few drinks ***upstairs*** in my room, and that began to be a habit.(p.464)

• He didn't have to lie in wait very long, but fortunately by that time, I had acquired friends ***upstairs*** and they covered me for quite a time.(p.519)

uptown

• There was loud talk in the jazz places ***uptown***.(p.3)

• When he was ***uptown*** -- we were living in the little town of Moscow – I went up to try to get some money from him to buy groceries.(p.193)

upward

• I would like to sketch for you the highlights of these sixteen years of a slow but steady and satisfying ***upward*** climb.(p.280)

urge

• When writing or speaking publicly about alcoholism, we ***urge*** each of our Fellowship to omit his personal name, designating himself instead as "a member of Alcoholics Anonymous."(p.xiii)

• There was a tremendous ***urge*** to cease forever.(p.34)

• It quiets the imperious ***urge***, when to yield would mean heartache.(p.70)

• Unless one's family expresses a desire to live upon spiritual principles we think we ought not to ***urge*** them.(p.83)

• But ***urge*** them not to be over-anxious, for that might spoil matters.(p.91)

• But ***urge*** upon a man's family that he has been a very sick person and should be treated accordingly.(p.100)

• They can ***urge*** action without arousing hostility.(p.113)

• We ***urge*** you to try our program, for nothing will be so helpful to your husband as the radically changed attitude toward him which God will show you how to have.(p.117)

• It will do little good if you point that out and ***urge*** more attention for yourself.(p.119)

• We think we are sensible when we ***urge*** that you stop this waste and give your worthwhile man a chance.(p.148)

• That job began a series of brief working spells, each one ending in a "drunk" and the ***urge*** to travel.(p.253)

• But I can remember the ***urge*** of the Prodigal Son to return to his Father.(p.260)

• I knew my wife didn't because I had been sincere in all my promises to her as well as to my mother and to my close friends, but the ***urge*** to take that drink was more powerful than anything else.(p.494)

• I suppose I had reached my spiritual gutter that night, but I have never had what you could call a real ***urge*** to drink again.(p.524)

• From that instant to this, nearly eight years later, I have not had the slightest ***urge*** to drink.(p.541)

urged

• Shortly after that, my brother, who had then become associated with a group of people and had stopped drinking, ***urged*** me to attend meetings with him.(p.205)

urgent

• We doctors have realized for a long time that some form of moral psychology was of ***urgent*** importance to alcoholics, but its application presented difficulties beyond our conception.(p.xxv)

• Hangovers began to assume monstrous proportions and the morning drink became an ***urgent*** necessity.(p.226)

• Therefore, no society of men and women ever had more ***urgent*** need for continuous effectiveness and permanent unity.(p.563)

• The "12 Traditions" of Alcoholics Anonymous are, we A.A.'s believe, the best answers that our experience has yet given to those ever ***urgent*** questions, "How can A.A. best function?" and, "How can A.A. best stay whole and so survive?"(p.563)

urges

• The times in which I grew up (the Prohibition era immortalized by Scott Fitzgerald and John Held Jr.) had taught me to be gay with the gayest; my own inner ***urges*** led me to outdo them all.(p.225)

• Following an injection I would have to keep one hand busy scratching my constantly itching nose and would also have sudden uncontrollable ***urges*** to vomit.(p.442)

urging

• Avoid ***urging*** him to follow our program.(p.113)

• For the next couple of hours a terrible battle went on between the good gremlins and the bad ones, one faction ***urging*** me to tell the truth, the other telling me to sit tight and say nothing.(p.366)

us

• Already," continues the early text, "twos and threes and fives of ***us*** have sprung up in other communities."(p.xv)

• Many of our friends encourage ***us*** by saying that this is but a beginning, only the augury of a much larger future ahead.(p.xv)

• Then Jack Alexander wrote a feature article in the Saturday Evening Post and placed such a compelling picture of A.A. before the general public that alcoholics in need of help really deluged ***us***.(p.xviii)

• More than 15% of ***us*** are women.(p.xx)

• Yet it is our great hope that all those who have as yet found no answer may begin to find one in the pages of this book and will presently join ***us*** on the highroad to a new freedom.(p.xxi)

• The physician who at our request, gave ***us*** this letter, has been kind enough to enlarge upon his views in another statement which follows.(p.xxiv)

• It did not satisfy ***us*** to be told that we could not control our drinking just because we were maladjusted to life, that we were in full flight from reality, or were outright mental defectives.(p.xxiv)

• These things were true to some extent, in fact, to a considerable extent with some of ***us***.(p.xxiv)

• The doctor's theory that we have an allergy to alcohol interests ***us***.(p.xxiv)

• If any feel that as psychiatrists directing a hospital for alcoholics we appear somewhat sentimental, let them stand with ***us*** a while on the firing line, see the tragedies, the despairing wives, the little children; let the solving of these problems become a part of their daily work, and even of their sleeping moments, and the most cynical will not wonder that we have accepted and encouraged this movement.(p.xxvi)

• This immediately precipitates ***us*** into a seething caldron of debate.(p.xxviii)

• War fever ran high in the New England town to which we new, young officers from Plattsburg were assigned, and we were flattered when the first citizens took ***us*** to their homes, making ***us*** feel heroic.(p.1)

• The exercise of an option brought in more money, leaving ***us*** with a profit of several thousand dollars for that year.(p.3)

• Thus was I convinced that God is concerned with ***us*** humans when we want Him enough.(p.12)

• I must turn in all things the Father of Light who presides over ***us*** all.(p.14)

• With ***us*** it is just like that.(p.15)

• We commenced to make many fast friends and a fellowship has grown up among ***us*** of which it is a wonderful thing to feel a part.(p.15)

• There is scarcely any form of trouble and misery which has not been overcome among ***us***.(p.15)

• In one western city and its environs there are one thousand of ***us*** and our families.(p.15)

• Faith has to work twenty-four hours a day in and through ***us***, or we perish.(p.16)

• Most of ***us*** feel we need look no further for Utopia.(p.16)

• We have it with ***us*** right here and now.(p.16)

• But there exists among ***us*** a fellowship, a friendliness, and an understanding which is indescribably wonderful.(p.17)

• The feeling of having shared in a common peril is one element in the powerful cement which binds ***us***.(p.17)

• But that in itself would never have held ***us*** together as we are now joined.(p.17)

• The tremendous fact for every one of ***us*** is that we have discovered a common solution.(p.17)

• An illness of this sort – and we have come to believe it an illness --involves those about ***us*** in a way no other human sickness can.(p.18)

• Highly competent psychiatrists who have dealt with ***us*** have found it sometimes impossible to persuade an alcoholic to discuss his situation without reserve.(p.18)

• Strangely enough, wives, parents and intimate friends usually find ***us*** even more unapproachable than do the psychiatrist and the doctor.(p.18)

• None of ***us*** makes a sole vocation of this work, nor do we think its effectiveness would be increased if we did.(p.19)

• A much more important demonstration of our principles lies before ***us*** in our respective homes, occupations and affairs.(p.19)

• All of ***us*** spend much of our spare time in the sort of effort which we are going to describe.(p.19)

• Those of ***us*** who live in large cities are overcome by the reflection that close by hundreds are dropping into oblivion every day.(p.19)

• How then shall we present that which has been so freely given ***us***?(p.19)

• Nothing would please ***us*** so much as to write a book which would contain no basis for contention or argument.(p.19)

• Most of ***us*** sense that real tolerance of other people's shortcomings and viewpoints and a respect for their opinions are attitudes which make ***us*** more useful to others.(p.19)

• You may already have asked yourself why it is that all of ***us*** became so very ill from drinking.(p.20)

• How many times people have said to ***us***: "I can take it or leave it alone.(p.20)

• The almost certain consequences that follow taking even a glass of beer do not crowd into the mind to deter ***us***.(p.24)

• How often have some of ***us*** begun to drink in this nonchalant way, and after the third or fourth, pounded on the bar and said to ourselves, "For God's sake, how did I ever get started again?"(p.24)

• Almost none of ***us*** liked the self-searching, the leveling of our pride, the confession of shortcomings which the process requires for its successful consummation.(p.25)

• When, therefore, we were approached by those in whom the problem had been solved, there was nothing left for ***us*** but to pick up the simple kit of spiritual tools laid at our feet.(p.25)

• He has commenced to accomplish those things for ***us*** which we could never do by ourselves.(p.25)

• Let ***us*** tell you the rest of the conversation our friend had with his doctor.(p.27)

• A new life has been given ***us*** or, if you prefer, "a design for living" that really works.(p.28)

• If what we have learned and felt and seen means anything at all, it means that all of ***us***, whatever our race, creed, or color are the children of a living Creator with whom we may form a relationship upon simple and understandable terms as soon as we are willing and honest enough to try.(p.28)

• There is no friction among ***us*** over such matters.(p.28)

• Not all of ***us*** join religious bodies, but most of ***us*** favor such memberships.(p.28)

• Most of ***us*** have been unwilling to admit we were real alcoholics.(p.30)

• All of ***us*** felt at times that we were regaining control, but such intervals – usually brief – were inevitably followed by still less control, which led in time to pitiful and incomprehensible demoralization.(p.30)

• Though there is no way of proving it, we believe that early in our drinking careers most of *us* could have stopped drinking.(p.32)
• Most of *us* have believed that if we remained sober for a long stretch, we could thereafter drink normally.(p.33)
• To be gravely affected, one does not necessarily have to drink a long time nor take the quantities some of *us* have.(p.33)
• Many of *us* felt that we had plenty of character.(p.34)
• How then shall we help our readers determine, to their own satisfaction, whether they are one of *us*?(p.34)
• On leaving the asylum he came into contact with *us*.(p.35)
• We asked him to tell *us* exactly how it happened.(p.36)
• To *us* it is not far-fetched, for this kind of thinking has been characteristic of every single one of *us*.(p.37)
• Our sound reasoning failed to hold *us* in check.(p.37)
• We, who have been through the wringer, have to admit if we substituted alcoholism for jay-walking, the illustration would fit *us* exactly.(p.38)
• Some of you are thinking: "Yes, what you tell *us* is true, but it doesn't fully apply.(p.38)
• We admit we have some of these symptoms, but we have not gone to the extremes you fellows did, nor are we likely to, for we understand ourselves so well after what you have told *us* that such things cannot happen again.(p.38)
• This is a point we wish to emphasize and re-emphasize, to smash home upon our alcoholic readers as it has been revealed to *us* out of bitter experience.(p.39)
• Let *us* take another illustration.(p.39)
• He soon indicated he was anxious to see *us*.(p.40)
• One of these men, staff member of a world-renowned hospital, recently made this statement to some of *us*: "What you say about the general hopelessness of the average alcoholic's plight is, in my opinion, correct.(p.43)
• At first some of *us* tried to avoid the issue, hoping against hope we were not true alcoholics.(p.44)
• But cheer up, something like half of *us* thought we were atheists or agnostics.(p.44)
• If a mere code of morals or a better philosophy of life were sufficient to overcome alcoholism, many of *us* would have recovered long ago.(p.44)
• But we found that such codes and philosophies did not save *us*, no matter how much we tried.(p.45)
• Some of *us* have been violently anti-religious.(p.45)
• Let *us* make haste to reassure you.(p.46)
• We found that as soon as we were able to lay aside prejudice and express even a willingness to believe in a Power greater than ourselves, we commenced to get results, even though it was impossible for any of *us* to fully define or comprehend that Power, which is God.(p.46)
• To *us*, the Realm of Spirit is broad, roomy, all inclusive; never exclusive or forbidding to those who earnestly seek.(p.46)
• It has been repeatedly proven among *us* that upon this simple cornerstone a wonderfully effective spiritual structure can be built.(p.47)
• That was great news to *us*, for we had assumed we could not make use of spiritual principles unless we accepted many things on faith which seemed difficult to believe.(p.47)
• When people presented *us* with spiritual approaches, how frequently did we all say, "I wish I had what that man has.(p.47)
• Many of *us* have been so touchy that even casual reference to spiritual things made *us* bristle with antagonism.(p.48)
• Though some of *us* resisted, we found no great difficulty in casting aside such feelings.(p.48)
• It finally beat *us* into a state of reasonableness.(p.48)
• Sometimes this was a tedious process; we hope no one else will be prejudiced for as long as some of *us* were.(p.48)
• Let *us* have a look at some of them.(p.48)
• Science tells *us* so.(p.49)
• Rather vain of *us*, wasn't it?(p.49)
• Experience has taught *us* that these are matters about which, for our purpose, we need not be worried.(p.50)
• Students of ancient history tell *us* that the intellect of men in those days was equal to the best of today.(p.51)
• We asked ourselves this: Are not some of *us* just as biased and unreasonable about the realm of the material?(p.51)
• When others showed *us* that "God-sufficiency" worked with them, we began to feel like those who had insisted the Wrights would never fly.(p.52)
• Some of *us* had already walked far over the Bridge of Reason toward the desired shore of faith.(p.53)
• We were grateful that Reason had brought *us* so far.(p.53)
• That was natural, but let *us* think a little more closely.(p.53)
• Who of *us* had not loved something or somebody?(p.54)
• Neither is reason, as most of *us* use it, entirely dependable, though it emanate from our best minds.(p.54)
• We found the Great Reality deep down within *us*.(p.55)
• It was so with *us*.(p.55)
• If our testimony helps sweep away prejudice, enables you to think honestly, encourages you to search diligently within yourself, then, if you wish, you can join *us* on the Broad Highway.(p.55)
• Even so has God restored *us* all to our right minds.(p.57)
• Some of *us* grow into it more slowly.(p.57)
• When we drew near to Him He disclosed Himself to *us*!(p.57)
• Some of *us* have tried to hold on to our old ideas and the result was nil until we let go absolutely.(p.58)
• Without help it is too much for *us*.(p.59)
• Half measures availed *us* nothing.(p.59)
• 2.Came to believe that a Power greater than ourselves could restore *us* to sanity.(p.59)
• 11.Sought through prayer and meditation to improve our conscious contact with God as we understood Him, praying only for knowledge of His will for *us* and the power to carry that out.(p.59)
• Many of *us* exclaimed, "What an order!(p.60)
• No one among *us* has been able to maintain anything like perfect adherence to these principles.(p.60)
• Whatever our protestations, are not most of *us* concerned with ourselves, our resentments, or our self-pity?(p.62)
• Sometimes they hurt *us*, seemingly without provocation, but we invariably find that at some time in the past we have made decisions based on self which later placed *us* in a position to be hurt.(p.62)
• We must, or it kills *us*!(p.62)
• Many of *us* had moral and philosophical convictions galore, but we could not live up to them even though we would have liked to.(p.62)
• Many of *us* said to our Maker, as we understood Him: "God, I offer myself to Thee -- to build with me and to do with me as Thou wilt.(p.63)
• Next we launched out on a course of vigorous action, the first step of which is a personal housecleaning, which many of *us* had never attempted.(p.63)
• Though our decision was a vital and crucial step, it could have little permanent effect unless at once followed by a strenuous effort to face, and to be rid of, the things in ourselves which had been blocking *us*.(p.64)
• Being convinced that self, manifested in various ways, was what had defeated *us*, we considered its common manifestations.(p.64)
• To conclude that others were wrong was as far as most of *us* ever got.(p.66)
• The usual outcome was that people continued to wrong *us* and we stayed sore.(p.66)
• And with *us*, to drink is to die.(p.66)
• The grouch and the brainstorm were not for *us*.(p.66)
• We began to see that the world and its people really dominated *us*.(p.66)
• This was our course: We realized that the people who wronged *us* were perhaps spiritually sick.(p.66)
• Though we did not like their symptoms and the way these disturbed *us*, they, like ourselves, were sick too.(p.67)
• We asked God to help *us* show them the same tolerance, pity, and patience that we would cheerfully grant a sick friend.(p.67)
• We cannot be helpful to all people, but at least God will show *us* how to take a kindly and tolerant view of each and every one.(p.67)
• We placed them before *us* in black and white.(p.67)
• It set in motion trains of circumstances which brought *us* misfortune we felt we didn't deserve.(p.67)
• Wasn't it because self-reliance failed *us*?(p.68)
• Some of *us* once had great self-confidence, but it didn't fully solve the fear problem, or any other.(p.68)
• When it made *us* cocky, it was worse.(p.68)
• Just to the extent that we do as we think He would have *us*, and humbly rely on Him, does He enable *us* to match calamity with serenity.(p.68)
• Instead we let Him demonstrate, through *us*, what He can do.(p.68)
• We ask Him to remove our fear and direct our attention to what He would have *us* be.(p.68)
• Many of *us* needed an overhauling there.(p.68)
• One school would allow man no flavor for his fare and the other would have *us* all on a straight pepper diet.(p.69)
• We asked God to mold our ideals and help *us* to live up to them.(p.69)
• Some people tell *us* so.(p.70)
• It depends on *us* and on our motives.(p.70)
• If we are sorry for what we have done, and have the honest desire to let God take *us* to better things, we believe we will be forgiven and will have learned our lesson.(p.70)
• This takes *us* out of ourselves.(p.70)
• In this book you read again and again that faith did for *us* what we could not do for ourselves.(p.70)
• This brings *us* to the Fifth Step in the program of recovery mentioned in the preceding chapter.(p.72)
• Many of *us* thought it necessary to go much further.(p.72)
• Psychologists are inclined to agree with *us*.(p.73)
• Those of *us* belonging to a religious denomination which requires confession must, and of course, will want to go to the properly appointed authority whose duty it is to receive it.(p.74)
• Our fears fall from *us*.(p.75)
• Are we now ready to let God remove from *us* all the things which we have admitted are objectionable?(p.76)
• If we still cling to something we will not let go, we ask God to help *us* be willing.(p.76)
• Let *us* be reassured.(p.76)
• Our real purpose is to fit ourselves to be of maximum service to God and the people about *us*.(p.77)
• It may be he has done *us* more harm than we have done him and, though we may have acquired a better attitude toward him, we are still not too keen about admitting our faults.(p.77)
• It is harder to go to an enemy than to a friend, but we find it much more beneficial to *us*.(p.77)
• Our former enemies sometimes praise what we are doing and wish *us* well.(p.78)
• It should not matter, however, if someone does throw *us* out of his office.(p.78)
• Approached in this way, the most ruthless creditor will sometimes surprise *us*.(p.78)
• Our drinking has made *us* slow to pay.(p.78)
• Perhaps we have committed a criminal offense which might land *us* in jail if it were known to the authorities.(p.78)
• Most of *us* have done that sort of thing.(p.78)
• Had this not been so, many of *us* would have no homes today, would perhaps be dead.(p.82)
• So we clean house with the family, asking each morning in meditation that our Creator show *us* the way of patience, tolerance, kindliness and love.(p.83)
• Fear of people and of economic insecurity will leave *us*.(p.84)
• We will intuitively know how to handle situations which used to baffle *us*.(p.84)
• We will suddenly realize that God is doing for *us* what we could not do for ourselves.(p.84)
• They are being fulfilled among *us* -- sometimes quickly, sometimes slowly.(p.84)
• This thought brings *us* to Step Ten, which suggests we continue to take personal inventory and continue to set right any new mistakes as we go along.(p.84)
• We will see that our new attitude toward liquor has been given *us* without any thought or effort on our part.(p.85)
• It does not exist for *us*.(p.85)
• These are thoughts which must go with *us* constantly.(p.85)
• If we have carefully followed directions, we have begun to sense the flow of His Spirit into *us*.(p.85)
• On awakening let *us* think about the twenty-four hours ahead.(p.86)
• Under these conditions we can employ our mental faculties with assurance, for after all God gave *us* brains to use.(p.86)
• Many of *us* have wasted a lot of time doing that and it doesn't work.(p.87)
• If circumstances warrant, we ask our wives or friends to join *us* in morning meditation.(p.87)
• So we let God discipline *us* in the simple way we have just outlined.(p.88)
• We have no monopoly on God; we merely have an approach that worked with *us*.(p.95)
• Some of *us* have taken very hard knocks to learn this truth: Job or no job -- wife or no wife -- we simply

do not stop drinking so long as we place dependence upon other people ahead of dependence on God.(p.98)
• When we look back, we realize that the things which came to *us* when we put ourselves in God's hands were better than anything we could have planned.(p.100)
• Many of *us* keep liquor in our homes.(p.102)
• Some of *us* still serve it to our friends provided they are not alcoholic.(p.102)
• But some of *us* think we should not serve liquor to anyone.(p.102)
• Every new alcoholic looks for this spirit among *us* and is immensely relieved when he finds we are not witch-burners.(p.103)
• Among *us* are wives, relatives and friends whose problem has been solved, as well as some who have not yet found a happy solution.(p.104)
• Some of *us* veered from extreme to extreme, ever hoping that one day our loved ones would be themselves once more.(p.105)
• We finally sought employment ourselves as destitution faced *us* and our families.(p.106)
• The alarming physical and mental symptoms, the deepening pall of remorse, depression and inferiority that settled down on our loved ones -- these things terrified and distracted *us*.(p.106)
• Most of *us* have entered the final stage with its commitment to health resorts, sanitariums, hospitals, and jails.(p.107)
• And just as we were being convinced of their heartlessness, they would surprise *us* with fresh resolves and new attentions.(p.107)
• Some, but not all of *us*, think it has its advantages when reasonably used.(p.110)
• Time after time, this apparent calamity has been a boon to *us*, for it opened up a path which led to the discovery of God.(p.116)
• At first, some of *us* did not believe we needed this help.(p.116)
• We women carry with *us* a picture of the ideal man, the sort of chap we would like our husbands to be.(p.118)
• If that is so we are sorry, for we ourselves don't always care for people who lecture *us*.(p.121)
• So to you out there -- who may soon be with *us* -- we say "Good luck and God bless you!"(p.121)
• A doctor said to *us*, "Years of living with an alcoholic is almost sure to make any wife or child neurotic.(p.122)
• Showing others who suffer how we were given help is the very thing which makes life seem so worth while to *us* now.(p.124)
• A few of *us* have had these growing pains and they hurt a great deal.(p.124)
• Among *us*, these are rare occurrences.(p.125)
• It takes some of *us* a long time to outgrow that serious handicap.(p.125)
• Although financial recovery is on the way for many of *us*, we found we could not place money first.(p.127)
• For *us*, material well-being always followed spiritual progress; it never preceded.(p.127)
• Many of *us* have experienced dad's elation.(p.128)
• Those of *us* who have spent much time in the world of spiritual make-believe have eventually seen the childishness of it.(p.130)
• We have come to believe He would like *us* to keep our heads in the clouds with Him, but that our feet ought to be firmly planted on earth.(p.130)
• These are the realities for *us*.(p.130)
• But those of *us* who have tried to shoulder the entire burden and trouble of others find we are soon overcome by them.(p.132)
• We are sure God wants *us* to be happy, joyous, and free.(p.133)
• We cannot subscribe to the belief that this life is a vale of tears, though it once was just that for many of *us*.(p.133)
• Try to remember that though God has wrought miracles among *us*, we should never belittle a good doctor or psychiatrist.(p.133)
• One of the many doctors who had the opportunity of reading this book in manuscript form told *us* that the use of sweets was often helpful, of course depending upon a doctor's advice.(p.133)
• Many of *us* have noticed a tendency to eat sweets and have found this practice beneficial.(p.134)
• Some of *us* had this experience, only to enjoy, in a few months, a finer intimacy than ever.(p.134)
• He left *us* a note saying you were the best boss he ever had, and that you were not to blame in any way."(p.136)
• And we, who have imposed on the best of employers, can scarcely blame them if they have been short with *us*.(p.138)
• Without much ado, he accepted the principles and procedure that had helped *us*.(p.139)
• A firm attitude at this point has helped many of *us*.(p.142)
• By no means do we offer it as the last word on this subject, but so far as we are concerned, it has worked with *us*.(p.144)
• As our work spreads and our numbers increase, we hope your employees may be put in personal contact with some of *us*.(p.144)
• The greatest enemies of *us* alcoholics are resentment, jealousy, envy, frustration, and fear.(p.145)
• Sometimes we alcoholics have an idea that people are trying to pull *us* down.(p.145)
• I don't see how you can be of any help to *us* for, as you see, we don't have any alcoholic problem."(p.148)
• But not so with *us* in those last days of heavy drinking.(p.151)
• There was an insistent yearning to enjoy life as we once did and a heartbreaking obsession that some new miracle of control would enable *us* to do it.(p.151)
• The less people tolerated *us*, the more we withdrew from society, from life itself.(p.151)
• Some of *us* sought out sordid places, hoping to find understanding companionship and approval.(p.151)
• The practical answer is that since these things have happened among *us*, they can happen with you.(p.153)
• The age of miracles is still with *us*.(p.153)
• Perhaps the best way of treating you to a glimpse of your future will be to describe the growth of the fellowship among *us*.(p.153)
• Many of *us* have felt, for the first time, the Presence and Power of God within its walls.(p.162)
• We are greatly indebted to the doctor in attendance there, for he, although it might prejudice his own work, has told *us* of his belief in ours.(p.162)
• Many of *us*, former patients, go there to help.(p.162)
• Some of *us* are salesmen and go about.(p.162)
• Little clusters of twos and threes and fives of *us* have sprung up in other communities, through contact with our two larger centers.(p.162)
• Those of *us* who travel drop in as often as we can.(p.162)
• This practice enables *us* to lend a hand, at the same time avoiding certain alluring distractions of the road, about which any traveling man can inform you.(p.162)
• God will constantly disclose more to you and to *us*.(p.164)
• This is the Great Fact for *us*.(p.164)
• Give freely of what you find and join *us*.(p.164)
• We shall be with you in the Fellowship of the Spirit, and you will surely meet some of *us* as you trudge the Road of Happy Destiny.(p.164)
• At that time I was not aware of the almost unlimited supply the government made it possible for *us* doctors to obtain, neither had I any knowledge of the bootlegger who soon appeared on the horizon.(p.175)
• It was bad news for *us*, and it will probably be bad news for you.(p.187)
• Bill lay on his hospital bed and looked at *us* in wonder.(p.188)
• Wouldn't you like to see *us* again?"(p.189)
• Eagerly he pointed to *us* saying, "These are the fellows I told you about; they are the ones who understand."(p.189)
• I was black and blue, with my lips all swollen, when they roused *us* to go into court in the morning.(p.204)
• You're never going to want another drink, are you?"; and this answer of his is very important to those of *us* who are victims of alcoholism.(p.206)
• Bill bought me a drink or two on the way, and Dorothy S. came with *us*, and the three of *us* went over to the City Hospital.(p.217)
• There was a concrete program, designed to secure the greatest possible inner security for *us* long-time escapists.(p.229)
• For the great majority of *us*, however, that condition didn't last.(p.232)
• All of *us* in A.A. know the tremendous happiness that is in our sobriety, but there are also tragedies.(p.239)
• There were four of *us* children, and although both of my brothers later became alcoholic -- one died of alcoholism -- my sister has never taken a drink in her life.(p.240)
• The same old routines seemed to be common to *us* all.(p.246)
• There was one meeting a week at Bill's home in Brooklyn, and we all took turns there spouting off about how we had changed our lives overnight, how many drunks we had saved and straightened out, and last, but not least, how God had touched each of *us* personally on the shoulder.(p.246)
• Around this time our big A.A. book was being written and it all became much simpler; we had a definite formula which some sixty of *us* agreed was the middle course for all alcoholics who wanted sobriety, and that formula has not been changed one iota down through the years.(p.248)
• They threw *us* in the jail.(p.264)
• He took his one hundred and seventeen dollars and let *us* go, and we proceeded.(p.264)
• My husband said that I said, "Can you imagine them giving *us* that jail fare?"(p.264)
• And another thing, it's a wonder they didn't throw *us* back in because I could become very dignified and sarcastic.(p.264)
• As we left, and they were escorting *us* across the bridge into Wheeling, I, with great dignity and sarcasm, told them if their wives were ever visiting in Akron, and they, too, were looking for their route sign as I was, that I hoped I could extend to them the hospitality that had been shown to me in Bellaire.(p.264)
• The next time vacation time rolled around that was a bitter lesson to *us*.(p.265)
• There was a very religious family that lived down the road from *us*, and we were on the same party line.(p.265)
• It was a thought that there might be some hope for *us*.(p.266)
• We always tried to buy him a drink, and he always told *us* he had liquor trouble -- couldn't drink.)(p.266)
• Russ said, "Mother, if this tells *us* how to do it, you'll have to read it."(p.268)
• And then he got *us* to laugh, which was what we needed.(p.269)
• I didn't know what they were going to do because he didn't tell *us* much.(p.269)
• He talked about his wife taking his little boy away from him because of his drinking, and how he got back together with them through A.A., and we began feeling grateful right then that all these things hadn't been taken from *us*.(p.270)
• They opened with a little prayer, and I thought it was very fine that we stood, all of *us* together, and closed with the Lord's Prayer.(p.270)
• I'd like to say here how important it was to *us* then that we do all the little things that people said were important, because later when Russ was so sick that I had to hold him up, they had a meeting out at the house.(p.270)
• Sometimes saying very little, but letting *us* say.(p.271)
• At that time they didn't let *us* know that people ever had trouble.(p.271)
• I can't express what A.A. meant to *us* during that year.(p.272)
• I don't ever remember that I was bored myself when we first came in, and they came out to the house and talked to *us* about these things.(p.273)
• It would be impossible for me to pass over this year without mentioning my love for, and my indebtedness to these two wonderful people who are no longer with *us*.(p.280)
• While there, two or three more "cash customers" (as Dr. Bob used to call them -- probably because they had so little cash) were shipped in to *us* from Detroit.(p.282)
• We are both depending upon God and our use of the A.A. program to help *us* make a success of this joint undertaking.(p.286)
• When I said yes, we both knelt at his desk and prayed, each of *us* asking to have these defects taken away.(p.292)
• A few months later one of the men who had been in touch with the group in Akron came to Chicago to live, and then there were three of *us* who continued to have informal meetings quite regularly.(p.294)
• The three of *us* did not feel up to the job, and after a few meetings we convinced the prospects that they too should go to Akron where they could see an older group in action.(p.295)
• In the meantime, another doctor in Evanston became convinced that the program had possibilities, and turned over a woman to *us* to do something about.(p.295)
• Occasionally, it is accorded to a few of *us* to watch something fine grow from a tiny kernel into something of gigantic goodness.(p.295)
• Some of *us* struggle with these people because we know that they are really very sick, but we also know that short of some miracle, we are not going to help them except temporarily, and that they will inevitably

get worse and worse until one of two things happens.(p.308)
• Shortly after I returned to Chicago, my doctor, encouraged by the results of my contact with A.A., sent *us* two more of his alcoholic patients.(p.310)
• Others may idle in a retrogressive groove without too much danger, but retrogression can spell death for *us*.(p.311)
• However, this isn't as rough as it sounds, as we do become grateful for the necessity that makes *us* toe the line, for we find that we are more than compensated for a consistent effort by the countless dividends we receive.(p.311)
• Actually, the bottom came up and hit *us*.(p.315)
• That sold *us* on Alcoholics Anonymous."(p.315)
• In the doorway stood a lovely young girl who said, "Are you one of *us* souses, too?"(p.321)
• I should have lost my husband, and I think that only the fact that he was an alcoholic too kept *us* together.(p.323)
• A.A. has given *us* that.(p.325)
• No prickling consciences to needle *us* with guilt feelings.(p.329)
• A.A. gives *us* alcoholics direction into a way of life without the need for alcohol.(p.340)
• And then it went on to say: "Half measures availed *us* nothing.(p.349)
• "Complete abandon"; "Half measures availed *us* nothing"; "Thoroughly follow our path"; "Completely give oneself to this simple program" -- rang in my swelled head.(p.349)
• Now they asked *us* to make a decision!(p.350)
• What can He do for *us* that we can't do for ourselves?"(p.350)
• And the clergy have tried hard to help *us*, but we haven't been helped.(p.352)
• And the psychiatrist has had thousands of couches, and has put you and me on them many, many times, but he hasn't helped *us* very much, though he has tried hard; and we owe the clergy and the doctor and the psychiatrist a deep debt of gratitude, but they haven't helped our alcoholism, except in a rare few instances.(p.352)
• It left *us* dazed, because he had seemed so indestructible.(p.370)
• To most of *us*, making amends will take the rest of our lives, but we can start immediately.(p.381)
• If we do a good job of living today, and if tomorrow comes for *us*, then the chances are we will do a good job when it arrives -- so why worry about it?(p.382)
• "Grant *us* the serenity to accept the things we cannot change, courage to change the things we can, and the wisdom to know the difference."(p.382)
• Dr. Bob said, "Love and service keep *us* dry," and Bill said, "Always we must remember that our first duty is face-to-face help for the alcoholic who still suffers."(p.395)
• It's the last thing I ever heard him say, and I think there are some of *us* who, at times, try to read extra messages and complexities into the Steps.(p.395)
• He said to me, gently and simply, "Do you think that you are one of *us*?"(p.413)
• Never in my entire life had anyone asked me "Are you one of *us*?"(p.413)
• However, I had phoned New York from the farm, appealing for help, and there in the station to meet *us* were two A.A.'s, John and Bud.(p.415)
• They did not seem ashamed to be with *us*, these strangers.(p.415)
• My second wife is a young A.A. member, too, and what a terrific adventure this is for *us*!(p.420)
• The sheriff bade *us* goodbye very happily.(p.424)
• I think He's on hand to see all of *us* through whatever may come to *us*.(p.437)
• A.A. and acceptance have taught me that there is a bit of good in the worst of *us* and a bit of bad in the best of *us*; that we are all children of God and we each have a right to be here.(p.449)
• Now sober for years, they tell *us* how they got well.(p.455)
• Most of *us* did not stay out of prison long enough to run the alcoholic gamut -- to develop the ongoing kind of alcoholism or alcoholic drinking you hear about in A.A. talks.(p.458)
• The poorest person has no less and the wealthiest has no more -- each of *us* has but one day.(p.473)
• What we do with it is our own business; how we use it is up to *us* individually.(p.473)
• Some of *us* always remember our big mouths when it comes to a drink, but somewhere along the line, we seem to have forgotten about taking care of our teeth.(p.479)
• We are so beautiful that it is never too much trouble to get some poor stranger to buy *us* a drink.(p.479)
• (Actually, he does it solely to get rid of *us*.)(p.480)
• You see how much work some of *us* have to do on ourselves when we finally come into A.A.!(p.480)
• She must have been real proud of *us*, I'm sure.(p.480)
• We are aware of the nice things around *us*, things we never noticed before in our drunken stupor.(p.481)
• But I will never be totally honest -- that would make me perfect, and none of *us* can claim to be perfect.(p.482)
• She was very possessive with *us* children.(p.483)
• We weren't even permitted to play cards in our home, but father would give *us* just a little toddy with whiskey and sugar and warm water now and then.(p.484)
• My mother resented it so that the first Christmas after our marriage, she didn't even invite *us* to dinner.(p.485)
• A very good friend of mine who owned a drug store across the street from *us*, came by only about two hours later and said that he had seen Vi down town.(p.487)
• My brother-in-law was living with *us* at that time and I said to Vi, "Maybe the bottles are brother's.(p.488)
• My practice at that juncture was just barely getting *us* a living.(p.488)
• So, finally, I went to the YMCA and they graciously permitted *us* to use a room at two dollars a night.(p.495)
• They came, many of them, and stuck by *us* and told *us* how to hold meetings.(p.495)
• They taught *us* a great deal about Twelve Step work too.(p.496)
• They saved *us* endless time and lost motion.(p.496)
• And, not only that, but they gave *us* financial help.(p.496)
• Even when we were paying that two dollars a night, they often paid it for *us* because our collection was so small.(p.496)
• I learn that when we act upon the highest conception of honesty which is given *us*, our sense of honesty becomes more acute.(p.507)
• I learn that honesty is truth, and that truth shall make *us* free!(p.507)
• When we first come into A.A., many of *us* are confused because as a general rule we're at the end of our respective ropes, and we don't know what to do.(p.512)
• Like many of *us* who went into the service, I thought it would be a cure-all, a new life.(p.513)
• I'd get downstairs to the gin mill, get enough in to hold me until eight o'clock in the morning, then I'd go out to join that "misery parade" that so many of *us* know so well.(p.514)
• I don't know if it's force of habit or something else that keeps them in one place, but I do know that in A.A. there is much work to do, and none of *us* can do it standing still.(p.529)
• If you give *us* a try, you will see that we are really human beings, and we will welcome you with open arms and hearts.(p.529)
• If I write with the air of one who has discovered the obvious, which is to say, the eternal truths which have been offered to *us* since the beginning, forgive my callowness; I had to find these things out for myself.(p.536)
• Alas for *us* men toward whom Shaw hurled his cry, "Must a Christ be crucified in every generation for the benefit of those who have no imagination?"(p.536)
• I've heard it said many times in A.A., "There is just one good drunk in every alcoholic's life, and that's the one that brings *us* into A.A.," and I believe it.(p.549)
• They suggested that I study the A.A. book and try to take the Twelve Steps according to the explanation in the Book, for it was their opinion that the application of these principles in our daily lives will get *us* sober and keep *us* sober.(p.550)
• It's been true in my case, nor could I quarrel with "restore *us* to sanity," for my actions drunk or sober, before A.A., were not those of a sane person.(p.550)
• And because it works for me, it will work for all of *us*.(p.552)
• "A.A. does not teach *us* how to handle our drinking," he said.(p.554)
• "It teaches *us* how to handle sobriety."(p.554)
• Alcoholics can stop drinking in many places and many ways -- but Alcoholics Anonymous offers *us* a way to stay sober.(p.559)
• We learn how to level out the emotional wings that got *us* into trouble both when we were up and when we were down.(p.560)
• We alcoholics see that we must work together and hang together, else most of *us* will finally die alone.(p.563)
• Six -- An A.A. group ought never endorse, finance or lend the A.A. name to any related facility or outside enterprise, lest problems of money, property and prestige divert *us* from our primary purpose.(p.564)
• Twelve -- Anonymity is the spiritual foundation of all our Traditions, ever reminding *us* to place principles before personalities.(p.564)
• Our A.A. experience has taught *us* that:(p.565)
• A.A. must continue to live or most of *us* will surely die.(p.565)
• 6. -- Problems of money, property, and authority may easily divert *us* from our primary spiritual aim.(p.565)
• Experience has often warned *us* that nothing can so surely destroy our spiritual heritage as futile disputes over property, money, and authority.(p.566)
• We feel it better to let our friends recommend *us*.(p.567)
• It reminds *us* that we are to place principles before personalities; that we are actually to practice a genuine humility.(p.568)
• This to the end that our great blessings may never spoil *us*; that we shall forever live in thankful contemplation of Him who presides over *us* all.(p.568)
• The terms "spiritual experience" and "spiritual awakening" are used many times in this book which, upon careful reading, shows that the personality change sufficient to bring about recovery from alcoholism has manifested itself among *us* in many different forms.(p.569)
• Most of *us* think this awareness of a Power greater than ourselves is the essence of spiritual experience.(p.570)
• Since Dr. Silkworth's first endorsement of Alcoholics Anonymous, medical societies and physicians throughout the world have set their approval upon *us*.(p.571)

use

• These allergic types can never safely *use* alcohol in any form at all; and once having formed the habit and found they cannot break it, once having lost their self-confidence, their reliance upon things human, their problems pile up on them and become astonishingly difficult to solve.(p.xxvi)
• At the end of it, my reports to Wall street procured me a position there and the *use* of a large expense account.(p.3)
• As matters grow worse, he begins to *use* a combination of high-powered sedative and liquor to quiet his nerves so he can go to work.(p.22)
• Or "What's the *use* anyhow?"(p.24)
• That was great news to us, for we had assumed we could not make *use* of spiritual principles unless we accepted many things on faith which seemed difficult to believe.(p.47)
• Simply because it is impossible to explain what we see, feel, direct, and *use*, without a reasonable assumption as a starting point.(p.48)
• Neither is reason, as most of us *use* it, entirely dependable, though it emanate from our best minds.(p.54)
• But we must not *use* this as a mere excuse to postpone.(p.75)
• We don't *use* this as an excuse for shying away from the subject of God.(p.77)
• It is the proper *use* of the will.(p.85)
• Under these conditions we can employ our mental faculties with assurance, for after all God gave us brains to *use*.(p.86)
• Make *use* of what they offer.(p.87)
• When dealing with such a person, you had better *use* everyday language to describe spiritual principles.(p.93)
• There is no *use* arousing any prejudice he may have against certain theological terms and conceptions about which he may already be confused.(p.93)
• But be sure you *use* discretion.(p.96)
• Some day we hope that Alcoholics Anonymous will help the public to a better realization of the gravity of the alcoholic problem, but we shall be of little *use* if our attitude is one of bitterness or hostility.(p.103)
• An alcoholic of this temperament may be quick to *use* this chapter as a club over your head.(p.108)
• He will *use* that as an excuse to drink more.(p.111)
• *Use* your energies to promote a better understanding all around.(p.115)
• Suppose we tell you some of the obstacles a family will meet; suppose we suggest how they may be avoided -- even converted to good *use* for others.(p.123)
• It is of little *use* to argue and only makes the impasse worse.(p.126)
• Nothing will help the man who is off on a spiritual tangent so much as the wife who adopts a sane spiri-

tual program, making a better practical *use* of it.(p.130)
• One of the many doctors who had the opportunity of reading this book in manuscript form told us that the *use* of sweets was often helpful, of course depending upon a doctor's advice.(p.133)
• Meanwhile, we are sure a great deal can be accomplished by the *use* of the book alone.(p.144)
• After your man has gone along without drinking for a few months, you may be able to make *use* of his services with other employees who are giving you the alcoholic run-around – provided, of course, they are willing to have a third party in the picture.(p.146)
• Should you wish them above all else, and be willing to make *use* of our experience, we are sure they will come.(p.153)
• The *use* of spiritual principles in such cases was not so well understood as it is now.(p.156)
• Hopelessness was written large on the man's face as he replied, "Oh, but that's no *use*.(p.157)
• I also made *use* of old trunks and chests, the old can container, and even the ash container.(p.176)
• I said, "In that case, there's no *use* of wasting this," and I got the last of that pint.(p.207)
• I would *use* barbiturates.(p.217)
• I had to persist in my attempts to get straightened out enough to be able to *use* the drinks I needed, without their turning on me.(p.227)
• In foreign parts many a soldier who has been abstemious at home learns to *use* new and potent drinks.(p.230)
• Then broke again, hiding out in cheap hotels all over the country, one night jail stands here and there, and always that horrible feeling "What's the *use* -- nothing is worth while."(p.244)
• Some of these were hard to believe, but it did not require a giant brain to perceive that they had something I could *use*.(p.279)
• We are both depending upon God and our *use* of the A.A. program to help us make a success of this joint undertaking.(p.286)
• My wife became pregnant and the doctor recommended the *use* of port or ale . . . so . . . I bought a six gallon crock and a few bottles, listened to advice from amateur brewmeisters, and was off on my beer manufacturing career on a small scale (for the time being).(p.297)
• My son had absolutely no *use* for me.(p.301)
• The Great Boss has given me diagnostic and surgical talent, and He has loaned it to me to *use* for the rest of my life.(p.350)
• I had to have enough to get drunk on, or what was the *use*?(p.397)
• I must *use* self-will, self-control.(p.408)
• But I was not able to make *use* of this knowledge until after I became sober.(p.409)
• My analyst was one of the first to learn of A.A. and to make subsequent *use* of it in her work.(p.412)
• "What's the *use*?(p.467)
• What we do with it is our own business; how we *use* it is up to us individually.(p.473)
• Even my family didn't have much *use* for me.(p.478)
• So, finally, I went to the YMCA and they graciously permitted us to *use* a room at two dollars a night.(p.495)
• No *use*.(p.499)
• No *use*.(p.501)
• There is no *use* trying any more, for there is nothing to try.(p.502)
• My life had become unmanageable due to the excessive *use* of alcohol.(p.515)
• We all *use* them differently.(p.516)
• I *use* that "Easy Does It" every day, to slow me down a little.(p.516)
• It was no *use* talking of putting myself into a home, a hospital, or of going to see a doctor again, or of going to see a priest or anyone else.(p.523)
• On the next page, A.A.'s "12 Traditions" are seen in their so-called "short form," the form in general *use* today.(p.563)
• We think, therefore, that any considerable property of genuine *use* to A.A. should be separately incorporated and managed, thus dividing the material from the spiritual.(p.565)
• Hence such facilities ought not to *use* the A.A. name.(p.566)
• There is something spiritual about an art museum or a symphony, and the Catholic Church approves of our *use* of them.(p.574)

used

• "Bill's Story," "Doctor Bob's Nightmare," and one other personal history from the first edition were retained intact; three were edited and one of these was retitled; new versions of two stories were written with new titles; thirty completely new stories were added; and the story section was divided into three parts, under the same headings that are *used* now.(p.xi)
• So we *used* our own conception, however limited it was.(p.47)
• Actually, we *used* to have no reasonable conception whatever.(p.49)
• We *used* to amuse ourselves by cynically dissecting spiritual beliefs and practices when we might have observed that many spiritually-minded persons of all races, colors, and creeds were demonstrating a degree of stability, happiness and usefulness which we should have sought ourselves.(p.49)
• Instead, we looked at the human defects of these people, and sometimes *used* their shortcomings as a basis of wholesale condemnation.(p.50)
• What a state of mental goose-flesh that *used* to bring on!(p.54)
• Our stories disclose in a general way what we *used* to be like, what happened, and what we are like now.(p.58)
• We remembered always that our sex powers were God-given and therefore good, neither to be *used* lightly or selfishly nor to be despised and loathed.(p.69)
• He subsequently denied having received the money and *used* the incident as a basis for discrediting the man.(p.80)
• He thus *used* his own wrong-doing as a means of destroying the reputation of another.(p.80)
• We will intuitively know how to handle situations which *used* to baffle us.(p.84)
• What *used* to be the hunch or the occasional inspiration gradually becomes a working part of the mind.(p.87)
• Some, but not all of us, think it has its advantages when reasonably *used*.(p.110)
• They expect him to give them the nice times they *used* to have before he drank so much, and to show his contrition for what they suffered.(p.126)
• But sometimes our drinking will be *used* politically.(p.145)
• He interrupted: "I *used* to be strong for the church, but that won't fix it.(p.157)
• This had little effect however for I kept on drinking and *used* a great deal more hard liquor than in former years.(p.174)
• The water tank on the toilet I never *used*, because that looked too easy.(p.176)
• I *used* to put eight or twelve ounce bottles of alcohol in a fur lined glove and toss it onto the back airing porch when winter days got dark enough.(p.176)
• I *used* also to put it up in four ounce bottles and stick several in my stocking tops.(p.177)
• I *used* to promise my wife, my friends, and my children that I would drink no more – promises which seldom kept me sober even through the day, though I was very sincere when I made them.(p.177)
• I *used* to get terribly upset when I saw my friends drink and knew I could not, but I schooled myself to believe that though I once had the same privilege, I had abused it so frightfully that it was withdrawn.(p.181)
• She had a hairdresser who *used* to tell her about a brother-in-law who had been quite a drinker and about some doctor in Akron who had straightened him out.(p.216)
• You can all remember that in the first few months after the change, a great many men, who had formerly been *used* to a few beers every day or an occasional drink of whiskey, simply quit all alcoholic drinks.(p.232)
• I knew the stuff I was making was a lot stronger than I had been *used* to, but I never suspected that steady drinking of it might develop a taste for something even stronger still.(p.233)
• I stayed so sober that I *used* to keep a quart of medicinal whiskey in my bureau which I *used* to taper off the occasional newspaper alcoholics who were sent to see me.(p.253)
• Lots of times, vain-gloriously, I *used* to take the bottle out, look at it and say, "I've got you licked."(p.253)
• They *used* a sound truck some.(p.265)
• She said to me, "You know, he *used* to own the Merry-Go-Round.(p.267)
• He *used* to drink, and then he found something that started up in Akron that helped him quit drinking."(p.267)
• Russ *used* to be very much pleased because he'd say, "I think Dr. Bob thoroughly enjoys coming out here.(p.271)
• I feel that one of the things that I still have to guard against is that I *used* to be set in my way about what I considered the old-time A.A.(p.272)
• I *used* to think I was cowardly because when things came out pertaining to the program that troubled me, I said to her many times, "Annie, am I being a coward because I lay those things away on the shelf and skip it?"(p.273)
• The details of the long road back to something resembling normal living -- the first short streetcar ride, the purchase of a *used* bike which enabled me to widen the narrow horizon of life, the first trip downtown – I will not dwell on.(p.276)
• While there, two or three more "cash customers" (as Dr. Bob *used* to call them – probably because they had so little cash) were shipped in to us from Detroit.(p.282)
• In the long ago past I *used* to start at the top as president or treasurer and end up with the sheriff breathing down my neck.(p.284)
• Some of the things which *used* to stop me in my tracks from fear still make me nervous in the anticipation of their doing, but once I kick myself into doing them nervousness disappears and I enjoy myself.(p.285)
• Where we *used* to run from responsibility, we find ourselves accepting it with gratitude that we can successfully shoulder it.(p.311)
• I *used* to make excuses to try and get George off the wagon.(p.325)
• He *used* to wonder, when he'd spot one of my bottles around the house, just how he could have overlooked that particular bottle.(p.325)
• Yet I recently recalled that each morning I *used* to talk to the bottle when I took it down from the closet.(p.332)
• One night, I was struck with the memory of a line Alan Ladd *used* in "Shane," a movie that I'd worked on.(p.333)
• I couldn't go to one wine store and look the man honestly in the face and buy a bottle, as I *used* to do when I had parties and entertained and did normal drinking.(p.336)
• I *used* to like to get it on my fingers so I could lick them and get another taste.(p.346)
• I needed alcohol from that night on, and it in turn *used* me, ruling my life for three years.(p.353)
• My sponsor *used* to say to me, "If I could only paint you a picture of how beautiful life can be without booze . . ."(p.355)
• I was living in constant fear that I would get caught while driving a car, so I *used* taxis part of the time.(p.375)
• So I was *used* to it, but I didn't know what the effect of alcohol was because I always had wine, usually with dinner, but always with a lot of ice and about two tablespoons of sugar in it.(p.385)
• Eighteen will be *used* as the starting point, because my drinking before was limited by age, the law, and money.(p.397)
• Showing all the courage and ingenuity that I had not *used* in a positive way, I covered my tracks and hid from my family so successfully that they did not find me for months.(p.401)
• My Quaker mother-in-law, bless her heart, *used* to set the Christmas pudding ablaze with lumps of sugar dipped in rubbing alcohol.(p.402)
• I *used* all those well-known phrases.(p.408)
• In my cups I *used* to tell them off, giving them lengthy advice on how to lead the right life.(p.410)
• Nor were those impossible dreams I *used* to have the things I really wanted.(p.416)
• The boys at the Post Office *used* to bring me my jugs; mail couldn't be opened for inspection at the gate.(p.426)
• I *used* to think, "Why live without whiskey?"(p.430)
• That's the stuff *used* when the oral surgeon puts the needle in your vein and says, "Count to ten," and before you get to two, you're asleep.(p.442)
• Today, I feel I have *used* up my right to chemical peace of mind.(p.448)
• We *used* to argue about our differing ideas, but we can't argue about our feelings.(p.451)
• During these seven years a thing called the Twenty-four Hour Program --a gadget I *used* to think was only a snare to trap the newcomer -- has come to mean much to me, not only as regards my drinking but in the whole pattern of my life.(p.473)
• I am learning that I cannot have my own way as I *used* to.(p.505)
• I *used* to think I was.(p.512)
• I would never admit that I was drinking too much, or spending money that I should have *used* to buy food for my two little boys.(p.526)
• Do it every day for two weeks and you will find you have come to mean it and to want it for them, and you will realize that where you *used* to feel bitter-

ness and resentment and hatred, you now feel compassionate understanding and love."(p.552)

• The terms "spiritual experience" and "spiritual awakening" are ***used*** many times in this book which, upon careful reading, shows that the personality change sufficient to bring about recovery from alcoholism has manifested itself among us in many different forms.(p.569)

useful

• This should suggest a ***useful*** program for anyone concerned with a drinking problem.(p.19)

• Most of us sense that real tolerance of other people's shortcomings and viewpoints and a respect for their opinions are attitudes which make us more ***useful*** to others.(p.19)

• I have since been brought into a way of living infinitely more satisfying and, I hope, more ***useful*** than the life I lived before.(p.42)

• Ministers and doctors are competent and you can learn much from them if you wish, but it happens that because of your own drinking experience you can be uniquely ***useful*** to other alcoholics.(p.89)

• If he gets the idea that you are a nag or a killjoy, your chance of accomplishing anything ***useful*** may be zero.(p.111)

• It is possible to have a full and ***useful*** life, though your husband continues to drink.(p.111)

• So we think that unless some good and ***useful*** purpose is to be served, past occurrences should not be discussed.(p.125)

• His present views ought to prove exceptionally ***useful*** to business men everywhere.(p.136)

• It may seem incredible that these men are to become happy, respected, and ***useful*** once more.(p.153)

• He too, has become a respected and ***useful*** member of his community.(p.158)

• An active member of A.A. since 1939, I feel myself a ***useful*** member of the human race at last.(p.229)

• (This is very ***useful*** knowledge in places where matches are prohibited.)(p.245)

• I never thought I could be ***useful*** to anyone except my husband and my children and perhaps a few friends.(p.326)

• Every day, I feel a little bit more ***useful***, more happy and more free.(p.417)

usefulness

• I was to know happiness, peace, and ***usefulness***, in a way of life that is incredibly more wonderful as time passes.(p.8)

• Never was I to pray for myself, except as my requests bore on my ***usefulness*** to others.(p.13)

• We used to amuse ourselves by cynically dissecting spiritual beliefs and practices when we might have observed that many spiritually-minded persons of all races, colors, and creeds were demonstrating a degree of stability, happiness and ***usefulness*** which we should have sought ourselves.(p.49)

• I pray that you now remove from me every single defect of character which stands in the way of my ***usefulness*** to you and my fellows.(p.76)

• But we must be careful not to drift into worry, remorse or morbid reflection, for that would diminish our ***usefulness*** to others.(p.86)

• We have found nothing incompatible between a powerful spiritual experience and a life of sane and happy ***usefulness***.(p.130)

• If he does not argue about religion, he will make new friends and is sure to find new avenues of ***usefulness*** and pleasure.(p.132)

• So we think cheerfulness and laughter make for ***usefulness***.(p.132)

• Universal respect is the key to their ***usefulness***.(p.567)

useless

• They probably felt that it was ***useless***, that surely I had enough intelligence to know what I was doing.(p.215)

• He did not know it was A.A., and it was ***useless*** to tell him, for he doesn't have our disease.(p.334)

uselessness

• We were having trouble with personal relationships, we couldn't control our emotional natures, we were a prey to misery and depression, we couldn't make a living, we had a feeling of ***uselessness***, we were full of fear, we were unhappy, we couldn't seem to be of real help to other people – was not a basic solution of these bedevilments more important than whether we should see newsreels of lunar flight?(p.52)

• That feeling of ***uselessness*** and self-pity will disappear.(p.84)

uses

• He ***uses*** his gifts to build up a bright outlook for his family and himself, and then pulls the structure down on his head by a senseless series of sprees.(p.21)

• Though it is entirely separate from Alcoholics Anonymous, it ***uses*** the general principles of the A.A. program as a guide for husbands, wives, relatives, friends, and others close to alcoholics.(p.121)

using

• Better men than we are ***using*** it constantly.(p.85)

• I remained with them for three weeks, ***using*** part of the time in making many amends, which I had had no earlier opportunity of making.(p.281)

• But when I cracked my leg with a sixteen-pound sledgehammer in the rock hole, I was fighting the system, ***using*** my body.(p.458)

• At one time, I was ***using*** twenty caps a day; I nearly died half a dozen times on the street.(p.480)

• I had been ***using*** paraldehyde more or less like ordinary drink for the last six years though, occasionally, I'd bounce back to phenobarbital and things like that.(p.524)

• We think that each group should soon achieve this ideal; that any public solicitation of funds ***using*** the name of Alcoholics Anonymous is highly dangerous, whether by groups, clubs, hospitals, or other outside agencies; that acceptance of large gifts from any source, or of contributions carrying any obligation whatever, is unwise.(p.566)

usual

• The ***usual*** outcome was that people continued to wrong us and we stayed sore.(p.66)

• The only answer I could make was that if the man followed the ***usual*** pattern, he would go on a bigger bust than ever.(p.138)

• It was the ***usual*** situation: home in jeopardy, wife ill, children distracted, bills in arrears and standing damaged.(p.155)

• Forty came and went and then the resolution was advanced to forty-one, forty-two, and so on in the ***usual*** pattern.(p.214)

• One evening I had gone out after dinner to take on a couple of double-headers and stayed a little later than ***usual***, and when I came home Clarence was sitting on the davenport with Bill W.(p.216)

• I'd only had two with her, but I'd managed four in the fifteen minutes I'd waited for her, and of course I'd had the ***usual*** uncounted swigs from the bottle as I painfully got up and did my slow spasmodic dressing.(p.223)

• That night I got very drunk, which was ***usual***, but I remembered everything, which was very unusual.(p.224)

• When I got back to Germany I settled down to finish my apprenticeship, drinking the wine of the country as ***usual***.(p.231)

• I had all the ***usual*** experiences of the alcoholic, for I was certainly one by this time.(p.233)

• After a couple of days in dollar hotels and one night in the pokey, I finally landed on my mother's doorstep -- shaking apart, with several days' beard and, of course, broke as ***usual***.(p.238)

• My wife made several attempts to get me to stop and I had the ***usual*** visits from persons who would always ask me "Why?" -- as if I knew!(p.254)

• Enduring all the hangover hells that every alcoholic experiences, I made the ***usual*** resolutions.(p.256)

• After a particularly bad Christmas and New Year's holiday, dad picked me up again early in January, 1937, to go through the ***usual*** sobering up routine.(p.289)

• And when I took that first drink, I was off on the ***usual*** merry-go-round.(p.339)

• The result was as ***usual***.(p.343)

• As ***usual***, I ran out of money, and, as ***usual***, I wired my father for funds to come home.(p.357)

• One night at the dinner table my wife said that tonight was my first birthday in A.A., and that the group would have the ***usual*** ice cream and cake for the "one year man."(p.365)

• As ***usual*** I got drunk and lost the money.(p.491)

• That was the ***usual*** pattern.(p.491)

• But if I came back in the ***usual*** state, then I'd have to go off for good the next day.(p.523)

• But our ***usual*** A.A. "12th Step" work is never to be paid for.(p.567)

usually

• Strangely enough, wives, parents and intimate friends ***usually*** find us even more unapproachable than do the psychiatrist and the doctor.(p.18)

• And the truth, strange to say, is ***usually*** that he has no more idea why he took that first drink than you have.(p.23)

• All of us felt at times that we were regaining control, but such intervals – ***usually*** brief – were inevitably followed by still less control, which led in time to pitiful and incomprehensible demoralization.(p.30)

• I reasoned I was not so far advanced as most of you fellows, that I had been ***usually*** successful in licking my other personal problems, and that I would therefore be successful where you men failed.(p.40)

• Those who do not recover are people who cannot or will not completely give themselves to this simple program, ***usually*** men and women who are constitutionally incapable of being honest with themselves.(p.58)

• What ***usually*** happens?(p.61)

• They arise out of ourselves, and the alcoholic is an extreme example of self-will run riot, though he ***usually*** doesn't think so.(p.62)

• A business which takes no regular inventory ***usually*** goes broke.(p.64)

• We were ***usually*** as definite as this example:(p.65)

• In actual practice, we ***usually*** find a solitary self-appraisal insufficient.(p.72)

• Telling them what we are trying to do, we make no bones about our drinking; they ***usually*** know it anyway, whether we think so or not.(p.78)

• ***Usually***, however, other people are involved.(p.79)

• Whatever the situation, we ***usually*** have to do something about it.(p.81)

• We ***usually*** conclude the period of meditation with a prayer that we be shown all through the day what our next step is to be, that we be given whatever we need to take care of such problems.(p.87)

• If there is any indication that he wants to stop, have a good talk with the person most interested in him -- ***usually*** his wife.(p.90)

• ***Usually*** the family should not try to tell your story.(p.91)

• If the alcoholic tries to shield himself he may succeed for a time, but he ***usually*** winds up with a bigger explosion than ever.(p.101)

• ***Usually*** we did not leave.(p.106)

• Of course, there is such a thing as incompatibility, but in nearly every instance the alcoholic only seems to be unloving and inconsiderate; it is ***usually*** because he is warped and sickened that he says and does these appalling things.(p.108)

• The problem with which you struggle ***usually*** falls within one of four categories:(p.108)

• If this kind of approach does not catch your husband's interest, it may be best to drop the subject, but after a friendly talk your husband will ***usually*** revive the topic himself.(p.112)

• When sober, father ***usually*** obeyed.(p.131)

• Is he not ***usually*** brilliant, fast-thinking, imaginative and likeable?(p.139)

• This may seem severe, but it is ***usually*** the best course.(p.142)

• But my friends ***usually*** found me and I would go home if they promised that I should not be scolded.(p.176)

• I think the longest drunk I was ever on was eleven days, but ***usually*** only two days with a complete blackout for a day, and then backing off by drinking as long as I could get anything.(p.203)

• The "speaks" ***usually*** sold whiskey.(p.233)

• Such thinking ***usually*** began with thoughts of the pleasant drinking of my youth.(p.285)

• He said the alcoholic seemed to possess a native acuteness and ***usually*** excelled in his field, regardless of environmental or educational advantages.(p.308)

• ***Usually***, the next morning I would be quite sick.(p.317)

• I ***usually*** passed out when I hit the bed.(p.319)

• By hook or crook I ***usually*** managed to sober up before I reached home, but always "terribly tired" from a "hard day's work," and just having to have one or two before dinner.(p.361)

• So I was used to it, but I didn't know what the effect of alcohol was because I always had wine, ***usually*** with dinner, but always with a lot of ice and about two tablespoons of sugar in it.(p.385)

• Any time I tried to kill myself, I was either drunk or pilled-up or both – ***usually*** the last.(p.479)

• And we ***usually*** have some kind of grimy sweater that we think we look sexy in, even if we weigh ninety-five pounds soaking wet and are not wearing a bra.(p.479)

• I've never seen him drunk in my life, although he'd take a shot in the morning and ***usually*** one in the evening, and so did I; but for the most part he kept his whiskey in his office.(p.484)

• I got a job by myself which suited me down to the ground, because there was nobody really to interfere with what I did, one way or the other, and I ***usually*** had my nerves in good trim when anybody was coming around to inspect.(p.519)

• For clubs, A.A. managers are ***usually*** preferred.(p.566)

Utah

• During this time I faithfully was writing my girl in *Utah*.(p.360)

utmost

• My talent for leadership, I imagined, would place me at the head of vast enterprises which I would manage with the ***utmost*** assurance.(p.1)

• I was to right all such matters to the ***utmost*** of my ability.(p.13)

• We shall do our ***utmost*** to achieve that ideal.(p.19)

• Simply we tell him that we will never get over drinking until we have done our ***utmost*** to straighten out the past.(p.77)

• Perhaps there are some cases where the ***utmost*** frankness is demanded.(p.82)

• If, on the contrary, you are sure he is doing his ***utmost***, you may wish to give him another chance.(p.147)

Utopia

• Most of us feel we need look no further for *Utopia*.(p.16)

• He is like the retired business man who lolls in the Florida sunshine in the winter complaining of the sad state of the nation; the minister who sighs over the sins of the twentieth century; politicians and reformers who are sure all would be *Utopia* if the rest of the world would only behave; the outlaw safe cracker who thinks society has wronged him; and the alcoholic who has lost all and is locked up.(p.61)

utter

• There was ***utter*** confidence.(p.14)

• This is the baffling feature of alcoholism as we know it – this ***utter*** inability to leave it alone, no matter how great the necessity or the wish.(p.34)

• And I remembered the creeping horror of the interminable night, in which I slept for short spells and woke up dripping with cold sweat and shaken with ***utter*** despair, to drink hastily from my bottle and mercifully pass out again, "You're mad, you're mad, you're mad!" pounded through my brain with each returning ray of consciousness, and I drowned the refrain with drink.(p.224)

• Suddenly I feel a wave of ***utter*** hopelessness sweep over me.(p.504)

• It has shown me, through the tragic stories of so many other alcoholics, the ***utter*** futility of self pity.(p.525)

utterance

• With that ***utterance*** I again made a wonderful discovery.(p.366)

utterly

• In the doctor's judgment he was ***utterly*** hopeless; he could never regain his position in society and he would have to place himself under lock and key or hire a bodyguard if he expected to live long.(p.26)

• Our human resources, as marshalled by the will were not sufficient; they failed ***utterly***.(p.45)

• We thought well before taking this step making sure we were ready; that we could at last abandon ourselves ***utterly*** to Him.(p.63)

• It would be wonderful were I able to tell you that my confidence in God and my application of the Twelve Steps to my daily living have ***utterly*** banished fear.(p.284)

Vv

vacated
• He consented, however, to go the hospital, where he occupied the very room recently *vacated* by the lawyer.(p.159)

vacation
• These vacations became quite something, and he always had two weeks *vacation* the first two weeks of every September.(p.264)
• The next time *vacation* time rolled around that was a bitter lesson to us.(p.265)
• I think that was the last *vacation* before sobriety.(p.265)
• I returned to my home in Lucknow, India, at the end of November last year from a *vacation* in one of the most famous beauty spots in our country, a mountain resort 6,800 feet up, with a wonderful lake.(p.342)
• Eight years ago, my wife and I decided to spend a *vacation* in Naini Tal, the mountain resort.(p.343)
• This was my first long *vacation* of sixty days since I had joined the army.(p.343)
• During this *vacation*, in the months of September and October, I decided to go on the water wagon.(p.343)
• Following this, I had a short *vacation*, during which time I read as much literature as my sponsor could send me.(p.343)
• Last year, I decided on an A.A. *vacation* in Naini Tal.(p.343)
• A year later, while we were on a *vacation* trip she packed up to go home because of my excessive drinking, and I talked her out of it with the promise I would go on the wagon for at least a year.(p.377)

vacations
• These *vacations* became quite something, and he always had two weeks vacation the first two weeks of every September.(p.264)
• *Vacations* from school and from work, spelled "travel" to me -- and I travelled with gusto.(p.275)
• I had the best schools, summer camps, resort *vacations* and travel.(p.304)
• The difference between the two *vacations* was this:(p.344)
• I did work of all kinds after school and during *vacations*, trying to find that which would appeal most as a goal for a life work.(p.373)
• Fear, love of dentistry, and an imitation of my father's periodic drinking pattern took me through dental college soberly, except for the few parties and *vacations* in those four years.(p.419)

vacuum
• And the mops would get out, the *vacuum* would get out, everything would get out, but nothing would get done.(p.337)

vagaries
• In the midst of an understanding and sympathetic family, these *vagaries* of dad's spiritual infancy will quickly disappear.(p.129)

vague
• In a *vague* way their families and friends sense that these drinkers are abnormal, but everybody hopefully awaits the day when the sufferer will rouse himself from his lethargy and assert his power of will.(p.23)
• It would be easy to be *vague* about this matter.(p.86)
• He added that occasionally in the night a *vague* craving arose which would be satisfied by candy.(p.134)
• My parents had some *vague* idea of making a priest out of me and for some years I attended the Franciscan school at Basle, Switzerland, just across the border, about six miles from my home.(p.230)
• Well, there I was, willing to try it, but I didn't know how, except in a *vague* way.(p.236)

vaguely
• I *vaguely* sensed I was not being any too smart, but felt reassured as I was taking the whiskey on a full stomach.(p.36)
• Coming to his senses, he is revolted at certain episodes he *vaguely* remembers.(p.73)
• As he talked I gathered *vaguely*, (because he was a faltering beginner then, just as I am now) that to be relieved of alcoholism I would have to be different.(p.257)
• I remember *vaguely* violent quarrels with my husband, his finding my liquor supply time and time again and throwing it out.(p.466)

vain
• Therefore, it is not surprising that our drinking careers have been characterized by countless *vain* attempts to prove we could drink like other people.(p.30)
• Rather *vain* of us, wasn't it?(p.49)
• There my drinking became so much worse that the boys in the fraternity house where I lived felt forced to send for my father, who made a long journey in the *vain* endeavor to get me straightened around.(p.174)
• An originator of Cleveland's Group No. 3, this one fought Prohibition in *vain*.(p.297)

vain-gloriously
• Lots of times, *vain-gloriously*, I used to take the bottle out, look at it and say, "I've got you licked."(p.253)

vainly
• I completely forgot myself in trying *vainly* to help Anne, whose misery I understood.(p.415)

vale
• We cannot subscribe to the belief that this life is a *vale* of tears, though it once was just that for many of us.(p.133)

valid
• And there may be a *valid* reason for postponement in some cases.(p.83)

valley
• And we went down through the *valley*, and I remembered reading about the Ku Klux Klan and how they burnt crosses, and I thought, "God alone knows what we are getting into this time!"(p.269)

valuable
• Yet, we believe we can make some definite and *valuable* suggestions.(p.86)
• It taught me a *valuable* lesson.(p.294)

value
• Henry Ford once made a wise remark to the effect that experience is the thing of supreme *value* in life.(p.124)
• This painful past may be of infinite *value* to other families still struggling with their problem.(p.124)
• He thought all alcoholics should constantly have chocolate available for its quick energy *value* at times of fatigue.(p.133)
• And when I place more *value* on my serenity and sobriety than on anything else, I can maintain them at a higher level -- at least for the time being.(p.452)
• When they saw me coming, they locked up the silverware and everything else of *value*.(p.478)
• Because the "long form" is more explicit and of possible historic *value*, it is also reproduced.(p.563)

values
• If the owner of the business is to be successful, he cannot fool himself about *values*.(p.64)
• If the family cooperates, dad will soon see that he is suffering from a distortion of *values*.(p.129)
• I learned a whole new sense of *values*.(p.409)
• I stood off and took a long look at life and the *values* I found in it: I saw a paradox, that he who loses his life does indeed find it.(p.542)
• My *values* became distorted.(p.556)
• To wear expensive clothes, to have bartenders know what to serve me before I ordered, to be recognized by headwaiters and shown to the best table, to play gin rummy for high stakes with the insouciance of a riverboat gambler -- these were the enduring *values* in life, I thought.(p.556)

valve
• He had taken up light work, and he had a safety *valve* and a pair of spurs and the clothes on his back, and that was all.(p.263)

vanish
• To watch people recover, to see them help others, to watch loneliness *vanish*, to see a fellowship grow up about you, to have a host of friends -- this is an experience you must not miss.(p.89)
• Now about health: A body badly burned by alcohol does not often recover overnight nor do twisted thinking and depression *vanish* in a twinkling.(p.133)
• The only kind of security I knew anything about at that time was material security and I decided that all these intruders would *vanish* immediately if I only had a lot of money.(p.545)

vanished
• Then I went on a prodigious bender, and that chance *vanished*.(p.5)
• My brilliant agnosticism *vanished*, and I saw for the first time that those who really believed, or at least honestly tried to find a Power greater than themselves, were much more composed and contented than I had ever been, and they seemed to have a degree of happiness which I had never known.(p.247)

vanishing
• Headstrong and willful, I rushed from pleasure to pleasure, and found the returns diminishing to the *vanishing* point.(p.226)

vanity
• We wives found that, like everybody else, we were afflicted with pride, self-pity, *vanity* and all the things which go to make up the self-centered person; and we were not above selfishness or dishonesty.(p.116)
• Dishonest thinking, prejudice, ego, antagonism toward anyone and everyone who dares to cross him, *vanity* and a critical attitude are character defects that gradually creep in and become a part of his life.(p.380)
• But as the years go by, the stretch becomes unbearable; and the man with the grown-up brain and the childish emotions -- *vanity*, self-interest, false pride, jealousy, longing for social approval, to name few -- becomes a prime candidate for alcohol.(p.534)
• I know there are some alcoholics who seem terribly, terribly grown-up, but I think that they are trying to make themselves think they are grown-up, and the strain of their effort is what is causing them to drink -- a sense of inadequacy, a childish *vanity* to be the most popular, the most sought after, the mostest of the most.(p.535)

vapor
• As we became subjects of King Alcohol, shivering denizens of his mad realm, the chilling *vapor* that is loneliness settled down.(p.151)

variation
• In our personal stories you will find a wide *variation* in the way each teller approaches and conceives of the Power which is greater than himself.(p.50)

varied
• But, as with most humans, he is more likely to have *varied* traits.(p.61)
• Brandishing my "motto," which was "A little man with a stick is equal to a big man," sometimes I *varied* the literary lecture by a fight with a big man, selected solely because he was big and I was little.(p.537)

varieties
• The distinguished American psychologist, William James, in his book "*Varieties* of Religious Experience," indicates a multitude of ways in which men have discovered God.(p.28)

variety
• To one who feels he is an atheist or agnostic such an experience seems impossible, but to continue as he is means disaster, especially if he is an alcoholic of the hopeless *variety*.(p.44)
• As a draftsman, I worked for several large companies and gained a *variety* of experience.(p.211)
• Most of our experiences are what the psychologist William James calls the "educational *variety*" because they develop slowly over a period of time.(p.569)

various
• He plans *various* ways of drinking.(p.xxviii)
• We have learned that whatever the human frailties of *various* faiths may be, those faiths have given purpose and direction to millions.(p.49)
• Being convinced that self, manifested in *various* ways, was what had defeated us, we considered its common manifestations.(p.64)
• He has begun to try, with or without your cooperation, *various* means of moderating or staying dry.(p.109)
• God has abundantly supplied this world with fine doctors, psychologists, and practitioners of *various* kinds.(p.133)
• None of the *various* cures of this kind were any good.(p.235)
• I moved in a gay crowd in the *various* "pubs" and sporting clubs.(p.251)
• The big A.A. book had not been written and there was no literature except *various* religious pamphlets.(p.291)
• In the *various* schools I attended, it was always a case of just getting by.(p.357)
• Looking back, it is surprising to me now that I managed to keep working and have enough money to squander at the *various* spots in the big city.(p.358)
• She tried reasoning with me, endeavored to work out *various* drinking schedules, in fact all the tricks

were practised faithfully for a short time somewhere along my shaky road to unhappiness.(p.361)

• The obsession of the mind was a little harder to understand and yet everyone has obsessions of ***various*** kinds.(p.380)

• They were bright and well read, they held ***various*** political views.(p.410)

• It started out as a good marriage, but it deteriorated over the years as she progressed through the ***various*** stages of qualifying for Al-Anon.(p.439)

• It is true that the doctors and nurses in the ***various*** institutions I attended knew too.(p.470)

• Like most other alcoholics I have known, I did quit drinking at ***various*** times – once for ten months on my own and during other interludes when I was hospitalized.(p.554)

variously

• Our struggles with them are ***variously*** strenuous, comic and tragic.(p.16)

• Had we not ***variously*** worshipped people, sentiment, things, money, and ourselves?(p.54)

vary

• This is by no means a comprehensive picture of the true alcoholic, as our behavior patterns ***vary***.(p.22)

• Opinions ***vary*** considerably as to why the alcoholic reacts differently from normal people.(p.22)

varying

• I seemed to react by developing a streak of ***varying*** meanness, which would cause me to do things to create excitement and to get attention.(p.211)

vast

• My talent for leadership, I imagined, would place me at the head of ***vast*** enterprises which I would manage with the utmost assurance.(p.1)

• My intellectual heroes, the chemists the astronomers, even the evolutionists, suggested ***vast*** laws and forces at work.(p.10)

• There is, however, a ***vast*** amount of fun about it all.(p.16)

• I had tried to be the center of my own little world, whereas God was the center of a ***vast*** universe of which I was perhaps an essential, but a very tiny, part.(p.280)

• Though it was not our intention to create such an impression, many alcoholics have nevertheless concluded that in order to recover they must acquire an immediate and overwhelming "God-consciousness" followed at once by a ***vast*** change in feeling and outlook.(p.569)

• Historians may one day recognize Alcoholics Anonymous to have been a great venture in social pioneering which forged a new instrument for social action; a new therapy based on the kinship of common suffering; one having a ***vast*** potential for the myriad other ills of mankind."(p.573)

vastly

• Yes, there is a substitute and it is ***vastly*** more than that.(p.152)

vaudeville

• For by now I had been exposed once to A.A., but I had treated it as a ***vaudeville*** and had taken friends to meetings so that they too could enjoy the fascination of the naked revelation of suffering and recovery.(p.539)

veered

• Some of us ***veered*** from extreme to extreme, ever hoping that one day our loved ones would be themselves once more.(p.105)

vehicles

• He gets a thrill out of skipping in front of fast-moving ***vehicles***.(p.37)

vein

• That's the stuff used when the oral surgeon puts the needle in your ***vein*** and says, "Count to ten," and before you get to two, you're asleep.(p.442)

• In the garage, I would put the needle in my ***vein*** and then try to figure out exactly how much medication to inject to overcome the pep pills while adding to the sleeping pills while ignoring the tranquilizers, in order to get just enough to be able to pull out the needle, jerk the tourniquet, throw it in the car, slam the car door shut, run down the hall, and fall in bed before I fell asleep.(p.442)

veins

• I didn't feel I could lie in bed and squirt the stuff in my ***veins*** while my kids and wife stood around watching me, so I kept the drug in my bag and the bag in the car and the car in the garage.(p.442)

venerable

• Maine newsletter (Boomerang) say: "With tireless devotion and humility, this ***venerable*** Indian gentleman traveled thousands of miles humbly pleading for sobriety.(p.476)

vengeful

• The thought came to me that if God, as my mother said, was a ***vengeful*** God, he couldn't be a loving God.(p.489)

venomous

• My tongue had become increasingly skilled at ***venomous*** home truths.(p.405)

vent

• It is better, however, that one does not needlessly name a person upon whom she can ***vent*** jealously.(p.82)

venture

• The broker had gone to Akron on a business ***venture*** which had collapsed, leaving him greatly in fear that he might start drinking again.(p.xvi)

• But his ***venture*** wound up in a law suit and bogged down completely.(p.154)

• Finally my father had to send a doctor out from my home town who managed to get me back there in some way, and I was in bed about two months before I could ***venture*** out of the house.(p.175)

• My last ***venture***, a book shop, was hastened to closed doors by my steady intoxication.(p.255)

• Once again I asked my girl to marry me and join me in this new ***venture***.(p.359)

• I was now head of a publishing ***venture*** in which nearly a million dollars had been invested.(p.435)

• Historians may one day recognize Alcoholics Anonymous to have been a great ***venture*** in social pioneering which forged a new instrument for social action; a new therapy based on the kinship of common suffering; one having a vast potential for the myriad other ills of mankind."(p.573)

ventured

• Looking sadder than ever, he wearily ***ventured***, "Well this is wonderful for you fellows, but it can't be for me.(p.188)

• Upon graduation, I ***ventured*** to New York to pursue my writing career.(p.555)

Venus

• Even when I was old enough to know better, I dreamed about being as beautiful as ***Venus***, as pure as the Madonna and as brilliant as the President of the United States is supposed to be.(p.400)

verbally

• I had contracted for half of it, at least ***verbally***, and the contractors were taking half of the second mortgage bond.(p.198)

verdict

• The ***verdict*** of the ages is that faith means courage.(p.68)

• However, a ***verdict*** was brought in of murder in the second degree.(p.508)

verge

• I had not yet lost my job or family, even though both were on the ***verge*** of going.(p.379)

veritable

• It is possible to dig up past misdeeds so they become a blight, a ***veritable*** plague.(p.124)

verity

• The statement fascinates me because of its simple ***verity***.(p.396)

Vermont

• In January 1938, I had the opportunity to go to northern ***Vermont*** to manage a small daytime radio station that was up against it financially, and was about to fold its antenna.(p.359)

• With new hope in my heart and new resolutions I set off for ***Vermont***.(p.360)

• My business reputation had reached from ***Vermont*** to Pennsylvania, but, thank goodness, my drinking reputation had not.(p.361)

verse

• In my twenties, I found Edna St. Vincent Millay's ***verse***:(p.534)

version

• There is another meaning for the Hebrew word that in the King James ***version*** of the Bible is translated "salvation."(p.228)

• This is a condensed ***version*** of the original "long form" A.A. Traditions as first printed in 1946.(p.563)

versions

• "Bill's Story," "Doctor Bob's Nightmare," and one other personal history from the first edition were retained intact; three were edited and one of these was retitled; new ***versions*** of two stories were written with new titles; thirty completely new stories were added; and the story section was divided into three parts, under the same headings that are used now.(p.xi)

vessel

• We are like the passengers of a great liner the moment after rescue from shipwreck when camaraderie, joyousness and democracy pervade the ***vessel*** from steerage to Captain's table.(p.17)

• Being wrecked in the same ***vessel***, being restored and united under one God, with hearts and minds attuned to the welfare of others, the things which matter so much to some people no longer signify much to them.(p.161)

vestiges

• Despite the living example of my friend there remained in me the ***vestiges*** of my old prejudice.(p.12)

veteran

• Twenty-two, and a ***veteran*** of foreign wars, I went home at last.(p.1)

• I went downstairs and there was the grizzly old ***veteran*** police officer in charge of the property desk, and as he gave me the stuff, he asked, "Are you going out in the street that way?"(p.204)

• My father was a railroad man and a Civil War ***veteran***.(p.210)

• A young ***veteran*** tells how a few rough experiences pushed him into A.A. – and how he was therefore spared years of suffering.(p.422)

veterinary

• We did, and spent a month boozing it up, popping pills, and smoking marijuana; taking shelter where we could, which included a ***veterinary*** hospital one night; accepting meals from anyone; actually begging; stealing anything we were in need of, which was about everything.(p.354)

Vi

• ***Vi*** was the first girl that I ever took out.(p.485)

• My father had purchased a restaurant, which he felt would take up some of my spare time, and that's how I met ***Vi***.(p.487)

• A very good friend of mine who owned a drug store across the street from us, came by only about two hours later and said that he had seen ***Vi*** down town.(p.487)

• The fear of the loss of ***Vi*** and the feeling that, though she had the right to do as she pleased, she should have told me the truth about it, upset me.(p.487)

• I'd go into my home with a bottle, and I remember clearly how I would look around to see if ***Vi*** was watching.(p.487)

• My brother-in-law was living with us at that time and I said to ***Vi***, "Maybe the bottles are brother's.(p.488)

• Nevertheless, I stayed sober there about six months, because I knew that ***Vi*** was to come later and bring the children.(p.490)

• ***Vi*** had secured work in Washington.(p.490)

• ***Vi*** thought I didn't want to stop.(p.490)

• So I went down to talk to the District Attorney, and the arrangement was made that I would go home to stay with my mother, and that meant ***Vi*** and I were separated.(p.491)

• I continued to work and continued to go to lunch with ***Vi***, and none of our acquaintances on the job knew that we had separated.(p.491)

• The one thing I can remember now was that ***Vi*** was on the corner of 8th and L, and I remember vividly that she had an envelope in her hand.(p.492)

• What actually happened was that I had taken a penknife and stabbed ***Vi*** three times with it.(p.492)

• ***Vi*** was very kind and explained to the jury that I was basically a fine fellow and a good husband, but that I drank too much and that she thought I had lost my mind and felt that I should be committed to an asylum.(p.492)

• I think the thing that galled me was that just after Easter I had drawn my salary for two weeks' work and had decided that I was going to send some money to ***Vi***; and above all else I was going to send my baby daughter an Easter outfit.(p.493)

• She didn't say anything about A.A. or getting me a sponsor at that time, but she did ask about ***Vi***, and I told her ***Vi*** was working and how she could locate her.(p.494)

• Of course, it wasn't very much of a meeting in the beginning; most of the time it was just ***Vi*** and myself.(p.495)

• ***Vi*** was taking care of me and I was devoting all my time to the building of that group.(p.496)

• ***VI***. How to Get in Touch With A.A.(p.563)

Vi's

• After the trial, I got big-hearted again and felt that I should do something in payment for ***Vi's*** kindness to me; so I left Washington and went to

Seattle to work.(p.492)

via

• And life keeps getting simpler and easier as we try to reverse my old idea, by taking care of the internal environment *via* the Twelve Steps, and letting the external environment take care of itself.)(p.446)

vicarious

• Or am I expecting to steal a little *vicarious* pleasure from the atmosphere of such places?"(p.101)

vice

• The other day an approach was made to the *vice* president of a large industrial concern.(p.148)
• What our friend, the *vice* president, had in mind was the habitual or whoopee drinker.(p.149)

vicious

• I wasn't mad or *vicious* – I was a sick person.(p.227)
• THE *VICIOUS* CYCLE(p.238)
• I wasn't entirely immoral; I wasn't bad; I wasn't *vicious*.(p.392)

viciously

• We have struck out *viciously*.(p.105)

vicissitude

• No later *vicissitude* has shaken it.(p.56)

victim

• Then he fell *victim* to a belief which practically every alcoholic has – that his long period of sobriety and self-discipline had qualified him to drink as other men.(p.32)
• Is he not a *victim* of the delusion that he can wrest satisfaction and happiness out of this world if he only manages well?(p.61)
• Can it be appreciated that he has been a *victim* of crooked thinking, directly caused by the action of alcohol on his brain?(p.140)
• The employer can many times protect the *victim* from this kind of talk.(p.145)
• I cannot remember just when I became the *victim* of insomnia, but I do know that the last year and a half I never went to bed sober a single night.(p.299)
• Nevertheless, there were a few doctors who saw alcoholism as a disease and felt that the alcoholic was a *victim* of something over which he had no control.(p.307)
• I told her that I was an alcoholic, *victim* of a disease, that there was no cure, only arrestment through total abstinence.(p.333)
• She was also the *victim* of my scolding and incessant nagging.(p.408)
• If he were still sober, chances are that very quickly I put him down as a Philistine with no appreciation of literary genius; and then I went on to another bar to find a new *victim*.(p.537)

victims

• You're never going to want another drink, are you?"; and this answer of his is very important to those of us who are *victims* of alcoholism.(p.206)

victor

• As in war, the *victor* only seemed to win.(p.66)

victory

• There was a sense of *victory*, followed by such a peace and serenity as I had never known.(p.14)
• Take away my difficulties, that *victory* over them may bear witness to those I would help of Thy Power, Thy Love, and Thy Way of life.(p.63)
• Remember it was agreed at the beginning we would go to any lengths for *victory* over alcohol.(p.76)
• Husbands and wives have sometimes been obliged to separate for a time until new perspective, new *victory* over hurt pride could be rewon.(p.125)
• But in the light of the new understanding that I have found in A.A., I have been able to interpret that defeat, and that failure, and that shame, as seeds of *victory*.(p.335)

Vietnam

• I got orders to go to *Vietnam*, and I spent most of the year over there either drunk or sick with a hangover.(p.317)

view

• Neither does A.A. take any particular medical point of *view*, though we cooperate widely with the men of medicine as well as with the men of religion.(p.xx)
• A new world came into *view*.(p.12)
• Each individual, in the personal stories, describes in his own language and from his own point of *view* the way he established his relationship with God.(p.29)
• We had to ask ourselves why we shouldn't apply to our human problems this same readiness to change our point of *view*.(p.52)
• We cannot be helpful to all people, but at least God will show us how to take a kindly and tolerant *view* of each and every one.(p.67)
• We think that such a *view* is self-centered and in direct conflict with the new way of living.(p.124)
• I really had a chance to see myself from a non-drinking point of *view*.(p.245)
• Another thing that mother drilled into me was a very Puritanical point of *view* as to sex relations and as to motherhood and womanhood.(p.483)
• About then too, I realized that my point of *view* on the opposite sex wasn't entirely like that of most of the boys I knew.(p.484)
• III. The Medical *View* on A.A.(p.563)
• V. The Religious *View* on A.A.(p.563)
• Then too, we *view* with much concern those A.A. treasuries which continue, beyond prudent reserves, to accumulate funds for no stated A.A. purpose.(p.566)
• THE MEDICAL *VIEW* ON A.A.(p.571)
• THE RELIGIOUS *VIEW* ON A.A.(p.574)

viewpoints

• Most of us sense that real tolerance of other people's shortcomings and *viewpoints* and a respect for their opinions are attitudes which make us more useful to others.(p.19)

views

• The physician who at our request, gave us this letter, has been kind enough to enlarge upon his *views* in another statement which follows.(p.xxiv)
• Do not contradict such *views*.(p.94)
• His present *views* ought to prove exceptionally useful to business men everywhere.(p.136)
• They were bright and well read, they held various political *views*.(p.410)
• In the course of drunken arguments, I found my own *views* and sense of responsibility as a citizen.(p.410)
• Concerning such matters they can express no *views* whatever.(p.567)

vigilance

• After such often-painful *vigilance* (and numerous phony stints of abstinence), retirement naturally created an impulse to live without restraints.(p.328)

vigor

• Instead of wanting to escape some perplexing problem, we experience a thrill of challenge in the opportunity it affords for another application of A.A. techniques, and we find ourselves tackling it with surprising *vigor*.(p.311)

vigorous

• Next we launched out on a course of *vigorous* action, the first step of which is a personal housecleaning, which many of us had never attempted.(p.63)
• The next day I went back to Chicago and started a *vigorous* campaign among my so-called friends or drinking companions.(p.293)

vigorously

• We *vigorously* commenced this way of living as we cleaned up the past.(p.84)

village

• I was born in a small New England *village* of about seven thousand souls.(p.171)
• But I can remember, in my teens, that there were a few characters who caused the *village* heads to nod pityingly and sometimes in anger as they paused to say, "That sot, Henri" and "Ce pauvre Jules," who drank too much.(p.230)
• They were undoubtedly the alcoholics of our *village*.(p.230)
• That was on a hot summer evening, down in the Greenwich *Village* Group, and there was a little porch out there in the old meeting place on Sullivan Street, and after the meeting I went out on the steps for some air.(p.321)
• I had met a bunch of gay young Bohemians who lived in the *Village*, and were sowing their wild oats.(p.407)
• Now it was semi-blackouts every night, outrageous behavior, passing out in some friend's *Village* studio or not knowing how I got home.(p.407)
• I saw that my *Village* friends, all of whom had small jobs, were living happily on about a tenth of my sinecure.(p.409)
• There was one *Village* bar in particular for which I formed an obsession.(p.410)
• I went to several *Village* bars, and drank cokes or tea.(p.414)
• I would never be like the *village* drunkard at home.(p.498)

villain

• He'd told a *villain*, "The trouble is, old man, you've lived too long."(p.333)

vin

• My four years of abstinence had something to do with it, but soldiering is a tough enough game for a sober man, and I had no yen for full-pack slogging through mud with a cognac or *vin* rouge hangover.(p.253)

vindicate

• (That condition was a distinct handicap to me in trying to *vindicate* myself with the not so patient wife.)(p.301)

vindictiveness

• We reverted to the old way of life we knew -- a life full of anger, *vindictiveness*, resentment, fear, dependence, denial, self-will, irresponsibility.(p.459)

violent

• In a few years he became so *violent* when intoxicated that he had to be committed.(p.35)
• If your man needs hospitalization, he should have it, but not forcibly unless he is *violent*.(p.91)
• You may have to fight with him if he is *violent*.(p.97)
• He is *violent*, or appears definitely insane when drunk.(p.110)
• My fright was real enough, but it didn't account for these *violent* reactions.(p.222)
• I am a young alcoholic with a drug problem, a doctor, the husband of an alcoholic, the son of an alcoholic, and a man once diagnosed as a *violent* manic-depressive.(p.421)
• I remember vaguely *violent* quarrels with my husband, his finding my liquor supply time and time again and throwing it out.(p.466)
• The idea behind it is that, having taken the treatment, your system is so "conditioned" that the mere sight or smell or taste of alcohol produces a *violent* reaction, and you become ill.(p.469)

violently

• This went on endlessly, and I began to waken very early in the morning shaking *violently*.(p.5)
• Some of us have been *violently* anti-religious.(p.45)
• But the firm became *violently* ill with my drunkenness and their course of treatment was to remove their ulcer, in the form of me, from the payroll, amid much fanfare and very personal and slighting remarks and insinuations.(p.300)

violins

• I was one of the star singers in the choir and one of the leading *violins* in the orchestra.(p.517)

Virgil

• There was the physical aspect; to be the youngest and the runt of the brood of children, to have to wear glasses very early and so to be teased, to be bookish and bored in school because the captain of the football team could not translate *Virgil* and yet was the school god while you, you, you little shrimp, were the school egghead, junior size and an early model.(p.533)

Virginia

• Still another experience: A woman's voice came faintly over long distance from *Virginia*.(p.137)
• At thirteen I was packed off to a very fine Protestant boarding school in *Virginia* where I stayed four years, graduating without any special achievements.(p.240)
• So, sometimes we'd end up in Charleston, West *Virginia*, or here or there, drinking all along the way.(p.264)
• A house in *Virginia*, during the fox hunting season; a little chalet in Switzerland during the summer or a place on Long Island – each house complete with cooks, butlers and maids.(p.403)
• This was in *Virginia*, where I had rented a house with stables and a swimming pool, and the fall fox hunting had begun.(p.404)
• I was born in a little town in *Virginia* in an average religious home.(p.483)
• Of course, when father finally came to *Virginia* to work his way through school, he resented the southern "cracker," as he often called them, so much that he didn't even go back to his mother's funeral.(p.486)
• Dad, due to having spent most of his time in a small *Virginia* town, didn't have any too much money, and the money he had saved and the property he had acquired were in Washington.(p.486)

virtually

• We are equally positive that once he takes any alcohol whatever into his system, something happens, both in the bodily and mental sense, which makes it *virtually* impossible for him to stop.(p.22)
• For most cases, there is *virtually* no other solution."(p.43)

virtue

• I remember the day when I decided to drink myself to death quietly, without bothering anyone, because I was tired of having been a dependable, trustworthy person for about thirty-nine years without having received what I thought was a proper reward for my ***virtue***.(p.531)

virtues
• Also, I believed I was the image of all domestic ***virtues***; secluded in my washday (any day) refuge.(p.369)

virtuous
• In trying to make these arrangements our actor may sometimes be quite ***virtuous***.(p.61)

vision
• Every day is a day when we must carry the ***vision*** of God's will into all of our activities.(p.85)
• It is the most natural thing in the world, once his liquor problem is solved, to feel that he will now measure up to that cherished ***vision***.(p.118)
• A *VISION* FOR YOU(p.151)
• But then, as I drank more and more, the alcohol seemed to affect my ***vision***: Instead of continuing to see what was good about my wife, I began to see her defects.(p.450)

visioned
• They had ***visioned*** the Great Reality – their loving and All Powerful Creator.(p.161)

visit
• When your man is better, the doctor might suggest a ***visit*** from you.(p.91)
• On your first ***visit*** tell him about the Fellowship of Alcoholics Anonymous.(p.94)
• Suppose now you are making your second ***visit*** to a man.(p.96)
• You should not hesitate to ***visit*** the most sordid spot on earth on such an errand.(p.102)
• They were willing, by day or night, to place a new man in the hospital and ***visit*** him afterward.(p.159)
• Before our ***visit*** was over, Bill suddenly turned to his wife and said, "Go fetch my clothes, dear.(p.189)
• During my ***visit*** there, renewing acquaintance with former friends, I soon spent most of my money.(p.252)
• I wanted to roam again and through relatives got a supercargo job on an Australian packet which allowed me to ***visit*** my people in Australia where I was born.(p.252)
• While there I was called to the hospital in my home town to see a former partner who had insisted that I ***visit*** him.(p.257)
• Singly and in groups of two or three, they came to ***visit*** me.(p.258)
• I got along fairly well with my party drinking for quite some time, but eventually I began to ***visit*** beer joints in between parties.(p.298)
• I didn't care to go visiting unless the parties we might ***visit*** had plenty of liquor on hand and I could get drunk.(p.301)
• Well . . . I had a job, and I really wanted desperately to stop drinking, but couldn't, so I readily agreed to ***visit*** the doctor she recommended.(p.301)
• My wife accompanied me on my ***visit*** and the doctor really told me some things that in my state of jitters nearly knocked me out of the chair.(p.302)
• The next day I received a ***visit*** from Mr. T., a recovered alcoholic.(p.309)
• He thought it would be helpful for me to ***visit*** the Akron group and meet many like himself.(p.309)
• Instead, I started going to a nice private sanitarium which, after the first ***visit***, turned out to be more like a country club than anything else.(p.468)
• Also, after that first ***visit*** I learned I could refuse to sign myself in unless they gave me a glass of whiskey in one hand and a glass of paraldehyde in the other.(p.468)
• I ***visit*** a friend who is awaiting orders.(p.499)
• Some men and women come to ***visit*** my friend of the night before.(p.504)
• I get out of the hospital and we ***visit*** some of these new-found friends.(p.505)
• I go to see a man I had been asked to ***visit*** and tell him my story.(p.505)
• I'd ***visit*** one bar after another, having one martini in each, and in each hoping to find someone interesting to talk to.(p.536)

visited
• I ***visited*** Winchester Cathedral.(p.1)
• My schoolmate ***visited*** me, and I fully acquainted him with my problems and deficiencies.(p.13)
• Many a distracted wife has ***visited*** this house to find loving and understanding companionship among women who knew her problem, to hear from the lips of their husbands what had happened to them, to be advised how her own wayward mate might be hospitalized and approached when next he stumbled.(p.160)
• Impressed by those who ***visited*** him at the hospital, he capitulated entirely when, later, in an upper room of this house, he heard the story of some man whose experience closely tallied with his own.(p.160)
• There were only seven or eight people in the group before me and they all ***visited*** me during my period in the hospital.(p.208)
• I ***visited*** my family just once in that time.(p.255)
• The next afternoon and evening, two other men ***visited*** me and each told me his story and the things that they were doing to try to recover from this tragic illness.(p.290)
• We ***visited*** most of that day and attended a meeting that night.(p.378)

visiting
• But life among Alcoholics Anonymous is more than attending gatherings and ***visiting*** hospitals.(p.161)
• We went to Akron for about six weeks and we did a lot of ***visiting*** among the people in Akron.(p.219)
• As we left, and they were escorting us across the bridge into Wheeling, I, with great dignity and sarcasm, told them if their wives were ever ***visiting*** in Akron, and they, too, were looking for their route sign as I was, that I hoped I could extend to them the hospitality that had been shown to me in Bellaire.(p.264)
• I didn't care to go ***visiting*** unless the parties we might visit had plenty of liquor on hand and I could get drunk.(p.301)
• Indeed, I was always well on my way before I would undertake to go ***visiting*** at all.(p.301)
• I also began ***visiting*** bars after work, with my older associates.(p.555)

visitor
• My ***visitor*** well knew, that as I tried to follow God I would get to studying these things out for myself.(p.236)

visitors
• Said one of the ***visitors***, "We're giving you a treatment for alcoholism."(p.157)
• At this both the ***visitors*** burst into a laugh.(p.157)
• He had three ***visitors***.(p.159)
• Now, this house will hardly accommodate its weekly ***visitors***, for they number sixty or eighty as a rule.(p.161)
• As time went on, I found that it was customary to open a few bottles whenever ***visitors*** dropped in.(p.297)
• Our home is always full of friends and ***visitors***.(p.303)
• This went on for thirteen weeks, the first eight of which I wasn't allowed ***visitors***.(p.425)

visits
• The ***visits*** from these men impressed me at once.(p.235)
• My wife made several attempts to get me to stop and I had the usual ***visits*** from persons who would always ask me "Why?" -- as if I knew!(p.254)
• ***Visits*** from friends which lasted over fifteen minutes exhausted me.(p.275)
• The example which they and Bill W., whose ***visits*** to Akron were fairly frequent, set me of service to their fellow men imbued me with a great desire to emulate them.(p.281)
• My ***visits*** to that sanitarium went on for nearly three years, until in March of 1944, my father died and I was too drunk to attend his funeral.(p.469)

vistas
• Whole new ***vistas*** were opened and life began to take on color and interest.(p.311)

visual
• Everybody nowadays, believes in scores of assumptions for which there is good evidence, but no perfect ***visual*** proof.(p.48)
• And does not science demonstrate that ***visual*** proof is the weakest proof?(p.48)

visualize
• By now it had become difficult to ***visualize*** a life without alcohol.(p.378)
• I don't know what I expected, but I most certainly didn't ***visualize*** a group of people talking about their drinking problems, making light of their personal tragedies and at the same time enjoying themselves.(p.378)
• My only hope was to try and get through what was left of life as best I could, but I could never ***visualize*** doing that without drinking.(p.522)

vital
• It also indicated that strenuous work, one alcoholic with another, was ***vital*** to permanent recovery.(p.xvii)
• I have seen men come out of asylums and resume a ***vital*** place in the lives of their families and communities.(p.15)
• Here and there, once in a while, alcoholics have had what are called ***vital*** spiritual experiences.(p.27)
• This hope, however, was destroyed by the doctor's telling him that while his religious convictions were very good, in his case they did not spell the necessary ***vital*** spiritual experience.(p.27)
• Though our decision was a ***vital*** and crucial step, it could have little permanent effect unless at once followed by a strenuous effort to face, and to be rid of, the things in ourselves which had been blocking us.(p.64)
• The best reason first: If we skip this ***vital*** step, we may not overcome drinking.(p.72)
• We have begun to develop this ***vital*** sixth sense.(p.85)
• To be ***vital***, faith must be accompanied by self sacrifice and unselfish, constructive action.(p.93)
• It is important for him to realize that your attempt to pass this on to him plays a ***vital*** part in your own recovery.(p.94)
• Hidden old-drunks can pass out on their beds and snooze unreproached, under the guise of taking those ***vital*** retirement-age naps.(p.330)
• It becomes ***vital***, also, that others not know of our defeats, nor suspect our loss of confidence.(p.331)
• And if I had been able to turn to the church at that time I'm sure they could not have convinced me my sickness was within myself, nor could they have shown me the need for self-analysis that A.A. has shown me is ***vital*** if I am to survive.(p.546)

vitally
• Had he been successful in his enterprise, he would have been set on his feet financially which at the time, seemed ***vitally*** important.(p.153)

vitamin
• There was a doctor in our church congregation who was interested in my case, and he thought it was a ***vitamin*** deficiency.(p.389)

vitamins
• You know those ***vitamins*** just don't keep you sober!(p.389)

vivid
• Instead, I quickly substituted one or another ***vivid*** scene from the nightmare of my later drinking.(p.286)
• This picture is still ***vivid***.(p.292)

vividly
• The one thing I can remember now was that Vi was on the corner of 8th and L, and I remember ***vividly*** that she had an envelope in her hand.(p.492)

vocation
• None of us makes a sole ***vocation*** of this work, nor do we think its effectiveness would be increased if we did.(p.19)

vodka
• It wasn't strong enough, so I added a shot of ***vodka*** -- and was right back to worse trouble than before.(p.556)
• Instead of drinking in fancy bars and clubs, I had to carry a bottle of ***vodka*** in my briefcase, duck into public toilets, and gulp from the bottle, trembling, in order to keep from falling apart.(p.557)
• Each time, I went back to drinking – even smuggling a bottle of ***vodka*** into the hospital as soon as the blood transfusions had ceased.(p.558)

voice
• The cheery ***voice*** of an old school friend asked if he might come over.(p.8)
• I could almost hear the sound of the preacher's ***voice*** as I sat, on still Sundays, way over there on the hillside; there was that proffered temperance pledge I never signed; my grandfather's good natured contempt of some church folk and their doings; his insistence that the spheres really had their music; but his denial of the preacher's right to tell him how he must listen; his fearlessness as he spoke of these things just before he died; these recollections welled up from the past.(p.10)
• Still another experience: A woman's ***voice*** came faintly over long distance from Virginia.(p.137)
• From far away, as if in a delirium, I heard my own ***voice*** -- calling someone "Dorothy," talking of dress shops, of jobs . . . the words came clearer . . . this sound of my own ***voice*** frightened me as it came closer . . . and suddenly, there I was, talking of I knew not what, to someone I'd never seen before this very moment.(p.222)
• This man faced the last ditch when his wife's ***voice*** from 1,300 miles away sent him to A.A.(p.356)
• I heard a lovely ***voice***, and a sympathetic ear listened to my plea.(p.363)

• At a large party in Geneva, with people from many countries represented, the kind of party that is "protocol" in the extreme, I swayed, laughed hysterically, made naughty remarks in an unhushed ***voice***, and was finally led from the scene.(p.406)

• Three weeks ago, my phone rang, and a ***voice*** I hadn't heard in over twenty-three years spoke.(p.462)

• The grand fellow who at my call made me a hail-fellow-well-met, who gave me such a fine ***voice***, as we sang "Hail, hail, the gang's all here," and "Sweet Adeline," who gave me freedom from fear and feelings of inferiority.(p.498)

• Then comes a thought that is like a ***Voice***.(p.504)

• My wife hears my ***voice*** and knows I have found the answer to life.(p.505)

voiced

• Our earliest printing ***voiced*** the hope "that every alcoholic who journeys will find the Fellowship of Alcoholics Anonymous at his destination.(p.xv)

voices

• One set of ***voices*** cry that sex is a lust of our lower nature, a base necessity of procreation.(p.68)

• Then we have the ***voices*** who cry for sex and more sex; who bewail the institution of marriage; who think that most of the troubles of the race are traceable to sex causes.(p.69)

• I heard ***voices*** when no one was around, and I saw things that weren't there.(p.319)

• Finally, he was drinking to keep away those little men, and those strange ***voices***, and the organ music that came out of the walls.(p.512)

• I was drinking to keep away the shakes, drinking to keep away those little men and those strange ***voices*** and the organ music that comes out of the walls.(p.514)

voicing

• The wording was, of course, quite optional so long as we expressed the idea, ***voicing*** it without reservation.(p.63)

volume

• Therefore, the first portion of this ***volume***, describing the A.A. recovery program, has been left untouched in the course of revisions made for both the second and the third editions.(p.xi)

• All changes made over the years in the Big Book (A.A. members' fond nickname for this ***volume***) have had the same purpose: to represent the current membership of Alcoholics Anonymous more accurately, and thereby to reach more alcoholics.(p.xii)

• This determination bore fruit in the spring of 1939 by the publication of this ***volume***.(p.xvii)

• We hope this ***volume*** will inform and comfort those who are, or who may be affected.(p.18)

• We have concluded to publish an anonymous ***volume*** setting forth the problem as we see it.(p.19)

• He has read this ***volume*** and says he is prepared to go through with the Twelve Steps of the program of recovery.(p.96)

• Being certain he wants to stop, you can go to him with this ***volume*** as joyfully as though you had struck oil.(p.113)

• When the man is presented with this ***volume*** it is best that no one tell him he must abide by its suggestions.(p.144)

• This company now does a ***volume*** of over three billion dollars annually.(p.242)

• I really worked for several weeks, and having had a fairly wide acquaintance with the dealer trade, it was not difficult for me to line up enough of them to give me a very substantial ***volume*** of business with a minimum of effort.(p.300)

volumes

• We gave up our positions and off we roared on a motorcycle, the sidecar stuffed with tent, blankets, a change of clothes, and three huge ***volumes*** of a financial reference service.(p.2)

voluntarily

• By this time I was beginning to pay very dearly physically and, in hope of relief, ***voluntarily*** incarcerated myself at least a dozen times in one of the local sanitariums.(p.174)

voluntary

• There were to be no fees or dues; our expenses were to be met by our own ***voluntary*** contributions.(p.xix)

• Here are some of the methods we have tried: Drinking beer only, limiting the number of drinks, never drinking alone, never drinking in the morning, drinking only at home, never having it in the house, never drinking during business hours, drinking only at parties, switching from scotch to brandy, drinking only natural wines, agreeing to resign if ever drunk on the job, taking a trip, not taking a trip, swearing off forever (with and without a solemn oath), taking more physical exercise, reading inspirational books, going to health farms and sanitariums, accepting ***voluntary*** commitment to asylums -- we could increase the list ad infinitum.(p.31)

• 7. – The A.A. groups themselves ought to be fully supported by the ***voluntary*** contributions of their own members.(p.566)

• They are the custodians of our A.A. Tradition and the receivers of ***voluntary*** A.A. contributions by which we maintain our A.A. General Service Office at New York.(p.567)

volunteer

• Many of my neighbors devoted time to ***volunteer*** work.(p.326)

• I said to her one day when I met her on the street, "What sort of ***volunteer*** work do you do?"(p.326)

• She said "Suppose I put your name down as a ***volunteer***.(p.326)

• So I never did any ***volunteer*** work.(p.326)

• He's now in A.A. and works as a ***volunteer*** for the local alcoholism council.(p.330)

• I tried ***volunteer*** activity.(p.410)

• But my attempts at community service ended in a drunken and abusive row with a fellow ***volunteer***.(p.410)

vomit

• Following an injection I would have to keep one hand busy scratching my constantly itching nose and would also have sudden uncontrollable urges to ***vomit***.(p.442)

vomited

• I ***vomited*** every morning.(p.558)

vomiting

• Suddenly, I began ***vomiting*** and losing rectally great quantities of blood.(p.558)

voted

• I was ***voted*** the man most likely to succeed.(p.345)

vow

• An offer of appreciation for not having had a drink for those few months and then and there, without anybody promising me anything or threatening me, I made a solemn ***vow*** that never so long as I lived would I take another drink.(p.200)

vowed

• I ***vowed*** that never again would any important person whom I wished to please and impress ever see me drunk.(p.328)

vows

• For, after those daily self-punishing sessions with myself, after the ***vows*** to stop, I would change entirely as evening came on.(p.408)

vows

• For, after those daily self-punishing sessions with myself, after the ***vows*** to stop, I would change entirely as evening came on.(p.408)

Ww

W

• They said is you want to know how this program works, take the first word of your question – the H is for honesty, the O is for open-mindedness and the *W* is for willingnes; these our Book calls the essentials of recovery.(p.550)

w-h-i-s-k-e-y

• At that time life to me was spelled "*w-h-i-s-k-e-y*."(p.430)

wad

• I suspect that those bartenders would wait until I shot my *wad*, then call a cab and send me home.(p.410)

wagon

• They are always "going on the *wagon* for keeps."(p.xxviii)
• Why can't he stay on the water *wagon*?(p.22)
• Two: Your husband is showing lack of control, for he is unable to stay on the water *wagon* even when he wants to.(p.109)
• I could take one drink and get right back on the *wagon*.(p.202)
• These periods became more frequent and I resolved that when I became forty, which was very shortly, I was going on the *wagon*.(p.213)
• "Anyhow, I'm on the *wagon* now," I said.(p.257)
• George tried many times to go on the *wagon*.(p.324)
• If I had been sincere in what I thought I wanted more than anything else in life – a sober husband and a happy, contented home – I would have gone on the *wagon* with him.(p.324)
• I used to make excuses to try and get George off the *wagon*.(p.325)
• And I was able to go on the *wagon* for long periods of time – once for four years, to cure an ulcer.(p.328)
• For this officer in the Indian Army, going on the *wagon* was not enough; attempts at control failed.(p.342)
• During this vacation, in the months of September and October, I decided to go on the water *wagon*.(p.343)
• On the first, though on the water *wagon*, I looked forward to my next drink.(p.344)
• I went on the *wagon* more to placate my wife than anything else.(p.344)
• I tried the *wagon* on numerous occasions but I always felt unhappy and abused.(p.375)
• A year later, while we were on a vacation trip she packed up to go home because of my excessive drinking, and I talked her out of it with the promise I would go on the *wagon* for at least a year.(p.377)
• I must go on the *wagon* for a while.(p.408)
• These things were carried out in moments of less severe hangover or short stretches on the *wagon*.(p.409)
• I had been on the *wagon* when I came to A.A. and this sobriety-tension eventually popped.(p.414)
• I got off the so-called *wagon*, and on the twenty-four hour plan.(p.415)
• I, who could never stay on the *wagon* for more than a week.(p.416)
• Climb on water *wagon* for few months.(p.475)
• I stay on *wagon* for while, but miserable.(p.475)
• I went on the *wagon*, with no outside help and with no real difficulty – except that I didn't enjoy life without drinking.(p.557)

wail

• Like most statistics, it doesn't prove anything – just satisfies a little curiosity engendered by the *wail* "Oh, those initiation fees" that prompted this investigation.(p.399)

wait

• Sometimes it is wise to *wait* till he goes on a binge.(p.90)
• *Wait* for the end of the spree, or at least for a lucid interval.(p.90)
• They should *wait* for the end of his next drinking bout.(p.90)
• *Wait* until repeated stumbling convinces him he must act, for the more you hurry him the longer his recovery may be delayed.(p.113)
• If he does not, you will probably not have long to *wait*.(p.113)
• There was nothing to do but *wait*.(p.139)
• I had to *wait* some time for the train.(p.179)
• Then when we got back to the apartment, he was willing to *wait* two or three days until I got my health back to be paid off for the liquor and fare.(p.289)
• I could not *wait* to tell him that I wanted help, that if these men in Akron had anything I wanted it, and would do anything to get it.(p.289)
• They realized that in the end alcoholism could be a mortal as cancer; certainly no sane man would *wait* for a malignant growth to become fatal before seeking help.(p.315)
• They sum it up like this: "We didn't *wait* to hit bottom because, thank God, we could see the bottom.(p.315)
• But then I thought, well, now *wait*, how will I feel next Tuesday?(p.326)
• They phoned my husband that I was in jail and in such terrible shape that they didn't know what I would do to myself; and they realized that jail was no place for me, but that he was to *wait* a while before he got me, because at the time they called him to come over for me I was beating a tin cup against the wall.(p.390)
• He said, "*Wait* until I get back and I will go with you to see this man."(p.393)
• I suspect that those bartenders would *wait* until I shot my wad, then call a cab and send me home.(p.410)
• But I do not *wait* for the charred keg to work.(p.501)
• Then a change in management took place in the regiment and the new O.C. didn't like me very much and I didn't like him, and he started to lie in *wait* for me.(p.519)
• He didn't have to lie in *wait* very long, but fortunately by that time, I had acquired friends upstairs and they covered me for quite a time.(p.519)
• I couldn't *wait* until the meeting was over to get a drink.(p.526)
• I would *wait* for the mailman each month, like any good mother, but as soon as he handed me my check, I put on my best dress and went looking for my alcoholic friend.(p.527)

waited

• I'd only had two with her, but I'd managed four in the fifteen minutes I'd *waited* for her, and of course I'd had the usual uncounted swigs from the bottle as I painfully got up and did my slow spasmodic dressing.(p.223)
• He *waited* until I was completely sober and the day before I was to head back for Chicago, he told me of a small group of men in Akron who apparently had the same problem that I had but were doing something about it.(p.289)
• I kept away from liquor and eagerly *waited*.(p.363)
• So he *waited* another week or two and I don't think I stayed sober hardly at all.(p.391)
• I went out to the West Coast, *waited* on table, washed dishes and sold newspaper subscriptions.(p.401)
• I *waited* all the rest of that day and paced the floor all that night.(p.467)
• By this time I was such a past master at kidding myself that I had convinced myself I had sat out a war and *waited* for this man to come home and, as my resentment and self-pity grew, so did my alcoholic problem.(p.548)

waiter

• I'd been sitting comfortably in a restaurant with Rita, drinking my sixth martini and hoping the *waiter* would forget about the lunch order – at least long enough for me to have a couple more.(p.223)

waiting

• This may take patient *waiting*, but it will be worth it.(p.112)
• I was still untrained for any work but washing dishes and *waiting* on table.(p.401)
• While *waiting* to depart I was selected – by giving a CPO five dollars – to be bartender in the Navy Chief's Club.(p.426)
• I never just sit and do nothing while *waiting* for Him to tell me what to do.(p.452)
• And then my *waiting* until I was sure he was asleep, and stealing money from him to replenish the supply.(p.466)
• I was taken out of the house and put bodily into a *waiting* car with nothing on but a robe and gown.(p.466)
• When I wended my way home four days later, on the 27th, there was a detective *waiting* for me.(p.508)
• You hit the street about ten minutes to eight, and you walk around the block, God knows how many times, *waiting* for that joint to open.(p.514)

waitress

• *Waitress* by day, barfly by night, she drifted down the years into jail.(p.478)

wake

• Many alcoholics have learned they can bring their bottle to a cheap movie theater and drink, sleep, *wake* up and drink again in the darkness.(p.244)
• For the last two years of my drinking I prayed on every drunk that I wouldn't *wake* up again.(p.245)
• I'd *wake* up covered with sweat.(p.319)
• I try to live today so that tomorrow I won't be ashamed when I *wake* up in the morning.(p.325)
• In the old days I hated to *wake* up and look back at what last night was like.(p.325)
• To *wake* up at home, not knowing how I got there, and to realize I had driven my car, became torture.(p.375)
• In the morning I would *wake* up with a dollar or two.(p.410)
• Then I found the solution: At the end of study time, I would drink two beers, jump in bed, sleep real fast, and *wake* up smart.(p.440)
• One morning I didn't *wake* up until after four o'clock.(p.515)
• I would *wake* to find myself in some beat-up rooming house, where roaches were crawling over everything.(p.527)
• But I would always *wake* up in the psychiatric ward to begin another long treatment.(p.528)
• Now I had gotten to the place where I would *wake* up with black eyes and not know where I got them, or *wake* up with a lot of money and not know where I got it.(p.528)
• I think I am dreaming and will soon *wake* up.(p.529)

waked

• I'd *waked* up in strange rooms before, fully dressed on a bed or a couch; I'd *waked* up in my own room, in or on my own bed, not knowing what hour or day it was, afraid to ask . . . but this was different.(p.222)

waken

• This went on endlessly, and I began to *waken* very early in the morning shaking violently.(p.5)

wakened

• The next morning, my wife came into my room and *wakened* me and said, "That man is downstairs and he said you said you'd go to Akron."(p.217)
• They, too, had taken a train to one town and had *wakened* hundreds of miles in the opposite direction, never knowing how they got there.(p.246)

waking

• Mom and I drank every *waking* moment because we felt so sorry for dad.(p.426)
• And then I went back home to live with my parents, and the merry-go-round started again – only this time I didn't have to worry about *waking* up behind bars in a psychiatric ward.(p.468)
• My personal definition, which I submit as applying only to myself (although everyone is welcome to it who wants it), includes every *waking* activity of the human being; to have a creative attitude towards things is a more exact meaning, to live and to deal with other human beings creatively, which to me means seeing the God in them, and respecting and worshipping this God.(p.535)

walk

• After such an approach many take up their beds and *walk* again.(p.19)
• After dinner I decided to take a *walk*.(p.41)
• Carefully reading the first five proposals we ask if we have omitted anything, for we are building an arch through which we shall *walk* a free man at last.(p.75)
• Both you and the new man must *walk* day by day in the path of spiritual progress.(p.100)
• Many mornings I have gone to classes, and even though fully prepared, would turn and *walk* back to the fraternity house because of my jitters, not daring to enter the classroom for fear of making a scene should I be called on for recitation.(p.173)
• The next thing they wanted to know was if I thought I could quit of my own accord, without any help, if I could just *walk* out of the hospital and never take another drink.(p.186)
• I could work a deal up to where all I had to do was

to go ahead with it; all the planning had been done, all the financing had been done, but then I'd say "Nuts to it!" and *walk* away.(p.197)
• At that time I could go into any saloon, have one or two beers, *walk* out and forget about it.(p.231)
• It was also an ending, for never since June 16th, 1938, have I had to *walk* alone.(p.248)
• As soon as I could get up and *walk* I started to drink again and kept it up until my friend of the hospital, who, in his first try at the new way of life had stubbed his toe in Chicago but had come back to the town to take counsel and make a new start, picked me up and got me into a hospital.(p.258)
• I went for my first *walk*.(p.276)
• He told me that it was imperative that I *walk* around the entire block, cost me what it might in mental agony.(p.276)
• It was February with snow and ice on the ground and I had a four blocks *walk* to the nearest cab stand, but I made it.(p.288)
• I couldn't *walk*, having it in a cast, and the doctor left the cast on three weeks longer than was necessary because he never found me sober enough to take it off.(p.390)
• One afternoon, the year after moving to Houston, I got as drunk as a skunk, and while I do not *walk* very straight sober, you should see me when I'm drunk!(p.390)
• I was just as drunk as I could be, getting ready to take an afternoon *walk*.(p.390)
• To me, A.A. is within the reach of every alcoholic, because it can be achieved in any *walk* of life and because the achievement is not ours but God's.(p.395)
• I would *walk* up and down under the 59th Street bridge, trying to get up the nerve to go up there and jump.(p.411)
• Then I know we *walk* same trail.(p.476)
• He planted many seeds, and it will be many moons before another rises to *walk* in his shoes."(p.476)
• *Walk* with me up Twelve Steps of A.A. to peace."(p.477)
• Then, of course, there are always the wrinkled slacks, which have been slept in and are so dirty, they could *walk* away by themselves.(p.479)
• I *walk* miles.(p.501)
• If something does come along that sort of upsets me, instead of walking in and throwing a buck at the barman and asking for a drink, I *walk* into a telephone booth, drop a dime in the box, and call somebody who was so kind as to give me his name and telephone number to meet such an emergency.(p.511)
• You hit the street about ten minutes to eight, and you *walk* around the block, God knows how many times, waiting for that joint to open.(p.514)
• We must learn to *walk* before we can run.(p.516)

walked

• One day I *walked* into a cafe to telephone.(p.6)
• Some of us had already *walked* far over the Bridge of Reason toward the desired shore of faith.(p.53)
• It would have been impressive heroics if he had *walked* up to the Judge and said, "Here I am."(p.79)
• With a shiver, he turned away and *walked* down the lobby to the church directory.(p.154)
• That afternoon he put on his clothes and *walked* from the hospital a free man.(p.158)
• Bill D. *walked* out of that hospital a free man never to drink again.(p.189)
• He *walked* to the hospital to save bus fare and did it gladly in order to be helpful to an individual he had never even seen.(p.208)
• Somehow I got out of there and *walked* five blocks past brownstone houses.(p.223)
• First, my new wife had *walked* out, bag, baggage and furniture; then the apartment landlord had thrown me out of the empty apartment and the finish was the loss of another job.(p.238)
• Sniffing at emotional religion, I *walked* away.(p.256)
• I jimmied the front door so that I could get back in, and *walked* out.(p.288)
• As we *walked* back through the hall, I, for the first time in my life, said to another human being, "I'm having trouble with my drinking, too."(p.321)
• I *walked* away from that girl grinding my teeth and cursing under my breath.(p.322)
• I recall, as I *walked* into that meeting, saying to myself, "Here I am, a fellow of the American College of Surgeons, a Fellow of the International College of Surgeons, a diplomate of one of the great specialty boards in these United States, a member of the American Psychiatric Society, and I have to go to the butcher, the baker and the carpenter to help make a man out of me!"(p.347)
• When I *walked* into the friendly atmosphere of my first A.A. meeting, I knew I was where I belonged.(p.355)
• I *walked* up that aisle just like Mae West in her prime.(p.385)
• So when he came for me, as he *walked* down the stairs, I could see him through the bars, and he was signing for me; I looked at him and said, "Don't you sign anything in this place!"(p.391)
• I planned to stay home the night before I left, but my folks got so drunk I *walked* off early in the evening and spent the night with my girl, getting very drunk myself.(p.425)
• One day as I sat there in the hospital, my psychiatrist *walked* up behind me and asked, "How'd you like to talk to the man from A.A.?"(p.446)
• I don't remember whether I went by streetcar, whether I *walked* or went in a taxicab.(p.492)
• About seven that evening my sponsor *walked* in, Charlie G.(p.494)
• When he left I *walked* with him to the streetcar line, which was just about a half a block, but there were two liquor stores, one on each corner from my home.(p.495)
• I was trying to remember where it came from, when two of the biggest cops I ever saw *walked* in and took me to jail.(p.528)

walking

• We feel we are on the Broad Highway, *walking* hand in hand with the Spirit of the Universe.(p.75)
• I remember well one fellow, Joe, *walking* nearly three miles through slush, wet and snow to come to the hospital to see a man that he had never seen before in his life, and that impressed me very much.(p.208)
• Need I say that in a very short time I was *walking* along a prairie highway with arm extended and thumb pointed?(p.255)
• This consisted of *walking* the floor for three or four days and nights until I could take nourishment.(p.289)
• I did go to A.A., two days later, *walking* in alone.(p.334)
• Scared that my dress wasn't going to fit right, that the church wasn't going to be filled, that I'd fall flat on my face *walking* up the aisle; in fact, I was afraid I wasn't going to be a prima donna in the place where I should be.(p.385)
• We headed out of town *walking* -- no money, cold and hungry.(p.424)
• If something does come along that sort of upsets me, instead of *walking* in and throwing a buck at the barman and asking for a drink, I walk into a telephone booth, drop a dime in the box, and call somebody who was so kind as to give me his name and telephone number to meet such an emergency.(p.511)

walks

• Friends who have reasoned with him after a spree which has brought him to the point of divorce or bankruptcy are mystified when he *walks* directly into a saloon.(p.35)
• We all one as Great Spirit *walks* through A.A. like sun *walks* through day.(p.474)

wall

• My work took me about *Wall* street and little by little I became interested in the market.(p.2)
• The inviting maelstrom of *Wall* Street had me in its grip.(p.2)
• At the end of it, my reports to *Wall* street procured me a position there and the use of a large expense account.(p.3)
• sometimes they were so inaccessible that it seemed as though a great *wall* had been built around them.(p.107)
• When I hear the more rugged stories of alcoholics who became sicker than I did with this affliction, I humbly thank God for showing me "the handwriting on the *wall*."(p.367)
• As I grow in A.A., I realize that a person with as much self-will as I had, as hard a head and as diseased an ego, had to try everything that I could think of, butting my head against every stone *wall* before I was ready to come in.(p.384)
• They phoned my husband that I was in jail and in such terrible shape that they didn't know what I would do to myself; and they realized that jail was no place for me, but that he was to wait a while before he got me, because at the time they called him to come over for me I was beating a tin cup against the *wall*.(p.390)
• In those days the A.A. Foundation was down in the *Wall* Street district of New York.(p.413)

Wallace

• This worked nicely until my wife and I went to see *Wallace* Beery in "Tugboat Annie," after which the pant-leg and stocking racket were out!(p.177)
• So I'd sit up, watch old *Wallace* Beery movies on all-night TV, and drink.(p.441)

wallet

• I'd lost my car again, pawned my *wallet* and all identification papers for a bottle, and gotten home somehow.(p.429)
• (I am pleased to state, however, that I had gone to only a very few A.A. meetings before I was able to make a really beautiful pair of moccasins -- and half a *wallet*.(p.445)
• Within a month, the police, the hospital authorities, several kind strangers, most of my friends, all of my close relatives, and a few adepts at rolling a drunk and removing his wrist watch and *wallet* had been involved.(p.532)

wallflower

• What had happened to the shy, lonely, churchgoing *wallflower*?(p.355)

Wallkill

• I remained there for about ten months, and then I was sent to a place called *Wallkill*, a so-called rehabilitation center.(p.509)
• I spent my last seventeen months in *Wallkill*, and it was there that I first got my introduction to A.A.(p.509)

wallowed

• Slowly, my life seemed to unfold before me, shedding insights on childhood resentments, jealousies, and fears that had mushroomed in adulthood, and also on the self-pity that I had *wallowed* in at every opportunity.(p.371)
• Under the skilled guidance of an expert practitioner I *wallowed* in the world's individual and collective mental agony.(p.434)

walls

• Many of us have felt, for the first time, the Presence and Power of God within its *walls*.(p.162)
• That armor had turned into prison *walls*, locking me in loneliness -- and fear.(p.226)
• Naturally, in spite of my good intentions, in spite of my protected life behind sanitarium *walls*, I several times got drunk, and was astounded . . . and badly shaken.(p.227)
• The *walls* crumpled -- and the light streamed in.(p.228)
• (And the church *walls* haven't tumbled down yet.)(p.482)
• Finally, he was drinking to keep away those little men, and those strange voices, and the organ music that came out of the *walls*.(p.512)
• I was drinking to keep away the shakes, drinking to keep away those little men and those strange voices and the organ music that comes out of the *walls*.(p.514)

Walter

• We went at once to the country, my wife to applaud while I started out to overtake *Walter* Hagen.(p.3)
• Liquor caught up with me much faster than I came up behind *Walter*.(p.3)

wander

• There will be alluring shortcuts and by-paths down which they may *wander* and lose their way.(p.123)
• I *wander* to a stable and drink five bottles of beer.(p.502)

wandered

• Much moved, I *wandered* outside.(p.1)
• I *wandered* from room to room, thinking, drinking, drinking, thinking.(p.337)
• She had looked for me last evening after I left the car and *wandered* off into the night.(p.502)
• I *wandered*, craving peace, from one spot to another of youthful happy memory, and loathed the man I had become.(p.539)

wandering

• There I was, unshaven, clothes torn and dirty with no recollection of *wandering* all over France but, of course, a hero to the local French.(p.242)
• I had completely forgotten the January 8th when I found the fellowship, and I spent the next four days *wandering* around New England half drunk, by which I mean I couldn't get drunk and I couldn't get sober.(p.247)

want

• Other thousands came to a few A.A. meetings and at first decided they didn't *want* the program.(p.xx)
• Thus was I convinced that God is concerned with us humans when we *want* Him enough.(p.12)
• So many *want* to stop but cannot.(p.25)
• We doubt if many of them can do it, because none will really *want* to stop, and hardly one of them, because of the peculiar mental twist already acquired, will find he can win out.(p.33)

• If you have decided you ***want*** what we have and are willing to go to any length to get it – then you are ready to take certain steps.(p.58)
• We ***want*** to stay out of this controversy.(p.69)
• We do not ***want*** to be the arbiter of anyone's sex conduct.(p.69)
• The right answer will come, if we ***want*** it.(p.69)
• Those of us belonging to a religious denomination which requires confession must, and of course, will ***want*** to go to the properly appointed authority whose duty it is to receive it.(p.74)
• She will ***want*** to know who the woman is and where she is.(p.81)
• We know you will not ***want*** to miss it.(p.89)
• Perhaps you are not acquainted with any drinkers who ***want*** to recover.(p.89)
• If he does not ***want*** to stop drinking, don't waste time trying to persuade him.(p.90)
• If he does not ***want*** to see you, never force yourself upon him.(p.90)
• Make it clear that he is not under pressure, that he needn't see you again if he doesn't ***want*** to.(p.94)
• Perhaps you will ***want*** to take the man into your home for a few days.(p.96)
• After they have seen tangible results, the family will perhaps ***want*** to go along.(p.99)
• We ***want*** the wives of Alcoholics Anonymous to address the wives of men who drink too much.(p.104)
• We ***want*** to analyze mistakes we have made.(p.104)
• We ***want*** to leave you with the feeling that no situation is too difficult and no unhappiness too great to be overcome.(p.104)
• As we say among ourselves, "He wants to ***want*** to stop."(p.109)
• Let him see that you ***want*** to be helpful rather than critical.(p.111)
• Say you do not ***want*** to be a wet blanket; that you only ***want*** him to take care of his health.(p.112)
• Your husband will sometimes be unreasonable and you will ***want*** to criticize.(p.117)
• They ***want*** him to make a fuss over them.(p.126)
• If newcomers could see no joy or fun in our existence, they wouldn't ***want*** it.(p.132)
• Whenever you ***want*** to, you control your drinking.(p.139)
• You, as a business man, ***want*** to know the necessities before considering the result.(p.140)
• If you are sure your man does not ***want*** to stop, he may as well be discharged, the sooner the better.(p.141)
• But there are many men who ***want*** to stop, and with them you can go far.(p.141)
• He wants to quit drinking and you ***want*** to help him, even if it be only a matter of good business.(p.141)
• Say that you believe he is a gravely ill person, with this qualification – being perhaps fatally ill, does he ***want*** to get well?(p.142)
• You ask, because many alcoholics, being warped and drugged, do not ***want*** to quit.(p.142)
• Do you ***want*** to stop drinking or not?(p.147)
• If he cannot or does not ***want*** to stop, he should be discharged.(p.148)
• The right kind of man, the kind who recovers, will not ***want*** this sort of thing.(p.149)
• You will ***want*** to know more of how to proceed from that point.(p.153)
• I did not ***want*** to disgrace myself so I then checked out.(p.179)
• I spend a great deal of time passing on what I learned to others who ***want*** and need it badly.(p.180)
• But if you really and truly ***want*** to quit drinking liquor for good and all, and sincerely feel that you must have some help, we know that we have an answer for you.(p.181)
• They said to me, "Do you ***want*** to quit drinking?(p.186)
• Now, if you don't ***want*** it, we'll not take up your time, and we'll be going and looking for someone else."(p.186)
• I thought of what liquor had done to me, the opportunities that I had discarded, the abilities that had been given me and how I had wasted them, and I finally came to the conclusion, that if I didn't ***want*** to quit, I certainly ought to ***want*** to, and that I was willing to do anything in the world to stop drinking.(p.186)
• One of the fellows, I think it was Doc, said, "Well, you ***want*** to quit?"(p.187)
• Bill looked across at my wife, and said to her, "Henrietta, the Lord has been so wonderful to me, curing me of this terrible disease, that I just ***want*** to keep talking about it and telling people."(p.191)
• That sentence, "The Lord has been so wonderful to me, curing me of this terrible disease, that I just ***want*** to keep telling people about it," has been sort of a golden text for the A.A. program and for me.(p.191)
• I'm so grateful for both the program and the people in it that I still ***want*** to go, and then probably the most wonderful thing that I learned from the program -- I've seen this in the 'A.A. Grapevine' a lot of times, and I've had people say it to me personally, and I've heard people get up in meetings and make the same statement: The statement is, "I came into A.A. solely for the purpose of sobriety, but it has been through A.A. that I have found God."(p.192)
• We boys drove out in somebody's car and went to the bar on the way do the dining room and I, in an effort to impress the other boys that I was city-bred, having lived in Scranton and Cleveland, asked them if they didn't ***want*** a drink.(p.194)
• Long since I had come to believe I was insane because I did so many things I didn't ***want*** to do.(p.199)
• I didn't ***want*** to neglect my children.(p.199)
• I didn't ***want*** to get into fights, but I did get into fights.(p.199)
• I didn't ***want*** to jeopardize the lives of innocent people by driving an automobile while intoxicated, but I did.(p.199)
• Everything in the world a man could possibly ***want***, and I was driving from Akron to Cleveland, having just been to the bank and discovered that I had approximately $5,000.(p.200)
• You're never going to ***want*** another drink, are you?"; and this answer of his is very important to those of us who are victims of alcoholism.(p.206)
• And I said, "Now you ***want*** to dry me up.(p.207)
• I'm not going to ***want*** another drink?"(p.207)
• I said, "Look, Bub, if I ***want*** those lights on, I'll turn them on."(p.207)
• And, because as I have discovered since, it is part of the "treatment" that these men be sent to see and talk with alcoholics who ***want*** to quit, he kept them busy.(p.235)
• I didn't ***want*** to be a fake.(p.237)
• We moved in from the country at the age when girls ***want*** all sorts of nice things.(p.261)
• When I came to my aunt, she knew that I had had an unhappy childhood, and she said, "Now, Ethel, you're welcome to have boy friends in our home, but there are two boys in this town that I don't ***want*** you to date, and one of them comes from a very fine family, one of the best.(p.262)
• But I don't believe now that it was with any deep feeling of resentment that I said to him, "The children are raised, and if this is the way you ***want*** it, this is the way we'll have it.(p.263)
• And Jim G. had such a wonderful sense of humor, and when he came I was in tears, and I told him, "I ***want*** to do this, but I can't.(p.269)
• Before I stop -- I always was a great talker – I ***want*** to say that nobody will ever know how I miss Annie's advice about things.(p.273)
• He mentioned lies and deceptions in the course of his story in the presence of the one person in the world I wouldn't ***want*** to know such things.(p.302)
• I was sent to a psychiatrist, for they didn't think it was normal for me to ***want*** to kill my platoon sergeant or to attempt suicide twice.(p.318)
• Karen didn't ***want*** to see me any more, and neither did two other girls I'd been going out with.(p.318)
• "It can't be my drinking," I thought, "because I can stop any time I ***want*** to.(p.318)
• I just don't ***want*** to."(p.318)
• All of them were so nice to me that I figured I must be careful – they were bound to ***want*** something, being that nice.(p.319)
• I was being very cagey, because I knew that if I did take one or two, I might ***want*** to take five or six or seven or eight.(p.323)
• I needed a drink, but I was afraid to take a morning drink, because I didn't ***want*** to be a drunk.(p.323)
• We're free at last to do our thing, to live uninhibited lives, to drink when and how and where we wish, when we ***want*** to and when we need to.(p.329)
• So I went to her and said, "There's only one thing I ***want*** in my whole life, and I don't ***want*** any commendation; I don't ***want*** any credit; I don't ***want*** anything from you or Janey for the rest of your life except one thing; and that is, the opportunity to do anything you ***want*** always, and I would like to start off by doing the dishes."(p.351)
• I had no idea what would happen -- I just knew I didn't ***want*** to live if life was going to go on like it was.(p.355)
• Why did I ***want*** increasingly greater quantities of alcohol?(p.374)
• There comes a time when you don't ***want*** to live and are afraid to die.(p.377)
• This suggestion had been made before on a number of occasions, but like all alcoholics I wanted to handle my problem my own way, which really meant I didn't ***want*** anything to interfere with my drinking.(p.378)
• I was told that I must ***want*** sobriety for my own sake and I am convinced this is true.(p.379)
• There may be many reasons which bring one to A.A. for the first time, but the lasting one must be to ***want*** sobriety and the A.A. way of living for oneself.(p.379)
• Frank found the doctor, but the doctor didn't ***want*** to take an alcoholic.(p.387)
• I don't ***want*** anybody ever to look at me like that again.(p.391)
• The next morning he came into my room and said, "Esther, I'm not going to lecture you any more, but I ***want*** you to read this article.(p.391)
• I know that when Frank came home, I said, "I ***want*** to try this thing," and he said, "There's a post office box to write to in New York."(p.392)
• I never ***want*** to forget that last drunk as long as I live.(p.393)
• I did not ***want*** to go and see her, but I went.(p.413)
• In the first year there were episodes such as kicking Priscilla in the shins, getting the lock changed on the desk in the A.A. Club, because I, as secretary, didn't ***want*** the Intergroup secretary "interfering," and taking an older woman member out to lunch for the express purpose of informing her that she was "a phony."(p.416)
• I ***want*** to write better and sell more.(p.417)
• I wasn't burdened with parental guidance and I didn't ***want*** any.(p.424)
• There wasn't much I could do about it, and I didn't ***want*** to do anything anyway.(p.427)
• But I didn't ***want*** to stop drinking – not at twenty-two.(p.429)
• "I've got to stop if I ***want*** to live," I told myself, and if I don't ***want*** to break my parents' hearts and maybe jeopardize their own carefully built up and hard-fought-for sobriety.(p.429)
• But if you ***want*** to, you're free to try them.(p.436)
• All I ***want*** to know is, why does that dog wet in my lap every time I hold him?"(p.440)
• I do not ***want*** to digress into the dynamics of penology.(p.458)
• Guess I'll never be a saint, but whatever I am, I ***want*** to be sober and in A.A.(p.463)
• My parents were due for the holidays that day, and she didn't ***want*** them to find their drunken daughter there.(p.467)
• I didn't ***want*** help.(p.468)
• I ***want*** to stop this bad life, but where to turn?(p.475)
• Tell him I ***want*** to get away from bottle and misery.(p.475)
• He old, sick, ***want*** to be alone with bottle.(p.476)
• This sober Indian say to sick, red-eyed alcoholic who ***want*** good medicine: "Put cork in bottle.(p.477)
• No drunk hopeless if he ***want*** to follow guide along right trail.(p.477)
• Vi thought I didn't ***want*** to stop.(p.490)
• She decided that she didn't ***want*** any more of that.(p.491)
• They cooked up a plan whereby she didn't have to be molested by me if she didn't ***want*** to be.(p.491)
• You take me, and all my troubles, and do anything you ***want*** with me.'(p.504)
• I ***want*** to sell the place and move away.(p.506)
• I ***want*** to get where I can find some alcoholics to help, and where I can have some fellowship.(p.506)
• It was their open night meeting, but of course I thought they were all alcoholics; I couldn't imagine why anybody else would ***want*** to go there, and my first reaction was, well, I've come to something that's not for me.(p.524)
• I didn't ***want*** that, so I stopped going to the psycho ward.(p.528)
• All they care about is that I am a human being and that I ***want*** to stay sober.(p.529)
• I just ***want*** to say that you don't have to be afraid, because no one at any A.A. meeting will bite you.(p.529)
• It's time to stop finding excuses for drinking and getting into trouble, because now there is a way out, and if you ***want*** what we have, try coming around and giving the program a chance.(p.530)
• It was my "secret garden" – bluntly, it was my retreat from life, and I didn't ***want*** to give it up.(p.534)
• I ***want*** to be one of His children, a member of the human race.(p.535)

• And, as a child is a part of his father, so do I now *want* to be a part of God.(p.535)
• The truth is, I did not know how to stop it, nor did I *want* to, really.(p.539)
• "Bob," he asked quietly, "do you *want* to live or die?"(p.540)
• But I said humbly, "I suppose I *want* to live."(p.540)
• I still *want* to write a fine play and to get it on.(p.542)
• I don't care too much about personal fame or glory, and I *want* only enough money to enable me to do the work I feel I can perhaps do best.(p.542)
• They said if you *want* to know how this program works, take the first word of your question – the H is for honesty, the O is for open-mindedness and the W is for willingness; these our Book calls the essentials of recovery.(p.550)
• One morning, however, I realized I had to get rid of it, for my reprieve was running out, and if I didn't get rid of it I was going to get drunk – and I didn't *want* to get drunk any more.(p.552)
• He said, in effect: "If you have a resentment you *want* to be free of, if you will pray for the person or the thing that you resent, you will be free.(p.552)
• If you will ask in prayer for everything you *want* for yourself to be given to them, you will be free.(p.552)
• Even when you don't really *want* it for them, and your prayers are only words and you don't mean it, go ahead and do it anyway.(p.552)
• Do it every day for two weeks and you will find you have come to mean it and to *want* it for them, and you will realize that where you used to feel bitterness and resentment and hatred, you now feel compassionate understanding and love."(p.552)
• As another great man says, "The only real freedom a human being can ever know is doing what you ought to do because you *want* to do it."(p.553)

wanted

• For a brief moment, I had needed and *wanted* God.(p.12)
• "He could stop if he *wanted* to."(p.20)
• This we did because we honestly *wanted* to, and were willing to make the effort.(p.25)
• For the type of alcoholic who is able and willing to get well, little charity, in the ordinary sense of the word, is needed or *wanted*.(p.97)
• Even when he *wanted* to assert himself he could not, for his drinking placed him constantly in the wrong.(p.130)
• I still expected a plea for clemency, but these words came through the receiver: "I just *wanted* to tell you Paul jumped from a hotel window in Hartford last Saturday.(p.136)
• She *wanted* to know if her husband's company insurance was still in force.(p.137)
• I *wanted* to throw up my hands in discouragement, for I saw that I had failed to help my banker friend understand.(p.138)
• He *wanted* so much to talk with someone, but whom?(p.154)
• He proved to be a devil-may-care young fellow whose parents could not make out whether he *wanted* to stop drinking or not.(p.158)
• My whole life seemed to be centered around doing what I *wanted* to do, without regard for the rights, wishes, or privileges of anyone else; a state of mind which became more and more predominant as the years passed.(p.172)
• I could drink all I *wanted* of that.(p.177)
• About this time a lady called up my wife one Saturday afternoon, saying she *wanted* me to come over that evening to meet a friend of hers who might help me.(p.179)
• All the other people that had talked to me *wanted* to help me, and my pride prevented me from listening to them, and caused only resentment on my part, but I felt as if I would be a real stinker if I did not listen to a couple of fellows for a short time, if that would cure them.(p.185)
• She also told me that I could not pay them even if I *wanted* to and had the money, which I did not.(p.185)
• The next thing they *wanted* to know was if I thought I could quit of my own accord, without any help, if I could just walk out of the hospital and never take another drink.(p.186)
• The next question, they *wanted* to know was if I believed in a Higher Power.(p.186)
• The next thing they *wanted* to know was would I be willing to go to this Higher Power and ask for help, calmly and without any reservations.(p.186)
• I wasn't afraid that the program wouldn't work, but I still was doubtful whether I would be able to hang on to the program, but I did come to the conclusion that I was willing to put everything I had into it, with God's power, and that I *wanted* to do just that.(p.189)
• I really *wanted* the program and I *wanted* to go along with it.(p.191)
• I had a crew of men working there and I *wanted* them to work Sunday afternoons so that I could sell lots on Sunday.(p.195)
• Naturally, I *wanted* no part of any meetings.(p.205)
• But me, I *wanted* no part of it!(p.206)
• After I was on the drafting board about two years I decided I *wanted* a technical education.(p.211)
• I went back to law school, and doubled up on the courses because I was then approaching thirty years of age and I *wanted* to get through as quickly as possible.(p.212)
• I was willful, full of will to do the things I *wanted* to do and to get the things that I *wanted* to have.(p.214)
• I do not recollect the specific conversation that went on but I believe I did challenge Bill to tell me something about A.A. and I do recall one other thing: I *wanted* to know what this was that worked so many wonders, and hanging over the mantel was a picture of Gethsemane and Bill pointed to it and said, "There it is," which didn't make much sense to me.(p.216)
• For me, work was only a different means to the same end, to be able to do exactly what I *wanted* to do.(p.225)
• I met all the people I *wanted* to meet; I saw all the places I *wanted* to see; I did all the things I *wanted* to do -- and I was increasingly miserable.(p.225)
• I *wanted* help, and I tried to cooperate.(p.226)
• I *wanted* to live, not in a desert, but in a normal world; and my idea of a normal world was among people who drank – teetotallers were not included.(p.227)
• I *wanted* to learn to stand on my own feet, not to change one prop for another, and an intangible and dubious one at that.(p.227)
• Like most immigrants I *wanted* to be somebody and have something and I was very happy and contented as I felt success crown my efforts.(p.232)
• My "periodics" became more frequent until I reached the point where I *wanted* to devote all my time to drinking, working as little as possible, and then only when the necessity of my family demanded it.(p.234)
• And yet, realizing at last that liquor really had me, I *wanted* to quit.(p.234)
• Instead he told me that some of them *wanted* to talk to me and would be over to see me.(p.235)
• At seventeen I entered the University, really to satisfy my father who *wanted* me to study medicine there as he had.(p.241)
• I refused to join any fraternity, as I *wanted* to be a free lance, and that year my drinking was confined to one-night stands, once or twice a week.(p.241)
• Around this time our big A.A. book was being written and it all became much simpler; we had a definite formula which some sixty of us agreed was the middle course for all alcoholics who *wanted* sobriety, and that formula has not been changed one iota down through the years.(p.248)
• I *wanted* to trade.(p.252)
• I *wanted* to roam again and through relatives got a supercargo job on an Australian packet which allowed me to visit my people in Australia where I was born.(p.252)
• I myself could see deterioration in my work from being physically and mentally affected by liquor, although I had not yet reached the point where all I *wanted* was more to drink.(p.254)
• I *wanted* to do nothing except what it pleased me to do when I *wanted* to do it.(p.256)
• The doctor who came to see me almost at once did not assail me with any new doctrines; he made sure that I had a need and that I *wanted* to have that need filled, and little by little I learned how my need could be met.(p.258)
• Whatever it was, I *wanted* it.(p.259)
• Finally, one morning, I got up and got in the car and cried all the way down to the M.'s – the people who owned the bar – and told her I was licked and *wanted* help.(p.267)
• I ate up every bit of it, because I *wanted* to find out how to stay sober.(p.273)
• During my first few months in Akron I was quite sure that I never *wanted* to see my home town again.(p.281)
• I *wanted* "ripe" prospects and I didn't feel that I would get very far chasing individual drunks in and out of bars.(p.281)
• At long last I am doing the kind of work I have always *wanted* to do, but never had the patience and emotional stability to train myself for.(p.284)
• Have I ever *wanted* a drink during these years?(p.285)
• Once dad came all the way to Florida to sober me up, after a hotel manager called him and said that if he *wanted* to see me alive he better get there fast.(p.288)
• I could not wait to tell him that I *wanted* help, that if these men in Akron had anything I *wanted* it, and would do anything to get it.(p.289)
• We went over these at great length and then he finally asked me if I *wanted* these defects of character removed.(p.292)
• Neither one of the two was interested for himself, one being a mother who *wanted* to do something for her son.(p.294)
• Well . . . I had a job, and I really *wanted* desperately to stop drinking, but couldn't, so I readily agreed to visit the doctor she recommended.(p.301)
• In all honesty though, I was skeptical, but I *wanted* so definitely to quit drinking that I would have welcomed any sort of physical torture or pain to accomplish the result.(p.302)
• By now I *wanted* to die, but had lost the courage even to take my life.(p.306)
• He asked me to read the book "Alcoholics Anonymous," and then he *wanted* me to talk with a man who was experiencing success with his own arrestment.(p.308)
• Now there is a sense of belonging, of being *wanted* and needed and loved.(p.312)
• They realized that repeated lack of drinking control, when they really *wanted* control, was the fatal symptom that spelled problem drinking.(p.315)
• One morning when I was feeling really bad, I was put on K.P. and the head cook *wanted* me to go out and scrub the garbage cans.(p.317)
• I also found out that all they *wanted* was to help me get sober and to stay sober themselves.(p.320)
• A.A.'s Twelve Steps showed me the way to sobriety if I *wanted* it.(p.320)
• I *wanted* it!(p.320)
• But we had to do a lot of entertaining, my husband liked to have a good time; I was very young; and I *wanted* to have a good time too.(p.322)
• I always *wanted* to drink too much, so I was watchful, always watchful, counting my drinks.(p.322)
• If I had been sincere in what I thought I *wanted* more than anything else in life – a sober husband and a happy, contented home – I would have gone on the wagon with him.(p.324)
• I *wanted* him to be sure that I wasn't the one who was going to drink the whole bottle.(p.336)
• I just *wanted* to live to a certain age, carry through with what I felt was my job with the children, and after that – no matter.(p.337)
• Since I gave my will over to A.A., whatever A.A. has *wanted* of me I've tried to do to the best of my ability.(p.340)
• I *wanted* so badly to see the picture as it was in her mind.(p.355)
• When I did make it home in 1920, I re-entered school and caught up with my class in a few short months – I actually did a year's work in three months, proving much to the disgust of my dad that I could do it when I *wanted* to.(p.358)
• I was going to prove to her that liquor wasn't necessary in my life, and above all that I still loved her more than anything else in the world and that I *wanted* her back.(p.362)
• This suggestion had been made before on a number of occasions, but like all alcoholics I *wanted* to handle my problem my own way, which really meant I didn't want anything to interfere with my drinking.(p.378)
• I knew that I *wanted* to try A.A. and if that didn't work, I didn't think anything would.(p.384)
• I *wanted* to do it all over again.(p.386)
• I *wanted* to go home.(p.387)
• I know now that I asked questions and told him what I *wanted* to learn, but I told him only what I *wanted* to believe about myself.(p.388)
• I wouldn't go to hospitals because I *wanted* my dog there, so I had to have a trained nurse.(p.390)
• I *wanted* a cigarette and room service, which I didn't get.(p.390)
• My husband couldn't tell whether I *wanted* to do something about my drinking.(p.391)
• It was such a feeling of relief that I *wanted* to know more about it and with that, I think for the first time, came the realization that there was something horribly, horribly wrong with me.(p.392)
• I *wanted* to try A.A. with my whole heart and soul.(p.393)
• I also *wanted* to be the queen of society, with a glittering salon, the bride of a dream prince and the mother of a happy brood.(p.400)
• Just what I *wanted*.(p.402)

• I *wanted* him to love me and make up to me for everything.(p.403)
• Even then I knew in my heart that I was unfit for the very things I *wanted* most, a happy marriage, security, a home and love.(p.403)
• Now I hid when I *wanted* to drink.(p.406)
• It combined running away from my world, and drinking all I *wanted* to.(p.407)
• Her father, quite rightly, *wanted* to put her in a school.(p.409)
• An obstreperous woman in a bar is a nuisance, and they *wanted* no trouble with the police.(p.410)
• I could not live on that tiny trust fund and still drink all I *wanted* to.(p.411)
• I *wanted* to die and often I would think of ways.(p.411)
• Nor were those impossible dreams I used to have the things I really *wanted*.(p.416)
• I *wanted* love and affection but I didn't get it.(p.424)
• I liked it and soon moved into the photo department which was what I *wanted* to do.(p.425)
• I *wanted* to get as far away from home as possible.(p.426)
• Meanwhile the letters from home were telling about how much my folks *wanted* to make up to me for some of the things I'd missed.(p.427)
• All I'd *wanted* was one more drink.(p.428)
• I merely *wanted* to cut down.(p.429)
• And the folks said A.A. was for people who *wanted* to quit, otherwise it wouldn't work.(p.429)
• They *wanted* me to make leather belts, of all things!(p.445)
• I *wanted* to talk about my many big problems; drinking seemed a small one.(p.447)
• And I was always glad to point it out, because I knew you *wanted* perfection, just as I did.(p.449)
• Others *wanted* to die.(p.455)
• It was my ex-wife, and she said my twenty-seven-year-old son, who has completed his Marine Corps training and graduated from college, *wanted* to see me privately, was getting married in three months, and *wanted* me at the wedding.(p.462)
• It was obvious even to me, in my drunken state, that I wasn't *wanted*.(p.466)
• He said he was finally and completely through -- that he never *wanted* to see me again.(p.467)
• I even *wanted* to -- but I wasn't allowed to, so I won't go now.(p.470)
• I had quite a heartache about her then because she wasn't the type of girl that my mother *wanted* me to marry.(p.485)
• He *wanted* to give me the very best and he thought that nothing but being a doctor would suffice.(p.485)
• He said he never *wanted* to set foot in the deep south again and he didn't.(p.486)
• I actually *wanted* a drink, besides feeling that I had to have a drink.(p.488)
• Anyhow, on the 24th, after drinking all day on the 23rd, I must have decided I *wanted* to see my wife and have some kind of reconciliation or at least talk with her.(p.491)
• I guess I felt, and he sensed it, that I *wanted* him to hurry up and say what he had to say and get out.(p.494)
• After he'd talked half an hour, I still *wanted* him to hurry up and get out so I could go and get some whiskey before the liquor store closed.(p.494)
• I just gathered up this and that alcoholic, because, in the back of my mind, I *wanted* to save all the world.(p.496)
• I had found this new "something," and I *wanted* to give it to everyone who had a problem.(p.496)
• Then I find myself thinking about myself, and a few things that I had *wanted* to forget.(p.503)
• After twenty years in prison for murder, he knew A.A. was the spot for him . . . if he *wanted* to stay on the outside.(p.508)
• My father was alive, and I had to do as he *wanted*, so I drank under cover.(p.508)
• It wasn't anything strange to me, and I knew if I *wanted* to stay on the outside, that would be the spot for me.(p.510)
• The Commanding Officer only spoke to me when he *wanted* to tell me exactly who I was and what I was and how little I counted in the scheme of things and how glad he would be if I went away.(p.520)
• Not least of my debts to A.A. is the knowledge that in that time when she *wanted* me most, I was there -- and that I wasn't drunk.(p.525)
• But I *wanted* a cosmos, a universe all my own which I had created and where I reigned as chief top reigner and ruler over everyone else.(p.535)
• Okay, I *wanted* to be God.(p.535)
• Actually, of course, I *wanted* someone to listen to me, because when I had a few martinis inside, I became the great author I longed to be; and the right listener was in for some pretty highflown theories of literature and of genius.(p.536)
• For a little while, I was the great man I *wanted* to be, and thought myself entitled to be just by reason of being.(p.537)
• I *wanted* to stop.(p.539)
• I thought that life was a pretty simple thing; you simply made a plan for your life, based upon what you *wanted*, and then you needed only the courage to go after it.(p.545)
• I thought I knew exactly what I *wanted* out of life and I thought I knew exactly how to get it.(p.545)
• I was married and divorced again before I was twenty-three years old, this time to a prominent band leader -- a man that many women *wanted*.(p.546)
• I thought this would give me ego-strength, make me feel *wanted* and secure, and alleviate my fears, but again nothing changed inside me.(p.546)
• This great experience that released me from the bondage of hatred and replaced it with love is really just another affirmation of the truth I know: I get everything I need in Alcoholics Anonymous – everything I need I get – and when I get what I need I invariably find that it was just what I *wanted* all the time.(p.553)
• Too often, I would overdo it and behave badly at the very time I *wanted* to be at my best!(p.556)

wanting

• As I look back on the events of two months, I can clearly see that I had been circling around, half-afraid of encountering the remedy for my situation, half *wanting* it, deferring fulfillment of my promise to get in touch with the doctor I had heard about.(p.258)
• I had been drinking heavily from one state of semi-coma to another and it was several days before I got "defogged," but subconsciously I was in earnest about *wanting* to quit liquor forever.(p.258)
• I remember starting to city school, coming from a country school, and *wanting* so very, very much to be like the other girls and trying flour on my face for powder because I wasn't able to have any real powder.(p.261)
• I landed him and shipped him by train to Akron, with a pint of whiskey in his pocket to keep him from *wanting* to get off the train in Toledo!(p.282)
• I had thought that I was completely different from other people, that I was beginning to become a little balmy, even to the point of withdrawing more and more from society and *wanting* to be alone with my bottle.(p.290)
• He had been *wanting* to do something about his drinking for a long time, but did not know how.(p.294)
• Instead of *wanting* to escape some perplexing problem, we experience a thrill of challenge in the opportunity it affords for another application of A.A. techniques, and we find ourselves tackling it with surprising vigor.(p.311)
• Living with fear and tension inevitably results in *wanting* to ease that tension, which alcohol seems to do temporarily.(p.380)
• Not understanding the twenty-four hour plan, or not *wanting* to, I began drinking and was off-again on-again, during that first month.(p.414)
• It didn't worry me very much, because at that time I could shut off for a couple of months without taking a drink or even *wanting* one, and without feeling that I was giving anything up.(p.518)
• The A.A. members who sponsored me told me in the beginning that I would not only find a way to live without having a drink, but that I would find a way to live without *wanting* to drink, if I would do these simple things.(p.550)

wants

• If you are an alcoholic who *wants* to get over it, you may already be asking – "What do I have to do?"(p.20)
• Each person is like an actor who *wants* to run the whole show; is forever trying to arrange the lights, the ballet, the scenery and the rest of the players in his own way.(p.60)
• Is it not evident to all the rest of the players that these are the things he *wants*?(p.61)
• *Wants* house put in her name.(p.65)
• He *wants* to enjoy a certain reputation, but knows in his heart he doesn't deserve it.(p.73)
• If there is any indication that he *wants* to stop, have a good talk with the person most interested in him -- usually his wife.(p.90)
• Then let his family or a friend ask him if he *wants* to quit for good and if he would go to any extreme to do so.(p.90)
• You should not be offended if he *wants* to call it off, for he has helped you more than you have helped him.(p.94)
• Unless your friend *wants* to talk further about himself, do not wear out your welcome.(p.95)
• Tell him that if he *wants* to get well you will do anything to help.(p.95)
• If he is sincerely interested and *wants* to see you again, ask him to read this book in the interval.(p.95)
• After doing that, he must decide for himself whether he *wants* to go on.(p.95)
• If you are with a person who *wants* to eat in a bar, by all means go along.(p.102)
• Especially when he has before him a way to stop his drinking and abuse if he really *wants* to pay the price.(p.108)
• Two: Your husband is showing lack of control, for he is unable to stay on the water wagon even when he *wants* to.(p.109)
• He is remorseful after serious drinking bouts and tells you he *wants* to stop.(p.109)
• As we say among ourselves, "He *wants* to want to stop."(p.109)
• He may have come to the point where he desperately *wants* to stop but cannot.(p.110)
• Being certain he *wants* to stop, you can go to him with this volume as joyfully as though you had struck oil.(p.113)
• It may convince your husband he *wants* to stop drinking forever.(p.116)
• He *wants* to make good.(p.118)
• If you are satisfied he really *wants* to get over drinking, you need not be alarmed.(p.120)
• Is it not because each *wants* to play the lead?(p.122)
• We are sure God *wants* us to be happy, joyous, and free.(p.133)
• He *wants* to quit drinking and you want to help him, even if it be only a matter of good business.(p.141)
• After satisfying yourself that your man *wants* to recover and that he will go to any extreme to do so, you may suggest a definite course of action.(p.142)
• The firm *wants* to help you get over it, and if you are interested, there is a way out.(p.147)
• If he *wants* to stop, he should be afforded a real chance.(p.148)
• Part of that program is that we take it to someone else, that needs it and *wants* it.(p.186)
• You should go out and take this program to somebody else that needs it and *wants* it."(p.190)
• Bill was very, very grateful that he had been released from this terrible thing and he had given God the credit for having done it, and he's so grateful about it he *wants* to tell other people about it.(p.191)
• He *wants* to go to the hospital, and I'm not paying for the hospital again!"(p.271)
• I was not able to hold a job -- no one *wants* a drunk around.(p.526)
• My personal definition, which I submit as applying only to myself (although everyone is welcome to it who *wants* it), includes every waking activity of the human being; to have a creative attitude towards things is a more exact meaning, to live and to deal with other human beings creatively, which to me means seeing the God in them, and respecting and worshipping this God.(p.535)
• We are taught to differentiate between our *wants* (which are never satisfied) and our needs (which are always provided for).(p.560)

war

• *War* fever ran high in the New England town to which we new, young officers from Plattsburg were assigned, and we were flattered when the first citizens took us to their homes, making us feel heroic.(p.1)
• Here was love, applause, *war*; moments sublime with intervals hilarious.(p.1)
• He had a commendable World *War* record.(p.35)
• As in *war*, the victor only seemed to win.(p.66)
• At the end of this selling of lots, just prior to World *War* I, I got into the crude rubber business, and six months later there was only one broker and myself left in Akron.(p.197)
• My father was a railroad man and a Civil *War* veteran.(p.210)
• With the *war* over, and back in Baltimore with the folks, there were several small jobs for three years and then I went to work soliciting as one of the first ten employees of a new national finance company.(p.242)
• The *war* was getting along.(p.253)
• I had run away from school to join the army in World *War* I, but missed it by one day since the Armistice was signed the very day I landed in Atlanta to

sign up with Uncle Sam.(p.357)
• Then there was wartime service to interrupt my plans, and an education to be picked up after the *war*.(p.373)
• At age twenty-one, I enlisted in the Navy for two reasons: (1) to avoid being drafted into the Army, and (2) out of a burst of patriotic fervor inspired by the advent of World *War* II and as the result of an all-night drinking binge which found me sitting on the doorstep of the Navy recruiting office when the chief petty officer arrived to open for business at nine o'clock Monday morning.(p.398)
• It looked as if the *war* would be over any day, but I had to go anyhow.(p.425)
• I don't know whether she was a pacifist or whether she just thought that in the event of another *war* it would have some bearing on my joining up.(p.484)
• True, I have recently recovered from pneumonia and have an alibi, but my friends are in the *war* or going, and I am not.(p.499)
• The *war* leaves me with a pair of blankets, a toilet kit, a sweater knit by my sister, and a still greater inferiority.(p.499)
• The *war* was on and it was a fairly short course, about eight months.(p.518)
• When the *war* was over, we had about a year in Germany, occupying the place.(p.518)
• Lots of the older people had taken to drinking quite a good deal more during the *war*, but the younger generation was, I think, about the same.(p.518)
• The Abyssinian *war* broke out just as things were going very badly for me, and I went off to Egypt on a job there.(p.519)
• Then Hitler's *war* broke out, and again, I was given a really important job on the Suez Canal, dealing with military shipping.(p.520)
• In part, it was a feeling of intense shame at having to leave the Army during the *war*, but mostly it was resentment that this kind of thing should happen to me for, strange as it may seem, up to then I still thought I could control drinking.(p.521)
• During this time, our country was at *war*.(p.547)
• By this time I was such a past master at kidding myself that I had convinced myself I had sat out a *war* and waited for this man to come home and, as my resentment and self-pity grew, so did my alcoholic problem.(p.548)

war-time
• That *war-time* day in old Winchester Cathedral came back again.(p.10)

ward
• Hence the two men set to work almost frantically upon alcoholics arriving in the *ward* of the Akron City Hospital.(p.xvii)
• I was always in a *ward* before."(p.157)
• Straightway, Bob called Akron's City Hospital and asked for the nurse on the receiving *ward*.(p.188)
• I remember looking longingly at the window as an easier solution, and shuddering at the memory of that other window, three years before, and the six agonizing months in a London hospital *ward*.(p.224)
• I lost my driver's license, was made a *ward* of the court, and was put on probation (not to mention the fact that I might have killed three friends and myself).(p.354)
• I could tell him a lot of reasons why I am here in an alky *ward* at the age of twenty.(p.423)
• So, when it ended up at a psycho *ward*, I wasn't all that surprised.(p.440)
• After nine days of tests at Mayo, I was put in the locked *ward* -- of all places!(p.444)
• I didn't like being on the nut *ward*, and I particularly didn't like being forced to ice cookies on Christmas Eve.(p.444)
• The people there insisted on putting me in a *ward*, when Max and I both knew I ought to have a private room.(p.445)
• Time went by very, very slowly on my second nut *ward*.(p.445)
• My reaction was that I'd already helped all the patients on the *ward*, and I still had plenty of problems of my own without trying to help some drunk from A.A.(p.446)
• This time I didn't put up any fight because I knew why they were there and where I was going, the psychopathic *ward* of the City Hospital, where I had been once before.(p.468)
• And then I went back home to live with my parents, and the merry-go-round started again – only this time I didn't have to worry about waking up behind bars in a psychiatric *ward*.(p.468)
• But I would always wake up in the psychiatric *ward* to begin another long treatment.(p.528)
• After a while, I found that the psycho *ward* was a good place to hide when I had taken something stolen to the pawnshop.(p.528)
• I didn't want that, so I stopped going to the psycho *ward*.(p.528)
• In those years I was in jail nine times, in an alcoholic *ward*, overnight, twice; and I was fired from three jobs, two of them very good ones.(p.536)
• What a revelation of ego and arrogance still remaining in me – as if anyone, instinct and training apart, likes to be in jail or in an alcoholic *ward* or fired from his job.(p.536)
• When I remark that I have been in jail nine times, and in an alcoholic *ward* twice, they think I'm kidding, or possibly dramatizing for the sake of a good yarn.(p.542)

warden
• I go back to my old alma mater occasionally to give A.A. talks, and -- just think! -- the *warden* is my friend.(p.462)

wards
• In all the sanitariums and psycho *wards* I had never met a single woman who said she was an alcoholic.(p.471)

warm
• Today I have Someone who will always hear me; I have a *warm* fellowship among men who understand my problems; I have tasks to do and am glad to do them, to see others who are alcoholics and to help them in any way I can to become sober men.(p.260)
• I had always hated beer, but now I grew to love it, bottle after bottle of it, *warm* or cold.(p.339)
• It was the first time in my life that I could not get a lift out of what I was drinking; and so one Friday night, at five minutes to six, I had half a water glass of *warm* gin, and that is when I first asked God to help me.(p.393)
• I remembered having had a little drink of whiskey with a can of *warm* beer as a chaser.(p.422)
• We weren't even permitted to play cards in our home, but father would give us just a little toddy with whiskey and sugar and *warm* water now and then.(p.484)
• But I am safe and *warm*.(p.497)

warming
• To go into a gathering of people was the sort of thing that all my life, from the time I left my private world of books and dreams to meet the real world of people and parties and jobs, had left me feeling an uncomfortable outsider, needing the *warming* stimulus of drinks to join in.(p.228)

warmly
• I was *warmly* welcomed by friends of my youth who had preceded me.(p.231)
• I was greeted *warmly*, honestly, and with a true ring of sincerity by everyone present.(p.259)

warmth
• I choose to believe that the Power greater than ourselves we ask for help, wrapped my shivering body in loving *warmth* and strength which has never left me.(p.541)

warn
• You should *warn* against arousing resentment or jealousy.(p.100)
• I would take a gulp, then *warn* the jug not to try to entice, lure, or seduce me into having more than one "medicinal" jolt.(p.332)

warned
• I had *warned* him several times that he had but one more chance.(p.136)
• There were times when I got to drinking, and I had been *warned* by Firestone that they wouldn't stand for this much longer, so, clearly, they were conscious of the fact that I drank too much and too often.(p.204)
• She had been *warned* numerous times, not only by her family but by my own mother, that I was a hopeless drunk, that there wasn't anything anybody could do with me, that I'd never stop, and that eventually I'd break her heart.(p.513)
• My doctor *warned* me that if I kept on, I might have esophageal hemorrhaging and die.(p.558)
• What my doctor had *warned* me about finally happened.(p.558)
• Experience has often *warned* us that nothing can so surely destroy our spiritual heritage as futile disputes over property, money, and authority.(p.566)

warning
• Ominous *warning* -- which I failed to heed.(p.1)
• If a sufficiently strong reason – ill health, falling in love, change of environment, or the *warning* of a doctor – becomes operative, this man can also stop or moderate, although he may find it difficult and troublesome and may even need medical attention.(p.21)
• My employer gave me one *warning*, then another.(p.558)

warnings
• I forgot the strong *warnings* and the prejudices of my people concerning drink.(p.1)
• He enjoys himself for a few years in spite of friendly *warnings*.(p.37)
• He has few worries, fewer *warnings*.(p.330)

warped
• It brings misunderstanding, fierce resentment, financial insecurity, disgusted friends and employers, *warped* lives of blameless children, sad wives and parents – anyone can increase the list.(p.18)
• Of course, there is such a thing as incompatibility, but in nearly every instance the alcoholic only seems to be unloving and inconsiderate; it is usually because he is *warped* and sickened that he says and does these appalling things.(p.108)
• You ask, because many alcoholics, being *warped* and drugged, do not want to quit.(p.142)
• And we found ourselves back in prison, where our personalities became even more *warped*.(p.459)

warps
• The man in the bed was told of the acute poisoning from which he suffered, how it deteriorates the body of an alcoholic and *warps* his mind.(p.157)

warrant
• She is indignant about it, and has a *warrant* out for our arrest.(p.79)
• If circumstances *warrant*, we ask our wives or friends to join us in morning meditation.(p.87)
• So let each family play together or separately, as much as their circumstances *warrant*.(p.132)

warranted
• Yet we do go to great extremes to provide each other with these very things, when such action is *warranted*.(p.98)

warring
• We looked upon this world of *warring* individuals, *warring* theological systems, and inexplicable calamity, with deep skepticism.(p.46)

wars
• Twenty-two, and a veteran of foreign *wars*, I went home at last.(p.1)
• The *wars* which had been fought, the burnings and chicanery that religious dispute had facilitated, made me sick.(p.11)
• People have *wars* and kill each other; they struggle and cut each other's throats for success and what does anyone get out of it?(p.244)

wartime
• Then there was *wartime* service to interrupt my plans, and an education to be picked up after the war.(p.373)
• Since it was *wartime*, I explained to the somewhat startled shopkeeper that I had many friends in the service whom I was remembering with a watch.(p.532)

wash
• Between classes I would run down to the *wash* room, take enough to steady my nerves and then go on to the next class.(p.183)
• I lost a lot of shirts that way, and sometimes I was minus a whole *wash*.(p.371)
• I still *wash* clothes, lots of them, but I no longer lose them at the Laundromat.(p.372)
• I tried to *wash* a little, but Anne refused to *wash* at all.(p.415)

washday
• Also, I believed I was the image of all domestic virtues, secluded in my *washday* (any day) refuge.(p.369)

washed
• In the next two years I *washed* more pans and peeled more potatoes than any other doughboy.(p.241)
• I halfway *washed* them, and he told me to do them again, and I did, and he yelled at me to do them again, and I picked up one of the cans and threw it at him and told him to do them himself.(p.317)
• I went out to the West Coast, waited on table, *washed* dishes and sold newspaper subscriptions.(p.401)

washing
• I do recall lying on a cold cement floor and shredding into little bits several pieces of stolen identification cards, and *washing* my face in the toilet bowl trying to sober up, and screaming hysterically while clinging to bars too high to see out of, and cursing everyone that came near me.(p.354)
• I was still untrained for any work but *washing* dishes and waiting on table.(p.401)

Washington

• One day I went to *Washington* to present some accounting evidence to a government bureau.(p.40)
• "As soon as I regained my ability to think, I went carefully over that evening in *Washington*.(p.41)
• They piled on me heaps of evidence to the effect that an alcoholic mentality, such as I had exhibited in *Washington*, was a hopeless condition.(p.42)
• By the time I had completed law school I had picked up some experience in patent law, for I remained with the patent law firm and worked too in *Washington* where they found that I was a capable infringement investigator.(p.213)
• January 8, 1938 -- that was my D-Day; the place, *Washington*, D.C.(p.238)
• And I still say that as long as I remember that January 8th in *Washington*, that is how long, by the grace of God as I understand Him, I will retain a happy sobriety.(p.250)
• *Washington*, D.C. and news-gathering agency work followed, along with many parties.(p.254)
• When it was closed through *Washington* edict I began with Federal Writers in San Antonio.(p.256)
• Can you picture two girls hitchhiking their way to Las Vegas from *Washington* State?(p.354)
• But now I was a young divorcee, leading a *Washington* social life.(p.402)
• It was in *Washington*, D.C. that this transition took place, and that the really bad part of alcoholism began happening.(p.465)
• The last Christmas I spent in *Washington*, fourteen years ago, comes to mind.(p.465)
• So we turned around and started back to *Washington*.(p.467)
• Even the Jack Alexander Saturday Evening Post article hadn't been written, and there was only a tiny group of people in *Washington*.(p.469)
• I went to elementary and high school in *Washington*, D.C. and then to Howard University.(p.486)
• My interneship was in *Washington*.(p.486)
• I had my own medical practice in *Washington* at that time, but the practice slackened and the mail order business started to fall off.(p.486)
• Dad, due to having spent most of his time in a small Virginia town, didn't have any too much money, and the money he had saved and the property he had acquired were in *Washington*.(p.486)
• Vi had secured work in *Washington*.(p.490)
• I think whiskey was cheaper there than it was in *Washington*.(p.490)
• Then I decided that I'd go back to *Washington*, which I did.(p.490)
• After the trial, I got big-hearted again and felt that I should do something in payment for Vi's kindness to me; so I left *Washington* and went to Seattle to work.(p.492)
• I haven't mentioned it, but Charlie, my sponsor, was white, and when we got our group started we got help from other white groups in *Washington*.(p.495)

washout

• Here I was, thirty-nine years old and a complete *washout*.(p.238)

wasp

• A *wasp* is crawling up the back of the lady in front of me.(p.497)

waste

• Following his physical rehabilitation, he had a talk with me in which he frankly stated he thought the treatment a *waste* of effort, unless I could assure him, which no one ever had, that in the future he would have the "will power" to resist the impulse to drink.(p.xxix)
• When we decide who is to hear our story, we *waste* no time.(p.75)
• If he does not want to stop drinking, don't *waste* time trying to persuade him.(p.90)
• We find it a *waste* of time to keep chasing a man who cannot or will not work with you.(p.96)
• This kind of *waste* goes on unabated.(p.137)
• If not, why *waste* time with him?(p.142)
• Alcoholism may be causing your organization considerable damage in its *waste* of time, men and reputation.(p.148)
• We think we are sensible when we urge that you stop this *waste* and give your worthwhile man a chance.(p.148)
• It was a *waste* of the doctors' time and the patients' money.(p.307)

wasted

• Many of us have *wasted* a lot of time doing that and it doesn't work.(p.87)
• I thought of what liquor had done to me, the opportunities that I had discarded, the abilities that had been given me and how I had *wasted* them, and I finally came to the conclusion, that if I didn't want to quit, I certainly ought to want to, and that I was willing to do anything in the world to stop drinking.(p.186)
• But the saddest, and thus the most consoling, drifted through from the country-music station – stories of broken hearts, *wasted* lives, lost loves, sung plaintively.(p.332)
• I was forty-four years old; my life had been *wasted*.(p.461)
• I *wasted* twenty years of my life, and there is nothing I can do about that, but there is something I can do about now.(p.480)

wasting

• But for every man who drinks others are involved -- the wife who trembles in fear of the next debauch; the mother and father who see their son *wasting* away.(p.104)
• I said, "In that case, there's no use of *wasting* this," and I got the last of that pint.(p.207)

watch

• Many times we talk to a new man and *watch* his hope rise as we discuss his alcoholic problems and explain our fellowship.(p.45)
• Continue to *watch* for selfishness, dishonesty, resentment, and fear.(p.84)
• To *watch* people recover, to see them help others, to *watch* loneliness vanish, to see a fellowship grow up about you, to have a host of friends – this is an experience you must not miss.(p.89)
• Members of a family should *watch* such matters carefully, for one careless, inconsiderate remark has been known to raise the very devil.(p.125)
• The shakes grew worse and I looked at my *watch* -- six o'clock.(p.223)
• At least three of those four years must have been a living hell for my wife, because she had to *watch* the man she loved disintegrate morally, mentally and financially.(p.277)
• Occasionally, it is accorded to a few of us to *watch* something fine grow from a tiny kernel into something of gigantic goodness.(p.295)
• "We *watch* the alcoholic performing in a position of responsibility and we know that because he is drinking heavily and daily he has cut his capacities by fifty per cent, and still he seems able to do a satisfactory job.(p.308)
• But, of course," he continued, "eventually the alcoholic loses all of his capacities as his disease gets progressively worse, and this is a tragedy that is painful to *watch*; the disintegration of a sound mind and body."(p.308)
• There was one girl especially, and I'd *watch* her from my window every morning, leaving faithfully to go to the hospital in the neighborhood.(p.326)
• I put my poor mother and father through agonies but, finally, I couldn't stand living with them and having them *watch* everything I did.(p.386)
• I cannot sit by and *watch* you destroy yourself."(p.391)
• So I'd sit up, *watch* old Wallace Beery movies on all-night TV, and drink.(p.441)
• I can again focus on my wife's good qualities and *watch* them grow and grow and grow.(p.451)
• I can *watch* my serenity level rise when I discard my expectations.(p.452)
• God must *watch* over me.(p.475)
• She continued to *watch* me, although she didn't say anything.(p.493)
• I have to *watch* myself all the time.(p.516)
• Within a month, the police, the hospital authorities, several kind strangers, most of my friends, all of my close relatives, and a few adepts at rolling a drunk and removing his wrist *watch* and wallet had been involved.(p.532)
• (There was a time, for about three months, when I bought a ten-dollar wrist *watch* every pay day – that is every two weeks.(p.532)
• Since it was wartime, I explained to the somewhat startled shopkeeper that I had many friends in the service whom I was remembering with a *watch*.(p.532)

watched

• The local banker *watched* me whirl fat checks in and out of his till with amused skepticism.(p.4)
• But I *watched* him, and he tossed off the rest of his, so I tossed off the rest of mine.(p.195)

watches

• This means trouble, unless the family *watches* for these tendencies in each other and comes to a friendly agreement about them.(p.131)

watchful

• I was afraid, and I had made my mind up that I would never get drunk, so I was *watchful* and careful.(p.322)
• I always wanted to drink too much, so I was *watchful*, always *watchful*, counting my drinks.(p.322)

watching

• I kept *watching* the man down the bar to see what he did with a contraption like that, and he just smelled of his drink and set it down again, so I did the same.(p.195)
• There was a man *watching*, and I turned to him and said with a defiant air I carried with me all the time, "If I don't quit this I'm going to have to join that alcoholic business they're talking about."(p.266)
• I didn't feel I could lie in bed and squirt the stuff in my veins while my kids and wife stood around *watching* me, so I kept the drug in my bag and the bag in the car and the car in the garage.(p.442)
• I'd go into my home with a bottle, and I remember clearly how I would look around to see if Vi was *watching*.(p.487)
• I can remember her *watching*.(p.487)

watchwords

• Patience, tolerance, understanding and love are the *watchwords*.(p.118)

water

• Why can't he stay on the *water* wagon?(p.22)
• It's *water* over the dam.(p.78)
• He had commenced our way of life, had secured a position, and was getting his head above *water*.(p.79)
• Two: Your husband is showing lack of control, for he is unable to stay on the *water* wagon even when he wants to.(p.109)
• The *water* tank on the toilet I never used, because that looked too easy.(p.176)
• I remember that my father kept whiskey around the house for medical purposes and entertainment, and I would drink from this when no one was about and then *water* it to keep my parents from knowing I was drinking.(p.183)
• But each drink after the "first" seemed to become less effective and after three or four they all seemed like *water*.(p.241)
• During this vacation, in the months of September and October, I decided to go on the *water* wagon.(p.343)
• On the first, though on the *water* wagon, I looked forward to my next drink.(p.344)
• Emma ran out to the kitchen and came back with a *water* glass full of bourbon and made me drink it down.(p.385)
• I dropped a two-quart *water* bottle on my big toe.(p.390)
• It was the first time in my life that I could not get a lift out of what I was drinking; and so one Friday night, at five minutes to six, I had half a *water* glass of warm gin, and that is when I first asked God to help me.(p.393)
• "You've got to space your drinks and take plenty of *water* in between," or "coat the stomach with a little olive oil," or "drink anything but those damn martinis."(p.433)
• Same thing when I let lye and *water* eat away at four of my toes and my foot for five hours.(p.458)
• Each ten-day period in the dark hole, I was fed bread and *water* daily, with one full meal on the third day only.(p.459)
• There, I received several soda crackers and *water* daily, and before I could have my third-day meal (again the only meal in ten days), I had to drink a glass of castor oil or mineral oil, depending on the cruelty of the person who was doing the dispensing.(p.459)
• Climb on *water* wagon for few months.(p.475)
• We weren't even permitted to play cards in our home, but father would give us just a little toddy with whiskey and sugar and warm *water* now and then.(p.484)
• I fix up a little apartment over the garage with books and drinking *water*.(p.506)

waterboy

• So did the *waterboy* on the high school football team attempt to revenge himself on the big brother who was the star quarterback; for I was the *waterboy* and my brother was the star quarterback, innocent of everything except the fact that he was a star quarterback.(p.537)

watering

• This secret drinker favored the local Laundromat as a *watering* hole.(p.369)

waterpipe

• If he can afford it, he may have liquor concealed all

over his house to be certain no one gets his entire supply away from him to throw down the *waterpipe*.(p.22)

waters

• I learned the true meaning of bread cast upon the *waters*.(p.541)

wave

• Suddenly I feel a *wave* of utter hopelessness sweep over me.(p.504)

waves

• I was not too well at the time, and was plagued by *waves* of self-pity and resentment.(p.15)

waxed

• The parties *waxed* more liquid and hilarious as time went on, and eventually I discovered that a little shot of liquor now and then between beers had the tendency to put me in a whacky mood much quicker than having to down several quarts of beer to obtain the same effect.(p.298)

way

• And besides, we are sure that our *way* of living has its advantages for all.(p.xiii)
• By the end of 1939, it was estimated that 800 alcoholics were on their *way* to recovery.(p.xviii)
• Of alcoholics who came to A.A. and really tried, 50% got sober at once and remained that *way*; 25% sobered up after some relapses, and among the remainder, those who stayed on with A.A. showed improvement.(p.xx)
• For the next few years fortune threw money and applause my *way*.(p.3)
• Someone had pushed a drink my *way*, and I had taken it.(p.5)
• I was to know happiness, peace, and usefulness, in a *way* of life that is incredibly more wonderful as time passes.(p.8)
• In a matter of fact *way* he told how two men had appeared in court, persuading the judge to suspend his commitment.(p.9)
• I could almost hear the sound of the preacher's voice as I sat, on still Sundays, *way* over there on the hillside; there was that proffered temperance pledge I never signed; my grandfather's good natured contempt of some church folk and their doings; his insistence that the spheres really had their music; but his denial of the preacher's right to tell him how he must listen; his fearlessness as he spoke of these things just before he died; these recollections welled up from the past.(p.10)
• I have since talked with scores of men who felt the same *way*.(p.12)
• My friend promised when these things were done I would enter upon a new relationship with my Creator; that I would have the elements of a *way* of living which answered all my problems.(p.13)
• Anything is better than the *way* you were."(p.14)
• He could not, or would not, see our *way* of life.(p.16)
• We have a *way* out on which we can absolutely agree, and upon which we can join in brotherly and harmonious action.(p.17)
• An illness of this sort – and we have come to believe it an illness –involves those about us in a *way* no other human sickness can.(p.18)
• If we keep on the *way* we are going there is little doubt that much good will result, but the surface of the problem would hardly be scratched.(p.19)
• In a vague *way* their families and friends sense that these drinkers are abnormal, but everybody hopefully awaits the day when the sufferer will rouse himself from his lethargy and assert his power of will.(p.23)
• The alcoholic may say to himself in the most casual *way*, "It won't burn me this time, so here's how!"(p.24)
• How often have some of us begun to drink in this nonchalant *way*, and after the third or fourth, pounded on the bar and said to ourselves, "For God's sake, how did I ever get started again?"(p.24)
• The central fact of our lives today is the absolute certainty that our Creator has entered into our hearts and lives in a *way* which is indeed miraculous.(p.25)
• We have no desire to convince anyone that there is only one *way* by which faith can be acquired.(p.28)
• Each individual, in the personal stories, describes in his own language and from his own point of view the *way* he established his relationship with God.(p.29)
• Though there is no *way* of proving it, we believe that early in our drinking careers most of us could have stopped drinking.(p.32)
• On the *way* I felt hungry so I stopped at a roadside place where they have a bar.(p.36)
• He was interested and conceded that he had some of the symptoms, but he was a long *way* from admitting that he could do nothing about it himself.(p.40)
• They had said that though I did raise a defense, it would one day give *way* before some trivial reason for having a drink.(p.42)
• I have since been brought into a *way* of living infinitely more satisfying and, I hope, more useful than the life I lived before.(p.42)
• Perhaps it is going to be that *way* with you.(p.44)
• As soon as a man can say that he does believe, or is willing to believe, we emphatically assure him that he is on his *way*.(p.47)
• In our personal stories you will find a wide variation in the *way* each teller approaches and conceives of the Power which is greater than himself.(p.50)
• They flatly declare that since they have come to believe in a Power greater than themselves, to take a certain attitude toward that Power, and to do certain simple things, there has been a revolutionary change in their *way* of living and thinking.(p.50)
• So, in one *way* or another, we discovered that faith had been involved all the time!(p.54)
• They are not at fault; they seem to have been born that *way*.(p.58)
• Our stories disclose in a general *way* what we used to be like, what happened, and what we are like now.(p.58)
• We thought we could find an easier, softer *way*.(p.58)
• Each person is like an actor who wants to run the whole show; is forever trying to arrange the lights, the ballet, the scenery and the rest of the players in his own *way*.(p.60)
• And there often seems no *way* of entirely getting rid of self without His aid.(p.62)
• Take away my difficulties, that victory over them may bear witness to those I would help of Thy Power, Thy Love, and Thy *Way* of life.(p.63)
• But the more we fought and tried to have our own *way*, the worse matters got.(p.66)
• Though we did not like their symptoms and the *way* these disturbed us, they, like ourselves, were sick too.(p.67)
• We wouldn't treat sick people that *way*.(p.67)
• Perhaps there is a better *way* -- we think so.(p.68)
• We can laugh at those who think spirituality the *way* of weakness.(p.68)
• Paradoxically, it is the *way* of strength.(p.68)
• It's so easy to get *way* off the track.(p.68)
• In this *way* we tried to shape a sane and sound ideal for our future sex life.(p.69)
• We have admitted certain defects; we have ascertained in a rough *way* what the trouble is; we have put our finger on the weak items in our personal inventory.(p.72)
• Most people approached in this *way* will be glad to help; they will be honored by our confidence.(p.75)
• I pray that you now remove from me every single defect of character which stands in the *way* of my usefulness to you and my fellows.(p.76)
• Approached in this *way*, the most ruthless creditor will sometimes surprise us.(p.78)
• He had commenced our *way* of life, had secured a position, and was getting his head above water.(p.79)
• If she knows in a general *way* that we have been wild, should we tell her in detail?(p.81)
• It may be that both will decide that the *way* of good sense and loving kindness is to let by-gones be bygones.(p.82)
• But he is yet a long *way* from making good to the wife or parents whom for years he has so shockingly treated.(p.82)
• The alcoholic is like a tornado roaring his *way* through the lives of others.(p.82)
• So we clean house with the family, asking each morning in meditation that our Creator show us the *way* of patience, tolerance, kindliness and love.(p.83)
• If we are painstaking about this phase of our development, we will be amazed before we are half *way* through.(p.83)
• We vigorously commenced this *way* of living as we cleaned up the past.(p.84)
• So we let God discipline us in the simple *way* we have just outlined.(p.88)
• Let the doctor, if he will, tell him he has something in the *way* of a solution.(p.91)
• If he thinks he can do the job in some other *way*, or prefers some other spiritual approach, encourage him to follow his own conscience.(p.95)
• The family should be offered your *way* of life.(p.97)
• The wife should fully understand his new *way* of life.(p.99)
• In this *way* you can set them on the right track without becoming critical of them.(p.100)
• Especially when he has before him a *way* to stop his drinking and abuse if he really wants to pay the price.(p.108)
• He clings to the notion that he will yet find a *way* to do so.(p.110)
• Sometimes he drinks on the *way* home from the hospital.(p.110)
• If such women adopt a spiritual *way* of life their road will be smoother.(p.114)
• A better *way* of life will emerge when they are overcome.(p.117)
• We had to learn these things the hard *way*.(p.121)
• There will be alluring shortcuts and by-paths down which they may wander and lose their *way*.(p.123)
• We think that such a view is self-centered and in direct conflict with the new *way* of living.(p.124)
• Although financial recovery is on the *way* for many of us, we found we could not place money first.(p.127)
• This may hang on for months, long after their mother has accepted dad's new *way* of living and thinking.(p.134)
• In time they will see that he is a new man and in their own *way* they will let him know it.(p.134)
• He left us a note saying you were the best boss he ever had, and that you were not to blame in any *way*."(p.136)
• In this *way* he was slyly carrying tales.(p.145)
• The firm wants to help you get over it, and if you are interested, there is a *way* out.(p.147)
• They will approach still other sick ones and fellowships of Alcoholics Anonymous may spring up in each city and hamlet, havens for those who must find a *way* out.(p.153)
• Suppose now that through you several families have adopted this *way* of life.(p.153)
• Perhaps the best *way* of treating you to a glimpse of your future will be to describe the growth of the fellowship among us.(p.153)
• He had a desperate desire to stop, but saw no *way* out, for he had earnestly tried many avenues of escape.(p.155)
• The last three times, I got drunk on the *way* home from here.(p.157)
• After a bit, he said, "The *way* you fellows put this spiritual stuff makes sense.(p.159)
• They experienced a few distressing failures, but in those cases they made an effort to bring the man's family into a spiritual *way* of living, thus relieving much worry and suffering.(p.159)
• In addition to these casual get-togethers, it became customary to set apart one night a week for a meeting to be attended by anyone or everyone interested in a spiritual *way* of life.(p.159)
• Finally my father had to send a doctor out from my home town who managed to get me back there in some *way*, and I was in bed about two months before I could venture out of the house.(p.175)
• I drank all the scotch they had on the train and bought several quarts on my *way* to the hotel.(p.179)
• I bought some more liquor on the *way* to the depot.(p.179)
• It hadn't worked out that *way* and I didn't know what the matter was and did not know what to do.(p.184)
• We boys drove out in somebody's car and went to the bar on the *way* do the dining room and I, in an effort to impress the other boys that I was city-bred, having lived in Scranton and Cleveland, asked them if they didn't want a drink.(p.194)
• And we stood there for twenty minutes, telling each other how much better we were, how much better we looked, how much better off we were financially, mentally, physically, morally, and in every *way*, shape and manner.(p.201)
• To show you the point to which this obsession went, there came an occasion when I had spent a most delightful week-end, and at nine o'clock on Sunday night I was on my *way* home, and I thought I would get a drink.(p.204)
• I went downstairs and there was the grizzly old veteran police officer in charge of the property desk, and as he gave me the stuff, he asked, "Are you going out in the street that *way*?"(p.204)
• Of course, it was always my aim to have my own *way* without being caught.(p.210)
• I could discipline myself but along the *way* there would be festivities and occasions when I got drunk.(p.211)
• It was not known to me as a group, but I later learned that my wife had known about it for nine months and had prayed constantly that I would stumble into Akron some *way* or another.(p.215)
• I was kind of shocked about anybody talking about themselves the *way* he did, and my impression was that the guy was a little "touched."(p.216)
• However, on a couple of other occasions, Clarence seemed to bob up at the last saloon that I would stop at on the *way* home every day.(p.216)

• Bill bought me a drink or two on the ***way***, and Dorothy S. came with us, and the three of us went over to the City Hospital.(p.217)
• He startled me by informing me that he was an alcoholic, that he had found a ***way*** which so far enabled him to live without taking a drink, and that the main idea was to find a ***way*** how not to take that first drink.(p.218)
• The name on it was unfamiliar and I had to ask the ***way*** to Grand Central.(p.223)
• If that was the ***way*** out, it wasn't for me.(p.227)
• "You can't win unless you try God's ***way***."(p.236)
• In a few sentences he made God seem personal to me, explained Him as a being who was interested in me, the alcoholic, and that all I needed to do was to be willing to follow His ***way***; that as long as I followed it I would be able to overcome my desire for liquor.(p.236)
• Well, there I was, willing to try it, but I didn't know how, except in a vague ***way***.(p.236)
• For a long time I kept on trying, in a pretty dumb ***way*** at first, I know, but very earnestly.(p.237)
• That is the ***way*** Jackie found me, lying on a cot in my skivvies, with hot and cold sweats, pounding heart and that awful itchy scratchiness all over.(p.238)
• He had also gone all the ***way*** through the wringer and had been dry two years when I saw him again.(p.243)
• I had repaired to one of these one morning with my jug and when I left late in the afternoon, I picked up a newspaper on the ***way*** home.(p.244)
• Much later I discovered the elders held many prayer meetings hoping to find a ***way*** to give me the heave-ho, but at the same time stay tolerant and spiritual.(p.247)
• So I rocked along my merry independent ***way*** until June, when I went out selling auto polish in New England.(p.247)
• I don't think the boys were completely convinced of my personality change, for they fought shy of including my story in the book, so my only contribution to their literary efforts was my firm conviction, being still a theological rebel, that the word God should be qualified with the phrase "as we understand him" -- for that was the only ***way*** I could accept spirituality.(p.248)
• She has been sober all the ***way*** through and for me that has been good.(p.249)
• We can share in the laughter and tears of our many friends, and most important, we can share our A.A. ***way*** of life and are given a daily opportunity to help others.(p.249)
• My boss, in his ***way***, was "big business."(p.251)
• Making my ***way*** to Pittsburgh, I met other former friends and got a job in a large factory where piecemakers were making good money.(p.252)
• As soon as I could get up and walk I started to drink again and kept it up until my friend of the hospital, who, in his first try at the new ***way*** of life had stubbed his toe in Chicago but had come back to the town to take counsel and make a new start, picked me up and got me into a hospital.(p.258)
• I began to read the Bible daily and to go over a simple devotional exercise as a ***way*** to begin each day.(p.259)
• It has been that ***way*** with some, but it has not been with me and may never be.(p.259)
• Today I have Someone who will always hear me; I have a warm fellowship among men who understand my problems; I have tasks to do and am glad to do them, to see others who are alcoholics and to help them in any ***way*** I can to become sober men.(p.260)
• But I don't believe now that it was with any deep feeling of resentment that I said to him, "The children are raised, and if this is the ***way*** you want it, this is the ***way*** we'll have it.(p.263)
• So, sometimes we'd end up in Charleston, West Virginia, or here or there, drinking all along the ***way***.(p.264)
• Time went on and the drinking got worse and worse, and I was in another barroom, down the road the other ***way***, a small one, and I took my glass -- that morning I'd been able to lift it from the bar -- and I said to the woman behind the bar, "I wish I might never take another drop of that stuff.(p.266)
• Finally, one morning, I got up and got in the car and cried all the ***way*** down to the M.'s -- the people who owned the bar -- and told her I was licked and wanted help.(p.267)
• I didn't know that anything was ever done for them in a medical ***way***.(p.267)
• I remember sometime, it was possibly six months after we had been going steadily to King School, that we were coming home from a meeting and saw a car along the ***way***, and a fellow in back drinking a bottle of beer.(p.271)
• We were so mad at her because she talked to him that ***way***.(p.271)
• I feel that one of the things that I still have to guard against is that I used to be set in my ***way*** about what I considered the old-time A.A.(p.272)
• Here was a tall, rugged, highly educated Yankee talking in a matter of course ***way*** about God and prayer.(p.279)
• In the spring of 1939, Bill stopped off in Akron on his ***way*** to Detroit on business.(p.281)
• The A.A. program showed me the ***way*** to come down to earth, start from the bottom and work up.(p.284)
• Once dad came all the ***way*** to Florida to sober me up, after a hotel manager called him and said that if he wanted to see me alive he better get there fast.(p.288)
• On the ***way*** home numerous places must be passed.(p.299)
• Indeed, I was always well on my ***way*** before I would undertake to go visiting at all.(p.301)
• I definitely liked it, everything about it, the taste, the effects; and I realize now that a drink did something for me or to me that was different from the ***way*** it affected others.(p.305)
• People didn't behave this ***way*** outside of an asylum.(p.306)
• Maybe I could find my ***way*** out of this agonizing existence.(p.309)
• It is a ***way*** of life, and the challenge contained in its principles is great enough to keep any human being striving for as long as he lives.(p.311)
• A.A.'s Twelve Steps showed me the ***way*** to sobriety if I wanted it.(p.320)
• I started to take A.A. seriously, and A.A. gave me a new ***way*** of life.(p.320)
• Fortunately, I didn't say a word to George on the ***way*** home.(p.322)
• The only ***way*** I knew to do it was to drink right along with him.(p.322)
• No ***way***!(p.331)
• Death seemed the only ***way*** out.(p.333)
• A.A. gives us alcoholics direction into a ***way*** of life without the need for alcohol.(p.340)
• Psychiatrist and surgeon, he had lost his ***way*** until he realized that God, not he, was the Great Healer.(p.345)
• The second ***way*** in which, perhaps, I differ from some other alcoholics is this; many alcoholics state that they didn't particularly like the taste of alcohol, but that they liked the effect.(p.345)
• In my stupid ***way*** I went up to see him with the idea in the back of my mind that I would investigate Alcoholics Anonymous from a medical standpoint.(p.346)
• And then we went up the side of a hill where we have a little barbecue area to make the fire for the barbecue, and on the ***way*** up, I thought to myself -- I'll go back down to the kitchen and refill this drink.(p.347)
• And the first thing you know I was lifted right out of the A.A. group, and I floated higher, and higher, and even higher, until I was ***way*** up on a pink cloud which is known as Pink Seven, and I felt miserable again.(p.348)
• "Well," he said, "you've been sober, but you've been floating ***way*** up on a cloud somewhere.(p.349)
• All I do in a very simple ***way***, is to help Him cure my patients.(p.351)
• Can you picture two girls hitchhiking their ***way*** to Las Vegas from Washington State?(p.354)
• I'd managed to drink my ***way*** through all my friends.(p.355)
• A.A. has become a ***way*** of life and living for me.(p.355)
• I was living in a small room on West 53rd Street right off Fifth Avenue, when I met a young lady who eventually was responsible for altering my entire ***way*** of living.(p.359)
• They told me their stories, which were much more rugged than mine -- yet what they said made sense, and the ***way*** they put it was easy for me to understand, with an understanding I had never had before.(p.363)
• She told me not to bother going "for her sake"; she told me in a nice ***way*** that it didn't make any difference to her -- and that really scared me -- so I went.(p.365)
• A whole new world of happiness and love began to unfold before my eyes, a truly new ***way*** of living.(p.365)
• I lost a lot of shirts that ***way***, and sometimes I was minus a whole wash.(p.371)
• That ***way***, I could spend most of my time at the Laundromat!(p.371)
• Rehearsals then became a part of the pattern, stopping at bars on the ***way*** to or from the place where drinks were to be served.(p.375)
• Whenever we went out she appeared to go out of her ***way*** to keep me from having more than one drink.(p.376)
• This suggestion had been made before on a number of occasions, but like all alcoholics I wanted to handle my problem my own ***way***, which really meant I didn't want anything to interfere with my drinking.(p.378)
• I was trying to find an easier, softer ***way***.(p.378)
• This was no ***way*** to live.(p.378)
• There may be many reasons which bring one to A.A. for the first time, but the lasting one must be to want sobriety and the A.A. ***way*** of living for oneself.(p.379)
• The Twelve Steps, which to me are a spiritual ***way*** of living, soon meant honest thinking, not wishful thinking, open mindedness, a willingness to try and a faith to accept.(p.381)
• The A.A. ***way*** of life is the ***way*** we always should have tried to live.(p.382)
• I had tried my ***way*** and had failed.(p.383)
• I didn't know which ***way*** to turn.(p.391)
• There are so many to whom I feel deeply grateful; to my husband (and best critic), whose generous love, compassion and understanding have helped me along the ***way***; to those before me in A.A. who inspired the first article I read, and the friend who sent that article to Frank; to Ruth for her personal note, and the first A.A. to talk to me; to my Bishop, whose loving and believing spirit inspired me; and to all the members of the Houston Group who were so patient, kind and helpful -- and to countless others.(p.393)
• It is a ***way*** of life that pays as it goes, every step of the ***way***, in compensations that have been wonderfully rich and rewarding.(p.394)
• But, as it was with drinking, this project will be entered into with enthusiasm and optimism -- and probably wind up the same ***way***, depressed.(p.396)
• Age and the law were still against me, but laws were not as strictly enforced in those days as they are now, and I discovered that as long as I had the green blood, there was always a ***way*** to get alcohol, either from a nondiscriminatory bartender or from an older friend who would be glad to purchase the joy juice for the privilege of sharing it.(p.397)
• I found out fast that the cheapest ***way*** to get drunk was on shots with beer chasers at two bits a crack.(p.397)
• Showing all the courage and ingenuity that I had not used in a positive ***way***, I covered my tracks and hid from my family so successfully that they did not find me for months.(p.401)
• So I did the right thing in the wrong ***way***.(p.409)
• I stopped at the cashier's any hour of the night on the ***way*** to the bar and cashed a check.(p.410)
• I am a part of A.A. which is a ***way*** of life.(p.417)
• Defeated by alcohol and pills, he found the ***way*** to a new life.(p.418)
• Three years later I was discharged in the same ***way***.(p.425)
• But I knew I'd never get that ***way***.(p.427)
• I'd thought of it in an offhand ***way***, of course.(p.429)
• I'd claw my ***way*** back to "respectability" and stay there -- until the inevitable next time.(p.432)
• Moreover, I am deeply convinced that so long as I continue to strive, in my bumbling ***way***, toward the principles I first encountered in the earlier chapters of this book, this remarkable power will continue to flow through me.(p.437)
• Max hadn't gotten that ***way*** because I didn't care.(p.440)
• I drank my ***way*** through schools and always got honors.(p.441)
• (Today, we don't have to live that ***way***.(p.446)
• "That's a devil of a ***way*** to run an organization," I thought, and I reported Frank to the psychiatrist, who didn't seem perturbed; he just got someone else to take me on Fridays.(p.447)
• When I am disturbed, it is because I find some person, place, thing, or situation -- some fact of my life -- unacceptable to me, and I can find no serenity until I accept that person, place, thing, or situation as being exactly the ***way*** it is supposed to be at this moment.(p.449)
• I can tell her she ought not to think a certain ***way***, but I certainly can't take away her right to feel however she does feel.(p.451)
• But it was the other ***way*** around.(p.452)
• Alcohol wrings the guts out of life, eats into the brain in such a ***way*** as to make the alcoholic blind to the truth.(p.457)
• Of course, an inmate must begin living the A.A.

way "inside," if he is to stand a chance "outside."(p.458)
• We reverted to the old ***way*** of life we knew -- a life full of anger, vindictiveness, resentment, fear, dependence, denial, self-will, irresponsibility.(p.459)
• After all, it was self (you, me) that stood in our own ***way***, that ran the show and ran ourselves into bankruptcy, that hurt the ones we loved.(p.459)
• This is difficult, but it is the only ***way*** it has worked for me.(p.463)
• This career girl preferred solitary drinking, the blackout kind, often hoping she'd stay that ***way*** for keeps.(p.464)
• On the day set for the extractions, on my ***way*** to the dentist's I felt a little nervous, so I had a couple of drinks, and after the teeth were out I was very nervous, so I had a few more.(p.466)
• We were on our ***way*** to New York where he planned to leave me with my sister.(p.466)
• On the ***way*** I tried, and I mean really tried, to throw myself out of the car.(p.466)
• I went out to a restaurant, found a booth ***way*** back in the rear, and started drinking.(p.467)
• Actually it had, ***way*** back in 1940.(p.469)
• In my screwed up mind I kept thinking I could have gone to A.A. ***way*** back there in 1940, and perhaps saved my marriage and home.(p.469)
• It came about in this ***way***.(p.472)
• She realized that, and the ***way*** I felt, and so for my own good she gradually began to pull away.(p.472)
• Met father (Tall Man) at fork in road -- one ***way*** to reservation, other ***way*** to State of Maine.(p.475)
• Men are supposed to be tough and rugged to start with, but if a woman becomes that ***way***, it is pretty hard to get back the niceties of womanhood.(p.480)
• We can have this new ***way*** of life – learning to live with our sickness and to be happy and content -- if we are willing to change our ***way*** of thinking and be honest, first with ourselves, then with others.(p.480)
• I can't begin to tell you of all the benefits I have derived from this new ***way*** of living.(p.481)
• That wasn't the ***way*** it was with my father.(p.485)
• Of course, when father finally came to Virginia to work his ***way*** through school, he resented the southern "cracker," as he often called them, so much that he didn't even go back to his mother's funeral.(p.486)
• The judge said that if she felt that ***way*** he would confine me for thirty days' examination and observation.(p.492)
• I have had experience in selling, collecting, and accounting, and am on my ***way*** up the ladder.(p.500)
• When you've been in a jam you've said, 'God, please do this or that,' and if it turned out your ***way*** that was the last of it, and if it didn't you've said 'There isn't any God' or 'He doesn't do anything for me.'(p.504)
• "That isn't the ***way***," he continued.(p.504)
• I am learning that I cannot have my own ***way*** as I used to.(p.505)
• I must find a ***way*** to make some money.(p.506)
• I will not be that ***way***.(p.506)
• I shall get myself "mellow" and stay that ***way***.(p.506)
• I rolled along with the mob this ***way***, that ***way*** and the other ***way***, but in those years nothing really bad happened to me.(p.508)
• When I wended my ***way*** home four days later, on the 27th, there was a detective waiting for me.(p.508)
• Yes, we find it rather confusing, but as we get around and get to know people in the group, they lead the ***way*** and all we have to do is to follow.(p.512)
• The realization came to me that I had to stop drinking, that I had to find a ***way***.(p.515)
• You went all the ***way***.(p.516)
• In this program there aren't any half ***way*** measures.(p.516)
• In here you must go all the ***way*** too."(p.516)
• For me, A.A. has become a ***way*** of life.(p.516)
• I got a job by myself which suited me down to the ground, because there was nobody really to interfere with what I did, one ***way*** or the other, and I usually had my nerves in good trim when anybody was coming around to inspect.(p.519)
• I stopped off just to have one drink to see if it tasted the same on the ***way*** back to London, and that night I was carried back to bed again.(p.522)
• I couldn't see that there was any ***way*** out of it, and I got absolutely despairing.(p.522)
• In time, I began to go out and forget the ***way*** back home.(p.527)
• It's time to stop finding excuses for drinking and getting into trouble, because now there is a ***way*** out, and if you want what we have, try coming around and giving the program a chance.(p.530)
• Perhaps a better ***way*** of saying it is that, on that day, with that decision, I no longer fought drinking as an escape.(p.531)
• Things weren't going as I thought they should, for my greater enjoyment, comfort and fame; therefore, if the universe wouldn't play my ***way***, I wouldn't play at all.(p.531)
• To my ***way*** of thinking, that is a definition of alcoholism; a state of being in which the emotions have failed to grow to the stature of the intellect.(p.535)
• Which is only another ***way*** of saying, I had to be right all the time, and only God can be that.(p.535)
• Still, I had had funds sufficient to get plastered because that, of course, was more important than paying my own ***way***.(p.538)
• And I am sure they would be right as far as they go, but A.A. has taught me I am the result of the ***way*** I reacted to what happened to me as a child.(p.544)
• The only ***way*** existence was possible was through rationalizing every sober moment and drinking myself into complete oblivion as often as I could.(p.547)
• The A.A. members who sponsored me told me in the beginning that I would not only find a ***way*** to live without having a drink, but that I would find a ***way*** to live without wanting to drink, if I would do these simple things.(p.550)
• In my prayers that morning I asked God to point out to me some ***way*** to be free of this resentment.(p.552)
• I guess I always knew that the ***way*** to handle my drinking was to quit.(p.554)
• Regarded as something of a "boy wonder," I began to see myself that ***way***.(p.555)
• Alcoholics can stop drinking in many places and many ways – but Alcoholics Anonymous offers us a ***way*** to stay sober.(p.559)
• 10. – No A.A. group or member should ever, in such a ***way*** as to implicate A.A., express any opinion on outside controversial issues – particularly those of politics, alcohol reform, or sectarian religion.(p.567)
• Dr. Harry M. Tiebout, psychiatrist: "As a psychiatrist, I have thought a great deal about the relationship of my specialty to A.A. and I have come to the conclusion that our particular function can very often lie in preparing the ***way*** for the patient to accept any sort of treatment or outside help.(p.571)

ways
• He plans various ***ways*** of drinking.(p.xxviii)
• Unlike the feelings of the ship's passengers, however, our joy in escape from disaster does not subside as we go our individual ***ways***.(p.17)
• The distinguished American psychologist, William James, in his book "Varieties of Religious Experience," indicates a multitude of ***ways*** in which men have discovered God.(p.28)
• He shuts himself up in an asylum, hoping to mend his ***ways***.(p.38)
• Being convinced that self, manifested in various ***ways***, was what had defeated us, we considered its common manifestations.(p.64)
• His ***ways*** of thinking and doing are the habit of years.(p.118)
• "You've been trying man's ***ways*** and they always fail," he told me.(p.236)
• Dr. Bob then led me through the restitution step, in which I made a list of all of the persons I had harmed, and worked out ***ways*** and means of slowly making restitution.(p.292)
• I have been very fortunate in many ***ways***.(p.323)
• In two ***ways*** I may be a little different from other alcoholics.(p.345)
• When it became noticeable to the point of comment, I devised ***ways*** of sneaking drinks on the side.(p.375)
• Resenting anyone and everyone who might interfere with my personal plans and ***ways*** of doing things, I was full of self pity, especially for any interference with my drinking.(p.376)
• She of course didn't realize how cunning an alcoholic can be and the lengths to which he will go in finding ***ways*** to satisfy the compulsion for more and more drinks after having had the first one.(p.377)
• There are no easy ***ways*** to sober up, but that's the most excruciating.(p.389)
• In all these ***ways*** I've experienced, in ever growing measure and beyond all expectations and rewards, a joy which I had never before imagined.(p.395)
• I wanted to die and often I would think of ***ways***.(p.411)
• One, the side I turned to myself and the world, was respectable – even, in some ***ways***, distinguished.(p.432)
• Alcoholics can stop drinking in many places and many ***ways*** -- but Alcoholics Anonymous offers us a way to stay sober.(p.559)

wayward
• By force of circumstances, she was often obliged to treat father as a sick or ***wayward*** child.(p.130)
• Many a distracted wife has visited this house to find loving and understanding companionship among women who knew her problem, to hear from the lips of their husbands what had happened to them, to be advised how her own ***wayward*** mate might be hospitalized and approached when next he stumbled.(p.160)

weak
• "His will power must be ***weak***."(p.20)
• We were bothered with the thought that faith and dependence upon a Power beyond ourselves was somewhat ***weak***, even cowardly.(p.45)
• We have admitted certain defects; we have ascertained in a rough way what the trouble is; we have put our finger on the ***weak*** items in our personal inventory.(p.72)
• You will no longer be self-conscious or feel that you must apologize as though your husband were a ***weak*** character.(p.115)
• In a ***weak*** moment he may take your dislike of his high-stepping friends as one of those insanely trivial excuses to drink.(p.120)
• When dealing with an alcoholic, there may be a natural annoyance that a man could be so ***weak***, stupid and irresponsible.(p.139)
• Can you discard the feeling that you are dealing only with habit, with stubbornness, or a ***weak*** will?(p.140)
• Still physically ***weak***, and sober but a few months, he saw that his predicament was dangerous.(p.154)
• With increasing guilt and never-ending depression, I was too ***weak*** to continue this day-by-day suicide.(p.355)
• I had no qualms, because I felt the source of a drinking problem was all in how ***weak*** one was, and I wasn't like my dad (I thought).(p.370)
• Other girls whom I had known all my life asked for one ***weak*** scotch after dinner.(p.406)
• Now, I am big and ***weak***, but Anne was bigger than I and strong.(p.414)
• I was too ***weak*** and exhausted to even try to throw myself out of the car.(p.467)
• I became so ***weak***, I could barely drag myself around.(p.558)

weakened
• It relieved me somewhat to learn that in alcoholics the will is amazingly ***weakened*** when it comes to combating liquor, though it often remains strong in other respects.(p.7)
• Being somewhat ***weakened***, and faced with physical and mental readjustment to a life which knows no alcohol, he may overdo.(p.146)

weakest
• And does not science demonstrate that visual proof is the ***weakest*** proof?(p.48)

weakling
• Again I swayed dizzily before an open window, or the medicine cabinet where there was poison, cursing myself for a ***weakling***.(p.6)

weaklings
• In those days, I trusted no church-goer, and thought A.A. was for ***weaklings***.(p.460)

weakness
• We can laugh at those who think spirituality the way of ***weakness***.(p.68)
• I had suppressed tendencies to overindulge and thus reveal my "moral ***weakness***," because false pride was so dominant.(p.327)
• While I sought the comforting arms of alcohol, I knew this was a sign of ***weakness*** on the part of a longtime-successful old codger with white hair, the image of dignity.(p.331)
• My mother was a lovely, sweet woman, whose only ***weakness*** was my father.(p.369)
• I thought he merely had a "***weakness***."(p.369)
• And I still felt it was a ***weakness*** -- plus, in her case, adverse circumstances.(p.370)
• At a women's halfway house, I became associated with Alcoholics Anonymous and became aware of alcoholism as a disease, not just a "***weakness***."(p.371)
• Strength has come from ***weakness***.(p.507)

wealth
• I have had my share of problems, heartaches and disappointments, because that is life, but also I have known a great deal of joy, and a peace that is the handmaiden of an inner freedom, I have a ***wealth*** of friends and, with my A.A. friends, an unusual quality of fellowship.(p.312)
• They inherited ***wealth*** and acquired more.(p.401)

wealthiest
• The poorest person has no less and the ***wealthiest*** has no more – each of us has but one day.(p.473)
wealthy
• They were neither poor nor ***wealthy***, but far better off than the average couple.(p.357)
weapon
• Out of this alloy of drink and speculation, I commenced to forge the ***weapon*** that one day would turn in its flight like a boomerang and all but cut me to ribbons.(p.2)
• I think our profession must take appreciative cognizance of this great therapeutic ***weapon***.(p.571)
wear
• Unless your friend wants to talk further about himself, do not ***wear*** out your welcome.(p.95)
• They sent me up with an attendant, and the attendant and I both arrived at the Egyptian Hospital rather the worse for ***wear***.(p.521)
• There was the physical aspect; to be the youngest and the runt of the brood of children, to have to ***wear*** glasses very early and so to be teased, to be bookish and bored in school because the captain of the football team could not translate Virgil and yet was the school god while you, you, you little shrimp, were the school egghead, junior size and an early model.(p.533)
• To ***wear*** expensive clothes, to have bartenders know what to serve me before I ordered, to be recognized by headwaiters and shown to the best table, to play gin rummy for high stakes with the insouciance of a riverboat gambler -- these were the enduring values in life, I thought.(p.556)
wearily
• The unselfishness of these men as we have come to know them, the entire absence of profit motive, and their community spirit, is indeed inspiring to one who has labored long and ***wearily*** in this alcoholic field.(p.xxv)
• As animals on a treadmill, we have patiently and ***wearily*** climbed, falling back in exhaustion after each futile effort to reach solid ground.(p.107)
• Looking sadder than ever, he ***wearily*** ventured, "Well this is wonderful for you fellows, but it can't be for me.(p.188)
wearing
• Thus mother, through no fault of her own, became accustomed to ***wearing*** the family trousers.(p.131)
• And we usually have some kind of grimy sweater that we think we look sexy in, even if we weigh ninety-five pounds soaking wet and are not ***wearing*** a bra.(p.479)
weary
• My ***weary*** and despairing wife was informed that it would all end with heart failure during delirium tremens, or I would develop a wet brain, perhaps within a year.(p.7)
• Maybe the doctor has been called in, and the ***weary*** round of sanitariums and hospitals has begun.(p.110)
weather
• Let families realize, as they start their journey, that all will not be fair ***weather***.(p.122)
• Where once I had casual acquaintances, all of whom were fair ***weather*** friends, I now have a host of friends who accept me for what I am.(p.296)
• High living, a great many fair ***weather*** friends, the 1929 stock market crash, and a couple of years of Depression, soon relieved me one by one of my worldly goods including my wife.(p.358)
• We worked in five below zero ***weather***, fixing on an elm tree a wrought iron device which modestly proclaimed that he was indeed a country doctor.(p.540)
weaving
• I got into slacks and out I went, ***weaving*** with the dog.(p.390)
wedding
• I believe the first time I ever realized what alcohol would do for me was at my own ***wedding***.(p.385)
• The night that I was married I had a big church ***wedding***.(p.385)
• I got right into the car and they drove me over, and just as soon as I got to the church they started the ***wedding***.(p.385)
• It was my ex-wife, and she said my twenty-seven-year-old son, who has completed his Marine Corps training and graduated from college, wanted to see me privately, was getting married in three months, and wanted me at the ***wedding***.(p.462)
• At the ***wedding***, I hope I will also get to see my daughter and their mother.(p.463)
• For instance, the fiftieth ***wedding*** anniversary of my wife's parents was the occasion for a huge family reunion at our home.(p.556)
weddings
• That includes bars, nightclubs, dances, receptions, ***weddings***, even plain ordinary whoopee parties.(p.101)
• At this school we had Bible readings before each meal, and church services four times on Sunday, and I became so rebellious at this that I swore I would never join or go to any church except for ***weddings*** or funerals.(p.240)
Wednesday
• From childhood through high school I was more or less forced to go to church, Sunday School and evening service, Monday night Christian Endeavor and sometimes to ***Wednesday*** evening prayer meeting.(p.172)
• I attended their meetings every Sunday and ***Wednesday*** for about nine months.(p.202)
• I left on a ***Wednesday*** afternoon, had dinner in Akron and then went to a house where I encountered my first meeting.(p.218)
• Jack said there was a meeting in Akron every ***Wednesday*** night and that it was very important that we go.(p.268)
• On ***Wednesday*** night Jack M. said, "You meet me at the Ohio Edison Building, and I will take you to the meeting."(p.269)
• We had never missed a ***Wednesday*** night at King School for a year.(p.270)
• The day before I was due to go back to Chicago, a ***Wednesday*** and Dr. Bob's afternoon off, he had me down to the office and we spent three or four hours formally going through the Six-Step program as it was at that time.(p.291)
week
• We are unable, at certain times, to bring into our consciousness with sufficient force the memory of the suffering and humiliation of even a ***week*** or a month ago.(p.24)
• Within a ***week*** after leaving the hospital a fast-moving trolley car breaks his arm.(p.38)
• In addition to these casual get-togethers, it became customary to set apart one night a ***week*** for a meeting to be attended by anyone or everyone interested in a spiritual way of life.(p.159)
• I know there was even more, something that I hadn't got, and I remember one day, a ***week*** or two after I had come out of the hospital, Bill was over to my house talking to my wife and me.(p.191)
• I can remember well thinking that I would quit drinking, really go to work hard, apply myself eight hours a day, five days a ***week***, make a lot of money, and then I could start drinking again.(p.199)
• When I left the hospital I tried this for a day and it worked, for a ***week*** and it worked, and for a month, and it worked – and then for a year and it still worked.(p.209)
• I believe though that it helped my family tremendously to have the A.A. meetings every ***week*** in my own home.(p.220)
• I refused to join any fraternity, as I wanted to be a free lance, and that year my drinking was confined to one-night stands, once or twice a ***week***.(p.241)
• Bill and Hank had just taken over a small automobile polishing company and they offered me a job -- ten dollars a ***week*** and keep at Hank's house.(p.246)
• There was one meeting a ***week*** at Bill's home in Brooklyn, and we all took turns there spouting off about how we had changed our lives overnight, how many drunks we had saved and straightened out, and last, but not least, how God had touched each of us personally on the shoulder.(p.246)
• After a very good ***week***, two of my customers took me to lunch on Saturday.(p.247)
• Then it was my turn – I ordered "Three beers," but this time it was different, I had a cash investment of thirty cents and, on a ten dollar a ***week*** salary, that's a big thing.(p.247)
• Very rarely do I miss the meetings of my neighborhood A.A. group, and my average has never been less than two meetings a ***week***.(p.249)
• Saying goodbye to my wife and baby, I was treading Manhattan's streets in a little more than a ***week***.(p.252)
• He introduced himself and began to tell me about a bunch of some sixty former drinkers and drunkards who met once a ***week***, and he invited me to go with him to the next meeting.(p.257)
• He knew too well that didn't mean a thing, just as I knew in my heart that it would be only a question of time -- a few days, a ***week***, or even a month, it was inevitable – till I would be off on another bender.(p.257)
• The time came just a ***week*** later.(p.258)
• I remember one instance when he took off and went down to Cincinnati and was gone a ***week*** on a drunk.(p.262)
• They spent at least an evening a ***week*** in our home out there for weeks and weeks.(p.270)
• But – I also stayed up ***week*** nights after they had retired and drank myself into bed.(p.277)
• I lived through a ***week*** of the fidgets because I had agreed to address a group of alcoholic inmates in one of our state mental hospitals.(p.283)
• A ***week*** later, I had to get an old friend from Akron to spend two days sobering me up.(p.293)
• Immediately on her return we began to have formal meetings once a ***week***, in the autumn of 1939, and we have continued to do this and to expand ever since.(p.295)
• A night or so a ***week*** in a joint, and a party or so a ***week*** at home or with friends, along with a little lone drinking, soon had me preparing for the existence of a top flight drunkard.(p.298)
• I went to A.A. meetings twice a ***week***.(p.320)
• After that I sat for a ***week***, a body in a chair, a mind off in space.(p.338)
• I went to work in Birmingham for a newspaper at fifteen dollars a ***week***.(p.357)
• Before too long, my husband (who seemed to prefer his shirts dirty) put his foot down, declaring that our family might have the cleanest clothes in town, but that I hadn't been out of the same old dirty slacks and blouse for a ***week***.(p.371)
• I think I actually read more contempt than was really there because just a ***week*** before someone had sent him the Saturday Evening Post article on A.A., and there was some glimmer of hope in it for him.(p.391)
• So he waited another ***week*** or two and I don't think I stayed sober hardly at all.(p.391)
• So I wrote this letter in very shaky handwriting, and in just one ***week*** came back a letter with A.A. literature from New York.(p.392)
• So Frank left town, and by Monday morning I had been sober for that whole ***week***.(p.393)
• Twelve dollars a ***week***.(p.397)
• Saying these sprees were limited to one a ***week*** (they were not), and saying that the average spree was ten of these drinks (sometimes more, sometimes less), we come up with the first boring statistic: two-fifty per ***week*** out of twelve dollars.(p.397)
• In those days there was only one big meeting a ***week*** in New York.(p.414)
• I, who could never stay on the wagon for more than a ***week***.(p.416)
• My experience has been active: three meetings a ***week***, many tapes, many A.A. conferences, much work on the Twelve Steps, and much work with other alcoholics and their families.(p.420)
• I was skipping classes about two days a ***week*** and doing no book work whatever.(p.423)
• I was released in a ***week***, a ***week*** of hell with no drinks.(p.428)
• A ***week*** after my decision to join A.A., she called it quits.(p.430)
• The rest of that ***week*** is pretty hazy.(p.466)
• I'd been home about a ***week*** or ten days when one of my friends asked if I could repair one of his electrical outlets.(p.493)
• The trial lasted about a ***week***, and whether or not I was going to the death house was anybody's guess.(p.508)
• Within a ***week***, I was feeling well enough to go home.(p.558)
week-end
• Unless he took some drinks, he might not have the courage to scrape an acquaintance and would have a lonely ***week-end***.(p.154)
• To show you the point to which this obsession went, there came an occasion when I had spent a most delightful ***week-end***, and at nine o'clock on Sunday night I was on my way home, and I thought I would get a drink.(p.204)
• All they talked of that first ***week-end*** was God, and how they were going to straighten out Jackie's and my life.(p.245)
• During that first ***week-end*** I decided to stay in New York and take all they gave out with, except the "God stuff."(p.246)
• Then I looked forward to the ***week-end*** of golf and the nineteenth hole.(p.374)
week-end's
• I got to the place where I'd look forward to the ***week-end's*** drinking and pacify myself by saying that the week-ends were mine, that it didn't interfere with my family or with my business if I drank on the week-ends.(p.488)
week-ends
• The second year my drinking was more or less restricted to ***week-ends***, but I was nearly kicked out for

scholastic failure.(p.241)
- I didn't know how to be a father; I don't know how to come home and work *week-ends* like other husbands; I don't know how to entertain my family.(p.351)
- I got to the place where I'd look forward to the week-end's drinking and pacify myself by saying that the *week-ends* were mine, that it didn't interfere with my family or with my business if I drank on the week-ends.(p.488)
- But the *week-ends* stretched on into Mondays and the time soon came when I drank every day.(p.488)

week-long
- After all, upon coming out of a *week-long* or ten-day drunk, it was hard enough to figure up just how much that one drunk cost, let alone trying to calculate the cost of approximately twenty-five years of active alcoholism.(p.396)
- Then I went on my first *week-long* bender of solitary drinking, locked up in a hotel room, because my family opposed my coming marriage.(p.464)

week's
- (I think my first feeling of fear came with my first *week's* solitary drinking, locked up in that hotel room.(p.465)

weekend
- I'm writing this during an A.A. convention, where I have spent the *weekend* with nothing but white people.(p.529)

weekends
- At this time I was holding what drinking I did down to *weekends*, but I hadn't had a drink at all in a month.(p.243)
- I confined drinking to *weekends*, and drank normally in college and for several years thereafter.(p.287)
- From my post, I'd go spend *weekends* with her.(p.318)
- After about three months, no more *weekends*.(p.318)
- Then my father fell down a flight of stairs on one of his lost *weekends*, at the peak of his career, and died.(p.370)
- On two occasions, over *weekends*, I decided I would take absolutely nothing.(p.443)
- I got to the place where I'd look forward to the week-end's drinking and pacify myself by saying that the week-ends were mine, that it didn't interfere with my family or with my business if I drank on the *week-ends*.(p.488)

weekly
- Now, this house will hardly accommodate its *weekly* visitors, for they number sixty or eighty as a rule.(p.161)
- This duty together with my *weekly* meetings with my fellow alcoholics, and my daily renewal of the contract I originally made with God, have kept me sober when nothing else ever did.(p.237)
- At our *weekly* meeting I was a menace to serenity those first few months, for I took every opportunity to lambaste the "spiritual angle" as we called it, or anything else that had any tinge of theology.(p.246)
- I asked this question *weekly* for the next couple of years.(p.359)
- I attended my *weekly* meetings with regularity, re-read the Big Book, attended other group meetings, gave leads when asked to and did some Twelve Step work whenever I was called upon to do so.(p.365)

weeks
- Some will be drunk the day after making their resolutions; most of them within a few *weeks*.(p.34)
- He tells you he has decided to stop jay-walking for good, but in a few *weeks* he breaks both legs.(p.38)
- Then, in days, *weeks*, or months, a fresh outburst.(p.105)
- We do not like the thought that the contents of a book or the work of another alcoholic has accomplished in a few *weeks* that for which we struggled for years.(p.118)
- After two *weeks* of drinking, he had placed his toe on the trigger of a loaded shotgun -- the barrel in his mouth.(p.137)
- I had discharged him for drinking six *weeks* before.(p.137)
- He had lived there but a few *weeks* when he found that the place probably contained more alcoholics per square mile than any city in the country.(p.163)
- This dry spell lasted for about three *weeks*; then I went to Atlantic City to attend several days' meeting of a national society of which I was a member.(p.179)
- Away from my office two or three *weeks* at a time; horrible days and nights when I would lie on the floor of my home, lying awake and reaching over to get the bottle, taking a drink and going back into oblivion.(p.184)
- So I had one double-header every night for about two or three *weeks*.(p.203)
- I was always interested in mechanics and after having about twenty miscellaneous jobs, lasting from one day to two *weeks*, I obtained a job as a toolmaker apprentice.(p.211)
- We went to Akron for about six *weeks* and we did a lot of visiting among the people in Akron.(p.219)
- And so on and on, for several *weeks*, while I grudgingly plowed through some more of the offending book, and felt more and more hopeless about myself.(p.227)
- For *weeks* after my arrival I was feted and entertained in the already large colony of Alsatians in the city, and among the Germans in their saloons and clubs.(p.231)
- Sometimes, after sobering up after a bout of several *weeks*, I would righteously resolve to quit.(p.233)
- I'd work like mad for three or four *weeks* without a single drink, save my money, pay a few bills and then "reward" myself with alcohol.(p.244)
- After being dry two *weeks* and sticking close to Jackie, all of a sudden I found I had become the sponsor of my sponsor, for he was suddenly taken drunk.(p.245)
- I'd been dry three *weeks*, had the wrinkles out and had sobered up my sponsor all by myself!(p.246)
- My wife and family stood by me for ten *weeks* and then, quite justifiably, ejected me.(p.257)
- I managed to maintain myself with odd jobs, did ten *weeks* in a social rescue institution, and at length wound up in a second-hand bookstore in an adjacent town as manager.(p.257)
- An accident while drunk laid me low for about three *weeks*.(p.258)
- These vacations became quite something, and he always had two *weeks* vacation the first two *weeks* of every September.(p.264)
- They spent at least an evening a week in our home out there for *weeks* and *weeks*.(p.270)
- I remained with them for three *weeks*, using part of the time in making many amends, which I had had no earlier opportunity of making.(p.281)
- Those three *weeks* left me completely exhausted and I had to return to Akron for three more months of rest.(p.282)
- I stayed in Akron two or three *weeks* on my initial trip trying to absorb as much of the program and philosophy as possible.(p.291)
- When I told them six *weeks*, they were polite and said that they would contact me in case they had anyone with an alcoholic problem.(p.293)
- So I suggested that he take a trip to Akron for a couple of *weeks*, which he did, living with one of the A.A. families there.(p.294)
- I really worked for several *weeks*, and having had a fairly wide acquaintance with the dealer trade, it was not difficult for me to line up enough of them to give me a very substantial volume of business with a minimum of effort.(p.300)
- We got along fine for about two *weeks*, until she told me where to go and to take my damn bottle with me.(p.318)
- Well, of course that was all I needed — to switch from wine to brandy for three *weeks*.(p.338)
- All I can remember about the Roaring Twenties is that I drank a great deal, thought I was having a grand time, managed to get to Europe for a few *weeks*, was very proud of the dozens of speak-easy cards entitling me to an entree in the better joints between Cleveland and New York, took on a wife, and built a home in a fashionable suburb of Cleveland.(p.358)
- In a few *weeks* I toed the line.(p.362)
- I stayed on in Florida for three *weeks*, enjoying our reunion, a new found health and a deeper love than I had ever experienced before.(p.364)
- One night, a few *weeks* after joining the Fellowship, much to my surprise and delight I saw a familiar but no longer frowning face.(p.371)
- He asked if I would cooperate with him after I went home, and if I would have a trained nurse stay with me for at least two *weeks*.(p.387)
- He said that because of my drinking, he shouldn't leave, but that he had to go to New York for two *weeks*.(p.388)
- I couldn't walk, having it in a cast, and the doctor left the cast on three *weeks* longer than was necessary because he never found me sober enough to take it off.(p.390)
- Two *weeks* later found me being sworn in, and the first payday in the Navy made me realize I had found a home.(p.398)
- This was how I had looked and acted a few short *weeks* ago.(p.415)
- This went on for thirteen *weeks*, the first eight of which I wasn't allowed visitors.(p.425)
- But my dad pulled some strings and got in to see me after three *weeks*.(p.425)
- *Weeks* would go by without further trouble, and I'd be assured I'd at last hit on the right formula.(p.433)
- Three *weeks* after an armed robbery in which one person received a superficial flesh wound (I could have killed someone!), I was apprehended.(p.460)
- Three *weeks* ago, my phone rang, and a voice I hadn't heard in over twenty-three years spoke.(p.462)
- Two *weeks* later, he come to A.A. meeting.(p.476)
- I was there about three *weeks*, and then I got restless and started to tramp across the country, here and there, until I finally wound up in Pennsylvania, in a steel mill.(p.492)
- Will I take a young fellow who has been drinking for two *weeks* to live with me?(p.506)
- I spent about six or seven *weeks* in Sing Sing, and was finally sent off to Dannemora in the Adirondacks.(p.509)
- Those poor stiffs probably went to a doctor and were told that if they quit they'd live three *weeks* and if they didn't they'd die in one."(p.510)
- My last binge followed the previous one by two *weeks*.(p.514)
- As I say, this specialist put a scare in me for about a fortnight or three *weeks*, then I started my last bout which went on and off for about three months.(p.523)
- (There was a time, for about three months, when I bought a ten-dollar wrist watch every pay day – that is every two *weeks*.(p.532)
- The children kept me sober for darn near three *weeks*, and then I went on (please God) my last drunk.(p.549)
- Do it every day for two *weeks* and you will find you have come to mean it and to want it for them, and you will realize that where you used to feel bitterness and resentment and hatred, you now feel compassionate understanding and love."(p.552)
- The days add up into *weeks*, the *weeks* into months and years."(p.572)

weeks'
- I think the thing that galled me was that just after Easter I had drawn my salary for two *weeks'* work and had decided that I was going to send some money to Vi; and above all else I was going to send my baby daughter an Easter outfit.(p.493)

weep
- I sat down on the side of one of their beds, and I started to *weep*, and I couldn't stop, and I was so startled, and I apologized again and again for it.(p.272)

weeping
- When I awoke in the middle of the night with shakes and sweats and fears, I would hear my wife *weeping* quietly in bed beside me.(p.558)

weeps
- (She no longer *weeps* in the night.)(p.559)

weigh
- And we usually have some kind of grimy sweater that we think we look sexy in, even if we *weigh* ninety-five pounds soaking wet and are not wearing a bra.(p.479)

weighed
- When I had known her years before she was rather slender, but at this time she *weighed* as much as she does now, which is up around in the two hundreds or very close to it.(p.493)

weighing
- A load *weighing* a thousand pounds came off my back.(p.414)

weight
- The message which can interest and hold these alcoholic people must have depth and *weight*.(p.xxvi)
- I could eat little or nothing when drinking, and I was forty pounds under *weight*.(p.7)
- I put on thirty pounds of *weight* in about two months, looked like a pig, and was uncomfortable from shortness of breath.(p.177)
- Ten days of this treatment the first time knocked me from 200 pounds to 130, and I seldom stayed out of the hole long enough to gain back my *weight*.(p.460)

welcome
- Friendly hands had stretched out in *welcome*.(p.53)
- Unless your friend wants to talk further about himself, do not wear out your *welcome*.(p.95)
- When I came to my aunt, she knew that I had had an unhappy childhood, and she said, "Now, Ethel, you're *welcome* to have boy friends in our home, but there are two boys in this town that I don't want you to date, and one of them comes from a very fine fam-

ily, one of the best.(p.262)
• Dad got out a jug for me and poured *welcome* home drinks.(p.428)
• There was a red plush carpet to *welcome* me, but even so it wasn't easy.(p.430)
• If you give us a try, you will see that we are really human beings, and we will *welcome* you with open arms and hearts.(p.529)
• My personal definition, which I submit as applying only to myself (although everyone is *welcome* to it who wants it), includes every waking activity of the human being; to have a creative attitude towards things is a more exact meaning, to live and to deal with other human beings creatively, which to me means seeing the God in them, and respecting and worshipping this God.(p.535)

welcomed

• Inquiry by scientific, medical, and religious societies will be *welcomed*.(p.xiv)
• I knew, and almost *welcomed* the idea.(p.7)
• Be certain he will be *welcomed* by your family, and that he is not trying to impose upon you for money, connections, or shelter.(p.96)
• No one is too discredited or has sunk too low to be *welcomed* cordially – if he means business.(p.161)
• I was warmly *welcomed* by friends of my youth who had preceded me.(p.231)
• From the top of the heap in a few years he had skidded to becoming a shuffling customer, still entering the better barrooms but *welcomed* by neither mine host nor his patrons.(p.236)
• I *welcomed* him with open arms.(p.263)
• In all honesty though, I was skeptical, but I wanted so definitely to quit drinking that I would have *welcomed* any sort of physical torture or pain to accomplish the result.(p.302)

welfare

• Unmindful of his *welfare*, I thought only of recapturing the spirit of other days.(p.9)
• Suggest how important it is that he place the *welfare* of other people ahead of his own.(p.94)
• Being wrecked in the same vessel, being restored and united under one God, with hearts and minds attuned to the *welfare* of others, the things which matter so much to some people no longer signify much to them.(p.161)
• But I am to learn later that it began with my desire for material success becoming greater than my interest in the *welfare* of my fellow man.(p.507)
• Since I have been in A.A., I have more friends than I ever had in my life – friends who care about me and my *welfare*, friends who don't care that I am black and that I have been in prison.(p.529)
• One – Our common *welfare* should come first; personal recovery depends upon A.A. unity.(p.564)
• Hence our common *welfare* comes first.(p.565)
• But individual *welfare* follows close afterward.(p.565)
• But when its plans concern the *welfare* of neighboring groups also, those groups ought to be consulted.(p.565)
• On such issues our common *welfare* is paramount.(p.565)

well

• Being mostly business or professional folk, we could not *well* carry on our occupations in such an event.(p.xiii)
• New groups started up and it was found, to the astonishment of everyone, that A.A.'s message could be transmitted in the mail as *well* as by word of mouth.(p.xviii)
• Neither does A.A. take any particular medical point of view, though we cooperate widely with the men of medicine as *well* as with the men of religion.(p.xx)
• These men may *well* have a remedy for thousands of such situations.(p.xxiv)
• But we are sure that our bodies were sickened as *well*.(p.xxiv)
• Though we work out our solution on the spiritual as *well* as an altruistic plane, we favor hospitalization for the alcoholic who is very jittery or befogged.(p.xxiv)
• What with our ultra-modern standards, our scientific approach to everything, we are perhaps not *well* equipped to apply the powers of good that lie outside our synthetic knowledge.(p.xxv)
• I studied economics and business as *well* as law.(p.2)
• As the whisky rose to my head I told myself I would manage better next time, but I might as *well* get good and drunk then.(p.6)
• *Well*, so had I.(p.6)
• I, who had thought so *well* of myself and my abilities, of my capacity to surmount obstacles, was cornered at last.(p.8)
• I was not too *well* at the time, and was plagued by waves of self-pity and resentment.(p.15)
• All sections of this country and many of its occupations are represented, as *well* as many political, economic, social, and religious backgrounds.(p.17)
• Before going into a detailed discussion, it may be *well* to summarize some points as we see them.(p.20)
• He is often perfectly sensible and *well* balanced concerning everything except liquor, but in that respect he is incredibly dishonest and selfish.(p.21)
• Only to have that thought supplanted by "*Well*, I'll stop with the sixth drink."(p.24)
• All went *well* for a time, but he failed to enlarge his spiritual life.(p.35)
• The experiment went so *well* that I ordered another whiskey and poured it into more milk.(p.36)
• We admit we have some of these symptoms, but we have not gone to the extremes you fellows did, nor are we likely to, for we understand ourselves so *well* after what you have told us that such things cannot happen again.(p.38)
• Fred is partner in a *well* known accounting firm.(p.39)
• To all appearance he is a stable, *well* balanced individual.(p.39)
• "In this frame of mind, I went about my business and for a time all was *well*.(p.40)
• My business came off *well*, I was pleased and knew my partners would be too.(p.41)
• *Well*, just that did happen and more, for what I had learned of alcoholism did not occur to me at all.(p.42)
• *Well*, that's exactly what this book is about.(p.45)
• That means we have written a book which we believe to be spiritual as *well* as moral.(p.45)
• The show doesn't come off very *well*.(p.61)
• Is he not a victim of the delusion that he can wrest satisfaction and happiness out of this world if he only manages *well*?(p.61)
• Being all powerful, He provided what we needed, if we kept close to Him and performed His work *well*.(p.63)
• We thought *well* before taking this step making sure we were ready; that we could at last abandon ourselves utterly to Him.(p.63)
• We think we have done *well* enough in admitting these things to ourselves.(p.72)
• Rightly and naturally, we think *well* before we choose the person or persons with whom to take this intimate and confidential step.(p.74)
• Though we have no religious connection, we may still do *well* to talk with someone ordained by an established religion.(p.74)
• Our former enemies sometimes praise what we are doing and wish us *well*.(p.78)
• Even though your protege may not have entirely admitted his condition, he has become very curious to know how you got *well*.(p.92)
• But he will be curious to learn why his own convictions have not worked and why yours seem to work so *well*.(p.93)
• Perhaps your story will help him see where he has failed to practice the very precepts he knows so *well*.(p.93)
• Tell him that if he wants to get *well* you will do anything to help.(p.95)
• For the type of alcoholic who is able and willing to get *well*, little charity, in the ordinary sense of the word, is needed or wanted.(p.97)
• Burn the idea into the consciousness of every man that he can get *well* regardless of anyone.(p.98)
• We have seen men get *well* whose families have not returned at all.(p.100)
• Among us are wives, relatives and friends whose problem has been solved, as *well* as some who have not yet found a happy solution.(p.104)
• Perhaps he can still tend to business fairly *well*.(p.109)
• Yet they got *well*.(p.110)
• You, as *well* as your husband, ought to think of what you can put into life instead of how much you can take out.(p.120)
• He is striving to recover fortune and reputation and feels he is doing very *well*.(p.126)
• Since the home has suffered more than anything else, it is *well* that a man exert himself there.(p.127)
• If the family will appreciate that dad's current behavior is but a phase of his development, all will be *well*.(p.129)
• Even if he displays a certain amount of neglect and irresponsibility towards the family, it is *well* to let him go as far as he likes in helping other alcoholics.(p.129)
• One more suggestion: Whether the family has spiritual convictions or not, they may do *well* to examine the principles by which the alcoholic member is trying to live.(p.130)
• This seemed to me like an opportunity to be helpful, so I spent two hours talking about alcoholism, the malady, and described the symptoms and results as *well* as I could.(p.138)
• If you desire to help it might be *well* to disregard your own drinking, or lack of it.(p.139)
• I *well* remember the shock I received when a prominent doctor in Chicago told me of cases where pressure of the spinal fluid actually ruptured the brain.(p.140)
• If you are sure your man does not want to stop, he may as *well* be discharged, the sooner the better.(p.141)
• Had they fired me first, and had they then taken steps to see that I was presented with the solution contained in this book, I might have returned to them six months later, a *well* man.(p.141)
• At this point, it might be *well* to explain alcoholism, the illness.(p.142)
• Say that you believe he is a gravely ill person, with this qualification – being perhaps fatally ill, does he want to get *well*?(p.142)
• Will he take every necessary step, submit to anything to get *well*, to stop drinking forever?(p.142)
• If he temporizes and still thinks he can ever drink again, even beer, he might as *well* be discharged after the next bender which, if an alcoholic, he is almost certain to have.(p.142)
• Either you are dealing with a man who can and will get *well* or you are not.(p.142)
• It might be *well* to have a long chat with him on his return.(p.143)
• But you should feel under no obligation to keep him on, for your obligation has been *well* discharged already.(p.147)
• They often jeopardize their own positions by trying to help serious drinkers who should have been fired long ago, or else given an opportunity to get *well*.(p.147)
• But alcoholism – *well*, they just don't believe they have it.(p.149)
• But what about his responsibilities – his family and the men who would die because they would not know how to get *well*, ah -- yes, those other alcoholics?(p.154)
• He found himself surprisingly *well* received, and learned that many knew of his drinking.(p.156)
• The use of spiritual principles in such cases was not so *well* understood as it is now.(p.156)
• In his prodigy of service, he was *well* assisted by Sister Ignatia at St. Thomas Hospital in Akron, Ohio, one of the greatest friends our Fellowship will ever know.(p.171)
• The town was *well* supplied with churches and schools in which I pursued my early educational activities.(p.171)
• Tuesday I started in the morning, getting *well* organized by noon.(p.179)
• I thought to myself, "*Well*, she is going to tell me this is the end," and I certainly couldn't blame her and did not intend to try to justify myself.(p.184)
• After a while, Bill said, "*Well*, now, you've been talking a good long time, let me talk a minute or two."(p.185)
• So, after hearing some more of my story, he turned around and said to Doc -- I don't think he knew I heard him, but I did -- he said, "*Well*, I believe he's worth saving and working on."(p.185)
• One of the fellows, I think it was Doc, said, "*Well*, you want to quit?"(p.187)
• Knowing Bob of old, she jokingly replied, "*Well*, Doctor, I suppose you've already tried it yourself?"(p.188)
• Looking sadder than ever, he wearily ventured, "*Well* this is wonderful for you fellows, but it can't be for me.(p.188)
• Then Dr. Bob said, "*Well*, Bill, maybe you'll feel better tomorrow.(p.189)
• Naturally, for quite a time, I wasn't too *well* physically, either.(p.190)
• It took me a year, or a year and a half to get to feeling physically *well*, and it was rather tough, but I soon found folks whose friendship I had once had, and I found, after I had been sober for quite some little time, that these people began to act like they had in previous years, before I had gotten so bad, so that I didn't pay too awful much attention to financial gains.(p.190)
• I went into the high school grades, but having missed all the intermediate grades, I didn't get along too *well*, so I developed the habit of going back to school just long enough for the football season and

then quitting.(p.193)
• Whether I could have done as *well* as he, I don't know.(p.194)
• I can *well* remember sitting with seven dollars in my pocket, planning on giving my family a hundred or two hundred dollars, when I made it next year.(p.197)
• I can *well* remember over a long period of years when I thought I was the only person in the world who knew that sooner or later I was going to get drunk.(p.198)
• In the meantime, the domestic situation was not getting along too *well*.(p.199)
• I can remember *well* thinking that I would quit drinking, really go to work hard, apply myself eight hours a day, five days a week, make a lot of money, and then I could start drinking again.(p.199)
• I had run into him, and he looked real prosperous; his face and eyes looked clear and he started to compliment me on my good front and how *well* I looked, and I said, "I haven't had a drink for nine months."(p.201)
• He said, "*Well*, I haven't had a drink for three months."(p.201)
• Then I got into the habit of having beers, and decided that a drink of whiskey was not any worse; so I would get the one drink of whiskey but, on second thought, I decided that as long as I was only going to have one, I might as *well* make it a double-header.(p.203)
• He said, "*Well*, why don't you take a cab?"(p.204)
• And I said, "*Well*, what about Paul, have you got him all dried up?"(p.207)
• "*Well*," the doctor said, "we have hopes in that direction."(p.207)
• I remember *well* one fellow, Joe, walking nearly three miles through slush, wet and snow to come to the hospital to see a man that he had never seen before in his life, and that impressed me very much.(p.208)
• My life was fairly *well* crowded and I didn't seem to need any stimulants to keep me going.(p.213)
• She said, "*Well*, he wouldn't be here if you didn't say so."(p.217)
• And being a big-shot man of my word, I said, "*Well*, if I said so, then I'll go."(p.217)
• I was doing very *well* with that and general upholstering work, and there was every indication that I would be financially independent by the time I reached middle age.(p.232)
• I was doing *well* in business, and in going around town I was frequently invited to have a drink in a speakeasy.(p.233)
• "Best in the business, when he's sober," my customers would say, and I still had a following who would give me work though they deplored my habits, because they knew the job would be *well* done when they eventually got it.(p.234)
• He had already imbued them with his own spirit until they were ready and willing at all times to go where sent, and as a doctor he *well* knew that this mission and duty would strengthen them as it later helped me.(p.235)
• *Well*, there I was, willing to try it, but I didn't know how, except in a vague way.(p.236)
• My visitor *well* knew, that as I tried to follow God I would get to studying these things out for myself.(p.236)
• In sports I made the track and tennis teams; I got along *well* with the other boys and had a fairly large circle of acquaintances but no intimate friends.(p.240)
• As long as things were tough and the job a challenge I could always manage to hold on pretty *well*, but as soon as I learned the combination, got the puzzle under control and the boss to pat me on the back, I was gone again.(p.243)
• He knew too *well* that didn't mean a thing, just as I knew in my heart that it would be only a question of time -- a few days, a week, or even a month, it was inevitable – till I would be off on another bender.(p.257)
• I'm sure his family felt that it was a marriage that -- *well*, I was a girl from the wrong side of the tracks -- definitely!(p.262)
• And I said, "*Well*, they brought a pitcher of coffee, and a sandwich wrapped up for me."(p.264)
• "*Well*, I'm nuts enough now," I said to him.(p.266)
• She said, "*Well*, you better talk to Jack."(p.266)
• "*Well*," I said to dad, when the A.A. people kept coming with these lovely cars and looked so nice, "I suppose the neighbors say, 'Now those old fools must have up and died, but where's the hearse?'"(p.269)
• *Well*, I wasn't sure I did, and it was awful foggy, and I wept and asked her what she thought I ought to do about it.(p.273)
• *Well*, suicide was a last straw matter, and I had not drawn the last straw yet.(p.278)
• It is *well* over sixteen years since I came back to life.(p.280)
• I *well* remember a session I had with myself soon after I returned.(p.282)
• At any rate the last great step toward a *well* rounded life still lay ahead of me.(p.286)
• He said they were sober, happy and had their self-respect back as *well* as the respect of their neighbors.(p.289)
• That was my lesson, that one could not take the moral inventory and then file it away; that the alcoholic has to continue to take inventory every day if he expects to get *well* and stay *well*.(p.293)
• I got along fairly *well* with my party drinking for quite some time, but eventually I began to visit beer joints in between parties.(p.298)
• Indeed, I was always *well* on my way before I would undertake to go visiting at all.(p.301)
• *Well* . . . I had a job, and I really wanted desperately to stop drinking, but couldn't, so I readily agreed to visit the doctor she recommended.(p.301)
• I was given every advantage in a *well* ordered home.(p.304)
• My broken home and broken heart fanned my smoldering self-pity into a fair-sized bonfire and this kept me *well* supplied with reasons for having another drink, and then another.(p.305)
• But this day my doctor gave it to me straight and said, "People like you are pretty *well* known to the medical profession.(p.307)
• I don't know what sort of person I was expecting, but I was very agreeably surprised to find Mr. T. a poised, intelligent, *well* groomed and mannered gentleman.(p.309)
• Since I didn't do *well* in school, I quit and joined the Army at age seventeen.(p.317)
• I said, "*Well*, I stood it to keep the home together, and for the children's sake."(p.322)
• But then I thought, *well*, now wait, how will I feel next Tuesday?(p.326)
• By the law of averages, some efforts came out *well*.(p.331)
• *Well*, at least I could drink myself to death.(p.333)
• I had to give him a story and ask him the same question over and over again, "*Well*, now, how many will that bottle serve?"(p.336)
• *Well*, of course that was all I needed – to switch from wine to brandy for three weeks.(p.338)
• And then one ill-defined day, one day that I can't recall, I stepped across the line that alcoholics know so *well*, and from that day on drinking was miserable.(p.346)
• I was *well* into the second fifth by this time.(p.347)
• So I thought to myself, I might just as *well* be drunk as feel like this.(p.348)
• "*Well*," he said, "you've been sober, but you've been floating way up on a cloud somewhere.(p.349)
• *Well*, I don't know who He is, but I've got my own idea.(p.350)
• *Well*, I could do the dishes.(p.351)
• *Well*, now I'm living it and trying to paint it for others.(p.355)
• I was active and did *well*, however, in school publications, dramatics (which came in handy during my drinking career), and Greek letter societies.(p.357)
• Of course I kept her posted on how *well* the station was doing and wrote convincing letters of how *well* I was doing with the liquor problem.(p.360)
• I achieved recognized and national standing in my profession, as *well* as becoming a director in many important institutions having to do with the civic life of a large city.(p.374)
• Early the next morning a man whose name I knew *well*, a lawyer, called on me.(p.378)
• I said, "*Well*, I don't know why."(p.387)
• I woke up in this bare room with nothing around me but bars; they wouldn't let me smoke and treated me, *well*, like I was nuts.(p.387)
• He was *well* behaved, and idealistic where women were concerned.(p.403)
• They were bright and *well* read, they held various political views.(p.410)
• He was *well* dressed; he was easy going.(p.413)
• They were doing very *well* -- at least a fifth apiece a day, except on dad's days off when they did some serious drinking.(p.425)
• *Well*, I'm willing, if it will curb this awful desire to drink, this fear of not having a drink, this feeling of always being alone, scared, deserted, sick.(p.430)
• I was never drunk on the job, never missed a day's work, was seldom rendered totally ineffective by a hangover and kept my liquor expenses *well* within my adequate budget.(p.433)
• "*Well*, Doc," I said, "what are we going to do?"(p.436)
• I remember very *well* saying, "There's only one person in the world whose guts I hate worse than yours, and those're my own."(p.440)
• After I had been around A.A. for seven months, tapering off alcohol and pills, not finding the program working very *well*, I was finally able to say, "Okay, God.(p.448)
• I have to discard my "rights," as *well* as my expectations, by asking myself, "How important is it, really?(p.452)
• Now sober for years, they tell us how they got *well*.(p.455)
• *Well*, this is understandable.(p.458)
• Finally they stopped and bought me a bottle; they knew so *well* that would keep me quiet.(p.466)
• I thought, "Oh *well*, these people are just like all the people I've known all my life.(p.472)
• *Well*, you know who I showed.(p.472)
• I have come to believe that my illness is spiritual as *well* as physical and mental, and I know that for help in the spiritual sphere I have to turn to a Higher Power.(p.473)
• There came a time when she spoke to me about it, and I would say that I had a bad cold or that I wasn't feeling *well*.(p.487)
• Nevertheless, we continued to work together and I continued to drink, but I guess, deep down within her heart as *well* as within mine, we both knew I couldn't stop drinking.(p.490)
• I knew my wife didn't because I had been sincere in all my promises to her as *well* as to my mother and to my close friends, but the urge to take that drink was more powerful than anything else.(p.494)
• "*Well*," said the older boy, "do you?"(p.498)
• *Well* – *well* -- look who's here!(p.500)
• "*Well*, you're not," says the man.(p.503)
• "*Well*," he answers, "You've probably tried praying like I have.(p.504)
• Things are not going so *well* at home.(p.505)
• He had gone through the windshields of cars a couple of times and was pretty *well* banged up.(p.510)
• I went along pretty *well* for the next ten months.(p.511)
• I'd get downstairs to the gin mill, get enough in to hold me until eight o'clock in the morning, then I'd go out to join that "misery parade" that so many of us know so *well*.(p.514)
• I got along *well* there.(p.517)
• I thought, *well*, now that I've been put out for drinking, I'll just show them that they were completely wrong, so I went off on the biggest bout I had been on up to then, involving about a fortnight's black-out.(p.521)
• I talked to him for quite a long time and at the end, he said, "*Well*, you're not quite mad enough to be shut up for good yet, but you soon will be if you live long enough."(p.522)
• It was their open night meeting, but of course I thought they were all alcoholics; I couldn't imagine why anybody else would want to go there, and my first reaction was, *well*, I've come to something that's not for me.(p.524)
• I, a man of steel, with very high ideals, *well* brought up, an honor student and the recipient of scholarships and prizes, a boy wonder in business -- I, Bob, the author of this essay, looked and saw that the universe was beneath my contempt, and that to remove myself from it was the only thing of dignity a man could do.(p.531)
• (*Well*!(p.536)
• This time, whoever had rolled me had taken my glasses as *well* (they were gold).(p.538)
• When the policeman released me to my stupefied and exasperated friend at four in the morning, I went to my traveling bag and groped until I found – *well*, let the officer speak: "Ah," said the policeman, "he's got anuder pair, t'ank God!"(p.538)
• I had no money – *well*, maybe a dime – and only the clothes I stood in.(p.540)
• One of the truly great things A.A. has taught me is that reality too has two sides; I had only known the grim side before the program, but now I had a chance to learn about the pleasant side as *well*.(p.550)
• Within a week, I was feeling *well* enough to go home.(p.558)
• But hospitals, as *well* as other places of recuperation, ought to be *well* outside A.A. -- and medically supervised.(p.566)
• Such special services may be *well* recompensed.(p.566)

well-balanced

• He seemed quite rational and *well-balanced* with respect to other problems.(p.26)

well-being

• For us, material *well-being* always followed spiritual progress; it never preceded.(p.127)

• Nearly every modern employer feels a moral responsibility for the *well-being* of his help, and he tries to meet these responsibilities.(p.137)

• There is a real interest, both humanitarian and business, in the *well-being* of employees.(p.149)

well-dressed

• Marty came in, looking clean, neat, *well-dressed* and, like Bill, she was neither a bloated wreck nor a reformer.(p.413)

well-integrated

• Father was a very *well-integrated* person, and while mother was highstrung and a bit selfish and demanding, our home life was reasonably harmonious.(p.240)

well-known

• A *well-known* doctor, chief physician at a nationally prominent hospital specializing in alcoholic and drug addiction, gave Alcoholics Anonymous this letter:(p.xxiii)

• After they have succumbed to the desire again, as so many do, and the phenomenon of craving develops, they pass through the *well-known* stages of a spree, emerging remorseful, with a firm resolution not to drink again.(p.xxvii)

• Understand he was once a *well-known* lawyer in town, but just now we've got him strapped down tight."(p.156)

• In one of these there is a *well-known* hospital for the treatment of alcoholic and drug addiction.(p.161)

• When I was eighteen, at the end of high school, the high school team had a banquet at a *well-known* roadhouse outside of Akron.(p.194)

• Shortly after I came to this conclusion, I was importuned by another *well-known* patent law firm to help them out on some trial work because their trial man had had a heart attack and had been forbidden to go into the courtroom.(p.220)

• I used all those *well-known* phrases.(p.408)

well-meaning

• So I married a nice, *well-meaning* young newspaper-man, so as not to have to go home.(p.402)

well-reviewed

• I have published a book covering certain aspects of this field which has been *well-reviewed* and which is helping other people.(p.541)

well-to-do

• I acquired the impeccable coat of tan one sees upon the *well-to-do*.(p.4)

• My parents were *well-to-do* people and their marriage was a happy one.(p.182)

well-trained

• My customers lost confidence in me to the point where I retained what business I had only because I was a *well-trained* and reputedly fine craftsman.(p.234)

welled

• I could almost hear the sound of the preacher's voice as I sat, on still Sundays, way over there on the hillside; there was that proffered temperance pledge I never signed; my grandfather's good natured contempt of some church folk and their doings; his insistence that the spheres really had their music; but his denial of the preacher's right to tell him how he must listen; his fearlessness as he spoke of these things just before he died; these recollections *welled* up from the past.(p.10)

wended

• When I *wended* my way home four days later, on the 27th, there was a detective waiting for me.(p.508)

wept

• We *wept* and Russ didn't go to work.(p.271)

• Well, I wasn't sure I did, and it was awful foggy, and I *wept* and asked her what she thought I ought to do about it.(p.273)

• I fled, finally, after having been fired from my job by a boss who *wept* a little (since I had worked hard) as he gave notice for me to clear out.(p.539)

weren't

• I avoided them rather than explain why they *weren't* seeing me.(p.203)

• The people in the group hadn't been around that day; part of my family was in Florida and the rest of them *weren't* speaking to me, so I spent a very lonesome day and by evening I was feeling very sorry for myself.(p.207)

• Suddenly I could accept myself, faults and all, as I was -- for *weren't* we all like that?(p.229)

• One of our gifts from the family was a very lovely Bible, but we'd let the bulldog chew it because we *weren't* too interested in it.(p.268)

• I heard voices when no one was around, and I saw things that *weren't* there.(p.319)

• The letter from A.A. had said this man would see me – there *weren't* any women.(p.393)

• Right from the start, I felt that they *weren't* doing anything for me, but they sure were helping Max.(p.447)

• I don't know whether it was right or wrong, but at least I know that people *weren't* thinking the same.(p.484)

• We *weren't* even permitted to play cards in our home, but father would give us just a little toddy with whiskey and sugar and warm water now and then.(p.484)

• They *weren't* quite so up-to-date on my history and I got away with about four years with them.(p.520)

• Things *weren't* going as I thought they should, for my greater enjoyment, comfort and fame; therefore, if the universe wouldn't play my way, I wouldn't play at all.(p.531)

west

• There is a good bit of travel between East and *West* and we foresee a great increase in this helpful interchange.(p.162)

• I came directly to a growing industrial city in the middle *west*, where I have lived practically ever since.(p.231)

• We now live in the *West* and are very fortunate in our area A.A.; it is good, simple and friendly, and our one desire is to stay in A.A. and not on it.(p.250)

• My migrations extended for over a year as far *west* as Omaha.(p.253)

• So, sometimes we'd end up in Charleston, *West* Virginia, or here or there, drinking all along the way.(p.264)

• Psychiatry might have helped, but psychiatrists had not penetrated the middle *west*.(p.276)

• I was living in a small room on *West* 53rd Street right off Fifth Avenue, when I met a young lady who eventually was responsible for altering my entire way of living.(p.359)

• I walked up that aisle just like Mae *West* in her prime.(p.385)

• I went out to the *West* Coast, waited on table, washed dishes and sold newspaper subscriptions.(p.401)

• I might go out *West* on a ranch where I couldn't get anything to drink.(p.502)

• We talked for a while, and then he sent me down to the Alanon House over on the *west* side, and there I had my introduction to A.A.(p.515)

• With no explanation at all, I was taken from my home in Florida to my grandparents' home in the middle *west*.(p.544)

West Virginia

• So, sometimes we'd end up in Charleston, *West Virginia*, or here or there, drinking all along the way.(p.264)

western

• In one *western* city and its environs there are one thousand of us and our families.(p.15)

• Years ago, in 1935, one of our number made a journey to a certain *western* city.(p.153)

• There are the same fast friendships, there is the same helpfulness to one another as you find among our *western* friends.(p.162)

• I conducted myself so creditably that I was able to secure a much coveted internship in a *western* city, where I spent two years.(p.174)

• I am a physician, licensed to practice in a *western* state.(p.345)

wet

• My weary and despairing wife was informed that it would all end with heart failure during delirium tremens, or I would develop a *wet* brain, perhaps within a year.(p.7)

• "Joykiller, nag, *wet* blanket" -- that's what they said.(p.106)

• Say you do not want to be a *wet* blanket; that you only want him to take care of his health.(p.112)

• On Sunday when I came to, it was a bad, *wet*, snowy day in February, 1937, and Paul and Doc and a lot of other fellows were in Cleveland on business.(p.207)

• I remember well one fellow, Joe, walking nearly three miles through slush, *wet* and snow to come to the hospital to see a man that he had never seen before in his life, and that impressed me very much.(p.208)

• Either they die of acute alcoholism or they develop *wet* brains and have to be put away permanently."(p.308)

• All I want to know is, why does that dog *wet* in my lap every time I hold him?"(p.440)

• (That dog hasn't *wet* my pants once since I joined A.A., and neither have I!)(p.440)

• Soon found *wet* canteens serve drinks to Indians in uniform.(p.474)

• And we usually have some kind of grimy sweater that we think we look sexy in, even if we weigh ninety-five pounds soaking *wet* and are not wearing a bra.(p.479)

whacky

• The parties waxed more liquid and hilarious as time went on, and eventually I discovered that a little shot of liquor now and then between beers had the tendency to put me in a *whacky* mood much quicker than having to down several quarts of beer to obtain the same effect.(p.298)

whammo

• Then one day, *whammo*!(p.319)

whatever

• That the man who is making the approach has had the same difficulty, that he obviously knows what he is talking about, that his whole deportment shouts at the new prospect that he is a man with a real answer, that he has no attitude of Holier Than Thou, nothing *whatever* except the sincere desire to be helpful; that there are no fees to pay, no axes to grind, no people to please, no lectures to be endured -- these are the conditions we have found most effective.(p.18)

• We are equally positive that once he takes any alcohol *whatever* into his system, something happens, both in the bodily and mental sense, which makes it virtually impossible for him to stop.(p.22)

• Yet he had no control *whatever* over alcohol.(p.26)

• If what we have learned and felt and seen means anything at all, it means that all of us, *whatever* our race, creed, or color are the children of a living Creator with whom we may form a relationship upon simple and understandable terms as soon as we are willing and honest enough to try.(p.28)

• Once he started, he had no control *whatever*.(p.32)

• *Whatever* the precise definition of the word may be, we call this plain insanity.(p.37)

• Not only had I been off guard, I had made no fight *whatever* against the first drink.(p.41)

• We have learned that *whatever* the human frailties of various faiths may be, those faiths have given purpose and direction to millions.(p.49)

• Actually, we used to have no reasonable conception *whatever*.(p.49)

• *Whatever* our protestations, are not most of us concerned with ourselves, our resentments, or our self-pity?(p.62)

• *Whatever* our ideal turns out to be, we must be willing to grow toward it.(p.69)

• We hope you are convinced now that God can remove *whatever* self-will has blocked you off from Him.(p.71)

• *Whatever* the situation, we usually have to do something about it.(p.81)

• We usually conclude the period of meditation with a prayer that we be shown all through the day what our next step is to be, that we be given *whatever* we need to take care of such problems.(p.87)

• I pointed out that I had had nothing to drink *whatever* for three years, and this in the face of difficulties that would have made nine out of ten men drink their heads off.(p.138)

• *Whatever* the method, its object is to thoroughly clear mind and body of the effects of alcohol.(p.143)

• We hope the doctor will tell the patient the truth about his condition, *whatever* that happens to be.(p.144)

• In fact, as I look back, I have often thought that they probably concluded that they would put up with me for a couple of years, that I couldn't live much longer, and that they would inherit *whatever* was left of the practice.(p.215)

• I resented it of course, and I offered Clarence his commission, *whatever* it might be, if he would please not bother me because I had arrived at the conclusion that he was a solicitor for some alcoholic institute.(p.216)

• I had no desire *whatever* to sit down at a table and stay a whole morning or afternoon drinking.(p.231)

• In conclusion, I can only say that *whatever* growth or understanding has come to me, I have no wish to graduate.(p.249)

• *Whatever* it was, I wanted it.(p.259)

• *Whatever* it was, it brushed all the heavy burdens off my back.(p.334)

• He said, "How I envy you for *whatever* you've found."(p.334)

• Since I gave my will over to A.A., ***whatever*** A.A. has wanted of me I've tried to do to the best of my ability.(p.340)
• A willingness to do ***whatever*** I was told to do simplified the program for me.(p.381)
• To me this meant telling my associates that I had joined Alcoholics Anonymous; that I didn't know what was expected of me by A.A., but that ***whatever*** it was, it was the most important thing in life for me; that sobriety meant more to me than anything in this world.(p.382)
• It has been a fellowship with God and man that has held good wherever I've turned and ***whatever*** I've done.(p.394)
• I was skipping classes about two days a week and doing no book work ***whatever***.(p.423)
• ***Whatever*** the root of my unhappiness might turn out to be, I thought, it could not possibly be booze.(p.433)
• I think He's on hand to see all of us through ***whatever*** may come to us.(p.437)
• It was as if I had, rather than a Midas touch which turned everything to gold, a magnifying mind that magnified ***whatever*** it focused on.(p.450)
• Rather, I do ***whatever*** is in front of me to be done, and I leave the results up to Him; however it turns out, that's God's will for me.(p.452)
• All found themselves headed for the same destruction, and it seemed they could to nothing ***whatever*** to stop it.(p.455)
• Guess I'll never be a saint, but ***whatever*** I am, I want to be sober and in A.A.(p.463)
• We think that each group should soon achieve this ideal; that any public solicitation of funds using the name of Alcoholics Anonymous is highly dangerous, whether by groups, clubs, hospitals, or other outside agencies; that acceptance of large gifts from any source, or of contributions carrying any obligation ***whatever***, is unwise.(p.566)
• Concerning such matters they can express no views ***whatever***.(p.567)

whatsoever

• There are no fees or dues ***whatsoever***.(p.xiv)

wheel

• Alone in the relative safety of my home because I knew I dare not risk the danger of blacking out in some public place or at the ***wheel*** of a car.(p.306)
• Sometimes I'd make it home and go to sleep at the ***wheel*** of my car, for all the neighbors to see next morning as they left for work.(p.429)

Wheeling

• As we left, and they were escorting us across the bridge into ***Wheeling***, I, with great dignity and sarcasm, told them if their wives were ever visiting in Akron, and they, too, were looking for their route sign as I was, that I hoped I could extend to them the hospitality that had been shown to me in Bellaire.(p.264)

wheels

• As part of this promotion, they sent me to their national convention in Atlantic City to tell the big ***wheels*** how I'd done it.(p.243)

whenever

• ***Whenever*** possible, let your husband explain.(p.115)
• We do not mean that you have to agree with your husband ***whenever*** there is an honest difference of opinion.(p.117)
• ***Whenever*** you want to, you control your drinking.(p.139)
• ***Whenever*** this man and I met – I didn't know his name then nor do I know it now – we would always get drunk.(p.201)
• ***Whenever*** a situation arose that fast talk wouldn't explain away, I simply withdrew.(p.214)
• In the Army, I became a periodic alcoholic – the periods always coming ***whenever*** I could make the opportunity.(p.241)
• I spent a great deal of time with Dr. Bob, ***whenever*** he had the time to spare, and in the homes of two or three other people, trying to see how the family lived the program.(p.291)
• As time went on, I found that it was customary to open a few bottles ***whenever*** visitors dropped in.(p.297)
• I attended my weekly meetings with regularity, reread the Big Book, attended other group meetings, gave leads when asked to and did some Twelve Step work ***whenever*** I was called upon to do so.(p.365)
• ***Whenever*** we went out she appeared to go out of her way to keep me from having more than one drink.(p.376)
• They said "Get active," so I helped ***whenever*** I could, and I still do.(p.381)
• It pays daily in more harmonious relations with my fellow men, in ever clearer insight into the true meaning of life, and in the answering love and gratitude wherever and ***whenever*** I have been the instrument of God's will in the lives of others.(p.394)
• And so, in those following years, ***whenever*** A.A. was mentioned I would have no part of it.(p.469)
• I have my brilliant moments yet, but ***whenever*** the boys catch me at it they tell me so very plainly.(p.512)
• But one was so outstanding that I like to pass it on ***whenever*** I can in the hope that it will help someone else as it has me.(p.551)

where

• ***Where*** had been my high resolve?(p.5)
• Again I swayed dizzily before an open window, or the medicine cabinet ***where*** there was poison, cursing myself for a weakling.(p.6)
• At a certain point in the drinking of every alcoholic, he passes into a state ***where*** the most powerful desire to stop drinking is of absolutely no avail.(p.24)
• We were in a position ***where*** life was becoming impossible, and if we had passed into the region from which there is no return through human aid we had but two alternatives: One was to go on to the bitter end, blotting out the consciousness of our intolerable situation as best we could; and the other, to accept spiritual help.(p.25)
• He can go anywhere on this earth ***where*** other free men may go without disaster, provided he remains willing to maintain a certain simple attitude.(p.26)
• I have never seen one single case recover, ***where*** that state of mind existed to the extent that it does in you."(p.27)
• We have heard of few instances ***where*** people, who showed definite signs of alcoholism, were able to stop for a long period because of an overpowering desire to do so.(p.32)
• But here is a man who at fifty-five years found he was just ***where*** he had left off at thirty.(p.33)
• As we look back, we feel we had gone on drinking many years beyond the point ***where*** we could quit on our will power.(p.34)
• On the way I felt hungry so I stopped at a roadside place ***where*** they have a bar.(p.36)
• However intelligent we may have been in other respects, ***where*** alcohol has been involved, we have been strangely insane.(p.38)
• We first saw Fred about a year ago in a hospital ***where*** he had gone to recover from a bad case of jitters.(p.39)
• I reasoned I was not so far advanced as most of you fellows, that I had been usually successful in licking my other personal problems, and that I would therefore be successful ***where*** you men failed.(p.40)
• I know little of ***where*** I went or what I said and did.(p.41)
• But ***where*** and how were we to find this Power?(p.45)
• Without knowing it, had we not been brought to ***where*** we stood by a certain kind of faith?(p.53)
• He attended church school, ***where*** he became rebellious at what he thought an overdose of religious education.(p.56)
• ***Where*** had we been selfish, dishonest, self-seeking and frightened?(p.67)
• ***Where*** were we to blame?(p.67)
• ***Where*** had we been selfish, dishonest, or inconsiderate?(p.69)
• ***Where*** were we at fault, what should we have done instead?(p.69)
• We must be willing to make amends ***where*** we have done harm, provided that we do not bring about still more harm in so doing.(p.69)
• We know but few instances ***where*** we have given these doctors a fair break.(p.73)
• Returning home we find a place ***where*** we can be quiet for an hour carefully reviewing what we have done.(p.75)
• She will want to know who the woman is and ***where*** she is.(p.81)
• Perhaps there are some cases ***where*** the utmost frankness is demanded.(p.82)
• Be quick to see ***where*** religious people are right.(p.87)
• You might place this book ***where*** he can see it in the interval.(p.90)
• Perhaps your story will help him see ***where*** he has failed to practice the very precepts he knows so well.(p.93)
• People have said we must not go ***where*** liquor is served; we must not have it in our homes; we must shun friends who drink; we must avoid moving pictures which show drinking scenes; we must not go into bars; our friends must hide their bottles if we go to their houses; we mustn't think or be reminded about alcohol at all.(p.100)
• So our rule is not to avoid a place ***where*** there is drinking, if we have a legitimate reason for being there.(p.101)
• Why sit with a long face in places ***where*** there is drinking, sighing about the good old days.(p.102)
• Your job now is to be at the place ***where*** you may be of maximum helpfulness to others, so never hesitate to go anywhere if you can be helpful.(p.102)
• Perhaps your husband has been living in that strange world of alcoholism ***where*** everything is distorted and exaggerated.(p.108)
• He may have come to the point ***where*** he desperately wants to stop but cannot.(p.110)
• Sometimes there are cases ***where*** alcoholism is complicated by other disorders.(p.114)
• Your desire to protect him should not cause you to lie to people when they have a right to know ***where*** he is and what he is doing.(p.115)
• Your husband will be the first to say it was your devotion and care which brought him to the point ***where*** he could have a spiritual experience.(p.118)
• While grateful that he drinks no more, they may not like the idea that God has accomplished the miracle ***where*** they failed.(p.128)
• That is ***where*** our fellow travelers are, and that is ***where*** our work must be done.(p.130)
• We do not know of many cases ***where*** this difficulty lasted long.(p.134)
• If this presents difficulty, re-reading chapters two and three, ***where*** the alcoholic sickness is discussed at length might be worth while.(p.140)
• I well remember the shock I received when a prominent doctor in Chicago told me of cases ***where*** pressure of the spinal fluid actually ruptured the brain.(p.140)
• But am I to be consigned to a life ***where*** I shall be stupid, boring and glum, like some righteous people I see?(p.152)
• "***Where*** am I to find these people?"(p.152)
• He consented, however, to go the hospital, ***where*** he occupied the very room recently vacated by the lawyer.(p.159)
• Aside from fellowship and sociability, the prime object was to provide a time and place ***where*** new people might bring their problems.(p.160)
• Then, in this eastern city, there are informal meetings such as we have described to you, ***where*** you may now see scores of members.(p.162)
• No beer or liquor was sold in the neighborhood, except at the State liquor agency ***where*** perhaps one might procure a pint if he could convince the agent that he really needed it.(p.171)
• After high school came four years in one of the best colleges in the country ***where*** drinking seemed to be a major extra-curricular activity.(p.172)
• There my drinking became so much worse that the boys in the fraternity house ***where*** I lived felt forced to send for my father, who made a long journey in the vain endeavor to get me straightened around.(p.174)
• I conducted myself so creditably that I was able to secure a much coveted internship in a western city, ***where*** I spent two years.(p.174)
• After three years of this, I wound up in the local hospital ***where*** they attempted to help me, but I would get my friends to smuggle me a quart, or I would steal the alcohol about the building, so that I got rapidly worse.(p.175)
• My bootlegger had hidden alcohol at the back steps ***where*** I could get it at my convenience.(p.176)
• My wife, a Kentucky girl, came with me to Akron ***where*** I completed my course in law at the Akron Law School.(p.182)
• It did help to certain extent, since I got in places ***where*** I could not obtain anything to drink, and so broke the habitual drinking.(p.183)
• During the first six months of 1935, I was hospitalized eight times for intoxication and shackled to the bed two or three days before I even knew ***where*** I was.(p.184)
• I could work a deal up to ***where*** all I had to do was to go ahead with it; all the planning had been done, all the financing had been done, but then I'd say "Nuts to it!" and walk away.(p.197)
• I was picked up at two-thirty that morning with my car smashed up by a street-car because I had run into a big concrete safety zone, and the street-car had run into me, and they took me out through the roof -- there's ***where*** I lost the suit.(p.202)
• I was arrested and taken to jail ***where*** I was beaten up by two or three fellows who were already in there and whom I tried to boss.(p.204)
• Then he started to talk to me about his drinking experiences, what his drinking had cost him, how much he had drunk and ***where***, things like that, and I remember I was quite bored because I had never seen

the guy before and had no interest at all in what, *where* and when he drank.(p.208)
• Not far from *where* I lived they built a new technical high school and one of the teachers sold me on the idea that I needed a little mechanical drawing if I were going to be a good toolmaker.(p.211)
• This experience sent me to law school *where* I went at night and which course I completed in less than three years, taking the highest state bar examinations and passing them.(p.212)
• By the time I had completed law school I had picked up some experience in patent law, for I remained with the patent law firm and worked too in Washington *where* they found that I was a capable infringement investigator.(p.213)
• My practice had advanced to the point *where* it could stand a lot of abuse and it got it.(p.214)
• I left on a Wednesday afternoon, had dinner in Akron and then went to a house *where* I encountered my first meeting.(p.218)
• I found in the fall of 1939, that I was not mentally impaired, so far as trial work was concerned, and thereafter took up *where* I had left off when I was about forty-five years old.(p.220)
• *Where* was I?(p.222)
• My daily consumption of wine was about a quart, but that was common *where* I lived.(p.230)
• I came directly to a growing industrial city in the middle west, *where* I have lived practically ever since.(p.231)
• My "periodics" became more frequent until I reached the point *where* I wanted to devote all my time to drinking, working as little as possible, and then only when the necessity of my family demanded it.(p.234)
• My customers lost confidence in me to the point *where* I retained what business I had only because I was a well-trained and reputedly fine craftsman.(p.234)
• I had never doubted the existence of the Supreme Being, but now I began to absent myself from my church *where* I had formerly been a member of the choir.(p.234)
• He had already imbued them with his own spirit until they were ready and willing at all times to go *where* sent, and as a doctor he well knew that this mission and duty would strengthen them as it later helped me.(p.235)
• *Where* preaching and prayers had touched me very little, I immediately desired further knowledge of these men.(p.235)
• Searching *where* I have been at fault, it is not hard to discover and get right again, for I have proven to myself and to many others who know me that God can keep a man sober if he will let Him.(p.237)
• My early life was spent in Baltimore *where* my father was a physician and a grain merchant.(p.240)
• At thirteen I was packed off to a very fine Protestant boarding school in Virginia *where* I stayed four years, graduating without any special achievements.(p.240)
• That is *where* I had my first drink and I still remember it, for every "first" drink afterwards did exactly the same trick -- I could feel it go right through every bit of my body and down to my very toes.(p.241)
• My next job was in sales promotion for an oil company in Mississippi *where* I promptly became high man and got lots of pats on the back.(p.242)
• (This is very useful knowledge in places *where* matches are prohibited.)(p.245)
• My wife traveled with me, but with a baby coming I decided to settle in a large city *where* I got a job with a commission agent which is a polite term for a handbook operator.(p.251)
• Making my way to Pittsburgh, I met other former friends and got a job in a large factory *where* piecemakers were making good money.(p.252)
• Following a big drunk on that sheet, *where* I was doing leg-work and rewrite, a feeling of nostalgia made me buy a ticket for Liverpool and I returned to Britain.(p.252)
• I wanted to roam again and through relatives got a supercargo job on an Australian packet which allowed me to visit my people in Australia *where* I was born.(p.252)
• I myself could see deterioration in my work from being physically and mentally affected by liquor, although I had not yet reached the point *where* all I wanted was more to drink.(p.254)
• "I'm doing a job I like and it's quiet *where* I live, practically no temptations.(p.257)
• I heard my son-in-law coming upstairs, and I asked him *where* dad was.(p.263)
• *Where* you go, I'll go, and what you drink, I'll drink."(p.263)
• Russ read a piece in the paper, and he kind of snickered, and said, "See here, *where* John D. has found something to keep him from drinking!"(p.265)
• I'll get you the password, and I can find out *where* they meet because I know a guy that belongs.(p.266)
• An attorney sat at the side of the bed *where* I was lying, and he sat on the edge of his chair and looked as innocent as a baby.(p.268)
• When I reached a point directly back of our house, *where* I could have cut through a friend's garden, I was almost overpowered by the desire to get home, but I made the whole journey.(p.276)
• Haunting me through each day's stupor -- and there were eighteen or nineteen such days in this man's home -- was the thought: "*Where* do I go when his family comes home?"(p.278)
• The next day he turned me over to a couple who, although neither was an alcoholic, knew Dr. Bob and were willing to drive me to Akron *where* they would turn me over to his care.(p.278)
• It took five years of A.A. living, and a substantial improvement in my health, before I could take a full-time office job *where* someone else was boss.(p.283)
• I do feel, though, that the fact that I finally grew up to a point *where* I could even tackle such a job is the apex of the story of a man who spent eighteen years running away from life.(p.286)
• I grew up in a small town outside Akron, Ohio, *where* the life was typical of any average small town.(p.287)
• I went to the sanitarium *where* this chap was incarcerated and found to my surprise that he was interested.(p.294)
• The three of us did not feel up to the job, and after a few meetings we convinced the prospects that they too should go to Akron *where* they could see an older group in action.(p.295)
• *Where* derision, contempt and pity were once shown me, I now enjoy the respect of many people.(p.296)
• *Where* once I had casual acquaintances, all of whom were fair weather friends, I now have a host of friends who accept me for what I am.(p.296)
• Above all, I have gained the greatest thing accorded to any man, the love and understanding of a gracious God, who has lifted me from the alcoholic scrap-heap to a position of trust *where* I have been able to reap the rich rewards that come from showing a little love for others and from serving them as I can.(p.296)
• I arrived at the stage *where* I couldn't quite make it to the office some mornings.(p.299)
• One is that I don't remember too many of them, as I was one of those drunks who could be on his feet and attend a meeting or a party, engage in a conversation with people and do things that any nearly normal person would do, and the next day not remember a thing about *where* I was, what I did, whom I saw, or how I got home.(p.301)
• Things eventually came to the point *where* I had no friends.(p.301)
• Even some of the saloon-keepers, *where* I had spent so much time and money, requested that I stay away from their places.(p.301)
• Mentally . . . I know *where* I was last night, the night before, and the nights before that.(p.303)
• *Where* we used to run from responsibility, we find ourselves accepting it with gratitude that we can successfully shoulder it.(p.311)
• We got along fine for about two weeks, until she told me *where* to go and to take my damn bottle with me.(p.318)
• Next, I was sent to Arizona, *where* my drinking picked up some more, and I started having blackouts, and I was thrown in jail for speeding and drunken driving.(p.318)
• I reached a stage *where* I couldn't go into my apartment without a drink.(p.324)
• We're free at last to do our thing, to live uninhibited lives, to drink when and how and *where* we wish, when we want to and when we need to.(p.329)
• *Where* were all those words coming from?(p.333)
• I had worked so long in a profession *where* fakery, deceit, and untruths are tools of trade that I instantly recognized honesty when I heard it, from the mouths of A.A. members.(p.334)
• To me, taking a bath was just being in a place with a bottle *where* I could drink in privacy.(p.337)
• And then we went up the side of a hill *where* we have a little barbecue area to make the fire for the barbecue, and on the way up, I thought to myself -- I'll go back down to the kitchen and refill this drink.(p.347)
• We did, and spent a month boozing it up, popping pills, and smoking marijuana; taking shelter *where* we could, which included a veterinary hospital one night; accepting meals from anyone; actually begging; stealing anything we were in need of, which was about everything.(p.354)
• When I walked into the friendly atmosphere of my first A.A. meeting, I knew I was *where* I belonged.(p.355)
• In 1940 another good opportunity came up and we moved to Pittsburgh *where* I was to manage two radio stations under the same ownership.(p.361)
• It was the first she had heard or read about it and she said she had considered sending it to me or trying to have someone in Pittsburgh send it to me so I wouldn't know *where* it came from.(p.366)
• After his death, my mother soon picked up drinking *where* Dad left off, and in a very short time she died of cirrhosis of the liver.(p.370)
• The ambition to succeed was instilled in me by my Scandinavian parents who came to this country *where* opportunities were so great.(p.373)
• I tried to hide my drinking by going places *where* I was unlikely to see anyone I knew.(p.375)
• Rehearsals then became a part of the pattern, stopping at bars on the way to or from the place *where* drinks were to be served.(p.375)
• Not knowing *where* I had been or how I got home was making me desperate.(p.375)
• That is *where* we are really fooled.(p.376)
• The following spring she left me one day without giving me any idea of *where* she had gone, hoping this would bring me to my senses.(p.377)
• It wasn't how far I had gone, but *where* I was headed.(p.379)
• Somehow our bodies had reached the point *where* we could no longer absorb alcohol in our systems.(p.380)
• I came from a family *where* alcohol was socially acceptable.(p.384)
• I lived in New Orleans *where*, at that time, cocktail parties, dances and night spots were almost the order of the day -- or rather the night.(p.384)
• Scared that my dress wasn't going to fit right, that the church wasn't going to be filled, that I'd fall flat on my face walking up the aisle; in fact, I was afraid I wasn't going to be a prima donna in the place *where* I should be.(p.385)
• He always thought that maybe I was safer in a building *where* there were other people.(p.388)
• *Where* have we heard this before?)(p.398)
• This was *where* I started my first drinking lessons.(p.402)
• He was well behaved, and idealistic *where* women were concerned.(p.403)
• This was in Virginia, *where* I had rented a house with stables and a swimming pool, and the fall fox hunting had begun.(p.404)
• I had a tiny trust fund, and I moved into a small apartment *where* I learned to cook, keep house, and do the things that normal people do.(p.409)
• I went to saloons *where* I could get drinks.(p.423)
• Now I own perhaps the most costly pair of moccasins anyone has ever seen, and they help me remember *where* I've been.)(p.445)
• And we found ourselves back in prison, *where* our personalities became even more warped.(p.459)
• I would rather talk about the good things A.A. has taught me; I feel that hitting on just a few sordid points should be sufficient to let those of you in institutions know *where* I came from.(p.459)
• Fortunately, I received only fifteen-twenty years, and I went back to my alma mater (*where* I had spent so much time in the hole).(p.461)
• I suddenly remembered one of my first A.A. meetings, *where* I heard, "If you are an alcoholic and if you continue to drink, the end is death or insanity."(p.461)
• Then I was transferred to the honor-grade unit, *where* I spent the most painful year of my life.(p.462)
• My pattern of drinking at that time had reached the point *where* once I really started, I would retire to my bed and drink myself into oblivion.(p.466)
• We were on our way to New York *where* he planned to leave me with my sister.(p.466)
• This time I didn't put up any fight because I knew why they were there and *where* I was going, the psychopathic ward of the City Hospital, *where* I had been once before.(p.468)
• You can help *where* no one else can."(p.473)
• I want to stop this bad life, but *where* to turn?(p.475)
• It is so beautiful to get up in the morning not being hung-over and being able to remember *where* we were the night before.(p.481)
• I got to the place *where* I'd look forward to the week-end's drinking and pacify myself by saying that the week-ends were mine, that it didn't interfere with my family or with my business if I drank on the week-ends.(p.488)
• I started inquiring *where* I could get a drink and, of

course, I found that it wasn't hard.(p.490)
• I return to the hotel ***where*** I am staying and get gin from the bellboy.(p.501)
• I go to the hospital, ***where*** I have made friends with the night superintendent.(p.501)
• I might go out West on a ranch ***where*** I couldn't get anything to drink.(p.502)
• I see ***where*** I have been wrong in some respects.(p.505)
• I want to get ***where*** I can find some alcoholics to help, and ***where*** I can have some fellowship.(p.506)
• I call my wife into a room ***where*** we can talk privately.(p.506)
• I'd say, "No, I don't know ***where*** they're at or when they meet.(p.510)
• I had no work to do and I was at an age ***where*** it seemed too late to start anything new.(p.522)
• That morning was the first time I really realized ***where*** I'd got to in my life.(p.523)
• When I arrived at The Country Shop, which was a restaurant ***where*** they met in Dublin, I found about thirty-five or forty people in the room.(p.524)
• I would wake to find myself in some beat-up rooming house, ***where*** roaches were crawling over everything.(p.527)
• My father was and still is a minister, and I was afraid that I might run into him, or that someone might tell him ***where*** I was, and I could still remember what he had done to me when I got drunk one Christmas when I was very young.(p.527)
• Now I had gotten to the place ***where*** I would wake up with black eyes and not know ***where*** I got them, or wake up with a lot of money and not know ***where*** I got it.(p.528)
• I was trying to remember ***where*** it came from, when two of the biggest cops I ever saw walked in and took me to jail.(p.528)
• I'm writing this during an A.A. convention, ***where*** I have spent the weekend with nothing but white people.(p.529)
• There was the father one lost respect for at the age of eleven, because the father broke his solemn word in a circumstance ***where*** you, eleven years old, had assumed guilt when you were innocent; but the father would not believe you, no matter what; and to ease his suffering you "confessed" and were "forgiven," only — months later — to have your "guilt" brought up — only he and you knew what he was talking bout -- brought up in front of the stern grandmother.(p.533)
• But I wanted a cosmos, a universe all my own which I had created and ***where*** I reigned as chief top reigner and ruler over everyone else.(p.535)
• I went back home, to a job of manual labor ***where*** for a little while I was able to keep away from alcohol.(p.539)
• But not for long; now, for five Friday nights in a row, I went to jail, picked up sodden with beer (which I always disliked, but which was the only drink available); in jail five consecutive Friday nights in the town ***where*** I had grown up, ***where*** I had been an honor student in high school, ***where*** a kindly uncle, bailing me out, said, "Bob, our family just doesn't do this sort of thing."(p.539)
• I stumbled agonizedly past the theatre ***where*** in years gone by a great star had played my play.(p.540)
• I wasn't afraid of anything or anybody after I learned about drinking, for it seemed right from the beginning that with liquor I could always retire to my little private world ***where*** nobody could get at me to hurt me.(p.547)
• I knew it didn't make any difference ***where*** I started, the inevitable end would be skid row.(p.548)
• Do it every day for two weeks and you will find you have come to mean it and to want it for them, and you will realize that ***where*** you used to feel bitterness and resentment and hatred, you now feel compassionate understanding and love."(p.552)
• I remember being dragged, drink in hand, from beneath the grand piano, ***where*** I had hidden, to be locked in my room in disgrace.(p.557)
• In my mind's eye, I played and replayed scenes in which I was plucked magically from the bar ***where*** I stood nursing a drink, and was instantly exalted to some position of power and prestige.(p.560)
• But we may employ alcoholics ***where*** they are going to perform those services for which we might otherwise have to engage nonalcoholics.(p.566)
• Following are excerpts from the comments of doctors present at the annual meeting of the Medical Society of the State of New York ***where*** a paper on A.A. was read:(p.571)
• Edward Dowling, S.J., of the Queen's Work staff says, "Alcoholics Anonymous is natural; it is natural at the point ***where*** nature comes closest to the supernatural, namely in humiliations and in consequent humility.(p.574)
• In large cities, groups often maintain local offices ***where*** alcoholics or their families may arrange for interviews or hospitalization.(p.575)

where's

• "Well," I said to dad, when the A.A. people kept coming with these lovely cars and looked so nice, "I suppose the neighbors say, 'Now those old fools must have up and died, but ***where's*** the hearse?'"(p.269)

whereas

• I had tried to be the center of my own little world, ***whereas*** God was the center of a vast universe of which I was perhaps an essential, but a very tiny, part.(p.280)
• But ***whereas*** my horse was always equipped with a flask, I merely endured the fox hunting so I could start drinking at lunch time.(p.404)

whereby

• Then she told me that these two drunks she had been talking to had a plan ***whereby*** they thought they could quit drinking, and part of that plan was that they tell it to another drunk.(p.185)
• We're not up here trying to take any of your rights or privileges away from you, but we have a program ***whereby*** we think we can stay sober.(p.186)
• Through going to meetings and listening, and occasionally speaking, through doing Twelve Step work, ***whereby*** in helping others you are both the teacher and the student, by making many wonderful A.A. friends, I have been taught all the things in life that are worth having.(p.416)
• They cooked up a plan ***whereby*** she didn't have to be molested by me if she didn't want to be.(p.491)

wherever

• 9.Made direct amends to such people ***wherever*** possible, except when to do so would injure them or others.(p.59)
• ***Wherever*** men are gathered together in business there will be rivalries and, arising out of these, a certain amount of office politics.(p.145)
• It has been a fellowship with God and man that has held good ***wherever*** I've turned and whatever I've done.(p.394)
• It pays daily in more harmonious relations with my fellow men, in ever clearer insight into the true meaning of life, and in the answering love and gratitude ***wherever*** and whenever I have been the instrument of God's will in the lives of others.(p.394)
• When sleep overtook me, my practice was to undress and go to bed, ***wherever***.(p.537)
• Thank you, Mr. Policeman, ***wherever*** you are now.(p.538)

whether

• A good soldier is ne'er forgot ***Whether*** he dieth by musket Or by pot."(p.1)
• I wondered ***whether*** I dared hide a full bottle of gin near the head of our bed.(p.8)
• I honestly doubted ***whether***, on balance, the religions of mankind had done any good.(p.11)
• If anyone questions ***whether*** he has entered this dangerous area, let him try leaving liquor alone for one year.(p.34)
• ***Whether*** such a person can quit upon a nonspiritual basis depends upon the extent to which he has already lost the power to choose ***whether*** he will drink or not.(p.34)
• How then shall we help our readers determine, to their own satisfaction, ***whether*** they are one of us?(p.34)
• ***Whether*** we agree with a particular approach or conception seems to make little difference.(p.50)
• We were having trouble with personal relationships, we couldn't control our emotional natures, we were a prey to misery and depression, we couldn't make a living, we had a feeling of uselessness, we were full of fear, we were unhappy, we couldn't seem to be of real help to other people — was not a basic solution of these bedevilments more important than ***whether*** we should see newsreels of lunar flight?(p.52)
• Telling them what we are trying to do, we make no bones about our drinking; they usually know it anyway, ***whether*** we think so or not.(p.78)
• Tell him you once felt as he does, but you doubt ***whether*** you would have made much progress had you not taken action.(p.94)
• After doing that, he must decide for himself ***whether*** he wants to go on.(p.95)
• A good doctor or psychiatrist can tell you ***whether*** these complications are serious.(p.114)
• One more suggestion: ***Whether*** the family has spiritual convictions or not, they may do well to examine the principles by which the alcoholic member is trying to live.(p.130)
• ***Whether*** the family goes on a spiritual basis or not, the alcoholic member has to if he would recover.(p.135)
• ***Whether*** you are a hard drinker, a moderated drinker or a teetotaler, you may have some pretty strong opinions, perhaps prejudices.(p.139)
• If your decision is yes, ***whether*** the reason be humanitarian or business or both, then the following suggestions may be helpful.(p.140)
• ***Whether*** you mention this book is a matter for your discretion.(p.142)
• ***Whether*** your employee likes it or not, he will learn the grim truth about alcoholism.(p.144)
• In case he does stumble, even once, you will have to decide ***whether*** to let him go.(p.147)
• He proved to be a devil-may-care young fellow whose parents could not make out ***whether*** he wanted to stop drinking or not.(p.158)
• Seventeen stories may help you decide ***whether*** you are alcoholic; also, ***whether*** A.A. is for you.(p.167)
• ***Whether*** you quit six days, months, or years, if you go out and take a drink or two you'll end up in this hospital tied down, just like you have been in these past six months.(p.187)
• I wasn't afraid that the program wouldn't work, but I still was doubtful ***whether*** I would be able to hang on to the program, but I did come to the conclusion that I was willing to put everything I had into it, with God's power, and that I wanted to do just that.(p.189)
• ***Whether*** I could have done as well as he, I don't know.(p.194)
• I don't know ***whether*** I drank to cover up being a failure, or ***whether*** I drank and then missed the deals.(p.198)
• After drinking one glass of beer at the end of my work period for about five days, I thought I'd better find out ***whether*** I really had the stuff licked.(p.203)
• He had no desire to know anything, except ***whether*** I was definite about my desire to quit drinking.(p.235)
• She said, "He's not going to the hospital, ***whether*** you pay for it or I pay for it, he's not going!"(p.271)
• It didn't bother me any more ***whether*** George was drinking or not.(p.324)
• Every breadwinner, ***whether*** trying to impress a boss or to hold customers in his own business, is fettered by people-pleasing.(p.329)
• All this while, I wondered ***whether*** I could do laundry for the neighbors as a part-time job.(p.371)
• They told me to go to meetings, and I still do at every available opportunity, ***whether*** I am at home or in some other city.(p.381)
• Yesterday is gone, and we don't know ***whether*** we will be here tomorrow.(p.382)
• My husband couldn't tell ***whether*** I wanted to do something about my drinking.(p.391)
• I didn't know ***whether*** I had told him to rush to the hospital and I'd meet him there, or to take two aspirin and call me in the morning.(p.441)
• The neurologist in charge of my case didn't think to ask me ***whether*** I drank, and I didn't think to tell him.(p.444)
• We got on the plane and immediately had a big fight over ***whether*** I'd drink the free booze.(p.444)
• At first, I wondered ***whether*** he was alcoholic himself, and was sending me to find out about A.A.(p.446)
• We lived just a few doors from the First Baptist Church and when they had funerals I remember very often asking my mother ***whether*** the person was good or bad and ***whether*** they were going to heaven or hell.(p.483)
• I don't know ***whether*** it was right or wrong, but at least I know that people weren't thinking the same.(p.484)
• I don't know ***whether*** she was a pacifist or ***whether*** she just thought that in the event of another war it would have some bearing on my joining up.(p.484)
• I don't remember ***whether*** I went by streetcar, ***whether*** I walked or went in a taxicab.(p.492)
• Then he asks me if I believe in a power greater than myself, ***whether*** I call that power God, Allah, Confucius, Prime Cause, Divine Mind, or any other name.(p.503)
• The trial lasted about a week, and ***whether*** or not I was going to the death house was anybody's guess.(p.508)
• Maybe I wouldn't be able to hold any job, or maybe (and this was my greatest fear) I wouldn't care ***whether*** I had a job or not.(p.548)
• We think that each group should soon achieve this ideal; that any public solicitation of funds using the name of Alcoholics Anonymous is highly dangerous, ***whether*** by groups, clubs, hospitals, or other outside agencies; that acceptance of large gifts from any source, or of contributions carrying any obligation whatever, is unwise.(p.566)

whichever

• Go or stay away, *whichever* seems best.(p.102)

while

• *While* the internal difficulties of our adolescent period were being ironed out, public acceptance of A.A. grew by leaps and bounds.(p.xix)

• Many years ago one of the leading contributors to this book came under our care in this hospital and *while* here he acquired some ideas which he put into practical application at once.(p.xxv)

• If any feel that as psychiatrists directing a hospital for alcoholics we appear somewhat sentimental, let them stand with us a *while* on the firing line, see the tragedies, the despairing wives, the little children; let the solving of these problems become a part of their daily work, and even of their sleeping moments, and the most cynical will not wonder that we have accepted and encouraged this movement.(p.xxvi)

• The sensation is so elusive that, *while* they admit it is injurious, they cannot after a time differentiate the true from the false.(p.xxvi)

• We went at once to the country, my wife to applaud *while* I started out to overtake Walter Hagen.(p.3)

• *While* I lay in the hospital the thought came that there were thousands of hopeless alcoholics who might be glad to have what had been so freely given me.(p.14)

• But not so with the alcoholic illness, for with it there goes annihilation of all the things worth *while* in life.(p.18)

• He does absurd, incredible, tragic things *while* drinking.(p.21)

• His disposition *while* drinking resembles his normal nature but little.(p.21)

• We know that *while* the alcoholic keeps away from drink, as he may do for months or years, he reacts much like other men.(p.22)

• Once in a *while* he may tell the truth.(p.23)

• Here and there, once in a *while*, alcoholics have had what are called vital spiritual experiences.(p.27)

• This hope, however, was destroyed by the doctor's telling him that *while* his religious convictions were very good, in his case they did not spell the necessary vital spiritual experience.(p.27)

• But the difficulty is that few alcoholics have enough desire to stop *while* there is yet time.(p.32)

• He tried to regulate his drinking for a *while*, making several trips to the hospital meantime.(p.32)

• We heard no more of Fred for a *while*.(p.40)

• But after a *while* we had to face the fact that we must find a spiritual basis of life -- or else.(p.44)

• We talked of intolerance, *while* we were intolerant ourselves.(p.50)

• *While* pondering the answer he felt as though he lived in hell.(p.56)

• To the precise extent that we permit these, do we squander the hours that might have been worth *while*.(p.66)

• We are there to sweep off our side of the street realizing that nothing worth *while* can be accomplished until we do so, never trying to tell him what he should do.(p.77)

• *While* drinking, he accepted a sum of money from a bitterly-hated business rival, giving him no receipt for it.(p.80)

• We are often surprised how the right answers come after we have tried this for a *while*.(p.86)

• Call on him *while* he is still jittery.(p.91)

• After a *while*, turn the talk to some phase of drinking.(p.91)

• A kindly act once in a *while* isn't enough.(p.97)

• *While* you were drinking, you were withdrawing from life little by little.(p.102)

• Our friends have counseled chucking the men and we have done so with finality, only to be back in a little *while* hoping, always hoping.(p.105)

• For a *while* they would be their old sweet selves, only to dash the new structure of affection to pieces once more.(p.107)

• Of those who keep on, a good number will become true alcoholics after a *while*.(p.109)

• *While* you need not discuss your husband at length, you can quietly let your friends know the nature of his illness.(p.115)

• Unless they actually need protection from their father, it is best not to take sides in any argument he has with them *while* drinking.(p.115)

• Showing others who suffer how we were given help is the very thing which makes life seem so worth *while* to us now.(p.124)

• He may tell mother, who has been religious all her life, that she doesn't know what it's all about, and that she had better get his brand of spirituality *while* there is yet time.(p.128)

• *While* grateful that he drinks no more, they may not like the idea that God has accomplished the miracle where they failed.(p.128)

• Their young minds were impressionable *while* he was drinking.(p.134)

• If this presents difficulty, re-reading chapters two and three, where the alcoholic sickness is discussed at length might be worth *while*.(p.140)

• *While* on the subject of confidence, can you adopt the attitude that so far as you are concerned this will be a strictly personal matter, that his alcoholic derelictions, the treatment about to be undertaken, will never be discussed without his consent?(p.143)

• If the book is read the moment the patient is able, *while* acutely depressed, realization of his condition may come to him.(p.144)

• You may need to encourage him to play once in a *while*.(p.146)

• A couple of hired hands were cleaning out the barn on the farm and I would ride to and fro on the sled, and *while* they were loading I would drink hard cider out of a barrel in the barn.(p.183)

• After a *while*, Bill said, "Well, now, you've been talking a good long time, let me talk a minute or two."(p.185)

• At that particular time, the boys put me on a shutter and took me out to the shed, and I lay in the car *while* they enjoyed their banquet.(p.195)

• This was a regular occurrence for a little *while*.(p.196)

• I didn't want to jeopardize the lives of innocent people by driving an automobile *while* intoxicated, but I did.(p.199)

• At three-thirty the next morning, I was in Champlain Street Station, in jail for driving *while* intoxicated and insulting an officer; and the suit of which I was so proud was in such shape that the turnkey had to get me a pair of trousers to go into court in the next morning.(p.201)

• I then began asking a lot of questions of both my brother and Dr. Bob about how this thing worked, and I suppose I was becoming more glassy-eyed all the *while*, for eventually I said to Bob, "You're all dried up.(p.206)

• I then entered Case School and worked *while* I went to school and finished there.(p.212)

• And so on and on, for several weeks, *while* I grudgingly plowed through some more of the offending book, and felt more and more hopeless about myself.(p.227)

• I came of good stock, of men and women who drank wine all their lives as a beverage, and *while* they occasionally got drunk at special celebrations, they were up and about their business the next day.(p.231)

• Little more of our talk stayed in my memory, but I do know I slept the rest of that night *while* before I had never known what a real night's sleep was.(p.239)

• My family lived in very prosperous circumstances, and *while* both my parents drank, sometimes too much, neither was an alcoholic.(p.240)

• Father was a very well-integrated person, and *while* mother was highstrung and a bit selfish and demanding, our home life was reasonably harmonious.(p.240)

• Then broke again, hiding out in cheap hotels all over the country, one night jail stands here and there, and always that horrible feeling "What's the use -- nothing is worth *while*."(p.244)

• We would follow one man's ideas for a *while*, decide he was wrong and switch to another's method.(p.246)

• *While* I went along with all that was done and attended the meetings, I never took an active job of leadership until February 1940.(p.249)

• *While* there I was called to the hospital in my home town to see a former partner who had insisted that I visit him.(p.257)

• An accident *while* drunk laid me low for about three weeks.(p.258)

• The next morning his wife came dragging him in before Russ went to work, *while* I was getting breakfast.(p.271)

• For a little *while*.(p.275)

• Here, *while* in a hospital bed, men with clear eyes, happy faces, and a look of assurance and purposefulness about them, came to see me and told me their stories.(p.279)

• *While* there, two or three more "cash customers" (as Dr. Bob used to call them -- probably because they had so little cash) were shipped in to us from Detroit.(p.282)

• The doctor, a young man, immediately took fire with the idea, and *while* he did not convince the son, he turned over two prospects who were anxious for the program.(p.294)

• *While* working in an office, there was some semblance of restraint, but, oh boy, when I got on the outside with this new company without supervision, did I go to town!(p.300)

• And all the *while* my fear fed a growing conviction that before long it would be necessary for me to be put away in some institution.(p.306)

• However, due to financial difficulties the whole printing was, for a *while*, held up and the book received no publicity, nor, of course, was it available in the stores, even if one knew it existed.(p.307)

• *While* I was in basic, I got high off booze almost every night.(p.317)

• Many retirees embrace alcoholism *while* secluded in motor trailers, rest homes, leisure-world bungalows, mountain cabins, or beach cottages, or even in penthouses, on yachts, and inside Palm Springs cabanas.(p.329)

• *While* I sought the comforting arms of alcohol, I knew this was a sign of weakness on the part of a longtime-successful old codger with white hair, the image of dignity.(p.331)

• Mere cessation from drinking is not enough for an alcoholic *while* the need for that drink goes on.(p.339)

• At the other side of the table sat one of the carpenters in our community, and at the further end of the table sat the man who ran the bakery, *while* on one side sat my friend who was a mechanic.(p.347)

• I do recall lying on a cold cement floor and shredding into little bits several pieces of stolen identification cards, and washing my face in the toilet bowl trying to sober up, and screaming hysterically *while* clinging to bars too high to see out of, and cursing everyone that came near me.(p.354)

• Many times have I heard the above expressions since I have been in A.A., and many times I have had to reply "Definitely I am an alcoholic, and *while* it may be hard for you to believe, it is not hard for me, for I have learned many things about alcohol and myself that would, perhaps, be difficult for you to understand."(p.356)

• *While* I was in Florida trying to convince my wife with all the A.A. literature that she should come back to me, she went over to her desk and picked up a clipping she had taken from the St. Petersburg Times about A.A.(p.366)

• There, I could be a proper mother and wife *while* drinking up a storm.(p.369)

• All this *while*, I wondered whether I could do laundry for the neighbors as a part-time job.(p.371)

• Never having enough, always craving more, the obsession for alcohol gradually dominated all my activities, particularly *while* travelling.(p.375)

• I was living in constant fear that I would get caught *while* driving a car, so I used taxis part of the time.(p.375)

• A year later, *while* we were on a vacation trip she packed up to go home because of my excessive drinking, and I talked her out of it with the promise I would go on the wagon for at least a year.(p.377)

• After all, I hadn't started to drink early in life, so I had some stability and maturity to guide me for a *while*.(p.379)

• One afternoon, the year after moving to Houston, I got as drunk as a skunk, and *while* I do not walk very straight sober, you should see me when I'm drunk!(p.390)

• They phoned my husband that I was in jail and in such terrible shape that they didn't know what I would do to myself; and they realized that jail was no place for me, but that he was to wait a *while* before he got me, because at the time they called him to come over for me I was beating a tin cup against the wall.(p.390)

• I returned from Europe a *while* after that encounter, and I never went back.(p.406)

• I must go on the wagon for a *while*.(p.408)

• Luckily a friend was with me, who dragged me out, screaming and cursing, *while* the bartender threatened to call the police.(p.411)

• Once in a *while* I stayed home for a night, to see how my folks were doing.(p.425)

• *While* waiting to depart I was selected -- by giving a CPO five dollars -- to be bartender in the Navy Chief's Club.(p.426)

• *While* I was at Pensacola my dad became dangerously ill and almost died of pneumonia plus a heart attack.(p.426)

• I don't know why I didn't fall out of the open cockpit of some of those planes I flew in *while* taking aerial pictures.(p.426)

• I seldom left the base any more except once in a *while* when I felt the need of talking to some girl.(p.427)

• For the leveling-off process, I just loved intravenous Demerol, but I found it hard to practice good medi-

cine *while* shooting morphine.(p.442)
• I didn't feel I could lie in bed and squirt the stuff in my veins *while* my kids and wife stood around watching me, so I kept the drug in my bag and the bag in the car and the car in the garage.(p.442)
• In the garage, I would put the needle in my vein and then try to figure out exactly how much medication to inject to overcome the pep pills *while* adding to the sleeping pills *while* ignoring the tranquilizers, in order to get just enough to be able to pull out the needle, jerk the tourniquet, throw it in the car, slam the car door shut, run down the hall, and fall in bed before I fell asleep.(p.442)
• Today, I find I can't work my A.A. program *while* taking pills, nor may I even have them around for dire emergencies only.(p.443)
• Much of my time was spent writing letters, notes, orders, and lists of things for Max, who was also my office nurse, to do to keep the world running *while* I was locked up.(p.445)
• But it quickly became obvious that he had this childish notion instead: If he could get me to go to enough meetings *while* in the hospital, I would continue to go after he let me out.(p.447)
• Before A.A., I judged myself by my intentions, *while* the world was judging me by my actions.(p.450)
• I never just sit and do nothing *while* waiting for Him to tell me what to do.(p.452)
• *While* I was taking inventory in the cold-storage locker one Sunday, a wooden sign bolted to the inside door stopped me in my tracks.(p.461)
• After a *while* I really did enjoy drinking and what it did to me, and I became dependent upon it for every occasion.(p.464)
• From that time on, fear was with me because I realized that not only would I not remember what happened to me *while* I was drinking, but apparently I couldn't control what happened.(p.465)
• On one occasion when I was serving time in my favorite drying-out place *while* I was having a session with the psychiatrist, she left my case history on her desk when she was called away from the room.(p.470)
• The Higher Power to whom I had turned, and who had sustained me, had once again been thrust into the background, *while* my emotions were running my life and, as always, my emotions ran me to the bottle.(p.472)
• *While* I was there I realized that I had missed something.(p.472)
• I stay on wagon for *while*, but miserable.(p.475)
• He did come, and I landed in the funny farm for a *while*.(p.479)
• After Charlie had talked a *while*, I knew that this man had something.(p.495)
• "Once in a *while*," I lied.(p.498)
• I have been drinking *while* the baby was arriving.(p.502)
• Can all the worth *while* people I have known be wrong about God?(p.503)
• We talked for a *while*, and then he sent me down to the Alanon House over on the west side, and there I had my introduction to A.A.(p.515)
• Oh yes, I get the dry jitters once in a *while*, but that isn't anything to worry about.(p.516)
• After a *while*, I found that the psycho ward was a good place to hide when I had taken something stolen to the pawnshop.(p.528)
• There was the physical aspect; to be the youngest and the runt of the brood of children, to have to wear glasses very early and so to be teased, to be bookish and bored in school because the captain of the football team could not translate Virgil and yet was the school god *while* you, you, you little shrimp, were the school egghead, junior size and an early model.(p.533)
• There was the love affair which was ridiculous -- "imagine that midget being able to fall in love!" -- and my head knew it *while* my heart pumped real, genuine anguish, for it hurt like hell, and since it was first love, things have never been quite the same.(p.534)
• For a *while*, for a long time, we can endure the intellect's being ahead of the emotions, which is the import of Millay's couplet.(p.534)
• For a little *while*, I was the great man I wanted to be, and thought myself entitled to be just by reason of being.(p.537)
• I went back home, to a job of manual labor where for a little *while* I was able to keep away from alcohol.(p.539)
• When I had been in A.A. only a short *while*, an oldtimer told me something that has affected my life ever since.(p.554)
• I sold my first article to a national magazine *while* still an undergraduate.(p.555)
• *While* there, I read the Big Book and the Grapevine and began the slow road back to health and sanity through the recovery program of A.A.(p.559)
• *While* an A.A. group may cooperate with anyone, such cooperation ought never go so far as affiliation or endorsement, actual or implied.(p.566)

whimper

• And having sung that phrase, I'd chuckle with amusement, turning into irony turning into self-contempt turning into self-pity, at the sad fate of Bob, that wonderful, poor little motherless boy who was so smart in school and who grew up to accept responsibility so early and so fast and who staggered under his burdens without a *whimper* until the time came when he thought he was too good for this world and so he ought to be out of it.(p.532)

whipped

• And I felt depleted, *whipped*.(p.326)

whirl

• The local banker watched me *whirl* fat checks in and out of his till with amused skepticism.(p.4)

whirled

• My brain *whirled*.(p.223)

whirling

• The prosaic steel girder is a mass of electrons *whirling* around each other at incredible speed.(p.48)
• Could we still say the whole thing was nothing but a mass of electrons, created out of nothing, meaning nothing, *whirling* on to a destiny of nothingness?(p.54)

whisked

• I found myself being lifted onto a stretcher and *whisked* away in an ambulance to a strange hospital.(p.558)

whiskey

• "Suddenly the thought crossed my mind that if I were to put an ounce of *whiskey* in my milk it couldn't hurt me on a full stomach.(p.36)
• I ordered a *whiskey* and poured it into the milk.(p.36)
• I vaguely sensed I was not being any too smart, but felt reassured as I was taking the *whiskey* on a full stomach.(p.36)
• The experiment went so well that I ordered another *whiskey* and poured it into more milk.(p.36)
• Yet all reasons for not drinking were easily pushed aside in favor of the foolish idea that he could take *whiskey* if only he mixed it with milk!(p.36)
• I remember that my father kept *whiskey* around the house for medical purposes and entertainment, and I would drink from this when no one was about and then water it to keep my parents from knowing I was drinking.(p.183)
• I felt having gotten married, I was an adult and one of the first things I did was to buy two cases of *whiskey* with no idea of drinking it.(p.196)
• I was a very young married man, having his *whiskey* in the cupboard over the sink, and when I helped my wife with the dishes at night I would take a cup of tea and spike it with *whiskey*.(p.196)
• Then I got into the habit of having beers, and decided that a drink of *whiskey* was not any worse; so I would get the one drink of *whiskey* but, on second thought, I decided that as long as I was only going to have one, I might as well make it a double-header.(p.203)
• In fact, after six months of living on food instead of on *whiskey*, I gained about thirty pounds.(p.220)
• You can all remember that in the first few months after the change, a great many men, who had formerly been used to a few beers every day or an occasional drink of *whiskey*, simply quit all alcoholic drinks.(p.232)
• The "speaks" usually sold *whiskey*.(p.233)
• I stayed so sober that I used to keep a quart of medicinal *whiskey* in my bureau which I used to taper off the occasional newspaper alcoholics who were sent to see me.(p.253)
• The next two years were simply a long drawn out process of less and less work and more and more *whiskey*.(p.278)
• I landed him and shipped him by train to Akron, with a pint of *whiskey* in his pocket to keep him from wanting to get off the train in Toledo!(p.282)
• The inevitable result of this discovery was that I soon learned that beer made a very good chaser for *whiskey*.(p.298)
• I entered the house, opened a new bottle of *whiskey* and sat down to drink myself into the right frame of mind to get in my car, start the motor and close the garage door behind me.(p.363)
• It was really medicinal that night, that *whiskey*, and it was a medication after that.(p.386)
• (It was the beer and cheap *whiskey* that was making me so sick.(p.398)
• The short tours could be taken care of by sneaking enough *whiskey* aboard ship so that it could be rationed out until another supply could be laid in.(p.398)
• I remembered having had a little drink of *whiskey* with a can of warm beer as a chaser.(p.422)
• I was drinking quite a bit of *whiskey* now.(p.425)
• I tried to control her drinking by pouring her *whiskey* down the sink before I'd leave for the night, to get drunker myself.(p.426)
• Pearl Harbor was a breeze of nine months, a gay Hawaiian paradise, drinking under the palms, listening to the surf beat on the shore, a bottle of *whiskey* near at hand.(p.426)
• I would drink all night in bars, come home about five a.m., down a good big glass of *whiskey* straight, and tumble into bed.(p.428)
• I used to think, "Why live without *whiskey*?"(p.430)
• Also, after that first visit I learned I could refuse to sign myself in unless they gave me a glass of *whiskey* in one hand and a glass of paraldehyde in the other.(p.468)
• We weren't even permitted to play cards in our home, but father would give us just a little toddy with *whiskey* and sugar and warm water now and then.(p.484)
• We had no *whiskey* in the house, other than my father's private stock.(p.484)
• I've never seen him drunk in my life, although he'd take a shot in the morning and usually one in the evening, and so did I; but for the most part he kept his *whiskey* in his office.(p.484)
• At this point I believe I had only been intoxicated on maybe three or four occasions, and certainly *whiskey* was no problem to me.(p.487)
• At that time the repeal whiskies were back, and I'd go to the store and buy my *whiskey* and take it to my office and put it under the desk, first in one place and then in another, and there soon was an accumulation of empty bottles.(p.488)
• I think *whiskey* was cheaper there than it was in Washington.(p.490)
• Thinking only of two or three dollars to buy some *whiskey*, I did the job and that's how I met Ella G., who was responsible for my coming into A.A.(p.493)
• She never mentioned anything about my *whiskey* drinking because if she had I would have told her, "No" right then.(p.494)
• Finally, he brought in the angle of *whiskey*.(p.494)
• After he'd talked half an hour, I still wanted him to hurry up and get out so I could go and get some *whiskey* before the liquor store closed.(p.494)
• I sneak downstairs and get a bottle of *whiskey* from the cellaret.(p.501)
• I was always able to get a boyfriend who had a drinking joint or sold *whiskey*, but it didn't last long.(p.526)
• I thought if they smelled *whiskey* on my breath, they would lock me up, and I couldn't live without my bottle.(p.526)
• But to me, *whiskey* meant more than a home for my sons.(p.527)
• Then the time came when I couldn't afford *whiskey*, so I turned to wine.(p.527)

whiskies

• At that time the repeal *whiskies* were back, and I'd go to the store and buy my whiskey and take it to my office and put it under the desk, first in one place and then in another, and there soon was an accumulation of empty bottles.(p.488)

whisky

• As the *whisky* rose to my head I told myself I would manage better next time, but I might as well get good and drunk then.(p.6)

whisper

• They would all stare at me and *whisper*!(p.413)

whistles

• It was November 11th and bells were ringing and *whistles* blowing for the real Armistice.(p.242)

whistling

• We know our friend is like a boy *whistling* in the dark to keep up his spirits.(p.152)

white

• We placed them before us in black and *white*.(p.67)
• I had *white* trousers on, *white* shoes and a *white* shirt that was streaked with blood.(p.204)
• I found some wool stockings, some *white* flannels that had shrunk to my knees, and an old jacket.(p.288)
• While I sought the comforting arms of alcohol, I knew this was a sign of weakness on the part of a longtime-successful old codger with *white* hair, the image of dignity.(p.331)
• I can't remember a dinner at home that we didn't

have ***white*** wine or claret on the table.(p.384)
• I was free, ***white*** and twenty-one and I had a time for myself.(p.386)
• I knew I wasn't capable of keeping the bulk of the money myself, so I gave it to a ***white*** fellow who owned the bar which I frequented.(p.493)
• I haven't mentioned it, but Charlie, my sponsor, was ***white,*** and when we got our group started we got help from other ***white*** groups in Washington.(p.495)
• I'm writing this during an A.A. convention, where I have spent the weekend with nothing but ***white*** people.(p.529)

who's
• Even obvious intoxication is excused by younger people as something "he's earned the right to do," and they say, "After all, ***who's*** he hurting?"(p.330)
• I was listed in "***Who's*** Who in America" as an American who, by distinguished achievement, had arrived.(p.432)
• Well – well – look ***who's*** here!(p.500)

whoever
• This time, ***whoever*** had rolled me had taken my glasses as well (they were gold).(p.538)

whole
• As we discovered the principles by which the individual alcoholic could live, so we had to evolve principles by which the A.A. groups and A.A. as a ***whole*** could survive and function effectively.(p.xix)
• Though the aggregate of recoveries resulting from psychiatric effort is considerable, we physicians must admit we have made little impression upon the problem as a ***whole.***(p.xxvii)
• There is the manic-depressive type, who is, perhaps, the least understood by his friends, and about whom a ***whole*** chapter could be written.(p.xxviii)
• We covered the ***whole*** eastern United States in a year.(p.3)
• That the man who is making the approach has had the same difficulty, that he obviously knows what he is talking about, that his ***whole*** deportment shouts at the new prospect that he is a man with a real answer, that he has no attitude of Holier Than Thou, nothing whatever except the sincere desire to be helpful; that there are no fees to pay, no axes to grind, no people to please, no lectures to be endured -- these are the conditions we have found most effective.(p.18)
• The great fact is just this, and nothing less: That we have had deep and effective spiritual experiences which have revolutionized our ***whole*** attitude toward life, toward our fellows and toward God's universe.(p.25)
• He begged the doctor to tell him the ***whole*** truth, and he got it.(p.26)
• Could we still say the ***whole*** thing was nothing but a mass of electrons, created out of nothing, meaning nothing, whirling on to a destiny of nothingness?(p.54)
• Each person is like an actor who wants to run the ***whole*** show; is forever trying to arrange the lights, the ballet, the scenery and the rest of the players in his own way.(p.60)
• We have seldom told them the ***whole*** truth nor have we followed their advice.(p.73)
• Of course she did not, and the ***whole*** situation has long since been adjusted.(p.79)
• Our ***whole*** attitude and outlook upon life will change.(p.84)
• Doctors are rightly loath to tell alcoholic patients the ***whole*** story unless it will serve some good purpose.(p.92)
• We thought, on the ***whole,*** we were pretty good women, capable of being nicer if our husbands stopped drinking.(p.116)
• My ***whole*** life seemed to be centered around doing what I wanted to do, without regard for the rights, wishes, or privileges of anyone else; a state of mind which became more and more predominant as the years passed.(p.172)
• At that particular stage, I lost interest in it, sold the option for $5,000 and forgot the ***whole*** deal.(p.198)
• (My mother and father were Catholics and I had been baptized, but at the end of my instructions for Confirmation I had not gone to church, and then when my mother remarried, she married a Protestant and the ***whole*** religious angle was forgotten.(p.201)
• Dr. Bob did not lay out the ***whole*** program.(p.218)
• I had no desire whatever to sit down at a table and stay a ***whole*** morning or afternoon drinking.(p.231)
• I had no resentments against individuals – the ***whole*** world was all wrong.(p.244)
• When I reached a point directly back of our house, where I could have cut through a friend's garden, I was almost overpowered by the desire to get home, but I made the ***whole*** journey.(p.276)
• However, due to financial difficulties the ***whole*** printing was, for a while, held up and the book received no publicity, nor, of course, was it available in the stores, even if one knew it existed.(p.307)
• ***Whole*** new vistas were opened and life began to take on color and interest.(p.311)
• And the ***whole*** merry-go-round would be on again.(p.325)
• Then, one night, my ***whole*** pattern for drinking was set.(p.328)
• I wanted him to be sure that I wasn't the one who was going to drink the ***whole*** bottle.(p.336)
• I made more money the last year of my drinking than I ever made before in my ***whole*** life.(p.345)
• We've got to turn the ***whole*** business over to some joker we can't even see!(p.350)
• Here he is powerless, unmanageable, in the grip of something bigger than he is, and he's got to turn the ***whole*** business over to someone else!(p.350)
• So I went to her and said, "There's only one thing I want in my ***whole*** life, and I don't want any commendation; I don't want any credit; I don't want anything from you or Janey for the rest of your life except one thing; and that is, the opportunity to do anything you want always, and I would like to start off by doing the dishes."(p.351)
• A ***whole*** new world of happiness and love began to unfold before my eyes, a truly new way of living.(p.365)
• I lost a lot of shirts that way, and sometimes I was minus a ***whole*** wash.(p.371)
• I only know that it does -- if you desire it with your ***whole*** heart and without reservation.(p.384)
• So Frank left town, and by Monday morning I had been sober for that ***whole*** week.(p.393)
• I wanted to try A.A. with my ***whole*** heart and soul.(p.393)
• It has changed not simply one department of my life – it has changed my ***whole*** life.(p.394)
• But my board, room, and clothing were free, and I could spend the ***whole*** ten bucks on booze.(p.398)
• A few stood by me, at least in their hearts, throughout the ***whole*** of my drinking career.(p.404)
• Now my ***whole*** thinking was crazy.(p.408)
• I learned a ***whole*** new sense of values.(p.409)
• Barleycorn's wringer squeezed this author – but he escaped quite ***whole.***(p.432)
• In other words, the kindest doctor in the ***whole*** world, and I had one such, couldn't help me because I always felt, "You can't know about me – you can't possibly know – you don't even drink!"(p.471)
• But by listening and talking to these A.A.'s – talking to them as I had never talked to anyone in my ***whole*** life, I saw that it was my life that was unmanageable – not just my drinking.(p.471)
• During these seven years a thing called the Twenty-four Hour Program --a gadget I used to think was only a snare to trap the newcomer -- has come to mean much to me, not only as regards my drinking but in the ***whole*** pattern of my life.(p.473)
• Then A.A. showed her the beauty of normal living, in a ***whole*** family reborn.(p.478)
• When I am through speaking, the ***whole*** idea has become absurd.(p.507)
• I was intensely unhappy the ***whole*** time, but I didn't seem to be able to do anything about it, and the worst part to me was the realization that all this was going to happen again and again until I died.(p.522)
• The "12 Traditions" of Alcoholics Anonymous are, we A.A.'s believe, the best answers that our experience has yet given to those ever urgent questions, "How can A.A. best function?" and, "How can A.A. best stay ***whole*** and so survive?"(p.563)
• Four – Each group should be autonomous except in matters affecting other groups or A.A. as a ***whole.***(p.564)
• 1. – Each member of Alcoholics Anonymous is but a small part of a great ***whole.***(p.565)
• And no group, regional committee, or individual should ever take any action that might greatly affect A.A. as a ***whole*** without conferring with the trustees of the General Service Board.(p.565)
• All such representatives are to be guided in the spirit of service, for true leaders in A.A. are but trusted and experienced servants of the ***whole.***(p.567)

whole-heartedly
• I went back to my group meetings, but not ***whole-heartedly,*** and I often skipped them with the excuse that I was too tired.(p.364)

wholeheartedly
• This happened soon after they ***wholeheartedly*** met a few simple requirements.(p.50)

wholesale
• Since the original Foreword to this book was written in 1939, a ***wholesale*** miracle has taken place.(p.xv)
• Instead, we looked at the human defects of these people, and sometimes used their shortcomings as a basis of ***wholesale*** condemnation.(p.50)

whom
• To ***whom*** it may concern:(p.xxiii)
• I personally know scores of cases who were of the type with ***whom*** other methods had failed completely.(p.xxiii)
• There is the manic-depressive type, who is, perhaps, the least understood by his friends, and about ***whom*** a whole chapter could be written.(p.xxviii)
• We made a list of people I had hurt or toward ***whom*** I felt resentment.(p.13)
• When, therefore, we were approached by those in ***whom*** the problem had been solved, there was nothing left for us but to pick up the simple kit of spiritual tools laid at our feet.(p.25)
• So he returned to this doctor, ***whom*** he admired, and asked him point-blank why he could not recover.(p.26)
• If what we have learned and felt and seen means anything at all, it means that all of us, whatever our race, creed, or color are the children of a living Creator with ***whom*** we may form a relationship upon simple and understandable terms as soon as we are willing and honest enough to try.(p.28)
• We think few, to ***whom*** this book will appeal, can stay dry anything like a year.(p.34)
• Moreover, he would lose his family for ***whom*** he had a deep affection.(p.35)
• We listed people, institutions or principles with ***whom*** we were angry.(p.64)
• ***Whom*** had we hurt?(p.69)
• Rightly and naturally, we think well before we choose the person or persons with ***whom*** to take this intimate and confidential step.(p.74)
• We have a list of all persons we have harmed and to ***whom*** we are willing to make amends.(p.76)
• It is better, however, that one does not needlessly name a person upon ***whom*** she can vent jealously.(p.82)
• But he is yet a long way from making good to the wife or parents ***whom*** for years he has so shockingly treated.(p.82)
• Four: You may have a husband of ***whom*** you completely despair.(p.110)
• He wanted so much to talk with someone, but ***whom?***(p.154)
• Why, he argued, should he lose the remainder of his business, only to bring still more suffering to his family by foolishly admitting his plight to people from ***whom*** he made his livelihood?(p.155)
• Of far more importance was the fact that he was the first living human with ***whom*** I had ever talked, who knew what he was talking about in regard to alcoholism from actual experience.(p.180)
• Did she have an alcoholic customer on ***whom*** it could be tried?(p.188)
• I spent most of my time trying to get back these friendships, and to make some recompense towards my wife, ***whom*** I had hurt a lot.(p.191)
• I was arrested and taken to jail where I was beaten up by two or three fellows who were already in there and ***whom*** I tried to boss.(p.204)
• At night, I woke up and the folks with ***whom*** I roomed were home by then.(p.205)
• Even then he went into no great detail about how he and a crowd of alcoholics, with ***whom*** he associated, had mastered their difficulty.(p.235)
• Jackie told me about a group of fellows in New York, of ***whom*** my old friend Fitz was one, who had the same problem I had, and who by working together to help each other were not now drinking and were happy like himself.(p.239)
• However, I made an SOS call to the New York Group, ***whom*** I hadn't met yet, and they suggested we both come there.(p.245)
• But in those days I had no one to ***whom*** I might take my troubles.(p.260)
• So six months ago I acquired a ready made family consisting of one charming wife, four grown children to ***whom*** I am devoted, and three grandchildren.(p.286)
• In the summer of 1938, almost a year from the time I made my original contact with Akron, the man for ***whom*** I was working and who knew about the program, approached me and asked if I could do anything about one of his salesmen who was drinking very heavily.(p.294)
• Where once I had casual acquaintances, all of ***whom*** were fair weather friends, I now have a host of

friends who accept me for what I am.(p.296)
• One is that I don't remember too many of them, as I was one of those drunks who could be on his feet and attend a meeting or a party, engage in a conversation with people and do things that any nearly normal person would do, and the next day not remember a thing about where I was, what I did, *whom* I saw, or how I got home.(p.301)
• Finally, an old business acquaintance of mine, *whom* I hadn't seen for several years offered me a job.(p.301)
• I vowed that never again would any important person *whom* I wished to please and impress ever see me drunk.(p.328)
• A spiritual awakening soon came to mean trying each day to be a little more thoughtful, more considerate, a little more courteous to those with *whom* I came in contact.(p.381)
• I could not identify myself with the people with *whom* I found myself and there was no understanding, and I can't stand confinement anyhow.(p.387)
• There are so many to *whom* I feel deeply grateful; to my husband (and best critic), whose generous love, compassion and understanding have helped me along the way; to those before me in A.A. who inspired the first article I read, and the friend who sent that article to Frank; to Ruth for her personal note, and the first A.A. to talk to me; to my Bishop, whose loving and believing spirit inspired me; and to all the members of the Houston Group who were so patient, kind and helpful -- and to countless others.(p.393)
• Other girls *whom* I had known all my life asked for one weak scotch after dinner.(p.406)
• I saw that my Village friends, all of *whom* had small jobs, were living happily on about a tenth of my sinecure.(p.409)
• I think now that a God, in *whom* I did not believe, was looking after me.(p.412)
• In fact, I was taken to A.A. by a woman *whom* my father had taken to A.A. thirteen years earlier.(p.419)
• I was an honor graduate in high school, and I was a "good boy" to *whom* mothers pointed when their sons went astray.(p.419)
• I teamed up with a cute little blonde with *whom* I was working at the office, and for about a year we were inseparable.(p.425)
• It seemed to me that those A.A.'s to *whom* I talked knew all about me.(p.470)
• The Higher Power to *whom* I had turned, and who had sustained me, had once again been thrust into the background, while my emotions were running my life and, as always, my emotions ran me to the bottle.(p.472)
• I'm sure my ideas as to what life should be like were quite different from that of the average person with *whom* I associated.(p.483)
• That year, on a Friday night, a man *whom* I had known for years came to my office.(p.488)
• I had a long talk with a psychiatrist, but nothing came of that, and I had also, just about that time, talked with a minister for *whom* I had a great deal of respect.(p.489)
• I knew it, and I turned for help to someone upon *whom* I had turned my back for many years.(p.515)
• Since it was wartime, I explained to the somewhat startled shopkeeper that I had many friends in the service *whom* I was remembering with a watch.(p.532)
• Alas for us men toward *whom* Shaw hurled his cry, "Must a Christ be crucified in every generation for the benefit of those who have no imagination?"(p.536)

whoop

• I just didn't give a *whoop* about myself or anyone else.(p.325)
• I didn't give a *whoop* about anything scholastic.(p.423)

whoopee

• That includes bars, nightclubs, dances, receptions, weddings, even plain ordinary *whoopee* parties.(p.101)
• What our friend, the vice president, had in mind was the habitual or *whoopee* drinker.(p.149)
• This phase was right down my alley; I had my master's degree in the art of making "*whoopee*."(p.359)

whose

• In that brief space, Alcoholics Anonymous has mushroomed into nearly 6,000 groups *whose* membership is far above 150,000 recovered alcoholics.(p.xv)
• He had also been greatly helped by the late Dr. William D. Silkworth, a New York specialist in alcoholism who is now accounted no less than a medical saint by A.A. members, and *whose* story of the early days of our Society appears in the next pages.(p.xvi)
• It melted the icy intellectual mountain in *whose* shadow I had lived and shivered many years.(p.12)
• It engulfs all *whose* lives touch the sufferer's.(p.18)
• We see that these expressions refer to people *whose* reactions are very different from ours.(p.20)
• As to two of you men, *whose* stories I have heard, there is no doubt in my mind that you were 100% hopeless, apart from divine help.(p.43)
• But with the alcoholic, *whose* hope is the maintenance and growth of a spiritual experience, this business of resentment is infinitely grave.(p.66)
• Those of us belonging to a religious denomination which requires confession must, and of course, will want to go to the properly appointed authority *whose* duty it is to receive it.(p.74)
• We have seen men get well *whose* families have not returned at all.(p.100)
• A spirit of intolerance might repel alcoholics *whose* lives could have been saved, had it not been for such stupidity.(p.103)
• Among us are wives, relatives and friends *whose* problem has been solved, as well as some who have not yet found a happy solution.(p.104)
• He proved to be a devil-may-care young fellow *whose* parents could not make out whether he wanted to stop drinking or not.(p.158)
• Impressed by those who visited him at the hospital, he capitulated entirely when, later, in an upper room of this house, he heard the story of some man *whose* experience closely tallied with his own.(p.160)
• It took me a year, or a year and a half to get to feeling physically well, and it was rather tough, but I soon found folks *whose* friendship I had once had, and I found, after I had been sober for quite some little time, that these people began to act like they had in previous years, before I had gotten so bad, so that I didn't pay too awful much attention to financial gains.(p.190)
• But I had never been a flippant, wise-cracking sneerer at the few persons I had met who had impressed me as Christian men and women, or at any institution *whose* sincerity of purpose I could see.(p.259)
• I ended up, homeless, jobless, penniless and rudderless, as the problem guest of a close friend *whose* family was out of town.(p.278)
• The example which they and Bill W., *whose* visits to Akron were fairly frequent, set me of service to their fellow men imbued me with a great desire to emulate them.(p.281)
• Sometimes during that year I rebelled inwardly at what seemed like lost time, and at having to be a burden to these good people *whose* means were limited.(p.281)
• On the last day I was drinking I went up to see a friend who had had a good deal of trouble with alcohol, and *whose* wife had left him a number of times.(p.346)
• My mother was a lovely, sweet woman, *whose* only weakness was my father.(p.369)
• Early the next morning a man *whose* name I knew well, a lawyer, called on me.(p.378)
• There are so many to whom I feel deeply grateful; to my husband (and best critic), *whose* generous love, compassion and understanding have helped me along the way; to those before me in A.A. who inspired the first article I read, and the friend who sent that article to Frank; to Ruth for her personal note, and the first A.A. to talk to me; to my Bishop, *whose* loving and believing spirit inspired me; and to all the members of the Houston Group who were so patient, kind and helpful -- and to countless others.(p.393)
• I completely forgot myself in trying vainly to help Anne, *whose* misery I understood.(p.415)
• I remember very well saying, "There's only one person in the world *whose* guts I hate worse than yours, and those're my own."(p.440)
• I left this home town, then, after I had made a public spectacle of myself in the presence of a revered teacher *whose* favorite pupil I had been.(p.539)
• The mental twists that led up to my drinking began many years before I ever took a drink for I am one of those *whose* history proves conclusively that my drinking was "a symptom of a deeper trouble."(p.544)

why

• *Why* not I?(p.2)
• He said, "*Why* don't you choose your own conception of God?"(p.12)
• You may already have asked yourself *why* it is that all of us became so very ill from drinking.(p.20)
• Doubtless you are curious to discover how and *why*, in the face of expert opinion to the contrary, we have recovered from a hopeless condition of mind and body.(p.20)
• *Why* can't he?"(p.20)
• "*Why* don't you drink like a gentleman or quit?"(p.20)
• "*Why* don't you try beer and wine?"(p.20)
• *Why* does he behave like this?(p.22)
• If hundreds of experiences have shown him that one drink means another debacle with all its attendant suffering and humiliation, *why* is it he takes that one drink?(p.22)
• *Why* can't he stay on the water wagon?(p.22)
• Opinions vary considerably as to *why* the alcoholic reacts differently from normal people.(p.22)
• We are not sure *why*, once a certain point is reached, little can be done for him.(p.22)
• If you ask him *why* he started on that last bender, the chances are he will offer you any one of a hundred alibis.(p.23)
• And the truth, strange to say, is usually that he has no more idea *why* he took that first drink than you have.(p.23)
• But in their hearts they really do not know *why* they do it.(p.23)
• So he returned to this doctor, whom he admired, and asked him point-blank *why* he could not recover.(p.26)
• *Why* was this?(p.26)
• *Why* does he?(p.35)
• The reader may still ask *why* he should believe in a Power greater than himself.(p.48)
• *Why* this ready acceptance?(p.48)
• Once confused and baffled by the seeming futility of existence they show the underlying reasons *why* they were making heavy going of life.(p.50)
• Leaving aside the drink question, they tell *why* living was so unsatisfactory.(p.51)
• When many hundreds of people are able to say that the consciousness of the Presence of God is today the most important fact of their lives, they present a powerful reason *why* one should have faith.(p.51)
• We had to ask ourselves *why* we shouldn't apply to our human problems this same readiness to change our point of view.(p.52)
• Hence we are at pains to tell *why* we think our present faith is reasonable, *why* we think it more sane and logical to believe than not to believe, *why* we say our former thinking was soft and mushy when we threw up our hands in doubt and said, "We don't know."(p.53)
• This is the how and *why* of it.(p.62)
• We asked ourselves *why* we were angry.(p.64)
• We asked ourselves *why* we had them.(p.68)
• We will be more reconciled to discussing ourselves with another person when we see good reasons *why* we should do so.(p.72)
• Having persevered with the rest of the program, they wondered *why* they fell.(p.73)
• We explain to our partner what we are about to do and *why* we have to do it.(p.75)
• *Why* lay ourselves open to being branded fanatics or religious bores?(p.77)
• You can easily see *why*.(p.87)
• But he will be curious to learn *why* his own convictions have not worked and *why* yours seem to work so well.(p.93)
• Outline the program of action, explaining how you made a self-appraisal, how you straightened out your past and *why* you are now endeavoring to be helpful to him.(p.94)
• Your candidate may give reasons *why* he need not follow all of the program.(p.94)
• Though an alcoholic does not respond, there is no reason *why* you should neglect his family.(p.97)
• *Why* sit with a long face in places where there is drinking, sighing about the good old days.(p.102)
• At proper time and place explain to all your friends *why* alcohol disagrees with you.(p.102)
• Asked *why* they commenced to drink again, they would reply with some silly excuse, or none.(p.107)
• *Why* could they not see that drink meant ruin to them?(p.107)
• *Why* was it, when these dangers were pointed out that they agreed, and then got drunk again immediately?(p.107)
• He admits he cannot drink like other people, but does not see *why*.(p.110)
• That is *why* we are anxious that you understand, and that you avoid these unnecessary difficulties.(p.121)
• And *why*?(p.122)
• They may not see *why* their love and devotion did not straighten him out.(p.128)
• If he means to right his past wrongs, *why* all this concern for everyone in the world but his family?(p.128)
• But *why* shouldn't we laugh?(p.132)
• *Why* not bring him into contact with some of our alcoholic crowd?(p.138)

• *Why* not at least afford him an opportunity to hear my story?(p.138)
• You cannot see *why* it should be to anyone else, save the spineless and stupid.(p.139)
• If not, *why* waste time with him?(p.142)
• But *why* not?(p.150)
• Of course he couldn't drink, but *why* not sit hopefully at a table, a bottle of ginger ale before him?(p.154)
• *Why*, he argued, should he lose the remainder of his business, only to bring still more suffering to his family by foolishly admitting his plight to people from whom he made his livelihood?(p.155)
• "Who are you fellows, and *why* this private room?(p.157)
• *Why* they should be subjected to the tortures we inflict upon them, I cannot explain.(p.178)
• We were eating lunch, and I was listening and trying to find out *why* they had this release that they seemed to have.(p.191)
• I drove towards Cleveland wondering *why* I found myself in such a changed set of conditions as compared with those of six months before.(p.200)
• I avoided them rather than explain *why* they weren't seeing me.(p.203)
• So having licked it, there was no reason *why* I shouldn't have a drink, and I stopped in before I got home and had one.(p.203)
• He said, "Well, *why* don't you take a cab?"(p.204)
• I could not see *why* I couldn't drink like a gentleman, and that was my primary ambition -- until I landed in A.A.(p.214)
• *Why* had "Dorothy" brought me here?(p.223)
• My wife made several attempts to get me to stop and I had the usual visits from persons who would always ask me "*Why*?" -- as if I knew!(p.254)
• And I said, "*Why* sure, that's what I'm here for."(p.270)
• If it isn't anything that's going to help you or anybody else, *why* should you become involved in it, and get all disturbed about it?"(p.273)
• My wife could not understand *why* I would sober up for dad but not for her.(p.288)
• My wife could not understand the next morning *why* I was drunker than the night before when she took my bottles.(p.289)
• *Why*, even a year ago, I had seen Howard, an exdoctor, mooching a dime for a drink.(p.289)
• I was trapped, and for the life of me I did not know how or *why* this had happened to me.(p.306)
• *Why* he bothered with me as long as he did I shall never know, for he knew there was no answer for me in medicine and he, like all doctors of his day, had been taught that the alcoholic was incurable and should be ignored.(p.307)
• *Why* do men and women like these join A.A.?(p.315)
• She said "*Why* don't you do it too?"(p.326)
• I knew *why* I identified.(p.333)
• He said, "*Why* don't you try Alcoholics Anonymous?"(p.340)
• And he said, "Earle, *why* don't you come on over and let me talk to you for a minute."(p.348)
• So he got me a cup of coffee, and a piece of cake, and sat me down and said, "*Why*, there's nothing wrong with you.(p.348)
• *Why* don't you join it?"(p.349)
• *Why* don't you go home and get the Big Book and open it at page fifty-eight and see what it says?"(p.349)
• *Why* should this happen to me -- hadn't I provided a good home -- wasn't I making a good living -- didn't I just get a substantial raise that had put me in the upper bracket class?(p.362)
• But for some reason -- she just didn't know *why* -- she just had to hold onto that clipping, with its thin hope.(p.367)
• *Why* did I want increasingly greater quantities of alcohol?(p.374)
• The *why* is not important; the fact is that one drink will set up a reaction in our system which requires more; that one drink was too much and one hundred drinks were not enough.(p.380)
• If we do a good job of living today, and if tomorrow comes for us, then the chances are we will do a good job when it arrives -- so *why* worry about it?(p.382)
• I wish I could tell you how and *why* A.A. works, but I don't know.(p.384)
• So finally, he said to me one morning, "Esther, *why* do you do this?"(p.386)
• I said, "Well, I don't know *why*."(p.387)
• I could see no reason *why* they should have any relationship to this problem of getting drunk every now and then.(p.388)
• So, as I have said, I don't know how or *why* A.A. works.(p.392)
• *Why* had I done it?(p.406)
• *Why*?(p.406)
• I was afraid to think *why*.(p.406)
• *Why* did I have to have at least three cocktails to sit through dinner?(p.406)
• Or: If I'm really a genius, I must produce a great work, to show *why* I act like a genius.(p.408)
• One day soon, the analyses would reveal *why* I drank and how to stop.(p.408)
• She, more than the others, showed me what ailed me basically, *why* I was immature and insecure.(p.409)
• "*Why* don't you just go down and see Mr. W.?" she asked.(p.412)
• *Why*?(p.415)
• *Why* am I alive, free, a respected member of my community?(p.421)
• "Do you know *why* you're in here?" he queried.(p.423)
• I could tell him a lot of reasons *why* I am here in an alky ward at the age of twenty.(p.423)
• I don't know *why* I didn't fall out of the open cockpit of some of those planes I flew in while taking aerial pictures.(p.426)
• *Why* I wasn't killed or how I got home I don't know.(p.429)
• I thought, "If this is A.A. *why* not go back to drinking, kill myself with booze in the next three years the doctor had given me, and call it a bad job?"(p.430)
• I used to think, "*Why* live without whiskey?"(p.430)
• "Then *why* in God's name haven't you told me so, during all these years?"(p.436)
• *Why* don't you admit it?"(p.439)
• *Why* don't you admit it?"(p.439)
• *Why* don't you admit you hate me?"(p.439)
• All I want to know is, *why* does that dog wet in my lap every time I hold him?"(p.440)
• I'd think, "I wonder *why* I'm saying that again -- I've already said it three times."(p.442)
• As a result, he couldn't figure out *why* I had the convulsions, and he decided to send me to the Mayo Clinic.(p.444)
• This time I didn't put up any fight because I knew *why* they were there and where I was going, the psychopathic ward of the City Hospital, where I had been once before.(p.468)
• You may wonder *why*, since I was having all this trouble, and was having to seek the assistance of others, A.A. hadn't come into the picture.(p.469)
• The same doctor who had sent me to the psycho had asked my husband, "*Why* don't you send her to this Alcoholics Anonymous?"(p.469)
• *Why* did it work for me when all other agencies had failed?(p.470)
• That was enough provocation to fight but I didn't fight, and I realized after recess *why* I didn't.(p.484)
• He started telling me how much trouble he had, and I said to myself, "I wonder *why* this guy is telling me all his troubles.(p.494)
• *Why*, I wasn't even ashamed of my skinny legs!(p.498)
• *Why* has God left me?(p.506)
• That's *why* we have these slogans.(p.516)
• It was their open night meeting, but of course I thought they were all alcoholics; I couldn't imagine *why* anybody else would want to go there, and my first reaction was, well, I've come to something that's not for me.(p.524)
• That's *why* I drank.(p.554)

wide

• Another reason for the *wide* acceptance of A.A. was the ministration of friends -- friends in medicine, religion, and the press, together with innumerable others who became our able and persistent advocates.(p.xx)
• In our personal stories you will find a *wide* variation in the way each teller approaches and conceives of the Power which is greater than himself.(p.50)
• I really worked for several weeks, and having had a fairly *wide* acquaintance with the dealer trade, it was not difficult for me to line up enough of them to give me a very substantial volume of business with a minimum of effort.(p.300)
• I screamed on the telephone for my mother to get up there; something was going to happen; I didn't know what, but if she didn't get there quick, I'd split *wide* open.(p.338)
• I thought that was bad until I hit the hole at a prison camp; it was just *wide* enough and long enough to lie down in.(p.459)

widely

• Though none of these principles had the force of rules or laws, they had become so *widely* accepted by 1950 that they were confirmed by our first International Conference held at Cleveland.(p.xix)
• Neither does A.A. take any particular medical point of view, though we cooperate *widely* with the men of medicine as well as with the men of religion.(p.xx)

widen

• The details of the long road back to something resembling normal living -- the first short streetcar ride, the purchase of a used bike which enabled me to *widen* the narrow horizon of life, the first trip downtown -- I will not dwell on.(p.276)

widened

• This *widened* the scope of my activities.(p.276)
• Of course, the more I drank, the more unrealistic my expectations became and the poorer my performance, and the gap *widened*.(p.557)

widening

• Each day my friend's simple talk in our kitchen multiplies itself in a *widening* circle of peace on earth and good will to men.(p.16)

wider

• Surveys of groups in the United States and Canada indicate that A.A. is reaching out, not only to more and more people, but to a *wider* and *wider* range.(p.xxii)
• My work with other alcoholics has led me, day by day, into ever *wider* and richer experiences.(p.394)

widespread

• His action met *widespread* approval, and today his is one of the most trusted citizens of his town.(p.80)

widow

• My wife, a sister member in A.A., had been a *widow* nine years and I had been single eighteen years.(p.286)

wife

• Though my drinking was not yet continuous, it disturbed my *wife*.(p.2)
• Living modestly, my *wife* and I saved $1,000.(p.2)
• I failed to persuade my broker friends to send me out looking over factories and managements, but my *wife* and I decided to go anyway.(p.2)
• There had been no real infidelity, for loyalty to my *wife*, helped at times by extreme drunkenness, kept me out of those scrapes.(p.3)
• We went at once to the country, my *wife* to applaud while I started out to overtake Walter Hagen.(p.3)
• My *wife* began to work in a department store, coming home exhausted to find me drunk.(p.4)
• The house was taken over by the mortgage holder, my mother-in-law died, and my *wife* and father-in-law became ill.(p.5)
• Before then, I had written lots of sweet promises, but my *wife* happily observed that this time I meant business.(p.5)
• There were flights from city to country and back, as my *wife* and I sought escape.(p.6)
• My weary and despairing *wife* was informed that it would all end with heart failure during delirium tremens, or I would develop a wet brain, perhaps within a year.(p.7)
• I thought of my poor *wife*.(p.8)
• My *wife* was at work.(p.8)
• My *wife* and I abandoned ourselves with enthusiasm to the idea of helping other alcoholics to a solution of their problems.(p.15)
• This man has a charming *wife* and family.(p.35)
• Finally, he can no longer work, his *wife* gets a divorce and he is held up to ridicule.(p.38)
• I have a shadowy recollection of being in an airplane bound for New York, and of finding a friendly taxicab driver at the landing field instead of my *wife*.(p.41)
• We found it very desirable to take this spiritual step with an understanding person, such as our *wife*, best friend or spiritual adviser.(p.63)
• His attention to my *wife*.(p.65)
• Told my *wife* of my mistress.(p.65)
• My *wife*(p.65)
• Notice that the word "fear" is bracketed alongside the difficulties with Mr. Brown, Mrs. Jones, the employer, and the *wife*.(p.67)
• Because of resentment and drinking, he had not paid alimony to his first *wife*.(p.79)
• We suggested he write his first *wife* admitting his faults and asking forgiveness.(p.79)
• After consulting with his *wife* and partner he came to the conclusion that it was better to take those risks than to stand before his Creator guilty of such ruinous slander.(p.80)
• After a few years with an alcoholic, a *wife* gets worn out, resentful and uncommunicative.(p.81)

- If we are sure our *wife* does not know, should we tell her?(p.81)
- It is as good for the *wife* as for the husband.(p.81)
- But he is yet a long way from making good to the *wife* or parents whom for years he has so shockingly treated.(p.82)
- To his *wife*, he remarked, "Don't see anything the matter here, Ma.(p.82)
- If there is any indication that he wants to stop, have a good talk with the person most interested in him -- usually his *wife*.(p.90)
- He should not be pushed or prodded by you, his *wife*, or his friends.(p.95)
- Your *wife* may sometimes say she is neglected.(p.97)
- Some of us have taken very hard knocks to learn this truth: Job or no job – *wife* or no *wife* -- we simply do not stop drinking so long as we place dependence upon other people ahead of dependence on God.(p.98)
- The *wife* should fully understand his new way of life.(p.99)
- In some cases the *wife* will never come back for one reason or another.(p.99)
- The story of how you and your *wife* settled your difficulties is worth any amount of criticism.(p.100)
- But for every man who drinks others are involved -- the *wife* who trembles in fear of the next debauch; the mother and father who see their son wasting away.(p.104)
- Meanwhile you might try to help the *wife* of another serious drinker.(p.112)
- It is probably true that you and your husband have been living too much alone, for drinking many times isolates the *wife* of an alcoholic.(p.119)
- Our women folk have suggested certain attitudes a *wife* may take with the husband who is recovering.(p.122)
- The alcoholic, his *wife*, his children, his "in-laws," each one is likely to have fixed ideas about the family's attitude toward himself or herself.(p.122)
- A doctor said to us, "Years of living with an alcoholic is almost sure to make any *wife* or child neurotic.(p.122)
- For example, we know of situations in which the alcoholic or his *wife* have had love affairs.(p.124)
- Nothing will help the man who is off on a spiritual tangent so much as the *wife* who adopts a sane spiritual program, making a better practical use of it.(p.130)
- Seeing this, and meaning to be helpful, his *wife* commenced to admonish him about it.(p.135)
- His *wife* is one of those persons who really feels there is something rather sinful about these commodities, so she nagged, and her intolerance finally threw him into a fit of anger.(p.135)
- Though he is now a most effective member of Alcoholics Anonymous, he still smokes and drinks coffee, but neither his *wife* or anyone else stands in judgment.(p.135)
- When his *wife* next calls saying he is sick, you might jump to the conclusion he is drunk.(p.146)
- It was the usual situation: home in jeopardy, *wife* ill, children distracted, bills in arrears and standing damaged.(p.155)
- His *wife* came, scarcely daring to be hopeful, though she thought she saw something different about her husband already.(p.158)
- One man and his *wife* placed their large home at the disposal of this strangely assorted crowd.(p.160)
- Many a distracted *wife* has visited this house to find loving and understanding companionship among women who knew her problem, to hear from the lips of their husbands what had happened to them, to be advised how her own wayward mate might be hospitalized and approached when next he stumbled.(p.160)
- He and his *wife* would leave elated by the thought of what they could now do for some stricken acquaintance and his family.(p.160)
- If my *wife* was planning to go out in the afternoon, I would get a large supply of liquor and smuggle it home and hide it in the coal bin, the clothes chute, over door jambs, over beams in the cellar and in cracks in the cellar tile.(p.176)
- I found out later that my *wife* inspected it frequently.(p.176)
- This worked nicely until my *wife* and I went to see Wallace Beery in "Tugboat Annie," after which the pant-leg and stocking racket were out!(p.177)
- We could not be invited out because I would surely get tight and my *wife* dared not invite people in for the same reason.(p.177)
- I used to promise my *wife*, my friends, and my children that I would drink no more – promises which seldom kept me sober even through the day, though I was very sincere when I made them.(p.177)
- So I filled the cellar full, with the permission of my good *wife*.(p.177)
- My *wife* became deeply interested and it was her interest that sustained mine, though I at no time sensed that it might be an answer to my liquor problem.(p.178)
- How my *wife* kept her faith and courage during all those years, I'll never know, but she did.(p.178)
- About this time a lady called up my *wife* one Saturday afternoon, saying she wanted me to come over that evening to meet a friend of hers who might help me.(p.179)
- Wishing to be polite, though I felt very badly, I said, "Let's make the call," and extracted from my *wife* a promise that we would not stay over fifteen minutes.(p.179)
- These good people notified my *wife*, who sent my newly made friend over to get me.(p.179)
- My *wife*, a Kentucky girl, came with me to Akron where I completed my course in law at the Akron Law School.(p.182)
- My *wife* and I belonged to some bridge clubs and they began to make wine and serve it.(p.184)
- I was moved into another room that morning and there was my *wife*.(p.184)
- I said, "Yes, Doc, I would like to quit, at least for five, six, or eight months, until I get things straightened up, and begin to get the respect of my *wife* and some other people back, and get my finances fixed up and so on."(p.187)
- Looking in later we found Bill with his *wife*, Henrietta.(p.189)
- Before our visit was over, Bill suddenly turned to his *wife* and said, "Go fetch my clothes, dear.(p.189)
- I spent most of my time trying to get back these friendships, and to make some recompense towards my *wife*, whom I had hurt a lot.(p.191)
- I know there was even more, something that I hadn't got, and I remember one day, a week or two after I had come out of the hospital, Bill was over to my house talking to my *wife* and me.(p.191)
- Bill looked across at my *wife*, and said to her, "Henrietta, the Lord has been so wonderful to me, curing me of this terrible disease, that I just want to keep talking about it and telling people."(p.191)
- I was a very young married man, having his whiskey in the cupboard over the sink, and when I helped my *wife* with the dishes at night I would take a cup of tea and spike it with whiskey.(p.196)
- As far as my home was concerned, I did not see then, though of course I can see now, that it was anything but a happy situation for my *wife*.(p.215)
- It was not known to me as a group, but I later learned that my *wife* had known about it for nine months and had prayed constantly that I would stumble into Akron some way or another.(p.215)
- So the story of my introduction into A.A. begins with the activities of my *wife*.(p.216)
- My *wife* didn't tell me this, but one Sunday afternoon when Mary was trying to get the cobwebs out of my mind, Clarence and his sister-in-law, the hairdresser, called at the house.(p.216)
- The next morning, my *wife* came into my room and wakened me and said, "That man is downstairs and he said you said you'd go to Akron."(p.217)
- My *wife* upbraided me often and plenty when she saw that my "periodics" were gradually losing me what business I could get.(p.233)
- My *wife* wrote away for advertised cures for the liquor habit and gave them to me in coffee.(p.235)
- First, my new *wife* had walked out, bag, baggage and furniture; then the apartment landlord had thrown me out of the empty apartment and the finish was the loss of another job.(p.238)
- After the oil job blew up, I went back to Baltimore and mother, my first *wife* having said a permanent "Goodbye."(p.243)
- My *wife* traveled with me, but with a baby coming I decided to settle in a large city where I got a job with a commission agent which is a polite term for a handbook operator.(p.251)
- Saying goodbye to my *wife* and baby, I was treading Manhattan's streets in a little more than a week.(p.252)
- My *wife* came over from Scotland and we started housekeeping in a large Ohio city.(p.254)
- My *wife* made several attempts to get me to stop and I had the usual visits from persons who would always ask me "Why?" -- as if I knew!(p.254)
- I arrived drunk, but I promised my *wife* I would keep sober, and I knew I could get work if I did.(p.256)
- My *wife* and family stood by me for ten weeks and then, quite justifiably, ejected me.(p.257)
- That night I was taken home by a former alcoholic and his *wife*.(p.259)
- Instead, over coffee cups, this man and his *wife* told me what had been done for them.(p.259)
- He talked about his *wife* taking his little boy away from him because of his drinking, and how he got back together with them through A.A., and we began feeling grateful right then that all these things hadn't been taken from us.(p.270)
- The next morning his *wife* came dragging him in before Russ went to work, while I was getting breakfast.(p.271)
- His *wife* was cussing him, raving at him, "I just brought him over to show you what kind of a guy he is!(p.271)
- At least three of those four years must have been a living hell for my *wife*, because she had to watch the man she loved disintegrate morally, mentally and financially.(p.277)
- When I got out of the hospital, I was invited to stay with Dr. Bob and his dear *wife*, Anne.(p.279)
- So six months ago I acquired a ready made family consisting of one charming *wife*, four grown children to whom I am devoted, and three grandchildren.(p.286)
- My *wife*, a sister member in A.A., had been a widow nine years and I had been single eighteen years.(p.286)
- That same year, my *wife* became fed up with my drinking around the house and called my dad in Akron to come and pick me up.(p.288)
- My *wife* could not understand why I would sober up for dad but not for her.(p.288)
- One time my *wife* decided to try this too.(p.288)
- On my ride to the nearest bar, I sold the driver on how misunderstood I was by my *wife* and what an unreasonable person she was.(p.288)
- My *wife* could not understand the next morning why I was drunker than the night before when she took my bottles.(p.289)
- A few months after I made my original trip to Akron I was feeling pretty cocky, and I didn't think my *wife* was treating me with proper respect, now that I was an outstanding citizen.(p.293)
- My *wife* became pregnant and the doctor recommended the use of port or ale . . . so . . . I bought a six gallon crock and a few bottles, listened to advice from amateur brewmeisters, and was off on my beer manufacturing career on a small scale (for the time being).(p.297)
- Somehow or other, I must have misunderstood the doctor's instructions, for I not only made the beer for my *wife*, I also drank it for her.(p.297)
- If I were alone I would stop at four or five of them, but only one or two in the event I had my mistrusting *wife* with me.(p.299)
- (That condition was a distinct handicap to me in trying to vindicate myself with the not so patient *wife*.)(p.301)
- After holding good positions, making better than an average income for over ten years, I was in debt, had no clothes to speak of, no money, no friends, and no one any longer tolerating me but my *wife*.(p.301)
- Just at this time my *wife* heard of a doctor in another city who had been very successful with drunks.(p.301)
- My *wife* accompanied me on my visit and the doctor really told me some things that in my state of jitters nearly knocked me out of the chair.(p.302)
- My *wife* is glad to see me come in.(p.303)
- I still had a *wife* and family, a home and a car, my driver's license, and a proper amount of insurance.(p.327)
- (My addiction bloomed within a small apartment I shared with my *wife*, a heart patient.)(p.329)
- Not wishing to disturb my *wife*, I slumped in a big red-leather chair and suffered.(p.332)
- I was gathering that cache for disposal when my *wife* woke up and caught me at it.(p.333)
- Three years and three months of sobriety, without a slip, has meant a lot to me, my *wife*, and my family.(p.342)
- Eight years ago, my *wife* and I decided to spend a vacation in Naini Tal, the mountain resort.(p.343)
- At Christmastime next year, I convinced my *wife* that I had alcohol under control and that I would do controlled drinking over Christmas and the New Year.(p.343)
- I went on the wagon more to placate my *wife* than anything else.(p.344)
- My *wife* never hinted that she would leave me.(p.345)
- On the last day I was drinking I went up to see a friend who had had a good deal of trouble with alcohol, and whose *wife* had left him a number of times.(p.346)

- This friend gave me a pamphlet, and I took it home and had my ***wife*** read it to me.(p.346)
- After my ***wife*** had read this to me, I said to her, as I had said many times in desperation, "I have got to do something."(p.346)
- She was doing fine, she was up and around, and that day her husband phoned me and said, "Doctor, thanks very much for curing my ***wife***," and I thanked him for his felicitations, and he hung up.(p.350)
- And then I scratched my head and said to myself, "What a fantastic thing for a man to say, that I cured his ***wife***.(p.350)
- I am not even there, and if I was there the only thing I could do would be to give her moral support, and yet he thanks me for curing his ***wife***."(p.350)
- So I went to my ***wife*** and asked her, wasn't there something that she and I could do to somehow get together, and she turned on her heel and looked me squarely in the eye, and said, "You don't care anything about my problem," and I could have smacked her, but I said to myself, "Grab on to your serenity!"(p.351)
- But I remembered that every night after dinner my ***wife*** would get up and do the dishes.(p.351)
- All I can remember about the Roaring Twenties is that I drank a great deal, thought I was having a grand time, managed to get to Europe for a few weeks, was very proud of the dozens of speak-easy cards entitling me to an entree in the better joints between Cleveland and New York, took on a ***wife***, and built a home in a fashionable suburb of Cleveland.(p.358)
- High living, a great many fair weather friends, the 1929 stock market crash, and a couple of years of Depression, soon relieved me one by one of my worldly goods including my ***wife***.(p.358)
- It was to be short lived, for on the day before Christmas I completely disillusioned my ***wife*** and ruined our first Christmas by coming home from the Rotary lunch dead drunk.(p.361)
- My wonderful ***wife*** did everything to play along with me.(p.361)
- On more than one occasion my ***wife*** would threaten to leave me.(p.362)
- In the very early spring of 1944, my frustrated ***wife*** couldn't take it any longer.(p.362)
- I had given her everything a ***wife*** could ask for.(p.362)
- Looking directly at me was a large oil painting of my ***wife***, and her very words seemed to shout at me -- "I am not leaving you because I don't love you; it's because I do love you.(p.363)
- After a few meetings I decided to drive to Florida unannounced to see my ***wife*** and tell her about my new found friends and association.(p.364)
- I had not only let my ***wife*** down but also a lot of other wonderful people who had helped me.(p.364)
- It was worrying my ***wife*** a little, but she had the good sense not to take me to task about it or goad me into going.(p.364)
- I had just raised the bottle to my lips when my ***wife*** opened the door and froze me completely in my tracks with "Happy New Year, dear."(p.365)
- One night at the dinner table my ***wife*** said that tonight was my first birthday in A.A., and that the group would have the usual ice cream and cake for the "one year man."(p.365)
- I had no trouble making the right decision when I saw my ***wife*** open her purse at the meeting that night and deposit a cute little angel in the middle of my birthday cake.(p.366)
- While I was in Florida trying to convince my ***wife*** with all the A.A. literature that she should come back to me, she went over to her desk and picked up a clipping she had taken from the St. Petersburg Times about A.A.(p.366)
- There, I could be a proper mother and ***wife*** while drinking up a storm.(p.369)
- With that, he told me to leave, because I was unfit as a mother, a ***wife***, and a laundress.(p.371)
- It seemed to me my ***wife*** was becoming more intolerant and narrow minded all the time.(p.376)
- Two years before I joined A.A. my ***wife*** took a long trip during which she wrote me she just couldn't return unless I did something about my drinking.(p.377)
- The glittering society belle, the modern Shakespeare, the happy ***wife***, the loving and beloved.(p.411)
- I had a lovely ***wife*** and three children.(p.418)
- My ***wife*** was in the Junior League, and I was on the board of directors of the local center for the mentally retarded.(p.418)
- In less than two years, I lost my practice, my home, my ***wife***, and my children.(p.418)
- The last time I drank, when I was twenty-nine, I drank for only four days, yet I threatened to kill my children; I beat my ***wife*** at home and on the church steps; I mistreated a child in my office; and I ran to a hospital for mental illness to avoid jail.(p.418)
- My life there was a nightmare of periodic binges on alcohol and pills, adultery, unhappy hours at the dental office, seeing my ***wife*** give birth to our second child and have several miscarriages, living in a turbulent household, and making continual attempts to be the respectable dentist, husband, father, and community leader.(p.419)
- After I came to A.A., I was divorced by my ***wife***; I lost my practice; I was legally restrained from seeing my children; I went broke; and the dental society threatened me with the loss of my license.(p.420)
- A.A. has given me a new ***wife***, a beautiful stepdaughter, a new practice, a new home, and a new relationship with my four children.(p.420)
- My second ***wife*** is a young A.A. member, too, and what a terrific adventure this is for us!(p.420)
- I have a lovely ***wife*** who understands my problem and helps me with it.(p.431)
- My ***wife*** loved to drink, and we tied on many a hooter in the name of marital bliss.(p.433)
- After a particularly ugly one-nighter, my ***wife*** suggested I try it, and I agreed.(p.434)
- My alcoholic ***wife*** took up someone else, divorced me, and took with her all my remaining property.(p.437)
- My new ***wife*** and I don't own any property to speak of, and the flashy successes of another day are no longer mine.(p.438)
- "If you had my ***wife***, you'd drink, too."(p.439)
- I didn't feel I could lie in bed and squirt the stuff in my veins while my kids and ***wife*** stood around watching me, so I kept the drug in my bag and the bag in the car and the car in the garage.(p.442)
- For my seventh A.A. birthday, my program-oriented, Al-Anon ***wife*** had my moccasins bronzed.(p.445)
- But then, as I drank more and more, the alcohol seemed to affect my vision: Instead of continuing to see what was good about my ***wife***, I began to see her defects.(p.450)
- It seems I should have learned to love my ***wife*** and family first; the newcomer to A.A., last.(p.451)
- He and his ***wife*** more than accepted me; he listened to all my woes; both of them treated me as a human being.(p.462)
- Things went from bad to worse, and since I had finally and completely failed at the job of being a ***wife*** and a mother, my marriage ended.(p.468)
- My ***wife*** and I have been married for some thirty years now.(p.485)
- This man's ***wife*** had been suffering for a couple of months and when he came in he owed me a little bill.(p.488)
- You know the prescription that you gave me for my ***wife*** last night."(p.488)
- The next morning I carried another prescription to this man's house and exchanged it for the bottle his ***wife*** had.(p.489)
- Then I said to my ***wife***, "Something has to be done."(p.489)
- My ***wife*** received me graciously, although she was living in a one room with kitchen affair.(p.490)
- Anyhow, on the 24th, after drinking all day on the 23rd, I must have decided I wanted to see my ***wife*** and have some kind of reconciliation or at least talk with her.(p.491)
- Around eight or nine o'clock there came two big detectives and a policeman to arrest me for assault; and I was the most amazed person in the world when they said I had assaulted someone, and especially that I had assaulted my ***wife***.(p.492)
- I knew my ***wife*** didn't because I had been sincere in all my promises to her as well as to my mother and to my close friends, but the urge to take that drink was more powerful than anything else.(p.494)
- My ***wife*** and new baby are fortunately staying with relatives.(p.500)
- My ***wife*** is extremely unhappy.(p.501)
- His ***wife*** dies that night.(p.501)
- I am at the hospital to see my ***wife***.(p.501)
- I tell my ***wife*** I cannot stop drinking.(p.502)
- My ***wife*** is in the living room.(p.502)
- I think of my ***wife***.(p.505)
- My ***wife*** hears my voice and knows I have found the answer to life.(p.505)
- I have left my ***wife*** at home, sick, and I have been unkind to her in leaving.(p.505)
- I blame my ***wife*** and children.(p.505)
- I'll tell my ***wife*** what I am going to do.(p.506)
- I call my ***wife*** into a room where we can talk privately.(p.506)
- He was drinking to hold on to his job, to hold on to his ***wife***, to hold on to his sanity.(p.512)
- I was drinking to try to hold on to a job, to try and hold on to my home, to try to hold on to my ***wife***, to try to hold on to my sanity.(p.514)
- When I awoke in the middle of the night with shakes and sweats and fears, I would hear my ***wife*** weeping quietly in bed beside me.(p.558)
- Hopeless now, I felt it would be better for my ***wife***, my children, and everyone in my life if I went ahead and died.(p.558)
- The relationship between my ***wife*** and me was restored to a love and happiness that we had not known even before my alcoholism became acute.(p.559)

wife's

- We went to live with my ***wife's*** parents.(p.4)
- Nevertheless, I still thought I could control the situation, and there were periods of sobriety which renewed my ***wife's*** hope.(p.5)
- Sometimes I stole from my ***wife's*** slender purse when the morning terror and madness were on me.(p.6)
- About two days later I was called by a friend of mine from Nevada City -- he's a brother of my ***wife's*** closest friend.(p.347)
- This man faced the last ditch when his ***wife's*** voice from 1,300 miles away sent him to A.A.(p.356)
- The final decision came when my daughter, following a drunk which ruined my ***wife's*** birthday, said, "It's Alcoholics Anonymous -- or else!"(p.378)
- I can again focus on my ***wife's*** good qualities and watch them grow and grow and grow.(p.451)
- My ***wife's*** parents come to our assistance.(p.501)
- We are staying with my ***wife's*** father.(p.501)
- For instance, the fiftieth wedding anniversary of my ***wife's*** parents was the occasion for a huge family reunion at our home.(p.556)
- Despite my ***wife's*** entreaties to take it easy that day, I arrived home in bad shape.(p.557)

wild

- If she knows in a general way that we have been ***wild***, should we tell her in detail?(p.81)
- Although, during this period I was not addicted to any pattern of alcohol consumption, when I did drink the drinking was pretty ***wild***.(p.212)
- It was all about Scott Fitzgerald's little lost debutante, abused, misunderstood and running ***wild***.(p.402)
- I had met a bunch of gay young Bohemians who lived in the Village, and were sowing their ***wild*** oats.(p.407)
- Or maybe I'd come home ***wild*** drunk, singing and raving about what a fine place home was and what grand parents I had since they joined A.A.(p.428)

wildest

- Never in my ***wildest*** moments had it occurred to me that I might like to be an alcoholic.(p.439)

wildly

- I would get ***wildly*** excited and look forward to another night of drinking.(p.408)

will

- For them, we hope these pages ***will*** prove so convincing that no further authentication ***will*** be necessary.(p.xiii)
- We think this account of our experiences ***will*** help everyone to better understand the alcoholic.(p.xiii)
- Inquiry by scientific, medical, and religious societies ***will*** be welcomed.(p.xiv)
- Our earliest printing voiced the hope "that every alcoholic who journeys ***will*** find the Fellowship of Alcoholics Anonymous at his destination.(p.xv)
- Some of the recommendations of A.A.'s early medical and religious friends ***will*** be found further on in this book.(p.xx)
- Yet it is our great hope that all those who have as yet found no answer may begin to find one in the pages of this book and ***will*** presently join us on the highroad to a new freedom.(p.xxi)
- We of Alcoholics Anonymous believe that the reader ***will*** be interested in the medical estimate of the plan of recovery described in this book.(p.xxiii)
- If any feel that as psychiatrists directing a hospital for alcoholics we appear somewhat sentimental, let them stand with us a while on the firing line, see the tragedies, the despairing wives, the little children; let the solving of these problems become a part of their daily work, and even of their sleeping moments, and the most cynical ***will*** not wonder that we have accepted and encouraged this movement.(p.xxvi)
- Following his physical rehabilitation, he had a talk with me in which he frankly stated he thought the

treatment a waste of effort, unless I could assure him, which no one ever had, that in the future he would have the "*will* power" to resist the impulse to drink.(p.xxix)
• It relieved me somewhat to learn that in alcoholics the *will* is amazingly weakened when it comes to combating liquor, though it often remains strong in other respects.(p.7)
• His human *will* had failed.(p.11)
• Each day my friend's simple talk in our kitchen multiplies itself in a widening circle of peace on earth and good *will* to men.(p.16)
• We hope this volume *will* inform and comfort those who are, or who may be affected.(p.18)
• If we keep on the way we are going there is little doubt that much good *will* result, but the surface of the problem would hardly be scratched.(p.19)
• Of necessity there *will* have to be discussion of matters medical, psychiatric, social, and religious.(p.19)
• "His *will* power must be weak."(p.20)
• What has become of the common sense and *will* power that he still sometimes displays with respect to other matters?(p.22)
• Perhaps there never *will* be a full answer to these questions.(p.22)
• The experience of any alcoholic *will* abundantly confirm this.(p.23)
• If you ask him why he started on that last bender, the chances are he *will* offer you any one of a hundred alibis.(p.23)
• If you draw this fallacious reasoning to the attention of an alcoholic, he *will* laugh it off, or become irritated and refuse to talk.(p.23)
• There is the obsession that somehow, someday, they *will* beat the game.(p.23)
• In a vague way their families and friends sense that these drinkers are abnormal, but everybody hopefully awaits the day when the sufferer *will* rouse himself from his lethargy and assert his power of *will*.(p.23)
• Our so-called *will* power becomes practically nonexistent.(p.24)
• Those having religious affiliations *will* find here nothing disturbing to their beliefs or ceremonies.(p.28)
• We hope no one *will* consider these self-revealing accounts in bad taste.(p.29)
• Our hope is that many alcoholic men and women, desperately in need, *will* see these pages, and we believe that it is only by fully disclosing ourselves and our problems that they *will* be persuaded to say, "Yes, I am one of them too; I must have this thing."(p.29)
• The idea that somehow, someday he *will* control and enjoy his drinking is the great obsession of every abnormal drinker.(p.30)
• Neither does there appear to be any kind of treatment which *will* make alcoholics of our kind like other men.(p.30)
• By every form of self-deception and experimentation, they *will* try to prove themselves exceptions to the rule, therefore nonalcoholic.(p.31)
• It *will* not take long for you to decide if you are honest with yourself about it.(p.32)
• If we are planning to stop drinking, there must be no reservation of any kind, nor any lurking notion that someday we *will* be immune to alcohol.(p.33)
• Young people may be encouraged by this man's experience to think that they can stop, as he did, on their own *will* power.(p.33)
• We doubt if many of them can do it, because none *will* really want to stop, and hardly one of them, because of the peculiar mental twist already acquired, *will* find he can win out.(p.33)
• As we look back, we feel we had gone on drinking many years beyond the point where we could quit on our *will* power.(p.34)
• We think few, to whom this book *will* appeal, can stay dry anything like a year.(p.34)
• Some *will* be drunk the day after making their resolutions; most of them within a few weeks.(p.34)
• Whether such a person can quit upon a nonspiritual basis depends upon the extent to which he has already lost the power to choose whether he *will* drink or not.(p.34)
• The experiment of quitting for a period of time *will* be helpful, but we think we can render an even greater service to alcoholic sufferers and perhaps to the medical fraternity.(p.34)
• But the actual or potential alcoholic, with hardly an exception, *will* be absolutely unable to stop drinking on the basis of self-knowledge.(p.39)
• I felt I had every right to be self-confident, that it would be only a matter of exercising my *will* power and keeping on guard.(p.40)
• I saw that *will* power and self-knowledge would not help in those strange mental blank spots.(p.42)
• If that be the case, you may be suffering from an illness which only a spiritual experience *will* conquer.(p.44)
• We could wish to be moral, we could wish to be philosophically comforted, in fact, we could *will* these things with all our might, but the needed power wasn't there.(p.45)
• Our human resources, as marshalled by the *will* were not sufficient; they failed utterly.(p.45)
• Its main object is to enable you to find a Power greater than yourself which *will* solve your problem.(p.45)
• Sometimes this was a tedious process; we hope no one else *will* be prejudiced for as long as some of us were.(p.48)
• In our personal stories you *will* find a wide variation in the way each teller approaches and conceives of the Power which is greater than himself.(p.50)
• Show any longshoreman a Sunday supplement describing a proposal to explore the moon by means of a rocket and he *will* say, "I bet they do it -- maybe not so long either."(p.52)
• In this book you *will* read the experience of a man who thought he was an atheist.(p.55)
• Those who do not recover are people who cannot or *will* not completely give themselves to this simple program, usually men and women who are constitutionally incapable of being honest with themselves.(p.58)
• 3.Made a decision to turn our *will* and our lives over to the care of God as we understood Him.(p.59)
• 11.Sought through prayer and meditation to improve our conscious contact with God as we understood Him, praying only for knowledge of His *will* for us and the power to carry that out.(p.59)
• Being convinced, we were at Step Three, which is that we decided to turn our *will* and our life over to God as we understood Him.(p.60)
• Relieve me of the bondage of self, that I may better do Thy *will*.(p.63)
• May I do Thy *will* always!"(p.63)
• Thy *will* be done."(p.67)
• We cannot be helpful to all people, but at least God *will* show us how to take a kindly and tolerant view of each and every one.(p.67)
• The right answer *will* come, if we want it.(p.69)
• If we are sorry for what we have done, and have the honest desire to let God take us to better things, we believe we *will* be forgiven and *will* have learned our lesson.(p.70)
• We have begun to learn tolerance, patience and good *will* toward all men, even our enemies, for we look on them as sick people.(p.70)
• This requires action on our part, which, when completed, *will* mean that we have admitted to God, to ourselves, and to another human being the exact nature of our defects.(p.72)
• We *will* be more reconciled to discussing ourselves with another person when we see good reasons why we should do so.(p.72)
• He hopes they *will* never see the light of day.(p.73)
• Those of us belonging to a religious denomination which requires confession must, and of course, *will* want to go to the properly appointed authority whose duty it is to receive it.(p.74)
• Perhaps our doctor or psychologist *will* be the person.(p.74)
• It may be one of our own family, but we cannot disclose anything to our wives or our parents which *will* hurt them and make them unhappy.(p.74)
• Such parts of our story we tell to someone who *will* understand, yet be unaffected.(p.74)
• It is important that he be able to keep a confidence; that he fully understand and approve what we are driving at; that he *will* not try to change our plan.(p.74)
• Most people approached in this way *will* be glad to help; they *will* be honored by our confidence.(p.75)
• The feeling that the drink problem has disappeared *will* often come strongly.(p.75)
• If we still cling to something we *will* not let go, we ask God to help us be willing.(p.76)
• If we haven't the *will* to do this, we ask until it comes.(p.76)
• He is going to be more interested in a demonstration of good *will* than in our talk of spiritual discoveries.(p.77)
• When it *will* serve any good purpose, we are willing to announce our convictions with tact and common sense.(p.77)
• The question of how to approach the man we hated *will* arise.(p.77)
• Simply we tell him that we *will* never get over drinking until we have done our utmost to straighten out the past.(p.77)
• If our manner is calm, frank, and open, we *will* be gratified with the result.(p.78)
• Occasionally, they *will* offer assistance.(p.78)
• Approached in this way, the most ruthless creditor *will* sometimes surprise us.(p.78)
• She *will* want to know who the woman is and where she is.(p.81)
• It may be that both *will* decide that the way of good sense and loving kindness is to let by-gones be by-gones.(p.82)
• Certainly he must keep sober, for there *will* be no home if he doesn't.(p.82)
• They *will* change in time.(p.83)
• Our behavior *will* convince them more than our words.(p.83)
• If we are painstaking about this phase of our development, we *will* be amazed before we are half way through.(p.83)
• We *will* not regret the past nor wish to shut the door on it.(p.83)
• We *will* comprehend the word serenity and we *will* know peace.(p.83)
• No matter how far down the scale we have gone, we *will* see how our experience can benefit others.(p.84)
• That feeling of uselessness and self-pity *will* disappear.(p.84)
• We *will* lose interest in selfish things and gain interest in our fellows.(p.84)
• Self-seeking *will* slip away.(p.84)
• Our whole attitude and outlook upon life *will* change.(p.84)
• Fear of people and of economic insecurity *will* leave us.(p.84)
• We *will* intuitively know how to handle situations which used to baffle us.(p.84)
• We *will* suddenly realize that God is doing for us what we could not do for ourselves.(p.84)
• They *will* always materialize if we work for them.(p.84)
• For by this time sanity *will* have returned.(p.84)
• We *will* seldom be interested in liquor.(p.84)
• We react sanely and normally, and we *will* find that this has happened automatically.(p.84)
• We *will* see that our new attitude toward liquor has been given us without any thought or effort on our part.(p.85)
• Every day is a day when we must carry the vision of God's *will* into all of our activities.(p.85)
• "How can I best serve Thee – Thy *will* (not mine) be done."(p.85)
• We can exercise our *will* power along this line all we wish.(p.85)
• It is the proper use of the *will*.(p.85)
• Our thought-life *will* be placed on a much higher plane when our thinking is cleared of wrong motives.(p.86)
• Nevertheless, we find that our thinking *will* as time passes, be more and more on the plane of inspiration.(p.87)
• We may ask for ourselves, however, if others *will* be helped.(p.87)
• We constantly remind ourselves we are no longer running the show, humbly saying to ourselves many times each day "Thy *will* be done."(p.87)
• Practical experience shows that nothing *will* so much insure immunity from drinking as intensive work with other alcoholics.(p.89)
• Life *will* take on new meaning.(p.89)
• We know you *will* not want to miss it.(p.89)
• They *will* be only too glad to assist you.(p.89)
• You *will* be handicapped if you arouse it.(p.89)
• You should be described to him as one of a fellowship who, as part of their own recovery, try to help others and who *will* be glad to talk to him if he cares to see you.(p.90)
• Let the doctor, if he *will*, tell him he has something in the way of a solution.(p.91)
• Under these conditions your prospect *will* see he is under no pressure.(p.91)
• He *will* feel he can deal with you without being nagged by his family.(p.91)
• You *will* thus get a better idea of how you ought to proceed.(p.91)
• If he is alcoholic, he *will* understand you at once.(p.92)
• He *will* match your mental inconsistencies with some of his own.(p.92)
• Show him, from your own experience, how the queer mental condition surrounding that first drink prevents normal functioning of the *will* power.(p.92)
• Doctors are rightly loath to tell alcoholic patients the

whole story unless it ***will*** serve some good purpose.(p.92)
• You ***will*** soon have your friend admitting he has many, if not all, of the traits of the alcoholic.(p.92)
• Let him ask you that question, if he ***will***.(p.93)
• But he ***will*** be curious to learn why his own convictions have not worked and why yours seem to work so well.(p.93)
• Perhaps your story ***will*** help him see where he has failed to practice the very precepts he knows so well.(p.93)
• Make it plain he is under no obligation to you, that you hope only that he ***will*** try to help other alcoholics when he escapes his own difficulties.(p.94)
• He ***will*** be more likely to follow your suggestions.(p.94)
• You ***will*** be most successful with alcoholics if you do not exhibit any passion for crusade or reform.(p.95)
• Tell him that if he wants to get well you ***will*** do anything to help.(p.95)
• We find it a waste of time to keep chasing a man who cannot or ***will*** not work with you.(p.96)
• Perhaps you ***will*** want to take the man into your home for a few days.(p.96)
• Be certain he ***will*** be welcomed by your family, and that he is not trying to impose upon you for money, connections, or shelter.(p.96)
• You ***will*** be making it possible for him to be insincere.(p.96)
• Sometimes you ***will*** have to call a doctor and administer sedatives under his direction.(p.97)
• Occasionally you ***will*** have to meet such conditions.(p.97)
• Should they accept and practice spiritual principles, there is a much better chance that the head of the family ***will*** recover.(p.97)
• And even though he continues to drink, the family ***will*** find life more bearable.(p.97)
• After they have seen tangible results, the family ***will*** perhaps want to go along.(p.99)
• These things ***will*** come to pass naturally and in good time provided, however, the alcoholic continues to demonstrate that he can be sober, considerate, and helpful, regardless of what anyone says or does.(p.99)
• When the time for living together has come, it ***will*** be apparent to both parties.(p.99)
• In some cases the wife ***will*** never come back for one reason or another.(p.99)
• If you persist, remarkable things ***will*** happen.(p.100)
• Follow the dictates of a Higher Power and you ***will*** presently live in a new and wonderful world, no matter what your present circumstances!(p.100)
• You ***will*** note that we made an important qualification.(p.101)
• Do not think of what you ***will*** get out of the occasion.(p.102)
• If you do this thoroughly, few people ***will*** ask you to drink.(p.102)
• Keep on the firing line of life with these motives and God ***will*** keep you unharmed.(p.102)
• Some day we hope that Alcoholics Anonymous ***will*** help the public to a better realization of the gravity of the alcoholic problem, but we shall be of little use if our attitude is one of bitterness or hostility.(p.103)
• Drinkers ***will*** not stand for it.(p.103)
• What they say ***will*** apply to nearly everyone bound by ties of blood or affections to an alcoholic.(p.104)
• What had become of their judgment, their common sense, their ***will*** power?(p.107)
• We realize some men are thoroughly bad-intentioned, that no amount of patience ***will*** make any difference.(p.108)
• Some ***will*** moderate or stop altogether, and some ***will*** not.(p.109)
• Of those who keep on, a good number ***will*** become true alcoholics after a while.(p.109)
• He admits this is true, but is positive that he ***will*** do better.(p.109)
• He clings to the notion that he ***will*** yet find a way to do so.(p.110)
• He ***will*** use that as an excuse to drink more.(p.111)
• He ***will*** tell you he is misunderstood.(p.111)
• We know these suggestions are sometimes difficult to follow, but you ***will*** save many a heartbreak if you can succeed in observing them.(p.111)
• If this kind of approach does not catch your husband's interest, it may be best to drop the subject, but after a friendly talk your husband ***will*** usually revive the topic himself.(p.112)
• This may take patient waiting, but it ***will*** be worth it.(p.112)
• If you think he ***will*** be shy of a spiritual remedy, ask him to look at the chapter on alcoholism.(p.112)
• Then perhaps he ***will*** be interested enough to continue.(p.113)
• If he is enthusiastic your cooperation ***will*** mean a great deal.(p.113)
• If he does not, you ***will*** probably not have long to wait.(p.113)
• Some men cannot or ***will*** not get over alcoholism.(p.114)
• If such women adopt a spiritual way of life their road ***will*** be smoother.(p.114)
• When you have carefully explained to such people that he is a sick person, you ***will*** have created a new atmosphere.(p.115)
• Barriers which have sprung up between you and your friends ***will*** disappear with the growth of sympathetic understanding.(p.115)
• You ***will*** no longer be self-conscious or feel that you must apologize as though your husband were a weak character.(p.115)
• Your new courage, good nature and lack of self-consciousness ***will*** do wonders for you socially.(p.115)
• Then that terrible tension which grips the home of every problem drinker ***will*** be lessened.(p.115)
• You may be afraid your husband ***will*** lose his position; you are thinking of the disgrace and hard times which ***will*** befall you and the children.(p.116)
• Maybe it ***will*** prove a blessing!(p.116)
• And now you know that he can stop if he ***will***!(p.116)
• We urge you to try our program, for nothing ***will*** be so helpful to your husband as the radically changed attitude toward him which God ***will*** show you how to have.(p.117)
• But all problems ***will*** not be solved at once.(p.117)
• In spite of your new-found happiness, there ***will*** be ups and downs.(p.117)
• Many of the old problems ***will*** still be with you.(p.117)
• The faith and sincerity of both you and your husband ***will*** be put to the test.(p.117)
• These work-outs should be regarded as part of your education, for thus you ***will*** be learning to live.(p.117)
• You ***will*** make mistakes, but if you are in earnest they ***will*** not drag you down.(p.117)
• Instead, you ***will*** capitalize them.(p.117)
• A better way of life ***will*** emerge when they are overcome.(p.117)
• Some of the snags you ***will*** encounter are irritation, hurt feeling and resentments.(p.117)
• Your husband ***will*** sometimes be unreasonable and you ***will*** want to criticize.(p.117)
• You and your husband ***will*** find that you can dispose of serious problems easier than you can the trivial ones.(p.118)
• If your husband is trying to live on a spiritual basis, he ***will*** also be doing everything in his power to avoid disagreement or contention.(p.118)
• Show him these things in yourself and they ***will*** be reflected back to you from him.(p.118)
• If you both show a willingness to remedy your own defects, there ***will*** be little need to criticize each other.(p.118)
• It is the most natural thing in the world, once his liquor problem is solved, to feel that he ***will*** now measure up to that cherished vision.(p.118)
• The chances are he ***will*** not for, like yourself, he is just beginning his development.(p.118)
• Your husband ***will*** be the first to say it was your devotion and care which brought him to the point where he could have a spiritual experience.(p.118)
• Sometimes he ***will*** be so interested that he becomes really neglectful.(p.119)
• It ***will*** do little good if you point that out and urge more attention for yourself.(p.119)
• If you cooperate, rather than complain, you ***will*** find that his excess enthusiasm ***will*** tone down.(p.119)
• Both of you ***will*** awaken to a new sense of responsibility for others.(p.119)
• Inevitably your lives ***will*** be fuller for doing so.(p.120)
• You ***will*** lose the old life to find one much better.(p.120)
• Perhaps your husband ***will*** make a fair start on the new basis, but just as things are going beautifully he dismays you by coming home drunk.(p.120)
• Your husband ***will*** see at once that he must redouble his spiritual activities if he expects to survive.(p.120)
• You need not remind him of his spiritual deficiency – he ***will*** know of it.(p.120)
• The slightest disposition on your part to guide his appointments or his affairs so he ***will*** not be tempted ***will*** be noticed.(p.120)
• Let families realize, as they start their journey, that all ***will*** not be fair weather.(p.122)
• There ***will*** be alluring shortcuts and by-paths down which they may wander and lose their way.(p.123)
• Suppose we tell you some of the obstacles a family ***will*** meet; suppose we suggest how they may be avoided – even converted to good use for others.(p.123)
• The good old days ***will*** soon be back, they think.(p.123)
• It ***will*** take time to clear away the wreck.(p.123)
• Though old buildings ***will*** eventually be replaced by finer ones, the new structures ***will*** take years to complete.(p.123)
• Perhaps he ***will*** never have much money again.(p.123)
• But the wise family ***will*** admire him for what he is trying to be, rather than for what he is trying to get.(p.123)
• Now and then the family ***will*** be plagued by spectres from the past, for the drinking career of almost every alcoholic has been marked by escapades, funny, humiliating, shameful or tragic.(p.123)
• The first impulse ***will*** be to bury these skeletons in a dark closet and padlock the door.(p.123)
• A man may criticize or laugh at himself and it ***will*** affect others favorably, but criticism or ridicule coming from another often produces the contrary effect.(p.125)
• At the beginning of recovery a man ***will*** take, as a rule, one of two directions.(p.125)
• In either case certain family problems ***will*** arise.(p.126)
• The family ***will*** be affected also, pleasantly at first, as they feel their money troubles are about to be solved, then not so pleasantly as they find themselves neglected.(p.126)
• If they sense these things, they ***will*** not take so seriously his periods of crankiness, depression, or apathy, which ***will*** disappear when there is tolerance, love, and spiritual understanding.(p.127)
• These family talks ***will*** be constructive if they can be carried on without heated argument, self-pity, self-justification or resentful criticism.(p.127)
• Little by little, mother and children ***will*** see they ask too much, and father ***will*** see he gives too little.(p.127)
• Giving, rather than getting, ***will*** become the guiding principle.(p.128)
• What about his talk that God ***will*** take care of them?(p.128)
• He may not see at once that he has barely scratched a limitless lode which ***will*** pay dividends only if he mines it for the rest of his life and insists on giving away the entire product.(p.129)
• If the family cooperates, dad ***will*** soon see that he is suffering from a distortion of values.(p.129)
• He ***will*** perceive that his spiritual growth is lopsided, that for an average man like himself, a spiritual life which does not include his family obligations may not be so perfect after all.(p.129)
• If the family ***will*** appreciate that dad's current behavior is but a phase of his development, all ***will*** be well.(p.129)
• In the midst of an understanding and sympathetic family, these vagaries of dad's spiritual infancy ***will*** quickly disappear.(p.129)
• During those first days of convalescence, this ***will*** do more to insure his sobriety than anything else.(p.129)
• Though some of his manifestations are alarming and disagreeable, we think dad ***will*** be on a firmer foundation than the man who is placing business or professional success ahead of spiritual development.(p.129)
• He ***will*** be less likely to drink again, and anything is preferable to that.(p.130)
• Nothing ***will*** help the man who is off on a spiritual tangent so much as the wife who adopts a sane spiritual program, making a better practical use of it.(p.130)
• There ***will*** be other profound changes in the household.(p.130)
• At the very beginning, the couple ought to frankly face the fact that each ***will*** have to yield here and there if the family is going to play an effective part in the new life.(p.131)
• Father ***will*** necessarily spend much time with other alcoholics, but this activity should be balanced.(p.131)
• Alcoholics who have derided religious people ***will*** be helped by such contacts.(p.131)

• Being possessed of a spiritual experience, the alcoholic ***will*** find he has much in common with these people, though he may differ with them on many matters.(p.131)
• If he does not argue about religion, he ***will*** make new friends and is sure to find new avenues of usefulness and pleasure.(p.132)
• In time they ***will*** see that he is a new man and in their own way they ***will*** let him know it.(p.134)
• From that point on, progress ***will*** be rapid.(p.134)
• If he has your ***will*** power and guts, he ***will*** make the grade."(p.138)
• Can you discard the feeling that you are dealing only with habit, with stubbornness, or a weak ***will***?(p.140)
• When drinking, or getting over a bout, an alcoholic, sometimes the model of honesty when normal, ***will*** do incredible things.(p.140)
• Afterward, his revulsion ***will*** be terrible.(p.141)
• Seeing your attempt to understand and help, some men ***will*** try to take advantage of your kindness.(p.141)
• Your understanding treatment of their cases ***will*** pay dividends.(p.141)
• ***Will*** he take every necessary step, submit to anything to get well, to stop drinking forever?(p.142)
• If he says yes, does he really mean it, or down inside does he think he is fooling you, and that after rest and treatment he ***will*** be able to get away with a few drinks now and then?(p.142)
• Either you are dealing with a man who can and ***will*** get well or you are not.(p.142)
• After satisfying yourself that your man wants to recover and that he ***will*** go to any extreme to do so, you may suggest a definite course of action.(p.142)
• Your man ***will*** fare better if placed in such physical condition that he can think straight and no longer craves liquor.(p.143)
• If you propose such a procedure to him, it may be necessary to advance the cost of treatment, but we believe it should be made plain that any expense ***will*** later be deducted from his pay.(p.143)
• To get over drinking ***will*** require a transformation of thought and attitude.(p.143)
• While on the subject of confidence, can you adopt the attitude that so far as you are concerned this ***will*** be a strictly personal matter, that his alcoholic derelictions, the treatment about to be undertaken, ***will*** never be discussed without his consent?(p.143)
• Whether your employee likes it or not, he ***will*** learn the grim truth about alcoholism.(p.144)
• We hope the doctor ***will*** tell the patient the truth about his condition, whatever that happens to be.(p.144)
• You are betting, of course, that your changed attitude plus the contents of this book ***will*** turn the trick.(p.144)
• In some cases it ***will***, and in others it may not.(p.144)
• But we think that if you persevere, the percentage of successes ***will*** gratify you.(p.144)
• If he feels free to discuss his problems with you, if he knows you understand and ***will*** not be upset by anything he wishes to say, he ***will*** probably be off to a fast start.(p.144)
• With this kind of employee such an attitude ***will*** command undying loyalty.(p.145)
• Wherever men are gathered together in business there ***will*** be rivalries and, arising out of these, a certain amount of office politics.(p.145)
• But sometimes our drinking ***will*** be used politically.(p.145)
• A reasonable amount of latitude ***will*** be helpful.(p.146)
• Being on a radically different basis of life, he ***will*** never take advantage of the situation.(p.146)
• If he is, and is still trying to recover, he ***will*** tell you about it even if it means the loss of his job.(p.146)
• He ***will*** appreciate knowing you are not bothering your head about him, that you are not suspicious nor are you trying to run his life so he ***will*** be shielded from temptation to drink.(p.146)
• In case he does stumble, even once, you ***will*** have to decide whether to let him go.(p.147)
• So, for one reason or another, they cover these men, hoping matters ***will*** take a turn for the better.(p.147)
• If you take it, your past ***will*** be forgotten and the fact that you went away for treatment ***will*** not be mentioned.(p.147)
• But if you cannot or ***will*** not stop drinking, I think you ought to resign."(p.148)
• But at least he ***will*** understand the problem and ***will*** no longer be misled by ordinary promises.(p.148)
• He ***will*** be able to take a position with such a man which is eminently fair and square.(p.148)
• He ***will*** have no further reason for covering up an alcoholic employee.(p.148)
• We think this method of approach ***will*** accomplish several things.(p.148)
• It ***will*** permit the rehabilitation of good men.(p.148)
• At the same time you ***will*** feel no reluctance to rid yourself of those who cannot or ***will*** not stop.(p.148)
• We hope our suggestions ***will*** help you plug up this sometimes serious leak.(p.148)
• It is not to be expected that an alcoholic employee ***will*** receive a disproportionate amount of time and attention.(p.149)
• The right kind of man, the kind who recovers, ***will*** not want this sort of thing.(p.149)
• He ***will*** not impose.(p.149)
• He ***will*** work like the devil and thank you to his dying day.(p.149)
• Unhappy drinkers who read this page ***will*** understand!(p.151)
• He ***will*** presently try the old game again, for he isn't happy about his sobriety.(p.152)
• Some day he ***will*** be unable to imagine life either with alcohol or without it.(p.152)
• Then he ***will*** know loneliness such as few do.(p.152)
• He ***will*** be at the jumping-off place.(p.152)
• He ***will*** wish for the end.(p.152)
• There you ***will*** find release from care, boredom and worry.(p.152)
• Your imagination ***will*** be fired.(p.152)
• Life ***will*** mean something at last.(p.152)
• Thus we find the fellowship, and so ***will*** you.(p.152)
• Among them you ***will*** make lifelong friends.(p.152)
• You ***will*** be bound to them with new and wonderful ties, for you ***will*** escape disaster together and you ***will*** commence shoulder to shoulder your common journey.(p.152)
• Then you ***will*** know what it means to give of yourself that others may survive and rediscover life.(p.153)
• You ***will*** learn the full meaning of "Love thy neighbor as thyself."(p.153)
• Should you wish them above all else, and be willing to make use of our experience, we are sure they ***will*** come.(p.153)
• Our hope is that when this chip of a book is launched on the world tide of alcoholism, defeated drinkers ***will*** seize upon it, to follow its suggestions.(p.153)
• Many, we are sure, ***will*** rise to their feet and march on.(p.153)
• They ***will*** approach still other sick ones and fellowships of Alcoholics Anonymous may spring up in each city and hamlet, havens for those who must find a way out.(p.153)
• You ***will*** want to know more of how to proceed from that point.(p.153)
• Perhaps the best way of treating you to a glimpse of your future ***will*** be to describe the growth of the fellowship among us.(p.153)
• When our friend related his experience, the man agreed that no amount of ***will*** power he might muster could stop his drinking for long.(p.155)
• Now, this house ***will*** hardly accommodate its weekly visitors, for they number sixty or eighty as a rule.(p.161)
• Being a large place, we think that some day its Fellowship ***will*** number many hundreds.(p.161)
• Some day we hope that every alcoholic who journeys ***will*** find a Fellowship of Alcoholics Anonymous at his destination.(p.162)
• We believe and hope it contains all you ***will*** need to begin.(p.163)
• So our fellow worker ***will*** soon have friends galore.(p.163)
• Some of them may sink and perhaps never get up, but if our experience is a criterion, more than half of those approached ***will*** become fellows of Alcoholics Anonymous.(p.163)
• When a few men in this city have found themselves, and have discovered the joy of helping others to face life again, there ***will*** be no stopping until everyone in that town has had his opportunity to recover -- if he can and ***will***.(p.163)
• Still you may say: "But I ***will*** not have the benefit of contact with you who write this book."(p.164)
• God ***will*** determine that, so you must remember that your real reliance is always upon Him.(p.164)
• He ***will*** show you how to create the fellowship you crave.(p.164)
• God ***will*** constantly disclose more to you and to us.(p.164)
• The answers ***will*** come, if your own house is in order.(p.164)
• See to it that your relationship with Him is right, and great events ***will*** come to pass for you and countless others.(p.164)
• We shall be with you in the Fellowship of the Spirit, and you ***will*** surely meet some of us as you trudge the Road of Happy Destiny.(p.164)
• In his prodigy of service, he was well assisted by Sister Ignatia at St. Thomas Hospital in Akron, Ohio, one of the greatest friends our Fellowship ***will*** ever know.(p.171)
• I ***will*** not take space to relate all my hospital or sanitarium experiences.(p.177)
• Your Heavenly Father ***will*** never let you down!(p.181)
• Each day I would try to find out what His ***will*** was, and try to follow that, rather than trying to get Him to always agree that the things I thought of myself were the things best for me.(p.187)
• It was bad news for us, and it ***will*** probably be bad news for you.(p.187)
• It was in the next two or three days after I had first met Doc and Bill, that I finally came to a decision to turn my ***will*** over to God and to go along with this program the best that I could.(p.189)
• I said, "Yes," reluctantly, "I probably ***will***."(p.190)
• "Who is convinced against his ***will*** is of the same opinion still."(p.193)
• The very simple program they advised me to follow was that I should ask to know God's ***will*** for me for that one day, and then, to the best of my ability, to follow that, and at night to express my gratefulness to God for the things that had happened to me during the day.(p.208)
• I was willful, full of ***will*** to do the things I wanted to do and to get the things that I wanted to have.(p.214)
• He then pulled up his chair with one of his knees touching mine and said, "***Will*** you pray with me for your success?"(p.218)
• I believe that my once over-weening self-will has finally found its proper place, for I can say many times daily, "Thy ***will*** be done, not mine" . . . and mean it.(p.229)
• Having regard for the law of the land, I resigned myself to the ***will*** of the national legislators and quit drinking altogether, not because I had found it harmful, but because I couldn't get what I was accustomed to drink.(p.232)
• That day I gave my ***will*** to God and asked to be directed.(p.237)
• Searching where I have been at fault, it is not hard to discover and get right again, for I have proven to myself and to many others who know me that God can keep a man sober if he ***will*** let Him.(p.237)
• So I always say that as long as I remember January 8th that is how long I ***will*** remain sober.(p.240)
• I checked into my hotel room and then noticed a placard tucked under the glass on the bureau stating "There ***will*** be positively NO drinking at this convention" signed by the president of the company.(p.243)
• And I still say that as long as I remember that January 8th in Washington, that is how long, by the grace of God as I understand Him, I ***will*** retain a happy sobriety.(p.250)
• They ***will*** never know how much their talk with me helped.(p.259)
• Today I have Someone who ***will*** always hear me; I have a warm fellowship among men who understand my problems; I have tasks to do and am glad to do them, to see others who are alcoholics and to help them in any way I can to become sober men.(p.260)
• He said, "I think this ***will*** tell you more.(p.268)
• On Wednesday night Jack M. said, "You meet me at the Ohio Edison Building, and I ***will*** take you to the meeting."(p.269)
• Before I stop -- I always was a great talker -- I want to say that nobody ***will*** ever know how I miss Annie's advice about things.(p.273)
• Probably only a few readers of this story ***will*** be able, from personal experiences of their own, to understand the exhilaration and sense of accomplishment which I felt after finishing this seemingly simple assignment.(p.276)
• The details of the long road back to something resembling normal living -- the first short streetcar ride, the purchase of a used bike which enabled me to widen the narrow horizon of life, the first trip downtown -- I ***will*** not dwell on.(p.276)
• You can't lose, and maybe God ***will*** help you -- just maybe, mind you.(p.280)
• I was supposed to be doing God's ***will***, not mine.(p.282)
• If I live to be a hundred, it ***will*** always stand out in my mind.(p.292)
• He would invariably reply, "When you are right

and the time is right, Providence *will* provide.(p.293)
• How I was able to discharge my duties at the office during those horrible mornings, I *will* never be able to explain.(p.299)
• Few doctors *will* tell a hopeless patient that there is no answer for him or for her.(p.307)
• Some of us struggle with these people because we know that they are really very sick, but we also know that short of some miracle, we are not going to help them except temporarily, and that they *will* inevitably get worse and worse until one of two things happens.(p.308)
• But then I thought, well, now wait, how *will* I feel next Tuesday?(p.326)
• How *will* I feel next Friday, if I make it a Friday?(p.326)
• How *will* I feel next Saturday morning?(p.326)
• He may even read in a newspaper that one out of every seven drinkers *will* become alcoholic, but he rarely is told that it holds true for all ages -- or that the tolerance to alcohol (and other drugs) decreases steadily, year after year, in the bodies of all persons.(p.330)
• I had to give him a story and ask him the same question over and over again, "Well, now, how many *will* that bottle serve?"(p.336)
• Since I gave my *will* over to A.A., whatever A.A. has wanted of me I've tried to do to the best of my ability.(p.340)
• When the time comes to solve them, God *will* give me strength for that day.(p.341)
• She's a good-natured soul and said, "I wouldn't worry about it; probably something *will* happen."(p.346)
• I *will* never forget the first meeting that I attended.(p.347)
• The Third Step said: "Made a decision to turn our *will* and our lives over to the care of God as we understood Him."(p.350)
• A lucky break, at least some *will* call it lucky, was in store for me at my group that night.(p.365)
• You *will* recall that I said the time that I got the idea out of a clear sky to call A.A. on a certain night was at about ten.(p.366)
• I *will* never know all the people I hurt, all the friends I abused, the humiliation of my family, the worry of my business associates, or how far reaching it was.(p.376)
• She of course didn't realize how cunning an alcoholic can be and the lengths to which he *will* go in finding ways to satisfy the compulsion for more and more drinks after having had the first one.(p.377)
• The why is not important; the fact is that one drink *will* set up a reaction in our system which requires more; that one drink was too much and one hundred drinks were not enough.(p.380)
• A "spiritual experience" to me meant attending meetings, seeing a group of people, all there for the purpose of helping each other; hearing the Twelve Steps and the Twelve Traditions read at a meeting, and hearing the Lord's Prayer, which in an A.A. meeting has such great meaning -- "Thy *will* be done, not mine."(p.381)
• To most of us, making amends *will* take the rest of our lives, but we can start immediately.(p.381)
• Just being sober *will* be making amends to many we have hurt by our drunken actions.(p.381)
• Yesterday is gone, and we don't know whether we *will* be here tomorrow.(p.382)
• If we do a good job of living today, and if tomorrow comes for us, then the chances are we *will* do a good job when it arrives -- so why worry about it?(p.382)
• I know that if I do daily what I have done for these last thirteen and a half years, I *will* stay sober.(p.384)
• He said, "If your father *will* come out and stay with you, you can have the house."(p.389)
• If you *will* try this thing, I'll go along with you.(p.391)
• If you don't, you *will* have to go home.(p.391)
• He said, "Wait until I get back and I *will* go with you to see this man."(p.393)
• It pays daily in more harmonious relations with my fellow men, in ever clearer insight into the true meaning of life, and in the answering love and gratitude wherever and whenever I have been the instrument of God's *will* in the lives of others.(p.394)
• It is also stated that we *will* never be able to figure out how much we have spent on alcohol.(p.396)
• But, as it was with drinking, this project *will* be entered into with enthusiasm and optimism -- and probably wind up the same way, depressed.(p.396)
• Eighteen *will* be used as the starting point, because my drinking before was limited by age, the law, and money.(p.397)
• Alcoholics being the argumentative lot that we are, the A.A. membership *will* undoubtedly come up with a few who *will* dispute these figures.(p.399)
• Well, I'm willing, if it *will* curb this awful desire to drink, this fear of not having a drink, this feeling of always being alone, scared, deserted, sick.(p.430)
• Moreover, I am deeply convinced that so long as I continue to strive, in my bumbling way, toward the principles I first encountered in the earlier chapters of this book, this remarkable power *will* continue to flow through me.(p.437)
• I can't say, "Thy *will* be done," and take a pill.(p.443)
• Rather, I do whatever is in front of me to be done, and I leave the results up to Him; however it turns out, that's God's *will* for me.(p.452)
• There go my good intentions, fear of consequences, *will* to care, responsibility for my behavior.(p.458)
• At the wedding, I hope I *will* also get to see my daughter and their mother.(p.463)
• I *will* be fifty years old next month, haven't seen my son or daughter yet, nor my daughter's two children, my grandchildren; but I am grateful.(p.463)
• This sound easy, so *will* try.(p.476)
• He planted many seeds, and it *will* be many moons before another rises to walk in his shoes.(p.476)
• Therefore, it *will* be the hardest to work on.(p.482)
• But I *will* never be totally honest -- that would make me perfect, and none of us can claim to be perfect.(p.482)
• If I work on it every day, it *will* be easier to be honest with myself.(p.482)
• Then getting and staying honest with other people *will* come automatically.(p.482)
• I know I *will* be grateful for a chance to make amends to everybody I have hurt in the past.(p.482)
• She said, "He has something of interest, if you *will* see him."(p.494)
• I wonder if it *will* reach her neck.(p.497)
• I hunt for my nickel to drop in the plate so that mine *will* be seen.(p.497)
• A little drink *will* put me on my feet.(p.500)
• I say I *will* go.(p.502)
• She makes the arrangements, but I *will* not go.(p.502)
• Maybe a few drinks when I get to the city *will* help.(p.505)
• I *will* not stand for it.(p.505)
• *Will* I take a young fellow who has been drinking for two weeks to live with me?(p.506)
• I *will* not go out and I *will* not enter into anything.(p.506)
• I *will* not be that way.(p.506)
• I talked to him for quite a long time and at the end, he said, "Well, you're not quite mad enough to be shut up for good yet, but you soon *will* be if you live long enough."(p.522)
• It continues to try to teach me the real charity, the charity that gives time and good *will* and service, and not just money.(p.525)
• I think I am dreaming and *will* soon wake up.(p.529)
• I just want to say that you don't have to be afraid, because no one at any A.A. meeting *will* bite you.(p.529)
• If you give us a try, you *will* see that we are really human beings, and we *will* welcome you with open arms and hearts.(p.529)
• What is much more important to me, A.A. has taught me that through this simple program I may experience a change in this reaction pattern that *will* indeed allow me to "match calamity with serenity."(p.544)
• The amount of *will* power exercised to control my drinking during working hours, diverted into a constructive channel, would have made me President, and the thing that made the *will* power possible was the knowledge that as soon as my day was finished I could drink myself into oblivion.(p.548)
• They suggested that I study the A.A. book and try to take the Twelve Steps according to the explanation in the Book, for it was their opinion that the application of these principles in our daily lives *will* get us sober and keep us sober.(p.550)
• A.A. has taught me that I *will* have peace of mind in exact proportion to the peace of mind I bring into the lives of other people, and it has taught me the true meaning of the admonition "happy are ye who know these things and do them."(p.551)
• But one was so outstanding that I like to pass it on whenever I can in the hope that it *will* help someone else as it has me.(p.551)
• He said, in effect: "If you have a resentment you want to be free of, if you *will* pray for the person or the thing that you resent, you *will* be free.(p.552)
• If you *will* ask in prayer for everything you want for yourself to be given to them, you *will* be free.(p.552)
• Ask for their health, their prosperity, their happiness, and you *will* be free.(p.552)
• Do it every day for two weeks and you *will* find you have come to mean it and to want it for them, and you *will* realize that where you used to feel bitterness and resentment and hatred, you now feel compassionate understanding and love."(p.552)
• It worked for me then, and it has worked for me many times since, and it *will* work for me every time I am willing to work it.(p.552)
• And because it works for me, it *will* work for all of us.(p.552)
• We alcoholics see that we must work together and hang together, else most of us *will* finally die alone.(p.563)
• A.A. must continue to live or most of us *will* surely die.(p.565)
• I now conceive the psychiatrist's job to be the task of breaking down the patient's inner resistance so that which is inside him *will* flower, as under the activity of the A.A. program."(p.571)
• If you cannot find A.A. in your locality, a letter addressed to Alcoholics Anonymous, Box 459, Grand Central Station, New York, NY 10163, U.S.A., *will* receive a prompt reply from this world center, referring you to the nearest A.A. group.(p.575)
• If there is none nearby, you *will* be invited to carry on a correspondence which *will* do much to insure your sobriety no matter how isolated you are.(p.575)
• This headquarters *will* give the location of the nearest family group and *will* if you wish, correspond with you about your special problems.(p.575)

willful

• I was *willful*, full of will to do the things I wanted to do and to get the things that I wanted to have.(p.214)
• Headstrong and *willful*, I rushed from pleasure to pleasure, and found the returns diminishing to the vanishing point.(p.226)

William

• The section called "The Doctor's Opinion" has been kept intact, just as it was originally written in 1939 by the late Dr. *William* D. Silkworth, our Society's great medical benefactor.(p.xi)
• He had also been greatly helped by the late Dr. *William* D. Silkworth, a New York specialist in alcoholism who is now accounted no less than a medical saint by A.A. members, and whose story of the early days of our Society appears in the next pages.(p.xvi)
• Very truly yours, *William* D. Silkworth, M.D.(p.xxiv)
• *William* D. Silkworth, M.D.(p.xxx)
• The distinguished American psychologist, *William* James, in his book "Varieties of Religious Experience," indicates a multitude of ways in which men have discovered God.(p.28)
• Most of our experiences are what the psychologist *William* James calls the "educational variety" because they develop slowly over a period of time.(p.569)

Willie

• I remembered going through what my sister assured me was my nightly procedure of trying to find *Willie* Seabrook's name in the telephone book.(p.224)

willing

• It was only a matter of being *willing* to believe in a Power greater than myself.(p.12)
• I ruthlessly faced my sins and became *willing* to have my new-found Friend take them away, root and branch.(p.13)
• This we did because we honestly wanted to, and were *willing* to make the effort.(p.25)
• He can go anywhere on this earth where other free men may go without disaster, provided he remains *willing* to maintain a certain simple attitude.(p.26)
• If what we have learned and felt and seen means anything at all, it means that all of us, whatever our race, creed, or color are the children of a living Creator with whom we may form a relationship upon simple and understandable terms as soon as we are *willing* and honest enough to try.(p.28)
• "Do I now believe, or am I even *willing* to believe, that there is a Power greater than myself?"(p.47)
• As soon as a man can say that he does believe, or is *willing* to believe, we emphatically assure him that he is on his way.(p.47)
• Circumstances made him *willing* to believe.(p.57)
• If you have decided you want what we have and are *willing* to go to any length to get it -- then you are ready to take certain steps.(p.58)
• 8.Made a list of all persons we had harmed, and became *willing* to make amends to them all.(p.59)

• The point is, that we are *willing* to grow along spiritual lines.(p.60)
• We admitted our wrongs honestly and were *willing* to set these matters straight.(p.67)
• Whatever our ideal turns out to be, we must be *willing* to grow toward it.(p.69)
• We must be *willing* to make amends where we have done harm, provided that we do not bring about still more harm in so doing.(p.69)
• We have listed the people we have hurt by our conduct, and are *willing* to straighten out the past if we can.(p.70)
• If we still cling to something we will not let go, we ask God to help us be *willing*.(p.76)
• When ready, we say something like this: "My Creator, I am now *willing* that you should have all of me, good and bad.(p.76)
• We have a list of all persons we have harmed and to whom we are *willing* to make amends.(p.76)
• When it will serve any good purpose, we are *willing* to announce our convictions with tact and common sense.(p.77)
• We may lose our position or reputation or face jail, but we are *willing*.(p.79)
• We thought he ought to be *willing* to do that if necessary, but if he were in jail he could provide nothing for either family.(p.79)
• He said he was perfectly *willing* to go to jail if she insisted.(p.79)
• We are sorry for what we have done and, God *willing*, it shall not be repeated.(p.81)
• If his own doctor is *willing* to tell him that he is alcoholic, so much the better.(p.92)
• The main thing is that he be *willing* to believe in a Power greater than himself and that he live by spiritual principles.(p.93)
• For the type of alcoholic who is able and *willing* to get well, little charity, in the ordinary sense of the word, is needed or wanted.(p.97)
• Your husband may be *willing* to talk to one of them.(p.112)
• That is true only if one is *willing* to turn the past to good account.(p.124)
• We think each family which has been relieved owes something to those who have not, and when the occasion requires, each member of it should be only too *willing* to bring former mistakes, no matter how grievous, out of their hiding places.(p.124)
• You are *willing* to overlook his past performances.(p.141)
• After your man has gone along without drinking for a few months, you may be able to make use of his services with other employees who are giving you the alcoholic run-around -- provided, of course, they are *willing* to have a third party in the picture.(p.146)
• You say, "Yes, I'm *willing*.(p.152)
• Should you wish them above all else, and be *willing* to make use of our experience, we are sure they will come.(p.153)
• On the third day the lawyer gave his life to the care and direction of his Creator, and said he was perfectly *willing* to do anything necessary.(p.158)
• They were *willing*, by day or night, to place a new man in the hospital and visit him afterward.(p.159)
• Understanding our work, he can do this with an eye to selecting those who are *willing* and able to recover on a spiritual basis.(p.162)
• Before very long we began to relate some incidents of our drinking and, naturally, pretty soon, I realized both of them knew what they were talking about because you can see things and smell things when you're drunk, that you can't other times, and, if I had thought they didn't know what they were talking about, I wouldn't have been *willing* to talk to them at all.(p.185)
• The next thing they wanted to know was would I be *willing* to go to this Higher Power and ask for help, calmly and without any reservations.(p.186)
• I thought of what liquor had done to me, the opportunities that I had discarded, the abilities that had been given me and how I had wasted them, and I finally came to the conclusion, that if I didn't want to quit, I certainly ought to want to, and that I was *willing* to do anything in the world to stop drinking.(p.186)
• I was *willing* to admit to myself that I had hit bottom, that I had gotten hold of something that I didn't know how to handle by myself.(p.187)
• So, after reviewing these things and realizing what liquor had cost me, I went to this Higher Power which, to me was God, without any reservation, and admitted that I was completely powerless over alcohol, and that I was *willing* to do anything in the world to get rid of the problem.(p.187)
• In fact, I admitted that from now on I was *willing* to let God take over, instead of me.(p.187)
• I wasn't afraid that the program wouldn't work, but I still was doubtful whether I would be able to hang on to the program, but I did come to the conclusion that I was *willing* to put everything I had into it, with God's power, and that I wanted to do just that.(p.189)
• Then I remember when the boys came back, that I told them, "I have gone to this Higher Power and I have told Him that I am *willing* to put His world first, above everything.(p.190)
• I have already done it, and I am *willing* to do it again here in the presence of you or I am *willing* to say it any place, anywhere in the world from now on and not be ashamed of it."(p.190)
• I apparently was *willing* to subdue these personality disturbances in a tremendous drive to succeed.(p.211)
• The afternoon that I was to leave the hospital, he came in to see me and asked me if I were *willing* to attempt to follow the program.(p.218)
• He had already imbued them with his own spirit until they were ready and *willing* at all times to go where sent, and as a doctor he well knew that this mission and duty would strengthen them as it later helped me.(p.235)
• In a few sentences he made God seem personal to me, explained Him as a being who was interested in me, the alcoholic, and that all I needed to do was to be *willing* to follow His way; that as long as I followed it I would be able to overcome my desire for liquor.(p.236)
• Well, there I was, *willing* to try it, but I didn't know how, except in a vague way.(p.236)
• This was the background that made me *willing* to listen on January 8th.(p.245)
• The next day he turned me over to a couple who, although neither was an alcoholic, knew Dr. Bob and were *willing* to drive me to Akron where they would turn me over to his care.(p.278)
• Having no one else to turn to, I was *willing* to give Him a chance, although with considerable doubt.(p.280)
• By the time we reached the bar, he was *willing* to buy me a quart with his own money.(p.288)
• Then when we got back to the apartment, he was *willing* to wait two or three days until I got my health back to be paid off for the liquor and fare.(p.289)
• You must always be *willing* and continue to make contacts."(p.293)
• It explained so much I had not understood about myself and, best of all, it promised recovery if I would do a few simple things and be *willing* to have the desire to drink removed.(p.309)
• By this time, with the doctor's explanation, the revelations contained in the book, and the hope-inspiring interview with Mr. T., I was ready and *willing* to go into the interior of the African jungles, if that was what it took, for me to find what these people had.(p.309)
• I could never be sure I'd have a clear head and hands that were *willing* to do some work.(p.326)
• I was *willing* to try anything.(p.340)
• My first meeting gave me a great deal of hope and lots of *willing* ears for my tale of woe and for my questions.(p.364)
• Well, I'm *willing*, if it will curb this awful desire to drink, this fear of not having a drink, this feeling of always being alone, scared, deserted, sick.(p.430)
• I must be ready and *willing* should I never see them.(p.463)
• We can have this new way of life -- learning to live with our sickness and to be happy and content -- if we are *willing* to change our way of thinking and be honest, first with ourselves, then with others.(p.480)
• Then he asks me if I am *willing* to right all the wrongs I have ever done to anyone, no matter how wrong I thought the others were.(p.503)
• Am I *willing* to be honest with myself about myself and tell someone about myself, and am I *willing* to think of other people, of their needs instead of myself, in order to get rid of the drink problem?(p.503)
• It had provided me with excuses for my lack of education, my marital failures, personal failures, inadequacy, and of course, my alcoholism and, though I really thought I had been *willing* to part with it, now I knew I was reluctant to let it go.(p.552)
• It worked for me then, and it has worked for me many times since, and it will work for me every time I am *willing* to work it.(p.552)
• "God *willing*, we . . . may never again have to deal with drinking, but we have to deal with sobriety every day."(p.554)
• God *willing*, we members of A.A. may never again have to deal with drinking, but we have to deal with sobriety every day.(p.560)

willingness

• But when the broker gave him Dr. Silkworth's description of alcoholism and its hopelessness, the physician began to pursue the spiritual remedy for his malady with a *willingness* he had never before been able to muster.(p.xvi)
• Upon a foundation of complete *willingness* I might build what I saw in my friend.(p.12)
• There had been a humble *willingness* to have Him with me -- and He came.(p.12)
• I expressed my entire *willingness* to approach these individuals, admitting my wrong.(p.13)
• Belief in the power of God, plus enough *willingness*, honesty and humility to establish and maintain the new order of things, were the essential requirements.(p.13)
• We found that as soon as we were able to lay aside prejudice and express even a *willingness* to believe in a Power greater than ourselves, we commenced to get results, even though it was impossible for any of us to fully define or comprehend that Power, which is God.(p.46)
• We have emphasized *willingness* as being indispensable.(p.76)
• If you both show a *willingness* to remedy your own defects, there will be little need to criticize each other.(p.118)
• We grow by our *willingness* to face and rectify errors and convert them into assets.(p.124)
• To duplicate, with such backing, what we have accomplished is only a matter of *willingness*, patience and labor.(p.163)
• And, accepting, I felt a new inner comfort, and the *willingness* and strength to do something about the traits I couldn't live with.(p.229)
• Here was something requiring a greater *willingness* to assume responsibility, and take a larger degree of cooperation and "give and take" than even business requires of one.(p.286)
• The Twelve Steps, which to me are a spiritual way of living, soon meant honest thinking, not wishful thinking, open mindedness, a *willingness* to try and a faith to accept.(p.381)
• A *willingness* to do whatever I was told to do simplified the program for me.(p.381)
• Mom has said the only requisite to start is *willingness*.(p.430)
• They said if you want to know how this program works, take the first word of your question -- the H is for honesty, the O is for open-mindedness and the W is for *willingness*; these our Book calls the essentials of recovery.(p.550)
• A.A. taught me that *willingness* to believe was enough for a beginning.(p.550)
• Sometimes I have to ask first for the *willingness*, but it too always comes.(p.552)
• *Willingness*, honesty and open mindedness are the essentials of recovery.(p.570)

willpower

• It helped me a great deal to become convinced that alcoholism was a disease, not a moral issue; that I had been drinking as a result of a compulsion, even though I had not been aware of the compulsion at the time; and that sobriety was not a matter of *willpower*.(p.448)

wills

• Max still works with me in the office, but we have turned our *wills* and our lives and our work over to the care of God.(p.446)

wilt

• Many of us said to our Maker, as we understood Him: "God, I offer myself to Thee -- to build with me and to do with me as Thou *wilt*.(p.63)

wilted

• The more I drank, the more she *wilted*.(p.451)

win

• As I drank, the old fierce determination to *win* came back.(p.4)
• But the ex-problem drinker who has found this solution, who is properly armed with facts about himself, can generally *win* the entire confidence of another alcoholic in a few hours.(p.18)
• We doubt if many of them can do it, because none will really want to stop, and hardly one of them, because of the peculiar mental twist already acquired, will find he can *win* out.(p.33)
• As in war, the victor only seemed to *win*.(p.66)
• "You can't *win* unless you try God's way."(p.236)

Winchester

• I visited *Winchester* Cathedral.(p.1)
• That war-time day in old *Winchester* Cathedral came back again.(p.10)

wind
• I felt lifted up, as though the great clean *wind* of a mountain top blew through and through.(p.14)
• Ain't it grand the *wind* stopped blowin'?"(p.82)
• The first definite indications of an alcoholic pattern began to arise when I would go to New York on business and disappear, and *wind* up in Philadelphia or Boston for two or three day periods.(p.213)
• In fact I was afraid to try it for fear that I would *wind* up like many examples I had seen of excessive drinking in the Army.(p.374)
• But, as it was with drinking, this project will be entered into with enthusiasm and optimism -- and probably *wind* up the same way, depressed.(p.396)
• But I can remember in post graduate days, and during interneship, that very often I'd go to a patient's bed and start a process of elimination and then, very often, I'd *wind* up guessing.(p.485)
• The *wind* is rising and howls around the house.(p.497)

windmills
• I have stopped tilting at *windmills*, and instead have tried to accomplish the little daily tasks, unimportant in themselves, but tasks that are an integral part of living fully.(p.295)

window
• Again I swayed dizzily before an open *window*, or the medicine cabinet where there was poison, cursing myself for a weakling.(p.6)
• Then came the night when the physical and mental torture was so hellish I feared I would burst through my *window*, sash and all.(p.6)
• It meant I would have to throw several lifelong conceptions out of the *window*.(p.42)
• I still expected a plea for clemency, but these words came through the receiver: "I just wanted to tell you Paul jumped from a hotel *window* in Hartford last Saturday.(p.136)
• I remember looking longingly at the *window* as an easier solution, and shuddering at the memory of that other *window*, three years before, and the six agonizing months in a London hospital ward.(p.224)
• There was one girl especially, and I'd watch her from my *window* every morning, leaving faithfully to go to the hospital in the neighborhood.(p.326)
• We broke open a *window* and got inside.(p.424)
• I'd deliberately smashed a *window*.(p.435)
• I must get out of the room or I shall jump out of the *window*.(p.501)

windows
• After my last binge I came home and smashed my dining room furniture to splinters, kicked out six *windows* and two balustrades.(p.435)

winds
• If the alcoholic tries to shield himself he may succeed for a time, but he usually *winds* up with a bigger explosion than ever.(p.101)

windshields
• He had gone through the *windshields* of cars a couple of times and was pretty well banged up.(p.510)

windward
• I was transferred to Kaneohe Bay, across the hump to the *windward* side of Oahu, to the aviation base.(p.426)

windy
• We read wordy books and indulge in *windy* arguments, thinking we believe this universe needs no God to explain it.(p.49)

wine
• "Why don't you try beer and *wine*?"(p.20)
• My wife and I belonged to some bridge clubs and they began to make *wine* and serve it.(p.184)
• I went over and bought a jug of hard cider and a gallon of *wine* that I gave these fellows to drink.(p.195)
• *Wine* and hard cider.(p.196)
• I became a specialist in making elderberry blossom *wine*.(p.213)
• Beer and *wine* were not the answer.(p.230)
• I was born in Europe, in Alsace to be exact, shortly after it had become German, and practically grew up with the "good Rhine *wine*" of song and story.(p.230)
• My daily consumption of *wine* was about a quart, but that was common where I lived.(p.230)
• Everybody drank *wine*.(p.230)
• When I got back to Germany I settled down to finish my apprenticeship, drinking the *wine* of the country as usual.(p.231)
• I early decided that the *wine* of America was very inferior stuff and took up beer instead.(p.231)
• I came of good stock, of men and women who drank *wine* all their lives as a beverage, and while they occasionally got drunk at special celebrations, they were up and about their business the next day.(p.231)
• I tried the beer diet, the *wine* diet, timing, measuring, and spacing of drinks.(p.305)
• We all have them, and I thought a little brandy or a little *wine* now and then could certainly hurt no one.(p.336)
• I had to have that *wine*.(p.336)
• I couldn't go to one *wine* store and look the man honestly in the face and buy a bottle, as I used to do when I had parties and entertained and did normal drinking.(p.336)
• Well, of course that was all I needed – to switch from *wine* to brandy for three weeks.(p.338)
• Near the Laundromat, I would buy one bottle of pop and a few bottles of beer or *wine*, and go into the rest room, empty the pop bottle, refill it with the booze, and proceed to do my laundering.(p.370)
• I can't remember a dinner at home that we didn't have white *wine* or claret on the table.(p.384)
• So I was used to it, but I didn't know what the effect of alcohol was because I always had *wine*, usually with dinner, but always with a lot of ice and about two tablespoons of sugar in it.(p.385)
• I displayed alcoholic tendencies actually from the age of fourteen, when I started to steal *wine* from the family jug, siphoning it off one drink at a time so it wouldn't be missed, not drinking it immediately, but saving it until about a pint was accumulated, so that I could get drunk.(p.397)
• I read sad poetry, cried, drank red *wine*, wrote sad poetry, and drank some more.(p.405)
• Drink only beer or *wine*.(p.408)
• The only time that I have ever seen my mother take anything alcoholic was around Christmas time, when she would drink some eggnog or light *wine*.(p.484)
• I went out and drank some German *wine* and it went to my head.(p.517)
• Then the time came when I couldn't afford whiskey, so I turned to *wine*.(p.527)
• I swore off hard liquor and turned to *wine*.(p.555)

wine-drinking
• You know the deteriorating effects, the disintegrating effects of chronic *wine-drinking*.(p.337)

wine-making
• It wasn't very long before home-brewing was an institution and men began to search feverishly for old recipe books on *wine-making*.(p.232)

wine-room
• Tom Sharkey's brawling bar on 14th Street and the famous *wine-room* at the back were headquarters for me.(p.251)

wine-tasting
• During this time, you are supposed to behave yourself, but I took a little *wine-tasting* tour through France, all by my lone, with car and chauffeur.(p.405)

wines
• Here are some of the methods we have tried: Drinking beer only, limiting the number of drinks, never drinking alone, never drinking in the morning, drinking only at home, never having it in the house, never drinking during business hours, drinking only at parties, switching from scotch to brandy, drinking only natural *wines*, agreeing to resign if ever drunk on the job, taking a trip, not taking a trip, swearing off forever (with and without a solemn oath), taking more physical exercise, reading inspirational books, going to health farms and sanitariums, accepting voluntary commitment to asylums -- we could increase the list ad infinitum.(p.31)

wing
• They told Annabelle to take me under her *wing*, and I shall never forget how she sort of curled up her nose and said, "They tell me you drink too."(p.269)

wings
• My writing career was described in the couplet "Alcohol gave me *wings* to fly,/And then it took away the sky."(p.331)
• I was certainly a complete surprise when I arrived at her family's home, but because I arrived on the *wings* of a tropical hurricane there wasn't much she could do but let me in.(p.364)
• We learn how to level out the emotional *wings* that got us into trouble both when we were up and when we were down.(p.560)

wins
• A FIVE-TIME LOSER *WINS*(p.457)

winter
• He is like the retired business man who lolls in the Florida sunshine in the *winter* complaining of the sad state of the nation; the minister who sighs over the sins of the twentieth century; politicians and reformers who are sure all would be Utopia if the rest of the world would only behave; the outlaw safe cracker who thinks society has wronged him; and the alcoholic who has lost all and is locked up.(p.61)
• I used to put eight or twelve ounce bottles of alcohol in a fur lined glove and toss it onto the back airing porch when *winter* days got dark enough.(p.176)
• I rented a beautiful apartment on the banks of the Seine in the *winter*, and a chalet in Switzerland in the summer.(p.405)
• There was no central heating, and this was the dead of *winter*.(p.415)
• But I don't remember that any of them ever went to sleep in joints and woke up with no shoes on in the *winter*, or fell out of chairs.(p.527)
• I don't remember any of them getting put out in the *winter* because they didn't pay their rent.(p.527)

wipe
• Only death could *wipe* out that security.(p.329)

wiped
• I have seen hundreds of families set their feet in the path that really goes somewhere; have seen the most impossible domestic situations righted; feuds and bitterness of all sorts *wiped* out.(p.15)
• I had some financial success through no ability of my own and, when jobless and almost *wiped* out in 1930, I began to trade and sell my collection; much of the proceeds went to keep my apartment stocked with liquor and almost every night saw me helpless to bed.(p.255)
• A twenty-three million dollar surplus *wiped* out.(p.500)

wired
• No one in that company saw me again – ten days later I *wired* my resignation.(p.243)
• As usual, I ran out of money, and, as usual, I *wired* my father for funds to come home.(p.357)

wireless
• We heard by *wireless* on the 5th that the Armistice would be signed the next day (this was a premature report) so I had a couple of cognacs to celebrate; then I hopped a truck and went AWOL.(p.242)

wires
• News of this got on the world *wires*; inquiries poured in again and many people went to the bookstores to get the book "Alcoholics Anonymous."(p.xviii)

wisdom
• I haven't written anything about that part of my story, but I believe in a Greater Power which I call God and I ask for His *wisdom* and guidance daily.(p.366)
• "Grant us the serenity to accept the things we cannot change, courage to change the things we can, and the *wisdom* to know the difference."(p.382)

wise
• Treatment seemed *wise*, for I showed signs of delirium tremens.(p.13)
• It is seldom *wise* to approach an individual, who still smarts from our injustice to him, and announce that we have gone religious.(p.77)
• Sometimes it is *wise* to wait till he goes on a binge.(p.90)
• But the *wise* family will admire him for what he is trying to be, rather than for what he is trying to get.(p.123)
• Henry Ford once made a *wise* remark to the effect that experience is the thing of supreme value in life.(p.124)
• She said, "I feel you're just being *wise*.(p.273)
• At this point, I was no longer the *wise* boy.(p.515)
• I suspect that if it is wisely handled – and it seems to be in *wise* and prudent hands -- there are doors of opportunity ahead of this project that may surpass our capacities to imagine."(p.574)

wise-cracking
• But I had never been a flippant, *wise-cracking* sneerer at the few persons I had met who had impressed me as Christian men and women, or at any institution whose sincerity of purpose I could see.(p.259)

wisely
• I suspect that if it is *wisely* handled – and it seems to be in wise and prudent hands – there are doors of opportunity ahead of this project that may surpass our capacities to imagine."(p.574)

wish
• We simply *wish* to be helpful to those who are afflicted.(p.xiv)
• I see him now and then and he is as fine a specimen of manhood as one could *wish* to meet.(p.xxx)

• This is the baffling feature of alcoholism as we know it -- this utter inability to leave it alone, no matter how great the necessity or the ***wish***.(p.34)
• This is a point we ***wish*** to emphasize and re-emphasize, to smash home upon our alcoholic readers as it has been revealed to us out of bitter experience.(p.39)
• We could ***wish*** to be moral, we could ***wish*** to be philosophically comforted, in fact, we could will these things with all our might, but the needed power wasn't there.(p.45)
• When people presented us with spiritual approaches, how frequently did we all say, "I ***wish*** I had what that man has.(p.47)
• If our testimony helps sweep away prejudice, enables you to think honestly, encourages you to search diligently within yourself, then, if you ***wish***, you can join us on the Broad Highway.(p.55)
• And do not his actions make each of them ***wish*** to retaliate, snatching all they can get out of the show?(p.61)
• We could not ***wish*** them away any more than alcohol.(p.66)
• Our former enemies sometimes praise what we are doing and ***wish*** us well.(p.78)
• Though there may be justifiable exceptions, and though we ***wish*** to lay down no rule of any sort, we have often found this the best course to take.(p.81)
• We will not regret the past nor ***wish*** to shut the door on it.(p.83)
• We can exercise our will power along this line all we ***wish***.(p.85)
• Ministers and doctors are competent and you can learn much from them if you ***wish***, but it happens that because of your own drinking experience you can be uniquely useful to other alcoholics.(p.89)
• Though the family has no religious connections, they may ***wish*** to make contact with or take membership in a religious body.(p.131)
• If he owes you money you may ***wish*** to make terms.(p.145)
• He may ***wish*** to do a lot for other alcoholics and something of the sort may come up during business hours.(p.146)
• If, on the contrary, you are sure he is doing his utmost, you may ***wish*** to give him another chance.(p.147)
• There is another thing you might ***wish*** to do.(p.147)
• He will ***wish*** for the end.(p.152)
• Should you ***wish*** them above all else, and be willing to make use of our experience, we are sure they will come.(p.153)
• In conclusion, I can only say that whatever growth or understanding has come to me, I have no ***wish*** to graduate.(p.249)
• In my early twenties the hardships of hobo life did not discourage me, but I had no ***wish*** to become just a tramp.(p.253)
• They did not show me to my room and ***wish*** me a good night's rest.(p.259)
• Time went on and the drinking got worse and worse, and I was in another barroom, down the road the other way, a small one, and I took my glass -- that morning I'd been able to lift it from the bar -- and I said to the woman behind the bar, "I ***wish*** I might never take another drop of that stuff.(p.266)
• It was very impressive and I ***wish*** that every A.A. could have the benefit of this type of sponsorship today.(p.292)
• We're free at last to do our thing, to live uninhibited lives, to drink when and how and where we ***wish***, when we want to and when we need to.(p.329)
• I ***wish*** I could tell you how and why A.A. works, but I don't know.(p.384)
• I ***wish*** I could tell you all that A.A. has done for me, all that I think and feel about A.A., but it's something that I have experienced and have never been able to put into words.(p.394)
• I ***wish*** I were home with the family and not in the dingy hotel.(p.500)
• I ***wish*** I were dead, as I have often wished before.(p.502)
• I ***wish*** I knew a short cut to maturity.(p.535)
• I ***wish*** we did not have to have jails; I ***wish*** everyone could be in A.A., and if everyone were there would be no need for jails, in my opinion.(p.542)
• At fifty-four, I have had come true for me the old ***wish***, "If only I could live my life over, knowing what I know."(p.543)
• Hence we may refuse none who ***wish*** to recover.(p.565)
• Most emphatically we ***wish*** to say that any alcoholic capable of honestly facing his problems in the light of our experience can recover, provided he does not close his mind to all spiritual concepts.(p.570)
• This headquarters will give the location of the nearest family group and will if you ***wish***, correspond with you about your special problems.(p.575)

wished

• He ***wished*** above all things to regain self-control.(p.26)
• That was growth, but if we ***wished*** to grow we had to begin somewhere.(p.47)
• If his arrangements would only stay put, if only people would do as he ***wished***, the show would be great.(p.60)
• My secretary returned to say that it was not Mr. B---- on the phone; it was Mr. B----'s brother, and he ***wished*** to give me a message.(p.136)
• I was, of course, soon on the carpet and the upshot was that I had to go back for two more quarters and remain absolutely dry, if I ***wished*** to graduate.(p.174)
• I vowed that never again would any important person whom I ***wished*** to please and impress ever see me drunk.(p.328)
• At noon on Christmas Day I called my family in New York, ***wished*** them a Merry Christmas, and assured them everything was fine with me.(p.467)
• I wish I were dead, as I have often ***wished*** before.(p.502)

wishes

• If he ***wishes*** to talk, let him do so.(p.91)
• Don't, at this stage, refer to this book, unless he has seen it and ***wishes*** to discuss it.(p.92)
• Let him know you are available if he ***wishes*** to make a decision and tell his story, but do not insist upon it if he prefers to consult someone else.(p.96)
• Each is interested in having his or her ***wishes*** respected.(p.122)
• If he feels free to discuss his problems with you, if he knows you understand and will not be upset by anything he ***wishes*** to say, he will probably be off to a fast start.(p.144)
• My whole life seemed to be centered around doing what I wanted to do, without regard for the rights, ***wishes***, or privileges of anyone else; a state of mind which became more and more predominant as the years passed.(p.172)

wishful

• The Twelve Steps, which to me are a spiritual way of living, soon meant honest thinking, not ***wishful*** thinking, open mindedness, a willingness to try and a faith to accept.(p.381)

wishing

• Neither could we reduce our self-centeredness much by ***wishing*** or trying on our own power.(p.62)
• When your husband is bad, you become a trembling recluse, ***wishing*** the telephone had never been invented.(p.115)
• ***Wishing*** to be polite, though I felt very badly, I said, "Let's make the call," and extracted from my wife a promise that we would not stay over fifteen minutes.(p.179)
• Not ***wishing*** to disturb my wife, I slumped in a big red-leather chair and suffered.(p.332)

witch-burners

• Every new alcoholic looks for this spirit among us and is immensely relieved when he finds we are not ***witch-burners***.(p.103)

withdraw

• Don't start to ***withdraw*** again just because your friends drink liquor.(p.102)

withdrawing

• While you were drinking, you were ***withdrawing*** from life little by little.(p.102)
• I had thought that I was completely different from other people, that I was beginning to become a little balmy, even to the point of ***withdrawing*** more and more from society and wanting to be alone with my bottle.(p.290)
• I woke up in jail, sick, ***withdrawing*** from alcohol and speed, already a four-time loser, and now with a fifth felony charge against me.(p.460)

withdrawn

• I used to get terribly upset when I saw my friends drink and knew I could not, but I schooled myself to believe that though I once had the same privilege, I had abused it so frightfully that it was ***withdrawn***.(p.181)

withdrew

• The less people tolerated us, the more we ***withdrew*** from society, from life itself.(p.151)
• Whenever a situation arose that fast talk wouldn't explain away, I simply ***withdrew***.(p.214)

withholding

• Once we have taken this step, ***withholding*** nothing, we are delighted.(p.75)

within

• My weary and despairing wife was informed that it would all end with heart failure during delirium tremens, or I would develop a wet brain, perhaps ***within*** a year.(p.7)
• But soon the sense of His presence had been blotted out by worldly clamors, mostly those ***within*** myself.(p.12)
• I was to test my thinking by the new God-consciousness ***within***.(p.13)
• In fact, I have been trying to produce some such emotional rearrangement ***within*** you.(p.27)
• Though a robust man at retirement, he went to pieces quickly and was dead ***within*** four years.(p.33)
• Some will be drunk the day after making their resolutions; most of them ***within*** a few weeks.(p.34)
• ***Within*** a week after leaving the hospital a fast-moving trolley car breaks his arm.(p.38)
• We found the Great Reality deep down ***within*** us.(p.55)
• If our testimony helps sweep away prejudice, enables you to think honestly, encourages you to search diligently ***within*** yourself, then, if you wish, you can join us on the Broad Highway.(p.55)
• If he is to find God, the desire must come from ***within***.(p.95)
• The problem with which you struggle usually falls ***within*** one of four categories:(p.108)
• Only a few knew of it at first but, ***within*** a short time, it was billboarded throughout the entire company.(p.145)
• Many of us have felt, for the first time, the Presence and Power of God ***within*** its walls.(p.162)
• If there was a lecture on the subject ***within*** a hundred miles of Akron, I attended.(p.202)
• ***Within*** a year of my return to Detroit, A.A. was a definitely established little group of about a dozen members and I too was established in a modest but steady job handling an independent dry-cleaning route of my own.(p.283)
• However, as there happened to be several saloons ***within*** that distance, I didn't find it necessary to patronize the same place each evening.(p.298)
• (My addiction bloomed ***within*** a small apartment I shared with my wife, a heart patient.)(p.329)
• You can never know the pure joy of recovering ***within*** the Fellowship of Alcoholics Anonymous."(p.334)
• ***Within*** a few months, I was admitted to a state hospital for the mentally ill.(p.370)
• I had nowhere else to go, and I knew something was terribly wrong, and the reason had to lie ***within*** myself.(p.371)
• I promised, but ***within*** two months, I began again.(p.377)
• ***Within*** thirty minutes I knew A.A. was the answer for me.(p.378)
• To me, A.A. is ***within*** the reach of every alcoholic, because it can be achieved in any walk of life and because the achievement is not ours but God's.(p.395)
• I was never drunk on the job, never missed a day's work, was seldom rendered totally ineffective by a hangover and kept my liquor expenses well ***within*** my adequate budget.(p.433)
• In fact it has been only ***within*** the last fifteen years that I changed from a fairly normal, controlled drinker into an alcoholic.(p.464)
• I felt very sorry for myself and attempted suicide on many occasions, making sure there was always somebody ***within*** reaching distance to see that I didn't finish the job.(p.478)
• Nevertheless, we continued to work together and I continued to drink, but I guess, deep down ***within*** her heart as well as ***within*** mine, we both knew I couldn't stop drinking.(p.490)
• ***Within*** about ten days I got locked up for being drunk and this same policeman was in the station house as I was being booked.(p.491)
• In that short period he built ***within*** me something that I had long since lost, which was hope.(p.495)
• ***Within*** a month, the police, the hospital authorities, several kind strangers, most of my friends, all of my close relatives, and a few adepts at rolling a drunk and removing his wrist watch and wallet had been involved.(p.532)
• And if I had been able to turn to the church at that time I'm sure they could not have convinced me my sickness was ***within*** myself, nor could they have shown me the need for self-analysis that A.A. has shown me is vital if I am to survive.(p.546)
• ***Within*** a week, I was feeling well enough to go home.(p.558)
• ***Within*** two months, I was drinking again.(p.558)
• ***Within*** a few days, I found myself drying out on a

drunk farm.(p.559)

without

- *Without* such support, A.A. could have made only the slowest progress.(p.xx)
- There is the type who always believes that after being entirely free from alcohol for a period of time he can take a drink *without* danger.(p.xxviii)
- All these, and many others, have one symptom in common: they cannot start drinking *without* developing the phenomenon of craving.(p.xxviii)
- I admitted for the first time that of myself I was nothing; that *without* Him I was lost.(p.13)
- Faith *without* works was dead, he said.(p.14)
- Highly competent psychiatrists who have dealt with us have found it sometimes impossible to persuade an alcoholic to discuss his situation *without* reserve.(p.18)
- We are *without* defense against the first drink.(p.24)
- He can go anywhere on this earth where other free men may go *without* disaster, provided he remains willing to maintain a certain simple attitude.(p.26)
- Some of our alcoholic readers may think they can do *without* spiritual help.(p.27)
- Here are some of the methods we have tried: Drinking beer only, limiting the number of drinks, never drinking alone, never drinking in the morning, drinking only at home, never having it in the house, never drinking during business hours, drinking only at parties, switching from scotch to brandy, drinking only natural wines, agreeing to resign if ever drunk on the job, taking a trip, not taking a trip, swearing off forever (with and *without* a solemn oath), taking more physical exercise, reading inspirational books, going to health farms and sanitariums, accepting voluntary commitment to asylums -- we could increase the list ad infinitum.(p.31)
- Everybody believes them *without* a murmur of doubt.(p.48)
- Simply because it is impossible to explain what we see, feel, direct, and use, *without* a reasonable assumption as a starting point.(p.48)
- *Without* that, nothing could have happened.(p.52)
- *Without* knowing it, had we not been brought to where we stood by a certain kind of faith?(p.53)
- Imagine life *without* faith!(p.54)
- *Without* help it is too much for us.(p.59)
- Sometimes they hurt us, seemingly *without* provocation, but we invariably find that at some time in the past we have made decisions based on self which later placed us in a position to be hurt.(p.62)
- And there often seems no way of entirely getting rid of self *without* His aid.(p.62)
- The wording was, of course, quite optional so long as we expressed the idea, voicing it *without* reservation.(p.63)
- One object is to disclose damaged or unsalable goods, to get rid of them promptly and *without* regret.(p.64)
- Have we tried to make mortar *without* sand?(p.75)
- Now we need more action, *without* which we find that "Faith *without* works is dead."(p.76)
- We should be sensible, tactful, considerate and humble *without* being servile or scraping.(p.83)
- We will see that our new attitude toward liquor has been given us *without* any thought or effort on our part.(p.85)
- "Faith *without* works is dead."(p.88)
- He will feel he can deal with you *without* being nagged by his family.(p.91)
- In this way you can set them on the right track *without* becoming critical of them.(p.100)
- He has begun to try, with or *without* your cooperation, various means of moderating or staying dry.(p.109)
- Perhaps you both like parties which would be dull *without* liquor.(p.110)
- Even though your husband becomes unbearable and you have to leave him temporarily, you should, if you can, go *without* rancor.(p.111)
- They can urge action *without* arousing hostility.(p.113)
- *Without* you he would have gone to pieces long ago.(p.119)
- In most cases, the alcoholic survived this ordeal *without* relapse, but not always.(p.125)
- These family talks will be constructive if they can be carried on *without* heated argument, self-pity, self-justification or resentful criticism.(p.127)
- *Without* saying so, they may cordially hate him for what he has done to them and to their mother.(p.134)
- When this happens, they can be invited to join in morning meditation and then they can take part in the daily discussion *without* rancor or bias.(p.134)
- *Without* much ado, he accepted the principles and procedure that had helped us.(p.139)
- We all had to place recovery above everything, for *without* recovery we would have lost both home and business.(p.143)
- While on the subject of confidence, can you adopt the attitude that so far as you are concerned this will be a strictly personal matter, that his alcoholic derelictions, the treatment about to be undertaken, will never be discussed *without* his consent?(p.143)
- After your man has gone along *without* drinking for a few months, you may be able to make use of his services with other employees who are giving you the alcoholic run-around -- provided, of course, they are willing to have a third party in the picture.(p.146)
- He cannot picture life *without* alcohol.(p.152)
- Some day he will be unable to imagine life either with alcohol or *without* it.(p.152)
- I know I must get along *without* liquor, but how can I?(p.152)
- To 1950, the year of his death, he carried the A.A. message to more than 5,000 alcoholic men and women, and to all these he gave his medical services *without* thought of charge.(p.171)
- *Without* this proof the expectant purchaser would be forced to depart empty handed with none of what I later came to believe was the great panacea for all human ills.(p.171)
- I did it more and more, and had lots of fun *without* much grief, either physical or financial.(p.172)
- My whole life seemed to be centered around doing what I wanted to do, *without* regard for the rights, wishes, or privileges of anyone else; a state of mind which became more and more predominant as the years passed.(p.172)
- During these years, I drank as much as my purse permitted, still *without* paying too great a penalty, although I was beginning to have morning jitters at times.(p.173)
- But they were much disgusted and told me they would attempt to struggle along *without* my presence.(p.173)
- The next thing they wanted to know was if I thought I could quit of my own accord, *without* any help, if I could just walk out of the hospital and never take another drink.(p.186)
- The next thing they wanted to know was would I be willing to go to this Higher Power and ask for help, calmly and *without* any reservations.(p.186)
- So, after reviewing these things and realizing what liquor had cost me, I went to this Higher Power which, to me was God, *without* any reservation, and admitted that I was completely powerless over alcohol, and that I was willing to do anything in the world to get rid of the problem.(p.187)
- And they said, "No, you have a disease, and it doesn't make any difference how long you do *without* it, after a drink or two you'll end up just like you are now."(p.187)
- Every time I'd start thinking about drinking, I would think of the long, dry years ahead *without* having a drink; but this idea of twenty-four hours, that it was up to me from then on, was a lot of help.(p.188)
- An offer of appreciation for not having had a drink for those few months and then and there, *without* anybody promising me anything or threatening me, I made a solemn vow that never so long as I lived would I take another drink.(p.200)
- Of course, it was always my aim to have my own way *without* being caught.(p.210)
- They suffered from my conduct *without* saying anything, but the reason for this was I still managed to hang onto a very substantial practice.(p.215)
- He startled me by informing me that he was an alcoholic, that he had found a way which so far enabled him to live *without* taking a drink, and that the main idea was to find a way how not to take that first drink.(p.218)
- I believe every member of the Akron Group did come to see me, which impressed me terrifically, not so much because of the stories they told, but because they would take the time to come and talk to me *without* even knowing who I was.(p.218)
- My husband was an alcoholic -- I had only contempt for those *without* my own amazing capacity -- the outcome was inevitable.(p.225)
- Alcohol was that prop, and I didn't see how I could live *without* it.(p.226)
- I had to persist in my attempts to get straightened out enough to be able to use the drinks I needed, *without* their turning on me.(p.227)
- And I was sure that I couldn't be with people who drank, *without* drinking.(p.227)
- In that I was correct: I couldn't be comfortable with any kind of people *without* drinking.(p.227)
- At thirteen I was packed off to a very fine Protestant boarding school in Virginia where I stayed four years, graduating *without* any special achievements.(p.240)
- I'd work like mad for three or four weeks *without* a single drink, save my money, pay a few bills and then "reward" myself with alcohol.(p.244)
- I was soon broke, this time *without* trainfare to go anywhere.(p.252)
- Curious about it, feeling I was missing something, absolutely *without* any illusions about the aftermath, with no pronounced feeling of patriotism, I joined up with a Canadian regiment, serving a little over two years.(p.253)
- He hardly ever went to anything like that *without* me.(p.263)
- It would be impossible for me to pass over this year *without* mentioning my love for, and my indebtedness to these two wonderful people who are no longer with us.(p.280)
- During the first three months I carried on all these activities *without* a car, depending entirely on buses and streetcars -- I, who had always to have a car at my immediate command.(p.283)
- I know now that sixty per cent of the time I drank alone *without* benefit of customers.(p.287)
- While working in an office, there was some semblance of restraint, but, oh boy, when I got on the outside with this new company *without* supervision, did I go to town!(p.300)
- I was *without* power to change the course my life had taken.(p.304)
- It wasn't long before any party *without* drinks was a dud for me.(p.305)
- Others may idle in a retrogressive groove *without* too much danger, but retrogression can spell death for us.(p.311)
- And, as the years go by, working together, sharing our experiences with one another, and also sharing a mutual trust, understanding and love -- *without* strings, *without* obligation -- we acquire relationships that are unique and priceless.(p.312)
- I still couldn't make it through the nights *without* drinking, so I went back into the hospital, this time to a rehabilitation center.(p.320)
- I reached a stage where I couldn't go into my apartment *without* a drink.(p.324)
- Through studied sneaky-drinking, I'd become a senior citizen *without* having lost a day's work because of booze.(p.327)
- After such often-painful vigilance (and numerous phony stints of abstinence), retirement naturally created an impulse to live *without* restraints.(p.328)
- He was close to tears in describing his boredom *without* an activity.(p.334)
- Because it was only through feeling defeat and feeling failure, the inability to cope with my life and with alcohol, that I was able to surrender and accept the fact that I had this disease, and that I had to learn to live again *without* alcohol.(p.335)
- I couldn't live *without* it.(p.337)
- I couldn't do anything *without* it.(p.337)
- And yet, how was I going to live *without* it?(p.338)
- Nevertheless, I began to try to live *without* alcohol.(p.338)
- But this second time, I found I couldn't live normally *without* it, and I was licked worse than ever.(p.340)
- A.A. gives us alcoholics direction into a way of life *without* the need for alcohol.(p.340)
- Three years and three months of sobriety, *without* a slip, has meant a lot to me, my wife, and my family.(p.342)
- I couldn't practice medicine *without* the Great Physician.(p.351)
- *Without* hesitation, I did the only logical thing -- ran away from home.(p.354)
- My sponsor used to say to me, "If I could only paint you a picture of how beautiful life can be *without* booze . . ."(p.355)
- The next steps were bottle hiding, and excuses for trips in order to drink *without* restraint.(p.375)
- We think we can drink to excess *without* anyone knowing it.(p.376)
- The following spring she left me one day *without* giving me any idea of where she had gone, hoping this would bring me to my senses.(p.377)
- By now it had become difficult to visualize a life *without* alcohol.(p.378)
- Could I be an alcoholic *without* some of the hair-raising experiences I had heard of in meetings?(p.379)
- I only know that it does -- if you desire it with your whole heart and *without* reservation.(p.384)
- Something went haywire and I got to depend on it so I could do nothing *without* it.(p.386)
- A "good boy" reached adulthood and success

without achieving maturity or fulfillment.(p.418)
• No one could live such an irresponsible, immature life as I had *without* consequences.(p.420)
• I used to think, "Why live *without* whiskey?"(p.430)
• Now I know I can't live *without* A.A.(p.430)
• Weeks would go by *without* further trouble, and I'd be assured I'd at last hit on the right formula.(p.433)
• But what a difference there is between going through hell *without* a power greater than one's self, and with it!(p.437)
• My reaction was that I'd already helped all the patients on the ward, and I still had plenty of problems of my own *without* trying to help some drunk from A.A.(p.446)
• I served twelve years in prison, never suspecting that *without* alcohol I would not have been in prison at all.(p.457)
• We do this by going to many A.A. meetings with an open mind and a desire to live the good-feeling life *without* chemicals – liquid or otherwise.(p.459)
• It is painful to grow, and *without* the help of my "civilian" A.A. companion, big Gene, I might not have survived that critical year of adjustment.(p.462)
• To this day I can't hear that song *without* remembering that awful Christmas.(p.468)
• My husband interrupted, "She's bad enough now *without* getting mixed up with a bunch of drunks."(p.469)
• It read something like this: "Faith *without* works is dead.(p.473)
• He is my best teacher; *without* him, I am sure I would never have made the progress I have.(p.481)
• If anyone had told me I would be enjoying a hockey game with my husband and my brother *without* being all boozed up, I would not have believed it.(p.481)
• I put Charlie on the car and when I left him I passed both of those liquor stores *without* even thinking about them.(p.495)
• Indeed, *without* their aid we couldn't possibly have gone on.(p.496)
• But I have not seen yet that I should do some constructive acts of love *without* expecting any return.(p.505)
• I was immediately arrested, arraigned in Homicide Court, held *without* bail, and remanded to the old Tombs Prison to await trial.(p.508)
• It didn't worry me very much, because at that time I could shut off for a couple of months *without* taking a drink or even wanting one, and *without* feeling that I was giving anything up.(p.518)
• My only hope was to try and get through what was left of life as best I could, but I could never visualize doing that *without* drinking.(p.522)
• Then it got to the place I couldn't drink *without* getting in jail.(p.526)
• I thought if they smelled whiskey on my breath, they would lock me up, and I couldn't live *without* my bottle.(p.526)
• I remember the day when I decided to drink myself to death quietly, *without* bothering anyone, because I was tired of having been a dependable, trustworthy person for about thirty-nine years *without* having received what I thought was a proper reward for my virtue.(p.531)
• Perhaps, *without* realizing it, I was.)(p.532)
• And having sung that phrase, I'd chuckle with amusement, turning into irony turning into self-contempt turning into self-pity, at the sad fate of Bob, that wonderful, poor little motherless boy who was so smart in school and who grew up to accept responsibility so early and so fast and who staggered under his burdens *without* a whimper until the time came when he thought he was too good for this world and so he ought to be out of it.(p.532)
• *Without* alcohol, I would be really alone.(p.539)
• I looked around me at people who seemed happy and tried to analyze their happiness, and it seemed to me that *without* exception these people had something or somebody they loved very much.(p.546)
• The A.A. members who sponsored me told me in the beginning that I would not only find a way to live *without* having a drink, but that I would find a way to live *without* wanting to drink, if I would do these simple things.(p.550)
• I went on the wagon, with no outside help and with no real difficulty -- except that I didn't enjoy life *without* drinking.(p.557)
• I had to cope with the demands of everyday living *without* my comforter, my anesthetic, my crutch.(p.557)
• But my thinking was still confused, and I was still unable to deal with the challenges of everyday living *without* help.(p.558)
• I have learned how to relate to people; before A.A., I could never do that comfortably *without* alcohol.(p.559)
• And no group, regional committee, or individual should ever take any action that might greatly affect A.A. as a whole *without* conferring with the trustees of the General Service Board.(p.565)
• If we do not do so, we shall stand convicted of emotional sterility and of having lost the faith that moves mountains, *without* which medicine can do little."(p.571)
• This self-insurance has resulted in the restoration of physical, mental and spiritual health and self-respect to hundreds of men and women who would be hopelessly down and out *without* its unique but effective therapy."(p.574)

witness

• Take away my difficulties, that victory over them may bear *witness* to those I would help of Thy Power, Thy Love, and Thy Way of life.(p.63)
• They bear *witness* that release from alcoholism can really be permanent.(p.169)
• We old-timers who get scattered and separated and then *witness* the construction of services to get in more people and to make this thing function, we think that A.A. has changed, but the root of it hasn't.(p.272)
• Each with the other as a *witness*, we took the Third Step out loud -- just as it says in the Big Book.(p.446)

witnessed

• Convincing testimony must surely come from the medical men who have had experience with the sufferings of our members and have *witnessed* our return to health.(p.xxiii)
• But in most fields our generation has *witnessed* complete liberation of our thinking.(p.52)

wits

• My associates, and all the *wits* and literary lights I so much admired, also drank.(p.433)

wits'

• It finally got such a hold on me that I was completely at my *wits'* end, not knowing what the result would be.(p.343)

witty

• I was *witty*.(p.498)

wives

• If any feel that as psychiatrists directing a hospital for alcoholics we appear somewhat sentimental, let them stand with us a while on the firing line, see the tragedies, the despairing *wives*, the little children; let the solving of these problems become a part of their daily work, and even of their sleeping moments, and the most cynical will not wonder that we have accepted and encouraged this movement.(p.xxvi)
• It brings misunderstanding, fierce resentment, financial insecurity, disgusted friends and employers, warped lives of blameless children, sad *wives* and parents – anyone can increase the list.(p.18)
• Strangely enough, *wives*, parents and intimate friends usually find us even more unapproachable than do the psychiatrist and the doctor.(p.18)
• It may be one of our own family, but we cannot disclose anything to our *wives* or our parents which will hurt them and make them unhappy.(p.74)
• Passing all understanding is the patience mothers and *wives* have had with alcoholics.(p.82)
• If circumstances warrant, we ask our *wives* or friends to join us in morning meditation.(p.87)
• It may mean sharing your money and your home, counseling frantic *wives* and relatives, innumerable trips to police courts, sanitariums, hospitals, jails and asylums.(p.97)
• TO *WIVES*(p.104)
• Among us are *wives*, relatives and friends whose problem has been solved, as well as some who have not yet found a happy solution.(p.104)
• We want the *wives* of Alcoholics Anonymous to address the *wives* of men who drink too much.(p.104)
• As *wives* of Alcoholics Anonymous, we would like you to feel that we understand as perhaps few can.(p.104)
• How could men who loved their *wives* and children be so unthinking, so callous, so cruel?(p.107)
• The *wives* and children of such men suffer horribly, but not more than the men themselves.(p.114)
• We *wives* found that, like everybody else, we were afflicted with pride, self-pity, vanity and all the things which go to make up the self-centered person; and we were not above selfishness or dishonesty.(p.116)
• We suggest that you direct some of your thought to the *wives* of his new alcoholic friends.(p.119)
• Though it is entirely separate from Alcoholics Anonymous, it uses the general principles of the A.A. program as a guide for husbands, *wives*, relatives, friends, and others close to alcoholics.(p.121)
• The foregoing pages (though addressed only to *wives*) indicate the problems such people may face.(p.121)
• Husbands and *wives* have sometimes been obliged to separate for a time until new perspective, new victory over hurt pride could be rewon.(p.125)
• We know there are difficult *wives* and families, but the man who is getting over alcoholism must remember he did much to make them so.(p.127)
• As we left, and they were escorting us across the bridge into Wheeling, I, with great dignity and sarcasm, told them if their *wives* were ever visiting in Akron, and they, too, were looking for their route sign as I was, that I hoped I could extend to them the hospitality that had been shown to me in Bellaire.(p.264)
• I hadn't been in too long when one of the men's *wives* called me one Sunday and told me she didn't think I had any part of the program.(p.273)
• The meeting consisted of perhaps eight or nine alcoholics and seven or eight *wives*.(p.291)
• That was when all the boys and Esther got drunk and the *wives* didn't.(p.386)
• This is a world clearing house for the Al-Anon Family Groups, composed largely of the *wives*, husbands and friends of A.A. members.(p.575)

wobbled

• After one of those days of inferno, I *wobbled* from a hotel bar to a brokerage office.(p.4)

woe

• My first meeting gave me a great deal of hope and lots of willing ears for my tale of *woe* and for my questions.(p.364)

woes

• He and his wife more than accepted me; he listened to all my *woes*; both of them treated me as a human being.(p.462)

woke

• I *woke* up.(p.5)
• I remember nothing from then on until I *woke* up at a friend's house, in a town near home.(p.179)
• The next morning I *woke* up in jail in Cleveland and the jailor had $1,175 of my money in an envelope.(p.196)
• At night, I *woke* up and the folks with whom I roomed were home by then.(p.205)
• And I remembered the creeping horror of the interminable night, in which I slept for short spells and *woke* up dripping with cold sweat and shaken with utter despair, to drink hastily from my bottle and mercifully pass out again, "You're mad, you're mad, you're mad!" pounded through my brain with each returning ray of consciousness, and I drowned the refrain with drink.(p.224)
• I was gathering that cache for disposal when my wife *woke* up and caught me at it.(p.333)
• I had to have it with me at night, in case I *woke* up and needed that drink.(p.337)
• I knew nothing about alcoholism or the D.T.'s, but when I *woke* up on this last morning of my son's illness, I taped the keyhole on my door because "everyone was out there."(p.338)
• So I got drunker and drunker, and then, suddenly, I *woke* up in the booby-hatch.(p.387)
• I *woke* up in this bare room with nothing around me but bars; they wouldn't let me smoke and treated me, well, like I was nuts.(p.387)
• They *woke* up with hangovers, but with no remorse.(p.407)
• I *woke* up filled with secret guilt and shame.(p.407)
• When I *woke* up sober, my handiwork confronted me.(p.435)
• I *woke* up in jail, sick, withdrawing from alcohol and speed, already a four-time loser, and now with a fifth felony charge against me.(p.460)
• I got drunk one night in October, went to sleep in the rain and *woke* up with pneumonia.(p.490)
• That *woke* me up.(p.511)
• But I don't remember that any of them ever went to sleep in joints and *woke* up with no shoes on in the winter, or fell out of chairs.(p.527)
• One morning, I *woke* up with a thousand dollars.(p.528)

wolf

• The remonstrances of my friends terminated in a row and I became a lone *wolf*.(p.3)

woman

• It was thought that no alcoholic man or *woman* could be excluded from our Society; that our leaders might serve but never govern; that each group was to be autonomous and there was to be no professional class of therapy.(p.xix)
• Actually we were fooling ourselves, for deep down

in every man, ***woman***, and child, is the fundamental idea of God.(p.55)
- She will want to know who the ***woman*** is and where she is.(p.81)
- Ask any ***woman*** who has sent her husband to distant places on the theory he would escape the alcohol problem.(p.101)
- In the midst of such pandemonium they may have rushed out threatening to live with the other ***woman*** forever.(p.106)
- These are some of the questions which race through the mind of every ***woman*** who has an alcoholic husband.(p.108)
- They need the counsel and love of a ***woman*** who has gone through what you have.(p.119)
- I offered them a drink, and they came to the bottom of the stairs and the good ***woman*** fainted, just looking at me.(p.205)
- She was a ***woman*** devoted to her family and loyal to her husband, but quarrels did not make a happy environment for her.(p.210)
- This time I seemed to be already awake, sitting upright in a big easy chair, in the middle of an animated conversation with a perfectly strange young ***woman***, who didn't appear to think it strange.(p.222)
- All I had left was an iron determination to live my own life in spite of the alien world -- and here I was, an inwardly frightened, outwardly defiant ***woman***, who desperately needed a prop to keep going.(p.226)
- A pioneer ***woman*** member of A.A.'s first Group.(p.261)
- Time went on and the drinking got worse and worse, and I was in another barroom, down the road the other way, a small one, and I took my glass -- that morning I'd been able to lift it from the bar -- and I said to the ***woman*** behind the bar, "I wish I might never take another drop of that stuff.(p.266)
- And that ***woman*** told me long after that was the surest proof to her that this program could work.(p.272)
- In the meantime, another doctor in Evanston became convinced that the program had possibilities, and turned over a ***woman*** to us to do something about.(p.295)
- Just an unstable ***woman***, undisciplined, poorly adjusted and filled with nameless fears.(p.305)
- My story happens to be a particular kind of woman's story; the story of the ***woman*** who drinks at home.(p.335)
- I was a ***woman***, tied to my home.(p.338)
- I heard one very ill ***woman*** say that she didn't believe in the surrender part of the A.A. program.(p.340)
- I was sitting in my office one time after I had operated on a ***woman***.(p.350)
- I thought to myself -- what is curing that ***woman***?(p.350)
- My mother was a lovely, sweet ***woman***, whose only weakness was my father.(p.369)
- This new analyst was a ***woman*** doctor, one of the best in the country.(p.409)
- An obstreperous ***woman*** in a bar is a nuisance, and they wanted no trouble with the police.(p.410)
- Nor was I the "worst ***woman*** who ever lived."(p.414)
- In the first year there were episodes such as kicking Priscilla in the shins, getting the lock changed on the desk in the A.A. Club, because I, as secretary, didn't want the Intergroup secretary "interfering," and taking an older ***woman*** member out to lunch for the express purpose of informing her that she was "a phony."(p.416)
- In fact, I was taken to A.A. by a ***woman*** whom my father had taken to A.A. thirteen years earlier.(p.419)
- And A.A. took this wreck of a ***woman*** and brought her back to life.(p.470)
- But to another ***woman***, the first ***woman*** I met in A.A., I could talk.(p.471)
- In all the sanitariums and psycho wards I had never met a single ***woman*** who said she was an alcoholic.(p.471)
- When I first came into A.A., the ***woman*** who was my sponsor was the first ***woman*** I had ever met who admitted that she was an alcoholic.(p.472)
- And so for three months this one ***woman*** was my A.A.(p.472)
- I went to meetings, I spent a lot of time at the clubroom, but it was all centered in this one ***woman***.(p.472)
- I not listen to old ***woman***.(p.474)
- This really makes for an attractive ***woman***!(p.479)
- I really do believe it is much harder for a ***woman*** to gain back her self-respect than it is for a man.(p.480)
- Men are supposed to be tough and rugged to start with, but if a ***woman*** becomes that way, it is pretty hard to get back the niceties of womanhood.(p.480)
- That was one of the worst things that could have happened to an alcoholic ***woman***.(p.527)
- It came out that I had sold a ***woman*** a fur coat.(p.528)

woman's

- Still another experience: A ***woman's*** voice came faintly over long distance from Virginia.(p.137)
- My story happens to be a particular kind of ***woman's*** story; the story of the woman who drinks at home.(p.335)

womanhood

- Men are supposed to be tough and rugged to start with, but if a woman becomes that way, it is pretty hard to get back the niceties of ***womanhood***.(p.480)
- Another thing that mother drilled into me was a very Puritanical point of view as to sex relations and as to motherhood and ***womanhood***.(p.483)

women

- Because this book has become the basic text for our Society and has helped such large numbers of alcoholic men and ***women*** to recover, there exists a sentiment against any radical changes being made in it.(p.xi)
- We, of Alcoholics Anonymous, are more than one hundred men and ***women*** who have recovered from a seemingly hopeless state of mind and body.(p.xiii)
- The membership had then reached about 100 men and ***women***.(p.xvii)
- More than 15% of us are ***women***.(p.xx)
- ***Women*** now make up more than one-fourth of the membership; among newer members, the proportion is nearly one-third.(p.xxii)
- Men and ***women*** drink essentially because they like the effect produced by alcohol.(p.xxvi)
- We of ALCOHOLICS ANONYMOUS, know thousands of men and ***women*** who were once just as hopeless as Bill.(p.17)
- Our hope is that many alcoholic men and ***women***, desperately in need, will see these pages, and we believe that it is only by fully disclosing ourselves and our problems that they will be persuaded to say, "Yes, I am one of them too; I must have this thing."(p.29)
- We alcoholics are men and ***women*** who have lost the ability to control our drinking.(p.30)
- This is particularly true of ***women***.(p.33)
- On one proposition, however, these men and ***women*** are strikingly agreed.(p.50)
- Here are thousands of men and ***women***, worldly indeed.(p.50)
- Those who do not recover are people who cannot or will not completely give themselves to this simple program, usually men and ***women*** who are constitutionally incapable of being honest with themselves.(p.58)
- Perhaps we are mixed up with ***women*** in a fashion we wouldn't care to have advertised.(p.80)
- But what we have said applies quite as much to ***women***.(p.104)
- Our activities in behalf of ***women*** who drink are on the increase.(p.104)
- There is every evidence that ***women*** regain their health as readily as men if they try our suggestions.(p.104)
- Sometimes there were other ***women***.(p.106)
- We know ***women*** who are unafraid, even happy under these conditions.(p.111)
- We know ***women*** who have done it.(p.114)
- If such ***women*** adopt a spiritual way of life their road will be smoother.(p.114)
- We thought, on the whole, we were pretty good ***women***, capable of being nicer if our husbands stopped drinking.(p.116)
- We ***women*** carry with us a picture of the ideal man, the sort of chap we would like our husbands to be.(p.118)
- Our ***women*** folk have suggested certain attitudes a wife may take with the husband who is recovering.(p.122)
- Seeing much of each other, scarce an evening passed that someone's home did not shelter a little gathering of men and ***women***, happy in their release, and constantly thinking how they might present their discovery to some newcomer.(p.159)
- Many a distracted wife has visited this house to find loving and understanding companionship among ***women*** who knew her problem, to hear from the lips of their husbands what had happened to them, to be advised how her own wayward mate might be hospitalized and approached when next he stumbled.(p.160)
- The expression on the faces of the ***women***, that indefinable something in the eyes of the men, the stimulating and electric atmosphere of the place, conspired to let him know that here was haven at last.(p.160)
- Dr. Bob and the twelve men and ***women*** who here tell their stories were among the early members of A.A.'s first groups.(p.169)
- To 1950, the year of his death, he carried the A.A. message to more than 5,000 alcoholic men and ***women***, and to all these he gave his medical services without thought of charge.(p.171)
- For some reason, we alcoholics seem to have the gift of picking out the world's finest ***women***.(p.178)
- One hundred for unmarried ***women*** at one end, one hundred for men at the other, and one hundred for married couples in the middle.(p.198)
- ***WOMEN*** SUFFER TOO(p.222)
- Early member, she spread the word among ***women*** in our pioneering period.(p.222)
- I came of good stock, of men and ***women*** who drank wine all their lives as a beverage, and while they occasionally got drunk at special celebrations, they were up and about their business the next day.(p.231)
- But I had never been a flippant, wise-cracking sneerer at the few persons I had met who had impressed me as Christian men and ***women***, or at any institution whose sincerity of purpose I could see.(p.259)
- I often think how that could have turned some people away, because there were no other ***women*** alcoholics there then.(p.269)
- There were two ***women*** in the St. Thomas Hospital at that time in a room.(p.272)
- I knew Doc and Anne were going to be there, and all of them thought it would be good for me, but the first thing I did was to go to St. Thomas and try to talk to those ***women***.)(p.272)
- Why do men and ***women*** like these join A.A.?(p.315)
- Many ***women*** who have reached the stage that I had reached in my drinking have lost husbands, children, homes, everything they hold dear.(p.323)
- I became one of the most active ***women*** in the community, what with P.T.A., other community organizations and drives.(p.339)
- My sister-in-law took me to a place she had heard about that helps ***women*** like me.(p.371)
- The letter from A.A. had said this man would see me -- there weren't any ***women***.(p.393)
- He was well behaved, and idealistic where ***women*** were concerned.(p.403)
- Shakespeare said, "All the world's a stage, all the men and ***women*** merely players."(p.449)
- (I've met some of these same ***women*** since in A.A.)(p.471)
- Some drunken ***women*** really are, you know.(p.479)
- I thought that all ***women*** should be perfect.(p.487)
- Some men and ***women*** come to visit my friend of the night before.(p.504)
- I was married and divorced again before I was twenty-three years old, this time to a prominent band leader -- a man that many ***women*** wanted.(p.546)
- Therefore, no society of men and ***women*** ever had more urgent need for continuous effectiveness and permanent unity.(p.563)
- This self-insurance has resulted in the restoration of physical, mental and spiritual health and self-respect to hundreds of men and ***women*** who would be hopelessly down and out without its unique but effective therapy."(p.574)

women's

- So I created a job for myself selling ***women's*** hosiery and men's made-to-order shirts.(p.282)
- At a ***women's*** halfway house, I became associated with Alcoholics Anonymous and became aware of alcoholism as a disease, not just a "weakness."(p.371)

won

- The insane idea ***won*** out.(p.37)
- Max ***won***; I didn't drink it.(p.444)

won't

- The alcoholic may say to himself in the most casual way, "It ***won't*** burn me this time, so here's how!"(p.24)
- A remorseful mumbling that we are sorry ***won't*** fill the bill at all.(p.83)
- That ***won't*** hurt him a bit, even though he does not go for this remedy.(p.144)
- He interrupted: "I used to be strong for the church, but that ***won't*** fix it.(p.157)
- "Sure I would," replied Bill, "Maybe it ***won't*** do any good, but I'd like to see you both, anyhow.(p.189)
- I try to live today so that tomorrow I ***won't*** be ashamed when I wake up in the morning.(p.325)
- Getting drunk ***won't*** solve them.(p.382)
- In the back of my mind, I probably thought, "They ***won't*** take me as drunk as I am."(p.398)

• I *won't* go into detail about that, but I can assure you it's no fun.(p.469)

• I even wanted to – but I wasn't allowed to, so I *won't* go now.(p.470)

• If I don't get started soon, I *won't* have time to finish.(p.499)

wonder

• If any feel that as psychiatrists directing a hospital for alcoholics we appear somewhat sentimental, let them stand with us a while on the firing line, see the tragedies, the despairing wives, the little children; let the solving of these problems become a part of their daily work, and even of their sleeping moments, and the most cynical will not *wonder* that we have accepted and encouraged this movement.(p.xxvi)

• I began to *wonder*, for such an appalling lack of perspective seemed near being just that.(p.5)

• He listened in *wonder* as I talked.(p.14)

• I had no trouble refusing drinks, and began to *wonder* if I had not been making too hard work of a simple matter.(p.40)

• There was a feeling of awe and *wonder*, but it was fleeting and soon lost.(p.46)

• Small *wonder* many in the medical profession have a low opinion of alcoholics and their chance for recovery!(p.73)

• In that case he is going to *wonder* how you can add anything to what he already knows.(p.93)

• No *wonder* an alcoholic is strangely irrational.(p.140)

• Bill lay on his hospital bed and looked at us in *wonder*.(p.188)

• When I look back on that last horrible year of constant drinking I *wonder* how I survived it either physically or mentally.(p.224)

• The lesson of his death still remains with me, yet I often *wonder* what would have happened if somebody else had made that first call on me.(p.239)

• And another thing, it's a *wonder* they didn't throw us back in because I could become very dignified and sarcastic.(p.264)

• On my trips back to Akron to get my spirits recharged and to work with other alcoholics, I would ask Dr. Bob about this delay and *wonder* just what was wrong with me.(p.293)

• And we *wonder* how much further this man could go if his alcoholic problem could be removed and he could throw one hundred per cent of his abilities into action.(p.308)

• He used to *wonder*, when he'd spot one of my bottles around the house, just how he could have overlooked that particular bottle.(p.325)

• I'd think, "I *wonder* why I'm saying that again -- I've already said it three times."(p.442)

• You may *wonder* why, since I was having all this trouble, and was having to seek the assistance of others, A.A. hadn't come into the picture.(p.469)

• He started telling me how much trouble he had, and I said to myself, "I *wonder* why this guy is telling me all his troubles.(p.494)

• I *wonder* if it will reach her neck.(p.497)

• But somehow or other, with my old alcoholic brain, sitting there in that chair, I kept saying to myself, "I *wonder* if it'll work?(p.515)

• I *wonder* if it'll work for me?"(p.516)

• Then I would go home full of remorse, and *wonder* what I was going to do until I got my next check.(p.527)

• I, a man of steel, with very high ideals, well brought up, an honor student and the recipient of scholarships and prizes, a boy *wonder* in business – I, Bob, the author of this essay, looked and saw that the universe was beneath my contempt, and that to remove myself from it was the only thing of dignity a man could do.(p.531)

• I *wonder* if ever there has been a sillier reason for getting drunk all the time.(p.537)

• Regarded as something of a "boy *wonder*," I began to see myself that way.(p.555)

• The early promise of the "boy *wonder*" faded, and my career began to drift.(p.556)

wondered

• I *wondered* whether I dared hide a full bottle of gin near the head of our bed.(p.8)

• I *wondered* how he had escaped.(p.9)

• Disappointed but curious, I *wondered* what had got into the fellow.(p.9)

• Having persevered with the rest of the program, they *wondered* why they fell.(p.73)

• I felt this was inevitable and *wondered* if the bank was doing the man an injustice.(p.138)

• All this while, I *wondered* whether I could do laundry for the neighbors as a part-time job.(p.371)

• However, after I heard a few stories of jails, sanitariums, broken homes and skid row, I *wondered* if I really was an alcoholic.(p.378)

• At first, I *wondered* whether he was alcoholic himself, and was sending me to find out about A.A.(p.446)

wonderful

• I was to know happiness, peace, and usefulness, in a way of life that is incredibly more *wonderful* as time passes.(p.8)

• We commenced to make many fast friends and a fellowship has grown up among us of which it is a *wonderful* thing to feel a part.(p.15)

• But there exists among us a fellowship, a friendliness, and an understanding which is indescribably *wonderful*.(p.17)

• Life would be *wonderful*.(p.61)

• Follow the dictates of a Higher Power and you will presently live in a new and *wonderful* world, no matter what your present circumstances!(p.100)

• When we do that, we find it solves our problems too; the ensuing lack of fear, worry and hurt feelings is a *wonderful* thing.(p.116)

• You will be bound to them with new and *wonderful* ties, for you will escape disaster together and you will commence shoulder to shoulder your common journey.(p.152)

• It is a most *wonderful* blessing to be relieved of the terrible curse with which I was afflicted.(p.180)

• If I could, that was *wonderful*, that was just fine, and they would very much appreciate a person who had that kind of power, but they were looking for a man that knew he had a problem, and knew that he couldn't handle it himself and needed outside help.(p.186)

• Looking sadder than ever, he wearily ventured, "Well this is *wonderful* for you fellows, but it can't be for me.(p.188)

• Bill looked across at my wife, and said to her, "Henrietta, the Lord has been so *wonderful* to me, curing me of this terrible disease, that I just want to keep talking about it and telling people."(p.191)

• That sentence, "The Lord has been so *wonderful* to me, curing me of this terrible disease, that I just want to keep telling people about it," has been sort of a golden text for the A.A. program and for me.(p.191)

• Of course, as time went on, and I began to get my health back and began to be so I didn't have to hide from people all the time, it's just been *wonderful*.(p.192)

• I'm so grateful for both the program and the people in it that I still want to go, and then probably the most *wonderful* thing that I learned from the program -- I've seen this in the 'A.A. Grapevine' a lot of times, and I've had people say it to me personally, and I've heard people get up in meetings and make the same statement: The statement is, "I came into A.A. solely for the purpose of sobriety, but it has been through A.A. that I have found God."(p.192)

• I feel that is about the most *wonderful* thing that a person can do.(p.192)

• And Jim G. had such a *wonderful* sense of humor, and when he came I was in tears, and I told him, "I want to do this, but I can't.(p.269)

• It would be impossible for me to pass over this year without mentioning my love for, and my indebtedness to these two *wonderful* people who are no longer with us.(p.280)

• It would be *wonderful* were I able to tell you that my confidence in God and my application of the Twelve Steps to my daily living have utterly banished fear.(p.284)

• For me it was a *wonderful* experience.(p.309)

• It took the help, understanding and *wonderful* companionship that was given so freely to me by my "exalkie" friends.(p.311)

• But I met a real *wonderful* girl I'll call Jean.(p.318)

• I thought it was *wonderful*, simply marvelous, for him.(p.321)

• Then I went to another meeting, and I still thought it was *wonderful* --for him, but not for me.(p.321)

• The regular flow of all the literature, which I keep meticulously and which, of course, I study, has been *wonderful*.(p.342)

• I returned to my home in Lucknow, India, at the end of November last year from a vacation in one of the most famous beauty spots in our country, a mountain resort 6,800 feet up, with a *wonderful* lake.(p.342)

• As these words are written at fifty-three years of age, with over nine years of A.A. behind me, with all its *wonderful* teachings, I haven't the slightest doubt about being an alcoholic.(p.356)

• My *wonderful* wife did everything to play along with me.(p.361)

• I had not only let my wife down but also a lot of other *wonderful* people who had helped me.(p.364)

• With that utterance I again made a *wonderful* discovery.(p.366)

• What a *wonderful* new feeling, what a *wonderful* relief!(p.366)

• I met a *wonderful* man.(p.403)

• I now said a lucky and *wonderful* thing.(p.412)

• Through going to meetings and listening, and occasionally speaking, through doing Twelve Step work, whereby in helping others you are both the teacher and the student, by making many *wonderful* A.A. friends, I have been taught all the things in life that are worth having.(p.416)

• This has been a *wonderful* thing in my life.(p.417)

• This was *wonderful*.(p.426)

• I headed home for the most *wonderful* experience of all time -- meeting my "new" parents -- mom and dad looked different than I had pictured them.(p.428)

• I have two *wonderful* little boys.(p.431)

• How exciting to learn the inward mysteries that govern the behavior of people, how *wonderful* to know, at last, all about myself!(p.434)

• There have been some *wonderful* things, too.(p.438)

• What a *wonderful* power he has over the mind!(p.499)

• What a *wonderful* idea!(p.505)

• So many *wonderful* things have happened to me that at times I can't believe this is me.(p.529)

• And having sung that phrase, I'd chuckle with amusement, turning into irony turning into self-contempt turning into self-pity, at the sad fate of Bob, that *wonderful*, poor little motherless boy who was so smart in school and who grew up to accept responsibility so early and so fast and who staggered under his burdens without a whimper until the time came when he thought he was too good for this world and so he ought to be out of it.(p.532)

wonderfully

• It has been repeatedly proven among us that upon this simple cornerstone a *wonderfully* effective spiritual structure can be built.(p.47)

• It is a way of life that pays as it goes, every step of the way, in compensations that have been *wonderfully* rich and rewarding.(p.394)

wondering

• One dismal afternoon he paced a hotel lobby *wondering* how his bill was to be paid.(p.154)

• I drove towards Cleveland *wondering* why I found myself in such a changed set of conditions as compared with those of six months before.(p.200)

• Just as I was *wondering* what on earth I could do -- I was too drunk even to pack a handkerchief – the memory of an A.A. write-up that I had seen in the Evening Mail flashed across my mind -- and I thought to myself, this is something I haven't tried yet.(p.523)

wonders

• Your new courage, good nature and lack of self-consciousness will do *wonders* for you socially.(p.115)

• I do not recollect the specific conversation that went on but I believe I did challenge Bill to tell me something about A.A. and I do recall one other thing: I wanted to know what this was that worked so many *wonders*, and hanging over the mantel was a picture of Gethsemane and Bill pointed to it and said, "There it is," which didn't make much sense to me.(p.216)

wooden

• While I was taking inventory in the cold-storage locker one Sunday, a *wooden* sign bolted to the inside door stopped me in my tracks.(p.461)

woodshed

• Four days before he had hanged himself in his *woodshed*.(p.137)

wool

• Perhaps they created the impression that he is to be wrapped in cotton *wool* and placed on a pedestal.(p.122)

• I found some *wool* stockings, some white flannels that had shrunk to my knees, and an old jacket.(p.288)

woolen

• I got a job in the *woolen* mills in Ravenna – very hard work.(p.262)

woos

• So long as a retiree *woos* his bottle at home, he stays out of public trouble.(p.330)

woozy

• I was still *woozy* from the night before.(p.323)

word

• We are not an organization in the conventional sense of the *word*.(p.xiii)

• New groups started up and it was found, to the astonishment of everyone, that A.A.'s message could be transmitted in the mail as well as by

word of mouth.(p.xviii)
• The ***word*** God still aroused a certain antipathy.(p.12)
• Whatever the precise definition of the ***word*** may be, we call this plain insanity.(p.37)
• To others, the ***word*** "God" brought up a particular idea of Him with which someone had tried to impress them during childhood.(p.45)
• Instead of regarding ourselves as intelligent agents, spearheads of God's ever advancing Creation, we agnostics and atheists chose to believe that our human intelligence was the last ***word***, the alpha and the omega, the beginning and end of all.(p.49)
• Notice that the ***word*** "fear" is bracketed alongside the difficulties with Mr. Brown, Mrs. Jones, the employer, and the wife.(p.67)
• This short ***word*** somehow touches about every aspect of our lives.(p.67)
• We will comprehend the ***word*** serenity and we will know peace.(p.83)
• For the type of alcoholic who is able and willing to get well, little charity, in the ordinary sense of the ***word***, is needed or wanted.(p.97)
• A ***word*** about sex relations.(p.134)
• By no means do we offer it as the last ***word*** on this subject, but so far as we are concerned, it has worked with us.(p.144)
• As far as I know that was the first time I had ever paid any attention to that ***word***.(p.187)
• I agreed with him and told him in no uncertain terms that I never broke my ***word*** in my life.(p.206)
• The man turned out to be Bill D., a very early member of A.A., and I couldn't tell you a ***word*** of what he said.(p.208)
• And being a big-shot man of my ***word***, I said, "Well, if I said so, then I'll go."(p.217)
• Early member, she spread the ***word*** among women in our pioneering period.(p.222)
• There is another meaning for the Hebrew ***word*** that in the King James version of the Bible is translated "salvation."(p.228)
• I don't think the boys were completely convinced of my personality change, for they fought shy of including my story in the book, so my only contribution to their literary efforts was my firm conviction, being still a theological rebel, that the ***word*** God should be qualified with the phrase "as we understand him" -- for that was the only way I could accept spirituality.(p.248)
• The program was carried on entirely by ***word*** of mouth.(p.291)
• Fortunately, I didn't say a ***word*** to George on the way home.(p.322)
• And "Think" -- that one important ***word*** means so much to me.(p.325)
• The ***word*** "insanity" came through clearly – and repugnantly.(p.332)
• The ***word*** "thoroughly" rang a bell.(p.349)
• I didn't say a ***word*** to anyone about my lapse.(p.364)
• I couldn't get a ***word*** in edgewise!(p.414)
• The ***word*** "alcoholic" does not turn me off any more; in fact, it is music to my ears when it applies to me.(p.463)
• Then in a couple of hours, when there was still no ***word*** from my husband and no sign of him, I had the feeling we alcoholics all know.(p.467)
• I know the biggest ***word*** for me in A.A. is "honesty."(p.482)
• Honesty is the easiest ***word*** for me to understand because it is the exact opposite of what I've been doing all my life.(p.482)
• How I hate that ***word***.(p.499)
• He never says an unkind ***word***.(p.501)
• There was the father one lost respect for at the age of eleven, because the father broke his solemn ***word*** in a circumstance where you, eleven years old, had assumed guilt when you were innocent; but the father would not believe you, no matter what; and to ease his suffering you "confessed" and were "forgiven," only – months later – to have your "guilt" brought up – only he and you knew what he was talking bout -- brought up in front of the stern grandmother.(p.533)
• The sacred ***word*** was broken and you never trusted your father again, and avoided him.(p.533)
• They said if you want to know how this program works, take the first ***word*** of your question – the H is for honesty, the O is for open-mindedness and the W is for willingness; these our Book calls the essentials of recovery.(p.550)
• During the day a friend of mine brought me some magazines to take to a hospital group I was interested in, and I looked through them and a "banner" across the front of one featured an article by a prominent clergyman in which I caught the ***word*** "resentment."(p.552)

wording

• The ***wording*** was, of course, quite optional so long as we expressed the idea, voicing it without reservation.(p.63)

words

• There was, therefore, a sense of real satisfaction when I was asked to contribute a few ***words*** on a subject which is covered in such masterly detail in these pages.(p.xxv)
• No ***words*** can tell of the loneliness and despair I found in that bitter morass of self-pity.(p.8)
• I had a few ***words*** with the boss, but nothing serious.(p.36)
• In other ***words***, we treat sex as we would any other problem.(p.69)
• Our behavior will convince them more than our ***words***.(p.83)
• I still expected a plea for clemency, but these ***words*** came through the receiver: "I just wanted to tell you Paul jumped from a hotel window in Hartford last Saturday.(p.136)
• In other ***words***, he talked my language.(p.180)
• In other ***words***, I was always safe from the discipline of my father, and having developed along that line, I had considerable difficulty in school.(p.210)
• In other ***words***, I fired the client before the client fired me.(p.214)
• From far away, as if in a delirium, I heard my own voice – calling someone "Dorothy," talking of dress shops, of jobs . . . the ***words*** came clearer . . . this sound of my own voice frightened me as it came closer . . . and suddenly, there I was, talking of I knew not what, to someone I'd never seen before this very moment.(p.222)
• He put me at ease with his first few ***words***.(p.309)
• Where were all those ***words*** coming from?(p.333)
• LIFESAVING ***WORDS***(p.342)
• As these ***words*** are written at fifty-three years of age, with over nine years of A.A. behind me, with all its wonderful teachings, I haven't the slightest doubt about being an alcoholic.(p.356)
• The next few years in New York can be described in a very few ***words***.(p.358)
• It was the first of many such experiences that became the only cause of harsh ***words***, tears and heartaches in an otherwise truly beautiful marriage.(p.361)
• Her parting ***words*** were "I am not leaving you because I don't love you; it's because I do love you.(p.362)
• Looking directly at me was a large oil painting of my wife, and her very ***words*** seemed to shout at me -- "I am not leaving you because I don't love you; it's because I do love you.(p.363)
• In other ***words***, I began contributing, and so, naturally, I began to get something more.(p.365)
• When I was called upon for a few ***words*** I had to tell my friends that I wasn't one year old in A.A. that evening but only a "nine month baby."(p.366)
• I could end my story here, but for the new man I would like to add a few ***words***.(p.366)
• These ***words*** may be difficult for you to understand now, but be patient and you'll know what I mean.(p.367)
• I wish I could tell you all that A.A. has done for me, all that I think and feel about A.A., but it's something that I have experienced and have never been able to put into ***words***.(p.394)
• The ***words*** of Dr. Bob and Bill are with me all the time.(p.395)
• I couldn't focus enough to make out the chart, but the card contained two ***words*** -- "ACUTE ALCOHOLISM."(p.422)
• Don't mince ***words***.(p.423)
• The ***words*** jumped out at me.(p.461)
• There at the top of the folder was my name, age and address, and underneath were the ***words***, "Periodic Drinker."(p.470)
• In other ***words***, the kindest doctor in the whole world, and I had one such, couldn't help me because I always felt, "You can't know about me – you can't possibly know – you don't even drink!"(p.471)
• Love has no ***words*** to spell or lines to start and stop.(p.474)
• Our language has few ***words*** to say many things.(p.474)
• My aunt had sharp ***words*** for me about drinking.(p.474)
• ***Words*** of truth and love are strong medicine.(p.476)
• As I write these ***words***, it seems incredible that these things should have happened to me, for they are, truly, against all my instincts and training.(p.536)
• Even when you don't really want it for them, and your prayers are only ***words*** and you don't mean it, go ahead and do it anyway.(p.552)

wordy

• We read ***wordy*** books and indulge in windy arguments, thinking we believe this universe needs no God to explain it.(p.49)

wore

• I ***wore*** a man's raincoat, turned inside out, a present from a friend, for now my funds were low.(p.411)
• I ***wore*** those moccasins every night for the next seven years, until they ***wore*** out.(p.445)
• I ***wore*** stripes and chains.(p.460)
• I remember in my early youth my mother dressed me just as she did my two sisters, and I ***wore*** curls until I was six years of age.(p.483)

work

• If you have a drinking problem, we hope that you may pause in reading one of the forty-four personal stories and think: "Yes, that happened to me"; or, more important, "Yes, I've felt like that"; or most important, "Yes, I believe this program can ***work*** for me, too."(p.xii)
• We would like it understood that our alcoholic ***work*** is an avocation.(p.xiii)
• We shall be interested to hear from those who are getting results from this book, particularly from those who have commenced ***work*** with other alcoholics.(p.xiv)
• It also indicated that strenuous ***work***, one alcoholic with another, was vital to permanent recovery.(p.xvii)
• Hence the two men set to ***work*** almost frantically upon alcoholics arriving in the ward of the Akron City Hospital.(p.xvii)
• This ***work*** at Akron continued through the summer of 1935.(p.xvii)
• The test that it faced was this: Could these large numbers of erstwhile erratic alcoholics successfully meet and ***work*** together?(p.xviii)
• Though we ***work*** out our solution on the spiritual as well as an altruistic plane, we favor hospitalization for the alcoholic who is very jittery or befogged.(p.xxiv)
• If any feel that as psychiatrists directing a hospital for alcoholics we appear somewhat sentimental, let them stand with us a while on the firing line, see the tragedies, the despairing wives, the little children; let the solving of these problems become a part of their daily ***work***, and even of their sleeping moments, and the most cynical will not wonder that we have accepted and encouraged this movement.(p.xxvi)
• My ***work*** took me about Wall street and little by little I became interested in the market.(p.2)
• My wife began to ***work*** in a department store, coming home exhausted to find me drunk.(p.4)
• My wife was at ***work***.(p.8)
• My intellectual heroes, the chemists the astronomers, even the evolutionists, suggested vast laws and forces at ***work***.(p.10)
• Here was something at ***work*** in a human heart which had done the impossible.(p.11)
• They in turn might ***work*** with others.(p.14)
• Particularly was it imperative to ***work*** with others as he had worked with me.(p.14)
• For if an alcoholic failed to perfect and enlarge his spiritual life through ***work*** and self-sacrifice for others, he could not survive the certain trials and low spots ahead.(p.14)
• If he did not ***work***, he would surely drink again, and if he drank, he would surely die.(p.15)
• It was fortunate, for my old business associates remained skeptical for a year and a half, during which I found little ***work***.(p.15)
• This sometimes nearly drove me back to drink, but I soon found that when all other measures failed, ***work*** with another alcoholic would save the day.(p.15)
• Faith has to ***work*** twenty-four hours a day in and through us, or we perish.(p.16)
• None of us makes a sole vocation of this ***work***, nor do we think its effectiveness would be increased if we did.(p.19)
• A few are fortunate enough to be so situated that they can give nearly all their time to the ***work***.(p.19)
• As matters grow worse, he begins to use a combination of high-powered sedative and liquor to quiet his nerves so he can go to ***work***.(p.22)
• His family was re-assembled, and he began to ***work*** as a salesman for the business he had lost through drinking.(p.35)
• This is his story: "I came to ***work*** on Tuesday morning.(p.36)
• Finally, he can no longer ***work***, his wife gets a divorce and he is held up to ridicule.(p.38)
• I had no trouble refusing drinks, and began to won-

der if I had not been making too hard *work* of a simple matter.(p.40)
• I'm sure it would *work* if I could only believe as he believes.(p.47)
• Is not our age characterized by the ease with which we discard old ideas for new, by the complete readiness with which we throw away the theory or gadget which does not *work* for something new which does?(p.52)
• Our ideas did not *work*.(p.52)
• It didn't *work*.(p.62)
• Being all powerful, He provided what we needed, if we kept close to Him and performed His *work* well.(p.63)
• We think of their needs and *work* for them.(p.70)
• Is our *work* solid so far?(p.75)
• They will always materialize if we *work* for them.(p.84)
• It works, if we have the proper attitude and *work* at it.(p.86)
• Many of us have wasted a lot of time doing that and it doesn't *work*.(p.87)
• Practical experience shows that nothing will so much insure immunity from drinking as intensive *work* with other alcoholics.(p.89)
• But he will be curious to learn why his own convictions have not worked and why yours seem to *work* so well.(p.93)
• We find it a waste of time to keep chasing a man who cannot or will not *work* with you.(p.96)
• He often says that if he had continued to *work* on them, he might have deprived many others, who have since recovered, of their chance.(p.96)
• The minute we put our *work* on a service plane, the alcoholic commences to rely upon our assistance rather than upon God.(p.98)
• If their old relationship is to be resumed it must be on a better basis, since the former did not *work*.(p.99)
• But if you are shaky, you had better *work* with another alcoholic instead!(p.102)
• Now we try to put spiritual principles to *work* in every department of our lives.(p.116)
• We do not like the thought that the contents of a book or the *work* of another alcoholic has accomplished in a few weeks that for which we struggled for years.(p.118)
• The fact is that he should *work* with other people to maintain his own sobriety.(p.119)
• We find it a real mistake to dampen his enthusiasm for alcoholic *work*.(p.119)
• Father knows he is to blame; it may take him many seasons of hard *work* to be restored financially, but he shouldn't be reproached.(p.123)
• That is where our fellow travelers are, and that is where our *work* must be done.(p.130)
• Because of the employee's special ability, or of his own strong personal attachment to him, the employer has sometimes kept such a man at *work* long beyond a reasonable period.(p.137)
• When sober, does he not *work* hard and have a knack of getting things done?(p.139)
• As our *work* spreads and our numbers increase, we hope your employees may be put in personal contact with some of us.(p.144)
• They *work* hard and they play hard.(p.146)
• You may have to curb his desire to *work* sixteen hours a day.(p.146)
• This *work* is necessary to maintain his sobriety.(p.146)
• He will *work* like the devil and thank you to his dying day.(p.149)
• *Work* better.(p.151)
• This couple has since become so fascinated that they have dedicated their home to the *work*.(p.160)
• We are greatly indebted to the doctor in attendance there, for he, although it might prejudice his own *work*, has told us of his belief in ours.(p.162)
• Understanding our *work*, he can do this with an eye to selecting those who are willing and able to recover on a spiritual basis.(p.162)
• I lost only a half day's *work* during these three years.(p.173)
• When I got the fog out of my brain, I decided that quitting school was very foolish and that I had better return and continue my *work*.(p.173)
• Occasionally, I would yield to the morning craving, but if I did, it would be only a few hours before I would be quite unfit for *work*.(p.176)
• I wasn't afraid that the program wouldn't *work*, but I still was doubtful whether I would be able to hang on to the program, but I did come to the conclusion that I was willing to put everything I had into it, with God's power, and that I wanted to do just that.(p.189)
• I immediately quit school and went to *work*, and from that time until I was high school age there was never a return to school.(p.193)
• I had a crew of men working there and I wanted them to *work* Sunday afternoons so that I could sell lots on Sunday.(p.195)
• When they got through the day's *work*, part was left which I proceeded to drink.(p.196)
• I could *work* a deal up to where all I had to do was to go ahead with it; all the planning had been done, all the financing had been done, but then I'd say "Nuts to it!" and walk away.(p.197)
• I can remember well thinking that I would quit drinking, really go to *work* hard, apply myself eight hours a day, five days a week, make a lot of money, and then I could start drinking again.(p.199)
• That was the reverse of my former pattern of fearing to go to *work* because I might drink!(p.199)
• And I continued to drink, on and off then, until every dollar I had in the world was gone again and I was right back living at my sister's, getting my cigarettes by calling her grocer and telling him to put in a couple of cartons with her order, exactly as I had before I started to *work* at Max's.(p.202)
• After drinking one glass of beer at the end of my *work* period for about five days, I thought I'd better find out whether I really had the stuff licked.(p.203)
• Three days later I went to *work*.(p.205)
• It has continued to *work* now for nearly eighteen years.(p.209)
• Being intensely interested in the *work*, I changed my conduct sufficiently to master the job.(p.211)
• A year later, after I completed the course in contracts, I quit the law school, and undertook some engineering *work* for a patent law firm on behalf of clients who were in difficulties and who desired to keep their troubles from their own engineering department.(p.212)
• This *work* consumed a period of about two-thirds of a year, and worked out successfully so I decided to follow patent law.(p.212)
• I was introduced to them and Clarence proceeded to put on his Twelve Step *work*.(p.216)
• That was an experience that I have never forgotten, and many times in my own *work* with A.A. newcomers I feel kind of guilty because I haven't done the same thing.(p.219)
• I still had enough practice to earn a good living if I would only *work*, so I resolved that in January of 1940 I would launch a patent law firm of my own.(p.220)
• Shortly after I came to this conclusion, I was importuned by another well-known patent law firm to help them out on some trial *work* because their trial man had had a heart attack and had been forbidden to go into the courtroom.(p.220)
• I found in the fall of 1939, that I was not mentally impaired, so far as trial *work* was concerned, and thereafter took up where I had left off when I was about forty-five years old.(p.220)
• My divorce coincided with my father's bankruptcy, and I went to *work*, casting off all allegiances and responsibilities to any other than myself.(p.225)
• For me, *work* was only a different means to the same end, to be able to do exactly what I wanted to do.(p.225)
• The fact that I can *work* again and earn my living, is important, but secondary.(p.229)
• We saw very early that Prohibition wasn't going to *work*.(p.232)
• I was doing very well with that and general upholstering *work*, and there was every indication that I would be financially independent by the time I reached middle age.(p.232)
• "Best in the business, when he's sober," my customers would say, and I still had a following who would give me *work* though they deplored my habits, because they knew the job would be well done when they eventually got it.(p.234)
• With the war over, and back in Baltimore with the folks, there were several small jobs for three years and then I went to *work* soliciting as one of the first ten employees of a new national finance company.(p.242)
• Routine jobs bored me, but I would take on the toughest one I could find, *work* day and night until I had it under control; then it would become tedious and I'd lose all interest in it.(p.243)
• I'd *work* like mad for three or four weeks without a single drink, save my money, pay a few bills and then "reward" myself with alcohol.(p.244)
• I had been too self-sufficient to write a moral inventory, but I discovered in pointing out to the new man his wrong attitudes and actions that I was really taking my own inventory, and that if I expected him to change I would have to *work* on myself too.(p.249)
• Drinking was all in the day's *work*.(p.251)
• Some college friends got me jobs when I finally had to go to *work*, but I didn't stick to them.(p.251)
• Drifting back to Ohio, I landed on a small newspaper and later was impressed into the direction of boy-welfare *work* at the local "Y."(p.253)
• I myself could see deterioration in my *work* from being physically and mentally affected by liquor, although I had not yet reached the point where all I wanted was more to drink.(p.254)
• Washington, D.C. and news-gathering agency *work* followed, along with many parties.(p.254)
• I did six years of newspaper advertising, and trade journal *work* with many, many drunks of drab and dreary hue woven into the pattern of my life.(p.254)
• I arrived drunk, but I promised my wife I would keep sober, and I knew I could get *work* if I did.(p.256)
• I got a job in the woolen mills in Ravenna – very hard *work*.(p.262)
• I looked much older than I was, I was always large, and I went back to *work* in this job.(p.262)
• He had taken up light *work*, and he had a safety valve and a pair of spurs and the clothes on his back, and that was all.(p.263)
• He got a job and went back to *work*.(p.263)
• The next morning his wife came dragging him in before Russ went to *work*, while I was getting breakfast.(p.271)
• We wept and Russ didn't go to *work*.(p.271)
• And that woman told me long after that was the surest proof to her that this program could *work*.(p.272)
• If, on Sunday, I could be there, trying to think of something that would help her with this problem, then we must have something that could *work*.(p.272)
• A low ebb in the family fortunes necessitated my going to *work* when I was twenty.(p.275)
• Vacations from school and from *work*, spelled "travel" to me – and I travelled with gusto.(p.275)
• I switched into real estate brokerage and property management *work*.(p.277)
• This happy combination of pleasant *work* and alcohol lasted for five years.(p.277)
• The next two years were simply a long drawn out process of less and less *work* and more and more whiskey.(p.278)
• When I finally returned to Detroit to find *work* and to learn to stand on my own feet, the ball was already rolling, however slowly.(p.282)
• But it took six more months of *work* and disappointments before a group of three men got together in my rooming house bedroom for their first A.A. meeting.(p.282)
• This gave me the freedom to do A.A. *work*, and to rest for periods of two or three days when I became too exhausted to carry on.(p.283)
• Seven years of *work* in this field brought an opportunity to affiliate myself actively with one of my clients, a fellow A.A.(p.284)
• At long last I am doing the kind of *work* I have always wanted to do, but never had the patience and emotional stability to train myself for.(p.284)
• The A.A. program showed me the way to come down to earth, start from the bottom and *work* up.(p.284)
• After I left school, I went to *work* in Akron, living at home with my parents.(p.287)
• 6.Continued *work* with other alcoholics.(p.292)
• On my trips back to Akron to get my spirits recharged and to *work* with other alcoholics, I would ask Dr. Bob about this delay and wonder just what was wrong with me.(p.293)
• Other days, I had to miss *work* because I was still too drunk to stand up.(p.318)
• Many of my neighbors devoted time to volunteer *work*.(p.326)
• I said to her one day when I met her on the street, "What sort of volunteer *work* do you do?"(p.326)
• I could never be sure I'd have a clear head and hands that were willing to do some *work*.(p.326)
• So I never did any volunteer *work*.(p.326)
• Through studied sneaky-drinking, I'd become a senior citizen without having lost a day's *work* because of booze.(p.327)
• My alcoholism-prone mind, however, reminded me that all great authors had needed a stimulus to build up inspiration and inventiveness before each day's *work*.(p.331)
• So that didn't *work*.(p.339)
• It's either all *work*, or I drink."(p.340)
• Surrender to me has meant the ability to run my home, to face my responsibilities as they should be faced, to take life as it comes to me day by day, and *work* my problems out.(p.340)
• Shortly after I was starting to *work* on the program I realized that I was not a good father; I wasn't a good husband, but, oh, I was a good provider.(p.351)

• I didn't know how to be a father; I don't know how to come home and ***work*** week-ends like other husbands; I don't know how to entertain my family.(p.351)
• They have contributed fantastic amounts of time and ***work*** to our problem, but they aren't able, it seems, to arrest either your alcoholism or mine.(p.352)
• I went to ***work*** in Birmingham for a newspaper at fifteen dollars a week.(p.357)
• When I did make it home in 1920, I re-entered school and caught up with my class in a few short months — I actually did a year's ***work*** in three months, proving much to the disgust of my dad that I could do it when I wanted to.(p.358)
• At this time, however, she had an opportunity to go to Salt Lake City on a new project for the government, but she did promise me that if I would curtail my drinking and buckle down to hard ***work*** she would give serious consideration to my latest proposal and maybe join me at a later date when I got settled.(p.359)
• My ***work*** kept me busy the first few months on the new job.(p.360)
• Since the radio station was getting on its feet, it didn't require so many nights of evening ***work***, and that permitted leisure time for drinking.(p.360)
• By hook or crook I usually managed to sober up before I reached home, but always "terribly tired" from a "hard day's ***work***," and just having to have one or two before dinner.(p.361)
• She tried reasoning with me, endeavored to ***work*** out various drinking schedules, in fact all the tricks were practised faithfully for a short time somewhere along my shaky road to unhappiness.(p.361)
• Of course, it didn't ***work***.(p.364)
• I attended my weekly meetings with regularity, reread the Big Book, attended other group meetings, gave leads when asked to and did some Twelve Step ***work*** whenever I was called upon to do so.(p.365)
• I'm very active in A.A. ***work*** and active at home, too, with my family.(p.372)
• I was raised like the majority of American boys, coming from a family of modest circumstances, attending public schools, having the social life of a small midwestern town, with part-time ***work*** and some athletics.(p.373)
• I did ***work*** of all kinds after school and during vacations, trying to find that which would appeal most as a goal for a life ***work***.(p.373)
• My hours of ***work*** were flexible so that returning to the office was not always important.(p.376)
• I knew that I wanted to try A.A. and if that didn't ***work***, I didn't think anything would.(p.384)
• I took that treatment three times and it didn't ***work*** -- at least, for me.(p.389)
• However, I threw myself into Twelve Step ***work***, and what I feared would be a calamity turned out to be the most blessed of blessings.(p.394)
• My ***work*** with other alcoholics has led me, day by day, into ever wider and richer experiences.(p.394)
• I know that I must ***work*** at it as long as I live; I know that it is only by working at it that I can stay sober and have a happy life.(p.394)
• I was still untrained for any ***work*** but washing dishes and waiting on table.(p.401)
• Or: If I'm really a genius, I must produce a great ***work***, to show why I act like a genius.(p.408)
• My analyst was one of the first to learn of A.A. and to make subsequent use of it in her ***work***.(p.412)
• Through going to meetings and listening, and occasionally speaking, through doing Twelve Step ***work***, whereby in helping others you are both the teacher and the student, by making many wonderful A.A. friends, I have been taught all the things in life that are worth having.(p.416)
• My experience has been active: three meetings a week, many tapes, many A.A. conferences, much ***work*** on the Twelve Steps, and much ***work*** with other alcoholics and their families.(p.420)
• I was skipping classes about two days a week and doing no book ***work*** whatever.(p.423)
• Sometimes I'd make it home and go to sleep at the wheel of my car, for all the neighbors to see next morning as they left for ***work***.(p.429)
• And the folks said A.A. was for people who wanted to quit, otherwise it wouldn't ***work***.(p.429)
• I was never drunk on the job, never missed a day's ***work***, was seldom rendered totally ineffective by a hangover and kept my liquor expenses well within my adequate budget.(p.433)
• It might ***work***."(p.436)
• My ***work*** is on a much deeper and more significant level than it ever was before, and I am today a fairly creative, relatively sane human being.(p.438)
• My drinking took place after ***work*** hours.(p.441)
• Today, I find I can't ***work*** my A.A. program while taking pills, nor may I even have them around for dire emergencies only.(p.443)
• Max still works with me in the office, but we have turned our wills and our lives and our ***work*** over to the care of God.(p.446)
• It hasn't been easy to ***work*** out this relationship with Max.(p.451)
• On the contrary, the hardest place to ***work*** this program has been in my own home, with my own children and, finally, with Max.(p.451)
• After nine months of training, all the rest of my class was paroled and I went to ***work*** in the Department of Corrections.(p.462)
• Then I, too, went to ***work*** as a counselor in Corrections.(p.462)
• Why did it ***work*** for me when all other agencies had failed?(p.470)
• My brother and me find ***work*** on turnpike in Maine.(p.475)
• To find ***work***, I have travel much.(p.476)
• You see how much ***work*** some of us have to do on ourselves when we finally come into A.A.!(p.480)
• I don't believe this program would ***work*** for me if I didn't get honest with myself about everything.(p.482)
• Therefore, it will be the hardest to ***work*** on.(p.482)
• If I ***work*** on it every day, it will be easier to be honest with myself.(p.482)
• Of course, when father finally came to Virginia to ***work*** his way through school, he resented the southern "cracker," as he often called them, so much that he didn't even go back to his mother's funeral.(p.486)
• I was able to get my ***work*** out.(p.486)
• Vi had secured ***work*** in Washington.(p.490)
• I was out of ***work*** for about four days.(p.490)
• Nevertheless, we continued to ***work*** together and I continued to drink, but I guess, deep down within her heart as well as within mine, we both knew I couldn't stop drinking.(p.490)
• I continued to ***work*** and continued to go to lunch with Vi, and none of our acquaintances on the job knew that we had separated.(p.491)
• Very often we rode to and from ***work*** together, but being separated really galled me deep down.(p.491)
• After the trial, I got big-hearted again and felt that I should do something in payment for Vi's kindness to me; so I left Washington and went to Seattle to ***work***.(p.492)
• I think the thing that galled me was that just after Easter I had drawn my salary for two weeks' ***work*** and had decided that I was going to send some money to Vi; and above all else I was going to send my baby daughter an Easter outfit.(p.493)
• They taught us a great deal about Twelve Step ***work*** too.(p.496)
• Father is an Episcopal minister and his ***work*** takes him over long drives on bad roads.(p.497)
• The doctor has told me that if I don't give up inside ***work***, I'll have tuberculosis.(p.500)
• I am happy in my ***work***.(p.500)
• But I do not wait for the charred keg to ***work***.(p.501)
• But somehow or other, with my old alcoholic brain, sitting there in that chair, I kept saying to myself, "I wonder if it'll ***work***?(p.515)
• I wonder if it'll ***work*** for me?"(p.516)
• But as long as you did your ***work*** and didn't disgrace yourself, you were socially acceptable and nobody really intruded on your private life very much.(p.518)
• I stayed there just long enough to ***work*** up a real good resentment against the doctor in charge, who I didn't think was doing anything at all except collecting fees, and I left there fully determined that I'd never put myself in the power of medical people again.(p.521)
• I had no ***work*** to do and I was at an age where it seemed too late to start anything new.(p.522)
• I don't know if it's force of habit or something else that keeps them in one place, but I do know that in A.A. there is much ***work*** to do, and none of us can do it standing still.(p.529)
• I had replied, "Uncle, give the judge ten dollars, or I'll have to ***work*** it out on the county road."(p.539)
• It is going strong still, these eight years later, and some of its members have been of great influence for good in state-wide A.A. ***work***.(p.541)
• I don't care too much about personal fame or glory, and I want only enough money to enable me to do the ***work*** I feel I can perhaps do best.(p.542)
• My mother went to a nearby city to go to ***work***, and my father, being an alcoholic, simply went.(p.544)
• It worked for me then, and it has worked for me many times since, and it will ***work*** for me every time I am willing to ***work*** it.(p.552)
• And because it works for me, it will ***work*** for all of us.(p.552)
• I also began visiting bars after ***work***, with my older associates.(p.555)
• We alcoholics see that we must ***work*** together and hang together, else most of us will finally die alone.(p.563)
• But our usual A.A. "12th Step" ***work*** is never to be paid for.(p.567)
• Learning to depend upon a higher power and absorb himself in his ***work*** with other alcoholics, he remains sober day by day.(p.572)
• Edward Dowling, S.J., of the Queen's ***Work*** staff says, "Alcoholics Anonymous is natural; it is natural at the point where nature comes closest to the supernatural, namely in humiliations and in consequent humility.(p.574)

work-houses

• I began to know the inside of jails and ***work-houses***.(p.255)

work-outs

• These ***work-outs*** should be regarded as part of your education, for thus you will be learning to live.(p.117)

workable

• The doctor proved to be able and exceedingly anxious to adopt any ***workable*** method of handling the situation.(p.163)

worked

• Prior to his journey to Akron, the broker had ***worked*** hard with many alcoholics on the theory that only an alcoholic could help an alcoholic, but he had succeeded only in keeping sober himself.(p.xvi)
• I have had many men who had, for example, ***worked*** a period of months on some problem or business deal which was to be settled on a certain date, favorable to them.(p.xxvii)
• I had had some success at speculation, so we had a little money, but we once ***worked*** on a farm for a month to avoid drawing on our small capital.(p.3)
• It ***worked***!(p.9)
• Particularly was it imperative to work with others as he had ***worked*** with me.(p.14)
• But we saw that it really ***worked*** in others, and we had come to believe in the hopelessness and futility of life as we had been living it.(p.25)
• On each of these occasions we ***worked*** with him, reviewing carefully what had happened.(p.35)
• When others showed us that "God-sufficiency" ***worked*** with them, we began to feel like those who had insisted the Wrights would never fly.(p.52)
• But he will be curious to learn why his own convictions have not ***worked*** and why yours seem to work so well.(p.93)
• Show him how they ***worked*** with you.(p.95)
• We have no monopoly on God; we merely have an approach that ***worked*** with us.(p.95)
• By no means do we offer it as the last word on this subject, but so far as we are concerned, it has ***worked*** with us.(p.144)
• This ***worked*** nicely until my wife and I went to see Wallace Beery in "Tugboat Annie," after which the pant-leg and stocking racket were out!(p.177)
• It hadn't ***worked*** out that way and I didn't know what the matter was and did not know what to do.(p.184)
• I ***worked*** along until I had really big names in rubber on a tentative contract, and then I neglected to go through with it.(p.198)
• I then began asking a lot of questions of both my brother and Dr. Bob about how this thing ***worked***, and I suppose I was becoming more glassy-eyed all the while, for eventually I said to Bob, "You're all dried up.(p.206)
• When I left the hospital I tried this for a day and it ***worked***, for a week and it ***worked***, and for a month, and it ***worked*** -- and then for a year and it still ***worked***.(p.209)
• As a draftsman, I ***worked*** for several large companies and gained a variety of experience.(p.211)
• I then entered Case School and ***worked*** while I went to school and finished there.(p.212)
• This work consumed a period of about two-thirds of a year, and ***worked*** out successfully so I decided to follow patent law.(p.212)
• By the time I had completed law school I had picked up some experience in patent law, for I remained with the patent law firm and ***worked*** too in Washington where they found that I was a capable infringement investigator.(p.213)
• I do not recollect the specific conversation that went on but I believe I did challenge Bill to tell me something about A.A. and I do recall one other thing: I

wanted to know what this was that ***worked*** so many wonders, and hanging over the mantel was a picture of Gethsemane and Bill pointed to it and said, "There it is," which didn't make much sense to me.(p.216)
• It ***worked***!(p.229)
• Nothing had ***worked***.(p.238)
• Federal Theatre in Texas gave me an administrative job which I held for a year, only because I ***worked*** hard and productively when I ***worked***, and because my very tolerant chief ascribed my frequent lapses to a bohemian temperament.(p.256)
• This first meeting was held in the living room of a home and was led by Bill D., the first man that Bill W. and Dr. Bob had ***worked*** with successfully.(p.291)
• Dr. Bob then led me through the restitution step, in which I made a list of all of the persons I had harmed, and ***worked*** out ways and means of slowly making restitution.(p.292)
• I really ***worked*** for several weeks, and having had a fairly wide acquaintance with the dealer trade, it was not difficult for me to line up enough of them to give me a very substantial volume of business with a minimum of effort.(p.300)
• Nothing ***worked***.(p.305)
• Then he told me there was a handful of people in Akron and New York who had ***worked*** out a technique for arresting their alcoholism.(p.308)
• I'd ***worked*** hard to be tops in my profession.(p.328)
• One night, I was struck with the memory of a line Alan Ladd used in "Shane," a movie that I'd ***worked*** on.(p.333)
• I had ***worked*** so long in a profession where fakery, deceit, and untruths are tools of trade that I instantly recognized honesty when I heard it, from the mouths of A.A. members.(p.334)
• As long as I ***worked***, as long as I got out, I didn't drink.(p.339)
• I had ***worked*** the previous summer on a New York fashion magazine, a job I really enjoyed.(p.405)
• I got a job after school pumping gas and ***worked*** until ten or eleven at night.(p.423)
• I got a job with the newspaper my dad ***worked*** for.(p.425)
• The harder I ***worked*** with Max, the sicker she got.(p.440)
• Nothing ***worked***.(p.455)
• This is difficult, but it is the only way it has ***worked*** for me.(p.463)
• This physician, the originator of A.A.'s first black group, but badly caught in the toils, tells of his release and of how freedom came as he ***worked*** among his own people.(p.483)
• I ***worked*** for the Government about a year and still maintained my evening office practice when the Government agencies were decentralized.(p.489)
• I ***worked*** in the steel mill for possibly two months, and then I became disgusted with myself and decided to go back home.(p.492)
• I ***worked*** at that alone for six months.(p.496)
• I fled, finally, after having been fired from my job by a boss who wept a little (since I had ***worked*** hard) as he gave notice for me to clear out.(p.539)
• A.A. had not ***worked*** for me.(p.539)
• The reason, as I learned later, was that I had not ***worked*** for A.A.(p.539)
• I ***worked*** when I could -- piddling jobs I thought them.(p.540)
• We ***worked*** in five below zero weather, fixing on an elm tree a wrought iron device which modestly proclaimed that he was indeed a country doctor.(p.540)
• But for the next years, I ***worked*** hard and exultantly in A.A.(p.541)
• I have been allowed to build an entirely new career in a field I had never ***worked*** in.(p.541)
• It ***worked*** for me then, and it has ***worked*** for me many times since, and it will work for me every time I am willing to work it.(p.552)

worker

• So our fellow ***worker*** will soon have friends galore.(p.163)
• After a few months there, I went to County Mental Health as an alcoholism ***worker***.(p.462)

workers

• There were business men, professional men, and factory ***workers***.(p.258)
• Offices closed up and ***workers*** discharged.(p.500)
• Eight — Alcoholics Anonymous should remain forever nonprofessional, but our service centers may employ special ***workers***.(p.564)

working

• What used to be the hunch or the occasional inspiration gradually becomes a ***working*** part of the mind.(p.87)
• *WORKING* WITH OTHERS(p.89)
• When ***working*** with a man and his family, you should take care not to participate in their quarrels.(p.100)
• For years we have been ***working*** with alcoholics committed to institutions.(p.114)
• After all, your family is reunited, alcohol is no longer a problem and you and your husband are ***working*** together toward an undreamed-of future.(p.119)
• In the chapter "***Working*** With Others" you gathered an idea of how we approach and aid others to health.(p.153)
• So, after hearing some more of my story, he turned around and said to Doc -- I don't think he knew I heard him, but I did — he said, "Well, I believe he's worth saving and ***working*** on."(p.185)
• I had a crew of men ***working*** there and I wanted them to work Sunday afternoons so that I could sell lots on Sunday.(p.195)
• I was moved in as Sales Manager and had four men ***working*** under me.(p.200)
• During the latter part of the Christian Science experience I had gotten a job and was ***working*** at Firestone.(p.203)
• The next day, they called me in for an examination, and the doctor wouldn't let me continue ***working*** and pardoned me from the plant for ten days because he said my eye had been injured.(p.205)
• My parents were hard ***working*** people.(p.210)
• My "periodics" became more frequent until I reached the point where I wanted to devote all my time to drinking, ***working*** as little as possible, and then only when the necessity of my family demanded it.(p.234)
• Jackie told me about a group of fellows in New York, of whom my old friend Fitz was one, who had the same problem I had, and who by ***working*** together to help each other were not now drinking and were happy like himself.(p.239)
• At that time the group in New York was composed of about twelve men who were ***working*** on the principle of every drunk for himself; we had no real formula and no name.(p.246)
• That job began a series of brief ***working*** spells, each one ending in a "drunk" and the urge to travel.(p.253)
• In the summer of 1938, almost a year from the time I made my original contact with Akron, the man for whom I was ***working*** and who knew about the program, approached me and asked if I could do anything about one of his salesmen who was drinking very heavily.(p.294)
• While ***working*** in an office, there was some semblance of restraint, but, oh boy, when I got on the outside with this new company without supervision, did I go to town!(p.300)
• And, as the years go by, ***working*** together, sharing our experiences with one another, and also sharing a mutual trust, understanding and love — without strings, without obligation — we acquire relationships that are unique and priceless.(p.312)
• You've been sober for three months, been ***working*** hard.(p.348)
• Looking back, it is surprising to me now that I managed to keep ***working*** and have enough money to squander at the various spots in the big city.(p.358)
• I was ***working*** for a Chicago firm that represented several large radio stations.(p.358)
• I sure had been ***working*** awfully hard of late.(p.360)
• I know that I must work at it as long as I live; I know that it is only by ***working*** at it that I can stay sober and have a happy life.(p.394)
• I teamed up with a cute little blonde with whom I was ***working*** at the office, and for about a year we were inseparable.(p.425)
• After going to school all day, ***working*** in the family drugstore all evening, and then studying until one or two in the morning, I would not be able to sleep soundly, with everything I had been studying going round in my head.(p.440)
• After I had been around A.A. for seven months, tapering off alcohol and pills, not finding the program ***working*** very well, I was finally able to say, "Okay, God.(p.448)
• After all, I had been ***working*** for eighteen years, slinging hash, and I was managing.(p.478)
• We were now both ***working*** in the same agency.(p.490)
• She didn't say anything about A.A. or getting me a sponsor at that time, but she did ask about Vi, and I told her Vi was ***working*** and how she could locate her.(p.494)
• At this time I wasn't ***working***.(p.496)
• I am ***working*** hard on the books of a subsidiary company of a large corporation.(p.500)
• I have no assistance and am ***working*** nights, Saturdays and Sundays.(p.500)
• Nothing seems to be ***working*** out right.(p.505)
• The only thing this changed, however, was my surroundings, and it was soon apparent that I could have the same uncomfortable emotions with an unlimited checking account that I could on a ***working*** girl's salary.(p.545)
• The amount of will power exercised to control my drinking during ***working*** hours, diverted into a constructive channel, would have made me President, and the thing that made the will power possible was the knowledge that as soon as my day was finished I could drink myself into oblivion.(p.548)

workings

• Above all, he believed he had acquired such a profound knowledge of the inner ***workings*** of his mind and its hidden springs that relapse was unthinkable.(p.26)

works

• Faith without ***works*** was dead, he said.(p.14)
• It is a design for living that ***works*** in rough going.(p.15)
• A new life has been given us or, if you prefer, "a design for living" that really ***works***.(p.28)
• HOW IT ***WORKS***(p.58)
• Now we need more action, without which we find that "Faith without ***works*** is dead."(p.76)
• It ***works***, if we have the proper attitude and work at it.(p.86)
• It ***works*** -- it really does.(p.88)
• "Faith without ***works*** is dead."(p.88)
• It ***works*** when other activities fail.(p.89)
• She tells how A.A. ***works*** when the going is rough.(p.261)
• And it ***works***.(p.320)
• He's now in A.A. and ***works*** as a volunteer for the local alcoholism council.(p.330)
• I wish I could tell you how and why A.A. ***works***, but I don't know.(p.384)
• So, as I have said, I don't know how or why A.A. ***works***.(p.392)
• Because A.A. really ***works*** for me!(p.421)
• Max still ***works*** with me in the office, but we have turned our wills and our lives and our work over to the care of God.(p.446)
• (God ***works*** through people.)(p.462)
• It read something like this: "Faith without ***works*** is dead.(p.473)
• "Let your light so shine before men that they may see your good ***works*** –."(p.497)
• They said if you want to know how this program ***works***, take the first word of your question -- the H is for honesty, the O is for open-mindedness and the W is for willingness; these our Book calls the essentials of recovery.(p.550)
• And because it ***works*** for me, it will work for all of us.(p.552)

workshop

• In four or five days I would be hunting all over the place, at home and in my ***workshop***, for the bottles I had destroyed, cursing myself for being a fool.(p.234)

world

• By late 1937, the number of members having substantial sobriety time behind them was sufficient to convince the membership that a new light had entered the dark ***world*** of the alcoholic.(p.xvii)
• It was now time, the struggling groups thought, to place their message and unique experience before the ***world***.(p.xvii)
• News of this got on the ***world*** wires; inquiries poured in again and many people went to the bookstores to get the book "Alcoholics Anonymous."(p.xviii)
• So far, upon the total problem of several million actual and potential alcoholics in the ***world***, we have made only a scratch.(p.xx)
• Each day, somewhere in the ***world***, recovery begins when one alcoholic talks with another alcoholic, sharing experience, strength, and hope.(p.xxii)
• I'd prove to the ***world*** I was important.(p.2)
• A new ***world*** came into view.(p.12)
• Back of them is a ***world*** of ignorance and misunderstanding.(p.20)
• He may be one of the finest fellows in the ***world***.(p.21)
• He had a commendable ***World*** War record.(p.35)
• We looked upon this ***world*** of warring individuals, warring theological systems, and inexplicable calamity, with deep skepticism.(p.46)
• It is being constantly revealed, as mankind studies the material ***world***, that outward appearances are not inward reality at all.(p.48)

• These tiny bodies are governed by precise laws, and these laws hold true throughout the material ***world***.(p.49)

• When, however, the perfectly logical assumption is suggested that underneath the material ***world*** and life as we see it, there is an All Powerful, Guiding, Creative Intelligence, right there our perverse streak comes to the surface and we laboriously set out to convince ourselves it isn't so.(p.49)

• This ***world*** of ours has made more material progress in the last century than in all the millenniums which went before.(p.51)

• Yet we had been seeing another kind of flight, a spiritual liberation from this ***world***, people who rose above their problems.(p.55)

• Is he not a victim of the delusion that he can wrest satisfaction and happiness out of this ***world*** if he only manages well?(p.61)

• He is like the retired business man who lolls in the Florida sunshine in the winter complaining of the sad state of the nation; the minister who sighs over the sins of the twentieth century; politicians and reformers who are sure all would be Utopia if the rest of the ***world*** would only behave; the outlaw safe cracker who thinks society has wronged him; and the alcoholic who has lost all and is locked up.(p.61)

• The first thing apparent was that this ***world*** and its people were often quite wrong.(p.65)

• We began to see that the ***world*** and its people really dominated us.(p.66)

• We are in the ***world*** to play the role He assigns.(p.68)

• To the outer ***world*** he presents his stage character.(p.73)

• We must be entirely honest with somebody if we expect to live long or happily in this ***world***.(p.73)

• We can look the ***world*** in the eye.(p.75)

• We have entered the ***world*** of the Spirit.(p.84)

• Follow the dictates of a Higher Power and you will presently live in a new and wonderful ***world***, no matter what your present circumstances!(p.100)

• Now you are getting back into the social life of this ***world***.(p.102)

• Perhaps your husband has been living in that strange ***world*** of alcoholism where everything is distorted and exaggerated.(p.108)

• This ***world*** is full of people like him.(p.109)

• It is the most natural thing in the ***world***, once his liquor problem is solved, to feel that he will now measure up to that cherished vision.(p.118)

• If there is no Al-Anon listing in your local telephone book, you may obtain further information on Al-Anon Family Groups by writing to its *World* Service Office: Box 182, Madison Square Station, New York, NY 10159.(p.121)

• They should be thankful he is sober and able to be of this ***world*** once more.(p.127)

• If he means to right his past wrongs, why all this concern for everyone in the ***world*** but his family?(p.128)

• Those of us who have spent much time in the ***world*** of spiritual make-believe have eventually seen the childishness of it.(p.130)

• This dream ***world*** has been replaced by a great sense of purpose, accompanied by a growing consciousness of the power of God in our lives.(p.130)

• Drinking isolates most homes from the outside ***world***.(p.131)

• He may bring new hope and new courage to many a priest, minister, or rabbi, who gives his all to minister to our troubled ***world***.(p.132)

• God has abundantly supplied this ***world*** with fine doctors, psychologists, and practitioners of various kinds.(p.133)

• Among many employers nowadays, we think of one member who has spent much of his life in the ***world*** of big business.(p.136)

• Here were three exceptional men lost to this ***world*** because I did not understand alcoholism as I do now.(p.137)

• Our hope is that when this chip of a book is launched on the ***world*** tide of alcoholism, defeated drinkers will seize upon it, to follow its suggestions.(p.153)

• I had some money, all the time in the ***world***, and considerable stomach trouble.(p.174)

• Pioneer member of Akron's Group No. 1, the first A.A. group in the ***world***.(p.182)

• I thought of what liquor had done to me, the opportunities that I had discarded, the abilities that had been given me and how I had wasted them, and I finally came to the conclusion, that if I didn't want to quit, I certainly ought to want to, and that I was willing to do anything in the ***world*** to stop drinking.(p.186)

• So, after reviewing these things and realizing what liquor had cost me, I went to this Higher Power which, to me was God, without any reservation, and admitted that I was completely powerless over alcohol, and that I was willing to do anything in the ***world*** to get rid of the problem.(p.187)

• Then I remember when the boys came back, that I told them, "I have gone to this Higher Power and I have told Him that I am willing to put His ***world*** first, above everything.(p.190)

• I have already done it, and I am willing to do it again here in the presence of you or I am willing to say it any place, anywhere in the ***world*** from now on and not be ashamed of it."(p.190)

• At the end of this selling of lots, just prior to *World* War I, I got into the crude rubber business, and six months later there was only one broker and myself left in Akron.(p.197)

• So in spite of anything that I might do, I prospered, being one of only two brokers in the rubber center of the ***world***.(p.197)

• I can well remember over a long period of years when I thought I was the only person in the ***world*** who knew that sooner or later I was going to get drunk.(p.198)

• Everything in the ***world*** a man could possibly want, and I was driving from Akron to Cleveland, having just been to the bank and discovered that I had approximately $5,000.(p.200)

• And I continued to drink, on and off then, until every dollar I had in the ***world*** was gone again and I was right back living at my sister's, getting my cigarettes by calling her grocer and telling him to put in a couple of cartons with her order, exactly as I had before I started to work at Max's.(p.202)

• All I had left was an iron determination to live my own life in spite of the alien ***world*** – and here I was, an inwardly frightened, outwardly defiant woman, who desperately needed a prop to keep going.(p.226)

• I wanted to live, not in a desert, but in a normal ***world***; and my idea of a normal ***world*** was among people who drank – teetotallers were not included.(p.227)

• I wasn't the only person in the ***world*** who felt and behaved like this!(p.227)

• To go into a gathering of people was the sort of thing that all my life, from the time I left my private ***world*** of books and dreams to meet the real ***world*** of people and parties and jobs, had left me feeling an uncomfortable outsider, needing the warming stimulus of drinks to join in.(p.228)

• I had no resentments against individuals – the whole ***world*** was all wrong.(p.244)

• At the time, I thought them just a swell pair of screwballs, for they were not only going to save all the drunks in the ***world*** but also all the so-called normal people!(p.245)

• I thought I had done that until Russ' second collapse, and the doctor told me very candidly that he wasn't long for this ***world***.(p.271)

• I entered the business ***world*** with every confidence that success lay ahead of me.(p.275)

• An hour later I awoke to a new ***world***.(p.280)

• I had tried to be the center of my own little ***world***, whereas God was the center of a vast universe of which I was perhaps an essential, but a very tiny, part.(p.280)

• From a mere handful in Akron we have spread throughout the ***world***.(p.295)

• Acceptance of things as they are has replaced the old impatient champing at the bit to conquer the ***world***.(p.295)

• He mentioned lies and deceptions in the course of his story in the presence of the one person in the ***world*** I wouldn't want to know such things.(p.302)

• If reasons for covering up are strong enough, secrets can be hidden from the ***world***.(p.327)

• I gave them everything, except the greatest thing in the ***world***, and that is peace of mind.(p.351)

• I had no one in the ***world*** to talk to.(p.355)

• I had run away from school to join the army in *World* War I, but missed it by one day since the Armistice was signed the very day I landed in Atlanta to sign up with Uncle Sam.(p.357)

• And deep in my heart I really meant what I said because I loved her more than anything else in the ***world***, yes – even more than liquor.(p.362)

• I was going to prove to her that liquor wasn't necessary in my life, and above all that I still loved her more than anything else in the ***world*** and that I wanted her back.(p.362)

• A whole new ***world*** of happiness and love began to unfold before my eyes, a truly new way of living.(p.365)

• A few months after that, I was released and left the ***world*** of insanity, only to return to the ***world*** of alcoholic insanity.(p.370)

• To me this meant telling my associates that I had joined Alcoholics Anonymous; that I didn't know what was expected of me by A.A., but that whatever it was, it was the most important thing in life for me; that sobriety meant more to me than anything in this ***world***.(p.382)

• No one individual can carry all the burdens of the ***world***.(p.382)

• I realized that there were other people in this ***world*** who behaved and acted as I did, and that I was a sick person, that I was suffering from an actual disease.(p.392)

• A few times at meetings, I have heard this statement: "Members of A.A. have paid the highest initiation fee of any club members in the ***world***."(p.396)

• At age twenty-one, I enlisted in the Navy for two reasons: (1) to avoid being drafted into the Army, and (2) out of a burst of patriotic fervor inspired by the advent of *World* War II and as the result of an all-night drinking binge which found me sitting on the doorstep of the Navy recruiting office when the chief petty officer arrived to open for business at nine o'clock Monday morning.(p.398)

• A titled lady, she still saw her ***world*** darkening.(p.400)

• I was always at odds with the entire ***world***, not to say the universe.(p.400)

• It combined running away from my ***world***, and drinking all I wanted to.(p.407)

• Except for one short slip, during the first eight months, which was an angry "the ***world*** can't do this to me" reaction to a personal tragedy in my life, I have been sober for twelve years.(p.416)

• My eyes opened onto a hazy ***world***.(p.422)

• One, the side I turned to myself and the ***world***, was respectable -- even, in some ways, distinguished.(p.432)

• I was club-man, athlete, artist, musician, author, editor, aircraft pilot and ***world*** traveller.(p.432)

• I came to understand the intricate processes of projection, by which we cast into our adult ***world*** the images of the horrors of our childhood.(p.434)

• With all this, it was becoming increasingly hard to maintain my front of distinction and respectability to the ***world***.(p.435)

• I remember very well saying, "There's only one person in the ***world*** whose guts I hate worse than yours, and those're my own."(p.440)

• Much of my time was spent writing letters, notes, orders, and lists of things for Max, who was also my office nurse, to do to keep the ***world*** running while I was locked up.(p.445)

• (Today, there is absolutely nothing in the ***world*** more important to me than my keeping this alcoholic sober; not taking a drink is by far the most important thing I do each day.)(p.447)

• Nothing, absolutely nothing happens in God's ***world*** by mistake.(p.449)

• I need to concentrate not so much on what needs to be changed in the ***world*** as on what needs to be changed in me and in my attitudes.(p.449)

• Before A.A., I judged myself by my intentions, while the ***world*** was judging me by my actions.(p.450)

• This was the end of my ***world***.(p.461)

• In other words, the kindest doctor in the whole ***world***, and I had one such, couldn't help me because I always felt, "You can't know about me – you can't possibly know – you don't even drink!"(p.471)

• It meant that I had to give up a lot of the things that I had been accustomed to and that wasn't the easiest thing in the ***world*** for me.(p.487)

• Around eight or nine o'clock there came two big detectives and a policeman to arrest me for assault; and I was the most amazed person in the ***world*** when they said I had assaulted someone, and especially that I had assaulted my wife.(p.492)

• I just gathered up this and that alcoholic, because, in the back of my mind, I wanted to save all the ***world***.(p.496)

• We didn't save the ***world***, but we did manage to help some individuals.(p.496)

• When I landed of course I hit a gin mill, and with three or four good shots under my belt the ***world*** began to go into that rosy glow.(p.513)

• I was in a ***world*** that I knew nothing at all about, and I felt intensely afraid.(p.521)

• It has made me understand that I must be one of my ***world***, that I cannot exist in any happiness as a rebel by myself.(p.524)

• And having sung that phrase, I'd chuckle with amusement, turning into irony turning into self-contempt turning into self-pity, at the sad fate of Bob, that wonderful, poor little motherless boy who was so smart in school and who grew up to accept responsibility so early and so fast and who staggered under his burdens without a whimper until the time came when he thought he was too good for this ***world*** and so he ought to be out of it.(p.532)

• There was the over-weening ambition to be the world's greatest author, when -- at thirty-nine -- I had nothing of importance to say to the ***world***.(p.534)

• I wasn't afraid of anything or anybody after I learned about drinking, for it seemed right from the beginning that with liquor I could always retire to my little private ***world*** where nobody could get at me to hurt me.(p.547)

• The only reality I was able to face had been forced upon me by its very repetition -- I had to drink; and I didn't know there was anything in the ***world*** that could be done about it.(p.548)

• He happened to be, by the grace of God, Dr. Harry Tiebout, the psychiatrist who probably knew more about alcoholism than any other in the ***world***.(p.559)

• I lived in a dream ***world***.(p.560)

• Since Dr. Silkworth's first endorsement of Alcoholics Anonymous, medical societies and physicians throughout the ***world*** have set their approval upon us.(p.571)

• The General Service Board of A.A. (the trustees) administers A.A.'s General Service Office, A.A. ***World*** Services, Inc., and our monthly magazine, the A.A. Grapevine.(p.575)

• If you cannot find A.A. in your locality, a letter addressed to Alcoholics Anonymous, Box 459, Grand Central Station, New York, NY 10163, U.S.A., will receive a prompt reply from this ***world*** center, referring you to the nearest A.A. group.(p.575)

• This is a ***world*** clearing house for the Al-Anon Family Groups, composed largely of the wives, husbands and friends of A.A. members.(p.575)

world-renowned

• One of these men, staff member of a ***world-renowned*** hospital, recently made this statement to some of us: "What you say about the general hopelessness of the average alcoholic's plight is, in my opinion, correct.(p.43)

world's

• With ministers, and ***world's*** religions, I parted right there.(p.10)

• We try not to indulge in cynicism over the state of the nations, nor do we carry the ***world's*** troubles on our shoulders.(p.132)

• For some reason, we alcoholics seem to have the gift of picking out the ***world's*** finest women.(p.178)

• My inability to accept the harsh realities of life had resulted in a disillusioned cynic, clothed in protective armor against the ***world's*** misunderstanding.(p.226)

• Under the skilled guidance of an expert practitioner I wallowed in the ***world's*** individual and collective mental agony.(p.434)

• Shakespeare said, "All the ***world's*** a stage, all the men and women merely players."(p.449)

• There was the over-weening ambition to be the ***world's*** greatest author, when -- at thirty-nine -- I had nothing of importance to say to the world.(p.534)

worldliness

• I suppose some would be shocked at our seeming ***worldliness*** and levity.(p.16)

worldly

• But soon the sense of His presence had been blotted out by ***worldly*** clamors, mostly those within myself.(p.12)

• Here are thousands of men and women, ***worldly*** indeed.(p.50)

• He may demand that the family find God in a hurry, or exhibit amazing indifference to them and say he is above ***worldly*** considerations.(p.128)

• This ***worldly*** lady helped to develop A.A. in Chicago and thus passed her keys to many.(p.304)

• High living, a great many fair weather friends, the 1929 stock market crash, and a couple of years of Depression, soon relieved me one by one of my ***worldly*** goods including my wife.(p.358)

• As might have been predicted, my teetering tower of ***worldly*** success collapsed.(p.437)

worldwide

• By March 1976, when this edition went to the printer, the total ***worldwide*** membership of Alcoholics Anonymous was conservatively estimated at more than 1,000,000, with almost 28,000 groups meeting in over 90 countries.(p.xxii)

worn

• After a few years with an alcoholic, a wife gets ***worn*** out, resentful and uncommunicative.(p.81)

• My tweed suit, once a very good one, was shapeless and baggy with bare places ***worn*** in the elbows from leaning on the bar.(p.411)

• Back to the big city, for another year of precarious living, paid for largely by one or two friends I still had not milked dry or ***worn*** to exhaustion with demands on their bounty.(p.540)

worried

• Experience has taught us that these are matters about which, for our purpose, we need not be ***worried***.(p.50)

• He is ***worried*** at times, and is becoming aware that he cannot drink like other people.(p.109)

• Tell him you have been ***worried***, though perhaps needlessly.(p.112)

• This ***worried*** me.(p.376)

• He kept the money for me, but I ***worried*** him to death for it.(p.493)

worries

• Neither did I have any pressing problems or ***worries***.(p.41)

• Many things happened; business trials, little ***worries***, and feelings of general despondency came near driving me to the bottle, but I made progress.(p.237)

• He has few ***worries***, fewer warnings.(p.330)

• Gradually the quantity increased, the occasions for a drink came more frequently; a hard day, ***worries*** and pressure, bad news, good news -- there were more and more reasons for a drink.(p.374)

• The same old problems and ***worries*** surround me.(p.505)

worry

• In some circumstances we have gone out deliberately to get drunk, feeling ourselves justified by nervousness, anger, ***worry***, depression, jealousy or the like.(p.37)

• We don't ***worry*** about them if we can honestly say to ourselves that we would right them if we could.(p.83)

• But we must be careful not to drift into ***worry***, remorse or morbid reflection, for that would diminish our usefulness to others.(p.86)

• We are then in much less danger of excitement, fear, anger, ***worry***, self-pity, or foolish decisions.(p.88)

• If your husband is a drinker, you probably ***worry*** over what other people are thinking and you hate to meet your friends.(p.114)

• When we do that, we find it solves our problems too; the ensuing lack of fear, ***worry*** and hurt feelings is a wonderful thing.(p.116)

• It means release from care, boredom and ***worry***.(p.151)

• There you will find release from care, boredom and ***worry***.(p.152)

• He told how he lived in constant ***worry*** about those who might find out about his alcoholism.(p.155)

• They experienced a few distressing failures, but in those cases they made an effort to bring the man's family into a spiritual way of living, thus relieving much ***worry*** and suffering.(p.159)

• If I could lay off it, that meant I didn't have to ***worry*** about a drinking problem, I thought.(p.317)

• Once I did have a slip -- tried drinking again -- but the A.A.'s tell me not to ***worry*** about yesterday, because nobody can change it, and not to ***worry*** about tomorrow, because it hasn't come yet.(p.320)

• Boredom was no ***worry*** to me when I went out to pasture.(p.330)

• I had to sleep, I had to clear my mind and free it from ***worry***, and I had to relax.(p.336)

• On the second, I knew -- as I know now -- that if I remained away from the first drink, then I had not to ***worry*** about the hundredth one.(p.344)

• She's a good-natured soul and said, "I wouldn't ***worry*** about it; probably something will happen."(p.346)

• Then I began to have blackouts and that was a constant ***worry***.(p.375)

• I will never know all the people I hurt, all the friends I abused, the humiliation of my family, the ***worry*** of my business associates, or how far reaching it was.(p.376)

• Broken promises, humiliation, hopelessness, ***worry***, anxiety -- but still not enough.(p.377)

• If we do a good job of living today, and if tomorrow comes for us, then the chances are we will do a good job when it arrives -- so why ***worry*** about it?(p.382)

• In six years of ***worry***, I hadn't learned anything.(p.387)

• And then I went back home to live with my parents, and the merry-go-round started again -- only this time I didn't have to ***worry*** about waking up behind bars in a psychiatric ward.(p.468)

• I didn't have to ***worry*** about him any longer.(p.508)

• I had a rough lot, but I don't ***worry*** about that, after hearing the stories of many others.(p.511)

• Of course I really didn't have to ***worry*** on that score, because I wasn't the type that got half drunk.(p.515)

• Oh yes, I get the dry jitters once in a while, but that isn't anything to ***worry*** about.(p.516)

• It didn't ***worry*** me very much, because at that time I could shut off for a couple of months without taking a drink or even wanting one, and without feeling that I was giving anything up.(p.518)

worrying

• It was ***worrying*** my wife a little, but she had the good sense not to take me to task about it or goad me into going.(p.364)

worse

• Gradually things got ***worse***.(p.5)

• As matters grow ***worse***, he begins to use a combination of high-powered sedative and liquor to quiet his nerves so he can go to work.(p.22)

• Over any considerable period we get ***worse***, never better.(p.30)

• In some instances there has been brief recovery, followed always by a still ***worse*** relapse.(p.31)

• The doctor intimated strongly that he might be ***worse*** than he realized.(p.39)

• But the more we fought and tried to have our own way, the ***worse*** matters got.(p.66)

• When it made us cocky, it was ***worse***.(p.68)

• The inconsistency is made ***worse*** by the things he does on his sprees.(p.73)

• We doubt if, in this respect, alcoholics are fundamentally much ***worse*** than other people.(p.81)

• Though once like number two he became ***worse***.(p.109)

• It is of little use to argue and only makes the impasse ***worse***.(p.126)

• This went from bad to ***worse*** until Sophomore spring when, after a prolonged period of drinking, I made up my mind that I could not complete my course, so I packed my grip and went South to spend a month on a large farm owned by a friend of mine.(p.173)

• There my drinking became so much ***worse*** that the boys in the fraternity house where I lived felt forced to send for my father, who made a long journey in the vain endeavor to get me straightened around.(p.174)

• After three years of this, I wound up in the local hospital where they attempted to help me, but I would get my friends to smuggle me a quart, or I would steal the alcohol about the building, so that I got rapidly ***worse***.(p.175)

• As time went on my drinking became progressively ***worse***.(p.184)

• Naturally, what little restraint I had exercised before was gone now, and my drinking became ***worse***.(p.199)

• Then I got into the habit of having beers, and decided that a drink of whiskey was not any ***worse***; so I would get the one drink of whiskey but, on second thought, I decided that as long as I was only going to have one, I might as well make it a double-header.(p.203)

• This pattern deepened and became ***worse***.(p.214)

• The shakes grew ***worse*** and I looked at my watch -- six o'clock.(p.223)

• And to my surprise, my drinking grew ***worse***.(p.226)

• My loneliness was ***worse*** than it had ever been before, for now even my own kind had turned against me.(p.247)

• It went on and grew ***worse*** and ***worse***.(p.262)

• I hated myself ***worse*** and ***worse***, and as I hated myself I became more defiant towards everything and everybody.(p.265)

• My defiant attitude became ***worse***.(p.265)

• One morning after a terrific drinking bout, I was in a little bar near our house, and I shook so that I was very much ashamed, because I was getting the shakes ***worse*** and ***worse***.(p.266)

• Time went on and the drinking got ***worse*** and ***worse***, and I was in another barroom, down the road the other way, a small one, and I took my glass -- that morning I'd been able to lift it from the bar -- and I said to the woman behind the bar, "I wish I might never take another drop of that stuff.(p.266)

• But I had my health back and besides, I reasoned, they were much ***worse*** than I would ever be.(p.289)

• Some of us struggle with these people because we know that they are really very sick, but we also know that short of some miracle, we are not going to help them except temporarily, and that they will inevitably get ***worse*** and ***worse*** until one of two things happens.(p.308)

• But, of course," he continued, "eventually the alcoholic loses all of his capacities as his disease gets progressively ***worse***, and this is a tragedy that is painful

to watch; the disintegration of a sound mind and body."(p.308)
- And when I looked at it, I knew I was just as much a drunk as George was, if not *worse*.(p.322)
- But this second time, I found I couldn't live normally without it, and I was licked *worse* than ever.(p.340)
- As someone in A.A. said to me once upon a time, there is nothing *worse* than a confused psychiatrist.(p.347)
- The more I drank, the *worse* it got and the more I had to drink.(p.354)
- My salesmanship was still good, for in the fall of 1938 she called me from Salt Lake and finally agreed to take me on for better or for *worse*.(p.360)
- IT MIGHT HAVE BEEN *WORSE*(p.373)
- I know that I was terribly screwed up inside, but I came out much *worse*.(p.387)
- But I got drunk that night and stayed drunk, getting increasingly *worse* until I found A.A. ten years later.(p.404)
- In the morning, because I was young and healthy, my remorse was *worse* than my hangover.(p.404)
- Her luck had been *worse* than mine, but not her drinking.(p.414)
- They had been drinking for many years and were getting progressively *worse*.(p.424)
- Drinking conditions at home were even *worse* than before.(p.424)
- To cut a long story short, I spent seven years and ten thousand dollars on my psychiatric adventure, and emerged in *worse* condition than ever.(p.434)
- Meanwhile, I was getting *worse*, both as regards my inward misery and my drinking.(p.434)
- I remember very well saying, "There's only one person in the world whose guts I hate *worse* than yours, and those're my own."(p.440)
- The more I focus my mind on its defects -- late start, long drunkalogues, cigarette smoke – the *worse* the meeting becomes.(p.451)
- There are many things *worse* than dying, but is there any death *worse* than the progressive, self-induced, slow suicide of the practicing alcoholic?(p.457)
- Things went from bad to *worse*, and since I had finally and completely failed at the job of being a wife and a mother, my marriage ended.(p.468)
- During the years 1930 to 1935, due to the Depression and its aftermath, business went from bad to *worse*.(p.486)
- Things had just gone from bad to *worse*.(p.487)
- Matters got *worse* all the time until finally they got so bad that I was reinvestigated by the Government.(p.490)
- "There are men on the streets of New York today who were *worse* than you, and they don't drink any more."(p.503)
- But I came out of the Army just as big a drunk as when I went in, if not *worse*, because now I had a lot more resentments.(p.513)
- They sent me up with an attendant, and the attendant and I both arrived at the Egyptian Hospital rather the *worse* for wear.(p.521)
- Things were getting *worse* and *worse*.(p.522)
- It wasn't strong enough, so I added a shot of vodka -- and was right back to *worse* trouble than before.(p.556)

worship
- It was impossible to say we had no capacity for faith, or love, or *worship*.(p.54)
- It may be obscured by calamity, by pomp, by *worship* of other things, but in some form or other it is there.(p.55)

worshipfully
- And then, with a better motive, had we not *worshipfully* beheld the sunset, the sea, or a flower?(p.54)

worshipped
- Had we not variously *worshipped* people, sentiment, things, money, and ourselves?(p.54)

worshippers
- We found, too, that we had been *worshippers*.(p.54)

worshipping
- My personal definition, which I submit as applying only to myself (although everyone is welcome to it who wants it), includes every waking activity of the human being; to have a creative attitude towards things is a more exact meaning, to live and to deal with other human beings creatively, which to me means seeing the God in them, and respecting and *worshipping* this God.(p.535)

worships
- How much did these feelings, these loves, these *worships*, have to do with pure reason?(p.54)

worst
- My old manner of life was by no means a bad one, but I would not exchange its best moments for the *worst* I have now.(p.43)
- They took inventory all right, but hung on to some of the *worst* items in stock.(p.73)
- We have been dealing with alcohol in its *worst* aspect.(p.132)
- It was one of the *worst* I ever had.(p.393)
- Nor was I the "*worst* woman who ever lived."(p.414)
- A.A. and acceptance have taught me that there is a bit of good in the *worst* of us and a bit of bad in the best of us; that we are all children of God and we each have a right to be here.(p.449)
- For years, I was sure the *worst* thing that could happen to a nice guy like me would be that I would turn out to be an alcoholic.(p.449)
- The thirteen stories in this group tell of alcoholism at its miserable *worst*.(p.455)
- The *worst* of prison treatment couldn't break this tough con.(p.457)
- I was intensely unhappy the whole time, but I didn't seem to be able to do anything about it, and the *worst* part to me was the realization that all this was going to happen again and again until I died.(p.522)
- That was one of the *worst* things that could have happened to an alcoholic woman.(p.527)
- Finally, I got so lowdown, I was ashamed of my friends' seeing me, so I went to the *worst* joints I could find.(p.527)

worth
- But not so with the alcoholic illness, for with it there goes annihilation of all the things *worth* while in life.(p.18)
- It may be *worth* a bad case of jitters if you get a full knowledge of your condition.(p.32)
- To the precise extent that we permit these, do we squander the hours that might have been *worth* while.(p.66)
- We are there to sweep off our side of the street realizing that nothing *worth* while can be accomplished until we do so, never trying to tell him what he should do.(p.77)
- The story of how you and your wife settled your difficulties is *worth* any amount of criticism.(p.100)
- This may take patient waiting, but it will be *worth* it.(p.112)
- Showing others who suffer how we were given help is the very thing which makes life seem so *worth* while to us now.(p.124)
- If he had these qualities and did not drink would he be *worth* retaining?(p.140)
- Is he *worth* salvaging?(p.140)
- If this presents difficulty, re-reading chapters two and three, where the alcoholic sickness is discussed at length might be *worth* while.(p.140)
- That was *worth* a lot even though I did not believe it.(p.185)
- So, after hearing some more of my story, he turned around and said to Doc -- I don't think he knew I heard him, but I did – he said, "Well, I believe he's *worth* saving and working on."(p.185)
- Then broke again, hiding out in cheap hotels all over the country, one night jail stands here and there, and always that horrible feeling "What's the use -- nothing is *worth* while."(p.244)
- The adjustments in such a case are difficult and take time, but we both feel that they are certainly *worth* it.(p.286)
- And of course a half empty bottle wasn't *worth* keeping, so I finished it up and naturally had to get more in right away for the people who "might come in unexpectedly."(p.336)
- Through going to meetings and listening, and occasionally speaking, through doing Twelve Step work, whereby in helping others you are both the teacher and the student, by making many wonderful A.A. friends, I have been taught all the things in life that are *worth* having.(p.416)
- Can all the *worth* while people I have known be wrong about God?(p.503)
- Finally, my mother came and said she had kept me at home for six years because she thought she could help me, but that now she had come to the conclusion that I wasn't even *worth* trying to help.(p.523)
- Poor, black, totally ruled by alcohol, she felt shut away from any life *worth* living.(p.526)
- On one of these trips, the judge must have thought I was *worth* saving, for instead of sending me to jail, he sent me to A.A. for one month.(p.526)

worthwhile
- He had lost everything *worthwhile* in life and was only living, one might say, to drink.(p.xxix)
- We think we are sensible when we urge that you stop this waste and give your *worthwhile* man a chance.(p.148)

wouldn't
- The market would recover, but I *wouldn't*.(p.6)
- Such a man would be crazy, *wouldn't* he?(p.38)
- Were nothing left but pure reason, it *wouldn't* be life.(p.54)
- We *wouldn't* treat sick people that way.(p.67)
- Perhaps we are mixed up with women in a fashion we *wouldn't* care to have advertised.(p.80)
- If newcomers could see no joy or fun in our existence, they *wouldn't* want it.(p.132)
- Who *wouldn't* be, with such a fevered brain?(p.140)
- Before very long we began to relate some incidents of our drinking and, naturally, pretty soon, I realized both of them knew what they were talking about because you can see things and smell things when you're drunk, that you can't other times, and, if I had thought they didn't know what they were talking about, I *wouldn't* have been willing to talk to them at all.(p.185)
- *Wouldn't* you like to see us again?"(p.189)
- I wasn't afraid that the program *wouldn't* work, but I still was doubtful whether I would be able to hang on to the program, but I did come to the conclusion that I was willing to put everything I had into it, with God's power, and that I wanted to do just that.(p.189)
- I knew that I had a helper that I could rely upon, who *wouldn't* fail me.(p.189)
- He *wouldn't* give me any money for the groceries, but he did take me across the street and buy me a bag of candy, which I later took back and traded for a loaf of bread.(p.193)
- I *wouldn't* put sufficient time on them.(p.194)
- I can remember occasions when friends recommended me for positions or business opportunities that I *wouldn't* take because I felt that at some future date I'd get drunk and they would be hurt.(p.198)
- I determined that I *wouldn't* drink.(p.200)
- There were times when I got to drinking, and I had been warned by Firestone that they *wouldn't* stand for this much longer, so, clearly, they were conscious of the fact that I drank too much and too often.(p.204)
- The next day, they called me in for an examination, and the doctor *wouldn't* let me continue working and pardoned me from the plant for ten days because he said my eye had been injured.(p.205)
- Paul measured the medicine out, but he figured that with my track record that little bit *wouldn't* be enough, so he doubled it and added a few drops more and then gave it to me.(p.207)
- I realized that I had a problem, although my realization was not very deep because my own conceit *wouldn't* admit that I had any personality problems.(p.214)
- Whenever a situation arose that fast talk *wouldn't* explain away, I simply withdrew.(p.214)
- I never left the church, but I was a fringe member, and the thought simply never occurred to me that through the exercise of what I had I might find the answer to my problem, simply because I *wouldn't* admit that I had a problem.(p.214)
- She said, "Well, he *wouldn't* be here if you didn't say so."(p.217)
- I might have done terrible things, and I *wouldn't* even know it!(p.223)
- For the last two years of my drinking I prayed on every drunk that I *wouldn't* wake up again.(p.245)
- They called the Mayor in so we *wouldn't* have to stay in there over the holiday.(p.264)
- Everyone had my number and *wouldn't* hire me at any price.(p.301)
- He mentioned lies and deceptions in the course of his story in the presence of the one person in the world I *wouldn't* want to know such things.(p.302)
- The doctor asked about my drinking, but I *wouldn't* talk to him.(p.319)
- I was sure I *wouldn't* belong in an A.A. group -- they were all old men, I thought, and all skid-row bums.(p.319)
- She decided she *wouldn't* let herself go in her drinking.(p.321)
- If we were invited to a formal party and I knew they were only going to have one or two drinks, I *wouldn't* have any.(p.323)
- I got so that I hid quite a bit of the time, *wouldn't* answer the phone, and stayed by myself as much as I could.(p.324)
- I couldn't keep up with any of my other friends, and I *wouldn't* go to anyone's house unless I knew they drank as heavily as I did.(p.324)
- And unless I had some rosy picture of what was

going to happen that day, I ***wouldn't*** even feel like getting up in the morning at all.(p.325)
• If I could only stop thinking, I ***wouldn't*** drink.(p.337)
• If I could only stop drinking, maybe I ***wouldn't*** think.(p.337)
• She's a good-natured soul and said, "I ***wouldn't*** worry about it; probably something will happen."(p.346)
• I ***wouldn't*** give it up or trade it for anything.(p.355)
• It was the first she had heard or read about it and she said she had considered sending it to me or trying to have someone in Pittsburgh send it to me so I ***wouldn't*** know where it came from.(p.366)
• However, knowing me, she thought it was a foolish idea, that I ***wouldn't*** be interested.(p.367)
• I woke up in this bare room with nothing around me but bars; they ***wouldn't*** let me smoke and treated me, well, like I was nuts.(p.387)
• I ***wouldn't*** go to hospitals because I wanted my dog there, so I had to have a trained nurse.(p.390)
• I displayed alcoholic tendencies actually from the age of fourteen, when I started to steal wine from the family jug, siphoning it off one drink at a time so it ***wouldn't*** be missed, not drinking it immediately, but saving it until about a pint was accumulated, so that I could get drunk.(p.397)
• I found I could boost my income by figuring out a lot of cute little tricks that the boss ***wouldn't*** be likely to notice – filching money from the Coke machine, short-sticking the customers on oil, and selling oil I'd drained out of other cars.(p.423)
• And the folks said A.A. was for people who wanted to quit, otherwise it ***wouldn't*** work.(p.429)
• That doctor in the Navy hospital told me I ***wouldn't*** live five years if I didn't quit.(p.429)
• Were I to revert to drinking, even now, I ***wouldn't*** give anything for these four years in A.A.(p.430)
• Second, you ***wouldn't*** have believed me even if I had told you."(p.436)
• But by God, I ***wouldn't*** talk or eat, either!(p.444)
• And I knew that giving up "one drink for one day" ***wouldn't*** really do any good.(p.448)
• I asked her just what this deal was, but she ***wouldn't*** say.(p.494)
• But I pointed out to him that as I was the first British boy who had been to the school, it ***wouldn't*** be a very good advertisement for him, so I got over that all right.(p.518)
• I have not seen a black face but mine since I've been here, and if I didn't look in the mirror, I ***wouldn't*** know that I was black, because these people treat me as one of them, which I am.(p.530)
• Things weren't going as I thought they should, for my greater enjoyment, comfort and fame; therefore, if the universe ***wouldn't*** play my way, I ***wouldn't*** play at all.(p.531)
• Maybe I ***wouldn't*** be able to hold any job, or maybe (and this was my greatest fear) I ***wouldn't*** care whether I had a job or not.(p.548)
• After my very first drink – a tiny glass of sherry my father gave me to celebrate the New Year when I was thirteen -- I went up to bed, dizzy with exhilaration and excitement, and I prayed I ***wouldn't*** drink any more!(p.554)

wound
• But his venture ***wound*** up in a law suit and bogged down completely.(p.154)
• After three years of this, I ***wound*** up in the local hospital where they attempted to help me, but I would get my friends to smuggle me a quart, or I would steal the alcohol about the building, so that I got rapidly worse.(p.175)
• I drank with moderation at first, but it took me only a relatively short time to drift back into the old habits which had ***wound*** up so disastrously before.(p.175)
• Yet I ***wound*** up at this place.(p.202)
• I managed to maintain myself with odd jobs, did ten weeks in a social rescue institution, and at length ***wound*** up in a second-hand bookstore in an adjacent town as manager.(p.257)
• Three weeks after an armed robbery in which one person received a superficial flesh ***wound*** (I could have killed someone!), I was apprehended.(p.460)
• I was there about three weeks, and then I got restless and started to tramp across the country, here and there, until I finally ***wound*** up in Pennsylvania, in a steel mill.(p.492)

woven
• I did six years of newspaper advertising, and trade journal work with many, many drunks of drab and dreary hue ***woven*** into the pattern of my life.(p.254)

wrapped
• Perhaps they created the impression that he is to be ***wrapped*** in cotton wool and placed on a pedestal.(p.122)
• And I said, "Well, they brought a pitcher of coffee, and a sandwich ***wrapped*** up for me."(p.264)
• I choose to believe that the Power greater than ourselves we ask for help, ***wrapped*** my shivering body in loving warmth and strength which has never left me.(p.541)

wreck
• From a trembling, despairing nervous ***wreck***, had emerged a man brimming over with self-reliance and contentment.(p.xxix)
• It will take time to clear away the ***wreck***.(p.123)
• There had been some occasions -- there was an automobile ***wreck***, for instance – when I had police escort home but not to jail, all of which, instead of doing me a favor, did me harm because I was then full of self-esteem as to the progress I had made both professionally and financially.(p.213)
• However, it finally caught up with me, and when it did, I was a mental, physical, and nervous ***wreck***.(p.299)
• Marty came in, looking clean, neat, well-dressed and, like Bill, she was neither a bloated ***wreck*** nor a reformer.(p.413)
• And A.A. took this ***wreck*** of a woman and brought her back to life.(p.470)

wreckage
• Clear away the ***wreckage*** of your past.(p.164)

wrecked
• Being ***wrecked*** in the same vessel, being restored and united under one God, with hearts and minds attuned to the welfare of others, the things which matter so much to some people no longer signify much to them.(p.161)

wrest
• Is he not a victim of the delusion that he can ***wrest*** satisfaction and happiness out of this world if he only manages well?(p.61)

wretched
• When a few drinks made me feel good before I went over that line, those same drinks now made me ***wretched***.(p.346)

Wright
• Even in the present century, American newspapers were afraid to print an account of the ***Wright*** brothers' first successful flight at Kitty Hawk.(p.51)
• The ***Wright*** brothers' almost childish faith that they could build a machine which would fly was the mainspring of their accomplishment.(p.52)

Wrights
• When others showed us that "God-sufficiency" worked with them, we began to feel like those who had insisted the ***Wrights*** would never fly.(p.52)

wringer
• We, who have been through the ***wringer***, have to admit if we substituted alcoholism for jay-walking, the illustration would fit us exactly.(p.38)
• He had felt only the first nip of the ***wringer***.(p.43)
• He had also gone all the way through the ***wringer*** and had been dry two years when I saw him again.(p.243)
• Barleycorn's ***wringer*** squeezed this author -- but he escaped quite whole.(p.432)

wrings
• Alcohol ***wrings*** the guts out of life, eats into the brain in such a way as to make the alcoholic blind to the truth.(p.457)

wrinkled
• Then, of course, there are always the ***wrinkled*** slacks, which have been slept in and are so dirty, they could walk away by themselves.(p.479)

wrinkles
• I'd been dry three weeks, had the ***wrinkles*** out and had sobered up my sponsor all by myself!(p.246)

wrist
• Within a month, the police, the hospital authorities, several kind strangers, most of my friends, all of my close relatives, and a few adepts at rolling a drunk and removing his ***wrist*** watch and wallet had been involved.(p.532)
• (There was a time, for about three months, when I bought a ten-dollar ***wrist*** watch every pay day – that is every two weeks.(p.532)

wrists
• Once, I phoned my brother-in-law and told him I was going to take a handful of pills (in fact, I already had) and I would slash my ***wrists*** if he didn't come over to stop me.(p.479)

wristwatch
• I had lost a hundred dollars I had in my pocket, and lost a ***wristwatch*** too.(p.202)

write
• At one of the finals I was too drunk to think or ***write***.(p.2)
• Nothing would please us so much as to ***write*** a book which would contain no basis for contention or argument.(p.19)
• We suggested he ***write*** his first wife admitting his faults and asking forgiveness.(p.79)
• Still you may say: "But I will not have the benefit of contact with you who ***write*** this book."(p.164)
• When I went in to ***write*** the examinations, my hand trembled so I could not hold a pencil.(p.174)
• As I ***write*** nearly four years have passed.(p.180)
• I had been too self-sufficient to ***write*** a moral inventory, but I discovered in pointing out to the new man his wrong attitudes and actions that I was really taking my own inventory, and that if I expected him to change I would have to work on myself too.(p.249)
• Lying on the divan, "getting in the mood" to ***write***, I cried openly or inwardly, as I listened to sad songs.(p.332)
• I know that when Frank came home, I said, "I want to try this thing," and he said, "There's a post office box to ***write*** to in New York."(p.392)
• I was shaking so, I asked my husband to ***write*** the letter for me, but he said no.(p.392)
• I had writing ambitions, and nothing would do but that I'd ***write*** like Shakespeare.(p.400)
• I have achieved the inner confidence to ***write*** quite unlike Shakespeare, and I have sold a good deal of what I've written.(p.416)
• I want to ***write*** better and sell more.(p.417)
• Forgive me -- I cannot ***write*** further about this latest turn of events, anticipating seeing the family I deserted so long ago.(p.463)
• This first story I ever ***write***.(p.474)
• I must ***write*** her.(p.505)
• If I ***write*** with the air of one who has discovered the obvious, which is to say, the eternal truths which have been offered to us since the beginning, forgive my callowness; I had to find these things out for myself.(p.536)
• As I ***write*** these words, it seems incredible that these things should have happened to me, for they are, truly, against all my instincts and training.(p.536)
• I ask the forgiveness of the reader; and from now on I shall try to ***write*** with the humility I honestly pray for.)(p.536)
• I still want to ***write*** a fine play and to get it on.(p.542)
• Then I joined the Navy and was commissioned as an ensign to ***write*** speeches for admirals.(p.555)
• Should you be the relative or friend of an alcoholic who shows no immediate interest in A.A., it is suggested that you ***write*** the Al-Anon Family Groups, Inc., Box 182, Madison Square Station, New York, NY 10159, U.S.A.(p.575)

write-up
• Just as I was wondering what on earth I could do -- I was too drunk even to pack a handkerchief – the memory of an A.A. ***write-up*** that I had seen in the Evening Mail flashed across my mind -- and I thought to myself, this is something I haven't tried yet.(p.523)

writers
• Show him that as alcoholics, the ***writers*** of the book understand.(p.112)
• When it was closed through Washington edict I began with Federal ***Writers*** in San Antonio.(p.256)

writes
• The doctor ***writes***:(p.xxv)

writhing
• My ***writhing*** nerves were stilled at last.(p.6)

writing
• When ***writing*** or speaking publicly about alcoholism, we urge each of our Fellowship to omit his personal name, designating himself instead as "a member of Alcoholics Anonymous."(p.xiii)
• If there is no Al-Anon listing in your local telephone book, you may obtain further information on Al-Anon Family Groups by ***writing*** to its World Service Office: Box 182, Madison Square Station, New York, NY 10159.(p.121)
• This was only a few days ago at this ***writing***.(p.163)
• A friend who knew I would soon be broke mounted guard over me when I left my job of ***writing*** the histories of Texas cities and put me aboard a bus for the town I had left almost five years before.(p.256)
• I still have my job, and just prior to the ***writing*** of this narrative, I received an advancement.(p.303)

• The movie racket had kept me too long from *writing* those novels, articles, short stories, and scripts on which I had copious notes.(p.330)
• My *writing* career was described in the couplet "Alcohol gave me wings to fly,/And then it took away the sky."(p.331)
• During this time I faithfully was *writing* my girl in Utah.(p.360)
• I had *writing* ambitions, and nothing would do but that I'd write like Shakespeare.(p.400)
• Much of my time was spent *writing* letters, notes, orders, and lists of things for Max, who was also my office nurse, to do to keep the world running while I was locked up.(p.445)
• I'm *writing* this during an A.A. convention, where I have spent the weekend with nothing but white people.(p.529)
• I am hoping that *writing* this may bring some poor, mixed-up soul into the program.(p.530)
• Upon graduation, I ventured to New York to pursue my *writing* career.(p.555)

written

• The section called "The Doctor's Opinion" has been kept intact, just as it was originally *written* in 1939 by the late Dr. William D. Silkworth, our Society's great medical benefactor.(p.xi)
• "Bill's Story," "Doctor Bob's Nightmare," and one other personal history from the first edition were retained intact; three were edited and one of these was retitled; new versions of two stories were *written* with new titles; thirty completely new stories were added; and the story section was divided into three parts, under the same headings that are used now.(p.xi)
• Since the original Foreword to this book was *written* in 1939, a wholesale miracle has taken place.(p.xv)
• There is the manic-depressive type, who is, perhaps, the least understood by his friends, and about whom a whole chapter could be *written*.(p.xxviii)
• Much has been *written* pro and con, but among physicians, the general opinion seems to be that most chronic alcoholics are doomed.(p.xxviii)
• Before then, I had *written* lots of sweet promises, but my wife happily observed that this time I meant business.(p.5)
• That means we have *written* a book which we believe to be spiritual as well as moral.(p.45)
• If we have been thorough about our personal inventory, we have *written* down a lot.(p.70)
• We have a *written* inventory and we are prepared for a long talk.(p.75)
• The fellowship of Al-Anon Family Groups was formed about thirteen years after this chapter was *written*.(p.121)
• Hopelessness was *written* large on the man's face as he replied, "Oh, but that's no use.(p.157)
• I remembered my loud resolution to find him and ask him to help me get into that "Asylum" he had *written* about.(p.224)
• Around this time our big A.A. book was being *written* and it all became much simpler; we had a definite formula which some sixty of us agreed was the middle course for all alcoholics who wanted sobriety, and that formula has not been changed one iota down through the years.(p.248)
• The big A.A. book had not been *written* and there was no literature except various religious pamphlets.(p.291)
• As these words are *written* at fifty-three years of age, with over nine years of A.A. behind me, with all its wonderful teachings, I haven't the slightest doubt about being an alcoholic.(p.356)
• I haven't *written* anything about that part of my story, but I believe in a Greater Power which I call God and I ask for His wisdom and guidance daily.(p.366)
• I got a novel *written*.(p.402)
• I have achieved the inner confidence to write quite unlike Shakespeare, and I have sold a good deal of what I've *written*.(p.416)
• Even the Jack Alexander Saturday Evening Post article hadn't been *written*, and there was only a tiny group of people in Washington.(p.469)
• Only they had been scratched out and over them was *written*, "Chronic Alcoholic."(p.470)
• Sobering up, the mind that was ahead of the emotions would impel the question: What have you *written* or done to be the great man?(p.537)

wrong

• I expressed my entire willingness to approach these individuals, admitting my *wrong*.(p.13)
• He has a positive genius for getting tight at exactly the *wrong* moment, particularly when some important decision must be made or engagement kept.(p.21)
• But later, alone in his room, he asked himself this question: "Is it possible that all the religious people I have known are *wrong*?"(p.56)
• 10.Continued to take personal inventory and when we were *wrong* promptly admitted it.(p.59)
• The first thing apparent was that this world and its people were often quite *wrong*.(p.65)
• To conclude that others were *wrong* was as far as most of us ever got.(p.66)
• The usual outcome was that people continued to *wrong* us and we stayed sore.(p.66)
• But our man is sure to be impressed with a sincere desire to set right the *wrong*.(p.77)
• He felt that he had done a *wrong* he could not possibly make right.(p.80)
• Our thought-life will be placed on a much higher plane when our thinking is cleared of *wrong* motives.(p.86)
• The men who cry for money and shelter before conquering alcohol, are on the *wrong* track.(p.98)
• Dad may feel that for years his drinking has placed him on the *wrong* side of every argument, but now he has become a superior person with God on his side.(p.129)
• Even when he wanted to assert himself he could not, for his drinking placed him constantly in the *wrong*.(p.130)
• Of course our friend was *wrong* -- dead *wrong*.(p.135)
• She sees she was *wrong* to make a burning issue out of such a matter when his more serious ailments were being rapidly cured.(p.135)
• Of course, we had talked over quite a number of the failings that I had and made a sort of an inventory, which wasn't too difficult, because I had an awful lot of things *wrong* that were very apparent to me, because I knew all about them.(p.190)
• They were *wrong*.(p.215)
• She gave no sign of recognizing anything *wrong*, but what had I been doing for those lost five hours?(p.223)
• I had no resentments against individuals – the whole world was all *wrong*.(p.244)
• Everything's all *wrong* and the hell with it."(p.245)
• They had also been periodic big shots who had goofed out repeatedly at the *wrong* time, and they also knew how to split one paper match into three separate matches.(p.245)
• We would follow one man's ideas for a while, decide he was *wrong* and switch to another's method.(p.246)
• I had been too self-sufficient to write a moral inventory, but I discovered in pointing out to the new man his *wrong* attitudes and actions that I was really taking my own inventory, and that if I expected him to change I would have to work on myself too.(p.249)
• I'm sure his family felt that it was a marriage that -- well, I was a girl from the *wrong* side of the tracks -- definitely!(p.262)
• I could never go and make up to all the people I've done *wrong* to."(p.269)
• I heard for the first time an expression which I was to grow to loathe: "There is nothing organically *wrong*."(p.276)
• On my trips back to Akron to get my spirits recharged and to work with other alcoholics, I would ask Dr. Bob about this delay and wonder just what was *wrong* with me.(p.293)
• (Now I know the answer – *wrong*.)(p.317)
• It would be a little thing that I'd think was *wrong*, and off I'd go, drinking.(p.324)
• When we begin to do things like that with alcohol, something's gone *wrong*.(p.336)
• So he got me a cup of coffee, and a piece of cake, and sat me down and said, "Why, there's nothing *wrong* with you.(p.348)
• At times, when I noticed other families, I felt something was very *wrong* with ours.(p.369)
• I had nowhere else to go, and I knew something was terribly *wrong*, and the reason had to lie within myself.(p.371)
• It was such a feeling of relief that I wanted to know more about it and with that, I think for the first time, came the realization that there was something horribly, horribly *wrong* with me.(p.392)
• In spite of knowing that my drunkenness was a symptom of the things that were *wrong* with me, and that I could never drink again, I thought I couldn't yet give it up, although I was going to try.(p.393)
• But I was *wrong*.(p.398)
• Underneath, I knew this was all *wrong*.(p.407)
• So I did the right thing in the *wrong* way.(p.409)
• Admitting that I am *wrong* or that I do not know is difficult for me.(p.420)
• But when I try to see what I can add to the meeting, rather than what I can get out of it, and when I focus my mind on what's good about it, rather than what's *wrong* with it, the meeting keeps getting better and better.(p.451)
• The hotel management, knowing that something was *wrong*, sent for a doctor.(p.465)
• How *wrong* I was!(p.481)
• I don't know whether it was right or *wrong*, but at least I know that people weren't thinking the same.(p.484)
• Then he asks me if I am willing to right all the wrongs I have ever done to anyone, no matter how *wrong* I thought the others were.(p.503)
• Can all the worth while people I have known be *wrong* about God?(p.503)
• I see where I have been *wrong* in some respects.(p.505)
• I return home and say I am sorry for my *wrong*.(p.505)
• I thought, well, now that I've been put out for drinking, I'll just show them that they were completely *wrong*, so I went off on the biggest bout I had been on up to then, involving about a fortnight's blackout.(p.521)
• But then one good doctor told me there was nothing *wrong* with me except drinking too much.(p.528)
• It was impossible for me to say at this point, "Maybe there is something *wrong* with my philosophy," and I certainly couldn't say, "Maybe there is something *wrong* with me."(p.545)

wrong-doing

• In that state, the *wrong-doing* of others, fancied or real, had power to actually kill.(p.66)
• He thus used his own *wrong-doing* as a means of destroying the reputation of another.(p.80)
• I was down to my shorts, unaware of *wrong-doing*, before the ambulance got there and hauled me off to a hospital from which anxious friends rescued me, later that night.(p.537)

wronged

• He is like the retired business man who lolls in the Florida sunshine in the winter complaining of the sad state of the nation; the minister who sighs over the sins of the twentieth century; politicians and reformers who are sure all would be Utopia if the rest of the world would only behave; the outlaw safe cracker who thinks society has *wronged* him; and the alcoholic who has lost all and is locked up.(p.61)
• This was our course: We realized that the people who *wronged* us were perhaps spiritually sick.(p.66)

wrongs

• 5.Admitted to God, to ourselves, and to another human being the exact nature of our *wrongs*.(p.59)
• Putting out of our minds the *wrongs* others had done, we resolutely looked for our own mistakes.(p.67)
• We admitted our *wrongs* honestly and were willing to set these matters straight.(p.67)
• There may be some *wrongs* we can never fully right.(p.83)
• If he means to right his past *wrongs*, why all this concern for everyone in the world but his family?(p.128)
• Then he asks me if I am willing to right all the *wrongs* I have ever done to anyone, no matter how wrong I thought the others were.(p.503)

wrote

• Then Jack Alexander *wrote* a feature article in the Saturday Evening Post and placed such a compelling picture of A.A. before the general public that alcoholics in need of help really deluged us.(p.xviii)
• My wife *wrote* away for advertised cures for the liquor habit and gave them to me in coffee.(p.235)
• Then I saw an A.A. advertisement in a newspaper, and I *wrote* to the address it gave.(p.343)
• Of course I kept her posted on how well the station was doing and *wrote* convincing letters of how well I was doing with the liquor problem.(p.360)
• Two years before I joined A.A. my wife took a long trip during which she *wrote* me she just couldn't return unless I did something about my drinking.(p.377)
• It was the A.A. General Service Office in New York that I *wrote* to, and that office has always meant a lot to me.(p.392)
• I *wrote* on Saturday.(p.392)
• So I *wrote* this letter in very shaky handwriting, and in just one week came back a letter with A.A. literature from New York.(p.392)
• They sent me the regular letter they send to everybody else, but along with it, Ruth Hock, the nonalcoholic secretary, *wrote* a longhand note because she could see from the letter that I really

needed help badly.(p.392)
• I read sad poetry, cried, drank red wine, ***wrote*** sad poetry, and drank some more.(p.405)
• I also ***wrote*** another novel, all about Scott Fitzgerald's poor, misbegotten, unloved, tipsy little debutante.(p.405)
• I ***wrote*** and sold some short stories.(p.409)
• They ***wrote*** me many long letters about it.(p.427)
• To this day I haven't been able to decipher what I ***wrote*** to them.(p.427)
• I think the Commanding Officer was rather tired of this particular chicken coming back to roost so often because he very soon ***wrote*** in to the medical authorities to tell them that they had to get me into hospital, to be thoroughly examined for drinking.(p.520)

wrought

• Let them remember that his drinking ***wrought*** all kinds of damage that may take long to repair.(p.127)
• Try to remember that though God has ***wrought*** miracles among us, we should never belittle a good doctor or psychiatrist.(p.133)
• We worked in five below zero weather, fixing on an elm tree a ***wrought*** iron device which modestly proclaimed that he was indeed a country doctor.(p.540)

Xx

X-rays
• ***X-rays*** showed that a couple of teeth had to come out.(p.465)

XYZ
• I was staring at an inch of the tape which bore the inscription ***XYZ***-32.(p.4)

Yy

yachts
• Many retirees embrace alcoholism while secluded in motor trailers, rest homes, leisure-world bungalows, mountain cabins, or beach cottages, or even in penthouses, on *yachts*, and inside Palm Springs cabanas.(p.329)

Yankee
• Here was a tall, rugged, highly educated *Yankee* talking in a matter of course way about God and prayer.(p.279)

Yankees
• Furthermore, I knew that I was looked upon as a city slicker from New York, and I had to be pretty cautious among small town, conservative *Yankees*.(p.360)

yard
• We drove my car and I left it down in the *yard*.(p.217)

yardstick
• Also, I was insane at times – according to society's *yardstick*.(p.458)

yarn
• When I remark that I have been in jail nine times, and in an alcoholic ward twice, they think I'm kidding, or possibly dramatizing for the sake of a good *yarn*.(p.542)

yawned
• They knew what to do about those black abysses that *yawned* ready to swallow me when I felt depressed, or nervous.(p.229)

ye
• A.A. has taught me that I will have peace of mind in exact proportion to the peace of mind I bring into the lives of other people, and it has taught me the true meaning of the admonition "happy are *ye* who know these things and do them."(p.551)

year
• At present, our membership is increasing at the rate of about seven per cent a *year*.(p.xx)
• About one *year* prior to this experience a man was brought in to be treated for chronic alcoholism.(p.xxix)
• One *year* later he called to see me, and I experienced a very strange sensation.(p.xxix)
• We covered the whole eastern United States in a *year*.(p.3)
• The exercise of an option brought in more money, leaving us with a profit of several thousand dollars for that *year*.(p.3)
• My weary and despairing wife was informed that it would all end with heart failure during delirium tremens, or I would develop a wet brain, perhaps within a *year*.(p.7)
• It was fortunate, for my old business associates remained skeptical for a *year* and a half, during which I found little work.(p.15)
• If anyone questions whether he has entered this dangerous area, let him try leaving liquor alone for one *year*.(p.34)
• In the early days of our drinking we occasionally remained sober for a *year* or more, becoming serious drinkers again later.(p.34)
• We think few, to whom this book will appeal, can stay dry anything like a *year*.(p.34)
• We first saw Fred about a *year* ago in a hospital where he had gone to recover from a bad case of jitters.(p.39)
• This same company spends millions for research every *year*.(p.149)
• He might be shocked if he knew how much alcoholism is costing his organization a *year*.(p.149)
• A *year* and six months later these three had succeeded with seven more.(p.159)
• To 1950, the *year* of his death, he carried the A.A. message to more than 5,000 alcoholic men and women, and to all these he gave his medical services without thought of charge.(p.171)
• I left the university in the latter part of my senior *year* and enlisted in the army.(p.183)
• It took me a *year*, or a *year* and a half to get to feeling physically well, and it was rather tough, but I soon found folks whose friendship I had once had, and I found, after I had been sober for quite some little time, that these people began to act like they had in previous years, before I had gotten so bad, so that I didn't pay too awful much attention to financial gains.(p.190)
• I think it was probably more than a *year* before I had anything more to do with liquor.(p.195)
• I can well remember sitting with seven dollars in my pocket, planning on giving my family a hundred or two hundred dollars, when I made it next *year*.(p.197)
• I remember one occasion when I did not drink for three hundred and sixty-four days, but I didn't quite make the *year*.(p.200)
• I knew I could quit because he had quit; he hadn't had a drink for over a *year*.(p.208)
• When I left the hospital I tried this for a day and it worked, for a week and it worked, and for a month, and it worked -- and then for a *year* and it still worked.(p.209)
• In the fall of the graduating *year*, I became involved in some litigation over the ownership of inventions and patents.(p.212)
• A *year* later, after I completed the course in contracts, I quit the law school, and undertook some engineering work for a patent law firm on behalf of clients who were in difficulties and who desired to keep their troubles from their own engineering department.(p.212)
• This work consumed a period of about two-thirds of a *year*, and worked out successfully so I decided to follow patent law.(p.212)
• There were, at that time, in the neighborhood of twelve or thirteen Cleveland members who had been sober anywhere from a *year* and a half to a couple of months.(p.219)
• So I enrolled at the university for night courses in religion, and I pursued those courses for a *year*.(p.221)
• I had been going on like that for over a *year*.(p.224)
• When I look back on that last horrible *year* of constant drinking I wonder how I survived it either physically or mentally.(p.224)
• The *year* after coming out, I married.(p.225)
• Unlike many other Catholics who frequently take pledges for definite periods – a *year*, two years or for good, I never had any desire to "take a pledge" before the priest.(p.234)
• This was my introduction to this "understanding fellowship" although it was to be more than a *year* later before our Society was to bear the name, Alcoholics Anonymous.(p.239)
• The first *year* in college I just got by in my studies, and that *year* I majored in poker and drinking.(p.241)
• I refused to join any fraternity, as I wanted to be a free lance, and that *year* my drinking was confined to one-night stands, once or twice a week.(p.241)
• The second *year* my drinking was more or less restricted to week-ends, but I was nearly kicked out for scholastic failure.(p.241)
• In June, 1945, with another member, I made my first – and only – Twelfth Step call on a female alcoholic and a *year* later I married her.(p.249)
• My migrations extended for over a *year* as far west as Omaha.(p.253)
• Federal Theatre in Texas gave me an administrative job which I held for a *year*, only because I worked hard and productively when I worked, and because my very tolerant chief ascribed my frequent lapses to a bohemian temperament.(p.256)
• I didn't see him for a *year*, or even hear from him.(p.262)
• At the end of a *year*, the children got a card from their father, which I still have and cherish.(p.262)
• I had gone to an attorney to see about getting a divorce during that *year*.(p.263)
• Our other daughter was in her last *year* of high school, and one night the new son-in-law and my husband went out to a prize fight.(p.263)
• One *year* we got as far as Bellaire, Ohio.(p.264)
• Of course, this *year* we decided on staying home and being sensible, doing a little drinking, and painting the house.(p.265)
• And he'd been dry a *year*.(p.267)
• We had never missed a Wednesday night at King School for a *year*.(p.270)
• Jack had been sober about a *year* and a half.(p.271)
• Russ lived a *year* longer than they expected him to live, and in that *year* he was in bed for at least six months.(p.272)
• I can't express what A.A. meant to us during that *year*.(p.272)
• During my first *year* out of college I had endless dates, and went to countless dances, balls and dinner parties.(p.275)
• A *year* later I was able to buy a Model T roadster and take a better job with a downtown printer.(p.276)
• My parents died, both in the same *year*, leaving me, a sheltered and somewhat immature man, on my own.(p.277)
• Poor health and a complete lack of money necessitated my remaining with Dr. Bob and Anne for very close to a *year*.(p.280)
• It would be impossible for me to pass over this *year* without mentioning my love for, and my indebtedness to these two wonderful people who are no longer with us.(p.280)
• Sometimes during that *year* I rebelled inwardly at what seemed like lost time, and at having to be a burden to these good people whose means were limited.(p.281)
• During that first *year*, however, I managed to make both ends meet, and to avoid ever going back to my old habit pattern of borrowing money when I could not earn it.(p.283)
• Within a *year* of my return to Detroit, A.A. was a definitely established little group of about a dozen members and I too was established in a modest but steady job handling an independent dry-cleaning route of my own.(p.283)
• I had been in A.A. a *year*, and the last thing in my mind was a drink.(p.285)
• That same *year*, my wife became fed up with my drinking around the house and called my dad in Akron to come and pick me up.(p.288)
• Why, even a *year* ago, I had seen Howard, an ex-doctor, mooching a dime for a drink.(p.289)
• Needless to say, it was a *year* or more before they did contact me.(p.293)
• In the summer of 1938, almost a *year* from the time I made my original contact with Akron, the man for whom I was working and who knew about the program, approached me and asked if I could do anything about one of his salesmen who was drinking very heavily.(p.294)
• I cannot remember just when I became the victim of insomnia, but I do know that the last *year* and a half I never went to bed sober a single night.(p.299)
• For about one *year*, prior to this time, there was one doctor who had continued to struggle with me.(p.306)
• I got orders to go to Vietnam, and I spent most of the *year* over there either drunk or sick with a hangover.(p.317)
• My guild had elected me president twice and later given me a "man of the *year*" award.(p.328)
• He may even read in a newspaper that one out of every seven drinkers will become alcoholic, but he rarely is told that it holds true for all ages -- or that the tolerance to alcohol (and other drugs) decreases steadily, *year* after *year*, in the bodies of all persons.(p.330)
• I returned to my home in Lucknow, India, at the end of November last *year* from a vacation in one of the most famous beauty spots in our country, a mountain resort 6,800 feet up, with a wonderful lake.(p.342)
• At Christmastime next *year*, I convinced my wife that I had alcohol under control and that I would do controlled drinking over Christmas and the New *Year*.(p.343)
• Last *year*, I decided on an A.A. vacation in Naini Tal.(p.343)
• I made more money the last *year* of my drinking than I ever made before in my whole life.(p.345)
• I was president of all my classes in high school and in my last *year* I was president of that student body.(p.345)
• I was in the fourth quarter of my senior *year* at high school, and my mother was quite sick in the hospital.(p.354)
• It took me a *year* to make it home.(p.357)
• In September of this same *year* I went to New York alone.(p.364)
• I had just raised the bottle to my lips when my wife opened the door and froze me completely in my tracks with "Happy New *Year*, dear."(p.365)
• One night at the dinner table my wife said that tonight was my first birthday in A.A., and that the group would have the usual ice cream and cake for the "one *year* man."(p.365)
• When I was called upon for a few words I had to tell my friends that I wasn't one *year* old in A.A. that evening but only a "nine month baby."(p.366)
• A *year* later, while we were on a vacation trip she packed up to go home because of my excessive drinking, and I talked her out of it with the promise I would go on the wagon for at least a *year*.(p.377)

• One afternoon, the *year* after moving to Houston, I got as drunk as a skunk, and while I do not walk very straight sober, you should see me when I'm drunk!(p.390)
• In my second *year* in A.A. we were transferred to Dallas.(p.394)
• For an estimate of salary from the twenty-one a month to start with, to over $400 per month upon my retirement after twenty years in the Navy, I believe that an average income of $2,000 a *year* over this period is low, but as I stated earlier, an underestimate is best.(p.399)
• $2,000 a *year* for twenty-five years is $50,000, twenty per cent of which is $10,000.(p.399)
• In the first *year* there were episodes such as kicking Priscilla in the shins, getting the lock changed on the desk in the A.A. Club, because I, as secretary, didn't want the Intergroup secretary "interfering," and taking an older woman member out to lunch for the express purpose of informing her that she was "a phony."(p.416)
• Awarded a scholarship to a famous old Eastern college, I began to drink at the end of my freshman *year*, and by junior *year*, I had to transfer to an easier state university to keep my grades up.(p.419)
• During my first *year* there, I married.(p.419)
• I teamed up with a cute little blonde with whom I was working at the office, and for about a *year* we were inseparable.(p.425)
• I spent eighteen hundred dollars fixing up that car in the first *year* I was home, after four bad smashups.(p.429)
• The end came next *year*.(p.429)
• I'd heard a lot about A.A. and met a great many A.A.'s during that *year* at home, but I hadn't thought of it for myself.(p.429)
• It was precisely a *year* before I spoke at an A.A. meeting.(p.447)
• Then I was transferred to the honor-grade unit, where I spent the most painful *year* of my life.(p.462)
• It is painful to grow, and without the help of my "civilian" A.A. companion, big Gene, I might not have survived that critical *year* of adjustment.(p.462)
• Now, I have been an alcoholism counselor for over a *year* and am off parole.(p.462)
• *Year* later, I go to Canada to carry message to Tall Man, but he not listen to son.(p.476)
• To tell you a small part of what my mother's life must have been like: Three of her kids were in jail that *year* -- two sons and a daughter.(p.480)
• I planted my first flower garden this *year* and am actually excited to see the results.(p.481)
• If someone had told me last *year* that I would be excited about gardening this *year*, I would have said he was off his rocker.(p.481)
• I remember in my first *year* in high school, that mother suggested that I do not join the cadet unit.(p.484)
• That *year*, on a Friday night, a man whom I had known for years came to my office.(p.488)
• I worked for the Government about a *year* and still maintained my evening office practice when the Government agencies were decentralized.(p.489)
• Final exams of my Senior *year* and I may somehow graduate.(p.499)
• A case of measles saved me from being kicked out during my Sophomore *year*.(p.499)
• Then I had a *year* in Germany at school – that was, incidentally, when I got drunk for the first time.(p.517)
• When the war was over, we had about a *year* in Germany, occupying the place.(p.518)
• I have been home for a *year*, and have not taken a drink in four years.(p.529)
• Repeated *year* on end, they are horrible -- frightening and degrading, a chronicle of tragedy which may be greater because the individual undergoing the tragedy, myself, knew what was happening, and yet refused to do anything to stop it.(p.538)
• Back to the big city, for another *year* of precarious living, paid for largely by one or two friends I still had not milked dry or worn to exhaustion with demands on their bounty.(p.540)
• It was not difficult to convince myself that my unhappiness was the fault of the man I had married, and I divorced him at the end of a *year*.(p.545)
• As I said earlier, self-pity and resentment were my constant companions and my inventory began to look like a thirty-three *year* diary, for I seemed to have a resentment against everybody I had ever known.(p.551)
• After my very first drink – a tiny glass of sherry my father gave me to celebrate the New *Year* when I was thirteen -- I went up to bed, dizzy with exhilaration and excitement, and I prayed I wouldn't drink any more!(p.554)
• In fact, I changed schools every *year* until high school.(p.555)
• In the last *year* of my navy service, I was married to a lovely, lively girl, who enjoyed drinking.(p.555)
• The American Psychiatric Association requested, in 1949, that a paper be prepared by one of the older members of Alcoholics Anonymous to be read at the Association's annual meeting of that *year*.(p.572)

year's

• After a particularly bad Christmas and New *Year's* holiday, dad picked me up again early in January, 1937, to go through the usual sobering up routine.(p.289)
• When I did make it home in 1920, I re-entered school and caught up with my class in a few short months – I actually did a *year's* work in three months, proving much to the disgust of my dad that I could do it when I wanted to.(p.358)
• I got through the holidays all right until New *Year's* Day.(p.365)
• The next recollection I have is of my husband coming into my room (later found out it was on New *Year's* Eve) accompanied by two policemen.(p.468)

yearbook

• An honor student in college, I became editor of the *yearbook*.(p.555)

yearned

• I was not beautiful or good, as I had *yearned* to be.(p.411)

yearning

• There was an insistent *yearning* to enjoy life as we once did and a heartbreaking obsession that some new miracle of control would enable us to do it.(p.151)

years

• The first edition appeared in April 1939, and in the following sixteen *years*, more than 300,000 copies went into circulation.(p.xi)
• All changes made over the *years* in the Big Book (A.A. members' fond nickname for this volume) have had the same purpose: to represent the current membership of Alcoholics Anonymous more accurately, and thereby to reach more alcoholics.(p.xii)
• Sixteen *years* have elapsed between our first printing of this book and the presentation in 1955 of our second edition.(p.xv)
• Seven percent of the A.A.'s surveyed are less than 30 *years* of age -- among them, many in their teens.(p.xxii)
• I have specialized in the treatment of alcoholism for many *years*.(p.xxiii)
• Many *years* ago one of the leading contributors to this book came under our care in this hospital and while here he acquired some ideas which he put into practical application at once.(p.xxv)
• We believe, and so suggested a few *years* ago, that the action of alcohol on these chronic alcoholics is a manifestation of an allergy; that the phenomenon of craving is limited to this class and never occurs in the average temperate drinker.(p.xxvi)
• We feel, after many *years* of experience, that we have found nothing which has contributed more to the rehabilitation of these men than the altruistic movement now growing up among them.(p.xxvi)
• He has not had a drink for a great many *years*.(p.xxx)
• For the next few *years* fortune threw money and applause my way.(p.3)
• Mercifully, no one could guess that I was to have no real employment for five *years*, or hardly draw a sober breath.(p.4)
• The mind and body are marvelous mechanisms, for mine endured this agony two more *years*.(p.6)
• It was *years* since I could remember his coming to New York in that condition.(p.9)
• It melted the icy intellectual mountain in whose shadow I had lived and shivered many *years*.(p.12)
• It may cause him to die a few *years* before his time.(p.21)
• We know that while the alcoholic keeps away from drink, as he may do for months or *years*, he reacts much like other men.(p.22)
• For *years* he had floundered from one sanitarium to another.(p.26)
• An exceptional man, he remained bone dry for twenty-five *years* and retired at the age of fifty-five, after a successful and happy business career.(p.32)
• Though a robust man at retirement, he went to pieces quickly and was dead within four *years*.(p.33)
• But here is a man who at fifty-five *years* found he was just where he had left off at thirty.(p.33)
• Several of our crowd, men of thirty or less, had been drinking only a few *years*, but they found themselves as helpless as those who had been drinking twenty *years*.(p.33)
• Potential female alcoholics often turn into the real thing and are gone beyond recall in a few *years*.(p.33)
• As we look back, we feel we had gone on drinking many *years* beyond the point where we could quit on our will power.(p.34)
• In a few *years* he became so violent when intoxicated that he had to be committed.(p.35)
• I also had the notion that I might find a customer for a car at this place, which was familiar for I had been going to it for *years*.(p.36)
• He enjoys himself for a few *years* in spite of friendly warnings.(p.37)
• On through the *years* this conduct continues, accompanied by his continual promises to be careful or to keep off the streets altogether.(p.38)
• Only thirty *years* later the conquest of the air was almost an old story and airplane travel was in full swing.(p.52)
• For *years* thereafter he was dogged by trouble and frustration.(p.56)
• The barriers he had built through the *years* were swept away.(p.56)
• That very night, *years* ago, it disappeared.(p.56)
• We reviewed our own conduct over the *years* past.(p.69)
• He attended church for the first time in many *years*.(p.80)
• This all happened *years* ago.(p.80)
• After a few *years* with an alcoholic, a wife gets worn out, resentful and uncommunicative.(p.81)
• But he is yet a long way from making good to the wife or parents whom for *years* he has so shockingly treated.(p.82)
• We must remember that ten or twenty *years* of drunkenness would make a skeptic out of anyone.(p.83)
• For *years* we have been working with alcoholics committed to institutions.(p.114)
• His ways of thinking and doing are the habit of *years*.(p.118)
• We do not like the thought that the contents of a book or the work of another alcoholic has accomplished in a few weeks that for which we struggled for *years*.(p.118)
• The fellowship of Al-Anon Family Groups was formed about thirteen *years* after this chapter was written.(p.121)
• A doctor said to us, "*Years* of living with an alcoholic is almost sure to make any wife or child neurotic.(p.122)
• Today's life is measured against that of other *years* and, when it falls short, the family may be unhappy.(p.123)
• But the head of the house has spent *years* in pulling down the structures of business, romance, friendship, health -- these things are now ruined or damaged.(p.123)
• Though old buildings will eventually be replaced by finer ones, the new structures will take *years* to complete.(p.123)
• Dad may feel that for *years* his drinking has placed him on the wrong side of every argument, but now he has become a superior person with God on his side.(p.129)
• Liquor incapacitated father for so many *years* that mother became head of the house.(p.130)
• Father may have laid aside for *years* all normal activities – clubs, civic duties, sports.(p.131)
• I pointed out that I had had nothing to drink whatever for three *years*, and this in the face of difficulties that would have made nine out of ten men drink their heads off.(p.138)
• The most satisfactory *years* of your existence lie ahead.(p.152)
• *Years* ago, in 1935, one of our number made a journey to a certain western city.(p.153)
• As we shall see, he now means a great deal to his community, and the major liabilities of thirty *years* of hard drinking have been repaired in four.(p.156)
• Six *years* ago one of our number was a patient there.(p.162)
• The periods of sobriety attained by these thirteen A.A.'s range from fifteen to forty-six *years*.(p.169)
• Today, hundreds of additional A.A. members can be found who have had no relapse for more than thirty *years*.(p.169)
• This resolution I kept steadfastly for the next forty *years*, except when circumstances made it seem unwise to absent myself.(p.172)
• After high school came four *years* in one of the best colleges in the country where drinking seemed to be a major extra-curricular activity.(p.172)

• My whole life seemed to be centered around doing what I wanted to do, without regard for the rights, wishes, or privileges of anyone else; a state of mind which became more and more predominant as the ***years*** passed.(p.172)
• The next three ***years*** I spent in Boston, Chicago, and Montreal in the employ of a large manufacturing concern, selling railway supplies, gas engines of all sorts, and many other items of heavy hardware.(p.172)
• During these ***years***, I drank as much as my purse permitted, still without paying too great a penalty, although I was beginning to have morning jitters at times.(p.173)
• I lost only a half day's work during these three ***years***.(p.173)
• This had little effect however for I kept on drinking and used a great deal more hard liquor than in former ***years***.(p.174)
• I conducted myself so creditably that I was able to secure a much coveted internship in a western city, where I spent two ***years***.(p.174)
• During these two ***years*** I was kept so busy that I hardly left the hospital at all.(p.174)
• When those two ***years*** were up, I opened an office downtown.(p.174)
• After three ***years*** of this, I wound up in the local hospital where they attempted to help me, but I would get my friends to smuggle me a quart, or I would steal the alcohol about the building, so that I got rapidly worse.(p.175)
• During the next few ***years***, I developed two distinct phobias.(p.175)
• During the subsequent fifteen ***years*** I had sense enough never to go to the hospital if I had been drinking, and very seldom did I receive patients.(p.176)
• This routine went on with few interruptions for seventeen ***years***.(p.177)
• I gave the matter much time and study for the next two and a half ***years***, but still got tight every night nevertheless.(p.178)
• How my wife kept her faith and courage during all those ***years***, I'll never know, but she did.(p.178)
• As I write nearly four ***years*** have passed.(p.180)
• But this was a man who had experienced many ***years*** of frightful drinking, who had had most all the drunkard's experiences known to man, but who had been cured by the very means I had been trying to employ, that is to say the spiritual approach.(p.180)
• Unlike most of our crowd, I did not get over my craving for liquor much during the first two and one-half ***years*** of abstinence.(p.181)
• Before my drinking had cut me down completely, I achieved a considerable measure of success, having been a City Councilman for five ***years*** and a financial director of Kenmore, a suburb later taken into the city itself.(p.182)
• The first time that I became intoxicated I was eight ***years*** old.(p.182)
• This continued until I enrolled in our state university and, at the end of four ***years***, I realized that I was a drunk.(p.183)
• Then Prohibition came into effect, and the facts that the stuff obtainable was so horrible and sometimes deadly, and that I had married and had a job which I had to look after, helped me for a period of some three or four ***years***, although I would get drunk every time I could get hold of enough to drink to get started.(p.183)
• Whether you quit six days, months, or ***years***, if you go out and take a drink or two you'll end up in this hospital tied down, just like you have been in these past six months.(p.187)
• Every time I'd start thinking about drinking, I would think of the long, dry ***years*** ahead without having a drink; but this idea of twenty-four hours, that it was up to me from then on, was a lot of help.(p.188)
• Nineteen ***years*** ago last summer, Dr. Bob and I saw him (Bill D.) for the first time.(p.188)
• It took me a year, or a year and a half to get to feeling physically well, and it was rather tough, but I soon found folks whose friendship I had once had, and I found, after I had been sober for quite some little time, that these people began to act like they had in previous ***years***, before I had gotten so bad, so that I didn't pay too awful much attention to financial gains.(p.190)
• Another reason I go is that I'm still grateful for the good ***years*** that I've had.(p.192)
• My father died in 1901 when I was eight ***years*** old and I was in the second or third grade at school.(p.193)
• When I was sixteen ***years*** old, my mother remarried and I was given the opportunity of going back to school.(p.193)
• Twenty-two ***years*** later, Doctor Bob told me that what I had done was like turning a switch and setting up a demand for more alcohol in my system.(p.195)
• Anyhow, I recognized the fact that I couldn't drink like normal people, but I tried hard and kept on trying for twenty-two ***years***.(p.196)
• The rubber prosperity went on for about six ***years*** -- 1916 to 1922.(p.197)
• I can well remember over a long period of ***years*** when I thought I was the only person in the world who knew that sooner or later I was going to get drunk.(p.198)
• It has continued to work now for nearly eighteen ***years***.(p.209)
• I can remember that in my childhood, he was ill at ease with the children because he attempted to assert an army discipline that had been ground into him during his three and a half ***years*** of army service.(p.210)
• My mother was eighty-nine ***years*** old when she died, and I was a full-blown alcoholic at the time of her death.(p.210)
• I was then about sixteen ***years*** old.(p.211)
• After I was on the drafting board about two ***years*** I decided I wanted a technical education.(p.211)
• I did not have a high school education so I went to night school to take the full high school course, which I finished in two ***years*** and nine months.(p.211)
• This experience sent me to law school where I went at night and which course I completed in less than three ***years***, taking the highest state bar examinations and passing them.(p.212)
• I went back to law school, and doubled up on the courses because I was then approaching thirty ***years*** of age and I wanted to get through as quickly as possible.(p.212)
• I married when I was twenty-eight ***years*** old, and started in law school after I was married.(p.212)
• My drinking career began about four ***years*** after I had moved up into partnership and had joined certain clubs, societies and so fourth, and during which period we had Prohibition.(p.213)
• After two or three ***years*** of effort along this line, I reached the point of actual despair that I ever would be able to drink only a harmless amount each day.(p.215)
• By that time, I had one boy in college, another a senior in high school, and a daughter about twelve ***years*** old.(p.215)
• In fact, as I look back, I have often thought that they probably concluded that they would put up with me for a couple of ***years***, that I couldn't live much longer, and that they would inherit whatever was left of the practice.(p.215)
• My children had lost respect for me and, in fact, it was only after three or four ***years*** of sobriety that any of them ever said anything to me to indicate that I had recouped even a little of their respect.(p.215)
• I was forty-nine and a half ***years*** old when I was first approached about the Akron Group.(p.215)
• Had anyone undertaken to explain to me what the A.A. movement was, what its real function was, I probably would have been set back several ***years*** and I doubt if I would have survived at all.(p.216)
• In fact, the last three ***years*** of my drinking was a routine of barbiturates in the morning, so that I could stop shaking enough to shave, and then alcohol beginning about four-thirty or five o'clock, with a struggle not to take a drink at noon or during the day, because I had the idea that if I took one drink, I would smell as though I had had a pint.(p.217)
• I found in the fall of 1939, that I was not mentally impaired, so far as trial work was concerned, and thereafter took up where I had left off when I was about forty-five ***years*** old.(p.220)
• I remember looking longingly at the window as an easier solution, and shuddering at the memory of that other window, three ***years*** before, and the six agonizing months in a London hospital ward.(p.224)
• I was thirty-two ***years*** old.(p.224)
• For the next ten ***years*** I did just that.(p.225)
• The feeling of impending disaster that had haunted me for ***years*** began to dissolve as I put into practice more and more of the Twelve Steps.(p.229)
• My parents had some vague idea of making a priest out of me and for some ***years*** I attended the Franciscan school at Basle, Switzerland, just across the border, about six miles from my home.(p.230)
• But I hardly tasted anything for two ***years*** and started in business for myself, founding a mattress factory which is today an important industrial enterprise in our city.(p.232)
• Unlike many other Catholics who frequently take pledges for definite periods -- a year, two ***years*** or for good, I never had any desire to "take a pledge" before the priest.(p.234)
• From the top of the heap in a few ***years*** he had skidded to becoming a shuffling customer, still entering the better barrooms but welcomed by neither mine host nor his patrons.(p.236)
• I have been sober for many ***years*** now.(p.237)
• Here I was, thirty-nine ***years*** old and a complete washout.(p.238)
• At thirteen I was packed off to a very fine Protestant boarding school in Virginia where I stayed four ***years***, graduating without any special achievements.(p.240)
• In the next two ***years*** I washed more pans and peeled more potatoes than any other dough-boy.(p.241)
• With the war over, and back in Baltimore with the folks, there were several small jobs for three ***years*** and then I went to work soliciting as one of the first ten employees of a new national finance company.(p.242)
• Three ***years*** later, at twenty-five, I opened and operated their Philadelphia office and was earning more than I ever have since.(p.242)
• I was the fair-haired boy all right, but two ***years*** later I was blacklisted as an irresponsible drunk.(p.242)
• He had also gone all the way through the wringer and had been dry two ***years*** when I saw him again.(p.243)
• In the eight ***years*** before A.A. found me, I had over forty jobs -- selling and travelling -- one thing after another, and the same old routine.(p.244)
• For the last two ***years*** of my drinking I prayed on every drunk that I wouldn't wake up again.(p.245)
• We checked into the home of Hank, the man who had fired me eleven ***years*** before in Mississippi, and there I met Bill, our founder.(p.245)
• Bill had then been dry three ***years*** and Hank, two.(p.245)
• Around this time our big A.A. book was being written and it all became much simpler; we had a definite formula which some sixty of us agreed was the middle course for all alcoholics who wanted sobriety, and that formula has not been changed one iota down through the ***years***.(p.248)
• This change had been a long, slow process for me, but through these latter ***years*** the dividends have been tremendous.(p.249)
• I have served on only one committee in the past nine ***years***, for I feel that I had my chance the first few ***years*** and that newer members should fill the jobs.(p.250)
• I stayed sober for four ***years*** except for a one-night carousal in Chicago.(p.253)
• Curious about it, feeling I was missing something, absolutely without any illusions about the aftermath, with no pronounced feeling of patriotism, I joined up with a Canadian regiment, serving a little over two ***years***.(p.253)
• My four ***years*** of abstinence had something to do with it, but soldiering is a tough enough game for a sober man, and I had no yen for full-pack slogging through mud with a cognac or vin rouge hang-over.(p.253)
• The new job lasted five ***years***.(p.254)
• I did six ***years*** of newspaper advertising, and trade journal work with many, many drunks of drab and dreary hue woven into the pattern of my life.(p.254)
• In the two succeeding ***years*** I held ten different jobs ranging from newspaper copy-desk and rewrite, to traffic director for an oil field equipment company.(p.255)
• A friend who knew I would soon be broke mounted guard over me when I left my job of writing the histories of Texas cities and put me aboard a bus for the town I had left almost five ***years*** before.(p.256)
• In five ***years*** a good many persons had forgotten that I had been somewhat notorious.(p.256)
• Some of them I had known for ***years***, good two-fisted drinkers who had disappeared from their former haunts.(p.258)
• I was sixteen when we were married and he was seven ***years*** older.(p.262)
• That was seven or eight ***years*** after we were married.(p.262)
• He stayed "dry" for thirteen ***years***!(p.263)
• At the end of these thirteen ***years*** I never dreamed that he'd ever take another drink.(p.263)
• We were in A.A. three and a half ***years*** when he was taken from me.(p.270)
• We are older in A.A., and we're older in ***years***.(p.273)
• He spent eighteen ***years*** in running away; and then found he didn't have to run.(p.275)
• For eighteen ***years***, from the age of twenty-one to thirty-nine, fear governed my life.(p.275)
• By the time I was twenty-one I had six ***years*** of life in foreign countries, spoke three languages fluently, and had attended college for two ***years***.(p.275)
• This happy combination of pleasant work and alcohol lasted for five ***years***.(p.277)

• All this changed when I was thirty *years* old.(p.277)
• The ensuing nine *years* were the Depression *years*, both nationally and personally.(p.277)
• Our marriage lasted four *years*.(p.277)
• At least three of those four *years* must have been a living hell for my wife, because she had to watch the man she loved disintegrate morally, mentally and financially.(p.277)
• The next two *years* were simply a long drawn out process of less and less work and more and more whiskey.(p.278)
• I have thanked God many times in the last sixteen *years* that that was just what he did not do!(p.278)
• I got down on my knees for the first time in thirty *years*.(p.280)
• It went something like this: "God, for eighteen *years* I have been unable to handle this problem.(p.280)
• It is well over sixteen *years* since I came back to life.(p.280)
• I would like to sketch for you the highlights of these sixteen *years* of a slow but steady and satisfying upward climb.(p.280)
• It took five *years* of A.A. living, and a substantial improvement in my health, before I could take a full-time office job where someone else was boss.(p.283)
• With this specialized training, and a liberal business education in the school of hard knocks, I was able to set up shop some two *years* later as an independent accountant.(p.284)
• Seven *years* of work in this field brought an opportunity to affiliate myself actively with one of my clients, a fellow A.A.(p.284)
• With God's help I am able, for one day at a time, to carry business responsibilities which, not many *years* ago, I would not have dreamed of assuming.(p.284)
• Never in sixteen *years* have I dodged anything because I was afraid of it.(p.285)
• In recent *years* I have had the happy combination of time and money to travel occasionally.(p.285)
• Have I ever wanted a drink during these *years*?(p.285)
• Twenty-odd *years* ago I made a mess out of my one and only marriage.(p.286)
• It was therefore not extraordinary that I should shy away from any serious thought of marriage for a great many *years* after joining A.A.(p.286)
• My wife, a sister member in A.A., had been a widow nine *years* and I had been single eighteen *years*.(p.286)
• I do feel, though, that the fact that I finally grew up to a point where I could even tackle such a job is the apex of the story of a man who spent eighteen *years* running away from life.(p.286)
• I confined drinking to weekends, and drank normally in college and for several *years* thereafter.(p.287)
• This was the beginning of five *years* of bounding back and forth between my home in Chicago and Akron to sober up.(p.288)
• He mentioned two of them that I had known through the *years* and suggested that I talk with them.(p.289)
• These last eighteen *years* have been the happiest of my life, trite though that statement may seem.(p.295)
• Fifteen of those *years* I would not have enjoyed had I continued drinking.(p.295)
• Doctors told me before I stopped that I had only three *years* at the outside to live.(p.295)
• Courage to face each day has replaced the fears and uncertainties of earlier *years*.(p.295)
• And over my A.A. *years* I have made many real, honest, sincere friendships that I shall always cherish.(p.296)
• Three *years* after I started on my drinking career, I lost my first job.(p.298)
• Up to this point I had spent six *years* in the business and had enjoyed the reputation of being very successful.(p.298)
• After holding good positions, making better than an average income for over ten *years*, I was in debt, had no clothes to speak of, no money, no friends, and no one any longer tolerating me but my wife.(p.301)
• Finally, an old business acquaintance of mine, whom I hadn't seen for several *years* offered me a job.(p.301)
• I feel as I did when I was fifteen *years* younger.(p.303)
• From a monetary standpoint . . . in the past few *years*, I have reduced my reckless debts to almost nothing, and have had money to get along on comfortably.(p.303)
• A little more than fifteen *years* ago, through a long and calamitous series of shattering experiences, I found myself being helplessly propelled toward total destruction.(p.304)
• I was thirty-three *years* old and my life was spent.(p.304)
• And still by the time I was thirty *years* old I was being pushed around with a compulsion to drink that was completely beyond my control.(p.305)
• The next three *years* saw me in sanitariums, once in a ten day coma, from which I very nearly did not recover, in and out of hospitals or confined at home with day and night nurses.(p.306)
• In describing his suffering, his fears, his many *years* of groping for some answer to that which always seemed to remain unanswerable, he could have been describing me, and nothing short of experience and knowledge could have afforded him that much insight!(p.309)
• He had been dry for two and a half *years* and had been maintaining his contact with a group of recovered alcoholics in Akron.(p.309)
• It had been so many *years* since I had not relied on some artificial crutch, either alcohol or sedatives.(p.310)
• The last fifteen *years* of my life have been rich and meaningful.(p.312)
• And, as the *years* go by, working together, sharing our experiences with one another, and also sharing a mutual trust, understanding and love — without strings, without obligation — we acquire relationships that are unique and priceless.(p.312)
• Therefore, these seventeen A.A.'s, and hundreds of thousands like them, have been saved *years* of infinite suffering.(p.315)
• The third time, after almost five *years* as an S.P. 4, I finally made sergeant.(p.318)
• I thought my problem was that I had been married to a drunk for twenty-seven *years*.(p.321)
• I said, "Twenty-seven *years*."(p.322)
• She said, "Twenty-seven *years* to an alcoholic!(p.322)
• I started my drinking nearly thirty *years* ago — right after I was married.(p.322)
• I did stay fairly good for a few *years*.(p.323)
• We have only been in A.A. a few *years*, but now we're trying to make up for lost time.(p.325)
• Twenty-seven *years* of confusion is what my early married life was.(p.325)
• THOSE GOLDEN *YEARS*(p.327)
• Until I took Social Security and a pension at the age of sixty-eight, after forty *years* in motion-picture-studio public relations, I had successfully hidden even any hints of approaching alcoholism.(p.327)
• Two *years* later, a month beyond age seventy, I was crying for help from A.A.(p.327)
• I'd been on the board of governors of the Academy of Motion Picture Arts and Sciences for six *years*.(p.328)
• A square from ultra-dry Kansas, I did not taste grog until I had finished college, done a stint on newspapers, married, become a father, and been in studio publicity two *years*.(p.328)
• And I was able to go on the wagon for long periods of time — once for four *years*, to cure an ulcer.(p.328)
• I could go on living and hurting ten *years* longer, or more."(p.333)
• Out of those forty *years* as a movie press agent came one blessing that granted me a blind faith in the program.(p.334)
• How full it has kept my retirement *years* -- the five I've lived since the first two lost in traveling a rocky road to hell, before I made a U-turn.(p.334)
• But during a period of particular stress and strain about thirteen *years* ago, I resorted to alcohol in my home, alone, as a means of temporary release, as a means of getting a little extra sleep.(p.335)
• Three *years* and three months of sobriety, without a slip, has meant a lot to me, my wife, and my family.(p.342)
• Eight *years* ago, my wife and I decided to spend a vacation in Naini Tal, the mountain resort.(p.343)
• During the next three *years*, I tried often again to give it up, but failed miserably.(p.343)
• I belong to more medical societies and honor societies than men ten to twenty *years* my senior.(p.345)
• *Years* earlier, I had gone into psychoanalysis to get relief.(p.349)
• I spent five and a half *years* in psychoanalysis and proceeded to become a drunk.(p.349)
• Just three *years* of drinking pushed a shy, lonely young girl to the depth of depression.(p.353)
• I needed alcohol from that night on, and it in turn used me, ruling my life for three *years*.(p.353)
• As these words are written at fifty-three *years* of age, with over nine *years* of A.A. behind me, with all its wonderful teachings, I haven't the slightest doubt about being an alcoholic.(p.356)
• I didn't particularly like it, but I loved the effects, and managed for the next twenty-five *years* to drink anything and everything, either handed to me or purchased, at the slightest excuse.(p.357)
• High living, a great many fair weather friends, the 1929 stock market crash, and a couple of *years* of Depression, soon relieved me one by one of my worldly goods including my wife.(p.358)
• The next few *years* in New York can be described in a very few words.(p.358)
• I asked this question weekly for the next couple of *years*.(p.359)
• Attending his fourth or fifth meeting was an old friend I had not seen for twenty *years*.(p.365)
• I have had many more reasons to drink since I have been in A.A. than I had in all the *years* of my drinking.(p.367)
• During three *years* in A.A., I haven't lost so much as one shirt.(p.372)
• The drive to get ahead, to succeed, kept me too busy for many *years* to have any great experience with social life.(p.374)
• The last two *years* of my drinking my entire personality changed to a cynical, intolerant and arrogant person completely different from my normal self.(p.376)
• Two *years* before I joined A.A. my wife took a long trip during which she wrote me she just couldn't return unless I did something about my drinking.(p.377)
• I know that if I do daily what I have done for these last thirteen and a half *years*, I will stay sober.(p.384)
• For some reason I can't remember, it finally dawned on me that I had a problem, and yet nobody was very critical about it except my family, and that was only because I decided, after seven *years* of marriage, that I would divorce my husband.(p.386)
• That went on for about three *years*, and then we moved back to Texas again.(p.386)
• In six *years* of worry, I hadn't learned anything.(p.387)
• Today, because of A.A.'s growth during the intervening *years*, it is of course much bigger than it was then.(p.392)
• A retired Navy man looks back over twenty *years* of drinking, to add up his A.A. "initiation fee."(p.396)
• After all, upon coming out of a week-long or ten-day drunk, it was hard enough to figure up just how much that one drunk cost, let alone trying to calculate the cost of approximately twenty-five *years* of active alcoholism.(p.396)
• Twenty-five *years* of drinking!(p.397)
• After a few more estimates as to income and expenditures for booze over a few sample *years*, taken at random, I conclude that this twenty per cent stayed fairly constant.(p.398)
• So I spent twenty *years* in the Navy.(p.398)
• For an estimate of salary from the twenty-one a month to start with, to over $400 per month upon my retirement after twenty *years* in the Navy, I believe that an average income of $2,000 a year over this period is low, but as I stated earlier, an underestimate is best.(p.399)
• $2,000 a year for twenty-five *years* is $50,000, twenty per cent of which is $10,000.(p.399)
• Incalculable are the intangible initiation fees that A.A. members have paid: the sick, sick hangovers, the remorse, guilt, broken homes, jails, and institutions, and the mental anguish in general that has been generated over the *years*.(p.399)
• It took me three psychoanalysts and several *years* in A.A. to really get this through my head.(p.401)
• With ten *years* of A.A. behind me, I was able to tell him that I'd have been alcoholic, no matter what; that I had been a sick person, unfit for marriage.(p.403)
• But I got drunk that night and stayed drunk, getting increasingly worse until I found A.A. ten *years* later.(p.404)
• During these *years*, I did acquire some good friends.(p.404)
• We went through two *years* of deadlock required by the English divorce laws.(p.405)
• *Years* of drinking and general high jinks had cut her off from old friends.(p.414)
• Except for one short slip, during the first eight months, which was an angry "the world can't do this to me" reaction to a personal tragedy in my life, I have been sober for twelve *years*.(p.416)
• My spiritual awakening in A.A. finally resulted in my joining a church some *years* ago.(p.417)
• I was twenty-eight *years* old.(p.418)
• In less than two *years*, I lost my practice, my home, my wife, and my children.(p.418)
• In fact, I was taken to A.A. by a woman whom my father had taken to A.A. thirteen *years* earlier.(p.419)

• I neither drank nor smoked until I was nineteen *years* old.(p.419)
• Fear, love of dentistry, and an imitation of my father's periodic drinking pattern took me through dental college soberly, except for the few parties and vacations in those four *years*.(p.419)
• Then came my tour in the U.S. Navy, part of it being two *years* in the Philippines.(p.419)
• A young veteran tells how a few rough experiences pushed him into A.A. – and how he was therefore spared *years* of suffering.(p.422)
• They had been drinking for many *years* and were getting progressively worse.(p.424)
• Three *years* later I was discharged in the same way.(p.425)
• I'd packed more drinking into seven *years* than many a heavy drinker does in a lifetime.(p.429)
• That doctor in the Navy hospital told me I wouldn't live five *years* if I didn't quit.(p.429)
• I thought, "If this is A.A. why not go back to drinking, kill myself with booze in the next three *years* the doctor had given me, and call it a bad job?"(p.430)
• Were I to revert to drinking, even now, I wouldn't give anything for these four *years* in A.A.(p.430)
• Four *years* ago I had nothing but a jumbled, mad existence.(p.430)
• In all the twenty-five *years* of my drinking there were only a few occasions when I took a morning drink.(p.432)
• To cut a long story short, I spent seven *years* and ten thousand dollars on my psychiatric adventure, and emerged in worse condition than ever.(p.434)
• In seven *years* the intervals between them decreased from eight months to ten days!(p.434)
• "Then why in God's name haven't you told me so, during all these *years*?"(p.436)
• Many times in the intervening *years* I have thanked God for that man, a man who had the courage to admit failure, a man who had the humility to confess that all the hard-won learning of his profession could not turn up the answer.(p.436)
• That was seven *years* ago – and many A.A. meetings ago -- and I haven't had a drink during those seven *years*.(p.437)
• Max and I had been married for twenty-eight *years* when I ended up in A.A.(p.439)
• It started out as a good marriage, but it deteriorated over the *years* as she progressed through the various stages of qualifying for Al-Anon.(p.439)
• I had begun to drink in the early *years* of pharmacy school, in order to get to sleep.(p.440)
• And that was how Max and I and our two daughters spent Christmas Day, eight *years* ago.(p.444)
• Had I gone to school all those *years* just to sit and make leather belts?(p.445)
• I wore those moccasins every night for the next seven *years*, until they wore out.(p.445)
• For *years*, I was sure the worst thing that could happen to a nice guy like me would be that I would turn out to be an alcoholic.(p.449)
• Max and I have been married now for thirty-five *years*.(p.450)
• Over the *years*, as I thought about Max, her good qualities grew and grew, and we married, and all these qualities became more and more apparent to me, and we were happier and happier.(p.450)
• Now sober for *years*, they tell us how they got well.(p.455)
• I served twelve *years* in prison, never suspecting that without alcohol I would not have been in prison at all.(p.457)
• The two *years* I spent there, I was incorrigible, and the records bear this out.(p.458)
• The first time I remember seeing or hearing of A.A. was twenty *years* ago.(p.460)
• Four *years* later, I was taken to my first A.A. meeting out of prison, in Los Angeles.(p.460)
• For the next five *years*, I was in and out of A.A. in Los Angeles, Phoenix, and San Francisco.(p.460)
• Fortunately, I received only fifteen-twenty *years*, and I went back to my alma mater (where I had spent so much time in the hole).(p.461)
• I was forty-four *years* old; my life had been wasted.(p.461)
• (I am looking at it now in my bedroom – a copy that was presented to me a couple of *years* ago by the A.A. group in that same prison.)(p.461)
• I was not eligible for parole, until -- with God's help, I'm sure – the governor cut five *years* off my sentence.(p.462)
• I was paroled when I had served less than three *years*.(p.462)
• Three weeks ago, my phone rang, and a voice I hadn't heard in over twenty-three *years* spoke.(p.462)
• I haven't seen my son since he was three and a half *years* old.(p.463)
• My daughter was one and a half *years* old when I last saw her.(p.463)
• I attempted nearly two *years* ago to make some amends and contact my children, but it wasn't God's time yet.(p.463)
• I will be fifty *years* old next month, haven't seen my son or daughter yet, nor my daughter's two children, my grandchildren; but I am grateful.(p.463)
• In fact it has been only within the last fifteen *years* that I changed from a fairly normal, controlled drinker into an alcoholic.(p.464)
• I started drinking socially and at parties and proms when I was about twenty *years* old.(p.464)
• Having passed over the border line, the next five *years* were filled with fear, failure and frustration.(p.465)
• Tragedies during those *years* that were caused by my drinking, such as the breaking up of my marriage, the death of my child, other things – had little restraining effect.(p.465)
• The last Christmas I spent in Washington, fourteen *years* ago, comes to mind.(p.465)
• My visits to that sanitarium went on for nearly three *years*, until in March of 1944, my father died and I was too drunk to attend his funeral.(p.469)
• And so, in those following *years*, whenever A.A. was mentioned I would have no part of it.(p.469)
• With their help I also saw that certainly, because of some of the things I had done during the *years*, I was bordering on insanity, and so, facing the record, I tried to believe that a Power greater than I could and would restore me to sanity.(p.471)
• Here was a book that said I could do something that all these doctors and priests and ministers and psychiatrists that I'd been going to for *years* couldn't do!(p.473)
• That was over seven *years* ago, and thank God and A.A., I haven't had a drink since.(p.473)
• During these seven *years* a thing called the Twenty-four Hour Program –a gadget I used to think was only a snare to trap the newcomer -- has come to mean much to me, not only as regards my drinking but in the whole pattern of my life.(p.473)
• I feel that I have been restored to health and sanity these past *years* not through my own efforts nor as a result of anything I may have done, but because I've come to believe -- to really believe – that alone I can do nothing.(p.473)
• Then many blackouts for next two *years*.(p.475)
• Next two *years*, I call them many times.(p.475)
• By grace of God I stop, think two things: This would kill good mother and father; then remember boys talk about Indian fellow who been sober three *years*.(p.475)
• Two *years* later, my brother take Tall Man to first A.A. meeting.(p.476)
• Tall Man die five *years* ago, a sober, peaceful, happy man.(p.476)
• Waitress by day, barfly by night, she drifted down the *years* into jail.(p.478)
• After all, I had been working for eighteen *years*, slinging hash, and I was managing.(p.478)
• Mind you, I had absolutely nothing to show for that eighteen *years*, except a beat-up car that I hadn't even paid for, but I was doing all right.(p.478)
• I wasted twenty *years* of my life, and there is nothing I can do about that, but there is something I can do about now.(p.480)
• For two *years*, I was also addicted to heroin.(p.480)
• A couple of *years* later, we lost our elder brother in a house fire, because of pills and booze.(p.480)
• I remember in my early youth my mother dressed me just as she did my two sisters, and I wore curls until I was six *years* of age.(p.483)
• My wife and I have been married for some thirty *years* now.(p.485)
• Father, through the *years*, had built up a very good mail order business because, at that time, there wasn't too much money in medicine.(p.485)
• During the *years* 1930 to 1935, due to the Depression and its aftermath, business went from bad to worse.(p.486)
• For the first couple of *years* it wasn't too bad because the momentum kept things going.(p.486)
• That year, on a Friday night, a man whom I had known for *years* came to my office.(p.488)
• My father had treated him many *years* prior to this.(p.488)
• When I had known her *years* before she was rather slender, but at this time she weighed as much as she does now, which is up around in the two hundreds or very close to it.(p.493)
• After twenty *years* in prison for murder, he knew A.A. was the spot for him . . . if he wanted to stay on the outside.(p.508)
• I rolled along with the mob this way, that way and the other way, but in those *years* nothing really bad happened to me.(p.508)
• For that crime I received a minimum of twenty *years* and a maximum of natural life.(p.508)
• I received an additional fifteen *years* for that, making a minimum of thirty-five *years* and a maximum of natural life.(p.509)
• On October 28th, I was sent to Sing Sing with a minimum of thirty-three and a half *years* to serve out of that thirty-five.(p.509)
• I have spent eighteen *years* in that institution.(p.509)
• I clung to the outfit for the balance of my time, and finally I was released, after having spent twenty *years* and nine months behind bars.(p.510)
• She was the one who really helped me to make a go of that twenty *years* and nine months in prison.(p.511)
• The days have grown into a little better than four *years* of sobriety.(p.511)
• I'm grateful because that Higher Power led me to A.A. a little over three *years* ago, when I needed it very badly.(p.512)
• And the guy said, "Heck, yes, I been married to her for *years*!"(p.512)
• A former employer of mine said to me a little over ten *years* ago, "Pat, you seem to be one of those unfortunate people who at least once every six months must go out and roll in the gutter."(p.513)
• I knew it, and I turned for help to someone upon whom I had turned my back for many *years*.(p.515)
• I had two *years* at Dublin University, and then in 1916, I got a nomination for Sandhurst, the British Military College.(p.518)
• Then I went over again to Germany for four *years* on an occupation job.(p.519)
• Strangely enough, right through to the end of my twenty-six *years* in the Army, I was still being offered very good and important jobs in spite of the fact that my superiors must have known that I wasn't thoroughly reliable.(p.519)
• However, I kept that job in Egypt and Palestine for about two *years*, and then I changed over to the other battalion in my regiment.(p.520)
• They weren't quite so up-to-date on my history and I got away with about four *years* with them.(p.520)
• That went on for about six *years*.(p.522)
• Finally, my mother came and said she had kept me at home for six *years* because she thought she could help me, but that now she had come to the conclusion that I wasn't even worth trying to help.(p.523)
• I had been using paraldehyde more or less like ordinary drink for the last six *years* though, occasionally, I'd bounce back to phenobarbital and things like that.(p.524)
• My mother lived on for five *years* after I joined A.A., the last two in complete blindness.(p.525)
• By the grace of God, I only served three *years*.(p.528)
• I have been home for a year, and have not taken a drink in four *years*.(p.529)
• I remember the day when I decided to drink myself to death quietly, without bothering anyone, because I was tired of having been a dependable, trustworthy person for about thirty-nine *years* without having received what I thought was a proper reward for my virtue.(p.531)
• There was the necessity for sticking to a job I hated, a dull, repetitive job performed in association with other men I had nothing in common with . . . performed for *years* on end, because the money was needed at home.(p.532)
• There was the father one lost respect for at the age of eleven, because the father broke his solemn word in a circumstance where you, eleven *years* old, had assumed guilt when you were innocent; but the father would not believe you, no matter what; and to ease his suffering you "confessed" and were "forgiven," only – months later – to have your "guilt" brought up – only he and you knew what he was talking bout -- brought up in front of the stern grandmother.(p.533)
• For by thirty-five I had been drinking for a few *years*.(p.533)
• But as the *years* go by, the stretch becomes unbearable; and the man with the grown-up brain and the childish emotions – vanity, self-interest, false pride, jealousy, longing for social approval, to name few -- becomes a prime candidate for alcohol.(p.534)
• My serious drinking covered about seven *years*.(p.536)
• In those *years* I was in jail nine times, in an alcoholic ward, overnight, twice; and I was fired from three jobs, two of them very good ones.(p.536)

• After nearly eight *years* of sobriety in A.A., I still can set down such thoughts, "against my instinct and training," showing that I still consider myself a "special" person, entitled to special privileges.(p.536)
• I stumbled agonizedly past the theatre where in *years* gone by a great star had played my play.(p.540)
• But I remembered the *years* of agony preceding the binge, I remembered the *years* I had thrown away.(p.540)
• From that instant to this, nearly eight *years* later, I have not had the slightest urge to drink.(p.541)
• But for the next *years*, I worked hard and exultantly in A.A.(p.541)
• It is going strong still, these eight *years* later, and some of its members have been of great influence for good in state-wide A.A. work.(p.541)
• All of my family and loved ones, all of my friends, are nearer and dearer to me than ever before and I have literally dozens of new friends who say they cannot believe that a short eight *years* ago I was ready for the scrap heap.(p.541)
• The mental twists that led up to my drinking began many *years* before I ever took a drink for I am one of those whose history proves conclusively that my drinking was "a symptom of a deeper trouble."(p.544)
• I am an only child, and when I was seven *years* old my parents separated very abruptly.(p.544)
• I was married and divorced again before I was twenty-three *years* old, this time to a prominent band leader -- a man that many women wanted.(p.546)
• It seems only fitting that when I did finally fall in love it was with an alcoholic, and for the next ten *years* I progressed as rapidly as is humanly possible into what I believed to be hopeless alcoholism.(p.547)
• Apparently I'd grown physically at the customary rate of speed, and I had acquired an average amount of intellectual training in the intervening *years*, but there had been no emotional maturity at all.(p.547)
• The last three *years* of my drinking, I drank on my job.(p.548)
• I attended my first A.A. meeting eight *years* ago, and it is with deep gratitude that I'm able to say I've not had a drink since that time, and that I take no sedation or narcotics, for this program is to me one of complete sobriety and I no longer need to escape reality.(p.549)
• I had only to reflect on the contrast between the plans I made so many *years* ago for my life with what really happened to know I couldn't manage my life drunk or sober.(p.550)
• It was against my mother and it was twenty-five *years* old.(p.551)
• Over the next two *years*, I sickened rapidly.(p.557)
• As the sober days grew into sober months and then into sober *years*, a new and beautiful life began to emerge from the shambles of my former existence.(p.559)
• What often takes place in a few months could seldom have been accomplished by *years* of self discipline.(p.569)
• The days add up into weeks, the weeks into months and *years*."(p.572)

years'
• I say this after many *years'* experience as Medical Director of one of the oldest hospitals in the country treating alcoholic and drug addiction.(p.xxv)
• Sometimes the man we are calling upon admits his own fault, so feuds of *years'* standing melt away in an hour.(p.78)

yelled
• I halfway washed them, and he told me to do them again, and I did, and he *yelled* at me to do them again, and I picked up one of the cans and threw it at him and told him to do them himself.(p.317)
• I *yelled* at Max, "What do you mean, 'The dog just needs more love'?(p.440)

yellow
• I am too *yellow* to kill myself.(p.502)

yells
• We heard some *yells* outside.(p.424)

yen
• My four years of abstinence had something to do with it, but soldiering is a tough enough game for a sober man, and I had no *yen* for full-pack slogging through mud with a cognac or vin rouge hangover.(p.253)

yes
• If you have a drinking problem, we hope that you may pause in reading one of the forty-four personal stories and think: "*Yes*, that happened to me"; or, more important, "*Yes*, I've felt like that"; or most important, "*Yes*, I believe this program can work for me, too."(p.xii)
• *Yes*, the old boy was on fire all right.(p.9)
• "*Yes*," replied the doctor, "there is.(p.27)
• Our hope is that many alcoholic men and women, desperately in need, will see these pages, and we believe that it is only by fully disclosing ourselves and our problems that they will be persuaded to say, "*Yes*, I am one of them too; I must have this thing."(p.29)
• Some of you are thinking: "*Yes*, what you tell us is true, but it doesn't fully apply.(p.38)
• *Yes*, we of agnostic temperament have had these thoughts and experiences.(p.46)
• *Yes*, we had been faithful, abjectly faithful to the God of Reason.(p.54)
• *Yes*, there is a long period of reconstruction ahead.(p.83)
• If he says *yes*, then his attention should be drawn to you as a person who has recovered.(p.90)
• If your decision is *yes*, whether the reason be humanitarian or business or both, then the following suggestions may be helpful.(p.140)
• If he says *yes*, does he really mean it, or down inside does he think he is fooling you, and that after rest and treatment he will be able to get away with a few drinks now and then?(p.142)
• You say, "*Yes*, I'm willing.(p.152)
• *Yes*, there is a substitute and it is vastly more than that.(p.152)
• But what about his responsibilities — his family and the men who would die because they would not know how to get well, ah — *yes*, those other alcoholics?(p.154)
• She replied, "*Yes*, we've got a corker.(p.156)
• "*Yes*, that's me," said the sick man, "the very image.(p.157)
• I said, "*Yes*, Doc, I would like to quit, at least for five, six, or eight months, until I get things straightened up, and begin to get the respect of my wife and some other people back, and get my finances fixed up and so on."(p.187)
• I said, "Sure, *yes*, anybody can do that, for twenty-four hours."(p.188)
• *Yes*, she did have a customer — a dandy.(p.188)
• I said, "*Yes*," reluctantly, "I probably will."(p.190)
• I said, "*Yes*."(p.266)
• When I said *yes*, we both knelt at his desk and prayed, each of us asking to have these defects taken away.(p.292)
• And she said, "Oh, *yes*.(p.321)
• I said, "*Yes*."(p.322)
• She said, "*Yes*, I know.(p.322)
• He said, "Earle?" and I said, "*Yes*."(p.347)
• *Yes*, I put in those stitches.(p.350)
• And deep in my heart I really meant what I said because I loved her more than anything else in the world, *yes* -- even more than liquor.(p.362)
• The time for decision had arrived, and it was a relief to say "*Yes*" when my family said they would call Alcoholics Anonymous for me.(p.378)
• So I called my father and he said, "*Yes*," he'd come out and stay with me for that time.(p.389)
• *Yes*, I, the queen of them all!(p.411)
• "*Yes*," he said, surprisingly, "you are."(p.436)
• *Yes*, I knew what the Serenity Prayer was — A.A. had taught me.(p.461)
• *Yes*, I even knew I was a "chronic alcoholic."(p.470)
• He said, "*Yes*.(p.488)
• I said, "*Yes*."(p.493)
• "*Yes*," I reply.(p.504)
• "*Yes*, it does," I answer.(p.504)
• And the guy said, "Heck, *yes*, I been married to her for years!"(p.512)
• *Yes*, we find it rather confusing, but as we get around and get to know people in the group, they lead the way and all we have to do is to follow.(p.512)
• Oh *yes*, I get the dry jitters once in a while, but that isn't anything to worry about.(p.516)
• Simply, *yes* it did end; for I had changed my mind about alcohol, and it stayed changed.(p.541)

yesterday
• Once I did have a slip – tried drinking again – but the A.A.'s tell me not to worry about *yesterday*, because nobody can change it, and not to worry about tomorrow, because it hasn't come yet.(p.320)
• *Yesterday* is gone, and we don't know whether we will be here tomorrow.(p.382)

yet
• *Yet* it is our great hope that all those who have as *yet* found no answer may begin to find one in the pages of this book and will presently join us on the highroad to a new freedom.(p.xxi)
• Though my drinking was not *yet* continuous, it disturbed my wife.(p.2)
• *Yet* let him drink for a day, and he frequently becomes disgustingly and even dangerously anti-social.(p.21)
• *Yet* early next morning he searches madly for the bottle he misplaced the night before.(p.21)
• The fact is that most alcoholics, for reasons *yet* obscure, have lost the power of choice in drink.(p.24)
• *Yet* he had no control whatever over alcohol.(p.26)
• Science may one day accomplish this, but it hasn't done so *yet*.(p.31)
• But the difficulty is that few alcoholics have enough desire to stop while there is *yet* time.(p.32)
• Though you may be able to stop for a considerable period, you may *yet* be a potential alcoholic.(p.34)
• *Yet* we found it impossible.(p.34)
• *Yet* he got drunk again.(p.36)
• *Yet* all reasons for not drinking were easily pushed aside in favor of the foolish idea that he could take whiskey if only he mixed it with milk!(p.36)
• *Yet*, he is alcoholic.(p.39)
• The story he told is most instructive, for here was a chap absolutely convinced he had to stop drinking, who had no excuse for drinking, who exhibited splendid judgment and determination in all his other concerns, *yet* was flat on his back nevertheless.(p.40)
• *Yet*, in other moments, we found ourselves thinking, when enchanted by a starlit night, "Who, then, made all this?"(p.46)
• *Yet* in ancient times material progress was painfully slow.(p.51)
• We could not prove life in the sense that you can prove a straight line is the shortest distance between two points, *yet*, there it was.(p.54)
• *Yet* we had been seeing another kind of flight, a spiritual liberation from this world, people who rose above their problems.(p.55)
• *Yet* its elements are simple.(p.57)
• Such parts of our story we tell to someone who will understand, *yet* be unaffected.(p.74)
• But he is *yet* a long way from making good to the wife or parents whom for years he has so shockingly treated.(p.82)
• *Yet*, we believe we can make some definite and valuable suggestions.(p.86)
• *Yet* we do go to great extremes to provide each other with these very things, when such action is warranted.(p.98)
• Among us are wives, relatives and friends whose problem has been solved, as well as some who have not *yet* found a happy solution.(p.104)
• He clings to the notion that he will *yet* find a way to do so.(p.110)
• *Yet* they got well.(p.110)
• *Yet* often such men had spectacular and powerful recoveries.(p.113)
• *Yet* you must not expect too much.(p.118)
• You have been starving for his companionship, *yet* he spends long hours helping other men and their families.(p.119)
• He may tell mother, who has been religious all her life, that she doesn't know what it's all about, and that she had better get his brand of spirituality while there is *yet* time.(p.128)
• Many a man, *yet* dazed from his hospital experience, has stepped over the threshold of that home into freedom.(p.160)
• *Yet*, as my record shows, I did become an extremely serious case.(p.182)
• *Yet* I wound up at this place.(p.202)
• And *yet*, realizing at last that liquor really had me, I wanted to quit.(p.234)
• *Yet* he was happy, relaxed, confident and laughing.(p.239)
• He brought in many of our original members, *yet* he himself could not make it and died of alcoholism.(p.239)
• The lesson of his death still remains with me, *yet* I often wonder what would have happened if somebody else had made that first call on me.(p.239)
• However, I made an SOS call to the New York Group, whom I hadn't met *yet*, and they suggested we both come there.(p.245)
• *Yet* we all had one really sincere purpose in our hearts and that was not to drink.(p.246)
• I myself could see deterioration in my work from being physically and mentally affected by liquor, although I had not *yet* reached the point where all I wanted was more to drink.(p.254)
• I'm pretty near afraid of Labor Day *yet*.(p.264)
• Well, suicide was a last straw matter, and I had not drawn the last straw *yet*.(p.278)
• Nothing had changed and *yet* everything had changed.(p.280)

- They saw that they had become actual or potential alcoholics, even though no serious harm had ***yet*** been done.(p.315)
- Once I did have a slip – tried drinking again – but the A.A.'s tell me not to worry about yesterday, because nobody can change it, and not to worry about tomorrow, because it hasn't come ***yet***.(p.320)
- ***Yet*** I recently recalled that each morning I used to talk to the bottle when I took it down from the closet.(p.332)
- And ***yet*** I had to have that drink.(p.337)
- And ***yet***, how was I going to live without it?(p.338)
- I am not even there, and if I was there the only thing I could do would be to give her moral support, and ***yet*** he thanks me for curing his wife."(p.350)
- They told me their stories, which were much more rugged than mine – ***yet*** what they said made sense, and the way they put it was easy for me to understand, with an understanding I had never had before.(p.363)
- I had not ***yet*** lost my job or family, even though both were on the verge of going.(p.379)
- The obsession of the mind was a little harder to understand and ***yet*** everyone has obsessions of various kinds.(p.380)
- For some reason I can't remember, it finally dawned on me that I had a problem, and ***yet*** nobody was very critical about it except my family, and that was only because I decided, after seven years of marriage, that I would divorce my husband.(p.386)
- In spite of knowing that my drunkenness was a symptom of the things that were wrong with me, and that I could never drink again, I thought I couldn't ***yet*** give it up, although I was going to try.(p.393)
- The last time I drank, when I was twenty-nine, I drank for only four days, ***yet*** I threatened to kill my children; I beat my wife at home and on the church steps; I mistreated a child in my office; and I ran to a hospital for mental illness to avoid jail.(p.418)
- ***Yet*** prisoners often can't identify with many A.A. members' drinking stories.(p.458)
- I attempted nearly two years ago to make some amends and contact my children, but it wasn't God's time ***yet***.(p.463)
- I will be fifty years old next month, haven't seen my son or daughter ***yet***, nor my daughter's two children, my grandchildren; but I am grateful.(p.463)
- I hadn't been drinking much about that time, for I had begun to realize that there was something abnormal about my drinking, although as ***yet***, I didn't realize that it was so out of control.(p.465)
- (And the church walls haven't tumbled down ***yet***.)(p.482)
- ***Yet*** I am fairly steady when I go to bed.(p.500)
- But I have not seen ***yet*** that I should do some constructive acts of love without expecting any return.(p.505)
- Each time I would make a report to the parole officer he would ask me, "Have you been to an A.A. meeting ***yet***?"(p.510)
- I have my brilliant moments ***yet***, but whenever the boys catch me at it they tell me so very plainly.(p.512)
- I talked to him for quite a long time and at the end, he said, "Well, you're not quite mad enough to be shut up for good ***yet***, but you soon will be if you live long enough."(p.522)
- Just as I was wondering what on earth I could do -- I was too drunk even to pack a handkerchief – the memory of an A.A. write-up that I had seen in the Evening Mail flashed across my mind -- and I thought to myself, this is something I haven't tried ***yet***.(p.523)
- They haven't eaten me ***yet***!(p.530)
- There was the physical aspect; to be the youngest and the runt of the brood of children, to have to wear glasses very early and so to be teased, to be bookish and bored in school because the captain of the football team could not translate Virgil and ***yet*** was the school god while you, you, you little shrimp, were the school egghead, junior size and an early model.(p.533)
- Repeated year on end, they are horrible -- frightening and degrading, a chronicle of tragedy which may be greater because the individual undergoing the tragedy, myself, knew what was happening, and ***yet*** refused to do anything to stop it.(p.538)
- And ***yet*** my ability to lie outwardly and to kid myself inwardly grew with every drink I took.(p.556)
- A.A. can, of course, mean just as much to uncounted alcoholics not ***yet*** reached.(p.563)
- The "12 Traditions" of Alcoholics Anonymous are, we A.A.'s believe, the best answers that our experience has ***yet*** given to those ever urgent questions, "How can A.A. best function?" and, "How can A.A. best stay whole and so survive?"(p.563)
- ***Yet*** it is true that our first printing gave many readers the impression that these personality changes, or religious experiences, must be in the nature of sudden and spectacular upheavals.(p.569)

yield

- It quiets the imperious urge, when to ***yield*** would mean heartache.(p.70)
- At the very beginning, the couple ought to frankly face the fact that each will have to ***yield*** here and there if the family is going to play an effective part in the new life.(p.131)
- Occasionally, I would ***yield*** to the morning craving, but if I did, it would be only a few hours before I would be quite unfit for work.(p.176)

yielding

- But at no time have I been anywhere near ***yielding***.(p.181)

YMCA

- So, finally, I went to the ***YMCA*** and they graciously permitted us to use a room at two dollars a night.(p.495)

you'd

- The next morning, my wife came into my room and wakened me and said, "That man is downstairs and he said you said ***you'd*** go to Akron."(p.217)
- I nudged George next morning, and I said, "I'm in," and he said, "Oh, I knew ***you'd*** make it."(p.322)
- Frank said, "If ***you'd*** like to talk to a psychiatrist, I'll see a doctor and find out who to go to here."(p.387)
- "If you had my problems, ***you'd*** drink, too" was my feeling.(p.439)
- "If you had my wife, ***you'd*** drink, too."(p.439)
- "If you had my responsibilities, if you needed the sleep like I do, ***you'd*** drink too."(p.441)
- Economic conditions had a great deal to do with it, because I've often heard my father say that his mother would take one of the old time flour sacks and cut a hole through the bottom and two corners of it and there ***you'd*** have a gown.(p.486)

you'll

- Whether you quit six days, months, or years, if you go out and take a drink or two ***you'll*** end up in this hospital tied down, just like you have been in these past six months.(p.187)
- And they said, "No, you have a disease, and it doesn't make any difference how long you do without it, after a drink or two ***you'll*** end up just like you are now."(p.187)
- Then Dr. Bob said, "Well, Bill, maybe ***you'll*** feel better tomorrow.(p.189)
- Russ said, "Mother, if this tells us how to do it, ***you'll*** have to read it."(p.268)
- Jack said, "Now you start and go to these meetings, and then ***you'll*** find out all about it."(p.268)
- ***You'll*** read and hear a great deal about the spiritual part of our program.(p.366)
- These words may be difficult for you to understand now, but be patient and ***you'll*** know what I mean.(p.367)
- But we have a baby who, if ***you'll*** pardon a little post-alcoholic sentimentality, is right out of Heaven.(p.438)

you're

- "Maybe ***you're*** right," he said.(p.158)
- Before very long we began to relate some incidents of our drinking and, naturally, pretty soon, I realized both of them knew what they were talking about because you can see things and smell things when ***you're*** drunk, that you can't other times, and, if I had thought they didn't know what they were talking about, I wouldn't have been willing to talk to them at all.(p.185)
- I remember telling them too that it was going to be awfully tough, because I did some other things, smoked cigarettes and played penny ante poker, sometimes bet on the horse races and they said, "Don't you think ***you're*** having more trouble with this drinking than with anything else at the present time?(p.190)
- I then began asking a lot of questions of both my brother and Dr. Bob about how this thing worked, and I suppose I was becoming more glassy-eyed all the while, for eventually I said to Bob, "***You're*** all dried up.(p.206)
- ***You're*** never going to want another drink, are you?"; and this answer of his is very important to those of us who are victims of alcoholism.(p.206)
- And I remembered the creeping horror of the interminable night, in which I slept for short spells and woke up dripping with cold sweat and shaken with utter despair, to drink hastily from my bottle and mercifully pass out again, "***You're*** mad, ***you're*** mad, ***you're*** mad!" pounded through my brain with each returning ray of consciousness, and I drowned the refrain with drink.(p.224)
- When I came to my aunt, she knew that I had had an unhappy childhood, and she said, "Now, Ethel, ***you're*** welcome to have boy friends in our home, but there are two boys in this town that I don't want you to date, and one of them comes from a very fine family, one of the best.(p.262)
- He said, "Sister, if you think ***you're*** a screwball now, all you have to do is join up with that.(p.266)
- She said, "I feel ***you're*** just being wise.(p.273)
- This girl and her husband are both in A.A., and she said to me, "Oh, but ***you're*** not the alcoholic; it's your husband."(p.322)
- ***You're*** just a martyr, aren't you?"(p.322)
- And I thought, "***You're*** some martyr, Jane!(p.322)
- ***You're*** not an alcoholic.(p.334)
- "Sure, I've seen you tight several times, but ***you're*** no alcoholic!"(p.356)
- But Frank turned around and looked at me and said, "Esther, remember ***you're*** in jail and not at home."(p.391)
- "Do you know why ***you're*** in here?" he queried.(p.423)
- But if you want to, ***you're*** free to try them.(p.436)
- That's the stuff used when the oral surgeon puts the needle in your vein and says, "Count to ten," and before you get to two, ***you're*** asleep.(p.442)
- "Well, ***you're*** not," says the man.(p.503)
- I talked to him for quite a long time and at the end, he said, "Well, ***you're*** not quite mad enough to be shut up for good yet, but you soon will be if you live long enough."(p.522)
- I had even borrowed money from her, over her protest: "Bob, please don't ask me to lend you money -- ***you're*** the only one who hasn't."(p.540)

you've

- After a while, Bill said, "Well, now, ***you've*** been talking a good long time, let me talk a minute or two."(p.185)
- And they both laughed very heartily, and said, "That's better than ***you've*** been doing, isn't it?"(p.187)
- Knowing Bob of old, she jokingly replied, "Well, Doctor, I suppose ***you've*** already tried it yourself?"(p.188)
- "***You've*** been trying man's ways and they always fail," he told me.(p.236)
- Now, if ***you've*** got a Bible around . . ."(p.268)
- He'd told a villain, "The trouble is, old man, ***you've*** lived too long."(p.333)
- He said, "How I envy you for whatever ***you've*** found."(p.334)
- ***You've*** been sober for three months, been working hard.(p.348)
- ***You've*** been doing all right."(p.348)
- "Well," he said, "***you've*** been sober, but ***you've*** been floating way up on a cloud somewhere.(p.349)
- "***You've*** got to space your drinks and take plenty of water in between," or "coat the stomach with a little olive oil," or "drink anything but those damn martinis."(p.433)
- "Well," he answers, "***You've*** probably tried praying like I have.(p.504)
- When ***you've*** been in a jam ***you've*** said, 'God, please do this or that,' and if it turned out your way that was the last of it, and if it didn't ***you've*** said 'There isn't any God' or 'He doesn't do anything for me.'(p.504)

young

- War fever ran high in the New England town to which we new, ***young*** officers from Plattsburg were assigned, and we were flattered when the first citizens took us to their homes, making us feel heroic.(p.1)
- ***Young*** people may be encouraged by this man's experience to think that they can stop, as he did, on their own will power.(p.33)
- We, who are familiar with the symptoms, see large numbers of potential alcoholics among ***young*** people everywhere.(p.33)
- Their ***young*** minds were impressionable while he was drinking.(p.134)
- He proved to be a devil-may-care ***young*** fellow whose parents could not make out whether he wanted to stop drinking or not.(p.158)
- I was a very ***young*** married man, having his whiskey in the cupboard over the sink, and when I helped my wife with the dishes at night I would take a cup of tea and spike it with whiskey.(p.196)
- I realized that there wasn't anything I could say to place myself in a more favorable light with my children, that it was going to be a matter of time; for I also understood the intolerance of ***young*** people towards deficiencies in their elders.(p.220)
- This time I seemed to be already awake, sitting upright in a big easy chair, in the middle of an animated conversation with a perfectly strange ***young*** woman, who didn't appear to think it strange.(p.222)
- The best boarding schools and a finishing school in

Europe had fitted me for the conventional role of debutante and ***young*** matron.(p.225)
• ***Young*** and able to travel with the best of them, I managed to hold my job and keep my end up in the barrooms.(p.252)
• There was a ***young*** fellow who led the meeting and that was a beautiful thing to me.(p.270)
• With the bravery born of desperation, and abetted by alcohol, I married a ***young*** and lovely girl.(p.277)
• The doctor, a ***young*** man, immediately took fire with the idea, and while he did not convince the son, he turned over two prospects who were anxious for the program.(p.294)
• Not only were they at peace with themselves, but they were getting a kick out of life such as one seldom encounters, except in the very ***young***.(p.310)
• TOO ***YOUNG***?(p.317)
• "I'm not crazy," I thought, "and I can't be an alcoholic – I'm too ***young***."(p.319)
• In the doorway stood a lovely ***young*** girl who said, "Are you one of us souses, too?"(p.321)
• But we had to do a lot of entertaining, my husband liked to have a good time; I was very ***young***; and I wanted to have a good time too.(p.322)
• Just three years of drinking pushed a shy, lonely ***young*** girl to the depth of depression.(p.353)
• I was living in a small room on West 53rd Street right off Fifth Avenue, when I met a ***young*** lady who eventually was responsible for altering my entire way of living.(p.359)
• The story is not very different from that of thousands of other ***young*** men in my generation.(p.373)
• So I married a nice, well-meaning ***young*** newspaperman, so as not to have to go home.(p.402)
• But now I was a ***young*** divorcee, leading a Washington social life.(p.402)
• In the morning, because I was ***young*** and healthy, my remorse was worse than my hangover.(p.404)
• I had met a bunch of gay ***young*** Bohemians who lived in the Village, and were sowing their wild oats.(p.407)
• My second wife is a ***young*** A.A. member, too, and what a terrific adventure this is for us!(p.420)
• I am a ***young*** alcoholic with a drug problem, a doctor, the husband of an alcoholic, the son of an alcoholic, and a man once diagnosed as a violent manic-depressive.(p.421)
• A ***young*** veteran tells how a few rough experiences pushed him into A.A. – and how he was therefore spared years of suffering.(p.422)
• When a big, healthy-looking ***young*** fellow stood up there and said, "I'm a success today if I don't drink today," I thought, "Man, I've got a thousand things to do today before I can brag about not taking a drink, for God's sake!"(p.447)
• Had first drink in ***young*** teens, but was scared of my father.(p.474)
• He was old, but now he grow ***young*** with new life in A.A. and travel all time.(p.476)
• Will I take a ***young*** fellow who has been drinking for two weeks to live with me?(p.506)
• My father was and still is a minister, and I was afraid that I might run into him, or that someone might tell him where I was, and I could still remember what he had done to me when I got drunk one Christmas when I was very ***young***.(p.527)
• For you learned that he had been guilty of the thing he had accused you of, and his guilt had brought suffering to his entire family; and he thought he saw his ***young*** son beginning his own tragic pattern.(p.533)
• ***Young*** when she joined, this A.A. believes her serious drinking was the result of even deeper defects.(p.544)

younger

• I feel as I did when I was fifteen years ***younger***.(p.303)
• Even obvious intoxication is excused by ***younger*** people as something "he's earned the right to do," and they say, "After all, who's he hurting?"(p.330)
• They were all kids, most of them ***younger*** than I was.(p.407)
• I attended meetings, I talked to my folks, I talked to ***younger*** people they had gotten in contact with to sponsor me.(p.430)
• For that reason, I believe, I married at a much ***younger*** age than I would have, had it not been for my home training.(p.485)
• Lots of the older people had taken to drinking quite a good deal more during the war, but the ***younger*** generation was, I think, about the same.(p.518)

youngest

• There was the physical aspect; to be the ***youngest*** and the runt of the brood of children, to have to wear glasses very early and so to be teased, to be bookish and bored in school because the captain of the football team could not translate Virgil and yet was the school god while you, you, you little shrimp, were the school egghead, junior size and an early model.(p.533)

youngster

• My ***youngster*** has adopted me.(p.303)
• The first had been as a ***youngster*** coming out from Ireland.(p.513)

your

• He said, "Why don't you choose ***your*** own conception of God?"(p.12)
• If ***your*** are an alcoholic who wants to get over it, you may already be asking – "What do I have to do?"(p.20)
• With many individuals the methods which I employed are successful, but I have never been successful with an alcoholic of ***your*** description."(p.27)
• It may be worth a bad case of jitters if you get a full knowledge of ***your*** condition.(p.32)
• I rather appreciated ***your*** ideas about the subtle insanity which precedes the first drink, but I was confident it could not happen to me after what I had learned.(p.40)
• Its main object is to enable you to find a Power greater than yourself which will solve ***your*** problem.(p.45)
• When, therefore, we speak to you of God, we mean ***your*** own conception of God.(p.47)
• The consciousness of ***your*** belief is sure to come to you.(p.55)
• If you have already made a decision, and an inventory of ***your*** grosser handicaps, you have made a good beginning.(p.71)
• Grant me strength, as I go out from here, to do ***your*** bidding.(p.76)
• Ministers and doctors are competent and you can learn much from them if you wish, but it happens that because of ***your*** own drinking experience you can be uniquely useful to other alcoholics.(p.89)
• Don't deal with him when he is very drunk, unless he is ugly and the family needs ***your*** help.(p.90)
• Usually the family should not try to tell ***your*** story.(p.91)
• If ***your*** man needs hospitalization, he should have it, but not forcibly unless he is violent.(p.91)
• When ***your*** man is better, the doctor might suggest a visit from you.(p.91)
• Under these conditions ***your*** prospect will see he is under no pressure.(p.91)
• See ***your*** man alone, if possible.(p.91)
• Tell him enough about ***your*** drinking habits, symptoms, and experiences to encourage him to speak of himself.(p.91)
• If he is not communicative, give him a sketch of ***your*** drinking career up to the time you quit.(p.91)
• If his mood is light, tell him humorous stories of ***your*** escapades.(p.91)
• He will match ***your*** mental inconsistencies with some of his own.(p.92)
• Show him, from ***your*** own experience, how the queer mental condition surrounding that first drink prevents normal functioning of the will power.(p.92)
• Keep his attention focussed mainly on ***your*** personal experience.(p.92)
• You will soon have ***your*** friend admitting he has many, if not all, of the traits of the alcoholic.(p.92)
• Even though ***your*** protege may not have entirely admitted his condition, he has become very curious to know how you got well.(p.92)
• If the man be agnostic or atheist, make it emphatic that he does not have to agree with ***your*** conception of God.(p.93)
• Don't raise such issues, no matter what ***your*** own convictions are.(p.93)
• ***Your*** prospect may belong to a religious denomination.(p.93)
• Perhaps ***your*** story will help him see where he has failed to practice the very precepts he knows so well.(p.93)
• Outline the program of action, explaining how you made a self-appraisal, how you straightened out ***your*** past and why you are now endeavoring to be helpful to him.(p.94)
• It is important for him to realize that ***your*** attempt to pass this on to him plays a vital part in ***your*** own recovery.(p.94)
• If ***your*** talk has been sane, quiet and full of human understanding, you have perhaps made a friend.(p.94)
• He will be more likely to follow ***your*** suggestions.(p.94)
• ***Your*** candidate may give reasons why he need not follow all of the program.(p.94)
• On ***your*** first visit tell him about the Fellowship of Alcoholics Anonymous.(p.94)
• If he shows interest, lend him ***your*** copy of this book.(p.94)
• Unless ***your*** friend wants to talk further about himself, do not wear out ***your*** welcome.(p.95)
• If he is not interested in ***your*** solution, if he expects you to act only as a banker for his financial difficulties or a nurse for his sprees, you may have to drop him until he changes his mind.(p.95)
• Do not be discouraged if ***your*** prospect does not respond at once.(p.96)
• Suppose now you are making ***your*** second visit to a man.(p.96)
• But you should not deprive ***your*** family or creditors of money they should have.(p.96)
• Perhaps you will want to take the man into ***your*** home for a few days.(p.96)
• Be certain he will be welcomed by ***your*** family, and that he is not trying to impose upon you for money, connections, or shelter.(p.96)
• Helping others is the foundation stone of ***your*** recovery.(p.97)
• It may mean the loss of many nights' sleep, great interference with ***your*** pleasures, interruptions to ***your*** business.(p.97)
• It may mean sharing ***your*** money and ***your*** home, counseling frantic wives and relatives, innumerable trips to police courts, sanitariums, hospitals, jails and asylums.(p.97)
• ***Your*** telephone may jangle at any time of the day or night.(p.97)
• ***Your*** wife may sometimes say she is neglected.(p.97)
• A drunk may smash the furniture in ***your*** home, or burn a mattress.(p.97)
• The family should be offered ***your*** way of life.(p.97)
• When ***your*** prospect has made such reparation as he can to his family, and has thoroughly explained to them the new principles by which he is living, he should proceed to put those principles into action at home.(p.98)
• Follow the dictates of a Higher Power and you will presently live in a new and wonderful world, no matter what ***your*** present circumstances!(p.100)
• You may spoil ***your*** chance of being helpful if you do.(p.100)
• If you have been successful in solving ***your*** own domestic problems, tell the newcomer's family how that was accomplished.(p.100)
• The story of how you and ***your*** wife settled ***your*** difficulties is worth any amount of criticism.(p.100)
• But be sure you are on solid spiritual ground before you start and that ***your*** motive in going is thoroughly good.(p.102)
• If it is a happy occasion, try to increase the pleasure of those there; if a business occasion, go and attend to ***your*** business enthusiastically.(p.102)
• Let ***your*** friends know they are not to change their habits on ***your*** account.(p.102)
• At proper time and place explain to all ***your*** friends why alcohol disagrees with you.(p.102)
• Don't start to withdraw again just because ***your*** friends drink liquor.(p.102)
• ***Your*** job now is to be at the place where you may be of maximum helpfulness to others, so never hesitate to go anywhere if you can be helpful.(p.102)
• Perhaps ***your*** husband has been living in that strange world of alcoholism where everything is distorted and exaggerated.(p.108)
• Try not to condemn ***your*** alcoholic husband no matter what he says or does.(p.108)
• An alcoholic of this temperament may be quick to use this chapter as a club over ***your*** head.(p.108)
• Is it right to let him ruin ***your*** life and the lives of ***your*** children?(p.108)
• One: ***Your*** husband may be only a heavy drinker.(p.108)
• Two: ***Your*** husband is showing lack of control, for he is unable to stay on the water wagon even when he wants to.(p.109)
• He has begun to try, with or without ***your*** cooperation, various means of moderating or staying dry.(p.109)
• You have passed happy evenings together chatting and drinking before ***your*** fire.(p.110)
• Even though ***your*** husband becomes unbearable and you have to leave him temporarily, you should, if you can, go without rancor.(p.111)
• If he gets the idea that you are a nag or a killjoy, ***your*** chance of accomplishing anything useful may be zero.(p.111)
• Be determined that ***your*** husband's drinking is not going to spoil ***your*** relations with ***your*** children or ***your*** friends.(p.111)

• They need ***your*** companionship and ***your*** help.(p.111)
• It is possible to have a full and useful life, though ***your*** husband continues to drink.(p.111)
• Do not set ***your*** heart on reforming ***your*** husband.(p.111)
• ***Your*** husband may come to appreciate ***your*** reasonableness and patience.(p.111)
• ***Your*** husband may be willing to talk to one of them.(p.112)
• If this kind of approach does not catch ***your*** husband's interest, it may be best to drop the subject, but after a friendly talk ***your*** husband will usually revive the topic himself.(p.112)
• If you act upon these principles, ***your*** husband may stop or moderate.(p.112)
• Suppose, however, that ***your*** husband fits the description of number two.(p.112)
• Show him ***your*** copy of this book and tell him what you have found out about alcoholism.(p.112)
• If he is enthusiastic ***your*** cooperation will mean a great deal.(p.113)
• He may not share ***your*** enthusiasm, but he is practically sure to read the book and he may go for the program at once.(p.113)
• If ***your*** husband is otherwise a normal individual, ***your*** chances are good at this stage.(p.113)
• In any event, try to have ***your*** husband read this book.(p.114)
• If he is already committed to an institution, but can convince you and ***your*** doctor that he means business, give him a chance to try our method, unless the doctor thinks his mental condition too abnormal or dangerous.(p.114)
• You may have the reverse situation on ***your*** hands.(p.114)
• If ***your*** husband is a drinker, you probably worry over what other people are thinking and you hate to meet ***your*** friends.(p.114)
• You draw more and more into yourself and you think everyone is talking about conditions at ***your*** home.(p.114)
• You avoid the subject of drinking, even with ***your*** own parents.(p.114)
• When ***your*** husband is bad, you become a trembling recluse, wishing the telephone had never been invented.(p.115)
• While you need not discuss ***your*** husband at length, you can quietly let ***your*** friends know the nature of his illness.(p.115)
• But you must be on guard not to embarrass or harm ***your*** husband.(p.115)
• Barriers which have sprung up between you and ***your*** friends will disappear with the growth of sympathetic understanding.(p.115)
• You will no longer be self-conscious or feel that you must apologize as though ***your*** husband were a weak character.(p.115)
• ***Your*** new courage, good nature and lack of self-consciousness will do wonders for you socially.(p.115)
• Use ***your*** energies to promote a better understanding all around.(p.115)
• Frequently, you have felt obliged to tell ***your*** husband's employer and his friends that he was sick, when as a matter of fact he was tight.(p.115)
• Whenever possible, let ***your*** husband explain.(p.115)
• ***Your*** desire to protect him should not cause you to lie to people when they have a right to know where he is and what he is doing.(p.115)
• You may be afraid ***your*** husband will lose his position; you are thinking of the disgrace and hard times which will befall you and the children.(p.116)
• It may convince ***your*** husband he wants to stop drinking forever.(p.116)
• If God can solve the age-old riddle of alcoholism, He can solve ***your*** problems too.(p.116)
• We urge you to try our program, for nothing will be so helpful to ***your*** husband as the radically changed attitude toward him which God will show you how to have.(p.117)
• Go along with ***your*** husband if you possibly can.(p.117)
• If you and ***your*** husband find a solution for the pressing problem of drink you are, of course, going to be very happy.(p.117)
• In spite of ***your*** new-found happiness, there will be ups and downs.(p.117)
• The faith and sincerity of both you and ***your*** husband will be put to the test.(p.117)
• These work-outs should be regarded as part of ***your*** education, for thus you will be learning to live.(p.117)
• ***Your*** husband will sometimes be unreasonable and you will want to criticize.(p.117)
• These family dissensions are very dangerous, especially to ***your*** husband.(p.117)
• We do not mean that you have to agree with ***your*** husband whenever there is an honest difference of opinion.(p.117)
• You and ***your*** husband will find that you can dispose of serious problems easier than you can the trivial ones.(p.118)
• If ***your*** husband is trying to live on a spiritual basis, he will also be doing everything in his power to avoid disagreement or contention.(p.118)
• ***Your*** husband knows he owes you more than sobriety.(p.118)
• If you both show a willingness to remedy ***your*** own defects, there will be little need to criticize each other.(p.118)
• ***Your*** husband will be the first to say it was ***your*** devotion and care which brought him to the point where he could have a spiritual experience.(p.118)
• When resentful thoughts come, try to pause and count ***your*** blessings.(p.119)
• After all, ***your*** family is reunited, alcohol is no longer a problem and you and ***your*** husband are working together toward an undreamed-of future.(p.119)
• ***Your*** house is filled with strangers.(p.119)
• We suggest that you direct some of ***your*** thought to the wives of his new alcoholic friends.(p.119)
• It is probably true that you and ***your*** husband have been living too much alone, for drinking many times isolates the wife of an alcoholic.(p.119)
• Therefore, you probably need fresh interests and a great cause to live for as much as ***your*** husband.(p.119)
• You, as well as ***your*** husband, ought to think of what you can put into life instead of how much you can take out.(p.120)
• Inevitably ***your*** lives will be fuller for doing so.(p.120)
• Perhaps ***your*** husband will make a fair start on the new basis, but just as things are going beautifully he dismays you by coming home drunk.(p.120)
• ***Your*** husband will see at once that he must redouble his spiritual activities if he expects to survive.(p.120)
• The slightest sign of fear or intolerance may lessen ***your*** husband's chance of recovery.(p.120)
• In a weak moment he may take ***your*** dislike of his high-stepping friends as one of those insanely trivial excuses to drink.(p.120)
• The slightest disposition on ***your*** part to guide his appointments or his affairs so he will not be tempted will be noticed.(p.120)
• God has either removed ***your*** husband's liquor problem or He has not.(p.120)
• Then you and ***your*** husband can get right down to fundamentals.(p.120)
• If there is no Al-Anon listing in ***your*** local telephone book, you may obtain further information on Al-Anon Family Groups by writing to its World Service Office: Box 182, Madison Square Station, New York, NY 10159.(p.121)
• Do not hesitate to take ***your*** health problems to such persons.(p.133)
• If he has ***your*** will power and guts, he will make the grade."(p.138)
• If you desire to help it might be well to disregard ***your*** own drinking, or lack of it.(p.139)
• Drinking occasionally, and understanding ***your*** own reactions, it is possible for you to become quite sure of many things which, so far as the alcoholic is concerned, are not always so.(p.139)
• As a moderate drinker, you can take ***your*** liquor or leave it alone.(p.139)
• Whenever you want to, you control ***your*** drinking.(p.139)
• Of an evening, you can go on a mild bender, get up in the morning, shake ***your*** head and go to business.(p.139)
• A look at the alcoholic in ***your*** organization is many times illuminating.(p.139)
• If ***your*** decision is yes, whether the reason be humanitarian or business or both, then the following suggestions may be helpful.(p.140)
• If you concede that ***your*** employee is ill, can he be forgiven for what he has done in the past?(p.140)
• ***Your*** man has probably been trying to conceal a number of scrapes, perhaps pretty messy ones.(p.140)
• Seeing ***your*** attempt to understand and help, some men will try to take advantage of ***your*** kindness.(p.141)
• If you are sure ***your*** man does not want to stop, he may as well be discharged, the sooner the better.(p.141)
• ***Your*** understanding treatment of their cases will pay dividends.(p.141)
• Whether you mention this book is a matter for ***your*** discretion.(p.142)
• After satisfying yourself that ***your*** man wants to recover and that he will go to any extreme to do so, you may suggest a definite course of action.(p.142)
• The matter of physical treatment should, of course, be referred to ***your*** own doctor.(p.143)
• ***Your*** man will fare better if placed in such physical condition that he can think straight and no longer craves liquor.(p.143)
• If ***your*** man accepts ***your*** offer, it should be pointed out that physical treatment is but a small part of the picture.(p.143)
• Whether ***your*** employee likes it or not, he will learn the grim truth about alcoholism.(p.144)
• We suggest you draw the book to the attention of the doctor who is to attend ***your*** patient during treatment.(p.144)
• You are betting, of course, that ***your*** changed attitude plus the contents of this book will turn the trick.(p.144)
• As our work spreads and our numbers increase, we hope ***your*** employees may be put in personal contact with some of us.(p.144)
• On ***your*** employee's return, talk with him.(p.144)
• He may, for example, reveal that he has padded his expense account or that he has planned to take ***your*** best customers away from you.(p.145)
• ***Your*** man should be on his mettle to make good.(p.146)
• After ***your*** man has gone along without drinking for a few months, you may be able to make use of his services with other employees who are giving you the alcoholic run-around -- provided, of course, they are willing to have a third party in the picture.(p.146)
• ***Your*** man may be trusted.(p.146)
• He will appreciate knowing you are not bothering ***your*** head about him, that you are not suspicious nor are you trying to run his life so he will be shielded from temptation to drink.(p.146)
• If he is conscientiously following the program of recovery he can go anywhere ***your*** business may call him.(p.147)
• But you should feel under no obligation to keep him on, for ***your*** obligation has been well discharged already.(p.147)
• If ***your*** organization is a large one, ***your*** junior executives might be provided with this book.(p.147)
• You might let them know you have no quarrel with the alcoholics of ***your*** organization.(p.147)
• If you take it, ***your*** past will be forgotten and the fact that you went away for treatment will not be mentioned.(p.147)
• ***Your*** junior executive may not agree with the contents of our book.(p.148)
• Alcoholism may be causing ***your*** organization considerable damage in its waste of time, men and reputation.(p.148)
• We think we are sensible when we urge that you stop this waste and give ***your*** worthwhile man a chance.(p.148)
• He remarked: "I'm mighty glad you fellows got over ***your*** drinking.(p.148)
• Even if you feel ***your*** organization has no alcoholic problem, it might pay to take another look down the line.(p.149)
• ***Your*** imagination will be fired.(p.152)
• The most satisfactory years of ***your*** existence lie ahead.(p.152)
• You are going to meet these new friends in ***your*** own community.(p.152)
• You will be bound to them with new and wonderful ties, for you will escape disaster together and you will commence shoulder to shoulder ***your*** common journey.(p.152)
• Perhaps the best way of treating you to a glimpse of ***your*** future will be to describe the growth of the fellowship among us.(p.153)
• You fellows know ***your*** stuff all right, but I don't see what good it'll do.(p.157)
• And so can you, though you be but one man with this book in ***your*** hand.(p.162)
• God will determine that, so you must remember that ***your*** real reliance is always upon Him.(p.164)
• Ask Him in ***your*** morning meditation what you can do each day for the man who is still sick.(p.164)
• The answers will come, if ***your*** own house is in order.(p.164)
• See to it that ***your*** relationship with Him is right, and great events will come to pass for you and countless others.(p.164)
• Admit ***your*** faults to Him and to ***your*** fellows.(p.164)
• Clear away the wreckage of ***your*** past.(p.164)

• The question which might naturally come into ***your*** mind would be: "What did the man do or say that was different from what others had done or said?"(p.180)
• If you still think you are strong enough to beat the game alone, that is ***your*** affair.(p.181)
• ***Your*** Heavenly Father will never let you down!(p.181)
• It's none of our business about ***your*** drinking.(p.186)
• We're not up here trying to take any of ***your*** rights or privileges away from you, but we have a program whereby we think we can stay sober.(p.186)
• Now, if you don't want it, we'll not take up ***your*** time, and we'll be going and looking for someone else."(p.186)
• Bill left me at the elevator and said, "***Your*** room is so and so," and I didn't see him again for six months.(p.217)
• He then pulled up his chair with one of his knees touching mine and said, "Will you pray with me for ***your*** success?"(p.218)
• This girl and her husband are both in A.A., and she said to me, "Oh, but you're not the alcoholic; it's ***your*** husband."(p.322)
• She said "Suppose I put ***your*** name down as a volunteer.(p.326)
• So I went to my wife and asked her, wasn't there something that she and I could do to somehow get together, and she turned on her heel and looked me squarely in the eye, and said, "You don't care anything about my problem," and I could have smacked her, but I said to myself, "Grab on to ***your*** serenity!"(p.351)
• So I went to her and said, "There's only one thing I want in my whole life, and I don't want any commendation; I don't want any credit; I don't want anything from you or Janey for the rest of ***your*** life except one thing; and that is, the opportunity to do anything you want always, and I would like to start off by doing the dishes."(p.351)
• They have contributed fantastic amounts of time and work to our problem, but they aren't able, it seems, to arrest either ***your*** alcoholism or mine.(p.352)
• I can't bear to be here when you lose the respect of others, and above all -- when you lose ***your*** own self respect."(p.362)
• I can't bear to be here when you lose the respect of others, and above all when you lose ***your*** own self respect."(p.363)
• Some crisis brings you to a point of making a decision to do something about ***your*** drinking problem.(p.377)
• I only know that it does -- if you desire it with ***your*** whole heart and without reservation.(p.384)
• Drinking it with ***your*** meals, you didn't feel it.(p.385)
• You didn't carry a little orchid up the aisle in those days; you carried a great big bouquet, like a funeral spray, and you didn't have ***your*** picture taken until just before you went to the church.(p.385)
• He said, "If ***your*** father will come out and stay with you, you can have the house."(p.389)
• "These people all had ***your*** problem," she told me.(p.412)
• He did not take out a folder and say, "What is the nature of ***your*** problem?"(p.413)
• "You've got to space ***your*** drinks and take plenty of water in between," or "coat the stomach with a little olive oil," or "drink anything but those damn martinis."(p.433)
• It wasn't until just lately that, in ***your*** case, I could draw it.(p.436)
• That's the stuff used when the oral surgeon puts the needle in ***your*** vein and says, "Count to ten," and before you get to two, you're asleep.(p.442)
• The idea behind it is that, having taken the treatment, ***your*** system is so "conditioned" that the mere sight or smell or taste of alcohol produces a violent reaction, and you become ill.(p.469)
• Finally she said, "Isn't ***your*** name Jim S.?"(p.493)
• "Let ***your*** light so shine before men that they may see ***your*** good works –."(p.497)
• You bet ***your*** life!(p.500)
• "Then all of ***your*** troubles are over," says the man and leaves the room.(p.503)
• When you've been in a jam you've said, 'God, please do this or that,' and if it turned out ***your*** way that was the last of it, and if it didn't you've said 'There isn't any God' or 'He doesn't do anything for me.'(p.504)
• Does that answer ***your*** question?"(p.504)
• But as long as you did ***your*** work and didn't disgrace yourself, you were socially acceptable and nobody really intruded on ***your*** private life very much.(p.518)
• There was the father one lost respect for at the age of eleven, because the father broke his solemn word in a circumstance where you, eleven years old, had assumed guilt when you were innocent; but the father would not believe you, no matter what; and to ease his suffering you "confessed" and were "forgiven," only – months later – to have ***your*** "guilt" brought up – only he and you knew what he was talking bout -- brought up in front of the stern grandmother.(p.533)
• The sacred word was broken and you never trusted ***your*** father again, and avoided him.(p.533)
• You were thirty-five before you understood ***your*** father's horrible anguish, and forgave him, and loved him again.(p.533)
• I thought that life was a pretty simple thing; you simply made a plan for ***your*** life, based upon what you wanted, and then you needed only the courage to go after it.(p.545)
• They said if you want to know how this program works, take the first word of ***your*** question – the H is for honesty, the O is for open-mindedness and the W is for willingness; these our Book calls the essentials of recovery.(p.550)
• Even when you don't really want it for them, and ***your*** prayers are only words and you don't mean it, go ahead and do it anyway.(p.552)
• If you cannot find A.A. in ***your*** locality, a letter addressed to Alcoholics Anonymous, Box 459, Grand Central Station, New York, NY 10163, U.S.A., will receive a prompt reply from this world center, referring you to the nearest A.A. group.(p.575)
• If there is none nearby, you will be invited to carry on a correspondence which will do much to insure ***your*** sobriety no matter how isolated you are.(p.575)
• This headquarters will give the location of the nearest family group and will if you wish, correspond with you about ***your*** special problems.(p.575)

yours

• Very truly ***yours***, William D. Silkworth, M.D.(p.xxiv)
• Exceptions to cases such as ***yours*** have been occurring since early times.(p.27)
• Though not a religious person, I have profound respect for the spiritual approach in such cases as ***yours***.(p.43)
• His religious education and training may be far superior to ***yours***.(p.93)
• But he will be curious to learn why his own convictions have not worked and why ***yours*** seem to work so well.(p.93)
• You feel he should now be ***yours***.(p.119)
• He gets stirred up about their troubles, but not at all about ***yours***.(p.119)
• I remember very well saying, "There's only one person in the world whose guts I hate worse than ***yours***, and those're my own."(p.440)

yourself

• You may already have asked ***yourself*** why it is that all of us became so very ill from drinking.(p.20)
• We do not like to pronounce any individual as alcoholic, but you can quickly diagnose ***yourself***.(p.31)
• It will not take long for you to decide if you are honest with ***yourself*** about it.(p.32)
• Its main object is to enable you to find a Power greater than ***yourself*** which will solve your problem.(p.45)
• Do not let any prejudice you may have against spiritual terms deter you from honestly asking ***yourself*** what they mean to you.(p.47)
• If our testimony helps sweep away prejudice, enables you to think honestly, encourages you to search diligently within ***yourself***, then, if you wish, you can join us on the Broad Highway.(p.55)
• That being so you have swallowed and digested some big chunks of truth about ***yourself***.(p.71)
• You need this information to put ***yourself*** in his place, to see how you would like him to approach you if the tables were turned.(p.90)
• If he does not want to see you, never force ***yourself*** upon him.(p.90)
• When he sees you know all about the drinking game, commence to describe ***yourself*** as an alcoholic.(p.91)
• Having had the experience ***yourself***, you can give him much practical advice.(p.96)
• Therefore, ask ***yourself*** on each occasion, "Have I any good social, business, or personal reason for going to this place?(p.101)
• Perhaps you enjoy drinking with him ***yourself*** when he doesn't go too far.(p.110)
• Attempt instead, to put ***yourself*** in his place.(p.111)
• You draw more and more into ***yourself*** and you think everyone is talking about conditions at your home.(p.114)
• Show him these things in ***yourself*** and they will be reflected back to you from him.(p.118)
• The chances are he will not for, like ***yourself***, he is just beginning his development.(p.118)
• It will do little good if you point that out and urge more attention for ***yourself***.(p.119)
• If he gets drunk, don't blame ***yourself***.(p.120)
• After satisfying ***yourself*** that your man wants to recover and that he will go to any extreme to do so, you may suggest a definite course of action.(p.142)
• At the same time you will feel no reluctance to rid ***yourself*** of those who cannot or will not stop.(p.148)
• Then you will know what it means to give of ***yourself*** that others may survive and rediscover life.(p.153)
• You are saying to ***yourself***: "I'm jittery and alone.(p.163)
• You forget that you have just now tapped a source of power much greater than ***yourself***.(p.163)
• Abandon ***yourself*** to God as you understand God.(p.164)
• Knowing Bob of old, she jokingly replied, "Well, Doctor, I suppose you've already tried it ***yourself***?"(p.188)
• The second one said, "Don't feel that you stop drinking for anyone other than ***yourself***," and this hit me between the eyes.(p.346)
• And the most important person to be honest with is ***Yourself***.(p.368)
• I cannot sit by and watch you destroy ***yourself***."(p.391)
• During this time, you are supposed to behave ***yourself***, but I took a little wine-tasting tour through France, all by my lone, with car and chauffeur.(p.405)
• But as long as you did your work and didn't disgrace ***yourself***, you were socially acceptable and nobody really intruded on your private life very much.(p.518)
• The less you think of ***yourself*** the more of a person you become.(p.542)
• If you will ask in prayer for everything you want for ***yourself*** to be given to them, you will be free.(p.552)

yourselves

• Had you offered ***yourselves*** as patients at this hospital, I would not have taken you, if I had been able to avoid it.(p.43)

youth

• Insofar as religion was concerned, I had a Catholic training in my ***youth***.(p.214)
• I was warmly welcomed by friends of my ***youth*** who had preceded me.(p.231)
• Such thinking usually began with thoughts of the pleasant drinking of my ***youth***.(p.285)
• I remember in my early ***youth*** my mother dressed me just as she did my two sisters, and I wore curls until I was six years of age.(p.483)
• I could not face the boy and ***youth*** I was in the reality of the contemptible man I had become.(p.540)

youthful

• I wandered, craving peace, from one spot to another of ***youthful*** happy memory, and loathed the man I had become.(p.539)

Zz

zeal
• It never fails, if you go about it with one half the ***zeal*** you have been in the habit of showing when you were getting another drink.(p.181)

zero
• If he gets the idea that you are a nag or a killjoy, your chance of accomplishing anything useful may be ***zero***.(p.111)
• We worked in five below ***zero*** weather, fixing on an elm tree a wrought iron device which modestly proclaimed that he was indeed a country doctor.(p.540)

zone
• I was picked up at two-thirty that morning with my car smashed up by a street-car because I had run into a big concrete safety ***zone***, and the street-car had run into me, and they took me out through the roof -- there's where I lost the suit.(p.202)

Appendices

Appendix I - Table of Footnotes • 891

Appendix II - Tables of dates • 892

Table 1: Dates by Year

Table 2: Dates by Month

Table 3: Miscellaneous Dates

Appendix III - Tables of Numbers • 900

Table 1: Numbers of Quantity

Table 2: Numbers of Enumeration

Table 3: Numbers As Percentages

Table 4: Numbers Expressing Geographical Locations

Table 5: Numbers As Denominations of Money

Table 6: Miscellaneous Numbers

Appendix IV - Frequency of Words: Alpha Sort • 908

Appendix V - Frequency of Words: Numerical Sort • 932

APPENDIX I

Table of Footnotes

Page Number	Footnote
xxii	[1]In 1985, over 58,500 groups, with A.A. activity in 114 countries.
xxii	[2]In 1985, almost one-third are women; about one-fifth, 30 and under.
16	*In 1985, A.A. is composed of approximately 58,000 groups.
25	*Fully explained -- Appendix II
27	*For amplification -- see Appendix II.
34	*True when this book was first published. But a 1983 U.S./Canada membership survey showed about one-fifth of A.A.'s were 30 and under.
47	*Please be sure to read Appendix II on "Spiritual Experience."
104	*Written in 1939, when there were few women in A.A., this chapter assumes that the alcoholic in the home is likely to be the husband. But many of the suggestions given here may be adapted to help the person who lives with a woman alcoholic -- whether she is still drinking or is recovering in A.A. A further source of help is noted on page 121.
150	*See Appendix VI -- We shall be happy to hear from you if we can be of help.
155	*This refers to Bill's first visit with Dr. Bob. These men later became co-founders of A.A. Bill's story opens the text of this book; Dr. Bob's heads the Story Section.
156	*This refers to Bill's and Dr. Bob's first visit to A.A. Number Three. See the Pioneer Section. This resulted in A.A.'s first group, at Akron, Ohio, in 1935.
161	*Written in 1939.
162	*Written in 1939. In 1985, there are about 58,500 groups. There is A.A. activity in 114 countries, with an estimated membership of over 1,000,000.
164	*Alcoholics Anonymous will be glad to hear from you. Address P.O. Box 459, Grand Central Station, New York, NY 10163.
235	*Written in 1939.
571	*1944
574	*Father Ed, an early and wonderful friend of A.A., died in the spring of 1960.

APPENDIX II

Tables Of Dates

Table 1: Dates by year.

1901
- My father died in 1901 when I was eight years old and I was in the second or third grade at school. (p.193)

1916
- The rubber prosperity went on for about six years -- 1916 to 1922.(p.197)
- I had two years at Dublin University, and then in 1916, I got a nomination for Sandhurst, the British Military College.(p.518)

1917
- This was in 1917.(p.183)
- In the spring of 1917, in order to beat being fired from school, I became "patriotic" and joined the Army.(p.241)

1918
- My last bout in the Army lasted from November 5th to 11th, 1918.(p.242)

1919
- Akron was really on the boom in those days, 1919-1920; expansion was terrific.(p.198)
- Discharged in 1919, I really made up for my dry spell.(p.253)

1920
- Akron was really on the boom in those days, 1919-1920; expansion was terrific.(p.198)
- When I did make it home in 1920, I re-entered school and caught up with my class in a few short months -- I actually did a year's work in three months, proving much to the disgust of my dad that I could do it when I wanted to.(p.358)

1922
- The rubber prosperity went on for about six years -- 1916 to 1922.(p.197)

1924
- In 1924, I had acquired enough clients of my own so that the firm made me a junior partner.(p.213)

1925
- I was divorced in 1925 or 1926.(p.199)
- This was about 1926.(p.519)

1926
- I was divorced in 1925 or 1926.(p.199)

1927
- It think this was about 1927.(p.199)

1928
- He was in his late fifties, and all that he had undertaken fell upon my shoulders at his death in 1928.(p.486)

1929
- In 1929 I contracted golf fever.(p.3)
- Abruptly in October 1929 hell broke loose on the New York stock exchange.(p.4)

(Table 1: Continued)

- High living, a great many fair weather friends, the 1929 stock market crash, and a couple of years of Depression, soon relieved me one by one of my worldly goods including my wife.(p.358)

1930

- I had some financial success through no ability of my own and, when jobless and almost wiped out in 1930, I began to trade and sell my collection; much of the proceeds went to keep my apartment stocked with liquor and almost every night saw me helpless to bed.(p.255)
- In 1930, I moved to Chicago.(p.287)
- During the years 1930 to 1935, due to the Depression and its aftermath, business went from bad to worse.(p.486)

1932

- Stocks were at the low point of 1932, and I had somehow formed a group to buy.(p.5)
- In 1932, some friends of mine advised me that I might try Christian Science, which had done a lot for some of their friends.(p.202)
- This Christian Science experience with a sobriety of fifteen months was in 1932.(p.203)
- By 1932, I was going on two or three day benders.(p.288)

1934

- In late 1934 I attended a patient who, though he had been a competent businessman of good earning capacity, was an alcoholic of a type I had come to regard as hopeless.(p.xxiii)

1935

- The birth of our Society dates from his first day of permanent sobriety, June 10, 1935.(p.v)
- The spark that was to flare into the first A.A. group was struck at Akron, Ohio, in June 1935, during a talk between a New York stockbroker and an Akron physician.(p.xv)
- This work at Akron continued through the summer of 1935.(p.xvii)
- When the broker returned to New York in the fall of 1935, the first A.A. group had actually been formed, though no one realized it at the time.(p.xvii)
- Then came the insidious insanity of that first drink, and on Armistice Day 1935, I was off again.(p.8)
- Years ago, in 1935, one of our number made a journey to a certain western city.(p.153)
- This resulted in A.A.'s first group, at Akron, Ohio, in 1935.(p.156)
- That was in June, 1935.(p.158)
- The birth of our Society dates from his first day of permanent sobriety, June 10, 1935.(p.171)
- That was June 10, 1935, and that was my last drink.(p.180)
- During the first six months of 1935, I was hospitalized eight times for intoxication and shackled to the bed two or three days before I even knew where I was.(p.184)
- On June 26, 1935, I came to in the hospital and to say I was discouraged is to put it mildly.(p.184)
- This was around 1935, and it was about this time that I actually started drinking.(p.486)
- During the years 1930 to 1935, due to the Depression and its aftermath, business went from bad to worse.(p.486)
- I don't think I actually started to drink pathologically until approximately 1935.(p.487)
- I think that was basically the thing that started me drinking in 1935.(p.487)

1937

- By late 1937, the number of members having substantial sobriety time behind them was sufficient to convince the membership that a new light had entered the dark world of the alcoholic.(p.xvii)
- On Sunday when I came to, it was a bad, wet, snowy day in February, 1937, and Paul and Doc and a lot of other fellows were in Cleveland on business.(p.207)
- I took my last drink in 1937.(p.260)

(Table 1: Continued)

- After a particularly bad Christmas and New Year's holiday, dad picked me up again early in January, 1937, to go through the usual sobering up routine.(p.289)

1938

- January 8, 1938 -- that was my D-Day; the place, Washington, D.C.(p.238)
- It was also an ending, for never since June 16th, 1938, have I had to walk alone.(p.248)
- The most accurate answer I can give you is this: Fear has never again ruled my life since that day in September, 1938, when I found that a Power greater than myself could not only restore me to sanity but could keep me both sober and sane.(p.285)
- In the summer of 1938, almost a year from the time I made my original contact with Akron, the man for whom I was working and who knew about the program, approached me and asked if I could do anything about one of his salesmen who was drinking very heavily.(p.294)
- In January 1938, I had the opportunity to go to northern Vermont to manage a small daytime radio station that was up against it financially, and was about to fold its antenna.(p.359)
- My salesmanship was still good, for in the fall of 1938 she called me from Salt Lake and finally agreed to take me on for better or for worse.(p.360)

1939

- The first edition appeared in April 1939, and in the following sixteen years, more than 300,000 copies went into circulation.(p.xi)
- The section called "The Doctor's Opinion" has been kept intact, just as it was originally written in 1939 by the late Dr. William D. Silkworth, our Society's great medical benefactor.(p.xi)
- This is the Foreword as it appeared in the first printing of the first edition in 1939.(p.xiii)
- Since the original Foreword to this book was written in 1939, a wholesale miracle has taken place.(p.xv)
- This determination bore fruit in the spring of 1939 by the publication of this volume.(p.xvii)
- In the fall of 1939, Fulton Oursler, then editor of Liberty, printed a piece in his magazine, called "Alcoholics and God."(p.xviii)
- By the end of 1939, it was estimated that 800 alcoholics were on their way to recovery.(p.xviii)
- Written in 1939, when there were few women in A.A., this chapter assumes that the alcoholic in the home is likely to be the husband.(p.104)
- Written in 1939.(p.161)
- Written in 1939.(p.162)
- (1939) The authorities were much concerned.(p.163)
- I went into the hospital in April, 1939.(p.217)
- It was finally decided to undertake the organization of a Cleveland group and toward the end of May, 1939, the first meeting was held in Cleveland in my home.(p.219)
- I found in the fall of 1939, that I was not mentally impaired, so far as trial work was concerned, and thereafter took up where I had left off when I was about forty-five years old.(p.220)
- An active member of A.A. since 1939, I feel myself a useful member of the human race at last.(p.229)
- Written in 1939.(p.235)
- In the spring of 1939, Bill stopped off in Akron on his way to Detroit on business.(p.281)
- In the spring of 1939, the Big Book was printed, and we had two inquiries from the New York office because of a fifteen-minute radio talk that was made.(p.294)
- Immediately on her return we began to have formal meetings once a week, in the autumn of 1939, and we have continued to do this and to expand ever since.(p.295)
- And then, in the spring of 1939, a very remarkable book was rolled off a New York press with the title "Alcoholics Anonymous."(p.307)
- By the latter part of September 1939, we had a nucleus of six and held our first official group meeting.(p.310)

(Table 1: Continued)

1940

- In the spring of 1940, John D. Rockefeller, Jr. gave a dinner for many of his friends to which he invited A.A. members to tell their stories.(p.xviii)
- I still had enough practice to earn a good living if I would only work, so I resolved that in January of 1940 I would launch a patent law firm of my own.(p.220)
- While I went along with all that was done and attended the meetings, I never took an active job of leadership until February 1940.(p.249)
- It was just about this time, in 1940, that we met up with A.A.(p.265)
- In 1940 another good opportunity came up and we moved to Pittsburgh where I was to manage two radio stations under the same ownership.(p.361)
- Actually it had, way back in 1940.(p.469)
- In my screwed up mind I kept thinking I could have gone to A.A. way back there in 1940, and perhaps saved my marriage and home.(p.470)
- A peculiar thing happened in 1940.(p.488)
- After this incident in 1940, I sought some other means of livelihood.(p.489)

1941

- By March 1941, the membership had shot up to 2,000.(p.xviii)
- By the close of 1941, A.A. numbered 8,000 members.(p.xviii)
- This was in 1941.(p.522)

1944

- In the very early spring of 1944, my frustrated wife couldn't take it any longer.(p.362)
- My visits to that sanitarium went on for nearly three years, until in March of 1944, my father died and I was too drunk to attend his funeral.(p.469)
- Finally, however, in November of 1944, at long last I went to A.A.(p.470)
- 1944.(p.571)

1945

- In June, 1945, with another member, I made my first -- and only -- Twelfth Step call on a female alcoholic and a year later I married her.(p.249)
- He gave my husband one and me one about ten-thirty on the eighth day of May in 1941.(p.267)

1946

- This is a condensed version of the original "long form" A.A. Traditions as first printed in 1946.(p.563)
- Dr. W.W. Bauer, broadcasting under the auspices of The American Medical Association in 1946, over the NBC network, said, in part: "Alcoholics Anonymous are no crusaders; not a temperance society.(p.572)

1947

- That was on the 28th of April, 1947.(p.523)

1949

- The American Psychiatric Association requested, in 1949, that a paper be prepared by one of the older members of Alcoholics Anonymous to be read at the Association's annual meeting of that year.(p.572)
- This was done, and the paper was printed in the American Journal of Psychiatry for November, 1949.(p.572)

1950

- He sobered, never to drink again up to the moment of his death in 1950.(p.xvi)
- Though none of these principles had the force of rules or laws, they had become so widely accepted by 1950 that they were confirmed by our first International Conference held at Cleveland.(p.xix)
- To 1950, the year of his death, he carried the A.A. message to more than 5,000 alcoholic men and women, and to all these he gave his medical services without thought of charge.(p.171)

(Table 1: Continued)

1951
- In 1951 the Lasker Award was given Alcoholics Anonymous.(p.573)
- "The American Public Health Association presents a Lasker Group Award for 1951 to Alcoholics Anonymous in recognition of its unique and highly successful approach to that age-old public health and social problem, alcoholism...(p.573)

1955
- The second edition, published in 1955, reached a total of more than 1,150,000 copies.(p.xi)
- Figures given in this foreword describe the Fellowship as it was in 1955.(p.xv)
- Sixteen years have elapsed between our first printing of this book and the presentation in 1955 of our second edition.(p.xv)

1960
- Father Ed, an early and wonderful friend of A.A., died in the spring of 1960.(p.574)

1971
- Bill W., co-founder of A.A., died January 24, 1971.(p.16)

1976
- By March 1976, when this edition went to the printer, the total worldwide membership of Alcoholics Anonymous was conservatively estimated at more than 1,000,000, with almost 28,000 groups meeting in over 90 countries.(p.xxii)

1983
- But a 1983 U.S./Canada membership survey showed about one-fifth of A.A.'s were 30 and under.(p.34)

1985
- In 1985, over 58,500 groups, with A.A. activity in 114 countries.(p.xxii)
- In 1985, almost one-third are women; about one-fifth, 30 and under.(p.xxii)
- In 1985, A.A. is composed of approximately 58,500 groups.(p.16)
- In 1985, there are about 58,500 groups.(p.162)

Table 2: Dates by Month.

January

- Bill W., co-founder of A.A., died January 24, 1971.(p.16)
- I still had enough practice to earn a good living if I would only work, so I resolved that in January of 1940 I would launch a patent law firm of my own.(p.220)
- January 8, 1938 -- that was my D-Day; the place, Washington, D.C.(p.238)
- So I always say that as long as I remember January 8th that is how long I will remain sober.(p.240)
- I had completely forgotten the January 8th when I found the fellowship, and I spent the next four days wandering around New England half drunk, by which I mean I couldn't get drunk and I couldn't get sober.(p.247)
- This was the background that made me willing to listen on January 8th.(p.245)
- And I still say that as long as I remember that January 8th in Washington, that is how long, by the grace of God as I understand Him, I will retain a happy sobriety.(p.250)
- After a particularly bad Christmas and New Year's holiday, dad picked me up again early in January, 1937, to go through the usual sobering up routine.(p.289)
- In January 1938, I had the opportunity to go to northern Vermont to manage a small daytime radio station that was up against it financially, and was about to fold its antenna.(p.359)

February

- On Sunday when I came to, it was a bad, wet, snowy day in February, 1937, and Paul and Doc and a lot of other fellows were in Cleveland on business.(p.207)
- While I went along with all that was done and attended the meetings, I never took an active job of leadership until February 1940.(p.249)
- It was February with snow and ice on the ground and I had a four blocks walk to the nearest cab stand, but I made it.(p.288)

March

- By March 1941, the membership had shot up to 2,000.(p.xviii)
- By March 1976, when this edition went to the printer, the total worldwide membership of Alcoholics Anonymous was conservatively estimated at more than 1,000,000, with almost 28,000 groups meeting in over 90 countries.(p.xxii)
- My visits to that sanitarium went on for nearly three years, until in March of 1944, my father died and I was too drunk to attend his funeral.(p.469)

April

- The first edition appeared in April 1939, and in the following sixteen years, more than 300,000 copies went into circulation.(p.xi)
- I went into the hospital in April, 1939.(p.217)
- That was on the 28th of April, 1947.(p.523)
- Since I joined on that April night, A.A. has done more for me than just stop me from drinking; it has brought me back to life again.(p.524)

May

- It was finally decided to undertake the organization of a Cleveland group and toward the end of May, 1939, the first meeting was held in Cleveland in my home.(p.219)
- He gave my husband one and me one about ten-thirty on the eighth day of May in 1941.(p.267)

June

- The birth of our Society dates from his first day of permanent sobriety, June 10, 1935.(p.v)
- The spark that was to flare into the first A.A. group was struck at Akron, Ohio, in June 1935, during a talk between a New York stockbroker and an Akron physician.(p.xv)
- The checking account melted like snow in June.(p.106)
- That was in June, 1935.(p.158)

(Table 2: Continued)

- The birth of our Society dates from his first day of permanent sobriety, June 10, 1935.(p.171)
- That was June 10, 1935, and that was my last drink.(p.180)
- On June 26, 1935, I came to in the hospital and to say I was discouraged is to put it mildly.(p.184)
- So I rocked along my merry independent way until June, when I went out selling auto polish in New England.(p.247)
- It was also an ending, for never since June 16th, 1938, have I had to walk alone.(p.248)
- In June, 1945, with another member, I made my first -- and only -- Twelfth Step call on a female alcoholic and a year later I married her.(p.249)

July
- I did divorce him in July.(p.386)
- By early July, I had tapered off alcohol completely, and I got off all pills in the ensuing few months.(p.448)
- It started July 23.(p.508)

September
- These vacations became quite something, and he always had two weeks vacation the first two weeks of every September.(p.264)
- The most accurate answer I can give you is this: Fear has never again ruled my life since that day in September, 1938, when I found that a Power greater than myself could not only restore me to sanity but could keep me both sober and sane.(p.285)
- By the latter part of September 1939, we had a nucleus of six and held our first official group meeting.(p.310)
- During this vacation, in the months of September and October, I decided to go on the water wagon.(p.343)
- In September of this same year I went to New York alone.(p.364)

October
- Abruptly in October 1929 hell broke loose on the New York stock exchange.(p.4)
- I got drunk one night in October, went to sleep in the rain and woke up with pneumonia.(p.490)
- It is the last day of the following October, a dark, rainy morning.(p.502)
- On October 28th, I was sent to Sing Sing with a minimum of thirty-three and a half years to serve out of that thirty-five.(p.509)

November
- Near the end of that bleak November, I sat drinking in my kitchen.(p.8)
- My last bout in the Army lasted from November 5th to 11th, 1918.(p.242)
- It was November 11th and bells were ringing and whistles blowing for the real Armistice.(p.242)
- I returned to my home in Lucknow, India, at the end of November last year from a vacation in one of the most famous beauty spots in our country, a mountain resort 6,800 feet up, with a wonderful lake.(p.342)
- We were married in Montreal in November.(p.361)
- Finally, however, in November of 1944, at long last I went to A.A.(p.470)
- The November following, I took a few days off after pay day to celebrate my birthday on the 25th of the month.(p.491)
- I am to go to camp on November 13th.(p.499)
- It is a cold, bleak day in November.(p.502)
- This was done, and the paper was printed in the American Journal of Psychiatry for November, 1949.(p.572)

Table 3: Miscellaneous Dates.

Page Number	Sentence
242	We heard by wireless on the 5th that the Armistice would be signed the next day (this was a premature report) so I had a couple of cognacs to celebrate; then I hopped a truck and went AWOL.
304	I was a product of the post-war prohibition era of the roaring '20's.
491	Anyhow, on the 24th, after drinking all day on the 23rd, I must have decided I wanted to see my wife and have some kind of reconciliation or at least talk with her.
499	The Armistice is signed on the 11th and the draft is called off.
508	When I wended my way home four days later, on the 27th, there was a detective waiting for me.

APPENDIX III

Tables of Numbers

Table 1: Numbers of Quantity

50
- All told, promising beginnings have been made in some 50 foreign countries and U.S. possessions.(p.xv)
- At these informal gatherings one may often see from 50 to 200 persons.(p.16)

90
- By March 1976, when this edition went to the printer, the total worldwide membership of Alcoholics Anonymous was conservatively estimated at more than 1,000,000, with almost 28,000 groups meeting in over 90 countries.(p.xxii)

100
- The membership had then reached about 100 men and women.(p.xvii)

114
- In 1985, over 58,500 groups, with A.A. activity in 114 countries.(p.xxii)
- There is A.A. activity in 114 countries, with an estimated membership of over 1,000,000.(p.162)

130
- Ten days of this treatment the first time knocked me from 200 pounds to 130, and I seldom stayed out of the hole long enough to gain back my weight.(p.460)

200
- At these informal gatherings one may often see from 50 to 200 persons.(p.16)
- Ten days of this treatment the first time knocked me from 200 pounds to 130, and I seldom stayed out of the hole long enough to gain back my weight.(p.460)

800
- This brought a rush of 800 frantic inquiries into the little New York office which meanwhile had been established.(p.xviii)
- By the end of 1939, it was estimated that 800 alcoholics were on their way to recovery.(p.xviii)

1,300
- This man faced the last ditch when his wife's voice from 1,300 miles away sent him to A.A.(p.viii)
- This man faced the last ditch when his wife's voice from 1,300 miles away sent him to A.A.(p.356)
- She said she cut this clipping from the paper at about ten on the same night, and at the same time as I called A.A. in Pittsburgh -- some 1300 miles away.(p.367)

2,000
- By March 1941, the membership had shot up to 2,000.(p.xviii)

5,000
- To 1950, the year of his death, he carried the A.A. message to more than 5,000 alcoholic men and women, and to all these he gave his medical services without thought of charge.(p.171)

6,000
- In that brief space, Alcoholics Anonymous has mushroomed into nearly 6,000 groups whose membership is far above 150,000 recovered alcoholics.(p.xv)

6,800
- I returned to my home in Lucknow, India, at the end of November last year from a vacation in one of the most famous beauty spots in our country, a mountain resort 6,800 feet up, with a wonderful lake.(p. 342)

(Table 1: continued)

8,000
- By the close of 1941, A.A. numbered 8,000 members.(p.xviii)

10,000
- Shortly thereafter, I was selected, with eight other inmates out of the 10,000 in the state's prisons at that time, to attend a school designed to take former "management problems" like me and convert them into paracounselors.(p.462)

28,000
- By March 1976, when this edition went to the printer, the total worldwide membership of Alcoholics Anonymous was conservatively estimated at more than 1,000,000, with almost 28,000 groups meeting in over 90 countries.(p.xxii)

58,500
- In 1985, over 58,500 groups, with A.A. activity in 114 countries.(p.xxii)
- In 1985, A.A. is composed of approximately 58,500 groups.(p.16)
- In 1985, there are about 58,500 groups.(p.162)

150,000
- In that brief space, Alcoholics Anonymous has mushroomed into nearly 6,000 groups whose membership is far above 150,000 recovered alcoholics.(p.xv)

300,000
- The first edition appeared in April 1939, and in the following sixteen years, more than 300,000 copies went into circulation.(p.xi)

1,000,000
- By March 1976, when this edition went to the printer, the total worldwide membership of Alcoholics Anonymous was conservatively estimated at more than 1,000,000, with almost 28,000 groups meeting in over 90 countries.(p.xxii)
- There is A.A. activity in 114 countries, with an estimated membership of over 1,000,000.(p.162)

1,150,000
- The second edition, published in 1955, reached a total of more than 1,150,000 copies.(p.xi)

Table 2: Numbers of Enumeration.

Page Number	Text
59	Here are the steps we took, which are suggested as a program of recovery: 1. We admitted we were powerless over alcohol -- that our lives had become unmanageable. 2. Came to believe that a Power greater than ourselves could restore us to sanity. 3. Made a decision to turn our will and our lives over to the care of God as we understood Him. 4. Made a searching and fearless moral inventory of ourselves. 5. Admitted to God, to ourselves, and to another human being the exact nature of our wrongs. 6. Were entirely ready to have God remove all these defects of character. 7. Humbly asked Him to remove our shortcomings. 8. Made a list of all persons we had harmed, and became willing to make amends to them all. 9. Made direct amends to such people wherever possible, except when to do so would injure them or others. 10. Continued to take personal inventory and when we were wrong promptly admitted it. 11. Sought through prayer and meditation to improve our conscious contact with God as we understood Him, praying only for knowledge of His will for us and the power to carry that out. 12. Having had a spiritual awakening as the result of these steps, we tried to carry this message to alcoholics, and to practice these principles in all our affairs.
181	I do it for four reasons: 1. Sense of duty. 2. It is a pleasure. 3. Because in so doing I am paying my debt to the man who took time to pass it on to me. 4. Because every time I do it I take out a little more insurance for myself against a possible slip.
292	The six steps were: 1. Complete deflation. 2. Dependence and guidance from a Higher Power. 3. Moral inventory. 4. Confession. 5. Restitution. 6. Continued work with other alcoholics.

(Table 2: Continued)

Page Number	Text
398	At age twenty-one, I elisted in the Navy for two reasons: (1) to avoid being drafted into the army, and (2) out of a burst of patriotic fervor inspired by the advent of World War II an as the result of an all-night drinking binge which found me sitting on the doorstep of the Navy recruiting office when the chief petty officer arrived to open for business at nine o'clock Monday morning.
565	Our A.A. experience has taught us that: 1. Each member of Alcoholics Anonymous is but a small part of a great whole. 2. For our group purpose there is but one ultimate authority -- a loving God as He may express Himself in our group conscience. 3. Our membership ought to include all who suffer from alcoholism. 4. With respect to its own affairs, each A.A group should be responsible to no other authority than its own conscience. 5. Each Alcoholics Anonymous group ought to be a spiritual entity having but one primary purpose -- that of carrying its message to the alcoholic who still suffers. 6. Problems of money, property, and authority may easily divert us from our primary spiritual aim. 7. The A.A. groups themselves ought to be fully supported by the voluntary contributions of their own members. 8. Alcoholics Anonymous should remain forever nonprofessional. 9. Each A.A. group needs the least possible organization. 10. No A.A. group or member should ever, in such a way as to implicate A.A., express any opinion on outside controversial issues-- particularly those of politics, alcohol reform, or sectarian religion. 11. Our relations with the general public should be characterized by personal anonymity. 12. And finally, we of Alcoholics Anonymous believe that the principle of anonymity has immense spiritual significance.

Table 3: Numbers as Percentages.

15%
- More than 15% of us are women.(p.xx)

25%
- Of alcoholics who came to A.A. and really tried, 50% got sober at once and remained that way; 25% sobered up after some relapses, and among the remainder, those who stayed on with A.A. showed improvement.(p.xx)

50%
- Of alcoholics who came to A.A. and really tried, 50% got sober at once and remained that way; 25% sobered up after some relapses, and among the remainder, those who stayed on with A.A. showed improvement.(p.xx)
- Any therapeutic or philosophic procedure which can prove a recovery rate of 50% to 60% must merit our consideration."(p.571)

60%
- Any therapeutic or philosophic procedure which can prove a recovery rate of 50% to 60% must merit our consideration."(p.571)

100%
- As to two of you men, whose stories I have heard, there is no doubt in my mind that you were 100% hopeless, apart from divine help.(p.43)

Table 4: Numbers Expressing Geographical Locations.

Page Number	Sentence
121	If there is no Al-Anon listing in your local telephone book, you may obtain further information on Al-Anon Family Groups by writing to its World Service Office: Box 182, Madison Square Station, New York, NY 10159.
164	Address P.O. Box 459, Grand Central Station, New York, NY 10163.
223	That had been in the center of New York, on noisy 42nd Street . . . this was obviously a quiet residential section.
251	Tom Sharkey's brawling bar on 14th Street and the famous wine-room at the back were headquarters for me.
359	I was living in a small room on West 53rd Street right off Fifth Avenue, when I met a young lady who eventually was responsible for altering my entire way of living.
411	I would walk up and down under the 59th Street bridge, trying to get up the nerve to go up there and jump.
492	The one thing I can remember now was that Vi was on the corner of 8th and L, and I remember vividly that she had an envelope in her hand.
572	(This address is now available in pamphlet form at nominal cost through most A.A. groups or from Box 459, Grand Central Station, New York, NY 10163, under the title "Three Talks to Medical Societies by Bill W." -- formerly called "Bill on Alcoholism" and earlier "Alcoholism the Illness.")
575	If you cannot find A.A. in your locality, a letter addressed to Alcoholics Anonymous, Box 459, Grand Central Station, New York, NY 10163, U.S.A., will receive a prompt reply from this world center, referring you to the nearest A.A. group.
575	Should you be the relative or friend of an alcoholic who shows no immediate interest in A.A., it is suggested that you write the Al-Anon Family Groups, Inc., Box 182, Madison Square Station, New York, NY 10159, U.S.A.

Table 5: Numbers as Denominations of Money

$400

- For an estimate of salary from the twenty-one a month to start with, to over $400 per month upon my retirement after twenty years in the Navy, I believe that an average income of $2,000 a year over this period is low, but as I stated earlier, an underestimate is best.(p.300)

$1,000

- Living modestly, my wife and I saved $1,000.(p.2)

$1,175

- The next morning I woke up in jail in Cleveland and the jailor had $1,175 of my money in an envelope.
- (p.196)

$2,000

- For an estimate of salary from the twenty-one a month to start with, to over $400 per month upon my retirement after twenty years in the Navy, I believe that an average income of $2,000 a year over this period is low, but as I stated earlier, an underestimate is best.(p.300)
- Some simple mathematics and more statistics: $2,000 a year for twenty-five years is $50,000, twenty per cent of which is $10,000.(p.399)

$5,000

- At that particular stage, I lost interest in it, sold the option for $5,000 and forgot the whole deal.(p.198)
- Everything in the world a man could possibly want, and I was driving from Akron to Cleveland, having just been to the bank and discovered that I had approximately $5,000.(p.200)

$10,000

- Some simple mathematics and more statistics: $2,000 a year for twenty-five years is $50,000, twenty per cent of which is $10,000.(p.399)

$40,000

- I had bought a piece of ground in Cuyahoga Falls and cut it into lots and had a profit of approximately $40,000 and that was a lot of money in those days.(p.194)

$50,000

- Some simple mathematics and more statistics: $2,000 a year for twenty-five years is $50,000, twenty per cent of which is $10,000.(p.399)

Table 6: Miscellaneous Numbers

Desgnation Numbers

- Pioneer member of Akron's Group **No. 1**, the first A.A. Group in the world.(p.vi)
- An originator of Cleveland's Group **No. 3**, this one fought Prohibition in vain.(p.vii)
- Pioneer member of Akron's Group **No. 1**, the first A.A. group in the world.(p.182)
- An originator of Cleveland's Group **No. 3**, this one fought Prohibition in vain.(p.297)
- The "**12 Traditions**" of Alcoholics Anonymous are, we A.A.'s believe, the best answers that our experience has yet given to those ever urgent questions, "how can A.A. best function?" and, "How can A.A. best stay whole and so survive?"(p.563)
- On the next page, A.A.'s "**12 Traditions**" are seen in their so-called "short form," the form in general use today.(p.563)

Miscellaneous Numbers

- I was staring at an inch of the tape which bore the inscription **XYZ-32**.(p.4)
- It had been **52** that morning.(p.4)
- The third time, after almost five years as an **S.P. 4**, I finally made sergeant.(p.318)

Page Numbers

- This was the substance of A.A.'s Twelve Traditions, which are stated in full on **page 564** of this book.(p.xix)
- A further source of help is noted on **page 121**.(p.104)

Time

- No matter how often I had gone into and come out of alcoholic lows during the day, the pattern bounced me out of bed each night about **2:00 a.m.**, shaking and hurting in the agitation that always follows a drug's sedation.(p.332)
- Instead, I had a **5:00 a.m.** shutoff time.(p.441)

APPENDIX IV

Frequency of Words: Alpha Sort

a	5132
A.A.	531
A.A.'s	25
abandon	5
abandoned	3
aberrations	1
abetted	2
abide	1
abilities	8
ability	18
abjectly	1
ablaze	1
able	102
abnormal	9
aboard	2
about	545
above	28
above-board	1
abroad	1
abruptly	5
absence	3
absent	3
absolute	4
absolutely	20
absorb	5
abstainer	1
abstemious	2
abstinence	5
absurd	5
absurdities	1
abundantly	2
abuse	2
abused	4
abusive	1
abysmal	1
abyss	1
abysses	1
Abyssinian	1
academic	1
academies	1
academy	1
accept	27
acceptable	3
acceptance	13
accepted	23
accepting	10
accepts	2
access	1
accident	1
accidentally	1
accommodate	1
accompanied	5
accompany	2
accomplish	5
accomplished	17
accomplishing	1
accomplishment	3
accomplishments	1
accord	2
accorded	2
according	3
accordingly	1
account	24
accountable	1
accountant	1
accounted	1
accounting	4
accounts	3
accumulate	1
accumulated	2
accumulating	1
accumulation	1
accurate	2
accurately	1
accused	2
accustomed	4
ace	1
ache	3
ached	1
achieve	2
achieved	5
achievement	3
achievements	1
achieving	1
acknowledge	1
acquaintance	10
acquaintances	6
acquainted	3
acquire	5
acquired	18
across	15
act	13
acted	4
action	33
actions	9
active	16
actively	2
activities	15
activity	8
actor	4
acts	1
actual	10
actually	32
acute	6
acutely	2
acuteness	1
ad infinitum	1
ad nauseam	1
adapt	1
add	6
added	11
addict	1
addicted	2
addiction	6
adding	1
addition	1
additional	4
address	5
addressed	4
adds	1
Adeline	1
adepts	1
adequate	2
adherence	1
adherents	1
Adirondacks	1
adjacent	1
adjusted	2
adjustment	2
adjustments	1
administer	1
administers	1
administration	1
administrative	1
admirals	1
admire	1
admired	2
admission	3
admit	25
admits	4
admitted	23
admitting	13
admonish	1
admonition	1
ado	1
adolescent	3
adopt	3
adopted	3
adopts	1
adored	1
adult	5
adultery	1
adulthood	2
advance	2
advanced	8
advancement	1
advancing	2
advantage	10
advantages	3
advent	1
adventure	4
adventures	2
adverse	1
adversity	1
advertised	2
advertisement	2
advertising	5
advice	15
advise	2
advised	7
adviser	1
advocates	1
aerial	1
affair	8
affairs	9
affect	4
affected	9
affecting	1
affection	4
affectionate	1
affections	3
affects	1
affiliate	1
affiliation	3
affiliations	1
affinity	1
affirmation	1
affixed	1
afflicted	5
affliction	2
affluence	1
afford	10
afforded	2
affords	1
afraid	34
afresh	1
African	1
Afro-American	1
after	303
aftermath	2
afternoon	21
afternoons	1
afterward	10
afterwards	5
again	219
against	42
age	44
age-old	3
agencies	4
agency	4
agent	3
agents	2
ages	4
aggregate	1
aggrieved	1
aghast	1
agitated	1
agitation	1
agitator	1
agnostic	8
agnostically	1
agnosticism	1
agnostics	6
ago	50
agonies	1
agonizedly	1
agonizing	2
agony	5
agree	10
agreeably	1
agreed	21
agreeing	1
agreement	1
ah	2
aha	1
ahead	24
aid	9
aided	2
aiding	1
aids	1
ailed	1
ailing	1
ailment	1
ailments	3
ails	1
aim	3
aimlessly	1
ain't	1
air	5
aircraft	1
airing	1
airplane	3
aisle	4
Akron	64
Akron's	2
Al-Anon	10
Alan	1
Alanon	1
alarm	1
alarmed	2
alarming	3
alas	2
Alaska	1
Alateen	1
alcohol	163
alcoholic	383
alcoholic's	6
alcoholics	239
Alcoholics Anonymous	88
alcoholism	118
alcoholism-prone	1
ale	6
alert	4
Alexander	2
Alexander's	1
alibi	1
alibis	1
Alice	1
alien	1
alimony	2
alive	5
alky	1
all	692
all-important	1
all-night	2
Allah	1
allegiances	1
allergic	5
allergy	9
alleviate	2
alley	1
alleys	3
alliances	1
allied	1
allies	1
allotment	1
allow	4
allowance	1
allowed	12
allows	2
alloy	1
alluring	2
alma mater	2
Almighty	1
almost	53
alone	61
aloneness	1
along	63
alongside	1
alpha	1
already	37
Alsace	1
Alsatians	1
also	84
altar	1
alter	1
alteration	1
altered	1
altering	1
alternately	1
alternative	2
alternatives	2
although	27
altogether	6
altruistic	2
always	163
am	141
Amarillo	1
amateur	1
amazed	6
amazing	4
amazingly	2
ambition	6
ambitions	5
ambitious	4
ambulance	4
Amen	1
Amendment	1
amends	12
America	8
American	16
American-sponsored	1
Americana	1
Americans	1
amid	1
among	49
amount	23
amounts	1
amuse	1
amused	1
amusement	1
amusing	3
an	575
analyses	1
analysis	1
analyst	11
analyze	3
analyzed	2
ancient	2
and	4874
anesthetic	1
anesthetize	1
anew	2
angel	1
anger	13
angers	1
angle	6
angling	1
angrily	1
angry	12
anguish	3
animals	1
animated	1
ankles	1
Annabelle	2
annals	1
Anne	14
Anne's	1
Annie	2
Annie's	1

annihilation	1
anniversary	1
announce	2
announced	1
annoy	2
annoyance	1
annoyed	1
annual	2
annually	1
anon	1
anonymity	4
anonymous	93
anonymously	1
another	171
another's	2
answer	72
answered	5
answering	3
answers	8
antagonism	2
ante	1
antenna	1
anti-religious	1
anti-social	1
anticipating	1
anticipation	2
anticipatory	1
antics	1
antipathy	1
antisocial	1
anuder	1
anxieties	1
anxiety	4
anxious	8
any	268
anybody	18
anybody's	1
anyhow	14
anyone	57
anyone's	4
anything	172
anyway	9
anywhere	10
apart	11
apartment	17
apathy	1
apex	2
apiece	1
apologize	3
apologized	1
apology	1
appalling	3
appallingly	1
apparent	9
apparently	7
appeal	6
appealed	1
appealing	1
appeals	1
appear	8
appearance	4
appearances	1
appeared	9
appears	5
appendices	2
appetite	1
applaud	1
applause	2
applecart	1
application	5
applied	8
applies	4
apply	8
applying	1
appointed	3
appointment	4
appointments	1
appraisal	1
appraise	1
appreciate	5
appreciated	3
appreciation	6
appreciative	1
apprehended	1
apprehension	2
apprentice	1
apprenticed	1
apprenticeship	2
approach	29
approached	10
approaches	2
approaching	2
appropriate	1
approval	5
approve	3
approves	1
approximately	6
April	4
apropos	1
apt	1
aptitudes	1
arbiter	1
arch	2
are	580
area	7
areas	1
aren't	6
argue	6
argued	1
argument	7
argumentative	1
arguments	3
arise	7
arises	2
arising	1
Arizona	1
arm	4
armed	2
armies	1
Armistice	5
armor	2
armored	1
arms	6
army	27
arose	3
around	84
arouse	2
aroused	1
arouses	1
arousing	3
arraigned	1
arraignment	1
arrange	5
arranged	2
arrangement	2
arrangements	5
arranging	1
arrears	1
arrest	4
arrested	8
arresting	1
arrestment	3
arrival	3
arrive	2
arrived	23
arrives	1
arriving	2
arrogance	1
arrogant	2
art	6
article	10
articles	2
artificial	1
artist	1
arts	3
as	937
ascertained	1
ascribed	1
ash	1
ashamed	9
ashes	1
ashore	1
Asia	1
aside	9
ask	70
askance	1
asked	78
askew	1
asking	14
asks	3
asleep	5
aspect	4
aspects	1
aspirin	1
assail	1
assault	1
assaulted	2
assert	4
asserting	1
assessment	1
asset	3
assets	3
assigned	2
assignment	1
assigns	1
assist	1
assistance	6
assistant	1
assisted	1
associated	8
associates	9
associating	1
association	9
association's	1
associations	3
assorted	1
assume	4
assumed	3
assuming	3
assumption	2
assumptions	1
assurance	5
assure	3
assured	4
astonished	2
astonishing	1
astonishingly	1
astonishment	1
astounded	1
astray	1
astronomers	1
astronomical	1
asylum	10
asylums	6
asymmetrical	1
at	845
ate	4
atheist	5
atheists	3
athlete	1
athletic	1
athletics	2
Atlanta	1
Atlantic City	2
atmosphere	7
atop	1
attached	1
attachment	1
attack	4
attacked	1
attained	1
attainment	1
attempt	14
attempted	8
attempts	8
attend	17
attendance	3
attendant	3
attended	25
attending	7
attends	1
attention	20
attentions	1
attic	1
attitude	32
attitudes	8
attorney	6
attracted	2
attraction	6
attractive	6
attributes	2
attuned	1
audience	1
auditorium	1
augury	1
aunt	3
aunt's	1
auspices	1
Australia	2
Australian	1
authentication	1
author	5
authorities	4
authority	9
authorized	1
authors	1
auto	2
automatically	2
automobile	7
automobiles	1
automotive	1
autonomous	2
autumn	1
avail	2
available	8
availed	3
avenue	2
avenues	2
average	25
averages	1
aversion	1
avert	1
aviation	1
avid	1
avocation	2
avoid	22
avoidance	1
avoided	8
avoiding	6
avoids	1
await	1
awaiting	1
awaits	1
awake	6
awaken	1
awakened	1
awakening	8
award	3
awarded	1
aware	11
awareness	2
away	126
awe	2
awful	12
awfully	5
awfulness	1
awoke	6
AWOL	1
axes	1
babe	1
babies	1
baby	12
bachelor	2
back	218
backfired	1
background	5
backgrounds	1
backing	2
backs	1
backwards	1
backyard	1
bad	62
bad-intentioned	1
bade	1
badly	20
baffle	1
baffled	4
baffling	7
bag	8
baggage	1
baggy	1
bags	1
bail	2
bailing	1
baker	2
bakery	1
balance	5
balanced	3
balked	1
ball	4
balls	1
balmy	2
Baltimore	3
balustrades	1
band	1
bang	1
banged	1
banished	1
bank	7
bankbook	1
banker	3
banker's	1
banking	1
bankroll	1
bankruptcy	4
banks	2
banner	1
banquet	2
Baptist	1
baptized	1
bar	46
Bar le Duc	1
barbecue	2
barbershop	1
barbiturates	3
bare	4
barely	5
barflies	3
barfly	1
bargain	3
Barleycorn	5
Barleycorn's	1
barman	1
barn	4
barracks	3
barred	1
barrel	2
barrier	2
barriers	2
barroom	5
barrooms	3
bars	25
barstool	1
barstools	1
bartender	5
bartenders	4
base	7
based	9
basement	2
basic	9
basically	4
basis	24
basketball	3
Basle	1
bat	1
bath	2
bathing	1
bathroom	4
bathrooms	1
bathtub	1
battalion	2
battery	1
battle	3
battle-grounds	1
Bauer	1
bay	2
be	1028
beach	1
beaches	1
beam	1
beams	1
bear	9
bearable	1
beard	1
bearing	3
beat	10
beat-up	2
beaten	8
beating	3
beats	1
beautiful	16
beautifully	3
beauty	6
became	136
because	280

become	94
becomes	17
becoming	19
bed	72
bed-time	1
bedevilments	1
bedraggled	1
bedroom	4
beds	3
bedside	3
been	519
beer	61
beers	11
Beery	2
befall	1
befell	2
befogged	1
before	233
beforehand	1
beg	3
began	112
begged	2
begging	1
begin	22
beginner	1
beginning	38
beginnings	1
begins	11
begotten	1
begrudged	1
begs	1
begun	15
behalf	2
behave	5
behaved	4
behavior	16
beheld	1
behind	23
behoove	1
being	158
beings	3
belief	12
beliefs	4
believe	121
believed	20
believes	6
believing	4
belittle	1
bell	3
belladonna	1
Bellaire	3
bellboy	1
belle	2
belligerent	1
bells	1
belong	7
belonged	3
belonging	3
belongs	1
beloved	2
below	2
belt	2
belts	3
bench	1
bend	1
bended	1
bender	9
benders	1
beneath	4
benefactor	1
beneficial	3
benefit	7
benefited	2
benefits	2
benevolent	1
benevolently	1
Benzedrine	2
beset	2
beside	7
besides	12
best	74
bestows	1
bet	6
bets	1
better	112
betting	1
betting-slips	1
between	42
beverage	1
Beverly Hills	1
bewail	1
bewildered	1
bewilderment	2
beyond	18
bias	1
biased	1
Bible	10
bidding	1
big	76
big-shot	1
big-hearted	1
bigger	8
biggest	5
bike	1
bill	6
Bill	44
Bill's	3
billboarded	1
billet	1
billion	1
bills	6
bin	1
bind	1
binds	1
Bing	1
binge	12
binges	7
bingo	2
birds	2
Birmingham	1
birth	4
birthday	7
Bishop	1
bit	31
bite	1
biting	1
bits	2
bitter	10
bitterly	3
bitterly-hated	1
bitterness	4
black	14
blacked	6
blacker	1
blacking	1
blacklisted	1
blackout	11
blackouts	6
blame	12
blamed	3
blameless	1
blaming	2
blank	2
blanket	2
blankets	3
blanks	1
blast	1
blazed	2
bleached	1
bleak	2
bless	5
blessed	3
blessing	5
blessings	5
blew	5
blight	1
blind	7
blindness	1
blinked	1
bliss	1
bloated	2
block	6
blocked	1
blocking	1
blocks	3
blonde	1
blood	9
bloomed	2
blossom	1
blotted	2
blotting	1
blouse	2
blow	7
blowin'	1
blowing	1
blown	1
blue	3
bluntly	1
blurry	1
board	10
boarding	2
boards	2
bob	2
Bob	48
Bob's	3
bodies	10
bodily	5
body	22
bodyguard	2
bogged	1
bohemian	2
Bohemians	1
boiled	2
boils	1
bologna	1
bolsterer	1
bolted	1
bond	2
bondage	3
bone	1
bones	1
bonfire	1
booby-hatch	1
book	112
booked	1
bookies	1
booking	1
bookish	1
bookmaker's	1
books	19
bookstore	2
bookstores	1
boom	2
boomerang	2
boon	1
boost	1
boot	1
booth	3
bootleg	1
bootlegger	4
bootleggers	1
booze	23
boozed	1
Boozeville	1
boozing	1
border	2
bordering	2
bore	4
bored	5
boredom	7
bores	1
boring	6
born	17
borrowed	3
borrowing	1
boss	14
Boston	3
both	71
bother	5
bothered	5
bothering	2
bothers	1
bottle	77
bottles	22
bottom	13
bought	11
bounce	2
bounced	3
bouncing	1
bound	5
bounding	3
bounds	2
bounty	1
bouquet	2
bourbon	2
bout	10
bouts	2
bowl	2
bowling	2
box	8
boxer	1
boy	28
boy-welfare	1
boyfriend	1
boyhood	1
boyish	1
boys	27
boys'	1
bra	1
bracket	1
bracketed	1
brag	2
brain	17
brains	7
brainstorm	1
brakes	1
branch	2
branches	1
brand	5
branded	1
brandishing	1
brandy	8
brat	2
bravery	1
brawl	2
brawling	1
brazen	2
bread	3
breadwinner	1
break	10
breakdown	4
breakfast	5
breaking	4
breaks	4
breath	4
breathing	3
breeze	1
brew	3
brewery	1
brewing	1
brewmeister	1
brewmeisters	1
bricks	1
bride	3
bridge	10
Bridgeport	1
brief	10
briefcase	1
bright	5
brilliant	9
brimming	1
bring	29
bringing	1
brings	6
bristle	1
Britain	1
British	6
British Isles	1
broad	3
broadcast	1
broadcasting	2
broadcasts	1
Broadway	1
broke	25
broken	11
broker	8
brokerage	3
brokers	1
bronzed	1
brood	2
Brooklyn	3
broomstick	1
brother	17
brother-executive	1
brother-in-law	3
brother's	1
Brotherhood	1
brotherly	2
brothers	3
brothers'	2
brought	54
Brown	4
brownstone	1
browsed	1
bruised	1
bruises	2
brushed	2
brushes	1
Bub	1
buck	2
buckle	1
bucks	3
buckwheat	1
Bud	2
Buddhists	1
buddy	1
budget	1
Buffalo	1
buggy	1
build	14
build-up	1
building	7
buildings	1
built	13
bulbs	1
bulk	1
bulky	1
bull	1
bulldog	1
bum	1
bumbling	1
bums	3
bunch	7
bungalows	2
bunk	1
burden	5
burdened	1
burdening	1
burdens	4
bureau	3
burgundy	1
buried	1
burlesque	1
burn	3
burned	2
burning	2
burnings	1
burnt	2
burst	6
bury	1
bus	3
buses	1
business	133
business-getters	1
businessman	1
businessmen	1
busload	1
bust	1
Buster	1
busts	1
busy	14
but	1043
butcher	4
butlers	1
butting	1
buttonholed	1
buy	24
buying	2
by	443
by-gones	2
by-paths	1
by-product	1
cab	6
cabanas	1
cabinet	1
cabins	1
cache	1
cadet	1
cafe	1
cagey	1
cajoling	1
cake	3
cakes	1
calamities	1
calamitous	1

calamity	7
calculate	2
calculated	1
calculating	1
calculation	2
calculations	1
caldron	1
California	1
call	55
called	63
calling	4
callous	1
callowness	1
calls	5
calm	2
calmly	1
camaraderie	1
came	244
camp	5
campaign	3
camps	2
can	401
can't	60
Canada	8
Canadian	3
canal	2
cancer	4
candidate	2
candidly	1
candle	1
candy	2
canned	1
cannot	73
cans	4
canteens	1
cap	1
capability	1
capable	6
capacities	3
capacity	11
capital	2
capitalize	2
capitulated	1
caps	1
captain	2
Captain's	1
car	44
card	5
cards	4
care	42
cared	8
career	26
careers	2
careful	16
carefully	12
careless	3
carelessly	1
carelessness	2
cares	3
caring	2
Carlyle	1
carom	1
carousal	1
carousing	1
carpenter	2
carpenters	1
carpet	3
carried	17
carries	1
carry	27
carrying	6
cars	5
cart	1
cartons	1
case	52
cases	29
cash	4
cashed	1
cashier's	1
cast	8
casting	2
castle	1
castor	1
casual	4
casually	2
casualties	1
cat-and-dog	1
catalyst	1
catapulted	1
catch	3
categories	1
cathedral	3
Catholic	8
Catholicism	1
Catholics	5
caught	14
cause	11
caused	14
causes	4
causing	3
caution	1
cautious	2
ce	1
cease	1
ceased	5
celebrate	4
celebrated	2
celebrations	1
cell	2
cellar	4
cellaret	1
cement	3
cent	10
center	10
centered	2
centers	4
central	6
cents	3
century	4
ceremonies	1
certain	63
certainly	40
certainty	4
certificate	1
cessation	2
chains	2
chair	9
chairman	1
chairs	1
chalet	2
challenge	7
challenges	1
champagne	1
champing	1
Champlain	1
chance	34
chances	12
change	52
changed	32
changes	10
changing	2
channel	1
channels	1
chaos	1
chap	9
Chaplain	1
chapter	24
chapters	5
character	15
characteristic	1
characterized	3
characters	1
charge	8
charged	1
charity	4
Charleston	1
Charlie	7
charm	2
charming	6
charred	2
chart	1
charted	1
chartered	1
Charybdis	1
chaser	2
chasers	2
chasing	3
chastened	1
chat	1
chatter	2
chattered	1
chattering	1
chatting	2
chauffeur	1
cheap	7
cheaper	1
cheapest	1
cheating	1
check	8
checked	4
checking	3
checks	1
checkup	2
cheekbone	1
cheeks	1
cheer	2
cheerfully	3
cheerfulness	1
cheery	1
chemical	2
chemicals	5
chemist	1
chemists	1
cherish	2
cherished	1
chest	1
chests	1
chew	2
Chicago	26
chicanery	1
chicken	1
chief	9
chief's	1
chiefly	1
child	33
childhood	14
childish	4
childishness	1
children	73
children's	1
chilling	1
chills	1
chin	1
China	1
chip	1
chocolate	1
choice	6
choir	2
choked	2
chokes	1
choose	6
chooses	1
choosing	2
chore	1
chose	2
chosen	6
Christ	2
Christ's	1
Christian	8
Christmas	21
Christmastime	1
chronic	9
chronically	1
chronicle	1
chucking	1
chuckle	1
chunks	1
church	47
church-goer	1
churches	4
churchgoing	1
churchman	1
chute	1
cider	3
cigarette	4
cigarettes	2
cinch	1
Cincinnati	1
cipher	1
circle	3
circles	1
circling	1
circuits	1
circulation	1
circumstance	1
circumstances	18
cirrhosis	2
citation	2
cited	1
cities	6
citing	1
citizen	3
citizens	2
citizenship	1
city	44
city-bred	1
civic	3
civil	2
civilian	2
civilization	1
claim	2
claimed	3
claiming	1
clamors	2
clang	1
Clarence	5
claret	1
Clark	2
class	14
classed	1
classes	4
classification	2
classroom	1
clattered	1
claw	1
clean	6
cleaned	1
cleanest	1
cleaning	2
clear	23
clear-cut	3
cleared	4
clearer	3
clearing	1
clearly	7
clears	1
clemency	1
clergy	2
clergyman	4
clergymen	1
clerk	1
Cleveland	20
Cleveland's	1
client	3
clients	3
climb	3
climbed	3
clinch	1
cling	2
clinging	1
clings	1
clinic	3
clipping	4
clock	2
clocks	1
close	17
close-mouthed	1
closed	13
closely	3
closer	6
closest	3
closet	3
closets	1
closing	2
clothed	1
clothes	22
clothing	1
cloud	4
clouds	1
clown	1
clowning	1
clowns	1
club	10
club-man	1
clubroom	1
clubs	11
clumsy	1
clung	1
clusters	1
clutches	1
co-founder	3
co-operation	1
coal	1
coast	1
coat	4
coats	2
coaxing	1
cobwebs	1
cock-sureness	1
cocker	1
cockiness	1
cockpit	1
cocktail	6
cocktails	6
cocky	3
coddle	1
code	2
codeine	1
codes	1
codger	1
coffee	11
cognac	1
cognacs	1
cognizance	1
coherent	1
coin	2
coincided	1
coined	1
Coke	1
cokes	1
cold	19
cold-blooded	1
cold-storage	1
cold-turkey	1
collapse	5
collapsed	5
colleagues	1
collect	1
collecting	3
collection	2
collections	1
collective	1
collectively	1
collectors	2
college	23
colleges	2
Collier	1
collision	1
colony	2
color	4
colored	1
colorful	1
colors	1
Columbus	1
coma	1
combat	1
combating	2
combed	1
combination	6
combined	4
come	149
comes	34
comfort	8
comfortable	3
comfortably	4
comforted	2
comforter	1
comforting	3
comic	1
coming	46
comings	1
command	5
commander	4
commanding	2
commence	6
commenced	12
commences	2
commencing	1
commendable	1
commendation	1
comment	3
comments	1
commercial	2
commission	3
commissioned	2

commit	1
commitment	4
committed	12
committee	7
committees	1
commodities	1
common	27
common-sense	1
commonly	1
commonplace	1
communicate	1
communicating	1
communicative	2
communities	4
community	22
commuting	1
companies	4
companion	1
companions	3
companionship	9
company	33
comparatively	1
compared	2
comparing	1
compassion	1
compassionate	1
compatible	1
compelling	1
compensate	1
compensated	1
compensation	1
compensations	1
competent	4
complain	3
complaining	2
complaints	1
complement	1
complete	30
completed	12
completely	38
complex	1
complexes	1
complexities	1
complicate	1
complicated	3
complication	1
complications	2
compliment	1
composed	4
comprehend	6
comprehensive	1
compromises	1
compulsion	8
compulsive	1
compulsory	1
comrades	1
con	2
conceal	1
concealed	2
concealment	1
concede	5
conceded	3
conceit	2
conceive	2
conceived	1
conceives	1
concentrate	5
concentrated	2
concentration	1
concept	1
conception	13
conceptions	5
concepts	1
concern	8
concerned	21
concerning	5
concerns	1
conclude	3
concluded	5
conclusion	14
conclusions	2
conclusively	1
concrete	2
concrete-and-steel	1
condemn	3
condemnation	1
condensed	1
condition	36
conditioned	3
conditions	16
condoned	1
conduct	10
conducted	1
conference	2
conferences	1
conferring	1
confess	1
confessed	1
confessing	1
confession	3
confidence	23
confident	2
confidential	1
confine	1
confined	5
confinement	2
confining	1
confirm	1
confirmation	1
confirmed	4
confirms	1
conflict	1
conflicts	1
conformity	1
confronted	2
Confucius	1
confuse	1
confused	9
confusing	1
confusion	5
congenial	1
congregation	1
congregations	1
Conn.	1
connected	1
Connecticut	2
connection	4
connections	4
conning	1
conquer	2
conquering	1
conquest	1
cons	1
conscience	8
consciences	1
conscientious	1
conscientiously	1
conscious	11
consciously	1
consciousness	12
consent	2
consented	2
consequences	8
consequent	1
consequently	3
conservative	2
conservatively	1
consider	5
considerable	13
considerably	2
considerate	5
consideration	6
considerations	1
considered	7
considering	1
consigned	1
consist	1
consisted	2
consistent	1
consisting	1
consolation	1
console	1
consoling	1
conspired	1
constant	10
constantly	11
consternation	1
constitutionally	1
constructed	1
construction	1
constructions	1
constructive	6
constructively	1
consult	3
consultation	1
consultations	1
consulted	4
consulting	2
consumed	1
consuming	1
consummation	1
consumption	9
contact	24
contacted	2
contacting	2
contacts	2
contain	1
contained	6
container	2
contains	6
contemplating	2
contemplation	1
contemporaries	1
contempt	9
contemptible	1
content	1
contented	4
contention	2
contentions	1
contentment	3
contents	3
contingent	1
continual	3
continually	3
continuance	1
continue	26
continued	28
continues	9
continuing	2
continuous	4
contract	2
contracted	2
contractors	1
contracts	3
contradict	1
contraption	1
contrary	5
contrast	2
contretemps	1
contribute	3
contributed	2
contributing	1
contribution	1
contributions	5
contributors	1
contrition	1
control	51
controlled	3
controls	1
controversial	2
controversies	1
controversy	3
convalescence	1
convalescing	1
convenience	1
convenient	1
convention	5
conventional	3
conversation	9
conversations	4
convert	2
converted	2
convicted	1
conviction	9
convictions	8
convince	10
convinced	30
convinces	1
convincing	5
conviviality	1
convulsion	1
convulsions	2
cook	4
cooked	1
cookies	1
cooks	1
cooled	1
coon	1
cooperate	6
cooperated	1
cooperates	1
cooperation	4
cop	1
cope	5
copies	2
coping	1
copious	1
cops	7
copy	4
copy-desk	1
cordially	2
cordials	1
core	1
cork	1
corker	1
corn	2
corner	5
cornered	2
corners	2
cornerstone	2
corporation	2
corps	1
corpsman	2
correct	3
correctional	1
corrections	2
corrective	1
correspondence	2
corroding	1
cosmos	1
cost	10
costing	1
costly	1
costs	1
cot	1
cottages	1
cotton	2
couch	1
couches	1
cough	1
coughed	1
could	466
couldn't	133
council	1
councilman	1
counsel	3
counseled	1
counseling	2
counselor	2
count	5
counted	3
countenance	1
counter	1
counteracted	1
counties	2
counting	2
countless	7
countries	5
country	31
country-music	1
counts	1
county	7
couple	52
couples	2
couplet	3
courage	21
courageous	1
course	121
courses	3
court	11
courteous	1
courteously	1
courtroom	1
courts	1
courtship	1
cousin	2
cover	3
covered	13
covering	3
coveted	1
coward	2
cowardly	2
cowboy	1
CPO	1
crack	1
crack-pot	1
crack-up	1
cracked	2
cracker	2
crackers	1
crackpot	1
cracks	1
craftsman	1
crafty	1
cram	1
crankiness	1
cranny	1
crash	1
crashed	1
crave	1
craved	2
craves	1
craving	14
crawl	3
crawled	2
crawling	2
craziest	2
crazy	10
cream	2
create	8
created	6
creates	2
Creation	1
creative	5
creatively	1
creativity	2
Creator	12
creature	1
credit	5
creditably	2
creditor	1
creditors	3
credits	1
creed	2
creeds	1
creep	1
creeping	3
creme de menthe	1
crew	2
cried	8
crime	4
criminal	1
crises	2
crisis	3
criterion	1
critic	2
critical	9
criticism	7
criticize	10
criticized	2
critics	1
crock	1
crockery	1
crocks	1
crook	1
crooked	1
crop	1
Crosby's	1
cross	6
cross-grained	1
crossbones	1
crossed	5
crosses	1
crowd	18
crowded	3
crown	1
crucial	2
crucified	1
crude	1
cruel	2
cruelty	1
crumbling	1
crumpled	1
crusade	1
crusaders	1

crush	2
crushed	1
crushing	1
crutch	4
crux	1
cry	6
crying	4
cryptic	1
cubicle	1
cuffed	1
Cunard	1
cunning	4
cup	4
cupboard	2
cups	5
curative	1
curb	2
cure	17
cure-all	2
cured	4
cures	2
curing	5
curiosity	2
curious	7
curled	1
curls	2
current	2
curse	1
cursed	1
cursing	5
curtail	1
curtain	1
curve	1
cussing	1
custodians	1
custody	1
customary	3
customer	5
customers	9
cut	16
cute	4
cutting	1
Cuyahoga	1
cycle	4
cyclone	1
cynic	1
cynical	2
cynically	1
cynicism	2
Czar	1
D-Day	1
dad	33
dad's	8
Daddy's	1
daily	37
daisies	1
Dallas	1
dam	1
damage	7
damaged	4
damn	3
damned	2
dampen	1
danced	1
dances	5
dancing	1
dandy	2
danger	8
dangerous	8
dangerously	2
dangers	2
Dannemora	1
dare	4
dared	6
dares	1
daring	2
dark	16
darken	1
darkening	1
darkness	1
darn	3
dash	2
date	11
dates	3
daughter	12
daughter's	1
daughters	2
davenport	1
dawn	3
dawned	1
day	285
day-by-day	1
day's	8
daylight	3
days	132
days'	3
daytime	1
daze	1
dazed	2
dazzling	1
deacon	2
dead	17
dead-end	1
deadlock	1
deadly	4
deal	54
dealer	1
dealers	2
dealing	12
deals	1
dealt	1
Dean	1
dear	8
dearer	1
dearly	4
death	41
deathly	2
debacle	1
debate	1
debauch	2
debit	1
debris	2
debt	3
debts	3
debutante	3
decade	1
decades	1
deceit	1
deceiving	1
decency	2
decent	1
decentralized	1
deceptions	1
decide	12
decided	65
decides	2
deciding	1
decimal	1
decipher	1
decision	26
decisions	3
deck	1
declaration	1
declare	1
declared	2
declaring	1
declining	2
decreased	2
decreases	1
dedicated	1
deducted	1
deeds	2
deep	27
deepened	1
deepening	1
deeper	6
deeply	7
defeat	6
defeated	5
defeats	1
defect	2
defectives	1
defects	19
defend	1
defense	6
deferring	1
defiant	5
deficiencies	2
deficiency	3
define	2
definite	12
definitely	10
definition	4
deflate	1
deflation	2
defogged	2
defunct	1
degenerated	1
degradation	1
degrading	1
degree	9
delay	3
delayed	2
delays	1
deliberate	1
deliberately	4
delicate	1
delicatessens	1
delight	1
delighted	1
delightedly	1
delightful	3
delinquencies	1
delirium	7
delivered	1
delivering	1
deluged	1
delusion	2
delve	1
demand	4
demanded	3
demanding	2
demands	6
Demerol	1
democracy	2
democratic	1
demonstrate	4
demonstrated	1
demonstrating	2
demonstration	5
demonstrations	2
demoralization	1
denial	4
denied	1
denizens	1
denomination	6
denominations	1
denounced	1
dental	5
dentist	4
dentist's	1
dentistry	1
deny	1
depart	2
department	11
depend	6
dependable	2
depended	2
dependence	6
dependent	6
depending	6
depends	3
deplored	1
deportment	2
deposit	1
deposits	1
depot	1
depressed	7
depressing	1
depression	17
Depression	17
deprive	1
deprived	2
depth	2
deranged	1
derelictions	1
derided	1
derision	1
derive	1
derived	3
derogatory	1
descended	2
describe	6
described	9
describes	1
describing	5
description	9
desert	2
deserted	3
desertion	1
deserts	1
deserve	3
design	4
designating	1
designed	4
designs	1
desirability	1
desirable	3
desire	44
desired	3
desires	2
desk	11
despair	14
despaired	1
despairing	5
desperate	9
desperately	6
desperation	9
despicable	1
despised	2
despite	9
despondency	1
despondently	1
destination	2
destined	1
destiny	2
destitution	1
destroy	4
destroyed	2
destroyer	1
destroying	1
destroys	1
destruction	5
destructiveness	1
detail	5
detailed	1
details	2
detective	1
detectives	1
deter	2
deteriorated	1
deteriorates	1
deteriorating	1
deterioration	2
determination	5
determine	4
determined	9
deterrent	1
detours	1
detrain	1
Detroit	6
devastating	3
develop	9
developed	11
developing	5
development	7
develops	1
device	1
devil	4
devil-may-care	2
devised	1
devising	1
devote	1
devoted	8
devoting	1
devotion	4
devotional	1
diabetes	2
diagnose	1
diagnosed	1
diagnosis	4
diagnostic	1
diagnostician	1
diary	1
dictates	1
dictation	1
dictionary	1
did	315
didn't	292
die	27
died	25
dies	1
diet	4
dieth	1
diets	1
differ	2
difference	23
differences	2
different	39
differentiate	2
differentiates	1
differently	4
differing	1
difficult	26
difficulties	13
difficulty	12
diffident	1
dig	1
digested	1
dignified	1
dignity	3
digress	1
dilemma	4
diligently	1
dim	1
dime	3
dimension	2
diminish	1
diminishing	1
dimly	1
dingy	1
dining	3
dinner	30
diploma	1
diplomate	1
dipped	1
dire	1
direct	6
directed	1
directing	3
direction	17
directions	6
directly	9
director	6
directories	1
directors	2
directory	4
dirty	7
disadvantage	1
disagree	1
disagreeable	1
disagreement	1
disagrees	1
disappear	6
disappeared	5
disappears	1
disappointed	2
disappointments	4
disaster	6
disastrously	1
discard	4
discarded	2
discharge	5
discharged	12
disciplinary	1
discipline	5
disclose	4
disclosed	1
disclosing	2
disconcerted	1
discontented	1
discord	1
discourage	1
discouraged	4
discouragement	1
discover	7
discovered	28
discoveries	2
discovery	9
discredited	2
discrediting	1
discreet	1
discretion	2
discuss	9
discussed	6

discussing	4
discussion	11
discussions	2
disease	17
diseased	1
disfavor	1
disgrace	6
disgraced	1
disgust	2
disgusted	5
disgusting	1
disgustingly	1
disheartening	1
dishes	7
dishonest	9
dishonesty	3
disillusioned	2
disillusionment	1
disinherited	1
disintegrate	1
disintegrating	1
disintegration	1
dislike	2
disliked	2
dislikes	1
disloyal	1
dismal	2
dismayed	1
dismays	1
dismissed	2
disorders	2
dispatched	1
dispensed	1
dispensing	1
displacements	1
display	1
displayed	2
displays	2
disposal	4
dispose	1
disposed	1
disposition	3
disproportionate	1
dispute	3
disputes	1
disregard	3
disregarded	1
disrupted	1
disrupting	1
dissecting	1
dissensions	1
dissipated	1
dissipation	2
dissolve	2
dissolved	2
distance	7
distances	2
distant	2
distinct	3
distinction	2
distinctions	1
distinctly	1
distinguish	1
distinguished	4
distorted	2
distortion	1
distract	1
distracted	3
distractions	1
distress	3
distressed	1
distressing	1
district	4
distrust	1
disturb	1
disturbances	2
disturbed	8
disturbing	1
ditch	1
dither	1
divan	2
dive	2
divert	2
diverted	2
divided	1
dividend	1
dividends	4
dividing	1
divine	4
division	1
divorce	14
divorced	9
divorcee	1
dizzily	1
dizzy	2
do	502
doc	13
doctor	131
Doctor	6
doctor's	9
doctors	29
doctors'	2
doctrine	1
doctrines	1
dodge	1
dodged	1
does	85
doesn't	26
dog	13
dogged	1
doggerel	1
doing	82
dollar	7
dollars	31
domestic	11
domesticity	1
dominant	1
dominate	1
dominated	3
dominates	1
domination	1
don't	165
done	105
doom	1
doomed	5
door	25
doors	7
doorstep	2
doorway	1
doorways	1
doped	1
Dorothy	3
doses	3
double	2
double-header	2
double-headers	1
doubled	2
doubt	21
doubted	3
doubtful	3
doubting	1
doubtless	1
doubts	1
doughboy	1
doughnuts	2
Dowling	1
down	153
downfall	1
downgrade	1
downs	3
downstairs	4
downtown	4
downward	1
dozen	10
dozens	2
Dr.	49
drab	1
draft	4
drafted	1
drafting	3
draftsman	2
drag	3
dragged	2
dragging	1
drained	1
drama	1
dramatic	1
dramatics	1
dramatizing	1
drank	92
drastic	8
drastically	1
draw	8
drawback	1
drawers	2
drawing	3
drawn	7
dreaded	1
dreadful	3
dream	6
dreamed	5
dreaming	1
dreamless	1
dreams	6
dreamy	1
dreary	2
drenched	1
dress	3
dressed	9
dresser	2
dresses	1
dressing	2
drew	4
dried	2
drift	3
drifted	3
drifting	2
drilled	1
drink	463
drinker	40
drinker's	2
drinkers	26
drinking	550
drinks	68
dripped	1
dripping	1
drive	13
driven	4
driver	5
driver's	3
drivers	1
drives	3
driveway	1
driving	10
drop	9
dropped	5
dropping	1
drops	1
drove	10
drowned	2
drowning	1
drug	8
drug's	1
drugged	1
drugs	6
drugstore	3
drugstore-home	1
drunk	186
drunk-driving	1
drunkalogues	2
drunkard	3
drunkard's	1
drunkards	2
drunken	15
drunkenness	6
drunker	6
drunkest	1
drunks	14
dry	29
dry-cleaning	2
drying	1
drying-out	1
dryness	1
dubious	3
Dublin	4
duck	2
dud	1
due	6
dues	3
dull	5
dulled	1
duly	1
dumb	2
dumped	1
duplex	2
duplicate	1
duplicated	1
DuPont	1
duration	1
during	97
duties	4
duty	8
dwell	3
dwelt	2
dying	5
dynamics	1
each	118
eager	2
eagerly	3
eagerness	1
ear	3
Earle	2
earlier	9
earliest	4
early	46
early-day	1
earmarks	1
earn	5
earned	4
earnest	4
earnestly	6
earnestness	4
earning	4
ears	4
earth	8
ease	13
eased	2
easier	11
easiest	2
easily	11
east	6
Easter	4
eastern	5
easy	34
eat	12
eaten	2
eating	3
eats	1
ebb	1
echoed	1
economic	7
economics	1
Ed	1
edge	1
edgewise	1
edict	1
Edison	1
edited	1
edition	13
editions	2
editor	5
editorially	1
editors	2
Edna	1
educated	3
education	14
educational	4
Edward	1
effect	28
effective	10
effectively	1
effectiveness	3
effects	6
efficiency	1
efficient	2
effort	19
efforts	11
egg	2
egghead	1
eggnog	1
ego	8
ego-centric	1
ego-strength	1
egocentric	1
egocentricity	1
egoism	1
egotism	1
egotistical	1
Egypt	5
Egyptian	1
eight	41
eighteen	23
eighteenth	1
eighth	2
eighty	1
eighty-nine	1
eighty-two	1
Eileen	1
Eire	1
either	36
ejected	1
elapsed	1
elated	1
elation	1
Elba	1
elbow	2
elbows	1
elder	1
elderberry	1
elderly	1
elders	2
elect	1
elected	4
electric	3
electrical	2
electricity	2
electrons	3
element	1
elementary	1
elements	3
elevator	2
eleven	11
eleventh	1
eligible	1
eliminate	3
eliminated	2
elimination	3
Ella	4
Ella's	1
elm	1
else	80
else's	1
elsewhere	1
eluding	1
elusive	1
emanate	1
embarrass	2
embarrassed	1
embarrassment	3
embassies	1
embittered	1
embodied	1
embodies	1
embrace	2
emerge	3
emerged	3
emergencies	1
emergency	2
emerging	3
Emerson	2
emigrated	1
eminently	1
Emma	1
Emmet	1
emotion	1
emotional	16
emotionalism	1
emotionally	1
emotions	12
emphasize	4
emphasized	3
emphasizing	1
emphatic	1
emphatically	3
employ	5
employed	2
employee	6
employee's	2
employees	9
employer	11
employers	6
employing	1
employment	4
employs	1
empties	1

empty	8
emulate	1
enable	4
enabled	4
enables	2
enacted	1
encased	1
enchanted	1
encounter	3
encountered	4
encountering	1
encounters	1
encourage	5
encouraged	6
encouragement	2
encourages	1
end	76
endangered	1
endeavor	2
endeavored	2
endeavoring	2
ended	16
ending	4
endless	6
endlessly	2
endorse	1
endorsement	2
endorsements	1
ends	2
endure	2
endured	3
enduring	2
enemies	3
enemy	2
energetic	1
energies	1
energy	3
enforced	2
engage	4
engaged	3
engagement	1
engagements	2
engendered	2
engine	1
engineering	3
engines	1
England	8
English	2
Englishman	1
engulfed	1
engulfs	1
enhanced	1
enjoy	13
enjoyable	1
enjoyed	17
enjoying	5
enjoyment	2
enjoys	3
enlarge	3
enlarged	2
enlargement	1
enlightened	2
enlightening	1
enlightenment	1
enlist	1
enlisted	3
enormous	1
enough	106
enquire	1
enquiring	1
enrolled	3
ensign	1
ensued	1
ensuing	4
enter	6
entered	19
enterprise	5
enterprises	2
entertain	4
entertained	2
entertaining	1
entertainment	2
enthralled	1
enthusiasm	8
enthusiast	1
enthusiastic	1
enthusiastically	1
enthusiasts	1
entice	1
entire	18
entirely	34
entitled	3
entitling	1
entity	2
entreaties	1
entree	1
entry	1
envelope	2
envelopes	1
environment	12
environmental	1
environs	1
envy	2
Episcopal	2
episode	1
episodes	5
epoch	1
equal	2
equalled	1
equally	3
equipment	2
equipped	2
equity	1
equivalent	1
era	3
eradicated	1
erase	1
errand	2
erratic	3
erroneous	1
errors	1
erstwhile	1
escapade	1
escapades	2
escape	19
escaped	2
escapes	2
escapism	1
escapists	1
escort	2
escorted	2
escorting	1
Eskimo	1
esophageal	2
especially	20
essay	1
essence	1
essential	4
essentially	3
essentials	2
establish	2
established	12
estate	1
Esther	5
estimate	7
estimated	3
estimates	1
estranged	1
eternal	1
Ethel	1
Europe	9
European	1
evade	2
evaded	1
evangelist	1
Evanston	1
Eve	2
even	186
evening	47
evening-up	1
evenings	5
event	7
events	4
eventual	2
eventually	26
ever	125
everlasting	1
every	176
everybody	21
everyday	5
everyone	47
everything	78
everything's	1
everywhere	4
evidence	5
evident	2
evidently	3
evil	2
evils	1
evolutionists	1
evolve	1
ex-alkie	1
ex-doctor	1
ex-husband	1
ex-incorrigible	1
ex-problem	4
ex-wife	1
exact	7
exactly	21
exaggerated	2
exalted	1
exam	2
examination	2
examinations	3
examine	2
examined	2
example	12
examples	1
exams	3
exasperated	1
exceed	1
exceedingly	1
excelled	1
excellent	3
except	46
exception	4
exceptional	3
exceptionally	1
exceptions	7
excerpts	1
excess	2
excessive	6
excessively	1
exchange	2
exchanged	1
exchequers	1
excited	4
excitement	5
exciting	3
exclaimed	1
excluded	1
exclusive	2
excruciating	1
excuse	14
excused	1
excuses	11
executive	4
executives	1
exempt	1
exercise	6
exercised	2
exercising	1
exert	2
exhausted	7
exhaustion	2
exhibit	2
exhibited	2
exhilarating	1
exhilaration	3
exile	1
exist	2
existed	3
existence	20
existing	2
exists	3
exonerating	1
expand	1
expanded	1
expansion	2
expect	6
expectant	1
expectations	8
expected	12
expecting	4
expects	3
expedient	1
expel	2
expelled	1
expenditures	1
expense	8
expenses	4
expensive	2
experience	106
experienced	12
experiences	30
experiencing	1
experiment	8
experimentally	1
experimentation	1
expert	2
expertly	1
explain	15
explained	19
explaining	2
explains	1
explanation	11
explicit	1
explodes	1
exploits	1
explore	1
explosion	1
explosions	1
exposed	2
express	10
expressed	4
expresses	1
expressing	1
expression	2
expressions	4
extend	1
extended	3
extensive	1
extent	12
external	3
extra	5
extra-curricular	1
extract	1
extracted	1
extractions	1
extraordinary	5
extravagant	1
extreme	10
extremely	5
extremes	5
exultantly	1
eye	8
eyes	27
fabric	2
facade	1
face	62
face-to-face	2
faced	11
faces	8
facilitated	1
facilities	4
facility	1
facing	3
fact	75
fact-facing	1
fact-finding	1
faction	1
factor	4
factories	1
factors	1
factory	5
facts	12
faculties	1
faculty	3
faded	2
fail	10
failed	30
failing	1
failings	1
fails	3
failure	19
failures	6
faint	2
fainted	1
faintly	1
fair	13
fair-haired	1
fair-sized	1
fair-weather	1
fairly	18
fairness	1
faith	54
faithful	2
faithfully	4
faiths	2
fake	1
faked	1
fakery	1
fall	23
fallacious	1
fallacy	1
fallen	1
falling	4
falls	4
false	5
faltering	1
fame	2
familiar	9
families	23
family	191
family's	2
famous	8
fanatic	3
fanatical	1
fanatics	1
fancied	3
fancy	1
fanfare	1
fanned	2
fantasized	1
fantasizing	3
fantastic	3
far	72
far-fetched	1
fare	9
fared	1
farm	10
farmer	2
farms	1
farther	1
fascinated	3
fascinates	1
fascinating	2
fascination	1
fashion	4
fashionable	2
fast	18
fast-moving	2
fast-thinking	1
faster	2
fat	2
fatal	7
fatality	1
fatally	2
fate	1
father	99
father-in-law	2
father's	5
fathers	2
fatigue	1
fault	11
fault-finding	1
faults	6
favor	5
favorable	2
favorably	1
favored	1
favorite	3
favorites	1
fear	84
feared	10
fearing	1
fearless	2
fearlessly	2
fearlessness	2
fears	15
fearsome	1
feature	5
featured	1
features	1
February	4

fed	5
Federal	2
fee	4
feeble	2
feel	108
feeling	70
feelings	17
feels	10
fees	7
feet	21
felicitations	1
fell	14
fellow	39
fellow-sufferer	1
fellow-sufferers	1
fellow-workers	1
fellow's	1
fellowman	1
fellows	38
fellowship	41
Fellowship's	1
fellowships	1
felony	3
felt	101
female	2
fence	1
fenced	1
fences	2
fervor	2
festering	1
festivities	1
fetch	1
feted	1
fettered	2
feuds	2
fever	2
fevered	1
feverishly	1
few	164
fewer	3
fictitious	1
fidgets	1
field	9
fields	1
fierce	2
fifteen	25
fifteen-minute	1
fifteen-twenty	1
fifth	9
fifties	1
fiftieth	1
fifty	6
fifty-eight	1
fifty-five	2
fifty-four	1
fifty-three	1
fight	17
fighting	5
fights	4
figure	6
figured	11
figures	3
figuring	1
filching	1
file	1
fill	5
filled	13
filling	1
fills	1
filmed	1
films	2
final	10
finality	1
finally	93
finals	1
finance	6
finances	2
financial	19
financially	10
financing	1
find	152
finding	12
finds	2
fine	31
finer	2
finest	3
finger	2
fingers	1
finish	8
finished	11
finishing	2
finite	1
fire	11
fired	20
fireside	1
Firestone	3
firewater	1
firing	3
firm	14
firmer	1
firmly	4
first	341
first-timers	1
fish	1
fish-wife	1
fishing	1
fist	1
fists	1
fit	11
fits	1
fitted	1
fitting	1
Fitz	2
Fitzgerald	2
Fitzgerald's	2
five	59
five-time	2
five-year-old	1
fives	2
fix	8
fixed	4
fixing	2
flagging	1
flame	1
flames	1
flank	1
flannels	1
flapper	1
flare	1
flare-ups	1
flash	1
flashed	2
flashing	1
flashy	1
flask	4
flat	3
flatly	1
flattered	1
flavor	1
flaw	1
flaws	1
fled	1
fledgling	1
fleeting	1
flesh	1
fleshpots	1
flew	1
flexible	1
flicker	2
flickered	1
flight	8
flights	1
flimsy	1
flippant	1
flipped	1
floated	2
floating	1
flood	1
floods	1
floor	9
floored	1
Florida	9
floundered	1
floundering	1
flour	2
flourishing	1
flow	4
flowed	1
flower	4
flowing	2
flown	1
flows	1
fluently	1
fluff-dry	1
fluid	1
flush	1
fly	5
flying	3
flying-blind	1
focus	11
focused	2
focussed	1
foe	1
fog	5
foggy	1
fold	3
folder	2
folk	4
folks	13
follow	27
follow-through	1
followed	29
follower	1
following	26
follows	4
fond	4
fondle	2
food	7
foods	1
fool	5
fooled	3
fooling	3
foolish	10
foolishly	4
fools	2
foot	9
football	4
foothills	1
footing	2
footsore	1
footsteps	1
for	1530
forbidden	2
forbidding	1
force	7
forced	6
forces	4
forcibly	1
Ford	1
foreboding	2
foregoing	3
foreign	4
foresaw	1
foresee	1
foresight	1
forest	1
forever	15
foreword	6
forfeit	1
forgave	2
forge	1
forged	1
forget	24
forgetfulness	2
forgive	4
forgiven	4
forgiveness	4
forgiving	1
forgot	7
forgotten	12
fork	2
form	21
formal	2
formally	1
formed	6
former	19
formerly	6
forming	2
forms	5
formula	5
forth	6
forthwith	1
fortified	1
fortify	2
fortnight	3
fortnight's	1
fortunate	11
fortunately	5
fortune	4
fortunes	1
forty	9
forty-five	3
forty-four	2
forty-nine	2
forty-one	1
forty-publicist	1
forty-seven	1
forty-six	2
forty-three	3
forty-two	1
forward	8
Fosdick	2
Foster	1
fought	10
found	200
foundation	10
founded	1
founder	1
founding	1
four	74
four-thirty	1
four-time	1
fourteen	4
fourteenth	1
fourth	9
fox	4
fraction	1
fractured	2
frailties	1
frame	4
France	3
Franciscan	1
frank	3
Frank	19
frankly	7
frankness	1
frantic	3
frantically	3
fraternity	7
freaks	1
Fred	5
Fred's	1
free	33
freed	1
freedom	22
freely	9
freights	1
French	1
frequency	2
frequent	9
frequented	1
frequenting	1
frequently	14
fresh	6
fresh-skinned	1
freshman	2
friction	1
Friday	10
Fridays	1
friend	89
friend's	7
friendliness	2
friendly	15
friends	171
friends'	1
friendship	4
friendships	5
fright	2
frightened	10
frightening	3
frightful	2
frightfully	1
fringe	2
fringes	1
fro	1
from	542
front	17
frothy	1
frown	1
frowned	1
frowning	1
froze	2
fruit	1
frustrated	1
frustrating	1
frustration	7
frustrations	2
fulfilled	1
fulfillment	4
full	38
full-blown	2
full-pack	1
full-time	2
fuller	2
fullest	1
fully	23
Fulton	1
fumed	1
fumes	1
fun	16
function	6
functioning	1
functions	1
fund	2
fundamental	1
fundamentally	1
fundamentals	1
funds	8
funeral	3
funerals	2
funniest	1
funny	6
fur	4
furious	2
furnish	1
furnished	1
furniture	3
further	23
furthermore	1
fuss	2
futile	4
futility	7
future	20
futures	1
fuzzy	1
gadget	2
gage	1
gaiety	1
gain	5
gained	9
gains	1
Galileo	1
gallantly	1
galled	2
gallon	4
gallons	1
galore	3
gambler	1
game	13
games	5
gamut	1
gang's	1
gangster's	1
gap	1
garage	6
garages	1
garbage	3
garden	3
gardening	1
garrison	1
gas	2
gasped	1
gastric	2
gate	1
gates	4
gather	2
gathered	5
gathering	5
gatherings	2
gaunt	1
gave	69
gay	9
gayest	1
gaze	2
Gene	1

general	33
generally	3
generalship	1
generated	1
generation	6
generations	1
generous	3
generously	2
Geneva	1
genius	6
gentle	1
gentleman	9
gentleman's	1
gentlemen	1
gently	2
genuine	5
geographical	1
geography	1
George	8
German	4
Germans	1
Germany	6
get	349
get-togethers	1
Gethsemane	1
gets	14
getting	82
ghastly	1
giant	1
gift	4
gifted	1
gifts	3
gigantic	1
giggle	1
gimmick	1
gin	17
ginger	3
gingerly	1
girder	1
girl	38
girl's	2
girls	8
give	85
given	57
gives	9
giving	23
glad	15
gladly	3
glaring	1
glass	18
glasses	7
glassful	1
glassily	1
glassy-eyed	1
glimmer	1
glimpse	1
glittering	2
gloom	1
glorious	1
glory	1
glove	1
glow	5
glowing	1
glued	1
glum	2
gluttonous	1
gnawing	1
go	296
goad	1
goal	3
God	242
God-conscious	1
God-consciousness	3
God-given	1
God-knows-who	1
God-sufficiency	1
God's	27
godly	1
goes	13
going	177
gold	5
golden	2
golf	5
gondola	1
gone	67
goner	1
good	252
good-feeling	1
good-natured	1
goodbye	3
goodness	3
goods	3
goofed	1
goose	1
goose-flesh	1
goose-stepping	1
gorge	1
gossip	2
got	273
Gotham	1
gotten	20
govern	4
governed	2
government	8
governor	2
governors	1
gown	2
grab	1
grace	8
gracious	2
graciously	3
graciousness	1
grade	8
grades	5
gradual	3
gradually	13
graduate	7
graduated	6
graduates	1
graduating	2
graduation	3
grain	2
grammar	2
grand	11
grandchildren	2
grandest	1
grandfather's	1
grandmother	1
grandparents	1
grandparents'	1
grant	3
granted	2
Grapevine	4
graph	1
grasp	1
grasped	1
grasping	1
grateful	18
gratefulness	1
gratified	1
gratify	1
gratitude	6
grave	4
gravely	2
gravitating	1
gravity	1
gray	1
great	152
greater	43
greatest	16
greatly	8
Greek	1
green	4
Greenland	1
Greenwich	1
greeted	1
gremlins	1
Grenadier	1
grew	24
grey	1
grief	3
grievous	1
grim	4
grimy	1
grind	1
grinding	1
grinned	1
grip	4
gripped	3
grips	1
grizzly	1
grocer	1
groceries	2
grocery	2
grog	2
groom	1
groomed	1
groove	1
groped	1
groping	2
grosser	1
grouch	1
ground	11
grounded	2
grounds	2
groundwork	1
group	109
group's	1
groupers	1
groups	36
grovelling	1
grow	23
growing	16
grown	7
grown-up	4
grows	3
growth	17
grudge	1
grudgingly	1
guarantee	1
guaranteed	1
guarantees	1
guard	8
guardhouse	1
guess	15
guessing	1
guest	1
guests	2
guidance	6
guide	5
guided	2
guides	1
guiding	4
guild	1
guilt	10
guilty	4
guise	1
guises	1
gulp	2
gulped	1
gun	1
gunnery	1
gurgles	1
gusto	1
guts	3
gutter	3
guy	15
guzzling	2
gym	1
H	1
ha-ha	1
ha-ha-ha	1
habit	15
habits	8
habitual	3
had	1814
hadn't	40
Hagen	1
hail	2
hail-fellow-well-met	1
hair	7
hair-raising	1
hairdresser	2
haired	2
half	59
half-afraid	1
half-bleached	1
half-truth	1
half-year	1
halfway	3
hall	4
Halloween	1
halves	1
hamburger	1
hamlet	1
hammer	1
hampers	3
Hampshire	1
hand	35
hand-book	1
handed	4
handful	4
handicap	2
handicapped	3
handicaps	1
handiwork	2
handkerchief	1
handle	21
handled	1
handling	3
handmaiden	1
hands	21
handwriting	2
handy	1
hang	9
hanged	1
hanger-on	1
hanging	4
hangout	1
hangover	15
hangovers	8
Hank	4
Hank's	1
happen	23
happened	76
happening	3
happens	9
happier	3
happiest	3
happily	6
happiness	32
happy	77
harbor	2
harboring	1
hard	78
hard-fought-for	1
hard-won	1
harder	9
hardest	2
hardly	20
hardness	1
hardships	1
hardware	1
harm	15
harmed	5
harmful	1
harmless	2
harmonious	3
harmony	1
harness	1
harness-making	1
harping	1
Harry	4
harsh	2
Hartford	2
has	362
hash	1
hasn't	8
haste	2
hastened	1
hastily	1
hasty	1
hat	2
hate	9
hated	13
hater	1
hates	1
hating	1
hatred	3
hats	1
hauled	1
hauling	1
haunted	1
haunting	1
haunts	1
have	1148
haven	1
haven't	29
havens	1
having	96
havoc	1
Hawaii	3
Hawaiian	2
hawk	2
hay	1
haywire	4
hazard	1
haze	1
hazy	3
he	1641
he'd	17
he'll	1
he's	27
head	45
headache	2
headaches	3
headed	8
headings	1
headlong	1
headmaster	2
headquarters	4
heads	5
headstrong	1
headwaiters	1
headway	1
heal	1
healed	2
healer	1
healing	2
health	37
healthy	5
healthy-looking	1
heap	3
heaps	1
hear	24
heard	44
hearing	11
hears	1
hearse	1
heart	32
heartache	2
heartaches	2
heartbreak	2
heartbreaking	4
heartening	1
heartily	1
heartlessness	1
hearts	10
heartsickness	1
heat	1
heated	2
heating	1
heave-ho	1
heaven	5
heavenly	1
heavens	2
heaves	1
heavier	1
heavily	8
heavy	16
Hebrew	1
heck	2
heckled	1
hectic	1
heed	1
heel	2
heels	1
height	1
held	22
hell	16
hellish	1
hells	1
help	174
helped	41
helper	1
helpful	36
helpfulness	4
helping	17
helpless	3
helplessly	3
helps	4
helter-skelter	1
hemorrhage	2
hemorrhages	1
hemorrhaging	1

hence	7
Henri	1
Henrietta	2
Henry	1
her	220
Herbert	1
herd	2
here	115
here's	3
hereafter	2
heresies	1
heritage	1
hero	1
heroes	2
heroic	1
heroics	1
heroin	2
hers	1
herself	2
hesitancy	1
hesitate	3
hesitated	3
hesitation	1
hid	6
hidden	13
hide	11
hideous	1
hiding	5
high	45
high-powered	1
high-stepping	1
highball	2
highballs	1
higher	25
Higher Power	18
highest	3
highflown	1
highlights	1
highly	5
highroad	1
highstrung	1
highway	3
hilarious	4
hilarity	1
Hilda	1
hill	3
hillside	1
hilltop	1
him	522
Himalaya	1
himself	95
Hindus	1
hint	1
hinted	3
hints	1
hip	2
hire	3
hired	2
his	652
historians	1
historic	1
historical	1
histories	2
history	7
hit	27
hitch-hiking	1
hitchhiking	1
Hitler's	1
hitting	3
hobbies	1
hobo	1
hobo's	1
hock	1
hockey	1
hoist	1
hold	44
holder	1
holding	3
holds	2
hole	9
holiday	2
holidays	3
holier	1
holler	1
home	295

home-brewers	1
home-brewing	1
homecoming	1
homeless	2
homelessness	1
homelife	1
homes	19
homesick	1
hometown	2
honest	31
honestly	23
honesty	18
honeymoon	2
Honolulu	1
honor	7
honor-grade	1
honored	1
honors	2
hooch	1
hook	2
hooked	1
hooter	1
hope	66
hope-inspiring	1
hoped	3
hopeful	2
hopefully	2
hopeless	25
hopelessly	2
hopelessness	9
hopes	3
hoping	13
hopped	1
hordes	1
horizon	4
horns	2
horrible	13
horribly	4
horrified	1
horror	2
horrors	3
horse	2
horsemen	1
hosiery	1
hospital	129
hospitality	2
hospitalization	5
hospitalized	6
hospitals	20
host	7
hostility	2
hot	5
hotel	19
hotels	3
hound	1
hour	19
hours	41
house	81
housecleaning	3
household	2
housekeeping	1
houses	6
housewife	2
housewives'	1
Houston	4
how	306
how'd	1
how's	1
Howard	3
however	72
howling	1
howls	1
huddle	1
hue	1
hug	1
huge	4
human	44
humanitarian	2
humanity	1
humanly	2
humans	2
humble	4
humbled	1
humbling	1
humbly	8

humiliated	2
humiliating	3
humiliation	7
humiliations	1
humility	9
humor	3
humorous	1
hump	1
hunch	2
hundred	29
hundreds	13
hundredth	1
hung	5
hung-over	1
hunger	1
hungry	2
hunt	2
hunting	5
hurled	1
hurricane	1
hurried	1
hurry	4
hurt	43
hurting	3
hurts	1
husband	109
husband's	7
husbands	16
husbands'	1
huts	1
Hyde	1
hydrotherapy	1
hymns	1
hypersensitive	2
hypodermic	1
hysterical	3
hysterically	3
hysterics	1
I	7214
I'd	150
I'll	45
I'm	84
I've	51
ice	7
ice-bag	2
iced	1
icy	2
idea	64
ideal	10
idealistic	2
idealists	1
ideals	3
ideas	28
identical	1
identification	2
identified	2
identify	5
identity	1
idle	2
if	581
Ignatia	2
ignorance	5
ignored	2
ignoring	2
ill	22
ill-defined	1
ill-temper	1
illness	27
ills	2
illuminating	2
illusion	1
illusions	1
illustrate	1
illustrates	1
illustration	3
image	5
images	1
imaginable	1
imagination	5
imaginative	1
imagine	9
imagined	5
imbued	2
imitation	1
immature	3

immaturity	2
immediate	5
immediately	26
immense	1
immensely	2
immersed	1
immigrants	1
immoral	1
immortalized	1
immune	1
immunity	1
immutable	1
impact	1
impair	1
impaired	3
impart	1
imparted	1
impartially	1
impasse	2
impatient	2
impeccable	1
impel	1
impending	6
imperative	5
imperious	1
implacably	1
implicate	2
implicit	1
implied	1
import	1
importance	6
important	64
importuned	1
impose	3
imposed	1
impossible	21
impotent	1
impress	4
impressed	13
impressing	1
impression	6
impressionable	1
impressions	1
impressive	3
imprisoned	1
improve	2
improved	1
improvement	2
impulse	3
impunity	1
in	2684
in-laws	1
inability	6
inaccessible	1
inadequacy	4
inadequate	4
inattention	1
Inc.	2
incalculable	1
incapable	2
incapacitated	1
incarcerated	2
incentive	1
incessant	1
incessantly	1
inch	1
incident	5
incidentally	1
incidents	2
inclined	4
include	3
included	2
includes	3
including	10
inclusive	1
income	11
incoming	1
incompatibility	1
incompatible	2
incomplete	1
incomprehensible	2
inconsiderate	4
inconsistencies	1
inconsistency	1
inconsistent	1

incorporated	2
incorrigible	2
increase	10
increased	10
increases	3
increasing	6
increasingly	5
incredible	6
incredibly	2
incurable	2
indebted	1
indebtedness	1
indecision	1
indeed	14
indefinable	1
independent	5
indescribable	1
indescribably	1
indestructible	1
India	3
Indian	10
Indiana	1
Indians	4
indicate	4
indicated	6
indicates	1
indication	4
indications	2
indicted	2
indifference	1
indignant	2
indispensable	3
individual	24
individually	1
individuals	10
indoctrination	1
induced	1
inducement	1
indulge	3
indulged	4
indulgence	1
indulgent	1
indulging	1
industrial	3
industry	1
ineffective	1
inescapable	1
inevitable	8
inevitably	6
inexperienced	1
inexplicable	1
inexplicably	1
infallibility	1
infancy	1
inferior	1
inferiorities	1
inferiority	4
inferno	1
infidelity	1
infinite	4
infinitely	3
inflict	1
influence	6
inform	2
informal	3
informality	1
information	6
informed	3
informing	2
infringement	1
ingenuity	1
ingredient	1
ingredients	1
inherent	1
inherit	1
inheritance	1
inherited	2
inhibitions	1
inhospitable	1
initial	1
initiation	6
inject	1
injecting	1
injection	1
injunction	1

injure	1
injured	2
injuries	1
injurious	1
injury	1
injustice	2
inmate	1
inmates	3
innate	1
inner	14
innermost	1
innocent	5
innumerable	4
inquire	1
inquired	2
inquiries	4
inquiring	1
inquiry	3
insane	13
insanely	4
insanity	19
inscription	1
insecure	2
insecurities	1
insecurity	5
inseparable	1
inside	24
inside-out	1
insidious	2
insidiousness	2
insight	2
insights	1
insincere	1
insinuations	1
insist	4
insisted	6
insistence	1
insistent	1
insists	1
insofar	1
insomnia	3
insouciance	1
inspect	1
inspected	2
inspection	2
inspiration	6
inspirational	1
inspire	1
inspired	6
inspiring	1
instance	6
instances	5
instant	4
instantly	4
instead	44
instilled	2
instinct	5
instincts	1
institute	1
institution	14
institutionalized	1
institutions	9
instruct	1
instruction	1
instructions	4
instructive	1
instrument	3
insufferably	1
insufficient	3
insult	1
insulted	3
insulting	1
insurance	5
insure	3
insurmountable	1
intact	2
intake	3
intangible	2
integral	1
integrity	1
intellect	3
intellect's	1
intellectual	8
intellectually	2
intelligence	8
intelligent	6
intend	6
intense	2
intensely	3
intensified	1
intensive	2
intent	1
intention	7
intentions	6
interchange	1
interest	25
interested	40
interesting	8
interests	5
interfere	7
interfered	3
interference	2
interferes	1
interfering	3
intergroup	3
interior	1
interludes	1
intermediate	1
interminable	2
intermingled	1
internal	3
international	4
interne	2
interneship	2
internship	2
interpersonal	1
interpret	1
interpretation	1
interpreted	1
interrupt	2
interrupted	3
interruptions	2
interval	4
intervals	8
intervening	3
intervention	1
interview	1
interviewed	1
interviews	1
intimacy	2
intimate	6
intimated	1
intimation	1
into	281
intolerable	3
intolerance	9
intolerant	4
intoxicated	7
intoxication	4
intravenous	1
intravenously	1
intricate	1
intrigued	3
intriguing	1
introduce	1
introduced	6
introduction	5
intrude	1
intruded	1
intruders	1
intuitive	2
intuitively	1
invariably	8
invented	1
invention	1
inventions	1
inventiveness	1
inventories	1
inventory	27
inversely	1
invested	1
investigate	2
investigation	4
investigator	2
investment	1
invitation	1
invitations	1
invite	3
invited	14
invites	1
inviting	1
involve	2
involved	13
involves	1
involving	1
inward	4
inwardly	8
iota	1
irate	1
Ireland	2
Irish	2
Irishman	3
irksome	1
iron	2
ironed	1
irony	2
irrational	2
irresistible	2
irresponsibility	2
irresponsible	4
irreversible	1
irritable	2
irritated	4
irritation	3
is	1007
island	2
isn't	25
isolated	1
isolates	2
issue	6
issues	4
it	1826
it'll	3
it's	38
its	72
itching	1
itchy	1
items	3
itself	14
Jack	17
jacket	1
Jackie	7
Jackie's	1
jackpot	1
jackrabbit	1
jag	1
jail	43
jailed	1
jailor	1
jails	12
jam	1
jambs	1
James	5
jams	1
Jane	1
Janey	1
jangle	1
January	9
jargon	1
jay-walking	4
jazz	1
jealous	3
jealousies	2
jealously	1
jealousy	8
Jean	3
Jekyll	1
Jekyll-and-Hyde	1
jeopardize	3
jeopardy	2
jerk	1
jest	1
Jesuits	1
jet	1
Jews	1
Jim	6
Jim's	1
jimmied	1
jinks	1
jitters	11
jittery	5
job	130
jobless	2
jobs	20
Joe	1
jogger	1
John	17
join	31
joined	24
joining	6
joint	7
joints	5
joker	1
jokes	1
jokingly	1
jolt	2
Jones	2
journal	2
journey	8
journeys	2
joy	14
joyfully	1
joykiller	1
joyous	4
joyousness	1
joys	2
Jr.	4
jubilant	1
judge	14
judged	2
judges	1
judging	2
judgment	7
jug	7
jugs	1
juice	1
juke	1
Jules	1
July	3
jumbled	1
jump	7
jumped	4
jumping	1
jumping-off	1
jumpy	1
juncture	1
June	9
Jung	1
jungles	1
junior	8
juniors	1
jury	1
just	245
justifiable	1
justifiably	1
justification	3
justified	3
justify	1
Kaneohe	1
kangaroo	1
Kansas	2
Karen	2
keen	2
keenly	1
keep	81
keeping	10
keeps	8
keg	2
Kenmore	1
Kennedy	1
Kent	1
Kentucky	2
kept	67
kernel	1
key	8
key-tapping	1
keyhole	1
keys	5
keystone	1
kick	3
kicked	6
kicking	1
kicks	1
kid	7
kidded	1
kidding	4
kids	5
kill	13
killed	8
killing	1
killjoy	1
killjoys	1
kills	2
kind	62
kindest	1
kindliness	1
kindly	4
kindness	5
kinds	8
king	5
kingdom	2
kinks	1
kinship	1
Kirby	1
kissed	2
kit	3
kitchen	9
Kitty Hawk	1
knack	2
knees	8
knelt	1
knew	176
knit	1
knitting	1
knock	1
knocked	6
knocks	3
know	279
knowing	24
knowledge	24
known	57
knows	24
Ku Klux Klan	1
lab	2
label	1
labor	8
labored	1
laboriously	1
lack	20
lacking	1
lad	3
Ladd	1
ladder	2
ladies	1
lads	1
lady	11
laid	9
lain	1
lake	3
lakes	1
lambaste	1
lance	1
land	6
landed	15
landing	1
landlord	1
lands	1
Langley's	1
language	8
languages	1
lap	1
lapse	2
lapses	1
large	48
largely	2
larger	5
largest	3
Las Vegas	1
Lasker	4
last	137
lasted	11
lasting	4
latched	1
late	20
lately	1
later	108
latest	3
latitude	1
latter	5
laugh	12
laughed	7
laughing	2
laughter	5
launch	1
launched	2

laundering	1
laundress	1
laundromat	7
laundry	2
laurels	1
law	33
laws	7
lawyer	7
lawyers	1
lay	23
laymen	1
lays	1
lead	6
leader	3
leaders	4
leadership	4
leading	8
leads	6
league	1
leak	1
leaning	3
leanings	1
leap	1
leaped	1
leaps	1
leapt	1
learn	36
learned	49
learning	10
learns	1
least	44
leather	2
leave	34
leaves	3
leaving	18
lecture	8
lectures	1
led	16
ledger	1
left	81
leg	2
leg-work	1
legally	1
legions	1
legislators	1
legitimate	1
legs	4
leisure	1
leisure-world	1
leisurely	1
lemon	1
lend	5
lending	1
length	8
lengths	2
lengthy	2
lenses	1
lent	2
less	39
lessen	3
lessened	1
lesson	8
lessons	1
lest	4
let	108
let's	9
lethargy	1
lets	1
letter	13
letters	8
letting	5
level	12
leveling	1
leveling-off	1
levity	1
liabilities	1
liable	1
liberal	2
liberation	3
liberty	2
librarians	1
license	3
licensed	1
lick	3
licked	10
licking	1
lie	13
lied	2
lies	6
lieutenant	2
life	352
life-and-death	1
life-styles	1
life's	2
lifelong	2
lifesaver	1
lifesaving	1
lifetime	5
lift	4
lifted	8
light	28
lightly	1
lightning	1
lights	5
likable	1
like	250
likeable	1
liked	17
likely	13
likes	13
likewise	1
liking	1
limburger	1
limitation	1
limited	8
limiting	3
limitless	2
line	26
lined	3
liner	1
lines	3
lips	3
liquid	3
liquor	107
list	12
listed	5
listen	15
listened	9
listener	2
listening	7
listing	3
lists	1
lit	1
literally	5
literary	4
literature	11
litigation	2
little	180
live	114
lived	38
livelihood	3
lively	1
liver	5
Liverpool	2
lives	49
living	117
load	2
loaded	2
loading	2
loads	1
loaf	1
loan	1
loaned	2
loath	1
loathe	1
loathed	3
lobby	4
local	18
locality	1
locate	1
located	2
location	1
lock	6
locked	15
locker	3
lockers	2
locking	1
lockups	1
lode	1
logic	1
logical	6
logically	1
lolling	1
lolls	1
London	2
lone	3
loneliness	14
lonely	9
lonesome	2
long	192
long-acting	1
long-time	1
longed	1
longer	49
longest	1
longhand	1
longing	1
longingly	1
longs	1
longshoreman	1
longtime-successful	1
look	56
looked	51
looking	28
looks	6
looming	1
loose	3
loosened	1
lopsided	1
Lord	2
Lord's	4
Los Angeles	2
los Douze Etapes	1
los Doce Pasos	1
lose	23
loser	5
loses	3
losing	5
loss	10
losses	1
lost	84
lot	61
lots	18
loud	3
loudly	1
louse	1
lousy	1
love	77
loved	26
lovely	11
loves	2
loving	15
low	12
lowdown	1
lower	5
lows	1
loyal	2
loyalty	4
lubricant	1
lucid	1
luck	7
luckily	2
Lucknow	1
lucky	10
lucrative	2
lukewarm	1
lull	1
lump	1
lumps	1
lunacy	1
lunar	1
lunch	11
luncheon	3
lunching	1
lure	1
lurking	1
Lusitania	1
lust	1
lustre	1
luxuries	1
luxury	3
lye	1
lying	8
Ma	2
machine	3
machinery	1
mad	14
made	200
made-to-order	1
Madison	2
madly	3
madman	1
madness	1
madonna	1
Mae	1
maelstrom	2
magazine	7
magazines	2
magic	2
magically	1
magnificent	1
magnified	1
magnifying	2
magnitude	1
maid	1
maids	1
mail	7
mailman	1
main	6
Maine	7
mainly	3
mainspring	1
mainstay	1
maintain	16
maintained	2
maintaining	3
maintains	2
maintenance	3
majestic	1
majesty	1
major	5
majored	1
majority	3
make	150
make-believe	1
make-up	2
Maker	3
makes	18
making	52
maladjusted	1
malady	8
malicious	1
Maliseet	1
mallet	1
man	271
man-sized	1
man's	17
manage	10
manageable	1
managed	18
management	7
managements	1
manager	5
managers	2
managership	1
manages	1
managing	2
mangled	1
manhandled	1
Manhattan's	1
manhood	1
manic-depressive	2
manifestation	3
manifestations	2
manifested	2
mankind	4
manner	6
mannered	1
mantel	2
manual	2
manufacture	3
manufacturing	3
manuscript	1
many	282
march	1
March	3
margin	1
marijuana	1
marine	1
marital	4
Maritimes	1
mark	4
marked	3
market	6
markets	1
marriage	26
marriages	1
married	52
marry	4
marshalled	1
martial	2
martini	6
martinis	7
Marty	7
Marty's	1
martyr	5
marvelous	4
marvelously	1
Mary	1
mass	4
master	5
master's	1
mastered	3
masterly	1
mastery	1
match	5
matches	3
mate	1
material	17
materialize	1
materially	2
mates	1
mathematical	1
mathematics	1
matron	1
Matteawan	1
matter	57
mattered	1
matters	20
mattress	4
mature	1
maturity	5
Maud	1
maudlin	2
Max	23
Max's	1
maximum	5
maximum-security	1
may	298
May	2
maybe	36
Mayo	4
mayor	1
me	1530
meager	1
meal	7
meals	3
mean	38
meaning	13
meaningful	3
meaningless	1
meanness	1
means	55
meant	35
meantime	5
meanwhile	6
measles	1
measure	5
measured	2
measures	8
measuring	1
mechanic	2
mechanical	1
mechanics	1
mechanisms	1
media	1
medical	38
medically	4
medication	2
medicinal	3
medicine	25
medicines	1
meditated	1
meditation	8
meet	33

meeting	90
meetings	72
mellow	2
melt	1
melted	2
member	36
members	44
members'	2
membership	18
memberships	1
memories	9
memorize	1
memory	10
men	162
men's	5
menace	3
mend	2
menial	1
mental	53
mental-health	1
mentality	1
mentally	21
mention	6
mentioned	10
mentioning	1
merchant	1
mercifully	2
mere	5
merely	8
merit	1
merriment	2
merry	4
merry-go-round	5
Mersey	1
mess	5
message	17
messages	1
messy	1
met	50
method	6
Methodist	1
methods	6
meticulously	1
metropolitan	1
mettle	1
Mexico	1
mid-week	1
Midas	1
middle	16
middle-of-the-road	1
midget	1
midnight	2
midst	3
midwestern	1
might	138
mighty	4
migrated	1
migrations	1
mike	1
mild	4
mildly	3
mile	2
miles	14
military	3
milk	6
milk-punch	1
milked	1
mill	7
Millay's	2
millenniums	1
milligrams	1
million	6
millionaire	1
millions	4
mills	2
Milwaukee	1
mimic	1
mince	1
mind	109
mind-affecting	1
mind's	2
minded	2
mindedness	2
minds	11
mine	39
mineral	1
mines	1
minimum	4
minister	9
minister's	2
ministers	8
ministration	1
minor	1
minus	2
minute	8
minutes	10
miracle	16
miracles	6
miraculous	3
miraculously	1
mire	1
Miriam	1
mirror	1
mirrored	1
misbegotten	1
miscarriages	1
miscellaneous	1
misdeeds	1
miserable	16
miserably	1
misery	14
misfortune	1
misfortunes	1
misgiving	1
misgivings	1
mishaps	1
misled	1
misplaced	1
miss	10
missed	12
missing	2
mission	2
Mississippi	2
mistake	7
mistaken	2
mistakes	7
mistreated	2
mistress	1
mistrusting	1
misunderstand	1
misunderstanding	5
misunderstands	1
misunderstood	5
misused	1
mix	1
mixed	10
mixed-up	1
mob	1
moccasins	4
mode	1
model	3
moderate	8
moderated	1
moderately	3
moderating	1
moderation	2
modern	4
modest	3
modestly	3
mold	1
molested	1
moll	1
mom	5
moment	22
momentarily	1
momentary	1
moments	13
momentum	1
Mommy	1
monastic	1
Monday	9
Mondays	1
monetary	2
money	99
monkeys	1
monopoly	2
monster	1
monstrous	1
month	33
monthly	2
months	143
Montreal	3
mooching	1
mood	4
moods	1
moon	1
moonlighting	1
moons	2
moonshine	1
mope	1
mops	1
moral	23
moralize	2
morally	3
morals	2
morass	1
morbid	1
more	410
moreover	2
morning	123
morning-after	2
mornings	4
morphine	2
mortal	3
mortar	1
mortgage	3
mortification	1
Moscow	1
Moslems	1
most	156
mostest	1
mostly	5
mother	79
mother-in-law	2
mother's	8
motherhood	1
motherless	2
mothers	3
motion	4
motion-picture-studio	1
motioned	1
motivated	1
motivation	1
motive	4
motives	6
motor	2
motorcycle	1
motto	1
mottoes	1
mount	2
mountain	6
mountains	2
mounted	3
mounting	1
mouth	8
mouths	2
move	9
moved	27
movement	5
moves	2
movie	6
movies	4
moving	3
Mr.	11
Mrs.	4
much	282
mud	1
muddled	1
mugged	1
multiplied	1
multiplies	1
multitude	1
mumbling	1
murder	4
murder	4
murmur	1
muscle	1
museum	1
mushroomed	2
mushrooming	1
mushy	1
music	7
musician	1
musing	1
musket	1
must	149
muster	2
mustn't	1
musty	1
mutual	3
mutually	1
my	2146
myriad	1
myself	278
mysteries	1
mysteriously	1
mystified	2
nadir	1
nag	2
nagged	2
nagging	1
nags	1
Naini Tal	3
naked	1
Nam	2
name	30
named	1
nameless	2
namely	2
names	2
Napoleon	1
naps	1
narcotics	2
narrative	1
narrow	3
nary	1
nasty	1
nation	1
national	8
nationalities	1
nationally	3
nationally-known	1
nations	1
native	4
natural	11
naturally	19
nature	20
natured	1
natures	1
naught	1
naughtier	1
naughty	3
nausea	3
navy	15
NBC	1
ne'er	1
near	24
near-wreck	1
nearby	5
nearer	4
nearest	6
nearing	1
nearly	43
nearness	1
neat	1
neatly	1
necessarily	4
necessary	26
necessitated	3
necessities	1
necessity	13
neck	3
necks	1
need	76
needed	46
needing	1
needle	4
needless	3
needlessly	3
needn't	1
needs	18
neglect	4
neglected	5
neglectful	1
negligible	1
Negro	1
Negroes	2
neighbor	2
neighbor's	1
neighborhood	6
neighboring	1
neighbors	5
neither	27
nerve	2
nerves	7
nervous	13
nervousness	3
nest	1
nest-egg	1
net	1
network	1
neurologist	3
neurosis	2
neurotic	4
neurotics	1
neutrality	1
Nevada City	1
never	340
never-ending	1
nevertheless	13
new	263
New Delhi	2
New England	6
New Orleans	1
New Year	3
New Year's	3
New York	65
new-found	4
newcomer	6
newcomer's	1
newcomers	7
newer	2
newly	1
news	12
news-gathering	1
newsletter	1
newsman	1
newspaper	16
newspaper-man	1
newspapers	3
newsreels	1
Newsweek	1
next	138
nice	16
nicely	1
nicer	1
niceties	1
nickel	1
nickname	1
night	177
night's	2
nightclubs	1
nightly	1
nightmare	7
nightmare-filled	1
nights	14
nights'	1
nil	1
nine	34
nineteen	7
nineteenth	1
ninety	2
ninety-five	1
ninth	1
no	455
No. 1	1
No. 3	1
nobody	19
nobody's	2
nod	1
nodding	1
noise	1
noisy	1
nominal	2
nomination	1
non-alcoholic	1
non-academic	1
non-denominational	1
non-drinking	1
non-existent	1
non-meeting	1
nonalcoholic	5
nonalcoholics	1
nonchalant	1
nondiscriminatory	1

none	21
nonexistent	1
nonprofessional	2
nonsense	1
nonspiritual	1
noon	12
noon-day	1
noonday	1
nor	48
normal	34
normalcy	1
normally	6
north	4
North Carolina	2
northern	1
nose	4
nosebleeds	1
nosey	1
nostalgia	1
nostrils	1
not	885
note	4
noted	1
notes	3
nothing	136
nothingness	1
notice	3
noticeable	1
noticed	11
notices	1
notified	1
notion	4
notorious	2
notoriously	1
notwithstanding	1
nourishment	2
novel	4
novels	1
November	10
now	253
nowadays	3
nowhere	7
nucleus	1
nudged	1
nuisance	2
number	35
numbered	1
numbers	9
numerous	6
nurse	7
nurses	5
nursing	2
nurtured	1
nut	4
nuts	3
NY	4
O	1
O.C.	1
O.K.	1
o'clock	19
Oahu	1
oasis	2
oath	1
oaths	1
oats	1
obesity	1
obey	1
obeyed	1
obituary	1
object	5
objectionable	1
objective	1
objectives	2
objects	2
obligation	6
obligations	1
obligatory	1
obliged	6
oblivion	12
obscure	1
obscured	1
observation	2
observations	2
observe	3
observed	3
observes	1
observing	1
obsession	15
obsessions	1
obstacle	2
obstacles	3
obstinacy	2
obstreperous	1
obtain	4
obtainable	1
obtained	5
obvious	6
obviously	10
occasion	20
occasional	8
occasionally	17
occasions	16
occupation	2
occupations	3
occupied	1
occupy	1
occupying	1
occur	4
occurred	11
occurrence	1
occurrences	4
occurring	2
occurs	1
October	5
odd	2
oddly	4
odds	1
of	3989
off	138
off-again	1
offended	2
offender	1
offending	1
offense	4
offer	16
offered	16
offers	1
offhand	1
office	49
officer	13
officer's	1
officers	1
offices	3
official	1
offset	1
often	94
often-painful	1
oh	16
Ohio	9
oil	10
oil-field	1
oilman	1
okay	4
Oklahoma	1
old	122
old-drunks	1
old-time	1
old-timers	1
older	13
oldest	6
oldsters	1
oldtimer	1
olive	3
Omaha	2
omega	1
ominous	1
omit	1
omitted	2
omnipotence	1
on	937
on-again	1
on-the-job	1
once	131
one	654
one-fourth	1
one-half	1
one-night	3
one-nighter	1
one-nighters	1
one-third	1
one-way	2
one's	7
ones	19
oneself	3
ongoing	1
only	305
onslaught	1
onto	8
open	25
open-mindedness	1
opened	17
opening	3
openly	3
operated	3
operation	2
operations	1
operative	1
operator	1
opined	1
opinion	18
opinions	5
opportunities	4
opportunity	32
oppose	2
opposed	2
opposite	6
optimism	2
option	2
optional	1
optioned	1
or	727
oral	1
orchestra	1
orchid	1
ordained	1
ordeal	2
order	25
ordered	13
orders	4
ordinary	10
organ	2
organically	1
organization	17
organizations	1
organized	3
organizers	1
original	6
originally	2
originated	3
originator	2
orthodox	1
ostracized	1
OTC	1
other	274
other's	3
others	115
others'	2
otherwise	8
ought	44
ounce	4
ounces	1
our	625
ours	8
ourself	1
ourselves	83
Oursler	1
out	523
out-grow	1
outburst	1
outcome	3
outdo	1
outer	1
outfit	4
outfits	1
outgrow	2
outlaw	1
outlet	1
outlets	1
outline	1
outlined	5
outlines	1
outlook	7
output	1
outrageous	1
outright	1
outset	1
outside	34
outsider	2
outsiders	3
outstanding	2
outward	2
outwardly	2
over	246
over-achiever	1
over-all	1
over-anxious	1
over-concentration	1
over-indulged	2
over-powering	1
over-remorseful	1
over-train	1
over-weening	2
overbearing	1
overboard	1
overcast	1
overcoat	2
overcome	14
overcomes	1
overdo	2
overdoing	1
overdose	1
overdue	1
overhauling	1
overindulge	1
overlook	1
overlooked	1
overnight	7
overpowered	1
overpowering	3
overseas	3
oversensitive	1
overshot	1
overtake	1
overtook	1
overwhelmed	2
overwhelming	2
overwork	1
owe	7
owed	1
owes	5
owl	1
own	166
owned	7
owner	3
owners	1
ownership	2
Oxford	3
pace	1
paced	4
pacifist	1
pacify	1
pack	5
packed	6
packet	1
packing	1
padded	1
padding	2
padlock	1
pagan	2
paganistic	1
page	8
pages	7
paid	20
pain	11
painful	9
painfully	5
pains	2
painstaking	1
painstakingly	1
paint	3
painting	2
pair	12
pal	1
palace	2
Palestine	1
pall	1
Palm Springs	1
palms	1
pals	2
pamphlet	2
pamphlets	3
panacea	1
pandemonium	1
panels	1
panic	4
pans	1
pant-leg	1
pants	4
panty-waist	1
paper	14
papers	3
paracounselors	1
parade	1
paradise	1
paradox	1
paradoxically	1
paragraph	1
paraldehyde	4
parallel	1
paralyzed	1
paralyzing	3
paramount	4
pardon	1
pardoned	1
parent	1
parental	3
parents	32
parents'	4
Paris	3
parishioners	1
park	1
parking	1
parlors	1
parole	3
paroled	2
part	95
part-time	3
parted	2
partially	2
participate	1
participation	1
particular	21
particularly	18
particulars	1
parties	21
parting	2
partly	2
partner	7
partners	3
partnership	2
parts	6
party	18
pass	16
passed	30
passengers	2
passes	4
passing	8
passion	2
password	1
past	50
pasture	1
pat	1
Pat	2
patent	8
patents	1
path	9
pathetic	1
pathological	1
pathologically	1
patience	12
patient	20
patient's	2
patiently	1
patients	15
patients'	1
patriotic	2
patriotism	2
patrol	2
patronize	1
patrons	1
pats	1
pattern	29
patterns	1
patting	1
Paul	8

pause	3
paused	1
pauvre	1
pawned	1
pawnshop	1
pay	33
payday	3
paying	6
payment	1
payroll	1
pays	2
peace	28
peaceful	1
peak	2
Pearl Harbor	1
peculiar	3
peculiarly	1
peddling	1
pedestal	2
peeled	1
pen	1
penalty	2
pencil	1
pencils	1
penetrated	1
penitentiaries	1
penknife	1
penniless	1
Pennsylvania	2
penny	1
penology	1
Pensacola	2
pension	1
pensioned	1
penthouses	1
pentothal	1
people	281
people-pleaser	2
people-pleasing	2
people's	2
pep	6
pepper	1
per	14
perceive	2
percent	3
percentage	1
percentages	1
percodan	1
perfect	12
perfection	2
perfectionists	1
perfectly	9
perform	1
performance	5
performances	1
performed	3
performing	2
perhaps	78
peril	1
period	42
periodic	9
periodics	2
periods	15
perish	1
permanent	7
permanently	4
permission	3
permit	3
permitted	6
peroxide	1
perpetually	1
perplexing	1
persevere	1
persevered	1
persist	2
persisted	1
persistence	2
persistent	1
persists	2
person	98
person's	1
personal	54
personalities	4
personality	20
personally	5
personnel	1
persons	16
perspective	3
perspiration	1
persuade	3
persuaded	3
persuader	1
persuading	1
pertaining	2
pertinent	1
perturbed	1
pervade	1
perverse	1
pet	3
petty	3
pew	2
pharmacist	2
pharmacy	2
phase	6
phenobarbital	1
phenomena	1
phenomenon	7
Philadelphia	7
Philander	1
Philippines	1
Philistine	1
philosophic	2
philosophical	1
philosophically	1
philosophies	1
philosophy	10
phobia	1
phobias	2
Phoenix	1
phone	11
phoned	4
phony	4
photo	3
photographer	1
phrase	3
phrases	2
physical	37
physically	20
physician	17
physician's	1
physicians	4
piano	1
pianos	1
pick	8
picked	20
picking	3
picnics	1
picture	22
pictured	1
pictures	5
piddling	1
piece	6
piecemakers	1
pieces	6
pier	1
pig	1
pile	5
piled	2
pill	10
pilled-up	1
pillhead	1
pills	19
pilot	1
pin	1
pinch	1
pine	1
pineapple	1
pineapples	3
pink	2
pint	12
pints	2
pioneer	3
pioneering	3
pioneers	4
pious	1
pit	3
pitcher	1
pitiful	1
pitiless	1
Pittsburgh	8
pity	7
pityingly	1
pizza	1
placard	1
placate	1
place	112
placed	16
places	23
placing	2
plague	2
plagued	3
plain	8
plainly	1
plaintively	1
plan	18
plane	6
planes	1
planned	5
planning	6
plans	9
plant	4
planted	4
plastered	3
platoon	1
Plattsburg	1
plausibility	1
play	21
played	9
players	4
playing	5
plays	1
playwright	1
plea	2
plead	1
pleaded	1
pleasant	10
pleasantly	3
please	12
pleased	9
pleasurable	2
pleasure	13
pleasures	2
pledge	2
pledges	2
plenty	13
plight	3
plowed	1
plucked	1
plug	1
plumber	1
plunge	2
plus	7
pluses	1
plush	2
pneumonia	4
pocket	10
pocketbooks	1
pockets	1
poetry	2
point	73
point-blank	2
pointed	10
pointing	2
pointless	1
points	4
poise	1
poised	1
poison	3
poisoning	1
poke	1
poker	3
poker-straight	1
pokey	1
police	9
policeman	7
policemen	2
policy	4
polish	3
polishing	1
polite	4
politely	1
political	3
politically	1
politicians	1
politics	2
pollens	1
pomp	1
pondered	1
pondering	1
pool	6
pooped	1
poor	23
poorer	1
poorest	1
poorly	2
pop	2
popped	1
popping	1
popular	4
porch	2
port	1
portion	1
portrayed	1
pose	1
posed	1
position	25
positions	5
positive	8
positively	1
possess	1
possessed	5
possesses	3
possession	3
possessions	1
possessive	1
possibilities	2
possible	38
possibly	23
post	10
post-alcoholic	1
post-operative	1
post-war	2
posted	1
postpone	2
postponed	1
postponement	1
pot	1
pot-belly	1
potatoes	2
potent	2
potential	11
Potomac	1
potted	1
pounded	2
pounding	1
pounds	7
pour	4
poured	7
pouring	1
powder	2
power	133
powerful	14
powerless	9
powers	3
practical	8
practically	12
practice	35
practiced	2
practices	1
practicing	5
practised	1
practitioner	1
practitioners	1
prairie	1
praise	4
praised	1
pray	12
prayed	7
prayer	25
prayers	4
praying	4
preached	1
preacher	1
preacher's	2
preachers	1
preaching	2
precarious	1
precede	1
preceded	2
precedence	1
precedes	1
preceding	4
precepts	1
precipitated	1
precipitates	1
precise	4
precisely	2
predicament	2
predicaments	1
predicted	1
predisposed	1
predominant	1
preface	1
prefer	2
preferable	1
preferably	1
preferred	2
prefers	2
pregnant	1
prejudice	15
prejudiced	1
prejudices	2
premature	1
premeditated	1
premeditation	1
preoccupied	1
prepared	6
preparing	2
preposterous	1
prescribed	5
prescribing	1
prescription	6
presence	10
present	24
presentation	2
presented	8
presently	8
presents	4
president	14
presides	2
press	6
pressed	1
pressing	2
pressure	7
pressures	4
prestige	3
presumption	1
pretend	1
pretense	3
pretty	43
prevails	1
prevalent	1
prevent	2
prevented	2
prevents	1
previous	4
previously	1
prey	1
price	7
priceless	1
pricked	1
prickling	1
pride	15
priest	7
priests	3
prim	1
prima donna	1
primarily	3
primary	5
prime	4
primitive	1
prince	2
principal	5
principle	10
principles	39
print	3
printed	6
printer	4
printing	6
prior	10
Priscilla	3
prison	31
prisoner	1
prisoners	2
prisons	1

privacy	1
private	16
privately	2
privilege	7
privileges	3
prize	2
prizes	1
pro	1
probability	1
probable	1
probably	36
probation	2
probed	1
problem	117
problems	79
procedure	7
proceed	6
proceeded	7
proceeding	1
proceeds	3
process	13
processes	1
procession	1
proclaimed	1
procrastination	1
procreation	1
procure	1
procured	1
prodded	1
Prodigal	1
prodigious	1
prodigy	1
produce	7
produced	1
producer	1
produces	3
product	2
production	1
productive	1
productively	1
profession	10
professional	9
professionalism	1
professionally	2
professor	1
proffered	1
profit	7
profited	1
profitably	1
profits	1
profound	6
program	106
program-oriented	1
programing	1
progress	14
progressed	5
progressing	1
progression	1
progressive	3
progressively	5
prohibited	1
prohibition	10
project	4
projection	1
projects	1
prolonged	2
prominent	7
promise	10
promised	15
promises	11
promising	6
promote	1
promoted	2
promotion	7
promotions	1
prompt	1
prompted	1
promptly	5
proms	1
prone	1
pronounce	1
pronounced	3
proof	8
prop	3
propelled	1
propensity	1
proper	11
properly	4
property	11
prophesied	1
proportion	4
proportional	2
proportionately	1
proportions	3
proposal	3
proposals	3
propose	1
proposes	1
proposition	3
propositions	1
prosaic	1
prospect	13
prospective	1
prospector	1
prospects	6
prospered	1
prosperity	2
prosperous	2
protect	6
protected	2
protecting	1
protection	3
protective	1
protege	1
protest	1
Protestant	2
Protestants	1
protested	1
protocol	1
proud	9
prove	15
proved	14
proven	2
proves	3
provide	7
provided	15
Providence	3
providentially	1
provider	1
provides	1
providing	1
provinces	1
proving	3
provocation	4
provoked	1
prowling	1
prudent	2
psalmist	1
pseudo-sophistication	1
psychiatric	10
psychiatrist	32
psychiatrist's	4
psychiatrists	9
psychiatry	7
psychic	3
psycho	5
psychoanalysis	3
psychoanalysts	1
psychological	2
psychologically	1
psychologist	4
psychologists	2
psychology	2
psychopathic	1
psychopaths	1
psychosis	1
psychosomatic	1
psychotherapy	2
pub	1
public	28
publication	4
publications	2
publicist	2
publicity	6
publicly	2
publish	1
published	4
publishing	1
pubs	1
pudding	1
puffs	2
pull	9
pulled	4
pulling	2
pulls	2
pumped	1
pumping	1
punch	1
pupil	1
pupils	1
purchase	2
purchased	2
purchaser	1
pure	4
Puritanical	1
purpose	30
purposefulness	1
purposes	2
purse	3
pursue	3
pursued	2
pushed	7
pushes	1
pushing	2
put	102
puts	2
putting	7
puzzle	1
puzzled	1
puzzling	2
quack	1
Quaker	2
qualification	2
qualified	3
qualifying	1
qualities	5
quality	4
qualms	1
quantities	4
quantity	2
quarrel	4
quarrels	4
quart	8
quarter	3
quarterback	3
quarters	1
quarts	2
queasy	2
Quebec	1
queen	3
queen's	1
queer	2
queerly	1
queried	2
question	26
questionable	2
questionnaire	1
questions	18
quick	11
quicker	1
quickly	13
quickness	1
quicksand	1
quiet	11
quieted	1
quieter	1
quietly	7
quiets	1
quit	54
quite	66
quits	1
quitting	4
quizzically	2
quota	1
quoted	1
rabbi	2
race	8
raced	1
races	3
racial	1
racing	1
racket	3
radical	1
radically	2
radio	12
rage	1
raging	1
railroad	2
railway	1
rain	1
raincoat	1
raining	1
rainstorm	1
rainy	1
raise	6
raised	8
raises	1
Ralph's	1
ramifications	1
ramming	1
ran	22
ranch	1
rancor	2
random	2
rang	4
range	2
ranging	1
rank	1
rant	1
ranting	2
rapid	3
rapidly	11
rare	6
rarely	6
rash	1
rat	1
rate	4
rated	1
rather	49
rational	1
rationalization	1
rationalize	2
rationalizing	2
rationed	1
Ravenna	1
raving	4
ray	1
re-assembled	1
re-create	1
re-emphasize	1
re-entered	1
re-establish	1
re-opened	1
re-organized	1
re-read	1
re-reading	1
reach	10
reached	38
reaches	1
reaching	5
reacquainted	1
react	6
reacted	1
reaction	12
reactions	3
reacts	2
read	63
reader	6
readers	6
readily	6
readiness	3
reading	19
readings	1
readjusted	1
readjustment	2
reads	2
ready	20
real	68
realities	3
reality	14
realization	9
realize	37
realized	42
realizes	1
realizing	8
really	138
realm	4
reap	1
reaped	1
rear	1
rearrangement	1
rearrangements	1
reason	50
reasonable	8
reasonableness	2
reasonably	2
reasoned	4
reasoning	5
reasons	27
reasserted	1
reassure	1
reassured	2
rebel	3
rebelled	3
rebellion	2
rebellious	2
rebels	1
reborn	2
recall	8
recalled	1
recapture	1
recapturing	1
receded	1
receipt	1
receive	7
received	17
receiver	2
receivers	1
receiving	3
recent	1
recently	6
receptions	1
receptive	2
recess	2
recharged	1
recipe	1
recipient	1
recitation	1
reckless	1
recluse	1
recognition	2
recognizable	1
recognize	4
recognized	9
recognizing	1
recoil	1
recollect	1
recollection	7
recollections	1
recommend	2
recommendation	1
recommendations	1
recommended	4
recompense	2
recompensed	1
reconcile	1
reconciled	1
reconciliation	2
reconstruct	1
reconstruction	1
record	9
recording	1
records	1
recount	1
recounts	1
recouped	1
recourse	1
recover	28
recovered	23
recoveries	3
recovering	2
recovers	2
recovery	45
recreational	1
recruit	1
recruiting	1
recruits	2
rectally	1
rectify	1
recuperation	1
red	7
red-eyed	1
red-leather	1
redeeming	1
rediscover	1

redo	1
redouble	1
reduce	1
reduced	5
reed	1
reenlisted	1
refer	2
reference	3
referred	3
referring	2
refers	1
refill	2
reflect	3
reflected	4
reflection	2
reflex	1
reform	4
reformer	2
reformers	2
reforming	1
refrain	1
refreshing	1
refuge	2
refusal	1
refuse	5
refused	9
refusing	1
regain	5
regained	4
regaining	2
regard	5
regarded	3
regarding	1
regardless	4
regards	2
regiment	6
region	1
regional	1
register	1
registered	2
registering	1
regret	3
regrets	1
regular	6
regularity	2
regularly	4
regulate	1
rehabilitation	8
rehearsals	1
reigned	1
reigner	1
reinvestigated	1
reject	1
rejected	3
rejection	3
rejections	1
relapse	6
relapses	1
relate	5
related	5
relating	1
relation	3
relations	18
relationship	14
relationships	4
relative	2
relatively	4
relatives	8
relax	5
relaxation	1
relaxed	1
relaxing	1
release	15
released	11
relegated	1
reliability	1
reliable	1
reliance	3
relied	1
relief	12
relieve	3
relieved	13
relieving	1
religion	21
religions	3
religious	47
relinquished	1
relish	1
relive	1
reluctance	1
reluctant	1
reluctantly	1
rely	5
relying	1
remain	12
remainder	2
remained	13
remaining	4
remains	5
remanded	1
remark	3
remarkable	7
remarkably	1
remarked	4
remarks	2
remarried	5
remedy	12
remember	112
remembered	19
remembering	3
remembers	2
remind	4
reminded	2
reminding	2
reminds	1
remonstrances	1
remorse	16
remorseful	5
remote	2
remove	11
removed	7
removing	1
render	1
rendered	1
rendezvous	1
renewal	2
renewed	1
renewing	2
renews	1
rent	3
rented	2
renting	1
reorganized	2
repair	5
repaired	3
repairs	1
reparation	1
reparations	1
repeal	1
repeat	1
repeated	6
repeatedly	4
repeats	1
repel	1
repetition	2
replaced	6
replayed	1
replenish	1
replied	6
reply	11
report	5
reported	3
reporter	1
reports	1
represent	2
representatives	1
represented	4
represents	1
reprieve	2
reprimanded	1
reproached	1
reproduce	1
reproduced	1
reproved	1
repugnantly	1
repulsive	1
reputation	9
reputations	1
repute	1
reputedly	1
request	3
requested	3
requests	1
require	6
required	4
requirement	3
requirements	2
requires	10
requiring	1
requisite	1
rescue	2
rescued	2
research	3
resemblance	1
resembles	1
resembling	1
resent	2
resented	7
resentful	10
resenting	1
resentment	31
resentments	15
reservation	9
reservations	1
reserve	1
reserved	1
reserves	1
reservoirs	1
residency	1
resident	1
residential	1
resign	2
resignation	2
resigned	2
resist	2
resistance	1
resisted	2
resolutely	2
resolution	5
resolutions	5
resolve	5
resolved	4
resolves	1
resort	4
resorted	1
resorts	1
resource	1
resources	3
respect	28
respectability	4
respectable	3
respected	6
respecter	3
respecting	1
respective	2
respects	6
respond	3
responded	1
response	1
responsibilities	14
responsibility	14
responsible	11
rest	37
restaurant	6
restitution	3
restless	2
restlessness	1
restoration	1
restorative	1
restore	6
restored	6
restrained	1
restraining	3
restraint	5
restraints	3
restricted	1
restrictions	1
result	28
resulted	3
resulting	1
results	14
resume	2
resumed	3
retain	1
retained	3
retaining	1
retaliate	2
retaliation	1
retaliatory	1
retarded	1
retire	3
retired	11
retiree	2
retirees	2
retirement	10
retirement-age	1
retitled	1
retreat	4
retreats	1
retrogression	1
retrogressive	1
return	33
returned	30
returning	6
returns	2
reunion	3
reunited	2
reveal	3
revealed	3
revelation	8
revelations	1
revenge	1
revered	1
reverse	4
revert	1
reverted	2
review	2
reviewed	4
reviewing	3
revised	1
revisions	1
revive	1
revolted	1
revolutionary	3
revolutionized	1
revulsion	2
reward	4
rewarding	1
rewards	2
rewon	1
rewrite	2
rewriting	1
Rhine	1
rhythm	1
ribald	1
ribaldry	1
ribbons	1
rich	6
richer	1
rid	16
riddle	2
ride	4
ridicule	2
ridiculous	2
riding	3
rids	1
right	139
right-about-face	1
righted	1
righteous	2
righteously	1
rightly	4
rights	6
rigorous	2
ring	2
ringing	1
rings	2
rinse	1
riot	1
ripe	1
ripened	1
ripped	1
rise	5
risen	1
rises	1
rising	3
risk	4
risked	1
risks	2
risky	1
Rita	1
rival	3
rivalries	2
river	1
riverbank	1
riverboat	1
roaches	1
road	18
roadhouse	1
roads	1
roadside	1
roadster	1
roam	1
roar	1
roared	1
roaring	4
robbed	1
robbery	1
robe	1
robust	1
rock	1
rocked	1
Rockefeller	2
rocker	1
rocket	1
rocketed	1
rocking	2
rocks	1
rocky	2
rode	2
rods	1
role	2
roll	2
rolled	7
rolling	5
romance	1
romantic	1
roof	3
rooftops	1
room	64
roomed	1
rooming	3
rooms	1
roomy	1
roost	1
root	4
roots	4
rope	2
ropes	1
rose	6
roses	1
rosy	2
Rotary	4
rotating	2
rotten	1
rouge	1
rough	10
roughly	1
round	6
rounded	2
rounds	4
rouse	1
roused	1
route	2
routine	9
routines	1
routing	1
row	11
rowed	1
rubber	9
rubbing	1
rudderless	1
rugged	4
ruin	5
ruined	7
ruinous	1
rule	12
ruled	2
ruler	1
rules	3
ruling	1
rum	2
rummy	3
rumor	1
rumor-mongers	1

run	33
run-around	1
running	17
runs	1
runt	1
ruptured	1
rush	3
rushed	5
rushes	2
Russ	15
rut	1
Ruth	2
ruthless	1
ruthlessly	1
sacks	1
sacred	1
sacrifice	3
sad	7
sadder	1
saddest	1
saddles	1
safe	7
safely	4
safer	1
safety	3
said	334
sail	1
sailed	2
sailor	1
sailors	1
saint	2
saints	1
sake	12
salary	6
sale	2
sales	4
salesman	9
salesmanship	2
salesmen	4
sally	1
salon	1
saloon	4
saloon-keepers	1
saloons	4
Salt Lake	2
Salt Lake City	1
salvaging	2
salvation	4
salve	1
Sam	1
Samaritan	3
Samaritans	1
same	100
sample	1
sampled	1
samples	1
San Antonio	1
San Diego	2
San Francisco	1
sand	1
Sandhurst	1
sandwich	5
sandwiches	1
sane	14
sanely	1
sang	2
sanitarium	12
sanitariums	11
sanity	15
sank	1
sarcasm	2
sarcastic	1
sash	1
sassy	1
sat	29
satisfaction	8
satisfactorily	1
satisfactory	7
satisfied	10
satisfies	1
satisfy	4
satisfying	4
Saturday	21
Saturdays	1
sausage	1
savagely	1
save	16
saved	13
saving	3
saw	75
sawdust	1
say	162
saying	31
says	21
scale	3
scales	2
scandalous	1
Scandinavian	2
scant	1
scarce	3
scarcely	5
scare	3
scared	17
scars	1
scattered	2
scene	4
scenery	1
scenes	4
schedule	2
scheduled	1
schedules	4
scheme	2
schisms	1
schizophrenia	1
scholarship	1
scholarships	1
scholastic	2
scholastically	1
school	113
schooled	1
schooling	1
schoolmaster	1
schoolmate	1
schools	12
science	13
sciences	1
scientific	4
scoff	2
scoffers	1
scold	1
scolded	1
scolding	2
scope	2
score	1
scores	4
scorn	1
scotch	6
Scotland	1
Scott	4
Scranton	1
scrap	2
scrap-heap	1
scrape	1
scrapes	7
scraping	1
scratch	1
scratched	4
scratchiness	1
scratching	1
scrawny	1
screamed	1
screaming	4
screwball	1
screwballs	1
screwed	2
screwy	1
scripts	1
scrub	1
Scylla	1
sea	3
Seabrook's	1
search	7
searched	1
searches	1
searching	4
season	2
seasons	1
seat	2
seated	1
Seattle	1
secluded	2
second	48
second-generation	1
second-hand	1
secondary	3
seconds	2
secret	5
secretary	8
secretive	1
secretly	1
secrets	2
sect	1
sectarian	1
section	7
sections	1
secure	5
secured	3
securing	1
securities	1
security	16
sedately	1
sedation	3
sedative	5
sedatives	6
seduce	1
seduction	1
see	217
seed	2
seeds	2
seeing	17
seek	7
seeking	4
seem	36
seemed	90
seeming	4
seemingly	7
seems	21
seen	48
sees	7
seesaw	1
seething	2
Seine	1
seize	1
seized	2
seizes	1
seldom	19
select	2
selected	3
selecting	2
self	26
self-analysis	1
self-appraisal	3
self-centered	5
self-centeredness	3
self-confidence	2
self-confident	1
self-conscious	3
self-consciousness	1
self-contempt	1
self-control	2
self-debasement	1
self-deception	2
self-delusion	1
self-destruction	2
self-discipline	1
self-esteem	8
self-evident	1
self-help	1
self-imposed	1
self-induced	1
self-insurance	2
self-interest	2
self-justification	1
self-knowledge	4
self-loathing	1
self-pity	26
self-pitying	1
self-possessed	1
self-propulsion	1
self-punishing	1
self-reliance	3
self-reproach	1
self-respect	6
self-revealing	1
self-righteous	1
self-sacrifice	1
self-sacrificing	2
self-searching	1
self-seeker	1
self-seeking	4
self-sufficient	3
self-sufficiency	1
self-supporting	1
self-will	10
selfish	16
selfishly	1
selfishness	7
sell	7
selling	11
selves	3
semblance	2
semi-blackouts	1
semi-coma	1
semi-hermit	1
semi-prostitution	1
send	18
sending	4
senior	7
senior-citizen	2
sensation	2
sensational	1
sense	60
sensed	5
senseless	1
senses	3
sensible	7
sensitive	3
sensitiveness	1
sensitivity	1
sent	41
sentence	10
sentences	2
sentient	1
sentiment	2
sentimental	1
sentimentality	1
separate	4
separated	7
separately	3
separation	3
September	5
serene	1
serenity	24
sergeant	4
sergeants	1
series	5
serious	37
seriously	7
seriousness	1
sermon	4
servant	1
servants	3
serve	15
served	10
service	41
services	9
servile	1
serving	5
session	2
sessions	1
set	51
set-up	3
setback	1
sets	2
setting	3
settle	4
settled	9
seven	35
seventeen	9
seventeenth	1
seventh	1
seventieth	1
seventy	2
several	56
severe	4
severely	2
sex	24
sexually	1
sexy	1
shackled	1
shackles	4
shadow	3
shadowy	1
shake	3
shaken	5
shakes	4
Shakespeare	5
shaking	7
shaky	4
shall	36
shambles	2
shame	9
shamed	1
shameful	1
Shane	1
shape	10
shapeless	1
share	5
shared	4
sharing	9
Sharkey's	2
sharp	1
shattering	4
shave	3
Shaw	1
she	328
she'd	4
she's	6
shed	1
shedding	1
sheer	3
sheet	1
shelf	2
shelter	4
sheltered	1
shelves	1
sheriff	3
sheriffs	1
sherry	3
shield	3
shielded	1
shifted	1
shine	1
shins	1
ship	5
ship's	1
shipped	6
shipping	1
shipwreck	1
shirt	2
shirts	3
shiver	1
shivered	1
shivering	2
shock	5
shocked	6
shocking	1
shockingly	1
shoes	9
shone	1
shook	4
shoot	2
shooting	2
shop	9
shopkeeper	1
shops	1
shore	4
short	42
short-acting	1
short-lived	1
short-sticking	1
shortcomings	4
shortcuts	1
shorter	4
shortest	1
shortly	12
shortness	1
shorts	1
shot	19
shotgun	1
shots	7
should	184
shoulder	5
shoulders	5
shouldn't	9

shout	1
shouted	1
shouting	2
shouts	1
show	48
showed	14
showing	11
shown	15
shows	12
shredding	1
shrewd	1
shrieks	1
shrimp	1
shrink	2
shrouded	1
shrubbery	1
shrunk	1
shucks	1
shuddering	1
shuffling	1
shun	1
shut	13
shutoff	1
shuts	1
shutter	1
shy	10
shying	1
shyness	1
sick	65
sickened	3
sickening	1
sicker	4
sickest	1
sickness	7
side	29
sidecar	1
sides	3
sidestepped	1
sighing	1
sighs	1
sight	5
sign	11
signed	5
significance	3
significant	3
signify	1
signing	1
signs	2
silences	1
silent	1
Silkworth	4
Silkworth's	2
sillier	1
silly	3
silverware	1
similar	2
similarly	1
simple	50
simpler	4
simplified	2
simply	30
simulated	1
simultaneously	1
since	91
sincere	12
sincerely	6
sincerity	6
sinecure	1
sinful	1
sing	6
singers	1
singing	4
single	10
singly	1
sinister	1
sink	3
sinking	2
sins	4
siphoning	1
sipped	1
sissies	1
sissy	2
sister	13
sister-in-law	2
sister's	2
sisters	4
sit	18
sitting	14
situated	2
situation	33
situations	6
six	67
six-step	1
sixteen	17
sixteen-pound	1
sixth	3
sixty	6
sixty-eight	1
sixty-four	1
sixty-six	1
size	2
skate	1
skeletons	2
skeptic	2
skeptical	3
skeptically	1
skepticism	2
sketch	2
ski	2
ski-jump	1
skid	7
skid-row	3
skidded	1
skids	2
skier	1
skilled	2
skills	1
skimped	1
skin	3
skinny	3
skip	2
skipped	1
skipping	2
skirt	1
skivvies	1
skull	2
skunk	1
sky	4
skyline	1
slackened	1
slacks	3
slam	1
slammed	2
slander	1
slash	1
slashing	1
sled	1
sledgehammer	1
sleep	33
sleeping	5
sleeplessness	1
slender	3
slept	7
slick	2
slicker	1
slide	1
slight	3
slightest	5
slighting	1
slightly	2
slinging	1
slip	10
slip-locked	1
slipped	2
slippers	1
slips	2
slogan	1
slogans	1
slogging	1
slow	12
slowest	1
slowing	1
slowly	12
slumped	1
slush	1
sly	1
slyly	1
smack	1
smacked	2
small	50
smart	5
smarter	1
smartest	1
smarts	1
smash	3
smash-up	1
smashed	7
smashups	1
smell	3
smelled	3
smile	4
smiled	1
smilingly	1
Smith	1
smoke	4
smoke-filled	1
smoked	3
smoker	1
smokes	1
smoking	1
smoldering	1
smoother	1
smote	1
smuggle	2
smuggled	1
smuggling	3
snag	1
snags	1
snap	2
snapped	1
snare	1
snatching	1
sneak	2
sneaked	1
sneaking	4
sneaky-drinking	1
sneerer	1
snickered	1
sniffing	1
snoops	1
snooze	1
snorts	1
snow	3
snowballed	1
snowing	1
snowy	1
snubbed	1
snuffed	1
so	631
so-called	10
soaking	1
soap	1
sober	137
sobered	6
soberest-seeming	1
sobering	5
soberly	1
sobriety	69
sobriety-tension	1
sociability	1
social	37
socially	11
societies	10
society	26
society's	2
sociologists	1
soda	1
sodas	1
sodden	1
soft	3
softer	2
soil	2
soiled	1
sojourn	1
solace	1
sold	22
soldier	3
soldiering	1
sole	3
solely	3
solemn	5
solicitation	1
soliciting	1
solicitor	1
solid	4
solitary	7
solution	23
solve	14
solved	8
solves	1
solving	5
some	356
somebody	12
somebody's	1
someday	3
somehow	25
someone	45
someone's	2
something	152
something's	1
somethingness	1
sometime	2
sometimes	83
somewhat	13
somewhere	15
son	19
son-in-law	2
son's	3
song	2
songs	2
sons	4
soon	91
sooner	5
sophomore	2
sordid	3
sore	3
sorrows	2
sorry	21
sort	32
sorts	13
SOS	1
sot	1
sots	1
sought	11
soul	8
souls	1
sound	12
sounded	1
soundly	1
soundness	1
sounds	2
source	4
souses	1
south	9
South Africa	1
South America	1
southern	4
southerner's	1
sowing	1
space	5
spaced	2
spacing	1
span	1
spaniel	1
spare	6
spared	1
spark	1
sparkle	1
spasm	1
spasmodic	1
speak	13
speak-easy	1
speakeasies	1
speakeasy	2
speaker	2
speaking	10
speaks	3
spearheads	1
special	15
specialist	4
specialized	2
specializing	1
specialty	3
specific	3
specifically	2
specimen	1
speck	1
spectacle	1
spectacular	2
spectres	1
speculation	2
speech	1
speeches	2
speed	4
speeding	1
speedy	1
spell	6
spelled	4
spells	4
Spencer	1
spend	12
spending	4
spends	3
spent	55
sphere	1
spheres	1
spike	1
spill	2
spinal	1
spine	1
spineless	1
spiral	1
spirit	28
spirits	6
spiritual	150
spirituality	4
spiritually	7
spiritually-minded	1
spite	12
splendid	2
splinters	1
split	3
splitting	1
spoil	5
spoiled	3
spoke	11
spoken	2
sponsor	17
sponsored	1
sponsors	2
sponsorship	1
sporting	1
sports	2
spot	12
spots	6
spotted	1
spouse	1
spout	1
spouting	1
spray	1
spread	2
spreads	1
spree	14
sprees	8
spring	12
springs	2
sprinkled	1
sprinkling	1
sprout	1
sprung	3
spurs	1
squad	1
squander	2
square	8
squarely	4
squawk	1
squeezed	1
squirt	1
St. Helena	1
St. Petersburg	1
St. Thomas	3
St. Vincent	1
stabbed	1
stability	3
stable	2
stables	1
staff	4
stage	13
stages	5
staggered	4
stairs	4
stake	3
stakes	1
stand	25
standard	4

standards	2
standing	11
standpoint	6
stands	6
star	6
stare	1
stared	2
staring	2
stark	2
starlit	1
starry-eyed	1
stars	2
start	50
started	109
starting	9
startled	4
starts	1
starving	1
state	38
state-wide	1
state's	1
stated	5
statement	14
states	11
statesman	1
stating	1
station	17
stations	4
statistic	1
statistics	4
stature	1
status	4
stay	71
stayed	37
staying	13
stays	2
steadfastly	1
steadily	3
steady	8
steal	3
stealing	4
steel	8
steer	1
steerage	1
stem	1
step	51
stepdaughter	1
stepped	8
stepping	1
steps	47
sterility	1
stern	1
stick	9
sticking	3
stickler	1
sticks	1
stiff	1
stiffs	1
stigma	2
still	157
stilled	1
stimulants	1
stimulating	2
stimulus	2
stinker	1
stint	1
stints	1
stipulation	1
stirred	1
stirring	1
stirs	1
stitches	1
stock	7
stock-in-trade	1
stockbroker	1
stocked	1
stocking	2
stockings	2
stocks	2
stole	5
stolen	3
stomach	10
stomach-pumped	1
stone	3
stones	1
stood	23
stop	119
stopped	34
stopping	3
store	11
storeroom	1
stores	4
stories	36
storm	1
story	61
Stouffer	1
stove	1
straggle	1
straight	13
straighten	7
straightened	7
straightway	1
strain	3
strained	2
straining	1
straitjacket	1
strange	23
strangely	6
stranger	5
strangers	10
strap	1
strapped	3
straw	2
streak	2
streaked	1
stream	2
streamed	1
street	25
street-car	2
street-corner	1
streetcar	3
streetcars	1
streets	3
strength	18
strengthen	1
strenuous	5
strenuously	1
stress	4
stressed	1
stretch	3
stretched	4
stretcher	1
stretches	1
stricken	2
strictly	4
strikes	2
strikingly	1
strings	2
stripes	1
strive	1
striving	2
strivings	1
strong	18
stronger	2
strongly	3
struck	12
structure	4
structures	2
struggle	10
struggled	2
struggles	2
struggling	2
stubbed	1
stubborn	1
stubbornness	2
stuck	6
student	7
students	1
studied	7
studies	3
studio	2
study	7
studying	5
stuff	23
stuffed	1
stumble	4
stumbled	3
stumbling	1
stupefied	1
stupid	7
stupidity	1
stupor	6
style	2
subconsciously	2
subdue	1
subject	16
subjected	3
subjects	1
sublime	1
submerge	1
submit	2
subscribe	1
subscriptions	1
subsequent	4
subsequently	2
subside	1
subsidiary	1
substance	2
substantial	5
substantially	2
substitute	4
substituted	3
subtle	2
suburb	2
subway	2
succeed	8
succeeded	6
succeeding	2
success	33
successes	2
successful	30
successfully	8
succession	3
successive	2
succumbed	3
such	176
Sudan	1
sudden	13
suddenly	24
sue	1
Suez	2
suffer	9
suffered	14
sufferer	1
sufferer's	1
sufferers	1
suffering	19
sufferings	1
suffers	5
suffice	1
suffices	1
sufficient	11
sufficiently	2
suffused	1
sugar	3
suggest	14
suggested	25
suggestion	8
suggestions	12
suggestive	1
suggests	4
suicidal	2
suicide	11
suit	7
suitable	1
suite	2
suited	2
suits	1
Sullivan	1
sum	5
summa cum laude	1
summarize	2
summer	12
summing	1
summoned	1
summons	2
sumptuous	1
sun	1
Sunday	21
Sunday-school	1
Sundays	2
sundry	1
sung	2
sunk	2
sunlight	2
sunset	2
sunshine	1
supercargo	1
superficial	1
superhuman	1
superintendent	1
superior	3
superiors	2
supernatural	1
superstition	1
supervised	1
supervision	1
supper	5
supplanted	2
supplement	2
supplied	4
supplies	3
supply	6
support	7
supported	1
supporters	1
supporting	1
suppose	20
supposed	10
supposing	1
suppressed	1
supreme	6
sure	73
surely	12
surest	1
surety	1
surf	1
surface	4
surgeon	3
surgeons	2
surgery	1
surgical	2
surgically	1
surmount	1
surpass	1
surpassed	1
surplus	1
surprise	9
surprised	5
surprising	4
surprisingly	3
surrender	8
surrendered	2
surround	1
surrounding	2
surroundings	2
surrounds	1
surveyed	1
surveys	1
survive	6
survived	6
surviving	1
survivors	1
suspect	5
suspected	4
suspecting	1
suspend	1
suspicion	2
suspicious	1
sustained	2
swallow	4
swallowed	1
sway	1
swayed	2
swear	1
swearing	3
sweat	2
sweater	2
sweats	4
sweep	4
sweet	7
sweetness	2
sweets	2
swell	2
swelled	1
swelling	1
swept	1
swig	1
swigs	1
swimming	1
swing	3
swinging	1
switch	4
switched	2
switching	1
Switzerland	3
swollen	1
swore	4
sworn	6
swung	1
symbol	1
sympathetic	8
sympathy	4
symphony	1
symptom	7
symptoms	11
synthetic	1
system	7
systematically	1
systems	2
table	22
tables	1
tablespoons	1
tack	1
tackle	1
tact	1
tactful	1
take	220
take-off	1
taken	58
takes	15
taking	51
tale	1
talebearers	1
talent	2
talented	1
talents	2
tales	3
talk	93
talked	47
talker	1
talking	36
talks	9
tall	11
tallied	1
tan	1
tangent	1
tangible	2
t'ank	1
tank	1
tap	1
tape	1
taped	1
taper	4
tapered	1
tapering	1
tapes	1
tapped	2
task	3
tasks	3
taste	11
tasted	3
tasting	1
taught	30
tavern	1
taverns	1
tax-free	1
taxi	3
taxicab	2
taxis	1
taxpayer	1
TB	1
tea	2
teach	5
teacher	5
teachers	2
teaches	1
teaching	1
teachings	2
team	3
teamed	1
teams	1
tearing	1
tears	7
teased	2

teaspoon	1
technical	2
technique	4
techniques	1
tedious	2
teen-aged	1
teen-ager's	1
teens	4
'teens	1
teetering	1
teeth	7
teetotaler	1
teetotallers	1
telegram	1
telegrams	1
telephone	15
telephoned	3
telephoning	1
television	1
tell	132
teller	1
telling	21
tells	9
temper	2
temperament	4
temperance	2
temperate	2
temporarily	5
temporary	6
temporizes	1
temptation	6
temptations	1
tempted	3
tempting	1
ten	54
ten-day	5
ten-dollar	1
ten-thirty	1
tend	3
tended	1
tendencies	4
tendency	3
tender	1
tends	1
tenets	1
tennis	1
tension	5
tensions	3
tent	1
tentative	1
tenth	3
term	3
terminal	1
terminated	1
terms	14
terrapin	1
terrible	25
terribly	12
terrific	14
terrifically	1
terrified	3
terrifying	1
territory	2
terror	3
test	6
Testament	1
tested	1
testimony	2
tests	2
Tex.	1
Texas	7
text	3
than	256
thank	18
thanked	5
thankful	3
thanks	3
that	2725
that's	36
the	6236
theater	2
theatre	4
theatrical	1
thee	2
theirs	1
them	365
themselves	42
then	386
theological	3
theology	1
theories	3
theorizing	1
theory	9
therapeutic	2
therapy	4
there	591
there's	12
thereafter	6
thereby	2
therefore	24
thereupon	1
these	304
they	740
they'd	4
they're	4
they've	1
thick	1
thickened	1
thin	2
thing	139
things	206
think	215
thinking	66
thinks	8
third	20
third-day	1
thirsty	1
thirteen	18
thirties	2
thirty	28
thirty-eight	1
thirty-five	8
thirty-nine	4
thirty-seven	1
thirty-three	3
thirty-two	3
this	1046
thorn	1
thorough	3
thoroughly	19
thoroughness	1
those	194
those're	1
thou	2
though	111
thought	219
thought-life	1
thoughtful	4
thoughtless	1
thoughts	14
thousand	13
thousands	18
thread	1
threadbare	1
threat	1
threaten	1
threatened	5
threatening	2
threatens	1
three	186
three-hundred	1
three-months	1
three-quarters	1
three-thirty	2
three-weeks'	1
three-year	1
threes	2
threshold	2
threw	11
thrill	4
thrilled	1
throat	2
throats	1
throes	1
through	192
throughout	9
throw	15
throwing	3
thrown	7
thrust	1
thumb	1
thunderbolt	1
thunderclouds	1
Thursday	1
thus	23
thy	13
thyself	3
ticker	1
ticket	3
tide	3
tidings	1
Tiebout	3
tied	3
ties	2
tiger	1
tight	14
Tijuana	1
tile	1
till	4
tilting	1
time	535
timed	1
times	109
timid	1
timing	1
tin	1
tinge	1
tinkering	1
tiny	8
tipped	1
tippler	1
tips	1
tipsy	1
tire	4
tired	8
tireless	1
tissue	1
tissues	2
title	4
titled	1
titles	2
to	5462
toast	1
toboggan	1
tobogganing	1
today	49
today's	2
toddy	1
toe	4
toed	1
toes	3
together	47
toilet	3
toilets	1
toils	1
token	1
told	178
Toledo	1
tolerance	12
tolerant	4
tolerantly	1
tolerated	2
tolerating	1
toll	1
Tom	2
tombs	1
tombstone	1
tomorrow	9
tone	1
tongue	2
tonight	1
too	206
took	128
tool	2
toolmaker	3
tools	3
top	9
topic	1
tops	2
torch	1
torches	1
torn	2
tornado	2
Toronto	1
torture	5
tortured	1
tortures	1
toss	1
tossed	4
tossing	2
total	10
totaling	1
totality	1
totally	5
tots	1
tottering	1
touch	16
touched	5
touches	1
touching	1
touchy	1
tough	10
toughest	1
tour	3
tourniquet	1
tours	2
toward	31
towards	8
towel	2
tower	1
towers	1
town	55
towns	3
townspeople	1
trace	2
traceable	1
track	5
tracks	6
trade	6
traded	1
trademark	1
tradition	3
traditionally	1
traditions	10
traffic	1
tragedies	4
tragedy	5
tragic	11
tragically	1
trail	3
trailers	1
train	12
trained	2
trainfare	1
training	14
trains	1
traits	5
tramp	2
tranquilizer	1
tranquilizers	3
transcended	1
transfer	1
transferred	5
transformation	1
transformations	2
transfusions	1
transgressions	1
transition	1
translate	1
translated	1
transmit	1
transmitted	1
trap	1
trapped	3
travel	13
traveled	5
travelers	1
traveling	6
travelled	1
traveller	1
travelling	2
treading	1
treadmill	1
treasure	1
treasured	1
treasurer	2
treasuries	1
treat	7
treated	8
treating	5
treatment	37
treatments	1
tree	1
trees	1
trembled	2
trembles	2
trembling	5
tremendous	9
tremendously	1
tremens	4
tremors	1
trial	7
trials	4
tribe	2
tribulations	1
trick	4
tricks	2
tried	96
tries	3
trifle	1
trigger	1
trim	2
trip	18
tripped	1
trips	6
trite	1
triumph	1
triumphant	1
trivial	4
trolley	1
troop	1
trooper	1
troops	1
tropical	1
trouble	54
troubled	2
troublemaker	1
troubles	18
troublesome	2
trousers	3
truck	3
trucks	1
trudge	1
true	39
truest	1
truly	8
trunks	1
trust	9
trusted	6
trustee	1
trustees	3
trusting	1
trustworthy	1
truth	31
truths	2
try	119
trying	77
tuberculosis	1
tubes	1
tucked	3
Tuesday	4
tugboat	1
tumble	3
tumbled	2
tumbler	2
tumor	2
tune	3
turbulent	1
turmoil	1
turn	53
turned	55
turning	9
turnkey	1
turnpike	1
turns	3
TV	2
tweed	1
twelfth	5
twelve	54
twelve-year	1
Twelve Steps	27
Twelve Traditions	6
twenties	6
twentieth	2
twenty	26

twenty-eight	4
twenty-five	13
twenty-four	14
twenty-four-year-old	2
twenty-nine	2
twenty-odd	1
twenty-one	7
twenty-seven	5
twenty-seven-year-old	1
twenty-six	2
twenty-three	6
twenty-two	7
twice	11
twinkling	2
twist	3
twisted	1
twists	1
two	260
two-fifty	1
two-fisted	2
two-forty-five	1
two-quart	1
two-thirds	2
two-thirty	2
twos	2
type	20
types	4
typewriter	2
typical	4
U.S.	4
U.S.A.	3
U-turn	1
uglier	1
ugliness	1
ugly	3
ulcer	2
ultimate	2
ultimately	2
ultra-dry	1
ultra-modern	1
unabated	1
unable	13
unacceptable	3
unaffected	2
unafraid	1
unaided	1
unannounced	1
unanswerable	1
unapproachable	1
unavailing	1
unaware	1
unbalanced	1
unbearable	6
uncanny	1
uncertain	4
uncertainties	2
unchanged	1
uncle	3
uncomfortable	4
uncommon	1
uncommunicative	1
unconscious	3
unconsciously	1
uncontrollable	4
uncontrollably	2
uncontrolled	1
uncounted	2
under	60
underestimate	1
underestimation	1
undergo	1
undergoing	1
undergone	2
undergraduate	1
underground	1
underlay	1
underlying	2
underneath	4
understand	59
understandable	2
understandably	1
understanding	48
understands	2
understood	23
undertake	2
undertaken	4
undertaker	1
undertaking	1
undertook	1
underweight	1
underwent	1
undisciplined	3
undisturbed	2
undo	1
undoubtedly	9
undreamed-of	1
undress	1
undue	1
undying	1
unearth	1
uneasy	1
unending	1
unexciting	1
unexpected	3
unexpectedly	2
unfailing	1
unfair	1
unfamiliar	1
unfavorably	1
unfit	4
unfold	2
unfolded	1
unforgettable	1
unfortunate	1
unfortunately	3
unfortunates	1
unguarded	1
unhappiness	10
unhappy	17
unharmed	1
unhushed	1
uniform	3
uniformity	1
unify	1
unimportant	2
uninhibited	1
unique	4
uniquely	1
unit	4
united	10
United States	9
unity	3
universal	3
universe	13
universities	3
university	8
unjust	1
unjustifiably	1
unkempt	1
unkind	2
unknown	2
unless	33
unlettered	1
unlike	7
unlikely	2
unlimited	3
unloved	1
unlovely	2
unloving	1
unmanageable	10
unmarried	1
unmentioned	1
unmindful	1
unmixed	1
unmoved	1
unnecessary	2
unpleasant	1
unpopular	1
unpredictable	1
unrealistic	1
unreasonable	6
unreasoning	1
unreproached	1
unreservedly	1
unsalable	1
unsatisfactory	1
unselfish	2
unselfishness	2
unsettled	1
unshaven	1
unstable	2
unsuccessful	1
unsuspected	1
unthinkable	1
unthinking	2
until	108
unto	2
untold	1
untouched	1
untrained	1
untruths	1
unusual	6
unusually	1
unwanted	1
unwelcome	1
unwilling	4
unwillingness	1
unwise	2
up	469
up-to-date	1
upbraided	1
upbringing	1
upheavals	1
uphold	1
upholsterer	1
upholstering	2
upholstery	1
uplift	1
upon	86
upper	4
uppermost	1
upright	2
uproar	1
uprooted	1
ups	3
upset	7
upsets	1
upshot	1
upstairs	5
uptown	2
upward	1
urge	15
urged	1
urgent	4
urges	2
urging	2
us	375
use	58
used	66
useful	14
usefulness	9
useless	2
uselessness	2
uses	2
using	6
usual	22
usually	38
Utah	1
utmost	6
Utopia	2
utter	5
utterance	1
utterly	4
vacated	1
vacation	10
vacations	6
vacuum	1
vagaries	1
vague	5
vaguely	4
vain	4
vain-gloriously	1
vainly	1
vale	1
valid	1
valley	1
valuable	2
value	6
values	6
valve	1
vanish	3
vanished	2
vanishing	1
vanity	4
vapor	1
variation	1
varied	2
varieties	1
variety	3
various	16
variously	2
vary	2
varying	1
vast	6
vastly	1
vaudeville	1
veered	1
vehicles	1
vein	2
veins	1
venerable	1
vengeful	1
venomous	1
vent	1
venture	7
ventured	2
Venus	1
verbally	1
verdict	2
verge	1
veritable	1
verity	1
Vermont	3
verse	1
version	2
versions	1
very	292
vessel	2
vestiges	1
veteran	4
veterinary	1
Vi	20
Vi's	1
via	1
vicarious	1
vice	2
vicious	3
viciously	1
vicissitude	1
victim	9
victims	1
victor	1
victory	5
Vietnam	1
view	14
viewpoints	1
views	6
vigilance	1
vigor	1
vigorous	2
vigorously	1
village	10
villain	1
vin	1
vindicate	1
vindictiveness	1
violent	8
violently	3
violins	1
Virgil	1
Virginia	8
virtually	2
virtue	1
virtues	1
virtuous	1
vision	4
visioned	1
visit	23
visited	8
visiting	6
visitor	1
visitors	7
visits	5
vistas	1
visual	2
visualize	3
vital	12
vitally	1
vitamin	1
vitamins	1
vivid	2
vividly	1
vocation	1
vodka	3
voice	12
voiced	1
voices	5
voicing	1
volume	10
volumes	1
voluntarily	1
voluntary	4
volunteer	7
vomit	1
vomited	1
vomiting	1
voted	1
vow	1
vowed	1
vows	1
vows	1
w-h-i-s-k-e-y	1
wad	1
wagon	24
wail	1
wait	20
waited	7
waiter	1
waiting	8
waitress	1
wake	14
waked	2
waken	1
wakened	2
waking	3
walk	26
walked	23
walking	8
walks	3
wall	8
Wallace	2
wallet	3
wallflower	1
Wallkill	2
wallowed	2
walls	7
Walter	2
wander	2
wandered	4
wandering	2
want	136
wanted	144
wanting	11
wants	35
war	23
war-time	1
ward	20
warden	1
wards	1
warm	6
warming	1
warmly	2
warmth	1
warn	2
warned	6
warning	3
warnings	3
warped	4
warps	1
warrant	3
warranted	1
warring	2
wars	3
wartime	2
was	2634
wash	5
washday	1
washed	3
washing	2
Washington	23
washout	1
wasn't	124
wasp	1
waste	9
wasted	5

wasting	2
watch	22
watched	2
watches	1
watchful	3
watching	5
watchwords	1
water	19
waterboy	2
watering	1
waterpipe	1
waters	1
wave	1
waves	1
waxed	1
way	257
ways	18
wayward	2
we	1659
we'd	6
we'll	5
we're	8
we've	4
weak	14
weakened	2
weakest	1
weakling	1
weaklings	1
weakness	8
wealth	2
wealthiest	1
wealthy	1
weapon	2
wear	4
wearily	3
wearing	2
weary	2
weather	4
weaving	1
wedding	6
weddings	2
Wednesday	7
week	47
week-end	5
week-end's	1
week-ends	4
week-long	2
week's	1
weekend	1
weekends	7
weekly	5
weeks	59
weeks'	1
weep	1
weeping	1
weeps	1
weigh	1
weighed	1
weighing	1
weight	4
welcome	7
welcomed	8
welfare	10
well	187
well-balanced	1
well-being	3
well-dressed	1
well-integrated	1
well-known	7
well-meaning	1
well-reviewed	1
well-to-do	2
well-trained	1
welled	1
wended	1
went	298
wept	3
were	539
weren't	11
west	12
West Virginia	1
western	5
wet	10
whacky	1
whammo	1
what	466
what's	16
whatever	37
whatsoever	1
wheel	2
Wheeling	1
wheels	1
when	594
whenever	15
where	191
where's	1
whereas	2
whereby	4
wherever	6
whether	52
which	409
whichever	1
while	123
whimper	1
whipped	1
whirl	1
whirled	1
whirling	2
whisked	1
whiskey	44
whiskies	1
whisky	1
whisper	1
whistles	1
whistling	1
white	12
who	527
who's	3
whoever	1
whole	52
whole-heartedly	1
wholeheartedly	1
wholesale	2
whom	50
whoop	2
whoopee	3
whose	27
why	127
wide	5
widely	2
widen	1
widened	2
widening	1
wider	3
widespread	1
widow	1
wife	196
wife's	11
wild	5
wildest	1
wildly	1
will	465
willful	2
William	6
Willie	1
willing	72
willingness	19
willpower	1
wills	1
wilt	1
wilted	1
win	5
Winchester	2
wind	7
windmills	1
window	10
windows	1
winds	1
windshields	1
windward	1
windy	1
wine	27
wine-drinking	1
wine-making	1
wine-room	1
wine-tasting	1
wines	1
wing	1
wings	3
wins	1
winter	6
wipe	1
wiped	3
wired	2
wireless	1
wires	1
wisdom	2
wise	8
wise-cracking	1
wisely	1
wish	39
wished	8
wishes	6
wishful	1
wishing	4
witch-burners	1
with	1160
withdraw	1
withdrawing	3
withdrawn	1
withdrew	2
withholding	1
within	35
without	141
witness	4
witnessed	2
wits	1
wits'	1
witty	1
wives	25
wobbled	1
woe	1
woes	1
woke	18
wolf	1
woman	41
woman's	2
womanhood	2
women	52
women's	2
won	2
won't	11
wonder	26
wondered	8
wonderful	44
wonderfully	2
wondering	3
wonders	2
wooden	1
woodshed	1
wool	2
woolen	1
woos	1
woozy	1
word	36
wording	1
words	35
wordy	1
wore	5
work	213
work-houses	1
work-outs	1
workable	1
worked	57
worker	2
workers	3
working	36
workings	1
works	21
workshop	1
world	115
world-renowned	1
world's	7
worldliness	1
worldly	6
worldwide	1
worn	3
worried	5
worries	5
worry	28
worrying	1
worse	62
worship	2
worshipfully	1
worshipped	1
worshippers	1
worshipping	1
worships	1
worst	12
worth	20
worthwhile	2
would	634
wouldn't	58
wound	7
woven	1
wrapped	3
wreck	6
wreckage	1
wrecked	1
wrest	1
wretched	1
Wright	2
Wrights	1
wringer	4
wrings	1
wrinkled	1
wrinkles	1
wrist	2
wrists	1
wristwatch	1
write	22
write-up	1
writers	2
writes	1
writhing	1
writing	13
written	21
wrong	52
wrong-doing	3
wronged	2
wrongs	6
wrote	15
wrought	3
X-rays	1
XYZ	1
yachts	1
Yankee	1
Yankees	1
yard	1
yardstick	1
yarn	1
yawned	1
ye	1
year	122
year's	4
yearbook	1
yearned	1
yearning	1
years	388
years'	2
yelled	2
yellow	1
yells	1
yen	1
yes	44
yesterday	2
yet	74
yield	3
yielding	1
YMCA	1
you	982
you'd	7
you'll	8
you're	23
you've	16
young	35
younger	6
youngest	1
youngster	2
your	252
yours	8
yourself	33
yourselves	1
youth	5
youthful	1
zeal	1
zero	2
zone	1

APPENDIX V

Frequency of Words: Numerical Sort

I	7214
the	6236
to	5462
a	5132
and	4874
of	3989
that	2725
in	2684
was	2634
my	2146
it	1826
had	1814
we	1659
he	1641
for	1530
me	1530
with	1160
have	1148
this	1046
but	1043
be	1028
is	1007
you	982
as	937
on	937
not	885
at	845
they	740
or	727
all	692
one	654
his	652
would	634
so	631
our	625
when	594
there	591
if	581
are	580
an	575
drinking	550
about	545
from	542
were	539
time	535
A.A.	531
who	527
out	523
him	522
been	519
do	502
up	469
could	466
what	466
will	465
drink	463
no	455
by	443
more	410
which	409
can	401
years	388
then	386
alcoholic	383
us	375
them	365
has	362
some	356
life	352
get	349
first	341
never	340
said	334
she	328
did	315
how	306
only	305
these	304
after	303
may	298
went	298
go	296
home	295
didn't	292
very	292
day	285
many	282
much	282
into	281
people	281
because	280
know	279
myself	278
other	274
got	273
man	271
any	268
new	263
two	260
way	257
than	256
now	253
good	252
your	252
like	250
over	246
just	245
came	244
God	242
alcoholics	239
before	233
her	220
take	220
again	219
thought	219
back	218
see	217
think	215
work	213
things	206
too	206
found	200
made	200
wife	196
those	194
long	192
through	192
family	191
where	191
well	187
drunk	186
even	186
three	186
should	184
little	180
told	178
going	177
night	177
every	176
knew	176
such	176
help	174
anything	172
another	171
friends	171
own	166
don't	165
few	164
alcohol	163
always	163
men	162
say	162
being	158
still	157
most	156
down	153
find	152
great	152
something	152
I'd	150
make	150
spiritual	150
come	149
must	149
wanted	144
months	143
am	141
without	141
right	139
thing	139
might	138
next	138
off	138
really	138
last	137
sober	137
became	136
nothing	136
want	136
business	133
couldn't	133
power	133
days	132
tell	132
doctor	131
once	131
job	130
hospital	129
took	128
why	127
away	126
ever	125
wasn't	124
morning	123
while	123
old	122
year	122
believe	121
course	121
stop	119
try	119
alcoholism	118
each	118
living	117
problem	117
here	115
others	115
world	115
live	114
school	113
began	112
better	112
book	112
place	112
remember	112
though	111
group	109
husband	109
mind	109
started	109
times	109
feel	108
later	108
let	108
until	108
liquor	107
enough	106
experience	106
program	106
done	105
able	102
put	102
felt	101
same	100
father	99
money	99
person	98
during	97
having	96
tried	96
himself	95
part	95
become	94
often	94
anonymous	93
finally	93
talk	93
drank	92
since	91
soon	91
meeting	90
seemed	90
friend	89
Alcoholics Anonymous	88
upon	86
does	85
give	85
also	84
around	84
fear	84
I'm	84
lost	84
ourselves	83
sometimes	83
doing	82
getting	82
house	81
keep	81
left	81
else	80
mother	79
problems	79
asked	78
everything	78
hard	78
perhaps	78
bottle	77
happy	77
love	77
trying	77
big	76
end	76
happened	76
need	76
fact	75
saw	75
best	74
four	74
yet	74
cannot	73
children	73
point	73
sure	73
answer	72
bed	72
far	72
however	72
its	72
meetings	72
willing	72
both	71
stay	71
ask	70
feeling	70
gave	69
sobriety	69
drinks	68
real	68
gone	67
kept	67
six	67
hope	66
quite	66
thinking	66
used	66
decided	65
New York	65
sick	65
Akron	64
idea	64
important	64
room	64
along	63
called	63
certain	63
read	63
bad	62
face	62
kind	62
worse	62
alone	61
beer	61
lot	61
story	61
can't	60
sense	60
under	60
five	59
half	59
understand	59
weeks	59
taken	58
use	58
wouldn't	58
anyone	57
given	57
known	57
matter	57
worked	57
look	56
several	56
call	55
means	55
spent	55
town	55
turned	55
brought	54
deal	54
faith	54
personal	54
quit	54
ten	54
trouble	54
twelve	54
almost	53
mental	53
turn	53
case	52
change	52
couple	52
making	52
married	52
whether	52
whole	52
women	52
wrong	52
control	51
I've	51
looked	51
set	51

step	51
taking	51
ago	50
met	50
past	50
reason	50
simple	50
small	50
start	50
whom	50
among	49
Dr.	49
learned	49
lives	49
longer	49
office	49
rather	49
today	49
Bob	48
large	48
nor	48
second	48
seen	48
show	48
understanding	48
church	47
evening	47
everyone	47
religious	47
steps	47
talked	47
together	47
week	47
bar	46
coming	46
early	46
except	46
needed	46
head	45
high	45
I'll	45
recovery	45
someone	45
age	44
Bill	44
car	44
city	44
desire	44
heard	44
hold	44
human	44
instead	44
least	44
members	44
ought	44
whiskey	44
wonderful	44
yes	44
greater	43
hurt	43
jail	43
nearly	43
pretty	43
against	42
between	42
care	42
period	42
realized	42
short	42
themselves	42
death	41
eight	41
fellowship	41
helped	41
hours	41
sent	41
service	41
woman	41
certainly	40
drinker	40
hadn't	40
interested	40
different	39
fellow	39
less	39
mine	39
principles	39
true	39
wish	39
beginning	38
completely	38
fellows	38
full	38
girl	38
it's	38
lived	38
mean	38
medical	38
possible	38
reached	38
state	38
usually	38
already	37
daily	37
health	37
physical	37
realize	37
rest	37
serious	37
social	37
stayed	37
treatment	37
whatever	37
condition	36
either	36
groups	36
helpful	36
learn	36
maybe	36
member	36
probably	36
seem	36
shall	36
stories	36
talking	36
that's	36
word	36
working	36
hand	35
meant	35
number	35
practice	35
seven	35
wants	35
within	35
words	35
young	35
afraid	34
chance	34
comes	34
easy	34
entirely	34
leave	34
nine	34
normal	34
outside	34
stopped	34
action	33
child	33
company	33
dad	33
free	33
general	33
law	33
meet	33
month	33
pay	33
return	33
run	33
situation	33
sleep	33
success	33
unless	33
yourself	33
actually	32
attitude	32
changed	32
happiness	32
heart	32
opportunity	32
parents	32
psychiatrist	32
sort	32
bit	31
country	31
dollars	31
fine	31
honest	31
join	31
prison	31
resentment	31
saying	31
toward	31
truth	31
complete	30
convinced	30
dinner	30
experiences	30
failed	30
name	30
passed	30
purpose	30
returned	30
simply	30
successful	30
taught	30
approach	29
bring	29
cases	29
doctors	29
dry	29
followed	29
haven't	29
hundred	29
pattern	29
sat	29
side	29
above	28
boy	28
continued	28
discovered	28
effect	28
ideas	28
light	28
looking	28
peace	28
public	28
recover	28
respect	28
result	28
spirit	28
thirty	28
worry	28
accept	27
although	27
army	27
boys	27
carry	27
common	27
deep	27
die	27
eyes	27
follow	27
God's	27
he's	27
hit	27
illness	27
inventory	27
moved	27
neither	27
reasons	27
Twelve Steps	27
whose	27
wine	27
career	26
Chicago	26
continue	26
decision	26
difficult	26
doesn't	26
drinkers	26
eventually	26
following	26
immediately	26
line	26
loved	26
marriage	26
necessary	26
question	26
self	26
self-pity	26
society	26
twenty	26
walk	26
wonder	26
A.A.'s	25
admit	25
attended	25
average	25
bars	25
broke	25
died	25
door	25
fifteen	25
higher	25
hopeless	25
interest	25
isn't	25
medicine	25
open	25
order	25
position	25
prayer	25
somehow	25
stand	25
street	25
suggested	25
terrible	25
wives	25
account	24
ahead	24
basis	24
buy	24
chapter	24
contact	24
forget	24
grew	24
hear	24
individual	24
inside	24
joined	24
knowing	24
knowledge	24
knows	24
near	24
present	24
serenity	24
sex	24
suddenly	24
therefore	24
wagon	24
accepted	23
admitted	23
amount	23
arrived	23
behind	23
booze	23
clear	23
college	23
confidence	23
difference	23
eighteen	23
fall	23
families	23
fully	23
further	23
giving	23
grow	23
happen	23
honestly	23
lay	23
lose	23
Max	23
moral	23
places	23
poor	23
possibly	23
recovered	23
solution	23
stood	23
strange	23
stuff	23
thus	23
understood	23
visit	23
walked	23
war	23
Washington	23
you're	23
avoid	22
begin	22
body	22
bottles	22
clothes	22
community	22
freedom	22
held	22
ill	22
moment	22
picture	22
ran	22
sold	22
table	22
usual	22
watch	22
write	22
afternoon	21
agreed	21
Christmas	21
concerned	21
courage	21
doubt	21
everybody	21
exactly	21
feet	21
form	21
handle	21
hands	21
impossible	21
mentally	21
none	21
particular	21
parties	21
play	21
religion	21
Saturday	21
says	21
seems	21
sorry	21
Sunday	21
telling	21
works	21
written	21
absolutely	20
attention	20
badly	20
believed	20
Cleveland	20
especially	20
existence	20
fired	20
future	20
gotten	20
hardly	20
hospitals	20
jobs	20
lack	20
late	20
matters	20
nature	20
occasion	20
paid	20
patient	20
personality	20
physically	20
picked	20
ready	20
suppose	20
third	20
type	20
Vi	20
wait	20
ward	20
worth	20
becoming	19

books	19
cold	19
defects	19
effort	19
entered	19
escape	19
explained	19
failure	19
financial	19
former	19
Frank	19
homes	19
hotel	19
hour	19
insanity	19
naturally	19
nobody	19
o'clock	19
ones	19
pills	19
reading	19
remembered	19
seldom	19
shot	19
son	19
suffering	19
thoroughly	19
water	19
willingness	19
ability	18
acquired	18
anybody	18
beyond	18
circumstances	18
crowd	18
entire	18
fairly	18
fast	18
glass	18
grateful	18
Higher Power	18
honesty	18
leaving	18
local	18
lots	18
makes	18
managed	18
membership	18
needs	18
opinion	18
particularly	18
party	18
plan	18
questions	18
relations	18
road	18
send	18
sit	18
strength	18
strong	18
thank	18
thirteen	18
thousands	18
trip	18
troubles	18
ways	18
woke	18
accomplished	17
apartment	17
attend	17
becomes	17
born	17
brain	17
brother	17
carried	17
close	17
cure	17
dead	17
Depression	17
depression	17
direction	17
disease	17
enjoyed	17
feelings	17
fight	17
front	17
gin	17
growth	17
he'd	17
helping	17
Jack	17
John	17
liked	17
man's	17
material	17
message	17
occasionally	17
opened	17
organization	17
physician	17
received	17
running	17
scared	17
seeing	17
sixteen	17
sponsor	17
station	17
unhappy	17
active	16
American	16
beautiful	16
behavior	16
careful	16
conditions	16
cut	16
dark	16
emotional	16
ended	16
fun	16
greatest	16
growing	16
heavy	16
hell	16
husbands	16
led	16
maintain	16
middle	16
miracle	16
miserable	16
newspaper	16
nice	16
occasions	16
offer	16
offered	16
oh	16
pass	16
persons	16
placed	16
private	16
remorse	16
rid	16
save	16
security	16
selfish	16
subject	16
touch	16
various	16
what's	16
you've	16
across	15
activities	15
advice	15
begun	15
character	15
drunken	15
explain	15
fears	15
forever	15
friendly	15
glad	15
guess	15
guy	15
habit	15
hangover	15
harm	15
landed	15
listen	15
locked	15
loving	15
navy	15
obsession	15
patients	15
periods	15
prejudice	15
pride	15
promised	15
prove	15
provided	15
release	15
resentments	15
Russ	15
sanity	15
serve	15
shown	15
somewhere	15
special	15
takes	15
telephone	15
throw	15
urge	15
whenever	15
wrote	15
Anne	14
anyhow	14
asking	14
attempt	14
black	14
boss	14
build	14
busy	14
caught	14
caused	14
childhood	14
class	14
conclusion	14
craving	14
despair	14
divorce	14
drunks	14
education	14
excuse	14
fell	14
firm	14
frequently	14
gets	14
indeed	14
inner	14
institution	14
invited	14
itself	14
joy	14
judge	14
loneliness	14
mad	14
miles	14
misery	14
nights	14
overcome	14
paper	14
per	14
powerful	14
president	14
progress	14
proved	14
reality	14
relationship	14
responsibilities	14
responsibility	14
results	14
sane	14
showed	14
sitting	14
solve	14
spree	14
statement	14
suffered	14
suggest	14
terms	14
terrific	14
thoughts	14
tight	14
training	14
twenty-four	14
useful	14
view	14
wake	14
weak	14
acceptance	13
act	13
admitting	13
anger	13
bottom	13
built	13
closed	13
conception	13
considerable	13
covered	13
difficulties	13
doc	13
dog	13
drive	13
ease	13
edition	13
enjoy	13
fair	13
filled	13
folks	13
game	13
goes	13
gradually	13
hated	13
hidden	13
hoping	13
horrible	13
hundreds	13
impressed	13
insane	13
involved	13
kill	13
letter	13
lie	13
likely	13
likes	13
meaning	13
moments	13
necessity	13
nervous	13
nevertheless	13
officer	13
older	13
ordered	13
pleasure	13
plenty	13
process	13
prospect	13
quickly	13
relieved	13
remained	13
saved	13
science	13
shut	13
sister	13
somewhat	13
sorts	13
speak	13
stage	13
staying	13
straight	13
sudden	13
thousand	13
thy	13
travel	13
twenty-five	13
unable	13
universe	13
writing	13
allowed	12
amends	12
angry	12
awful	12
baby	12
belief	12
besides	12
binge	12
blame	12
carefully	12
chances	12
commenced	12
committed	12
completed	12
consciousness	12
Creator	12
daughter	12
dealing	12
decide	12
definite	12
difficulty	12
discharged	12
eat	12
emotions	12
environment	12
established	12
example	12
expected	12
experienced	12
extent	12
facts	12
finding	12
forgotten	12
jails	12
laugh	12
level	12
list	12
low	12
missed	12
news	12
noon	12
oblivion	12
pair	12
patience	12
perfect	12
pint	12
please	12
practically	12
pray	12
radio	12
reaction	12
relief	12
remain	12
remedy	12
rule	12
sake	12
sanitarium	12
schools	12
shortly	12
shows	12
sincere	12
slow	12
slowly	12
somebody	12
sound	12
spend	12
spite	12
spot	12
spring	12
struck	12
suggestions	12
summer	12
surely	12
terribly	12
there's	12
tolerance	12
train	12
vital	12
voice	12
west	12
white	12
worst	12
added	11
analyst	11
apart	11
aware	11
beers	11
begins	11
blackout	11
bought	11
broken	11
capacity	11
cause	11
clubs	11
coffee	11
conscious	11
constantly	11
court	11
date	11

department	11
desk	11
developed	11
discussion	11
domestic	11
easier	11
easily	11
efforts	11
eleven	11
employer	11
excuses	11
explanation	11
faced	11
fault	11
figured	11
finished	11
fire	11
fit	11
focus	11
fortunate	11
grand	11
ground	11
hearing	11
hide	11
income	11
jitters	11
lady	11
lasted	11
literature	11
lovely	11
lunch	11
minds	11
Mr.	11
natural	11
noticed	11
occurred	11
pain	11
phone	11
potential	11
promises	11
proper	11
property	11
quick	11
quiet	11
rapidly	11
released	11
remove	11
reply	11
responsible	11
retired	11
row	11
sanitariums	11
selling	11
showing	11
sign	11
socially	11
sought	11
spoke	11
standing	11
states	11
store	11
sufficient	11
suicide	11
symptoms	11
tall	11
taste	11
threw	11
tragic	11
twice	11
wanting	11
weren't	11
wife's	11
won't	11
accepting	10
acquaintance	10
actual	10
advantage	10
afford	10
afterward	10
agree	10
Al-Anon	10
anywhere	10
approached	10
article	10
asylum	10
beat	10
Bible	10
bitter	10
board	10
bodies	10
bout	10
break	10
bridge	10
brief	10
cent	10
center	10
changes	10
club	10
conduct	10
constant	10
convince	10
cost	10
crazy	10
criticize	10
definitely	10
dozen	10
driving	10
drove	10
effective	10
express	10
extreme	10
fail	10
farm	10
feared	10
feels	10
final	10
financially	10
foolish	10
fought	10
foundation	10
Friday	10
frightened	10
guilt	10
hearts	10
ideal	10
including	10
increase	10
increased	10
Indian	10
individuals	10
keeping	10
learning	10
licked	10
loss	10
lucky	10
manage	10
memory	10
mentioned	10
minutes	10
miss	10
mixed	10
November	10
obviously	10
oil	10
ordinary	10
philosophy	10
pill	10
pleasant	10
pocket	10
pointed	10
post	10
presence	10
principle	10
prior	10
profession	10
prohibition	10
promise	10
psychiatric	10
reach	10
requires	10
resentful	10
retirement	10
rough	10
satisfied	10
self-will	10
sentence	10
served	10
shape	10
shy	10
single	10
slip	10
so-called	10
societies	10
speaking	10
stomach	10
strangers	10
struggle	10
supposed	10
total	10
tough	10
traditions	10
unhappiness	10
united	10
unmanageable	10
vacation	10
village	10
volume	10
welfare	10
wet	10
window	10
abnormal	9
actions	9
affairs	9
affected	9
aid	9
allergy	9
anyway	9
apparent	9
appeared	9
ashamed	9
aside	9
associates	9
association	9
authority	9
based	9
basic	9
bear	9
bender	9
blood	9
brilliant	9
chair	9
chap	9
chief	9
chronic	9
companionship	9
confused	9
consumption	9
contempt	9
continues	9
conversation	9
conviction	9
critical	9
customers	9
degree	9
described	9
description	9
desperate	9
desperation	9
despite	9
determined	9
develop	9
directly	9
discovery	9
discuss	9
dishonest	9
divorced	9
doctor's	9
dressed	9
drop	9
earlier	9
employees	9
Europe	9
familiar	9
fare	9
field	9
fifth	9
floor	9
Florida	9
foot	9
forty	9
fourth	9
freely	9
frequent	9
gained	9
gay	9
gentleman	9
gives	9
hang	9
happens	9
harder	9
hate	9
hole	9
hopelessness	9
humility	9
imagine	9
institutions	9
intolerance	9
January	9
June	9
kitchen	9
laid	9
let's	9
listened	9
lonely	9
memories	9
minister	9
Monday	9
move	9
numbers	9
Ohio	9
painful	9
path	9
perfectly	9
periodic	9
plans	9
played	9
pleased	9
police	9
powerless	9
professional	9
proud	9
psychiatrists	9
pull	9
realization	9
recognized	9
record	9
refused	9
reputation	9
reservation	9
routine	9
rubber	9
salesman	9
services	9
settled	9
seventeen	9
shame	9
sharing	9
shoes	9
shop	9
shouldn't	9
south	9
starting	9
stick	9
suffer	9
surprise	9
talks	9
tells	9
theory	9
throughout	9
tomorrow	9
top	9
tremendous	9
trust	9
turning	9
undoubtedly	9
United States	9
usefulness	9
victim	9
waste	9
abilities	8
activity	8
advanced	8
affair	8
agnostic	8
America	8
answers	8
anxious	8
appear	8
applied	8
apply	8
arrested	8
associated	8
attempted	8
attempts	8
attitudes	8
available	8
avoided	8
awakening	8
bag	8
beaten	8
bigger	8
box	8
brandy	8
broker	8
Canada	8
cared	8
cast	8
Catholic	8
charge	8
check	8
Christian	8
comfort	8
compulsion	8
concern	8
conscience	8
consequences	8
convictions	8
create	8
cried	8
dad's	8
danger	8
dangerous	8
day's	8
dear	8
devoted	8
disturbed	8
drastic	8
draw	8
drug	8
duty	8
earth	8
ego	8
empty	8
England	8
enthusiasm	8
expectations	8
expense	8
experiment	8
eye	8
faces	8
famous	8
finish	8
fix	8
flight	8
forward	8
funds	8
George	8
girls	8
government	8
grace	8
grade	8
greatly	8
guard	8
habits	8
hangovers	8
hasn't	8
headed	8
heavily	8
humbly	8
inevitable	8
intellectual	8
intelligence	8
interesting	8
intervals	8
invariably	8
inwardly	8
jealousy	8
journey	8
junior	8
keeps	8
key	8
killed	8
kinds	8
knees	8
labor	8

language	8
leading	8
lecture	8
length	8
lesson	8
letters	8
lifted	8
limited	8
lying	8
malady	8
measures	8
meditation	8
merely	8
ministers	8
minute	8
moderate	8
mother's	8
mouth	8
national	8
occasional	8
onto	8
otherwise	8
ours	8
page	8
passing	8
patent	8
Paul	8
pick	8
Pittsburgh	8
plain	8
positive	8
practical	8
presented	8
presently	8
proof	8
quart	8
race	8
raised	8
realizing	8
reasonable	8
recall	8
rehabilitation	8
relatives	8
revelation	8
satisfaction	8
secretary	8
self-esteem	8
solved	8
soul	8
sprees	8
square	8
steady	8
steel	8
stepped	8
succeed	8
successfully	8
suggestion	8
surrender	8
sympathetic	8
thinks	8
thirty-five	8
tiny	8
tired	8
towards	8
treated	8
truly	8
university	8
violent	8
Virginia	8
visited	8
waiting	8
walking	8
wall	8
we're	8
weakness	8
welcomed	8
wise	8
wished	8
wondered	8
you'll	8
yours	8
advised	7
apparently	7
area	7
argument	7
arise	7
atmosphere	7
attending	7
automobile	7
baffling	7
bank	7
base	7
belong	7
benefit	7
beside	7
binges	7
birthday	7
blind	7
blow	7
boredom	7
brains	7
building	7
bunch	7
calamity	7
challenge	7
Charlie	7
cheap	7
clearly	7
committee	7
considered	7
cops	7
countless	7
county	7
criticism	7
curious	7
damage	7
deeply	7
delirium	7
depressed	7
development	7
dirty	7
discover	7
dishes	7
distance	7
dollar	7
doors	7
drawn	7
economic	7
estimate	7
event	7
exact	7
exceptions	7
exhausted	7
fatal	7
fees	7
food	7
force	7
forgot	7
frankly	7
fraternity	7
friend's	7
frustration	7
futility	7
glasses	7
graduate	7
grown	7
hair	7
hence	7
history	7
honor	7
host	7
humiliation	7
husband's	7
ice	7
intention	7
interfere	7
intoxicated	7
Jackie	7
joint	7
judgment	7
jug	7
jump	7
kid	7
laughed	7
laundromat	7
laws	7
lawyer	7
listening	7
luck	7
magazine	7
mail	7
Maine	7
management	7
martinis	7
Marty	7
meal	7
mill	7
mistake	7
mistakes	7
music	7
nerves	7
newcomers	7
nightmare	7
nineteen	7
nowhere	7
nurse	7
one's	7
outlook	7
overnight	7
owe	7
owned	7
pages	7
partner	7
permanent	7
phenomenon	7
Philadelphia	7
pity	7
plus	7
policeman	7
pounds	7
poured	7
prayed	7
pressure	7
price	7
priest	7
privilege	7
procedure	7
proceeded	7
produce	7
profit	7
prominent	7
promotion	7
provide	7
psychiatry	7
pushed	7
putting	7
quietly	7
receive	7
recollection	7
red	7
remarkable	7
removed	7
resented	7
rolled	7
ruined	7
sad	7
safe	7
satisfactory	7
scrapes	7
search	7
section	7
seek	7
seemingly	7
sees	7
selfishness	7
sell	7
senior	7
sensible	7
separated	7
seriously	7
shaking	7
shots	7
sickness	7
skid	7
slept	7
smashed	7
solitary	7
spiritually	7
stock	7
straighten	7
straightened	7
student	7
studied	7
study	7
stupid	7
suit	7
support	7
sweet	7
symptom	7
system	7
tears	7
teeth	7
Texas	7
thrown	7
treat	7
trial	7
twenty-one	7
twenty-two	7
unlike	7
upset	7
venture	7
visitors	7
volunteer	7
waited	7
walls	7
Wednesday	7
weekends	7
welcome	7
well-known	7
wind	7
world's	7
wound	7
you'd	7
acquaintances	6
acute	6
add	6
addiction	6
agnostics	6
alcoholic's	6
ale	6
altogether	6
amazed	6
ambition	6
angle	6
appeal	6
appreciation	6
approximately	6
aren't	6
argue	6
arms	6
art	6
assistance	6
asylums	6
attorney	6
attraction	6
attractive	6
avoiding	6
awake	6
awoke	6
beauty	6
believes	6
bet	6
bill	6
bills	6
blacked	6
blackouts	6
block	6
boring	6
brings	6
British	6
burst	6
cab	6
capable	6
carrying	6
central	6
charming	6
choice	6
choose	6
chosen	6
cities	6
clean	6
closer	6
cocktail	6
cocktails	6
combination	6
commence	6
comprehend	6
consideration	6
constructive	6
contained	6
contains	6
cooperate	6
created	6
cross	6
cry	6
dared	6
deeper	6
defeat	6
defense	6
demands	6
denomination	6
depend	6
dependence	6
dependent	6
depending	6
describe	6
desperately	6
Detroit	6
direct	6
directions	6
director	6
disappear	6
disaster	6
discussed	6
disgrace	6
Doctor	6
dream	6
dreams	6
drugs	6
drunkenness	6
drunker	6
due	6
earnestly	6
east	6
effects	6
employee	6
employers	6
encouraged	6
endless	6
enter	6
excessive	6
exercise	6
expect	6
failures	6
faults	6
fifty	6
figure	6
finance	6
forced	6
foreword	6
formed	6
formerly	6
forth	6
fresh	6
function	6
funny	6
garage	6
generation	6
genius	6
Germany	6
graduated	6
gratitude	6
guidance	6
happily	6
hid	6
hospitalized	6
houses	6
impending	6
importance	6
impression	6
inability	6
increasing	6
incredible	6
indicated	6
inevitably	6
influence	6
information	6
initiation	6
insisted	6
inspiration	6
inspired	6
instance	6
intelligent	6
intend	6
intentions	6

intimate	6
introduced	6
issue	6
Jim	6
joining	6
kicked	6
knocked	6
land	6
lead	6
leads	6
lies	6
lock	6
logical	6
looks	6
main	6
manner	6
market	6
martini	6
meanwhile	6
mention	6
method	6
methods	6
milk	6
million	6
miracles	6
motives	6
mountain	6
movie	6
nearest	6
neighborhood	6
New England	6
newcomer	6
normally	6
numerous	6
obligation	6
obliged	6
obvious	6
oldest	6
opposite	6
original	6
packed	6
parts	6
paying	6
pep	6
permitted	6
phase	6
piece	6
pieces	6
plane	6
planning	6
pool	6
prepared	6
prescription	6
press	6
printed	6
printing	6
proceed	6
profound	6
promising	6
prospects	6
protect	6
publicity	6
raise	6
rare	6
rarely	6
react	6
reader	6
readers	6
readily	6
recently	6
regiment	6
regular	6
relapse	6
repeated	6
replaced	6
replied	6
require	6
respected	6
respects	6
restaurant	6
restore	6
restored	6
returning	6
rich	6
rights	6
rose	6
round	6
salary	6
scotch	6
sedatives	6
self-respect	6
she's	6
shipped	6
shocked	6
sincerely	6
sincerity	6
sing	6
situations	6
sixty	6
sobered	6
spare	6
spell	6
spirits	6
spots	6
standpoint	6
stands	6
star	6
strangely	6
stuck	6
stupor	6
succeeded	6
supply	6
supreme	6
survive	6
survived	6
sworn	6
temporary	6
temptation	6
test	6
thereafter	6
tracks	6
trade	6
traveling	6
trips	6
trusted	6
Twelve Traditions	6
twenties	6
twenty-three	6
unbearable	6
unreasonable	6
unusual	6
using	6
utmost	6
vacations	6
value	6
values	6
vast	6
views	6
visiting	6
warm	6
warned	6
we'd	6
wedding	6
wherever	6
William	6
winter	6
wishes	6
worldly	6
wreck	6
wrongs	6
younger	6
abandon	5
abruptly	5
absorb	5
abstinence	5
absurd	5
accompanied	5
accomplish	5
achieved	5
acquire	5
address	5
adult	5
advertising	5
afflicted	5
afterwards	5
agony	5
air	5
alive	5
allergic	5
ambitions	5
answered	5
appears	5
application	5
appreciate	5
approval	5
Armistice	5
arrange	5
arrangements	5
asleep	5
assurance	5
atheist	5
author	5
awfully	5
background	5
balance	5
barely	5
Barleycorn	5
barroom	5
bartender	5
behave	5
biggest	5
bless	5
blessing	5
blessings	5
blew	5
bodily	5
bored	5
bother	5
bothered	5
bound	5
brand	5
breakfast	5
bright	5
burden	5
calls	5
camp	5
card	5
cars	5
Catholics	5
ceased	5
chapters	5
chemicals	5
Clarence	5
collapse	5
collapsed	5
command	5
concede	5
concentrate	5
conceptions	5
concerning	5
concluded	5
confined	5
confusion	5
consider	5
considerate	5
contrary	5
contributions	5
convention	5
convincing	5
cope	5
corner	5
count	5
countries	5
creative	5
credit	5
crossed	5
cups	5
curing	5
cursing	5
customer	5
dances	5
defeated	5
defiant	5
demonstration	5
dental	5
describing	5
despairing	5
destruction	5
detail	5
determination	5
developing	5
disappeared	5
discharge	5
discipline	5
disgusted	5
doomed	5
dreamed	5
driver	5
dropped	5
dull	5
dying	5
earn	5
eastern	5
editor	5
Egypt	5
employ	5
encourage	5
enjoying	5
enterprise	5
episodes	5
Esther	5
evenings	5
everyday	5
evidence	5
excitement	5
extra	5
extraordinary	5
extremely	5
extremes	5
factory	5
false	5
father's	5
favor	5
feature	5
fed	5
fighting	5
fill	5
fly	5
fog	5
fool	5
forms	5
formula	5
fortunately	5
Fred	5
friendships	5
gain	5
games	5
gathered	5
gathering	5
genuine	5
glow	5
gold	5
golf	5
grades	5
guide	5
harmed	5
heads	5
healthy	5
heaven	5
hiding	5
highly	5
hospitalization	5
hot	5
hung	5
hunting	5
identify	5
ignorance	5
image	5
imagination	5
imagined	5
immediate	5
imperative	5
incident	5
increasingly	5
independent	5
innocent	5
insecurity	5
instances	5
instinct	5
insurance	5
interests	5
introduction	5
James	5
jittery	5
joints	5
keys	5
kids	5
kindness	5
king	5
larger	5
latter	5
laughter	5
lend	5
letting	5
lifetime	5
lights	5
listed	5
literally	5
liver	5
loser	5
losing	5
lower	5
major	5
manager	5
martyr	5
master	5
match	5
maturity	5
maximum	5
meantime	5
measure	5
men's	5
mere	5
merry-go-round	5
mess	5
misunderstanding	5
misunderstood	5
mom	5
mostly	5
movement	5
nearby	5
neglected	5
neighbors	5
nonalcoholic	5
nurses	5
object	5
obtained	5
October	5
opinions	5
outlined	5
owes	5
pack	5
painfully	5
performance	5
personally	5
pictures	5
pile	5
planned	5
playing	5
positions	5
possessed	5
practicing	5
prescribed	5
primary	5
principal	5
progressed	5
progressively	5
promptly	5
psycho	5
qualities	5
reaching	5
reasoning	5
reduced	5
refuse	5
regain	5
regard	5
relate	5
related	5
relax	5
rely	5
remains	5
remarried	5
remorseful	5
repair	5
report	5
resolution	5
resolutions	5
resolve	5
restraint	5
rise	5
rolling	5
ruin	5
rushed	5
sandwich	5
scarcely	5

secret	5
secure	5
sedative	5
self-centered	5
sensed	5
September	5
series	5
serving	5
shaken	5
Shakespeare	5
share	5
ship	5
shock	5
shoulder	5
shoulders	5
sight	5
signed	5
sleeping	5
slightest	5
smart	5
sobering	5
solemn	5
solving	5
sooner	5
space	5
spoil	5
stages	5
stated	5
stole	5
stranger	5
strenuous	5
studying	5
substantial	5
suffers	5
sum	5
supper	5
surprised	5
suspect	5
teach	5
teacher	5
temporarily	5
ten-day	5
tension	5
thanked	5
threatened	5
torture	5
totally	5
touched	5
track	5
tragedy	5
traits	5
transferred	5
traveled	5
treating	5
trembling	5
twelfth	5
twenty-seven	5
upstairs	5
utter	5
vague	5
victory	5
visits	5
voices	5
wash	5
wasted	5
watching	5
we'll	5
week-end	5
weekly	5
western	5
wide	5
wild	5
win	5
wore	5
worried	5
worries	5
youth	5
absolute	4
abused	4
accounting	4
accustomed	4
acted	4
actor	4
additional	4
addressed	4
admits	4
adventure	4
affect	4
affection	4
agencies	4
agency	4
ages	4
aisle	4
alert	4
allow	4
amazing	4
ambitious	4
ambulance	4
anonymity	4
anxiety	4
anyone's	4
appearance	4
applies	4
appointment	4
April	4
arm	4
arrest	4
aspect	4
assert	4
assume	4
assured	4
ate	4
attack	4
authorities	4
baffled	4
ball	4
bankruptcy	4
bare	4
barn	4
bartenders	4
basically	4
bathroom	4
bedroom	4
behaved	4
beliefs	4
believing	4
beneath	4
birth	4
bitterness	4
bootlegger	4
bore	4
breakdown	4
breaking	4
breaks	4
breath	4
Brown	4
burdens	4
butcher	4
calling	4
cancer	4
cans	4
cards	4
cash	4
casual	4
causes	4
celebrate	4
cellar	4
centers	4
century	4
certainty	4
charity	4
checked	4
childish	4
churches	4
cigarette	4
classes	4
cleared	4
clergyman	4
clipping	4
cloud	4
coat	4
color	4
combined	4
comfortably	4
commander	4
commitment	4
communities	4
companies	4
competent	4
composed	4
confirmed	4
connection	4
connections	4
consulted	4
contented	4
continuous	4
conversations	4
cook	4
cooperation	4
copy	4
crime	4
crutch	4
crying	4
cunning	4
cup	4
cured	4
cute	4
cycle	4
damaged	4
dare	4
deadly	4
dearly	4
definition	4
deliberately	4
demand	4
demonstrate	4
denial	4
dentist	4
design	4
designed	4
destroy	4
determine	4
devil	4
devotion	4
diagnosis	4
diet	4
differently	4
dilemma	4
directory	4
disappointments	4
discard	4
disclose	4
discouraged	4
discussing	4
disposal	4
distinguished	4
district	4
dividends	4
divine	4
downstairs	4
downtown	4
draft	4
drew	4
driven	4
Dublin	4
duties	4
earliest	4
earned	4
earnest	4
earnestness	4
earning	4
ears	4
Easter	4
educational	4
elected	4
Ella	4
emphasize	4
employment	4
enable	4
enabled	4
encountered	4
ending	4
engage	4
ensuing	4
entertain	4
essential	4
events	4
everywhere	4
ex-problem	4
exception	4
excited	4
executive	4
expecting	4
expenses	4
expressed	4
expressions	4
facilities	4
factor	4
faithfully	4
falling	4
falls	4
fashion	4
February	4
fee	4
fights	4
firmly	4
fixed	4
flask	4
flow	4
flower	4
folk	4
follows	4
fond	4
foolishly	4
football	4
forces	4
foreign	4
forgive	4
forgiven	4
forgiveness	4
fortune	4
fourteen	4
fox	4
frame	4
friendship	4
fulfillment	4
fur	4
futile	4
gallon	4
gates	4
German	4
gift	4
govern	4
Grapevine	4
grave	4
green	4
grim	4
grip	4
grown-up	4
guiding	4
guilty	4
hall	4
handed	4
handful	4
hanging	4
Hank	4
Harry	4
haywire	4
headquarters	4
heartbreaking	4
helpfulness	4
helps	4
hilarious	4
horizon	4
horribly	4
Houston	4
huge	4
humble	4
hurry	4
impress	4
inadequacy	4
inadequate	4
inclined	4
inconsiderate	4
Indians	4
indicate	4
indication	4
indulged	4
inferiority	4
infinite	4
innumerable	4
inquiries	4
insanely	4
insist	4
instant	4
instantly	4
instructions	4
international	4
interval	4
intolerant	4
intoxication	4
investigation	4
inward	4
irresponsible	4
irritated	4
issues	4
jay-walking	4
joyous	4
Jr.	4
jumped	4
kidding	4
kindly	4
Lasker	4
lasting	4
leaders	4
leadership	4
legs	4
lest	4
lift	4
literary	4
lobby	4
Lord's	4
loyalty	4
mankind	4
marital	4
mark	4
marry	4
marvelous	4
mass	4
mattress	4
Mayo	4
medically	4
merry	4
mighty	4
mild	4
millions	4
minimum	4
moccasins	4
modern	4
mood	4
mornings	4
motion	4
motive	4
movies	4
Mrs.	4
murder	4
murder	4
native	4
nearer	4
necessarily	4
needle	4
neglect	4
neurotic	4
new-found	4
north	4
nose	4
note	4
notion	4
novel	4
nut	4
NY	4
obtain	4
occur	4
occurrences	4
oddly	4
offense	4
okay	4
opportunities	4
orders	4
ounce	4
outfit	4
paced	4
panic	4
pants	4
paraldehyde	4
paramount	4
parents'	4
passes	4
permanently	4
personalities	4
phoned	4
phony	4
physicians	4
pioneers	4
plant	4

planted	4
players	4
pneumonia	4
points	4
policy	4
polite	4
popular	4
pour	4
praise	4
prayers	4
praying	4
preceding	4
precise	4
presents	4
pressures	4
previous	4
prime	4
printer	4
project	4
properly	4
proportion	4
provocation	4
psychiatrist's	4
psychologist	4
publication	4
published	4
pulled	4
pure	4
quality	4
quantities	4
quarrel	4
quarrels	4
quitting	4
rang	4
rate	4
raving	4
realm	4
reasoned	4
recognize	4
recommended	4
reflected	4
reform	4
regained	4
regardless	4
regularly	4
relationships	4
relatively	4
remaining	4
remarked	4
remind	4
repeatedly	4
represented	4
required	4
resolved	4
resort	4
respectability	4
retreat	4
reverse	4
reviewed	4
reward	4
ride	4
rightly	4
risk	4
roaring	4
root	4
roots	4
Rotary	4
rounds	4
rugged	4
safely	4
sales	4
salesmen	4
saloon	4
saloons	4
salvation	4
satisfy	4
satisfying	4
scene	4
scenes	4
schedules	4
scientific	4
scores	4
Scott	4
scratched	4
screaming	4
searching	4
seeking	4
seeming	4
self-knowledge	4
self-seeking	4
sending	4
separate	4
sergeant	4
sermon	4
settle	4
severe	4
shackles	4
shakes	4
shaky	4
shared	4
shattering	4
she'd	4
shelter	4
shook	4
shore	4
shortcomings	4
shorter	4
sicker	4
Silkworth	4
simpler	4
singing	4
sins	4
sisters	4
sky	4
smile	4
smoke	4
sneaking	4
solid	4
sons	4
source	4
southern	4
specialist	4
speed	4
spelled	4
spells	4
spending	4
spirituality	4
squarely	4
staff	4
staggered	4
stairs	4
standard	4
startled	4
stations	4
statistics	4
status	4
stealing	4
stores	4
stress	4
stretched	4
strictly	4
structure	4
stumble	4
subsequent	4
substitute	4
suggests	4
supplied	4
surface	4
surprising	4
suspected	4
swallow	4
sweats	4
sweep	4
switch	4
swore	4
sympathy	4
taper	4
technique	4
teens	4
temperament	4
tendencies	4
theatre	4
therapy	4
they'd	4
they're	4
thirty-nine	4
thoughtful	4
thrill	4
till	4
tire	4
title	4
toe	4
tolerant	4
tossed	4
tragedies	4
tremens	4
trials	4
trick	4
trivial	4
Tuesday	4
twenty-eight	4
types	4
typical	4
U.S.	4
uncertain	4
uncomfortable	4
uncontrollable	4
underneath	4
undertaken	4
unfit	4
unique	4
unit	4
unwilling	4
upper	4
urgent	4
utterly	4
vaguely	4
vain	4
vanity	4
veteran	4
vision	4
voluntary	4
wandered	4
warped	4
we've	4
wear	4
weather	4
week-ends	4
weight	4
whereby	4
wishing	4
witness	4
wringer	4
year's	4
abandoned	3
absence	3
absent	3
acceptable	3
accomplishment	3
according	3
accounts	3
ache	3
achievement	3
acquainted	3
admission	3
adolescent	3
adopt	3
adopted	3
advantages	3
affections	3
affiliation	3
age-old	3
agent	3
ailments	3
aim	3
airplane	3
alarming	3
alleys	3
amusing	3
analyze	3
anguish	3
answering	3
apologize	3
appalling	3
appointed	3
appreciated	3
approve	3
arguments	3
arose	3
arousing	3
arrestment	3
arrival	3
arts	3
asks	3
asset	3
assets	3
associations	3
assumed	3
assuming	3
assure	3
atheists	3
attendance	3
attendant	3
aunt	3
availed	3
award	3
balanced	3
Baltimore	3
banker	3
barbiturates	3
barflies	3
bargain	3
barracks	3
barrooms	3
basketball	3
battle	3
bearing	3
beating	3
beautifully	3
beds	3
bedside	3
beg	3
beings	3
bell	3
Bellaire	3
belonged	3
belonging	3
belts	3
beneficial	3
Bill's	3
bitterly	3
blamed	3
blankets	3
blessed	3
blocks	3
blue	3
Bob's	3
bondage	3
booth	3
borrowed	3
Boston	3
bounced	3
bounding	3
bread	3
breathing	3
brew	3
bride	3
broad	3
brokerage	3
Brooklyn	3
brother-in-law	3
brothers	3
bucks	3
bums	3
bureau	3
burn	3
bus	3
cake	3
campaign	3
Canadian	3
capacities	3
careless	3
cares	3
carpet	3
catch	3
cathedral	3
causing	3
cement	3
cents	3
characterized	3
chasing	3
checking	3
cheerfully	3
cider	3
circle	3
citizen	3
civic	3
claimed	3
clear-cut	3
clearer	3
client	3
clients	3
climb	3
climbed	3
clinic	3
closely	3
closest	3
closet	3
co-founder	3
cocky	3
collecting	3
comfortable	3
comforting	3
comment	3
commission	3
companions	3
complain	3
complicated	3
conceded	3
conclude	3
condemn	3
conditioned	3
confession	3
consequently	3
consult	3
contentment	3
contents	3
continual	3
continually	3
contracts	3
contribute	3
controlled	3
controversy	3
conventional	3
correct	3
counsel	3
counted	3
couplet	3
courses	3
cover	3
covering	3
crawl	3
creditors	3
creeping	3
crisis	3
crowded	3
customary	3
damn	3
darn	3
dates	3
dawn	3
daylight	3
days'	3
debt	3
debts	3
debutante	3
decisions	3
deficiency	3
delay	3
delightful	3
demanded	3
depends	3
derived	3
deserted	3
deserve	3
desirable	3
desired	3
devastating	3
dignity	3
dime	3
dining	3
directing	3
dishonesty	3
disposition	3
dispute	3
disregard	3
distinct	3
distracted	3
distress	3
dominated	3
Dorothy	3
doses	3
doubted	3
doubtful	3
downs	3

drafting	3
drag	3
drawing	3
dreadful	3
dress	3
drift	3
drifted	3
driver's	3
drives	3
drugstore	3
drunkard	3
dubious	3
dues	3
dwell	3
eagerly	3
ear	3
eating	3
educated	3
effectiveness	3
electric	3
electrons	3
elements	3
eliminate	3
elimination	3
embarrassment	3
emerge	3
emerged	3
emerging	3
emphasized	3
emphatically	3
encounter	3
endured	3
enemies	3
energy	3
engaged	3
engineering	3
enjoys	3
enlarge	3
enlisted	3
enrolled	3
entitled	3
equally	3
era	3
erratic	3
essentially	3
estimated	3
evidently	3
examinations	3
exams	3
excellent	3
exceptional	3
exciting	3
exhilaration	3
existed	3
exists	3
expects	3
extended	3
external	3
facing	3
faculty	3
fails	3
fanatic	3
fancied	3
fantasizing	3
fantastic	3
fascinated	3
favorite	3
felony	3
fewer	3
figures	3
finest	3
Firestone	3
firing	3
flat	3
flying	3
fold	3
fooled	3
fooling	3
foregoing	3
fortnight	3
forty-five	3
forty-three	3
France	3
frank	3
frantic	3
frantically	3
frightening	3
funeral	3
furniture	3
galore	3
garbage	3
garden	3
generally	3
generous	3
gifts	3
ginger	3
gladly	3
goal	3
God-consciousness	3
goodbye	3
goodness	3
goods	3
graciously	3
gradual	3
graduation	3
grant	3
grief	3
gripped	3
grows	3
guts	3
gutter	3
habitual	3
halfway	3
hampers	3
handicapped	3
handling	3
happening	3
happier	3
happiest	3
harmonious	3
hatred	3
Hawaii	3
hazy	3
headaches	3
heap	3
helpless	3
helplessly	3
here's	3
hesitate	3
hesitated	3
highest	3
highway	3
hill	3
hinted	3
hire	3
hitting	3
holding	3
holidays	3
hoped	3
hopes	3
horrors	3
hotels	3
housecleaning	3
Howard	3
humiliating	3
humor	3
hurting	3
hysterical	3
hysterically	3
ideals	3
illustration	3
immature	3
impaired	3
impose	3
impressive	3
impulse	3
include	3
includes	3
increases	3
India	3
indispensable	3
indulge	3
industrial	3
infinitely	3
informal	3
informed	3
inmates	3
inquiry	3
insomnia	3
instrument	3
insufficient	3
insulted	3
insure	3
intake	3
intellect	3
intensely	3
interfered	3
interfering	3
intergroup	3
internal	3
interrupted	3
intervening	3
intolerable	3
intrigued	3
invite	3
Irishman	3
irritation	3
it'll	3
items	3
jealous	3
Jean	3
jeopardize	3
July	3
justification	3
justified	3
kick	3
kit	3
knocks	3
lad	3
lake	3
largest	3
latest	3
leader	3
leaning	3
leaves	3
lessen	3
liberation	3
license	3
lick	3
limiting	3
lined	3
lines	3
lips	3
liquid	3
listing	3
livelihood	3
loathed	3
locker	3
lone	3
loose	3
loses	3
loud	3
luncheon	3
luxury	3
machine	3
madly	3
mainly	3
maintaining	3
maintenance	3
majority	3
Maker	3
manifestation	3
manufacture	3
manufacturing	3
March	3
marked	3
mastered	3
matches	3
meals	3
meaningful	3
medicinal	3
menace	3
midst	3
mildly	3
military	3
miraculous	3
model	3
moderately	3
modest	3
modestly	3
Montreal	3
morally	3
mortal	3
mortgage	3
mothers	3
mounted	3
moving	3
mutual	3
Naini Tal	3
narrow	3
nationally	3
naughty	3
nausea	3
necessitated	3
neck	3
needless	3
needlessly	3
nervousness	3
neurologist	3
New Year	3
New Year's	3
newspapers	3
notes	3
notice	3
nowadays	3
nuts	3
observe	3
observed	3
obstacles	3
occupations	3
offices	3
olive	3
one-night	3
oneself	3
opening	3
openly	3
operated	3
organized	3
originated	3
other's	3
outcome	3
outsiders	3
overpowering	3
overseas	3
owner	3
Oxford	3
paint	3
pamphlets	3
papers	3
paralyzing	3
parental	3
Paris	3
parole	3
part-time	3
partners	3
pause	3
payday	3
peculiar	3
percent	3
performed	3
permission	3
permit	3
perspective	3
persuade	3
persuaded	3
pet	3
petty	3
photo	3
phrase	3
picking	3
pineapples	3
pioneer	3
pioneering	3
pit	3
plagued	3
plastered	3
pleasantly	3
plight	3
poison	3
poker	3
polish	3
political	3
possesses	3
possession	3
powers	3
prestige	3
pretense	3
priests	3
primarily	3
print	3
Priscilla	3
privileges	3
proceeds	3
produces	3
progressive	3
pronounced	3
prop	3
proportions	3
proposal	3
proposals	3
proposition	3
protection	3
proves	3
Providence	3
proving	3
psychic	3
psychoanalysis	3
purse	3
pursue	3
qualified	3
quarter	3
quarterback	3
queen	3
races	3
racket	3
rapid	3
reactions	3
readiness	3
realities	3
rebel	3
rebelled	3
receiving	3
recoveries	3
reference	3
referred	3
reflect	3
regarded	3
regret	3
rejected	3
rejection	3
relation	3
reliance	3
relieve	3
religions	3
remark	3
remembering	3
rent	3
repaired	3
reported	3
request	3
requested	3
requirement	3
research	3
resources	3
respectable	3
respecter	3
respond	3
restitution	3
restraining	3
restraints	3
resulted	3
resumed	3
retained	3
retire	3
reunion	3
reveal	3
revealed	3
reviewing	3
revolutionary	3
riding	3
rising	3
rival	3
roof	3
rooming	3
rules	3
rummy	3
rush	3
sacrifice	3
safety	3
Samaritan	3
saving	3
scale	3
scarce	3
scare	3
sea	3

secondary	3
secured	3
sedation	3
selected	3
self-appraisal	3
self-centeredness	3
self-conscious	3
self-reliance	3
self-sufficient	3
selves	3
senses	3
sensitive	3
separately	3
separation	3
servants	3
set-up	3
setting	3
shadow	3
shake	3
shave	3
sheer	3
sheriff	3
sherry	3
shield	3
shirts	3
sickened	3
sides	3
significance	3
significant	3
silly	3
sink	3
sixth	3
skeptical	3
skid-row	3
skin	3
skinny	3
slacks	3
slender	3
slight	3
smash	3
smell	3
smelled	3
smoked	3
smuggling	3
snow	3
soft	3
soldier	3
sole	3
solely	3
someday	3
son's	3
sordid	3
sore	3
speaks	3
specialty	3
specific	3
spends	3
split	3
spoiled	3
sprung	3
St. Thomas	3
stability	3
stake	3
steadily	3
steal	3
sticking	3
stolen	3
stone	3
stopping	3
strain	3
strapped	3
streetcar	3
streets	3
stretch	3
strongly	3
studies	3
stumbled	3
subjected	3
substituted	3
succession	3
succumbed	3
sugar	3
superior	3
supplies	3
surgeon	3
surprisingly	3
swearing	3
swing	3
Switzerland	3
tales	3
task	3
tasks	3
tasted	3
taxi	3
team	3
telephoned	3
tempted	3
tend	3
tendency	3
tensions	3
tenth	3
term	3
terrified	3
terror	3
text	3
thankful	3
thanks	3
theological	3
theories	3
thirty-three	3
thirty-two	3
thorough	3
throwing	3
thyself	3
ticket	3
tide	3
Tiebout	3
tied	3
toes	3
toilet	3
toolmaker	3
tools	3
tour	3
towns	3
tradition	3
trail	3
tranquilizers	3
trapped	3
tries	3
trousers	3
truck	3
trustees	3
tucked	3
tumble	3
tune	3
turns	3
twist	3
U.S.A.	3
ugly	3
unacceptable	3
uncle	3
unconscious	3
undisciplined	3
unexpected	3
unfortunately	3
uniform	3
unity	3
universal	3
universities	3
unlimited	3
ups	3
vanish	3
variety	3
Vermont	3
vicious	3
violently	3
visualize	3
vodka	3
waking	3
walks	3
wallet	3
warning	3
warnings	3
warrant	3
wars	3
washed	3
watchful	3
wearily	3
well-being	3
wept	3
who's	3
whoopee	3
wider	3
wings	3
wiped	3
withdrawing	3
wondering	3
workers	3
worn	3
wrapped	3
wrong-doing	3
wrought	3
yield	3
abetted	2
aboard	2
abstemious	2
abundantly	2
abuse	2
accepts	2
accompany	2
accord	2
accorded	2
accumulated	2
accurate	2
accused	2
achieve	2
actively	2
acutely	2
addicted	2
adequate	2
adjusted	2
adjustment	2
admired	2
adulthood	2
advance	2
advancing	2
adventures	2
advertised	2
advertisement	2
advise	2
affliction	2
afforded	2
aftermath	2
agents	2
agonizing	2
ah	2
aided	2
Akron's	2
alarmed	2
alas	2
Alexander	2
alimony	2
all-night	2
alleviate	2
allows	2
alluring	2
alma mater	2
alternative	2
alternatives	2
altruistic	2
amazingly	2
analyzed	2
ancient	2
anew	2
Annabelle	2
Annie	2
announce	2
annoy	2
annual	2
another's	2
antagonism	2
anticipation	2
apex	2
appendices	2
applause	2
apprehension	2
apprenticeship	2
approaches	2
approaching	2
arch	2
arises	2
armed	2
armor	2
arouse	2
arranged	2
arrangement	2
arrive	2
arriving	2
arrogant	2
articles	2
assaulted	2
assigned	2
assumption	2
astonished	2
athletics	2
Atlantic City	2
attracted	2
attributes	2
Australia	2
auto	2
automatically	2
autonomous	2
avail	2
avenue	2
avenues	2
avocation	2
awareness	2
awe	2
bachelor	2
backing	2
bail	2
baker	2
balmy	2
banks	2
banquet	2
barbecue	2
barrel	2
barrier	2
barriers	2
basement	2
bath	2
battalion	2
bay	2
beat-up	2
Beery	2
befell	2
begged	2
behalf	2
belle	2
beloved	2
below	2
belt	2
benefited	2
benefits	2
Benzedrine	2
beset	2
bewilderment	2
bingo	2
birds	2
bits	2
blaming	2
blank	2
blanket	2
blazed	2
bleak	2
bloated	2
bloomed	2
blotted	2
blouse	2
boarding	2
boards	2
bob	2
bodyguard	2
bohemian	2
boiled	2
bond	2
bookstore	2
boom	2
boomerang	2
border	2
bordering	2
bothering	2
bounce	2
bounds	2
bouquet	2
bourbon	2
bouts	2
bowl	2
bowling	2
brag	2
branch	2
brat	2
brawl	2
brazen	2
broadcasting	2
brood	2
brotherly	2
brothers'	2
bruises	2
brushed	2
buck	2
Bud	2
bungalows	2
burned	2
burning	2
burnt	2
buying	2
by-gones	2
calculate	2
calculation	2
calm	2
camps	2
canal	2
candidate	2
candy	2
capital	2
capitalize	2
captain	2
careers	2
carelessness	2
caring	2
carpenter	2
casting	2
casually	2
cautious	2
celebrated	2
cell	2
centered	2
cessation	2
chains	2
chalet	2
changing	2
charm	2
charred	2
chaser	2
chasers	2
chatter	2
chatting	2
checkup	2
cheer	2
chemical	2
cherish	2
chew	2
choir	2
choked	2
choosing	2
chose	2
Christ	2
cigarettes	2
cirrhosis	2
citation	2
citizens	2
civil	2
civilian	2
claim	2
clamors	2
Clark	2
classification	2
cleaning	2
clergy	2
cling	2
clock	2
closing	2
coats	2
code	2
coin	2
collection	2
collectors	2
colleges	2
colony	2
combating	2
comforted	2
commanding	2
commences	2
commercial	2

commissioned	2
communicative	2
compared	2
complaining	2
complications	2
con	2
concealed	2
conceit	2
conceive	2
concentrated	2
conclusions	2
concrete	2
conference	2
confident	2
confinement	2
confronted	2
Connecticut	2
conquer	2
consent	2
consented	2
conservative	2
considerably	2
consisted	2
consulting	2
contacted	2
contacting	2
contacts	2
container	2
contemplating	2
contention	2
continuing	2
contract	2
contracted	2
contrast	2
contributed	2
controversial	2
convert	2
converted	2
convulsions	2
copies	2
cordially	2
corn	2
cornered	2
corners	2
cornerstone	2
corporation	2
corpsman	2
corrections	2
correspondence	2
cotton	2
counseling	2
counselor	2
counties	2
counting	2
couples	2
cousin	2
coward	2
cowardly	2
cracked	2
cracker	2
craved	2
crawled	2
crawling	2
craziest	2
cream	2
creates	2
creativity	2
creditably	2
creed	2
crew	2
crises	2
critic	2
criticized	2
crucial	2
cruel	2
crush	2
cupboard	2
curb	2
cure-all	2
cures	2
curiosity	2
curls	2
current	2
cynical	2
cynicism	2
damned	2
dandy	2
dangerously	2
dangers	2
daring	2
dash	2
daughters	2
dazed	2
deacon	2
dealers	2
deathly	2
debauch	2
debris	2
decency	2
decides	2
declared	2
declining	2
decreased	2
deeds	2
defect	2
deficiencies	2
define	2
deflation	2
defogged	2
delayed	2
delusion	2
demanding	2
democracy	2
demonstrating	2
demonstrations	2
depart	2
dependable	2
depended	2
deportment	2
deprived	2
depth	2
descended	2
desert	2
desires	2
despised	2
destination	2
destiny	2
destroyed	2
details	2
deter	2
deterioration	2
devil-may-care	2
diabetes	2
differ	2
differences	2
differentiate	2
dimension	2
directors	2
disappointed	2
discarded	2
disclosing	2
discoveries	2
discredited	2
discretion	2
discussions	2
disgust	2
disillusioned	2
dislike	2
disliked	2
dismal	2
dismissed	2
disorders	2
displayed	2
displays	2
dissipation	2
dissolve	2
dissolved	2
distances	2
distant	2
distinction	2
distorted	2
disturbances	2
divan	2
dive	2
divert	2
diverted	2
dizzy	2
doctors'	2
doorstep	2
double	2
double-header	2
doubled	2
doughnuts	2
dozens	2
draftsman	2
dragged	2
drawers	2
dreary	2
dresser	2
dressing	2
dried	2
drifting	2
drinker's	2
drowned	2
drunkalogues	2
drunkards	2
dry-cleaning	2
duck	2
dumb	2
duplex	2
dwelt	2
eager	2
Earle	2
eased	2
easiest	2
eaten	2
editions	2
editors	2
egg	2
eighth	2
elbow	2
elders	2
electrical	2
electricity	2
elevator	2
eliminated	2
embarrass	2
embrace	2
emergency	2
Emerson	2
employed	2
employee's	2
enables	2
encouragement	2
endeavor	2
endeavored	2
endeavoring	2
endlessly	2
endorsement	2
ends	2
endure	2
enduring	2
enemy	2
enforced	2
engagements	2
engendered	2
English	2
enjoyment	2
enlarged	2
enlightened	2
enterprises	2
entertained	2
entertainment	2
entity	2
envelope	2
envy	2
Episcopal	2
equal	2
equipment	2
equipped	2
errand	2
escapades	2
escaped	2
escapes	2
escort	2
escorted	2
esophageal	2
essentials	2
establish	2
evade	2
Eve	2
eventual	2
evident	2
evil	2
exaggerated	2
exam	2
examination	2
examine	2
examined	2
excess	2
exchange	2
exclusive	2
exercised	2
exert	2
exhaustion	2
exhibit	2
exhibited	2
exist	2
existing	2
expansion	2
expel	2
expensive	2
expert	2
explaining	2
exposed	2
expression	2
fabric	2
face-to-face	2
faded	2
faint	2
faithful	2
faiths	2
fame	2
family's	2
fanned	2
farmer	2
fascinating	2
fashionable	2
fast-moving	2
faster	2
fat	2
fatally	2
father-in-law	2
fathers	2
favorable	2
fearless	2
fearlessly	2
fearlessness	2
Federal	2
feeble	2
female	2
fences	2
fervor	2
fettered	2
feuds	2
fever	2
fierce	2
fifty-five	2
films	2
finances	2
finds	2
finer	2
finger	2
finishing	2
Fitz	2
Fitzgerald	2
Fitzgerald's	2
five-time	2
fives	2
fixing	2
flashed	2
flicker	2
floated	2
flour	2
flowing	2
focused	2
folder	2
fondle	2
fools	2
footing	2
forbidden	2
foreboding	2
forgave	2
forgetfulness	2
fork	2
formal	2
forming	2
fortify	2
forty-four	2
forty-nine	2
forty-six	2
Fosdick	2
fractured	2
frequency	2
freshman	2
friendliness	2
fright	2
frightful	2
fringe	2
froze	2
frustrations	2
full-blown	2
full-time	2
fuller	2
fund	2
funerals	2
furious	2
fuss	2
gadget	2
galled	2
gas	2
gastric	2
gather	2
gatherings	2
gaze	2
generously	2
gently	2
girl's	2
glittering	2
glum	2
golden	2
gossip	2
governed	2
governor	2
gown	2
gracious	2
graduating	2
grain	2
grammar	2
grandchildren	2
granted	2
gravely	2
groceries	2
grocery	2
grog	2
groping	2
grounded	2
grounds	2
guests	2
guided	2
gulp	2
guzzling	2
hail	2
hairdresser	2
haired	2
handicap	2
handiwork	2
handwriting	2
harbor	2
hardest	2
harmless	2
harsh	2
Hartford	2
haste	2
hat	2
Hawaiian	2
hawk	2
headache	2
headmaster	2
healed	2
healing	2
heartache	2
heartaches	2
heartbreak	2
heated	2
heavens	2
heck	2
heel	2
hemorrhage	2
Henrietta	2
herd	2
hereafter	2
heroes	2
heroin	2
herself	2

highball	2
hip	2
hired	2
histories	2
holds	2
holiday	2
homeless	2
hometown	2
honeymoon	2
honors	2
hook	2
hopeful	2
hopefully	2
hopelessly	2
horns	2
horror	2
horse	2
hospitality	2
hostility	2
household	2
housewife	2
humanitarian	2
humanly	2
humans	2
humiliated	2
hunch	2
hungry	2
hunt	2
hypersensitive	2
ice-bag	2
icy	2
idealistic	2
identification	2
identified	2
idle	2
Ignatia	2
ignored	2
ignoring	2
ills	2
illuminating	2
imbued	2
immaturity	2
immensely	2
impasse	2
impatient	2
implicate	2
improve	2
improvement	2
Inc.	2
incapable	2
incarcerated	2
incidents	2
included	2
incompatible	2
incomprehensible	2
incorporated	2
incorrigible	2
incredibly	2
incurable	2
indications	2
indicted	2
indignant	2
inform	2
informing	2
inherited	2
injured	2
injustice	2
inquired	2
insecure	2
insidious	2
insidiousness	2
insight	2
inspected	2
inspection	2
instilled	2
intact	2
intangible	2
intellectually	2
intense	2
intensive	2
interference	2
interminable	2
interne	2
interneship	2
internship	2
interrupt	2
interruptions	2
intimacy	2
intuitive	2
investigate	2
investigator	2
involve	2
Ireland	2
Irish	2
iron	2
irony	2
irrational	2
irresistible	2
irresponsibility	2
irritable	2
island	2
isolates	2
jealousies	2
jeopardy	2
jobless	2
jolt	2
Jones	2
journal	2
journeys	2
joys	2
judged	2
judging	2
Kansas	2
Karen	2
keen	2
keg	2
Kentucky	2
kills	2
kingdom	2
kissed	2
knack	2
lab	2
ladder	2
lapse	2
largely	2
laughing	2
launched	2
laundry	2
leather	2
leg	2
lengths	2
lengthy	2
lent	2
liberal	2
liberty	2
lied	2
lieutenant	2
life's	2
lifelong	2
limitless	2
listener	2
litigation	2
Liverpool	2
load	2
loaded	2
loading	2
loaned	2
located	2
lockers	2
London	2
lonesome	2
Lord	2
Los Angeles	2
loves	2
loyal	2
luckily	2
lucrative	2
Ma	2
Madison	2
maelstrom	2
magazines	2
magic	2
magnifying	2
maintained	2
maintains	2
make-up	2
managers	2
managing	2
manic-depressive	2
manifestations	2
manifested	2
mantel	2
manual	2
martial	2
materially	2
maudlin	2
May	2
measured	2
mechanic	2
medication	2
mellow	2
melted	2
members'	2
mend	2
mercifully	2
merriment	2
midnight	2
mile	2
Millay's	2
mills	2
mind's	2
minded	2
mindedness	2
minister's	2
minus	2
missing	2
mission	2
Mississippi	2
mistaken	2
mistreated	2
moderation	2
monetary	2
monopoly	2
monthly	2
moons	2
moralize	2
morals	2
moreover	2
morning-after	2
morphine	2
mother-in-law	2
motherless	2
motor	2
mount	2
mountains	2
mouths	2
moves	2
mushroomed	2
muster	2
mystified	2
nag	2
nagged	2
Nam	2
nameless	2
namely	2
names	2
narcotics	2
Negroes	2
neighbor	2
nerve	2
neurosis	2
New Delhi	2
newer	2
night's	2
ninety	2
nobody's	2
nominal	2
nonprofessional	2
North Carolina	2
notorious	2
nourishment	2
nuisance	2
nursing	2
oasis	2
objectives	2
objects	2
observation	2
observations	2
obstacle	2
obstinacy	2
occupation	2
occurring	2
odd	2
offended	2
Omaha	2
omitted	2
one-way	2
operation	2
oppose	2
opposed	2
optimism	2
option	2
ordeal	2
organ	2
originally	2
originator	2
others'	2
outgrow	2
outsider	2
outstanding	2
outward	2
outwardly	2
over-indulged	2
over-weening	2
overcoat	2
overdo	2
overwhelmed	2
overwhelming	2
ownership	2
padding	2
pagan	2
pains	2
painting	2
palace	2
pals	2
pamphlet	2
paroled	2
parted	2
partially	2
parting	2
partly	2
partnership	2
passengers	2
passion	2
Pat	2
patient's	2
patriotic	2
patriotism	2
patrol	2
pays	2
peak	2
pedestal	2
penalty	2
Pennsylvania	2
Pensacola	2
people's	2
people-pleaser	2
people-pleasing	2
perceive	2
perfection	2
performing	2
periodics	2
persist	2
persistence	2
persists	2
pertaining	2
pew	2
pharmacist	2
pharmacy	2
philosophic	2
phobias	2
phrases	2
piled	2
pink	2
pints	2
placing	2
plague	2
plea	2
pleasurable	2
pleasures	2
pledge	2
pledges	2
plunge	2
plush	2
poetry	2
point-blank	2
pointing	2
policemen	2
politics	2
poorly	2
pop	2
porch	2
possibilities	2
post-war	2
postpone	2
potatoes	2
potent	2
pounded	2
powder	2
practiced	2
preacher's	2
preaching	2
preceded	2
precisely	2
predicament	2
prefer	2
preferred	2
prefers	2
prejudices	2
preparing	2
presentation	2
presides	2
pressing	2
prevent	2
prevented	2
prince	2
prisoners	2
privately	2
prize	2
probation	2
product	2
professionally	2
prolonged	2
promoted	2
proportional	2
prosperity	2
prosperous	2
protected	2
Protestant	2
proven	2
prudent	2
psychological	2
psychologists	2
psychology	2
psychotherapy	2
publications	2
publicist	2
publicly	2
puffs	2
pulling	2
pulls	2
purchase	2
purchased	2
purposes	2
pursued	2
pushing	2
puts	2
puzzling	2
Quaker	2
qualification	2
quantity	2
quarts	2
queasy	2
queer	2
queried	2
questionable	2
quizzically	2
rabbi	2
radically	2
railroad	2
rancor	2
random	2
range	2
ranting	2
rationalize	2
rationalizing	2
reacts	2
readjustment	2
reads	2
reasonableness	2
reasonably	2
reassured	2
rebellion	2
rebellious	2
reborn	2

receiver	2
receptive	2
recess	2
recognition	2
recommend	2
recompense	2
reconciliation	2
recovering	2
recovers	2
recruits	2
refer	2
referring	2
refill	2
reflection	2
reformer	2
reformers	2
refuge	2
regaining	2
regards	2
registered	2
regularity	2
relative	2
remainder	2
remarks	2
remembers	2
reminded	2
reminding	2
remote	2
renewal	2
renewing	2
rented	2
reorganized	2
repetition	2
represent	2
reprieve	2
requirements	2
rescue	2
rescued	2
resent	2
resign	2
resignation	2
resigned	2
resist	2
resisted	2
resolutely	2
respective	2
restless	2
resume	2
retaliate	2
retiree	2
retirees	2
returns	2
reunited	2
reverted	2
review	2
revulsion	2
rewards	2
rewrite	2
riddle	2
ridicule	2
ridiculous	2
righteous	2
rigorous	2
ring	2
rings	2
risks	2
rivalries	2
Rockefeller	2
rocking	2
rocky	2
rode	2
role	2
roll	2
rope	2
rosy	2
rotating	2
rounded	2
route	2
ruled	2
rum	2
rushes	2
Ruth	2
sailed	2
saint	2
sale	2
salesmanship	2
Salt Lake	2
salvaging	2
San Diego	2
sang	2
sarcasm	2
scales	2
Scandinavian	2
scattered	2
schedule	2
scheme	2
scholastic	2
scoff	2
scolding	2
scope	2
scrap	2
screwed	2
season	2
seat	2
secluded	2
seconds	2
secrets	2
seed	2
seeds	2
seething	2
seized	2
select	2
selecting	2
self-confidence	2
self-control	2
self-deception	2
self-destruction	2
self-insurance	2
self-interest	2
self-sacrificing	2
semblance	2
senior-citizen	2
sensation	2
sentences	2
sentiment	2
session	2
sets	2
seventy	2
severely	2
shambles	2
Sharkey's	2
shelf	2
shirt	2
shivering	2
shoot	2
shooting	2
shouting	2
shrink	2
signs	2
Silkworth's	2
similar	2
simplified	2
sinking	2
sissy	2
sister's	2
sister-in-law	2
situated	2
size	2
skeletons	2
skeptic	2
skepticism	2
sketch	2
ski	2
skids	2
skilled	2
skip	2
skipping	2
skull	2
slammed	2
slick	2
slightly	2
slipped	2
slips	2
smacked	2
smuggle	2
snap	2
sneak	2
society's	2
softer	2
soil	2
someone's	2
sometime	2
son-in-law	2
song	2
songs	2
sophomore	2
sorrows	2
sounds	2
spaced	2
speakeasy	2
speaker	2
specialized	2
specifically	2
spectacular	2
speculation	2
speeches	2
spill	2
splendid	2
spoken	2
sponsors	2
sports	2
spread	2
springs	2
squander	2
stable	2
standards	2
stared	2
staring	2
stark	2
stars	2
stays	2
stigma	2
stimulating	2
stimulus	2
stocking	2
stockings	2
stocks	2
strained	2
straw	2
streak	2
stream	2
street-car	2
stricken	2
strikes	2
strings	2
striving	2
stronger	2
structures	2
struggled	2
struggles	2
struggling	2
stubbornness	2
studio	2
style	2
subconsciously	2
submit	2
subsequently	2
substance	2
substantially	2
subtle	2
suburb	2
subway	2
succeeding	2
successes	2
successive	2
Suez	2
sufficiently	2
suicidal	2
suite	2
suited	2
summarize	2
summons	2
Sundays	2
sung	2
sunk	2
sunlight	2
sunset	2
superiors	2
supplanted	2
supplement	2
surgeons	2
surgical	2
surrendered	2
surrounding	2
surroundings	2
suspicion	2
sustained	2
swayed	2
sweat	2
sweater	2
sweetness	2
sweets	2
swell	2
switched	2
systems	2
talent	2
talents	2
tangible	2
tapped	2
taxicab	2
tea	2
teachers	2
teachings	2
teased	2
technical	2
tedious	2
temper	2
temperance	2
temperate	2
territory	2
testimony	2
tests	2
theater	2
thee	2
therapeutic	2
thereby	2
thin	2
thirties	2
thou	2
threatening	2
three-thirty	2
threes	2
threshold	2
throat	2
ties	2
tissues	2
titles	2
today's	2
tolerated	2
Tom	2
tongue	2
tool	2
tops	2
torn	2
tornado	2
tossing	2
tours	2
towel	2
trace	2
trained	2
tramp	2
transformations	2
travelling	2
treasurer	2
trembled	2
trembles	2
tribe	2
tricks	2
trim	2
troubled	2
troublesome	2
truths	2
tumbled	2
tumbler	2
tumor	2
TV	2
twentieth	2
twenty-four-year-old	2
twenty-nine	2
twenty-six	2
twinkling	2
two-fisted	2
two-thirds	2
two-thirty	2
twos	2
typewriter	2
ulcer	2
ultimate	2
ultimately	2
unaffected	2
uncertainties	2
uncontrollably	2
uncounted	2
undergone	2
underlying	2
understandable	2
understands	2
undertake	2
undisturbed	2
unexpectedly	2
unfold	2
unimportant	2
unkind	2
unknown	2
unlikely	2
unlovely	2
unnecessary	2
unselfish	2
unselfishness	2
unstable	2
unthinking	2
unto	2
unwise	2
upholstering	2
upright	2
uptown	2
urges	2
urging	2
useless	2
uselessness	2
uses	2
Utopia	2
valuable	2
vanished	2
varied	2
variously	2
vary	2
vein	2
ventured	2
verdict	2
version	2
vessel	2
vice	2
vigorous	2
virtually	2
visual	2
vivid	2
waked	2
wakened	2
Wallace	2
Wallkill	2
wallowed	2
Walter	2
wander	2
wandering	2
warmly	2
warn	2
warring	2
wartime	2
washing	2
wasting	2
watched	2
waterboy	2
wayward	2
weakened	2
wealth	2
weapon	2
wearing	2
weary	2
weddings	2
week-long	2
well-to-do	2
wheel	2
whereas	2
whirling	2
wholesale	2
whoop	2
widely	2
widened	2
willful	2
Winchester	2
wired	2
wisdom	2
withdrew	2
witnessed	2

woman's	2
womanhood	2
women's	2
won	2
wonderfully	2
wonders	2
wool	2
worker	2
worship	2
worthwhile	2
Wright	2
wrist	2
writers	2
wronged	2
years'	2
yelled	2
yesterday	2
youngster	2
zero	2
'teens	1
aberrations	1
abide	1
abjectly	1
ablaze	1
above-board	1
abroad	1
abstainer	1
absurdities	1
abusive	1
abysmal	1
abyss	1
abysses	1
Abyssinian	1
academic	1
academies	1
academy	1
access	1
accident	1
accidentally	1
accommodate	1
accomplishing	1
accomplishments	1
accordingly	1
accountable	1
accountant	1
accounted	1
accumulate	1
accumulating	1
accumulation	1
accurately	1
ace	1
ached	1
achievements	1
achieving	1
acknowledge	1
acts	1
acuteness	1
ad infinitum	1
ad nauseam	1
adapt	1
addict	1
adding	1
addition	1
adds	1
Adeline	1
adepts	1
adherence	1
adherents	1
Adirondacks	1
adjacent	1
adjustments	1
administer	1
administers	1
administration	1
administrative	1
admirals	1
admire	1
admonish	1
admonition	1
ado	1
adopts	1
adored	1
adultery	1
advancement	1
advent	1
adverse	1
adversity	1
adviser	1
advocates	1
aerial	1
affecting	1
affectionate	1
affects	1
affiliate	1
affiliations	1
affinity	1
affirmation	1
affixed	1
affluence	1
affords	1
afresh	1
African	1
Afro-American	1
afternoons	1
aggregate	1
aggrieved	1
aghast	1
agitated	1
agitation	1
agitator	1
agnostically	1
agnosticism	1
agonies	1
agonizedly	1
agreeably	1
agreeing	1
agreement	1
aha	1
aiding	1
aids	1
ailed	1
ailing	1
ailment	1
ails	1
aimlessly	1
ain't	1
aircraft	1
airing	1
Alan	1
Alanon	1
alarm	1
Alaska	1
Alateen	1
alcoholism-prone	1
Alexander's	1
alibi	1
alibis	1
Alice	1
alien	1
alky	1
all-important	1
Allah	1
allegiances	1
alley	1
alliances	1
allied	1
allies	1
allotment	1
allowance	1
alloy	1
Almighty	1
aloneness	1
alongside	1
alpha	1
Alsace	1
Alsatians	1
altar	1
alter	1
alteration	1
altered	1
altering	1
alternately	1
Amarillo	1
amateur	1
Amen	1
Amendment	1
American-sponsored	1
Americana	1
Americans	1
amid	1
amounts	1
amuse	1
amused	1
amusement	1
analyses	1
analysis	1
anesthetic	1
anesthetize	1
angel	1
angers	1
angling	1
angrily	1
animals	1
animated	1
ankles	1
annals	1
Anne's	1
Annie's	1
annihilation	1
anniversary	1
announced	1
annoyance	1
annoyed	1
annually	1
anon	1
anonymously	1
ante	1
antenna	1
anti-religious	1
anti-social	1
anticipating	1
anticipatory	1
antics	1
antipathy	1
antisocial	1
anuder	1
anxieties	1
anybody's	1
apathy	1
apiece	1
apologized	1
apology	1
appallingly	1
appealed	1
appealing	1
appeals	1
appearances	1
appetite	1
applaud	1
applecart	1
applying	1
appointments	1
appraisal	1
appraise	1
appreciative	1
apprehended	1
apprentice	1
apprenticed	1
appropriate	1
approves	1
apropos	1
apt	1
aptitudes	1
arbiter	1
areas	1
argued	1
argumentative	1
arising	1
Arizona	1
armies	1
armored	1
aroused	1
arouses	1
arraigned	1
arraignment	1
arranging	1
arrears	1
arresting	1
arrives	1
arrogance	1
artificial	1
artist	1
ascertained	1
ascribed	1
ash	1
ashes	1
ashore	1
Asia	1
askance	1
askew	1
aspects	1
aspirin	1
assail	1
assault	1
asserting	1
assessment	1
assignment	1
assigns	1
assist	1
assistant	1
assisted	1
associating	1
association's	1
assorted	1
assumptions	1
astonishing	1
astonishingly	1
astonishment	1
astounded	1
astray	1
astronomers	1
astronomical	1
asymmetrical	1
athlete	1
athletic	1
Atlanta	1
atop	1
attached	1
attachment	1
attacked	1
attained	1
attainment	1
attends	1
attentions	1
attic	1
attuned	1
audience	1
auditorium	1
augury	1
aunt's	1
auspices	1
Australian	1
authentication	1
authorized	1
authors	1
automobiles	1
automotive	1
autumn	1
averages	1
aversion	1
avert	1
aviation	1
avid	1
avoidance	1
avoids	1
await	1
awaiting	1
awaits	1
awaken	1
awakened	1
awarded	1
awfulness	1
AWOL	1
axes	1
babe	1
babies	1
backfired	1
backgrounds	1
backs	1
backwards	1
backyard	1
bad-intentioned	1
bade	1
baffle	1
baggage	1
baggy	1
bags	1
bailing	1
bakery	1
balked	1
balls	1
balustrades	1
band	1
bang	1
banged	1
banished	1
bankbook	1
banker's	1
banking	1
bankroll	1
banner	1
Baptist	1
baptized	1
Bar le Duc	1
barbershop	1
barfly	1
Barleycorn's	1
barman	1
barred	1
barstool	1
barstools	1
Basle	1
bat	1
bathing	1
bathrooms	1
bathtub	1
battery	1
battle-grounds	1
Bauer	1
beach	1
beaches	1
beam	1
beams	1
bearable	1
beard	1
beats	1
bed-time	1
bedevilments	1
bedraggled	1
befall	1
befogged	1
beforehand	1
begging	1
beginner	1
beginnings	1
begotten	1
begrudged	1
begs	1
beheld	1
behoove	1
belittle	1
belladonna	1
bellboy	1
belligerent	1
bells	1
belongs	1
bench	1
bend	1
bended	1
benders	1
benefactor	1
benevolent	1
benevolently	1
bestows	1
bets	1
betting	1
betting-slips	1
beverage	1
Beverly Hills	1
bewail	1
bewildered	1
bias	1
biased	1
bidding	1
big-hearted	1
big-shot	1
bike	1
billboarded	1
billet	1
billion	1
bin	1
bind	1
binds	1
Bing	1
Birmingham	1

Bishop	1
bite	1
biting	1
bitterly-hated	1
blacker	1
blacking	1
blacklisted	1
blameless	1
blanks	1
blast	1
bleached	1
blight	1
blindness	1
blinked	1
bliss	1
blocked	1
blocking	1
blonde	1
blossom	1
blotting	1
blowin'	1
blowing	1
blown	1
bluntly	1
blurry	1
bogged	1
Bohemians	1
boils	1
bologna	1
bolsterer	1
bolted	1
bone	1
bones	1
bonfire	1
booby-hatch	1
booked	1
bookies	1
booking	1
bookish	1
bookmaker's	1
bookstores	1
boon	1
boost	1
boot	1
bootleg	1
bootleggers	1
boozed	1
Boozeville	1
boozing	1
bores	1
borrowing	1
bothers	1
bouncing	1
bounty	1
boxer	1
boy-welfare	1
boyfriend	1
boyhood	1
boyish	1
boys'	1
bra	1
bracket	1
bracketed	1
brainstorm	1
brakes	1
branches	1
branded	1
brandishing	1
bravery	1
brawling	1
breadwinner	1
breeze	1
brewery	1
brewing	1
brewmeister	1
brewmeisters	1
bricks	1
Bridgeport	1
briefcase	1
brimming	1
bringing	1
bristle	1
Britain	1
British Isles	1
broadcast	1
broadcasts	1
Broadway	1
brokers	1
bronzed	1
broomstick	1
brother's	1
brother-executive	1
Brotherhood	1
brownstone	1
browsed	1
bruised	1
brushes	1
Bub	1
buckle	1
buckwheat	1
Buddhists	1
buddy	1
budget	1
Buffalo	1
buggy	1
build-up	1
buildings	1
bulbs	1
bulk	1
bulky	1
bull	1
bulldog	1
bum	1
bumbling	1
bunk	1
burdened	1
burdening	1
burgundy	1
buried	1
burlesque	1
burnings	1
bury	1
buses	1
business-getters	1
businessman	1
businessmen	1
busload	1
bust	1
Buster	1
busts	1
butlers	1
butting	1
buttonholed	1
by-paths	1
by-product	1
cabanas	1
cabinet	1
cabins	1
cache	1
cadet	1
cafe	1
cagey	1
cajoling	1
cakes	1
calamities	1
calamitous	1
calculated	1
calculating	1
calculations	1
caldron	1
California	1
callous	1
callowness	1
calmly	1
camaraderie	1
candidly	1
candle	1
canned	1
canteens	1
cap	1
capability	1
capitulated	1
caps	1
Captain's	1
carelessly	1
Carlyle	1
carom	1
carousal	1
carousing	1
carpenters	1
carries	1
cart	1
cartons	1
cashed	1
cashier's	1
castle	1
castor	1
casualties	1
cat-and-dog	1
catalyst	1
catapulted	1
categories	1
Catholicism	1
caution	1
ce	1
cease	1
celebrations	1
cellaret	1
ceremonies	1
certificate	1
chairman	1
chairs	1
challenges	1
champagne	1
champing	1
Champlain	1
channel	1
channels	1
chaos	1
Chaplain	1
characteristic	1
characters	1
charged	1
Charleston	1
chart	1
charted	1
chartered	1
Charybdis	1
chastened	1
chat	1
chattered	1
chattering	1
chauffeur	1
cheaper	1
cheapest	1
cheating	1
checks	1
cheekbone	1
cheeks	1
cheerfulness	1
cheery	1
chemist	1
chemists	1
cherished	1
chest	1
chests	1
chicanery	1
chicken	1
chief's	1
chiefly	1
childishness	1
children's	1
chilling	1
chills	1
chin	1
China	1
chip	1
chocolate	1
chokes	1
chooses	1
chore	1
Christ's	1
Christmastime	1
chronically	1
chronicle	1
chucking	1
chuckle	1
chunks	1
church-goer	1
churchgoing	1
churchman	1
chute	1
cinch	1
Cincinnati	1
cipher	1
circles	1
circling	1
circuits	1
circulation	1
circumstance	1
cited	1
citing	1
citizenship	1
city-bred	1
civilization	1
claiming	1
clang	1
claret	1
classed	1
classroom	1
clattered	1
claw	1
cleaned	1
cleanest	1
clearing	1
clears	1
clemency	1
clergymen	1
clerk	1
Cleveland's	1
clinch	1
clinging	1
clings	1
clocks	1
close-mouthed	1
closets	1
clothed	1
clothing	1
clouds	1
clown	1
clowning	1
clowns	1
club-man	1
clubroom	1
clumsy	1
clung	1
clusters	1
clutches	1
co-operation	1
coal	1
coast	1
coaxing	1
cobwebs	1
cock-sureness	1
cocker	1
cockiness	1
cockpit	1
coddle	1
codeine	1
codes	1
codger	1
cognac	1
cognacs	1
cognizance	1
coherent	1
coincided	1
coined	1
Coke	1
cokes	1
cold-blooded	1
cold-storage	1
cold-turkey	1
colleagues	1
collect	1
collections	1
collective	1
collectively	1
Collier	1
collision	1
colored	1
colorful	1
colors	1
Columbus	1
coma	1
combat	1
combed	1
comforter	1
comic	1
comings	1
commencing	1
commendable	1
commendation	1
comments	1
commit	1
committees	1
commodities	1
common-sense	1
commonly	1
commonplace	1
communicate	1
communicating	1
commuting	1
companion	1
comparatively	1
comparing	1
compassion	1
compassionate	1
compatible	1
compelling	1
compensate	1
compensated	1
compensation	1
compensations	1
complaints	1
complement	1
complex	1
complexes	1
complexities	1
complicate	1
complication	1
compliment	1
comprehensive	1
compromises	1
compulsive	1
compulsory	1
comrades	1
conceal	1
concealment	1
conceived	1
conceives	1
concentration	1
concept	1
concepts	1
concerns	1
conclusively	1
concrete-and-steel	1
condemnation	1
condensed	1
condoned	1
conducted	1
conferences	1
conferring	1
confess	1
confessed	1
confessing	1
confidential	1
confine	1
confining	1
confirm	1
confirmation	1
confirms	1
conflict	1
conflicts	1
conformity	1
Confucius	1
confuse	1
confusing	1
congenial	1
congregation	1
congregations	1
Conn.	1
connected	1
conning	1
conquering	1
conquest	1
cons	1
consciences	1
conscientious	1
conscientiously	1
consciously	1
consequent	1
conservatively	1
considerations	1
considering	1
consigned	1

consist	1
consistent	1
consisting	1
consolation	1
console	1
consoling	1
conspired	1
consternation	1
constitutionally	1
constructed	1
construction	1
constructions	1
constructively	1
consultation	1
consultations	1
consumed	1
consuming	1
consummation	1
contain	1
contemplation	1
contemporaries	1
contemptible	1
content	1
contentions	1
contingent	1
continuance	1
contractors	1
contradict	1
contraption	1
contretemps	1
contributing	1
contribution	1
contributors	1
contrition	1
controls	1
controversies	1
convalescence	1
convalescing	1
convenience	1
convenient	1
convicted	1
convinces	1
conviviality	1
convulsion	1
cooked	1
cookies	1
cooks	1
cooled	1
coon	1
cooperated	1
cooperates	1
cop	1
coping	1
copious	1
copy-desk	1
cordials	1
core	1
cork	1
corker	1
corps	1
correctional	1
corrective	1
corroding	1
cosmos	1
costing	1
costly	1
costs	1
cot	1
cottages	1
couch	1
couches	1
cough	1
coughed	1
council	1
councilman	1
counseled	1
countenance	1
counter	1
counteracted	1
country-music	1
counts	1
courageous	1
courteous	1
courteously	1
courtroom	1
courts	1
courtship	1
coveted	1
cowboy	1
CPO	1
crack	1
crack-pot	1
crack-up	1
crackers	1
crackpot	1
cracks	1
craftsman	1
crafty	1
cram	1
crankiness	1
cranny	1
crash	1
crashed	1
crave	1
craves	1
Creation	1
creatively	1
creature	1
creditor	1
credits	1
creeds	1
creep	1
creme de menthe	1
criminal	1
criterion	1
critics	1
crock	1
crockery	1
crocks	1
crook	1
crooked	1
crop	1
Crosby's	1
cross-grained	1
crossbones	1
crosses	1
crown	1
crucified	1
crude	1
cruelty	1
crumbling	1
crumpled	1
crusade	1
crusaders	1
crushed	1
crushing	1
crux	1
cryptic	1
cubicle	1
cuffed	1
Cunard	1
curative	1
curled	1
curse	1
cursed	1
curtail	1
curtain	1
curve	1
cussing	1
custodians	1
custody	1
cutting	1
Cuyahoga	1
cyclone	1
cynic	1
cynically	1
Czar	1
D-Day	1
Daddy's	1
daisies	1
Dallas	1
dam	1
dampen	1
danced	1
dancing	1
Dannemora	1
dares	1
darken	1
darkening	1
darkness	1
daughter's	1
davenport	1
dawned	1
day-by-day	1
daytime	1
daze	1
dazzling	1
dead-end	1
deadlock	1
dealer	1
deals	1
dealt	1
Dean	1
dearer	1
debacle	1
debate	1
debit	1
decade	1
decades	1
deceit	1
deceiving	1
decent	1
decentralized	1
deceptions	1
deciding	1
decimal	1
decipher	1
deck	1
declaration	1
declare	1
declaring	1
decreases	1
dedicated	1
deducted	1
deepened	1
deepening	1
defeats	1
defectives	1
defend	1
deferring	1
deflate	1
defunct	1
degenerated	1
degradation	1
degrading	1
delays	1
deliberate	1
delicate	1
delicatessens	1
delight	1
delighted	1
delightedly	1
delinquencies	1
delivered	1
delivering	1
deluged	1
delve	1
Demerol	1
democratic	1
demonstrated	1
demoralization	1
denied	1
denizens	1
denominations	1
denounced	1
dentist's	1
dentistry	1
deny	1
deplored	1
deposit	1
deposits	1
depot	1
depressing	1
deprive	1
deranged	1
derelictions	1
derided	1
derision	1
derive	1
derogatory	1
describes	1
desertion	1
deserts	1
designating	1
designs	1
desirability	1
despaired	1
despicable	1
despondency	1
despondently	1
destined	1
destitution	1
destroyer	1
destroying	1
destroys	1
destructiveness	1
detailed	1
detective	1
detectives	1
deteriorated	1
deteriorates	1
deteriorating	1
deterrent	1
detours	1
detrain	1
develops	1
device	1
devised	1
devising	1
devote	1
devoting	1
devotional	1
diagnose	1
diagnosed	1
diagnostic	1
diagnostician	1
diary	1
dictates	1
dictation	1
dictionary	1
dies	1
dieth	1
diets	1
differentiates	1
differing	1
diffident	1
dig	1
digested	1
dignified	1
digress	1
diligently	1
dim	1
diminish	1
diminishing	1
dimly	1
dingy	1
diploma	1
diplomate	1
dipped	1
dire	1
directed	1
directories	1
disadvantage	1
disagree	1
disagreeable	1
disagreement	1
disagrees	1
disappears	1
disastrously	1
disciplinary	1
disclosed	1
disconcerted	1
discontented	1
discord	1
discourage	1
discouragement	1
discrediting	1
discreet	1
diseased	1
disfavor	1
disgraced	1
disgusting	1
disgustingly	1
disheartening	1
disillusionment	1
disinherited	1
disintegrate	1
disintegrating	1
disintegration	1
dislikes	1
disloyal	1
dismayed	1
dismays	1
dispatched	1
dispensed	1
dispensing	1
displacements	1
display	1
dispose	1
disposed	1
disproportionate	1
disputes	1
disregarded	1
disrupted	1
disrupting	1
dissecting	1
dissensions	1
dissipated	1
distinctions	1
distinctly	1
distinguish	1
distortion	1
distract	1
distractions	1
distressed	1
distressing	1
distrust	1
disturb	1
disturbing	1
ditch	1
dither	1
divided	1
dividend	1
dividing	1
division	1
divorcee	1
dizzily	1
doctrine	1
doctrines	1
dodge	1
dodged	1
dogged	1
doggerel	1
domesticity	1
dominant	1
dominate	1
dominates	1
domination	1
doom	1
doorway	1
doorways	1
doped	1
double-headers	1
doubting	1
doubtless	1
doubts	1
doughboy	1
Dowling	1
downfall	1
downgrade	1
downward	1
drab	1
drafted	1
dragging	1
drained	1
drama	1
dramatic	1
dramatics	1
dramatizing	1
drastically	1
drawback	1
dreaded	1
dreaming	1
dreamless	1
dreamy	1
drenched	1
dresses	1
drilled	1
dripped	1
dripping	1
drivers	1
driveway	1
dropping	1
drops	1
drowning	1

drug's	1
drugged	1
drugstore-home	1
drunk-driving	1
drunkard's	1
drunkest	1
drying	1
drying-out	1
dryness	1
dud	1
dulled	1
duly	1
dumped	1
duplicate	1
duplicated	1
DuPont	1
duration	1
dynamics	1
eagerness	1
early-day	1
earmarks	1
eats	1
ebb	1
echoed	1
economics	1
Ed	1
edge	1
edgewise	1
edict	1
Edison	1
edited	1
editorially	1
Edna	1
Edward	1
effectively	1
efficiency	1
efficient	1
egghead	1
eggnog	1
ego-centric	1
ego-strength	1
egocentric	1
egocentricity	1
egoism	1
egotism	1
egotistical	1
Egyptian	1
eighteenth	1
eighty	1
eighty-nine	1
eighty-two	1
Eileen	1
Eire	1
ejected	1
elapsed	1
elated	1
elation	1
Elba	1
elbows	1
elder	1
elderberry	1
elderly	1
elect	1
element	1
elementary	1
eleventh	1
eligible	1
Ella's	1
elm	1
else's	1
elsewhere	1
eluding	1
elusive	1
emanate	1
embarrassed	1
embassies	1
embittered	1
embodied	1
embodies	1
emergencies	1
emigrated	1
eminently	1
Emma	1
Emmet	1
emotion	1
emotionalism	1
emotionally	1
emphasizing	1
emphatic	1
employing	1
employs	1
empties	1
emulate	1
enacted	1
encased	1
enchanted	1
encountering	1
encounters	1
encourages	1
endangered	1
endorse	1
endorsements	1
energetic	1
energies	1
engagement	1
engine	1
engines	1
Englishman	1
engulfed	1
engulfs	1
enhanced	1
enjoyable	1
enlargement	1
enlightening	1
enlightenment	1
enlist	1
enormous	1
enquire	1
enquiring	1
ensign	1
ensued	1
entertaining	1
enthralled	1
enthusiast	1
enthusiastic	1
enthusiastically	1
enthusiasts	1
entice	1
entitling	1
entreaties	1
entree	1
entry	1
envelopes	1
environmental	1
environs	1
episode	1
epoch	1
equalled	1
equity	1
equivalent	1
eradicated	1
erase	1
erroneous	1
errors	1
erstwhile	1
escapade	1
escapism	1
escapists	1
escorting	1
Eskimo	1
essay	1
essence	1
estate	1
estimates	1
estranged	1
eternal	1
Ethel	1
European	1
evaded	1
evangelist	1
Evanston	1
evening-up	1
everlasting	1
everything's	1
evils	1
evolutionists	1
evolve	1
ex-alkie	1
ex-doctor	1
ex-husband	1
ex-incorrigible	1
ex-wife	1
exalted	1
examples	1
exasperated	1
exceed	1
exceedingly	1
excelled	1
exceptionally	1
excerpts	1
excessively	1
exchanged	1
exchequers	1
exclaimed	1
excluded	1
excruciating	1
excused	1
executives	1
exempt	1
exercising	1
exhilarating	1
exile	1
exonerating	1
expand	1
expanded	1
expectant	1
expedient	1
expelled	1
expenditures	1
experiencing	1
experimentally	1
experimentation	1
expertly	1
explains	1
explicit	1
explodes	1
exploits	1
explore	1
explosion	1
explosions	1
expresses	1
expressing	1
extend	1
extensive	1
extra-curricular	1
extract	1
extracted	1
extractions	1
extravagant	1
exultantly	1
facade	1
facilitated	1
facility	1
fact-facing	1
fact-finding	1
faction	1
factories	1
factors	1
faculties	1
failing	1
failings	1
fainted	1
faintly	1
fair-haired	1
fair-sized	1
fair-weather	1
fairness	1
fake	1
faked	1
fakery	1
fallacious	1
fallacy	1
fallen	1
faltering	1
fanatical	1
fanatics	1
fancy	1
fanfare	1
fantasized	1
far-fetched	1
fared	1
farms	1
farther	1
fascinates	1
fascination	1
fast-thinking	1
fatality	1
fate	1
fatigue	1
fault-finding	1
favorably	1
favored	1
favorites	1
fearing	1
fearsome	1
featured	1
features	1
felicitations	1
fellow's	1
fellow-sufferer	1
fellow-sufferers	1
fellow-workers	1
fellowman	1
Fellowship's	1
fellowships	1
fence	1
fenced	1
festering	1
festivities	1
fetch	1
feted	1
fevered	1
feverishly	1
fictitious	1
fidgets	1
fields	1
fifteen-minute	1
fifteen-twenty	1
fifties	1
fiftieth	1
fifty-eight	1
fifty-four	1
fifty-three	1
figuring	1
filching	1
file	1
filling	1
fills	1
filmed	1
finality	1
finals	1
financing	1
fingers	1
finite	1
fireside	1
firewater	1
firmer	1
first-timers	1
fish	1
fish-wife	1
fishing	1
fist	1
fists	1
fits	1
fitted	1
fitting	1
five-year-old	1
flagging	1
flame	1
flames	1
flank	1
flannels	1
flapper	1
flare	1
flare-ups	1
flash	1
flashing	1
flashy	1
flatly	1
flattered	1
flavor	1
flaw	1
flaws	1
fled	1
fledgling	1
fleeting	1
flesh	1
fleshpots	1
flew	1
flexible	1
flickered	1
flights	1
flimsy	1
flippant	1
flipped	1
floating	1
flood	1
floods	1
floored	1
floundered	1
floundering	1
flourishing	1
flowed	1
flown	1
flows	1
fluently	1
fluff-dry	1
fluid	1
flush	1
flying-blind	1
focussed	1
foe	1
foggy	1
follow-through	1
follower	1
foods	1
foothills	1
footsore	1
footsteps	1
forbidding	1
forcibly	1
Ford	1
foresaw	1
foresee	1
foresight	1
forest	1
forfeit	1
forge	1
forged	1
forgiving	1
formally	1
forthwith	1
fortified	1
fortnight's	1
fortunes	1
forty-one	1
forty-publicist	1
forty-seven	1
forty-two	1
Foster	1
founded	1
founder	1
founding	1
four-thirty	1
four-time	1
fourteenth	1
fraction	1
frailties	1
Franciscan	1
frankness	1
freaks	1
Fred's	1
freed	1
freights	1
French	1
frequented	1
frequenting	1
fresh-skinned	1
friction	1
Fridays	1
friends'	1
frightfully	1
fringes	1
fro	1
frothy	1
frown	1
frowned	1
frowning	1
fruit	1
frustrated	1
frustrating	1
fulfilled	1
full-pack	1
fullest	1
Fulton	1

fumed	1
fumes	1
functioning	1
functions	1
fundamental	1
fundamentally	1
fundamentals	1
funniest	1
furnish	1
furnished	1
furthermore	1
futures	1
fuzzy	1
gage	1
gaiety	1
gains	1
Galileo	1
gallantly	1
gallons	1
gambler	1
gamut	1
gang's	1
gangster's	1
gap	1
garages	1
gardening	1
garrison	1
gasped	1
gate	1
gaunt	1
gayest	1
Gene	1
generalship	1
generated	1
generations	1
Geneva	1
gentle	1
gentleman's	1
gentlemen	1
geographical	1
geography	1
Germans	1
get-togethers	1
Gethsemane	1
ghastly	1
giant	1
gifted	1
gigantic	1
giggle	1
gimmick	1
gingerly	1
girder	1
glaring	1
glassful	1
glassily	1
glassy-eyed	1
glimmer	1
glimpse	1
gloom	1
glorious	1
glory	1
glove	1
glowing	1
glued	1
gluttonous	1
gnawing	1
goad	1
God-conscious	1
God-given	1
God-knows-who	1
God-sufficiency	1
godly	1
gondola	1
goner	1
good-feeling	1
good-natured	1
goofed	1
goose	1
goose-flesh	1
goose-stepping	1
gorge	1
Gotham	1
governors	1
grab	1
graciousness	1
graduates	1
grandest	1
grandfather's	1
grandmother	1
grandparents	1
grandparents'	1
graph	1
grasp	1
grasped	1
grasping	1
gratefulness	1
gratified	1
gratify	1
gravitating	1
gravity	1
gray	1
Greek	1
Greenland	1
Greenwich	1
greeted	1
gremlins	1
Grenadier	1
grey	1
grievous	1
grimy	1
grind	1
grinding	1
grinned	1
grips	1
grizzly	1
grocer	1
groom	1
groomed	1
groove	1
groped	1
grosser	1
grouch	1
groundwork	1
group's	1
groupers	1
grovelling	1
grudge	1
grudgingly	1
guarantee	1
guaranteed	1
guarantees	1
guardhouse	1
guessing	1
guest	1
guides	1
guild	1
guise	1
guises	1
gulped	1
gun	1
gunnery	1
gurgles	1
gusto	1
gym	1
H	1
ha-ha	1
ha-ha-ha	1
Hagen	1
hail-fellow-well-met	1
hair-raising	1
half-afraid	1
half-bleached	1
half-truth	1
half-year	1
Halloween	1
halves	1
hamburger	1
hamlet	1
hammer	1
Hampshire	1
hand-book	1
handicaps	1
handkerchief	1
handled	1
handmaiden	1
handy	1
hanged	1
hanger-on	1
hangout	1
Hank's	1
harboring	1
hard-fought-for	1
hard-won	1
hardness	1
hardships	1
hardware	1
harmful	1
harmony	1
harness	1
harness-making	1
harping	1
hash	1
hastened	1
hastily	1
hasty	1
hater	1
hates	1
hating	1
hats	1
hauled	1
hauling	1
haunted	1
haunting	1
haunts	1
haven	1
havens	1
havoc	1
hay	1
hazard	1
haze	1
he'll	1
headings	1
headlong	1
headstrong	1
headwaiters	1
headway	1
heal	1
healer	1
healthy-looking	1
heaps	1
hears	1
hearse	1
heartening	1
heartily	1
heartlessness	1
heartsickness	1
heat	1
heating	1
heave-ho	1
heavenly	1
heaves	1
heavier	1
Hebrew	1
heckled	1
hectic	1
heed	1
heels	1
height	1
hellish	1
hells	1
helper	1
helter-skelter	1
hemorrhages	1
hemorrhaging	1
Henri	1
Henry	1
Herbert	1
heresies	1
heritage	1
hero	1
heroic	1
heroics	1
hers	1
hesitancy	1
hesitation	1
hideous	1
high-powered	1
high-stepping	1
highballs	1
highflown	1
highlights	1
highroad	1
highstrung	1
hilarity	1
Hilda	1
hillside	1
hilltop	1
Himalaya	1
Hindus	1
hint	1
hints	1
historians	1
historic	1
historical	1
hitch-hiking	1
hitchhiking	1
Hitler's	1
hobbies	1
hobo	1
hobo's	1
hock	1
hockey	1
hoist	1
holder	1
holier	1
holler	1
home-brewers	1
home-brewing	1
homecoming	1
homelessness	1
homelife	1
homesick	1
Honolulu	1
honor-grade	1
honored	1
hooch	1
hooked	1
hooter	1
hope-inspiring	1
hopped	1
hordes	1
horrified	1
horsemen	1
hosiery	1
hound	1
housekeeping	1
housewives'	1
how'd	1
how's	1
howling	1
howls	1
huddle	1
hue	1
hug	1
humanity	1
humbled	1
humbling	1
humiliations	1
humorous	1
hump	1
hundredth	1
hung-over	1
hunger	1
hurled	1
hurricane	1
hurried	1
hurts	1
husbands'	1
huts	1
Hyde	1
hydrotherapy	1
hymns	1
hypodermic	1
hysterics	1
iced	1
idealists	1
identical	1
identity	1
ill-defined	1
ill-temper	1
illusion	1
illusions	1
illustrate	1
illustrates	1
images	1
imaginable	1
imaginative	1
imitation	1
immense	1
immersed	1
immigrants	1
immoral	1
immortalized	1
immune	1
immunity	1
immutable	1
impact	1
impair	1
impart	1
imparted	1
impartially	1
impeccable	1
impel	1
imperious	1
implacably	1
implicit	1
implied	1
import	1
importuned	1
imposed	1
impotent	1
impressing	1
impressionable	1
impressions	1
imprisoned	1
improved	1
impunity	1
in-laws	1
inaccessible	1
inattention	1
incalculable	1
incapacitated	1
incentive	1
incessant	1
incessantly	1
inch	1
incidentally	1
inclusive	1
incoming	1
incompatibility	1
incomplete	1
inconsistencies	1
inconsistency	1
inconsistent	1
indebted	1
indebtedness	1
indecision	1
indefinable	1
indescribable	1
indescribably	1
indestructible	1
Indiana	1
indicates	1
indifference	1
individually	1
indoctrination	1
induced	1
inducement	1
indulgence	1
indulgent	1
indulging	1
industry	1
ineffective	1
inescapable	1
inexperienced	1
inexplicable	1
inexplicably	1
infallibility	1
infancy	1
inferior	1
inferiorities	1
inferno	1
infidelity	1
inflict	1
informality	1
infringement	1
ingenuity	1
ingredient	1
ingredients	1
inherent	1
inherit	1
inheritance	1
inhibitions	1
inhospitable	1
initial	1

inject	1
injecting	1
injection	1
injunction	1
injure	1
injuries	1
injurious	1
injury	1
inmate	1
innate	1
innermost	1
inquire	1
inquiring	1
inscription	1
insecurities	1
inseparable	1
inside-out	1
insights	1
insincere	1
insinuations	1
insistence	1
insistent	1
insists	1
insofar	1
insouciance	1
inspect	1
inspirational	1
inspire	1
inspiring	1
instincts	1
institute	1
institutionalized	1
instruct	1
instruction	1
instructive	1
insufferably	1
insult	1
insulting	1
insurmountable	1
integral	1
integrity	1
intellect's	1
intensified	1
intent	1
interchange	1
interferes	1
interior	1
interludes	1
intermediate	1
intermingled	1
interpersonal	1
interpret	1
interpretation	1
interpreted	1
intervention	1
interview	1
interviewed	1
interviews	1
intimated	1
intimation	1
intravenous	1
intravenously	1
intricate	1
intriguing	1
introduce	1
intrude	1
intruded	1
intruders	1
intuitively	1
invented	1
invention	1
inventions	1
inventiveness	1
inventories	1
inversely	1
invested	1
investment	1
invitation	1
invitations	1
invites	1
inviting	1
involves	1
involving	1
iota	1
irate	1
irksome	1
ironed	1
irreversible	1
isolated	1
itching	1
itchy	1
jacket	1
Jackie's	1
jackpot	1
jackrabbit	1
jag	1
jailed	1
jailor	1
jam	1
jambs	1
jams	1
Jane	1
Janey	1
jangle	1
jargon	1
jazz	1
jealously	1
Jekyll	1
Jekyll-and-Hyde	1
jerk	1
jest	1
Jesuits	1
jet	1
Jews	1
Jim's	1
jimmied	1
jinks	1
Joe	1
jogger	1
joker	1
jokes	1
jokingly	1
joyfully	1
joykiller	1
joyousness	1
jubilant	1
judges	1
jugs	1
juice	1
juke	1
Jules	1
jumbled	1
jumping	1
jumping-off	1
jumpy	1
juncture	1
Jung	1
jungles	1
juniors	1
jury	1
justifiable	1
justifiably	1
justify	1
Kaneohe	1
kangaroo	1
keenly	1
Kenmore	1
Kennedy	1
Kent	1
kernel	1
key-tapping	1
keyhole	1
keystone	1
kicking	1
kicks	1
kidded	1
killing	1
killjoy	1
killjoys	1
kindest	1
kindliness	1
kinks	1
kinship	1
Kirby	1
Kitty Hawk	1
knelt	1
knit	1
knitting	1
knock	1
Ku Klux Klan	1
label	1
labored	1
laboriously	1
lacking	1
Ladd	1
ladies	1
lads	1
lain	1
lakes	1
lambaste	1
lance	1
landing	1
landlord	1
lands	1
Langley's	1
languages	1
lap	1
lapses	1
Las Vegas	1
latched	1
lately	1
latitude	1
launch	1
laundering	1
laundress	1
laurels	1
lawyers	1
laymen	1
lays	1
league	1
leak	1
leanings	1
leap	1
leaped	1
leaps	1
leapt	1
learns	1
lectures	1
ledger	1
leg-work	1
legally	1
legions	1
legislators	1
legitimate	1
leisure	1
leisure-world	1
leisurely	1
lemon	1
lending	1
lenses	1
lessened	1
lessons	1
lethargy	1
lets	1
leveling	1
leveling-off	1
levity	1
liabilities	1
liable	1
librarians	1
licensed	1
licking	1
life-and-death	1
life-styles	1
lifesaver	1
lifesaving	1
lightly	1
lightning	1
likable	1
likeable	1
likewise	1
liking	1
limburger	1
limitation	1
liner	1
lists	1
lit	1
lively	1
loads	1
loaf	1
loan	1
loath	1
loathe	1
locality	1
locate	1
location	1
locking	1
lockups	1
lode	1
logic	1
logically	1
lolling	1
lolls	1
long-acting	1
long-time	1
longed	1
longest	1
longhand	1
longing	1
longingly	1
longs	1
longshoreman	1
longtime-successful	1
looming	1
loosened	1
lopsided	1
los Doce Pasos	1
los Douze Etapes	1
losses	1
loudly	1
louse	1
lousy	1
lowdown	1
lows	1
lubricant	1
lucid	1
Lucknow	1
lukewarm	1
lull	1
lump	1
lumps	1
lunacy	1
lunar	1
lunching	1
lure	1
lurking	1
Lusitania	1
lust	1
lustre	1
luxuries	1
lye	1
machinery	1
made-to-order	1
madman	1
madness	1
madonna	1
Mae	1
magically	1
magnificent	1
magnified	1
magnitude	1
maid	1
maids	1
mailman	1
mainspring	1
mainstay	1
majestic	1
majesty	1
majored	1
make-believe	1
maladjusted	1
malicious	1
Maliseet	1
mallet	1
man-sized	1
manageable	1
managements	1
managership	1
manages	1
mangled	1
manhandled	1
Manhattan's	1
manhood	1
mannered	1
manuscript	1
march	1
margin	1
marijuana	1
marine	1
Maritimes	1
markets	1
marriages	1
marshalled	1
Marty's	1
marvelously	1
Mary	1
master's	1
masterly	1
mastery	1
mate	1
materialize	1
mates	1
mathematical	1
mathematics	1
matron	1
Matteawan	1
mattered	1
mature	1
Maud	1
Max's	1
maximum-security	1
mayor	1
meager	1
meaningless	1
meanness	1
measles	1
measuring	1
mechanical	1
mechanics	1
mechanisms	1
media	1
medicines	1
meditated	1
melt	1
memberships	1
memorize	1
menial	1
mental-health	1
mentality	1
mentioning	1
merchant	1
merit	1
Mersey	1
messages	1
messy	1
Methodist	1
meticulously	1
metropolitan	1
mettle	1
Mexico	1
mid-week	1
Midas	1
middle-of-the-road	1
midget	1
midwestern	1
migrated	1
migrations	1
mike	1
milk-punch	1
milked	1
millenniums	1
milligrams	1
millionaire	1
Milwaukee	1
mimic	1
mince	1
mind-affecting	1
mineral	1
mines	1
ministration	1
minor	1
miraculously	1
mire	1
Miriam	1
mirror	1
mirrored	1
misbegotten	1
miscarriages	1
miscellaneous	1
misdeeds	1
miserably	1
misfortune	1
misfortunes	1
misgiving	1
misgivings	1

mishaps	1
misled	1
misplaced	1
mistress	1
mistrusting	1
misunderstand	1
misunderstands	1
misused	1
mix	1
mixed-up	1
mob	1
mode	1
moderated	1
moderating	1
mold	1
molested	1
moll	1
momentarily	1
momentary	1
momentum	1
Mommy	1
monastic	1
Mondays	1
monkeys	1
monster	1
monstrous	1
mooching	1
moods	1
moon	1
moonlighting	1
moonshine	1
mope	1
mops	1
morass	1
morbid	1
mortar	1
mortification	1
Moscow	1
Moslems	1
mostest	1
motherhood	1
motion-picture-studio	1
motioned	1
motivated	1
motivation	1
motorcycle	1
motto	1
mottoes	1
mounting	1
mud	1
muddled	1
mugged	1
multiplied	1
multiplies	1
multitude	1
mumbling	1
murmur	1
muscle	1
museum	1
mushrooming	1
mushy	1
musician	1
musing	1
musket	1
mustn't	1
musty	1
mutually	1
myriad	1
mysteries	1
mysteriously	1
nadir	1
nagging	1
nags	1
naked	1
named	1
Napoleon	1
naps	1
narrative	1
nary	1
nasty	1
nation	1
nationalities	1
nationally-known	1
nations	1
natured	1
natures	1
naught	1
naughtier	1
NBC	1
ne'er	1
near-wreck	1
nearing	1
nearness	1
neat	1
neatly	1
necessities	1
necks	1
needing	1
needn't	1
neglectful	1
negligible	1
Negro	1
neighbor's	1
neighboring	1
nest	1
nest-egg	1
net	1
network	1
neurotics	1
neutrality	1
Nevada City	1
never-ending	1
New Orleans	1
newcomer's	1
newly	1
news-gathering	1
newsletter	1
newsman	1
newspaper-man	1
newsreels	1
Newsweek	1
nicely	1
nicer	1
niceties	1
nickel	1
nickname	1
nightclubs	1
nightly	1
nightmare-filled	1
nights'	1
nil	1
nineteenth	1
ninety-five	1
ninth	1
No. 1	1
No. 3	1
nod	1
nodding	1
noise	1
noisy	1
nomination	1
non-academic	1
non-alcoholic	1
non-denominational	1
non-drinking	1
non-existent	1
non-meeting	1
nonalcoholics	1
nonchalant	1
nondiscriminatory	1
nonexistent	1
nonsense	1
nonspiritual	1
noon-day	1
noonday	1
normalcy	1
northern	1
nosebleeds	1
nosey	1
nostalgia	1
nostrils	1
noted	1
nothingness	1
noticeable	1
notices	1
notified	1
notoriously	1
notwithstanding	1
novels	1
nucleus	1
nudged	1
numbered	1
nurtured	1
O	1
O.C.	1
O.K.	1
Oahu	1
oath	1
oaths	1
oats	1
obesity	1
obey	1
obeyed	1
obituary	1
objectionable	1
objective	1
obligations	1
obligatory	1
obscure	1
obscured	1
observes	1
observing	1
obsessions	1
obstreperous	1
obtainable	1
occupied	1
occupy	1
occupying	1
occurrence	1
occurs	1
odds	1
off-again	1
offender	1
offending	1
offers	1
offhand	1
officer's	1
officers	1
official	1
offset	1
often-painful	1
oil-field	1
oilman	1
Oklahoma	1
old-drunks	1
old-time	1
old-timers	1
oldsters	1
oldtimer	1
omega	1
ominous	1
omit	1
omnipotence	1
on-again	1
on-the-job	1
one-fourth	1
one-half	1
one-nighter	1
one-nighters	1
one-third	1
ongoing	1
onslaught	1
open-mindedness	1
operations	1
operative	1
operator	1
opined	1
optional	1
optioned	1
oral	1
orchestra	1
orchid	1
ordained	1
organically	1
organizations	1
organizers	1
orthodox	1
ostracized	1
OTC	1
ounces	1
ourself	1
Oursler	1
out-grow	1
outburst	1
outdo	1
outer	1
outfits	1
outlaw	1
outlet	1
outlets	1
outline	1
outlines	1
output	1
outrageous	1
outright	1
outset	1
over-achiever	1
over-all	1
over-anxious	1
over-concentration	1
over-powering	1
over-remorseful	1
over-train	1
overbearing	1
overboard	1
overcast	1
overcomes	1
overdoing	1
overdose	1
overdue	1
overhauling	1
overindulge	1
overlook	1
overlooked	1
overpowered	1
oversensitive	1
overshot	1
overtake	1
overtook	1
overwork	1
owed	1
owl	1
owners	1
pace	1
pacifist	1
pacify	1
packet	1
packing	1
padded	1
padlock	1
paganistic	1
painstaking	1
painstakingly	1
pal	1
Palestine	1
pall	1
Palm Springs	1
palms	1
panacea	1
pandemonium	1
panels	1
pans	1
pant-leg	1
panty-waist	1
paracounselors	1
parade	1
paradise	1
paradox	1
paradoxically	1
paragraph	1
parallel	1
paralyzed	1
pardon	1
pardoned	1
parent	1
parishioners	1
park	1
parking	1
parlors	1
participate	1
participation	1
particulars	1
password	1
pat	1
pasture	1
patents	1
pathetic	1
pathological	1
pathologically	1
patiently	1
patients'	1
patronize	1
patrons	1
pats	1
patterns	1
patting	1
paused	1
pauvre	1
pawned	1
pawnshop	1
payment	1
payroll	1
peaceful	1
Pearl Harbor	1
peculiarly	1
peddling	1
peeled	1
pen	1
pencil	1
pencils	1
penetrated	1
penitentiaries	1
penknife	1
penniless	1
penny	1
penology	1
pension	1
pensioned	1
penthouses	1
pentothal	1
pepper	1
percentage	1
percentages	1
percodan	1
perfectionists	1
perform	1
performances	1
peril	1
perish	1
peroxide	1
perpetually	1
perplexing	1
persevere	1
persevered	1
persisted	1
persistent	1
person's	1
personnel	1
perspiration	1
persuader	1
persuading	1
pertinent	1
perturbed	1
pervade	1
perverse	1
phenobarbital	1
phenomena	1
Philander	1
Philippines	1
Philistine	1
philosophical	1
philosophically	1
philosophies	1
phobia	1
Phoenix	1
photographer	1
physician's	1
piano	1
pianos	1
picnics	1
pictured	1
piddling	1
piecemakers	1
pier	1
pig	1
pilled-up	1
pillhead	1
pilot	1
pin	1
pinch	1
pine	1
pineapple	1
pious	1
pitcher	1
pitiful	1

pitiless	1
pityingly	1
pizza	1
placard	1
placate	1
plainly	1
plaintively	1
planes	1
platoon	1
Plattsburg	1
plausibility	1
plays	1
playwright	1
plead	1
pleaded	1
plowed	1
plucked	1
plug	1
plumber	1
pluses	1
pocketbooks	1
pockets	1
pointless	1
poise	1
poised	1
poisoning	1
poke	1
poker-straight	1
pokey	1
polishing	1
politely	1
politically	1
politicians	1
pollens	1
pomp	1
pondered	1
pondering	1
pooped	1
poorer	1
poorest	1
popped	1
popping	1
port	1
portion	1
portrayed	1
pose	1
posed	1
positively	1
possess	1
possessions	1
possessive	1
post-alcoholic	1
post-operative	1
posted	1
postponed	1
postponement	1
pot	1
pot-belly	1
Potomac	1
potted	1
pounding	1
pouring	1
practices	1
practised	1
practitioner	1
practitioners	1
prairie	1
praised	1
preached	1
preacher	1
preachers	1
precarious	1
precede	1
precedence	1
precedes	1
precepts	1
precipitated	1
precipitates	1
predicaments	1
predicted	1
predisposed	1
predominant	1
preface	1
preferable	1
preferably	1
pregnant	1
prejudiced	1
premature	1
premeditated	1
premeditation	1
preoccupied	1
preposterous	1
prescribing	1
pressed	1
presumption	1
pretend	1
prevails	1
prevalent	1
prevents	1
previously	1
prey	1
priceless	1
pricked	1
prickling	1
prim	1
prima donna	1
primitive	1
prisoner	1
prisons	1
privacy	1
prizes	1
pro	1
probability	1
probable	1
probed	1
proceeding	1
processes	1
procession	1
proclaimed	1
procrastination	1
procreation	1
procure	1
procured	1
prodded	1
Prodigal	1
prodigious	1
prodigy	1
produced	1
producer	1
production	1
productive	1
productively	1
professionalism	1
professor	1
proffered	1
profitably	1
profited	1
profits	1
program-oriented	1
programing	1
progressing	1
progression	1
prohibited	1
projection	1
projects	1
promote	1
promotions	1
prompt	1
prompted	1
proms	1
prone	1
pronounce	1
propelled	1
propensity	1
prophesied	1
proportionately	1
propose	1
proposes	1
propositions	1
prosaic	1
prospective	1
prospector	1
prospered	1
protecting	1
protective	1
protege	1
protest	1
Protestants	1
protested	1
protocol	1
providentially	1
provider	1
provides	1
providing	1
provinces	1
provoked	1
prowling	1
psalmist	1
pseudo-sophistication	1
psychoanalysts	1
psychologically	1
psychopathic	1
psychopaths	1
psychosis	1
psychosomatic	1
pub	1
publish	1
publishing	1
pubs	1
pudding	1
pumped	1
pumping	1
punch	1
pupil	1
pupils	1
purchaser	1
Puritanical	1
purposefulness	1
pushes	1
puzzle	1
puzzled	1
quack	1
qualifying	1
qualms	1
quarters	1
Quebec	1
queen's	1
queerly	1
questionnaire	1
quicker	1
quickness	1
quicksand	1
quieted	1
quieter	1
quiets	1
quits	1
quota	1
quoted	1
raced	1
racial	1
racing	1
radical	1
rage	1
raging	1
railway	1
rain	1
raincoat	1
raining	1
rainstorm	1
rainy	1
raises	1
Ralph's	1
ramifications	1
ramming	1
ranch	1
ranging	1
rank	1
rant	1
rash	1
rat	1
rated	1
rational	1
rationalization	1
rationed	1
Ravenna	1
ray	1
re-assembled	1
re-create	1
re-emphasize	1
re-entered	1
re-establish	1
re-opened	1
re-organized	1
re-read	1
re-reading	1
reaches	1
reacquainted	1
reacted	1
readings	1
readjusted	1
realizes	1
reap	1
reaped	1
rear	1
rearrangement	1
rearrangements	1
reasserted	1
reassure	1
rebels	1
recalled	1
recapture	1
recapturing	1
receded	1
receipt	1
receivers	1
recent	1
receptions	1
recharged	1
recipe	1
recipient	1
recitation	1
reckless	1
recluse	1
recognizable	1
recognizing	1
recoil	1
recollect	1
recollections	1
recommendation	1
recommendations	1
recompensed	1
reconcile	1
reconciled	1
reconstruct	1
reconstruction	1
recording	1
records	1
recount	1
recounts	1
recouped	1
recourse	1
recreational	1
recruit	1
recruiting	1
rectally	1
rectify	1
recuperation	1
red-eyed	1
red-leather	1
redeeming	1
rediscover	1
redo	1
redouble	1
reduce	1
reed	1
reenlisted	1
refers	1
reflex	1
reforming	1
refrain	1
refreshing	1
refusal	1
refusing	1
regarding	1
region	1
regional	1
register	1
registering	1
regrets	1
regulate	1
rehearsals	1
reigned	1
reigner	1
reinvestigated	1
reject	1
rejections	1
relapses	1
relating	1
relaxation	1
relaxed	1
relaxing	1
relegated	1
reliability	1
reliable	1
relied	1
relieving	1
relinquished	1
relish	1
relive	1
reluctance	1
reluctant	1
reluctantly	1
relying	1
remanded	1
remarkably	1
reminds	1
remonstrances	1
removing	1
render	1
rendered	1
rendezvous	1
renewed	1
renews	1
renting	1
repairs	1
reparation	1
reparations	1
repeal	1
repeat	1
repeats	1
repel	1
replayed	1
replenish	1
reporter	1
reports	1
representatives	1
represents	1
reprimanded	1
reproached	1
reproduce	1
reproduced	1
reproved	1
repugnantly	1
repulsive	1
reputations	1
repute	1
reputedly	1
requests	1
requiring	1
requisite	1
resemblance	1
resembles	1
resembling	1
resenting	1
reservations	1
reserve	1
reserved	1
reserves	1
reservoirs	1
residency	1
resident	1
residential	1
resistance	1
resolves	1
resorted	1
resorts	1
resource	1
respecting	1
responded	1
response	1
restlessness	1
restoration	1
restorative	1
restrained	1
restricted	1
restrictions	1
resulting	1
retain	1
retaining	1
retaliation	1
retaliatory	1
retarded	1
retirement-age	1
retitled	1
retreats	1

retrogression	1
retrogressive	1
revelations	1
revenge	1
revered	1
revert	1
revised	1
revisions	1
revive	1
revolted	1
revolutionized	1
rewarding	1
rewon	1
rewriting	1
Rhine	1
rhythm	1
ribald	1
ribaldry	1
ribbons	1
richer	1
rids	1
right-about-face	1
righted	1
righteously	1
ringing	1
rinse	1
riot	1
ripe	1
ripened	1
ripped	1
risen	1
rises	1
risked	1
risky	1
Rita	1
river	1
riverbank	1
riverboat	1
roaches	1
roadhouse	1
roads	1
roadside	1
roadster	1
roam	1
roar	1
roared	1
robbed	1
robbery	1
robe	1
robust	1
rock	1
rocked	1
rocker	1
rocket	1
rocketed	1
rocks	1
rods	1
romance	1
romantic	1
rooftops	1
roomed	1
rooms	1
roomy	1
roost	1
ropes	1
roses	1
rotten	1
rouge	1
roughly	1
rouse	1
roused	1
routines	1
routing	1
rowed	1
rubbing	1
rudderless	1
ruinous	1
ruler	1
ruling	1
rumor	1
rumor-mongers	1
run-around	1
runs	1
runt	1
ruptured	1
rut	1
ruthless	1
ruthlessly	1
sacks	1
sacred	1
sadder	1
saddest	1
saddles	1
safer	1
sail	1
sailor	1
sailors	1
saints	1
sally	1
salon	1
saloon-keepers	1
Salt Lake City	1
salve	1
Sam	1
Samaritans	1
sample	1
sampled	1
samples	1
San Antonio	1
San Francisco	1
sand	1
Sandhurst	1
sandwiches	1
sanely	1
sank	1
sarcastic	1
sash	1
sassy	1
satisfactorily	1
satisfies	1
Saturdays	1
sausage	1
savagely	1
sawdust	1
scandalous	1
scant	1
scars	1
scenery	1
scheduled	1
schisms	1
schizophrenia	1
scholarship	1
scholarships	1
scholastically	1
schooled	1
schooling	1
schoolmaster	1
schoolmate	1
sciences	1
scoffers	1
scold	1
scolded	1
score	1
scorn	1
Scotland	1
Scranton	1
scrap-heap	1
scrape	1
scraping	1
scratch	1
scratchiness	1
scratching	1
scrawny	1
screamed	1
screwball	1
screwballs	1
screwy	1
scripts	1
scrub	1
Scylla	1
Seabrook's	1
searched	1
searches	1
seasons	1
seated	1
Seattle	1
second-generation	1
second-hand	1
secretive	1
secretly	1
sect	1
sectarian	1
sections	1
securing	1
securities	1
sedately	1
seduce	1
seduction	1
seesaw	1
Seine	1
seize	1
seizes	1
self-analysis	1
self-confident	1
self-consciousness	1
self-contempt	1
self-debasement	1
self-delusion	1
self-discipline	1
self-evident	1
self-help	1
self-imposed	1
self-induced	1
self-justification	1
self-loathing	1
self-pitying	1
self-possessed	1
self-propulsion	1
self-punishing	1
self-reproach	1
self-revealing	1
self-righteous	1
self-sacrifice	1
self-searching	1
self-seeker	1
self-sufficiency	1
self-supporting	1
selfishly	1
semi-blackouts	1
semi-coma	1
semi-hermit	1
semi-prostitution	1
sensational	1
senseless	1
sensitiveness	1
sensitivity	1
sentient	1
sentimental	1
sentimentality	1
serene	1
sergeants	1
seriousness	1
servant	1
servile	1
sessions	1
setback	1
seventeenth	1
seventh	1
seventieth	1
sexually	1
sexy	1
shackled	1
shadowy	1
shamed	1
shameful	1
Shane	1
shapeless	1
sharp	1
Shaw	1
shed	1
shedding	1
sheet	1
sheltered	1
shelves	1
sheriffs	1
shielded	1
shifted	1
shine	1
shins	1
ship's	1
shipping	1
shipwreck	1
shiver	1
shivered	1
shocking	1
shockingly	1
shone	1
shopkeeper	1
shops	1
short-acting	1
short-lived	1
short-sticking	1
shortcuts	1
shortest	1
shortness	1
shorts	1
shotgun	1
shout	1
shouted	1
shouts	1
shredding	1
shrewd	1
shrieks	1
shrimp	1
shrouded	1
shrubbery	1
shrunk	1
shucks	1
shuddering	1
shuffling	1
shun	1
shutoff	1
shuts	1
shutter	1
shying	1
shyness	1
sickening	1
sickest	1
sidecar	1
sidestepped	1
sighing	1
sighs	1
signify	1
signing	1
silences	1
silent	1
sillier	1
silverware	1
similarly	1
simulated	1
simultaneously	1
sinecure	1
sinful	1
singers	1
singly	1
sinister	1
siphoning	1
sipped	1
sissies	1
six-step	1
sixteen-pound	1
sixty-eight	1
sixty-four	1
sixty-six	1
skate	1
skeptically	1
ski-jump	1
skidded	1
skier	1
skills	1
skimped	1
skipped	1
skirt	1
skivvies	1
skunk	1
skyline	1
slackened	1
slam	1
slander	1
slash	1
slashing	1
sled	1
sledgehammer	1
sleeplessness	1
slicker	1
slide	1
slighting	1
slinging	1
slip-locked	1
slippers	1
slogan	1
slogans	1
slogging	1
slowest	1
slowing	1
slumped	1
slush	1
sly	1
slyly	1
smack	1
smarter	1
smartest	1
smarts	1
smash-up	1
smashups	1
smiled	1
smilingly	1
Smith	1
smoke-filled	1
smoker	1
smokes	1
smoking	1
smoldering	1
smoother	1
smote	1
smuggled	1
snag	1
snags	1
snapped	1
snare	1
snatching	1
sneaked	1
sneaky-drinking	1
sneerer	1
snickered	1
sniffing	1
snoops	1
snooze	1
snorts	1
snowballed	1
snowing	1
snowy	1
snubbed	1
snuffed	1
soaking	1
soap	1
soberest-seeming	1
soberly	1
sobriety-tension	1
sociability	1
sociologists	1
soda	1
sodas	1
sodden	1
soiled	1
sojourn	1
solace	1
soldiering	1
solicitation	1
soliciting	1
solicitor	1
solves	1
somebody's	1
something's	1
somethingness	1
SOS	1
sot	1
sots	1
souls	1
sounded	1
soundly	1
soundness	1
souses	1
South Africa	1
South America	1
southerner's	1
sowing	1
spacing	1
span	1
spaniel	1
spared	1
spark	1
sparkle	1
spasm	1
spasmodic	1

speak-easy	1
speakeasies	1
spearheads	1
specializing	1
specimen	1
speck	1
spectacle	1
spectres	1
speech	1
speeding	1
speedy	1
Spencer	1
sphere	1
spheres	1
spike	1
spinal	1
spine	1
spineless	1
spiral	1
spiritually-minded	1
splinters	1
splitting	1
sponsored	1
sponsorship	1
sporting	1
spotted	1
spouse	1
spout	1
spouting	1
spray	1
spreads	1
sprinkled	1
sprinkling	1
sprout	1
spurs	1
squad	1
squawk	1
squeezed	1
squirt	1
St. Helena	1
St. Petersburg	1
St. Vincent	1
stabbed	1
stables	1
stakes	1
stare	1
starlit	1
starry-eyed	1
starts	1
starving	1
state's	1
state-wide	1
statesman	1
stating	1
statistic	1
stature	1
steadfastly	1
steer	1
steerage	1
stem	1
stepdaughter	1
stepping	1
sterility	1
stern	1
stickler	1
sticks	1
stiff	1
stiffs	1
stilled	1
stimulants	1
stinker	1
stint	1
stints	1
stipulation	1
stirred	1
stirring	1
stirs	1
stitches	1
stock-in-trade	1
stockbroker	1
stocked	1
stomach-pumped	1
stones	1
storeroom	1
storm	1
Stouffer	1
stove	1
straggle	1
straightway	1
straining	1
straitjacket	1
strap	1
streaked	1
streamed	1
street-corner	1
streetcars	1
strengthen	1
strenuously	1
stressed	1
stretcher	1
stretches	1
strikingly	1
stripes	1
strive	1
strivings	1
stubbed	1
stubborn	1
students	1
stuffed	1
stumbling	1
stupefied	1
stupidity	1
subdue	1
subjects	1
sublime	1
submerge	1
subscribe	1
subscriptions	1
subside	1
subsidiary	1
Sudan	1
sue	1
sufferer	1
sufferer's	1
sufferers	1
sufferings	1
suffice	1
suffices	1
suffused	1
suggestive	1
suitable	1
suits	1
Sullivan	1
summa cum laude	1
summing	1
summoned	1
sumptuous	1
sun	1
Sunday-school	1
sundry	1
sunshine	1
supercargo	1
superficial	1
superhuman	1
superintendent	1
supernatural	1
superstition	1
supervised	1
supervision	1
supported	1
supporters	1
supporting	1
supposing	1
suppressed	1
surest	1
surety	1
surf	1
surgery	1
surgically	1
surmount	1
surpass	1
surpassed	1
surplus	1
surround	1
surrounds	1
surveyed	1
surveys	1
surviving	1
survivors	1
suspecting	1
suspend	1
suspicious	1
swallowed	1
sway	1
swear	1
swelled	1
swelling	1
swept	1
swig	1
swigs	1
swimming	1
swinging	1
switching	1
swollen	1
swung	1
symbol	1
symphony	1
synthetic	1
systematically	1
t'ank	1
tables	1
tablespoons	1
tack	1
tackle	1
tact	1
tactful	1
take-off	1
tale	1
talebearers	1
talented	1
talker	1
tallied	1
tan	1
tangent	1
tank	1
tap	1
tape	1
taped	1
tapered	1
tapering	1
tapes	1
tasting	1
tavern	1
taverns	1
tax-free	1
taxis	1
taxpayer	1
TB	1
teaches	1
teaching	1
teamed	1
teams	1
tearing	1
teaspoon	1
techniques	1
teen-aged	1
teen-ager's	1
teetering	1
teetotaler	1
teetotallers	1
telegram	1
telegrams	1
telephoning	1
television	1
teller	1
temporizes	1
temptations	1
tempting	1
ten-dollar	1
ten-thirty	1
tended	1
tender	1
tends	1
tenets	1
tennis	1
tent	1
tentative	1
terminal	1
terminated	1
terrapin	1
terrifically	1
terrifying	1
Testament	1
tested	1
Tex.	1
theatrical	1
theirs	1
theology	1
theorizing	1
thereupon	1
they've	1
thick	1
thickened	1
third-day	1
thirsty	1
thirty-eight	1
thirty-seven	1
thorn	1
thoroughness	1
those're	1
thought-life	1
thoughtless	1
thread	1
threadbare	1
threat	1
threaten	1
threatens	1
three-hundred	1
three-months	1
three-quarters	1
three-weeks'	1
three-year	1
thrilled	1
throats	1
throes	1
thrust	1
thumb	1
thunderbolt	1
thunderclouds	1
Thursday	1
ticker	1
tidings	1
tiger	1
Tijuana	1
tile	1
tilting	1
timed	1
timid	1
timing	1
tin	1
tinge	1
tinkering	1
tipped	1
tippler	1
tips	1
tipsy	1
tireless	1
tissue	1
titled	1
toast	1
toboggan	1
tobogganing	1
toddy	1
toed	1
toilets	1
toils	1
token	1
Toledo	1
tolerantly	1
tolerating	1
toll	1
tombs	1
tombstone	1
tone	1
tonight	1
topic	1
torch	1
torches	1
Toronto	1
tortured	1
tortures	1
toss	1
totaling	1
totality	1
tots	1
tottering	1
touches	1
touching	1
touchy	1
toughest	1
tourniquet	1
tower	1
towers	1
townspeople	1
traceable	1
traded	1
trademark	1
traditionally	1
traffic	1
tragically	1
trailers	1
trainfare	1
trains	1
tranquilizer	1
transcended	1
transfer	1
transformation	1
transfusions	1
transgressions	1
transition	1
translate	1
translated	1
transmit	1
transmitted	1
trap	1
travelers	1
travelled	1
traveller	1
treading	1
treadmill	1
treasure	1
treasured	1
treasuries	1
treatments	1
tree	1
trees	1
tremendously	1
tremors	1
tribulations	1
trifle	1
trigger	1
tripped	1
trite	1
triumph	1
triumphant	1
trolley	1
troop	1
trooper	1
troops	1
tropical	1
troublemaker	1
trucks	1
trudge	1
truest	1
trunks	1
trustee	1
trusting	1
trustworthy	1
tuberculosis	1
tubes	1
tugboat	1
turbulent	1
turmoil	1
turnkey	1
turnpike	1
tweed	1
twelve-year	1
twenty-odd	1
twenty-seven-year-old	1
twisted	1
twists	1
two-fifty	1
two-forty-five	1
two-quart	1
U-turn	1
uglier	1
ugliness	1
ultra-dry	1
ultra-modern	1
unabated	1
unafraid	1
unaided	1
unannounced	1
unanswerable	1
unapproachable	1

unavailing	1
unaware	1
unbalanced	1
uncanny	1
unchanged	1
uncommon	1
uncommunicative	1
unconsciously	1
uncontrolled	1
underestimate	1
underestimation	1
undergo	1
undergoing	1
undergraduate	1
underground	1
underlay	1
understandably	1
undertaker	1
undertaking	1
undertook	1
underweight	1
underwent	1
undo	1
undreamed-of	1
undress	1
undue	1
undying	1
unearth	1
uneasy	1
unending	1
unexciting	1
unfailing	1
unfair	1
unfamiliar	1
unfavorably	1
unfolded	1
unforgettable	1
unfortunate	1
unfortunates	1
unguarded	1
unharmed	1
unhushed	1
uniformity	1
unify	1
uninhibited	1
uniquely	1
unjust	1
unjustifiably	1
unkempt	1
unlettered	1
unloved	1
unloving	1
unmarried	1
unmentioned	1
unmindful	1
unmixed	1
unmoved	1
unpleasant	1
unpopular	1
unpredictable	1
unrealistic	1
unreasoning	1
unreproached	1
unreservedly	1
unsalable	1
unsatisfactory	1
unsettled	1
unshaven	1
unsuccessful	1
unsuspected	1
unthinkable	1
untold	1
untouched	1
untrained	1
untruths	1
unusually	1
unwanted	1
unwelcome	1
unwillingness	1
up-to-date	1
upbraided	1
upbringing	1
upheavals	1
uphold	1
upholsterer	1
upholstery	1
uplift	1
uppermost	1
uproar	1
uprooted	1
upsets	1
upshot	1
upward	1
urged	1
Utah	1
utterance	1
vacated	1
vacuum	1
vagaries	1
vain-gloriously	1
vainly	1
vale	1
valid	1
valley	1
valve	1
vanishing	1
vapor	1
variation	1
varieties	1
varying	1
vastly	1
vaudeville	1
veered	1
vehicles	1
veins	1
venerable	1
vengeful	1
venomous	1
vent	1
Venus	1
verbally	1
verge	1
veritable	1
verity	1
verse	1
versions	1
vestiges	1
veterinary	1
Vi's	1
via	1
vicarious	1
viciously	1
vicissitude	1
victims	1
victor	1
Vietnam	1
viewpoints	1
vigilance	1
vigor	1
vigorously	1
villain	1
vin	1
vindicate	1
vindictiveness	1
violins	1
Virgil	1
virtue	1
virtues	1
virtuous	1
visioned	1
visitor	1
vistas	1
vitally	1
vitamin	1
vitamins	1
vividly	1
vocation	1
voiced	1
voicing	1
volumes	1
voluntarily	1
vomit	1
vomited	1
vomiting	1
voted	1
vow	1
vowed	1
vows	1
vows	1
w-h-i-s-k-e-y	1
wad	1
wail	1
waiter	1
waitress	1
waken	1
wallflower	1
war-time	1
warden	1
wards	1
warming	1
warmth	1
warps	1
warranted	1
washday	1
washout	1
wasp	1
watches	1
watchwords	1
watering	1
waterpipe	1
waters	1
wave	1
waves	1
waxed	1
weakest	1
weakling	1
weaklings	1
wealthiest	1
wealthy	1
weaving	1
week's	1
week-end's	1
weekend	1
weeks'	1
weep	1
weeping	1
weeps	1
weigh	1
weighed	1
weighing	1
well-balanced	1
well-dressed	1
well-integrated	1
well-meaning	1
well-reviewed	1
well-trained	1
welled	1
wended	1
West Virginia	1
whacky	1
whammo	1
whatsoever	1
Wheeling	1
wheels	1
where's	1
whichever	1
whimper	1
whipped	1
whirl	1
whirled	1
whisked	1
whiskies	1
whisky	1
whisper	1
whistles	1
whistling	1
whoever	1
whole-heartedly	1
wholeheartedly	1
widen	1
widening	1
widespread	1
widow	1
wildest	1
wildly	1
Willie	1
willpower	1
wills	1
wilt	1
wilted	1
windmills	1
windows	1
winds	1
windshields	1
windward	1
windy	1
wine-drinking	1
wine-making	1
wine-room	1
wine-tasting	1
wines	1
wing	1
wins	1
wipe	1
wireless	1
wires	1
wise-cracking	1
wisely	1
wishful	1
witch-burners	1
withdraw	1
withdrawn	1
withholding	1
wits	1
wits'	1
witty	1
wobbled	1
woe	1
woes	1
wolf	1
wooden	1
woodshed	1
woolen	1
woos	1
woozy	1
wording	1
wordy	1
work-houses	1
work-outs	1
workable	1
workings	1
workshop	1
world-renowned	1
worldliness	1
worldwide	1
worrying	1
worshipfully	1
worshipped	1
worshippers	1
worshipping	1
worships	1
woven	1
wreckage	1
wrecked	1
wrest	1
wretched	1
Wrights	1
wrings	1
wrinkled	1
wrinkles	1
wrists	1
wristwatch	1
write-up	1
writes	1
writhing	1
X-rays	1
XYZ	1
yachts	1
Yankee	1
Yankees	1
yard	1
yardstick	1
yarn	1
yawned	1
ye	1
yearbook	1
yearned	1
yearning	1
yellow	1
yells	1
yen	1
yielding	1
YMCA	1
youngest	1
yourselves	1
youthful	1
zeal	1
zone	1